PENGUIN BOOKS

THE PENGUIN PRICE GUIDE FOR RECORD AND COMPACT DISC COLLECTORS

Nick Hamlyn is the co-proprietor of Pied Piper Records, the well-known collectors' record shop in Northampton. He has been a record collector himself for nearly forty years (having started very young!) and a dealer for nearly twenty. He has contributed to various rock magazines over the years and currently writes a monthly feature for the newly established record collecting magazine, *Record Mart and Buyer*. He provides record valuation advice in regular phone-in programmes on a number of BBC local radio stations. In his spare time, Nick writes fiction and plays lead guitar, both for rock'n'roll soul band Loose Covers and in a free-improvisation duo with saxophonist Richard Powell. Four Bop Drop, an improv quartet having both Nick and Richard as members, has a CD currently available on SLAM.

The Penguin Price Guide for Record and Compact Disc Collectors

Nick Hamlyn

PENGUIN BOOKS

PENGUIN BOOKS

Published by the Penguin Group
Penguin Books Ltd, 27 Wrights Lane, London W8 5TZ, England
Penguin Putnam Inc., 375 Hudson Street, New York, New York 10014, USA
Penguin Books Australia Ltd, Ringwood, Victoria, Australia
Penguin Books Canada Ltd, 10 Alcorn Avenue, Toronto, Ontario, Canada M4V 3B2
Penguin Books (NZ) Ltd, Private Bag 102902, NSMC Auckland, New Zealand

Penguin Books Ltd, Registered Offices: Harmondsworth, Middlesex, England

First published as *The MusicMaster Price Guide for Record Collectors* by Retail Entertainment Data Publishing Ltd 1991
Published in Penguin Books 1997
New edition 2000
10 9 8 7 6 5 4 3 2 1

Set in Monotype Bembo and ITC Officina
Typeset by Rowland Phototypesetting Ltd, Bury St Edmunds, Suffolk
Printed in England by Clays Ltd, St Ives plc

Contents

Introduction

For all those record collectors who believe the year 2000 to be the first of the new millennium, this updated and improved edition of the *Penguin Price Guide for Record and Compact Disc Collectors* is the perfect celebration. Personally, I prefer to view the year as the climax of the last millennium – it *is*, after all, the thousandth year – and the new *Penguin Price Guide* to be perfectly placed to look back over the years of recording history that are a significant feature of the end part of that millennium.

Either way, this *Penguin Price Guide for Record and CD Collectors* is definitely the first such guide to be published in the year 2000. Its indisputable claim to the milestone is appropriate, because the very first edition of the *Nick Hamlyn Price Guide*, which appeared in the shops near the beginning of 1991, was itself a milestone in the world of record collecting. It was the very first comprehensive record price guide ever to be compiled in the UK. Through the nineties, both this and the subsequent Nick Hamlyn price guides charted the undulating landscape – the rise and rise – of what has become one of the most exciting and widely followed of all collectors' markets. The edition that you now hold in your hand is the fifth in the line. It remains the only UK price guide that can fairly claim to represent the concerns of the modern record collector. Gone are the days when the only records to make an enthusiast's pulse quicken were items from the obscurer reaches of the London label catalogue. In the year 2000, there are collectors keenly searching for the legendary American psychedelic albums by the West Coast Pop Art Experimental Band or Lothar And The Hand People; for the pioneering German electronic LPs by Cluster and Kraftwerk; for the sixties beat EPs made by vital UK groups like the In Betweens and the Creation, but issued only in France; and for imported Blue Note jazz records by John Patton and Horace Silver. And alongside them are more traditional collectors whose no less ambitious desires revolve around attempts to acquire all the London gold singles or else a complete set of mint condition Beatles originals. All of these records – and the thousands like them – are included in the new *Penguin Price Guide*.

Four or five years ago, it seemed as though record collecting was beginning to follow the lead set by the shops selling new releases, which have almost entirely swept vinyl off their display racks. The general upwards trend in values that had been apparent over the previous decade had largely halted, and indeed, in some areas, prices were beginning to fall. Today, it is still the case that records at the bottom end of the value scale continually teeter and fall off it altogether. Many of the LPs listed at £10 in earlier editions of the *Price Guide* are no longer included in this new edition. A considerably larger number of singles formerly listed at £4 have also been dropped. At one time, for example, it seemed to make sense that virtually any original single from the fifties or sixties would be worth a minimum of £4 – especially if its status as a chart hit meant that it was likely to appeal to a wide range of collectors. This is not, however, an argument that can any longer be realistically sustained. The fact is that common singles – even ones that are around thirty-five or forty years old, like 'What Do You Want' by Adam Faith or 'I Like It' by Gerry And The Pacemakers – no longer sell for anything like £4, no matter how much a dealer or collector may feel that they should.

Further up the value scale, however, I am happy to report that the prices of a large number of items are continuing to move upwards. Within the key areas of original fifties rock'n'roll and R&B and the currently fashionable freakbeat genre of the sixties there have been some quite startling price jumps in recent years, particularly in the case of very rare singles. Led by a small number of keen collectors who are seemingly prepared to pay almost anything for a record that they do not already own, the auction prices for some singles titles have on occasion far exceeded the previously listed values. As explained below, one must always be very cautious where the results of auctions are concerned, since one or two high bids for a particular record do not necessarily imply that further copies of the same record will attract equal enthusiasm. Nevertheless, this edition of the *Price Guide* does list many greatly increased values, with records showing the greatest movement and likely to continue doing so being indicated by the advisory phrase 'best auctioned'.

Meanwhile, the albums of certain perennially popular artists – notably the Beatles, the Small Faces, the Who, Jimi Hendrix and some other sixties stars – have maintained the often strikingly high values they acquired in the late nineties and have even continued to show increases in value in many cases. This is a response, no doubt, to the deeper interest in sixties music originally opened up by successful modern artists like Oasis, Blur, Paul Weller and the late lamented Kula Shaker, who have been only too happy to display their sixties influences openly.

With more specialist genres like jazz, folk and seventies Euro-rock continuing to attract converts keen to acquire original issues, the market for vinyl can only be described as remarkably buoyant.

At the same time, the inclusion of 'Compact Disc' in the *Price Guide*'s title is highly significant. Although a few die-hard vinyl specialists will complain bitterly about the fact, the silver disc has now established a significant place within the collectors' arena. A large number of collectable CD albums and singles are included in the listings and while their values cannot compete, in general, with those of the most collectable vinyl items, that they are here at all is a demonstration of the way that the market in collectable recorded music is continuing to develop.

The *Penguin Price Guide* presents the record and compact disc collectors' market as it is now. Like its predecessors, it is an essential work of reference for collectors, dealers and researchers alike.

HOW ACCURATE ARE THE VALUES LISTED IN THE GUIDE?

The title of this book means what it says: it is a guide to the values of collectable records. Within any collectors' field, an item is essentially worth whatever a collector is prepared to pay for it. When considering items of which several copies are potentially available, however, as is the case with collectors' records, then a few points need to be kept in mind. Let us suppose that Steve Crick, a collector of extraordinary tastes, is desperate to obtain a copy of 'My Old Killarney Hat' by Sister Mary Gertrude. This is not a record that features very often in dealers' lists, so Steve advertises that he is prepared to pay fifty pounds for a copy. Four dealers eventually manage to come across the elusive record: one is delighted to receive fifty pounds from an equally delighted Steve Crick, but the other three find that they are unable to interest anyone at all in the record, at any price. So what is the value of 'My Old Killarney Hat'?

At the other end of the scale, there must be numerous collectors who would like to obtain a copy of the Beatles fan club album *From Then To You*. This is a record with a listed value of £250 – it is scarce, but copies do turn up, and most dealers will have had at least one passing through their hands. Dave Conroy is a keen Beatles collector and he does not have a copy of *From Then To You*. On the other hand, he does have the actual music in his collection, as he was able to buy an American counterfeit of the record quite cheaply a few years ago. When he sees the real thing in his local collectors' record shop with a price tag of £250, he argues that he has waited thirty years for the record, so he might as well wait a little longer for a copy that is more 'reasonably' priced. In the event, the shop is unable to find a customer for the record. The manager reduces the price to £225, and after a few weeks, with the record still unsold, Dave Conroy offers £200, which is accepted. So again, what is the value of *From Then To You*?

A junk shop, selling all kinds of second-hand goods from shabby premises, and with a box of old records in the corner, would find in all probability that the records would remain unsold if priced according to the values given in this guide. An efficient specialist mail-order company, on the other hand, with a large number of customers in Scandinavia, Germany and Japan, could well be regularly managing to obtain prices in excess of those listed in the guide.

The above arguments apply equally well in the case of known rarities being sold at auction. As every rare-record dealer is aware, offers made on these occasions can often climb way above the 'book values' of the records in question. There are a number of collectors who, like Steve Crick, are prepared to pay well over the odds to gain the rare records they need. There are also a much larger number of collectors who are of the Dave Conroy persuasion and prepared to temper their enthusiasm. It is important, therefore, to resist the temptation to assume that, simply because one copy of, for example, 'Addicted Man' by the Game has successfully been auctioned for £600, then all subsequent copies of the record will also sell for that figure.

To these considerations must be added the fact that the collectors' market is a volatile one. The success of a new group in the charts can send the values of their back catalogue shooting upwards (although a later fall from favour can just as easily send them tumbling back down again); an influential disc jockey can create a collectors' item out of an obscurity simply by deciding to play it (particularly in the case of soul records); or else the reissue of a scarce album can increase the value of the original by making more people aware of its existence. On the other hand, the discovery of a warehouse full of copies of a previously rare record is likely to make the price fall dramatically; or a similar effect can simply result from several people deciding to sell their cherished copies of the same record at the same time. It happens!

To repeat, therefore, this book is a *guide* to the values of collectable records. A large amount of research, however, has gone into making it as accurate as possible, much of it being first-hand – the result of actually selling the records through a successful collectors' record shop to both the home and the international market over a period of several years. The values are based on actual sales and, within the constraints detailed above, the margin of error is not likely to be large. Comments and corrections are always welcome, however. It should be noted that a definite price structure is used throughout, along the lines of the discrete price levels used by auctioneers. It starts with the sequence 4, 5, 6, 8, 10, 12, 15, 20 and carries on from there, so that no record is listed as having values such as £7 or £11 or £19. The two values listed for each item refer to two condition categories – 'near mint' (excellent) and the significantly lower 'very good'.

To qualify as collectable, a lower price limit was set for near-mint items. All the LPs included in the guide are valued at ten pounds or over; double LPs and CD albums are twelve pounds or over; 7″ singles are four pounds or over; 7″ EPs and CD and cassette singles are five pounds and over; 12″ singles start at six pounds.

HOW IS THE PRICE GUIDE ORGANIZED?

The artists are listed alphabetically, and for each one the collectable records are also listed alphabetically. Where more than one listing appears under the same name, then these are actually the recordings of different artists. It must be remembered that the listings are not complete discographies, but only a catalogue of those items that are valuable enough to be considered collectable. As far as possible, it is the A-side that is listed in the case of singles, but if a certain title cannot be found, it is always worth checking to see if the B-side has been listed instead. Similarly, where a record has a different artist on each side (a common practice with sixties reggae and ska singles), it will only be listed under one of them. Records featuring several different artists are usually listed under the 'Various' heading. A small number of abbreviations have been used. These are as follows:

cass: cassette; **cass-s**: cassingle; **CD-s**: compact disc single; **r-reel**: reel to reel tape.

The extract below shows the different parts of an entry:

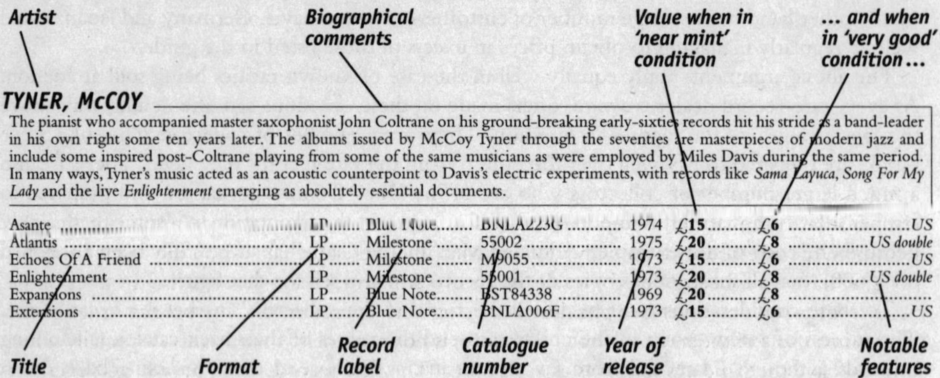

TYNER, McCOY

The pianist who accompanied master saxophonist John Coltrane on his ground-breaking early-sixties records hit his stride as a band-leader in his own right some ten years later. The albums issued by McCoy Tyner through the seventies are masterpieces of modern jazz and include some inspired post-Coltrane playing from some of the same musicians as were employed by Miles Davis during the same period. In many ways, Tyner's music acted as an acoustic counterpoint to Davis's electric experiments, with records like *Sama Layuca*, *Song For My Lady* and the live *Enlightenment* emerging as absolutely essential documents.

Title	Format	Label	Catalogue number	Year	Near mint	Very good	Notes
Asante	LP	Blue Note	BNLA223G	1974	**£15**	£6	*US*
Atlantis	LP	Milestone	55002	1975	**£20**	£8	*US double*
Echoes Of A Friend	LP	Milestone	M9055	1973	**£15**	£6	*US*
Enlightenment	LP	Milestone	55001	1973	**£20**	£8	*US double*
Expansions	LP	Blue Note	BST84338	1969	**£20**	£8	
Extensions	LP	Blue Note	BNLA006F	1973	**£15**	£6	*US*

As a finale to this introduction I would like to offer my grateful thanks to the various dealers and collectors who have helped with information, advice and record sleeves for photographing. An enormous number of people have contacted me after reading the earlier editions of the *Price Guide* and I have talked with a large number of dealers and collectors at different record fairs. I hope that they will have the satisfaction of seeing some of their information included, even if there are far too many names for me to list here! Particular thanks are due, however, to Natalie Round, whose efficient management of Pied Piper Records gives me the time to work on the *Price Guide* database; to Peter Green (the jazz fan, not the guitarist!), Steve Moulin, Allen Souster, Jon Taylor, Phil Walker and David Walker-Collins, who have continually helped me to fill the obscurer corners of the discography and have given me access to their extensive record collections for photographing; and to my family – Liz, David and Eileen, Catherine, Fred and Sarah.

Nick Hamlyn

Record-collecting Charts

The volatile nature of the top end of the collectors' market, combined with the fact that, by definition, the rarest records are only very occasionally offered for sale (or, in the case of number 4 below, have *never* been offered for sale, so far as is known), means that the listed values of the rarest records can only ever be considered as being very approximate. The precise order of the records in a chart of the most valuable, therefore, is not particularly important – especially when so many have the same guide values as each other. The fifty records listed below, however, are definitely amongst the rarest and most sought-after of all. A sensible owner wishing to sell any of these would be very well advised to auction them to the highest bidder!

The Rarest Records

1. Bob Dylan: Freewheelin' LP Columbia CS8786 1963 US stereo with 4 different tracks **£12,000**
2. Beatles: Beatles (White Album) LP Apple PMC/PCS7067/8 1968 cover number 000001–000010 **£5000**
3. Bob Dylan: Freewheelin' LP Columbia CL1986 1963 US mono with 4 different tracks **£5000**
4. Quarrymen: In Spite Of All The Danger 7″ or 78 Percy Phillips no number 1981 **£5000**
5. Elvis Presley: TV Guide Presents Elvis Presley 7″ RCA GBMW8705 1956 US interview promo **£4000**
6. Beatles: The Beatles At The Beeb CD Apple 1980s promotional only, 140 CD set **£3000**
7. Beatles: Yesterday And Today LP Capitol ST 2553 1966 US stereo, peeled butcher sleeve **£3000**
8. Prisonaires: There Is Love In You 7″ US Sun 207 1954 **£3000**
9. Queen: Bohemian Rhapsody 7″ EMI EMI2375 1978 blue vinyl, with envelope, boxed goblets and assorted other goodies **£3000**
10. Bob Dylan: Blood On The Tracks LP Columbia PC33235 1974 US test pressing with different versions of 5 tracks **£2500**
11. Beatles: Beatles (White Album) LP Apple PMC/PCS7067/8 1968 cover number 000011–000020 **£2000**
12. David Bowie: Space Oddity 7″ Philips BF1801 1969 with picture sleeve **£2000**
13. Bobby Charles: See You Later Alligator 7″ London HLU8247 **£2000**
14. Cold Sun: Dark Shadows LP US private pressing 1969 **£2000**
15. Dragonwyck: Dragonwyck LP US private pressing 1972 **£2000**
16. Ron Hargrave: Latch On 7″ MGM MGM956 1957 **£2000**
17. Music Emporium: Music Emporium LP US Sentinel 100 1969 **£2000**
18. Search Party: Montgomery's Chapel LP US private pressing 1969 **£2000**
19. T Rex: Ride A White Swan 7″ Octopus OCTO1 1970 test pressing **£2000**
20. Barons: Don't Walk Out 7″ London HLP8391 1957 **£1500**
21. Beatles: From Me To You 7″ EP French Odeon SOE3739 1963 sleeve showing the Beatles in French costume **£1500**
22. Beatles: Please Please Me LP Parlophone PCS3042 1963 stereo, label with gold print **£1500**
23. Christopher: Whatcha Gonna Do LP US Chris-tee PRP12411 1970 **£1500**

24. Crows: Gee 7″ Columbia SCM5119 1954 £1500
25. Damon: Song Of A Gypsy LP US ANKH 1970 £1500
26. Willie Dixon: Walking The Blues 7″ London HLU8297 1956 £1500
27. Harmonica Frank: Rockin' Chair Daddy 7″ US Sun 205 1954 £1500
28. John's Children: Midsummer Night's Scene 7″ Track 604005 1967 test pressing £1500
29. John Lennon: You Know My Name 7″ Apple 1002 1969 test pressing £1500
30. Mariani: Perpetuum Mobile LP US Sonobeat 1004 1970s £1500
31. Odyssey: Setting Forth LP US private pressing year unknown £1500
32. Penguins: Best Vocal Groups – Rhythm And Blues LP US DooTone DTL204 1950s with other artists, red vinyl £1500
33. Phafner: Overdrive LP US Dragon no number 1971 £1500
34. Elvis Presley: Elvis And Janis 10″ LP South African Teal T31077 1958 with Janis Martin £1500
35. Sex Pistols: God Save The Queen 7″ A&M AMS7284 1977 £1500
36. West Coast Pop Art Experimental Band: West Coast Pop Art Experimental Band LP US Fifo M101 1966 £1500
37. Beatles: Beatles Vs The Four Seasons LP US Vee Jay DX30 1964 double £1250
38. C.A. Quintet: A Trip Thru' Hell LP US Candy 7764 1968 £1250
39. Dark: Round The Edges LP S.I.S. SR0102S 1972 £1250
40. Forever Amber: Love Cycle LP Advance no number 1969 £1250
41. Other Half: Other Half LP US 7/2 Records HS12 1966 £1250
42. Touch: Street Suite LP US Mainline LP2001 1969 £1250
43. Ike And Tina Turner: River Deep And Mountain High LP US Philles PHLP4011 1966 no cover £1250
44. Rolling Stones: Their Satanic Majesties Request LP Decca TXL/TXS103 1967 promo with padded silk sleeve £1000
45. Jimi Hendrix: Electric Ladyland LP Track 612008/9 1968 mono double £1000
46. Elton John: Warlock Sampler LP Warlock Music WMM101/2 1970 demo, with Linda Peters £1000
47. Jokers Wild: Jokers Wild LP Regent Sound RSLP007 1966 1-sided £1000
48. Blue Men: I Hear A New World LP Triumph TRXST9000 1960 demo £1000
49. Kate Bush: Eat The Music 7″ EMI EM280 1993 £1000
50. Michael Jackson: Dangerous LP US Epic 1991 sample picture disc £1000

Another 57 items are also valued at £1000!

Some of the artists in the chart above are not exactly household names. A quick count of the number of lines devoted to each artist in the *Price Guide* produces fewer surprises, perhaps. The pre-eminence of the Beatles and Elvis Presley in the list confirms the instinctive suspicion that these are the most collected artists of all. A rather different result would be produced further down the chart, however, by totalling the values of the artists' rare records. Frank Sinatra and the reggae singers Prince Buster, Derrick Morgan and Laurel Aitken released a large number of records over the years, but comparatively few of them reach particularly high values.

Artists with the Largest Number of Rare Records

1. Beatles (465)
2. Elvis Presley (430)
3. Cliff Richard (301)
4. Rolling Stones (236)
5. Prince Buster (163)

6. Queen (148)
7. James Brown (143)
8.= Frank Sinatra (135)
8.= U2 (135)
10. Everly Brothers (125)
11. Connie Francis (116)
12. Fats Domino (112)
13. Derrick Morgan (111)
14. Bob Marley (108)
15. Michael Jackson (106)
16. Buddy Holly (104)
17. Miles Davis (101)
18. David Bowie (100)
19. Laurel Aitken (96)
20.= John Barry (95)
20.= Ray Charles (95)

At the start of the 1950s, pop music in Britain did not have the central position of importance in our culture that it has undoubtedly acquired today. Far from there being an early version of *Top Of The Pops* to publicize the latest and biggest hits, there were actually no hits, because there was no pop music chart. The first chart was a top twelve published in the *New Musical Express* in November 1952. Al Martino had the number one slot and, certainly in terms of chart success, his kind of light-ballad material was the dominant sound of the fifties. Singers like Frankie Laine, Ruby Murray and, of course, Frank Sinatra were huge stars.

The arrival at number one of an uptempo song called 'Rock Around The Clock' by Bill Haley and his Comets seemed like a mere novelty at the time. Before long, however, it was followed by the first hits from a new singer with a new quality – teen appeal – and after Elvis Presley, things were never quite the same again. The impact of the new music – rock'n'roll – on the charts in Britain was considerable, although it was rivalled by a home-grown equivalent, skiffle, while the ballad singers continued to take the greater number of chart placings. In America, however, artists like Presley, Buddy Holly and the Everly Brothers were just the tip of the iceberg. There was a wealth there of new teen-oriented music, described within several different categories. Elvis Presley and Johnny Burnette played rockabilly; Chuck Berry and Fats Domino were rhythm and blues; the Flamingos and the Five Royales sung doo-wop – all of these being areas of music of immense interest to record collectors today. It should also be remembered that modern jazz, as created by the likes of Miles Davis, Sonny Rollins and Art Blakey's Jazz Messengers, flourished through the fifties even if it seldom troubled the charts. Roots music too – the blues of Muddy Waters and the country of Hank Williams – music that lay behind the more commercial rock'n'roll, remained a continual presence.

The Rarest UK Singles of the Fifties

1. Bobby Charles: See You Later Alligator London HLU8247 1956 **£2000**
2. Ron Hargrave: Latch On MGM MGM956 1957 **£2000**
3. Willie Dixon: Walking The Blues London HLU8297 1956 **£1500**
4. Crows: Gee Columbia SCM5119 1954 **£1500**
5. Barons: Don't Walk Out London HLP8391 1957 **£1500**
6. Chords: Sh'boom Columbia SCM5133 1954 **£1000**
7. Jackie Lee Cochran: Mama Don't You Think I Know Brunswick 05669 1957 **£1000**

8. Cupids: Lillie Mae Vogue V9102 1958 £1000
9. Mac Curtis: You Ain't Treating Me Right Parlophone R4279 1957 £1000
10. Penguins: Earth Angel London HL8114 1955 £1000
11. Commodores: Riding On A Train London HLD8209 1955 £750
12. Drifters: Soldier Of Fortune London HLE8344 1956 £750
13. Werly Fairburn: All The Time London HLC8349 1956 £750
14. Willows: Church Bells May Ring London HLL8290 1956 £600
15. Clovers: Nip Sip London HLE8229 1956 £600
16. Commodores: Speedo London HLD8251 1956 £600
17. Johnny Carroll & The Hot Rocks: Hot Rock Brunswick 05603 1956 £600
18. Johnny Carroll & The Hot Rocks: Wild Wild Women Brunswick 05580 1956 £600
19. Smiley Lewis: One Night London HLU8312 1956 £600
20. Smiley Lewis: Don't Be That Way HLU8337 1956 £600

The Rarest 10" LPs

1. Elvis Presley: Elvis And Janis South African Teal T31077 1958 £1500
2. Billy Ward And The Dominoes: Billy Ward And His Dominoes US Federal 29594 1954 £1000
3. Ruth Brown: Ruth Brown Sings US Atlantic 115 1956 £750
4. Johnny Burnette: Rock'n'Roll Trio Coral LVC10041 1956 £600
5. Billy Ward And The Dominoes: Billy Ward And The Dominoes Parlophone PMD1061 1958 £500
6. Hank Ballard And The Midnighters: Midnighters US Federal 29590 1954 £400
7. Charles Brown: Mood Music US Aladdin 702 1954 red vinyl £400
8. Frankie Lymon & The Teenagers: Rockin' With Frankie Columbia 33S1134 1957 £400
9. Bill Haley: Shake, Rattle And Roll US Decca DL5560 1954 £350
10. Marty Robbins: Rock'n'Roll'n'Robbins US Columbia CL2601 1956 £350
11. Johnny Ace: Memorial Album US Duke DLP70 1955 £300
12. Wynonie Harris & others: Party After Hours US Aladdin 703 1956 red vinyl £300
13. Saints: Saints MJB BEV73/4 1964 £300
14. Beatles With Tony Sheridan: Meet The Beat German Polydor J74557 1965 £250
15. Cyril Davies: The Legendary Cyril Davies 77 LP2 1957 £250
16. Amos Milburn: Rockin' The Boogie US Aladdin 704 1956 red vinyl £250
17. Platters: Platters Parlophone PMD1058 1958 £250
18. Elvis Presley: The Best Of Elvis HMV DLP1159 1956 £250
19. Don Rendell: Meet Don Rendell Tempo LAP1 1955 £200
20. Black vinyl issues of the 3 red vinyl albums listed above £200

The Rarest 12" LPs of the Fifties

1. Penguins and others: Best Vocal Groups – Rhythm And Blues US DooTone DTL204 1950s red vinyl £1500
2. Elvis Presley: Elvis US RCA LPM1382 1956 with alternate 'Old Shep' £750
3. Boyd Bennett & His Rockets: Boyd Bennett US King 594 1957 £600
4. Johnny Burnette: Rock'n'Roll Trio US Coral CRL57080 1956 £600
5. Esther Phillips: Memory Lane US King LP622 1956 £600
6. Five Keys: Best Of The Five Keys US Aladdin 806 1956 £500
7. Five Satins: Five Satins Sing US Ember ELP100 1957 blue vinyl £500
8. Four Lovers: Joyride US RCA LPM1317 1956 £500
9. Screaming Jay Hawkins: At Home US Epic LN3448 1956 £500
10. Billy Ward & The Dominoes: Billy Ward & His Dominoes US Federal 395548 1956 £500

11. Billy Ward & The Dominoes: Clyde McPhatter With Billy Ward US Federal 395559 1957 £500
12. Five Keys: Five Keys On The Town US Score LP4003 1957 £400
13. Five Royales: Rockin' Five Royales US Apollo LP488 1956 £400
14. Buddy Holly: That'll Be The Day US Decca DL8707 1958 £400
15. Lavern Baker: Rock And Roll With Lavern Baker London HAE2107 1958 £350
16. Jim Reeves: Jim Reeves Sings US Abbott LP5001 1956 £350
17. Chantels: We're The Chantels US End LP301 1958 group photo cover £300
18. Clovers: Clovers US Atlantic LP1248 1956 £300
19. Esquerita: Esquerita US Capitol T1186 1959 £300
20. Dale Hawkins: Susie-Q US Chess 1429 1958 £300
21. Penguins: Cool Cool Penguins US DooTone DTL242 1959 £300
22. Platters: Platters US Federal 395549 1955 £300
23. Elvis Presley: Rock'n'Roll No. 2 HMV CLP1105 1956 £300
24. Spaniels: Goodnite, It's Time To Go US Vee Jay LP1002 1958 £300
25. Teddy Bears: Teddy Bears Sing US Imperial SLP12067 1959 stereo £300
26. Eddie 'Cleanhead' Vinson: Battle Of The Blues Vol. 3 US King 634 1959 £300

25 Doo-wop Singles to Die For

Cadets: Stranded In The Jungle London HLU8313 1956 £400
Chantels: Maybe London HLU8561 1958 £300
Chords: Sh'Boom Columbia SCM5133 1954 £1000
Cleftones: Heart And Soul Columbia DB4678 1961 £100
Clovers: Love Potion No.9 London HLT8949 1959 £30
Crests: Sixteen Candles London HL8794 1959 £30
Crows: Gee Columbia SCM5119 1954 £1500
Danleers: One Summer Night Mercury AMT1003 1958 £150
Danny & The Juniors: At The Hop HMV POP436 1958 £10
Dion & The Belmonts: I Wonder Why London HLH8646 1958 £50
Drifters: Moonlight Bay London HLE8686 1958 £100
Dubs: Could This Be Magic London HLU8526 1957 £150
Elegants: Little Star HMV POP520 1958 £15
Five Royales: Dedicated To The One I Love Ember EMBS124 1960 £75
Flamingos: I Only Have Eyes For You Top Rank JAR263 1960 £75
Four Seasons: Sherry Stateside SS122 1962 £4
Harvey & The Moonglows: Ten Commandments Of Love London HLM8730 1958 £200
Frankie Lymon & The Teenagers: Why Do Fools Fall In Love? Columbia SCM5265 1956 £30
Monotones: Book Of Love London HLM8625 1958 £40
Penguins: Earth Angel London HL8114 1955 £1000
Phil Phillips & Twilights: Sea Of Love Mercury AMT1059 1959 £25
Randy & The Rainbows: Denise Stateside SS214 1963 £25
Shep & The Limelites: Daddy's Home Pye 7N25090 1961 £60
Silhouettes: Get A Job Parlophone R4407 1958 £30
Skyliners: Since I Don't Have You London HLB8829 1959 £150

Several classic singles ('Goodnight, It's Time To Go' by the Spaniels; 'Speedo' by the Cadillacs; 'A Thousand Miles Away' by the Heartbeats; 'In The Still Of The Night' by the Five Satins; 'Mary Lee' by the Rainbows; and 'The Closer You Are' by the Channells, to name just six) were not issued in the UK, although the songs are available on original albums listed in the *Guide*.

Correspondence is welcome on the subject of the above list, which is obviously an entirely personal selection (and the same applies to the three similar lists to be found later in this section).

It has been said that anyone who can remember the sixties was not actually there. I am told that, as far as pop music is concerned, the sixties began late – at the end of 1962. For it was then that the Beatles released their first single. The Beatles had an impact on their decade, the force of which has never been quite matched by any artist since. It was not just that they dominated the charts, with virtually every record climbing straight to the top. The Beatles were a major influence too on fashion, they filled the newspaper gossip columns and often the headlines, and in music they almost single-handedly acquired for pop an artistic credibility that it had not enjoyed previously. By the end of the decade, pop musicians were producing rock operas, staging elaborate multimedia events, and displaying an unparalleled virtuosity on their instruments. The inspiration for all of this can be easily traced back to the Beatles' own love of growth and experiment.

The development of rock music through the sixties, from beat to psychedelia to progressive, was underscored too by an interest in American blues. The other leading beat group, the Rolling Stones, psychedelic pioneers Pink Floyd and the progressive icon Jimi Hendrix all took their love of the blues as a starting point. Advances in technology played a key role too. Amplification became more powerful, enabling guitarists in particular to find a range of exciting sounds that had never been revealed by the instrument previously. Recording techniques became increasingly sophisticated, with the introduction of multi-track recording allowing for the mixing of separately recorded parts in an effort to add depth and extra interest to the finished product. Meanwhile, a large number of fans discovered their musical roots in folk music. Folk clubs prospered and one performer in particular, Bob Dylan, began to exert an influence almost as great as that of the Beatles, even if he did not manage to match their extreme popularity.

Jazz continued to find an enthusiastic if increasingly minority following, with its avant garde exploring stranger avenues than even the most outrageous of the psychedelic rock groups. The popular sound of Black America was soul music, although its appeal soon began to stretch much further. With major centres of activity based in Detroit (Tamla Motown) and Memphis (Stax), soul had become a mass-market music by the end of the decade.

Through it all, and despite having little or no connection with any of the exciting new rock sounds that defined the swinging sixties, middle-of-the-road ballad singers continued to do well, with Tom Jones and Engelbert Humperdinck in particular scoring a number of big chart hits. It remains the case, however, that even despite Tom Jones gaining a surprising street credibility in the nineties, collectors' interest in the middle-of-the-road music of the sixties (or any other decade) remains slight.

The Rarest UK Singles of the Sixties

1. David Bowie: Space Oddity Philips BF1801 1969 picture sleeve **£2000**
2. John's Children: Midsummer Night's Scene Track 604005 1967 test pressing **£1500**
3. John Lennon: You Know My Name Apple 1001 1969 test pressing **£1500**
4. Beatles: Love Me Do Parlophone R4949 1962 demo **£1000**
5. Status Quo: Technicolour Dreams Pye 7N17650 1968 **£1000**
6. Beatles: Our First Four Apple no number 1968 4-single promo pack **£750**
7. Beatles: Please Please Me Parlophone R4983 1963 demo **£600**
8. David Bowie (as Davy Jones & The King Bees): Liza Jane Vocalion V9221 1964 **£600**
9. Mike & The Modifiers: I Found Myself A Brand New Baby Oriole CB1775 1962 **£600**

10. Valadiers: I Found A Girl Oriole CBA1809 1963 £600
11. Beatles: Something Apple R5814 1969 demo £500
12. Marc Bolan: Hippy Gumbo Parlophone R5539 1966 £500
13. Marc Bolan: Third Degree Decca F12413 1966 £500
14. David Bowie (as Davy Jones & The Lower Third): You've Got A Habit Of Leaving Parlophone R5315 1965 £500
15. Farinas: Bye Bye Johnny Victor Buckland Sound Studio 1964 £500
16. Jokers Wild: Don't Ask Me Why Regent Sound RSR0031 1966 £500
17. Pink Floyd: Arnold Layne Columbia DB8156 1967 demo in picture sleeve £500
18. Pink Floyd: See Emily Play Columbia DB8214 1967 demo in picture sleeve £500
19. Pink Floyd: Apples And Oranges Columbia DB8310 1967 demo in picture sleeve £500
20. Sweet: Slow Motion Fontana TF958 1968 £500

The Rarest 7" EPs

1. Beatles: From Me To You French Odeon SOE3739 1963 sleeve showing the Beatles in French costume £1500
2. Bo Street Runners: Bo Street Runners Oak RGJ131 1964 £750
3. Thirteenth Floor Elevators: Reverberation French Riviera 231240 1966 £750
4. Wild Oats: Wild Oats Oak RGJ117 1964 £750
5. Muleskinners: Muleskinners Keepoint KEEEP7104 1960s £600
6. Thor's Hammer: Thor's Hammer Parlophone CGEP62 1966 export, with bonus single £600
7. Kinks: Kinks Pye NEP5039 1964 export £500
8. Clique: Clique private pressing 1960s £500
9. Pharoahs: Pharoahs Decca DFE6522 1958 £500
10. Ptolomy Psycon: Loose Capacitor private pressing 1970s £400
11. Joe Cocker: Joe Cocker Oak 1960s £400
12. Blue Men: I Hear A New World Triumph RGXST5000 1960 £400
13. Apex Rhythm & Blues All Stars: Tall Girl John Lever JLEP1 1964 £400
14. Eyes: Arrival Of The Eyes Mercury MCE10035 1966 £400
15. Glenn Athens & The Trojans: Glenn Athens & The Trojans Spot 7E1018 1965 £350

The Rarest UK LPs of the Sixties

1. Beatles: Beatles (White Album) Apple PMC/PCS7067/8 1968 cover number 000001–000010 £5000
2. Beatles: Beatles (White Album) Apple PMC/PCS7067/8 1968 cover number 000011–000020 £2000
3. Beatles: Please Please Me Parlophone PCS3042 1963 stereo, label with gold print £1500
4. Forever Amber: Love Cycle Advance no number 1969 £1250
5. Beatles: Beatles (White Album) Apple PMC/PCS7067/8 1968 cover number 000021–000100 £1000
6. Beatles: Beatles (White Album) Parlophone PPCS7067/8 1968 export £1000
7. Beatles: Yellow Submarine Odeon PPCS7070 1969 export £1000
8. Blue Men: I Hear A New World Triumph TRXST9000 1960 demo £1000
9. Jimi Hendrix: Electric Ladyland Track 612008/9 1968 mono double £1000
10. Jokers Wild: Jokers Wild Regent Sound RSLP007 1966 1 sided £1000
11. Rolling Stones: Their Satanic Majesties Request Decca TXL/TXS103 1967 promo with padded silk sleeve £1000
12. Tinkerbell's Fairydust: Tinkerbell's Fairydust Decca LK/SKL5028 1969 demo only £1000
13. Beatles: Something New Parlophone CPCS101 1965 export £750
14. Beatles: Abbey Road Parlophone PPCS7088 1969 export £750

15. Beatles: Beatles (White Album) Apple PMC/PCS7067/8 1968 cover number 000101–001000 £750
16. Beatles: Yellow Submarine Parlophone PPCS7070 1969 export £750
17. John Lennon & Yoko Ono: Unfinished Music No. 1 – Two Virgins Apple APCOR2 1968 mono £750
18. Billy Nicholls: Would You Believe Immediate IMLP009 £750
19. Beatles: Beatles' Second Album Parlophone CPCS103 1966 export £600
20. Beatles: Beatles VI Parlophone CPCS104 1966 export £600
21. Delaney & Bonnie: Accept No Substitute Apple SAPCOR7 1969 test pressing with no sleeve £600
22. Dr Isaiah Ross: Flying Eagle Blue Horizon LP1 1966 £600
23. Rolling Stones: The Promotional LP Decca RSM1 1969 promo £600
24. Left Handed Marriage: On The Right Side Of The Left Handed Marriage private pressing 1967 £600

The Rarest US Company LPs of the Sixties

1. Bob Dylan: Freewheelin' Columbia CS8786 1963 stereo with 4 different tracks £12,000
2. Bob Dylan: Freewheelin' Columbia CL1986 1963 mono with 4 different tracks £5000
3. Beatles: Yesterday And Today Capitol ST2553 1966 stereo, peeled butcher sleeve £3000
4. Beatles: Beatles Vs The Four Seasons Vee Jay DX30 1964 double £1250
5. Ike And Tina Turner: River Deep And Mountain High Philles PHLP4011 1966 no cover £1250
6. Beatles: Beatles & Frank Ifield On Stage Vee Jay LP1085 1964 Beatles picture on cover £1000
7. Beatles: Yesterday And Today Capitol T2553 1966 mono, peeled butcher sleeve £1000
8. Bow Street Runners: Bow Street Runners B.T. Puppy BTPS1026 1969 £1000
9. Rolling Stones: 12 x 5 London LL3402 1964 blue vinyl £1000
10. Beatles: Introducing The Beatles Vee Jay LPS1062 1963 stereo, with 'Love Me Do', blank back cover £600
11. Beatles: Yesterday And Today Capitol ST2553 1966 mono, unpeeled butcher sleeve £600
12. Bob Dylan: Nine Song Publisher's Sampler Warner Brothers ZTD221567 1963 promo £600
13. Elvis Presley: Special Palm Sunday Programme RCA SP33461 1967 promo £600
14. Frank Frost & The Nighthawks: Hey Boss Man! Philips 1975 1961 £400
15. Elvis Presley. Speedway RCA LPM3989 1968 mono £400
16. Hank Ballard & The Midnighters: Mr Rhythm And Blues King 700 1960 £350
17. Elvis Presley: Golden Records Vol. 4 RCA LPM3921 1968 mono, with photo £350
18. Beatles: Introducing The Beatles Vee Jay mono, with 'Love Me Do', blank back cover £300
19. Beatles: Introducing The Beatles Vee Jay stereo, with 'Please Please Me' £300
20. Roy Brown, Wynonie Harris & Eddie Vinson: Battle Of The Blues Vol. 4 King 668 1960 £300
21. Carl Mann: Like Mann Philips 1960 1960 £300
22. Gatemouth Moore: I'm A Fool To Care King 684 1960 £300

The Rarest US Private and Small Label LPs of the Sixties

1. Cold Sun: Dark Shadows LP US private pressing 1969 £2000
2. Music Emporium: Music Emporium LP US Sentinel 100 1969 £2000
3. Search Party: Montgomery's Chapel LP US private pressing 1969 £2000
4. West Coast Pop Art Experimental Band: West Coast Pop Art Experimental Band LP US Fifo M101 1966 £1500
5. C.A. Quintet: A Trip Thru' Hell LP US Candy 7764 1968 £1250
6. Other Half: Other Half LP US 7/2 Records HS12 1966 £1250

7. Touch: Street Suite LP US Mainline LP2001 1969 £1250
8. Bachs: Out Of The Bachs private pressing 1968 £1000
9. Steve Ellis & The Starfires: Steve Ellis Songbook IGL105 1967 £1000
10. Fapardokly: Fapardokly V.I.P. 250 1966 £1000
11. Fugitives: Fugitives At Dave's Hideout Hideout 1001 1965 £1000
12. Haymarket Square: Magic Lantern Chaparral CRM201 1968 £1000
13. Hickory Wind: Hickory Wind Gigantic 1969 £1000
14. Index: Index private pressing 1968 £1000
15. Lazy Smoke: Corridor Of Faces Onyx ES6903 1967 £1000
16. Marble Phrogg: Marble Phrogg Derrick 8868 1968 £1000
17. Country Joe McDonald: Joe McDonald Custom Fidelity 1965 £1000
18. New Tweedy Brothers: New Tweedy Brothers Ridon 234 1966 £1000
19. Nightshadows: Square Root Of Two Spectrum Sounds 1968 £1000
20. Rising Storm: Calm Before The Rising Storm Remnant BBA3571 1966 £1000
21. Shaggs: Wink MCM 6311 1967 £1000
22. Smack: Smack Audio House no number 1967 £1000

The Rarest European LPs of the Sixties

1. Elvis Presley: Golden Boy Elvis Swiss RCA 25037 1965 £750
2. Beatles: Impression German Parlophone 6086 1965 club pressing £600
3. Beatles: Impression German Parlophone 6279 1965 club pressing £400
4. Bad Boys: Best Of The Bad Boys Italian Style STLP8061 1966 £300
5. Five Liverpools: Tokio International German CBS 62460 1965 £250
6. Iveys: Maybe Tomorrow European Apple SAPCOR8 1969 £250
7. Scotch: Scotch Italian R.T. Club LP25002 1966 £250
8. Shakespears: Give It To Me Dutch Philips QU625276 1960s £250
9. Beatles: Help! German Odeon SMO984008 1965 club pressing £200
10. Didi & His ABC Boys: Beat Aus Berlin German Telefunken BLE14340P 1966 £200
11. Rolling Stones: Rolling Stones Swiss Decca 25014 1965 club pressing £200
12. Système Crapoutchik: Aussi Loin Que Je Me Souvienne French Flamophone FL3301 1969 £200
13. Various Artists: Folk Centrum Utrecht '69 private pressing 1969 £200
14. Beatles: Please Please Me German Odeon ZTOX5550 1963 export £175
15. Various Artists: Star Club Information Record German Starclub 111371L 1964 £175

35 Definitive Psychedelic Singles

Beach Boys: Heroes And Villains Capitol CL15510 1967 £4
Beatles: Penny Lane/Strawberry Fields Forever Parlophone R5570 1967 picture sleeve £15
Blossom Toes: What On Earth Marmalade 598002 1967 £20 picture sleeve £40
Byrds: Eight Miles High CBS 202067 1966 £4
Crazy World of Arthur Brown: Devil's Grip Track 604008 1967 £4
Creation: Making Time Planet PLF116 1966 £30
Dantalian's Chariot: Madman Running Through The Fields Columbia DB8260 1967 £60
Julie Driscoll & Brian Auger: This Wheel's On Fire Marmalade 598006 1968 £4
Electric Prunes: Get Me To The World On Time Reprise RS20564 1967 £6
Family: Scene Thru The Eye Of A Lens Liberty LBF15031 1967 £100
Fever Tree: San Francisco Girls MCA MU1043 1968 £6
Fire: Father's Name Is Dad Decca F12753 1968 £100
Grateful Dead: Born Cross-Eyed Warner Brothers WB7186 1967 £30
Jimi Hendrix Experience: Burning Of The Midnight Lamp Track 604007 1967 £4
Idle Race: Imposters Of Life's Magazine Liberty LBF15026 1967 £25

Jefferson Airplane: White Rabbit RCA RCA1631 1967 £5
Kaleidoscope: Flight From Ashiya Fontana TF863 1967 £25 picture sleeve £60
Love: Laughing Stock Elektra EKSN45038 1968 £8
David McWilliams: Days Of Pearly Spencer Major Minor MM533 1968 £6
Misunderstood: I Can Take You To The Sun Fontana TF777 1966 £30
Moby Grape: Omaha CBS 2935 1967 £6
Monkees: Porpoise Song RCA RCA1862 1969 £5
Nazz: Open My Eyes Screen Gems SGC219001 1968 £6
Pink Floyd: See Emily Play Columbia DB8214 1967 £25
Pretty Things: Defecting Grey Columbia DB8300 1967 £30
Rolling Stones: We Love You Decca F12654 1967 £4
Sands: Mrs Gillespie's Refrigerator Reaction 591017 1967 £125
Smoke: My Friend Jack Columbia DB8115 1966 £20
Sorrows: Pink, Purple, Yellow, Red Piccadilly 7N35385 1967 £75
SRC: Black Sheep Capitol CL15576 1969 £10
Sharon Tandy & Fleur De Lys: Our Day Will Come Atlantic 584137 1967 £15
Tomorrow: Revolution Parlophone R5627 1967 £20
Traffic: Here We Go Round The Mulberry Bush Island WIP6025 1967 picture sleeve £5
Who: I Can See For Miles Track 604011 1967 £4
Yardbirds: Happening Ten Years Time Ago Columbia DB8024 1966 £20

The Rarest Blues LPs

1. Dr Isaiah Ross: Flying Eagle Blue Horizon LP1 1966 **£600**
2. Alexis Korner: Sky High Spot JW551 1965 **£500**
3. Cyril Davies: The Legendary Cyril Davies 77 LP2 10" LP **£250**
4. Jo-Ann Kelly: Jo-Ann Kelly Meets Dick Wellstood BBC Radioplay TSRP7726 1970s **£200**
5. Alexis Korner: Blues At The Roundhouse 77 1957 **£200**
6. Lightnin' Hopkins: Lightnin' And The Blues US Herald 1012 1960 **£150**
7. Jellybread: Jellybread Liphook IBCLP3627 1969 **£125**
8. Dave Kelly: Black Blue Kelly Mercury 6310001 1971 **£125**
9. Eddie Boyd: And His Blues Band Decca LK/SKL4872 1967 **£100**
10. Jo-Ann Kelly: Jo-Ann Kelly CBS 63841 1969 **£100**
11. Alexis Korner: At The Cavern Oriole PS40058 1964 **£100**
12. Alexis Korner: Red Hot From Alex Transatlantic TRA117 1964 **£100**
13. Piano Red: In Concert US Groove 1002 1964 **£100**
14. Piano Red: Jump Man Jump US Groove 1001 1964 **£100**
15. Smokey Smothers: Backporch Blues US King 779 1962 **£100**

The Rarest Jazz LPs

1. London Jazz Quartet: London Jazz Quartet Tempo TAP28 1960 **£300**
2. Newcastle Big Band: Newcastle Big Band Impulse ISSNBB106 1972 **£300**
3. Tubby Hayes: Late Spot At Scott's Fontana TL5200 1964 **£250**
4. Tubby Hayes: Tubby's Groove Tempo TAP29 1961 **£250**
5. Don Rendell & Ian Carr Quintet: Shades Of Blue Columbia 33SX1733 1965 **£250**
6. Howard Riley: Discussions Opportunity CP2500 1967 **£250**
7. Jazz Couriers: Jazz Couriers Tempo TAP15 1957 **£200**
8. Jazz Couriers: Last Word Tempo TAP26 1959 **£200**
9. Dizzy Reece: Progress Report Tempo TAP9 1957 **£200**
10. Don Rendell: Meet Don Rendell Tempo LAP1 1955 10" LP **£200**
11. Don Rendell & Ian Carr Quintet: Change Is Columbia SCX6368 1969 **£200**

12. Don Rendell & Ian Carr Quintet: Dusk Fire Columbia SX6064 1966 £200
13. Mike Taylor: Pendulum Columbia SX6042 1965 £200
14. Mike Taylor: Trio Columbia SX6137 1966 £200

It is intriguing to note that all of the rarest jazz albums are by British artists. Sun Ra and Charlie Parker, as representatives of the American jazz scene that forms the major part of the genre, put in an appearance at the £100 mark.

25 Cornerstones of a Modern Jazz Collection

Cannonball Adderley: Them Dirty Blues Riverside RLP12322/1170 1960 £15
Albert Ayler: Spiritual Unity US ESP-Disk 1002 1964 £30
Art Blakey: Buhaina's Delight Blue Note BLP/BST84104 1963 £20
Dave Brubeck: Jazz At Oberlin Vogue LAE12048 1957 £20
Ornette Coleman: Free Jazz US Atlantic (SD)1364 1961 £25
John Coltrane: A Love Supreme HMV CLP1869/CSD1605 1965 £20
Miles Davis: Milestones Fontana TFL5035 1958 £20
Miles Davis: Kind Of Blue Fontana TFL5072/STFL513 1960 £20
Miles Davis: Nefertiti CBS 63248 1968 £10
Duke Ellington: At Newport Philips BBL7133 1957 £15
Don Ellis: Electric Bath CBS 63230 1968 £15
Bill Evans: Portrait In Jazz Riverside RLP12315/1162 1959 £15
Gil Evans: Out Of The Cool HMV CLP1456 1961 £15
Stan Getz: Getz–Gilberto Verve VLP9065 1964 £12
Charlie Haden: Liberation Music Orchestra Probe SPB1037 1969 £20
Herbie Hancock: Maiden Voyage Blue Note BLP/BST84195 1966 £25
Charles Mingus: Mingus Ah Um Philips BBL7352 1960 £20
Charles Mingus: Mingus At Monterey Liberty LDS84002 1969 double £20
Thelonious Monk: Brilliant Corners London LTZU15097 1957 £25
Gerry Mulligan: Gerry Mulligan Quartet Vogue LAE12050 1957 £20
Charlie Parker/Quintet Of The Year: Jazz At Massey Hall Vogue LAE12031 1957 £100
Max Roach: Percussion Bitter Suite HMV CLP1522 1962 £12
Sonny Rollins: Saxophone Colossus Esquire 32045 1958 £25
Horace Silver: Song For My Father Blue Note BLP/BST84185 1964 £25
Cecil Taylor: Nefertiti, The Beautiful One Has Come Fontana SFJL926 1969 £20

Rock and pop music had become very diverse by the start of the seventies and became even more so as the decade proceeded. Progressive rock groups sought artistic satisfaction while disdaining the charts. One of them, Led Zeppelin, released no singles at all yet managed to become the most successful group in the world through album and concert ticket sales. As jazz artists like Miles Davis and Weather Report adopted rock rhythms and instrumentation, while rock groups like King Crimson and Colosseum incorporated lengthy improvised sections, it sometimes seemed quite difficult to tell the musics apart. Critics today continue to have something of a problem with progressive rock, although it is within this genre that many of the major collectors' items are to be found.

Of course, Led Zeppelin apart, the progressive musicians were never as generally popular as the glam rock groups. Attired in a range of elaborate and impractical costumes, Gary Glitter and the Sweet, David Bowie and T Rex held sway over the charts with their pop-rock fancies. Singer-songwriters were popular too, particularly in America, where the likes of Joni Mitchell and James Taylor were major stars. Adapted into a group setting and combined with country and modern rock'n'roll, this music developed into the kind of commercial easy-listening rock typified by the Eagles and Fleetwood Mac that Americans call AOR (adult oriented rock).

As a reaction to all of this, a growing back-to-basics pub-rock style provided a context for the eventual rock revolution that was punk. The Sex Pistols and the Clash changed many people's perceptions of how rock music should be put together, at least for a while, although its influence was perhaps ultimately less profound than that of the other seventies newcomer – disco. Evolving out of sixties soul, via the rhythmic funk workouts of James Brown and his disciples, disco set the ball rolling for the wealth of beat-based dance music that has followed. It also, through its fondness for extending the length of the dance experience, provided a music perfectly suited for a new format, the twelve-inch single, which became very popular at the end of the decade.

One artist, Bob Marley, succeeded in directing the focus of attention away from the UK and America for a while, and was responsible for making the sound and the rhythms of reggae into part of the basic rock music vocabulary. Abba managed something similar for Sweden, although their highly successful music was set firmly in the UK pop mould from the beginning.

The Rarest UK Singles of the Seventies

1. Queen: Bohemian Rhapsody EMI EMI2375 1978 blue vinyl, with envelope, boxed goblets and assorted other goodies £3000
2. T Rex: Ride A White Swan Octopus OCTO1 1970 test pressing £2000
3. Sex Pistols: God Save The Queen A&M AMS7284 1977 £1500
4. T Rex: Christmas Bop EMI MARC12 1975 £1000
5. Thin Lizzy: Farmer Irish Parlophone DIP513 1970 £750
6. XTC: 3D EP (Science Friction) Virgin VS188 1977 picture sleeve £750
7. Blondie: X Offender Private Stock PVT90 1977 £600
8. U2: Out Of Control (U2:3) Irish CBS 1979 brown vinyl £400
9. Black Sabbath: Children Of The Grave Phonogram DJ005 1974 promo with Status Quo B-side £350
10. Paul McCartney: Love Is Strange Apple R5932 1972 test pressing £350
11. John Lennon: Woman Is The Nigger Of The World Apple R5953 1972 demo only £350
12. T Rex: Chariot Choogle EMI SPRS346 1972 promo £300
13. Genesis: Looking For Someone Charisma GS1 1970 promo £300
14. Genesis: The Knife Charisma CB152 1971 picture sleeve £250
15. Genesis: Happy The Man CB181 1972 picture sleeve £250
16. Billy Harner: What About The Music Kama Sutra 2013029 1971 instrumental B-side £250

The Rarest UK Company LPs of the Seventies

1. Jimi Hendrix: The Cry Of Love Track 2408101 1971 red vinyl £1000
2. Paul McCartney: Back To The Egg Parlophone PCTCP257 1979 promo picture disc £1000
3. Beatles: Let It Be Parlophone PPCS7096 1970 export £750
4. Rolling Stones: History Of The Rolling Stones Decca ZAL12996–13001 1975 3 LP test pressings £750
5. Leafhound: Growers Of Mushrooms Decca SKLR5094 1971 £600
6. Marc Bolan: Hard On Love Track 2406101 1972 test pressing £500
7. Paul McCartney: MPL Presents Capitol no number 1979 promo 6 LP boxed set £500
8. Mellow Candle: Swaddling Songs Deram SDL7 1972 £500
9. Red Dirt: Red Dirt Fontana STL5540 1970 £500
10. Rolling Stones: Golden B-Sides Decca SKL5165 1973 test pressing £500
11. Rolling Stones: Live Stones Decca ROST3/4 1975 double test pressing £500
12. T Rex: Electric Warrior Fly HIFLY6 1971 test pressing with 'Jeepster' £500

13. Vashti Bunyan: Just Another Diamond Day Philips 6308019 1971 £400
14. Norman Haines: Den Of Iniquity Parlophone PCS7130 1971 £400
15. Who: Who Did It Track 2856001 1971 £350
16. Zakarrias: Zakarrias Deram SML1091 1971 £350

The Rarest UK Privately Pressed and Small Label LPs of the Seventies

1. Dark: Round The Edges S.I.S. SR0102S 1972 £1250
2. Elton John & Linda Peters: Warlock Sampler LP Warlock Music WMM101/2 1970 £1000
3. Spriguns Of Tolgus: Jack With A Feather Alida Star Cottage ASC7755A 1975 £1000
4. Five Day Rain: Five Day Rain private £750
5. Isolation: Isolation Riverside HASLP2083 1973 £750
6. Oberon: Midsummer Night's Dream Acorn no number 1971 £750
7. Various Artists: Samantha Promotions Vols. 1 & 2 Transworld SPLP101/2 1970 each £750
8. Charge: Charge SRT 1973 £600
9. Complex: Complex Halpix CLPM001 1970 £600
10. Complex: The Way We Feel Deroy 1971 £600
11. Ithaca: A Game For All Who Know Merlin HF6 1972 £600
12. Vulcan's Hammer: True Hearts And Sound Bottoms Brown BVH1 1973 £600

The Rarest US Company LPs of the Seventies

1. Bob Dylan: Blood On The Tracks Columbia PC33235 1974 test pressing with different versions of 5 tracks £2500
2. Brute Force: Extemporaneous B.T. Puppy BTPS1015 1971 £1000
3. Frank Zappa: Lather Columbia 41500 1976 4 LP test pressings £1000
4. Elvis Presley: International Hotel, Las Vegas, Presents Elvis Presley RCA LSP6020 boxed double with 7″ £500
5. Rolling Stones: Trident Mixes ABKCO PR164 1971 promo double £500
6. Fats Domino: Fats Reprise RS6439 1971 £300
7. Beatles: Beatles' Christmas Album Apple SBC100 1970 £200
8. David Bowie: Station To Station RCA APLI1327 1976 multicoloured vinyl £200
9. Kate Bush: Self-Portrait EMI SSA3020 1979 promo £200
10. George Harrison: Dark Horse Radio Special Dark Horse SP22002 1974 promo £200
11. Bruce Springsteen: Born To Run Columbia PC33795 1975 cover titles in script £200

The Rarest US Private and Small Label LPs of the Seventies

1. Dragonwyck: Dragonwyck private pressing 1972 £2000
2. Christopher: Whatcha Gonna Do Chris-tee PRP12411 1970 £1500
3. Damon: Song Of A Gypsy ANKH 1970 £1500
4. Mariani: Perpetuum Mobile Sonobeat 1004 1970s £1500
5. Phafner: Overdrive Dragon no number 1971 £1500
6. Apache: Maitreya Kali Akashic CF2777 1971 £1000
7. Azitis: Help Elco SCEC5555 1971 £1000
8. Bent Wind: Sussex Trend 1972 Canadian £1000
9. Big Lost Rainbow: Big Lost Rainbow private pressing 1973 £1000
10. Bolder Damn: Mourning private pressing 1971 £1000
11. Brigade: Last Laugh Band N Vocal 1066 1970 £1000
12. Fraction: Moon Blood Angelus 571 1971 £1000
13. Khazad Doom: Level Six And A Half LPL LPL892 1970 £1000
14. Kreed: Kreed! Visions Of Sound 7156 1971 £1000
15. Stonewall: Stonewall private pressing 1974 £1000

The Rarest European LPs of the Seventies

1. Elluffant: Release Concert Dutch Disko Thiel 1972 £1000
2. Lang'Syne: Lang'Syne German Dusselton TS2737 1976 £750
3. Les Gosses: 1 April 1963–31 Mei 1971 Dutch private pressing 1971 £750
4. Surprieze: Zeer Oude Klanken En Heel Nieuwe Geluiden Dutch private pressing 1973 £600
5. Avalanche: Perseverance Kills Our Game Dutch Starlet 1979 £500
6. Jam: From The Road Dutch private pressing 1976 £500
7. Necromonicon: Tips Zum Selbstmord German Best Prehodi F60634 1972 £500
8. Paul Van Der Ree: In The Balancing Of Night And Day Dutch Goldfish LP0001 1970 £500
9. Loudest Whisper: Children Of Lir Irish Polydor 1975 £400
10. Pacific Sound: Forget Your Dream Swiss Splendid 50104 1972 £400
11. Irish Coffee: Irish Coffee Belgian Triangle BE920321 1971 £350
12. David Bowie: The Man Who Sold The World German Mercury 6338041 1970 round sleeve £300
13. Oriental Sunshine: Dedicated To The Bird We Love Swedish Fontana 1971 £300
14. Mammut: Mammut German Mouse TTM5022 1971 £300
15. Fire: Could You Understand Me Dutch Killroy 1973 £250
16. Chicken Bones: Hard Rock In Concert German Procom 027606 £250
17. Fragile: Fragile Dutch private pressing 1976 £250
18. Old Man & The Sea: Old Man & The Sea Danish Sonet SLPS1539 1972 £250

The Rarest Folk LPs

1. Spriguns Of Tolgus: Jack With A Feather Alida Star Cottage ASC7755A 1975 £1000
2. Oberon: A Midsummer Night's Dream Acorn no number 1971 £750
3. Shide & Acorn: Under The Tree private pressing 1973 £500
4. Mushroom: Early One Morning Hawk HALPX116 with poster £350
5. Trevor Lucas: Overlander Reality RY1002 1966 £300
6. Tickawinda: Rosemary Lane Pennine PSS153 1975 £300
7. Barry Dransfield: Barry Dransfield Polydor 2383160 1972 £250
8. Fairport Convention: Full House Island ILPS9130 test pressing £250
9. Folkal Point: Folkal Point Midas MR003 1972 £250
10. Gospelfolk: Prodigal Emblem 7DR324 1969 £200
11. Christy Moore: Paddy On The Road Mercury 20170SMCL 1969 £200
12. Parcel Of Rogues And The Villagers: Parcel Of Folk Deroy 1973 £200
13. Ragged Heroes: Ragged Heroes Annual Celtic Music CM013 1983 £200
14. Silver Birch: Silver Birch Brayford BR02 1974 £200
15. Various Artists: Folk Centrum Utrecht 1970 Dutch private pressing £200
16. Stained Glass: Open Road Sweet Folk And Country SFA019 1975 £200
17. Booze Hoister Folk Group: The More You Booze, The Double You See Crossroad 1978 Dutch £200
18. Beggar's Hill: Beggar's Hill Moonshine MS60 1976 £200
19. Various Artists: Folk Centrum Utrecht 1969 Dutch private pressing £200

25 Progressive Rock Albums You Cannot Live Without

Blossom Toes: If Only For A Moment Marmalade 608010 1969 £75
Caravan: Caravan Verve (S)VLP6011 1968 stereo £75, mono £100
Colosseum: Daughter Of Time Vertigo 6360017 1970 £10
Comus: First Utterance Dawn DNLS3019 1971 £100
Culpeper's Orchard: Culpeper's Orchard German Polydor 2390006 1971 £100
East Of Eden: Snafu Deram SML1050 1970 £15

Egg: Egg Nova SDN14 1970 £15
Family: Family Entertainment Reprise R(S)LP6340 1969 stereo £15, mono £30
Gentle Giant: Octopus Vertigo 6360080 1972 £15
Gnidrolog: Lady Lake RCA SF8322 1972 £75
Gong: Shamal Virgin V2046 1976 £10
Hannibal: Hannibal B&C CAS1022 1970 £30
Jimi Hendrix: Electric Ladyland Track 613008/9 1968 double £50
King Crimson: In The Court Of The Crimson King Island ILPS9111 1969 £30
Mighty Baby: Mighty Baby Head HDLS6002 1969 £75
Pink Floyd: A Saucerful Of Secrets Columbia SX/SCX6258 1968 stereo £60, mono £150
Sandrose: Sandrose Polydor 2480137 1972 £125
Second Hand: Death May Be Your Santa Claus Mushroom 200MR6 1972 £100
Soft Machine: Third CBS 66246 1970 double £15
T2: It'll All Work Out In Boomland Decca SKL5050 1970 £50
Tonton Macoute: Tonton Macoute Neon NE4 1971 £50
Traffic: Traffic Island ILP981/ILPS9081 1968 stereo £15, mono £30
Van Der Graaf Generator: H To He Who Am The Only One Charisma CAS1027 1970 £12
Yes: The Yes Album Atlantic 2400101 1971 £12
Frank Zappa: Uncle Meat Transatlantic TRA197 1969 double with booklet £30

In the eighties, the heirs of punk continued trading under the banner 'new wave', but the original shock ethic was very quickly replaced by a keen pop sensibility. Different styles came and went in rapid succession as various influences were tried on for size as a main ingredient in the new wave sound – most notably reggae (UB40 and the Police), its sixties antecedent ska (Madness and the Specials) and glam rock, which was reborn with an eighties slant as the new romantic movement (Duran Duran and Spandau Ballet). Eventually, the new wave settled on a guitar-centred sound, as defined by the Smiths, and, known by now as indie music, it has hardly departed from this formula ever since.

Most significant, however, was the adoption of the synthesizer as a new staple instrument for rock. One of the leading post-punk outfits, Joy Division, switched almost entirely to a synthesizer-driven music as New Order, while a number of new groups emerged sporting just two active members, a synthesizer player and a singer. The rhythmic possibilities of the instrument were just as important as the ability to create soundscapes and, as the decade progressed, the first synthesizer-based dance tracks were produced. Associated with these developments was the changing role of record producers, some of whom began to take on a creative approach to record making rivalling that of the ostensible artists themselves. The key figure here was Trevor Horn, whose productions and multiple remixes for the group Frankie Goes To Hollywood were lovingly created extravaganzas that completely transcended the nature of the original song material.

In America, the rap groups found a new way to present the human voice, while a number of West Indian poets working in Britain achieved something similar with their music. At the same time, disc jockeys began to find a new role as performing musicians. Equipped with two or more turntables, these scratch mixers developed impressive techniques of record manipulation, thereby turning all their discs into sound effect libraries.

In contrast to these new experiments with keyboards, mixing desks and such, the most guitar-driven style of all, the heavy metal of Led Zeppelin and their contemporaries, underwent a considerable renaissance. Def Leppard and Iron Maiden presented the music in a stylized, theatrical form, with the latter group in particular making a connection with a kind of gothic cartoon horror. By the end of the decade, the association of heavy metal with violence was complete, with a number of grotesquely named groups competing to see who could produce the most raucous and extreme music.

Despite all of which, it is the Beatles, or the group's members, that continue to dominate the lists of the rarest records.

The Rarest UK Singles of the Eighties

1. Quarrymen: In Spite Of All The Danger Percy Phillips no number 1981 £5000
2. Manic Street Preachers: Suicide Alley SBS SD3002 1988 hand-made sleeve £500
3. Queen: Radio Ga Ga EMI QUEEN1 1984 video shoot proof sleeve £400
4. Manic Street Preachers: Suicide Alley SBS 002 1989 picture sleeve £400
5. Jean-Jacques Burnel: Girl From The Snow Country United Artists BP361 1980 £300
6. George Harrison & Vicki Brown: Shanghai Surprise Ganga Publishing SHANGHAI1 1986 promo only £300
7. George Harrison: Songs By George Harrison Genesis Publications SGH777 1988 issued with limited edition book £250
8. Smiths: Hand In Glove Rough Trade RT131 1987 silver photo on blue sleeve £250
9. Smiths: Reel Around The Fountain Rough Trade RT136 1983 test pressing £250
10. U2: 4 U2 Play CBS PAC1 1982 Irish, yellow vinyl 4 pack £250
11. Abba: Anniversary Boxed Set Epic ABBA26 1984 26 blue vinyl singles £200
12. Justified Ancients Of Mu Mu KLF JAMSDS1 1987 flexi £200
13. U2: Joshua Tree Collection Island U261–65 1987 promo 5 single set £200
14. Paul McCartney: All The Best Parlophone PMBOX11–19 1988 boxed set with autographed print £175
15. Paul McCartney: Boxed Set Of 9 Promo Singles Parlophone PMBOX1 1986 numbered and signed £150
16. Various Artists: Anniversary Issue Recommended RRR&RE 1985 15 single set £150
17. Jam: Beat Surrender Polydor PODJ540 1982 autographed double with handwritten lyrics £125
18. Madonna: Lucky Star Sire W9522 1983 sunglasses picture sleeve £125
19. Bruce Springsteen: Sherry Darling/Independence Day CBS A9568 1980 promo with picture sleeve £125
20. U2: I Will Follow Island 9065 1980 Irish, white vinyl £125

The Rarest LPs of the Eighties

1. Beatles: The Beatles At The Beeb BBC CN3970 1982 transcription disc £500
2. Kraftwerk: Technopop EMI EMC3407 1983 £500
3. Level 42: Strategy Elite LEVLP1 1981 test pressing only £400
4. Pet Shop Boys: Introspective Parlophone PCSX7325 1988 on 3 clear vinyl 12" singles £400
5. Queen: The Complete Works EMI QB1 1985 autographed 14 LP boxed set £400
6. Beatles: Original Master Records Mobile Fidelity 0575 1984 US audiophile 13 LP boxed set £350
7. Beatles: Beatles Collection Mobile Fidelity 1982 US audiophile 14 LP boxed set £300
8. Status Quo: From The Makers Of Phonogram PROBX1 1982 promo bronze tin £300
9. Various Artists: Psilotripitaka United Dairies UD134 1980s 4 LP set in leather bag £300
10. Beatles: Sgt Pepper's Lonely Hearts Club Band Mobile Fidelity UHQR1100 1982 US audiophile, quarter-inch-thick vinyl £200
11. David Bowie: Let's Dance RCA UK83 1983 numbered promo £200
12. David Bowie: Scary Monsters RCA BOWLP2 1980 purple vinyl £200
13. Kate Bush: Interview With Kate Bush EMI SPRO282 1985 Canadian promo £200

14. Coil: Gold Is The Metal Threshold House LOCI1 1988 boxed with 7″, poster and booklet in linen folder £200
15. Josef K: Sorry For Laughing Postcard 81–1 1981 test pressing with proof sleeve £200
16. Life After Life: Life After Life Time Track SRTSKL453 1985 £200
17. Nirvana: Bleach Tupelo TUPLP6 1989 white vinyl £200
18. Elvis Presley: Pure Elvis RCA DJL13455 1980 US promo £200
19. Ragged Heroes: Ragged Heroes Annual Celtic Music CM013 1983 £200
20. Rolling Stones: First Eight Studio Albums Decca ROLL1 boxed set of 8 LPs with book £200

The Rarest Picture Discs

1. Michael Jackson: Dangerous LP US Epic 1991 sample disc £1000
2. Paul McCartney: Back To The Egg LP Parlophone PCTCP257 1979 promo £1000
3. Madonna: Erotica Maverick W0138TP 12″ 1992 gold insert £500
4. Beatles: Abbey Road LP Apple PHO7088 1979 UK issue £250
5. Pink Floyd: First XI LP set Harvest PF11 1979 includes 2 picture discs not available separately £200
6. Queen: Jazz LP French EMI PIC3 1978 £200
7. Elvis Costello: My Aim Is True/This Year's Model LP US Columbia no number 1978 promo £150
8. Electric Light Orchestra: Xanadu 10″ LP US MCA 2315 1980 promo £150
9. Bruce Springsteen: Darkness On The Edge Of Town LP US Columbia PAL35318 1978 promo £125
10. Queen: Live At The BBC LP US Hollywood SPRO62005 1995 promo £100
11. Roxette: Look Sharp LP European EMI 1989 £100
12. Kate Bush: The Kick Inside LP EMI EMCP3223 same picture both sides 1978 £100
13. AC/DC: Japan Tour '81 LP Atlantic SAM155 1981 promo £75
14. Madonna: You Can Dance LP Sire PROMAD1 1987 promo £60
15. Culture Club: War Song 7″ Virgin VSY694 1984 £60

The Rarest CDs

1. Beatles: The Beatles At The Beeb Apple 1980s promotional only 140 CD set £3000
2. Nirvana: Penny Royal Tea Geffen no number 1994 promo only single £750
3. Kate Bush: Best Works 1978–1993 EMI SPCD1402/3 1994 Japanese promo double £500
4. Elton John: Plays The Siran Happenstance HAPP001 1993 private pressing £500
5. Elton John: Fishing Trip Happenstance HAPP002 1993 private pressing, 4 CD set £500
6. Rolling Stones: Pleasure Of Pain Rolling Stones XDDP930823 1990 Japanese promo double £500
7. Michael Jackson: Smile Epic 1997 withdrawn single £400
8. Oasis: Vox Box Creation no number 1997 9 single set in amplifier-shaped box £400
9. Queen: Highlander EMI EMCDV2 1986 CD video £400
10. U2: Rattle And Hum Island U27 1988 promo set with LP, CD & cassette £400
11. David Bowie: All Saints 1993 private pressing £300
12. Pearl Jam: Rarified And Live Epic SAMP656 1995 Australian promo double £300
13. U2: Achtung Baby Island U28 1991 promo set with CD and cassette £300
14. Various Artists: Psilotripitaka United Dairies UD134CD 1980s 4 CD set in leather bag £300
15. Beatles: Abbey Road Japanese Odeon CP353016 1986 £250
16. David Bowie: BBC Sessions 1969–1972 Sampler BBC NMCD0072 1996 promo only £250
17. George Harrison: Songs By George Harrison Genesis Publications SGHCD777 1988 issued with limited edition book £250

18. George Harrison: Songs By George Harrison Vol. 2 Genesis Publications SGHCD778 1992 issued with limited edition book £250
19. Pet Shop Boys: Pet Shop Boys Compiled Abbey Road 1993 autographed promo CD-R £250
20. Elvis Presley: Legend RCA PD89000 1983 boxed set of 3 gold or 3 silver discs £250
21. Rolling Stones: Out Of Tears Virgin VSCDG1524 1994 withdrawn single £250

Many of the musical strands from previous decades have been teased out and either improved or desecrated, depending on the listener's point of view, by artists in the nineties. Most notable has been a revival of interest in the mainstream of sixties music, led by successful artists like Oasis and Paul Weller. The spirit of punk too was revived, in the early years of the decade, and given a heavy-metal slant by groups like Nirvana, whose music became christened grunge. Singer-songwriters are back, with the likes of Sheryl Crow and Tori Amos receiving plaudits for their perceptive lyrics, just like their predecessors in the seventies. The indie bands, still sounding much like the Smiths, have to compete for concert-goers' money with tribute bands, who try to create a note-for-note facsimile of some great group that is no longer touring. The atmosphere of nostalgia has even encouraged many names from the past to have another go themselves, so that it sometimes seems as though virtually every hit-making artist from the sixties and early seventies who has not actually died can be seen playing live somewhere in the country. Meanwhile, of course, many of the biggest stars from the eighties – Madonna, Elton John and the rest – are still big stars in the nineties.

Of course, rock and pop music has a long history now, so that the different kinds of artist performing and recording in the nineties are often appealing to quite different audiences. And the fact that the market has grown so vast that it can accommodate various different genres from the past should not make anyone believe that the decade of the nineties has nothing new to offer for itself. Bands that consist entirely of singers, with completely anonymous backroom support, are very much a recent phenomenon. The sparkling pop produced by the likes of Take That, Boyzone and the Spice Girls does not just stand comparison with similarly conceived chart music from previous decades, it beats it hands down in terms of production, sound quality and sheer professionalism. Dance music, meanwhile, has grown in influence and authority to the point where its values touch almost every record made. Little escapes the attentions of the remix producer, who can draw on a range of computer-aided techniques and a whole new instrument, the sampler, to enhance the impact of a song. Anyone who doubts the reality of the skills employed has only to listen to 'Brimful Of Asher' by Cornershop or 'What Can I Do' by the Corrs in versions before and after remixing. When these studio wizards – people like Underworld, Massive Attack and Fatboy Slim – make their own records, the results are exciting and utterly contemporary.

It is, of course, a little too early to assess the nineties properly, but for this critic the decade's ability to draw on the music's considerable history, to filter it through modern technology, tie the whole thing together with a creativity that is timeless, and produce a result that could only have been achieved now is perfectly encapsulated by the experience, in early 1999, of seeing Björk on stage. Accompanied only by a string octet and a man standing behind a big black box, Björk delivered her own very personal version of the singer-songwriter's art. The music was, at times, as powerful as any piece of heavy metal and, at other times, as delicate as any folk song. And none of it could have been produced in any other decade than the nineties

Rarest Records of the Nineties

	Record	Value
1.	Kate Bush: Eat The Music 7″ EMI EM280 1993	£1000
2.	Michael Jackson: Dangerous LP US Epic 1991 sample picture disc	£1000
3.	Nirvana: Penny Royal Tea 7″ Geffen no number 1994 test pressing	£750
4.	Madonna: Erotica Maverick W0138TP 12″ 1992 picture disc, gold insert	£500
5.	Queen: Heaven For Everyone & 6 other titles 12″ Parlophone VIRGIN2–8 1996 1 sided Virgin Radio prizes each	£500
6.	Elton John: Club At The End Of The Street 7″ or 12″ Rocket EJS21(12) 1990	£400
7.	Kraftwerk: Kraftwerk 12″ EMI KLANG BOX 101 1997 4 single promo box set with T-shirt	£400
8.	Oasis: I Am The Walrus 12″ Creation CTP190 1994 promo only	£300
9.	Pet Shop Boys: Can You Forgive Her? 7″ Parlophone R6348 red vinyl 1993	£300
10.	George Harrison: Songs By George Harrison Vol. 2 7″ Genesis SGH778 1992 with limited-edition book	£250
11.	Oasis: Columbia 12″ Creation CTP8 1993 1 sided promo	£250
12.	Queen: The Show Must Go On/Bohemian Rhapsody 7″ Parlophone QUEEN19/20 1991 no picture sleeve	£250
13.	Take That: The Yellow Tape cassette private issue 1990	£250
14.	Prodigy: Minefields XL XLT76 12″ 1996 test pressing only	£200
15.	U2: Best Of 1980–1990 LP Island 1998 promo boxed set of 14 singles	£200

The chart below shows how the values of a fairly random assortment of collectable records from different genres have changed over the years. The 1986 values are taken from sales lists of the time – the majority being from those of the author's own shop, Pied Piper Records, which opened in 1986. The subsequent values for these records are those printed in each of the successive Nick Hamlyn *Price Guides*.

The Changing Fortunes of Some Collectable Records

1986 values	PG1 1991	PG2 1992	PG3 1994	PG4 1997	PG5 2000
Fifties					
Jimmy Bowen: Meet Jimmy Bowen EP					
£20	£20	£30	£50	£50	£60
Cadets: Stranded In The Jungle 7″					
£60	£70	£150	£150	£350	£400
Bobby Darin: Queen Of The Hop 7″					
£6	£8	£8	£20	£20	£20
Elvis Presley: Good Rocking Tonight EP					
£40	£40	£50	£90	£100	£100
Billy Ward & The Dominoes: Three Coins In A Fountain					
£40	£50	£60	£75	£100	£100
Mac Wiseman: Step It Up And Go 7″					
£40	£40	£60	£120	£250	£250

1986 values	PG1 1991	PG2 1992	PG3 1994	PG4 1997	PG5 2000

Sixties

Mike Berry: Tribute To Buddy Holly EP
£10 £10 £20 £20 £25 £30

Blues Magoos: Psychedelic Lollipop LP
£15 £20 £20 £25 £40 £50

David Bowie: Man Who Sold The World dress cover LP
£150 £150 £170 £170 £200 £200

David Bowie: Memory Of A Free Festival 7″
£75 £80 £80 £80 £150 £150

Manfred Mann: Mann Made LP
£8 £15 £15 £15 £20 £20

Move: Something Else EP
£20 £20 £25 £25 £25 £30

Pink Floyd: Apples And Oranges 7″
£10 £10 £10 £20 £25 £30

Sam Apple Pie: Sam Apple Pie LP
£10 £30 £70 £70 £75 £75

Sands: Mrs Gillespie's Refrigerator 7″
£8 £10 £60 £75 £125 £125

Skip Bifferty: Skip Bifferty LP
£15 £50 £50 £75 £75 £75

Who: Sell Out stereo LP
£15 £20 £20 £20 £30 £30

Soul

Martha & The Vandellas: Riding High LP
£12 £12 £12 £12 £12 £15

Mike & The Modifiers: I Found Myself A Brand New Baby 7″
£100 £120 £180 £400 £600 £600

Miracles: Hi We're The Miracles LP
£35 £40 £50 £60 £100 £125

Edwin Starr: 25 Miles LP
£10 £12 £12 £12 £12 £15

Supremes: Hits EP
£7.50 £8 £10 £10 £10 £15

Progressive

Audience: Audience LP
£30 £70 £70 £70 £60 £60

Clark–Hutchinson: A=MH2 LP
£6 £15 £15 £15 £15 £25

Gnidrolog: Lady Lake LP
£15 £60 £60 £60 £75 £75

Jade Warrior: Last Autumn's Dream LP
£10 £30 £30 £30 £30 £30

1986 values	PG1 1991	PG2 1992	PG3 1994	PG4 1997	PG5 2000
July: July LP					
£75	£200	£300	£300	£300	£300
Writing On The Wall: Power Of The Picts LP					
£40	£80	£130	£130	£125	£125

New Wave

Alarm: Unsafe Buildings 7"					
£40	£60	£80	£50	£40	£40
Cure: Charlotte Sometimes 12"					
£15	£15	£15	£12	£12	£12
Johnny & The Self-Abusers: Saints & Sinners 7"					
£8	£12	£15	£10	£10	£10
U2: Unforgettable Fire shaped picture disc					
£12	£12	£20	£20	£15	£25

A comparison between the New Wave section of the above chart and the other sections suggests that, in general, it is the older collectors' records that provide the best investment. Of course, buying records with their investment potential in mind is an activity particularly fraught with danger. At least in the case of long-established rarities, it is possible to make some kind of guess as to their likely direction of movement in the future. Certainly in the medium term, original doo-wop singles, to name one obvious example, are unlikely to have peaked in value yet. With more recent recordings, however, the whole collecting arena is much more problematic. Values of such items are particularly susceptible to changes in fashion. At the time of writing, for instance, the Manic Street Preachers are riding on a crest of both cult and general popularity, with a consequential large rise in the values of the group's earliest and rarest records. Arguably, this popularity is well deserved. It is almost inevitable, however, that it will decline in the next few years and it is extremely likely, therefore, that the group's most collectable records will not retain their present values. The examples given in the cases of All About Eve, Jesus And Mary Chain, the Orb and Take That, all of whom were much more popular and collectable a few years ago than they are now, are typical. (The increase in the number of items for some artists in the fourth *Price Guide* is due to the addition of several CD-singles for the first time.)

Collecting Modern Artists as an Investment?

All About Eve

PG1 33 items: D For Desire 12" £60; In The Clouds 12" with poster £40
PG2 34 items: D For Desire 12" £60; In The Clouds 12" with poster £50
PG3 12 items: D For Desire 12" £40; In The Clouds 12" with poster £25
PG4 20 items: D For Desire 12" £30; In The Clouds 12" with poster £20
PG5 13 items: D For Desire 12" £15; In The Clouds 12" with poster £12

Jesus And Mary Chain

PG1 14 items: Upside Down 12" demo £80; Just Like Honey 7" double £10
PG2 17 items: Upside Down 12" demo £80; Just Like Honey 7" double £10
PG3 12 items: Upside Down 12" demo £50; Just Like Honey 7" double £6
PG4 18 items: Upside Down 12" demo £50; Just Like Honey 7" double £6
PG5 16 items: Upside Down 12" demo £30; Just Like Honey 7" double £5

The Orb

PG1 0 items
PG2 8 items: Perpetual Dawn remix 12" £10

PG3 29 items: Perpetual Dawn remix 12″ £8; Huge Ever Growing 12″ £40 (Orbital Dance Mix)

PG4 29 items: Perpetual Dawn remix 12″ £8; Huge Ever Growing 12″ £30 (Orbital Dance Mix)

PG5 23 items: Perpetual Dawn remix 12″ not included; Huge Ever Growing 12″ £20 (Orbital Dance Mix)

Take That

PG1 0 items

PG2 0 items

PG3 3 items: Once You've Tasted Love 12″ pic disc £20

PG4 24 items: Once You've Tasted Love 12″ pic disc £25; Do What U Like 12″ £40

PG5 24 items: Once You've Tasted Love 12″ pic disc £15; Do What U Like 12″ £15

Manic Street Preachers

PG1 0 items

PG2 9 items: Suicide Alley with pic sleeve 7″ £50; Feminine Is Beautiful 7″ £12

PG3 9 items: Suicide Alley with pic sleeve 7″ £70; Feminine Is Beautiful 7″ £15

PG4 14 items: Suicide Alley with pic sleeve 7″ £100; Feminine Is Beautiful 7″ £15

PG5 59 items: Suicide Alley with pic sleeve 7″ £400; Feminine Is Beautiful 7″ £100

Labels

ACTION

Action was a specialist soul label, whose singles issued in 1968 and 1969 (with a distinctive red and black label bearing a shooting star logo) are all very much in demand. Soul collectors, more than those in other fields, tend to prefer demo copies of singles, arguing that these are the true first pressings. This is particularly true of the Action label, where demos typically have a value of three times that of the standard issues.

ACT4500 Wilmer & The Dukes: Give Me One More Chance £4
ACT4501 Little Carl Carlton: Competition Ain't Nothing £15
ACT4502 Ernie K. Doe: Dancing Man £5
ACT4503 Minnie Epperson: Grab Your Clothes £6
ACT4504 Buddy Ace: Got To Get Myself Together £5
ACT4505 O. V. Wright: Oh Baby Mine £8
ACT4506 Al 'TNT' Braggs: Earthquake £5
ACT4507 Harmonica Fats: Tore Up £8
ACT4508 Vernon Garrett: Shine It On £4
ACT4509 Bobby Williams: Baby I Need Your Love £15
ACT4510 Bell Brothers: Tell Him No £5
ACT4511 John Roberts: I'll Forget About You £6
ACT4512 Ernie K. Doe: Gotta Pack My Bags £4
ACT4513 Brothers Two: Here I Am In Love Again £5
ACT4514 Little Carl Carlton: 46 Drums 1 Guitar £4
ACT4515 Roosevelt Grier: People Make The World £4
ACT4516 Rubaiyats: Omar Khayam £5
ACT4517 Chuck Chuck: Call On You £5
ACT4518 Roy Lee Johnson: So Anna Just Love Me £5
ACT4519 Eddie Buster Forehand: Young Boy Blues £5
ACT4520 Alice Clarke: You Got A Deal £5
ACT4522 Dee Dee Sharp: What Kinda Lady £20
ACT4523 Intruders: Slow Drag £8
ACT4524 Bobby Bland: Rockin' In The Same Old Boat £6
ACT4525 Della Humphrey: Don't Make The Good Girls So Bad £4
ACT4526 Al 'TNT' Braggs: I'm A Good Man £4
ACT4527 O. V. Wright: I Want Everyone To Know £5
ACT4528 Little Richard: Baby What You Want Me To Do £5
ACT4529 Norman Johnson: You're Everything £10
ACT4531 Melvin Davis: Save It £10
ACT4532 Z. Z. Hill: Make Me Yours £10
ACT4533 Bobby Marchan: Ain't No Reason For Girls To Be Lonely £5
ACT4534 Jeanette Williams: Stuff £8
ACT4535 Betty Harris: Ride Your Pony £6
ACT4536 Eddie Wilson: Shing A Ling A Stroll £6
ACT4537 Little Carl Carlton: Look At Mary Wonder £5

ACT4538 Bobby Bland: Gotta Get To Know You £10
ACT4539 Olympics: Baby Do The Philly Dog £5
ACT4540 Al Green: Don't Hurt Me No More £4
ACT4541 Brenda & The Tabulations: That's In The Past £12
ACT4542 Barbara Mason: Slipping Away £8
ACT4543 Fantastic Johnny C: New Love £4
ACT4544 Hideaways: Hideout £4
ACT4545 Norman Johnson: Take It Baby £15
ACT4547 Eddie Holman: I Surrender £25
ACT4548 Bobby Bland: Share Your Love With Me £6
ACT4549 Clifford Curry: She Shot A Hole In My Soul £4
ACT4550 Clifton Chenier: Black Girl £4
ACT4551 Gene Chandler: I Can't Save It £20
ACT4552 Performers: I Can't Stop You £5
ACT4553 Bobby Bland: Chains Of Love £6
ACT4555 Eddie Wilson: Get Out On The Street £4
ACT4556 Olympics: I'll Do A Little Bit More £5
ACT4557 Jeanette Williams: Hound Dog £8

These are the collectable singles on the revived Action label from 1971–4:

ACT4601 Norman Johnson: You're Everything £6
ACT4602 Billy Sharae: Do It £4
ACT4603 Bobbettes: That's A Bad Thing To Know £6
ACT4604 Bobby Patterson: I'm In Love With You £6
ACT4605 Hoagy Lands: Why Didn't You Let Me Know £4
ACT4607 Joe S. Maxey: Sign Of The Crab £5
ACT4616 Backyard Heavies: Just Keep On Truckin' £5
ACT4621 Tom Green: Rock Springs Railroad Station £10
ACT4622 Bobbi Houston: I Want To Make It With You £5
ACT4624 Wee Willie & The Winners: Get Some £5

There are also a few Action LPs:

ACLP6001 Fantastic Johnny C: Boogaloo Down Broadway £15
ACLP6002 Barbara Mason: Oh How It Hurts £25
ACLP6003 Brenda & The Tabulations: Dry Your Eyes £20
ACLP6004 Z. Z. Hill: Whole Lot Of Soul £20
ACLP6005 Various Artists: Action Packed Soul £15
ACLP6006 Bobby Bland: Piece Of Gold £20
ACLP6007 Betty Harris: Soul Perfection £20
ACLP6008 Al Green: Back Up Train £20
ACLP6009 Various Artists: These Kind Of Blues Vol.1 £15
ACLP6010 Gene Chandler: Live On Stage £25
ACLP6011 Jimmy Reed: Down In Virginia £20
ACMP100 Eddie 'Guitar' Burns: Bottle Up And Go £12

APPLE

The label set up and run by the Beatles is viewed as a legitimate area of interest by Beatles collectors. Quite apart from the records of the Beatles themselves, there are a few considerable rarities on the label, by such names as the Iveys, Delaney and Bonnie, Richard Brautigan and

John Tavener. The enormous musical range represented by these and the other names on the label reflects the fact that the Beatles were wealthy enough to issue whatever music took their individual fancies, without commercial success being a particular consideration. The records issued by the Beatles themselves from 1968 onwards were on the Apple label as far as label design was concerned, but the catalogue numbers were actually part of the main Parlophone series.

The original sequence of Apple label singles from 1968 to 1974 is as follows:

(no number) Beatles and other artists: Our First Four promo pack with 4 x 7″ £750
CT1 Various Artists: Walls Ice Cream Presents EP £40
1001 John Lennon: Cold Turkey picture sleeve £10; Dutch or promo two skulls picture sleeve £200
1002 John Lennon: You Know My Name test pressing £1500
1003 John Lennon: Instant Karma picture sleeve £6
3 Jackie Lomax: Sour Milk Sea £5
4 Black Dyke Mills Band: Thingumybob £25
5 Iveys: Maybe Tomorrow £25
6 White Trash: Road To Nowhere £8
7 Mary Hopkin: Lontana Dagli Occhi European £6
8 Brute Force: King Of Fuh £400
9 Mary Hopkin: Prince En Avignon European £6
11 Jackie Lomax: New Day £8
12 Billy Preston: That's The Way God Planned It £4 picture sleeve £6
13 John Lennon: Give Peace A Chance picture sleeve £6
14 Iveys: Dear Angie European £150
15 Radha Krishna Temple: Hare Krishna Mantra £5; picture sleeve, insert £12
17 Trash: Golden Slumbers £8
18 Hot Chocolate: Give Peace A Chance £20
20 Badfinger: Come And Get It picture sleeve £4
21 Billy Preston: All That I've Got picture sleeve £10
23 Jackie Lomax: How The Web Was Woven picture sleeve £8
24 Doris Troy: Ain't That Cute £4 picture sleeve £8
25 Radha Krishna Temple: Govinda picture sleeve £10
27 Mary Hopkin: Qué Será Será European £6
28 Doris Troy: Jacob's Ladder £5
30 Mary Hopkin: Think About Your Children picture sleeve £4
31 Badfinger: No Matter What picture sleeve £8
32 James Taylor: Carolina In My Mind £5
33 Ronnie Spector: Try Some Buy Some picture sleeve £20
34 Mary Hopkin: Let My Name Be Sorrow picture sleeve £8
36 Bill Elliott & The Elastic Oz Band: God Save Us £6 picture sleeve £15
37 Ravi Shankar: Joi Bangla picture sleeve £8
38 Yoko Ono: Mrs Lennon £8
39 Mary Hopkin: Water, Paper And Clay picture sleeve £12
40 Badfinger: Day After Day picture sleeve £6
41 Yoko Ono: Mind Train £5 picture sleeve £12
43 Chris Hodge: We're On Our Way picture sleeve £15
44 Sundown Playboys: Saturday Night Special picture sleeve £15; promo 78 £200
46 Lon & Derrek Van Eaton: Warm Woman £4; picture sleeve £25
47 Yoko Ono: Death Of Samantha £10
48 Yoko Ono: Run Run Run £12
49 Badfinger: Apple Of My Eye £8

And the albums:

CORE2001 John Lennon & Yoko Ono: Live Peace In Toronto with calendar £50
(S)APCOR1 George Harrison: Wonderwall mono £60; stereo £25
(S)APCOR2 John Lennon & Yoko Ono: Unfinished Music No.1: Two Virgins mono £750; stereo £200
(S)APCOR3 James Taylor: James Taylor mono £30; stereo £12
(S)APCOR4 Modern Jazz Quartet: Under The Jasmine Tree mono £40; stereo £30
(S)APCOR5 Mary Hopkin: Postcard mono £12; stereo £10
(S)APCOR6 Jackie Lomax: Is This What You Want mono £30; stereo £15
SAPCOR7 Delaney & Bonnie: Accept No Substitute test pressing, no sleeve £600
SAPCOR8 Iveys: Maybe Tomorrow European £250
SAPCOR9 Billy Preston: That's The Way God Planned It £15
SAPCOR10 Modern Jazz Quartet: Space single or gatefold sleeve £30
SAPCOR11 John Lennon & Yoko Ono: Wedding Album boxed, inserts £150
SAPCOR12 Badfinger: Magic Christian Music £30
SAPCOR13 Doris Troy: Doris Troy £20
SAPCOR14 Billy Preston: Encouraging Words £20
SAPCOR15 John Tavener: The Whale £40
SAPCOR16 Badfinger: No Dice £30
SAPCOR17 Yoko Ono: Plastic Ono Band £30
SAPCOR18 Radha Krishna Temple: Radha Krishna Temple £30
SAPCOR19 Badfinger: Straight Up £30
SAPCOR20 John Tavener: Celtic Requiem £125
SAPCOR21 Mary Hopkin: Earth Song/Ocean Song £15
SAPCOR22 Elephant's Memory: Elephant's Memory £10
SAPCOR23 Mary Hopkin: Those Were The Days £60
APCOR24 Phil Spector: Christmas Album £15
SAPCOR25 Lon & Derrek Van Eaton: Brother with insert £25
SAPCOR26 Yoko Ono: Feeling The Space £25
SAPCOR27 Badfinger: Ass £20
SAPDO1001 Yoko Ono: Approximately Infinite Universe double £12
SAPDO1002 Ravi Shankar: In Concert 1972 double £100
SPTU101/2 Yoko Ono: Fly LP double £30
ZAPPLE1 John Lennon & Yoko Ono: Unfinished Music No.2: Life With The Lions £60; with card insert £75
ZAPPLE2 George Harrison: Electronic Sound £50
ZAPPLE03 Richard Brautigan: Listening To Richard Brautigan test pressing £250

US Apple albums unreleased in the UK:

SWAO3384 Ravi Shankar: Raga £20
SWAO3388 Alexandro Jodorowsky: El Topo £15
SW3391 David Peel & The Lower East Side The Pope Smokes Dope £15

ATLANTIC

The Atlantic label's status as one of the most successful independents (until its incorporation within the Kinney organization in 1971) depended on the skill with which its founders, the Ertegun brothers, were able to identify the key developments in jazz and R&B. In the UK, Atlantic releases were originally distributed via the London label, but from 1964 the Atlantic label was issued in its own right. Identification of original pressings is not a problem, since

Atlantic obligingly used new catalogue numbers whenever a reissue was made. In particular, the Kinney take-over resulted in the use of a 'K' as prefix to all UK catalogue numbers – so that, *Led Zeppelin IV*, for example, changed from 2401012 to K50008. (There was also a label design change at this time, with the red and plum LP labels becoming green and orange.)

BLUE HORIZON

Producer Mike Vernon formed the Blue Horizon label as an outlet for his beloved blues music and virtually the entire catalogue is now collectable (the label's one sore thumb, an album by the group Focus, just makes it by the skin of its teeth). The very earliest records to make use of the Blue Horizon name were ten singles and a pair of albums (one by Dr Ross and one a various artists collection) that were sold by mail order in 1965–6. The albums in particular are now extremely rare. In 1967 the signing of Peter Green's new group, Fleetwood Mac, prompted a distribution deal with CBS. The first single releases by Fleetwood Mac and Aynsley Dunbar bore a Blue Horizon logo on an orange CBS label, but by the start of 1968 the familiar light blue label was in use.

The Blue Horizon singles are as follows:

451000 Hubert Sumlin: Across The Board £100
451001 Woodrow Adams: Baby You Just Don't Know £100
451002 George Harmonica Smith: Blues In The Dark £100
451003 Snooky & Moody: Snooky And Moody's Blues £100
451004 J. B. Lenoir: Mojo Boogie £100
451005 Drifting Slim: Good Morning Baby £100
451006 Houston Boines: Superintendant Blues £100
451007 Champion Jack Dupree: Get Your Head Happy (with T. S. McPhee) £100
451008 Sonny Boy Williamson: From The Bottom £100
451009 Eddie Eddie: It's So Miserable To Be Alone £100
453109 Aynsley Dunbar: Warning picture sleeve £30 (£12 without)
573051 Fleetwood Mac: I Believe My Time Ain't Long picture sleeve £40 (£6 without)
573135 Chicken Shack: It's OK With Me Baby £6
573136 Arthur K. Adams: She Drives Me Out Of My Mind £10
573137 Eddie Boyd: Big Boat £12
573138 Fleetwood Mac: Black Magic Woman £5
573139 Fleetwood Mac: Need Your Love So Bad £4
573140 Champion Jack Dupree: I Haven't Done No One No Harm £10
573141 Duster Bennett: It's A Man Down There £6
573142 Otis Spann: Can't Do Me No Good £6
573143 Chicken Shack: Worried About My Woman £6
573144 B. B. King: Woman I Love £8
573145 Fleetwood Mac: Albatross £4
573146 Chicken Shack: When The Train Comes Back £4
573147 Buster Brown: Sugar Babe £10
573148 Duster Bennett: Raining In My Heart £8
573149 Guitar Crusher & Jimmy Spruill: Since My Baby Hit The Numbers £15
573150 Garfield Love & Jimmy Spruill: Next Time You See Me £15
573151 Bobby Parker: It's Hard But It's Fair £20
573152 Champion Jack Dupree: Ba' La Fouche £10
573153 Chicken Shack: I'd Rather Go Blind £4
573154 Duster Bennett: Bright Lights, Big City £6
573155 Otis Spann: Walkin' (with Fleetwood Mac) £10
573156 Gordon Smith: Too Long £8

573157 Fleetwood Mac: Need Your Love So Bad £4
573158 Champion Jack Dupree: I Want To Be A Hippy £10
573159 Otis Rush: All Your Love £10
573160 Chicken Shack: Tears In The Wind £4
573161 B. B. King: Every Day I Have The Blues £8
573162 Jellybread: Chairman Mao's Boogaloo £5
573163 Juke Boy Bonner: Runnin' Shoes £15
573164 Duster Bennett: I'm Gonna Wind Up Endin' Up £10
573165 Christine Perfect: When You Say £6
573166 Earl Hooker: Boogie Don't Blot £15
573167 Top Topham: Christmas Cracker £10
573168 Chicken Shack: Maudie £4
573169 Jellybread: Comment £5
573170 George Harmonica Smith: Someday You're Gonna Learn £10
573171 Bacon Fat: Nobody But You £5
573172 Christine Perfect: I'm Too Far Gone £8
573173 Duster Bennett: I Chose To Sing The Blues £5
573174 Jellybread: Rockin' Pneumonia & The Boogie Woogie Flu £5
573175 Slim Harpo: Folsom Prison Blues £15
573176 Chicken Shack: Sad Clown £4
573177 Kelly Brothers: That's What You Mean To Me £15
573178 Key Largo: Voodoo Rhythm £8
573179 Duster Bennett: Act Nice And Gentle £5
573180 Jellybread: Old Man Hank £5
573181 Bacon Fat: Evil £5
2096001 Jellybread: Creeepin' And Crawlin' £5
2096002 Marshall Hooks & Co: I Want The Same Thing Tomorrow £8
2096003 Mighty Baby: Devil's Whisper £40
2096004 Focus: Hocus Pocus £5
2096005 Fugi: Red Moon £12
2096006 Jellybread: Down Along The Cove £6
2096007 Mike Vernon: Let's Try It Again £15
2096008 Focus: Tommy £6
2096009 Michigan Rag: Don't Run Away £10
2096010 Martha Velez: Boogie Kitchen £8
2096013 Lightnin' Slim: Just A Little Bit £15

These are the Blue Horizon albums:

LP1 Dr Isaiah Ross: Flying Eagle £600
LP2 Various Artists: Let Me Tell You About The Blues £250
763200 Fleetwood Mac: Fleetwood Mac mono £30; stereo £25
763201 Roosevelt Holts: Presenting The Country Blues £40
763202 Eddie Boyd: 7936 South Rhodes £60
763203 Chicken Shack: 40 Blue Fingers Freshly Packed And Ready To Serve £30
763204 Elmore James & John Brim: Tough £30
763205 Fleetwood Mac: Mr Wonderful £25
763206 Champion Jack Dupree: When You Feel The Feeling You Was Feeling £50
763207 Curtis Jones: Now Resident In Europe £40
763208 Duster Bennett: Smiling Like I'm Happy £30
763209 Chicken Shack: O.K. Ken? £25
763210 Various Artists: 1968 Memphis Country Music Festival £30

763211 Gordon Smith: Long Overdue £40
763212 Johnny Shines: Last Night's Dream £50
763213 Sunnyland Slim: Midnight Jump £40
763214 Champion Jack Dupree: Scooby Dooby Doo £50
763215 Fleetwood Mac: Pious Bird Of Good Omen £15
763216 B. B. King: B. B. King Story Vol. 1 £40
763217 Otis Spann: Biggest Thing Since Colossus (with Fleetwood Mac) £60
763218 Chicken Shack: 100 Ton Chicken £25
763221 Duster Bennett: Bright Lights £40
763222 Otis Rush: This One's A Good Un £50
763223 Magic Sam: Magic Sam 1937–69 £50
763226 B. B. King: B. B. King Story Vol. 2 £40
763227 Mississippi Joe Callicott: Presenting The Country Blues £30
763228 Furry Lewis: Presenting The Country Blues £50
763229 Bukka White: Memphis Hot Shots £40
763850 Earl Hooker: Sweet Black Angel £75
763851 Larry Johnson: Presenting The Country Blues £40
763852 Johnny Young: Fat Mandolin £50
763853 Jellybread: First Slice £25
763854 Slim Harpo: He Knew The Blues £50
763855 Arthur Crudup: Mean Ole Frisco £40
763856 George Harmonica Smith: No Time To Jive £60
763857 Top Topham: Ascension Heights £75
763858 Bacon Fat: Grease One For Me £30
763859 Key Largo: Key Largo £20
763860 Christine Perfect: Christine Perfect £40
763861 Chicken Shack: Accept £25
763863 Lightnin' Slim: Rooster Blues £50
763864 Lonesome Sundown: Lonesome Lonely Blues £50
763866 Jellybread: 65 Parkway £25
763867 Martha Velez: Fiends And Angels Again £40
763868 Duster Bennett: 12 dBs £25
763875 Fleetwood Mac: Original Fleetwood Mac £10
766227 Fleetwood Mac and other artists: Blues Jam At Chess double £40
766230 Elmore James: To Know A Man double £50
766263 Various Artists: Swamp Blues double £40
2431001 Bacon Fat: Tough Dude £40
2431002 Jellybread: 65 Parkway £20
2431003 Marshall Hooks & Co: Marshall Hooks & Co. £40
2431004 B. B. King: Take A Swing With Me £40
2431005 Lightnin' Hopkins: Let's Work Awhile £60
2431006 Rick Hayward: Rick Hayward £60
2431007 Lazy Lester: Made Up My Mind £60
2431008 Silas Hogan: Trouble At Home £50
2431009 Whalefeathers: Whalefeathers £40
2431012 Arthur Gunter: Blues After Hours £40
2431013 Billy Harner: Trigger Finger £12
2431013 Slim Harpo: Trigger Finger £60
2431015 Whispering Smith: Over Easy £40
2683007 Various Artists: Excello Story double £60
2931001 Mighty Baby: Jug Of Love £75
2931002 Focus: Moving Waves with poster £10

2931003 Mike Vernon: Bring It Back Home £60
2931004 Jellybread: Back To Begin Again £60
2931005 Lightnin' Slim: London Gumbo £50
PR31 Various Artists: Super Duper Blues £12
PR37 Various Artists: In Our Own Way/Oldies But Goodies £15
PR45/46 Various Artists: How Blue Can We Get? double £20

BLUE NOTE

Blue Note is the most collected jazz label in the UK, with every sixties release being of value (and listed in the *Guide*). The label was founded in 1939 in the US, and the earliest album releases now command high prices. A mint copy of *Genius Of Modern Music Vol. 1* by Thelonious Monk (Blue Note BLP5002 1951) sells for £250, for example. Starting in 1961, records released on the label became available in the UK as direct imports. Within this *Guide*, the issue date given often refers to the date of import rather than to the actual release date in the US, which may well have been a few years earlier (this is true for all of the LPs in the BLP15 series). These original US pressings will be worth significantly more than the values listed, which apply to the import copies. Original Blue Note records issued during 1961–6 have a blue and white label design with the legend 'Blue Note Records Inc ★ New York USA'; from 1966 to 1970 the legend 'A Division Of Liberty Records' appears. The same label design reappeared in 1985, but apart from the fact that the reissues from this time have a generally newer appearance, they also carry the new wording 'The Finest In Jazz Since 1939'.

CAPITOL

Capitol singles had purple labels in the fifties and black in the sixties. The LPs had turquoise labels in the fifties and black labels with a rainbow border in the sixties. In 1968, the rainbow border was dropped for a short time, before the company switched to a lime green label, with a new deep pink logo.

CBS

The label that is called Columbia in the US became abbreviated to CBS in the UK (standing for Columbia Broadcasting Systems) to avoid conflict with the UK Columbia label, whose links with its American ancestor became severed during the fifties. The plain orange labels used by CBS on both its singles and LPs in 1962, when the first UK records were released, remained essentially unchanged until 1975, when a new label on which orange shaded into yellow was introduced. As a result, the label design is of limited use in identifying original pressings of records by the likes of Bob Dylan. (The rear fold-over sixties cover design, however, remains a reliable guide in these circumstances.) The BPG prefix used for LPs (SBPG for stereo) was dropped at the start of 1968 and reissues from that date onwards have their catalogue numbers amended accordingly.

CHARISMA

The Charisma label began in 1969 as something of a progressive rock specialist label. Most of the early albums are collectable, although the label lacked the sureness of touch of Island or Vertigo, and a few releases are hardly sought after at all. Until 1972, the label design featured a large scroll logo on a deep-pink background and first pressings of early albums by the likes of Audience, Van Der Graaf Generator and Genesis have this label. A new design, featuring a cartoon mad hatter on a pale-pink label, began with the album *Foxtrot* by Genesis (CAS1058).

Albums bearing this label but with lower catalogue numbers are therefore second issues and are worth no more than 50 per cent of the first issue values.

COLUMBIA

Labels for the main Columbia SX series were green with gold print until 1963, when they were changed to match the style of EMI's sister label, Parlophone. From 1963 to 1969, this resulted in a black label with silver print and a blue 'Columbia' logo; from 1969 the 'EMI' logo was added to a redesigned black and silver label, with a silver 'Columbia' logo now appearing in a box. Singles also changed from a green to a black label in 1963, with some earlier singles being given later, black label, reissues. Much later reissues using a very similar design to the original green label are easily identifiable by the references to EMI, which are not present on the early labels.

DANDELION

The Dandelion label was set up and co-financed by disc jockey John Peel in 1969 to enable him to promote the work of artists he felt were worthy of wider exposure, but who may have found some difficulty in gaining record contracts with anyone else! None of the records sold particularly well and the entire catalogue is now collectable. Initially the label was distributed by CBS – the labels for these issues are crimson overlaid with dandelion seed parachutes. In 1971, distribution was taken over by Warner Brothers, whose new label design featured a multi-coloured picture of dandelion flowers on a beige background. None of the CBS records was reissued by Warner Brothers. The label folded in 1972.

These are the albums:

63750 Bridget St John: Ask Me No Questions £25
63751 Beau: Beau £20
63752 Principal Edward's Magic Theatre: Soundtrack £15
63753 Occasional Word Ensemble: Year Of The Great Leap Sideways £15
63754 Gene Vincent: I'm Back & I'm Proud £20
63755 Siren: Siren £15
63756 Mike Hart: Mike Hart Bleeds £15
63757 Medicine Head: New Bottles Old Medicine £20
69001 Lol Coxhill: Ear Of Beholder double £40
DAN8001 Siren: Strange Locomotion £15
DAN8002 Principal Edward's Magic Theatre: Asmoto Running Band £12
DAN8004 Way We Live: Candle For Judith £100
DAN8005 Medicine Head: Heavy On The Drum £20
DAN8006 Beau: Creation £20
DAN8007 Bridget St John: Songs For The Gentle Man £25
2310145 Burnin' Red Ivanhoe: W.W.W. £15
2310146 Supersister: To The Highest Bidder £20
2310154/DAN8003 Stackwaddy: Stackwaddy £40
2310165 David Bedford: Nurses Song With Elephants £20
2310193 Bridget St John: Thank You For £25
2310216 Clifford T. Ward: Singer Songwriter £10
2310217 Tractor: Tractor £75
2310228 Kevin Coyne: Case History £40
2310231 Stackwaddy: Bugger Off £50
2485021 Various: There Is Some Fun Going Forward (with poster) £50

And the singles:

K4403 Beau: 1917 Revolution £4
K4404 Bridget St John: To B Without A Hitch £4
K4405 Principal Edward's Magic Theatre: Ballad Of The Big Girl Now £4
K4493 Clague: Bottle Up And Go £4
K4494 Clague: Stride £4
4596 Gene Vincent: Be Bop A Lula £5
4661 Medicine Head: His Guiding Hand £10
4971 Gene Vincent: White Lightning £6
5075 Medicine Head: Coast To Coast £6
5119 Stackwaddy: Roadrunner £6
DS7001 Various: Dandelion Sampler £4
DAN7003 Medicine Head: Pictures In The Sky (picture sleeve) £5
2001327 Clifford T. Ward: Carrie £5
2001331 Stackwaddy: You Really Got Me £5
2001382 Clifford T. Ward: Coathanger £4

DAWN

Dawn was the specialist progressive label set up by Pye. The label's list of signings somehow lacked the class of rival concerns like Vertigo and Harvest, but the majority of the albums released from 1969 to 1975 are collectable, even if only a handful have managed to reach high values.

DNLS3002 John Kongos: Confusions About Goldfish £10
DNLS3003 Man: 2oz Of Plastic With A Hole In The Middle £15
DNLS3004 Trader Horne: Morning Way £60
DNLS3005 Mike Cooper: Do I Know You £12
DNLS3006 Trio: Trio double £40
DNLS3007 Quiet World: Road £50
DNLS3008 Mungo Jerry: Mungo Jerry (with 3D glasses) £10
DNLS3009 Donovan: Open Road £15
DNLS3010 Heron: Heron £40
DNLS3011 Mike Cooper: Trout Steel £12
DNLS3012 Titus Groan: Titus Groan £50
DNLS3013 Demon Fuzz: Afreaka £25
DNLS3014 Atlantic Bridge: Atlantic Bridge £12
DNLS3015 Harvey Mandel: Baby Batter £10
DNLS3016 Potliquor: First Taste £60
DNLS3017 Trifle: First Meeting £15
DNLS3018 John McLaughlin, John Surman et al.: Where Fortune Smiles £30
DNLS3019 Comus: First Utterance £100
DNLS3021 Paul Brett: Jubilation Foundry £10
DNLS3022 Trio: Conflagration £30
DNLS3023 Jackie McAuley: Jackie McAuley £40
DNLS3025 Heron: Twice As Nice double £40
DNLS3026 Mike Cooper: Places I Know £12
DNLS3029 Noir: We Had To Let You Have It £15
DNLS3030 Pluto: Pluto £75
DNLS3031 Mike Cooper: Machine Gun Company £12
DNLS3032 Paul Brett: Schizophrenia £12
DNLS3034 Bronx Cheer: Greatest Hits £10

DNLS3035 Paul King: Been In The Pen Too Long £12
DNLS3037 Finbar & Eddie Furey: Dawning Of The Day £25
DNLS3038 Atomic Rooster: Made In England denim cover £30; picture cover £10
DNLS3040 King Earl Boogie Band: Trouble At Mill £10
DNLS3042 Jonesy: No Alternative £25
DNLS3043 Peter Franc: Profile £10
DNLS3044 Stephen Jameson: Stephen Jameson £10
DNLS3046 Gravy Train: Second Birth £30
DNLS3048 Jonesy: Keeping Up £15
DNLS3049 Atomic Rooster: Nice And Greasy £25
DNLS3050 Mason: Mason £10
DNLS3051 Peter Franc: En Route £10
DNLS3053 Fruupp: Future Legends £25
DNLS3055 Jonesy: Growing £15
DNLS3056 Quicksand: Home Is Where I Belong £40
DNLS3058 Fruupp: Seven Secrets £25
DNLS3060 Curtis Knight: Zeus, The Second Coming £10
DNLS3062 Tim Rose: Tim Rose £10
DNLS3068 Sahara: Sunrise £10
DNLS3070 Fruupp: Modern Masquerades £25
DNLD4001 Donovan: H.M.S. Donovan double with poster £75; without poster £40
DNLH1 Gravy Train: Staircase To The Day £30
DNLH2 Fruupp: Prince Of Heaven's Eyes with booklet £25

DECCA

Until 1970, Decca used a red label for its mono LPs (LK series) and a blue label for its stereo LPs (SKL series). A few of the mono LPs from the early sixties were still in the catalogue at the end of the decade, but although these later pressings have the same label design as the originals, they no longer use the cover construction in which the edges of the front sheet are folded over the back. From 1970, a blue label is used, but with significantly changed details as compared with the earlier stereo label. The earlier label has a circular 'ffss' logo at the top and a relatively wide 'full frequency stereophonic sound' band immediately adjacent to the centre hole. The later label has a narrow band, with a gap between itself and the hole; there is no circular logo, and the 'Decca' logo is now inside a box. The sleeves for albums released during 1968–70 have a small hole on the back, at the top-right corner. The inner sleeves have a red (for mono) or blue (for stereo) coloured band which can be seen through the hole to identify immediately which kind of record it is! Decca singles have a blue label from the early fifties – switching from a tri-centre to a round centre at the end of the decade, and starting to use the boxed Decca logo during 1966.

DERAM

Decca was the first company to start a specialist progressive label with the release of the first Deram records towards the end of 1966. Of course, in 1966 it was by no means clear what music should actually be included in the definition, with the result that some fairly odd records were given Deram releases (such as those by Whistling Jack Smith and Lionel Bart). Nevertheless, the proportion of musically adventurous releases is high and the label's sixties records are widely collected. Both singles and LPs had a brown and white label – albums bearing a 1970 or 1971 release date with red and white labels are later pressings.

ECM

ECM is a jazz and contemporary music label run by producer Manfred Eicher, whose direct involvement in the creation of his company's releases is unparalleled in the world of music. From the label's start in 1970, Eicher was determined to enhance the music with as high a recording quality as was possible, combined with superior standards of record pressing. Although there are exceptions – particularly in the early days when avant-garde improvisers like Derek Bailey were recorded – ECM's music is well known for having something of a house style (described in the label's own advertising slogan as 'the most beautiful sound next to silence'). Particularly since the tremendous success (in jazz terms) of Keith Jarrett and, later, that of Pat Metheny and Jan Garbarek, fans of music that somehow manages to be both cutting edge and attractively mellow are content in the knowledge that any record bearing the ECM name is likely to be one that they will like.

ELEKTRA

From its beginnings as a US folk and roots specialist company, Elektra was held in high regard as a label that could be relied on to issue only artistically worthwhile records. Even when the company began to branch out into the developing rock market, it still seemed to have the knack of finding artists whose role in the development was destined to be a key one – such as the Butterfield Blues Band, the Doors, Love and the Incredible String Band. The earliest Elektra records have gold labels, changing briefly to white in 1966, and then orange to the end of the decade. In 1970, a red label was used, then, following the absorption of the label into the Kinney group in 1971, a mottled green label featuring a butterfly logo was introduced.

EMBASSY

Embassy was the record label sold by Woolworth's during the late fifties and early sixties. Its policy was to issue sound-alike cover versions of the hits of the day, with the result that the label scarcely features in the collectors' market today. A handful of Embassy artists eventually made it on to 'proper' labels – Johnny Worth, Hal Munro and, most notably, Maureen Evans.

FACTORY

The label that provided a home for the music of Joy Division and New Order is one of the few modern labels to attract collectors trying to put together a complete run. In practice, however, it is impossible for anyone to collect every Factory catalogue item, due to the label's eccentric habit of giving numbers to assorted items other than music releases. The very first Factory item, in fact, is a concert poster (FAC1). Later catalogue oddities include a badge (FAC21), a computer program (FAC91), the Hacienda club's first birthday party (FAC83), and, indeed, the Hacienda club itself (FAC51).

HARVEST

Harvest was set up as EMI's specialist progressive rock label in 1969. Many of the original releases on each of the two number series (SHSP and SHVL) are now collectable, although EMI's high success rate means that there are fewer high-value items than are found on many of the other progressive labels. Unfortunately for collectors, Harvest retained its distinctive lime-green label throughout the seventies, so that the first pressings of albums selling well enough to stay in the catalogue cannot easily be identified. This is the reason for the low values attaching to such well-known albums as Pink Floyd's *Ummagumma* and *Atom Heart Mother* and the omission from the listings altogether of Deep Purple's *Deep Purple*, *Concerto For Group And Orchestra* and *In Rock*, original copies of all of which might be expected to be sought after.

SHVL752 Pete Brown: A Meal You Can Shake Hands With In The Dark 1969 £75
SHVL753 Panama Ltd Jug Band: Panama Ltd Jug Band 1969 £30
SHVL754 Shirley & Dolly Collins: Anthems In Eden 1969 £50
SHVL755 Michael Chapman: Rainmaker 1969 £12
SHVL756 Third Ear Band: Alchemy 1969 £20
SHVL757 Edgar Broughton Band: Wasa Wasa 1969 £15
SHVL758 Battered Ornaments: Mantle Piece 1969 £60
SHVL760 Forest: Forest 1969 £60
SHVL761 Tea & Symphony: Asylum For The Musically Insane 1969 £60
SHVL762 Bakerloo: Bakerloo 1969 £60
SHVL763 Kevin Ayers: Joy Of A Toy 1970 £15
SHVL764 Michael Chapman: Fully Qualified Survivor 1969 £12
SHVL765 Syd Barrett: Madcap Laughs 1970 £20
SHVL768 Pete Brown: Art School Dance Goes On Forever 1970 £75
SHVL769 Greatest Show on Earth: Horizons 1970 £25
SHVL770 Barclay James Harvest: Barclay James Harvest 1970 £10
SHVL771 Shirley & Dolly Collins: Love, Death And The Lady 1970 £50
SHVL772 Edgar Broughton Band: Sing Brother Sing 1970 £15
SHVL773 Third Ear Band: Third Ear Band 1970 £15
SHVL774 Pretty Things: Parachute 1970 £15
SHVL775 Quatermass: Quatermass 1970 £40
SHVL776 Roy Harper: Flat Baroque And Beserk 1970 £10
SHVL779 Panama Ltd Jug Band: Indian Summer 1970 £40
SHVL781 Pink Floyd: Atom Heart Mother 1970 £10
SHVL782 Pete Brown: Thousands On A Raft 1970 £50
SHVL783 Greatest Show on Earth: Going's Easy 1970 £25
SHVL784 Forest: Full Circle 1970 £75
SHVL785 Tea & Symphony: Jo Sago 1970 £60
SHVL786 Michael Chapman: Window 1971 £12
SHVL787 Love: False Start 1971 £20
SHVL789 Roy Harper: Stormcock 1971 £10
SHVL790 Grease Band: Grease Band 1971 £10
SHVL791 Edgar Broughton Band: Edgar Broughton Band 1971 £12
SHVL792 East of Eden: East Of Eden 1971 £15
SHVL795 Pink Floyd: Meddle 1971 £10
SHVL796 East of Eden: New Leaf 1971 £10
SHVL797 Electric Light Orchestra: Electric Light Orchestra 1971 £10
SHVL798 Michael Chapman: Wrecked Again 1971 £12
SHVL800 Kevin Ayers: Whatevershebringswesing 1973 £10
SHVL801 Spontaneous Combustion: Spontaneous Combustion 1972 £25
SHVL804 Pink Floyd: Dark Side Of The Moon 1973 with inserts & stickers £10
SHVL805 Spontaneous Combustion: Triad 1972 £25
SHVL807 Kevin Ayers: Bananamour 1973 with booklet £20; without £10
SHVL808 Roy Harper: Lifemask 1973 £10
SHVL810 Edgar Broughton Band: Oora 1973 £15
SHVL812 Babe Ruth: Amar Caballero 1973 £10
SHVL814 Pink Floyd: Wish You Were Here 1976 black polythene wrapper £10

SHSP4001 Ike & Tina Turner: Hunter 1970 £25

SHSP4002 Clifton Chenier: Very Best 1970 £20
SHSP4004 Chris Spedding: Backwoods Progression 1970 £15
SHSP4005 Kevin Ayers: Shooting At The Moon 1971 £15
SHSP4006 Buddy Guy: Buddy And The Juniors 1970 £15
SHSP4007 Syd Barrett: Barrett 1970 £20
SHSP4008 Ron Geesin & Roger Waters: The Body 1970 £12
SHSP4009 Climax Blues Band: Lot Of Bottle 1970 £10
SHSP4010 Flying Circus: Prepared In Peace 1970 £10
SHSP4011 Mark Almond: Mark Almond 1971 £10
SHSP4013 Move: Message From The Country 1971 £10
SHSP4014 Nine Days Wonder: Nine Days Wonder 1971 £25
SHSP4015 Climax Blues Band: Tightly Knit 1971 £10
SHSP4016 Formerly Fat Harry: Formerly Fat Harry 1971 £12
SHSP4017 Chris Spedding: Only Lick I Know 1972 £15
SHSP4019 Third Ear Band: Music From Macbeth 1972 £12
SHSP4020 Pink Floyd: Obscured By Clouds 1972 rounded sleeve £12
SHSP4022 Babe Ruth: First Base 1972 £10
SHSP4024 Climax Blues Band: Rich Man 1972 £10
SHSP4027 Roy Harper: Valentine 1974 with lyric booklet £12
SHSP4033 Kayak: See See The Sun 1973 £10
SHSP4036 Kayak: Kayak 1974 £10
SHSP4038 Babe Ruth: Babe Ruth 1975 £10
SHSP4044 Soft Machine: Bundles 1975 £10
SHSP4056 Soft Machine: Softs 1976 £10
SHSP4059 Albion Band: Prospect Before Us 1976 £12
SHSP4060 Roy Harper: Bullinamingvase 1977 with 'Watford Gap' £12; with 7" £20
SHSP4073 Ashley Hutchings: Kickin' Up The Sawdust 1977 £40
SHSP4077 Roy Harper: Commercial Break 1977 test pressing £200
SHSP4083 Soft Machine: Alive And Well 1978 £10
SHSP4086 Professor Longhair: Live On The Queen Mary 1978 £10
SHSP4090 Matumbi: Seven Seals 1978 £10
SHSP4092 Albion Band: Rise Up Like The Sun 1978 £10
SHSP4099 Israel Vibration: Same Song 1979 £10
SHSP4105 Wire: 154 1979 with 7" (PSR444) £10

HMV

HMV's turquoise-blue labels are a welcome sight on Elvis Presley singles from the fifties, indicating an early release of some value. Sixties HMV labels were black. The LP labels changed from crimson in 1963, acquiring the EMI house-style shown in the Columbia and Parlophone labels of the period. In the case of HMV, this meant a black label with a red 'His Masters Voice' logo. There is no problem with regard to later reissues, since in 1967 HMV became a classical label only (though its pop wing was revived in the late eighties for Morrissey's benefit).

INCUS

The Incus label was set up in 1970 by avant-garde improvisers Evan Parker and Derek Bailey as a means of ensuring that rather more of their own difficult music, as well as that of other like-minded musicians, would be recorded than might otherwise be the case. With typically self-deprecating humour, the duo elected to call their parent company Compatible Recording And Publishing Ltd, with the initial capital letters picked out in bold print. The label's releases are, however, definitive statements within their free improvisation genre and are consequently all collected by fans of the style, who know exactly what to expect from an Incus album. The majority of these stayed in the catalogue until the changeover to CDs, but original copies of the earliest issues are particularly sought after, being easily identified by their Edward Road, Bromley, company address, and dark-blue record labels.

ISLAND

The Island record company was formed in 1962 as an outlet for Caribbean music in the UK – the catalogue number prefix used for singles being 'WI', standing for 'West Indies'. These singles, with their white and red labels, are all very collectable. During 1967, Island began issuing rock LPs, gaining a significant boost by their successful signing of Stevie Winwood's new group, Traffic. The change in musical emphasis was matched by a change in label design. From 1967 until 1970, Island labels were pink, a fact which easily enables the identification of first pressings. Collectors are not often concerned about the fine differences, but there are actually three different pink label designs. From 1967 until 1969 (beginning with ILP952 by John Martyn), the labels have a distinctive red and black 'eye' logo on the left-hand side. The last album to be issued with this label was ILPS9106 by Dr Strangely Strange, although ILPS9099 (White Noise), ILPS9100 (Clouds), ILPS9104 (Free), and ILPS9105 (Nick Drake) all have the later pink label designs. During 1969 a few issues used a pink label on which an enlarged black-only version of the 'eye' logo appeared at the centre. A few singles, plus copies of *Holidays* and *Unhalfbricking* by Fairport Convention, *Ahead Rings Out* by Blodwyn Pig and *This Was* by Jethro Tull have been spotted with this label design. The albums are therefore second pressings, although they are actually rarer than the earlier issues. The Clouds and Nick Drake albums mentioned above were first issued with this second pink label design. From 1969 to 1970 the pink labels have a large white 'i' logo below the centre. The last album to be issued with this label was ILPS9135 by Cat Stevens, although one number down, Nick Drake's *Bryter Layter* is not pink, and it is probable that Alan Bown's *Listen* (ILPS9131) is not pink either. From 1970 to 1974, the pink colour was relegated to a circular border for a multi-coloured label bearing a stylized picture of an island in the sun. Many of the earlier albums were reissued with this label, but the values of these later pressings are seldom more than 50 per cent of the original pink-label copies. Some albums appear with even later label designs, but unless stated otherwise in the listings, these late issues are of no interest to collectors.

The complete listing of Island ILP pink label albums is as follows:

ILP952 John Martyn: London Conversation £40
ILP953 Millie: Best Of Millie Small £40
ILP955 Derrick Harriott: Rock Steady Party £100
ILP957 Hopeton Lewis: Take It Easy £100
ILP958 Various Artists: Duke Reid's Rock Steady £100
ILP959/ILPS9059 Nirvana: The Story Of Simon Simopath £40
ILP960/ILPS9060 Jackie Edwards: Premature Golden Sands £40
ILP961/ILPS9061 Traffic: Mr Fantasy (mono) £50; (stereo) £25
ILP962 Jimmy Cliff: Hard Road To Travel £40
ILP963 Jackie Edwards & Millie: Best Of Jackie & Millie Vol. 2 £60
ILP964 Various Artists: Club Soul £25
ILP965 Various Artists: Club Rock Steady '68 £60
ILP966/ILPS9066 Various Artists: British Blue Eyed Soul £30
ILP967 Art: Supernatural Fairytales £60
ILP968 Joyce Bond: Soul And Ska £75
ILP969 Lyn Taitt: Sounds Rock Steady £60
ILP970/ILPS9070 Spencer Davis Group: Best Of £25
ILP971 Granville Williams Orchestra: Hi Life £40

ILP972 Sonny Burke: Sounds Of Sonny Burke £50
ILP974 Bobby Bland: Touch Of The Blues £25
ILP975 O. V. Wright: 8 Men, 4 Women £30
ILP976 Various Artists: Duke And The Peacock £50
ILP977 Various: Guy Stevens' Testament Of Rock'n'Roll £20
ILP978 Various Artists: Put It On, It's Rock Steady £50
ILPS9079 Spontaneous Music Ensemble: Karyobin £50
ILP980/ILPS9080 Spooky Tooth: It's All About £30
ILP981/ILPS9081 Traffic: Traffic (mono) £30; (stereo) £15
ILP982/ILPS9082 Wynder K. Frog: Out Of The Frying Pan £30
ILP983 Derrick Harriott: Best Of Derrick Harriott Vol. 2 £75
ILP984 Merrymen: Caribbean Treasure Chest £30
ILP985/ILPS9085 Jethro Tull: This Was (mono) £30; (stereo) £25
ILP986 Bunny Lee All Stars: Leaping With Mr Lee £100
ILP987/ILPS9087 Nirvana: All Of Us £40
ILPS9088 Tramline: Somewhere Down The Line £40
ILPS9089 Free: Tons Of Sobs £25
ILP990 Derrick Morgan: Derrick Morgan & His Friends £60
ILP991/ILPS9091 John Martyn: The Tumbler £40
ILPS9092 Fairport Convention: What We Did On Our Holidays £20
ILPS9093 Unfolding Book Of Life: Vol. 1 £20
ILPS9094 Unfolding Book Of Life: Vol. 2 £20
ILPS9095 Tramline: Moves Of Vegetable Centuries £40
ILPS9096 Bama Winds: Windy £10
ILPS9097 Traffic: Last Exit £15
ILPS9098 Spooky Tooth: Spooky Two £20
ILPS9099 White Noise: Electric Storm £15
ILPS9100 Clouds: Scrapbook £30
ILPS9101 Blodwyn Pig: Ahead Rings Out £20
ILPS9102 Fairport Convention: Unhalfbricking £20
ILPS9103 Jethro Tull: Stand Up £15
ILPS9104 Free: Free £25
ILPS9105 Nick Drake: Five Leaves Left £75
ILPS9106 Dr Strangely Strange: Kip Of The Serenes £75
ILPS9107 Spooky Tooth & Pierre Henry: Ceremony £15
ILPS9108 Mott The Hoople: Mott The Hoople £15 (1st version with 'Road To Birmingham' £30)
ILPS9110 Quintessence: In Blissful Company £25
ILPS9111 King Crimson: In The Court Of The Crimson King £30
ILPS9112 Traffic: Best Of Traffic £15
ILPS9113 John & Beverley Martyn: Stormbringer £40
ILPS9114 Renaissance: Renaissance £20
ILPS9115 Fairport Convention: Liege And Lief £15
ILPS9116 Traffic: John Barleycorn Must Die £12
ILPS9117 Spooky Tooth: Last Puff £15
ILPS9118 Cat Stevens: Mona Bone Jakon £10
ILPS9119 Mott The Hoople: Mad Shadows £10
ILPS9120 Free: Fire And Water £20
ILPS9123 Jethro Tull: Benefit £25
ILPS9124 Bronco: Country Home £20 (The number was originally issued to Traffic: Live At The Fillmore. Demos of this are worth £100)
ILPS9125 Fotheringay: Fotheringay £20
ILPS9126 McDonald & Giles: McDonald & Giles £20

ILPS9127 King Crimson: In The Wake Of Poseidon £20
ILPS9128 Quintessence: Quintessence £25
ILPS9129 If: If £25
ILPS9130 Fairport Convention: Full House £15 (Test pressings with 'Poor Will And The Jolly Hangman' are worth £250)
ILPS9132 Emerson, Lake & Palmer: Emerson, Lake and Palmer £15
ILPS9133 John & Beverley Martyn: Road To Ruin £20
ILPS9135 Cat Stevens: Tea For The Tillerman £20

Two of the the missing numbers are LPs with the earlier white label:

ILP954 Various Artists: Dr Kitch £40
ILP956 Various Artists: Club Ska '67 Vol. 2 £60

Another two have the pink rim label:

ILPS9131 Alan Bown: Listen £10
ILPS9134 Nick Drake: Bryter Layter £50

KEY

Records issued on the Key label during the early seventies were all Christian in content, but many have become collectable as a by-product of the interest in progressive rock and folk music of the period. Most notable in this respect is the album by Out Of Darkness, which continues to be one of the more sought-after progressive rarities.

KINNEY

In 1971, three major US record labels, Elektra, Reprise and Warner Brothers, amalgamated under the Kinney company name – Atlantic joined the fold in early 1972. Records still in the catalogue at that time were immediately given new numbers beginning with a 'K', a change which is immensely useful to collectors in that it enables the easy identification of original pressings – those without the K numbers. Today the company continues under the name W.E.A.

LIBERTY

The bright blue labels on late sixties Liberty LPs were changed to black during 1970. Collectable albums like the second by the Groundhogs and the first by Hawkwind, which stayed in the catalogue long enough to be issued with both label designs, are only worth the full values listed in this *Guide* if they are the first pressings with the bright blue labels. Second-issue, black-label copies typically fetch no more than two thirds of this value. The black label design was short-lived, however, as in 1971 Liberty was absorbed into the United Artists record company.

LONDON

London was the first label to receive serious attention from collectors owing to its policy of issuing in the UK the best of American rock'n'roll and rhythm and blues records. Many collectors try to obtain complete runs of London singles at least up until the mid-sixties, when the rise of British beat effectively put an end to the label's importance. Their task in this respect is hindered by the extreme rarity of some of the issues, but they are also safe in the knowledge that a complete collection will contain remarkably few dud recordings. The earliest London singles have gold writing on a black label and these 'gold label' singles are the most highly prized and the most valuable. Where gold label singles have been reissued as later 'silver label' pressings (i.e. they have silver writing on a black label), these are generally only worth around half the value of the first issues. Unfortunately, the London label did not appear to be particularly systematic in its procedures, so that during the early months of 1957 some records were issued on gold labels and some on silver. There are, however, no gold label issues after HLP8420 (which happens to be by Slim Whitman). Within these listings, London singles with gold labels are specifically indicated where it might not be clear whether the first issue is gold or silver. A further design change occurs at the end of the decade, when the original triangular single centres were replaced by a round centre. As before, a round-centre issue of a record that was first issued with a tri-centre is only worth about half the value of the original. The first round-centre issue was HLU8903 (Gloria Smith), but the last tri-centre was HLW9050 (Duane Eddy). There is a period of some five months between these two, during which both kinds of centre were being used for new releases. Again, where it would not otherwise be clear in these listings, the existence of a tri-centre is indicated. London EPs have the same label design changes as the singles, but complications with regard to London LPs are restricted to the fact that a few were reissued after 1967 with black labels replacing the original plum-coloured labels.

The collectable 8000 and 9000 series are as follows (the missing early numbers are records that were issued on the 78 rpm format only):

HL8004 Mitchell Torok: Caribbean 1954 tri-centre £25
HL8012 Floyd Cramer: Fancy Pants 1954 £30
HL8013 Woody Herman: Wooftie 1954 £15
HL8014 Jim Reeves: Bimbo 1954 £125
HL8015 Norman Brooks: I'd Like To Be In Your Shoes Baby 1954 £15
HL8017 Jerry Fielding Orchestra: When I Grow Too Old To Dream 1954 £15
HL8018 Slim Whitman: Stairway To Heaven 1954 £40
HL8026 Hilltoppers: From The Vine Came The Grape 1954 £30
HL8027 Lancers: Stop Chasing Me Baby 1954 £30
HL8029 John Sebastian: Inca Dance 1954 £15
HL8030 Jim Reeves: Mexican Joe 1954 £125
HL8031 Woody Herman: Fancy Woman 1954 £15
HL8032 Teddy Phillips: Ridin' To Tennessee 1954 £25
HL8033 Rue Barclay & Peggy Duncan: Tongue Tied Boy 1954 £20
HL8035 Archie Bleyer: Amber 1954 £15
HL8036 Del Wood: Ragtime Annie 1954 £25
HL8039 Slim Whitman: Secret Love 1954 gold label £25
HL8041 Norman Brooks: I Can't Give You Anything But Love 1954 £15
HL8042 Claude Thornhill: Pussyfooting 1954 £20
HL8043 Lorry Raine: You Broke My Broken Heart 1954 £20
HL8048 Mitchell Torok: Hootchy Coochy 1954 £25
HL8051 Norman Brooks: My Three D Sweetie 1954 £15
HL8055 Jim Reeves: Butterfly Love 1954 £125
HL8061 Slim Whitman: Rose Marie 1954 £10
HL8062 Floyd Cramer: Jolly Cholly 1954 £40
HL8064 Jim Reeves: Echo Bonita 1954 £125
HL8070 Hilltoppers: Poor Butterfly 1954 £30
HL8071 Smiley Burnette: Lazy Locomotive 1954 £30
HL8076 Al Lombardy: Blues 1954 £25
HL8078 Bill Stegmeyer: On The Waterfront 1954 £20
HL8079 Lancers: So High So Low So Wide 1954 £30
HL8080 Slim Whitman: Beautiful Dreamer 1954 £20
HL8081 Hilltoppers: Will You Remember 1954 £30

HL8082 Bob Trow: Soft Squeeze Baby 1954 £15
HL8083 Mitchell Torok: Haunting Waterfall 1954 £25
HL8085 Smiley Burnette: Chugging On Down Sixty Six 1954 £30
HL8091 Slim Whitman: Singing Hills 1954 gold label £20
HL8092 Hilltoppers: If I Didn't Care 1954 £30
HL8093 Ginny Wright: Wonderful World 1954 with Tommy Cutrer £25
HL8094 Rudy Grayzell: Looking At The Moon 1954 £150
HL8099 Fontane Sisters: Happy Days And Lonely Nights 1954 £60
HL8100 Songsters: Bahama Buggy Ride 1954 £12
HL8101 Laurie Loman: Whither Thou Goest 1954 £20
HL8102 Kitty White & David Howard: Jesse James 1954 £25
HL8103 Merle Kilgore: It Can't Rain All The Time 1954 £100
HL8104 De Castro Sisters: Teach Me Tonight 1954 £25
HL8105 Jim Reeves: Padre Of Old San Antone 1954 £75
HL8107 Hal Hoppers: Do Nothing Blues 1954 £15
HL8109 Sandy Coker: Meadowlark Melody 1954 £50
HL8111 Archie Bleyer: Naughty Lady Of Shady Lane 1954 £15
HL8112 Billy Vaughn: Melody Of Love 1955 £15
HL8113 Fontane Sisters: Hearts Of Stone 1955 £75
HL8114 Penguins: Earth Angel 1955 £1000
HL8115 Norman Brooks: Back In Circulation 1955 £15
HL8116 Hilltoppers: You Try Somebody Else 1955 £30
HL8117 Don, Dick & Jimmy: You Can't Have Your Cake . . . 1955 £10
HL8118 Jim Reeves: Penny Candy 1955 £100
HL8119 Ginny Wright: Indian Moon 1955 £25
HL8120 Rosalind Paige: When The Saints 1955 £10
HL8121 Two Ton Baker: Clink Clank 1955 £40
HL8122 Woody Herman: Sorry 'Bout The Whole Darned Thing 1955 £12
HL8123 Jim Edward & Maxine Brown: Itsy Witsy Bitsy Me 1955 £20
HL8124 Fats Domino: Love Me 1955 £125
HL8125 Slim Whitman: When I Grow Too Old To Dream 1955 £20
HL8126 Fontane Sisters: Rock Love 1955 £75
HL8127 Al Lombardy: In A Little Spanish Town 1955 £25
HL8128 Dooley Sisters: Ko Ko Mo 1955 £25
HL8129 Hal Hoppers: Baby I've Had It 1955 £12
HL8130 Oscar McLollie Honeyjumpers: Love Me Tonight 1955 £150
HL8131 John Sebastian: Stranger In Paradise 1955 £12
HL8132 Lorry Raine: Love Me Tonight 1955 £20
HL8133 Fats Domino: I Know 1955 £100
HL8134 Johnny Maddox: Crazy Otto Medley 1955 £10
HL8135 Sunnysiders: Hey Mister Banjo 1955 £40
HL8136 Eddie Albert: Come Pretty Little Girl 1955 £20
HL8137 De Castro Sisters: Boom Boom Boomerang 1955 £25
HL8138 John Laurenz: Goodbye Stranger Goodbye 1955 £20
HL8139 Bon Bons: That's The Way Love Goes 1955 £25
HL8140 Ferko String Band: Alabama Jubilee 1955 £12
HL8141 Slim Whitman: Haunted Hungry Heart 1955 £20
HL8142 Bill Haley: Greentree Boogie 1955 £100
HL8143 Jerry Colonna: Chicago Style 1955 £12
HL8144 Don, Dick & Jimmy: Make Yourself Comfortable 1955 £10
HL8145 Nappy Brown: Don't Be Angry 1955 £500
HL8146 Thunderbirds: Ayuh Ayuh 1955 £60

HL8147 David Houston: Blue Prelude 1955 £20
HL8148 Janr Morgan: Why Oh Why 1955 £20
HL8149 Bill Hayes: Berry Tree 1955 £15
HL8150 Tom Tall & Ginny Wright: Are You Mine 1955 £15
HL8151 Four Tunes: I Sold My Heart To The Junkman 1955 £75
HL8152 Four Esquires: Sphinx Won't Tell 1955 £25
HL8153 Ruth Brown: Mambo Baby 1955 £200
HL8154 Julius La Rosa: Mobile 1955 £20
HL8155 Sir Hubert Pimm: Goodnight And Cheerio 1955 £20
HL8156 Bob Jaxon: Ali Baba 1955 £20
HL8157 Jerry Cornell: Please Don't Talk About Me 1955 £25
HL8158 De Castro Sisters: I'm Bewildered 1955 £25
HL8159 Jim Reeves: Drinking Tequila 1955 £150
HL8160 Sunnysiders: Oh Me Oh My 1955 £25
HL8184 Al Hibbler: Now I Lay Me Down To Dream 1955 £10
HL8227 Eydie Gorme: Sincerely Yours 1956 £10
HL8254 Bobby Scott: Chain Gang 1956 £25
HL8358 Johnny Cash: I Walk The Line 1957 gold label £60
HL8361 George Hamilton IV: Rose And A Candy Bar 1957 gold label £100
HL8363 Lee Tully: Around The World With Elwood Pretzel 1957 gold label £50
HL8376 Four Esquires: Look Homeward Angel 1957 demo £30
HL8426 Jack Haskell: Around The World 1957 £10
HL8430 Bill Hayes: Wringle Wrangle 1957 £8
HL8438 Lloyd Price: Just Because 1957 £75
HL8443 Randy Starr: After School 1957 £25
HL8456 Jodie Sands: With All My Heart 1957 £6
HL8467 Charlie Gracie: Wandering Eyes 1957 £15
HL8481 Micki Marlo: That's Right 1957 B-side with Paul Anka £15
HL8482 Dale Hawkins: Susie Q 1957 £300
HL8501 Five Satins: To The Aisle 1957 £500
HL8503 Tuneweavers: Happy Happy Birthday Baby 1957 B-side by Paul Gayten £100
HL8530 Jodie Sands: Please Don't Tell Me 1957 £8
HL8545 Hollywood Flames: Buzz Buzz Buzz 1958 £40
HL8547 Wayne Handy: Say Yeah 1958 £400
HL8548 Georgettes: Love Like A Fool 1958 £25
HL8636 Frankie Avalon: Darling 1958 £20
HL8651 Jody Reynolds: Endless Sleep 1958 £15
HL8652 Pets: Cha Hua Hua 1958 £15
HL8653 Jan & Arnie: Jennie Lee 1958 £30
HL8655 Champs: El Rancho Rock 1958 £6
HL8668 Gerry Granahan: No Chemise Please 1958 £20
HL8669 Duane Eddy: Rebel Rouser 1958 £6
HL8673 Stu Phillips: Champlain & St Lawrence Line 1958 £6
HL8677 Chuck Berry: Beautiful Delilah 1958 £25
HL8684 Dubs: Gonna Make A Change 1958 £250
HL8697 Jerry Butler: For Your Precious Love 1958 £75
HL8712 Chuck Berry: Carol 1958 £25
HL8714 Bobby Hendricks: Itchy Twitchy Feeling 1958 £40
HL8715 Champs: Chariot Rock 1958 £6
HL8718 Dion: I Can't Go On 1958 £30
HL8719 Jerry Wallace: With This Ring 1958 £10
HL8723 Duane Eddy: Ramrod 1958 £5

HL8726 Bobby Day: Rockin' Robin 1958 £12
HL8731 Jimmy Starr: It's Only Make Believe 1958 £25
HL8746 Four Esquires: Hideaway 1958 £5
HL8747 Donnie Owens: Need You 1958 £15
HL8750 Cozy Cole: Topsy 1958 £5
HL8764 Duane Eddy: Cannonball 1958 £5
HL8794 Crests: Sixteen Candles 1959 £30
HL8798 Bill Parsons: All American Boy 1959 £8
HL8799 Dion: Don't Pity Me 1959 £25
HL8800 Bobby Day: Bluebird Buzzard And Oriole 1959 £25
HL8802 Dee Clark: When I Call On You 1959 £12
HL8803 Ritchie Valens: Donna 1959 £15
HL8807 Linda Laurie: Ambrose 1959 £6
HL8843 Cozy Cole: Turvy 1959 £4
HL8848 Little Anthony & The Imperials: Oh Yeah 1959 £20
HL8850 Frankie Ford: Sea Cruise 1959 £40
HL8866 Watusi Warriors: Wa chi bam ba 1959 £8
HL8870 Fiestas: So Fine 1959 £20
HL8872 Rockin' Rs: Crazy Baby 1959 £25
HL8873 Jimmy Lytell: Hot Cargo 1959 £5
HL8885 Tassels: To A Soldier Boy 1959 £60
HL8886 Ritchie Valens: That's My Little Suzie 1959 £20
HL8899 Johnny & The Hurricanes: Crossfire 1959 £15
HL8915 Dee Clark: Just Keep It Up 1959 £15
HL8922 Addrissi Brothers: Cherry Stone 1959 £8
HL8933 Tony Bellus: Robbing The Cradle 1959 £25
HL8940 Eugene Church: Miami 1959 £30
HL8947 Vinnie Monte: Summer Spree 1959 £6
HL8948 Johnny & The Hurricanes: Red River Rock 1959 tri-centre £5
HL8954 Crests: Angels Listened In 1959 £30
HL8956 Gene & Eunice: Poco Loco 1959 £25
HL8958 Wailers: Tall Cool One 1959 £12
HL8964 Bobby Day: Love Is A One Time Affair 1959 £12
HL8972 Rusty & Doug: I Like You 1959 £20
HL8973 Addrissi Brothers: Saving My Kisses 1959 £8
HL8985 Ernie Fields: In The Mood 1959 £4
HL8994 Wailers: Mau Mau 1959 tri-centre £100
HL8995 Eternals: Rocking In The Jungle 1959 tri-centre £75
HL9017 Johnny & The Hurricanes: Reveille Rock 1959 tri-centre £6
HL9051 Ray Smith: Rocking Little Angel 1960 £50
HL9052 Champs: Too Much Tequila 1960 £4
HL9096 Billy Bland: Let The Little Girl Dance 1960 £8
HL9100 Ernie Fields: Chattanooga Choo Choo 1960 £5
HL9132 Sonny James: Jenny Lou 1960 £5
HL9191 Barry Darvell: How Will It End 1960 £50
HL9227 Ernie Fields: Raunchy 1960 £4
HL9233 Shirelles: Tonight's The Night 1960 £10
HL9270 Gene Pitney: I Wanna Love My Life Away 1961 £8
HL9276 Miracles: Shop Around 1961 £40
HL9345 Ronnie & The Rainbows: Loose Ends 1961 £6
HL9366 Miracles: Ain't It Baby 1961 £60
HL9450 Duals: Stick Shift 1961 £20

HL9451 Ike & Tina Turner: It's Gonna Work Out Fine 1961 £10
HL9476 Troy & The T Birds: Twistle 1961 £6
HL9494 Ritchie Valens: La Bamba 1962 £12
HL9513 Barbara George: I Know 1962 £8
HL9537 Dennis Turner: Lover Please 1962 £6
HL9548 Eddie Reeves: Cry Baby 1962 £6
HL9577 Bobby Curtola: Fortune Teller 1962 £4
HL9605 Johnny Crawford: Your Nose Is Gonna Grow 1962 £4
HL9638 Johnny Crawford: Rumours 1962 £4
HL9639 Bobby Curtola: Aladdin 1962 £4
HL9662 Trade Martin: Hula Hula Dancin' Doll 1963 £5
HL9666 Danny & The Juniors: Oo La La Limbo 1963 £4
HL9668 Troy Shondell: I Got A Woman 1963 £6
HL9669 Johnny Crawford: Proud 1963 £4
HL9680 Jimmy Hughes: I'm Qualified 1963 £10
HL9686 Sherrys: Slop Time 1963 £8
HL9700 Wade Ray: Burning Desire 1963 £6
HL9702 Earls: Never 1963 £25
HL9718 Raindrops: What A Guy 1963 £8
HL9730 James Brown: Prisoner Of Love 1963 £15
HL9733 Volumes: Sandra 1963 £30
HL9737 Hawkshaw Hawkins: Lonesome 7-7203 1963 £5
HL9743 Righteous Brothers: Little Latin Lupe Lu 1963 £4
HL9747 Miriam Makeba: Click Song 1963 £4
HL9757 Garnell Cooper & Kinfolk: Green Monkey 1963 £8
HL9769 Raindrops: Kind Of Boy You Can't Forget 1963 £8
HL9775 James Brown: These Foolish Things 1963 £12
HL9780 Bruce Johnston: Original Surfer Stomp 1963 £20
HL9792 Sunny & The Sunglows: Talk To Me 1963 £15
HL9796 Betty Harris: Cry To Me 1963 £6
HL9807 Dale & Grace: I'm Leaving It Up To You 1963 £6
HL9808 Trini Lopez: Jean Marie 1963 £4
HL9814 Righteous Brothers: My Babe 1963 £4
HL9825 Raindrops: That Boy John 1964 £6
HL9831 Jim & Joe: Fireball Mail 1964 £8
HL9836 Johnny Crawford: Judy Loves Me 1964 £4
HL9857 Dale & Grace: Stop And Think It Over 1964 £5
HL9892 Wailers: Tall Cool One 1964 £6
HL9896 Little Richard: Bama Lama Bama Loo 1964 £5
HL9897 Don & Dewey: Get Your Hat 1964 £12
HL9921 Bobby Jameson: I Wanna Love You 1964 £15
HL9937 Ned Miller: Do What You Do Do Well 1964 £4
HL9941 Big Maybelle: Careless Love 1965 £6
HL9943 Righteous Brothers: You've Lost That Lovin' Feelin' 1965 £4
HL9945 James Brown: Have Mercy Baby 1965 £10
HL9953 Dobie Gray: In Crowd 1965 £5
HL9959 Carolyn Carter: I'm Thru 1965 £10
HL9962 Righteous Brothers: Just Once In My Life 1965 demo only £40
HL9975 Righteous Brothers: Unchained Melody 1965 £4
HL9977 Barbara Mason: Yes I'm Ready 1965 £15
HL9988 Beach Nuts: Out In The Sun 1965 £8
HL9990 James Brown: Papa's Got A Brand New Bag 1965 £8

HLA8163 Four Tophatters: Go Baby Go 1955 £200
HLA8165 Chris Dane: Cynthia's In Love 1955 £15
HLA8169 Chordettes: Hummingbird 1955 £25
HLA8170 Julius La Rosa: Domani 1955 £15
HLA8176 Archie Bleyer: Hernando's Hideaway 1955 £12
HLA8193 Julius La Rosa: Suddenly There's A Valley 1955 £20
HLA8198 Four Tophatters: Wild Rosie 1955 £200
HLA8199 Lavern Baker: That Lucky Old Sun 1955 £200
HLA8201 Mariners: I Love You Fair Dinkum 1955 £12
HLA8217 Chordettes: Duddlesack Polka 1956 £25
HLA8220 Bill Hayes: Ballad Of Davy Crockett 1956 £25
HLA8224 Four Esquires: Adorable 1956 £25
HLA8239 Bill Hayes: Kwela Kwela 1956 £12
HLA8243 Archie Bleyer: Nothin' To Do 1956 £6
HLA8248 Barry Sisters: Baby Come A Little Closer 1956 £20
HLA8263 Archie Bleyer: Bridge Of Happiness 1956 £6
HLA8264 Chordettes: Our Melody 1956 £30
HLA8268 Kay Thompson: Eloise 1956 £15
HLA8272 Julius La Rosa: No Other Love 1956 £12
HLA8284 Andy Williams: Walk Hand In Hand 1956 gold label £20
HLA8300 Bill Hayes: Das Ist Musik 1956 £10
HLA8302 Chordettes: Born To Be With You 1956 £25
HLA8304 Barry Sisters: Intrigue 1956 £20
HLA8306 Marion Marlowe: Hands Of Time 1956 £50
HLA8315 Andy Williams: Canadian Sunset 1956 £20
HLA8323 Chordettes: Lay Down Your Arms 1956 £15
HLA8325 Bill Hayes: Legend Of Wyatt Earp 1956 £20
HLA8353 Julius La Rosa: Jingle Bells 1956 £8
HLA8360 Andy Williams: Baby Doll 1956 £20
HLA8397 Harvey Boys: Nothing Is Too Good For You 1957 £20
HLA8399 Andy Williams: Butterfly 1957 £12
HLA8418 Tommy Furtado: Sun Tan Sam 1957 £20
HLA8437 Andy Williams: I Like Your Kind Of Love 1957 £10
HLA8440 Everly Brothers: Bye Bye Love 1957 £15
HLA8453 Joyce Hahn: Gonna Find Me A Bluebird 1957 £8
HLA8473 Chordettes: Just Between You And Me 1957 £15
HLA8474 Bobbsey Twins: Change Of Heart 1957 £15
HLA8480 Ocie Smith: Lighthouse 1957 £50
HLA8487 Andy Williams: Lips Of Wine 1957 £10
HLA8497 Chordettes: Like A Baby 1957 £15
HLA8498 Everly Brothers: Wake Up Little Suzie 1957 £6
HLA8554 Everly Brothers: This Little Girl Of Mine 1958 £15
HLA8566 Chordettes: Baby Of Mine 1958 £12
HLA8584 Chordettes: Lollipop 1958 £8
HLA8587 Andy Williams: Are You Sincere 1958 £8
HLA8618 Everly Brothers: All I Have To Do Is Dream 1958 £5
HLA8623 Link Wray: Rumble 1958 £15
HLA8654 Chordettes: Love Is A Two Way Street 1958 £8
HLA8685 Everly Brothers: Bird Dog 1958 £5
HLA8693 Anita Carter: Blue Doll 1958 £10
HLA8710 Andy Williams: Promise Me, Love 1958 £8
HLA8781 Everly Brothers: Problems 1958 £5

HLA8784 Andy Williams: House Of Bamboo 1959 £5
HLA8809 Chordettes: No Other Arms No Other Lips 1959 £5
HLA8863 Everly Brothers: Poor Jenny 1959 £6
HLA8926 Chordettes: Girl's Work Is Never Done 1959 £12
HLA8930 Johnny Tillotson: True True Happiness 1959 £40
HLA8934 Everly Brothers: Till I Kissed You 1959 tri-centre £6
HLA8957 Andy Williams: Lonely Street 1959 £4
HLA9018 Andy Williams: Village Of St Bernadette 1959 £4
HLA9039 Everly Brothers: Let It Be Me 1960 tri-centre £10
HLA9048 Johnny Tillotson: Why Do I Love You So 1960 £20
HLA9099 Andy Williams: Wake Me When It's Over 1960 £4
HLA9101 Johnny Tillotson: Earth Angel 1960 £20
HLA9157 Everly Brothers: When Will I Be Loved 1960 £5
HLA9216 Johnnie Ray: In The Heart Of A Fool 1960 £4
HLA9231 Johnny Tillotson: Poetry In Motion 1960 £4
HLA9250 Everly Brothers: Like Strangers 1960 £5
HLA9275 Johnny Tillotson: Jimmy's Girl 1961 £4
HLA9305 Eddie Hodges: Bandit Of My Dreams 1962 £8
HLA9369 Eddie Hodges: I'm Gonna Knock On Your Door 1961 £6
HLA9400 Chordettes: Never On Sunday 1961 £4
HLA9412 Johnny Tillotson: Without You 1961 £4
HLA9514 Johnny Tillotson: Dreamy Eyes 1962 £4
HLA9550 Johnny Tillotson: It Keeps Right On A Hurtin' 1962 £4
HLA9576 Eddie Hodges: Made To Love 1962 £4
HLA9598 Johnny Tillotson: Send Me The Pillow You Dream On 1962 £4
HLA9642 Johnny Tillotson: I Can't Help It 1962 £4
HLA9695 Johnny Tillotson: Out Of My Mind 1963 £4
HLA9811 Johnny Tillotson: Funny How Time Slips Away 1963 £4
HLA9944 Ernie Freeman: Raunchy '65 1965 £5
HLB8175 Dave Burgess: I Love Paris 1955 £20
HLB8190 Bert Convy & The Thunderbirds: Come On Back 1955 £125
HLB8192 Gogi Grant: Suddenly There's A Valley 1955 £12
HLB8257 Gogi Grant: We Believe In Love 1956 £10
HLB8282 Gogi Grant: Wayward Wind 1956 £10
HLB8364 Gogi Grant: You're In Love 1957 £8
HLB8406 Russell Arms: Cinco Robles 1957 £8
HLB8507 Bobby Please: Your Driver's License Please 1957 demo £200
HLB8508 Lee Lamar: Sophia 1957 £40
HLB8550 Gogi Grant: Golden Ladder 1958 £6
HLB8568 Gloria March: Baby Of Mine 1958 £10
HLB8620 Art & Dottie Todd: Chanson D'Amour 1958 £10
HLB8829 Skyliners: Since I Don't Have You 1959 £150
HLB9957 Johnny Bond: Ten Little Bottles 1965 £5
HLC8182 Nappy Brown: Pitter Patter 1955 £300
HLC8285 Al Caiola: Flamenco Love 1956 £12
HLC8349 Werly Fairburn: All The Time 1956 £750
HLC8384 Nappy Brown: Little By Little 1957 £200
HLC8447 Big Maybelle: All Of Me 1957 £25
HLC8760 Nappy Brown: It Don't Hurt No More 1958 £40
HLC8854 Big Maybelle: Baby Won't You Please Come Home 1959 £15
HLC9970 Soul Sisters: Good Time Tonight 1965 £15
HLC9971 Inez & Charlie Foxx: My Momma Told Me 1965 £5

HLC9974 Tina Britt: Real Thing 1965 £20
HLC9987 Baby Washington: Only Those In Love 1965 £10
HLD8168 Hilltoppers: Kentuckian Song 1955 £30
HLD8171 Jim Lowe: Close The Door 1955 £30
HLD8172 Pat Boone: Ain't That A Shame 1955 £15
HLD8174 Mac Wiseman: Kentuckian Song 1955 £40
HLD8177 Fontane Sisters: Seventeen 1955 £60
HLD8197 Pat Boone: No Arms Could Ever Hold You 1955 £20
HLD8203 Johnny Maddox: Do Do Do 1955 £10
HLD8205 Ken Nordine: Shifting Whispering Sands 1955 £10
HLD8208 Hilltoppers: Searching 1955 £40
HLD8209 Commodores: Riding On A Train 1955 £750
HLD8211 Fontane Sisters: Rolling Stone 1955 £60
HLD8221 Hilltoppers: Only You 1956 £10
HLD8222 Gale Storm: I Hear You Knocking 1956 £25
HLD8223 Snooky Lanson: It's Almost Tomorrow 1956 £75
HLD8225 Fontane Sisters: Adorable 1956 £40
HLD8226 Mac Wiseman: My Little Home In Tennessee 1956 £30
HLD8232 Gale Storm: Memories Are Made Of This 1956 £25
HLD8233 Pat Boone: Gee Whittakers 1956 £20
HLD8235 Beasley Smith: Goodnight Sweet Dreams 1956 £15
HLD8236 Snooky Lanson: Last Minute Love 1956 £125
HLD8238 Billy Vaughn: Theme From Threepenny Opera 1956 £8
HLD8249 Snooky Lanson: Seven Days 1956 £125
HLD8251 Commodores: Speedo 1956 £600
HLD8253 Pat Boone: I'll Be Home 1956 £6
HLD8255 Hilltoppers: My Treasure 1956 £20
HLD8259 Mac Wiseman: Fireball Mail 1956 £40
HLD8265 Fontane Sisters: Eddie My Love 1956 £40
HLD8266 Lois Winters: Japanese Farewell Song 1956 £15
HLD8270 Jimmy Work: When She Said You All 1956 £50
HLD8273 Beasley Smith: My Foolish Heart 1956 £15
HLD8276 Jim Lowe: Blue Suede Shoes 1956 £60
HLD8277 Johnny Maddox: Hands Off 1956 £20
HLD8278 Hilltoppers: Do The Bop 1956 £50
HLD8281 Marc Fredericks: Mystic Midnight 1956 £12
HLD8283 Gale Storm: Ivory Tower 1956 £25
HLD8286 Gale Storm: Why Do Fools Fall In Love 1956 £25
HLD8288 Jim Lowe: Love Is A $64,000 Question 1956 £40
HLD8289 Fontane Sisters: I'm In Love Again 1956 £25
HLD8291 Pat Boone: Long Tall Sally 1956 £10
HLD8298 Hilltoppers: Tryin' 1956 £15
HLD8303 Pat Boone: I Almost Lost My Mind 1956 £6
HLD8308 Jimmy Work: Heart Like A Merry Go Round 1956 £30
HLD8311 Gale Storm: Don't Be That Way 1956 £20
HLD8316 Pat Boone: Rich In Love 1956 £8
HLD8317 Jim Lowe: Green Door 1956 £30
HLD8318 Fontane Sisters With Pat Boone: Voices 1956 £20
HLD8319 Billy Vaughn: When The Lilac Blooms Again 1956 £6
HLD8320 Sanford Clark: Fool 1956 £75
HLD8329 Gale Storm: Heart Without A Sweetheart 1956 £15
HLD8333 Hilltoppers: So Tired 1956 £15

HLD8338 Nervous Norvus: Ape Call 1956 £50
HLD8342 Billy Vaughn: Petticoats Of Portugal 1956 £6
HLD8343 Fontane Sisters: Silver Bells 1956 £15
HLD8346 Pat Boone: Friendly Persuasion 1956 £5
HLD8347 Johnny Maddox: Dixieland Band 1956 £6
HLD8348 Dick Lory: Cool It Baby 1956 £400
HLD8362 Sonny Knight: Confidential 1957 £250
HLD8368 Jim Lowe: By You By You By You 1957 £20
HLD8370 Pat Boone: Don't Forbid Me 1957 £5
HLD8378 Fontane Sisters: Banana Boat Song 1957 £15
HLD8380 Tab Hunter: Young Love 1957 £15
HLD8381 Hilltoppers: Marianne 1957 £10
HLD8383 Nervous Norvus: Bullfrog Hop 1957 £75
HLD8393 Gale Storm: Lucky Lips 1957 £25
HLD8400 Molly Bee: Since I Met You Baby 1957 £25
HLD8402 Shirley Forwood: Two Hearts 1957 £20
HLD8404 Pat Boone: Why Baby Why 1957 £5
HLD8405 Del Vikings: Come Go With Me 1957 gold label £100
HLD8410 Tab Hunter: Ninety Nine Ways 1957 £8
HLD8412 Mac Wiseman: Step It Up And Go 1957 £250
HLD8413 Gale Storm: Orange Blossoms 1957 £10
HLD8415 Fontane Sisters: Please Don't Leave Me 1957 £15
HLD8417 Ken Nordine: Ship That Never Sailed 1957 £4
HLD8421 Anna Valentino: Calypso Joe 1957 £15
HLD8424 Gale Storm: Dark Moon 1957 £10
HLD8431 Jim Lowe: Four Walls 1957 £15
HLD8439 Ronnie O'Dell: Melody Of Napoli 1957 £8
HLD8441 Hilltoppers: I'm Serious 1957 £12
HLD8445 Pat Boone: Love Letters In The Sand 1957 £4
HLD8451 Margaret Whiting: Kill Me With Kisses 1957 £8
HLD8455 Hilltoppers: Fallen Star 1957 £12
HLD8460 Jimmy Newman: Fallen Star 1957 £15
HLD8464 Del Vikings: Whispering Bells 1957 £30
HLD8479 Pat Boone: Remember You're Mine 1957 £4
HLD8488 Fontane Sisters: Fool Around 1957 £12
HLD8500 Nick Todd: Plaything 1957 £25
HLD8511 Billy Vaughn: Johnny Tremain 1957 £5
HLD8512 Pat Boone: April Love 1957 £4
HLD8520 Pat Boone: White Christmas 1957 £4
HLD8522 Billy Vaughn: Raunchy 1957 £5
HLD8528 Hilltoppers: Joker 1957 £15
HLD8534 Hal March: Hear Me Good 1958 £12
HLD8535 Tab Hunter: Don't Let It Get Around 1958 £10
HLD8537 Nick Todd: At The Hop 1958 £12
HLD8538 Jim Lowe: Rock A Chicka 1958 £75
HLD8540 Johnny Maddox: Yellow Dog Blues 1958 £6
HLD8553 Mills Brothers: Get A Job 1958 £15
HLD8562 Margaret Whiting: I Can't Help It 1958 £6
HLD8570 Gale Storm: Farewell To Arms 1958 £8
HLD8576 Frank De Rosa: Big Guitar 1958 £20
HLD8591 Bonnie Guitar: Very Precious Love 1958 £8
HLD8603 Hilltoppers: You Sure Look Good To Me 1958 £8

HLD8612 Billy Vaughn: Tumbling Tumbleweeds 1958 £5
HLD8621 Fontane Sisters: Chanson D'Amour 1958 £8
HLD8632 Gale Storm: You 1958 £8
HLD8662 Margaret Whiting: Hot Spell 1958 £8
HLD8676 Robin Luke: Susie Darling 1958 £6
HLD8706 Shields: You Cheated 1958 £30
HLD8771 Robin Luke: Chicka Chicka Honey 1958 £10
HLD8791 Clark Sisters: Chicago 1959 £6
HLD8824 Pat Boone: Good Rockin' Tonight 1959 £4
HLD8826 Johnny Maddox: Hurdy Gurdy Song 1959 £4
HLD8828 Bob Crosby: Petite Fleur 1959 £4
HLD8834 Dodie Stevens: Pink Shoe Laces 1959 £12
HLD8858 Treniers: When Your Hair Has Turned Silver 1959 £25
HLD8861 Fontane Sisters: Billy Boy 1959 £8
HLD8902 Nick Todd: Tiger 1959 £20
HLD8923 Louis Prima & Keely Smith: Bei Mir Bist Du Schön 1959 £4
HLD8931 Sonny Williams: Bye Bye Baby Goodbye 1959 £15
HLD8937 Don Cornell: This Earth Is Mine 1959 £4
HLD8962 Wink Martindale: Deck Of Cards 1959 £4
HLD8984 Keely Smith: If I Knew I'd Find You 1959 £6
HLD9037 Fontane Sisters: Listen To Your Heart 1960 £5
HLD9038 Hilltoppers: Alone 1960 £5
HLD9042 Wink Martindale: Life Gets Teejus Don't It? 1960 £4
HLD9043 Jim Lowe: He'll Have To Go 1960 £8
HLD9078 Fontane Sisters: Theme From A Summer Place 1960 £5
HLD9084 Louis Prima & Keely Smith: I'm Confessin' 1960 £4
HLD9148 Walter Brennan: Dutchman's Gold 1960 £4
HLD9228 Bob Crosby: Dark At The Top Of The Stairs 1960 £4
HLD9230 Louis Prima: Ol' Man Moses 1960 £5
HLD9240 Keely Smith: Here In My Heart 1960 £5
HLD9272 Ronnie Love: Chills And Fever 1961 £15
HLD9280 Dodie Stevens: Yes I'm Lonesome Tonight 1961 £5
HLD9381 Tab Hunter: Wild Side Of Life 1961 £6
HLD9417 Lennon Sisters: Sad Movies 1961 £5
HLD9419 Wink Martindale: Black Land Farmer 1961 £4
HLD9431 Alvino Rey: Original Mama Blues 1961 £5
HLD9455 Billy Joe Tucker: Boogie Woogie Bill 1961 £50
HLD9496 Robert Knight: Free Me 1962 £6
HLD9523 Arthur Alexander: You Better Move On 1962 £25
HLD9535 Stringalongs: Twistwatch 1962 £5
HLD9559 Tab Hunter: I Can't Stop Loving You 1962 £5
HLD9566 Arthur Alexander: Soldiers Of Love 1962 £25
HLD9588 Stringalongs: Spinnin' My Wheels 1962 £5
HLD9632 Jimmy Gilmer: I'm Gonna Go Walkin' 1962 £5
HLD9641 Arthur Alexander: Anna 1962 £25
HLD9652 Stringalongs: Matilda 1963 £6
HLD9667 Arthur Alexander: Go Home Girl 1963 £20
HLD9684 Rumblers: Boss 1963 £12
HLD9696 Chantays: Pipeline 1963 £5
HLD9719 Dartells: Dartell Stomp 1963 £8
HLD9751 Surfaris: Wipe Out 1963 £4
HLD9789 Jimmy Gilmer: Sugar Shack 1963 £5

HLD9821 Robin Ward: Wonderful Summer 1963 £6
HLD9827 Jimmy Gilmer: Daisy Petal Picking 1964 £4
HLD9835 Dale Ward: Letter from Shirley 1964 £8
HLD9869 Bob Osburn: Bound To Happen 1964 £10
HLD9872 Jimmy Gilmer: Ain't Gonna Tell Nobody 1964 £4
HLD9898 Jimmy Gilmer: Look At Me 1964 £5
HLD9899 Arthur Alexander: Black Night 1964 £15
HLE8210 Ruth Brown: As Long As I'm Moving 1955 £200
HLE8229 Clovers: Nip Sip 1956 £600
HLE8250 Clyde McPhatter: Seven Days 1956 £300
HLE8260 Lavern Baker: Get Up Get Up 1956 £250
HLE8261 Ivory Joe Hunter: Tear Fell 1956 £250
HLE8293 Clyde McPhatter: Treasure Of Love 1956 £175
HLE8301 Joe Turner: Corrine Corrina 1956 £250
HLE8310 Ruth Brown: I Want To Do More 1956 £100
HLE8314 Clovers: Love Love Love 1956 £400
HLE8332 Joe Turner: Boogie Woogie Country Girl 1956 £500
HLE8334 Clovers: From The Bottom Of My Heart 1956 £400
HLE8344 Drifters: Soldier Of Fortune 1956 £750
HLE8357 Joe Turner: Lipstick Powder And Paint 1957 £300
HLE8396 Lavern Baker: I Can't Love You Enough 1957 £75
HLE8401 Ruth Brown: Mom Oh Mom 1957 £100
HLE8442 Lavern Baker: Game Of Love 1957 £150
HLE8444 Chuck Willis: C.C. Rider 1957 £50
HLE8450 Coasters: Searchin' 1957 £25
HLE8462 Clyde McPhatter: Just To Hold Your Hand 1957 £100
HLE8463 Dean Beard & The Crewcuts: On My Mind Again 1957 £300
HLE8476 Clyde McPhatter: Long Lonely Nights 1957 £75
HLE8477 Bobbettes: Mr Lee 1957 £30
HLE8483 Ruth Brown: One More Time 1957 £50
HLE8486 Ivory Joe Hunter: Love's A Hurting Game 1957 £100
HLE8489 Chuck Willis: That Train Has Gone 1957 £40
HLE8490 Jimmy Breedlove: Over Somebody Else's Shoulder 1957 £60
HLE8496 Jerry Diamond: Sunburned Lips 1957 £20
HLE8524 Lavern Baker: Humpty Dumpty Heart 1957 £75
HLE8525 Clyde McPhatter: Rock And Cry 1957 £60
HLE8544 Young Jessie: Shuffle In The Gravel 1958 £200
HLE8552 Ruth Brown: New Love 1958 £50
HLE8557 Betty Johnson: Little Blue Man 1958 £25
HLE8595 Chuck Willis: Betty And Dupree 1958 £40
HLE8597 Bobbettes: Come A Come A Come A 1958 £30
HLE8616 Otis Blackwell: Make Ready For Love 1958 £30
HLE8635 Chuck Willis: What Am I Living For 1958 £25
HLE8637 Ganim's Asia Minors: Daddy Lolo 1958 £5
HLE8638 Lavern Baker: Learning To Love 1958 £60
HLE8645 Ruth Brown: Just Too Much 1958 £40
HLE8665 Coasters: Yakety Yak 1958 £10
HLE8666 Bobby Darin: Splish Splash 1958 £20
HLE8667 Hutch Davie & His Honky Tonkers: At The Woodchoppers' Ball 1958 £6
HLE8672 Lavern Baker: Whipper Snapper 1958 £50
HLE8678 Betty Johnson: Dream 1958 £12
HLE8679 Bobby Darin & Rinky Dinks: Early in The Morning 1958 £30

HLE8683 Sandy Stewart: Certain Smile 1958 £10
HLE8686 Drifters: Moonlight Bay 1958 £100
HLE8701 Betty Johnson: There's Never Been A Night 1958 £30
HLE8707 Clyde McPhatter: Come What May 1958 £40
HLE8725 Betty Johnson: Hoopa Hula 1958 £25
HLE8729 Coasters: The Shadow Knows 1958 £30
HLE8735 Kingsmen: Better Believe It 1958 £15
HLE8737 Bobby Darin: Queen Of The Hop 1958 £20
HLE8755 Clyde McPhatter: Lover's Question 1958 £25
HLE8757 Ruth Brown: This Little Girl's Gone Rocking 1958 £40
HLE8768 Ray Charles: Rockhouse 1958 £20
HLE8790 Lavern Baker: I Cried A Tear 1959 £25
HLE8793 Bobby Darin & Rinky Dinks: Mighty Mighty Man 1959 £25
HLE8812 Kingsmen: Conga Rock 1959 £20
HLE8815 Bobby Darin: Plain Jane 1959 £20
HLE8818 Chuck Willis: My Life 1959 £25
HLE8819 Coasters: Charlie Brown 1959 £5
HLE8839 Betty Johnson: Does Your Heart Beat For Me 1959 £20
HLE8869 Chris Connor: Hallelujah I Love Him So 1959 £4
HLE8871 Lavern Baker: I've Waited Too Long 1959 £25
HLE8878 Clyde McPhatter: Lovey Dovey 1959 £25
HLE8882 Coasters: Along Came Jones 1959 £8
HLE8887 Ruth Brown: Jack Of Diamonds 1959 £30
HLE8892 Drifters: There Goes My Baby 1959 £12
HLE8906 Clyde McPhatter: Since You've Been Gone 1959 £25
HLE8917 Ray Charles: What I Say 1959 £10
HLE8938 Coasters: Poison Ivy 1959 £8
HLE8939 Bobby Darin: Mack The Knife 1959 £4
HLE8945 Lavern Baker: So High So Low 1959 £25
HLE8946 Ruth Brown: I Don't Know 1959 £25
HLE8988 Drifters: Dance With Me 1959 £10
HLE9000 Clyde McPhatter: You Went Back On Your Word 1959 £30
HLE9009 Ray Charles: I'm Movin' On 1959 £5
HLE9020 Coasters: What About Us 1960 £5
HLE9023 Lavern Baker: Tiny Tim 1960 £25
HLE9054 Mickey & Kitty: Buttercup 1960 £15
HLE9055 Joe Turner: Honey Hush 1960 £30
HLE9058 Ray Charles: Let The Good Times Roll 1960 £5
HLE9071 Hollywood Flames: If I Thought You Needed Me 1960 £15
HLE9079 Clyde McPhatter: Just Give Me A Ring 1960 £30
HLE9080 Bobby Comstock: Jambalaya 1960 £10
HLE9081 Drifters: This Magic Moment 1960 £6
HLE9093 Ruth Brown: Don't Deceive Me 1960 £15
HLF8161 Bill Haley: Farewell So Long Goodbye 1955 £100
HLF8179 Dinning Sisters: Drifting And Dreaming 1955 £25
HLF8181 Billy Butterfield: Magnificent Matador 1955 £10
HLF8183 Ferko String Band: Ma She's Making Eyes At Me 1955 £10
HLF8186 Don Costa: Love Is A Many-Splendored Thing 1955 £15
HLF8188 Mulcays: Harbour Lights 1955 £15
HLF8194 Bill Haley: Rockin' Chair On The Moon 1955 £125
HLF8213 Ken Carson: Hawkeye 1955 £20
HLF8215 Ferko String Band: Happy Days Are Here Again 1955 £10

HLF8218 Dinning Sisters: Hold Me Tight 1956 £25
HLF8237 Ken Carson: Daniel Boone 1956 £15
HLF8244 Jackie Riggs: Great Pretender 1956 £20
HLF8371 Bill Haley: Rock The Joint 1957 gold label £100
HLG8245 Simon Bolivar: Merengue Holiday 1956 £8
HLG9066 Smiley Wilson: Running Bear 1960 £30
HLG9115 Eddie Cochran: Three Steps To Heaven 1960 £8
HLG9147 Joiner, Arkansas, Junior High School Band: National City 1960 £4
HLG9155 Garry Miles: Look For A Star 1960 £6
HLG9172 Johnny Burnette: Dreamin' 1960 £4
HLG9179 Bobby Vee: Devil Or Angel 1960 £15
HLG9185 Gogi Grant: Goin' Home 1960 £4
HLG9192 Statues: Blue Velvet 1960 £30
HLG9196 Eddie Cochran: Sweetie Pie 1960 £10
HLG9232 Ventures: Perfidia 1960 £4
HLG9254 Johnny Burnette: You're Sixteen 1960 £4
HLG9255 Bobby Vee: Rubber Ball 1961 £5
HLG9268 Buddy Knox: Lovey Dovey 1961 £10
HLG9269 Little Dippers: Lonely 1961 £8
HLG9284 Dick Lory: My Last Date 1961 £15
HLG9292 Ventures: Ram Bunk Shush 1961 £4
HLG9315 Johnny Burnette: Little Boy Sad 1961 £4
HLG9316 Bobby Vee: More Than I Can Say 1961 £4
HLG9319 Gene McDaniels: Hundred Pounds Of Clay 1961 £5
HLG9321 Billy Strange: Where Your Arms Used To Be 1961 £5
HLG9331 Buddy Knox: Ling Ting Tong 1961 £6
HLG9340 Rollers: Continental Walk 1961 £8
HLG9341 Fleetwoods: Tragedy 1961 £6
HLG9344 Ventures: Lullaby Of The Leaves 1961 £4
HLG9352 Cornbread & Jerry: L'il Ole Me 1961 £4
HLG9360 Julie London: Sanctuary 1961 £4
HLG9362 Eddie Cochran: Weekend 1961 £8
HLG9388 Johnny Burnette: Girls 1961 £4
HLG9389 Bobby Vee: How Many Tears 1961 £4
HLG9396 Gene McDaniels: Tear 1961 £5
HLG9403 Timi Yuro: Hurt 1961 £6
HLG9408 Dick & Dee Dee: Mountain's High 1961 £5
HLG9411 Ventures: Theme From Silver City 1961 £4
HLG9426 Fleetwoods: He's The Great Imposter 1961 £6
HLG9432 Troy Shondell: This Time 1961 £4
HLG9438 Bobby Vee: Take Good Care Of My Baby 1961 £4
HLG9448 Gene McDaniels: Tower Of Strength 1961 £5
HLG9453 Johnny Burnette: God, Country And My Baby 1961 £6
HLG9458 Johnny Burnette: Setting The Woods On Fire 1961 £6
HLG9459 Bobby Vee: Love's Made A Fool Of You 1961 £8
HLG9460 Eddie Cochran: Jeannie Jeannie Jeannie 1961 £15
HLG9464 Eddie Cochran: Pretty Girl 1961 £20
HLG9465 Ventures: Blue Moon 1961 £6
HLG9467 Eddie Cochran: Stockings And Shoes 1961 £20
HLG9470 Bobby Vee: Run To Him 1961 £4
HLG9472 Buddy Knox: Three Eyed Man 1961 £6
HLG9473 Johnny Burnette: Fool 1961 £6

HLG9483 Dick & Dee Dee: Goodbye To Love 1962 £5
HLG9484 Johnnie Ray: I Believe 1962 Timi Yuro B-side £5
HLG9486 Crickets: He's Old Enough To Know Better 1961 £5
HLH8274 Cathy Carr: Ivory Tower 1956 £25
HLH8295 Dick Noel: Birds And The Bees 1956 £15
HLH8573 Dale Wright: She's Neat 1958 £125
HLH8646 Dion: I Wonder Why 1958 £50
HLH8704 Little Anthony & Imperials: Tears On My Pillow 1958 £40
HLH8811 Champs: Beatnick 1959 £5
HLH8864 Champs: Caramba 1959 £5
HLH8943 Jerry Wallace: Primrose Lane 1959 £4
HLH8982 Jerry Fuller: Tennessee Waltz 1959 £5
HLH9040 Jerry Wallace: Little Coco Palm 1960 £4
HLH9110 Jerry Wallace: You're Singing Our Love Song 1960 £4
HLH9395 Jan & Dean: Heart And Soul 1961 £10
HLH9430 Champs: Cantina 1961 £4
HLH9506 Champs: Limbo Rock 1962 £4
HLH9539 Champs: Experiment In Terror 1962 £4
HLH9604 Champs: Latin Limbo 1962 £4
HLH9705 George McCurn: I'm Just A Country Boy 1963 £5
HLH9804 Galens: Baby I Do Love You 1963 £5
HLI9072 Johnny & The Hurricanes: Beatnik Fly 1959 £4
HLI9153 Videls: Mister Lonely 1960 £30
HLI9186 Shirley & Lee: I've Been Loved Before 1960 £15
HLI9209 Shirley & Lee: Let The Good Times Roll 1960 £12
HLJ8164 Four Tunes: Tired Of Waiting 1955 £30
HLJ8207 Coney Island Kids: Baby Baby You 1955 £15
HLJ8466 Don Rondo: White Silver Sands 1957 £5
HLJ8549 Moe Koffman: Swingin' Shepherd Blues 1958 £6
HLJ8567 Don Rondo: What A Shame 1958 £6
HLJ8610 Don Rondo: I've Got Bells On My Heart 1958 £5
HLJ8633 Moe Koffman: Little Pixie 1958 £5
HLJ8641 Don Rondo: Blonde Bombshell 1958 £8
HLJ8644 Bobby Freeman: Do You Wanna Dance 1958 £20
HLJ8674 Jim Backus: Delicious 1958 £4
HLJ8687 Della Reese: You Gotta Love Everybody 1958 £6
HLJ8688 Upbeats: My Foolish Heart 1958 £12
HLJ8721 Bobby Freeman: Betty Lou Got A New Pair Of Shoes 1958 £25
HLJ8744 Royaltones: Poor Boy 1958 £10
HLJ8782 Bobby Freeman: Need Your Love 1959 £20
HLJ8786 Cadillacs: Peek A Boo 1959 £30
HLJ8813 Moe Koffman: Shepherd's Cha Cha 1959 £5
HLJ8814 Della Reese: Sermonette 1959 £5
HLJ8898 Bobby Freeman: Mary Ann Thomas 1959 £15
HLJ8987 Tony Reese: Just About This Time Tomorrow 1959 £5
HLJ9031 Bobby Freeman: Ebb Tide 1960 £6
HLJ9118 Sylvia Robbins: Frankie And Johnny 1960 £10
HLK9111 Coasters: Besame Mucho 1960 £5
HLK9119 Joe Turner: My Little Honeydripper 1960 £30
HLK9124 Chris Connor: I Only Want Some 1960 £4
HLK9140 Teddy Redell: Judy 1960 £50
HLK9145 Drifters: Lonely Winds 1960 £6

HLK9151 Coasters: Stewball 1960 £5
HLK9173 Bobbettes: I Shot Mr Lee 1960 £20
HLK9181 Ray Charles: Tell The Truth 1960 £5
HLK9197 Bobby Darin: Beachcomber 1960 £4
HLK9201 Drifters: Save The Last Dance For Me 1960 £4
HLK9208 Coasters: Shopping For Clothes 1960 £5
HLK9236 Billy Storm: Sure As You're Born 1960 £5
HLK9251 Ray Charles: Come Rain Or Come Shine 1960 £4
HLK9252 Lavern Baker: Bumble Bee 1960 £20
HLK9258 Ben E. King: Spanish Harlem 1961 £6
HLK9274 Danny Reid: Teenager Feels It Too 1961 £4 as 'Denny Reed' £10
HLK9287 Drifters: I Count The Tears 1961 £4
HLK9293 Coasters: Thumbin' A Ride 1961 £4
HLK9300 Lavern Baker: You're The Boss 1961 with Jimmy Ricks £15
HLK9304 Ruth Brown: Sure Nuff 1961 £20
HLK9310 Carla Thomas: Gee Whiz 1961 £10
HLK9326 Drifters: Some Kind Of Wonderful 1961 £6
HLK9343 Lavern Baker: Saved 1961 £20
HLK9349 Coasters: Little Egypt 1961 £4
HLK9358 Ben E. King: Stand By Me 1961 £6
HLK9359 Carla Thomas: Love Of My Own 1961 £8
HLK9364 Ray Charles: Early In The Mornin' 1961 £4
HLK9382 Drifters: Please Stay 1961 £5
HLK9399 Markeys: Last Night 1961 £5
HLK9407 Bobby Darin: Theme From Come September 1961 £6
HLK9413 Coasters: Girls Girls Girls 1961 £4
HLK9416 Ben E. King: Amor Amor 1961 £4
HLK9427 Drifters: Sweets For My Sweet 1961 £5
HLK9435 Ray Charles: I Wonder Who 1961 £4
HLK9449 Markeys: Morning After 1961 £4
HLK9454 Solomon Burke: Just Out Of Reach 1961 £15
HLK9457 Ben E. King: Here Comes The Night 1961 £5
HLK9468 Lavern Baker: Voodoo Voodoo 1961 £40
HLK9493 Coasters: Ain't That Just Like Me 1962 £4
HLK9500 Drifters: Room Full Of Tears 1962 £5
HLK9508 Ikettes: I'm Blue 1962 £8
HLK9510 Markeys: Foxy 1962 £4
HLK9512 Solomon Burke: Cry To Me 1962 £25
HLK9517 Ben E. King: Yes 1962 £4
HLK9522 Drifters: When My Little Girl Is Smiling 1962 £4
HLK9544 Ben E. King: Don't Play That Song 1962 £4
HLK9552 Ritchie Barrett: Some Other Guy 1962 £25
HLK9554 Drifters: Stranger On The Shore 1962 £4
HLK9560 Solomon Burke: Down In The Valley 1962 £8
HLK9565 Falcons: I Found A Love 1962 £30
HLK9580 Nino Tempo & April Stevens: Sweet And Lovely 1962 £5
HLK9586 Ben E. King: Too Bad 1962 £4
HLK9595 Booker T & The MGs: Green Onions 1962 £5
HLK9618 Carla Thomas: I'll Bring It On Home To You 1962 £8
HLK9626 Drifters: Up On The Roof 1962 £4
HLK9631 Ben E. King: I'm Standing By 1962 £6
HLK9643 Mel Tormé: Comin' Home Baby 1962 £5

HLK9649 Lavern Baker: See See Rider 1963 £25
HLK9663 Bobby Darin: Keep A Walking 1963 £4
HLK9670 Booker T & The MGs: Jelly Bread 1963 £5
HLK9681 Shepherd Sisters: What Makes Little Girls Cry 1963 £10
HLK9691 Ben E. King: How Can I Forget 1963 £4
HLK9699 Drifters: On Broadway 1963 £5
HLK9708 Little Richard: Crying In The Chapel 1963 £5
HLK9715 Solomon Burke: If You Need Me 1963 £8
HLK9724 Barbara Lewis: Hello Stranger 1963 £10
HLK9748 Betty Carter: Good Life 1963 £4
HLK9749 Doris Troy: Just One Look 1963 £10
HLK9750 Drifters: Rat Race 1963 £5
HLK9756 Little Richard: Travelling Shoes 1963 £5
HLK9758 Shepherd Sisters: Talk Is Cheap 1963 £8
HLK9763 Solomon Burke: Can't Nobody Love You 1963 £8
HLK9768 High Keys: Qué Será Será 1963 £10
HLK9778 Ben E. King: I (Who Have Nothing) 1963 £4
HLK9779 Barbara Lewis: Straighten Up Your Heart 1963 £10
HLK9782 Nino Tempo & April Stevens: Deep Purple 1963 £4
HLK9784 Booker T & The MGs: Chinese Checkers 1963 £5
HLK9785 Drifters: I'll Take You Home 1963 £4
HLK9799 Rufus Thomas: Walking The Dog 1963 £10
HLK9819 Ben E. King: I Could Have Danced All Night 1963 £4
HLK9829 Nino Tempo & April Stevens: Whispering 1964 £4
HLK9832 Barbara Lewis: Snap Your Fingers 1964 £8
HLK9833 Otis Redding: Pain In My Heart 1964 £10
HLK9840 Ben E. King: Grooving 1964 £4
HLK9848 Drifters: In The Land Of Make Believe 1964 £4
HLK9849 Solomon Burke: He'll Have To Go 1964 £8
HLK9850 Rufus Thomas: Can Your Monkey Do The Dog 1964 £6
HLK9859 Nino Tempo & April Stevens: Stardust 1964 £4
HLK9863 Coasters: T'ain't Nothing To Me 1964 £4
HLK9875 Vibrations: My Girl Sloopy 1964 £8
HLK9876 Otis Redding: Come To Me 1964 £10
HLK9884 Rufus Thomas: Somebody Stole My Dog 1964 £6
HLK9886 Drifters: One Way Love 1964 £4
HLK9887 Solomon Burke: Someone To Love 1964 £8
HLK9890 Nino Tempo & April Stevens: I'm Confessing 1964 £4
HLL8290 Willows: Church Bells May Ring 1956 £600
HLL8774 Charlie Margulis: Gigi 1959 £5
HLL8785 Jesse Lee Turner: Shake Baby Shake 1959 £40
HLL8825 Arlyne Tye: Universe 1959 £10
HLL8851 Jack Scott: I Never Felt Like This 1959 £8
HLL8881 Gary Stites: Lonely For You 1959 £15
HLL8912 Jack Scott: Way I Walk 1959 tri-centre £15
HLL8968 Paul Evans: Seven Little Girls Sitting In The Back Seat 1959 £6
HLL8970 Jack Scott: There Comes A Time 1959 tri-centre £10
HLL8983 Anita Bryant: Six Boys And Seven Girls 1959 £4
HLL9003 Gary Stites: Starry Eyed 1959 £6
HLL9019 Nelson Trio: All In Good Time 1960 £5
HLL9045 Paul Evans: Midnight Special 1960 £8
HLL9075 Anita Bryant: Little George 1960 £4

HLL9082 Gary Stites: Lawdy Miss Clawdy 1960 £10
HLL9129 Paul Evans: Happy Go Lucky Me 1960 £5
HLL9171 Anita Bryant: My Little Corner Of The World 1960 £4
HLL9183 Paul Evans: Brigade Of Broken Hearts 1960 £5
HLL9239 Paul Evans: Hushabye Little Guitar 1960 £8
HLL9336 Strollers: Come On Over 1961 £10
HLL9428 Chantels: Look In My Eyes 1961 £15
HLL9478 Danny Peppermint: Peppermint Twist 1961 £4
HLL9480 Chantels: Still 1962 £12
HLL9510 Danny Peppermint: One More Time 1962 £4
HLL9532 Chantels: Summertime 1962 £12
HLL9614 Danny Peppermint: Maybe Tomorrow 1962 £4
HLL9729 Orval Prophet: Run Run Run 1963 £5
HLM8531 Chuck Berry: Rock & Roll Music 1957 £40
HLM8546 Lee Andrews & The Hearts: Teardrops 1958 £200
HLM8585 Chuck Berry: Sweet Little Sixteen 1958 £20
HLM8598 Jimmy McCracklin: Walk 1958 £30
HLM8622 Kendall Sisters: Won't You Be My Baby 1958 £40
HLM8625 Monotones: Book Of Love 1958 £40
HLM8629 Chuck Berry: Johnny B. Goode 1958 £15
HLM8664 Wendall Tracey: Who's To Know 1958 £20
HLM8682 Johnnie & Joe: Over the Mountain Across The Sea 1958 £200
HLM8698 Dean Allen: Ooh Ooh Baby Baby 1958 £20
HLM8711 Eddie Fontaine: Nothing Shaking 1958 £20
HLM8728 Dale Hawkins: La Do Da Da 1958 £30
HLM8730 Harvey & The Moonglows: Ten Commandments Of Love 1958 £200
HLM8745 Solitaires: Walking Along 1958 £100
HLM8767 Chuck Berry: Sweet Little Rock and Roller 1958 £15
HLM8801 Tab Smith: My Happiness Cha Cha 1959 £5
HLM8842 Dale Hawkins: Yea Yea Classcutter 1959 £30
HLM8849 Rod Bernard: This Should Go On Forever 1959 £20
HLM8853 Chuck Berry: Little Queenie 1959 £15
HLM8913 Bo Diddley: Great Grandfather 1959 £30
HLM8921 Chuck Berry: Memphis Tennessee 1959 £20
HLM8966 Mel Robbins: Save It 1959 tri-centre £300
HLM8975 Bo Diddley: Say Man 1959 £30
HLM8998 Paul Gayten: Hunch 1959 £100
HLM9016 Dale Hawkins: Liza Jane 1959 £25
HLM9035 Bo Diddley: Say Man Back Again 1960 £30
HLM9053 Larry Williams: Baby Baby 1960 £15
HLM9060 Dale Hawkins: Hot Dog 1960 £25
HLM9069 Chuck Berry: Let It Rock 1960 £10
HLM9112 Bo Diddley: Road Runner 1960 £40
HLM9139 Etta James: All I Could Do Was Cry 1960 £15
HLM9159 Chuck Berry: Bye Bye Johnny 1960 £10
HLM9175 Little Walter: My Babe 1960 £15
HLM9180 Etta & Harvey: If I Can't Have You 1960 £30
HLM9234 Etta James: My Dearest Darling 1960 £12
HLN8305 Mel Tormé: Lulu's Back In Town 1956 £6
HLN8322 Mel Tormé: Lullaby Of Birdland 1956 £6
HLN8340 Vince Martin with the Tarriers: Cindy Oh Cindy 1956 £20
HLN8354 Pearl Bailey: That Certain Feeling 1956 £8

HLN8372 Ivy Schulman & The Bowties: Rock Pretty Baby 1957 £40
HLN8373 Flamingos: Just For A Kick 1957 £400
HLN8374 Moonglows: I Knew From The Start 1957 £400
HLN8375 Chuck Berry: You Can't Catch Me 1957 £150
HLN8389 Clarence 'Frogman' Henry: Ain't Got No Home 1957 £150
HLN8472 Larry Williams: Short Fat Fannie 1957 £25
HLN8694 Tony & Joe: Freeze 1958 £30
HLN8733 Teddy Bears: To Know Him Is To Love Him 1958 £5
HLN8838 Art & Dottie Todd: Straight As An Arrow 1959 £10
HLN8936 Jan & Dean: Baby Talk 1959 £15
HLN9047 Dorsey Burnette: Tall Oak Tree 1960 £10
HLN9074 Johnny Bachelor: Mumbles 1960 £30
HLN9160 Dorsey Burnette: Hey Little One 1960 £12
HLN9168 Donnie Brooks: Mission Bell 1960 £4
HLN9194 Larry Verne: Mr Custer 1960 £4
HLN9253 Donnie Brooks: Doll House 1960 £4
HLN9263 Larry Verne: Mr Livingston 1961 £4
HLN9361 Donnie Brooks: That's Why 1961 £4
HLN9365 Dorsey Burnette: It's No Sin 1961 £8
HLN9392 Castells: Sacred 1961 £15
HLN9439 Jerry Fuller: Guilty Of Loving You 1961 £4
HLN9527 Ketty Lester: Love Letters 1962 £4
HLN9551 Castells: So This Is Love 1962 £15
HLN9572 Donnie Brooks: Oh You Beautiful Doll 1962 £4
HLN9619 Carol Connors: Big Big Love 1962 £6
HLN9647 Toy Dolls: Little Tin Soldier 1963 £10
HLN9656 Moments: Walk Right In 1963 £5
HLN9851 Crescents: Pink Dominoes 1964 £6
HLN9894 Bermudas: Donnie 1964 £6
HLN9954 Jewel Akens: Birds And The Bees 1965 £4
HLO8336 Little Richard: Rip It Up 1956 £75
HLO8366 Little Richard: Long Tall Sally 1957 £75
HLO8382 Little Richard: Girl Can't Help It 1957 £75
HLO8435 Gladiolas: Little Darling 1957 £200
HLO8446 Little Richard: Lucille 1957 £15
HLO8470 Little Richard: Jenny Jenny 1957 £15
HLO8509 Little Richard: Keep A Knocking 1957 £15
HLO8533 Four Esquires: Love Me Forever 1958 £10
HLO8579 Four Esquires: Always And Forever 1958 £6
HLO8631 Aquatones: You 1958 £30
HLO8647 Little Richard: Ooh My Soul 1958 £8
HLP8367 Smiley Lewis: Shame Shame Shame 1957 £500
HLP8377 Fats Domino: Blue Monday 1957 £30
HLP8391 Barons: Don't Walk Out 1957 £1500
HLP8392 Merle Kilgore: Ernie 1957 £200
HLP8398 Roy Brown: Party Doll 1957 £350
HLP8403 Slim Whitman: I'll Take You Home Again Kathleen 1957 £10
HLP8407 Fats Domino: I'm Walking 1957 £15
HLP8416 Slim Whitman: Curtain Of Tears 1957 £8
HLP8420 Slim Whitman: Gone 1957 gold label £20
HLP8423 Ken Copeland: Pledge Of Love 1957 Mints B-side £250
HLP8434 Slim Whitman: Many Times 1957 £8

HLP8448 Roy Brown: Saturday Night 1957 £500
HLP8449 Fats Domino: Valley Of Tears 1957 £15
HLP8459 Slim Whitman: Lovesick Blues 1957 £8
HLP8471 Fats Domino: When I See You 1957 £15
HLP8499 Rick Nelson: Be Bop Baby 1957 £20
HLP8518 Slim Whitman: Unchain My Heart 1957 £8
HLP8519 Fats Domino: Wait And See 1957 £12
HLP8523 Ernie Freeman: Raunchy 1957 £8
HLP8542 Rick Nelson: Stood Up 1958 £12
HLP8558 Ernie Freeman: Dumplin's 1958 £6
HLP8575 Fats Domino: Big Beat 1958 £10
HLP8578 Irving Ashby: Big Guitar 1958 £12
HLP8588 Jackie Walker: Oh Lonesome Me 1958 £150
HLP8590 Slim Whitman: Very Precious Love 1958 £8
HLP8594 Rick Nelson: Believe What You Say 1958 £10
HLP8628 Fats Domino: Sick And Tired 1958 £10
HLP8642 Slim Whitman: Candy Kisses 1958 £6
HLP8660 Ernie Freeman: Indian Love Call 1958 £5
HLP8663 Fats Domino: Little Mary 1958 £12
HLP8670 Rick Nelson: Poor Little Fool 1958 £4
HLP8708 Slim Whitman: Wherever You Are 1958 £6
HLP8727 Fats Domino: Young School Girl 1958 £15
HLP8732 Rick Nelson: Someday 1958 £4
HLP8738 Rick Nelson: My Babe 1958 £6
HLP8759 Fats Domino: Whole Lotta Loving 1958 £12
HLP8817 Rick Nelson: Never Be Anyone Else But You 1959 £5
HLP8822 Fats Domino: When The Saints Go Marching In 1959 £8
HLP8830 Jimmie & The Night Hoppers: Night Hop 1959 £15
HLP8835 Slim Whitman: I Never See Maggie Alone 1959 £5
HLP8836 Teddy Bears: Oh Why 1959 £10
HLP8865 Fats Domino: Margie 1959 £6
HLP8889 Teddy Bears: If Only You Knew 1959 £20
HLP8927 Rick Nelson: Just A Little Too Much 1959 £6
HLP8942 Fats Domino: I Want To Walk You Home 1959 £8
HLP8967 Jules Farmer: Love Me Now 1959 £5
HLP8997 Sammy Salvo: Afraid 1959 £6
HLP9005 Fats Domino: Be My Guest 1959 tri-centre £25; round centre £5
HLP9015 Sandy Nelson: Drum Party 1959 £5
HLP9021 Rick Nelson: I Wanna Be Loved 1960 £4
HLP9036 Sonny Anderson: Lonely Lonely Train 1960 £30
HLP9041 Ernie Freeman: Big River 1960 £4
HLP9073 Fats Domino: Country Boy 1960 £6
HLP9098 Georgia Gibbs: Stroll That Stole My Heart 1960 £4
HLP9103 Slim Whitman: Roll River Roll 1960 £4
HLP9108 Jesse Lee Turner: I'm The Little Space Girl's Father 1960 £20
HLP9121 Rick Nelson: Young Emotions 1960 £4
HLP9133 Fats Domino: Tell Me That You Love Me 1960 £10
HLP9163 Fats Domino: Walking To New Orleans 1960 £6
HLP9188 Rick Nelson: Yes Sir That's My Baby 1960 £4
HLP9198 Fats Domino: Three Nights A Week 1960 £6
HLP9214 Sandy Nelson: Bouncy 1960 £4
HLP9222 Frankie Ford: You Talk Too Much 1960 £15

HLP9244 Fats Domino: My Girl Josephine 1960 £5
HLP9260 Rick Nelson: Milkcow Blues 1961 £6
HLP9301 Fats Domino: Ain't That Just Like A Woman 1961 £8
HLP9302 Slim Whitman: Vaya Con Dios 1961 £4
HLP9327 Fats Domino: Shurah 1961 £8
HLP9347 Rick Nelson: Hello Mary Lou 1961 £4
HLP9374 Fats Domino: It Keeps Raining 1961 £15
HLP9377 Sandy Nelson: Get With It 1961 £4
HLP9415 Fats Domino: Let The Four Winds Blow 1961 £6
HLP9440 Rick Nelson: Everlovin' 1961 £4
HLP9456 Fats Domino: What A Party 1961 £6
HLP9481 Showmen: It Will Stand 1962 £50
HLP9487 Ernie K. Doe: Certain Girl 1962 £8
HLP9499 Clay Cole: Twist Around The Clock 1962 £4
HLP9520 Fats Domino: Jambalaya 1962 £5
HLP9524 Rick Nelson: Young World 1962 £4
HLP9557 Fats Domino: My Real Name 1962 £8
HLP9558 Sandy Nelson: Drummin' Up A Storm 1962 £4
HLP9562 Lloyd George: Sing Real Loud 1962 £25
HLP9570 Benny Spellman: Fortune Teller 1962 £30
HLP9571 Showmen: Wrong Girl 1962 £75
HLP9583 Rick Nelson: Teenage Idol 1962 £4
HLP9590 Fats Domino: Nothing New 1962 £8
HLP9602 Majors: Wonderful Dream 1962 £8
HLP9612 Sandy Nelson: And Then There Were Drums 1962 £4
HLP9616 Fats Domino: Stop The Clock 1962 £8
HLP9627 Majors: She's A Troublemaker 1962 £10
HLP9648 Rick Nelson: It's Up To You 1963 £4
HLP9693 Majors: What In The World 1963 £8
HLP9717 Sandy Nelson: Ooh Poo Pah Doo 1963 £4
HLP9738 Fats Domino: You Always Hurt The One You Love 1963 £6
HLR8395 Jane Morgan: From The First Hello 1957 £15
HLR8422 Roger Williams: Almost Paradise 1957 £4
HLR8436 Jane Morgan: Around The World 1957 £10
HLR8452 Buddy Greco: With All My Heart 1957 £10
HLR8454 Armenian Jazz Quartet: Harem Dance 1957 £8
HLR8458 Jose Duval: Message Of Love 1957 £10
HLR8468 Jane Morgan: Fascination 1957 £8
HLR8469 Troubadours: Fascination 1957 £8
HLR8516 Roger Williams: Till 1957 £4
HLR8539 Jane Morgan: I'm New At The Game Of Romance 1958 £6
HLR8541 Troubadours: Lights Of Paris 1958 £8
HLR8543 Mark Stone: Stroll 1958 £60
HLR8572 Roger Williams: Arrivederci Roma 1958 £4
HLR8577 Chuck Sims: Little Pigeon 1958 best auctioned £250
HLR8611 Jane Morgan: I've Got Bells On My Heart 1958 £6
HLR8613 Buddy Greco: I've Grown Accustomed To Her Face 1958 £4
HLR8649 Jane Morgan: Enchanted Island 1958 £5
HLR8696 Jo March: Dormi, Dormi, Dormi 1958 £4
HLR8763 Jo March: Virgin Mary Had One Son 1958 £4
HLR8805 X Rays: Out Of Control 1959 £25
HLR8833 Bill Hayes: Wimoweh 1959 £6

HLR8837 Carmen McRae: Play For Keeps 1959 £5
HLR8890 Jerry Keller: Here Comes Summer 1959 tri-centre £4
HLR8969 Eartha Kitt: Love Is A Gamble 1959 £4
HLR8980 Jerry Keller: If I Had A Girl 1959 £4
HLR8981 Barbara Carroll: North By Northwest 1959 £5
HLR9106 Jerry Keller: Now Now Now 1960 £4
HLR9113 Brian Hyland: Rosemary 1960 £10
HLR9150 Lane Brothers: Mimi 1960 £10
HLR9161 Brian Hyland: Itsy Bitsy Teeny Weeny . . . 1960 £4
HLR9203 Brian Hyland: Four Little Heels 1960 £4
HLR9262 Brian Hyland: I Gotta Go 1961 £4
HLR9271 Eileen Rodgers: Sailor 1961 £6
HLR9589 Babs Tino: Forgive Me 1962 £10
HLR9640 Emotions: Come Dance Baby 1962 £20
HLR9679 Ruby & The Romantics: Our Day Will Come 1963 £5
HLR9682 Johnny Cymbal: Mister Bass Man 1963 £4
HLR9689 Jerry Jackson: Gypsy Eyes 1963 £10
HLR9701 Emotions: Love 1963 £20
HLR9731 Johnny Cymbal: Teenage Heaven 1963 £8
HLR9734 Ruby & The Romantics: My Summer Love 1963 £6
HLR9762 Johnny Cymbal: Dum Dum De Dum 1963 £5
HLR9770 Paul Evans: Even Tan 1963 £6
HLR9771 Ruby & The Romantics: Hey There Lonely Boy 1963 £8
HLR9801 Ruby & The Romantics: Young Wings Can Fly 1963 £6
HLR9802 Linda Scott: Let's Fall In Love 1963 £4
HLR9820 Charmettes: Please Don't Kiss Me Again 1963 £10
HLR9823 Barbara Chandler: Do You Really Love Me Too 1963 £5
HLR9824 Shirley Ellis: Nitty Gritty 1963 £4
HLR9860 Initials: School Days 1964 £6
HLR9861 Barbara Chandler: Lonely New Year 1964 £5
HLR9881 Ruby & The Romantics: Our Everlasting Love 1964 £5
HLR9893 Simon Sisters: Winkin' Blinkin' And Nod 1964 £6
HLR9911 Johnny Cymbal: Robinson Crusoe On Mars 1964 £8
HLR9916 Ruby & The Romantics: Baby Come Home 1964 £6
HLR9935 Ruby & The Romantics: When You're Young And In Love 1964 £6
HLR9946 Shirley Ellis: Name Game 1965 £4
HLR9947 You Know Who Group: Roses Are Red My Love 1965 £8
HLR9949 Sammy Masters: Big Man Cried 1965 £6
HLR9961 Shirley Ellis: Clapping Song 1965 £4
HLR9972 Ruby & The Romantics: Your Baby Doesn't Love You Anymore 1965 £8
HLR9973 Shirley Ellis: Puzzle Song 1965 £4
HLR9981 Lenny Welch: Darling Take Me Back 1965 £5
HLR9983 Tony Middleton & Burt Bacharach: My Little Red Book 1965 £12
HLR9984 Simon Sisters: Cuddlebug 1965 £5
HLR9993 Kids Next Door: Inky Dinky Spider 1965 £4
HLS8408 Carl Perkins: Matchbox 1957 £100
HLS8409 Ernie Chaffin: Lonesome For My Baby 1957 £100
HLS8427 Johnny Cash: Train Of Love 1957 £30
HLS8457 Jerry Lee Lewis: Whole Lotta Shaking Going On 1957 £15
HLS8461 Johnny Cash: Next In Line 1957 £20
HLS8514 Johnny Cash: Home Of The Blues 1957 £12
HLS8517 Bill Justis: Raunchy 1957 £10

HLS8527 Carl Perkins: Glad All Over 1957 £75
HLS8529 Jerry Lee Lewis: Great Balls Of Fire 1957 £10
HLS8559 Jerry Lee Lewis: You Win Again 1958 £15
HLS8586 Johnny Cash: Ballad Of A Teenage Queen 1958 £10
HLS8592 Jerry Lee Lewis: Breathless 1958 £6
HLS8608 Carl Perkins: That's Right 1958 £75
HLS8614 Bill Justis: College Man 1958 £10
HLS8656 Johnny Cash: Guess Things Happen That Way 1958 £8
HLS8691 Jack Clement: Ten Years 1958 £30
HLS8699 Jimmy Clanton: Just A Dream 1958 £8
HLS8700 Jerry Lee Lewis: Break Up 1958 £6
HLS8709 Johnny Cash: Ways Of A Woman In Love 1958 £6
HLS8779 Jimmy Clanton: Letter To An Angel 1959 £20
HLS8780 Jerry Lee Lewis: High School Confidential 1959 £12
HLS8789 Johnny Cash: It's Just About Time 1959 £6
HLS8832 Jimmy Isle: Diamond Ring 1959 £50
HLS8840 Jerry Lee Lewis: Loving Up A Storm 1959 £10
HLS8847 Johnny Cash: Luther Played The Boogie 1959 £10
HLS8928 Johnny Cash: Katy Too 1959 £6
HLS8935 Carl Mann: Mona Lisa 1959 £15
HLS8941 Jerry Lee Lewis: Let's Talk About Us 1959 tri-centre £6
HLS8979 Johnny Cash: You Tell Me 1959 £5
HLS8993 Jerry Lee Lewis: Little Queenie 1959 tri-centre £8
HLS9006 Carl Mann: Pretend 1959 £15
HLS9025 Vernon Taylor: Mystery Train 1960 £50
HLS9059 Tracy Pendarvis: Thousand Guitars 1960 £15
HLS9064 Sonny Burgess: Sadie's Back In Town 1960 £150
HLS9070 Johnny Cash: Straight A's In Love 1960 £6
HLS9083 Jerry Lee Lewis: I'll Sail My Ship Alone 1960 £5
HLS9131 Jerry Lee Lewis: Baby Baby Bye Bye 1960 £8
HLS9167 Rayburn Anthony: There's No Tomorrow 1960 £20
HLS9170 Carl Mann: South Of The Border 1960 £12
HLS9182 Johnny Cash: Down The Street To 301 1960 £5
HLS9202 Jerry Lee Lewis: Hang Up My Rock & Roll Shoes 1960 £5
HLS9213 Tracy Pendarvis: South Bound Line 1960 £15
HLS9314 Johnny Cash: Oh Lonesome Me 1961 £4
HLS9386 Harold Dorman: There They Go 1961 £15
HLS9414 Jerry Lee Lewis: It Won't Happen With Me 1961 £4
HLS9446 Jerry Lee Lewis: When I Get Paid 1961 £4
HLS9482 Charlie Rich: Just A Little Bit Sweet 1962 £20
HLS9526 Jerry Lee Lewis: Rambling Rose 1962 £4
HLS9584 Jerry Lee Lewis: Sweet Little Sixteen 1962 £4
HLS9585 Anita Wood: I'll Wait Forever 1962 £15
HLS9688 Jerry Lee Lewis: Good Golly Miss Molly 1963 £4
HLS9722 Jerry Lee Lewis: Teenage Letter 1963 £5
HLS9867 Jerry Lee Lewis: Lewis Boogie 1964 £6
HLS9980 Jerry Lee Lewis: Carry Me Back To Old Virginia 1965 £5
HLT8692 Hal Schaefer Orchestra: March Of The Vikings 1958 £4
HLT8705 Joe Valino: God's Little Acre 1958 £8
HLT8717 Tunerockers: Green Mosquito 1958 £20
HLT8724 Bob Carroll: Hi Ho Silver 1958 £8
HLT8787 Wildcats: Gazachstahagen 1959 £10

HLT8788 Diahann Carroll: Big Country 1959 £5
HLT8856 Marv Johnson: Come To Me 1959 £75
HLT8862 Marilyn Monroe: I Wanna Be Loved By You 1959 £15
HLT8876 Falcons: You're So Fine 1959 £60
HLT8888 Bob Carroll: I Can't Get You Out Of My Life 1959 £6
HLT8914 Kings IV: Some Like It Hot 1959 £8
HLT8949 Clovers: Love Potion No. 9 1959 £30
HLT8953 Delicates: Ronnie Is My Lover 1959 £75
HLT8992 Don Costa: I Walk The Line 1959 £5
HLT9011 Jaye Sisters: Sure Fire Love 1959 £30
HLT9013 Marv Johnson: You Got What It Takes 1959 £6
HLT9109 Marv Johnson: I Love The Way You Love Me 1960 £12
HLT9122 Clovers: One Mint Julep 1960 £25
HLT9154 Clovers: Easy Loving 1960 £20
HLT9165 Marv Johnson: Ain't Gonna Be That Way 1960 £12
HLT9176 Delicates: Too Young To Date 1960 £30
HLT9187 Marv Johnson: Move Two Mountains 1960 £10
HLT9265 Marv Johnson: Happy Days 1961 £12
HLT9290 Eydie Gorme & Steve Lawrence: Facts Of Life 1961 £5
HLT9311 Marv Johnson: Merry Go Round 1961 £20
HLT9325 Al Caiola: Bonanza 1961 £8
HLU8162 Dusty Rose: Birds And The Bees 1955 £30
HLU8166 Jim Edward & Maxine Brown: Your Love Is Wild As The West Wind 1955 £20
HLU8167 Slim Whitman: I'll Never Stop Loving You 1955 £20
HLU8173 Fats Domino: Ain't That A Shame 1955 £40
HLU8178 Vonnie Fritchie: Sugar Booger Avenue 1955 £25
HLU8180 Sunnysiders: Banjo Woogie 1955 £25
HLU8185 Jim Reeves: Tahiti 1955 £100
HLU8187 Myrna Lorrie: Underway 1955 £25
HLU8189 De Castro Sisters: If I Ever Fall In Love 1955 £20
HLU8191 Alvadean Coker: We're Gonna Bop 1955 £200
HLU8195 Floyd Cramer: Rag A Tag 1955 £20
HLU8196 Slim Whitman: Song Of The Wild 1955 £20
HLU8200 Jim Edward & Maxine Brown: Here Today And Gone Tomorrow 1955 £15
HLU8202 Sunnysiders: I Love You Fair Dinkum 1955 £20
HLU8204 Bill Darnell: My Little Mother 1955 £20
HLU8206 Duke & Duchess: Get Ready For Love 1955 £15
HLU8212 De Castro Sisters: Christmas Is Coming 1955 £20
HLU8214 Roger Williams: Autumn Leaves 1955 £8
HLU8216 Tom Tall: Give Me A Chance 1955 £25
HLU8219 Tommy Davidson: Half Past Kissing Time 1956 £50
HLU8228 De Castro Sisters: Give Me Time 1956 £20
HLU8230 Slim Whitman: Tumbling Tumbleweeds 1956 £15
HLU8231 Tom Tall: Underway 1956 £25
HLU8234 Bill Darnell: Last Frontier 1956 £25
HLU8240 Julie London: Cry Me A River 1956 £30
HLU8241 Eddie Albert & Sandra Lee: Jenny Kissed Me 1956 £12
HLU8242 Alfie & Harry: Trouble With Harry 1956 £10
HLU8246 Sunnysiders: Doesn't He Love Me 1956 £25
HLU8247 Bobby Charles: See You Later Alligator 1956 £2000
HLU8252 Slim Whitman: I'm A Fool 1956 £15
HLU8256 Fats Domino: Bo Weevil 1956 £75

HLU8258 Bill Krenz Ragtimers: Goofus 1956 £15
HLU8262 Bon Bons: Circle 1956 £25
HLU8267 Bill Darnell: Guilty Lips 1956 £20
HLU8269 Larry Evans: Crazy About My Baby 1956 £400
HLU8271 Carl Perkins: Blue Suede Shoes 1956 £150
HLU8275 Chuck Berry: No Money Down 1956 gold label £500
HLU8279 Julie London: Baby Baby All The Time 1956 £15
HLU8280 Fats Domino: My Blue Heaven 1956 £60
HLU8287 Slim Whitman: Serenade 1956 £15
HLU8292 Bill Darnell: Tell Me More 1956 £20
HLU8294 Myrna Lorrie: Life's Changing Scene 1956 £40
HLU8296 De Castro Sisters: No One To Blame But You 1956 £20
HLU8297 Willie Dixon: Walking The Blues 1956 £1500
HLU8299 Bob Carroll: Red Confetti, Pink Balloons & Tambourines 1956 £20
HLU8307 Betty Johnson: I'll Wait 1956 £30
HLU8309 Fats Domino: When My Dreamboat Comes Along 1956 £40
HLU8312 Smiley Lewis: One Night 1956 £600
HLU8313 Cadets: Stranded In The Jungle 1956 £400
HLU8321 Patience & Prudence: Tonight You Belong To Me 1956 £15
HLU8324 Dave Barry & Sarah Berner: Out Of This World With Flying Saucers 1956 £25
HLU8326 Betty Johnson: Honky Tonk Rock 1956 £100
HLU8327 Slim Whitman: Dear Mary 1956 £20
HLU8328 Judy Kileen: Just Walking In The Rain 1956 £20
HLU8330 Fats Domino: Blueberry Hill 1956 £40
HLU8331 Mack Sisters: Long Range Love 1956 £25
HLU8335 Lonnie Coleman & Jesse Robertson: Dolores Diana 1956 £25
HLU8337 Smiley Lewis: Don't Be That Way 1956 £600
HLU8339 Faye Adams: I'll Be True 1956 £500
HLU8341 Roger Williams & Jane Morgan: Two Different Worlds 1956 £10
HLU8345 Six Teens: Casual Look 1956 £300
HLU8350 Slim Whitman: I'm Casting My Lasso 1956 £15
HLU8351 Jim Reeves: Wilder Your Heart Beats 1956 £100
HLU8352 Rosanne June: Charge Of The Light Brigade 1956 £12
HLU8355 Muzzy Marcellino: Mary Lou 1956 Mr Ford & Mr Goon Bones B-side £15
HLU8356 Fats Domino: Honey Chile 1957 gold label £40
HLU8359 David Seville: Armen's Theme 1957 gold label £6
HLU8365 Betty Johnson: I Dreamed 1957 £30
HLU8369 Patience & Prudence: Gonna Get Along Without You Now 1957 £12
HLU8379 Roger Williams: Anastasia 1957 £5
HLU8385 Dom Frontiere: Jet Rink Ballad 1957 £20
HLU8386 Eddie Cochran: Twenty Flight Rock 1957 £100
HLU8387 Nino Tempo: Tempo's Tempo 1957 £200
HLU8388 Johnny Olenn: My Idea Of Love 1957 £250
HLU8390 Rod McKuen: Happy Is A Boy Named Me 1957 £25
HLU8394 Julie London: Meaning Of The Blues 1957 gold label £10
HLU8411 David Seville: Gift 1957 £5
HLU8414 Julie London: Boy On A Dolphin 1957 £6
HLU8425 Patience & Prudence: Dreamers' Bay 1957 £8
HLU8428 Chuck Berry: Roll Over Beethoven 1957 £75
HLU8429 Tom Tall & Ruckus Taylor: Don't You Know 1957 £20
HLU8432 Betty Johnson: 1492 1957 £25
HLU8433 Eddie Cochran: Sitting In The Balcony 1957 £200

HLU8465 Billy Ward & The Dominoes: Stardust 1957 £15
HLU8478 Jimmy Gavin: I Sit In My Window 1957 £50
HLU8484 Jeff Chandler: Half Of My Heart 1957 £6
HLU8485 David Seville: Got To Get To Your House 1957 £5
HLU8491 Robert Wagner: Almost Eighteen 1957 £12
HLU8493 Patience & Prudence: You Tattletale 1957 £6
HLU8494 Alfie & Harry: Closing Time 1957 £5
HLU8495 Lincoln Chase: Johnny Klingeringding 1957 £10
HLU8502 Billy Ward & The Dominoes: Deep Purple 1957 £15
HLU8505 Rays: Silhouettes 1957 £25
HLU8506 Sam Cooke: You Send Me 1957 £25
HLU8510 Timmie Rogers: Back To School Again 1957 £50
HLU8515 Margie Rayburn: I'm Available 1957 £10
HLU8521 Charlie Gracie: Cool Baby 1957 £20
HLU8526 Dubs: Could This Be Magic 1957 £150
HLU8532 Larry Williams: Bony Moronie 1958 £20
HLU8536 Jo Ann Campbell: Wait A Minute 1958 £25
HLU8551 Laura K. Bryant: Bobby 1958 £15
HLU8555 Tommy Fredericks: Prince Of Players 1958 £30
HLU8556 Four Winds: Short Shorts 1958 £25
HLU8560 Little Richard: Good Golly Miss Molly 1958 £15
HLU8561 Chantels: Maybe 1958 best auctioned £300
HLU8563 Crescendos: Oh Julie 1958 £30
HLU8564 Billie & Lillie: La Dee Dah 1958 £15
HLU8565 Billy Scott: You're The Greatest 1958 £10
HLU8569 Johnny Faire: Bertha Lou 1958 best auctioned £300
HLU8571 Storey Sisters: Bad Motorcycle 1958 £75
HLU8580 Champs: Tequila 1958 £6
HLU8581 Rene Hall: Twitchy 1958 £30
HLU8582 David Seville: Bonjour Tristesse 1958 £4
HLU8583 Kuff Linx: So Tough 1958 £125
HLU8589 Dickie Doo & The Donts: Click Clack 1958 £25
HLU8593 Bob Hope & Bing Crosby: Paris Holiday 1958 £6
HLU8596 Charlie Gracie: Crazy Girl 1958 £25
HLU8599 John Zacherley: Dinner With Drac 1958 £25
HLU8600 Tarriers: Lonesome Traveller 1958 £8
HLU8601 Timmie Rogers: Take Me To Your Leader 1958 £60
HLU8602 Julie London: Saddle The Wind 1958 £6
HLU8604 Larry Williams: Dizzy Miss Lizzy 1958 £30
HLU8605 Gene Allison: Hey Hey I Love You 1958 £60
HLU8606 Johnny Brantley: Place 1958 £15
HLU8607 Wes Bryan: Lonesome Lover 1958 £20
HLU8609 Titans: Don't You Just Know It 1958 £60
HLU8615 Sam Cooke: That's All I Need To Know 1958 £25
HLU8617 Carl McVoy: Tootsie 1958 £150
HLU8619 David Seville: Witch Doctor 1958 £4
HLU8624 Chiefs: Apache 1958 £20
HLU8626 Jack Scott: My True Love 1958 £5
HLU8627 Noble Thin Man Watts: Hard Times 1958 £40
HLU8630 Billie & Lillie: Creeping Crawling Crying 1958 £20
HLU8634 Billy Ward & The Dominoes: Jennie Lee 1958 £20
HLU8648 Margie Rayburn: I Would 1958 £10

HLU8650 Johnny Janis: Better To Love You 1958 £8
HLU8657 Julie London: My Strange Affair 1958 £6
HLU8658 Kingpins: Ungaua 1958 £10
HLU8659 David Seville: Bird On My Head 1958 £4
HLU8661 Lee Andrews & The Hearts: Try The Impossible 1958 £300
HLU8681 Playboys: Over The Weekend 1958 £25
HLU8689 Billie & Lillie: Hanging On To You 1958 £12
HLU8702 Eddie Cochran: Summertime Blues 1958 £20
HLU8716 Rondells: Good Good 1958 £75
HLU8720 Chiefs: Enchiladas 1958 £12
HLU8722 Royal Holidays: Margaret 1958 £60
HLU8734 Gainors: Secret 1958 £100
HLU8741 Al Morgan: Jealous Heart 1958 £5
HLU8748 Georgie Young: Nine More Miles 1958 £6
HLU8752 Billy Grammer: Gotta Travel On 1958 £8
HLU8753 Applejacks: Mexican Hat Rock 1958 £10
HLU8754 Dickie Doo & The Donts: Leave Me Alone 1958 £25
HLU8756 Nu Tornados: Philadelphia USA 1958 £10
HLU8761 Andy Rose: Just Young 1958 £15
HLU8765 Jack Scott: With Your Love 1958 £8
HLU8769 Julie London: Man Of The West 1958 £6
HLU8770 Little Richard: Baby Face 1958 £4
HLU8773 Patience & Prudence: Tom Thumb's Tune 1958 £6
HLU8792 Eddie Cochran: C'mon Everybody 1959 £20
HLU8795 Billie & Lillie: Lucky Ladybug 1959 £12
HLU8796 Quaker City Boys: Teasin' 1959 £6
HLU8804 Jack Scott: Goodbye Baby 1959 £8
HLU8806 Applejacks: Rock A Conga 1959 £10
HLU8831 Little Richard: By The Light Of The Silvery Moon 1959 £4
HLU8841 Fleetwoods: Come Softly To Me 1959 £8
HLU8844 Larry Williams: She Said Yeah 1959 £15
HLU8846 Thomas Wayne: Tragedy 1959 £25
HLU8852 Dave Baby Cortez: Happy Organ 1959 £8
HLU8868 Little Richard: Kansas City 1959 £6
HLU8874 Dion: Teenager In Love 1959 £20
HLU8875 Felix & His Guitar: Chili Beans 1959 £6
HLU8880 Eddie Cochran: Teenage Heaven 1959 £25
HLU8883 Billy Ward & The Dominoes: Please Don't Say No 1959 £10
HLU8891 Julie London: Must Be Catchin' 1959 £8
HLU8895 Fleetwoods: Graduation's Here 1959 £8
HLU8903 Gloria Smith: Playmates 1959 £6
HLU8911 Larry Williams: I Can't Stop Loving You 1960 £15
HLU8919 Dave Baby Cortez: Whistling Organ 1959 £8
HLU8924 Skyliners: This I Swear 1959 £50
HLU8944 Eddie Cochran: Somethin' Else 1959 tri-centre £40
HLU8951 Chuck Veddar: Spanky Boy 1959 £20
HLU8971 Skyliners: It Happened Today 1959 £25
HLU8978 Wes Bryan: Honey Baby 1959 £25
HLU8990 Jan & Dean: There's A Girl 1959 £15
HLU9001 Gene Autry: Nine Little Reindeer 1958 £4
HLU9024 Titus Turner: We Told You Not To Marry 1960 £15
HLU9030 Dion: Where Or When 1960 £8

HLU9046 Sam Cooke: I Need You Now 1960 £15
HLU9057 Fireflies: I Can't Say Goodbye 1960 £8
HLU9063 Jan & Dean: Clementine 1960 £10
HLU9065 Little Richard: I Got It 1960 £10
HLU9088 Barrett Strong: Money 1960 £100
HLU9097 Teddy Vann: Cindy 1960 £10
HLU9107 Charlie Rich: Lonely Weekends 1960 £25
HLU9116 Ron Holden: Love You So 1960 £30
HLU9117 Jesse Hill: Ooh Poo Pah Doo 1960 £10
HLU9126 Dave Baby Cortez: Deep In The Heart Of Texas 1960 £8
HLU9146 Hollywood Argyles: Alley Oop 1960 £20
HLU9149 Roy Orbison: Only The Lonely 1960 £4
HLU9189 Johnny Bond: Hot Rod Jalopy 1960 £8
HLU9200 Ritchie Adams: Back To School 1960 £20
HLU9205 Paul Chaplain & The Emeralds: Shortning Bread 1960 £15
HLU9206 Jimmy Charles: Million To One 1960 £5
HLU9207 Roy Orbison: Blue Angel 1960 £4
HLU9220 Ronnie Mitchell: How Many Times 1960 £4
HLU9226 Ike & Tina Turner: Fool In Love 1960 £6
HLU9245 Dee Dee Ford: Good Morning Blues 1960 £30
HLU9248 Bobbettes: Have Mercy Baby 1960 £15
HLU9266 Rosie & The Originals: Angel Baby 1961 £25
HLU9282 Ramrods: Riders In The Sky 1961 £4
HLU9283 Chimes: Once In A While 1961 £15
HLU9285 Paul Clayton: Wings Of A Dove 1961 £5
HLU9286 Maxine Brown: All In My Mind 1961 £10
HLU9288 Shells: Baby Oh Baby 1961 £25
HLU9291 Al Tousan: Naomi 1961 £5
HLU9296 Royaltones: Flamingo Express 1961 £8
HLU9307 Roy Orbison: I'm Hurtin' 1961 £4
HLU9312 Jack Eubanks: What'd I Say 1961 £4
HLU9328 Velvets: That Lucky Old Sun 1961 £15
HLU9330 Ernie K. Doe: Mother In Law 1961 £8
HLU9333 Pentagons: To Be Loved 1961 £50
HLU9338 Salt & Pepper: High Noon 1961 £4
HLU9354 Stringalongs: Brass Buttons 1961 £4
HLU9355 Ramrods: Loch Lomond Rock 1961 £6
HLU9367 Eddy & Teddy: Bye Bye Butterfly 1961 £5
HLU9368 Dreamtimers: Dancin' Lady 1961 £8
HLU9372 Velvets: Tonight 1961 £15
HLU9384 Electric Johnny: Black Eyes Rock 1961 £20
HLU9387 Altecs: Easy 1961 £5
HLU9390 Ernie K. Doe: Te Ta Te Ta Ta 1961 £6
HLU9393 Bobby Parker: Watch Your Step 1961 £20
HLU9404 Rondells: Backbeat Number One 1961 £10
HLU9410 Chris Kenner: I Like It Like That 1961 £8
HLU9424 Halos: Nag 1961 £20
HLU9433 G-Clefs: I Understand 1961 £4
HLU9436 Bill Black Combo: Moving 1961 £5
HLU9441 Flares: Foot Stomping 1961 £15
HLU9444 Velvets: Laugh 1961 £15
HLU9447 Marvin Rainwater: I Can't Forget 1961 £75

HLU9452 Stringalongs: Mina Bird 1961 £5
HLU9463 Justin Jones: Dance By Yourself 1961 £30
HLU9471 Bill Haley: Spanish Twist 1961 £8
HLU9490 Flips: Rockin' Twist 1962 £6
HLU9492 Tony Gunner: Rough Road 1962 £8
HLU9495 Chuck Foote: You're Running Out Of Kisses 1962 £5
HLU9501 Jack Eubanks: Searchin' 1962 £4
HLU9530 G-Clefs: Girl Has To Know 1962 £8
HLU9531 Ernie Maresca: Shout Shout 1962 £8
HLU9542 Tad & The Small Fry: Checkered Continental Pants 1962 £5
HLU9545 Frank Starr: Little Bitty Feeling 1962 £8
HLU9547 King Curtis: Soul Twist 1962 £8
HLU9555 Khans: New Orleans 2 a.m. 1962 £5
HLU9556 Raging Storms: Dribble 1962 £15
HLU9563 G-Clefs: Make Up Your Mind 1962 £8
HLU9579 Ernie Maresca: Mary Jane 1962 £8
HLU9591 Carole King: It Might As Well Rain Until September 1962 £4
HLU9592 Bobby Vinton: I Love The Way You Are 1962 £6
HLU9597 Bobby Pickett & The Crypt Kickers: Monster Mash 1962 £6
HLU9599 Marcie Blane: Bobby's Girl 1962 £12
HLU9603 Charlie Gracie: Night And Day USA 1962 £10
HLU9606 Ricky Shaw: No Love But Your Love 1962 £4
HLU9607 Roy Orbison: Workin' For The Man 1962 £4
HLU9610 Young Sisters: Cassanova Brown 1962 £5
HLU9611 Crystals: He's A Rebel 1962 £8
HLU9613 Larry Finnegan: It's Walking Talking Time 1962 £6
HLU9621 Nick Woods: Ballad Of Billy Bud 1962 £4
HLU9633 Little Eva: Keep Your Hands Off My Baby 1962 £4
HLU9634 Cookies: Chains 1962 £6
HLU9644 Shells: It's A Happy Holiday 1962 £25
HLU9646 Bob B. Soxx & The Blue Jeans: Zip A Dee Doo Dah 1963 £6
HLU9651 Pastel Six: Cinnamon Cinder 1963 £5
HLU9661 Crystals: He Sure Is The Boy I Love 1963 £10
HLU9671 Crests: Guilty 1963 £8
HLU9673 Marcie Blane: How Can I Tell Him 1963 £5
HLU9677 Buck Ram: Benfica 1963 £6
HLU9678 Duprees: I'd Rather Be Here In Your Arms 1963 £10
HLU9685 Boots Randolph: Yakety Sax 1963 £5
HLU9687 Little Eva: Let's Turkey Trot 1963 £4
HLU9690 Danny Dexter: Sweet Mama 1963 £8
HLU9692 Jerry Martin: Shake A Take A 1963 £5
HLU9694 Bob B. Soxx & The Blue Jeans: Why Do Lovers Break Each Others' Hearts 1963 £8
HLU9704 Cookies: Don't Say Nothing Bad About My Baby 1963 £8
HLU9707 Bryan Keith: Mean Mama 1963 £6
HLU9709 Duprees: Gone With the Wind 1963 £8
HLU9711 Bette Davis & Debbie Burton: Whatever Happened To Baby Jane 1963 £4
HLU9712 Maxine Starr: Wishing Star 1963 £4
HLU9720 Ernie Maresca: Love Express 1963 £6
HLU9725 Darlene Love: Boy I'm Gonna Marry 1963 £15
HLU9732 Crystals: Da Doo Ron Ron 1963 £4
HLU9739 Cliff Rivers: True Lips 1963 £15
HLU9744 Marcie Blane: Little Miss Fool 1963 £5

HLU9753 Sylte Sisters: Summer Magic 1963 £5
HLU9754 Bob B. Soxx & The Blue Jeans: Not Too Young To Get Married 1963 £10
HLU9760 Randells: Martian Hop 1963 £15
HLU9765 Darlene Love: Wait Till My Bobby Gets Home 1963 £15
HLU9767 Bob Davies: Rock And Roll Show 1963 £15
HLU9773 Crystals: Then He Kissed Me 1963 £4
HLU9774 Duprees: Why Don't You Believe Me 1963 £8
HLU9776 Bruce Channel: Blue And Lonesome 1963 £4
HLU9783 Alice Wonderland: He's Mine 1963 £4
HLU9786 Rusty Draper: That's Why I Love You Like I Do 1963 £8
HLU9787 Marcie Blane: You Gave My Number To Billy 1963 £6
HLU9793 Ronettes: Be My Baby 1963 £4
HLU9795 Amos Milburn Jr: Gloria 1963 £10
HLU9797 Dixie Belles: Down At Poppa Joe's 1963 £4
HLU9803 Permanents: Oh Dear, What Can The Matter Be 1983 £4
HLU9813 Duprees: Have You Heard 1963 £8
HLU9815 Darlene Love: Fine Fine Boy 1963 £15
HLU9826 Ronettes: Baby I Love You 1964 £4
HLU9830 Murray Kellum: Long Tall Texan 1964 Glen Sutton B-side £10
HLU9834 Ernie Maresca: Rovin' Kind 1964 £5
HLU9837 Crystals: Little Boy 1964 £30
HLU9841 Bruce Channel: Going Back To Louisiana 1964 £4
HLU9843 Duprees: It's No Sin 1964 £8
HLU9847 Pyramids: Penetration 1964 £20
HLU9852 Crystals: I Wonder 1964 £8
HLU9856 Vicky Baker: No More Foolish Stories 1964 £5
HLU9862 Monarchs: Look Homeward Angel 1964 £20
HLU9871 Terry Stafford: Suspicion 1964 £4
HLU9874 David Box: Sweet Sweet Day 1964 £8
HLU9885 Scott McKay: Cold Cold Heart 1964 £4
HLU9889 Ray Ruff & The Checkmates: I Took A Liking To You 1964 £12
HLU9891 Boots Randolph: Hey Mr Sax Man 1964 £4
HLU9902 Terry Stafford: I'll Touch A Star 1964 £5
HLU9905 Ronettes: The Best Part Of Breaking Up 1964 £6
HLU9906 Chartbusters: She's The One 1964 £6
HLU9908 Round Robin: Kick That Little Foot Sally Ann 1964 £25
HLU9909 Crystals: All Grown Up 1964 £8
HLU9913 Jumpin' Gene Simmons: Haunted House 1964 £8
HLU9922 Ronettes: Do I Love You 1964 £5
HLU9923 Terry Stafford: Follow The Rainbow 1964 £5
HLU9924 David Box: Little Lonely Summer Girl 1964 £8
HLU9925 Bill Black Combo: Little Queenie 1964 £12
HLU9926 Willie Mitchell: 20 75 1964 £4
HLU9931 Ronettes: Walking In The Rain 1964 £5
HLU9932 Tommy Tucker: Oh What A Feeling 1964 £20
HLU9933 Jumpin' Gene Simmons: Jump 1964 £8
HLU9934 Chartbusters: Why 1964 £5
HLU9936 Clarence 'Frogman' Henry: Little Green Frog 1964 £4
HLU9940 Novas: Crusher 1965 £20
HLU9942 Bobby Skel: Kiss And Run 1964 £5
HLU9952 Ronettes: Born To Be Together 1965 £8
HLU9955 Stokes: Whipped Cream 1965 £5

HLU9964 Sir Douglas Quintet: She's About A Mover 1965 £4
HLU9976 Ronettes: Is This What I Get For Loving You 1965 £8
HLU9982 Sir Douglas Quintet: Tracker 1965 £4
HLU9989 Rusty Draper: Folsom Prison Blues 1965 £5
HLU9992 Twilights: Take What I Got 1965 £8
HLU9996 Vogues: You're The One 1965 £5
HLU9997 John & Paul: People Say 1965 £6
HLU9998 Bonnie & The Treasures: Home Of The Brave 1965 £20
HLU9999 Al De Lory: Yesterday 1965 £10
HLW8821 Duane Eddy: Lonely One 1959 tri-centre £5
HLW8827 Scamps: Petite Fleur 1959 £5
HLW8884 Don French: Goldilocks 1959 £100
HLW8904 Tu Tones: Still In Love With You 1959 £75
HLW8908 Jordan Brothers: Never Never 1959 £20
HLW8932 Ray Sharpe: Linda Lu 1959 tri-centre £25
HLW8950 Earl Nelson: No Time To Cry 1959 £8
HLW8955 Hollywood Flames: Much Too Much 1959 £40
HLW8959 Sanford Clark: Run Boy Run 1959 £15
HLW8961 Neil Sedaka: Ring A Rocking 1959 £25
HLW8977 Atmospheres: Fickle Chicken 1959 £12
HLW8989 Don French: Little Blonde Girl 1959 £75
HLW8991 Steve Wright: Wild Wild Women 1959 £125
HLW9008 Joe London: It Might Have Been 1959 £5
HLW9012 Sheiks: Très Chic 1959 £6
HLW9022 Eddie Cochran: Hallelujah I Love Her So 1960 tri-centre £40; round £8
HLW9026 Sanford Clark: Son Of A Gun 1960 £8
HLW9091 Atmospheres: Telegraph 1960 £8
HLW9095 Sanford Clark: Pledging My Love 1960 £8
HLW9102 Anita Carter: Moon Girl 1960 £6
HLW9130 Mitchell Torok: Pink Chiffon 1960 £6
HLW9135 Blackwells: Unchained Melody 1960 £5
HLW9178 Ivy Three: Yogi 1960 £6
HLW9223 Lee Hazelwood: Words Mean Nothing 1960 £8
HLW9224 Craig Alden: Crazy Little Horn 1960 £4
HLW9235 Jordan Brothers: Things I Didn't Say 1960 £8
HLW9308 Jordan Brothers: No Wings On My Angel 1961 £5
HLW9334 Blackwells: Love Or Money 1961 £5
HLW9337 Mirriam Johnson: Lonesome Road 1961 £6
HLW9625 Sherrys: Pop Pop Popeye 1962 £6
HLW9657 Billie & The Essentials: Maybe You'll be There 1963 £30
HLW9918 Barbara Lynn: Oh Baby 1964 £10
HLX8671 Honeytones: Don't Look Now But 1958 £40
HLX8713 Shades: Sun Glasses 1958 B-side Knott Sisters £25
HLX8740 Bobby Pedricks: White Bucks And Saddle Shoes 1958 £25
HLX8845 Jackson Brothers: Tell Him No 1959 £15
HLX8918 Sammy Turner: Lavender Blue 1959 £8
HLX8963 Sammy Turner: Always 1959 £5
HLX9002 Kenny & Corky: Nuttin' For Christmas 1959 £4
HLX9062 Sammy Turner: Paradise 1960 £5
HLX9105 Mel Gadson: Comin' Down With Love 1960 £4
HLX9134 Johnny & The Hurricanes: Down Yonder 1960 £4
HLX9237 Azie Mortimer: Lips 1960 £8

HLX9246 Ray Peterson: Corrine Corrina 1960 £6
HLX9313 Curtis Lee: Pledge Of Love 1961 £12
HLX9317 Del Shannon: Runaway 1961 £4; B-side mispress plays 'Snake' £10
HLX9332 Ray Peterson: Sweet Little Kathy 1961 £5
HLX9356 Maximilian: Snake 1961 £25
HLX9379 Ray Peterson: You Thrill Me 1961 £4
HLX9397 Curtis Lee: Pretty Little Angel Eyes 1961 £10
HLX9398 Mickey Denton: Steady Kind 1961 £5
HLX9402 Del Shannon: Hats Off To Larry 1961 £4
HLX9443 Curtis Lee: Under The Moon Of Love 1961 £10
HLX9488 Sammy Turner: Raincoat In The River 1962 £10
HLX9489 Ray Peterson: I Could Have Loved You So Well 1962 £6
HLX9491 Johnny & The Hurricanes: Traffic Jam 1962 £4
HLX9529 Don & Juan: What's Your Name 1962 £15
HLX9533 Curtis Lee: Night At Daddy Gees 1962 £10
HLX9536 Johnny & The Hurricanes: Salvation 1962 £5
HLX9569 Ray Peterson: You Didn't Care 1962 £4
HLX9587 Del Shannon: Cry Myself To Sleep 1962 £4
HLX9609 Del Shannon: Swiss Maid 1962 £4
HLX9617 Johnny & The Hurricanes: Minnesota Fats 1962 £4
HLX9653 Del Shannon: Little Town Flirt 1963 £4
HLX9660 Johnny & The Hurricanes: Greens And Jeans 1963 £4
HLX9713 Jamie Coe: Fool 1963 £8
HLX9719 Del Shannon: Two Kinds Of Teardrops 1963 £4
HLX9746 Ray Peterson: Give Us Your Blessing 1963 £5
HLX9759 Gerri Granger: Just Tell Him Jane Said Hello 1963 £4
HLX9761 Del Shannon: Two Silhouettes 1963 £4
HLX9772 Andrea Carroll: It Hurts To Be Sixteen 1963 £5
HLX9800 Del Shannon: Sue's Gonna Be Mine 1963 £4
HLX9805 Lou Johnson: Magic Potion 1963 £15
HLX9809 Dynamics: Misery 1963 £20
HLX9858 Del Shannon: That's The Way Love Is 1964 £4
HLX9917 Lou Johnson: Always Something There To Remind Me 1964 £15
HLX9929 Lou Johnson: Message To Martha 1964 £6
HLX9965 Lou Johnson: Please Stop The Wedding 1965 £5
HLX9994 Lou Johnson: Unsatisfied 1965 £30
HLY9044 Bobby Day: My Blue Heaven 1960 £12
HLY9056 Googie Rene: Forever 1960 £8
HLY9868 Jimmy Holiday: I Lied 1964 £8
HLZ8419 Lou Stein: Almost Paradise 1957 £10
HLZ8475 Norma Douglas: Be It Resolved 1957 £15

A collector wishing to acquire a complete set, assuming they could be found, would have to pay out at least £54,500 to complete his ambition! In practice, many of the higher-value items would be auctioned and might well cost more than the listed price.

MARMALADE

The short-lived (from 1967 to 1969) and collectable Marmalade label was set up and run by impresario Giorgio Gomelsky, who was the original manager of the Yardbirds amongst other things. The company found some interesting artists to record – Blossom Toes, Julie Driscoll and

Brian Auger, and John McLaughlin among them – but the label never really recovered from the failure (or refusal) of Julie Driscoll to become the huge star she could have been.

The Marmalade albums:

607/608001 Blossom Toes: We Are Ever So Clean £75
607/608002 Julie Driscoll & Brian Auger: Open £20
607003 Brian Auger: Definitely What £15
607/608004 Brian Auger/Jimmy Page/Sonny Boy Williamson: Don't Send Me No Flowers £30
608005/6 Julie Driscoll & Brian Auger: Streetnoise double £25
608007 John McLaughlin: Extrapolation £15
608008 John Stevens: Spontaneous Music Ensemble £25
608009 Chris Barber: Battersea Rain Dance £20
608010 Blossom Toes: If Only For A Moment £75
608011 Ottilie Patterson: 3000 Years With Ottilie £15
608012 Gordon Jackson: Thinking Back £40
608013 Gary Farr: Take Something With You £30
608014 Julie Driscoll & Brian Auger: Streetnoise Part 1 £10
608015 Julie Driscoll & Brian Auger: Streetnoise Part 2 £10

The collectable singles:

598001 Roaring Sixties: We Love The Pirates £25
598002 Blossom Toes: What On Earth £20 picture sleeve £40
598003 Brian Auger: Red Beans And Rice £5
598004 Julie Driscoll & Brian Auger: Save Me £4
598005 Chris Barber: Catcall £30
598006 Julie Driscoll & Brian Auger: This Wheel's On Fire £4
598007 Gary Farr: Everyday with Kevin Westlake £4
598009 Blossom Toes: I'll Be Your Baby Tonight £15
598010 Gordon Jackson: Me And My Zoo £4
598012 Blossom Toes: Postcard £15
598013 Chris Barber: Battersea Rain Dance £4
598014 Blossom Toes: Peace Loving Man £15
598015 Brian Auger: What You Gonna Do £4
598016 Keith Meehan: Darkness Of My Life Tony Meehan B-side £8
598017 Gary Farr: Hey Daddy £5
598019 Frabjoy & The Runcible Spoon: I'm Beside Myself £10
598021 Gordon Jackson: Song For Freedom £4
598022 Blossom Toes: New Day test pressing only £100

MUSHROOM

Four companies have adopted the Mushroom name. A late seventies US label released albums by the group Heart, a long-lived Australian Mushroom label is still going, while in the UK Mushroom is the name of the record company handling releases by the group Garbage. The Mushroom of most interest to collectors, however, is a tiny concern that issued a handful of LPs during 1970–72. The label's varied catalogue of progressive rock, Indian music and jazz was never available in ordinary record shops, but was advertised in the underground press (notably *Oz* magazine) for sale by mail order. The original asking price of a pound for the '100' prefix albums is now multiplied many times over!

100MR1 Andreas Thomopoulous: Songs Of The Street LP 1970 £75

100MR2 Simon Finn: Pass The Distance LP 1970 £60
50MR3(?) Andreas Thomopoulous: So Long Suzanne 7" 1970 £40
150MR4 Andreas Thomopoulous: Born Out Of The Tears Of The Sun LP 1971 £75
200MR6 Second Hand: Death May Be Your Santa Claus LP 1972 £100
100MR7 Pandit Kanwar Sain Trikha: Three Sitar Pieces LP 1970 £40
150MR9 Liverpool Fishermen: Swallow The Anchor LP 1971 £100
100MR10 Bach Two Bach: Bach Two Bach LP 1971 £100
100MR11 Chillum: Chillum LP 1971 £40
100MR13 Les Flambeaux: Les Flambeaux LP 1971 £30
100MR14 Ustad Ali Akbar Khan: Peaceful Music LP 1971 £40
100MR16 Various Artists: Mushroom Folk Sampler LP 1971 £50
50MR17 Callinan Flynn: We Are The People 7" 1972 £50
150MR18 Callinan Flynn: Freedom's Lament LP 1972 £200
200MR20 Magic Carpet: Magic Carpet LP 1972 £100
100MR22 Natai Dasgupta: Songs Of India LP 1972 £40
150MR23 Lol Coxhill: Toverbal Sweet LP 1972 £75

NEON

Neon was the specialist progressive label set up by RCA at a time when all the majors were doing something similar. RCA was actually a little slow off the mark – the first Neon album was released in 1971 – and although some of the records are rather fine (and have the attractive gatefold sleeves typical of the genre), they sold poorly. All the Neon albums are now collectable – there being just eleven of them in the series:

NE1 Fairweather: Beginning From An End £10
NE2 Chris McGregor: Brotherhood Of Breath £40
NE3 Indian Summer: Indian Summer £30
NE4 Tonton Macoute: Tonton Macoute £50
NE5 Dando Shaft: Dando Shaft £40
NE6 Spring: Spring £100
NE7 Shape Of The Rain: Riley, Riley, Wood & Waggett £25
NE8 Raw Material: Time Is £250
NE9 Centipede: Septober Energy double £50
NE10 Mike Westbrook: Metropolis £30
NE11 Running Man: Running Man £125

There are also three Neon singles:

NE1001 Shape Of The Rain: Woman £4
NE1002 Raw Material: Ride On Pony £15
NE1003 Quintessence Sweet Jesus picture sleeve £10 (without £4)

NEPENTHA

The short-lived Nepentha label is often described as being a subsidiary to Vertigo, with whom it shared a house-style. In reality, of course, Vertigo is itself a subsidiary of Phonogram, who presumably felt that if one specialist progressive label could prove to be a success, then it was worth trying a second one. In fact, Nepentha never managed to achieve the strong corporate image that Vertigo did (its label design featured a blue quill, whose link with the music's powers of making the listener forget all grief – for such is the label name's arcane meaning – is not a striking one) and it was abandoned after just five album releases. In fact, the label was lucky to even last that long. After minimal sales of the first three Nepentha albums, the cancelled matrix number visible on the fourth, *Earth And Fire*, shows that the record was originally intended for the Mercury label.

6437001 Pete Dello: Into Your Ears £60
6437002 Robin Lent: Scarecrow's Journey £30
6437003 Dulcimer: And I Turned As I Had Turned As A Boy £50
6437004 Earth & Fire: Earth And Fire £150
6437005 Zior: Zior £40

There are also three singles:

6129001 Earth & Fire: Invitation £20
6129002 Zior: Za Za Za Zilda £8
6129003 Zior: Cat's Eyes £8

NOVA

Although Deram had originally been conceived as something of a progressive offshoot for Decca records, the flowering of the music in 1969, accompanied by the birth of several specialist labels to feature it, encouraged Decca to try the tactic for a second time. The link with the parent company was made explicit from the outset, and records were issued on labels described either as 'Decca Nova' or 'Deram Nova', although there was only one catalogue number series. Unfortunately, the albums always seemed to convey the impression that Decca's heart was not really in the exercise. Few of the artists were particularly inspiring, and the elaborate gatefold sleeves that were so much a part of the package in the case of rival labels like Vertigo, Harvest and Island were never used. The label was abandoned at the start of 1971 – later albums on a German label called Nova have no connection with these.

(S)RNR1 Ashkan: In From The Cold £50
(S)DNR2 Clark–Hutchinson: A=MH2 £25
SDN4 Galliard: Strange Pleasures £20
(S)DN5 Bulldog Breed: Made In England £40
DN/SND6 Elastic Band: Expansions On Life £30
SDN7 Sunforest: Sound Of Sunforest £60
SDN8 Jan Dukes De Grey: Sorcerers £25
DN/SND9 Harvey Andrews: Places And Faces £20
SDN10 Denny Gerrard: Sinister Morning with High Tide £30
SDN11 Alan Skidmore: Once Upon A Time £40
SDN12 Bill Fay: Bill Fay £25
(S)DN13 Pacific Drift: Feelin' Free £25
SDN14 Egg: Egg £15
SDN15 Black Cat Bones: Barbed Wire Sandwich £60
SDN17 Aardvark: Aardvark £75
SDN19 Jazz Rock Experience: Jazz Rock Experience £15
SDN20 Hunter Muskett: Every Time You Move £100
SDN21 Peter Collins: First Album £10
SDN22 Patricia Cahill: Summer's Daughter £15

OAK

Of the many small private recording studios, catering mainly to young bands without a record contract, that run by R. G. Jones in South London has become the subject of considerable cult interest. Part of this interest derives from the studio's association with the Rolling Stones and the Yardbirds, both of which groups made early recordings there. More, however, is due to the current fascination with any records from the sixties or early seventies that are sufficiently obscure to be suitable candidates for high-priced collectors' items. Oak was the label name given to the small number of records actually pressed up by the R. G. Jones studio. These were paid for by the artists concerned for use as demos – in the same way as modern groups will produce cassettes of their songs in order to obtain a record contract or gigs (or just to sell at those gigs). The small number of collectable Oak records of this kind are listed in the *Guide*. The Bo Street Runners and the Thyrds found some very limited success via the TV rock group contest organized by the *Ready Steady Go* programme, but the majority of the Oak artists were never heard of again. There were also a larger number of Oak label acetates, which occasionally come on to the market at upwards of £25 each (one featuring two unreleased songs by a youthful David Bowie is worth nearer a hundred times this value). Although many of the Oak recordings are decent beat group performances, there is a considerable danger in assuming that everything on the label is worthwhile (and collectable). A recent discovery of an unsuspected Oak album may have whetted a few appetites, but the MOR pop selection that makes up *Wilf Todd And His Music* is not the kind of thing normally to set collectors' pulses racing – a fact which nevertheless proved to be no curb on the hyperbole of one specialist dealer, who managed to describe the record as a 'monster rare Oak label 60s private LP – £400' with a straight face. The R. G. Jones studio is still in operation, incidentally, one of its more recent successes being the number one single recorded by Mr Blobby.

A-Jaes: I'm Leaving You 7" RGJ132 1964 £200
Act: Act 7" EP RGJ407 1965 £125
Bo Street Runners: Bo Street Runners 7" EP RGJ131 1964 £750
Joe Cocker: Joe Cocker 7" EP 196– £400
Daisy Planet: Daisy Planet 7" EP no number 196– £40
Factory: Time Machine 7" RGJ718 1970 £150
Five Of Diamonds: Five Of Diamonds 7" EP RGJ150FD 1965 £300
Four Degrees: Four Degrees LP RGJ187 1965 1 sided, no sleeve £300
Four Leaved Clover: Why 7" RGJ207 1965 £250
Free 'n' Easy: Free 'n' Easy LP RGJ628 1968 £100
Hickory Stix: Hello My Darling 7" RGJ149 1964 £100
Hoboken: Hoboken LP no number 1973 £500
Jill & The Y'verns: My Soulful Dress 7" RGJ503 196– £40
Karoo: Mama's Out Of Town 7" RGJ193 1965 £100
Miller: Baby I Got News For You 7" RGJ190 1965 £200
Valerie Mitchell: There Goes My Heart Again 7" RGJ160 1965 picture sleeve £30
Roy North: Blues In Three 7" RGJ107 1963 £25
Peter & The Persuaders: Wanderer 7" EP RGJ197 1965 £25
Plebs: Plebs LP 196– 1 sided £500
Pneumonia: I Can See Your Face 7" RGJ625 1968 £100
Malcolm Price: Pickin' On The Country Strings 7" EP RGJ106 196 £15
Princess & The Swineherd: Princess And The Swineherd LP RGJ633 1968 £25
Rats: Spoonful 7" RGJ145 1964 1 sided £150; with picture sleeve £250
Roulettes: I Can't Stop 7" RGJ205 1965 1 sided £50; with picture sleeve £100
Derek Sarjeant: Folk Songs 7" EP RGJ101 1961 £20

Derek Sarjeant: Folk Songs Vol. 2 7″ EP RGJ105 1961 £20
Derek Sarjeant: Man Of Kent 7″ EP RGJ117 1963 £20
Derek Sarjeant: Songs We Like To Sing 7″ EP RGJ103 1961 £15
Sons Of Man: Sons Of Man 7″ EP RGJ612 1967 £250
Soupherbs: Soupherbs LP RGJ601 1965 £200
Thyrds: Hide'n'Seek 7″ RGJ133 1964 £150
Wilf Todd: Wilf Todd And His Music LP WT101 1966 £12
Trendsetters: At The Hotel De France 7″ EP RGJ999 196– £20
Truth Of Truths: Truth Of Truths LP OR1001 1971 double £25
Velvet Hush: Broken Heart 7″ RGJ648 1968 £75
Wild Oats: Wild Oats 7″ EP RGJ117 1963 £750

The records have been listed in artist order because the number sequence is all over the place! There appear to be two records with the number RGJ117 – it is likely that at least one of them is incorrectly listed.

PARLOPHONE

The changes in Parlophone label designs are of particular importance with regard to records by the Beatles. In early 1963, the label used for singles was changed from red to black, so that early pressings of *Please Please Me* are found with the earlier design and later pressings with the later design. The black-label singles, incidentally, all carry the message 'Made In Gt Britain', which is not present on reissue copies from the seventies. Parlophone LPs were also given a label change in 1963. The original labels are black, with all the print being in gold ink. The 'Parlophone' logo is written in gold 3-D effect capitals. The replacement labels were still black, but the print was now silver. 'Parlophone', now in simple flat capitals, was a bright canary yellow, as was the company's pound-sign logo. Again, the change took place at just the right time for the earliest copies of the Beatles LP *Please Please Me* to have the original label, while most have the newer one. In 1969, the LP labels were changed again, with the yellow 'Parlophone' now being replaced by a silver one in a box.

PYE

Pye was the third major British record company (after EMI and Decca) and by the early sixties it was issuing singles on a number of related labels – Pye, Pye International, Pye Jazz and Piccadilly (as well as a large number of subsidiary labels licensed from US originals, including Cameo Parkway, Colpix, Red Bird, Chess and Kama Sutra). Only the main Pye and Pye International labels cause much trouble with regard to reissues. Pye labels are purple until 1962; then deep pink until the end of 1967 (with a change of layout at the beginning of 1965, when the 'Pye' moved from the left to the top of the label and gained a wide black band); then sky blue into the seventies. Pye International labels change in tandem: from a greenish-blue, to red and yellow, to red, to sky blue. In both cases, LPs follow through the same label design changes as the corresponding singles. Records by the likes of the Kinks with labels coloured pink shading to mauve, or grey shading to white, or any records mentioning the PRT company, are later pressings from the seventies or eighties and are not collectable.

RCA

RCA was the company that launched the 45rpm single in the United States in 1949, as an initial response to its rival Columbia's invention of the LP. During the 1950s, the company's records were issued by HMV in the UK (both labels used the distinctive dog and gramophone logo), but in 1957 RCA set up its own UK company. Both singles and LPs used a black label until late 1968, when this was replaced by an orange label.

RECOMMENDED RECORDS

Some of the most interesting records from the late seventies and early eighties are to be found on the Recommended Records label, co-founded by Henry Cow drummer, Chris Cutler. The company's manifesto included the statement: 'We do not operate R.R. as a business which means we do not have to play the market. We just do what we like.' What they liked was a range of artists who had in common their originality and their defiantly uncommercial bias. The records were often housed in hand-decorated sleeves that were almost works of art in their own right; they were frequently limited editions, and were given catalogue numbers whose logic is hard to identify. They are only just beginning to attract the attention of collectors, but the values are set to rise in the future.

REGAL ZONOPHONE

The label that was used for Salvation Army records during the fifties was revived by EMI in 1967 as something of a specialist progressive label. The majority of the records released on the label, until its demise in early 1975, are collectable. It is not generally realized that a handful of records were actually issued on Regal Zonophone during 1964–7. Only one of these is listed in the *Guide* (that by the Innocents and the Leroys) – the others continued the label's earlier tradition by featuring the Salvation Army's pop group, the Joystrings.

REPRISE

Frank Sinatra's Reprise was one of the labels becoming part of the Kinney company in 1971. In addition to its catalogue numbers changing from the RSLP series to the new K series, the label design also changed from yellow and pale green, with a distinctive drawing of a steamboat, to a plain tawny or orange-yellow.

STIFF

The Stiff label made an enviable start with its best-selling releases by Elvis Costello, Ian Dury and the Damned and looked set to become one of the most successful of the new breed of record companies to emerge along with punk. The company's unconventional, irreverent approach served as a role model for many later record labels and helped to endear itself to the collectors who tried to amass complete runs of Stiff releases a few years ago. Unfortunately, the label lost much of its prominence when its original stars moved elsewhere and only the Pogues have succeeded in providing much of a boost since. One result is that Stiff is now much less collected than it was and the values of its records have fallen across the board.

STUDIO 36

The equivalent of Oak records in Northampton was the Studio 36 label, used to issue songs by a tiny number of local beat groups in the sixties made at Northampton Sound Recording. Four records are listed in this *Price Guide* – those by Tony Sands And The Drumbeats, the Quakers, the Blues Five and the Skyliners – and all are extremely scarce, even in the label's home town. There is also an acetate – 'Running Away From Love' by Phoenix – and there are likely to be others as yet unknown to the author.

SUE

The British Sue label was formed in 1963 as a subsidiary of Island Records, with a policy of leasing US soul records, in contrast to the parent label's West Indian bias. Initially, the label concentrated on records from the American Sue company, but it soon began to cast its net wider. With a label manager, Guy Stevens, who was himself very much a soul fan, the Sue catalogue soon became one of the most impressive of all – and is collected as such by soul enthusiasts today.

WI301 Inez & Charlie Foxx: Mockingbird £12
WI302 Baby Washington: That's How Heartaches Are Made £20
WI303 Jimmy McGriff: All About My Girl £15
WI304 Inez & Charlie Foxx: Jaybirds £12
WI305 Russell Byrd: Hitch Hike £20
WI306 Ike & Tina Turner: It's Gonna Work Out Fine £10
WI307 Inez & Charlie Foxx: Here We Go Round £12
WI308 Derak Martin: Daddy Rolling Stone £15
WI309 Ernestine Anderson: Keep An Eye On Love £20
WI310 Jimmy McGriff: Last Minute £12
WI311 Mary Lou Williams: Chug A Lug Jug £12
WI312 Soul Sisters: I Can't Stand It £20
WI313 Hank Jacobs: Monkey Hips And Rice £15
WI314 Inez & Charlie Foxx: Hi Diddle Diddle £12
WI315 Bobby Hendricks: Itchy Twitchy Feeling £8
WI316 Barbara George: Send For Me £12
WI317 Jimmy McGriff: I've Got A Woman £12
WI318 Tim Whitsett: Macks By The Tracks £12
WI319 Homesick James: Crossroads £12
WI320 Willie Mabon: Got To Have Some £12
WI321 Baby Washington: I Can't Wait Until I See My Baby £20
WI322 Ike & Tina Turner: Poor Fool £10
WI323 Inez & Charlie Foxx: Hurt By Love £10
WI324 Patti Labelle & The Bluebelles: Down The Aisle £12
WI325 Megatons: Shimmy Shimmy Walk £15
WI326 Bobby Lee Trammell: New Dance In France £15
WI327 Tony Washington: Show Me How £8
WI328 Anita Wood: Dream Baby £10
WI329 Jackie Edwards: Stagger Lee £10
WI330 Homesick James: Set A Date £15
WI331 Willie Mabon: Just Got Some £12
WI332 Doug Sheldon: Take It Like A Man £8
WI333 Jimmy McGriff: Round Midnight £10
WI334 Wallace Brothers: Precious Words £12
WI335 Elmore James: Dust My Blues £12
WI336 Soul Sisters: Loop De Loop £20
WI337 Louisiana Red: I Done Woke Up £15
WI339 J. B. Lenoir: I Sing The Way I Feel £15
WI340 Bobby Parker: Watch Your Step £15
WI341 Al Downing: Yes I'm Loving You £12
WI342 Bobby Peterson: Rocking Charlie £10
WI343 Daylighters: Oh Mom Teach Me How £10
WI344 Paul Revere & The Raiders: Like Long Hair £10

WI345 Willie Mae (Big Mama) Thornton: Tom Cat £75
WI346 Bobby Peterson: Piano Rock £10
WI347 Noble Thin Man Watts: Noble's Theme June Bateman B-side £15
WI348 Olympics: The Bounce £12
WI349 Freddie King: Driving Sideways £15
WI350 Ike & Tina Turner: I Can't Believe What You Say £10
WI351 Chris Kenner: Land Of A Thousand Dances £15
WI352 Betty Everett: I've Got A Claim On You £15
WI353 Harold Burrage: I'll Take One £12
WI354 Roscoe Shelton: Question £12
WI355 Wallace Brothers: Lover's Prayer £15
WI356 Inez & Charlie Foxx: La De Dah I Love You £12
WI357 Pleasures: Music City £12
WI358 B. B. King: You Never Know £8
WI359 Etta James: Rock With Me Henry £12
WI360 James Brown: Night Train £20
WI361 John Lee Hooker: I'm In The Mood £15
WI362 Otis Redding: Shout Bamalama £15
WI363 Wilbert Harrison: Let's Stick Together £10
WI364 Huey 'Piano' Smith: If It Ain't One Thing It's Another £12
WI365 Sonny Boy Williamson: No Nights By Myself £10
WI366 Frankie Ford: Sea Cruise £8
WI367 Lee Dorsey: Ya Ya £10
WI368 Buster Brown: Fannie Mae £12
WI369 Frankie Ford: What's Going On £15
WI370 Joe Tex: Yum Yum Yum £12
WI371 Larry Williams: Strange £10
WI372 Irma Thomas: Don't Mess With My Man £15
WI373 Big Jay McNeely: Something On Your Mind £15
WI374 Bob & Earl: Harlem Shuffle £10
WI375 Lowell Fulson: Too Many Drivers £12
WI376 Ike & Tina Turner: Please Please Please £10
WI377 Donnie Elbert: Little Piece Of Leather £12
WI378 Harold Betters: Do Anything You Wanna £10
WI379 Screaming Jay Hawkins: I Hear Voices £15
WI380 Huey 'Piano' Smith: Rockin' Pneumonia £12
WI381 Larry Williams: Turn On Your Lovelight £12
WI382 Willie Mabon: I'm The Fixer £12
WI383 Elmore James: It Hurts Me Too £12
WI384 Manhattans: I Wanna Be Your Everything £15
WI385 Little Joe Cook (Chris Farlowe): Stormy Monday Blues £25
WI386 Alexander Jackson & The Turnkeys: Whip £20
WI387 Jimmy Johnson: Don't Answer The Door £12
WI388 Bobby Day: Rockin' Robin £12
WI389 Ikettes: Prisoner Of Love £15
WI390 Tarheel Slim & Little Ann: You Make Me Feel So Good £12
WI391 Dorsets: Pork Chops £12
WI392 Elmore James: Calling The Blues £60
WI393 Bob & Earl: Baby I'm Satisfied £12
WI394 Gladys Knight & The Pips: Letter Full Of Tears £12
WI395 Esther Phillips: Chains £12
WI396 Donnie Elbert: You Can Push It Or Pull It £12

WI397 Professor Longhair: Baby Let Me Hold Your Hand £15
WI398 Baron & His Pounding Piano: Is A Bluebird Blue £15
WI399 Lee Dorsey: Messed Around £10
WI4001 Little Richard: Without Love £15
WI4002 Tommy Duncan: Dance Dance Dance £15
WI4003 Jerry Butler: I Stand Accused £15
WI4004 Jimmy Reed: Odds And Ends £12
WI4005 Phil Upchurch: You Can't Sit Down £12
WI4006 Jimmy Hughes: Goodbye My Love £12
WI4007 Elmore James: I Need You £12
WI4009 Jerry Butler: Just For You £10
WI4010 Effie Smith: Dial That Phone £10
WI4011 Ritchie Valens: La Bamba demo £30
WI4012 Billy Preston: Billy's Bag £8
WI4013 Jaybirds: Somebody Help Me £12
WI4014 Birdlegs & Pauline: Spring £10
WI4015 Little Richard: It Ain't What You Do £15
WI4016 Thurston Harris: Little Bitty Pretty One £12
WI4017 Phil Upchurch: Nothing But Soul £12
WI4018 Righteous Brothers: You Can Have Her £10
WI4019 Spidells: Find Out What's Happening £15
WI4020 Santells: So Fine £12
WI4021 Little Milton: Early In The Morning £15
WI4022 Shades Of Blue: Oh How Happy £10
WI4023 Lowell Fulson: Talking Woman £20
WI4024 Raymond Parker: Ring Around The Roses £12
WI4025 Lydia Marcelle: Another Kind Of Fellow £20
WI4026 Gerri Hall: Who Can I Run To demo £50
WI4027 Mr Dynamite: Sh'mon £20
WI4028 Barbara Lynn: Letter To Mommy And Daddy £15
WI4029 Sugar Simone: Suddenly £10
WI4030 Bob & Earl: Don't Ever Leave Me £12
WI4031 Danny White: Keep My Woman Home £20
WI4032 Don & Dewey: Soul Motion £12
WI4033 Anglos: Incense demo only £20
WI4034 Kelly Brothers: Falling In Love Again £30
WI4035 Theola Kilgore: I'll Keep Trying £10
WI4036 Wallace Brothers: I'll Step Aside £15
WI4037 Edgewood Smith & Fabulous Tailfeathers: Ain't That Lovin' You £10
WI4038 Barbara Lynn: You'll Lose A Good Thing £15
WI4039 Claudine Clark: Strength To Be Strong £12
WI4040 Jackie Day: Before It's Too Late £60
WI4041 Paul Martin: Snake In The Grass £15
WI4042 John Roberts: Sockin' 1, 2, 3, 4 £10
WI4043 O. V. Wright: What About You £12
WI4044 Bobby Bland: Touch Of The Blues £15
WI4045 Al King: Think Twice Before You Speak £15
WI4046 Joe Matthews: Sorry Ain't Good Enough £25
WI4047 Thelma Jones: Stranger £10
WI4048 Lamp Sisters: Woman With The Blues £20
WI4049 Fascinations: Girls Are Out To Get You £15

TAMLA MOTOWN

The consistency of Tamla Motown's single release policy during the sixties means that, today, virtually every one of those records is a collectors' item. As with many other specialist soul labels, the most sought-after items are the demonstration copies of the singles. Collectors take the not unreasonable attitude that only these can really be considered to be the first pressings. The consequence for the value of these is that a tripling of the value of the standard issue is a realistic procedure (except in the case of the very rarest singles, where doubling is more appropriate), but only where this takes the value above the following minimum values for demonstration singles: Stateside singles by Motown artists – £50; TMG501–599 – £50; TMG600–635 – £30; TMG636–680 – £20.

TMG501 Supremes: Stop In The Name Of Love £4
TMG502 Martha & The Vandellas: Nowhere to Run £8
TMG503 Miracles: Ooh Baby Baby £20
TMG504 Temptations: It's Growing £20
TMG505 Stevie Wonder: Kiss Me Baby £25
TMG506 Earl Van Dyke: All For You £50
TMG507 Four Tops: Ask The Lonely £25
TMG508 Brenda Holloway: When I'm Gone £60
TMG509 Junior Walker & The All Stars: Shotgun £20
TMG510 Marvin Gaye: I'll Be Doggone £25
TMG511 Kim Weston: I'm Still Loving You £60
TMG512 Shorty Long: Out To Get You £50
TMG513 Hit Pack: Never Say No To Your Baby £50
TMG514 Detroit Spinners: Sweet Thing £40; demo as by Spinners £100
TMG515 Four Tops: I Can't Help Myself £6
TMG516 Supremes: Back In My Arms Again £8
TMG517 Choker Campbell: Mickey's Monkey £60
TMG518 Marvelettes: I'll Keep Holding On £25
TMG519 Brenda Holloway: Operator £40
TMG520 Junior Walker & The All Stars: Do The Boomerang £40
TMG521 Velvelettes: Lonely Lonely Girl Am I £75
TMG522 Miracles: Tracks Of My Tears £25
TMG523 Detroit Spinners: I'll Always Love You £30
TMG524 Marvin Gaye: Pretty Little Baby £15
TMG525 Marv Johnson: Why Do You Want To Let Me Go £50
TMG526 Temptations: Since I Lost My Baby £15
TMG527 Supremes: Nothing But Heartaches £12
TMG528 Four Tops: It's The Same Old Song £8
TMG529 Junior Walker & The All Stars: Shake And Fingerpop £15
TMG530 Martha & The Vandellas: You've Been In Love Too Long £12
TMG531 Contours: First I Look At The Purse £25
TMG532 Stevie Wonder: Hi Heel Sneakers £25
TMG533 Billy Eckstine: Had You Been Around £40
TMG534 Dorsey Burnette: Jimmy Brown £40
TMG535 Marvelettes: Danger Heartbreak Dead Ahead £15
TMG536 Lewis Sisters: You Need Me £50
TMG537 Tony Martin: Bigger Your Heart Is £50
TMG538 Kim Weston: Take Me In Your Arms £30
TMG539 Marvin Gaye: Ain't That Peculiar £10

TMG540 Miracles: My Girl Has Gone £12
TMG541 Temptations: My Baby £15
TMG542 Four Tops: Something About You £8
TMG543 Supremes: I Hear A Symphony £5
TMG544 Barbara McNair: You're Gonna Love My Baby £200
TMG545 Stevie Wonder: Uptight £6
TMG546 Marvelettes: Don't Mess With Bill £20
TMG547 Miracles: Going To A Go Go £6
TMG548 Supremes: My World Is Empty Without You £10
TMG549 Martha & The Vandellas: My Baby Loves Me £10
TMG550 Junior Walker & The All Stars: Cleo's Mood £12
TMG551 Elgins: Put Yourself In My Place £30
TMG552 Marvin Gaye: One More Heartache £10
TMG553 Four Tops: Shake Me Wake Me £15
TMG554 Kim Weston: Helpless £60
TMG555 Isley Brothers: This Old Heart Of Mine £4
TMG556 Brenda Holloway: Together Till The End Of Time £30
TMG557 Temptations: Get Ready £12
TMG558 Stevie Wonder: Nothing's Too Good For My Baby £15
TMG559 Junior Walker & The All Stars: Road Runner £6
TMG560 Supremes: Love Is Like An Itching In My Heart £20
TMG561 Tammi Terrell: Come On And See Me £50
TMG562 Marvelettes: You're The One £15
TMG563 Marvin Gaye: Take This Heart Of Mine £10
TMG564 Contours: Determination £25
TMG565 Temptations: Ain't Too Proud To Beg £8
TMG566 Isley Brothers: Take Some Time Out For Love £10
TMG567 Martha & The Vandellas: What Am I Going To Do £8
TMG568 Four Tops: Loving You Is Sweeter Than Ever £5
TMG569 Miracles: Whole Lotta Shakin' In My Heart £12
TMG570 Stevie Wonder: Blowin' In The Wind £8
TMG571 Junior Walker & The All Stars: How Sweet It Is £6
TMG572 Isley Brothers: I Guess I'll Always Love You £10
TMG573 Shorty Long: Function At The Junction £12
TMG574 Marvin Gaye: Little Darling £10
TMG575 Supremes: You Can't Hurry Love £4
TMG576 Gladys Knight & The Pips: Just Walk In My Shoes £25
TMG577 Jimmy Ruffin: What Becomes Of The Broken Hearted £4
TMG578 Temptations: Beauty is Only Skin Deep £6
TMG579 Four Tops: Reach Out & I'll Be There £4
TMG580 Velvelettes: These Things Keep Me Loving You £15
TMG581 Brenda Holloway: Hurt A Little Everyday £25 demo as by Brenda Holliday £75
TMG582 Martha & The Vandellas: I'm Ready For Love £4
TMG583 Elgins: Heaven Must Have Sent You £20
TMG584 Miracles: I'm The One You Need £6
TMG585 Supremes: You Keep Me Hanging On £4
TMG586 Junior Walker & The All Stars: Money £8
TMG587 Temptations: I'm Losing You £5
TMG588 Stevie Wonder: Place In The Sun £8
TMG589 Four Tops: Standing In The Shadows Of Love £4
TMG590 Marvin Gaye & Kim Weston: It Takes Two £6
TMG591 Chris Clark: Love's Gone Bad £20

TMG592 Originals: Good Night Irene £40
TMG593 Jimmy Ruffin: I've Passed This Way Before £5
TMG594 Marvelettes: Hunter Gets Captured By The Game £10
TMG595 Velvelettes: Needle In A Haystack £8
TMG596 Junior Walker & The All Stars: Pucker Up Buttercup £10
TMG597 Supremes: Love Is Here And Now You're Gone £4
TMG598 Smokey Robinson & The Miracles: Love I Saw In You Was Just A Mirage £8
TMG599 Martha & The Vandellas: Jimmy Mack £4
TMG600 Shorty Long: Chantilly Lace £6
TMG601 Four Tops: Bernadette £3
TMG602 Stevie Wonder: Travelling Man £4
TMG603 Jimmy Ruffin: Gonna Give Her All The Love I Got £4
TMG604 Gladys Knight & The Pips: Take Me In Your Arms And Love Me £5
TMG605 Contours: It's So Hard Being A Loser £15
TMG606 Isley Brothers: Got To Have You Back £6
TMG607 Supremes: Happening £4
TMG608 Brenda Holloway: Just Look What I've Done £15
TMG609 Marvelettes: When You're Young And In Love £5
TMG610 Temptations: All I Need £6
TMG611 Marvin Gaye & Tammi Terrell: Ain't No Mountain High Enough £6
TMG612 Four Tops: 7 Rooms Of Gloom £5
TMG613 Stevie Wonder: I Was Made To Love Her £4
TMG614 Smokey Robinson & The Miracles: More Love/Swept For You Baby £10; with Come Spy With Me B-side £60
TMG615 Elgins: It's Been A Long Time £15
TMG616 Diana Ross & The Supremes: Reflections £4
TMG617 Jimmy Ruffin: Don't You Miss Me A Little Bit Baby £5
TMG618 Marvin Gaye: Your Unchanged Love £8
TMG619 Gladys Knight & The Pips: Everybody Needs Love £5; demo with Stepping Closer To Your Heart B-side £50
TMG620 Temptations: You're My Everything £4
TMG621 Martha & The Vandellas: Love Bug Leave My Heart Alone £5
TMG622 Brenda Holloway: You've Made Me So Very Happy £15
TMG623 Four Tops: You Keep Running Away £4
TMG624 Chris Clark: From Head To Toe £15
TMG625 Marvin Gaye & Tammi Terrell: Your Precious Love £5
TMG626 Stevie Wonder: I'm Wondering £4
TMG627 Detroit Spinners: For All We Know £8
TMG628 Barbara Randolph: I Got A Feeling £25
TMG629 Gladys Knight & The Pips: I Heard It Through The Grapevine £6
TMG630 Edwin Starr: I Want My Baby Back £10
TMG631 Smokey Robinson & The Miracles: I Second That Emotion £4
TMG632 Diana Ross & The Supremes: In And Out of Love £4
TMG633 Temptations: It's You That I Need £20
TMG634 Four Tops: Walk Away Renée £3
TMG635 Marvin Gaye & Tammi Terrell: If I Could Build My Whole World Around You £4
TMG636 Martha & The Vandellas: Honey Chile £6
TMG637 Junior Walker & The All Stars: Come See About Me £5
TMG638 Chris Clark: I Want To Go Back There Again £12
TMG639 Marvelettes: My Baby Must Be A Magician £8
TMG640 Marvin Gaye: You £6
TMG641 Temptations: I Wish It Would Rain £5

TMG642 Elgins: Put Yourself In My Place £8
TMG643 Rita Wright: I Can't Give Back The Love £15
TMG644 Shorty Long: Night Fo' Last £6
TMG645 Gladys Knight & The Pips: End Of Our Road £4
TMG646 Edwin Starr: I Am The Man For You Baby £10
TMG647 Four Tops: If I Were A Carpenter £3
TMG648 Smokey Robinson & The Miracles: If You Can Want £5
TMG649 Jimmy Ruffin: I'll Say Forever My Love £4
TMG650 Diana Ross & The Supremes: Forever Came Today £4
TMG651 Chuck Jackson: Girls Girls Girls £8
TMG652 Isley Brothers: Take Me In Your Arms £8
TMG653 Stevie Wonder: Shoo Be Doo Be Doo Da Day £4
TMG654 Bobby Taylor: Does Your Mama Know About Me with the Vancouvers £25
TMG655 Marvin Gaye & Tammi Terrell: Ain't Nothing Like The Real Thing £4
TMG656 R. Dean Taylor: Gotta See Jane £4
TMG657 Martha & The Vandellas: I Promise To Wait My Love £4
TMG658 Temptations: I Could Never Love Another £4
TMG659 Marvelettes: Here I Am Baby £8
TMG660 Gladys Knight & The Pips: It Should Have Been Me £5
TMG661 Smokey Robinson & The Miracles: Yester Love £4
TMG662 Diana Ross & The Supremes: Some Things You Never Get Used To £4
TMG663 Shorty Long: Here Comes The Judge £4
TMG664 Jimmy Ruffin: Don't Let Him Take Your Love From Me £4
TMG665 Four Tops: Yesterday's Dreams £3
TMG666 Stevie Wonder: You Met Your Match £4
TMG667 Junior Walker & The All Stars: Hip City £6
TMG668 Marvin Gaye & Tammi Terrell: You're All I Need To Get By £4
TMG669 Martha & The Vandellas: I Can't Dance To The Music You're Playing £5
TMG670 Paul Peterson: Little Bit Of Sandy £15
TMG671 Temptations: Why Did You Leave Me Darling £4
TMG672 Edwin Starr: 25 Miles £4
TMG673 Smokey Robinson & The Miracles: Special Occasion £4
TMG674 Gladys Knight & The Pips: I Wish It Would Rain £4
TMG675 Four Tops: I'm In A Different World £4
TMG676 Marvin Gaye: Chained £6
TMG677 Diana Ross & The Supremes: Love Child £4
TMG678 Fantastic Four: I Love You Madly £10
TMG679 Stevie Wonder: For Once In My Life £4
TMG680 Marv Johnson: I'll Pick A Rose For My Rose £4

TOPIC

Topic is the oldest specialist folk label, with its first releases appearing on 78rpm recordings in the mid-fifties, and it is by far the most successful. All the fifties and sixties issues are collectable to a greater or lesser extent, and many of the later issues are of interest too. Although the vinyl catalogue has now been deleted in favour of CDs, many of the records remained available for many years. Topic used a plain dark-blue label until the mid-seventies, however, and the listed values refer to this label design.

VERTIGO

The Vertigo label has been of interest to collectors for several years, with many enthusiasts trying to put together a complete run of the original album releases. These are all characterized by a black-and-white label design intended to induce vertigo when watched spinning round on a turntable. This design is commonly referred to as a 'spiral', although it is actually nothing of the kind – the alternative 'swirl' description is marginally more accurate for a design made up of overlapping circles. Most albums used the 'spiral' design as the entire side-one label, with all the track information being included on the side-two label, although a few albums have conventional labels on both sides, with the spiral reduced to the status of a logo. The spiral label albums were nearly all housed in extravagantly designed gatefold sleeves (those by Dr Z and Mike Absalom are more elaborate opening-out creations), which play an essential part in giving these records the special appeal that they have. Vertigo was set up in 1969 as a specialist progressive label for Phonogram (Philips/Fontana) and, from the outset, the high proportion of albums by musically interesting artists was a strong indication that the label was destined for long-term success. In fact, it continues today, although inevitably no longer linked to music that might be described as 'progressive'.

VO1 Colosseum: Valentyne Suite 1969 £12
VO2 Juicy Lucy: Juicy Lucy 1969 £20
VO3 Manfred Mann Chapter Three: Manfred Mann Chapter Three 1969 £20
VO4 Rod Stewart: An Old Raincoat Won't Ever Let You Down 1970 £10
VO6 Black Sabbath: Black Sabbath 1970 £20
VO7 Cressida: Cressida 1970 £50
6360001 Fairfield Parlour: From Home To Home 1970 £60
6360002 Gracious: Gracious 1970 £50
6360003 Magna Carta: Seasons 1970 £12
6360004 Affinity: Affinity 1970 £60
6360005 Bob Downes: Electric City 1970 £25
6360006 Uriah Heep: Very 'Umble, Very 'Eavy 1970 £30
6360007 May Blitz: May Blitz 1970 £30
6360008 Nucleus: Elastic Rock 1970 £25
6360009 Dr Strangely Strange: Heavy Petting 1970 £60
6360010 Jimmy Campbell: Half Baked 1970 with Merseybeats £15
6360011 Black Sabbath: Paranoid 1970 £20
6360012 Manfred Mann Chapter Three: Volume 2 1970 £25
6360013 Clear Blue Sky: Clear Blue Sky 1971 £60
6360014 Juicy Lucy: Lie Back & Enjoy It 1970 £20
6360015 Warhorse: Warhorse 1970 £30
6360016 Patto: Patto 1970 £30
6360017 Colosseum: Daughter Of Time 1970 £10
6360018 Beggars Opera: Act One 1970 £20
6360019 Legend: Red Boot Album 1971 £50
6360020 Gentle Giant: Gentle Giant 1970 £15
6360021 Graham Bond: Holy Magick 1971 £25
6360023 Gravy Train: Gravy Train 1970 £30
6360024 Keith Tippett: Dedicated To You But You Weren't Listening 1971 £25
6360025 Cressida: Asylum 1971 £75
6360026 Still Life: Still Life 1971 £75
6360027 Nucleus: We'll Talk About It Later 1970 £30
6360028 Uriah Heep: Salisbury 1971 £40

6360029 Catapilla: Catapilla 1971 £40
6360030 Assagai: Assagai 1971 £15
6360031 Nirvana: Local Anaesthetic 1971 £30
6360032 Patto: Hold Your Fire 1971 £100
6360033 Jade Warrior: Jade Warrior 1971 £30
6360034 Ian Matthews: If You Saw Through My Eyes 1971 £12
6360037 May Blitz: Second Of May 1971 £60
6360038 Daddy Longlegs: Oakdown Farm 1971 £15
6360039 Nucleus: Solar Plexus 1971 £25
6360040 Magna Carta: Songs From Wasties Orchard 1971 £15
6360041 Gentle Giant: Acquiring The Taste 1971 £15
6360042 Graham Bond: We Put Our Magick On You 1971 £25
6360043 Tudor Lodge: Tudor Lodge 1971 £150
6360045 Various Artists: Heads Together, First Round 1971 double £12
6360046 Ramases: Space Hymns 1971 £25
6360048 Dr Z: Three Parts To My Soul 1971 £250
6360049 Freedom: Through The Years 1971 £40
6360050 Black Sabbath: Master Of Reality 1971 with poster £40
6360051 Gravy Train: Ballad Of A Peaceful Man 1971 £150
6360052 Ben: Ben 1971 £150
6360053 Mike Absalom: Mike Absalom 1971 £60
6360054 Beggars Opera: Waters Of Change 1971 £20
6360055 John Dummer: Blue 1972 £60
6360056 Ian Matthews: Tigers Will Survive 1972 £12
6360058 Assagai: Assagai II 1971 test pressing £50 (would have been spiral if released)
6360059 Paul Jones: Crucifix In A Horseshoe 1971 £25
6360060 Linda Hoyle: Pieces Of Me 1971 £125
6360062 Jade Warrior: Released 1971 £40
6360063 Legend: Moonshine 1972 £50
6360064 Hokus Poke: Earth Harmony 1972 £50
6360066 Warhorse: Red Sea 1972 £50
6360067 Jackson Heights: Fifth Avenue Bus 1972 £20
6360068 Magna Carta: In Concert 1972 £10
6360069 Gordon Waller: Gordon 1972 £100
6360070 Gentle Giant: Three Friends 1972 £15
6360071 Black Sabbath: Black Sabbath 4 1972 with booklet £20
6360072 Freedom: Is More Than A Word 1972 £60
6360073 Beggars Opera: Pathfinder 1972 £20
6360074 Catapilla: Changes 1972 £200
6360076 Nucleus: Belladonna 1972 £40
6360077 Jackson Heights: Ragamuffin's Fool 1973 £20
6360079 Jade Warrior: Last Autumn's Dream 1972 £30
6360080 Gentle Giant: Octopus 1972 £15
6360081 Alex Harvey: Framed 1972 £40
6360082 Status Quo: Piledriver 1973 £8
6360083 John Dummer: Oobleedooblee Jubilee 1973 £30
6342010 Lighthouse: One Fine Morning 1971 £20
6342011 Lighthouse: Thoughts Of Moving On 1971 £20
6343700 Thomas F. Browne: Wednesday's Child 1972 £40
6360500 Rod Stewart: Gasoline Alley 1970 £10
6360609 Atlantis: Atlantis 1973 £10
6360700 Jim Croce: You Don't Mess Around With Jim 1971 £12

6499407/8 Various Artists: Vertigo Annual 1970 1970 double £12
6641077 Kraftwerk: Kraftwerk 1973 double £75
6673001 Aphrodite's Child: 666 1972 double £25

Rumours and foreigners:

6360087 Manfred Mann's Earth Band: Messin' 1973 German £8
6360093 Magna Carta: Lord Of The Ages 1973 German £8
6360602 Lucifer's Friend: Where The Groupies Killed The Blues 1973 German £10
6360604 Frumpy: By The Way 1972 German £12
6360605 Jean Jacques Kravetz: Kravetz 1972 German £20
6360606 Brave New World: Impressions On Reading Aldous Huxley 1972 German £50
6360607 Agitation Free: Malesch 1972 German £25
6360608 Odin: Odin 1972 German £20
6360610 Tiger B. Smith: Tigerrock 1972 German £25
6360612 Between: And The Waters Opened 1973 German £15
6360613 Peter Michael Hamel: Voice Of Silence 1973 German £12
6360615 Agitation Free: Second Album 1973 German £25
6360616 Kraftwerk: Ralf And Florian 1973 £75
6360902 Dragon: Universal Radio 1971 New Zealand £60
67641055 Peter Michael Hamel: Hamel 1972 German double £20

WARNER BROTHERS

The record division of the well-known American film company was begun in 1958, but despite early success with the Everly Brothers and Peter, Paul And Mary, the label did not really start to become a significant force within the industry until its incorporation within the Kinney company in 1971. The green labels in use at the time were not changed until after several months, with the result that some early K series albums can be easily distinguished from the later pressings bearing the 'tree-lined avenue' label.

ZTT

Both the fortunes and the collectability of the Zang Tumb Tuum label were inextricably linked with the popularity of the company's major asset, Frankie Goes To Hollywood. Whereas at the height of Frankie-mania, it was possible to point to a breed of collector that was interested in the dull music of Andrew Poppy purely because it was to be found on the same label as the star group, this would no longer seem to be the case.

Glossary

ACETATES

Acetates are records made either of hard, brittle plastic or else of metal with a thin vinyl coating. There are two sources of these. Song pluggers in the early sixties would often operate acetate disc-cutters to enable them easily to produce convenient demonstration recordings at a time when cassettes did not exist. Within recording studios, meanwhile, similar quickly produced acetates would be made in order to give the artist or some other interested party some idea of how the finished recording would sound. Where such acetates feature artists whose regular records are collectable, they can also acquire a considerable collectors' interest, especially bearing in mind the fact that, at most, only a handful of copies of any one recording are likely to be in existence. Many commercially released records can be found in acetate form, but values for these tend to be modest, apart from those made by the most collected artists. Examples that have been sold at the well-known London auction housess include the following:

Beatles: All My Loving £260 (1991)
Penny Lane/Strawberry Fields Forever £400 (1990)
Get Back/Don't Let Me Down £225 (1995)
I Should Have Known Better £425 (1998)
Marc Bolan: Hot Love £120 (1990)
David Bowie: Up The Hill Backwards £35 (1990)
Cream: Wrapping Paper £125 (1994)
Jimi Hendrix: The Wind Cries Mary £50 (1986)
Buddy Holly: Peggy Sue £380 (1987)
Michael Jackson: Bad £220 (1989)
Madonna: True Blue £65 (1989)
Bob Marley: Jamming £90 (1988)
Pink Floyd: See Emily Play £154 (1989)
Elvis Presley: Heartbreak Hotel 78 £380 (1994)
Rolling Stones: The Last Time £330 (1990)
Sex Pistols: Pretty Vacant £200 (1987)

At an American auction of Elvis Presley material held at the end of 1999, a 10" double sided acetate of 'Hound Dog'/'Don't Be Cruel' fetched $2875, while a 10" acetate of the *Elvis Sails* EP sold for $1955.

Inevitably, the acetates that are of most interest to collectors are those that contain songs or versions of songs that did not end up as commercial releases. It is in this area that the highest prices have been reached, as the following auction examples make clear:

Beatles: Hey Little Girl/Like Dreamers Do £2500 (1986)
Twelve Bar Original 13.12.65 £1300 (1988)
Yesterday (alternate take) £770 (1989)
Strawberry Fields Forever (alternate take) £560 (1995)
Bob Dylan: Live With The Hawks (2-sided 12") £1125 (1995)
Cliff Richard: Breathless/Lawdy Miss Clawdy £2800 (1985)
Breathless/Lawdy Miss Clawdy £1000 (1986)
Rolling Stones: Road Runner/Diddley Daddy £1500 (1988)
Soon Forgotten/Close Together/Can't Judge A Book £6000 (1988)
Soon Forgotten/Close Together/Can't Judge A Book £4000 (1989)

It is interesting to see how different acetates of the same recordings can realize quite different prices on different occasions. While some of this discrepancy may be explicable in terms of different playing surface conditions, it also highlights the extent to which the demands of just one or two individual collectors can produce a result that confounds general expectations. A third copy of 'Soon Forgotten' (pre-dating the Rolling Stones' earliest Decca recordings) was subsequently auctioned and failed to reach its reserve price. Perhaps there were, after all, only two collectors prepared to pay substantial four-figure sums for this small chunk of rock music history.

AUCTIONS

For some time now, rock music auctions have been held once or twice a year by all the major London auction houses. These have tended to concentrate on memorabilia rather than records as such, and they have become the foremost marketplace for star instruments, stage clothing, star autographs, gold disc awards and the like. A number of scarce acetate recordings have also been sold at auction, but commercial recordings, even when very rare, have played a very limited part on such occasions. At a more private level, however, record auctions are often the most appropriate means of sale for the rarest records. While there is little point in asking for offers on an item whose £20 value is well established and which is relatively often offered for sale, there are a number of more valuable items (notably the rarest rock'n'roll and R&B singles from the fifties) where the demand by individual collectors can be such as to make them prepared to offer considerably more than the *Guide* value on occasion. Such records are identified in this edition of the *Price Guide* with the cautionary phrase 'best auctioned'.

AUDIOPHILE PRESSINGS

Hi-fi enthusiasts inevitably maintain that a vinyl record played on a quality system will always sound better than a compact disc. A better sound still is intended to be obtainable from the 'super-stereo', audiophile albums that were issued in the late seventies and eighties. These are mastered at half the usual speed from a tape playing at half the usual speed, which is supposed to create a superior sound quality when played back normally. The records are also pressed on to virgin vinyl, with a high degree of quality control. Despite this, it is actually quite difficult to distinguish most audiophile recordings from their ordinary stereo equivalents on a blindfold test. Curiously, in view of the hype that was originally used to promote the supposedly superior sound quality of compact discs, there also exist a number of audiophile CDs, which are meant to sound even more superior.

AUTOGRAPHS

Autographs are unfortunately the easiest collecting feature to counterfeit, for which reason autographed records will often attract no more than a slight premium over the normal value of the item, particularly in the case of a modern artist who is still touring and is not of the first stellar magnitude. The situation is different in the case of star or historic names, where the value of an artist's rarest records provides an indication of the likely value of a genuine autograph. The most valuable – by artists like the Beatles and Elvis Presley – are regular features of the London rock auctions, where the authenticity of the autographs will have been verified by experts with experience of what the star signatures actually look like. Other dealers will require some kind of provenance, which may comprise nothing more complicated than a convincing story as to how the autograph was obtained, if the estimated value is not too high. It should be realized, to mention just one area of possible confusion, that signed photographs issued by the Beatles fan club had often never actually been in contact with the pen of a real Beatle, although Ringo Starr apparently quite enjoyed this aspect of fame and would sometimes sign all four names himself! There are, of course, a number of limited-edition releases bearing autographs, and these are listed in the *Guide* where appropriate.

BBC TRANSCRIPTION DISCS

These records are not listed within the *Guide*, although they are actually highly collectable. In order to sell its programmes to radio stations abroad, the BBC records them on to LPs (CDs in recent times), which can be easily used for broadcast purposes. The records of interest to rock music collectors consist of live recordings from programmes like Radio 1's *In Concert*. Essentially, anyone who is anyone in the eighties and nineties has at least one side of one of these records devoted to their music, while a large number of seventies artists are also represented. Unfortunately, the BBC itself does not approve of the sale of its transcription discs. It will not provide any kind of discography and indeed it actively operates to prevent such records being advertised for sale. Copies do change hands on the collectors' market notwithstanding, although values are kept relatively low by the existence of bootlegs and counterfeits, the average being around £50 to £60. Exceptions to this average are the artists one would expect – *The Beatles At The Beeb* set would be likely to sell for around £500, for example. Any BBC record with a black-and-white label is definitely a counterfeit, as original labels are green and white (early issues are green and yellow). Also counterfeit are the records that apparently have correct labels, but have hand-scratched matrix numbers on the vinyl.

BOOTLEGS

A bootleg recording is one that consists of either a live performance or else a set of studio out-takes. Such recordings do not duplicate any official record-company release and, unlike the situation with regard to counterfeits, the issue of whether or not they are genuine does not arise. They are illegal because of the lack of record company involvement, although occasionally the artist is involved and may even get some royalty payment. Lowell George, for example, is known to have mixed two Little Feat live bootlegs himself. Bootlegs are, nevertheless, often keenly sought by collectors for the sake of the otherwise unavailable music they contain. Popular titles are constantly reissued by different manufacturers, but there is some collectors' interest in original labels like Trade Mark of Quality, the Amazing Kornyphone Label and Wizardo Records. Such records, however, have not been listed in this edition of the *Price Guide*.

CASSETTES

Cassettes are not very well favoured by collectors. Many of the highly priced progressive albums from the early seventies were also issued on cassette, and these are at least as rare as their vinyl equivalents. Despite this, the cassettes do not have a significant collectors' value at all. To illustrate the point, only one such cassette is actually listed in this *Guide*. David Bowie's *The Man Who Sold The World* with the dress cover is listed at £200 for the LP, but a mere £25 for the cassette that was issued at the same time. In the case of modern releases, too, cassette-singles have noticeably failed to maintain an initial interest from collectors, while even the limited privately produced items from early in the careers of subsequently successful groups have much lower values than would vinyl versions if these existed.

CLASSICAL MUSIC

Although considerations of time and space prevent their inclusion in this edition of the *Price Guide*, collectors and dealers generally should be aware of the high prices being demanded and paid for certain classical records. Realistically, a complete listing of all the collectable classical records would fill a second volume as large as this one. The market as a whole, however, is smaller at present than the rock collectors' market, with many fewer specialist dealers serving the appetites of a small but active body of enthusiasts. (Many of these live in the Far East, within a market that has become much less buoyant during the last couple of years.) The most sought-after are the early stereo recordings made by Decca, the company that pioneered the LP in Britain. Decca were always very concerned to deliver the highest sound quality possible and the stereo records in the SXL2000 and SXL6000 series, together with the boxed sets in the SET200 series, are collected as being among the finest classical recordings ever made. Also in demand are the later Decca issues on the Phase Four label (PFS series) and on all the Argo subsidiary series. The Decca labels, Eclipse (ECS series), Ace Of Diamonds (SDD and GOS series) and World Of (SPA series) reissued the early Decca recordings at a bargain price, but the sound quality is as good as the originals. These records are therefore collected as well, although the values are inevitably rather lower. (Anything in 'electronic stereo', however, is immediately shunned, as such recordings do not have the high sound quality that collectors demand.) The Decca company was also responsible for pressing records on certain other labels, which again have become collectable. These are Capitol (CTL series), Lyrita (SRCS series, until as late as 1980), London (American CS, OS, OSA and STS series), and RCA (SB2000, SB6500 and SER4000 series until 1970, together with the 'bargain' Victrola releases bearing a ruby label, VICS1000 series). Mercury 'Living Presence' recordings are also renowned for their impressive sound quality, many of them being the result of recordings on to 35 mm magnetic film. The American SR series is very collectable in consequence, as is the British AMS series, whose records were made by EMI, using American masters and machine parts. Other collectable early stereo recordings are to be found on the Angel (SAN and American 35000 series), Columbia (SAX series until 1967, SCX3000 series, TWO series), HMV (ASD series until 1969, CSD series, SLS series of boxed sets), Philips (SABL series) and RCA (LSC 'Living Stereo' series) labels. Some early mono recordings on all these labels are also sought after by some collectors, although in general the demand for mono records is quite limited, other than for key items that never were issued in stereo.

COLOURED VINYL

Records made of plastic in colours other than black are considerably older than many collectors appreciate. Though not particularly common, there are 78s made of various different colours. In the rock era, coloured vinyl issues were an occasional occurrence during the fifties and sixties and all of the coloured records with a rock or blues content are now collectable. (A large number of singles and EPs aimed at children were also issued on coloured vinyl – usually red – but these are of no more than novelty value.) During the late seventies the use of coloured vinyl became something of an epidemic, to the extent that it ceases to be any guarantee of a record's collectability – a situation that remains true through the eighties, although coloured vinyl had become fairly unusual again by the end of the decade. It remains the case, however, that if an artist's records are collectable anyway, then their coloured vinyl releases are likely to be worth a little more than the equivalent black vinyl issues. With CDs, coloration seems to be restricted so far to the plastic packaging rather than being used for the CDs themselves.

COMPACT DISCS

Research into the feasibility of the compact disc format began as early as the sixties, but it was not until March 1979 that the first public demonstration took place. In June 1981 a European press conference was held at which some specially produced CDs of opera extracts were on show. These, therefore, are the likely candidates for the first CDs to be made. The first generally available CDs, however, were issued by Sony in Japan in October 1982, after which March 1983 saw the simultaneous release of some 200 different titles in the UK by all the major record companies. The contrast between this and the situation over two decades earlier, when the LP was adopted by different companies at quite different times (some showing a marked reluctance to invest in a medium with what appeared to be an uncertain future), is quite remarkable. CD singles crept on to the market much more surreptitiously than the albums. The first was 'If You're Ready' by Ruby Turner (Jive JIVEX109 1986), although its value has stayed low owing to the lack of collectors' interest in Ms Turner. The penetration of the collectors' market by compact discs remains relatively limited, but it continues to grow. There *are* some major collectors' items on compact disc these days, however, as the table of the rarest items included elsewhere in this *Guide* makes clear. Candidates for future CD collectability include the limited-edition double-CD sets created by adding a bonus disc of live recordings or out-takes to an album made by a major artist (some of these are already to be found in the listings); the multiple-disc boxed sets designed to provide an overview of the careers of important artists and typically including a number of previously unreleased tracks; and the two-part CD single releases that aim to boost a single's performance in the charts by persuading fans effectively to buy the single twice (many of these can also be already found in the listings).

CONDITION

As a description of the condition of a record, the word 'mint' tends to be one of the most misused of all. A record with a light surface mark or two is not mint, even if the marks produce no audible effect. A record whose cover is slightly creased at the corners is not mint – and neither is one where the cover has torn slightly along the top or bottom edge (a condition that is actually suffered by some records bought new from regular record shops). Some collectors would argue that a record ceases to be mint the moment it is played; others would merely insist on a completely blemish-free playing surface and cover. For records with conditions lower than mint, a scale of descriptions operates. The higher values quoted in this *Guide* are for records in excellent (or NM = near-mint) condition. Such a record has no scratches or any other mark producing an audible effect that should not be there. The cover is free from tearing and has no more than very slight scuffing or creasing. For a record in worse condition than this, the value will be substantially less than the figure listed. This cannot be stressed too strongly. A record whose music is interrupted by a click that repeats thirty-three or forty-five times every minute is likely to be of interest to a collector only as a stop-gap until he can obtain a better copy. He will certainly not pay a price anywhere approaching the near-mint value for such a record. A record whose music is accompanied by what sounds like a frying breakfast is practically worthless. Nor is it possible to use a record's age as an excuse. In many cases, hundreds of thousands of copies of a record may have been sold originally, but a relatively high value is given in the *Guide* precisely because copies in excellent condition are scarce. At the other end of the scale, a record in truly mint condition may sometimes fetch a little more than the listed value. The term VG (very good) is used by dealers to indicate a record that, in practice, has several marks on its surface, some of which are audible. The lower values listed in the *Guide* are for VG records. Typically, these are 50 per cent of the near-mint values, although the figure is lower than this for the relatively common records at the lower end of the value scale, and higher for the more valuable records, where an appearance on the market in any condition at all is a relatively unusual occurrence. The terms G (good) and F (fair) are seldom used – in most cases they refer to a record from which few collectors would gain much listening pleasure. Exactly the same condition grades are applicable to CDs. It is unfortunate that many CD purchasers have been too ready to take at face value the original company claims with regard to the indestructability of the discs. Scratches do not always cause problems, but they often do make the music on CDs stick or jump.

COUNTERFEITS

It is a sad fact that some of the rarer records have been counterfeited by unscrupulous individuals wishing to pass off their copies as the real thing. Recognizing a counterfeit can sometimes be a problem. Often the label or the cover simply look 'too new', or the colour or some feature of the design simply does not look quite right. This is no help, however, where one has no idea what the original record should look like. In the case of UK pressings, a good indication is provided by the matrix number, which is to be found on the vinyl in the space occupied by the run-out groove, next to the label. If this is machine printed, then the record is likely to be genuine. If, however, the number is hand scratched, then the record is likely to be a counterfeit. One should also always be suspicious of a record offered for sale far too cheaply, especially if the record is a well-known collectors' item and the dealer is not one with a reputable name. (Although genuine bargains can always be found, of course, amongst the stock of dealers who are simply unaware of its value. It is a matter of judgement.) High-value collectors' items from the eighties are a particular target for the counterfeiters, as age discrepancies are less likely to arise. 'Mutant Moments' by Soft Cell, 'Damage Done' by the Sisters of Mercy and 'So Young' by the Stone Roses are three rarities of which counterfeits are definitely in circulation, but there are undoubtedly others. In the last few years, a large number of unofficial reissues of scarce albums from the sixties and early seventies have appeared on the market, but the manufacturers of these take care to remove the original record company names from the cover and identification is not a problem.

DEALERS

The values of the records listed in this *Guide* are the prices that a collector might be expected to pay for a copy of the record concerned in NM (near-mint) or VG (very good) condition. The price that a dealer might pay for the record is another matter altogether. A dealer has to cover the cost of his overheads (which include the rent, rates, and other running expenses of the shop; staff salaries; advertising expenses; and the time and effort spent acquiring the knowledge that he must have) before he can even begin to make a profit. A 10 or 20 per cent slice of the record's value is too little to justify the outlay involved. In general, dealers expect to pay around half the anticipated selling price for a record, but this figure may be increased in the case of an item for which there is a waiting customer and decreased for an item whose appeal is rather specialized. It is also likely to be decreased (often considerably) for items at the bottom of the collectors' price scale.

DEMONSTRATION RECORDS

Demonstration records, or 'demos', are the earliest pressings of a record, used as samples and often made available in advance of the regular commercial copies. Review copies tend to be demos, as do the records sent to radio stations, and collectors' interest centres on those examples where a distinct label design is used. At its most boring, the design simply adds a few printed words to the normal label – something along the lines of 'Demonstration sample. Not for sale'. More excitingly, however, record companies in the sixties, particularly, used demo labels that were striking variations of the issue labels. The EMI group of companies, for example, favoured a white label for their singles, dominated by a big red 'A' on the side that was intended to be the hit. During 1966, this was changed to a green label with a big white 'A'. Pye also favoured a white label, with a black 'A' across the record's centre. The Decca group of companies liked to use a pattern of short radial lines around the edge of the label, and sometimes a colour change – Brunswick from black to red and London from black to orange or yellow, although the Decca label itself retained its blue colour for both issues and demos. Deram kept the same label layout, but replaced its brown colour with light blue. The value and collectability of demos varies considerably. Soul collectors prefer demo copies and will pay double the listed price for them (but see the entries for the Action and Tamla Motown labels). This doubling formula works well for other kinds of single too, but only where the artist is generally collectable. A demo copy of 'Bad Blood' by the Paramounts, for example, would be worth around £15, rather than the £8 figure that applies to an issue copy. In the case of one-off or genre singles, however, where the song rather than the singer is important, a demo copy is likely to attract only a modest premium. A copy of 'War Machine' by Leviathan is valued at £30: a demo copy of the record would, perhaps, push the price up to £35. This rule is even more relevant in the case of particularly rare singles, which may originally have sold so poorly that demo copies are actually more common than issue copies. 'She Just Satisfies' by Jimmy Page seldom turns up at all – both demo and issue copies are worth the listed value of £300. To collectors of singles from the fifties, demos are actually inferior to issue copies, so that demonstration copies of rare London singles are worth considerably less than the listed values – probably no more than 50 per cent. Note that fifties demos are often one-sided, a pair of such records being made to demonstrate the A- and B-sides of the commercial single. (This format is prevalent later in the case of demos of LP releases.) In all periods, demo copies of common singles by star artists defy all the usual rules. The values of Beatles demos are listed separately in the *Guide* – hit single demos by the likes of Billy Fury, the Kinks and the Who would fetch around £100 each. Where demos are specifically indicated in the *Guide*, then this is either to draw attention to a value that departs significantly from the guidelines given above or else it is a reference to a record that was withdrawn from issue, with the demonstration copies, therefore, being the only kind in existence. Demonstration albums are less common, but where they do occur, the general guidelines above apply once more. Often the demonstration copies are marked by a label stuck on the sleeve, with the cover and record label being in every other respect identical to those on the issue copies. This procedure is the one commonly followed today in the case of demonstration CDs. Such labels could, of course, be mass-produced by a counterfeiter and stuck on to quantities of regular releases, for which reason demonstration items of this kind attract little or no premium.

DISCO MIX CLUB

The Disco Mix Club, run by disc jockey Tony Prince, has issued a series of special LPs (now CDs) to accredited DJs who pay to join the club, at the rate of two albums per month from the early eighties. The first of these monthly issues is of no interest to collectors, being merely a compilation of recently issued tracks. The second, however, contains various remixes and megamixes of previously released material, much of it being unavailable in this form anywhere else. Although the individual albums are not listed in the *Guide*, they sell for prices in the range of £10–£50, depending on the artists involved, on the infrequent occasions when they come on to the open market.

EXPORT ISSUES

The major British record companies have, from time to time, pressed up special editions of selected domestic records for release overseas. Such records are inevitably scarce in their home country and tend to be sought after by collectors. Usually identifiable by their catalogue numbers, such records are distinguishable from releases made by the actual overseas branches of the record companies concerned, by being marked as 'Manufactured in Great Britain'.

EXTENDED-PLAY RECORDS

As far as most record collectors are concerned, 'EP' is a technical term. It refers to the 7" records that were issued during the fifties and sixties with a playing time around twice that of the standard single. In most cases these had four tracks (though some, like *The Spotnicks On The Air*, had six), played at 45rpm (though some, like *Something Else By The Move*, played at 33rpm), and had picture sleeves constructed out of thin card, with the front-cover edges folded over the back, like the LP sleeves of the time (though many of the early fifties EPs have company covers without pictures). These mini-LPs are widely collected for their own sake, with the result that these listings include many EPs by artists who are otherwise only marginally collectable. During the late seventies, many of the tiny independent labels that emerged in the wake of punk released records containing four or more tracks, often using the 12" format. Sometimes (though not in this *Price Guide*), these too are described as EPs, but they are not collected as such by EP specialists, and they do not serve the mini-LP function of the earlier records.

FLEXI-DISCS

Flexi-discs are 7" singles pressed on to plastic so thin that it is extremely bendy – and extremely easy to damage! Two companies are primarily responsible for making these discs – Lyntone and Sound for Industry – but these are essentially manufacturers and not record companies as such. A variety of sources are responsible for commissioning the flexi-discs in the first place. Record companies use them as promotional devices, typically advertising a forthcoming boxed album set, or else including them as a free extra within the packaging of another record. Magazines, too, use them as a free extra, either on an occasional basis, or with every issue (as in the case of the eighties *Flexipop* magazine). Fan clubs issue them as an exclusive product for their members (the most famous examples of these being the Beatles Christmas flexi-discs). Occasionally, independent record companies will use the flexi-disc format for a cheap, limited-edition run. A few of these different flexi-discs are collectable and are listed in the *Guide*. In many cases, test pressings are made on ordinary hard vinyl and these records are typically worth around three to four times the value of the flexi-disc.

FOAM-EDGE COVERS

For a few months in 1970–71, one manufacturer of album sleeves decided that it would be a good idea to employ a design in which a cardboard cover like a book cover housed the record in a clear plastic sleeve, along the edge of which was fastened a strip of plastic foam. *Colosseum Live* was one album given such a sleeve; the Pentangle's *Basket Of Light* was another. Sensible purchasers of these records immediately placed a standard paper sleeve inside the plastic one, because although the strip of foam was intended to clean the record as it was pulled out of the sleeve, in practice the foam used was so coarse that it actually damaged the vinyl surface. A similar problem is sometimes found in the case of LPs using polythene-lined inner sleeves. Where the record has not been removed from its sleeve for a period of years, a reaction can take place between the polythene and the vinyl, leaving a thin but visible deposit on the surface of the record. Unlike the foam-edge marking, however, this deposit normally wipes clean and causes minimal effect to the record's sound quality.

FOLK

Folk music is a collectors' area that tends to get ignored by many people, but there are a large number of valuable albums to be found on the specialist labels. As always, the records issued during the sixties and early seventies are the ones in which there is most interest (a tiny number of folk records dating from the fifties also exist), with anything issued on the Topic label being worth investigating. Other key labels are Acorn, Argo (Decca's home for non-commercial music of various kinds – classical and some jazz as well as folk, and also some spoken-word material), Broadside, Cottage, Claddagh (from Ireland), Dolphin (also from Ireland), Folkways (from the US), Free Reed, Leader, Rubber, Saydisc, Tradition, Trailer, Transatlantic (most collectors and dealers do know about that one) and Village Thing. There are also a number of labels responsible for only a handful or fewer releases, which are effectively private pressings.

FOREIGN RELEASES

The majority of items listed in the *Guide* are UK issues. A substantial number of releases from other countries, however, have also been included, wherever it is felt that these are of particular interest to the UK collector. Some of these consist of recordings by British artists (by birth or by adoption) that were not actually released in Britain. The rest are a selection of records by artists from other countries that are of particular appeal to collectors in the UK. In particular, a large number of US albums have been included. American LPs have always been imported into Britain in quite large numbers so that they frequently turn up for sale in the collectors' market. Moreover, with so much rock music being American in origin, the first pressing of a large number of releases is actually an American record. In addition, there are key areas of interest (the obscurer regions of West Coast rock, for example), as well as several particularly collectable records, that are exclusively American, yet whose omission in a book seeking to describe the collectors' market would be a nonsense. As a general rule, US albums have been included in this *Guide* either if they have no exact UK equivalent or if the American pressing has a higher value than its British counterpart. (It should be noted that American pressings of many UK original albums are actually less valuable in the UK, especially where the label is a key factor in the collectability of the British record.) In the last few years, there has been an escalation of interest in collectable European albums from the seventies, particularly those originating in Germany. Once again, it would be a nonsense to exclude these records from a comprehensive record *Price Guide* and it is hoped that every such album has in fact been listed.

FREAKBEAT

During their brief career, the Beatles presided over a rock music scene that was growing and developing so fast that it was able to move from British beat to psychedelia to progressive rock in the space of just seven years. Of course, rock analysts love categories, and not content with these three to cover the major sixties trends, some have sought to define yet another. 'Freakbeat' attempts to find a genre in the space between British beat and psychedelia – a space that hardly seems big enough to accommodate it. The term is a recent one – no one in the sixties thought it necessary to modify the 'Beat' idea until the sounds heard on such records as the Yardbirds' 'Shapes Of Things' and Jimi Hendrix's 'Purple Haze' made it clear that the description had become inadequate. There is also much disagreement over which records should properly be described as freakbeat, which only goes to highlight the artificial nature of the term.

FRENCH EPs

France has always been highly resistant to Anglo-American cultural imports and it was not until 1962 that the local record industry paid any attention to the rock music phenomenon. Even then, the French response was typically idiosyncratic. Spurning singles entirely (until 1967), the French record companies decided to concentrate instead on four-track extended-play records. Between 1962 and 1968 a large number of these 7″ EPs were issued, featuring both French and some well-known (and not so well-known) British and American artists. The consequence of this was that groups like the Beatles, the Animals and the Rolling Stones had many more EP releases than they did in the UK, and the novelty of both the cover art and the availability of

UK album tracks in a unique 7″ format has made these records extremely collectable today. Even more sought after are the EPs by groups like the Creation, the Tony Jackson Group and the Primitives, who had no picture-cover releases at all in the UK. The majority of the French EP catalogue is therefore included within this *Guide*.

GATEFOLD SLEEVES

Single-record LP sleeves that open out like a book cover were occasionally used in the fifties and sixties to give a touch of extra class to the records of the biggest stars. Elvis Presley's *Golden Records* and *Elvis Is Back*, Frank Sinatra's *Sinatra–Basie* and the Beatles *Beatles For Sale* are notable examples. For ten years from the mid-sixties, these double sleeves became a common feature and help to make the albums of the period into attractive artefacts in their own right. With the declining influence of progressive rock in the later seventies, however, gatefold sleeves fell out of use and returned to their role of highlighting certain star issues.

GOLD DISCS

Although there are more copies made of the average gold-disc award (or silver or platinum) than many people realize, they are still comparatively uncommon items in the collectors' marketplace. Most often, therefore, they tend to be auctioned rather than offered for a fixed price. In most cases, the values reached are actually quite modest (for items in much shorter supply than the average valuable collectors' record), as the following list of recent auction house sales indicates:

Bryan Adams: Waking Up (platinum) £200
Beatles: Abbey Road (gold) £850
Get Back (gold) £580
Hey Jude (gold) £780
Bee Gees: Too Much Heaven (platinum) £315
Boomtown Rats: A Tonic For The Troops (gold) £130
Carpenters: Please Mr Postman (platinum) £280
Def Leppard: Hysteria (platinum) £200
Dire Straits: Brothers In Arms (platinum) £320
Frankie Goes To Hollywood: Relax (gold) £130
Guns 'N' Roses: Appetite For Destruction (platinum) £350
House Of Love: House Of Love (silver) £100
Inspiral Carpets: Life (gold – presented to the group's roadie, Noel Gallagher) £460
Janet Jackson: Control (gold) £400
James: Gold Mother (gold) £100
Elton John: The Very Best Of Elton John (platinum) £350
Paul McCartney: Tripping The Live Fantastic (platinum) £320
Metallica: Metallica (gold) £350
Sinead O'Connor: The Lion And The Cobra (gold) £140
Pet Shop Boys: Heart (platinum) £90
Pink Floyd: Dark Side Of The Moon (platinum) £280
Pretenders: Pretenders II (silver) £170
Prince: Batdance (gold) £400
Tears For Fears: Seeds Of Love (platinum) £110

Most valuable are those awards presented to the artists themselves, but these are very seldom offered for sale. The products of those companies that offer to make a 'gold disc from your favourite record' are not the same thing at all, of course, and have no value to collectors.

GOLD LABEL

Just as in the case of the London label, the earliest pressings of singles issued by Columbia, HMV and Parlophone are described as being 'gold label' copies. It is actually the print on the label that is coloured gold, rather than the label itself, but its presence is a good indication of likely value. (Within the industry itself, the colour was actually referred to as bronze, the responsible dye being known as bronzing powder.) If the original issue of a single should have a gold label, then this is indicated in the listings if later pressings bearing the same catalogue number exist. In such cases, the later pressing will have a value of only half the value given.

INTERVIEW RECORDS

As far as copyright law in the UK and US is concerned, the rules that apply to recordings of music do not apply to the spoken word. Accordingly, anyone can issue records containing interviews with the famous, without worrying about the fact that the artists in question have contracts elsewhere. Companies like Baktabak capitalize on this by producing attractive interview picture discs, which can appear to the unwary to be highly desirable collectors' items. In fact, however, few collectors are actually much interested in these items and their values never rise above the cost when new. A small exception to this rule occurs in the case of interview material issued by the artist's record company as a promotional device, although even here interview recordings seldom reach the values of promotional releases containing music.

JAZZ

For the third edition of the *Price Guide*, a large number of collectable jazz albums by American artists were included for the first time. This did not reflect a new development within the realm of record collecting, but was rather a belated acknowledgement of a collectors' market that had actually been in existence for some time. The emphasis was deliberately placed on UK issues via labels such as Esquire, Vogue and London Jazz, although the highest prices are actually paid for the original American albums that these British labels merely repackaged. The jazz list has been expanded further still for this fifth edition.

JAZZ IN BRITAIN

British jazz is a somewhat different animal to its American cousin. From the outset, the restricted market for the music, together with a typically British myopia with regard to the position of jazz's cutting edge, led to a much more intimate relationship between jazz and rock than was ever the case in America. The popularity of traditional jazz was a piece of British idiosyncrasy, for music that was inclined to view jazz as a kind of music hall entertainment could have little in common with what had been going on in New York's 52nd Street (the difference between Acker Bilk and Charlie Parker being as great as the difference between Brotherhood of Man and Kurt Cobain's Nirvana). But it was out of trad that the success of Lonnie Donegan was made; out of trad too that Alexis Korner was able to form his launching pad for much of the British R&B and beat boom that followed. During the sixties, musicians like Jack Bruce, Dick Heckstall-Smith, Jon Hiseman and Henry Lowther proved themselves to be equally at home playing both jazz and rock – partly out of necessity, but partly too because they were able to make worthwhile musical statements in both areas. Records by people like Neil Ardley, Mike Westbrook and Ian Carr on the one hand, and Colosseum, Soft Machine and the Battered Ornaments on the other, contain so many overlapping personnel (who feel little need to compromise their playing styles in either area), that it hardly makes sense to differentiate between the two kinds of music. As far as the collectors' market is concerned, it is the overlapping of musical styles and personnel that makes some of the late-sixties/early-seventies British jazz albums so desirable. Most of these are rare and prices remain high – especially since little in this field has ever been reissued.

LASER-ETCHED RECORDS

In 1980 the first records appeared with laser-etched surfaces. As it happens, neither *True Colours* by Split Enz nor *Paradise Theatre* by Styx is of much more than novelty value these days, despite the attractive designs visible on the playing surface when the records are tilted towards the light. (Neither record was a limited edition, incidentally – all copies have the surface pictures.) The technique has been used very infrequently since 1980, possibly because, although the effect is undoubtedly interesting, it is nevertheless a lot less spectacular than one would imagine.

LONG-PLAY RECORDS

The first LPs were issued in the United States in early 1949 by the Columbia (CBS) record company. In the UK, however, EMI, which was responsible for distributing the Columbia label, prevaricated – and it was Decca which issued the first LPs in June 1950. The company's initial release sheet comprised fifty-three records, the majority of which were classical, with a sprinkling of light orchestral items, together with gems by such popular artists as Edmundo Ros, the Galloway-Ruault Old Time Dance Orchestra and Troise and His Banjoliers. The claims made on behalf of the new format by advertisers at the time make interesting reading. Superb sound quality, with 'almost silent' playing surfaces, negligible wear during play, unbreakability, and ease of storage are all cited as reasons for purchasing LPs – and all of these will sound very familiar to those who remember the promotion of CDs nearly three and a half decades later.

MATRIX NUMBERS

The matrix numbers that are to be found on the vinyl surface of a record in between the playing area and the label are sometimes of considerable help in providing information about the record itself. Much of the number will consist of the record's catalogue number, which is itself a piece of vital information in the case of test pressings issued with nothing useful written on the labels themselves. Extra digits, however, provide information about the stampers used to press the records (the 'matrix' being the mould from which the stampers were made). On some occasions, the recorded version of a song has been changed during an extended pressing run, and the corresponding change in the matrix number enables identification of the different versions without the record having to be played (collectable examples of this appear in the listings – see, for example, the Frankie Goes To Hollywood variations where the relevant matrix number differences are given in brackets after the catalogue numbers). In principle, the matrix number can be used to distinguish first and later pressings where the catalogue number is the same, although only classical record collectors seem to be much interested in these fine distinctions. In the case of UK releases, matrix numbers are generally machine-stamped. There may also be one or more slogans or messages hand-scratched in the vinyl. A random inspection, for example, reveals the words 'Everything's Jelly' on a Spritualised 12″ test pressing, 'Bilbo' on a copy of the Who's *Live At Leeds* album and both 'Loosely From The Stiff Beach' and 'With Pink Warmth' on a copy of *Psonic Psunspot* by the Dukes of Stratosphear. The ubiquitous 'Townhouse' refers to one of the major studios, while 'A Porky Prime Cut' indicates that the master has been made by the most highly respected cutting engineer, George Peckham.

MISPRESSED RECORDS

Whenever a record plays music that is not what the label or cover would lead the listener to expect, then this record is said to be a mispress. When pressing plants are producing several different records at the same time, it is an unfortunate but easily understood error if the occasional batch of vinyl is passed under the wrong stamper. Accordingly, records where one side plays what it should, but the other plays something quite different do turn up from time to time. In general, such records are of novelty but little monetary value. The exceptions are those records involving the major collectable artists – a number of Beatles mispressings, for instance, are listed in the *Guide*, as are a few other interesting examples. In the CD age, incidentally, mispressings continue – discs where the musical content bears no relation to what is printed on the disc are in circulation. Errors involving labels on otherwise correctly pressed records are comparatively common. A record may have a side-one (or side-two) label on both sides; or else the labels for the two sides may be interchanged; or one or both labels may be missing altogether. None of these occurrences creates any increase in value, however, if only because they could be easily reproduced by a counterfeiter. Records where the label is displaced on to the playing surface, preventing play, are virtually worthless, of course.

NM CONDITION

NM, standing for Near Mint, is used in this *Guide* synonymously with Excellent, to indicate a record in played, but aurally perfect, condition. Further details are given under the heading 'Condition'.

ORIGINAL PRESSINGS

The date of publication or the copyright date given on a record usually relates to the original release date, which is not necessarily the date of issue of the particular piece of vinyl in question. Where a record is given a reissue, after having been unavailable for a time, it is usually (though not always, unfortunately) given a new catalogue number. Catalogue numbers are therefore a considerable aid in identifying original pressings, and these are given in the *Guide* wherever possible. Where a record remains in a company's catalogue over an extended period of time, changes in label design can make the first issues distinctive. Some of the most important of these are described under the appropriate record company headings within this *Guide*. Values given in this *Guide* are for original pressings. Later pressings may not be collectable at all, although if the record in question is not easily available in any form, then a later pressing may still command some kind of collectors' value. This, however, will obviously be rather less than for the original.

PICTURE DISCS

The first picture disc, a 10″ 78rpm recording of 'Cowhand's Last Ride' by Jimmie Rodgers, was issued in America in 1933. At various times after that, further picture discs were issued, but all suffered from the fundamental problem of having poor sound quality, which prevented them from achieving much commercial success. The first rock picture discs (and the earliest to be listed in this *Guide*) date from 1969-70 and comprise two compilation albums alongside LPs by Curved Air and Saturnalia. The sound quality of these was also poor, due to the fact that they are essentially thin, clear flexi-discs glued to a piece of card on which the actual pictures are printed. From the late seventies, picture discs became very much more common and although the sound quality is still inferior compared to the conventional black vinyl equivalents, it is good enough to allow the inherent attractiveness of the discs to become the major consideration. There tends to be a natural bias towards picture discs within the collectors' market, to the extent that for artists who are collected anyway, their picture discs are all sought after. The first shaped picture discs were a series of singles by the Police issued in the US (and widely available on import, albeit at quite high prices). These were cut into the shapes of police badges and were issued within special cardboard folders. For some reason, shaped picture discs did not really catch on in a big way until 1982-3, but they were a common record company gimmick throughout the rest of the eighties. Some of these explicitly recognize their primary function as display items, rather than serious sources of music, by including pieces of cardboard within the packaging that are intended to be folded into stands ('plinths') for the records. Uncut shaped picture discs consist of the twelve-inch record (with seven-inch grooves), from which the shaped disc is cut. They are collected rather in the same way as demonstration copies of regular singles are collected and typically sell for around three times the value of the finished shaped discs.

PRIVATE PRESSINGS

When a group is unable to gain a recording contract with any established record company and decides to finance the production and distribution of a record itself, then the result is a private pressing. Many singles issued in the post-punk era conform to this description, but the term is most generally used in connection with a fairly large number of more-or-less progressive albums issued during the seventies. Many of these albums have been sold or exchanged for extraordinarily high amounts in the past and although the values of many such items have fallen a little, prices are still high, as reference to the entries for such groups as the Dark, Ithaca, Toby Jug and Complex will confirm. Arguably, the high values of these records are entirely the result of a skilful exercise in hype on the part of a few specialist dealers, but there have been a few transactions to confirm these as genuine market values. Nevertheless, collectors should be aware that this whole area is something of a minefield, especially if ideas of investment and making a profit are a priority.

PROMOTIONAL RECORDS

The term 'promo' is often used interchangeably with the term 'demo', even by the record companies themselves. Within this *Guide*, however, the terms have specific, and different, meanings. A demo is a regular commercial release given a special label for the purposes of radio play or review. A promo, on the other hand, is a record (or other item) specially manufactured for advertising or promotional purposes. While being clearly related to a commercial release, the promo will be different in some major way from any version of the release that could be bought in a shop. Such items have long been a feature of the record industry and in the eighties and nineties in particular, a large number have been issued. Sometimes they consist of mixes not available to the general public, to enable radio stations to present something to their listeners that seems exclusive. It is also common for sampler recordings to be issued containing a small number of tracks from a forthcoming album, while the albums themselves may be provided with special packaging as a promotional device. This may range from a simple box containing one of each of the available formats, to the more elaborate affair typified by Talk Talk's *Laughing Stock*, where a picture CD is housed in a wooden box, along with pencils, rubber, ruler and other items of stationery, most stamped with the group's name. The majority of such releases have not been included in this *Guide*, although the intention has been to include collectable items containing music that is not otherwise available, providing that they have values greater than twice any equivalent regular release.

QUADRAPHONIC RECORDINGS

During the early seventies a number of quadraphonic LPs were issued. When played on a suitable system, incorporating a special decoder, such records enable sounds to be heard from each of four speakers. These are intended to be arranged with two in front of the listener, as in stereo, and a further two behind the listener. The extra two speakers deliver ambient sound in the case of recordings designed to re-create the sound of a live performance; otherwise they can be essential ingredients in a surround-sound experience. Few collectors possess a quadraphonic system – nevertheless, the records are often sought after, since they were designed to be playable on conventional stereo systems and although they do not then provide a quadraphonic effect, they often do contain mixes that sound noticeably different from their stereo equivalents. It should be noted that some US albums – such as many of those on the Impulse label – deliver quadraphonic sound on appropriate systems, even though there is no mention of the fact on either record label or sleeve.

R.G.M.

The initials 'R.G.M' on a sixties record (whether in a Triumph record catalogue number or a reference to production by R.G.M. Sound) are indicative of the guiding hand of producer Robert George (Joe) Meek. Beginning as an engineer in the fifties, Joe Meek worked on numerous records by the likes of Frankie Vaughan, Shirley Bassey, Petula Clark and Lonnie Donegan, before setting himself up as an independent producer. His concern with creating unusual and distinctive sounds led him continually to push the primitive sound equipment of the time to its limits and it is his reputation as an innovator that is responsible for the considerable interest in his records today. Meek's experiments with speeded-up tape, distortion, close miking, echo and even multi-tracking were certainly some years before his time, but the fact that all this imagination and inventiveness was directed towards the production of what was, for the most part, crassly commercial material, tends to blunt the impact, for modern listeners, of what Meek was achieving. As it happens, Joe Meek did score some considerable commercial successes, including 'Johnny Remember Me' by John Leyton, 'Don't You Think It's Time' by Mike Berry, 'Have I The Right' by the Honeycombs, 'Just Like Eddie' by Heinz and 'Telstar' by the Tornados.

RADIO TRANSCRIPTION DISCS

The American equivalents of the BBC transcription discs, used to syndicate rock music programmes across a large number of radio stations, are mostly the products of two companies: Westwood One and King Biscuit Flour Hour. Originally issued as two- and three-LP sets, they now come out as compact discs. Either way, the values are on a par with the BBC discs, at around £50 to £60 for the average album set or CD (with the same obvious exceptions). These recordings consist of live concerts interspersed with advertisements, ready for broadcast in the US. Other radio show albums contain a mixture of music (some of it previously issued studio material) and interviews. These have lower values than the all-live sets, going down to as little as £10, depending on the amount of unreleased live material they contain.

REGGAE

Reggae (or ska or rock steady) from the sixties is very collectable and every record released is of value. Listing the records is in some cases quite problematic due to the chaotic nature of the specialist record labels involved. It is common practice for different artists to appear on either side of a single, but it is not always apparent which is intended to be the A side. Artists' names are frequently misspelt or simply change from record to record. Lloyd Charmers, Lloyd Chalmers, Lloyd Tyrell and Lloyd Terrel, for example, are all the same person; so are Roland Alphonso and Rolando Al; so are Jackie, Jackie Edwards, Wilfred, Wilfred Edwards and Wilfred Jackie Edwards! Sometimes the B side of a record changes during the lifetime of a single; sometimes a song is reattributed to a different artist; and there are numerous examples where the name that appears on the record is simply wrong. It would even appear to be the case that, on occasion, more than one single has been issued with the same catalogue number. The reggae listings in this *Guide* represent the best attempt at making sense of these various difficulties. In practice, sixties reggae collectors are interested in the entire output of the relevant labels and, apart from the special case of records by Bob Marley, which are worth considerably more than their fellows, all the records issued on any particular label have similar values. Singles on the Studio One and Blue Beat labels sell for £12–£15 each. Other key labels are Black Swan, Coxsone, Dice, Doctor Bird, Island, Port-O-Jam, R&B, Rio (from 1963–5), Ska Beat, and Treasure Isle (from 1967–8), all of whose singles sell for £10–£12. The small number of albums on these labels range from expensive to very expensive – typically £50–£100. Further sixties reggae labels worth looking out for, with singles in the price range £5–£8, are: Aladdin, Amalgamated, Bamboo, Big Shot, Blue Cat, Caltone, Camel, Clan Disc, Columbia Bluebeat (a unique example of a major label taking an interest in the music), Crab, Double D, Duke, Duke Reid, Escort, Gas, Giant, High Note, Jackpot, Jolly, Jump Up, Nu Beat, Pama, Pressure Beat, Punch, Pyramid, Rainbow, Randys, Rio (from 1966), Treasure Isle (1969), Unity and Upsetter. Many of these labels continued into the seventies, but collectors' interest falls off dramatically.

REMIXES

Ever since Trevor Horn and Frankie Goes To Hollywood hit upon the idea of using multiple remixes as a marketing device, it has been standard practice for modern artists to release several slightly different versions of the same song. A cynic might suggest that the reason for this is primarily to avoid the creative energy necessary in writing more songs and point to the nadir of the practice as being Prince's decision to issue an album-length collection of alternative arrangements of a song that only really consists of a single repeated line in the first place ('The Beautiful Experience'). Many collectors, on the other hand, delight in seeking out different mixes, and some of these can reach quite high prices.

SEVENTY-EIGHTS

To most collectors, 78rpm recordings are of little interest. They break much too easily for one thing; and hardly anyone has the means to play them these days for another. The age of these records is of no consequence in this respect – indeed it is actually part of the problem, for most 78s contain music from before the rock'n'roll era, which is itself subject to only slight collectors' interest. Even within the rock'n'roll era, the 45rpm singles are much more collectable than their 78rpm equivalents, despite what is sometimes suggested by the (non-specialist) media. A small number can be found listed within the pages of this *Guide*, these being either records by particularly collectable artists, like Elvis Presley and Cliff Richard, or else the handful of significant rock'n'roll and R&B songs that were not given a 45rpm release in the fifties. Apart from these, the general rule is that 78s have a value of about one-quarter of their seven-inch equivalent. It is suggested elsewhere that there is a growing market for 78s from 1959–60, when the format was rapidly dying out. These records are not actually as rare as is sometimes suggested and neither is it true that many were available by special mail order only. It should be realized that many parts of Scotland, for example, were still without mains electricity at this time, so that demand for 78s in these areas was still high. If, however, there really are collectors around who are prepared to pay a three-figure sum for 78s by the likes of Neil Sedaka and Duane Eddy – artists whose other records sell for extremely modest amounts – then the author would be grateful if they could let him know. Once he has recovered from the shock, he could add them to the listing for the next *Price Guide*!

SLEEVES

LPs and EPs are supposed to be in sleeves and it should go without saying that a damaged or missing sleeve has a serious effect on the value of a record. As a general rule, the cover should be considered as being responsible for half the value of an item, while the disc is responsible for the other half. An exception to this principle is where a particular sleeve variation is the major factor in a record's rarity – such cases are mentioned explicitly in the listings. Picture sleeves for singles were a comparative rarity prior to the late seventies and were often reserved for promotional issues. In these cases, the effect of the sleeve on the value of a record can be dramatic (see, for example, the Pink Floyd and Tyrannosaurus Rex discographies). Increasingly from about 1978 onwards, it became standard practice for the first several thousand copies of a single to be issued with a picture sleeve. For these, therefore, collectors expect to find such a sleeve and are not very interested in copies without one. Within these listings, singles from 1980 onwards are presumed to come with picture sleeves and no explicit mention is made of the fact. Collectors like to see a company sleeve on singles from the fifties, sixties or seventies, where a picture sleeve is not appropriate, but the absence of a company sleeve has a very minor effect on a single's value. It is possible to obtain very good reproductions of many of the major fifties and sixties company sleeves and many collectors are happy to accept these as an alternative to the real thing. It is worth noting that the construction of LP and EP sleeves made in the UK is a considerable aid in the identification of original issues. During the fifties and sixties, the cardboard edges of the front cover were turned over the outside of the back cover; from the late sixties the edges were glued inside the back cover. In addition, LP covers from the fifties seem to be made of a much thinner, flimsier cardboard than used subsequently.

STEREO

At the annual Audio Fair held in New York in October 1957, Decca demonstrated the results of its research into the reproduction of stereo sound by records. EMI had, in fact, been recording many of its artists in stereo for over two years previously and was issuing the results on what it called 'stereosonic' tapes. One company in America had issued twin-track stereo discs, which had to be played with two pickups. The first stereo LPs to be issued commercially in the UK were intended to demonstrate the system – Pye CSCL70007, EMI SDD1 and Decca SKL4001 all appearing in mid-1958 and all comprising extracts from various light and classical pieces, together with assorted sound effect recordings. In August, a large number of stereo records, covering various kinds of music, were given a simultaneous release by several different companies, with the first UK stereo LPs appearing a month later (courtesy of EMI and Decca). As a general rule, stereo records from the early years of the medium are worth a little more to collectors than their mono equivalents, owing to the rather smaller numbers of them sold at the time. (It should be noted, however, that many jazz collectors prefer the mono versions, as being more faithful to the intentions of the musicians in the studio, so that stereo jazz LPs from the early years are worth a little less than their mono equivalents.) Towards the end of the sixties, when stereo recordings were rapidly becoming the norm, it is the mono versions that are scarcer and in consequence worth a little more to collectors. Mono recordings (other than reissues of earlier material) died out altogether after 1970. There tend to be many differences of detail between mono and stereo versions of the same LP – sometimes different takes are used and on occasion, the artist went back to the studio and re-recorded all the music for stereo. With the advent of multi-track recording, musicians began to take increasing liberties with the technology at their disposal. In order, for example, to record more than four parts on a four-track machine, the technique of mixing tracks and bouncing them down to create free tape was invented. The final overdubs would be added at the final mixing stage, so that these would inevitably be different in the case of separately prepared mono and stereo mixes. Well-known examples of different mono and stereo versions resulting from this include the Beatles' *White Album* (the two recordings of 'Don't Pass Me By' are completely different takes; the mono 'Helter Skelter' lacks Ringo's shouted complaint at the end); Jimi Hendrix's *Axis: Bold As Love* (the stereo 'EXP' is twice as long as the mono); Traffic's *Mr Fantasy* (Stevie Winwood plays wildly divergent guitar solos at the ends of 'Heaven Is In Your Mind'); and Pink Floyd's *Saucerful Of Secrets* (the instrumental texture of the two versions of 'Let There Be More Light' is markedly different).

TEST PRESSINGS

A test pressing is an earlier stage in the production of a record than even the advance demonstration discs. It is made on ordinary vinyl literally to test the fidelity of each component involved, from the master tape itself through to the setting of the cutting equipment. Alternatively, a test pressing may represent a try-out for a proposed record release, the most collectable of these being records that did not, after all, become finished commercial releases. Where these pressings are albums, they may have proof or even finished covers. Test pressings generally, however, are distinguished by their plain (usually white) labels. Apart from certain test pressings that are particularly collectable, and are listed as such in the *Guide*, the values for these records are on a par with the values for demonstration records.

TRI-CENTRES

The earliest singles have triangular centres, which identify original pressings in the case of fifties singles that were reissued with the same catalogue numbers. For most companies, tri-centres were used until the end of 1959, at which time round centres replaced them (the precise situation with regard to London singles is described under the London heading). Capitol, however, were using round centres from as early as 1956.

TWELVE-INCH SINGLES

The first twelve-inch single was conceived very much as a gimmick. This was a 1976 reissue of the Who's 'Substitute', using exactly the same version as on the original 7″ single. The popularity of late-seventies disco music, however, turned the twelve-inch single into a staple format, since the lengthy playing times possible were ideal for coping with extended dance mixes. The early releases did not often have picture sleeves (RCA used what was essentially a company sleeve for its disco records, with a small picture of the artist at the top). From 1980, however, the majority of twelve-inch singles did have picture sleeves, which form an essential part of the collectors' package.

VG CONDITION

VG, standing for Very Good is a description of a record's condition that is actually less complimentary than it sounds. Further details are given under the heading 'Condition'.

VINYL

The great majority of dealers will complain that during the last few years, the public demand for vinyl records has plummeted. The collectors' market has actually been less affected than the general second-hand market in records, but it is definitely the case that collectable records sell more reluctantly than they used to. The spiralling upward rise in the values of progressive albums has halted in general and, in some cases, prices have begun to fall. In many other areas too, values are a little lower than they used to be. In the case of fifties and sixties records, however, demand is still high and in these areas there are a number of trend-bucking price rises. The rarest singles, in particular, are becoming increasingly difficult to find in any condition and several collectors are deciding that they had better buy them now while they still can. As a result, the values of these are climbing, most noticeably in the case of the highest-price items, where the results of auctions frequently produce very happy surprises for the vendors. Other areas of increasing interest are sixties albums by key artists like the Beatles, the Who and the Small Faces; European progressive albums by artists like Faust, Can and Amon Düül; and a range of jazz albums.

List of Illustrations

First Section

Second Section

a

A – AUSTR

It is appropriate that the first record listed in this guide should be one that typifies exactly what collecting rare records is all about. Produced as a labour of love on an independent label created for the purpose, the record came complete with lavish packaging and sold hardly at all! The music, which is thoughtful and pastoral, is interesting enough to give the record a cult reputation, and the mystique is enhanced for record collectors today by the album being reissued in a very limited facsimile edition, itself being sold at something of a collectors' price.

A – Austr	LP	Holyground	HG113	1970	**£350**	**£210**	
A – Austr	LP	Magic Mixture	MM1	1989	**£20**	**£8**	

A B SKHY

A B Skhy	LP	MGM	SE4628	1969	**£10**	**£4**	*US*
Ramblin' On	LP	MGM	SE4676	1970	**£10**	**£4**	*US*

A. C. MARIAS

Drop	7"	Dome	DOM451	1981	**£5**	**£2**	

A CERTAIN RATIO

All Night Party	7"	Factory	FAC5	1979	**£5**	**£2**	*limited-edition sticker*
Backs To The Wall	CD-s	A&M	ACRCD517	1989	**£5**	**£2**	
Big E	CD-s	A&M	ACRCD514	1989	**£5**	**£2**	
Four For The Floor EP	CD-s	A&M	ACRCD550	1990	**£5**	**£2**	
I Need Someone Tonite	7"	Factory	FAC727	1983	**£4**	**£1.50**	*promo*
Life's A Scream	7"	Factory	FAC112P	1984	**£8**	**£4**	*promo only pack*
Planet	CD-s	A&M	CDROB2	1991	**£5**	**£2**	
Shack Up	12"	A&M	ACRY590	1990	**£8**	**£4**	*promo only*
Shack Up	7"	A&M	ACR590	1990	**£5**	**£2**	*promo only*
Twenty Seven Forever	CD-s	A&M	CDROB5	1991	**£5**	**£2**	
Won't Stop Loving You	CD-s	A&M	ACDCD540	1990	**£5**	**£2**	

A HOUSE

Kick Me Again Jesus	12"	Rip	ARIPT1	1987	**£6**	**£2.50**	

A II Z

I'm The One Who Loves You	7"	Polydor	POSP314	1981	**£10**	**£5**	
No Fun After Midnight	12"	Polydor	POSPX243	1981	**£10**	**£5**	*red vinyl*
No Fun After Midnight	7"	Polydor	POSP243	1981	**£5**	**£2**	
Witch Of Berkeley – Live	LP	Polydor	2383587	1980	**£15**	**£6**	

AARDVARK

Aardvark	LP	Nova	SDN17	1970	**£75**	**£37.50**	

ABACUS

Abacus	LP	Polydor	2371215	1971	**£25**	**£10**	
Everything You Need	LP	Zebra	2949002	1972	**£20**	**£8**	*German*
Indian Dancer	7"	York	YR207	1973	**£5**	**£2**	
Just A Day's Journey Away	LP	Polydor	2371270	1972	**£20**	**£8**	*German*
Midway	LP	Zebra	2949013	1974	**£20**	**£8**	*German*

ABBA

Scandinavia's most successful pop export continue to enthral a large and loyal following a decade and a half after disbanding. As is well-known, all four members were established artists before joining together in Abba. In addition to the items listed below, therefore, Abba collectors are also interested in the records listed under the Anni-Frid Lyngstad, Agnetha Faltskog, Björn Ulvaeus, Hootenanny Singers, Northern Lights, and Hep Stars headings.

Anniversary Boxed Set	7"	Epic	ABBA26	1984	**£200**	**£100**	*26 blue vinyl singles*
Anniversary Boxed Set	7"	Epic	ABBA26	1984	**£75**	**£37.50**	*26 singles*
Arrival	LP	Nautilus	NR20	1981	**£12**	**£5**	*US audiophile*
Best Of Abba	cass	Readers Digest	GABCC112	1986	**£30**	**£15**	*5 tape set*
Best Of Abba	LP	Readers Digest	GABA112	1986	**£25**	**£10**	*5 LP set*
Chiquitita (Spanish version)	7"	Vogue	45X1188	1978	**£5**	**£2**	*French*
Dream World	CD-s	Polydor	8538912	1994	**£40**	**£20**	*promo*
Dream World	CD-s	Polydor	8538912	1994	**£20**	**£10**	*promo*
Estoy Sonando	7"	Vogue	101235	1979	**£5**	**£2**	*French*
Hit Collection	cass	St Michael	13615704	1984	**£20**	**£8**	*with book*
I Have A Dream	7"	Epic	EPC8088	1979	**£4**	**£1.50**	*gatefold picture sleeve*
I Have A Dream (Shakin' Stevens B side)	7"	Kelloggs	KELL1	1984	**£6**	**£2.50**	
Interview	CD	Polar	ABBAINT	1999	**£25**	**£10**	*promo*

Ring Ring	7"	Polar	POS1171	1973	**£10**	**£5**	*Swedish label & language*
Ring Ring	7"	Epic	EPC1793	1973	**£20**	**£10**	
Ring Ring	7"	Polydor	2040105	1973	**£20**	**£10**	*sung in German*
Ring Ring	LP	Polar	POLS242	1973	**£12**	**£5**	*Swedish*
Singles, The First Ten Years	LP	Epic	ABBOX2	1983	**£40**	**£20**	*2 picture discs, boxed*
Slipping Through My Fingers	12"	Discomate	PD1005	1981	**£60**	**£30**	*Japanese, red vinyl*
Slipping Through My Fingers	7"	Discomate	PD105	1981	**£30**	**£15**	*Japanese Coca-Cola picture disc*
So Long	7"	Epic	EPC2848	1974	**£8**	**£4**	
Summer Night City	12"	Polydor	ABBA1DJ	1993	**£15**	**£7.50**	*1 sided promo*
Super Trouper	CD	Epic	CDEPC10022	1983	**£12**	**£5**	
Super Trouper	LP	Epic	ABBOX1	1980	**£40**	**£20**	*boxed, book, poster*
Thank You For The Music	7"	Epic	WA3894	1983	**£15**	**£7.50**	*shaped picture disc*
Under Attack	7"	Epic	EPCA112971	1982	**£10**	**£5**	*picture disc*
Visitors	CD	Epic	CDEPC10032	1983	**£12**	**£5**	
Voulez Vous	LP	Epic	EPC86086	1979	**£50**	**£25**	*picture disc*
Waterloo	7"	Polar	POS1187	1974	**£10**	**£5**	*Swedish label & language*
Waterloo	7"	Polydor	2040116	1974	**£20**	**£10**	*sung in German*
Waterloo	7"	Vogue	103104	1974	**£20**	**£10**	*sung in French*
Winner Takes It All	12"	Epic	EPC128835	1980	**£30**	**£15**	*gatefold picture sleeve*

ABBEY TAVERN SINGERS

Collectors of records on a particular label often find themselves buying albums or singles that are not at all to their taste! *We're Off To Dublin In The Green* by the Abbey Tavern Singers is an LP of Irish pub songs that just happens to have been released on a subsidiary of Tamla Motown.

We're Off To Dublin In The Green	LP	VIP	VS402	1966	**£12**	**£5**	*US*

ABBOTT, BILL & THE JEWELS

Groovy Baby	7"	Cameo Parkway	P874	1963	**£8**	**£4**	

ABC

King Without A Crown	CD-s	Neutron	NTCD113	1987	**£5**	**£2**	
Look Of Love	CD-s	Neutron	NTCD116	1990	**£5**	**£2**	
One Better World	CD-s	Neutron	NTCD114	1989	**£5**	**£2**	
Real Thing	CD-s	Neutron	NTCD115	1989	**£5**	**£2**	
When Smokey Sings	CD-s	Neutron	NTCD111	1987	**£5**	**£2**	

ABERCROMBIE, JOHN

Gateway	LP	ECM	ECM1061ST	1975	**£12**	**£5**	*with Dave Holland & Jack DeJohnette*
Sargasso Sea	LP	ECM	ECM1080ST	1976	**£10**	**£4**	*with Ralph Towner*
Timeless	LP	ECM	ECM1047ST	1974	**£12**	**£5**	

ABICAIR, SHIRLEY

In the quest to find increasingly rare grooves, some very strange artists become included within the domain of Northern Soul. Hence the unlikely inclusion here of Shirley Abicair, a lady who used to sing rather twee songs on children's television, to the accompaniment of a strummed autoharp.

Am I Losing You	7"	Piccadilly	7N35364	1967	**£5**	**£2**	
Fair Dinkum	7" EP	Parlophone	GEP8612	1957	**£8**	**£4**	
Willie Can	7"	Parlophone	MSP6224	1956	**£5**	**£2**	

ABLUTION

Ablution	LP	CBS	80536	1974	**£25**	**£10**	*Swedish*

ABRAHAMS, MICK

At Last	LP	Chrysalis	CHR1005	1972	**£25**	**£10**	*round cover*
Learning To Play Guitar With	LP	SRT	SRT73313	1975	**£10**	**£4**	
Mick Abrahams	LP	Chrysalis	ILPS9147	1971	**£15**	**£6**	

ABRAMS, DAVE

If I'd Stayed Around	LP	Folksound	FS103	1975	**£75**	**£37.50**	

ABRAMS, RICHARD

Levels And Degrees Of Light	LP	Delmark	DS413	1968	**£12**	**£5**	

ABRASIVE WHEELS

Army Song	7"	Abrasive	ABW1	1981	**£6**	**£2.50**	

ABSALOM, MIKE

Hector And Other Peccadillos	LP	Philips	6308131	1972	**£20**	**£8**	
Mighty Absalom Sings Bathroom Ballads	LP	Sportsdisc	ILP1081	196–	**£10**	**£4**	
Mike Absalom	LP	Vertigo	6360053	1971	**£60**	**£30**	*spiral label*
Save The Last Gherkin For Me	LP	Saydisc	SDL162	1969	**£40**	**£20**	

ABSOLUTE

Can't You See	LP	Reset	7REST8	1987	**£60**	**£30**	
TV Glare	12"	Reset	12REST5	1985	**£25**	**£12.50**	
TV Glare	7"	Reset	7REST5	1985	**£20**	**£10**	

ABSOLUTELY FABULOUS

Absolutely Fabulous	CD-s	Parlophone	CDR6332	1994	**£15**	**£7.50**	

ABSTRACT TRUTH

Title	Format	Label	Cat. No.	Year	Value	Value	Notes
Abstract Truth	LP	Parlophone	PCSJ12065	1970	**£100**	**£50**	*South African*

ABYSSINIAN BAPTIST CHOIR

Title	Format	Label	Cat. No.	Year	Value	Value	Notes
Abyssinian Baptist Choir	LP	Philips	847095BY	1963	**£30**	**£15**	

ABYSSINIANS

Title	Format	Label	Cat. No.	Year	Value	Value	Notes
Arise	LP	Front Line	FL1019	1978	**£12**	**£5**	
Forward To Zion	LP	Klik	KLP9023	1977	**£12**	**£5**	
Yim Mas Gan	7"	Harry J	HJ6652	1973	**£10**	**£5**	

AC DONNCA, SEAN

Title	Format	Label	Cat. No.	Year	Value	Value	Notes
An Aill Bain (The White Rock)	LP	Claddagh	CC9	1971	**£12**	**£5**	*Irish*

ACADEMY

Title	Format	Label	Cat. No.	Year	Value	Value	Notes
Pop Lore According To	LP	Morgan Blue Town	BT5001	1969	**£75**	**£37.50**	
Rachel's Dream	7"	Morgan Blue Town	BTS2	1969	**£6**	**£2.50**	

ACCENT

The Accent's one single was produced by Mike Vernon, but it is quite unlike the blues-based material in which Vernon specialized. Instead, crashing guitars and a warbling, distorted guitar solo frame a mysterious unison vocal for a performance that is nowadays described as being psychedelic. The record has a similar feel to the Smoke's greatly superior 'My Friend Jack', which is perhaps the classic of the genre, but it is hardly surprising that the record sunk without trace, given that the Smoke's record was not a UK hit either.

Title	Format	Label	Cat. No.	Year	Value	Value	Notes
Red Sky At Night	7"	Decca	F12679	1967	**£100**	**£50**	

ACCENTS

Title	Format	Label	Cat. No.	Year	Value	Value	Notes
Wiggle Wiggle	7"	Coral	Q72351	1959	**£20**	**£10**	

ACCIDENTS

Title	Format	Label	Cat. No.	Year	Value	Value	Notes
Blood Spattered With Guitars	7"	Hook, Line 'n' Sinker	HOOK1	1980	**£4**	**£1.50**	
Kiss Me On The Apocalypse	LP	Hook Line 'n' Sinker		1980	**£60**	**£30**	*test pressing*

ACCOLADE

Title	Format	Label	Cat. No.	Year	Value	Value	Notes
Accolade	LP	Columbia	SCX6405	1970	**£20**	**£8**	
Accolade 2	LP	Regal Zonophone	SLRZ1024	1971	**£30**	**£15**	
Natural Day	7"	Columbia	DB8688	1970	**£4**	**£1.50**	

AC/DC

Title	Format	Label	Cat. No.	Year	Value	Value	Notes
AC/DC Live	CD	Atlantic	PRCD48182	1992	**£40**	**£20**	*US promo*
Albert Archives	LP	Albert	APLP037	1979	**£12**	**£5**	*Australian*
Ballbreakers	CD	East West	SAM1693	1995	**£30**	**£15**	*promo compilation*
Can I Sit Next To You Girl	7"	Albert	AP10551	1974	**£75**	**£37.50**	*Australian*
Danger	7"	Atlantic	A9532	1985	**£4**	**£1.50**	
Danger	7"	Atlantic	A9532P	1985	**£12**	**£6**	*shaped picture disc*
Danger	7"	Atlantic	A9532W	1985	**£4**	**£1.50**	*poster sleeve*
Dirty Deeds Done Cheap	12"	Atco	SAM1127	1992	**£6**	**£2.50**	*promo*
Dirty Deeds Done Dirt Cheap	7"	Atlantic	K10899	1977	**£20**	**£10**	*cartoon schoolboy picture sleeve*
Flick Of The Switch Interview Album	LP	Atlantic	PR562	1983	**£12**	**£5**	*US promo*
For Those About To Rock	12"	Atlantic	SAM143	1982	**£30**	**£15**	*promo*
Girl's Got Rhythm	7"	Atlantic	K11406	1979	**£5**	**£2**	
Girl's Got Rhythm	7"	Atlantic	K11406E	1979	**£6**	**£2.50**	*envelope sleeve*
Guns For Hire	7"	Atlantic	A9774P	1983	**£10**	**£5**	*shaped picture disc*
Hail Caesar	CD-s	East West	3BALLCD	1995	**£20**	**£10**	*promo*
Heat Seeker	12"	Atlantic	A9136TP	1988	**£8**	**£4**	*picture disc*
Heatseeker	CD-s	Atlantic	A9136CD	1988	**£8**	**£4**	*3" single*
High Voltage	7"	Atlantic	K10960	1976	**£8**	**£4**	*no picture sleeve*
High Voltage	7"	Atlantic	K10860	1976	**£50**	**£25**	*picture sleeve*
Highway To Hell	12"	Atco	SAM1089	1992	**£6**	**£2.50**	*promo*
Highway To Hell	7"	Atlantic	K11321	1979	**£5**	**£2**	
Highway To Hell	LP	Atlantic	ATL50628	1979	**£100**	**£50**	*German, yellow vinyl*
Highway To Hell	LP	Atlantic	K50628	1979	**£300**	**£180**	*test pressing with different sleeve*
If You Want Blood	LP	Atlantic	ATL50532	1978	**£200**	**£100**	*Dutch, red and white vinyl*
It's A Long Way To The Top	7"	Atlantic	K10745	1976	**£8**	**£4**	
Jailbreak	7"	Atlantic	K10805	1976	**£8**	**£4**	
Japan Tour '81	LP	Atlantic	SAM155	1981	**£75**	**£37.50**	*promo picture disc*
Let There Be Rock	7"	Atlantic	K11018	1977	**£5**	**£2**	
Let There Be Rock	LP	Atlantic	K50366	1977	**£150**	**£75**	*mispress – 2 side ones*
Live From The Atlantic Studios	LP	Atlantic	LAAS001	1978	**£75**	**£37.50**	*US promo*
Money Talks	CD-s	East West	B8886CD	1990	**£5**	**£2**	
Nervous Shakedown	7"	Atlantic	A9651P	1984	**£12**	**£6**	*shaped picture disc*
Powerage	LP	Atlantic	KSD19180	1978	**£40**	**£20**	*Canadian red vinyl*
Razor's Edge	CD	Atlantic	ACDC1	1990	**£20**	**£8**	*interview promo*
Rock'n'Roll Ain't Noise Pollution	12"	Atlantic	K11630T	1980	**£8**	**£4**	*with badge*
Rock'n'Roll Damnation	12"	Atlantic	K11142T	1978	**£10**	**£5**	
Rock'n'Roll Damnation	7"	Atlantic	K11142	1978	**£4**	**£1.50**	
Shake A Leg	7"	Atlantic	K11600	1979	**£30**	**£15**	*wrong A side*

Title	Format	Label	Cat. No.	Year	Mint	Good	Notes
Shake Your Foundations	7"	Atlantic	A9474C	1986	£4	£1.50	*poster sleeve*
Shake Your Foundations	7"	Atlantic	A9474P	1986	£10	£5	*shaped picture disc*
Shake Your Foundations	CD-s	Atlantic	A9474CD	198–	£5	£2	
That's The Way I Wanna Rock'n'Roll	12"	Atlantic	A9098TP	1988	£6	£2.50	*picture disc*
That's The Way I Wanna Rock'n'Roll	CD-s	Atlantic	A9098CD	1988	£8	£4	*3" single*
Thunderstruck	12"	Atco	SAM693	1990	£12	£6	*red vinyl promo*
Thunderstruck	CD-s	Atco	B8907CD	1990	£5	£2	
Touch Too Much	7"	Atlantic	K11435	1980	£6	£2.50	*back-to-front sleeve*
Who Made Who	7"	Atlantic	A9425P	1986	£10	£5	*shaped picture disc*
Who Made Who	CD-s	Atlantic	A9425CD	198–	£5	£2	
Who Made Who (Collectors Mix)	12"	Atlantic	A9425TW	1986	£10	£5	*with poster*
Whole Lotta Rosie	12"	Atlantic	K11207T	1978	£10	£5	
Whole Lotta Rosie	7"	Atlantic	K11207	1978	£5	£2	
You Shook Me All Night Long	7"	Atlantic	A9377P	1986	£10	£5	*shaped picture disc*
You Shook Me All Night Long	7"	Atlantic	K11600	1980	£4	£1.50	
You Shook Me All Night Long	7"	Atlantic	K11600	1980	£60	£30	*mispress – plays Shake A Leg*

ACE, BUDDY

Title	Format	Label	Cat. No.	Year	Mint	Good	Notes
Buddy Ace	7" EP	Vocalion	VEP170164	1965	£50	£25	
Got To Get Myself Together	7"	Action	ACT4504	1968	£5	£2	

ACE, CHARLIE

Title	Format	Label	Cat. No.	Year	Mint	Good	Notes
Creeper	7"	Upsetter	US359	1971	£8	£4	*Upsetters B side*
Need No Whip	7"	Smash	SMA2325	1971	£8	£4	

ACE, JOHNNY

Title	Format	Label	Cat. No.	Year	Mint	Good	Notes
Johnny Ace	7" EP	Vogue	VE170150	1962	£75	£37.50	
Memorial Album	10" LP	Duke	DLP70	1955	£300	£180	*US*
Memorial Album	LP	Vocalion	VA160177	1961	£75	£37.50	
Memorial Album	LP	Duke	DLP71	1956	£100	£50	*US*
My Song	7"	Vogue	V9200	1962	£60	£30	*demo only*
Pledging My Love	7"	Vocalion	V9180	1961	£30	£15	
Pledging My Love	7"	Vogue	V9180	1961	£60	£30	

ACE, RICHARD

Title	Format	Label	Cat. No.	Year	Mint	Good	Notes
Don't Let The Sun Catch You Crying	7"	Coxsone	CS7031	1967	£12	£6	*Viceroys B side*
Hang 'Em High	7"	Trojan	TR654	1969	£4	£1.50	*Black & George B side*
I Need You	7"	Studio One	SO2022	1967	£12	£6	*Soul Vendors B side*
More Reggae	7"	Studio One	SO2072	1969	£12	£6	*Gladiators B side*

ACES

Title	Format	Label	Cat. No.	Year	Mint	Good	Notes
But Say It Isn't So	7"	Parlophone	R5108	1964	£4	£1.50	
Wait Till Tomorrow	7"	Parlophone	R5094	1963	£4	£1.50	

ACES (2)

Title	Format	Label	Cat. No.	Year	Mint	Good	Notes
One Way Street	7"	Etc.	ETC1	1982	£10	£5	

ACHE

Title	Format	Label	Cat. No.	Year	Mint	Good	Notes
Bla Som Altid	LP	KHF	ROLP6570	1977	£12	£5	*Danish*
De Homine Urbano	LP	Philips	841906	1970	£15	£6	*German*
Green Man	LP	Philips	6318005	1971	£25	£10	*German*
Pictures From Cyclus 7	LP	CBS	81216	1974	£10	£4	*Dutch*

ACHES & PAINS

Title	Format	Label	Cat. No.	Year	Mint	Good	Notes
Again And Again	7"	Page One	POF008	1966	£4	£1.50	

ACHOR

Title	Format	Label	Cat. No.	Year	Mint	Good	Notes
End Of My Day	LP	Cedar	CEDAR1	1978	£100	£50	
Hosanna To The Son Of David	LP	Dove	DOVE54	1978	£75	£37.50	

ACID GALLERY

Title	Format	Label	Cat. No.	Year	Mint	Good	Notes
Dance Around The Maypole	7"	CBS	4608	1969	£30	£15	

ACID SYMPHONY

Title	Format	Label	Cat. No.	Year	Mint	Good	Notes
Acid Symphony	LP	private		1969	£150	£75	*US, 3 LP set*

ACINTYA

Title	Format	Label	Cat. No.	Year	Mint	Good	Notes
La Cité Des Dieux Oubliés	LP	SRC	161754	1978	£30	£15	*French*

ACKLES, DAVID

Title	Format	Label	Cat. No.	Year	Mint	Good	Notes
American Gothic	LP	Elektra	K42112	1972	£10	£4	
David Ackles	LP	Elektra	EKL4022/ EKS74022	1968	£15	£6	
Five and Dime	LP	CBS	32466	1973	£15	£6	*US*
Subway To The Country	LP	Elektra	EKS74060	1970	£15	£6	

ACKLIN, BARBARA

Title	Format	Label	Cat. No.	Year	Mint	Good	Notes
Am I The Same Girl	7"	MCA	MU1071	1969	£4	£1.50	
Love Makes A Woman	7"	MCA	MU1038	1968	£4	£1.50	
Love Makes A Woman	LP	MCA	MUP(S)366	1969	£12	£5	
Seven Days Of Night	LP	MCA	MUPS410	1971	£20	£8	
Somebody Else's Arms	LP	MCA	MUPS416	1971	£15	£6	

ACQUA FRAGILE

Title	Format	Label	Cat. No.	Year	Mint	Good	Notes
Acqua Fragile	LP	Numero Uno	DZSLN55656	1973	£25	£10	*Italian*
Mass Media Stars	LP	Dischi	6150	1974	£15	£6	*Italian*

ACRE, SEPH & THE PETS

Title	Format	Label	Cat. No.	Year	Mint	Half	Notes
Rock And Roll Cha Cha	7"	Pye	7N25001	1958	**£5**	**£2**	

ACT

Title	Format	Label	Cat. No.	Year	Mint	Half	Notes
Absolutely Immune	12"	ZTT	VIMM1	1987	**£12**	**£6**	
Chance	12"	ZTT	BETT1	1988	**£60**	**£30**	
Chance	7"	ZTT	BET1	1988	**£40**	**£20**	
Chance	CD-s	ZTT	CDBET1	1988	**£100**	**£50**	
I Can't Escape From You	CD-s	ZTT	CDIMM2	1987	**£10**	**£5**	
Laughter, Tears And Rage	CD	ZTT	ZQCD1	1988	**£15**	**£6**	
Snobbery And Decay	12"	ZTT	CT01	1987	**£20**	**£10**	*promo*
Snobbery And Decay	12"	ZTT	12XACT28	1987	**£10**	**£5**	*with poster*
Snobbery And Decay	CD-s	ZTT	CID28	1987	**£15**	**£7.50**	*gatefold card sleeve*

ACT (2)

Title	Format	Label	Cat. No.	Year	Mint	Half	Notes
Cobbled Streets	7"	Columbia	DB8179	1967	**£12**	**£6**	
Here Come Those Tears	7"	Columbia	DB8261	1967	**£12**	**£6**	
Just A Little Bit	7"	Columbia	DB8331	1968	**£40**	**£20**	

ACT (3)

Title	Format	Label	Cat. No.	Year	Mint	Half	Notes
Act	7" EP	Oak	RGJ407	1965	**£125**	**£62.50**	

ACTION

The Action were a mod group with a similar soul/R&B sound to the Who, except that, according to those who saw the group live, the Action were better. Not that this is particularly apparent from the group's records, which are, for the most part, worthy cover versions, but lacking the extra spark of star quality. Sadly, the Action never did get to make an album, although a later incarnation of the group made two, as Mighty Baby.

Title	Format	Label	Cat. No.	Year	Mint	Half	Notes
Action Speaks Louder Than . . .	LP	Dojo	DOJOLOP3	1985	**£12**	**£5**	
Baby You've Got It	7"	Parlophone	R5474	1966	**£40**	**£20**	
Harlem Shuffle	7"	Hansa	14321AT	1968	**£40**	**£20**	*German*
Hey Sah-Lo-Ney	7"	Edsel	E5008	1984	**£5**	**£2**	
I'll Keep On Holding On	7"	Edsel	E5001	1981	**£4**	**£1.50**	
I'll Keep On Holding On	7"	Parlophone	R5410	1966	**£40**	**£20**	
Land Of 1000 Dances	7"	Parlophone	R5354	1965	**£40**	**£20**	
Never Ever	7"	Parlophone	R5572	1967	**£40**	**£20**	
Shadows And Reflections	7"	Edsel	E5003	1982	**£5**	**£2**	
Shadows And Reflections	7"	Parlophone	R5610	1967	**£40**	**£20**	
Shadows And Reflections	7" EP	Odeon	MOE149	1967	**£300**	**£180**	*French, best auctioned*
Since I Lost My Baby	7"	Edsel	E5002	1981	**£4**	**£1.50**	
Ultimate Action	LP	Edsel	ED101	1980	**£12**	**£5**	

ACTIONS

Title	Format	Label	Cat. No.	Year	Mint	Half	Notes
Wepp	7"	Studio One	SO2065	1968	**£12**	**£6**	*Larry & Alvin B side*

ACTIVE RESTRAINT

Title	Format	Label	Cat. No.	Year	Mint	Half	Notes
Terror In My Home	7"	Sticky	PEELOFF3	1983	**£5**	**£2**	

ACTRESS

Title	Format	Label	Cat. No.	Year	Mint	Half	Notes
Good Job With Prospects	7"	CBS	4016	1969	**£40**	**£20**	

ACUFF, ROY

Title	Format	Label	Cat. No.	Year	Mint	Half	Notes
Favorite Hymns	LP	MGM	E3707	1958	**£12**	**£5**	*US*
I Like Mountain Music	7"	Brunswick	05635	1957	**£4**	**£1.50**	
Old Time Barn Music	10" LP	Columbia	CL9010	195–	**£20**	**£8**	*US*
Songs Of The Smokey Mountains	10" LP	Columbia	CL9004	195–	**£20**	**£8**	*US*
Songs Of The Smokey Mountains	LP	Capitol	T617	1955	**£15**	**£6**	*US*

AD CONSPIRACY

Title	Format	Label	Cat. No.	Year	Mint	Half	Notes
Ad Conspiracy	LP	Diamond Age		1979	**£15**	**£6**	

ADAM & THE ANTS

Title	Format	Label	Cat. No.	Year	Mint	Half	Notes
Goody Two Shoes	7"	CBS	A112367	1982	**£6**	**£2.50**	*not credited to 'Adam Ant'*
Young Parisians	12"	Damaged Goods	FNARR7	1989	**£6**	**£2.50**	*picture disc*
Young Parisians	12"	Damaged Goods	FNARR7	1989	**£6**	**£2.50**	*white vinyl, with fanzine*

ADAM, MIKE & TIM

Title	Format	Label	Cat. No.	Year	Mint	Half	Notes
Most Peculiar Man	7"	Columbia	DB7902	1966	**£4**	**£1.50**	

ADAMO

Title	Format	Label	Cat. No.	Year	Mint	Half	Notes
'66	LP	Electrola	E84070	1966	**£15**	**£6**	*German*
Adamo	LP	HMV	1044	1962	**£20**	**£8**	*Dutch*
Belgium's Top Recording Star	7" EP	HMV	7EG8860	1963	**£5**	**£2**	
Hits Of Adamo	LP	HMV	CLP3601	1966	**£12**	**£5**	
Olympia '67	LP	HMV	DF321	1967	**£30**	**£15**	*French*
Salvatore Adamo	LP	Columbia	SCX6254	1968	**£12**	**£5**	
Sensational Adamo	LP	HMV	CLP3635	1967	**£12**	**£5**	

ADAMS, ALICIA

Title	Format	Label	Cat. No.	Year	Mint	Half	Notes
Love Bandit	7"	Capitol	CL15195	1961	**£5**	**£2**	

ADAMS, ARTHUR K.

She Drives Me Out Of My Mind	7"	Blue Horizon	573136	1968	£10	£5	

ADAMS, BILLY

Count Every Star	7"	Capitol	CL15107	1959	£10	£5	

ADAMS, BRYAN

Can't Stop This Thing We Started	CD-s	A&M	AMCD812	1991	£5	£2	
Eighteen Til I Die – The Interview	CD	A&M	BRYANINTCD1	1996	£20	£8	*promo*
Everything I Do I Do It For You	CD-s	A&M	AMCD789	1991	£5	£2	
Hidin' From Love	7"	A&M	AMS7520	1980	£10	£5	*picture sleeve*
Let Me Take You Dancing	12"	A&M	AMSP7460	1979	£15	£6	
Let Me Take You Dancing	7"	A&M	AMS7460	1979	£10	£5	
Lonely Nights	7"	A&M	AMS8183	1981	£8	£4	
One Good Reason	7"	A&M	AM170	1984	£50	£25	
Reckless	CD	Mobile Fidelity	UDCD544	1991	£15	£6	*US audiophile*
Run To You	12"	A&M	AMY224	1984	£6	£2.50	*poster sleeve*
Somebody	12"	A&M	AMY236	1985	£6	£2.50	*with tour poster*
Somebody	7"	A&M	AMP236	1985	£4	£1.50	*picture disc*
There Will Never Be Another Tonight	CD-s	A&M	AMCD838	1991	£5	£2	
Waking Up The Neighbourhood	CD	A&M	3971642	1991	£30	£15	*CD & cassette in promo pack*
Waking Up The Neighbourhood	CD	A&M	POCM3023/4	1991	£25	£10	*Japanese with bonus rarities CD*

ADAMS, CLIFF

Lonely Man Theme	7"	Pye	7N25056	1960	£4	£1.50	

ADAMS, DANNY & THE CHALLENGERS

Bye Bye Baby, Bye Bye	7"	Philips	BF1346	1964	£4	£1.50	

ADAMS, DERROLL

Feelin' Fine	LP	Village Thing	VTS17	1972	£20	£8	

ADAMS, FAYE

I'll Be True	7"	London	HLU8339	1956	£500	£330	*best auctioned*
Shake A Hand	LP	Warwick	2031	1961	£50	£25	*US*

ADAMS, GLADSTON

Dollars And Cents	7"	Trojan	TR659	1969	£6	£2.50	

ADAMS, GLEN

Cool Cool Rocksteady	7"	Collins Downbeat	CR006	1968	£15	£7.50	*Owen Gray B side*
Hold Down Miss Winey	7"	Island	WI3100	1967	£12	£6	*Vincent Gordon B side*
My Girl	7"	Duke	DU58	1969	£4	£1.50	*Gladiators B side*
Never Fall In Love	7"	Explosion	EX2048	1971	£4	£1.50	
Rent Too High	7"	Trojan	TR621	1968	£8	£4	
She	7"	Island	WI3083	1967	£12	£6	*Sonny Burke B side*
She Is Leaving	7"	Blue Cat	BS126	1968	£8	£4	*Uniques B side*
She Is So Fine	7"	Island	WI3120	1967	£12	£6	*Roy Shirley B side*
She's So Fine	7"	Amalgamated	AMG837	1969	£4	£1.50	*Ernest Wilson B side*
Silent Lover	7"	Island	WI3072	1967	£12	£6	

ADAMS, JOHNNY

Come On	7"	Top Rank	JAR192	1959	£4	£1.50	
Heart And Soul	LP	SSS	SSS5	196–	£12	£5	*US*
Reconsider Me	7"	Polydor	56775	1969	£6	£2.50	

ADAMS, JUNE

River Keep Movin'	7"	King	KG1038	1966	£10	£5	

ADAMS, LLOYD

I Wish Your Picture Was You	7"	Blue Beat	BB366	1966	£12	£6	*Creepers B side*

ADAMS, MARIE

What Do You Want To Make Those Eyes At Me For	7"	Capitol	CL14963	1958	£15	£7.50	

ADAMS, MIKE & THE REDJACKETS

Surfers Beat	LP	Crown	CST312	1963	£30	£15	*US*

ADAMS, PAUL & LINDA

Far Over The Fell	LP	Sweet Folk & Country	SFA27	1975	£30	£15	

ADAMS, PEPPER

Cool Sound	LP	Pye	NPL28007	1959	£25	£10	
Critics' Choice	LP	Vogue	LAE12134	1958	£20	£8	

ADAMS, RITCHIE

Back To School	7"	London	HLU9200	1960	£20	£10	

ADAMS, RUSH

Birds And The Bees	7"	MGM	SP1176	1956	£5	£2	
I'm Sorry Dear	7"	Parlophone	MSP6101	1954	£6	£2.50	
Then I'll Be Happy	7"	Parlophone	CMSP33	1955	£10	£5	

ADAMS, STEVE

Steve Adams	LP	Mind's Ear		1977	£15	£6	

ADAMS, SUZIE & HELEN WATSON

Songbird	LP	Dingles	DIN327	1983	£12	£5	

ADAMS, WOODROW

Baby You Just Don't Know	7"	Blue Horizon	451001	1965	£100	£50	

ADAMSON, BARRY

Achieved In The Valley Of The Dolls	CD-s	Mute	RCDSTUMM134	1996	£5	£2	*promo*

ADDERLEY, CANNONBALL

Accent On Africa	LP	Capitol	(S)T2987	1969	£12	£5	
African Waltz	LP	Riverside	RLP377	1961	£15	£6	
Alabama Concerto	LP	Riverside	RLP12276	196–	£15	£6	
At The Lighthouse	LP	Riverside	RLP344	1960	£15	£6	
Cannonball	LP	London	LTZC15015	1956	£20	£8	
Cannonball Adderley	LP	Emarcy	EJL1261	1957	£20	£8	
Cannonball Adderley And John Coltrane	LP	Philips	6336242	1973	£12	£5	
Cannonball Adderley And The Pollwinners	LP	Riverside	RLP355	1961	£15	£6	
Cannonball Adderley Quintet Plus	LP	Riverside	RLP388	1961	£15	£6	
Cannonball In Europe	LP	Riverside	RLP499	1963	£12	£5	
Cannonball Plays Bossa Nova	LP	Riverside	RM455	1963	£12	£5	
Cannonball Takes Charge	LP	Riverside	RLP12303	1959	£15	£6	
Cannonball's Sharpshooters	LP	Mercury	MMB12008	1959	£12	£5	
Country Preacher	LP	Capitol	EST404	1970	£12	£5	
In New York	LP	Riverside	RLP(9)404	1962	£15	£6	
In San Francisco	LP	Riverside	RLP12311	1962	£15	£6	
Inside Straight	LP	Fantasy	FT517	1973	£12	£5	
Know What I Mean?	LP	Riverside	RLP433	1962	£12	£5	
Mercy Mercy Mercy!	LP	Capitol	ST2663	1967	£10	£4	
Portrait Of Cannonball	LP	Riverside	RLP12269	1958	£15	£6	
Quintet And Orchestra	LP	Capitol	EST484	1970	£12	£5	
San Francisco Revisited	LP	Riverside	RM444	1963	£12	£5	
Somethin' Else	LP	Blue Note	BLP/BST81595	196–	£25	£10	*with Miles Davis*
Them Dirty Blues	LP	Riverside	RLP12322/1170	1960	£15	£6	
Things Are Getting Better	LP	Riverside	RLP12286	1958	£15	£6	
With Sergio Mendes And The Bossa Rio Sextet	LP	Capitol	(S)T2877	1968	£12	£5	
Wow!	LP	Fontana	FJL107	1965	£12	£5	

ADDERLEY, NAT

Nat Adderley	LP	London	LTZC15018	1956	£25	£10	
That's Right	LP	Riverside	RLP330	1960	£15	£6	
Work Song	LP	Riverside	RLP12318/1167	1960	£15	£6	

ADDICTS

Here She Comes	7"	Decca	F11902	1964	£15	£7.50	

ADDICTS (2)

Lunch With The Addicts	7"	Dining Out	TUX1	1981	£12	£6	

ADDRISSI BROTHERS

Cherry Stone	7"	London	HL8922	1959	£8	£4	
It's Love	7"	Columbia	DB4370	1959	£6	£2.50	
Saving My Kisses	7"	London	HL8973	1959	£8	£4	

ADENO, BOBBY

Hands Of Time	7"	Vocalion	VP9279	1966	£15	£7.50	

ADLAM, BETH

Seventeen	7"	Starlite	ST45024	1960	£6	£2.50	

ADLER, LARRY

Weeping Willows	7"	HMV	POP405	1958	£5	£2	

ADLIBS

Boy From New York City	7"	Red Bird	RB10102	1966	£20	£10	
Giving Up	7"	Deep Soul	DS9102	1970	£8	£4	

ADLIBS (2)

Neighbour Neighbour	7"	Fontana	TF584	1965	£25	£12.50	

ADMIRALS

Promised Land	7"	Fontana	TF597	1965	£25	£12.50	

ADRIAN & THE SUNSETS

Breakthrough	LP	Sunset	(SE)63601	1963	£50	£25	*US, multi-coloured vinyl*

Breakthrough	LP	Sunset	(SE)63601	1963	**£30**	**£15**	*US*

ADRIATICO, DALE

I Hurt Too Easy	7"	Parlophone	R5583	1967	**£5**	**£2**	

ADULT NET

Honey Tangle	CD	Fontana	8381252	1989	**£12**	**£5**	
Take Me	CD-s	Fontana	BRXCD1	1989	**£5**	**£2**	
Waking Up In The Sun	CD-s	Fontana	BRXCD3	1989	**£5**	**£2**	
Where Were You	CD-s	Fontana	BRXCD2	1989	**£5**	**£2**	

ADVANCEMENT

Advancement	LP	Philips	PHS600328	1969	**£30**	**£15**	*US*

ADVENTURERS

Can't Stop Twisting	LP	Columbia	CL2147/CS8547	1961	**£15**	**£6**	*US*

ADVERTS

Crossing The Red Sea	LP	Bright	BRL201	1978	**£10**	**£4**	
Crossing The Red Sea	LP	Bright	BRL201	1978	**£12**	**£5**	*red vinyl*
Crossing The Red Sea	LP	Butt	ALSO002	1981	**£10**	**£4**	*red vinyl*
One Chord Wonders	7"	Stiff	BUY13	1977	**£5**	**£2**	*push-out centre*

ADVOCATES

Advocates	LP	Dovetail	DOVE1	1973	**£25**	**£10**	

AERA

Aera Humanum Est	LP	Erikonig	ERL2001	1974	**£10**	**£4**	*German*
Hand Und Fuss	LP	Erikonig	ERL2002	1976	**£10**	**£4**	*German*

AEROSMITH

Angel	12"	Geffen	GEF34TP	1988	**£6**	**£2.50**	*picture disc*
Angel	CD-s	Geffen	GEF34CD	1988	**£8**	**£4**	*3" single*
Done With Mirrors	CD	WEA	9240912	1989	**£12**	**£5**	
Dream On	7"	CBS	1898	1973	**£5**	**£2**	
Dude Looks Like A Lady	12"	Geffen	GEF29TP	1987	**£6**	**£2.50**	*picture disc*
Dude Looks Like A Lady	CD-s	Geffen	GEF72CD	1990	**£5**	**£2**	
Get A Grip	CD	Geffen	24444	1994	**£20**	**£8**	*US promo in calfskin case*
Get Your Wings	LP	Columbia	KCQ32847	1974	**£10**	**£4**	*US quad*
Gripping Stuff	CD	Geffen	CDGRIP1	1994	**£20**	**£8**	*promo sampler*
Janie's Got A Gun	7"	Geffen	GEF68P	1989	**£4**	**£1.50**	*shaped picture disc*
Janie's Got A Gun	CD-s	Geffen	GEF68CD	1989	**£8**	**£4**	*3" single*
Livin' On The Edge	CD-s	Geffen	GFSTD35	1993	**£10**	**£5**	*with interview disc*
Love In An Elevator	CD-s	Geffen	GEF63CD	1989	**£8**	**£4**	*3" single*
Other Side	CD-s	Geffen	GEF79CD	1990	**£5**	**£2**	
Pump	CD	Geffen	22469DJ	1989	**£20**	**£8**	*US promo in leather case*
Rag Doll	CD-s	Geffen	GEF76CD	1990	**£5**	**£2**	
Rats In The Cellar	7"	CBS	AS1	1976	**£6**	**£2.50**	*promo*
Rock This Way	CD	Columbia		1989	**£20**	**£8**	*US promo compilation*
Rocks	LP	Columbia	PCQ34165	1976	**£10**	**£4**	*US quad*
Toys In The Attic	LP	Columbia	JCQ33479	1975	**£10**	**£4**	*US quad*

AESOP'S FABLES

In Due Time	LP	Cadet Concept	LPS323	1969	**£100**	**£50**	*US*

AFEX

She Got The Time	7"	King	KG1058	1967	**£50**	**£40**	

AFFINITY

Affinity	LP	Vertigo	6360004	1970	**£60**	**£30**	*spiral label*
Eli's Comin'	7"	Vertigo	6059018	1970	**£8**	**£4**	
I Wonder If I Care As Much	7"	Vertigo	6059007	1970	**£6**	**£2.50**	

AFFLICTED

All Right Boy	7"	Bonk	AFF2	1982	**£6**	**£2.50**	
I'm Afflicted	7"	Bonk	AFF1	1981	**£6**	**£2.50**	
untitled	7"	Bonk	AFF4	1982	**£5**	**£2**	

AFO EXECUTIVES

Compendium	LP	AFO	LP0002		**£75**	**£37.50**	*US*

AFRICAN MUSIC MACHINE

Black Water Gold	7"	Mojo	2092046	1972	**£4**	**£1.50**	

AFRIQUE

Soul Makossa	LP	Mainstream	MSL1018	1974	**£12**	**£5**	

AFRO ENCHANTERS

Peace And Love	7"	Island	WI071	1963	**£8**	**£4**	

AFROTONES

All For One	7"	High Note	HS023	1969	**£4**	**£1.50**	
Freedom Sound	7"	Duke	DU19	1969	**£4**	**£2**	*Boys B side*
Things I Love	7"	Trojan	TR655	1969	**£5**	**£2**	*Eric Fratter B side*

AFTER ALL

After All	LP	Athena		1970	**£15**	**£6**	*US*

AFTER DARK

Deathbringer	7"	Lazer	PROMO1	1983	**£30**	**£15**	*promo picture disc*
Evil Woman	7"	After Dark	AD001	1981	**£50**	**£25**	

AFTER TEA

After Tea	LP	Ace Of Clubs	ACL/SCL1251	1967	**£15**	**£6**	

AFTER THE FIRE

80F	7"	Epic	XPR104	1980	**£6**	**£2.50**	*promo*
80F	cass	Epic	EPC84545	1980	**£10**	**£4**	*test pressing*
Love Will Always Make You Cry	7"	Epic	EPC8394	1980	**£5**	**£2**	
Signs Of Change	LP	Rapid	RR001	1978	**£30**	**£15**	

AFTERGLOW

Afterglow	LP	MTA	MTS5010	1967	**£60**	**£30**	*US*

AFTERSHAVE

Skin Deep	LP	Splendid	SLP50106	1972	**£125**	**£62.50**	*Swiss, gatefold sleeve*

AFX

Hangable Autobulb	12"	Warp	WAP67	1995	**£20**	**£10**	
Hangable Autobulb II	12"	Warp	WAP69	1995	**£10**	**£5**	

AGAPE

Gospel Hard Rock	LP	Mark	2170	1971	**£150**	**£75**	*US*
Victims Of Tradition	LP	Renrut		1972	**£150**	**£75**	*US*

AGE OF REASON

Age Of Reason	LP	Georgetowne		1969	**£150**	**£75**	*US*

AGGREGATION

Mind Odyssey	LP	L.H.I.	12008	1967	**£300**	**£180**	*US*

AGGROVATORS

Big Red Ball	7"	Smash	SMA2302	1970	**£4**	**£1.50**	
One More Bottle Of Beer	7"	Smash	SMA2312	1971	**£4**	**£1.50**	
Straight To Jackson Head	7"	Smash	SMA2339	1973	**£6**	**£2.50**	

AGINCOURT (ITHACA)

Fly Away	LP	Merlin	HF3	1970	**£400**	**£250**	

AGITATION FREE

At Last	LP	Barclay	XBLY80612	1976	**£25**	**£10**	*French*
Malesch	LP	Vertigo	6360607	1972	**£25**	**£10**	*German*
Second Album	LP	Vertigo	6360615	1973	**£25**	**£10**	*German*

AGNES STRANGE

Can't Make Up My Mind	7"	Baal	BDN38048	1977	**£5**	**£2**	
Clever Fool	7"	Birdsnest	BN1	1975	**£10**	**£5**	
Strange Flavour	LP	Birdsnest	BRL9000	1975	**£100**	**£50**	

AGONY BAG

Rabies Is A Killer	7"	Monza	MON2	1980	**£10**	**£5**	

AGORA

Agora 2	LP	Atlantic	T50324	1976	**£10**	**£4**	*Italian*
Live In Montreux	LP	Atlantic	T50171	1975	**£12**	**£5**	*Italian*

A-HA

Blood That Moves The Body	CD-s	WEA	W7840CD	1988	**£5**	**£2**	
Cry Wolf	12"	Warner Bros	W8500TP	1986	**£6**	**£2.50**	*picture disc*
Crying In The Rain	CD-s	WEA	W9547CD	1990	**£5**	**£2**	
Dark Is The Night	CD-s	WEA	W0175CD1/2	1993	**£8**	**£4**	*2 CD set*
Early Morning	CD-s	WEA	W0012CD	1991	**£5**	**£2**	
East Of The Sun, West Of The Moon	CD	Warner Bros	263142DJ	1990	**£15**	**£6**	*US promo picture disc*
Hunting High And Low	12"	Warner Bros	W6663TP	1986	**£6**	**£2.50**	*picture disc*
Hunting High And Low	12"	Warner Bros	W8663T	1986	**£6**	**£2.50**	*with poster*
I Call Your Name	CD-s	WEA	W9462CD	1990	**£5**	**£2**	
Living Daylights	12"	Warner Bros	W8305TP	1987	**£8**	**£4**	*picture disc*
Manhattan Skyline	12"	Warner Bros	W8405TP	1987	**£8**	**£4**	*picture disc*
Move To Memphis	CD-s	WEA	W0070CD	1991	**£5**	**£2**	
Stay On These Roads	CD	Warner Bros	9257336	1988	**£15**	**£6**	*promo picture disc*
Stay On These Roads	CD-s	Warner Bros	9256162	1988	**£6**	**£2.50**	*picture disc*
Sun Always Shines On TV	7"	Warner Bros	W8846P	1986	**£8**	**£4**	*shaped picture disc*
Take On Me	12"	Warner Bros	W9146T	1984	**£60**	**£30**	*with poster*

Take On Me	12"	Warner Bros	W9146T	1984	**£40**	**£20**	
Take On Me	7"	Warner Bros	W9146	1984	**£25**	**£12.50**	
Touchy	CD-s	Warner Bros	W7749CD	1988	**£6**	**£2.50**	*3" single*
Train Of Thought	7"	Warner Bros	W8736P	1986	**£8**	**£4**	*shaped picture disc*
You Are The One	CD-s	Warner Bros	W7636CD	1988	**£6**	**£2.50**	

AHAB

Party Girl	7"	Chicken Jazz	JAZZ5	1982	**£**	**£2.00**	

AHAB & THE WAILERS

Cleopatra's Needle	7"	Pye	7N15553	1963	**£6**	**£2.50**	

AHORA MAZDA

Ahora Mazda	LP	Catfish	5C05424184	1970	**£100**	**£50**	*Dutch*

AILEACH

Ard Ri	LP	Leaf	7014	1977	**£12**	**£5**	*Irish*

AINIGMA

Diluvium	LP	Arc	ALPS151715	1973	**£125**	**£62.50**	*German*

AIRFORCE

Airforce was put together by Ginger Baker as the archetypal supergroup. Graham Bond, Denny Laine, Stevie Winwood, Harold McNair, Rick Grech, and Chris Wood rubbed shoulders within a big band – and achieved very much less than their talents might suggest they should have.

Airforce	LP	Polydor	2662001	1970	**£15**	**£6**	*double*
Airforce 2	LP	Polydor	2383029	1970	**£10**	**£4**	

AIRTO

Fingers	LP	CTI	CTI18	1973	**£10**	**£4**	
Free	LP	CTI	6020	1972	**£12**	**£5**	*US*
In Concert	LP	CTI	CTI21	1974	**£10**	**£4**	
Seeds On The Ground	LP	Polydor	2310040	1972	**£12**	**£5**	
Virgin Land	LP	CTI	CTI23	1974	**£10**	**£4**	

AITKEN, BOBBY

Baby Baby	7"	Island	WI028	1962	**£12**	**£6**	
Don't Leave Me	7"	Blue Beat	BB146	1963	**£12**	**£6**	
Garden Of Eden	7"	Rio	R40	1964	**£10**	**£5**	
I've Told You	7"	Rio	R14	1963	**£10**	**£5**	
It Takes A Friend	7"	Rio	R15	1963	**£10**	**£5**	*Laurel Aitken B side*
Jericho	7"	Black Swan	WI441	1965	**£10**	**£5**	*Lester Sterling B side*
Kiss Bam Bam	7"	Island	WI3028	1967	**£12**	**£6**	*Cynthia Richards B side*
Let Them Have A Home	7"	Doctor Bird	DB1072	1967	**£10**	**£5**	
Little Girl	7"	Rio	R50	1964	**£10**	**£5**	
Mr Judge	7"	Rio	R64	1965	**£10**	**£5**	
Never Never	7"	Blue Beat	BB93	1962	**£12**	**£6**	
Rain Came Tumbling Down	7"	Rio	R52	1965	**£10**	**£5**	*Shenley Lunan B side*
Rolling Stone	7"	Rio	R34	1964	**£10**	**£5**	*Lester Sterling B side*
Shame And Scandal	7"	Blue Beat	BB369	1966	**£12**	**£6**	
Sweets For My Sweet	7"	Doctor Bird	DB1077	1967	**£10**	**£5**	
Thunderball	7"	Ska Beat	JB252	1966	**£10**	**£5**	*Originators B side*
What A Fool	7"	Giant	GN11	1967	**£5**	**£2**	

AITKEN, LAUREL

Adam And Eve	7"	Rio	R11	1963	**£10**	**£5**	*Bobby Aitken B side*
Aitken's Boogie	7"	Kalypso	XX16	1960	**£8**	**£4**	
Baby Don't Do It	7"	Rio	R92	1966	**£8**	**£4**	
Bachelor Life	7"	R&B	JB171	1964	**£10**	**£5**	
Bad Minded Woman	7"	Rio	R13	1963	**£10**	**£5**	
Be Mine	7"	Columbia	DB7280	1964	**£8**	**£4**	
Bewildered And Blue	7"	Rainbow	RAI106	1966	**£8**	**£4**	
Boogie In My Bones	7"	Island	WI198	1965	**£10**	**£5**	
Boogie In My Bones	7"	Starlite	ST45011	1960	**£12**	**£6**	
Boogie Rock	7"	Blue Beat	BB1	1960	**£15**	**£7.50**	
Bossa Nova Hop	7"	Dice	CC13	1963	**£10**	**£5**	
Brother David	7"	Blue Beat	BB84	1962	**£12**	**£6**	
Carolina	7"	Doctor Bird	DB1203	1969	**£10**	**£5**	
Clementine	7"	Blue Beat	BB340	1966	**£12**	**£6**	
Daniel Saw The Stone	7"	Blue Beat	BB194	1963	**£12**	**£6**	
Devil Or Angel	7"	Rio	R17	1963	**£10**	**£5**	
Don't Be Cruel	7"	Nu Beat	NB040	1969	**£4**	**£1.50**	
Drinking Whisky	7"	Starlite	ST45014	1960	**£12**	**£6**	
Fire	LP	Doctor Bird	DLM5012	1967	**£75**	**£37.50**	
Fire In Your Wire	7"	Doctor Bird	DB1187	1969	**£10**	**£5**	
For Sentimental Reasons	7"	Fab	FAB45	1968	**£8**	**£4**	
Freedom Train	7"	Rio	R18	1963	**£10**	**£5**	
Green Banana	7"	Ska Beat	JB239	1966	**£10**	**£5**	
Haile Haile (The Lion)	7"	Doctor Bird	DB1202	1969	**£10**	**£5**	*Seven Letters B side*
Hailie Selasie	7"	Nu Beat	NB032	1969	**£5**	**£2**	
High Priest Of Reggae	LP	Pama	PSP1012	1969	**£40**	**£20**	
How Can I Forget You	7"	Rio	R91	1966	**£8**	**£4**	
I Shall Remove	7"	Island	WI092	1963	**£12**	**£6**	
I'm Still In Love With You Girl	7"	Columbia	DB106	1967	**£8**	**£4**	

Title	Format	Label	Number	Year	Mint	VG+	Notes
In My Soul	7"	Island	WI099	1963	£12	£6	
Jamaica	7"	Dice	CC28	1964	£10	£5	
Jamboree	7"	Ska Beat	JB232	1966	£10	£5	
Jeannie Is Back	7"	Blue Beat	BB10	1960	£12	£6	
Jesse James	7"	Nu Beat	NB045	1969	£4	£1.50	
John Saw Them Coming	7"	Rio	R37	1964	£10	£5	
Judgement Day	7"	Blue Beat	BB14	1960	£12	£6	
La La La	7"	Doctor Bird	DB1161	1968	£10	£5	*Detours B side*
Landlords And Tenants	7"	Nu Beat	NB044	1969	£5	£2	
Last Night	7"	Rainbow	RAI101	1966	£8	£4	
Lawd Doctor	7"	Nu Beat	NB033	1969	£5	£2	
Let's Be Lovers	7"	Rio	R65	1965	£10	£5	
Love Me Baby	7"	Starlite	ST45034	1961	£12	£6	
Low Down Dirty Girl	7"	Duke	DK1002	1963	£8	£4	*Duke Reid B side*
Lucille	7"	Blue Beat	BB109	1962	£12	£6	
Mabel	7"	Dice	CC1	1962	£10	£5	
Mary	7"	Rio	R12	1963	£10	£5	
Mary Don't You Weep	7"	Rio	R53	1965	£10	£5	
Mary Lee	7"	Melodisc	1570	1960	£12	£6	
Mary Lou	7"	Rio	R54	1965	£10	£5	
Mash Potato Boogie	7"	Blue Beat	BB40	1961	£12	£6	
Mighty Redeemer	7"	Blue Beat	BB70	1961	£12	£6	
Moon Rock	7"	Bamboo	BAM16	1970	£4	£1.50	
More Whiskey	7"	Blue Beat	BB25	1960	£12	£6	*Lloyd Clarke B side*
Mr Lee	7"	Doctor Bird	DB1160	1968	£10	£5	
Nebuchnezer	7"	Kalypso	XX15	1960	£8	£4	
Never You Hurt	7"	Fab	FAB5	1967	£8	£4	
Nursery Rhyme Boogie	7"	Blue Beat	BB52	1961	£12	£6	
One More Time	7"	Rio	R56	1965	£10	£5	
Pick Up Your Bundle And Go	7"	R&B	JB170	1964	£10	£5	
Propaganda	7"	Ska Beat	JB236	1966	£10	£5	
Pussy Got Thirteen Life	7"	Ackee	ACK104	1970	£4	£1.50	
Pussy Price	7"	Nu Beat	NB046	1969	£5	£2	
Railroad Track	7"	Blue Beat	BB22	1960	£12	£6	
Reggae Prayer	7"	Doctor Bird	DB1196	1969	£10	£5	
Remember My Darling	7"	Black Swan	WI401	1964	£10	£5	
Revival	7"	Rio	R99	1966	£8	£4	
Rice And Peas	7"	Doctor Bird	DB1190	1969	£10	£5	*Classics B side*
Rise And Fall	7"	Doctor Bird	DB1197	1969	£10	£5	
Rise And Fall	LP	J.J.		1969	£60	£30	
Rock Of Ages	7"	Rio	R35	1964	£10	£5	
Rock Steady	7"	Columbia	DB102	1967	£8	£4	
Run Powell Run	7"	Nu Beat	NB035	1969	£5	£2	*Rico B side*
Saint	7"	Black Swan	WI411	1964	£10	£5	
Save The Last Dance	7"	Nu Beat	NB039	1969	£4	£1.50	
Scandal In Brixton Market	LP	Pama	ECO8	1969	£40	£20	
Seven Lonely Nights	7"	Rio	R60	1965	£10	£5	
Shoo Be Doo	7"	Nu Beat	NB043	1969	£4	£1.50	
Sin Pon You	7"	Ackee	ACK106	1970	£4	£1.50	
Sixty Days Sixty Nights	7"	Blue Beat	BB120	1962	£12	£6	
Ska With Laurel	LP	Rio	LR1	1966	£100	£50	
Skinhead Invasion	7"	Nu Beat	NB048	1970	£8	£4	*test pressing*
Skinhead Train	7"	Nu Beat	NB047	1969	£4	£1.50	
Suffering Still	7"	Nu Beat	NB025	1969	£5	£2	
Sweet Precious Love	7"	Rainbow	RAI111	1966	£8	£4	
Think Me No Know	7"	Junior	JR105	1969	£5	£2	*Rico B side*
This Great Day	7"	Blue Beat	BB249	1964	£12	£6	
Tribute To Collie Smith	7"	Kalypso	XX19	1960	£8	£4	
We Shall Overcome	7"	Rio	R97	1966	£8	£4	
Weary Wanderer	7"	Blue Beat	BB142	1962	£12	£6	*Bandits B side*
West Indian Cricket Test	7"	J.N.A.C.	1	1964	£5	£2	
What A Weeping	7"	Island	WI095	1963	£12	£6	
Woppi King	7"	Nu Beat	NB024	1969	£5	£2	
You Can't Stop Me From Loving You	7"	R&B	JB167	1964	£10	£5	
You Left Me Standing	7"	Dice	CC31	1965	£10	£5	
You Left Me Standing	7"	Rio	R36	1964	£10	£5	
Zion	7"	Blue Beat	BB164	1963	£12	£6	

A-JAES

Title	Format	Label	Number	Year	Mint	VG+	Notes
I'm Leaving You	7"	Oak	RGJ132	1964	£200	£100	*best auctioned*

AKA & THE CHARLATANS

Title	Format	Label	Number	Year	Mint	VG+	Notes
Heroes Are Losers	12"	Vanity	VANE1	1978	£8	£4	

AKENS, JEWEL

Title	Format	Label	Number	Year	Mint	VG+	Notes
Birds And The Bees	7"	London	HLN9954	1965	£4	£1.50	
Birds And The Bees	7" EP	London	RE10170	1965	£8	£4	*French*
Birds And The Bees	LP	London	HAN8234	1965	£10	£4	
Dancing Jenny	7"	Ember	EMBS219	1966	£5	£2	

AKIYOSHI, TOSHIKO

Title	Format	Label	Number	Year	Mint	VG+	Notes
Newport Jazz Festival 1957	LP	Columbia	33CX10101	1958	£15	£6	*side 2 by Leon Sash*

AKRYLYKZ

Title	Format	Label	Number	Year	Mint	VG+	Notes
Spyderman	7"	Red Rhino	RED2	1980	£4	£1.50	

AKTUALA

Title	Format	Label	Number	Year	Mint	VG+	Notes
Tappeto Volante	LP	Bla-Bla	BBXL10009	1976	£25	£10	*Italian*

AL, ROLANDO & THE SOUL BROTHERS

Title	Format	Label	Cat. No.	Year	Mint	VG	Notes
Doctor Ring A Ding	7"	Doctor Bird	DB1023	1966	£10	£5	Freddie & The Heartaches B side
From Russia With Love	7"	Doctor Bird	DB1010	1966	£10	£5	
I Love You	7"	Doctor Bird	DB1035	1966	£10	£5	
Phoenix City	7"	Doctor Bird	DB1020	1966	£10	£5	Deacons B side
Sufferer's Choice	7"	Doctor Bird	DB1011	1966	£10	£5	Soulettes B side
Sugar And Spice	7"	Doctor Bird	DB1017	1966	£10	£5	
VC10	7"	Doctor Bird	DB1008	1966	£10	£5	Larry Marshall B side

AL & THE VIBRATORS

Title	Format	Label	Cat. No.	Year	Mint	VG	Notes
Check Up	7"	High Note	HS005	1969	£4	£1.50	
Move Up	7"	Doctor Bird	DB1085	1967	£10	£5	
Move Up Calypso	7"	High Note	HS007	1969	£4	£1.50	Patsy Todd B side

ALABAMA JUG BAND

Title	Format	Label	Cat. No.	Year	Mint	VG	Notes
Alabama Jug Band	7" EP	Brunswick	OE9161	1955	£8	£4	

ALABAMA STATE TROUPERS

Title	Format	Label	Cat. No.	Year	Mint	VG	Notes
Alabama State Troupers	LP	Elektra	EKS75022	1972	£12	£5	US

ALAIMO, STEVE

Title	Format	Label	Cat. No.	Year	Mint	VG	Notes
Every Day I Have To Cry	LP	Checker	LP2986	1963	£25	£10	US
Everyday I Have To Cry	7"	Pye	7N25174	1963	£15	£7.50	
It's A Long Long Way To Happiness	7"	Pye	7N25199	1963	£4	£1.50	
Mashed Potatoes	LP	Checker	LP2983	1962	£20	£8	US
My Friends	7"	Pye	7N25161	1962	£4	£1.50	
Sings And Swings	LP	ABC	(S)551	1966	£12	£5	US
So Much Love	7"	HMV	POP1531	1966	£5	£2	
Starring Steve Alaimo	LP	ABC	(S)501	1965	£12	£5	US
Steve Alaimo	LP	Crown	CLP5382	1963	£12	£5	US
Twist With Steve Alaimo	LP	Checker	LP2981	1961	£20	£8	US
Where The Action Is	LP	ABC	(S)531	1965	£12	£5	US

ALAMO

Title	Format	Label	Cat. No.	Year	Mint	VG	Notes
Alamo	LP	Atlantic	SD8279	1971	£12	£5	US

ALARCEN, JEAN PIERRE

Title	Format	Label	Cat. No.	Year	Mint	VG	Notes
Alarcen	LP	L'Escargot	ESC371	1978	£25	£10	French
Tableau No. 1	LP	Scoppuzle	ZZ001	1980	£25	£10	French

ALARM

Title	Format	Label	Cat. No.	Year	Mint	VG	Notes
68 Guns	7"	IRS	PFPC1023	1983	£5	£2	with cassette (CS70504)
Compact Hits	CD-s	A&M	AMCD906	1988	£5	£2	
Curtain Call	CD	IRS	POPPY1	1988	£25	£10	US promo sampler
Deceiver	7"	IRS	IRS103	1984	£25	£12.50	mustard vinyl
Deceiver	7"	IRS	IRSD103	1984	£5	£2	double
Love Don't Come Easy	CD-s	IRS	EIRSCD134	1990	£5	£2	
Marching On	7"	IRS	ILS0032	1982	£12	£6	
New South Wales	CD-s	IRS	EIRSCD129	1989	£5	£2	
Presence Of Love	CD-s	IRS	DIRM155	1988	£5	£2	
Rain In The Summertime	CD-s	IRS	DIRM144	1987	£5	£2	promo only
Raw	CD-s	IRS	ALARMCD3	1991	£5	£2	
Sold Me Down The River	CD-s	IRS	EIRSCD123	1989	£5	£2	
Unsafe Building 1990	CD-s	IRS	ALARMCD2	1990	£5	£2	
Unsafe Buildings	7"	White Cross	001	1981	£40	£20	gatefold picture sleeve

ALBA

Title	Format	Label	Cat. No.	Year	Mint	VG	Notes
Alba	LP	Rubber	RUB021	1978	£20	£8	

ALBAM, MANNY

Title	Format	Label	Cat. No.	Year	Mint	VG	Notes
And The Jazz Greats Of Our Time Vol. 1	LP	Coral	LVA9064	1958	£12	£5	
West Side Story	LP	Coral	LVA9097	1959	£12	£5	

ALBAM, MANNY & ERNIE WILKINS

Title	Format	Label	Cat. No.	Year	Mint	VG	Notes
Drum Suite	LP	HMV	CLP1107	1957	£12	£5	

ALBERT, BILLY

Title	Format	Label	Cat. No.	Year	Mint	VG	Notes
Black Jack	7"	Vogue Coral	Q72214	1956	£6	£2.50	

ALBERT, EDDIE

Title	Format	Label	Cat. No.	Year	Mint	VG	Notes
Come Pretty Little Girl	7"	London	HL8136	1955	£20	£10	
Jenny Kissed Me	7"	London	HLU8241	1956	£12	£6	with Sandra Lee

ALBERTO Y LOS TRIOS PARANOIAS

Title	Format	Label	Cat. No.	Year	Mint	VG	Notes
Snuff Rock	12"	Stiff	LAST2	1977	£8	£4	promo

ALBION BAND

Title	Format	Label	Cat. No.	Year	Mint	VG	Notes
Battle Of The Field	LP	Island	HELP25	1976	£12	£5	
Prospect Before Us	LP	Harvest	SHSP4059	1976	£12	£5	
Rise Up Like The Sun	LP	Harvest	SHSP4092	1978	£10	£4	

ALCAPONE, DENNIS

Title	Format	Label	Cat. No.	Year	Mint	VG	Notes
Alpha And Omega	7"	Upsetter	US377	1971	£5	£2	Junior Byles B side

Dread Capone	LP	Live And Love	LALP104	1975	£25	£10	
Duppy Serenade	7"	Banana	BA328	1971	£6	£2.50	
Fine Style	7"	Attack	ATT8027	1972	£4	£1.50	*Winston Scotland B side*
Forever Version	7"	Banana	BA341	1971	£6	£2.50	
Great Woggie	7"	Treasure Isle	TI7069	1971	£5	£2	
Guns Don't Argue	LP	Trojan	TRL187	1971	£15	£6	
Investigator Rock	LP	Third World	TWS911	1977	£12	£5	
King Of The Track	LP	Magnet	MGT001	1973	£15	£6	
Let It Roll	7"	Prince Buster	PB12	1971	£4	£1.50	*test pressing, Ansell Collins B side*
Master Key	7"	Upsetter	US388	1972	£5	£2	
Power Version	7"	Ackee	ACK146	1971	£4	£1.50	*Bluesblasters B side*
Rasta Dub	7"	Grape	GR3035	1972	£4	£1.50	*Upsetters B side*
Revelation Version	7"	Explosion	EX2039	1970	£8	£4	
Shades Of Hudson	7"	Big Shot	BI565	1971	£8	£4	
Six Million Dollar Man	LP	Third World	TWS801	1977	£12	£5	
Wake Up Jamaica	7"	Treasure Isle	TI7074	1971	£5	£2	*Tommy McCook B side*
Well Dread	7"	Upsetter	US373	1971	£5	£2	*Upsetters B side*
Wonderman	7"	Upsetter	US381	1972	£5	£2	
You Must Believe Me	7"	Supreme	SUP214	1970	£10	£5	

ALDEN, CRAIG

Crazy Little Horn	7"	London	HLW9224	1960	£4	£1.50	

ALDO, STEVE

Can I Get A Witness	7"	Decca	F12041	1964	£30	£15	
Everybody Has To Cry	7"	Parlophone	R5432	1966	£30	£15	

ALDRICH, RONNIE

Big Band Beat	7"	Columbia	DB3945	1957	£5	£2	
Coach Call Boogie	7"	Decca	F10248	1954	£4	£1.50	
Ko Ko Mo	7"	Decca	F10494	1955	£5	£2	
Rhythm 'n Blues	7"	Decca	F10564	1955	£5	£2	
Right Now, Right Now	7"	Columbia	DB3882	1957	£8	£4	
Rock Candy	7"	Decca	F10544	1955	£5	£2	
Wolf On The Prowl	7"	Decca	F10274	1954	£4	£1.50	

ALEANNA

Aleanna	LP	Inchecronin	INC7421	1978	£40	£20	

ALEONG, AKI

Trade Wins, Trade Wins	7"	Reprise	R20021	1961	£4	£1.50	

ALEONG, AKI & THE NOBLES

C'mon Baby Let's Dance	LP	Reprise	R(9)6020	1962	£10	£4	*US*
Come Surf With Me	LP	Vee Jay	LP/SR1060	1963	£12	£5	*US*
Twistin' The Hits	LP	Reprise	R(9)6011	1962	£10	£4	*US*

ALESSI, DON

Guitar Spectacular	LP	Salvo	SLO5521	1966	£12	£5	

ALEX

Alex	LP	Pan	87305	1974	£25	£10	*German*
That's The Deal	LP	Pan	88831	1976	£15	£6	*German*

ALEXANDER, ARTHUR

Alexander The Great	7" EP	London	RED1364	1963	£100	£50	
Anna	7"	London	HLD9641	1962	£25	£12.50	
Black Night	7"	London	HLD9899	1964	£15	£7.50	
For You	7"	London	HLU10023	1966	£15	£7.50	
Go Home Girl	7"	London	HLD9667	1963	£20	£10	
Soldier Of Love	7" EP	London	RED1401	1963	£100	£50	
Soldiers Of Love	7"	London	HLD9566	1962	£25	£12.50	
You Better Move On	7"	London	HLD9523	1962	£25	£12.50	
You Better Move On	LP	London	HAD2457	1962	£125	£62.50	

ALEXANDER'S TIMELESS BLOOZBAND

Alexander's Timeless Bloozband	LP	Smack	1001	1967	£100	£50	*US*
For Sale	LP	Uni	73021	1968	£20	£8	*US*

ALEXANDRIA, LOREZ

Lorez Sings Pres	10" LP	Parlophone	PMD1062	1958	£25	£10	

ALFIE & HARRY

Closing Time	7"	London	HLU8494	1957	£5	£2	
Trouble With Harry	7"	London	HLU8242	1956	£10	£5	

ALFONSO, CARLTON

I Have Changed	7"	Nu Beat	NB004	1968	£5	£2	

ALFORD, CLEM

India	LP	KPM	KPM1183	1975	£20	£8	
Mirror Image	LP	Columbia	SCX6571	1974	£30	£15	

ALFRED, SANDRA

Rocket And Roll	7"	Oriole	CB1408	1958	**£40**	**£20**	

ALFRED & MELMOTH

I Want Someone	7"	Island	WI3130	1967	**£8**	**£4**	

ALI, RASHIED

Exchange	LP	Survival	SR101	1974	**£20**	**£8**	*US, with Frank Lowe*
New Directions In Modern Music	LP	Survival	SR104	1974	**£20**	**£8**	*US*
Rashied Ali Quintet	LP	Survival	SR102	1974	**£20**	**£8**	*US*

ALICE

Alice	LP	Byg	529016	1970	**£20**	**£8**	*French*
Arretez Le Monde	LP	Polydor	2393043	1972	**£15**	**£6**	*French*

ALICE ISLAND BAND

Splendid Isolation	LP	Warren	WAR341	1974	**£100**	**£50**	

ALICE THROUGH THE LOOKING GLASS (ITHACA)

Alice Through The Looking Glass	LP	SNP	no number	1969	**£400**	**£250**	

ALIEN SEX FIEND

ASF Box	12"	Windsong	02	1990	**£20**	**£10**	*3 coloured vinyl singles, boxed*
First Alien Sex Fiend Compact Disc	CD	Anagram	CDGRAM25	1987	**£12**	**£5**	*with poster*
Haunted House	CD-s	Anagram	CDANA46	1989	**£5**	**£2**	
I Walk The Line	CD-s	Anagram	CDANA53	1991	**£5**	**£2**	
Ignore The Machine	CD-s	Anagram	CDANA11	1988	**£5**	**£2**	
Now I'm feeling Zombiefied	CD-s	Anagram	CDANA52	1990	**£5**	**£2**	

ALISON & JILL

Alison And Jill	LP	Profile	GMOR103	1973	**£20**	**£8**	

ALL ABOUT EVE

A comparison between the present edition of the *Price Guide* and the earlier versions will reveal that many bands from the eighties have passed out of fashion, with a corresponding drop in the values of their rarest records. Most dramatic in this respect is perhaps All About Eve, whose list of collector's items is now only a third as long as it used to be.

D For Desire	12"	Eden	EDEN1	1985	**£15**	**£7.50**	
December	CD-s	Mercury	EVCDX11	1989	**£5**	**£2**	*picture disc*
Every Angel	CD-s	Mercury	EVNCD7	1988	**£5**	**£2**	
In The Clouds	12"	Eden	EDEN2	1986	**£12**	**£6**	*with poster*
In The Clouds	CD-s	Mercury	EVCDX13	1991	**£5**	**£2**	*picture disc*
Martha's Harbour	12"	Mercury	EVNXB8	1988	**£6**	**£2.50**	*boxed with poster, autographed*
Martha's Harbour	CD-s	Mercury	EVNCD8	1988	**£5**	**£2**	
Martha's Harbour	CD-s	Mercury	EVNCD8	1988	**£6**	**£2.50**	*gatefold sleeve*
Martha's Harbour	CDV	Mercury	0805222	1988	**£8**	**£3**	
Road To Your Soul	CD-s	Mercury	EVCDX10	1989	**£5**	**£2**	*gold wallet*
What Kind Of Fool	CD-s	Mercury	EVNCD99	1988	**£10**	**£5**	*with cards*
What Kind Of Fool	CDV	Mercury	0806182	1988	**£20**	**£10**	
Wild Hearted Woman	CD-s	Mercury	EVNCD6	1988	**£5**	**£2**	

ALL DAY

York Pop Music Project	LP	private		1973	**£200**	**£100**	

ALL SAINTS

The ZTT songs are the work of Melanie Blatt and Shaznay T. Lewis, together with a third girl, Simone Rainford, who sang lead on 'Silver Shadow', but left to start an abortive solo career. The well-known quartet came together in time to sign a deal with London records and are unlikely to have looked back since.

All Saints	CD	London		1997	**£40**	**££20**	*promo box set, with cassette & inserts*
I Know Where It's At	12"	London	BLUE1	1997	**£6**	**£2.50**	
I Know Where It's At	12"	London	RED1	1997	**£6**	**£2.50**	
I Know Where It's At	CD-s	London	LOCDP398	1997	**£10**	**£5**	
If You Wanna Party	CD-s	ZTT	ZANG71CD	1995	**£10**	**£5**	
Let's Get Started	CD-s	ZTT	ZANG63CD	1995	**£12**	**£6**	
Never Ever	CD-s	London	LOCDP407	1997	**£10**	**£5**	
Open Ended Interview	CD	London	ASINT1	1997	**£20**	**£8**	*promo*
Silver Shadow	12"	ZTT	SAM1372	1994	**£20**	**£10**	*promo double*
Silver Shadow	CD-s	ZTT	ZANG53CD	1995	**£15**	**£7.50**	

ALL STARS

All Stars	LP	Capitol	LCT6110	1956	**£15**	**£6**	
Season At Riverside	LP	Capitol	T761	1957	**£12**	**£5**	

ALLAN, RICHARD

As Time Goes By	7"	Parlophone	R4634	1960	**£4**	**£1.50**	

ALLEN, ANNISTEEN

Don't Nobody Move	7"	Brunswick	05639	1957	**£10**	**£5**	
Fujiyama Mama	7"	Capitol	CL14264	1955	**£100**	**£50**	

ALLEN, BOBBY

I'll Forget About You ... 7" ... Fontana ... 267252TF ... 1962 £4 ... £1.50

ALLEN, CHAD & THE EXPRESSIONS

Chad Allen And The Expressions ... LP ... Scepter ... SP533 ... 1966 £12 ... £5 ... US

ALLEN, CLAY

Crazy Crazy World ... 7" ... Starlite ... ST45106 ... 1963 £6 ... £2.50
I Can't Stop The Blues From Moving ... 7" ... Starlite ... ST45096 ... 1963 £6 ... £2.50
This Time It's Really Goodbye ... 7" ... Starlite ... ST45086 ... 1962 £6 ... £2.50

ALLEN, DAEVID

Banana Moon ... LP ... BYG ... 529345 ... 1971 £15 ... £6 ... *French*
Banana Moon ... LP ... Caroline ... C1512 ... 1975 £10 ... £4
Good Morning ... LP ... Virgin ... V2054 ... 1976 £10 ... £4
It's The Time Of Your Life ... 7" ... Virgin ... VS123 ... 1975 £6 ... £2.50 ... *promo*

ALLEN, DAVE

Color Blind ... LP ... International Artist ... IALP11 ... 1969 £40 ... £20 ... US

ALLEN, DAVIE & THE ARROWS

Apache '65 ... LP ... Tower ... T5002 ... 1965 £15 ... £6 ... US
Blues Theme ... LP ... Tower ... (D)T5078 ... 1967 £15 ... £6 ... US
Cycledelic Sounds ... LP ... Tower ... DT5094 ... 1968 £15 ... £6 ... US
Wild In The Streets ... LP ... Tower ... DT5099 ... 1968 £15 ... £6 ... US

ALLEN, DEAN

Ooh Ooh Baby Baby ... 7" ... London ... HLM8698 ... 1958 £20 ... £10

ALLEN, HENRY RED

Newport Jazz Festival 1957 ... LP ... Columbia ... 33CX10106 ... 1958 £15 ... £6 ... *with Jack Teagarden & Kid Ory*
Ride, Red, Ride In Hi Fi ... LP ... RCA ... RD27045 ... 1958 £20 ... £8

ALLEN, JEFF

That'll Be The Day ... 7" ... HMV ... JO477 ... 1957 £15 ... £7.50 ... *export*

ALLEN, LEE

Cat Walk ... 7" ... Top Rank ... JAR265 ... 1960 £8 ... £4
Down On Bourbon Street ... LP ... NoLa ... LP16 ... 1978 £10 ... £4
Mood Music Library ... LP ... Ember ... ELR3312 ... 1962 £40 ... £20 ... *Lee Allen not credited*
Walking With Mr Lee ... 7" ... HMV ... POP452 ... 1958 £25 ... £12.50
Walking With Mr Lee ... 7" EP ... Top Rank ... JKR8020 ... 1959 £15 ... £7.50
Walking With Mr Lee ... LP ... Ember ... ELP200 ... 1958 £100 ... £50 ... US

ALLEN, MAURICE

Oooh Baby ... 7" ... Pye ... 7N15128 ... 1958 £6 ... £2.50

ALLEN, RAY & THE UPBEATS

Tribute To Six ... LP ... Blast ... BLP6804 ... £30 ... £15 ... US

ALLEN, REX

Country And Western Aces ... 7" EP ... Mercury ... 10011MCE ... 1964 £8 ... £4
Little White Horses ... 7" ... Brunswick ... 05675 ... 1957 £4 ... £1.50
This Ole House ... 7" ... Brunswick ... 05341 ... 1954 £8 ... £4
Westward Ho The Wagons ... 7" EP ... Brunswick ... OE9317 ... 1957 £8 ... £4
Wringle Wrangle ... 7" ... Brunswick ... 05677 ... 1957 £4 ... £1.50

ALLEN, RITCHIE

Rising Surf ... LP ... Imperial ... LP9229/LP12229 ... 1963 £25 ... £10 ... US
Stranger From Durango ... LP ... Imperial ... LP9212/LP12212 ... 1963 £25 ... £10 ... US
Surfer's Slide ... LP ... Imperial ... LP9243/LP12243 ... 1963 £25 ... £10 ... US

ALLEN, STEVE

Ballad Of Davy Crockett ... 7" ... Vogue Coral ... Q72118 ... 1956 £4 ... £1.50

ALLEN, TONY

Rock And Roll With Tony Allen ... LP ... Crown ... CLP5231 ... 1960 £75 ... £37.50 ... US
Time To Swing ... 7" EP ... Philips ... BBE12522 ... 1962 £15 ... £7.50

ALLEN, VERNON

Babylon ... 7" ... R&B ... JB169 ... 1964 £8 ... £4

ALLEN, WOODY

Spot Floyd ... 7" ... Colpix ... PX775 ... 1964 £4 ... £1.50
Third Woody Allen Album ... LP ... Capitol ... T2986 ... 1968 £12 ... £5 ... US
Wonderful Wacky World ... LP ... Bell ... 6008 ... 1968 £10 ... £4 ... US
Woody Allen ... LP ... Colpix ... PXL488 ... 1964 £12 ... £5
Woody Allen 2 ... LP ... Colpix ... PXL518 ... 1965 £12 ... £5

ALLEN & MILTON

It Is I ... 7" ... Blue Beat ... BB348 ... 1966 £12 ... £6
Someone Like You ... 7" ... Blue Beat ... BB353 ... 1966 £12 ... £6

ALLEY CATS

Title	Format	Label	Cat. No.	Year	Mint	VG	Notes
Snap Crackle And Pop	7"	Vogue	V9155	1959	**£15**	**£7.50**	

ALLISON, BOB

Title	Format	Label	Cat. No.	Year	Mint	VG	Notes
You've Got Everything	7"	Solar	SRP103	1964	**£6**	**£2.50**	

ALLISON, GENE

Title	Format	Label	Cat. No.	Year	Mint	VG	Notes
Gene Allison	LP	Vee Jay	VJLP1009	1959	**£60**	**£30**	*US*
Hey Hey I Love You	7"	London	HLU8605	1958	**£60**	**£30**	

ALLISON, KEITH

Title	Format	Label	Cat. No.	Year	Mint	VG	Notes
In Action	LP	Columbia	CL2641/CS9441	1967	**£10**	**£4**	*US*

ALLISON, LUTHER

Title	Format	Label	Cat. No.	Year	Mint	VG	Notes
Luther Allison	LP	Delmark	DS625	1971	**£10**	**£4**	

ALLISON, MOSE

Pianist and singer Mose Allison has a distinctively laid-back approach to bluesy jazz (somewhat like a jazz J. J. Cale) that has made him a highly regarded and influential figure. His 'Parchman Farm' was a staple of the sixties R&B scene in Britain, with Georgie Fame in particular borrowing elements of Allison's style wholesale.

Title	Format	Label	Cat. No.	Year	Mint	VG	Notes
Autumn Song	LP	Transatlantic	PR7189	1967	**£15**	**£6**	
Baby Please Don't Go	7"	Fontana	H292	1961	**£8**	**£4**	
Back Country Suite	7" EP	Esquire	EP221	1959	**£15**	**£7.50**	
Back Country Suite	LP	Esquire	32051	1959	**£20**	**£8**	
Best Of Mose Allison	LP	Atlantic	SD1542	1970	**£12**	**£5**	*US*
Blueberry Hill	7" EP	Esquire	EP224	1960	**£15**	**£7.50**	
Creek Bank	LP	Esquire	32094	1960	**£20**	**£8**	
Hello There, Universe	LP	Atlantic	SD1550	1970	**£12**	**£5**	*US*
I Don't Worry About A Thing	LP	Atlantic	SD1389	1962	**£20**	**£8**	*US*
I Love The Life I Live	7"	Columbia	DB7330	1964	**£6**	**£2.50**	
I Love The Life I Live	LP	Realm	RM52318	1966	**£25**	**£10**	
I've Been Doin' Some Thinkin'	LP	Atlantic	SD1511	1969	**£15**	**£6**	*US*
Local Color	LP	Esquire	32071	1959	**£20**	**£8**	
Mose Alive!	LP	Atlantic	587/588007	1966	**£20**	**£8**	
Mose Allison	LP	Prestige	PR24002	1972	**£15**	**£6**	*double*
Mose In Your Ear	LP	Atlantic	K40460	1973	**£12**	**£5**	
Parchman Farm	7" EP	Esquire	EP214	1959	**£15**	**£7.50**	
Ramblin' With Mose	LP	Esquire	32171	1962	**£20**	**£8**	
Sings	LP	Stateside	SL10106	1964	**£20**	**£8**	
Sings	LP	Transatlantic	PR7279	1968	**£15**	**£6**	
Sings The Blues	7" EP	Columbia	SEG8353	1964	**£15**	**£7.50**	
Swingin' Machine	LP	London	HAK8083	1963	**£20**	**£8**	
That Man Mose Again	7" EP	Esquire	EP231	1960	**£15**	**£7.50**	
V8 Ford	LP	Columbia	SX6058	1964	**£20**	**£8**	
Western Man	LP	Atlantic	2400205	1971	**£12**	**£5**	
Wild Man On The Loose	LP	Atlantic	587/588031	1966	**£15**	**£6**	
Word From Mose	LP	Atlantic	SD1424	1966	**£15**	**£6**	*US*
Young Man Mose	LP	Esquire	32083	1959	**£20**	**£8**	

ALLISONS

Title	Format	Label	Cat. No.	Year	Mint	VG	Notes
Allisons	7" EP	Fontana	TFE17339	1961	**£20**	**£10**	
Are You Sure	LP	Fontana	TFL5135/ STFL558	1961	**£30**	**£15**	
What A Mess	7"	Fontana	H336	1961	**£5**	**£2**	*picture sleeve*

ALLISONS (2)

Title	Format	Label	Cat. No.	Year	Mint	VG	Notes
Surfer Street	7"	Stateside	SS289	1964	**£5**	**£2**	

ALLMAN, DUANE

Title	Format	Label	Cat. No.	Year	Mint	VG	Notes
Anthology	LP	Capricorn	K67502	1972	**£12**	**£5**	*double*
Anthology Vol. 2	LP	Capricorn	2659037	1974	**£12**	**£5**	*double*

ALLMAN BROTHERS BAND

Title	Format	Label	Cat. No.	Year	Mint	VG	Notes
Allman Brothers Band	LP	Capricorn	228033	1969	**£10**	**£4**	
At Fillmore East	LP	Atlantic	2659005	1971	**£12**	**£5**	*double*
Brothers And Sisters	CD	Mobile Fidelity	UDCD617	1994	**£15**	**£6**	*US audiophile*
Eat A Peach	CD	Mobile Fidelity	UDCD513	1989	**£15**	**£6**	*US audiophile*
Eat A Peach	LP	Capricorn	K67501	1972	**£12**	**£5**	*double*
Eat A Peach	LP	Capricorn	CP40102	1972	**£15**	**£6**	*US quad*
Eat A Peach	LP	Mobile Fidelity	MFSL2157	1983	**£15**	**£6**	*US audiophile*
Idlewild South	LP	Capricorn	2400032	1970	**£10**	**£4**	

ALLMAN JOYS

Title	Format	Label	Cat. No.	Year	Mint	VG	Notes
Allman Joys	LP	Mercury	6398005	1973	**£10**	**£4**	

ALLSUP, TOMMY

Title	Format	Label	Cat. No.	Year	Mint	VG	Notes
Buddy Holly Songbook	LP	London	HAU8218	1965	**£25**	**£10**	

ALMEIDA, LAURINDO

Title	Format	Label	Cat. No.	Year	Mint	VG	Notes
Laurindo Almeida Quartet	LP	Brunswick	LAE12019	1956	**£25**	**£10**	

ALMIGHTY

Destroyed	12"	Polydor	PZP60	1989	£6	**£2.50**	*picture disc*
Little Lost Sometimes	CD-s	Polydor	PZCD151	1991	£5	**£2**	
Power	CD-s	Polydor	PZCD66	1990	£5	**£2**	
Power Trippin'/Live From Donington '92	CD	Polydor	5192262	1993	£20	**£10**	*double*

ALMOND, JOHNNY

Hollywood Blues	LP	Deram	SML1057	1970	£15	**£6**	
Patent Pending	LP	Deram	DML/SML1043	1969	£20	**£8**	
Solar Level	7"	Deram	DM266	1969	£4	**£1.50**	

ALMOND, MARC

Bitter Sweet	CD-s	Parlophone	CDR6194	1988	£8	**£4**	
Boy Who Came Back	10"	Some Bizarre	BZS2310	1984	£8	**£3**	
Days Of Pearly Spencer	12"	Some Bizarre	YZ638T	1992	£8	**£4**	
Days Of Pearly Spencer	CD-s	WEA	YZ638CDX	1992	£5	**£2**	*holographic disc*
Desperate Hours	CD-s	Parlophone	CDR6252	1990	£5	**£2**	
Jacky	CD-s	WEA	YZ610CD	1991	£5	**£2**	
Kept Boy	7"	Parlophone	PSR500	1988	£15	**£7.50**	*1 side etched*
Love Letter	10"	Some Bizarre	BONK210	1985	£6	**£2.50**	
Lover Spurned	CD-s	Parlophone	CDR6229	1990	£5	**£2**	
My Death	7"	Gutterhearts	LYN14210	1984	£8	**£4**	*flexi*
Only The Moment	CD-s	Parlophone	CDR6210	1989	£5	**£2**	
Ruby Red	12"	Some Bizarre	GLOW313	1986	£8	**£4**	
Something's Gotten Hold Of My Heart	CD-s	Parlophone	CDR6201	1989	£5	**£2**	*with Gene Pitney*
Stories Of Johnny	10"	Some Bizarre	BONK110	1985	£6	**£2.50**	
Tears Run Rings	CD-s	Offbeat	1	1989	£8	**£4**	*3" single*
Tears Run Rings	CD-s	Parlophone	CDR6186	1988	£10	**£5**	
Tenderness Is A Weakness	10"	Some Bizarre	BZS2510	1984	£8	**£3**	
Violent Silence/Flesh Volcano	CD	Some Bizarre	SBZCD022	1997	£15	**£6**	
Waifs And Strays	CD-s	Parlophone	CDR6263	1990	£5	**£2**	
Woman's Story	10"	Some Bizarre	GLOW210	1986	£8	**£3**	
Woman's Story	12"	Some Bizarre	GLOWY212	1986	£10	**£5**	
You Have	10"	Some Bizarre	BZS2410	1984	£8	**£3**	
You Have	12"	Some Bizarre	BZS2412	1984	£8	**£4**	
Your Aura	7"	Gutterhearts		1986	£8	**£4**	*flexi*

ALMOND LETTUCE

Magic Circle	7"	Philips	BF1764	1969	£6	**£2.50**	

ALONE AGAIN OR

Drum The Beat	7"	All One	ALG1	1984	£4	**£1.50**	

ALOVE & PAXTON

Wickeder	7"	Blue Cat	BS168	1969	£5	**£2**	

ALPERT, TRIGGER

Trigger Happy	LP	Riverside	RLP12225	196–	£15	**£6**	
Trigger Happy	LP	London	LTZU15096	1957	£25	**£10**	

ALPHONSO, CARLTON

Where In This World	7"	Pama	PM700	1967	£8	**£4**	

ALPHONSO, CLYDE

Good Enough	7"	Studio One	SO2076	1969	£12	**£6**	

ALPHONSO, ORVILLE

Belly Lick	7"	Caribou	CRC1	1965	£4	**£1.50**	

ALPHONSO, ROLAND

Blackberry Brandy	7"	Blue Beat	BB58	1961	£12	**£6**	
Cat	7"	Pyramid	PYR6008	1967	£8	**£4**	*Desmond Dekker B side*
Crime Wave	7"	R&B	JB164	1964	£20	**£10**	
Devoted To You	7"	Island	WI264	1966	£12	**£6**	*Jackie Opel B side*
El Pussy Cat	7"	Island	WI217	1965	£12	**£6**	*Lord Brynner B side*
Federal Special	7"	R&B	JB122	1963	£20	**£10**	
Feeling Fine	7"	Island	WI146	1964	£12	**£6**	*Leon & Owen B side*
Four Corners Of The World	7"	Blue Beat	BB112	1962	£12	**£6**	*Shiners B side*
Green Door	7"	Blue Beat	BB63	1961	£12	**£6**	*Monty & Roy B side*
Guantanamera Ska	7"	Pyramid	PYR6009	1967	£8	**£4**	*Spanishtonians B side*
Jazz Ska	7"	Rio	R58	1965	£10	**£5**	*Hyacinth B side*
Jericho Chain	7"	Blue Beat	BB356	1966	£12	**£6**	
Jungle Bit	7"	Pyramid	PYR6007	1967	£8	**£4**	*Norman Grant B side*
Middle East	7"	Pyramid	PYR6003	1967	£8	**£4**	*Desmond Dekker B side*
Never To Be Mine	7"	Trojan	TR001	1967	£10	**£5**	*Duke Reid B side*
Nimblefoot	7"	Ska Beat	JB210	1965	£20	**£10**	*Andy And Joey B side*
Nothing For Nothing	7"	Pyramid	PYR6011	1967	£8	**£4**	*Desmond Dekker B side*
Nuclear Weapon	7"	Ska Beat	JB216	1965	£20	**£10**	*Stranger Cole B side*
On The Move	7"	Pyramid	PYR6006	1967	£8	**£4**	*Desmond Dekker B side*

Peace And Love	7"	Pyramid	PYR6023	1968	£8	£4	
Phoenix City	7"	Trojan	TRM9010	1974	£4	£1.50	
Reggae In The Grass	7"	Coxsone	CS7077	1968	£12	£6	*Roy Richards B side*
Rinky Dink	7"	Ska Beat	JB231	1966	£10	£5	*Scratch & The Dynamites B side*
Roland Plays The Prince	7"	Blue Beat	BB286	1965	£12	£6	*Gaynor & Errol B side*
Roll On	7"	Punch	PH39	1970	£4	£1.50	
Shanty Town Curfew	7"	Island	WI3055	1967	£10	£5	*Hopeton Lewis B side*
Ska Au Go-Go	LP	Coxsone	CSL8003	1967	£100	£50	
Sock It To Me	7"	Pyramid	PYR6018	1967	£8	£4	*Spanishtonians B side*
Stream Of Life	7"	Pyramid	PYR6016	1967	£8	£4	*Austin Faithful B side*
Thousand Tons Of Megaton	7"	[illegible]	CA3112	1969	£4	£1.50	
Whiter Shade Of Pale	7"	Pyramid	PYR6022	1968	£8	£4	
Woman Of The World	7"	Pyramid	PYR6005	1967	£8	£4	*Spanishtonians B side*
Yard Broom	7"	Ska Beat	JB183	1965	£20	£10	*Dotty & Bonnie B side*

ALPINES

Get Ready	7"	Double D	DD110	1968	£8	£4	

ALRUNE ROD

Alrune Rock	LP	Sonet	SLPS1537	1971	£15	£6	*Danish*
Alrune Rod	LP	Sonet	SLPS1516	1969	£50	£25	*Danish*
Dansk Beat	LP	Sonet	SLPS2413	1975	£12	£5	*Danish*
Four	LP	Mandragora	MGLP2	1973	£12	£5	*Danish*
Hey Du	LP	Sonet	SLPS1524	1970	£15	£6	*Danish*
Spredt For Vinden	LP	Mandragora	MGLP1	1973	£12	£5	*Danish*
Tatuba Tapes	LP	Mandragora	MGLP3	1975	£12	£5	*Danish*

ALTECS

Easy	7"	London	HLU9387	1961	£5	£2	

ALTERED IMAGES

Despite Claire Grogan's regular appearances as a presenter on MTV and her cameo slot in EastEnders, the group of which she was lead singer remains obstinately uncollectable, apart from this solitary oddity.

Happy New Year	7"	Lyntone	LYN10795	1983	£8	£4	

ALTERNATIVE TV

Knights Of The Future	7"	Nice	NICE2	1980	£10	£5	

ALTON & EDDY

Muriel	7"	Blue Beat	BB17	1960	£12	£6	
My Love Divine	7"	Island	WI009	1962	£12	£6	

ALTON & PHYLLIS

Love Letters	7"	Trojan	TR622	1968	£6	£2.50	

ALTONA

Altona	LP	RCA	PPL11049	1974	£12	£5	*German*
Chicken Farm	LP	RCA	PPL14129	1975	£15	£6	*German*

ALVARO

Drinkin My Own Sperm	LP	Squeaky Shoes	SSRDR1	1977	£12	£5	
Mum's Milk Not Powder	LP	Squeaky Shoes	SSRM2	1979	£10	£4	
Working Class	LP	Squeaky Shoes	SSR3	1981	£10	£4	

ALVYN

You've Gotta Have An Image	7"	Morgan Bluetown	MR18	1969	£4	£1.50	

AMALGAM

Another Time	LP	Vinyl	VS100	1976	£15	£6	
Close To You	LP	Ogun	OG528	1978	£15	£6	
Deep	LP	Vinyl	VS108	1977	£15	£6	
Innovation	LP	Tangent	TGS121	1974	£15	£6	
Mad	LP	Syntohn	VR20020	1976	£15	£6	
Over The Rainbow	LP	Arc	ARC01	1979	£15	£6	
Play Blackwell And Higgins	LP	A Records	A002	1973	£20	£8	
Prayer For Peace	LP	Transatlantic	TRA196	1969	£30	£15	
Samanna	LP	Vinyl	VS106	1977	£15	£6	
Wipe Out	LP	Impetus	IMP47901	1979	£50	£25	*4 LP set*

AMAZIAH

Straight Talker	LP	Sunrise	SR001	1973	£150	£75	

AMAZING BLONDEL

Alleluia	7"	Island	WIP6153	1972	£4	£1.50	
Amazing Blondel	LP	Bell	SBLL131	1970	£100	£50	
Blondel	LP	Island	ILPS9257	1973	£10	£4	
England	LP	Island	ILPS9205	1972	£10	£4	

Evensong	LP	Island	ILPS9136	1970	£12	£5	
Fantasia Lindum	LP	Island	ILPS9156	1971	£12	£5	
Mulgrave Street	LP	DJM	DJF20442	1974	£10	£4	

AMAZING CATSFIELD STEAMERS

United Friends	LP	Fat Hen	FH002LP	1983	£10	£4	

AMAZING DANCE BAND

Amazing Dance Band	LP	Verve	SVLP9214	1967	£12	£5	
Deep Blue Train	7"	Verve	VS567	1968	£10	£5	

AMAZING FRIENDLY APPLE

Water Woman	7"	Decca	F12887	1969	£20	£10	

AMAZING RHYTHM ACES

Full House – Aces High	LP	A&M	AMJ2001/2	1978	£40	£20	*US double*

AMBER SQUAD

Can We Go Dancing?	7"	Deadgood	DEAD17	1980	£10	£5	
Put My Finger On You	7"	Sound Of Leicester	ST1	1980	£12	£6	

AMBOY DUKES

Marriage On The Rocks	LP	Polydor	244012	1970	£15	£6	*US*

AMBOY DUKES (2)

In order to appreciate the Amboy Dukes' tendency to overdo everything, one need look no further than the seminal punk (sixties-style) compilation, *Nuggets*. Here the group turns 'Tobacco Road' into a totally unsuitable vehicle for guitar excess. Lead guitarist Ted Nugent has followed more or less the same approach ever since.

Amboy Dukes	LP	Fontana	(S)TL5468	1968	£40	£20	
Journey To The Centre Of The Mind	LP	London	HAT/SHT8378	1968	£20	£8	
Let's Go Get Stoned	7"	Fontana	TF971	1968	£8	£4	
Migration	LP	London	HAT/SHT8392	1969	£20	£8	*credited to American Amboy Dukes*

AMBROSE, SAM

Monkey See Monkey Do	7"	Stateside	SS399	1965	£60	£30	
This Diamond Ring	7"	Stateside	SS385	1965	£40	£20	

AMBROSE SLADE

Ambrose Slade was the original name of Slade, back in the days when they were being marketed as the first skinhead group (despite the fact that the group's music had nothing in common with the likes of 'Skinhead Moonstomp'). The reissue of the group's LP, on Contour, is as rare as the original – it was withdrawn shortly after release – but the US version of the record, retitled *Ballzy* and given an appropriate cover, is rather more common.

Ballzy	LP	Fontana	SRF67598	1969	£60	£30	*US*
Beginnings	LP	Contour	6870678	1975	£40	£20	
Beginnings	LP	Fontana	STL5492	1969	£200	£100	
Genesis	7"	Fontana	TF1015	1969	£175	£87.50	

AMBROSIA

Ambrosia	LP	20th Century	BT434	1975	£10	£4	
Somewhere I've Never Travelled	LP	20th Century	BT510	1976	£10	£4	

AME SON

Ame Son	LP	Byg	529324	1970	£15	£6	*French*

AMECHE, LOLA

Rock The Joint	78	Oriole	CB1143	1953	£5	£2	

AMEN CORNER

Farewell Magnificent Seven	LP	Immediate	IMSP028	1969	£10	£4	
National Welsh Coast Live	LP	Immediate	IMSP023	1969	£10	£4	
Round Amen Corner	LP	Deram	DML/SML1021	1968	£10	£4	
So Fine	7"	Immediate	AS3	1969	£15	£7.50	*promo*

AMERICAN BLUES

The only UK release of the second American Blues album is a 1987 reissue on the See For Miles label. Although the record is a typically inventive chunk of psychedelia, its real interest, and the reason for the collectibility of the original, lies in the fact that two-thirds of American Blues later became two-thirds of ZZ Top.

American Blues Is Here	LP	Karma	KLP1001	1968	£150	£75	*US*
Do Their Thing	LP	Uni	73044	1969	£40	£20	*US*

AMERICAN BLUES EXCHANGE

Blueprints	LP	Taylus	TLS1	1969	£300	£180	*US*

AMERICAN BREED

American Breed	LP	Dot	DOLP255	1967	£10	£4	
Bend Me Shape Me	7"	Stateside	SS2078	1968	£4	£1.50	
Bend Me Shape Me	LP	Dot	(S)LPD502	1968	£10	£4	
Lonely Side Of The City	LP	Dot	(S)LPD526	1969	£10	£4	
No Way To Treat A Lady	LP	Dot	(S)LPD507	1968	£15	£6	
Pumpkin Powder, Scarlet & Green	LP	Dot	(S)LPD518	1968	£10	£4	
Step Out Of Your Mind	7"	CBS	2888	1967	£4	£1.50	

AMERICAN DREAM

Title	Format	Label	Cat. No.	Year	Price	Price	Notes
American Dream	LP	Ampex	A10101	1968	**£25**	**£10**	*US*

AMERICAN EAGLE

Title	Format	Label	Cat. No.	Year	Price	Price	Notes
American Eagle	LP	Decca	DL75258	1970	**£10**	**£4**	*US*

AMERICAN FOUR

Both Arthur Lee and fellow Love guitarist John Echols were members of the American Four, which stayed together just long enough to make this rare single.

Title	Format	Label	Cat. No.	Year	Price	Price	Notes
Luci Baines	7"	Selma	2001	1964	**£100**	**£50**	*US*

AMERICAN GYPSY

Title	Format	Label	Cat. No.	Year	Price	Price	Notes
American Gypsy	LP	BTM	BTM1001GG	1975	**£10**	**£4**	
Anithesis	LP	RCA	LSP4775	1972	**£10**	**£4**	*US*
Gypsy	LP	CBS	66270	1970	**£12**	**£5**	*double*
In The Garden	LP	Metromedia	1044	1972	**£10**	**£4**	*US*
Unlock The Dead Gates	LP	RCA	APL10093	1973	**£10**	**£4**	*US*

AMERICAN POETS

Title	Format	Label	Cat. No.	Year	Price	Price	Notes
She Blew A Good Thing	7"	London	HLC10037	1966	**£40**	**£20**	

AMERICAN REVOLUTION

Title	Format	Label	Cat. No.	Year	Price	Price	Notes
American Revolution	LP	Flick	45002	1968	**£10**	**£4**	*US*

AMERICAN SPRING

Title	Format	Label	Cat. No.	Year	Price	Price	Notes
American Spring	LP	United Artists	UAS29363	1972	**£15**	**£6**	

AMERICAN TEARS

Title	Format	Label	Cat. No.	Year	Price	Price	Notes
Branded Bad	LP	CBS	33038	1974	**£20**	**£8**	*US*
Powerhouse	LP	CBS	34676	1977	**£20**	**£8**	*US*
Teargas	LP	CBS	33847	1975	**£20**	**£8**	*US*

AMERICAN YOUTH CHOIR

Title	Format	Label	Cat. No.	Year	Price	Price	Notes
Together We Can Make It	7"	Polydor	2066013	1971	**£10**	**£5**	

AMES, NANCY

Title	Format	Label	Cat. No.	Year	Price	Price	Notes
Cry Softly	7"	Columbia	DB8039	1966	**£30**	**£15**	
Friends And Lovers Forever	7"	Columbia	DB7809	1966	**£5**	**£2**	

AMES BROTHERS

Title	Format	Label	Cat. No.	Year	Price	Price	Notes
Best Of The Ames Brothers	7" EP	RCA	RCX1047	1959	**£6**	**£2.50**	
Boogie Woogie Maxine	7"	HMV	7M179	1954	**£5**	**£2**	
Exactly Like You	7" EP	HMV	7EG8237	1957	**£6**	**£2.50**	
I'm Gonna Love You	7"	HMV	POP242	1956	**£5**	**£2**	
If You Wanna See Mamie Tonight	7"	HMV	7MC46	1956	**£4**	**£1.50**	*export*
Naughty Lady Of Shady Lane	7"	HMV	7M281	1955	**£12**	**£6**	
Rockin' Shoes	7"	RCA	RCA1015	1957	**£5**	**£2**	
You You You	7"	HMV	7M153	1953	**£5**	**£2**	

AMITY

Title	Format	Label	Cat. No.	Year	Price	Price	Notes
Amity	LP	Red Rag		1976	**£30**	**£15**	

AMM

Apart from being the rarest album on the orange Elektra label, *AMMMusic*, with its distinctive yellow lorry cover, is also a crucial, pioneering landmark within the genre of free improvisation. Instruments like guitar, cello, and saxophone are credited, but so are transistor radios, and in truth it is extremely hard to identify the individual contributions within the maelstrom of sound that the group produces. The album was sponsored by Pink Floyd's management, the kinship with Floyd pieces like *A Saucerful Of Secrets* being clear, but AMM's music proved to be too extreme even in the heady days of the late sixties. Versions of the group have nevertheless continued to perform on occasion ever since.

Title	Format	Label	Cat. No.	Year	Price	Price	Notes
AMM Music	LP	Elektra	EUK(S7)256	1966	**£100**	**£50**	
At The Roundhouse	7"	Incus	EP1	1973	**£50**	**£25**	
Crypt – 12th June 1968	LP	Matchless	MR5	1981	**£30**	**£15**	*boxed double*
Generative Themes	LP	Matchless	MR6	1982	**£15**	**£6**	
Inexhaustible Document	LP	Matchless	MR13	198–	**£15**	**£6**	
It Had Been An Ordinary Enough Day In Pueblo	LP	ECM	60031	1979	**£15**	**£6**	
Live Electronic Music Improvised	LP	Mainstream	MS5002	1968	**£40**	**£20**	*US, with MEV*
To Hear And Back Again	LP	Matchless	MR3	1978	**£15**	**£6**	

AMMONS, ALBERT

Title	Format	Label	Cat. No.	Year	Price	Price	Notes
Albert Ammons	7" EP	Vogue	EPV1071	1955	**£30**	**£15**	
And His Rhythm Kings	LP	Mercury	MG25012	1954	**£25**	**£10**	
Boogie Woogie Stomp	7" EP	Brunswick	OE9325	1957	**£15**	**£7.50**	

AMMONS, ALBERT, PETE JOHNSON & MEADE LUX LEWIS

Title	Format	Label	Cat. No.	Year	Price	Price	Notes
Boogie Woogie Trio	LP	Storyville	SLP184	1966	**£10**	**£4**	
Giants Of Boogie Woogie	LP	Riverside	RLP12106	1963	**£15**	**£7.50**	
Shout For Joy	7" EP	Columbia	SEG7528	1954	**£20**	**£10**	

AMMONS, GENE

Title	Format	Label	Cat. No.	Year	Price	Price	Notes
Ammons Boogie	7"	Starlite	ST45017	1960	**£40**	**£20**	
Anna	7"	Starlite	ST45097	1963	**£6**	**£2.50**	
Bad! Bossa Nova	LP	Esquire	32178	1963	**£20**	**£8**	
Blue Gene	LP	Esquire	32147	1962	**£20**	**£8**	

Boss Tenor	LP	Esquire	32177	1963	**£20**	**£8**	
Bossa Nova By The Boss	7" EP	Esquire	EP249	1962	**£8**	**£4**	
Hi Fidelity Jam Session	LP	Esquire	32047	1958	**£30**	**£15**	
Jammin' With Gene	LP	Esquire	32097	1960	**£15**	**£6**	
Soul Summit	LP	Transatlantic	PR7234	1968	**£12**	**£5**	*with Sonny Stitt*

AMON DÜÜL

Collapsing	LP	Metronome	SMLP012	1969	**£30**	**£15**	*German*
Disaster	LP	BASF	29290794	1971	**£30**	**£15**	*German double*
Minnelied	LP	Brain	0040149	1975	**£25**	**£10**	*German*
Paradieswärts	LP	Ohr	OMM56008	1969	**£40**	**£20**	*German*
Psychedelic Underground	LP	Metronome	MLP15332	1969	**£30**	**£15**	*German*
This Is Amon Düül	LP	Brain	21046	1973	**£25**	**£10**	*German double*

AMON DÜÜL II

Amon Düül II were originally a splinter group away from Amon Düül, following an ideological disagreement, but they rapidly became rather better known than the parent group. Essentially, the group is a German version of Hawkwind, with a similar mystical outlook and fascination with spacey noises. Equally, the music is at root very simply constructed, with single chords being worried half to death for minutes at a time.

Almost Live	LP	Nova	623305	1977	**£12**	**£5**	*German*
Archangel's Thunderbird	7"	Liberty	LBF15355	1970	**£5**	**£2**	
Carnival In Babylon	LP	United Artists	UAG29327	1972	**£15**	**£6**	
Dance Of The Lemmings	LP	United Artists	60003/4	1971	**£15**	**£6**	*double*
Hi Jack	LP	Atlantic	K50136	1974	**£12**	**£5**	
Lemmingmania	LP	United Artists	UAS29723	1975	**£12**	**£5**	
Live In London	LP	United Artists	USP102	1973	**£15**	**£6**	
Made In Germany	LP	Atlantic	K50182	1975	**£12**	**£5**	
Made In Germany	LP	Nova	628350	1975	**£20**	**£8**	*German, double*
Only Human	LP	Vinyl	LV1004	1978	**£12**	**£5**	
Phallus Dei	LP	Liberty	LBS83279	1969	**£40**	**£20**	
Pyragony	LP	Nova	622890	1976	**£12**	**£5**	*German*
Vive La Trance	LP	United Artists	UAS29504	1973	**£15**	**£6**	
Wolf City	LP	United Artists	UAG29406	1972	**£15**	**£6**	
Yeti	LP	Liberty	LSP101/2	1970	**£20**	**£8**	*double*

AMOR VIVI

Dirty Dog	7"	Big Shot	BI534	1970	**£4**	**£1.50**	

AMORPHOUS ANROGYNOUS

Tales Of Ephidrina	LP	Quigley	LPEBV1	1993	**£12**	**£5**	

AMOS, TORI

Five years before releasing her acclaimed *Little Earthquakes* album, Tori Amos signed a contract with Atlantic, but only made one record with them. *Y Kant Tori Read* presents a startlingly different Tori Amos, casting her in the same mould as Pat Benatar (at least, visually: much of the actual music is close in style to that of her subsequent recordings). The record is extremely scarce, however, and Tori Amos herself disowns it. Even scarcer is the US single 'Baltimore', recorded when Ms Amos was just seventeen. The listed value has to be viewed as highly approximate, since few copies are ever likely to appear on the market.

Baltimore	7"	MEA	5290	1980	**£500**	**£330**	*US, credited to Ellen Amos*
China	CD-s	East West	A7531CD	1992	**£20**	**£10**	
Cornflake Girl	CD-s	East West	A7281CDX	1994	**£15**	**£7.50**	*digipak*
Crucify Live EP	CD-s	East West	A7479CDX	1992	**£25**	**£12.50**	
Little Drummer Boy	CD-s	East West	no number	1992	**£75**	**£37.50**	*promo*
Me And A Gun EP (Silent All These Years)	12"	East West	YZ618T	1991	**£10**	**£5**	
Me And A Gun EP (Silent All These Years)	CD-s	East West	YZ618CD	1991	**£20**	**£10**	
New Music From Tori Amos	CD	Atlantic	PRCD65352	1996	**£15**	**£6**	*US promo compilation*
Precious Things	CD-s	Atlantic	PRCD47422	1992	**£60**	**£30**	*US promo picture disc*
Silent All These Years	12"	East West	YZ618T	1991	**£8**	**£4**	
Silent All These Years	7"	East West	YZ618	1991	**£6**	**£2.50**	
Silent All These Years	CD-s	East West	YZ618CD	1991	**£12**	**£6**	
Silent All These Years	CD-s	East West	A7433CDX	1992	**£25**	**£12.50**	*fold-out digipak*
Tea With The Waitress	CD	Atlantic	PRCD5498	1994	**£30**	**£15**	*US interview promo*
Under The Pink/ More Pink	CD	East West	7567806072	1994	**£25**	**£10**	*Australian with bonus disc*
Winter	CD-s	East West	A7504CD	1992	**£6**	**£2.50**	
Winter	CD-s	East West	A7504CDX	1992	**£20**	**£10**	
Y Kant Tori Read	CD	Atlantic	81845	1988	**£100**	**£50**	*US*
Y Kant Tori Read	LP	Atlantic	81845	1988	**£75**	**£37.50**	*US*

AMPS

Bragging Party	7"	4AD	AMP1	1995	**£5**	**£2**	*promo*

AMRAM–BARROW QUARTET

Jazz Studio Six	LP	Brunswick	LAT8239	1958	**£20**	**£8**	

AMY, CURTIS

Katanga	LP	Fontana	688136ZL	1966	**£12**	**£5**	

ANAN

Haze Woman	7"	Pye	7N17571	1968	**£20**	**£10**	
Madena	7"	Pye	7N17642	1968	**£15**	**£7.50**	

ANCIENT GREASE

Women And Children First	LP	Mercury	6338033	1970	**£30**	**£15**	

ANCIENT MORNING

Ancient Morning	LP	Cocaine		1979	**£40**	**£20**	*Swiss*

AND ALSO THE TREES

House Of The Heart	CD-s	Reflex	RE14CD	1988	**£5**	**£2**	
Lady D'Arbanville	CD-s	Reflex	RE15CD	1989	**£5**	**£2**	
Secret Sea	12"	Reflex	12RE6	1984	**£6**	**£2.50**	
Secret Sea	7"	Reflex	RE6	1984	**£5**	**£2**	
Shantell	7"	Reflex	FS9	1984	**£6**	**£2.50**	

ANDERS, CHRISTIAN

Beat Gitarren Schule 1	LP	Joker	SM3037	1965	**£30**	**£15**	*German*

ANDERSEN, ARILD

Clouds In My Head	LP	ECM	ECM1059ST	1975	**£15**	**£6**	

ANDERSEN, ERIC

'Bout Changes & Things	LP	Fontana	STFL6068	1968	**£12**	**£5**	
Avalanche	LP	Warner Bros	WS1748	1970	**£12**	**£5**	*US*
Best Of Eric Andersen	LP	Vanguard	VSD7/8	1973	**£12**	**£5**	*US, double*
Blue River	LP	CBS	65145	1973	**£10**	**£4**	
Country Dream	LP	Vanguard	VSD6540	1969	**£12**	**£5**	*US*
Eric Andersen	LP	Warner Bros	WS1806	1970	**£12**	**£5**	*US*
More Hits From Tin Can Alley	LP	Vanguard	VSD79271	1968	**£12**	**£5**	*US*
Stage	LP	CBS	65571	1974	**£10**	**£4**	*US*
Today Is The Highway	LP	Fontana	TFL6061	1965	**£12**	**£5**	

ANDERSON, ALISTAIR

Concertina Workshop	LP	Free Reed	FRS501	1974	**£10**	**£4**	
Plays English Concertina	LP	Trailer	LER2074	1972	**£10**	**£4**	
Traditional Tunes	LP	Front Hall	FHR08	1976	**£15**	**£6**	*US*

ANDERSON, BRUFORD, WAKEMAN & HOWE

Anderson, Bruford, Wakeman And Howe	CD	Arista	ARCD90126	1989	**£15**	**£6**	*US promo picture disc*
Brother Of Mine	CD-s	Arista	662379	1989	**£5**	**£2**	*picture disc*
Order Of The Universe	CD-s	Arista	662693	1989	**£5**	**£2**	

ANDERSON, CASEY

Bag I'm In	LP	Atco	(SD)33149	1962	**£15**	**£6**	*US*
Blues Is A Woman Gone	LP	Atco	(SD)33176	1965	**£12**	**£5**	*US*
Goin' Places	LP	Elektra	EKL/EKS7192	1960	**£15**	**£6**	*US*
Live At The Ice House	LP	Atco	(SD)33172	1965	**£12**	**£5**	*US*
More Pretty Girls Than One	LP	Atco	(SD)33166	1964	**£12**	**£5**	*US*

ANDERSON, CAT

Cat On A Hot Tin Horn	LP	Mercury	MMB12006	1959	**£15**	**£6**	

ANDERSON, ERNESTINE

Azure-Te	7" EP	Mercury	ZEP10105	1961	**£5**	**£2**	
By Special Request	LP	Pye	NPT19025	1958	**£10**	**£4**	
Ernestine Anderson	7" EP	Mercury	10007MCE	1964	**£6**	**£2.50**	
Ernestine Anderson	LP	Columbia	SX/SCX6145	1967	**£10**	**£4**	
Fascinating Ernestine	LP	Mercury	MMC14037	1960	**£10**	**£4**	
Jerk And Twine	7"	Mercury	MF912	1965	**£5**	**£2**	
Just A Swinging	7" EP	Mercury	ZEP10124	1962	**£5**	**£2**	
Keep An Eye On Love	7"	Sue	WI309	1964	**£20**	**£10**	
Moanin'	LP	Mercury	MMC14062	1961	**£10**	**£4**	
New Sound Of Ernestine Anderson	LP	Sue	ILP914	1964	**£60**	**£30**	
Runnin' Wild	LP	Mercury	MMC14016	1959	**£15**	**£6**	
Running Wild	7" EP	Mercury	ZEP10057	1960	**£6**	**£2.50**	
Somebody Told You	7"	Stateside	SS455	1965	**£5**	**£2**	
Welcome To The Club	7" EP	Mercury	ZEP10089	1960	**£6**	**£2.50**	

ANDERSON, GLADSTONE

Judas	7"	Blue Cat	BS172	1969	**£4**	**£1.50**	

ANDERSON, HARLEY & BATT

Whatever You Believe	12"	Epic	PEEPS12P1	1988	**£6**	**£2.50**	
Whatever You Believe	7"	Epic	PEEPS1	1988	**£6**	**£2.50**	

ANDERSON, IAN A.

Almost The Country Blues	7" EP	Saydisc	EPSD134	1969	**£12**	**£6**	
Book Of Changes	LP	Fontana	STL5542	1970	**£20**	**£8**	
Inverted World	LP	Matchbox	SDM159	1968	**£40**	**£20**	*with Mike Cooper*
One More Chance	7"	Village Thing	VTSX1002	1971	**£10**	**£5**	
Royal York Crescent	LP	Village Thing	VTS3	1970	**£12**	**£5**	
Singer Sleeps On As Blaze Rages	LP	Village Thing	VTS18	1972	**£10**	**£4**	
Stereo Death Breakdown	LP	Liberty	LBS83242	1969	**£25**	**£10**	
Vulture Is Not A Bird You Can Trust	LP	Village Thing	VTS9	1971	**£10**	**£4**	

ANDERSON, JON

Change We Must	CD	EMI	CDC5550882	1994	**£25**	**£10**	*promo CD and video boxed set*

Evening With Jon Anderson	LP	Atlantic	PR285	1976	**£15**	**£6**	*US promo*
Hold On To Love	CD-s	Epic	6515142	1988	**£5**	**£2**	
In The City Of Angels	CD	Epic	4606932	1988	**£12**	**£5**	
Is It Me	CD-s	Epic	6529472	1988	**£5**	**£2**	

ANDERSON, JONES, JACKSON

Anderson, Jones, Jackson	7" EP	Saydisc	EPSD125	1968	**£15**	**£7.50**	

ANDERSON, LAURIE

United States Live	LP	Warner Bros	9251921	1984	**£40**	**£20**	*5 LP set*

ANDERSON, LEROY

Anderson Compositions	7" EP	Brunswick	OE9021	1954	**£5**	**£2**	
Forgotten Dreams	7"	Brunswick	05485	1955	**£4**	**£1.50**	
Pops Concert Pt 1	7" EP	Brunswick	OE9356	1958	**£5**	**£2**	
Pops Concert Pt 2	7" EP	Brunswick	OE9357	1958	**£5**	**£2**	

ANDERSON, MILLER

Miller Anderson was the lead guitarist and singer with the Keef Hartley Band. His solo LP uses the band musicians (but not Hartley himself) to rather less effect than on *Little Big Band*, which was released at the same time.

Bright City	7"	Deram	DM337	1971	**£4**	**£1.50**	
Bright City	LP	Deram	SDL3	1971	**£30**	**£15**	

ANDERSON, PINK

Ballad And Folk Singer	LP	Bluesville	BV1071	1963	**£12**	**£5**	*US*
Carolina Blues Man	LP	Bluesville	BV1038	1961	**£12**	**£5**	*US*
Medicine Show Man	LP	Bluesville	BV1051	1962	**£12**	**£5**	*US*

ANDERSON, REUBEN

Christmas Time Again	7"	Doctor Bird	DB1045	1966	**£10**	**£5**	

ANDERSON, SONNY

Lonely Lonely Train	7"	London	HLP9036	1960	**£30**	**£15**	

ANDERSON, VICKI

Super Good	7"	Polydor	2001150	1971	**£4**	**£1.50**	

ANDERSON'S ALL STARS

Intensified Girls	7"	Blue Cat	BS133	1968	**£8**	**£4**	

ANDREWS, CATHERINE

Fruits	LP	Cat Tracks	PURRLP2	1982	**£100**	**£50**	

ANDREWS, DAVE & SUGAR

I'm On My Way	7"	Jewel	JL04	1968	**£25**	**£12.50**	

ANDREWS, ERNIE

In The Dark	LP	Vogue	VA160147	1959	**£12**	**£5**	
Round Midnight	7"	Vogue	V9166	1960	**£8**	**£4**	
Where Were you	7"	Capitol	CL15407	1965	**£10**	**£5**	

ANDREWS, HARVEY

Brand New Day	LP	Polydor	2383595	1980	**£10**	**£4**	
Fantasies From A Corner Seat	LP	Transatlantic	TRA298	1975	**£10**	**£4**	
Friends Of Mine	LP	Fly	HIFLY15	1973	**£10**	**£4**	
Harvey Andrews	7" EP	Transatlantic	TRAEP133	1965	**£15**	**£7.50**	
Places And Faces	LP	Nova	DN/SND9	1969	**£20**	**£8**	
Soldier	7"	Cube	BUG20	1971	**£4**	**£1.50**	
Someday	LP	Transatlantic	TRA329	1976	**£10**	**£4**	
Writer Of Songs	LP	Cube	HIFLY10	1972	**£10**	**£4**	

ANDREWS, INEZ & THE ANDREWETTES

Inez Andrews And The Andrewettes	7" EP	Vogue	EDVP1283	1965	**£20**	**£10**	

ANDREWS, JOHN & THE LONELY ONES

Rose Grows In The Ruins	7"	Parlophone	R5455	1966	**£30**	**£15**	

ANDREWS, LEE & THE HEARTS

Teardrops	7"	London	HL7031	1957	**£100**	**£50**	*export*
Teardrops	7"	London	HLM8546	1958	**£200**	**£100**	*best auctioned*
Try The Impossible	7"	London	HLU8661	1958	**£300**	**£210**	*best auctioned*

ANDREWS, PATTY

Suddenly There's A Valley	7"	Capitol	CL14374	1955	**£6**	**£2.50**	
Where To My Love?	7"	Capitol	CL14324	1955	**£6**	**£2.50**	

ANDREWS, WILLIAM & LIAM WALSH

Classics Of Irish Piping Vol. 2	LP	Topic	12T262	1976	**£12**	**£5**	

ANDREWS SISTERS

Rum And Coca-Cola	7"	Capitol	CL14705	1957	**£6**	**£2.50**	

ANDROIDS OF MU

Blood Robots	LP	Fuck Off	FLP001	1980	**£10**	**£4**	

ANDROMEDA

Andromeda's self-titled progressive hard rock rarity is something of a genre classic and deserves its collectable status. Guitarist John Cann subsequently joined Atomic Rooster and scored a top five hit with them, 'The Devil's Answer', in 1971. Bass player Mick Hawksworth joined a late line-up of Ten Years After.

Andromeda	LP	RCA	SF8031	1969	**£125**	**£62.50**	
Go Your Way	7"	RCA	RCA1854	1969	**£10**	**£5**	

ANDWELLA

Are You Ready	7"	Reflection	RS6	1970	**£4**	**£1.50**	
Peoples People	LP	Reflection	REFL10	1971	**£12**	**£5**	
World's End	LP	Reflection	REF1010	1970	**£12**	**£5**	

ANDWELLA'S DREAM

Every Little Minute	7"	Reflection	RS1	1970	**£4**	**£1.50**	
Love And Poetry	LP	CBS	63673	1969	**£250**	**£150**	
Midday Sun	7"	CBS	4301	1969	**£20**	**£10**	
Mr Sunshine	7"	CBS	4634	1969	**£10**	**£5**	
Mrs Man	7"	CBS	4469	1969	**£10**	**£5**	

ANDY, BOB

Born A Man	7"	Coxsone	CS7074	1968	**£12**	**£6**	*Marcia Griffiths B side*
Experience	7"	Studio One	SO2063	1968	**£12**	**£6**	
Going Home	7"	Studio One	SO2075	1969	**£12**	**£6**	*Sound Dimension B side*
Lots Of Love	LP	Sky Note	SKLP15	1978	**£12**	**£5**	
Way I Feel	7"	Doctor Bird	DB1183	1969	**£12**	**£6**	*Ethiopians B side*

ANDY, HORACE

Don't Think About Me	7"	Randys	RAN533	1973	**£8**	**£4**	
You Are My Angel	LP	Trojan	TBL197	1972	**£10**	**£4**	

ANDY & CLYDE

I'm So Lonesome	7"	Rio	R69	1965	**£10**	**£5**	
Never Be A Slave	7"	Rio	R62	1965	**£10**	**£5**	
We All Have To Part	7"	Rio	R71	1965	**£10**	**£5**	

ANDY & JOEY

Have You Ever	7"	Island	WI056	1962	**£12**	**£6**	
I Want To Know	7"	Port-O-Jam	PJ4009	1964	**£10**	**£5**	
You'll Never	7"	R&B	JB162	1964	**£10**	**£5**	

ANGE

Au Delà Du Délire	LP	Philips	9101004	1974	**£10**	**£4**	*French*
Caricatures	LP	Philips	6325181	1972	**£12**	**£5**	*French*
Cimetière Des Arlequins	LP	Philips	9101022	1973	**£12**	**£5**	*French*
Emile Jacotey	LP	Philips	9101012	1975	**£10**	**£4**	*French*
Par Le Fils Du Mandarin	LP	Philips	9101090	1976	**£10**	**£4**	*French*

ANGEL, JOHNNY

Better Luck Next Time	7"	Parlophone	R4948	1962	**£4**	**£1.50**	
Chinese Butterfly	7"	Parlophone	R4642	1960	**£4**	**£1.50**	
Look, Look Little Angel	7"	Parlophone	R4874	1962	**£4**	**£1.50**	
Too Young To Go Steady	7"	Parlophone	R4679	1960	**£4**	**£1.50**	
Touch Of Venus	7"	Parlophone	R5026	1963	**£4**	**£1.50**	
Trocadero Double-Nine-One-O	7"	Parlophone	R4795	1961	**£4**	**£1.50**	
What Happens To Love	7"	Parlophone	R4750	1961	**£4**	**£1.50**	

ANGEL, MARION

It's Gonna Be Alright	7"	Columbia	DB7537	1965	**£5**	**£2**	

ANGEL

Angel's claim to fame lies not so much in their status as the poor man's Kiss, but rather in being home to Punky Meadows, the guitarist who took exception to being lampooned in Frank Zappa's song, 'Punky's Whips'.

Angel	LP	Casablanca	CBC4007	1976	**£20**	**£8**	
Helluva Band	LP	Casablanca	CBC4010	1976	**£10**	**£4**	
Live Without A Net	LP	Casablanca	CALH2703	1980	**£15**	**£6**	*double*
On Earth As It Is In Heaven	LP	Casablanca	CAL2002	1977	**£10**	**£4**	
Sinful	LP	Casablanca	CAL2046	1979	**£12**	**£5**	
White Hot	LP	Casablanca	CSL2023	1978	**£12**	**£5**	

ANGEL (2)

Little Boy Blue	7"	Cube	BUG51	1974	**£6**	**£2.50**	

ANGEL PAVEMENT

Baby You've Gotta Stay	7"	Fontana	TF1059	1969	**£4**	**£1.50**	
Tell Me What I've Got To Do	7"	Fontana	TF1072	1970	**£4**	**£1.50**	

ANGELA & THE FANS

This tribute/cash-in song in praise of Illya Kuryakin, the character played by David McCallum in TV's *The Man From U.N.C.L.E.*, was actually performed by Alma Cogan.

Love Ya Illya	7"	Pye	7N17108	1966	**£12**	**£6**	

ANGELIC UPSTARTS

Title	Format	Label	Cat. No.	Year	Price	Price	Notes
Brighton Bomb	12"	Gas	GM3010	1985	£6	£2.50	*Thatcher sleeve*
England	7"	Regal Zonophone	Z12	1980	£6	£2.50	
Murder Of Liddle Towers	7"	Angelic Upstarts	AU1024	1978	£20	£10	

ANGELINA

Title	Format	Label	Cat. No.	Year	Price	Price	Notes
I Just Don't Know How	7"	Fontana	TF648	1965	£4	£1.50	

ANGELO, BOBBY & THE TUXEDOS

Title	Format	Label	Cat. No.	Year	Price	Price	Notes
Baby Sitting	7"	HMV	POP892	1961	£15	£7.50	
Don't Stop	7"	HMV	POP982	1961	£15	£7.50	

ANGELO, MICHAEL

Title	Format	Label	Cat. No.	Year	Price	Price	Notes
Rocco's Theme	7"	Columbia	DB4705	1961	£6	£2.50	
Tears	7"	Columbia	DB4800	1962	£8	£4	

ANGELOU, MAYA

Title	Format	Label	Cat. No.	Year	Price	Price	Notes
Miss Calypso	LP	London	HAU2062	1957	£10	£4	

ANGELS

Title	Format	Label	Cat. No.	Year	Price	Price	Notes
And The Angels Sing	LP	Caprice	(S)LP1001	1962	£40	£20	*US*
Everybody Loves A Lover	7"	Pye	7N25150	1962	£4	£1.50	
Greatest Hits	LP	Ascot	AM13009/ ALS6009	1964	£20	£8	*US*
Halo To You	LP	Smash	MGS27048/ SRS67048	1964	£25	£10	*US*
I Adore Him	7"	Mercury	AMT1215	1963	£6	£2.50	
My Boyfriend's Back	7"	Mercury	AMT1211	1963	£4	£1.50	
My Boyfriend's Back	LP	Smash	MGS27039/ SRS67039	1963	£25	£10	*US*
Wow Wow Wee	7"	Philips	BF1312	1964	£4	£1.50	

ANGELWITCH

Title	Format	Label	Cat. No.	Year	Price	Price	Notes
Angel Witch	7"	Bronze	BRO108	1980	£5	£2	
Goodbye	7"	Killerwatt	KIL3001	1985	£5	£2	
Loser	7"	Bronze	BRO121	1981	£10	£5	
Sweet Danger	12"	EMI	125064	1980	£20	£10	
Sweet Danger	7"	EMI	EMI5064	1980	£8	£4	

ANGLIANS

Title	Format	Label	Cat. No.	Year	Price	Price	Notes
Friend Of Mine	7"	CBS	202489	1967	£5	£2	

ANGLOS

The marvelous 'Incense' by the Anglos was issued several times during the sixties and by some means still managed to avoid becoming a hit. The group, however, was purely a studio creation, the intensely soulful singer being Stevie Winwood (who also used the name Steve Anglo for his guest recording with John Mayall, included on the *Raw Blues* compilation album).

Title	Format	Label	Cat. No.	Year	Price	Price	Notes
Incense	7"	Brit	WI1004	1965	£20	£10	
Incense	7"	Sue	WI4033	1967	£20	£10	*demo only*
Incense	7"	Fontana	TF589	1965	£10	£5	
Incense	7"	Fontana	TF561	1965	£30	£15	*demo only*
Incense	7"	Island	WIP6061	1969	£5	£2	

ANIMALS

As with the Beatles and the Rolling Stones, the British and American LPs by the Animals have numerous differences, even where the titles are the same. Five tracks on the first UK album were replaced in the US by the songs from the first two singles, together with a track, 'Blue Feeling', that never did get a British release. The second album, called *Animal Tracks* in the UK, had three of its songs removed and four different ones added for the US version, which was retitled *The Animals On Tour*. An American LP called *Animal Tracks* was also issued, but this was a different record altogether, being a compilation of various singles and LP tracks not already released in the US. The two hits anthologies are inevitably different – the British *Most Of The Animals* (not to be confused with a later Music For Pleasure release with a greatly inferior selection) has fourteen tracks, while the American *Best Of The Animals* has only eleven – and only nine are to be found on both records. *Animalisms* and *Animalization* have four differences in their running orders; the American *Animalism* LP has no British equivalent at all. Of its eleven tracks, nine were not released in the UK, while a tenth, 'Outcast', is a different take to the version found on *Animalisms*.

Title	Format	Label	Cat. No.	Year	Price	Price	Notes
Animal Tracks	7" EP	Columbia	SEG8499	1966	£20	£10	
Animal Tracks	LP	MGM	(S)E4305	1965	£25	£10	*US*
Animal Tracks	LP	Columbia	33SX1708	1965	£30	£15	
Animalism	LP	MGM	(S)E4414	1966	£25	£10	*US*
Animalisms	LP	Decca	LK4797	1966	£25	£10	
Animalization	LP	MGM	(S)E4384	1966	£25	£10	*US*
Animals	7" EP	Columbia	SEG8400	1965	£12	£6	
Animals	LP	Regal	SREG104	196–	£20	£8	*export*
Animals	LP	MGM	(S)E4264	1964	£25	£10	*US*
Animals	LP	Columbia	33SX1669	1964	£20	£8	
Animals Are Back	7" EP	Columbia	SEG8452	1965	£12	£6	
Animals Is Here	7" EP	Columbia	SEG8374	1964	£12	£6	
Animals No. 2	7" EP	Columbia	SEG8439	1965	£12	£6	
Animals On Tour	LP	MGM	(S)E4281	1965	£25	£10	*US*
Baby Let Me Take You Home	7"	Columbia	DB7247	1964	£4	£1.50	
Best Of The Animals	LP	MGM	(S)E4324	1966	£15	£6	*US*
Best Of The Animals Vol. 2	LP	MGM	(S)E4454	1967	£15	£6	*US*
Boom Boom	7" EP	Columbia	ESRF1632	1964	£20	£10	*French*
Bring It On Home To Me	7"	Columbia	DB7539	1965	£4	£1.50	

Title	Format	Label	Catalogue No.	Year	Mint	VG	Notes
Bring It On Home To Me	7" EP	Columbia	ESRF1671	1965	**£20**	**£10**	*French*
Don't Bring Me Down	7"	Decca	F12407	1966	**£4**	**£1.50**	
Don't Bring Me Down	7" EP	Barclay	071043	1966	**£20**	**£10**	*French*
Don't Let Me Be Misunderstood	7"	Columbia	DB7445	1965	**£20**	**£10**	*demo A side – matrix 1N*
Don't Let Me Be Misunderstood	7"	Columbia	DB7445	1965	**£4**	**£1.50**	
Get Yourself A College Girl	LP	MGM	(S)E4273	1964	**£15**	**£6**	*US, with other artists*
Help Me Girl	7"	Decca	F12502	1966	**£4**	**£1.50**	
House Of The Rising Sun	7"	Columbia	DB7301	1964	**£4**	**£1.50**	
House Of The Rising Sun	7" EP	Columbia	ESRF1571	1964	**£20**	**£10**	*French*
I Just Want To Make Love To You	12" EP	Graphic Sound	ALO10867	1963	**£300**	**£180**	*credited to Alan Price R&B Group*
I'm Crying	7"	Columbia	DB7354	1964	**£4**	**£1.50**	
I'm Crying	7" EP	Columbia	ESRF1593	1964	**£20**	**£10**	*French*
In The Beginning There Was Early Animals	7" EP	Decca	DFE8643	1965	**£20**	**£10**	
Inside Looking Out	7"	Decca	F12332	1966	**£4**	**£1.50**	
It's My Life	7"	Columbia	DB7741	1965	**£4**	**£1.50**	
It's My Life	7" EP	Columbia	ESRF1717	1965	**£20**	**£10**	*French*
Mama Told Me Not To Come	7"	Decca	F12502	1966	**£40**	**£20**	
Most Of The Animals	LP	Columbia	SX6035	1966	**£20**	**£8**	
Outcast	7" EP	Barclay	070970	1966	**£20**	**£10**	*French*
We've Gotta Get Out Of This Place	7"	Columbia	DB7639	1965	**£4**	**£1.50**	
We've Gotta Get Out Of This Place	CD-s	EMI	CDEM154	1990	**£5**	**£2**	
We've Gotta Get Out This Place	7" EP	Columbia	ESRF1692	1965	**£20**	**£10**	*French*

ANIMATED EGG

Title	Format	Label	Catalogue No.	Year	Mint	VG	Notes
Animated Egg	LP	Alshire	SF5104	1967	**£30**	**£15**	*US*
Animated Egg	LP	Marble Arch	MAL 890	1969	**£25**	**£10**	

ANKA, PAUL

Title	Format	Label	Catalogue No.	Year	Mint	VG	Notes
Anka Again	7" EP	Columbia	SEG7801	1958	**£10**	**£5**	
At The Copa	LP	ABC	(S)353	1960	**£15**	**£6**	*US*
Can't Get You Out Of My Mind	7"	RCA	RCA1676	1968	**£15**	**£7.50**	
Crazy Love	7"	Columbia	DB4110	1958	**£4**	**£1.50**	
Diana	7"	Columbia	DB3980	1957	**£4**	**£1.50**	
Diana	7" EP	Columbia	SEG7747	1957	**£15**	**£7.50**	
Diana	LP	ABC	(S)420	1962	**£20**	**£8**	*US*
Excitement On Park Avenue	LP	RCA	RD7700	1964	**£12**	**£5**	
Fly Me To The Moon	7" EP	RCA	RCX7127	1964	**£8**	**£4**	
Four Golden Hits	7" EP	RCA	RCX7152	1964	**£8**	**£4**	
I Love You Baby	7"	Columbia	DB4022	1957	**£4**	**£1.50**	
I Miss You So	7"	Columbia	DB4286	1959	**£4**	**£1.50**	
It's Christmas Everywhere	LP	Columbia	33SX1287	1960	**£15**	**£6**	
Let's Sit This One Out	LP	RCA	RD/SF7533	1962	**£12**	**£5**	
Lonely Boy	7"	Columbia	DB4324	1959	**£4**	**£1.50**	
My Heart Sings	LP	Columbia	33SX1196	1959	**£15**	**£6**	
Our Man Around The World	LP	RCA	RD/SF7547	1963	**£12**	**£5**	
Paul Anka	LP	Columbia	33SX1092	1958	**£30**	**£15**	
Puppy Love	7"	Columbia	DB4434	1960	**£4**	**£1.50**	
Sing Sing Sing	7" EP	Columbia	SEG7890	1959	**£10**	**£5**	
Sings His Big 15	LP	Columbia	33SX1282	1960	**£12**	**£5**	
Sings His Big 15 Vol. 2	LP	Columbia	33SX1395	1961	**£12**	**£5**	
Sings His Big 15 Vol. 3	LP	Columbia	33SX1432	1962	**£12**	**£5**	
Sings Songs From Girls Town	7" EP	Columbia	SEG7985	1960	**£10**	**£5**	
Songs I Wish I'd Written	LP	RCA	RD/SF7613	1963	**£12**	**£5**	
Strictly Instrumental	LP	ABC	(S)371	1961	**£20**	**£8**	*US*
Strictly Nashville	LP	RCA	LPM/LSP3580	1966	**£10**	**£4**	*US*
Swings For Young Lovers	LP	Columbia	33SX1268	1960	**£15**	**£6**	
Sylvia	7" EP	RCA	RCX7170	1964	**£8**	**£4**	
Twenty-One Golden Hits	LP	RCA	RD/SF7573	1963	**£12**	**£5**	
You Are My Destiny	7"	Columbia	DB4063	1958	**£4**	**£1.50**	
Young Alive And In Love	LP	RCA	RD27257/SF5129	1962	**£12**	**£5**	

ANKA, PAUL, SAM COOKE & NEIL SEDAKA

Title	Format	Label	Catalogue No.	Year	Mint	VG	Notes
Three Great Guys	LP	RCA	RD/SF7608	1963	**£10**	**£4**	

ANNETTE

Title	Format	Label	Catalogue No.	Year	Mint	VG	Notes
Annette	LP	Buena Vista	BV3301	1959	**£30**	**£15**	*US*
Annette And Hayley Mills	LP	Buena Vista	BV3508	196–	**£50**	**£25**	*US*
Annette At Bikini Beach	LP	Buena Vista	BV/STER3324	1964	**£25**	**£10**	*US*
Annette Funicello	LP	Buena Vista	BV4037	1962	**£30**	**£15**	*US*
Annette On Campus	LP	Buena Vista	BV/STER3320	1964	**£25**	**£10**	*US*
Annette Sings Anka	LP	Buena Vista	BV3302	1960	**£30**	**£15**	*US*
Annette Sings Golden Surfin' Hits	LP	Buena Vista	BV/STER3327	1964	**£25**	**£10**	*US*
Annette's Beach Party	LP	HMV	CLP1782	1963	**£30**	**£15**	
Annette's Pajama Party	LP	Buena Vista	BV/STER3325	1964	**£25**	**£10**	*US*
Babes In Toyland	LP	Decca	LKR4416/ SKLR4148	1961	**£20**	**£8**	*soundtrack recording*
Best Of Broadway	LP	Disneyland	DQ1267	1965	**£20**	**£8**	*US*
Dance Annette	LP	Buena Vista	BV3305	1961	**£25**	**£10**	*US*
First Name Initial	7"	Top Rank	JAR233	1959	**£5**	**£2**	
Hawaiiannette	LP	Buena Vista	BV3303	1960	**£25**	**£10**	*US*
How To Stuff A Wild Bikini	LP	Wand	(S)671	1965	**£15**	**£6**	*US*
Italiannette	LP	Buena Vista	BV3304	1960	**£25**	**£10**	*US*
Lonely Guitar	7"	Top Rank	JAR137	1959	**£6**	**£2.50**	
Merlin Jones	7"	HMV	POP1322	1964	**£4**	**£1.50**	
Monkey's Uncle	7"	HMV	POP1447	1965	**£12**	**£6**	*with the Beach Boys*

Title	Format	Label	Cat. No.	Year	Mint	VG	Notes
Muscle Beach Party	7"	HMV	POP1270	1964	£6	£2.50	
Muscle Beach Party	LP	Buena Vista	BV/STER3314	1963	£25	£10	US
O Dio Mio	7"	Top Rank	JAR343	1960	£5	£2	
Parent Trap	LP	Buena Vista	BV(S)3309	1961	£20	£8	US
Pineapple Princess	7"	Pye	7N25061	1960	£4	£1.50	
Something Borrowed, Something Blue	LP	Buena Vista	BV3328	1964	£25	£10	US
Songs From Annette	LP	Mickey Mouse	MM24	196–	£30	£15	US
State And College Songs	LP	Disneyland	DQ(S)1293	1967	£20	£8	US
Story Of My Teens	LP	Buena Vista	BV3312	1962	£30	£15	US
Tall Paul	7" EP	Gala	45XP1046	196–	£10	£5	
Teen Street	LP	Buena Vista	BV3313	1962	£25	£10	US
Thunder Alley	LP	Sidewalk	(S)T5902	1967	£15	£6	US
Tubby The Tuba	LP	Disneyland	DQ(S)1287	1966	£15	£6	US
Walt Disney's Wonderful World Of Color	LP	Disneyland	DQ(S)1245	1964	£15	£6	US

ANNETTE & THE KEYMEN

Title	Format	Label	Cat. No.	Year	Mint	VG	Notes
Look Who's Blue	7"	King	KG1006	1964	£4	£1.50	

ANNEXUS QUAM

Title	Format	Label	Cat. No.	Year	Mint	VG	Notes
Beziehungen	LP	Ohr	OMM56028	1972	£20	£8	German
Osmose	LP	Ohr	OMM56007	1970	£30	£15	German

ANNIS

Title	Format	Label	Cat. No.	Year	Mint	VG	Notes
Don't Play Your Games	7"	GTO	266	1979	£5	£2	

ANNIVERSARY

Title	Format	Label	Cat. No.	Year	Mint	VG	Notes
Give Me A Smile	7"	Aerco	AERE102	1978	£20	£10	

ANNO DOMINI

Title	Format	Label	Cat. No.	Year	Mint	VG	Notes
On The New Day	LP	Deram	SML1085	1971	£100	£50	

ANONYMOUS

Title	Format	Label	Cat. No.	Year	Mint	VG	Notes
Inside The Shadow	LP	A Major Label	AMLS1002	1976	£100	£50	US

ANOREXIA

Title	Format	Label	Cat. No.	Year	Mint	VG	Notes
Rapist In The Park	7"	Slim	SJP812	1980	£15	£7.50	

ANOTHER DREAM

Title	Format	Label	Cat. No.	Year	Mint	VG	Notes
Forever In Darkness	7"	Sticky	PEELOFF2	198–	£5	£2	

ANOTHER PRETTY FACE

Title	Format	Label	Cat. No.	Year	Mint	VG	Notes
All The Boys Love Carrie	7"	New Pleasures	Z1	1979	£10	£5	*green & white sleeve*
All The Boys Love Carrie	7"	New Pleasures	Z1	1979	£5	£2	*red & white sleeve*
Heaven Gets Closer Every Day	7"	Chicken Jazz	JAZZ1	1980	£10	£5	
I'm Sorry That I Beat You	cass	Chicken Jazz	JAZZ2	1981	£40	£20	*with badge & book*
Soul To Soul	7"	Chicken Jazz	JAZZ3	1981	£15	£7.50	*gatefold picture sleeve*

ANOTHER SUNNY DAY

Title	Format	Label	Cat. No.	Year	Mint	VG	Notes
Anorak City	7"	Sarah	SARAH4	1988	£8	£4	*flexi*
Genetic Engineering	7"	Caff	CAFF7	1989	£10	£5	
I'm In Love With A Girl	7"	Sarah	SARAH7	1988	£8	£4	

ANSWERS

Lead guitarist with the Answers was Tony Hill, whose talents are heard to best advantage on the more collectable of the group's two singles. Subsequently, Hill was a member of two cult bands, the Misunderstood and High Tide.

Title	Format	Label	Cat. No.	Year	Mint	VG	Notes
It's Just A Fear	7"	Columbia	DB7847	1966	£75	£37.50	
That's What You're Doing To Me	7"	Columbia	DB7953	1966	£10	£5	

ANT, ADAM

Title	Format	Label	Cat. No.	Year	Mint	VG	Notes
Apollo 9	12"	CBS	TA4719	1984	£6	£2.50	
Can't Set Rules About Love	CD-s	MCA	DMCAT1404	1990	£5	£2	
Desperate But Not Serious	7"	CBS	A2892	1982	£20	£10	*single sleeve*
Room At The Top	CD-s	MCA	DMCAT1387	1990	£5	£2	

ANT TRIP CEREMONY

Title	Format	Label	Cat. No.	Year	Mint	VG	Notes
24 Hours	LP	Resurrection		1983	£25	£10	US
Twenty-Four Hours	LP	C.R.C.	2129	1967	£150	£75	US

ANTEEKS

Title	Format	Label	Cat. No.	Year	Mint	VG	Notes
I Don't Want You	7"	Philips	BF1471	1966	£60	£30	

ANTHEM

Title	Format	Label	Cat. No.	Year	Mint	VG	Notes
Anthem	LP	Buddah	BDS5071	1970	£10	£4	US

ANTHONY, BILLIE

Title	Format	Label	Cat. No.	Year	Mint	VG	Notes
Banjo's Back In Town	7"	Columbia	SCM5191	1955	£5	£2	
Bring Me A Bluebird	7"	Columbia	SCM5210	1955	£5	£2	
Lay Down Your Arms	7"	Columbia	DB3818	1956	£5	£2	
No More	7"	Columbia	SCM5164	1955	£5	£2	
Rock A Billy	7"	Columbia	DB3935	1957	£10	£5	
Something's Gotta Give	7"	Columbia	SCM5184	1955	£5	£2	
Sweet Old Fashioned Girl	7"	Columbia	SCM5286	1956	£6	£2.50	

Title	Format	Label	Cat. No.	Year			Notes
Teach Me Tonight	7"	Columbia	SCM5155	1954	**£6**	**£2.50**	
This Ole House	7"	Columbia	SCM5143	1954	**£15**	**£7.50**	
Tweedle Dee	7"	Columbia	SCM5174	1955	**£10**	**£5**	

ANTHONY, DAVE

Title	Format	Label	Cat. No.	Year			Notes
All Night	7"	Island	WI3148	1968	**£10**	**£5**	
Race With The Wind	7"	Mercury	MF1031	1968	**£5**	**£2**	

ANTHONY, DAVE MOODS

Title	Format	Label	Cat. No.	Year			Notes
New Directions	7"	Parlophone	R5438	1966	**£15**	**£7.50**	

ANTHONY, RAY

Title	Format	Label	Cat. No.	Year			Notes
Arthur Murray Swing Foxtrots	10" LP	Capitol	LC6692	1955	**£10**	**£4**	
Bunny Hop	7"	Capitol	CL14769	1957	**£4**	**£1.50**	
Flip Flop	7"	Capitol	CL14525	1956	**£5**	**£2**	
Girl Can't Help It	7" EP	Capitol	EAP1823	1957	**£15**	**£7.50**	
Heat Wave	7"	Capitol	CL14243	1955	**£5**	**£2**	
Hernando's Hideaway	7"	Capitol	CL14354	1955	**£5**	**£2**	
House Party	10" LP	Capitol	LC6617	1953	**£10**	**£4**	
I Remember Glenn Miller	10" LP	Capitol	LC6653	1954	**£10**	**£4**	
Learning The Blues	7"	Capitol	CL14321	1955	**£4**	**£1.50**	
Longest Walk	7" EP	Capitol	EAP1008	1957	**£6**	**£2.50**	
Pete Kelly's Blues	7"	Capitol	CL14345	1955	**£4**	**£1.50**	
Peter Gunn	7" EP	Capitol	EAP11181	1959	**£5**	**£2**	
Plymouth Rock	7"	Capitol	CL14703	1957	**£4**	**£1.50**	
Ray Anthony's Orchestra	10" LP	Capitol	LC6570	1953	**£10**	**£4**	
Rock And Roll With Ray Anthony	7" EP	Capitol	EAP1958	1957	**£10**	**£5**	
Rock Around The Rockpile	7"	Capitol	CL14689	1957	**£10**	**£5**	
Rockin' Through Dixie	7"	Capitol	CL14567	1956	**£4**	**£1.50**	
Sweet And Lovely	10" LP	Capitol	LC6615	1953	**£10**	**£4**	

ANTHONY, RAYBURN

Title	Format	Label	Cat. No.	Year			Notes
There's No Tomorrow	7"	London	HLS9167	1960	**£20**	**£10**	

ANTHRAX

Title	Format	Label	Cat. No.	Year			Notes
Anti-Social	CD-s	Island	CIDX409	1989	**£5**	**£2**	
Armed And Dangerous	12"	Megaforce	MRS05P	1987	**£6**	**£2.50**	*picture disc*
Bring The Noise	CD-s	Island	CID490	1991	**£5**	**£2**	*with Chuck D*
Got The Time	CD-s	Island	CID476	1990	**£5**	**£2**	
In My World	CD-s	Island	CID470	1990	**£5**	**£2**	
Make Me Laugh	CD-s	Island	CIDP379	1988	**£5**	**£2**	*picture disc*

ANTHRAX (2)

Title	Format	Label	Cat. No.	Year			Notes
They've Got It All Wrong	7"	Small Wonder	SMALL27	1983	**£5**	**£2**	

ANTI ESTABLISHMENT

Title	Format	Label	Cat. No.	Year			Notes
1980	7"	Charnel House	CADAV1	1980	**£5**	**£2**	

ANTI GROUP

Title	Format	Label	Cat. No.	Year			Notes
Big Sex	7"	Sweatbox	OX011	1987	**£5**	**£2**	
Ha	12"	Sweatbox	SOX009	1985	**£6**	**£2.50**	*with booklet*

ANTI SOCIAL

Title	Format	Label	Cat. No.	Year			Notes
Made In England	7"	Lightbeat	SOCIAL1	1982	**£5**	**£2**	

ANTISOCIAL

Title	Format	Label	Cat. No.	Year			Notes
Traffic Lights	7"	Dynamite	DRO1	1978	**£5**	**£2**	

ANTOINETTE

Title	Format	Label	Cat. No.	Year			Notes
Jenny Let Him Go	7"	Decca	F11820	1964	**£6**	**£2.50**	
Lullaby Of Love	7"	Piccadilly	7N35310	1966	**£4**	**£1.50**	
There He Goes	7"	Piccadilly	7N35201	1964	**£6**	**£2.50**	
Why Don't I Run Away From You	7"	Piccadilly	7N35293	1966	**£4**	**£1.50**	

ANTON, REY

Title	Format	Label	Cat. No.	Year			Notes
Don't Worry Boy	7"	Parlophone	R5420	1966	**£10**	**£5**	
Girl You Don't Know Me	7"	Parlophone	R5274	1965	**£10**	**£5**	
Heard It All Before	7"	Parlophone	R5172	1964	**£10**	**£5**	
Hey Good Looking	7"	Oriole	CB1771	1962	**£5**	**£2**	
How Long Can This Last	7"	Oriole	CB1843	1963	**£5**	**£2**	
Nothing Comes Easy	7"	Parlophone	R5310	1965	**£10**	**£5**	
Peppermint Man	7"	Oriole	CB1811	1963	**£5**	**£2**	
Premeditation	7"	Parlophone	R5358	1965	**£10**	**£5**	
Things Get Better	7"	Parlophone	R5487	1966	**£10**	**£5**	
Wishbone	7"	Parlophone	R5245	1965	**£10**	**£5**	
You Can't Judge A Book By The Cover	7"	Parlophone	R5132	1964	**£20**	**£10**	

ANTON, TERRY

Title	Format	Label	Cat. No.	Year			Notes
Leave A Little Love	7"	Pye	7N15857	1965	**£4**	**£1.50**	

ANTS

Title	Format	Label	Cat. No.	Year			Notes
Christmas Star	7"	Parlophone	R5082	1963	**£4**	**£1.50**	

ANVIL FLUTES & CAPRICORN VOICES

Title	Format	Label	Cat. No.	Year			Notes
April Showers	7"	Deram	DM208	1968	**£4**	**£1.50**	
Something New Is Coming	LP	Deram	DML/SML1026	1968	**£10**	**£4**	

ANY TROUBLE

Any Trouble's first LP was released to a fanfare of critical acclaim. It was as though after bravely withstanding the onslaught of punk for three years or so, the rock weeklies were delighted to find a new group that actually played 'real tunes'. Unfortunately, Any Trouble's material was not really strong enough to take the weight of the praise heaped on it, and although the group carried on for a few years, it was with diminishing success. Clive Gregson, the group's leader, has since established himself in the folk circuit as half a duo with Christine Collister – the pair also finding useful employment as part of the Richard Thompson band.

Live At The Venue	LP	Stiff	TRUBZ1	1980	£10	£4	
Nice Girls	7"	Pennine	PSS165	1979	£10	£5	

AORTA

Aorta	LP	Columbia	CS9785	1968	£15	£6	US
Aorta 2	LP	Happy Tiger	HT1010	1970	£30	£15	US

APACHE

Maitreya Kali	LP	Akashic	CF2777	1971	£1000	£700	US

APARTMENT ONE

Open House	LP	Pink Elephant	877013	1970	£25	£10	Dutch

APEX GROUP

Until the arrival of the chain stores forced its closure, the best-known record shop in Northampton was owned and run by John Lever. As a drummer, Lever was also a member of the Apex Group and Apex Rhythm & Blues All Stars, whose rare singles were recorded privately and sold through the shop. Much of the high value achieved by the All Stars' EP is attributable to a connection with Ian Hunter, the only member of the group to eventually live up to its optimistic name. Unfortunately, Hunter had long departed the group by the time that 'Tall Girl' and its companions were recorded.

Caravan	7"	John Lever	AP100	1959	£25	£12.50	

APEX RHYTHM & BLUES ALL STARS

Tall Girl	7" EP	John Lever	JLEP1	1964	£400	£250	best auctioned

APHEX TWIN

Analogue Bubblebath Vol. 1	12"	Mighty Force	01	1991	£10	£5	
Analogue Bubblebath Vol. 1	12"	Rabbit City	CUT001	1991	£30	£15	
Analogue Bubblebath Vol. 2	12"	Rabbit City	009	1991	£30	£15	white label
Analogue Bubblebath Vol. 2	12"	Rabbit City	CUT002	1993	£20	£10	
Analogue Bubblebath Vol. 3	12"	Rephlex	CAT008	1994	£8	£4	
Didgeridoo	12"	Outer Rhythm	R+SRSUK	1992	£10	£5	
Didgeridoo	CD-s	Outer Rhythm	R+SRSUK	1992	£40	£20	

APHRODITE'S CHILD

To choose a name taken from Greek mythology was rather par for the course in the late sixties – but since the members of Aphrodite's Child did actually come from Greece, they were more entitled than most. Best known for the pop hit, 'Rain And Tears', the group was perhaps an unlikely signing to the progressive Vertigo label. But the group was always something of a compromise between the diverse interests of the singer and the keyboards player – the pop sensibilities of Demis Roussos versus the ambition of Vangelis. Both, of course, became rather better known after the group split up.

666	LP	Vertigo	6673001	1972	£25	£10	spiral label, double
666	LP	Vertigo	6641581	1977	£12	£5	double
Break	7"	Vertigo	6032900	1972	£5	£2	
End Of The World	LP	Mercury	SMCL20140	1969	£15	£7.50	
It's Five O'Clock	LP	Mercury	138351	1969	£12	£5	

APOLLO XI

Peace	12"	Wau!Mr.Modo	APOLLO11	1991	£6	£2.50	

APOLLOS

Rocking Horse	7"	Mercury	AMT1096	1960	£5	£2	

APOSTLES

Hour Of Prayer	LP	Sound Recording	1245		£75	£37.50	US

APOSTOLIC INTERVENTION

Steve Marriott and Ronnie Lane of the Small Faces wrote and produced the single by the Apostolic Intervention. When Marriott formed Humble Pie two years later, he called on the services of the group's drummer, Jerry Shirley.

Have You Ever Seen Me	7"	Immediate	IM043	1967	£125	£62.50	

APPALACHIANS

Bony Moronie	7"	HMV	POP1158	1963	£4	£1.50	

APPALOOSA

Appaloosa	LP	Columbia	CS9819	1971	£20	£8	US

APPELL, DAVE

Alone Together	LP	Cameo	C1004	1959	£40	£20	US
Happy Jose	7"	Columbia	DB4763	1962	£5	£2	

APPELL, DAVE & APPLEJACKS

Applejack	7"	Columbia	DB3894	1957	£40	£20	
Smarter	7"	Brunswick	05396	1955	£15	£7.50	

APPLE

Apple A Day	LP	Page One	POLS016	1968	**£500**	**£330**	
Dr Rock	7"	Page One	POF110	1968	**£50**	**£25**	
Let's Take A Trip Down The Rhine	7"	Page One	POF101	1968	**£50**	**£25**	
Thank U Very Much	7"	Smash	2143	1968	**£50**	**£25**	US

APPLEJACKS

Applejacks	LP	Decca	LK4635	1964	**£75**	**£37.50**	
Chim Chim Cheree	7"	Decca	F12050	1965	**£75**	**£37.50**	
I Go To Sleep	7"	Decca	F12216	1965	**£10**	**£5**	
I'm Through	7"	Decca	F12301	1965	**£5**	**£2**	
It's Not A Game	7"	Decca	F12106	1965	**£6**	**£2.50**	
Three Little Words	7"	Decca	F11981	1964	**£4**	**£1.50**	
You've Been Cheatin'	7"	CBS	202615	1967	**£8**	**£4**	

APPLEJACKS (2)

Circle Dance	7"	Top Rank	JAR273	1960	**£5**	**£2**	
Mexican Hat Rock	7"	London	HLU8753	1958	**£10**	**£5**	
Mexican Hat Rock	7"	London	HL7063	1958	**£6**	**£2.50**	*export*
Rock A Conga	7"	London	HLU8806	1959	**£10**	**£5**	

APPLETREE THEATRE

Playback	LP	MGM	2353051	1972	**£12**	**£5**	
Playback	LP	Polydor	2353051	1968	**£20**	**£8**	

APPLEWHITE, CHARLIE

Blue Star	7"	Brunswick	05416	1955	**£10**	**£5**	

AQUARIAN AGE

This is the first version of a song that Twink – drummer with the Pretty Things and the Pink Fairies and main performer here – later re-recorded for his *Think Pink* album.

Ten Thousand Words In A Cardboard Box	7"	Parlophone	R5700	1968	**£60**	**£30**	

AQUARIANS

Circy Cap	7"	Ackee	ACK135	1971	**£6**	**£2.50**	
Rebel	7"	Ackee	ACK137	1971	**£6**	**£2.50**	

AQUATONES

Aquatones Sing	LP	Fargo	FLP3001	1964	**£125**	**£62.50**	US
You	7"	London	HLO8631	1958	**£30**	**£15**	

AQUILA

Aquila	LP	RCA	SF8126	1970	**£30**	**£15**	

AR LOG

Ar Log	LP	Dingles	DIN305	1979	**£10**	**£4**	
Ar Log II	LP	Dingles	DIN310	1980	**£10**	**£4**	
Ar Log II	LP	Sain	1187M	1980	**£12**	**£5**	
Ar Log III	LP	Dingles	DIN315	1981	**£10**	**£4**	
Ar Log III	LP	Sain	1218M	1981	**£12**	**£5**	
Celtic Folk Festival	LP		CAL30588		**£15**	**£6**	
Meillionen	LP	Dingles	DID715	1983	**£10**	**£4**	
Pedwar	LP	Recordiau Ar Log	RAL001	1985	**£10**	**£4**	
Rhwng Hwyl A Thaith	LP	Sain	1252M	1982	**£12**	**£5**	
Yma O Hyd	LP	Sain	1275M	1983	**£12**	**£5**	

ARABIS

Jump High Jump Low	7"	Doctor Bird	DB1204	1969	**£8**	**£4**	

ARANBEE POP SYMPHONY ORCHESTRA

Today's Pop Symphony	LP	Immediate	IMLP/IMSP003	1966	**£125**	**£62.50**	

ARBETE & FRITID

Arbete & Fritid	LP	Sonet	SLP2513	1970	**£25**	**£10**	*Swedish*
Arbete Och Fritid	LP	MNW	MNW39P	1973	**£15**	**£6**	*Swedish*
Se Danser Vi Nt	LP	MNW	KRLP3	1973	**£12**	**£5**	*Swedish double*
Se Up For Livat	LP	MNW	MNW75P	1975	**£12**	**£5**	*Swedish double*
Ur Spar	LP	MNW	MNW5F	1975	**£15**	**£6**	*Swedish*

ARC

Arc At This	LP	Decca	SKLR5077	1971	**£30**	**£15**	

ARC (2)

Tribute	7"	Orchrist	ORC1	1980	**£40**	**£20**	

ARCADIA

Arcadia	video	PMI	MVP9911382	1987	**£20**	**£10**	
Election Day	12"	EMI	12NSRX1	1985	**£50**	**£25**	*promo*
Election Day	12"	EMI	12NSR1	1985	**£15**	**£7.50**	*promo, foil picture sleeve*
Election Day (Cryptic Cut)	12"	EMI	12NSRA1	1985	**£10**	**£5**	
Election Day (Re-election Day)	12"	EMI	PSLP393	1985	**£30**	**£15**	*1 sided promo*
Promise	12"	EMI	12NSR2	1986	**£6**	**£2.50**	*with poster*
Say The Word	12"	Atlantic	PR939	1986	**£75**	**£37.50**	*US promo*

ARCADIUM

Title	Format	Label	Cat. No.	Year	Mint	Good	Notes
Breathe Awhile	LP	Middle Earth	MDLS302	1969	**£250**	**£150**	
Sing My Song	7"	Middle Earth	MDS102	1969	**£20**	**£10**	

ARCHITECTS OF DISASTER

Title	Format	Label	Cat. No.	Year	Mint	Good	Notes
Cucumber Sandwich	7"	Neuter	NEU1	1982	**£5**	**£2**	*with insert, polythene bag*

ARCOCHA, JUAN & LESLIE MACKENZIE

Title	Format	Label	Cat. No.	Year	Mint	Good	Notes
Book Of Am: Part One	LP	Labo Lab	LTM1016	1978	**£75**	**£37.50**	*French*

ARDEN, TONI

Title	Format	Label	Cat. No.	Year	Mint	Good	Notes
Little By Little	7"	Brunswick	05645	1957	**£4**	**£1.50**	

ARDLEY, NEIL

The high prices being fetched by British jazz albums from the sixties and early seventies reflects the fact that, with many of the same musicians being involved in both jazz and rock recordings, LPs like those of Neil Ardley are very much part of the progressive rock scene. Certainly, drummer Jon Hiseman viewed his role within Neil Ardley's big band as being no different from that in his own group, Colosseum (most of whose members also played with Neil Ardley). Side two of *Symphony of Amaranths* includes, by way of a contrast, the delightfully eccentric Ivor Cutler reciting Edward Lear's 'The Dong With The Luminous Nose', with Ardley's band performing a suitable accompaniment.

Title	Format	Label	Cat. No.	Year	Mint	Good	Notes
Déjeuner Sur L'Herbe	LP	Verve	SVLP9236	1969	**£100**	**£50**	
Greek Variations	LP	Columbia	SCX6414	1970	**£100**	**£50**	*with Ian Carr and Don Rendell*
Mediterranean Intrigue	LP	KPM	KPM1084	1971	**£25**	**£10**	*B side by John Leach*
Symphony Of Amaranths	LP	Regal Zonophone	SLRZ1028	1972	**£100**	**£50**	
Western Reunion London 1965	LP	Decca	LK/SKL4690	1965	**£100**	**£50**	
Will Power	LP	Argo	ZDA164/5	1974	**£150**	**£75**	*double, with Ian Carr and Mike Gibbs*

ARDO DOMBEC

Title	Format	Label	Cat. No.	Year	Mint	Good	Notes
Ardo Dombec	LP	BASF	2021095	1971	**£15**	**£6**	*German*

AREA

Title	Format	Label	Cat. No.	Year	Mint	Good	Notes
Arbeit Macht Frei	LP	Cramps	5205101	1973	**£12**	**£5**	*Italian*
Areazione	LP	Cramps	5205104	1975	**£12**	**£5**	*Italian*
Caution Nacht Frei	LP	Cramps	5205102	1974	**£12**	**£5**	*Italian*
Crac	LP	Cramps	5205103	1975	**£12**	**£5**	*Italian*
Maledetti	LP	Cramps	5205105	1976	**£12**	**£5**	*Italian*

ARENA TWINS

Title	Format	Label	Cat. No.	Year	Mint	Good	Notes
Mama, Care Mama	7"	London	HL7071	1959	**£10**	**£5**	*export*

ARGENT

Argent was formed by the Zombies' keyboard player, Rod Argent, and the group's first LP takes the earlier group's posthumous hit, 'Time Of The Season', as a stylistic jumping-off point. *Argent* emerges, in effect, as the follow up to the Zombies' excellent *Odessey and Oracle*. Subsequent Argent releases were less distinctive, although the group was quite successful in sales terms. Rod Argent's colleagues included Russ Ballard and Bob Henrit, both of whom had been members of the Roulettes.

Title	Format	Label	Cat. No.	Year	Mint	Good	Notes
Argent	LP	CBS	63781	1970	**£10**	**£4**	
In Deep	LP	Epic	Q65475	1974	**£10**	**£4**	*quad*

ARGONAUTS

Title	Format	Label	Cat. No.	Year	Mint	Good	Notes
Apeman	7"	Lyntone	LYN18249/50	1986	**£6**	**£2.50**	

ARGOSY

Title	Format	Label	Cat. No.	Year	Mint	Good	Notes
Mr Boyd	7"	DJM	DJS214	1969	**£4**	**£1.50**	

ARIEL

Ariel was the first group formed by Tom Rowlands, now known as one half of the Chemical Brothers, who played guitar in the line-up.

Title	Format	Label	Cat. No.	Year	Mint	Good	Notes
Let It Slide	CD-s	DeConstruction	74321134512	1993	**£25**	**£12.50**	
Rollercoaster	12"	DeConstruction	PT44888	1991	**£25**	**£12.50**	
Rollercoaster	7"	DeConstruction	PB44887	1991	**£20**	**£10**	
Rollercoaster	CD-s	DeConstruction	PD44888	1991	**£25**	**£12.50**	
Sea Of Beats	12"	Eastern Bloc	CREED8T	1991	**£40**	**£20**	
Sea Of Beats	12"	private		1990	**£50**	**£25**	
T-Baby	12"	DeConstruction	AR2	1994	**£25**	**£12.50**	*promo*

ARISTOCATS

Title	Format	Label	Cat. No.	Year	Mint	Good	Notes
Boogie And Blues	LP	Hifi	R610		**£75**	**£37.50**	*US*

ARISTOCRATS

Title	Format	Label	Cat. No.	Year	Mint	Good	Notes
Girl With The Laughing Eyes	7"	Oriole	CB1928	1964	**£5**	**£2**	

ARIZONA SWAMP COMPANY

With their hit-making days some way behind them, the Nashville Teens tried an experimental name change: sadly to no great effect.

Title	Format	Label	Cat. No.	Year	Mint	Good	Notes
Train Keeps Rollin'	7"	Parlophone	R5841	1970	**£20**	**£10**	

ARKTIS

Title	Format	Label	Cat. No.	Year	Mint	Good	Notes
Arktis	LP	Bonnbons	BBR4040	1974	**£60**	**£30**	*German*
Arktis Tapes	LP	Bonnbons	BBR7502	1975	**£40**	**£20**	*German*

ARKUS

Title	Format	Label	Cat. No.	Year	Mint	Good	Notes
1914	LP	Arkus		1981	**£15**	**£6**	*Dutch*

ARLEN, STEVE

That's Love	7"	Melodisc	1458	1958	£6	£2.50	

ARLON, DEKE

Can't Make Up My Mind	7"	Columbia	DB7194	1964	£20	£10	
Hard Times For Young Lovers	7"	Columbia	DB7841	1966	£4	£1.50	
I Need You	7"	HMV	POP1340	1964	£15	£7.50	
If I Didn't Have A Dime	7"	Columbia	DB7487	1965	£5	£2	
Little Piece Of Paper	7"	Columbia	DB7753	1965	£4	£1.50	

ARMAGEDDON

Armageddon	LP	A&M	AMLH64513	1975	£25	£10	

ARMAGEDDON (2)

Armageddon	LP	Amos	AA37009	1969	£25	£10	US

ARMAGEDDON (3)

Armageddon	LP	Kuckuck	2375003	1970	£60	£30	German

ARMATRADING, JOAN

Compact Hits	CD-s	A&M	AMCD903	1988	£5	£2	
Live At The Bijou, Philadelphia	LP	A&M	SP8414	1977	£25	£10	US promo
Talk Under Ladders	LP	A&M	SAMP12	1981	£12	£5	promo

ARMENIAN JAZZ QUARTET

Harem Dance	7"	London	HLR8454	1957	£8	£4	

ARMS, RUSSELL

Cinco Robes	7"	London	HL7018	1957	£5	£2	export
Cinco Robles	7"	London	HLB8406	1957	£8	£4	

ARMS & LEGS

Heat Of The Night	7"	MAM	MAM147	1976	£5	£2	
Is There Any More Wine	7"	MAM	MAM156	1977	£5	£2	
Janice	7"	MAM	MAM140	1976	£5	£2	

ARMSTRONG, FRANKIE

And The Music Plays So Grand	LP	Briar	SBR4211	1980	£10	£4	US
Lovely On The Water	LP	Topic	12TS216	1972	£10	£4	

ARMSTRONG, FRANKIE, KATHY HENDERSON, SANDRA KERR, ALISON McMORLAND

My Song Is My Own	LP	Plane	TPL0001	1979	£12	£5	

ARMSTRONG, JACK

Celebrated Minstrel	LP	Saydisc	SDL252	1974	£12	£5	
Northumbrian Pipe Music	7" EP	Beltona	SEP43	1957	£25	£12.50	

ARMSTRONG, JACK & PATRICIA JENNINGS

Northumbrian Small Pipes	LP	Morton	MTN3073	1969	£10	£4	

ARMSTRONG, LOUIS

Ambassador Satch	LP	Philips	BBL7091	1956	£10	£4	
At Pasadena	LP	Brunswick	LAT8019	1952	£12	£5	
At Symphony Hall Vol. 1	LP	Brunswick	LAT8017	1952	£12	£5	
At Symphony Hall Vol. 2	LP	Brunswick	LAT8018	1952	£12	£5	
At The Crescendo Vol. 1	LP	Brunswick	LAT8084	1956	£15	£6	
At The Crescendo Vol. 2	LP	Brunswick	LAT8085	1956	£15	£6	
Basin Street Blues	10" LP	Brunswick	LA8691	1954	£12	£5	
Basin Street Blues	7"	Brunswick	05303	1954	£5	£2	
Blueberry Hill	10" LP	Brunswick	LA8700	1955	£12	£5	
Chicago Breakdown	7"	Columbia	SCM5118	1954	£5	£2	
Christmas Night In Harlem	7"	Brunswick	05505	1955	£5	£2	
Classics	10" LP	Brunswick	LA8528	1951	£12	£5	
I'm Not Rough	7"	Columbia	SCM5142	1954	£5	£2	
I've Got The World On A String	LP	HMV	CLP1388/ CSD1317	1960	£15	£6	
Jazz Classics	10" LP	Brunswick	LA8597	1953	£12	£5	
Jazz Concert	10" LP	Brunswick	LA8534	1951	£12	£5	
Jazzin' With Armstrong	10" LP	Columbia	33S1007	1953	£12	£5	
King Of The Zulus	7"	Columbia	SCM5061	1953	£5	£2	
Ko Ko Mo	7"	Brunswick	05400	1955	£5	£2	
Laughin' Louis	10" LP	HMV	DLP1036	1954	£12	£5	
Louis And The Good Book	LP	Brunswick	LAT8270	1958	£12	£5	
Louis Armstrong	10" LP	Columbia	33S1069	1955	£12	£5	
Louis Armstrong And Earl Hines	LP	Philips	BBL7046	1955	£10	£4	
Louis Armstrong And His Hot Five	10" LP	Fontana	TFR6003	1958	£10	£4	
Louis Armstrong And His Hot Five	LP	Columbia	33SX1029	1954	£12	£5	
Louis Armstrong Andf His Hot Seven	10" LP	Columbia	33S1041	1954	£12	£5	
Louis Armstrong Story Vol. 1	LP	Philips	BBL7134	1957	£12	£5	
Louis Armstrong Story Vol. 2	LP	Philips	BBL7189	1958	£12	£5	
Louis Under The Stars	LP	HMV	CLP1247	1959	£15	£6	
Meets Oscar Peterson	LP	HMV	CLP1328	1960	£15	£6	
Musical Autobiography	LP	Brunswick	LAT8211-14	1958	£40	£20	4 LPs, boxed
New Orleans Days	10" LP	Brunswick	LA8537	1952	£12	£5	
New York Town Hall Concert 1947	10" LP	HMV	DLP1015	1953	£12	£5	
Plays The Blues	10" LP	London	AL3501	1953	£15	£6	
Plays W. C. Handy	LP	Philips	BBL7017	1955	£10	£4	

Rendezvous At The Sunset Café	10" LP	Columbia	33S1058	1955	**£12**	**£5**	
Satch Plays Fats	LP	Philips	BBL7064	1956	**£10**	**£4**	
Satchmo Plays King Oliver	LP	Audio Fidelity	AFLP1930/ AFSD5930	1960	**£10**	**£4**	
Satchmo Serenades	10" LP	Brunswick	LA8679	1954	**£12**	**£5**	
Satchmo Session	10" LP	HMV	DLP1105	1955	**£12**	**£5**	
Satchmo Sings	LP	Brunswick	LAT8243	1958	**£15**	**£6**	
Satchmo The Great	LP	Philips	BBL7216	1958	**£10**	**£4**	
We Have All The Time In The World	7"	United Artists	UP35059	1969	**£15**	**£7.50**	
We Have All The Time In The World	7"	United Artists	UA3172	1969	**£25**	**£12.50**	*picture sleeve*
We Have All The Time In The World	7"	United Artists	JB001	1969	**£15**	**£7.50**	*1 sided promo*

ARMY

The solitary single recorded by the Army features guitarist Adrian Utley, who re-emerged some thirteen years later as a member of Portishead.

Kick It Down	7"	Map	MAP3	1981	**£10**	**£5**	

ARMY OF LOVERS

Love Me Like A Loaded Gun	12"	Ton Son Ton	SONL7	1988	**£8**	**£4**	
Love Me Like A Loaded Gun	7"	Ton Son Ton	SON7	1988	**£4**	**£1.50**	

ARNAU, B. J.

Live And Let Die	7"	RCA	RCA2365	1973	**£5**	**£2**	

ARNELL, GINNY

Carnival	7"	Brunswick	05836	1960	**£5**	**£2**	
Just Like A Boy	7"	MGM	MGM1270	1965	**£5**	**£2**	
Little Bit Of Love	7"	MGM	MGM1270	1965	**£4**	**£1.50**	

ARNEZ, CHICO

From Chico With Love	LP	Columbia	SX/SCX6265	1968	**£10**	**£4**	
This Is Chico	LP	Pye	NPL18035	1959	**£20**	**£8**	
Yashmak	7"	Pye	7N15196	1959	**£20**	**£10**	

ARNOLD, BOB

Mornin' All	LP	Argo	ZFB83	1972	**£10**	**£4**	*with the Yetties*

ARNOLD, EDDIE

All-Time Favorites	10" LP	RCA	LPM3117	1953	**£20**	**£8**	*US*
All-Time Favorites	LP	RCA	LPM1223	1955	**£15**	**£6**	*US*
All-Time Hits From The Hills	10" LP	RCA	LPM3031	1952	**£20**	**£8**	*US*
American Institution	10" LP	RCA	LPM3230	1954	**£20**	**£8**	*US*
Anytime	10" LP	RCA	LPM3027	1952	**£20**	**£8**	*US*
Anytime	LP	RCA	LPM1224	1955	**£15**	**£6**	*US*
Chapel On The Hill	10" LP	RCA	LPM3219	1954	**£20**	**£8**	*US*
Chapel On The Hill	7" EP	HMV	7EG8080	1955	**£10**	**£5**	
Chapel On The Hill	LP	RCA	LPM1225	1955	**£15**	**£6**	*US*
Dozen Hits	LP	RCA	LPM1293	1956	**£15**	**£6**	*US*
Eddie Arnold	7" EP	HMV	7EG8020	1954	**£10**	**£5**	
Free Home Demonstrations	7"	HMV	7MC16	1954	**£6**	**£2.50**	*export*
Gonna Find Me A Bluebird	7"	RCA	RCA1008	1957	**£4**	**£1.50**	
Have Guitar, Will Travel	LP	RCA	LPM/LSP1928	1959	**£12**	**£5**	*US*
Hep Cat Baby	7"	HMV	7MC22	1954	**£6**	**£2.50**	*export*
In Time	7"	HMV	7MC32	1955	**£6**	**£2.50**	*export*
Little On The Lonely Side	LP	RCA	LPM1377	1956	**£15**	**£6**	*US*
My Darling, My Darling	LP	RCA	LPM1575	1957	**£15**	**£6**	*US*
Praise Him, Praise Him	LP	RCA	LPM1733	1958	**£12**	**£5**	*US*
Prayer	7"	HMV	7MC10	1954	**£6**	**£2.50**	*export*
Richest Man	7"	HMV	7M339	1955	**£4**	**£1.50**	
Second Fling	7"	HMV	7MC19	1954	**£6**	**£2.50**	*export*
Tennessee Stud	7"	RCA	RCA1138	1959	**£4**	**£1.50**	
Thereby Hangs A Tale	LP	RCA	RD27155	1959	**£10**	**£4**	
Wanderin'	LP	RCA	LPM1111	1955	**£15**	**£6**	*US*
When They Were Young	LP	RCA	LPM1484	1957	**£15**	**£6**	*US*

ARNOLD, KOKOMO

Kokomo Arnold	LP	Saydisc	SDR163	1969	**£15**	**£6**	

ARNOLD, P. P.

Pat Arnold tried hard for solo success with a number of releases on the Immediate label. Despite producing several fondly remembered tracks, however, it was her backing group, the Nice, that achieved the most success. P. P. Arnold returned to session work, although she achieved a brief revival at the end of the eighties. She had originally been a member of Ike and Tina Turner's backing group, the Ikettes.

Angel Of The Morning	7"	Immediate	IM067	1968	**£4**	**£1.50**	
Everything's Gonna Be Alright	7"	Immediate	IM040	1966	**£50**	**£25**	
First Cut Is The Deepest	7"	Immediate	IM047	1967	**£4**	**£1.50**	
First Cut Is The Deepest	7" EP	Columbia	ESRF1877	1967	**£15**	**£7.50**	*French*
First Lady Of Immediate	LP	Immediate	IMLP/IMSP11	1967	**£30**	**£15**	
If You Think You're Groovy	7"	Immediate	IM061	1968	**£4**	**£1.50**	
Kafunta	LP	Immediate	IMSP17	1968	**£20**	**£8**	
Time Has Come	7"	Immediate	IM055	1967	**£4**	**£1.50**	

ARNOLD, PAUL

Bon Soir Dame	7"	Pye	7N17473	1968	**£4**	**£1.50**	
Somewhere In A Rainbow	7"	Pye	7N17317	1967	**£4**	**£1.50**	

ARROWS

Title	Format	Label	Cat. No.	Year	Mint	VG	Notes
Apache '65	7"	Capitol	CL15386	1965	**£4**	**£1.50**	
Apache '65	7" EP	Capitol	EAP60000	1965	**£10**	**£5**	*French*

ARS NOVA

Title	Format	Label	Cat. No.	Year	Mint	VG	Notes
Ars Nova	LP	Elektra	EKS74020	1968	**£10**	**£4**	
Sunshine And Shadows	LP	Atlantic	588196	1969	**£10**	**£4**	

ART

When Chris Blackwell of Island records decided to expand his sphere of operations by entering the rock market place, he demonstrated from the start a remarkable sureness of touch in his decisions regarding which artists to sign. If Island albums seldom reach the high prices regularly achieved by Vertigo and Deram releases, then that is not because their music is uninteresting, but because the company was rather more successful at selling it. The Art LP is a relative obscurity, however, perhaps because the group itself immediately added an extra member and mutated into the rather better-known Spooky Tooth.

Title	Format	Label	Cat. No.	Year	Mint	VG	Notes
Supernatural Fairytales	LP	Island	ILP967	1975	**£12**	**£5**	*pink rim label*
Supernatural Fairytales	LP	Island	ILP967	1968	**£60**	**£30**	*pink label*
What's That Sound	7"	Island	WIP6019	1967	**£10**	**£5**	
What's That Sound	7"	Island	WIP6224	1975	**£4**	**£1.50**	

ART ATTACKS

Title	Format	Label	Cat. No.	Year	Mint	VG	Notes
I Am A Dalek	7"	Albatross	TIT1	1978	**£10**	**£5**	
Punk Rock Stars	7"	Fresh	FRESH3	1979	**£8**	**£4**	

ART BEARS

Title	Format	Label	Cat. No.	Year	Mint	VG	Notes
Coda To Man And Boy	7"	Recommended	RE+H	1981	**£8**	**£4**	*1 side painted*
Hopes And Fears	LP	Recommended	RE2188	1978	**£15**	**£6**	*2 different covers*
Winter Songs	LP	Recommended	RE0618	1979	**£15**	**£6**	
World As It Is Today	LP	Recommended	RE6622	1981	**£15**	**£6**	

ART ENSEMBLE OF CHICAGO

The musicians of the Art Ensemble combined virtuoso avant-garde playing with a highly developed sense of theatricality to emerge as one of the premier jazz groups of the seventies and beyond. Saxophonists Joseph Jarman and Roscoe Mitchell have solo albums listed in the *Guide*, while trumpeter Lester Bowie has appeared on numerous records over the years, including several of his own and one by his namesake, David Bowie. The trumpeter's wife, Fontella Bass, scored a big hit in the sixties with 'Rescue Me' and appears on a couple of the albums made by the Art Ensemble.

Title	Format	Label	Cat. No.	Year	Mint	VG	Notes
Bap Tizum	LP	Atlantic	SD1639	1973	**£15**	**£6**	*US*
Certain Blacks	LP	America	30AM6098	1970	**£25**	**£10**	*French*
Chi Congo	LP	Paula	LPS4001	1970	**£20**	**£8**	*US*
Fanfare For The Warriors	LP	Atlantic	SD1651	1974	**£15**	**£6**	*US*
Jackson In Your House	LP	BYG	529302	1969	**£25**	**£10**	*French*
Kabalaba	LP	AECO		1974	**£15**	**£6**	*US*
Les Stances A Sophie	LP	Nessa	N4	1970	**£40**	**£20**	*US*
Live At Mundell Hall	LP	Delmark	DS432/3	1975	**£20**	**£8**	*US double*
Message To Our Folks	LP	BYG	529328	1969	**£25**	**£10**	*French*
People In Sorrow	LP	Nessa	N3	1969	**£25**	**£10**	*US*
Phase One	LP	Prestige	PR10064	1971	**£20**	**£8**	*US*
Rees And The Smooth Ones	LP	BYG		1969	**£25**	**£10**	*French*
Spiritual	LP	Polydor	2383098	1974	**£12**	**£5**	
With Fontella Bass	LP	America	30AM6117	1972	**£25**	**£10**	*French*

ART MOVEMENT

Title	Format	Label	Cat. No.	Year	Mint	VG	Notes
Game Of Love	7"	Decca	F12768	1968	**£4**	**£1.50**	

ART NOUVEAUX

Title	Format	Label	Cat. No.	Year	Mint	VG	Notes
Extra Terrestrial Visitations	7"	Fontana	TF483	1964	**£8**	**£4**	

ART OF LOVIN'

Title	Format	Label	Cat. No.	Year	Mint	VG	Notes
Art Of Lovin'	LP	Mainstream	6613	1968	**£30**	**£15**	*US*

ART OF NOISE

Title	Format	Label	Cat. No.	Year	Mint	VG	Notes
Couldn't Say Goodbye	CD-s	Dover	ROJCD10	1991	**£5**	**£2**	*with Tom Jones*
Kiss	CD-s	China	CHICD11	1988	**£5**	**£2**	*with Tom Jones*
Paranoimia '89	CD-s	China	CHICD14	1989	**£5**	**£2**	
Yebo	CD-s	China	CHICD18	1989	**£5**	**£2**	*with Mahotella Queens*

ART SCIENCE TECHNOLOGY

Title	Format	Label	Cat. No.	Year	Mint	VG	Notes
A.S.T.	12"	Debut	DEBTX3100	1990	**£8**	**£4**	

ART ZOYD

Title	Format	Label	Cat. No.	Year	Mint	VG	Notes
Manege	7"	Recommended	RR14.15	1982	**£8**	**£4**	*1 side painted*

ARTERY

Title	Format	Label	Cat. No.	Year	Mint	VG	Notes
Mother Moon	7"	Limited Edition	TAKE1	1979	**£8**	**£4**	
Unbalanced	7"	Aardvark	STEAL3	1980	**£6**	**£2.50**	*double*

ARTHUR

Title	Format	Label	Cat. No.	Year	Mint	VG	Notes
Dreams And Images	LP	LHI	12000	1968	**£25**	**£10**	*US*

ARTHUR, DAVE & TONI

Title	Format	Label	Cat. No.	Year	Mint	VG	Notes
Bushes And Briars	7"	Trailer	LER1	1970	**£4**	**£1.50**	
Hearken To The Witches' Rune	LP	Trailer	LER2017	1970	**£30**	**£15**	
Lark In The Morning	LP	Topic	12T190	1969	**£25**	**£10**	

Morning Stands On Tiptoe	LP	Transatlantic	TRA154	1967	£30	£15	
Sing A Story	LP	Decca	SPA509	1977	£10	£4	

ARTHURS, ANDY

I Can Detect You For A Million Miles	7"	Radar	ADA7	1978	£8	£4	

ARTI & MESTIERI

Tilt	LP	Cramps	5501	1974	£12	£5	*Italian*

ARTISTICS

Girl I Need you	7"	Coral	Q72492	1967	£15	£7.50	
I'm Gonna Miss You	7"	Coral	Q72488	1966	£15	£7.50	

ARTWOODS

The Artwoods were typical of the many R&B and beat groups that spent years slogging round the British club circuit without ever really gaining much success. Unlike many, however, two of the group's members did achieve success later – drummer Keef Hartley, who used his stint with John Mayall's Bluesbreakers as a springboard to forming his own band; and organist Jon Lord, the founder member of Deep Purple and Whitesnake. As for poor Art Wood himself, he has been rather eclipsed by his more famous brother, Ron Wood.

Art Gallery	LP	Decca	LK4830	1966	£300	£180	
Art Gallery	LP	Eclipse	ECS2025	1974	£40	£20	
Artwoods	LP	Spark	SRLM2006	1973	£25	£10	
Goodbye Sisters	7"	Decca	F12206	1965	£50	£25	
I Feel Good	7"	Decca	F12465	1966	£50	£25	
I Take What I Want	7"	Decca	F12384	1966	£50	£25	
Jazz In Jeans	7" EP	Decca	DFE8654	1966	£300	£180	*best auctioned*
Oh My Love	7"	Decca	F12091	1965	£50	£25	
Oh My Love	7" EP	Decca	457076	1965	£300	£180	*French*
Sweet Mary	7"	Decca	F12015	1964	£50	£25	
What Shall I Do	7"	Parlophone	R5590	1967	£75	£37.50	

ARZACHEL

The Arzachel LP only received a limited release, but it is a fine and innovative recording – despite being recorded to order on a very tight budget. As would be expected from the musicians involved – guitarist Steve Hillage and keyboard wizard Dave Stewart, with Clive Brooks and Hugh Montgomery-Campbell in support. In other words, this is Egg, augmented by guitar. At least one reference book lists an entirely different personnel for the group – these names are taken from the record's sleeve, which includes a set of biographies that are clearly intended as a gentle leg-pull!

Arzachel	LP	Evolution	Z1003	1969	£250	£150	
Arzachel	LP	Roulette	SR42036	1969	£50	£25	*US*

ASGARD

In The Realm Of Asgard	LP	Threshold	THS6	1972	£30	£15	

ASH

Angel Interceptor	7"	Infectious	INFECT27C	1995	£8	£4	*blue vinyl promo*
Angel Interceptor	7"	Infectious	INFECT27J	1995	£5	£2	*juke box issue*
Get Ready	7"	Fantastic Plastic	FP004	1995	£6	£2.50	*red vinyl*
Girl From Mars	CD-s	Infectious	INFECT24CD	1995	£5	£2	*promo, with dust jacket*
Jack Names The Planets	7"	La La Land	LALA001	1994	£10	£5	
Kung Fu	7"	Infectious	INFECT21J	1995	£6	£2.50	
Kung Fu	7"	Infectious	INFECT21C	1995	£8	£4	*red vinyl promo*
Petrol	7"	Infectious	INFECT13S	1994	£12	£6	
Trailer	LP	Infectious	INFECT14LP	1994	£20	£8	*with yellow vinyl 7"*
Uncle Pat	7"	Infectious	INFECT16S	1994	£12	£6	

ASH, MARVIN

New Orleans At Midnight	LP	Brunswick	LAT8191	1957	£12	£5	

ASH, VIC

Hoagy	7" EP	Nixa	NJE1002	1956	£10	£5	
Session For Four	7" EP	Polygon	JTE100	1955	£10	£5	
Vic Ash And Four	7" EP	Nixa	NJE1032	1956	£10	£5	

ASH RA TEMPLE

Although synthesizer pioneer Klaus Schulze was involved in the group in the early days, Ash Ra Temple is essentially a vehicle for the playing of German guitarist Manuel Göttsching. Using an E-bow to generate infinite sustain and a fluent playing technique, Göttsching seeks to emulate on guitar what groups like Tangerine Dream and Kraftwerk achieve with synthesizers. Later albums on the Virgin label are quite common and do not qualify for inclusion here, but the early records are becoming increasingly sought after.

Ash Ra Temple	LP	Ohr	OMM556013	1971	£30	£15	*German*
Discover Music	LP	Ohr	940101/02X	1977	£40	£20	*French double*
Inventions For Electric Guitar	LP	Komische	KM58015	1975	£20	£8	*German*
Join In	LP	Ohr	OMM556032	1973	£25	£10	*German*
Schwingungen	LP	Ohr	OMM556020	1972	£30	£15	*German*
Seven Up	LP	Komische	KK58001	1973	£25	£10	*German, with Timothy Leary*
Starring Rosi	LP	Komische	KM58007	1973	£25	£10	*German*

ASHBY, HAROLD

Born To Swing	LP	Columbia	33SX1257	1960	£10	£4	

ASHBY, IRVING

Big Guitar	7"	London	HLP8578	1958	£12	£6	

ASHCROFT, JOHNNY

Little Boy Lost .... 7" .... HMV .... POP759 .... 1960 **£5** .... **£2** ....

ASHCROFT, STEVE

Keys Of Tomorrow .... LP .... Wild Dog .... DOGLR15 .... 1978 **£20** .... **£8** ....

ASHES

Ashes .... LP .... Vault .... 125 .... 1966 **£30** .... **£15** .... *US*

ASHKAN

In From The Cold .... LP .... Nova .... (S)RNR1 .... 1970 **£50** .... **£25** ....

ASHLEY, STEVE

Stroll On .... LP .... Gull .... GULP1003 .... 1974 **£10** .... **£4** ....

ASHMAN, MICKEY

Taking The Mickey .... LP .... Pye .... NJL25 .... 1960 **£20** .... **£8** ....
Through Darkest Ashman .... LP .... Pye .... NJL29 .... 1961 **£20** .... **£8** ....

ASHTON, BUD

More Swinging Guitars .... 7" EP .. Embassy .... WEP1088 .... 1963 **£5** .... **£2** ....
Swinging Guitars .... 7" EP .. Embassy .... WEP1058 .... 1961 **£5** .... **£2** ....

ASHTON, TONY

Celebration .... 7" .... Purple .... PUR109 .... 1972 **£4** .... **£1.50** ....

ASHTON & LORD

We're Gonna Make It .... 7" .... Purple .... PUR121 .... 1974 **£4** .... **£1.50** ....

ASIA

Asia .... LP .... Geffen .... GEF1185577 .... 1982 **£10** .... **£4** .... *picture disc*
Don't Cry .... 7" .... Geffen .... WA3580 .... 1982 **£4** .... **£1.50** .... *shaped picture disc*
Who Will Stop The Rain .... 10" .... Musidisc .... 109526 .... 1992 **£6** .... **£2.50** .... *picture disc*
Who Will Stop The Rain .... CD-s ... Musidisc .... 109522 .... 1992 **£5** .... **£2** ....

ASKEW, ED

Ed Askew .... LP .... Fontana .... STL5519 .... 1969 **£15** .... **£6** ....

ASKEY, ARTHUR

Hello Playmates .... 7" EP .. HMV .... 7EG8294 .... 1957 **£5** .... **£2** ....
Hello Playmates .... LP .... Oriole .... MG20017 .... 1957 **£12** .... **£5** ....

ASLAN

Paws For Thought .... LP .... Profile .... GMOR006 .... 1976 **£150** .... **£75** ....
Second Helpings .... LP .... Profile .... GMOR144 .... 1977 **£150** .... **£75** ....

ASMUSSEN, SVEND

Hot Fiddle .... 10" LP Parlophone .... CPMD1 .... 1955 **£20** .... **£8** ....

ASOKA

Asoka .... LP .... Sonet .... SLP2527 .... 1973 **£175** .. **£87.50** .... *Swedish*

ASPEY, GARY & VERA

From The North .... LP .... Topic .... 12TS255 .... 1975 **£10** .... **£4** ....
Taste Of Hotpot .... LP .... Topic .... 12TS299 .... 1976 **£10** .... **£4** ....

ASPEY, VERA

Blackbird .... LP .... Topic .... 12TS356 .... 1977 **£10** .... **£4** ....

ASPHALT RIBBONS

Good Love .... 7" .... In Tape .... IT068 .... 1989 **£8** .... **£4** ....
Good Love .... 7" .... In Tape .... ITTI068 .... 1989 **£10** .... **£5** ....
Old Horse .... LP .... ETT .... E1012 .... 1991 **£10** .... **£4** ....
Orchard .... 12" .... In Tape .... ITTI063 .... 1989 **£10** .... **£5** ....
Orchard .... 7" .... In Tape .... IT063 .... 1989 **£8** .... **£4** ....
Over Again .... 7" .... In Tape .... IT65451 .... 1989 **£8** .... **£4** .... *promo*
Passion, Coolness, Indifference .... 12" .... Lily .... LILY002 .... 1988 **£15** .... **£7.50** ....

ASQUITH, MARY

Closing Time .... LP .... Mother Earth ... MUM1204 .... 1978 **£60** .... **£30** ....

ASSAGAI

Assagai .... LP .... Vertigo .... 6360030 .... 1971 **£15** .... **£6** .... *spiral label*
Assagai II .... LP .... Vertigo .... 6360058 .... 1971 **£50** .... **£25** .... *test pressing*
Zimbabwe .... LP .... Philips .... 6308079 .... 1972 **£15** .... **£6** ....

ASSOCIATES

Affectionate Punch .... 7" .... Fiction .... FICS11 .... 1980 **£4** .... **£1.50** ....
Boys Keep Swinging .... 7" .... MCA .... MCA537 .... 1980 **£20** .... **£10** ....
Boys Keep Swinging .... 7" .... Double Hip .... DHR1 .... 1980 **£40** .... **£20** ....
Country Boy .... 12" .... WEA .... YZ329T .... 1988 **£50** .... **£25** .... *test pressing*
Country Boy .... CD-s ... WEA .... YZ329CD .... 1988 **£40** .... **£20** .... *3" single*
Fever .... CD-s ... Circa .... YRCD46 .... 1990 **£5** .... **£2** ....
Fire To Ice .... CD-s ... Circa .... YRCD49 .... 1990 **£5** .... **£2** ....
Heart Of Glass .... 12" .... WEA .... YZ310TX .... 1988 **£10** .... **£5** .... *with 3D glasses*
Heart Of Glass .... CD-s ... WEA .... YZ310CD .... 1988 **£5** .... **£2** ....
Just Can't Say Goodbye .... CD-s ... Circa .... YRCD56 .... 1991 **£5** .... **£2** ....

Peel Sessions	CD-s	Strange Fruit	SFPSCD075	1989	£5	£2	
Tell Me Easter's On Friday	7"	Beggars Banquet	BEG86	1984	£15	£7.50	test pressing
Wild And Lonely	CD-s	Circa	BILLY1	1990	£6	£2.50	album sampler

ASSOCIATION

Most of the successful Californian groups that emerged during the late sixties had backgrounds rooted in folk music and naturally tended to favour melodic material and close-harmony singing. The Association were very much a case in point, sustaining a six-year career on the back of four tuneful singles, which if not exactly classics, are at any rate fondly remembered. 'Along Comes Mary', 'Cherish', 'Windy', and 'Never My Love' are to be found scattered through their LP releases alongside similar fare, although, the vagaries of the pop charts being what they are, it was the much less well-known 'Time For Living' that scored in a small way in the UK.

Along Comes Mary	7"	London	HLT10054	1966	£4	£1.50	
And Then . . . Along Came Association	LP	London	HAT8305	1966	£15	£6	
Association	LP	Warner Bros	W(S)1800	1969	£10	£4	
Birthday	LP	Warner Bros	W(S)1733	1968	£10	£4	
Cherish	7" EP	Riviera	231209	1966	£10	£5	French
Goodbye Columbus	LP	Warner Bros	W(S)1786	1969	£10	£4	
Greatest Hits	LP	Warner Bros	W(S)1767	1969	£10	£4	
Insight Out	LP	London	HAT/SHT8342	1967	£15	£6	
Live	LP	Warner Bros	2WS1868	1970	£15	£6	US double
No Fair At All	7" EP	Riviera	231241	1967	£10	£5	French
Pandora's Golden Heebie Jeebies	7"	London	HLT10098	1966	£4	£1.50	
Renaissance	LP	London	HAT8313	1967	£15	£6	
Stop The Motor	LP	Warner Bros	WS1927	1971	£10	£4	US
Windy	7" EP	Riviera	231243	1967	£10	£5	French

ASSOCIATION P. C.

Earwax	LP	Munich	6802634	1969	£30	£15	Dutch

ASTAIRE, FRED

Funny Face	7"	HMV	POP337	1957	£4	£1.50	Audrey Hepburn B side
Mr Top Hat	LP	HMV	CLP1100	1956	£10	£4	with Oscar Peterson
Ritz Roll And Rock	7"	MGM	MGM964	1957	£8	£4	

ASTERIX

Asterix	LP	Decca	SLK16695P	1970	£10	£4	German
Everybody	7"	Decca	F13075	1970	£6	£2.50	

ASTLEY, EDWIN ORCHESTRA

Danger Man Theme	7"	RCA	RCA1492	1965	£40	£20	
Saint	LP	RCA	LPM/LSP3631	1966	£30	£15	US
Secret Agent (Danger Man)	LP	RCA	LPM/LSP3630	1966	£30	£15	US
Secret Agent Meets The Saint	LP	RCA	LPM/LSP3467	1965	£30	£15	US

ASTLEY, TED

Baron	7"	Decca	F12389	1966	£20	£10	

ASTORS

Candy	7"	Atlantic	AT4037	1965	£20	£10	

ASTRAL NAVIGATIONS

The music on the rare *Astral Navigations* album is actually the work of two different bands, who take a side each. Lightyears Away and Thundermother made no other records, although the guitarist with the former band was Bill Nelson. He has recorded prolifically since, as the leader of Bebop Deluxe and as a solo artist.

Astral Navigations	LP	Holyground	HG114	1971	£200	£100	
Astral Navigations	LP	Magic Mixture	MM2	1989	£20	£8	

ASTRONAUTS

Banana	7"	Hala Gala	HG14	196–	£6	£2.50	
Before You Leave	7"	Island	WI3065	1967	£5	£2	
Before You Leave	7"	Hala Gala	HG9	1966	£6	£2.50	
I'll Be There	7"	Hala Gala	HG13	196–	£6	£2.50	
Oh Why I Still Love You	7"	Hala Gala	HG12	196–	£6	£2.50	

ASTRONAUTS (2)

Go Go Go	LP	RCA	LPM/LSP3307	1965	£15	£6	US
Baja	7" EP	RCA	86328	1963	£15	£7.50	French
Baju	7"	RCA	RCA1349	1963	£15	£7.50	
Big Boss Man	7" EP	RCA	86367	1963	£15	£7.50	French
Competition Coupe	LP	RCA	LPM/LSP2858	1964	£20	£8	US
Down The Line	LP	RCA	LPM/LSP3454	1965	£15	£6	US
Everything Is A-OK	LP	RCA	LPM/LSP2782	1964	£20	£8	US
Favorites For You, Our Fans, From Us	LP	RCA	LPM/LSP3359	1965	£15	£6	US
I'm A Rollin' Stone	7" EP	RCA	86457	1964	£15	£7.50	French
Kuk	7" EP	RCA	86334	1963	£15	£7.50	French
Orbit Campus	LP	RCA	RD7662	1964	£30	£15	
Rockin' With The Astronauts	LP	RCA	PRM183	1964	£20	£8	US
Surf Party	LP	Stateside	SL10089	1964	£25	£10	with other artists
Surfin' With The Astronauts	LP	RCA	LPM/LSP2760	1963	£25	£10	US
Travelin' Men	LP	RCA	LPM/LSP3733	1967	£12	£5	US
Wild On The Beach	LP	RCA	LPM/LSP3441	1965	£15	£6	US
Wild Wild Winter	LP	Decca	DL(7)4699	1966	£15	£6	US

ASTRONAUTS (3)

Title	Format	Label	Number	Year	Mint	Excellent	Notes
All Night Party	7″	Bugle	BLAST1	1979	£8	£4	
It's All Done By Mirrors	LP	Bugle		1982	£25	£10	
Peter Pan Hits The Suburbs	LP	Bugle	GENIUS001	1981	£30	£15	
We Were Talking	7″	Bugle	BLAST5	1979	£5	£2	

AT LAST THE 1958 ROCK'N'ROLL SHOW

This single was the work of pianist Freddie Fingers Lee, whose backing group included future Mott The Hoople front-man, Ian Hunter.

Title	Format	Label	Number	Year	Mint	Excellent	Notes
I Can't Drive	7″	CBS	3349	1968	£12	£6	

ATACAMA

Title	Format	Label	Number	Year	Mint	Excellent	Notes
Atacama	LP	Charisma	CAS1039	1971	£10	£4	
Sun Burns Up Above	LP	Charisma	CAS1060	1972	£10	£4	

ATHENIANS

Title	Format	Label	Number	Year	Mint	Excellent	Notes
I've Got Love If You Want It	7″	Waverley	SLP532	1964	£40	£20	
I've Got Love If You Want It	7″	Waverley	SLP532	1964	£75	£37.50	*picture sleeve*
Thinking Of Our Love	7″	Waverley	SLP533	1965	£50	£25	*picture sleeve*
Thinking Of Your Love	7″	Waverley	SLP533	1965	£30	£15	
You Tell Me	7″	Edinburgh Students C	ESC1	1964	£75	£37.50	*picture sleeve*
You Tell Me	7″	Edinburgh Students C	ESC1	1964	£50	£25	

ATHENS, GLENN & THE TROJANS

Title	Format	Label	Number	Year	Mint	Excellent	Notes
Glenn Athens And The Trojans	7″ EP	Spot	7E1018	1965	£350	£210	*best auctioned*

ATILA

Title	Format	Label	Number	Year	Mint	Excellent	Notes
Intención	LP	BASF		1976	£125	£62.50	*Spanish*
Revlure	LP	Odeon		1978	£125	£62.50	*Spanish*

ATKIN, PETE

Pete Atkin was the author of some half-dozen LPs, whose stylish and intelligent singer-songwriting was somehow never as popular as it should have been. In the collectors' market too this remains the case, as such classics of the genre as *A King At Nightfall* and *The Road Of Silk* steadfastly refuse to fetch even moderate collectors' prices, despite being long deleted. Not that Atkin himself should worry, having forged a satisfying career as a television producer. The lyricist on the records has done rather well for himself too – his name is Clive James – yes, it is the same one!

Title	Format	Label	Number	Year	Mint	Excellent	Notes
Beware Of The Beautiful Stranger	LP	Fontana	6309011	1970	£10	£4	
Driving Through Mythical America	LP	Philips	6308070	1971	£10	£4	

ATKINS, CHET

Title	Format	Label	Number	Year	Mint	Excellent	Notes
At Home	LP	RCA	LPM1544	1957	£15	£6	*US*
Chet Atkins' Gallopin' Guitar	10″ LP	RCA	LPM3079	1952	£30	£15	*US*
Chet Atkins' Workshop	LP	RCA	RD27214	1960	£10	£4	
Finger Style Guitar	LP	RCA	LPM1383	1956	£15	£6	*US*
Guitar Genius	7″ EP	RCA	RCX7118	1963	£8	£4	
Hi Fi In Focus	LP	RCA	LPM1577	1957	£15	£6	*US*
In Three Dimensions	LP	RCA	LPM1197	1956	£15	£6	*US*
Other Chet Atkins	LP	RCA	RD27194	1960	£10	£4	
Picks On The Beatles	LP	RCA	RD/SF7813	1966	£10	£4	
Session With Chet Atkins	LP	RCA	LPM1090	1955	£15	£6	*US*
String Dustin'	10″ LP	RCA	LPM3167	1953	£25	£10	*US*
Stringin' Along	10″ LP	RCA	LPM3169	1953	£25	£10	*US*
Stringin' Along	LP	RCA	LPM1236	1956	£15	£6	*US*
Teensville	LP	RCA	RD27168	1960	£10	£4	

ATLANTIC BRIDGE

Title	Format	Label	Number	Year	Mint	Excellent	Notes
Atlantic Bridge	LP	Dawn	DNLS3014	1970	£12	£5	

ATLANTIC OCEAN

Title	Format	Label	Number	Year	Mint	Excellent	Notes
Tranquility Bay	LP	Love		1970	£60	£30	*Swedish*

ATLANTICS

Title	Format	Label	Number	Year	Mint	Excellent	Notes
Bomborra	LP	CBS	233066	1972	£15	£6	*Australian*

ATLANTIS

Title	Format	Label	Number	Year	Mint	Excellent	Notes
Atlantis	LP	Vertigo	6360609	1973	£10	£4	*spiral label*

ATLAS

Title	Format	Label	Number	Year	Mint	Excellent	Notes
Against All The Odds	LP	Atlas	WIL001	1978	£15	£6	

ATMOSFEAR

Title	Format	Label	Number	Year	Mint	Excellent	Notes
Dancing In Outer Space	12″	Elite	DAZZ47	1986	£6	£2.50	

ATMOSPHERES

Title	Format	Label	Number	Year	Mint	Excellent	Notes
Fickle Chicken	7″	London	HLW8977	1959	£12	£6	
Telegraph	7″	London	HLW9091	1960	£8	£4	

ATOLL

Title	Format	Label	Number	Year	Mint	Excellent	Notes
L'araignée Mal	LP	Eurodisc	913002	1975	£10	£4	*French*
Musiciens Et Magiciens	LP	Eurodisc	87008	1974	£10	£4	*French*

ATOMIC ROOSTER

Title	Format	Label	Number	Year	Mint	Excellent	Notes
Atomic Rooster	LP	B&C	CAS1010	1970	£20	£8	
Death Walks Behind You	LP	B&C	CAS1026	1970	£15	£6	

Title	Format	Label	Cat. No.	Year	Mint	VG	Notes
Friday The 13th	7"	B&C	CB121	1970	£5	£2	picture sleeve
In Hearing Of	LP	Pegasus	PEG1	1971	£12	£5	
Made In England	LP	Dawn	DNLS3038	1972	£30	£15	denim cover
Made In England	LP	Dawn	DNLS3038	1972	£10	£4	
Nice And Greasy	LP	Dawn	DNLS3049	1973	£25	£10	
Tell Your Story – Sing Your Song	7"	Decca	FR13503	1974	£5	£2	export

ATTACK

The Attack were best known as the performers of the other version of 'Hi Ho Silver Lining', but unfortunately for them, despite receiving fairly extensive radio play, they lost out to Jeff Beck. The guitarist with the Attack was David O'List, who subsequently became a member of the Nice.

Title	Format	Label	Cat. No.	Year	Mint	VG	Notes
Created By Clive	7"	Decca	F12631	1967	£30	£15	
Hi Ho Silver Lining	7"	Decca	F12578	1967	£30	£15	
Magic In The Air	LP	Reflection	MM08	1990	£12	£5	
Neville Thumbcatch	7"	Decca	F12725	1968	£40	£20	
Try It	7"	Decca	F12550	1967	£60	£30	

ATTACK (2)

Title	Format	Label	Cat. No.	Year	Mint	VG	Notes
Please Mr Phil Spector	7"	Philips	BF1585	1967	£15	£7.50	

ATTAK

Title	Format	Label	Cat. No.	Year	Mint	VG	Notes
Today's Generation: Murder In The Subway	7"	No Future	OI17	1982	£5	£2	

ATTILA

Title	Format	Label	Cat. No.	Year	Mint	VG	Notes
Attila	LP	Epic	E30030	1970	£15	£6	US

ATTRACTION

Title	Format	Label	Cat. No.	Year	Mint	VG	Notes
Party Line	7"	Columbia	DB8010	1966	£50	£25	
Stupid Girl	7"	Columbia	DB7936	1966	£25	£12.50	

ATTRITION

Title	Format	Label	Cat. No.	Year	Mint	VG	Notes
Fear	7"	Sound For Industry	SFI671	1981	£5	£2	flexi
Monkey In A Bin	12"	Uniton	19841	1984	£10	£5	
Shrinkwrap	12"	Third Mind	TMS04	1985	£8	£4	
Two Traces	7"	Adventures In Realit	AINR2	1982	£8	£4	flexi
Voice Of God	12"	Third Mind	TMS03	1984	£8	£4	

ATWELL, WINIFRED

Title	Format	Label	Cat. No.	Year	Mint	VG	Notes
Boogie With Winifred Atwell	7" EP	Decca	DFE6099	1955	£5	£2	
Poor People Of Paris	7"	Decca	F10681	1956	£5	£2	

AU GO-GO SINGERS

Title	Format	Label	Cat. No.	Year	Mint	VG	Notes
San Francisco Bay Blues	7"	Columbia	DB7493	1965	£5	£2	
They Call Us The Au Go-Go Singers	LP	Columbia	33SX1696	1964	£50	£25	

AUBREY SMALL

Title	Format	Label	Cat. No.	Year	Mint	VG	Notes
Aubrey Small	LP	Polydor	2383048	1971	£40	£20	

AUDIENCE

As label-mates of Genesis and Van Der Graaf Generator, Audience played very much the same kind of complex structured but essentially melodic material, although with rather less commercial success. The real Audience rarity, however, is the first LP, recorded for Polydor. The scarcity of this record has led some dealers to conclude that the record was withdrawn soon after its release, although the truth is that it was simply deleted after a short time, due to its sales being rather poor.

Title	Format	Label	Cat. No.	Year	Mint	VG	Notes
Audience	LP	Polydor	583065	1969	£60	£30	
Friends Friends Friends	LP	Charisma	CAS1012	1970	£10	£4	
House On The Hill	LP	Charisma	CAS1032	1971	£10	£4	
Indian Summer	7"	Charisma	CB141	1971	£4	£1.50	picture sleeve
Lunch	LP	Charisma	CAS1054	1972	£10	£4	

AUDREY

Title	Format	Label	Cat. No.	Year	Mint	VG	Notes
Love Me Tonight	7"	Downtown	DT414	1969	£4	£1.50	Brother Dan Allstars B side
Lovers' Concerto	7"	Downtown	DT418	1969	£4	£1.50	Brother Dan Allstars B side
Oh I Was Wrong	7"	Downtown	DT454	1969	£4	£1.50	
Someday We'll Be Together	7"	Downtown	DT457	1969	£4	£1.50	Music Doctors B side
Sweeter Than Sugar	7"	Downtown	DT452	1969	£4	£1.50	
You'll Lose A Good Thing	7"	Downtown	DT436	1969	£4	£1.50	Desmond Riley B side

AUDSLEY, MICK

Title	Format	Label	Cat. No.	Year	Mint	VG	Notes
Dark And Devil Waters	LP	Sonet	SNTF641	1973	£10	£4	
Storyboard	LP	Sonet	SNTF659	1974	£10	£4	

AUGER, BRIAN

Brian Auger's long career as a jazz-rock organist peaked on the recordings made jointly with singer Julie Driscoll. For just a short while, Auger was more than just the skilled craftsman of his recordings before and since, becoming part of a group with real innovative power. Nothing Julie Driscoll and the Brian Auger Trinity recorded together could quite match the brilliance of 'This Wheel's On Fire', but all the Marmalade recordings contain much worthwhile and memorable music.

Title	Format	Label	Cat. No.	Year	Mint	VG	Notes
Befour	LP	RCA	SF8101	1970	£10	£4	
Definitely What	LP	Marmalade	607003	1968	£15	£6	

Don't Send Me No Flowers	LP	Marmalade	607/608004	1968	**£30**	**£15**	*with Jimmy Page & Sonny Boy Williamson*
Fool Killer	7"	Columbia	DB7590	1965	**£12**	**£6**	
Green Onions '65	7"	Columbia	DB7715	1965	**£10**	**£5**	
Oblivion Express	LP	RCA	SF8170	1971	**£10**	**£4**	
Red Beans And Rice	7"	Marmalade	598003	1967	**£5**	**£2**	
Tiger	7"	Columbia	DB8163	1967	**£20**	**£10**	
What You Gonna Do	7"	Marmalade	598015	1969	**£4**	**£1.50**	

AULD, GEORGIE

Dancing In The Land Of Hi-Fi	LP	Emarcy	EJL1266	1958	**£12**	**£5**	
Georgie Auld	LP	Vogue Coral	LVA9023	1956	**£12**	**£5**	
In The Land Of Hi-Fi	LP	Emarcy	EJL1251	1957	**£12**	**£5**	*with Sarah McLawler*
Manhattan	7"	Vogue Coral	Q2002	1954	**£[illegible]**	**£1.50**	
With The André Previn Orchestra	LP	Vogue Coral	LVA9012	1956	**£12**	**£5**	

AULD TRIANGLE

Auld Triangle	LP	Castle	CASLP008		**£30**	**£15**	

AULDRIDGE, MIKE

Blues And Bluegrass	LP	Sonet	SNTF673	1974	**£10**	**£4**	

AUM

For a few minutes during the group's long version of 'Tobacco Road' on the *Bluesvibes* album, one could almost imagine that this was a live recording by Cream. Sadly, the rest of the group's output is not in the same league, consisting of formulaic blues performances delivered with little of the spark needed to transcend the limitations of the material.

Bluesvibes	LP	London	HAK/SHK8401	1969	**£30**	**£15**	
Resurrection	LP	Fillmore	30002	1969	**£20**	**£8**	*US*

AUNT MARY

Aunt Mary	LP	Polydor	2380002	1971	**£75**	**£37.50**	*German*
Best Of Vol. 1	LP	Polydor	6478009	1974	**£50**	**£25**	*German*
Best Of Vol. 2	LP	Polydor	6478055	1975	**£50**	**£25**	*German*
Janus	LP	Vertigo	6317750	1973	**£100**	**£50**	*Norwegian*
Live Reunion	LP	Philips	6327059	1980	**£30**	**£15**	*Swedish*
Loaded	LP	Philips	6317010	1971	**£150**	**£75**	*Danish*
Whispering Farewell	LP	Polydor	2499083	1974	**£50**	**£25**	*German*

AURA

Aura	LP	Mercury	SRM1620	1971	**£12**	**£5**	

AUSTIN, CHARLES

Home From Home	LP	Ogun	OG522	1979	**£12**	**£5**	*with Roy Babbington & Joe Gallivan*
Peace On Earth	LP	Compendium	FIDARDO5	1977	**£10**	**£4**	*with Joe Gallivan*

AUSTIN, CLAIRE

Claire Austin Sings The Blues	10" LP	Good Time Jazz	LDG185	1956	**£40**	**£20**	
When Your Lover Has Gone	LP	Contemporary	LAC12139	1959	**£20**	**£8**	

AUSTIN, LOVEY BLUE SERENADERS

Small Jazz Bands Vol. 1	7" EP	Collector	JE123	1960	**£5**	**£2**	*with the State Street Ramblers*

AUSTIN, PATTI

Are We Ready For Love	7"	CBS	7180	1971	**£6**	**£2.50**	

AUSTIN, PETER

Your Love	7"	Caltone	TONE125	1968	**£6**	**£2.50**	

AUSTIN, REG

My Saddest Day	7"	Pye	7N15885	1965	**£30**	**£15**	

AUSTIN, SIL

Band With The Beat	7" EP	Mercury	MEP9540	1958	**£25**	**£12.50**	
Don't You Just Know It	7"	Mercury	7MT220	1958	**£8**	**£4**	
Go Sil Go	7" EP	Mercury	MEP9541	1958	**£25**	**£12.50**	
Hey Eula	7"	Mercury	7MT225	1958	**£8**	**£4**	
Slow Walk Rock	LP	Mercury	MPL6534	1958	**£30**	**£15**	

AUSTRALIAN JAZZ QUARTET

Australian Jazz Quartet	LP	London	LTZN15054	1957	**£12**	**£5**	
Australian Jazz Quartet	LP	London	LTZN15065	1957	**£12**	**£5**	

AUSTRALIAN JAZZ QUINTET

Australian Jazz Quintet Plus One	LP	London	LTZN15089	1957	**£12**	**£5**	

AUSTRALIAN PLAYBOYS

Black Sheep	7"	Immediate	IM054	1967	**£300**	**£180**	*best auctioned*

AUTECHRE

Cavity Job	12"	Hardcore	HARD003	1992	**£10**	**£5**	
Incunabula	LP	Warp	LP17LTD	1993	**£15**	**£6**	*double, silver vinyl*

AUTOSALVAGE

The one LP recorded by Autosalvage is a little like Jefferson Airplane and a little like the Lovin' Spoonful, but with more ambitious arranging than either (including the use of medieval instruments, though not a medieval sound). Unfortunately, the songs are not as strong as they might be, but the record is still very interesting. Frank Zappa is supposed to have had a hand in the group's discovery.

Title	Format	Label	Cat. No.	Year	Mint	Good	Notes
Autosalvage	LP	RCA	LSP3940	1968	**£30**	**£15**	*US*

AUTRY, GENE

Title	Format	Label	Cat. No.	Year	Mint	Good	Notes
At The Rodeo	10" LP	Columbia	JL8001	1949	**£25**	**£10**	*US*
Champion Western Adventures	LP	Columbia	CL677	1955	**£15**	**£6**	*US*
Christmas With Gene Autry	LP	Challenge	CHL600	1958	**£15**	**£6**	*US*
Gene Autry Sings Peter Cottontail	10" LP	Columbia	CL2568	1955	**£25**	**£10**	*US*
Golden Hits	LP	RCA	LPM/LSP2623	1962	**£12**	**£5**	*US*
Greatest Hits	LP	Columbia	CL1575	1961	**£15**	**£6**	*US*
Little Johnny Pilgrim	10" LP	Columbia	MJV83	195–	**£25**	**£10**	*US*
Merry Christmas	10" LP	Columbia	CL2547	1955	**£25**	**£10**	*US*
Nine Little Reindeer	7"	London	HLU9001	1958	**£4**	**£1.50**	
Rusty The Rocking Horse	10" LP	Columbia	MJV94	195–	**£25**	**£10**	*US*
Stampede	10" LP	Columbia	JL8009	195–	**£25**	**£10**	*US*
Story Of The Nativity	10" LP	Columbia	MJV82	195–	**£25**	**£10**	*US*
Western Classic, Vol. 1	10" LP	Columbia	HL9001	195–	**£25**	**£10**	*US*
Western Classic, Vol. 2	10" LP	Columbia	HL9002	195–	**£25**	**£10**	*US*

AUTUMN

Title	Format	Label	Cat. No.	Year	Mint	Good	Notes
My Little Girl	7"	Pye	7N45090	1970	**£4**	**£1.50**	

AUTUMN PEOPLE

Title	Format	Label	Cat. No.	Year	Mint	Good	Notes
Autumn People	LP	Soundtech	3020	1976	**£60**	**£30**	*US*

AVALANCHE

Title	Format	Label	Cat. No.	Year	Mint	Good	Notes
Perseverance Kills Our Game	LP	Starlet		1979	**£500**	**£330**	*Dutch*

AVALANCHE (2)

Title	Format	Label	Cat. No.	Year	Mint	Good	Notes
Finding My Way Home	7"	Parlophone	R5890	1971	**£25**	**£12.50**	

AVALANCHES

Title	Format	Label	Cat. No.	Year	Mint	Good	Notes
Ski Surfin'	LP	Warner Bros	WS1525	1963	**£15**	**£6**	*US*

AVALON, FRANKIE

Title	Format	Label	Cat. No.	Year	Mint	Good	Notes
And Now About Mr Avalon	LP	Chancellor	CHL(S)5022	1961	**£12**	**£5**	*US*
Bobby Sox To Stockings	7"	HMV	POP636	1959	**£4**	**£1.50**	
Christmas Album	LP	Chancellor	CHL(S)5031	1962	**£15**	**£6**	*US*
Cleopatra	LP	Chancellor	CHL(S)5032	1963	**£15**	**£6**	*US*
Darling	7"	London	HL8636	1958	**£20**	**£10**	
Dede Dinah	7"	HMV	POP453	1958	**£10**	**£5**	
Fifteen Greatest Hits	LP	United Artists	UAL3382/ UAS6382	1964	**£10**	**£4**	*US*
Frankie Avalon	7" EP	HMV	7EG8471	1958	**£12**	**£6**	
Frankie Avalon	LP	Chancellor	CHL5001	1958	**£20**	**£8**	*US*
Frankie Avalon No. 2	7" EP	HMV	7EG8482	1958	**£12**	**£6**	
Frankie Avalon No. 3	7" EP	HMV	7EG8507	1958	**£12**	**£6**	
Gingerbread	7"	HMV	POP517	1958	**£5**	**£2**	
I'll Wait For You	7"	HMV	POP569	1959	**£4**	**£1.50**	
Italiano	LP	Chancellor	CHL(S)5025	1962	**£12**	**£5**	*US*
Songs From Muscle Beach Party	LP	United Artists	ULP1078	1964	**£15**	**£6**	
Songs Of The Alamo	7" EP	HMV	7EG8632	1960	**£8**	**£4**	
Summer Scene	LP	HMV	CLP1423	1960	**£15**	**£6**	
Swingin' On A Rainbow	LP	HMV	CLP1346	1959	**£15**	**£6**	
Venus	7"	HMV	POP603	1959	**£4**	**£1.50**	
Whole Lot Of Frankie	LP	Chancellor	CHL5018	1961	**£15**	**£6**	*US*
Why	7"	HMV	POP688	1960	**£4**	**£1.50**	
You Are Mine	LP	Chancellor	CHL(S)5027	1962	**£12**	**£5**	*US*
Young And In Love	LP	HMV	CLP1440/ CSD1358	1960	**£15**	**£6**	
Young Frankie Avalon	LP	Chancellor	CHL5002	1959	**£15**	**£6**	*US*

AVALONS

Title	Format	Label	Cat. No.	Year	Mint	Good	Notes
Every Day	7"	Island	WI263	1966	**£6**	**£2.50**	

AVANT-GARDE

Title	Format	Label	Cat. No.	Year	Mint	Good	Notes
Naturally Stoned	7"	CBS	3704	1968	**£4**	**£1.50**	

AVENGERS

Title	Format	Label	Cat. No.	Year	Mint	Good	Notes
Everyone's Gonna Wonder	7"	Parlophone	R5661	1968	**£4**	**£1.50**	

AVENGERS (2)

Title	Format	Label	Cat. No.	Year	Mint	Good	Notes
American In Me	12"	White Noise	WNR002	1979	**£12**	**£6**	*different picture sleeves*

AVENGERS (3)

The cult TV programme is represented on vinyl by recordings of its theme tunes. The first series with Patrick McNee and Honor Blackman had a theme by Johnny Dankworth. The second and third series with McNee and Diana Rigg, followed by McNee and Linda Thorson had a theme by Laurie Johnson, and since these series were the ones that achieved the biggest cult following, it is Johnson's music that is most readily associated with the programme. The New Avengers revival in the seventies was rather less popular, but its theme was also by Laurie Johnson. Details of all these records can be found in the *Guide* under the appropriate artist headings.

AVENGERS VI

Real Cool Hits	LP	Mark 56 Records		1965	**£60**	**£30**	*US*

AVERAGE WHITE BAND

Show Your Hand	LP	MCA	MUPS486	1973	**£10**	**£4**	*white golliwog sleeve*

AVON, ALAN & THE TOY SHOP

Night To Remember	7"	Concord	CONC005	1974	**£60**	**£30**	

AVON, VALERIE

He Knows I Love Him Too Much	7"	Columbia	DB8201	1967	**£4**	**£1.50**	

AVON CITIES JAZZ BAND

Avon Cities Jazz Band	10" LP	Tempo	LAP10	1956	**£25**	**£10**	

AVON CITIES SKIFFLE GROUP

Hey Hey Daddy Blues	7"	Tempo	A146	1956	**£15**	**£7.50**	
How Long Blues	7"	Tempo	A156	1957	**£12**	**£6**	
Lonesome Day Blues	7"	Tempo	A157	1957	**£10**	**£5**	
Ray Bush & The Avon Cities Skiffle Group	7" EP	Tempo	EXA40	1957	**£15**	**£7.50**	
Ray Bush & The Avon Cities Skiffle Group No. 2	7" EP	Tempo	EXA50	1957	**£15**	**£7.50**	
This Little Light Of Mine	7"	Tempo	A149	1956	**£15**	**£7.50**	

AVON SISTERS

Jerri-Lee	7"	Columbia	DB4236	1959	**£4**	**£1.50**	

AVONS

Avons	LP	Hull	HLP1000	1960	**£150**	**£75**	*US*

AWAY FROM THE SAND

Away From The Sand	LP	Beaujangle	DB0003	1973	**£125**	**£62.50**	

AXELROD, DAVID

Earth Rot	LP	Capitol	SKAO456	1970	**£12**	**£5**	*US*
Rock Messiah	LP	RCA	4636	1972	**£12**	**£5**	*US*
Songs Of Experience	LP	Capitol	SKAP338	1969	**£12**	**£5**	*US*
Songs Of Innocence	LP	Capitol	ST2982	1968	**£10**	**£4**	

AXIOM

Fools' Gold	LP	Parlophone	PCSO7561	1970	**£15**	**£6**	*Australian*

AXIS

Axis	LP	Riviera	421088	1973	**£15**	**£6**	*French*
Axis	LP	Riviera	95010	1971	**£15**	**£6**	*French*
Ela Ela	LP	Riviera	521192	1971	**£15**	**£6**	*French*

AXTON, HOYT

Apart from being quite well known as a folk and country singer in his own right, Hoyt Axton is also the son of the woman who wrote 'Heartbreak Hotel'. Intending the song as a smooth, sentimental ballad, Mrs Axton was apparently quite upset when she heard what Elvis Presley had done to it – although she cheered up considerably when the royalties started to arrive!

Best Of Hoyt Axton	LP	London	HAF/SHF8276	1966	**£15**	**£7.50**	
Country Anthem	LP	Capitol	SMAS850	1971	**£10**	**£4**	*US*
Explodes	LP	Vee Jay	VJS1098	1964	**£15**	**£6**	*US*
Greenback Dollar	LP	Stateside	SL10082	1964	**£15**	**£7.50**	
Joy To The World	LP	Capitol	EST788	1970	**£10**	**£4**	*US*
Less Than A Song	LP	A&M	AMLH64376	1973	**£10**	**£4**	
Saturday's Child	LP	Vee Jay	VJS1127	1965	**£15**	**£6**	*US*
Sings Betty Smith	LP	Exodus	301	1965	**£12**	**£5**	*US*
Thunder And Lightnin'	LP	Stateside	SL10096	1964	**£15**	**£7.50**	

AYERS, KEVIN

As one of the founders of the 'English eccentric' school of rock music, Kevin Ayers still makes records for the loyal army of fans who have followed his activities since his days as bass player for the Soft Machine. The two earliest albums contain what is arguably his most interesting music, with telling contributions from the supporting musicians, who include Soft Machine on *Joy Of A Toy*, and on *Shooting At The Moon*, saxophonist Lol Coxhill, composer/arranger David Bedford (here playing keyboards), and the youthful Mike Oldfield.

As Close As You Think	LP	Illuminated	AMA25	1986	**£10**	**£4**	
Bananamour	LP	Harvest	SHVL807	1973	**£10**	**£4**	
Bananamour	LP	Harvest	SHVL807	1973	**£20**	**£8**	*with booklet*
Caribbean Moon	7"	Harvest	HAR5071	1973	**£6**	**£2.50**	*picture sleeve*
Caribbean Moon	7"	Harvest	HAR5109	1976	**£6**	**£2.50**	*picture sleeve*
Joy Of A Toy	LP	Harvest	SHVL763	1970	**£15**	**£6**	
Joy Of A Toy/Shooting At The Moon	LP	Harvest	SHDW407	1975	**£12**	**£5**	*double*
Puis-je?	7"	Harvest	HAR5027	1970	**£4**	**£1.50**	
Shooting At The Moon	LP	Harvest	SHSP4005	1971	**£15**	**£6**	
Singing A Song In The Morning	7"	Harvest	HAR5011	1970	**£6**	**£2.50**	
Stepping Out	7"	Illuminated	LEV71	1986	**£4**	**£1.50**	
Whatevershebringswesing	LP	Harvest	SHVL800	1973	**£10**	**£4**	

AYERS, ROY

Africa Centre Of The World	LP	Polydor	2391157	1981	**£10**	**£4**	
Best Of Roy Ayers	LP	Polydor	2391429	1979	**£10**	**£4**	
Crystal Reflection	LP	Muse	MR5101	1977	**£10**	**£4**	

Daddy Bug And Friend	LP	Atco	SD1692	1973	**£15**	**£6**	*US*
Everybody Loves The Sunshine	LP	Polydor	PD16070	1976	**£10**	**£4**	*US*
Evolution	7"	Polydor	2066671	1976	**£4**	**£1.50**	
Feelin' Good	LP	Polydor	2391539	1982	**£20**	**£8**	
Fever	LP	Polydor	2391396	1979	**£10**	**£4**	
He's Coming	LP	Polydor	PD5022/2391027	1972	**£100**	**£50**	
Let's Do It	LP	Polydor	2490145	1978	**£10**	**£4**	
Lifeline	LP	Polydor	2391292	1977	**£10**	**£4**	
Mystic Voyage	LP	Polydor	PD6057	1975	**£12**	**£5**	*US*
Red, Black And Green	LP	Polydor	PD16078	1976	**£10**	**£4**	*US*
Running Away	12"	Polydor	POSPX135	1980	**£6**	**£2.50**	
Step Into Our Life	LP	Polydor	2391380	1978	**£10**	**£4**	
Ubiquity	LP	Polydor	PD6046	1974	**£15**	**£6**	*US*
Vibrations	LP	Polydor	2391256	1976	**£10**	**£4**	
Virgo Vibes	LP	Atlantic	SD1488	1967	**£20**	**£8**	*US*
You Send Me	LP	Polydor	2391365	1978	**£10**	**£4**	

AYLER, ALBERT

At St Paul De Vence Vol. 1	LP	Shandar	SR10000	1973	**£20**	**£8**	*French*
At St Paul De Vence Vol. 2	LP	Shandar	SR10004	1973	**£20**	**£8**	*French*
Bells	LP	ESP-Disk	1010	1965	**£30**	**£15**	*US*
Ghosts	LP	Fontana	SFJL925	1969	**£25**	**£10**	
Ghosts	LP	Debut	DEB144	1956	**£50**	**£25**	*US*
In Greenwich Village	LP	Impulse	AS9155	1967	**£25**	**£10**	*US*
Last Album	LP	Impulse	AS9208	1971	**£25**	**£10**	*US*
Love Cry	LP	Impulse	AS9165	1968	**£25**	**£10**	*US*
Music Is The Healing Force Of The Universe	LP	Impulse	AS9191	1969	**£25**	**£10**	*US*
My Name Is Albert Ayler	LP	Fantasy	FS6016	1965	**£25**	**£10**	*US*
My Name Is Albert Ayler	LP	Debut	DEB140	1956	**£50**	**£25**	*US*
New Grass	LP	Impulse	AS9175	1968	**£25**	**£10**	*US*
New York Eye And Ear Control	LP	ESP-Disk	1016	1966	**£30**	**£15**	*US*
Nuits De La Fondation Maeght	LP	Shandar	SHAN83503/4	1978	**£25**	**£10**	*French*
Spirits	LP	Debut	DEB146	1956	**£50**	**£25**	*US*
Spirits Rejoice	LP	ESP-Disk	1020	1966	**£30**	**£15**	*US*
Spiritual Unity	LP	Fontana	SFJL933	1969	**£25**	**£10**	
Spiritual Unity	LP	ESP-Disk	1002	1964	**£30**	**£15**	*US*
Vibrations	LP	Freedom		196–	**£20**	**£8**	
Witches And Devils	LP	Freedom	FLP40101	1967	**£20**	**£8**	

AYRSHIRE FOLK

Ayrshire Folk	LP	Deroy		1974	**£50**	**£25**	

AYSHEA

Ayshea	LP	Polydor	2384026	1970	**£15**	**£6**	
Lift Off With Ayshea	LP	DJM	DJLPS445	1974	**£10**	**£4**	
Only Your Love Can Save Me	7"	Polydor	56276	1968	**£10**	**£5**	
Peep My Love	7"	Fontana	TF627	1965	**£4**	**£1.50**	

AZITIS

Help	LP	Elco	SCEC5555	1971	**£1000**	**£700**	*US*

AZTEC CAMERA

Crying Scene	CD-s	WEA	YZ492CD	1990	**£5**	**£2**	
Deep And Wide And Tall	CD-s	WEA	YZ154CD	1988	**£5**	**£2**	
Good Morning Britain	CD-s	WEA	YZ521CD	1990	**£5**	**£2**	*with Mick Jones*
How Men Are	CD-s	WEA	2480282	1988	**£5**	**£2**	*Dutch import*
Just Like Gold	7"	Postcard	81-3	1981	**£10**	**£5**	*lyric postcard*
Just Like Gold	7"	Postcard	81-3	1981	**£5**	**£2**	
Mattress Of Wire	7"	Postcard	81-8	1981	**£10**	**£5**	*picture sleeve*
Oblivious (Langer/Winstanley Remix)	7"	Rainhill	ACFC1	1983	**£10**	**£5**	
Retrospect	CD	Sire		1993	**£20**	**£8**	*US promo compilation*
Somewhere In My Heart	CD-s	WEA	YZ181CD	1988	**£5**	**£2**	
Working In A Goldmine	CD-s	WEA	YZ7199CD	1988	**£5**	**£2**	

AZTECS

Live At The Ad-Lib Club	LP	World Artists	WAM2001	1964	**£50**	**£25**	*US*

B. B. BLUNDER

Worker's Playtime is the often overlooked third LP by the Blossom Toes, but sadly it shares few of the inventive qualities of its predecessors. The cover, however, is a delight, being a parody of the Radio Times, with all the song lyrics and credits disguised as programme information.

Title	Format	Label	Cat. No.	Year	Mint	VG	Notes
Workers Playtime	LP	United Artists	UAS29156	1971	**£10**	**£4**	

B-52s

Title	Format	Label	Cat. No.	Year	Mint	VG	Notes
Channel Z	CD-s	WEA	W2831CD	1989	**£5**	**£2**	
Deadbeat Club	CD-s	WEA	W9526CD	1990	**£5**	**£2**	
Love Shack	CD-s	WEA	W9917CD	1990	**£5**	**£2**	
Roam	CD-s	WEA	W9827CD	1990	**£5**	**£2**	
Rock Lobster	7"	Island	BFTP1/BFTL1/ BFTR1	1986	**£10**	**£5**	*set of 3 rectangular picture discs*
Wild Planet	LP	Island	ILPS9622	1980	**£10**	**£4**	*with carrying bag, badge*

B-MOVIE

Title	Format	Label	Cat. No.	Year	Mint	VG	Notes
Dead Good Tapes	CD	Wax	WAXCD1	1988	**£15**	**£6**	
Nowhere Girl	12"	Dead Good	BIGDEAD9	1980	**£15**	**£7.50**	
Nowhere Girl	12"	Wax	12WAX3	1988	**£6**	**£2.50**	*orange vinyl*
Nowhere Girl	12"	Wax	12WAX3	1988	**£6**	**£2.50**	*pink vinyl*
Take Three	7"	Dead Good	DEAD9	1980	**£15**	**£7.50**	

BABASIN, HARRY

Title	Format	Label	Cat. No.	Year	Mint	VG	Notes
For Moderns Only	LP	Emarcy	EJL1265	1958	**£20**	**£8**	

BABE RUTH

Title	Format	Label	Cat. No.	Year	Mint	VG	Notes
Amar Caballero	LP	Harvest	SHVL812	1973	**£10**	**£4**	
Babe Ruth	LP	Harvest	SHSP4038	1975	**£10**	**£4**	
First Base	LP	Harvest	SHSP4022	1972	**£10**	**£4**	

BABES IN TOYLAND

Title	Format	Label	Cat. No.	Year	Mint	VG	Notes
Live At The Academy	CD	Warner Bros	PROCD5838	1992	**£20**	**£8**	*promo*

BABY

Title	Format	Label	Cat. No.	Year	Mint	VG	Notes
Baby	LP	Lone Star	6264	1974	**£10**	**£4**	*US*

BABY BIRD

Title	Format	Label	Cat. No.	Year	Mint	VG	Notes
Bad Shave	CD	Baby Bird	CD2	1995	**£20**	**£8**	
Bad Shave	LP	Baby Bird	LP2	1995	**£15**	**£6**	
Fatherhood	CD	Baby Bird	CD3	1995	**£20**	**£8**	
Fatherhood	LP	Baby Bird	LP3	1995	**£15**	**£6**	
Happiest Man Alive	CD	Baby Bird	CD4	1995	**£20**	**£8**	
Happiest Man Alive	LP	Baby Bird	LP4	1995	**£15**	**£6**	
I Was Born A Man	CD	Baby Bird	CD1	1995	**£25**	**£10**	
Snake Caves	7"	Gorgonzola	REEL01	1996	**£15**	**£7.50**	*blue vinyl*
You're Gorgeous	7"	Echo	ECS026	1996	**£5**	**£2**	*gold vinyl*
You're Gorgeous	CD-s	Echo	ECSCX026	1996	**£6**	**£2.50**	

BABY HUEY

Title	Format	Label	Cat. No.	Year	Mint	VG	Notes
Living Legend	LP	Buddah	2365001	1971	**£20**	**£8**	

BABY JANE & THE ROCKABYES

Title	Format	Label	Cat. No.	Year	Mint	VG	Notes
How Much Is That Doggie In The Window	7"	United Artists	UP1010	1963	**£5**	**£2**	

BABY RAY & THE FERNS

The single by Baby Ray and the Ferns is one of the early steps in the career of Frank Zappa, who wrote the songs on both sides.

Title	Format	Label	Cat. No.	Year	Mint	VG	Notes
How's Your Bird?	7"	Donna	1378	1963	**£150**	**£75**	*US*

BABY SUNSHINE

Title	Format	Label	Cat. No.	Year	Mint	VG	Notes
Baby Sunshine	LP	Deroy	DER1301	1975	**£60**	**£30**	

BABYLON

Babylon's lead singer was Carol Grimes, who has managed to maintain a lengthy if unspectacular career in rock since then.

Title	Format	Label	Cat. No.	Year	Mint	VG	Notes
Into The Promised Land	7"	Polydor	BM56356	1969	**£6**	**£2.50**	*picture sleeve*

BACH TWO BACH

Bach Two Bach	LP	Mushroom	100MR10	1971	£100	£50	

BACHARACH, BURT

Alfie	7"	A&M	AMS702	1969	£10	£5	
Casino Royale	LP	RCA	RD/SF7874	1967	£40	£20	
Hit Maker!	LP	London	HAR/SHR8233	1965	£10	£4	

BACHDENKEL

Lemmings	LP	Initial	IRL001	1977	£20	£8	with 7"
Stalingrad	LP	Initial	IRL002	1977	£10	£4	

BACHELOR, JOHNNY

Mumbles	7"	London	HLN9074	1960	£30	£15	

BACHELORS

Ding Ding	7"	Parlophone	R4547	1959	£15	£7.50	
Lovin' Babe	7"	Decca	F11300	1960	£30	£15	
Platter Party	7"	Parlophone	R4454	1958	£15	£7.50	

BACHS

Out Of The Bachs	LP	private		1968	£1000	£700	US

BACK ALLEY CHOIR

Back Alley Choir	LP	York	FYK406	1972	£300	£180	
Nursery Rhyme Song	7"	York	SYK547	1973	£12	£6	
Smile Born Of Courtesy	7"	York	SYK517	1972	£12	£6	

BACK DOOR

Back Door	LP	Blakey	BLP5989	1972	£20	£8	
Back Door	LP	Warner Bros	K46231	1973	£10	£4	

BACKBEAT PHILHARMONIC

Rock And Roll Symphony	7"	Top Rank	JAR576	1961	£4	£1.50	

BACKHOUSE, MIRIAM

Gypsy Without A Road	LP	Mother Earth	MUM1203	1977	£200	£100	

BACKUS, JIM

Delicious	7"	London	HLJ8674	1958	£4	£1.50	

BACKYARD HEAVIES

Just Keep On Truckin'	7"	Action	ACT4616	1973	£5	£2	

BACON, GAR

Chains Of Love	7"	Felsted	AF107	1958	£8	£4	
Marshall Marshall	7"	Fontana	H196	1959	£15	£7.50	

BACON FAT

Evil	7"	Blue Horizon	573181	1971	£5	£2	
Grease One For Me	LP	Blue Horizon	763858	1970	£30	£15	
Nobody But You	7"	Blue Horizon	573171	1970	£5	£2	
Tough Dude	LP	Blue Horizon	2431001	1971	£40	£20	

BAD BOYS

Best Of The Bad Boys	LP	Style	STLP8061	1966	£300	£180	Italian
Owl And The Pussycat	7"	Piccadilly	7N35208	1964	£20	£10	

BAD COMPANY

Bad Co	LP	Island	ILPS9279	1974	£10	£4	
Can't Get Enough	CD-s	Atlantic	A7954CD	1990	£5	£2	
Deal With The Preacher	7"	Island	BCDJ1	1976	£15	£7.50	1 sided promo
Straight Shooter	LP	Island	ILPS9304	1975	£10	£4	

BAD EDGE

Bad Edge	LP	private		1981	£20	£8	Dutch

BAD NEWS

Bohemian Rhapsody	12"	EMI	12EM24X	1987	£6	£2.50	scratch 'n' sniff sleeve

BAD NEWS REUNION

Live Im Logo	LP	Oktave	JFF33781	1978	£20	£8	German

BADFINGER

Apple Of My Eye	7"	Apple	49	1974	£8	£4	
Ass	LP	Apple	SAPCOR27	1974	£20	£8	
Badfinger	LP	Warner Bros	K56023	1974	£10	£4	
Come And Get It	7"	Apple	20	1969	£4	£1.50	picture sleeve
Day After Day	7"	Apple	40	1972	£6	£2.50	picture sleeve
Magic Christian Music	LP	Apple	SAPCOR12	1970	£30	£15	
No Dice	LP	Apple	SAPCOR16	1970	£30	£15	
No Matter What	7"	Apple	31	1970	£8	£4	picture sleeve
Straight Up	LP	Apple	SAPCOR19	1972	£30	£15	
Wish You Were Here	LP	Warner Bros	K56076	1974	£30	£15	

BADGE

Silver Woman	7"	Metal Minded	MM2	1981	£15	£7.50	

BADGER

Badger was the group formed by Tony Kaye after his departure from Yes. *One Live Badger* has a pop-up cover – a badger (naturally) stands up when the gatefold sleeve is opened.

Title	Format	Label	Cat. No.	Year	Mint	VG	Notes
One Live Badger	LP	Atlantic	K40473	1973	**£15**	**£6**	

BADGER'S MATE

Title	Format	Label	Cat. No.	Year	Mint	VG	Notes
Brighter Than Usual	LP	Cottage	COT521	197–	**£15**	**£6**	

BAEZ, JOAN

Title	Format	Label	Cat. No.	Year	Mint	VG	Notes
Any Day Now	LP	Vanguard	VSD79306/7	1968	**£12**	**£5**	*double*
Baptism	LP	Vanguard	SVRL19000	1968	**£10**	**£4**	
Blessed Are	LP	Vanguard	VSD6570/1	1971	**£12**	**£5**	*double*
Carry It On	LP	Vanguard	VSD519042	1972	**£10**	**£4**	
Come From The Shadows	LP	A&M	AMLH64339	1972	**£10**	**£4**	
David's Album	LP	Vanguard	SVRL19050	1969	**£10**	**£4**	
Don't Think Twice	7" EP	Fontana	TFE18007	1964	**£5**	**£2**	
Farewell Angelina	LP	Fontana	(S)TFL6058	1965	**£10**	**£4**	
First Ten Years	LP	Vanguard	VSD6560	1970	**£12**	**£5**	*double*
Hard Rain's Gonna Fall	7" EP	Fontana	TFE18013	1966	**£5**	**£2**	
In Concert	LP	Fontana	(S)TFL6033	1962	**£10**	**£4**	
In Concert Part 2	LP	Fontana	(S)TFL6035	1962	**£10**	**£4**	
Joan	LP	Fontana	(S)TFL6082	1967	**£10**	**£4**	
Joan Baez	7" EP	Fontana	TFE18000	1964	**£5**	**£2**	
Joan Baez	LP	Fontana	(S)TFL6002	1960	**£10**	**£4**	
Joan Baez 2	LP	Fontana	(S)TFL6025	1961	**£10**	**£4**	
Joan Baez 5	LP	Fontana	(S)TFL6043	1964	**£10**	**£4**	
Joan Baez No. 2	7" EP	Fontana	TFE18001	1964	**£5**	**£2**	
Joan Baez Sings Silver Dagger & Other Songs	7" EP	Fontana	TFE18005	1964	**£5**	**£2**	
Noel	LP	Fontana	(S)TFL6078	1966	**£10**	**£4**	
Once I Had A Sweetheart	7" EP	Fontana	TFE18006	1964	**£5**	**£2**	
One Day At A Time	LP	Vanguard	VSD23010	1970	**£10**	**£4**	
Portrait	LP	Fontana	(S)TFL6077	1966	**£10**	**£4**	
Pretty Boy Floyd	7" EP	Fontana	TFE18008	1965	**£5**	**£2**	
With God On Our Side	7" EP	Fontana	TFE18012	1965	**£5**	**£2**	

BAGDASARIAN, ROSS

Title	Format	Label	Cat. No.	Year	Mint	VG	Notes
Crazy, Mixed-Up World	LP	Liberty	LRP3451/ LST7451	1966	**£20**	**£8**	*US*

BAGLEY, DON

Title	Format	Label	Cat. No.	Year	Mint	VG	Notes
Jazz On The Rocks	LP	Pye	NPL28008	1959	**£20**	**£8**	

BAILEY, BURR

Title	Format	Label	Cat. No.	Year	Mint	VG	Notes
San Francisco Bay	7"	Decca	F11686	1963	**£15**	**£7.50**	
You Made Me Cry	7"	Decca	F11846	1964	**£20**	**£10**	

BAILEY, BUSTER

Title	Format	Label	Cat. No.	Year	Mint	VG	Notes
All About Memphis	LP	Felsted	FAJ7003	1959	**£15**	**£6**	

BAILEY, CLIVE & RICO

Title	Format	Label	Cat. No.	Year	Mint	VG	Notes
Evening Train	7"	Blue Beat	BB92	1962	**£12**	**£6**	

BAILEY, DEREK

Title	Format	Label	Cat. No.	Year	Mint	VG	Notes
Aida	LP	Incus	INCUS40	1982	**£12**	**£5**	
Compatibles	LP	Incus	INCUS50	1986	**£12**	**£5**	*with Evan Parker*
Dart Drug	LP	Incus	INCUS41	1983	**£12**	**£5**	*with Jamie Muir*
Duo	LP	Incus	INCUS20	1976	**£12**	**£5**	*with Tristan Honsinger*
Duo	LP	Emanem	601	1975	**£20**	**£8**	*double, with Anthony Braxton*
Improvisations	LP	ECM	ECM1013ST	1971	**£20**	**£8**	
London Concert	LP	Incus	INCUS16	197–	**£12**	**£5**	*with Evan Parker*
Lot 74 Solo Improvisations	LP	Incus	INCUS12	1974	**£12**	**£5**	
Notes	LP	Incus	INCUS48	1986	**£12**	**£5**	
One Music Ensemble	LP	Nondo	002		**£15**	**£6**	
Royal Vol. 1	LP	Incus	INCUS43	1984	**£12**	**£5**	*with Anthony Braxton*
Selections From Live Performances At Verity's Place	LP	Incus	INCUS9	1972	**£15**	**£6**	
Solo Guitar	LP	Incus	INCUS2	1971	**£30**	**£15**	

BAILEY, MILDRED

Title	Format	Label	Cat. No.	Year	Mint	VG	Notes
Mildred Bailey And Her Alley Cats	7" EP	Parlophone	GEP8600	1957	**£10**	**£5**	
Rockin' Chair Lady	10" LP	Brunswick	LA8692	1954	**£20**	**£8**	

BAILEY, PEARL

Title	Format	Label	Cat. No.	Year	Mint	VG	Notes
She's Something Spanish	7"	Vogue Coral	Q2026	1954	**£4**	**£1.50**	
That Certain Feeling	7"	London	HLN8354	1956	**£8**	**£4**	

That Certain Feeling	7" EP	London	REU1104	1957	£10	£5	

BAILEY, ROY

New Bell Wake	LP	Fuse	AC262	1976	£10	£4	
Roy Bailey	LP	Trailer	LER3021	1971	£12	£5	

BAILEY, ROY & LEON ROSSELSON

Love, Loneliness, Laundry	LP	Acorn	CF271	1976	£10	£4	

BAILEY, ROY & VAL & LEON ROSSELSON

Oats And Beans And Kangaroos	LP	Fontana	SFL13061	1968	£20	£8	

BAIN, ALY & MIKE WHELLANS

Aly Bain And Mike Whellans	LP	Trailer	LER2022	1971	£12	£5	

BAIN, ALY & TOM ANDERSON

Shetland Folk Fiddling Vol. 1	LP	Topic	12TS281	1976	£10	£4	
Shetland Folk Fiddling Vol. 2	LP	Topic	12TS379	1978	£10	£4	

BAIN, BOB

Rockin', Rollin'	LP	Capitol	T965	1958	£30	£15	*US*

BAIRD, ARTHUR SKIFFLE GROUP

Union Train	7"	Beltona	BL2669	1956	£15	£7.50	

BAKER, CHET

At Ann Arbor	LP	Vogue	LAE12044	1957	£25	£10	
Chet Baker And Crew	LP	Vogue	LAE12076	1958	£20	£8	
Chet Baker And His Crew	7" EP	Vogue	EPV1186	1957	£5	£2	
Chet Baker And His Crew	LP	Vogue	LAE12076/ SEA5005	1958	£25	£10	
Chet Baker And Strings	10" LP	Philips	BBL7022	1955	£20	£8	
Chet Baker Ensemble	10" LP	Vogue	LDE163	1956	£30	£15	
Chet Baker Ensemble Vol. 1	7" EP	Vogue	EPV1131	1956	£5	£2	
Chet Baker Ensemble Vol. 2	7" EP	Vogue	EPV1132	1956	£5	£2	
Chet Baker Plays Standards	7" EP	Felsted	ESD3069	1959	£5	£2	
Chet Baker Quartet	10" LP	Vogue	LDE116	1955	£30	£15	
Chet Baker Quartet	10" LP	Vogue	LDE045	1954	£30	£15	
Chet Baker Quartet	7" EP	Vogue	EPV1007	1954	£5	£2	
Chet Baker Quartet Vol. 1	LP	Felsted	PDL85008	1956	£25	£10	
Chet Baker Quartet Vol. 2	LP	Felsted	PDL85013	1956	£25	£10	
Chet Baker Sextet	10" LP	Vogue	LDE159	1955	£30	£15	
Chet Baker Sextet	7" EP	Vogue	EPV1121	1956	£5	£2	
Chet Baker Sings	10" LP	Vogue	LDE182	1956	£30	£15	
Chet Baker Sings	LP	Vogue	LAE12164	1959	£20	£8	
Chet Baker Sings	LP	Vogue	LAE12018	1956	£25	£10	
Chet Baker Sings And Plays Vol. 1	7" EP	Vogue	EPV1137	1956	£5	£2	
Chet Baker Sings And Plays Vol. 2	7" EP	Vogue	EPV1138	1956	£5	£2	
Fabulous Chet Baker Quartet	7" EP	Vogue	EPV1032	1955	£5	£2	
I Get Chet	LP	Felsted	PDL85036	1957	£25	£10	
Michelle	LP	Fontana	TL5326	1966	£10	£4	
Myth	7" EP	Felsted	ESD3034	1957	£5	£2	
Phil's Blues	LP	Vogue	LAE12109	1958	£20	£8	
Playboys	LP	Vogue	LAE12183	1959	£20	£8	*with Art Pepper*

BAKER, DESMOND

Rude Boy Gone Jail	7"	Island	WI295	1966	£12	£6	*Sharks B side*

BAKER, GEORGE SELECTION

Little Green Bag	LP	Penny Farthing	PELS503	1970	£10	£4	
Love In The World	LP	Ariola	85132	1970	£20	£8	*German*

BAKER, GINGER

Eleven Sides Of Baker	LP	Mountain	5005	1977	£10	£4	
Fela Ransome Kuti with Ginger Baker	LP	Regal Zonophone	SLRZ1023	1972	£10	£4	
Stratavarious	LP	Polydor	2383133	1972	£10	£4	

BAKER, JEANETTE

Crazy With You	7"	Vogue	V9143	1959	£150	£75	

BAKER, KENNY

Baker Plays McHugh	10" LP	Pye	NJT517	1959	£15	£6	
Baker's Dozen	10" LP	Nixa	NPT19003	1956	£15	£6	
Blowin' Up A Storm	10" LP	Columbia	33S1140	1959	£25	£10	
Date With The Dozen	10" LP	Nixa	NPT19020	1957	£15	£6	
Kenny Baker Half Dozen	LP	Nixa	NJL10	1957	£25	£10	
Operation Jam Session	LP	Polygon	JTL1	1955	£40	£20	

BAKER, LAVERN

Best Of Lavern	7" EP	Atlantic	AET6009	1965	£40	£20	
Best Of Lavern Baker	LP	Atlantic	ATL5002	1964	£60	£30	
Blues Ballads	LP	Atlantic	8030	1959	£75	£37.50	*US*
Bumble Bee	7"	London	HLK9252	1960	£20	£10	
Game Of Love	7"	London	HLE8442	1957	£150	£75	
Get Up Get Up	7"	London	HLE8260	1956	£250	£150	*best auctioned*
Humpty Dumpty Heart	7"	London	HLE8524	1957	£75	£37.50	

Title	Format	Label	Cat. No.	Year	Value		Notes
I Can't Love You Enough	7"	London	HLE8396	1957	**£75**	**£37.50**	
I Cried A Tear	7"	London	HLE8790	1959	**£25**	**£12.50**	
I've Waited Too Long	7"	London	HLE8871	1959	**£25**	**£12.50**	
Jim Dandy	7"	Columbia	DB3879	1957	**£250**	**£150**	*best auctioned*
Lavern	LP	Atlantic	8002	1956	**£150**	**£75**	*US*
Lavern Baker	LP	Atlantic	8007	1957	**£100**	**£50**	*US*
Learning To Love	7"	London	HLE8638	1958	**£60**	**£30**	
Precious Memories	LP	Atlantic	8036	1959	**£60**	**£30**	*US*
Rock And Roll With Lavern Baker	LP	London	HAE2107	1958	**£350**	**£210**	
Saved	7"	London	HLK9343	1961	**£20**	**£10**	
Saved	LP	London	HAE2422	1961	**£75**	**£37.50**	
See See Rider	7"	London	HLK9649	1963	**£25**	**£12.50**	
See See Rider	LP	Atlantic	587/588133	1968	**£20**	**£8**	
See See Rider	LP	London	HAK8074	1963	**£75**	**£37.50**	
Sings Bessie Smith	LP	London	LTZK15139	1958	**£60**	**£[illegible]**	
So High So Low	7"	London	HLE8945	1959	**£25**	**£12.50**	
That Lucky Old Sun	7"	London	HLA8199	1955	**£200**	**£100**	*best auctioned*
Tiny Tim	7"	London	HLE9023	1960	**£25**	**£12.50**	
Tweedle Dee	7"	Columbia	SCM5172	1955	**£300**	**£180**	*best auctioned*
Voodoo Voodoo	7"	London	HLK9468	1961	**£40**	**£20**	
Whipper Snapper	7"	London	HLE8672	1958	**£50**	**£25**	
You're The Boss	7"	London	HLK9300	1961	**£15**	**£7.50**	*with Jimmy Ricks*

BAKER, MICKEY

Title	Format	Label	Cat. No.	Year	Value		Notes
But Wild	LP	King	K(S)839	1963	**£30**	**£15**	*US*
In Blunderland	LP	Major Minor	SMLP67	1970	**£15**	**£6**	
Wildest Guitar	LP	Atlantic	(SD)8035	1959	**£60**	**£30**	*US*

BAKER, ROBERT

Title	Format	Label	Cat. No.	Year	Value		Notes
Pardon Me For Being So Friendly	LP	Crescendo	GNP2027	1966	**£20**	**£8**	*US*

BAKER, SAM

Title	Format	Label	Cat. No.	Year	Value		Notes
I Believe In You	7"	Monument	MON1009	1968	**£6**	**£2.50**	

BAKER, TWO TON

Title	Format	Label	Cat. No.	Year	Value		Notes
Clink Clank	7"	London	HL8121	1955	**£40**	**£20**	

BAKER, VICKY

Title	Format	Label	Cat. No.	Year	Value		Notes
No More Foolish Stories	7"	London	HLU9856	1964	**£5**	**£2**	

BAKER STREET PHILHARMONIC

Title	Format	Label	Cat. No.	Year	Value		Notes
By The Light Of The Moon	LP	Pye	NSPL28131	1970	**£25**	**£10**	

BAKERLOO

Bakerloo (originally Bakerloo Blues Line) was one of the many guitarist-led blues groups to surface in the wake of the pioneering work carried out by the various editions of John Mayall's Bluesbreakers. This one featured Dave 'Clem' Clempson, whose name has graced many album sleeves since – most notably during his time as a member of Humble Pie.

Title	Format	Label	Cat. No.	Year	Value		Notes
Bakerloo	LP	Harvest	SHVL762	1969	**£60**	**£30**	
Driving Backwards	7"	Harvest	HAR5004	1969	**£25**	**£12.50**	

BAKERLOO JUNCTION

Title	Format	Label	Cat. No.	Year	Value		Notes
Emigrant's Return	LP	Emerald	GES1187	1978	**£10**	**£4**	
Next Stop	LP	Emerald	GES1156	1976	**£10**	**£4**	

BALANCE

Title	Format	Label	Cat. No.	Year	Value		Notes
Balance	LP	Incus	INCUS11	1973	**£20**	**£8**	
In For The Count	LP	private		1973	**£20**	**£8**	

BALANCE, BILL

Title	Format	Label	Cat. No.	Year	Value		Notes
Bill Balance And The Feminine Look	LP	Mark 56	NO578	1978	**£25**	**£10**	*US picture disc*

BALDHEAD GROWLER

Title	Format	Label	Cat. No.	Year	Value		Notes
Sausage	7"	Jump Up	JU531	1967	**£4**	**£1.50**	

BALDO, CHRIS

Title	Format	Label	Cat. No.	Year	Value		Notes
Living For Your Love	7"	Vogue	VRS7029	1968	**£10**	**£5**	

BALDRY, LONG JOHN

John Baldry, known as 'long' because he is indeed something like six-foot-six tall, has for most of his career sung the blues, for which his distinctive, smokey voice is an ideal instrument. He is featured on Alexis Korner's *R&B At The Marquee* album, and was a member of Cyril Davies's group. When Davies died, Baldry became the leader of the group, which now became called the Hoochie Coochie Men. The earliest recordings in Baldry's name are by this group. With the switch to Pye, Baldry made what was probably a wrong career move when he decided to start singing middle-of-the-road ballad material. Four hits followed, but then nothing, and his attempts to recapture his blues audience in the seventies were not very successful.

Title	Format	Label	Cat. No.	Year	Value		Notes
Cuckoo	7" EP	United Artists	36108	1966	**£15**	**£7.50**	*French*
Drifter	7"	United Artists	UP1136	1966	**£20**	**£10**	
Everything Stops For Tea	LP	Warner Bros	K46160	1972	**£10**	**£4**	
How Long Will It Last	7"	United Artists	UP1107	1965	**£15**	**£7.50**	
I'm On To You Baby	7"	United Artists	UP1078	1965	**£5**	**£2**	
It Ain't Easy	LP	Warner Bros	K46088	1971	**£10**	**£4**	
Let Him Go	7"	United Artists	UP1204	1967	**£8**	**£4**	
Let The Heartaches Begin	LP	Pye	N(S)PL18208	1967	**£15**	**£6**	
Let There Be Long John	LP	Pye	N(S)PL18228	1968	**£15**	**£6**	
Long John Baldry And The Hoochie Coochie Men	LP	Hallmark	HM560	1970	**£10**	**£4**	

Title	Format	Label	Cat. No.	Year	Price	Price	Notes
Long John's Blues	7" EP	United Artists	UEP1013	1965	**£40**	**£20**	
Long John's Blues	LP	United Artists	ULP1081	1964	**£60**	**£30**	
Looking At Long John	LP	United Artists	(S)ULP1146	1966	**£20**	**£8**	
Unseen Hands	7"	United Artists	UP1124	1966	**£5**	**£2**	
Up Above My Head	7"	United Artists	UP1056	1964	**£12**	**£6**	
Wait For Me	LP	Pye	N(S)PL18306	1969	**£15**	**£6**	

BALES, BURT

Title	Format	Label	Cat. No.	Year	Price	Price	Notes
Burt Bales	10" LP	Good Time Jazz	LDG136	1955	**£12**	**£5**	
Jazz From The San Francisco Waterfront	LP	HMV	CLP1218	1958	**£15**	**£6**	

BALFOUR, KEITH

Title	Format	Label	Cat. No.	Year	Price	Price	Notes
Dreaming	7"	Studio One	SO2079	1969	**£12**	**£6**	

BALIN, MARTY

Title	Format	Label	Cat. No.	Year	Price	Price	Notes
I Specialize In Love	7"	Challenge	9156	1962	**£20**	**£10**	*US*
Nobody But You	7"	Challenge	9146	1962	**£20**	**£10**	*US*

BALL, DAVE

Title	Format	Label	Cat. No.	Year	Price	Price	Notes
In Strict Tempo	LP	Some Bizarre	BIZL5	1983	**£10**	**£4**	

BALL, KENNY

Title	Format	Label	Cat. No.	Year	Price	Price	Notes
Invitation To The Ball	LP	Pye	NJL24	1960	**£12**	**£5**	
Kenny Ball And His Jazzmen	LP	Pye	NJL28	1961	**£12**	**£5**	
Waterloo	7"	Collector	JDN101	1959	**£10**	**£5**	

BALLARD, FLORENCE

Title	Format	Label	Cat. No.	Year	Price	Price	Notes
Doesn't Matter How I Say It	7"	Stateside	SS2113	1968	**£20**	**£10**	

BALLARD, FRANK

Title	Format	Label	Cat. No.	Year	Price	Price	Notes
Rhythm And Blues Party	LP	Philips	1985	1962	**£250**	**£150**	*US*

BALLARD, HANK & THE MIDNIGHTERS

Title	Format	Label	Cat. No.	Year	Price	Price	Notes
1963 Sound Of Hank Ballard	LP	King	815	1963	**£25**	**£10**	*US*
Biggest Hits	LP	King	867	1963	**£25**	**£10**	*US*
Continental Walk	7"	Parlophone	R4771	1961	**£6**	**£2.50**	
Finger Popping Time	7"	Parlophone	R4682	1960	**£12**	**£6**	
Glad Songs, Sad Songs	LP	King	927	1966	**£20**	**£8**	*US*
Hoochi Coochi Coo	7"	Parlophone	R4728	1961	**£15**	**£7.50**	*Little Willie John B side*
Jumpin' Hank Ballard	LP	London	HA8101	1963	**£40**	**£20**	
Let's Go Again	7"	Parlophone	R4762	1961	**£6**	**£2.50**	
Let's Go Again	LP	King	748	1961	**£40**	**£20**	*US*
Let's Go Let's Go Let's Go	7"	Parlophone	R4707	1960	**£15**	**£7.50**	
Midnighters	10" LP	Federal	29590	1954	**£400**	**£250**	*US*
Midnighters	LP	King	395541	1958	**£60**	**£30**	*US*
Midnighters	LP	Federal	395541	1956	**£150**	**£75**	*US*
Midnighters Vol. 2	LP	King	395581	1958	**£60**	**£30**	*US*
Midnighters Vol. 2	LP	Federal	395581	1957	**£100**	**£50**	*US*
Mr Rhythm And Blues	LP	King	700	1960	**£350**	**£210**	*US*
One And Only Hank Ballard	LP	King	674	1960	**£40**	**£20**	*US*
Sing Along	LP	King	759	1961	**£40**	**£20**	*US*
Singin' And Swingin'	LP	King	618	1959	**£40**	**£20**	*US*
Spotlight On Hank Ballard	LP	Parlophone	PMC1158	1961	**£50**	**£25**	
Star In Your Eyes	LP	King	896	1964	**£25**	**£10**	*US*
Those Lazy Lazy Days	LP	King	913	1965	**£20**	**£8**	*US*
Twenty-Four Great Songs	LP	King	981	1968	**£15**	**£6**	*US*
Twenty-Four Hit Tunes	LP	King	950	1966	**£20**	**£8**	*US*
Twist	7"	Parlophone	R4558	1959	**£25**	**£12.50**	
Twist	7"	Parlophone	R4688	1960	**£15**	**£7.50**	
Twistin' Fools	LP	King	781	1962	**£30**	**£15**	*US*
You Can't Keep A Good Man Down	LP	King	KSD1052	1969	**£12**	**£5**	*US*

BALLETTO DIBRONZO

Title	Format	Label	Cat. No.	Year	Price	Price	Notes
Ys	LP	Polydor	2480127	1972	**£25**	**£10**	*German*

BALLOON FARM

Title	Format	Label	Cat. No.	Year	Price	Price	Notes
Question Of Temperature	7"	London	HLP10185	1968	**£40**	**£20**	

BALLS

Much was expected of the alliance between Denny Laine and the Move's Trevor Burton, but in the end, Balls could only manage one single. This was later reissued under Burton's name.

Title	Format	Label	Cat. No.	Year	Price	Price	Notes
Fight For My Country	7"	Wizard	WIZ101	1971	**£10**	**£5**	

BALMER, LORI

Title	Format	Label	Cat. No.	Year	Price	Price	Notes
Treacle Brown	7"	Polydor	56293	1968	**£6**	**£2.50**	

BALTIK

Title	Format	Label	Cat. No.	Year	Price	Price	Notes
Baltik	LP	CBS	65581	1973	**£20**	**£8**	*Swedish*

BALTIMORE & OHIO MARCHING BAND

Title	Format	Label	Cat. No.	Year	Price	Price	Notes
Lapland	7"	Stateside	SS2065	1967	**£60**	**£30**	
Lapland	LP	Stateside	SL/SSL10231	1968	**£25**	**£10**	

BAMA WINDS

Title	Format	Label	Cat. No.	Year	Mint	VG	Notes
Windy	LP	Island	ILPS9096	1969	£10	£4	pink label

BAMBIS

Title	Format	Label	Cat. No.	Year	Mint	VG	Notes
Baby Blue	7"	CBS	201778	1965	£10	£5	
Not Wrong	7"	Oriole	CB1965	1964	£10	£5	

BAMBOO SHOOTS

Title	Format	Label	Cat. No.	Year	Mint	VG	Notes
Fox Has Gone To Ground	7"	Columbia	DB8370	1968	£100	£50	

BANANA & THE BUNCH

Title	Format	Label	Cat. No.	Year	Mint	VG	Notes
Mid Mountain Ranch	LP	Warner Bros	BS2626	1973	£15	£6	US

BANANARAMA

Title	Format	Label	Cat. No.	Year	Mint	VG	Notes
Aie A Mwana	12"	Deram	DMX446	1981	£6	£2.50	
Cruel Summer '89	CD-s	London	NANCD19	1989	£5	£2	
Help	CD-s	London	LONCD222	1989	£5	£2	with French & Saunders
I Can't Help It	CD-s	London	NANCD15	1988	£5	£2	
I Want You Back	CD-s	London	NANCD16	1988	£5	£2	
It's Only Your Love	CD-s	London	NANCD21	1990	£5	£2	
Long Train Running	CD-s	London	NANCD24	1991	£5	£2	
Love In The First Degree	CD-s	London	0804802	1988	£15	£7.50	CD video
Love, Truth And Honesty	CD-s	London	NANCD17	1988	£5	£2	
Nathan Jones	CD-s	London	NANCD18	1988	£5	£2	
Preacher Man	CD-s	London	NANCD23	1990	£5	£2	

BANCHEE

Title	Format	Label	Cat. No.	Year	Mint	VG	Notes
Banchee	LP	Atlantic	8240	1969	£20	£8	US
Thinkin'	LP	Polydor	244066	1971	£40	£20	US

BANCO

Title	Format	Label	Cat. No.	Year	Mint	VG	Notes
Banco Del Mutuo Soccorso	LP	Orizzonte	ORL8041	1972	£20	£8	Italian
Carofano Rosso	LP	Orizzonte	ORL8334	1976	£15	£6	Italian
Come In Un Ultima Cena	LP	Manticore	28004	1976	£20	£8	
Darwin	LP	Orizzonte	ORL8094	1972	£25	£10	Italian
Lo Sono Nato Libero	LP	Orizzonte	ORL8202	1973	£20	£8	Italian

BAND

Title	Format	Label	Cat. No.	Year	Mint	VG	Notes
Across The Great Divide	CD	Capitol		1994	£15	£6	US promo sampler
Band	LP	Capitol	EST132	1969	£10	£4	
Band On CD	CD	Capitol	DPRO79379	1990	£20	£8	US promo sampler
Cahoots	LP	Capitol	EAST651	1971	£10	£4	
Moondog Matinee	LP	Capitol	ESW11241	1973	£10	£4	
Music From Big Pink	CD	Mobile Fidelity	UDCD527	1989	£15	£6	US audiophile
Music From Big Pink	LP	Capitol	(S)T2955	1968	£10	£4	
Rock Of Ages	LP	Capitol	ESTSP11	1972	£12	£5	double
Stage Fright	CD	DCC	GZS1061	1994	£15	£6	US audiophile
Stage Fright	LP	Capitol	EASW425	1970	£10	£4	

BAND AID

Title	Format	Label	Cat. No.	Year	Mint	VG	Notes
Do They Know It's Christmas?	7"	Mercury	FEEDP1	1985	£6	£2.50	shaped picture disc

BAND OF ANGELS

A Band of Angels wore straw boaters to emphasize their Harrow origins, and it would have been surprising if at least some of them had not achieved success. First up was singer Mike D'Abo, who became the lead singer with Manfred Mann after the departure of Paul Jones. Later, however, the group's guitarist and manager founded EG management, amongst whose signings were King Crimson and Roxy Music.

Title	Format	Label	Cat. No.	Year	Mint	VG	Notes
Gonna Make A Woman Of You	7"	United Artists	UP1066	1964	£12	£6	
Invitation	7"	Piccadilly	7N35292	1966	£12	£6	
Invitation	7" EP	Pye	PNV24162	1966	£30	£15	French
Leave It To Me	7"	Piccadilly	7N35279	1966	£12	£6	
Not True As Yet	7"	United Artists	UP1049	1964	£12	£6	
She'll Never Be You	7" EP	United Artists	36050	1964	£30	£15	French

BANDOGGS

Title	Format	Label	Cat. No.	Year	Mint	VG	Notes
Bandoggs	LP	Transatlantic	LTRA504	1978	£12	£5	

BANDY LEGS

Title	Format	Label	Cat. No.	Year	Mint	VG	Notes
Ride Ride	7"	WWW	WWS01	1974	£15	£7.50	

BANERJEE, JAYASRI

Title	Format	Label	Cat. No.	Year	Mint	VG	Notes
Classical Indian Ragas	LP	Polydor	583010	1967	£10	£4	

BANGLES

Title	Format	Label	Cat. No.	Year	Mint	VG	Notes
Be With You	CD-s	CBS	BANGSD6	1989	£5	£2	picture disc
Eternal Flame	CD-s	CBS	BANGSC5	1989	£5	£2	
Everything	CD	Columbia	CSK1520	1988	£15	£6	US promo picture disc
Greatest Hits	CD	CBS	4666869	1990	£12	£5	picture disc
Hazy Shade Of Winter	CD-s	CBS	BANGSC3	1988	£5	£2	

I'll Set You Free	CD-s	CBS	BANGSC7	1989	£5	£2	
In Your Room	CD-s	CBS	BANGSC4	1988	£5	£2	
Walk Like An Egyptian	CD-s	CBS	BANGSC8	1990	£5	£2	

BANGOR FLYING CIRCUS

Bangor Flying Circus	LP	Stateside	SSL5022	1969	£10	£4	

BANGS

Debbi and Vicki Peterson and Susanna Hoffs first recorded as the Bangs, before expanding both the size of the group and its name – becoming the Bangles.

Getting Out Of Hand	7"	Downkiddie	001	1981	£25	£12.50	*US*

BANJO BOYS

Hey Mr Banjo	7"	Capitol	CL14298	1955	£4	£1.50	

BANJO KINGS

Nostalgia Revisited	LP	Good Time Jazz	LAG12174	1959	£12	£5	

BANKS, BESSIE

Go Now	7"	Soul City	SC105	1968	£5	£2	
Go Now	7"	Red Bird	BC106	1964	£20	£10	
I Can't Make It	7"	Verve	VS563	1967	£20	£10	

BANKS, DARRELL

Angel Baby	7"	Atlantic	584120	1967	£15	£7.50	
Here To Stay	LP	Stax	SXATS1011	1969	£25	£10	
Just Because Your Love Is Gone	7"	Stax	STAX124	1969	£20	£10	
Open The Door To Your Heart	7"	London	HL10070	1966	£200	£100	*demo only, best auctioned*
Open The Door To Your Heart	7"	Stateside	SS536	1966	£10	£5	

BANKS, HOMER

Hooked By Love	7"	Liberty	LIB12060	1967	£10	£5	
Lot Of Love	7"	Liberty	LIB12028	1966	£12	£6	
Me Or Your Mama	7"	Minit	MLF11015	1969	£5	£2	
Round The Clock Lover Man	7"	Minit	MLF11004	1968	£5	£2	
Sixty Minutes Of Your Love	7"	Minit	MLF11007	1968	£4	£1.50	
Sixty Minutes Of Your Love	7"	Liberty	LIB12047	1967	£10	£5	

BANKS, LARRY

I Don't Wanna Do It	7"	Stateside	SS579	1967	£10	£5	

BANKS, LLOYD

We'll Meet Again	7"	Reaction	591008	1966	£5	£2	

BANKS, PETER

Peter Banks	LP	Sovereign	SVNA7256	1973	£20	£8	

BANNED

Little Girl	7"	Can't Eat	EAT1UP	1977	£6	£2.50	

BANSHEES

Bryan Ferry sung with the Banshees for a time, although he cannot be heard on any of the group's records.

Big Buildin'	7"	Columbia	DB7530	1965	£20	£10	
I Got A Woman	7"	Columbia	DB7361	1964	£20	£10	
Yes Indeed	7"	Columbia	DB7752	1965	£20	£10	

BANTAMS

Beware The Bantams	LP	Warner Bros	W(S)1625	1966	£20	£8	*US*
Over You	7" EP	Warner Bros	WEP1448	1966	£10	£5	*French*

BARA MENYN

Bara Menyn	7" EP	Wren	WRE1065	1969	£15	£7.50	
Rhagor O'r Bara Menyn	7" EP	Wren	WRE1072	1969	£15	£7.50	

BARBARA & BRENDA

Never Love A Robin	7"	Direction	583799	1968	£4	£1.50	

BARBARIANS

Are You A Boy Or Are You A Girl	7"	Stateside	SS449	1965	£20	£10	
Are You A Boy Or Are You A Girl	7" EP	Vogue	INT18027	1965	£100	£50	*French*
Barbarians	LP	Laurie	LLP/SLP2033	1966	£60	£30	*US*
Moulty	7"	Stateside	SS497	1966	£20	£10	

BARBARIN, PAUL

New Orleans Band	10" LP	Vogue	LDE013	1952	£20	£8	
New Orleans Jazz	LP	London	LTZK15032	1957	£15	£6	

BARBARIN, PAUL & PUNCH MILLER

Jazz At Preservation Hall Vol. 4	LP	London	HAK/SHK8164	1964	£10	£4	

BARBECUE BOB

Georgia Blues No. 1	LP	Kokomo	K1002	1967	£75	£37.50	

BARBEE, JOHN HENRY

Portraits In Blues Vol. 9	LP	Storyville	670171	1967	£10	£4	

BARBER, CHRIS

American Jazz Band	LP	Columbia	33SX1321/ SCX3376	1961	£10	£4	
At The London Palladium	LP	Columbia	33SX1346	1961	£40	£20	
At The Royal Festival Hall	7" EP	Decca	DFE6252	1956	£6	£2.50	
At The Royal Festival Hall No. 2	7" EP	Decca	DFE6344	1956	£6	£2.50	
Band Box Vol. 1	LP	Columbia	33SX1158	1959	£10	£4	
Band Box Vol. 2	LP	Columbia	33SX1245/ SCX3310	1960	£10	£4	
Bandbox Vol. 1	7" EP	Columbia	ESG7789	1960	£6	£2.50	stereo
Bandbox Vol. 1	7" EP	Columbia	SEG7980	1960	£5	£2	
Bandbox Vol. 1 No. 2	7" EP	Columbia	ESG7901	1963	£6	£2.50	stereo
Bandbox Vol. 1 No. 2	7" EP	Columbia	SEG7994	1960	£5	£2	
Barber In Copenhagen	7" EP	Columbia	SEG8182	1962	£5	£2	
Barber's Best	7" EP	Decca	DFE6382	1956	£6	£2.50	
Barber's Best	LP	Decca	LK4246	1958	£10	£4	
Barber's Blues Book Vol. 1	7" EP	Columbia	SEG8214	1962	£5	£2	
Battersea Rain Dance	7"	Marmalade	598013	1969	£4	£1.50	
Battersea Rain Dance	LP	Polydor	2384020	197–	£20	£8	
Battersea Rain Dance	LP	Marmalade	608009	1969	£20	£8	
Best Of Chris Barber	LP	Ace Of Clubs	ACL1037	1960	£10	£4	
Best Yet	LP	Columbia	33SX1401	1961	£25	£10	
Blues Book	LP	Columbia	33SX1333/ SCX3384	1961	£10	£4	
Bobby Shafto	7"	Decca	F10492	1955	£4	£1.50	
Can't You Line 'Em	7"	Pye	7NJ2017	1958	£4	£1.50	
Catcall	7"	Marmalade	598005	1967	£30	£15	
Chimes Blues	7"	Decca	F10417	1954	£4	£1.50	
Chris Barber Plays Vol. 1	10" LP	Polygon	JTL3	1955	£20	£8	
Chris Barber Plays Vol. 1	10" LP	Nixa	NJT500	1956	£15	£6	
Chris Barber Plays Vol. 2	10" LP	Nixa	NJT502	1956	£15	£6	
Chris Barber Plays Vol. 3	10" LP	Nixa	NJT505	1957	£12	£5	
Chris Barber Plays Vol. 4	10" LP	Nixa	NJT508	1957	£12	£5	
Chris Barber Skiffle Group	7" EP	Pye	NJE1025	1957	£15	£7.50	
Chris Barber Special	7" EP	Pye	NJE1007	1956	£5	£2	
Chris Barber's Jazz Band	7" EP	Tempo	EXA22	1956	£5	£2	
Chris Barber's New Orleans Jazz Band	7" EP	Tempo	EXA6	1955	£5	£2	
Echoes Of Harlem	LP	Nixa	NJL1	1955	£12	£5	
Extracts From Barber In Berlin	7" EP	Columbia	ESG7821	1960	£6	£2.50	stereo
Extracts From Barber In Berlin	7" EP	Columbia	SEG8030	1960	£5	£2	
Finishing Straight	7"	Columbia	DB7461	1965	£15	£7.50	
Folk Barber Style	LP	Decca	LK4742	1965	£25	£10	
Folk Barber Style	LP	Decca	PFS4070	1965	£15	£6	
Good Mornin' Blues	LP	Columbia	33SX1657	1965	£30	£15	
I Never Knew Just What A Girl Could Do	7"	Decca	FJ10790	1956	£4	£1.50	
Ice Cream	7"	Tempo	A160	1957	£5	£2	
In Berlin Vol. 1	LP	Columbia	33SX1189	1959	£10	£4	
In Berlin Vol. 2	LP	Columbia		1959	£10	£4	
In Concert	LP	Nixa	NJL6	1957	£10	£4	
In Concert Vol. 2	LP	Pye	NJL15	1958	£10	£4	
In Concert Vol. 3	LP	Pye	NJL17	1958	£10	£4	
In Copenhagen	LP	Columbia	33SX1274/ SCX3342	1961	£10	£4	
Introducing Ian	7" EP	Columbia	SEG8110	1961	£5	£2	
It's Tight Like That	7"	Decca	F10666	1955	£4	£1.50	
Jazz At The Royal Festival Hall	7" EP	Decca	DFE6238	1955	£8	£4	
Jazz Sacred And Secular	10" LP	Columbia	33S1112	1957	£20	£8	
New Orleans Blues	7" EP	Decca	DFE6463	1958	£10	£5	
New Orleans Joys	10" LP	Decca	LF1198	1954	£20	£8	
Pat	7" EP	Columbia	ESG7846	1961	£6	£2.50	stereo
Pat	7" EP	Columbia	SEG8081	1961	£5	£2	
Plays Spirituals	7" EP	Columbia	SEG7568	1955	£6	£2.50	
Plus/Minus 1	7" EP	Pye	NJE1013	1956	£8	£4	
Plus/Minus One	7" EP	Polygon	JTE103	1956	£10	£5	
Precious Lord, Lead Me On	7"	Tempo	A116	1956	£10	£5	
Saratoga Swing	7"	Tempo	A132	1956	£5	£2	
White Christmas	7"	Columbia	SCMC10	1954	£20	£10	export
World Is Waiting For The Sunrise	7"	Decca	FJ10724	1956	£4	£1.50	

BARBIERI, GATO

Caliente	LP	A&M	AMLH64597	1976	£10	£4	
Chapter Four: Alive In New York	LP	Impulse	AQD9303	1975	£12	£5	US
Chapter One: Latin America	LP	Impulse	AS9248	1973	£12	£5	US
Chapter Three: Viva Emiliano	LP	Impulse	ASD9279	1974	£12	£5	US
Chapter Two: Hasta Siempre	LP	Impulse	AS9263	1974	£12	£5	US
El Pampero	LP	Philips	6369418	1973	£12	£5	
Fenix	LP	Philips	6369409	1973	£12	£5	
In Search Of Mystery	LP	ESP-Disk	1049	1966	£25	£10	US
Last Tango In Paris	LP	United Artists	UAGC29440	1973	£12	£5	
Third World	LP	Philips	6369403	1969	£15	£6	

Under Fire	LP	Philips	6369419	1973	£12	£5	

BARBOUR, DAVE

Tough	7"	Oriole	CB1507	1959	£4	£1.50	

BARCLAY, EDDIE

Eddie And Quincy	LP	Felsted	PDL85056	1959	£12	£5	*with Quincy Jones*
James Dean – Music From His Films	7" EP	Felsted	ESD3041	1957	£15	£7.50	

BARCLAY, RUE & PEGGY DUNCAN

Tongue Tied Boy	7"	London	HL8033	1954	£20	£10	

BARCLAY JAMES HARVEST

In their day, Barclay James Harvest were one of the major players in the progressive rock league, with music that sounded like a sometimes inspired collision between Moody Blues-style melody (complete with the obligatory mellotron) and the guitar histrionics of someone like Procol Harum's Robin Trower. Albums like *Once Again* and *Barclay James Harvest And Other Short Stories* are worthy period pieces, but they sold too well to be particularly collectable now – indeed they sold well enough to enable the group to maintain a career through to the nineties. Sadly, however, Barclay James Harvest are likely to be best remembered for being virtually bankrupted by a short-sighted attempt to fight the court action of the Enid's Robert John Godfrey, who was determined to claim payment and credit for the vital work he contributed to the 'Once Again' album.

Barclay James Harvest	LP	Harvest	SHVL770	1970	£10	£4	
Brother Thrush	7"	Harvest	HAR5003	1969	£5	£2	
Cheap The Bullet	CD-s	Polydor	PZCD67	1990	£5	£2	
Early Morning	7"	Parlophone	R5693	1968	£8	£4	
Harvest Years	CD	Nova Lepidoptera		1991	£25	£10	*double, fan club issue*
Just A Day Away	7"	Polydor	POPPX585	1983	£4	£1.50	*shaped picture disc*
Once Again	LP	Harvest	Q4SHVL0788	1971	£15	£6	*quad*
Taking Some Time On	7"	Harvest	HAR5025	1970	£5	£2	
Victims Of Circumstance	7"	Polydor	POSPP674	1984	£4	£1.50	*picture disc*

BARDENS, PETER

Answer	LP	Transatlantic	TRA222	1970	£10	£4	
Peter Bardens	LP	Transatlantic	TRA243	1971	£10	£4	

BARDOLINI, BAKADI

Songs	LP	private		1983	£150	£75	*Austrian*

BARDOT, BRIGITTE

Brigitte Bardot	LP	Philips	BL7561	1963	£50	£25	
Harley Davidson	7"	Pye	7N25450	1968	£60	£30	*picture sleeve*
Harley Davidson	7"	Pye	7N25450	1968	£6	£2.50	
Mr Sun	7"	Vogue	VRS7018	1966	£20	£10	
Mr Sun	7"	Vogue	VRS7018	1966	£100	£50	*picture sleeve*
Very Private Affair	7" EP	MGM	MGMEP768	1962	£50	£25	

BARE, BOBBY

Constant Sorrow	LP	RCA	RD7783	1966	£10	£4	
Detroit City	7" EP	RCA	RCX7139	1964	£8	£4	
Five Hundred Miles Away From Home	LP	RCA	LPM/LSP2835	1963	£10	£4	*US*
I'm Hanging Up My Rifle	7"	Top Rank	JAR310	1960	£6	£2.50	

BAREFOOT BLUES BAND

Can't You See	7"	Beacon	BEA163	1970	£10	£5	
Spirit Of Joe Hill	7"	Deram	DM353	1972	£5	£2	

BARELLI, MINOUCHE

Boum Bababoum	7"	CBS	2806	1967	£10	£5	

BARGE, GENE

Dance With Daddy G	LP	Checker	2994	1965	£20	£8	*US*

BARHAM, TINY

Tiny Barham	10" LP	Audubon		195–	£20	£8	

BARK PSYCHOSIS

Nothing Feels I Know	CD-s	Cheree	CHEREE010CD	1990	£5	£2	

BARKAN, MARK

Pity The Woman	7"	Stateside	SS2064	1967	£5	£2	

BARKAYS

Black Rock	LP	Polydor	2362003	1971	£12	£5	
Cold Blooded	LP	Stax	STX1033	1976	£10	£4	
Do You See What I See?	LP	Polydor	2325087	1972	£10	£4	
Gotta Groove	LP	Stax	STATS1009	1969	£12	£5	
Soul Finger	7"	Stax	601014	1967	£4	£1.50	
Soul Finger	LP	Atlantic	K40184	1972	£10	£4	
Soul Finger	LP	Atco	228030	1969	£12	£5	

BARKEE, JOHN HENRY

Portraits In Blues	LP	Storyville	SLP171	1965	£12	£5	

BARKER, DAVE

Fastest Man Alive	7"	Jackpot	JP736	1970	£4	£1.50	
Funky Reggae	7"	Duke	DU74	1970	£5	£2	

Girl Of My Dreams	7"	Jackpot	JP745	1970	£4	£1.50	
Groove Me	7"	Upsetter	US362	1971	£6	£2.50	
October	7"	Randys	RAN503	1970	£4	£1.50	
Prisoner Of Love	7"	Punch	PH20	1970	£4	£1.50	*Busty & Upsetters B side*
Prisoner Of Love	LP	Trojan	TRL127	1976	£20	£8	
Shocks '71	7"	Upsetter	US358	1971	£6	£2.50	
Shocks Of Mighty	7"	Punch	PH25	1970	£4	£1.50	
Shocks Of Mighty	7"	Upsetter	US331	1970	£6	£2.50	
Some Sympathy	7"	Upsetter	US344	1970	£6	£2.50	*Untouchables B side*
Sound Underground	7"	Upsetter	US347	1970	£6	£2.50	
Wet Version	7"	Jackpot	JP742	1970	£4	£1.50	
What A Confusion	7"	Upsetter	US364	1971	£6	£2.50	
You Betray Me	7"	Punch	PH22	1970	£4	£1.50	

BARKER, LES

Mrs Ackroyd Superstar!	LP	Free Reed	FRR015	1977	£12	£5	

BARNABY BYE

Room To Grow	LP	Atlantic	SD7273	1973	£20	£8	US

BARNES, BARNEY J.

It Must Be Love	7"	Decca	F12662	1967	£6	£2.50	

BARNES, J. J.

Baby Please Come Back Home	7"	Stax	STAX130	1969	£8	£4	
Daytripper	7"	Polydor	56722	1967	£10	£5	
Rare Stamps	LP	Stax	SXATS1012	1969	£20	£8	*with Steve Mancha*

BARNES, JEFF

Wake The Nation	7"	Smash	SMA2313	1971	£5	£2	

BARNES, LLOYD

Time Is Hard	7"	Blue Beat	BB235	1964	£12	£6	*Buster's Allstars B side*

BARNES, MAE

Songs By Mae Barnes	10" LP	Atlantic	ALS404	195–	£100	£50	US

BARNES, MYRA

Message For The Soul Sisters	12"	Urban		1988	£6	£2.50	

BARNET, CHARLIE

Cherokee	LP	Top Rank	35037	1960	£10	£4	
Classics In Jazz	LP	Capitol	LCT6018	1955	£20	£8	
Dance Session	10" LP	Columbia	33C9024	1956	£20	£8	
Hop On The Skyliner	LP	Brunswick	LAT8094	1956	£20	£8	

BARNET, ERIC

Horse	7"	Gas	GAS100	1969	£4	£1.50	
Quaker City	7"	Crab	CRAB37	1969	£4	£1.50	
Te Ta Toe	7"	Gas	GAS106	1969	£4	£1.50	*Milton Boothe B side*

BARNETT, BARRY

Book Of Love	7"	HMV	POP487	1958	£4	£1.50	
Susie Darlin'	7"	HMV	POP532	1958	£4	£1.50	

BARNETT, DON

Maria	LP	Ovation	OV1725	1976	£20	£8	

BARNSTORMERS SPASM BAND

Stormin' The Barn	7"	Tempo	A168	1959	£5	£2	
Whistling Rufus	7"	Parlophone	R4416	1958	£5	£2	

BARNUM, H. B.

Big Voice Of Barnum	LP	RCA	RD/SF7500	1962	£10	£4	
Everybody Loves H. B.	LP	RCA	RD/SF7543	1963	£10	£4	
Great	7" EP	RCA	RCX7147	1964	£100	£50	
Lost Love	7"	Fontana	H299	1961	£4	£1.50	
Record	7"	Capitol	CL15391	1965	£15	£7.50	

BAROCK & ROLL ENSEMBLE

Eine Kleine Beatlemusik by the Barock and Roll Ensemble consists of tunes written by the Beatles arranged for a small group of strings as though the music was by Mozart. The joke – perpetrated by musicologist Fritz Spiegl – is a good one, and the record works as music too. The B side is less successful, however; Spiegl knows his Mozart but not his rock music and his arrangements of themes by Wagner as if they were pieces by the Shadows are simply feeble.

Eine Kleine Beatlemusik	7" EP	HMV	7EG8887	1965	£5	£2	

BARON, CARL & THE CHEETAHS

Beg Borrow Or Steal	7"	Columbia	DB7162	1963	£8	£4	

BARON & HIS POUNDING PIANO

Is A Bluebird Blue	7"	Sue	WI398	1965	£15	£7.50	*with the V.I.P.s*

BARONS

Don't Walk Out	7"	London	HLP8391	1957	**£1500**	**£1000**	*best auctioned*

BARONS (2)

Cossack	7"	Oriole	CB1608	1961	**£6**	**£2.50**	
Samurai	7"	Oriole	CB1620	1961	**£8**	**£4**	

BAROQUES

Barbarians With Love	LP	Job	1002	1966	**£20**	**£8**	*Dutch*
Baroques	LP	Whamm	PS10001	1966	**£30**	**£15**	*Dutch*
With Love	LP	Whamm	PS10003	1967	**£20**	**£8**	*Dutch*

BAROQUES (2)

Baroques	LP	Chess	(S)1516	1967	**£40**	**£20**	*US*

BARRACUDAS

Plane View	LP	Justice	143	1968	**£200**	**£100**	*US*

BARRACUDAS (2)

1965 Again	7"	Zonophone	Z11	1980	**£6**	**£2.50**	
His Last Summer	7"	Zonophone	Z8	1980	**£6**	**£2.50**	
I Can't Pretend	7"	Zonophone	Z17	1981	**£6**	**£2.50**	
I Want My Woody Back	7"	Cells	CELLOUT1	1979	**£8**	**£4**	
Summer Fun	7"	Zonophone	Z5	1980	**£6**	**£2.50**	*with sticker sheet*

BARRETT, DICKIE

Smoke Gets In Your Eyes	7"	MGM	MGM976	1958	**£5**	**£2**	

BARRETT, RICHARD

Come Softly To Me	7"	HMV	POP609	1959	**£6**	**£2.50**	

BARRETT, RITCHIE

Some Other Guy	7"	London	HLK9552	1962	**£25**	**£12.50**	

BARRETT, SYD

Syd Barrett was eased out of the Pink Floyd due to his increasingly unreliable behaviour – a guitarist with a tendency to stand still on stage without actually playing anything was something of a liability. Nevertheless, the rest of the Floyd bore him no malice and were happy to turn up to lend support to Barrett's solo recordings (as did Soft Machine too). Whether these records are the work of a brilliant eccentric or merely the last gasp of semi-coherency from an unmitigated loony probably depends on the listener's point of view.

Barrett	LP	Harvest	SHSP4007	1970	**£20**	**£8**	
Madcap Laughs	LP	Harvest	SHVL765	1970	**£20**	**£8**	
Madcap Laughs/Barrett	LP	Harvest	SHDW404	1974	**£15**	**£6**	*double*
Octopus	7"	Harvest	HAR5009	1969	**£60**	**£30**	
Peel Sessions	12"	Strange Fruit	SFPS043	1988	**£6**	**£2.50**	
Peel Sessions	CD-s	Strange Fruit	SFPSCD043	1988	**£6**	**£2.50**	

BARRETT, WILD WILLY

Organic Bondage	LP	Galvanised	DIP1	1986	**£20**	**£8**	*wooden sleeve*

BARRETTO, RAY

Acid	7"	London	HL10262	1969	**£4**	**£1.50**	
Acid	LP	London	HA/SH8383	1969	**£20**	**£8**	
El Watusi	7"	Columbia	DB7051	1963	**£6**	**£2.50**	
El Watusi	7"	Columbia	DB7684	1965	**£5**	**£2**	
El Watusi	LP	Island	ILP946	1967	**£30**	**£15**	

BARRIER

Georgie Brown	7"	Eyemark	EMS1013	1968	**£60**	**£30**	
Spot The Lights	7"	Philips	BF1731	1968	**£30**	**£15**	
Tide Is Turning	7"	Philips	BF1692	1968	**£4**	**£1.50**	

BARRON KNIGHTS

Barron Knights	LP	Columbia	SX6007	1966	**£12**	**£5**	
Call Up The Groups	LP	Columbia	33SX1648	1964	**£15**	**£7.50**	
Guying The Top Pops	7" EP	Columbia	SEG8424	1965	**£6**	**£2.50**	
Lazy Fat People	7" EP	Festival	FX1537	196–	**£8**	**£4**	*French*
Let's Face It	7"	Fontana	H368	1962	**£5**	**£2**	
Scribed	LP	Columbia	SX/SCX6176	1967	**£12**	**£5**	
Those Versatile Barron Knights	7" EP	Columbia	SEG8526	1966	**£6**	**£2.50**	

BARROW POETS

The Barrow Poets were a poetry and music group, a little like the Liverpool Scene, but with much less of a rock sound. Where the Liverpool Scene played on the John Peel programme, the Barrow Poets would have turned up on Radio Four. Essentially the records are an extension of the fifties and sixties jazz-and-poetry experiments, in which the words are by far the most important element. Fortunately, they are always well worth hearing. Group member Jim Parker is still very much around, his name being frequently credited as the composer for TV programme themes.

At The Printer's Devil	7" EP	Barrow	BR1	1967	**£20**	**£10**	
Barrow Collection	LP	Argo	PLP1072	197–	**£15**	**£6**	
Entertainment Of Poetry And Music	LP	Argo	RG360	1963	**£25**	**£10**	
Folk Rhymes Tunes And Verses	LP	Fontana	STL5479	1968	**£20**	**£8**	
Joker	LP	RCA	SF8110	1970	**£15**	**£6**	
Letter In A Bottle	7"	Fontana	TF939	1968	**£4**	**£1.50**	
Magic Egg	LP	Argo	ZSW511	1972	**£15**	**£6**	

Outpatients	LP	Argo	ZSW508	1972	£15	£6	

BARRY, AL

Morning Sun	7"	Doctor Bird	DB1502	1970	£4	£1.50	

BARRY, DAVE & SARAH BERNER

Out Of This World With Flying Saucers	7"	London	HLU8324	1956	£25	£12.50	

BARRY, JOE

Fool To Care	7" EP	Mercury	ZEP10130	1962	£100	£50	
I Started Loving You Again	7"	Stateside	SS2127	1969	£4	£1.50	
I'm A Fool To Care	7"	Mercury	AMT1149	1961	£4	£1.50	

BARRY, JOHN

007	7"	Ember	EMBS243	1967	£4	£1.50	
007	7"	Ember	EMBS243	1967	£5	£2	*picture sleeve*
Americans	LP	Polydor	2383405	1976	£15	£6	
Barry Theme Successes	7" EP	Columbia	SEG8255	1963	£15	£7.50	
Beat For Beatniks	7"	Columbia	DB4446	1960	£4	£1.50	
Best Of Bond	LP	United Artists	LAS29021	1967	£10	£4	*mono*
Best Of Bond	LP	United Artists	UAS29021	1969	£10	£4	*stereo*
Big Beat	7" EP	Parlophone	GEP8737	1958	£25	£12.50	
Big Guitar	7"	Parlophone	R4418	1958	£20	£10	
Black Stockings	7"	Columbia	DB4554	1960	£4	£1.50	
Boom	LP	MCA	MUPS360	1969	£60	£30	*with Georgie Fame*
Born Free	LP	MGM	C8010	1966	£10	£4	
Chase	LP	CBS	(S)BPG62665	1966	£25	£10	
Concert John Barry	LP	Polydor	2383156	1971	£10	£4	
Cutty Sark	7"	Columbia	DB4806	1962	£4	£1.50	
Day Of The Locust	LP	Decca	PFS4339	1974	£10	£4	
Deadfall	LP	Stateside	(S)SL10263	1968	£30	£15	
Deep	LP	Casablanca	CAL2018	1977	£10	£4	
Diamonds Are For Ever	7"	Polydor	2058216	1972	£6	£2.50	
Diamonds Are For Ever	LP	United Artists	UAS29216	1971	£15	£6	
Every Which Way	7"	Parlophone	R4394	1958	£30	£15	
Farrago	7"	Parlophone	R4488	1958	£5	£2	
Film Themes	LP	CBS	64816	1972	£10	£4	
Four In The Morning	LP	Ember	NR56088	1965	£30	£15	
From Russia With Love	7"	Ember	EMBS181	1963	£4	£1.50	
From Russia With Love	7"	Ember	EMBS181	1963	£8	£4	*picture sleeve*
From Russia With Love	7" EP	United Artists	UEP1011	1965	£15	£7.50	
From Russia With Love	LP	United Artists	(S)ULP1052	1963	£15	£6	
Funeral In Berlin	LP	RCA	RD7860	1966	£15	£6	
Goldfinger	7"	United Artists	UP1068	1964	£4	£1.50	
Goldfinger	7" EP	United Artists	UEP1012	1965	£15	£7.50	
Goldfinger	LP	United Artists	(S)ULP1076	1964	£15	£6	
Great Screen Themes	7" EP	CBS	WEP1131	1961	£6	£2.50	
High Road To China	LP	A&R	FILM001	1983	£15	£6	
Hit And Miss	7"	Columbia	DB4414	1960	£4	£1.50	
Human Jungle	7"	Columbia	DB7003	1963	£4	£1.50	
Human Jungle	7"	Columbia	DB7003	1963	£8	£4	*picture sleeve*
Ingersoll Trendsetters	7"	Lyntone	LYN378	1963	£10	£5	*flexi*
Ipcress File	LP	CBS	BPG62530	1966	£40	£20	
James Bond Collection	LP	United Artists	UAD60027/8	1973	£15	£6	*double*
James Bond Is Back	7" EP	Ember	EMBEP4551	1964	£12	£6	
James Bond Theme	7"	Columbia	DB4898	1962	£4	£1.50	
James Bond Theme	7"	CBS	WB730	1968	£5	£2	*Ray Conniff B side*
John Barry Sound	7" EP	Columbia	SEG8069	1961	£15	£7.50	
King Kong	LP	Reprise	K54090	1976	£12	£5	*with poster*
King Rat	LP	Fontana	(S)TL5302	1966	£30	£15	
Kinky	7"	Ember	EMBS178	1963	£4	£1.50	
Knack	LP	United Artists	ULP1104	1965	£40	£20	
Last Valley	LP	Probe	SPB1027	1971	£25	£10	
Lion In Winter	7"	CBS	3935	1969	£12	£6	
Lion In Winter	LP	CBS	70049	1969	£20	£8	
Little John	7"	Parlophone	R4560	1959	£4	£1.50	
Living Daylights	CD	Warner Bros	9256162	1987	£50	£25	
London Theme	7"	Ember	EMBS183	1963	£4	£1.50	
Loneliness Of Autumn	7" EP	Ember	EMBEP4544	1964	£15	£7.50	
Long John	7"	Parlophone	R4530	1959	£4	£1.50	
Magnificent Seven	7"	Columbia	DB4598	1961	£4	£1.50	
Man Alone	7"	CBS	201747	1965	£6	£2.50	
Man In The Middle	7"	Stateside	SS296	1964	£12	£6	
Man In The Middle	LP	Stateside	(S)SL10087	1964	£40	£20	
March Of The Mandarins	7"	Columbia	DB4941	1962	£5	£2	
Mary Queen Of Scots	LP	MCA	MUPS441	1972	£20	£8	
Meets Chad And Jeremy	LP	Ember	NR5032	1965	£15	£6	
Menace	7"	Columbia	DB4659	1961	£4	£1.50	
Music Of John Barry	LP	CBS	22014	1976	£15	£6	*double*
Never Let Go	7"	Columbia	DB4480	1960	£4	£1.50	
On Her Majesty's Secret Service	7"	CBS	4680	1969	£8	£4	
On Her Majesty's Secret Service	LP	United Artists	UAS29020	1969	£25	£10	*gatefold sleeve*
Pancho	7"	Parlophone	R4453	1958	£5	£2	
Passion Flower Hotel	LP	CBS	BPG62598	1965	£25	£10	
Play It Again	LP	Polydor	2383300	1974	£10	£4	
Plays 007	LP	Ember	NR5025	1964	£25	£10	
Quiller Memorandum	LP	CBS	62869	1966	£20	£8	*with Matt Monro*
Ready When You Are JB	LP	CBS	63952	1970	£10	£4	

Revisited	LP	Ember	SE8008	1971	£15	£6	
Seance On A Wet Afternoon	7"	United Artists	UP1060	1964	£15	£7.50	
Seven Faces	7"	Columbia	DB7414	1964	£15	£7.50	
Starfire	7"	Columbia	DB4699	1961	£4	£1.50	
Stringbeat	LP	Columbia	33SX1358/ SCX3401	1961	£30	£15	
Syndicate	7"	CBS	201822	1965	£10	£5	
Thunderball	7" EP	United Artists	UEP1015	1966	£12	£6	
Thunderball	LP	United Artists	(S)ULP1110	1965	£15	£6	
Twelfth Street Rag	7"	Parlophone	R4582	1959	£12	£6	
Walk Don't Run	7"	Columbia	DB4505	1960	£4	£1.50	
Watch Your Step	7"	Columbia	DB4746	1961	£4	£1.50	
Wednesday's Child	7"	CBS	202451	1967	£6	£2.50	
Whisperers	LP	United Artists	(S)ULP1168	1967	£30	£15	
Wrong Box	LP	Mainstream	5/S6088	1966	£150	£75	US
You Only Live Twice	7"	CBS	2825	1967	£6	£2.50	
You Only Live Twice	LP	United Artists	(S)ULP1171	1967	£15	£6	
Zip Zip	7"	Parlophone	R4363	1957	£50	£25	
Zulu	LP	Ember	NR5012	1964	£20	£8	
Zulu Stamp	7"	Ember	EMBS185	1963	£6	£2.50	picture sleeve
Zulu Stamp	7"	Ember	EMBS185	1963	£4	£1.50	

BARRY, LEN

1-2-3	7" EP	Brunswick	10672	1965	£12	£6	French
1-2-3	7" EP	Decca	60001	1965	£12	£6	French
1-2-3	LP	Brunswick	LAT8637	1965	£15	£6	
Having A Good Time	7" EP	Cameo Parkway	CPE556	1966	£10	£5	with the Dovells
Hearts Are Trumps	7"	Cameo Parkway	P969	1965	£6	£2.50	
It's A Crying Shame	7" EP	Decca	60005	1966	£10	£5	French
Moving Finger Writes	7"	RCA	RCA1588	1967	£4	£1.50	
My Kind Of Soul	LP	RCA	LSP/LSP3823	1967	£10	£4	US
Sings With The Dovells	LP	Cameo Parkway	C1082	1966	£10	£4	

BARRY, MARGARET

Come Back Paddy Reilly	LP	Emerald	GEM1003	1968	£12	£5	
Street Songs And Fiddle Tunes Of Ireland	10" LP	Topic	10T6	1958	£20	£8	

BARRY, MARGARET & MICHAEL GORMAN

Blarney Stone	LP	XTRA	XTRA5037	1967	£12	£5	
Her Mantle So Green	LP	Topic	12T123	1958	£20	£8	
Her Mantle So Green	LP	Topic	12T123	1965	£12	£5	reissue with different sleeve
Ireland's Queen Of The Tinkers Sings	LP	Top Rank	25020	1960	£25	£10	
Margaret Barry And Michael Gorman	LP	Folkways	FW8729	1975	£12	£5	US

BARRY, SANDRA

'Really Gonna Shake' by Sandra Barry and the Boys represents the first recording by the group that became (without Ms Barry) the Action.

End Of The Line	7"	Pye	7N15753	1965	£5	£2	
Question	7"	Pye	7N15840	1965	£5	£2	
Really Gonna Shake	7"	Decca	F11851	1964	£20	£10	with the Boys
Stop Thief	7"	Pye	7N17102	1966	£5	£2	

BARRY & THE TAMERLANES

Butterfly	7"	Warner Bros	WB124	1964	£5	£2	
I Wonder What She's Doing Tonight	7"	Warner Bros	WB116	1963	£20	£10	
I Wonder What She's Doing Tonight	LP	A&M	W406	1963	£50	£25	US
What She's Doing Tonight	7" EP	Warner Bros	WEP1429	1964	£40	£20	French

BARRY SISTERS

Baby Come A Little Closer	7"	London	HLA8248	1956	£20	£10	
Intrigue	7"	London	HLA8304	1956	£20	£10	
Side By Side	LP	Columbia	33SX1309	1960	£12	£5	
Sing Me A Sentimental Love Song	7"	Columbia	DB3843	1956	£5	£2	

BARRY SISTERS (2)

Jo Jo	7"	Decca	F11141	1959	£4	£1.50	
Tall Paul	7"	Decca	F11118	1959	£4	£1.50	

BART, LIONEL

Bart For Bart's Sake	10" LP	Decca	LF1324	1959	£12	£5	
Isn't This Where We Came In	LP	Deram	DML/SML1028	1967	£12	£5	

BARTHOLOMEW, DAVE

Fats Domino Presents Dave Bartholomew	LP	Imperial	LP9162/LP12076	1961	£30	£15	US
New Orleans House Party	LP	Imperial	LP9217/LP12217	1963	£30	£15	US

BARTLEY, CHRIS

I Found A Goodie	7"	Bell	BLL1031	1968	£5	£2	
Sweetest Thing This Side Of Heaven	7"	Cameo Parkway	P101	1962	£30	£15	

BARTOK

Title	Format	Label	Cat. No.	Year	Mint	VG	Notes
Insanity	7"	On	ON1	1982	£5	£2	

BARTON, EILEEN

Title	Format	Label	Cat. No.	Year	Mint	VG	Notes
Cry Me A River	7"	Vogue Coral	Q72122	1956	£8	£4	
Fujiyama Mama	7"	Vogue Coral	Q72075	1955	£20	£10	
Spring It Was	7"	Vogue Coral	Q72205	1956	£4	£1.50	
Teenage Heart	7"	Vogue Coral	Q72148	1956	£4	£1.50	
Too Close For Comfort	7"	Vogue Coral	Q72250	1957	£4	£1.50	
Without Love	7"	Vogue Coral	Q72270	1957	£4	£1.50	
Year We Fell In Love	7"	Vogue Coral	Q72060	1955	£5	£2	

BARTY, ALAN

Title	Format	Label	Cat. No.	Year	Mint	VG	Notes
Barty's Bow	LP	Kettle	KOP4	1980	£10	£4	

BARTZ, GARY

Title	Format	Label	Cat. No.	Year	Mint	VG	Notes
Another Earth	LP	Milestone	MSP901	1971	£15	£6	
I've Known Rivers And Other Bodies	LP	Prestige	66001	1974	£15	£6	US

BASES

Title	Format	Label	Cat. No.	Year	Mint	VG	Notes
Home Sweet Home	7"	Coxsone	CS7062	1968	£10	£5	*Marcia Griffiths B side*
I Don't Mind	7"	Studio One	SO2056	1968	£12	£6	*Jackie Mittoo B side*

BASHFUL BROTHER OSWALD

Title	Format	Label	Cat. No.	Year	Mint	VG	Notes
Bashful Brother Oswald	LP	London	HAB/SHB8104	1964	£10	£4	

BASHO, ROBBIE

Title	Format	Label	Cat. No.	Year	Mint	VG	Notes
Basho Sings!	LP	Takoma	C1012	1967	£10	£4	US
Falconer's Arm 1	LP	Takoma	C1017	1967	£10	£4	US
Falconer's Arm 2	LP	Takoma	C1018	1968	£10	£4	US
Grail And The Lotus	LP	Takoma	C1007	1967	£10	£4	US
Seal Of The Blue Lotus	LP	Takoma	C1005	1965	£10	£4	US
Song Of The Stallion	LP	Takoma	C1031	1972	£10	£4	US
Venus In Cancer	LP	Blue Thumb	BTS10	1969	£10	£4	US
Zarthus	LP	Vanguard	VSD79339	1972	£10	£4	US

BASIC BLACK & PEARL

Title	Format	Label	Cat. No.	Year	Mint	VG	Notes
There'll Come A Time	7"	Bus Stop	BUS1030	1975	£5	£2	

BASIE, COUNT

Title	Format	Label	Cat. No.	Year	Mint	VG	Notes
April In Paris	LP	Columbia	33CX10088	1957	£15	£6	
At Newport	LP	Columbia	33CX10110	1958	£15	£6	
Atomic Mr Basie	LP	Columbia	33SX1084/ SCX3265	1958	£12	£5	
Atomic Mr Basie	LP	Columbia	33SX1084	1958	£15	£6	
Band Of Distinction	LP	HMV	CLP1428	1961	£10	£4	
Basie	LP	Columbia	33CX10065	1957	£15	£6	
Basie At Birdland	LP	Columbia	33SX1404	1961	£10	£4	
Basie Meets Bond	LP	United Artists	(S)ULP1127	1966	£15	£6	
Basie Plays Hefti	LP	Columbia	33SX1135	1958	£10	£4	
Basie's Back In Town	LP	Philips	BBL7141	1957	£15	£6	
Basie's Best	10" LP	Brunswick	LA8589	1953	£20	£8	
Blues By Basie	LP	Philips	BBL7190	1957	£15	£6	
Breakfast Dance And Barbecue	LP	Columbia	33SX1209/ SCX3294	1959	£10	£4	
Chairman Of The Board	LP	Columbia	33SX1224/ SCX3304	1960	£10	£4	
Count	10" LP	Columbia	33S1054	1955	£20	£8	
Count Basie	LP	Brunswick	LAT8028	1954	£25	£10	
Count Basie Classics	LP	Fontana	TFL5077	1960	£10	£4	
Count Basie Sextet	10" LP	Columbia	33C9010	1955	£20	£8	
Count Basie Story Vol. 1	LP	Columbia	33SX1316/ SCX3372	1961	£10	£4	
Count Basie Story Vol. 2	LP	Columbia	33SX1317/ SCX3373	1961	£10	£4	
Count Basie Swings And Joe Williams Sings	LP	Columbia	33CX10026	1956	£15	£6	
Count Basie Swings, Tony Bennett Sings	LP	Columbia	33SX1174	1959	£10	£4	
Count Basie/Lester Young	10" LP	Mercury	MG25015	1954	£20	£8	
Dance Along With Basie	LP	Columbia	33SX1264/ SCX3333	1960	£10	£4	
Dance Session	LP	Columbia	33CX10007	1955	£15	£6	
Dance Session No. 2	LP	Columbia	33CX10044	1956	£15	£6	
Just The Blues	LP	Columbia	33SX1326/ SCX3380	1961	£10	£4	
Night At Count Basie's	LP	Vanguard	PPL11005	1957	£15	£6	
Not Now – I'll Tell You When	LP	Columbia	33SX1293/ SCX3356	1961	£10	£4	
Old Count And The New Count	10" LP	Philips	BBR8036	1955	£20	£8	
One More Time	LP	Columbia	33SX1183/ SCX3284	1959	£10	£4	
One O'Clock Jump	LP	Fontana	TFL5046	1959	£10	£4	
String Along With Basie	LP	Columbia	33SX1151	1959	£10	£4	

BASS, BILLY

I'm Coming Too	7"	Pama	PM761	1969	£8	£4	

BASS, FONTELLA

Don't Mess Up A Good Thing	7"	Chess	CRS8007	1965	£10	£5	*with Bobby McClure, 2 different B sides*
Fontella Bass & Bobby McClure	7" EP	Chess	CRE6025	1966	£15	£7.50	
Fontella's Hits	7" EP	Chess	CRE6015	1966	£15	£7.50	
Free	LP	Mojo	2916018	1972	£12	£5	
I Can't Rest	7"	Chess	CRS8032	1966	£5	£2	
I Can't Rest	7" EP	Chess	CRE6020	1966	£15	£7.50	
New Look	LP	Chess	CRL4517	1966	£15	£6	
Recovery	7"	Chess	CRS8027	1966	£4	£1.50	
Rescue Me	7"	Chess	CRS8023	1965	£4	£1.50	
Safe And Sound	7"	Chess	CRS8042	1966	£4	£1.50	

BASSES

River Jordan	7"	Coxsone	CS7030	1967	£12	£6	

BASSEY, SHIRLEY

Banana Boat Song	7"	Philips	JK1006	1957	£8	£4	
Born To Sing The Blues	10" LP	Philips	BBR8130	1957	£10	£4	
Don't Take The Lovers From The World	7"	United Artists	UP1134	1966	£5	£2	
Goldfinger	7"	Columbia	DB7360	1964	£4	£1.50	
If I Had A Needle And Thread	7"	Philips	JK1018	1957	£6	£2.50	
Puh-leeze Mister Brown	7"	Philips	JK1034	1957	£6	£2.50	
To Give	7"	United Artists	UP2254	1968	£6	£2.50	

BASSMAN, JOHN GROUP

Filthy Sky	LP	ASP	60600	1971	£75	£37.50	*Dutch*

BATAAN, JOE

Riot!	LP	London	HA/SH8386	1969	£10	£4	

BATES, COLIN

Brew	LP	Fontana	SFJL913	1968	£10	£4	

BATES, MARTYN

Letters Written	10"	Cherry Red	TRED38	1982	£6	£2.50	

BATMAN

In 1966 the *Batman* TV series started, complete with its catchy double-note riff theme. A large number of different artists recorded it, entries in this guide being found under the following names: Neal Hefti, Jan and Dean, The Marketts, Nelson Riddle, the Riddlers, the Spacemen, the Spotlights, the Ventures, Link Wray (a latecomer from 1978), and the Who (on their *Ready Steady Who* EP). The stars of the show, Adam West and Burt Ward, made an LP themselves, while Ward followed this up with a single the next year (masterminded by Frank Zappa). A reggae tribute was issued in 1970 by the Sydney All Stars, while the 1989 *Batman* film also turns up in the guide, represented by Prince's LP picture disc.

BATORS, STIV

It's Cold Outside	7"	London	HLZ10575	1979	£5	£2	

BATS

Accept It	7"	Columbia	DB7429	1964	£4	£1.50	
Listen To My Heart	7"	Decca	F22534	1966	£4	£1.50	
Take Me As I Am	7"	Decca	F22616	1967	£4	£1.50	
You Will Won't You	7"	Decca	F22568	1967	£4	£1.50	

BATT, MIKE

I See Wonderful Things In You	7"	Liberty	LBF15122	1968	£4	£1.50	
Mr Poem	7"	Liberty	LBF15093	1968	£4	£1.50	
Your Mother Should Know	7"	Liberty	LBF15210	1969	£4	£1.50	

BATTERED ORNAMENTS

The Battered Ornaments was the group originally brought together by poet Pete Brown. Without him, they did not have an effective vocalist, but the *Mantle Piece* LP is an interesting and worthwhile addition to the Harvest catalogue.

Mantle Piece	LP	Harvest	SHVL758	1969	£60	£30	

BATTIN, SKIP

Skip	LP	Signpost	SG4255	1972	£10	£4	

BATTLEAXE

Burn This Town	7"	Guardian	GRC132	1982	£10	£5	

BATTLEFIELD BAND

Scottish Folk	LP	Arfolk	SB349	1976	£12	£5	*French*

BAUER, JOE

Moonset	LP	Raccoon	N3	1971	£20	£8	*US*

BAUHAUS

1979–1983	CD	Beggars Banquet	BAUCDBOX1	1988	£25	£10	*boxed double*
Bela Lugosi's Dead	12"	Small Wonder	TEENY2	1979	£10	£5	*white vinyl*

Bela Lugosi's Dead	12"	Small Wonder	TEENY2	1989	£6	£2.50	green, blue, pink, purple, or clear vinyl
Bela Lugosi's Dead	12"	Small Wonder	TEENY2P	1988	£6	£2.50	picture disc
Bela Lugosi's Dead	CD-s	Small Wonder	TEENY2CD	1988	£6	£2.50	
Burning From The Inside	LP	Beggars Banquet	BEGA45P	1983	£10	£4	picture disc
Dark Entries	7"	Beggars Banquet	BEG37	1980	£5	£2	
Dark Entries	7"	Axis	AXIS3	1980	£8	£4	
Dark Entries	7"	4AD	AD3	1980	£4	£1.50	blue label
Dark Entries	7"	4AD	BEG37	1980	£5	£2	
Kick In The Eye	12"	Beggars Banquet	BEG74TA1	1983	£20	£10	mispress with 'Poison Pen'
Sanity Assassin	7"	Lyntone	LYN13777/8	1983	£100	£50	
She's In Parties	7"	Beggars Banquet	BEG91P	1983	£5	£2	picture disc
Spirit	7"	Beggars Banquet	BEG79P	1982	£5	£2	picture disc
Terror Couple Kill Colonel	7"	4AD	AD7	1980	£15	£7.50	with alternative version of track 3

BAUMSTAM

On Tour	LP	private	BS6232855	1976	£150	£75	German

BAXTER, ART

Don't Knock The Rock	78	Philips	PB666	1957	£6	£2.50	
Jingle Rock	78	Philips	PB652	1956	£6	£2.50	
Rock You Sinners	10" LP	Philips	BBR8107	1957	£75	£37.50	

BAXTER, DAVID

Goodbye Dave	LP	Reflection	REFL9	1970	£20	£8	

BAXTER, LES

Cherry Pink And Apple Blossom White	7"	Capitol	CL14337	1955	£5	£2	
Earth Angel	7"	Capitol	CL14239	1955	£10	£5	
I Ain't Mad At You	7"	Capitol	CL14249	1955	£5	£2	
Teen Drums	LP	Capitol	(S)T1355	1960	£10	£4	
Unchained Melody	7"	Capitol	CL14257	1955	£8	£4	
Wake The Town And Tell The People	7"	Capitol	CL14344	1955	£5	£2	

BAXTER, RONNIE

I Finally Found You	7"	Top Rank	JAR293	1960	£4	£1.50	

BAY CITY JAZZ BAND

Bay City Jazz Band	LP	Vogue	LAG12093	1958	£12	£5	

BAY CITY ROLLERS

Keep On Dancing	7"	Bell	BLL1164	1971	£5	£2	
We Can Make Music	7"	Bell	BLL1220	1972	£5	£2	
You Made Me Believe In Magic	7"	Arista	ARIST127	1977	£5	£2	picture sleeve

BAYSIDERS

Over The Rainbow	LP	Everest	LPBR/BRST5124	1961	£30	£15	US

BAYTOWN SINGERS

Walkin' Down The Line	7"	Decca	F12160	1965	£4	£1.50	

BBC RADIOPHONIC WORKSHOP

Doctor Who	7"	PRT	RESL80	1980	£5	£2	3 different picture sleeves
Dr Who	7"	Decca	F11837	1964	£10	£5	
Dr Who	7"	BBC	RESL11	1974	£5	£2	picture sleeve, Delia Derbyshire credit
Moonbase 3	7"	BBC	RESL13	1973	£10	£5	
Radiophonic Music	LP	BBC	REC25M	1971	£10	£4	by John Baker, David Cain, Delia Derbyshire

BEACH BOYS

For a group as long-lived and as popular as the Beach Boys, there are surprisingly few hard-core rarities, although all their original issues from the sixties are inevitably collectable. The ultimate Beach Boys rarity has still not been released in full – the LP *Smile* was cancelled by Brian Wilson and would perhaps have included tracks to rival the masterworks 'Good Vibrations', 'Heroes and Villains', and 'Surf's Up', which were all destined for inclusion on the lost album. For collectors who do not actually feel the need to own every note that the group has produced, it should be noted that the World Record Club boxed set *The Capitol Years* is a particularly well-assembled compilation of the group's sixties work, with no major omissions. A bonus LP, moreover, assembles a number of Brian Wilson productions which are otherwise rather difficult to find.

20 Golden Greats	LP	EMI	EMTV1	1977	£10	£4	blue vinyl
20 Golden Greats Promo	7"	EMI	PSR402	1976	£8	£4	promo
20/20	LP	Capitol	ET133	1969	£10	£4	mono
All Summer Long	7"	Capitol	CL15384	1965	£4	£1.50	
All Summer Long	LP	Capitol	(S)T2110	1964	£15	£6	
Ballad Of An Old Car	7" EP	Capitol	EAP120576	1964	£20	£10	French
Barbara Ann	7"	Capitol	CL15432	1966	£4	£1.50	
Barbara Ann	7" EP	Capitol	EAP120762	1965	£15	£7.50	French
Beach Boy Interviews	LP	Caribou	XPR1204	1980	£15	£6	promo

Beach Boys	CD	Caribou	CD26378	1985	**£12**	**£5**	
Beach Boys	CD	Capitol	DPRO79168	1990	**£25**	**£10**	*US promo sampler*
Beach Boys Concert	7" EP	Capitol	EAP42198	1964	**£15**	**£7.50**	
Beach Boys Concert	LP	Capitol	(S)T2198	1964	**£15**	**£6**	
Beach Boys Party	LP	Capitol	(S)T2398	1965	**£12**	**£5**	
Beach Boys Today	LP	Capitol	(S)T2269	1965	**£15**	**£6**	
Beach Boys' Hits	7" EP	Capitol	EAP120781	1964	**£12**	**£6**	
Bluebirds Over The Mountain	7"	Capitol	CL15572	1968	**£4**	**£1.50**	
Break Away	7"	Capitol	CL15598	1969	**£4**	**£1.50**	
California Girls	7"	Capitol	CL15409	1965	**£4**	**£1.50**	
California Girls	7" EP	Capitol	EAP42354	1965	**£15**	**£7.50**	*French*
Capitol Years	LP	World Record Club	SM651-7	1981	**£50**	**£25**	*7 LPs, boxed*
Carl And The Passions, So Tough	CD	Epic	4683492	1991	**£12**	**£5**	
Christmas Album	LP	Capitol	(S)T2164	1964	**£25**	**£10**	
Cottonfields	7"	Capitol	CL15640	1970	**£4**	**£1.50**	
Dance Dance Dance	7"	Capitol	CL15370	1965	**£4**	**£1.50**	
Dance Dance Dance	7" EP	Capitol	EAP120648	1965	**£15**	**£7.50**	*French*
Darlin'	7"	Capitol	CL15527	1968	**£4**	**£1.50**	
Deluxe Set	LP	Capitol	TCL2813	1967	**£60**	**£30**	*US, triple, mono*
Deluxe Set	LP	Capitol	DTCL2813	1967	**£40**	**£20**	*US, triple, stereo*
Do It Again	7"	Capitol	CL15554	1968	**£4**	**£1.50**	
Do It Again	CD-s	Capitol	CDEMCT1	1991	**£5**	**£2**	
Don't Go Near The Water	7"	Stateside	SS2194	1971	**£10**	**£5**	*demo, picture sleeve*
Driving Cars	7" EP	Capitol	EAP41998	1964	**£20**	**£10**	*French*
Four By The Beach Boys	7" EP	Capitol	EAP15267	1964	**£12**	**£6**	
Friends	7"	Capitol	CL15545	1968	**£4**	**£1.50**	
Friends	LP	Capitol	T2895	1968	**£10**	**£4**	*mono*
Fun Fun Fun	7"	Capitol	CL15339	1964	**£30**	**£15**	
Fun Fun Fun	7" EP	Capitol	EAP120603	1964	**£15**	**£7.50**	
God Only Knows	7"	Capitol	CL15459	1966	**£4**	**£1.50**	
God Only Knows	7" EP	Capitol	EAP62458	1967	**£12**	**£6**	
Good Vibrations	7"	Capitol	CL15475	1966	**£4**	**£1.50**	
Help Me Rhonda	7"	Capitol	CL15392	1965	**£4**	**£1.50**	
Help Me Ronda	7" EP	Capitol	EAP42269	1965	**£15**	**£7.50**	*French*
Heroes And Villains	7"	Capitol	CL15510	1967	**£4**	**£1.50**	
Holland	LP	Reprise	MS2118	1973	**£150**	**£75**	*US test pressing with 'We Got Love'*
Holland	LP	Reprise	K54008	1973	**£10**	**£4**	*with 7"*
I Can Hear Music	7"	Capitol	CL15584	1969	**£4**	**£1.50**	
I Get Around	7"	Capitol	CL15350	1964	**£4**	**£1.50**	
I Get Around	7" EP	Capitol	EAP120620	1964	**£15**	**£7.50**	*French, 2 different sleeves*
L.A. (Light Album)	LP	Caribou	CRB1186081	1979	**£10**	**£4**	*picture disc*
Little Deuce Coupe	LP	Capitol	(S)T1998	1963	**£15**	**£6**	
Little Girl I Once Knew	7"	Capitol	CL15425	1965	**£4**	**£1.50**	
Louie Louie	7" EP	Capitol	EAP120658	1965	**£15**	**£7.50**	*French*
Pet Sounds	CD	Capitol	CCM74618	1987	**£25**	**£10**	*US*
Pet Sounds	LP	Capitol	T2458	1966	**£20**	**£8**	*mono*
Pet Sounds	LP	Capitol	ST2458	1966	**£15**	**£7.50**	*stereo*
Shut Down Vol. 2	LP	Capitol	(S)T2027	1964	**£15**	**£6**	
Singles Collection	7"	Capitol	BBP26	1979	**£50**	**£25**	*26 singles, boxed*
Sloop John B	7"	Capitol	CL15441	1966	**£4**	**£1.50**	
Sloop John B	7" EP	Capitol	EAP120812	1966	**£15**	**£7.50**	*French*
Smiley Smile	LP	Capitol	(S)T9001	1967	**£10**	**£4**	
Smiley Smile	LP	Capitol	ST82891	1968	**£75**	**£37.50**	*US, record club issue*
Stack-O-Tracks	LP	Capitol	DKAO2893	1968	**£60**	**£30**	*US, with booklet*
Still Cruisin'	CD-s	Capitol	CDCL549	1989	**£5**	**£2**	
Summer Days & Summer Nights	LP	Capitol	(S)T2354	1965	**£12**	**£5**	
Summertime Blues	LP	Sears	SPS609	1970	**£50**	**£25**	*US*
Sunflower	LP	Capitol	SKAO93352	1970	**£20**	**£8**	*US, record club issue*
Sunflower	LP	Stateside	SSLA8251	1970	**£10**	**£4**	
Surf's Up	LP	Asylum	R113793	1971	**£50**	**£25**	*US, record club issue*
Surfer Girl	LP	Capitol	(S)T1981	1963	**£15**	**£6**	
Surfer Party	7" EP	Capitol	EAP120561	1963	**£20**	**£10**	*French*
Surfin'	7"	Candix	301	1961	**£150**	**£75**	*US*
Surfin'	7"	X	301	1961	**£200**	**£100**	*US, best auctioned*
Surfin'	7"	Candix	331	1961	**£125**	**£62.50**	*US*
Surfin' Safari	7"	Capitol	CL15273	1962	**£15**	**£7.50**	
Surfin' Safari	7" EP	Capitol	EAP51808	1962	**£20**	**£10**	*French*
Surfin' Safari	LP	Capitol	T1808	1962	**£20**	**£8**	
Surfin' USA	7"	Capitol	CL15305	1963	**£12**	**£6**	
Surfin' USA	7" EP	Capitol	EAP120504	1963	**£20**	**£10**	*French*
Surfin' USA	7" EP	Capitol	EAP120540	1963	**£15**	**£7.50**	
Surfin' USA	LP	Capitol	(S)T1890	1963	**£15**	**£6**	
Surfin' USA/Surfer Girl	CD	Mobile Fidelity	UDCD521	1989	**£15**	**£6**	*US audiophile*
Susie Cincinnatti	7"	Reprise	K14411	1976	**£30**	**£15**	*demo*
Ten Little Indians	7"	Capitol	CL15285	1963	**£40**	**£20**	
Then I Kissed Her	7"	Capitol	CL15502	1967	**£4**	**£1.50**	
When I Grow Up	7"	Capitol	CL15361	1964	**£4**	**£1.50**	
Wild Honey	7"	Capitol	CL15517	1967	**£60**	**£30**	
Wild Honey	7"	Capitol	CL15521	1967	**£4**	**£1.50**	
Wild Honey	LP	Capitol	T2859	1968	**£10**	**£4**	*mono*
Wouldn't It Be Nice	7" EP	Capitol	EAP502458	1967	**£15**	**£7.50**	*French*
Wouldn't It Be Nice	CD-s	Capitol	CDCL579	1990	**£5**	**£2**	
You Need A Mess of Help	7"	Reprise	K14173	1972	**£5**	**£2**	*picture sleeve*

BEACH NUTS

Title	Format	Label	Number	Year	Mint	VG	Notes
Out In The Sun	7"	London	HL9988	1965	**£8**	**£4**	

BEACHCOMBERS

An instrumental group whose drummer was Keith Moon, who left to join the High Numbers just as the latter decided to revert to their earlier name of the Who. His presence on these singles, however, is doubtful.

Title	Format	Label	Number	Year	Mint	VG	Notes
Mad Goose	7"	Columbia	DB7124	1963	**£15**	**£7.50**	
Night Train	7"	Columbia	DB7200	1964	**£15**	**£7.50**	

BEACON STREET UNION

Title	Format	Label	Number	Year	Mint	VG	Notes
Clown Died In Marvin Gardens	LP	MGM	SE4568	1968	**£15**	**£6**	*US*
Eyes Of The Beacon Street Union	LP	MGM	8069	1968	**£15**	**£6**	

BEAD GAME

Title	Format	Label	Number	Year	Mint	VG	Notes
Welcome	LP	Avco	33009	1970	**£30**	**£15**	*US*

BEAN, GEORGE

Title	Format	Label	Number	Year	Mint	VG	Notes
Privilege	7" EP	Vogue	INT18137	1967	**£10**	**£5**	*French, B side by Mike Leander Orchestra*
Sad Story	7"	Decca	F11922	1964	**£8**	**£4**	
She Belongs To Me	7"	Decca	F12228	1965	**£4**	**£1.50**	
Will You Be My Lover Tonight	7"	Decca	F11808	1964	**£8**	**£4**	

BEAN & LOOPY'S LOT

Title	Format	Label	Number	Year	Mint	VG	Notes
Haywire	7"	Parlophone	R5458	1966	**£12**	**£6**	

BEANS

Title	Format	Label	Number	Year	Mint	VG	Notes
Hey Janey	7"	Starlite	ST45075	1962	**£4**	**£1.50**	
Jumping Beans	7"	Starlite	ST45071	1962	**£4**	**£1.50**	

BEAR

Title	Format	Label	Number	Year	Mint	VG	Notes
Greetings Children Of Paradise	LP	Verve	FTS3059	1969	**£20**	**£8**	

BEARCATS

Title	Format	Label	Number	Year	Mint	VG	Notes
Beatlemania	LP	Somerset	P20800	1964	**£20**	**£8**	*US*

BEARD, DEAN & THE CREWCUTS

Title	Format	Label	Number	Year	Mint	VG	Notes
On My Mind Again	7"	London	HLE8463	1957	**£300**	**£180**	*best auctioned*

BEARZ

Title	Format	Label	Number	Year	Mint	VG	Notes
Darwin	7"	Occult	OCC1	1984	**£5**	**£2**	
She's My Girl	7"	Axis	AXIS2	1980	**£10**	**£5**	

BEAS

Title	Format	Label	Number	Year	Mint	VG	Notes
Dr Goodfoot And His Bikini Machine	7"	Pama	PM744	1968	**£12**	**£6**	

BEASLEY, JIMMY

Title	Format	Label	Number	Year	Mint	VG	Notes
Fabulous Jimmy Beasley	LP	Modern	LMP1214	1956	**£50**	**£25**	*US*
Fabulous Jimmy Beasley	LP	Crown	CLP5014	1957	**£30**	**£15**	*US*
Twist With Jimmy Beasley	LP	Crown	CLP5247	1961	**£20**	**£8**	*US*

BEASTIE BOYS

Title	Format	Label	Number	Year	Mint	VG	Notes
Cookie Puss	CD-s	Rat Cage	MOTR26CD	198–	**£5**	**£2**	
Frozen Metal Head EP	12"	Capitol	12CL665	1992	**£6**	**£2.50**	*white vinyl*
Frozen Metal Head EP	CD-s	Capitol	CDCL665	1992	**£15**	**£7.50**	
Girls	7"	Def Jam	BEASTQ3	1987	**£8**	**£4**	*shaped picture disc*
Hey Ladies	CD-s	Capitol	CDCL540	1989	**£10**	**£5**	
No Sleep Till Brooklyn	7"	Def Jam	BEASTP1	1987	**£8**	**£4**	*shaped picture disc*
Pass The Mic	CD-s	Capitol	CDCL653	1992	**£10**	**£5**	
Polly Wog Stew	12"	Rat Cage	MOTR21T	1982	**£8**	**£4**	
Polly Wog Stew	7"	Rat Cage	MOTR21	1982	**£6**	**£2.50**	
Sampler	CD	Capitol	GRAND1	1994	**£15**	**£6**	*promo compilation*

BEAT BOYS

Title	Format	Label	Number	Year	Mint	VG	Notes
That's My Plan	7"	Decca	F11730	1963	**£20**	**£10**	

BEAT BROTHERS

Title	Format	Label	Number	Year	Mint	VG	Notes
Nick Nack Hully Gully	7"	Polydor	NH52185	1963	**£20**	**£10**	

BEAT CHICS

Title	Format	Label	Number	Year	Mint	VG	Notes
Skinny Minny	7"	Decca	F12016	1964	**£6**	**£2.50**	

BEAT MERCHANTS

Title	Format	Label	Number	Year	Mint	VG	Notes
Pretty Face	7"	Columbia	DB7367	1964	**£30**	**£15**	
So Fine	7"	Columbia	DB7492	1965	**£30**	**£15**	

BEAT MIXERS

Title	Format	Label	Number	Year	Mint	VG	Notes
Beat	LP	Baccarola	72662	1964	**£15**	**£6**	*German*

BEAT OF THE EARTH

Title	Format	Label	Number	Year	Mint	VG	Notes
This Record Is An Artistic Statement	LP	Radish	AS0001	1968	**£150**	**£75**	*US*

BEAT SIX

Title	Format	Label	Cat. No.	Year	Mint	VG	Notes
Bernadine	7"	Decca	F12011	1964	**£5**	**£2**	

BEATHOVENS

Title	Format	Label	Cat. No.	Year	Mint	VG	Notes
Happy To Be Happy	LP	Somerset	650	1965	**£50**	**£25**	*German*

BEATLES

The Beatles sold so many copies of their singles that it should come as no surprise that few of them have acquired much of a value in the collectors' market. It is a different matter with their LPs, however, especially as so many original copies have been extremely well played over the years! There are also a number of rarer items. The Polydor singles and LP are the first pressings of the material that the Beatles recorded in Germany in 1962 – mainly as a backing group to singer Tony Sheridan, although 'Ain't She Sweet' features a typically gritty John Lennon vocal, and 'Cry For A Shadow' is George Harrison's instrumental tribute to Hank Marvin and company. This material has been reissued on a number of occasions, along with live recordings by the Beatles in Hamburg without Sheridan, but few of these records fetch any kind of collectors' prices, despite the historical importance of the music they present. The Christmas flexi-disc singles were issued each year to members of the fan club and feature specially recorded material not otherwise available, although not very much of this is actually musical. *From Then To You* gathers all these singles together on a highly sought-after LP – inevitably this has been frequently bootlegged, but the copies in recent circulation do not have the Apple label of the original. The US version of the LP has a different cover and title (*The Beatles Christmas Album*) and has also been bootlegged – original copies are on black vinyl, with a clear Apple label and a typically thick cardboard sixties American cover. The limited edition package which combined the *Let It Be* album (whose cover should have a small green apple on the back) with a substantial book has become quite scarce. The catalogue number PXS1 was used in advertising material at the time, but appears nowhere on the package! First pressings of the *Please Please Me* LP have the old Parlophone label design, with gold lettering (the stereo version of this is especially rare) – further details are given in this guide under the Parlophone heading. The infamous American 'butcher cover', hastily withdrawn after the initial release of *Yesterday And Today*, varies considerably in value depending on whether it is mono or stereo and on whether it is 'unpeeled' (i.e. with the replacement cover design pasted on top) or 'peeled' (i.e. with the replacement cover design either successfully removed or never pasted on to begin with). The conversion of an unpeeled copy into a more valuable peeled one is fraught with danger, needless to say, and should be left to a specialist, or not done at all. Reissue copies of the US album *Introducing The Beatles* are common – these have assorted label variants which have a silver VJ logo in large straight brackets. The situation with regard to valuable original pressings is complicated. The values given here are an average for a range of prices attaching to subtle label variations, all of which are extremely rare, especially in the UK. Essentially, however, original pressings have an oval Vee Jay logo, together with a machine-stamped matrix identification ('Audio Matrix', 'MR', or 'ARP'). The much sought-after UK export issues of various of the Beatles' recordings have long been the subject of rumour and misinformation as to what does and does not exist. Claims have been made for the existence of various export albums and singles other than those listed here, but until such time as a collector can confirm ownership of these, one can only remain sceptical. It should be noted, finally, that all original copies of *The Beatles* double album (usually referred to as 'The White Album', after its cover design) were stamped with a unique issue number. Low-numbered copies inevitably come on to the market from time to time and can be expected to fetch considerably higher prices than the norm. Number 000001, autographed by Ringo Starr, was sold at auction in 1985 for $715 and was sold again in November 1999, when it realized an impressive £8500. The values listed below for these records should be taken as points on a sliding scale and are highly approximate – they are all best auctioned.

Title	Format	Label	Cat. No.	Year	Mint	VG	Notes
1962–1966	LP	Apple	PCSPR717	1978	**£15**	**£6**	*red vinyl, double*
1962–1970	7"	Lyntone	no number	1977	**£8**	**£4**	*promo flexi*
1967–1970	LP	Apple	PCSPR718	1978	**£15**	**£6**	*blue vinyl, double*
4 Garçons Dans Le Vent	7" EP	Odeon	SOE3757	1964	**£20**	**£10**	*French*
4 Garçons Dans Le Vent	7" EP	Odeon	SOE3756	1964	**£20**	**£10**	*French*
Abbey Road	r-reel	Apple	TAPMC7088	1970	**£100**	**£50**	*mono*
Abbey Road	r-reel	Apple	TDPCS7088	1970	**£60**	**£30**	*stereo*
Abbey Road	LP	Apple	PCS7088	1969	**£20**	**£8**	*dark green label*
Abbey Road	LP	Apple	PCS7088	1978	**£75**	**£37.50**	*green vinyl*
Abbey Road	LP	Apple	PHO7088	1979	**£250**	**£150**	*picture disc*
Abbey Road	LP	Apple	SO383	1969	**£10**	**£4**	*US*
Abbey Road	LP	Capitol	SEAX11900	1978	**£20**	**£8**	*US picture disc*
Abbey Road	LP	EMI	5CP06204243	1979	**£15**	**£6**	*Dutch picture disc*
Abbey Road	LP	Mobile Fidelity	MFSL1023	1978	**£30**	**£15**	*US audiophile*
Abbey Road	LP	Parlophone	PPCS7088	1969	**£300**	**£180**	*export, silver & black label*
Abbey Road	LP	Parlophone	PPCS7088	1969	**£750**	**£500**	*export, yellow & black label*
Abbey Road	CD	EMI	BEACD25/7	1987	**£20**	**£8**	*HMV box, badge, booklet, 2 posters*
Abbey Road	CD	Odeon	CP353016	1986	**£250**	**£150**	*Japanese*
Abbey Road	CD	Parlophone	CDP7464462	1987	**£40**	**£20**	*mispressing – plays Edith Piaf*
Album Set	LP	Parlophone/ Apple		1988	**£200**	**£100**	*complete set of LPs in black wooden box*
All My Loving	7" EP	Parlophone	GEP8891	1964	**£12**	**£6**	
All My Loving	7" EP	Odeon	SOE3751	1964	**£20**	**£10**	*French*
All You Need Is Love	7"	Parlophone	R5620	1967	**£20**	**£10**	*no reference to TV transmission*
All You Need Is Love	7"	Parlophone	RP5620	1987	**£15**	**£7.50**	*picture disc*
All You Need Is Love	7"	Parlophone	R5620	1967	**£250**	**£150**	*demo*
All You Need Is Love	CD-s	Parlophone	CD3R5620	1989	**£8**	**£4**	*3" single*
Amazing Beatles	LP	Clarion	601	1966	**£40**	**£20**	*US, mono*
Amazing Beatles	LP	Clarion	SD601	1966	**£60**	**£30**	*US, stereo*
Another Beatles Christmas Record	7"	Lyntone	LYN757	1964	**£20**	**£10**	*picture sleeve, flexi*
Another Beatles Christmas Record	7"	Lyntone	LYN757	1964	**£40**	**£20**	*picture sleeve, flexi, newsletter*
Anthology 2	CD	Apple	no number	1996	**£75**	**£37.50**	*US promo CD-ROM press kit*
Anthology 2	CD	Apple	CDANTH2	1996	**£25**	**£10**	*10 track promo sampler, booklet*
Anthology 3	CD	Apple	CDANTH3	1996	**£25**	**£10**	*5 track promo sampler, press kit*
Baby It's You	CD-s	Capitol	DPRO79553	1995	**£50**	**£25**	*US promo, Valentine's card sleeve*

Back In The USSR	7"	Parlophone	R6016	1976	£25	£12.50	*demo*
Ballad Of John And Yoko	7"	Apple	R5786	1969	£1000	£700	*demo, existence doubtful*
Ballad Of John And Yoko	7"	Apple	RP5786	1989	£15	£7.50	*picture disc*
Ballad Of John And Yoko	CD-s	Parlophone	CD3R5786	1989	£8	£4	*3" single*
Beatles	LP	Deutscher Bücherclub	H052	1965	£60	£30	*German, club pressing*
Beatles	LP	Deutscher Bücherclub	J033	1964	£75	£37.50	*German, club pressing*
Beatles & Frank Ifield On Stage	LP	Vee Jay	LPS1085	1964	£150	£75	*US, old man on cover, stereo*
Beatles & Frank Ifield On Stage	LP	Vee Jay	LP1085	1964	£1000	£700	*US, Beatles on cover*
Beatles & Frank Ifield On Stage	LP	Vee Jay	LP1085	1964	£50	£25	*US, old man on cover, mono*
Beatles (White Album)	r-reel	Apple	DTAPMC/ DTDPCS7067/8	1968	£75	£37.50	
Beatles (White Album)	LP	Apple	PCS7067/8	1968	£40	£20	*stereo*
Beatles (White Album)	LP	Apple	PCS7067/8	1978	£75	£37.50	*white vinyl*
Beatles (White Album)	LP	Apple	PMC/PCS7067/8	1968	£5000	£3500	*cover number 000001–00010*
Beatles (White Album)	LP	Apple	PMC/PCS7067/8	1968	£2000	£1400	*cover number 000011–00020*
Beatles (White Album)	LP	Apple	PMC/PCS7067/8	1968	£1000	£700	*cover number 000021–00100*
Beatles (White Album)	LP	Apple	PMC/PCS7067/8	1968	£750	£500	*cover number 000101–01000*
Beatles (White Album)	LP	Apple	PMC/PCS7067/8	1968	£500	£330	*cover number 001001–10000*
Beatles (White Album)	LP	Apple	PMC7067/8	1968	£150	£75	*mono*
Beatles (White Album)	LP	Apple	SWBO101	1968	£25	£10	*US, double*
Beatles (White Album)	LP	Mobile Fidelity	MFSL2072	1982	£40	£20	*US audiophile*
Beatles (White Album)	LP	Parlophone	PCSJ7067/8	1969	£400	£250	*double export*
Beatles (White Album)	LP	Parlophone	PPCS7067/8	1968	£1000	£700	*export, yellow & black label*
Beatles (White Album)	LP	Parlophone	PPCS7067/8	1969	£400	£250	*double export, silver & black label*
Beatles (White Album)	CD	EMI	BEACD25/4	1987	£50	£25	*HMV box, badge, booklet*
Beatles '65	LP	Odeon	SMO83917	1965	£100	£50	*German, white & gold label*
Beatles '65	LP	Capitol	T2228	1964	£25	£10	*US, mono*
Beatles '65	LP	Capitol	ST2228	1964	£20	£8	*US, stereo*
Beatles 1962	7"	Baktabak	TABOKS1001	1988	£50	£25	*15 singles, boxed*
Beatles At The Beeb	CD	Apple			£3000	£2000	*promo only 140 CD set*
Beatles At The Beeb	LP	BBC	CN3970	1982	£500	£330	*transcription disc*
Beatles At The Hollywood Bowl	7"	Parlophone	EMTV4	1977	£50	£25	*promo boxed set*
Beatles Beat	LP	Odeon	O83692	1964	£75	£37.50	*German, green label*
Beatles Box	LP	World Record Club	SM701-8	1980	£50	£25	*8 LPs, boxed*
Beatles Collection	LP	Mobile Fidelity		1982	£300	£180	*US audiophile, 14 LPs, boxed*
Beatles Collection	LP	Parlophone	BC13	1978	£100	£50	*13 LPs (1 double), boxed*
Beatles Collection	7"	Lyntone	LYN9657	1978	£8	£4	*flexi*
Beatles Collection	7"	Lyntone	LYNSF165	1978	£8	£4	*promo flexi, poster*
Beatles Collection	7"	World Record Club		1977	£40	£20	*24 singles, boxed*
Beatles Collection	7"	World Record Club		1978	£40	£20	*25 singles, boxed*
Beatles Conquer America	7"	Baktabak	BAKPAK1004	1989	£8	£4	*4 single pack*
Beatles EP Collection	7" EP	Parlophone	BEP14	1981	£60	£30	*14 EPs*
Beatles Fifth Christmas Record	7"	Lyntone	LYN1360	1967	£50	£25	*picture sleeve, flexi, newsletter*
Beatles Fifth Christmas Record	7"	Lyntone	LYN1360	1967	£30	£15	*picture sleeve, flexi*
Beatles For Sale	r-reel	Parlophone	TAPMC1240/ TDPCS3062	1965	£25	£10	
Beatles For Sale	LP	Mobile Fidelity	MFSL1104	1984	£20	£8	*US audiophile*
Beatles For Sale	LP	Parlophone	PCS3062	1964	£60	£30	*stereo*
Beatles For Sale	LP	Parlophone	PCS3062	1969	£12	£5	*reissue, exposed edges on inside of cover, 'Made in Gt Britain' on label*
Beatles For Sale	LP	Parlophone	PMC1240	1964	£30	£15	*mono*
Beatles For Sale	7" EP	Parlophone	GEP8931	1965	£15	£7.50	
Beatles For Sale No. 2	7" EP	Parlophone	GEP8938	1965	£20	£10	
Beatles Fourth Christmas Record	7"	Lyntone	LYN1145	1966	£50	£25	*picture sleeve, flexi, newsletter*
Beatles Fourth Christmas Record	7"	Lyntone	LYN1145	1966	£30	£15	*picture sleeve, flexi*
Beatles Greatest Hits	LP	Parlophone	EMTVS34	1982	£100	£50	*double, test pressing*
Beatles Hits	7" EP	Parlophone	GEP8880	1963	£15	£7.50	
Beatles Million Sellers	7" EP	Parlophone	GEP8946	1965	£15	£7.50	
Beatles Mono Collection	LP	Parlophone	BMC10	1982	£175	£87.50	*10 LPs, boxed*
Beatles No. 1	7" EP	Parlophone	GEP8883	1963	£15	£7.50	
Beatles Second Album	LP	Capitol	ST2080	1964	£20	£8	*US, stereo*

Beatles Second Album	LP	Capitol	ST82080	1964	**£50**	**£25**	*US, Record Club issue*
Beatles Second Album	LP	Capitol	T2080	1964	**£25**	**£10**	*US, mono*
Beatles Second Album	LP	Parlophone	CPCS103	1969	**£200**	**£100**	*export, silver & black label*
Beatles Seventh Christmas Record	7"	Lyntone	LYN1970/1	1969	**£50**	**£25**	*picture sleeve, flexi, newsletter*
Beatles Seventh Christmas Record	7"	Lyntone	LYN1970/1	1969	**£30**	**£15**	*picture sleeve, flexi*
Beatles Singles Collection	7"	EMI	BSC1	1982	**£40**	**£20**	*26 singles, boxed*
Beatles Singles Collection	7"	EMI	BSCP1	1982	**£50**	**£25**	*27 singles, boxed, export*
Beatles Singles Collection	7"	Lyntone	LYNSF1291	1977	**£20**	**£10**	*promo flexi, poster, letter*
Beatles Singles Collection	7"	Parlophone	BSCP1	1982	**£75**	**£37.50**	*box set with mispressed picture disc – 'Love Me Do' both sides*
Beatles Singles Collection	7"	Parlophone/ Apple	BS24	1976	**£50**	**£25**	*24 singles, boxed*
Beatles Sixth Christmas Record	7"	Lyntone	LYN1743/4	1968	**£50**	**£25**	*picture sleeve, flexi, sales insert*
Beatles Sixth Christmas Record	7"	Lyntone	LYN1743/4	1968	**£40**	**£20**	*picture sleeve, flexi*
Beatles Story	LP	Capitol	STBO2222	1964	**£20**	**£8**	*US, stereo*
Beatles Story	LP	Capitol	TBO2222	1964	**£25**	**£10**	*US, mono*
Beatles Tapes (David Wigg Interviews)	LP	Polydor	2683068	1976	**£12**	**£5**	*double*
Beatles Third Christmas Record	7"	Lyntone	LYN948	1965	**£40**	**£20**	*picture sleeve, flexi, newsletter*
Beatles Third Christmas Record	7"	Lyntone	LYN948	1965	**£20**	**£10**	*picture sleeve, flexi*
Beatles VI	LP	Capitol	ST2358	1965	**£20**	**£8**	*US, stereo*
Beatles VI	LP	Capitol	ST82358	1965	**£50**	**£25**	*US, Record Club issue*
Beatles VI	LP	Capitol	T2358	1965	**£25**	**£10**	*US, mono*
Beatles VI	LP	Parlophone	CPCS104	1966	**£600**	**£400**	*export*
Beatles VI	LP	Parlophone	CPCS104	1969	**£250**	**£150**	*export, black & silver label*
Beatles Vs The Four Seasons	LP	Vee Jay	DX30	1964	**£1250**	**£875**	*US double*
Beatles With Tony Sheridan	LP	MGM	SE4215	1964	**£100**	**£50**	*US, stereo*
Beatles With Tony Sheridan	LP	MGM	E4215	1964	**£50**	**£25**	*US, mono*
Beatles' Christmas Album	LP	Apple	SBC100	1970	**£200**	**£100**	*US*
Beatles' Christmas Record	7"	Lyntone	LYN492	1963	**£75**	**£37.50**	*picture sleeve, flexi*
Beatles' Rock'n'Roll Medley	7"	EMI	SPSR401	1976	**£200**	**£100**	*1 sided promo*
Beatles' Second Album	LP	Parlophone	CPCS103	1966	**£600**	**£400**	*export*
Can't Buy Me Love	7"	Parlophone	R5114	1964	**£350**	**£210**	*demo*
Can't Buy Me Love	7"	Parlophone	RP5114	1984	**£10**	**£5**	*picture disc*
Can't Buy Me Love	7" EP	Odeon	SOE3750	1964	**£20**	**£10**	*French*
Can't Buy Me Love	CD-s	Parlophone	CD3R5114	1989	**£8**	**£4**	*3" single*
Chansons Du Film Help	7" EP	Odeon	SOE3771	1965	**£20**	**£10**	*French*
Collection Of Beatles Oldies	r-reel	Parlophone	TAPMC/ TDPCS7016	1967	**£25**	**£10**	
Collection Of Beatles Oldies	LP	Parlophone	PMC7016	1967	**£25**	**£12**	*mono*
Collection Of Beatles Oldies	LP	Parlophone	PCS7016	1967	**£50**	**£25**	*stereo*
Collection Of Beatles Oldies	LP	Parlophone	PCS7016	1969	**£12**	**£5**	*reissue, exposed edges on back cover, 'Made in Gt Britain' on label*
Complete Silver Beatles	LP	Audiofidelity	AFELP1047	1982	**£10**	**£4**	
Day Tripper	7"	Parlophone	RP5389	1985	**£10**	**£5**	*picture disc*
Day Tripper	7"	Parlophone	R5389	1965	**£350**	**£210**	*demo*
Day Tripper	78	Parlophone	R5389	196–	**£400**	**£250**	*Indian, best auctioned*
Devil In Her Heart	7" EP	Odeon	SOE3777	1965	**£30**	**£15**	*French*
Dizzy Miss Lizzy	78	Parlophone	DPE183	196–	**£400**	**£250**	*Indian, best auctioned*
Do You Want To Know A Secret	7"	Odeon	22710	1964	**£10**	**£5**	*German import*
Early Beatles	LP	Capitol	T2309	1965	**£25**	**£10**	*US, mono*
Early Beatles	LP	Capitol	ST2309	1965	**£20**	**£8**	*US, stereo*
Eight Days A Week	7" EP	Odeon	SOE3764	1965	**£20**	**£10**	*French*
Excerpts From David Wigg Interviews	7"	Polydor	PPSP1	1976	**£60**	**£30**	*promo*
Free As A Bird	7"	Apple	RDJ6422	1995	**£10**	**£5**	*jukebox issue*
Free As A Bird	CD-s	Apple	CDFREEDJ1	1995	**£10**	**£5**	*promo*
From Me To You	7"	Parlophone	RP5015	1983	**£12**	**£6**	*picture disc*
From Me To You	7"	Parlophone	R5015	1963	**£350**	**£210**	*demo*
From Me To You	7" EP	Odeon	SOE3739	1963	**£1500**	**£1050**	*French, Beatles in French costume on sleeve*
From Me To You	7" EP	Odeon	SOE3739	1963	**£20**	**£10**	*French*
From Me To You	CD-s	Parlophone	CD3R5015	1988	**£8**	**£4**	*3" single*
From Them To You	LP	Apple	LYN2153/4	1970	**£250**	**£150**	*green Apple label*
Get Back	7"	Apple	R5777	1978	**£15**	**£7.50**	*mispress – B side plays 'I've Had Enough' by Wings*
Get Back	7"	Apple	RP5777	1989	**£15**	**£7.50**	*picture disc*
Get Back	7"	Apple	R5779	1969	**£1000**	**£700**	*demo, existence doubtful*
Get Back	CD-s	Parlophone	CD3R5777	1989	**£8**	**£4**	*3" single*
Girl	78	Parlophone	DPE188	196–	**£400**	**£250**	*Indian, best auctioned*

Title	Format	Label	Cat. No.	Year	Mint	VG	Notes
Hard Day's Night	r-reel	Parlophone	TAPMC1230/ TDPCS3058	1964	**£25**	**£10**	
Hard Day's Night	LP	Mobile Fidelity	MFSL1103	1984	**£20**	**£8**	*US audiophile*
Hard Day's Night	LP	Parlophone	PCS3058	1964	**£60**	**£30**	*stereo*
Hard Day's Night	LP	Parlophone	PCS3058	1969	**£12**	**£5**	*reissue, exposed edges on back cover, 'Made in Gt Britain' on label*
Hard Day's Night	LP	Parlophone	PMC1230	1964	**£30**	**£15**	*mono*
Hard Day's Night	LP	United Artists	SP2359	1964	**£250**	**£150**	*US promo with script*
Hard Day's Night	LP	United Artists	UAL3366	1964	**£30**	**£15**	*US, mono*
Hard Day's Night	LP	United Artists	UAS6366	1964	**£25**	**£10**	*US, stereo*
Hard Day's Night	CD-s	Parlophone	CD3R5160	1989	**£8**	**£4**	*3" single*
Hard Day's Night	CD	Liberty	CDP7460792	1987	**£40**	**£20**	*mispressed on to James Bond CD*
Hard Day's Night	7" EP	Parlophone	GEP8920	1964	**£15**	**£7.50**	
Hard Day's Night	7"	Parlophone	R5160	1964	**£350**	**£210**	*demo*
Hard Day's Night	7"	Parlophone	RP5160	1984	**£12**	**£6**	*picture disc*
Hard Day's Night No. 2	7" EP	Parlophone	GEP8924	1964	**£25**	**£12.50**	
Hello Goodbye	7"	Parlophone	R5655	1967	**£250**	**£150**	*demo*
Hello Goodbye	7"	Parlophone	RP5655	1987	**£15**	**£7.50**	*picture disc*
Hello Goodbye	CD-s	Parlophone	CD3R5655	1989	**£8**	**£4**	*3" single*
Help!	r-reel	Parlophone	TAPMC1255/ TDPCS3071	1965	**£25**	**£10**	
Help!	LP	Capitol	MAS2386	1965	**£25**	**£10**	*US, mono*
Help!	LP	Capitol	SMAS2386	1965	**£20**	**£8**	*US, stereo*
Help!	LP	Capitol	SMAS82386	1965	**£50**	**£25**	*US, Record Club issue*
Help!	LP	Mobile Fidelity	MFSL1105	1984	**£20**	**£8**	*US audiophile*
Help!	LP	Odeon	SMO84008	1965	**£75**	**£37.50**	*German, white and gold label*
Help!	LP	Odeon	SMO984008	1965	**£200**	**£100**	*German, club pressing*
Help!	LP	Parlophone	PCS3071	1965	**£60**	**£30**	*stereo*
Help!	LP	Parlophone	PCS3071	1969	**£12**	**£5**	*reissue, exposed edges on back cover, 'Made in Gt Britain' on label*
Help!	LP	Parlophone	PMC1255	1965	**£30**	**£15**	*mono*
Help!	CD-s	Parlophone	CD3R5305	1989	**£8**	**£4**	*3" single*
Help!	78	Parlophone	R5305	196–	**£500**	**£250**	*Indian, best auctioned*
Help!	7" EP	Odeon	SOE3769	1965	**£20**	**£10**	*French*
Help!	7"	Parlophone	R5305	1965	**£350**	**£210**	*demo*
Help!	7"	Parlophone	RP5305	1985	**£10**	**£5**	*picture disc*
Help!/Rubber Soul/Revolver	CD	EMI	BEACD25/2	1987	**£75**	**£37.50**	*HMV red box, magazine*
Here, There And Everywhere	78	Parlophone	DPE189	196–	**£400**	**£250**	*Indian, best auctioned*
Hey Jude	LP	Apple	CPCS106	197–	**£30**	**£15**	*export*
Hey Jude	LP	Apple	CPCS106	1970	**£50**	**£25**	*dark green Apple label*
Hey Jude	LP	Parlophone	CPCS106	1970	**£250**	**£150**	*export, silver & black label*
Hey Jude	LP	Parlophone	PCSJ149	1970	**£20**	**£8**	*export*
Hey Jude	CD-s	Parlophone	CD3R5722	1989	**£8**	**£4**	*3" single*
Hey Jude	78	Parlophone	DPE190	196–	**£400**	**£250**	*Indian, best auctioned*
Hey Jude	7"	Apple	RP5722	1988	**£15**	**£7.50**	*picture disc*
Hey Jude	7"	Parlophone	DP570	1968	**£30**	**£15**	*export*
Hey Jude	7"	Parlophone	R5722	1968	**£1000**	**£700**	*demo, existence doubtful*
Hey Jude	12"	Apple	12RP5722	1988	**£12**	**£6**	*picture disc*
Hey Jude/The Beatles Again	LP	Apple	SO/SW385	1970	**£15**	**£6**	*US, labels read 'The Beatles Again'*
History Of Rock Vol. 26	LP	Orbis	HRL026	1984	**£15**	**£6**	*double*
Honey Don't	7" EP	Odeon	SOE3779	1965	**£30**	**£15**	*French*
I Feel Fine	7"	Parlophone	R5200	1964	**£350**	**£210**	*demo*
I Feel Fine	7"	Parlophone	RP5200	1984	**£10**	**£5**	*picture disc*
I Feel Fine	7" EP	Odeon	SOE3760	1964	**£20**	**£10**	*French*
I Feel Fine	78	Parlophone	R5200	196–	**£400**	**£250**	*Indian, best auctioned*
I Feel Fine	CD-s	Parlophone	CD3R5200	1989	**£8**	**£4**	*3" single*
I Saw Her Standing There	78	Parlophone	DPE159	196–	**£400**	**£250**	*Indian, best auctioned*
I Should Have Known Better	78	Parlophone	DPE168	196–	**£400**	**£250**	*Indian, best auctioned*
I Wanna Be Your Man	7"	Odeon	22681	1964	**£10**	**£5**	*German import*
I Want To Hold Your Hand	7"	Parlophone	RP5084	1983	**£10**	**£5**	*picture disc*
I Want To Hold Your Hand	7"	Parlophone	R5084	1963	**£350**	**£210**	*demo*
I Want To Hold Your Hand	7"	Odeon	22623	1964	**£10**	**£5**	*German import*
I Want To Hold Your Hand	7" EP	Odeon	SOE3745	1963	**£20**	**£10**	*French*
I Want To Hold Your Hand	CD-s	Parlophone	CD3R5084	1989	**£8**	**£4**	*3" single*
I'm A Loser	7"	HMV	MQ20007	1964	**£10**	**£5**	*Italian import*
I'm A Loser	78	Parlophone	DPE178	196–	**£400**	**£250**	*Indian, best auctioned*
I'm Looking Through You	78	Parlophone	DPE193	196–	**£400**	**£250**	*Indian, best auctioned*

Title	Format	Label	Number	Year	Mint	Fair	Notes
If I Fell	7"	Parlophone	DP562	1964	£30	£15	export
If I Fell	78	Parlophone	DPE167	196–	£400	£250	Indian, best auctioned
Impression	LP	Parlophone	6086	1965	£600	£400	German, club pressing
Impression	LP	Parlophone	6279	1965	£400	£250	German, club pressing
In The Beginning	LP	Polydor	244504	1970	£15	£6	US, red label
Introducing The Beatles	LP	Vee Jay	LP1062	1963	£300	£180	US, with 'Love Me Do', blank back cover, mono
Introducing The Beatles	LP	Vee Jay	LPS1062	1963	£600	£400	US, with 'Love Me Do', blank back cover, stereo
Introducing The Beatles	LP	Vee Jay	LP1062	1963	£100	£50	US, with 'Love Me Do', songs listed on back
Introducing The Beatles	LP	Vee Jay	LP1062	1964	£50	£25	US, with 'Please Please Me', mono
Introducing The Beatles	LP	Vee Jay	LPS1062	1964	£300	£180	US, with 'Please Please Me', stereo
Kansas City	7" EP	Odeon	SOE3776	1965	£30	£15	French
Komm Gib Mir Deine Hand	7"	Odeon	22671	1964	£50	£25	German import, picture sleeve
Lady Madonna	7"	Parlophone	RP5675	1988	£15	£7.50	picture disc
Lady Madonna	7"	Parlophone	R5675	1968	£250	£150	demo
Lady Madonna	CD-s	Parlophone	CD3R5675	1989	£8	£4	3" single
Les Beatles	LP	Odeon	OSX222	1963	£75	£37.50	French
Let It Be	r-reel	Apple	TAPMC7096	1970	£100	£50	mono
Let It Be	r-reel	Apple	TDPCS7096	1970	£60	£30	stereo
Let It Be	LP	Apple	AR34001	1970	£10	£4	US, 'a subsidiary of Capitol'
Let It Be	LP	Apple	PCS7096	1970	£12	£5	
Let It Be	LP	Apple	PCS7096	1978	£60	£30	white vinyl
Let It Be	LP	Apple	PPCS7096	1970	£40	£20	export
Let It Be	LP	Apple	PXS1/PCS7096	1970	£200	£100	boxed with book
Let It Be	LP	Mobile Fidelity	MFSL1109	1984	£20	£8	US audiophile
Let It Be	LP	Parlophone	PPCS7096	1970	£300	£180	export, silver & black label
Let It Be	LP	Parlophone	PPCS7096	1970	£750	£500	export, yellow & black label
Let It Be	CD-s	Parlophone	CD3R5833	1989	£8	£4	3" single
Let It Be	CD	EMI	BEACD25/8	1987	£20	£8	HMV boxed set, poster, booklet, badge
Let It Be	CD	Parlophone	CDP7464472	1988	£125	£62.50	promo, green disc, boxed
Let It Be	7"	Apple	PR5833	1970	£75	£37.50	export
Let It Be	7"	Apple	R5833	1970	£1000	£700	demo, existence doubtful
Let It Be	7"	Apple	R5833	1970	£8	£4	picture sleeve, APPLES1002 scratched out matrix number
Let It Be	7"	Apple	RP5833	1990	£15	£7.50	picture disc
Let It Be	7"	Parlophone	PR5833	1970	£50	£25	export
Live At The BBC	CD	Apple	CDPCSPDJ7261	1994	£30	£15	promo sampler in fold-out package
Live At The BBC	CD	Apple	724383179626	1994	£20	£8	double, mistitled track 17, disc 2
Live At The Star Club Hamburg	CD	Lingasong	LING95	1995	£15	£6	LP-sized box
Live At The Star Club Hamburg	LP	Lingasong	LNS1	1977	£12	£5	double
Long Tall Sally	7"	Odeon	22745	1964	£12	£6	German import
Long Tall Sally	7" EP	Parlophone	GEP8913	1964	£12	£6	
Long Tall Sally	7" EP	Odeon	SOE3755	1964	£15	£7.50	French
Long Tall Sally	78	Parlophone	DPE164	196–	£400	£250	Indian, best auctioned
Love Me Do	CD-s	Parlophone	CD3R4949	1988	£8	£4	3" single
Love Me Do	7"	Parlophone	R4949	1962	£1000	£700	demo
Love Me Do	7"	Parlophone	R4949	1962	£25	£12.50	red label
Love Me Do	7"	Parlophone	R4949	1963	£50	£25	black label, 2 versions
Love Me Do	7"	Parlophone	R4949	1982	£12	£6	Ardmore & Beechwood credit
Love Me Do	7"	Parlophone	RP4949	1982	£15	£7.50	Ardmore & Beechwood credit, picture disc
Love Me Do	7"	Parlophone	RP4949	1982	£10	£5	picture disc
Love Me Do	7"	Parlophone	RP4949	1982	£20	£10	picture disc mispress – 2 A sides
Love Me Do	12"	Parlophone	12R4949	1982	£6	£2.50	
Magical Mystery Tour	LP	Capitol	MAL2835	1967	£60	£30	US, mono
Magical Mystery Tour	LP	Capitol	SMAL2835	1967	£15	£6	US, stereo
Magical Mystery Tour	LP	Mobile Fidelity	MFSL1047	1981	£25	£10	US audiophile
Magical Mystery Tour	LP	Parlophone	PCTC255	1978	£50	£25	yellow vinyl
Magical Mystery Tour	CD	EMI	BEACD25/6	1987	£30	£15	HMV box, badge, booklet, poster
Magical Mystery Tour	7" EP	Odeon	MEOHS39501/2	1967	£20	£10	French double

Magical Mystery Tour	7" EP	Parlophone	MMT1	1967	**£20**	**£10**	*double, mono, blue lyric sheet*
Magical Mystery Tour	7" EP	Parlophone	MMT1	1967	**£30**	**£15**	*mispress, Beach Boys 'Darlin'' on B side of 'Walrus'*
Magical Mystery Tour	7" EP	Parlophone	SMMT1	1967	**£20**	**£10**	*double, stereo, blue lyric sheet*
Magical Mystery Tour	7" EP	Parlophone	SMMT1	197–	**£10**	**£5**	*yellow lyric sheet*
Meet The Beatles	LP	Capitol	ST2047	1964	**£20**	**£8**	*US, green title, stereo*
Meet The Beatles	LP	Capitol	ST2047	1964	**£25**	**£10**	*US, brown title, stereo*
Meet The Beatles	LP	Capitol	T2047	1964	**£25**	**£10**	*US, green title, mono*
Meet The Beatles	LP	Capitol	ST82047	1964	**£50**	**£25**	*US, Record Club issue*
Meet The Beatles	LP	Capitol	T2047	1964	**£30**	**£15**	*US, brown title, mono*
Michelle	7"	Parlophone	DP564	1966	**£75**	**£37.50**	*export*
Michelle	7" EP	Odeon	MEO102	1966	**£15**	**£7.50**	*French*
Michelle	78	Parlophone	DPE187	196–	**£400**	**£250**	*Indian, best auctioned*
Michelle	78	Parlophone	DPE186	196–	**£400**	**£250**	*Indian, best auctioned*
Misery	7" EP	Odeon	SOE3778	1965	**£30**	**£15**	*French*
Money	7"	Odeon	22638	1964	**£10**	**£5**	*German import*
No Reply	7"	Odeon	22893	1964	**£10**	**£5**	*German import*
No. 1	LP	Odeon	OSX225	1963	**£125**	**£62.50**	*French*
Nowhere Man	7" EP	Parlophone	GEP8952	1966	**£40**	**£20**	
Ob-La-Di, Ob-La-Da	78	Parlophone	DPE192	196–	**£400**	**£250**	*Indian, best auctioned*
Only The Beatles	cass	EMI	SMMC151	1986	**£10**	**£4**	*Heineken promotion*
Original Master Records	LP	Mobile Fidelity	0575	1984	**£350**	**£210**	*US 13 LP box set, audiophile*
Our First Four	7"	Apple	no number	1968	**£750**	**£500**	*promo, pack with 4 x 7" by Beatles and other artists*
Paperback Writer	CD-s	Parlophone	CD3R5452	1989	**£8**	**£4**	*3" single*
Paperback Writer	7" EP	Odeon	MEO119	1966	**£15**	**£7.50**	*French*
Paperback Writer	7"	Parlophone	R5452	1966	**£350**	**£210**	*demo*
Paperback Writer	7"	Parlophone	RP5452	1986	**£15**	**£7.50**	*picture disc*
Paperback Writer	7"	Parlophone	RP5452	1986	**£50**	**£25**	*picture disc mispress – A side plays Queen track*
Past Masters Vol. 1	CD	EMI	BEACD25/9	1987	**£20**	**£8**	*HMV box, booklet, badge*
Past Masters Vol. 2	CD	EMI	BEACD25/10	1987	**£20**	**£8**	*HMV box, booklet, badge*
Penny Lane	7"	Parlophone	R5570	1967	**£15**	**£7.50**	*picture sleeve*
Penny Lane	7"	Parlophone	R5570	1967	**£300**	**£180**	*demo*
Penny Lane	7"	Parlophone	RP5570	1987	**£15**	**£7.50**	*picture disc*
Penny Lane	CD-s	Parlophone	CD3R5570	1989	**£8**	**£4**	*3" single*
Please Please Me	r-reel	Parlophone	TAPMC1202/ TDPCS3042	1963	**£25**	**£10**	
Please Please Me	LP	Mobile Fidelity	MFSL1101	1984	**£20**	**£8**	*US audiophile*
Please Please Me	LP	Odeon	ZTOX5550	1963	**£175**	**£87.50**	*German export*
Please Please Me	LP	Parlophone	PCS3042	1963	**£1500**	**£1000**	*gold label stereo*
Please Please Me	LP	Parlophone	PCS3042	1963	**£150**	**£75**	*stereo*
Please Please Me	LP	Parlophone	PCS3042	1969	**£12**	**£5**	*reissue, exposed edges on back cover, 'Made in Gt Britain' on label*
Please Please Me	LP	Parlophone	PMC1202	1963	**£30**	**£15**	*mono*
Please Please Me	LP	Parlophone	PMC1202	1963	**£250**	**£150**	*mono, gold label*
Please Please Me	CD-s	Parlophone	CD3R4983	1988	**£8**	**£4**	*3" single*
Please Please Me	CD	Parlophone	CDP7463452	1987	**£50**	**£25**	*mispressing – plays A Hard Day's Night*
Please Please Me	CD	Parlophone	CDP7463452	1987	**£50**	**£25**	*mispressing – plays Beatles For Sale*
Please Please Me	78	Parlophone		196–	**£400**	**£250**	*Indian, best auctioned*
Please Please Me	7"	Parlophone	R4983	1963	**£5**	**£2**	*black label*
Please Please Me	7"	Parlophone	R4983	1963	**£600**	**£400**	*demo*
Please Please Me	7"	Parlophone	R4983	1963	**£30**	**£15**	*red label*
Please Please Me	7"	Parlophone	RP4983	1982	**£15**	**£7.50**	*picture disc mispress, plays 'From Me To You'*
Please Please Me	7"	Parlophone	RP4983	1983	**£10**	**£5**	*picture disc*
Please Please Me/With . . ./ Hard Day's Night/For Sale	CD	EMI	BEACD25/1	1987	**£175**	**£87.50**	*HMV black box, book, leaflet*
Rarities	LP	Capitol	SN12009	1978	**£40**	**£20**	*US green label*
Real Love	7"	Apple	RDJ6425	1995	**£10**	**£5**	*jukebox issue*
Real Love	CD-s	Apple	CDREALDJ1	1995	**£10**	**£5**	*promo*
Reel Music	LP	Capitol	SV12199	1982	**£20**	**£8**	*US gold vinyl*
Reel Music	LP	Capitol	SV12199	1982	**£30**	**£15**	*US gold vinyl, numbered*
Revolver	r-reel	Parlophone	TAPMC/ TDPCS7009	1966	**£25**	**£10**	
Revolver	LP	Capitol	ST2576	1966	**£20**	**£8**	*US, stereo*
Revolver	LP	Capitol	ST82576	1966	**£50**	**£25**	*US, Record Club issue*

Title	Format	Label	Cat. No.	Year	Mint	VG	Notes
Revolver	LP	Capitol	T2576	1966	**£25**	**£10**	*US, mono*
Revolver	LP	Mobile Fidelity	MFSL1107	1984	**£20**	**£8**	*US audiophile*
Revolver	LP	Odeon	SMO74161	1966	**£75**	**£37.50**	*German, white and gold label*
Revolver	LP	Parlophone	PCS7009	1966	**£60**	**£30**	*stereo*
Revolver	LP	Parlophone	PCS7009	1969	**£12**	**£5**	*reissue, exposed edges on back cover, 'Made in Gt Britain' on label*
Revolver	LP	Parlophone	PMC7009	1966	**£30**	**£15**	*mono*
Revolver	CD	Decca	4177182	1987	**£40**	**£20**	*mispressed on to Haydn CD*
Rock And Roll Music	78	Parlophone	DPE179	196–	**£400**	**£250**	*Indian, best auctioned*
Roll Over Beethoven	7" EP	Odeon	SOE3746	1963	**£20**	**£10**	*French*
Rubber Soul	r-reel	Parlophone	TAPMC1267/ TDPCS3075	1966	**£25**	**£10**	
Rubber Soul	LP	Capitol	ST2442	1965	**£20**	**£8**	*US, stereo*
Rubber Soul	LP	Capitol	ST82442	1965	**£50**	**£25**	*US, Record Club issue*
Rubber Soul	LP	Capitol	T2442	1965	**£25**	**£10**	*US, mono*
Rubber Soul	LP	Mobile Fidelity	MFSL1106	1984	**£20**	**£8**	*US audiophile*
Rubber Soul	LP	Odeon	SMO984066	1965	**£150**	**£75**	*German, club pressing*
Rubber Soul	LP	Parlophone	PCS3075	1966	**£60**	**£30**	*stereo*
Rubber Soul	LP	Parlophone	PCS3075	1969	**£12**	**£5**	*reissue, exposed edges on back cover, 'Made in Gt Britain' on label*
Rubber Soul	LP	Parlophone	PMC1267	1966	**£30**	**£15**	*mono*
Rubber Soul	CD	Parlophone	CDP7464402	1987	**£40**	**£20**	*mispressing – plays Wilson-Phillips*
Searchin'	7"	AFE	AFS1	1982	**£8**	**£4**	
Second Album	LP	Odeon	ZTOX5558	1964	**£100**	**£50**	*German, export*
Sgt Pepper's Lonely Hearts Club Band	r-reel	Parlophone	TAPMC7027	1967	**£25**	**£10**	
Sgt Pepper's Lonely Hearts Club Band	LP	Capitol	MAS2653	1967	**£50**	**£25**	*US, mono*
Sgt Pepper's Lonely Hearts Club Band	LP	Capitol	SEAV11840	1978	**£25**	**£10**	*Canadian, marbled vinyl*
Sgt Pepper's Lonely Hearts Club Band	LP	Capitol	SEAX11840	1978	**£25**	**£10**	*US picture disc*
Sgt Pepper's Lonely Hearts Club Band	LP	Capitol	SMAS2653	1967	**£25**	**£10**	*US, stereo*
Sgt Pepper's Lonely Hearts Club Band	LP	Mobile Fidelity	MFSL1100	1982	**£20**	**£8**	*US audiophile*
Sgt Pepper's Lonely Hearts Club Band	LP	Mobile Fidelity	UHQR1100	1982	**£200**	**£100**	*US audiophile, ¼" thick vinyl*
Sgt Pepper's Lonely Hearts Club Band	LP	Parlophone	PCS7027	1967	**£30**	**£15**	*stereo*
Sgt Pepper's Lonely Hearts Club Band	LP	Parlophone	PCS7027	1969	**£12**	**£5**	*reissue, exposed edges on inside of cover, 'Made in Gt Britain' on label*
Sgt Pepper's Lonely Hearts Club Band	LP	Parlophone	PHO7027	1979	**£25**	**£10**	*picture disc*
Sgt Pepper's Lonely Hearts Club Band	LP	Parlophone	PMC7027	1967	**£50**	**£25**	*mono*
Sgt Pepper's Lonely Hearts Club Band	LP	Parlophone	PMC7027	1982	**£12**	**£5**	*from BMC10, but with stereo B side*
Sgt Pepper's Lonely Hearts Club Band	7"	Parlophone	R6022	1978	**£25**	**£12.50**	*demo*
Sgt Pepper's Lonely Hearts Club Band	CD	EMI	BEACD25/3	1987	**£30**	**£15**	*HMV box, badge, booklet, cutouts*
Sgt Pepper's Lonely Hearts Club Band	CD	Parlophone	CDP7464422	1987	**£40**	**£20**	*mispressing – plays classical album*
Sgt Pepper's Lonely Hearts Club Band	CD	Parlophone	CDP7464422	1987	**£40**	**£20**	*mispressing – plays Now 18*
Sgt Pepper's Lonely Hearts Club Band	CD	Parlophone	CDP7464422	1987	**£50**	**£25**	*mispressing – plays Revolver*
Sgt Pepper's Lonely Hearts Club Band	CD	Virgin	CDV2421	1987	**£40**	**£20**	*mispressed on to In Tua Nua CD*
She Loves You	7"	Parlophone	RP5055	1983	**£12**	**£6**	*picture disc*
She Loves You	7"	Parlophone	R5055	1963	**£350**	**£210**	*demo*
She Loves You	7" EP	Odeon	SOE3741	1963	**£20**	**£10**	*French, 2 slightly different sleeves*
She Loves You	CD-s	Parlophone	CD3R5055	1988	**£8**	**£4**	*3" single*
Silver Beatles	LP	Exclusive	AR30003	1983	**£12**	**£5**	*picture disc*
Singles Collection	CD-s	Parlophone/ Apple	CDBSC1	1989	**£200**	**£100**	*boxed set of 22 3" singles*
Something	7"	Apple	R5814	1969	**£500**	**£330**	*demo*
Something	7"	Apple	RP5814	1989	**£15**	**£7.50**	*picture disc*
Something	CD-s	Parlophone	CD3R5814	1989	**£8**	**£4**	*3" single*
Something New	LP	Capitol	ST2108	1964	**£20**	**£8**	*US, stereo*
Something New	LP	Capitol	ST82108	1964	**£50**	**£25**	*US, Record Club issue*
Something New	LP	Capitol	T2108	1964	**£25**	**£10**	*US, mono*
Something New	LP	Parlophone	CPCS101	1965	**£750**	**£500**	*export*
Something New	LP	Parlophone	CPCS101	1969	**£250**	**£150**	*export, silver & black label*
Songs, Pictures And Stories	LP	Vee Jay	LP1092	1964	**£75**	**£37.50**	*US, fold-open cover*
Strawberry Fields Forever	7" EP	Odeon	MEO134	1967	**£15**	**£7.50**	*French*
Tell Me What You See	7" EP	Odeon	SOE3775	1965	**£20**	**£10**	*French*
Tell Me Why	78	Parlophone	DPE172	196–	**£400**	**£250**	*Indian, best auctioned*
Their Greatest Hits	cass	St Michael	13615701	1984	**£25**	**£10**	*boxed with book*

Title	Format	Label	Cat. No.	Year	Mint	Value	Notes
Ticket To Ride	7"	Parlophone	R5265	1965	**£350**	**£210**	*demo*
Ticket To Ride	7"	Parlophone	RP5265	1985	**£10**	**£5**	*picture disc*
Ticket To Ride	7"	Parlophone	RP5265	1985	**£15**	**£7.50**	*picture disc mispress, B side plays Power Station track*
Ticket To Ride	7" EP	Odeon	SOE3766	1965	**£20**	**£10**	*French*
Ticket To Ride	CD-s	Parlophone	CD3R5265	1989	**£8**	**£4**	*3" single*
Twist And Shout	7"	Lingasong	NB1	1977	**£8**	**£4**	
Twist And Shout	7"	Odeon	22581	1964	**£10**	**£5**	*German import*
Twist And Shout	7" EP	Parlophone	GEP8882	1963	**£15**	**£7.50**	
Volume 1	7" EP	Odeon	MOE21001	1965	**£60**	**£30**	*French*
Volume 2	7" EP	Odeon	MOE21002	1965	**£60**	**£30**	*French*
Volume 3	7" EP	Odeon	MOE21003	1965	**£75**	**£37.50**	*French*
Volume 4	7" EP	Odeon	MOE21004	1965	**£60**	**£30**	*French*
We Can Work It Out	7" EP	Odeon	MEO107	1965	**£15**	**£7.50**	*French*
We Can Work It Out	CD-s	Parlophone	CD3R5389	1989	**£8**	**£4**	*3" single*
With The Beatles	r-reel	Parlophone	TAPMC1206/ TDPCS3045	1964	**£25**	**£10**	
With The Beatles	LP	Mobile Fidelity	MFSL1102	1984	**£40**	**£20**	*US audiophile*
With The Beatles	LP	Parlophone	PCS3045	1963	**£150**	**£75**	*stereo*
With The Beatles	LP	Parlophone	PCS3045	1969	**£12**	**£5**	*reissue, exposed edges on back cover, 'Made in Gt Britain' on label*
With The Beatles	LP	Parlophone	PMC1206	1963	**£30**	**£15**	*mono*
With The Beatles	LP	Parlophone	PMC1206	1963	**£100**	**£50**	*Swedish, gold label*
Words Of Love	78	Parlophone	DPE180	196–	**£400**	**£250**	*Indian, best auctioned*
World Records Presents The Music Of The Beatles	7"	Lyntone	LYN8982	1980	**£8**	**£4**	*promo flexi*
Yellow Submarine	r-reel	Apple	TAPMC/ TDPCS7070	1969	**£100**	**£50**	
Yellow Submarine	LP	Apple	PCS7070	1969	**£25**	**£15**	*stereo*
Yellow Submarine	LP	Apple	PMC7070	1969	**£150**	**£75**	*mono*
Yellow Submarine	LP	Apple	SW153	1968	**£12**	**£5**	*US*
Yellow Submarine	LP	Mobile Fidelity	MFSL1108	1984	**£20**	**£8**	*US audiophile*
Yellow Submarine	LP	Odeon	PPCS7070	1969	**£1000**	**£700**	*export*
Yellow Submarine	LP	Parlophone	PPCS7070	1969	**£300**	**£180**	*export, silver & black label*
Yellow Submarine	LP	Parlophone	PPCS7070	1969	**£750**	**£500**	*export, yellow & black label*
Yellow Submarine	CD-s	Parlophone	CD3R5493	1989	**£8**	**£4**	*3" single*
Yellow Submarine	CD	EMI	BEACD25/5	1987	**£60**	**£30**	*HMV box, badge, cutout, leaflet*
Yellow Submarine	CD	Parlophone	CDP7464452	1987	**£50**	**£25**	*mispressing – plays Sgt Pepper*
Yellow Submarine	7" EP	Odeon	MEO126	1966	**£15**	**£7.50**	*French*
Yellow Submarine	7"	Parlophone	R5493	1966	**£300**	**£180**	*demo*
Yellow Submarine	7"	Parlophone	RP5493	1986	**£15**	**£7.50**	*picture disc*
Yesterday	7"	Parlophone	DP563	1965	**£60**	**£30**	*export*
Yesterday	7"	Parlophone	R6013	1976	**£25**	**£12.50**	*demo*
Yesterday	7" EP	Odeon	SOE3772	1965	**£20**	**£10**	*French*
Yesterday	7" EP	Odeon	MEO105	1965	**£15**	**£7.50**	*French*
Yesterday	7" EP	Parlophone	GEP8948	1966	**£30**	**£15**	
Yesterday	78	Parlophone	DPE184	196–	**£400**	**£250**	*Indian, best auctioned*
Yesterday And Today	LP	Capitol	ST2553	1966	**£3000**	**£2100**	*US, peeled butcher sleeve, stereo*
Yesterday And Today	LP	Capitol	ST2553	1966	**£20**	**£8**	*US, stereo*
Yesterday And Today	LP	Capitol	ST2553	1966	**£600**	**£400**	*US, unpeeled butcher sleeve, stereo*
Yesterday And Today	LP	Capitol	ST2553	198–	**£200**	**£100**	*Japanese butcher sleeve reissue*
Yesterday And Today	LP	Capitol	ST82553	1966	**£50**	**£25**	*US, Record Club issue*
Yesterday And Today	LP	Capitol	T2553	1966	**£1000**	**£700**	*US peeled butcher sleeve*
Yesterday And Today	LP	Capitol	T2553	1966	**£200**	**£100**	*US unpeeled butcher sleeve*
Yesterday And Today	LP	Capitol	T2553	1966	**£25**	**£10**	*US, mono*
You Like Me Too Much	78	Parlophone	DPE185	196–	**£400**	**£250**	*Indian, best auctioned*
You've Got To Hide Your Love Away	7" EP	Odeon	SOE3772	1965	**£30**	**£15**	*French*

BEATLES WITH TONY SHERIDAN

Title	Format	Label	Cat. No.	Year	Mint	Value	Notes
Ain't She Sweet	7"	Polydor	NH52317	1967	**£20**	**£10**	*red label*
Ain't She Sweet	7"	Polydor	NH52317	1964	**£100**	**£50**	*picture sleeve*
Ain't She Sweet	7"	Polydor	NH52317	1964	**£40**	**£20**	*orange label*
Ain't She Sweet	7" EP	Polydor	21965	1964	**£40**	**£20**	*French*
Ain't She Sweet	LP	Atco	SD33169	1964	**£75**	**£37.50**	*US, stereo*
Ain't She Sweet	LP	Atco	33169	1964	**£60**	**£30**	*US, mono*
Beatles' First	CD	Polydor	8237012	1984	**£50**	**£25**	*withdrawn sleeve with wrong line-up*
Beatles' First	LP	Polydor	236201	1964	**£75**	**£37.50**	
Beatles' First	LP	Polydor	236201	1967	**£60**	**£30**	*stereo*
Beatles' First	LP	Polydor	POLD666	1982	**£60**	**£30**	

Cry For A Shadow	7"	Polydor	NH52275	1964	**£40**	**£20**	*orange label*
Cry For A Shadow	7"	Polydor	NH52275	1967	**£8**	**£4**	*red label*
Cry For A Shadow	7"	Polydor	NH52275	1964	**£100**	**£50**	*picture sleeve*
Meet The Beat	10" LP	Polydor	J74557	1965	**£250**	**£150**	*German*
Mister Twist	7" EP	Polydor	21914	1962	**£50**	**£25**	*French*
My Bonnie	7"	Polydor	NH66833	1962	**£50**	**£25**	*orange label*
My Bonnie	7"	Polydor	NH66833	1967	**£8**	**£4**	*red label*
Savage Young Beatles	10" LP	Charly	CFM701	1982	**£15**	**£6**	
Sweet Georgia Brown	7"	Polydor	NH52906	1967	**£25**	**£12.50**	*red label, German import*
Sweet Georgia Brown	7"	Polydor	NH52906	1964	**£75**	**£37.50**	*orange label, German import*
Tony Sheridan With The Beatles	7" EP	Polydor	EPH21610	196–	**£30**	**£15**	*red label*
Tony Sheridan With The Beatles	7" EP	Polydor	EPH21610	1963	**£60**	**£30**	*orange label*
When The Saints	7" EP	Polydor	21914	1963	**£40**	**£20**	*French, 2 different sleeves*

BEATMEN

Now The Sun Has Gone	7"	Pye	7N15792	1965	**£4**	**£1.50**	
You Can't Sit Down	7"	Pye	7N15659	1964	**£6**	**£2.50**	

BEATSTALKERS

Everybody's Talkin' About My Baby	7"	Decca	F12259	1965	**£20**	**£10**	
Everything Is You	7"	CBS	3557	1968	**£20**	**£10**	
Left Right Left	7"	Decca	F12352	1966	**£20**	**£10**	
Love Like Yours	7"	Decca	F12460	1966	**£20**	**£10**	
My One Chance	7"	CBS	2732	1967	**£25**	**£12.50**	
Silver Tree Top School For Boys	7"	CBS	3105	1967	**£40**	**£20**	
When I'm Five	7"	CBS	3936	1969	**£20**	**£10**	
You'd Better Get A Better Hold On	7" EP	Decca	457112	1966	**£200**	**£100**	*French*

BEATTY, E. C.

Ski King	7"	Felsted	AF127	1959	**£8**	**£4**	

BEAU

C. J. T. Midgley (Beau) was a singer-songwriter whose songs would have benefited from more fully worked-out arrangements than they actually got. No doubt John Peel's Dandelion label could not afford the expense of a cast of session musicians. Nevertheless, '1917 Revolution' with its taut strummed twelve-string guitar echoing across the sound-stage is quite wonderful.

1917 Revolution	7"	Dandelion	K4403	1970	**£4**	**£1.50**	
Beau	LP	Dandelion	63751	1969	**£20**	**£8**	
Creation	LP	Dandelion	DAN8006	1971	**£20**	**£8**	

BEAU BRUMMELS

The natural response of America to the initial furore surrounding the Beatles was for the record-buying public to embrace a number of home-grown talents, whose sound and style owed everything to their Liverpudlian rivals. The Beau Brummels were probably the most successful of these, although they inevitably meant little in Britain. As a result, one of the classic albums of the late sixties has been largely ignored – for *Triangle* is an immaculate collection of imaginatively arranged songs to rival Love's *Forever Changes.*

Beau Brummels	LP	Pye	NPL28062	1965	**£30**	**£15**	
Beau Brummels 66	LP	Warner Bros	W(S)1644	1966	**£30**	**£15**	*US*
Beau Brummels Vol. 2	LP	Autumn	(S)LP104	1966	**£25**	**£10**	*US*
Best Of The Beau Brummels	LP	Vault	LPS114	1967	**£30**	**£15**	*US*
Bradley's Barn	LP	Warner Bros	WS1760	1968	**£25**	**£10**	*US*
Don't Talk To Strangers	7"	Pye	7N25333	1965	**£5**	**£2**	
Here We Are Again	7" EP	Warner Bros	WB112	1966	**£25**	**£12.50**	*French*
Just A Little	7"	Pye	7N25306	1965	**£5**	**£2**	
Just A Little	7" EP	Vogue	INT18010	1965	**£25**	**£12.50**	*French*
Laugh Laugh	7"	Pye	7N25293	1965	**£5**	**£2**	
Laugh Laugh	7" EP	Vogue	INT18002	1965	**£25**	**£12.50**	*French*
Triangle	LP	Warner Bros	W(S)1692	1967	**£25**	**£10**	*US*
Vol. 44	LP	Vault	LPS121	1967	**£25**	**£10**	*US*
You Tell Me Why	7"	Pye	7N25318	1965	**£5**	**£2**	

BEAUMARKS

Clap Your Hands	7"	Top Rank	JAR377	1960	**£10**	**£5**	

BEAUMONT, JIMMY

You Got Too Much Going For You	7"	London	HLZ10059	1966	**£25**	**£12.50**	

BEAUREGARDE

Beauregarde	LP	F-Empire	1001	1969	**£60**	**£30**	*US*

BEAUTIFUL SOUTH

Carry On Continues . . .	CD	Go! Discs	TNTBS1	1996	**£20**	**£8**	*promo compilation*
Cary On Up The Charts	CD	Go! Discs	8285692	1994	**£15**	**£6**	*double*
I'll Sail This Ship Alone	CD-s	Go! Discs	GODCD38	1989	**£5**	**£2**	
Little Time	CD-s	Go! Discs	GODCD47	1990	**£5**	**£2**	
My Book	CD-s	Go! Discs	GODCD48	1990	**£5**	**£2**	
Song For Whoever	CD-s	Go! Discs	GODCD32	1989	**£5**	**£2**	
You Keep It All In	CD-s	Go! Discs	GODCD35	1989	**£5**	**£2**	

BEAVER, PAUL

Perchance To Dream	LP	Rapture	11111		**£15**	**£6**	*US*

BEAVER–KRAUSE

Paul Beaver and Bernie Krause were the other pair of synthesizer pioneers, but, unlike the records by Tonto's Expanding Headband, theirs mix the electronics with conventional instruments. Particularly recommended is the music to be found on side two of *Gandharva*, where saxophonist Gerry Mulligan meets the duo in church to glorious effect. The *Nonesuch Guide To Electronic Music* is by way of being an aural handbook, recorded for an avant-garde classical label.

All Good Men	LP	Warner Bros	K46184	1972	**£10**	**£4**	
Gandharva	LP	Warner Bros	K46130	1971	**£12**	**£5**	
In A Wild Sanctuary	LP	Warner Bros	WS1850	1970	**£12**	**£5**	*US*
Nonesuch Guide To Electronic Music	LP	Nonesuch	HC73018	1968	**£15**	**£6**	*2 LP boxed set*
Ragnarok Electronic Funk	LP	Limelight	86069	1969	**£12**	**£5**	*US*

BEAZERS (CHRIS FARLOWE)

Blue Beat	7"	Decca	F11827	1964	**£15**	**£7.50**	

BEBOP DELUXE

Between Two Worlds	7"	Harvest	HAR5091	1975	**£30**	**£15**	
Teenage Archangel	7"	Smile	LAFS001	1973	**£15**	**£7.50**	

BECHET, SIDNEY

At Storyville	10" LP	Vogue	LDE132	1955	**£40**	**£20**	
At Storyville	10" LP	Vogue	LDE149	1955	**£40**	**£20**	
Blue Note Jazz Men	10" LP	Vogue	LDE025	1953	**£50**	**£25**	
Blue Note Jazzmen	10" LP	Vogue	LDE127	1955	**£40**	**£20**	
Blue Note Jazzmen Vol. 2	10" LP	Vogue	LDE086	1954	**£40**	**£20**	
Fabulous	LP	Blue Note	BLP/BST81207	196–	**£20**	**£8**	
Festival de Jazz 1958	LP	Vogue	LAE12168	1959	**£15**	**£6**	
Giant Of Jazz Vol. 1	LP	Blue Note	BLP/BST81203	196–	**£20**	**£8**	
Giant Of Jazz Vol. 2	LP	Blue Note	BLP/BST81204	196–	**£20**	**£8**	
Golden Disc Concert	LP	Vogue	LAE12010	1956	**£25**	**£10**	
Golden Disc Concert	LP	Vogue	LAE12011	1956	**£25**	**£10**	
Hot Six	10" LP	Vogue	LDE138	1955	**£40**	**£20**	
Jazz Classics Vol. 1	LP	Blue Note	BLP/BST81201	196–	**£20**	**£8**	
Jazz Classics Vol. 2	LP	Blue Note	BLP/BST81202	196–	**£20**	**£8**	
Jazz Concert Vol. 1	10" LP	Vogue	LDE018	1953	**£40**	**£20**	
Jazz Concert Vol. 2	10" LP	Vogue	LDE019	1953	**£40**	**£20**	
Jazz Concert Vol. 3	10" LP	Vogue	LDE027	1953	**£40**	**£20**	
Last Show	LP	Pye	NPL28006	1959	**£15**	**£6**	
New Orleans In Paris	10" LP	Vogue	LDE069	1954	**£40**	**£20**	
Shake It And Break It	10" LP	HMV	DLP1042	1954	**£40**	**£20**	
Sidney Bechet	10" LP	Vogue	LDE001	1952	**£40**	**£20**	
Sidney Bechet	10" LP	Columbia	33S1042	1954	**£40**	**£20**	
Vogue Jazzmen	10" LP	Vogue	LDE119	1955	**£40**	**£20**	
With Humphrey Lyttelton's Band	7" EP	Melodisc	EPM751	1955	**£6**	**£2.50**	
With Sammy Price's Bluesicians	LP	Vogue	LAE12037	1957	**£25**	**£10**	
With The Claude Luter Orchestra	LP	Vogue	LAE12003	1955	**£25**	**£10**	
With The Claude Luter Orchestra	LP	Vogue	LAE12024	1956	**£25**	**£10**	

BECK

Loser	7"	Geffen	GFS67	1994	**£5**	**£2**	
Loser	CD-s	Geffen	GFSTD67	1994	**£5**	**£2**	
Pay No Mind	12"	Geffen	GFST74	1994	**£12**	**£6**	
Pay No Mind	CD-s	Geffen	GFSTD74	1994	**£8**	**£4**	

BECK, BOGERT & APPICE

Beck, Bogert & Appice	LP	CBS	Q65455	1975	**£10**	**£4**	*quad*
Live In Japan	LP	CBS/Sony	ECPJ11/12	1973	**£20**	**£8**	*Japanese double*

BECK, ELDER CHARLES

RCA Victor Race Series Vol. 5	7" EP	RCA	RCX7176	1965	**£5**	**£2**	

BECK, GORDON

All In The Morning	cass	Jaguar	JS1	1974	**£12**	**£5**	
Beck–Matthewson–Humair Trio	LP	Dire	FO341	1972	**£30**	**£15**	
Experiments With Pops	LP	Major Minor	MMLP/SMLP21	1969	**£30**	**£15**	
Gyroscope	LP	Morgan	MJ1	1968	**£40**	**£20**	
Half A Jazz Sixpence	LP	Major Minor	MMLP/SMLP22	1968	**£30**	**£15**	
One, Two, Three . . . Go!	cass	Jaguar	JS2	1974	**£12**	**£5**	*credited to Gyroscope*
Plays Dr Doolittle	LP	Major Minor	SML88	1968	**£30**	**£15**	
Seven Ages Of Man	LP	Rediffusion	ZS115	1972	**£40**	**£20**	

BECK, JEFF

When the *Observer* surveyed a number of well-known rock guitarists to discover who the 'guitarists' guitarist' was, the consensus of opinion was Jeff Beck. Notoriously difficult to work with, Beck's career has been notable for the instability of his group line-ups and also for his apparent difficulty in deciding on the best music style to display his talents. He has, nevertheless, managed to create the occasional masterpiece along the way, of which the most obvious examples are the electric jazz album *Blow By Blow* (too common to be valuable, unfortunately) and the blues-rock *Truth*. This record, which included Rod Stewart and Ron Wood as members of a fine band, was a direct influence on Led Zeppelin, not least with regard to Jimmy Page's guitar playing, in which the Jeff Beck approach is very apparent.

Beck-ola	LP	Columbia	SCX6351	1969	**£10**	**£4**	
Beck-ola	LP	Columbia	SX6351	1969	**£15**	**£6**	*mono*
Beckology	CD	Epic	4692622	1992	**£40**	**£20**	*boxed 3 CD set*
Beckology – The Sampler	CD	Epic	ESK4275	1992	**£20**	**£8**	*US promo sampler*
Blow By Blow	LP	Epic	PEQ33409	1975	**£15**	**£6**	*US quad*
Day In The House	CD-s	Epic	BECK1CD	1989	**£5**	**£2**	

Fire Meets The Fury	CD	Epic	ESK1901	1989	£20	£8	US promo sampler, with Stevie Ray Vaughan
Guitar Shop	CD-s	Epic	CDBECK1	1989	£5	£2	
Hi Ho Silver Lining	7"	Columbia	DB8151	1967	£5	£2	
Hi Ho Silver Lining	7"	RAK	RRP3	1982	£4	£1.50	picture disc
Jeff Beck Group	LP	Epic	EQ31331	1974	£12	£5	US quad
Live	LP	Epic	PEQ34433	1977	£12	£5	US quad
Love Is Blue	7"	Columbia	DB8359	1968	£4	£1.50	
Mustang Sally	CD-s	Silvertone	ORECD30	1991	£5	£2	with Buddy Guy
Plinth	7"	Columbia	DB8590	1968	£40	£20	demo only
Rough And Ready	LP	Epic	Q64619	1974	£12	£5	quad
Tallyman	7"	Columbia	DB8227	1967	£6	£2.50	
Truth	7"	Columbia	PSR317	1968	£15	£7.50	promo
Truth	LP	Columbia	SCX6293	1968	£15	£6	
Truth	LP	Columbia	SX6293	1968	£25	£10	mono
Wired	CD	Mobile Fidelity	MFCD531	1988	£15	£6	US audiophile
Wired	LP	Epic	PEQ33849	1976	£15	£6	US quad

BECKETT, HAROLD

Harold Beckett is a jazz trumpeter whose playing seems to be included somewhere on most British rock LPs made in the early seventies! His own records, which feature the usual familiar jazz faces of the period, are actually remarkably free from rock influence, which is the reason for their relatively low collectors' values today.

Flare Up	LP	Philips	6308026	1971	£20	£8	
Got It Made	LP	Ogun	OG020	1977	£12	£5	
Joy Unlimited	LP	Cadillac	SGC1004	1975	£15	£6	
Memories Of Bacares	LP	Ogun	OG800	1976	£12	£5	
Theme For Fega	LP	RCA	SF8264	1973	£20	£8	
Warm Smiles	LP	RCA	SF8225	1972	£20	£8	

BECKFORD, KEITH

Suzy Wong	7"	Big Shot	BI521	1969	£5	£2	

BECKFORD, LYN

Combination	7"	Island	WI3144	1968	£12	£6	
Kiss Me Quick	7"	Jackpot	JP707	1969	£4	£1.50	Mr Miller B side

BECKFORD, THEO

Bollerman	7"	Island	WI106	1963	£12	£6	
Bringing In The Sheep	7"	Blue Beat	BB132	1962	£12	£6	
Brother Ram Goat	7"	Crab	CRAB25	1969	£4	£1.50	Starlights B side
Dig The Dig	7"	Blue Beat	BB303	1965	£12	£6	
Don't Worry To Cry	7"	Blue Beat	BB257	1964	£12	£6	
Easy Snappin'	7"	Nu Beat	NB009	1968	£5	£2	Eric Morris B side
Easy Snapping	7"	Blue Beat	BB15	1960	£12	£6	
Georgie And The Old Shoes	7"	Blue Beat	BB50	1961	£12	£6	
I Don't Want You	7"	Island	WI026	1962	£12	£6	
If Life Was A Thing	7"	Island	WI246	1965	£10	£5	Lloyd Clarke B side
Jack And Jill Shuffle	7"	Blue Beat	BB33	1961	£12	£6	
On Your Knees	7"	Blue Beat	BB287	1965	£12	£6	
She's Gone	7"	Blue Beat	BB250	1964	£12	£6	
Take Your Time	7"	Black Swan	WI452	1965	£12	£6	Stranger Cole B side
Trench Town People	7"	Island	WI238	1965	£10	£5	Pioneers B side
Walking Down King Street	7"	Blue Beat	BB87	1962	£12	£6	Sir Dee's Group B side
What A Woe	7"	Island	WI248	1965	£10	£5	
You Are The One	7"	Island	WI243	1965	£10	£5	

BEDFORD, DAVID

David Bedford is an avant-garde composer whose sympathy for rock music has led to his gaining much employment as an arranger. In particular, he has worked extensively with Mike Oldfield, producing an orchestral version of *Tubular Bells* and writing a guitar concerto for him (the superb *Star's End*, which should be required listening for Jon Lord, Keith Emerson and other rock-classical fusionists whose ideas of how classical music is constructed are still rooted in the nineteenth century). *Nurses Song With Elephants* is less accessible than later Bedford works, but is still crammed with original ideas.

Music For Albion Moonlight	LP	Argo	ZRG638	1970	£20	£8	other side Elizabeth Lutyens
Nurses Song With Elephants	LP	Dandelion	2310165	1972	£20	£8	

BEDLAM

Bedlam	LP	Chrysalis	CHR1048	1973	£15	£6	
I Believe In You	7"	Chrysalis	CFB1	1973	£4	£1.50	

BEE, EDWIN

I've Been Loving You	7"	Decca	F12781	1968	£4	£1.50	

BEE, MOLLY

Since I Met You Baby	7"	London	HLD8400	1957	£25	£12.50	

BEE GEES

Despite a long and very successful hit-making career, the Bee Gees have proved to be of limited interest to collectors. There are one or two high-priced items, but the albums issued prior to the leap into the premier division occasioned by the *Saturday Night Fever* soundtrack struggle to be included in the list below (many are not) despite being quite hard to find. The first UK album is actually something of a period classic, standing shoulder-to-shoulder with other post-Sgt Pepper albums like the Hollies' *Butterfly* or the Rainbow Ffolly's *Sallies Forth*.

Bee Gees First	LP	Polydor	582/583012	1967	£10	£4	

Boogie Child	7"	RSO	2090224	1977	**£8**	**£4**	*promo only*
Horizontal	LP	Polydor	582/583020	1968	**£10**	**£4**	
How Deep Is Your Love	CD-s	Polydor	PZCD110	1990	**£5**	**£2**	
Idea	LP	Polydor	582/583036	1968	**£10**	**£4**	
Inception And Nostalgia	LP	Karussell	2674002	1973	**£75**	**£37.50**	*German double*
New York Mining Disaster 1941	7" EP	Polydor	27806	1967	**£15**	**£7.50**	*French*
Odessa	LP	Polydor	583049/050	1969	**£20**	**£8**	*felt sleeve, double*
One	CD-s	WEA	W2916CD	1989	**£5**	**£2**	
Ordinary Lives	CD-s	WEA	W7523CD	1989	**£5**	**£2**	
Rare Precious & Beautiful Vol. 1	LP	Polydor	236221	1968	**£10**	**£4**	
Rare Precious & Beautiful Vol. 2	LP	Polydor	236513	1968	**£10**	**£4**	
Rare Precious & Beautiful Vol. 3	LP	Polydor	236556	1969	**£10**	**£4**	
Secret Love	CD-s	WEA	W0014CD	1991	**£5**	**£2**	
Short Cuts	LP	RSO	BGPLP1	1979	**£10**	**£4**	*promo*
Sing & Play 14 Barry Gibb Songs	LP	Calendar	R66241	1968	**£40**	**£20**	*Australian reissue*
Sing & Play 14 Barry Gibb Songs	LP	London	LL31801	1965	**£100**	**£50**	*Australian*
Spicks And Specks	7"	Polydor	56727	1967	**£4**	**£1.50**	
Spicks And Specks	LP	Spin	EL32031	1966	**£50**	**£25**	*Australian*
Spirits Having Flown	LP	Nautilus	NR17	1981	**£10**	**£4**	*US audiophile*
To Love Somebody	7" EP	Polydor	27811	1967	**£15**	**£7.50**	*French*

BEEFEATERS

Please Let Me Love You	7"	Pye	7N25277	1964	**£60**	**£30**	
Please Let Me Love You	7"	Elektra	2101007	1970	**£15**	**£7.50**	

BEEFEATERS (2)

Beefeaters	LP	Sonet	SLPS1242	1967	**£25**	**£10**	*Danish*
Meet You There	LP	Sonet	SPLP1509	1969	**£12**	**£5**	
Meet You There	LP	Sonet	SLPS1509	1967	**£12**	**£5**	*Danish*
Soul In	LP	Karussell	635078	1968	**£30**	**£15**	*German*

BEER, MARK

Dust On The Road	LP	My China	TAO001	1981	**£20**	**£8**	

BEES

Jesse James Rides Again	7"	Columbia	DB101	1967	**£5**	**£2**	
Jesse James Rides Again	7"	Blue Beat	BB386	1967	**£12**	**£6**	
Prisoner From Alcatraz	7"	Columbia	DB111	1968	**£5**	**£2**	

BEES MAKE HONEY

Music Every Night	LP	EMI	EMC3013	1972	**£15**	**£6**	

BEETHOVEN SOUL

Beethoven Soul	LP	Dot	DLP25821	1967	**£15**	**£6**	*US*

BEEZ

Beez EP	7"	Edible	SNACK002	1979	**£15**	**£7.50**	
Easy	7"	Edible	SNACK001	1979	**£15**	**£7.50**	

B.E.F.

Free	7"	Ten	TEN386	1991	**£40**	**£20**	
Music For Stowaways	LP	Virgin	V2888	1980	**£25**	**£10**	*test pressing*

BEGGARS FARM

Depth Of A Dream	LP	White Rabbit	WR1001	1984	**£30**	**£15**	

BEGGAR'S HILL

Beggar's Hill	LP	Moonshine	MS60	1976	**£200**	**£100**	

BEGGARS MANTLE

Beggars Mantle	LP	Milestone	CM5001R	1984	**£25**	**£10**	

BEGGARS OPERA

Act One	LP	Vertigo	6360018	1970	**£20**	**£8**	*spiral label*
Get Your Dog Off Me	LP	Vertigo	6360090	1973	**£10**	**£4**	
Pathfinder	LP	Vertigo	6360073	1972	**£20**	**£8**	*spiral label*
Sagittary	LP	Jupiter	88907	1974	**£15**	**£6**	*German*
Sarabande	7"	Vertigo	6059026	1970	**£5**	**£2**	
Waters Of Change	LP	Vertigo	6360054	1971	**£20**	**£8**	*spiral label*

BEGINNING OF THE END

Funky Nassau	LP	Atlantic	K40304	1971	**£20**	**£8**	

BEHAN, BRENDAN

Hostage	LP	Argo	RG239	1960	**£20**	**£8**	

BEHAN, DOMINIC

Arkle	7"	Piccadilly	7N35238	1965	**£4**	**£1.50**	
Arkle	LP	Marble Arch	MAL1123	1969	**£10**	**£4**	
Bells Of Hell	7"	Decca	F11147	1959	**£4**	**£1.50**	
Cosmopolitan Man	LP	Folklore	FLEUT4	1962	**£40**	**£20**	
Down By The Liffeyside	LP	Topic	12T35	1960	**£30**	**£15**	
Easter Week And After	LP	Topic	12T44	1961	**£30**	**£15**	
Finnegan's Wake	7" EP	Collector	JEI4	1960	**£15**	**£7.50**	
Ireland Sings	LP	Pye	NPL18134	1965	**£25**	**£10**	
Irish Rover	LP	Folklore	FLEUT2	1961	**£40**	**£20**	
Liverpool Lou	7"	Piccadilly	7N35172	1964	**£4**	**£1.50**	
Lots Of Fun At Finnegan's Wake	7" EP	Collector	JEI1	1959	**£15**	**£7.50**	

McCafferty ... 7" EP .. Collector ... JEI2 ... 1959 £15 ... £7.50
Patriot Game ... 7" ... Topic ... STOP115 ... 1964 £4 ... £1.50
Rifles Of The IRA ... 7" ... Major Minor ... MM575 ... 1968 £4 ... £1.50
Songs Of The Streets ... 7" EP .. Collector ... JEI3 ... 1959 £15 ... £7.50

BEIDERBECKE, BIX
Bix Beiderbecke ... 7" EP .. Columbia ... SEG7577 ... 1956 £5 ... £2
Bix Beiderbecke And His Orchestra ... 7" EP .. Columbia ... SEG7523 ... 1955 £5 ... £2
Bix Beiderbecke And The Wolverines ... 10" LP London ... AL3532 ... 1954 £25 ... £10
Great Bix ... 10" LP Columbia ... 33S1035 ... 1954 £15 ... £6

BEIRACH, RICHARD
Eon ... LP ... ECM ... ECM1054ST ... 1975 £15 ... £6

BEL CANTOS
Feel Alright ... 7" ... R&B ... MRB5003 ... 1965 £8 ... £4

BELAFONTE, HARRY
Banana Boat Song ... 7" ... HMV ... POP308 ... 1957 £5 ... £2
Calypso ... 7" EP .. HMV ... 7EG8211 ... 1957 £5 ... £2
Close Your Eyes ... 7" ... Capitol ... CL14312 ... 1955 £4 ... £1.50
Close Your Eyes ... 7" EP .. Capitol ... EAP1619 ... 1956 £5 ... £2
Hold 'Em Joe ... 7" ... HMV ... 7M202 ... 1954 £4 ... £1.50
I'm Just A Country Boy ... 7" ... HMV ... 7M224 ... 1954 £4 ... £1.50
Mathilda Mathilda ... 7" EP .. HMV ... 7EG8259 ... 1957 £5 ... £2
Midnight Special ... LP ... RCA ... LPM/LSP2499 ... 1962 £15 ... £6 ... US
Scarlet Ribbons ... 7" ... HMV ... POP360 ... 1957 £4 ... £1.50
Versatile Mr Belafonte ... 10" LP HMV ... DLP1147 ... 1957 £10 ... £4

BELFAST GYPSIES
Belfast Gypsies ... LP ... Grand Prix ... GP9923 ... 1967 £50 ... £25 ... *Swedish*
Gloria's Dream ... 7" ... Island ... WI3007 ... 1966 £15 ... £7.50
Gloria's Dream ... 7" EP .. Vogue ... INT18079 ... 1966 £60 ... £30 ... *French*
Them Belfast Gypsies ... LP ... Sonet ... SNTF738 ... 1977 £20 ... £8

BELIN, ED TEX
Ed Tex Belin ... 7" EP .. Starlite ... STEP39 ... 1963 £8 ... £4
Ed Tex Belin ... 7" EP .. Starlite ... GRK509 ... 1966 £5 ... £2

BELL, ALEXANDER
Alexander Bell Believes ... 7" ... CBS ... 2977 ... 1967 £4 ... £1.50

BELL, ARCHIE & THE DRELLS
Tighten Up ... 7" ... Atlantic ... 584185 ... 1968 £4 ... £1.50
Tighten Up ... LP ... Atlantic ... ... 1968 £25 ... £10

BELL, BELINDA
Stone Valley ... LP ... Columbia ... SCXA9255 ... 1973 £15 ... £6

BELL, BENNY & THE BLOCKBUSTERS
Sack Dress ... 7" ... Parlophone ... R4372 ... 1957 £4 ... £1.50

BELL, CAREY
Carey Bell ... LP ... Delmark ... DS622 ... 1971 £12 ... £5

BELL, CHARLES & CONTEMPORARY JAZZ QUARTET
Another Dimension ... LP ... London ... HAK/SHK8095 ... 1963 £15 ... £6

BELL, DEREK
Carolan's Favourite ... LP ... Claddagh ... CC28 ... 1979 £10 ... £4
Carolan's Receipt ... LP ... Claddagh ... CC18 ... 1975 £12 ... £5

BELL, ERIC
Lonely Man ... 7" ... Hobo ... HOS016 ... 1981 £20 ... £10

BELL, FREDDY & THE BELL BOYS
Bells Are Swinging ... LP ... 20th Century ... (S)4146 ... 1964 £15 ... £6 ... US
Big Bad Wolf ... 78 ... Mercury ... MT149 ... 1957 £6 ... £2.50
Giddy-Up-A-Ding-Dong ... 78 ... Mercury ... MT122 ... 1956 £6 ... £2.50
Hucklebuck ... 78 ... Mercury ... MT141 ... 1957 £6 ... £2.50
Rock And Roll – All Flavors ... LP ... Mercury ... MG20289 ... 1958 £50 ... £25 ... US
Rock With The Bell Boys ... 7" EP .. Mercury ... MEP9508 ... 1956 £20 ... £10
Rock With The Bell Boys Vol. 2 ... 7" EP .. Mercury ... MEP9512 ... 1957 £30 ... £15
Rockin' Is My Business ... 78 ... Mercury ... MT159 ... 1957 £6 ... £2.50
Teach You To Rock ... 78 ... Mercury ... MT146 ... 1957 £6 ... £2.50

BELL, FREDERICK
Rocksteady Cool ... 7" ... Nu Beat ... NB004 ... 1968 £5 ... £2

BELL, GRAHAM
Graham Bell ... LP ... Charisma ... CAS1061 ... 1972 £10 ... £4
How Can You Say I Don't Love You ... 7" ... Polydor ... 56067 ... 1966 £4 ... £1.50

BELL, MADELINE
Because You Didn't Care ... 7" ... HMV ... POP1215 ... 1963 £4 ... £1.50
Bells A-Poppin' ... LP ... Philips ... (S)BL7818 ... 1967 £12 ... £5
Daytime ... 7" ... Columbia ... DB7512 ... 1965 £4 ... £1.50
Doin' Things ... LP ... Philips ... SBL7865 ... 1969 £10 ... £4

Don't Come Running To Me	7"	Philips	BF1501	1966	£5	£2	
I'm Gonna Make You Love Me	7"	Philips	BF1656	1968	£4	£1.50	
One Step At A Time	7"	Philips	BF1526	1966	£4	£1.50	
Picture Me Gone	7"	Philips	BF1611	1967	£8	£4	
What The World Needs Now	7"	Philips	BF1448	1965	£8	£4	
You Don't Love Me No More	7"	Columbia	DB7257	1964	£5	£2	

BELL, PADDIE

I Know Where I'm Going	LP	Waverley	(S)ZLP2104	1968	£15	£6	

BELL, WILLIAM

Bound To Happen	LP	Stax	2362002	1971	£10	£4	
Bound To Happen	LP	Stax	SXATS1016	1970	£12	£5	
Happy	7"	Stax	STAX128	1969	£5	£2	
Phases Of Reality	LP	Stax	2362027	1972	£10	£4	
Tribute To A King	LP	Atco	[illegible]	[illegible]	[illegible]	£4	
Wow	LP	Stax	2362009	1971	£10	£4	

BELL & ARC

Bell And Arc	LP	Charisma	CAS1053	1971	£10	£4	

BELL BROTHERS

Tell Him No	7"	Action	ACT4510	1968	£5	£2	

BELL-TONES

Selina	7"	Columbia	DB4848	1962	£5	£2	

BELLA & ME

Whatever Happened To The Seven Day Week	7"	Columbia	DB8243	1967	£5	£2	

BELLAMY, GEORGE

Maman	7"	Chapter One	CH167	1972	£5	£2	
Where I'm Bound	7"	Parlophone	R5282	1965	£12	£6	

BELLAMY, PETER

Barrack Room Ballads	LP	Free Reed	FRR014	1977	£12	£5	
Both Sides Then	LP	Topic	12TS400	1979	£10	£4	
Fair England's Shore	LP	XTRA	XTRA1075	1969	£25	£10	
Fox Jumps Over The Parson's Gate	LP	Topic	12T200	1970	£25	£10	
Keep On Kipling	LP	Fellside	FE032	1982	£12	£5	
Mainly Norfolk	LP	XTRA	XTRA1060	1968	£20	£8	
Merlin's Isle Of Gramarye	LP	Argo	ZFB81	1972	£25	£10	
Oak, Ash And Thorn	LP	Argo	ZFB11	1970	£20	£8	
Peter Bellamy	LP	Green Linnet	SIF1001	1975	£12	£5	*US*
Rudyard Kipling Made Exceedingly Good Songs	LP	Dambuster	DAM019	1989	£10	£4	
Second Wind	LP	EFDSS	ES002	1985	£10	£4	
Tell It Like It Was	LP	Trailer	LER2089	1975	£12	£5	
Transports	LP	Free Reed	FRR021/2	1977	£20	£8	*double*
Won't You Go My Way	LP	Argo	ZFB37	1970	£20	£8	*with Louis Killen*

BELLE & SEBASTIAN

Tigermilk	LP	Elektric Honey	EHRLP5	1996	£100	£50	

BELLETTO, AL

Half And Half	LP	Capitol	T751	1957	£15	£6	

BELLINE, DENNY & THE RICH KIDS

Denny Belline And The Rich Kids	LP	RCA	LPM/LSP3655	1966	£30	£15	*US*

BELLSON, LOUIS

At The Flamingo	LP	Columbia	33CX10142	1959	£15	£6	
Brilliant Bellson Sound	LP	HMV	CLP1343	1960	£15	£6	
Louis Bellson	10" LP	Columbia	33C9017	1956	£40	£20	
Louis Bellson	LP	Columbia	33CX10083	1957	£15	£6	
Louis In London	LP	Pye	NSPL18349	1970	£12	£5	

BELLUS, TONY

Robbing The Cradle	7"	London	HL8933	1959	£25	£12.50	
Robbing The Cradle	LP	NRC	LPA8	1960	£50	£25	*US*

BELMONTS

Carnival Of Hits	LP	Sabina	SALP5001	1962	£75	£37.50	*US*
Cigars, Acappella, Candy	LP	Buddah	BDS5123	1972	£12	£5	*US*
Come On Little Angel	7"	Stateside	SS128	1962	£6	£2.50	
Summer Love	LP	Dot	DLP25949	1969	£12	£5	*US*
Tell Me Why	7"	Pye	7N25094	1961	£15	£7.50	

BELOVED

Deliver Me	CD-s	East West	EW043CD	1996	£10	£5	
Hello	CD-s	WEA	YZ426CD	1990	£6	£2.50	
It's Alright Now	CD-s	East West	YZ541CD	1990	£10	£5	
Loving Feeling	12"	WEA	YZ311T	1988	£6	£2.50	
Loving Feeling	CD-s	WEA	YZ311CD	1989	£20	£10	*3" single*
Sun Rising	12"	WEA	YZ414TX	1989	£12	£6	
Sun Rising	12"	WEA	YZ414TP	1989	£8	£4	*picture disc*

Sun Rising	CD-s	WEA	YZ414CD	1989	**£10**	**£5**	*3" single*
Time After Time	CD-s	East West	YZ482CD	1990	**£5**	**£2**	
Where It Is	CD	Orange	HARPCD2	1990	**£25**	**£10**	
Your Love Takes Me Higher	12"	WEA	YZ357TX	1989	**£10**	**£5**	*with transfer*
Your Love Takes Me Higher	CD-s	WEA	YZ357CD	1989	**£20**	**£10**	*3" single*
Your Love Takes Me Higher	CD-s	WEA	YZ463CD	1990	**£5**	**£2**	

BELT & BRACES ROADSHOW BAND

Belt And Braces Roadshow Band	LP	private		1975	**£12**	**£5**	

BELTONES

Home Without You	7"	Duke	DU17	1969	**£4**	**£1.50**	
Mary Mary	7"	High Note	HS017	1969	**£4**	**£1.50**	
No More Heartaches	7"	Trojan	TR628	1968	**£5**	**£2**	
No More Heartaches	7"	Blue Cat	BS142	1968	**£6**	**£2.50**	

BELVIN, JESSE

Best Of Jesse Belvin	LP	Camden	CAS960	1966	**£15**	**£6**	*US*
But Not Forgotten	LP	United	7220	1968	**£15**	**£6**	*US*
Casual	LP	Crown	CLP5145	1960	**£20**	**£8**	*US*
Funny	7"	RCA	RCA1119	1959	**£8**	**£4**	
Just Jesse Belvin	LP	RCA	LPM/LSP2089	1959	**£40**	**£20**	*US*
Mr Easy	LP	RCA	LPM/LSP2105	1960	**£30**	**£15**	*US*
Unforgettable	LP	Crown	CLP5187	1960	**£20**	**£8**	*US*

BEN

Ben	LP	Vertigo	6360052	1971	**£150**	**£75**	*spiral label*

BENATAR, PAT

Don't Walk Away	CD-s	Chrysalis	PATCD6	1988	**£5**	**£2**	
If You Think You Know How To Love Me	7"	Chrysalis	CHS2373	1979	**£4**	**£1.50**	
In The Heat Of The Night	LP	Mobile Fidelity	MFSL1057	1981	**£12**	**£5**	*US audiophile*
One Love	CD-s	Chrysalis	PATCD7	1988	**£5**	**£2**	
True Love	CD-s	Chrysalis	PATCD8	1991	**£5**	**£2**	

BENBOW, STEVE

Captain Kidd	7" EP	Collector	JEB2	1960	**£5**	**£2**	
I Travel The World	LP	HMV	CLP1687	1963	**£15**	**£6**	
Of Situations And Predicaments	LP	Decca	LK4881	1967	**£12**	**£5**	
Steve Benbow Sings	LP	HMV	CLP1603	1962	**£15**	**£6**	
Whaling In Greenland	7" EP	Collector	JEB1	1959	**£5**	**£2**	

BENNETT, BOBBY

You're Ready Now	7"	Columbia	DB8532	1969	**£15**	**£7.50**	

BENNETT, BOBBY (2)

Big New York	7"	London	HLZ10274	1969	**£5**	**£2**	

BENNETT, BOYD & HIS ROCKETS

Banjo Rock And Roll	7"	Parlophone	MSP6203	1956	**£200**	**£100**	
Blue Suede Shoes	7"	Parlophone	MSP6233	1956	**£175**	**£87.50**	
Boogie At Midnight	7"	Parlophone	MSP6161	1955	**£200**	**£100**	*best auctioned*
Boyd Bennett	LP	King	594	1957	**£600**	**£400**	*US*
Hi That Jive Jack	7"	Parlophone	R4214	1956	**£175**	**£87.50**	*with Big Moe*
Move	7"	Parlophone	R4423	1958	**£100**	**£50**	
Rocking Up A Storm	7"	Parlophone	R4252	1957	**£175**	**£87.50**	*with Big Moe*
Seventeen	7"	Parlophone	MSP6180	1955	**£175**	**£87.50**	
Tight Tights	7"	Mercury	AMT1031	1959	**£50**	**£25**	

BENNETT, BRIAN

Brian Bennett replaced the original drummer with the Shadows, Tony Meehan, in 1962, and has played with the group ever since. He has also done a considerable amount of production and session work, of which the collectable records issued under his own name and listed below are but a small fraction.

Canvas	7"	Columbia	DB8294	1967	**£10**	**£5**	
Change Of Direction	LP	Columbia	SX/SCX6144	1968	**£20**	**£8**	
Chase Side Shoot Up	7"	Fontana	6007040	1974	**£5**	**£2**	
Illustrated London Noise	LP	Studio Two	TWO268	1969	**£40**	**£20**	
Saturday Night Special	7"	DJM	DJS10756	1977	**£5**	**£2**	*promo, picture sleeve*
Thunderbolt	7"	DJM	DJS10714	1976	**£5**	**£2**	*promo, picture sleeve*

BENNETT, CLIFF

Branches Out	LP	Parlophone	PMC/PCS7054	1968	**£40**	**£20**	
Cliff Bennett's Rebellion	LP	CBS	64487	1971	**£10**	**£4**	
I'll Take Good Care Of You	7" EP	Odeon	MEO149	1967	**£25**	**£12.50**	*French*
One More Heartache	7"	Parlophone	R5728	1968	**£4**	**£1.50**	

BENNETT, CLIFF & REBEL ROUSERS

Cliff Bennett	LP	Regal	REG1039	1966	**£15**	**£6**	*export*
Cliff Bennett & The Rebel Rousers	7" EP	Parlophone	GEP8923	1964	**£25**	**£12.50**	
Cliff Bennett & The Rebel Rousers	LP	Parlophone	PMC1242	1964	**£40**	**£20**	
Drivin' You Wild	LP	MFP	MFP1121	1966	**£10**	**£4**	
Everybody Loves A Lover	7"	Parlophone	R5046	1963	**£20**	**£10**	
Got My Mojo Working	7"	Parlophone	R5119	1964	**£4**	**£1.50**	
Got To Get You Into Our Lives	LP	Parlophone	PMC/PCS7017	1967	**£30**	**£15**	

I'll Take Good Care Of You	7"	Parlophone	R5565	1967	£4	£1.50	
Poor Joe	7"	Parlophone	DP560	1963	£60	£30	*export*
Poor Joe	7"	Parlophone	R4895	1962	£15	£7.50	
Try It Baby	7" EP	Parlophone	GEP8936	1965	£25	£12.50	
We're Gonna Make It	7" EP	Parlophone	GEP8955	1966	£50	£20	
When I Get Paid	7"	Parlophone	DP561	1964	£60	£30	*export*
When I Get Paid	7"	Parlophone	R4836	1961	£15	£7.50	
You Got What I Like	7"	Parlophone	R4793	1961	£15	£7.50	
You Really Got A Hold On Me	7"	Parlophone	R5080	1963	£4	£1.50	

BENNETT, DICKIE

Dungaree Doll	7"	Decca	F10697	1956	£5	£2	

BENNETT, DUSTER

Using his nickname to avoid an obvious confusion, Tony Bennett was a one-man band who played the blues, and played it rather well. Although a few supporting musicians are used in places on his records, what one hears is essentially Duster Bennett's voice and harmonica, his guitar, and his bass drum. If the format sounds limited, then Bennett proves that it need not be. He was an unlikely addition to John Mayall's band in the early seventies, but this facet of his career was never recorded.

12 dBs	LP	Blue Horizon	763868	1970	£25	£10	
Act Nice And Gentle	7"	Blue Horizon	573179	1970	£5	£2	
Bright Lights	LP	Blue Horizon	763221	1969	£40	£20	
Bright Lights, Big City	7"	Blue Horizon	573154	1969	£6	£2.50	
Comin' Home	7"	RAK	RAK177	1974	£8	£4	
Fingertips	LP	Mushroom	L35436	1974	£20	£8	*Australian*
I Chose To Sing The Blues	7"	Blue Horizon	573173	1970	£5	£2	
I'm Gonna Wind Up Endin' Up	7"	Blue Horizon	573164	1969	£10	£5	
It's A Man Down There	7"	Blue Horizon	573141	1967	£6	£2.50	
Raining In My Heart	7"	Blue Horizon	573148	1967	£8	£4	
Smiling Like I'm Happy	LP	Blue Horizon	763208	1968	£30	£15	

BENNETT, JO JO

Groovy Jo Jo	LP	Trojan	TBL133	1970	£15	£6	
Leaving Rome	7"	Trojan	TR7774	1970	£4	£1.50	
Lecture	7"	Doctor Bird	DB1097	1967	£10	£5	
Rocksteady	7"	Doctor Bird	DB1117	1967	£10	£5	

BENNETT, JOE & THE SPARKLETONES

Black Slacks	7"	HMV	POP399	1957	£75	£37.50	
Rocket	7"	HMV	POP445	1958	£100	£50	

BENNETT, RAY

Introducing Ray Bennett	7" EP	Decca	DFE8516	1962	£8	£4	

BENNETT, TONY

Cloud Seven	10" LP	Philips	BBR8051	1955	£12	£5	
Congratulations To Someone	7"	Columbia	SCM5048	1953	£6	£2.50	
Stranger In Paradise	7" EP	Philips	BBE12009	1955	£6	£2.50	
Voice Of Your Choice	10" LP	Philips	BBR8089	1956	£12	£5	
Whatever Lola Wants	7"	Philips	JK1008	1957	£5	£2	

BENNETT, VAL

All In The Game	7"	Trojan	TR625	1968	£6	£2.50	*George Penny B side*
Any More	7"	Fab	FAB131	1970	£4	£1.50	
Baby Baby	7"	Trojan	TR640	1968	£6	£2.50	
Jumping With Mr Lee	7"	Island	WI3113	1967	£12	£6	*Roy Shirley B side*
Midnight Spin	7"	Camel	CA24	1969	£4	£1.50	*Soul Cats B side*
My Girl	7"	Trojan	TR649	1969	£4	£1.50	*Clancy Eccles B side*
Reggae City	7"	Crab	CRAB6	1969	£4	£1.50	*Cannon King B side*
Russians Are Coming	7"	Island	WI3146	1968	£12	£6	*Lester Stirling B side*
Soul Survivor	7"	Island	WI3116	1967	£12	£6	*Lloyd Clarke B side*
South Parkway Rock	7"	Trojan	TR626	1968	£6	£2.50	*Derrick Morgan B side*
Spanish Harlem	7"	Trojan	TR611	1968	£6	£2.50	*Roy Shirley B side*

BENNINGS, JOHN & HIS RHYTHM & BLUES BAND

Timber	78	Esquire	10376	1954	£15	£7.50	

BENSON, BARRY

Stay A Little While	7"	Parlophone	R5446	1966	£8	£4	
Sunshine Child	7"	Parlophone	R5484	1966	£4	£1.50	

BENSUSAN, PIERRE

Solilai	LP	Rounder	3068	1982	£25	£10	*US*

BENT WIND

Sussex	LP	Trend		1972	£1000	£700	*Canadian*

BENTINE, MICHAEL

It's A Square World	LP	Parlophone	PMC1179/PCS3031	1962	£15	£6	
Square Bashing	LP	RCA	RD785	1967	£10	£4	

BENTLEY, BRIAN & THE BACHELORS

Caramba	7"	Salvo	SLO1813	1962	£8	£4	

BENTLEY, JAY & THE JET SET

Watusi 64	7" EP	Vogue	18006	1964	**£20**	**£10**	*French*

BENTLEY, RAY

Ray Bentley	7" EP	Disc-A-Fran	AVE44	1967	**£5**	**£2**	

BENTON, BROOK

At His Best	7" EP	Fontana	TFE17151	1958	**£6**	**£2.50**	
Boll Weevil Song	LP	Mercury	MMC14090/ CMS18060	1961	**£12**	**£5**	
Born To Sing The Blues	LP	Mercury	20024MCL	1962	**£10**	**£4**	
Brook Benton	7" EP	RCA	RCX169	1958	**£15**	**£7.50**	
Brook Benton & Jesse Belvin	LP	Crown	CST350	1963	**£15**	**£6**	*US*
Caressing Voice Of Brook Benton	7" EP	Mercury	ZEP10023	1959	**£5**	**£2**	
Endlessly	LP	Mercury	MMC14022	1959	**£15**	**£6**	
Golden Hits	LP	Mercury	MMC14124	1962	**£10**	**£4**	
I Love You In So Many Ways	LP	Mercury	MMC14042	1960	**£12**	**£5**	
It's Just A Matter Of Time	LP	Mercury	20040MCL	1963	**£10**	**£4**	
It's Just A Matter Of Time	LP	Mercury	MMC14015	1958	**£15**	**£6**	
Make A Date With Brook Benton	7" EP	Mercury	ZEP10046	1959	**£5**	**£2**	
So Warm	7" EP	Mercury	SEZ19024	1962	**£5**	**£2**	*stereo*
Songs I Love To Sing	LP	Mercury	MMC14060/ CMS18041	1960	**£12**	**£5**	
There Goes That Song Again	LP	Mercury	MMC14108/ CMS18068	1961	**£12**	**£5**	
This Bitter Earth	LP	Mercury	20053MCL	1963	**£10**	**£4**	
When I Fall In Love	7" EP	Mercury	SEZ19009	1961	**£5**	**£2**	*stereo*
When You're In Love	7" EP	Mercury	SEZ19019	1961	**£5**	**£2**	*stereo*

BENTON, BROOK & DINAH WASHINGTON

Baby	7"	Mercury	AMT1083	1960	**£5**	**£2**	
Rockin' Good Way	7"	Mercury	AMT1099	1960	**£12**	**£6**	
Rockin' Good Way	7" EP	Mercury	SEZ19022	1961	**£25**	**£12.50**	*stereo*
Rockin' Good Way	7" EP	Mercury	ZEP10120	1961	**£20**	**£10**	

BENTON, OSCAR BLUES BAND

Benton '71	LP	Decca	641900	1971	**£10**	**£4**	*Dutch*
Blues Is Gonna Wreck My Life	LP	Decca	XBY846521	1969	**£12**	**£5**	*Dutch*
Feel So Good	LP	Decca	XBY846510	1969	**£12**	**£5**	*Dutch*

BENTON, WALTER

Out Of This World	LP	Jazzland	JLP28	1960	**£20**	**£8**	*with Freddie Hubbard*

BERBERIAN, JOHN

Impressions East	LP	Mainstream	S6123	1969	**£60**	**£30**	*US*
Middle Eastern Rock	LP	Verve	FTS3073	1969	**£40**	**£20**	*US*

BERETS

Mass For Peace	LP	Avant Garde	AVS116	1970	**£15**	**£6**	

BERGER, GABY

Die Grossen Erfolge	LP	Ariola	80886AT	1970	**£15**	**£6**	*German*

BERGIN, MARY

Feadoga Stain	LP	Gael-Linn	CEF071	1979	**£10**	**£4**	

BERIGAN, BUNNY

Plays Again	10" LP	HMV	DLP1018	1953	**£20**	**£8**	
Take It, Bunny	LP	Philips	BBL7086	1956	**£20**	**£8**	

BERKERS, JERRY

Unterwegs	LP	Pilz	20291316	1972	**£20**	**£8**	*German*

BERLE, MILTON

In The Middle Of The House	7"	Vogue Coral	Q72197	1956	**£6**	**£2.50**	

BERMUDAS

Donnie	7"	London	HLN9894	1964	**£6**	**£2.50**	

BERNARD, KENNY

Ain't No Sole Left In These Old Shoes	7"	Pye	7N17233	1967	**£12**	**£6**	
I Do	7"	Pye	7N17284	1967	**£4**	**£1.50**	
Nothing Can Change That Love	7"	Pye	7N17131	1966	**£15**	**£7.50**	
Somebody	7"	CBS	2936	1967	**£30**	**£15**	
Tracker	7"	Pye	7N15920	1965	**£6**	**£2.50**	
Victim Of Perfume And Lace	7"	CBS	3860	1968	**£5**	**£2**	

BERNARD, ROD

One More Chance	7"	Mercury	AMT1070	1959	**£5**	**£2**	
Rod Bernard	LP	Jin	LP4007	1966	**£40**	**£20**	*US*
This Should Go On Forever	7"	London	HLM8849	1959	**£20**	**£10**	

BERNHARDT, CLYDE

Sittin' On Top Of The World	LP	Wam	780061	1975	**£25**	**£10**	*German*

BERNIE & THE BUZZ BAND

House That Jack Built	7"	Decca	F22829	1968	£8	£4	B side by Pete Kelly's Soulution

BERNSTEIN, ELMER

Baby, The Rain Must Fall	LP	Fontana	TL5306	1967	£25	£10	
Carpetbaggers	LP	MGM	C984	1964	£10	£4	
Carpetbaggers	LP	London	HAA/SHA8219	1964	£10	£4	
Cast A Giant Shadow	LP	United Artists	(S)ULP1140	1966	£10	£4	
Clark Street	7"	Brunswick	05544	1956	£6	£2.50	gold label
Desire Under The Elms	LP	London	HAD2111	1958	£10	£4	
God's Little Acre	LP	London	HAT2125	1958	£10	£4	
Great Escape	LP	United Artists	ULP1041	1963	£10	£4	
Men In War	LP	London	HAP2076	1957	£50	£25	
Rat Race	7"	MGM	MGM1238	1963	£5	£2	
Silencers	LP	RCA	RD7792	1967	£25	£10	
Staccato	7" EP	Capitol	EAP11287	1960	£5	£2	
Ten Commandments	LP	London	HAD2074/5	1958	£25	£10	double
True Grit	LP	Capitol	EST263	1969	£10	£4	
Walk On The Wild Side	LP	MGM	C891	1962	£10	£4	
Where's Jack?	LP	Paramount	SPFL254	1969	£10	£4	

BERNSTEIN, LEONARD

What Is Jazz?	LP	Philips	BBL7149	1957	£15	£6	

BERRY, CHU

Stompy Stevedores	LP	Philips	BBL7054	1955	£25	£10	

BERRY, CHUCK

Although Elvis Presley defined the rock'n'roll image, it was Chuck Berry who invented the actual music – a fact recognized both by the enormous number of cover versions of his best-known songs and by the inclusion of 'Johnny B. Goode' among the cultural artefacts on board the Voyagers I and II spacecraft.

After School Session	LP	Chess	LP1426	1958	£60	£30	US
Beautiful Delilah	7"	London	HL8677	1958	£25	£12.50	
Berry Is On Top	LP	Chess	LP1435	1959	£50	£25	US
Best Of Chuck Berry	7" EP	Pye	NEP44018	1964	£8	£4	
Blue Mood	7" EP	Pye	NEP44033	1964	£8	£4	
Bye Bye Johnny	7"	London	HLM9159	1960	£10	£5	
Carol	7"	London	HL7055	1958	£25	£12.50	export
Carol	7"	London	HL8712	1958	£25	£12.50	
Chuck Berry	7" EP	Pye	NEP44011	1963	£8	£4	
Chuck Berry	LP	Pye	NPL28024	1963	£12	£5	
Chuck Berry Hits	7" EP	Pye	NEP44028	1964	£8	£4	
Chuck In London	LP	Chess	CRL4005	1965	£10	£4	
Come On	7" EP	Chess	CRE6005	1965	£15	£7.50	
Concerto In B. Goode	LP	Mercury	20162SMCL	1969	£10	£4	
Dear Dad	7"	Chess	CRS8012	1965	£4	£1.50	
Fresh Berrys	LP	Chess	CRL4506	1965	£10	£4	
Go Go Go	7"	Pye	7N25209	1963	£4	£1.50	
Golden Decade	LP	Chess	6641018	1972	£12	£5	double
I Got A Booking	7" EP	Chess	CRE6012	1966	£15	£7.50	
I'm Talking About You	7"	Pye	7N25100	1961	£8	£4	
In Memphis	LP	Mercury	(S)MCL20110	1967	£10	£4	
It Wasn't Me	7"	Chess	CRS8022	1965	£4	£1.50	
Johnny B. Goode	7"	London	HLM8629	1958	£15	£7.50	
Johnny B. Goode	7"	Chess	CRS8075	1968	£4	£1.50	
Juke Box Hits	LP	Pye	NPL28019	1962	£20	£8	
Latest And The Greatest	LP	Pye	NPL28031	1964	£12	£5	
Let It Rock	7"	London	HLM9069	1960	£10	£5	
Little Marie	7"	Pye	7N25271	1964	£4	£1.50	
Little Queenie	7"	London	HLM8853	1959	£15	£7.50	
Live At Fillmore Auditorium	LP	Mercury	20112MCL	1967	£10	£4	with the Steve Miller Band
Lonely School Days	7"	Chess	CRS8006	1965	£4	£1.50	
Memphis Tennessee	7"	London	HLM8921	1959	£20	£10	
Memphis Tennessee	7"	Pye	7N25218	1963	£4	£1.50	
More Chuck Berry	LP	Pye	NPL28028	1963	£10	£4	
Nadine	7"	Pye	7N25236	1964	£4	£1.50	
No Money Down	7"	London	HLU8275	1956	£200	£100	silver label, tri-centre
No Money Down	7"	London	HLU8275	1956	£500	£330	gold label, best auctioned
No Particular Place To Go	7"	Chess	CRS8089	1969	£4	£1.50	
No Particular Place To Go	7"	Pye	7N25242	1964	£4	£1.50	
On Stage	LP	Pye	NPL28027	1963	£10	£4	
One Dozen Berrys	LP	London	HAM2132	1958	£60	£30	
Promised Land	7"	Pye	7N25285	1965	£4	£1.50	
Promised Land	7" EP	Chess	CRE6002	1965	£15	£7.50	
Ramona Say Yes	7"	Chess	CRS8037	1966	£4	£1.50	
Reeling And Rocking	7" EP	London	REM1188	1960	£125	£62.50	tri-centre
Rhythm And Blues With Chuck Berry	7" EP	London	REU1053	1956	£125	£62.50	gold label
Rock & Roll Music	7"	London	HLM8531	1957	£40	£20	
Rockin' At The Hops	LP	Chess	LP1448	1960	£50	£25	US
Roll Over Beethoven	7"	London	HLU8428	1957	£75	£37.50	
Run Rudolph Run	7"	Pye	7N25228	1963	£4	£1.50	
Schooldays	7"	Columbia	DB3951	1957	£75	£37.50	

Title	Format	Label	Number	Year	Mint	Good	Notes
Sweet Little Rock and Roller	7"	London	HLM8767	1958	**£15**	**£7.50**	
Sweet Little Sixteen	7"	London	HLM8585	1958	**£20**	**£10**	
This Is Chuck Berry	7" EP	Pye	NEP44013	1963	**£8**	**£4**	
You Came A Long Way From Saint Louis	7" EP	Chess	CRE6016	1966	**£15**	**£7.50**	
You Can't Catch Me	7"	London	HLN8375	1957	**£150**	**£75**	*gold label*
You Never Can Tell	7"	Pye	7N25257	1964	**£4**	**£1.50**	
You Never Can Tell	LP	Pye	NPL28039	1964	**£12**	**£5**	

BERRY, CHUCK & BO DIDDLEY

Title	Format	Label	Number	Year	Mint	Good	Notes
Chuck And Bo Vol. 1	7" EP	Pye	NEP44009	1963	**£10**	**£5**	
Chuck And Bo Vol. 2	7" EP	Pye	NEP44012	1963	**£10**	**£5**	
Chuck And Bo Vol. 3	7" EP	Pye	NEP44017	1964	**£10**	**£5**	
Two Great Guitars	LP	Pye	NPL28047	1964	**£15**	**£6**	

BERRY, DAVE

Title	Format	Label	Number	Year	Mint	Good	Notes
Baby It's You	7"	Decca	F11876	1964	**£4**	**£1.50**	
Can I Get It From You	7" EP	Decca	DFE8625	1965	**£15**	**£7.50**	
Dave Berry	7" EP	Decca	DFE8601	1964	**£15**	**£7.50**	
Dave Berry	LP	Decca	LK4653	1964	**£30**	**£15**	
Dave Berry '68	LP	Decca	LK/SKL4932	1968	**£20**	**£8**	
Dozen Berrys	LP	Ace Of Clubs	ACL/SCL1218	1966	**£12**	**£5**	
Little Things	7" EP	Decca	457071	1965	**£15**	**£7.50**	*French*
Mama	7" EP	Decca	457124	1966	**£15**	**£7.50**	*French*
Memphis Tennessee	7"	Decca	F11734	1963	**£5**	**£2**	
My Baby Left Me	7"	Decca	F11803	1963	**£4**	**£1.50**	
Special Sound Of Dave Berry	LP	Decca	LK4823	1966	**£20**	**£8**	

BERRY, EMMETT

Title	Format	Label	Number	Year	Mint	Good	Notes
Beauty And The Blues	LP	Columbia	33SX1246	1960	**£12**	**£5**	*side 2 by Buddy Tate*
Emmett Berry Orchestra	10" LP	Columbia	33S1107	1957	**£10**	**£4**	

BERRY, HEIDI

Title	Format	Label	Number	Year	Mint	Good	Notes
Below The Waves	CD-s	Creation	CRE047CD	1989	**£5**	**£2**	

BERRY, MIKE

Title	Format	Label	Number	Year	Mint	Good	Notes
Don't Try To Stand In My Way	7"	HMV	POP1362	1964	**£4**	**£1.50**	
Don't You Think It's Time	7"	HMV	POP1105	1962	**£4**	**£1.50**	
Every Little Kiss	7"	HMV	POP1042	1962	**£15**	**£7.50**	
It Comes And Goes	7"	HMV	POP1494	1965	**£4**	**£1.50**	
It Really Doesn't Matter	7"	HMV	POP1194	1963	**£6**	**£2.50**	
It's Just A Matter Of Time	7"	HMV	POP979	1962	**£6**	**£2.50**	
It's Time For Mike Berry	7" EP	HMV	7EG8793	1963	**£25**	**£12.50**	
Lovesick	7"	HMV	POP1284	1964	**£6**	**£2.50**	
My Little Baby	7"	HMV	POP1142	1963	**£8**	**£4**	
Raining In My Heart	7"	Polydor	56182	1967	**£4**	**£1.50**	
Talk	7"	HMV	POP1314	1964	**£6**	**£2.50**	
That's All I Ever Wanted From You	7"	HMV	POP1449	1965	**£4**	**£1.50**	
This Little Girl	7"	HMV	POP1257	1964	**£6**	**£2.50**	
Tribute To Buddy Holly	7"	HMV	POP912	1961	**£8**	**£4**	
Tribute To Buddy Holly	7" EP	HMV	7EG8808	1963	**£30**	**£15**	
Warm Baby	7"	HMV	POP1530	1966	**£4**	**£1.50**	
Will You Love Me Tomorrow	7"	Decca	F11314	1961	**£15**	**£7.50**	

BERRY, RICHARD

Title	Format	Label	Number	Year	Mint	Good	Notes
Live At The Century Club	LP	Pam	1001		**£40**	**£20**	*US*
Rhythm And Blues Vol. 3	7" EP	Ember	EMBEP4527	1964	**£150**	**£75**	
Richard Berry And The Dreamers	LP	Crown	CLP5371	1963	**£20**	**£8**	*US*
Wild Berry	LP	Pam	1002		**£40**	**£20**	*US*

BERRYMAN, PETE

Title	Format	Label	Number	Year	Mint	Good	Notes
Pete Berryman And Guitar	LP	Autogram	FLLP509	1978	**£12**	**£5**	*German*

BERT, EDDIE

Title	Format	Label	Number	Year	Mint	Good	Notes
Encore	LP	London	LTZC15060	1957	**£20**	**£8**	
Musician Of The Year	LP	London	LTZC15040	1957	**£20**	**£8**	

BESSON, CLAUDE

Title	Format	Label	Number	Year	Mint	Good	Notes
Instrumental	LP	Pendes	13NP609	197–	**£25**	**£10**	*French*
Instrumental Vol. 2	LP	Pendes	13NP637	197–	**£25**	**£10**	*French*
N'Oubliez Pas L'Amour	LP	Pendes	13NP605	197–	**£25**	**£10**	*French*

BEST, JON

Title	Format	Label	Number	Year	Mint	Good	Notes
Young Boy Blues	7"	Decca	F12077	1965	**£6**	**£2.50**	

BEST, PETE

Pete Best was the original drummer with the Beatles, and is still understandably bitter at the way he was sacked to make way for Ringo Starr just as the group was about to make its first record for Parlophone. The American LP was given a deliberately misleading title – these are not Beatles recordings.

Title	Format	Label	Number	Year	Mint	Good	Notes
Anyway	7"	Beatles	800	1964	**£50**	**£25**	*US*
Best Of The Beatles	LP	Savage	BM71	1965	**£75**	**£37.50**	*US*
Boys	7"	Cameo	391	1966	**£25**	**£12.50**	*US*
Casting My Spell	7"	Mr.Maestro	712	1965	**£25**	**£12.50**	*US*
I Can't Do Without You Now	7"	Mr.Maestro	711	1964	**£50**	**£25**	*US*
I'm Gonna Knock On Your Door	7"	Decca	F11929	1964	**£40**	**£20**	

If You Can't Get Her	7"	Happening	405	1964	£50	£25	US
If You Can't Get Her	7"	Happening	117/8	1964	£50	£25	US

BETHEA, H. & THE AGENTS

Got To Find A Sweet Name	LP	Reprise	MS3239	1972	£20	£8	US

BETHNAL

Fiddler	7"	Bethnal	VIOL1	1977	£6	£2.50	

BETTERDAYS

Don't Want That	7"	Polydor	56024	1965	£150	£75	
Down On The Waterfront	7" EP	NTB	1002	1992	£5	£2	
Howl Of The Streets	7" EP	NTB	001	1991	£5	£2	

BETTERS, HAROLD

Do Anything You Wanna	7"	Sue	WI378	1965	£10	£5	

BETWEEN

And The Waters Opened	LP	Vertigo	6360612	1973	£15	£6	German
Contemplation	LP	Wergo	WER1012	1976	£15	£6	German
Dharana	LP	Vertigo	6360619	1974	£15	£6	German
Einstieg	LP	Wergo	WER1001	1971	£20	£8	German
Hesse Between Music	LP	EMI	1C06229546	1974	£15	£6	German

BEVERLEY

Beverley became Beverley Martyn when she married John Martyn. The pair recorded two fine albums together.

Happy New Year	7"	Deram	DM101	1966	£5	£2	
Museum	7"	Deram	DM137	1967	£5	£2	

BEVERLEY SISTERS

Beverley Sisters	7" EP	Decca	DFE6307	1956	£6	£2.50	
Beverley Sisters No. 2	7" EP	Decca	DFE6401	1957	£8	£4	
Beverley Sisters No. 3	7" EP	Decca	DFE6402	1957	£5	£2	
Beverley Sisters No. 4	7" EP	Decca	DFE6512	1958	£6	£2.50	
Bevs For Christmas	7" EP	Decca	DFE6611	1959	£5	£2	
Born To Be With You	7"	Decca	F10770	1956	£4	£1.50	
Bye Bye Love	7"	Decca	F10909	1957	£4	£1.50	
Date With The Bevs	10" LP	Philips	BBR8052	1955	£15	£6	
Enchanting Beverley Sisters	LP	Columbia	33SX1285	1960	£10	£4	
Long Black Nylons	7"	Decca	F10971	1958	£5	£2	
Those Beverley Sisters	LP	Ace Of Clubs	ACL1048	1960	£10	£4	
Three's Company	7" EP	Columbia	SEG7602	1956	£6	£2.50	
Willie Can	7"	Decca	F10705	1956	£5	£2	

BEVERLEY'S ALL STARS

Double Shot	7"	Trojan	TR683	1969	£4	£1.50	
Go Home	7"	Black Swan	WI449	1965	£10	£5	

BEVIS FROND

Nick Salomon knows about record collecting from two different sides. Starting as a dealer, he was able to put his love and knowledge of psychedelic music to good use. As an artist, demonstrating that love by playing the same style himself, he has seen his limited-edition record releases acquiring a cult reputation and hence an increase in value. Woronzow is Salomon's own label, which he uses to issue recordings by several like-minded groups as well as his own efforts, which appear under the name of the Bevis Frond.

Bevis Through The Looking Glass	LP	Woronzow	WOO51/2	1987	£30	£15	*double, booklet*

BIANCHI, MAURICIO

Sympathy For A Genocide	LP	Sterile	SR2	1981	£50	£25	

BIANCO, GENE

Alarm Clock Boogie	7"	Vogue	V9167	1960	£12	£6	

BIBBY

Rub It Down	7"	Blue Beat	BB289	1965	£12	£6	

BIBLE

Crystal Palace	CD-s	Chrysalis	BIBCD2	1988	£5	£2	
Graceland (New Version)	CD-s	Chrysalis	BIBCD4	1989	£5	£2	
Honey Be Good	CD-s	Ensign	BIBCD5	1989	£5	£2	
Honey Be Good	CD-s	Chrysalis	BIBCD3	1988	£5	£2	

BIFF BANG POW!

Creation was that true rarity – a record label with a player-manager. For Alan McGee, when not keeping an eye on the likes of Teenage Fanclub and Ride, played guitar and sang for his own group, Biff Bang Pow!

Fifty Years Of Fun	7"	Creation	CRE003	1984	£5	£2	
Sleep	7"	Caff	CAFF13	1991	£12	£6	*Times B side*
There Must Be A Better Life	7"	Creation	CRE007	1984	£10	£5	

BIG AUDIO DYNAMITE

Ally Pally Paradiso	CD	Columbia	CSK4271	1991	£20	£8	*US promo*
Ally Pally Paradiso	LP	CBS	BIG11	1990	£10	£4	*promo*
Contact	CD-s	CBS	CDBAAD6	1989	£5	£2	
Just Play Music	CD-s	CBS	CDBAAD4	1988	£5	£2	
Looking For A Song	CD	Epic	ZSK6587	1994	£25	£10	*US double promo*

Other 99	CD-s	CBS	CDBAAD5	1988	£5	£2	
Rush	CD-s	CBS	6576402	1991	£5	£2	

BIG BEATS

Live	LP	Liberty	LRP/LST7407	1965	**£15**	**£6**	*US*

BIG BEN ACCORDION BAND

Rock'n'Roll Medley No. 1	7"	Columbia	DB3835	1956	£5	£2	
Rock'n'Roll Medley No. 2	7"	Columbia	DB3856	1957	£5	£2	

BIG BERTHA

This group was formed by the original Move bass player, Ace Kefford, as the Ace Kefford Stand, becoming Big Bertha when Kefford himself left. The drummer for a short while was Cozy Powell. The single would appear to have been withdrawn – or else never given a full release in the first place – as it bears the same catalogue number as a single by Yes.

Munich City	7"	United Artists	UA35142	1969	**£12**	**£6**	*German, picture sleeve*
World's An Apple	7"	Atlantic	584298	1969	**£15**	**£7.50**	

BIG BLACK

Headache	12"	Blast First	BFFP14T	1987	**£40**	**£20**	*red vinyl, with booklet, poster, 7"*
Il Duce	7"	Homestead	HMS042	1986	£5	£2	
Pigpile	LP	Touch & Go	TG81	1992	**£20**	**£8**	*with video & T-shirt, boxed*
Sound Of Impact	LP		NOT2(BUT1)	1986	**£30**	**£15**	*nos. 1–1000*
Sound Of Impact	LP		NOT2(BUT1)	1987	**£15**	**£6**	*nos. 1001–1500*

BIG BOB

Your Line Was Busy	7"	Top Rank	JAR185	1959	**£20**	**£10**	

BIG BOPPER

Big Bopper	7" EP	Mercury	ZEP10004	1959	**£100**	**£50**	
Big Bopper's Wedding	7"	Mercury	AMT1017	1958	**£10**	**£5**	
Chantilly Lace	7"	Mercury	AMT1002	1958	**£6**	**£2.50**	
Chantilly Lace	LP	Mercury	MMC14008	1958	**£150**	**£75**	
Chantilly Lace	LP	Contour	6870531	1974	**£10**	**£4**	
It's The Truth Ruth	7"	Mercury	AMT1046	1959	**£15**	**£7.50**	
Pink Petticoats	7" EP	Mercury	ZEP10027	1959	**£175**	**£87.50**	

BIG BOY PETE

Cold Turkey	7"	Camp	602005	1968	**£50**	**£25**	

BIG BROTHER

Confusion	LP	All American	5570	1970	**£75**	**£37.50**	*US*

BIG BROTHER & THE HOLDING CO.

Big Brother and the Holding Co. had Janis Joplin as their lead singer, but were far from being just her backing group. The first LP, recorded before Cream toured America with their amplifiers turned up to maximum, sounds weak. The partly live *Cheap Thrills*, however, is an exciting and vital recording. Janis Joplin without the Holding Co. failed to achieve this power, but equally, the Holding Co. without Janis Joplin (as on the 1971 recordings) lacked distinction.

Be A Brother	LP	CBS	64118	1971	**£10**	**£4**	
Big Brother & The Holding Co.	LP	Fontana	STL5457	1967	**£20**	**£8**	*stereo*
Big Brother & The Holding Co.	LP	London	HAT/SHT8377	1968	**£15**	**£7.50**	
Big Brother & The Holding Co.	LP	Fontana	TL5457	1967	**£25**	**£10**	*mono*
Bye Bye Baby	7"	Fontana	TF881	1967	**£6**	**£2.50**	
Cheap Thrills	LP	CBS	63392	1968	**£40**	**£20**	*mono*
Cheap Thrills	LP	CBS	63392	1968	**£12**	**£5**	*stereo*
Down On Me	7"	London	HLT10226	1969	**£4**	**£1.50**	
How Hard It Is	LP	CBS	30738	1971	**£12**	**£5**	*US*
Light Is Faster Than Sound	7" EP	Vogue	INT18147	1967	**£25**	**£12.50**	*French*
Piece Of My Heart	7"	CBS	3683	1968	**£10**	**£5**	*picture sleeve*

BIG CARROT

The single credited to Big Carrot is actually the work of T Rex, being designed as a showcase for Marc Bolan's increasing desire to be taken seriously as a lead guitarist.

Blackjack	7"	EMI	EMI2047	1973	**£20**	**£10**	

BIG CHARLIE

Red Sea	7"	Blue Beat	BB241	1964	**£12**	**£6**	

BIG COUNTRY

Broken Heart	CD-s	Mercury	BIGCD6	1988	£5	£2	
King Of Emotion	CD-s	Mercury	BIGCD5	1988	£5	£2	
One Great Thing	CD-s	Mercury	BIGCD3	1986	£5	£2	
Peace In Our Time	CD-s	Mercury	BIGCD7	1989	£5	£2	

BIG DADDY

Big Daddy's Blues	LP	Gee	(S)G704	1960	**£20**	**£8**	*US*
Twist Party	LP	Regent	6106	1962	**£15**	**£6**	*US*

BIG DAVE & HIS ORCHESTRA

Cat From Coos Bay	7"	Capitol	CL14195	1954	**£8**	**£4**	
Rock And Roll Party	7"	Capitol	CL14245	1955	**£20**	**£10**	
Rock, Roll, Ball And Wail	78	Capitol	CL14156	1954	**£8**	**£3**	

BIG FLAME

Sink	7"	Plaque	001	1984	£10	£5	

BIG FOOT

Big Foot	LP	Winro	1004	1968	£20	£8	US

BIG GROUP

Big Hammer	LP	Peer International Library	PIL9009	1971	£100	£50	

BIG IN JAPAN

Various people passing through the ranks of Big In Japan went on to be fairly big in lots of places – most notably Budgie (Siouxsie and the Banshees), David Balfe (Teardrop Explodes, then founder of the Food label), Holly Johnson (Frankie Goes To Hollywood), Bill Drummond (KLF and manager of Zoo label), and Ian Broudie (production work and the Lightning Seeds).

Big In Japan	7"	Erics	ERICS001	1977	£6	£2.50	
From Y To Z And Never Again	7"	Zoo	CAGE001	1978	£8	£4	

BIG LOST RAINBOW

Big Lost Rainbow	LP	private		1973	£1000	£700	US

BIG MAYBELLE

All Of Me	7"	London	HLC8447	1957	£25	£12.50	
Baby Won't You Please Come Home	7"	London	HLC8854	1959	£15	£7.50	
Blues, Candy And Big Maybelle	LP	Savoy	MG14011	1958	£40	£20	US
Careless Love	7"	London	HL9941	1965	£6	£2.50	
Gospel Soul	LP	Brunswick	BL754142	1968	£15	£6	US
Got A Brand New Bag	LP	Rajac	(S)S122	1967	£15	£6	US
Mama He Treats Your Daughter Mean	7"	CBS	2926	1967	£5	£2	
Pure Soul Of Big Maybelle	LP	CBS	62999	1967	£25	£10	
Quittin' Time	7"	Direction	583312	1968	£15	£7.50	
Sings	LP	Savoy	MG14005	1958	£40	£20	US
Soul Of Big Maybelle	LP	Scepter	(S)S522	1964	£20	£8	US
Turn The World Around	7"	CBS	2735	1967	£15	£7.50	
What More Can A Woman Do	LP	Brunswick	BL(7)54107	1962	£25	£10	US

BIG MOOSE

Puppy Howl Blues	7"	Python	PKM1	1968	£8	£4	

BIG SLEEP

Bluebell Wood	LP	Pegasus	PEG4	1971	£40	£20	

BIG STAR

Big Star, the group led by Alex Chilton following the disbanding of the Box Tops, has acquired a formidable cult reputation wholly unjustified by the actual music to be found on the records. The songs are rather ordinary and Big Star's lack of success is not at all surprising.

Radio City	LP	Ardent	ADS1501	1971	£25	£10	US
# 1 Record	LP	Ardent	ADS2803	1971	£25	£10	US
Radio City/Big Star	LP	Stax	SXSP302	1978	£20	£8	*double*
Third Album	LP	Aura	AUL703	1978	£10	£4	

BIG THREE

By all accounts, the Big Three were, on stage, the most impressive Liverpool group of them all. Their records, however, never did them justice – even with the live *At The Cavern* EP, it is clearly a case of 'you had to be there'. Bass player Johnny Gustafson has been ubiquitous ever since, however, playing, among others, with Quatermass, Hard Stuff, Gillan and Roxy Music.

At The Cavern	7" EP	Decca	DFE8552	1963	£25	£12.50	
By The Way	7"	Decca	F11689	1963	£4	£1.50	
I'm With You	7"	Decca	F11752	1963	£6	£2.50	
If You Ever Change Your Mind	7"	Decca	F11927	1964	£10	£5	
Resurrection	LP	Polydor	2383199	1973	£20	£8	
Some Other Guy	7"	Decca	F11614	1963	£6	£2.50	
What'd I Say	7" EP	Decca	457029	1964	£25	£12.50	*French*

BIG THREE (CASS ELLIOTT, JIM HENDRICKS, TIM ROSE)

Big Three	LP	FM	(FS)307	1963	£15	£6	US
Big Three Featuring Cass Elliott	LP	Roulette	RCP1003	1967	£10	£4	
Live At The Recording Studio	LP	FM	(FS)311	1964	£15	£6	US

BIG YOUTH

Of the many toasting DJs to emerge in the wake of U Roy's first successes, Big Youth was the most idiosyncratic and the most spectacular. His 'Ace 90 Skank' set the pattern – a roaring motor bike engine is overlaid by thickly accented Jamaican voices; then a lanky bass guitar begins its deep descent as Big Youth unleashes a stream of words that manage to sound lazy even while tumbling over each other.

A So We Say	7"	Summit	SUM8542	1973	£4	£1.50	*Winston Scotland B side*
Ace 90 Skank	7"	Downtown	DT492	1972	£8	£4	
Can You Keep A Secret	7"	Pyramid	PYR7015	1974	£10	£5	*with Keith Hudson*
Cane And Abel	7"	Prince Buster	PB50	1973	£4	£1.50	
Chi Chi Run	7"	Blue Beat	BB424	1972	£12	£6	*John Holt B side*
Chi Chi Run	7"	Prince Buster	PB46	1972	£4	£1.50	
Chi Chi Run	LP	Fab	MS8	1972	£20	£8	
Concrete Jungle	7"	Grape	GR3061	1973	£4	£1.50	
Cool Breeze	7"	Green Door	GD4051	1973	£4	£1.50	*Crystalites B side*
Dock Of The Bay	7"	Downtown	DT497	1972	£8	£4	*Crystalites B side*
Dreadlocks Dread	LP	Front Line	FL1014	1978	£12	£5	

Dreadlocks Dread ... LP ... Klik ... KLP9001 ... 1976 **£15** ... **£6**
Foreman v. Frazier ... 7" ... Grape ... GR3040 ... 1973 **£4** ... **£1.50**
Hit The Road Jack ... LP ... Trojan ... TRLS137 ... 1976 **£15** ... **£6**
Isaiah First Prophet Of Old ... LP ... Front Line ... FL1011 ... 1978 **£12** ... **£5**
JA To UK ... 7" ... Grape ... GR3044 ... 1973 **£4** ... **£1.50**
Leggo Beast ... 7" ... Prince Buster ... PB48 ... 1973 **£4** ... **£1.50**
Medicine Doctor ... 7" ... Gayfeet ... CS206 ... 1969 **£4** ... **£1.50**
Natty Cultural Dread ... LP ... Trojan ... TRLS123 ... 1976 **£15** ... **£6**
Opportunity Rock ... 7" ... Grape ... GR3051 ... 1973 **£4** ... **£1.50**
Reggae Phenomenon ... LP ... Big Youth ... BYD1 ... 1977 **£12** ... **£5**
Screaming Target ... LP ... Trojan ... TRLS61 ... 1973 **£15** ... **£6**

BIGLIETTO PER L'INFERNO

Biglietto Per L'Inferno ... LP ... Trident ... TRI1005 ... 1973 **£150** ... **£75** ... *Italian*

BIKINIS

Bikini ... 7" ... Columbia ... DB4149 ... 1958 **£8** ... **£4**

BILK, ACKER

Ack's Back ... LP ... Columbia ... 33SX1747 ... 1965 **£15** ... **£6**
Acker ... LP ... Columbia ... 33SX1248 ... 1960 **£15** ... **£6**
Acker Bilk Sings ... 7" EP ... Pye ... NJE1067 ... 1959 **£6** ... **£2.50**
Acker's Away ... 7" EP ... Columbia ... SEG7940 ... 1959 **£6** ... **£2.50**
Band Of Thieves ... 7" EP ... Columbia ... SEG8178 ... 1962 **£6** ... **£2.50**
Beau Jazz ... LP ... Columbia ... 33SX1456 ... 1962 **£15** ... **£6**
Call Me Mister ... LP ... Columbia ... 33SX1525 ... 1963 **£15** ... **£6**
Dippermouth Blues ... 7" ... Tempo ... A134 ... 1956 **£4** ... **£1.50**
Four Hits And A Mister ... 7" EP ... Columbia ... SEG8156 ... 1962 **£6** ... **£2.50**
Golden Treasury Of Bilk ... LP ... Columbia ... 33SX1304 ... 1961 **£15** ... **£6**
Goodnight Sweet Prince ... 7" ... Melodisc ... 1547 ... 1960 **£12** ... **£6**
Landsdowne Folio ... LP ... Columbia ... 33SX1348 ... 1961 **£15** ... **£6**
Master Acker Bilk ... 7" EP ... Esquire ... EP213 ... 1959 **£8** ... **£4**
Mr Acker Bilk Omnibus ... LP ... Pye ... NJL22 ... 1960 **£15** ... **£6**
My Early Days ... LP ... Society ... SOC908 ... 1960 **£10** ... **£4**
Noble Art Of Acker Bilk ... 10" LP ... Columbia ... 33S1141 ... 1959 **£15** ... **£6**
Requests ... 10" LP ... Pye ... NJT513 ... 1958 **£15** ... **£6**
Seven Ages Of Acker ... LP ... Columbia ... 33SX1205 ... 1960 **£15** ... **£6**
Veritable Mr Bilk ... LP ... Columbia ... SX/SCX6241 ... 1967 **£15** ... **£6**

BILL, TOPO D.

Witchi Tai To ... 7" ... Charisma ... CB116 ... 1970 **£5** ... **£2** ... *picture sleeve*

BILLIE & EDDIE

King Is Coming Back ... 7" ... Top Rank ... JAR249 ... 1959 **£8** ... **£4**

BILLIE & LILLIE

Bells Bells Bells ... 7" ... Top Rank ... JAR157 ... 1959 **£4** ... **£1.50**
Creeping Crawling Crying ... 7" ... London ... HLU8630 ... 1958 **£20** ... **£10**
Hanging On To You ... 7" ... London ... HLU8689 ... 1958 **£12** ... **£6**
La Dee Dah ... 7" ... London ... HLU8564 ... 1958 **£15** ... **£7.50**
Lucky Ladybug ... 7" ... London ... HLU8795 ... 1959 **£12** ... **£6**

BILLIE & THE ESSENTIALS

Maybe You'll be There ... 7" ... London ... HLW9657 ... 1963 **£30** ... **£15**

BIM & BAM

Fatty ... 7" ... Gayfeet ... GS201 ... 1973 **£10** ... **£5**

BIM, BAM & CLOVER

Party Time ... 7" ... Trojan ... TR7754 ... 1970 **£4** ... **£1.50**

BINTANGS

Blues On The Ceiling ... LP ... Decca ... XBY846514 ... 1969 **£15** ... **£6** ... *Dutch*
Down South Blues ... LP ... Decca ... PD12032 ... 1973 **£12** ... **£5** ... *German*
Genuine Bull ... LP ... RCA ... YHPL10982 ... 1975 **£10** ... **£4** ... *Dutch*
Ridin' With The Bintangs ... LP ... Decca ... 6454420 ... 1970 **£15** ... **£6** ... *Dutch*
Travelling In The USA ... LP ... Decca ... 6440677 ... 1970 **£15** ... **£6** ... *Dutch*

BIOTA

The albums issued by the musicians and artists involved in both Biota and Mnemonists are conceived as general art packages, in which the cover art, the elaborate art print inserts, and the music itself are of equal importance. The concept becomes a little subverted in the compact disc age, so that although the majority of the albums listed are available on CD, along with some more recent releases, the original vinyl issues are definitely the ones to get. The music itself is instrumental and consists of dense, fascinating soundscapes produced by a large number of different instrumental sounds, without, however, including anything that might be described as a synthesizer.

Bellowing Room ... LP ... Recommended ... RRC27 ... 1987 **£12** ... **£5**
Biota ... LP ... Dys ... BIOTA ... 1982 **£15** ... **£6** ... *US*
Rackabones ... LP ... Dys ... DYS12/13 ... 1985 **£30** ... **£15** ... *US double*
Tinct ... LP ... Recommended ... RRC31 ... 1988 **£12** ... **£5**

BIRD, IVOR

Over The Wall We Go ... 7" ... RSO ... 2090270 ... 1978 **£4** ... **£1.50**

BIRD, RONNIE

Adieu A Un Ami ... 7" EP ... Decca ... 460844 ... 196– **£25** ... **£12.50** ... *French*
Chante ... 7" EP ... Philips ... 437220 ... 196– **£15** ... **£7.50** ... *French*
Elle M'Attend ... 7" EP ... Decca ... 460918 ... 196– **£15** ... **£7.50** ... *French*

Title	Format	Label	Number	Year	Price	Price	Note
Elle M'Attend	LP	Decca	154134	196–	**£50**	**£25**	*French*
L'Amour Nous Rend Fou	7" EP	Decca	460889	196–	**£15**	**£7.50**	*French*
La Surprise	7" EP	Philips	437353	196–	**£15**	**£7.50**	*French*
Le Pivert	7" EP	Philips	437403	196–	**£15**	**£7.50**	*French*
N'Ecoute Pas Ton Coeur	7" EP	Philips	437239	196–	**£15**	**£7.50**	*French*
Où va-t-elle?	7" EP	Decca	460946	196–	**£15**	**£7.50**	*French*
Tu En Dis Trop	7" EP	Philips	437327	196–	**£15**	**£7.50**	*French*

BIRD, TONY

Title	Format	Label	Number	Year	Price	Price	Note
Bird Of Paradise	LP	CBS	82498	1978	**£10**	**£4**	
Tony Bird	LP	CBS	81183	1976	**£10**	**£4**	

BIRDLEGS & PAULINE

Title	Format	Label	Number	Year	Price	Price	Note
Spring	7"	Sue	WI4014	1966	**£10**	**£5**	

BIRDS

The Birds started playing together at art college in Middlesex, the three singles featuring their typical British R&B. They had shortened their name from the Thunderbirds, a move that brought the group into legal conflict with the more successful Byrds. This gave them a modicum of publicity, but it was not translated into sales. A fourth single was credited to Bird's Birds, but the group split up soon afterwards. Bass player Kim Gardner achieved chart success a few years later as a member of Ashton, Gardner and Dyke, while the Birds' guitarist did even better when he joined successively the Jeff Beck Group, the Faces and the Rolling Stones – his name being Ron Wood.

Title	Format	Label	Number	Year	Price	Price	Note
Leavin' Here	7"	Decca	F12140	1965	**£40**	**£20**	
No Good Without You Baby	7"	Decca	F12257	1965	**£40**	**£20**	
No Good Without You Baby	7" EP	Decca	457114	1966	**£200**	**£100**	*French, best auctioned*
You're On My Mind	7"	Decca	F12031	1964	**£75**	**£37.50**	

BIRDS OF A FEATHER

Title	Format	Label	Number	Year	Price	Price	Note
Birds Of A Feather	LP	Page One	POLS027	1970	**£30**	**£15**	

BIRD'S BIRDS

Title	Format	Label	Number	Year	Price	Price	Note
Say Those Magic Words	7"	Reaction	591005	1966	**£400**	**£250**	*best auctioned*

BIRKIN, JANE & SERGE GAINSBOURG

Title	Format	Label	Number	Year	Price	Price	Note
Jane Birkin And Serge Gainsbourg	LP	Fontana	STL5493	1969	**£20**	**£8**	
Je T'Aime . . . Moi Non Plus	7"	Antic	K11511	1974	**£4**	**£1.50**	*picture sleeve*
Je T'Aime . . . Moi Non Plus	7"	Fontana	TF1042	1969	**£4**	**£1.50**	*picture sleeve*

BIRMINGHAM

Title	Format	Label	Number	Year	Price	Price	Note
Birmingham	LP	Grosvenor	GRS1011	1971	**£125**	**£62.50**	

BIRTH CONTROL

Title	Format	Label	Number	Year	Price	Price	Note
Backdoor Possibilities	LP	Brain	60019	1976	**£12**	**£5**	*German*
Believe In The Pill	LP	Ohr	OMM556025	1972	**£15**	**£6**	*German*
Birth Control	LP	Charisma	CAS1036	1971	**£15**	**£6**	
Birth Control	LP	Metronome	MLP15366	1970	**£30**	**£15**	*German*
Hoodoo Man	LP	CBS	65316	1972	**£15**	**£6**	*German*
Live	LP	CBS	88088	1974	**£20**	**£8**	*German double*
Operation	LP	Ohr	OMM556015	1971	**£20**	**£8**	*German double*
Plastic People	LP	CBS	80921	1975	**£12**	**£5**	*German*
Re-birth	LP	CBS	65963	1974	**£15**	**£6**	*German*

BIRTHDAY PARTY

Title	Format	Label	Number	Year	Price	Price	Note
Friend Catcher	7"	4AD	AD12	1980	**£5**	**£2**	
Mr Clarinet	7"	4AD	AD114	1981	**£5**	**£2**	
Peel Sessions	CD-s	Strange Fruit	SFPSCD020	1988	**£5**	**£2**	
Release The Bats	7"	4AD	AD111	1981	**£4**	**£1.50**	

BISCAYNES

The recordings by the Biscaynes are the first by the group that found success when they changed their name to the Walker Brothers.

Title	Format	Label	Number	Year	Price	Price	Note
Church Key	7"	Northridge	1001	1963	**£20**	**£10**	*US*
Midnight In Montevideo	7"	Co-En	01	196–	**£20**	**£10**	*US*

BISHOP, DICKIE & HIS SIDEKICKS

Title	Format	Label	Number	Year	Price	Price	Note
Cumberland Gap	7"	Decca	F10869	1957	**£8**	**£4**	
Jumping Judy	7"	Decca	F11028	1958	**£5**	**£2**	
No Other Baby	7"	Decca	F10981	1958	**£5**	**£2**	
Prisoners Song	7"	Decca	F10959	1957	**£8**	**£4**	

BISHOP, ELVIN

Title	Format	Label	Number	Year	Price	Price	Note
Elvin Bishop	LP	Fillmore	30001	1969	**£12**	**£5**	*US*

BISHOP, JOHN

Title	Format	Label	Number	Year	Price	Price	Note
Plays His Guitar (Doesn't He?)	LP	Tangerine	6495002	1971	**£10**	**£4**	

BISHOPS

Title	Format	Label	Number	Year	Price	Price	Note
Mr Jones	7"	Chiswick	NS35	1978	**£12**	**£6**	*test pressing*

BIT 'A SWEET

Title	Format	Label	Number	Year	Price	Price	Note
Hypnotic 1	LP	ABC	ABCS640	1968	**£25**	**£10**	*US*

BITCHES SIN

Title	Format	Label	Number	Year	Price	Price	Note
No More Chances	12"	Quiet	QT001	1983	**£6**	**£2.50**	
Predator	LP	Heavy Metal	HMRLP4	1982	**£10**	**£4**	

BJÖRK

Björk's strikingly distinctive voice – capable of rising from a tender caress to a violent banshee wail within the same song – would have been enough to attract attention on its own. The fact that Björk was from Iceland and had, what was to British ears, an attractive and unusual accent to prove it, only served to broaden her appeal. When, however, these facets were matched to an eccentric punk-ballerina image and a taste for adventurous dance, classical- and jazz-inspired arrangements to enhance the impact of her powerful melodies, the combination became quite irresistible for fans and critics alike. Other collectable items involving her can be found under the Tappi Tikarrass, Kukl, Sugarcubes, and Eight-O-Eight State headings. Of those listed here, the album *Björk* was recorded when the singer was just eleven years old, while *Gling-Glo* is a reasonably straightforward vocal and piano jazz record, only with the bulk of the lyrics delivered in Icelandic.

Title	Format	Label	Cat. No.	Year	Mint	VG	Notes
Army Of Me	12"	One Little Indian	162TP12P	1995	**£10**	**£5**	*promo double*
Army Of Me	12"	One Little Indian	162TP12GM	1995	**£10**	**£5**	*promo*
Bachelorette	CD-s	One Little Indian	20TP7BOX212	1997	**£30**	**£15**	*3 singles, video, boxed*
Best Mixes From Debut	12"	One Little Indian	152TP12	1994	**£10**	**£5**	
Big Time Sensuality	12"	One Little Indian	BJDJ124/5	1993	**£20**	**£10**	*promo double*
Björk	LP	Falkinn	FA006	1977	**£200**	**£100**	*Icelandic, credited to Björk Gudmundsdottir*
Come To Me	10"	One Little Indian	BJDJ103	1993	**£12**	**£6**	*promo*
Debut	CD	One Little Indian	TPLP31CDL	1993	**£15**	**£6**	*without PlayDead*
Debut	LP	One Little Indian	TPLP31L	1993	**£10**	**£4**	*with lyric booklet*
Gling-Glo	LP	Smekkleysa	SM27	1990	**£20**	**£8**	*Icelandic*
Human Behaviour	10"	One Little Indian	BJDJ104	1993	**£12**	**£6**	*promo*
Human Behaviour	12"	One Little Indian	112TP12DJ	1993	**£10**	**£5**	*promo*
Human Behaviour	12"	One Little Indian	112TP12P	1993	**£10**	**£5**	*promo*
Joga	CD-s	One Little Indian	20TP7BOX	1997	**£30**	**£15**	*3 singles, video, boxed*
One Day	10"	One Little Indian	BJDJ101	1993	**£12**	**£6**	*promo*
One Day	12"	One Little Indian	BJDJ123	1993	**£20**	**£10**	*promo*
Possibly Maybe	12"	One Little Indian	193TP12TD	1996	**£25**	**£12.50**	
Post	LP	One Little Indian	TPLP51L	1994	**£12**	**£5**	*pink vinyl*
Violently Happy	10"	One Little Indian	BJDJ102	1993	**£12**	**£6**	*promo*

BLACK

Title	Format	Label	Cat. No.	Year	Mint	VG	Notes
Human Features	7"	Rox	ROX17	1981	**£8**	**£4**	

BLACK, BILL

Title	Format	Label	Cat. No.	Year	Mint	VG	Notes
Beat Goes On	LP	London	HAU/SHU8367	1968	**£10**	**£4**	

BLACK, BILL COMBO

Title	Format	Label	Cat. No.	Year	Mint	VG	Notes
Bill Black's Combo	7" EP	London	REU1277	1960	**£15**	**£7.50**	
Goes Big Band	LP	Hi	HLP32020	1964	**£12**	**£5**	US
Greatest Hits	LP	London	HAU8113	1963	**£12**	**£5**	
Let's Twist	LP	London	HAU2427/SAHU6222	1962	**£15**	**£6**	
Little Queenie	7"	London	HLU9925	1964	**£12**	**£6**	
More Solid And Raunchy	LP	Hi	HLP32023	1965	**£10**	**£4**	US
Movin'	LP	London	HAU2433	1962	**£15**	**£6**	
Moving	7"	London	HLU9436	1961	**£5**	**£2**	
Mr Beat	LP	Hi	HLP32027	1965	**£10**	**£4**	US
Plays Chuck Berry	LP	London	HAU8187	1964	**£20**	**£8**	
Plays The Blues	LP	Hi	HLP32015	1964	**£15**	**£6**	US
Record Hop	LP	Hi	HLP32006	1961	**£20**	**£8**	US
Saxy Jazz	LP	Hi	HLP32002	1960	**£20**	**£8**	US
Smokie	7"	Felsted	AF129	1959	**£5**	**£2**	
Smokie	LP	Hi	HLP12001	1960	**£20**	**£8**	US
Solid & Raunchy	LP	London	HAU2310	1962	**£20**	**£8**	
That Wonderful Feeling	LP	Hi	HLP32004	1962	**£15**	**£6**	US
Untouchable Sound	7" EP	London	REU1369	1963	**£15**	**£7.50**	
Untouchable Sound Of Bill Black	LP	London	HAU8080	1963	**£15**	**£6**	

BLACK, CILLA

Nothing detracts from an artist's collectability as much as their becoming a popular entertainer and interest in Cilla Black's recordings has plummeted since her emergence as a television personality. She was, however, an integral part of the Merseybeat phenomenon and her first LP, in particular, stands up well.

Title	Format	Label	Cat. No.	Year	Mint	VG	Notes
Alfie	7" EP	Odeon	MEO114	1966	**£8**	**£4**	*French*
Anyone Who Had A Heart	7" EP	Parlophone	GEP8901	1964	**£6**	**£2.50**	
Anyone Who Had A Heart	7" EP	Odeon	SOE3747	1963	**£6**	**£2.50**	*French*
Cilla	LP	Parlophone	PCS3063	1965	**£12**	**£5**	*stereo*
Cilla	LP	Parlophone	PMC1243	1965	**£10**	**£4**	*mono*

Cilla	LP	World Record Club	STP1036	1966	£**10**	£**4**	
Cilla Sings A Rainbow	LP	Parlophone	PCS7004	1966	£**12**	£**5**	*stereo*
Cilla Sings A Rainbow	LP	Parlophone	PMC7004	1966	£**10**	£**4**	*mono*
Cilla's Hits	7" EP	Parlophone	GEP8954	1966	£**8**	£**4**	
It's For You	7" EP	Parlophone	GEP8916	1964	£**8**	£**4**	
Love Of The Loved	7"	Parlophone	R5065	1963	£**4**	£**1.50**	
Sheroo!	LP	Parlophone	PMC/PCS7041	1968	£**10**	£**4**	
Time For Cilla	7" EP	Parlophone	GEP8967	1967	£**15**	£**7.50**	
You're My World	7" EP	Odeon	SOE3758	1964	£**8**	£**4**	*French*
You've Lost That Lovin' Feelin'	7" EP	Odeon	SOE3765	1965	£**8**	£**4**	*French*

BLACK, FRANK

Conversation	CD	Elektra	PRCD88292	1993	£**20**	£**8**	*US promo*
Teenager Of The Year	CD	Elektra	PRCD9000	1994	£**20**	£**8**	*US promo*

BLACK, MATT & THE DOODLEBUGS

Punky Xmas	7"	Punk	BCS0005	1976	£**5**	£**2**	

BLACK, STANLEY

Hand In Hand	7"	Decca	F11624	1963	£**8**	£**4**	

BLACK ABBOTTS

Love Is Alive	7"	Evolution	E3004	1971	£**10**	£**5**	

BLACK ACE

Black Ace	7" EP	XX	MIN701	1961	£**8**	£**4**	
Black Ace	LP	Heritage	HLP1006	1962	£**25**	£**10**	

BLACK AXE

Red Lights	7"	Metal	MELT1	1980	£**10**	£**5**	*picture sleeve*

BLACK CAT BONES

Barbed Wire Sandwich	LP	Nova	SDN15	1970	£**60**	£**30**	

BLACK COUNTRY THREE

Black Country Three	LP	Transatlantic	TRA140	1966	£**30**	£**15**	

BLACK CROWES

Grits'n'Gravy	CD	Reprise	PROCD7102	1994	£**20**	£**8**	*US promo compilation*
Hard To Handle	12"	Def American	DEFAP612	1990	£**10**	£**5**	*shaped picture disc*
Hard To Handle	7"	Def American	DEFAP10	1991	£**6**	£**2.50**	*shaped picture disc*
Hard To Handle	CD-s	Def American	DEFAC6	1990	£**6**	£**2.50**	
Jealous Again	12"	Def American	DEFA812	1991	£**8**	£**4**	*with patch*
Jealous Again	12"	Def American	DEFAP412	1990	£**6**	£**2.50**	*picture disc*
Jealous Again	CD-s	Def American	DEFAC8	1991	£**5**	£**2**	
Jealous Again	CD-s	Def American	DEFAC4	1990	£**8**	£**4**	
Twice As Hard	12"	Def American	DEFAP712	1991	£**6**	£**2.50**	*picture disc*
Twice As Hard	CD-s	Def American	DEFAC7	1991	£**5**	£**2**	

BLACK DYKE MILLS BAND

Thingumybob	7"	Apple	4	1968	£**25**	£**12.50**	

BLACK DYNAMITES

Brush Those Tears	7"	Top Rank	JAR319	1960	£**15**	£**7.50**	

BLACK FLAG

Annihilate This Week	CD-s	SST	SST081CD	1988	£**5**	£**2**	
I Can See You	CD-s	SST	SST226CD	1990	£**5**	£**2**	
Six Pack	7"	Alternative Tentacles	VIRUS9	1981	£**4**	£**1.50**	

BLACK KNIGHTS

I Got A Woman	7"	Columbia	DB7443	1965	£**12**	£**6**	

BLACK MERDA

Black Merda	LP	Chess	569517	1970	£**30**	£**15**	*US*
Long Burn The Fire	LP	Janus	JLS3042	1971	£**20**	£**8**	*US*

BLACK OAK ARKANSAS

Black Oak Arkansas	LP	Atlantic	2400180	1971	£**10**	£**4**	

BLACK PEARL

Live	LP	Prophesy	PRS1001	1970	£**12**	£**5**	*US*

BLACK ROSE

Boys Will Be Boys	7"	Bullet	BOL9	1984	£**10**	£**5**	
No Point Runnin'	7"	Teesbeat	TB5	1982	£**25**	£**12.50**	

BLACK SABBATH

Black Sabbath were hated by the critics in the early days, so that the latter were disconcerted to see the group's first LP release climb high in the album charts. The achievement was based on the group's sheer hard work in building up a large and loyal following through live performance. Essentially, the group also invented the heavy metal genre, or at any rate solidified the style into the riff-based music that it has remained ever since.

Am I Going Insane?	7"	NEMS	6165300	1975	£**4**	£**1.50**	

Black Sabbath	LP	Vertigo	VO6	1970	£20	£8	*spiral label*
Black Sabbath 4	LP	Vertigo	6360071	1972	£20	£8	*spiral label, booklet*
Children Of The Grave	7"	Phonogram	DJ005	1974	£350	£210	*promo, Status Quo B side*
Cross Purposes Live	CD	EMI		1994	£30	£15	*promo CD and video boxed set*
Evil Woman	7"	Fontana	TF1067	1970	£50	£25	
Evil Woman	7"	Vertigo	V2	1970	£8	£4	
Feels Good To Me	CD-s	IRS	EIRSCD148	1990	£5	£2	
Four Songs From The Eternal Idol	12"	Vertigo	SABAF1	1987	£6	£2.50	*promo*
Greatest Hits	LP	Nems	NEP6009	1985	£10	£4	*picture disc*
In For The Kill	12"	Vertigo	SABDJ12	1986	£10	£5	*promo*
Master Of Insanity	CD-s	IRS	EIRSDJ180	1992	£8	£4	*promo only*
Master Of Reality	LP	Vertigo	6360050	1971	£40	£20	*spiral label, poster*
Paranoid	12"	NEMS	12NEX01	1982	£8	£4	*clear vinyl*
Paranoid	7"	Vertigo	6059010	1970	£5	£2	
Paranoid	7"	NEMS	NEP1	1982	£4	£1.50	*picture disc*
Paranoid	CD-s	Castle Communications	CD35	1988	£5	£2	*3" single*
Paranoid	LP	Vertigo	6360011	1970	£20	£8	*spiral label*
Paranoid	LP	Warner Bros	K3104	1970	£12	£5	*US quad*
Paranoid	LP	Nems	NEP6003	1977	£10	£4	*picture disc*
Sabbath Bloody Sabbath	7"	WWA	WWS002	1973	£4	£1.50	
Tomorrow's Dream	7"	Vertigo	6059061	1972	£6	£2.50	
Turn Up The Night	12"	Vertigo	SABP612	1982	£6	£2.50	*picture disc*
Turn Up The Night	7"	Vertigo	SABP6	1982	£4	£1.50	*picture disc*

BLACK SHEEP

Black Sheep	LP	Capitol	11369	1975	£15	£6	*US*

BLACK SPIRIT

Black Spirit	LP	Brutkasten	850006	1978	£60	£30	*German*

BLACK UHURU

Love Crisis	LP	Third World	TWS925	1978	£12	£5	

BLACK VELVET

Can You Feel It	LP	Seven Sun	SUNLP1	1973	£40	£20	
People Of The World	LP	Pye	NSPL18392	1972	£30	£15	
This Is Black Velvet	LP	Beacon	BEAS16	1971	£25	£10	

BLACK WIDOW

Black Widow	LP	CBS	64133	1970	£20	£8	
Come To The Sabbat	7"	CBS	5031	1970	£15	£7.50	
Sacrifice	LP	CBS	63948	1970	£20	£8	
Three	LP	CBS	64562	1971	£20	£8	
Wish You Would	7"	CBS	7596	1971	£8	£4	

BLACKBIRDS

No Destination	7"	Saga	OPP3	1968	£15	£7.50	
No Destination	LP	Saga	FID2113	1968	£25	£10	
Touch Of Music	LP	Opp	534	1971	£25	£10	*German*

BLACKBURDS

Play The Bugaloo	7" EP	Philips	437323	196–	£8	£4	*French*

BLACKBURN, TONY

Don't Get Off That Train	7"	Fontana	TF562	1965	£5	£2	
Meets Matt Monro	LP	Fontana	SFL13161	1966	£10	£4	
Tony Blackburn Sings	LP	MGM	C(S)8062	1968	£10	£4	

BLACKBYRDS

Action	LP	Fantasy	FT534	1977	£10	£4	
Blackbyrds	LP	Fantasy	FT9444	1975	£15	£6	
City Life	LP	Fantasy	FTA3003	1976	£12	£5	
Flying Start	LP	Fantasy	FT522	1974	£15	£6	
Night Grooves	LP	Fantasy	FT555	1979	£10	£4	

BLACKFEATHER

At The Mountains Of Madness	LP	Festival	34159	1970	£50	£25	*Australian*
Boppin' The Blues	LP	Infinity	34731	1972	£50	£25	*Australian*
Live	LP	Festival	25095	1972	£50	£25	*Australian*

BLACKFOOT

Send Me An Angel	7"	Atco	B9880P	1983	£5	£2	*shaped picture disc*

BLACKFOOT, J. D.

Song Of Crazy Horse	LP	Fantasy	9468	1974	£15	£6	*US*
Southbound And Gone	LP	Fantasy	9487	1975	£12	£5	*US*
Ultimate Prophecy	LP	Mercury	6338031	1970	£40	£20	

BLACKFOOT SUE

Gun Running	LP	DJM	DJLPS455	1975	£40	£20	
Nothing To Hide	LP	Jam	JAL104	1973	£15	£6	

BLACKJACK

The lead singer of this otherwise obscure American AOR group was Michael Bolton.

Title	Format	Label	Cat. No.	Year	Mint	VG	Notes
Blackjack	LP	Polydor	2391411	1979	**£10**	**£4**	
Worlds Apart	LP	Polydor	PD16279	1980	**£10**	**£4**	*US*

BLACKJACKS

Title	Format	Label	Cat. No.	Year	Mint	VG	Notes
Woo Hoo	7"	Pye	7N15586	1963	**£8**	**£3**	
Woo Hoo	7" EP	Pye	PNV24117	1964	**£12**	**£6**	*French*

BLACKMAN, HONOR

Title	Format	Label	Cat. No.	Year	Mint	VG	Notes
Before Today	7"	CBS	3896	1968	**£30**	**£15**	*picture sleeve*
Before Today	7"	CBS	3896	1968	**£10**	**£5**	
Everything I've Got	LP	Decca	LK4642	1964	**£25**	**£10**	
Kinky Boots	7"	Decca	F11843	1964	**£20**	**£10**	*with Patrick MacNee*
Kinky Boots	CD-s	London	KINCD1	1990	**£5**	**£2**	*with Patrick MacNee*

BLACKMORE, RITCHIE

Title	Format	Label	Cat. No.	Year	Mint	VG	Notes
Getaway	7"	Oriole	CB314	1965	**£400**	**£250**	*best auctioned*

BLACKTHORN

Title	Format	Label	Cat. No.	Year	Mint	VG	Notes
Blackthorn	LP	WHM	1921	1977	**£50**	**£25**	
Blackthorn II	LP	WHM	1923	1978	**£50**	**£25**	

BLACKTHORN (2)

Title	Format	Label	Cat. No.	Year	Mint	VG	Notes
Blackthorn	LP	Homespun	HRL118	1976	**£10**	**£4**	*Irish*

BLACKWATER PARK

Title	Format	Label	Cat. No.	Year	Mint	VG	Notes
Dirt Box	LP	BASF	20212386	1971	**£60**	**£30**	*German*

BLACKWELL, CHARLES

Title	Format	Label	Cat. No.	Year	Mint	VG	Notes
Freight Train	7"	Columbia	DB4919	1962	**£4**	**£1.50**	
Supercar	7"	Columbia	DB4839	1962	**£12**	**£6**	
Taboo	7"	HMV	POP977	1962	**£20**	**£10**	
Those Plucking Strings	LP	Triumph	TRY4000	1960	**£400**	**£250**	*test pressing*

BLACKWELL, OTIS

Title	Format	Label	Cat. No.	Year	Mint	VG	Notes
Make Ready For Love	7"	London	HLE8616	1958	**£30**	**£15**	
Singin' The Blues	LP	Davis	109	1956	**£100**	**£50**	*US*

BLACKWELL, RORY & THE BLACKJACKS

Title	Format	Label	Cat. No.	Year	Mint	VG	Notes
Bye Bye love	7"	Parlophone	R4326	1957	**£25**	**£12.50**	

BLACKWELL, SCRAPPER

Title	Format	Label	Cat. No.	Year	Mint	VG	Notes
Blues Before Sunrise	LP	77	LA124	1961	**£20**	**£8**	
Longtime Blues	7" EP	Collector	JEN7	1962	**£6**	**£2.50**	
Mr Scrapper's Blues	LP	XTRA	XTRA5011	1966	**£15**	**£6**	

BLACKWELLS

Title	Format	Label	Cat. No.	Year	Mint	VG	Notes
Love Or Money	7"	London	HLW9334	1961	**£5**	**£2**	
Unchained Melody	7"	London	HLW9135	1960	**£5**	**£2**	

BLACKWELLS (2)

Title	Format	Label	Cat. No.	Year	Mint	VG	Notes
Why Don't You Love Me	7"	Columbia	DB7442	1965	**£20**	**£10**	

BLAH BLAH BLAH

Title	Format	Label	Cat. No.	Year	Mint	VG	Notes
Blah Blah Blah	LP	Some Bizarre		1981	**£30**	**£15**	*test pressing*

BLAINE, HAL

Title	Format	Label	Cat. No.	Year	Mint	VG	Notes
Deuces, T's, Roadsters And Drums	LP	RCA	RD7624	1964	**£25**	**£10**	
Gear Stripper	7"	RCA	RCA1379	1963	**£8**	**£4**	

BLAIR

Title	Format	Label	Cat. No.	Year	Mint	VG	Notes
Night Life	12"	Miracle	M4	1979	**£6**	**£2.50**	

BLAIR, HENRY

Title	Format	Label	Cat. No.	Year	Mint	VG	Notes
Sparky's Magic Piano	7" EP	Capitol	EAP13003	195–	**£5**	**£2**	

BLAIR, SALLIE

Title	Format	Label	Cat. No.	Year	Mint	VG	Notes
Squeeze Me	LP	Parlophone	PMC1083	1959	**£15**	**£6**	

BLAKE, ERIC

Title	Format	Label	Cat. No.	Year	Mint	VG	Notes
Sin City	7"	Carrere	CAR141	1980	**£5**	**£2**	

BLAKE, KEITH

Title	Format	Label	Cat. No.	Year	Mint	VG	Notes
Musically	7"	Blue Cat	BS102	1968	**£8**	**£4**	
Woo Oh Oh	7"	Amalgamated	AMG809	1968	**£8**	**£4**	*Overtakers B side*

BLAKE, RALPH

Title	Format	Label	Cat. No.	Year	Mint	VG	Notes
High Blood Pressure	7"	Coxsone	CS7063	1968	**£10**	**£5**	

BLAKE, SONNY

Title	Format	Label	Cat. No.	Year	Mint	VG	Notes
Harmonica Blues	7" EP	Rooster	R706	1980	**£5**	**£2**	

BLAKE, TIM

Going under the name of Hi-T Moonweed when a member of Gong, Tim Blake contributed greatly to that group's science-fiction ambience with his arsenal of synthesizer sounds. For his solo recordings, the synthesizer takes over completely, with Blake covering similar territory to that explored by Tangerine Dream.

Title	Format	Label	Cat. No.	Year			Notes
Blake's New Jerusalem	LP	Barclay	CLAY7005	1978	**£15**	£6	
Crystal Machine	LP	Egg	900545	1977	**£15**	£6	*French*
Generator Laserbeam	7"	Barclay	BAR711	1978	**£5**	£2	*picture sleeve*

BLAKEY, ART

Title	Format	Label	Cat. No.	Year			Notes
'S Make It	LP	Mercury	(S)LML4000	1965	**£12**	£5	
African Beat	LP	Blue Note	BLP/BST84097	196–	**£20**	£8	
Are You Real	7" EP	Fontana	TFE17364	1961	**£5**	£2	
Art Blakey Jazz Messengers	LP	HMV	CLP1532/ CSD1423	1962	**£15**	£6	
Art Blakey's Big Band	LP	Parlophone	PMC1099	1959	**£25**	£10	
At The Café Bohemia Vol. 1	LP	Blue Note	BLP/BST81507	196–	**£25**	£10	
At The Café Bohemia Vol. 2	LP	Blue Note	BLP/BST81508	196–	**£25**	£10	
At The Jazz Corner Of The World Vol. 1	LP	Blue Note	BLP/BST84015	196–	**£25**	£10	
At The Jazz Corner Of The World Vol. 2	LP	Blue Note	BLP/BST84016	196–	**£25**	£10	
Big Beat	LP	Blue Note	BLP/BST84029	196–	**£25**	£10	
Blue Monk	LP	Atlantic	590009	1967	**£12**	£5	*with Thelonious Monk*
Blues March	7" EP	Fontana	TFE17257	1960	**£5**	£2	
Buhaina's Delight	LP	Blue Note	BLP/BST84104	1963	**£20**	£8	
Buttercorn Lady	LP	Mercury	(S)LML4021	1966	**£12**	£5	
Caravan	LP	Riverside	RLP438	1964	**£15**	£6	
Child's Dance	LP	Prestige	PR10047	1974	**£10**	£4	
Cu-Bop	LP	London	LTZJ15110	1958	**£20**	£8	
Drum Suite	LP	Philips	BBL7196	1958	**£15**	£6	
Free For All	LP	Blue Note	BLP/BST84170	1966	**£20**	£8	
Freedom Rider	LP	Blue Note	BLP/BST84156	1964	**£20**	£8	
Hard Bop	LP	Philips	BBL7212	1958	**£20**	£8	
Hard Bop	LP	Philips	BBL7220	1958	**£20**	£8	
Hard Drive	LP	Parlophone	PMC1084	1959	**£20**	£8	
Hold On, I'm Comin'	LP	Mercury	(S)LML4023	1967	**£12**	£5	
Holiday For Skins Vol. 1	LP	Blue Note	BLP/BST84004	196–	**£25**	£10	
Holiday For Skins Vol. 2	LP	Blue Note	BLP/BST84005	196–	**£25**	£10	
I Remember Clifford	7" EP	Fontana	TFE17337	1961	**£5**	£2	
Indestructable	LP	Blue Note	BLP/BST84193	1965	**£20**	£8	
Jazz Message	LP	HMV	CLP1760	1964	**£15**	£6	
Jazz Messengers	LP	Philips	BBL7121	1957	**£20**	£8	
Jazz Messengers With Thelonious Monk	LP	London	LTZK15157/ SAHK6017	1959	**£20**	£8	
Kyoto	LP	Storyville	673013	1969	**£10**	£4	
Les Liaisons Dangereuses	LP	Fontana	TFL5184	1962	**£15**	£6	
Like Someone In Love	LP	Blue Note	BLP/BST84245	1967	**£15**	£6	
Meet You At The Jazz Corner Of The World Vol. 1	LP	Blue Note	BLP/BST84054	196–	**£20**	£8	
Meet You At The Jazz Corner Of The World Vol. 2	LP	Blue Note	BLP/BST84055	196–	**£20**	£8	
Message From Kenya	7"	Blue Note	451626	1964	**£4**	£1.50	
Moanin'	7"	Blue Note	451735	1962	**£4**	£1.50	
Moanin'	LP	Blue Note	BLP/BST84003	1963	**£25**	£10	
Mosaic	LP	Blue Note	BLP/BST84090	1962	**£20**	£8	
Night At Birdland Vol. 1	LP	Blue Note	BLP/BST81521	1964	**£25**	£10	
Night At Birdland Vol. 2	LP	Blue Note	BLP/BST81522	1964	**£25**	£10	
Night In Tunisia	7"	Blue Note	451796	1961	**£4**	£1.50	
Night In Tunisia	LP	Blue Note	BLP/BST84049	1962	**£25**	£10	
Olympia Concert	LP	Fontana	TFL5116	1961	**£15**	£6	
Orgy In Rhythm Vol. 1	LP	Blue Note	BLP/BST81554	1962	**£25**	£10	
Orgy In Rhythm Vol. 2	LP	Blue Note	BLP/BST81555	1965	**£25**	£10	
Right Down Front	LP	Polydor	545116	1970	**£12**	£5	
Ritual	LP	Vogue	LAE12096	1958	**£25**	£10	
Roots And Herbs	LP	Blue Note	BST84347	1969	**£12**	£5	
Soul Finger	LP	Mercury	(S)LML4012	1966	**£12**	£5	
Thermo	LP	Milestone	ML47008	1974	**£10**	£4	
Three Blind Mice	LP	United Artists	(S)ULP1017	1963	**£20**	£8	
Ugetsu	LP	Riverside	RLP464	1964	**£15**	£6	
Witch Doctor	LP	Blue Note	BLP/BST84258	1967	**£15**	£6	

BLANC, MEL

Title	Format	Label	Cat. No.	Year			Notes
Bugs Bunny	7" EP	Capitol	EAP56	1958	**£5**	£2	
I Taut I Taw A Puddy Tat	7"	Capitol	CL14950	1958	**£5**	£2	
Tweety Pie	7" EP	Capitol	EAP59	1958	**£5**	£2	
Tweety Pie	7" EP	Capitol	EAP57	1958	**£5**	£2	
Woody Woodpecker	7" EP	Capitol	EAP58	1958	**£5**	£2	
Woody Woodpecker's Family Album No. 1	7" EP	Brunswick	OE9397	1959	**£5**	£2	
Woody Woodpecker's Family Album No. 2	7" EP	Brunswick	OE9398	1959	**£5**	£2	
Woody Woodpecker's Family Album No. 3	7" EP	Brunswick	OE9399	1959	**£5**	£2	

BLANCA, BURT

Texas Rider ... 7" ... Zodiac ... ZR004 ... 1960 £**8** ... £**4**

BLANCMANGE

Irene And Mavis ... 7" ... Blahh ... no number ... 1979 £**10** ... £**5**

BLAND, BILLY

Let The Little Girl Dance ... 7" ... London ... HL9096 ... 1960 £**8** ... £**4**

BLAND, BOBBY

Ain't Doing Too Bad ... 7" EP ... Vocalion ... VEP170157 ... 1964 £**30** ... £**15**
Ain't Nothin' You Can Do ... LP ... Vocalion ... VAP8027 ... 1964 £**30** ... £**15**
Best Of Bobby Bland ... LP ... Duke ... DLP(S)84 ... 1967 £**15** ... £**6** ... *US*
Best Of Bobby Bland Vol. 2 ... LP ... Duke ... DLP(S)86 ... 1968 £**15** ... £**6** ... *US*
Blue Moon ... 7" ... Vogue ... V9192 ... 1962 £**15** ... £**7.50**
Blues For Mr Crump ... LP ... Polydor ... 2383257 ... 1974 £**12** ... £**5**
Call On Me ... LP ... Vocalion ... VAP8034 ... 1965 £**30** ... £**15**
Chains Of Love ... 7" ... Action ... ACT4553 ... 1969 £**6** ... £**2.50**
Cry Cry Cry ... 7" ... Vogue ... V9178 ... 1961 £**15** ... £**7.50**
Don't Cry No More ... 7" ... Vogue ... V9188 ... 1961 £**15** ... £**7.50**
Good Time Charlie ... 7" ... Vocalion ... VP9273 ... 1966 £**8** ... £**4**
Gotta Get To Know You ... 7" ... Action ... ACT4538 ... 1969 £**10** ... £**5**
Here's The Man ... LP ... Vocalion ... VAP8041 ... 1962 £**30** ... £**15**
His California Album ... LP ... Probe ... SPB1088 ... 1973 £**10** ... £**4**
His California Album ... LP ... ABC ... ABCL5044 ... 1973 £**10** ... £**4**
Honey Child ... 7" ... Vocalion ... VP9222 ... 1964 £**8** ... £**4**
I Wouldn't Treat A Dog ... 7" ... ABC ... ABC4030 ... 1975 £**5** ... £**2**
I'm Too Far Gone ... 7" ... Vocalion ... VP9262 ... 1966 £**8** ... £**4**
If Loving You Is Wrong ... LP ... Duke ... X90 ... 1970 £**15** ... £**6** ... *US*
Lead Me On ... 7" ... Vogue ... V9182 ... 1961 £**15** ... £**7.50**
Piece Of Gold ... LP ... Action ... ACLP6006 ... 1969 £**20** ... £**8**
Rockin' In The Same Old Boat ... 7" ... Action ... ACT4524 ... 1969 £**6** ... £**2.50**
Share Your Love With Me ... 7" ... Vocalion ... VP9229 ... 1964 £**8** ... £**4**
Share Your Love With Me ... 7" ... Action ... ACT4548 ... 1969 £**6** ... £**2.50**
Soul Of The Man ... LP ... Duke ... DLP(S)79 ... 1966 £**25** ... £**10** ... *US*
Spotlighting The Man ... LP ... Duke ... DLPS89 ... 1969 £**20** ... £**8** ... *US*
These Hands ... 7" ... Vocalion ... VP9251 ... 1965 £**8** ... £**4**
Together For The First Time ... LP ... ABC ... ABCD605 ... 1974 £**12** ... £**5** ... *double, with B. B. King*
Touch Of The Blues ... 7" ... Sue ... WI4044 ... 1968 £**15** ... £**7.50**
Touch Of The Blues ... LP ... Island ... ILP974 ... 1968 £**25** ... £**10** ... *pink label*
Two Steps From The Blues ... LP ... Vogue ... VAP160183 ... 1961 £**30** ... £**15**
Yield Not To Temptation ... 7" ... Vocalion ... VP9232 ... 1965 £**8** ... £**4**
Yield Not To Temptation ... 7" EP ... Vocalion ... VEP170153 ... 1963 £**30** ... £**15**
You're The One That I Need ... 7" ... Vogue ... V9190 ... 1962 £**15** ... £**7.50**

BLANE, MARCIE

Bobby's Girl ... 7" ... London ... HLU9599 ... 1962 £**12** ... £**6**
How Can I Tell Him ... 7" ... London ... HLU9673 ... 1963 £**5** ... £**2**
Little Miss Fool ... 7" ... London ... HLU9744 ... 1963 £**5** ... £**2**
Marcie Blane ... 7" EP ... London ... REU1413 ... 1964 £**60** ... £**30**
You Gave My Number To Billy ... 7" ... London ... HLU9787 ... 1963 £**6** ... £**2.50**

BLANKE, TOTO

Spider's Dance ... LP ... Vertigo ... 6360623 ... 1975 £**15** ... £**6** ... *German*

BLANKS

Northern Ripper ... 7" ... Void ... SRTS79CUS560 ... 1979 £**10** ... £**5**

BLAST FURNACE

Blast Furnace ... LP ... Polydor ... 2380013 ... 1971 £**75** ... £**37.50** ... *Danish*

BLASTERS

American Music ... LP ... Rollin' Rock ... 021 ... 1980 £**25** ... £**10** ... *US*

BLAZER BLAZER

Cecil B. Devine ... 7" ... Logo ... GO362 ... 1978 £**15** ... £**7.50**

BLAZERS

Rock And Roll ... 10" LP ... Fontana ... TFR6010 ... 1958 £**40** ... £**20**

BLAZING SONS

Chant Down The National Front ... 7" ... Cool Ghoul ... COOL002 ... 1983 £**6** ... £**2.50**

BLEACH BOYS

Chloroform ... 7" ... Tramp ... THF002 ... 1978 £**20** ... £**10**
Gimme That Neutron Taste ... 12" ... Zombie International ... ZOMBO103010 ... 1985 £**15** ... £**7.50**

BLEAK HOUSE

Chase The Wind ... 7" ... Buzzard ... BUZZ2 ... 1982 £**30** ... £**15**
Rainbow Warrior ... 7" ... Buzzard ... BUZZ1 ... 198– £**60** ... £**30** ... *picture sleeve*

BLEECHERS

Come Into My Parlour ... 7" ... Upsetter ... US314 ... 1969 £**5** ... £**2** ... *Melotones B side*
Ease Up ... 7" ... Trojan ... TR679 ... 1969 £**5** ... £**2**
Send Me The Pillow ... 7" ... Columbia ... DB118 ... 1970 £**5** ... £**2**

BLEGVAD, PETER

Title	Format	Label	Number	Year	Mint	VG	Notes
Alcohol	7"	Recommended	RR5.75	1981	£4	£1.50	*1 side engraved*

BLENDELLS

Title	Format	Label	Number	Year	Mint	VG	Notes
Dance With Me	7"	Reprise	R20340	1964	£4	£1.50	
Lalalalalala	7"	Reprise	R20291	1964	£4	£1.50	

BLESSED END

Title	Format	Label	Number	Year	Mint	VG	Notes
Movin' On	LP	Tns	J248	1971	£150	£75	*US*

BLESSING, MICHAEL

Before becoming a Monkee, Mike Nesmith recorded as Michael Blessing.

Title	Format	Label	Number	Year	Mint	VG	Notes
New Recruit	7"	Colpix	787	1965	£25	£12.50	*US, probably promo only*
Until It's Time For You To Go	7"	Colpix	792	1965	£25	£12.50	*US, probably promo only*

BLEY, CARLA

Carla Bley's *Escalator Over The Hill* is a jazz opera, covering a range of musical styles, and bringing together some unlikely combinations of musicians. Linda Ronstadt and John McLaughlin, Don Cherry and Jack Bruce, Paul Jones and Gato Barbieri all have key roles in a work that continues to grow in stature. Carla Bley has never quite achieved this greatness again, and few other composers have either.

Title	Format	Label	Number	Year	Mint	VG	Notes
Escalator Over The Hill	LP	JCOA	EOTH3	1972	£25	£10	*triple, boxed*

BLEY, PAUL

Pianist Paul Bley is a major, though often unheralded, figure within jazz. Playing with Ornette Coleman in the fifties (documented rather belatedly on the *Fabulous Paul Bley Quintet* album), Bley went on to become a very early synthesizer pioneer, touring with the huge, distinctly user-unfriendly machines that were the early seventies state of the art.

Title	Format	Label	Number	Year	Mint	VG	Notes
Ballads	LP	ECM	ECM1010ST	1971	£20	£8	
Barrage	LP	ESP-Disk	1008	1965	£20	£8	*US*
Fabulous Paul Bley Quintet	LP	America	30AM6120	1972	£15	£6	
Mr Joy	LP	Mercury	SMWL21050	1969	£20	£8	
Open, To Love	LP	ECM	ECM1023ST	1973	£12	£5	
Pastorius/Metheny/Ditmas/Bley	LP	Improvising Artists	373846	1976	£12	£5	*US*
Paul Bley	10" LP	Vogue	LDE171	1956	£50	£25	
Paul Bley Synthesizer Show	LP	Milestone	MSP9033	1971	£30	£15	*US*
Paul Bley With Gary Peacock	LP	ECM	ECM1003ST	1970	£12	£5	
Scorpio	LP	Milestone	MSP9046	1973	£15	£6	*US*
Touching	LP	Fontana	SFJL929	1969	£25	£10	

BLEY, PAUL & ANNETTE PEACOCK

Title	Format	Label	Number	Year	Mint	VG	Notes
Dual Unity	LP	Freedom	2383105	1972	£30	£15	
Improvisie	LP	America	30AM6121	1973	£30	£15	*French*
Revenge	LP	Polydor	2425043	1971	£40	£20	

BLEYER, ARCHIE

Title	Format	Label	Number	Year	Mint	VG	Notes
Amber	7"	London	HL8035	1954	£15	£7.50	
Bridge Of Happiness	7"	London	HLA8263	1956	£6	£2.50	
Hernando's Hideaway	7"	London	HLA8176	1955	£12	£6	
Naughty Lady Of Shady Lane	7"	London	HL8111	1954	£15	£7.50	
Nothin' To Do	7"	London	HLA8243	1956	£6	£2.50	

BLIND BLAKE

Title	Format	Label	Number	Year	Mint	VG	Notes
Blind Blake	10" LP	Collector	JFL2001	1960	£20	£8	
Blind Blake 1927–30	LP	Whoopee	101	196–	£10	£4	
Blues In Chicago	LP	Riverside	RLP8804	1967	£15	£6	
Hey Hey Daddy Blues	78	Tempo	R23	1950	£5	£2	
Legendary Blind Blake	10" LP	Ristic	LP18	1958	£30	£15	

BLIND BLAKE & CHARLIE JACKSON

Title	Format	Label	Number	Year	Mint	VG	Notes
Blind Blake And Charlie Jackson	LP	Heritage	HLP1011	1960	£25	£10	

BLIND BLAKE & RAMBLING THOMAS

Title	Format	Label	Number	Year	Mint	VG	Notes
Male Blues Vol. 3	7" EP	Collector	JEL4	1959	£8	£4	

BLIND FAITH

Title	Format	Label	Number	Year	Mint	VG	Notes
Blind Faith	CD	Mobile Fidelity	UDCD507	1988	£15	£6	*US audiophile*
Blind Faith	LP	Polydor	583059	1969	£12	£5	*gatefold sleeve*
Instrumental (Change Of Address)	7"	Island	no number	1969	£150	£75	*promo*

BLIND RAVAGE

Title	Format	Label	Number	Year	Mint	VG	Notes
Blind Ravage	LP	Crescent Street	CS1874	1972	£25	£10	*Canadian*

BLINKERS

Title	Format	Label	Number	Year	Mint	VG	Notes
Original Sin	7"	Pye	7N17752	1969	£40	£20	

BLISS

Title	Format	Label	Number	Year	Mint	VG	Notes
Bliss	LP	Canyon	7707	1969	£60	£30	*US*
Castles In Castille	7"	Chapter One	CH107	1969	£5	£2	

BLISS, MELVIN

Title	Format	Label	Cat. No.	Year	Mint	VG+	Notes
Reward	7"	Contempo	CS2013	1977	**£8**	**£4**	

BLITZ

Title	Format	Label	Cat. No.	Year	Mint	VG+	Notes
All Out Attack	7"	No Future	OI1	1982	**£15**	**£7.50**	
All Out Attack	7"	No Future	OI1	1981	**£5**	**£2**	*white label*
Never Surrender	7"	No Future	OI6	1982	**£5**	**£2**	
Voice Of A Generation	LP	No Future	PUNK1	1982	**£10**	**£4**	
Warriors	7"	No Future	OI16	1982	**£5**	**£2**	

BLITZ BOYS

Title	Format	Label	Cat. No.	Year	Mint	VG+	Notes
Eddy's New Shoes	12"	Told You So	TYS001	1981	**£30**	**£15**	

BLITZKRIEG

Title	Format	Label	Cat. No.	Year	Mint	VG+	Notes
Buried Alive	7"	Neat	NEAT10	1981	**£25**	**£12.50**	
Time Of Changes	LP	Neat	NEAT1023	1985	**£15**	**£6**	

BLITZKRIEG(2)

Title	Format	Label	Cat. No.	Year	Mint	VG+	Notes
Lest We Forget	7"	No Future	OI8	1982	**£5**	**£2**	

BLITZKRIEG BOP

Title	Format	Label	Cat. No.	Year	Mint	VG+	Notes
Let's Go	7"	Lightning	GTL504	1977	**£20**	**£10**	
Let's Go	7"	Mortonsound	MTN3172/3	1977	**£30**	**£15**	
U.F.O.	7"	Lightning	GTL543	1978	**£12**	**£6**	

BLIZZARDS

Title	Format	Label	Cat. No.	Year	Mint	VG+	Notes
I'm Your Guy	LP	Fontana	885424	1966	**£100**	**£50**	*German*

BLODWYN PIG

The natural successor to the bluesy, jazzy music to be found on Jethro Tull's first LP, *This Was*, is Blodwyn Pig's *Ahead Rings Out*, rather than the later recordings of Ian Anderson and his cohorts. The common factor, of course, is guitarist Mick Abrahams, whose distinctive playing-style dominates both records. For Blodwyn Pig, he found an ideal foil in Jack Lancaster, whose fluent work on saxophones and flute is far more noteworthy than Ian Anderson's flautistry.

Title	Format	Label	Cat. No.	Year	Mint	VG+	Notes
Ahead Rings Out	LP	Island	ILPS9101	1969	**£20**	**£8**	*pink label*
Dear Jill	7"	Island	WIP6059	1969	**£5**	**£2**	
Getting To This	LP	Chrysalis	ILPS9122	1970	**£12**	**£5**	
Same Old Story	7"	Island	WIP6078	1969	**£5**	**£2**	
Walk On The Water	7"	Island	WIP6069	1969	**£5**	**£2**	

BLOND

Title	Format	Label	Cat. No.	Year	Mint	VG+	Notes
Blond	LP	Fontana	SRF67607	1969	**£30**	**£15**	*US*
Lilac Years	LP	Fontana	STL5515	1969	**£100**	**£50**	
Wake Up And Call	7"	Fontana	TF1040	1969	**£5**	**£2**	

BLONDE ON BLONDE

Title	Format	Label	Cat. No.	Year	Mint	VG+	Notes
All Day All Night	7"	Pye	7N17637	1968	**£40**	**£20**	
Blonde On Blonde	LP	Ember	LP7005	1972	**£100**	**£50**	*test pressing only*
Castles In The Sky	7"	Ember	EMBS279	1970	**£12**	**£6**	*picture sleeve*
Castles In The Sky	7"	Ember	EMBS279	1970	**£5**	**£2**	
Contrasts	LP	Pye	NSPL18288	1969	**£40**	**£20**	
Rebirth	LP	Ember	NR5049	1970	**£25**	**£10**	
Reflections On A Life	LP	Ember	NR5058	1971	**£25**	**£10**	

BLONDIE

Title	Format	Label	Cat. No.	Year	Mint	VG+	Notes
Auto-American Interview	7"	Fan Club	FLX146	1980	**£10**	**£5**	*flexi*
Blondie	LP	Private Stock	PVLP1017	1977	**£10**	**£4**	
Call Me	CD-s	Chrysalis	CHSCD3342	1989	**£5**	**£2**	
Denis 88	CD-s	Chrysalis	CHSCD3328	1988	**£5**	**£2**	
Encounters With Blondie	LP	Chrysalis	CDMR1		**£50**	**£25**	*double*
Hunter	LP	Chrysalis	PCDL1384	1982	**£10**	**£4**	*picture disc*
In The Flesh	7"	Private Stock	PVT105	1977	**£12**	**£6**	*no picture sleeve*
Parallel Lines	LP	Chrysalis	PCDL1192	1978	**£12**	**£5**	*US picture disc*
Parallel Lines	LP	Mobile Fidelity	MFSL1050	1981	**£12**	**£5**	*US audiophile*
Rip Her To Shreds	7"	Chrysalis	CHS2180	1977	**£5**	**£2**	*picture sleeve*
X Offender	7"	Private Stock	PVT90	1977	**£600**	**£400**	*best auctioned*

BLOOD

Title	Format	Label	Cat. No.	Year	Mint	VG+	Notes
Megalomania	7"	No Future	OI22	1983	**£5**	**£2**	
Stark Raving Normal	7"	Noise	NOY1	1983	**£5**	**£2**	

BLOOD, SWEAT & TEARS

Title	Format	Label	Cat. No.	Year	Mint	VG+	Notes
Blood, Sweat & Tears	LP	Columbia	CQ30994	1973	**£10**	**£4**	*US quad*
Child Is Father To The Man	LP	CBS	63296	1968	**£10**	**£4**	
Child Is Father To The Man	LP	Columbia	HC49619	1981	**£10**	**£4**	*US audiophile*
Greatest Hits	LP	Columbia	CQ31170	1973	**£10**	**£4**	*US quad*
I Can't Quit Her	7"	CBS	3563	1968	**£4**	**£1.50**	

BLOODY MARY

Title	Format	Label	Cat. No.	Year	Mint	VG+	Notes
Bloody Mary	LP	Family	2707	1972	**£30**	**£15**	*US*

BLOOM, ROGER HAMMER

Title	Format	Label	Cat. No.	Year	Mint	VG+	Notes
Out Of The Blue	7"	CBS	202654	1967	**£6**	**£2.50**	

BLOOMFIELD, MIKE

Analine	LP	Sonet	SNTF749	1977	**£10**	**£4**	
If You Love Those Blues	LP	Sonet	SNTF726	1977	**£10**	**£4**	
It's Not Killing Me	LP	CBS	63652	1969	**£12**	**£5**	
Live At Bill Graham's Fillmore West	LP	CBS	63816	1969	**£10**	**£4**	
Try It Before You Buy It	LP	Columbia	PC33173	1973	**£10**	**£4**	*US*

BLOOMFIELD, MIKE & AL KOOPER

Live Adventures	LP	CBS	66216	1969	**£20**	**£8**	*double*
Weight	7"	CBS	4094	1969	**£5**	**£2**	

BLOOMFIELD, MIKE, DR JOHN, JOHN HAMMOND

Triumvirate	LP	CBS	65659	1973	**£10**	**£4**	

BLOSSOM TOES

Blossom Toes was one of the most interesting groups to emerge out of the psychedelic period, but failed to find the success it deserved. The first album contains inspired pop, imaginatively arranged in the *Sgt Pepper* manner. The second is very different in sound, presenting guitar-based rock with a hard edge, but with all the creative imagination still intact. The group members all managed to sustain subsequent careers, especially guitarists Jim Cregan and Brian Godding – the former playing for Family and Rod Stewart amongst others, while the latter has placed his increasingly finely honed technique and imagination at the disposal of such diverse employers as Keith Tippett, Mike Westbrook and Kevin Coyne, before recording an impressive solo album in 1988. What is in effect a third Blossom Toes LP was issued under the name of B. B. Blunder in 1971.

I'll Be Your Baby Tonight	7"	Marmalade	598009	1968	**£15**	**£7.50**	
If Only For A Moment	LP	Marmalade	608010	1969	**£75**	**£37.50**	
New Day	7"	Marmalade	598022	1969	**£100**	**£50**	*test pressing only*
Peace Loving Man	7"	Marmalade	598014	1969	**£15**	**£7.50**	
Postcard	7"	Marmalade	598012	1969	**£15**	**£7.50**	
We Are Ever So Clean	LP	Marmalade	607/608001	1967	**£75**	**£37.50**	
What On Earth	7"	Marmalade	598002	1967	**£40**	**£20**	*picture sleeve*
What On Earth	7"	Marmalade	598002	1967	**£20**	**£10**	

BLOSSOMS

Led by Darlene Love, the Blossoms provided backing vocals for a vast number of other artists, including Elvis Presley. The high value of 'Things Are Changing', however, derives from the fact that it is a rare collaboration between Phil Spector, who produced, and Brian Wilson, who played piano.

Baby Daddy-O	7"	Capitol	CL14947	1958	**£30**	**£15**	
Blossoms	LP	MGM	LN1007	1972	**£20**	**£8**	*US*
Little Louie	7"	Capitol	CL14856	1958	**£30**	**£15**	
Move On	7"	Capitol	CL14833	1958	**£25**	**£12.50**	
Things Are Changing	7"	EOEOC		1965	**£200**	**£100**	*US*

BLOSSOMS (2)

Stand By	7"	Pama	PM814	1971	**£10**	**£5**	

BLOUNT, MICHAEL

Fantasies	LP	York	FYK414	1973	**£12**	**£5**	
Patchwork	LP	CBS	64230	1970	**£15**	**£6**	
Souvenirs	LP	York	FYK401	1972	**£12**	**£5**	

BLOW MONKEYS

Celebrate The Day	CD-s	RCA	MONKC6	1989	**£5**	**£2**	
Celebrate The Day After You	10"	RCA	MONKX6	1987	**£10**	**£5**	
Choice	CD-s	RCA	PD42886	1989	**£5**	**£2**	
It Pays To Belong	CD-s	RCA	PD42232	1988	**£5**	**£2**	*in tin box*
Live Today Love Tomorrow	7"	Parasol	PAR1	1980	**£4**	**£1.50**	
Out With Her	CD-s	RCA	MONKC5	1987	**£5**	**£2**	
Passionara	CD-s	RCA	PD43864	1990	**£5**	**£2**	
Slaves No More	CD-s	RCA	PD43202	1989	**£5**	**£2**	*with Sylvia Tella*
Springtime For The World	CD-s	RCA	PD43624	1990	**£5**	**£2**	
This Is Your Life	CD-s	RCA	PD42696	1989	**£5**	**£2**	
This Is Your Life	CD-s	RCA	PD42150	1988	**£5**	**£2**	

BLUE, BABBITY

Don't Hurt Me	7"	Decca	F12149	1965	**£4**	**£1.50**	
Don't Make Me	7"	Decca	F12053	1965	**£4**	**£1.50**	

BLUE, BOBBY

Going In Circles	7"	Duke	DU86	1970	**£4**	**£1.50**	

BLUE, DAVID

23 Days In September	LP	Reprise	RS6293	1968	**£15**	**£6**	*US*
David Blue	LP	Elektra	EKL4003	1966	**£20**	**£8**	
Me	LP	Reprise	RS6375	1970	**£12**	**£5**	*US*
Nice Baby And The Angel	LP	Asylum	SYL9009	1973	**£10**	**£4**	
Stories	LP	Asylum	SYL9001	1972	**£10**	**£4**	

BLUE, PAMELA

My Friend Bobby	7"	Decca	F11761	1963	**£60**	**£30**	

BLUE, TIMOTHY

Room At The Top Of The Stairs	7"	Spark	SRL1014	1968	**£10**	**£5**	

BLUE ACES

All I Want	7"	Columbia	DB7755	1965	**£20**	**£10**	

I Beat You To It	7"	Pye	7N15713	1964	**£4**	**£1.50**	
Land Of Love	7"	Pye	7N15672	1964	**£4**	**£1.50**	
Talk About My Baby	7"	Columbia	DB7954	1966	**£50**	**£25**	
You Don't Care	7"	Pye	7N15821	1965	**£4**	**£1.50**	

BLUE & FERRIS

You Stole My Money	7"	Blue Cat	BS147	1968	**£6**	**£2.50**	

BLUE ANGEL

Blue Angel made an album and two singles, but the group's lead singer only found success once she had decided to go solo. Her name: Cyndi Lauper.

Blue Angel	LP	Polydor	2391486	1980	**£15**	**£6**	
I Had A Love	7"	Polydor	POSP241	1981	**£12**	**£6**	
I'm Gonna Be Strong	7"	Polydor	POSP212	1984	**£6**	**£2.50**	*reissue, picture sleeve*
I'm Gonna Be Strong	7"	Polydor	POSP212	1980	**£12**	**£6**	

BLUE BARONS

Twist To The Great Blues Hits	LP	Philips	PHM2/ PHS600017	1962	**£25**	**£10**	*US*

BLUE BEATS

Beatle Beat	LP	A.A.	133	1964	**£30**	**£15**	*US*

BLUE BLOOD

Blue Blood	LP	Sonet	SNTF615	1970	**£15**	**£6**	

BLUE CATS

Beat Beat Beat	LP	Starlet	3261	1965	**£20**	**£8**	*German*

BLUE CHEER

Blue Cheer	LP	Philips	6336001	1969	**£15**	**£6**	
Feathers From Your Tree	7"	Philips	BF1711	1968	**£4**	**£1.50**	
Just A Little Bit	7"	Philips	BF1684	1968	**£4**	**£1.50**	
New Improved	LP	Philips	SBL7896	1969	**£15**	**£6**	
Oh Pleasant Hope	LP	Philips	PHS600350	1971	**£30**	**£15**	*US*
Original Human Being	LP	Philips	6336004	1970	**£20**	**£8**	
Outside Inside	LP	Philips	SBL7860	1968	**£30**	**£15**	
Pilot	7"	Philips	6051010	1971	**£4**	**£1.50**	
Summertime Blues	7"	Philips	BF1646	1968	**£6**	**£2.50**	
Vincebus Eruptum	LP	Philips	BL7839	1968	**£30**	**£15**	*mono*
Vincebus Eruptum	LP	Philips	SBL7839	1967	**£25**	**£10**	*stereo*
West Coast Child Of Sunshine	7"	Philips	BF1778	1969	**£4**	**£1.50**	

BLUE CHIPS

I'm On The Right Side	7"	Pye	7N15970	1965	**£15**	**£7.50**	
Some Kind Of Lovin'	7"	Pye	7N17111	1966	**£15**	**£7.50**	
Tell Her	7"	Pye	7N17155	1966	**£15**	**£7.50**	

BLUE DIAMONDS

Always	10" LP	Decca	60413	1962	**£40**	**£20**	*Dutch*
I'm Forever Blowing Bubbles	7" EP	Decca	DFE6675	1960	**£6**	**£2.50**	
Ramona	LP	Fontana	ST701595	1969	**£15**	**£6**	*German*
Weltschlager	LP	Fontana	680517	1963	**£40**	**£20**	*German*

BLUE EFFECT

Kingdom Of Life	LP	Supraphon	1131023	1971	**£25**	**£10**	*Czechoslovakian*

BLUE EPITAPH

Ode	LP	Holyground	HG117	1974	**£200**	**£100**	

BLUE FLAMES

The two instrumental singles credited to the Blue Flames are the earliest recordings made by Georgie Fame's band, with Fame himself on the organ.

J.A. Blues	7"	R&B	JB114	1963	**£25**	**£12.50**	
Stop Right Here	7"	R&B	JB126	1963	**£25**	**£12.50**	

BLUE GOOSE

Blue Goose's guitarist was Eddie Clarke, who subsequently became one third of the classic Motorhead line-up.

Blue Goose	LP	Anchor	ANCL2005	1975	**£10**	**£4**	

BLUE JEANS

Hey Mrs Housewife	7"	Columbia	DB8555	1969	**£15**	**£7.50**	

BLUE MEN

I Hear A New World	7" EP	Triumph	RGXST5000	1960	**£400**	**£250**	*best auctioned*
I Hear A New World	LP	Triumph	TRXST9000	1960	**£1000**	**£700**	*demo, best auctioned*
I Hear A New World Part Two	7" EP	Triumph	RGXST5001	1960	**£60**	**£30**	*sleeve only*

BLUE MOUNTAIN EAGLE

Blue Mountain Eagle	LP	Atco	SD33324	1970	**£10**	**£4**	*US*

BLUE NILE

Downtown Lights	CD-s	Linn	LKSCD3	1989	**£8**	**£4**	*3" single*
Hats	CD	Linn	LKHCD2	1990	**£15**	**£6**	*promo in round box*

Title	Format	Label	Cat. No.	Year	Mint	VG	Notes
Headlights On The Parade	CD-s	Linn	LKSCD4	1990	£5	£2	
I Love This Life	7"	RSO	RSO84	1981	£15	£7.50	
Saturday Night	CD-s	Linn	LKSCD5	1991	£5	£2	

BLUE NOTES

Title	Format	Label	Cat. No.	Year	Mint	VG	Notes
For Johnny	LP	Ogun	OG532	1987	£12	£5	
For Mongezi	LP	Ogun	OGD001/002		£20	£8	*double*
In Concert Vol. 1	LP	Ogun	OG220	1978	£15	£6	

BLUE OYSTER CULT

Title	Format	Label	Cat. No.	Year	Mint	VG	Notes
Astronomy	CD-s	CBS	6529852	1988	£5	£2	
Don't Fear The Reaper/Tattoo Vampire	7"	CBS	4483	1976	£6	£2.50	*demo*
Live Bootleg	10" LP	Columbia	AS40	1973	£15	£6	*US promo*
Secret Treaties	LP	CBS	PCQ32858	1974	£10	£4	*US quad*
Tyranny and Mutation	LP	CBS	PCQ32017	1973	£10	£4	*US quad*

BLUE PHANTOM

Title	Format	Label	Cat. No.	Year	Mint	VG	Notes
Distortions	LP	Kaleidoscope	KAL101	1972	£60	£30	

BLUE RONDOS

Title	Format	Label	Cat. No.	Year	Mint	VG	Notes
Don't Want Your Lovin'	7"	Pye	7N15833	1965	£30	£15	
Little Baby	7"	Pye	7N15734	1964	£50	£25	

BLUE STARS

Title	Format	Label	Cat. No.	Year	Mint	VG	Notes
I Can Take It	7"	Decca	F12303	1965	£100	£50	

BLUE SUN

Title	Format	Label	Cat. No.	Year	Mint	VG	Notes
Blue Sun	LP	Parlophone	1019	1971	£20	£8	*Danish*
Peace Be Unto You	LP	Spectator	SL1013	1970	£20	£8	*Danish*

BLUE THINGS

Title	Format	Label	Cat. No.	Year	Mint	VG	Notes
Blue Things	LP	RCA	LPM/LSP3603	1966	£75	£37.50	*US*

BLUE VELVET BAND

Title	Format	Label	Cat. No.	Year	Mint	VG	Notes
Sweet Moments	LP	Warner Bros	WS1802	1969	£20	£8	*US*

BLUE YOGURT

Title	Format	Label	Cat. No.	Year	Mint	VG	Notes
Lydia	7"	Penny Farthing	PEN732	1970	£5	£2	

BLUE ZONE

Title	Format	Label	Cat. No.	Year	Mint	VG	Notes
On Fire	CD-s	Rockin' Horse	RHCD116	1987	£6	£2.50	*3" single*
Thinking About His Baby	CD-s	Rockin' Horse	RHCD115	1987	£6	£2.50	*3" single*

BLUEBEARD

Title	Format	Label	Cat. No.	Year	Mint	VG	Notes
Bluebeard	LP	Ember	LT7004	1971	£400	£250	*test pressing*
Country Man	7"	Ember	EMBS302	1971	£10	£5	*picture sleeve*

BLUEBEATS

Title	Format	Label	Cat. No.	Year	Mint	VG	Notes
Fabulous Bluebeats Vol. 1	7" EP	Ember	EMBEP4525	1962	£40	£20	
Fabulous Bluebeats Vol. 2	7" EP	Ember	EMBEP4526	1962	£40	£20	

BLUEBELLS

Title	Format	Label	Cat. No.	Year	Mint	VG	Notes
Young At Heart	7"	London	LON49	1984	£4	£1.50	*shaped picture disc*

BLUEBERRIES

Title	Format	Label	Cat. No.	Year	Mint	VG	Notes
It's Gonna Work Out Fine	7"	Mercury	MF894	1965	£20	£10	

BLUES ADDICTS

Title	Format	Label	Cat. No.	Year	Mint	VG	Notes
Blues Addicts	LP	Spectator	1015	1970	£150	£75	*Danish*

BLUES BAND

Title	Format	Label	Cat. No.	Year	Mint	VG	Notes
Official Bootleg Album	LP	Arista	BBBP101	1980	£10	£4	*autographed*

BLUES BLENDERS

Title	Format	Label	Cat. No.	Year	Mint	VG	Notes
Girl Next Door	7"	Rio	R93	1966	£6	£2.50	

BLUES BROTHERS

Title	Format	Label	Cat. No.	Year	Mint	VG	Notes
Everybody Needs Somebody To Love	CD-s	Atlantic	A7951CD	1990	£5	£2	
Soul Man	CD-s	Atlantic	A7897CD	1990	£5	£2	

BLUES BUSTERS

Title	Format	Label	Cat. No.	Year	Mint	VG	Notes
Behold!	LP	Island	ILP923	1965	£100	£50	
Behold!	LP	Trojan	TTl42	1970	£20	£8	
Blues Busters	LP	Doctor Bird	DLM5008	1966	£75	£37.50	
Donna	7"	Blue Beat	BB55	1961	£12	£6	
How Sweet It Is	7"	Island	WI214	1965	£10	£5	
I've Been Trying	7"	Doctor Bird	DB1030	1966	£10	£5	
Little Vilma	7"	Limbo	XL101	1960	£12	£6	
Oh Baby	7"	Island	WI023	1962	£10	£5	
Philip And Lloyd	LP	Dynamic	DYLP3007	1976	£10	£4	
Spiritual	7"	Starlite	ST45031	1961	£12	£6	
Tell Me Why	7"	Blue Beat	BB102	1962	£12	£6	
There's Always A Sunshine	7"	Doctor Bird	DB1078	1967	£10	£5	
There's Always Sunshine	7"	Blue Beat	BB73	1962	£12	£6	
Wings Of A Dove	7"	Island	WI222	1965	£10	£5	*Byron Lee B side*

Your Love	7"	Starlite	ST45072	1962	£12	£6	

BLUES BY FIVE

Boom Boom	7"	Decca	F12029	1964	£40	£20	

BLUES CLIMAX

Blues Climax	LP	Horn	JC888	1972	£15	£6	*US*

BLUES COUNCIL

Baby Don't Look Down	7"	Parlophone	R5264	1965	£50	£25	

BLUES DIMENSION

Blues Dimension	LP	Decca	ND254	1969	£12	£5	*German*

BLUES FIVE

Running Away From Love	7"	Studio 36		1965	£75	£37.50	

BLUES MAGOOS

Basic Blues Magoos	LP	Mercury	MG2/SR61167	1968	£40	£20	*US*
Blues Magoos	LP	Fontana	(S)TL5402	1966	£40	£20	
Electric Comic Book	LP	Mercury	MG2/SR61104	1967	£50	£25	*US, with comic*
Gulf Coast Bound	LP	Probe	SPB1024	1971	£20	£8	
Never Going Back To Georgia	LP	ABC	S697	1969	£25	£10	*US*
One By One	7"	Fontana	TF848	1967	£12	£6	
Psychedelic Lollipop	LP	Mercury	MG2/SR61096	1966	£50	£25	*US*
We Ain't Got Nothin' Yet	7"	Mercury	MF954	1966	£20	£10	
We Ain't Got Nothin' Yet	7" EP	Mercury	126221	1967	£50	£25	*French*

BLUES MESSAGE

Golden Cups Album	LP	Capitol	CPC8005	1969	£30	£15	*Japanese*

BLUES PROJECT

The Blues Project had an important role within the growing maturity of rock music during the sixties, which the loss of credibility of leading member Al Kooper in the succeeding years should do nothing to diminish. The group had a loose, improvisational approach to the blues, in which Andy Kulberg's flute playing was an effective element. *Lazarus* and *Blues Project* represent an attempt to revive the group in the seventies, but by then the spark had inevitably gone.

Blues Project	LP	Capitol	EST11017	1972	£10	£4	
Flanders, Kalb, Katz . . .	LP	Verve	FTS3069	1969	£15	£6	*US*
I Can't Keep From Crying	7"	Verve	VS1505	1967	£10	£5	
Lazarus	LP	Capitol	ST872	1971	£15	£6	*US*
Live At The Café Au Go-Go	LP	Verve	FT(S)3000	1966	£30	£15	*US*
Live At Town Hall	LP	Verve	FT(S)3025	1967	£30	£15	*US*
No Time Like The Right Time	7" EP	Verve	519905	1967	£50	£25	*French*
Planned Obsolescence	LP	Verve	FTS3046	1968	£25	£10	*US*
Projections	LP	Verve	(S)VLP6009	1967	£25	£10	
Reunion In Central Park	LP	MCA	8003	1973	£15	£6	*US*

BLUES SECTION

Once More On The Road	LP	Love	2	1967	£20	£8	*Finnish*

BLUESBREAKERS

Curly	7"	Decca	F12588	1967	£5	£2	

BLUESOLOGY

Bluesology worked as the backing group for Long John Baldry when the singer was still performing rhythm and blues. The group's pianist was Reg Dwight – or rather Elton John, as he subsequently chose to be known.

Come Back Baby	7"	Fontana	TF594	1965	£250	£150	*best auctioned*
Mr Frantic	7"	Fontana	TF668	1966	£250	£150	*best auctioned*
Since I Found You Baby	7"	Polydor	56195	1967	£250	£150	*with Stu Brown, best auctioned*

BLUETONES

Are You Blue Or Are You Blind?	12"	Superior Quality Rec.	BLUE001T	1995	£10	£5	
Are You Blue Or Are You Blind?	7"	Superior Quality Rec.	BLUE001X	1995	£5	£2	
Are You Blue Or Are You Blind?	CD-s	Superior Quality Rec.	BLUE001CD	1995	£10	£5	
Bluetonic	12"	Superior Quality Rec.	BLUE002T	1995	£6	£2.50	
Bluetonic	7"	Superior Quality Rec.	BLUE002X	1995	£4	£1.50	
Bluetonic	CD-s	Superior Quality Rec.	BLUE002CD	1995	£5	£2	
Expecting To Fly	LP	Superior Quality Rec.	BLUELPX004	1996	£15	£6	*with plastic sleeve*
Slight Return	7"	Superior Quality Rec.	BLUE003X	1996	£50	£25	*red vinyl*
Slight Return	7"	Superior Quality Rec.	TONE001	1995	£25	£12.50	*blue vinyl*
Slight Return	7"	Superior Quality Rec.	TONE001	1995	£40	£20	*red vinyl, export*

BLUEWATER FOLK

Bluewater Folk	LP	Folk Heritage	FH24	197–	£150	£75	

Bugs, Black Puddings And Clogs	LP	Moonraker	MOO1	197–	**£20**	**£8**	
Lancashire Life	LP	Moonraker	MOO2	197–	**£20**	**£8**	

BLUNSTONE, COLIN

Ennismore	LP	Epic	EPC65278	1972	**£10**	**£4**	
One Year	LP	Epic	EPC64557	1971	**£10**	**£4**	

BLUR

The media-provoked competition between Blur and Oasis in 1995 did Blur few favours, since their more thoughtful, less bombastic material was always likely to be overshadowed in such a contest. In fact, however, Blur's development from the laddish guitar pop of their first singles to the carefully constructed arrangements of their more recent music has been remarkable. It is likely that Damon Albarn and his colleagues will be a musical force to be reckoned with for a considerable time to come.

Bang	12"	Food	12FOOD31	1991	**£10**	**£5**	
Bang	7"	Food	FOOD31	1991	**£5**	**£2**	
Bang	CD-s	Food	CDFOOD31	1991	**£25**	**£12.50**	
Basically Blur	CD	SBK		1992	**£30**	**£15**	*US promo*
Bet Bet Bet	CD-s	EMI	SPCD1736	1995	**£60**	**£30**	*4 track French promo*
Blue To Go	CD	SBK	DPRO5455	1993	**£15**	**£6**	*US promo*
Blurb	CD	Food	CDIN106	1997	**£20**	**£8**	*interview promo*
Chemical World	12"	Food	12FOOD45	1993	**£12**	**£6**	
Chemical World	7"	Food	FOODS45	1993	**£10**	**£5**	*red vinyl*
Chemical World	CD-s	Food	CDFOOD(S)45	1993	**£20**	**£10**	*2 versions*
Country House	12"	Food	12FOODDJ63	1995	**£8**	**£4**	*promo*
Death Of A Party	CD-s	Food	CDFOODDJ109	1997	**£6**	**£2.50**	*promo*
Death Of A Party	CD-s	Fan Club	DEATH1	1996	**£8**	**£4**	
Focusing In With Blur	CD	SBK	DPRO5424	1993	**£15**	**£6**	*US promo*
For Tomorrow	12"	Food	12FOOD40	1992	**£10**	**£5**	
For Tomorrow	CD-s	Food	CD(S)FOOD40	1993	**£20**	**£10**	*2 versions*
Girls And Boys	CD-s	Food	CDFOOD(S)47	1994	**£6**	**£2.50**	*2 versions*
High Cool	12"	Food	12BLUR4	1991	**£20**	**£10**	*promo*
I Love Her	CD-s	Fan Club	LOVE001	1997	**£8**	**£4**	
On Your Own	12"	Food	12BLURDJ7	1997	**£10**	**£5**	*promo*
Parklife	CD	Food	PCD0476	1994	**£50**	**£25**	*Japanese electronic pack with 5 extra tracks*
Parklife	CD-s	Food	CDFOOD53	1994	**£5**	**£2**	
Parklife	CD-s	Food	CDFOODS53	1994	**£5**	**£2**	
Popscene	12"	Food	12FOOD37	1992	**£15**	**£7.50**	
Popscene	7"	Food	FOOD37	1992	**£10**	**£5**	
Popscene	CD-s	Food	CDFOOD37	1992	**£30**	**£15**	
She's So High	12"	Food	12FOOD26	1990	**£15**	**£7.50**	
She's So High	7"	Food	FOOD26	1990	**£8**	**£4**	
She's So High	CD-s	Food	CDFOOD26	1990	**£25**	**£12.50**	
Special Collectors' Edition	CD	Food	TOCP8395	1994	**£30**	**£15**	*Japanese compilation from first 3 albums*
Sunday Sunday	12"	Food	12FOODS46	1993	**£10**	**£5**	*with print*
Sunday Sunday	7"	Food	FOODS46	1993	**£10**	**£5**	*yellow vinyl*
Sunday Sunday	CD-s	Food	CDFOOD(X)46	1993	**£20**	**£10**	*2 versions*
There's No Other Way	12"	Food	12FOOD29	1991	**£12**	**£6**	
There's No Other Way	7"	Food	FOOD29	1991	**£6**	**£2.50**	
There's No Other Way	CD-s	Food	CDFOOD29	1991	**£25**	**£12.50**	
There's No Other Way (Remix)	12"	Food	12FOODX29	1991	**£20**	**£10**	
This Is A Low	CD-s	Food	CDFOODDJ59	1995	**£8**	**£4**	*promo*
To The End	CD-s	Food	CDFOOD50	1994	**£8**	**£4**	
Universal	12"	Food	12FOODDJ69	1995	**£8**	**£4**	*promo*
Wassailing Song	7"	Food	BLUR6	1992	**£60**	**£30**	*1 sided promo*

BLYTHE, HENRY

Investigation Into Reincarnation	LP	Oriole	MG20009	1956	**£15**	**£6**	

BLYTHE, JIMMY

South Side Blues Piano	10" LP	London	AL3527	1954	**£20**	**£8**	
South Side Chicago Jazz	10" LP	London	AL3529	1954	**£20**	**£8**	

BLYTON, ENID

Noddy Stories	7" EP	HMV	7EG8260	1957	**£5**	**£2**	

BMX BANDITS

Sad?	12"	53rd & 3rd	AGARR312	1986	**£6**	**£2.50**	
Sad?	7"	53rd & 3rd	AGARR3	1986	**£6**	**£2.50**	*with comic*

BO & PEEP

Young Love	7"	Decca	F11968	1964	**£20**	**£10**	

BO STREET RUNNERS

When the cult TV show *Ready Steady Go* organized a beat group talent contest in 1964, the Bo Street Runners were the winners. (The various-artists' LP *Ready Steady Win* documents the affair). As is usually the case with talent contests, however, the win yielded nothing in terms of subsequent success for the Bo Street Runners. The group was led by organist Tim Hinkley, while both Mick Fleetwood and Mike Patto were members for a time.

Baby Never Say Goodbye	7"	Columbia	DB7640	1965	**£30**	**£15**	
Bo Street Runner	7"	Decca	F11986	1964	**£40**	**£20**	
Bo Street Runners	7" EP	Oak	RGJ131	1964	**£750**	**£500**	*best auctioned*
Drive My Car	7"	Columbia	DB7901	1966	**£30**	**£15**	
Tell Me What You're Gonna Do	7"	Columbia	DB7488	1965	**£50**	**£25**	

BOA

Wrong Road	LP	Snakefield	SN001	1969	**£250**	**£150**	*US*

BOARDMAN, HARRY

Lancashire Mon	LP	Topic	12TS236	1974	**£10**	**£4**	

BOARDMAN, HARRY & DAVE HILLERY

Trans Pennine	LP	Topic	12TS215	1971	**£20**	**£8**	

BOARDWALKERS

Miracle	7"	private	JC1	196–	**£100**	**£50**	

BOB

Esmerelda Brooklyn	7"	House Of Teeth	HOT003	1988	**£6**	**£[illegible].50**	
Prune	7"	House Of Teeth		1988	**£5**	**£2**	*flexi*

BOB & BOBBY

The single by Bob and Bobby is one of the small number of outside productions undertaken by Beach Boy Brian Wilson in the sixties.

Twelve-O-Four	7"	Tower	154	1965	**£25**	**£12.50**	*US*

BOB & EARL

Baby I'm Satisfied	7"	Sue	WI393	1965	**£12**	**£6**	
Don't Ever Leave Me	7"	Sue	WI4030	1967	**£12**	**£6**	
Harlem Shuffle	7"	Sue	WI374	1965	**£10**	**£5**	
Harlem Shuffle	LP	Sue	ILP951	1967	**£30**	**£15**	

BOB & JERRY

Ghost Satellite	7"	Pye	7N25003	1958	**£6**	**£2.50**	

BOB & MARCIA

Pied Piper	LP	Trojan	TRLS26	1971	**£10**	**£4**	
Really Together	7"	Bamboo	BAM40	1970	**£6**	**£2.50**	
Young Gifted And Black	7"	Harry J	HJ6605	1970	**£4**	**£1.50**	
Young, Gifted And Black	LP	Trojan	TBL122	1970	**£12**	**£5**	

BOB & SHERI

The ultra-rare single by Bob and Sheri is a Brian Wilson production.

Surfer Moon	7"	Safari	101	1962	**£750**	**£500**	*US, blue label, best auctioned*

BOB & TYRONE

I Don't Care	7"	Coxsone	CS7086	1969	**£12**	**£6**	

BOBBETTES

Come A Come A Come A	7"	London	HLE8597	1958	**£30**	**£15**	
Have Mercy Baby	7"	London	HLU9248	1960	**£15**	**£7.50**	
I Shot Mr Lee	7"	London	HLK9173	1960	**£20**	**£10**	
I Shot Mr Lee	7"	Pye	7N25060	1960	**£20**	**£10**	
Mr Lee	7"	London	HLE8477	1957	**£30**	**£15**	
That's A Bad Thing To Know	7"	Action	ACT4603	1972	**£6**	**£2.50**	

BOBBSEY TWINS

Change Of Heart	7"	London	HLA8474	1957	**£15**	**£7.50**	

BOBBY & DAVE

Build My World Around You	7"	Ackee	ACK116	1971	**£5**	**£2**	

BOBBY & LAURIE

Hitch Hiker	7"	Parlophone	R5480	1966	**£6**	**£2.50**	

BOBBY & THE MIDNITES

Where The Beat Meets The Street	LP	CBS	26046	1984	**£12**	**£5**	

BOBCATS

Can't See For Looking	7"	Pye	7N17242	1967	**£8**	**£4**	

BOBO MR SOUL

Hitch Hiking To Heartbreak	7"	London	HLU10418	1973	**£4**	**£1.50**	

BOCCARA, FRIDA

Through The Eyes Of A Child	7"	Philips	BF1765	1969	**£10**	**£5**	

BOCKY & THE VISIONS

I Go Crazy	7"	Atlantic	AT4049	1965	**£12**	**£6**	

BODGER'S MATE

Brighter Than Usual	LP	Cottage	COT521	1978	**£25**	**£10**	

BODINES

God Bless	7"	Creation	CRE016	1985	**£5**	**£2**	

BODKIN

Bodkin	LP	West	CSA104	1972	**£400**	**£250**	

BODY

Body Album	LP	Recession	REC01	1981	**£40**	**£20**	

BOFFALONGO

Beyond Your Head	LP	United Artists	UAG29130	1970	**£10**	**£4**	
Boffalongo	LP	United Artists	6726	1969	**£12**	**£5**	US

BOGARDE, DIRK

Darling	7"	Fontana	TF615	1965	**£4**	**£1.50**	
Lyrics For Lovers	LP	Decca	LK4373	1960	**£15**	**£6**	

BOGIES

'Bye 'Bye	LP	private	no number	1964	**£200**	**£100**	
On Campus	LP	private	no number	1964	**£200**	**£100**	

BOHEMIAN VENDETTA

Bohemian Vendetta	LP	Mainstream	(S)6106	1968	**£75**	**£37.50**	US

BOINES, HOUSTON

Superintendant Blues	7"	Blue Horizon	451006	1966	**£100**	**£50**	

BOKAJ RETSIEM

Psychedelic Underground	LP	Fass	1532WY	1969	**£15**	**£6**	German

BOLAN, MARC

For an artist with an essentially rather limited talent, Marc Bolan has managed to attract an extraordinarily devoted following. Part of this is no doubt the direct consequence of Bolan's premature death. In any event, there are a number of quite valuable recordings to be found scattered through Bolan's catalogue. These include the original issue of his *Zinc Alloy* LP, which has an individually numbered poster sleeve, and the early solo singles (whose lack of chart success is not hard to understand once they are heard; they are somewhat less than inspiring). Records made with John's Children and Tyrannosaurus Rex are listed under those headings.

Beginning Of Doves	LP	Track	2410201	1974	**£15**	**£6**	
Hard On Love	LP	Track	2406101	1972	**£500**	**£330**	*test pressing*
Hippy Gumbo	7"	Parlophone	R5539	1966	**£500**	**£330**	*best auctioned*
Jasper C. Debussy	7"	Track	2094013	1974	**£12**	**£6**	*picture sleeve*
Road I'm On	7"	Archive Jive	TOBY1	1990	**£8**	**£4**	*as Toby Tyler*
Sailor Of The Highway	7"	Cube	BUG99	1984	**£6**	**£2.50**	*promo*
Third Degree	7"	Decca	F12413	1966	**£500**	**£330**	*best auctioned*
To Know Him Is To Love Him	7"	EMI	EMI2572	1977	**£8**	**£4**	*with Gloria Jones*
Wizard	7"	Decca	F12288	1965	**£300**	**£180**	*best auctioned*
You Scare Me To Death	7"	Cherry Red	CHERRYP29	1981	**£4**	**£1.50**	*picture disc*
You Scare Me To Death	7"	Cherry Red	CHERRY29	1981	**£4**	**£1.50**	*with flexi (LYN10086)*
You Scare Me To Death	CD-s	Cherry Red	CDCHERRY29	1989	**£5**	**£2**	
You Scare Me To Death	LP	Cherry Red	PERED20	1981	**£10**	**£4**	*picture disc*

BOLAN, MARC & T REX

Bolan Boogie	LP	Fly	HIFLY8	1971	**£250**	**£150**	*test pressing with The Visit*
Celebrate Summer	7"	EMI	MARC18	1977	**£4**	**£1.50**	*picture sleeve*
Chariot Choogle	7"	EMI	SPSR346	1972	**£200**	**£100**	*promo, white label*
Chariot Choogle	7"	EMI	SPRS346	1972	**£300**	**£180**	*promo, picture label*
Children Of Rarn	10"	Marc	ABOLAN2	1982	**£15**	**£6**	*with book*
Christmas Bop	7"	EMI	MARC12	1975	**£1000**	**£700**	
Christmas Time	7"	Lyntone		1972	**£20**	**£10**	*flexi*
Christmas Time	7"	Lyntone		1972	**£30**	**£15**	*flexi with letter*
Electric Warrior	LP	Fly	HIFLY6	1971	**£500**	**£330**	*test pressing with Jeepster*
Electric Warrior	LP	Fly	HIFLY6	1971	**£10**	**£4**	*with inner & poster*
Essential Collection	CD	Relativity		1991	**£20**	**£8**	*US promo sampler*
Get It On	7"	Fly	BUG10	1971	**£8**	**£4**	*picture sleeve, silver fly on label, handwritten credits*
Great Hits	LP	EMI	BLN5003	1972	**£10**	**£4**	*with poster*
Hard On Love	LP	Track	2406101	1972	**£200**	**£100**	*test pressing*
History Of T Rex	LP	Marc On Wax	WARRIOR1-4	1986	**£20**	**£8**	*4 picture discs, boxed*
Jeepster	7"	Fly	GRUB1	1971	**£100**	**£50**	*promo*
Jeepster	7"	Fly	GRUB1	1971	**£150**	**£75**	*promo, pink sleeve*
Life's A Gas	12"	Cube	ANTS001	1979	**£8**	**£4**	
Megarex 2	7"	Marc	PTANX1	1985	**£4**	**£1.50**	*shaped picture disc*
Metal Guru	CD-s	Total	CDMARC502	1991	**£5**	**£2**	
One Inch Rock	7"	Magnifly	ECHO102	1972	**£100**	**£50**	*test pressing*
Ride A White Swan	7"	Fly	BUG1	1970	**£10**	**£5**	*picture sleeve, purple label*
Ride A White Swan	7"	Octopus	OCTO1	1970	**£2000**	**£1400**	*test pressing, best auctioned*
Sing Me A Song	12"	Rarn	MBFS001P	1981	**£10**	**£5**	*picture disc, black rim*
Sing Me A Song	12"	Rarn	MBFS001P	1981	**£15**	**£7.50**	*back-to-front picture disc*
Solid Gold Easy Action	7"	EMI	MARC3	1972	**£10**	**£5**	*mispressings with other artist B side*
Solid Gold Easy Action	CD-s	Old Gold	OG6134	1989	**£5**	**£2**	
T REX	CD-s	Edsel	MBPROMO1	1994	**£12**	**£6**	*promo*
T Rex EP	CD-s	Special Edition	CD313	1988	**£5**	**£2**	
T Rex In Concert	LP	Marc	ABOLAN1	1981	**£15**	**£6**	*promo, no applause*

Title	Format	Label	Cat. No.	Year	Mint	VG	Notes
Tanx	LP	EMI	BLN5002	1972	**£10**	**£4**	*with inner & poster*
Twentieth Century Boy	CD-s	Total	CDMARC501	1991	**£5**	**£2**	
Words And Music Of Marc Bolan	LP	Cube	HIFLY1	1978	**£15**	**£6**	*double, with 7" (BINT1)*
Zinc Alloy & Hidden Riders Of Tomorrow	LP	EMI	BLNA7751	1974	**£10**	**£4**	*with inner*
Zinc Alloy & Hidden Riders Of Tomorrow	LP	EMI	BLNA7751	1974	**£175**	**£87.50**	*fold-out numbered sleeve*
Zinc Alloy And The Hidden Riders Of Tomorrow	LP	EMI	BNLA7751	1974	**£200**	**£100**	*fold-out sleeve with magazine letter*
Zinc Alloy And The Hidden Riders Of Tomorrow	LP	EMI	BNLA7751	1974	**£125**	**£62.50**	*fold-out sleeve, no letter or number*
Zip Gun	LP	EMI	BLNA7752	1975	**£12**	**£5**	*diamond cut sleeve, inner*

BOLD

Title	Format	Label	Cat. No.	Year	Mint	VG	Notes
Bold	LP	ABC	ABCS705	1969	**£15**	**£6**	*US*

BOLDER DAMN

Title	Format	Label	Cat. No.	Year	Mint	VG	Notes
Mourning	LP	private		1971	**£1000**	**£700**	*US*

BOLIN, TOMMY

Title	Format	Label	Cat. No.	Year	Mint	VG	Notes
Grind	7"	Nemperor	K10730	1976	**£6**	**£2.50**	
Teaser	LP	Atlantic	K50208	1975	**£10**	**£4**	

BOLIVAR, SIMON

Title	Format	Label	Cat. No.	Year	Mint	VG	Notes
Merengue Holiday	7"	London	HLG8245	1956	**£8**	**£4**	

BOLOTIN, MICHAEL

Bolotin is, of course, Michael Bolton, performing in much the same style as was successful for him several years later.

Title	Format	Label	Cat. No.	Year	Mint	VG	Notes
Every Day Of My Life	LP	RCA	APL11550	1976	**£12**	**£5**	*US*
Michael Bolotin	LP	RCA	SF8451	1975	**£12**	**£5**	

BOLTON, POLLY

Title	Format	Label	Cat. No.	Year	Mint	VG	Notes
No Going Back	LP	Making Waves	SPIN134	1989	**£30**	**£15**	

BOMBAY DUCKS

Title	Format	Label	Cat. No.	Year	Mint	VG	Notes
Dance Music	LP	United Dairies	UP05	198–	**£15**	**£6**	
Sympathy For The Devil	7"	Complete Control	CON1	1980	**£5**	**£2**	

BON BONS

Title	Format	Label	Cat. No.	Year	Mint	VG	Notes
Circle	7"	London	HLU8262	1956	**£25**	**£12.50**	
That's The Way Love Goes	7"	London	HL8139	1955	**£25**	**£12.50**	

BON JOVI

The music of Bon Jovi defines modern American stadium rock. Histrionic lead vocals, with stirring chorus support, declaim anthems that are custom-written for arenas holding thousands of fans, while the lead guitar delivers the sustain-drenched tone, with all the whammy bar dives and tricky tapped figures that are expected of the style. *Slippery When Wet* was the biggest-selling rock album of 1987, the group's continued success since inspiring considerable collectors' interest in its growing back catalogue.

Title	Format	Label	Cat. No.	Year	Mint	VG	Notes
Always	7"	Vertigo	JOVJB14	1994	**£5**	**£2**	*jukebox issue*
Always	CD-s	Vertigo	JOVCD14	1994	**£10**	**£5**	
Bad Medicine	12"	Vertigo	JOVR312	1988	**£6**	**£2.50**	
Bad Medicine	7"	Vertigo	JOVS3	1988	**£6**	**£2.50**	*fold-out sleeve*
Bad Medicine	CD-s	Vertigo	JOVCD3	1988	**£12**	**£6**	
Bed Of Roses	7"	Vertigo	JOVLH9	1992	**£5**	**£2**	*jukebox issue*
Bed Of Roses	CD-s	Vertigo	JOVCD9	1992	**£8**	**£4**	
Blaze Of Glory	CD-s	Vertigo	JBJCD1	1990	**£5**	**£2**	
Born To Be My Baby	12"	Vertigo	JOVR412	1988	**£6**	**£2.50**	
Born To Be My Baby	12"	Vertigo	JOVP412	1988	**£12**	**£6**	*picture disc*
Born To Be My Baby	7"	Vertigo	JOVS4	1988	**£6**	**£2.50**	*envelope pack*
Born To Be My Baby	CD-s	Vertigo	JOVCD4	1988	**£12**	**£6**	
Dry County	CD-s	Vertigo	JOVBX13	1994	**£6**	**£2.50**	
Essential Bon Jovi	CD	Mercury	JOVI1989	1989	**£25**	**£10**	*promo*
Hardest Part Is The Night	12"	Vertigo	VERX22	1985	**£10**	**£5**	
Hardest Part Is The Night	12"	Vertigo	VERXR22	1985	**£25**	**£12.50**	*red vinyl*
Hardest Part Is The Night	7"	Vertigo	VER22	1985	**£10**	**£5**	
Hardest Part Is The Night	7"	Vertigo	VERDP22	1985	**£15**	**£7.50**	*double*
I'll Be There For You	CD-s	Vertigo	JOVCD5	1989	**£12**	**£6**	
In And Out Of Love	12"	Vertigo	VERX19	1985	**£15**	**£7.50**	
In And Out Of Love	7"	Vertigo	VERP19	1985	**£30**	**£15**	*picture disc*
In And Out Of Love	7"	Vertigo	VER19	1985	**£8**	**£4**	
In These Arms	CD-s	Vertigo	JOVCD10	1993	**£5**	**£2**	
Interview	CD	Mercury	CDP1371	1995	**£20**	**£8**	*US promo*
Keep The Faith	CD	Mercury	PHCR16003	1993	**£25**	**£10**	*Japanese, with bonus live disc*
Keep The Faith	CD-s	Vertigo	VOBCB8	1992	**£5**	**£2**	*boxed CD*
Keep The Faith	CD-s	Vertigo	VOBCD8	1992	**£8**	**£4**	
Lay Your Hands On Me	10"	Vertigo	JOVP610	1989	**£10**	**£5**	*picture disc*

Lay Your Hands On Me	7"	Vertigo	JOV6	1989	**£20**	**£10**	*triple pack, red, white, blue vinyls*
Lay Your Hands On Me	CD-s	Vertigo	JOVCD6	1989	**£12**	**£6**	
Livin' On A Prayer	CD-s	Vertigo	0800422	1987	**£20**	**£10**	*CD video*
Living In Sin	12"	Vertigo	JOVR712	1989	**£10**	**£5**	*white vinyl*
Living In Sin	CD-s	Vertigo	JOVCD7	1989	**£15**	**£7.50**	*boxed*
Living On A Prayer	12"	Vertigo	VERXG28	1986	**£15**	**£7.50**	
Living On A Prayer	12"	Vertigo	VERXR28	1986	**£12**	**£6**	*green vinyl*
Living On A Prayer	7"	Vertigo	VERPA28	1986	**£8**	**£4**	*with patch*
Living On A Prayer	7"	Vertigo	VERP28	1986	**£15**	**£7.50**	*picture disc*
Miracle	CD-s	Vertigo	JBJCD2	1990	**£15**	**£7.50**	*picture disc*
Never Say Goodbye	12"	Vertigo	JOVR212	1987	**£10**	**£5**	*yellow vinyl*
Never Say Goodbye	CD-s	Polygram	0802262	1987	**£30**	**£15**	*CD video*
New Jersey	LP	Vertigo	VERHP62	1988	**£12**	**£5**	*picture disc*
Please Come Home For Christmas	7"	Vertigo	JOVJB16	1994	**£5**	**£2**	*jukebox issue*
Please Come Home For Christmas	7"	Vertigo	JOVP16	1994	**£5**	**£2**	*picture disc*
Runaway	12"	Vertigo	VERX14	1984	**£30**	**£15**	
Runaway	7"	Vertigo	VER14	1984	**£15**	**£7.50**	
She Don't Know Me	12"	Vertigo	VERX11	1984	**£30**	**£15**	
She Don't Know Me	7"	Vertigo	VER11	1984	**£15**	**£7.50**	
Sleep When I'm Dead	CD-s	Vertigo	JOVD11	1993	**£8**	**£4**	
Sleep When I'm Dead	CD-s	Vertigo	JOVCD11	1993	**£5**	**£2**	
Slippery When Wet	LP	Vertigo	VERHP38	1988	**£12**	**£5**	*picture disc, poster*
Someday I'll Be Saturday Night	7"	Vertigo	JOVJB15	1994	**£5**	**£2**	*jukebox issue*
Someday I'll Be Saturday Night	CD-s	Vertigo	JOVDD15	1994	**£6**	**£2.50**	*in tin*
These Days	CD	Mercury		1995	**£30**	**£15**	*interview promo*
These Days	CD	Mercury	5326442	1996	**£15**	**£6**	*double*
Volkswagen Presents These Days	CD-s	Mercury	JOVVW1	1996	**£30**	**£15**	*promo*
Wanted Dead Or Alive	12"	Vertigo	JOVPB112	1987	**£15**	**£7.50**	*poster sleeve*
Wanted Dead Or Alive	12"	Vertigo	JOVR112	1987	**£15**	**£7.50**	*silver vinyl*
Wanted Dead Or Alive	7"	Vertigo	JOVS1	1987	**£6**	**£2.50**	*with stickers*
Wanted Dead Or Alive	CD-s	Vertigo	JOVCD1	1987	**£30**	**£15**	
Wanted Dead Or Alive	CD-s	Mercury	0800522	1987	**£30**	**£15**	*CD video*
You Give Love A Bad Name	10"	Vertigo	VERP26	1986	**£25**	**£12.50**	*shaped picture disc*
You Give Love A Bad Name	12"	Vertigo	VERXR26	1986	**£15**	**£7.50**	*blue vinyl*
You Give Love A Bad Name	12"	Vertigo	VERX26	1986	**£10**	**£5**	*with poster*

BON JOVI, JON

Miracle	12"	Vertigo	JBJ212	1990	**£10**	**£5**	*with poster*
Miracle	12"	Vertigo	JBJP212	1990	**£12**	**£6**	*picture disc*

BONANO, SHARKEY

At The Round Table	LP	Columbia	33SX1255/ SCX3327	1960	**£10**	**£4**	

BOND, BOBBY

Sweet Love	7"	Pye	7N25081	1961	**£5**	**£2**	

BOND, BRIGITTE

Blue Beat Baby	7"	Blue Beat	BB212	1964	**£12**	**£6**	

BOND, EDDIE

Greatest Country Gospel Hits	LP	Philips	1980	1961	**£50**	**£25**	US

BOND, GRAHAM

Although he was undoubtedly a major influence within the development of sixties rock, Bond's tragedy was to see his ideas developed more successfully by others. Few of his records really do justice to his undoubted talents, partly because, despite being a good jazz alto sax player (as his work on both the Don Rendell Quintet LP of 1962 and on the early Organization tracks included on *Solid Bond* prove), he constantly compromised his art in a desperate search for commercial success. Unfortunately, he never did find it, and yet all his sixties sidemen managed to – Ginger Baker and Jack Bruce with Cream; Jon Hiseman and Dick Heckstall-Smith with Colosseum; and John McLaughlin with Mahavishnu Orchestra. Bond himself stumbled through increasingly marginal musical projects, in which personal and drug problems did not help, until he fell under a train in 1974.

Bond In America	LP	Mercury	6499200/1	1971	**£25**	**£10**	*double*
Holy Magick	LP	Vertigo	6360021	1971	**£25**	**£10**	*spiral label*
Lease On Love	7"	Columbia	DB7647	1965	**£30**	**£15**	
Long Tall Shorty	7"	Decca	F11909	1964	**£40**	**£20**	
Love Is The Law	LP	Pulsar	AR10604	1968	**£25**	**£10**	US
Mighty Graham Bond	LP	Pulsar	AR10606	1968	**£25**	**£10**	US
Solid Bond	LP	Warner Bros	WS3001	1970	**£25**	**£10**	*double*
Sound Of '65	LP	Columbia	33SX1711	1965	**£75**	**£37.50**	
Sound Of '65	LP	Columbia	SX1711	1969	**£30**	**£15**	*silver and black label*
St James Infirmary	7"	Columbia	DB7838	1966	**£30**	**£15**	
Tammy	7"	Columbia	DB7471	1965	**£30**	**£15**	
Tell Me	7"	Columbia	DB7528	1965	**£30**	**£15**	
There's A Bond Between Us	LP	Columbia	33SX1750	1966	**£75**	**£37.50**	
There's A Bond Between Us	LP	Columbia	SX1750	1969	**£30**	**£15**	*silver and black label*
This Is Graham Bond	LP	Philips	6382010	1972	**£10**	**£4**	
Twelve Gates To The City	7"	Vertigo	6059042	1971	**£5**	**£2**	
Walking In The Park	7"	Warner Bros	WB8004	1970	**£10**	**£5**	
We Put Our Magick On You	LP	Vertigo	6360042	1971	**£25**	**£10**	*spiral label*
You've Gotta Have Love Babe	7"	Page One	POF014	1967	**£30**	**£15**	

BOND, GRAHAM & PETE BROWN

Lost Tribe	7"	Greenwich	GSS104	1972	**£30**	**£15**	
Two Heads Are Better Than One	LP	Chapter One	CHSR813	1972	**£60**	**£30**	

BOND, ISABELLA

Title	Format	Label	Cat. No.	Year	Mint	VG	Notes
Surfin' 66	LP	Decca	SLK16410	1966	**£25**	**£10**	*German*

BOND, JACKI

Title	Format	Label	Cat. No.	Year	Mint	VG	Notes
He Say	7"	Strike	JH320	1966	**£15**	**£7.50**	
Tell Him To Go Away	7"	Strike	JH302	1966	**£5**	**£2**	

BOND, JAMES

Records associated with the James Bond films are widely collected and are listed in the *Price Guide* under the names of the relevant artists. Much of the soundtrack music has been written and recorded by John Barry. Other relevant entries are as follows: Monty Norman (*Dr No*); Matt Monro (*From Russia With Love*); Shirley Bassey (*Goldfinger* and *Diamonds Are Forever*); Tom Jones (*Thunderball*); Burt Bacharach (*Casino Royale*); Dusty Springfield ('The Look Of Love', from *Casino Royale*, is the B side of 'Give Me Time'); Nancy Sinatra (*You Only Live Twice*); Louis Armstrong ('We Have All The Time In The World' from *On Her Majesty's Secret Service*); Lulu (*The Man With The Golden Gun*); Michel Legrand (*Never Say Never Again*); and A-Ha (*The Living Daylights*). A large number of other artists have also issued cover versions of the various Bond theme songs and other songs associated with, or inspired by James Bond.

BOND, JOHNNY

Title	Format	Label	Cat. No.	Year	Mint	VG	Notes
Famous Hot Rodders I Have Known	LP	London	HAB8272	1966	**£10**	**£4**	
Hot Rod Jalopy	7"	London	HLU9189	1960	**£8**	**£4**	
Hot Rod Lincoln	7"	London	HL7100	1960	**£15**	**£7.50**	*export*
Live It Up	LP	London	HAB8098	1963	**£10**	**£4**	
Songs That Made Him Famous	LP	London	HAB8228	1965	**£15**	**£6**	
Ten Little Bottles	7"	London	HLB9957	1965	**£5**	**£2**	
That Wild, Wicked But Wonderful West	LP	Stateside	SL10008	1962	**£10**	**£4**	

BOND, JOYCE

Title	Format	Label	Cat. No.	Year	Mint	VG	Notes
Back To School	7"	Pama	PM718	1968	**£4**	**£1.50**	
Do The Teasy	7"	Island	WIP6010	1967	**£4**	**£1.50**	
Help Me Make It Through The Night	7"	Trojan	TR7837	1971	**£6**	**£2.50**	
It's Alright	7"	Airborn	NBP0011	1967	**£8**	**£4**	
Mr Pitiful	7"	Pama	PM770	1969	**£4**	**£1.50**	
Ob La Di Ob La Da	7"	Island	WIP6051	1968	**£4**	**£1.50**	
Soul And Ska	LP	Island	ILP968	1968	**£75**	**£37.50**	*pink label*
Tell Me What It's All About	7"	Island	WI3019	1966	**£5**	**£2**	
This Train	7"	Island	WIP6018	1967	**£4**	**£1.50**	

BOND, MARGARET

Title	Format	Label	Cat. No.	Year	Mint	VG	Notes
Your Love Is My Love	7"	Parlophone	R4283	1957	**£4**	**£1.50**	

BOND, OLIVER

Title	Format	Label	Cat. No.	Year	Mint	VG	Notes
Let Me Love You	7"	Parlophone	R5476	1966	**£8**	**£4**	

BOND, PETER

Title	Format	Label	Cat. No.	Year	Mint	VG	Notes
Awkward Age	LP	Totem	STO813	1983	**£15**	**£6**	
It's Alright For Some	LP	Trailer	LER2108	1977	**£15**	**£6**	

BOND, RONNIE

Title	Format	Label	Cat. No.	Year	Mint	VG	Notes
Anything For You	7"	Page One	POF123	1969	**£20**	**£10**	

BONDS, GARY (U.S.)

Title	Format	Label	Cat. No.	Year	Mint	VG	Notes
Dance Till Quarter To Three	LP	Top Rank	35114	1961	**£40**	**£20**	
Dear Lady Twist	7"	Top Rank	JAR602	1962	**£4**	**£1.50**	
Do The Limbo With Me	7"	Stateside	SS179	1963	**£4**	**£1.50**	
Ella Is Yella	7"	Stateside	SS308	1964	**£4**	**£1.50**	
Greatest Hits	LP	Stateside	SL10037	1962	**£20**	**£8**	
New Orleans	7"	Top Rank	JAR527	1961	**£4**	**£1.50**	
Not Me	7"	Top Rank	JAR566	1961	**£4**	**£1.50**	
Quarter To Three	7"	Top Rank	JAR575	1961	**£4**	**£1.50**	
School Is In	7"	Top Rank	JAR595	1961	**£4**	**£1.50**	
School Is Out	7"	Top Rank	JAR581	1961	**£4**	**£1.50**	
Send Her To Me	7"	Stateside	SS2025	1967	**£8**	**£4**	
Seven Day Weekend	7"	Stateside	SS111	1962	**£4**	**£1.50**	
Twist Twist Senora	7"	Top Rank	JAR615	1962	**£4**	**£1.50**	
Twist Up Calypso	LP	Stateside	SL10001	1962	**£25**	**£10**	

BONE, OLIVER

Title	Format	Label	Cat. No.	Year	Mint	VG	Notes
Knock On Wood	7"	Parlophone	R5527	1966	**£5**	**£2**	

BONFIRE, MARS

Title	Format	Label	Cat. No.	Year	Mint	VG	Notes
Faster Than The Speed Of Life	LP	Columbia	CS9834	1969	**£15**	**£6**	*US*
Mars Bonfire	LP	UNI	73027	1968	**£15**	**£6**	*US*

BONGO LES & BUNNY

Title	Format	Label	Cat. No.	Year	Mint	VG	Notes
Feel Nice	7"	Attack	ATT8041	1972	**£5**	**£2**	*Winston Scotland B side*

BONNER, JUKE BOY

Title	Format	Label	Cat. No.	Year	Mint	VG	Notes
More Down Home Blues	7" EP	Jan & Dil	JR451	196–	**£6**	**£2.50**	
One Man Trio	LP	Flyright	LP3501	1968	**£20**	**£8**	
Runnin' Shoes	7"	Blue Horizon	573163	1969	**£15**	**£7.50**	
Things Ain't Right	LP	Liberty	LBS83319	1969	**£12**	**£5**	

BONNET, GRAHAM

Title	Format	Label	Cat. No.	Year	Mint	VG	Notes
Back Row In The Stalls	7"	DJM	DJS328	1974	**£5**	**£2**	
Danny	7"	Ring O'	2017106	1977	**£6**	**£2.50**	*picture sleeve*
Goodnight And Good Morning	7"	Ring O'	2017110	1977	**£4**	**£1.50**	

Graham Bonnet	LP	Ring O'	2320103	1977	£10	£4	
Rare Specimen	7"	RCA	RCA2230	1972	£5	£2	
Trying To Say Goodbye	7"	RCA	RCA2280	1973	£5	£2	
Warm Ride	12"	Ring O'	POSP002	1978	£6	£2.50	

BONNEVILLES

Meet The Bonnevilles	LP	Drum Boy	DLM/LS1001	1963	£25	£10	US

BONNEY, GRAHAM

Get Ready	7"	Columbia	DB8531	1969	£4	£1.50	
No One Knows	7"	Columbia	DB8005	1966	£4	£1.50	
Sign On The Dotted Line	7"	Columbia	DB8648	1970	£4	£1.50	
Super Girl	7"	Columbia	DB7843	1966	£4	£1.50	
Supergirl	LP	Columbia	SX6052	1966	£12	£5	

BONNIE

Did You Get The Message	7"	Ska Beat	JB270	1967	£10	£5	

BONNIE & THE TREASURES

Home Of The Brave	7"	London	HLU9998	1965	£20	£10	

BONNIWELL, T. S.

Close	LP	Capitol	ST277	1969	£30	£15	US

BONO & GAVIN FRIDAY

In The Name Of The Father	CD-s	Island	CID593	1994	£10	£5	

BONUS, JACK

Jack Bonus	LP	Grunt	FTR1005	1972	£15	£6	US

BONZO DOG (DOO-DAH) BAND

Alberts, The Bonzo Dog Band, & The Temperance Seven	LP	Starline	SRS5151	1973	£10	£4	*with other artists*
Alley Oop	7"	Parlophone	R5499	1966	£20	£10	
Best Of The Bonzos	LP	Liberty	LBS83332	1970	£10	£4	
Doughnut In Granny's Greenhouse	LP	Liberty	LBL/LBS83158	1968	£20	£8	*with booklet*
Equestrian Statue	7"	Liberty	LBF15040	1967	£5	£2	
Gorilla	LP	Liberty	LBL/LBS83056	1967	£20	£8	*with booklet*
History Of The Bonzos	LP	United Artists	UAD60071/2	1974	£15	£6	*double*
I Want To Be With You	7"	Liberty	LBF15273	1969	£4	£1.50	
Keynsham	LP	Liberty	LBS83290	1969	£15	£6	
Let's Make Up & Be Friendly	LP	United Artists	UAS29288	1972	£12	£5	
Mr Apollo	7"	Liberty	LBF15201	1969	£4	£1.50	
My Brother Makes The Noises For The Talkies	7"	Parlophone	R5430	1966	£20	£10	
No Matter Who You Vote For	7"	China	WOK2021	1992	£4	£1.50	*promo*
No Matter Who You Vote For	CD-s	China	WOKCD2021	1992	£8	£4	
Tadpoles	LP	Liberty	LBS83257	1969	£20	£8	
Urban Spaceman	7"	Liberty	LBF15144	1968	£4	£1.50	*2 versions of B side*
You Done My Brain In	7"	Liberty	LBF15314	1970	£4	£1.50	

BOO RADLEYS

Boo Up!	CD-s	Rough Trade	R2753	1991	£5	£2	
Every Heaven	CD-s	Rough Trade	R20112713	1991	£8	£4	
Ichabod And I	LP	Action	TAKE4	1990	£15	£6	
Kaleidoscope	12"	Rough Trade	RTT241	1990	£6	£2.50	
Kaleidoscope	CD-s	Rough Trade	RTT241CD	1990	£8	£4	

BOOGIE KINGS

Blue Eyed Soul	LP	Montel-Michelle	109	1967	£12	£5	US
Boogie Kings	LP	Montel-Michelle	104	1966	£12	£5	US

BOOGIE WOOGIE COMPANY

Live For Dancing	LP	Electrola	1C06291783	1971	£40	£20	*German*

BOOK OF A.M.

Dawn And Morning	LP	LMT	1016	1978	£15	£6	*French*

BOOKER T & THE MGs

And Now	LP	Stax	589002	1966	£12	£5	
Back To Back	LP	Stax	(STS)720	1967	£10	£4	*with Markeys; US*
Best Of Booker T And The MG's	LP	Atlantic	228015	1968	£10	£4	
Booker T Set	LP	Stax	SXATS1015	1970	£10	£4	
Bootleg	7"	Atlantic	AT4033	1965	£5	£2	
Chinese Checkers	7"	London	HLK9784	1963	£5	£2	
Chinese Checkers	7"	Stax	601026	1967	£4	£1.50	
Doin' Our Thing	LP	Atlantic	2464011	1968	£12	£5	
Get Ready	LP	Atco	228004	1969	£10	£4	
Green Onions	7"	Atlantic	584088	1967	£4	£1.50	
Green Onions	7"	London	HLK9595	1962	£5	£2	
Green Onions	LP	London	HAK8182	1964	£25	£10	
Green Onions	LP	Atlantic	587/588033	1966	£10	£4	
Hip Hug-Her	LP	Stax	(STS)717	1967	£10	£4	US
Hip Hugger	7"	Stax	601009	1967	£4	£1.50	
In The Christmas Spirit	LP	Stax	(STS)713	1966	£10	£4	US
Jelly Bread	7"	London	HLK9670	1963	£5	£2	

Jingle Bells	7"	Atlantic	584060	1966	£4	£1.50	
McLemore Avenue	LP	Stax	SXATS1031	1970	£10	£4	
My Sweet Potato	7"	Atlantic	584044	1966	£4	£1.50	
R&B With Booker T Vol. 1	7" EP	London	REK1367	1963	£12	£6	
R&B With Booker T Vol. 2	7" EP	Atlantic	AET6002	1964	£12	£6	
Red Beans And Rice	7"	Atlantic	AT4063	1966	£5	£2	
Slim Jenkins' Place	7"	Stax	601018	1967	£4	£1.50	
Soul Christmas	LP	Stax	589013	1967	£10	£4	
Soul Dressing	LP	Atlantic	ATL5027	1965	£15	£6	
Soul Dressing	LP	Atlantic	587047	1967	£10	£4	
Soul Limbo	LP	Stax	(S)XATS1001	1968	£12	£5	
Uptight	LP	Stax	(S)XATS1005	1968	£12	£5	

BOOKER, BERYL

Beryl Booker Trio	10" LP	London	HBA1054	1956	£40	£20	

BOOKER, JAMES

Cool Turkey	7"	Vogue	V9177	1961	£12	£6	
Gonzo	7" EP	Vocalion	VEP170154	1963	£40	£20	

BOOMERANGS

Another Tear Falls	7"	Fontana	TF555	1965	£12	£6	
Rockin' Robin	7"	Fontana	TF507	1964	£20	£10	

BOOMERANGS (2)

Beat Live	LP	Baccarola	S72660	1966	£15	£6	*German*
Dream World	7"	Pye	7N17049	1966	£5	£2	

BOOMTOWN RATS

Bob Geldof's continuing status as a media celebrity has sadly done nothing for the collectability of his former group. The only item to be listed here rather emphasizes the general lack of interest in the Boomtown Rats heritage – a six-single set by anyone else might be expected to be worth much more than this.

Rat Pack	7"	Ensign		1978	£8	£4	*6 singles in plastic wallet*

BOONE, PAT

Ain't That A Shame	7"	London	HLD8172	1955	£15	£7.50	
All Hands On Deck	7" EP	London	RED1294	1961	£5	£2	
Always You And Me	7" EP	London	RED1384	1963	£5	£2	
April Love	7"	London	HLD8512	1957	£4	£1.50	
April Love	LP	London	HAD2078	1958	£10	£4	
Beach Girl	7"	Dot	DS16658	1964	£4	£1.50	
Boss Beat	LP	Dot	(D)DLP3594	1965	£10	£4	
Don't Forbid Me	7"	London	HLD8370	1957	£5	£2	
Down Lovers Lane	7" EP	London	RED1359	1963	£5	£2	
Easy	7" EP	London	RED1255	1960	£5	£2	
For A Penny	7"	London	SLD4002	1959	£20	£10	*export, stereo*
Four By Pat	7" EP	London	RED1109	1957	£5	£2	
Friendly Persuasion	7"	London	HLD8346	1956	£5	£2	
Gee Whittakers	7"	London	HLD8233	1956	£20	£10	
Golden Hits	LP	London	HAD/SHD8031	1962	£10	£4	
Good Rockin' Tonight	7"	London	HLD8824	1959	£4	£1.50	
Hey Baby	7" EP	Dot	DEP20008	1966	£5	£2	
Howdy	LP	London	HAD2030	1957	£10	£4	
Howdy Part 1	7" EP	London	RED1081	1957	£5	£2	
Howdy Part 2	7" EP	London	RED1082	1957	£5	£2	
Howdy Part 3	7" EP	London	RED1119	1958	£5	£2	
I Almost Lost My Mind	7"	London	HL7012	1956	£5	£2	*export*
I Almost Lost My Mind	7"	London	HLD8303	1956	£6	£2.50	
I Love You Truly	LP	London	HAD/SHD8053	1963	£10	£4	
I'll Be Home	7"	London	HL7007	1956	£6	£2.50	*export*
I'll Be Home	7"	London	HLD8253	1956	£6	£2.50	
I'll See You In My Dreams	LP	London	HAD2452/ SAHD6240	1962	£10	£4	
Journey To The Centre Of The Earth	7" EP	London	RED1244	1959	£6	£2.50	
Just A Closer Walk With Thee	7" EP	London	RED1095	1957	£5	£2	
Latest And Greatest	7" EP	London	RED1281	1961	£5	£2	
Latest And Greatest No. 2	7" EP	London	RED1335	1962	£5	£2	
Long Tall Sally	7"	London	HL7010	1956	£6	£2.50	*export*
Long Tall Sally	7"	London	HLD8291	1956	£10	£5	
Love Letters In The Sand	7"	London	HLD8445	1957	£4	£1.50	
Make The World Go Away	7" EP	Dot	DEP20012	1966	£5	£2	
Merry Christmas	7" EP	London	RED1128	1958	£5	£2	
Mexican Joe	7"	London	HLD7121	1963	£8	£4	*export*
Moody River	7" EP	London	RED1302	1961	£5	£2	
Moody River	LP	London	HAD2382/ SAHD6182	1961	£10	£4	
Moonglow	LP	London	HAD2265/ SAHD6085	1960	£10	£4	
Moonglow Pt 1	7" EP	London	RED1267	1961	£5	£2	
Moonglow Pt 2	7" EP	London	RED1268	1961	£5	£2	
No Arms Could Ever Hold You	7"	London	HLD8197	1955	£20	£10	
On Mike	7" EP	London	RED1069	1957	£5	£2	
Pat Boone Hits	7" EP	Dot	DEP20001	1965	£5	£2	
Pat Boone Sings The Hits	7" EP	London	RED1063	1956	£5	£2	
Pat Boone Sings The Hits No. 2	7" EP	London	RED1086	1957	£5	£2	

Title	Format	Label	Cat. No.	Year	Mint	VG	Notes
Pat Boone Sings The Hits No. 3	7" EP	London	RED1112	1958	£5	£2	
Pat Boone's Hits Vol. 2	7" EP	Dot	DEP20005	1965	£5	£2	
Pat Part 1	7" EP	London	RED1132	1958	£6	£2.50	
Pat Part 2	7" EP	London	RED1133	1958	£5	£2	
Pat Sings	LP	London	HAD2161/ SAHD6013	1959	£10	£4	
Pat Sings Movie Themes	7" EP	London	RED1391	1963	£5	£2	
Pat!	LP	London	HAD2049	1957	£10	£4	
Pat's Big Hits	7" EP	London	RED1118	1958	£5	£2	
Pat's Big Hits	LP	London	HAD2024	1957	£12	£5	
Pat's Big Hits Vol. 2	LP	London	HAD2098	1958	£12	£5	
Remember You're Mine	7"	London	HLD8479	1957	£4	£1.50	
Rich In Love	7"	London	HLD8316	1956	£8	£4	
Send Me The Pillow You Dream On	7"	London	HL7118	1963	£6	£2.50	*export*
Side By Side	7" EP	London	RED1220	1959	£5	£2	*with Shirley Boone*
Side By Side	LP	London	HAD2210/ SAHD6057	1960	£10	£4	*with Shirley Boone*
Sings Guess Who?	LP	London	HAD/SHD8109	1963	£20	£8	
Sings Irving Berlin	LP	London	HAD2082/ SAHD6038	1958	£10	£4	
Sings Irving Berlin Pt 1	7" EP	London	RED1164	1958	£5	£2	
Sings Irving Berlin Pt 2	7" EP	London	RED1165	1958	£5	£2	
Sings Irving Berlin Pt 3	7" EP	London	RED1166	1958	£5	£2	
Songs From Friendly Persuasion	7" EP	London	RED1068	1957	£5	£2	
Songs From Mardi Gras	7" EP	London	RED1194	1959	£5	£2	
Stardust	LP	London	HAD2127/ SAHD6001	1958	£10	£4	
Stardust Part 1	7" EP	London	RED1177	1959	£5	£2	
Stardust Part 2	7" EP	London	RED1178	1959	£5	£2	
Stardust Part 3	7" EP	London	RED1179	1959	£5	£2	
State Fair	LP	London	HAD2453/ SAHD6241	1962	£10	£4	
Sweet Little Sixteen	7" EP	Dot	DEP20013	1966	£5	£2	
Tenderly	LP	London	HAD2204/ SAHD6053	1960	£10	£4	
This And That	LP	London	HAD2305	1961	£10	£4	
Touch Of Your Lips	LP	London	HAD/SHD8153	1964	£10	£4	
White Christmas	7"	London	HLD8520	1957	£4	£1.50	
Why Baby Why	7"	London	HLD8404	1957	£5	£2	
Yes Indeed	LP	London	HAD2144/ SAHD6010	1959	£10	£4	
Yes Indeed Part 1	7" EP	London	RED1190	1959	£5	£2	
Yes Indeed Part 2	7" EP	London	RED1191	1959	£5	£2	
Yes Indeed Part 3	7" EP	London	RED1192	1959	£5	£2	

BOOT

Title	Format	Label	Cat. No.	Year	Mint	VG	Notes
Boot	LP	Agape	2601	1972	£20	£8	*US*

BOOTH, BARRY

Title	Format	Label	Cat. No.	Year	Mint	VG	Notes
Diversions!	LP	Pye	NPL18216	1968	£10	£4	

BOOTHE, KEN

Title	Format	Label	Cat. No.	Year	Mint	VG	Notes
Artibella	7"	Punch	PH30	1970	£5	£2	
Be Yourself	7"	Bamboo	BAM8	1969	£5	£2	*Sound Dimension B side*
Drums Of Freedom	7"	Trojan	TR7780	1970	£4	£1.50	
Everybody Knows	7"	Coxsone	CS7041	1968	£12	£6	*Gaylads B side*
Feel Good	7"	Studio One	SO2000	1967	£12	£6	
Freedom Street	7"	Trojan	TR7756	1970	£4	£1.50	
Girl I Left Behind	7"	Studio One	SO2041	1968	£12	£6	*Termites B side*
Give To Me	7"	Gas	GAS169	1970	£4	£1.50	
Home Home Home	7"	Coxsone	CS7020	1967	£12	£6	*Soul Brothers B side*
I Remember Someone	7"	Fab	FAB63	1968	£12	£6	
It's Gonna Take A Miracle	7"	Trojan	TR7772	1970	£4	£1.50	
Lady With The Starlight	7"	High Note	HS003	1969	£12	£6	*Leslie Butler & Count Ossie B side*
Lonely Teardrops	7"	Coxsone	CS7006	1967	£12	£6	
Mr Rock Steady	LP	Studio One	SOL9001	1967	£100	£50	
One I Love	7"	Caltone	TONE107	1967	£8	£4	
Original Six	7"	Banana	BA352	1971	£8	£4	
Pleading	7"	Bamboo	BAM4	1969	£8	£4	*Sound Dimension B side*
Puppet On A String	7"	Studio One	SO2012	1967	£12	£6	*Roland Alphonso B side*
Say You	7"	Doctor Bird	DB1110	1967	£12	£6	*Lyn Taitt B side*
Sherry	7"	Coxsone	CS7094	1969	£12	£6	
Tomorrow	7"	Studio One	SO2053	1968	£12	£6	
Train Is Coming	7"	Island	WI3020	1966	£10	£5	
When I Fall In Love	7"	Studio One	SO2039	1968	£12	£6	*Heptones B side*
Why Baby Why	7"	Trojan	TR7716	1970	£4	£1.50	
You Keep Me Hanging On	7"	Coxsone	CS7043	1968	£12	£6	*Charmers B side*
You Left The Water Running	7"	Jackpot	JP748	1970	£8	£4	
You're No Good	7"	Ska Beat	JB248	1966	£10	£5	*Soulettes B side*
You're On My Mind	7"	Studio One	SO2073	1969	£12	£6	*Richard Ace B side*

BOOTHE, MILTON

Title	Format	Label	Cat. No.	Year	Mint	VG	Notes
Lonely And Blue	7"	Gas	GAS106	1969	£5	£2	

BOOTLES

Title	Format	Label	Cat. No.	Year	Mint	VG	Notes
I'll Let You Hold My Hand	7"	Vocalion	VN9216	1964	**£8**	**£4**	

BOOTS

Title	Format	Label	Cat. No.	Year	Mint	VG	Notes
Animal In Me	7"	CBS	3550	1968	**£8**	**£4**	
Beat With The Boots	LP	Telefunken	SLE14457	1965	**£100**	**£50**	*German*
Here Are The Boots	LP	Telefunken	SLE14399	1966	**£75**	**£37.50**	*German*
Keep Your Lovelight Burning	7"	CBS	3833	1968	**£10**	**£5**	

BOOTS, DAVE

Title	Format	Label	Cat. No.	Year	Mint	VG	Notes
Green Satin And Gold	LP	Solent	SM013	196–	**£100**	**£50**	

BOOTSY'S RUBBER BAND

Title	Format	Label	Cat. No.	Year	Mint	VG	Notes
Ahh . . . The Name Is Bootsy, Baby	LP	Warner Bros	K56302	1977	**£10**	**£4**	
Bootsy? Player Of The Year	LP	Warner Bros	K56424	1978	**£10**	**£4**	
One Giveth, The Count Taketh Away	LP	Warner Bros	K56998	1981	**£10**	**£4**	
Stretchin' Out	LP	Warner Bros	K56200	1976	**£10**	**£4**	
This Boot Is Made For Fonk-n	LP	Warner Bros	K56615	1979	**£10**	**£4**	
Ultra Wave	LP	Warner Bros	BSK3433	1980	**£10**	**£4**	*US*

BOOZE HOISTER BAND

Title	Format	Label	Cat. No.	Year	Mint	VG	Notes
Tavern Tales	LP	Peace Pie		1980	**£40**	**£20**	*Dutch*

BOOZE HOISTER FOLK GROUP

Title	Format	Label	Cat. No.	Year	Mint	VG	Notes
More You Booze, The Double You See	LP	Crossroad		1978	**£200**	**£100**	*Dutch*

BOOZERS

Title	Format	Label	Cat. No.	Year	Mint	VG	Notes
No No No	7" EP	DiscAZ		1967	**£8**	**£4**	*French*

BOP & THE BELTONES

Title	Format	Label	Cat. No.	Year	Mint	VG	Notes
Smile Like An Angel	7"	Coxsone	CS7007	1967	**£12**	**£6**	*Soul Agents B side*

BORBETOMAGUS

Borbetomagus are a band of extreme noise terrorists with a side-line in vaguely unsettling album covers, typically involving worms. Depending on one's point of view, the music is either extremely exhilarating or else nothing but a racket, but it has proved to be remarkably influential. The group's two saxophonists, Jim Sauter and Donald Dietrich, can also be found on an album (*Barefoot In The Head*) with Sonic Youth's Thurston Moore, who has no difficulty slotting his abrasive guitar into the general mêlée.

Title	Format	Label	Cat. No.	Year	Mint	VG	Notes
Barbed Wire Maggots	LP	Agaric	AG1983	1983	**£20**	**£8**	*US*
Borbeto Jam	LP	Cadence	1026	198–	**£20**	**£8**	*US*
Borbetomagus	LP	Agaric	AG1982	1982	**£25**	**£10**	*US*
Borbetomagus	LP	Agaric	AG1980	1980	**£25**	**£10**	*US*
Fish That Sparkling Bubble	LP	Agaric	AG1987	1987	**£20**	**£8**	*US*
Industrial Strength	LP	Leo	113	1984	**£20**	**£8**	
New York Performances	LP	Agaric	AG1986	1986	**£20**	**£8**	*US*
Seven Reasons For Tears	LP	Purge	027	1986	**£20**	**£8**	*US*
Work On What Has Been Spoiled	LP	Agaric	AG1981	1981	**£25**	**£10**	*US*
Zurich	LP	Agaric	AG1984	1984	**£25**	**£10**	*US double*

BORDERSONG

Title	Format	Label	Cat. No.	Year	Mint	VG	Notes
Morning	LP	Real Good	1001	1975	**£20**	**£8**	*US*

BOSS ATTACK

Title	Format	Label	Cat. No.	Year	Mint	VG	Notes
Hell-El	7"	Fab	FAB187	1971	**£4**	**£1.50**	

BOSS COMBO

Title	Format	Label	Cat. No.	Year	Mint	VG	Notes
Golden Rock And Roll Instrumentals	LP	Coral	LVA9205	1962	**£10**	**£4**	

BOSTIC, EARL

Title	Format	Label	Cat. No.	Year	Mint	VG	Notes
Alto Magic	7" EP	Parlophone	GEP8754	1958	**£6**	**£2.50**	
Alto Magic In Hi-Fi	LP	King	597	1958	**£20**	**£8**	*US*
Alto Sax And Mambo Strings	7" EP	Parlophone	GEP8565	1956	**£5**	**£2**	
Alto-Tude	LP	King	515	195–	**£20**	**£8**	*US*
Best Of Bostic	LP	King	500	195–	**£20**	**£8**	*US*
Beyond The Blue Horizon	7"	Parlophone	R4232	1956	**£4**	**£1.50**	
Big Bostic Beat	7" EP	Parlophone	GEP8701	1958	**£5**	**£2**	
Blue Skies	7"	Parlophone	MSP6119	1954	**£6**	**£2.50**	
Bo Do Rock	7"	Parlophone	R4208	1956	**£5**	**£2**	
Bostic In Harlem	7" EP	Parlophone	GEP8637	1957	**£5**	**£2**	
Bostic Meets Doggett	10" LP	Parlophone	PMD1054	1958	**£20**	**£8**	
Bostic Rocks	10" LP	Parlophone	PMD1068	1958	**£20**	**£8**	
Bostic Rocks	LP	King	571	1958	**£20**	**£8**	*US*
Bostic Showcase Of Swinging Dance Hits	LP	King	583	1958	**£20**	**£8**	*US*
Bostic Workshop	LP	King	613	1959	**£20**	**£8**	*US*
Bubbin's Rock	7"	Parlophone	R4278	1957	**£5**	**£2**	
C'mon Dance With Earl Bostic	LP	King	558	1958	**£20**	**£8**	*US*
Cherokee	7"	Parlophone	CMSP8	1954	**£15**	**£7.50**	*export*
Dance Time	LP	King	525	195–	**£20**	**£8**	*US*
Deep Purple	7"	Parlophone	MSP6089	1954	**£8**	**£4**	
Don't You Do It	7"	Parlophone	MSP6105	1954	**£6**	**£2.50**	
Earl Bostic	10" LP	Parlophone	PMD1016	1954	**£20**	**£8**	
Earl Bostic	7" EP	Parlophone	GEP8520	1955	**£6**	**£2.50**	
Earl Bostic	7" EP	Vogue	EPV1010	1955	**£10**	**£5**	
Earl Bostic And His Alto Sax No. 2	10" LP	Parlophone	PMD1040	1956	**£20**	**£8**	
Earl Bostic And His Orchestra	10" LP	Vogue	LDE100	1954	**£20**	**£8**	
Earl's Imagination	7" EP	Parlophone	GEP8548	1956	**£5**	**£2**	

Flamingo	7"	Vogue	V2145	1956	£8	£4	
Flamingo	7" EP	Parlophone	GEP8506	1954	£6	£2.50	
For You	LP	King	503	195–	£20	£8	*US*
Harlem Nocturne	7"	Parlophone	R4263	1957	£4	£1.50	
Honeymoon Night	7"	Island	WI271	1966	£6	£2.50	
Invitation To Dance	LP	King	547	1957	£20	£8	*US*
Jungle Drums	7"	Parlophone	MSP6110	1954	£6	£2.50	
Let's Dance With Earl Bostic	LP	King	529	195–	£20	£8	*US*
Linger Awhile	7" EP	Parlophone	GEP8513	1955	£6	£2.50	
Mambostic	7"	Parlophone	MSP6131	1954	£8	£4	
Melody Of love	7"	Parlophone	MSP6162	1955	£6	£2.50	
Moonglow	7"	Vogue	V2148	1956	£8	£4	
Music A La Bostic No. 1	7" EP	Parlophone	GEP8571	1956	£5	£2	
Music A La Bostic No. 2	7" EP	Parlophone	GEP8574	1956	£6	£2.50	
Music A La Bostic No. 3	7" EP	Parlophone	GEP8603	1957	£6	£2.50	
Off Shore	7"	Parlophone	MSP6075	1954	£8	£4	
Over The Waves Rock	7"	Parlophone	R4460	1958	£5	£2	
Plays The Hit Tunes Of The Big Broadway Shows	LP	Parlophone	PMC1125	1960	£10	£4	
Plays The Sweet Side Of The Fantastic 50's	LP	King	602	1959	£20	£8	*US*
Rocking With Bostic	7" EP	Parlophone	GEP8741	1958	£6	£2.50	
Showcase Of Swinging Dance Hits	10" LP	Parlophone	PMD1071	1959	£12	£5	
Sweet Tunes Of The Fantastic Fifties	10" LP	Parlophone	PMD1074	1959	£12	£5	
Temptation	7"	Parlophone	R4370	1957	£4	£1.50	
Too Fine For Crying	7"	Parlophone	R4305	1957	£4	£1.50	
Tuxedo Junction	7"	Ember	JBS708	1962	£6	£2.50	
Velvet Sunset	7" EP	Vogue	EPV1111	1956	£6	£2.50	
Wrap It Up	7" EP	Parlophone	GEP8539	1955	£6	£2.50	

BOSTON

Boston	LP	Epic	EPCH81611	1976	£10	£4	*audiophile*
Boston	LP	Epic	E99-34188	1978	£10	£4	*US picture disc*
Can'tcha Say	CD-s	MCA	DMCA1150	1987	£5	£2	

BOSTON CRABS

In an effort to make themselves stand out from the mass of mid-sixties British beat groups, the Boston Crabs favoured an intriguing assortment of stage costumes – the lead guitarist dressed as a country bumpkin, the drummer wore an asbestos fire-fighting suit, and the lead singer posed as a blind man in a wheelchair! Uniform red shirts and blue jeans for the second half proved the last to be indeed a pose. Not that any of this did the group much good, for even substantial airplay on pirate radio for their cover of the Lovin' Spoonful's 'You Didn't Have To Be So Nice' failed to give the Boston Crabs the success they sought.

As Long As I Have You	7"	Columbia	DB7679	1965	£8	£4	
Down In Mexico	7"	Columbia	DB7586	1965	£8	£4	
You Didn't Have To Be So Nice	7"	Columbia	DB7830	1966	£6	£2.50	

BOSTON DEXTERS

I've Got Something To Tell You	7"	Columbia	DB7498	1965	£20	£10	
I've Got Troubles Of My Own	7"	Contemporary	CR103	1964	£75	£37.50	
La Bamba	7"	Contemporary	CR101	1964	£75	£37.50	
Try Hard	7"	Columbia	DB7641	1965	£20	£10	
You've Been Talking About Me	7"	Contemporary	CR102	1964	£75	£37.50	

BOSWELL, CONNIE

If I Give My Heart To You	7"	Brunswick	05319	1954	£4	£1.50	

BOSWELL, EVE

Chantez Chantez	7"	Parlophone	R4299	1957	£5	£2	
Cookie	7"	Parlophone	MSP6220	1956	£6	£2.50	
Enchanting Eve	7" EP	Parlophone	GEP8601	1957	£10	£5	
Following The Sun Around	LP	Parlophone	PMC1105	1959	£20	£8	
Gypsy In My Soul	7"	Parlophone	R4341	1957	£4	£1.50	
Keeping Cool With Lemonade	7"	Parlophone	MSP6245	1956	£5	£2	
Love Me Again	7"	Parlophone	R4414	1958	£4	£1.50	
Pam-Poo-Dey	7"	Parlophone	MSP6158	1955	£6	£2.50	
Saries Marais	7"	Parlophone	MSP6250	1956	£5	£2	
Sentimental Eve	LP	Parlophone	PMC1038	1957	£20	£8	
Showcase	7" EP	Parlophone	GEP8690	1958	£10	£5	
Showcase No. 2	7" EP	Parlophone	GEP8717	1958	£10	£5	
Sugar And Spice	10" LP	Parlophone	PMD1039	1957	£25	£10	
Sugar Bush	7"	Parlophone	MSP6006	1953	£12	£6	
Tika Tika Tok	7"	Parlophone	MSP6160	1955	£6	£2.50	
Tra La La	7"	Parlophone	R4275	1957	£8	£4	
True Love	7"	Parlophone	R4230	1956	£5	£2	
With All My Heart	7"	Parlophone	R4328	1957	£4	£1.50	
Young And Foolish	7"	Parlophone	MSP6208	1956	£6	£2.50	

BOTHWELL, JOHNNY

Whatever Happened To Johnny Bothwell?	LP	Bob Thiele Music	BBM10641	1974	£15	£6	

BOTHY BAND

Afterhours	LP	Polydor	2383530	1979	£10	£4	
Bothy Band	LP	Polydor	2383379	1975	£12	£5	
Old Hag You Have Killed Me	LP	Polydor	2383417	1976	£10	£4	
Out Of The Wind And Into The Sun	LP	Polydor	2383456	1977	£10	£4	

BOTTCHER, GERD

Die Grossen Efolge	LP	Decca	357	1966	£40	£20	German
Gerd Bottcher	LP	Decca	BLK16217P	1963	£40	£20	German

BOUDEWIJN DE GROOT

Nacht En Outiz	LP	Decca		1969	£60	£30	Dutch

BOULEVARD

Dawn Raid	7"	Boulevard	VARD1	1981	£40	£20	

BOURBON STREET ALL STAR DIXIELANDERS

Bourbon Street All Star Dixielanders	LP	HMV	CLP1121	1957	£10	£4	

BOW STREET RUNNERS

Bow Street Runners	LP	B.T.Puppy	BTPS1026	1969	£1000	£700	US

BOW WOW WOW

C-30 C-60 C-90 Go!	cass	EMI	EMI5088	1980	£10	£5	in can
Mile High Club	7"	Tour D'Eiffel	TE001	1981	£5	£2	

BOWEN, JIMMY

Crossover	7"	Columbia	DB4027	1957	£15	£7.50	
I'm Sticking With You	7"	Columbia	DB3915	1957	£40	£20	
Jimmy Bowen	LP	Roulette	R25004	1957	£60	£30	US
Meet Jimmy Bowen	7" EP	Columbia	SEG7757	1958	£60	£30	
Meet Jimmy Bowen No. 2	7" EP	Columbia	SEG7793	1958	£60	£30	
Spanish Cricket	7"	Reprise	RS23043	1965	£15	£7.50	
Sunday Morning With The Comics	LP	Reprise	R(S)6210	1966	£20	£8	US
Two Step	7"	Columbia	DB4184	1958	£10	£5	
Warm Up To Me Baby	7"	Columbia	DB3984	1957	£30	£15	

BOWERS, BEN

Big Ben Blues	7" EP	Pye	NJE1001	1956	£6	£2.50	
Country Boy	7"	Parlophone	R4317	1957	£4	£1.50	
Kentuckian Song	7"	Columbia	SCM5192	1955	£6	£2.50	
Kings Of Calypso Vol. 4	7" EP	Pye	NEP24069	1958	£5	£2	

BOWIE, DAVID

David Bowie achieved popularity a fairly long time after starting to make records, so that there are a considerable number of rare and expensive records from the early years of his career for the Bowie completist to obtain. Perhaps the most famous of these is the original cover of the LP *The Man Who Sold The World*, which portrays Bowie casually attired in a dress. 'It's a man's dress,' he explained at the time. The uncensored cover of *Diamond Dogs*, on which Bowie is painted as a creature half man and half dog, has the dog's genitalia intact – these were airbrushed out on all but the first issues. More recently, Bowie's RCA albums were issued on compact disc and then speedily withdrawn due to a royalty dispute. These became, in consequence, among the first CDs to acquire collectors' values.

1980 All Clear	LP	RCA	DJL13545	1980	£20	£8	US promo
Absolute Beginners	7"	Virgin	VSS838	1986	£4	£1.50	square picture disc
Absolute Beginners	CD-s	Virgin	CDT20	1988	£6	£2.50	3" single
Aladdin Sane	CD	RCA	PD83890	1985	£30	£15	
Aladdin Sane	LP	RCA	BOPIC1	1984	£15	£6	picture disc
All Saints	CD	private		1993	£300	£180	
BBC Sessions 1969–1972 (Sampler)	CD	BBC	NMCD0072	1996	£250	£150	promo
Black Tie, White Noise	CD	Savage		1993	£50	£25	US promo with interview
Black Tie, White Noise	CD	Savage		1994	£40	£20	Japanese with 4 extra tracks
Can't Help Thinking About Me	7"	Pye	7N17020	1966	£150	£75	
ChangesOneBowie	CD	RCA	PD81732	1985	£30	£15	
ChangesOneBowie	LP	RCA	RS1055	1976	£20	£8	with sax version of 'John'
ChangesTwoBowie	CD	RCA	PD84202	1985	£30	£15	
ChangesTwoBowie	LP & cass	RCA	DF1	1983	£15	£6	LP & cassette in holder
China Girl	CD-s	Virgin	VVCS8	1990	£5	£2	
David Bowie	CD	Deram	8000872	1984	£60	£30	white title
David Bowie	LP	Deram	DML1007	1967	£200	£100	mono
David Bowie	LP	Deram	SML1007	1967	£250	£150	stereo
David Bowie	LP	Philips	SBL7912	1969	£150	£75	
David Bowie Now	LP	RCA	DJL12697	1977	£25	£10	US promo
David Bowie Radio Special Vol. 1	LP	RCA	DJL13829	1980	£25	£10	US promo
David Live	CD	RCA	PD80771	1985	£30	£15	
Diamond Dogs	CD	RCA	PD83859	1985	£30	£15	
Diamond Dogs	LP	RCA	APL10576	1974	£250	£150	uncensored cover
Diamond Dogs	LP	RCA	BOPIC5	1984	£15	£6	picture disc
DJ	7"	RCA	BOW3	1979	£15	£7.50	picture sleeve, green vinyl
Do Anything You Say	7"	Pye	7N17079	1966	£350	£210	best auctioned
Do Anything You Say	7"	Pye	7NX8002	1972	£10	£5	picture sleeve
Evening With David Bowie	LP	RCA	DJL13016	1978	£25	£10	US promo
Fame 90	CD-s	EMI	CDFAME90	1990	£5	£2	
Fame And Fashion	CD	RCA	PD84919	1985	£60	£30	
Fashions	7"	RCA	BOW100	1982	£40	£20	set of 10 picture discs in folder
Golden Years	CD	RCA	PD84792	1985	£20	£8	
Heart's Filthy Lesson	CD-s	fan club		1995	£10	£5	shaped disc
Helden	7"	RCA	PB9168	1978	£5	£2	sung in German

Title	Format	Label	Cat. No.	Year	Mint	VG+	Notes
Heroes	CD	RCA	PD83857	1985	**£20**	**£8**	
Héros	7"	RCA	PB9167	1978	**£5**	**£2**	*sung in French*
Holy Holy	7"	Mercury	6052049	1971	**£150**	**£75**	
Hunky Dory	CD	RCA	PD84623	1985	**£30**	**£15**	
Hunky Dory	LP	RCA	BOPIC2	1984	**£15**	**£6**	*picture disc*
I Dig Everything	7"	Pye	7N17157	1966	**£350**	**£210**	*best auctioned*
I Pity The Fool	7"	Parlophone	R5250	1965	**£350**	**£210**	*credited to the Manish Boys, best auctioned*
I Pity The Fool	CD-s	See For Miles	SEACD1	1985	**£5**	**£2**	*credited to the Manish Boys*
Laughing Gnome	7"	Deram	DM123	1967	**£75**	**£37.50**	*matrix no. upside down on label*
Let's Dance	LP	RCA	UK83	1983	**£200**	**£100**	*numbered promo*
Let's Dance	LP	Mobile Fidelity	MFSL1083	1982	**£12**	**£5**	*US audiophile*
Let's Talk	LP	EMI	SPRO9960/1	1983	**£25**	**£10**	*US promo*
Life On Mars	7"	RCA	RCA2316	1973	**£6**	**£2.50**	*picture sleeve*
Lifetimes	LP	RCA	LIFETIMES1	1983	**£25**	**£10**	*promo*
Liza Jane	7"	Vocalion	V9221	1964	**£600**	**£400**	*credited to Davie Jones & The King Bees, best auctioned*
Lodger	CD	RCA	PD84234	1985	**£20**	**£8**	
Love You Till Tuesday	7"	Deram	DM135	1967	**£150**	**£75**	
Loving The Alien	7"	EMI	EAP195	1984	**£4**	**£1.50**	*shaped picture disc*
Low	CD	RCA	PD83856	1985	**£25**	**£10**	
Man Of Words, Man Of Music	LP	Mercury	SR61246	1969	**£100**	**£50**	*US*
Man Who Sold The World	cass	Mercury	6338041	1971	**£25**	**£10**	*dress cover*
Man Who Sold The World	CD	RCA	PD84654	1985	**£30**	**£15**	
Man Who Sold The World	LP	Mercury	61325	1971	**£25**	**£10**	*US, cartoon cover, stamped matrix no.*
Man Who Sold The World	LP	Mercury	6338041	1970	**£300**	**£180**	*German, round sleeve*
Man Who Sold The World	LP	RCA	LSP4816	1971	**£10**	**£4**	*with inner and poster*
Man Who Sold The World	LP	Mercury	6338041	1971	**£200**	**£100**	*dress cover*
Memory Of A Free Festival	7"	Mercury	6052026	1970	**£150**	**£75**	
Narrates Peter And The Wolf	CD	RCA	PD82743	1985	**£20**	**£8**	
Narrates Peter And The Wolf	LP	RCA	ARLI2743	1978	**£10**	**£4**	*US green vinyl*
Pin-Ups	CD	RCA	PD84653	1985	**£30**	**£15**	
Pin-Ups	LP	RCA	BOPIC4	1984	**£15**	**£6**	*picture disc*
Portrait Of A Star	LP	RCA	PL37700	1982	**£25**	**£10**	*French 3 LP boxed set*
Prettiest Star	7"	Mercury	MF1135	1970	**£150**	**£75**	
Ragazza Sola, Ragazza Solo	7"	Philips	BW704208	1969	**£150**	**£75**	*sung in Italian, picture sleeve, black label*
Ragazza Sola, Ragazza Solo	7"	Philips	BW704208	1969	**£125**	**£62.50**	*sung in Italian, picture sleeve, blue label*
Ragazza Sola, Ragazza Solo	7"	Philips	BW704208	1969	**£100**	**£50**	*sung in Italian*
Rare Bowie	LP	RCA	PL45406	1982	**£20**	**£8**	*hand stamped edition*
Rubber Band	7"	Deram	DM107	1966	**£150**	**£75**	
Scary Monsters	CD	RCA	PD83647	1985	**£30**	**£15**	
Scary Monsters	LP	RCA	BOWLP2	1980	**£200**	**£100**	*purple vinyl*
Scary Monsters Interview	LP	RCA	DJL13840	1980	**£25**	**£10**	*US promo*
Selections From The Singles Collection	CD	EMI	BOWIE1	1993	**£20**	**£8**	*promo sampler*
Sound And Vision	CD	Ryko		1989	**£200**	**£100**	*US triple plus CDV box set, wooden box, signed certificate*
Space Oddity	7"	Philips	BF1801	1969	**£5**	**£2**	
Space Oddity	7"	Philips	BF1801	1969	**£6**	**£2.50**	*stereo*
Space Oddity	7"	Philips	BF1801	1969	**£2000**	**£1400**	*picture sleeve, best auctioned*
Space Oddity	7"	RCA	RCA2593	1975	**£5**	**£2**	*picture sleeve*
Space Oddity	CD	RCA	PD84813	1985	**£30**	**£15**	
Stage	CD	RCA	PD89002	1985	**£30**	**£15**	
Stage	LP	RCA	PL02913	1978	**£20**	**£8**	*double, green or blue vinyl*
Stage	LP	RCA	PL02913	1978	**£15**	**£6**	*double, yellow vinyl*
Starman	7"	RCA	RCA2199	1972	**£30**	**£15**	*picture sleeve*
Station To Station	CD	RCA	PD81327	1985	**£30**	**£15**	
Station To Station	LP	RCA	APLI1327	1976	**£200**	**£100**	*US multicoloured vinyl*
Suffragette City	7"	RCA	RCA2726	1976	**£8**	**£4**	*picture sleeve*
Underground	7"	EMI	EAP216	1986	**£5**	**£2**	*shaped picture disc*
World Of David Bowie	LP	Decca	PA58	1970	**£15**	**£6**	*mono*
You've Got A Habit Of Leaving	7"	Parlophone	R5315	1965	**£500**	**£330**	*credited to Davy Jones & The Lower Third, best auctioned*
Young Americans	CD	RCA	PD80998	1985	**£30**	**£15**	
Ziggy Stardust	CD	RCA	PD84702	1985	**£30**	**£15**	
Ziggy Stardust	CD	Ryko	LSD4702	1990	**£100**	**£50**	*US promo boxed set, picture disc & scratched album!*
Ziggy Stardust	LP	Mobile Fidelity	MFSL1064	1982	**£15**	**£6**	*US audiophile*
Ziggy Stardust	LP	RCA	BOPIC3	1984	**£15**	**£6**	*picture disc*
Ziggy Stardust: The Motion Picture	CD	RCA	PD84862	1985	**£20**	**£8**	
Ziggy Stardust: The Motion Picture	LP	RCA	CPL24862	1983	**£60**	**£30**	*US clear vinyl*

BOWMAN–HYDE PLAYERS

Sing Me A Souvenir	LP	Parlophone	PMC1155	1961	**£25**	**£10**	

BOWN, ALAN

Alan Bown	LP	Deram	DML/SML1049	1970	**£15**	**£7.50**	
Baby Don't Push Me	7"	Pye	7N17084	1966	**£8**	**£4**	
Can't Let Her Go	7"	Pye	7N15934	1965	**£6**	**£2.50**	
Emergency	7"	Pye	7N17192	1966	**£6**	**£2.50**	
First Album – Outward Bown	LP	Music Factory	CUBLM/LS1	1968	**£15**	**£6**	
Gonna Fix You Good	7"	Pye	7N17256	1967	**£10**	**£5**	
Headline News	7"	Pye	7N17148	1966	**£5**	**£2**	
Jeu De Massacre	7" EP	Vogue	EPL8537	1967	**£15**	**£7.50**	*French, with tracks by Jacques Loussier*
Listen	LP	Island	ILPS9131	1970	**£10**	**£4**	
Outward Bown	LP	Music Factory	MF12000	1967	**£25**	**£10**	
Stretching Out	LP	Island	ILPS9163	1971	**£10**	**£4**	
We Can Help You	7"	Music Factory	CUB1	196–	**£4**	**£1.50**	

BOWN, ALAN & JIMMY JAMES

London Swings	LP	Pye	N(S)PL18156	1966	**£25**	**£10**	*1 side each*

BOWN, ANDREW

Tarot	7"	Parlophone	R5856	1970	**£25**	**£12.50**	

BOWN, ANDY

Gone To My Head	LP	Mercury	6310002	1972	**£10**	**£4**	
Sweet William	LP	GM	GML1001	1973	**£10**	**£4**	

BOX, DAVID

Little Lonely Summer Girl	7"	London	HLU9924	1964	**£8**	**£4**	
Sweet Sweet Day	7"	London	HLU9874	1964	**£8**	**£4**	

BOX TOPS

Cry Like A Baby	LP	Bell	MBLL/SBLL105	1968	**£10**	**£4**	
Dimensions	LP	Bell	SBLL120	1969	**£10**	**£4**	
Letter	7"	Stateside	SS2044	1967	**£4**	**£1.50**	
Letter/Neon Rainbow	LP	Stateside	(S)SL10218	1968	**£15**	**£6**	
Lifetime Believing	LP	Cotillon	SD057	1971	**£10**	**£4**	*US*
Mi Sento Felice	7"		SIR20072	1967	**£8**	**£4**	*sung in Italian*
Non Stop	LP	Bell	MBLL/SBLL108	1968	**£10**	**£4**	
Soul Deep	7"	Bell	BLL1068	1969	**£4**	**£1.50**	
Super Hits	LP	Bell	S6025	1968	**£12**	**£5**	*US*

BOXER

Bloodletting	LP	Virgin	V2073	1976	**£60**	**£30**	*demo only*

BOY GEORGE

Crying Game	CD-s	Polydor	CIOCD6	1992	**£5**	**£2**	
Devil In Sister George EP	CD-s	Virgin	VSCDG1490	1994	**£8**	**£4**	
Don't Cry	CD-s	Virgin	BOYCD107	1989	**£8**	**£4**	*3" single*
Don't Take My Mind On A Trip	CD-s	Virgin	BOYCD108	1989	**£10**	**£5**	
Live My Life	12"	Virgin	BOY10512	1988	**£6**	**£2.50**	
No Clause 28	CD-s	Virgin	BOYCD106	1988	**£6**	**£2.50**	
No Clause 28	CD-s	Virgin	BOYT106	1988	**£8**	**£4**	*3" single*
To Be Reborn	CD-s	Virgin	CDEP9	1987	**£10**	**£5**	

BOY HAIRDRESSERS

Golden Shower	12"	53rd & 3rd	AGARR12T	1987	**£12**	**£6**	

BOYCE, DENNIS

Bad Boy	7"	Oriole	CB1458	1958	**£4**	**£1.50**	

BOYCE, TOMMY

Twofold Talent	LP	Camden	CAL/CAS2202	1967	**£10**	**£4**	*US*

BOYCE, TOMMY & BOBBY HART

I Wonder What She's Doing Tonight	LP	A&M	SP4143	1968	**£10**	**£4**	*US*
It's All Happening On The Inside	LP	A&M	SP4162	1968	**£10**	**£4**	*US*
Out And About	7" EP	A&M	EAM1001	1967	**£5**	**£2**	*French*
Test Patterns	LP	A&M	AML907	1967	**£10**	**£4**	

BOYD, EDDIE

7936 South Rhodes	LP	Blue Horizon	763202	1968	**£60**	**£30**	
Big Boat	7"	Blue Horizon	573137	1967	**£12**	**£6**	
Boyd's Blues	7" EP	Esquire	EP247	1962	**£40**	**£20**	
Dust My Broom	LP	London	PS554	1969	**£15**	**£6**	*US*
Eddie Boyd And His Blues Band	LP	Decca	LK/SKL4872	1967	**£100**	**£50**	
Five Long Years	LP	Fontana	STJL905	1965	**£25**	**£10**	
In Concert	LP	Storyville	SLP4054	1968	**£15**	**£6**	
It's So Miserable To Be Alone	7"	Blue Horizon	451009	1966	**£100**	**£50**	
With the Blues	7" EP	Chess	CRE6009	1966	**£15**	**£7.50**	*2 tracks by Buddy Guy*

BOYD, JIMMY

I Saw Mommy Kissing Santa Claus	7"	Columbia	SCM5072	1953	**£20**	**£10**	

BOYLE, BILLY

Title	Format	Label	Number	Year	Mint	VG	Notes
My Baby's Crazy About Elvis	7"	Decca	F11503	1962	**£12**	**£6**	
Walk Walk Walkin'	7"	Columbia	DB7294	1964	**£5**	**£2**	

BOYLES BROTHERS

Title	Format	Label	Number	Year	Mint	VG	Notes
Introducing The Boyles Brothers	LP	International Artist	6801	1968	**£125**	**£62.50**	*US*

BOYS

The Boys, who released 'It Ain't Fair' in 1964, became the Action shortly afterwards.

Title	Format	Label	Number	Year	Mint	VG	Notes
It Ain't Fair	7"	Pye	7N15726	1964	**£30**	**£15**	

BOYS (2)

Title	Format	Label	Number	Year	Mint	VG	Notes
Kamikaze	7"	Safari	SAFE21	1979	**£4**	**£1.50**	*with booklet*

BOYS (3)

Title	Format	Label	Number	Year	Mint	VG	Notes
Polaris	7"	Parlophone	R5027	1963	**£15**	**£7.50**	

BOYS (4)

No doubt deliberately named after the Boys who became the Action, this mod revival group included Ocean Colour Scene guitarist Steve Craddock within its line-up.

Title	Format	Label	Number	Year	Mint	VG	Notes
Happy Days	7"	private		1988	**£8**	**£4**	

BOYS BLUE

Title	Format	Label	Number	Year	Mint	VG	Notes
Take A Heart	7"	HMV	POP1427	1965	**£50**	**£25**	

BOYS OF THE LOUGH

Title	Format	Label	Number	Year	Mint	VG	Notes
Boys Of The Lough	LP	Trailer	LER2086	1973	**£10**	**£4**	
Good Friends Good Music	LP	Transatlantic	TRA354	1977	**£10**	**£4**	
Piper's Broken Finger	LP	Transatlantic	TRA333	1976	**£10**	**£4**	
Recorded Live	LP	Transatlantic	TRA296	1975	**£10**	**£4**	
Regrouped	LP	Topic	12TS409	1980	**£10**	**£4**	
Second Album	LP	Trailer	LER2090	1974	**£10**	**£4**	

BOYZONE

Title	Format	Label	Number	Year	Mint	VG	Notes
Love Me For A Reason	CD-s	Polydor	8512802	1995	**£6**	**£2.50**	
Working My Way Back To You	CD-s	Polydor	8532462	1994	**£15**	**£7.50**	*Irish*

BOZ

Title	Format	Label	Number	Year	Mint	VG	Notes
Baby Song	7"	Columbia	DB7972	1966	**£4**	**£1.50**	
I Shall Be Released	7"	Columbia	DB8406	1968	**£4**	**£1.50**	
Isn't That So	7"	Columbia	DB7832	1966	**£4**	**£1.50**	
Light My Fire	7"	Columbia	DB8468	1968	**£4**	**£1.50**	
Meeting Time	7"	Columbia	DB7889	1966	**£4**	**£1.50**	
Pinnochio	7"	Columbia	DB7941	1966	**£4**	**£1.50**	

BRACEY, ISHMAN

Title	Format	Label	Number	Year	Mint	VG	Notes
RCA Victor Race Series Vol. 1	7" EP	RCA	RCX7167	1964	**£5**	**£2**	

BRACKEN

Title	Format	Label	Number	Year	Mint	VG	Notes
Prince Of The Northlands	LP	Look	LKLP6438	1979	**£75**	**£37.50**	

BRADFORD, BOBBY

Title	Format	Label	Number	Year	Mint	VG	Notes
Love's Dream	LP	Emanem	302	1974	**£15**	**£6**	

BRADFORD, PROFESSOR ALEX

Title	Format	Label	Number	Year	Mint	VG	Notes
Angel On Vacation	LP	Stateside	SL10083	1964	**£10**	**£4**	
One Step	LP	Stateside	SL10047	1963	**£10**	**£4**	
Too Close To Heaven	7" EP	London	REU1357	1963	**£10**	**£5**	

BRADLEY, JAN

Title	Format	Label	Number	Year	Mint	VG	Notes
Mama Didn't Lie	7"	Pye	7N25182	1963	**£10**	**£5**	

BRADLEY, OWEN

Title	Format	Label	Number	Year	Mint	VG	Notes
Big Guitar	7"	Brunswick	05736	1958	**£6**	**£2.50**	
Big Guitar	LP	Brunswick	LAT8327	1960	**£20**	**£8**	

BRADSHAM-LEATHER, DON

Title	Format	Label	Number	Year	Mint	VG	Notes
Distance Between Us	LP	Distance	DIST101	1972	**£40**	**£20**	*double*

BRADSHAW, SONNY

Title	Format	Label	Number	Year	Mint	VG	Notes
Festival Jump Up	7"	Duke	DK1003	1963	**£5**	**£2**	

BRADSHAW, TINY

Title	Format	Label	Number	Year	Mint	VG	Notes
Bradshaw Boogie	78	Parlophone	DP418	1952	**£5**	**£2**	
Breaking Up The House	78	Vogue	V2146	1952	**£5**	**£2**	
Great Composer	LP	King	653	1959	**£30**	**£15**	*US*
Off And On	10" LP	King	29574	195–	**£150**	**£75**	*US*
Overflow	7"	Parlophone	MSP6145	1955	**£10**	**£5**	
Pompton Turnpike	7" EP	Parlophone	GEP8552	1956	**£15**	**£7.50**	
Selections	LP	King	395501	195–	**£50**	**£25**	*US*
South Of The Orient	7"	Parlophone	CMSP3	1954	**£15**	**£7.50**	*export*
Spider Web	7"	Parlophone	MSP6118	1954	**£10**	**£5**	
Train Kept A Rolling	7" EP	Parlophone	GEP8507	1954	**£25**	**£12.50**	

Twenty-Four Great Songs	LP	King	953	1966	**£15**	**£6**	*US*

BRADSHAW, TINY & WYNONIE HARRIS

Kings Of Rhythm And Blues	LP	Polydor	623273	1970	**£10**	**£4**	

BRADY, BOB & THE CONCHORDS

Everybody Goin' To A Love-In	7"	Bell	BLL1025	1968	**£4**	**£1.50**	

BRADY, PAUL

Welcome Here Kind Stranger	LP	Mulligan	LUN024	1974	**£12**	**£5**	*Irish*

BRADY, VICTOR

Brown Rain	LP	Polydor	2489010	1970	**£25**	**£10**	

BRAFF, RUBY

Hustlin' And Bustlin'	LP	Vogue	LAE12051	1957	**£25**	**£10**	
Inventions In Jazz Part 2	10" LP	Vanguard	PPT12022	1958	**£25**	**£10**	*with Ellis Larkins*
Newport Jazz Festival 1957	LP	Columbia	33CX10104	1958	**£15**	**£6**	*side 2 by Bobby Henderson*
Ruby Braff All Stars	LP	Philips	BBL7130	1957	**£12**	**£5**	
Ruby Braff And The Dixie Victors	LP	HMV	CLP1091	1956	**£15**	**£6**	
Ruby Braff Orchestra	10" LP	London	LZN14022	1956	**£25**	**£10**	
Ruby Braff Sextet	10" LP	London	LZN14028	1956	**£25**	**£10**	
Ruby Braff Special	LP	Vanguard	PPL11003	1956	**£15**	**£6**	

BRAGG, BILLY

Peel Sessions	CD-s	Strange Fruit	SFPSCD027	1988	**£5**	**£2**	
Sexuality	CD-s	Go! Discs	GODCD56	1991	**£5**	**£2**	
You Woke Up My Neighbourhood	CD-s	Go! Discs	GODCD60	1991	**£5**	**£2**	

BRAGGS, AL TNT

Al TNT Braggs	7" EP	Vocalion	VEP170163	1965	**£30**	**£15**	
Earthquake	7"	Vocalion	VP9278	1966	**£6**	**£2.50**	
Earthquake	7"	Action	ACT4506	1968	**£5**	**£2**	
I'm A Good Man	7"	Action	ACT4526	1969	**£4**	**£1.50**	

BRAHAM, ERNEL

Musical Fight	7"	Rio	R79	1966	**£6**	**£2.50**	

BRAIN

The Brain's 'Nightmares In Red' is not so much psychedelic as lunatic. It is in fact an early recorded effort by the brothers Giles – prior to them joining forces with guitarist Robert Fripp and beginning the rehearsals that led to the debut of King Crimson.

Nightmares In Red	7"	Parlophone	R5595	1967	**£75**	**£37.50**	

BRAINBOX

Best Of Brainbox	LP	EMI	05424327	1972	**£15**	**£6**	*German*
Brainbox	LP	Parlophone	PCS7094	1970	**£30**	**£15**	
Down Man	7"	Parlophone	R5775	1969	**£5**	**£2**	
Parts	LP	Harvest	05624551	1972	**£15**	**£6**	*German*
To You	7"	Parlophone	R5842	1970	**£4**	**£1.50**	

BRAINCHILD

Healing Of The Lunatic Owl	LP	A&M	AMLS979	1970	**£40**	**£20**	

BRAINIAC FIVE

Mushy Doubt	7"	Roach	RREP5001	1978	**£6**	**£2.50**	
Working	7"	Roach	RR5002	1980	**£5**	**£2**	

BRAINSTORM

Second Smile	LP	Spiegelei	28596	1974	**£10**	**£4**	*German*
Smile A While	LP	Spiegelei	28505	1972	**£10**	**£4**	*German*

BRAINTICKET

Celestial Ocean	LP	RCA	SF8398	1974	**£15**	**£6**	
Cotton Wood Hill	LP	Bellaphon	BLPS19019	1971	**£20**	**£8**	*German double*
Psychonaut	LP	Bellaphon	BLPS19104	1972	**£15**	**£6**	*German*

BRAITH, GEORGE

Extension	LP	Blue Note	BLP/BST84171	1964	**£30**	**£15**	
Soul Dream	LP	Blue Note	BLP/BST84161	1964	**£30**	**£15**	
Two Souls In One	LP	Blue Note	BLP/BST84148	1963	**£30**	**£15**	

BRAM STOKER

Hard Rock Spectacular	LP	Windmill	WMD117	1972	**£40**	**£20**	

BRAMBELL, WILFRED

Secondhand	7"	Parlophone	R5058	1963	**£6**	**£2.50**	

BRAMBELL, WILFRED & HARRY H. CORBETT

Gems From The Steptoe Scrap Heap	LP	Pye	NPL18153	1966	**£12**	**£5**	
Love And Harold Steptoe	LP	Pye	NPL18135	1965	**£12**	**£5**	
Steptoe A La Carte	LP	Pye	NPL18101	1964	**£10**	**£4**	
Steptoe And Son	LP	Pye	NPL18081	1964	**£10**	**£4**	

BRAMLETT, DELANEY

Heartbreak Hotel	7"	Vocalion	VN9227	1964	**£8**	**£4**	

Liverpool Lou	7"	Vocalion	VN9237	1965	**£10**	**£5**	

BRAN

Ail Ddechra	LP	Sain	1038M	1974	**£25**	**£10**	
Gwrach Y Hos	LP	Sain	1120M	1978	**£20**	**£8**	
Hedfan	LP	Sain	1070M	1976	**£25**	**£10**	

BRAND

I'm A Lover Not A Fighter	7"	Piccadilly	7N35216	1965	**£75**	**£37.50**	

BRAND, DOLLAR

Anatomy Of A South African Village	LP	Fontana	688314ZL	1964	**£10**	**£4**	

BRANDO, MARLON & JEAN SIMMONS

Guys And Dolls	7" EP	Brunswick	OE9241	1955	**£6**	**£2.50**	

BRANDON, JOHNNY

Hits	7" EP	Pye	NEP24003	1955	**£12**	**£6**	
Rock-A-Bye Baby	7"	Parlophone	MSP6238	1956	**£4**	**£1.50**	
Shim Sham Shuffle	7"	Parlophone	R4207	1956	**£8**	**£4**	

BRANDON, KIRK

Kirk Brandon And The Pack Of Lies	7"	SS	SS1N2/SS2N1	1987	**£6**	**£2.50**	

BRANDON, VERN

Gotta Know The Reason	7"	Decca	F11472	1962	**£10**	**£5**	

BRANDY BOYS

Gale Winds	7"	Columbia	DB7507	1965	**£6**	**£2.50**	

BRANDYWINE BRIDGE

English Meadow	LP	Cottage	COT321	1978	**£20**	**£8**	
Grey Lady	LP	Cottage	COT311	1977	**£20**	**£8**	

BRANTLEY, JOHNNY

Place	7"	London	HLU8606	1958	**£15**	**£7.50**	

BRASS MONKEY

Brass Monkey	LP	Topic	12TS431	1983	**£10**	**£4**	

BRASS TACKS

I'll Keep Holding On	7"	Transatlantic	BIG110	1968	**£4**	**£1.50**	
Maxwell Ferguson	7"	Transatlantic	BIG114	1968	**£10**	**£5**	

BRASSEUR, ANDRE

Early Bird	7"	Pye	7N25332	1965	**£5**	**£2**	

BRAUN, CHRIS

Both Sides	LP	BASF	20213994	1972	**£10**	**£4**	*German*
Foreign Lady	LP	Pan	87586	1973	**£10**	**£4**	*German*

BRAUTIGAN, RICHARD

Richard Brautigan is an American writer whose whimsically poetic prose style struck something of a chord in the late sixties and early seventies. *Trout Fishing In America* is perhaps his best-known book, but his reading of extracts from it failed to achieve the success on Apple that was intended.

Listening To Richard Brautigan	LP	Apple	ZAPPLE03	1969	**£250**	**£150**	*test pressing*
Listening To Richard Brautigan	LP	Straight	ST424	1969	**£20**	**£8**	*US*

BRAVE NEW WORLD

Impressions On Reading Aldous Huxley	LP	Vertigo	6360606	1972	**£50**	**£25**	*German*

BRAVO, CEDRIC

Merry Christmas	7"	Ska Beat	JB229	1965	**£10**	**£5**	

BRAXTON, ANTHONY

Anthony Braxton's forbiddingly intellectual approach to jazz improvisation and composition is shot through with a pleasing eccentricity. Many of his pieces have titles that are like molecular diagrams or mathematical formulae – some even comprise little pictures of people and buildings and suchlike. Then there is his plan to write music for orchestras situated on different planets . . . The collectable albums listed here are just the earliest in a huge and still growing catalogue.

Anthony Braxton	LP	BYG	529315	1970	**£15**	**£6**	*French*
Donna Lee	LP	America	30AM6122	1972	**£12**	**£5**	
For Alto	LP	Delmark	DS420/1	1971	**£20**	**£8**	*double*
This Time	LP	BYG	529347	1971	**£15**	**£6**	*French*
Three Compositions Of New Jazz	LP	Delmark	DS415	1968	**£15**	**£6**	

BRAZIER, PRISCILLA

Priscilla Brazier	LP	Dovetail	DOVE9	1974	**£20**	**£8**	
Something Beautiful	LP	Key	KL038	1976	**£20**	**£8**	

BREAD, LOVE & DREAMS

Amarylis	LP	Decca	SKL5081	1971	**£250**	**£150**	
Bread, Love & Dreams	LP	Decca	SKL5008	1969	**£40**	**£20**	
Strange Tale Of Captain Shannon	LP	Decca	LK/SKL5048	1970	**£40**	**£20**	
Switch Out The Sun	7"	Decca	F12958	1969	**£5**	**£2**	

BREAD & BEER BAND

The high value of the Bread and Beer Band's single derives from the fact that the band's pianist was one Reg Dwight (who was shortly to adopt the stage name Elton John). There is an LP by the band, but it is believed that only one copy of this exists. It came up for sale at one of the London rock auctions at the end of the eighties and fetched £1700.

Title	Format	Label	Number	Year	Value	Value	Notes
Dick Barton Theme	7"	Decca	F13354	1973	**£40**	**£20**	
Dick Barton Theme	7"	Decca	F12891	1969	**£100**	**£50**	

BREAKAWAYS

Title	Format	Label	Number	Year	Value	Value	Notes
Danny Boy	7"	Pye	7N15973	1965	**£4**	**£1.50**	
He Doesn't Love Me	7"	Pye	7N15618	1964	**£5**	**£2**	
He's A Rebel	7"	Pye	7N15471	1962	**£4**	**£1.50**	
Here She Comes	7"	Pye	7N15585	1963	**£5**	**£2**	
Sacred Love	7"	CBS	2833	1967	**£5**	**£2**	
Santo Domingo	7"	MCA	MU1018	1968	**£4**	**£1.50**	
That Boy Of Mine	7" EP	Pye	PNV24119	1964	**£20**	**£10**	*French*

BREAKDOWN

Title	Format	Label	Number	Year	Value	Value	Notes
Meet Me On The Highway	LP	private	MCP001	1977	**£40**	**£20**	

BREAKTHRU

Title	Format	Label	Number	Year	Value	Value	Notes
Ice Cream Tree	7"	Mercury	MF1066	1968	**£6**	**£2.50**	

BREATHLESS

Title	Format	Label	Number	Year	Value	Value	Notes
Nobody Leaves This Song Alive	LP	EMI	SW17041	1980	**£50**	**£25**	*US*

BRECKER, RANDY

Title	Format	Label	Number	Year	Value	Value	Notes
Score	LP	Solid State	18051	1968	**£20**	**£8**	*US*

BREEDLOVE, JIMMY

Title	Format	Label	Number	Year	Value	Value	Notes
Over Somebody Else's Shoulder	7"	London	HLE8490	1957	**£60**	**£30**	
You're Following Me	7"	Pye	7N25121	1962	**£5**	**£2**	

BREEZIN

Title	Format	Label	Number	Year	Value	Value	Notes
Breezin	LP	Plahadima		1983	**£15**	**£6**	*Dutch*

BREGMAN, BUDDY

Title	Format	Label	Number	Year	Value	Value	Notes
Buddy Bregman And His Orchestra	LP	HMV	CLP1154	1958	**£15**	**£6**	
Theme From Picnic	7"	HMV	7MC40	1956	**£6**	**£2.50**	*export*

BREL, JACQUES

Title	Format	Label	Number	Year	Value	Value	Notes
A L'Olympia	LP	Fontana	SFJL967	1968	**£15**	**£6**	
Alive And Well And Living In Paris	LP	CBS	66207	1968	**£20**	**£8**	*double*
Jacques Brel	LP	Fontana	TL5330	1965	**£15**	**£6**	
Jacques Brel '67	LP	Fontana	STL5429	1967	**£15**	**£6**	
Jacques Brel Vol. 2	LP	Fontana	TL5391	1965	**£15**	**£6**	
Personally	LP	Barclay	90037	1975	**£10**	**£4**	*French*

BRENDA & THE TABULATIONS

Title	Format	Label	Number	Year	Value	Value	Notes
Baby You're So Right For Me	7"	Direction	583678	1968	**£4**	**£1.50**	
Dry Your Eyes	7"	London	HL10127	1967	**£8**	**£4**	
Dry Your Eyes	LP	Action	ACLP6003	1969	**£20**	**£8**	
That's In The Past	7"	Action	ACT4541	1969	**£12**	**£6**	
When You're Gone	7"	London	HL10174	1967	**£8**	**£4**	

BRENDON

Title	Format	Label	Number	Year	Value	Value	Notes
Gimme Some	7"	Magnet	MAG80	1976	**£10**	**£5**	

BRENNAN, ROSE

Title	Format	Label	Number	Year	Value	Value	Notes
Band Of Gold	7"	HMV	7M383	1956	**£4**	**£1.50**	
Courtin' In The Kitchen	7"	HMV	7M392	1956	**£4**	**£1.50**	
Sincerely	7"	HMV	7M299	1955	**£5**	**£2**	
Ten Little Kisses	7"	HMV	7M328	1955	**£4**	**£1.50**	
Tra La La	7"	HMV	POP302	1957	**£5**	**£2**	
You Are My Love	7"	HMV	7M360	1956	**£4**	**£1.50**	

BRENNAN, WALTER

Title	Format	Label	Number	Year	Value	Value	Notes
Dutchman's Gold	7"	London	HLD9148	1960	**£4**	**£1.50**	
Gunfight At The OK Corral	LP	Liberty	LBY1249	1964	**£15**	**£6**	

BRENT, FRANKIE

Title	Format	Label	Number	Year	Value	Value	Notes
Be My Girl	78	Pye	N15103	1957	**£5**	**£2**	
Rockin' Shoes	78	Pye	N15102	1957	**£5**	**£2**	

BRENT, TONY

Title	Format	Label	Number	Year	Value	Value	Notes
Amore	7"	Columbia	DB3884	1957	**£6**	**£2.50**	
Big Hits	LP	Columbia	33SX5001	195–	**£20**	**£8**	
Butterfly	7"	Columbia	DB3918	1957	**£8**	**£4**	
Cindy, Oh Cindy	7"	Columbia	DB3844	1956	**£8**	**£4**	
Dark Moon	7"	Columbia	DB3950	1957	**£5**	**£2**	
Deep Within Me	7"	Columbia	DB3987	1957	**£5**	**£2**	
Ding Dong Boogie	7"	Columbia	SCM5029	1953	**£15**	**£7.50**	
Have You Heard	7"	Columbia	SCM5042	1953	**£15**	**£7.50**	
I Understand Just How You Feel	7"	Columbia	SCM5135	1954	**£10**	**£5**	
It's A Woman's World	7"	Columbia	SCM5160	1955	**£10**	**£5**	
Love By The Jukebox Light	7"	Columbia	DB4043	1957	**£5**	**£2**	

Mirror Mirror	7"	Columbia	SCM5188	1955	£8	£4	
My Little Angel	7"	Columbia	SCM5272	1956	£8	£4	
Nicolette	7"	Columbia	SCM5146	1954	£8	£4	
Off Stage	10" LP	Columbia	33S1125	1958	£25	£10	
Off Stage	7" EP	Columbia	SEG8019	1960	£15	£7.50	
Off Stage No. 2	7" EP	Columbia	SEG8040	1960	£15	£7.50	
Open Up Your Heart	7"	Columbia	SCM5170	1955	£12	£6	
Sooner Or Later	7"	Columbia	SCM5245	1956	£6	£2.50	
Time For Tony	7" EP	Columbia	SEG7869	1957	£15	£7.50	
Tony Calls The Tune	7" EP	Columbia	SEG7824	1958	£15	£7.50	
Tony Takes Five	LP	Columbia	33SX1200/ SCX3288	1960	£20	£8	
Which Way The Wind Blows	7"	Columbia	SCM5057	1953	£12	£6	
With Your Love	7"	Columbia	SCM5200	1955	£8	£4	

BRENTWOOD ROAD ALL STARS

Love At First Sight	7"	Bamboo	BAM23	1970	£5	£2	
Soul Shake	7"	Bamboo	BAM25	1970	£5	£2	

BRESSLAW, BERNARD

I Only Arsked	7" EP	HMV	7EG8439	1957	£6	£2.50	

BRETT, PAUL

Jubilation Foundry	LP	Dawn	DNLS3021	1971	£10	£4	
Music Manifold	LP	private		197–	£15	£6	
Paul Brett	LP	Bradleys	BRAD1001	1973	£10	£4	
Paul Brett Sage	LP	Pye	NSPL18347	1970	£12	£5	
Phoenix Future	LP	Phoenix Future	PF001	1975	£12	£5	
Schizophrenia	LP	Dawn	DNLS3032	1972	£12	£5	
Very Strange Brew	LP	ABC	672	1969	£15	£6	US

BRETT, STEVE & THE MAVERICKS

Chains On My Heart	7"	Columbia	DB7794	1965	£125	£62.50	
Sad Lonely And Blue	7"	Columbia	DB7581	1965	£100	£50	
Wishing	7"	Columbia	DB7470	1965	£100	£50	

BREVETT, LLOYD

Wayward Ska	7"	Ska Beat	JB213	1965	£10	£5	Winston Samuels B side

BREWER & FARNER

Monumental Funk	LP	Quadico	QLP7401	1974	£12	£5	US

BREWER, TERESA

Aloha From Teresa	LP	Coral	LVA9152	1962	£12	£5	
And The Dixieland Band	LP	Coral	LVA9107	1959	£12	£5	
And The Dixieland Band Pt 1	7" EP	Coral	FEP2047	1960	£10	£5	
And The Dixieland Band Pt 2	7" EP	Coral	FEP2048	1960	£10	£5	
At Christmas Time	LP	Coral	LVA9091	1958	£15	£6	
Au Revoir	7"	Vogue Coral	Q2029	1954	£10	£5	
Banjo's Back In Town	7"	Vogue Coral	Q72098	1955	£6	£2.50	
Bouquet Of Hits	LP	Coral	CRL56072	1954	£15	£6	US
Crazy With Love	7"	Vogue Coral	Q72213	1956	£5	£2	
Don't Mess Around With Tess	LP	Coral	LVA9204	1962	£12	£5	
Empty Arms	7"	Vogue Coral	Q72251	1957	£4	£1.50	
For Teenagers In Love	LP	Coral	LVA9075	1957	£15	£6	
Good Man Is Hard To Find	7"	Vogue Coral	Q72130	1956	£6	£2.50	
How Do You Know It's Love	7" EP	Coral	FEP2061	1960	£10	£5	
How Important Can It Be?	7"	Vogue Coral	Q72065	1955	£8	£4	
Hula Hoop Time	7" EP	Coral	FEP2013	1959	£10	£5	
I'm Drowning My Sorrows	7"	Vogue Coral	Q72239	1957	£4	£1.50	
Jingle Bell Rock	7"	Coral	Q72349	1958	£4	£1.50	
Keep Your Cotton Pickin' Paddies	7"	Vogue Coral	Q72199	1956	£4	£1.50	
Let Me Go Lover	7"	Vogue Coral	Q72043	1955	£12	£6	
Lula Rock-A-Hula	7"	Vogue Coral	Q72278	1957	£6	£2.50	
Music! Music! Music!	LP	Coral	LVA9020	1956	£15	£6	
My Golden Favourites	LP	Coral	LVA9131	1960	£10	£4	
Naughty Naughty Naughty	LP	Coral	LVA9138	1960	£12	£5	
Nora Malone	7"	Vogue Coral	Q72224	1957	£5	£2	
Pledging My Love	7"	Vogue Coral	Q72077	1955	£10	£5	
Remembering	7"	Vogue Coral	Q72139	1956	£8	£4	
Ridin' High	LP	Coral	LVA9129	1960	£12	£5	
Rock Love	7"	Vogue Coral	Q72066	1955	£12	£6	
Showcase	10" LP	London	HAPB1006	1951	£25	£10	
Skinny Minnie	7"	Vogue Coral	Q2011	1954	£12	£6	
Songs Everybody Knows	LP	Coral	LVA9145	1961	£12	£5	
Sweet Old-Fashioned Girl	7"	Vogue Coral	Q72172	1956	£8	£4	
Tear Fell	7"	Vogue Coral	Q72146	1956	£10	£5	
Till I Waltz Again With You	LP	Coral	CRL56093	1954	£15	£6	US
Time For Teresa Brewer	LP	Coral	LVA9095	1959	£12	£5	
When Your Lover Has Gone	LP	Coral	LVA9100/ SVL3003	1959	£12	£5	
When Your Lover Has Gone Pt 1	7" EP	Coral	FEP2036	1959	£10	£5	
When Your Lover Has Gone Pt 2	7" EP	Coral	FEP2037	1959	£10	£5	
When Your Lover Has Gone Pt 3	7" EP	Coral	FEP2038	1959	£10	£5	
You Send Me	7"	Vogue Coral	Q72292	1957	£5	£2	
You're Telling Our Secret	7"	Vogue Coral	Q72083	1955	£8	£4	

BREWERS DROOP

Opening Time	LP	RCA	SF8301	1972	£10	£4	

BRIAR

Edge Of A Broken Heart	7"	PRT	BRIARP1	1987	£5	£2	*shaped picture disc*
Gimme All You Got	7"	Shotgun Charlie	SCR1	1989	£6	£2.50	*picture sleeve*
Rainbow	7"	Happy Face	MM142	1982	£6	£2.50	
Too Young	LP	Heavy Metal	HMRLP41	1985	£10	£4	*with single and poster*

BRIDES OF FUNKENSTEIN

Funk Or Walk	LP	Atlantic	K50545	1978	£15	£6	

BRIDGES

Fakkeltog	LP	Vakenatt	VN01	1979	£100	£50	*Norwegian*

BRIERLEY, MARC

Autograph Of Time	7"	CBS	3857	1968	£4	£1.50	
Hello	LP	CBS	63835	1969	£25	£10	
Marc Brierley	7" EP	Transatlantic	TRAEP147	1966	£30	£15	
Welcome To The Citadel	LP	CBS	63478	1967	£20	£8	

BRIGADE

Last Laugh	LP	Band N Vocal	1066	1970	£1000	£700	*US*

BRIGG

Brigg	LP	private		1972	£300	£180	*US*

BRIGGS, ANNE

Richard Thompson's song, 'Beeswing', the tale of a woman possessed of an incurable restlessness, is supposed to be inspired by the life of Anne Briggs. Her handful of recordings (which include 'Bird In The Bush', a collaboration with A. L. Lloyd, listed in this guide under his name) are widely regarded as folk masterpieces. Her treatments of traditional material are definitive, while her own songs – some of which were covered by Bert Jansch – are highly memorable. Her version of the traditional tune 'Blackwater Side' inspired Bert Jansch to record the piece also, from where it found its way into the repertoire of Led Zeppelin (as 'Black Mountain Side'). Anne Briggs's lack of interest in establishing any kind of career as a singer, however, is highlighted by the fact that her own daughter apparently only discovered her mother's recordings when a compilation CD was issued in 1990.

Anne Briggs	LP	Topic	12TS207	1971	£100	£50	
Hazards Of Love	7" EP	Topic	TOP94	1963	£60	£30	
Time Has Come	LP	CBS	64612	1971	£100	£50	

BRIGGS, BILLY

Chew Tobacco Rag	78	Columbia	DB2938	1951	£5	£2	

BRIGHT, GREG

Room By Greg	LP	private		1969	£100	£50	

BRIGHT, RONNELL

Bright Flight	LP	Vanguard	PPL11016	1958	£12	£5	

BRIGMAN, GEORGE

Jungle Rot	LP	Solid	SR001	1975	£75	£37.50	*US*
Second Album	cass			1977	£25	£10	*US*

BRILLIANT, ASHLEIGH

In The Haight-Ashbury	LP	Dorash	1001	1967	£40	£20	*US*

BRILLIANT CORNERS

She's Got Fever	7"	SS20	SS21	1984	£10	£5	

BRIMSTONE

Paper Winged Dreams	LP	Brimstone		196–	£100	£50	*US*

BRIMSTONE, DEREK

Derek Brimstone	LP	Fontana	STL5478	1969	£12	£5	

BRINDLEY BRAE

Village Music	LP	Harmony	DB0002	197–	£25	£10	

BRINSLEY SCHWARZ

Forever damned as the group whose manager virtually invented the concept of hype (when he chartered a plane-load of journalists to watch his clients perform at the bottom of the Fillmore bill), Brinsley Schwarz never quite managed to find the acclaim that their frequently fine material deserved. Bassist Nick Lowe, however, went on to do quite well for himself, while other members of the group, including guitarist Schwarz himself, found employment as members of Graham Parker's Rumour.

Brinsley Schwarz	LP	United Artists	UAS29111	1970	£15	£6	
Country Girl	7"	Liberty	LBY15419	1970	£4	£1.50	
Despite It All	LP	Liberty	LBG83427	1970	£15	£6	
Nervous On The Road	LP	United Artists	UAS29374	1972	£10	£4	
New Favourites	LP	United Artists	UAS29641	1974	£10	£4	
Please Don't Ever Change	LP	United Artists	UAS29489	1973	£15	£6	
Shining Brightly	7"	United Artists	UP35118	1970	£4	£1.50	
Silver Pistol	LP	United Artists	UAS29217	1972	£12	£5	*with poster*

BRITISH WALKERS

I Found You	7"	Pye	7N25298	1965	£20	£10	

BRITT

Title	Format	Label	Cat. No.	Year	Mint	Good	Notes
Leave My Baby Alone	7"	Piccadilly	7N35273	1966	£6	£2.50	

BRITT, ELTON

Title	Format	Label	Cat. No.	Year	Mint	Good	Notes
Wandering Cowboy	LP	ABC-Paramount	(S)293	1959	£12	£5	US
Yodel Songs	10" LP	RCA	LPM3222	1954	£25	£10	US
Yodel Songs	LP	RCA	LPM1288	1956	£15	£6	US

BRITT, TINA

Title	Format	Label	Cat. No.	Year	Mint	Good	Notes
Real Thing	7"	London	HLC9974	1965	£20	£8	

BRITTEN, BUDDY & THE REGENTS

Title	Format	Label	Cat. No.	Year	Mint	Good	Notes
Don't Spread It Around	7"	Decca	F11435	1962	£4	£1.50	
Hey There	7"	Oriole	CB1839	1963	£5	£2	
I Guess I'm In The Way	7"	Oriole	CB1911	1964	£6	£2.50	
If You've Gotta Make A Fool Of Somebody	7"	Oriole	CB1827	1963	£6	£2.50	
Money	7"	Oriole	CB1889	1963	£6	£2.50	
My Pride And Joy	7"	Piccadilly	7N35075	1962	£5	£2	
My Resistance Is Low	7"	Oriole	CB1859	1963	£5	£2	
Right Now	7"	Piccadilly	7N35257	1965	£4	£1.50	
She's About A Mover	7"	Piccadilly	7N35241	1965	£5	£2	

BRITTON, CHRIS

Title	Format	Label	Cat. No.	Year	Mint	Good	Notes
As I Am	LP	Page One	POLS022	1969	£100	£50	

BROADBENT, TIM

Title	Format	Label	Cat. No.	Year	Mint	Good	Notes
Female Drummer	LP	Longman	LM4004	1976	£30	£15	

BROADSIDE

Title	Format	Label	Cat. No.	Year	Mint	Good	Notes
Gipsy's Wedding Day	10" LP	Lincolnshire Associa	LA4	1971	£50	£25	
Moon Shone Bright	LP	Topic	12TS228	1973	£10	£4	
Songs From The Stocks	LP	Guildhall	GHS5	1975	£75	£37.50	
To Drive The Dark Away	LP	Guildhall	12	1975	£12	£5	

BROCK, B. & THE SULTANS

Title	Format	Label	Cat. No.	Year	Mint	Good	Notes
Do The Beetle	LP	Crown	CST399	1964	£20	£8	US

BROCK, DAVE

Title	Format	Label	Cat. No.	Year	Mint	Good	Notes
Social Alliance	7"	Flicknife	FLS024P	1983	£5	£2	*picture disc*

BROCKETT, JAIME

Title	Format	Label	Cat. No.	Year	Mint	Good	Notes
Remember The Wind And The Rain	LP	Capitol	ST678	1968	£10	£4	US

BROCKSTEDT, NORAH

Title	Format	Label	Cat. No.	Year	Mint	Good	Notes
Big Boy	7"	Top Rank	JAR353	1960	£6	£2.50	

BROGUES

Greg Elmore and Gary Duncan played as members of the Brogues before helping to form the Quicksilver Messenger Service.

Title	Format	Label	Cat. No.	Year	Mint	Good	Notes
But Now I'm Fine	7"	Challenge		1965	£25	£12.50	US
But Now I'm Fine	7"	Twilight	408	1965	£40	£20	US
I Ain't No Miracle Worker	7"	Challenge	59316	1965	£15	£12.50	US

BROMLEY, JOHN

Title	Format	Label	Cat. No.	Year	Mint	Good	Notes
Sing	LP	Polydor	583048	1969	£15	£6	

BRONCO

Jess Roden, former singer with Alan Bown, hit on the idea of a group that could rock hard on acoustic guitars. Live, Bronco played sitting down, which was certainly a novelty, and their records, particularly *Country Home*, still have a remarkable freshness. Guitarist Robbie Blunt is also an impressive electric player, as he later proved as a member of the Robert Plant band.

Title	Format	Label	Cat. No.	Year	Mint	Good	Notes
Ace Of Sunlight	LP	Island	ILPS9161	1971	£10	£4	
Country Home	LP	Island	ILPS9124	1970	£20	£8	*pink label*

BRONSKI BEAT

Title	Format	Label	Cat. No.	Year	Mint	Good	Notes
Love To Love You Baby	10"	Forbidden Fruit	BITET4	1985	£6	£2.50	*with Marc Almond*

BRONX CHEER

Title	Format	Label	Cat. No.	Year	Mint	Good	Notes
Greatest Hits	LP	Dawn	DNLS3034	1972	£10	£4	

BROOK BROTHERS

Title	Format	Label	Cat. No.	Year	Mint	Good	Notes
Brook Brothers	7" EP	Pye	NEP24155	1962	£15	£7.50	
Brook Brothers	LP	Pye	NPL18067	1961	£30	£15	
Hit Parade	7" EP	Pye	NEP24140	1961	£20	£10	
Hit Parade Vol. 2	7" EP	Pye	NEP24148	1961	£20	£10	

BROOK, PATTI

'I Love You, I Need You' has the rare songwriting credit, 'Cliff Richard'. The song is not especially distinguished, and Cliff Richard's own opinion of it can be gauged by the fact that he did not record it himself.

Title	Format	Label	Cat. No.	Year	Mint	Good	Notes
I Love You, I Need You	7"	Pye	7N15422	1962	£10	£5	

BROOK, TONY & THE BREAKERS

Title	Format	Label	Cat. No.	Year	Mint	VG	Notes
Love Dances On	7"	Columbia	DB7444	1965	£5	£2	
Meanie Genie	7"	Columbia	DB7279	1964	£60	£30	
Meanie Genie	7"	Columbia	DB7279	1964	£100	£50	picture sleeve

BROOKLYN

Title	Format	Label	Cat. No.	Year	Mint	VG	Notes
Hollywood	7"	Rondelet	ROUND6	1981	£5	£2	
I Wanna Be A Detective	7"	Rondelet	ROUND3	1980	£5	£2	
You Never Know What You'll Find	LP	Rondelet	ABOUT3	1980	£12	£5	

BROOKMEYER, BOB

Title	Format	Label	Cat. No.	Year	Mint	VG	Notes
Blues Hot And Cold	LP	HMV	CLP1438/ CSD1356	1961	£15	£6	
Bob Brookmeyer Quartet	10" LP	Vogue	LDE131	1955	£40	£20	
Bob Brookmeyer Quartet	10" LP	Vogue	LDE164	1956	£40	£20	
Dual Roll	10" LP	Esquire	20084	1957	£25	£10	
Portrait Of The Artist	LP	London	LTZK15208/ SAHK6125	1961	£15	£6	
Street Swingers	LP	Vogue	LAE12147	1959	£20	£8	
Tonight's Jazz Today	LP	Vogue	LAE12047	1957	£25	£10	with Zoot Sims
Traditionalism Revisited	LP	Vogue	LAE12108	1958	£20	£8	
Whooeeee	LP	Vogue	LAE12053	1957	£25	£10	with Zoot Sims

BROOKS, BABA

Title	Format	Label	Cat. No.	Year	Mint	VG	Notes
Baby Elephant Walk	7"	Black Swan	WI466	1965	£12	£6	Don Drummond B side
Bank To Bank	7"	Island	WI096	1963	£12	£6	
Catch A Fire	7"	Island	WI150	1964	£12	£6	Eric Morris B side
Clock	7"	Doctor Bird	DB1042	1966	£10	£5	Lyn Taitt B side
Cork Foot	7"	Black Swan	WI438	1964	£12	£6	Hersang Combo B side
Duck Soup	7"	Island	WI235	1965	£12	£6	Zodiacs B side
Eighth Games	7"	Doctor Bird	DB1043	1966	£10	£5	Joe White B side
Ethiopia	7"	Black Swan	WI451	1965	£12	£6	Archibald Trott B side
Faberge	7"	Doctor Bird	DB1081	1967	£10	£5	Monty Morris B side
First Session	7"	Doctor Bird	DB1001	1966	£10	£5	Joe White B side
Girls Town Ska	7"	Ska Beat	JB218	1965	£10	£5	Derrick Morgan B side
Guns Fever	7"	Island	WI229	1965	£12	£6	Dotty & Bonnie B side
Independence Ska	7"	Island	WI233	1965	£12	£6	Strangher & Claudette B side
Jelly Beans	7"	Black Swan	WI412	1964	£12	£6	Eric Morris B side
King Size	7"	Doctor Bird	DB1009	1966	£10	£5	Saints B side
Mattie Rag	7"	Ska Beat	JB217	1965	£10	£5	Lord Tanamo B side
Musical Workshop	7"	Black Swan	WI442	1965	£12	£6	Duke White B side
One Eyed Giant	7"	Ska Beat	JB220	1965	£10	£5	Dynamites B side
One Eyed Giant	7"	Ska Beat	JB268	1967	£10	£5	Dynamites B side
Open The Door	7"	Doctor Bird	DB1067	1966	£10	£5	Monty Morris B side
Our Man Flint	7"	High Note	HS030	1969	£4	£1.50	Hippy Boys B side
Party Time	7"	Doctor Bird	DB1064	1966	£10	£5	Aston & Yen B side
Roll Call	7"	Doctor Bird	DB1062	1966	£10	£5	
Scratch	7"	Doctor Bird	DB1065	1966	£10	£5	Valentines B side
Shock Resistance	7"	Island	WI078	1963	£12	£6	
Skank J. Sheck	7"	Rio	R61	1965	£10	£5	Shenley & Hiacinth B side
Spider	7"	Black Swan	WI434	1964	£12	£6	
Teenage Ska	7"	Island	WI241	1965	£10	£5	Alton Ellis B side
Three Blind Mice	7"	Island	WI127	1963	£12	£6	Billy & Bobby B side
Virginia Ska	7"	Island	WI247	1965	£10	£5	Riots B side
Water Melon Man	7"	R&B	JB125	1963	£10	£5	Stranger Cole B side

BROOKS, CHUCK

Title	Format	Label	Cat. No.	Year	Mint	VG	Notes
Black Sheep	7"	Soul City	SC116	1969	£5	£2	

BROOKS, DALE

Title	Format	Label	Cat. No.	Year	Mint	VG	Notes
Army Green	7"	King	KG1025	1965	£4	£1.50	
I Wanna Be Your Girl	7"	Stateside	SS553	1966	£5	£2	

BROOKS, DONNIE

Title	Format	Label	Cat. No.	Year	Mint	VG	Notes
Doll House	7"	London	HLN9253	1960	£4	£1.50	
Happiest	LP	London	HAN2391	1961	£25	£10	
Mission Bell	7"	London	HLN9168	1960	£4	£1.50	
Oh You Beautiful Doll	7"	London	HLN9572	1962	£4	£1.50	
That's Why	7"	London	HLN9361	1961	£4	£1.50	

BROOKS, ELKIE

Title	Format	Label	Cat. No.	Year	Mint	VG	Notes
All Of My Life	7"	HMV	POP1480	1965	£6	£2.50	
Baby Let Me Love You	7"	HMV	POP1512	1966	£6	£2.50	
Elkie Brooks	LP	A&M	ELKIE1	1978	£15	£6	promo compilation
He's Gotta Love Me	7"	HMV	POP1431	1965	£15	£7.50	
Nothing Left To Do But Cry	7"	Decca	F11983	1964	£10	£5	
Something's Got A Hold On Me	7"	Decca	F11928	1964	£6	£2.50	
Way You Do The Things You do	7"	Decca	F12061	1965	£8	£4	

BROOKS, HADDA

Boogie	LP	Crown	CLP5058	1958	**£20**	**£8**	US
Femme Fatale	LP	Crown	CLP5010	1957	**£20**	**£8**	US
Femme Fatale	LP	Modern	LMP1210	1956	**£60**	**£30**	US
Sings And Swings	LP	Crown	CLP5374	1963	**£15**	**£6**	US

BROOKS, MEL

To Be Or Not To Be	7"	Island	ISP158	1983	**£6**	**£2.50**	*picture disc*

BROOKS, NORMAN

Baby Mine	7" EP	London	REP1021	1955	**£30**	**£15**	
Back In Circulation	7"	London	HL8115	1955	**£15**	**£7.50**	
Hello Sunshine	7"	London	L1166	1954	**£15**	**£7.50**	
I Can't Give You Anything But Love	7"	London	HL8041	1954	**£15**	**£7.50**	
I'd Like To Be In Your Shoes Baby	7"	London	HL8015	1954	**£15**	**£7.50**	
My Three D Sweetie	7"	London	HL8051	1954	**£15**	**£7.50**	
Skyblue Shirt & A Rainbow Tie	7"	London	L1228	1954	**£20**	**£10**	
Vol. 1	7" EP	London	REP1004	1954	**£30**	**£15**	
You Shouldn't Have Kissed Me	7"	London	L1202	1954	**£15**	**£7.50**	

BROOKS, ROSA LEE

The collaboration between Love's Arthur Lee and Jimi Hendrix, which produced, in the song 'The Everlasting First', a particularly noteworthy addition to the careers of both musicians, was not the first time they worked together. 'My Diary' was written by Arthur Lee and features Jimi Hendrix's guitar. Like all of Hendrix's early work, it is not exactly essential, but the single has not been reissued and seldom appears in the market place.

My Diary	7"	Revis	1013	1964	**£300**	**£180**	*US, best auctioned*

BROOKS, TERRY & STRANGE

High Flyer	LP	Star People		198–	**£20**	**£8**	US
Raw Power	LP	Outer Galaxie	OG1001	1976	**£75**	**£37.50**	US
Translucent World	LP	Outer Galaxie	TW1000	1973	**£75**	**£37.50**	US

BROOKS, TINA

True Blue	LP	Blue Note	BLP/BST84041	196–	**£125**	**£62.50**	

BROONZY, BIG BILL

Back Water Blues	78	Vogue	V2068	1951	**£6**	**£2.50**	
Big Bill Blues	78	Vogue	V2075	1951	**£6**	**£2.50**	
Big Bill Blues	LP	Vogue	LAE12009	1956	**£20**	**£8**	
Big Bill Broonzy	7" EP	Columbia	SEG7674	1957	**£10**	**£5**	
Big Bill Broonzy	LP	Philips	BBL7113	1957	**£30**	**£15**	
Big Bill Broonzy & Washboard Sam	LP	Chess	LP1468	1962	**£20**	**£8**	US
Big Bill Broonzy No. 2	7" EP	Columbia	SEG7790	1958	**£10**	**£5**	
Big Bill Broonzy Sings	10" LP	Period	1114	195–	**£20**	**£8**	US
Big Bill Broonzy, Sonny Terry & Brownie McGhee	LP	Folkways	FA3817	1959	**£12**	**£5**	US
Big Bill's Blues	LP	Columbia	WL111	1958	**£20**	**£8**	US
Bill Bailey Won't You Please Come Home	7" EP	Tempo	EXA61	1957	**£6**	**£2.50**	
Black, Brown And White	78	Vogue	V2077	1951	**£6**	**£2.50**	
Blues	LP	Vogue	LAE12063	1958	**£20**	**£8**	
Blues Anthology Vol. 3	7" EP	Storyville	SEP383	1962	**£6**	**£2.50**	
Blues By Broonzy	LP	EmArcy	MG26137	1957	**£20**	**£8**	US
Blues Gospel Spiritual	7" EP	Mercury	10003MCE	1964	**£8**	**£4**	
Country Blues	LP	Folkways	FA2326	195–	**£12**	**£5**	US
Do You Remember Big Bill Broonzy?	7" EP	Emarcy	YEP9508	1959	**£6**	**£2.50**	
Evening With Big Bill Broonzy	LP	Tempo	TAP23	1959	**£30**	**£15**	
Evening With Big Bill Broonzy	LP	Storyville	SLP114	1964	**£10**	**£4**	
Five Foot Seven	78	Melodisc	1203	1952	**£6**	**£2.50**	
Folk Blues	LP	EmArcy	MG26034	1957	**£20**	**£8**	US
Guitar Shuffle	7"	Vogue	V2351	1958	**£12**	**£6**	
Guitar Shuffle	7" EP	Vogue	EPV1107	1956	**£12**	**£6**	
Hey Bud Blues	7" EP	Vogue	EPV1024	1955	**£10**	**£5**	
His Songs And Story	LP	Folkways	FA3586	195–	**£12**	**£5**	US
Hollering Blues	7" EP	Mercury	ZEP10093	1960	**£6**	**£2.50**	
House Rent Stomp	78	Vogue	V2076	1951	**£6**	**£2.50**	
In Concert	LP	XTRA	XTRA1006	1965	**£15**	**£6**	*with Pete Seeger*
In Concert	LP	Verve	VLP5006/SVLP506	1966	**£12**	**£5**	*with Pete Seeger*
In Paris	LP	Vogue	LO60530	1956	**£20**	**£8**	US
In The Evenin'	78	Vogue	V2073	1951	**£6**	**£2.50**	
John Henry	78	Vogue	V2074	1951	**£6**	**£2.50**	
Keep Your Hands Off	7" EP	Melodisc	EPM765	1956	**£6**	**£2.50**	
Keep Your Hands Off	78	Melodisc	1191	1951	**£6**	**£2.50**	
Last Session Part 1	LP	HMV	CLP1544	1961	**£10**	**£4**	
Last Session Part 2	LP	HMV	CLP1551	1961	**£10**	**£4**	
Last Session Part 3	LP	HMV	CLP1562	1961	**£10**	**£4**	
Make My Getaway	78	Vogue	V2078	1952	**£6**	**£2.50**	
Memorial	LP	Mercury	MG2/SR60822	1963	**£10**	**£4**	US
Midnight Special	7"	Storyville	A45053	1961	**£5**	**£2**	
Mississippi Blues Vol. 1	7" EP	Pye	NJE1005	1956	**£6**	**£2.50**	
Mississippi Blues Vol. 2	7" EP	Pye	NJE1015	1956	**£6**	**£2.50**	
Portraits In Blues	LP	Storyville	SLP154	1964	**£10**	**£4**	
Portraits In Blues Vol. 2	LP	Storyville	670154	1967	**£10**	**£4**	
Remembering Broonzy	LP	Mercury	20044MCL	1966	**£10**	**£4**	

Sings The Blues	7" EP	Vogue	EPV1074	1956	**£12**	**£6**	
South Bound Train	78	Pye	NJ2016	1957	**£6**	**£2.50**	
Southern Saga	7" EP	Pye	NJE1047	1957	**£6**	**£2.50**	
Tribute To Big Bill	LP	Nixa	NJL16	1958	**£20**	**£8**	
Trouble In Mind	LP	Fontana	688206ZL	1965	**£15**	**£6**	
Walking Down A Lonesome Road	7" EP	Mercury	ZEP10065	1960	**£6**	**£2.50**	
Walking Down A Lonesome Road	7" EP	Mercury	10003MCE	1964	**£6**	**£2.50**	
When Do I Get To Be Called A Man?	78	Pye	NJ2012	1957	**£6**	**£2.50**	

BROONZY, BIG BILL & JOSH WHITE

Blues	7" EP	Pieces Of 8	PEP605	1961	**£6**	**£2.50**	

BROONZY, BIG BILL & SONNY BOY WILLIAMSON

Big Bill And Sonny Boy	LP	RCA	RD7685	1965	**£30**	**£15**	*with Sonny Boy Williamson I*

BROSELMASCHINE

Broselmaschine	LP	Pilz	20211002	1971	**£25**	**£10**	*German*

BROTH

Broth	LP	Mercury	6338032	1970	**£15**	**£6**	

BROTHER BUNG

Blues Crusade	7" EP	Avenue	BEV1054	1968	**£10**	**£5**	

BROTHER DAN ALL STARS

Another Saturday Night	7"	Trojan	TR608	1968	**£6**	**£2.50**	
Donkey Returns	7"	Trojan	TR601	1968	**£6**	**£2.50**	
Eastern Organ	7"	Trojan	TR602	1968	**£6**	**£2.50**	
Follow That Donkey	LP	Trojan	TRL1	1969	**£15**	**£6**	
Hold Pon Them	7"	Trojan	TR603	1968	**£6**	**£2.50**	
Let's Catch The Beat	LP	Trojan	TBL101	1968	**£25**	**£10**	
Read Up	7"	Trojan	TR607	1968	**£6**	**£2.50**	

BROTHER FOX & THE TAR BABY

Brother Fox And The Tar Baby	LP	Capitol	ST544	1969	**£15**	**£6**	*US*

BROTHERHOOD

Brotherhood	LP	RCA	LSP4092	1968	**£15**	**£6**	*US*
Brotherhood Brotherhood	LP	RCA	LSP4228	1969	**£15**	**£6**	*US*
Paper Man	7"	Philips	BF1766	1969	**£5**	**£2**	

BROTHERHOOD OF MAN

United We Stand	LP	Deram	SML1066	1970	**£12**	**£5**	

BROTHERS

Disco Soul	LP	People	PLEO25	1975	**£20**	**£8**	

BROTHERS AND SISTERS

Are Watching You	LP	private		1968	**£50**	**£25**	

BROTHERS FOUR

Sing Bob Dylan	7" EP	CBS	EP6063	1965	**£5**	**£2**	
Song Book	LP	CBS	BPG62012	1961	**£10**	**£4**	

BROTHERS GRIMM

Looky Looky	7"	Ember	EMBS222	1966	**£50**	**£25**	

BROTHERS KANE

Walking In The Sand	7"	Decca	F12448	1966	**£6**	**£2.50**	

BROTHERS TWO

Here I Am In Love Again	7"	Action	ACT4513	1968	**£5**	**£2**	

BROUGHTON, EDGAR BAND

The Edgar Broughton Band were a staple feature of the open-air festivals and free concerts of 1969–70. They were supremely good at giving an audience a good time, but on record their musical limitations become rather glaringly obvious. The crowd-pleasing chant, 'Out Demons Out', with which they always ended their stage act, sounds rather weak on cold vinyl, while the fusion of Captain Beefheart with the Shadows on 'Apache Drop Out' sounds silly. Nevertheless, the track 'Love In The Rain', on the first LP, provides for an exhilarating three minutes or so, and would do Motorhead proud.

Apache Drop Out	7"	Harvest	HAR5032	1970	**£4**	**£1.50**	
Bandages	LP	Nems	NEL6006	1975	**£10**	**£4**	
Edgar Broughton Band	LP	Harvest	SHVL791	1971	**£12**	**£5**	
Evil	7"	Harvest	HAR5001	1969	**£4**	**£1.50**	
Inside Out	LP	Harvest	SHTC252	1972	**£15**	**£6**	
Legendary	LP	Babylon	DB80073	1984	**£15**	**£6**	*German double*
Live Hits Harder	LP	BB	BB201009	1979	**£10**	**£4**	
Oora	LP	Harvest	SHVL810	1973	**£15**	**£6**	
Out Demons Out	7"	Harvest	HAR5015	1970	**£4**	**£1.50**	
Sing Brother Sing	LP	Harvest	SHVL772	1970	**£15**	**£6**	
Super Chip	LP	Sheet	SHEET2	1982	**£10**	**£4**	
Wasa Wasa	LP	Harvest	SHVL757	1969	**£15**	**£6**	

BROWN, AL

Ain't Got No Soul	7"	Fab	FAB186	1971	**£4**	**£1.50**	
No Soul Today	7"	Banana	BA360	1971	**£6**	**£2.50**	

BROWN, AL & HIS TUNE TOPPERS

Madison Dance Party	LP	Amy	A(S)1	1960	**£20**	**£8**	US

BROWN, ARTHUR

Arthur Brown's stage act, which began with his being lowered on to the stage with his head-dress on fire, was legendary during 1967–8. His album, *The Crazy World Of Arthur Brown* (which was actually the name of his group) easily matches the visual bombast, emerging as one of the classic recordings of the period. The music is guitar-free, which is often a recipe for dullness, but Vincent Crane's organ playing is so full of imagination, and Arthur Brown's singing so powerful, that guitars are not missed. The non-album 'Devil's Grip' is in the same league, although the jokey B side, 'Give Him A Flower', is a bit of a throw-away. Brown's contribution to the soundtrack record of the Roger Vadim film *The Game Is Over/La Curée* is uncredited, but consists of two songs in a style close to that of the Crazy World.

Complete Tapes Of Atoya	LP	Plexus	KMH709223	1984	**£10**	**£4**	*Dutch*
Crazy World Of Arthur Brown	LP	Track	612/613005	1968	**£15**	**£6**	
Devil's Grip	7"	Track	604008	1967	**£4**	**£1.50**	
Faster Than The Speed Of Sound	LP	WEA	58088	1980	**£10**	**£4**	*Dutch*
Game Is Over (La Curée)	LP	Atco	33205	1966	**£60**	**£30**	*US*
La Curée	7" EP	Barclay	71026	1966	**£75**	**£37.50**	*French*
Nightmare	7"	Track	604026	1968	**£4**	**£1.50**	
Six Pack	7"	Gull	SIXPACK4	1977	**£4**	**£1.50**	*picture disc*
You Don't Know	7"	Reading Rag Record	LYN771	1965	**£60**	**£30**	*flexi, with the Diamonds*

BROWN, BEN

Ask The Lonely	7"	Polydor	56198	1967	**£15**	**£7.50**	

BROWN, BOBBY

Enlightening Beam Of Axonda	LP	Destiny	4002	1972	**£100**	**£50**	*US*
Live	LP	Destiny	4001	1972	**£60**	**£30**	*US*

BROWN, BOOTS

Cerveza	7"	RCA	RCA1078	1958	**£4**	**£1.50**	
Rock That Beat	LP	RCA	LG1000	1958	**£20**	**£8**	*US*

BROWN, BUSTER

B. & Buster Brown	7" EP	XX	MIN713	196–	**£8**	**£4**	*with B. Brown*
Fannie Mae	7"	Melodisc	1559	1960	**£40**	**£20**	
Fannie Mae	7"	Sue	WI368	1965	**£12**	**£6**	
My Blue Heaven	7"	Island	WI3031	1967	**£15**	**£7.50**	
New King Of The Blues	LP	Fire	FLP102	1960	**£75**	**£37.50**	*US*
Sugar Babe	7"	Blue Horizon	573147	1969	**£10**	**£5**	

BROWN, BUSTY

Broken Heart	7"	Punch	PH10	1969	**£4**	**£1.50**	
Here Comes The Night	7"	Doctor Bird	DB1158	1968	**£10**	**£5**	
To Love Somebody	7"	Upsetter	US308	1969	**£5**	**£2**	*Bleechers B side*
What A Price	7"	Upsetter	US304	1969	**£5**	**£2**	

BROWN, CHARLES

Ballads My Way	LP	Mainstream	6035	1965	**£15**	**£6**	*US*
Christmas Question	7"	Parlophone	R4848	1961	**£20**	**£10**	
Confidential	7"	Vogue	V9065	1957	**£300**	**£180**	*best auctioned*
Driftin' Blues	LP	Score	SLP4011	1957	**£75**	**£37.50**	*US*
Great Charles Brown	LP	King	878	1963	**£30**	**£15**	*US*
Legend	LP	Bluesway	6039	1970	**£12**	**£5**	*US*
Million Sellers	LP	Imperial	A9178	1961	**£40**	**£20**	*US*
Mood Music	10" LP	Aladdin	702	1954	**£200**	**£100**	*US*
Mood Music	10" LP	Aladdin	702	1954	**£400**	**£250**	*US, red vinyl*
Mood Music	LP	Aladdin	809	1956	**£125**	**£62.50**	*US*
Sings Christmas Songs	LP	King	775	1961	**£30**	**£15**	*US*
Soothe Me	7"	Vogue	V9061	1956	**£300**	**£180**	*best auctioned*

BROWN, CLARENCE 'GATEMOUTH'

Clarence 'Gatemouth' Brown	7" EP	Vocalion	VE170161	1965	**£50**	**£25**	
Vol. 1: 1948–1953	LP	Python	PLP26	1972	**£20**	**£8**	
Vol. 2: 1956–1965	LP	Python	PLP27	1972	**£20**	**£8**	

BROWN, CLIFFORD

At Basin Street	LP	Emarcy	EJL1253	1957	**£30**	**£15**	*with Max Roach*
Clifford Brown And Art Farmer Vol. 1	7" EP	Esquire	EP3	1954	**£5**	**£2**	
Clifford Brown And Art Farmer Vol. 2	7" EP	Esquire	EP4	1954	**£5**	**£2**	
Clifford Brown And Max Roach	7" EP	Emarcy	ERE1572	1958	**£5**	**£2**	
Clifford Brown And Tadd Dameron	7" EP	Esquire	EP71	1955	**£5**	**£2**	
Clifford Brown Ensemble	10" LP	Vogue	LDE158	1955	**£40**	**£20**	
Clifford Brown Ensemble	7" EP	Vogue	EPV1119	1956	**£5**	**£2**	
Clifford Brown Quartet	10" LP	Vogue	LDE042	1954	**£25**	**£10**	
Clifford Brown Sextet	10" LP	Vogue	LDE121	1955	**£25**	**£10**	
Clifford Brown–Gigi Gryce Orchestra	7" EP	Vogue	EPV1027	1955	**£5**	**£2**	
Conception	7" EP	Vogue	EPV1041	1955	**£5**	**£2**	
I Remember Clifford	LP	Mercury	MMC14041	1960	**£15**	**£6**	*with Max Roach*
Memorial Album	LP	Blue Note	BLP/BST81526	1963	**£25**	**£10**	
Remember Clifford	LP	Mercury	20022MCL	1964	**£15**	**£6**	
Study In Brown	LP	Emarcy	EJL1278	1958	**£20**	**£8**	
Sudy In Brown Vol. 1	7" EP	Emarcy	ERE1565	1958	**£5**	**£2**	
Sudy In Brown Vol. 2	7" EP	Emarcy	ERE1566	1958	**£5**	**£2**	
Sweet Clifford	7" EP	Emarcy	ERE1501	1956	**£5**	**£2**	

BROWN, DAVID

Title	Format	Label	Cat. No.	Year	Price	Price	Notes
All My Life	7"	Island	WI3112	1967	**£10**	**£5**	*Ron Wilson B side*

BROWN, DENNIS

Title	Format	Label	Cat. No.	Year	Price	Price	Notes
Black Magic Woman	7"	Explosion	EX2068	1972	**£8**	**£4**	
Cheater	7"	Randys	RAN526	1972	**£4**	**£1.50**	
Concentration	7"	Smash	SMA2327	1973	**£4**	**£1.50**	
He Can't Spell	7"	Jackpot	JP813	1973	**£5**	**£2**	
It's Too Late	7"	Ashanti	ASH402	1973	**£5**	**£2**	
Just Dennis	LP	Trojan	TRLS107	1975	**£10**	**£4**	
Little Green Apples	7"	Ocean	OC001	1971	**£5**	**£2**	*Sound Dimension B side*
Love Grows	7"	Bamboo	BAM56	1970	**£6**	**£2.50**	*Sound Dimension B side*
Meet Me On The Corner	7"	Randys	RAN528	1972	**£4**	**£1.50**	
Money In My Pocket	7"	Pressure Beat	PB5513	1972	**£4**	**£1.50**	*Joe Gibbs B side*
Never Fall In Love	7"	Banana	BA336	1971	**£6**	**£2.50**	
No Man Is An Island	7"	Banana	BA309	1970	**£6**	**£2.50**	*Soul Sisters B side*
Silhouettes	7"	Songbird	SB1074	1972	**£4**	**£1.50**	
Super Reggae And Soul Hits	LP	Trojan	TRLS57	1973	**£12**	**£5**	
Visions	LP	Lightning	LIP7	1978	**£10**	**£4**	
West Bound Train	LP	Third World	TWS934	1977	**£10**	**£4**	
What About The Half	7"	Duke	DU139	1972	**£8**	**£4**	
Words Of Wisdom	LP	Laser	LASL1	1979	**£10**	**£4**	

BROWN, DUSTY

Title	Format	Label	Cat. No.	Year	Price	Price	Notes
Please Don't Go	7"	Starlite	ST45058	1961	**£20**	**£10**	

BROWN, FAY

Title	Format	Label	Cat. No.	Year	Price	Price	Notes
Unchained Melody	7"	Columbia	SCM5185	1955	**£6**	**£2.50**	

BROWN, FRANK

Title	Format	Label	Cat. No.	Year	Price	Price	Notes
Some Come Some Go	7"	Island	WI3103	1967	**£10**	**£5**	

BROWN, GERRY

Title	Format	Label	Cat. No.	Year	Price	Price	Notes
It's Trad Time	LP	Fontana	TFL5165	1961	**£15**	**£6**	

BROWN, GLEN, JOE WHITE & TREVOR

Title	Format	Label	Cat. No.	Year	Price	Price	Notes
Way Of Life	7"	Blue Cat	BS131	1968	**£6**	**£2.50**	*Carl Bryan & Lyn Taitt B side*

BROWN, GLENMORE & HOPETON LEWIS

Title	Format	Label	Cat. No.	Year	Price	Price	Notes
Girl You're Cold	7"	Fab	FAB42	1968	**£6**	**£2.50**	

BROWN, HENRY

Title	Format	Label	Cat. No.	Year	Price	Price	Notes
Blues	LP	77	LA125	1961	**£15**	**£6**	

BROWN, HUX & SCOTTY

Title	Format	Label	Cat. No.	Year	Price	Price	Notes
Unbelievable Sounds	7"	High Note	HS056	1971	**£8**	**£4**	

BROWN, IRVING

Title	Format	Label	Cat. No.	Year	Price	Price	Notes
I'm Still Around	7"	Bamboo	BAM58	1970	**£6**	**£2.50**	
Let's Make It Up	7"	Bamboo	BAM61	1970	**£8**	**£4**	
Now I'm Alone	7"	Bamboo Now	BN1003	1971	**£4**	**£1.50**	
Today	7"	Bamboo	BAM36	1970	**£6**	**£2.50**	

BROWN, JAMES

James Brown is the most sampled artist of all for the simple reason that, as the inventor of funk, he has also made the records that are the best examples of it. From 'Think' to 'Papa's Got A Brand New Bag' to 'Cold Sweat' to 'Give It Up Or Turn It A-Loose' and beyond, Brown's skill at winding up the rhythmic tension has always been totally unsurpassed. Of course, within the mêlee of brittle drum beats, scratchy guitar patterns, and moon-booted bass riffs, Brown apparently does nothing more than oversee. He does, of course, have an emotion-wrenching soul voice, as early ballads like 'Prisoner Of Love' and 'It's A Man's Man's Man's World' confirm, but he more often chooses to employ a series of ecstatic calls and rhythmic vocal adjuncts than to deliver anything resembling a melody. In reality, however, the music is as much in his control as that of an orchestra which stands or falls according to the talents of its conductor. The proof of this is easily found in the lower level of inspiration apparent in the work of Brown's musicians playing without the man himself (Maceo and the King's Men, the JBs, and even Bootsy Collins's groups cannot compare to the man they call the Godfather for the rhythmic impact, the sheer funk of the music).

Title	Format	Label	Cat. No.	Year	Price	Price	Notes
Ain't It Funky	LP	Polydor	2343010	1970	**£25**	**£10**	
Ain't It Funky Now	7"	Polydor	56793	1970	**£4**	**£1.50**	
Ain't That A Groove	7"	Pye	7N25367	1966	**£5**	**£2**	
Always Amazing James Brown	LP	King	LP743	1961	**£40**	**£20**	*US*
At The Apollo	LP	Polydor	582703	1967	**£15**	**£6**	
At The Apollo	LP	London	HA8184	1964	**£30**	**£15**	
At The Apollo Vol. 2	LP	Polydor	583729/730	1969	**£25**	**£10**	*double*
Best Of James Brown	LP	Polydor	583765	1969	**£12**	**£5**	
Black Caesar	LP	Polydor	2490117	1974	**£30**	**£15**	
Bodyheat	7"	Polydor	2066763	1977	**£4**	**£1.50**	
Bodyheat	LP	Polydor	2391258	1977	**£10**	**£4**	
Bring It Up	7"	Pye	7N25411	1967	**£5**	**£2**	
Bring It Up	7" EP	Pye	NEP44088	1967	**£15**	**£7.50**	
Christmas Album	LP	Pye	NPL28097	1966	**£25**	**£10**	
Cold Sweat	7"	Pye	7N25430	1967	**£6**	**£2.50**	
Don't Be A Drop-Out	7"	Pye	7N25394	1966	**£6**	**£2.50**	
Everybody's Doin' The Hustle	LP	Polydor	2391197	1975	**£12**	**£5**	
Exciting James Brown	LP	King	LP780	1962	**£40**	**£20**	*US*

Title	Format	Label	Number	Year	Mint	VG	Notes
Eyesight	7"	Polydor	2066915	1978	£4	£1.50	
Funky President	7"	Polydor	2066520	1975	£4	£1.50	
Get Involved	7"	Polydor	2001190	1971	£4	£1.50	
Get It Together	7"	Pye	7N25441	1967	£5	£2	
Get On The Good Foot	7"	Polydor	2066231	1972	£4	£1.50	
Get On The Good Foot	LP	Polydor	2659018	1973	£30	£15	double
Get Up Offa That Thing	7"	Polydor	2066687	1976	£4	£1.50	
Get Up Offa That Thing	LP	Polydor	2391228	1976	£10	£4	
Gettin' Down To It	LP	Polydor	583742	1970	£25	£10	
Greatest Hits	LP	Polydor	623017	1968	£12	£5	
Grits And Soul	LP	Philips	BL7664	1965	£25	£10	
Handful Of Soul	LP	Philips	(S)BL7761	1967	£20	£8	
Have Mercy Baby	7"	London	HL9945	1965	£10	£5	
Hell	LP	Polydor	2659036	1974	£40	£20	double
Hey America	7"	Mojo	2093006	1971	£4	£1.50	
Honky Tonk	7"	Polydor	2066216	1972	£4	£1.50	
Honky Tonk	7"	Polydor	2066834	1977	£4	£1.50	
Hot	7"	Polydor	2066642	1976	£4	£1.50	
Hot	LP	Polydor	2391214	1976	£12	£5	
Hot Pants	7"	Polydor	2001213	1971	£4	£1.50	
Hot Pants	LP	Polydor	2425086	1971	£15	£6	
How Long Darling	7" EP	Pye	NEP44076	1967	£15	£7.50	
I Can't Stand Myself	7"	Polydor	56787	1970	£5	£2	
I Can't Stand Myself	LP	Polydor	184136	1968	£25	£10	
I Do Just What I Want	7" EP	Ember	EMBEP4549	1964	£20	£10	
I Got A Bag Of My Own	7"	Polydor	2066285	1973	£4	£1.50	
I Got A Feeling	7"	Polydor	56743	1968	£6	£2.50	
I Got Ants In My Pants	7"	Polydor	2066296	1973	£4	£1.50	
I Got You	7"	Pye	7N25350	1966	£8	£4	
I Got You	7" EP	Pye	NEP44059	1966	£15	£7.50	
I Got You (I Feel Good)	LP	Pye	NPL28074	1966	£25	£10	
I'll Go Crazy	7" EP	Pye	NEP44068	1966	£15	£7.50	
I'm A Greedy Man	7"	Polydor	2066153	1971	£4	£1.50	
In The Jungle Groove	LP	Urban	URBLP11	1988	£15	£6	double
It's A Man's Man's Man's World	7"	Pye	7N25371	1966	£8	£4	
It's A Man's Man's Man's World	LP	Pye	NPL28079	1966	£20	£8	
It's A Mother	LP	Polydor	583768	1969	£25	£10	
It's A New Day	7"	Polydor	2001018	1970	£4	£1.50	
It's A New Day	LP	Polydor	2310029	1971	£25	£10	
It's Hell	7"	Polydor	2066513	1974	£4	£1.50	
Jump Around	LP	King	LP/KS771	1962	£40	£20	US
Kansas City	7"	Pye	7N25418	1967	£6	£2.50	
King Heroin	7"	Polydor	2066185	1972	£4	£1.50	
King Of Soul	LP	Polydor	184159	1969	£20	£8	
Let A Man Come In	7"	Polydor	56783	1969	£5	£2	
Let Yourself Go	7"	Pye	7N25423	1967	£6	£2.50	
Licking Stick	7"	Polydor	56744	1968	£5	£2	
Live At The Apollo	LP	Polydor	2482184	1975	£10	£4	
Live At The Apollo 1962	CD	Mobile Fidelity	UDCD583	1993	£15	£6	US audiophile
Live At The Apollo Vol. 2	LP	Polydor	2612005	1970	£15	£6	double
Live At The Garden	LP	Pye	NPL28104	1967	£25	£10	
Make It Funky	7"	Polydor	2001223	1971	£4	£1.50	
Mighty Instrumentals	LP	Pye	NPL28093	1967	£20	£8	
Money Won't Change You	7"	Pye	7N25379	1966	£6	£2.50	
Mother Popcorn	7"	Polydor	56776	1969	£4	£1.50	
Mr Dynamite	LP	Polydor	623032	1968	£20	£8	
Mr Excitement	LP	Pye	NPL28100	1967	£20	£8	
Mr Soul	LP	Polydor	184100	1968	£20	£8	
Mutha Nature	LP	Polydor	2391300	1977	£12	£5	
My Thing	7"	Polydor	2066485	1974	£4	£1.50	
Nature	7"	Polydor	2066984	1978	£4	£1.50	
New Breed	7"	Philips	BF1481	1966	£6	£2.50	
Night Train	7"	Parlophone	R4922	1962	£20	£10	
Night Train	7"	Sue	WI360	1964	£20	£10	
Out Of Sight	7"	Philips	BF1368	1964	£10	£5	
Out Of Sight	LP	Mercury	SMCL20133	1969	£20	£8	
Papa's Got A Brand New Bag	7"	London	HL9990	1965	£8	£4	
Papa's Got A Brand New Bag	7"	Polydor	2141008	1973	£4	£1.50	
Papa's Got A Brand New Bag	LP	Pye	NPL28099	1967	£20	£8	
Papa's Got A Brand New Bag	LP	London	HA8262	1966	£25	£10	
Papa's Got A Brand New Bag	LP	Polydor	2334009	1970	£15	£6	
Payback	LP	Polydor	2659030	1974	£40	£20	double
Plays James Brown Today & Yesterday	LP	Philips	BL7697	1966	£20	£8	
Plays New Breed	LP	Philips	BL7718	1966	£20	£8	
Plays The Real Thing	LP	Philips	(S)BL7823	1967	£20	£8	
Please Please Please	LP	London	HA8231	1965	£25	£10	
Please Please Please	LP	King	395610	1959	£75	£37.50	US
Popcorn	LP	Polydor	184319	1970	£30	£15	
Prisoner Of Love	7"	London	HL9730	1963	£15	£7.50	
Prisoner Of Love	7" EP	London	RE1410	1964	£25	£12.50	
Prisoner Of Love	7" EP	Pye	NEP44072	1967	£15	£7.50	
Prisoner Of Love	LP	King	LP/KS851	1963	£40	£20	US
Pure Dynamite	LP	London	HA8177	1964	£25	£10	
Raw Soul	LP	Pye	NPL28103	1967	£20	£8	
Reality	LP	Polydor	2391164	1975	£15	£6	
Revolution Of The Mind	LP	Polydor	2659011	1972	£30	£15	double
Say It Loud I'm Black & I'm Proud	LP	Polydor	583741	1969	£25	£10	

Say It Loud, I'm Black And I'm Proud	7"	Polydor	56752	1968	**£6**	**£2.50**	
Sex Machine	7"	Polydor	2001071	1970	**£4**	**£1.50**	
Sex Machine	LP	Polydor	2625004	1971	**£25**	**£10**	*double*
Sex Machine Today	LP	Polydor	2391175	1975	**£12**	**£5**	
Shout And Shimmy	7"	Parlophone	R4952	1962	**£15**	**£7.50**	
Showtime	LP	Philips	BL7630	1964	**£25**	**£10**	
Slaughter's Big Rip-Off	LP	Polydor	2391084	1973	**£30**	**£15**	
Soul Brother No. 1	LP	Polydor	2343036	1971	**£12**	**£5**	
Soul Classics	LP	Polydor	2391057	1973	**£12**	**£5**	
Soul Classics Vol. 2	LP	Polydor	2391116	1974	**£12**	**£5**	
Soul Classics Vol. 3	LP	Polydor	2391166	1975	**£12**	**£5**	
Soul Fire	LP	Polydor	184148	1969	**£20**	**£8**	
Soul On Top	LP	Polydor	2310022	1971	**£25**	**£10**	
Soul Power	7"	Polydor	2001163	1971	**£4**	**£1.50**	
Stone To The Bone	7"	Polydor	2066411	1974	**£4**	**£1.50**	
Super Bad	7"	Polydor	2001097	1970	**£4**	**£1.50**	
Super Bad	LP	Polydor	2310089	1971	**£20**	**£8**	
Tell Me What You're Gonna Do	7"	Ember	EMBS216	1965	**£10**	**£5**	
Tell Me What You're Gonna Do	LP	Ember	EMB3357	1964	**£25**	**£10**	
That's Life	7"	Polydor	56540	1970	**£4**	**£1.50**	
There It Is	7"	Polydor	2066210	1972	**£4**	**£1.50**	
There It Is	LP	Polydor	2391033	1972	**£30**	**£15**	
There Was A Time	7"	Polydor	56740	1968	**£6**	**£2.50**	
These Foolish Things	7"	London	HL9775	1963	**£12**	**£6**	
Think	7"	Parlophone	R4667	1960	**£20**	**£10**	
Think	7"	Polydor	2066329	1973	**£4**	**£1.50**	
Think	LP	King	LP683	1960	**£60**	**£30**	*US*
This Is James Brown	LP	Polydor	643317	1969	**£15**	**£6**	
This Is James Brown	LP	Philips	6336201	1972	**£10**	**£4**	
This Old Heart	7"	Fontana	H273	1960	**£20**	**£10**	
Tours The USA	LP	London	HA8240	1965	**£25**	**£10**	
Try Me	7"	Philips	BF1458	1965	**£6**	**£2.50**	
Try Me	LP	King	395635	1959	**£75**	**£37.50**	*US*
Turn It Loose	7" EP	Polydor	580701	1970	**£20**	**£10**	
Unbeatable Sixteen Hits	LP	London	HA8203	1965	**£25**	**£10**	
What My Baby Needs Now	7"	Polydor	2066283	1972	**£4**	**£1.50**	
Woman	7"	Polydor	2066370	1973	**£4**	**£1.50**	
World	7"	Polydor	56780	1969	**£4**	**£1.50**	

BROWN, JIM EDWARD

Introducing	7" EP	RCA	RCX7179	1965	**£5**	**£2**	

BROWN, JIM EDWARD & MAXINE

Country Songs	7" EP	London	REP1024	1955	**£15**	**£7.50**	
Country Songs Vol. 3	7" EP	London	REU1044	1955	**£15**	**£7.50**	
Here Today And Gone Tomorrow	7"	London	HLU8200	1955	**£15**	**£7.50**	
Itsy Witsy Bitsy Me	7"	London	HL8123	1955	**£20**	**£10**	
Your Love Is Wild As The West Wind	7"	London	HLU8166	1955	**£20**	**£10**	

BROWN, JOE

As the guitarist on Billy Fury's highly regarded *Sound Of Fury* album, Joe Brown had considerable credibility, yet his own records are wildly variable in quality. The problem was that Brown seemed to be determined to prove his versatility, but when this included the performance of old music-hall songs and an instrumental version of 'All Things Bright And Beautiful', then the effort did not seem to be particularly worthwhile. At his best, however, such as on the succession of hit singles begun with 'A Picture Of You', Brown created an effective form of robust pop-country that could, perhaps, have become a significant influence if only he had developed it further.

All Things Bright And Beautiful	7" EP	Piccadilly	NEP34026	1962	**£8**	**£4**	
Darktown Strutters Ball	7"	Decca	F11207	1960	**£6**	**£2.50**	
Good Luck And Goodbye	7"	Pye	7N35005	1961	**£4**	**£1.50**	
Here Comes Joe Brown	LP	Golden Guinea	GGL0231	1963	**£10**	**£4**	
Hit Parade	7" EP	Piccadilly	NEP34025	1962	**£8**	**£4**	
Jellied Eels	7"	Decca	F11246	1960	**£5**	**£2**	
Live	LP	Piccadilly	NPL38006	1963	**£15**	**£7.50**	
Mrs O's Theme	7" EP	Pye	PNV24195	1967	**£10**	**£5**	*French*
People Gotta Talk	7"	Decca	F11185	1959	**£8**	**£4**	
Picture Of Joe Brown	7" EP	Decca	DFE8500	1962	**£10**	**£5**	
Picture Of Joe Brown	LP	Ace Of Clubs	ACL1127	1962	**£12**	**£5**	
Picture Of You	LP	Golden Guinea	GGL0146	1962	**£10**	**£4**	
Satisfied Mind	7"	Pye	7N17184	1966	**£4**	**£1.50**	
Shine	7"	Pye	7N15322	1960	**£5**	**£2**	

BROWN, JOE & MARK WYNTER

Big Hits	7" EP	Golden Guinea	WO1	1963	**£5**	**£2**	
Just For Fun	7" EP	Pye	NEP24167	1963	**£6**	**£2.50**	

BROWN, K.

Pocket Money	7"	Blue Beat	BB66	1961	**£12**	**£6**	

BROWN, KENT & THE RAINBOWS

Come Ya Come Ya	7"	Fab	FAB53	1968	**£5**	**£2**	

BROWN, LAWRENCE

Inspired Abandon	LP	HMV	CLP1913	1965	**£10**	**£4**	

Slide Trombone	LP	Columbia	33CX10046	1956	£15	£6	

BROWN, LES

Dancers' Choice	LP	Capitol	T812	1957	£10	£4	
Forty Cups Of Coffee	7"	Vogue Coral	Q72242	1957	£5	£2	
Les Brown Band	10" LP	Vogue Coral	LVC10033	1956	£10	£4	
Les Brown Band	10" LP	Vogue Coral	LVC10017	1955	£10	£4	
Les Brown Orchestra	10" LP	Vogue Coral	LVC10002	1955	£10	£4	

BROWN, MARION

Afternoon Of A Georgia Faun	LP	ECM	ECM1004ST	1970	£12	£5	
Geechee Recollections	LP	Impulse	AS9252	1973	£15	£6	US
Marion Brown Quartet	LP	Fontana	SFJL930	1967	£15	£6	
Porto Novo	LP	Polydor	583724	1969	£20	£8	

BROWN, MARK

Brown Low Special	7"	Island	WI3097	1967	£10	£5	Dawn Penn B side

BROWN, MAXINE

All In My Mind	7"	London	HLU9286	1961	£10	£5	
Fabulous Sound Of Maxine Brown	LP	Wand	WD656	1963	£12	£5	US
Greatest Hits	LP	Wand	WD(S)684	1967	£12	£5	US
I've Got A Lot Of Love Left In Me	7"	Pye	7N25410	1967	£5	£2	
It's Gonna Be Alright	7"	Pye	7N25299	1965	£5	£2	
Oh No Not My Baby	7"	Pye	7N25272	1964	£8	£4	
One Step At A Time	7"	Pye	7N25317	1965	£8	£4	
Promise Me Anything	7"	HMV	POP1102	1962	£40	£20	
Reason To Believe	7"	Major Minor	MM709	1970	£4	£1.50	
Since I Found You	7"	Pye	7N25434	1967	£6	£2.50	
Spotlight On Maxine Brown	LP	Wand	WD(S)663	1965	£12	£5	US
Yesterday's Kisses	7"	Stateside	SS188	1963	£10	£5	

BROWN, NAPPY

Don't Be Angry	7"	London	HL8145	1955	£500	£330	best auctioned
It Don't Hurt No More	7"	London	HLC8760	1958	£40	£20	
Little By Little	7"	London	HLC8384	1957	£200	£100	best auctioned
Nappy Brown Sings	LP	Savoy	MG14002	1958	£100	£50	US
Pitter Patter	7"	London	HLC8182	1955	£300	£210	best auctioned
Right Time	LP	Savoy	MG14025	1960	£60	£30	US

BROWN, NOEL

By The Time I Get To Phoenix	7"	Songbird	SB1012	1969	£4	£1.50	
Man's Temptation	7"	Island	WI3149	1968	£10	£5	

BROWN, PAMELA

People Are Running	7"	Joe	JRS8	1970	£5	£2	

BROWN, PETE

Pete Brown was one of the first poets to attempt to make a living by giving readings of his work, but achieved his greatest success as lyricist for Cream and for Jack Bruce solo. His own rock groups – Battered Ornaments and Piblokto – were interesting and featured strong contributions from musicians with their feet in both the jazz and rock camps, such as Chris Spedding, Jim Mullen and George Khan. They were ultimately handicapped, however, by their vocalist's (Brown himself) inability to sing.

Art School Dance Goes On Forever	LP	Harvest	SHVL768	1970	£75	£37.50	
Can't Get Off The Planet	7"	Harvest	HAR5023	1970	£5	£2	
Flying Hero Sandwich	7"	Harvest	HAR5028	1970	£5	£2	
Living Life Backwards	7"	Harvest	HAR5008	1970	£6	£2.50	
Meal You Can Shake Hands With In The Dark	LP	Harvest	SHVL752	1969	£75	£37.50	
My Last Band	LP	Harvest	SHSM2017	1977	£15	£6	
Not Forgotten Association	LP	Deram	SML1103	1973	£60	£30	
Thousands On A Raft	LP	Harvest	SHVL782	1970	£50	£25	
Week Looked Good On Paper	7"	Parlophone	R5767	1969	£15	£7.50	
Week Looked Good On Paper	7"	Parlophone	R5767	1969	£50	£25	demo, picture sleeve

BROWN, PETE & IAN LYNN

Party In The Rain	LP	Discs International	INTLP1	1982	£40	£20	

BROWN, PETE (2)

Pete Brown Sextet	10" LP	London	LZN14002	1955	£30	£15	

BROWN, RAY

Bass Hit	10" LP	Columbia	33C9037	1957	£20	£8	

BROWN, RICKY & THE HI-LITES

Liverpool Beat!	LP	CBS	62262	1965	£100	£50	German

BROWN, ROY

Blues Are All Brown	LP	Bluesway	BLS6019	1968	£15	£6	US
Hard Luck Blues	LP	King	KS1130	1971	£12	£5	US
Hard Times	LP	Bluesway	BLS6056	1973	£12	£5	US
Live At Monterey	LP	Epic	BG30473	1971	£12	£5	US
Party Doll	7"	London	HLP8398	1957	£350	£210	best auctioned
Saturday Night	7"	London	HLP8448	1957	£500	£330	best auctioned
Sings 24 Hits	LP	King	(KS)956	1966	£20	£8	US

BROWN, ROY & WYNONIE HARRIS

Battle Of The Blues Vol. 1	LP	King	607	1958	**£150**	**£75**	*US*
Battle Of The Blues Vol. 2	LP	King	627	1959	**£150**	**£75**	*US*

BROWN, ROY, WYNONIE HARRIS & EDDIE VINSON

Battle Of The Blues Vol. 4	LP	King	668	1960	**£300**	**£180**	*US*

BROWN, RUTH

Along Comes Ruth	LP	Philips	652012BL	1962	**£30**	**£15**	
As Long As I'm Moving	7"	London	HLE8210	1955	**£200**	**£100**	*best auctioned*
Best Of Ruth Brown	LP	Atlantic	ATL5007	1964	**£50**	**£25**	
Don't Deceive Me	7"	London	HLE9093	1960	**£15**	**£7.50**	
Gospel Time	7" EP	Philips	BE12537	1963	**£25**	**£12.50**	
Gospel Time	LP	Philips	652020BL	1963	**£25**	**£10**	
I Don't Know	7"	London	HLE8946	1959	**£25**	**£12.50**	
I Want To Do More	7"	London	HLE8310	1956	**£100**	**£50**	
Jack Of Diamonds	7"	London	HLE8887	1959	**£30**	**£15**	
Just Too Much	7"	London	HLE8645	1958	**£40**	**£20**	
Late Date	LP	Atlantic	(S)1308	1959	**£60**	**£30**	*US*
Late Date	LP	London	LTZK15187	1960	**£40**	**£20**	
Lucky Lips	7"	Columbia	DB3913	1957	**£200**	**£100**	*best auctioned*
Mambo Baby	7"	London	HL8153	1955	**£200**	**£100**	*best auctioned*
Miss Rhythm	LP	Atlantic	8026	1959	**£60**	**£30**	*US*
Mom Oh Mom	7"	London	HLE8401	1957	**£100**	**£50**	
New Love	7"	London	HLE8552	1958	**£50**	**£25**	
One More Time	7"	London	HLE8483	1957	**£50**	**£25**	
Queen Of R&B	7" EP	London	REE1038	1955	**£125**	**£62.50**	
Rockin' With Ruth	LP	London	HAE2106	1958	**£100**	**£50**	
Ruth Brown	LP	Atlantic	8004	1957	**£100**	**£50**	*US*
Ruth Brown '65	LP	Mainstream	1/S6044	1965	**£15**	**£6**	*US*
Ruth Brown Sings	10" LP	Atlantic	115	1956	**£750**	**£500**	*US*
Sugar Babe	LP	President	PTLS1067	1976	**£10**	**£4**	
Sure Nuff	7"	London	HLK9304	1961	**£20**	**£10**	
This Little Girl's Gone Rocking	7"	London	HLE8757	1958	**£40**	**£20**	
This Little Girl's Gone Rocking	7"	London	HL7061	1958	**£25**	**£12.50**	*export*
Yes Sir That's My Baby	7"	Brunswick	05904	1964	**£10**	**£5**	

BROWN, RUTH & JOE TURNER

King And Queen Of R&B	7" EP	London	REE1047	1956	**£150**	**£75**	

BROWN, SANDY

African Queen	7"	Tempo	A124	1958	**£4**	**£1.50**	
Afro McJazz	7" EP	Nixa	NJE1056	1957	**£8**	**£4**	
Blue McJazz	7" EP	Nixa	NJE1054	1957	**£8**	**£4**	
Doctor McJazz	LP	Columbia	33SX1306/ SCX3367	1961	**£12**	**£5**	*with Al Fairweather*
Hair At Its Hairiest	LP	Fontana	SFJL921	1969	**£30**	**£15**	
McJazz	LP	Nixa	NJL9	1957	**£15**	**£6**	
Playing Compositions By Al Fairweather	LP	Tempo	TAP3	1956	**£30**	**£15**	
Sandy Brown All Stars	LP	Fontana	TEI7473	1966	**£20**	**£8**	
Sandy Brown's Jazz Band	7" EP	Esquire	EP28	1954	**£10**	**£5**	
Sandy Brown's Jazz Band	7" EP	Tempo	EXA33	1955	**£10**	**£5**	
Sandy Brown's Jazz Band	7" EP	Tempo	EXA13	1955	**£10**	**£5**	
Traditional Jazz Scene '56	7" EP	Tempo	EXA49	1956	**£10**	**£5**	
Traditional Jazz Vol. 2	10" LP	Esquire	20022	1953	**£20**	**£8**	
With The Brian Lemon Trio	LP	77	SEU1249	1971	**£15**	**£6**	

BROWN, TINY

No More Blues	78	Capitol	CL13306	1950	**£12**	**£6**	

BROWN, VIC

Swanee River	7"	Rio	R7	1963	**£6**	**£2.50**	

BROWN BROTHERS

Let The Good Times Roll	7"	Vogue	V9131	1959	**£100**	**£50**	

BROWN SUGAR

I'm In Love With A Dreadlocks	7"	Lovers Rock	CJ613	197–	**£10**	**£5**	

BROWNE, DUNCAN

Duncan Browne	LP	Rak	SRKA6754	1973	**£10**	**£4**	
Give Me Take You	LP	Immediate	IMSP018	1968	**£150**	**£75**	
On The Bombsite	7"	Immediate	IM070	1968	**£6**	**£2.50**	

BROWNE, FRIDAY

Ask Any Woman	7"	Fontana	TF851	1967	**£4**	**£1.50**	
Getting Nowhere	7"	Parlophone	R5396	1966	**£4**	**£1.50**	
Thirty Second Love Affair	7"	Fontana	TF736	1966	**£4**	**£1.50**	

BROWNE, GEORGE

Calypso Mambo	7"	Parlophone	CMSP6	1954	**£5**	**£2**	*export*
Somebody Bad Stole De Wedding Bell	7"	Parlophone	CMSP17	1954	**£5**	**£2**	*export*

BROWNE, JACKSON

Jackson Browne	LP	Asylum	SD5051	1972	**£12**	**£5**	*canvas cover, US*
Late For The Sky	LP	Asylum	K243007	1974	**£10**	**£4**	*quad*

Pretender	LP	Mobile Fidelity	MFSL1055	1981	£10	£4	US audiophile

BROWNE, SANDRA

Johnny Boy	7"	Columbia	DB4998	1963	£5	£2	
Knock On Any Door	7"	Columbia	DB7465	1965	£5	£2	
You'd Think He Didn't Know Me	7"	Columbia	DB7109	1963	£4	£1.50	

BROWNE, TEDDY

Pretty Little Baby	7"	Starlite	ST45033	1961	£6	£2.50	

BROWNE, THOMAS F.

Wednesday's Child	LP	Vertigo	6343700	1972	£40	£20	spiral label

BROWNS

In The Country	7" EP	RCA	RCX187	1960	£10	£5	
Sweet Sounds By The Browns	LP	RCA	RD27153/SF5052	1959	£15	£6	

BROWNSVILLE STATION

Brownsville Station	LP	Palladium	P1004	1970	£10	£4	US

BROX, VICTOR & ANNETTE

Rollin' Back	LP	Sonet	SNTF663	1974	£12	£5	
Wake Me And Shake Me	7"	Fontana	TF536	1965	£4	£1.50	

BRUBECK, DAVE

At Storyville	LP	Philips	BBL7018	1955	£15	£6	
Bernstein Plays Brubeck Plays Bernstein	LP	Fontana	TFL5114/ STFL542	1960	£10	£4	
Best Of Brubeck	LP	Fontana	TFL5136	1961	£10	£4	
Brubeck And Rushing	LP	Fontana	TFL5126/ STFL550	1961	£10	£4	
Countdown – Time In Outer Space	LP	CBS	(S)BPG62013	1962	£10	£4	
Dave Brubeck	LP	Philips	BBL7116	1957	£12	£5	
Dave Brubeck And Jay And Kai At Newport	LP	Philips	BBL7147	1957	£15	£6	with J. J. Johnson & Kai Winding
Dave Brubeck Quartet	10" LP	Vogue	LDE095	1954	£25	£10	
Dave Brubeck Quartet	LP	Philips	BBL7060	1956	£15	£6	
Dave Brubeck Quartet	LP	Vogue	LAE12105	1959	£10	£4	
Dave Brubeck Quartet	LP	Philips	BBL7041	1955	£15	£6	
Dave Brubeck Quartet Featuring Paul Desmond	LP	Vogue	LAE12114	1959	£15	£6	
Dave Brubeck Quartet Vol. 2	10" LP	Vogue	LDE104	1954	£25	£10	
Dave Brubeck Quartet Vol. 3	10" LP	Vogue	LDE114	1955	£25	£10	
Dave Brubeck Trio	10" LP	Vogue	LDE090	1954	£25	£10	
Dave Digs Disney	LP	Fontana	TFL5017	1957	£12	£5	
Fabulous Trio And Octet	LP	Vogue	LAE12008	1956	£20	£8	
Gone With The Wind	LP	Fontana	TFL5071/ STFL501	1959	£12	£5	
In Europe	LP	Fontana	TFL5034	1959	£10	£4	
Jazz At Oberlin	LP	Vogue	LAE12048	1957	£20	£8	
Jazz At The Black Hawk	LP	Vogue	LAE12094	1958	£12	£5	
Jazz At The College Of The Pacific	LP	Vogue	LAE12110	1960	£12	£5	
Jazz Goes To College	LP	Philips	BBL7447	1960	£10	£4	
Jazz Goes To Junior College	LP	Fontana	TFL5002	1958	£12	£5	
Jazz Impressions Of Eurasia	LP	Fontana	TFL5051	1959	£10	£4	
Jazz Impressions Of The USA	LP	Philips	BBL7171	1957	£12	£5	
Newport 1958	LP	Fontana	TFL5059	1959	£10	£4	
Riddle	LP	Fontana	TFL5101/ STFL532	1960	£10	£4	
Southern Scene	LP	Fontana	TFL5099/ STFL530	1960	£10	£4	
Time Changes	LP	CBS	BPG62253	1964	£10	£4	
Time Further Out	LP	CBS	(S)BPG62078	1962	£10	£4	
Time In	LP	CBS	62757	1966	£10	£4	
Time Out	LP	CBS	(S)BPG62068	1962	£10	£4	
Time Out	LP	Fontana	TFL5085/ STFL523	1960	£12	£5	
Tonight Only!	LP	Fontana	STFL566	1961	£10	£4	with Carmen McRae

BRUCE, JACK

As a member of the Graham Bond Organization, John Mayall's Bluesbreakers (briefly) and Cream, Jack Bruce was perhaps the first rock bass player to attract notice for the excellence of his musicianship. At the same time, he was playing jazz with the likes of Mike Taylor, Mike Gibbs and John McLaughlin, as well as developing a fruitful songwriting partnership with poet Pete Brown. The solo albums from 1969 and 1971 (as well as the impressive *Out Of The Storm* from 1974) combine all these talents in magnificent fashion and make it all the more regrettable that Bruce's career since then has consisted largely of a catalogue of lost opportunities.

Consul At Sunset	7"	Polydor	2058153	1971	£4	£1.50	
Harmony Row	LP	Polydor	2310107	1971	£10	£4	
I'm Gettin' Tired	7"	Polydor	56036	1965	£60	£30	
Songs For A Tailor	LP	Polydor	583058	1969	£12	£5	
Things We Like	LP	Polydor	2343033	1970	£10	£4	

BRUCE, LENNY

Berkeley Concert	LP	Transatlantic	TRA195	1969	£20	£8	double
Best Of Lenny Bruce	LP	Fantasy	7012	1962	£20	£8	US
Carnegie Hall February 4, 1961	LP	United Artists	UAS9800	1971	£20	£8	US triple

Essential Lenny Bruce	LP	Douglas	SD788	1968	**£15**	**£6**	*US*
I Am Not A Nut, Elect Me	LP	Fantasy	7007	1959	**£20**	**£8**	*US*
Interviews Of Our Times	LP	Fantasy	7001	1958	**£20**	**£8**	*US*
Law, Language And Lenny Bruce	LP	Phil Spector	2307001	1974	**£12**	**£5**	
Lenny Bruce	LP	United Artists	UAL3580	1967	**£15**	**£6**	*US*
Lenny Bruce Is Out Again	LP	Philles	PHLP4010	1966	**£60**	**£30**	*US*
Lenny Bruce, American	LP	Fantasy	7011	1962	**£20**	**£8**	*US*
Live At The Curran Theatre	LP	Fantasy	34201	1972	**£12**	**£5**	*US*
Midnight Concert	LP	United Artists	UAS6794	196–	**£12**	**£5**	*US*
Recordings Submitted As Evidence	10" LP	private		1962	**£75**	**£37.50**	*US*
Sick Humor Of Lenny Bruce	LP	Fantasy	7003	1958	**£20**	**£8**	*US*
Thank You, Masked Man	LP	Fantasy	F7017	1972	**£12**	**£5**	*US*
To Is A Preposition, Come Is A Verb	LP	Douglas	2KZ30872	1970	**£15**	**£6**	*US*
What I Was Arrested For	LP	Douglas	2KZ30872	1971	**£12**	**£5**	*US*

BRUCE, TOMMY

Boom Boom	7"	Polydor	BM56006	1965	**£6**	**£2.50**	
Broken Doll	7"	Columbia	DB4498	1960	**£4**	**£1.50**	
Knockout	7" EP	Columbia	SEG8077	1961	**£75**	**£37.50**	

BRUCE & ROBIN ROCKERS

Batman Theme	LP	Marble Arch	MAL626	1966	**£12**	**£5**	

BRUCKEN, CLAUDIA

Absolute	CD-s	Island	CID471	1990	**£10**	**£5**	
Kiss Like Ether	CD-s	Island	CID479	1991	**£10**	**£5**	
Love And A Million Other Things	CD	Island	CID9971	1991	**£20**	**£8**	

BRUHL, HEIDI

Marcel	7"	Philips	345579BF	1963	**£8**	**£4**	
Ring Of Gold	7"	Philips	PB1095	1960	**£6**	**£2.50**	*picture sleeve*

BRUISERS

Blue Girl	7"	Parlophone	R5042	1963	**£4**	**£1.50**	
Your Turn To Cry	7"	Parlophone	R5092	1963	**£4**	**£1.50**	

BRUMBEATS

Cry Little Girl, Cry	7"	Decca	F11834	1964	**£10**	**£5**	

BRUMMELL, BEAU

Better Man Than I	7"	Columbia	DB7675	1965	**£4**	**£1.50**	
I Know Know Know	7"	Columbia	DB7447	1965	**£4**	**£1.50**	
Next Kiss	7"	Columbia	DB7538	1965	**£4**	**£1.50**	

BRUNNING HALL SUNFLOWER BLUES BAND

Saga was a bargain-priced label, specializing in cheaply produced cash-ins of the prevailing trends. The Brunning Hall Band was Saga's blues band, and by having their records released on the label, the group was fighting a losing battle from the outset with regard to being taken as serious rivals for the likes of Fleetwood Mac or Savoy Brown. In fact, Bob Brunning had been the original bass player with Fleetwood Mac (and plays on one track on the group's debut LP), while Bob Hall played piano on all Savoy Brown's early records, albeit without ever being counted as a member of the group.

Bullen Street Blues	LP	Saga	FID2118	1968	**£12**	**£5**	
Bullen Street Blues	LP	Boulevard	4032	1971	**£10**	**£4**	
I Wish You Would	LP	Saga	SAGA8150	1970	**£40**	**£20**	
Sunflower Blues Band	LP	Gemini	GM2010	1969	**£50**	**£25**	
Trackside Blues	LP	Saga	EROS8132	1969	**£25**	**£10**	

BRUNO, TONY

What's Yesterday	7"	Capitol	CL15534	1968	**£10**	**£5**	

BRUT

Brut	LP	Philips	6305045	1970	**£15**	**£6**	*German*

BRUTE FORCE

Extemporaneous	LP	B.T.Puppy	BTPS1015	1971	**£1000**	**£700**	*US*
King Of Fuh	7"	Apple	8	1969	**£400**	**£250**	*best auctioned*

BRUTUS

Payroll	7"	Purple	PUR126	1975	**£4**	**£1.50**	

BRYAN, CANNONBALL

Man About The Town	7"	Amalgamated	AMG829	1968	**£6**	**£2.50**	*Hugh Malcolm B side*
Red Ash	7"	Trojan	TR673	1969	**£5**	**£2**	*Silvertones B side*

BRYAN, CARL

Run For Your Life	7"	Camel	CA22	1969	**£4**	**£1.50**	*Two Sparks B side*
Soul Pipe	7"	Duke	DU13	1969	**£5**	**£2**	

BRYAN, FITZVAUGHN ORCHESTRA

Evening News	7"	Melodisc	1560	1960	**£5**	**£2**	

BRYAN, WES

Honey Baby	7"	London	HLU8978	1959	**£25**	**£12.50**	
Lonesome Lover	7"	London	HLU8607	1958	**£20**	**£10**	

BRYAN & THE BRUNELLES

Title	Format	Label	Cat. No.	Year	Mint	VG	Notes
Jacqueline	7"	HMV	POP1394	1965	**£30**	**£15**	

BRYANT, ANITA

Title	Format	Label	Cat. No.	Year	Mint	VG	Notes
In My Little Corner Of The World	LP	London	HAL2381	1961	**£25**	**£10**	
Kisses Sweeter Than Wine	7" EP	CBS	AGG20005	1962	**£8**	**£4**	
Little George	7"	London	HLL9075	1960	**£4**	**£1.50**	
My Little Corner Of The World	7"	London	HLL9171	1960	**£4**	**£1.50**	
My Mind's Playing Tricks On Me Again	7"	CBS	202026	1966	**£20**	**£10**	
Six Boys And Seven Girls	7"	London	HLL8983	1959	**£4**	**£1.50**	

BRYANT, LAURA K.

Title	Format	Label	Cat. No.	Year	Mint	VG	Notes
Bobby	7"	London	HLU8551	1958	**£15**	**£7.50**	

BRYANT, MARIE

Title	Format	Label	Cat. No.	Year	Mint	VG	Notes
Calypso's Too Hot To Handle	7" EP	Kalypso	XXEP7	1963	**£8**	**£4**	
Don't Touch Me Nylons	LP	Melodisc	MLP12132	1963	**£20**	**£8**	
Don't Touch My Nylon	7"	Kalypso	XX28	1961	**£4**	**£1.50**	
Water Melon	7"	Kalypso	XX27	1961	**£4**	**£1.50**	

BRYANT, RAY

Title	Format	Label	Cat. No.	Year	Mint	VG	Notes
Alone With The Blues	LP	Esquire	32106	1960	**£20**	**£8**	
Ray Bryant Trio	LP	Esquire	32066	1958	**£25**	**£10**	

BRYANT, RUSTY

Title	Format	Label	Cat. No.	Year	Mint	VG	Notes
All Night Long	LP	Dot	DLP3006	1956	**£40**	**£20**	US
Rock'n'Roll With Rusty Bryant	10" LP	London	HBD1066	1956	**£50**	**£25**	

BRYARS, GAVIN

Title	Format	Label	Cat. No.	Year	Mint	VG	Notes
Sinking Of The Titanic/Jesus Blood	LP	Obscure	OBS1	1975	**£12**	**£5**	

BRYCE, CALUM

Title	Format	Label	Cat. No.	Year	Mint	VG	Notes
Love Maker	7"	Condor	PS1001	1968	**£75**	**£37.50**	

BRYDEN, BERYL

Title	Format	Label	Cat. No.	Year	Mint	VG	Notes
Casey Jones	7"	Decca	F10823	1956	**£15**	**£7.50**	

Bs

Title	Format	Label	Cat. No.	Year	Mint	VG	Notes
In Your Bonnet	LP	private		1974	**£150**	**£75**	

BUBBLE PUPPY

Title	Format	Label	Cat. No.	Year	Mint	VG	Notes
Gathering Of Promises	LP	International Artist	IALP10	1969	**£40**	**£20**	US

BUBBLEMEN

Title	Format	Label	Cat. No.	Year	Mint	VG	Notes
Bubblemen Rap!	CD-s	Beggars Banquet	BULB1CD	1988	**£5**	**£2**	

BUBBLES

Title	Format	Label	Cat. No.	Year	Mint	VG	Notes
Bopping In The Barnyard	7"	Duke	DK1001	1963	**£6**	**£2.50**	

BUCCHI, J.-L.

Title	Format	Label	Cat. No.	Year	Mint	VG	Notes
Sunflower	LP	De L'Autre	0047	1978	**£15**	**£6**	*French*

BUCHANAN, ROY

Title	Format	Label	Cat. No.	Year	Mint	VG	Notes
In The Beginning	LP	Polydor	PD6035	1975	**£10**	**£4**	US
Live Stock	LP	Polydor	2391192	1975	**£10**	**£4**	
Loading Zone	LP	Polydor	2391295	1977	**£10**	**£4**	
Rescue Me	LP	Polydor	2391152	1975	**£10**	**£4**	
Roy Buchanan	LP	Polydor	2482275	1976	**£10**	**£4**	
Roy Buchanan	LP	Polydor	2391042	1972	**£12**	**£5**	
Second Album	LP	Polydor	2391062	1973	**£12**	**£5**	
Street Called Straight	LP	Polydor	2391233	1976	**£10**	**£4**	
That's What I'm Here For	LP	Polydor	2391114	1974	**£10**	**£4**	
You're Not Alone	LP	Atlantic	SD19170	1978	**£10**	**£4**	US

BUCHANAN BROTHERS

Title	Format	Label	Cat. No.	Year	Mint	VG	Notes
Medicine Man	LP	Event	ES101	1969	**£20**	**£8**	US

BUCKINGHAM, LINDSEY

Title	Format	Label	Cat. No.	Year	Mint	VG	Notes
Countdown	CD-s	Mercury	MERCD371	1992	**£5**	**£2**	
Go Insane	12"	Mercury	MERX168	1984	**£8**	**£4**	
Holiday Road	7"	Mercury	MER150	1983	**£5**	**£2**	
Soul Drifter	CD-s	Mercury	MERCD380	1992	**£5**	**£2**	

BUCKINGHAM–NICKS

Lindsey Buckingham and Stevie Nicks achieved little success with their LP, yet its sound is almost exactly that of the LPs *Fleetwood Mac* and *Rumours*, with which the Buckingham–Nicks team managed so spectacularly to restore Fleetwood Mac's fortunes. The earlier LP was reissued in 1981, when it might have been expected to do very well, and yet once again the record sank without a trace.

Title	Format	Label	Cat. No.	Year	Mint	VG	Notes
Buckingham–Nicks	LP	Polydor	2482378	1981	**£20**	**£8**	
Buckingham–Nicks	LP	Polydor	2391093	1973	**£30**	**£15**	
Don't Let Me Down Again	7"	Polydor	2066700	1976	**£6**	**£2.50**	
Don't Let Me Down Again	7"	Polydor	2066398	1974	**£10**	**£5**	

BUCKINGHAMS

Back In Love Again	7"	CBS	3559	1968	£4	£1.50	
Don't You Care	7"	CBS	2640	1968	£6	£2.50	
Greatest Hits	LP	Columbia	CS9812	1969	£15	£6	US
Hey Baby	7"	CBS	2995	1967	£4	£1.50	
I Call Your Name	7"	Stateside	SS529	1966	£4	£1.50	
In One Ear And Gone Tomorrow	LP	Columbia	CS9703	1968	£15	£6	US
Kind Of A Drag	7"	Stateside	SS588	1967	£4	£1.50	
Kind Of A Drag	7" EP	Columbia	ESRF1841	1967	£20	£10	French
Kind Of A Drag	LP	USA	107	1967	£20	£8	US
Kind Of A Drag	LP	USA	107	1967	£25	£10	US, with 'I'm A Man'
Making Up And Breaking Up	7"	Stateside	SS2011	1967	£4	£1.50	
Mercy Mercy Mercy	7"	CBS	[illegible]	1967	£4	£1.50	
Portraits	LP	Columbia	CL2798/CS9598	1968	£12	£5	US
Susan	7"	CBS	3195	1967	£4	£1.50	
Time And Charges	LP	Columbia	CL2669/CS9469	1967	£12	£5	US

BUCKINGHAMS (2)

I'll Never Hurt You No More	7"	Pye	7N15848	1965	£4	£1.50	

BUCKLE, BOB

Come Listen To Bob Buckle	LP	Ash	ALP1075	1973	£10	£4	

BUCKLEY, JEFF

Although he disliked the comparison, Jeff Buckley inherited his father's astonishing voice and was able to flex its powers on a set of self-composed songs that, for melodic invention allied to emotional strength, make most others sound a little inadequate. *Grace* is one of the towering albums of the nineties, while the live tours that Buckley undertook in its support showed him to have the same kind of charisma and vitality as the young Bruce Springsteen. The promotional *Album Sampler* emphasizes Columbia's faith in their signing by actually consisting of the entire *Grace* album. Jeff Buckley will be greatly missed.

Album Sampler	CD	Columbia	SAMPCD2281	1994	£20	£8	promo

BUCKLEY, SEAN & THE BREADCRUMBS

It Hurts Me When I Cry	7"	Stateside	SS421	1965	£50	£25	

BUCKLEY, TIM

It would have been easy for Tim Buckley to stay as the conventional singer-songwriter of *Goodbye And Hello* and his first LP. Instead, he chose to let the incredible range and power of his tenor voice lead him into unexplored territory. *Lorca* and *Starsailor*, with members of the Mothers of Invention amongst its cast of backing musicians, are brave, inspirational recordings, in which Buckley's voice really does function as an instrument – its player an improvising virtuoso of the highest order.

Aren't You The Girl?	7"	Elektra	EKSN45008	1967	£4	£1.50	
Blue Afternoon	LP	Straight	STS1060	1969	£30	£15	
Goodbye And Hello	LP	Elektra	EKL/EKS318	1967	£15	£6	
Greetings From L.A.	LP	Warner Bros	K46176	1972	£10	£4	
Happy Sad	LP	Elektra	EKS74045	1968	£20	£8	
Happy Time	7"	Straight	4799	1970	£4	£1.50	
Look At The Fool	LP	Discreet	K59204	1974	£10	£4	
Lorca	LP	Elektra	2410005	1970	£25	£10	
Morning Glory	7"	Elektra	EKSN45018	1967	£4	£1.50	
Once I Was	7"	Elektra	EKSN45023	1968	£4	£1.50	
Peel Sessions	CD-s	Strange Fruit	SFPSCD082	1991	£5	£2	
Pleasant Street	7"	Elektra	EKSN45041	1968	£4	£1.50	
Sefronia	LP	Discreet	K49201	1973	£10	£4	
Starsailor	LP	Straight	STS1064	1970	£25	£10	
Tim Buckley	LP	Elektra	EKL/EKS4004	1966	£30	£15	
Wings	7"	Elektra	EKSN45031	1968	£4	£1.50	

BUCKNER, MILT

Night Mist	7"	Capitol	CL14662	1956	£4	£1.50	
Rockin' Hammond	10" LP	Capitol	T722	1956	£12	£5	
Rocking With Milt	7" EP	Capitol	EAP1000	1956	£5	£2	

BUCKNER, TEDDY

Dixieland Jubilee	10" LP	Vogue	LDE175	1956	£10	£4	
Salute To Louis Armstrong	LP	Vogue	LAE12129	1958	£10	£4	
Teddy Buckner	LP	Vogue	LAE12026	1957	£10	£4	

BUCKY & THE STRINGS

Lolitas On The Loose	7"	Salvo	SLO1807	1962	£10	£5	

BUD & TRAVIS

In Concert	LP	London	SAHG6128	1961	£10	£4	stereo

BUDD, HAROLD

Pavilion Of Dreams	LP	Obscure	OBS10	1978	£10	£4	

BUDD, ROY

At Newport	LP	Pye	NPL18212	1968	£10	£4	
Birth Of The Budd	7"	Pye	7N15807	1965	£4	£1.50	
Carter	7"	Pye	7N45051	1970	£12	£6	
Carter	7"	Pye	7N45051	1970	£30	£15	picture sleeve
Concerto For Harry – Something To Hide	LP	Pye	NSPL18389	1972	£30	£15	
Diamonds	LP	Bradleys	BRADS8002	1976	£50	£25	

Fear Is The Key	LP	Pye	NSPL18398	1973	£**50**	£**25**	
Great Songs And Themes From Great Films	LP	Pye	NSPL18373	1971	£**40**	£**20**	
Kidnapped	LP	Polydor	2383102	1972	£**30**	£**15**	
Plays Soldier Blue And Other Themes	LP	Pye	NSPL18348	1971	£**50**	£**25**	

BUDDIES

Buddies And The Compacts	LP	Wing	MGW12293/ SRW16293	1965	£**15**	£**6**	*US*
Go Go	LP	Wing	MGW12306/ SRW16306	1965	£**15**	£**6**	*US*

BUDGIE

Budgie	LP	MCA	MKPS2018	1971	£**20**	£**8**	*pink and red label*
Budgie	LP	MCA	MKPS2018	1971	£**30**	£**15**	*pink and red label, poster*
Budgie	LP	MCA	MKPS2018	1971	£**15**	£**6**	*blue and black label*
Crash Course In Brain Surgery	7"	MCA	MK5072	1971	£**10**	£**5**	
Crime Against The World	12"	Active	BUDGIE2	1980	£**6**	£**2.50**	
Crime Against The World	7"	Active	BUDGE2	1980	£**5**	£**2**	
I Ain't No Mountain	7"	MCA	MCA175	1975	£**5**	£**2**	
If Swallowed Do Not Induce Vomiting	12"	Active	BUDGE1	1980	£**8**	£**4**	
If Swallowed Do Not Induce Vomiting	12"	Active	BUDGIE1	1980	£**6**	£**2.50**	
Never Turn Your Back On A Friend	LP	MCA	MDKS8010	1973	£**12**	£**5**	
Smile Boy Smile	7"	A&M	AMS7342	1978	£**5**	£**2**	
Squawk	LP	MCA	MKPS2023	1972	£**12**	£**5**	
Whisky River	7"	MCA	MK5085	1972	£**6**	£**2.50**	
Wildfire	7"	Active	BUDGE	1980	£**8**	£**4**	*promo*
Zoom Club	7"	MCA	MCA133	1974	£**5**	£**2**	

BUENA VISTAS

Hot Shot	7"	Stateside	SS525	1966	£**6**	£**2.50**	

BUFFALO

Average Rock'n'Roller	LP	Vertigo	6357104	1977	£**40**	£**20**	*Australian*
Dead Forever	LP	Vertigo	6357007	1971	£**60**	£**30**	*Australian*
Mother's Choice	LP	Vertigo	6357103	1976	£**50**	£**25**	*Australian*
Volcanic Rock	LP	Vertigo	6357101	1973	£**60**	£**30**	*Australian*

BUFFALO (2)

Battle Torn Heroes	7"	Heavy Metal	HEAVY3	1981	£**10**	£**5**	
Mean Machine	7"	Heavy Metal	HEAVY15	1982	£**10**	£**5**	

BUFFALO NICKEL JUGBAND

Buffalo Nickel Jugband	LP	Happy Tiger	1018	1971	£**12**	£**5**	*US*

BUFFALO SPRINGFIELD

The uneasy alliance that existed between Buffalo Springfield's three major talents – Neil Young, Steve Stills and Richie Furay – meant that the group was never destined to last very long. The competition, however, inspired the three into producing some particularly inventive material, which turns *Buffalo Springfield Again* into one of the key albums of the late sixties. By comparison, the eponymous first album is strictly formative, while *Last Time Around*, released when the group had already split, suffers from being compiled from the material that the three songwriters did not particularly want to keep for their next projects.

Beginning	LP	Atlantic	K30028	1973	£**10**	£**4**	
Best Of/Retrospective	LP	Atlantic	K40071	1972	£**10**	£**4**	
Bluebird	7"	Atlantic	K10237	1972	£**4**	£**1.50**	*picture sleeve*
Buffalo Springfield	LP	Atlantic	587/588070	1967	£**25**	£**10**	
Buffalo Springfield	LP	Atlantic	K70001	1973	£**15**	£**6**	*double*
Buffalo Springfield	LP	Atlantic	587/588070	1967	£**40**	£**20**	*with 'Baby Don't Scold Me'*
Buffalo Springfield Again	LP	Atlantic	587/588091	1968	£**20**	£**8**	
Buffalo Springfield Again	LP	Atlantic	K40014	1971	£**10**	£**4**	
Expecting To Fly	7"	Atlantic	584165	1968	£**4**	£**1.50**	
Expecting To Fly	LP	Atlantic	2462012	1970	£**10**	£**4**	
For What It's Worth	7"	Atlantic	584077	1967	£**4**	£**1.50**	
For What It's Worth	7" EP	Atco	123	1967	£**75**	£**37.50**	*French*
Last Time Around	LP	Atlantic	K40077	1971	£**12**	£**5**	
Last Time Around	LP	Atco	228024	1969	£**15**	£**6**	
Pretty Girl Why	7"	Atco	226006	1969	£**4**	£**1.50**	
Retrospective	LP	Atco	228012	1969	£**12**	£**5**	
Rock'n'Roll Woman	7"	Atlantic	584145	1967	£**4**	£**1.50**	
Uno Mundo	7"	Atlantic	584189	1968	£**4**	£**1.50**	

BUFFALO TOM

Enemy	7"	Caff	CAFF6	1989	£**12**	£**6**	

BUFFOONS

Girls Beat	LP	Hör Zu	SHZE234	1967	£**25**	£**10**	*German*
My World Fell Down	7"	Columbia	DB8317	1967	£**5**	£**2**	

BUGGS

Beetle Beat	LP	Coronet	212	1964	£**20**	£**8**	*US*

BULL

This Is Bull	LP	Paramount	PAS5028	1970	£**20**	£**8**	*US*

BULL, SANDY

E Pluribus Unum	LP	Vanguard	SVRL19040	1969	£**10**	£**4**	

Fantasias	LP	Vanguard	VSD79119	1963	**£15**	**£6**	US
Inventions	LP	Vanguard	VSD79191	1965	**£15**	**£6**	US

BULLDOG BREED

Made In England	LP	Nova	(S)DN5	1970	**£40**	**£20**	
Portcullis Gate	7"	Deram	DM270	1969	**£20**	**£10**	

BULLDOGS

John, Paul, George, and Ringo	7"	Mercury	MF808	1964	**£6**	**£2.50**	

BULLET

Hobo	7"	Purple	PUR101	1971	**£4**	**£1.50**	

BULLET (2)

Hanged Man	LP	Contour	2870437	1975	**£25**	**£10**	

BULLY WEE BAND

Bully Wee	LP	Folksound	FS102AB	1975	**£25**	**£10**	
Enchanted Lady	LP	Red Rag	RRR007	1976	**£15**	**£6**	
Madmen Of Gotham	LP	Red Rag		1981	**£15**	**£6**	
Silvermines	LP	Red Rag	RRR017	1978	**£15**	**£6**	

BUMBLE, B. & THE STINGERS

Bumble Boogie	7"	Top Rank	JAR561	1961	**£4**	**£1.50**	
Nut Rocker	7" EP	Pathe	EMF316	1962	**£25**	**£12.50**	*French*
Piano Stylings Of B. Bumble	7" EP	Stateside	SE1001	1962	**£25**	**£12.50**	

BUMBLE BEE SLIM

Bee's Back In Town	LP	Fontana	688138ZL	1966	**£15**	**£6**	

BUMBLES

Beep Beep	7"	Purple	PUR107	1972	**£20**	**£10**	*picture sleeve*
Beep Beep	7"	Purple	PUR107	1972	**£5**	**£2**	

BUMP

Bump	LP	Pioneer	PRSD2150	1970	**£400**	**£250**	US

BUNCH

The Bunch was not a real group as such, but rather members and friends of Fairport Convention on holiday. *Rock On* contains their versions of a number of rock'n'roll classics – and it has to be admitted that once the novelty of hearing these particular musicians tackling this kind of material has worn off, the results are not especially impressive.

Rock On	LP	Island	ILPS9189	1972	**£25**	**£10**	*with flexi*

BUNCH (2)

Birthday	7"	CBS	3692	1968	**£8**	**£4**	
Birthday	7"	CBS	3709	1968	**£6**	**£2.50**	
Spare A Shilling	7"	CBS	3060	1967	**£50**	**£25**	
You Can't Do This	7"	CBS	2740	1967	**£10**	**£5**	
You Never Came Home	7"	CBS	202506	1967	**£30**	**£15**	

BUNCH OF FIVES

Go Home Baby	7"	Parlophone	R5494	1966	**£20**	**£10**	

BUNN, ROGER

Piece Of Mind	LP	Major Minor	SMLP70	1971	**£15**	**£6**	

BUNNY & RUDDY

On The Town	7"	Nu Beat	NB011	1968	**£6**	**£2.50**	*Monty Morris B side*
True Romance	7"	Nu Beat	NB007	1968	**£6**	**£2.50**	*Bobby Kalphat B side*

BUNTING, BOB

You've Got To Go Down This Way	LP	Transatlantic	TRA166	1968	**£25**	**£10**	

BUNYAN, VASHTI

Just Another Diamond Day	LP	Philips	6308019	1971	**£400**	**£250**	

BURCHETTE, WILBURN

Guitar Grimoire	LP	Burchette	001	1973	**£100**	**£50**	US
Mind Storm	LP	Burchette	007	1977	**£100**	**£50**	US
Music Of The Godhead	LP	Burchette	003	1975	**£100**	**£50**	US
Occult Concert	LP	Ames	7014	1971	**£100**	**£50**	US
Opens The Seven Gates	LP	Ebos	0001	1972	**£100**	**£50**	US
Psychic Meditation Music	LP	Burchette	002	1974	**£100**	**£50**	US
Transcendental Music For Meditation	LP	Burchette	004	1976	**£100**	**£50**	US

BURDON, ERIC

Guilty	LP	United Artists	UAG29251	1971	**£12**	**£5**	*with Jimmy Witherspoon*

BURDON, ERIC & THE ANIMALS

Eric Is Here	LP	MGM	(S)E4433	1967	**£20**	**£8**	US
Everyone Of Us	LP	MGM	(S)E4553	1968	**£20**	**£8**	US
Good Times	7"	MGM	MGM1344	1967	**£4**	**£1.50**	
Hey Gyp	7" EP	Barclay	071121	1967	**£20**	**£10**	*French*
Love Is	LP	MGM	SE4591/2	1968	**£30**	**£15**	*US double*
Love Is	LP	MGM	CS8105	1968	**£15**	**£6**	

Love Is	LP	MGM	2354006/7	1971	£25	£10	double
Monterey	7"	MGM	MGM1412	1968	£4	£1.50	
Ring Of Fire	7"	MGM	MGM1461	1969	£6	£2.50	
River Deep Mountain High	7"	MGM	MGM1481	1969	£8	£4	
San Franciscan Nights	7"	MGM	MGM1359	1967	£4	£1.50	
See See Rider	7" EP	Barclay	071081	1966	£20	£10	French
Sky Pilot	7"	MGM	MGM1373	1968	£4	£1.50	
Twain Shall Meet	LP	MGM	CS8074	1968	£15	£6	
When I Was Young	7"	MGM	MGM1340	1967	£4	£1.50	
Winds Of Change	LP	MGM	C(S)8052	1967	£15	£6	
Winds Of Change	LP	MGM	2354001	1971	£10	£4	

BURDON, ERIC & WAR

Blackman's Burdon	LP	Liberty	LDS8400	1970	£15	£6	double
Eric Burdon Declares War	LP	Polydor	2310041	1970	£10	£4	

BURGESS, DAVE

I Love Paris	7"	London	HLB8175	1955	£20	£10	
I'm Available	7"	Oriole	CB1413	1957	£60	£30	

BURGESS, JOHN

King Of Highland Pipers	LP	Topic	12T199	1969	£12	£5	

BURGESS, SONNY

Sadie's Back In Town	7"	London	HLS9064	1960	£150	£75	

BURGETT, JIM

Let's Investigate	7"	Philips	PB1133	1961	£15	£7.50	

BURKE, JOE, ANDY MCGANN & FELIX DOLAN

Tribute To Michael Coleman	LP	Shaskeen	05360	1970	£15	£6	

BURKE, KEVIN

If The Cap Fits	LP	Rockburgh	ROC105	1978	£15	£6	

BURKE, KEVIN & JACKIE DALY

Eavesdropper	LP	Mulligan	LUN039	1981	£12	£5	Irish

BURKE, KEVIN & MICHAEL O DOMHNAILL

Promenade	LP	Mulligan	LUN028	1979	£12	£5	Irish

BURKE, SOLOMON

Baby Come On Home	7"	Atlantic	AT4073	1966	£4	£1.50	
Best Of Solomon Burke	LP	Atlantic	587/588016	1966	£20	£8	
Can't Nobody Love You	7"	London	HLK9763	1963	£8	£4	
Cry To Me	7"	London	HLK9512	1962	£25	£12.50	
Down In The Valley	7"	London	HLK9560	1962	£8	£4	
Everybody Needs Somebody To Love	7"	Atlantic	AT4004	1964	£5	£2	
Greatest	LP	London	HAK8018	1963	£40	£20	
He'll Have To Go	7"	London	HLK9849	1964	£8	£4	
I Feel A Sin Comin' On	7"	Atlantic	584005	1966	£4	£1.50	
I Wish I Knew	7"	Atlantic	584191	1968	£4	£1.50	
I Wish I Knew	LP	Atlantic	587/588117	1968	£15	£6	
If You Need Me	7"	London	HLK9715	1963	£8	£4	
If You Need Me	LP	Atlantic	(SD)8085	1963	£30	£15	US
Just Out Of Reach	7"	London	HLK9454	1961	£15	£7.50	
Keep A Light In The Window	7"	Atlantic	584100	1967	£4	£1.50	
Keep Lookin'	7"	Atlantic	584026	1966	£4	£1.50	
King Of Rock'n'Soul	LP	Atlantic	590004	1966	£12	£5	
King Of Rock'n'Soul	LP	Atlantic	ATL5009	1964	£30	£15	
King Solomon	LP	Atlantic	587105	1968	£15	£6	
Maggie's Farm	7"	Atlantic	AT4030	1965	£5	£2	
More Rocking Soul	7"	Atlantic	AT4014	1964	£5	£2	
Only Love	7"	Atlantic	AT4061	1965	£5	£2	
Peepin'	7"	Atlantic	AT4022	1965	£4	£1.50	
Proud Mary	7"	Bell	BLL1062	1969	£4	£1.50	
Proud Mary	LP	Bell	MBLL/SBLL118	1969	£12	£5	
Rock'n'Soul	7" EP	Atlantic	AET6008	1965	£30	£15	
Save It	7"	Atlantic	584204	1968	£4	£1.50	
Solomon Burke	LP	Apollo	ALP498	1962	£50	£25	US
Someone Is Watching	7"	Atlantic	AT4044	1965	£4	£1.50	
Someone To Love	7"	London	HLK9887	1964	£8	£4	
Take Me	7"	Atlantic	584122	1967	£4	£1.50	
Tonight My Heart She Is Crying	7" EP	London	REK1379	1963	£40	£20	
Uptight Good Woman	7"	Bell	BLL1047	1968	£4	£1.50	

BURKE, SONNY

Blue Island	7"	Blue Beat	BB363	1966	£12	£6	
Choo Choo Train	7"	Island	WI3082	1967	£10	£5	*Ken Parker B side*
Dance With Me	7"	Black Swan	WI470	1965	£10	£5	
Glad	7"	Black Swan	WI469	1965	£10	£5	
Grandpa	7"	Island	WI221	1965	£10	£5	
Have Faith	7"	Ska Beat	JB272	1967	£10	£5	
Life Without Fun	7"	Island	WI134	1963	£10	£5	
Rudy Girl	7"	Island	WI3040	1967	£10	£5	*Bob Andy B side*
Sounds Of Sonny Burke	LP	Island	ILP972	1968	£50	£25	*pink label*
Wicked People	7"	Black Swan	WI471	1965	£10	£5	
You Rule My Heart	7"	Island	WI3022	1966	£10	£5	*Gaylads B side*

BURKE, VINNIE

String Jazz Quartet	LP	HMV	CLP1163	1958	**£15**	**£6**	
Vinnie Burke All Stars	LP	HMV	CLP1217	1958	**£15**	**£6**	

BURLAND, DAVE

Dalesman's Litany	LP	Trailer	LER2029	1971	**£12**	**£5**	
Dave Burland	LP	Trailer	LER2082	1972	**£12**	**£5**	
Double Take	LP	Rubber	RUB012/036	1980	**£20**	**£8**	*double*
Rollin'	LP	Moonraker	MOO6	1985	**£10**	**£4**	
Songs And Buttered Haycocks	LP	Rubber	RUB012	1975	**£12**	**£5**	
You Can't Fool The Fat Man	LP	Rubber	RUB036	1979	**£12**	**£5**	

BURLAND, DAVE, TONY CAPSTICK & DICK GAUGHAN

Songs Of Ewan MacColl	LP	Rubber	RUB027	1978	**£10**	**£4**	

BURMOE BROTHERS

Skin	12"	Some Bizarre	WBY121	1985	**£10**	**£5**	

BURNEL, JEAN-JACQUES

Euroman Cometh	LP	Mau Mau	PMAU601	1988	**£10**	**£4**	*picture disc*
Girl From The Snow Country	7"	United Artists	BP361	1980	**£300**	**£180**	

BURNETT, FRANCES

Please Remember Me	7"	Coral	Q72374	1959	**£30**	**£15**	*tri-centre*

BURNETT, KING

I Man Free	7"	Dip	DL5056	1975	**£4**	**£1.50**	
Key Card	7"	Dip	DL5073	1975	**£4**	**£1.50**	

BURNETTE, DORSEY

Dorsey Burnette	LP	London	HAD8050	1963	**£50**	**£25**	
Dorsey Burnette Sings	7" EP	London	RED1402	1963	**£30**	**£15**	
Greatest Hits	LP	Era	ES800	1969	**£15**	**£6**	*US*
Greatest Love	7"	Liberty	LIB15190	1969	**£5**	**£2**	
Hey Little One	7"	London	HLN9160	1960	**£12**	**£6**	
It's No Sin	7"	London	HLN9365	1961	**£8**	**£4**	
Jimmy Brown	7"	Tamla Motown	TMG534	1965	**£40**	**£20**	
Tall Oak Tree	7"	London	HLN9047	1960	**£10**	**£5**	
Tall Oak Tree	LP	Era	EL(S)102	1960	**£75**	**£37.50**	*US*

BURNETTE, JAN

All At Once	7"	Oriole	CB1742	1962	**£5**	**£2**	
Boy I Used To Know	7"	Oriole	CB1807	1963	**£6**	**£2.50**	
I Could Have Loved You So Well	7"	Oriole	CB1716	1962	**£6**	**£2.50**	
Let Me Make You Smile Again	7"	Oriole	CB1905	1964	**£6**	**£2.50**	
Love, Let Me Not Hunger	7"	Oriole	CB1949	1964	**£5**	**£2**	
Teddy	7"	Oriole	CB1761	1962	**£5**	**£2**	
Till I Hear The Truth From You	7"	Oriole	CB1841	1963	**£4**	**£1.50**	
Too Young	7"	Oriole	CB1920	1964	**£6**	**£2.50**	

BURNETTE, JOHNNY

Johnny Burnette's original rock'n'roll trio played rockabilly to rival that of Elvis Presley. Like Presley, however, Burnette rapidly descended into trite pop music – there is simply no comparison between 'You're Sixteen' and 'Train Kept A-Rollin''. Not for nothing has the latter song inspired furious cover versions by the Yardbirds and Motorhead.

All Week Long	7"	Capitol	CL15322	1963	**£10**	**£5**	
Big Big World	7" EP	London	REG1309	1961	**£50**	**£25**	
Clown Shoes	7"	Liberty	LIB55416	1962	**£4**	**£1.50**	
Damn The Defiant	7"	Liberty	LIB55489	1962	**£5**	**£2**	
Dreamin'	7"	London	HLG9172	1960	**£4**	**£1.50**	
Dreamin'	7"	Liberty	LIB10235	1966	**£5**	**£2**	
Dreamin'	7" EP	London	REG1263	1960	**£50**	**£25**	
Dreamin'	LP	Sunset	SLS50007	1969	**£10**	**£4**	
Dreamin'	LP	London	HAG2306	1961	**£60**	**£30**	
Eager Beaver Baby	7"	Vogue Coral	Q72283	1957	**£175**	**£87.50**	
Fool	7"	London	HLG9473	1961	**£6**	**£2.50**	
Four By Johnny Burnette	7" EP	Capitol	EAP120645	1964	**£75**	**£37.50**	
Girls	7"	London	HLG9388	1961	**£4**	**£1.50**	
God, Country And My Baby	7"	London	HLG9453	1961	**£6**	**£2.50**	
Hit After Hit	7" EP	Liberty	LEP2091	1963	**£30**	**£15**	
Hits And Other Favourites	LP	Liberty	LBY1006	1961	**£30**	**£15**	
I Wanna Thank Your Folks	7"	Pye	7N25158	1962	**£5**	**£2**	
I'm The One Who Loves You	7"	Pye	7N25187	1963	**£5**	**£2**	
Johnny Burnette	7" EP	London	REG1327	1961	**£50**	**£25**	
Johnny Burnette Sings	LP	London	HAG2375	1961	**£60**	**£30**	
Johnny Burnette Sings	LP	London	SAHG6175	1961	**£75**	**£37.50**	*stereo*
Johnny Burnette Story	LP	Liberty	LBY1231	1964	**£40**	**£20**	
Johnny Burnette/You're 16	LP	London	HAG2349	1961	**£60**	**£30**	
Little Boy Sad	7"	London	HLG9315	1961	**£4**	**£1.50**	
Little Boy Sad	7" EP	London	REG1291	1961	**£50**	**£25**	
Lonesome Train	7"	Vogue Coral	Q72227	1957	**£400**	**£250**	*best auctioned*
Rock'n'Roll Trio	10" LP	Coral	LVC10041	1956	**£600**	**£400**	
Rock'n'Roll Trio	LP	Ace Of Hearts	AH120	1966	**£15**	**£6**	
Rock'n'Roll Trio	LP	Coral	CRL57080	1956	**£600**	**£400**	*US*

Title	Format	Label	Cat. No.	Year	Mint	VG	Notes
Roses Are Red	LP	Liberty	LRP3255/ LST7255	1962	£30	£15	US
Setting The Woods On Fire	7"	London	HLG9458	1961	£6	£2.50	
Tear It Up	7"	Vogue Coral	Q72177	1956	£400	£250	best auctioned
Tear It Up	LP	Coral	CP15	1969	£10	£4	
Walking Talking Doll	7"	Capitol	CL15347	1964	£12	£6	
You're Sixteen	7"	London	HLG9254	1960	£4	£1.50	
You're Undecided	7"	Von	1006	1954	£500	£330	US, best auctioned

BURNETTE, JOHNNY & DORSEY

Title	Format	Label	Cat. No.	Year	Mint	VG	Notes
Hey Sue	7"	Reprise	R20153	1963	£25	£12.50	

BURNETTE, SMILEY

Title	Format	Label	Cat. No.	Year	Mint	VG	Notes
Chugging On Down Sixty-Six	7"	London	HL8085	1954	£30	£15	
Lazy Locomotive	7"	London	HL8071	1954	£30	£15	
Rudolph The Red-Nosed Reindeer	78	Capitol	CL13388	1950	£5	£2	

BURNIN' RED IVANHOE

Title	Format	Label	Cat. No.	Year	Mint	VG	Notes
6 Elefantskovcikadeviser	LP	Sonet	SLSP1528	1971	£25	£10	Danish
Burnin' Red Ivanhoe	LP	Warner Bros	K44062	1970	£15	£6	
Dansk Beat	LP	Sonet	SLPS2140	1974	£20	£8	Danish
M144	LP	Sonet	SLPS1512/3	1969	£25	£10	Danish double
Miley Smile/Stage Recall	LP	Sonet	SLSP1540	1972	£20	£8	Danish
Right On	LP	Sonet	SLSP1549	1974	£25	£10	Danish
W.W.W.	LP	Dandelion	2310145	1971	£15	£6	

BURNING PLAGUE

Title	Format	Label	Cat. No.	Year	Mint	VG	Notes
Burning Plague	LP	CBS	65664	1973	£20	£8	Dutch

BURNING SPEAR

Title	Format	Label	Cat. No.	Year	Mint	VG	Notes
Dry And Heavy	LP	Island	ILPS9431	1977	£12	£5	
Foggy Road	7"	Fab	FAB240	1975	£5	£2	
Garvey's Ghost	LP	Island	ILPS9382	1976	£15	£6	
Hail HIM	LP	Radic	RDC2003	1980	£10	£4	
Harder Than The Rest	LP	Island	ILPS9567	1979	£10	£4	
Live	LP	Island	ILPS9513	1977	£12	£5	
Man In The Hills	LP	Island	ILPS9412	1976	£12	£5	
Marcus Garvey	LP	Island	ILPS9377	1975	£12	£5	
Social Living	LP	Island	ILPS9556	1980	£10	£4	

BURNS, EDDIE 'GUITAR'

Title	Format	Label	Cat. No.	Year	Mint	VG	Notes
Bottle Up And Go	LP	Action	ACMP100	1972	£12	£5	

BURNS, JACKIE & THE BELLS

Title	Format	Label	Cat. No.	Year	Mint	VG	Notes
He's My Guy	7"	MGM	MGM1226	1963	£40	£20	

BURNS, RALPH

Title	Format	Label	Cat. No.	Year	Mint	VG	Notes
Jazz Studio Five	LP	Brunswick	LAT8121	1956	£25	£10	
Ralph Burns Group	LP	Columbia	33CX10017	1955	£25	£10	
Very Warm For Jazz	LP	Brunswick	LAT8289	1959	£15	£6	

BURNS, RANDY

Title	Format	Label	Cat. No.	Year	Mint	VG	Notes
Evening Of The Magician	LP	Fontana	STL5520	1968	£10	£4	

BURNS, RAY

Title	Format	Label	Cat. No.	Year	Mint	VG	Notes
Condemned For Life	7"	Columbia	DB3811	1956	£5	£2	
Ray Burns	7" EP	Columbia	SEG7594	1955	£10	£5	

BURNT SUITE

Title	Format	Label	Cat. No.	Year	Mint	VG	Notes
Burnt Suite	LP	B.J.W.	CSS9	1968	£100	£50	US

BURRAGE, HAROLD

Title	Format	Label	Cat. No.	Year	Mint	VG	Notes
I'll Take One	7"	Sue	WI353	1965	£12	£6	
You Made Me So Happy	7"	President	PT130	1968	£5	£2	

BURRELL, KENNY

Title	Format	Label	Cat. No.	Year	Mint	VG	Notes
All Day Long	LP	Esquire	32107	1960	£25	£10	
All Night Long	LP	Esquire	32140	1961	£15	£6	
Asphalt Canyon Suite	LP	Verve	SVLP9250	1970	£10	£4	
Blue Bash	LP	Verve	VLP9058	1964	£12	£5	with Jimmy Smith
Blue Nights Vol. 1	LP	Blue Note	BLP/BST81596	196–	£25	£10	
Blue Nights Vol. 2	LP	Blue Note	BLP/BST81597	196–	£25	£10	
Blues, The Common Ground	LP	Verve	(S)VLP9217	1968	£15	£6	
Bluesy Burrell	LP	XTRA	XTRA5048	1968	£12	£5	
Crash	LP	Stateside	SL10163	1966	£15	£6	with Jack McDuff
Guitar Forms	LP	Verve	VLP9099	1965	£12	£5	
Introducing	LP	Blue Note	BLP/BST81523	196–	£25	£10	
Kenny Burrell Vol. 2	LP	Blue Note	BLP/BST81543	196–	£25	£10	
Midnight Blue	LP	Blue Note	BLP/BST84123	1964	£20	£8	
Night Song	LP	Verve	SVLP9246	1969	£15	£6	
On View At The Five Spot Café	LP	Blue Note	BLP/BST84021	1961	£25	£10	

BURROUGHS, WILLIAM

Title	Format	Label	Cat. No.	Year	Mint	VG	Notes
Call Me Burroughs	LP	ESP-Disk	1050	1968	£25	£10	US
Nothing Here Now But The Recordings	LP	Industrial	IR0016	1980	£20	£8	

BURTON, GARY

The track 'General Mojo Cuts Up' on the album *Lofty Fake Anagram* has the dubious distinction of featuring the first burst of guitar feedback on a jazz record. Courtesy of Larry Coryell, the sound is actually a fairly modest one, more reminiscent of what the Beatles had pioneered some years earlier on 'I Feel Fine' than the extravagances of the contemporary Jimi Hendrix. Burton himself is a vibraphone player of astonishing virtuosity – he is capable of playing with three mallets in each hand. His own skill, together with his knack for finding inspirational colleagues to work with – bass player Steve Swallow, composer/arranger Michael Gibbs, and guitarist Pat Metheny among them – has assured Burton's status as a premier-league jazz musician.

Title	Format	Label	Cat. No.	Year	Mint	VG	Notes
Alone At Last	LP	Atlantic	K40305	1972	**£10**	**£4**	
Country Roads And Other Places	LP	RCA	SF8042	1969	**£10**	**£4**	
Crystal Silence	LP	ECM	ECM1024ST	1972	**£12**	**£5**	*with Chick Corea*
Dreams So Real	LP	ECM	ECM1072ST	1975	**£15**	**£6**	
Duster	LP	RCA	LPM/LSP3835	1967	**£15**	**£6**	*US*
Gary Burton And Keith Jarrett	LP	Atlantic	K40208	1971	**£12**	**£5**	*US*
Genuine Tong Funeral	LP	RCA	SF8015	1969	**£15**	**£6**	*with Carla Bley*
Good Vibes	LP	Atlantic	2400107	1971	**£12**	**£5**	
Groovy Sound Of Music	LP	RCA	LPM/LSP3360	1965	**£15**	**£6**	*US*
Hotel Hello	LP	ECM	ECM1055ST	1975	**£15**	**£6**	*with Steve Swallow*
Hotel Hello/Matchbook	LP	ECM	ECM1055/6ST	1975	**£30**	**£15**	*special double sleeve*
In Concert	LP	RCA	LPM/LSP3985	1968	**£15**	**£6**	*US*
Lofty Fake Anagram	LP	RCA	RD/SF7923	1968	**£10**	**£4**	
Matchbook	LP	ECM	ECM1056ST	1975	**£12**	**£5**	*with Ralph Towner*
New Quartet	LP	ECM	ECM1030ST	1973	**£15**	**£6**	
New Vibe Man In Town	LP	RCA	LPM/LSP2420	1961	**£20**	**£8**	*US*
Paris Encounter	LP	Atlantic	K40378	1972	**£10**	**£4**	*with Stephane Grappelli*
Passengers	LP	ECM	ECM1092ST	1976	**£10**	**£4**	
Ring	LP	ECM	ECM1051ST	1974	**£15**	**£6**	
Seven Songs For Quartet And Chamber Orchestra	LP	ECM	ECM1040ST	1974	**£20**	**£8**	*with Michael Gibbs*
Something's Coming	LP	RCA	LPM/LSP2880	1964	**£15**	**£6**	*US*
Tennessee Firebird	LP	RCA	LPM/LSP3719	1966	**£15**	**£6**	*US*
Throb	LP	Atlantic	588203	1969	**£15**	**£6**	
Time Machine	LP	RCA	LPM/LSP3642	1966	**£15**	**£6**	*US*
Who Is Gary Burton?	LP	RCA	LPM/LSP2665	1963	**£20**	**£8**	*US*

BURTON, JAMES

James Burton's legendary reputation as an ace guitarist is entirely justified by his playing on record. Largely content to work for others – most notably Rick Nelson and Elvis Presley – his two solo LPs are quite scarce (and undervalued).

Title	Format	Label	Cat. No.	Year	Mint	VG	Notes
Corn Pickin' And Slick Slidin'	LP	Capitol	ST2822	1968	**£50**	**£25**	*US*
Guitar Sounds Of James Burton	LP	A&M	AMLS64293	1971	**£40**	**£20**	

BURTON, LORI

Title	Format	Label	Cat. No.	Year	Mint	VG	Notes
Breakout	LP	Mercury	SR61136	1967	**£25**	**£10**	*US*

BURTON, TOMMY

Title	Format	Label	Cat. No.	Year	Mint	VG	Notes
I'm Walking	7"	Blue Beat	BB237	1964	**£12**	**£6**	

BURTON, TREVOR

Title	Format	Label	Cat. No.	Year	Mint	VG	Notes
Fight For My Country	7"	Wizard	WIZ103	1971	**£6**	**£2.50**	

BUSCH, LOU

Title	Format	Label	Cat. No.	Year	Mint	VG	Notes
Zambesi	7"	Capitol	CL14504	1956	**£6**	**£2.50**	

BUSH

Title	Format	Label	Cat. No.	Year	Mint	VG	Notes
Bush	LP	Dunhill	DS50086	1970	**£20**	**£8**	*US*

BUSH, KATE

When Kate Bush first appeared on TV's *Top Of The Pops* wailing to Heathcliff in that extraordinary high voice, it seemed impossible that she could ever turn out to be more than a one-hit-wonder novelty act. Instead, of course, it turned out that she was possessed of a rare talent – as a singer, as a dancer, as a performance artist, and above all as a composer and musician. Each of her album releases has been more impressive than the one before it and she is without doubt one of the most important rock artists of the eighties and nineties. Many of her records have become collectable, with picture-sleeve copies of all her early singles rising steadily in value.

Title	Format	Label	Cat. No.	Year	Mint	VG	Notes
Amiga	LP	EMI	856072	1984	**£30**	**£15**	*German*
And So Is Love	7"	EMI	EMPD355	1994	**£20**	**£10**	*numbered picture disc*
And So Is Love	7"	EMI	EMPD355	1994	**£6**	**£2.50**	*picture disc*
Best Works 1978–1993	CD	EMI	SPCD1402/3	1994	**£500**	**£330**	*Japanese double promo compilation*
Big Sky	7"	EMI	KB4P	1986	**£10**	**£5**	*picture disc*
Breathing	7"	EMI	EMI5058	1980	**£40**	**£20**	*bat picture sleeve*
Dreaming	7"	EMI	EMI5296	1982	**£4**	**£1.50**	*picture sleeve*
Eat The Music	7"	EMI	EM280	1993	**£1000**	**£700**	*best auctioned*
Eat The Music	CD-s	EMI	MUSIC1	1993	**£100**	**£50**	*promo*
Hammer Horror	7"	EMI	EMI2887	1978	**£6**	**£2.50**	*picture sleeve*
Hounds Of Love	CD	EMI	CDP7461642	1986	**£12**	**£5**	*cover reference to 12" mix of 'Running Up That Hill'*
Hounds Of Love	CD	EMI	CDP7461642	1987	**£50**	**£25**	*US mispressing – plays the Beatles' A Hard Day's Night*
Hounds Of Love	LP	EMI	ST17171	1985	**£30**	**£15**	*US, coloured vinyl*
Interview With Kate Bush	LP	EMI	SPRO282	1985	**£200**	**£100**	*Canadian promo*

Kate Bush	LP	EMI	MLP19004	1984	**£60**	**£30**	*Canadian 6 track LP, brown or clear vinyl*
Kate Bush	LP	EMI	MLP19004	1984	**£30**	**£15**	*Canadian 6 track LP, green, yellow, blue, or white vinyl*
Kick Inside	LP	EMI	EMCP3223	1979	**£40**	**£20**	*picture disc*
Kick Inside	LP	EMI	EMCP3223	1978	**£100**	**£50**	*picture disc, same picture both sides*
Kick Inside	LP	EMI/ Harvest	EMC3223/ SW11761	1978	**£15**	**£6**	*different US sleeve on UK record*
Kick Inside	LP	EMI	5C06206603	1978	**£50**	**£25**	*coloured vinyl, Dutch*
Love And Anger	CD-s	EMI	CDEM134	1990	**£6**	**£2.50**	
Man With The Child In His Eyes	7"	EMI	EMI2806	1978	**£10**	**£5**	*picture sleeve*
Moments Of Pleasure	CD-s	EMI	CDEM297	1993	**£5**	**£2**	*boxed with 4 prints*
Ne T'En Fui Pas	7"	EMI	PM102	1983	**£10**	**£5**	*sung in French*
Never For Ever	7"	EMI	SFI562	1980	**£15**	**£7.50**	*promo, flexi*
Never For Ever	7"	EMI	SFI562	1980	**£75**	**£37.50**	*pink flexi*
Night Of The Swallow	7"	EMI	1EMI9001	1983	**£50**	**£25**	*Irish*
On Stage	7"	EMI	PSR442/443	1979	**£60**	**£30**	*promo, double*
Red Shoes	CD	EMI	CDEMD1047	1993	**£175**	**£87.50**	*promo shoe box with CD, video, slide, pen, biog*
Rocket Man	CD-s	Mercury	TRICD2	1991	**£6**	**£2.50**	
Rubberband Girl	CD-s	EMI	GIRL1	1993	**£10**	**£5**	*promo*
Self Portrait	LP	EMI	SSA3020	1979	**£200**	**£100**	*US promo*
Sensual World	CD	EMI	CDEMD1010	1989	**£125**	**£62.50**	*promo box set, with cassette, biog, lyric book*
Sensual World	CD-s	EMI	EMCD102	1989	**£6**	**£2.50**	
Single File	7"	EMI	KBS1	1984	**£100**	**£50**	*boxed with booklet*
There Goes A Tenner	7"	EMI	EMI5350	1982	**£6**	**£2.50**	*picture sleeve*
This Woman's Work	7"	EMI	EMPD119	1989	**£4**	**£1.50**	*picture disc*
This Woman's Work	CD	EMI	CDKBBX1	1990	**£100**	**£50**	*box set*
This Woman's Work	CD-s	EMI	CDEM119	1989	**£6**	**£2.50**	
This Woman's Work	LP	EMI	KBBX1	1990	**£75**	**£37.50**	*box set*
Wow	7"	EMI	EMI2911	1979	**£4**	**£1.50**	*picture sleeve*
Wuthering Heights	7"	EMI	EMI2719	1978	**£20**	**£10**	*picture sleeve*

BUSHKIN, JOE

Joe Bushkin Orchestra	LP	Capitol	LCT6126	1957	**£10**	**£4**	
Nightsounds	LP	Capitol	T983	1958	**£10**	**£4**	
Piano After Midnight	LP	Fontana	TFL5014	1958	**£10**	**£4**	

BUSINESS

1980–81 Official Bootlegs	LP	Syndicate	SYNLP2	1983	**£20**	**£8**	
Drinking 'n Driving	12"	Diamond	DIA001T	1985	**£15**	**£7.50**	
Drinking 'n Driving	7"	Diamond	DIA001	1985	**£10**	**£5**	
Get Out Of My House	12"	Wonderful World	121	1985	**£15**	**£7.50**	
Harry May	7"	Secret	SHH123	1981	**£8**	**£4**	
In And Out Of Business	LP	Link	LRMO1	1990	**£15**	**£6**	
Loud, Proud 'n Punk, Live	LP	Syndicate	SYNLP6	1984	**£15**	**£6**	
Out Of Business	12"	Secret	SHH150	1983	**£50**	**£25**	*promo*
Saturday Heroes	LP	Harry May	SE13	1985	**£15**	**£6**	
Singalongabusiness	LP	Dojo	DOJOLP35	1986	**£10**	**£4**	
Smash The Disco	7"	Secret	SHH132	1982	**£6**	**£2.50**	
Suburban Rebels	LP	Secret	SEC11	1983	**£15**	**£6**	

BUSKER

Mowrey Junior And Watson	LP	Riverdale		1976	**£75**	**£37.50**	

BUSKERS

Buskers	LP	Hawk	HALPX142	1975	**£12**	**£5**	
Life Of A Man	LP	Rubber	RUB007	1973	**£12**	**£5**	

BUSTERS

Bust Out	7"	Stateside	SS231	1963	**£5**	**£2**	

BUTALA, TONY

Long Black Stockings	7"	Salvo	SLO1801	1962	**£15**	**£7.50**	

BUTCHER, EDDIE

I Once Was A Daysman	LP	Free Reed	FRR003	1976	**£12**	**£5**	
Shamrock, Rose And Thistle	LP	Leader	LED2070	1976	**£10**	**£4**	

BUTERA, SAM & THE WITNESSES

Big Horn	LP	Capitol	T1098	1959	**£15**	**£6**	
Bim Bam	7"	Capitol	CL14913	1958	**£100**	**£50**	
Good Gracious Baby	7"	HMV	POP476	1958	**£25**	**£12.50**	
Handle With Care	7"	Capitol	CL14988	1959	**£10**	**£5**	
Rat Race	LP	London	HAD2288	1960	**£15**	**£6**	
Sax Serenade	7" EP	HMV	7EG8087	1955	**£25**	**£12.50**	

BUTLER, BILLY

Right Track	7"	Soul City	SC113	1969	**£8**	**£4**	
Right Track	LP	Soul City		196–	**£20**	**£8**	

BUTLER, JERRY

Are You Happy	7"	Mercury	MF1078	1969	**£4**	**£1.50**	
Aware Of Love	LP	Vee Jay	LP/SR1038	1961	**£20**	**£8**	*US*
Best Of Jerry Butler	LP	Vee Jay	LP/SR1048	1962	**£15**	**£6**	*US*
Brand New Me	7"	Mercury	MF1132	1969	**£4**	**£1.50**	
Folk Songs	LP	Stateside	SL10050	1963	**£25**	**£10**	
For Your Precious Love	7"	London	HL8697	1958	**£75**	**£37.50**	
For Your Precious Love	LP	Vee Jay	LP/VJS1075	1963	**£20**	**£8**	*US*
Give Me Your Love	7"	Stateside	SS252	1964	**£8**	**£4**	
Giving Up On Love	LP	Vee Jay	LP/VJS1076	1963	**£20**	**£8**	*US*
Good Times	7"	Fontana	TF553	1965	**£6**	**£2.50**	
He Will Break Your Heart	7"	Top Rank	JAR531	1961	**£30**	**£15**	
He Will Break Your Heart	LP	Stateside	SL10032	1963	**£30**	**£15**	
Hey Mr Western Union Man	7"	Mercury	MF1058	1968	**£5**	**£2**	
Hey Mr Western Union Man	7"	Mercury	MF1058	1968	**£4**	**£1.50**	
I Can't Stand To See You Cry	7"	Fontana	TF588	1965	**£6**	**£2.50**	
I Dig You Baby	7"	Mercury	MF964	1967	**£5**	**£2**	
I Found A Love	7"	Top Rank	JAR389	1960	**£15**	**£7.50**	
I Stand Accused	7"	Sue	WI4003	1966	**£15**	**£7.50**	
I've Been Trying	7"	Stateside	SS300	1964	**£8**	**£4**	
Ice Man Cometh	LP	Mercury	20154SML	1969	**£12**	**£5**	
Jerry Butler Esquire	LP	Vee Jay	LP1027	1961	**£25**	**£10**	*US*
Jerry Butler Esquire	LP	Abner	R2001	1959	**£75**	**£37.50**	*US*
Just For You	7"	Sue	WI4009	1966	**£10**	**£5**	
Love	7"	Mercury	MF932	1965	**£6**	**£2.50**	
Love Me	LP	Fontana	(S)TL5264	1968	**£15**	**£6**	
Make It Easy On Yourself	7"	Stateside	SS121	1962	**£10**	**£5**	
Make It Easy On Yourself	7"	President	PT299	1970	**£4**	**£1.50**	
Moody Woman	7"	Mercury	MF1122	1969	**£4**	**£1.50**	
Moon River	7"	Columbia	DB4743	1961	**£10**	**£5**	
Moon River	LP	Vee Jay	LP/SR1046	1962	**£20**	**£8**	*US*
More Of The Best Of Jerry Butler	LP	Vee Jay	(VJS)1119	1965	**£15**	**£6**	*US*
Mr Dream Merchant	7"	Mercury	MF1005	1967	**£4**	**£1.50**	
Mr Dream Merchant	LP	Mercury	20118(S)MCL	1968	**£15**	**£6**	
Never Give You up	7"	Mercury	MF1035	1968	**£4**	**£1.50**	
Only The Strong Survive	7"	Mercury	MF1094	1969	**£4**	**£1.50**	
Soul Goes On	LP	Mercury	20144(S)MCL	1969	**£15**	**£6**	
Spice Of Life	LP	Mercury	6338102	1972	**£12**	**£5**	
When Trouble Calls	7"	Top Rank	JAR562	1961	**£12**	**£6**	
You Can Run	7"	Stateside	SS158	1963	**£8**	**£4**	
You Go Right Through Me	7"	Stateside	SS170	1963	**£8**	**£4**	
You Won't Be Sorry	7"	Stateside	SS195	1963	**£8**	**£4**	

BUTLER, LESLIE

Ramona	7"	Doctor Bird	DB1083	1967	**£10**	**£5**	
Revival	7"	High Note	HS009	1969	**£6**	**£2.50**	
Soul Drums	7"	High Note	HS001	1969	**£6**	**£2.50**	*Gaylads B side*
Top Cat	7"	High Note	HS008	1969	**£6**	**£2.50**	
You Don't Have To Say You Love Me	7"	Island	WI3069	1967	**£10**	**£5**	

BUTTERCUPS

Come Put My Life In Order	7"	Pama	PM760	1969	**£5**	**£2**	
If I Love You	7"	Pama	PM742	1968	**£8**	**£4**	

BUTTERFIELD, BILLY

Ballads For Sweethearts	10" LP	Nixa	WLPY6729	1955	**£12**	**£5**	
Billy Butterfield Orchestra	10" LP	London	HBF1043	1956	**£12**	**£5**	
Classics In Jazz	10" LP	Capitol	LC6684	1955	**£15**	**£6**	
Magnificent Matador	7"	London	HLF8181	1955	**£10**	**£5**	
That Butterfield Bounce	10" LP	Nixa	WLPY6720	1955	**£12**	**£5**	

BUTTERFIELD, PAUL BLUES BAND

Paul Butterfield occupied a very similar position within American rock music to that of John Mayall in Britain. Both were virtuoso harmonica players; both chose to surround themselves with a continually evolving team of inspirational musicians; and both adopted an imaginative approach to the blues, in which improvised solos were a key element. Butterfield's masterpiece came early – *East West* is an essential sixties album, if only for the freshness of the guitar-playing by Michael Bloomfield and Elvin Bishop on the two long instrumental tracks.

All These Blues	7"	Elektra	EKSN45007	1967	**£4**	**£1.50**	
Come On In	7"	London	HLZ10100	1966	**£6**	**£2.50**	
East West	LP	Elektra	K42006	1971	**£10**	**£4**	
East West	LP	Elektra	EKL/EKS315	1966	**£25**	**£10**	
Get Yourself Together	7"	Elektra	EKSN45047	1968	**£4**	**£1.50**	
Golden Butter	LP	Elektra	K62011	1972	**£12**	**£5**	*double*
I Got My Mojo Working	7" EP	Vogue	INT18063	1965	**£25**	**£12.50**	*French*
In My Own Dream	LP	Elektra	EKL/EKS74025	1968	**£15**	**£6**	
In My Own Dream	LP	Elektra	K42042	1971	**£10**	**£4**	
Keep On Moving	LP	Elektra	K42033	1971	**£10**	**£4**	
Keep On Moving	LP	Elektra	EKS74053	1969	**£12**	**£5**	
Live	LP	Elektra	EKS2001	1970	**£12**	**£5**	*double*
Live	LP	Elektra	K62001	1971	**£12**	**£5**	*double*
Offer You Can't Refuse	LP	Red Lightnin'	R008	1972	**£10**	**£4**	
Paul Butterfield Blues Band	LP	Elektra	EKL/EKS7294	1965	**£20**	**£8**	
Paul Butterfield Blues Band	LP	Elektra	K42004	1971	**£10**	**£4**	
Resurrection Of Pigboy Crabshaw	LP	Elektra	K42017	1971	**£10**	**£4**	
Resurrection Of Pigboy Crabshaw	LP	Elektra	EKL/EKS74015	1967	**£15**	**£6**	

Run Out Of Time	7"	Elektra	EKSN45020	1967	£4	£1.50	
Where Did My Baby Go	7"	Elektra	EKSN45069	1968	£4	£1.50	

BUTTERFLYS

Goodnight Baby	7"	Red Bird	RB10009	1964	£10	£5	

BUTTHOLE SURFERS

Double Live	LP	LBV		198–	£15	£6	double
Hurdy Gurdy Man	CD-s	Rough Trade	RTT240CD	1990	£5	£2	
Widowermaker	CD-s	Blast First	BFFP41CD	1989	£5	£2	

BUTTONDOWN BRASS

Funk In Hell	LP	DJM	DJS22046	1976	£15	£6	

BUXTON, SHEILA

Charm	7"	Columbia	DB4051	1957	£4	£1.50	
Perfect Love	7"	Columbia	DB3887	1957	£4	£1.50	
Sixteen Reasons	7"	Top Rank	JAR356	1960	£4	£1.50	
Thank You For The Waltz	7"	Columbia	SCM5193	1955	£4	£1.50	

BUZZ

You're Holding Me Down	7"	Columbia	DB7887	1966	£200	£100	

BUZZ (2)

Insanity	7"	Redball	RR06	1979	£5	£2	

BUZZ & BUCKY

Tiger A-Go-Go	7"	Stateside	SS428	1965	£10	£5	

BUZZCOCKS

The Buzzcocks' *Spiral Scratch* EP was the first self-produced record to emerge out of punk and was an early collectors' item. A reissue brought the record's value down to its current level, although the two issues are easily distinguished by the original making no specific reference to Howard Devoto on the front cover.

Another Music In A Different Kitchen	LP	United Artists	UAG30159	1978	£20	£8	with printed carrier bag
Fab Four	CD-s	EMI	CDEM104	1989	£5	£2	
Moving Away From The Pulsebeat	12"	United Artists	UALP15	1978	£15	£7.50	1 sided promo
Spiral Scratch	7" EP	New Hormones	ORG1	1977	£12	£6	no Devoto reference on sleeve
Spiral Scratch	7" EP	Document	DPRO1	1991	£5	£2	promo

BYARD, JAKI

Freedom Together	LP	Transatlantic	PR7463	1968	£10	£4	

BYAS, DON

Don Byas	10" LP	Esquire	20005	1953	£40	£20	
Don Byas	10" LP	Felsted	EDL87004	1954	£40	£20	
On 52nd Street	LP	Realm	RM230	1965	£10	£4	

BYLES, JUNIOR

Beat Down Babylon	7"	Bullet	BU499	1971	£4	£1.50	Upsetters B side
Beat Down Babylon	LP	Trojan	TRL52	1972	£30	£15	
Curly Locks	7"	Dip	DL5035	1974	£5	£2	
Curly Locks	7"	Magnet	MAG27	1974	£4	£1.50	
Festival Da Da	7"	Upsetter	US387	1971	£4	£1.50	Upsetters B side
Fever	7"	Pama	PM857	1972	£4	£1.50	Groovers B side
King Of Babylon	7"	Randys	RAN523	1972	£5	£2	
Long Way	7"	Dip	DL5074	1975	£5	£2	
Mumbling And Grumbling	7"	Ethnic	ETH26	1975	£4	£1.50	

BYRD, BOBBY

Back From The Dead	7"	Seville	SEV1003	1975	£4	£1.50	
I Know You Got Soul	12"	Urban	URBX8	1987	£6	£2.50	
I Know You Got Soul	7"	Mojo	2027003	1971	£5	£2	
I Need Help	7"	Polydor	2001118	1971	£4	£1.50	
I Need Help – Live	LP	Mojo	2918002	1972	£50	£25	

BYRD, CHARLIE

Blues Sonata	LP	Riverside	OLP(9)3009	1963	£10	£4	
Bossa Nova Pelos Passaros	LP	Riverside	RLP436	1962	£12	£5	
Guitar Artistry	LP	Riverside	OLP(9)3007	1963	£10	£4	

BYRD, DONALD

And Then Some	LP	Eros	ERL50067	1962	£10	£4	
At The Half Note Café	LP	Blue Note	BLP/BST84060	1961	£25	£10	
At The Half Note Café Vol. 2	LP	Blue Note	BLP/BST84061	1961	£30	£15	
Black Byrd	LP	Blue Note	BNLA047F	1973	£15	£6	US
Black Jack	LP	Blue Note	BLP/BST84259	1967	£15	£6	
Boom Boom	7"	Verve	VS532	1966	£4	£1.50	
Byrd In Flight	LP	Blue Note	BLP/BST84048	196–	£25	£10	
Caricatures	LP	Blue Note	UAG20008	1978	£10	£4	
Cat Walk	LP	Blue Note	BLP/BST84075	1961	£20	£8	
Child's Play	LP	Polydor	423/623224	1967	£12	£5	
Donald Byrd And Gigi Gryce	7" EP	Philips	BBE12274	1959	£5	£2	
Donald Byrd Group	LP	Esquire	32013	1956	£30	£15	
Donald Byrd Group	LP	London	LTZC15039	1957	£30	£15	

Donald Byrd Sextet	LP	Esquire	32019	1956	£30	£15	
Donald Byrd's Jazz Group	7" EP	Esquire	EP149	1957	£5	£2	
Donald Byrd's Jazz Group	7" EP	Esquire	EP139	1957	£5	£2	
Electric Byrd	LP	Blue Note	BST84349	1970	£15	£6	
Ethiopian Nights	LP	Blue Note	BST84380	1970	£15	£6	
Fancy Free	LP	Blue Note	BST84319	1969	£15	£6	
Free Form	LP	Blue Note	BLP/BST84118	1962	£20	£8	
Fuego	7"	Blue Note	451764	1962	£4	£1.50	
Fuego	LP	Blue Note	BLP/BST84026	1961	£25	£10	
I'm Trying To Get Home	LP	Blue Note	BLP/BST84188	1965	£20	£8	
Jazz Lab	LP	Philips	BBL7210	1958	£25	£10	*with Gigi Gryce*
Modern Jazz Perspective	LP	Philips	BBL7244	1958	£20	£8	*with Gigi Gryce*
Mustang	LP	Blue Note	BLP/BST84238	1966	£20	£8	
New Perspective	LP	Blue Note	BLP/BST84124	1963	£25	£10	
Places And Spaces	LP	United Artists	UAG20001	197–	£20	£8	
Royal Flush	LP	Blue Note	BLP/BST84101	1962	£20	£8	
Slow Drag	LP	Blue Note	BST84292	1968	£15	£6	
Street Lady	LP	Blue Note	BNLA140F	1974	£15	£6	*US*
Three Trumpets	LP	Esquire	32093	1960	£15	£6	*with Art Farmer & Idrees Sulieman*
Up With Byrd	LP	Vintage Jazz	VLP9104	1965	£12	£5	
Up With Donald Byrd	LP	Verve	VLP9104	1965	£15	£6	

BYRD, JOE & THE FIELD HIPPIES

American Metaphysical Circus is, in effect, the follow-up to the innovative LP made by the United States Of America. With only Joe Byrd remaining from the original line-up, however, a change of name was clearly appropriate.

American Metaphysical Circus	LP	CBS	7317	1969	£30	£15	*US*

BYRD, RUSSELL

Hitch Hike	7"	Sue	WI305	1964	£20	£10	

BYRDS

Back Pages	CD	Columbia	CSK2239	1990	£20	£8	*US promo sampler*
Ballad Of Easy Rider	LP	CBS	63795	1970	£10	£4	
Byrdmaniax	LP	CBS	64389	1971	£10	£4	
Byrds	LP	Asylum	SYLA8754	1973	£10	£4	
Dr Byrds And Mr Hyde	LP	CBS	63545	1969	£10	£4	
Dr Byrds And Mr Hyde	LP	CBS	63545	1969	£15	£6	*mono*
Early Flight	LP	Together	ST1014	1969	£20	£8	*US*
Eight Miles High	7"	CBS	202067	1966	£4	£1.50	
Eight Miles High	7" EP	CBS	EP6077	1966	£15	£7.50	
Farther Along	LP	CBS	64676	1972	£10	£4	
Fifth Dimension	LP	CBS	BPG62783	1966	£25	£10	*mono*
Fifth Dimension	LP	CBS	SBPG62783	1966	£20	£8	
Four Dimensions	CD-s	CBS	6565445	1990	£5	£2	*picture disc*
It Won't Be Wrong	7" EP	CBS	5668	1966	£20	£10	*French*
Lady Friend	7"	CBS	2924	1967	£8	£4	
Mr Spaceman	7"	CBS	202295	1966	£4	£1.50	
Mr Tambourine Man	7" EP	CBS	6100	1965	£20	£10	*French, 2 different track listings*
Mr Tambourine Man	LP	CBS	BPG62571	1965	£20	£8	*mono*
Mr Tambourine Man	LP	CBS	SBPG62571	1965	£15	£6	
Notorious Byrd Brothers	LP	CBS	BPG63169	1968	£20	£8	*mono*
Notorious Byrd Brothers	LP	CBS	SBPG63169	1968	£15	£6	
Preflyte	LP	Together	ST1001	1969	£25	£10	*US*
Preflyte	LP	CBS	KC32183	1972	£20	£8	*US*
Preflyte	LP	Bumble	GEXP8001	196–	£25	£10	*US*
Set You Free This Time	7"	CBS	202037	1966	£5	£2	
So You Want To Be A Rock'n'Roll Star	7"	CBS	202559	1967	£4	£1.50	
Sweetheart Of The Rodeo	LP	CBS	63353	1968	£25	£10	*mono*
Sweetheart Of The Rodeo	LP	CBS	63353	1968	£10	£4	
Things Will Be Better	7"	Asylum	AYM516	1973	£10	£5	*demo, picture sleeve*
Times They Are A Changing	7" EP	CBS	EP6069	1966	£12	£6	
Turn! Turn! Turn!	7" EP	CBS	6521	1965	£20	£10	*French*
Turn! Turn! Turn!	LP	CBS	SBPG62652	1966	£20	£8	
Turn! Turn! Turn!	LP	CBS	BPG62652	1966	£25	£10	*mono*
Untitled	LP	CBS	66253	1970	£12	£5	*double*
Younger Than Yesterday	LP	CBS	BPG62988	1967	£25	£10	*mono*
Younger Than Yesterday	LP	CBS	SBPG62988	1967	£20	£8	

BYRNE, BRIAN

Brian Byrne	LP	Hawk	HALP105	1976	£12	£5	*Irish*

BYRNE, DAVID

Rei Momo	CD	Sire		1989	£20	£8	*US promo with artwork on case*
Words And Music	CD	Sire	PROCD3820	1989	£20	£8	*US interview promo*

BYRNE, JERRY

Lights Out	7"	Speciality	SON5011	1976	£4	£1.50	

BYRNE, PACKIE

Packie Byrne	LP	EFDSS	LP1009	1969	£12	£5	
Songs Of A Donegal Man	LP	Topic	12TS257	1975	£12	£5	

BYRNE, PACKIE & BONNIE SHALJEAN

Title	Format	Label	Cat. No.	Year	Mint	VG	Notes
Half Door	LP	Dingles	DIN302	1977	£10	£4	
Roundtower	LP	Dingles	DIN311	1981	£10	£4	

BYRNES, EDDIE

Title	Format	Label	Cat. No.	Year	Mint	VG	Notes
Kookie	7" EP	Warner Bros	WSEP2010	1960	£10	£5	stereo
Kookie	7" EP	Warner Bros	WEP6010	1960	£8	£4	
Kookie	LP	Warner Bros	W(S)1309	1959	£15	£6	US
Kookie Vol. 2	7" EP	Warner Bros	WEP6108	1963	£8	£4	
Kookie, Kookie, Lend Me Your Comb	7"	Warner Bros	WB5	1960	£4	£1.50	

BYRNES, MARTIN

Title	Format	Label	Cat. No.	Year	Mint	VG	Notes
Martin Byrnes	LP	Leader	LEA2004	1969	£15	£6	

BYRON, PAUL

Title	Format	Label	Cat. No.	Year	Mint	VG	Notes
Pale Moon	7"	Decca	F11210	1960	£5	£2	

BYRON, SOL & THE IMPACTS

Title	Format	Label	Cat. No.	Year	Mint	VG	Notes
Pride And Joy	7"	Flamingo	PR5027	196–	£10	£5	

BYSTANDERS

There were a number of sixties groups who eventually achieved some measure of success in the seventies by effecting a dramatic change of style. Status Quo are the obvious example, yet the Bystanders are another good one. In their case, the change from their original harmony vocal approach was so great that they found it necessary to change their name too – to Man.

Title	Format	Label	Cat. No.	Year	Mint	VG	Notes
98.6	7"	Piccadilly	7N35363	1967	£6	£2.50	
My Love Come Home	7"	Piccadilly	7N35351	1966	£12	£6	
Pattern People	7"	Piccadilly	7N35399	1967	£8	£4	
Royal Blue Summer Sunshine Day	7"	Piccadilly	7N35382	1967	£12	£6	
That's The End	7"	Pylot	501	1965	£100	£50	
This World Is My World	7"	Pye	7N17540	1968	£10	£5	
When Jezamine Goes	7"	Pye	7N17476	1968	£20	£10	
You're Gonna Hurt Yourself	7"	Piccadilly	7N35330	1966	£10	£5	

BYZANTIUM

The group's first album, *Live And Studio* was a private pressing of 99 copies, and is considerably more interesting than the material they subsequently recorded for A&M. Guitarist Chas Jankel was later the main man in Ian Dury's Blockheads.

Title	Format	Label	Cat. No.	Year	Mint	VG	Notes
Byzantium	LP	A&M	AMLH68104	1972	£40	£20	with poster
Byzantium	LP	A&M	AMLH68104	1972	£20	£8	
Live and Studio	LP	private		1972	£100	£50	
Seasons Changing	LP	A&M	AMLH68163	1972	£40	£20	
What A Coincidence	7"	A&M	AMS7064	1973	£4	£1.50	

C

C, FANTASTIC JOHNNY

Title	Format	Label	Number	Year	Mint	VG	Notes
Boogaloo Down Broadway	7"	London	HL10169	1967	**£4**	**£1.50**	
Boogaloo Down Broadway	LP	Action	ACLP6001	1969	**£15**	**£6**	
Hitch It To The Horse	7"	London	HL10212	1968	**£4**	**£1.50**	
New Love	7"	Action	ACT4543	1969	**£4**	**£1.50**	

C, ROY

Title	Format	Label	Number	Year	Mint	VG	Notes
Shotgun Wedding	7"	Island	WI273	1966	**£6**	**£2.50**	*2 different B sides*
That Shotgun Wedding Man	LP	Ember	NR5055	1966	**£15**	**£6**	
Twistin' Pneumonia	7"	Ember	EMBS230	1967	**£4**	**£1.50**	

C. A. QUINTET

Title	Format	Label	Number	Year	Mint	VG	Notes
Live	LP	private		1985	**£25**	**£10**	*US*
Trip Thru' Hell	LP	Candy Floss	7764	1968	**£1250**	**£875**	*US*
Trip Thru' Hell	LP	Psycho	PSYCHO12	1983	**£15**	**£6**	

C JAM BLUES

Title	Format	Label	Number	Year	Mint	VG	Notes
Candy	7"	Columbia	DB8064	1966	**£10**	**£5**	

CABARET VOLTAIRE

Title	Format	Label	Number	Year	Mint	VG	Notes
Easy Life	CD-s	Parlophone	CDR6261	1990	**£5**	**£2**	
Here To Go	CD-s	Parlophone	CDR6166	1987	**£15**	**£7.50**	
Hypnotised	CD-s	Parlophone	CDR6227	1989	**£5**	**£2**	
Keep On	CD-s	Parlophone	CDR6250	1990	**£5**	**£2**	
Limited Edition	cass	private		1976	**£30**	**£15**	
What Is Real	CD-s	Crepuscule	TWI9482	1991	**£5**	**£2**	

CABLES

Title	Format	Label	Number	Year	Mint	VG	Notes
Be A Man	7"	Studio One	SO2060	1968	**£12**	**£6**	
Got To Find Someone	7"	Studio One	SO2085	1969	**£12**	**£6**	
How Can I Trust You?	7"	Bamboo	BAM19	1970	**£4**	**£1.50**	
Love Is A Pleasure	7"	Studio One	SO2071	1968	**£12**	**£6**	
So Long	7"	Bamboo	BAM12	1969	**£4**	**£1.50**	
What Kind Of World	7"	Coxsone	CS7072	1968	**£12**	**£6**	

CACCIAPAGEIA, ROBERTO

Title	Format	Label	Number	Year	Mint	VG	Notes
Sonanze	LP	Cosmic Music	PDU6025	1975	**£30**	**£15**	*Italian*

CACTUS

Title	Format	Label	Number	Year	Mint	VG	Notes
Cactus	LP	Atlantic	2400020	1970	**£10**	**£4**	

CADDICK, BILL

Title	Format	Label	Number	Year	Mint	VG	Notes
Duck On His Head	LP	Highway	SHY7012	1980	**£10**	**£4**	
Rough Music	LP	Park	SHP102	1976	**£10**	**£4**	
Sunny Memories	LP	Trailer	LER2097	1977	**£10**	**£4**	

CADDY, ALAN

Title	Format	Label	Number	Year	Mint	VG	Notes
Workout	7"	HMV	POP1286	1964	**£20**	**£10**	

CADETS

Title	Format	Label	Number	Year	Mint	VG	Notes
Cadets	LP	Crown	CLP5370/CST370	1963	**£30**	**£15**	*US*
Rockin' 'n' Reelin'	LP	Crown	CLP5015	1957	**£100**	**£50**	*US*
Stranded In The Jungle	7"	London	HLU8313	1956	**£400**	**£250**	*gold label, best auctioned*

CADILLAC, EARL

Title	Format	Label	Number	Year	Mint	VG	Notes
Fish Seller	7"	Vogue	V9138	1959	**£8**	**£4**	
Zon, Zon, Zon	7"	Vogue	V9133	1959	**£8**	**£4**	

CADILLACS

Title	Format	Label	Number	Year	Mint	VG	Notes
Cadillacs Meet The Orioles	LP	Jubilee	JGM1117	1961	**£75**	**£37.50**	*US*
Crazy Cadillacs	LP	Jubilee	JGM1089	1959	**£125**	**£62.50**	*US*
Fabulous Cadillacs	LP	Jubilee	JGM1045	1957	**£150**	**£75**	*US*
Peek A Boo	7"	London	HLJ8786	1959	**£30**	**£15**	
Twisting With The Cadillacs	LP	Jubilee	JGM5009	1962	**£60**	**£30**	*US*

CAEDMON

Title	Format	Label	Number	Year	Mint	VG	Notes
Caedmon	LP	private		1978	**£300**	**£180**	*with 7"*

CAERN FOLK TRIO

Title	Format	Label	Number	Year	Mint	VG	Notes
Irish Folk Favourites	LP	Emerald	GES1058	1971	**£10**	**£4**	

CAESAR & CLEO

Love Is Strange	7"	Reprise	R20419	1965	£4	£1.50	
Love Is Strange	7"	Reprise	R20419	1965	£8	£4	*picture sleeve*

CAESARS

Five In The Morning	7"	Decca	F12462	1966	£5	£2	
On The Outside Looking In	7"	Decca	F12251	1965	£6	£2.50	

CAFE SOCIETY

Café Society included Tom Robinson in its line-up, but the collectability of the group's records has more to do with the fact that they were among the few releases on the label founded by the Kinks' Ray Davies.

Café Society	LP	Konk	KONK102	1975	£10	£4	

CAGE, BUTCH

Raise A Ruckus Tonight	LP	Flyright	LP545	1978	£10	£4	

CAGE, BUTCH & MABEL LEE WILLIAMS

Country Blues	LP	Storyville	SLP129	1964	£10	£4	

CAGE, JOHN

Cartridge Music	LP	Deutsche Grammophon	137009	1969	£15	£6	
Concerto For Piano & Orchestra	LP	EMI	C165289547		£15	£6	
Concerto For Prepared Piano & Orchestra	LP	Nonesuch	H71202	1968	£15	£6	*other side by Lukas Foss*
Fontana Mix	LP	Turnabout	TV34046	196–	£15	£6	
HPSCHD	LP	Nonesuch	H71224	1970	£15	£6	*other side by Ben Johnston*
Sonatas & Interludes For Prepared Piano	LP	Decca	HEAD9	1976	£15	£6	
Variations	LP	Everest	3132		£15	£6	
Variations II	LP	Columbia	MS7051		£15	£6	*US*

CAGLE, AUBREY

Come Along Little Girl	7"	Starlite	ST45082	1962	£200	£100	*best auctioned*

CAHILL, JEREMY

September Blues	7"	Solent		197–	£10	£5	

CAHILL, PATRICIA

Summer's Daughter	LP	Nova	SDN22	1970	£15	£6	

CAIN

Her Emotion	7"	Page One	POF054	1968	£6	£2.50	

CAIN, JACKIE & ROY KRAL

Bits And Pieces	LP	HMV	CLP1187	1958	£15	£6	
Free And Easy	LP	HMV	CLP1232	1959	£15	£6	
Glory Of Love	LP	HMV	CLP1219	1958	£15	£6	

CAIN, JEFFREY

For You	LP	Warner Bros	WS1880	1970	£20	£8	*US*
Whispering Thunder	LP	Raccoon	12	1972	£15	£6	*US*

CAIOLA, AL

Bonanza	7"	London	HLT9325	1961	£8	£4	
Deep In A Dream	LP	London	HAC2017	1956	£10	£4	
Flamenco Love	7"	London	HLC8285	1956	£12	£6	
Hit TV Themes	7" EP	United Artists	UEP1018	1966	£6	£2.50	
Serenade In Blue	LP	London	HAC2022	1957	£10	£4	
Sounds For Spies And Private Eyes	LP	United Artists	(S)ULP1115	1966	£15	£6	
Tuff Guitar	LP	United Artists	ULP1090	1964	£10	£4	

CAJUN MOON

Cajun Moon	LP	Chrysalis	CHR1116	1976	£10	£4	

CAKE

Cake	LP	MCA	MUPS303	1968	£10	£4	
Slice Of Cake	LP	MCA	MUPS390	1969	£10	£4	

CALDWELL, LOUISE HARRISON

All About The Beatles	LP	Recar	2012	1964	£100	£50	*US*

CALE, J. J.

J. J. Cale	LP	Shelter	ISADJ1	1976	£10	£4	*promo*
Outside Looking In	7"	Liberty	LBY55881	1966	£6	£2.50	

CALE, JOHN

Hear Fear	LP	Island	IXP2	1976	£15	£6	*US promo*
Jack The Ripper	7"	Illegal	IL006	1977	£15	£7.50	*demo*
Vintage Violence	LP	CBS	64256	1970	£10	£4	

CALEB

Caleb is top session guitarist Caleb Quaye, the uncle of nineties hit singer Finley Quaye. The single's freakbeat credentials give it the high value that it has, although it is quite likely that Elton John is the keyboard player.

Title	Format	Label	Cat. No.	Year	Mint	VG	Notes
Woman Of Distinction	7"	Philips	BF1588	1967	**£150**	**£75**	

CALEDONIANS

Title	Format	Label	Cat. No.	Year	Mint	VG	Notes
Funny Way Of Laughing	7"	Fab	FAB103	1969	**£5**	**£2**	

CALIFORNIA IN CROWD

Title	Format	Label	Cat. No.	Year	Mint	VG	Notes
Questions And Answers	7"	Fontana	TF779	1966	**£20**	**£10**	

CALIFORNIANS

Title	Format	Label	Cat. No.	Year	Mint	VG	Notes
Cooks Of Cake And Kindness	7"	Fontana	TF991	1969	**£30**	**£15**	
Follow Me	7"	Decca	F12678	1967	**£5**	**£2**	
Golden Apples	7"	CBS	202263	1967	**£15**	**£7.50**	

CALL GIRLS

Title	Format	Label	Cat. No.	Year	Mint	VG	Notes
Primal World	7"	Bold and 3rd	AGAR001	1988	**£6**	**£2.50**	

CALLAN & JOHN

Title	Format	Label	Cat. No.	Year	Mint	VG	Notes
House Of Delight	7"	CBS	4447	1969	**£10**	**£5**	

CALLENDER, BOBBY

Title	Format	Label	Cat. No.	Year	Mint	VG	Notes
Rainbow	LP	MGM	SE4557	1968	**£60**	**£30**	*US*
Way	LP	MGM		1971	**£30**	**£15**	*US double*

CALLICOTT, MISSISSIPPI JOE

Title	Format	Label	Cat. No.	Year	Mint	VG	Notes
Deal Gone Down	LP	Revival	RVS1002	1972	**£12**	**£5**	
Presenting The Country Blues	LP	Blue Horizon	763227	1968	**£30**	**£15**	

CALLIER, TERRY

The records made by Terry Callier in the seventies have recently become very fashionable, and the man himself has emerged from retirement to sing on disc with Beth Orton. His ethereal approach to soul, however (like a lightweight Bill Withers), is definitely not for all tastes and it is not that hard to understand why his records sold so poorly the first time around.

Title	Format	Label	Cat. No.	Year	Mint	VG	Notes
Fire On Ice	LP	Elektra	K52096	1978	**£20**	**£8**	
I Don't Want To See Myself	12"	Acid Jazz	JAZID27T	1990	**£6**	**£2.50**	
I Just Can't Help Myself	LP	Cadet	CA50041	1975	**£30**	**£15**	*US*
Occasional Rain	LP	Cadet	CA50007	1972	**£30**	**£15**	*US*
Turn You To Love	LP	Elektra	K52140	1979	**£20**	**£8**	
Very Best Of Terry Callier On Cadet	LP	Charly	ARC514	1994	**£15**	**£6**	*double*
What Color Is Love?	LP	Cadet	CA50019	1973	**£30**	**£15**	*US*

CALLIES

Title	Format	Label	Cat. No.	Year	Mint	VG	Notes
On Your Side	LP	Rubber	RUB001	1971	**£20**	**£8**	

CALLINAN FLYNN

Title	Format	Label	Cat. No.	Year	Mint	VG	Notes
Freedom's Lament	LP	Mushroom	150MR18	1972	**£200**	**£100**	
We Are The People	7"	Mushroom	50MR17	1972	**£50**	**£25**	

CALLIOPE

Title	Format	Label	Cat. No.	Year	Mint	VG	Notes
Steamed	LP	Buddah	203016	1968	**£10**	**£4**	

CALLOWAY, CAB

Title	Format	Label	Cat. No.	Year	Mint	VG	Notes
Cab Calloway	7" EP	Fontana	TFE17216	1960	**£15**	**£7.50**	
Cab Calloway	7" EP	Gala	45XP1016	1958	**£5**	**£2**	
Cabulous Calloway	7" EP	Vintage Jazz	VEP22	196–	**£5**	**£2**	
Cabulous Calloway Vol. 2	7" EP	Vintage Jazz	VEP35	196–	**£5**	**£2**	
Minnie The Moocher	78	Brunswick	05022	1952	**£8**	**£4**	

CALVERT, EDDIE

Title	Format	Label	Cat. No.	Year	Mint	VG	Notes
Cherry Pink And Apple Blossom White	7"	Columbia	SCM5168	1955	**£6**	**£2.50**	

CALVERT, ROBERT

Title	Format	Label	Cat. No.	Year	Mint	VG	Notes
At The Queen Elizabeth Hall	LP	Clear	BLACK1	1989	**£20**	**£8**	*with badge & T-shirt*
Captain Lockheed & The Starfighters	LP	United Artists	UAG29507	1974	**£20**	**£8**	*inner sleeve, booklet*
Cricket Star	7"	Wake Up	WUR5	1979	**£6**	**£2.50**	*flexi*
Ejection	7"	United Artists	UP35543	1973	**£6**	**£2.50**	*different mix*
Ejection	7"	United Artists	UP35543	1973	**£15**	**£7.50**	*picture sleeve, credited to Captain Lockheed*
Hype	LP	A Side	IFO311	1980	**£10**	**£4**	
Lord Of The Hornets	7"	Flicknife	FLS204	1980	**£6**	**£2.50**	*purple print sleeve*
Lucky Leif & The Longships	LP	United Artists	UAG29852	1975	**£12**	**£5**	

CALVIN, TABBY & THE ROUNDERS

Title	Format	Label	Cat. No.	Year	Mint	VG	Notes
False Alarm	7"	Capitol	CL14640	1956	**£4**	**£1.50**	

CALYX

Title	Format	Label	Cat. No.	Year	Mint	VG	Notes
Just A Dream	LP	ALG		1976	**£75**	**£37.50**	*Dutch*

CAMARATA

Title	Format	Label	Cat. No.	Year	Mint	VG	Notes
Sleeping Beauty Love Theme	7"	Top Rank	JAR160	1959	**£6**	**£2.50**	
Think Young	LP	London	SHU8257	1965	**£10**	**£4**	
Velvet Gentleman	LP	Deram	SML1101	1973	**£50**	**£25**	

CAMBODIANS

Title	Format	Label	Cat. No.	Year	Mint	VG	Notes
Coolie Man	7"	Duke	DU101	1970	**£5**	**£2**	

CAMEL

Title	Format	Label	Cat. No.	Year	Mint	VG	Notes
Camel	LP	MCA	MUPS473	1973	**£10**	**£4**	

Title	Format	Label	Cat. No.	Year	Mint	VG+	Notes
Mirage	LP	Deram	SML1107	1974	£10	£4	
Never Let Go	7"	MCA	MU1177	1973	£4	£1.50	

CAMEO

Title	Format	Label	Cat. No.	Year	Mint	VG+	Notes
Cardiac Arrest	LP	Casablanca	CAL2015	1977	£10	£4	

CAMEOS

Title	Format	Label	Cat. No.	Year	Mint	VG+	Notes
My Baby's Coming Home	7"	Columbia	DB7201	1964	£25	£12.50	
Powercut	7"	Columbia	DB7092	1963	£25	£12.50	

CAMERON, DION

Title	Format	Label	Cat. No.	Year	Mint	VG+	Notes
Get Ready	7"	Rio	R111	1966	£8	£4	
Miserable Friday	7"	Doctor Bird	DB1101	1967	£10	£5	

CAMERON, ISLA

Title	Format	Label	Cat. No.	Year	Mint	VG+	Notes
Lost Love	7" EP	Transatlantic	TRAEP109	1964	£12	£6	

CAMERON, ISLA, GUY CARAWAN, PEGGY SEEGER

Title	Format	Label	Cat. No.	Year	Mint	VG+	Notes
Origins Of Skiffle	7" EP	Pye	NJE1043	1957	£8	£4	

CAMERON, JOHN

Title	Format	Label	Cat. No.	Year	Mint	VG+	Notes
Cover Lover	LP	Columbia	SCX6116	1967	£40	£20	
Off Centre	LP	Deram	DML/SML1044	1969	£40	£20	

CAMERON, JOHNNY

Title	Format	Label	Cat. No.	Year	Mint	VG+	Notes
I Double Dare You	7"	Top Rank	JAR396	1960	£4	£1.50	

CAMERON, RAY

Title	Format	Label	Cat. No.	Year	Mint	VG+	Notes
Doin' My Time	7"	Island	WIP6003	1967	£4	£1.50	

CAMERON, TED & THE DEEJAYS

Title	Format	Label	Cat. No.	Year	Mint	VG+	Notes
Early In The Morning	7"	Pye	7N15292	1960	£20	£10	

CAMPBELL, AL & THE THRILLERS

Title	Format	Label	Cat. No.	Year	Mint	VG+	Notes
Heart For Sale	7"	Blue Cat	BS118	1968	£8	£4	*Zoot Sims B side*

CAMPBELL, ALEX

Title	Format	Label	Cat. No.	Year	Mint	VG+	Notes
Alex Campbell	LP	XTRA	XTRA1014	1965	£12	£5	
Alex Campbell And Friends	LP	Saga	EROS8021	1967	£20	£8	*with Sandy Denny*
At His Best	LP	Boulevard	4073	1972	£10	£4	
Been On The Road So Long	7"	Transatlantic	TRASP4	1965	£4	£1.50	*picture sleeve*
Best Loved Songs Of Bonnie Scotland	LP	Society	SOC936	1963	£10	£4	
Big Daddy Of Folk Music	LP	Antagon	LP3206	1976	£12	£5	*German*
Folk Session	LP	Fidelity	FID2171	1964	£10	£4	
Folk Session	LP	Society	SOC960	1963	£10	£4	
In Copenhagen	LP	Polydor	623035	1965	£20	£8	
No Regrets	LP	Look	LKLP6043	1976	£15	£6	
Out West	7"	Arc	ARC36	1963	£4	£1.50	
This Is Alex Campbell 1	LP	Ad Rhythm-Tepee	ARPS1	1971	£30	£15	
This Is Alex Campbell 2	LP	Ad Rhythm-Tepee	ARPS2	1971	£30	£15	
Way Out West	LP	Society	SOC912	1963	£10	£4	
With The Greatest Respect	LP	Sundown	SDLP2048	1987	£12	£5	*double*

CAMPBELL, ALEX, ALAN ROBERTS, DOUGIE MACLEAN

Title	Format	Label	Cat. No.	Year	Mint	VG+	Notes
Alex Campbell, Alan Roberts, Dougie Maclean	LP	Burlington	BURL002	1979	£12	£5	

CAMPBELL, ALEX, COLIN WILKIE & SHIRLEY HART

Title	Format	Label	Cat. No.	Year	Mint	VG+	Notes
Sing Folk	LP	Presto	PRE648	1965	£12	£5	

CAMPBELL, CAT & NICKY

Title	Format	Label	Cat. No.	Year	Mint	VG+	Notes
Hammering	7"	Pressure Beat	PB5511	1972	£10	£5	*Peter Tosh B side*

CAMPBELL, CHOKER

Title	Format	Label	Cat. No.	Year	Mint	VG+	Notes
Hits Of The Sixties	LP	Tamla Motown	TML11011	1965	£100	£50	
Mickey's Monkey	7"	Tamla Motown	TMG517	1965	£60	£30	

CAMPBELL, CHRISTINE

Title	Format	Label	Cat. No.	Year	Mint	VG+	Notes
Wherever I Go	7" EP	Parlophone	GEP8874	1963	£6	£2.50	

CAMPBELL, CORNELL

Title	Format	Label	Cat. No.	Year	Mint	VG+	Notes
Cornell Campbell	LP	Trojan	TBL199	1972	£20	£8	
Dearest Darling	7"	Green Door	GD4042	1972	£5	£2	
Each Lonely Night	7"	Island	WI083	1963	£12	£6	
Give Me Love	7"	Green Door	GD4057	1973	£5	£2	
Gloria	7"	Rio	R38	1964	£10	£5	
Gorgan	LP	Angen	ANGL3	1976	£12	£5	
Jericho Road	7"	Port-O-Jam	PJ4008	1964	£15	£7.50	
My Confession	7"	Dynamic	DYN446	1972	£5	£2	
Pity The Children	7"	Jackpot	JP809	1973	£5	£2	
Rosahelle	7"	Island	WI039	1962	£12	£6	

CAMPBELL, DAVID

Sun Wheel	LP	Decca	SKL5139	1972	£10	£4	
Young Blood	LP	Transatlantic	TRA141	1967	£25	£10	

CAMPBELL, DICK

This obscure American singer-songwriter would have loved to be hailed as a second Bob Dylan and, indeed, he somehow managed to persuade members of the Butterfield Blues Band (together with a pre-Chicago Peter Cetera) to perform on his album. Mike Bloomfield periodically delivers a facsimile of his lead guitar work on 'Like A Rolling Stone', but can do little to redeem Campbell's extraordinarily arrogant and patronizing lyrics, mostly directed at the singer's unfortunate girlfriend.

Sings Where It's At	LP	Mercury	MG2/SR61060	1965	£12	£5	*US*

CAMPBELL, DOREEN

Rude Girls	7"	Rainbow	RAI117	1967	£6	£2.50	

CAMPBELL, ETHNA

What's Easy For Two	7"	Mercury	MF804	1964	£6	£2.50	

CAMPBELL, GLEN

Glen Campbell is dismissed as irredeemably middle-of-the-road by rock music collectors, yet his versions of songs by Jimmy Webb are always worth hearing, and include at least one genuine classic in 'Wichita Lineman'. In 1965 he turned down the chance to become a full-time Beach Boy, but did record Brian Wilson's 'Guess I'm Dumb' (without intending it to be any kind of comment on himself!) with the writer in the producer's chair.

Guess I'm Dumb	7"	Capitol	5441	1965	£30	£15	*US*
Turn Around, Look At Me	7"	Top Rank	JAR596	1961	£8	£4	

CAMPBELL, IAN

The Ian Campbell Folk Group recorded prolifically during the sixties to considerable acclaim, but lost momentum thereafter – finally disbanding in 1978. Star fiddler Dave Swarbrick was a member of the group on the majority of the recordings listed below, while bass player Dave Pegg was a member during the late sixties. Swarbrick and Pegg went on to play together in Fairport Convention. Ian Campbell's sons have gained considerable success with their group UB40, although it is said that the father did not really approve of the commercial direction they decided to take.

Across The Hills	LP	Transatlantic	TRA118	1964	£20	£8	
Adam's Rib	LP			1976	£40	£20	
Break My Mind	7"	Major Minor	MM639	1969	£4	£1.50	
Ceilidh At The Crown	7" EP	Topic	TOP76	1962	£20	£10	
Circle Game	LP	Transatlantic	TRA163	1968	£15	£6	
Coaldust Ballads	LP	Transatlantic	TRA123	1965	£25	£10	
Cock Doth Craw	LP	XTRA	XTRA1061	1968	£15	£6	
Come Kiss Me	7"	Transatlantic	TRASP6	1966	£4	£1.50	
Contemporary Campbells	LP	Transatlantic	TRA137	1965	£20	£8	
Guantanamera	7"	Transatlantic	TRASP7	1966	£4	£1.50	
Ian Campbell Folk Group	7" EP	Decca	DFE8592	1964	£8	£4	
Ian Campbell Folk Group	LP	MFP	MFP1349	1969	£10	£4	
Kelly From Killane	7"	Transatlantic	TRASP2	1965	£4	£1.50	
Lover Let Me In	7"	Transatlantic	BIG103	1968	£4	£1.50	
Marilyn Monroe	7"	Decca	F11802	1964	£4	£1.50	
New Impressions	LP	Transatlantic	TRA151	1967	£15	£6	
One Eyed Reilly	7"	Transatlantic	TRASP10	1966	£4	£1.50	
Presenting The Ian Campbell Folk Group	LP	Contour	2870314	197–	£10	£4	
Sampler	7" EP	Transatlantic	TRAEP128	1965	£6	£2.50	
Sampler	LP	Transatlantic	TRASAM4	1969	£12	£5	
Sampler 2	LP	Transatlantic	TRASAM12	1969	£12	£5	
Something To Sing About	LP	Pye	PKL5506	1972	£20	£8	
Sun Is Burning	7"	Topic	STOP102	1964	£8	£4	*picture sleeve*
Sun Is Burning	LP	Argo	ZFB13	1971	£20	£8	
Tam O'Shanter	LP	XTRA	XTRA1074	1968	£15	£6	
This Is The Ian Campbell Folk Group	LP	Transatlantic	TRA110	1963	£20	£8	
Times They Are A-Changin'	7"	Transatlantic	TRASP5	1965	£4	£1.50	

CAMPBELL, JIMMY

Album	LP	Philips	6308100	1972	£10	£4	
Half Baked	LP	Vertigo	6360010	1970	£15	£6	*with the Merseybeats*
On A Monday	7"	Fontana	TF1009	1969	£4	£1.50	*picture sleeve*
Songs Of Anastasia	LP	Fontana	STL5508	1969	£10	£4	

CAMPBELL, JO ANN

All The Hits	LP	Cameo	(S)C1026	1962	£20	£8	*US*
I Changed My Mind Jack	7"	HMV	POP1003	1962	£5	£2	
I'm Nobody's Baby	LP	End	LP306	1959	£30	£15	*US*
Kookie Little Paradise	7"	HMV	POP776	1960	£5	£2	
Mister Fixit Man	7"	Cameo Parkway	C237	1962	£5	£2	
Mother Please	7"	Cameo Parkway	C249	1963	£5	£2	
Motorcycle Michael	7"	HMV	POP873	1961	£6	£2.50	
Starring	LP	Coronet	CX(S)199	1964	£25	£10	*US*
Twistin' And Listenin'	LP	ABC	(S)393	1962	£25	£10	*US*
Wait A Minute	7"	London	HLU8536	1958	£25	£12.50	

CAMPBELL, NOLA

Pictures Of You	7"	Gas	GAS107	1969	£4	£1.50	

CAMPBELL, ROY

Title	Format	Label	Number	Year	Mint	Value	Notes
Another Saturday Night	7"	Giant	GN41	1968	**£4**	**£1.50**	
Engine Number Nine	7"	Jolly	JY003	1968	**£4**	**£1.50**	

CAMPBELL FAMILY

Title	Format	Label	Number	Year	Mint	Value	Notes
Singing Campbells	LP	Topic	12T120	1965	**£25**	**£10**	

CAMPBELL-LYONS, PATRICK

Title	Format	Label	Number	Year	Mint	Value	Notes
Electric Plough	LP	Public	PUBL1	1981	**£12**	**£5**	
Everybody Should Fly A Kite	7"	Sovereign	SOV115	1973	**£8**	**£4**	
Me And My Friend	LP	Sovereign	SVNA7258	1973	**£100**	**£50**	
Out On The Road	7"	Sovereign	SOV119	1973	**£8**	**£4**	

CAN

Title	Format	Label	Number	Year	Mint	Value	Notes
Cannibalism	LP	United Artists	UDM105/6	1978	**£20**	**£8**	*double*
Ege Bamyasi	LP	United Artists	UAS29414	1972	**£15**	**£6**	
Flow Motion	CD	Virgin	CDV2071	1988	**£12**	**£5**	
Flow Motion	LP	Virgin	V2071	1976	**£10**	**£4**	
Future Days	LP	United Artists	UAS29505	1973	**£12**	**£5**	
Landed	LP	Virgin	V2041	1975	**£12**	**£5**	
Limited Edition	LP	United Artists	USP103	1974	**£12**	**£5**	
Monster Movie	LP	United Artists	UAS29094	1969	**£20**	**£8**	
Monster Movie	LP	Music Factory	SRS001	1969	**£75**	**£37.50**	*German*
Onlyou	cass	Pure Freude	PF23	1982	**£30**	**£15**	*tin container*
Opener	LP	Sunset	SLS50400	1976	**£10**	**£4**	
Saw Delight	CD	Virgin	CDV2079	1988	**£12**	**£5**	
Saw Delight	LP	Virgin	V2079	1977	**£10**	**£4**	
Soon Over Babaluma	LP	United Artists	UAG29673	1974	**£12**	**£5**	
Soundtracks	LP	United Artists	UAS29283	1970	**£20**	**£8**	
Tago Mago	LP	United Artists	UAD60009/10	1971	**£25**	**£10**	*double*
Unlimited Edition	LP	Caroline	CAD3001	1976	**£20**	**£8**	*double*

CANAAN

Title	Format	Label	Number	Year	Mint	Value	Notes
Canaan	LP	Dovetail	DOVE3	1973	**£50**	**£25**	
Out Of The Wilderness	LP	Myrrh	MYR1042	1976	**£30**	**£15**	

CANADIAN BEATLES

Title	Format	Label	Number	Year	Mint	Value	Notes
Three Faces North	LP	Tide	2005	1964	**£40**	**£20**	*US*

CANADIAN SQUIRES

Levon and the Hawks – later to become the Band – recorded as the Canadian Squires for one single.

Title	Format	Label	Number	Year	Mint	Value	Notes
Uh Uh Uh	7"	Ware	6002	1965	**£20**	**£10**	*US*

CANARIES

Title	Format	Label	Number	Year	Mint	Value	Notes
Flying High	LP	B.T.Puppy	BTPS1007	1970	**£12**	**£5**	*US*

CANDIDO

Title	Format	Label	Number	Year	Mint	Value	Notes
Beautiful	LP	Blue Note	BST84357	1970	**£12**	**£5**	
Candido In Indigo	LP	HMV	CLP1265	1959	**£15**	**£6**	
Candido The Volcanic	10" LP	HMV	DLP1182	1958	**£15**	**£6**	

CANDLE FACTORY

Title	Format	Label	Number	Year	Mint	Value	Notes
Nightshift	LP	Cavs		197–	**£50**	**£25**	

CANDOLI, CONTE

Title	Format	Label	Number	Year	Mint	Value	Notes
Sincerely, Conte	10" LP	London	LZN14010	1956	**£20**	**£8**	
Toots Sweet	LP	London	LTZN15036	1957	**£15**	**£6**	

CANDOLI, PETE

Title	Format	Label	Number	Year	Mint	Value	Notes
St Louis Blues Boogie	7"	Capitol	CL14615	1956	**£5**	**£2**	

CANDY & THE KISSES

Title	Format	Label	Number	Year	Mint	Value	Notes
Do The 81	7"	Cameo Parkway	C336	1965	**£50**	**£25**	
Mr Creator	7"	Kent	TOWN104	1985	**£6**	**£2.50**	*Chuck Jackson B side*

CANDY CHOIR

Title	Format	Label	Number	Year	Mint	Value	Notes
Shake Hands And Come Out Crying	7"	Parlophone	R5472	1966	**£8**	**£4**	

CANDY DATES

Title	Format	Label	Number	Year	Mint	Value	Notes
Day Just Like That	7"	Pye	7N15944	1965	**£4**	**£1.50**	
Some Other Time	7"	Pye	7N17000	1965	**£4**	**£1.50**	

CANDYMEN

Title	Format	Label	Number	Year	Mint	Value	Notes
De Manchester A Paris	7" EP	Barclay	70806	1965	**£10**	**£5**	*French*
Georgia Pines	7"	HMV	POP1612	1967	**£4**	**£1.50**	

CANE

Title	Format	Label	Number	Year	Mint	Value	Notes
3 x 3	7"	Lightning	GIL531	1978	**£5**	**£2**	

CANNED HEAT

At their best (*Boogie With Canned Heat*), Canned Heat were one of the most interesting white blues groups. Bob Hite and Henry Vestine had a collection of blues records of legendary proportions, so they were not short of good examples to follow. They did have a liking, however, for what they called 'boogie', by which they meant a string of extremely long and extremely tedious instrumental solos played over an elemental riff. Both extremes can be found on the double *Living The Blues*. There is a boogie of record-breaking length, but also some short experimental tracks that take interesting liberties with the blues format. The record made with John Lee Hooker, listed under that name, also shows Canned Heat's abilities well. They let Hooker run the show, but by virtue of their telling support, they push him into making one of his very best records.

Title	Format	Label	Number	Year	Mint	VG	Notes
Boogie With Canned Heat	LP	Liberty	LBL/LBS83103	1968	**£15**	**£6**	
Canned Heat	LP	Liberty	LBL/LBS83059	1967	**£15**	**£6**	
Canned Heat '70: Live In Europe	LP	Liberty	LBS83333	1970	**£12**	**£5**	
Cookbook	LP	Liberty	LBS83303	1970	**£10**	**£4**	
Future Blues	LP	Liberty	LBS83364	1970	**£12**	**£5**	
Gate's On Heat	LP	Barclay	80603	1973	**£15**	**£6**	*French, with Clarence 'Gatemouth' Brown*
Hallelujah	LP	Liberty	LBS83239	1969	**£12**	**£5**	
Let's Work Together	CD-s	Liberty	CDEM100	1989	**£5**	**£2**	
Live At Topanga Canyon	LP	Wand	WD[illegible]	1970	**£15**	**£6**	*US*
Living The Blues	LP	Liberty	LDS84001	1969	**£20**	**£8**	*double*
Living The Blues	LP	United Artists	UAS29258/9	1972	**£15**	**£6**	*double*
Memphis Heat	LP	Barclay	80607	1975	**£15**	**£6**	*French, with Memphis Slim*
Spoonful	7"	Pye	7N25513	1970	**£4**	**£1.50**	
Vintage Heat	LP	Pye	NSPL28129	1970	**£12**	**£5**	

CANNIBAL & THE HEADHUNTERS

Title	Format	Label	Number	Year	Mint	VG	Notes
Land Of 1000 Dances	7"	Stateside	SS403	1965	**£10**	**£5**	
Land Of 1000 Dances	LP	CBS	62942	1967	**£20**	**£8**	

CANNIBALS

Title	Format	Label	Number	Year	Mint	VG	Notes
Good Guys	7"	Big Cock	FUK1	1978	**£5**	**£2**	

CANNON, ACE

Title	Format	Label	Number	Year	Mint	VG	Notes
Tuff	LP	Hi	HLP32007	1961	**£12**	**£5**	*US*

CANNON, FREDDIE

Title	Format	Label	Number	Year	Mint	VG	Notes
Action	LP	Warner Bros	W(S)1612	1965	**£20**	**£8**	*US*
Bang On	LP	Stateside	SL10013	1963	**£30**	**£15**	
Blast Off	7" EP	Stateside	SE1002	1962	**£15**	**£7.50**	
Buzz Buzz A Diddle It	7"	Top Rank	JAR568	1961	**£10**	**£5**	
Dedication Song	7"	Warner Bros	WB5693	1966	**£4**	**£1.50**	
Explosive Freddie Cannon	7" EP	Top Rank	JKP2058	1960	**£20**	**£10**	
Explosive Freddie Cannon	LP	Top Rank	25018	1960	**£25**	**£10**	
Four Direct Hits	7" EP	Top Rank	JKP2066	1960	**£15**	**£7.50**	
Freddie Cannon	LP	Warner Bros	WM/WS8153	1964	**£20**	**£8**	
Freddie Cannon Favourites	LP	Top Rank	35113	1961	**£30**	**£15**	
Greatest Hits	LP	Warner Bros	W(S)1628	1966	**£20**	**£8**	*US*
Happy Shades Of Blue	LP	Top Rank	35106	1961	**£30**	**£15**	
Okefenokee	7"	Top Rank	JAR207	1959	**£5**	**£2**	
On Target	7" EP	Top Rank	JKP3010	1961	**£15**	**£7.50**	
Patty Baby	7"	Stateside	SS201	1963	**£4**	**£1.50**	
Steps Out	LP	Stateside	SL10062	1964	**£40**	**£20**	
Tallahassee Lassie	7"	Top Rank	JAR135	1959	**£4**	**£1.50**	

CANNON, GUS

Title	Format	Label	Number	Year	Mint	VG	Notes
Cannon's Jug Stompers/Clifford's Louisville Jug Band	LP	Tax	LP2	1966	**£15**	**£6**	
Kings Of The Blues Vol. 1	7" EP	RCA	RCX202	1961	**£5**	**£2**	
Walk Right In	LP	Stax	702	1962	**£20**	**£8**	*US*

CANNON, JUDY

Title	Format	Label	Number	Year	Mint	VG	Notes
Very First Day I Met You	7"	Pye	7N15900	1965	**£20**	**£10**	

CANNON, SEAN

Title	Format	Label	Number	Year	Mint	VG	Notes
Erin The Green	LP	Ogham	BLB5004	1979	**£10**	**£4**	*Irish*
Roving Journey Man	LP	Cottage	COT411	1977	**£10**	**£4**	

CANNON BROTHERS

Title	Format	Label	Number	Year	Mint	VG	Notes
Turn Your Eyes To Me	7"	Brit	WI1003	1965	**£8**	**£4**	

CANNONBALL & JOHNNY MELODY

Title	Format	Label	Number	Year	Mint	VG	Notes
Cool Hand Luke	7"	Big Shot	BI518	1969	**£4**	**£1.50**	

CANNONBALLS

Title	Format	Label	Number	Year	Mint	VG	Notes
Calliope Boogie	7"	Coral	Q72431	1961	**£8**	**£4**	
New Orleans Beat	7"	Coral	Q72428	1961	**£8**	**£4**	

CANNONS

Title	Format	Label	Number	Year	Mint	VG	Notes
Bush Fire	7"	Columbia	DB4724	1961	**£8**	**£4**	
I Didn't Know The Gun Was Loaded	7"	Decca	F11269	1960	**£8**	**£4**	

CANNY FETTLE

Title	Format	Label	Number	Year	Mint	VG	Notes
Trip To Harrogate	LP	Tradition	TSR027	1977	**£15**	**£6**	
Varry Canny	LP	Tradition	TSR023	1975	**£20**	**£8**	

CANTELON, WILLARD

Title	Format	Label	Number	Year	Mint	VG	Notes
LSD Battle For The Mind	LP	Supreme	M/S113	1966	**£15**	**£6**	*US*

CANTOR, EDDIE

Title	Format	Label	Number	Year	Mint	VG	Notes
Ma He's Making Eyes At Me	7" EP	Capitol	EAP120113	1961	**£5**	**£2**	

CAPABILITY BROWN

Title	Format	Label	Number	Year	Mint	VG	Notes
From Scratch	LP	Charisma	CAS1056	1972	**£10**	**£4**	
Voice	LP	Charisma	CAS1068	1973	**£10**	**£4**	

CAPE KENNEDY CONSTRUCTION CO.

Title	Format	Label	Number	Year	Mint	VG	Notes
First Step On The Moon	7"	President	PT265	1969	**£25**	**£12.50**	

CAPERCAILLIE

Title	Format	Label	Number	Year	Mint	VG	Notes
Cascade	LP	SRT	4KL178	1984	**£15**	**£6**	
Coisich A Ruin	CD-s	Survival	ZD44594	1991	**£5**	**£2**	
Four Stone Walls	CD-s	Survival	no number	1993	**£5**	**£2**	*promo*
Waiting For The Wheel To Turn	CD-s	Survival	74321115872	1992	**£8**	**£4**	

CAPITOLS

Title	Format	Label	Number	Year	Mint	VG	Notes
Cool Jerk	7"	Atlantic	584004	1966	**£5**	**£2**	
Dance The Cool Jerk	LP	Atlantic	587/588019	1966	**£15**	**£6**	
We Got A Thing	LP	Atco	(SD33)201	1966	**£15**	**£6**	*US*

CAPITOLS (2)

Title	Format	Label	Number	Year	Mint	VG	Notes
Honey And Wine	7"	Pye	7N17025	1966	**£5**	**£2**	

CAPRIS

Title	Format	Label	Number	Year	Mint	VG	Notes
There's A Moon Out Tonight	7"	Columbia	DB4605	1961	**£60**	**£30**	

CAPSTICK, TONY

Title	Format	Label	Number	Year	Mint	VG	Notes
Punch And Judy Man	LP	Rubber	RUB008	1974	**£10**	**£4**	

CAPTAIN BEEFHEART

Don Van Vliet followed his own wayward path through rock music, before deciding that he would much rather make a living as a full-time artist (and has apparently become far wealthier through his painting than he ever did through his music). Evolving from an idiosyncratic approach to the blues, the music made by the Magic Band on the ground-breaking albums *Strictly Personal* and *Trout Mask Replica* has strong parallels within a rock context to the harmelodic jazz approach developed by Ornette Coleman. The rhythms and harmonies sound fractured and chaotic at first, but they have their own logic and are very far from being dismissable as the weird ramblings of an eccentric. Indeed, Van Vliet's influence has become increasingly noticeable in the work of various adventurous post-punk groups. As it happens, *Trout Mask Replica*, produced by Van Vliet's schoolfriend Frank Zappa, sold well enough to enter the lower reaches of the album charts, and later pressings are fairly common.

Title	Format	Label	Number	Year	Mint	VG	Notes
Bluejeans And Moonbeams	LP	Virgin	V2123	1974	**£10**	**£4**	
Clear Spot	LP	Reprise	K54007	1972	**£10**	**£4**	
Diddy Wah Diddy	7" EP	A&M	AME600	1971	**£300**	**£180**	*best auctioned*
Dropout Boogie	LP	Buddah	2349002	1970	**£10**	**£4**	
Legendary A & M Sessions	12"	A&M	AMY226	1984	**£6**	**£2.50**	
Lick My Decals Off	LP	Reprise	K44244	1973	**£15**	**£7.50**	
Lick My Decals Off	LP	Straight	STS1063	1970	**£25**	**£10**	
Light Reflected Off The Oceans Of The Moon	12"	Virgin	VS53412	1982	**£6**	**£2.50**	
Mirror Man	LP	Buddah	BDLP4004	1974	**£10**	**£4**	
Mirror Man	LP	Buddah	2365022	1971	**£20**	**£8**	
Moonchild	7"	A&M	AMS726	1968	**£25**	**£12.50**	
Safe As Milk	LP	Pye	NPL28110	1968	**£25**	**£10**	
Safe As Milk	LP	Buddah	623171	1969	**£10**	**£4**	
Sixpack	7"	Virgin	SIXPACK1	1979	**£15**	**£7.50**	*picture disc*
Spotlight Kid	LP	Reprise	K44162	1972	**£10**	**£4**	
Spotlight Kid/Clear Spot	CD	Reprise	26249	1990	**£15**	**£6**	*US promo picture disc*
Stand Up To Be Discontinued	CD	Cantz	398013203X	1993	**£50**	**£25**	*German, with hard-cover book*
Strictly Personal	LP	Liberty	LBL/LBS83172	1968	**£25**	**£10**	
Sure'Nuff 'n Yes I Do	7"	Buddah	BDS466	1978	**£4**	**£1.50**	
Too Much Time	7"	Reprise	K14233	1973	**£4**	**£1.50**	
Trout Mask Replica	LP	Straight	STS1053	1969	**£25**	**£10**	*double*
Trout Mask Replica	LP	Reprise	K64026	1975	**£15**	**£7.50**	*double*
Unconditionally Guaranteed	LP	Virgin	V2015	1974	**£10**	**£4**	
Upon The My-Oh-My	7"	Virgin	VS110	1974	**£4**	**£1.50**	
Yellow Brick Road	7"	Pye	7N25443	1968	**£20**	**£10**	

CAPTAIN BEYOND

Title	Format	Label	Number	Year	Mint	VG	Notes
Captain Beyond	LP	Capricorn	K47503	1972	**£12**	**£5**	*3D cover*

CAPTAIN NOAH & HIS FLOATING ZOO

Title	Format	Label	Number	Year	Mint	VG	Notes
Captain Noah & His Floating Zoo	LP	Argo	ZDA149	1972	**£10**	**£4**	

CARAVAN

The unrecorded Canterbury group, Wilde Flowers, evolved into both Soft Machine and Caravan. Not surprisingly, therefore, these two groups have many similarities in their sound, although Caravan always had rather more of a pop sensibility. Unusual time signatures and improvised solos abound in Caravan's music, but always wedded to easily attractive melodies. Like Soft Machine too, Caravan's long career was distinguished by numerous personnel changes, which served to dilute the group's impact. The most effective recordings are the first three albums, made by the original line-up. The Verve LP has become quite scarce, although it is an essential sixties document. Like many albums of the period, the mono and stereo mixes are noticeably different.

Title	Format	Label	Number	Year	Mint	VG	Notes
Caravan	LP	Verve	VLP6011	1968	**£100**	**£50**	*mono*
Caravan	LP	Verve	SVLP6011	1968	**£75**	**£37.50**	*stereo*
Caravan	LP	MGM	2353058	1972	**£25**	**£10**	
For Girls Who Grow Plump In The Night	LP	Deram	SDL12	1973	**£10**	**£4**	
If I Could Do It All Over Again	7"	Decca	F13063	1970	**£6**	**£2.50**	
If I Could Do It All Over Again . . .	LP	Decca	SKL5052	1970	**£15**	**£6**	

In The Land Of Grey And Pink	LP	Deram	SDLR1	1971	**£12**	**£5**	
Love To Love You	7"	Decca	F23125	1971	**£6**	**£2.50**	
Place Of My Own	7"	Verve	VS1518	1968	**£20**	**£10**	
Waterloo Lily	LP	Deram	SDL8	1972	**£12**	**£5**	

CARAVELLES

Caravelles	LP	Decca	LK4565	1963	**£25**	**£10**	
Hey Mama You've Been On My Mind	7"	Polydor	BM56137	1966	**£6**	**£2.50**	
You Are Here	7"	Fontana	TF466	1964	**£4**	**£1.50**	

CARAWAN, GUY

Guy Carawan Sings	LP	Folkways	3548	1959	**£15**	**£6**	*US*
Old Man Atom	7"	Pye	7N15132	1958	**£4**	**£1.50**	
Songs From The South	7" EP	Collector	JEA1	1961	**£5**	**£2**	

CARDALE TRIO

Follow On	7" EP	Pilgrim		1968	**£10**	**£5**	

CARDBOARD ORCHESTRA

Nothing But A Sad Sad Show	7"	CBS	4633	1969	**£4**	**£1.50**	
Zebady Zak	7"	CBS	4176	1969	**£4**	**£1.50**	

CARDEILHAC

Cardeilhac	LP	Olabel	703721	1972	**£100**	**£50**	*Swiss*

CARDEW, CORNELIUS

Thalmann Variations	LP	Matchless	MR10	1986	**£12**	**£5**	

CARDIAC ARREST

Bus For A Bus On A Bus	7"	Tortch	TOR002	1979	**£8**	**£4**	
Running In The Street	7"	Another Record	AN1	1981	**£5**	**£2**	

CARDIACS

Little Man, A House And The Whole World Window	CD	Torso	CD060	1988	**£20**	**£8**	
Obvious Identity	cass	private		1981	**£10**	**£4**	
Rude Bootleg – Live At Reading '86	LP	Alphabet	ALPH005	1987	**£10**	**£4**	
Seaside	cass	Alphabet	ALPH01	1983	**£10**	**£4**	
Toy World	cass	Cardiacs		1981	**£10**	**£4**	

CARDIGANS

Poor Boy	7"	Mercury	AMT1007	1958	**£5**	**£2**	

CAREFREES

We Love You All	LP	London	LL3/PS379	1964	**£40**	**£20**	*US*
We Love You Beatles	7"	Oriole	CB1916	1964	**£6**	**£2.50**	

CAREY, DAVE

Broken Wings	7"	Columbia	SCM5030	1953	**£4**	**£1.50**	
Dave Carey Jazz Band	7" EP	Tempo	EXA38	1956	**£10**	**£5**	
Dave Carey Jazz Band	LP	Tempo	LAP4	1955	**£20**	**£8**	
Jazz At The Railway Arms	LP	Tempo	TAP16	1957	**£20**	**£8**	

CAREY, MARIAH

12s	LP	Sony	MARIAH1	1998	**£100**	**£50**	*promo boxed set of 12 x 12" singles*
Can't Let Go	CD-s	CBS	6576622	1991	**£15**	**£7.50**	
Emotions	CD-s	CBS	6574032	1991	**£12**	**£6**	
Fly Away	12"	Columbia	XPR2378	1997	**£10**	**£5**	*promo*
I'll Be There	CD-s	CBS	6581379	1992	**£20**	**£10**	*picture disc, live tracks*
I'll Be There	CD-s	CBS	6581372	1992	**£8**	**£4**	
Joy To The World	12"	Columbia	XPR2129	1995	**£10**	**£5**	*promo*
Love And Dreams – The Best Collection 1990–1995	CD	Sony	XACS90032	1996	**£150**	**£75**	*Japanese promo*
Love Takes Time	12"	Columbia	6563646	1990	**£6**	**£2.50**	
Love Takes Time	CD-s	CBS	6563642	1990	**£15**	**£7.50**	
Love Takes Time	CD-s	CBS	6563645	1990	**£20**	**£10**	*picture disc*
Make It Happen	CD-s	CBS	6579412	1992	**£12**	**£6**	
My All	12"	Columbia	XPR2409	1998	**£10**	**£5**	*promo*
Roof	12"	Columbia	XPR2396	1998	**£10**	**£5**	*promo*
Roof	12"	Columbia	XPR2380	1997	**£10**	**£5**	*promo*
Roof	12"	Columbia	XPR2398	1998	**£10**	**£5**	*promo*
Someday	12"	Columbia	6565836	1991	**£8**	**£4**	
Someday	CD-s	CBS	6565832	1991	**£15**	**£7.50**	
Someday	CD-s	CBS	6565835	1991	**£25**	**£12.50**	*picture disc*
There's Got To Be A Way	CD-s	CBS	6569312	1991	**£15**	**£7.50**	
There's Got To Be A Way	CD-s	CBS	6569315	1991	**£30**	**£15**	*picture disc*
Vision Of Love	CD-s	CBS	6559322	1990	**£15**	**£7.50**	

CARGO

Cargo	LP	Harvest	5C05224582	1971	**£200**	**£100**	*Dutch*

CARIBBEANS

Let Me Walk By	7"	Doctor Bird	DB1181	1969	**£10**	**£5**	*Amblings B side*
Please Please	7"	Crab	CRAB14	1969	**£4**	**£1.50**	*Matadors B side*

CARIBBEATS

Title	Format	Label	Cat. No.	Year	Mint	VG	Notes
Bells Of Saint Mary's Ska	7"	Ska Beat	JB246	1966	£10	£5	*Winston Richards B side*
Highway 300	7"	Double D	DD101	1967	£8	£4	
I'll Try	7"	Double D	DD103	1967	£8	£4	

CARIBS

Title	Format	Label	Cat. No.	Year	Mint	VG	Notes
Taboo	7"	Starlite	ST45012	1960	£4	£1.50	

CARIFTA ALL STARS

Title	Format	Label	Cat. No.	Year	Mint	VG	Notes
Harder They Come	7"	Green Door	GD4040	1972	£4	£1.50	

CARL & THE COMMANDERS

Title	Format	Label	Cat. No.	Year	Mint	VG	Notes
Farmer John	7"	Columbia	DB4719	1961	£8	£4	

CARLISLE, BELINDA

Title	Format	Label	Cat. No.	Year	Mint	VG	Notes
Belinda	CD	MCA	DMIRL1505	1990	£12	£5	
Circle In The Sand	12"	Virgin	VSTY1074	1988	£10	£4	*picture disc*
Circle In The Sand	CD-s	Virgin	VSCD1074	1987	£20	£10	
Half The World	CD-s	Virgin	VSCDG1388	1992	£5	£2	*digipak*
Heaven Is A Place On Earth	CD-s	Virgin	VSCD1036	1987	£20	£10	
Heaven On Earth	CD	Virgin	CDVP2496	1988	£12	£5	*picture disc*
I Get Weak	CD-s	Virgin	VSCD1046	1988	£15	£7.50	*picture disc*
La Luna	CD-s	Virgin	VSCD1230	1989	£5	£2	*3" single*
La Luna	CD-s	Virgin	VSCD1230DJ	1989	£40	£20	*promo picture disc*
Leave A Light On	7"	Virgin	VSP1210	1989	£4	£1.50	*poster picture sleeve*
Leave A Light On	CD-s	Virgin	VSCD1210	1989	£6	£2.50	
Little Black Book	CD-s	Virgin	VSCDG1428	1992	£6	£2.50	*digipak*
Live Your Life Be Free	CD-s	Virgin	VSCDG1370	1991	£5	£2	*digipak*
Love Never Dies	CD-s	Virgin	VSCD1150	1988	£8	£4	
Mad About You	CD-s	IRS	DIRM118	1988	£40	£20	*3" single*
Real	CD	Virgin	CDVDJ2725	1993	£20	£8	*promo in rubber case*
Runaway Horses	CD	Virgin	CDV2599	1989	£12	£5	
Runaway Horses	CD-s	Virgin	VSCD1244	1990	£6	£2.50	
Summer Rain	CD-s	Virgin	VSCDT1323	1990	£8	£4	*boxed*
Summer Rain	CD-s	Virgin	VSCDX1323	1990	£6	£2.50	*digipak*
Vision Of You	CD-s	Virgin	VSCDT1264	1990	£6	£2.50	
We Want The Same Thing (Summer Mix)	CD-s	Virgin	VSCDP1291	1990	£5	£2	
Woman And A Man	CD	Chrysalis		1996	£60	£30	*promo box set, with video*
World Without You	12"	Virgin	VST1114	1988	£8	£4	*poster sleeve*
World Without You	7"	Virgin	VSX1114	1988	£8	£4	*boxed*
World Without You	CD-s	Virgin	VSCD1114	1988	£10	£5	

CARLISLE, BILLY

Title	Format	Label	Cat. No.	Year	Mint	VG	Notes
Down Boy	7"	Mercury	AMT1063	1959	£20	£10	

CARLISLE BROTHERS

Title	Format	Label	Cat. No.	Year	Mint	VG	Notes
Fresh From The Country	7" EP	Parlophone	GEP8799	1959	£12	£6	

CARLSEN, DAVE

Title	Format	Label	Cat. No.	Year	Mint	VG	Notes
Pale Horse	LP	Spark	SRLP110	1973	£15	£6	

CARLTON, EDDIE

Title	Format	Label	Cat. No.	Year	Mint	VG	Notes
It Will Be Done	7"	Cream	5001	1976	£5	£2	

CARLTON, LITTLE CARL

Title	Format	Label	Cat. No.	Year	Mint	VG	Notes
46 Drums 1 Guitar	7"	Action	ACT4514	1968	£4	£1.50	
Competition Ain't Nothing	7"	Action	ACT4501	1968	£15	£7.50	
Look At Mary Wonder	7"	Action	ACT4537	1969	£5	£2	

CARLTON & HIS SHOES

Title	Format	Label	Cat. No.	Year	Mint	VG	Notes
Love Me Forever	7"	Coxsone	CS7065	1968	£12	£6	
Love Me Forever	LP	Studio One	PSOL003	197–	£50	£25	
This Feeling	7"	Studio One	SO2062	1968	£12	£6	

CARMEN

Title	Format	Label	Cat. No.	Year	Mint	VG	Notes
Dancing On A Cold Wind	LP	Regal Zonophone	SLRZ1040	1975	£20	£8	
Fandangos In Space	LP	Regal Zonophone	SRZA8518	1973	£15	£6	

CARMICHAEL, HOAGY

Title	Format	Label	Cat. No.	Year	Mint	VG	Notes
Crazy Otto Rag	7"	Vogue Coral	Q72078	1955	£4	£1.50	
Hoagy Carmichael	7" EP	Vogue	VE170113	1958	£5	£2	
Hong Kong Blues	7"	Vogue Coral	Q72123	1956	£4	£1.50	
I Walk The Line	7"	Vogue Coral	Q72206	1956	£4	£1.50	
Lazy River	7"	Vogue Coral	Q72095	1955	£4	£1.50	
Stardust	7" EP	HMV	7EG8037	1954	£5	£2	
Stardust Road	7" EP	Brunswick	OE9023	1954	£5	£2	

CARMICHAEL, IAN

Title	Format	Label	Cat. No.	Year	Mint	VG	Notes
Lucky Jim	7"	HMV	POP406	1957	£5	£2	

CARNABY

Title	Format	Label	Cat. No.	Year	Mint	VG	Notes
Jump And Dance	7"	Piccadilly	7N35272	1965	£50	£25	

CARNABY STREET POP
Carnaby Street Pop ... LP ... Carnaby ... CNLS6003 ... 1969 **£50** ... **£25**

CARNATIONS
Mighty Man ... 7" ... Blue Beat ... BB285 ... 1965 **£12** ... **£6**

CARNEGY HALL
Bells Of San Francisco ... 7" ... Polydor ... 56224 ... 1968 **£10** ... **£5**

CARNES, KIM
Rest On Me ... LP ... Amos ... 7016 ... 1970 **£10** ... **£4** ... *US*

CAROL & THE MEMORIES
Tears On My Pillow ... 7" ... CBS ... 202006 ... 1966 **£5** ... **£2**

CAROLINA SLIM
Carolina Blues And Boogie ... LP ... Flyright ... LP4702 ... 1972 **£12** ... **£5**

CARPENTER, IKE
Lights Out ... LP ... Score ... SLP4010 ... 1957 **£60** ... **£30** ... *US*
Lights Out ... LP ... Aladdin ... LP811 ... 1956 **£100** ... **£50** ... *US*

CARPENTER, KAREN
I'll Be Yours ... 7" ... Magic Lamp ... 704 ... 196– **£250** ... **£150** ... *US, best auctioned*

CARPENTER, THELMA
Yes I'm Lonesome Tonight ... 7" ... Coral ... Q72422 ... 1961 **£4** ... **£1.50**

CARPENTERS
Carpenters ... LP ... A&M ... QU53502 ... 1971 **£10** ... **£4** ... *US quad*
Close To You ... CD-s ... A&M ... AMCD558 ... 1990 **£5** ... **£2**
Close To You ... LP ... A&M ... QU54271 ... 1970 **£10** ... **£4** ... *US quad*
Compact Hits ... CD-s ... A&M ... AMCD901 ... 1988 **£5** ... **£2**
Horizon ... LP ... A&M ... QU54530 ... 1975 **£10** ... **£4** ... *US quad*
Now And Then ... LP ... A&M ... QU53519 ... 1973 **£10** ... **£4** ... *US quad*
Singles 1969–1973 ... LP ... A&M ... QU53601 ... 1973 **£10** ... **£4** ... *US quad*
Song For You ... CD ... Mobile Fidelity ... UDCD525 ... 1990 **£15** ... **£6** ... *US audiophile*
Song For You ... LP ... A&M ... QU53511 ... 1972 **£10** ... **£4** ... *US quad*

CARPENTER'S APPRENTICE
Changes ... LP ... SRS ... 12107 ... 1972 **£75** ... **£37.50**

CARPET BAGGERS
Flea Teacher ... 7" ... Spin ... SP2006 ... 1967 **£5** ... **£2**

CARPETTES
I Don't Mean It ... 7" ... Beggars Banquet ... BEG27 ... 1979 **£4** ... **£1.50**
Johnny Won't Hurt You ... 7" ... Beggars Banquet ... BEG32 ... 1980 **£4** ... **£1.50**
Nothing Ever Changes ... 7" ... Beggars Banquet ... BEG47 ... 1980 **£4** ... **£1.50**
Radio Wunderbar ... 7" ... Small Wonder ... SMALL3 ... 1977 **£5** ... **£2**
Small Wonder ... 7" ... Small Wonder ... SMALL9 ... 1978 **£5** ... **£2**

CARR, CATHY
Ivory Tower ... 7" ... London ... HLH8274 ... 1956 **£25** ... **£12.50**

CARR, GEORGIA
Rocks In My Bed ... LP ... Vee Jay ... LP/VJS1105 ... 1964 **£15** ... **£6** ... *US*
Shy ... LP ... Roulette ... (S)R25077 ... 196– **£15** ... **£6** ... *US*
Songs By A Moody Miss ... LP ... Tops ... 1617 ... 1958 **£20** ... **£8** ... *US*

CARR, HELEN
Why Do I Love You? ... LP ... London ... HAN2065 ... 1957 **£10** ... **£4**

CARR, JAMES
Baby You've Got My Mind Messed Up ... 7" ... Stateside ... SS507 ... 1966 **£30** ... **£15**
Dark End Of The Street ... 7" ... Stateside ... SS2001 ... 1967 **£6** ... **£2.50**
Freedom Train ... 7" ... B&C ... CB101 ... 1969 **£4** ... **£1.50**
I'm A Fool For You ... 7" ... Stateside ... SS2052 ... 1967 **£5** ... **£2**
Let It Happen ... 7" ... Stateside ... SS2038 ... 1967 **£10** ... **£5**
Love Attack ... 7" ... Stateside ... SS535 ... 1966 **£8** ... **£4**
Man Needs A Woman ... LP ... Bell ... MBLL/SBLL113 ... 1968 **£15** ... **£6**
Pouring Water On A Drowning Man ... 7" ... Stateside ... SS545 ... 1966 **£6** ... **£2.50**
You Got My Mind Messed Up ... LP ... Stateside ... SL10205 ... 1967 **£40** ... **£20**

CARR, JOE 'FINGERS'
Barky-Roll Stomp ... 7" ... Capitol ... CL14359 ... 1955 **£5** ... **£2**
Piccadilly Rag ... 7" ... Capitol ... CL14169 ... 1954 **£6** ... **£2.50**

CARR, JOHNNY
Do You Love That Girl ... 7" ... Fontana ... TF600 ... 1965 **£6** ... **£2.50**
Respectable ... 7" ... Decca ... F11854 ... 1964 **£8** ... **£4**
Then So Do I ... 7" ... Fontana ... TF681 ... 1966 **£5** ... **£2**
Things Get Better ... 7" ... Fontana ... TF823 ... 1967 **£10** ... **£5**

CARR, LEROY

Title	Format	Label	Number	Year	Mint	VG	Notes
Blues Before Sunrise	LP	CBS	BPG62206	1963	**£20**	**£8**	
RCA Victor Race Series Vol. 2	7" EP	RCA	RCX7168	1964	**£10**	**£5**	
Treasures Of North American Negro Music	7" EP	Fontana	TFE17051	1958	**£12**	**£6**	

CARR, LINDA

Title	Format	Label	Number	Year	Mint	VG	Notes
Everytime	7"	Stateside	SS2058	1967	**£10**	**£5**	

CARR, MIKE

Title	Format	Label	Number	Year	Mint	VG	Notes
Hammond Under Pressure	LP	Columbia	S(C)X6248	1968	**£15**	**£6**	*with Tony Crombie*
Mike Carr	LP	Ad-Rhythm	ARPS1020	1973	**£15**	**£6**	
Mike Carr And His Trio	LP	Spotlite	SPJ517	1980	**£12**	**£5**	

CARR, ROMEY

Title	Format	Label	Number	Year	Mint	VG	Notes
These Things Will Keep Me Loving You	7"	Columbia	DB8710	1970	**£10**	**£5**	

CARR, VALERIE

Title	Format	Label	Number	Year	Mint	VG	Notes
Every Hour, Every Day Of My Life	LP	Columbia	33SX1228/ SCX3307	1961	**£10**	**£4**	

CARR, WYNONA

Title	Format	Label	Number	Year	Mint	VG	Notes
I Gotta Stand Tall	7"	Reprise	R20033	1961	**£10**	**£5**	

CARRADINE, DAVID

Title	Format	Label	Number	Year	Mint	VG	Notes
Grasshopper	LP	Jet	JETLP10	1975	**£10**	**£4**	

CARRAGEEN

Title	Format	Label	Number	Year	Mint	VG	Notes
From Clare To Here	LP	Homespun	HRL173	1979	**£10**	**£4**	

CARROLL, ANDREA

Title	Format	Label	Number	Year	Mint	VG	Notes
It Hurts To Be Sixteen	7"	London	HLX9772	1963	**£5**	**£2**	

CARROLL, BARBARA

Title	Format	Label	Number	Year	Mint	VG	Notes
North By Northwest	7"	London	HLR8981	1959	**£5**	**£2**	

CARROLL, BERNADETTE

Title	Format	Label	Number	Year	Mint	VG	Notes
Party Girl	7"	Stateside	SS311	1964	**£4**	**£1.50**	

CARROLL, BOB

Title	Format	Label	Number	Year	Mint	VG	Notes
Hi Ho Silver	7"	London	HLT8724	1958	**£8**	**£4**	
I Can't Get You Out Of My Life	7"	London	HLT8888	1959	**£6**	**£2.50**	
I Love You So Much It Hurts	7"	MGM	SP1132	1955	**£4**	**£1.50**	
Red Confetti, Pink Balloons, & Tambourines	7"	London	HLU8299	1956	**£20**	**£10**	

CARROLL, CATHY

Title	Format	Label	Number	Year	Mint	VG	Notes
Poor Little Puppet	7"	Warner Bros	WB72	1962	**£4**	**£1.50**	

CARROLL, DIAHANN

Title	Format	Label	Number	Year	Mint	VG	Notes
Big Country	7"	London	HLT8788	1959	**£5**	**£2**	
Sings Harold Arlen	LP	RCA	LPM1467	1956	**£20**	**£8**	*US*

CARROLL, JOHNNY & THE HOT ROCKS

Title	Format	Label	Number	Year	Mint	VG	Notes
Hot Rock	7"	Brunswick	05603	1956	**£600**	**£400**	*best auctioned*
Wild Wild Women	7"	Brunswick	05580	1956	**£600**	**£400**	*best auctioned*

CARROLL, RONNIE

Title	Format	Label	Number	Year	Mint	VG	Notes
From Ten Till One	10" LP	Philips	BBR8105	1956	**£15**	**£6**	*with Bill McGuffie*
Lucky Thirteen	LP	Philips	BBL7236	1958	**£12**	**£5**	
Mr And Mrs Is The Name	LP	Philips	(S)BL7591	1964	**£10**	**£4**	*with Millicent Martin*
Sometimes I'm Happy, Sometimes I'm Blue	LP	Philips	BL7563	1963	**£10**	**£4**	
Walk Hand In Hand	7" EP	Philips	BBE12074	1956	**£6**	**£2.50**	

CARROLLS

Title	Format	Label	Number	Year	Mint	VG	Notes
Carrolls	10" LP	Electrocord	EDD1150	1966	**£100**	**£50**	*Romanian*
Come On	7"	CBS	3710	1968	**£4**	**£1.50**	
Surrender Your Love	7"	Polydor	BM56081	1966	**£5**	**£2**	

CARRUTHERS, BEN AND THE DEEP

The 'Jack O'Diamonds' single is of special interest to Bob Dylan collectors, as the song consists of a setting of part of the poetry written by Bob Dylan as sleeve notes for his *Another Side* album. An effective version of the song was also recorded by Fairport Convention on their debut LP.

Title	Format	Label	Number	Year	Mint	VG	Notes
Jack O'Diamonds	7"	Parlophone	R5295	1965	**£25**	**£12.50**	

CARS

Title	Format	Label	Number	Year	Mint	VG	Notes
Candy O	LP	Nautilus	NR49	1981	**£10**	**£4**	*US audiophile*
Cars	LP	Nautilus	NR14	1981	**£10**	**£4**	*US audiophile*
Just What I Needed	7"	Elektra	K12301	1978	**£5**	**£2**	

CARSON, CHAD

Title	Format	Label	Number	Year	Mint	VG	Notes
Don't Pick On Me	7"	HMV	POP1156	1963	**£25**	**£12.50**	

CARSON, JOHNNY

Title	Format	Label	Number	Year	Mint	VG	Notes
Fräulein	7"	Fontana	H243	1960	**£4**	**£1.50**	

Tears Came Rolling Down	7"	Ember	EMBS161	1963	£5	£2	
Teenage Bachelor	7"	Ember	EMBS150	1962	£5	£2	
Train Of Love	7"	Fontana	H259	1960	£4	£1.50	
You Talk Too Much	7"	Fontana	H277	1960	£4	£1.50	

CARSON, KEN

Daniel Boone	7"	London	HLF8237	1956	£15	£7.50	
Hawkeye	7"	London	HLF8213	1955	£20	£10	

CARSON, KIT

Band Of Gold	7"	Capitol	CL14524	1956	£5	£2	

CARTER, ANITA

Blue Doll	7"	London	HLA8693	1958	£10	£5	
Moon Girl	7"	London	HLW9102	1960	£6	£2.50	

CARTER, BENNY

Aspects	LP	London	LTZT15169	1959	£15	£6	
Benny Carter Orchestra	10" LP	Columbia	33C9002	1955	£40	£20	
Jazz Giant	LP	Contemporary	LAC12188	1959	£15	£6	
Swingin' The Twenties	LP	Contemporary	LAC12225	1959	£15	£6	

CARTER, BETTY

Good LIfe	7"	London	HLK9748	1963	£4	£1.50	

CARTER, CALVIN

Twist Along	LP	Vee Jay	LP/SR1041	1962	£15	£6	US

CARTER, CAROLYN

I'm Thru	7"	London	HL9959	1965	£10	£5	

CARTER, CLARENCE

Dynamic	LP	Atlantic	588172	1968	£12	£5	
Looking For A Fox	7"	Atlantic	584176	1968	£5	£2	
Testifyin'	LP	Atlantic	588191	1969	£12	£5	
This Is Clarence Carter	LP	Atlantic	588152	1968	£12	£5	
Thread The Needle	7"	Atlantic	584154	1968	£4	£1.50	

CARTER, HERBIE

Happy Time	7"	Duke	DU4	1968	£6	£2.50	

CARTER, JEAN

No Good Jim	7"	Stateside	SS2114	1968	£4	£1.50	

CARTER, JOHN & RUSS ALQUIST

Laughing Man	7"	Spark	SRL1017	1968	£20	£10	

CARTER, MARTIN

Ups And Downs	LP	Tradition	TSR012	1972	£40	£20	

CARTER, MEL

Easy Listening	LP	Imperial	12319	1966	£10	£4	US
Hold Me, Thrill Me, Kiss Me	7"	Liberty	LIB66113	1966	£15	£7.50	
Hold Me, Thrill Me, Kiss Me	LP	Imperial	12289	1965	£10	£4	US
My Heart Sings	LP	Imperial	12300	1965	£10	£4	US
When A Boy Falls In Love	7"	Pye	7N25212	1963	£4	£1.50	
When A Boy Falls In Love	LP	Derby	LPM702	1963	£50	£25	US

CARTER, MOTHER MAYBELLE

Queen Of The Autoharp	LP	London	HAR8214	1964	£10	£4	

CARTER, SONNY

There Is No Greater Love	7"	Parlophone	MSP6167	1955	£20	£10	*with Earl Bostic*

CARTER, SYDNEY

Lord Of The Dance	7" EP	Elektra	EPK801	1966	£12	£6	

CARTER, SYDNEY & JEREMY TAYLOR

At Eton	LP	Fontana	TL5418	1967	£20	£8	

CARTER FAMILY

Mean As Hell	7" EP	CBS	EP6073	1966	£5	£2	
Mountain Music Vol. 2	7" EP	Brunswick	OE9168	1955	£8	£4	
Original And Great Carter Family Vol. 1	7" EP	RCA	RCX7100	1962	£6	£2.50	
Original And Great Carter Family Vol. 2	7" EP	RCA	RCX7101	1962	£6	£2.50	
Original And Great Carter Family Vol. 3	7" EP	RCA	RCX7102	1962	£6	£2.50	
Original And Great Carter Family Vol. 4	7" EP	RCA	RCX7109	1963	£6	£2.50	
Original And Great Carter Family Vol. 5	7" EP	RCA	RCX7110	1963	£6	£2.50	
Original And Great Carter Family Vol. 6	7" EP	RCA	RCX7111	1963	£6	£2.50	

CARTER LEWIS & THE SOUTHERNERS

Poor Joe	7"	Piccadilly	7N35085	1962	£20	£10	
Skinnie Minnie	7"	Oriole	CB1919	1964	£15	£7.50	
So Much in Love	7"	Piccadilly	7N35004	1961	£15	£7.50	
Sweet And Tender Romance	7"	Oriole	CB1835	1963	£10	£5	
Tell Me	7"	Ember	EMBS165	1962	£30	£15	
Two Timing Baby	7"	Ember	EMBS145	1961	£30	£15	
Your Mama's Out Of Town	7"	Oriole	CB1868	1963	£10	£5	

CARTER THE UNSTOPPABLE SEX MACHINE

Christmas Shoppers Paradise ...... 7" ...... Rough Trade ...... GIFT1 ...... 1990 **£8** ...... **£4** ......

CARTHY, MARTIN

Brigg Fair ...... LP ...... Fontana ...... 6857010 ...... 1967 **£15** ...... **£6** ...... *same LP as Byker Hill*
But Two Came By ...... LP ...... Fontana ...... STL5477 ...... 1968 **£25** ...... **£10** .. *with Dave Swarbrick*
Byker Hill ...... LP ...... Fontana ...... (S)TL5434 ...... 1967 **£25** ...... **£10** .. *with Dave Swarbrick*
Landfall ...... LP ...... Philips ...... 6308049 ...... 1971 **£15** ...... **£6** ......
Martin Carthy ...... LP ...... Fontana ...... (S)TL5269 ...... 1965 **£25** ...... **£10** ......
No Songs ...... 7" EP .. Fontana ...... TE17490 ...... 1967 **£30** ...... **£15** .. *with Dave Swarbrick*
Prince Heathen ...... LP ...... Fontana ...... STL5529 ...... 1969 **£15** ...... **£6** .. *with Dave Swarbrick*
Second Album ...... LP ...... Fontana ...... (S)TL5362 ...... 1966 **£25** ...... **£10** ......
Selections ...... LP ...... Pegasus ...... PEG6 ...... 1971 **£15** ...... **£6** .. *with Dave Swarbrick*
Shearwater ...... LP ...... Mooncrest ...... CREST25 ...... 1974 **£10** ...... **£4** ......
Shearwater ...... LP ...... Pegasus ...... PEG12 ...... 1972 **£15** ...... **£6** ......
Sweet Wivelsfield ...... LP ...... Deram ...... SML1111 ...... 1974 **£15** ...... **£6** ......
This Is Martin Carthy ...... LP ...... Philips ...... 6282022 ...... 1972 **£10** ...... **£4** ......

CARTLAND, BARBARA

Sings An Album Of Love Songs ...... LP ...... State ...... ETAT22 ...... 1978 **£10** ...... **£4** ......

CARTOONE

Cartoone ...... LP ...... Atlantic ...... 588174 ...... 1969 **£20** ...... **£8** ......
Penny for The Sun ...... 7" ...... Atlantic ...... 584240 ...... 1969 **£4** ...... **£1.50** ......

CARTRIDGE, FLIP

Dear Mrs Applebee ...... 7" ...... London ...... HLU10076 ...... 1966 **£4** ...... **£1.50** ......

CARTWRIGHT, DAVE

In The Middle Of The Road ...... LP ...... Harmony ...... DB0001 ...... 1970 **£40** ...... **£20** ......

CARTY, PADDY & MICK O'CONNOR

Traditional Music of Ireland ...... LP ...... Morning Star ... 1 ...... 1974 **£12** ...... **£5** ...... *US*

CASCADES

Maybe The Rain Will Fall ...... LP ...... Uni ...... 73069 ...... 1969 **£15** ...... **£6** ...... *US*
Rhythm Of The Rain ...... 7" EP .. Warner Bros .... WEP1419 ...... 1963 **£20** ...... **£10** ...... *French*
Rhythm Of The Rain ...... 7" EP .. Warner Bros .... WEP6106 ...... 1963 **£20** ...... **£10** ......
Rhythm Of The Rain ...... LP ...... Warner Bros .... WM8127 ...... 1963 **£30** ...... **£15** ......
Vol. 2 ...... 7" EP .. Warner Bros .... WEP1421 ...... 1963 **£20** ...... **£10** ...... *French*
What Goes On ...... LP ...... Cascade ...... 681001 ...... 1968 **£25** ...... **£10** ...... *US*

CASEY, AL & THE K.C.ETTES

Surfing Hootenanny ...... 7" ...... Pye ...... 7N25215 ...... 1963 **£10** ...... **£5** ......

CASEY, HOWIE & THE SENIORS

Bony Moronie ...... 7" ...... Fontana ...... TF403 ...... 1963 **£10** ...... **£5** ......
Double Twist ...... 7" ...... Fontana ...... H364 ...... 1962 **£15** ...... **£7.50** ......
I Ain't Mad At You ...... 7" ...... Fontana ...... H381 ...... 1962 **£10** ...... **£5** ......
Let's Twist ...... LP ...... Wing ...... WL1022 ...... 1965 **£15** ...... **£6** ......
Twist At The Top ...... LP ...... Fontana ...... TFL5180 ...... 1962 **£30** ...... **£15** ......

CASH, ALVIN

Philly Freeze ...... 7" ...... Stateside ...... SS543 ...... 1966 **£10** ...... **£5** ......
Philly Freeze ...... LP ...... President ...... PTL1000 ...... 1966 **£12** ...... **£5** ......
Twine Time ...... 7" ...... Stateside ...... SS386 ...... 1965 **£15** ...... **£7.50** ......

CASH, JOHNNY

All Aboard the Blue Train ...... LP ...... Sun ...... 1270 ...... 1963 **£15** ...... **£6** ...... *US*
All Over Again ...... 7" ...... Philips ...... PB874 ...... 1958 **£5** ...... **£2** ......
Ballad Of A Teenage Queen ...... 7" ...... London ...... HLS8586 ...... 1958 **£10** ...... **£5** ......
Ballad Of A Teenage Queen ...... 7" ...... London ...... HL7032 ...... 1958 **£8** ...... **£4** ...... *export*
Bitter Tears ...... LP ...... CBS ...... (S)BPG62463 ...... 1964 **£10** ...... **£4** ......
Blood, Sweat And Tears ...... LP ...... CBS ...... BPG62119 ...... 1963 **£10** ...... **£4** ......
Christmas Spirit ...... LP ...... CBS ...... (S)BPG62284 ...... 1963 **£10** ...... **£4** ......
Country Boy ...... 7" EP .. London ...... RES1212 ...... 1959 **£20** ...... **£10** ...... *tri-centre*
Don't Take Your Guns To Town ...... 7" ...... Philips ...... PB897 ...... 1959 **£5** ...... **£2** ......
Down The Street To 301 ...... 7" ...... London ...... HLS9182 ...... 1960 **£5** ...... **£2** ......
Fabulous Johnny Cash ...... LP ...... CBS ...... (S)BPG62042 ...... 1961 **£10** ...... **£4** ......
Fabulous Johnny Cash ...... LP ...... Philips ...... BBL7298/ SBBL554 ...... 1959 **£12** ...... **£5** ......
Folsom Prison Blues ...... 7" EP .. CBS ...... EP6601 ...... 1969 **£8** ...... **£4** ......
Forty Shades Of Green ...... 7" ...... Philips ...... PB1148 ...... 1961 **£4** ...... **£1.50** ......
Forty Shades Of Green ...... 7" EP .. CBS ...... AGG20050 ...... 1964 **£10** ...... **£5** ......
Frankie's Man, Johnny ...... 7" ...... Philips ...... PB928 ...... 1959 **£5** ...... **£2** ......
Going To Memphis ...... 7" ...... Philips ...... PB1075 ...... 1960 **£4** ...... **£1.50** ......
Guess Things Happen That Way ...... 7" ...... London ...... HLS8656 ...... 1958 **£8** ...... **£4** ......
Holy Land ...... LP ...... Columbia ...... CS9726 ...... 1969 **£12** ...... **£5** ...... *US, 3D cover*
Holy Land ...... LP ...... CBS ...... 63428 ...... 1968 **£10** ...... **£4** ......
Home Of The Blues ...... 7" ...... London ...... HLS8514 ...... 1957 **£12** ...... **£6** ......
Home Of The Blues ...... 7" ...... London ...... HL7023 ...... 1957 **£10** ...... **£5** ...... *export*
Hymns By Johnny Cash ...... LP ...... Philips ...... BBL7373 ...... 1960 **£10** ...... **£4** ......
I Got Stripes ...... 7" ...... Philips ...... PB953 ...... 1959 **£5** ...... **£2** ......
I Walk The Line ...... 7" ...... London ...... HL8358 ...... 1957 **£60** ...... **£30** ...... *gold label*
I Walk The Line ...... LP ...... CBS ...... (S)BPG62371 ...... 1964 **£10** ...... **£4** ......
It Ain't Me Babe ...... 7" EP .. CBS ...... EP6061 ...... 1965 **£8** ...... **£4** ......

Title	Format	Label	Cat. No.	Year	Mint	VG	Notes
It's Just About Time	7″	London	HLS8789	1959	**£6**	**£2.50**	
Johnny Cash	7″ EP	London	RES1120	1958	**£25**	**£12.50**	*tri-centre*
Johnny Cash No. 2	7″ EP	London	RES1230	1959	**£20**	**£10**	*tri-centre*
Johnny Cash Sings Hank Williams	7″ EP	London	RES1193	1959	**£20**	**£10**	*tri-centre*
Johnny Cash Sings Hank Williams	LP	Sun	1245	1960	**£20**	**£8**	*US*
Johnny Cash With His Hot And Blue Guitar	LP	Sun	1220	1956	**£40**	**£20**	*US*
Johnny Cash's Greatest	LP	Sun	1240	1959	**£30**	**£15**	*US*
Katy Too	7″	London	HLS8928	1959	**£6**	**£2.50**	
Little Drummer Boy	7″	Philips	PB979	1959	**£4**	**£1.50**	
Live At San Quentin	LP	CBS	Q63629	1973	**£10**	**£4**	*quad*
Lonesome Me	LP	London	HAS8253	1966	**£12**	**£5**	
Lure Of The Grand Canyon	LP	Columbia	CL1622/CS8422	1961	**£15**	**£6**	*US*
Luther Played The Boogie	7″	London	HLS8847	1959	**£10**	**£5**	
Mean As Hell	7″ EP	CBS	EP6073	1966	**£8**	**£4**	
Next In Line	7″	London	HLS8461	1957	**£20**	**£10**	
Next In Line	7″	London	HL7020	1957	**£10**	**£5**	*export*
Now Here's Johnny Cash	LP	Sun	1255	1961	**£20**	**£8**	*US*
Now There Was A Song	LP	Philips	BBL7358/ SBBL580	1960	**£10**	**£4**	
Oh Lonesome Me	7″	London	HLS9314	1961	**£4**	**£1.50**	
Original Sun Sound Of Johnny Cash	LP	London	HAS8220	1965	**£12**	**£5**	
Ride This Train	LP	Philips	BBL7417	1960	**£10**	**£4**	
Ring Of Fire	LP	CBS	(S)BPG62171	1963	**£10**	**£4**	
Rock Island Line	LP	London	HAS2179	1959	**£15**	**£6**	
Seasons Of My Heart	7″	Philips	PB1017	1960	**£4**	**£1.50**	
Songs Of Our Soil	7″ EP	Philips	BBE12395	1960	**£10**	**£5**	
Songs Of Our Soil	LP	Philips	BBL7353	1959	**£10**	**£4**	
Songs That Made Him Famous	LP	London	HAS2157	1959	**£20**	**£8**	
Songs That Made Him Famous	LP	Sun	1235	1958	**£30**	**£15**	*US*
Sound Of Johnny Cash	LP	CBS	(S)BPG62073	1962	**£10**	**£4**	
Straight A's In Love	7″	London	HLS9070	1960	**£6**	**£2.50**	
Strictly Cash	7″ EP	Philips	BBE12494	1961	**£10**	**£5**	
Train Of Love	7″	London	HLS8427	1957	**£30**	**£15**	
Troubadour	7″ EP	Philips	BBE12377	1960	**£10**	**£5**	
Ways Of A Woman In Love	7″	London	HLS8709	1958	**£6**	**£2.50**	
Ways Of A Woman In Love	7″	London	HL7053	1958	**£6**	**£2.50**	*export*
You Tell Me	7″	London	HLS8979	1959	**£5**	**£2**	

CASINOS

Title	Format	Label	Cat. No.	Year	Mint	VG	Notes
That's The Way	7″	Ember	EMBS241	1967	**£20**	**£10**	
Then You Can Tell Me Goodbye	7″	President	PT123	1968	**£4**	**£1.50**	
Then You Can Tell Me Goodbye	LP	President	PTL1007	1967	**£10**	**£4**	

CASSIBER

Title	Format	Label	Cat. No.	Year	Mint	VG	Notes
Beauty And The Beast	LP	Recommended	RE0110	1984	**£12**	**£5**	
Perfect Worlds	LP	Recommended	RE0000	1986	**£10**	**£4**	
Time Running Out	7″	Recommended	RE21	1984	**£8**	**£4**	*blue vinyl, 1 side painted*

CASSIDY, JAMES

Title	Format	Label	Cat. No.	Year	Mint	VG	Notes
Empty Road	LP	Claddagh	CCF14	198–	**£20**	**£8**	

CASSIDY, TED

Title	Format	Label	Cat. No.	Year	Mint	VG	Notes
Lurch	7″	Capitol	CL15423	1965	**£12**	**£6**	

CAST

Title	Format	Label	Cat. No.	Year	Mint	VG	Notes
All Change	CD	Polydor	CASTCD1	1995	**£20**	**£8**	*promo sampler in tin*
Cast Sampler	10″	private	GRA001	1994	**£60**	**£30**	*promo*
Finetime	7″	Polydor	5795067	1995	**£5**	**£2**	*green vinyl, with stencil*
Finetime	CD-s	Polydor	5795072	1995	**£8**	**£4**	
Sandstorm	CD-s	Polydor	5779032	1995	**£8**	**£4**	*in tin*

CAST OF THOUSANDS

Title	Format	Label	Cat. No.	Year	Mint	VG	Notes
My Jeannie Wears A Mini	7″	Stateside	SS546	1966	**£10**	**£5**	

CASTANARC

Title	Format	Label	Cat. No.	Year	Mint	VG	Notes
Journey To The East	LP	Peninsula	PENCIL010	1974	**£25**	**£10**	

CASTAWAYS

Title	Format	Label	Cat. No.	Year	Mint	VG	Notes
Liar Liar	7″	London	HL10003	1965	**£12**	**£6**	

CASTELL, JOEY

Title	Format	Label	Cat. No.	Year	Mint	VG	Notes
I'm Left, You're Right, She's Gone	7″	Decca	F10966	1957	**£60**	**£30**	

CASTELLS

Title	Format	Label	Cat. No.	Year	Mint	VG	Notes
Sacred	7″	London	HLN9392	1961	**£15**	**£7.50**	
So This Is Love	7″	London	HLN9551	1962	**£15**	**£7.50**	
So This Is Love	LP	Era	EL/ES109	1962	**£50**	**£25**	*US*

CASTLE, LEE & THE BARONS

Title	Format	Label	Cat. No.	Year	Mint	VG	Notes
Love She Can Count On	7″	Parlophone	R5151	1964	**£6**	**£2.50**	

CASTLE, ROY

Title	Format	Label	Cat. No.	Year	Mint	VG	Notes
Castlewise	LP	Philips	BBL7457/ SBBL626	1961	**£10**	**£4**	
Doctor Terror's House Of Horrors	7″	CBS	201736	1965	**£8**	**£4**	

Title	Format	Label	Cat. No.	Year	Mint	VG	Notes
Little White Berry	7"	Philips	PB1087	1960	£4	£1.50	

CASTLE FARM

Title	Format	Label	Cat. No.	Year	Mint	VG	Notes
Mascot	7"	private		1972	£20	£10	

CASTLE JAZZ BAND

Title	Format	Label	Cat. No.	Year	Mint	VG	Notes
Famous Castle Jazz Band In Hi Fi	LP	Good Time Jazz	LAG12176	1959	£12	£5	
Five Pennies	LP	Good Time Jazz	LAG12207	1960	£12	£5	

CASTLE SISTERS

Title	Format	Label	Cat. No.	Year	Mint	VG	Notes
Stop Your Lying	7"	Ska Beat	JB257	1966	£10	£5	

CASTOR, JIMMY

Title	Format	Label	Cat. No.	Year	Mint	VG	Notes
Hey Leroy	7"	Philips	BF1543	1967	£4	£1.50	
Hey Leroy	LP	Smash	MGS2/SRW67091	1967	£15	£6	US
Magic Saxophone	7"	Philips	BF1590	1967	£10	£5	

CASUAL FOUR

Title	Format	Label	Cat. No.	Year	Mint	VG	Notes
I Can Tell	7"	private	102	196–	£30	£15	

CASUALS

Title	Format	Label	Cat. No.	Year	Mint	VG	Notes
Hour World	LP	Decca	SKL5001	1969	£15	£6	
If You Walk Out	7"	Fontana	TF635	1965	£4	£1.50	
Toy	7"	Decca	F22852	1968	£5	£2	*picture sleeve*

CAT

Title	Format	Label	Cat. No.	Year	Mint	VG	Notes
Run Run Run	7"	Reaction		196–	£125	£62.50	

CAT IRON

Title	Format	Label	Cat. No.	Year	Mint	VG	Notes
Cat Iron	LP	XTRA	XTRA1087	1969	£30	£15	

CAT MOTHER & THE ALL NIGHT NEWSBOYS

The first LP by Cat Mother and the All Night Newsboys was produced by Jimi Hendrix, a fact which once gave the record a higher collectors' value than it now has. The problem is that the group sounds extremely ordinary. Hendrix does not play on the record and the production wizardry that he brought to his own records is nowhere in evidence.

Title	Format	Label	Cat. No.	Year	Mint	VG	Notes
Street Giveth	LP	Polydor	184300	1969	£10	£4	

CATALINAS

Title	Format	Label	Cat. No.	Year	Mint	VG	Notes
Fun Fun Fun	LP	Ric	M1006	1964	£50	£25	US

CATAPILLA

Title	Format	Label	Cat. No.	Year	Mint	VG	Notes
Catapilla	LP	Vertigo	6360029	1971	£40	£20	*spiral label*
Changes	LP	Vertigo	6360074	1972	£200	£100	*spiral label*

CATATONIA

Title	Format	Label	Cat. No.	Year	Mint	VG	Notes
Bleed	7"	Blanco Y Negro	NEG97CD1	1996	£5	£2	
Bleed	7"	Nursery	NYS12L	1995	£15	£7.50	*red vinyl*
Bleed	CD-s	Nursery	NYSCD12	1995	£15	£7.50	
Blow The Millenium Blow	7"	Blanco Y Negro	SAM1746	1995	£15	£7.50	*white vinyl*
For Tinkerbell	CD-s	Crai	CD039	1993	£5	£2	
Hooked	CD-s	Crai	CRAICD042	1994	£5	£2	
Whale	7"	Rough Trade	45rev33	1994	£20	£10	

CATCH

Title	Format	Label	Cat. No.	Year	Mint	VG	Notes
Borderline	7"	Logo	GO103	1977	£30	£15	

CATES, GEORGE

Title	Format	Label	Cat. No.	Year	Mint	VG	Notes
Moonglow	7"	Vogue Coral	Q72162	1956	£6	£2.50	

CATHARSIS

Title	Format	Label	Cat. No.	Year	Mint	VG	Notes
32 Mars	LP	Galloway	GB600507	1973	£10	£4	*French*
Catharsis	LP	Explosive	558004	1971	£15	£6	*French*
Catharsis	LP	Saravah	SH10035	1971	£12	£5	*French*
Et S'Aimer Et Mourir	LP	Festival	678	1978	£10	£4	*French*
Illuminations	LP	Festival	655	1974	£10	£4	*French*
Le Boléro	LP	Festival	676	1976	£10	£4	*French*
Les Chevrons	LP	Festival	651	1972	£12	£5	*French*
Mars	LP	Festival	652	1973	£10	£4	*French*

CATHODE, RAY

Title	Format	Label	Cat. No.	Year	Mint	VG	Notes
Time Beat	7"	Parlophone	R4901	1962	£4	£1.50	

CATHY JEAN & THE ROOMATES

Title	Format	Label	Cat. No.	Year	Mint	VG	Notes
At The Hop!	LP	Valmor	789	1961	£100	£50	US

CATS EYES

Title	Format	Label	Cat. No.	Year	Mint	VG	Notes
Where Is She Now	7"	Deram	DM251	1969	£10	£5	
Wizard	7"	MCA	MK5056	1970	£6	£2.50	

CATS PYJAMAS

Title	Format	Label	Cat. No.	Year	Mint	VG	Notes
Camera Man	7"	Direction	583482	1968	£10	£5	

Title	Format	Label	Cat. No.	Year	Mint	VG+	Notes
Virginia Waters	7"	Direction	583235	1968	**£10**	**£5**	

CATTINI, CLEM

Title	Format	Label	Cat. No.	Year	Mint	VG+	Notes
No Time To Think	7"	Decca	F12135	1965	**£20**	**£10**	

CATTOUSE, NADIA

Title	Format	Label	Cat. No.	Year	Mint	VG+	Notes
Beautiful Barbados	7"	Reality	RE503	1966	**£4**	**£1.50**	
Earth Mother	LP	RCA	SF8070	1969	**£50**	**£6**	
Nadia Cattouse	LP	Reality	RY1001	1966	**£75**	**£37.50**	

CAUSTIC WINDOW

Title	Format	Label	Cat. No.	Year	Mint	VG+	Notes
Joyrex J4	12"	Rephlex	CAT004	1992	**£12**	**£6**	
Joyrex J5	12"	Rephlex	CAT005	1992	**£20**	**£10**	*white vinyl*
Joyrex J5	12"	Rephlex	CAT005	1992	**£12**	**£6**	
Joyrex J9	10"	Rephlex	CAT009i	1993	**£20**	**£10**	*picture disc*
Joyrex J9	12"	Rephlex	CAT009ii	1993	**£6**	**£2.50**	

CAVALLI, PIERRE

Title	Format	Label	Cat. No.	Year	Mint	VG+	Notes
Strictly Guitar	7" EP	HMV	7EG8817	1963	**£5**	**£2**	

CAVE, EDDIE & THE FIX

Title	Format	Label	Cat. No.	Year	Mint	VG+	Notes
Fresh Out Of Tears	7"	Pye	7N17161	1966	**£20**	**£10**	

CAVE, NICK

Title	Format	Label	Cat. No.	Year	Mint	VG+	Notes
Murder Ballads – The Interview	CD	Mute	CAVESPEAK1CD	1996	**£15**	**£6**	*promo*
Scum	7"	Lyntone	LYN18038	1986	**£6**	**£2.50**	*green flexi, poster*
Ship Song	CD-s	Mute	CDMUTE108	1990	**£5**	**£2**	
Weeping Song	CD-s	Mute	CDMUTE118	1990	**£5**	**£2**	*4 track single*

CAVELL, ANDY

Title	Format	Label	Cat. No.	Year	Mint	VG+	Notes
Always On Saturday	7"	HMV	POP1080	1962	**£20**	**£10**	
Andy	7"	Pye	7N15539	1963	**£20**	**£10**	
Hey There Cruel Heart	7"	HMV	POP1024	1962	**£20**	**£10**	
Tell The Truth	7"	Pye	7N15610	1964	**£20**	**£10**	

CAVELLO, JIMMY & THE HOUSE ROCKERS

Title	Format	Label	Cat. No.	Year	Mint	VG+	Notes
Footstomping	7"	Vogue Coral	Q72240	1957	**£200**	**£100**	*best auctioned*
Rock Rock Rock	7"	Vogue Coral	Q72226	1957	**£175**	**£87.50**	

CAZAZZA, MONTE

Title	Format	Label	Cat. No.	Year	Mint	VG+	Notes
Something For Nobody	7"	Industrial	IR0010	1980	**£5**	**£2**	
To Mom On Mother's Day	7"	Industrial	IR0005	1979	**£8**	**£4**	

CCS

Title	Format	Label	Cat. No.	Year	Mint	VG+	Notes
CCS	LP	RAK	SRKA6751	1970	**£10**	**£4**	

CECCARELLI, ANDRE

Title	Format	Label	Cat. No.	Year	Mint	VG+	Notes
André Ceccarelli	LP	Carla	CAR500002	1977	**£25**	**£10**	*French*

CEDARS

Title	Format	Label	Cat. No.	Year	Mint	VG+	Notes
For Your Information	7"	Decca	F22720	1968	**£25**	**£12.50**	
I Like The Way	7"	Decca	F22772	1968	**£20**	**£10**	

CELEBRATED RATLIFFE STOUT BAND

The Celebrated Ratliffe Stout Band was formed by eccentric folk singer-songwriter Tom Hall, and includes the playing of Gerald Claridge, Mark Griffiths and other stalwarts of the Northampton music scene. The earliest recording, *Songs And Tales*, is a duo Hall/Jay Woodhall venture, and is sufficiently rare that Tom Hall himself does not have a copy.

Title	Format	Label	Cat. No.	Year	Mint	VG+	Notes
Behind The Mask	LP	Plant Life	PLR020	1981	**£25**	**£10**	
Dan Half Dan And The Spaceman	LP	private		1976	**£125**	**£62.50**	
Songs And Tales From Greenwood Edge	LP	private	DT21	1976	**£150**	**£75**	
Vanlag	LP	Plant Life	PLR030	1981	**£25**	**£10**	

CELESTIN, OSCAR 'PAPA'

Title	Format	Label	Cat. No.	Year	Mint	VG+	Notes
New Orleans Band	10" LP	Melodisc	MLP506	1956	**£15**	**£6**	

CELIA & THE MUTATIONS

Title	Format	Label	Cat. No.	Year	Mint	VG+	Notes
You Better Believe Me	7"	United Artists	UP36318	1977	**£5**	**£2**	*picture sleeve*

CELTIC FOLKWEAVE

Title	Format	Label	Cat. No.	Year	Mint	VG+	Notes
Celtic Folkweave	LP	Polydor	2908013	1974	**£30**	**£15**	

CENOTAPH CORNER

Title	Format	Label	Cat. No.	Year	Mint	VG+	Notes
Every Day But Wednesday	LP	Cottage	COT031	1979	**£20**	**£8**	
Ups And Downs	LP	Cottage	COT501	1976	**£20**	**£8**	

CENTAURUS

Title	Format	Label	Cat. No.	Year	Mint	VG+	Notes
Centaurus	LP	Azra	61549	1978	**£40**	**£20**	*US picture disc*

CENTIPEDE

Centipede was so named because of its huge line-up: fifty-five people play on the record, not including Robert Fripp, who played guitar with the band on stage, but who remains in the producer's chair here. Centipede was the inspiration of jazz pianist Keith Tippett, as a piece of mad indulgence that would be unlikely to make anyone's fortune. *Septober Energy* is a single piece of music spread over four sides of vinyl, but it falls naturally into sections, which enable different combinations of musicians to be highlighted.

Title	Format	Label	Cat. No.	Year	Mint	VG+	Notes
Septober Energy	LP	Neon	NE9	1971	**£50**	**£25**	*double*
Septober Energy	LP	RCA	DPS2054	1974	**£30**	**£15**	*different cover*

CENTURIANS

Surfers' Pajama Party	LP	Del Fi	DFST128	1964	£30	£15	US

CENTURY 21

Alias Mister Hackenbacker	7" EP	Century 21	MA123	1967	£20	£10	
Atlantic Inferno	7" EP	Century 21	MA125	1967	£20	£10	
Brink Of Disaster	7" EP	Century 21	MA124	1967	£20	£10	
Captain Scarlet & The Mysterons	7" EP	Century 21	MA132	1967	£20	£10	
Captain Scarlet Is Indestructible	7" EP	Century 21	MA133	1967	£20	£10	
Captain Scarlet Of Spectrum	7" EP	Century 21	MA134	1967	£20	£10	
Captain Scarlet Vs Captain Black	7" EP	Century 21	MA135	1967	£20	£10	
Chain Chain	7" EP	Century 21	MA122	1967	£20	£10	
Daleks	7" EP	Century 21	MA106	1966	£30	£15	
Day Of Disaster	7" EP	Century 21	MA121	1967	£20	£10	
Desperate Intruder	7" EP	Century 21	MA119	1966	£20	£10	
Fab	7" EP	Century 21	MA107	1966	£12	£6	
Favourite Television Themes	LP	Century 21	LA6	1966	£25	£10	
Great Themes From Thunderbirds	7" EP	Century 21	MA116	1966	£15	£7.50	
Imposters	7" EP	Century 21	MA120	1966	£15	£7.50	
Into Action With Troy Tempest	7" EP	Century 21	MA101	1965	£10	£5	
Introducing Captain Scarlet	7" EP	Century 21	MA131	1967	£20	£10	
Introducing Thunderbirds	7" EP	Century 21	MA103	1965	£10	£5	
Jeff Tracy Introduces International Rescues	LP	Century 21	LA3	1966	£30	£15	
Journey To The Moon	7" EP	Century 21	MA100	1965	£10	£5	
Journey To The Moon	LP	Century 21	LA100	1965	£40	£20	
Lady Penelope & Other TV Themes	7" EP	Century 21	MA111	1966	£15	£7.50	
Lady Penelope Investigates	LP	Century 21	LA4	1966	£30	£15	
Lady Penelope Presents	LP	Century 21	LA2	1966	£30	£15	
Marina Speaks	7" EP	Century 21	MA104	1965	£10	£5	
One Move And You're Dead	7" EP	Century 21	MA128	1967	£20	£10	
Perils Of Penelope	7" EP	Century 21	MA114	1966	£15	£7.50	
Ricochet	7" EP	Century 21	MA126	1967	£20	£10	
Space Age Nursery Rhymes	7" EP	Century 21	MA117	1966	£20	£10	
Stately Home Robberies	7" EP	Century 21	MA110	1966	£15	£7.50	
Thirty Minutes After Noon	7" EP	Century 21	MA129	1967	£20	£10	
Thunderbird Four	7" EP	Century 21	MA113	1966	£12	£6	
Thunderbird One	7" EP	Century 21	MA108	1966	£12	£6	
Thunderbird Three	7" EP	Century 21	MA112	1966	£12	£6	
Thunderbird Two	7" EP	Century 21	MA109	1966	£12	£6	
Thunderbirds And Captain Scarlet	LP	Hallmark	HMA227	1973	£10	£4	
Tingha And Tucker And The Wombaville Band	7" EP	Century 21	MA127	1967	£20	£10	
Tingha And Tucker Club Song Book	LP	Century 21	LA5	1966	£25	£10	
Tingha And Tucker In Nursery Rhyme Time	7" EP	Century 21	MA130	1967	£20	£10	
Topo Gigio In London	7" EP	Century 21	MA115	1966	£20	£10	
Trip To Marineville	7" EP	Century 21	MA102	1965	£10	£5	
TV Favourites Vol. 1	LP	Marble Arch	MAL770	1968	£15	£6	
TV Favourites Vol. 2	LP	Marble Arch	MAL771	1968	£15	£8	
TV Themes	7" EP	Century 21	MA136	1967	£20	£10	
TV21 Themes	7" EP	Century 21	MA105	1965	£10	£5	
Vault Of Death	7" EP	Century 21	MA118	1966	£20	£10	
World Of Tomorrow	LP	Century 21	LA1	1965	£30	£15	

CESANA

Tender Emotions	LP	Modern	M100	1964	£12	£5	US

CEYLEIB PEOPLE

Tanyet	LP	Vault	LP117	1968	£100	£50	US

CHAFFIN, ERNIE

Lonesome For My Baby	7"	London	HLS8409	1957	£100	£50	

CHAINO

Africana	LP	London	SAHD6078	1959	£10	£4	

CHAINSAW

Police And Politicians	7"	Square	SQSP2	1980	£50	£25	

CHAIRMEN OF THE BOARD

Bittersweet	LP	Invictus	SVT1006	1972	£12	£5	
Chairmen Of The Board	LP	Invictus	SVT1002	1970	£12	£5	
Greatest Hits	LP	Invictus	SVT1009	1973	£12	£5	
In Session	LP	Invictus	SVT1003	1971	£12	£5	
Skin I'm In	LP	Invictus	65868	1974	£12	£5	

CHAKACHAS

Jungle Fever	LP	Polydor	2489050	1972	£10	£4	

CHAKIRIS, GEORGE

Cool	7"	Saga	SAG452905	1959	£5	£2	
I'm Always Chasing Rainbows	7"	Triumph	RGM1010	1960	£25	£12.50	

CHALIBAUCHE

Les Noces Du Papillon	LP	CEZ	1017	1976	£15	£6	French

CHALKER, BRYAN

Title	Format	Label	Cat. No.	Year	Mint	VG	Notes
Bryan Chalker	LP	Chapter One	CMS1017	1973	**£10**	**£4**	
Daddy Sing Me A Song	LP	Chapter One	CMS1020	1974	**£10**	**£4**	
Early Days	LP	Sweet Folk & Country	SFAO20	1975	**£10**	**£4**	
From Waters Of The Medway	LP	BBC	REC206	1975	**£10**	**£4**	
Hanging Of Samuel Hall	LP	Avenue	AVE071	1971	**£150**	**£75**	
New Frontier	LP	Chapter One	CMS1010	1972	**£25**	**£10**	
Songs And Ballads	LP	Sweet Folk & Country	SFAO25	1975	**£10**	**£4**	

CHALLENGER

Title	Format	Label	Cat. No.	Year	Mint	VG	Notes
So Sure Of Yourself	7"	CMC	CM0001	1981	**£10**	**£5**	

CHALLENGERS

Title	Format	Label	Cat. No.	Year	Mint	VG	Notes
At The Teenage Fair	LP	GNP-Crescendo	(S)2010	1965	**£25**	**£10**	*US*
Billy Strange And The Challengers	LP	GNP-Crescendo	(S)2030	1966	**£20**	**£8**	*US*
Bulldog	7"	Stateside	SS177	1963	**£5**	**£2**	
California Kicks	LP	GNP-Crescendo	(S)2025	1966	**£25**	**£10**	*US*
Challengers Au Go-Go	LP	Vault	LP/VS110	1966	**£25**	**£10**	*US*
Greatest Hits	LP	Vault	LP/VS111	1967	**£20**	**£8**	*US*
K-39	LP	Vault	LP107	1964	**£25**	**£10**	*US*
Light My Fire	LP	GNP-Crescendo	S2045	1968	**£20**	**£8**	*US*
Man From UNCLE	7"	Vocalion	VN9253	1965	**£8**	**£4**	
Man From UNCLE	LP	GNP-Crescendo	(S)2018	1965	**£25**	**£10**	*US*
On The Move	LP	Vault	LP/VS102	1963	**£25**	**£10**	*US*
Sidewalk Surfing	LP	Triumph	(TR)100	1965	**£25**	**£10**	*US*
Surf's Up	LP	Vault	LP/VS109	1965	**£25**	**£10**	*US*
Surfbeat	LP	Stateside	SL10030	1963	**£30**	**£15**	
Surfing	LP	Vault	LP/VS101	1963	**£30**	**£15**	*US*
Twenty-Five Great Instrumental Hits	LP	GNP-Crescendo	(S)609	1967	**£20**	**£8**	*US*
Vanilla Funk	LP	GNP-Crescendo	S2056	1970	**£15**	**£6**	*US*
Walk With Me	7"	Vocalion	VN9270	1966	**£4**	**£1.50**	
Wipe Out	7" EP	Vogue	INT18094	1966	**£20**	**£10**	*French*
Wipe Out	LP	Vocalion	VAN/SAVN8069	1967	**£25**	**£10**	

CHALLENGERS *(2)*

Title	Format	Label	Cat. No.	Year	Mint	VG	Notes
Cry Of The Wild Goose	7"	Parlophone	R4773	1961	**£5**	**£2**	

CHALMERS, LLOYD

Title	Format	Label	Cat. No.	Year	Mint	VG	Notes
Big Red Bum Ball	7"	Smash	SMA2302	1970	**£4**	**£1.50**	
Cooyah	7"	Duke	DU15	1969	**£4**	**£1.50**	*Uniques B side*
Death A Come	7"	Explosion	EX2001	1969	**£4**	**£1.50**	
Dollars And Bonds	7"	Bullet	BU435	1970	**£4**	**£1.50**	
Duckey Luckey	7"	Songbird	SB1007	1969	**£4**	**£1.50**	
Five To Five	7"	Duke	DU25	1969	**£4**	**£1.50**	
Follow This Sound	7"	Duke	DU16	1969	**£4**	**£1.50**	
For The Good Times	7"	Duke	DU162	1973	**£4**	**£1.50**	
Hi Shan	7"	Escort	ES836	1970	**£5**	**£2**	
House In Session	LP	Pama	SECO25	1970	**£25**	**£10**	
I'm Gonna Love You Just A Little	7"	Trojan	MJ6662	1974	**£4**	**£1.50**	
Ling Tong Tong	7"	Songbird	SB1001	1969	**£4**	**£1.50**	
Oh Me Oh My	7"	Trojan	TR7788	1970	**£5**	**£2**	
Ready Talk	7"	Explosion	EX2034	1970	**£4**	**£1.50**	
Reggae A Bye Bye	7"	Bullet	BU442	1970	**£4**	**£1.50**	
Reggae Charm	LP	Trojan	TTL30	1970	**£12**	**£5**	
Reggae Is Tight	LP	Trojan	TTL25	1970	**£12**	**£5**	
Safari	7"	Duke	DU36	1969	**£4**	**£1.50**	
Save The People	7"	Green Door	GD4064	1973	**£5**	**£2**	
Time Is Getting Hard	7"	Coxsone	CS7023	1967	**£10**	**£5**	*Tony Gregory B side*
Vengeance	7"	Explosion	EX2032	1970	**£5**	**£2**	
Why Baby	7"	Gas	GAS114	1969	**£5**	**£2**	

CHALOFF, SERGE

Title	Format	Label	Cat. No.	Year	Mint	VG	Notes
Blue Serge	LP	Capitol	T742	1956	**£20**	**£8**	
Fable Of Mabel	LP	Vogue	LAE12052	1957	**£40**	**£20**	
Lestorian Mode	LP	Realm	RM113	1963	**£12**	**£5**	*with tracks by Stan Getz & Brew Moore*

CHAMAELEON CHURCH

Film star Chevy Chase was the drummer and keyboard player with this obscure pop band (who come on like a less inspired version of the Left Banke), while the two guitarists became part of the line-up of the second, less interesting, version of cult band Ultimate Spinach.

Title	Format	Label	Cat. No.	Year	Mint	VG	Notes
Chamaeleon Church	LP	MGM	SE4574	1968	**£30**	**£15**	*US*

CHAMBER POP ENSEMBLE

Title	Format	Label	Cat. No.	Year	Mint	VG	Notes
Chamber Pop Ensemble	LP	Decca	SKL4933	1968	**£10**	**£4**	

CHAMBERLAIN, RICHARD

Title	Format	Label	Cat. No.	Year	Mint	VG	Notes
Richard Chamberlain Hits	7" EP	MGM	MGMEP776	1963	**£5**	**£2**	

Title	Format	Label	Cat. No.	Year	Mint	VG	Notes
Richard Chamberlain Sings	LP	MGM	C923	1963	£10	£4	

CHAMBERS BROTHERS

Title	Format	Label	Cat. No.	Year	Mint	VG	Notes
Call Me	7"	Vocalion	VP9276	1966	£5	£2	
Feelin' The Blues	LP	Liberty	LBS83276	1970	£10	£4	
Greatest Hits	LP	Vault	135	1970	£10	£4	US
Love Me Like The Rain	7"	Vocalion	VP9267	1966	£5	£2	
Love, Peace And Happiness	LP	CBS	66228	1970	£12	£5	double
New Generation	LP	CBS	64156	1971	£10	£4	
New Time – A New Day	LP	Direction	863451	1969	£10	£4	
Now	LP	Vault	115	1967	£15	£6	US
Oh My God	LP	Columbia	KC31158	1972	£10	£4	US
People Get Ready	LP	Vocalion	VAL/SAVL8058	1966	£20	£8	
Shout!	LP	Liberty	LBS83272	1969	£15	£6	
Time Has Come Today	LP	Direction	863407	1968	£10	£4	

CHAMBERS, JACK & RALPH HODGE

Title	Format	Label	Cat. No.	Year	Mint	VG	Notes
Country & Western Express Vol. 2	7" EP	Top Rank	JKP2056	1960	£5	£2	

CHAMBERS, PAUL

Title	Format	Label	Cat. No.	Year	Mint	VG	Notes
Bass On Top	LP	Blue Note	BLP/BST81569	196–	£25	£10	
Whims Of Chambers	LP	Blue Note	BLP/BST81534	196–	£25	£10	

CHAMBLEE, EDDIE

Title	Format	Label	Cat. No.	Year	Mint	VG	Notes
Blues For Eddie	78	Esquire	10330	1953	£8	£3	
Chamblee Music	LP	Emarcy	EJL1281	1958	£15	£6	
Cradle Rock	78	Esquire	10340	1953	£8	£3	

CHAMELEONS

Title	Format	Label	Cat. No.	Year	Mint	VG	Notes
In Shreds	12"	Statik	TAK2912	1985	£6	£2.50	
In Shreds	7"	Epic	EPCA2210	1982	£10	£5	
In Shreds	7"	Statik	TAK29	1985	£4	£1.50	
Person Isn't Safe Anywhere These Days	7"	Statik	TAK6	1983	£4	£1.50	
Script Of The Bridge	LP	Statik	STATP17	1985	£15	£6	picture disc
Tears	7"	Geffen	GEF4/SAM287	1986	£5	£2	double
Tony Fletcher Walked On Water	12"	Glass Pyramid	EMC1	1990	£12	£6	
Tony Fletcher Walked On Water	CD-s	Glass Pyramid	EMCD1	1990	£15	£7.50	

CHAMPIONS

Title	Format	Label	Cat. No.	Year	Mint	VG	Notes
Circlorama	7"	Oriole	CB1854	1963	£5	£2	

CHAMPS

Title	Format	Label	Cat. No.	Year	Mint	VG	Notes
All American Music	LP	Challenge	CHL/CHS614	1962	£25	£10	US
Another Four By The Champs	7" EP	London	REH1209	1959	£25	£12.50	
Beatnick	7"	London	HLH8811	1959	£5	£2	
Cantina	7"	London	HLH9430	1961	£4	£1.50	
Caramba	7"	London	HLH8864	1959	£5	£2	
Chariot Rock	7"	London	HL8715	1958	£6	£2.50	
El Rancho Rock	7"	London	HL8655	1958	£6	£2.50	
Everybody's Rockin'	LP	London	HAH2184	1959	£30	£15	
Experiment In Terror	7"	London	HLH9539	1962	£4	£1.50	
Four By The Champs	7" EP	London	RE1176	1959	£25	£12.50	
Go Champs Go	LP	London	HAH2152	1958	£30	£15	
Great Dance Hits	LP	London	HAH2451	1962	£20	£8	
Knockouts	7" EP	London	REH1250	1961	£25	£12.50	
Latin Limbo	7"	London	HLH9604	1962	£4	£1.50	
Limbo Rock	7"	London	HLH9506	1962	£4	£1.50	
Still More By The Champs	7" EP	London	REH1223	1959	£25	£12.50	
Tequila	7"	London	HLU8580	1958	£6	£2.50	
Too Much Tequila	7"	London	HL9052	1960	£4	£1.50	

CHAMPS (2)

Title	Format	Label	Cat. No.	Year	Mint	VG	Notes
Walk Between Your Enemies	7"	Blue Beat	BB267	1964	£12	£6	

CHANCE, ROB & CHANCES R

Title	Format	Label	Cat. No.	Year	Mint	VG	Notes
At The End Of The Day	7"	CBS	3130	1967	£4	£1.50	

CHANCES ARE

Title	Format	Label	Cat. No.	Year	Mint	VG	Notes
Fragile Child	7"	Columbia	DB8144	1967	£20	£10	

CHANCES R

Title	Format	Label	Cat. No.	Year	Mint	VG	Notes
Do It Yourself	7"	CBS	2940	1967	£4	£1.50	
Talking Out The Back Of My Head	7"	CBS	202614	1967	£4	£1.50	

CHANDELLE, DANY

Title	Format	Label	Cat. No.	Year	Mint	VG	Notes
Lying Awake	7"	Columbia	DB7540	1965	£10	£5	

CHANDLER, BARBARA

Title	Format	Label	Cat. No.	Year	Mint	VG	Notes
Do You Really Love Me Too	7"	London	HLR9823	1963	£5	£2	
Lonely New Year	7"	London	HLR9861	1964	£5	£2	

CHANDLER, GENE

Title	Format	Label	Cat. No.	Year	Mint	VG	Notes
Bless Our Love	7"	Stateside	SS364	1964	£6	£2.50	
Duke Of Earl	7"	Columbia	DB4793	1962	£20	£10	
Duke Of Earl	LP	Fontana	TL5247	1962	£40	£20	
Duke Of Soul	LP	Checker	LP(S)3003	1967	£15	£6	US
Fool For You	7"	Stateside	SS500	1966	£8	£4	
Girl Don't Care	7"	Coral	Q72490	1967	£10	£5	

Girl Don't Care	LP	Coral	LVA9236	1967	**£25**	**£10**	
Good Times	7"	Stateside	SS458	1965	**£8**	**£4**	
Greatest Hits	LP	Constellation	LP1421	1964	**£20**	**£8**	*US*
I Can't Save It	7"	Action	ACT4551	1969	**£20**	**£10**	
Just Be True	LP	Constellation	LP1423	1964	**£20**	**£8**	*US*
Live On Stage	LP	Action	ACLP6010	1969	**£25**	**£10**	
Nothing Can Stop Me	7"	Soul City	SC102	1968	**£6**	**£2.50**	
Nothing Can Stop Me	7"	Stateside	SS425	1965	**£30**	**£15**	
Song Called Soul	7"	Stateside	SS331	1964	**£8**	**£4**	
Such A Pretty Thing	7"	Chess	CRS8047	1966	**£15**	**£7.50**	
There Was A Time	LP	MCA	MUPS367	1968	**£12**	**£5**	
What Now	7"	Stateside	SS388	1965	**£8**	**£4**	
You Can't Hurt Me No More	7"	Stateside	SS401	1965	**£6**	**£2.50**	
You Threw A Lucky Punch	7"	Stateside	SS185	1963	**£10**	**£5**	
You're A Lady	7"	Mercury	6052098	1971	**£4**	**£1.50**	

CHANDLER, JEFF

Half Of My Heart	7"	London	HLU8484	1957	**£6**	**£2.50**	
I Should Care	7"	Brunswick	05264	1954	**£6**	**£2.50**	
Sings To You	LP	London	HAU2100	1958	**£20**	**£8**	

CHANDLER, KAREN

My Own True Love	7"	Salvo	SLO1803	1962	**£10**	**£5**	

CHANDLER, KENNY

Beyond Love	7"	Stateside	SS2110	1968	**£30**	**£15**	

CHANNEL, BRUCE

Blue And Lonesome	7"	London	HLU9776	1963	**£4**	**£1.50**	
Going Back To Louisiana	7"	London	HLU9841	1964	**£4**	**£1.50**	
Hey Baby!	LP	Mercury	MMC14104	1962	**£20**	**£8**	
Keep On	LP	Bell	MBLL/SBLL111	1969	**£12**	**£5**	

CHANNEL 3

I've Got A Gun	7"	No Future	OI11	1982	**£5**	**£2**	

CHANTAYS

Beyond	7"	King	KG1018	1965	**£8**	**£4**	
Pipeline	7"	London	HLD9696	1963	**£5**	**£2**	
Pipeline	7"	Dot	DS26757	1967	**£4**	**£1.50**	
Pipeline	7" EP	London	RED1397	1963	**£40**	**£20**	
Pipeline	LP	London	HAD/SHD8087	1963	**£30**	**£15**	
Pipeline	LP	Downey	DLP1002	1963	**£100**	**£50**	*US*
Two Sides Of The Chantays	LP	Dot	DLP3771/25771	1966	**£30**	**£15**	*US*

CHANTELLES

Blue Moon	7"	CBS	2777	1967	**£5**	**£2**	
Gonna Get Burned	7"	Parlophone	R5350	1965	**£5**	**£2**	
I Think Of You	7"	Parlophone	R5431	1966	**£4**	**£1.50**	
I Want That Boy	7"	Parlophone	R5271	1965	**£6**	**£2.50**	
Secret Of My Success	7"	Parlophone	R5303	1965	**£4**	**£1.50**	
There's Something About You	7"	Polydor	56119	1966	**£6**	**£2.50**	

CHANTELS

Eternally	7"	Capitol	CL15297	1963	**£5**	**£2**	
Look In My Eyes	7"	London	HLL9428	1961	**£15**	**£7.50**	
Maybe	7"	London	HLU8561	1958	**£300**	**£180**	*best auctioned*
On Tour	LP	Carlton	(ST)LP144	1961	**£75**	**£37.50**	*US*
Still	7"	London	HLL9480	1962	**£12**	**£6**	
Summertime	7"	London	HLL9532	1962	**£12**	**£6**	
There's Our Song Again	LP	End	LP312	1962	**£30**	**£15**	*US*
We're The Chantels	LP	End	LP301	1958	**£300**	**£180**	*US, group photo cover*
We're The Chantels	LP	End	LP301	1959	**£150**	**£75**	*US, jukebox cover*

CHANTER

Suburban Ethnia	LP	Expert	ELP1	1977	**£15**	**£6**	

CHANTERS

Every Night I Sit And Cry	7"	CBS	202454	1966	**£4**	**£1.50**	
My Love Is For You	7"	CBS	3668	1968	**£4**	**£1.50**	
What's Wrong With You	7"	CBS	3400	1968	**£4**	**£1.50**	
You Can't Fool Me	7"	CBS	202616	1967	**£6**	**£2.50**	

CHANTS

The Chants were a black Merseybeat group with a style that took rather more from fifties doo-wop than did any of their contemporaries. They found little success then, but, with a name change to the Real Thing, in the seventies and eighties the group scored numerous big chart hits, including a UK number one.

Ain't Nobody Home	7"	Page One	POF016	1967	**£4**	**£1.50**	
Come Back & Get This Loving Boy	7"	Fontana	TF716	1966	**£5**	**£2**	
I Could Write A Book	7"	Pye	7N15591	1964	**£4**	**£1.50**	
I Don't Care	7"	Pye	7N15557	1963	**£4**	**£1.50**	
I Get The Sweetest Feeling	7"	RCA	RCA1823	1969	**£5**	**£2**	
I've Been Trying	7"	Chipping Norton	CHIP2	1976	**£15**	**£7.50**	
Love Is A Playground	7"	Fresh Air	6121109	1974	**£5**	**£2**	

Lover's Story	7"	Decca	F12650	1967	£4	£1.50	
Man Without A Face	7"	RCA	RCA1754	1968	£40	£20	
She's Mine	7"	Pye	7N15643	1964	£4	£1.50	
Sweet Was The Wine	7"	Pye	7N15691	1964	£4	£1.50	

CHANTS (2)

Close Friends	7"	Capitol	CL14876	1958	£6	£2.50	

CHAPIN BROTHERS

Chapin Music	LP	Rockland	66	1967	£40	£20	US

CHAPLAIN, PAUL & THE EMERALDS

Shortning Bread	7"	London	HLU9205	1960	£15	£7.50	

CHAPMAN, GENE

Oklahoma Blues	7"	Starlite	ST45102	1963	£200	£100	best auctioned

CHAPMAN, MICHAEL

Almost Alone	LP	Black Crow	CRO202	1981	£10	£4	
Deal Gone Down	LP	Deram	SML1114	1974	£10	£4	
Fully Qualified Survivor	LP	Harvest	SHVL764	1969	£12	£5	
Guitars	LP	Standard	ESL146	197–	£50	£25	
Lady On The Rocks	LP	Intercord	126309	1980	£10	£4	German
Life On The Ceiling	LP	Criminal	STEAL5	1978	£10	£4	
Lived Here	LP	Cube	GNAT1	1977	£10	£4	
Looking For Eleven	LP	Criminal	STEAL9	1980	£10	£4	
Man Who Hated Mornings	LP	Decca	SKLR5290	1977	£10	£4	
Millstone Grit	LP	Deram	SML1105	1973	£12	£5	
Playing Guitar The Easy Way	LP	Criminal	STEAL2	1978	£10	£4	
Pleasures Of The Street	LP	Nova	622321	1975	£10	£4	German
Rainmaker	LP	Harvest	SHVL755	1969	£12	£5	
Savage Amusement	LP	Decca	SKLR5242	1976	£12	£5	
Window	LP	Harvest	SHVL786	1971	£12	£5	
Wrecked Again	LP	Harvest	SHVL798	1971	£12	£5	

CHAPMAN, TRACY

Baby Can I Hold You	CD-s	Elektra	EKR82CD	1988	£5	£2	
Fast Car	CD-s	Elektra	EKR73CD	1988	£5	£2	3" single
Talkin' 'Bout A Revolution	CD-s	Elektra	EKR78CD	1988	£5	£2	

CHAPS

Popping Medley	7"	Parlophone	R4979	1962	£10	£5	

CHAPTER FIVE

Anything That You Do	7"	CBS	202395	1966	£400	£250	best auctioned
One In A Million	7"	CBS	2696	1967	£150	£75	

CHAPTER FOUR

In My Life	7"	United Artists	UP1143	1966	£150	£75	

CHAPTER FOUR (2)

Chapter Four	7" EP	GSP	11009/10	196–	£60	£30	

CHAPTER FOUR (3)

Hanging Around Sterling	LP	Bridge	BR001	1980	£25	£10	

CHAPTER TWO

Page One	LP	Philips	655023	1966	£40	£20	Dutch

CHAPTERS

Can't Stop Thinking About Her	7"	Pye	7N15815	1965	£25	£12.50	

CHARGE

Zeugma	7"	private		1970	£15	£7.50	

CHARGE (2)

Charge	LP	SRT		1973	£600	£400	

CHARGE (3)

Charge	LP	Fresh Air	6308900	1974	£20	£8	

CHARIG, MARC

Pipedream	LP	Ogun	OG710	1977	£12	£5	with Keith Tippett & Ann Winter

CHARIOT

Chariot	LP	National General	NG2003	1968	£60	£30	US

CHARLATANS

The original Charlatans were one of the great, pioneering San Francisco groups, but only the Kapp single comes anywhere near to capturing them at their peak. By the time the Charlatans got to make an album, several of the founder members had departed and the moment had passed.

32:20	7"	Kapp	779	1966	£20	£10	US
Alabama Bound	LP	Eva	12017	1983	£12	£5	French
Charlatans	LP	Philips	SBL7903	1969	£60	£30	

Title	Format	Label	Cat. No.	Year	Mint	VG	Notes
Charlatans	LP	Groucho Marx		1979	£**20**	£**8**	*Italian*

CHARLATANS (2)

Title	Format	Label	Cat. No.	Year	Mint	VG	Notes
Between 10th And 11th	CD	Situation Two	SITU37	1992	£**25**	£**10**	*promo box with cassette and video*
Chemical Brothers Remixes	12″	Beggars Banquet	CHAR13	1995	£**6**	£**2.50**	
Happen To Die	7″	Beggars Banquet	CHAR1	1991	£**6**	£**2.50**	*promo*
I Never Want An Easy Life	CD-s	Beggars Banquet	BBQ31CD1	1994	£**10**	£**5**	*boxed with 3 cards*
Indian Rope	12″	Dead Dead Good	GOOD ONE	1990	£**12**	£**6**	[illegible]
Indian Rope	CD-s	Dead Dead Good	GOOD1CD	1991	£**6**	£**2.50**	
Isolation (Live At Chicago Metro)	LP	Live Live Good	CB2	1991	£**12**	£**5**	*fan club issue*
Isolation 21.2.91	LP	Live Live Good	CB2	1991	£**15**	£**6**	
Me In Time	CD-s	Situation 2	SIT84CD	1991	£**5**	£**2**	
Melting Pot	CD	Beggars Banquet	CHAR14	1995	£**20**	£**8**	*promo sampler*
October '89	cass	Dead Dead Good	no number	1989	£**15**	£**6**	
Only One I Know	CD-s	Situation 2	SIT70CD	1990	£**5**	£**2**	
Over Rising	CD-s	Situation 2	SIT76CD	1991	£**5**	£**2**	
Polar Bear	12″	Situation Two	SIT74T	1990	£**60**	£**30**	*test pressing*
Subterranean	CD-s	Beggars Banquet	CHAR7	1993	£**5**	£**2**	
Subterranean (Live)	CD-s	Beggars Banquet	CHAR7	1993	£**8**	£**4**	*with fan club magazine*
Then	CD-s	Situation 2	SIT74CD	1990	£**5**	£**2**	
Up To Our Hips	CD	Beggars Banquet	BBCD147	1994	£**25**	£**10**	*promo box with cassette and video*
Weirdo	CD-s	Situation Two	SIT88CD	1992	£**5**	£**2**	

CHARLEE

Title	Format	Label	Cat. No.	Year	Mint	VG	Notes
Charlee	LP	RCA	LSP4809	1972	£**40**	£**20**	*Canadian*
Charlee	LP	Mind Dust	MDM1001	1976	£**15**	£**6**	*Canadian*

CHARLES, BOBBY

'See You Later Alligator' by Bobby Charles has the distinction of being the most valuable single issued commercially in the UK. One of the few copies to appear on the market has sold for £2000 and one London dealer maintains that this copy is the only surviving one, having changed hands on a number of occasions, with the price climbing steadily each time. Another dealer, however, insists with equal certainty that he has personally handled six different copies!

Title	Format	Label	Cat. No.	Year	Mint	VG	Notes
Bobby Charles	LP	Bearsville	K45516	1972	£**10**	£**4**	
See You Later Alligator	7″	London	HLU8247	1956	£**2000**	£**1400**	*best auctioned*

CHARLES, DON

Title	Format	Label	Cat. No.	Year	Mint	VG	Notes
Angel Of Love	7″	Decca	F11602	1963	£**12**	£**6**	
Don Charles	7″ EP	Decca	DFE8530	1963	£**100**	£**50**	
Drifter	7″	Parlophone	R5688	1968	£**20**	£**10**	
Have I Told You Lately	LP	Parlophone	PMC/PCS7021	1967	£**20**	£**8**	
Heart's Ice Cold	7″	Decca	F11645	1963	£**20**	£**10**	
Hermit Of Misty Mountain	7″	Decca	F11464	1962	£**10**	£**5**	
It's My Way Of Loving You	7″	Decca	F11528	1962	£**10**	£**5**	
She's Mine	7″	HMV	POP1332	1964	£**8**	£**4**	
Walk With Me My Angel	7″	Decca	F11424	1962	£**10**	£**5**	

CHARLES, JIMMY

Title	Format	Label	Cat. No.	Year	Mint	VG	Notes
Million To One	7″	London	HLU9206	1960	£**5**	£**2**	

CHARLES, RAY

Ray Charles is the man who invented soul music, brought it into the entertainment mainstream, and, some would say, sold out. Charles himself sees it differently – he has never deliberately sought to be a champion for black culture, but has simply played what he enjoys. Having been exposed to a wide range of styles during childhood – across blues, jazz and country – he does in fact enjoy an equally wide range and has been happy to perform it all. It is fair to say, however, that the influence and reputation that he enjoys amongst rock musicians and collectors is based on the earlier, blacker material. Even so, the music played by Ray Charles in the fifties has nothing to do with rock'n'roll and has little in common with the work of most other R&B artists – the main reason, no doubt, for the values of his records remaining relatively low. The songs and instrumental pieces on Charles's recordings for Atlantic (issued on London in the UK) swing rather than rock, have a line-up modelled on that of Count Basie, and include many straightforward hard bop pieces, with Charles playing fluent solos on the alto saxophone.

Title	Format	Label	Cat. No.	Year	Mint	VG	Notes
Baby Don't You Cry	7″	HMV	POP1272	1964	£**4**	£**1.50**	
Baby It's Cold Outside	7″ EP	HMV	7EG8807	1963	£**5**	£**2**	
Ballad Style Of Ray Charles	7″ EP	HMV	7EG8783	1963	£**5**	£**2**	
Busted	7″	HMV	POP1221	1963	£**4**	£**1.50**	
Busted	7″ EP	HMV	7EG8841	1964	£**5**	£**2**	
C&W Meets R&B	LP	HMV	CLP1914/ CSD1630	1965	£**10**	£**4**	
Cincinnati Kid	7″	HMV	POP1484	1965	£**4**	£**1.50**	
Cincinnati Kid	LP	MGM	(S)E4313	1965	£**10**	£**4**	*US*
Come Rain Or Come Shine	7″	London	HLK9251	1960	£**4**	£**1.50**	
Cry	7″	HMV	POP1392	1965	£**4**	£**1.50**	

Cryin' Time	7"	HMV	POP1502	1966	£4	£1.50	
Crying Time	LP	HMV	CLP/CSD3533	1966	£10	£4	
Dedicated To You	LP	HMV	CLP1449/ CSD1362	1961	£10	£4	
Don't Set Me Free	7"	HMV	POP1133	1963	£4	£1.50	
Early In The Mornin'	7"	London	HLK9364	1961	£4	£1.50	
Genius After Hours	LP	London	HAK8035	1963	£12	£5	
Genius Hits The Road	LP	HMV	CLP1387/ CSD1320	1960	£10	£4	
Genius Of Ray Charles	LP	London	LTZK15190	1960	£20	£8	
Genius Sings The Blues	LP	London	LTZK15238	1960	£15	£6	
Genius+Soul=Jazz	LP	HMV	CLP1475/ CSD1384	1961	£10	£4	
Georgia On My Mind	7"	HMV	POP792	1960	£4	£1.50	
Great Ray Charles	7" EP	London	EZK19043	1959	£8	£4	
Great Ray Charles	LP	London	LTZK15134	1958	£25	£10	
Greatest Hits	LP	HMV	CLP1626/ CSD1482	1962	£10	£4	
Have A Smile With Me	LP	HMV	CLP1795/ CSD1566	1964	£10	£4	
Hide Nor Hair	7"	HMV	POP1017	1962	£4	£1.50	
Hit The Road Jack	7"	HMV	POP935	1961	£4	£1.50	
Hit the Road Jack	7" EP	HMV	7EG8729	1962	£5	£2	
I Can't Stop Loving You	7"	HMV	POP1034	1962	£4	£1.50	
I Can't Stop Loving You	7" EP	HMV	7EG8781	1962	£5	£2	
I Chose To Sing The Blues	7"	HMV	POP1551	1966	£4	£1.50	
I Gotta Woman	7"	HMV	POP1437	1965	£4	£1.50	
I Wonder Who	7"	London	HLK9435	1961	£4	£1.50	
I'm Movin' On	7"	London	HLE9009	1959	£5	£2	
In Person	LP	London	HAK2284	1960	£15	£6	
In The Heat Of The Night	LP	United Artists	(S)ULP1181	1967	£30	£15	
Ingredients In A Recipe For Soul	LP	HMV	CLP1678	1963	£10	£4	
Let The Good Times Roll	7"	London	HLE9058	1960	£5	£2	
Let's Go Get Stoned	7"	HMV	POP1537	1966	£4	£1.50	
Light Out Of Darkness	7"	HMV	POP1414	1965	£4	£1.50	
Listen	LP	HMV	CLP/CSD3630	1967	£10	£4	
Live In Concert	LP	HMV	CLP1872/ CSD1606	1965	£10	£4	
Love's Gonna Live Here	7"	HMV	POP1457	1965	£4	£1.50	
Makin' Whoopee	7"	HMV	POP1383	1965	£4	£1.50	
Man And His Soul	LP	ABC	(S)590	1967	£10	£4	*US*
Memories Of A Middle-Aged Man	LP	Atlantic	SD263	1968	£10	£4	*US*
Modern Sounds In C&W	LP	HMV	CLP1580/ CSD1451	1961	£12	£5	
Modern Sounds In C&W 2	LP	HMV	CLP1613/ CSD1477	1962	£10	£4	
My Baby Don't Dig Me	7"	HMV	POP1315	1964	£4	£1.50	
No One	7"	HMV	POP1202	1963	£4	£1.50	
No One To Cry To	7"	HMV	POP1333	1964	£4	£1.50	
One Mint Julep	7"	HMV	POP862	1961	£4	£1.50	
Original Ray Charles	LP	London	HAB8022	1962	£15	£6	
Original Ray Charles Vol. 1	7" EP	London	REB1407	1963	£8	£4	
Original Ray Charles Vol. 2	7" EP	London	REB1408	1963	£8	£4	
Original Ray Charles Vol. 3	7" EP	London	REB1409	1963	£8	£4	
Please Say You're Fooling	7"	HMV	POP1566	1966	£20	£10	
Ray Charles & Betty Carter	LP	HMV	CLP1520/ CSD1414	1961	£10	£4	
Ray Charles At Newport	7" EP	London	REK1317	1961	£6	£2.50	
Ray Charles At Newport	LP	London	LTZK15149/ SAHK6008	1959	£15	£6	
Ray Charles Live	7" EP	HMV	7EG8932	1966	£5	£2	
Ray Charles Sextet	LP	London	LTZK15178	1960	£15	£6	
Ray Charles Sings	7" EP	HMV	7EG8861	1964	£5	£2	
Ray Charles Story Vol. 1	LP	London	HAK8023	1962	£10	£4	
Ray Charles Story Vol. 2	LP	London	HAK8024	1962	£10	£4	
Ray Charles Story Vol. 3	LP	Atlantic	(SD)8083	1963	£10	£4	*US*
Ray Charles Story Vol. 4	LP	Atlantic	(SD)8094	1964	£10	£4	*US*
Ray Charles/Rock And Roll	LP	Atlantic	8006	1957	£25	£10	*US*
Ray's Moods	LP	HMV	CLP/CSD3574	1966	£10	£4	
Rockhouse	7"	London	HLE8768	1958	£20	£10	
Ruby	7"	HMV	POP825	1961	£4	£1.50	
Sings Songs Of Buck Owens	7" EP	HMV	7EG8951	1966	£5	£2	
Smack Dab In The Middle	7"	HMV	POP1350	1964	£4	£1.50	
Soul Brothers	7" EP	London	EZK19048	1959	£8	£4	
Soul Brothers	LP	London	LTZK15146/ SAHK6030	1959	£15	£6	
Soul Meeting	LP	London	HAK/SHK8045	1963	£12	£5	*with Milt Jackson*
Sticks And Stones	7"	HMV	POP774	1960	£4	£1.50	
Sweet & Sour Tears	LP	HMV	CLP1728/ CSD1537	1963	£10	£4	
Swinging Style Of Ray Charles	7" EP	HMV	7EG8801	1963	£5	£2	
Take These Chains From My Heart	7"	HMV	POP1161	1963	£4	£1.50	
Take These Chains From My Heart	7" EP	HMV	7EG8812	1963	£5	£2	
Tell The Truth	7"	London	HLK9181	1960	£5	£2	
That Lucky Old Sun	7"	HMV	POP1251	1964	£4	£1.50	
Them That Got	7"	HMV	POP838	1961	£4	£1.50	
Together Again	7"	HMV	POP1519	1966	£4	£1.50	
Together Again	LP	ABC	(S)520	1966	£10	£4	*US*

Unchain My Heart 7" HMV POP969 1962 £4 £1.50
What I Say 7" Atlantic 584093 1967 £4 £1.50
What I Say 7" London HLE8917 1959 £10 £5
What'd I Say 7" EP London REK1306 1961 £6 £2.50
What'd I Say LP London HAK2226 1959 £15 £6
Yes Indeed LP London HAE2168 1958 £15 £6
You Don't Know Me 7" HMV POP1064 1962 £4 £1.50
Young Ray Charles 7" EP Realm REP4001 1964 £6 £2.50
Your Cheating Heart 7" HMV POP1099 1962 £4 £1.50

CHARLES, SONNY

Mastered The Art Of Love 7" Ember EMBS240 1967 £12 £6

CHARLES, TEDDY

New Directions 10" LP Esquire 20034 1951 £10 £20
New Directions Quartet 10" LP Esquire 20043 1955 £40 £20
Teddy Charles Quartet 10" LP Atlantic ATLLP3 1955 £50 £25
Teddy Charles Tentet LP London LTZK15034 1957 £15 £6
Three For Duke LP London LTZJ15119 1958 £15 £6 *...with Hal Overton & Oscar Pettiford*

CHARLESWORTH, DICK

Yes Indeed It's The Gents LP HMV CLP1495 1962 £15 £6

CHARLIE PARKAS

Ballad Of Robin Hood 7" Paranoid Plastics PPS1 1980 £5 £2

CHARMERS

Oh Yes 7" Vogue V9095 1958 £300 £180 *best auctioned*

CHARMERS (2)

Angel Love 7" R&B JB118 1963 £10 £5
Back To Back 7" Melodisc CAL9 1963 £8 £4
Dig Them Prince 7" Blue Beat BB251 1964 £12 £6
Done Me Wrong 7" Blue Beat BB157 1963 £12 £6
Glamour Girl 7" Blue Beat BB256 1964 £12 £6 *Prince Buster B side*
I Am Through 7" R&B JB151 1964 £10 £5
I'm Back 7" Blue Beat BB204 1964 £12 £6
In My Soul 7" R&B JB156 1964 £10 £5
Keep On Going 7" Treasure Isle TI7036 1968 £10 £5
Lonely Boy 7" Blue Beat BB42 1961 £12 £6
Now You Want To Cry 7" Blue Beat BB114 1962 £12 £6
Oh My Baby 7" Blue Beat BB315 1965 £12 £6 *Spanishtonians B side*
Oh Why Baby 7" R&B JB121 1963 £10 £5 *Roland Alphonso B side*
One Big Unhappy Family 7" Green Door GD4001 1971 £10 £5
Skinhead Train 7" Explosion EX2045 1970 £8 £4
Stone Cold Man 7" Melodisc CAL8 1963 £8 £4
Waiting For You 7" Blue Beat BB238 1964 £12 £6
You Don't Know 7" Rio R78 1966 £8 £4

CHARMETTES

Please Don't Kiss Me Again 7" London HLR9820 1963 £10 £5

CHARMS

Carry, Go, Bring, Come 7" Island WI154 1964 £10 £5
Everybody Say Yeah 7" Rio R98 1966 £8 £4

CHARMS (2)

The rare single, 'Hearts Of Stone', is listed in the *Guide* under the name used on other singles by the group – Otis Williams and the Charms.

CHARMS, TEDDY

I Want It Girl 7" Blue Cat BS141 1968 £8 £4

CHARTBUSTERS

She's The One 7" London HLU9906 1964 £6 £2.50
Why 7" London HLU9934 1964 £5 £2

CHASE

Chase LP Epic EQ30472 1971 £12 £5 *US quad*

CHASE, LINCOLN

Explosive LP Liberty LRP3076 1958 £15 £6 *US*
Johnny Klingeringding 7" London HLU8495 1957 £10 £5

CHASERS

Hey Little Girl 7" Decca F12302 1965 £50 £25
Hey Little Girl 7" Decca F12302 1965 £60 £30 *picture sleeve*
Inspiration 7" Parlophone R5451 1966 £75 £37.50
Ways Of A Man 7" Philips BF1546 1967 £15 £7.50

CHAUSETTES

Noire's Party LP Barclay 80197 1963 £20 £8 *French*

CHEAP TRICK

Title	Format	Label	Cat. No.	Year	Mint	VG	Notes
Don't Be Cruel	CD-s	Epic	6530053	1988	£5	£2	3" single
Don't Be Cruel	CD-s	Epic	6528962	1988	£5	£2	
Flame	CD-s	Epic	6514662	1988	£5	£2	
So Good To See You	7"	Epic	EPC6199	1978	£6	£2.50	
Solid Gold	CD-s	Epic	6548513	1988	£5	£2	3" single

CHEATIN' HEARTS

Title	Format	Label	Cat. No.	Year	Mint	VG	Notes
Bad Kind	7"	Columbia	DB8048	1966	£4	£1.50	

CHECKER, CHUBBY

Title	Format	Label	Cat. No.	Year	Mint	VG	Notes
All The Hits	LP	Cameo Parkway	P7014	1963	£12	£5	
Beach Party	LP	Parkway	(S)P7030	1963	£12	£5	US
Biggest Hits	LP	Parkway	(S)P7022	1962	£12	£5	US
Chubby Checker	LP	Cameo Parkway	P7036	1963	£12	£5	
Chubby Checker	LP	Parkway	5001	1960	£30	£15	US
Class	7"	Top Rank	JAR154	1959	£25	£12.50	
Dancing Party	7"	Columbia	DB4876	1962	£4	£1.50	
Dancing Party	7" EP	Cameo Parkway	CPE550	1963	£8	£4	
Discotheque	7"	Cameo Parkway	P949	1965	£20	£10	
Discotheque	LP	Parkway	(S)P7045	1965	£12	£5	US
Don't Knock The Twist	LP	Columbia	33SX1446	1962	£20	£8	
Eighteen Golden Hits	LP	Parkway	(S)P7048	1966	£12	£5	US
Everything's Wrong	7"	Cameo Parkway	P959	1965	£12	£6	
Fly	7"	Columbia	DB4728	1961	£4	£1.50	
Folk Album	LP	Parkway	(S)P7040	1963	£12	£5	US
For Twisters Only	LP	Columbia	33SX1341	1961	£15	£6	
Good Good Loving	7"	Columbia	DB4652	1961	£4	£1.50	
Hey You Little Boogaloo	7"	Cameo Parkway	P989	1965	£8	£4	
Hucklebuck	7"	Columbia	DB4541	1960	£8	£4	
In Person	LP	Parkway	(S)P7026	1963	£12	£5	US
It's Pony Time	LP	Columbia	33SX1365	1961	£15	£6	
King Of The Twist	7" EP	Columbia	SEG8155	1962	£8	£4	
Let's Limbo Some More	LP	Parkway	(S)P7027	1963	£12	£5	US
Let's Twist Again	7"	Columbia	DB4691	1961	£4	£1.50	
Let's Twist Again	7"	Cameo Parkway	P824	1961	£4	£1.50	
Let's Twist Again	LP	Columbia	33SX1411	1961	£12	£5	
Limbo Party	LP	Cameo Parkway	P7020	1963	£12	£5	
Limbo Rock	7"	Cameo Parkway	P849	1962	£4	£1.50	
Loddy Lo	7"	Cameo Parkway	P890	1964	£4	£1.50	
Lovely Lovely	7"	Cameo Parkway	P936	1965	£5	£2	
Pony Time	7"	Columbia	DB4591	1961	£4	£1.50	
Slow Twisting	7"	Columbia	DB4808	1962	£4	£1.50	
Twist	7"	Columbia	DB4503	1960	£4	£1.50	
Twist Along With Chubby Checker	LP	Columbia	33SX1445	1962	£12	£5	
Twist With Chubby Checker	LP	Columbia	33SX1315	1961	£20	£8	
Twistin' Around The World	LP	Golden Guinea	GGL0236	1962	£12	£5	
Twistin' Around The World	LP	Parkway	P7008	1962	£12	£5	US
Two Hearts Make One Love	7"	Cameo Parkway	P965	1965	£75	£37.50	
Your Twist Party	LP	Parkway	P7007	1961	£15	£6	US

CHECKER, CHUBBY & BOBBY RYDELL

Title	Format	Label	Cat. No.	Year	Mint	VG	Notes
Chubby Checker & Bobby Rydell In London	7" EP	Cameo Parkway	CPE554	1964	£12	£6	
Chubby Checker And Bobby Rydell	LP	Columbia	33SX1424	1962	£20	£8	
Golden Hits	LP	Cameo Parkway	C1063	1963	£10	£4	
Jingle Bell Rock	7"	Cameo Parkway	C205	1962	£4	£1.50	
Teach Me To Twist	7"	Columbia	DB4802	1962	£4	£1.50	

CHECKER, CHUBBY & DEE DEE SHARP

Title	Format	Label	Cat. No.	Year	Mint	VG	Notes
Down To Earth	LP	Cameo Parkway	C1029	1963	£20	£8	

CHECKMATES

Title	Format	Label	Cat. No.	Year	Mint	VG	Notes
Around	7"	Decca	F12114	1965	£8	£4	
Checkmates	LP	Pye	NPL18061	1961	£20	£8	
Every Day Is Just The Same	7"	Parlophone	R5495	1966	£8	£4	
Rocking Minstrel	7"	Piccadilly	7N35010	1961	£5	£2	
Sticks And Stones	7"	Decca	F11844	1964	£20	£10	
Stop That Music	7"	Parlophone	R5337	1965	£8	£4	
You Got The Gamma Goochie	7"	Parlophone	R5402	1966	£10	£5	
You've Gotta Have A Gimick Today	7"	Decca	F11603	1963	£15	£7.50	

CHECKMATES (2)

Invisible Ska	7"	Ska Beat	JB225	1965	**£10**	**£5**	*Winston Richards B side*

CHECKMATES LTD

Do The Walk	7"	Ember	EMBS235	1967	**£5**	**£2**	
I Keep Forgettin'	7"	A&M	AMS780	1970	**£4**	**£1.50**	
Live At Caesar's Palace	LP	Ember	NR5048	1967	**£10**	**£4**	
Love Is All We Have To Give	LP	A&M	AMLS943	1969	**£12**	**£5**	

CHECKPOINT CHARLY

Frühling Der Krüppel	LP	Schneeball	2015	1978	**£20**	**£8**	*German*
Grüss Gott Mit Hellem Klang	LP	CPM	LPS003	1970	**£25**	**£10**	*German*

CHEECH & CHONG

Big Bambu	LP	A&M	AMLH67014	1972	**£10**	**£4**	
Cheech And Chong	LP	A&M	AMLS67010	1972	**£12**	**£5**	
Los Cochinos	LP	Ode	ODE77019	1973	**£10**	**£4**	
Sleeping Beauty	LP	Ode	ODE77040	1976	**£10**	**£4**	
Wedding Album	LP	Ode	ODE77025	1974	**£10**	**£4**	

CHEERS

Bazoom I Need Your Loving	7"	Capitol	CL14189	1954	**£25**	**£12.50**	
Black Denim Trousers	7"	Capitol	CL14377	1955	**£25**	**£12.50**	
Blueberries	7"	Capitol	CL14280	1955	**£15**	**£7.50**	
Cheers	7" EP	Capitol	EAP1584	1956	**£50**	**£25**	
Chicken	7"	Capitol	CL14561	1956	**£10**	**£5**	
I Must Be Dreaming	7"	Capitol	CL14337	1955	**£20**	**£10**	
Qué Pasa Muchacha?	7"	Capitol	CL14601	1956	**£12**	**£6**	*Bert Convy B side*
Whadya Want	7"	Capitol	CL14248	1955	**£15**	**£7.50**	

CHEETAHS

Goodbye Baby	7"	Philips	BF1412	1965	**£5**	**£2**	
Mecca	7"	Philips	BF1362	1964	**£5**	**£2**	
Russian Boat Song	7"	Philips	BF1499	1966	**£5**	**£2**	
Soldier Boy	7"	Philips	BF1383	1965	**£5**	**£2**	
Whole Lotta Love	7"	Philips	BF1453	1965	**£5**	**£2**	

CHELSEA

Alternative Hits	LP	Step Forward	SFLP5	1981	**£12**	**£5**	
Chelsea	LP	Step Forward	SFLP2	1979	**£12**	**£5**	
Evacuate	LP	Step Forward	SFLP7	1982	**£10**	**£4**	

CHEMICAL BROTHERS

All those ageing cynics, who maintain that rock music in the nineties owes everything to its sixties and seventies predecessors and has nothing new to offer, have simply been listening to the wrong records. Inspired by the need to find ever more exciting beats for the dance floor and armed with samplers rather than guitars, a number of artists have emerged in recent years with music that sets its sights firmly on the here and now. For them, the sounds of the past are a source of plunder rather than of reverence and if they can be rendered close to unrecognizable, then so much the better. Prime movers amongst these innovators are the duo known as the Chemical Brothers. Their music is built almost entirely out of samples – a staggering three hundred of them making up the eight minutes of their definitive track 'Electrobank' – yet the results have an energy and, above all, a freshness that succeeds in trampling all over the arguments of the cynics.

Anti-Nazi Mix	CD	Virgin	ANNIVDJ97	1997	**£30**	**£15**	*promo double*
Leave Home	12"	Junior Boys Own	CHEMSTX1	1995	**£15**	**£7.50**	
Leave Home	12"	Junior Boys Own	CHEMST1	1995	**£15**	**£7.50**	
Leave Home	CD-s	Junior Boys Own	CHEMSD1	1995	**£10**	**£5**	
Loops Of Fury	12"	Junior Boys Own	CHEMST3	1996	**£10**	**£5**	
Loops Of Fury	CD-s	Junior Boys Own	CHEMSD3	1996	**£10**	**£5**	

CHENE NOIR

Orphee 2000	LP	Disque Chene Noir	CN002	1977	**£20**	**£8**	*French*

CHENIER, CLIFTON

Bayou Blues	LP	Sonet	SNTF5012	1970	**£10**	**£4**	
Black Girl	7"	Action	ACT4550	1969	**£4**	**£1.50**	
Very Best	LP	Harvest	SHSP4002	1970	**£20**	**£8**	

CHER

3614 Jackson Highway	LP	Atlantic	226026	1969	**£10**	**£4**	
After All	CD-s	Geffen	GEF52CD	1989	**£5**	**£2**	*with Peter Cetera*
Alfie	7" EP	Polydor	27788	1966	**£6**	**£2.50**	*French*
All I Really Want To Do	7" EP	Polydor	27771	1965	**£6**	**£2.50**	*French*
All I Really Want To Do	LP	Liberty	LBY3058	1965	**£10**	**£4**	
Baby I'm Yours	CD-s	Geffen	GEF84CD	1990	**£5**	**£2**	
Backstage	LP	Liberty	LBL/LBS83156	1968	**£10**	**£4**	
Bang Bang	7" EP	Polydor	27782	1966	**£8**	**£4**	*French, 2 different sleeves*
Cher	LP	Liberty	(S)LBY3081	1967	**£10**	**£4**	
Cher	LP	MCA	MUPS438	1971	**£10**	**£4**	
Golden Greats	LP	Liberty	LBL/LBS83105	1968	**£10**	**£4**	

Heart Of Stone	CD-s	Geffen	GEF75CD	1990	£5	£2	
Hits Of Cher	7" EP	Liberty	LEP4047	1966	£8	£4	
If I Could Turn Back Time	CD-s	Geffen	GEF59CD	1989	£5	£2	
Just Like Jesse James	CD-s	Geffen	GEF69CD	1990	£5	£2	
Love And Understanding	CD-s	Geffen	GFSXD5	1991	£5	£2	*heart-shaped pack*
Love Hurts	CD	Geffen	243692DJ	1991	£20	£8	*US promo picture disc in wooden box*
Mama	7" EP	Polydor	27797	1966	£5	£2	*French*
Skin Deep	CD-s	Geffen	GEF44CD	1988	£5	£2	
Sonny Side Of Cher	LP	Liberty	(S)LBY3072	1966	£10	£4	
Take Me Home	LP	Casablanca	NBPIX7133	1979	£12	£5	*picture disc*
Turning Back Time	CD	Geffen	CHERCD1	1992	£20	£8	*promo sampler*
We All Sleep Alone	CD-s	Geffen	GEF35CD	1988	£5	£2	
With Love	LP	Liberty	LBL/LBS83051	1967	£10	£4	
You Wouldn't Know Love	CD-s	Geffen	GEF77CD	1990	£5	£2	

CHEROKEES

Dig A Little Deeper	7"	Columbia	DB7704	1965	£5	£2	
Land Of A Thousand Dances	7"	Columbia	DB7822	1966	£5	£2	
Seven Daffodils	7"	Columbia	DB7341	1964	£5	£2	
Wondrous Place	7"	Columbia	DB7473	1965	£5	£2	
You've Done It Again Little Girl	7"	Decca	F11915	1964	£5	£2	

CHEROKEES (2)

Cherokee	7"	Pye	7N25066	1961	£5	£2	

CHERRY, DON

The Don Cherry who recorded pop songs during the fifties has no connection at all with the jazz trumpeter who participated in pioneering recordings by Ornette Coleman and John Coltrane, before embarking on his own solo career. Much of this has taken trumpeter Cherry out of a strictly jazz context, embracing instead a range of influences taken directly from African and Oriental music. Cherry's role as one of the first Western musicians to be seriously interested in World Music has clearly been well understood by his step-daughter Neneh. Recently, his son has also gained some acclaim as a performer, under the name of Eagle-Eye.

Complete Communion	LP	Blue Note	BLP/BST84226	1966	£20	£8	
Don Cherry	LP	Horizon	SP717	1976	£12	£5	*US*
Eternal Now	LP	Sonet	SNTF653	1973	£15	£6	
Eternal Rhythm	LP	BASF	20680	1968	£20	£8	*German*
Mu First Part	LP	BYG	529301	1970	£20	£8	*French*
Mu Second Part	LP	BYG	529331	1970	£20	£8	*French*
Symphony For Improvisors	LP	Blue Note	BLP/BST84247	1966	£20	£8	
Where Is Brooklyn?	LP	Blue Note	BST84311	1969	£20	£8	

CHERRY, DON (2)

Last Dance	7"	Philips	JK1013	1957	£5	£2	
Wanted Someone To Love	7"	Brunswick	05538	1956	£4	£1.50	

CHERRY, NENEH

Buffalo Stance	CD-s	Circa	YRCD21	1989	£5	£2	*3" single*
I've Got You Under My Skin	CD-s	Circa	YRCD53	1990	£5	£2	
Inna City Mamma	CD-s	Circa	YRCD42	1989	£5	£2	
Kisses On The Wind	CD-s	Circa	YRCD33	1989	£5	£2	*3" single*
Manchild	CD-s	Circa	YRCD30	1989	£5	£2	*3" single*

CHERRY PEOPLE

And Suddenly	7"	MGM	MGM1438	1968	£20	£10	
Cherry People	LP	Heritage	HTS35000	1968	£15	£6	*US*
Gotta Get Back	7"	MGM	MGM1472	1969	£4	£1.50	
Light Of Love	7"	MGM	MGM1489	1969	£4	£1.50	

CHERRY SMASH

Much of this group's material was written by Manfred Mann's Mike Hugg – guitarist Bryan Sebastian was his brother – although the songs were perhaps not among his best.

Fade Away Maureen	7"	Decca	F12884	1969	£8	£4	
Goodtime Sunshine	7"	Decca	F12838	1968	£8	£4	
Sing Songs Of Love	7"	Track	604017	1967	£5	£2	

CHERVAL, FRANKIE

How Come	7"	MGM	MGM1183	1962	£6	£2.50	

CHESTER, GARY

Yeah Yeah Yeah	LP	DCP	D(S)6803	1964	£10	£4	*US*

CHESTER, PETE

Forest Fire	7"	Pye	7N25074	1961	£15	£7.50	
Ten Swinging Bottles	7"	Pye	7N15305	1960	£15	£7.50	

CHESTER, VIC

Rock A Billy	7"	Decca	F10882	1957	£12	£6	

CHEVIOT RANTERS

Cheviot Barn Dance	LP	Topic	12TS245	1974	£12	£5	
Cheviot Hills	LP	Topic	12TS222	1973	£12	£5	
Sound Of The Cheviots	LP	Topic	12T214	1972	£12	£5	

CHEVRONS

Lullaby	7"	Top Rank	JAR308	1960	£5	£3	

Sing Along Rock And Roll	LP	Time	T10008	1961	£20	£8	US

CHEVY

Just Another Day	7"	Avatar	AAA114	1981	£8	£4	
Taker	7"	Avatar	AAA107	1980	£10	£5	
Taker	LP	Avatar	AALP5001	1980	£10	£4	
Too Much Loving	7"	Avatar	AAA104	1980	£5	£2	

CHEYNES

A well-respected but ultimately unsuccessful R&B group, the Cheynes included Peter Bardens and Mick Fleetwood, whose next project was the Peter Bs, and Phil Sawyer, who later turned up as a member of the second Spencer Davis Group.

Down And Out	7"	Columbia	DB7464	1965	£40	£20	
Going To The River	7"	Columbia	DB7368	1964	£40	£20	
Respectable	7"	Columbia	DB7153	1963	£40	£20	

CHICAGO

Chicago have fallen into almost as much disfavour as Blood, Sweat and Tears, but many of their records are actually rather fine. The presence of brass instruments, however, does not make the group's music jazz-rock. The primary function of the brass is to give the music power, in the manner of the Atlantic recordings by Otis Redding and Wilson Pickett. Meanwhile, the most dominant solo voice is that of Terry Kath's guitar, which is fluent and exciting, though without, perhaps, being particularly individual.

Chicago At Carnegie Hall	LP	Columbia	CQ30865	1974	£25	£10	*US quad, 4 LPs*
Chicago II	LP	Columbia	GQ33258	1975	£12	£5	*US quad, double*
Chicago III	LP	Columbia	C2Q30110	1974	£12	£5	*US quad, double*
Chicago Transit Authority	LP	CBS	66221	1969	£12	£5	*double*
Chicago Transit Authority	LP	Columbia	GQ33255	1975	£12	£5	*US quad, double*
Chicago Transit Authority	LP	Mobile Fidelity	MFSL2218	1983	£12	£5	*US audiophile, double*
I'm A Man	7"	CBS	4503	1969	£6	£2.50	
Live In Japan 1972	LP	CBS/Sony	SCPS31	1975	£12	£5	*Japanese*

CHICAGO LINE

Shimmy Shimmy Ko Ko Bop	7"	Philips	BF1488	1966	£100	£50	

CHICKEN BONES

Hard Rock In Concert	LP	Procom	027606	1973	£250	£150	*German*

CHICKEN SHACK

As the second most successful group signed to Blue Horizon (behind Fleetwood Mac), Chicken Shack relied heavily on the blues guitar of Stan Webb. He was not, however, as talented as he thought he was, as his embarrassing attempts to prove his versatility via live versions of Davey Graham's tricky instrumental 'Angie' showed only too clearly. The real talent in the group was singer and pianist Christine Perfect (later Christine McVie), but she defected to Fleetwood Mac after the first two LPs.

Early in 1999 a representative of Stan Webb telephoned the author of this *Price Guide* to object to this assessment of the man's prowess. It seems that Eric Clapton had been given a copy of the book and had laughingly said to Webb, on an occasion when they met, 'You'll never guess what someone has said about you!' Webb's sensitivity would seem to be rather curious in the circumstances – no judgement was being passed on any of his more recent playing than thirty years ago and one would have thought that he had done well enough since then to be able to brush off the occasional criticism! As it happens, however, the author was earlier approached at a record fair by a man who identified himself as a former Webb sideman. He referred to the above Chicken Shack entry, which has been included in every edition of the *Price Guide* since the first and smiled. 'I agree with you!' he said.

100 Ton Chicken	LP	Blue Horizon	763218	1969	£25	£10	
40 Blue Fingers Freshly Packed And Ready To Serve	LP	Blue Horizon	763203	1968	£30	£15	
Accept	LP	Blue Horizon	763861	1970	£25	£10	
Goodbye (Live)	LP	Nova	621579	1974	£12	£5	
Goodbye Chicken Shack	LP	Deram	SDL8008	1974	£10	£4	
I'd Rather Go Blind	7"	Blue Horizon	573153	1969	£4	£1.50	
Imagination Lady	LP	Deram	SDL5	1971	£20	£8	
It's OK With Me Baby	7"	Blue Horizon	573135	1967	£6	£2.50	
Maudie	7"	Blue Horizon	573168	1970	£4	£1.50	
O.K. Ken?	LP	Blue Horizon	763209	1968	£25	£10	
Sad Clown	7"	Blue Horizon	573176	1970	£4	£1.50	
Tears In The Wind	7"	Blue Horizon	573160	1969	£4	£1.50	
Unlucky Boy	LP	Deram	SML1100	1973	£15	£7.50	
When The Train Comes Back	7"	Blue Horizon	573146	1968	£4	£1.50	
Worried About My Woman	7"	Blue Horizon	573143	1968	£6	£2.50	

CHICKEN SHED

Alice	LP	Colby	AJ370	1977	£50	£25	
Rock	LP	Colby	AJ371	1978	£15	£6	

CHICKS

What Are Boys Made Of?	7"	Oriole	CB1828	1963	£4	£1.50	

CHIEFS

Apache	7"	London	HLU8624	1958	£20	£10	
Enchiladas	7"	London	HLU8720	1958	£12	£6	

CHIEFTAINS

Chieftains	LP	Claddagh	CC2	1965	£15	£6	
Chieftains Vol. 2	LP	Claddagh	CC7	1969	£12	£5	
Chieftains Vol. 3	LP	Claddagh	CC10	1971	£12	£5	
Chieftains Vol. 4	LP	Claddagh	CC14	1973	£12	£5	

CHIFFONS

Chiffons	LP	Stateside	SL10040	1963	£40	£20	

Title	Format	Label	Cat. No.	Year	Mint	VG	Notes
He's So Fine	7"	Stateside	SS172	1963	£4	£1.50	
He's So Fine	LP	Laurie	LLP2018	1963	£40	£20	US
I Have A Boyfriend	7"	Stateside	SS254	1964	£5	£2	
Love So Fine	7"	Stateside	SS230	1963	£4	£1.50	
My Boyfriend's Back	7"	Stateside	SS578	1967	£8	£4	
My Secret Love	LP	B.T.Puppy	S1011	1970	£20	£8	US
Nobody Knows What's Goin' On	7"	Stateside	SS437	1965	£10	£5	
One Fine Day	7"	Stateside	SS202	1963	£4	£1.50	
One Fine Day	LP	Laurie	LLP2020	1963	£40	£20	US
Out Of This World	7"	Stateside	SS533	1966	£6	£2.50	
Sailor Boy	7"	Stateside	SS332	1964	£5	£2	
Stop, Look, & Listen	7"	Stateside	SS559	1966	£6	£2.50	
Sweet Talkin' Guy	7"	Stateside	SS512	1966	£4	£1.50	
Sweet Talkin' Guy	LP	Stateside	(S)SL10190	1966	£30	£15	
They're So Fine	7" EP	Stateside	SE1012	1964	£40	£20	

CHILD

Title	Format	Label	Cat. No.	Year	Mint	VG	Notes
Child	LP	Jubilee	JGS5673	1969	£30	£15	US

CHILD, LORRAINE

Title	Format	Label	Cat. No.	Year	Mint	VG	Notes
You	7"	Decca	F11969	1964	£6	£2.50	

CHILD HAROLDS

Title	Format	Label	Cat. No.	Year	Mint	VG	Notes
Diary Of My Mind	7"	Trident	TRA201	1968	£20	£10	

CHILDE, SONNY

Title	Format	Label	Cat. No.	Year	Mint	VG	Notes
Giving Up On Love	7"	Decca	F12218	1965	£10	£5	
Heartbreak	7"	Polydor	56141	1966	£10	£5	
To Be Continued	LP	Polydor	582003	1966	£12	£5	
Two Lovers	7"	Polydor	56108	1966	£10	£5	

CHILDREN

Bass player with the Children was Cassell Webb, who has subsequently enjoyed a moderately successful solo career.

Title	Format	Label	Cat. No.	Year	Mint	VG	Notes
Rebirth	LP	Cinema	CLP1	1967	£100	£50	US
Rebirth	LP	Atco	SD33271	1968	£50	£25	US

CHILDREN OF ONE

Title	Format	Label	Cat. No.	Year	Mint	VG	Notes
Children Of One	LP	Real	101	1968	£100	£50	US

CHILDREN OF THE NIGHT

Title	Format	Label	Cat. No.	Year	Mint	VG	Notes
Dinner With Dracula	LP	Pip	PIP6822	1977	£20	£8	US

CHI-LITES

Title	Format	Label	Cat. No.	Year	Mint	VG	Notes
Pretty Girl	7"	Beacon	BEA119	1968	£15	£7.50	

CHILLI WILLI & THE RED HOT PEPPERS

Title	Format	Label	Cat. No.	Year	Mint	VG	Notes
Bongos Over Balham	LP	Mooncrest	CREST21	1974	£10	£4	
Kings Of The Robot Rhythm	LP	Revelation	REV002	1972	£12	£5	

CHILLUM

Title	Format	Label	Cat. No.	Year	Mint	VG	Notes
Chillum	LP	Mushroom	100MR11	1971	£40	£20	

CHIMERA

Title	Format	Label	Cat. No.	Year	Mint	VG	Notes
Obstakel	LP	Spoof		1981	£60	£30	Dutch

CHIMES

Title	Format	Label	Cat. No.	Year	Mint	VG	Notes
Once In A While	7"	London	HLU9283	1961	£15	£7.50	

CHIMES FEATURING DENISE

Title	Format	Label	Cat. No.	Year	Mint	VG	Notes
I'll Be Waiting, I'll Be There	7"	Decca	F11885	1964	£4	£1.50	
Say It Again	7"	Decca	F11783	1963	£4	£1.50	

CHIN, TSAI

Title	Format	Label	Cat. No.	Year	Mint	VG	Notes
World Of Tsai Chin	LP	Decca	LK4501	1962	£10	£4	

CHINA DOLLS

Title	Format	Label	Cat. No.	Year	Mint	VG	Notes
One Hit Wonder	7"	Speed	FIRED001	1982	£25	£12.50	

CHINATOWN

Title	Format	Label	Cat. No.	Year	Mint	VG	Notes
Play It To Death	LP	Airship	AP343	1981	£50	£25	
Short And Sweet	7"	Airship	AP138	1981	£20	£10	

CHINAWITE

Title	Format	Label	Cat. No.	Year	Mint	VG	Notes
Blood On The Streets	7"	Future Earth	FER014	1983	£8	£4	

CHIPMUNKS

Title	Format	Label	Cat. No.	Year	Mint	VG	Notes
All My Loving	7"	Liberty	LIB10170	1964	£4	£1.50	
Sing The Beatles	LP	Liberty	LBY1218	1964	£10	£4	
Sing The Beatles Hits	7" EP	Liberty	LEP2188	1964	£8	£4	French

CHIRCO

Title	Format	Label	Cat. No.	Year	Mint	VG	Notes
Visitation	LP	Crested Butte	701598	1972	£40	£20	US

CHISHOLM, GEORGE

Title	Format	Label	Cat. No.	Year	Mint	VG	Notes
George Chisholm Sextet	LP	Decca	LK4147	1956	£12	£5	
Honky Tonk	7"	Beltona	BL2671	1956	£4	£1.50	
Stars Play Jazz	LP	Embassy	WLP6047	1962	£12	£5	

CHITINOUS ENSEMBLE

Title	Format	Label	Cat. No.	Year			Notes
Chitinous Ensemble	LP	Deram	SML1093	1971	**£60**	**£30**	

CHOCOLATE FROG

This was actually the Fleur De Lys, recording under a pseudonym for, apparently, no good reason.

Title	Format	Label	Cat. No.	Year			Notes
Butchers And Bakers	7"	Atlantic	584207	1968	**£60**	**£30**	

CHOCOLATE MILK

Title	Format	Label	Cat. No.	Year			Notes
Actions Speak Louder Than Words	7"	RCA	RCA2592	1975	**£4**	**£1.50**	
Comin'	LP	RCA	PL11830	1977	**£20**	**£8**	

CHOCOLATE WATCH BAND

Title	Format	Label	Cat. No.	Year			Notes
Inner Mystique	LP	Tower	ST510[illegible]	1968	**£250**	**£150**	*US*
No Way Out	LP	Tower	(S)T5096	1967	**£250**	**£150**	*US*
One Step Beyond	LP	Tower	ST5153	1969	**£100**	**£50**	*US*

CHOCOLATE WATCH BAND *(2)*

Title	Format	Label	Cat. No.	Year			Notes
Requiem	7"	Decca	F12704	1967	**£15**	**£7.50**	
Sound Of The Summer	7"	Decca	F12649	1967	**£15**	**£7.50**	

CHOIR

Title	Format	Label	Cat. No.	Year			Notes
It's Cold Outside	7"	Major Minor	MM537	1968	**£25**	**£12.50**	
When You Were With Me	7"	Major Minor	MM557	1968	**£20**	**£10**	

CHOPYN

Title	Format	Label	Cat. No.	Year			Notes
Grand Slam	LP	Jet	LP08	1975	**£15**	**£6**	
In The Midnight Hour	7"	Jet	JET751	1975	**£5**	**£2**	

CHORDETTES

Title	Format	Label	Cat. No.	Year			Notes
Baby Of Mine	7"	London	HLA8566	1958	**£12**	**£6**	
Born To Be With You	7"	London	HLA8302	1956	**£25**	**£12.50**	
Born To Be With You	7"	London	HA7011	1956	**£15**	**£7.50**	*export*
Chordettes	7" EP	London	REA1228	1960	**£40**	**£20**	
Chordettes	LP	London	HAA2088	1958	**£40**	**£20**	
Chordettes Sing	LP	London	HAA2441	1962	**£30**	**£15**	
Close Harmony	LP	Cadence	CLP3002	1957	**£50**	**£25**	*US*
Duddlesack Polka	7"	London	HLA8217	1956	**£25**	**£12.50**	
Girl's Work Is Never Done	7"	London	HLA8926	1959	**£12**	**£6**	
Harmony Encores	10" LP	Columbia	CL6218	1953	**£40**	**£20**	*US*
Harmony Time	10" LP	Columbia	CL6111	1950	**£40**	**£20**	*US*
Harmony Time Vol. 2	10" LP	Columbia	CL6170	1951	**£40**	**£20**	*US*
Hummingbird	7"	London	HLA8169	1955	**£25**	**£12.50**	
Just Between You And Me	7"	London	HLA8473	1957	**£15**	**£7.50**	
Lay Down Your Arms	7"	London	HLA8323	1956	**£15**	**£7.50**	
Like A Baby	7"	London	HLA8497	1957	**£15**	**£7.50**	
Listen	LP	Columbia	CL956	1954	**£50**	**£25**	*US*
Lollipop	7"	London	HLA8584	1958	**£8**	**£4**	
Love Is A Two Way Street	7"	London	HLA8654	1958	**£8**	**£4**	
Mister Sandman	7"	Columbia	SCM5158	1954	**£150**	**£75**	
Never On Sunday	7"	London	HLA9400	1961	**£4**	**£1.50**	
Never On Sunday	LP	Cadence	CLP3062/25062	1962	**£30**	**£15**	*US*
No Other Arms No Other Lips	7"	London	HLA8809	1959	**£5**	**£2**	
Our Melody	7"	London	HLA8264	1956	**£30**	**£15**	
Your Requests	10" LP	Columbia	CL6285	1953	**£40**	**£20**	*US*

CHORDS

Title	Format	Label	Cat. No.	Year			Notes
Sh'boom	7"	Columbia	SCM5133	1954	**£1000**	**£700**	*best auctioned*

CHORDS *(2)*

Title	Format	Label	Cat. No.	Year			Notes
Now It's Gone	7"	Polydor	2059141	1979	**£4**	**£1.50**	
One More Minute	7"	Polydor	POSP270	1981	**£5**	**£2**	
So Far Away	LP	Polydor	POLS1019	1980	**£10**	**£4**	*with 7"*
Turn Away Again	7"	Polydor	POSP288	1981	**£5**	**£2**	

CHORDS FIVE

Title	Format	Label	Cat. No.	Year			Notes
I'm Only Dreaming	7"	Island	WI3044	1967	**£30**	**£15**	
Same Old Fat Man	7"	Polydor	56261	1968	**£40**	**£20**	
Some People	7"	Jayboy	BOY6	1968	**£20**	**£10**	

CHOSEN FEW

The Chosen Few eventually evolved into Skip Bifferty. The guitarist, however, who was the composer of all the songs on the two singles, went his own way, eventually forming a successful folk-rock group. They were Lindisfarne – he, of course, was Alan Hull.

Title	Format	Label	Cat. No.	Year			Notes
I Won't Be Around You Anymore	7"	Pye	7N15905	1965	**£8**	**£4**	
So Much To Look Forward To	7"	Pye	7N15942	1965	**£8**	**£4**	

CHOSEN FEW *(2)*

Title	Format	Label	Cat. No.	Year			Notes
I Can Make Your Dreams Come True	7"	Polydor	2058721	1976	**£6**	**£2.50**	
You Mean Everything To Me	7"	Polydor	2058975	1978	**£6**	**£2.50**	

CHOSEN FEW *(3)*

Title	Format	Label	Cat. No.	Year			Notes
Going Back Home	7"	Songbird	SB1032	1970	**£4**	**£1.50**	
Hit After Hit	LP	Trojan	TRLS56	1973	**£15**	**£6**	
Time Is Hard	7"	Songbird	SB1031	1970	**£4**	**£1.50**	
Why Can't I Touch You	7"	Songbird	SB1046	1970	**£4**	**£1.50**	

CHRIS, PETER & THE OUTCASTS

Over The Hill	7"	Columbia	DB7923	1966	£20	£10	

CHRIS & COSEY

Gift Of Tongues	12"	C.T.I.	CTI2	1984	£6	£2.50	
Hammer House	12"	C.T.I.	CTI1	1984	£6	£2.50	
Sweet Surprise	cass	Electronic Soundmake		198–	£15	£6	*with magazine*

CHRIS & STUDENTS

Lass Of Richmond Hill	7"	Parlophone	R4806	1961	£15	£7.50	

CHRISTIAN, BOBBY

Crickets On Parade	7"	Oriole	CB1384	1957	£15	£7.50	

CHRISTIAN, CHARLIE

Profoundly Blue	7"	Blue Note	451634	1964	£4	£1.50	*Ike Quebec B side*
With The Benny Goodman Sextet And Orchestra	LP	Philips	BBL7172	1957	£12	£5	

CHRISTIAN, HANS

This was, for a short time, the stage name of the future lead singer of Yes, Jon Anderson.

Mississippi Hobo	7"	Parlophone	R5698	1968	£60	£30	
Never My Love	7"	Parlophone	R5676	1968	£60	£30	

CHRISTIAN, LIZ

Suddenly You Find Love	7"	CBS	202520	1967	£30	£15	

CHRISTIAN, NEIL

Lead guitarist for a time with Neil Christian's group, the Crusaders, was the young Jimmy Page (or Elmer Twitch, as he liked to be known at the time), although he does not play on many of the singles.

All Things Bright And Beautiful	7"	Pye	7N17372	1967	£5	£2	
Big Beat Drum	7"	Columbia	DB4938	1962	£15	£7.50	
Get A Load Of This	7"	Columbia	DB7075	1963	£5	£2	
Honey Hush	7"	Columbia	DB7289	1964	£10	£5	
Little Bit Of Something Else	7" EP	Columbia	SEG8492	1966	£40	£20	
Oops	7"	Strike	JH313	1966	£4	£1.50	
That's Nice	7"	Strike	JH301	1966	£4	£1.50	
That's Nice	7" EP	Riviera	231161	1966	£30	£15	*French*
Two At A Time	7"	Strike	JH319	1966	£4	£1.50	

CHRISTIAN DEATH

Official Anthology Of Live Bootlegs	LP	Jungle	NOS006	1986	£20	£8	*black & yellow cover*
Only Theatre Of Pain	LP	No Future	FL2	1983	£20	£8	
Zero Sex	CD-s	Jungle	JUNG050CD	1989	£5	£2	

CHRISTIE, JOHN

Fourth Of July	7"	Polydor	2058496	1974	£12	£6	*picture sleeve*
Fourth Of July	7"	Polydor	2058496	1974	£6	£2.50	

CHRISTIE, KEITH

Homage To The Duke	10" LP	Esquire	20047	1955	£15	£6	

CHRISTIE, LOU

All That Glitters Isn't Gold	7"	King	KG1036	1966	£4	£1.50	
Gina	7"	CBS	2922	1967	£4	£1.50	
Gypsy Cried	7"	Columbia	DB4983	1963	£6	£2.50	
How Many Teardrops	7"	Columbia	DB7096	1963	£5	£2	
If My Car Could Only Talk	7"	MGM	MGM1325	1966	£5	£2	
Lightnin' Strikes	7"	MGM	MGM1297	1966	£4	£1.50	
Lightnin' Strikes	LP	MGM	C(S)8008	1966	£15	£6	
Lou Christie	LP	Roulette	(S)R25208	1963	£15	£6	*US*
Lou Christie Strikes Back	LP	Co & Ce	LP1231	1966	£12	£5	*US*
Merry Go Round	7"	Colpix	PX735	1966	£4	£1.50	
Outside The Gates Of Heaven	7"	King	KG1036	1967	£4	£1.50	
Painter	7"	MGM	MGM1317	1966	£4	£1.50	
Strikes Again	LP	Colpix	PXL551	1966	£12	£5	
Two Faces Have I	7"	Columbia	DB7031	1963	£6	£2.50	

CHRISTMAS

Lies To Live By	LP	Daffodil	10047	1974	£50	£25	*US*

CHRISTMAS, JOHNNY & THE SUNSPOTS

I'm Gonna Sing Sing Sing	7" EP	Starlite	STEP5	1958	£5	£2	

CHRISTMAS, KEITH

Fable Of The Wings	LP	B&C	CAS1015	1971	£12	£5	
Pigmy	LP	B&C	CAS1041	1971	£12	£5	
Stimulus	LP	RCA	SF8059	1969	£40	£20	
Stories From The Human Zoo	LP	Manticore	K53509	1976	£12	£5	

CHRISTOPHER

Whatcha Gonna Do	LP	Rockadelic		1991	£12	£5	*US*
Whatcha Gonna Do	LP	Chris-tee	PRP12411	1970	£1500	£1000	*US*

CHRISTOPHER (2)

Title	Format	Label	Cat. No.	Year	Price	Price	Notes
Christopher	LP	Metromedia	1024	1970	**£150**	**£75**	US

CHRISTY, JUNE

Title	Format	Label	Cat. No.	Year	Price	Price	Notes
Ballads For Night People	LP	Capitol	(S)T1308	1960	**£12**	**£5**	
Cool School	LP	Capitol	(S)T1398	1961	**£12**	**£5**	
Duet	LP	Capitol	T656	1955	**£15**	**£6**	US
Gone For The Day	LP	Capitol	T902	1957	**£15**	**£6**	
June Fair And Warmer	LP	Capitol	T833	1957	**£15**	**£6**	
June's Got Rhythm	LP	Capitol	T1076	1959	**£12**	**£5**	
Misty Miss Christy	LP	Capitol	T725	1956	**£15**	**£6**	
Recalls Those Kenton Days	LP	Capitol	T1202	1959	**£12**	**£5**	
Something Cool	10" LP	Capitol	LC6682	1954	**£20**	**£8**	
Something Cool	7" EP	Capitol	EAP1516	1955	**£5**	**£2**	
Something Cool	LP	Capitol	1516	1955	**£15**	**£6**	US
Song Is June	LP	Capitol	(S)T1114	1959	**£12**	**£5**	
This Is June Christy	LP	Capitol	T1006	1959	**£15**	**£6**	

CHROME

Title	Format	Label	Cat. No.	Year	Price	Price	Notes
Alien Soundtracks	LP	Siren	DE2100	1978	**£15**	**£6**	US
Firebomb	7"	Don't Fall Off The M	Z17	1982	**£5**	**£2**	
Inworlds	12"	Don't Fall Off The M	Y3	1981	**£8**	**£4**	
No Humans Allowed	LP	Siren	7140	1981	**£15**	**£6**	US
Read Only Memory	12"	Siren	RS12007	1980	**£8**	**£4**	*with poster*
Visitation	LP	Siren	DE1000	1977	**£15**	**£6**	US

CHRYSTAL BAND

Title	Format	Label	Cat. No.	Year	Price	Price	Notes
Chrystal Band	LP	Carole			**£50**	**£25**	

CHUBBY & THE HONEYSUCKERS

Title	Format	Label	Cat. No.	Year	Price	Price	Notes
Emergency Ward	7"	Rio	R75	1966	**£6**	**£2.50**	

CHUCK & BETTY

Title	Format	Label	Cat. No.	Year	Price	Price	Notes
Sissy Britches	7"	Brunswick	05815	1959	**£20**	**£10**	

CHUCK & DOBBY

Title	Format	Label	Cat. No.	Year	Price	Price	Notes
Cool School	7"	Blue Beat	BB23	1960	**£12**	**£6**	
Do Du Wap	7"	Blue Beat	BB39	1961	**£12**	**£6**	
Lovey Dovey	7"	Starlite	ST45044	1961	**£10**	**£5**	
Oh Fanny	7"	Blue Beat	BB59	1961	**£12**	**£6**	
Sweeter Than Honey	7"	Starlite	ST45043	1961	**£10**	**£5**	
Till The End Of Time	7"	Blue Beat	BB19	1960	**£12**	**£6**	

CHUCK & GARY

Title	Format	Label	Cat. No.	Year	Price	Price	Notes
Teenie Weenie Jeannie	7"	HMV	POP466	1958	**£30**	**£15**	

CHUCKS

Title	Format	Label	Cat. No.	Year	Price	Price	Notes
Chucks	7" EP	Decca	DFE8562	1964	**£20**	**£10**	

CHURCH

Title	Format	Label	Cat. No.	Year	Price	Price	Notes
Sing Songs	12"	Carrere	CHURCH5	1983	**£6**	**£2.50**	
Starfish	LP	Arista	208895	1988	**£10**	**£4**	*with bonus 12"*
Under The Milky Way	CD-s	Arista	659778	1988	**£5**	**£2**	

CHURCH, EUGENE

Title	Format	Label	Cat. No.	Year	Price	Price	Notes
Miami	7"	London	HL8940	1959	**£30**	**£15**	

CHURLS

Title	Format	Label	Cat. No.	Year	Price	Price	Notes
Churls	LP	A&M	SP4169	1969	**£12**	**£5**	US

CHWYS

Title	Format	Label	Cat. No.	Year	Price	Price	Notes
Gwr Bonheddig Hael	7"	Afon	RAS001	1975	**£6**	**£2.50**	

CICERO

Dave Cicero's handful of single releases bear the Pet Shop Boys' Spaghetti Recordings imprint. Apart from the first, the singles are also produced by the duo, the connection being the reason for collectors seeking them out.

Title	Format	Label	Cat. No.	Year	Price	Price	Notes
Future Boy	CD	Spaghetti	5134282	1993	**£15**	**£6**	
Heaven Must Have Sent You Back To Me	12"	Spaghetti	CIAOX1	1992	**£6**	**£2.50**	
Heaven Must Have Sent You Back To Me	CD-s	Polydor	CIOCD1	1991	**£8**	**£4**	
Heaven Must Have Sent You Back To Me	CD-s	Polydor	CIOCD5	1992	**£5**	**£2**	
Live For Today	CD-s	Polydor	CIOCD7	1992	**£6**	**£2.50**	
Love Is Everywhere	CD-s	Polydor	CIOCD3	1992	**£5**	**£2**	
That Loving Feeling	CD-s	Polydor	CIOCD4	1992	**£6**	**£2.50**	

CIGARETTES

Title	Format	Label	Cat. No.	Year	Price	Price	Notes
Can't Sleep At Night	7"	Dead Good	DEAD10	1980	**£15**	**£7.50**	
They're Back Again, Here They Come	7"	Company	CIGCO008	1979	**£20**	**£10**	

CIMARONS

Title	Format	Label	Cat. No.	Year	Price	Price	Notes
Bad Day At Black Rock	7"	Reggae	REG3003	1970	**£4**	**£1.50**	
Funky Fight	7"	Big Shot	BI562	1971	**£4**	**£1.50**	

In Time	LP	Trojan	TRLS87	1974	**£10**	**£4**	
Soul For Sale	7"	Spinning Wheel	SW107	1971	**£4**	**£1.50**	

CINDERELLAS

Baby Baby I Still Love You	7"	Colpix	PX11126	1964	**£15**	**£7.50**	
Mr Dee-Jay	7"	Brunswick	05794	1959	**£20**	**£10**	
Trouble With Boys	7"	Philips	PB1012	1960	**£8**	**£4**	

CINDY

Let Me Serve You	LP	York	FYK418	1973	**£60**	**£30**	

CINEMA FACE

Cinema Face	LP		RS2		**£20**	**£8**	*Canadian*

CINEMATICS

Farewell To The Playground	7" EP	Pulsebeat	CINE001	198–	**£15**	**£7.50**	

CINNAMON QUILL

Candy	7"	Morgan	MRS21	1969	**£5**	**£2**	
Girl On A Swing	7"	Morgan	MRS17	1969	**£5**	**£2**	

CINNAMOND, ROBERT

You Rambling Boys Of Pleasure	LP	Topic	12T269	1976	**£10**	**£4**	

CIRCLE

Paris Concert	LP	ECM	ECM1018/9ST	1972	**£15**	**£6**	*double*

CIRCLE (2)

In Aid Of The Millfield Building Fund	7" EP	Circle	GR1	196–	**£150**	**£75**	

CIRCLES

Take Your Time	7"	Island	WI279	1966	**£40**	**£20**	

CIRCLES (2)

Angry Voices	7"	Vertigo	ANGRY1	1980	**£5**	**£2**	
Circles	7"	Graduate	GRAD17	1985	**£6**	**£2.50**	
Opening Up	7"	Chrysalis	CHS2418	1980	**£5**	**£2**	
Opening Up	7"	Graduate	GRAD4	1979	**£6**	**£2.50**	

CIRCULATION

Circulation	LP	Deroy		1969	**£500**	**£330**	

CIRCUS

Circus played a serviceable rock style with jazz overtones and were chiefly notable for launching the career of Mel Collins, whose saxophone and flute have been used to spice literally dozens of records since.

Circus	LP	Transatlantic	TRA207	1969	**£50**	**£25**	
Do You Dream	7"	Parlophone	R5672	1968	**£25**	**£12.50**	
Sink Or Swim	7"	Parlophone	R5633	1967	**£6**	**£2.50**	

CIRCUS 2000

Circus 2000	LP	Rift	RFLLP14049	1969	**£150**	**£75**	*Italian*
Escape From A Box	LP	Rift		1970	**£100**	**£50**	

CIRCUS MAXIMUS

Circus Maximus	LP	Vanguard	VSD79260	1967	**£25**	**£10**	*US*
Neverland Revisited	LP	Vanguard	VSD79274	1968	**£20**	**£8**	*US*

CIRKEL

First Goodbye	LP	Goodbye		1983	**£20**	**£8**	*Dutch*

CIRKUS

Future Shock	LP	Shock	SHOCK1	1977	**£50**	**£25**	
Melissa	7"	Guardian	GRCA4	1970	**£20**	**£10**	
One	LP	RCB	RCB1	1973	**£100**	**£50**	

CITATIONS

Moon Race	7"	Columbia	DB7068	1963	**£12**	**£6**	

CITY

Carole King's first LP was issued under the name of a group, City, but the sound is the same as on its successors. Following her success with *Tapestry*, the City album was counterfeited – copies with black and white covers are the unofficial ones.

Now That Everything's Been Said	LP	Ode	Z1244012	1969	**£15**	**£6**	*colour cover*

CITY PREACHERS

Back To The City	LP	Hör Zu	SHZM265	1972	**£15**	**£6**	*German*
City Preachers	LP	Decca	SLK16435	1966	**£20**	**£8**	*German*
Cool Water	LP	Decca	SLK16482P	1966	**£20**	**£8**	*German*
Folk Songs	LP	Decca	SLK16382	1966	**£20**	**£8**	*German*
Warum	LP	Philips	843798PY	1966	**£25**	**£10**	*German*

CITY RAMBLERS SKIFFLE GROUP

Delia's Gone	7"	Tempo	A165	1957	**£8**	**£4**	
Delia's Gone	7" EP	Tempo	EXA77	1958	**£20**	**£10**	
Ella Speed	7"	Tempo	A158	1957	**£8**	**£4**	

Title	Format	Label	Cat. No.	Year	Mint	VG	Notes
Good Morning Blues	7" EP	Tempo	EXA71	1957	**£20**	**£10**	
I Shall Not Be Moved	7" EP	Storyville	SEP345	1957	**£25**	**£12.50**	
I Want A Girl	7" EP	Tempo	EXA59	1957	**£20**	**£10**	
I Want A Girl	7" EP	Storyville	SEP327	1957	**£25**	**£12.50**	
Mama Don't Allow	7"	Tempo	A161	1957	**£6**	**£2.50**	

CITY WAITES

Title	Format	Label	Cat. No.	Year	Mint	VG	Notes
City Waites	LP	Decca	SKL5264	1976	**£50**	**£25**	
Gorgeous Gallery Of Gallant Inventions	LP	EMI	EMC3017	1974	**£40**	**£20**	
How The World Wags	LP	Hyperion	A66008	1981	**£60**	**£30**	

CLAGUE

The two singles credited to Clague were the work of the same band that played on John Peel's radio show as Coyne-Clague and then made two LPs as Siren.

Title	Format	Label	Cat. No.	Year	Mint	VG	Notes
Bottle Up And Go	7"	Dandelion	K4493	1970	**£4**	**£1.50**	
Stride	7"	Dandelion	K4494	1970	**£4**	**£1.50**	

CLANCY, WILLIE

Title	Format	Label	Cat. No.	Year	Mint	VG	Notes
Minstrel From Clare	LP	Topic	12T175	1967	**£15**	**£6**	

CLANCY, WILLY & MICHAEL GORMAN

Title	Format	Label	Cat. No.	Year	Mint	VG	Notes
Irish Jigs, Reels And Hornpipes	10" LP	Folkways	FW6819	1956	**£30**	**£15**	*US*

CLANCY BROTHERS & TOMMY MAKEM

Title	Format	Label	Cat. No.	Year	Mint	VG	Notes
At Home With The Clancy Brothers	LP	Emerald	GEM/S1006	1968	**£10**	**£4**	
Boys Won't Leave The Girls Alone	LP	CBS	(S)BPG62164	1963	**£10**	**£4**	
First Hurrah!	LP	CBS	(S)BPG62283	1964	**£10**	**£4**	
Freedom's Sons	LP	CBS	62775	1967	**£10**	**£4**	
Hearty And Hellish	LP	CBS	BPG62020	1962	**£10**	**£4**	
In Concert	LP	CBS	(S)BPG63070	1967	**£10**	**£4**	
In Ireland!	LP	CBS	(S)BPG62479	1965	**£10**	**£4**	
In Person At Carnegie Hall	LP	CBS	(S)BPG62192	1963	**£10**	**£4**	
Isn't It Grand Boys	LP	CBS	62674	1966	**£10**	**£4**	
Sing Of The Sea	LP	CBS	63393	1968	**£10**	**£4**	

CLANNAD

Title	Format	Label	Cat. No.	Year	Mint	VG	Notes
Clannad	LP	Philips	6392013	1973	**£15**	**£6**	*Irish*
Clannad 2	LP	Gael-Linn	CEF041	1974	**£15**	**£6**	*Irish*
Dulaman	LP	Gael Linn	CEF058	1976	**£10**	**£4**	*Irish*
Hourglass	CD-s	RCA	PD43076	1989	**£5**	**£2**	
In A Lifetime	12"	RCA	PA42995	1989	**£6**	**£2.50**	*picture disc, with Bono*
In A Lifetime	12"	RCA	PB4035T	1986	**£8**	**£4**	*poster, with Bono*
In A Lifetime	CD-s	RCA	PD42874	1989	**£6**	**£2.50**	*with Bono*
In Concert	LP	Ogham	BLB5001	1978	**£10**	**£4**	*Irish*

CLANTON, JIMMY

Title	Format	Label	Cat. No.	Year	Mint	VG	Notes
Another Sleepless Night	7"	Top Rank	JAR382	1960	**£4**	**£1.50**	
Best Of Jimmy Clanton	LP	Philips	PHM2/PHS600154	1964	**£25**	**£10**	*US*
Come Back	7"	Top Rank	JAR509	1960	**£4**	**£1.50**	
Go Jimmy Go	7"	Top Rank	JAR269	1960	**£5**	**£2**	
Hurting Each Other	7"	Stateside	SS410	1965	**£12**	**£6**	
Jimmy's Blue	LP	Ace	1008	1960	**£30**	**£15**	*US*
Jimmy's Blue	LP	Ace	1008	1960	**£50**	**£25**	*US, blue vinyl*
Jimmy's Happy	LP	Ace	1007	1960	**£30**	**£15**	*US*
Jimmy's Happy	LP	Ace	1007	1960	**£50**	**£25**	*US, red vinyl*
Just A Dream	7"	London	HLS8699	1958	**£8**	**£4**	
Just A Dream	7" EP	London	RES1224	1959	**£50**	**£25**	
Just A Dream	LP	Ace	1001	1959	**£40**	**£20**	*US*
Letter To An Angel	7"	London	HLS8779	1959	**£20**	**£10**	
Letter To An Angel	7"	London	HL7066	1958	**£10**	**£5**	*export*
My Best To You	LP	Ace	1011	1961	**£40**	**£20**	*US*
My Own True Love	7"	Top Rank	JAR189	1959	**£4**	**£1.50**	
Teenage Millionaire	LP	Ace	1014	1961	**£40**	**£20**	*US*
Venus In Blue Jeans	7"	Stateside	SS120	1962	**£5**	**£2**	
Venus In Blue Jeans	LP	Ace	1026	1962	**£40**	**£20**	*US*
What Am I Gonna Do	7"	Top Rank	JAR544	1961	**£4**	**£1.50**	

CLAP

Title	Format	Label	Cat. No.	Year	Mint	VG	Notes
Have You Reached Yet?	LP	Nova Sol	1001		**£100**	**£50**	*US*

CLAPHAM SOUTH ESCALATORS

Title	Format	Label	Cat. No.	Year	Mint	VG	Notes
Get Me To The World On Time	7"	Upright	UPYOUR1	1981	**£5**	**£2**	

CLAPTON, ERIC

Anyone attempting to collect a complete set of the records with which Eric Clapton has been involved is facing an extremely difficult task. For Clapton probably holds the prize for the highest number of guest appearances, including some on records that have become extremely rare. The compilation album *Clapton* was withdrawn and supposedly only four copies were left undestroyed. In fact many more than this have appeared on the market and the value of the record remains stubbornly low.

Title	Format	Label	Cat. No.	Year	Mint	VG	Notes
461 Ocean Boulevard	CD	Mobile Fidelity	UDCD594	1993	**£15**	**£6**	*US audiophile*
461 Ocean Boulevard	LP	RSO	QD4801	1974	**£15**	**£6**	*US quad*
After Midnight	7"	Polydor	2001096	1970	**£6**	**£2.50**	
After Midnight	CD-s	Polydor	PZCD8	1988	**£8**	**£4**	

Title	Format	Label	Cat. No.	Year	Mint	VG	Notes
Another Ticket	7"	RSO	RSO75	1981	£5	£2	
Bad Love	CD-s	Duck	W2644CD	1990	£8	£4	
Behind The Mask	7"	Duck	W8461F	1987	£5	£2	*double*
Clapton	LP	RSO	2479702	1978	£25	£10	
Cream Of Eric Clapton	CD	Polydor	8335192	1987	£60	£30	*promo box set with album & cassette*
Edge Of Darkness	12"	BBC	12RSL178	1985	£8	£4	
Edge Of Darkness	CD-s	BBC	CDRSL178	1989	£20	£10	*3" single*
Hello Old Friend	7"	RSO	2090208	1976	£8	£4	
It's In The Way That You Use It	7"	Duck	W8397F	1987	£5	£2	*double*
Journeyman	7"	Duck	ECBOX2	1989	£60	£30	*promo 6 single boxed set*
Just One Night	CD	Mobile Fidelity	UDCD2608	1994	£25	£10	*US audiophile double*
Just One Night	LP	Nautilus	NR32	1981	£15	£6	*US audiophile double*
Layla	CD-s	Polydor	PZCD163	1991	£5	£2	
Layla And Other Assorted Love Songs	CD	Mobile Fidelity	UDCD585	1993	£20	£8	*US audiophile, original mix*
No Alibis	CD-s	WEA	W9981CD	1990	£6	£2.50	
Pretending	CD-s	Duck	W9970CD	1990	£6	£2.50	
Shape You're In	7"	Duck	W9701P	1983	£5	£2	*picture disc*
Slowhand	CD	Mobile Fidelity	UDCD553	1991	£15	£6	*US audiophile*
Slowhand	LP	Mobile Fidelity	MFSL1030	1979	£12	£5	*US audiophile*
Tearing Us Apart	12"	WEA	W8299TP	1987	£6	£2.50	*with Tina Turner, picture disc*
Tears In Heaven	CD-s	Reprise	W0081CD	1992	£5	£2	
There's One In Every Crowd	LP	RSO	QD4806	1974	£12	£5	*US quad*
Twenty-Four Nights	7"	Duck	ECB3/ECL1/7	1991	£40	£20	*promo 7 single boxed set*
Willie And The Hand Jive	7"	RSO	2090139	1974	£8	£4	
Wonderful Tonight	7"	RSO	JON1	1979	£10	£5	*promo*
Wonderful Tonight (Live)	12"	RSO	JONX1	1979	£10	£5	*promo*

CLARE, ALAN

Title	Format	Label	Cat. No.	Year	Mint	VG	Notes
Jazz Around The Clock	LP	Decca	LK4260	1959	£15	£6	
Young Girl	LP	Decca	SKL4965	1968	£10	£4	

CLARE, KENNY

Title	Format	Label	Cat. No.	Year	Mint	VG	Notes
Drum Spectacular	LP	Columbia	TWO146	1967	£10	£4	*with Ronnie Stephenson*

CLARENDONIANS

Title	Format	Label	Cat. No.	Year	Mint	VG	Notes
Baby Baby	7"	Caltone	TONE114	1968	£8	£4	
Baby Don't Do It	7"	Trojan	TR7719	1970	£4	£1.50	
Come Along	7"	Duke	DU97	1970	£4	£1.50	
Goodbye Forever	7"	Island	WI3041	1967	£10	£5	
He Who Laughs Last	7"	Studio One	SO2007	1967	£12	£6	*Gaylads B side*
I Can't Go On	7"	Studio One	SO2004	1967	£12	£6	
I'll Never Change	7"	Island	WI3005	1966	£10	£5	
Jerk	7"	Ska Beat	JB261	1966	£10	£5	
Lick It Back	7"	Trojan	TR7714	1970	£4	£1.50	
Little Girl	7"	Island	WI180	1965	£10	£5	
Ma Bien	7"	Ska Beat	JB219	1965	£10	£5	
Musical Train	7"	Rio	R115	1967	£8	£4	
Rudie Bam Bam	7"	Rio	R112	1966	£8	£4	
Sweetheart Of Beauty	7"	Island	WI3032	1967	£10	£5	
Try Me One More Time	7"	Island	WI284	1966	£10	£5	
When I Am Gone	7"	Gas	GAS131	1969	£4	£1.50	

CLARK, ALICE

Title	Format	Label	Cat. No.	Year	Mint	VG	Notes
You Got A Deal	7"	Action	ACT4520	1969	£4	£1.50	

CLARK, CHRIS

Title	Format	Label	Cat. No.	Year	Mint	VG	Notes
C C Rides Again	LP	Weed	WS801		£50	£25	*US*
From Head To Toe	7"	Tamla Motown	TMG624	1967	£15	£7.50	
I Want To Go Back There Again	7"	Tamla Motown	TMG638	1968	£12	£6	
Love's Gone Bad	7"	Tamla Motown	TMG591	1967	£20	£10	
Soul Sounds	LP	Tamla Motown	(S)TML11069	1968	£50	£25	

CLARK, CLAUDINE

Title	Format	Label	Cat. No.	Year	Mint	VG	Notes
Party Lights	7"	Pye	7N25157	1962	£4	£1.50	
Party Lights	LP	Chancellor	CHL5029	1962	£40	£20	*US*
Strength To Be Strong	7"	Sue	WI4039	1967	£12	£6	
Walk Me Home From The Party	7"	Pye	7N25186	1963	£4	£1.50	

CLARK, DAVE FIVE

Anyone watching the repeat showings of the influential *Ready Steady Go* TV programme would be forgiven for presuming that the biggest stars of the sixties were the Dave Clark Five. In truth, the group was very successful, particularly in America, but the reason for their dominance of the *RSG* videos lies in Clark's astute purchase of the rights to the show back when few people would have predicted a nostalgia boom for all things sixties. At the time, Clark had apparently epitomized the rock music cliché of the thick drummer, with singer

Mike Smith appearing to be the group's real leader. However, Dave Clark was actually highly adept at managing the fortunes of his own group. Unlike many of the sixties stars, who fell victim to highly disadvantageous royalty deals, Clark was clever enough to retain the rights to his own material and merely leased it to his record company.

Title	Format	Label	Cat. No.	Year	Mint	Near mint	Notes
5 By 5 – Go!	LP	Epic	LN24/BN26236	1967	**£20**	**£8**	*US*
5 By 5 – Go! (14 Titles By Dave Clark)	LP	Columbia	SCX6309	1968	**£15**	**£6**	
All Time Greats	7"	Columbia	DB8963	1972	**£5**	**£2**	*picture sleeve*
American Tour	LP	Epic	LN24/BN26117	1964	**£20**	**£8**	*US*
Bits And Pieces	7"	Columbia	DB7210	1964	**£4**	**£1.50**	
Bits And Pieces	7" EP	Columbia	ESRF1525	1964	**£20**	**£10**	*French*
Catch Us If You Can	7" EP	Columbia	ESRF1699	1965	**£20**	**£10**	*French*
Catch Us If You Can	LP	Columbia	SX1756	1965	**£25**	**£10**	
Chaquita	7"	Ember	EMBS156	1962	**£25**	**£12.50**	
Coast To Coast	LP	Epic	LN24/BN26128	1965	**£20**	**£8**	*US*
Come Home	7"	Columbia	DB7580	1965	**£6**	**£2.50**	*picture sleeve*
Dave Clark 5 & Washington DC	LP	Ember	FA2003	1965	**£25**	**£10**	
Dave Clark And Friends	LP	Columbia	SCX6494	1972	**£12**	**£5**	
Dave Clark Five	7" EP	Columbia	SEG8289	1964	**£10**	**£5**	
Dave Clark Five	LP	Epic	EG30434	1971	**£20**	**£8**	*US double*
Do You Love Me	7"	Columbia	DB7112	1963	**£4**	**£1.50**	
Everybody Knows	7"	Polydor	2058953	1977	**£6**	**£2.50**	*picture sleeve*
Everybody Knows	7"	Columbia	DB7453	1965	**£4**	**£1.50**	
Everybody Knows	7"	Polydor	2058953	1977	**£8**	**£4**	*picture sleeve*
Everybody Knows	LP	Columbia	SX6207	1968	**£15**	**£6**	
First Love	7"	Piccadilly	7N35088	1962	**£25**	**£12.50**	
Get It On Now	7"	Columbia	DB8591	1969	**£75**	**£37.50**	*test pressing*
Glad All Over	7"	Columbia	DB7154	1963	**£4**	**£1.50**	
Glad All Over	7" EP	Columbia	ESRF1489	1964	**£20**	**£10**	*French*
Glad All Over	LP	Epic	LN24/BN26093	1964	**£20**	**£8**	*US*
Good Old Rock'n'Roll	7"	Columbia	DB8638	1969	**£4**	**£1.50**	*picture sleeve*
Greatest Hits	LP	Columbia	SX6105	1966	**£12**	**£5**	
Having A Wild Weekend	LP	Epic	LN24/BN26162	1965	**£20**	**£8**	*US*
Hits Of The Dave Clark Five	7" EP	Columbia	SEG8381	1965	**£15**	**£7.50**	
I Knew It All The Time	7"	Piccadilly	7N35500	1962	**£25**	**£12.50**	
I Like It Like That	LP	Epic	LN24/BN26178	1966	**£20**	**£8**	*US*
If Somebody Loves You	LP	Columbia	SCX6437	1971	**£12**	**£5**	
In Session	LP	Regal	REG2017	1965	**£25**	**£10**	*export*
Julia	7"	Columbia	DB8681	1970	**£4**	**£1.50**	
More Greatest Hits	LP	Epic	LN24/BN26221	1966	**£15**	**£6**	*US*
Mulberry Bush	7"	Columbia	DB7011	1963	**£15**	**£7.50**	
Over And Over	7" EP	Columbia	ESRF1727	1965	**£20**	**£10**	*French*
Please Tell Me Why	7" EP	Columbia	ESRF1795	1966	**£20**	**£10**	*French*
Reelin' And Rockin'	7" EP	Columbia	ESRF1647	1964	**£20**	**£10**	*French*
Return	LP	Epic	LN24/BN26104	1964	**£20**	**£8**	*US*
Satisfied With You	LP	Epic	LN24/BN26212	1966	**£20**	**£8**	*US*
Session With The Dave Clark Five	LP	Columbia	33SX1598	1964	**£20**	**£8**	
Tabatha Twitchit	7"	Columbia	DB8194	1967	**£6**	**£2.50**	*picture sleeve*
Think Of Me	7"	Columbia	DB8862	1972	**£5**	**£2**	
Thinking Of You Baby	7" EP	Columbia	ESRF1581	1964	**£20**	**£10**	*French*
Try Too Hard	LP	Epic	LN24/BN26198	1966	**£20**	**£8**	*US*
Weekend In London	LP	Epic	LN24/BN26139	1965	**£20**	**£8**	*US*
Wild Weekend	7" EP	Columbia	SEG8447	1965	**£15**	**£7.50**	
You Got What It Takes	7" EP	Columbia	ESRF1871	1967	**£20**	**£10**	*French*
You Got What It Takes	LP	Epic	LN24/BN26312	1967	**£20**	**£8**	*US*
You Knew It All The Time	7" EP	Palette	22009	1963	**£20**	**£10**	*French, B side by the Ravens*

CLARK, DEE

Title	Format	Label	Cat. No.	Year	Mint	Near mint	Notes
At My Front Door	7"	Top Rank	JAR373	1960	**£12**	**£6**	
Best Of Dee Clark	LP	Vee Jay	LP/SR1047	1964	**£20**	**£8**	*US*
Dee Clark	LP	Vee Jay	LP1028	1961	**£25**	**£10**	*US*
Dee Clark	LP	Abner	LP/SR2000	1959	**£30**	**£15**	*US*
Don't Walk Away From Me	7"	Columbia	DB4768	1962	**£10**	**£5**	
Heartbreak	7"	Stateside	SS355	1964	**£5**	**£2**	
Hey Little Girl	7"	Top Rank	JAR196	1959	**£12**	**£6**	
Hold On, It's Dee Clark	LP	Vee Jay	LP/SR1037	1961	**£25**	**£10**	*US*
How About That	7"	Top Rank	JAR284	1960	**£6**	**£2.50**	
How About That	LP	Top Rank	BUY044	1960	**£25**	**£10**	
I'm A Soldier Boy	7"	Stateside	SS180	1963	**£10**	**£5**	
Just Keep It Up	7"	London	HL8915	1959	**£15**	**£7.50**	
Raindrops	7"	Top Rank	JAR570	1961	**£6**	**£2.50**	
T.C.B.	7"	Stateside	SS400	1965	**£10**	**£5**	
When I Call On You	7"	London	HL8802	1959	**£12**	**£6**	
Where Did All The Good Times Go?	7"	Liberty	LBF15334	1970	**£5**	**£2**	
You're Looking Good	7"	Top Rank	JAR501	1960	**£4**	**£1.50**	
You're Looking Good	LP	Vee Jay	LP1019	1960	**£25**	**£10**	*US*
Your Friends	7"	Top Rank	JAR551	1961	**£4**	**£1.50**	

CLARK, GENE

Title	Format	Label	Cat. No.	Year	Mint	Near mint	Notes
Early L.A. Sessions	LP	CBS	31123	1972	**£15**	**£6**	*US*
Echoes	7"	CBS	202523	1967	**£5**	**£2**	
Gene Clark And The Gosdin Brothers	LP	CBS	62934	1967	**£15**	**£6**	
Road Master	LP	Ariola	87584	1973	**£15**	**£6**	*Dutch*
Three Songs By The Byrds	CD-s	Demon	GENE1	1992	**£6**	**£2.50**	*promo, with Carla Olson*
White Light	LP	A&M	AMLS64297	1972	**£12**	**£5**	

CLARK, GUY

Old No. 1	LP	RCA	APL1130	1975	£12	£5	
Texas Cookin'	LP	RCA	RS1097	1976	£12	£5	

CLARK, MICHAEL

None Of These Girls	7"	Liberty	LIB5893	1966	£6	£2.50	

CLARK, PETULA

A Date With Pet	10" LP	Pye	NPT19014	1956	£75	£37.50	
Alone	7"	Pye	7N15112	1957	£4	£1.50	
Baby Lover	7"	Pye	7N15126	1958	£4	£1.50	
Beautiful Sounds	LP	Pet Projects	PP2	1976	£20	£8	
C'Est Ma Chanson	7" EP	Pye-Vogue	VRE5025	1967	£8	£4	
C'Est Ma Chanson	LP	Pye-Vogue	VRL3030	1967	£10	£4	
Call Me	7" EP	Pye	NEP24237	1966	£6	£2.50	
Chante En Italian	7" EP	Vogue	VRE5007	1965	£8	£4	
Children's Choice	7" EP	Pye	NEP24006	1956	£20	£10	
Christmas Carol	7" EP	Pye	NSEP85001	1958	£15	£7.50	*stereo*
Christmas Carol	7" EP	Pye	NEP24094	1958	£10	£5	
Cinderella Jones	7"	Pye	7N15281	1960	£4	£1.50	
Colour My World	LP	Pye	N(S)PL18171	1967	£10	£4	*with 'England Swings' & 'Reach Out'*
Devotion	7"	Pye	7N15152	1958	£4	£1.50	
Dis Moi Au Revoir	7" EP	Vogue	VRE5028	1968	£8	£4	
Don't Give Up	7" EP	Pye	NEP24301	1968	£8	£4	
Downtown	7" EP	Pye	NEP24206	1965	£6	£2.50	
Downtown	LP	Pye	NPL18114	1965	£10	£4	
Downtown '88	CD-s	PRT	PYD19	1988	£5	£2	
En Francais	7" EP	Pye	NEP24182	1963	£10	£5	
Encore	7" EP	Pye	NEP24121	1959	£6	£2.50	
Encore En Francais	7" EP	Pye	NEP24189	1964	£10	£5	
Ever Been In Love	7"	Pye	7N15182	1959	£4	£1.50	
Fibbin'	7"	Pye	7N15168	1958	£4	£1.50	
Finian's Rainbow	LP	Warner Bros	WF(S)2550	1968	£15	£6	
Goodbye Mr Chips	LP	MGM	CS8113	1969	£15	£6	
Hello Dolly In French	7" EP	Pye	NEP24194	1964	£10	£5	
Hello Mr Brown	7" EP	Pye-Vogue	VRE5023	1966	£8	£4	
Hello Paris Vol. 1	LP	Pye-Vogue	VRL3016	1966	£12	£5	
Hello Paris Vol. 2	LP	Pye-Vogue	VRL3019	1966	£10	£4	
Here, There And Everywhere	7" EP	Pye	NEP24286	1968	£6	£2.50	
Hit Parade	7" EP	Pye	NEP24016	1956	£15	£7.50	
Hit Parade 4	7" EP	Pye	NEP24137	1961	£8	£4	
Hit Parade 5	7" EP	Pye	NEP24150	1961	£6	£2.50	
Hit Parade No. 2	7" EP	Pye	NEP24056	1957	£6	£2.50	
Hit Parade No. 3	7" EP	Pye	NEP24080	1958	£6	£2.50	
Hits	7" EP	Pye	NEP24163	1962	£5	£2	
I Am Your Song	7"	Polydor	2058560	1975	£6	£2.50	
I Couldn't Live Without Your Love	7" EP	Pye	NEP24266	1966	£6	£2.50	
I Couldn't Live Without Your Love	LP	Pye	N(S)PL18148	1966	£10	£4	
I Couldn't Live Without Your Love ('89 Mix)	CD-s	Legacy	LGYCD100	1989	£6	£2.50	
I Love A Violin	7"	Pye	7N15244	1960	£4	£1.50	
I'm The Woman You Need	LP	Polydor	2383324	1975	£12	£5	
In Other Words	LP	Pye	NPL18070	1962	£15	£6	
Jumble Sale	7"	Pye	7N15456	1962	£4	£1.50	
Just Say Goodbye	7" EP	Pye	NEP24259	1966	£6	£2.50	
L'Agent Secret	7" EP	Pye-Vogue	VRE5019	1966	£8	£4	
L'Amour Viendra	7" EP	Vogue	VRE5026	1968	£8	£4	
Lead Me On	7"	Polydor	2058413	1973	£10	£5	
Les Disques D'Or De La Chanson	7" EP	Vogue	VRE5004	1965	£5	£2	
Les James Dean	LP	Pye-Vogue	VRL3001	1964	£10	£4	
Let's Sing A Love Song	7"	Polydor	2058519	1974	£5	£2	
Live In London	LP	Polydor	2383303	1974	£10	£4	
Many Faces	7" EP	Pye	NEP24280	1967	£6	£2.50	
My Love	7" EP	Pye	NEP24246	1966	£5	£2	
My Love	LP	Pye	NPL18141	1966	£10	£4	
New Petula Clark Album	LP	Pye	N(S)PL18118	1965	£10	£4	
Noel	LP	Pet Projects	PP1	1975	£20	£8	
Pet Ooh La La	7" EP	Pye	NEP24157	1962	£6	£2.50	
Petula	LP	Pye	NPL18089	1962	£10	£4	
Petula '65	LP	Pye-Vogue	VRL3010	1965	£15	£6	
Petula '66	LP	Pye-Vogue	VRL3022	1966	£10	£4	
Petula '71	LP	Pye	NSPL18370	1971	£10	£4	
Petula Clark In Hollywood	LP	Pye	NPL18039	1959	£30	£15	
Petula Clark Sings	10" LP	Pye	NPT19002	1956	£75	£37.50	
Road	7"	Pye	7N15478	1962	£4	£1.50	
Sign Of The Times	7"	Pye	7N17071	1966	£4	£1.50	
Sings In French	7" EP	Pye	NEP24089	1958	£10	£5	
Sings The International Hits	LP	Pye	NPL18123	1965	£10	£4	
This Is My Song	7" EP	Pye	NEP24279	1967	£5	£2	
Today	LP	Pye	PKL5502	1971	£10	£4	
Valentino	7"	Pye	7N15517	1963	£8	£4	
Watch Your Heart	7"	Pye	7N15191	1959	£4	£1.50	
Where Do I Go From Here?	7"	Pye	7N15208	1959	£4	£1.50	
Whistlin' For The Moon	7"	Pye	7N15437	1962	£4	£1.50	

With All My Heart	7"	Pye	7N15096	1957	**£10**	**£5**	
You Are My Lucky Star	LP	Pye	NPL18007	1957	**£30**	**£15**	
You Are My Lucky Star Part 1	7" EP	Pye	NEP24060	1957	**£12**	**£6**	
You Are My Lucky Star Part 2	7" EP	Pye	NEP24061	1957	**£12**	**£6**	
You Are My Lucky Star Part 3	7" EP	Pye	NEP24062	1957	**£12**	**£6**	
You're the One	7" EP	Pye	NEP24233	1965	**£25**	**£12.50**	

CLARK, ROY

Lightning Fingers	LP	Capitol	(S)T1780	1962	**£10**	**£4**	
Please Mr Mayor	7"	HMV	POP581	1959	**£40**	**£20**	
Texas Twist	7"	Capitol	CL15288	1963	**£5**	**£2**	
Tips Of My Fingers	7"	Capitol	CL15317	1963	**£4**	**£1.50**	

CLARK, SANFORD

Fool	7"	London	HLD8320	1956	**£75**	**£37.50**	
Fool	7"	London	HL7014	1956	**£25**	**£12.50**	*export*
Lowdown Blues	7" EP	London	REW1256	1960	**£40**	**£20**	
Pledging My Love	7"	London	HLW9095	1960	**£8**	**£4**	
Presenting Sanford Clark	7" EP	London	RED1105	1957	**£60**	**£30**	
Run Boy Run	7"	London	HLW8959	1959	**£15**	**£7.50**	
Shades	7"	Ember	EMBS250	1968	**£4**	**£1.50**	
Son Of A Gun	7"	London	HLW9026	1960	**£8**	**£4**	
They Call Me Country	LP	Ember	CW131	1972	**£10**	**£4**	

CLARK, SONNY

Cool Struttin'	LP	Blue Note	BLP/BST81588	196–	**£25**	**£10**	
Leapin' And Lopin'	LP	Blue Note	BLP/BST84091	1961	**£30**	**£15**	

CLARK, TREVOR

Sufferer	7"	Studio One	SO2082	1969	**£12**	**£6**	*Jackie Mittoo B side*

CLARK–HUTCHINSON

The Clark–Hutchinson LP, *A=MH2*, was probably the best selling record on Decca's progressive offshoot, Nova, although, as most of the records on the label sank without trace, this is not saying very much. The duo turned themselves into a group by extensive multitracking, concentrating on Mick Hutchinson's efficient guitar playing to provide a focus of interest. After two decades of silence, during which he worked as a guitar teacher, Hutchinson re-emerged in late 1998 with an album of guitar instrumentals called 'Eclecticus'.

A=MH2	LP	Nova	(S)DNR2	1970	**£25**	**£10**	
Gestalt	LP	Deram	SML1090	1971	**£20**	**£8**	
Retribution	LP	Deram	SML1076	1970	**£20**	**£8**	

CLARK SISTERS

Beauty Shop Beat	LP	Coral	CRL(7)57290	1960	**£15**	**£6**	*US*
Chicago	7"	London	HLD8791	1959	**£6**	**£2.50**	
Sing Sing Sing	7" EP	London	RED1198	1959	**£10**	**£5**	
Sing Sing Sing	LP	London	HAD2128	1958	**£15**	**£6**	
Swing Again	LP	London	HAD2177/ SAHD6025	1959	**£15**	**£6**	

CLARKE, ALICE

You Got A Deal	7"	Action	ACT4520	1969	**£5**	**£2**	

CLARKE, ALLAN

You're Losing Me	7"	RCA	RCA2244	1972	**£5**	**£2**	

CLARKE, JOHNNY

Authorised Versions	LP	Virgin	V2076	1977	**£12**	**£5**	
Enter Into His Gates	LP	Attack	ATLP1015	1975	**£15**	**£6**	
Put It On	LP	Vulcan	VULP001	1975	**£15**	**£6**	
Rockers Time Now	LP	Virgin	V2058	1976	**£12**	**£5**	

CLARKE, KENNY

Jacksonville	LP	Realm	RM124	1963	**£12**	**£5**	
Jazz International	LP	Vogue	LAE12029	1957	**£25**	**£10**	
Jazz Is Universal	LP	London	HAK8085	1963	**£15**	**£6**	
Kenny Clarke	LP	London	LTZC15047	1957	**£25**	**£10**	
Kenny Clarke	LP	London	LTZC15038	1957	**£25**	**£10**	
Kenny Clarke Quartet	7" EP	Columbia	SEG7830	1957	**£5**	**£2**	
Kenny Clarke Sextet	LP	London	LTZC15004	1956	**£25**	**£10**	
Klook's Clique	LP	Realm	RM156	1963	**£12**	**£5**	
Plenty For Kenny	LP	London	LTZC15008	1956	**£25**	**£10**	*with Ernie Wilkins*
What's New	LP	Realm	RM115	1963	**£12**	**£5**	

CLARKE, KENNY & FRANCY BOLAND

All Blues	LP	BASF	BMP29747	1973	**£12**	**£5**	
All Smiles	LP	Polydor	583727	1969	**£15**	**£6**	
At Her Majesty's Pleasure	LP	Black Lion	2460131	1971	**£12**	**£5**	
Faces	LP	Polydor		1968	**£15**	**£6**	
Fellini 712	LP	Polydor		1968	**£15**	**£6**	
Golden Eight	LP	Blue Note	BLP/BST84092	1961	**£30**	**£15**	
Latin Kaleidoscope	LP	Polydor	583726	1969	**£12**	**£5**	
Live At Ronnie Scott's Vol. 1	LP	Polydor		1969	**£15**	**£6**	
Live At Ronnie Scott's Vol. 2	LP	Polydor		1969	**£15**	**£6**	
More	LP	Polydor		1968	**£15**	**£6**	
More Smiles	LP	BASF	BMP29746	1972	**£12**	**£5**	
Off Limits	LP	Polydor	2310147	1972	**£12**	**£5**	

CLARKE, LLOYD

Fellow Jamaican	7"	Rio	R24	1964	**£10**	**£5**	Patrick & George B side
Fools Day	7"	Blue Beat	BB104	1962	**£12**	**£6**	
Good Morning	7"	Blue Beat	BB99	1962	**£12**	**£6**	
Japanese Girl	7"	Island	WI045	1962	**£12**	**£6**	
Love Is Strange	7"	Blue Beat	BB371	1967	**£12**	**£6**	Sonny Burke B side
Love Me	7"	Rio	R16	1963	**£10**	**£5**	
Love You The Most	7"	Island	WI007	1962	**£12**	**£6**	Lloyd Robinson B side
Stop Your Talking	7"	Rio	R23	1964	**£10**	**£5**	
Young Love	7"	Blue Cat	BS136	1968	**£8**	**£4**	Untouchables B side

CLARKE, STANLEY

Stanley Clarke	LP	Atlantic	K5010	1975	**£10**	**£4**	

CLARKE, TONY

Ain't Love Good Ain't Love Proud	7"	Pye	7N25251	1964	**£8**	**£4**	
Entertainer	7"	Chess	CRS8011	1965	**£10**	**£5**	
Entertainer	7"	Chess	CRS8091	1969	**£6**	**£2.50**	

CLASH

As one of the pivotal punk groups, the early recordings of the Clash have actually gained in stature in the years since. The video that accompanied their posthumous hit, 'Should I Stay Or Should I Go', showed a group whose understanding of the essential modern rock'n'roll stance was total. The Clash did not have to have hits to be stars – they had the poise, the dress and above all they had attitude.

Black Market Clash	10" LP	Epic	4E36846	1980	**£12**	**£5**	US
Capital Radio	7"	CBS	CL1	1977	**£25**	**£12.50**	promo
Combat Rock	LP	Epic	FE37689	1982	**£25**	**£10**	US promo camoflague vinyl
Combat Rock	LP	Epic	AS991592	1982	**£25**	**£10**	US promo picture disc
Give 'Em Enough Rope	LP	CBS	82431	1978	**£25**	**£10**	promo with poster
I Fought The Law	CD-s	CBS	CLASHC1	1988	**£5**	**£2**	
If Music Could Talk	LP	Epic	AS952	1981	**£20**	**£8**	US promo
London Calling	CD-s	CBS	6569465	1991	**£5**	**£2**	in round tin
London Calling	CD-s	CBS	CLASHC2	1988	**£5**	**£2**	
Remote Control	12"	CBS	125293	1978	**£15**	**£7.50**	promo
Return To Brixton	CD-s	CBS	6560722	1990	**£5**	**£2**	
Rock The Casbah	CD-s	CBS	6568145	1991	**£8**	**£4**	in round tin
Rock The Casbah	CD-s	CBS	6568142	1991	**£5**	**£2**	
Sandinista Now!	LP	Epic	AS913	1980	**£20**	**£8**	US single LP promo
Should I Stay Or Should I Go	7"	CBS	A112646	1982	**£4**	**£1.50**	picture disc
Should I Stay Or Should I Go	CD-s	CBS	6566675	1991	**£8**	**£4**	in round tin
Should I Stay Or Should I Go	CD-s	CBS	6566672	1991	**£5**	**£2**	
Take A Gamble	12"	CBS		1980	**£6**	**£2.50**	promo
Train In Vain	CD-s	CBS	6574302	1991	**£5**	**£2**	
World According To The Clash	LP	Epic	AS1574	1982	**£40**	**£20**	US promo

CLASSICS

Life Is But A Dream	7"	Mercury	AMT1152	1961	**£50**	**£25**	
Pollyanna	7"	Capitol	CL15470	1966	**£5**	**£2**	
Till Then	7"	Stateside	SS215	1963	**£5**	**£2**	

CLASSICS IV

Golden Greats	LP	Imperial	16000	1969	**£12**	**£5**	US
Mamas And Papas Soul Train	LP	Imperial	12407	1968	**£12**	**£5**	US
Spooky	7"	Liberty	LBF15051	1968	**£4**	**£1.50**	
Spooky	LP	Imperial	12371	1968	**£15**	**£6**	US

CLASSMATES

Go Away	7"	Decca	F12047	1964	**£6**	**£2.50**	

CLAUDETTE & THE CORPORATION

Skinheads A Bash Them	7"	Grape	GR3020	1970	**£12**	**£6**	

CLAY, CASSIUS

If the idea of Cassius Clay (or Mohammed Ali as he became better known) wailing 'Stand By Me' seems hard to take, then the single's B side may be more to the point – 'I Am The Greatest', it is called.

I Am The Greatest!	LP	Columbia	BPG62274	1963	**£25**	**£10**	
Stand By Me	7"	CBS	AAG190	1964	**£10**	**£5**	
Stand By Me	7"	CBS	202190	1966	**£6**	**£2.50**	

CLAY, JUDY

You Can't Run Away From Your Heart	7"	Stax	601022	1967	**£4**	**£1.50**	

CLAY, JUDY & WILLIAM BELL

Private Number	7"	Stax	STAX101	1968	**£4**	**£1.50**	

CLAY, OTIS

Baby Jane	7"	Atlantic	584282	1969	**£30**	**£15**	
Trying To Live My Life Without You	LP	London	SHU8446	1973	**£10**	**£4**	

CLAYRE, ALASDAIR

Adam And The Beasts	LP	Acorn	CF252	1976	**£15**	**£6**	
Alasdair Clayre	LP	Elektra	EUK255	1967	**£30**	**£15**	

CLAYTON, ADAM & LARRY MULLEN

Theme From Mission: Impossible	12"	Mother	12MUMDJ751	1996	**£10**	**£5**	*promo*
Theme From Mission: Impossible	12"	Mother	12MUMDJ752	1996	**£10**	**£5**	*promo*
Theme From Mission: Impossible	7"	Mother	MUM75	1996	**£5**	**£2**	*promo*
Theme From Mission: Impossible	CD-s	Mother	MUMCD75DJ	1996	**£8**	**£4**	*promo*

CLAYTON, BUCK

All The Cats Join In	LP	Philips	BBL7129	1957	**£12**	**£5**	
Buck	LP	Vogue	LAE12032	1957	**£12**	**£5**	
Buck Clayton	10" LP	Vogue	LDE140	1955	**£20**	**£8**	
Buck Clayton	LP	Philips	BBL7068	1956	**£15**	**£6**	
Buck Clayton Special	LP	Philips	BBL7217	1958	**£12**	**£5**	
Buck Meets Ruby	10" LP	Vanguard	PPT12006	1956	**£20**	**£8**	*with Ruby Braff*
Buckin' The Blues	LP	Vanguard	PPT11010	1958	**£12**	**£5**	
How Hi The Fi	LP	Philips	BBL7040	1955	**£15**	**£6**	
Jam Session	LP	Philips	BBL7446	1961	**£10**	**£4**	
Jam Session	LP	Philips	BBL7032	1955	**£15**	**£6**	
Jumpin' At The Woodside	LP	Philips	BBL7087	1956	**£12**	**£5**	
Newport Jazz Festival All Stars	LP	London	LTZK15202/ SAHK6116	1961	**£10**	**£4**	
Songs For Swingers	LP	Philips	BBL7317	1959	**£10**	**£4**	

CLAYTON, PAUL

Paul Clayton	7" EP	London	REU1276	1960	**£40**	**£20**	
Wings Of A Dove	7"	London	HLU9285	1961	**£5**	**£2**	

CLAYTON, PAUL *(2)*

Dulcimer Songs And Solos	LP	Folkways	FG3571	1962	**£15**	**£6**	*US*

CLAYTON, VIKKI

Lost Lady Found	LP	Dambuster	DAM021	1988	**£100**	**£50**	

CLAYTON SQUARES

Come And Get It	7"	Decca	F12250	1965	**£15**	**£7.50**	
There She Is	7"	Decca	F12456	1966	**£30**	**£15**	

CLEANERS FROM VENUS

Anyone who has read Giles Smith's entertaining book, *Lost In Music*, knows all about the Cleaners From Venus, the group in which Smith played. Despite good reviews, the album did not sell well in 1987 and has consequently become rather scarce. It is, however, well worth seeking out.

Going To England	LP	Ammunition	CLEANLP1	1987	**£10**	**£4**	

CLEANLINESS & GODLINESS SKIFFLE BAND

Greatest Hits	LP	Vanguard	SVRL19043	1968	**£10**	**£4**	

CLEAR BLUE SKY

Clear Blue Sky	LP	Vertigo	6360013	1971	**£60**	**£30**	*spiral label*

CLEAR LIGHT

Black Roses	7"	Elektra	EKSN45019	1967	**£6**	**£2.50**	
Clear Light	LP	Elektra	EKL/EKS74011	1967	**£20**	**£8**	
Night Sounds Loud	7"	Elektra	EKSN45027	1968	**£4**	**£1.50**	

CLEARLIGHT

Clearlight Symphony	LP	Virgin	V2029	1975	**£12**	**£5**	
Forever Blowing Bubbles	LP	Virgin	V2039	1975	**£12**	**£5**	
Les Contes Du Singe Fou	LP	Isadora	9009	1976	**£12**	**£5**	*French*
Visions	LP	Polydor	2393185	1978	**£12**	**£5**	*French*

CLEARWAYS

I'll Be Here	7"	Columbia	DB7333	1964	**£4**	**£1.50**	

CLEESE, JOHN & OTHERS

I'm Sorry, I'll Read That Again	LP	Parlophone	PMC7024	1967	**£10**	**£4**	

CLEFS

Dream Train Special	7"	Salvo	SLO1810	1962	**£10**	**£5**	

CLEFTONES

For Sentimental Reasons	LP	Gee	(S)GLP707	1962	**£125**	**£62.50**	*US*
Heart And Soul	7"	Columbia	DB4678	1961	**£100**	**£50**	
Heart And Soul	LP	Gee	(S)GLP705	1961	**£125**	**£62.50**	*US*
I Love You For Sentimental Reasons	7"	Columbia	DB4720	1961	**£60**	**£30**	
Little Girl Of Mine	7"	Columbia	DB3801	1956	**£300**	**£180**	*best auctioned*
Lover Come Back To Me	7"	Columbia	DB4988	1963	**£60**	**£30**	

CLEMENT, JACK

Ten Years	7"	London	HLS8691	1958	**£30**	**£15**	

CLEMENTS, SOUL JOE

Never Never	7"	Plexium	PXM10	1968	**£150**	**£75**	

CLEMENTS, VASSAR

Bluegrass Session	LP	Sonet	SNTF748	1977	**£10**	**£4**	

CLEVELAND, JIMMY

Jimmy Cleveland	LP	Mercury	MMB12012	1959	**£20**	**£8**	
Map Of Jimmy Cleveland	LP	Mercury	MMC14023	1959	**£12**	**£5**	
Trombones	LP	London	LTZC15088	1958	**£20**	**£8**	*with Henry Coker, Bill Hughes, Benny Powell*

CLIFF, JIMMY

Another Cycle	LP	Island	ILPS9159	1971	**£10**	**£4**	
Give And Take	7"	Island	WIP6004	1967	**£4**	**£1.50**	
Hard Road To Travel	LP	Trojan	TTl36	1970	**£10**	**£4**	
Hard Road To Travel	LP	Island	ILP962	1968	**£40**	**£20**	*pink label*
Harder They Come	7"	Island	WIP6139	1972	**£4**	**£1.50**	
Harder They Come	LP	Island	ILPS9202	1972	**£10**	**£4**	*with other artists*
Huricane Hatty	7"	Island	WI012	1962	**£10**	**£5**	
I Got A Feeling	7"	Island	WIP6011	1967	**£4**	**£1.50**	
I'm Sorry	7"	Blue Beat	BB78	1962	**£12**	**£6**	*Red Price B side*
Jimmy Cliff	LP	Trojan	TRLS16	1969	**£15**	**£6**	
King Of Kings	7"	Island	WI070	1963	**£10**	**£5**	*Sir Percy B side*
Man	7"	Black Swan	WI403	1964	**£10**	**£5**	
Miss Jamaica	7"	Island	WI016	1962	**£10**	**£5**	
Miss Universe	7"	Island	WI112	1963	**£10**	**£5**	
My Lucky Day	7"	Island	WI062	1962	**£10**	**£5**	
One Eyed Jacks	7"	Stateside	SS342	1964	**£6**	**£2.50**	
Pride And Passion	7"	Fontana	TF641	1966	**£6**	**£2.50**	
Since Lately	7"	Island	WI025	1962	**£10**	**£5**	
Struggling Man	LP	Island	ILPS9235	1974	**£10**	**£4**	
That's The Way Life Goes	7"	Island	WIP6024	1967	**£4**	**£1.50**	
Trapped	7"	Island	WIP6132	1972	**£4**	**£1.50**	
Unlimited	LP	EMI	EMA757	1973	**£10**	**£4**	
Vietnam	7"	Trojan	TR7722	1970	**£4**	**£1.50**	
Waterfall	7"	Island	WIP6039	1968	**£6**	**£2.50**	
Wild World	7"	Island	WIP6087	1970	**£4**	**£1.50**	
Wonderful World	LP	A&M	SP4251	1970	**£10**	**£4**	*US*
Wonderful World Beautiful People	7"	Trojan	TR690	1969	**£4**	**£1.50**	

CLIFFORD, BILLY

Irish Traditional Flute Solos	LP	Topic	12TS312	1977	**£10**	**£4**	

CLIFFORD, BUZZ

Baby Sittin' Boogie	7"	Fontana	H297	1961	**£6**	**£2.50**	
Baby Sittin' With Buzz	LP	Fontana	TFL5147/ STFL567	1961	**£50**	**£25**	
Nobody Loves Me Like You	7"	Columbia	DB4903	1962	**£5**	**£2**	
Three Little Fishes	7"	Fontana	H312	1961	**£4**	**£1.50**	

CLIFFORD, JOHN & JULIA

Humours Of Lisheen	LP	Topic	12TS311	1977	**£20**	**£8**	

CLIFFORD, MIKE

For The Love Of Mike	LP	United Artists	UAL/UAS6409	1965	**£10**	**£4**	*US*

CLIFTERS

Amapola	7"	Philips	PB1242	1962	**£5**	**£2**	

CLIFTON, BILL

Beatle Crazy	7"	Decca	F11793	1963	**£4**	**£1.50**	
Bill Clifton	7" EP	Mercury	MEP9546	1958	**£6**	**£2.50**	
Blue River Hoedown	7" EP	Melodisc	EPM7102	195–	**£8**	**£4**	*with Jim Eanes*
Bluegrass Sound	LP	London	HAB8020	1962	**£10**	**£4**	
Carter Family Memorial Album	LP	London	HAB8004	1962	**£10**	**£4**	
Code Of The Mountains	LP	London	HAB8193	1964	**£10**	**£4**	
Mountain Ramblings	LP	London	HAU8325	1967	**£10**	**£4**	
Soldier Sing Me A Song	LP	London	HAB8070	1963	**£10**	**£4**	
You Don't Think About Me	7"	Melodisc	1554	1960	**£4**	**£1.50**	

CLIFTON, BILL & GEORGE JONES

Country & Western Trailblazers No. 2	7" EP	Mercury	ZEP10052	1960	**£6**	**£2.50**	

CLIMAX BLUES BAND

Climax Chicago Blues Band	LP	Parlophone	PMC/PCS7069	1969	**£40**	**£20**	*yellow & black label*
Like Uncle Charlie	7"	Parlophone	R5809	1969	**£4**	**£1.50**	
Lot Of Bottle	LP	Harvest	SHSP4009	1970	**£10**	**£4**	
Plays On	LP	Parlophone	PCS7084	1969	**£75**	**£37.50**	*yellow & black label*
Plays On	LP	Parlophone	PCS7084	1969	**£15**	**£6**	
Rich Man	LP	Harvest	SHSP4024	1972	**£10**	**£4**	
Tightly Knit	LP	Harvest	SHSP4015	1971	**£10**	**£4**	

CLINE, PATSY

Always	LP	MCA	MUP(S)350	1969	**£10**	**£4**	
Crazy	7"	Brunswick	05861	1961	**£15**	**£7.50**	
Cry Not For Me	7" EP	Ember	EMBEP4552	1964	**£5**	**£2**	
Heartaches	7"	Brunswick	05878	1962	**£4**	**£1.50**	
Heartaches	LP	MCA	MUP(S)326	1968	**£10**	**£4**	
I Can't Forget You	LP	Fontana	FJL309	1966	**£10**	**£4**	
I Fall To Pieces	7"	Brunswick	05855	1961	**£6**	**£2.50**	
In Memoriam	LP	Ember	CW16	1965	**£10**	**£4**	

Title	Format	Label	Number	Year	Price 1	Price 2	Notes
Leaving On Your Mind	7"	Brunswick	05883	1963	£4	£1.50	
Patsy Cline	LP	Decca	DL8611	1957	£25	£10	*US*
Patsy Cline Showcase	LP	Brunswick	LAT8344	1959	£15	£6	
Patsy Cline Story	LP	Decca	D(S)XB(7)176	1963	£15	£6	*US, with booklet*
Portrait Of Patsy Cline	LP	Brunswick	LAT/STA8589	1964	£15	£6	
Sentimentally Yours	LP	Brunswick	LAT/STA8510	1962	£15	£6	
She's Got You	7"	Brunswick	05866	1962	£4	£1.50	
So Wrong	7"	Brunswick	05874	1962	£4	£1.50	
Sound Of Patsy Cline	LP	MCA	MUP316	1968	£10	£4	
Sweet Dreams	7"	Brunswick	05888	1963	£5	£2	
Sweet Dreams	7" EP	Brunswick	OE9490	1962	£15	£7.50	
That's How A Heartache Begins	LP	Decca	DL(7)4586	1964	£12	£5	*US*
That's How A Heartache Begins	LP	MCA	MUPS378	1970	£10	£4	
Today Tomorrow And Forever	LP	Fontana	FJL302	1965	£10	£4	
Tribute To Patsy Cline	LP	Brunswick	LAT8540	1963	£12	£5	
Walkin' After Midnight	7"	Brunswick	05660	1957	£30	£15	
Walking After Midnight	LP	Ember	CW134	1968	£10	£4	
When I Get Through With You	7"	Brunswick	05869	1962	£4	£1.50	

CLIQUE

Title	Format	Label	Number	Year	Price 1	Price 2	Notes
Clique	7" EP	private		196–	£500	£330	*promo, best auctioned*
She Ain't No Good	7"	Pye	7N15786	1965	£60	£30	
We Didn't Kiss	7"	Pye	7N15853	1965	£150	£75	

CLIQUE (2)

Title	Format	Label	Number	Year	Price 1	Price 2	Notes
Clique	LP	White Whale	WW7126	1969	£20	£8	*US*
Sugar On Sunday	7"	London	HLU10286	1969	£12	£6	

CLIVE ALL STARS

Title	Format	Label	Number	Year	Price 1	Price 2	Notes
Donkey Trot	7"	Big Shot	BI501	1968	£8	£4	*Tennors B side*

CLIVE & GLORIA

Title	Format	Label	Number	Year	Price 1	Price 2	Notes
Change Of Plan	7"	R&B	JB113	1963	£10	£5	
Do The Ska	7"	King	KG1004	1964	£10	£5	
Have I Told You Lately That I Love You?	7"	Ska Beat	JB173	1964	£10	£5	

CLIVE & NAOMI

Title	Format	Label	Number	Year	Price 1	Price 2	Notes
Open The Door	7"	Ska Beat	JB181	1965	£10	£5	

CLOCK DVA

Title	Format	Label	Number	Year	Price 1	Price 2	Notes
Four Hours	7"	Fetish	FET008	1981	£5	£2	
White Souls In Black Suits	cass	Indutrial	IRC31	1981	£10	£4	

CLOCKWORK CRIMINALS

Title	Format	Label	Number	Year	Price 1	Price 2	Notes
Young And Bold	7"	Ace	ACE38	1982	£8	£4	

CLOCKWORK ORANGES

Title	Format	Label	Number	Year	Price 1	Price 2	Notes
Ready Steady	7"	Ember	EMBS227	1966	£8	£4	

CLOONEY, BETTY

Title	Format	Label	Number	Year	Price 1	Price 2	Notes
I Love You A Mountain	7"	HMV	7M311	1955	£4	£1.50	

CLOONEY, ROSEMARY

Title	Format	Label	Number	Year	Price 1	Price 2	Notes
At The London Palladium	10" LP	Philips	BBR8073	1956	£15	£6	
Blues In The Night	7"	Columbia	SCM5049	1953	£6	£2.50	
Children's Favourites	LP	Philips	BBL7191	1957	£10	£4	
Date With The King	10" LP	Columbia	CL2572	195–	£20	£8	*US*
Half As Much	7"	Columbia	SCM5019	1953	£10	£5	
Hey Baby	LP	Philips	BBL7090	1956	£10	£4	
I Still Feel The Same About You	7"	Columbia	SCM5093	1954	£4	£1.50	
I'm The One Who Loves You	7"	Columbia	SCM5040	1953	£4	£1.50	
If I Had A Penny	7"	Columbia	SCM5027	1953	£5	£2	
Mangos	7"	Philips	JK1010	1957	£8	£4	
On The First Warm Day	7"	Columbia	SCM5028	1953	£6	£2.50	
Ring Around Rosie	LP	Philips	BBL7156	1957	£10	£4	*with the Hi-Lo's*
Rosemary Clooney	10" LP	Philips	BBR8047	1955	£15	£6	
Rosemary Clooney	7" EP	Philips	BBE12004	1955	£8	£4	
Rosemary Clooney	7" EP	Philips	BBE12051	1956	£8	£4	
Rosemary Clooney & Benny Goodman	7" EP	Philips	BBE12038	1956	£5	£2	
Rosemary Clooney & Harry James	7" EP	Columbia	SEG7552	1954	£6	£2.50	
Showcase Of Hits	LP	Philips	BBL7301	1958	£10	£4	
Sings For You	7" EP	MGM	MGMEP721	1960	£5	£2	
Swing Around Rosie	LP	Coral	LVA9112	1959	£10	£4	
Swing Around Rosie Vol. 1	7" EP	Coral	FEP2045	1960	£6	£2.50	
Swing Around Rosie Vol. 2	7" EP	Coral	FEP2046	1960	£6	£2.50	
Swings Softly No. 1	7" EP	MGM	MGMEP758	1961	£5	£2	
Swings Softly No. 1	7" EP	MGM	ES3514	1961	£5	£2	*stereo*
Tenderly	10" LP	Columbia	CL2525	195–	£20	£8	*US*
Too Old To Cut The Mustard	7"	Columbia	SCM5010	1953	£10	£5	*with Marlene Dietrich*
White Christmas	10" LP	Philips	BBR8022	1954	£20	£8	

CLOSE LOBSTERS

Title	Format	Label	Number	Year	Price 1	Price 2	Notes
Just Too Bloody Stupid	7"	Caff	CAFF4	1989	£5	£2	

CLOUD

Title	Format	Label	Number	Year	Price 1	Price 2	Notes
Free To Fly	LP	Dovetail	DOVE16	1975	£30	£15	

Promise	LP	Songs Of Fellowship	SFR103	1985	£15	£6	
Resting Place	LP	private		197–	£30	£15	
Watered Garden	LP	Dovetail	DOVE44	1977	£40	£20	

CLOUD, CLAUDE

Beat	7"	MGM	MGM946	1957	£6	£2.50	
Let's Get Catstatic No. 1	7" EP	MGM	MGMEP517	1955	£20	£10	
Rock'n'Roll Music For Dancing	10" LP	MGM	D142	1956	£50	£25	

CLOUDS

As 1-2-3, the organ trio that became Clouds pioneered a brand of underground music that was unfortunately not properly represented by the records that the group made. To quote organist Billy Ritchie, 'The records are a very poor record of a good live group. On a good night, we could kill anybody, and often did, especially in the States.' It seems that Clouds suffered from the sadly familiar record company behaviour whereby they were signed on the basis of an exciting live sound and then forced to change style for their records.

Make No Bones About It	7"	Island	WIP6055	1969	£4	£1.50	
Scrapbook	7"	Island	WIP6067	1969	£4	£1.50	
Scrapbook	LP	Island	ILPS9100	1969	£30	£15	*pink label*
Up Above Our Heads	LP	Deram	DES18044	1969	£25	£10	*US*
Watercolour Days	LP	Island	ILPS9151	1971	£20	£8	

CLOUGH, TOM, NED PEARSON, BILLY BALLANTINE

Holey Ha'penny	LP	Topic	12T283	1978	£10	£4	

CLOUT

We'll Bring The House Down	7"	Mooncrest	JWL1000	1990	£4	£1.50	

CLOVEN HOOF

Opening Ritual	7"	Cloven Hoof	TOA1402	1982	£20	£10	

CLOVER

Clover	LP	Liberty	LBS83340	1970	£10	£4	
Forty-Niner	LP	Liberty	LBS83487	1971	£10	£4	
Wade In The Water	7"	Liberty	LBF15341	1970	£4	£1.50	

CLOVERLEAFS

Step Right Up And Say Howdy	7"	MGM	MGM933	1956	£4	£1.50	

CLOVERS

Clovers	LP	Atlantic	LP8009	1957	£200	£100	*US*
Clovers	LP	Atlantic	LP1248	1956	£300	£180	*US*
Dance Party	LP	Atlantic	LP8034	1959	£150	£75	*US*
Easy Loving	7"	London	HLT9154	1960	£20	£10	
From The Bottom Of My Heart	7"	London	HLE8334	1956	£400	£250	*best auctioned*
Honey Dripper	7"	HMV	POP883	1961	£10	£5	
In Clover	LP	Poplar	1001	1958	£150	£75	*US*
In Clover	LP	United Artists	UAL3033/ UAS6033	1959	£150	£75	*US*
In The Good Old Summertime	7"	HMV	POP542	1958	£15	£7.50	
Love Bug	LP	Atlantic	587162	1969	£25	£10	
Love Love Love	7"	London	HLE8314	1956	£400	£250	*best auctioned*
Love Potion No. 9	7"	London	HLT8949	1959	£30	£15	
Love Potion No. 9	LP	United Artists	UAL3/UAS6099	1960	£125	£62.50	*US*
Nip Sip	7"	London	HLE8229	1956	£600	£400	*gold label, best auctioned*
One Mint Julep	7"	London	HLT9122	1960	£25	£12.50	
Original Love Potion No. 9	LP	Grand Prix	K428	1964	£25	£10	*US*
Wishing For Your Love	7"	London	HL7048	1958	£175	£87.50	*export*
Your Cash Ain't Nothin' But Trash	7"	Atlantic	584160	1968	£6	£2.50	

CLUE J & HIS BLUES BUSTERS

Little Willie	7"	Blue Beat	BB60	1961	£12	£6	
Lovers' Jive	7"	Blue Beat	BB37	1961	£12	£6	

CLUSTER

After The Heat	LP	Sky	SKY021	1979	£12	£5	*German*
Cluster	LP	Philips	6305074	1971	£20	£8	*German*
Cluster 2	LP	Brain	1006	1972	£20	£8	*German*
Cluster And Eno	LP	Sky	SKY010	1977	£12	£5	*German*
Curiosum	LP	Sky	SKY063	1981	£10	£4	*German*
Grosses Wasser	LP	Sky	SKY027	1979	£12	£5	*German*
Klopfzeichen	LP	Schwann	STUDIO511	1970	£30	£15	*German*
Sowieso	LP	Sky	SKY005	1976	£12	£5	*German*
Stimmungen	LP	Sky	SKY093	1984	£10	£4	*German*
Zuckerzeit	LP	Brain	0001065	1974	£15	£6	*German*
Zwei Osterie	LP	Schwann	STUDIO512	1970	£30	£15	*German*

CLUTHA

Bonnie Mill Dams	LP	Topic	12TS330	1977	£10	£4	
Scotia!	LP	Argo	ZFB18	1971	£15	£6	

CLYDE VALLEY STOMPERS

Clyde Valley Stompers	10" LP	Beltona	ABL524	1958	£15	£6	
Have Tartan Will Trad	LP	Pye	NJL23	1960	£15	£6	

CLYNE, JEFF & OTHERS

Springboard .... LP .... Polydor .... 545007 .... 1966 **£40** .... **£20** ....

C.M.J.

C.M.J. Trio .... 7" EP .. Impression .... EPIM501 .... 1965 **£150** .... **£75** ....
I Can't Do It All By Myself .... 7" .... Impression .... IMP102 .... 1968 **£30** .... **£15** ....
La La La .... 7" .... Mother .... MOT3 .... 1971 **£6** .... **£2.50** ....
Live At The Bankhouse .... LP .... Impression .... IMPL1001 .... 1969 **£200** .... **£100** ....

CMU

Heart Of The Sun .... 7" .... Transatlantic .... BIG508 .... 1972 **£5** .... **£2** ....
Open Spaces .... LP .... Transatlantic .... TRA237 .... 1971 **£60** .... **£30** ....
Space Cabaret .... LP .... Transatlantic .... TRA259 .... 197[illegible] **£10** .... **£20** ....

COACHMEN

Here Come The Coachmen .... 7" EP .. Vogue .... VE170149 .... 1962 **£6** .... **£2.50** ....
Here Come The Coachmen .... LP .... Vogue .... VA16062 .... 1960 **£10** .... **£4** ....
Those Brown Eyes .... 7" .... Vogue .... V9154 .... 1959 **£5** .... **£2** ....

COAST ROAD DRIVE

Delicious And Refreshing .... LP .... Deram .... SML1113 .... 1974 **£30** .... **£15** ....

COASTERS

Ain't That Just Like Me .... 7" .... London .... HLK9493 .... 1962 **£4** .... **£1.50** ....
All Time Great Hits .... LP .... Atlantic .... 590015 .... 1967 **£15** .... **£6** ....
Along Came Jones .... 7" .... London .... HLE8882 .... 1959 **£8** .... **£4** ....
Besame Mucho .... 7" .... London .... HLK9111 .... 1960 **£5** .... **£2** ....
Charlie Brown .... 7" .... London .... HLE8819 .... 1959 **£5** .... **£2** ....
Charlie Brown .... 7" .... London .... HL7073 .... 1959 **£4** .... **£1.50** .... *export*
Coasters .... 7" EP .. London .... REE1203 .... 1959 **£40** .... **£20** ....
Coasters .... LP .... Atco .... 33101 .... 1958 **£125** .. **£62.50** .... *US*
Coastin' Along .... LP .... Atlantic .... 587134 .... 1968 **£15** .... **£6** ....
Coastin' Along .... LP .... London .... HAK8033 .... 1963 **£40** .... **£20** ....
Cool Jerk .... 7" .... Stateside .... SS2201 .... 1972 **£6** .... **£2.50** ....
Girls Girls Girls .... 7" .... London .... HLK9413 .... 1961 **£4** .... **£1.50** ....
Greatest Hits .... LP .... Atco .... 33111 .... 1959 **£60** .... **£30** .... *US*
Greatest Hits .... LP .... London .... HAE2237 .... 1960 **£40** .... **£20** ....
Hungry .... LP .... Joy .... JOYS189 .... 1971 **£10** .... **£4** ....
Little Egypt .... 7" .... London .... HLK9349 .... 1961 **£4** .... **£1.50** ....
One By One .... LP .... Atco .... (SD)33123 .... 1960 **£30** .... **£15** .... *US*
Poison Ivy .... 7" .... London .... HLE8938 .... 1959 **£8** .... **£4** ....
Searchin' .... 7" .... London .... HLE8450 .... 1957 **£25** .... **£12.50** ....
Searchin' .... 7" .... London .... HL7021 .... 1957 **£10** .... **£5** .... *export*
Searchin' .... 7" .... Atlantic .... 584087 .... 1967 **£4** .... **£1.50** ....
Shadow Knows .... 7" .... London .... HLE8729 .... 1958 **£30** .... **£15** ....
She Can .... 7" .... Direction .... 583701 .... 1968 **£4** .... **£1.50** ....
She's A Yum Yum .... 7" .... Atlantic .... 584033 .... 1966 **£4** .... **£1.50** ....
Shopping For Clothes .... 7" .... London .... HLK9208 .... 1960 **£5** .... **£2** ....
Soul Pad .... 7" .... CBS .... 2749 .... 1967 **£4** .... **£1.50** ....
Stewball .... 7" .... London .... HLK9151 .... 1960 **£5** .... **£2** ....
T'ain't Nothing To Me .... 7" .... London .... HLK9863 .... 1964 **£4** .... **£1.50** ....
Thumbin' A Ride .... 7" .... London .... HLK9293 .... 1961 **£4** .... **£1.50** ....
What About Us .... 7" .... London .... HLE9020 .... 1960 **£5** .... **£2** ....
Yakety Yak .... 7" .... London .... HLE8665 .... 1958 **£10** .... **£5** ....

C.O.B. (CLIVE'S OWN BAND)

Singer and banjo player Clive Palmer seemed to be a man who was scared of success. As a founder member of the Incredible String Band, he played on their first album, yet left just as they began to gain a following. He then formed the Famous Jug Band, recorded a promising LP, but again left when it began to seem as though the band might actually live up to its name. Finally, he formed C.O.B., and was no doubt highly gratified when neither of the group's albums sold more than a handful of copies.

Blue Morning .... 7" .... Polydor .... 2058260 .... 1972 **£15** .... **£7.50** ....
Moyshe McStiff .... LP .... Polydor .... 2383161 .... 1972 **£200** .... **£100** ....
Spirit Of Love .... LP .... CBS .... 69010 .... 1971 **£60** .... **£30** ....

COBB, ARNETT

Blow Arnett, Blow .... LP .... Esquire .... 32114 .... 1961 **£20** .... **£8** . *with Eddie 'Lockjaw' Davis*

COBBLERS LAST

Boot In The Door .... LP .... Banshee .... BAN1012 .... 1979 **£150** .... **£75** ....

COBBS

Hot Buttered Corn .... 7" .... Amalgamated ... AMG845 .... 1969 **£5** .... **£2** ....
Space Doctor .... 7" .... Amalgamated ... AMG849 .... 1969 **£5** .... **£2** ....

COBHAM, BILLY

Crosswinds .... LP .... Atlantic .... K50037 .... 1974 **£10** .... **£4** ....
Spectrum .... LP .... Atlantic .... K40406 .... 1973 **£10** .... **£4** ....
Stratus .... LP .... In-Akustic .... INAK813 .... 1981 **£15** .... **£6** .... *German, direct to disc*
Total Eclipse .... LP .... Atlantic .... K50098 .... 1974 **£10** .... **£4** ....

COBRA

Graveyard Boogie .... 7" .... Rip Off .... RIP3 .... 1978 **£40** .... **£20** ....

COCHISE

Title	Format	Label	Cat. No.	Year	Mint	VG	Notes
Cochise	LP	United Artists	UAS29117	1970	£10	£4	
So Far	LP	United Artists	UAS29286	1972	£10	£4	
Swallow Tales	LP	Liberty	LBS83428	1970	£10	£4	

COCHRAN, DIB & THE EARWIGS

This mysterious pseudonym actually hides the identity of Tyrannosaurus Rex, having fun with Rick Wakeman and Tony Visconti. It has often been thought that David Bowie appears on the record too, but this would seem not to be the case.

Title	Format	Label	Cat. No.	Year	Mint	VG	Notes
Oh Baby	7"	Bell	BLL1121	1970	£150	£75	

COCHRAN, EDDIE

Title	Format	Label	Cat. No.	Year	Mint	VG	Notes
C'mon Again	7" EP	Liberty	LEP2165	1964	£40	£20	
C'mon Everybody	7"	Liberty	LBF15366	1970	£6	£2.50	
C'mon Everybody	7"	Liberty	LIB10233	1966	£15	£7.50	
C'mon Everybody	7"	London	HLU8792	1959	£20	£10	
C'mon Everybody	7" EP	London	REU1214	1959	£60	£30	*tri-centre*
C'mon Everybody	7" EP	Liberty	LEP2111	1963	£25	£12.50	
Cherished Memories	LP	Liberty	LBY1109	1962	£20	£8	
Cherished Memories	LP	Liberty	LBL/LBS83072	1967	£12	£5	
Cherished Memories Of Eddie Cochran	7" EP	London	REG1301	1961	£60	£30	
Cherished Memories Of Eddie Cochran	7" EP	Liberty	LEP2123	1963	£25	£12.50	
Cherished Memories Vol. 1	7" EP	Liberty	LEP2090	1963	£30	£15	
Drive In Show	7"	Liberty	LIB10108	1963	£15	£7.50	
Eddie's Hits	7" EP	London	REG1262	1960	£60	£30	
Eddie's Hits	7" EP	Liberty	LEP2124	1963	£25	£12.50	
Hallelujah I Love Her So	7"	London	HLW9022	1960	£8	£4	
Hallelujah I Love Her So	7"	London	HLW9022	1960	£40	£20	*tri-centre*
Jeannie Jeannie Jeannie	7"	London	HLG9460	1961	£15	£7.50	
Legendary Masters	LP	United Artists	UAD60017/8	1972	£15	£6	*double*
Memorial Album	LP	London	HAG2267	1960	£50	£25	
Memorial Album	LP	Liberty	LBY1127	1963	£20	£8	
Memorial Album	LP	Liberty	LBL/LBS83009	1967	£10	£4	
My Way	7"	Liberty	LIB10088	1963	£8	£4	
My Way	LP	Liberty	LBY1205	1964	£30	£15	
My Way	LP	Liberty	LBL83104	1968	£10	£4	
Never To Be Forgotten	7" EP	Liberty	LEP2052	1962	£30	£15	
Never To Be Forgotten	LP	Liberty	LRP3220	1962	£30	£15	*US*
Pretty Girl	7"	London	HLG9464	1961	£20	£10	
Singing To My Baby	LP	Liberty	LBY1158	1963	£25	£10	
Singing To My Baby	LP	Liberty	LBL/LBS83152	1968	£12	£5	
Singing To My Baby	LP	London	HAU2093	1958	£100	£50	
Singing To My Baby	LP	Liberty	LRP3061	1958	£125	£62.50	*US*
Sitting In The Balcony	7"	London	HLU8433	1957	£200	£100	*best auctioned*
Skinny Jim	7"	Liberty	LIB10151	1964	£25	£12.50	
Skinny Jim	7"	Crest	1026	1956	£175	£87.50	*US*
Skinny Jim	7"	Crest	1026	1956	£500	£330	*US, red vinyl, best auctioned*
Somethin' Else	7"	Liberty	LBF15109	1968	£6	£2.50	
Somethin' Else	7"	London	HLU8944	1959	£40	£20	*tri-centre*
Somethin' Else	7" EP	London	REU1239	1960	£60	£30	
Somethin' Else	7" EP	Liberty	LEP2122	1963	£25	£12.50	
Stockings And Shoes	7"	London	HLG9467	1961	£20	£10	
Stockings And Shoes	7" EP	Liberty	LEP2180	1964	£30	£15	
Summertime Blues	7"	London	HLU8702	1958	£20	£10	
Summertime Blues	7"	Liberty	LBF15071	1968	£6	£2.50	
Sweetie Pie	7"	London	HLG9196	1960	£10	£5	
Teenage Heaven	7"	London	HLU8880	1959	£25	£12.50	
Teenage Heaven	7"	London	HL7082	1959	£60	£30	*export*
Think Of Me	7"	Liberty	LIB10049	1962	£10	£5	
Three Stars	7"	Liberty	LIB10249	1966	£30	£15	
Three Steps To Heaven	7"	Liberty	LIB10276	1967	£25	£12.50	
Three Steps To Heaven	7"	London	HLG9115	1960	£8	£4	
Twentieth Anniversary Album	LP	United Artists	ECSP20	1980	£30	£15	*4 LPs, boxed*
Twenty Flight Rock	7"	London	HLU8386	1957	£100	£50	*tri-centre*
Weekend	7"	London	HLG9362	1961	£8	£4	

COCHRAN, JACKIE LEE

Title	Format	Label	Cat. No.	Year	Mint	VG	Notes
Mama Don't You Think I Know	7"	Brunswick	05669	1957	£1000	£700	*best auctioned*

COCHRAN, WAYNE

Title	Format	Label	Cat. No.	Year	Mint	VG	Notes
Wayne Cochran	LP	Chess	LP(S)1519	1967	£15	£6	*US*

COCHRAN BROTHERS

Though sharing a surname, Hank and Eddie Cochran were not actually related at all.

Title	Format	Label	Cat. No.	Year	Mint	VG	Notes
Guilty Conscience	7"	Ekko	1005	1955	£150	£75	*US*
Mr Fiddle	7"	Ekko	1003	1955	£150	£75	*US*
Tired And Sleepy	7"	Ekko	3001	1956	£175	£87.50	*US*

COCK SPARRER

Title	Format	Label	Cat. No.	Year	Mint	VG	Notes
Cock Sparrer	LP	Decca	TXS3103	1978	£40	£20	*Spanish*
England Belongs To Me	7"	Carrere	CAR255	1982	£25	£12.50	
Runnin' Riot In '84	LP	Syndicate	SYNLP7	1984	£12	£5	
Running Riot	7"	Decca	FR13710	1977	£75	£37.50	*picture sleeve*
Running Riot	7"	Decca	FR13710	1977	£15	£7.50	
Shock Troops	LP	Razor	RAZ9	1983	£15	£6	

Title	Format	Label	Cat. No.	Year	Price	Price	Notes
True Grit	LP	Razor	RAZ26	1986	**£10**	**£4**	
We Love You	12"	Decca	FR13732	1977	**£10**	**£5**	
We Love You	7"	Decca	FR13732	1977	**£10**	**£5**	

COCKBURN, BRUCE

Bruce Cockburn is a Canadian singer-songwriter who, since first issuing LPs on his own True North label at the start of the seventies, seems to have grown in stature with each passing year. His most impressive recordings are the most recent ones, the earliest records being interesting mainly for the glimpses they afford of a great artist in the making. This, of course, is the exact reverse of the usual state of affairs where rock performers are concerned.

Title	Format	Label	Cat. No.	Year	Price	Price	Notes
Bruce Cockburn	LP	True North	TN1	1970	**£15**	**£6**	*Canadian*
Circles In The Stream	LP	Island	ILTA9475	1977	**£15**	**£6**	*US double*
Further Adventures	LP	True North	TN33	1976	**£15**	**£6**	*Canadian*
Hand Dancing	LP	True North	TN13	1974	**£15**	**£6**	*Canadian*
High Winds White Sky	LP	True North	TN3	1971	**£15**	**£6**	*Canadian*
In The Falling Dark	LP	True North	TN26	1976	**£15**	**£6**	*Canadian*
Joy Will Find A Way	LP	True North	TN23	1975	**£15**	**£6**	*Canadian*
Night Vision	LP	True North	TN11	1973	**£15**	**£6**	*Canadian*
Salt, Sun And Time	LP	True North	TN16	1974	**£15**	**£6**	*Canadian*
Sunwheel Dance	LP	Epic	65187	1972	**£15**	**£6**	

COCKER, JOE

Title	Format	Label	Cat. No.	Year	Price	Price	Notes
Best Of Joe Cocker Live	CD	EMI		1994	**£25**	**£10**	*CD & video boxed set*
Don't You Love Me Anymore	CD-s	Capitol	CDCL493	1988	**£5**	**£2**	
I'll Cry Instead	7"	Decca	F11974	1964	**£40**	**£20**	
Joe Cocker	7" EP	Oak		196–	**£400**	**£250**	*best auctioned*
Joe Cocker	LP	Regal Zonophone	SLRZ1011	1969	**£12**	**£5**	
Luxury You Can Afford	LP	Asylum	DP400	1978	**£12**	**£5**	*US promo picture disc*
Marjorine	7"	Regal Zonophone	RZ3006	1968	**£4**	**£1.50**	
Rag Goes Mad At The Mojo	7"	Action	ACT002	1967	**£60**	**£30**	*with other artists*
Sheffield Steel	CD	Mobile Fidelity		1995	**£15**	**£6**	*US audiophile*
Unchain My Heart	CD-s	Capitol	CDCL465	1987	**£5**	**£2**	
When The Night Comes	CD-s	Capitol	CDCL535	1989	**£5**	**£2**	
With A Little Help From My Friends	7"	Regal Zonophone	RZ3013	1968	**£4**	**£1.50**	
With A Little Help From My Friends	7"	MagniFly	ECHO103	1972	**£4**	**£1.50**	*picture sleeve*
With A Little Help From My Friends	LP	Regal Zonophone	SLRZ1006	1969	**£15**	**£6**	

COCKNEY REBEL

Title	Format	Label	Cat. No.	Year	Price	Price	Notes
Best Years Of Our Lives	7"	EMI	EMI2673	1977	**£6**	**£2.50**	*picture sleeve*
Human Menagerie	LP	EMI	EMA759	1973	**£20**	**£8**	*with booklet*
Psychomodo	7"	EMI	EMI2191	1974	**£50**	**£25**	*demo*

COCKNEY REJECTS

Title	Format	Label	Cat. No.	Year	Price	Price	Notes
Greatest Hits Vol. 1	LP	Zonophone	ZONO101	1980	**£10**	**£4**	
Greatest Hits Vol. 2	LP	Zonophone	ZONO102	1980	**£10**	**£4**	
Greatest Hits Vol. 3	LP	Zonophone	ZEM101	1981	**£10**	**£4**	

COCKNEYS

Title	Format	Label	Cat. No.	Year	Price	Price	Notes
After Tomorrow	7"	Philips	BF1338	1964	**£6**	**£2.50**	
After Tomorrow	7"	Philips	BF1303	1964	**£6**	**£2.50**	
I Know You're Gonna Be Mine	7"	Philips	BF1360	1964	**£6**	**£2.50**	

COCKTAIL CABINET

Title	Format	Label	Cat. No.	Year	Price	Price	Notes
Puppet On A String	7"	Page One	POF23046	1967	**£10**	**£5**	

COCTEAU TWINS

Title	Format	Label	Cat. No.	Year	Price	Price	Notes
Blue Bell Knoll	DAT	4AD	CADT807	1987	**£20**	**£8**	
Cocteau Twins	CD	Capitol	DPRO79065	1991	**£25**	**£10**	*US promo sampler*
Echoes In A Shallow Bay	CD-s	4AD	BAD511CD	1985	**£5**	**£2**	
EP Box Set	CD-s	4AD	CTBOX1	1991	**£20**	**£10**	
Ice Blink Luck	CD-s	4AD	BADCD0011	1990	**£5**	**£2**	
Peppermint Pig	7"	4AD	AD303	1983	**£12**	**£6**	
Sugar Hiccup	7"	4AD	AD314	1984	**£10**	**£5**	*1 sided promo*
Tiny Dynamite	CD-s	4AD	BAD510CD	1988	**£5**	**£2**	

CODA

Title	Format	Label	Cat. No.	Year	Price	Price	Notes
Sounds Of Passion	LP	Boni	2860481	1986	**£15**	**£6**	*Dutch*

CODE III

Title	Format	Label	Cat. No.	Year	Price	Price	Notes
Planet Of Man	LP	Delta-Akustik	251251	1974	**£50**	**£25**	*German*

C.O.D.S

Title	Format	Label	Cat. No.	Year	Price	Price	Notes
Michael	7"	Stateside	SS489	1966	**£15**	**£7.50**	

COE, DAVID ALAN

Title	Format	Label	Cat. No.	Year	Price	Price	Notes
Penitentiary Blues	LP	SSS	9	1968	**£12**	**£5**	*US*
Requiem For A Harlequin	LP	SSS	31	1969	**£12**	**£5**	*US*

COE, JAMIE

Title	Format	Label	Cat. No.	Year	Price	Price	Notes
Fool	7"	London	HLX9713	1963	**£8**	**£4**	

How Low Is Low	7"	HMV	POP991	1961	£8	£4	
Schoolday Blues	7"	Parlophone	R4621	1960	£40	£20	
Summertime Symphony	7"	Parlophone	R4600	1959	£100	£50	

COE, PETE & CHRIS

Game Of All Fours	LP	Highway	SHY7007	1979	£12	£5	
Open The Door And Let Us In	LP	Leader	LER2077	1972	£15	£6	
Out Of Season Out Of Rhyme	LP	Trailer	LER2098	1976	£12	£5	

COE, TONY

Existence	LP	Leelambert	LAM100	1978	£15	£6	
Le Chat Se Retourne	LP	Nato	257	1984	£12	£5	
Nutty On Willisau	LP	Hat Art	2004	1983	£12	£5	
Pop Makes Progress	LP	Chapter One	CHS804	1970	£30	£15	*with Robert Farnon*
Swingin' Till The Girls Come Home	LP	Philips	B10784L	1962	£30	£15	
Tony Coe And The Brian Lemon Trio	LP	77	SEU1241	1971	£25	£10	
Tony's Basement	LP	Columbia	S(C)X6170	1967	£100	£50	
Tournée Du Chat	LP	Nato	19	1982	£12	£5	
Zeitgeist	LP	EMI	EMC3207	1977	£15	£6	

COE, TONY & DEREK BAILEY

Time	LP	Incus	INCUS34	1979	£12	£5	

COEN, JACK & CHARLIE

Branch Line	LP	Topic	12TS337	1977	£15	£6	

COEUR MAGIQUE

Wankan Tanka	LP	Byg	529018	1971	£20	£8	*French*

COFFEY, DENNIS

Evolution	LP	A&M	AMLS68035	1970	£10	£4	
Goin' For Myself	LP	A&M	AMLS68072	1971	£10	£4	
Instant Coffey	LP	Sussex	LPSX9	1974	£10	£4	

COGAN, ALMA

Alma	LP	Columbia	SX6130	1967	£30	£15	
Alma Sings With You In Mind	LP	Columbia	SCX3391	1961	£60	£30	*stereo*
Alma Sings With You In Mind	LP	Columbia	33SX1345	1961	£40	£20	
Bell Bottom Blues	7"	HMV	7M188	1954	£25	£12.50	
Birds And The Bees	7"	HMV	7M415	1956	£20	£10	
Chantez Chantez	7"	HMV	POP336	1957	£10	£5	
Chee Chee Oo Chee	7"	HMV	7M293	1955	£15	£7.50	
Do Do Do Do Do Do Do It Again	7"	HMV	7M226	1954	£10	£5	*with Frankie Vaughan*
Eight Days A Week	7"	Columbia	DB7786	1965	£4	£1.50	
Fabulous	7"	HMV	POP367	1957	£10	£5	
Fly Away Lovers	7"	HMV	POP500	1958	£4	£1.50	
Girl With A Laugh In Her Voice No. 2	7" EP	HMV	7EG8151	1955	£12	£6	
Girl With The Laugh In Her Voice	7" EP	HMV	7EG8122	1955	£15	£7.50	
Girl With The Laugh In Her Voice	LP	MFP	MFP1377	1970	£10	£4	
Girl With The Laugh In Her Voice No. 3	7" EP	HMV	7EG8169	1956	£12	£6	
Got 'n Idea	7"	HMV	7M316	1955	£15	£7.50	
Hits From My Fair Lady	7" EP	HMV	7EG8352	1957	£6	£2.50	*with Ronnie Hilton*
How About Love	LP	Columbia	SCX3459	1962	£60	£30	*stereo*
How About Love	LP	Columbia	33SX1465	1962	£40	£20	
I Can't Tell A Waltz From A Tango	7"	HMV	7M271	1954	£15	£7.50	
I Love To Sing	LP	HMV	CLP1152	1958	£40	£20	
I Went To Your Wedding	7"	HMV	7M106	1953	£20	£10	
In The Middle Of The House	7"	HMV	POP261	1956	£20	£10	
It's All Been Done Before	7"	HMV	7M390	1956	£20	£10	*with Ronnie Hilton*
It's You	7"	Columbia	DB7390	1964	£4	£1.50	
Last Night On The Back Porch	7"	HMV	POP573	1959	£5	£2	
Little Shoemaker	7"	HMV	7M219	1954	£20	£10	
Little Things Mean A Lot	7"	HMV	7M228	1954	£20	£10	
Love And Marriage	7"	HMV	7M367	1956	£15	£7.50	
Make Love To Me	7"	HMV	7M196	1954	£15	£7.50	
Mama Teach Me To Dance	7"	HMV	POP239	1956	£10	£5	
More Than Ever Now	7"	HMV	7M301	1955	£15	£7.50	
Must Be Santa	7"	HMV	POP815	1960	£4	£1.50	
Never Do A Tango With An Eskimo	7"	HMV	7M337	1955	£20	£10	
Now That I've Found You	7"	Columbia	DB8088	1966	£4	£1.50	
O Dio Mio	7"	HMV	POP728	1960	£4	£1.50	
Oliver	LP	HMV	CSD1370	1961	£40	£20	*stereo*
Oliver	LP	HMV	CLP1459	1961	£30	£15	*mono*
Over And Over Again	7"	HMV	7M166	1953	£15	£7.50	*with Les Howard*
Paper Kisses	7"	HMV	7M286	1955	£15	£7.50	
Party Time	7"	HMV	POP415	1957	£6	£2.50	
Pink Shoelaces	7"	HMV	POP608	1959	£5	£2	
Ricochet	7"	HMV	7M173	1954	£20	£10	
She Loves To Sing	7" EP	HMV	7EG8437	1957	£20	£10	
Snakes And Snails	7"	Columbia	DB7652	1965	£4	£1.50	
Stairway Of Love	7"	HMV	POP482	1958	£8	£4	
Story Of My Life	7"	HMV	POP433	1958	£8	£4	
Sugartime	7"	HMV	POP450	1958	£10	£5	
Tennessee Waltz	7"	Columbia	DB7233	1964	£6	£2.50	
That's Happiness	7"	HMV	POP392	1957	£6	£2.50	
There's Never Been A Night	7"	HMV	POP531	1958	£5	£2	

This Ole House	7"	HMV	7M269	1954	**£20**	**£10**	
To Be Loved By You	7"	HMV	7M107	1953	**£20**	**£10**	
Train Of Love	7"	HMV	POP760	1960	**£5**	**£2**	
We Got Love	7"	HMV	POP670	1959	**£4**	**£1.50**	
What Am I Gonna Do, Ma?	7"	HMV	7M239	1954	**£30**	**£15**	
Whatever Lola Wants	7"	HMV	POP317	1957	**£10**	**£5**	
You Me And Us	7"	HMV	POP284	1957	**£10**	**£5**	

COGAN, SHAYE

Billy Be Sure	7"	Columbia	DB4055	1958	**£5**	**£2**	
Mean To Me	7"	MGM	MGM1063	1960	**£20**	**£10**	

COHEN, ALAN

Duke Ellington's Black, Brown & Beige	LP	Argo	ZDA159	1973	**£12**	**£5**	

COHEN, LEONARD

Ain't No Cure For Love	CD-s	CBS	6515992	1988	**£5**	**£2**	
First We Take Manhattan	CD-s	CBS	6513522	1988	**£5**	**£2**	
Live From The Complex, Los Angeles	CD	Columbia	CSK5249	1993	**£20**	**£8**	*US promo*
McCabe & Mrs Miller	7" EP	CBS	7684	1972	**£5**	**£2**	
Songs From A Room	LP	CBS	63587	1968	**£10**	**£4**	
Songs Of Leonard Cohen	LP	Columbia	CL2733	1968	**£100**	**£50**	*US, mono*
Songs Of Leonard Cohen	LP	CBS	63241	1968	**£10**	**£4**	
Songs Of Love And Hate	LP	CBS	69004	1970	**£10**	**£4**	*with booklet*

COHEN, LEONARD & OTHERS

Canadian Poets 1	LP	CBC		1966	**£50**	**£25**	*Canadian*
Six Montreal Poets	LP	Folkways	FL9805	1957	**£50**	**£25**	*US*

COHN, AL

Al Cohn Orchestra	10" LP	HMV	DLP1107	1955	**£40**	**£20**	

COIL

Anal Staircase	12"	Force & Form	ROTA121	1986	**£6**	**£2.50**	
Anal Staircase	12"	Force & Form	ROTA121	1986	**£10**	**£5**	*clear vinyl*
Gold Is The Metal	CD	Threshold House	LOCICD1	1987	**£12**	**£5**	
Gold Is The Metal	LP	Threshold House	LOCI1	1988	**£20**	**£8**	*red or clear vinyl, with bonus 7"*
Gold Is The Metal	LP	Threshold House	LOCI1	1988	**£15**	**£6**	*red or clear vinyl*
Gold Is The Metal	LP	Threshold House	LOCI1	1988	**£200**	**£100**	*boxed with 7", poster, booklet, linen folder*
Hellraiser	10"	Solar Lodge	COIL001	198–	**£6**	**£2.50**	*clear or pink vinyl*
How To Destroy Angels	CD-s	Laylah	LAY005CD	1988	**£5**	**£2**	
Panic	12"	Force & Form	FFK512	1985	**£6**	**£2.50**	
Panic	12"	Force & Form	FFK512	1985	**£10**	**£5**	*red vinyl*
Wrong Eye	7"	Shock	SX002	1989	**£8**	**£4**	*individually numbered*
Wrong Eye	7"	Shock	SX002	1989	**£20**	**£10**	*individually lettered*

COIL (2)

Motor Industry	7"	Northampton Wood Hil	HAV1	1979	**£5**	**£2**	

COINCIDENCE

Coincidence	LP	Tromblas	1133	1976	**£15**	**£6**	*French*

COKER, ALVADEAN

We're Gonna Bop	7"	London	HLU8191	1955	**£200**	**£100**	*best auctioned*

COKER, SANDY

Meadowlark Melody	7"	London	HL8109	1954	**£50**	**£25**	

COLA BOY

Seven Ways 2 Love	12"	Cola	COLA1	1991	**£10**	**£5**	*promo, with Sarah Cracknell*

COLBECK, RIC

Sun Is Coming Up	LP	Fontana	63883001	1970	**£20**	**£8**	

COLD BLOOD

First Blood	LP	Atlantic	588218	1970	**£10**	**£4**	
First Taste Of Sin	LP	Reprise	2074	1972	**£10**	**£4**	*US*
Lydia	LP	Warner Bros	K56047	1974	**£10**	**£4**	
Sisyphus	LP	Atlantic	2400102	1971	**£10**	**£4**	

COLD CUTS

Cold Cuts	LP	Pink Elephant	8777099	1973	**£15**	**£6**	*Dutch*

COLD STEEL

Cold Steel	LP	Ariola	87736	1974	**£10**	**£4**	*Dutch*

COLD SUN

Dark Shadows	LP	Rockadelic		1991	**£30**	**£15**	*US*
Dark Shadows	LP	private		1969	**£2000**	**£1400**	*US acetate*

COLDER, BEN

Title	Format	Label	Cat. No.	Year	Mint	VG	Notes
Make The World Go Away	7" EP	MGM	MGMEP791	1964	**£8**	**£4**	

COLDMAN, RICHARD & JOHN RUSSELL

Title	Format	Label	Cat. No.	Year	Mint	VG	Notes
Homecooking . . . and Richard Coldman	LP	Incus	INCUS31	1979	**£12**	**£5**	

COLDWATER ARMY

Title	Format	Label	Cat. No.	Year	Mint	VG	Notes
Peace	LP	Agape	2600	1972	**£20**	**£8**	*US*

COLE, B. J.

Title	Format	Label	Cat. No.	Year	Mint	VG	Notes
New Hovering Dog	LP	United Artists	UAS29418	1972	**£10**	**£4**	

COLE, CINDY

Title	Format	Label	Cat. No.	Year	Mint	VG	Notes
Just Being Your Baby	7"	Columbia	DB7973	1966	**£5**	**£2**	
Love Like Yours	7"	Columbia	DB7519	1965	**£4**	**£1.50**	

COLE, CLAY

Title	Format	Label	Cat. No.	Year	Mint	VG	Notes
Twist Around The Clock	7"	London	HLP9499	1962	**£4**	**£1.50**	

COLE, COZY

Title	Format	Label	Cat. No.	Year	Mint	VG	Notes
Cozy Cole All Stars	7" EP	MGM	MGMEP622	1957	**£8**	**£4**	
Father Cooperates	7"	Mercury	AMT1015	1958	**£4**	**£1.50**	
Topsy	7"	London	HL8750	1958	**£5**	**£2**	
Topsy	7"	London	HL7065	1958	**£4**	**£1.50**	*export*
Turvy	7"	London	HL8843	1959	**£4**	**£1.50**	

COLE, JERRY

Title	Format	Label	Cat. No.	Year	Mint	VG	Notes
Every Window In The City	7"	Capitol	CL15397	1965	**£4**	**£1.50**	
Hot Rod Dance Party	LP	Capitol	(S)T2061	1964	**£15**	**£6**	*US*
Outer Limits	LP	Capitol	(S)T2044	1963	**£15**	**£6**	*US*
Surf Age	LP	Capitol	(S)T2112	1964	**£25**	**£10**	*US, with bonus Dick Dale 7"*

COLE, LLOYD & THE COMMOTIONS

Title	Format	Label	Cat. No.	Year	Mint	VG	Notes
Are You Ready To Be Heartbroken?	7"	Welcome To Las Vegas	LC1	1984	**£20**	**£10**	

COLE, NAT 'KING'

Title	Format	Label	Cat. No.	Year	Mint	VG	Notes
After Midnight	LP	Capitol	LCT6133	1957	**£10**	**£4**	
After Midnight Part 1	7" EP	Capitol	EAP1782	1957	**£5**	**£2**	
After Midnight Part 2	7" EP	Capitol	EAP2782	1957	**£5**	**£2**	
After Midnight Part 3	7" EP	Capitol	EAP3782	1957	**£5**	**£2**	
After Midnight Part 4	7" EP	Capitol	EAP4782	1958	**£5**	**£2**	
Annabelle	7"	Capitol	CL14317	1955	**£6**	**£2.50**	
Around The World	7" EP	Capitol	EAP1813	1957	**£5**	**£2**	
At The Piano	10" LP	Capitol	H156	1952	**£20**	**£8**	*US*
Ballads Of The Day	10" LP	Capitol	LC6818	1956	**£10**	**£4**	
Ballads Of The Day	LP	Capitol	T680	1956	**£12**	**£5**	*US*
Blossom Fell	7"	Capitol	CL14235	1955	**£8**	**£4**	
Capitol Presents Nat King Cole	10" LP	Capitol	LC6569	1953	**£15**	**£6**	
Capitol Presents Nat King Cole & His Trio Vol. 1	10" LP	Capitol	LC6587	1953	**£10**	**£4**	
Capitol Presents Nat King Cole & His Trio Vol. 2	10" LP	Capitol	LC6594	1953	**£10**	**£4**	
Capitol Presents Nat King Cole At The Piano	10" LP	Capitol	LC6593	1953	**£10**	**£4**	
Christmas Song	7" EP	Capitol	EAP1036	1956	**£5**	**£2**	
Cole Espanol	LP	Capitol	LCT6166	1958	**£10**	**£4**	
Cole Espanol Part 1	7" EP	Capitol	EAP11031	1959	**£5**	**£2**	
Cole Espanol Part 2	7" EP	Capitol	EAP21031	1959	**£5**	**£2**	
Dreams Can Tell A Lie	7"	Capitol	CL14513	1956	**£5**	**£2**	
Every Time I Feel The Spirit	LP	Capitol	LCT6187	1959	**£10**	**£4**	
I Am In Love	7"	Capitol	CL14172	1954	**£6**	**£2.50**	
If I Give My Heart To You	7"	Capitol	CL14203	1954	**£6**	**£2.50**	
If I May	7"	Capitol	CL14295	1955	**£6**	**£2.50**	
In The Beginning	LP	Brunswick	LAT8123	1956	**£15**	**£6**	
Instrumental Classics	LP	Capitol	T592	1955	**£12**	**£5**	*US*
Just One Of Those Things	LP	Capitol	(S)LCT6149	1958	**£10**	**£4**	
King Cole Trio	10" LP	Capitol	H8	1950	**£20**	**£8**	*US*
King Cole Trio	10" LP	Score	SLP4019	1950	**£60**	**£30**	*US*
King Cole Trio Vol. 2	10" LP	Capitol	H29	1950	**£20**	**£8**	*US*
King Cole Trio Vol. 3	10" LP	Capitol	H59	1950	**£20**	**£8**	*US*
King Cole Trio Vol. 4	10" LP	Capitol	H139	1951	**£20**	**£8**	*US*
Long Long Ago	7"	Capitol	CL14215	1955	**£8**	**£4**	
Looking Back	7" EP	Capitol	EAP1960	1958	**£5**	**£2**	
Love Is A Many Splendoured Thing	7"	Capitol	CL14364	1955	**£6**	**£2.50**	
Love Is A Many Splendoured Thing	7" EP	Capitol	EAP1010	1956	**£6**	**£2.50**	
Love Is Here To Stay	7" EP	Capitol	EAP120151	1961	**£5**	**£2**	
Love Is The Thing	LP	Capitol	(S)LCT6129	1957	**£10**	**£4**	
Love Is The Thing Part 1	7" EP	Capitol	EAP1824	1957	**£5**	**£2**	
Love Is The Thing Part 2	7" EP	Capitol	EAP2824	1957	**£5**	**£2**	
Love Is The Thing Part 3	7" EP	Capitol	EAP3824	1957	**£5**	**£2**	
Love Me As Though There Were No Tomorrow	7"	Capitol	CL14621	1956	**£5**	**£2**	
Midnight Flyer	7" EP	Capitol	EAP11317	1960	**£5**	**£2**	
Moods In Song	7" EP	Capitol	EAP1633	1956	**£6**	**£2.50**	
My One Sin	7"	Capitol	CL14327	1955	**£8**	**£4**	

Title	Format	Label	Cat. No.	Year	Mint	VG	Notes
Nat King Cole And George Shearing Part 1	7" EP	Capitol	EAP41675	1961	£5	£2	
Nat King Cole And George Shearing Part 2	7" EP	Capitol	EAP51675	1963	£5	£2	
Nat King Cole Trio	10" LP	Capitol	H220	1952	£20	£8	US
Nat King Cole Trio	10" LP	Capitol	H177	1952	£20	£8	US
Night Lights	7" EP	Capitol	EAP1801	1957	£5	£2	
Night Of The Quarter Moon	7" EP	Capitol	EAP11211	1959	£5	£2	
Non Domenticar	7" EP	Capitol	EAP11138	1959	£5	£2	
Penthouse Serenade	10" LP	Capitol	H332	1953	£20	£8	US
Penthouse Serenade	LP	Capitol	T332	1953	£12	£5	US
Piano Style Of Nat King Cole	10" LP	Capitol	LC6830	1956	£10	£4	
Piano Style Of Nat King Cole	LP	Capitol	W689	1956	£12	£5	US
Ramblin' Rose	7" EP	Capitol	EAP51793	1963	£5	£2	
Sand And The Sea	7"	Capitol	CL14251	1955	£6	£2.50	
Sings For Two In Love	10" LP	Capitol	LC6627	1953	£10	£4	
Sings For Two In Love	LP	Capitol	T420	1954	£12	£5	US
Smile	7"	Capitol	CL14149	1954	£8	£4	
Someone You Love	7"	Capitol	CL14378	1955	£6	£2.50	
St Louis Blues	LP	Capitol	(S)LCT6156	1958	£10	£4	
St Louis Blues Part 1	7" EP	Capitol	EAP1993	1958	£5	£2	
St Louis Blues Part 2	7" EP	Capitol	EAP2993	1958	£5	£2	
St Louis Blues Part 3	7" EP	Capitol	EAP3993	1958	£5	£2	
Strip For Action	7" EP	Capitol	EAP1040	1956	£5	£2	
Teach Me Tonight	7"	Capitol	CL14207	1954	£8	£4	
Tenderly	7" EP	Capitol	EAP120108	1961	£5	£2	
Tenth Anniversary Album	LP	Capitol	LCT6003	1954	£15	£6	
Tenth Anniversary Album Part 1	7" EP	Capitol	EAP1514	1955	£6	£2.50	
Tenth Anniversary Album Part 2	7" EP	Capitol	EAP2514	1955	£6	£2.50	
Tenth Anniversary Album Part 3	7" EP	Capitol	EAP3514	1955	£6	£2.50	
Tenth Anniversary Album Part 4	7" EP	Capitol	EAP4514	1955	£6	£2.50	
This Is Nat King Cole	LP	Capitol	LCT6142	1957	£10	£4	
To Whom It May Concern	LP	Capitol	(S)LCT6182	1959	£10	£4	
To Whom It May Concern Part 1	7" EP	Capitol	EAP11190	1959	£5	£2	
To Whom It May Concern Part 2	7" EP	Capitol	EAP21190	1959	£5	£2	
To Whom It May Concern Part 3	7" EP	Capitol	EAP31190	1959	£5	£2	
Too Young To Go Steady	7"	Capitol	CL14573	1956	£4	£1.50	
Unbelievable	7"	Capitol	CL14155	1954	£6	£2.50	
Unforgettable	10" LP	Capitol	H357	1953	£20	£8	US
Unforgettable	7" EP	Capitol	EAP120053	1961	£5	£2	
Unforgettable	LP	Capitol	T357	1953	£12	£5	US
Very Thought Of You	LP	Capitol	(S)LCT6173	1959	£10	£4	
Very Thought Of You Part 1	7" EP	Capitol	EAP11084	1959	£5	£2	
Very Thought Of You Part 2	7" EP	Capitol	EAP21084	1959	£5	£2	
Vocal Classics	LP	Capitol	T591	1955	£12	£5	US
Welcome To The Club	7" EP	Capitol	EAP11120	1959	£5	£0	
Welcome To The Club	LP	Capitol	(S)LCT6176	1959	£10	£4	
When I Fall In Love	7"	Capitol	CL14709	1957	£4	£1.50	
When Rock And Roll Came To Trinidad	7"	Capitol	CL14733	1957	£4	£1.50	

COLE, NATALIE

Title	Format	Label	Cat. No.	Year	Mint	VG	Notes
Party Lights	7"	Capitol	CL15929	1977	£4	£1.50	*demo only*

COLE, STRANGER

Title	Format	Label	Cat. No.	Year	Mint	VG	Notes
All Your Friends	7"	R&B	JB120	1963	£10	£5	*with Ken*
Cherry May	7"	Island	WI162	1964	£10	£5	*Don Drummond B side*
Cow In A Pasture	7"	Island	WI169	1965	£10	£5	*Gloris & Dreamletts B side*
Crying Every Night	7"	Camel	CA72	1971	£8	£4	
Darling Please	7"	Songbird	SB1008	1969	£4	£1.50	
Down The Train Line	7"	Doctor Bird	DB1087	1967	£10	£5	*with Patsy Todd*
Drop The Rachet	7"	Doctor Bird	DB1040	1966	£10	£5	
Give Me One More Chance	7"	Rio	R81	1966	£8	£4	*with Patsy Cole*
Give Me The Right	7"	Doctor Bird	DB1050	1966	£10	£5	*with Patsy Todd*
Glad You're Living	7"	Duke	DU27	1969	£4	£1.50	
Hey Little Girl	7"	Black Swan	WI462	1965	£10	£5	*with Patsy Todd, Cornell Campbell B side*
I Want To Go Home	7"	Black Swan	WI465	1965	£10	£5	
Jeboza Macod	7"	Island	WI3154	1968	£10	£5	
Just Like A River	7"	Amalgamated	AMG801	1968	£8	£4	*Leaders B side*
Last Love	7"	Island	WI114	1963	£10	£5	*Stranger & Ken B side*
Leana Leana	7"	Escort	ES819	1969	£4	£1.50	
Little Boy Blue	7"	Black Swan	WI435	1964	£10	£5	*Eric Morris B side*
Morning Star	7"	R&B	JB129	1963	£10	£5	
Night After Night	7"	Black Swan	WI461	1965	£10	£5	
Oh Oh I Need You	7"	Island	WI141	1964	£10	£5	*Don Drummond B side*
Out Of Many	7"	R&B	JB133	1963	£10	£5	
Over And Over Again	7"	Island	WI3128	1967	£10	£5	
Pretty Cottage	7"	Escort	ES810	1969	£4	£1.50	
Pussy Cat	7"	Ska Beat	JB192	1965	£10	£5	*Maytals B side*
Remember	7"	Escort	ES826	1969	£4	£1.50	
Rolling On	7"	Island	WI126	1963	£10	£5	
Run Joe	7"	Island	WI177	1965	£10	£5	

Title	Format	Label	Cat. No.	Year	Mint	VG	Notes
Seeing Is Knowing	7"	Amalgamated	AMG806	1968	£8	£4	Roy Shirley B side
Senor Senorita	7"	Island	WI113	1963	£10	£5	with Patsy Todd, Don Drummond B side
Stranger At The Door	7"	Island	WI110	1963	£10	£5	
Summer Day	7"	Black Swan	WI415	1964	£10	£5	
Tell It To Me	7"	Doctor Bird	DB1084	1967	£10	£5	with Patsy Todd
Things Come To Those Who Wait	7"	Island	WI160	1964	£10	£5	with Patsy Todd
Till My Dying Days	7"	Island	WI133	1963	£10	£5	Stranger & Patsy B side
Tom Dick And Harry	7"	Island	WI144	1964	£10	£5	with Patsy Todd
Uno-Dos-Tres	7"	Black Swan	WI413	1964	£10	£5	
We Shall Overcome	7"	Doctor Bird	DB1025	1966	£10	£5	
What Moma No Want She Get	7"	Amalgamated	AMG838	1969	£6	£2.50	
When I Get My Freedom	7"	Unity	UN514	1969	£4	£1.50	
When The Party Is Over	7"	Blue Beat	BB345	1966	£12	£6	Charmers B side
Yea Yea Baby	7"	Island	WI152	1964	£10	£5	with Patsy Todd, Baba Brooks B side
You Took My Love	7"	Doctor Bird	DB1066	1966	£10	£5	

COLEMAN, BOBBY

Title	Format	Label	Cat. No.	Year	Mint	VG	Notes
You Don't Have To Tell Me	7"	Pye	7N25365	1966	£40	£20	

COLEMAN, FITZROY

Title	Format	Label	Cat. No.	Year	Mint	VG	Notes
Lucille	7"	Starlite	ST45064	1961	£4	£1.50	

COLEMAN, LONNIE & JESSE ROBERTSON

Title	Format	Label	Cat. No.	Year	Mint	VG	Notes
Dolores Diana	7"	London	HLU8335	1956	£25	£12.50	

COLEMAN, MICHAEL

Title	Format	Label	Cat. No.	Year	Mint	VG	Notes
Irish Jigs And Reels	LP	Ace Of Hearts	AH56	1963	£25	£10	
Legacy Of Michael Coleman	LP	Shanachie	33002	1976	£10	£4	US

COLEMAN, ORNETTE

Title	Format	Label	Cat. No.	Year	Mint	VG	Notes
Art Of The Improvisors	LP	Atlantic	2400109	1971	£15	£6	
At The Golden Circle, Stockholm, Vol. 1	LP	Blue Note	BLP/BST84224	1966	£20	£8	
At The Golden Circle, Stockholm, Vol. 2	LP	Blue Note	BLP/BST84225	1966	£20	£8	
Change Of The Century	LP	London	LTZK15199/SAHK6099	1961	£25	£10	
Chappaqua Suite	LP	CBS	66203	1967	£30	£15	double
Crisis	LP	Impulse	AS9187	1972	£15	£6	US
Dancing In Your Head	LP	Horizon	SP722	1977	£15	£6	US
Empty Foxhole	LP	Blue Note	BLP/BST84246	1967	£20	£8	
Evening With Ornette Coleman	LP	Polydor	623246/7	1968	£30	£15	boxed double
Free Jazz	LP	Atlantic	(SD)1364	1961	£25	£10	US
Love Call	LP	Blue Note	BST84356	1970	£25	£10	
Music Of Ornette Coleman	LP	RCA	RD/SF7944	1970	£15	£6	
New York Is Now	LP	Blue Note	BST84287	1968	£25	£10	
Ornette	LP	London	LTZK15241/SAHK6235	1962	£25	£10	
Ornette At Twelve	LP	Impulse	M/SIPL518	1969	£15	£6	
Ornette On Tenor	LP	Atlantic	588121	1968	£15	£6	
Ornette On Tenor	LP	Atlantic	(SD)1394	1962	£25	£10	US
Science Fiction	LP	CBS	64774	1972	£15	£6	
Shape Of Jazz To Come	LP	Atlantic	587/588022	1966	£15	£6	
Shape Of Jazz To Come	LP	Atlantic	(SD)1317	1959	£25	£10	US
Skies Of America	LP	CBS	64147	1972	£20	£8	
Something Else	LP	Contemporary	LAC12170	1959	£25	£10	
This Is Our Music	LP	London	LTZK15228/SAHK6181	1961	£25	£10	
Tomorrow Is The Question	LP	Contemporary	LAC12228	1960	£25	£10	
Town Hall 1962	LP	Fontana	SFJL923	1969	£15	£6	
Twins	LP	Atlantic	K40278	1972	£15	£6	

COLEMAN TRADITIONAL SOCIETY

Title	Format	Label	Cat. No.	Year	Mint	VG	Notes
Music From The Coleman Country	LP	Leader	LEA2044	1972	£10	£4	

COLES, JOHNNY

Title	Format	Label	Cat. No.	Year	Mint	VG	Notes
Little Johnny C	LP	Blue Note	BLP/BST84144	1963	£40	£20	

COLEY

Title	Format	Label	Cat. No.	Year	Mint	VG	Notes
Goodbye Brains	LP	private		1971	£100	£50	

COLLAGE

Title	Format	Label	Cat. No.	Year	Mint	VG	Notes
Misty	LP	Studio Two	TWO410	1973	£15	£6	

COLLECTORS

Title	Format	Label	Cat. No.	Year	Mint	VG	Notes
Collectors	LP	Warner Bros	WS1746	1968	£25	£10	US
Grass And Wild Strawberries	LP	Warner Bros	WS1774	1968	£20	£8	

COLLEGE BOYS

Title	Format	Label	Cat. No.	Year	Mint	VG	Notes
Someone Will Be There	7"	Blue Beat	BB202	1963	£12	£6	

COLLEGE BOYS (2)

Title	Format	Label	Cat. No.	Year	Mint	VG	Notes
I Just Don't Understand	7"	Columbia	DB7306	1964	£10	£5	

COLLEN, SHARON

Title	Format	Label	Number	Year	Mint	VG	Notes
Travelling People	LP	HMV	CLP3592	1966	**£10**	**£4**	

COLLETTE, BUDDY

Title	Format	Label	Number	Year	Mint	VG	Notes
Man Of Many Parts	LP	Contemporary	LAC12090	1958	**£15**	**£6**	
Nice Day With Buddy Collette	LP	Contemporary	LAC12092	1958	**£15**	**£6**	
Porgy And Bess	LP	Top Rank	25003	1960	**£12**	**£5**	
Swinging Shepherds	LP	Mercury	MMB12001	1959	**£12**	**£5**	

COLLIER, GRAHAM

Title	Format	Label	Number	Year	Mint	VG	Notes
Darius	LP	Mosaic	GCM741	1974	**£12**	**£5**	
Day Of The Dead	LP	Mosaic	GCMD783/4	1978	**£20**	**£8**	*double*
Deep Dark Blue Centre	LP	Deram	DML/SML1005	1967	**£60**	**£30**	
Down Another Road	LP	Fontana	SFJL922	1960	**£[illegible]**	**£20**	
Jazz Illustrations	LP	Cambridge University	521205646	1975	**£20**	**£8**	
Jazz Lecture Concert	LP	Cambridge University	051205638	1975	**£20**	**£8**	
Jazz Rhythm Section	LP	Cambridge University	05212056033	1976	**£20**	**£8**	
Midnight Blue	LP	Mosaic	GCM751	1975	**£12**	**£5**	
Mosaics	LP	Philips	6308051	1971	**£40**	**£20**	
New Conditions	LP	Mosaic	GCM761	1976	**£12**	**£5**	
Portraits	LP	Saydisc	SDL244	1972	**£30**	**£15**	
Songs For My Father	LP	Polydor	6309006	1970	**£50**	**£25**	
Symphony Of Scorpions	LP	Mosaic	GCM773	1977	**£12**	**£5**	

COLLIER, MITTY

Title	Format	Label	Number	Year	Mint	VG	Notes
I Had A Talk With My Man	7"	Pye	7N25275	1964	**£15**	**£7.50**	

COLLINS, AL JAZZBO

Title	Format	Label	Number	Year	Mint	VG	Notes
East Coast Jazz Scene	LP	Vogue Coral	LVA9030	1956	**£30**	**£15**	

COLLINS, ALBERT

Albert Collins was one of the great blues guitarists, with an easily recognizable sound of his own derived from an oddly tuned Telecaster played without a plectrum. After some success with his earliest recordings, Collins hardly recorded at all during the seventies, but found himself becoming a considerable blues star towards the end of his life, thanks in no small part to the enthusiastic support of Robert Cray and Gary Moore, who featured him on their records, and jazz composer John Zorn, who wrote an extended showcase for his guitar playing (included on the album *Spillane*).

Title	Format	Label	Number	Year	Mint	VG	Notes
Compleat Albert Collins	LP	Imperial	12445	1969	**£20**	**£8**	*US*
Cool Sound Of Albert Collins	LP	TCF Hall	8002	1965	**£25**	**£10**	*US*
Love Can Be Found Anywhere	LP	Liberty	LBS83238	1969	**£20**	**£8**	
There's Gotta Be A Change	LP	Tumbleweed	TW3501	1971	**£15**	**£6**	
Trash Talkin'	LP	Imperial	12438	1969	**£20**	**£8**	*US*
Truckin'	LP	Blue Thumb	8758	197–	**£15**	**£6**	*US*

COLLINS, ANSELL

Title	Format	Label	Number	Year	Mint	VG	Notes
Cock Robin	7"	J-Dan	JDN4401	1970	**£4**	**£1.50**	
My Last Waltz	7"	Amalgamated	AMG851	1969	**£6**	**£2.50**	*Immortals B side*
Night Of Love	7"	Trojan	TR699	1969	**£4**	**£1.50**	
Nuclear Weapon	7"	Technique	TE913	1971	**£4**	**£1.50**	
Top Secret	7"	Technique	TE907	1970	**£4**	**£1.50**	

COLLINS, DAVE & ANSELL

Title	Format	Label	Number	Year	Mint	VG	Notes
Double Barrel	7"	Technique	TE901	1971	**£4**	**£1.50**	
Double Barrel	LP	Trojan	TBL162	1971	**£10**	**£4**	
Monkey Spanner	7"	Technique	TE914	1971	**£4**	**£1.50**	

COLLINS, DONNIE SHOW BAND

Title	Format	Label	Number	Year	Mint	VG	Notes
Get Down With It	7"	Pye	7N17628	1968	**£5**	**£2**	

COLLINS, DOROTHY

Title	Format	Label	Number	Year	Mint	VG	Notes
At Home With Dorothy And Raymond	LP	Coral	LVA9058	1957	**£12**	**£5**	
Baby Can Rock	7"	Vogue Coral	Q72232	1957	**£10**	**£5**	
Cool It Baby	7"	Vogue Coral	Q72198	1956	**£20**	**£10**	
Dorothy Collins Sings	7" EP	London	REP1025	1955	**£15**	**£7.50**	
Four Walls	7"	Vogue Coral	Q72262	1957	**£4**	**£1.50**	
Moments To Remember	7"	Vogue Coral	Q72116	1956	**£6**	**£2.50**	
Mr Wonderful	7"	Vogue Coral	Q72252	1957	**£4**	**£1.50**	
My Boy Flat Top	7"	Vogue Coral	Q72111	1955	**£20**	**£10**	
Rock And Roll Train	7"	Vogue Coral	Q72193	1956	**£20**	**£10**	
Seven Days	7"	Vogue Coral	Q72137	1956	**£10**	**£5**	
Soft Sands	7"	Vogue Coral	Q72287	1957	**£4**	**£1.50**	
Treasure Of Love	7"	Vogue Coral	Q72173	1956	**£12**	**£6**	
Twelve Gifts Of Christmas	7"	Vogue Coral	Q72208	1956	**£8**	**£4**	

COLLINS, EDWYN

Title	Format	Label	Number	Year	Mint	VG	Notes
Don't Shilly Shally	12"	Creation	CRE047T	1987	**£25**	**£12.50**	*test pressing*
Fifty Shades Of Blue	CD-s	Demon	D1065CD	1989	**£5**	**£2**	
My Beloved Girl	7"	Elevation	ACID6B	1987	**£5**	**£2**	*boxed with 3 cards*

COLLINS, GLENDA

Title	Format	Label	Number	Year	Mint	VG	Notes
Age For Love	7"	Decca	F11321	1961	**£10**	**£5**	
Baby It Hurts	7"	HMV	POP1283	1964	**£40**	**£20**	
Head Over Heels In Love	7"	Decca	F11417	1961	**£6**	**£2.50**	
I Lost My Heart In The Fairground	7"	HMV	POP1163	1963	**£60**	**£30**	

If You've Got To Pick A Baby	7"	HMV	POP1233	1963	£30	£15	
It's Hard To Believe It	7"	Pye	7N17150	1966	£60	£30	
Johnny Loves Me	7"	HMV	POP1439	1965	£40	£20	
Lollipop	7"	HMV	POP1323	1964	£30	£15	
Something I've Got To Tell You	7"	Pye	7N17044	1966	£40	£20	
Take A Chance	7"	Decca	F11280	1960	£8	£4	
Thou Shalt Not Steal	7"	HMV	POP1475	1965	£30	£15	

COLLINS, JOHNNY

Johnny's Private Army	LP	Tradition	TSR020	1975	£10	£4	
Traveller's Rest	LP	Tradition	TSR014	1973	£10	£4	

COLLINS, JUDY

Concert	LP	Elektra	EKL/EKS7280	1964	£10	£4	
Fifth Album	LP	Elektra	EKL/EKS7300	1965	£10	£4	
Golden Apples Of The Sun	LP	Elektra	EKL/EKS7222	1962	£10	£4	
I'll Keep It With Mine	7"	London	HLZ10029	1966	£4	£1.50	
In My Life	LP	Elektra	EKL/EKS7320	1967	£10	£4	
Maid Of Constant Sorrow	LP	Elektra	EKL/EKS7209	1962	£15	£6	
Third Album	LP	Elektra	EKL/EKS7243	1964	£10	£4	
Who Knows Where The Time Goes	LP	Elektra	EKL/EKS74033	1969	£12	£5	
Wild Flowers	LP	Elektra	EKL/EKS74012	1968	£12	£5	

COLLINS, LYN

Check Me Out If You Don't Know Me By Now	LP	People	PE6605	1975	£30	£15	US
Female Preacher	LP	Urban	URBLP7	1988	£10	£4	
Rock Me Again And Again	7"	Polydor	2066490	1974	£6	£2.50	
Think	7"	Mojo	2093029	1974	£5	£2	
Think	LP	Polydor	2918006	1972	£30	£15	
What Am I Gonna Do Without You?	7"	Sabre	SA0002	1964	£6	£2.50	

COLLINS, PETER

First Album	LP	Nova	SDN21	1970	£10	£4	

COLLINS, PHIL

Another Day In Paradise	CD-s	Virgin	VSC1234	1989	£5	£2	
Do You Remember (Live)	CD-s	Virgin	VSCDX1305	1990	£10	£5	picture disc
Do You Remember (Live)	CD-s	Virgin	VSCD1305	1990	£5	£2	
Groovy Kind Of Love	CD-s	Virgin	VSCD1117	1988	£5	£2	
Hang In Long Enough	CD-s	Virgin	VSCDX1300	1990	£6	£2.50	picture disc
I Wish It Would Rain Down	CD-s	Virgin	VSCD1240	1990	£5	£2	
In The Air Tonight	7"	Virgin	VSK102	1981	£5	£2	with booklet
In The Air Tonight	CD-s	Virgin	VSCD102	1988	£5	£2	
One More Night	7"	Virgin	VSS755	1985	£5	£2	shaped picture disc
Profiled!	CD	Atlantic	PR30922	1989	£20	£8	US interview promo
Separate Lives	7"	Virgin	VSSD818	1985	£6	£2.50	2 picture discs
Serious Hits	CD	Virgin	PCVCD1	1990	£60	£30	promo box set with video, tour programme
Something Happened On The Way To Heaven	CD-s	Virgin	VSCDT1251	1990	£5	£2	
Story Interview Disc	CD	Atlantic	PR53702	1993	£20	£8	US interview promo
Story So Far	CD	Virgin	PC001	1993	£30	£15	promo compilation
Sussudio	7"	Virgin	VSY73612	1985	£5	£2	shaped picture disc
That's Just The Way It Is	CD-s	Virgin	VSCD1277	1990	£5	£2	
Thru' These Walls	7"	Virgin	VSY524	1982	£4	£1.50	picture disc
Twelve Inchers	CD-s	Virgin	CDEP4	1988	£5	£2	
Two Hearts	CD-s	Virgin	VSCD1142	1988	£5	£2	3" single
You Can't Hurry Love	7"	Virgin	VSY531	1982	£5	£2	picture disc

COLLINS, ROGER

She's Looking Good	7"	Vocalion	VP9285	1967	£6	£2.50	

COLLINS, SHIRLEY

Adieu To Old England	LP	Topic	12T238	1974	£25	£10	
Amaranth	LP	Harvest	SHSM2008	1976	£20	£8	
Anthems In Eden	LP	Harvest	SHVL754	1969	£50	£25	with Dolly Collins
English Songs Vol. 2	7" EP	Collector	JEB9	1964	£50	£25	
False True Lovers	LP	Folkways	FG3564	1959	£150	£75	US
Favourite Garland	LP	Deram	SML1117	1975	£15	£6	
Foggy Dew	7" EP	Collector	JEB3	1960	£50	£25	
For As Many As Will	LP	Topic	12T380	1978	£10	£4	with Dolly Collins
Heroes In Love	7" EP	Topic	TOP95	1963	£50	£25	
Love, Death And The Lady	LP	Harvest	SHVL771	1970	£50	£25	with Dolly Collins
No Roses	LP	Pegasus	PEG7	1971	£25	£10	with Albion Band
No Roses	LP	Mooncrest	CREST11	1974	£10	£4	with Albion Band
Power Of The True Love Knot	LP	Polydor	583025	1968	£60	£30	
Power Of The True Love Knot	LP	Hannibal	HNBL1327	198–	£10	£4	
Sings Irish	7" EP	Collector	JEI1508	1960	£50	£25	
Sweet England	LP	Argo	RG150	1960	£100	£50	
Sweet Primroses	LP	Topic	12TS170	1967	£40	£20	
Unquiet Grave	7" EP	Collector	JEB5	1961	£50	£25	

COLLINS, TOMMY

Dynamic Tommy Collins	LP	Columbia	CL2510/CS9310	1966	£20	£8	US
Let Down	7"	Capitol	CL14894	1958	£4	£1.50	
Let's Live A Little	LP	Tower	(D)T5021	1966	£12	£5	US

Title	Format	Label	Catalogue No.	Year	Mint	VG	Notes
Light Of The Lord	LP	Capitol	T1125	1959	**£25**	**£10**	*US*
Little June	7"	Capitol	CL15076	1959	**£5**	**£2**	
On Tour	LP	Columbia	CL2778/CS9578	1968	**£20**	**£8**	*US*
Shindig	LP	Tower	(D)T5107	1968	**£12**	**£5**	*US*
Songs I Love To Sing	LP	Capitol	(S)T1436	1961	**£20**	**£8**	*US*
Think It Over Boys	7"	Capitol	CL14838	1958	**£5**	**£2**	
This Is Tommy Collins	LP	Capitol	T1196	1959	**£20**	**£8**	
Words And Music Country Style	LP	Capitol	T776	1957	**£20**	**£8**	
Wreck Of The Old '97	7"	Capitol	CL15118	1960	**£4**	**£1.50**	

COLONEL

Title	Format	Label	Catalogue No.	Year	Mint	VG	Notes
Cokey Cokey	7"	Ring O'	2017104	1975	**£5**	**£2**	

COLONEL (2)

Title	Format	Label	Catalogue No.	Year	Mint	VG	Notes
Too Many Cooks	7"	Virgin	VS380	1980	**£10**	**£5**	

COLONNA, JERRY

Title	Format	Label	Catalogue No.	Year	Mint	VG	Notes
Chicago Style	7"	London	HL8143	1955	**£12**	**£6**	
Ebb Tide	7"	Brunswick	05243	1954	**£8**	**£4**	
It Might As Well Be Spring	7"	Brunswick	05342	1954	**£6**	**£2.50**	
Let Me Go Lover	7"	Parlophone	MSP6165	1955	**£4**	**£1.50**	
Let's All Sing	LP	London	HAU2190	1959	**£15**	**£7.50**	
Shifting Whispering Sands	7"	HMV	7M369	1956	**£4**	**£1.50**	

COLORADOS

Title	Format	Label	Catalogue No.	Year	Mint	VG	Notes
Lips Are Redder On You	7"	Oriole	CB1972	1964	**£6**	**£2.50**	

COLOSSEUM

Arguably the finest of the jazz-rock groups, Colosseum was only together for three years originally, but made a big impact. The members all had a long pedigree, having played with the likes of John Mayall's Bluesbreakers and Graham Bond, and nearly all have remained in music since. Jon Hiseman, in particular, led the rockier Colosseum II with Gary Moore, and has since been the drummer and producer for his wife, jazz saxophonist Barbara Thompson. In the nineties, the classic line-up of Colosseum re-formed and has played a number of dynamic, enthusiastically received concerts as well as recording an album of new material.

Title	Format	Label	Catalogue No.	Year	Mint	VG	Notes
Collectors' Colosseum	LP	Bronze	ILPS9173	1971	**£10**	**£4**	
Daughter Of Time	LP	Vertigo	6360017	1970	**£10**	**£4**	*spiral label*
Live	LP	Bronze	ICD1	1971	**£12**	**£5**	*double*
Those About To Die Salute You	LP	Fontana	STL5510	1969	**£12**	**£5**	
Those Who Are About To Die	7"	Fontana	TF1029	1969	**£4**	**£1.50**	
Valentyne Suite	LP	Vertigo	VO1	1969	**£12**	**£5**	*spiral label*

COLOURBOX

Title	Format	Label	Catalogue No.	Year	Mint	VG	Notes
Breakdown	12"	4AD	BAD215	1982	**£6**	**£2.50**	
Breakdown	7"	4AD	AD215	1982	**£4**	**£1.50**	
Colourbox	LP	4AD	CAD508/MAD509	1985	**£15**	**£6**	*double*

COLOURFIELD

Title	Format	Label	Catalogue No.	Year	Mint	VG	Notes
Deception	CD	Chrysalis	CCD1546	1987	**£20**	**£8**	
Virgins And Philistines	CD	Chrysalis	CCD1480	1985	**£25**	**£10**	

COLOURS OF LOVE

Although collectors' interest in the singles made by Colours of Love is slight, one of the singers was Elaine Page.

Title	Format	Label	Catalogue No.	Year	Mint	VG	Notes
I'm A Train	7"	Page One	POF060	1968	**£4**	**£1.50**	
Just Another Fly	7"	Page One	POF086	1968	**£4**	**£1.50**	
Mother Of Convention	7"	Page One	POF124	1969	**£4**	**£1.50**	

COLT, CHRISTOPHER

Title	Format	Label	Catalogue No.	Year	Mint	VG	Notes
Virgin Sunrise	7"	Decca	F12726	1968	**£15**	**£7.50**	

COLTON, TONY

Title	Format	Label	Catalogue No.	Year	Mint	VG	Notes
I Stand Accused	7"	Pye	7N15886	1965	**£100**	**£50**	
I've Laid Some Down In My Time	7"	Pye	7N17117	1966	**£15**	**£7.50**	
In The World Of Marnie Dreaming	7"	Columbia	DB8385	1968	**£6**	**£2.50**	
Lose My Mind	7"	Decca	F11879	1964	**£6**	**£2.50**	
You're Wrong There Baby	7"	Pye	7N17046	1966	**£15**	**£7.50**	

COLTRANE, ALICE

John Coltrane's wife played piano on her husband's last recordings, and expanded her range to include organ and harp on the music she made after his death. Her albums tend to have a mystical slant which makes them fit well into the ethos of much seventies progressive music, although the sound is closer to the emotional out-pouring of John Coltrane than to a superficially similar hippy group like Gong. Nevertheless, Alice Coltrane did later make an album with Carlos Santana, though it is not listed here.

Title	Format	Label	Catalogue No.	Year	Mint	VG	Notes
Eternity	LP	Warner Bros	BS2916	1976	**£12**	**£5**	*US*
Journey In Satchidananda	LP	Impulse	AS9203	1971	**£20**	**£8**	*US*
Lord Of Lords	LP	Impulse	AS9224	1973	**£15**	**£6**	*US*
Monastic Trio	LP	Impulse	AS9156	1968	**£20**	**£8**	*US*
Ptah The El Daoud	LP	Impulse	AS9196	1970	**£20**	**£8**	*US*
Reflection On Creation And Space	LP	Impulse	AS92322	1973	**£25**	**£10**	*US*
Universal Consciousness	LP	Impulse	AS9210	1971	**£20**	**£8**	*US*

COLTRANE, JOHN

In the sixties, John Coltrane's passionate brand of modal improvisation often appealed to rock fans who did not otherwise like jazz. And when rock groups started to introduce long improvised solos, it was invariably the Coltrane style that they adopted. (This was made explicit by Mike Bloomfield and Al Kooper in their Coltrane tribute track 'His Holy Modal Majesty'.) There is one oddity in the Coltrane discography – some copies of *Kulu Se Mama* actually play the album *Om*, which was not otherwise given a UK release. There are likely to be some owners of *Kulu Se Mama* who are unaware that the music they know by that title is actually something totally different!

Title	Format	Label	Number	Year	Mint	VG	Notes
Africa/Brass	LP	HMV	CLP1548/ CSD1431	1962	**£20**	**£8**	
Afro Blue	LP	Probe	SPB1025	1971	**£15**	**£6**	
Alternate Takes	LP	Atlantic	SD1668	1975	**£12**	**£5**	*US*
Ascension	LP	HMV	CLP/CSD3543	1966	**£20**	**£8**	
Atlantic Years	LP	Atlantic	K60052	1974	**£15**	**£6**	*double*
Avant-Garde	LP	Atlantic	587/588004	1966	**£20**	**£8**	*with Don Cherry*
Bags And Trane	LP	London	LTZK15232/ SAHK6192	1962	**£25**	**£10**	*with Milt Jackson*
Bahia	LP	Stateside	SL10162	1966	**£15**	**£6**	
Ballads	LP	HMV	CLP1647/ CSD1496	1963	**£20**	**£8**	
Bass Blues	7" EP	Esquire	EP239	1961	**£5**	**£2**	
Black Pearls	LP	Stateside	SL10124	1965	**£15**	**£6**	
Black Pearls	LP	Prestige	PR24037	1974	**£12**	**£5**	*double*
Blue Train	LP	Blue Note	BLP/BST81577	1961	**£30**	**£15**	
Cattin'	LP	Esquire	32101	1960	**£20**	**£8**	
Coltrane	LP	HMV	CLP1629/ CSD1483	1963	**£20**	**£8**	
Coltrane Jazz	LP	Atlantic	ATL/SAL1354	1967	**£15**	**£6**	
Coltrane Jazz	LP	London	LTZK15219/ SAHK6162	1961	**£25**	**£10**	
Coltrane Plays The Blues	LP	London	HAK/SHK8017	1963	**£25**	**£10**	
Coltrane Time	LP	United Artists	(S)ULP1018	1963	**£20**	**£8**	
Coltrane's Sound	LP	Atlantic	587/588039	1966	**£15**	**£6**	
Concert In Japan	LP	Impulse	AS9246	1973	**£30**	**£15**	*US triple*
Cosmic Music	LP	Impulse	M/SIPL515	1969	**£20**	**£8**	*with Alice Coltrane*
Crescent	LP	HMV	CLP1799/ CSD1567	1965	**£20**	**£8**	
Dakar	LP	Transatlantic	PR7280	1968	**£15**	**£6**	
Duke Ellington And John Coltrane	LP	HMV	CLP1657/ CSD1502	1963	**£20**	**£8**	
Expression	LP	Impulse	M/SIPL502	1968	**£20**	**£8**	
First Trane	LP	Esquire	32079	1958	**£25**	**£10**	
Giant Steps	LP	London	LTZK15197	1960	**£25**	**£10**	
Giant Steps	LP	Atlantic	ATL1311	1967	**£15**	**£6**	
Giant Steps	LP	Atlantic	588168	1969	**£10**	**£4**	
Impressions	LP	HMV	CLP1695/ CSD1509	1964	**£20**	**£8**	
Infinity	LP	Impulse	AS9225	1973	**£15**	**£6**	*US*
Interstellar Space	LP	Impulse	ASD9277	1974	**£15**	**£6**	*US*
John Coltrane	LP	Prestige	PR24003	1973	**£12**	**£5**	*double*
John Coltrane Quartet Plays	LP	HMV	CLP1897/ CSD1619	1965	**£20**	**£8**	
John Coltrane With Johnny Hartman	LP	HMV	CLP1700	1964	**£20**	**£8**	
Kulu Se Mama	LP	HMV	CLP/CSD3617	1967	**£25**	**£10**	*mispress – plays Coltrane's Om LP*
Kulu Se Mama	LP	HMV	CLP/CSD3617	1967	**£20**	**£8**	
Last Trane	LP	Transatlantic	PR7378	1968	**£15**	**£6**	
Live At Birdland	LP	HMV	CLP1741/ CSD1544	1964	**£20**	**£8**	
Live At The Village Vanguard	LP	HMV	CLP1590/ CSD1456	1962	**£20**	**£8**	
Live At The Village Vanguard Again	LP	HMV	CLP/CSD3599	1967	**£20**	**£8**	
Live In Seattle	LP	Impulse	AS92022	1971	**£25**	**£10**	*US double*
Love Supreme	LP	HMV	CLP1869/ CSD1605	1965	**£20**	**£8**	
Lush Life	LP	Esquire	32129	1961	**£25**	**£10**	
Meditation	LP	HMV	CLP/CSD3575	1966	**£20**	**£8**	
Moment's Notice	7"	Blue Note	451718	1964	**£5**	**£2**	
More Lasting Than Bronze	LP	Prestige	PR24014	1973	**£12**	**£5**	*double*
My Favorite Things	LP	Atlantic	588146	1969	**£10**	**£4**	
My Favorite Things	LP	Atlantic	ATL/SAL5022	1965	**£15**	**£6**	
New Thing At Newport	LP	HMV	CLP/CSD3551	1966	**£20**	**£8**	*with Archie Shepp*
Olé Coltrane	LP	London	LTZK15239/ SAHK6223	1962	**£25**	**£10**	
On West 42nd Street	LP	Realm	RM157	1963	**£15**	**£6**	
Other Village Vanguard Tapes	LP	Impulse	AS9325	1977	**£12**	**£5**	*US*
Selflessness	LP	Impulse	SIPL522	1969	**£20**	**£8**	
Soul Of Trane	7" EP	Esquire	EP229	1960	**£5**	**£2**	
Soultrane	LP	Esquire	32089	1959	**£25**	**£10**	
Soultrane	LP	Transatlantic	PR7531	1968	**£12**	**£5**	
Standard Coltrane	LP	Esquire	32179	1963	**£20**	**£8**	
Sun Ship	LP	Impulse	AS9211	1973	**£15**	**£6**	*US*
Tanganyika Strut	LP	Realm	RM52226	1965	**£15**	**£6**	
Tenor Conclave	LP	Esquire	32059	1958	**£20**	**£8**	
Trane Ride	LP	Realm	RM181	1964	**£15**	**£6**	
Traneing In	LP	Esquire	32091	1959	**£25**	**£10**	
Transition	LP	Impulse	AS9195	1970	**£20**	**£8**	*US*
While My Lady Sleeps	7" EP	Fontana	469203TE	1964	**£5**	**£2**	

COLWELL BROTHERS

Title	Format	Label	Number	Year	Mint	VG	Notes
Africa's Got The Answer	7" EP	Philips	NBE11117	1959	**£5**	**£2**	
Colwell Brothers	7" EP	Philips	NBE11048	195–	**£5**	**£2**	

Colwell Brothers	7" EP	Philips	NBE11047	195–	**£5**	**£2**	
There'll Be A New World	7" EP	Philips	NBE11118	1959	**£5**	**£2**	

COLWELL–WINFIELD BLUES BAND

Live Bust	LP	Zazoo	1	1971	**£15**	**£6**	*US*

COLYER, KEN

And Back To New Orleans Vol. 1	7" EP	Decca	DFE6268	1955	**£5**	**£2**	
And Back To New Orleans Vol. 2	7" EP	Decca	DFE6299	1956	**£5**	**£2**	
And His Omega Brass	7" EP	Decca	DFE6435	1957	**£5**	**£2**	
At The Thames Hotel	LP	Joy	JOYS170	1970	**£10**	**£4**	
Back To The Delta	10" LP	Decca	LF1196	1954	**£20**	**£8**	
Club Session	LP	Decca	LK4178	1957	**£12**	**£5**	
Colyer's Pleasure	LP	Society	SOC914	1963	**£10**	**£4**	
Dippermouth Blues	7"	Decca	FJ107[illegible]	19[illegible]	**£4**	**£1.50**	
Early Hours	7"	Decca	F10504	1955	**£4**	**£1.50**	
If I Ever Cease To Love	7"	Decca	F10519	1955	**£4**	**£1.50**	
In Hamburg	10" LP	Decca	LF1319	1959	**£15**	**£6**	
In New Orleans	10" LP	Vogue	LDE161	1955	**£20**	**£8**	
In New Orleans	7" EP	Vogue	EPV1102	1956	**£5**	**£2**	
In New Orleans	7" EP	Tempo	EXA53	1957	**£6**	**£2.50**	
In New Orleans Pt 2	7" EP	Vogue	EPV1202	1958	**£5**	**£2**	
Isle Of Capri	7"	Tempo	A120	1956	**£4**	**£1.50**	
Ken Colyer	7" EP	Melodisc	EPM7105	195–	**£5**	**£2**	
Ken Colyer Jazzmen	7" EP	Storyville	SEP301	1960	**£5**	**£2**	
Ken Colyer Jazzmen	7" EP	Tempo	EXA26	1956	**£6**	**£2.50**	
Ken Colyer Jazzmen	7" EP	Tempo	EXA31	1956	**£6**	**£2.50**	
Ken Colyer Jazzmen & Crane River Jazz Band	7" EP	Melodisc	EPM759	1956	**£5**	**£2**	
Ken Colyer's Jazzmen	10" LP	Tempo	LAP11	1956	**£30**	**£15**	
Ken Colyer's Jazzmen	7" EP	Storyville	SEP305	196–	**£5**	**£2**	
Ken Colyer's Jazzmen	7" EP	Storyville	SEP309	196–	**£5**	**£2**	
Marching To New Orleans	10" LP	Decca	LF1301	1958	**£15**	**£6**	
Maryland My Maryland	7"	Tempo	A136	1956	**£4**	**£1.50**	
New Orleans To London	10" LP	Decca	LF1152	1954	**£20**	**£8**	
Plays Standards	LP	Decca	LK4294	1959	**£12**	**£5**	
Real Ken Colyer	LP	77	LEU1210	1964	**£20**	**£8**	
Red Wing	7"	Decca	F10565	1955	**£4**	**£1.50**	
Rum And Coca Cola	7" EP	Esquire	EP233	1960	**£5**	**£2**	
Sheik Of Araby	7"	Tempo	A117	1956	**£4**	**£1.50**	
Stomping	7" EP	Esquire	EP243	1961	**£5**	**£2**	
They All Played Ragtime	7" EP	Decca	DFE6466	1958	**£5**	**£2**	
This Is Jazz	7" EP	Columbia	SEG8038	1960	**£5**	**£2**	
This Is Jazz	LP	Columbia	33SX1220	1960	**£10**	**£4**	
This Is Jazz Vol. 1 No. 2	7" EP	Columbia	SEG8104	1961	**£5**	**£2**	
This Is Jazz Vol. 2	7" EP	Columbia	SEG8145	1962	**£5**	**£2**	
This Is Jazz Vol. 2	LP	Columbia	33SX1297/ SCX3360	1961	**£10**	**£4**	
This Is The Blues Vol. 1	LP	Columbia	33SX1363	1961	**£40**	**£20**	
Too Busy	7" EP	Columbia	SEG8180	1962	**£5**	**£2**	
Trad Jazz Scene In Europe Vol. 2	7" EP	Storyville	SEP392	1961	**£5**	**£2**	
Wabash Blues	7"	Tempo	A126	1956	**£4**	**£1.50**	
Walking The Blues	7" EP	Decca	STO143	1960	**£5**	**£2**	
Walking The Blues	7" EP	Decca	DFE6645	1960	**£5**	**£2**	
Wandering	LP	K.C.	KCS1001	1965	**£20**	**£8**	
Watch That Dirty Tone	LP	Joy	JOYS164	1970	**£10**	**£4**	
Wildcat Blues	7" EP	Storyville	SEP412	1961	**£5**	**£2**	

COLYER, KEN SKIFFLE GROUP

Downbound Train	7"	Decca	FJ10751	1956	**£5**	**£2**	
Ella Speed	7"	Decca	FJ10972	1958	**£4**	**£1.50**	
Green Corn	7" EP	KC	KCS11EP	1966	**£5**	**£2**	
Grey Goose	7"	Decca	FJ10889	1957	**£4**	**£1.50**	
House Rent Stomp	7"	Decca	FJ10926	1957	**£4**	**£1.50**	
Ken Colyer Skiffle Group In Hamburg	7" EP	Decca	DFE6563	1959	**£8**	**£4**	
Ken Colyer's Skiffle Group	7" EP	Decca	DFE6286	1956	**£6**	**£2.50**	
Ken Colyer's Skiffle Group No. 2	7" EP	Decca	DFE6444	1957	**£6**	**£2.50**	
Ole Riley	7"	Decca	FJ10772	1956	**£5**	**£2**	
Streamline Train	7"	Decca	F10711	1956	**£5**	**£2**	
Take This Hammer	7"	Decca	F10631	1955	**£5**	**£2**	

COMBAT 84

Orders Of The Day	7"	Victory	VIC1	1983	**£12**	**£6**	
Rapist	7"	Victory	VIC2	1983	**£12**	**£6**	

COMBINE HARVESTER

Combine Harvester	LP	Folk Heritage	FHR009	1970	**£15**	**£6**	

COME

Come Sunday	7"	Come Org.	WDC88001	1979	**£10**	**£5**	
I'm Jack	LP	Come Org.	WDC880012	1981	**£25**	**£10**	*orange vinyl*
Rampton	LP	Come Org.	WDC88002	1979	**£30**	**£15**	

COMFORTABLE CHAIR

Comfortable Chair	LP	Ode	21244005	1969	**£25**	**£10**	*US*

COMMANCHES

Tomorrow	7"	Pye	7N15609	1964	**£4**	**£1.50**	

COMMANDERS

Cat From Coos Bay	7"	Brunswick	05433	1955	**£4**	**£1.50**	
Meet The Commanders	7" EP	Brunswick	OE9037	1955	**£5**	**£2**	
Monster	7"	Brunswick	05467	1955	**£4**	**£1.50**	

COMMODORES

Riding On A Train	7"	London	HLD8209	1955	**£750**	**£500**	*best auctioned*
Speedo	7"	London	HLD8251	1956	**£600**	**£400**	*best auctioned*

COMMON BOND

Faces	LP	Word	WST9569	1975	**£30**	**£15**	

COMMON PEOPLE

Of The People, By The People, For The People	LP	Capitol	ST266	1969	**£75**	**£37.50**	*US*

COMMON ROUND

Four Pence A Day	LP	Galliard	GAL4015	197–	**£12**	**£5**	

COMMUNARDS

Don't Leave Me This Way	CD-s	Polygram	0804782	1988	**£8**	**£4**	*CD video*
For A Friend	CD-s	London	LONCD166	1988	**£5**	**£2**	
Never Can Say Goodbye	CD-s	London	LONCD158	1988	**£5**	**£2**	
There's More To Love	CD-s	London	LONCD173	1988	**£5**	**£2**	
You Are My World	CD-s	London	LONFC123	1988	**£5**	**£2**	

COMO, PERRY

All At Once You Love Her	7"	HMV	POP394	1957	**£4**	**£1.50**	
Bushel And A Peck	7"	HMV	7M138	1953	**£10**	**£5**	
Como Sings	7" EP	HMV	7EG8192	1956	**£5**	**£2**	
Don't Let The Stars Get In Your Eyes	7"	HMV	7M118	1953	**£12**	**£6**	
Door Of Dreams	7"	HMV	7M305	1955	**£6**	**£2.50**	
Frosty The Snowman	7"	HMV	7M278	1954	**£6**	**£2.50**	
Glendora	7"	HMV	7MC49	1956	**£10**	**£5**	
Hello Young Lovers	7"	HMV	7M155	1953	**£6**	**£2.50**	
Hot Diggity	7"	HMV	7M404	1956	**£8**	**£4**	
Idle Gossip	7"	HMV	7M200	1954	**£8**	**£4**	
If You Were Only Mine	7"	HMV	7M241	1954	**£8**	**£4**	
Juke Box Baby	7"	HMV	7MC39	1956	**£25**	**£12.50**	*export*
Ko Ko Mo	7"	HMV	7M296	1955	**£8**	**£4**	
Moonlight Love	7"	HMV	POP271	1956	**£5**	**£2**	
More	7"	HMV	POP240	1956	**£8**	**£4**	
Papa Loves Mambo	7"	HMV	7M263	1954	**£10**	**£5**	
Perry Como	7" EP	HMV	7EG8013	1954	**£5**	**£2**	
Perry Como Sings	10" LP	HMV	DLP1026	1954	**£10**	**£4**	
Rose Tattoo	7"	HMV	7M366	1956	**£6**	**£2.50**	
Round And Round	7"	HMV	POP328	1957	**£5**	**£2**	
Ruby And The Pearl	7"	HMV	7M102	1953	**£6**	**£2.50**	
Say You're Mine Again	7"	HMV	7M149	1953	**£8**	**£4**	
Silk Stockings	7"	HMV	POP369	1957	**£4**	**£1.50**	
So Smooth	7" EP	HMV	7EG8171	1956	**£5**	**£2**	
Some Enchanted Evening	7"	HMV	7M110	1953	**£8**	**£4**	
Somebody Up There Likes Me	7"	HMV	7MC51	1957	**£8**	**£4**	*export*
Somebody Up There Likes Me	7"	HMV	POP304	1957	**£5**	**£2**	
Tina Marie	7"	HMV	7M326	1955	**£8**	**£4**	
Wanted	7"	HMV	7M215	1954	**£8**	**£4**	
Why Did You Leave Me?	7"	HMV	7M163	1953	**£6**	**£2.50**	
Wild Horses	7"	HMV	7M124	1953	**£8**	**£4**	
With A Song In My Heart	7" EP	HMV	7EG8244	1957	**£5**	**£2**	
You Alone	7"	HMV	7M175	1954	**£8**	**£4**	

COMPANY

Company 1	LP	Incus	INCUS21	1977	**£12**	**£5**	
Company 2	LP	Incus	INCUS23	1977	**£12**	**£5**	
Company 3	LP	Incus	INCUS25	1977	**£12**	**£5**	
Company 4	LP	Incus	INCUS26	1977	**£12**	**£5**	
Company 5	LP	Incus	INCUS28	1978	**£12**	**£5**	
Company 6	LP	Incus	INCUS29	1978	**£12**	**£5**	
Company 7	LP	Incus	INCUS30	1978	**£12**	**£5**	
Epiphany	LP	Incus	INCUS46/7	1985	**£20**	**£8**	*double*
Fables	LP	Incus	INCUS36	1980	**£12**	**£5**	
Fictions	LP	Incus	INCUS38	1981	**£12**	**£5**	
Trios	LP	Incus	INCUS51	1986	**£12**	**£5**	

COMPANY (2)

We Wish You Well	7"	United Artists	BP326	1979	**£15**	**£7.50**	

COMPETITORS

Hits Of The Street And Strip	LP	Dot	DLP3542/25542	1963	**£25**	**£10**	*US*

COMPLEX

Complex	LP	Halpix	CLPM001	1970	**£600**	**£400**	
Way We Feel	LP	Deroy		1971	**£600**	**£400**	

COMPROMISE

You Will Think Of Me	7"	CBS	202050	1966	**£4**	**£1.50**	

COMSAT ANGELS

Title	Format	Label	Cat. No.	Year	Mint	VG	Notes
Red Planet	7"	Junta	JUNTA1	1979	**£5**	**£2**	*red vinyl*

COMSTOCK, BOBBY

Title	Format	Label	Cat. No.	Year	Mint	VG	Notes
I'm A Man	7"	United Artists	UP1086	1965	**£10**	**£5**	
Jambalaya	7"	London	HLE9080	1960	**£10**	**£5**	
Let's Stomp	7"	Stateside	SS163	1963	**£6**	**£2.50**	
Out Of Sight	LP	Ascot	ALM13/ALS16026	1966	**£15**	**£6**	*US*
Susie Baby	7"	Stateside	SS221	1963	**£4**	**£1.50**	
Tennessee Waltz	7"	Top Rank	JAR223	1959	**£4**	**£1.50**	

COMTON, PETER BIG BAND

Title	Format	Label	Cat. No.	Year	Mint	VG	Notes
Sound Of Eleven	LP	77	77LEU1214	196–	**£20**	**£8**	

COMUS

Comus were like a folky version of Family, with the group's singer adopting the same gargling tones as Roger Chapman. The largely acoustic instrumentation, however, gives the vocals a considerable dramatic emphasis, especially when underscored by a female singer. *First Utterance* is not exactly a classic, but it is certainly interesting.

Title	Format	Label	Cat. No.	Year	Mint	VG	Notes
Diana	7"	Dawn	DNX2506	1971	**£10**	**£5**	*picture sleeve*
First Utterance	LP	Dawn	DNLS3019	1971	**£100**	**£50**	
To Keep From Crying	LP	Virgin	V2018	1974	**£10**	**£4**	

CONCEPT

Title	Format	Label	Cat. No.	Year	Mint	VG	Notes
Invasion	LP	RC	772	1977	**£30**	**£15**	*Canadian*

CONCHORDS

Title	Format	Label	Cat. No.	Year	Mint	VG	Notes
You Can't Take It Away	7"	Polydor	BM56059	1965	**£5**	**£2**	

CONCORDE

Title	Format	Label	Cat. No.	Year	Mint	VG	Notes
Let Me Out	7"	Attack	ATT8020	1970	**£5**	**£2**	

CONCORDS

Title	Format	Label	Cat. No.	Year	Mint	VG	Notes
I Need Your Loving	7"	Blue Cat	BS170	1969	**£5**	**£2**	

CONDELLO, MIKE

Title	Format	Label	Cat. No.	Year	Mint	VG	Notes
Phase One	LP	Scepter	SPS542	1968	**£25**	**£10**	*US*

CONDON, EDDIE

Title	Format	Label	Cat. No.	Year	Mint	VG	Notes
Chicago Style Jazz	LP	Philips	BBL7061	1956	**£15**	**£6**	
Condon A La Carte	LP	Stateside	SL10010	1962	**£10**	**£4**	
Dixieland	LP	Philips	BBL7109	1957	**£15**	**£6**	
Dixieland Dance Party	LP	London	LTZD15158/SAHD6014	1959	**£12**	**£5**	
Eddie Condon All Stars	LP	Philips	BBL7031	1955	**£15**	**£6**	
Eddie Condon Is Uptown Now	LP	MGM	C768	1958	**£10**	**£4**	
Eddie Condon Orchestra	10" LP	London	LZC14024	1956	**£15**	**£6**	
Gershwin Jazz	10" LP	Brunswick	LA8518	1951	**£20**	**£8**	
Jam Sessions At Commodore	LP	Stateside	SL10005	1962	**£10**	**£4**	
Jazz Band Ball Vol. 1	10" LP	Brunswick	LA8549	1952	**£20**	**£8**	
Jazz Concert	10" LP	Brunswick	LA8577	1953	**£20**	**£8**	
Ringside At Condon's Vol. 1	10" LP	London	LZC14004	1955	**£15**	**£6**	
Roaring Twenties	LP	Philips	BBL7227	1958	**£15**	**£6**	
That Toddlin' Town	LP	Warner Bros	WM4009/WS8009	1960	**£12**	**£5**	
Treasury Of Jazz	LP	Philips	BBL7131	1957	**£15**	**£6**	
We Called It Music	10" LP	Brunswick	LA8542	1952	**£20**	**£8**	

CONDOR, HOWIE G.

Title	Format	Label	Cat. No.	Year	Mint	VG	Notes
Big Noise From Winnetka	7"	Fontana	TF613	1965	**£5**	**£2**	

CONEY ISLAND KIDS

Title	Format	Label	Cat. No.	Year	Mint	VG	Notes
Baby Baby You	7"	London	HLJ8207	1955	**£15**	**£7.50**	

CONLEY, ARTHUR

Title	Format	Label	Cat. No.	Year	Mint	VG	Notes
Aunt Dora's Love Soul Shack	7"	Atlantic	584224	1968	**£4**	**£1.50**	
Funky Street	7"	Atlantic	584175	1968	**£4**	**£1.50**	
More Sweet Soul	LP	Atco	228019	1969	**£12**	**£5**	
People Sure Act Funny	7"	Atlantic	584197	1968	**£4**	**£1.50**	
Shake Rattle And Roll	7"	Atlantic	584121	1967	**£4**	**£1.50**	
Shake, Rattle And Roll	LP	Atlantic	587084	1967	**£12**	**£5**	
Soul Directions	LP	Atlantic	587128	1968	**£12**	**£5**	
Sweet Soul Music	7"	Atlantic	584083	1967	**£4**	**£1.50**	
Sweet Soul Music	LP	Atlantic	587069	1967	**£15**	**£6**	
Whole Lotta Woman	7"	Atlantic	584143	1967	**£4**	**£1.50**	

CONNELL, BRIAN & THE ROUND SOUND

Considerable confusion exists as to whether Brian Connell is the same person as Brian Connolly, the lead singer of the Sweet. Some authorities state that Connell is Connolly, while others are equally certain that he is not. Brian Connolly himself was no help in the matter, unfortunately, having made contrary statements to his Dutch fan club when they tried to determine the facts once and for all!

Title	Format	Label	Cat. No.	Year	Mint	VG	Notes
I Know	7"	Philips	BF1718	1968	**£5**	**£2**	
Just My Kind Of Loving	7"	Mercury	MF956	1966	**£5**	**£2**	
Same Thing Happened To Me	7"	Mercury	MF991	1966	**£5**	**£2**	

Title	Format	Label	Number	Year	Mint	VG	Notes
What Good Am I	7"	Philips	BF1661	1968	£5	£2	

CONNIFF, RAY

Title	Format	Label	Number	Year	Mint	VG	Notes
How To Save A Marriage And Ruin Your Life	LP	CBS	(S)BPG63276	1968	£10	£4	

CONNIFF, RAY & HIS ROCKING RHYTHM BOYS

Title	Format	Label	Number	Year	Mint	VG	Notes
Piggy Bank Boogie	7"	Vogue Coral	QW5001	1955	£8	£4	

CONNOLLY, BRIAN

Title	Format	Label	Number	Year	Mint	VG	Notes
Hypnotised	7"	Carrere	CAR231	1981	£10	£5	

CONNOR, CHRIS

Title	Format	Label	Number	Year	Mint	VG	Notes
Ballad Of The Sad Café	LP	London	LTZK15183	1960	£10	£4	
Bethlehem Girls	LP	Bethlehem	BCP6006	1956	£15	£6	US
Chris	10" LP	London	HBN1074	1956	£15	£6	
Chris	LP	Bethlehem	BCP56	1956	£15	£6	US
Chris Connor	LP	Atlantic	1228	1957	£15	£6	US
Chris Craft	LP	London	LTZK15151	1959	£15	£6	
Chris In Person	LP	London	LTZK15195/ SAHK6088	1960	£10	£4	
George Gershwin Almanac Of Songs	LP	Atlantic	2601	1957	£20	£8	US
Hallelujah I Love Him So	7"	London	HLE8869	1959	£4	£1.50	
He Loves Me, He Loves Me Not	LP	London	HAK2066	1957	£15	£6	
I Miss You So	LP	Atlantic	8014	1956	£15	£6	US
I Only Want Some	7"	London	HLK9124	1960	£4	£1.50	
Jazz Date	LP	London	LTZK15142	1959	£15	£6	
London's Girl Friends No. 2	7" EP	London	REN1093	1957	£6	£2.50	
Lullaby Of Birdland	7" EP	London	EZN19010	1956	£6	£2.50	
Lullabys For Lovers	LP	Bethlehem	BCP6005	1956	£15	£6	US
Lullabys Of Birdland	10" LP	Bethlehem	1001	1954	£20	£8	US
Lullabys Of Birdland	LP	Parlophone	PMC1082	1959	£15	£6	
Meets J And Kai	7" EP	Parlophone	GEP8767	1958	£5	£2	
Presenting	LP	London	HAK2020/ SHK6032	1957	£15	£6	
Sings Lullabys For Lovers	10" LP	London	LZN14007	1956	£20	£8	
This Is Chris	7" EP	Parlophone	GEP8778	1958	£5	£2	
This Is Chris	LP	Bethlehem	BCP20	1955	£15	£6	US
Witchcraft	LP	London	LTZK15185	1960	£10	£4	

CONNORS, BILL

Title	Format	Label	Number	Year	Mint	VG	Notes
Theme To The Guardian	LP	ECM	ECM1057ST	1975	£12	£5	

CONNORS, CAROL

Title	Format	Label	Number	Year	Mint	VG	Notes
Big Big Love	7"	London	HLN9619	1962	£6	£2.50	

CONNORS, NORMAN

Title	Format	Label	Number	Year	Mint	VG	Notes
Best Of Norman Connors And Friends	LP	Buddah	BDS5716	1977	£10	£4	US
Dance Of Magic	LP	Cobblestone	CST9024	1973	£20	£8	US
Dark Of Light	LP	Buddah	BDS5675	1977	£12	£5	US
Dark Of Light	LP	Cobblestone	CST9035	1973	£20	£8	US
Love From The Sun	LP	Buddah	BDS5142	1974	£15	£6	US
Romantic Journey	LP	Buddah	BDS5682	1977	£12	£5	US
Saturday Night Special	LP	Buddah	BDS5643	1976	£12	£5	US
Slewfoot	LP	Buddah	BDS5611	1975	£12	£5	US
This Is Your Life	LP	Buddah	BDLP4058	1978	£10	£4	
You Are My Starship	LP	Buddah	BDS5655	1977	£12	£5	US

CONNY

Title	Format	Label	Number	Year	Mint	VG	Notes
Gino	7"	Columbia	DB4845	1962	£10	£5	

CONQUERORS

Title	Format	Label	Number	Year	Mint	VG	Notes
If You Can't Beat Them Join Them	7"	High Note	HS016	1969	£5	£2	
Jumpy Jumpy Girl	7"	Amalgamated	AMG832	1968	£6	£2.50	
Lonely Street	7"	Treasure Isle	TI7035	1968	£12	£6	
Mr D.J.	7"	High Note	HS025	1969	£5	£2	
What A Agony	7"	Doctor Bird	DB1046	1966	£10	£5	*Baba Brooks B side*
Won't You Come Home Now	7"	Doctor Bird	DB1119	1967	£10	£5	

CONRAD, JESS

Title	Format	Label	Number	Year	Mint	VG	Notes
Hey Little Girl	7"	Decca	F11412	1961	£5	£2	*picture sleeve*
Human Jungle	7" EP	Decca	DFE8524	1963	£8	£4	
Hurt Me	7"	Pye	7N15849	1965	£20	£10	
Jess Conrad	7" EP	Decca	DFE6666	1960	£10	£5	
Jess For You	LP	Decca	LK4390	1961	£25	£10	
Twist My Wrist	7" EP	Decca	DFE6702	1962	£8	£4	

CONRAD, TONY AND FAUST

Tony Conrad was a member of La Monte Young's Theatre Of Eternal Music in 1962, playing violin and bowed guitar alongside John Cale. Later, he played in a group called the Primitives, with both Cale and Lou Reed. Despite these Velvet Underground connections, however, the increasing interest in Conrad's album derives mainly from the fact that it is a collaborative work with the German avant-garde group Faust.

Title	Format	Label	Number	Year	Mint	VG	Notes
Outside The Dream Syndicate	LP	Caroline	C1501	1972	£20	£8	

CONROY

The value of the once-legendary *London's Underground* LP has been steadily falling since collectors have realized that this is not actually the work of a forgotten progressive group. The 'Conroy Recorded Music Library' is not a group at all, in fact, but a series of records produced by anonymous session musicians for use in film and TV work.

Background Action	LP	Berry Music Co.		197–	£50	£25	
Far West/Far East	LP	Berry Music Co.	BMLP155	1976	£10	£4	
Indian Suite	LP	Berry Music Co.		197–	£10	£4	
London's Underground	LP	Berry Music Co.	BMLP092	1972	£50	£25	
London's Underground No. 2	LP	Berry Music Co.	BMLP115	1975	£30	£15	
Psychosis Suite	LP	Berry Music Co.		197–	£10	£4	
Way In Way Out	LP	Berry Music Co.		197–	£10	£4	

CONSCIOUS MINDS

Jamaican Boy	7"	Big	BG318	1971	£4	£1.50	

CONSUMATES

What Is It	7"	Coxsone	CS7054	1968	£12	£6	

CONTINENTALS

Going Crazy	7"	Island	WI010	1962	£10	£5	

CONTINUUM

Autumn Grass	LP	RCA	SF8196	1971	£15	£6	
Continuum	LP	RCA	SF8157	1970	£10	£4	

CONTOURS

Can You Do It	7"	Stateside	SS299	1964	£25	£12.50	
Can You Jerk Like Me	7"	Stateside	SS381	1965	£20	£10	
Contours	7" EP	Tamla Motown	TME2002	1965	£50	£25	
Determination	7"	Tamla Motown	TMG564	1966	£25	£12.50	
Do You Love Me	7"	Oriole	CBA1763	1962	£15	£7.50	
Do You Love Me	LP	Oriole	PS40043	1963	£100	£50	
Don't Let Her Be Your Baby	7"	Oriole	CBA1831	1963	£30	£15	
First I Look At The Purse	7"	Tamla Motown	TMG531	1965	£25	£12.50	
It's So Hard Being A Loser	7"	Tamla Motown	TMG605	1967	£15	£7.50	
Shake Sherry	7"	Oriole	CBA1799	1963	£25	£12.50	

CONTRABAND

Contraband	LP	Transatlantic	TRA278	1974	£15	£6	

CONTROLLED BLEEDING

Headcrack	LP	Sterile	SR11	1986	£20	£8	

CONVAIRS

Mignight Mary	7"	HMV	POP1549	1966	£5	£2	

CONVY, BERT & THE THUNDERBIRDS

Come On Back	7"	London	HLB8190	1955	£125	£62.50	

CONWAY, CONNIE

Connie Conway	LP	London	HAW2214	1960	£10	£4	

COODER, RY

Borderlive	LP	Warner Bros		1981	£15	£6	*US promo*
Chicken Skin Music	7"	Reprise	PRO644	1977	£4	£1.50	*promo*
Jazz	LP	Mobile Fidelity	MFSL1085	1982	£10	£4	*US audiophile*
Ry Cooder	LP	Reprise	RSLP6402	1971	£10	£4	
Ry Cooder Radio Show	LP	Reprise	PRO558	1976	£15	£6	*US promo*

COOK, LITTLE JOE

Don't You Have Feelings	7"	Sonet	SON2002	1968	£6	£2.50	

COOK, LITTLE JOE (CHRIS FARLOWE)

Stormy Monday Blues	7"	Sue	WI385	1965	£25	£12.50	

COOK, PETER

Ballad Of Spotty Muldoon	7"	Decca	F12182	1965	£6	£1.50	
Beyond The Fringe	LP	Parlophone	PMC1145	1961	£12	£5	*with other artists*
Bridge On The River Wye	LP	Parlophone	PMC1190/ PCS3036	1962	£12	£5	*with other artists*
Peter Cook Presents The Establishment	LP	Parlophone	PMC1198	1963	£10	£4	*with other artists*
Presents Misty Mr Wisty	LP	Decca	LK4722	1965	£12	£5	
Private Eye's Blue Record	LP	Transatlantic	TRA131	1965	£10	£4	*with others*
Sitting On The Bench	7"	Parlophone	R4969	1962	£5	£2	*with others*

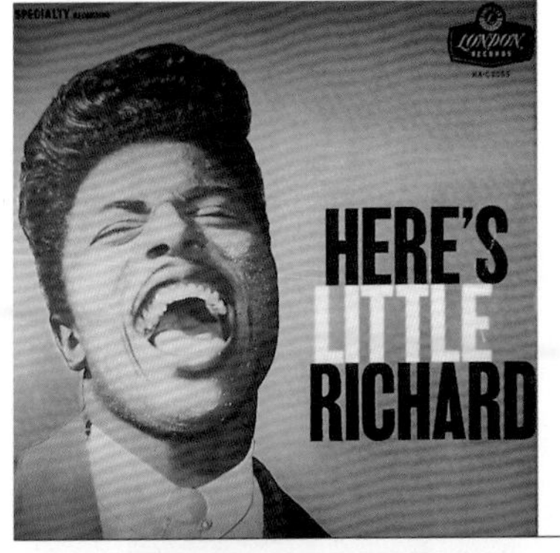

LITTLE RICHARD
Here's Little Richard
£40/£25

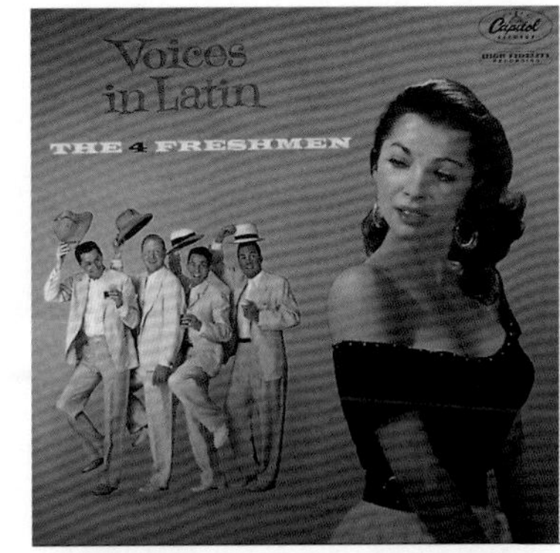

FOUR FRESHMEN
Voices In Latin
£10

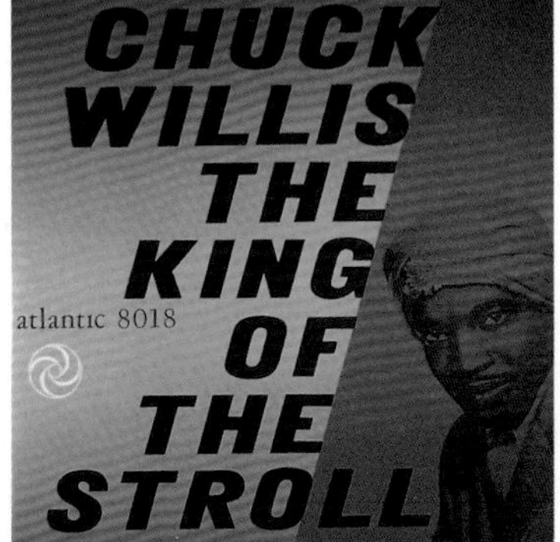

CHUCK WILLIS
King Of The Stroll
£100/£50

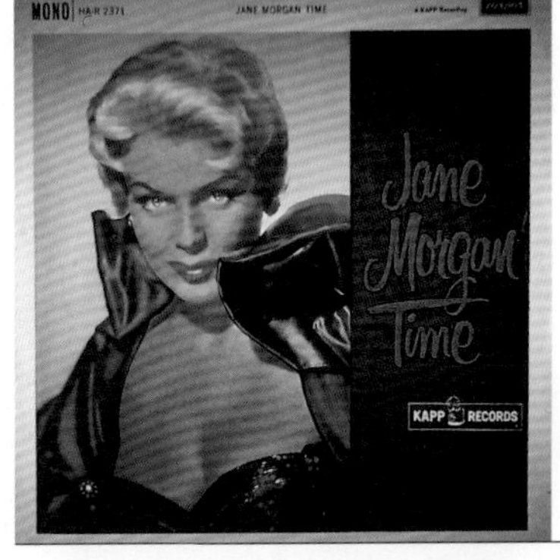

JANE MORGAN
Jane Morgan Time
£12

EVERLY BROTHERS
Both Sides Of An Evening
£25/£20

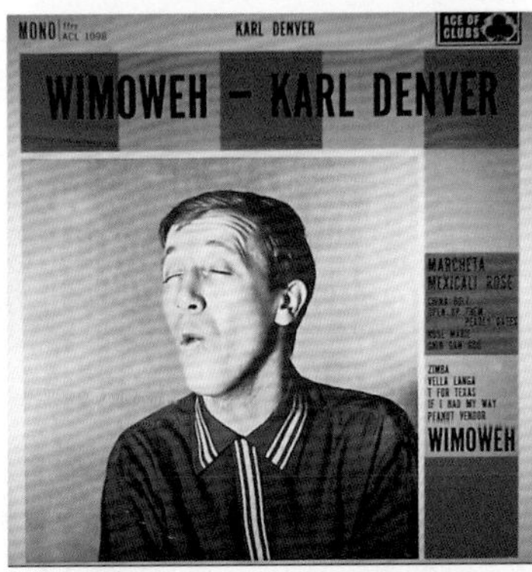

KARL DENVER
Wimoweh
£12

LES PAUL AND MARY FORD
Hits Of Les And Mary
£10

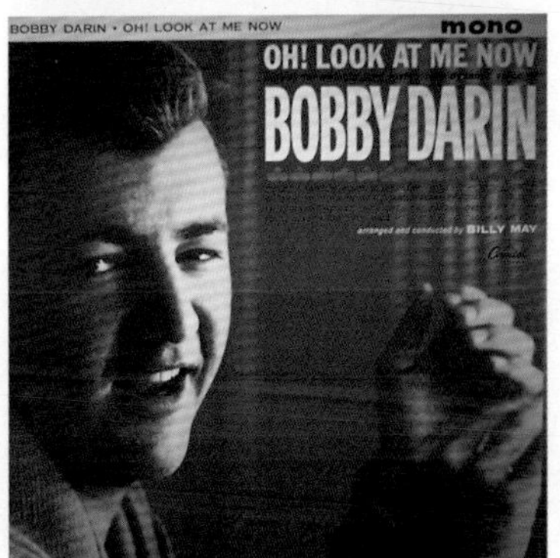

BOBBY DARIN
Oh! Look At Me Now
£15

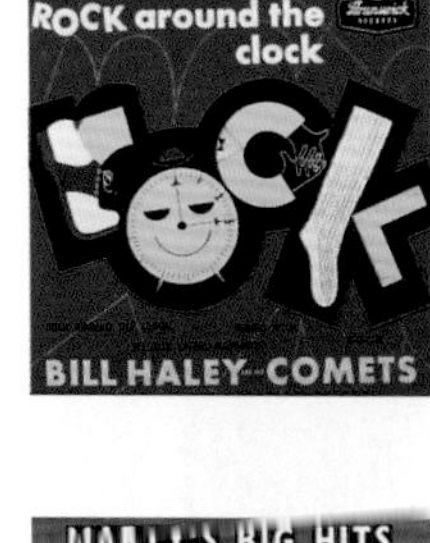

BILL HALEY
Rock Around The Clock
7" EP £15

THEM
Them
7" EP £60

CHRIS FARLOWE
Hits
7" EP £15

MARTY ROBBINS
Marty's Big Hits
7" EP £25

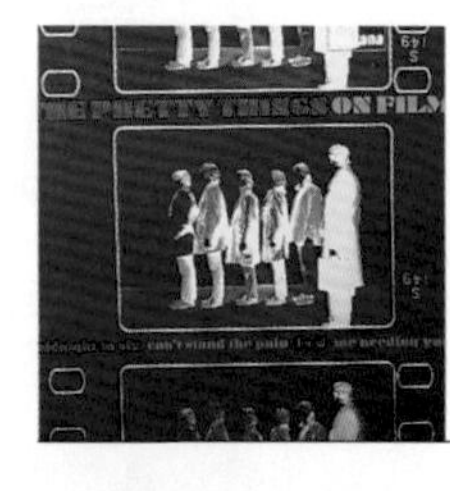

PRETTY THINGS
On Film
7" EP £75

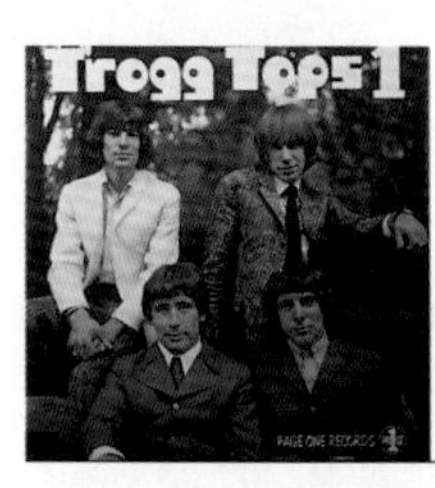

TROGGS
Trogg Tops 1
7" EP £12

CONNIE STEVENS
As Cricket
7" EP £12/£8

BYRDS
The Times They Are A Changin'
7" EP £12

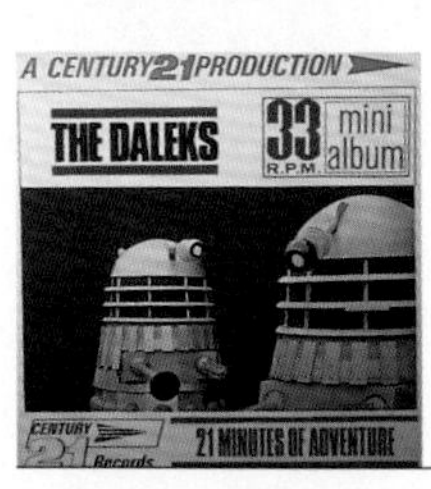

CENTURY 21
The Daleks
7" EP £30

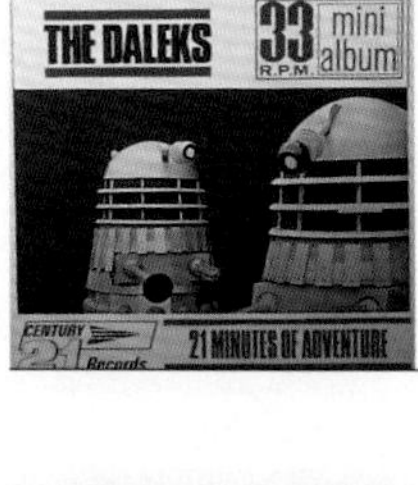

SHADOWS
To The Fore
7" EP £6

JOHN MAYALL'S BLUESBREAKERS
With Paul Butterfield
7" EP £25

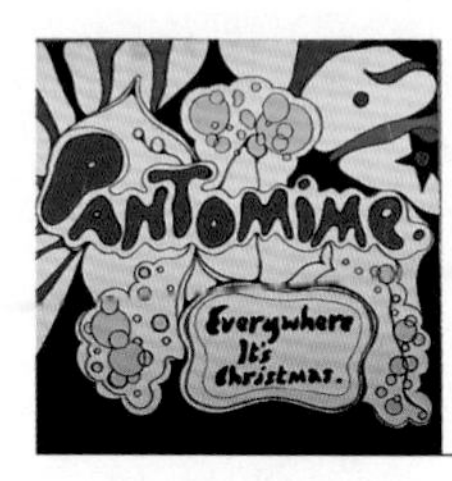

BEATLES
The Beatles' Fourth Christmas Record
7" flexi £50/£30

GERRY & THE PACEMAKERS
You'll Never Walk Alone
7" EP £10

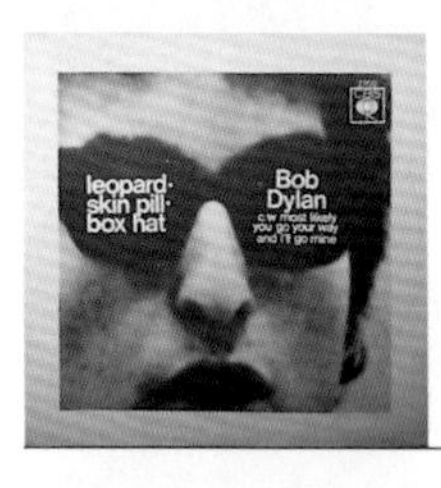

FRANÇOISE HARDY
C'est Fab
7" EP £6

BOB DYLAN
Leopard-Skin Pill-Box Hat
7" single £40

NASHVILLE TEENS
Nashville Teens
7" EP £30

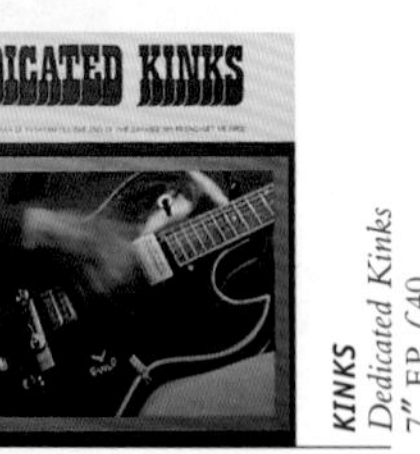

KINKS
Dedicated Kinks
7" EP £40

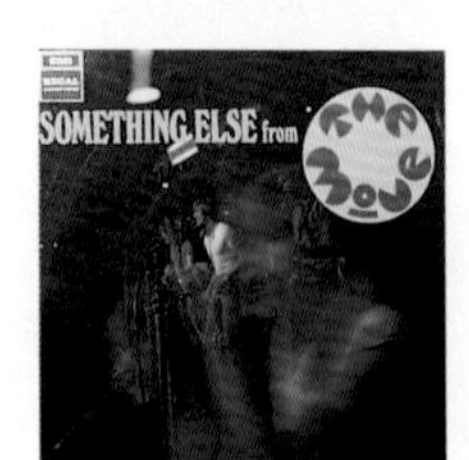

MOVE
Something Else From The Move
7" EP £30

DOVELLS
For Your Hully Gully Party
£25

DOWNLINERS SECT
The Sect
£50

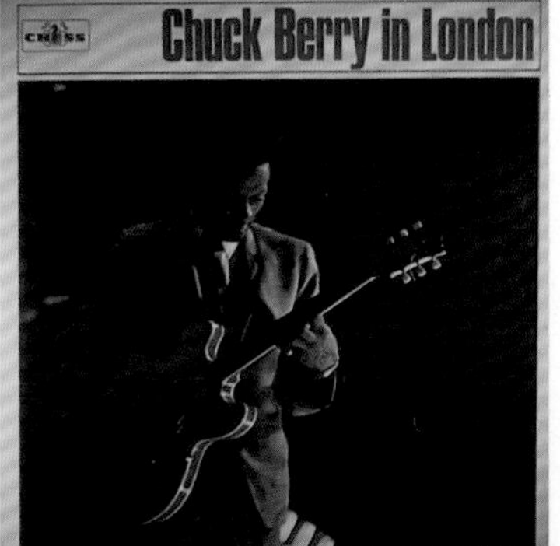

CHUCK BERRY
In London
£10

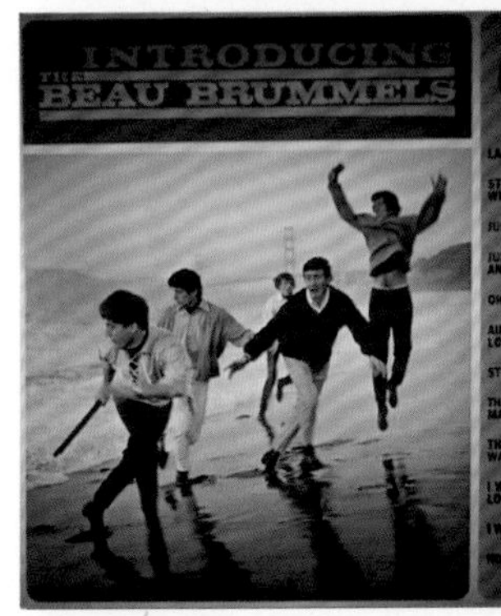

BEAU BRUMMELS
Introducing The Beau Brummels
£30

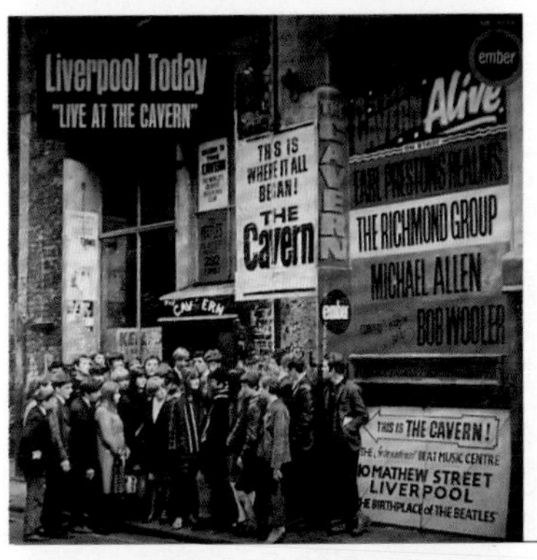

VARIOUS
Liverpool Today – Live At The Cavern
£20

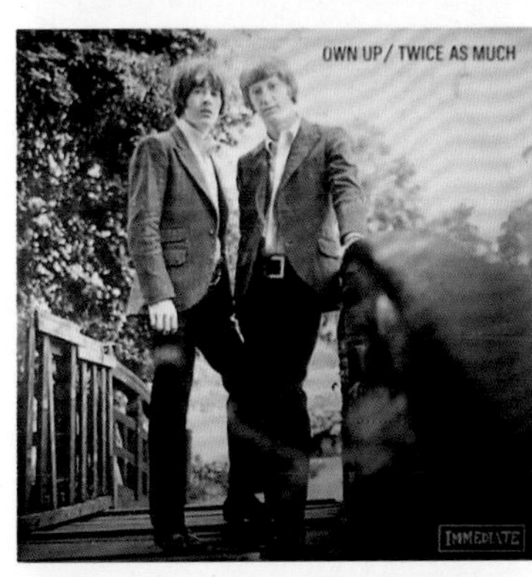

TWICE AS MUCH
Own Up
£25

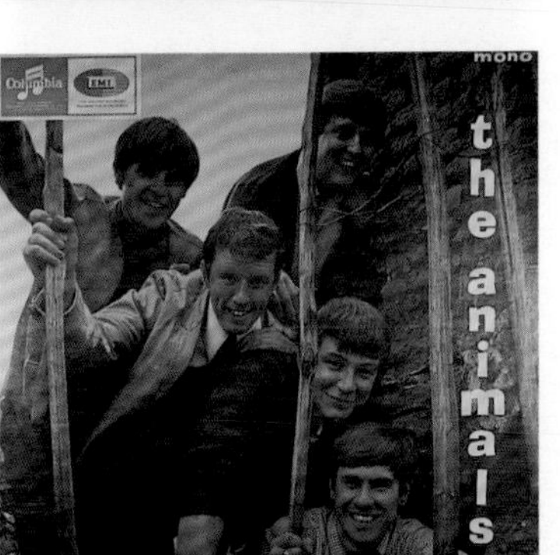

ANIMALS
Animals
£20

DECCA
NORTH COUNTRY MAID

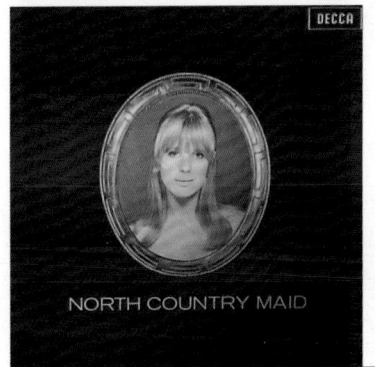

MARIANNE FAITHFULL
North Country Maid
£30

HERD
Paradise Lost
£30

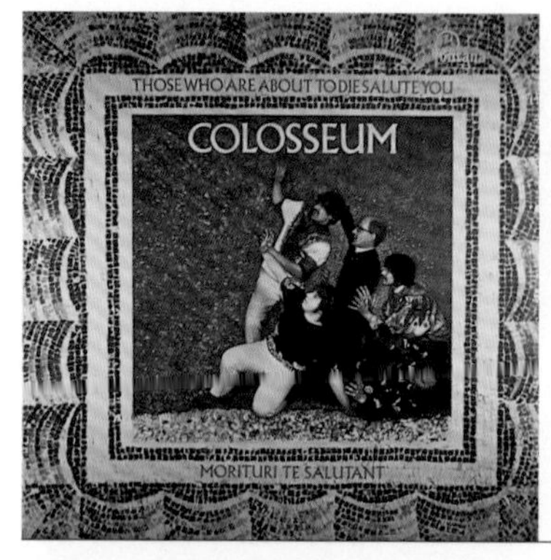

COLOSSEUM
Those Who Are About To Die Salute You
£12

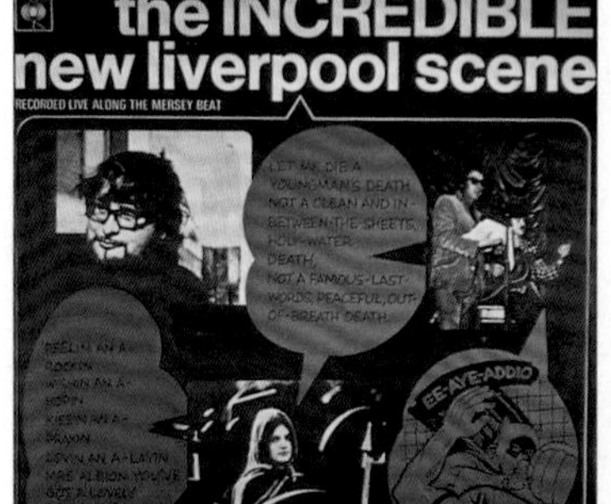

LIVERPOOL SCENE
Incredible New Liverpool Scene
£30

STEAMHAMMER
Mk II
£25

FAIRPORT CONVENTION
What We Did On Our Holidays
£20

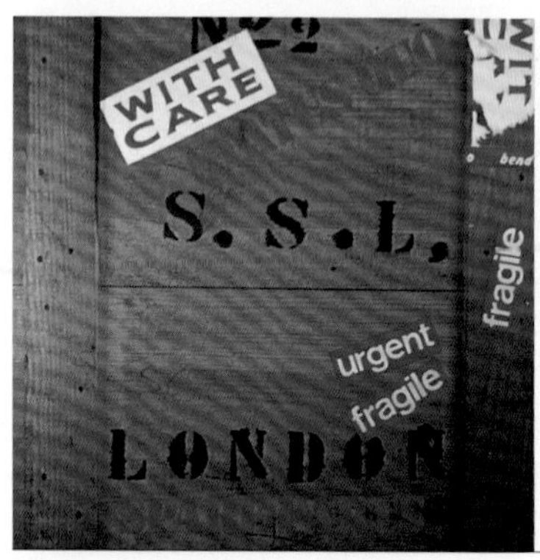

STATUS QUO
Spare Parts
£100

JETHRO TULL
This Was
£30/£25

IDLE RACE
Idle Race
£50

PINK FLOYD
Piper At The Gates Of Dawn
£150/£75

TEN YEARS AFTER
Ten Years After
£25/£20

ARTHUR BROWN
The Crazy World Of Arthur Brown
£15

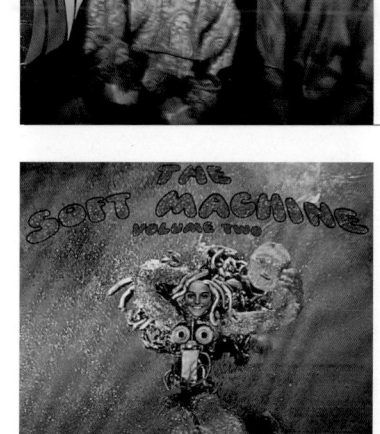

SOFT MACHINE
Volume Two
£25

GUN
Gun
£15

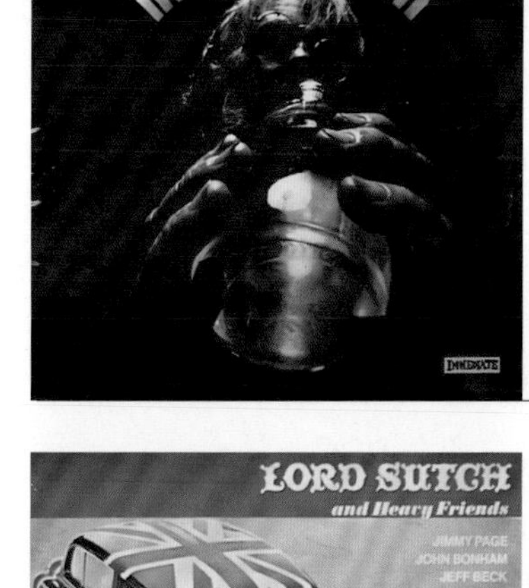

SMALL FACES
In Memoriam
£250/£40

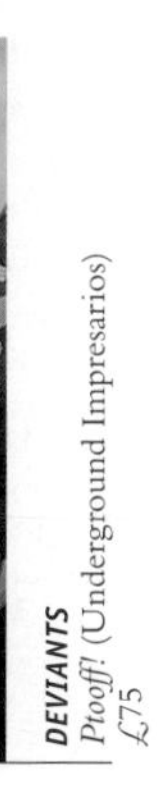

DEVIANTS
Ptooff! (Underground Impresarios)
£75

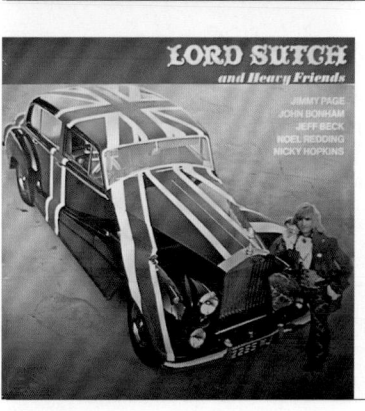

SCREAMING LORD SUTCH
And Heavy Friends
£20

SAVOY BROWN
Getting To The Point
£30

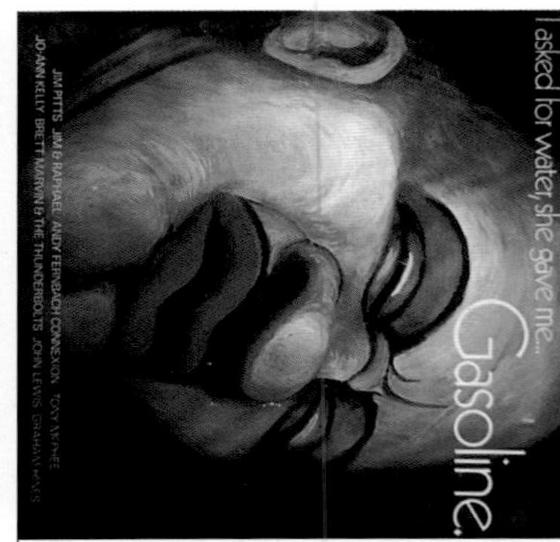

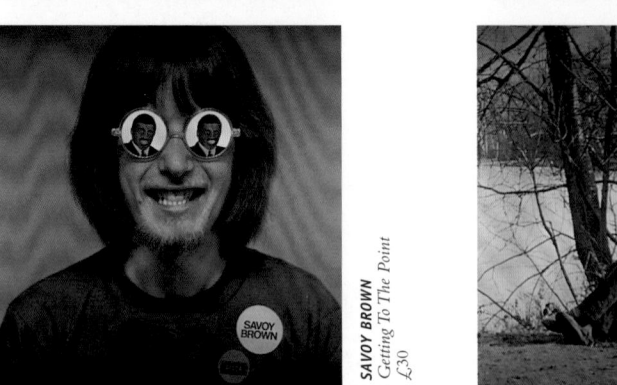

TONY MCPHEE & OTHER ARTISTS
I Asked For Water, She Gave Me Gasoline
£60

FLEETWOOD MAC
Fleetwood Mac (Blue Horizon)
£25

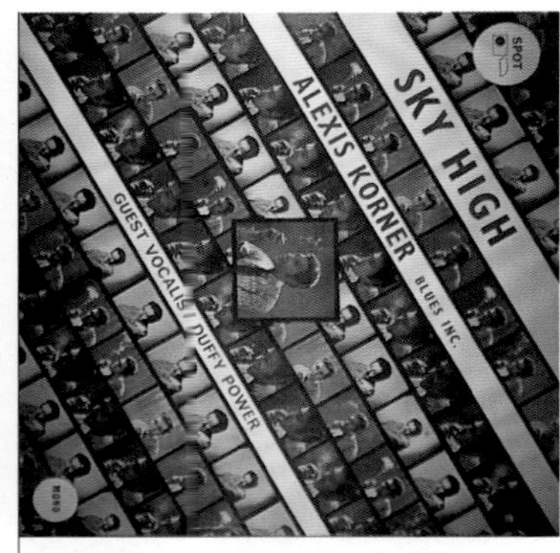

ALEXIS KORNER
Sky High
£500

CHRISTINE PERFECT
Christine Perfect
£40

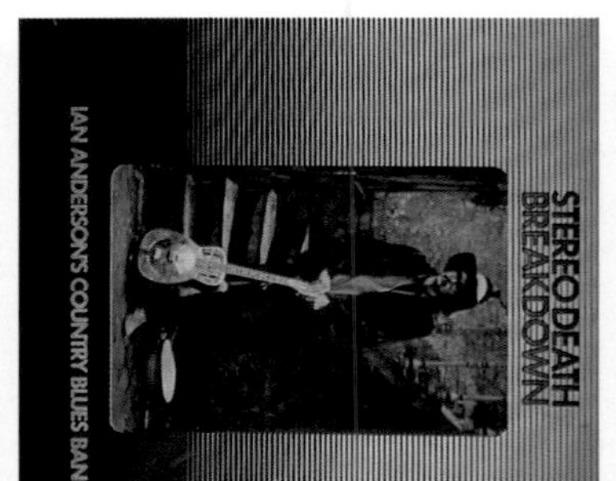

IAN A. ANDERSON
Stereo Death Breakdown
£25

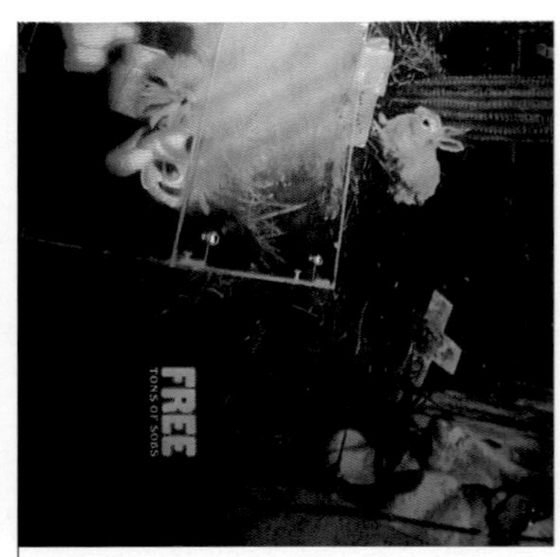

FREE
Tons Of Sobs
£25

AYNSLEY DUNBAR RETALIATION
Doctor Dunbar's Prescription
£30

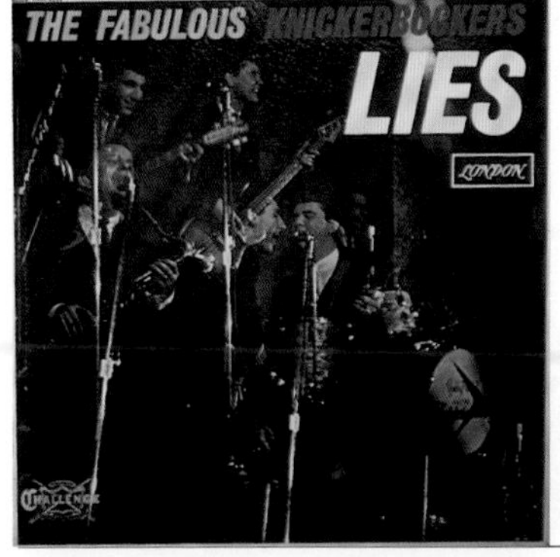

KNICKERBOCKERS
The Fabulous Knickerbockers – Lies
£60

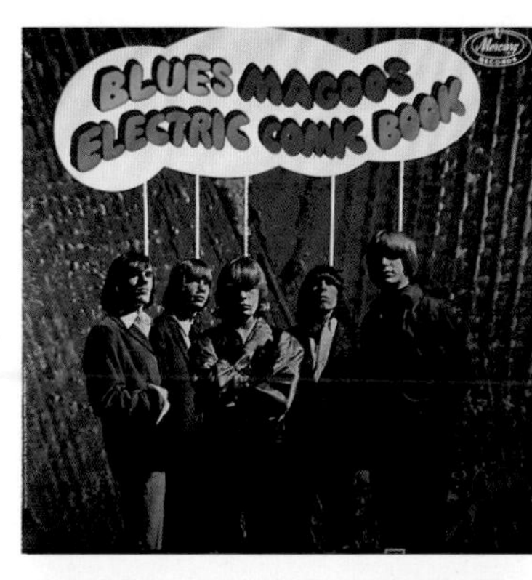

BLUES MAGOOS
Electric Comic Book
£50

SHADOWS OF KNIGHT
Gloria
£60

ELECTRIC PRUNES
I Had Too Much To Dream
£50

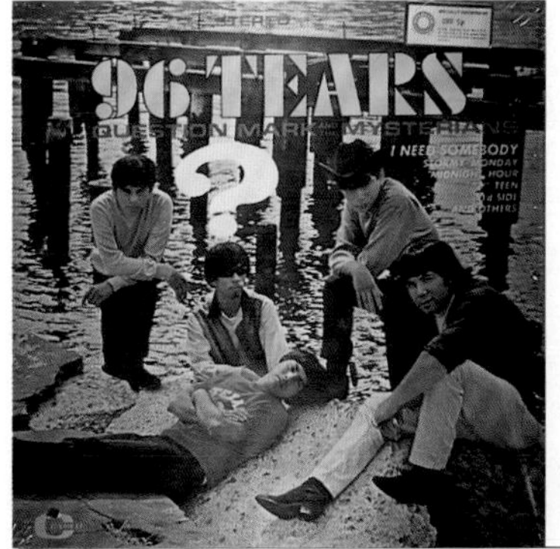

QUESTION MARK & THE MYSTERIANS
96 Tears
£75

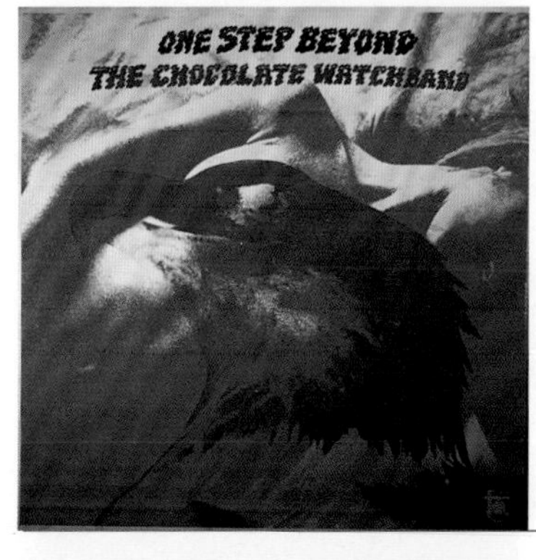

CHOCOLATE WATCH BAND
One Step Beyond
£100

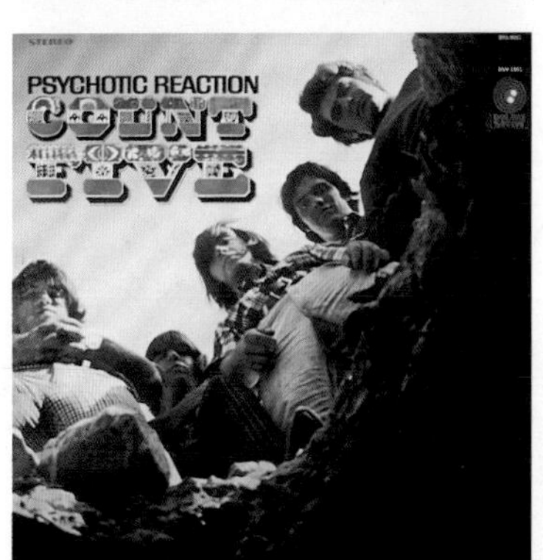

COUNT FIVE
Psychotic Reaction
£50

NAZZ
Nazz Nazz
£75

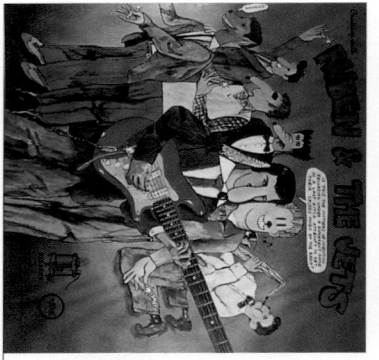

FRANK ZAPPA & THE MOTHERS OF INVENTION
Ruben And The Jets
£40/£30

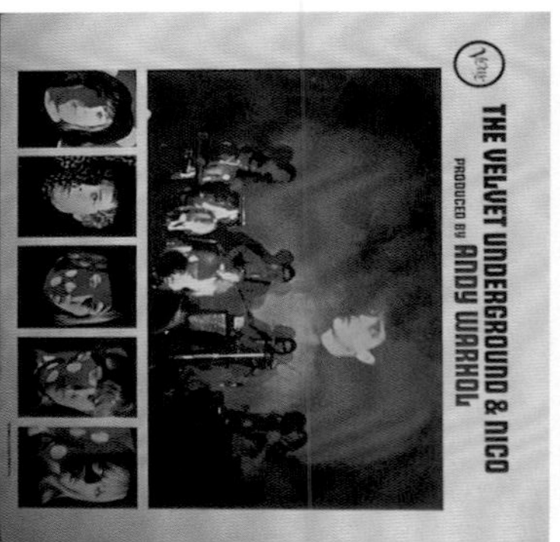

VELVET UNDERGROUND
Velvet Underground And Nico
£60/£40

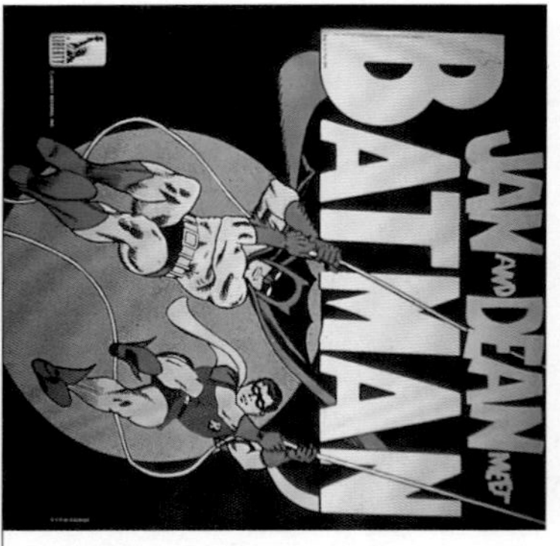

JAN AND DEAN
Meet Batman
£20

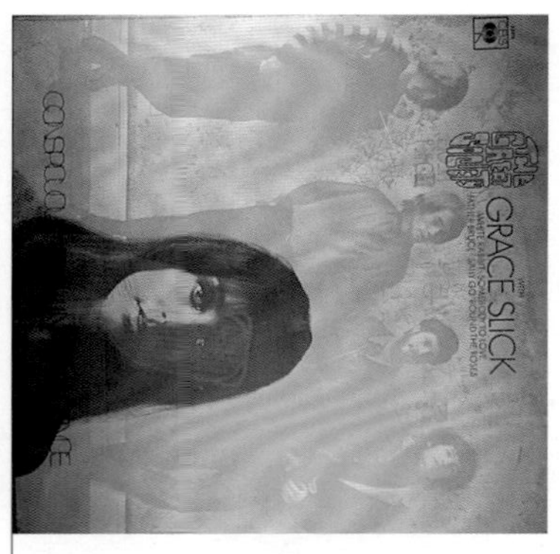

GREAT SOCIETY
Conspicuous Only In Its Absence
£15

MC5
Kick Out The Jams
£40/£30

BUFFALO SPRINGFIELD
Again
£20

KALEIDOSCOPE
A Beacon From Mars
£60

CAPTAIN BEEFHEART
Trout Mask Replica
£25

COOK, PETER & DUDLEY MOORE

The duo's comedy records include a drug-culture spoof, 'L. S. Bumble Bee', that was given a perfect punch-line by being included on several Beatles bootleg albums in the seventies under the guise of a supposed *Sgt Pepper* out-take.

Title	Format	Label	Cat. No.	Year			
Bedazzled	7"	Decca	F12710	1967	**£8**	**£4**	
Bedazzled	LP	Decca	LK/SKL4923	1968	**£50**	**£25**	
By Appointment	7" EP	Decca	DFE8644	1965	**£6**	**£2.50**	
Goodbye-ee	7"	Decca	F12158	1965	**£5**	**£2**	
Isn't She A Sweetie	7"	Decca	F12380	1966	**£5**	**£2**	
L. S. Bumble Bee	7"	Decca	F12551	1967	**£10**	**£5**	
Not Only But Also	LP	Decca	LK4703	1965	**£12**	**£5**	
Not Only But Also	LP	Decca	LK5080	1971	**£10**	**£4**	
Once Moore With Cook	LP	Decca	LK4785	1966	**£12**	**£5**	
Peter Cook & Dudley Moore	7" EP	Parlophone	GEP8940	1965	**£8**	**£4**	

COOK, PETER (2)

Title	Format	Label	Cat. No.	Year			
Georgia	7"	Pye	7N15847	1965	**£15**	**£7.50**	

COOK, ROGER

Title	Format	Label	Cat. No.	Year			
Meanwhile Back At The World	LP	Regal Zonophone	SRZA8508	1972	**£10**	**£4**	
Minstrel In Flight	LP	Regal Zonophone	SLRZ1035	1973	**£10**	**£4**	
Study	LP	Columbia	SCX6388	1970	**£10**	**£4**	

COOKE, SAM

Title	Format	Label	Cat. No.	Year			
Ain't That Good News	LP	RCA	RD/SF7635	1964	**£20**	**£8**	
Another Saturday Night	7"	RCA	RCA1701	1968	**£8**	**£4**	*Duane Eddy B side*
Another Saturday Night	7"	RCA	RCA1341	1963	**£4**	**£1.50**	
At The Copa	LP	RCA	RD/SF7674	1965	**£20**	**£8**	
Best Of Sam Cooke	LP	RCA	LPM/LSP2625	1962	**£20**	**£8**	*US*
Best Of Sam Cooke Vol. 2	LP	RCA	LPM/LSP3373	1965	**£20**	**£8**	*US*
Bring It On Home To Me	7"	RCA	RCA1296	1962	**£4**	**£1.50**	
Chain Gang	7"	RCA	RCA1202	1960	**£4**	**£1.50**	
Cooke's Tour	LP	RCA	RD27190/SF5076	1961	**£30**	**£15**	
Cousin Of Mine	7"	RCA	RCA1420	1964	**£4**	**£1.50**	
Cupid	7"	RCA	RCA1242	1961	**£4**	**£1.50**	
Encore	LP	HMV	CLP1273	1959	**£50**	**£25**	
Feel It	7"	RCA	RCA1260	1961	**£4**	**£1.50**	
Frankie And Johnny	7"	RCA	RCA1361	1963	**£4**	**£1.50**	
Good News	7"	RCA	RCA1386	1964	**£4**	**£1.50**	
Good Times	7"	RCA	RCA1405	1964	**£4**	**£1.50**	
Heart And Soul	7" EP	RCA	RCX7117	1963	**£15**	**£7.50**	
Hit Kit	LP	Keen	86101	1959	**£50**	**£25**	*US*
Hits Of The Fifties	LP	RCA	RD27215/SF5098	1961	**£30**	**£15**	
I Need You Now	7"	London	HLU9046	1960	**£15**	**£7.50**	
I Thank God	LP	Keen	86103	1960	**£30**	**£15**	*US*
It's Got The Whole World Shakin'	7"	RCA	RCA1452	1965	**£4**	**£1.50**	
Little Red Rooster	7"	RCA	RCA1367	1963	**£4**	**£1.50**	
Little Things You Do	7"	HMV	POP610	1959	**£20**	**£10**	
Love Me	7"	RCA	RCA1221	1961	**£5**	**£2**	
Love You Most Of All	7"	HMV	POP568	1958	**£20**	**£10**	
Man Who Invented Soul	LP	RCA	LSP3991	1968	**£15**	**£6**	*US*
Mr Soul	LP	RCA	RD/SF7539	1963	**£25**	**£10**	
My Kind Of Blues	LP	RCA	RD27245/SF5120	1962	**£25**	**£10**	
Night Beat	LP	RCA	RD/SF7583	1963	**£30**	**£15**	
Nothing Can Change This Love	7"	RCA	RCA1310	1962	**£4**	**£1.50**	
One Hour Ahead	7"	HMV	POP675	1959	**£15**	**£7.50**	
Only Sixteen	7"	HMV	POP642	1959	**£10**	**£5**	
Sam Cooke	LP	HMV	CLP1261	1958	**£60**	**£30**	
Send Me Some Loving	7"	RCA	RCA1327	1963	**£4**	**£1.50**	
Shake	7"	RCA	RCA1436	1965	**£4**	**£1.50**	
Shake	LP	RCA	RD7730	1965	**£20**	**£8**	
Sugar Dumpling	7"	RCA	RCA1476	1965	**£4**	**£1.50**	
Swing Low	LP	RCA	RD27222	1960	**£30**	**£15**	
Swing Sweetly	7" EP	RCA	RCX7128	1964	**£20**	**£10**	
Teenage Sonata	7"	RCA	RCA1184	1960	**£4**	**£1.50**	
That's All I Need To Know	7"	London	HLU8615	1958	**£25**	**£12.50**	
That's Heaven To Me	7"	Immediate		1966	**£25**	**£12.50**	*demo only*
That's It I Quit, I'm Moving On	7"	RCA	RCA1230	1961	**£4**	**£1.50**	
Tribute To The Lady	LP	Keen	2004	1959	**£50**	**£25**	*US*
Try A Little Love	LP	RCA	RD/SF7764	1966	**£20**	**£8**	
Twistin' The Night Away	LP	RCA	RD27263/SF5133	1962	**£20**	**£8**	
Unforgettable Sam Cooke	LP	RCA	LPM/LSP3517	1966	**£20**	**£8**	*US*
Wonderful World	7"	HMV	POP754	1960	**£15**	**£7.50**	
Wonderful World Of Sam Cooke	LP	Immediate	IMLP002	1966	**£20**	**£8**	
You Send Me	7"	London	HLU8506	1957	**£25**	**£12.50**	

COOKIES

Title	Format	Label	Cat. No.	Year			
Chains	7"	London	HLU9634	1962	**£6**	**£2.50**	
Don't Say Nothing Bad About My Baby	7"	London	HLU9704	1963	**£8**	**£4**	
Girls Grow Up Faster Than Boys	7"	Colpix	PX11020	1964	**£8**	**£4**	
Willpower	7"	Colpix	PX11012	1963	**£8**	**£4**	

COOL

Title	Format	Label	Cat. No.	Year			
Pop Sounds	LP	DeWolfe	DWLP3136	1969	**£20**	**£8**	

COOL BREEZE

Title	Format	Label	Cat. No.	Year	Value		Notes
People Ask What Love Is	7"	Patheway	PAT103	1971	**£10**	**£5**	

COOL CATS

Title	Format	Label	Cat. No.	Year	Value		Notes
Hold Your Love	7"	Jolly	JY009	1968	**£8**	**£4**	*Helmsley Morris B side*
What Kind Of Man	7"	Jolly	JY007	1968	**£12**	**£6**	

COOL MEN

Title	Format	Label	Cat. No.	Year	Value		Notes
Cool For Cats No. 1	7" EP	Parlophone	GEP8739	1958	**£10**	**£5**	
Cool For Cats No. 2	7" EP	Parlophone	GEP8752	1958	**£10**	**£5**	

COOL SPOON

Title	Format	Label	Cat. No.	Year	Value		Notes
Yakety Yak	7"	Coxsone	CS7032	1967	**£10**	**£5**	

COOL STICKY

Title	Format	Label	Cat. No.	Year	Value		Notes
Train To Soulville	7"	Amalgamated	AMG825	1968	**£8**	**£4**	*Eric Morris B side*

COOLEY, EDDIE & THE DIMPLES

Title	Format	Label	Cat. No.	Year	Value		Notes
Got A Little Woman	7"	Columbia	DB3873	1957	**£125**	**£62.50**	

COOMBES, CHRIS

Title	Format	Label	Cat. No.	Year	Value		Notes
Where It's At	7" EP	Holyground	HG110	1965	**£25**	**£12.50**	

COOPER, ALICE

Title	Format	Label	Cat. No.	Year	Value		Notes
Alice Cooper Reads Stoopid News	CD	Epic		1991	**£20**	**£8**	*US promo*
Be My Lover	7"	Warner Bros	K16154	1972	**£4**	**£1.50**	
Bed Of Nails	CD-s	Epic	ALICEC3	1989	**£5**	**£2**	
Billion Dollar Babies	LP	Warner Bros	BS42685	1973	**£10**	**£4**	*US quad*
Clones	7"	Warner Bros	K17598	1980	**£4**	**£1.50**	
Easy Action	LP	Straight	STS1061	1969	**£25**	**£10**	
Eighteen	7"	Straight	S7209	1971	**£60**	**£30**	
Elected	7"	Warner Bros	K16214	1972	**£6**	**£2.50**	*picture sleeve*
For Britain Only	7"	Warner Bros	K17940	1982	**£5**	**£2**	
Greatest Hits	LP	Warner Bros	W42803	1974	**£10**	**£4**	*US quad*
Hey Stoopid	CD-s	Epic	6569839	1991	**£5**	**£2**	
House Of Fire	7"	Epic	ALICEP4	1989	**£4**	**£1.50**	*shaped picture disc*
House Of Fire	CD-s	Epic	ALICEC4	1989	**£5**	**£2**	
I Love America	12"	Warner Bros	ALICE1T	1983	**£6**	**£2.50**	
I Never Cry	7"	Warner Bros	K16792	1976	**£6**	**£2.50**	
I'm Flash	7"	Chrysalis	CHS2069	1974	**£20**	**£10**	*promo, Elkie Brooks B side*
Killer	LP	Warner Bros	K56005	1971	**£10**	**£4**	*calendar cover*
Last Temptation	CD	Epic	EPC4765942	1994	**£12**	**£5**	*with comic*
Last Temptation	CD	Epic		1994	**£25**	**£10**	*Japanese, with bonus live CD*
Love It To Death	LP	Straight	STS1065	1971	**£25**	**£10**	
Love It To Death	LP	Warner Bros	K46177	1975	**£10**	**£4**	
Love's Like A Loaded Gun	CD-s	Epic	6574389	1991	**£10**	**£5**	*gun-shaped sleeve*
Muscle Of Love	LP	Warner Bros	BS42748	1974	**£10**	**£4**	*US quad*
Poison	CD-s	Epic	6551652	1989	**£10**	**£5**	*bottle sleeve*
Pretties For You	LP	Straight	STS1051	1969	**£25**	**£10**	
School's Out	7"	Warner Bros	K16188	1972	**£5**	**£2**	*picture sleeve*
School's Out	LP	Warner Bros	K56007	1972	**£15**	**£6**	*with panties*
Schooldays	LP	Warner Bros	K66021	1973	**£12**	**£5**	*double*
Trash	CD	Epic		1989	**£50**	**£25**	*US promo trash can with tape, video, biog*
Under My Wheels	7"	Warner Bros	K16127	1971	**£4**	**£1.50**	
Welcome To My Nightmare	12"	Anchor	ANE12001	1977	**£6**	**£2.50**	
Welcome To My Nightmare	LP	Mobile Fidelity	MFSL1063	1980	**£10**	**£4**	*US audiophile*
Who Do You Think We Are?	12"	Warner Bros	K17940T	1982	**£8**	**£4**	

COOPER, BOB

Title	Format	Label	Cat. No.	Year	Value		Notes
Bob Cooper Sextet	10" LP	Capitol	KPL102	1955	**£20**	**£8**	
Coop	LP	Contemporary	LAC12157	1959	**£15**	**£6**	

COOPER, GARNELL & KINFOLK

Title	Format	Label	Cat. No.	Year	Value		Notes
Green Monkey	7"	London	HL9757	1963	**£8**	**£4**	

COOPER, JIM

Title	Format	Label	Cat. No.	Year	Value		Notes
Jim Cooper Band	LP	Jim Cooper Band	JCB1	1979	**£20**	**£8**	

COOPER, JIMMY

Title	Format	Label	Cat. No.	Year	Value		Notes
Dulcimer Player	LP	Forest Tracks	FTS3009	1976	**£10**	**£4**	

COOPER, LES & THE SOUL ROCKERS

Title	Format	Label	Cat. No.	Year	Value		Notes
Wiggle Wobble	7"	Stateside	SS142	1962	**£6**	**£2.50**	

COOPER, LINDSAY

Title	Format	Label	Cat. No.	Year	Value		Notes
Pictures From The Great Exhibition	7"	Recommended	RE1851	1983	**£8**	**£4**	*1 side painted*

COOPER, MARTY

Title	Format	Label	Cat. No.	Year	Value		Notes
If You Were A Singer	LP	EMI	1C06445413	1979	**£15**	**£6**	*German*

COOPER, MIKE

Title	Format	Label	Number	Year	Mint	VG	Notes
Do I Know You	LP	Dawn	DNLS3005	1970	**£12**	**£5**	
Life & Death In Paradise	LP	Fresh Air	6370500	1974	**£10**	**£4**	
Machine Gun Company	LP	Dawn	DNLS3031	1972	**£12**	**£5**	
Oh Really	LP	Pye	NSPL18281	1969	**£20**	**£8**	
Places I Know	LP	Dawn	DNLS3026	1971	**£12**	**£5**	
Trout Steel	LP	Dawn	DNLS3011	1970	**£12**	**£5**	
Up The Country Blues	7" EP	Saydisc	SD137	196–	**£20**	**£10**	

COOPER, TOMMY

Title	Format	Label	Number	Year	Mint	VG	Notes
Don't Jump Off The Roof Dad	7"	Palette	PG9019	1961	**£8**	**£4**	

COPAS, COWBOY

Title	Format	Label	Number	Year	Mint	VG	Notes
Alabam	7"	Melodisc	1566	1960	**£5**	**£2**	
Best Of American Country Music Vol. 3	7" EP	Ember	EMBEP4547	1964	**£5**	**£2**	
Country Entertainer No. 1	LP	London	HAB8088	1963	**£10**	**£4**	
Country Hits	7" EP	Stateside	SE1003	1963	**£8**	**£4**	
Country Music	7" EP	Top Rank	JKP3014	1962	**£8**	**£4**	
Cowboy Copas	LP	Melodisc	MLP12119	1961	**£10**	**£4**	
Favourite Cowboy Songs	7" EP	Parlophone	GEP8527	1955	**£8**	**£4**	
Heartbreak Ago	7"	Parlophone	MSP6109	1954	**£12**	**£6**	
I Can't Go On	7"	Parlophone	CMSP10	1954	**£20**	**£10**	*export*
Return To Sender	7"	Parlophone	MSP6164	1955	**£12**	**£6**	
Star Of The Grand Ole Opry	LP	London	HAB8180	1964	**£10**	**£4**	
Tennessee Senorita	7"	Parlophone	MSP6079	1954	**£12**	**£6**	
Unforgettable . . . Vol. 1	7" EP	London	REB1418	1964	**£8**	**£4**	
Unforgettable . . . Vol. 2	7" EP	London	REB1419	1964	**£8**	**£4**	
Unforgettable . . . Vol. 3	7" EP	London	REB1420	1964	**£8**	**£4**	
Western Style	7" EP	Parlophone	GEP8575	1956	**£8**	**£4**	

COPE, JULIAN

Title	Format	Label	Number	Year	Mint	VG	Notes
Charlotte Anne	CD-s	Island	CIDP380	1988	**£5**	**£2**	*picture disc*
China Doll	CD-s	Island	CID406	1989	**£5**	**£2**	
Droolian	CD	Mofo	MOFOCOCD90	1990	**£15**	**£6**	
Droolian	LP	Mofo	MOFOCOLP90	1990	**£10**	**£4**	
Eve's Volcano	CD-s	Island	CID318	1987	**£5**	**£2**	
Five O'Clock World	CD-s	Island	CIDP399	1988	**£5**	**£2**	*picture disc*
Interview	7"	Antar	4503	1987	**£5**	**£2**	*boxed set*
Paranormal In The West Country	7"	K.A.K.	no number	1994	**£10**	**£5**	
Safesurfer	7"	Island	JC1	1991	**£10**	**£5**	
Saint Julian	LP	Island	ILPS9861	1987	**£10**	**£4**	*with bonus interview LP*
Skellington	CD	Copeco	JUCD89	1989	**£15**	**£6**	
Skellington	LP	Copeco	JULP89	1989	**£10**	**£4**	
Sunspots	7"	Mercury	MER1822	1985	**£5**	**£2**	*double*
World Shut Your Mouth	7"	Island	ISBN290	1986	**£6**	**£2.50**	*boxed double*

COPE, SUZY

Title	Format	Label	Number	Year	Mint	VG	Notes
Biggity Big	7"	HMV	POP1167	1963	**£4**	**£1.50**	
Not Never Not Now	7"	HMV	POP1047	1962	**£4**	**£1.50**	
Teenage Fool	7"	HMV	POP941	1961	**£5**	**£2**	
You Can't Say I Never Told You	7"	CBS	201792	1965	**£5**	**£2**	

COPELAND, ALAN

Title	Format	Label	Number	Year	Mint	VG	Notes
Feeling Happy	7"	Vogue Coral	Q72237	1957	**£6**	**£2.50**	
Flip Flop	7"	Pye	7N25007	1959	**£10**	**£5**	
How Will I Know?	7"	Vogue Coral	Q72277	1957	**£4**	**£1.50**	

COPELAND, JOHNNY

Title	Format	Label	Number	Year	Mint	VG	Notes
Sufferin' City	7"	Atlantic	K10242	1972	**£4**	**£1.50**	

COPELAND, KEN

Title	Format	Label	Number	Year	Mint	VG	Notes
Pledge Of Love	7"	London	HLP8423	1957	**£250**	**£150**	*Mints B side, best auctioned*

COPELAND, MARTHA

Title	Format	Label	Number	Year	Mint	VG	Notes
RCA Victor Race Series Vol. 8	7" EP	RCA	RCX7183	1966	**£5**	**£2**	

COPPER, BOB

Title	Format	Label	Number	Year	Mint	VG	Notes
Sweet Rose In June	LP	Topic	12TS328	1977	**£10**	**£4**	

COPPER FAMILY

Title	Format	Label	Number	Year	Mint	VG	Notes
Song For Every Season	LP	Leader	LEAB404	1971	**£100**	**£50**	*4 LP box set*

COPPERFIELD

Title	Format	Label	Number	Year	Mint	VG	Notes
Any Old Time	7"	Instant	IN004	1969	**£6**	**£2.50**	

COPS & ROBBERS

Title	Format	Label	Number	Year	Mint	VG	Notes
I Could Have Danced All Night	7"	Pye	7N15870	1965	**£15**	**£7.50**	
I Could Have Danced All Night	7" EP	Pye	PNV24148	1965	**£50**	**£25**	*French*
It's All Over Now Baby Blue	7"	Pye	7N15928	1965	**£12**	**£6**	
St James Infirmary	7"	Decca	F12019	1964	**£25**	**£12.50**	

CORBAN

Title	Format	Label	Number	Year	Mint	VG	Notes
Break In The Clouds	LP	Acorn	AC002	1978	**£20**	**£8**	

CORBETT, HARRY H.

Title	Format	Label	Cat. No.	Year	Mint	VG	Notes
Flower Power Fred	7"	Decca	F12714	1967	**£5**	**£2**	

CORBETT, MIKE & JAY HIRSH

Title	Format	Label	Cat. No.	Year	Mint	VG	Notes
Mike Corbett And Jay Hirsh	LP	Atlantic	2400141	1971	**£15**	**£6**	
Mike Corbett And Jay Hirsh	LP	Atlantic	K40242	1971	**£10**	**£4**	

CORBITT, JERRY

Title	Format	Label	Cat. No.	Year	Mint	VG	Notes
Jerry Corbitt	LP	Capitol	ST771	1971	**£20**	**£8**	*US*

CORDELL, FRANK

Title	Format	Label	Cat. No.	Year	Mint	VG	Notes
Black Bear	7"	HMV	POP824	1961	**£5**	**£2**	

CORDELL, PHIL

Title	Format	Label	Cat. No.	Year	Mint	VG	Notes
Chevy Van	7"	Mowest	MW3026	1975	**£5**	**£2**	*demo*

CORDES

Title	Format	Label	Cat. No.	Year	Mint	VG	Notes
Give Her Time	7"	Cavern Sound	IMSTL1	1965	**£30**	**£15**	

CORDET, LOUISE

Title	Format	Label	Cat. No.	Year	Mint	VG	Notes
Don't Let The Sun Catch You Crying	7"	Decca	F11824	1964	**£4**	**£1.50**	
Don't Make Me Over	7"	Decca	F11875	1964	**£5**	**£2**	
I'm Just A Baby	7"	Decca	F11476	1962	**£4**	**£1.50**	
Sweet Beat Of Louise Cordet	7" EP	Decca	DFE8515	1962	**£30**	**£15**	
Sweet Enough	7"	Decca	F11524	1962	**£4**	**£1.50**	
Which Way The Wind Blows	7"	Decca	F11673	1963	**£4**	**£1.50**	

CORDUROYS

Title	Format	Label	Cat. No.	Year	Mint	VG	Notes
Tick Tock	7"	Planet	PLF122	1966	**£20**	**£10**	

COREA, CHICK

Title	Format	Label	Cat. No.	Year	Mint	VG	Notes
ARC	LP	ECM	ECM1009ST	1971	**£12**	**£5**	
Hymn Of The Seventh Galaxy	LP	Polydor	2310283	1973	**£15**	**£6**	*credited to Return To Forever*
Inner Space	LP	Atlantic	K60081	1974	**£15**	**£6**	*double*
Is	LP	Solid State	SS18055	1969	**£20**	**£8**	*US*
Light As A Feather	LP	Polydor	2310247	1972	**£15**	**£6**	*credited to Return To Forever*
Now He Sings Now He Sobs	LP	Solid State	SS18039	1968	**£20**	**£8**	*US*
Piano Improvisations Vol. 1	LP	ECM	ECM1014ST	1971	**£12**	**£5**	
Piano Improvisations Vol. 2	LP	ECM	ECM1020ST	1972	**£12**	**£5**	
Return To Forever	LP	ECM	ECM1022ST	1972	**£12**	**£5**	
Round Trip	LP	Epic	EPC65558	1974	**£10**	**£4**	
Song Of Singing	LP	Blue Note	BST84353	1971	**£15**	**£6**	*US*
Sundance	LP	People	PLEO9	1974	**£15**	**£6**	
Tones For Joan's Bones	LP	Vortex	2004	1966	**£40**	**£20**	*US*
Where Have I Known You Before	LP	Polydor	2310354	1974	**£12**	**£5**	*credited to Return To Forever*

CORKSCREW

Title	Format	Label	Cat. No.	Year	Mint	VG	Notes
For Openers	LP	Highway	SHY7005	1979	**£25**	**£10**	

CORNBREAD & JERRY

Title	Format	Label	Cat. No.	Year	Mint	VG	Notes
L'il Ole Me	7"	London	HLG9352	1961	**£4**	**£1.50**	

CORNELIUS BROTHERS & SISTER ROSE

Title	Format	Label	Cat. No.	Year	Mint	VG	Notes
Too Late To Turn Back Now	7"	United Artists	UP35378	1972	**£8**	**£4**	

CORNELL, DON

Title	Format	Label	Cat. No.	Year	Mint	VG	Notes
But Love Me	7"	Vogue Coral	Q72164	1956	**£6**	**£2.50**	
Don Cornell	7" EP	HMV	7EG8105	1955	**£5**	**£2**	
For You	10" LP	Vogue Coral	LVC10004	1955	**£20**	**£8**	
Heaven Only Knows	7"	Vogue Coral	Q72203	1956	**£5**	**£2**	
Hold My Hand	7"	Vogue Coral	Q2013	1954	**£20**	**£10**	
I've Got Bells On My Heart	7"	Coral	Q72313	1958	**£4**	**£1.50**	
Let's Be Friends	7"	Vogue Coral	Q72234	1957	**£5**	**£2**	
Let's Get Lost	LP	Coral	LVA9037	1956	**£20**	**£8**	
Love Is A Many Splendoured Thing	7"	Vogue Coral	Q72104	1955	**£10**	**£5**	
Mailman Bring Me No More Blues	7"	Coral	Q72308	1958	**£8**	**£4**	
Mama Guitar	7"	Vogue Coral	Q72276	1957	**£12**	**£6**	
No Man Is An Island	7"	Vogue Coral	Q72058	1955	**£6**	**£2.50**	
Rock Island Line	7"	Vogue Coral	Q72152	1956	**£10**	**£5**	
S'posin'	7"	Vogue Coral	Q2037	1954	**£8**	**£4**	
See-saw	7"	Vogue Coral	Q72218	1956	**£8**	**£4**	
Sempre Amore	7"	Pye	7N25041	1959	**£4**	**£1.50**	
Sittin' In The Balcony	7"	Vogue Coral	Q72257	1957	**£12**	**£6**	
Size Twelve	7"	Vogue Coral	Q72071	1955	**£6**	**£2.50**	
Stranger In Paradise	7"	Vogue Coral	Q72073	1955	**£20**	**£10**	
Teenage Meeting	7"	Vogue Coral	Q72144	1956	**£15**	**£7.50**	
There Once Was A Beautiful	7"	Vogue Coral	Q72132	1956	**£6**	**£2.50**	
There's Only You	7"	Vogue Coral	Q72291	1957	**£4**	**£1.50**	
This Earth Is Mine	7"	London	HLD8937	1959	**£4**	**£1.50**	
Unchained Melody	7"	Vogue Coral	Q72080	1955	**£8**	**£4**	
When You Are In Love	7"	Vogue Coral	Q72070	1955	**£6**	**£2.50**	

CORNELL, JERRY

Title	Format	Label	Cat. No.	Year	Mint	VG	Notes
Please Don't Talk About Me	7"	London	HL8157	1955	**£25**	**£12.50**	

CORNELL, LYN

I Sold My Heart To The Junkman	7"	Decca	F11469	1962	£**5**	£**2**	

CORNELLS

Beach Bound	LP	Garex	100	1963	£**150**	£**75**	*US*

CORNERSHOP

Brimful Of Asha	12"	Wiiija	ROOT014T	1997	£**8**	£**4**	*etched B side*
Naii Zindagi	7"	NME	NMEPS001	1993	£**5**	£**2**	
Waterlogged	7"	Wiiija	WIJ19V	1993	£**4**	£**1.50**	*coloured vinyl*

CORNS, ARNOLD

The records issued by Arnold Corns are actually songwriting demos recorded by David Bowie (and re-recorded later for inclusion on his *Ziggy Stardust* album).

Hang On To Yourself	7"	B&C	CB189	1971	£**20**	£**10**	
Hang On To Yourself	7"	Mooncrest	MOON25	1974	£**10**	£**5**	
Moonage Daydream	7"	B&C	CB149	1971	£**40**	£**20**	

CORNUCOPIA

Full Horn	LP	Brain	1030	1973	£**12**	£**5**	*German*

CORNWELL, HUGH

Another KInd Of Love	CD-s	Virgin	VSCD94512	1988	£**5**	£**2**	*3" single*
Dreaming Again	CD-s	Virgin	VSCD1093	1988	£**5**	£**2**	

CORONETS

Do Do Do It Again	7"	Columbia	SCM5117	1954	£**6**	£**2.50**	
Lizzie Borden	7"	Columbia	SCM5235	1956	£**4**	£**1.50**	
Magic Touch	7"	Columbia	SCM5261	1956	£**8**	£**4**	
Perfect Combination	7" EP	Columbia	SEG7621	1956	£**6**	£**2.50**	
Rhythm And Blues	7" EP	Columbia	SEG7603	1956	£**6**	£**2.50**	
Someone To Love	7"	Columbia	DB3827	1956	£**4**	£**1.50**	

CORONETS (2)

I Wonder Why	7"	Stresa	BEVSP1104/5	1968	£**25**	£**12.50**	

CORPORATION

Corporation	LP	Capitol	ST175	1969	£**30**	£**15**	
Get On Our Swing	LP	Age Of Aquarius	4150	1969	£**30**	£**15**	*US*
Hassels In My Mind	LP	Age Of Aquarius	4250	1969	£**30**	£**15**	*US*

CORPORATION (2)

Sweet Musille	7"	Grape	GR3022	1970	£**5**	£**2**	

CORPUS

Creation A Child	LP	Acorn	1001	1970	£**100**	£**50**	*US*

CORRIB FOLK

Corrib Folk	LP	Homespun	HRL107	1975	£**10**	£**4**	*Irish*

CORRIE FOLK TRIO

Cam Ye By Atholl	LP	Philips	6382083	1973	£**10**	£**4**	*reissue of Those Wild Corries!*
Corrie Folk Trio	7" EP	Waverley	ELP129	1963	£**15**	£**7.50**	
Corrie Folk Trio And Paddie Bell	LP	Waverley	ZLP2042/ SZLP2043	1964	£**15**	£**6**	
In Retrospect	LP	Talisman	STAL5005	1970	£**15**	£**6**	*with Paddie Bell*
More Folk Songs For The Burds	7" EP	Waverley	ELP132	1963	£**15**	£**7.50**	*with Paddie Bell*
Promise Of The Day	LP	Waverley	(S)ZLP2050	1965	£**15**	£**6**	
Those Wild Corries!	LP	Fontana	STL5337	1966	£**15**	£**6**	
Yon Folk Songs For The Burds	7" EP	Waverley	ELP131	1963	£**15**	£**7.50**	*with Paddie Bell*

CORRIES

Bonnet, Belt And Sword	LP	Philips	8220841		£**10**	£**4**	
Bonnet, Belt And Sword	LP	Fontana	STL5401	1967	£**15**	£**6**	
In Concert	LP	Fontana	STL5484	1969	£**12**	£**5**	
Kishmul's Galley	LP	Fontana	STL5465	1968	£**15**	£**6**	
Little Of What You Fancy	LP	Columbia	SCX6546	1973	£**10**	£**4**	
Live At The Royal Lyceum Theatre Edinburgh	LP	EMI	NTS109	197–	£**10**	£**4**	
Live At The Royal Lyceum Theatre Edinburgh	LP	Columbia	SCX6468	1971	£**15**	£**6**	
Scottish Love Songs	LP	Fontana		1970	£**12**	£**5**	
Sound The Pibroch	LP	Columbia	SCX6511	1972	£**10**	£**4**	
Spotlight On The Corries	LP	Philips	6625035	1977	£**15**	£**6**	*double*
Strings And Things	LP	Columbia	SCX6442	1970	£**10**	£**4**	
These Are The Corries Vol. 2	LP	Philips	6382059	1969	£**10**	£**4**	

CORRS

Live	CD	Atlantic	PRCD390	1996	£**20**	£**8**	*promo*
Six Songs From Talk On Corners	CD	East West	19417	1997	£**20**	£**8**	*promo*

CORSAIRS

I'll Take You Home | 7" | Pye | 7N25142 | 1962 | **£4** | **£1.50** |

CORSAIRS (2)

I'm Gonna Shut You Down | 7" | CBS | 202624 | 1967 | **£5** | **£2** |

CORT, BOB

Ain't It A Shame | LP | Decca | LK4222 | 1958 | **£20** | **£8** |
Ark | 7" | Decca | F10989 | 1958 | **£5** | **£2** |
Barrack Room Ballads | 7" EP | Decca | DFE6630 | 1959 | **£5** | **£2** |
Bob Cort's Gentlefolk | 7" EP | Decca | DFE6686 | 1961 | **£5** | **£2** |
Don't You Rock Me Daddy-O | 7" | Decca | FJ10831 | 1957 | **£8** | **£4** |
El Paso | 7" | Decca | F11197 | 1960 | **£4** | **£1.50** |
Eskimo Nell | LP | Decca | LK4301 | 1959 | **£15** | **£6** |
Kissin' Time | 7" | Decca | F11160 | 1959 | **£4** | **£1.50** |
Maggie May | 7" | Decca | F10899 | 1957 | **£4** | **£1.50** |
Mule Skinner Blues | 7" | Decca | F11256 | 1960 | **£4** | **£1.50** |
On Top Of Old Smokey | 7" | Decca | F11109 | 1959 | **£4** | **£1.50** |
Schoolday | 7" | Decca | F10905 | 1957 | **£8** | **£4** |
Six Five Special | 7" | Decca | F10892 | 1957 | **£8** | **£4** |
Skiffle Party | 7" | Decca | F10951 | 1957 | **£5** | **£2** |
Waterloo | 7" | Decca | F11145 | 1959 | **£4** | **£1.50** |
Yes! Suh! | LP | Ace Of Clubs | ACL1197 | 1965 | **£10** | **£4** |

CORTEZ, DAVE BABY

And His Happy Organ | LP | RCA | LPM/LSP2099 | 1959 | **£20** | **£8** | US
Countdown | 7" | Roulette | RK7001 | 1966 | **£4** | **£1.50** |
Dave Baby Cortez | 7" EP | London | REU1233 | 1960 | **£25** | **£12.50** |
Dave Baby Cortez | LP | Clock | C331 | 1960 | **£20** | **£8** | US
Deep In The Heart Of Texas | 7" | London | HLU9126 | 1960 | **£8** | **£4** |
Golden Hits | LP | London | HAU8142 | 1964 | **£25** | **£10** |
Happy Organ | 7" | London | HLU8852 | 1959 | **£8** | **£4** |
In Orbit | LP | Roulette | (S)R25328 | 1966 | **£10** | **£4** | US
Organ Shindig | LP | Roulette | (S)R25298 | 1965 | **£15** | **£6** | US
Piano Shuffle | 7" | Columbia | DB4404 | 1960 | **£5** | **£2** |
Rinky Dink | 7" | Pye | 7N25159 | 1962 | **£10** | **£5** |
Rinky Dink | LP | Chess | LP1473 | 1962 | **£20** | **£8** | US
Tweety Pie | LP | Roulette | (S)R25315 | 1966 | **£10** | **£4** | US
Whistling Organ | 7" | London | HLU8919 | 1959 | **£8** | **£4** |

CORTINAS

Phoebe's Flower Shop | 7" | Polydor | 56255 | 1968 | **£4** | **£1.50** |

CORYELL, LARRY

Larry Coryell caused much comment as the first guitarist in a jazz group to employ feedback, but the offending track, Gary Burton's 'General Mojo Cuts Up', is actually a very mild-mannered affair. Ever since, Coryell has languished in the shade of John McLaughlin, who is the real innovator where the use of a highly amplified guitar in jazz is concerned. There is a reasonable sampler of his work – the double *Essential Larry Coryell* on Vanguard. Otherwise, he has made a great many records, of which the scarcer, earlier ones listed here are just the start.

Back Together Again | LP | Atlantic | K50382 | 1977 | **£10** | **£4** | *with Alphonse Mouzon*
Coryell | LP | Vanguard | SVRL19059 | 1969 | **£10** | **£4** |
Introducing The Eleventh House | LP | Vanguard | VSD79342 | 1974 | **£10** | **£4** | *quad*
Lady Coryell | LP | Vanguard | SVRL19051 | 1969 | **£10** | **£4** |
Live At The Village Gate | LP | Vanguard | VSD6573 | 1971 | **£10** | **£4** | *quad*
Offering | LP | Vanguard | VSD79319 | 1972 | **£10** | **£4** | *quad*
Spaces | LP | Philips | 6359005 | 1970 | **£10** | **£4** | *with John McLaughlin*

COSBY, BILL

Little Ole Man | 7" | Warner Bros | WB7072 | 1967 | **£6** | **£2.60** | *picture sleeve*

COSMIC DEALER

Crystallization | LP | Negram | NQ20015 | 1971 | **£150** | **£75** | *Dutch*

COSMIC EYE

Cosmic Eye represented an attempt on the part of some of the second division of British jazz musicians – basically John Mayer's Indo-jazz group – to break directly into the progressive rock market.

Dream Sequence | LP | Regal Zonophone | SLRZ1030 | 1972 | **£125** | **£62.50** |

COSMIC JOKERS

Cosmic Jokers | LP | Metronome | KM58008 | 1974 | **£20** | **£8** | *German*
Planet Sit In | LP | Metronome | KM58013 | 1974 | **£15** | **£6** | *German*

COSMIC SOUNDS

The Zodiac was the first electronic rock record and featured spoken verses, one for each Zodiacal sign, behind which Paul Beaver put his new synthesizer through its paces.

Zodiac | LP | Elektra | EKL/EKS74009 | 1967 | **£15** | **£6** |

COSMO, FRANK

Alone | 7" | Black Swan | WI446 | 1965 | **£10** | **£5** |

Better Get Right	7"	Island	WI135	1964	£10	£5	
Gypsy Woman	7"	Blue Beat	BB175	1963	£12	£6	
I Love You	7"	R&B	JB119	1963	£10	£5	*Don Drummond B side*
Merry Christmas	7"	Island	WI100	1963	£10	£5	
Revenge	7"	Island	WI058	1963	£12	£6	

COSMO & DENZIL

Bed Of Roses	7"	Blue Beat	BB145	1962	£12	£6	
Come On Come On	7"	Blue Beat	BB312	1965	£12	£6	
Sweet Rosemarie	7"	Blue Beat	BB296	1965	£12	£6	

COSTA, DON

I Walk The Line	7"	London	HLT8992	1959	£5	£2	
Love Is A Many Splendored Thing	7"	London	HLF8186	1955	£15	£7.50	
Theme From The Unforgiven	7"	London	HLT7103	1960	£6	£2.50	*export*

COSTA, EDDIE

Eddie Costa Quintet	10" LP	Top Rank	25017	1960	£15	£6	
Newport Jazz Festival 1957	LP	Columbia	33CX10108	1958	£15	£6	*with Mat Matthews & Don Elliott*

COSTANZO, JACK

Mr Bongo	LP	Vogue	VA160150	1959	£20	£8	

COSTELLO, CECILIA

Recordings From The Sound Archives Of The BBC	LP	Leader	LEE4054	1975	£12	£5	

COSTELLO, DAY

Despite its early date, the Beatles cover credited to 'Day Costello' was long thought to have been attributable to the young Declan McManus. It is not, but the guess was not so very wide of the mark, as the name actually hides the identity of Elvis Costello's father, the former singer with the Joe Loss Orchestra, Ross McManus.

Long And Winding Road	7"	Spark	SRL1042	1970	£5	£2	

COSTELLO, ELVIS

Two of Elvis Costello's limited-edition releases are vital additions to any collection of his work. *A Conversation With Elvis Costello* spreads the contents of his *Imperial Bedroom* LP over two records, adding a substantial amount of interview material in which Costello explains the genesis of each of the songs, prior to each one being heard. (The promo version of *Almost Blue* gives the same treatment to that album, but the interview segments are much shorter and much less interesting.) *Live At The El Mocambo*, meanwhile, contains a brilliant live reworking of some of the songs from Costello's first two LPs. Most copies that appear on the market are actually counterfeits, although this has little effect on their value. (As usual, the counterfeits are readily identified by their hand-written matrix numbers.) The original pressing of the *Armed Forces* LP, complete with its opening-out cover and its EP record and postcard inserts, is nothing like as rare as some people seem to imagine. The record was included in earlier editions of the *Price Guide*, but has now become a victim of the general fall in vinyl prices at the bottom end of the market.

Alison	7"	Stiff	BUY14	1977	£200	£100	*white vinyl A side*
Armed Forces	CD	Demon	IMPFIENDCD21	1986	£12	£5	*with 'Peace, Love and Understanding'*
Armed Forces	LP	CBS	JC35709	1979	£10	£4	*Canadian, yellow vinyl*
Baby Plays Around	CD-s	WEA	W2949CD	1989	£5	£2	
Big Sister	7"	F-Beat		1982	£5	£2	*1 sided promo*
Blood And Chocolate	cass	Demon	XFIENDCASS80	1986	£12	£5	*'chocolate bar' package*
Conversation With Elvis Costello	LP	F-Beat	ECCHAT2	1982	£50	£25	*double promo*
Costello Hour	CD	Warner Bros	PROCD3426	1989	£20	£8	*US promo*
Don't Let Me Be Misunderstood (Live)	12"	Columbia	CAS2310	1986	£15	£7.50	*US promo*
Excerpts from Almost Blue	7"	F-Beat	EC1	1981	£25	£12.50	*promo*
Excerpts from Trust	12"	F-Beat	EL2	1981	£30	£15	*promo*
Get Happy	LP	F-Beat	XXPROMO1	1980	£40	£20	*double 12" promo*
Good Year For The Roses	7"	F-Beat	XX17	1981	£15	£7.50	*picture sleeve*
Highlights From Blood And Chocolate	7"	Imp	CHOC1	1986	£6	£2.50	*red vinyl promo*
I Can't Stand Up For Falling Down	7"	2-Tone	CHSTT7	1980	£8	£4	*matrix no. XX1*
I Can't Stand Up For Falling Down	7"	2-Tone	CHSTT7	1980	£12	£6	
I Wanna Be Loved (Radio Version)	12"	F-Beat	XX35Z	1984	£10	£5	*promo*
I Wanna Be Loved (Radio Version)	7"	F-Beat	XX35DJ	1984	£5	£2	*promo*
Imperial Bedroom	LP	Columbia	HC48157	1982	£12	£5	*US audiophile*
Imperial Bedroom/Almost Blue	CD	Demon	ECPROMO2	1994	£15	£6	*promo sampler*
Introduces The Tracks From Almost Blue	LP	F-Beat	ECCHAT1	1981	£50	£25	*promo*
Live At Hollywood High	12"	Columbia	AS529	1979	£15	£7.50	*US promo*
Live At The El Mocambo	LP	Columbia	CDN10	1978	£50	£25	*Canadian promo*
Mighty Like A Rose	CD	Warner Bros		1991	£15	£6	*US promo picture disc*
My Aim Is True/This Year's Model	LP	Columbia	no number	1978	£150	£75	*US promo picture disc*
New Amsterdam	7"	F-Beat	XX5P	1980	£4	£1.50	*picture disc, white rim*
New Amsterdam	7"	F-Beat	XX5P	1980	£6	£2.50	*picture disc, black rim*
Other Side Of Summer	CD-s	WEA	W0025CD	1991	£5	£2	
Punch The Clock	7"	F-Beat		1983	£25	£12.50	*2 x 7" in plastic wallet, promo*
Radio Radio	12"	Columbia	AS443	1978	£12	£6	*US promo, orange vinyl, with other artists*
Radio Radio	12"	Radar	ADA24	1978	£12	£6	*promo*

Spike	CD	Warner Bros	PROCD3426	1989	**£15**	**£6**	*US promo in tartan cover*
Stiff Singles Four Pack	7"	Stiff	GRAB3	1980	**£12**	**£6**	
Taking Liberties	12"	Columbia	AS847	1980	**£15**	**£7.50**	*US promo, Costello label*
Taking Liberties	LP	Columbia	JC36939	1980	**£10**	**£4**	*US*
Talking In The Dark	7"	Radar	RG1	1978	**£6**	**£2.50**	
Ten Bloody Marys And Ten How's Your Fathers	cass	F-Beat	XXC6	1980	**£10**	**£4**	*gold cassette & case*
Tom Snyder Interview	12"	Columbia	AS958	1980	**£15**	**£7.50**	*US promo*
Two And A Half Years In Thirty-One Minutes	CD	Demon		1993	**£20**	**£8**	*promo sampler*
Veronica	CD-s	WEA	W7558CD	1989	**£5**	**£2**	
Words And Music	CD	Warner Bros	PROCD6955	1994	**£20**	**£8**	*US promo*

COTSWOLD FOLK

Collection	LP	Deroy		1977	**£50**	**£25**	

COTTON, BILLY

Friends And Neighbours	7"	Decca	F10299	1954	**£4**	**£1.50**	

COTTON, JAMES BLUES BAND

Cotton In Your Ears	LP	Verve	FTS3060	1969	**£12**	**£5**	*US*
Cut You Loose	LP	Vanguard	SVRL19035	1968	**£15**	**£6**	
James Cotton Blues Band	LP	Verve	FT(S)3023	1967	**£15**	**£6**	*US*
Pure Cotton	LP	Verve	FTS3038	1968	**£15**	**£6**	*US*
Taking Care Of Business	LP	Capitol	SM814	1970	**£12**	**£5**	*US*

COTTON, JIMMY

Chris Barber Presents Jimmy Cotton	7" EP	Columbia	SEG8141	1962	**£10**	**£5**	
Chris Barber Presents Jimmy Cotton No. 2	7" EP	Columbia	SEG8189	1962	**£10**	**£5**	

COTTON, MIKE SOUND

Cotton Picking	7" EP	Columbia	SEG8144	1962	**£20**	**£10**	
Harlem Shuffle	7"	Polydor	56096	1966	**£15**	**£7.50**	
I Don't Wanna Know	7"	Columbia	DB7267	1964	**£20**	**£10**	
Make Up Your Mind	7"	Columbia	DB7623	1965	**£15**	**£7.50**	
Make Up Your Mind	7" EP	Festival	452433	1965	**£50**	**£25**	*French*
Midnight Flyer	7"	Columbia	DB7134	1963	**£5**	**£2**	
Mike Cotton Sound	LP	Columbia	33SX1647	1964	**£300**	**£180**	
Round And Round	7"	Columbia	DB7382	1964	**£30**	**£15**	
Swing That Hammer	7"	Columbia	DB7029	1963	**£5**	**£2**	*credited to the Mike Cotton Jazzmen*
Wild And The Willing	7" EP	Columbia	SEG8190	1962	**£20**	**£10**	

COUGARS

Caviare And Chips	7"	Parlophone	R5115	1964	**£8**	**£4**	
Red Square	7"	Parlophone	R5038	1963	**£5**	**£2**	
Saturday Night At The Duckpond	7"	Parlophone	R4989	1963	**£5**	**£2**	
Saturday Night With The Cougars	7" EP	Parlophone	GEP8886	1963	**£30**	**£15**	

COUGHLAN, CATHAL

I'm Long Me Measaim	7"	Caff	CAFF1	198–	**£5**	**£2**	*flexi, East Village B side*

COULAM, ROGER

Blow Hot Blow Cold	LP	Fontana	16009	1970	**£10**	**£4**	
Organ In Orbit	LP	CBS	52399	1967	**£10**	**£4**	

COULDRY, DENIS & SMILE

James In The Basement	7"	Decca	F12734	1968	**£4**	**£1.50**	
Penny For The Wind	7"	Decca	F12786	1968	**£4**	**£1.50**	

COULSON, DEAN, MCGUINESS, FLINT

Lo And Behold	LP	DJM	DJLPS424	1972	**£10**	**£4**	

COUNCE, CURTIS

Carl's Blues	LP	Contemporary	LAC12263	1961	**£20**	**£8**	
Curtis Counce Group	LP	Contemporary	LAC12073	1958	**£20**	**£8**	
You Get More Bounce With Curtis Counce	LP	Contemporary	LAC12133	1959	**£20**	**£8**	

COUNT

Gazaroody	7"	Purple	PUR122	1974	**£5**	**£2**	

COUNT BUSTY & THE RUDIES

You Like It	7"	Melody	MRC003	1968	**£5**	**£2**	

COUNT DOWN & THE ZEROS

Hello My Angel	7"	Ember	EMBS189	1964	**£25**	**£12.50**	

COUNT FIVE

Psychotic Reaction	7"	Pye	7N25393	1966	**£15**	**£7.50**	
Psychotic Reaction	7" EP	DiscAZ	1058	1966	**£50**	**£25**	*French*
Psychotic Reaction	LP	Double Shot	DSM1001/ DSS5001	1966	**£50**	**£25**	*US*

COUNT OSSIE

Count Ossie and the Mystic Revelation of Rastafari are members of an isolated rural Rastafarian community in Jamaica. Their music is rather different from that of other reggae groups – the several percussionists that form the central strand give it a pronounced African flavour; the horns and acoustic double bass add a jazz flavour; the poets and chanters turn the whole thing into pure Count Ossie.

Title	Format	Label	Number	Year	Mint	VG	Notes
Grounation	LP	Ashanti	NTI301	1973	£25	£10	*triple, with the Mystic Revelation Of Rastafari*
Nyiah Bongo	7"	Doctor Bird	DB1086	1967	£10	£5	
Pure Soul	7"	Doctor Bird	DB1113	1967	£10	£5	*Patsy Todd B side*
Rasta Reggae	7"	Ashanti	ASH404	1971	£4	£1.50	
Tales Of Mozambique	LP	Dynamic	DNYLS1001	1975	£15	£6	*with the Mystic Revelation Of Rastafari*
Turn Me On	7"	Doctor Bird	DB1018	1966	£10	£5	
Whispering Drums	7"	Moodisc	MU3515/HM105	1971	£4	£1.50	

COUNT VICTORS

Title	Format	Label	Number	Year	Mint	VG	Notes
Peeping And Hiding	7"	Coral	Q72456	1962	£5	£2.50	
Road Runner	7"	Coral	Q72462	1963	£8	£4	

COUNTRY BOY

Title	Format	Label	Number	Year	Mint	VG	Notes
I'm A Lonely Boy	7"	Blue Beat	BB236	1964	£12	£6	

COUNTRY FUNK

Title	Format	Label	Number	Year	Mint	VG	Notes
Country Funk	LP	Polydor	2482018	1970	£15	£6	

COUNTRY GENTLEMEN

Title	Format	Label	Number	Year	Mint	VG	Notes
Greensleeves	7"	Decca	F11766	1963	£25	£12.50	

COUNTRY HAMS

Title	Format	Label	Number	Year	Mint	VG	Notes
Walking In The Park With Eloise	7"	EMI	EMI2220	1974	£25	£12.50	*red & brown label*
Walking In The Park With Eloise	7"	EMI	EMI2220	1982	£5	£2	*straw label*

COUNTRY JOE & THE FISH

The album that most clearly epitomizes the spirit of the 1967 'summer of love' is *I Feel Like I'm Fixin' To Die* by Country Joe and the Fish. The combination of electric guitar wizardry, political protest, and general psychedelia lends credence to the legend that the whole thing was recorded while the band was tripping on acid, but it also happens to be one of the finest albums of the period. Country Joe McDonald himself had a background in folk and country – and returned to this as a solo artist after the Fish disbanded in 1970. His early career is documented by the self-produced Rag Baby series of EPs and also by a recently discovered solo album from 1965 – listed under his own name.

Title	Format	Label	Number	Year	Mint	VG	Notes
Best Of Country Foe And The Fish	LP	Vanguard	SVRL19058	1969	£10	£4	
C. J. Fish	LP	Vanguard	6369002	1970	£10	£4	
Country Joe And The Fish	7" EP	Rag Baby	RAG1002	1965	£50	£25	*US*
Electric Music For The Mind & Body	LP	Vanguard	SVRL19026	1967	£12	£5	
Electric Music For The Mind & Body	LP	Fontana	(S)TFL6081	1967	£25	£10	
Electric Music For The Mind And Body	LP	Vanguard	VSD79244	1972	£10	£4	
Here I Go Again	7"	Vanguard	VA3	1969	£5	£2	
Here We Are Again	LP	Vanguard	SVRL19048	1969	£12	£5	
I Feel Like I'm Fixin' To Die	7"	Vanguard	6076250	1970	£5	£2	
I Feel Like I'm Fixin' To Die	LP	Vanguard	VSD79266	1971	£10	£4	
I Feel Like I'm Fixing To Die	LP	Vanguard	SVRL19029	1967	£12	£5	
I Feel Like I'm Fixing To Die	LP	Fontana	(S)TFL6087	1967	£20	£8	
Life And Times Of Country Joe And The Fish	LP	Vanguard	VSD27/28	1973	£15	£6	*double*
Life And Times Of Country Joe And The Fish	LP	Vanguard	VSQ40004/5	1973	£25	£10	*quad, double*
Not So Sweet Martha Lorraine	7"	Fontana	TF882	1967	£6	£2.50	
Rag Baby Talking Issue	7" EP	Rag Baby	RAG1001	1965	£50	£25	*US*
Resist	7" EP	Rag Baby	RAG1003	1971	£30	£15	*US*
Together	LP	Vanguard	SVRL19006	1968	£12	£5	

COUNTRY JUG

Title	Format	Label	Number	Year	Mint	VG	Notes
I'm Sorry	7"	Decca	F13270	1972	£15	£7.50	

COUNTRY LANE

Title	Format	Label	Number	Year	Mint	VG	Notes
Substratum	LP	Splendid	SLP50108	1973	£200	£100	*Swiss*

COUNTRYMEN

Title	Format	Label	Number	Year	Mint	VG	Notes
I Know Where I'm Going	7"	Piccadilly	7N34012	1962	£5	£2	

COURIERS

Title	Format	Label	Number	Year	Mint	VG	Notes
Pack Up Your Sorrows	LP	Ash	ALP201	1969	£20	£8	
Take Away	7"	Ember	EMBS218	1966	£75	£37.50	*picture sleeve*
Take Away	7"	Ember	EMBS218	1966	£60	£30	

COURTNEY, PETER

Title	Format	Label	Number	Year	Mint	VG	Notes
Docteur David's Private Papers	7" EP	Fontana	469210	1967	£8	£4	*French*

COURTYARD MUSIC GROUP

Title	Format	Label	Number	Year	Mint	VG	Notes
Just Our Way Of Saying Hello	LP	Deroy		1974	£200	£100	

COUSIN EMMY & HER KINFOLK

Title	Format	Label	Number	Year	Mint	VG	Notes
Kentucky Mountain Ballads Vol. 1	7" EP	Brunswick	OE9258	1956	£10	£5	
Kentucky Mountain Ballads Vol. 2	7" EP	Brunswick	OE9259	1956	£10	£5	

COUSINS

Title	Format	Label	Number	Year	Mint	Good	Notes
Anda	7"	Palette	PG9035	1962	**£5**	**£2**	
Bouddha	7"	Palette	PG9017	1961	**£5**	**£2**	
Greatest Hits	LP	Palette	PPB225	1966	**£20**	**£8**	*Belgian*
Kili Watch	7"	Palette	PG9011	1961	**£5**	**£2**	
Live	LP	Palette	MGPB9449	1964	**£20**	**£8**	*Dutch*

COUSINS, DAVE

Title	Format	Label	Number	Year	Mint	Good	Notes
Old School Songs	LP	Slurp	1	1980	**£20**	**£8**	
Old School Songs	LP	Passport	PVC8901	1980	**£10**	**£4**	
Two Weeks Last Summer	LP	A&M	AMLS68118	1972	**£25**	**£10**	

COVAY, DON

Title	Format	Label	Number	Year	Mint	Good	Notes
Different Strokes	LP	Janus	3030	1970	**£12**	**£5**	*US*
Forty Days – Forty Nights	7"	Atlantic	584114	1967	**£4**	**£1.50**	
House Of Blue Light	LP	Atlantic	K50225	1969	**£12**	**£5**	
Mercy	LP	Atlantic	ATL5025	1965	**£40**	**£20**	
Mercy Mercy	7"	Atlantic	AT4006	1964	**£4**	**£1.50**	
Mercy Mercy	7"	Atlantic	584094	1967	**£4**	**£1.50**	
Pony Time	7"	Pye	7N25075	1961	**£5**	**£2**	
Popeye Waddle	7"	Cameo Parkway	C239	1962	**£15**	**£7.50**	
See Saw	7"	Atlantic	AT4056	1965	**£4**	**£1.50**	
See Saw	7"	Atlantic	584059	1966	**£4**	**£1.50**	
See-Saw	LP	Atlantic	587062	1967	**£15**	**£6**	
Shake Wid The Shake	7"	Philips	PB1140	1961	**£15**	**£7.50**	
Shing-A-Ling '67	7"	Atlantic	584082	1967	**£4**	**£1.50**	
Sookie Sookie	7"	Atlantic	AT4078	1966	**£4**	**£1.50**	
Take This Hurt Off Me	7"	Atlantic	AT4016	1965	**£4**	**£1.50**	
You Put Something On Me	7"	Atlantic	584025	1966	**£4**	**£1.50**	

COVERDALE, DAVID

Title	Format	Label	Number	Year	Mint	Good	Notes
Breakdown	7"	Purple	PUR136	1978	**£8**	**£4**	
Hole In The Sky	7"	Purple	PUR133	1977	**£8**	**£4**	
Last Note Of Freedom	CD-s	Epic	6562922	1990	**£5**	**£2**	

COVEY, JULIAN & THE MACHINE

Title	Format	Label	Number	Year	Mint	Good	Notes
Little Bit Hurt	7"	Island	WIP6009	1967	**£15**	**£7.50**	

COVINGTON, JULIE

Title	Format	Label	Number	Year	Mint	Good	Notes
Beautiful Changes	LP	Columbia	SCX6466	1971	**£100**	**£50**	
Magic Wasn't There	7"	Columbia	DB8649	1970	**£8**	**£4**	
Tonight Your Love Is Over	7"	Columbia	DB8705	1970	**£8**	**£4**	

COVINGTON, JULIE & PETE ATKIN

Title	Format	Label	Number	Year	Mint	Good	Notes
While The Music Lasts	LP	MJB	BEVLP1009	1967	**£100**	**£50**	

COWELL, STANLEY

Title	Format	Label	Number	Year	Mint	Good	Notes
Illusion Suite	LP	ECM	ECM1026ST	1973	**£15**	**£6**	

COWSILLS

Title	Format	Label	Number	Year	Mint	Good	Notes
Captain Sad And His Ship Of Fools	LP	MGM	CS8095	1968	**£10**	**£4**	
Cowsills	LP	MGM	C(S)8059	1967	**£10**	**£4**	
Cowsills And The Lincoln Park Zoo	LP	Fontana	SFL13055	1968	**£10**	**£4**	
In Concert	LP	MGM	SE4619	1969	**£10**	**£4**	*US*
On My Side	LP	London	SHU8421	1971	**£10**	**£4**	
Rain, The Park And Other Things	7"	MGM	MGM1353	1967	**£4**	**£1.50**	
Two By Two	LP	MGM	SE4639	1970	**£10**	**£4**	*US*
We Can Fly	LP	MGM	CS8077	1968	**£10**	**£4**	

COX, BILLY

Immediately after the death of his employer, Jimi Hendrix, bassist Billy Cox recorded what amounts to a tribute LP before effectively vanishing from the music scene. For *Nitro Function*, he recruited a rather fine lady guitarist, who manages to convey the spirit of Jimi Hendrix rather better than most, although she too subsequently disappeared. The record cover, incidentally, is a creation by the same man who was responsible for the series of distinctive Yes sleeves – Roger Dean.

Title	Format	Label	Number	Year	Mint	Good	Notes
Nitro Function	LP	Pye	NSPL28158	1971	**£25**	**£10**	

COX, HARRY

Title	Format	Label	Number	Year	Mint	Good	Notes
English Folk Singer	LP	EFDSS	LP1004	1965	**£20**	**£8**	
Sings English Love Songs	LP	DTS	LFX4	1965	**£20**	**£8**	

COX, IDA

Title	Format	Label	Number	Year	Mint	Good	Notes
Blues For Rampart Street	LP	Riverside	RLP374	1961	**£15**	**£6**	
Female Blues Vol. 1	7" EP	Collector	JEL12	1960	**£10**	**£5**	*with Ma Rainey*
Ida Cox	7" EP	Fontana	TFE17136	1959	**£10**	**£5**	
Ida Cox Vol. 1	LP	Fountain	FB301	1974	**£10**	**£4**	
Ida Cox Vol. 2	LP	Fountain	FB304	1975	**£10**	**£4**	
Sings The Blues	10" LP	London	AL3517	1954	**£25**	**£10**	

COX, IDA & ETHEL WATERS

Title	Format	Label	Number	Year	Mint	Good	Notes
Ida Cox And Ethel Waters	LP	Poydras	104	195–	**£25**	**£10**	

COX, KENNY

Title	Format	Label	Number	Year	Mint	Good	Notes
Introducing	LP	Blue Note	BST84302	1968	**£12**	**£5**	
Multidirection	LP	Blue Note	BST84339	1969	**£12**	**£5**	

COX, MICHAEL

Title	Format	Label	Cat. No.	Year	Mint	VG+	Notes
Along Came Caroline	7"	HMV	POP789	1960	£10	£5	
Angela Jones	7"	Triumph	RGM1011	1960	£8	£4	
Angela Jones	7"	Ember	EMBS103	1960	£30	£15	
Boy Meets Girl	7"	Decca	F11166	1959	£10	£5	
Don't You Break My Heart	7"	HMV	POP1137	1963	£12	£6	
Gee What A Party	7"	HMV	POP1220	1963	£12	£6	
Gypsy	7"	HMV	POP1417	1965	£12	£6	
I Hate Getting Up In The Morning	7"	Parlophone	R5436	1966	£4	£1.50	
Rave On	7"	HMV	POP1293	1964	£15	£7.50	
Stand Up	7"	HMV	POP1065	1962	£12	£6	
Sweet Little Sixteen	7"	HMV	POP905	1961	£8	£4	
Teenage Love	7"	HMV	POP830	1961	£8	£4	
Too Hot To Handle	7"	Decca	F11182	1959	£10	£5	
Young Only Once	7"	HMV	POP972	1962	£12	£6	

COX, WALLY

Title	Format	Label	Cat. No.	Year	Mint	VG+	Notes
I Can't Help It	7"	Vogue	V9175	1961	£12	£6	

COXHILL, LOL

Lol Coxhill is as great an eccentric as he is a saxophone player – and his work on that instrument is very fine indeed! The Dandelion double album *Ear Of Beholder* is the ideal introduction to both the man and the musician. It contains free group improvisation; recordings of Coxhill busking on the streets of London (he is supposed to be the inspiration behind Joni Mitchell's 'For Free', although he was apparently mildly insulted by this); Victorian music-hall songs interpreted by the Coxhill-Bedford duo; and a group of school children singing 'I Am The Walrus'. The later *Murder In The Air* consists of a radio play with all the parts accompanied by what amount to saxophone sub-titles!

Title	Format	Label	Cat. No.	Year	Mint	VG+	Notes
10:02	LP	Nato	439	1986	£12	£5	
Café De La Place	LP	Nato		1988	£12	£5	
Chantenay '80	LP	Nato	10	1980	£12	£5	
Couscous	LP	Nato	157	1983	£12	£5	
Coxhill–Miller	LP	Caroline	C1503	1973	£10	£4	*with Stephen Miller*
Digwell Duets	LP	Random Radar	RR005	1979	£12	£5	
Diverse	LP	Ogun	OG510	1976	£12	£5	
Dunois Solos	LP	Nato	95	1981	£12	£5	
Ear Of Beholder	LP	Dandelion	69001	1971	£40	£20	*double*
Fleas In The Custard	LP	Caroline	C1515	1975	£10	£4	
French Gigs	LP	AAA	A02	1982	£12	£5	
Frogdance	LP	Impetus	1085	1984	£12	£5	
Inimitable	LP	Chabada	OH9	1986	£12	£5	*French*
Instant Replay	LP	Nato	25/32	1982	£12	£5	
Johnny Rondo Duo Plus Mike Cooper	LP	FMP	SAJ29	1982	£12	£5	*German, with David Holland*
Joy Of Paranoia	LP	Ogun	OG525	1978	£12	£5	
Lid	LP	Ictus	0011	1978	£15	£6	
Lol Coxhill & Welfare State	LP	Caroline	C1514	1975	£10	£4	
Moot	LP	Ictus	0008	1978	£15	£6	
Murder In The Air	12"	Chiltern Sound	CS100	1978	£10	£5	
Slow Music	LP	Pipe	1	1980	£12	£5	*with Morgan Fisher*
Story So Far . . . Oh Really?	LP	Caroline	C1507	1974	£10	£4	*with Stephen Miller*
Toverbal Sweet	LP	Mushroom	150MR23	1972	£75	£37.50	

COXHILL, LOL & DAVID BEDFORD

Title	Format	Label	Cat. No.	Year	Mint	VG+	Notes
Pretty Little Girl	7"	Polydor	2001253	1971	£4	£1.50	

COXSONE, LLOYD

Title	Format	Label	Cat. No.	Year	Mint	VG+	Notes
Cruising	7"	Pyramid	PYR7003	1973	£4	£1.50	

COYNE, KEVIN

Title	Format	Label	Cat. No.	Year	Mint	VG+	Notes
Blame It On The Night	LP	Virgin	V2012	1974	£10	£4	
Case History	LP	Dandelion	2310228	1972	£40	£20	
Heartburn	LP	Virgin	V2047	1976	£10	£4	
In Living Black And White	LP	Virgin	VD2505	1976	£12	£5	*double*
Marjory Razorblade	LP	Virgin	VD2501	1973	£12	£5	*double*
Matching Head And Feet	LP	Virgin	V2033	1975	£10	£4	

CRACK

Title	Format	Label	Cat. No.	Year	Mint	VG+	Notes
All Or Nothing	7"	RCA	CRACK1	1983	£6	£2.50	
Don't You Ever Let Me Down	7"	RCA	RCA214	1982	£5	£2	
Going Out	7"	RCA	RCA255	1982	£5	£2	

CRACKED MIRROR

Title	Format	Label	Cat. No.	Year	Mint	VG+	Notes
Cracked Mirror	LP	private	CMLP001	1983	£50	£25	

CRACKNELL, SARAH

Title	Format	Label	Cat. No.	Year	Mint	VG+	Notes
Goldie	CD-s	Gut	CDGUT7	1997	£15	£7.50	
Love Is All You Need	7"	Three Bears	TED001	1987	£6	£2.50	

CRADDOCK, BILLY 'CRASH'

Title	Format	Label	Cat. No.	Year	Mint	VG+	Notes
Boom Boom Baby	7"	Philips	PB966	1959	£10	£5	
Goodtime Billy	7"	Philips	PB1092	1961	£8	£4	
I'm Tore Up	LP	King	912	1964	£30	£15	*US*
Since She Turned Seventeen	7"	Philips	PB1006	1960	£10	£5	
Truly True	7"	Mercury	AMT1146	1961	£6	£2.50	

CRAIG

I Must Be Mad	7"	Fontana	TF715	1966	£175	£87.50	
Little Bit Of Soap	7"	Fontana	TF665	1966	£60	£30	

CRAIG (2)

Ain't That A Shame	7"	King	KG1022	1965	£8	£4	

CRAIG, PAUL

Midnight Girl	7"	CBS	202406	1966	£4	£1.50	

CRAMER, FLOYD

Fancy Pants	7"	London	HL8012	1954	£30	£15	
Flip Flop And Bop	7"	RCA	RCA1050	1958	£15	£7.50	
Jolly Cholly	7"	London	HL8062	1954	£40	£20	
Last Date	7"	RCA	RCA1211	1960	£4	£1.50	
On The Rebound	LP	RCA	RD27221/SF5103	1961	£10	£4	
Piano Hayride	7" EP	London	REP1023	1955	£25	£12.50	
Rag A Tag	7"	London	HLU8195	1955	£20	£10	
That Handsome Piano	7" EP	RCA	RCX7120	1963	£10	£5	

CRAMP

She Doesn't Love Me	7"	Rip Off	RIP7	1978	£5	£2	

CRAMPS

All Women Are Bad	CD-s	Enigma	ENVCD19	1990	£5	£2	
Bikini Girls With Machine Guns	CD-s	Enigma	ENVCD17	1990	£5	£2	
Creature From The Black Leather Lagoon	CD-s	Enigma	ENVCD22	1990	£5	£2	
Crusher	12"	IRS	PFSX1008	1981	£8	£4	
Drug Train	7"	Illegal	ILS021	1980	£8	£4	
Eyeball In My Martini	CD-s	Big Beat	CDNST135	1991	£5	£2	
Fever	7"	Illegal	ILS017	1980	£10	£5	*band picture sleeve*
Flamejob	CD	Creation	CRECD170	1994	£20	£8	*US promo with extra tracks*
Garbageman/Mystery Plane	7"	Illegal	ILS017	1980	£12	£6	*demo*
Goo Goo Muck	7"	IRS	PFS1003	1981	£8	£4	*yellow vinyl*
Gravest Hits	12"	Illegal	ILS12013	1979	£10	£5	*blue vinyl*
Lux	12"	Windsong	WINDSONG4	1991	£40	£20	*3 disc boxed set*
Off The Bone	LP	Illegal	ILP012	1983	£10	£4	*picture disc*
Smell Of Female	LP	Big Beat	BEDP6	1984	£10	£4	*picture disc*
Songs The Lord Taught Us	LP	Illegal	ILP005	1980	£50	£25	*test pressing with 'Drug Train'*

CRANBERRIES

Seldom has the Irish accent found so mellifluous a setting as in the singing of Dolores O'Riordan with the music of the Cranberries. Whether her songwriting abilities will prove sufficient to sustain the group through a long career remains to be proved, but the Cranberries have already earned their place within the rock encyclopaedias of the next century – if only for the powerful 'Zombie', whose reverberations continue to be felt. In addition to the collectables listed below, there is also supposed to be a demo three-track tape, including the song 'Nothing Left At All', issued in 1991 when the group still used the original punning version of their name, the Cranberry Saw Us. Further information on this item will be gratefully received.

Dreams	CD-s	Island	CID548	1992	£5	£2	
Everybody Else Is Doing It	CD	Island	CRAN1	1996	£20	£8	*promo with Linger CD-s*
No Need To Argue	CD-s	Island	4373	1994	£20	£10	*French live promo*
To The Faithful Departed Interview	CD	Island	CDINTCRAN	1996	£25	£10	*promo*
Uncertain	12"	Xeric	XER014T	1991	£20	£10	
Uncertain	7"	Xeric	XER014	1991	£10	£5	
Uncertain	CD-s	Xeric	XER014CD	1991	£30	£15	
Zombie	CD-s	Island	CID600/ CIDX600	1994	£10	£5	*boxed double*

CRANE, DON & THE NEW DOWNLINERS SECT

I Can't Get Away From You	7"	Pye	7N17261	1967	£75	£37.50	

CRANE, TONY

Anonymous Mr Brown	7"	Pye	7N17337	1967	£4	£1.50	
Even The Bravest	7"	CBS	202022	1965	£4	£1.50	
Ideal Love	7"	Polydor	BM56008	1965	£4	£1.50	
Scratchin' Ma Head	7"	Pye	7N17517	1968	£4	£1.50	

CRANE, VINCENT & CHRIS FARLOWE

Can't Find A Reason	7"	Dawn	DNS1034	1972	£4	£1.50	

CRANE RIVER JAZZ BAND

Crane River Jazz Band	7" EP	Parlophone	GEP8652	1957	£5	£2	
Lily Of The Valley	7"	Parlophone	MSP6008	1953	£5	£2	

CRANES

Fuse	cass	Biteback		1987	£20	£10	

CRANNOG

Crannog	LP	private	CR1	1980	£50	£25	

CRASHERS

Off Track	7"	Amalgamated	AMG834	1969	£4	£1.50	

CRASS

Feeding Of The Five Thousand	12"	Small Wonder	WEENY2	1978	£6	£2.50	
Reality Asylum	7"	Crass	5219841	1979	£6	£2.50	*brown card picture sleeve*

CRAVINKEL

Cravinkel	LP	Philips	6305055	1970	£15	£6	*German*
Garden Of Loneliness	LP	Philips	6305124	1971	£12	£5	*German*

CRAWFORD, CAROLYN

When Someone's Good To You	7"	Stateside	SS384	1965	£100	£50	

CRAWFORD, GLORIA

Sad Movies	7"	Doctor Bird	DB1057	1966	£10	£5	*Lester Sterling B side*

CRAWFORD, HANK

We Got A Good Thing Going	LP	Kudu	KUL7	1973	£10	£4	

CRAWFORD, JIMMY

Long Stringy Baby	7"	Columbia	DB4525	1960	£15	£7.50	

CRAWFORD, JOHNNY

Captivating Johnny Crawford	LP	Del-Fi	LP1220	1962	£25	£10	*US*
Cindy's Birthday	7"	Pye	7N25145	1962	£4	£1.50	
Greatest Hits	LP	Del-Fi	LP/ST1229	1963	£20	£8	*US*
Greatest Hits Vol. 2	LP	Del-Fi	LP/ST1248	1964	£20	£8	*US*
His Greatest Hits	LP	London	HA8197	1964	£15	£6	
Johnny Crawford	7" EP	London	RE1343	1962	£15	£7.50	
Judy Loves Me	7"	London	HL9836	1964	£4	£1.50	
Proud	7"	London	HL9669	1963	£4	£1.50	
Rumors	LP	London	HA8060	1963	£20	£8	
Rumours	7"	London	HL9638	1962	£4	£1.50	
When I Fall In Love	7" EP	London	RE1416	1964	£15	£7.50	
Young Man's Fancy	LP	Del-Fi	LP/ST1223	1963	£20	£8	*US*
Your Nose Is Gonna Grow	7"	London	HL9605	1962	£4	£1.50	

CRAWFORD, RANDY

Knocking On Heaven's Door	CD-s	Warner Bros	W2865CD	1989	£8	£4	*3" single*

CRAWFORD BROTHERS

I Ain't Guilty	7"	Vogue	V9140	1959	£150	£75	
Midnight Mover Groover	7"	Vogue	V9077	1957	£150	£75	

CRAYTON, PEE WEE

Pee Wee Crayton	LP	Crown	CLP5175	1959	£25	£10	*US*
Things I Used To Do	LP	Vanguard	VSD6566	1978	£10	£4	

CRAZY CASEY

Beast And I	LP	Polydor	236148	1967	£20	£8	*Dutch*

CRAZY ELEPHANT

Crazy Elephant	LP	Major MInor	SMLP62	1969	£10	£4	

CRAZY HORSE

Crazy Horse	LP	Reprise	RSLP6438	1972	£10	£4	
Loose	LP	Reprise	K44171	1972	£10	£4	

CRAZY ROCKERS

Best Of Crazy Rockers	LP	Negram	NYN218	1973	£30	£15	*Dutch*
Out Of Sight	LP	CNR	657580	1981	£15	£6	*Dutch*
Successen Van Crazy Rockers	LP	Delta	HJD102	1964	£60	£30	*Dutch*
Third Man Theme	7"	King	KG1001	1964	£4	£1.50	

CREAM

Cream are not highly regarded by those who feel that improvisation has no place in rock music, but on a good night the interplay between the three virtuoso musicians, each trying to outplay the others, was thrilling. Inevitably this approach does not always work, but when it does, the risks are entirely justified. 'Crossroads' is an electric blues masterpiece, while the long modal improvisation on 'Spoonful' (also included on *Wheels Of Fire*) is as inspirational as the lengthy drum solo on 'Toad' is tedious. The other side of Cream was their ability to create intelligent pop music with an attractive blues edge – *Disraeli Gears* was quite rightly hailed as one of the most impressive recordings of 1967 – in a year when the competition was extremely stiff.

Anyone For Tennis	7"	Polydor	56258	1968	£4	£1.50	
Cream	LP	RSO	2658142	1980	£40	£20	*German 6 LP boxed set*
Disraeli Gears	CD	Mobile Fidelity	UDCD562	1992	£20	£8	*US audiophile, mono & stereo mixes*
Disraeli Gears	LP	Reaction	593003	1967	£25	£10	*mono*
Disraeli Gears	LP	Reaction	594003	1967	£20	£8	*stereo*
Fresh Cream	CD	DCC	GZS1022	1992	£15	£6	*US audiophile*
Fresh Cream	LP	Reaction	593001	1966	£30	£15	*mono*
Fresh Cream	LP	Reaction	594001	1966	£25	£10	*stereo*
Goodbye	LP	Polydor	583053	1969	£10	£4	
I Feel Free	7"	Reaction	591011	1966	£5	£2	
I Feel Free	7" EP	Polydor	27798	1966	£30	£15	*French*
Live Cream Vols. 1 & 2	CD	Mobile Fidelity	UDCD2625	1995	£25	£10	*US double audiophile*

Title	Format	Label	Cat. No.	Year	Mint	VG	Notes
On Top	LP	Polydor	2855002	1969	**£12**	**£5**	
Strange Brew	7"	Reaction	591015	1967	**£4**	**£1.50**	
Strange Brew	7" EP	Polydor	27810	1967	**£30**	**£15**	*French*
Wheels Of Fire	CD	DCC	GZS21020	1992	**£25**	**£10**	*US double audiophile*
Wheels Of Fire	LP	Polydor	582031/2	1968	**£40**	**£20**	*double, mono*
Wheels Of Fire	LP	Polydor	583031/2	1968	**£30**	**£15**	*double, stereo*
Wheels Of Fire	LP	Mobile Fidelity	MFSL2066	1982	**£20**	**£8**	*US audiophile*
Wheels Of Fire In The Studio	LP	Polydor	582033	1968	**£15**	**£6**	*mono*
Wheels Of Fire In The Studio	LP	Polydor	583033	1968	**£12**	**£5**	*stereo*
Wheels Of Fire Live At Fillmore	LP	Polydor	582040	1968	**£15**	**£6**	*mono*
Wheels Of Fire Live At Fillmore	LP	Polydor	583040	1968	**£12**	**£5**	*stereo*
Wrapping Paper	7"	Reaction	591007	1966	**£5**	**£2**	
Wrapping Paper	7" EP	Polydor	27791	1966	**£30**	**£15**	*French*

CREAMERS

Title	Format	Label	Cat. No.	Year	Mint	VG	Notes
Sunday Head	7"	Fierce	FRIGHT045	1989	**£6**	**£2.50**	

CREARY SISTERS

Title	Format	Label	Cat. No.	Year	Mint	VG	Notes
Oh What A Glory	7"	High Note	HS020	1969	**£4**	**£1.50**	

CREATION

The Creation have acquired the status of one of the great groups of the sixties, with guitarist Eddie Phillips being a pioneer in the use of feedback and violin bow techniques. The group failed to find much success, however, and in all honesty they are not well served by their records, which are much less impressive than those of their rivals, the Who.

Title	Format	Label	Cat. No.	Year	Mint	VG	Notes
1966–67	LP	Charisma	CS8	1973	**£25**	**£10**	
Best Of The Creation	LP	Pop Schallplaten	ZS10168	1968	**£75**	**£37.50**	*German*
How Does It Feel To Feel	7"	Polydor	56230	1968	**£15**	**£7.50**	
How Does It Feel To Feel	LP	Edsel	ED106	1982	**£10**	**£4**	
If I Stay Too Long	7"	Polydor	56177	1967	**£15**	**£7.50**	
Making Time	7"	Charisma	CB213	1973	**£4**	**£1.50**	
Making Time	7"	Planet	PLF116	1966	**£30**	**£15**	
Making Time	7" EP	Vogue	INT18098	1966	**£300**	**£180**	*French, best auctioned*
Midway Down	7"	Polydor	56246	1968	**£15**	**£7.50**	
Painter Man	7"	Planet	PLF119	1966	**£30**	**£15**	
Through My Eyes	7"	Polydor	56207	1967	**£20**	**£10**	
Tom Tom	7" EP	Vogue	INT18144	1967	**£300**	**£180**	*French, best auctioned*
We Are The Paintermen	LP	Sonet	SLPS1251	1967	**£150**	**£75**	*Danish*
We Are The Paintermen	LP	Hitton	HTSLP340037	1967	**£150**	**£75**	*German*

CREATION (2)

Title	Format	Label	Cat. No.	Year	Mint	VG	Notes
I Got The Fever	7"	Stateside	SS2205	1972	**£4**	**£1.50**	

CREATION OF SUNLIGHT

Title	Format	Label	Cat. No.	Year	Mint	VG	Notes
Creation Of Sunlight	LP	Windi	1001	1968	**£300**	**£180**	*US*

CREATIONS

Title	Format	Label	Cat. No.	Year	Mint	VG	Notes
Get On Up	7"	Amalgamated	AMG818	1968	**£8**	**£4**	
Meet Me At Eight	7"	Rio	R133	1967	**£8**	**£4**	

CREATIVE ROCK

Title	Format	Label	Cat. No.	Year	Mint	VG	Notes
Gorilla	LP	Brain	1017	1973	**£12**	**£5**	*German*
Lady Pig	LP	Brain	1061	1974	**£12**	**£5**	*German*

CREATURES

Title	Format	Label	Cat. No.	Year	Mint	VG	Notes
Fury Eyes	CD-s	Polydor	SHECD18	1990	**£5**	**£2**	
Standing There	CD-s	Polydor	SHECD17	1989	**£5**	**£2**	

CREATURES (2)

Title	Format	Label	Cat. No.	Year	Mint	VG	Notes
Looking At Tomorrow	7"	CBS	2666	1967	**£4**	**£1.50**	
String Along	7"	CBS	202350	1966	**£4**	**£1.50**	
Turn Out The Light	7"	CBS	202048	1966	**£4**	**£1.50**	

CREEDENCE CLEARWATER REVIVAL

Title	Format	Label	Cat. No.	Year	Mint	VG	Notes
Bayou Country	LP	Liberty	LBS83261	1969	**£10**	**£4**	
Cosmo's Factory	CD	DCC	GZS1031	1992	**£15**	**£6**	*US audiophile*
Cosmo's Factory	LP	Liberty	LBS83388	1970	**£10**	**£4**	
Cosmo's Factory	LP	Mobile Fidelity	MFSL1037	1979	**£12**	**£5**	*US audiophile*
Creedence Clearwater Revival	LP	Liberty	LBS83259	1969	**£10**	**£4**	
Green River	CD	DCC	GZS1064	1994	**£15**	**£6**	*US audiophile*
Green River	LP	Liberty	LBS83273	1969	**£10**	**£4**	
Long As I Can See The Light	7"	Liberty	LBF15384	1970	**£5**	**£2**	*picture sleeve*
Pendulum	LP	Liberty	LBS83400	1971	**£10**	**£4**	
Porterville	7"	Scorpio	412	1967	**£25**	**£12.50**	*US*
Proud Mary/I Put A Spell On You	7"	Liberty	LBF15223	1969	**£15**	**£7.50**	
Up Around The Bend	7"	Liberty	LBF15354	1970	**£5**	**£2**	*picture sleeve*
Willy And The Poor Boys	LP	Liberty	LBS83338	1970	**£10**	**£4**	
Willy And The Poor Boys	CD	DCC	GZS1070	1994	**£15**	**£6**	*US audiophile*

CREME SODA

Title	Format	Label	Cat. No.	Year	Mint	VG	Notes
Tricky Zingers	LP	Trinity	CST11	1975	£300	£180	US

CRESCENDOES

Title	Format	Label	Cat. No.	Year	Mint	VG	Notes
Crescendoes	LP	Metronome	MLP15200	1966	£50	£25	German

CRESCENDOS

Title	Format	Label	Cat. No.	Year	Mint	VG	Notes
Oh Julie	7"	London	HLU8563	1958	£30	£15	
Oh Julie	LP	Guest Star	G1453	196–	£40	£20	US

CRESCENDOS (2)

Title	Format	Label	Cat. No.	Year	Mint	VG	Notes
Presenting	LP	Gallotone	GALP1458	1966	£100	£50	South African

CRESCENTS

Title	Format	Label	Cat. No.	Year	Mint	VG	Notes
Baby Baby Baby	7"	Columbia	DB4093	1958	£50	£25	

CRESCENTS (2)

Title	Format	Label	Cat. No.	Year	Mint	VG	Notes
Pink Dominoes	7"	London	HLN9851	1964	£6	£2.50	

CRESSIDA

Title	Format	Label	Cat. No.	Year	Mint	VG	Notes
Asylum	LP	Vertigo	6360025	1971	£75	£37.50	spiral label
Cressida	LP	Vertigo	VO7	1970	£50	£25	spiral label

CRESTAS

Title	Format	Label	Cat. No.	Year	Mint	VG	Notes
I Want To Be Loved	7"	Fontana	TF551	1965	£12	£6	

CRESTERS

Title	Format	Label	Cat. No.	Year	Mint	VG	Notes
I Just Don't Understand	7"	HMV	POP1249	1964	£5	£2	
Put Your Arms Around Me	7"	HMV	POP1296	1964	£5	£2	

CRESTS

Title	Format	Label	Cat. No.	Year	Mint	VG	Notes
Angels Listened In	7"	London	HL8954	1959	£30	£15	
Best Of The Crests	LP	Coed	LPC/LPS904	1961	£125	£62.50	US
Crests Sing All The Biggies	LP	Coed	LPC901	1960	£150	£75	US
Flower Of Love	7"	Top Rank	JAR150	1959	£10	£5	
Gee	7"	Top Rank	JAR372	1960	£15	£7.50	
Guilty	7"	London	HLU9671	1963	£8	£4	
Isn't It Amazing	7"	HMV	POP808	1960	£10	£5	
Little Miracles	7"	HMV	POP976	1962	£10	£5	
Model Girl	7"	HMV	POP848	1961	£10	£5	
Paper Crown	7"	Top Rank	JAR302	1960	£15	£7.50	
Six Nights A Week	7"	Top Rank	JAR168	1959	£12	£6	
Sixteen Candles	7"	London	HL8794	1959	£30	£15	
Trouble in Paradise	7"	HMV	POP768	1960	£15	£7.50	

CREW

Title	Format	Label	Cat. No.	Year	Mint	VG	Notes
Cecilia	7"	Decca	F13000	1970	£4	£1.50	
Marty	7"	Plexium	PXM12	1969	£4	£1.50	

CREWCUTS

Title	Format	Label	Cat. No.	Year	Mint	VG	Notes
Angels In The Sky	7"	Mercury	7MT2	1956	£15	£7.50	export
Crewcut Capers	LP	Mercury	MG20143	1954	£40	£20	US
Crewcuts	7" EP	Mercury	MEP9002	1956	£30	£15	
Crewcuts	LP	Wing	MGW12177	1959	£25	£10	US
Crewcuts Go Longhair	LP	Mercury	MG20067	1954	£40	£20	US
Crewcuts On The Campus	LP	Mercury	MG20140	1954	£40	£20	US
Crewcuts Sing	LP	RCA	LPM/LSP2037	1959	£25	£10	US
Crewcuts Sing Folk	LP	Camay	CA1/CA3002	196–	£20	£8	US
Hey Stella	7"	RCA	RCA1075	1958	£20	£10	
High School Favorites	LP	Wing	MGW12180	1959	£25	£10	US
Music A La Carte	LP	Mercury	MG20199	1955	£40	£20	US
On Parade	10" LP	Mercury	MPT7501	1956	£40	£20	
Rock And Roll Bash	LP	Mercury	MG21044	1955	£50	£25	US
Surprise Package	LP	RCA	LPM/LSP1933	1958	£25	£10	US
Susie-Q	78	Mercury	MT161	1957	£6	£2.50	
You Must Have Been A Beautiful Baby	LP	RCA	LPM/LSP2067	1960	£20	£8	US

CREWE, BOB

Title	Format	Label	Cat. No.	Year	Mint	VG	Notes
Music To Watch Girls By	LP	Stateside	SL10210	1967	£10	£4	

CRIBBINS, BERNARD

Title	Format	Label	Cat. No.	Year	Mint	VG	Notes
Combination Of Cribbins	LP	Parlophone	PMC1186	1962	£10	£4	
Hole In The Ground	7" EP	Parlophone	GEP8859	1962	£6	£2.50	

CRICKETS

Title	Format	Label	Cat. No.	Year	Mint	VG	Notes
April Avenue	7"	Liberty	LIB55603	1966	£5	£2	
Baby My Heart	7"	Coral	Q72395	1960	£6	£2.50	
Bubblegum, Pop, Ballads & Boogies	LP	Philips	6308149	1973	£10	£4	
Collection	LP	Liberty	LBY1258	1965	£10	£8	
Come On	7" EP	Liberty	LEP2173	1964	£15	£7.50	
Crickets	7" EP	Coral	FEP2053	1960	£40	£20	tri-centre
Crickets Don't Ever Change	7" EP	Coral	FEP2064	1961	£20	£10	
Don't Try To Change Me	7"	Liberty	LIB10092	1963	£5	£2	
Hayride	7"	Philips	6006294	1973	£12	£6	picture sleeve
Hayride	7"	Philips	6006294	1973	£6	£2.50	
He's Old Enough To Know Better	7"	London	HLG9486	1961	£5	£2	
I Fought The Law	7"	Coral	Q72440	1961	£6	£2.50	

I Think I've Got The Blues	7"	Liberty	LIB10174	1964	**£4**	**£1.50**	
In Style With	LP	Coral	LVA9142	1959	**£30**	**£15**	
La Bamba	7"	Liberty	LIB55696	1964	**£4**	**£1.50**	
Little Hollywood Girl	7"	Liberty	LIB55495	1962	**£5**	**£2**	
Long Way From Lubbock	LP	Mercury	6310007	1974	**£10**	**£4**	
Love's Made A Fool Of You	7"	Coral	Q72365	1959	**£6**	**£2.50**	
Now Hear This	7"	Liberty	LIB10196	1965	**£4**	**£1.50**	
Peggy Sue Got Married	7"	Coral	Q72417	1961	**£6**	**£2.50**	
Rockin' Fifties Rock'n'Roll	LP	CBS	64301	1971	**£10**	**£4**	
Something Old Something New	LP	Liberty	(S)LBY1120	1962	**£20**	**£8**	
Straight No Strings	7" EP	Liberty	SLEP2094	1963	**£25**	**£12.50**	*stereo*
Straight No Strings	7" EP	Liberty	LEP2094	1963	**£15**	**£7.50**	
When You Ask About Love	7"	Coral	Q72382	1959	**£6**	**£2.50**	

CRIMINAL CLASS

Fighting The System	7"	Inferno	HELL7	1982	**£10**	**£5**	

CRIMSON BRIDGE

Crimson Bridge	LP	Myrrh	MST6503	1972	**£15**	**£6**	

CRISIS

Alienation	7"	Ardkor	CRI004	1981	**£8**	**£4**	
Holocaust	12"	Crisis	NOTH1/CRI002	1982	**£12**	**£6**	
Hymns Of Faith	12"	Ardkor	CRI003	1980	**£15**	**£7.50**	
No Town Hall (Southwark)	7"	Peckham Action Group	NOTH1	1982	**£10**	**£5**	
UK '79	7"	Ardkor	CRI002	1979	**£5**	**£2**	

CRISIS (2)

Another Fine Mess	LP	private		197–	**£50**	**£25**	

CRISPY AMBULANCE

Four Minutes From The Frontline	7"	Aural Assault	AAR001	1976	**£6**	**£2.50**	

CRISS, GARY

Our Favourite Melodies	7"	Stateside	SS104	1962	**£5**	**£2**	

CRISS, SONNY

Sonny Criss Plays Cole Porter	LP	London	LTZP15094	1957	**£50**	**£25**	

CRISTINA

Is That All There Is	12"	Ze	WIP6560T	1980	**£6**	**£2.50**	

CRISTO, BOBBY & THE REBELS

Other Side Of The Track	7"	Decca	F11913	1964	**£25**	**£12.50**	

CRISTY, MARY

Thank You For Rushing Into My Life	7"	Polydor	2056513	1976	**£6**	**£2.50**	

CRITICS & NYAH SHUFFLE

Behold	7"	Joe	JRS1	1970	**£4**	**£1.50**	

CRITICS GROUP

Female Frolic	LP	Argo	(Z)DA82	1968	**£25**	**£10**	
Merry Progress To London	LP	Argo	(Z)DA46	1966	**£25**	**£10**	
Merry Progress To London	LP	Argo	ZFB60	1972	**£15**	**£6**	
Sweet Thames Flow Softly	LP	Argo	(Z)DA47	1966	**£25**	**£10**	
Sweet Thames Flow Softly	LP	Argo	ZFB61	1972	**£15**	**£6**	
Waterloo Peterloo	LP	Argo	DA86	1968	**£25**	**£10**	

CRITTERS

Bad Misunderstanding	7"	London	HLR10101	1966	**£4**	**£1.50**	
Don't Let The Rain Fall Down On Me	7"	London	HLR10149	1967	**£4**	**£1.50**	
Heart Of Love, Head Of Stone	7" EP	Kapp	KEV13028	1966	**£15**	**£7.50**	*French*
Marryin' Kind Of Love	7"	London	HLR10119	1967	**£4**	**£1.50**	
Mr Dieingly Sad	7"	London	HLR10071	1966	**£4**	**£1.50**	
Mr Dieingly Sad	7" EP	Kapp	KEV13031	1966	**£15**	**£7.50**	*French*
Younger Girl	7"	London	HLR10047	1966	**£4**	**£1.50**	
Younger Girl	LP	London	HAR8302	1966	**£15**	**£6**	

CROCE, JIM

Croce	LP	Capitol	ST315	1969	**£25**	**£10**	*with Ingrid Croce; US*
You Don't Mess Around With Jim	LP	Vertigo	6360700	1971	**£12**	**£5**	*spiral label*

CROCHETED DOUGHNUT RING

Havana Anna	7"	Deram	DM169	1967	**£20**	**£10**	
Maxine's Parlour	7"	Deram	DM180	1968	**£10**	**£5**	
Two Little Ladies	7"	Polydor	56204	1967	**£20**	**£10**	

CROFTERS

Crofters	LP	Beltona	SBE103	1969	**£30**	**£15**	

CROMAGNON

Cromagnon	LP	ESP-Disk	2001	1969	**£30**	**£15**	*US*

CROMBIE, TONY

Title	Format	Label	Cat. No.	Year	Price	Price	Notes
Atmosphere	7" EP	Columbia	SEG7918/ ESG7753	1959	**£5**	**£2**	
Atmosphere	LP	Columbia	33SX1119	1958	**£30**	**£15**	
Brighton Rock	7"	Columbia	DB3921	1957	**£20**	**£10**	
Drums! Drums! Drums!	LP	Top Rank	BUY027	1960	**£15**	**£6**	
Dumplin's	7"	Columbia	DB4076	1958	**£5**	**£2**	
Flying Hickory	7"	Decca	F10592	1955	**£6**	**£2.50**	
Flying Home	7"	Decca	F10547	1955	**£5**	**£2**	
Four Favourite Film Themes	7" EP	Decca	DFE6670	1960	**£5**	**£2**	
Gigglin' Gurgleburp	7"	Columbia	DB4189	1958	**£4**	**£1.50**	
Gutbucket	7"	Ember	JBS706	1962	**£4**	**£1.50**	
I Want You To Be My Baby	7"	Decca	F10637	1955	**£6**	**£2.50**	
Jazz Inc	LP	Tempo	TAP30	1960	**£25**	**£10**	
Let's You And I Rock	7"	Columbia	DB3859	1956	**£15**	**£7.50**	
Let's You And I Rock	7" EP	Columbia	SEG7686	1957	**£40**	**£20**	
Lonesome Train	7"	Columbia	DB3881	1957	**£15**	**£7.50**	
Man From Interpol	LP	Top Rank	35043	1959	**£15**	**£6**	
Perdido	7"	Decca	F10454	1955	**£8**	**£4**	
Presenting Tony Crombie No. 1	7" EP	Decca	DFE6247	1956	**£8**	**£4**	
Presenting Tony Crombie No. 2	7" EP	Decca	DFE6281	1956	**£8**	**£4**	
Rock Rock Rock	7"	Columbia	DB3880	1957	**£15**	**£7.50**	
Rock Rock Rock	7" EP	Columbia	SEG7676	1957	**£40**	**£20**	
Rockin' With The Rockets	10" LP	Columbia	33S1108	1957	**£100**	**£50**	
Stop It	7"	Decca	F10424	1954	**£5**	**£2**	
Sweet And Rhythmic	7" EP	Columbia	SEG7769	1958	**£5**	**£2**	
Sweet Beat	7"	Columbia	DB4000	1957	**£6**	**£2.50**	
Sweet, Wild And Blue	LP	Decca	SKL4114	1961	**£15**	**£6**	
Swinging Dance Beat No. 1	7" EP	Columbia	SEG7882/ ESG7768	1959	**£5**	**£2**	
Swinging Dance Beat No. 2	7" EP	Columbia	SEG7896	1959	**£5**	**£2**	
Teach You To Rock	7"	Columbia	DB3822	1956	**£20**	**£10**	
Twelve Favourite Film Themes	LP	Decca	LK4385/SKL4127	1961	**£10**	**£4**	
Ungaua	7"	Columbia	DB4145	1958	**£4**	**£1.50**	
Whole Lotta Tony	LP	Ember	EMB3336	1961	**£15**	**£6**	

CROME CYRCUS

Title	Format	Label	Cat. No.	Year	Price	Price	Notes
Love Cycle	LP	Command	925	1968	**£30**	**£15**	*US*

CROMPTON, BILL

Title	Format	Label	Cat. No.	Year	Price	Price	Notes
Hoot An' A Holler	7"	Fontana	H152	1958	**£4**	**£1.50**	

CROMWELL

This pleasant but unexceptional album is undoubtedly rare, but its value has been considerably boosted by claims that the music is like that of the Rolling Stones on *Exile On Main Street*. In fact, the resemblance is limited to the fact that both groups play guitars and drums and sing. If a comparison is really required for Cromwell, then a name like Edison Lighthouse would be far more appropriate.

Title	Format	Label	Cat. No.	Year	Price	Price	Notes
At The Gallop	LP	private	WELL005	1975	**£150**	**£75**	
First Day	7"	Cromwell	WELL006	1975	**£15**	**£7.50**	

CROMWELL, LINK

Title	Format	Label	Cat. No.	Year	Price	Price	Notes
Crazy Like A Fox	7"	London	HLB10040	1966	**£6**	**£2.50**	

CRONSHAW, ANDREW

Title	Format	Label	Cat. No.	Year	Price	Price	Notes
A Is For Andrew Z Is For Zither	LP	Transatlantic	XTRA1139	1974	**£15**	**£6**	
Wade In The Flood	LP	Transatlantic	LTRA508	1978	**£10**	**£4**	

CROOKED OAK

Title	Format	Label	Cat. No.	Year	Price	Price	Notes
Foot O'Wor Stairs	LP	Eron	019	1979	**£30**	**£15**	
From Little Acorns Grow	LP	Folkland	FL0102	1976	**£175**	**£87.50**	

CROOKS

Title	Format	Label	Cat. No.	Year	Price	Price	Notes
All The Time In The World	7"	Blue Print	BLU2006	1980	**£5**	**£2**	

CROPPER, STEVE

Title	Format	Label	Cat. No.	Year	Price	Price	Notes
With A Little Help From My Friends	LP	Stax	SXATS1008	1971	**£10**	**£4**	

CROPPER, STEVE, ALBERT KING & POP STAPLES

Title	Format	Label	Cat. No.	Year	Price	Price	Notes
Jammed Together	LP	Stax	SXATS1020	1971	**£10**	**£4**	

CROSBY, BING

Title	Format	Label	Cat. No.	Year	Price	Price	Notes
Changing Partners	7"	Brunswick	05244	1954	**£5**	**£2**	
Count Your Blessings Instead Of Sheep	7"	Brunswick	05339	1954	**£4**	**£1.50**	
Crosby Classics	10" LP	Columbia	33S1036	1954	**£10**	**£4**	
El Bingo	10" LP	Brunswick	LA8529	1951	**£10**	**£4**	
Secret Love	7"	Brunswick	05269	1954	**£5**	**£2**	
Silent Night	7"	Brunswick	03929	1954	**£4**	**£1.50**	
Sings Cole Porter Songs	10" LP	Brunswick	LA8513	1951	**£10**	**£4**	
Sings Jerome Kern Songs	10" LP	Brunswick	LA8505	1951	**£10**	**£4**	
Stardust	10" LP	Brunswick	LA8514	1951	**£10**	**£4**	
Straight Down The Middle	7"	Philips	PB817	1958	**£4**	**£1.50**	
Stranger In Paradise	7"	Brunswick	05410	1955	**£4**	**£1.50**	
White Christmas	7"	Brunswick	03384	1954	**£4**	**£1.50**	

CROSBY, BOB

Title	Format	Label	Cat. No.	Year	Price	Price	Notes
Bob Crosby And His Bobcats	10" LP	Capitol	LC6553	1952	**£15**	**£6**	

Bob Crosby's Bobcats	LP	Brunswick	LAT8050	1955	**£12**	**£5**	
Dark At The Top Of The Stairs	7"	London	HLD9228	1960	**£4**	**£1.50**	
Great Hits	LP	London	HAD2293/ SAHD6105	1960	**£10**	**£4**	
In Hi-Fi	LP	Coral	LVA9083	1958	**£10**	**£4**	
Petite Fleur	7"	London	HLD8828	1959	**£4**	**£1.50**	

CROSBY, DAVID

If I Could Only Remember My Name	LP	Atlantic	2401005	1971	**£10**	**£4**	

CROSBY, GARY

Ayuh Ayuh	7"	Brunswick	05446	1955	**£5**	**£2**	
Gary Crosby	LP	Vogue	VA160118	1957	**£10**	**£4**	
Give Me A Band And My Baby	7"	Brunswick	05496	1955	**£5**	**£2**	
Judy Judy	7"	HMV	POP330	1958	**£10**	**£5**	
Ko Ko Mo	7"	Brunswick	05400	1955	**£8**	**£4**	*with Louis Armstrong*
Mambo In The Moonlight	7"	Brunswick	05340	1954	**£5**	**£2**	
Palsy Walsy	7"	Brunswick	05365	1955	**£5**	**£2**	
Ready, Willing And Able	7"	Brunswick	05378	1955	**£8**	**£4**	

CROSBY, STILLS & NASH

Crosby, Stills And Nash	CD	Atlantic	PR4283	1991	**£20**	**£8**	*US promo sampler*
Crosby, Stills And Nash	LP	Atlantic	588189	1969	**£10**	**£4**	*lyric sheet*

CROSBY, STILLS, NASH & YOUNG

American Dream	CD	Atlantic	PR24972	1988	**£15**	**£6**	*US promo picture disc, hard-cloth cover*
Celebration Record	LP	Atlantic	PR165	1971	**£25**	**£10**	*US promo*
Déjà Vu	LP	Mobile Fidelity	MFSL1088	1982	**£12**	**£5**	*US audiophile*
Déjà Vu	LP	Atlantic	2401001	1970	**£12**	**£5**	
Déjà Vu	LP	Atlantic	SD19118	197–	**£15**	**£6**	*Dutch, brown vinyl*
Four Way Street	LP	Atlantic	2657004	1972	**£12**	**£5**	*double*
In Synch	CD	Atlantic	PR2575	1988	**£15**	**£6**	*US interview promo*
Ohio	7"	Atlantic	2091023	1970	**£4**	**£1.50**	
Our House	7"	Atlantic	2091039	1970	**£4**	**£1.50**	
Rap With Crosby, Stills, Nash And Young	LP	Atlantic	18102	1973	**£15**	**£6**	*US promo*
Teach Your Children	7"	Atlantic	2091002	1970	**£4**	**£1.50**	
Woodstock	7"	Atlantic	2091010	1970	**£4**	**£1.50**	

CROSS

Cowboys And Indians	12"	Virgin	VST1007	1987	**£8**	**£4**	
Cowboys And Indians	7"	Virgin	VS1007	1987	**£6**	**£2.50**	
Cowboys And Indians	CD-s	Virgin	CDEP10	1987	**£50**	**£25**	*promo*
Heaven For Everyone	12"	Virgin	VST1062	1988	**£15**	**£7.50**	
Heaven For Everyone	7"	Virgin	VS1062	1988	**£4**	**£1.50**	
Life Changes	CD-s	Electrola	5602045472	1991	**£60**	**£30**	*Dutch*
Love On The Tightrope	CD-s	Virgin	VVCS7	1988	**£6**	**£2.50**	*3" single*
Mad, Bad And Dangerous To Know	CD	Parlophone	CDPCS7342	1990	**£50**	**£25**	
Mad, Bad And Dangerous To Know	LP	Parlophone	PCS7342	1990	**£15**	**£6**	
Manipulator	12"	Virgin	VST1100	1988	**£20**	**£10**	
Manipulator	7"	Virgin	VS1100	1988	**£10**	**£5**	
Power To Love	12"	Parlophone	12R6251	1990	**£10**	**£5**	
Power To Love	7"	Parlophone	R6251	1990	**£6**	**£2.50**	
Power To Love	CD-s	Parlophone	CDR6251	1990	**£30**	**£15**	
Shove It	12"	Virgin	VST1026	1988	**£12**	**£6**	
Shove It	7"	Virgin	VS1026	1988	**£5**	**£2**	
Shove It	CD	Virgin	CDV2477	1988	**£15**	**£6**	
Shove It	CD-s	Virgin	CDEP20	1988	**£30**	**£15**	

CROSS, JIMMIE

Super Duper Man	7"	Red Bird	RB10042	1966	**£10**	**£5**	

CROSS, KEITH & PETER ROSS

Bored Civilians	LP	Decca	SKL5129	1972	**£50**	**£25**	
Can You Believe It?	7"	Decca	F13224	1971	**£4**	**£1.50**	
Peace In The End	7"	Decca	F13316	1972	**£4**	**£1.50**	

CROSSBEATS

Busy Man	7"	Pilgrim	PSR7004	1967	**£4**	**£1.50**	
Crazy Mixed Up Generation	LP	Pilgrim	KLP12	1967	**£20**	**£8**	
Step Aside	7"	Pilgrim	PSR7003	1967	**£5**	**£2**	

CROW

Crow By Crow	LP	Stateside	SSL10310	1970	**£15**	**£6**	
Crow Music	LP	Stateside	SSL10301	1970	**£15**	**£6**	

CROW, SHERYL

Having apparently had to fend off the unwelcome advances of Michael Jackson's bodyguard while on tour as one of the star's backing singers, and having been told, in effect, that failure to give in to the advances would seriously affect the success of her music career (as described in the song 'What I Can Do For You'), it must have been particularly gratifying for Sheryl Crow when her debut album and its attendant singles managed to catapult her into the ranks of stardom in her own right. The album's success has produced two interesting variations. A limited-edition double-disc package, issued some time after the original release of the studio album, adds a set of six live recordings made by the BBC at a London concert. A limited US version, meanwhile, houses the disc in an envelope glued inside the front cover of a ring-bound book, printed to look like Sheryl Crow's own scrapbook, with photographs, song lyrics, and even a printed coffee-cup stain on the front.

If It Makes You Happy	7"	A&M	5819027	1996	£4	**£1.50**	*jukebox issue*
Leaving Las Vegas	CD-s	A&M	5806452	1994	£6	**£2.50**	
Run Baby Run	7"	A&M	5803807	1993	£4	**£1.50**	
Run Baby Run	CD-s	A&M	5811472	1994	£10	**£5**	*boxed set*
Run Baby Run	CD-s	A&M	5805692	1994	£6	**£2.50**	
Run Baby Run	CD-s	A&M	5803812	1993	£10	**£5**	
Strong Enough	7"	A&M	SCJB2	1996	£4	**£1.50**	*jukebox issue*
Tuesday Night Music Club	CD	A&M	5401262/5403682	1991	£20	**£8**	*double*
Tuesday Night Music Club	CD	A&M	3145401262	1993	£15	**£6**	*US, scrapbook packaging*
What Can I Do For You	CD-s	A&M	5804627	1994	£6	**£2.50**	

CROWBAR

Hippie Punks	7"	Skinhead	SKIN1	1984	£20	**£10**	

CROWDED HOUSE

Better Be Home Soon	12"	Capitol	12CL498	1988	£8	**£4**	
Better Be Home Soon	CD-s	Capitol	CDCL498	1988	£20	**£10**	
Chocolate Cake	CD-s	EMI	CDCL618	1991	£6	**£2.50**	
Conversation With Neil Finn	CD	EMI	FINNTERVIEW1	1993	£20	**£8**	*promo*
Don't Dream It's Over	12"	Capitol	12CL438	1987	£8	**£4**	
Fall At Your Feet	CD-s	Capitol	CDCL626	1991	£5	**£2**	
Fall At Your Feet	CD-s	Capitol	CDCLX626	1991	£5	**£2**	
Final Interview . . . ?	CD	EMI	FINNTERVIEW2	1996	£20	**£8**	*promo*
Four Seasons In One Day	CD-s	Capitol	CDCLS655	1992	£10	**£5**	*with collectors' box*
Four Seasons In One Day	CD-s	Capitol	CDCLS655	1992	£5	**£2**	
Full House	CD	Capitol	CDCHDJ1	1994	£25	**£10**	*promo compilation*
It's Only Natural	CD-s	Capitol	CDCL661	1992	£5	**£2**	
It's Only Natural	CD-s	Capitol	CDCLS661	1992	£5	**£2**	
Live At The Town And Country Club	CD	Capitol	CH1	1992	£60	**£30**	*double promo*
Locked Out	CD	Capitol	DPRO79297	1993	£40	**£20**	*US promo with bonus CD album*
Recurring Dream	CD	Capitol	724385224829	1996	£15	**£6**	*double*
Sister Madly	12"	Capitol	12CL509	1988	£6	**£2.50**	
Sister Madly	CD-s	Capitol	CDCL509	1988	£20	**£10**	
Something So Strong	12"	Capitol	12CL456	1987	£8	**£4**	
Weather With You	CD-s	Capitol	CDCLS643	1992	£12	**£6**	*double*
Woodface	CD	Capitol	CDP7935592	1991	£15	**£6**	*foldout pack*
Woodface – The Singles Collection	CD-s	Capitol		1991	£75	**£37.50**	*8 CD single boxed set*
World Where You Live	12"	Capitol	12CL416	1986	£8	**£4**	
World Where You Live	7"	Capitol	CL416	1986	£4	**£1.50**	
World Where You Live	CD-s	Capitol	CDCL416	1986	£20	**£10**	

CROWDY CRAWN

No Song To Sing	LP	Sentinel	SENS1021	1974	£75	**£37.50**	

CROWNS

Made Of Gold	LP	Pama	PMLP6	1968	£12	**£5**	

CROWS

Gee	7"	Columbia	SCM5119	1954	£1500	**£1000**	*best auctioned*

CROWS (2)

Crows	LP	Dingles	DIN317	1981	£10	**£4**	

CROZIER, TREVOR BROKEN CONSORT

Parcel Of Old Crams	LP	Argo	AFB60	1972	£25	**£10**	

CRUCIFIXION

Fox	7"	Miramar	MIR4	1980	£50	**£25**	
Green Eyes	12"	Neat	NEAT3712	1984	£12	**£6**	*purple vinyl*

CRUDUP, ARTHUR

Crudup's Mood	LP	Delmark	DS621	1971	£12	**£5**	
Father Of Rock'n'Roll	LP	RCA	RD8224	1971	£10	**£4**	
Look On Yonder's Wall	LP	Delmark	DS614	1970	£12	**£5**	
Mean Ole Frisco	LP	Blue Horizon	763855	1969	£40	**£20**	
My Baby Left Me	7"	RCA	RCA1401	1964	£15	**£7.50**	
Rhythm And Blues Vol. 4	7" EP	RCA	RCX7161	1964	£12	**£6**	

CRUISERS

It Ain't Me Babe	7"	Decca	F12098	1965	£8	**£4**	

CRUM, SIMON

Enormity In Motion	7"	Capitol	CL15183	1961	£8	**£4**	
Morgan Poisoned The Waterhole	7"	Capitol	CL15077	1959	£8	**£4**	
Stand Up Sit Down	7"	Capitol	CL14965	1958	£20	**£10**	

CRUSADERS

Crusaders	LP	Blue Thumb	ILPS9218	1972	£12	**£5**	*double*
Hollywood	LP	Mowest	MWS7004	1973	£15	**£6**	
Old Socks, New Shoes	LP	Rare Earth	SRE3001	1971	£10	**£4**	
Southern Comfort	LP	ABC	ABCD607	1975	£12	**£5**	*double*

CRYAN SHAMES

Scratch In The Sky	LP	CBS	CL/CS9586	1967	**£30**	**£15**	*US*
Sugar And Spice	7"	CBS	202344	1966	**£15**	**£7.50**	
Sugar And Spice	LP	CBS	CL2589/CS9389	1966	**£30**	**£15**	*US*
Synthesis	LP	CBS	CS9719	1968	**£30**	**£15**	*US*

CRYCH, TALCEN

Angharad	7"	Afon	RAS002	1975	**£5**	**£2**	

CRYER, BARRY

Angelina	7"	Fontana	H177	1959	**£5**	**£2**	
Nothin' Shakin'	7"	Fontana	H151	1958	**£5**	**£2**	
Purple People Eater	7"	Fontana	H139	1958	**£4**	**£1.50**	

CRYIN' SHAMES

Nobody Waved Goodbye	7"	Decca	F12425	1966	**£15**	**£7.50**	
Please Stay	7"	Decca	F12340	1966	**£10**	**£5**	

CRYING SHAMES

That's Rock'n'Roll	7"	Logo	GO385	1980	**£12**	**£6**	

CRYSTALITES

Bad	7"	Explosion	EX2010	1970	**£4**	**£1.50**	
Barefoot Brigade	7"	Explosion	EX2003	1969	**£5**	**£2**	
Biafra	7"	Big Shot	BI510	1969	**£4**	**£1.50**	
Bombshell	7"	Explosion	EX2005	1969	**£4**	**£1.50**	
Doctor Who	7"	Explosion	EX2002	1969	**£5**	**£2**	
Fistful Of Dollars	7"	Explosion	EX2006	1969	**£4**	**£1.50**	
Fistful Of Dollars	7"	Bullet	BU424	1970	**£4**	**£1.50**	
Ilya Kuryakin	7"	Island	WI3134	1968	**£10**	**£5**	
Isies	7"	Songbird	SB1024	1970	**£4**	**£1.50**	
James Ray	7"	Island	WI3153	1968	**£8**	**£4**	*Derrick Harriott B side*
Lady Madonna	7"	Songbird	SB1020	1970	**£4**	**£1.50**	
Overtaker	7"	Songbird	SB1034	1970	**£4**	**£1.50**	
Sic Him Rover	7"	Songbird	SB1030	1970	**£4**	**£1.50**	
Smokey Eyes	7"	Songbird	SB1081	1972	**£4**	**£1.50**	
Splashdown	7"	Nu Beat	NB036	1969	**£4**	**£1.50**	
Stranger In Town	7"	Songbird	SB1025	1970	**£4**	**£1.50**	
Try A Little Merriness	7"	Island	WI3151	1968	**£10**	**£5**	
Undertaker	7"	Songbird	SB1015	1969	**£4**	**£1.50**	
Undertaker	7"	Songbird	SB1017	1970	**£4**	**£1.50**	

CRYSTALS

All Grown Up	7"	London	HLU9909	1964	**£8**	**£4**	
Da Doo Ron Ron	7"	London	HLU9732	1963	**£4**	**£1.50**	
Da Doo Ron Ron	7" EP	London	REU1381	1963	**£50**	**£25**	
Do The Screw	7"	Philles	111	1963	**£1000**	**£700**	*US, promo only, best auctioned*
Greatest Hits	LP	Philles	PHLP4003	1963	**£125**	**£62.50**	*US*
He Sure Is The Boy I Love	7"	London	HLU9661	1963	**£10**	**£5**	
He's A Rebel	7"	London	HLU9611	1962	**£8**	**£4**	
He's A Rebel	LP	London	HAU8120	1963	**£75**	**£37.50**	
I Wonder	7"	London	HLU9852	1964	**£8**	**£4**	
Little Boy	7"	London	HLU9837	1964	**£30**	**£15**	
My Place	7"	United Artists	UP1110	1965	**£20**	**£10**	
Then He Kissed Me	7"	London	HLU9773	1963	**£4**	**£1.50**	
There's No Other	7"	Parlophone	R4867	1962	**£75**	**£37.50**	
Twist Uptown	LP	Philles	PHLP4000	1962	**£125**	**£62.50**	*US*

CUBA, JOE

Bang! Bang!	7"	Pye	7N25401	1966	**£6**	**£2.50**	

CUBY & THE BLIZZARDS

Afscheids-Koncert	LP	Philips	6343229	1974	**£15**	**£6**	*Dutch*
Appleknockers Flophouse	7"	Philips	BF1827	1969	**£5**	**£2**	
Appleknockers Flophouse	LP	Philips	SBL7918	1969	**£20**	**£8**	
Best Of 66–68	LP	Philips	6677023	1974	**£15**	**£6**	*Dutch double*
Desolation	LP	Philips	SBL7874	1968	**£30**	**£15**	
Distant Smile	7"	Philips	BF1638	1968	**£5**	**£2**	
Groeten Uit Grollo	LP	Philips	855040XPY	1967	**£25**	**£10**	*Dutch*
King Of The World	LP	Philips	6314002	1970	**£20**	**£8**	*Dutch*
Live	LP	Philips	6440091	1968	**£25**	**£10**	*Dutch*
On The Road	LP	Philips	K1014	1968	**£25**	**£10**	*Dutch*
Praise The Blues	LP	Philips	6440308	1968	**£25**	**£10**	*Dutch*
Simple Man	LP	Philips	6413014	1971	**£15**	**£6**	*Dutch*
Sometimes	LP	Philips	6413026	1972	**£15**	**£6**	*Dutch*
Soul	LP	Philips	044054	1968	**£25**	**£10**	*Dutch*
Too Blind To See	LP	Philips	6413002	1969	**£20**	**£8**	*Dutch*
Trippin' Thru A Midnight Blues	LP	Philips	6343228	1967	**£25**	**£10**	*Dutch*
Windows Of My Eyes	7"	Philips	BF1719	1968	**£4**	**£1.50**	
With Regards From Grollo	LP	Philips	6343227	1967	**£25**	**£10**	*Dutch*

CUDDLY DUDLEY

Blarney Blues	7"	Oriole	ICB9	1964	**£5**	**£2**	
Later	7"	HMV	POP586	1959	**£6**	**£2.50**	
Monkey Party	7"	Piccadilly	7N35090	1962	**£4**	**£1.50**	

Sitting On A Train	7"	Ember	EMBS136	1961	£4	£1.50	
Too Pooped To Pop	7"	HMV	POP725	1960	£6	£2.50	
Way Of Life	7"	Oriole	ICB10	1964	£5	£2	

CUES

Burn That Candle	7"	Capitol	CL14501	1956	£150	£75	
Crackerjack	7"	Capitol	CL14651	1956	£125	£62.50	
Prince Or Pauper	7"	Capitol	CL14682	1957	£100	£50	

CUGAT, XAVIER

Dance Party	LP	Brunswick	STA8647	1965	£12	£5	
Viva Cugat!	LP	Mercury	MMC14067	1961	£15	£6	

CULPEPER'S ORCHARD

Terrific guitar-centred progressive rock from Denmark – the rare first album in particular deserves to be very much better known than it currently is.

1971–73	LP	Polydor	2444032	1975	£20	£8	*Danish*
All Dressed Up And Nowhere To Go	LP	Sonet	SLP1558	1977	£20	£8	*Danish*
Culpeper's Orchard	LP	Polydor	2380006	1971	£100	£50	*German*
Going For A Song	LP	Polydor	2308020	1972	£40	£20	*German*
Second Sight	LP	Polydor	2480123	1972	£60	£30	

CULT

Ceremony	CD-s	Beggars Banquet	CULT14	1991	£6	£2.50	*promo only*
Edie (Ciao Baby)	CD-s	Beggars Banquet	BEG230CD	1989	£5	£2	
Edie (Ciao Baby)	CD-s	Beggars Banquet	BEG230CP	1989	£6	£2.50	*picture disc*
Fire Woman	CD-s	Beggars Banquet	BEG228CD	1989	£5	£2	*black plastic wallet*
Li'l Devil	CD-s	Beggars Banquet	BEG188CD	1987	£8	£4	
Singles Collection	CD-s	Beggars Banquet	CBOX1	1991	£30	£15	*10 picture disc singles, boxed*
Soldier Blue	CD-s	Beggars Banquet	BEG205CD	1987	£5	£2	
Sun King	CD-s	Beggars Banquet	BEG235CD	1989	£5	£2	
Wildflower	CD-s	Beggars Banquet	BEG195CD	1987	£5	£2	

CULT HERO

I'm A Cult Hero	7"	Fiction	FICS006	1979	£30	£15	

CULTURE

Baldhead Bridge	LP	Laser	LASL7	1980	£10	£4	
Cumbolo	LP	Front Line	FL1040	1979	£10	£4	
Harder Than The Rest	LP	Front Line	FL1016	1978	£12	£5	
International Herb	LP	Front Line	FL1047	1979	£10	£4	
Two Sevens Clash	LP	Lightning	LIP1	1977	£12	£5	

CULTURE CLUB

Church Of The Poison Mind	7"	Virgin	VSY571	1983	£4	£1.50	*picture disc*
Colour By Numbers	LP	Virgin	VP2285	1983	£10	£4	*picture disc*
Do You Really Want To Hurt Me	7"	Virgin	VSY518	1982	£4	£1.50	*picture disc*
God Thank You Woman	7"	Virgin	VSY861	1986	£10	£5	*picture disc*
I'm Afraid Of Me	12"	Virgin	VS50912	1982	£8	£4	
It's A Miracle	7"	Virgin	VSY657	1984	£4	£1.50	*picture disc*
Karma Chameleon	7"	Virgin	VSY612	1983	£4	£1.50	*picture disc*
Kissing To Be Clever	LP	Virgin	VP2232	1982	£10	£4	*picture disc*
Move Away	5"	Virgin	VSX845	1986	£4	£1.50	*picture disc*
Time (Clock Of My Heart)	7"	Virgin	VSY558	1983	£4	£1.50	*picture disc*
Victims	7"	Virgin	VSY641	1983	£4	£1.50	*picture disc*
Waking Up With The House On Fire	LP	Virgin	VP2330	1984	£10	£4	*picture disc*
War Song	7"	Virgin	VSY694	1984	£60	£30	*picture disc*
White Boy	12"	Virgin	VS49612	1982	£8	£4	

CULVER STREET PLAYGROUND

Alley Pond Park	7"	President	PT145	1968	£5	£2	

CUMBERLAND THREE

Civil War Almanac – Rebels Vol. 2	LP	Columbia	33SX1325	1961	£10	£4	
Civil War Almanac – Yankees Vol. 1	LP	Columbia	33SX1318	1961	£10	£4	
Cumberland Three	LP	Parlophone	PMC1223	1964	£10	£4	
Folk Scene USA	LP	Columbia	33SX1302/ SCX3364	1961	£10	£4	

CUNNINGHAM, JOHN

Against The Storm	LP	Highway	SHY7011	1980	£10	£4	*with Phil Cunningham*
Thoughts From Another World	LP	Highway	SHY7013	1981	£10	£4	

CUNNINGHAM, PORTER

Observations	LP	Folk Heritage	FHR027	1972	£75	£37.50	

CUPIDS

Title	Format	Label	Cat. No.	Year	Mint	VG	Notes
Lillie Mae	7"	Vogue	V9102	1958	**£1000**	**£700**	*best auctioned*

CUPID'S INSPIRATION

Title	Format	Label	Cat. No.	Year	Mint	VG	Notes
Yesterday Has Gone	LP	Nems	63553	1968	**£10**	**£4**	

CUPOL

Title	Format	Label	Cat. No.	Year	Mint	VG	Notes
Like This For Ages	12"	4AD	BAD9	1980	**£6**	**£2.50**	

CUPPA T

Title	Format	Label	Cat. No.	Year	Mint	VG	Notes
Miss Pinkerton	7"	Deram	DM144	1967	**£8**	**£4**	
Streatham Hippodrome	7"	Deram	DM185	1968	**£8**	**£4**	

CUPS

Title	Format	Label	Cat. No.	Year	Mint	VG	Notes
Good As Gold	7"	Polydor	56777	1968	**£6**	**£2.50**	

CURE

Title	Format	Label	Cat. No.	Year	Mint	VG	Notes
Boys Don't Cry	7"	Fiction	FICS002	1979	**£10**	**£5**	
Boys Don't Cry	CD-s	Fiction	8150112	1986	**£12**	**£6**	*non-picture disc*
Catch	7"	Fiction	FICSC26	1987	**£8**	**£4**	*clear vinyl*
Catch	7"	Fiction	FICS26	1987	**£4**	**£1.50**	
Catch	CD-s	Fiction	0801862	1987	**£30**	**£15**	*CD video*
Caterpillar	7"	Fiction	FICSP20	1984	**£20**	**£10**	*picture disc*
Charlotte Sometimes	12"	Fiction	FICSX14	1981	**£12**	**£6**	
Charlotte Sometimes	7"	Fiction	FICS14	1981	**£5**	**£2**	
Close To Me	10"	Fiction	FICST23	1985	**£10**	**£4**	
Close To Me	7"	Fiction	FICSG23	1985	**£4**	**£1.50**	*poster picture sleeve*
Close To Me	7"	Fiction	FICSP23	1985	**£6**	**£2.50**	*poster sleeve, sticker*
Close To Me	CD-s	Fiction	0801802	1989	**£30**	**£15**	*CD video*
Close To Me	CD-s	Fiction	FICCD36	1990	**£6**	**£2.50**	*poster pack*
Close To Me	CD-s	Fiction	FICCD36	1990	**£5**	**£2**	*picture disc single*
Disintegration	CD	Fiction	8393532	1989	**£30**	**£15**	*promo pack*
Disintegration	LP	Fiction	FIXHP14	1990	**£10**	**£4**	*picture disc*
Entreat	CD	Fiction	FIXCD17	1990	**£15**	**£6**	*promo*
Faith	CD	Fiction	8276872	1985	**£12**	**£5**	*non-picture disc*
Forest	12"	Fiction	FICSX10	1980	**£20**	**£10**	
Forest	7"	Fiction	FICS10	1980	**£8**	**£4**	*picture sleeve, blue label*
Forest	7"	Fiction	FICS10	1980	**£5**	**£2**	*'radio' sleeve, silver label*
Friday I'm In Love	CD-s	Fiction	8630012	1992	**£8**	**£4**	
Grinding Halt	12"	Fiction	CUR1	1979	**£40**	**£20**	*promo*
Hanging Garden	7"	Fiction	FICG15	1982	**£12**	**£6**	*double*
Hanging Garden	7"	Fiction	FICS15	1982	**£6**	**£2.50**	
Hot! Hot! Hot!	7"	Fiction	FICS28	1988	**£6**	**£2.50**	*promo*
Hot! Hot! Hot!	CD-s	Fiction	FIXCD28	1988	**£8**	**£4**	
In Between Days	CD-s	Polygram	0801822	1988	**£30**	**£15**	*CD video*
Interview	CD	Fiction	CUREPROCD3	1990	**£30**	**£15**	*promo*
Japanese Whispers	CD	Fiction	8174702	1987	**£12**	**£5**	*non-picture disc*
Jumping Someone Else's Train	7"	Fiction	FICS005	1979	**£12**	**£6**	
Just Like Heaven	7"	Fiction	FICSW27	1987	**£5**	**£2**	*white vinyl*
Just Like Heaven	7"	Fiction	FICSP27	1987	**£8**	**£4**	*picture disc*
Just Like Heaven	CD-s	Fiction	FIXCD27	1987	**£12**	**£6**	
Killing An Arab	7"	Fiction	FICS001	1979	**£10**	**£5**	
Killing An Arab	7"	Small Wonder	SMALL11	1978	**£12**	**£6**	
Killing An Arab (Peel Sessions)	7"	Strange Fruit	671002	1991	**£4**	**£1.50**	*shaped picture disc*
Kiss Me Kiss Me Kiss Me	CD	Elektra		1987	**£150**	**£75**	*US promo box set, with LP and cassette*
Kiss Me Kiss Me Kiss Me	LP	Fiction	FIXH13	1987	**£15**	**£6**	*with orange vinyl disc in cellophane*
Kiss Me Kiss Me Kiss Me Interview	LP	Fiction	KSME2	1987	**£10**	**£4**	*promo*
Lament	7"	Lyntone	LYN12011	1982	**£6**	**£2.50**	*Flexipop green flexi*
Lament	7"	Lyntone	LYN12011	1982	**£8**	**£4**	*Flexipop red flexi*
Let's Go To Bed	12"	Fiction	FICSX17	1982	**£6**	**£2.50**	
Limited Edition CD Box	CD	Fiction	5136000	1992	**£150**	**£75**	*15 CD boxed set*
Love Cats	7"	Fiction	FICSP19	1983	**£25**	**£12.50**	*picture disc*
Love Song	CD-s	Fiction	FICCD30	1989	**£8**	**£4**	
Lovesong	12"	Fiction	FICSX30	1989	**£40**	**£20**	*picture disc test pressing*
Lovesong	CD-s	Fiction	0813982	1989	**£30**	**£15**	*CD video*
Lullaby	12"	Fiction	FICVX29	1989	**£8**	**£4**	*pink vinyl*
Lullaby	7"	Fiction	FICSP29	1989	**£6**	**£2.50**	*clear vinyl*
Lullaby	CD-s	Fiction	0809822	1989	**£30**	**£15**	*CD video*
Lullaby (Remix)	CD-s	Fiction	FICCD29	1989	**£5**	**£2**	*3" single*
Never Enough	CD-s	Fiction	FICCD35	1990	**£8**	**£4**	
One Hundred Years	12"	Fiction	CURE1	1982	**£30**	**£15**	*promo*
Peel Sessions	CD-s	Strange Fruit	SFPSCD050	1988	**£5**	**£2**	
Pictures Of You	12"	Fiction	FIXPB34	1990	**£8**	**£4**	*purple vinyl*
Pictures Of You	7"	Fiction	FICPB34	1990	**£5**	**£2**	*purple vinyl*
Pictures Of You	CD-s	Fiction	FICDB34	1990	**£8**	**£4**	
Pictures Of You	CD-s	Fiction	FICDA34	1990	**£6**	**£2.50**	
Pornography	CD	Fiction	8276882	1986	**£12**	**£5**	*non-picture disc*
Primary	12"	Fiction	FICSX12	1981	**£15**	**£7.50**	
Primary	7"	Fiction	FICS12	1981	**£6**	**£2.50**	
Retrospective	CD	Elektra	PRCD95522	1996	**£20**	**£8**	*US promo compilation*
Seventeen Seconds	CD	Fiction	8253542	1985	**£12**	**£5**	*non-picture disc*

Stranger Than Fiction	CD	Fiction	SCIFCD301	1989	£75	£37.50	*promo sampler*
Three Imaginary Boys	LP	Fiction	FIX1	1979	£10	£4	*with postcard*
Top	LP	Fiction	FIXS9	1984	£10	£4	*with badge and poster*
Walk	12"	Fiction	FICSX18	1983	£6	£2.50	
Walk	7"	Fiction	FICS18	1983	£8	£4	*poster sleeve*
Walk	7"	Fiction	FICSP18	1983	£25	£12.50	*picture disc*
Why Can't I Be You?	7"	Fiction	FICSG25	1987	£6	£2.50	*double*
Why Can't I Be You?	CD-s	Fiction	0801842	1990	£30	£15	*CD video*
Wish	CD	Fiction	PK1	1992	£40	£20	*promo box set, with cassette and video*
Wish Interview	CD	Fiction	CID1	1992	£20	£8	*promo*

CURE, MARTIN & THE PEEPS

It's All Over Now	7"	Philips	BF1605	1967	£20	£10	

CURFEW

Let There Be Dark And There Was Dark	LP	United Artists	UAS6746	1970	£15	£6	*US*

CURIOSITY SHOPPE

Baby I Need You	7"	Deram	DM220	1968	£20	£10	

CURIOUS, JOHNNY & THE STRANGERS

In Tune	7"	Illegal	IL009	1978	£4	£1.50	
Someone Else's Home	7"	Bugle	BLAST2	1979	£8	£4	

CURLY CURVE

Curly Curve	LP	Brain	1040	1974	£30	£15	*German*

CURRANT KRAZE

Lady Pearl	7"	Deram	DM292	1970	£5	£2	

CURRENT 93

1888	LP	New European	BADVC693	1990	£30	£15	*clear or red vinyl, with Death In June*
1888	LP	New European	BADVC693	1990	£20	£8	*with Death In June*
Broken Birds Fly	7"	Ptolemaic Terrascope	POT6	1994	£5	£2	*other artists on B side*
Christ And The Pale Queen	LP	Maldorer	MAL666	1988	£50	£25	
Crowleymass	12"	Maldorer	MAL108	1987	£15	£7.50	
Dawn	LP	Maldorer	MAL093	1989	£40	£20	
Earth Covers Earth	LP	United Dairies	UD029	1990	£40	£20	*with card and 7"*
Earth Covers Earth	LP	United Dairies	UD029	1990	£10	£4	
Faith's Favourites	7"	Yangki	002	1988	£15	£7.50	
Imperium	LP	Maldorer	MAL777	1988	£15	£6	
In Menstrual Night	LP	Maldorer	UDO22M	1986	£30	£15	*picture disc*
In Menstrual Night	LP	United Dairies	UD022	1986	£10	£4	
In Menstrual Night	LP	United Dairies	UD022	1986	£75	£37.50	*handmade cover and inserts*
Island	LP	Durtro	DURTRO006	1992	£15	£6	
Live At Bar Maldorer	LP	Durtro	DURTRO001	1989	£40	£20	
Looney Runes	12"	Durtro	DURTRO004	1992	£12	£6	*with poster*
Lucifer Over London	12"	Durtro	DURTRO019	1994	£10	£5	*red vinyl, insert*
Nature Unveiled	LP	Maldorer	MAL123	1990	£20	£8	*with insert*
No Hiding From The Blackbird	7"	Harbinger	001	1990	£8	£4	
Of Ruine, Or Some Blazing Starre	LP	Durtro	DURTRO018	1994	£20	£8	*blue vinyl*
Red Face Of God	12"	Maldorer	MAL088	1988	£15	£7.50	
She Is Dead And All Fall Down	7"	Shock	SX003	1990	£20	£10	*individually lettered*
She Is Dead And All Fall Down	7"	Shock	SX003	1990	£12	£6	
Tamlin	12"	Durtro	DURTRO025	1995	£8	£4	*with insert*
Tamlin	CD-s	Durtro	DURTRO025	1995	£10	£5	
This Ain't The Summer Of Love	7"	Cerne	004	1990	£12	£6	*Sol Invictus B side*
Thunder Perfect Mind	LP	Durtro	DURTRO011	1992	£20	£8	*double*
Where The Long Shadows Fall	12"	Durtro	DURTRO028	1995	£12	£6	*clear vinyl*

CURRIE, CHERIE & MARIE

Messin' With The Boys	7"	Capitol	CL16119	1980	£6	£2.50	

CURRY, CLIFFORD

I Can't Get A Hold Of Myself	7"	Pama	PM797	1969	£8	£4	
She Shot A Hole In My Soul	7"	Action	ACT4549	1969	£4	£1.50	
You Turn Out The Light	7"	Pama	PM793	1969	£4	£1.50	

CURSON, TED

Tears For Dolphy	LP	Fontana	688310ZL	1964	£10	£4	

CURTIS, CHRIS

Aggravation	7"	Pye	7N17132	1966	£25	£12.50	

CURTIS, JOHNNY

Jack And The Beanstalk	7"	Parlophone	R5582	1967	£10	£5	
Our Love's Disintegrating	7"	Parlophone	R5529	1966	£20	£10	

CURTIS, KING

Arthur Murray's Music For Dancing – The Twist	LP	RCA	RD27252	1962	£15	£6	
Azure	LP	Everest	DBR1121	1961	£20	£8	US
Best Of King Curtis	LP	Atlantic	228002	1968	£12	£5	
Doin' The Dixie Twist	LP	Tru-Sound	(S)TS15009	1962	£15	£6	US
Good To Me	7"	Atlantic	584109	1967	£4	£1.50	
Have Tenor Sax, Will Blow	7" EP	London	REK1307	1961	£25	£12.50	
Have Tenor Sax, Will Blow	LP	London	HAK2247	1960	£25	£10	
Hits Made Famous By Sam Cooke	LP	Capitol	(S)T2341	1965	£15	£6	US
Instant Groove	LP	Atlantic	228027	1968	£12	£5	
It's Party Time	LP	Tru-Sound	(S)TS15008	1962	£15	£6	US
Kingsize Soul	LP	Atlantic	587043	1967	£10	£4	
La Jeanne	7"	Atlantic	584287	1969	£4	£1.50	
Live At Small's Paradise	LP	Atco	(SD)33198	1966	£15	£6	US
Memphis Soul Stew	7"	Atlantic	584134	1967	£4	£1.50	
New Scene	LP	Esquire	32161	1962	£15	£6	
Plays Great Memphis Hits	LP	Atlantic	587067	1967	£10	£4	
Soul Battle	LP	Esquire	32189	1963	£15	£6	*with Oliver Nelson & Jimmy Forrest*
Soul Serenade	7"	Capitol	CL15346	1964	£6	£2.50	
Soul Serenade	LP	Capitol	(S)T2095	1964	£15	£6	US
Soul Serenade	LP	Ember	SPE/LP6600	1968	£10	£4	
Soul Twist	7"	London	HLU9547	1962	£8	£4	
Sweet Soul	LP	Atlantic	587115	1968	£12	£5	
That Lovin' Feeling	LP	Atco	(SD)33189	1966	£15	£6	US
Wiggle Wobble	7"	Speciality	SPE1000	1967	£5	£2	

CURTIS, LEE & THE ALL STARS

Ecstasy	7"	Philips	BF1385	1964	£10	£5	
It's Lee	LP	Star-Club	158017STY	1965	£75	£37.50	German
Let's Stomp	7"	Decca	F11690	1963	£10	£5	
Little Girl	7"	Decca	F11622	1963	£8	£4	
Star-Club Show 3	LP	Star-Club	158002STY	1965	£75	£37.50	German
What About Me	7"	Decca	F11830	1964	£8	£4	

CURTIS, MAC

Rockabilly Kings	LP	Polydor	2310293	1974	£10	£4	*with Charlie Feathers*
You Ain't Treating Me Right	7"	Parlophone	R4279	1957	£1000	£700	*best auctioned*

CURTIS, SONNY

Beatle Hits Flamenco Guitar Style	LP	Imperial	LP9276/LP12276	1964	£20	£8	US
Beatle I Want To Be	7"	Colpix	PX11024	1964	£8	£4	
Bo Diddley Bach	7"	Liberty	LIB55710	1964	£8	£4	
Red Headed Stranger	7"	Coral	Q72400	1960	£15	£7.50	

CURTISS, DAVE & THE TREMORS

Summertime Blues	7"	Philips	BF1330	1964	£4	£1.50	
What Kind of Girl Are You	7"	Philips	BF1285	1963	£4	£1.50	
You Don't Love Me	7"	Philips	BF1257	1963	£4	£1.50	

CURTISS, ROCKY & THE HARMONY FLAMES

USA Hit Parade	7" EP	Fontana	TFE17172	1959	£25	£12.50	

CURTOLA, BOBBY

Aladdin	7"	London	HL9639	1962	£4	£1.50	
Don't You Sweethaert Me	7"	Columbia	DB4672	1961	£5	£2	
Fortune Teller	7"	London	HL9577	1962	£4	£1.50	

CURVE

BlackerThreeTrackerTwo EP	CD-s	Anxious	ANXCDS42	1993	£5	£2	
Blindfold	CD-s	Anxious	ANXCD27	1991	£5	£2	
Clipped	CD-s	Anxious	ANXCD35	1991	£5	£2	
Coast Is Clear	CD-s	Anxious	ANXCD30	1991	£5	£2	
Ten Little Girls	7"	Anxious	ANXP27	1991	£4	£1.50	*picture disc*

CURVED AIR

Curved Air (named after the Terry Riley piece) were more successful than most at integrating elements of classical music within a rock format and both Francis Monkman and Darryl Way have worked extensively with the same approach ever since the group's first release. The first LP, *Air Conditioning*, was issued as a limited-edition picture disc – probably the first rock record to be released in this form. Its value has been kept low, however, by the fact that a small number of playings causes a drastic deterioration in sound quality.

Air Conditioning	LP	Warner Bros	WSX3012	1970	£15	£6	*picture disc*
Air Conditioning	LP	Warner Bros	WSX3012	1970	£10	£4	
Air Cut	LP	Warner Bros	K46224	1973	£10	£4	
Phantasmagoria	LP	Warner Bros	K46158	1972	£10	£4	
Second Album	LP	Warner Bros	K46092	1971	£10	£4	

CUT AND DRY BAND

Cut And Dry Dolly	LP	Topic	12TS278	1976	£10	£4	
Cut And Dry No. 2	LP	Topic	12TS413	1980	£10	£4	

CUTLER, CHRIS & FRED FRITH

Limoges	7"	Recommended	REDUO	1983	£8	£4	*clear vinyl*
Live In Prague And Washington	LP	Recommended	RE1729	1983	£12	£5	

CUTLER, CHRIS & LINDSAY COOPER

Title	Format	Label	Cat. No.	Year	Mint	VG	Notes
News From Babel	LP	Recommended	RE6116	1984	£12	£5	
News From Babel: Contraries	7"	Recommended	RE	1984	£8	£4	1 side painted

CUTLER, IVOR

Title	Format	Label	Cat. No.	Year	Mint	VG	Notes
Get Away From The Wall	7" EP	Decca	DFE6677	1961	£20	£10	
Great Grey Grasshopper	7"	Parlophone	R5624	1967	£4	£1.50	
Ludo	LP	Parlophone	PCS7040	1967	£30	£15	
Of Y'hup	7" EP	Fontana	TFE17144	1959	£20	£10	
Who Tore Your Trousers	LP	Decca	LK4405	1961	£30	£15	

CUTTERS

Title	Format	Label	Cat. No.	Year	Mint	VG	Notes
I've Had It	7"	Decca	F11110	1959	£6	£2.50	

CUTTY, GORDON

Title	Format	Label	Cat. No.	Year	Mint	VG	Notes
Grand Old Fashioned Dance	LP	Free Reed	FRR006	1976	£12	£5	

CWT

Title	Format	Label	Cat. No.	Year	Mint	VG	Notes
Hundredweight	LP	Kuckuck	2375022	1973	£60	£30	German

CYAN THREE

Title	Format	Label	Cat. No.	Year	Mint	VG	Notes
Since I Lost My Baby	7"	Decca	F12371	1966	£10	£5	

CYANIDE

Title	Format	Label	Cat. No.	Year	Mint	VG	Notes
Cyanide	LP	Pye	NSPL18554	1978	£25	£10	
Fireball	7"	Pinnacle	PIN23	1979	£15	£7.50	
I'm A Boy	7"	Pye	7N46048	1978	£20	£10	
Mac The Flash	7"	Pye	7N46094	1978	£15	£7.50	

CYBERMEN

Title	Format	Label	Cat. No.	Year	Mint	VG	Notes
Cybermen	7"	Rockaway	AERE101	1978	£25	£12.50	
You're To Blame	7"	Rockaway	LUV002	1979	£20	£10	

CYCLONES

Title	Format	Label	Cat. No.	Year	Mint	VG	Notes
Nobody	7"	Oriole	CB1898	1964	£25	£12.50	

CYKLE

Title	Format	Label	Cat. No.	Year	Mint	VG	Notes
Cykle	LP	Label	9261	1969	£500	£330	US

CYMANDE

Title	Format	Label	Cat. No.	Year	Mint	VG	Notes
Cymande	LP	Alaska	ALKA100	1973	£15	£6	
Promised Height	LP	Contempo	CLP508	1974	£15	£6	

CYMBAL, JOHNNY

Title	Format	Label	Cat. No.	Year	Mint	VG	Notes
Cymbal Smashes	7" EP	London	RER1406	1963	£30	£15	
Dum Dum De Dum	7"	London	HLR9762	1963	£5	£2	
Go VW Go	7"	United Artists	UP1093	1965	£12	£6	
It'll Be Me	7"	MGM	MGM1106	1960	£8	£4	
Mister Bass Man	7"	London	HLR9682	1963	£4	£1.50	
Mister Bass Man	7" EP	London	RER1375	1963	£30	£15	
Mister Bass Man	LP	Kapp	KL1324/KS3324	1963	£40	£20	US
Robinson Crusoe On Mars	7"	London	HLR9911	1964	£8	£4	
Teenage Heaven	7"	London	HLR9731	1963	£8	£4	

CYMBALINE

Title	Format	Label	Cat. No.	Year	Mint	VG	Notes
Down By The Seaside	7"	Philips	BF1681	1968	£4	£1.50	
I Don't Want It	7"	Mercury	MF961	1967	£4	£1.50	
Matrimonial Fears	7"	Philips	BF1624	1967	£25	£12.50	
Peanuts And Chewy Macs	7"	Mercury	MF975	1967	£4	£1.50	
Please Little Girl	7"	Pye	7N15916	1965	£20	£10	
Top Girl	7"	Mercury	MF918	1965	£12	£6	
Turn Around	7"	Philips	BF1749	1969	£4	£1.50	

CYMERONS

Title	Format	Label	Cat. No.	Year	Mint	VG	Notes
Everyday	7"	Polydor	56098	1966	£4	£1.50	
I'll Be There	7"	Decca	F11976	1964	£8	£4	

CYNARA

Title	Format	Label	Cat. No.	Year	Mint	VG	Notes
Cynara	LP	Capitol	ST547	1968	£40	£20	US

CYRKLE

Title	Format	Label	Cat. No.	Year	Mint	VG	Notes
Neon	LP	CBS	62977	1967	£20	£8	
Red Rubber Ball	7"	CBS	202064	1966	£4	£1.50	
Red Rubber Ball	LP	CBS	CL2544/CS9344	1966	£30	£15	US

CZAR

Title	Format	Label	Cat. No.	Year	Mint	VG	Notes
Oh Lord I'm Getting Heavy	7"	Philips	6006071	1970	£20	£10	
Tread Softly On My Dreams	LP	Fontana	6309009	1970	£150	£75	

CZUKAY, HOLGER & ROLF DAMMERS

Title	Format	Label	Cat. No.	Year	Mint	VG	Notes
Canaxis 5	LP	Music Factory	SRS002	1969	£150	£75	

D, KIM

Title	Format	Label	Number	Year	Mint	Good	Notes
Real Thing	7"	Pye	7N15953	1965	**£5**	**£2**	

D, TONY & THE SHAKEDOWNS

Title	Format	Label	Number	Year	Mint	Good	Notes
Is It True	7"	Piccadilly	7N35168	1964	**£5**	**£2**	

D JUNIOR, DON

Title	Format	Label	Number	Year	Mint	Good	Notes
Dirty Dozen	7"	Caltone	TONE124	1968	**£10**	**£5**	*Phil Pratt B side*

D'ABO, MIKE

Title	Format	Label	Number	Year	Mint	Good	Notes
D'Abo	LP	Uni	UNLS114	1970	**£12**	**£5**	
Down At Rachel's Place	LP	A&M	AMLH68097	1972	**£10**	**£4**	
Gulliver's Travels	7"	Immediate	IM075	1969	**£8**	**£4**	

DADA

Dada was an ambitious big band that unfortunately found the costs of maintaining a large line-up too great to continue when their LP failed to set the country alight. A slimmed-down version of the group continued as Vinegar Joe. The singer in both cases was Elkie Brooks and, at the end, Dada's second singer was Robert Palmer, although he makes no more than a passing appearance on the album.

Title	Format	Label	Number	Year	Mint	Good	Notes
Dada	LP	Atco	2400030	1970	**£15**	**£6**	

DADDY LONGLEGS

Title	Format	Label	Number	Year	Mint	Good	Notes
Daddy Longlegs	LP	Warner Bros	WS3004	1970	**£10**	**£4**	
Oakdown Farm	LP	Vertigo	6360038	1971	**£15**	**£6**	*spiral label*
Shifting Sands	LP	Polydor	2371323	1972	**£12**	**£5**	
Three Musicians	LP	Polydor	2371261	1972	**£12**	**£5**	

DADDY-Os

Title	Format	Label	Number	Year	Mint	Good	Notes
Got A Match?	7"	Oriole	CB1454	1958	**£6**	**£2.50**	

DADDY'S ACT

Title	Format	Label	Number	Year	Mint	Good	Notes
Eight Days A Week	7"	Columbia	DB8242	1967	**£6**	**£2.50**	

DAFOS, CALVIN

Title	Format	Label	Number	Year	Mint	Good	Notes
Brown Sugar	7"	Blue Beat	BB347	1966	**£12**	**£6**	
Lash Them	7"	Doctor Bird	DB1174	1969	**£10**	**£5**	

DAFT PUNK

Title	Format	Label	Number	Year	Mint	Good	Notes
Alive – The New Wave	12"	Soma	014	1994	**£10**	**£5**	
Da Funk	12"	Soma	025	1995	**£8**	**£4**	

DAGABAND

Title	Format	Label	Number	Year	Mint	Good	Notes
Second Time Around	7"	MHM	AM094	1983	**£15**	**£7.50**	
Test Flight	7"	Rutland	RX100	1980	**£12**	**£6**	

DAGGERMEN

Title	Format	Label	Number	Year	Mint	Good	Notes
Introducing The Daggermen	7"	Empire	UPW258J	1986	**£6**	**£2.50**	

DAHO, ETIENNE

Title	Format	Label	Number	Year	Mint	Good	Notes
Stay With Me	7"	Virgin	VS1180	1989	**£10**	**£5**	

DAILY, PETE

Title	Format	Label	Number	Year	Mint	Good	Notes
Dixie By Daily	10" LP	Capitol	LC6603	1953	**£12**	**£5**	
Dixieland Band	10" LP	Capitol	LC6525	1951	**£12**	**£5**	
Pete Daily And Phil Napoleon	10" LP	Brunswick	LA8515	1951	**£15**	**£6**	

DAILY FLASH

Title	Format	Label	Number	Year	Mint	Good	Notes
I Flash Daily	LP	Psycho	PSYCHO32	1984	**£10**	**£4**	

DAISY PLANET

Title	Format	Label	Number	Year	Mint	Good	Notes
Daisy Planet	7" EP	Oak	no number	196–	**£40**	**£20**	*no picture sleeve*

DAKOTAS

Title	Format	Label	Number	Year	Mint	Good	Notes
Cruel Sea	7"	Parlophone	R5044	1963	**£4**	**£1.50**	
I Can't Break The News To Myself	7"	Philips	BF1645	1968	**£40**	**£20**	
I'm An 'Ardworkin' Barrow Boy	7"	Page One	POF018	1967	**£15**	**£7.50**	
Magic Carpet	7"	Parlophone	R5064	1963	**£4**	**£1.50**	
Meet The Dakotas	7" EP	Parlophone	GEP8888	1963	**£30**	**£15**	
Oyeh	7"	Parlophone	R5203	1964	**£15**	**£7.50**	

DAKOTA'S ALL STARS

Call Me Master	7"	Blue Beat	BB358	1966	£12	£6	

D'ALBUQUERQUE, MICHAEL

We May Be Cattle But We All Have Names	LP	RCA	SF8383	1974	£10	£4	

DALE, ALAN

Cherry Pink And Apple Blossom White	7"	Vogue Coral	Q72072	1955	£6	£2.50	
Don't Knock The Rock	7"	Vogue Coral	Q72225	1957	£12	£6	
Lonesome Road	7"	Vogue Coral	Q72231	1957	£12	£6	
Robin Hood	7"	Vogue Coral	Q72121	1956	£15	£7.50	
Rockin' The Cha-Cha	7"	Vogue Coral	Q72105	1955	£6	£2.50	
Sweet And Gentle	7"	Vogue Coral	Q72089	1955	£8	£4	
Test Of Time	7"	Vogue Coral	Q72194	1956	£4	£1.50	

DALE, DICK & THE DELTONES

The man who claims to have been a major influence on Jimi Hendrix certainly managed to deliver some ferocious playing on his early-sixties recordings, although the casual investigator should be warned that his vocal tracks are fairly awful. His tune 'Miserlou' from 1962 was played over the opening credits of the film 'Pulp Fiction', which was enough to revive his career and enabled him to make a number of new recordings. These revealed the skating of his fingers down the fretboard to be a lasting feature of his playing technique.

Checkered Flag	LP	Capitol	(S)T2002	1963	£50	£25	US
King Of The Surf Guitar	LP	Capitol	(S)T1930	1963	£50	£25	
Mr Eliminator	LP	Capitol	(S)T2053	1964	£50	£25	US
Peppermint Man	7"	Capitol	CL15296	1963	£8	£4	
Rock Out	LP	Capitol	(S)T2293	1965	£50	£25	US
Scavenger	7"	Capitol	CL15320	1963	£8	£4	
Summer Surf	LP	Capitol	(S)T2111	1964	£40	£20	US
Surfer's Choice	LP	Capitol	T1886	1963	£50	£25	
Surfer's Choice	LP	Deltone	LPM1001	1962	£60	£30	US

DALE, GLEN

Good Day Sunshine	7"	Decca	F12475	1966	£4	£1.50	

DALE, JIM

Be My Girl	7"	Parlophone	R4343	1957	£5	£2	
Gotta Find A Girl	7"	Parlophone	R4522	1959	£4	£1.50	
Jim	10" LP	Parlophone	PMD1055	1958	£40	£20	
Jim Dale	7" EP	Parlophone	GEP8656	1957	£20	£10	
Just Born	7"	Parlophone	R4376	1957	£4	£1.50	
Piccadilly Line	7"	Parlophone	R4329	1957	£6	£2.50	
Somewhere There's A Someone	7"	Academy	AD001	196–	£4	£1.50	
Somewhere There's A Someone	7"	Academy	AD001	1960	£4	£1.50	
Sugartime	7"	Parlophone	R4402	1958	£4	£1.50	
Top Ten Special	7"	Parlophone	R4356	1957	£8	£4	*with the Vipers & King Brothers*
Tread Softly	7"	Parlophone	R4424	1958	£4	£1.50	

DALE & GRACE

Dale And Grace No. 1	7" EP	London	RE1428	1964	£20	£10	
Dale And Grace No. 2	7" EP	London	RE1429	1964	£20	£10	
Dale And Grace No. 3	7" EP	London	RE1430	1964	£20	£10	
I'm Leaving It Up To You	7"	London	HL10249	1969	£4	£1.50	
I'm Leaving It Up To You	7"	London	HL9807	1963	£6	£2.50	
I'm Leaving It Up To You	LP	Montel	LP100	1964	£50	£25	US
Stop And Think It Over	7"	London	HL9857	1964	£5	£2	

DALE SISTERS

Kiss	7"	HMV	POP781	1960	£5	£2	
My Sunday Baby	7"	Ember	EMBS140	1961	£6	£2.50	
Secrets	7"	Ember	EMBS151	1962	£4	£1.50	

DALEY, BASIL

Born To Love	7"	Studio One	SO2054	1968	£12	£6	

DALEY, JIMMY & THE DING-A-LINGS

Rock, Pretty Baby	7"	Brunswick	05648	1957	£75	£37.50	
Rock, Pretty Baby	LP	Brunswick	LAT8162	1957	£75	£37.50	

DALI, SALVADOR

Dali In Venice	LP	Decca	SET230	1962	£60	£30	

DALLON, MIKI

Cheat And Lie	7"	Strike	JH306	1966	£5	£2	
Do You Call That Love?	7"	RCA	RCA1438	1965	£20	£10	
I Care About You	7"	RCA	RCA1478	1965	£30	£15	
What Will Your Mama Say	7"	Strike	JH318	1966	£4	£1.50	

DALMOUR, DAVID & MARIANNE

Introducing	LP	Columbia	33SX1715	1965	£40	£20	

DALTONS

Never Kiss You Again	7"	Fab	FAB30	1967	£8	£4	*Righteous Flames B side*

DALTREY, ROGER

McVicar	LP	Polydor	POLD5034	1980	£**10**	£**4**	*clear vinyl*
Say It Ain't So/Satin And Lace	7"	Polydor	2058948	1976	£**10**	£**5**	
Under A Raging Moon	10"	10	TEN(G)8112	1986	£**6**	£**2.50**	*double*

DALY, JACKIE

Music From Sliabh Luachra Vol. 6	LP	Topic	12TS358	1977	£**10**	£**4**	

DAMASCUS

Open Your Eyes	12"	private		198–	£**40**	£**20**	

DAMERON, TADD

Fontainebleau	LP	Esquire	32034	1957	£**25**	£**10**	
Tadd Dameron Band	10" LP	Esquire	20044	1955	£**40**	£**20**	
Tadd's Delight	7" EP	Capitol	EAP120388	1962	£**5**	£**2**	

DAMIAN

Time Warp	12"	Jive	JIVET160	1987	£**6**	£**2.50**	
Time Warp	12"	Sedition	EDITL3311	1986	£**6**	£**2.50**	
Time Warp	7"	Jive	JIVE182	1988	£**4**	£**1.50**	
Time Warp	7"	Jive	JIVE160	1987	£**4**	£**1.50**	

DAMNED

The thing about the Damned is that, for all their anti-progressive rock establishment stance and their iconic status as the first punk group to issue a record, they were actually pretty good musicians. Punk classics like 'I Just Can't Be Happy Today' and 'Smash It Up' work on wider terms too, because they are interesting songs, well played. Even that first punk record, 'New Rose', has an authority – a grandeur even – that is lacking in most of the records made by the style's camp followers. These days, of course, punk – and especially the Damned – has taken its own place within the rock establishment. This was emphasized by the sight of Captain Sensible making star appearances at a number of VIP record fairs during 1997 – playing wah-wah lead-guitar solos of a distinctly virtuoso nature.

Alone Again Or	CD-s	MCA	DGRIM7	1987	£**5**	£**2**	*7" sleeve*
Damned Damned Damned	LP	Stiff	SEEZ1	1977	£**40**	£**20**	*Eddie & The Hot Rods photo, with red sticker*
Damned Damned Damned	LP	Stiff	SEEZ1	1977	£**30**	£**15**	*Eddie & The Hot Rods photo*
Damned Damned Damned/Music For Pleasure	LP	Stiff	MAIL2	1986	£**12**	£**5**	*double, yellow vinyl*
Damned Damned Damned/Music For Pleasure	LP	Stiff	MAIL2	1983	£**15**	£**6**	*double*
Don't Cry Wolf	7"	Stiff	BUY24	1977	£**4**	£**1.50**	*pink vinyl*
Four Pack	7"	Stiff	GRAB2	1981	£**20**	£**10**	*BUY6,10,18,24 in plastic wallet*
Fun Factory	CD-s	Deltic	DELT7C	1991	£**5**	£**2**	
Generals	7"	Bronze	BRO159	1982	£**5**	£**2**	
Grimly Fiendish	12"	MCA	GRIMT1	1985	£**6**	£**2.50**	*autographed*
Grimly Fiendish	7"	MCA	GRIM1	1985	£**5**	£**2**	*gatefold picture sleeve, autographed*
Live In Newcastle	LP	Damned	DAMU2	1983	£**12**	£**5**	
Live In Newcastle	LP	Damned	PDAMU2	1983	£**12**	£**5**	*picture disc*
Lively Arts	7"	Big Beat	NS80	1982	£**5**	£**2**	*green vinyl*
Love Song	7"	Dodgy Demo	SGS105	1978	£**15**	£**7.50**	
Neat Neat Neat	7"	Stiff	BUY10	1977	£**5**	£**2**	*gothic lettering*
New Rose	7"	Stiff	BUY6	1976	£**8**	£**4**	*press-out centre*
Peel Sessions	CD-s	Strange Fruit	SFPSCD002	1988	£**5**	£**2**	
Problem Child	7"	Stiff	BUY18	1977	£**4**	£**1.50**	*press-out centre*
Stretcher Case Baby	7"	Stiff	DAMNED1	1977	£**25**	£**12.50**	
Thanks For The Night	12"	Plus One	DAMNED1T	1984	£**6**	£**2.50**	*multicoloured vinyl*
Thanks For The Night	7"	Plus One	DAMNED1P	1986	£**10**	£**5**	*shaped picture disc, plinth*
White Rabbit	7"	Chiswick	CHIS130	1980	£**100**	£**50**	*2 x 1 sided test pressings only*

DAMON

Song Of A Gypsy	LP	private		1993	£**12**	£**5**	*US*
Song Of A Gypsy	LP	ANKH		1970	£**1500**	£**1000**	*US*

DAMON, RUSS

Hip Huggers	7"	Stateside	SS258	1964	£**4**	£**1.50**	

DAMONE, VIC

All-Time Song Hits	10" LP	Mercury	MPT7514	1957	£**15**	£**6**	
Closer Than A Kiss	LP	Philips	BBL7259	1958	£**10**	£**4**	
Damone Favourites	7" EP	Philips	BBE12197	1958	£**5**	£**2**	
Do I Love You	7" EP	Philips	BBE12245	1959	£**5**	£**2**	
Linger Awhile	7" EP	Capitol	EAP11646	1962	£**5**	£**2**	
On The Swingers Side	7" EP	Philips	BBE12502	1961	£**5**	£**2**	
That Towering Feeling	LP	Philips	BBL7144	1957	£**10**	£**4**	
Vic Damone	7" EP	Philips	BBE12099	1957	£**5**	£**2**	
Vic Damone	7" EP	Philips	BBE12222	1958	£**5**	£**2**	
Voice Of Vic Damone	7" EP	Mercury	MEP9534	1958	£**5**	£**2**	
Walking My Baby Back Home	7" EP	Mercury	EP13121	1954	£**8**	£**4**	
Yours For A Song	7" EP	Mercury	ZEP10022	1959	£**5**	£**2**	

DANCE CHAPTER

Anonymity	7"	4AD	AD18	1980	£5	£2	insert
Chapter II	12"	4AD	BAD115	1981	£6	£2.50	

DANCING DID

Dancing Did	7"	Fruit And Veg	F&V1	1979	£5	£2	

DANDO SHAFT

Cold Wind	7"	Youngblood	YB1012	1970	£4	£1.50	
Dando Shaft	LP	Neon	NE5	1971	£40	£20	
Evening With	LP	Youngblood	SSYB6	1970	£40	£20	
Kingdom	LP	Rubber	RUB034	1978	£60	£30	
Lantaloon	LP	RCA	SF8256	1972	£60	£30	with poster
Sun Clog Dance	7"	RCA	RCA2246	1972	£5	£2	

DANDY

Baby Don't Go	7"	Dice	CC21	1963	£10	£5	
Be Natural Be Proud	7"	Downtown	DT434	1969	£4	£1.50	
Build Your Love	7"	Downtown	DT458	1970	£4	£1.50	
Charlie Brown	7"	Giant	GN20	1968	£5	£2	
Come On Home	7"	Downtown	DT437	1969	£4	£1.50	
Dandy Livingstone	LP	Trojan	TRL45	1972	£10	£4	
Everybody Loves A Winner	7"	Downtown	DT442	1969	£4	£1.50	
Fight	7"	Ska Beat	JB247	1966	£10	£5	
Games People Play	7"	Downtown	DT421	1969	£4	£1.50	
Hey Boy Hey Girl	7"	Blue Beat	BB319	1965	£12	£6	
How Glad I Am	7"	Downtown	DT468	1970	£4	£1.50	
I Found Love	7"	Blue Beat	BB336	1966	£12	£6	
I Need You	LP	Trojan	TRL17	1969	£12	£5	with Audrey
I'm Back with A Bang Bang	7"	Giant	GN36	1968	£5	£2	
I'm In The Mood	7"	Giant	GN19	1968	£5	£2	
I'm Looking For Love	7"	Blue Beat	BB308	1965	£12	£6	
I'm Your Puppet	7"	Downtown	DT416	1969	£4	£1.50	
In The Mood	7"	Caltone	TONE103	1967	£8	£4	Honeyboy Martin B side
Let's Go Rocksteady	7"	Giant	GN7	1967	£5	£2	
Little More Ska	7"	Dice	CC29	1964	£10	£5	
Morning Side Of The Mountain	7"	Downtown	DT462	1970	£4	£1.50	
Morning Side Of The Mountain	LP	Trojan	TBL118	1970	£12	£5	with Audrey
Move Your Mule	7"	Downtown	DT401	1969	£4	£1.50	
My Babe	7"	Blue Beat	BB327	1965	£12	£6	
My Time Now	7"	Giant	GN3	1967	£5	£2	
Now I Have You	7"	Dice	CC24	1964	£10	£5	
One Scotch, One Bourbon, One Beer	7"	Ska Beat	JB269	1967	£10	£5	
People Get Ready	7"	Downtown	DT429	1969	£4	£1.50	
Play It Cool	7"	Columbia	DB112	1969	£6	£2.50	
Propogandist	7"	Giant	GN23	1968	£5	£2	
Puppet On A String	7"	Giant	GN5	1967	£5	£2	
Raining In My Heart	7"	Downtown	DT456	1970	£4	£1.50	
Reggae In Your Jeggae	7"	Downtown	DT410	1969	£4	£1.50	
Returns	LP	Trojan	TRL2	1969	£15	£6	
Rocksteady With Dandy	LP	Giant	GNL1000	1967	£40	£20	
Rudy A Message To You	7"	Ska Beat	JB273	1967	£10	£5	
Sentence	7"	Trojan	TR629	1968	£6	£2.50	Lee Perry B side
Shake Me Wake Me	7"	Downtown	DT402	1969	£4	£1.50	
Somewhere My Love	7"	Giant	GN10	1967	£5	£2	
Sweet Ride	7"	Giant	GN27	1968	£5	£2	
Tears On My Pillow	7"	Giant	GN30	1968	£5	£2	
Tell Me Darling	7"	Downtown	DT404	1969	£4	£1.50	
There Is A Mountain	7"	Giant	GN15	1967	£5	£2	
Toast	7"	Trojan	TR618	1968	£6	£2.50	
Trier	7"	Downtown	DT411	1969	£4	£1.50	
Vipers	7"	Carnival	CV7020	1965	£8	£4	
Won't You Come Home	7"	Downtown	DT453	1969	£4	£1.50	
You're No Hustler	7"	Ska Beat	JB279	1967	£10	£5	
Your Musical Doctor	LP	Trojan	TTL26	1970	£12	£5	

DANE, CHRIS

Cynthia's In Love	7"	London	HLA8165	1955	£15	£7.50	

DANE, SHELLEY

Hannah Lee	7"	Pye	7N25064	1960	£4	£1.50	

D'ANGELO, MICHAEL

Rocco's Theme	7"	Columbia	DSB4705	1961	£10	£5	

DANGER

Danger	LP	Cow		1973	£100	£50	Dutch

DANGER, CAL

Teenage Girlie Blues	7"	Fontana	267225TF	1962	£30	£15	

DANGERFIELD, A. P.

Conversations	7"	Fontana	TF935	1968	£10	£5	

DANGERFIELD, KEITH

The Keith Dangerfield single owes its high value to the once-held belief that the Dangerfield name was a pseudonym for the Yardbirds' vocalist, Keith Relf. This was very much a case of wishful thinking, however. Relf did attempt a solo career while still with the Yardbirds, but his singles have the obvious credit – Keith Relf.

No Life Child	7"	Plexium	P1237	1968	£100	£50	

DANGERFIELD, TONY

She's Too Way Out	7"	Pye	7N15695	1964	£30	£15	

D'ARBY, TERENCE TRENT

Sign Your Name	CD-s	CBS	TRENTC4	1988	£5	£2	*picture disc*

DANI

That Old Familiar Feeling	7"	Pye	7N25667	1974	£8	£4	

DANIELLE

I'm Gonna Marry The Boy	7"	Philips	BF1532	1966	£4	£1.50	

DANIELS, BILLY

At The Crescendo	LP	Vogue	LAE12021	1956	£10	£4	
Best Of Billy Daniels	7" EP	HMV	7EG8485	1958	£5	£2	
Songs At Midnight	10" LP	Mercury	MG25163	1954	£20	£8	
Songs At Midnight	10" LP	Mercury	MPT7505	1956	£12	£5	
That Old Black Magic	7"	Vogue	V9172	1960	£6	£2.50	
That Old Black Magic	7" EP	Mercury	ZEP10066	1960	£6	£2.50	
That Old Black Magic	7" EP	Mercury	MEP9001	1956	£8	£4	
Torch Hour	10" LP	Mercury	MG10003	1953	£20	£8	
Torch Hour	10" LP	Mercury	MPT7006	1956	£10	£4	
Torch Hour	10" LP	Mercury	MG25103	1954	£15	£6	
You Go To My Head	10" LP	HMV	DLP1174	1958	£10	£4	

DANIELS, JULIUS

RCA Victor Race Series Vol. 4	7" EP	RCA	RCX7175	1965	£12	£6	

DANIELS, MAXINE

Coffee-Bar Calypso	7"	Oriole	CB1366	1957	£4	£1.50	
I Never Realised	7"	Oriole	CB1402	1957	£4	£1.50	
Passionate Summer	7"	Oriole	CB1462	1958	£4	£1.50	
When It's Springtime In The Rockies	7"	Oriole	CB1449	1958	£4	£1.50	
You Brought A New Kind Of Love To Me	7"	Oriole	CB1440	1958	£4	£1.50	

DANIELS, ROLY 'YO YO'

Yo Yo Boy	7"	Stardisc	SD101	196–	£8	£4	*picture sleeve*
Yo Yo Boy	7"	Decca	F11501	1962	£4	£1.50	

DANIELS, SAM

Tell Me Baby	7"	Sway	SW003	1963	£5	£2	

DANISH SHARKS

Ready Steady Go	LP	Ariola	TD209	196–	£15	£6	*German*

DANKWORTH, JOHNNY

African Waltz	7" EP	Columbia	SEG8137	1961	£5	£2	
Avengers	7"	Fontana	TF422	1963	£6	£2.50	
Avengers	7"	Columbia	DB4695	1961	£6	£2.50	
Criminal	7" EP	Columbia	SEG8037/ESG7825	1960	£5	£2	
Curtain Up	LP	Columbia	33SX1572	1963	£25	£10	
Dankworth Workshop No. 1	7" EP	Parlophone	GEP8653	1958	£5	£2	
Dankworth Workshop No. 2	7" EP	Parlophone	GEP8697	1958	£5	£2	
Experiments With Mice	7"	Parlophone	MSP6255	1956	£4	£1.50	
Fathom	LP	Stateside	(S)SL10213	1967	£20	£8	
Five Steps To Dankworth	LP	Parlophone	PMC1043	1957	£20	£8	
Jazz Routes	LP	Columbia	33SX1280/SCX3347	1961	£15	£6	
London To Newport	LP	Top Rank	25019	1960	£15	£6	
Million Dollar Collection	LP	Fontana	TL5445	1968	£12	£5	
Modesty Blaise Theme	7"	Fontana	TF700	1966	£4	£1.50	
Movies And Me	LP	Sepia	RSR1005	1974	£10	£4	
Vintage Years	LP	Parlophone	PMC1076	1959	£20	£8	
What The Dickens	LP	Fontana	TL/STL5203	1964	£20	£8	
Zodiac Variations	LP	Fontana	TL5229	1965	£60	£30	

DANLEERS

One Summer Night	7"	Mercury	AMT1003	1958	£150	£75	

DANNY & THE JUNIORS

At The Hop	7"	HMV	POP436	1958	£10	£5	
Back To The Hop	7"	Top Rank	JAR587	1961	£6	£2.50	
Dottie	7"	HMV	POP504	1958	£12	£6	
Oo-La-La-Limbo	7"	London	HL9666	1963	£4	£1.50	
Pony Express	7"	Top Rank	JAR552	1961	£6	£2.50	
Rock And Roll Is Here To Stay	7"	HMV	POP467	1958	£25	£12.50	
Twisting All Night Long	7"	Top Rank	JAR604	1962	£5	£2	

Twisting USA	7"	Top Rank	JAR510	1960	£6	**£2.50**	

DANSE SOCIETY

Clock	7"	North	SOC381	1981	**£8**	**£4**	
There Is No Shame In Death	12"	Pax	PAX2	1981	**£15**	**£7.50**	*blue vinyl*
Woman's Own	12"	Pax	PAX5	1982	**£8**	**£4**	
Woman's Own	7"	Pax	PAX5	1982	**£6**	**£2.50**	

DANSETTE DAMAGE

New Musical Express	7"	Shoestring	LACE001	1978	**£30**	**£15**	

DANTALIAN'S CHARIOT

With the arrival of psychedelia, Zoot Money was able to indulge his penchant for on-stage flamboyance and, with the aid of his latest re-named version of the Big Roll Band, recorded one of the classic singles of the genre. The drummer, Colin Allen, subsequently played with John Mayall and Stone the Crows; bassist Pat Donaldson joined Fotheringay and has been a busy session musician ever since; while guitarist Andy Summers eventually found mega-stardom as a member of the Police.

Madman Running Through The Fields	7"	Columbia	DB8260	1967	**£60**	**£30**	

DANTE, TROY & THE INFERNOS

This Little Girl	7"	Fontana	TF477	1964	**£6**	**£2.50**	

DANTE & THE EVERGREENS

Alley Oop	7"	Top Rank	JAR402	1960	**£15**	**£7.50**	
Dante & The Evergreens	LP	Madison	MA1002	1961	**£175**	**£87.50**	*US*

DARIEN SPIRIT

Elegy To Marilyn	LP	Charisma	CAS1065	1973	**£10**	**£4**	

DARIN, BOBBY

25th Day Of December	7" EP	London	REK1321	1961	**£25**	**£12.50**	
At The Copa	LP	London	HAK2291	1960	**£15**	**£6**	
At The Copa	LP	London	SAHK6103	1960	**£20**	**£8**	*stereo*
Be Mad Little Girl	7"	Capitol	CL15328	1963	**£4**	**£1.50**	
Be Mad Little Girl	7"	Capitol	CL15328	1963	**£4**	**£1.50**	
Beachcomber	7"	London	HLK9197	1960	**£4**	**£1.50**	
Best Of Bobby Darin	LP	Capitol	T2571	1966	**£15**	**£6**	
Bobby Darin	7" EP	London	REE1173	1959	**£40**	**£20**	
Bobby Darin	LP	London	HAE2140	1958	**£50**	**£25**	
Bobby Darin	LP	Motown	M753L	1972	**£10**	**£4**	*US*
Bobby Darin No. 2	7" EP	London	REE1225	1959	**£30**	**£15**	
Bobby Darin Story	LP	Atlantic	587065	1967	**£12**	**£5**	
Bobby Darin Story	LP	London	HAK2372	1961	**£25**	**£10**	
Born Robert Walden Cassotto	LP	Bell	MBLL/SBLL112	1969	**£10**	**£4**	
Commitment	LP	Bell	SBLL128	1970	**£10**	**£4**	
Early in The Morning	7"	London	HLE8679	1958	**£30**	**£15**	*with the Rinky Dinks*
Earthy	LP	Capitol	T1826	1963	**£20**	**£8**	
Eighteen Yellow Roses	LP	Capitol	(S)T1942	1963	**£20**	**£8**	
For Teenagers Only	7" EP	London	REK1286	1961	**£20**	**£10**	
For Teenagers Only	LP	London	HAK2311	1960	**£25**	**£10**	
From Hello Dolly To Goodbye Charlie	LP	Capitol	T2194	1964	**£10**	**£4**	
Golden Folk Hits	LP	Capitol	(S)T2007	1963	**£20**	**£8**	
Hear Them Bells	7"	Brunswick	05831	1960	**£6**	**£2.50**	
I Wanna Be Around	LP	Capitol	T2322	1965	**£20**	**£8**	
If I Were A Carpenter	LP	Atlantic	587/588051	1966	**£10**	**£4**	
In A Broadway Bag	LP	Atlantic	587/588020	1966	**£12**	**£5**	
Inside Out	LP	Atlantic	587076	1967	**£12**	**£5**	
It's You Or No One	LP	London	HAK8102	1963	**£15**	**£6**	
It's You Or No One	LP	London	SHK8102	1963	**£20**	**£8**	*stereo*
Keep A Walking	7"	London	HLK9663	1963	**£4**	**£1.50**	
Love Swings	7" EP	London	REK1334	1961	**£12**	**£6**	
Love Swings	LP	London	HAK2394	1961	**£15**	**£6**	*mono*
Love Swings	LP	London	SAHK6194	1961	**£20**	**£8**	*stereo*
Mack The Knife	7"	London	HLE8939	1959	**£4**	**£1.50**	
Mighty Mighty Man	7"	London	HLE8793	1959	**£25**	**£12.50**	*with the Rinky Dinks*
Milord	7"	Atlantic	AT4002	1964	**£4**	**£1.50**	
Milord	7" EP	Atlantic	AET6013	1965	**£12**	**£6**	
Oh Look At Me Now	LP	Capitol	T1791	1962	**£15**	**£6**	
Plain Jane	7"	London	HLE8815	1959	**£20**	**£10**	
Plain Jane	7"	London	HL7078	1959	**£10**	**£5**	*export*
Queen Of The Hop	7"	London	HLE8737	1958	**£20**	**£10**	
Queen Of The Hop	7"	London	HL7060	1958	**£10**	**£5**	*export*
Rock Island Line	7"	Brunswick	05561	1956	**£100**	**£50**	
Shadow Of Your Smile	LP	Atlantic	587/588014	1966	**£15**	**£6**	
Sings Dr Doolittle	LP	Atlantic	587089	1968	**£10**	**£4**	
Sings Ray Charles	LP	London	HAK2456	1962	**£20**	**£8**	
Sings Ray Charles	LP	London	SAHK6243	1962	**£25**	**£10**	*stereo*
Something Special	LP	Atlantic	587073	1967	**£30**	**£15**	
Splish Splash	7"	London	HLE8666	1958	**£20**	**£10**	
That's All	7" EP	London	REK1243	1960	**£20**	**£10**	
That's All	LP	London	HAE2172	1959	**£20**	**£8**	
Theme From Come September	7"	London	HLK9407	1961	**£6**	**£2.50**	
Things	7" EP	London	REK1342	1962	**£12**	**£6**	
Things And Other Things	LP	London	HAK8030	1962	**£15**	**£6**	
This Is Bobby Darin	LP	London	HAK2235	1959	**£15**	**£6**	

This Is Bobby Darin	LP	London	SAHK6067	1960	**£20**	**£8**	*stereo*
Twist With Bobby Darin	7" EP	London	REK1338	1962	**£12**	**£6**	
Two Of A Kind	7" EP	London	REK1310	1961	**£15**	**£7.50**	*with Johnny Mercer*
Two Of A Kind	LP	London	HAK2363	1961	**£15**	**£6**	*with Johnny Mercer*
Two Of A Kind	LP	London	SAHK6164	1961	**£20**	**£8**	*with Johnny Mercer, stereo*
Up A Lazy River	7" EP	London	REK1290	1961	**£12**	**£6**	
We Didn't Ask To Be Brought Here	7"	Atlantic	AT4046	1965	**£4**	**£1.50**	
Winners	LP	Atlantic	ATL5014	1965	**£20**	**£8**	
You're The Reason I'm Living	LP	Capitol	T1866	1963	**£15**	**£6**	

DARIUS

Darius	LP	Chartmaker	1102	1968	**£100**	**£50**	US

DARK

The high value attaching to privately pressed progressive albums by groups like the Dark, Forever Amber and Complex depends in part on the mystique woven around them by collectors and dealers alike. The records are certainly rare and when so few people have actually heard them, it is difficult to gainsay claims that they are masterpieces. Now these records are being reissued, but in tiny limited editions and at prices that are often themselves well into the realm of serious collecting. Thus the mystique continues. Original copies of the Dark album exist in four different forms. The first ten or twelve copies came in a colour gatefold sleeve; the next edition of around thirty copies had a black and white gatefold sleeve; and a final run of about thirty-five copies had a black and white single sleeve. Meanwhile, just one eight-track cartridge was made for a friend who wanted it to play in his car! The record's status as the most valuable of the private pressings is supported by the fact that it is actually a very decent set of progressive hard rock performances – certainly at least as good as many records of the period that were issued by major record companies. Encouraged by the publicity surrounding their rare private pressing, the Dark reformed in 1994 and recorded *Anonymous Days*, a long-delayed follow-up that does the legend no harm at all.

Round The Edges	LP	S.I.S.	SR0102S	1972	**£1250**	**£875**	
Round The Edges	LP	Darkside	001	1991	**£25**	**£10**	

DARK (2)

Living End	LP	Fallout	FALLLP005	1982	**£10**	**£4**	

DARK STAR

Dark Star	LP	Avatar	AALP5003	1981	**£15**	**£6**	*with patch*
Lady Of Mars	7"	Avatar	AAA105	1981	**£5**	**£2**	

DARKSIDE

Waiting For The Angels	CD-s	Situation 2	SIT72CD	1990	**£5**	**£2**	

DARLING BUDS

Burst	CD-s	Epic	BLONDC1	1988	**£5**	**£2**	
Hit The Ground	CD-s	Epic	BLONDC2	1988	**£5**	**£2**	
If I Said	7"	Darling Buds	DAR1	1987	**£10**	**£5**	*with insert*
Let's Go Round There	CD-s	Epic	BLONDC3	1989	**£5**	**£2**	
You've Gotta Choose	CD-s	Epic	BLONDC4	1989	**£5**	**£2**	

DARNELL, BILL

Guilty Lips	7"	London	HLU8267	1956	**£20**	**£10**	
Last Frontier	7"	London	HLU8234	1956	**£25**	**£12.50**	
My Little Mother	7"	London	HLU8204	1955	**£20**	**£10**	
Tell Me More	7"	London	HLU8292	1956	**£20**	**£10**	

DARRELL, GUY

Evil Woman	7"	Piccadilly	7N35406	1967	**£10**	**£5**	
Go Home Girl	7"	Oriole	CB1932	1964	**£5**	**£2**	
Guy Darrell	LP	CBS	53364	196–	**£10**	**£4**	
I've Been Hurt	7"	CBS	202082	1966	**£8**	**£4**	
Sorry	7"	Oriole	CB1964	1964	**£5**	**£2**	

DARREN, JAMES

Album No. 1	LP	Colpix	CP406	1960	**£15**	**£6**	US
All	LP	Warner Bros	WS1688	1967	**£12**	**£5**	US
Angel Face	7"	Pye	7N25034	1959	**£5**	**£2**	
Gidget	7"	Pye	7N25019	1959	**£5**	**£2**	
James Darren Hit Parade	7" EP	Pye	NEP44008	1962	**£10**	**£5**	
Love Among The Young	LP	Pye	NPL28021	1963	**£12**	**£5**	
P.S. I Love You	7" EP	Pye	NEP44004	1959	**£8**	**£4**	
Sings For All Sizes	LP	Colpix	CP424	1962	**£15**	**£6**	US
Sings The Movies	LP	Colpix	CP418	1961	**£15**	**£6**	US

DARREN, MAXINE

How Can I Hide It From My Heart	7"	Pye	7N15796	1965	**£5**	**£2**	

DARROW, CHRIS

Chris Darrow	LP	United Artists	UAG29453	1973	**£10**	**£4**	
Under My Own Disguise	LP	United Artists	UAG29634	1974	**£10**	**£4**	

DARTELLS

Dartell Stomp	7"	London	HLD9719	1963	**£8**	**£4**	
Hot Pastrami	LP	Dot	DLP3522/25522	1963	**£20**	**£8**	US

DARTS

Hollywood Drag	LP	Del-Fi	DF(ST)1244	1963	**£15**	**£6**	US

DARVELL, BARRY

How Will It End	7"	London	HL9191	1960	**£50**	**£25**	

DARWIN'S THEORY

Daytime	7"	Major Minor	MM503	1967	**£25**	**£12.50**	

DAS FENSTER

Doch wir	LP	BASF		1970	**£50**	**£25**	*German*

DASGUPTA, NATAI

Songs Of India	LP	Mushroom	100MR22	1972	**£40**	**£20**	

DATE WITH SOUL

This single is a reissue of one originally credited to Hale and the Hushabyes.

Yes Sir That's My Baby	7"	Stateside	SS2062	1967	**£20**	**£10**	

DAUGHTERS OF THE ALBION

Daughters Of The Albion	LP	Fontana	STL5486	1968	**£15**	**£6**	

DAUNER, WOLFGANG

Et Cetera	LP	Intercord	26001	1971	**£12**	**£5**	*German*
Et Cetera Live	LP	MPS	2921754	1973	**£12**	**£5**	*German double*
Khirsh	LP	MPS	2121432	1972	**£12**	**£5**	*German*
Output	LP	ECM	ECM1006ST	1971	**£20**	**£8**	
Rischkas Soul	LP	Brain	1016	1972	**£12**	**£5**	*German*

DAVANI, DAVE

Don't Fool Around	7"	Columbia	DB7125	1963	**£6**	**£2.50**	
Four Faced	LP	Parlophone		1962	**£25**	**£10**	
Fused	LP	Parlophone	PMC1258	1965	**£25**	**£10**	
King Kong Blues	7"	Philips	6006195	1972	**£5**	**£2**	
Midnight Special	7"	Decca	F11896	1964	**£8**	**£4**	
One Track Mind	7"	Parlophone	R5525	1966	**£10**	**£5**	
Top Of The Pops	7"	Parlophone	R5329	1965	**£8**	**£4**	
Tossin' And Turnin'	7"	Parlophone	R5490	1966	**£8**	**£4**	

DAVE & THE DIAMONDS

I Walk The Lonely Night	7"	Columbia	DB7692	1965	**£5**	**£2**	
I Walk The Lonely Night	7"	Columbia	DB7692	1965	**£20**	**£10**	*picture sleeve*

DAVE DEE, DOZY, BEAKY, MICK & TICH

All I Want	7"	Fontana	TF586	1965	**£10**	**£5**	
Bend It	7" EP	Fontana	465324	1966	**£8**	**£4**	*French*
Dave Dee, Dozy, Beaky, Mick & Tich	LP	Fontana	(S)TL5350	1966	**£12**	**£5**	
DDDBMT	LP	Fontana	SFL13002	1968	**£10**	**£4**	
Golden Hits	LP	Fontana	(S)TL5441	1967	**£10**	**£4**	
Hideaway	7" EP	Fontana	465312	1966	**£8**	**£4**	*French*
If Music Be The Food Of Love	LP	Fontana	(S)TL5388	1966	**£12**	**£5**	
If No One Sang	LP	Fontana	(S)TL5471	1968	**£12**	**£5**	
Legend Of	LP	Fontana	SFL13063	1969	**£10**	**£4**	
Loos Of England	7" EP	Fontana	TE17488	1967	**£8**	**£4**	
No Time	7"	Fontana	TF531	1965	**£12**	**£6**	
Save Me	7" EP	Fontana	465349	1966	**£8**	**£4**	*French*
Together	LP	Fontana	SFL13173	1969	**£10**	**£4**	
Touch Me Touch Me	7" EP	Fontana	465372	1966	**£8**	**£4**	*French*
You Make It Move	7"	Fontana	TF630	1965	**£4**	**£1.50**	

DAVENPORT, BOB

And The Marsden Rattlers	LP	Trailer	LER3008	1971	**£25**	**£10**	
Bob Davenport And The Rakes	LP	Columbia	SX1786	1965	**£25**	**£10**	
Bob Davenport And The Rakes	LP	Topic	12TS350	1977	**£10**	**£4**	
Down The Long Road	LP	Topic	12TS274	1975	**£12**	**£5**	
Geordie Songs	7" EP	Collector	JEB4	1959	**£10**	**£5**	
Postcards Home	LP	Topic	12TS318	1977	**£10**	**£4**	
Wor Geordie	7" EP	Topic	TOP83	1962	**£10**	**£5**	

DAVEY, ALAN

Elf	7"	Hawkfan	HWFB3/4	1987	**£6**	**£2.50**	*double*

DAVEY & MORRIS

Davey & Morris	LP	York	FYK417	1973	**£50**	**£25**	

DAVEY & THE BADMEN

Wanted	LP	KRW	WA63054		**£30**	**£15**	*US*

DAVID

Another Day, Another Lifetime	LP	Vance Music Co.	VS124	1967	**£75**	**£37.50**	*US*

DAVID (2)

Please Mr Postman	7"	Philips	BF1776	1969	**£30**	**£10**	

DAVID, ALAN

Alan David	LP	Decca	LK4674	1965	**£10**	**£4**	

DAVID AND JONATHAN

David & Jonathan	LP	Columbia	SX/SCX6031	1967	£12	£5	
Lovers Of The World Unite	7" EP	Columbia	ESRF1807	1966	£10	£5	*French*
Ten Storeys High	7"	Columbia	DB8035	1966	£4	£1.50	

DAVID AND ROZAA

Spark That Lights The Flame	7"	Philips	6006094	1971	£8	£4	
Time Of Our Life	7"	Philips	6006040	1970	£8	£4	

DAVIDSON, DIANE

Sympathy	7"	Janus	no number	1972	£8	£4	*demo, plus 2 tracks by other artists*

DAVIDSON, FRANKIE & THE HI MARKS

You're Driving Me Crazy	7"	Starlite	ST45037	1961	£12	£6	

DAVIDSON, TOMMY

Half Past Kissing Time	7"	London	HLU8219	1956	£50	£25	

DAVIE, HUTCH & HIS HONKY TONKERS

At The Woodchoppers' Ball	7"	London	HLE8667	1958	£6	£2.50	

DAVIES, BOB

Rock And Roll Show	7"	London	HLU9767	1963	£15	£7.50	

DAVIES, CYRIL

Country Line Special	7"	Pye	7N25194	1963	£15	£7.50	
Country Line Special	7"	Pye	7N17663	1969	£6	£2.50	
Legendary Cyril Davies	10" LP	77	LP2	1957	£250	£150	
Legendary Cyril Davies	LP	Folklore	FLEUT9	1970	£60	£30	
Preaching The Blues	7"	Pye	7N25221	1963	£15	£7.50	
Sound Of Davies	7" EP	Pye	NEP44025	1964	£40	£20	

DAVIES, DAVE

Dave Davies Hits	7" EP	Pye	NEP24289	1968	£300	£180	*best auctioned*
Death Of A Clown	7" EP	Pye	PNV24196	1967	£30	£15	*French, B side by the Kinks*
Hold My Hand	7"	Pye	7N17678	1969	£8	£4	
Lincoln County	7"	Pye	7N17514	1968	£6	£2.50	
Susannah's Still Alive	7"	Pye	7N17429	1967	£4	£1.50	

DAVIES, MIAR

I Hear You Knocking	7"	Decca	F11894	1964	£4	£1.50	

DAVIES, RAY & BUTTON DOWN BRASS

Flashpoint	LP	Philips	6382111	1975	£12	£5	
Funk In Hell	LP	DJM	DJSLP22046	1976	£20	£8	
I Believe In Music	LP	Pye	NSPL41021	1973	£15	£6	
Themes From The Exorcist And Other Great Films	LP	Philips	6382103	1974	£10	£4	

DAVIS, BARRINGTON

Tracks Of Mind	LP	Montague	MONS2	1972	£200	£100	

DAVIS, BETTE

Miss Bette Davis	LP	EMI	EMA778	1976	£10	£4	
Whatever Happened To Baby Jane	7"	London	HLU9711	1963	£4	£1.50	*with Debbie Burton*

DAVIS, BETTY

Betty Davis	LP	Just Sunshine	JSS5	1973	£15	£6	*US*
Nasty Gal	LP	Island	ILPS9329	1975	£12	£5	
They Say I'm Different	LP	Polydor	2933402	1974	£12	£5	

DAVIS, BILLIE

Angel Of The Morning	7"	Decca	F12696	1967	£4	£1.50	
Billie Davis	LP	Decca	SKL5029	1970	£30	£15	
He's The One	7"	Decca	F11658	1963	£4	£1.50	
Heart And Soul	7"	Piccadilly	7N35308	1966	£5	£2	
I Can Remember	7"	Decca	F12923	1969	£6	£2.50	
I Want You To Be My Baby	7"	Decca	F12823	1968	£4	£1.50	
I'll Come Home	7"	Decca	F12870	1969	£4	£1.50	
Just Walk In My Shoes	7"	Piccadilly	7N35350	1966	£8	£4	
Last One To Be Loved	7"	Piccadilly	7N35227	1965	£4	£1.50	
No Other Baby	7"	Piccadilly	7N35266	1965	£4	£1.50	
Say Nothing	7"	Columbia	DB7195	1964	£4	£1.50	
School Is Over	7"	Columbia	DB7246	1964	£4	£1.50	
Tell Him	7"	Decca	F11572	1963	£4	£1.50	
Wasn't It You	7"	Decca	F12620	1967	£4	£1.50	
Whatcha Gonna Do	7"	Columbia	DB7346	1964	£4	£1.50	
You And I	7"	Columbia	DB7115	1963	£5	£2	

DAVIS, BLIND JOHNNY

Your Love Belongs To Me	7"	MGM	MGM463	1952	£10	£5	

DAVIS, BOBBY

Hype You Into Selling Your Head	7"	Starlite	ST45056	1961	£20	£10	
Return Your Love	7"	Banana	BA344	1971	£4	£1.50	

DAVIS, BONNIE

Title	Format	Label	Number	Year	Mint	VG	Notes
Pepperhot Baby	7"	Brunswick	05507	1955	**£25**	**£12.50**	

DAVIS, CLIFFORD

Title	Format	Label	Number	Year	Mint	VG	Notes
Before the Beginning	7"	Reprise	RS27003	1969	**£6**	**£2.50**	
Before The Beginning	7"	Reprise	K14282	1973	**£4**	**£1.50**	
Come On Down And Follow Me	7"	Reprise	RS27008	1970	**£4**	**£1.50**	

DAVIS, DANNY

Title	Format	Label	Number	Year	Mint	VG	Notes
Rome Wasn't Built In A Day	7"	Pye	7N15427	1962	**£4**	**£1.50**	

DAVIS, DANNY ORCHESTRA

Title	Format	Label	Number	Year	Mint	VG	Notes
Main Theme From The Saint	7"	MGM	MGM1277	1965	**£6**	**£2.50**	
They're Playing Our Song	LP	London	HAR8204	1964	**£15**	**£6**	*with Ruby & The Romantics*

DAVIS, EDDIE 'LOCKJAW'

Title	Format	Label	Number	Year	Mint	VG	Notes
Count Basie Presents The Eddie Davis Trio	LP	Columbia	33SX1117	1959	**£15**	**£6**	
Eddie 'Lockjaw' Davis Cookbook	LP	Esquire	32104	1960	**£15**	**£6**	
Eddie Lockjaw Davis	7" EP	Esquire	EP217	1959	**£5**	**£2**	
Eddie Lockjaw Davis Quartet	7" EP	Esquire	EP237	1961	**£5**	**£2**	
Eddie Lockjaw Davis Trio	7" EP	Parlophone	GEP8587	1956	**£5**	**£2**	
Eddie Lockjaw Davis Trio	7" EP	Parlophone	GEP8685	1958	**£5**	**£2**	
First Set (Live At Minton's)	LP	Stateside	SL10102	1964	**£15**	**£6**	
Jaws In Orbit	LP	Esquire	32128	1961	**£15**	**£6**	
Lockjaw	7" EP	Parlophone	GEP8678	1957	**£5**	**£2**	
Very Saxy	LP	Esquire	32117	1960	**£15**	**£6**	

DAVIS, JACKIE

Title	Format	Label	Number	Year	Mint	VG	Notes
Land Of Make Believe	7"	Pye		196–	**£10**	**£5**	

DAVIS, JIMMY

Title	Format	Label	Number	Year	Mint	VG	Notes
Maxwell Street Jimmy Davis	LP	Bounty	BY6009	1966	**£20**	**£8**	

DAVIS, KIM

Title	Format	Label	Number	Year	Mint	VG	Notes
Don't Take Your Lovin' Away	7"	Decca	F12387	1966	**£10**	**£5**	
Tell It Like It Is	7"	CBS	202568	1967	**£5**	**£2**	

DAVIS, LARRY & FENTON ROBINSON

Title	Format	Label	Number	Year	Mint	VG	Notes
Larry Davis And Fenton Robinson	LP	Python	PLP24	1972	**£25**	**£10**	

DAVIS, MAXWELL

Title	Format	Label	Number	Year	Mint	VG	Notes
Batman Theme And Other Bat Songs	LP	Ember	FA2040	1966	**£25**	**£10**	

DAVIS, MELVIN

Title	Format	Label	Number	Year	Mint	VG	Notes
Save It	7"	Action	ACT4531	1969	**£10**	**£5**	

DAVIS, MILES

The changing styles of jazz presented by Miles Davis during his four-and-a-half-decade career give his many fans a uniquely varied listening experience if they follow it all through. During the forties, Davis was a member of Charlie Parker's crucially important quintet, helping to invent the modern jazz music called bebop. Through the fifties, leading his own groups, Miles Davis began by developing the cool jazz style (*Birth Of The Cool*). The formation of his first permanent line-up – a quintet with saxophonist John Coltrane – sparked a lucrative recording deal with CBS. The four albums still owed to Prestige were dashed off in just two sessions, yet such was the level of inspiration in the quintet, that these four – *Cookin'*, *Relaxin'*, *Workin'* and *Steamin'* – emerged as the definitive hard bop recordings. The big band albums made with Gil Evans (notably *Miles Ahead*, *Porgy And Bess* and *Sketches Of Spain*) set new standards in harmonic and textural invention, while the sextet recording with John Coltrane and Cannonball Adderley (*Kind Of Blue*) pioneered a new, modal approach to improvisation. The live recordings of the early sixties (particularly *My Funny Valentine* and *Four And More*) stretched the concept of improvising around jazz standards as far as it could go. Then the formation of the second great Miles Davis quintet, with Wayne Shorter and Herbie Hancock, spurred a succession of magisterial albums (*Miles Smiles*, *ESP*, and their successors) that define a free jazz alternative to the jagged music of Ornette Coleman and Cecil Taylor – free, yet still clearly melodic. From the late sixties until a serious car crash put a temporary halt to his career in 1975, Miles Davis maintained a remarkable creative run in which he not only invented the fusion genre, but also began to explore most of the possibilities inherent in it. He released an unusually large number of records during this period, and every one is different. Of the rarities listed here, the quadraphonic mix of *Bitches Brew* is significantly different from the stereo, with extra percussion and a frequent doubling-up of melodic phrases to create an echo effect. The Japanese double albums are all live recordings – *Black Beauty*, with Chick Corea, Jack DeJohnette and Steve Grossman, is close to the jazz avant-garde in places; *Dark Magus* is a densely rhythmic work-out from a 1974 Carnegie Hall concert; while *Pangaea* is a companion set to the UK released *Agharta* – the second set from the same evening's performance. It is magnificent, powerful music, though not for the faint-hearted. The Session Disc LP, a poorly recorded set from 1971, would qualify as a bootleg if it was a rock album – in the jazz world, however, such live recordings have always been accepted as part of the natural scheme of things.

Title	Format	Label	Number	Year	Mint	VG	Notes
Back To Back	LP	Fontana	FJL135	1966	**£20**	**£8**	*side 2 by Art Blakey*
Bags' Groove	LP	Esquire	32090	1959	**£25**	**£10**	
Birth Of The Cool	LP	Capitol	T762	1957	**£40**	**£20**	
Birth Of The Cool	LP	Capitol	T1974	1966	**£12**	**£5**	
Bitches Brew	LP	CBS	QBL30998/9	1971	**£25**	**£10**	*quad double*
Bitches Brew	LP	CBS	66236	1970	**£12**	**£5**	*double*
Black Beauty	LP	CBS-Sony	SOPJ39/40	1973	**£30**	**£15**	*Japanese double*
Blue Changes	7" EP	Esquire	EP242	1961	**£5**	**£2**	
Blue Haze	LP	Esquire	32088	1960	**£30**	**£15**	
Blue Miles	7" EP	Esquire	EP232	1960	**£5**	**£2**	
Blue Moods	LP	Vocalion	LAEF584	1964	**£20**	**£8**	
Changes	LP	Esquire	32028	1957	**£25**	**£10**	
Classics In Jazz	10" LP	Capitol	LC6683	1954	**£30**	**£15**	
Collectors' Item	LP	Esquire	32030	1957	**£40**	**£20**	

Title	Format	Label	Cat. No.	Year	Mint	VG	Notes
Cookin'	LP	Esquire	32048	1958	**£25**	**£10**	
Dark Magus	LP	CBS-Sony	40AP741/2	1977	**£30**	**£15**	*Japanese double*
Davis Cup	7" EP	Philips	BBE12418	1961	**£5**	**£2**	
Dig	10" LP	Esquire	20017	1953	**£30**	**£15**	
E.S.P.	LP	CBS	(S)BPG62577	1966	**£12**	**£5**	
Early Miles	LP	Esquire	32118	1961	**£25**	**£10**	
Essential Miles Davis	LP	CBS	66310	1973	**£40**	**£20**	*3 LP boxed set, bonus single*
Ezz-thetic	LP	XTRA	XTRA5004	1966	**£12**	**£5**	*with Lee Konitz, B side by Teddy Charles*
Filles de Kilimanjaro	LP	CBS	63551	1969	**£10**	**£4**	
Four And More	LP	CBS	(S)BPG62655	1966	**£12**	**£5**	
Friday Night At The Blackhawk	LP	Fontana	TFL5163/ STFL580	1961	**£20**	**£8**	
Friday Night At The Blackhawk	LP	CBS	(S)BPG62306	1964	**£12**	**£5**	
HiFi Modern Jazz Jam Session	10" LP	Esquire	20052	1955	**£30**	**£15**	
Hooray For Miles Davis	LP	Session Disc	123	1972	**£15**	**£6**	
In A Silent Way	LP	CBS	63630	1970	**£10**	**£4**	
Isle Of Wight	LP	CBS	4504721	1987	**£20**	**£8**	*French*
Jazz Track	LP	Fontana	TFL5081	1960	**£25**	**£10**	
Kind Of Blue	LP	Fontana	TFL5072/ STFL513	1960	**£20**	**£8**	
Kind Of Blue	LP	CBS	(S)BPG62066	1966	**£10**	**£4**	
Live/Evil	LP	CBS	QBL30954	1973	**£25**	**£10**	*quad double*
Miles Ahead	LP	CBS	(S)BPG62496	1966	**£10**	**£4**	
Miles Ahead	LP	Fontana	TFL5007	1957	**£25**	**£10**	
Miles And Monk At Newport	LP	CBS	(S)BPG62389	1964	**£15**	**£6**	*with Thelonious Monk*
Miles Davis	7" EP	Vogue	EPV1191	1958	**£5**	**£2**	
Miles Davis	7" EP	Philips	BBE12351	1960	**£5**	**£2**	
Miles Davis	7" EP	Esquire	EP152	1957	**£5**	**£2**	
Miles Davis	7" EP	Philips	BBE12266	1959	**£5**	**£2**	
Miles Davis	7" EP	Fontana	TFE17119	1959	**£5**	**£2**	
Miles Davis	LP	Esquire	32021	1957	**£40**	**£20**	
Miles Davis All Stars	10" LP	Vogue	LDE028	1953	**£50**	**£25**	
Miles Davis All Stars	10" LP	Esquire	20021	1953	**£30**	**£15**	
Miles Davis All Stars Sextet	10" LP	Esquire	20062	1956	**£30**	**£15**	
Miles Davis And His Orchestra	10" LP	Vogue	LDE064	1954	**£30**	**£15**	
Miles Davis And John Coltrane Play Richard Rogers	LP	Stateside	SL10111	1965	**£15**	**£6**	
Miles Davis And John Coltrane Play Richard Rogers	LP	Pacific Jazz	688204ZL	1965	**£15**	**£6**	
Miles Davis And John Coltrane Play Richard Rogers	LP	Transatlantic	PR7322	1968	**£12**	**£5**	
Miles Davis And The Modern Jazz Giants	LP	Esquire	32100	1960	**£25**	**£10**	
Miles Davis At Carnegie Hall	LP	CBS	(S)BPG62081	1962	**£15**	**£6**	
Miles Davis In Europe	LP	CBS	(S)BPG62390	1964	**£15**	**£6**	
Miles Davis New Quartet	7" EP	Esquire	EP212	1959	**£5**	**£2**	
Miles Davis No. 2	7" EP	Fontana	TFE17223	1960	**£5**	**£2**	
Miles Davis No. 3	7" EP	Fontana	TFE17225	1960	**£5**	**£2**	
Miles Davis Orchestra	7" EP	Capitol	EAP2459	1954	**£5**	**£2**	
Miles Davis Orchestra	7" EP	Capitol	EAP1459	1954	**£5**	**£2**	
Miles Davis Plays For Lovers	LP	Stateside	SL10168	1966	**£15**	**£6**	
Miles Davis Quartet	7" EP	Esquire	EP132	1957	**£5**	**£2**	
Miles Davis Quartet	7" EP	Esquire	EP12	1954	**£5**	**£2**	
Miles Davis Quartet	7" EP	Fontana	TFE17359	1961	**£5**	**£2**	
Miles Davis Quartet	7" EP	Esquire	EP172	1958	**£5**	**£2**	
Miles Davis Quintet	10" LP	Esquire	20072	1956	**£30**	**£15**	
Miles Davis Quintet	10" LP	Esquire	20041	1955	**£30**	**£15**	
Miles Davis Sextet	7" EP	Vogue	EPV1075	1956	**£5**	**£2**	
Miles Davis Vol. 1	LP	Blue Note	BLP/BST81501	1961	**£25**	**£10**	
Miles Davis Vol. 2	LP	Blue Note	BLP/BST81502	1964	**£25**	**£10**	
Miles In The Sky	LP	CBS	63352	1969	**£10**	**£4**	
Miles Smiles	LP	CBS	(S)BPG62933	1967	**£12**	**£5**	
Miles Theme	7" EP	Esquire	EP222	1959	**£5**	**£2**	
Milestones	LP	Fontana	TFL5035	1958	**£20**	**£8**	
Milestones	LP	CBS	62308	1967	**£10**	**£4**	
Modern Jazz Giants	LP	Transatlantic	PR7150	1967	**£12**	**£5**	
More Miles	7" EP	Fontana	TFE17195	1959	**£5**	**£2**	
Most Of Miles	LP	Fontana	TFL5089	1960	**£15**	**£6**	
Musings Of Miles	LP	Esquire	32012	1956	**£30**	**£15**	
My Funny Valentine	LP	CBS	(S)BPG62510	1965	**£12**	**£5**	
Nature Boy	10" LP	Vogue	LDE191	1957	**£40**	**£20**	
Nefertiti	LP	CBS	63248	1968	**£10**	**£4**	
Odyssey!	LP	XTRA	XTRA5050	1968	**£12**	**£5**	
Pangaea	LP	CBS-Sony	36AP1789/90	1975	**£30**	**£15**	*Japanese double*
Porgy And Bess	7" EP	Fontana	TFE17247	1960	**£5**	**£2**	
Porgy And Bess	LP	Fontana	TFL5056	1959	**£20**	**£8**	
Porgy And Bess	LP	CBS	(S)BPG62108	1966	**£10**	**£4**	
Quiet Nights	LP	CBS	(S)BPG62213	1964	**£15**	**£6**	
Relaxin'	LP	Esquire	32068	1958	**£25**	**£10**	
Round About Midnight	LP	Philips	BBL7140	1957	**£20**	**£8**	
Saturday Night At The Blackhawk	LP	Fontana	TFL5164/ STFL581	1961	**£20**	**£8**	
Saturday Night At The Blackhawk	LP	CBS	(S)BPG62307	1964	**£12**	**£5**	
Second HiFi Modern Jazz Jam Session	10" LP	Esquire	20056	1955	**£30**	**£15**	

Seven Steps To Heaven	LP	CBS	(S)BPG62170	1964	£15	£6	
Sketches Of Spain	LP	CBS	(S)BPG62327	1964	£10	£4	
Sketches Of Spain	LP	Fontana	TFL5100/ STFL531	1961	£25	£10	
Someday My Prince Will Come	LP	Fontana	TFL5172/ STFL587	1962	£20	£8	
Someday My Prince Will Come	LP	CBS	(S)BPG62104	1966	£10	£4	
Sorcerer	LP	CBS	63097	1968	£10	£4	
Steamin' With The Miles Davis Quintet	LP	Esquire	32138	1961	£25	£10	
Straight No Chaser	7" EP	Fontana	TFE17197	1959	£5	£2	
Walkin'	LP	Esquire	32098	1960	£25	£10	
Workin' With The Miles Davis Quintet	LP	Esquire	32108	1960	£25	£10	

DAVIS, REV. GARY

Bring Your Money Honey	LP	Fontana	SFJL914	1969	£12	£5	
Children Of Zion	LP	Transatlantic	TRA249	1972	£10	£4	
Harlem Street Singer	LP	Fontana	688303ZL	1964	£12	£5	
Little More Faith	LP	XTRA	XTRA5042	1968	£20	£8	
Lo I Be With You Always	LP	Kicking Mule	SNKD1	1974	£12	£5	*double*
Lord I Wish I Could See	LP	Biograph	BLP12034	1971	£10	£4	*US*
Pure Religion And Bad Company	LP	77	LA1214	1963	£20	£8	
Ragtime Guitar	LP	Transatlantic	TRA244	1971	£10	£4	
Rev. Gary Davis/Short Stuff Macon	LP	XTRA	XTRA1009	1965	£10	£4	*1 side each artist*
Say No To The Devil	LP	XTRA	XTRA5014	1966	£20	£8	

DAVIS, SAMMY JR

All Of You	7"	Brunswick	05629	1956	£4	£1.50	
Because Of You	7"	Brunswick	05326	1954	£4	£1.50	
Birth Of The Blues	7"	Brunswick	05383	1955	£4	£1.50	
Hey There	7"	Brunswick	05469	1955	£8	£4	
In A Persian Market	7"	Brunswick	05518	1956	£4	£1.50	
Just For Lovers	LP	Brunswick	LAT8088	1956	£10	£4	
Love Me Or Leave Me	7"	Brunswick	05428	1955	£8	£4	
Not For Me	7"	Reprise	R20289	1964	£5	£2	
Porgy And Bess	LP	Brunswick	STA3017	1959	£10	£4	*stereo, with Carmen McRae*
Rhythm Of Life	7"	MCA	MK5016	1969	£10	£5	
Sammy At The Town Hall, New York	LP	Brunswick	STA3012	1959	£10	£4	*stereo*
Six Bridges To Cross	7"	Brunswick	05389	1955	£4	£1.50	
Something For Everyone	LP	Tamla Motown	STML11160	1970	£15	£6	
Starring Sammy Davis	LP	Brunswick	LAT8153	1956	£10	£4	
That Old Black Magic	7"	Brunswick	05450	1955	£8	£4	

DAVIS, SKEETER

Cloudy, With Occasional Tears	LP	RCA	RD/SF7604	1963	£12	£5	
End Of The World	7"	RCA	RCA1328	1963	£4	£1.50	
End Of The World	LP	RCA	RD/SF7563	1963	£12	£5	
Here's The Answer	LP	RCA	LPM2327	1961	£12	£5	*US*
I Can't Stay Mad At You	7"	RCA	RCA1363	1963	£4	£1.50	
I'll Sing You A Song And Harmonize Too	LP	RCA	LPM2197	1960	£12	£5	*US*
I'm Falling Too	7"	RCA	RCA1201	1960	£5	£2	
Let Me Get Close To You	LP	RCA	RD7676	1964	£10	£4	
My Last Date With You	7"	RCA	RCA1222	1961	£4	£1.50	
Silver Threads And Golden Needles	7" EP	RCA	RCX7153	1964	£8	£4	

DAVIS, SKEETER & BOBBY BARE

Tunes For Two	LP	RCA	RD7711	1965	£10	£4	

DAVIS, SKEETER & PORTER WAGONER

Duets	LP	RCA	LPM/LSP2529	1962	£12	£5	*US*

DAVIS, SPENCER GROUP

Spencer Davis had no dominant role within the group that bore his name, which is probably why his solo career in the seventies and eighties was such a low-key affair. Originally, the Spencer Davis Group focused on its dynamic young singer, Stevie Winwood, who was also a talented guitarist and keyboard player. Winwood shines throughout the group's sturdy R&B material and in particular on the impressive series of singles, which include some real classics. Remarkably, when Winwood left to form Traffic, Spencer Davis was able to find a replacement, Eddie Hardin, whose singing and keyboard playing was almost as fine. 'Time Seller' and 'Mr.Second Class' are a worthy continuation of the singles series, being soulful performances tinged with psychedelia. They are included on the album *With Their New Face On*, which is itself a very under-rated recording.

Autumn 66	LP	Fontana	STL5359	1966	£25	£10	
Best Of The Spencer Davis Group	LP	Island	ILP970/ILPS9070	1968	£25	£10	*pink label*
Dimples	7"	Fontana	TF471	1964	£6	£2.50	
Every Little Bit Hurts	7"	Fontana	TF530	1965	£5	£2	
Every Little Bit Hurts	7" EP	Fontana	TE17450	1965	£15	£7.50	
Gimme Some Lovin'	LP	United Artists	UAL3578/ UAS6578	1967	£20	£8	*US*
Gimme Some Loving	7" EP	Fontana	465337	1966	£20	£10	*French*
Hits Of The Spencer Davis Group	cass-s	Philips	MCF5003	1968	£8	£3	
I Can't Stand It	7"	Fontana	TF499	1964	£5	£2	
I'm A Man	7"	Fontana	TF785	1967	£4	£1.50	
I'm A Man	7" EP	Fontana	465360	1966	£20	£10	*French*
I'm A Man	LP	United Artists	UAL3589/ UAS6589	1967	£20	£8	*US*

Title	Format	Label	Cat. No.	Year	Mint	VG	Notes
Keep On Running	7" EP	Fontana	465297	1965	£20	£10	*French*
Keep On Running	CD-s	Island	CID487	1991	£5	£2	
Letters From Edith	LP	CBS	63842	1969	£200	£100	*test pressing*
Mr Second Class	7"	United Artists	UP1203	1967	£4	£1.50	
Second Album	LP	Fontana	TL5295	1966	£30	£15	
Sitting And Thinking	7" EP	Fontana	TE17463	1966	£20	£10	
Somebody Help Me	7" EP	Fontana	465305	1966	£20	£10	*French*
Strong Love	7"	Fontana	TF571	1965	£4	£1.50	
Their First Album	LP	Fontana	TL5242	1965	£25	£10	
Their First Album	LP	Wing	WL1165	1968	£10	£4	
Time Seller	7"	Fontana	TF854	1967	£4	£1.50	
When I Come Home	7" EP	Fontana	465318	1966	£20	£10	*French*
With Their New Face On	LP	United Artists	SULP1192	1968	£20	£8	
You Put The Hurt On Me	7" EP	Fontana	TE17444	[illegible]	£[illegible]0	£10	

DAVIS, SPENCER GROUP & TRAFFIC

Title	Format	Label	Cat. No.	Year	Mint	VG	Notes
Here We Go Round The Mulberry Bush	LP	United Artists	SULP1186	1968	£20	£8	

DAVIS, STEVE

Title	Format	Label	Cat. No.	Year	Mint	VG	Notes
Takes Time To Know Her	7"	Fontana	TF922	1968	£30	£15	

DAVIS, TYRONE

Title	Format	Label	Cat. No.	Year	Mint	VG	Notes
Can I Change My Mind	7"	Atlantic	584253	1969	£4	£1.50	
Can I Change My Mind	LP	Atlantic	588209	1970	£12	£5	
Is It Something You've Got	7"	Atlantic	584265	1969	£4	£1.50	
Turn Back The Hands Of Time	7"	Atlantic	2091003	1970	£4	£1.50	
Turn Back The Hands Of Time	LP	Atlantic	2465021	1970	£10	£4	
What If A Man	7"	Stateside	SS2092	1968	£6	£2.50	

DAVIS, WALTER

Title	Format	Label	Cat. No.	Year	Mint	VG	Notes
RCA Victor Race Series Vol. 3	7" EP	RCA	RCX7169	1964	£10	£5	
Think You Need A Shot	LP	RCA	INTS1085	1970	£12	£5	

DAVIS, WARREN MONDAY BAND

Title	Format	Label	Cat. No.	Year	Mint	VG	Notes
Love Is A Hurting Thing	7"	Columbia	DB8270	1967	£6	£2.50	
Wait For Me	7"	Columbia	DB8190	1967	£10	£5	

DAVIS, WILD BILL

Title	Format	Label	Cat. No.	Year	Mint	VG	Notes
Wild Bill Davis	10" LP	Philips	BBR8079	1956	£20	£8	

DAVIS SISTERS

Title	Format	Label	Cat. No.	Year	Mint	VG	Notes
Rock-a-Bye Boogie	78	HMV	B10582	1953	£10	£5	

DAVISON, BRIAN

Title	Format	Label	Cat. No.	Year	Mint	VG	Notes
Every Which Way	LP	Charisma	CAS1021	1970	£10	£4	

DAVISON, WILD BILL

Title	Format	Label	Cat. No.	Year	Mint	VG	Notes
Greatest Of The Greats	LP	Vogue	LAE12217	1960	£10	£4	
Wild BIll Davison	LP	London	LTZU15068	1957	£12	£5	
Wild Bill Davison Band	10" LP	Melodisc	MLP501	1955	£20	£8	
With Strings Attached	LP	Philips	BBL7104	1957	£12	£5	

DAWE, TIM

Title	Format	Label	Cat. No.	Year	Mint	VG	Notes
Penrod	LP	Straight	ST1058	1969	£20	£8	*US*

DAWKINS, CARL

Title	Format	Label	Cat. No.	Year	Mint	VG	Notes
All Of A Sudden	7"	Rio	R136	1967	£8	£4	
Baby I Love You	7"	Rio	R137	1967	£8	£4	
Get Together	7"	Duke	DU93	1970	£4	£1.50	
Hot And Sticky	7"	Rio	R138	1967	£8	£4	*Rulers B side*
I Love The Way You Are	7"	Blue Cat	BS114	1968	£8	£4	*Dermott Lynch B side*
I'll Make It Up	7"	Duke	DU3	1968	£6	£2.50	*J. J. Allstars B side*
Perseverence	7"	Big Shot	BI570	1971	£5	£2	
Rodney's History	7"	Nu Beat	NB030	1969	£4	£1.50	*Dynamites B side*
Satisfaction	7"	Trojan	TR7765	1970	£4	£1.50	
This Land	7"	Duke	DU95	1970	£4	£1.50	

DAWKINS, HORELL

Title	Format	Label	Cat. No.	Year	Mint	VG	Notes
Butterfly	7"	Ska Beat	JB240	1966	£10	£5	

DAWKINS, JIMMY

Title	Format	Label	Cat. No.	Year	Mint	VG	Notes
Fast Fingers	LP	Delmark	DS623	1971	£12	£5	

DAWN, JULIE

Title	Format	Label	Cat. No.	Year	Mint	VG	Notes
Wild Horses	7"	Columbia	SCM5035	1953	£5	£2	

DAWNWIND

Title	Format	Label	Cat. No.	Year	Mint	VG	Notes
Looking Back On The Future	LP	Amron	ARD5003	1976	£100	£50	

DAWSON, JULIET

Title	Format	Label	Cat. No.	Year	Mint	VG	Notes
Boo	LP	Sovereign		1972	£40	£20	

DAWSON, LES SYNDICATE

Title	Format	Label	Cat. No.	Year	Mint	VG	Notes
Last Chicken In The Shop	7"	Melodisc	1586	1964	£5	£2	

DAWSON, LESLEY

Title	Format	Label	Cat. No.	Year	Mint	VG	Notes
Just Say Goodbye	7"	Mercury	MF946	1967	**£4**	**£1.50**	
Run For Shelter	7"	Mercury	MF965	1967	**£8**	**£4**	

DAX, DANIELLE

Title	Format	Label	Cat. No.	Year	Mint	VG	Notes
Pop-Eyes	LP	Initial	IRC009	1983	**£25**	**£10**	
Tomorrow Never Knows	CD-s	Sire	W9529CD	1990	**£5**	**£2**	

DAY, BING

Title	Format	Label	Cat. No.	Year	Mint	VG	Notes
I Can't Help It	7"	Mercury	AMT1047	1959	**£50**	**£25**	

DAY, BOBBY

Title	Format	Label	Cat. No.	Year	Mint	VG	Notes
Bluebird Buzzard And Oriole	7"	London	HL8800	1959	**£25**	**£12.50**	
Little Bitty Pretty One	7"	HMV	POP425	1957	**£100**	**£50**	
Love Is A One Time Affair	7"	London	HL8964	1959	**£12**	**£6**	
My Blue Heaven	7"	London	HLY9044	1960	**£12**	**£6**	
Over And Over	7"	Top Rank	JAR538	1961	**£8**	**£4**	
Rockin' Robin	7"	London	HL8726	1958	**£12**	**£6**	
Rockin' Robin	7"	Sue	WI388	1965	**£12**	**£6**	
Rockin' With Robin	LP	Class	LP5002	1959	**£125**	**£62.50**	*US*

DAY, DORIS

Title	Format	Label	Cat. No.	Year	Mint	VG	Notes
Annie Get Your Gun	LP	CBS	(S)BPG62129	1963	**£10**	**£4**	
April In Paris	7"	Columbia	SCM5038	1953	**£8**	**£4**	
Boys And Girls Together	10" LP	Columbia	CL2530	195–	**£15**	**£6**	*US*
Bright And Shiny	LP	Philips	BBL7471/ SBBL619	1961	**£15**	**£6**	
Bushel And A Peck	7"	Columbia	SCM5044	1953	**£10**	**£5**	
By The Light Of The Silvery Moon	10" LP	Columbia	CL6248	1953	**£25**	**£10**	*US*
Calamity Jane	10" LP	Philips	BBR8104	1956	**£15**	**£6**	*with Howard Keel*
Canadian Capers	7" EP	Columbia	SEG7507	1954	**£8**	**£4**	
Cherries	7"	Columbia	SCM5059	1953	**£6**	**£2.50**	
Christmas Album	LP	CBS	(S)BPG62712	1966	**£10**	**£4**	
Cuttin' Capers	LP	Philips	BBL7296/ SBBL540	1959	**£10**	**£4**	
Day By Day	LP	Philips	BBL7142	1957	**£25**	**£10**	
Day By Night	LP	Philips	BBL7211	1958	**£25**	**£10**	
Day By Night	LP	Philips	SBBL548	1959	**£15**	**£6**	*stereo, 1 different track*
Day Dreams	7" EP	Philips	BBE12151	1957	**£8**	**£4**	
Day Dreams	LP	Philips	BBL7120	1957	**£15**	**£6**	
Day In Hollywood	LP	Philips	BBL7175	1957	**£15**	**£6**	
Doris	7" EP	Philips	BBE12167	1958	**£8**	**£4**	
Doris And Frank	LP	Philips	BBL7137	1957	**£12**	**£5**	*with Frank Sinatra*
Doris Day	7" EP	Philips	BBE12007	1955	**£8**	**£4**	
Doris Day No. 2	7" EP	Philips	BBE12089	1956	**£8**	**£4**	
Dream A Little Dream Of Me	7" EP	Philips	BBE12213	1958	**£8**	**£4**	
Duet	7" EP	CBS	AGG20018	1962	**£6**	**£2.50**	*with André Previn*
Duet	LP	CBS	(S)BPG62010	1962	**£10**	**£4**	*with André Previn*
Duet No. 2	7" EP	CBS	AGG20029	1963	**£6**	**£2.50**	*with André Previn*
Favourites	10" LP	Philips	BBR8094	1956	**£15**	**£6**	
Hooray For Hollywood	LP	Philips	SBBL519	1959	**£12**	**£5**	*stereo*
Hooray For Hollywood Vol. 1	LP	Philips	BBL7247	1958	**£15**	**£6**	
Hooray For Hollywood Vol. 2	LP	Philips	BBL7248	1958	**£15**	**£6**	
Hot Canaries	10" LP	Columbia	CL2534	195–	**£15**	**£6**	*US, with Peggy Lee*
I Have Dreamed	7" EP	CBS	AGG20009	1962	**£6**	**£2.50**	
I Have Dreamed	LP	Philips	BBL7496/ SBBL643	1961	**£15**	**£6**	
I'll Never Stop Loving You	7" EP	Philips	BBE12011	1955	**£8**	**£4**	
I'll See You In My Dreams	10" LP	Columbia	CL6198	1951	**£25**	**£10**	*US*
In The Still Of The Night	LP	Philips	SBBL537	1960	**£15**	**£6**	
Jumbo	LP	CBS	(S)BPG62118	1962	**£10**	**£4**	
Just One Of Those Things	7"	Columbia	SCM5171	1955	**£8**	**£4**	
Latin For Lovers	LP	CBS	(S)BPG62502	1965	**£10**	**£4**	
Let's Fly Away	7" EP	Philips	SBBE9006	1960	**£10**	**£5**	*stereo*
Let's Fly Away	7" EP	Philips	BBE12298	1959	**£8**	**£4**	
Lights, Cameras, Action	10" LP	Columbia	CL2518	195–	**£15**	**£6**	*US*
Load Of Hay	7"	Columbia	SCM5087	1954	**£8**	**£4**	
Love Him	LP	CBS	(S)BPG62226	1964	**£25**	**£10**	
Love Me Or Leave Me	LP	Philips	BBL7047	1955	**£25**	**£10**	
Love Me Or Leave Me/Young At Heart	LP	CBS	63528	1969	**£25**	**£10**	
Lullaby Of Broadway	10" LP	Columbia	CL6168	1951	**£25**	**£10**	*US*
Lullaby Of Broadway (Doris Day Hits)	10" LP	Columbia	33S1038	1954	**£20**	**£8**	
Ma Says, Pa Says	7"	Columbia	SCM5033	1953	**£15**	**£7.50**	*with Johnnie Ray*
Mister Tap-Toe	7"	Columbia	SCM5062	1953	**£8**	**£4**	
Move Over Darling	7" EP	CBS	AGG20048	1964	**£5**	**£2**	
Nobody's Sweetheart	7" EP	Columbia	SEG7531	1954	**£8**	**£4**	
On Moonlight Bay	10" LP	Columbia	CL6186	1951	**£25**	**£10**	*US*
Oowee Baby	7"	CBS	AAG219	1964	**£6**	**£2.50**	
Party's Over	7"	Philips	JK1031	1957	**£8**	**£4**	*jukebox issue*
Pillow Talk	7" EP	Philips	BBE12339	1959	**£8**	**£4**	
Pyjama Game	LP	Philips	BBL7197	1957	**£10**	**£4**	
Second Star To The Right	7"	Columbia	SCM5045	1953	**£6**	**£2.50**	
Sentimental Journey	LP	CBS	(S)BPG62562	1966	**£10**	**£4**	
Show Time	LP	Philips	BBL7392/ SBBL577	1960	**£10**	**£4**	
Show Time No. 1	7" EP	Philips	SBBE9034	1961	**£8**	**£4**	*stereo*

Showcase Of Hits	LP	Philips	BBL7297	1959	£10	£4	
Sings Her Great Movie Hits	LP	CBS	BPG62785	1966	£10	£4	
Sometimes I'm Happy	7" EP	Columbia	SEG7546	1954	£8	£4	
Song Is You	7" EP	Philips	BBE12187	1958	£8	£4	
Tea For Two	10" LP	Columbia	CL6149	1950	£25	£10	US
That's The Way He Does It	7"	Columbia	SCM5075	1953	£8	£4	
That's What Makes Paris Paree	7"	Columbia	SCM5039	1953	£6	£2.50	
Twelve O'Clock Tonight	7"	Philips	JK1020	1957	£8	£4	*jukebox issue*
Vocal Gems From The Film Young Man Of Music	7" EP	Columbia	SEG7572	1955	£8	£4	
Voice Of Your Choice	10" LP	Philips	BBR8026	1954	£15	£6	
We Kiss In A Shadow	7"	Columbia	SCM5067	1953	£6	£2.50	
We Kiss In A Shadow	7" EP	Columbia	SEG7515	1954	£8	£4	
What Every Girl Should Know	LP	Philips	BBL7377/ SBBL563	1960	£10	£4	
With A Smile And A Song	LP	CBS	(S)BPG62461	1965	£20	£8	
You Can't Have Everything	7" EP	Philips	SBBE9021	1960	£10	£5	*stereo*
You Can't Have Everything	7" EP	Philips	BBE12388	1960	£8	£4	
You'll Never Walk Alone	LP	CBS	(S)BPG62101	1963	£25	£10	
You're My Thrill	10" LP	Columbia	CL6071	1949	£20	£8	US
Young At Heart	10" LP	Philips	BBR8040	1955	£15	£6	*with Frank Sinatra*
Young Man With A Horn	10" LP	Columbia	CL6106	1950	£25	£10	US
Young Man With A Horn	LP	Columbia	CL582	1954	£15	£6	US

DAY, JACKIE

Before It's Too Late	7"	Sue	WI4040	1967	£60	£30	

DAY, JILL

I Hear You Knocking	7"	HMV	7M362	1956	£8	£4	
Mangos	7"	HMV	POP320	1957	£4	£1.50	
Promises	7"	Parlophone	MSP6177	1955	£5	£2	
Sincerely	7"	Parlophone	MSP6169	1955	£6	£2.50	
Tear Fell	7"	HMV	7M391	1956	£5	£2	

DAY, KENNY

Teenage Sonata	7"	Top Rank	JAR339	1960	£5	£2	*picture sleeve*
Why Don't We Do This More Often	7"	Top Rank	JAR400	1961	£5	£2	*picture sleeve*

DAY, MURIEL

Nine Times Out Of Ten	7"	Page One	POF151	1969	£15	£7.50	
Wages Of Love	7"	CBS	4115	1969	£5	£2	

DAY, TANYA

His Lips Get In The Way	7"	Polydor	NH52331	1964	£4	£1.50	

DAY, TERRY

That's All I Want	7"	CBS	AAG104	1962	£5	£2	

DAY BLINDNESS

Day Blindness	LP	Studio 10	DBX101	1969	£60	£30	US

DAY BROTHERS

Angel	7"	Oriole	CB1575	1960	£5	£2	

DAY OF THE PHOENIX

Neighbour's Son	LP	Chapter One	CNSR812	1972	£40	£20	
Wide Open N-Way	LP	Greenwich	GSLPR1002	1970	£30	£15	

DAYLIGHT

Daylight	LP	RCA	SF8194	1971	£30	£15	
Lady Of St Clare	7"	RCA	RCA2106	1971	£4	£1.50	

DAYLIGHTERS

Oh Mom Teach Me How	7"	Sue	WI343	1964	£10	£5	

DAYS

Bacchus Is Back	LP	Sonet	SLPS1701	1975	£50	£25	*Danish*

D.C.10s

Bermuda	7"	Certain Euphoria	ACE451	1980	£5	£2	

DE BURGH, CHRIS

Compact Hits	CD-s	A&M	AMCD915	1988	£5	£2	
Missing You	CD-s	A&M	CDEE474	1988	£5	£2	*3" single*
Tender Hands	CD-s	A&M	CDEE486	1988	£5	£2	*3" single*

DE BYL, FRANZ

Franz De Byl	LP	Metronome	MLP15383	1970	£20	£8	*German*
Und	LP	Thorofon	ATH114	1972	£20	£8	*German*

DE CASTRO SISTERS

Boom Boom Boomerang	7"	London	HL8137	1955	£25	£12.50	
Christmas Is Coming	7"	London	HLU8212	1955	£20	£10	
Give Me Time	7"	London	HLU8228	1956	£20	£10	
I'm Bewildered	7"	London	HL8158	1955	£25	£12.50	
If I Ever Fall In Love	7"	London	HLU8189	1955	£20	£10	
No One To Blame But You	7"	London	HLU8296	1956	£20	£10	

Red Sails In The Sunset	7"	Capitol	CL15199	1961	£4	£1.50	
Teach Me Tonight	7"	London	HL8104	1954	£25	£12.50	
Teach Me Tonight Cha-Cha	7"	HMV	POP583	1959	£5	£2	
Who Are They To Say	7"	HMV	POP527	1958	£5	£2	

DE DANANN

Banks Of The Nile	LP	Decca	SKL5318	1980	£10	£4	
De Danann	LP	Polydor	2904005	1975	£15	£6	*Irish*
De Danann	LP	Decca	SKL5287	1977	£15	£6	

DE FRANCO, BUDDY

Buddy DeFranco	10" LP	Columbia	33C9022	1956	£25	£10	
Buddy DeFranco Wailers	LP	Columbia	33CX10091	1957	£20	£8	
King Of The Clarinet	10" LP	MGM	D112	1953	£30	£15	
Plays Benny Goodman	LP	HMV	CLP1215	1958	£15	£6	
Takes You To The Stars	10" LP	Vogue	LDE077	1954	£30	£15	
With Oscar Peterson	LP	Columbia	33CX10003	1955	£25	£10	

DE GALLIER, ZION

Dream Dream Dream	7"	Parlophone	R5710	1968	£10	£5	
Winter Will Be Cold	7"	Parlophone	R5686	1968	£8	£4	

DE LITTLE, JOHNNY

Knack	7"	CBS	201790	1965	£4	£1.50	
Wind And The Rain	7"	Columbia	DB7044	1963	£4	£1.50	

DE LORY, AL

Yesterday	7"	London	HLU9999	1965	£10	£5	

DE LUGG, MILTON ORCHESTRA

Addams Family Theme	7"	Columbia	DB7474	1965	£5	£2	
Munsters Theme	7"	Columbia	DB7762	1966	£6	£2.50	

DE MARCO SISTERS

Bouillabasse	7"	MGM	SP1043	1953	£5	£2	
Dreamboat	7"	Brunswick	05425	1955	£6	£2.50	
Hot Barcarolle	7"	Brunswick	05474	1955	£5	£2	
Love Me	7"	Brunswick	05349	1954	£6	£2.50	
Romance Me	7"	Brunswick	05526	1956	£5	£2	

DE PARIS, SIDNEY

DeParis Dixie	LP	Blue Note	B6501	1969	£10	£4	

DE PARIS, WILBUR

At Symphony Hall	LP	London	LTZK15086/ SAHK6016	1957	£15	£6	
New Orleans Jazz	LP	London	LTZK15024	1957	£15	£6	
Plays Cole Porter	LP	London	LTZK15156	1959	£12	£5	
Something Old, New, Gay Blue	LP	London	LTZK15175/ SAHK6060	1960	£12	£5	
That's A Plenty	LP	London	LTZK15192/ SAHK6079	1960	£12	£5	
Wild Jazz Age	LP	London	LTZK15201/ SAHK6115	1961	£10	£4	

DE ROSA, FRANK

Big Guitar	7"	London	HLD8576	1958	£20	£10	

DE VIVRE, JOY

Our Wedding	7"	Crass	ENVY1	1981	£15	£7.50	*white flexi*

DE VORZON, BARRY

Barbara Jean	7"	RCA	RCA1066	1958	£50	£25	*B side by Jimmy Bell*
Betty Betty	7"	Philips	PB993	1960	£6	£2.50	

DEACON, BOBBY

Fool Was I	7"	Pye	7N15270	1960	£6	£2.50	
I Love You So	7"	Pye	7N15299	1960	£5	£2	

DEACON, GEORGE & MARION ROSS

Sweet William's Ghost	LP	XTRA	XTRA1130	1973	£100	£50	

DEACON BLUE

Chocolate Girl	CD-s	CBS	CDDEAC6	1988	£5	£2	
Dignity	CD-s	CBS	CDDEAC4	1988	£5	£2	
Fergus Sings The Blues	CD-s	CBS	CDDEAC9	1989	£5	£2	
Love And Regret	CD-s	CBS	DEACC10	1989	£5	£2	
Raintown/Riches	CD	CBS	4505490/ XPCD277	1988	£30	£15	*double*
Raintown/Riches	LP	CBS	4505491/ XPR1361	1988	£25	£10	*double*
Real Gone Kid	CD-s	CBS	CDDEAC7	1988	£5	£2	
Riches	LP	CBS	XPR1361	1988	£15	£6	
Wages Day	CD-s	CBS	CDDEAC8	1989	£5	£2	*wallet sleeve*
When Will You Make My Telephone Ring	CD-s	CBS	CDDEAC5	1988	£5	£2	
When Will You Make My Telephone Ring	CD-s	CBS	CPDEAC5	1988	£5	£2	*picture disc*

DEAD BOYS

Sonic Reducer	12"	Sire	6078609	1977	£10	£5	
Tell Me	7"	Sire	SRE1029	1978	£8	£4	
We Have Come For Your Children	LP	Sire	SRK6054	1978	£10	£4	
Young Loud And Snotty	LP	Sire	9103329	1977	£10	£4	

DEAD CAN DANCE

Host Of Seraphim	CD-s	4AD	DCD1	1993	£10	£5	*promo*

DEAD KENNEDYS

Holiday In Cambodia	CD-s	Cherry Red	CDCHERRY13	1988	£5	£2	

DEAD OR ALIVE

Baby Don't Say Goodbye	CD-s	Epic	BURNSC6	1989	£5	£2	
Come Home With Me Baby	CD-s	Epic	BURNSC5	1989	£10	£5	
I'd Do Anything	10"	Epic	QA4069	1984	£8	£3	
I'd Do Anything	7"	Epic	A4069	1984	£4	£1.50	
I'm Falling	7"	Inevitable	INEV005	1980	£8	£4	
Lover Come Back To Me	12"	Epic	QTA6086	1985	£8	£4	*poster sleeve*
Lover Come Back To Me	7"	Epic	WA6086	1985	£5	£2	*shaped picture disc*
Lover Come Back To Me	7"	Epic	A6086	1985	£25	£12.50	
Mighty Mix	12"	Epic	XPR1257	1984	£25	£10	*promo*
Misty Circles	12"	Epic	TA3399	1983	£10	£5	
Misty Circles	7"	Epic	A3399	1983	£5	£2	
My Heart Goes Bang	7"	Epic	DA6571	1985	£4	£1.50	*double*
Nowhere To Nowhere	12"	Black Eyes	BE1	1982	£10	£5	
Number Eleven	7"	Inevitable	INEV008	1981	£5	£2	
Something In My House (Clean & Dirty Mix)	12"	Epic	XPR1328	1987	£60	£30	*promo*
Stranger	7"	Black Eyes	BE2	1982	£6	£2.50	
That's The Way	7"	Epic	WA4271	1984	£4	£1.50	*picture disc*
Turn Around And Count To Ten	12"	Epic	BURNSQ4	1988	£30	£15	
Turn Around And Count To Ten	CD-s	Epic	BURNSC4	1988	£20	£10	*picture disc*
What I Want	12"	Epic	TA3676	1983	£6	£2.50	
What I Want	12"	Epic	TA3676	1983	£10	£5	*with poster*
What I Want	7"	Epic	A3676	1983	£20	£10	*floppy hat picture sleeve*
What I Want	7"	Epic	A3676	1983	£10	£5	*black picture sleeve*
What I Want (Dance Mix)	12"	Epic	TA4510	1984	£6	£2.50	*with poster*
What I Want (Remix)	7"	Epic	A4510	1984	£6	£2.50	*poster sleeve*
You Spin Me Round	7"	Epic	DA4861	1984	£4	£1.50	*double*
Youthquake	CD	Epic	EPC26420	1985	£30	£15	*2 extra 12" mixes*

DEAD SEA FRUIT

Dead Sea Fruit	LP	Camp	603001	1967	£40	£20	
Kensington High Street	7"	Camp	602001	1967	£8	£4	
Loulou Put Another Record On	7" EP	DiscAZ	1126	1967	£20	£10	*French, 2 different sleeves*
Love At The Hippiedrome	7"	Camp	602004	1968	£8	£4	

DEADLY ONES

It's Monster Surfing Time	LP	Vee Jay	LP/VS1090	1964	£20	£8	*US*

DEAL, BILL & THE RHONDELLS

I've Been Hurt	7"	MGM	MGM1479	1969	£5	£2	

DEALER

Better Things To Do	7"	Windrush	WR1030	1983	£40	£20	
First Strike	LP	Ebony	EBON42	1986	£10	£4	

DEAN, ALAN

Rock'n'Roll Tarantella	7"	Columbia	DB3932	1957	£8	£4	

DEAN, ALAN & THE PROBLEMS

Thunder And Rain	7"	Pye	7N15749	1965	£40	£20	
Time It Takes	7"	Decca	F11947	1964	£8	£4	

DEAN, ELTON

Elton Dean (from whom Reg Dwight pinched half of his stage name) was the saxophonist with Soft Machine during the early seventies. Since leaving the group he has followed a busy jazz career, including the recording of several albums in his own name.

Bologna Tapes	LP	Ogun	OG530	1985	£10	£4	
Boundaries	LP	Japo	60033	1980	£10	£4	
Cheque Is In The Mail	LP	Ogun	OG610	1977	£12	£5	
Elton Dean	LP	CBS	64539	1971	£30	£15	
Happy Daze	LP	Ogun	OG910	1977	£12	£5	
Mercy Dash	LP	Culture Press	CP2001	1985	£10	£4	
Oh! For The Edge	LP	Ogun	OG900	1976	£12	£5	
They All Be On This Old Road	LP	Ogun	OG410	1977	£12	£5	
Welcome Live In Brazil 1986	LP	Impetus	IMP18126	1987	£10	£4	

DEAN, JIMMY

Best Of Jimmy Dean	7" EP	CBS	EP6075	1966	£8	£4	
Big Bad John	LP	Philips	BBL7537	1961	£20	£8	
Hour Of Prayer	LP	Columbia	CL1025	1957	£12	£5	*US*

Jimmy Dean	7" EP	Philips	BBE12501	1961	**£10**	**£5**	
Little Black Book	7"	CBS	AAG122	1962	**£4**	**£1.50**	
Smoke Smoke That Cigarette	7"	Philips	PB1223	1962	**£4**	**£1.50**	
Weekend Blues	7"	Philips	PB940	1959	**£5**	**£2**	

DEAN, JOHNNY & THE APACHES

Johnny Dean And The Apaches	LP	Rave	RMG1194	1964	**£100**	**£50**	*South African*

DEAN, LITTLE BILLY

That's Always Like You	7"	Strike	JH325	1967	**£15**	**£7.50**	

DEAN, NORA

Same Thing You Gave To Daddy	7"	Upsetter	US322	1969	**£4**	**£1.50**	*Upsetter Pilgrims B side*

DEAN, PAUL

Although these singles sank without trace, Paul Beuselinck went on to achieve considerable success as an actor and a singer, after changing his stage surname from Dean to Nicholas.

She Can Build A Mountain	7"	Reaction	591002	1966	**£5**	**£2**	*with the Soul Savages*
You Don't Own Me	7"	Decca	F12136	1965	**£8**	**£4**	*with the Thoughts*

DEAN, PAULA & NYAH SHUFFLE

Since I Met You Baby	7"	Joe	JRS2	1970	**£4**	**£1.50**	

DEAN, ROGER

Roger Dean is a painter, whose science-fantasy landscapes were commissioned on several occasions through the seventies for use on LP sleeves. The most well-known of these are the series he produced for Yes, but Dean's sleeves are also to be found on records by the likes of Osibisa, Greenslade, Badger, Keith Tippett, Billy Cox, Paladin, The Gun, Ramases, and, more recently, Asia. All of these are collected by fans of Dean. As it happens, he can also be heard on record – he is the guitarist with John Mayall's Bluesbreakers on the group's first album, *John Mayall Plays John Mayall.*

DEAN, ROGER & LYSIS

Cycle	LP	Mosaic	GCM774	1977	**£12**	**£5**	
Lysis Live	LP	Mosaic	GCM762	1977	**£12**	**£5**	

DEAN & JEAN

Hey Jean Hey Dean	7"	Stateside	SS283	1964	**£6**	**£2.50**	
I Love The Summertime	7"	Stateside	SS249	1964	**£8**	**£4**	
I Wanna Be Loved	7"	Stateside	SS313	1964	**£8**	**£4**	

DEAN & MARK

Just A Step Away	7"	Hickory	451294	1965	**£4**	**£1.50**	
When I Stop Dreaming	7"	Hickory	451249	1964	**£4**	**£1.50**	
With Tears In My Eyes	7"	Hickory	451227	1964	**£4**	**£1.50**	

DEANE, JASON

Down In The Street	7"	King	KG1060	1967	**£30**	**£15**	
Make Believe	7"	King	KG1049	1966	**£15**	**£7.50**	

DEAR MR TIME

Grandfather	LP	Square	SQA101	1970	**£75**	**£37.50**	
Prayer For Her	7"	Square	SQ3	1970	**£6**	**£2.50**	

DEARIE, BLOSSOM

The eccentric name has led more than one collector into supposing that this is some kind of sixties psychedelic group but, in fact, Blossom Dearie is a jazz singer, accompanying her fragile, little girl voice with her own piano playing. Her gushing tribute to Georgie Fame attracted a fair amount of attention when it was first issued, though not enough to actually make it into a hit.

Hey John	7"	Fontana	TF986	1968	**£4**	**£1.50**	
I'm Hip	7"	Fontana	TF719	1966	**£4**	**£1.50**	
Plays For Dancing	10" LP	Felsted	SDL86034	1956	**£15**	**£6**	
Soon It's Gonna Rain	LP	Fontana	STL5454	1968	**£12**	**£5**	
Sweet Blossom Dearie	LP	Fontana	TL5399	1967	**£12**	**£5**	
Sweet Georgie Fame	7"	Fontana	TF788	1967	**£4**	**£1.50**	
That's The Way I Want It To Be	LP	Fontana	6309015	1970	**£10**	**£4**	

DEARLY BELOVED

Peep Peep Pop Pop	7"	CBS	202398	1966	**£6**	**£2.50**	

DEATH ADDICT

Killing Time	7"	Stench	STN1	1983	**£8**	**£4**	

DEATH IN JUNE

And Murder Love	12"	New European	BADVC73T	1985	**£10**	**£5**	
And Murder Love	7"	New European	BADVC73	1985	**£8**	**£4**	
Born Again	12"	New European	BADVC69	1985	**£10**	**£5**	
Born Again	12"	Cenaz	CENAZ09	1988	**£8**	**£4**	*picture disc*
Burial	LP	New European	UBADVC4	199–	**£25**	**£10**	*coloured vinyl*
Heaven Street	12"	New European	SA29634	1984	**£20**	**£10**	*blue & white sleeve*

Heaven Street	12"	New European	SA29634	1984	**£30**	**£15**	*brown & gold sleeve*
Heaven Street	7"	New European	SA29634	1984	**£20**	**£10**	
Holy Water	7"	New European	SA30634	1982	**£15**	**£7.50**	
Nada	LP	New European	BADVC13	1985	**£20**	**£8**	*blue sleeve*
Nada	LP	New European	BADVC13	1985	**£10**	**£4**	*brown sleeve*
She Said Destroy	12"	New European	BADVC6T	1984	**£15**	**£7.50**	
She Said Destroy	7"	New European	BADVC6	1984	**£10**	**£5**	
To Drown A Rose	10"	New European	BADVC10	1987	**£8**	**£3**	
Wall Of Sacrifice	LP	New European	BADVC88	1988	**£30**	**£15**	*green & yellow sleeve*
Wall Of Sacrifice	LP	New European	BADVC88	1988	**£40**	**£20**	*red sleeve*
World That Summer	LP	New European	BADVC9	1988	**£12**	**£5**	*double*

DEBONAIRES

I'm In Love Again	7"	Track	604035	1970	**£10**	**£5**	

DEBRIS

Debris	LP	Static Disposal	PIG0000	1976	**£75**	**£37.50**	*US*

DEBS

Sloopy's Gonna Hang On	7"	Mercury	MF888	1965	**£4**	**£1.50**	

DEB-TONES

Knock, Knock, Who's There?	7"	RCA	RCA1137	1959	**£15**	**£7.50**	

DECEMBER'S CHILDREN

December's Children	LP	Mainstream	6128	1968	**£60**	**£30**	*US*

DECKER, DIANA

Abracadabra	7"	Columbia	SCM5145	1954	**£6**	**£2.50**	
Apples, Peaches And Cherries	7"	Columbia	SCM5173	1955	**£4**	**£1.50**	
Happy Wanderer	7"	Columbia	SCM5096	1954	**£4**	**£1.50**	
Kitty In The Basket	7"	Columbia	SCM5123	1954	**£4**	**£1.50**	
Mama Mia	7"	Columbia	SCM5130	1954	**£5**	**£2**	
Man With The Banjo	7"	Columbia	SCM5120	1954	**£5**	**£2**	
Oh My Papa	7"	Columbia	SCM5083	1954	**£6**	**£2.50**	
Open The Window Of Your Heart	7"	Columbia	SCM5166	1955	**£4**	**£1.50**	
Rock-A-Boogie Baby	7"	Columbia	SCM5246	1956	**£12**	**£6**	

DEDE LIND

Io Non So Da	LP	Mercury	6323093	1972	**£150**	**£75**	*Italian*

DEDICATED MEN'S JUG BAND

Boodle Am Shake	7"	Piccadilly	7N35245	1965	**£4**	**£1.50**	
Don't Come Knocking	7"	Piccadilly	7N35283	1966	**£4**	**£1.50**	

DEE, JEANNIE

Don't Come Home My Little Darling	7"	Beacon	BEA142	1969	**£5**	**£2**	

DEE, JOEY & THE STARLIGHTERS

All The World Is Twistin'	LP	Columbia	33SX1502	1962	**£15**	**£6**	
Back To The Peppermint Lounge Twistin'	LP	Columbia	33SX1461	1962	**£15**	**£6**	
Dance Dance Dance	7"	Columbia	DB7102	1963	**£4**	**£1.50**	
Dance, Dance, Dance	LP	Columbia	33SX1607	1963	**£15**	**£6**	
Doin' The Twist	LP	Columbia	33SX1406	1961	**£15**	**£6**	
Down By The Riverside	7"	Columbia	DB7277	1963	**£4**	**£1.50**	
Hey Let's Twist	LP	Columbia	33SX1421	1962	**£15**	**£6**	
Joey Dee	LP	Columbia	33SX1532	1963	**£15**	**£6**	
Peppermint Twist	7"	Columbia	DB4758	1962	**£4**	**£1.50**	
Two Tickets To Paris	LP	Columbia	33SX1482	1962	**£15**	**£6**	

DEE, JOHNNY

Sitting In The Balcony	7"	Oriole	CB1367	1957	**£100**	**£50**	

DEE, KIKI

Baby I Don't Care	7"	Fontana	TF490	1964	**£4**	**£1.50**	
Early Night	7"	Fontana	TF394	1963	**£5**	**£2**	
En Français	7" EP	Fontana	465323	1966	**£15**	**£7.50**	*French*
Great Expectations	LP	Tamla Motown	STML11158	1970	**£30**	**£15**	
I Was Only Kidding	7"	Fontana	TF414	1963	**£4**	**£1.50**	
I'm Going Out	7"	Fontana	TF792	1967	**£4**	**£1.50**	
I'm Kiki Dee	LP	Fontana	(S)TL5455	1968	**£20**	**£8**	
Kiki Dee	7" EP	Fontana	TE17443	1965	**£20**	**£10**	
Kiki Dee In Clover	7" EP	Fontana	TE17470	1966	**£15**	**£7.50**	
Now The Flowers Cry	7"	Fontana	TF983	1968	**£40**	**£20**	

Our Day Will Come Between Monday & Sunday	7"	Tamla Motown	TMG739	1970	**£5**	**£2**	
Running Out Of Fools	7"	Fontana	TF596	1965	**£4**	**£1.50**	
That's Right Walk On By	7"	Fontana	TF443	1964	**£6**	**£2.50**	
Why Don't I Run Away From You	7"	Fontana	TF669	1966	**£5**	**£2**	

DEE, LENNY

Plantation Boogie	7"	Brunswick	05440	1955	**£4**	**£1.50**	

DEE, RICKY & THE EMBERS

Workout	7"	Stateside	SS136	1962	**£5**	**£2**	

DEE, SANDRA

Tammy Tell Me	7"	Brunswick	05858	1961	**£4**	**£1.50**	

DEE, TOMMY & THE TEEN TONES

Three Stars	7"	Melodisc	1516	1959	**£50**	**£25**	*tri-centre*

DEE & THE DYNAMITES

Blaze Away	7"	Philips	PB1081	1960	**£5**	**£2**	

DEE DEE

Love Is Always	7"	Palette	PB25579	1968	**£15**	**£7.50**	

DEE SET

I Know A Place	7"	Blue Cat	BS146	1968	**£6**	**£2.50**	

DEEJAYS

Black-Eyed Woman	7"	Polydor	56501	1965	**£75**	**£37.50**	
Blackeyed Woman	7" EP	Polydor	27773	1965	**£100**	**£50**	*French*
Deejays	LP	Polydor	LPHM46254	1966	**£100**	**£50**	*Swedish*
Dimples	7"	Polydor	56034	1965	**£40**	**£20**	
Haze	LP	Hep House	HLP02	1967	**£60**	**£30**	*Swedish*

DEELEY, ANTHONY

Anytime Man	7"	Pama	PM728	1968	**£4**	**£1.50**	

DEENE, CAROL

Love Affair	LP	World Records	ST1031	1970	**£20**	**£8**	

DEEP

Psychedelic Moods	LP	Parkway	7051	1966	**£250**	**£150**	*US*

DEEP END

Begged And Borrowed	LP	private	CPLP016	1978	**£10**	**£4**	

DEEP FEELING

Deep Feeling	LP	DJM	DJLPS419	1971	**£25**	**£10**	

DEEP FREEZE MICE

Gates Of Lunch	LP	Mole Embalming	MOLE3	1981	**£10**	**£4**	
Hang On Constance Let Me Hear The News	7"	Cordelia	ERICAT004	198–	**£5**	**£2**	
I Love You Little Bo Bo With Your Delicate Golden Lions	LP	Cordelia	ERICAT001	198–	**£12**	**£5**	*double*
My Geraniums Are Bulletproof	LP	Mole Embalming	MOLE1	1979	**£25**	**£10**	
My Geraniums Are Bulletproof	LP	Mole Embalming	MOLE1	1979	**£50**	**£25**	*various inserts, DIY sleeve*
Rain Is When The Earth Is Television	7"	Cordelia	ERICAT013	198–	**£4**	**£1.50**	
Saw A Ranch Burning Last Night	LP	Mole Embalming	MOLE4	1983	**£10**	**£4**	
Teenage Head In My Refrigerator	LP	Mole Embalming	MOLE2	1981	**£25**	**£10**	
These Floors Are Smooth	7"	Cordelia	ERICAT002	198–	**£6**	**£2.50**	

DEEP PURPLE

Deep Purple are one of the definitive founding fathers of heavy metal, if only for having created the bane of guitar-shop proprietors, 'Smoke On The Water'. The earliest Deep Purple recordings, however, follow much more of a progressive rock policy, with keyboard player Jon Lord trying very hard, if seldom very successfully, to integrate rock with classical music. The group underwent numerous personnel changes during its long life, with only Lord and drummer Ian Paice giving continuity to the different line-ups. What is viewed as the classic version of Deep Purple, with Ian Gillan and Ritchie Blackmore, came together when Gillan joined the band just in time to contribute to Lord's failed experiment, *Concerto For Group And Orchestra*, following which the group turned towards Blackmore's preferred direction, delivering the heavy metal master-work, *Deep Purple In Rock*.

Anthology	LP	EMI	PUR1	1985	**£20**	**£8**	*blue vinyl double*
Bad Attitude	CD-s	Polygram	0800882	1988	**£40**	**£20**	*CD video*
Battle Rages On	LP	BMG	74321154201	1993	**£15**	**£6**	
Concerto For Group And Orchestra	7"	Harvest	PSR325	1970	**£25**	**£12.50**	*promo*
Deep Purple Mark 2 Singles	LP	Purple	TPS3514	1979	**£10**	**£4**	*purple vinyl*
Emmaretta	7"	Parlophone	R5763	1969	**£30**	**£15**	
Fireball	LP	EMI	EJ2603440	1984	**£10**	**£4**	*picture disc, poster*
Hallelujah	7"	Harvest	HAR5006	1969	**£8**	**£4**	
Hallelujah	7"	Harvest	HAR5006	1969	**£200**	**£100**	*promo, picture sleeve*

Title	Format	Label	Cat. No.	Year	£	£	Notes
Hush	7"	Parlophone	R5708	1968	£30	£15	
Hush	7"	Parlophone	R5708	1968	£200	£100	*demo, picture sleeve*
Hush	CD-s	Polydor	PZCD4	1988	£8	£4	
In Rock	LP	EMI	EJ2603430	1984	£10	£4	*picture disc, poster*
Kentucky Woman	7"	Parlophone	R5745	1968	£40	£20	
King Of Dreams	CD-s	RCA	PD49248	1990	£5	£2	
Love Conquers All	CD-s	RCA	PD49226	1991	£5	£2	
Machine Head	LP	EMI	EJ2603450	1984	£10	£4	*picture disc, poster*
Machine Head	LP	Harvest	Q4SHVL7504	1974	£30	£15	*quad*
Shades Of Deep Purple	LP	Parlophone	PMC7055	1968	£75	£37.50	*mono*
Shades Of Deep Purple	LP	Parlophone	PCS7055	1968	£40	£20	*stereo*
Shades Of Deep Purple	LP	Parlophone	PMC/PCS7055	1968	£15	£6	*black & white label*
Shades Of Deep Purple	LP	Harvest	SHSM2016	1980	£15	£6	*sleeve with doll limbs*
Singles A's And B's	LP	Harvest	SHSM2026	1978	£10	£4	*purple vinyl*
Stormbringer	LP	Warner Bros	[illegible]	1975	£20	£8	*US quad*
Woman From Tokyo	7"	Purple	PUR112	1973	£20	£10	

DEEP RIVER BOYS

Title	Format	Label	Cat. No.	Year	£	£	Notes
Deep River Boys	7" EP	HMV	7EG8133	1955	£5	£2	
Deep River Boys	LP	Vik	LXA1019	1956	£50	£25	*US*
Ezikiel Saw The Wheel	7" EP	Nixa	45EP131	1955	£5	£2	
Go On Board Little Children	7" EP	Nixa	45EP113	1955	£5	£2	
Itchy Twitchy Feeling	7"	HMV	POP537	1958	£8	£4	
Midnight Magic	LP	Que	FLS104	1957	£40	£20	*US*
Negro Spirituals	7" EP	HMV	7EG8445	1957	£5	£2	
Nola	7"	Top Rank	JAR172	1959	£4	£1.50	
Not Too Old To Rock And Roll	7"	HMV	POP449	1958	£10	£5	
Presenting The Deep River Boys	LP	Camden	CAL303	1956	£40	£20	*US*
Presenting The Deep River Boys	LP	Capitol	T6050	195–	£20	£8	*US*
Rock A Beating Boogie	7"	HMV	7M361	1956	£15	£7.50	
Romance A La Mode	7" EP	HMV	7EG8321	1957	£5	£2	
Settle Down	7"	HMV	POP1081	1962	£5	£2	
Shake Rattle And Roll	7"	HMV	7M280	1954	£15	£7.50	
Spirituals	10" LP	Waldorf	120	1956	£50	£25	*US*
Spirituals	10" LP	Pye	XLTY138	1954	£12	£5	
Spirituals	10" LP	Nixa	XLPY135	1954	£12	£5	
Spirituals And Jubilees	10" LP	Waldorf	108	1956	£50	£25	*US*
Sweet Mama Tree Top Tall	7"	HMV	7M174	1954	£12	£6	
Swing Low Sweet Chariot	7" EP	Nixa	45EP114	1955	£5	£2	
That's Right	7"	HMV	POP263	1956	£12	£6	
Timbers Gotta Roll	7"	Top Rank	JAR174	1959	£4	£1.50	
Walk Together Children	7" EP	Nixa	45EP130	1955	£5	£2	
Whole Lotta Shaking Going On	7"	HMV	POP395	1957	£15	£7.50	

DEEP SET

Title	Format	Label	Cat. No.	Year	£	£	Notes
I Started A Joke	7"	Major Minor	MM607	1969	£4	£1.50	

DEEP SIX

Title	Format	Label	Cat. No.	Year	£	£	Notes
Deep Six	LP	Liberty	LRP3475/ LST7475	1966	£15	£6	*US*

DEERFIELD

Title	Format	Label	Cat. No.	Year	£	£	Notes
Nil Desperandum	LP	Flat Rock		1971	£100	£50	*US*

DEES, SAM

Title	Format	Label	Cat. No.	Year	£	£	Notes
Handle With Care	7"	Atlantic	K10676	1975	£10	£5	
If It's All Wrong	7"	Major Minor	MM655	1969	£8	£4	
Show Must Go On	LP	Atlantic	K50142	1975	£15	£6	
Storybook Children	7"	Atlantic	K10719	1976	£5	£2	*with Bettye Swann*

DEF LEPPARD

It would be nice to think that the rise to megastardom of Def Leppard had at least something to do with the public's appreciation of the way the group stood by their drummer, Rick Allen, when he lost an arm in an accident. In any event, as with other rock stars of the eighties, Def Leppard have released a multitude of picture discs and special packages geared directly at the collector. There is also a genuine rarity (i.e. one not expressly created by the record company) in the first single, 'Getcha Rocks Off', which was a private pressing running to three separate issues.

Title	Format	Label	Cat. No.	Year	£	£	Notes
Action	CD-s	Phonogram	LEPCD13	1994	£10	£5	*boxed with booklet*
Adrenalize Collectors Box	CD	Bludgeon Riffola	ACB1/2	1994	£200	£100	*2 CD wooden boxed set, Honorary Edition*
Adrenalize Collectors Box	CD	Bludgeon Riffola	ACB1/2	1994	£150	£75	*2 CD wooden boxed set with booklets, certificate, plectrum*
Adrenalize Interview With Joe Elliott	CD	Mercury	SACD508	1992	£15	£6	*US promo*
Adrenalize Mega Edition	CD	Mercury	PHCR16001	1993	£25	£10	*Japanese with bonus live disc*
Animal	12"	Vertigo	LEPC1	1987	£12	£6	*red vinyl*
Animal	CD-s	Polygram	0806262	1989	£60	£30	*CD video*
Animal	CD-s	Phonogram	LEPCD1	1987	£15	£7.50	
Armageddon It	12"	Phonogram	LEPXB4	1988	£10	£5	*boxed, poster, badge, 5 cards*
Armageddon It	CD-s	Phonogram	LEPCD4	1988	£20	£10	
Bringin' On The Heartbreak	12"	Vertigo	LEPP312	1982	£12	£6	
Bringin' On The Heartbreak	7"	Vertigo	LEPP3	1982	£20	£10	
First Strike	LP	Flash	843007	1984	£75	£37.50	*Belgian*
Four Albums	CD	Phonogram	8366062	1989	£40	£20	*4 CD boxed set*

Getcha Rocks Off .... 7" .... Bludgeon Riffola .... SRTS78CUS232 ..... 1979 £**200** ...... £**100** ...... *picture sleeve, lyric insert, red label*
Getcha Rocks Off .... 7" .... Bludgeon Riffola .... MSB001 .... 1979 £**10** .... £**5** .... *yellow label, no picture sleeve*
Getcha Rocks Off .... 7" .... Bludgeon Riffola .... SRTS78CUS232 ..... 1979 £**100** .... £**50** *picture sleeve, red label*
Getcha Rocks Off .... 7" .... Vertigo .... 6059240 .... 1979 £**5** .... £**2** .... *no picture sleeve*
Getcha Rocks Off .... 7" .... Phonogram ...... 6059240 .... 1979 £**15** ...... £**7.50** *mispress with 2 B sides*
Greatest Hits – Vault 1980–1995 .... CD ...... Mercury .... 5286572 .... 1995 £**15** .... £**6** .... *double*
Hello America .... 7" .... Vertigo .... LEPP1 .... 1980 £**6** .... £**2.50** ....
Hysteria .... 12" ...... Phonogram ...... LEPX313 .... 1987 £**8** .... £**4** *envelope sleeve, poster*
Hysteria .... CD ...... Mobile Fidelity .... UDCD580 .... 1993 £**15** .... £**6** .... *US audiophile*
Hysteria .... CD-s ... Phonogram ...... LEPCD3 .... 1988 £**12** .... £**6** ....
Hysteria .... LP .... Phonogram ...... HYSPD1 .... 1987 £**12** .... £**5** .... *picture disc*
Interview With Joe Elliott and Rick Savage .... CD ...... Mercury .... DLINT3 .... 1996 £**20** .... £**8** .... *promo*
Let It Go .... 7" .... Vertigo .... LEPP2 .... 1981 £**6** .... £**2.50** ....
Let It Go .... 7" .... Vertigo .... LEPP2 .... 1981 £**10** .... £**5** .... *with patch*
Let's Get Rocked .... 12" ...... Phonogram ...... DEFXP7 .... 1992 £**6** .... £**2.50** .... *picture disc*
Let's Get Rocked .... CD-s ... Phonogram ...... DEFCD7 .... 1992 £**40** .... £**20** .. *boxed set of 4 picture discs*
Love Bites .... 12" ...... Phonogram ...... LEPXB5 .... 1988 £**10** .... £**5** .... *boxed, 4 cards*
Love Bites .... CD-s ... Phonogram ...... LEPCD5 .... 1988 £**15** ...... £**7.50** ....
Photograph .... 12" ...... Vertigo .... VERX9 .... 1984 £**12** .... £**6** .... *same sleeve as VERX5*
Photograph .... 12" ...... Vertigo .... VERX5 .... 1983 £**12** .... £**6** ....
Photograph .... 7" .... Vertigo .... VER9 .... 1984 £**5** .... £**2** ..... *wallet picture sleeve*
Photograph .... 7" .... Vertigo .... VERP5 .... 1983 £**20** .... £**10** .... *3D sleeve*
Photograph .... 7" .... Vertigo .... VER5 .... 1983 £**6** .... £**2.50** ....
Photograph .... 7" .... Vertigo .... VERQ5 .... 1983 £**15** ...... £**7.50** .... *3D sleeve*
Photograph .... 7" .... Vertigo .... VERG9 .... 1984 £**30** .... £**15** .. *gatefold wallet picture sleeve*
Pour Some Sugar On Me .... 7" .... Phonogram ...... LEPS2 .... 1987 £**8** .... £**4** ...... *shaped picture disc*
Pyromania .... CD ...... Mobile Fidelity .... UDCD520 .... 1989 £**15** .... £**6** .... *US audiophile*
Release Me (Stumpus Maximus) .... 12" ...... Phonogram ...... LEPDK6 .... 1989 £**8** .... £**4** .... *promo*
Rock Of Ages .... 12" ...... Vertigo .... VERX6 .... 1983 £**10** .... £**5** ....
Rock Of Ages .... 7" .... Vertigo .... VERQ6 .... 1983 £**25** .... £**12.50** .... *cube sleeve*
Rock Of Ages .... 7" .... Vertigo .... VERP6 .... 1983 £**8** .... £**4** ...... *shaped picture disc*
Rock Of Ages .... CD ...... Polygram .... 0800342 .... 1989 £**20** .... £**8** .... *CD video*
Rocket .... 12" ...... Phonogram ...... LEPXP6 .... 1989 £**12** .... £**6** .. *numbered picture disc*
Rocket .... 12" ...... Phonogram ...... LEPXP6 .... 1989 £**6** .... £**2.50** .... *picture disc*
Rocket .... CD ...... Polygram .... 0809902 .... 1989 £**15** .... £**6** .... *CD video*
Rocket .... CD-s ... Phonogram ...... LEPCD6 .... 1989 £**20** .... £**10** ....
Slang .... CD ...... Mercury .... 5324932 .... 1996 £**15** .... £**6** .... *double*
Tonight .... CD-s ... Phonogram ...... LEPCD10 .... 1993 £**25** .... £**12.50** .... *double single, etched case*
Too Late For Love .... 12" ...... Vertigo .... VERX8 .... 1983 £**10** .... £**5** ....
Too Late For Love .... 7" .... Vertigo .... VER8 .... 1983 £**6** .... £**2.50** ....
Too Late For Love .... 7" .... Vertigo .... VER8 .... 1983 £**40** .... £**20** .... *soccer strip picture sleeve*
Two Steps Behind .... CD-s ... Phonogram ...... LEPTN12 .... 1993 £**5** .... £**2** .... *metal tin*
Wasted .... 7" .... Vertigo .... 6059247 .... 1979 £**6** .... £**2.50** .... *picture sleeve*

DEFENDANTS

Headmaster .... 7" .... Edible .... EAT001 .... 198– £**10** .... £**5** ....

DEFENDERS

Drag Beat .... LP .... Del-Fi .... DFLP1242 .... 1964 £**40** .... £**20** .... *US*

DEFENDERS (2)

Set Them Free .... 7" .... Doctor Bird ..... DB1104 .... 1967 £**10** .... £**5** ....

DEFINITION OF SOUND

Now Is Tomorrow .... CD-s ... Circa .... YRCD54 .... 1990 £**5** .... £**2** ....
Wear Your Love Like Heaven .... CD-s ... Circa .... YRCD61 .... 1991 £**5** .... £**2** ....

DE-HEMS

Don't Cross That Line .... 7" .... President .... PT388 .... 1972 £**5** .... £**2** ....

DEINING

Deining .... LP .... Crossroad .... 1982 £**50** .... £**25** .... *Dutch*

DEIRDRE

Deirdre .... LP .... Polydor .... 1972 £**150** .... £**75** .... *Irish*
Deirdre .... LP .... Philips .... 1977 £**100** .... £**50** .... *Dutch*

DEJOHNETTE, JACK

Untitled .... LP .... ECM .... ECM1074ST .... 1976 £**15** .... £**6** ....

DEKKER, DESMOND

007 .... 7" .... Pyramid .... PYR6004 .... 1967 £**4** .... £**1.50** .... *Roland Alphonso B side*
007 Shanty Town .... LP .... Doctor Bird ..... DLM5007 .... 1967 £**60** .... £**30** ....
Beautiful And Dangerous .... 7" .... Pyramid .... PYR6031 .... 1968 £**8** .... £**4** ....

Title	Format	Label	Cat. No.	Year			Notes
Bongo Gal	7"	Pyramid	PYR6035	1968	**£8**	**£4**	
Christmas Day	7"	Pyramid	PYR6059	1969	**£5**	**£2**	
Double Dekker	LP	Trojan	TRLD401	1973	**£12**	**£5**	*double*
Dracula	7"	Black Swan	WI455	1965	**£12**	**£6**	*Don Drummond B side*
Get Up Edna	7"	Island	WI181	1965	**£10**	**£5**	
Hey Grandma	7"	Pyramid	PYR6047	1968	**£8**	**£4**	
Honour Your Mother And Father	7"	Island	WI054	1963	**£10**	**£5**	
Israelites	7"	Pyramid	PYR6058	1969	**£4**	**£1.50**	*Beverley's Allstars B side*
Israelites	LP	Doctor Bird	DLM5013	1969	**£40**	**£20**	
It Mek	7"	Pyramid	PYR6054	1968	**£8**	**£4**	
It Mek	7"	Pyramid	PYR6068	1969	**£4**	**£1.50**	
It Pays	7"	Pyramid	PYR6026	1968	**£8**	**£4**	
J[illegible]	7"	Island	WI158	1964	**£10**	**£5**	
Mother Pepper	7"	Pyramid	PYR6044	1968	**£8**	**£4**	
Mother's Young Gal	7"	Pyramid	PYR6012	1967	**£8**	**£4**	*Soul Brothers B side*
Music Like Dirt	7"	Pyramid	PYR6051	1968	**£8**	**£4**	
Parents	7"	Island	WI111	1963	**£10**	**£5**	
Pickney Girl	7"	Pyramid	PYR6078	1970	**£4**	**£1.50**	
Sabotage	7"	Pyramid	PYR6020	1967	**£8**	**£4**	
This Is Desmond Dekker	LP	Trojan	TTL4	1969	**£12**	**£5**	
This Woman	7"	Island	WI202	1965	**£10**	**£5**	*Lee Perry B side*
To Sir With Love	7"	Pyramid	PYR6037	1968	**£8**	**£4**	
Unity	7"	Pyramid	PYR6017	1967	**£8**	**£4**	
You Can Get It If You Really Want	7"	Trojan	TR7777	1970	**£4**	**£1.50**	
You Can Get It If You Really Want	LP	Trojan	TBL146	1970	**£12**	**£5**	

DEL AMITRI

Title	Format	Label	Cat. No.	Year			Notes
Hammering Heart	12"	Chrysalis	CHS122925	1985	**£6**	**£2.50**	
Kiss This Thing Goodbye	CD-s	A&M	AMCD551	1990	**£5**	**£2**	
Medicine	CD-s	A&M	5823652/3672	1997	**£10**	**£5**	*2 versions*
Move Away Jimmy Blue	CD-s	A&M	AMCD555	1990	**£5**	**£2**	
Nothing Ever Happens	CD-s	A&M	AMCD536	1990	**£6**	**£2.50**	
Sense Sickness	7"	No Strings	NOSP1	1983	**£20**	**£10**	
Spit In The Rain	CD-s	A&M	AMCD589	1990	**£5**	**£2**	
Sticks And Stones Girl	12"	Chrysalis	CHS122859	1985	**£6**	**£2.50**	
Sticks And Stones Girl	7"	Chrysalis	CHS2859	1985	**£4**	**£1.50**	
Stone Cold Sober	CD-s	A&M	CDEE527	1989	**£5**	**£2**	
Twisted	CD	A&M	5403962	1995	**£15**	**£6**	*double*

DEL FUEGO, TERESA

Title	Format	Label	Cat. No.	Year			Notes
Don't Hang Up	7"	Satril	HH155	1981	**£5**	**£2**	

DEL SATINS

Title	Format	Label	Cat. No.	Year			Notes
Out To Lunch	LP	B.T.Puppy	BTPS1019	1972	**£20**	**£8**	*US*

DEL VIKINGS

Title	Format	Label	Cat. No.	Year			Notes
Angel Up In Heaven	7"	HMV	POP1145	1963	**£6**	**£2.50**	
Come Go With Me	7"	London	HLD8405	1957	**£100**	**£50**	*gold label*
Come Go With Me	LP	Dot	DLP3695	1966	**£75**	**£37.50**	*US*
Come Go With The Del Vikings	LP	Luniverse	LP1000	1957	**£250**	**£150**	*US*
Confession Of Love	7"	HMV	POP1072	1962	**£6**	**£2.50**	
Cool Shake	78	Mercury	MT169	1957	**£10**	**£5**	
Del Vikings And The Sonnets	LP	Crown	CLP5368	1963	**£25**	**£10**	*US*
Flat Tyre	7"	Mercury	AMT1027	1959	**£40**	**£20**	
Swinging, Singing Record Session	LP	Mercury	MG20353	1958	**£150**	**£75**	*US*
They Sing They Swing	LP	Mercury	MG20314	1957	**£150**	**£75**	*US*
Voodoo Man	7"	Mercury	7MT199	1958	**£40**	**£20**	
Whispering Bells	7"	London	HLD8464	1957	**£30**	**£15**	

DELACARDOS

Title	Format	Label	Cat. No.	Year			Notes
Mister Dillon	7"	HMV	POP890	1961	**£15**	**£7.50**	

DELANEY, ERIC

Title	Format	Label	Cat. No.	Year			Notes
Hi-Fi Delaney	10" LP	Pye		195–	**£15**	**£6**	

DELANEY & BONNIE

The sense of well-being and fun that spills over from Delaney and Bonnie's records attracted some famous names to their cause – George Harrison, Dave Mason and Eric Clapton were all perfectly content to play as sidemen within the band for a while. The LP *Accept No Substitute* was to have appeared on the Apple label, but was eventually released on Elektra. Apple test pressings exist, but no cover has ever been found. Meanwhile, Eric Clapton's thrilling contributions to the Delaney and Bonnie sound can be sampled on the LP *On Tour*.

Title	Format	Label	Cat. No.	Year			Notes
Accept No Substitute (The Original Delaney & Bonnie)	LP	Apple	SAPCOR7	1969	**£600**	**£400**	*test pressing, no sleeve*
Accept No Substitute (The Original Delaney & Bonnie)	LP	Elektra	EKS74039	1969	**£10**	**£4**	
Get Ourselves Together	7"	Elektra	EKSN45066	1969	**£5**	**£2**	
On Tour	LP	Atlantic	2400013	1970	**£10**	**£4**	

DELFONICS

Title	Format	Label	Cat. No.	Year			Notes
La La Means I Love You	LP	Bell	SBLL106	1968	**£10**	**£4**	
Sound Of Sexy Soul	LP	Bell	SBLL121	1969	**£10**	**£4**	

DELICATES

Title	Format	Label	Number	Year	Mint	VG	Notes
Ronnie Is My Lover	7"	London	HLT8953	1959	£75	£37.50	
Too Young To Date	7"	London	HLT9176	1960	£30	£15	

DELIRIUM

Title	Format	Label	Number	Year	Mint	VG	Notes
Three	LP	Fonit	LPX29	1974	£100	£50	*Italian*

D'ELL, DENNIS

Title	Format	Label	Number	Year	Mint	VG	Notes
It Breaks My Heart In Two	7"	CBS	202605	1967	£75	£37.50	*demo*
It Breaks My Heart In Two	7"	CBS	202605	1967	£150	£75	

DELLO, PETE

Title	Format	Label	Number	Year	Mint	VG	Notes
Into Your Ears	LP	Nepentha	6437001	1971	£60	£30	

DELLS

Title	Format	Label	Number	Year	Mint	VG	Notes
Bossa Nova Bird	7"	Pye	7N25178	1963	£8	£4	
Greatest Hits	LP	Chess	CRLS4554	1968	£12	£5	
It's All Up To You	7"	Chess	6145008	1972	£4	£1.50	
It's Not Unusual	LP	Vee Jay	LP(S)1141	1965	£15	£6	*US*
Like It Is	LP	Cadet	837	1969	£10	£4	*US*
Love Is Blue – I Can Sing A Rainbow	LP	Chess	CRLS4555	1969	£12	£5	
Musical Menu	LP	Cadet	822	1968	£12	£5	*US*
Oh What A Nite	LP	Vee Jay	VJLP1010	1959	£100	£50	*US*
Oo I Love You	7"	Chess	CRS8066	1967	£4	£1.50	
Stay In My Corner	7"	Chess	CRS8079	1968	£4	£1.50	
There Is	LP	Cadet	804	1968	£12	£5	*US*
Wear It On Our Face	7"	Chess	CRS8071	1968	£5	£2	

DELMORE BROTHERS

Title	Format	Label	Number	Year	Mint	VG	Notes
Country And Western	7" EP	Parlophone	GEP8728	1958	£15	£7.50	
In Memory	LP	King	910	1964	£12	£5	*US*
In Memory Vol. 2	LP	King	920	1964	£12	£5	*US*
Songs By The Delmore Brothers	LP	King	589	1958	£30	£15	*US*
Thirtieth Anniversary Album	LP	King	785	1962	£25	£10	*US*
Twenty-Four Great Country Songs	LP	King	(S)983	1966	£12	£5	*US*

DELTA BLUES BAND

Title	Format	Label	Number	Year	Mint	VG	Notes
Delta Blues Band	LP	Parlophone	6E06237038	1969	£150	£75	*Danish*
No Overdubs	LP	KB	KBLP4	1979	£20	£8	*Danish*
Rave On	LP	Medley	6031	1979	£20	£8	*Danish*

DELTA CATS

Title	Format	Label	Number	Year	Mint	VG	Notes
I Can't Re-Live	7"	Bamboo	BAM3	1969	£5	£2	
Unworthy Baby	7"	Blue Cat	BS128	1968	£8	£4	*Thrillers B side*

DELTA KINGS

Title	Format	Label	Number	Year	Mint	VG	Notes
At Sundown	7" EP	London	RER1318	1961	£5	£2	
Down The River	LP	London	LTZR15180	1960	£10	£4	

DELTA RHYTHM BOYS

Title	Format	Label	Number	Year	Mint	VG	Notes
Mood Indigo	7"	Brunswick	05353	1954	£4	£1.50	
Sixteen Tons	7" EP	Felsted	ESD3064	1958	£5	£2	
With The Metronome All Stars	10" LP	Esquire	15001	1952	£12	£5	

DELTA SKIFFLE GROUP

Title	Format	Label	Number	Year	Mint	VG	Notes
Delta Skiffle Group	7" EP	Esquire	EP162	1958	£30	£15	

DELTAS

Title	Format	Label	Number	Year	Mint	VG	Notes
Georgia	7"	Blue Beat	BB265	1964	£12	£6	
Visitor	7"	Blue Beat	BB275	1965	£12	£6	*Skatalites B side*

DELTONES

Title	Format	Label	Number	Year	Mint	VG	Notes
Rocking Blues	7"	Top Rank	JAR171	1959	£40	£20	

DELUSION

Title	Format	Label	Number	Year	Mint	VG	Notes
Pessimists Paradise	7"	Wizzo	WIZZO2	198–	£5	£2	

DEMENSIONS

Title	Format	Label	Number	Year	Mint	VG	Notes
Count Your Blessings Instead Of Sheep	7"	Coral	Q72437	1961	£6	£2.50	
Over The Rainbow	7"	Top Rank	JAR505	1960	£30	£15	

DEMIAN

Title	Format	Label	Number	Year	Mint	VG	Notes
Demian	LP	ABC	ABC5718	1971	£40	£20	*US*

DEMOB

Title	Format	Label	Number	Year	Mint	VG	Notes
Anti Police	7"	Round Ear	ROUND1	1981	£6	£2.50	*fold-out sleeve*

DEMON FUZZ

Title	Format	Label	Number	Year	Mint	VG	Notes
Afreaka	LP	Dawn	DNLS3013	1971	£25	£10	
I Put A Spell On You	7"	Sawn	DNX2504	1970	£6	£2.50	*picture sleeve*

DEMON PACT

Title	Format	Label	Number	Year	Mint	VG	Notes
Eaten Alive	7"	Slime	PACT1	1981	£20	£10	

DEMON PREACHER

Title	Format	Label	Number	Year	Mint	VG	Notes
Little Miss Perfect	7"	Small Wonder	SMALL10	1978	£5	£2	
Royal Northern	7"	Illegal	SRTS78110	1978	£10	£5	

DEMON THOR

Title	Format	Label	Cat. No.	Year	Mint	VG	Notes
Anno 1972	LP	United Artists	UAS29393	1972	£25	£10	
Written In The Sky	LP	United Artists	UAS29496	1974	£25	£10	

DEMONS

Title	Format	Label	Cat. No.	Year	Mint	VG	Notes
Bless You	7"	Big Shot	BI523	1969	£4	£1.50	

DEMONS (2)

Title	Format	Label	Cat. No.	Year	Mint	VG	Notes
Action By Example	7"	Crypt Music	DEM1	1980	£5	£2	

DEMPSEY, TOMMY & JOHN SWIFT

Title	Format	Label	Cat. No.	Year	Mint	VG	Notes
Green Grow The Laurel	LP	Trailer	LER2096	1976	£10	£4	

DENE, TERRY

Title	Format	Label	Cat. No.	Year	Mint	VG	Notes
Bimbombey	7"	Decca	F11100	1959	£5	£2	
Call To The Wind	LP	Pilgrim	JLPS188	1973	£10	£4	
Come And Get It	7"	Decca	F10938	1957	£10	£5	
Come In And Be Loved	7"	Decca	F10977	1958	£10	£5	
Feminine Look	7"	Aral	PS107	1963	£6	£2.50	*picture sleeve*
Geraldine	7"	Oriole	CB1562	1960	£8	£4	
Golden Disc	7" EP	Decca	DFE6427	1957	£25	£12.50	
I Thought Terry Dene Was Dead	LP	Decca	SPA368	1974	£10	£4	
I've Come Of Age	7"	Decca	F11136	1959	£5	£2	
If That Isn't Love	LP	Pilgrim	JLPS175	1972	£10	£4	
Like A Baby	7"	Oriole	CB1594	1961	£8	£4	
Lucky Lucky Bobby	7"	Decca	F10964	1957	£10	£5	
Pretty Little Pearly	7"	Decca	F11076	1958	£8	£4	
Seven Steps To Love	7"	Decca	F11037	1958	£6	£2.50	
Stairway Of Love	7"	Decca	F11016	1958	£6	£2.50	
Start Moving	7"	Decca	F10914	1957	£12	£6	
Terry Dene No. 1	7" EP	Decca	DFE6459	1958	£25	£12.50	
Terry Dene No. 2	7" EP	Decca	DFE6507	1958	£25	£12.50	
Terry Dene Now	7" EP	Herald	ELR107	1966	£8	£4	
Thank You Pretty Baby	7"	Decca	F11154	1959	£8	£4	
White Sports Coat	7"	Decca	F10895	1957	£20	£10	

DENE BOYS

Title	Format	Label	Cat. No.	Year	Mint	VG	Notes
Bye Bye Love	7"	HMV	POP374	1957	£6	£2.50	

DENE FOUR

Title	Format	Label	Cat. No.	Year	Mint	VG	Notes
Hush-A-Bye	7"	HMV	POP666	1959	£8	£4	

DENIGH

Title	Format	Label	Cat. No.	Year	Mint	VG	Notes
No Way	7"	Ace	ACE16	1980	£30	£15	

DENIMS

Title	Format	Label	Cat. No.	Year	Mint	VG	Notes
I'm Your Man	7"	CBS	201807	1965	£30	£15	

DENISON, ROGER

Title	Format	Label	Cat. No.	Year	Mint	VG	Notes
I'm On An Island	7"	Parlophone	R5545	1966	£6	£2.50	
She Wanders Through My Mind	7"	Parlophone	R5566	1967	£4	£1.50	

DENNING, WADE & THE PORT WASHINGTONS

Title	Format	Label	Cat. No.	Year	Mint	VG	Notes
Tarzan's March	7"	MGM	MGM1339	1967	£5	£2	

DENNIS, CATHY

Title	Format	Label	Cat. No.	Year	Mint	VG	Notes
Irresistible	12"	Polydor	CATHX7	1992	£15	£7.50	
Just Another Dream	12"	Polydor	CATHR1	1989	£6	£2.50	

DENNIS, D. D., PAT RHODEN & BROTHER LLOYD'S ALL STARS

Title	Format	Label	Cat. No.	Year	Mint	VG	Notes
Rock Steady Hits Of '69	LP	Fontana	SFL13116	1969	£12	£5	

DENNIS, DENZIL

Title	Format	Label	Cat. No.	Year	Mint	VG	Notes
Donkey Train	7"	Trojan	TR614	1968	£6	£2.50	
Hush Don't You Cry	7"	Trojan	TR615	1968	£6	£2.50	
Oh Carol	7"	Jolly	JY011	1968	£5	£2	
Seven Nights In Rome	7"	Blue Beat	BB181	1963	£12	£6	

DENNIS, JACKIE

Title	Format	Label	Cat. No.	Year	Mint	VG	Notes
Gingerbread	7"	Decca	F11090	1958	£4	£1.50	
Jackie Dennis No. 1	7" EP	Decca	DFE6513	1958	£20	£10	
La Dee Dah	7"	Decca	F10992	1958	£4	£1.50	
Miss Valerie	7"	Decca	F11011	1958	£6	£2.50	
More Than Ever	7"	Decca	F11060	1958	£4	£1.50	
Purple People Eater	7"	Decca	F11033	1958	£8	£4	

DENNIS & LIZZY

Title	Format	Label	Cat. No.	Year	Mint	VG	Notes
Everybody Bawlin'	7"	Camel	CA56	1970	£5	£2	

DENNISONS

Title	Format	Label	Cat. No.	Year	Mint	VG	Notes
Be My Girl	7"	Decca	F11691	1963	£8	£4	
Nobody Like My Babe	7"	Decca	F11990	1964	£8	£4	
Walking The Dog	7"	Decca	F11880	1964	£8	£4	

DENNY, MARTIN

Title	Format	Label	Cat. No.	Year	Mint	VG	Notes
Afrodesia	LP	London	HAU2196/ SAHU6048	1959	£20	£8	

Enchanted Sea	LP	London	HAG2281/ SAHG6098	1960	£15	£6	
Exotic Percussion	LP	London	HAG2387/ SAHG6187	1961	£12	£5	
Exotic Sounds	7" EP	London	REU1241	1960	£15	£7.50	
Exotica	10" LP	London	HBU1079	1957	£25	£10	
Exotica	LP	London	SAHW6062	1960	£20	£8	
Exotica Vol. 2	LP	London	HAG2254/ SAHG6076	1960	£15	£6	
Exotica Vol. 3	LP	London	HAW2239/ SAHW6089	1960	£15	£6	
Forbidden Island	LP	London	SAHU6004	1958	£25	£10	
Hawaii Tattoo	LP	Liberty	LBY1241	1964	£12	£5	
Hawaii Touch	LP	Liberty	(S)LBY1354	1966	£10	£4	
Latin Village	LP	Liberty	(S)LBY1221	1965	£10	£4	
Martin Denny Plays	LP	Liberty	(S)LBY1301	1966	£10	£4	
Quiet Village	7"	London	SLW4004	1959	£15	£7.50	*stereo*
Quiet Village	LP	London	HAU2208/ SAHU6055	1960	£15	£6	
Romantica	LP	London	HAG2417/ SAHG6215	1962	£12	£5	
Silver Screen	LP	London	HAG2317/ SAHG6122	1961	£12	£5	
Spanish Village	LP	Liberty	(S)LBY1267	1965	£10	£4	
Twenty Golden Hawaiian Hits	LP	Liberty	(S)LBY1276	1966	£10	£4	

DENNY, SANDY

Despite the acclaim she continues to receive, Sandy Denny was something of a limited singer. She is hopeless on uptempo rock material, but she does indeed sound gorgeous on a slow ballad – as her recording of 'The Sea' with Fotheringay proves at a stroke. The small number of early, pre-Fairport Convention tracks are spread somewhat thinly over various LPs. The album with Johnny Silvo, for example, is not a collaboration, but merely includes songs recorded by each separately. The Strawbs LP, however, is a true joint effort.

All Our Own Work	LP	Pickwick	SHM813	1973	£12	£5	*with the Strawbs*
Candle In The Wind	7"	Island	WIP6391	1977	£50	£25	*demo only*
Like An Old Fashioned Waltz	LP	Island	ILPS9258	1973	£15	£6	
Listen Listen	7"	Island	WIP6142	1972	£4	£1.50	
Make Me A Pallet On Your Floor	7"	Mooncrest	MOON54	1976	£4	£1.50	
Northstar Grass Man & The Ravens	LP	Island	ILPS9165	1971	£15	£6	
Pass Of Arms EP	7"	Island	WIP6141	1972	£75	£37.50	*picture sleeve*
Rendezvous	LP	Island	ILPS9433	1977	£10	£4	*with insert*
Sandy	LP	Island	ILPS9207	1972	£15	£6	
Sandy And Johnny	LP	Saga	EROS8041	1967	£30	£15	*with Johnny Silvo*
Sandy Denny	LP	Mooncrest	CREST28	1978	£25	£10	*1 extra track*
Sandy Denny	LP	Saga	EROS8153	1970	£30	£15	
Whispering Grass	7"	Island	WIP6176	1973	£5	£2	*picture sleeve*
Who Knows Where The Time Goes	LP	Island	SDSP100	1985	£25	£10	*4 LP box set*

DENNY, SUSAN

Don't Touch Me	7"	Melodisc	MEL1596	1965	£6	£2.50	

DENTON, MICKEY

Steady Kind	7"	London	HLX9398	1961	£5	£2	

DENTON, RICHARD & MARTIN COOK

Quiller	7"	BBC	RESL25	1975	£5	£2	

DENVER, KARL

At The Yew Tree	LP	Decca	LK4540	1963	£12	£5	
By A Sleepy Lagoon	7" EP	Decca	DFE8501	1962	£8	£4	
Karl Denver	LP	Ace Of Clubs	ACL1131	1962	£12	£5	
Karl Denver Hits	7" EP	Decca	DFE8504	1962	£8	£4	
Wimoweh	LP	Ace Of Clubs	ACL1098	1961	£12	£5	
With Love	LP	Decca	LK4596	1964	£15	£6	

DENVER, NIGEL

Borderline	LP	Decca	LK5014	1969	£10	£4	
Folk, Old And New	LP	Decca	SKL4943	1968	£12	£5	
Movin' On	LP	Decca	LK4728	1966	£15	£6	
Rebellion	LP	Decca	SKL4844	1967	£12	£5	
Scottish Nationalist Songs	LP	Major Minor	MMLP1	1967	£12	£5	
There Was A Lad	LP	Major Minor	MMLP38	1968	£12	£5	

DENVERS

Do You Love Me	7" EP	Polydor	27114	1964	£10	£5	*French*
Liverpool Party	LP	Polydor	46144	1964	£50	£25	*French*

DENZIL & PAT

Dream	7"	Downtown	DT403	1969	£4	£1.50	

DEPECHE MODE

Behind The Wheel	CD-s	Mute	CDBONG15	1988	£5	£2	
Behind The Wheel (Beatmasters Mix)	12"	Mute	L12BONG15	1988	£6	£2.50	
Behind The Wheel (Shep Pettibone Mix)	12"	Mute	DBONG15	1987	£6	£2.50	*promo*
Blasphemous Rumours	CD-s	Mute	INT826839	1987	£5	£2	*German import*
Depeche Mode	CD-s	Mute	DMBX2	1991	£20	£10	*6 CD singles, boxed*
Depeche Mode	CD-s	Mute	DMBX1	1991	£20	£10	*6 CD singles, boxed*

Depeche Mode	CD-s	Mute	DMBX3	1991	**£20**	**£10**	*6 CD singles, boxed*
Enjoy The Silence	12"	Mute	P12BONG18	1990	**£6**	**£2.50**	*promo*
Enjoy The Silence	CD-s	Mute	CDBONG18	1990	**£5**	**£2**	
Enjoy The Silence	CD-s	Mute	LCDBONG18	1990	**£10**	**£5**	
Enjoy The Silence (The Quad)	CD-s	Mute	XLCDBONG18	1990	**£15**	**£7.50**	*3" single*
Everything Counts (Absolute Mix)	10"	Mute	10BONG16	1989	**£6**	**£2.50**	
Everything Counts (Edit)	7"	Mute	7BONG16R	1989	**£5**	**£2**	*promo*
Everything Counts (Live)	CD-s	Mute	CDBONG16	1989	**£5**	**£2**	
Everything Counts (Simenon & Saunders Mix)	12"	Mute	P12BONG16	1989	**£6**	**£2.50**	*promo*
Everything Counts (Simenon & Saunders Mix)	CD-s	Mute	LCDBONG16	1989	**£20**	**£10**	*3" single*
Leave In Silence	CD-s	Intercord	INT826807	1988	**£5**	**£2**	
Love In Itself	CD-s	Mute	INT826836	1987	**£5**	**£2**	*German import*
Master And Servant	12"	Mute	L12BONG6	1984	**£6**	**£2.50**	
Music For The Masses	CD	Mute	CDSTUMM47	1987	**£20**	**£8**	*test pressing with 10 tracks*
Music For The Masses	LP	Mute	STUMM47	1987	**£10**	**£4**	*HMV limited edition with promo 12" (HMV1)*
Music For The Masses	LP	Mute	STUMM47	1987	**£10**	**£4**	*clear or blue vinyl*
Never Let Me Down Again	12"	Mute	P12BONG14	1987	**£6**	**£2.50**	*promo*
Never Let Me Down Again	CD-s	Mute	CDBONG14	1987	**£6**	**£2.50**	
People Are People (On U Sound Mix)	12"	Mute	L12BONG5	1984	**£6**	**£2.50**	
Personal Jesus	12"	Mute	P12BONG17	1989	**£6**	**£2.50**	*promo*
Personal Jesus	CD-s	Mute	CDBONG17	1989	**£5**	**£2**	*3" single*
Personal Jesus	CD-s	Mute	LCDBONG17	1989	**£12**	**£6**	
Policy Of Truth	CD-s	Mute	CDBONG19	1990	**£5**	**£2**	
Policy Of Truth (Capitol Mix)	12"	Mute	P12BONG19	1990	**£6**	**£2.50**	*promo*
Policy Of Truth (Trancentral Mix)	CD-s	Mute	LCDBONG19	1990	**£6**	**£2.50**	
Sometimes I Wish I Was Dead	7"	Lyntone	LYN10209	1981	**£6**	**£2.50**	*Flexipop flexi*
Strangelove	CD-s	Mute	CDBONG13	1987	**£5**	**£2**	
Strangelove (Blind Mix)	12"	Mute	L12BONG13	1987	**£6**	**£2.50**	
Strangelove (Fresh Ground Mix)	12"	Mute	DANCEBONG13	1987	**£25**	**£12.50**	*promo*
Strangelove (Hijack Mix)	12"	Mute	PP12BONG16	1989	**£8**	**£4**	*promo*
Strangelove (Maxi-Mix)	12"	Mute	S12BONG13	1987	**£6**	**£2.50**	*promo*
Stripped	12"	Mute	12BONG10	1986	**£6**	**£2.50**	*promo*
Violator	12"	Mute	PSTUMM64	1990	**£8**	**£4**	*promo sampler*
Violator	CD	Mute	CDSTUMM64	1989	**£100**	**£50**	*promo box set, with LP and cassette*
World In My Eyes	CD-s	Mute	CDBONG20	1990	**£5**	**£2**	
World In My Eyes (Dub In My Eyes)	CD-s	Mute	LCDBONG20	1990	**£20**	**£10**	
World In My Eyes (Mayhem Mode)	12"	Mute	P12BONG20	1990	**£6**	**£2.50**	*promo*

DEPUTIES

Given Half A Chance	7"	Strike	JH305	1966	**£5**	**£2**	

DEREK, JON

Songs I Have Written	LP	Westwood	WR5098	1976	**£20**	**£8**	

DEREK & THE DOMINOES

Layla And Other Assorted Love Songs	LP	Polydor	2625005	1971	**£12**	**£5**	*double*
Tell The Truth	7"	Polydor	2058057	1970	**£30**	**£15**	

DEREK & THE FRESHMEN

Gone Away	7"	Oriole	CB305	1965	**£5**	**£2**	

DES, HENRI

Return	7"	United Artists	UP35109	1970	**£8**	**£4**	

DES ALL STARS

Henry The Great	7"	Grape	GR3016	1970	**£4**	**£1.50**	
If I Had A Hammer	7"	Grape	GR3015	1970	**£4**	**£1.50**	
Night Food Reggae	7"	Grape	GR3014	1970	**£4**	**£1.50**	

DES BARRES, MICHAEL

Leon	7"	Purple	PUR123	1974	**£5**	**£2**	

DESANTO, SUGAR PIE

I Don't Wanna Fuss	7"	Pye	7N25267	1964	**£8**	**£4**	
Soulful Dress	7"	Pye	7N25249	1964	**£10**	**£5**	
Soulful Dress	7"	Chess	CRS8093	1969	**£4**	**£1.50**	
Sugar Pie	LP	Checker	LP2979	1961	**£30**	**£15**	*US*
There's Gonna Be Trouble	7"	Chess	CRS8034	1966	**£6**	**£2.50**	

DESCENDANTS

Garden Of Eden	7"	CBS	202545	1967	**£40**	**£20**	

DESHANNON, JACKIE

Are You Ready For This?	LP	Liberty	(S)BLY3085	1966	**£12**	**£5**	
Breakin' It Up On The Beatles Tour	LP	Liberty	LRP3390/ LST7390	1964	**£20**	**£8**	*US*
C'Mon Let's Live A Little	LP	Liberty	LRP3430/ LST7430	1966	**£10**	**£4**	*US*
Come On Down	7"	Liberty	LIB66224	1966	**£6**	**£2.50**	
Don't Turn Your Back On Me	7"	Liberty	LIB10175	1964	**£4**	**£1.50**	
Don't Turn Your Back On Me	LP	Liberty	LBY1245	1965	**£12**	**£5**	
Great Performances	LP	Liberty	LBS83117	1968	**£12**	**£5**	

In The Wind	LP	Imperial	LP9296/12296	1965	£10	£4	US
Jackie	7" EP	Liberty	LEP2233	1965	£15	£7.50	
Jackie	LP	Atlantic	K40396	1972	£10	£4	
Jackie DeShannon	LP	Liberty	LBY1182	1963	£15	£6	
Me About You	LP	Liberty	LBS83148E	1969	£10	£4	
Needles And Pins	7"	Liberty	LIB55563	1963	£5	£2	
Put A Little Love In Your Heart	LP	Liberty	LBS83304	1970	£10	£4	
This Is Jackie DeShannon	LP	Liberty	LBY3063	1965	£10	£4	
When You Walk In The Room	7"	Liberty	LIB55645	1964	£5	£2	
You Won't Forget Me	LP	Imperial	LP9294/12294	1965	£10	£4	US

DESIGN

Day Of The Fox	LP	Regal Zonophone	SLRZ1037	1973	£15	£6	
Design	LP	Epic	64322	1970	£20	£8	
Tomorrow Is So Far Away	LP	Epic	64653	1971	£20	£8	

DESMOND, ANDY

Living On A Shoe String	LP	Konk	KONK103	1975	£10	£4	

DESMOND, JOHNNY

Bushel And A Peck	7"	MGM	SP1042	1953	£4	£1.50	*B side by Art Lund*
Eighteenth Century Music Box	7"	Vogue Coral	Q72235	1957	£4	£1.50	
Sixteen Tons	7"	Vogue Coral	Q72115	1956	£4	£1.50	
White Sports Coat	7"	Vogue Coral	Q72261	1957	£4	£1.50	
Yellow Rose Of Texas	7"	Vogue Coral	Q72099	1955	£4	£1.50	

DESMOND, LORRAE

Ding Dong Rock-A-Billy	7"	Parlophone	R4361	1957	£10	£5	
Heartbroken	7"	Decca	F10533	1955	£6	£2.50	
Hold My Hand	7"	Decca	F10375	1954	£8	£4	
House With Love In It	7"	Parlophone	R4239	1956	£5	£2	
I Can't Tell A Waltz From A Tango	7"	Decca	F10404	1954	£8	£4	
Kansas City Special	7"	Parlophone	R4320	1957	£5	£2	
No One But You	7"	Decca	F10398	1954	£8	£4	
Secret Of Happiness	7"	Parlophone	R4430	1958	£4	£1.50	
Soda Pop Hop	7"	Parlophone	R4463	1958	£6	£2.50	
Tall Paul	7"	Parlophone	R4534	1959	£8	£4	
Two Ships	7"	Parlophone	R4400	1958	£4	£1.50	
Wake The Town And Tell The People	7"	Decca	F10612	1955	£6	£2.50	
Where Will The Dimple Be?	7"	Decca	F10510	1955	£8	£4	
Why Oh Why?	7"	Decca	F10461	1955	£8	£4	
You Won't Be Around	7"	Parlophone	R4287	1957	£5	£2	

DESMOND, PAUL

Glad To Be Unhappy	LP	RCA	SF7761	1966	£10	£4	
Paul Desmond And Friends	LP	Warner Bros	WM4020/ WS8020	1961	£15	£6	
Two Of A Mind	LP	RCA	RD7525	1962	£15	£6	*with Gerry Mulligan*

DESOLATION ANGELS

Desolation Angels	LP	Thameside	TRR111	1985	£20	£8	
Valhalla	7"	AM	AM266	1984	£8	£4	

DESPERATE BICYCLES

Grief Is Very Private	7"	Refill	RR7	1978	£5	£2	
Medium Was Tedium	7"	Refill	RR2	1977	£5	£2	
New Cross New Cross	7"	Refill	RR3	1978	£4	£1.50	
Occupied Territory	7"	Refill	RR4	1978	£4	£1.50	
Remorse Code	LP	Refill	RR6	1978	£10	£4	
Smokescreen	7"	Refill	RR1	1977	£5	£2	

DESTROYER

Evil Place	7"	Clean Kill	SJP829	1981	£25	£12.50	

DESTROYERS

Niney Special	7"	Amalgamated	AMG856	1969	£4	£1.50	
Pressure Tonic	7"	Pressure Beat	PB5505	1970	£4	£1.50	

DETERGENTS

I Don't Know	7"	Columbia	DB7591	1965	£4	£1.50	
Leader Of The Laundromat	7"	Columbia	DB7513	1965	£8	£4	
Many Faces Of The Detergents	LP	Roulette	(S)R25308	1965	£25	£10	US

DETOURS

Run To Me Baby	7"	CBS	3213	1968	£20	£10	
Whole Lotta Lovin'	7"	CBS	3401	1968	£30	£15	

DETROIT

Detroit	LP	Paramount	SPFL277	1971	£15	£6	

DETROIT EMERALDS

Do Me Right	LP	Janus	6310204	1971	£10	£4	
You Want It, You Got It	LP	Janus	6310207	1972	£10	£4	

DETROIT SPINNERS

Detroit Spinners	LP	Tamla Motown	(S)TML11060	1968	£30	£15	

Title	Format	Label	Cat. No.	Year			Notes
For All We Know	7"	Tamla Motown	TMG627	1967	**£8**	**£4**	
I'll Always Love You	7"	Tamla Motown	TMG523	1965	**£30**	**£15**	
Sweet Thing	7"	Tamla Motown	TMG514	1965	**£40**	**£20**	

DEUCHAR, JIMMY

Title	Format	Label	Cat. No.	Year			Notes
Jimmy Deuchar Ensemble	10" LP	Tempo	LAP2	1955	**£40**	**£20**	
Jimmy Deuchar Quartet	10" LP	Esquire	20059	1956	**£20**	**£8**	
Pal Jimmy	LP	Tempo	TAP20	1958	**£40**	**£20**	
Showcase	10" LP	Vogue	LDE023	1953	**£30**	**£15**	

DEUTER

Title	Format	Label	Cat. No.	Year			Notes
Aum	LP	Kuckuck	2375017	1972	**£15**	**£6**	*German*
Celebration	LP	Kuckuck	2375040	1976	**£12**	**£5**	*German*
Deuter	LP	Kuckuck	2375009	1971	**£15**	**£6**	*German*

DEUTSCHER, DRAFI

Title	Format	Label	Cat. No.	Year			Notes
Drafi	LP	Decca	SLK16380	1966	**£30**	**£15**	*German*

DEVIANTS

The Deviants, masterminded (if the word is appropriate to such a chaotic organization) by Mick Farren, were more about social revolution than about music. Pieces like 'Let's Loot The Supermarket' describe the group's stance, although they were too disorganized and too full of drugs and alcohol to have ever achieved even this much of a blow against society. Amazingly, many of the original group members managed to continue with some kind of career in rock music – Farren with new versions of the Deviants (and he also became a successful writer) and Duncan Sanderson, Russ Hunter, and Paul Rudolph with the Pink Fairies.

Title	Format	Label	Cat. No.	Year			Notes
Deviants	LP	Transatlantic	TRA204	1969	**£40**	**£20**	
Deviants	LP	Transatlantic	TRA204	1969	**£50**	**£25**	*with booklet*
Disposable	LP	Stable	SLP7001	1968	**£50**	**£25**	
Ptooff	LP	Decca	LKR/SKLR4993	1969	**£40**	**£20**	
Ptooff	LP	Underground Impressarios	IMP1	1967	**£75**	**£37.50**	*poster sleeve*
Ptooff!	LP	Psycho	PSYCHO16	1983	**£12**	**£5**	
You've Got To Hold On	7"	Stable	STA5601	1968	**£20**	**£10**	

DEVILED HAM

Title	Format	Label	Cat. No.	Year			Notes
I Had Too Much To Dream Last Night	LP	Super K	6003	1968	**£12**	**£5**	*US*

DEVIL'S ANVIL

Title	Format	Label	Cat. No.	Year			Notes
Hardrock From The Middle East	LP	Columbia	CL2664/CS9464	1968	**£25**	**£10**	*US*

DEVON

Title	Format	Label	Cat. No.	Year			Notes
Making Love	7"	Nu Beat	NB021	1968	**£5**	**£2**	
What A Sin Thing	7"	Blue Cat	BS158	1969	**£5**	**£2**	

DEVOTED

Title	Format	Label	Cat. No.	Year			Notes
I Love George Best	7"	Page One	POF076	1968	**£5**	**£2**	*picture sleeve*

DEVOTIONS

Title	Format	Label	Cat. No.	Year			Notes
For Sentimental Reasons	7"	Columbia	DB7256	1964	**£20**	**£10**	

DEW DROPS

Title	Format	Label	Cat. No.	Year			Notes
Somebody Is Knocking	7"	Blue Beat	BB381	1967	**£12**	**£6**	

DEWHURST, BRIAN

Title	Format	Label	Cat. No.	Year			Notes
Hunter And The Hunted	LP	Folk Heritage	FHR075	1975	**£20**	**£8**	

DEXTER, DANNY

Title	Format	Label	Cat. No.	Year			Notes
Sweet Mama	7"	London	HLU9690	1963	**£8**	**£4**	

DEXTER, RAY & THE LAYABOUTS

Title	Format	Label	Cat. No.	Year			Notes
Coalman's Lament	7"	Decca	F11538	1962	**£12**	**£6**	

DEXY'S MIDNIGHT RUNNERS

It seems incredible that a group with the inspiration and brilliance that Dexy's Midnight Runners had at the beginning of the eighties could so rapidly and so completely fall from favour in the aftermath of a number one hit. The group is now represented by just two collectors' items, the rarity of the listed LP being considerably greater than might be suggested by its low value. On the eve of the group's second album being released, Kevin Rowland had still not come up with his Celtic Soul identity, although the actual music was in place. Accordingly, test pressings of the album that was actually issued as *Too Rye Aye* have a different title and completely different artwork.

Title	Format	Label	Cat. No.	Year			Notes
Come On Eileen	CD-s	Mercury	MERCD347	1991	**£5**	**£2**	
Hey Where Are You Going With That Suitcase	LP	Mercury	MERS5	1982	**£20**	**£8**	*promo of 2nd LP*

DEY, TRACY

Title	Format	Label	Cat. No.	Year			Notes
Go Away	7"	Stateside	SS287	1964	**£8**	**£4**	

DHARMA BLUES

The music of the Dharma Blues is a reasonably faithful copy of the country blues – piano and harmonica to the fore – but suffers badly from the perennial problem of white blues records: the vocals are totally unconvincing. The sleeve notes go on at length about how exciting the music is and how relevant it is to the present age, but in truth these versions of some well-known traditional songs are a bit boring. That anyone should be willing to pay a substantial collectors' price for the record, when for a fraction of the sum they could buy a good compilation of music by the likes of Memphis Slim or Sonny Terry and Brownie McGhee, is one of the mysteries of record collecting.

Dharma Blues	LP	Major Minor	SMCP5017	1969	£60	£30	

DIALOGUE

Dialogue	LP	Cold Studio	DM68425	1968	£200	£100	

DIALS

Bye Bye Love	7"	Duke	DU48	1969	£4	£1.50	
Love Is A Treasure	7"	Duke	DU49	1969	£4	£1.50	

DIAMOND, BRIAN & THE CUTTERS

Big Bad Wolf	7"	Pye	7N15779	1965	£5	£2	
Bone Idol	7"	Pye	7N15952	1965	£5	£2	
Jealousy Will Get You Nowhere	7"	Decca	F11724	1963	£6	£2.50	
Shake Shout And Go	7"	Fontana	TF452	1964	£6	£2.50	

DIAMOND, GREGG & BIONIC BOOGIE

Chains	12"	Polydor	POSPX50	1979	£6	£2.50	

DIAMOND, JERRY

Sunburned Lips	7"	London	HLE8496	1957	£20	£10	

DIAMOND, LEE

I'll Step Down	7"	Fontana	H310	1961	£6	£2.50	
Stop Your Crying	7"	Fontana	H345	1961	£6	£2.50	

DIAMOND, NEIL

Best Years Of Our Lives	CD	CBS	XPCD113	1989	£20	£8	*promo compilation*
Brother Love's Travelling Salvation Show	LP	MCA	MUPS382	1969	£10	£4	
Clown Town	7"	Columbia	42809	1963	£125	£62.50	*US*
Feel Of Neil Diamond	LP	London	HAZ8307	1966	£20	£8	
Heartlight	12"	Columbia	AS991586	1982	£10	£5	*US 1 sided promo picture disc*
Hot August Night	CD	Mobile Fidelity	UDCD589	1993	£15	£6	*US audiophile*
Hot August Night	LP	Mobile Fidelity	MFSL2024	1978	£12	£5	*US audiophile, double*
In My Lifetime Sampler	CD	Columbia	CSK8877	1996	£20	£8	*promo*
Jazz Singer	LP	Mobile Fidelity	MFSL2071	1982	£10	£4	*US audiophile*
Jonathan Livingstone Seagull	LP	Columbia	HC42550	1981	£10	£4	*US audiophile*
Neil Diamond Songbook	CD	CBS	XPCD708	1996	£20	£8	*promo*
Open Ended Interview	LP	Uni	LP1913	1968	£15	£6	*US promo*
Solitary Man	7"	London	HLZ10049	1966	£4	£1.50	
This Time And All The Hits	CD	Columbia		1989	£20	£8	*US promo compilation*
Velvet Gloves And Spit	LP	MCA	MUPS365	1968	£10	£4	
You Don't Bring Me Flowers	LP	Columbia	HC45625	1980	£10	£4	*US audiophile*

DIAMOND BOYS

Fool In Love	7"	Parlophone	GIB102	1962	£20	£10	*export*
Hey Little Girl	7"	RCA	RCA1351	1963	£4	£1.50	

DIAMOND HEAD

Diamond Lights	12"	Windsong	DHM005	1981	£8	£4	
Kingmaker	7"	MCA	DHMP104	1983	£4	£1.50	*picture disc*
Lightning To The Nations	LP	Happy Face	MMDHLP105	1981	£25	£10	*plain white sleeve*
Living On Borrowed Time	LP	MCA	DH1001	1981	£12	£5	*with poster*
Out Of Phase	12"	MCA	DHMT104	1983	£6	£2.50	
Shoot Out the Lights	7"	Happy Face	MMDH120	1980	£6	£2.50	
Sweet And Innocent	7"	Media	SCREEN1	1980	£5	£2	
Waited Too Long	7"	DHM	DHM004	1981	£4	£1.50	

DIAMONDS

Black Denim Trousers & Motorcycle Boots	7"	Vogue Coral	Q72109	1955	£30	£15	
Collection Of Golden Hits	LP	Mercury	MG20213	1956	£60	£30	*US*
Diamonds	10" LP	Mercury	MPT7526	1957	£75	£37.50	
Diamonds	LP	Mercury	MG20309	1958	£50	£25	*US*
Diamonds	LP	Wing	MGW12114	1958	£25	£10	*US*
Diamonds Are Trumps	7" EP	Mercury	ZEP10026	1959	£25	£12.50	
Diamonds Meet Pete Rugulo	7" EP	Mercury	ZEP10020	1959	£15	£7.50	
Diamonds Meet Pete Rugulo	LP	Mercury	MG20368/ SR60076	1958	£25	£10	*US*
Diamonds Vol. 1	7" EP	Mercury	MEP9523	1957	£20	£10	
Diamonds Vol. 2	7" EP	Mercury	MEP9527	1958	£20	£10	
Diamonds Vol. 3	7" EP	Mercury	MEP9530	1958	£20	£10	
Dig The Diamonds	7" EP	Mercury	ZEP10003	1959	£25	£12.50	
Don't Say Goodbye	78	Mercury	MT167	1957	£5	£2	
Eternal Lovers	7"	Mercury	AMT1004	1958	£8	£4	
High Sign	7"	Mercury	7MT207	1958	£20	£10	
Kathy O	7"	Mercury	7MT233	1958	£5	£2	
Love Love Love	78	Mercury	MT121	1956	£6	£2.50	
Oh How I Wish	78	Mercury	MT179	1957	£6	£2.50	
One Summer Night	7"	Mercury	AMT1156	1961	£10	£5	
Pete Rugolo Leads The Diamonds	7" EP	Mercury	SEZ19012	1961	£20	£10	*stereo*
Pete Rugolo Leads The Diamonds	7" EP	Mercury	ZEP10097	1961	£15	£7.50	

Pop Hits By The Diamonds	LP	Wing	MGW12178	1959	**£20**	**£8**	US
Presenting The Diamonds	7" EP	Mercury	MEP9515	1957	**£15**	**£7.50**	
She Say Oom Dooby Oom	7"	Mercury	AMT1024	1959	**£8**	**£4**	
Silhouettes	7"	Mercury	7MT187	1958	**£20**	**£10**	
Songs From The Old West	LP	Mercury	MMC14039	1960	**£15**	**£6**	
Star Studded Diamonds	7" EP	Mercury	ZEP10053	1960	**£20**	**£10**	
Straight Skirts	7"	Mercury	7MT208	1958	**£20**	**£10**	
Stroll	7"	Mercury	7MT195	1958	**£15**	**£7.50**	
Surprise Package	7" EP	Mercury	ZEP10088	1960	**£20**	**£10**	*with Ben Hewitt*
Tell The Truth	7"	Mercury	AMT1086	1960	**£10**	**£5**	

DIAMONDS (2)

Lost City	7"	Philips	BF1264	1963	**£6**	**£2.50**	

DIANE & THE JAVELINS

Heart And Soul	7"	Columbia	DB7819	1966	**£30**	**£15**	

DI'ANNO, PAUL

Di'Anno	LP	FM	WKFMPD1	1984	**£10**	**£4**	*picture disc*

DIATONES

Ruby Has Gone	7"	Starlite	ST45057	1961	**£6**	**£2.50**	

DIBANGO, MANU

Soul Makossa	LP	Atlantic	SD7267	1972	**£10**	**£4**	US

DICE THE BOSS

Brixton Cat	7"	Joe	DU50	1969	**£6**	**£2.50**	
Brixton Cat	LP	Trojan	TBL106	1969	**£15**	**£6**	
But Officer	7"	Joe	DU52	1969	**£6**	**£2.50**	
Funky Duck	7"	Explosion	EX2020	1970	**£4**	**£1.50**	
Funky Monkey	7"	Explosion	EX2017	1970	**£4**	**£1.50**	
Gun The Man Down	7"	Duke	DU51	1969	**£4**	**£1.50**	
Honky Tonk Popcorn	7"	Jackpot	JP715	1969	**£4**	**£1.50**	
Informer	7"	Joe	JRS17	1970	**£4**	**£1.50**	
Sin, Sun And Sex	7"	Jackpot	JP716	1969	**£4**	**£1.50**	
Trial Of Pama Dice	7"	Joe	JRS5	1970	**£4**	**£1.50**	
Your Boss DJ	7"	Joe	DU57	1969	**£6**	**£2.50**	

DICK & DEE DEE

All My Trials	7"	Warner Bros	WB126	1964	**£4**	**£1.50**	
Be My Baby	7"	Warner Bros	WB156	1965	**£4**	**£1.50**	
Goodbye To Love	7"	London	HLG9483	1962	**£5**	**£2**	
Mountain's High	7"	London	HLG9408	1961	**£5**	**£2**	
Remember When	7"	Warner Bros	WB138	1964	**£4**	**£1.50**	
Songs We've Sung On Shindig	LP	Warner Bros	W(S)1623	1965	**£12**	**£5**	US
Tell Me	LP	Liberty	LRP3236/ LST7236	1962	**£15**	**£6**	US
Thou Shalt Not Steal	LP	Warner Bros	W(S)1586	1965	**£12**	**£5**	US
Turn Around	LP	Warner Bros	WM/WS8150	1963	**£15**	**£6**	
Young And In Love	LP	Warner Bros	WM/WS8132	1963	**£15**	**£6**	

DICKENS

Standing Out	LP	Hawkmoon	ROCK101P	1985	**£20**	**£8**	

DICKENS, CHARLES

So Much In Love	7"	Immediate	IM025	1966	**£6**	**£2.50**	

DICKENSON, VIC

Mainstream	LP	London	LTZK15182/ SAHK6066	1960	**£15**	**£6**	*with Joe Thomas*
Showcase	LP	Fontana	FJL404	1967	**£12**	**£5**	
Vic Dickenson Septet	10" LP	Vanguard	PPT12000	1955	**£20**	**£8**	
Vic Dickenson Septet	10" LP	Vanguard	PPT12005	1956	**£20**	**£8**	
Vic Dickenson Septet	10" LP	Vanguard	PPT12015	1957	**£20**	**£8**	
Vol. 4	10" LP	Vanguard	PPT12019	1958	**£20**	**£8**	

DICKINSON, BRUCE

All The Young Dudes	CD-s	EMI	CDEM142	1990	**£5**	**£2**	
Dive Dive Dive	CD-s	EMI	CDEM151	1990	**£5**	**£2**	
Tattooed Millionaire	CD-s	EMI	CDEM138	1990	**£5**	**£2**	

DICKSON, BARBARA

At the start of her career, Barbara Dickson was a folk singer, this being the style to be found on her collectable Trailer and Decca albums. Her commercial breakthrough came when she was asked to perform the music for the hit stage show about the Beatles – *John, Paul, George, Ringo and Bert.* Her subsequent recordings have found their way into far too many people's homes to have any kind of rarity value.

Do Right Woman	LP	Decca	SKL5058	1970	**£50**	**£25**	
Fate O' Charlie	LP	Trailer	LER3002	1969	**£30**	**£15**	*with Archie Fisher & John MacKinnon*
From The Beggar's Mantle	LP	Decca	SKL5116	1972	**£50**	**£25**	
From The Beggar's Mantle	LP	Celtic	CM029	198–	**£10**	**£4**	
Golden Bird	LP	Oliver And Boyd		1969	**£100**	**£50**	
John, Paul, George, Ringo, & Bert	LP	RSO	2394167	1975	**£10**	**£4**	
Through The Recent Years	LP	Decca	SKL5041	1970	**£30**	**£15**	*with Archie Fisher*

DICTATORS WITH TONY & HOWARD

So Long Little Girl	7"	Oriole	CB1934	1963	£5	£2	

DIDDLEY, BO

Although he has recorded numerous songs that do not use it, Bo Diddley's name will for ever be associated with a particular rhythm – the one used on his eponymous first single and translated by band-leader Johnny Otis as 'shave and a haircut, two bits'. It is extremely unlikely that Bo Diddley thought of the rhythm himself – indeed there is evidence that it goes right back to Africa – but it has become his anyway. The 'Bo Diddley beat' has been borrowed at intervals ever since by artists as varied as the Rolling Stones, Bruce Springsteen, the Smiths, and George Michael. Bo Diddley is also famous for his unusual guitars – one was covered in fake fur, one was rectangular in shape – but he is not a lead player and his playing has not been an influence on anyone else. Apart, that is, from that rhythm.

16 All Time Greatest Hits	LP	Pye	NPL28049	1964	£15	£6	
500 Per Cent More Man	7"	Chess	CRS8026	1966	£4	£1.50	
Another Sugar Daddy	7"	Chess	CRS8078	1968	£4	£1.50	
Beach Party	LP	Pye	NPL28032	1963	£12	£5	
Beach Party	LP	Checker	LP(S)2988	1963	£30	£15	US
Black Gladiator	LP	Checker	LP(S)3013	1969	£12	£5	US
Bo Diddley	7"	Pye	7N25210	1963	£6	£2.50	
Bo Diddley	LP	Chess	LP1431	1957	£50	£25	US
Bo Diddley	LP	Checker	LP2984	1962	£20	£8	US
Bo Diddley	LP	Pye	NPL28026	1963	£15	£6	
Bo Diddley 1969	7"	Chess	CRS8088	1969	£4	£1.50	
Bo Diddley And Company	LP	Checker	LP2985	1963	£40	£20	US
Bo Diddley Is A Gunslinger	LP	Pye	NJL33	1963	£25	£10	
Bo Diddley Is A Gunslinger	LP	Checker	LP2977	1961	£40	£20	US
Bo Diddley Is A Lover	7"	Pye	7N25227	1963	£5	£2	
Bo Diddley Is A Lover	LP	Checker	LP2980	1961	£30	£15	US
Bo Diddley Is A Twister	LP	Checker	LP2982	1962	£20	£8	US
Bo Diddley Rides Again	LP	Pye	NPL28029	1963	£15	£6	
Bo's A Lumberjack	7" EP	Pye	NEP44031	1964	£12	£6	
Boss Man	LP	Checker	LP(S)3007	1967	£30	£15	US
Diddling	7" EP	Pye	NEP44036	1964	£12	£6	
Five Hundred Per Cent More Man	LP	Checker	LP(S)2996	1964	£15	£6	US
Go Bo Diddley	LP	London	HAM2230	1959	£100	£50	
Great Grandfather	7"	London	HLM8913	1959	£30	£15	
Have Guitar, Will Travel	LP	Checker	LP2974	1959	£30	£15	US
Hey Bo Diddley	7" EP	Pye	NEP44014	1963	£10	£5	
Hey Bo Diddley	LP	Pye	NPL28025	1963	£15	£6	
Hey Good Looking	7"	Chess	CRS8000	1965	£4	£1.50	
Hey Good Looking	LP	Chess	CRL4002	1964	£12	£5	
I'm A Man	7" EP	Chess	CRE6008	1965	£10	£5	
I'm A Man	LP	MF	2002	1977	£50	£25	US
In The Spotlight	LP	Pye	NPL28034	1964	£15	£6	
In The Spotlight	LP	Checker	LP2976	1960	£20	£8	US
Let Me Pass	LP	Chess	CRL4507	1965	£12	£5	
Let The Kids Dance	7"	Chess	CRS8021	1965	£4	£1.50	
Mama Keep Your Big Mouth Shut	7"	Pye	7N25258	1964	£5	£2	
Memphis	7"	Pye	7N25235	1964	£5	£2	
Mona	7"	Pye	7N25243	1964	£6	£2.50	
Ooh Baby	7"	Chess	CRS8053	1967	£4	£1.50	
Originator	LP	Chess	CRL4526	1967	£12	£5	
Rhythm And Blues With Bo Diddley	7" EP	London	REU1054	1956	£150	£75	
Road Runner	7"	Pye	7N25217	1963	£6	£2.50	
Road Runner	7"	London	HLM9112	1960	£40	£20	
Road Runner	LP	Checker	LP2982	1962	£30	£15	US
Rooster Stew	7" EP	Chess	CRE6023	1966	£10	£5	
Say Man	7"	London	HLM8975	1959	£30	£15	
Say Man Back Again	7"	London	HLM9035	1960	£30	£15	
Somebody Beat Me	7"	Chess	CRS8014	1965	£4	£1.50	
Story Of Bo Diddley	7" EP	Pye	NEP44019	1964	£10	£5	
Surfin' With Bo Diddley	LP	Checker	LP(S)2987	1963	£20	£8	US
We're Gonna Get Married	7"	Chess	CRS8036	1966	£4	£1.50	
Where It All Began	LP	Chess	CH50016	1972	£20	£8	US
Who Do You Love	7"	Pye	7N25193	1963	£6	£2.50	
Wrecking My Love Life	7"	Chess	CRS8057	1967	£4	£1.50	
You Can't Judge A Book By Its Cover	7"	Pye	7N25165	1962	£8	£4	
You Can't Judge A Book By The Cover	7"	Pye	7N25216	1963	£5	£2	

DIDI & HIS ABC BOYS

Beat Aus Berlin	LP	Telefunken	BLE14340P	1966	£200	£100	German
Beat Beat Beat	LP	Gong	74999	1967	£40	£20	German

DIE ELECTRIC EELS

Agitated	7"	Rough Trade	RT008	1979	£6	£2.50	

DIED PRETTY

Whitlam Square	CD-s	Beggars Banquet	BEG238CD	1990	£5	£2	

DIES IRAE

First	LP	Pilz	20201147	1971	£15	£6	German

DIETRICH, MARLENE

At The Café De Paris	10" LP	Philips	BBR8006	1954	£10	£4	
Marlene Dietrich	7" EP	London	RED1146	1958	£6	£2.50	
Marlene Dietrich	7" EP	HMV	7EG8257	1957	£5	£2	

Title	Format	Label	Number	Year	Mint	VG	Notes
Marlene Returns To Germany	7" EP	HMV	7EG8844	1964	**£5**	**£2**	
Souvenir Album	10" LP	Brunswick	LA8591	1953	**£10**	**£4**	

DIF JUZ

Title	Format	Label	Number	Year	Mint	VG	Notes
Huremics	12"	4AD	BAD109	1981	**£10**	**£5**	
Vibrating Air	12"	4AD	BAD116	1981	**£8**	**£4**	

DIGA RHYTHM BAND

Title	Format	Label	Number	Year	Mint	VG	Notes
Diga	LP	Round	UAS29975	1976	**£12**	**£5**	

DILLARD, DOUG

Title	Format	Label	Number	Year	Mint	VG	Notes
Banjo Album	LP	Together	STT1003	1970	**£30**	**£15**	*US*

DILLARD, MOSES & JOSHUA

Title	Format	Label	Number	Year	Mint	VG	Notes
My Elusive Dreams	7"	Stateside	SS2059	1967	**£6**	**£2.50**	

DILLARD & CLARK

Title	Format	Label	Number	Year	Mint	VG	Notes
Fantastic Expedition Of Dillard And Clark	LP	A&M	AMLS939	1969	**£10**	**£4**	
Kansas City Southern	LP	Ariola	86436	1975	**£10**	**£4**	*Dutch*
Through The Morning	LP	A&M	AMLS966	1969	**£10**	**£4**	

DILLARDS

Title	Format	Label	Number	Year	Mint	VG	Notes
Back Porch Blue Grass	LP	Elektra	EKL/EKS7232	1963	**£20**	**£8**	*US*
Copperfields	LP	Elektra	EKS74054	1970	**£10**	**£4**	
Live Almost	LP	Elektra	EKL/EKS7265	1964	**£20**	**£8**	*US*
Pickin' And Fiddlin'	LP	Elektra	EKL/EKS7285	1965	**£20**	**£8**	*US*
Wheatsheaf Suite	LP	Elektra	EKS74035	1968	**£10**	**£4**	

DILLINGER

Title	Format	Label	Number	Year	Mint	VG	Notes
Answer Me Question	LP	Third World	TWS928	1978	**£10**	**£4**	
Bionic Dread	LP	Island	ILPS9455	1976	**£12**	**£5**	
CB200	LP	Island	ILPS9385	1976	**£12**	**£5**	
Clash	LP	Burning Sounds	BSLP1003	1978	**£10**	**£4**	*as Dillinger vs Trinity*
Headquarters	7"	Duke	DU149	1973	**£8**	**£4**	
Talking Blues	LP	Magnum	DEAD1001	1977	**£10**	**£4**	
Tighten Up Skank	7"	Downtown	DT512	1973	**£8**	**£4**	
Top Ranking	LP	Third World	TWS919	1977	**£10**	**£4**	

DILLON, PHYLLIS

Title	Format	Label	Number	Year	Mint	VG	Notes
Don't Stay Away	7"	Doctor Bird	DB1061	1966	**£10**	**£5**	*Tommy McCook B side*
Get On The Right Track	7"	Trojan	TR671	1969	**£6**	**£2.50**	*Tommy McCook B side*
I Wear This Ring	7"	Treasure Isle	TI7041	1968	**£10**	**£5**	
In The Ghetto	7"	Sioux	SI009	1972	**£5**	**£2**	
It's Rocking Time	7"	Treasure Isle	TI7015	1967	**£10**	**£5**	
Lipstick On Your Collar	7"	Trojan	TR686	1969	**£5**	**£2**	*Tommy McCook B side*
Love Is All I Had	7"	Trojan	TR651	1969	**£6**	**£2.50**	
Midnight Confession	7"	Treasure Isle	TI7070	1971	**£4**	**£1.50**	*Tommy McCook B side*
One Life To Live	LP	Trojan	TRL41	1972	**£20**	**£8**	
One Life To Live One Love To Give	7"	Treasure Isle	TI7058	1970	**£4**	**£1.50**	*Tommy McCook B side*
Things Of The Past	7"	Treasure Isle	TI7003	1967	**£10**	**£5**	
This Is A Lovely Way	7"	Trojan	TR006	1967	**£8**	**£4**	
This Is Me	7"	Duke Reid	DR2508	1970	**£4**	**£1.50**	

DIMENSIONS

Title	Format	Label	Number	Year	Mint	VG	Notes
Tears On My Pillow	7"	Parlophone	R5294	1965	**£10**	**£5**	

DIMENSIONS (2)

Title	Format	Label	Number	Year	Mint	VG	Notes
From All Dimensions	LP	private	1666	1966	**£750**	**£500**	*US*

DIMPLES

Title	Format	Label	Number	Year	Mint	VG	Notes
Love Of A Lifetime	7"	Decca	F12537	1966	**£20**	**£10**	

DIMPLES & EDDIE

Title	Format	Label	Number	Year	Mint	VG	Notes
Fleet Street	7"	Planetone	RC3	1962	**£10**	**£5**	

DINGER

Title	Format	Label	Number	Year	Mint	VG	Notes
Air Of Mystery	7"	SRT	SRT394	1985	**£25**	**£12.50**	
Air Of Mystery	7"	Face Value	FVRA221	1985	**£25**	**£12.50**	

DINGLE BROTHERS

Title	Format	Label	Number	Year	Mint	VG	Notes
Tank De Lard	7"	Doctor Bird	DB1026	1966	**£10**	**£5**	

DINGLE SPIKE

Title	Format	Label	Number	Year	Mint	VG	Notes
Dingle Spike	LP	SRTX	78CUS185	1978	**£12**	**£5**	

DINNING, MARK

Mark Dinning is responsible for what is undoubtedly the worst record ever released. Forget all the other candidates for the accolade – 'Teen Angel' is the one! The song has one of those lyrics that deal with death – on this occasion, the singer's girlfriend has apparently rushed back into a burning building in order to save a ring that the singer had bought her. The symbol of the romance was more important than the romance itself! Meanwhile, the singer laments: 'I'll never kiss your lips again, they buried you today'. The epitome of bad taste – and all delivered in a thin, quavery voice so as to pile the pathos on really thick. Needless to say, the record was an American number one!

Title	Format	Label	Cat. No.	Year	Mint	VG	Notes
Teen Angel	7"	MGM	MGM1053	1960	£5	£2	
Teen Angel	LP	MGM	(S)E3828	1960	£40	£20	US
Wanderin'	LP	MGM	(S)E3855	1960	£25	£10	US

DINNING SISTERS

Title	Format	Label	Cat. No.	Year	Mint	VG	Notes
Drifting And Dreaming	7"	London	HLF8179	1955	£25	£12.50	
Hold Me Tight	7"	London	HLF8218	1956	£25	£12.50	

DINO, DESI & BILLY

Title	Format	Label	Cat. No.	Year	Mint	VG	Notes
I'm A Fool	7" EP	Reprise	RVEP60072	1965	£5	£2	French

DINO, KENNY

Title	Format	Label	Cat. No.	Year	Mint	VG	Notes
Your Ma Said You Cried In Your Sleep Last Night	7"	HMV	POP960	1961	£4	£1.50	

DINO & DEL

Title	Format	Label	Cat. No.	Year	Mint	VG	Notes
Hey Little Girl Hey Little Boy	7"	Carnival	CV7026	1965	£4	£1.50	

DINOSAUR

Title	Format	Label	Cat. No.	Year	Mint	VG	Notes
Kiss Me Again	12"	Sire	SRE1034	1979	£8	£4	
Kiss Me Again	7"	Sire	SRE1034	1979	£5	£2	

DINOSAUR JR

Title	Format	Label	Cat. No.	Year	Mint	VG	Notes
Dinosaur Jr	CD-s	SST	SST152CD	1988	£5	£2	
Just Like Heaven	CD-s	Blast First	BFFP47CD	1989	£5	£2	
Just Like Heaven	CD-s	SST	SST244CD	1990	£5	£2	
Wagon	CD-s	Blanco Y Negro	NEG48CD	1991	£5	£2	
Without A Sound	CD	Warner Bros		1994	£25	£10	Australian double tour CD

DIO

Title	Format	Label	Cat. No.	Year	Mint	VG	Notes
Hey Angel	CD-s	Vertigo	DIOCD9	1990	£5	£2	
Sitting In A Dream	7"	Purple	PUR128	1975	£6	£2.50	

DION

Title	Format	Label	Cat. No.	Year	Mint	VG	Notes
Abraham, Martin And John	7"	London	HLP10229	1968	£4	£1.50	
Alone With Dion	LP	Laurie	LLP2004	1960	£30	£15	US
Be Careful Of The Stones That You Throw	7"	CBS	AAG161	1963	£5	£2	
Berimbau	7"	HMV	POP1565	1966	£4	£1.50	
Both Sides Now	7"	London	HLP10277	1969	£4	£1.50	
By Special Request	LP	Laurie	LLP2016	1963	£30	£15	US
Come Go With Me	7"	Stateside	SS209	1963	£6	£2.50	
Dion	LP	London	HAP/SHP8390	1969	£10	£4	
Dion Sings The Fifteen Million Sellers	LP	Laurie	LLP2019	1963	£25	£10	US
Dion Sings To Sandy & All Other Girls	LP	Laurie	LLP2017	1963	£25	£10	US
Dion's Hits	7" EP	Stateside	SE1006	1963	£30	£15	
Don't Pity Me	7"	London	HL8799	1959	£25	£12.50	
Donna La Prima Donna	7"	CBS	121053	1963	£6	£2.50	sung in Italian
Donna The Prima Donna	7"	CBS	AAG169	1963	£4	£1.50	
Donna The Prima Donna	LP	CBS	(S)BPG62203	1964	£15	£6	
Drip Drop	7"	CBS	AAG177	1963	£5	£2	
Greatest Hits	LP	Laurie	LLP2013	1962	£25	£10	US
Having Fun	7"	Top Rank	JAR545	1961	£6	£2.50	
I Can't Go On	7"	London	HL8718	1958	£30	£15	
I Wonder Why	7"	London	HLH8646	1958	£50	£25	
I'm Your Hoochie Coochie Man	7"	CBS	AAG188	1964	£6	£2.50	
In The Still Of The Night	7"	Top Rank	JAR503	1960	£8	£4	
Johnny B. Goode	7"	CBS	AAG224	1964	£6	£2.50	
Little Diane	7"	Stateside	SS115	1962	£4	£1.50	
Lonely Teenager	7"	Top Rank	JAR521	1960	£8	£4	
Love Came To Me	7"	Stateside	SS139	1962	£4	£1.50	
Love Came To Me	LP	Laurie	LLP2015	1963	£25	£10	US
Lover's Prayer	7"	Pye	7N25038	1959	£15	£7.50	
Lovers Who Wander	7"	HMV	POP1020	1962	£5	£2	
Lovers Who Wander	LP	Stateside	SL10034	1962	£40	£20	
More Greatest Hits	LP	Laurie	LLP2022	1963	£20	£8	US
Movin' Man	7"	HMV	POP1586	1967	£5	£2	
Presenting Dion And The Belmonts	LP	Laurie	LLP2002	1959	£100	£50	US
Presenting Dion And The Belmonts	LP	London	HAU2194	1959	£150	£75	
Ruby Baby	7"	CBS	AAG133	1963	£5	£2	
Ruby Baby	LP	CBS	(B)PG62137	1963	£15	£6	
Runaround Sue	7"	Top Rank	JAR586	1961	£5	£2	
Runaround Sue	LP	HMV	CLP1539	1961	£40	£20	
Runaround Sue	LP	Laurie	LLP2009	1961	£60	£30	US, blue vinyl
Sanctuary	LP	Warner Bros	K46122	1972	£10	£4	
Sandy	7"	Stateside	SS161	1963	£8	£4	
Sit Down Old Friend	LP	Warner Bros	WS1826	1970	£10	£4	
Spoonful	7"	CBS	201780	1965	£5	£2	
Suite For Late Summer	LP	Warner Bros	K46199	1972	£10	£4	
Sweet Sweet Baby	7"	CBS	201728	1965	£5	£2	
Swing Along With Dion	7" EP	HMV	7EG8745	1962	£50	£25	
Teenager In Love	7"	London	HLU8874	1959	£20	£10	

Title	Format	Label	Cat. No.	Year	Mint	Good	Notes
This Little Girl	7"	CBS	AAG145	1963	£5	£2	
Together Again	LP	HMV	CLP/CSD3618	1967	£20	£8	
Toppermost Vol. 1	LP	Top Rank	25027	1960	£50	£25	
Wanderer	7"	HMV	POP971	1962	£5	£2	
When You Wish Upon A Star	7"	Top Rank	JAR368	1960	£8	£4	
Where Or When	7"	London	HLU9030	1960	£8	£4	
Wish Upon A Star	LP	Laurie	LLP2006	1960	£30	£15	*US*
You're Not Alone	LP	Warner Bros	WS1872	1971	£10	£4	

DION, CELINE

Title	Format	Label	Cat. No.	Year	Mint	Good	Notes
Beauty And The Beast	CD-s	Epic	6576605	1992	£10	£5	
Beauty And The Beast	CD-s	Epic	6576602	1992	£5	£2	
Celine Dion	CD	Epic	4715082	1992	£15	£6	
Celine Dion	LP	Epic	4715081	1992	£10	£4	
If You Asked Me To	[illegible]	Epic	[illegible]	[illegible]	[illegible]	£2.50	
Last To Know	CD-s	Epic	6573332	1991	£8	£4	
Love Can Move Mountains	CD-s	Epic	6587782	1992	£10	£5	
Misled	CD-s	Epic	6602922	1994	£5	£2	
Unison	LP	Epic	4672031	1991	£10	£4	
Where Does My Heart Beat Now?	CD-s	Epic	6563262/5	1991	£10	£5	*2 versions*

DIONYSOS

Title	Format	Label	Cat. No.	Year	Mint	Good	Notes
Le Grand Jeu	LP	Jupiter	8032	1970	£15	£6	*Canadian*

DIPLOMATS

Title	Format	Label	Cat. No.	Year	Mint	Good	Notes
I Can Give You Love	7"	Direction	583899	1968	£4	£1.50	

DIRE STRAITS

One of the most popular groups of the eighties was responsible for the earliest CD rarity: a promotional sampler taken from the best-selling *Brothers In Arms* album. The live album from 1980, meanwhile, is thoroughly recommended as a demonstration of the sparky appeal that helped to catapult Dire Straits to international success, despite their playing music based on all the old-fashioned principles that punk and new wave were supposed to have rendered irrelevant.

Title	Format	Label	Cat. No.	Year	Mint	Good	Notes
Brothers In Arms	7"	Vertigo	DSPIC11	1985	£8	£4	*shaped picture disc*
Brothers In Arms	CD-s	Vertigo	0801322	1989	£15	£7.50	*CD video*
Brothers In Arms Special Edition	CD	Vertigo	8842852	1985	£30	£15	*promo*
Calling Elvis	CD-s	Vertigo	DSCD16	1991	£5	£2	
Dire Straits Live	LP	Warner Bros	WBMS109	1980	£25	£10	*US promo*
Heavy Fuel	CD-s	Vertigo	DSHAM17	1991	£5	£2	
Money For Nothing	7"	Vertigo	DSPIC10	1985	£5	£2	*shaped picture disc*
Money For Nothing	CD-s	Vertigo	0801302	1988	£15	£7.50	*CD video*
On Every Street	CD	Vertigo	5101602	1991	£50	£25	*promo box set with cassette*
Sultans Of Swing	CD	Vertigo	DST1	1998	£40	£20	*promo 3 CD set*
Sultans Of Swing	CD-s	Vertigo	DSCD15	1988	£8	£4	*card sleeve*
Sultans Of Swing	CD-s	Vertigo	0801282	1989	£15	£7.50	*CD video*
Twisting By The Pool	CD-s	Vertigo	0801362	1989	£15	£7.50	*CD video*
Walk Of Life	CD-s	Vertigo	0801342	1989	£15	£7.50	*CD video*

DIRECT HITS

Title	Format	Label	Cat. No.	Year	Mint	Good	Notes
Blow Up	LP	Whaam	BIG7	1984	£25	£10	
Christopher Cooper	7"	Direct	POP001	1985	£4	£1.50	
Modesty Blaise	7"	Whaam	WHAAM7	1982	£10	£5	

DIRECTIONS

Title	Format	Label	Cat. No.	Year	Mint	Good	Notes
Three Bands Tonite	7"	Tortch	TOR004	1979	£40	£20	

DIRK & STIG

Title	Format	Label	Cat. No.	Year	Mint	Good	Notes
Ging Gang Goolie	7"	EMI	EMI2852	1979	£6	£2.50	*with the Rutles, khaki vinyl*
Ging Gang Goolie	7"	EMI	EMI2852	1979	£4	£1.50	*with the Rutles*

DIRTY BLUES BAND

Title	Format	Label	Cat. No.	Year	Mint	Good	Notes
Dirty Blues Band	LP	Stateside	(S)SL10234	1968	£15	£6	
Stone Dirt	LP	Stateside	(S)SL10268	1969	£10	£4	

DIRTY DOG

Title	Format	Label	Cat. No.	Year	Mint	Good	Notes
Let Go Of My Hand	7"	Lightning	GIL511	1978	£10	£5	

DIRTY FILTHY MUD

Title	Format	Label	Cat. No.	Year	Mint	Good	Notes
Dirty Filthy Mud	7" EP	Worex	2340	1967	£300	£180	*US*

DISCO 2000

Title	Format	Label	Cat. No.	Year	Mint	Good	Notes
I Gotta CD	12"	KLF	D2000	1987	£8	£4	
I Gotta CD	7"	KLF	D2001	1987	£7	£4	*white label*
One Love Nation	12"	KLF	D2002	1988	£6	£2.50	
Uptight	12"	KLF	D2003T	1989	£6	£2.50	

DISCO STUDENTS

Title	Format	Label	Cat. No.	Year	Mint	Good	Notes
Boy With A Penchant For Open-Necked Shirts	7"	Yeah Yeah Yeah	UHHUH2	1980	£8	£4	
South Africa House	7"	Yeah Yeah Yeah	UHHUH1	1979	£8	£4	

DISCO ZOMBIES

Title	Format	Label	Cat. No.	Year	Mint	Good	Notes
Drums Over London	7"	South Circular	SGS106	1979	£10	£5	

Title	Format	Label	Cat. No.	Year	Mint	VG	Notes
Here Come The Buts	7"	Dining Out	TUX2	1981	**£5**	**£2**	
Invisible EP	7"	Wizzo	WIZZO1	1979	**£8**	**£4**	

DISGUISE IN LOVE

Title	Format	Label	Cat. No.	Year	Mint	VG	Notes
Ross Was My Best Friend	7"	Purple Snow	FLAKE1	1982	**£5**	**£2**	*purple vinyl*

DISORDER

Title	Format	Label	Cat. No.	Year	Mint	VG	Notes
Reality Crisis	7"	Durham Book Centre	BOOK1	1980	**£10**	**£5**	
Singles Collection	12"	Disorder	12ORDER5	1984	**£6**	**£2.50**	

DISSING, POVL

Title	Format	Label	Cat. No.	Year	Mint	VG	Notes
Dansk Beat	LP	Sonet	SLPS2412	1975	**£15**	**£6**	*Danish*
Mor Danmark	LP	Hookfarm	HKLP3	1973	**£15**	**£6**	*Danish*
Svantes Visir	LP	Metronome	BP7739	1973	**£20**	**£8**	*Danish*

DISSIVELT, TOM

Title	Format	Label	Cat. No.	Year	Mint	VG	Notes
Fantasy In Orbit	LP	Philips	BL7681	1965	**£10**	**£4**	

DISTANT COUSINS

Title	Format	Label	Cat. No.	Year	Mint	VG	Notes
She Ain't Loving You	7"	CBS	202352	1966	**£10**	**£5**	

DISTRACTIONS

Title	Format	Label	Cat. No.	Year	Mint	VG	Notes
You're Not Going Out Dressed Like That	12"	TJM	TJM2	1979	**£6**	**£2.50**	

DIVINE

Title	Format	Label	Cat. No.	Year	Mint	VG	Notes
Walk Like A Man	7"	Proto	ENAP125	1985	**£4**	**£1.50**	*shaped picture disc*

DIVINE COMEDY

Title	Format	Label	Cat. No.	Year	Mint	VG	Notes
Europop: New Wave	12"	Setanta	SET011	1992	**£20**	**£10**	
Europop: New Wave	CD-s	Setanta	SET011CD	1992	**£30**	**£15**	
Fanfare For The Comic Muse	CD	Setanta	SETCD002	1990	**£50**	**£25**	
Fanfare For The Comic Muse	LP	Setanta	SETLPM002	1990	**£40**	**£20**	
Indulgence No. 1	7"	Setanta	DC1	1993	**£12**	**£6**	*picture disc*
Indulgence No. 2	7"	Setanta	DC002	1994	**£20**	**£10**	
Lucy	7"	Setanta	CAO008	1991	**£6**	**£2.50**	
Promenade	CD	Setanta	SETCD013	1994	**£25**	**£10**	*with bonus live CD*
Timewatch	12"	Setanta	SET008	1991	**£15**	**£7.50**	

DIXIE BELLES

Title	Format	Label	Cat. No.	Year	Mint	VG	Notes
Dixie Belles	7" EP	London	REU1434	1964	**£10**	**£5**	
Down At Papa Joe's	LP	London	HAU/SHU8152	1964	**£15**	**£6**	
Down At Poppa Joe's	7"	London	HLU9797	1963	**£4**	**£1.50**	

DIXIE CUPS

Title	Format	Label	Cat. No.	Year	Mint	VG	Notes
Chapel Of Love	7"	Pye	7N25245	1964	**£5**	**£2**	
Chapel Of Love	LP	Red Bird	RB20100	1964	**£30**	**£15**	
Gee The Moon Is Shining Bright	7"	Red Bird	RB10032	1965	**£10**	**£5**	
Iko Iko	7"	Red Bird	RB10024	1965	**£4**	**£1.50**	
Iko Iko	LP	Red Bird	RB(S)20103	1965	**£25**	**£10**	*US*
Little Bell	7"	Red Bird	RB10017	1964	**£5**	**£2**	
Love Ain't So Bad	7"	HMV	POP1557	1966	**£4**	**£1.50**	
People Say	7"	Red Bird	RB10006	1964	**£5**	**£2**	
Riding High	LP	HMV	CLP1916	1966	**£20**	**£8**	
Two Way Poc-A-Way	7"	HMV	POP1453	1965	**£4**	**£1.50**	
What Kind Of Fool	7"	HMV	POP1524	1966	**£5**	**£2**	
You Should Have Seen The Way He Looked At Me	7"	Red Bird	RB10012	1964	**£4**	**£1.50**	

DIXIE DRIFTER

Title	Format	Label	Cat. No.	Year	Mint	VG	Notes
Soul Heaven	7"	Columbia	DB7710	1965	**£8**	**£4**	

DIXIE FOUR

Title	Format	Label	Cat. No.	Year	Mint	VG	Notes
Dixie Four	7" EP	Rarities	RA3	196–	**£15**	**£7.50**	

DIXIE HUMMINGBIRDS

Title	Format	Label	Cat. No.	Year	Mint	VG	Notes
Dixie Hummingbirds	7" EP	Vocalion	EPVP1277	1964	**£8**	**£4**	
Final Edition	7" EP	Vocalion	EPVP1281	1964	**£8**	**£4**	
Have A Talk With Jesus	7"	Vogue	V2422	1964	**£6**	**£2.50**	

DIXIELAND ALL STARS

Title	Format	Label	Cat. No.	Year	Mint	VG	Notes
Dixiecats	LP	Columbia	33SX1080	1958	**£12**	**£5**	

DIXIELAND JUG BLOWERS

Title	Format	Label	Cat. No.	Year	Mint	VG	Notes
Boodle-Am-Shake	7"	HMV	7M223	1954	**£5**	**£2**	
Hen Party Blues	7"	HMV	7M233	1954	**£5**	**£2**	

DIXIELANDERS

Title	Format	Label	Cat. No.	Year	Mint	VG	Notes
Cyclone	7"	Vocalion	V9209	1963	**£15**	**£7.50**	

DIXON, BILLY & THE TOPICS

This was one of a number of names tried out by the group that eventually settled on the Four Seasons.

Title	Format	Label	Cat. No.	Year	Mint	VG	Notes
I Am All Alone	7"	Topix	6002	1960	**£60**	**£30**	*US*
Lost Lullabye	7"	Topix	6008	1960	**£60**	**£30**	*US*

DIXON, ERROL

Title	Format	Label	Cat. No.	Year	Price	Price	Notes
Back To The Chicken Shack	7"	Decca	F12826	1968	**£8**	**£4**	
Bad Bad Woman	7"	Blue Beat	BB86	1962	**£12**	**£6**	
Blues In The Pot	LP	Decca	LK/SKL4962	1968	**£50**	**£25**	*with Chicken Shack*
Errol Sings Fats	7" EP	Decca	DFE8626	1965	**£30**	**£15**	
Gloria	7"	Blue Beat	BB337	1966	**£12**	**£6**	
Hoop	7"	Direct	DS5002	1967	**£6**	**£2.50**	
I Love You	7"	Island	WI069	1963	**£10**	**£5**	
I Need Someone To Love Me	7"	Rainbow	RAI104	1966	**£6**	**£2.50**	
I Want	7"	Fab	FAB1	1966	**£5**	**£2**	
Mama Shut Your Door	7"	Blue Beat	BB46	1961	**£12**	**£6**	
Mean And Evil Woman	7"	Carnival	CV7004	1963	**£8**	**£4**	
Midnight Party	7"	Ska Beat	JB271	1967	**£10**	**£5**	
Midnight Train	7"	Blue Beat	BB27	1960	**£12**	**£6**	
Morning Train	7"	Island	WI017	1962	**£10**	**£5**	
Oo Wee Baby	7"	Carnival	CV7001	1963	**£8**	**£4**	
Rocks In My Pillow	7"	Oriole	CB1914	1964	**£15**	**£7.50**	
Six Questions	7"	Decca	F12613	1967	**£8**	**£4**	
That's How You Got Killed	LP	Transatlantic	TRA225	1970	**£20**	**£8**	
True Love Never Runs Smooth	7"	Decca	F12717	1967	**£8**	**£4**	
Why Hurt Yourself	7"	Doctor Bird	DB1197	1969	**£10**	**£5**	
You're No Good	7"	Blue Beat	BB344	1966	**£12**	**£6**	

DIXON, HUGH

Title	Format	Label	Cat. No.	Year	Price	Price	Notes
Frantic Guitars	LP	London	HAU8188	1964	**£10**	**£4**	

DIXON, JEFF

Title	Format	Label	Cat. No.	Year	Price	Price	Notes
Rock	7"	Coxsone	CS7015	1967	**£12**	**£6**	
Tickle Me	7"	Studio One	SO2051	1968	**£12**	**£6**	

DIXON, WILLIE

Title	Format	Label	Cat. No.	Year	Price	Price	Notes
Catalyst	LP	Ovation	OVQD1433	1973	**£50**	**£25**	*US quad*
I Am The Blues	LP	Columbia	CS9987	1970	**£15**	**£6**	*US*
Walking The Blues	7"	London	HLU8297	1956	**£1500**	**£1000**	*best auctioned*
Walking The Blues	7"	Pye	7N25270	1964	**£12**	**£6**	

DIXON, WILLIE & MEMPHIS SLIM

Title	Format	Label	Cat. No.	Year	Price	Price	Notes
Blues Every Which Way	LP	Verve	V(6)3007	1961	**£15**	**£6**	*US*
In Paris	LP	Battle	BV(S)6122	1963	**£15**	**£6**	*US*
Willie's Blues	LP	Bluesville	BV1003	1960	**£20**	**£8**	*US*

DIXXY SISTERS

Title	Format	Label	Cat. No.	Year	Price	Price	Notes
Game Of Broken Hearts	7"	Columbia	SCM5105	1954	**£5**	**£2**	

DIZZY, JOHNNY

Title	Format	Label	Cat. No.	Year	Price	Price	Notes
Sudden Destruction	7"	Ska Beat	JB204	1965	**£10**	**£5**	*Soulettes B side*

D'JURANN JURANN

Interesting that someone thought of using the name of the angel character from the film *Barbarella* before the New Romantics and 'Planet Earth'. This lot only managed the one single, however, and appear in none of the reference books.

Title	Format	Label	Cat. No.	Year	Price	Price	Notes
Streakin'	7"	Dawn	DNS1068	1974	**£6**	**£2.50**	

DMOCHOWSKI, JED

Title	Format	Label	Cat. No.	Year	Price	Price	Notes
Sha La La	7"	Whaam!	WHAAM9	1983	**£6**	**£2.50**	

DNA

Title	Format	Label	Cat. No.	Year	Price	Price	Notes
La Serenissima	12"	Raw Bass	12RBASS006	1990	**£6**	**£2.50**	

DNV

Title	Format	Label	Cat. No.	Year	Price	Price	Notes
Mafia	7"	New Pleasures	Z2	1979	**£15**	**£7.50**	*fold-out picture sleeve*

D.O.A.

Title	Format	Label	Cat. No.	Year	Price	Price	Notes
Disco Sucks	7"	Quintessence	QEP002	1979	**£20**	**£10**	
Disco Sucks	7"	Sudden Death	3097	1978	**£25**	**£12.50**	
Hardcore '81	LP	Friends	FR010	1981	**£60**	**£30**	
Something Better Change	LP	Friends	FR003	1980	**£40**	**£20**	
Triumph Of The Ignoroids	12"	Friends		198–	**£40**	**£20**	

DOBKINS, CARL

Title	Format	Label	Cat. No.	Year	Price	Price	Notes
Exclusively Yours	7"	Brunswick	05832	1960	**£4**	**£1.50**	
If You Don't Want My Lovin'	7"	Brunswick	05811	1959	**£15**	**£7.50**	
Lucky Devil	7"	Brunswick	05817	1960	**£5**	**£2**	
My Heart Is An Open Book	7"	Brunswick	05804	1959	**£5**	**£2**	
My Heart Is An Open Book	LP	Brunswick	LAT8329	1959	**£30**	**£15**	

DOBSON, ANITA

It might be assumed that the collectors' interest in these items by actress Anita Dobson is related to her former role as Angie in BBC TV's EastEnders. In fact, however, it has rather more to do with the presence of her boyfriend, guitarist Brian May.

Title	Format	Label	Cat. No.	Year	Price	Price	Notes
In One Of My Weaker Moments	12"	MCA	MCAT1260	1988	**£10**	**£5**	
In One Of My Weaker Moments	7"	MCA	MCA1260	1988	**£8**	**£4**	
Talking Of Love	12"	Parlophone	12RP6159	1987	**£15**	**£7.50**	*picture disc*
To Know Him Is To Love Him	7"	Odeon	ODO111	1988	**£15**	**£7.50**	

DOBSON, BONNIE

It was Bonnie Dobson who wrote the song 'Morning Dew', only to watch helplessly while Tim Rose added a verse and then claimed all the credit for himself. The fact that her own polite version of the song is completely upstaged by Rose's recording can have been no help at all.

Bonnie Dobson	LP	Argo	ZFB79	1972	£30	£15	
Bonnie Dobson	LP	RCA	SF8079	1970	£10	£4	
Morning Dew	LP	Polydor	2383400	1976	£10	£4	

DOBSON, DOBBY

Cry A Little Cry	7"	King	KG1008	1965	£5	£2	
Loving Pauper	7"	Trojan	TR011	1967	£10	£5	*Tommy McCook B side*
Seems To Me I'm Losing You	7"	Coxsone	CS7058	1968	£10	£5	*Gaylads B side*
Strange	7"	Blue Cat	BS171	1969	£5	£2	
Strange	LP	Pama	SECO33	1969	£20	£8	
Tell Me	7"	Blue Beat	BB246	1964	£12	£6	
That Wonderful Sound	LP	Trojan	TBL145	1970	£15	£6	
Walking In The Footsteps	7"	Studio One	SO2068	1968	£12	£6	*Soul Vendors B side*

DOCKER, ROY

I'm An Outcast	7"	Pama	PM756	1968	£4	£1.50	
When	7"	Pama	PM750	1968	£4	£1.50	

DOCTOR ALIMANTADO

Best Dressed Chicken In Town	LP	Greensleeves	GREL1	1978	£10	£4	
King's Bread	LP	Ital Sounds	ISDA5000	1979	£10	£4	

DOCTOR & THE MEDICS

Druids Are Here	7"	Whaam!	WHAAM6	1982	£8	£4	

DOCTOR CLAYTON

Pearl Harbor Blues	LP	RCA	INTS1176	1970	£10	£4	
RCA Victor Race Series Vol. 6	7" EP	RCA	RCX7177	1965	£12	£6	

DOCTOR FATHER

Umbopo	7"	Pye	7N17977	1970	£4	£1.50	

DOCTOR FEELGOOD

Something To Take Up Time	LP	Number One		1969	£25	£10	*US*

DODD, DICK

First Evolution Of Dick Dodd	LP	Tower	ST5142	1968	£25	£10	*US*

DODD, PAT

Stag Party	7"	Pye	7N25030	1959	£4	£1.50	

DODD ALL STARS

Hip Shuffle	7"	Coxsone	CS7076	1968	£10	£5	
Mother Aitken	7"	Coxsone	CS7096	1969	£10	£5	

DODDS, JOHNNY

Johnny Dodds And Kid Ory	LP	Philips	BBL7136	1957	£15	£6	
Johnny Dodds Vol. 1	10" LP	Vogue Coral	LRA10025	1955	£20	£8	
Johnny Dodds Vol. 1	10" LP	London	AL3505	1953	£20	£8	
Johnny Dodds Vol. 2	10" LP	London	AL3513	1954	£20	£8	
Johnny Dodds Vol. 3	10" LP	London	AL3555	1956	£20	£8	
Johnny Dodds Vol. 4	10" LP	London	AL3560	1957	£20	£8	
Johnny Dodds Washboard Band	10" LP	HMV	DLP1073	1955	£20	£8	

DODDS, NELLA

Come See About Me	7"	Pye	7N25281	1965	£12	£6	
Finders Keepers Losers Weepers	7"	Pye	7N25291	1965	£10	£5	

DODGERS

Let's Make A Whole Lot Of Love	7"	Downbeat	CHA2	1960	£15	£7.50	

DODGY

Black And White Single	CD-s	Bostin	BTN003CDS	1992	£5	£2	
Easy Way	7"	Bostin	BTN002	1991	£6	£2.50	
Summer Fayre	7"	Bostin	BTN001	1991	£8	£3	

DODO RESURRECTION

Supposedly a sadly underrated progressive rock band based in Kettering, Dodo Resurrection are, in reality, a Mushroom Soup for the nineties – and readers are referred to the entry in the M section. The group was created as an April Fool's joke by a record collectors' magazine that really should have known better – especially when the resulting confusion has been compounded through the inclusion of Dodo Resurrection's 'album' within listings of the rarest and most valuable records. Unwary progressive rock fans will search in vain for a copy to add to their collections – it does not exist!

DODOS

I Made Up My Mind	7"	Polydor	56153	1967	£5	£2	

DOE, ERNIE K

Certain Girl	7"	London	HLP9487	1962	£8	£4	
Dancing Man	7"	Action	ACT4502	1968	£5	£2	
Gotta Pack My Bags	7"	Action	ACT4512	1968	£4	£1.50	

Title	Format	Label	Cat. No.	Year	Mint	VG	Notes
Mother In Law	7"	London	HLU9330	1961	£8	£4	
Mother In Law	LP	Minit	LP0002	1961	£50	£25	US
My Mother In Law	7"	Vocalion	VP9233	1965	£5	£2	
Te Ta Te Ta Ta	7"	London	HLU9390	1961	£6	£2.50	

DOG THAT BIT PEOPLE

Title	Format	Label	Cat. No.	Year	Mint	VG	Notes
Dog That Bit People	LP	Parlophone	PCS7125	1971	£300	£180	
Lovely Lady	7"	Parlophone	R5880	1971	£15	£7.50	

DOGFEET

Title	Format	Label	Cat. No.	Year	Mint	VG	Notes
Dogfeet	LP	Reflection	REFL8	1970	£300	£180	
Sad Story	7"	Reflection	RS7	1970	£25	£12.50	
Since I Went Away	7"	Reflection	HRS12	1971	£25	£12.50	

DOGGEREL BANK

The two little-known LPs by Doggerel Bank continue the experiments in mixing poetry, wit, and music carried out by the Barrow Poets, with many of the same personnel.

Title	Format	Label	Cat. No.	Year	Mint	VG	Notes
Mister Skillicorn Dances	LP	Charisma	CAS1102	1975	£10	£4	
Silver Faces	LP	Charisma	CAS1079	1973	£10	£4	

DOGGETT, BILL

Title	Format	Label	Cat. No.	Year	Mint	VG	Notes
3046 People Danced Till 4 a.m.	LP	Warner Bros	WM4042	1961	£10	£4	
As You Desire Me	LP	King	523	1955	£30	£15	US
Back Again With More	LP	King	723	1960	£15	£6	US
Back With More Bill Doggett	LP	Parlophone	PMC1165	1962	£15	£6	
Band With The Beat	LP	Warner Bros	WS8056	1962	£10	£4	*stereo*
Best Of Bill Doggett	LP	King	908	1964	£10	£4	US
Big City Dance Party	LP	King	641	1959	£20	£8	US
Bill Doggett	7" EP	Parlophone	GEP8711	1958	£8	£4	
Candle Glow	LP	King	563	1958	£20	£8	US
Christmas	LP	King	600	1959	£20	£8	US
Dame Dreaming	10" LP	Parlophone	PMD1067	1958	£20	£8	
Dame Dreaming	LP	King	532	1956	£30	£15	US
Dance Awhile	10" LP	Parlophone	PMD1073	1959	£20	£8	
Dance Awhile	LP	King	585	1958	£20	£8	US
Doggett Beat	LP	King	557	1958	£30	£15	US
Doggett's Big City Dance Party	LP	Parlophone	PMC1118	1960	£15	£6	
Everybody Dance The Honky Tonk	LP	King	531	1956	£30	£15	US
Flute Cocktail	7" EP	Parlophone	GEP8694	1958	£5	£2	
For Reminiscent Lovers	LP	King	706	1960	£20	£8	US
High And Wide	LP	King	633	1959	£20	£8	US
Hold It	LP	King	609	1959	£20	£8	US
Honky Tonk	7"	Parlophone	R4231	1956	£10	£5	*gold label*
Honky Tonk	7"	Parlophone	CMSP39	1956	£8	£4	*export*
Honky Tonk	7" EP	Parlophone	GEP8644	1957	£8	£4	
Hot Doggett	LP	King	514	1954	£30	£15	US
Hot Ginger	7"	Parlophone	R4379	1957	£10	£5	
Jolly Christmas	7" EP	Parlophone	GEP8771	1958	£8	£4	
Leaps And Bounds	7"	Parlophone	R4413	1958	£6	£2.50	
Many Moods	LP	King	778	1961	£15	£6	US
Moondust	LP	King	502	1954	£30	£15	US
On Tour	LP	Parlophone	PMC1124	1960	£15	£6	
Plays Duke Ellington	7" EP	Parlophone	GEP8674	1957	£6	£2.50	
Prelude To The Blues	LP	Columbia	1942	1962	£12	£5	US
Rainbow Riot	7" EP	Parlophone	GEP8727	1958	£6	£2.50	
Ram Bunk Shush	7"	Parlophone	R4306	1957	£6	£2.50	
Salute To Ellington	LP	King	533	1956	£30	£15	US
Slow Walk	7"	Parlophone	R4265	1957	£8	£4	
Smoke	7"	Parlophone	R4629	1960	£5	£2	
Swingin' Easy	LP	King	582	1958	£20	£8	US
Swings	LP	Warner Bros	1452	1963	£10	£4	US
Wow	LP	HMV	CLP1884	1965	£10	£4	
You Can't Sit Down	7"	Warner Bros	WB46	1961	£4	£1.50	

DOGROSE

Title	Format	Label	Cat. No.	Year	Mint	VG	Notes
All For The Love Of Dogrose	LP	Satril	SATL4002	1972	£25	£10	

DOGS D'AMOUR

Title	Format	Label	Cat. No.	Year	Mint	VG	Notes
(Un)authorised Bootleg	LP	China	WOL7	1988	£15	£6	
Back On The Juice	CD-s	China	CHICD30	1990	£5	£2	
Empty World	CD-s	China	CHICD27	1990	£5	£2	
How Come It Never Rains	CD-s	China	CHICD13	1989	£5	£2	
Satellite Kid	CD-s	China	CHICD17	1989	£5	£2	
State We're In	LP	Kumibeat		1984	£25	£10	Finnish
Trail Of Tears	CD-s	China	CHICD20	1989	£5	£2	

DOGWATCH

Title	Format	Label	Cat. No.	Year	Mint	VG	Notes
Penfriend	LP	Bridgehouse	BHLP002	1979	£50	£25	

DOLBY, THOMAS

Title	Format	Label	Cat. No.	Year	Mint	VG	Notes
Airhead	CD-s	EMI	CDMT38	1988	£5	£2	
Hot Sauce	CD-s	EMI	CDMT59	1988	£5	£2	
My Brain Is Like A Sieve	CD-s	EMI	CDMT71	1989	£5	£2	

DOLDINGER, KLAUS

Title	Format	Label	Cat. No.	Year	Mint	VG	Notes
Blues Happening	LP	World Pacific	20167	1968	£15	£6	German

Title	Format	Label	Cat. No.	Year	Mint	VG	Notes
Doldinger's Motherhood	LP	Liberty	LBS83426	1970	**£15**	**£6**	*German*
In Südamerika	LP	Philips	843728	1965	**£15**	**£6**	*German*
Made In Germany	LP	Philips	48024	1963	**£15**	**£6**	*German*

DOLE

Title	Format	Label	Cat. No.	Year	Mint	VG	Notes
New Wave Love	7"	Ultimate	ULT402	1978	**£10**	**£5**	

DOLENZ, JONES, BOYCE & HART

Title	Format	Label	Cat. No.	Year	Mint	VG	Notes
Dolenz, Jones, Boyce & Hart	LP	Capitol	ST11513	1976	**£12**	**£5**	*US*

DOLENZ, MICKEY

Title	Format	Label	Cat. No.	Year	Mint	VG	Notes
Don't Do It	7"	London	HLH10117	1967	**£8**	**£4**	*B side by Finders Keepers*
Huff Puff	7"	London	HLH10152	1967	**£8**	**£4**	*Obvious B side*

DOLENZ, MICKY

Title	Format	Label	Cat. No.	Year	Mint	VG	Notes
Daybreak	7"	MGM	2006265	1973	**£6**	**£2.50**	
Ooh She's Young	7"	MGM	2006392	1974	**£6**	**£2.50**	
Tomorrow	7"	A&M	BUGSY1	1983	**£6**	**£2.50**	*with poster*

DOLL, ANDY

Title	Format	Label	Cat. No.	Year	Mint	VG	Notes
On Stage	LP	Starlite	STLP11	1963	**£15**	**£6**	
Wild Desire	7"	Starlite	ST45068	1962	**£6**	**£2.50**	

DOLL, LINDA & THE SUNDOWNERS

Title	Format	Label	Cat. No.	Year	Mint	VG	Notes
Bonie Maronie	7"	Piccadilly	7N35166	1964	**£4**	**£1.50**	

DOLLIES

Title	Format	Label	Cat. No.	Year	Mint	VG	Notes
You Touch Me Baby	7"	CBS	201788	1965	**£4**	**£1.50**	

DOLPHIN

Title	Format	Label	Cat. No.	Year	Mint	VG	Notes
Molecules	LP	Gale	LP02	1980	**£15**	**£6**	

DOLPHY, ERIC

Title	Format	Label	Cat. No.	Year	Mint	VG	Notes
At The Five Spot	LP	Transatlantic	PR7294	1967	**£15**	**£6**	
Eric Dolphy And Booker Little Memorial Album	LP	Stateside	SL10160	1966	**£15**	**£6**	
Out To Lunch	LP	Blue Note	BLP/BST84163	1964	**£25**	**£10**	
Outward Bound	LP	Transatlantic	PR7311	1969	**£15**	**£6**	
Screamin' The Blues	LP	XTRA	XTRA5039	1968	**£12**	**£5**	*with Oliver Nelson*
Screamin' The Blues	LP	Esquire		1962	**£20**	**£8**	*with Oliver Nelson*

DOM

Title	Format	Label	Cat. No.	Year	Mint	VG	Notes
Edge Of Time	LP	Melocord	STLPD001	1971	**£100**	**£50**	*German*

DOME

Title	Format	Label	Cat. No.	Year	Mint	VG	Notes
3R4	12"	4AD	CAD16	1980	**£6**	**£2.50**	
Dome	LP	Dome	DOME1	1980	**£10**	**£4**	
Dome 2	LP	Dome	DOME2	1980	**£10**	**£4**	
Dome 3	LP	Dome	DOME3	1981	**£10**	**£4**	

DOMINO, FATS

With a hit-making career that began as early as 1949 (with music that differs hardly at all from the rock'n'roll that exploded into the American charts some half a dozen years later), Fats Domino had achieved more million-selling gold discs than any other artist apart from Elvis Presley by the time that the arrival of the Beatles effectively consigned him to the nostalgia circuit. The fact that his records were issued in the UK on the London label would have made him a collectable artist in any case, but the matter is clinched by the status of songs like 'Blue Monday', 'Ain't That A Shame', and above all, 'Blueberry Hill', as classic recordings of the fifties.

Title	Format	Label	Cat. No.	Year	Mint	VG	Notes
Ain't That A Shame	7"	London	HLU8173	1955	**£40**	**£20**	*gold label*
Ain't That Just Like A Woman	7"	London	HLP9301	1961	**£8**	**£4**	
Be My Guest	7"	London	HLP9005	1959	**£25**	**£12.50**	*tri-centre*
Be My Guest	7"	London	HLP9005	1959	**£5**	**£2**	
Be My Guest	7" EP	London	REP1261	1960	**£20**	**£10**	
Big Beat	7"	London	HLP8575	1958	**£10**	**£5**	
Big Beat	7"	London	HL7054	1958	**£12**	**£6**	*export*
Blue Monday	7"	London	HLP8377	1957	**£30**	**£15**	*gold label*
Blueberry Hill	7"	London	HLU8330	1956	**£40**	**£20**	*gold label*
Blues For Love Vol. 1	7" EP	London	REP1022	1955	**£50**	**£25**	*gold label*
Blues For Love Vol. 2	7" EP	London	REU1062	1956	**£40**	**£20**	*gold label*
Blues For Love Vol. 3	7" EP	London	REP1117	1958	**£25**	**£12.50**	
Blues For Love Vol. 4	7" EP	London	REP1121	1958	**£25**	**£12.50**	
Bo Weevil	7"	London	HLU8256	1956	**£75**	**£37.50**	*gold label*
Carry On Rocking	LP	London	HAU2041	1956	**£60**	**£30**	
Carry On Rocking Part 1	7" EP	London	REP1115	1958	**£25**	**£12.50**	
Carry On Rocking Part 2	7" EP	London	REP1116	1958	**£25**	**£12.50**	
Country Boy	7"	London	HLP9073	1960	**£6**	**£2.50**	
Domino '65	LP	Mercury	(S)MCL20070	1965	**£10**	**£4**	
Don't Leave Me This Way	78	London	HL8096	1954	**£20**	**£10**	
Everybody's Got Something To Hide . . .	7"	Reprise	RS20810	1969	**£4**	**£1.50**	
Fabulous Mr D	LP	London	HAP2135	1958	**£30**	**£15**	
Fantastic Fats	LP	Stateside	(S)SL10240	1968	**£10**	**£4**	
Fats	7" EP	London	REU1073	1957	**£75**	**£37.50**	*gold label*
Fats	LP	Reprise	RS6439	1971	**£300**	**£180**	*US*
Fats Domino	LP	Imperial	LP9009	1956	**£60**	**£30**	*US*
Fats Domino Swings	LP	Imperial	LP9062	1959	**£30**	**£15**	*US*

Fats On Fire	LP	HMV	CLP1740/ CSD1543	1963	**£20**	**£8**	
Getaway With Fats	LP	HMV	CLP1821/ CSD1580	1966	**£15**	**£6**	
Here Comes Fats	LP	HMV	CLP1690/ CSD1520	1963	**£20**	**£8**	
Here Comes Fats Vol. 1	7" EP	London	REP1079	1957	**£25**	**£12.50**	
Here Comes Fats Vol. 2	7" EP	London	REP1080	1957	**£25**	**£12.50**	
Here Comes Fats Vol. 3	7" EP	London	REP1138	1958	**£25**	**£12.50**	
Here He Comes Again	LP	Imperial	LP9248	1963	**£20**	**£8**	*US*
Here Stands Fats Domino	LP	London	HAU2052	1957	**£60**	**£30**	
Here Stands Fats Domino	LP	Imperial	LP9038	1957	**£60**	**£30**	*US*
Honest Mamas Love Their Papas	7"	Reprise	R20696	1968	**£6**	**£2.50**	
Honey Chile	7"	London	HLU8356	1957	**£40**	**£20**	*gold label*
I Don't Want To Set The World On Fire	7"	HMV	POP1281	1964	**£4**	**£1.50**	
I Know	7"	London	HL8133	1955	**£100**	**£50**	*gold label*
I Left My Heart In San Francisco	7"	Mercury	MF869	1965	**£6**	**£2.50**	
I Miss You So	LP	London	HAP2364	1961	**£30**	**£15**	
I Want To Walk You Home	7"	London	HLP8942	1959	**£8**	**£4**	
I'm Livin' Right	7"	HMV	POP1582	1967	**£4**	**£1.50**	
I'm Ready	7"	Liberty	LIB15274	1969	**£6**	**£2.50**	
I'm Walking	7"	London	HLP8407	1957	**£15**	**£7.50**	
It Keeps Raining	7"	Liberty	LIB12055	1967	**£4**	**£1.50**	
It Keeps Raining	7"	London	HLP9374	1961	**£15**	**£7.50**	
Jambalaya	7"	London	HLP9520	1962	**£5**	**£2**	
Just A Lonely Man	7"	HMV	POP1265	1963	**£4**	**£1.50**	
Just Domino	LP	London	HAP8039	1963	**£30**	**£15**	
Kansas City	7"	HMV	POP1370	1964	**£4**	**£1.50**	
Lady Madonna	7"	Reprise	RS20763	1968	**£4**	**£1.50**	
Let The Four Winds Blow	7"	London	HLP9415	1961	**£6**	**£2.50**	
Let The Four Winds Blow	LP	London	HAP2420	1961	**£30**	**£15**	
Let's Dance With Domino	LP	Imperial	LP9239	1963	**£25**	**£10**	*US*
Let's Play Fats Domino	LP	London	HAP2223	1959	**£30**	**£15**	
Little Mary	7"	London	HLP8663	1958	**£12**	**£6**	
Lot Of Domino's	LP	London	HAP2312	1960	**£30**	**£15**	
Love Me	7"	London	HL8124	1955	**£125**	**£62.50**	*gold label*
Margie	7"	London	HLP8865	1959	**£6**	**£2.50**	
Mary Oh Mary	7"	HMV	POP1324	1964	**£4**	**£1.50**	
Million Record Hits	LP	Imperial	LP9103/12103	1960	**£25**	**£10**	*US*
Million Sellers Vol. 1	LP	Liberty	LBY3033	1965	**£10**	**£4**	
Million Sellers Vol. 2	LP	Liberty	LBY3046	1965	**£10**	**£4**	
Million Sellers Vol. 3	LP	Liberty	LBL83101	1968	**£10**	**£4**	
My Blue Heaven	7"	London	HLU8280	1956	**£60**	**£30**	*gold label*
My Blue Heaven	7" EP	Liberty	LEP4026	1965	**£15**	**£7.50**	
My Girl Josephine	7"	London	HLP9244	1960	**£5**	**£2**	
My Real Name	7"	London	HLP9557	1962	**£8**	**£4**	
Nothing New	7"	London	HLP9590	1962	**£8**	**£4**	
Red Sails In The Sunset	7"	HMV	POP1219	1963	**£4**	**£1.50**	
Red Sails In The Sunset	7" EP	HMV	7EG8862	1964	**£15**	**£7.50**	
Rock And Rollin'	LP	London	HAU2028	1956	**£60**	**£30**	
Rock And Rollin'	LP	Imperial	LP9004	1956	**£60**	**£30**	*US*
Rocking Mister D Vol. 1	7" EP	London	REP1206	1959	**£25**	**£12.50**	
Rocking Mister D Vol. 2	7" EP	London	REP1207	1959	**£25**	**£12.50**	
Rocking Mister D Vol. 3	7" EP	London	REP1265	1960	**£20**	**£10**	
Rolling	7" EP	Liberty	LEP4045	1966	**£15**	**£7.50**	
Shurah	7"	London	HLP9327	1961	**£8**	**£4**	
Sick And Tired	7"	London	HLP8628	1958	**£10**	**£5**	
Sick And Tired	7"	London	HL7040	1958	**£12**	**£6**	*export*
Something You Got Baby	7"	HMV	POP1303	1964	**£15**	**£7.50**	
Stop The Clock	7"	London	HLP9616	1962	**£8**	**£4**	
Tell Me That You Love Me	7"	London	HLP9133	1960	**£10**	**£5**	
There Goes My Heart Again	7"	HMV	POP1164	1963	**£6**	**£2.50**	
This Is Fats	LP	London	HAP2087	1958	**£30**	**£15**	
This Is Fats	LP	Imperial	LP9040	1957	**£50**	**£25**	*US*
This Is Fats Domino	LP	London	HAP2073	1956	**£30**	**£15**	
This Is Fats Domino	LP	Imperial	LP9028	1957	**£50**	**£25**	*US*
Three Nights A Week	7"	London	HLP9198	1960	**£6**	**£2.50**	
Twistin' The Stomp	LP	London	HAP2447	1962	**£30**	**£15**	
Valley Of Tears	7"	London	HLP8449	1957	**£15**	**£7.50**	
Wait And See	7"	London	HL7028	1957	**£12**	**£6**	*export*
Wait And See	7"	London	HLP8519	1957	**£12**	**£6**	
Walking To New Orleans	7"	London	HLP9163	1960	**£6**	**£2.50**	
Walking To New Orleans	LP	London	HAP8084	1963	**£30**	**£15**	
What A Party	7"	London	HLP9456	1961	**£6**	**£2.50**	
What A Party	7" EP	London	REP1340	1962	**£20**	**£10**	
What A Party	LP	London	HAP2426	1961	**£30**	**£15**	
What's That You Got	7"	Mercury	MF873	1965	**£5**	**£2**	
What's That You Got	7"	Mercury	MF1104	1969	**£5**	**£2**	
When I See You	7"	London	HLP8471	1957	**£15**	**£7.50**	
When I'm Walking	7"	HMV	POP1197	1963	**£5**	**£2**	
When My Dreamboat Comes Along	7"	London	HLU8309	1956	**£40**	**£20**	*gold label*
When The Saints Go Marching In	7"	London	HLP8822	1959	**£8**	**£4**	
Whole Lotta Loving	7"	London	HLP8759	1958	**£12**	**£6**	
Why Don't You Do Right	7"	HMV	POP1421	1965	**£4**	**£1.50**	
You Always Hurt The One You Love	7"	London	HLP9738	1963	**£6**	**£2.50**	
You Done Me Wrong	78	London	HL8063	1954	**£25**	**£12.50**	
You Said You Loved Me	78	London	HL8007	1954	**£25**	**£12.50**	
Young School Girl	7"	London	HLP8727	1958	**£15**	**£7.50**	

DOMINOES

Title	Format	Label	Number	Year	Mint	VG	Notes
Tribute	7"	Melody	MRC002	1968	£6	£2.50	

DOMINOES (2)

Title	Format	Label	Number	Year	Mint	VG	Notes
Bye Bye Johnny	7"	Reading Rag	LYN545	1958	£6	£2.50	

DOMINOES & SWALLOWS

Title	Format	Label	Number	Year	Mint	VG	Notes
Rhythm And Blues	7" EP	Vogue	EPV1113	1956	£200	£100	

DON, DICK & JIMMY

Title	Format	Label	Number	Year	Mint	VG	Notes
Angela Mia	7"	Columbia	SCM5110	1954	£8	£4	
Don, Dick & Jimmy	7" EP	London	REU1043	1955	£20	£10	
Make Yourself Comfortable	7"	London	HL8144	1955	£10	£5	
Spring Fever	LP	Modern	LMP1205	1956	£25	£10	US
That's The Way I Feel	7"	HMV	POP280	1956	£5	£2	
You Can't Have Your Cake & Eat It Too	7"	London	HL8117	1955	£10	£5	

DON & DANDY & THE SUPERBOYS

Title	Format	Label	Number	Year	Mint	VG	Notes
Keep On Fighting	7"	Giant	GN24	1968	£4	£1.50	

DON & DEWEY

Title	Format	Label	Number	Year	Mint	VG	Notes
Get Your Hat	7"	London	HL9897	1964	£12	£6	
Soul Motion	7"	Sue	WI4032	1967	£12	£6	
Soul Motion	7"	Cameo Parkway	CP750	1966	£12	£6	

DON & JUAN

Title	Format	Label	Number	Year	Mint	VG	Notes
What's Your Name	7"	London	HLX9529	1962	£15	£7.50	

DON & THE GOODTIMES

Title	Format	Label	Number	Year	Mint	VG	Notes
Greatest Hits	LP	Burdette	300	1966	£25	£10	US
So Good	LP	Epic	BN26311	1967	£20	£8	US
Where The Action Is	LP	Wand	WDS679	1966	£25	£10	US

DON BRADSHAW LEATHER

Title	Format	Label	Number	Year	Mint	VG	Notes
Distance Between Us	LP	Distance	no number	1972	£40	£20	*double*

DONAHUE, JERRY

Title	Format	Label	Number	Year	Mint	VG	Notes
Telecasting	LP	Musicmaker	MML880011	1986	£12	£5	
Theme From Catlow	7"	Philips	6006219	1972	£5	£2	

DONAHUE, SAM

Title	Format	Label	Number	Year	Mint	VG	Notes
Sam Donahue Orchestra	10" LP	Capitol	LCT6019	1955	£15	£6	
Saxaboogie	7"	Capitol	CL14349	1955	£8	£4	

DONALD, MIKE

Title	Format	Label	Number	Year	Mint	VG	Notes
North By North East	LP	Galliard	GAL4020	1972	£15	£6	
Yorkshire Songs Of The Broad Acres	LP	Folk Heritage	FHR021	1971	£15	£6	

DONALDSON, BOBBY

Title	Format	Label	Number	Year	Mint	VG	Notes
Dixieland – New York!	LP	London	SAHC6007	1959	£12	£5	

DONALDSON, ERIC

Title	Format	Label	Number	Year	Mint	VG	Notes
Cherry Oh Baby	7"	Dynamic	DYN420	1971	£4	£1.50	*Lloyd Charmers B side*
Eric Donaldson	LP	Trojan	TRL42	1972	£15	£6	

DONALDSON, JULIA & MICHAEL

Title	Format	Label	Number	Year	Mint	VG	Notes
First Fourteen	LP	Longmans		1979	£30	£15	

DONALDSON, LOU

Title	Format	Label	Number	Year	Mint	VG	Notes
Alligator Boogaloo	LP	Blue Note	BLP/BST84263	1967	£20	£8	
Blues Walk	LP	Blue Note	BLP/BST81593	196–	£25	£10	
Cosmos	LP	Blue Note	BST84370	1970	£12	£5	
Everything I Play Is Funky	LP	Blue Note	BST84337	1969	£15	£6	
Good Gracious	LP	Blue Note	BLP/BST84125	1963	£30	£15	
Gravy Train	LP	Blue Note	BLP/BST84079	196–	£25	£10	
Here 'Tis	LP	Blue Note	BLP/BST84066	196–	£25	£10	
Hot Dog	LP	Blue Note	BST84318	1969	£15	£6	
Light Foot	LP	Blue Note	BLP/BST84053	196–	£30	£15	
Midnight Creeper	LP	Blue Note	BST84280	1968	£15	£6	
Mr Shing-A-Ling	LP	Blue Note	BLP/BST84271	1967	£20	£8	
Natural Soul	LP	Blue Note	BLP/BST84108	1962	£25	£10	
Pretty Things	LP	Blue Note	BST84359	1970	£12	£5	
Say It Loud	LP	Blue Note	BST84299	1968	£15	£6	
Sunny Side Up	LP	Blue Note	BLP/BST84036	196–	£30	£15	
Sweet Slumber	LP	Blue Note	BLP/BST84254	1967	£20	£8	
Time Is Right	LP	Blue Note	BLP/BST84025	196–	£30	£15	

DONAYS

Title	Format	Label	Number	Year	Mint	VG	Notes
Devil In His Heart	7"	Oriole	CB1770	1962	£100	£50	

DONEGAN, DOROTHY

Title	Format	Label	Number	Year	Mint	VG	Notes
Dorothy Donegan Trio	7" EP	MGM	MGMEP532	1956	£5	£2	

DONEGAN, LONNIE

To anyone who grew up with the rock music of the sixties, Lonnie Donegan was essentially a novelty figure – the man who recorded weak musical jokes like 'My Old Man's A Dustman' and 'Does Chewing Gum Lose Its Flavour On The Bedpost Overnight?'. In fact, Donegan actually deserves as much respect as Elvis Presley as a vital rock pioneer. Musicians like Brian May and Rory Gallagher have spoken in glowing terms of the man who introduced the sound of the blues to British listeners, single-handedly inventing the skiffle genre in the process, and thereby inspiring them to pick up a guitar. As the banjo player with Chris Barber's traditional jazz band in the early fifties, Donegan would also entertain audiences during set breaks by trading his banjo for an acoustic guitar and bashing his way through enthusiastic renditions of Leadbelly songs. Someone decided that one of these, an extraordinary and rather thrilling version of 'Rock Island Line' included on Barber's LP, *New Orleans Joys*, would make a good single. It became the first of an incredible run of twenty-six British chart hits that ended only with the arrival of the Beatles.

Backstairs Session	7" EP	Polygon	JTE107	1956	**£20**	**£10**	
Backstairs Session	7" EP	Pye	NJE1014	1956	**£8**	**£4**	
Comancheros	7"	Pye	7N3109	1962	**£6**	**£2.50**	*export, 2 picture sleeves*
Digging My Potatoes	7"	Decca	FJ10695	1956	**£10**	**£5**	
Folk Album	LP	Pye	NPL18126	1965	**£15**	**£6**	
Grand Coulee Dam	7"	Pye	7N15129	1958	**£6**	**£2.50**	
Jack O'Diamonds	7"	Pye	7N15116	1957	**£4**	**£1.50**	
Kevin Barry	7"	Pye	7N15219	1959	**£15**	**£7.50**	
Lonesome Traveller	7"	Pye	7N15158	1958	**£4**	**£1.50**	
Lonnie	10" LP	Pye	NPT19027	1958	**£15**	**£6**	
Lonnie	10" LP	Pye	NSPT84000	1957	**£40**	**£20**	*stereo*
Lonnie Donegan Hit Parade	7" EP	Pye	NEP24031	1957	**£6**	**£2.50**	
Lonnie Donegan Hit Parade Vol. 2	7" EP	Pye	NEP24040	1957	**£6**	**£2.50**	
Lonnie Donegan Hit Parade Vol. 3	7" EP	Pye	NEP24067	1958	**£6**	**£2.50**	
Lonnie Donegan Hit Parade Vol. 4	7" EP	Pye	NEP24081	1958	**£6**	**£2.50**	
Lonnie Donegan Hit Parade Vol. 5	7" EP	Pye	NEP24104	1959	**£6**	**£2.50**	
Lonnie Donegan Hit Parade Vol. 6	7" EP	Pye	NEP24114	1959	**£6**	**£21.50**	
Lonnie Donegan Hit Parade Vol. 7	7" EP	Pye	NEP24134	1961	**£8**	**£4**	
Lonnie Donegan Hit Parade Vol. 8	7" EP	Pye	NEP24149	1961	**£8**	**£4**	
Lonnie Donegan On Stage	7" EP	Pye	NEP24075	1958	**£8**	**£4**	
Lonnie Donegan Skiffle Group	7" EP	Decca	DFE6345	1956	**£10**	**£5**	*tri-centre*
Lonnie's Skiffle Party	7"	Pye	7N15165	1958	**£4**	**£1.50**	
Lonniepops	LP	Decca	SKL5068	1970	**£10**	**£4**	
Midnight Special	7"	Pye	7NJ2006	1958	**£10**	**£5**	
More Tops With Lonnie	LP	Pye	NPL18063	1961	**£12**	**£5**	
Passing Stranger	78	Oriole	CB1329	1956	**£8**	**£4**	*B side by Tommy Reilly*
Pick A Bale Of Cotton	7"	Pye	7N15455	1962	**£10**	**£5**	*picture sleeve*
Relax With Lonnie	7" EP	Pye	NEP24107	1959	**£8**	**£4**	
Rides Again	LP	Pye	NPL18043	1959	**£12**	**£5**	
Rock Island Line	7"	Decca	FJ10647	1955	**£12**	**£6**	
Sally Don't You Grieve	7"	Pye	7N15148	1958	**£4**	**£1.50**	
Showcase	10" LP	Pye	NPT19012	1956	**£15**	**£6**	
Sing Hallelujah	LP	Pye	NPL18073	1962	**£15**	**£6**	
Skiffle Session	7" EP	Pye	NJE1017	1956	**£5**	**£2**	
Take My Hand	7"	Columbia	DB3850	1956	**£15**	**£7.50**	
Tops With Lonnie	LP	Pye	NPL18034	1958	**£12**	**£5**	
Yankee Doodle Donegan	7" EP	Pye	NEP24127	1960	**£6**	**£2.50**	

DONKEYS

Don't Go	7"	Rhesus	GOAPE105	1980	**£5**	**£2**	
No Way	7"	Rhesus	GOAPE103	1980	**£5**	**£2**	
What I Want	7"	Rhesus	GOAPE102	1980	**£5**	**£2**	

DONLEY, JIMMY

Shape You Left Me In	7"	Brunswick	05807	1959	**£75**	**£37.50**	
South Of The Border	7"	Brunswick	05715	1957	**£8**	**£4**	

DONNA & THE FREEDOM SINGERS

Oh Me Oh My	7"	Bamboo	BAM53	1970	**£5**	**£2**	

DONNER, RAL

Bells Of Love	7"	Stateside	SS109	1962	**£8**	**£4**	
I Don't Need You	7"	Parlophone	R4889	1962	**£8**	**£4**	
I Got Burned	7"	Reprise	R20141	1963	**£15**	**£7.50**	
Please Don't Go	7"	Parlophone	R4859	1961	**£6**	**£2.50**	
Takin' Care Of Business	LP	Gone	LP5012	1961	**£100**	**£50**	*US*
You Don't Know What You Got	7"	Parlophone	R4820	1961	**£5**	**£2**	

DONNIE & THE DREAMERS

Count Every Star	7"	Top Rank	JAR571	1961	**£15**	**£7.50**	

DONOVAN

Donovan is often viewed as a bit of a joke these days, seeming to epitomize all the more pretentious, self-conscious aspects of hippy culture. His achievement in moving onwards from being a pale shadow of Bob Dylan into creating music of genuine invention and charm is considerable, however. The UK album, *Sunshine Superman*, which combines the best tracks of two albums issued in America, is like a folk version of *Sgt Pepper*, while the double *Gift From A Flower To A Garden*, despite being inevitably too long, is almost as good. This latter album, which was issued as a boxed set, is becoming increasingly scarce, especially with its numerous poetic inserts intact.

7-Tease	LP	Epic	SEPC69104	1974	**£10**	**£4**	
Barabajagal	LP	Epic	BN26481	1968	**£15**	**£6**	*US*
Brother Sun, Sister Moon	LP	HMV	3C06493393	1970	**£30**	**£15**	*German*
Catch The Wind	7" EP	Pye	NEP24287	1968	**£8**	**£4**	
Catch The Wind	7" EP	Pye	PNV24138	1965	**£8**	**£4**	*French*

Colours	7" EP	Pye	NEP24229	1965	£10	£5	
Colours	7" EP	Pye	PNV24153	1965	£10	£5	*French*
Cosmic Wheels	LP	Epic	SEPC65450	1973	£10	£4	
Donovan	LP	World Records	ST951	1965	£10	£4	
Donovan Rising	LP	Permanent	PERMLP2	1990	£10	£4	
Donovan Vol. 1	7" EP	Pye	NEP24239	1966	£8	£4	
Epistle To Dippy	7" EP	Epic	9064	1967	£12	£6	*French*
Essence To Essence	LP	Epic	SEPC69050	1973	£10	£4	
Fairytale	LP	Pye	NPL18128	1965	£15	£6	
For Little Ones	LP	Epic	LN24/BN26350	1967	£15	£6	*US*
Four Shades	LP	Pye	11PP102	1973	£50	£25	*4 LP boxed set*
Gift From A Flower To A Garden	LP	Pye	N(S)PL20000	1968	£40	£20	*double, boxed*
Greatest Hits	LP	Pye	N(S)PL18283	1969	£10	£4	
HMS Donovan	LP	Dawn	DNLD4001	1971	£75	£37.50	*with poster*
HMS Donovan	LP	Dawn	DNLD4001	1971	£40	£20	*double*
Hurdy Gurdy Donovan	7" EP	Pye	NEP24299	1968	£10	£5	
Hurdy Gurdy Man	LP	Epic	BN26420	1968	£10	£4	*US*
In Concert	LP	Pye	N(S)PL18237	1968	£10	£4	
Jennifer Juniper	7"	Epic		1967	£8	£4	*sung in Italian*
Live In Japan, Spring Tour 1973	LP	Epic	ECPM25	1973	£25	£10	*Japanese*
Mellow Yellow	LP	Epic	LN24/BN26239	1967	£15	£6	*US*
Open Road	LP	Dawn	DNLS3009	1970	£15	£6	
Remember The Alamo	7"	Pye	7N17088	1966	£10	£5	
Rock'n'roll With Me	7"	Epic	EPC2661	1975	£12	£6	*picture sleeve*
Slow Down World	LP	Epic	SEPC86011	1976	£10	£4	
Summer Day Reflection Song	7" EP	Pye	PNV24170	1966	£12	£6	*French*
Sunshine Superman	CD-s	EMI	CDEM98	1989	£5	£2	
Sunshine Superman	LP	Pye	NPL18181	1967	£15	£6	
Sunshine Superman	LP	Epic	LN24/BN26217	1966	£15	£6	*US, different tracks*
Turquoise	7" EP	Pye	PNV24158	1965	£10	£5	*French*
Universal Soldier	7" EP	Pye	NEP24219	1965	£6	£2.50	
Universal Soldier	7" EP	Pye	PNV24149	1965	£8	£4	*French*
Wear Your Love Like Heaven	LP	Epic	LN24/BN26349	1967	£15	£6	*US*
What's Bin Did And What's Bin Hid	LP	Pye	NPL18117	1965	£20	£8	

DONOVAN & JEFF BECK GROUP

Goo Goo Barabajagal	7"	Pye	7N17778	1969	£4	£1.50	
Goo Goo Barabajagal	7"	Pye	7N17778	1969	£5	£2	*'Bed With Me' B side*

DONOVAN, JASON

Angel	CD-s	Polydor	PZCD295	1994	£10	£5	
Every Day	CD-s	PWL	PWCD43	1989	£5	£2	
Nothing Can Divide Us	CD-s	PWL	PWLCD17	1988	£8	£4	
Sealed With A Kiss	CD-s	PWL	PWCD39	1989	£5	£2	
Too Many Broken Hearts	CD-s	PWL	PWCD32	1989	£8	£4	

DONTELLS

In Your Heart	7"	Fontana	TF566	1965	£25	£12.50	

DOO, DICKIE & THE DONTS

Click Clack	7"	London	HLU8589	1958	£25	£12.50	
Leave Me Alone	7"	London	HLU8754	1958	£25	£12.50	
Madison	LP	United Artists	UAL3094/UAS6094	1960	£25	£10	*US*
Teen Scene	LP	United Artists	UAL3097/UAS6097	1960	£25	£10	*US*
Wabash Cannonball	7"	Top Rank	JAR318	1960	£4	£1.50	

DOOLEY SISTERS

Ko Ko Mo	7"	London	HL8128	1955	£25	£12.50	

DOONAN, JOHN

At The Feis	LP	Topic	12TS368	1978	£25	£10	
Flute For The Feis	LP	Leader	LEA2043	1972	£12	£5	

DOORFIELD

Nil Desperandum	LP	Flatrock		1971	£30	£15	*US*

DOORS

For the most part, the success of the Doors represented a triumph of image over content. Certainly to British ears, the simple blues-based material in which the group specialized sounded distinctly ordinary in comparison with either the other West Coast bands or the more searching local groups. The Doors had two effective hit singles – 'Light My Fire' and 'Riders On The Storm', together with a first album that was interesting in parts, but the rest was largely built on the repetition of a few tried formulae. Live, however, the group had an aggressive macho image, with lead singer Jim Morrison wearing an all-leather outfit and gaining a reputation for exposing himself on stage. His stance at the microphone has become widely copied by charismatic singers in groups like the Stone Roses and Oasis, so that, in combination with the fact that fans have never become disillusioned by seeing Morrison grow old and tired, the Doors are made to seem like a more important sixties group than they were at the time.

13	LP	Elektra	K42062	1971	£10	£4	
Absolutely Live	CD	Elektra	K262005	1987	£20	£8	*double*
Absolutely Live	LP	Elektra	2665002	1970	£15	£6	*double*
Alabama Song	7"	Elektra	EKSN45012	1967	£10	£5	
American Prayer	LP	Elektra	K52111	1978	£10	£4	*with booklet*
Best Of The Doors	LP	Elektra	K242143	1974	£12	£5	*quad*
Break On Through	7"	Elektra	EKSN45009	1967	£15	£7.50	

Break On Through	7" EP	Vogue	INT18129	1967	£**200**	£**100**	*French*
Break On Through	CD-s	Elektra	EKR121CD	1991	£**5**	£**2**	
Doors	CD	DCC	GZS1023	1992	£**15**	£**6**	*US audiophile*
Doors	LP	Mobile Fidelity	MFSL1051	1980	£**12**	£**5**	*US audiophile*
Doors	LP	Elektra	EKS74007	1970	£**10**	£**4**	*red label*
Doors	LP	Elektra	EKS74007	1967	£**25**	£**10**	*stereo*
Doors	LP	Elektra	EKL4007	1967	£**30**	£**15**	*mono*
Hello I Love You	7"	Elektra	EKSN45037	1968	£**4**	£**1.50**	
L.A. Woman	CD	Elektra	C8816	1988	£**12**	£**5**	*HMV boxed set*
L.A. Woman	CD	DCC	GZS1034	1993	£**15**	£**6**	*US audiophile*
L.A. Woman	LP	Elektra	K42090	1971	£**15**	£**6**	*clear window sleeve*
Light My Fire	7"	Elektra	EKSN45014	1967	£**10**	£**5**	
Light My Fire	7" EP	Vogue	INT18145	1967	£**100**	£**50**	*French*
Light My Fire	CD-s	Elektra	EKR125CD	1991	£**5**	£**2**	
Live At The Hollywood Bowl	LP	Elektra	EKT40F	1987	£**20**	£**8**	*promo with interview LP*
Love Her Madly	7"	Elektra	EK45726	1971	£**4**	£**1.50**	
Love Me Two Times	7"	Elektra	EKSN45022	1967	£**6**	£**2.50**	
Love Me Two Times	7"	Elektra	K12215	1979	£**4**	£**1.50**	*double*
Morrison Hotel	LP	Elektra	EKS75007	1970	£**12**	£**5**	
Other Voices	LP	Elektra	K42104	1971	£**10**	£**4**	
Peace Frog	CD-s	Elektra	PRCD947	1997	£**25**	£**12.50**	*promo*
People Are Strange	7"	Elektra	EKSN45017	1967	£**10**	£**5**	
Riders On The Storm	CD-s	Elektra	EKR131CD	1991	£**5**	£**2**	
Roadhouse Blues	7"	Elektra	2101008	1970	£**4**	£**1.50**	
Soft Parade	LP	Elektra	EKS75005	1969	£**15**	£**6**	
Strange Days	CD	DCC	GZS1026	1992	£**15**	£**6**	*US audiophile*
Strange Days	LP	Elektra	EKS74014	1968	£**20**	£**8**	*stereo*
Strange Days	LP	Elektra	EKL4014	1968	£**30**	£**15**	*mono*
Tell All The People	7"	Elektra	EKSN45065	1969	£**5**	£**2**	
Touch Me	7"	Elektra	EKSN45050	1969	£**5**	£**2**	
Unknown Soldier	7"	Elektra	EKSN45030	1968	£**6**	£**2.50**	
Waiting For The Sun	LP	Elektra	EKL4024	1968	£**30**	£**15**	*mono*
Waiting For The Sun	LP	Elektra	EKS74024	1968	£**20**	£**8**	*stereo*
Weird Scenes Inside The Goldmine	LP	Elektra	K62009	1972	£**12**	£**5**	*double*
Wishful Sinful	7"	Elektra	EKSN45059	1969	£**5**	£**2**	
You Make Me Real	7"	Elektra	2101004	1970	£**4**	£**1.50**	

DORAN, FELIX

Last Of The Travelling Pipers	LP	Topic	12TS288	1976	£**10**	£**4**	

DOREEN

Rude Girls	7"	Rainbow	RAI114	1967	£**6**	£**2.50**	

DOREEN & JACKIE

Welcome Home	7"	Ska Beat	JB208	1965	£**10**	£**5**	

DORHAM, KENNY

Jazz Contrasts	LP	London	LTZU15133	1958	£**20**	£**8**	
Kenny Dorham And The Jazz Prophets	10" LP	HMV	DLP1184	1958	£**20**	£**8**	
Trompeta Toccata	LP	Blue Note	BLP/BST84181	1964	£**25**	£**10**	
Unas Mas	LP	Blue Note	BLP/BST84127	1963	£**20**	£**8**	
Whistle Stop	LP	Blue Note	BLP/BST84063	1961	£**25**	£**10**	

DORIAN GRAY

Idaho Transfer	LP	New Blood	PA476	1976	£**100**	£**50**	*German*

DORMAN, HAROLD

Mountain Of Love	7"	Top Rank	JAR357	1960	£**8**	£**4**	
There They Go	7"	London	HLS9386	1961	£**15**	£**7.50**	

DOROTHY

I Confess	7"	Industrial	IR0014	1980	£**6**	£**2.50**	

DORPER, RALPH

Eraserhead	12"	Operation Twilight	OPT18	1983	£**6**	£**2.50**	

DORS, DIANA

April Heart	7"	Pye	7N15242	1960	£**4**	£**1.50**	
Security	7"	Polydor	BM56111	1966	£**4**	£**1.50**	
So Little Time	7"	Fontana	TF506	1964	£**5**	£**2**	
Swingin' Dors	LP	Pye	NPL18044	1960	£**40**	£**20**	

DORSET, RAY

Cold Blue Excursion	7"	Dawn	DNS1018	1972	£**5**	£**2**	
Dancin' In The Street	7"	Polydor	2059127	1979	£**4**	£**1.50**	*with Mungo Jerry*
Forgotten Land	7"	Satellite	RAY001	1979	£**8**	£**4**	*promo*
Knocking On Heaven's Door	7"	Stagecoach	TRI101	1981	£**4**	£**1.50**	*with Mungo Jerry*
Mungo Box	7"	Polydor	2230103	1977	£**5**	£**2**	*with Mungo Jerry*

DORSETS

Pork Chops	7"	Sue	WI391	1965	£**12**	£**6**	

DORSEY, GERRY

Baby Turn Around	7"	Hickory	451337	1965	£**6**	£**2.50**	

DORSEY, JACK ORCHESTRA

Dance Of The Daleks	7"	Polydor	56020	1965	£6	£2.50	

DORSEY, JIMMY

Dixie By Dorsey	10" LP	Columbia	33S1026	1954	£15	£6	
Jay Dee's Boogie Woogie	7"	HMV	POP383	1957	£10	£5	

DORSEY, LEE

Best Of Lee Dorsey	LP	Sue	ILP924	1965	£40	£20	
Confusion	7"	Stateside	SS506	1966	£4	£1.50	
Do Re Mi	7"	Top Rank	JAR606	1962	£8	£4	
Get Out Of My Life Woman	7"	Stateside	SS485	1966	£4	£1.50	
Holy Cow	7"	Stateside	SS552	1966	£4	£1.50	
Lee Dorsey	LP	Stateside	(S)SL10177	1966	£15	£6	
Messed Around	7"	Sue	WI399	1966	£10	£5	
New Lee Dorsey	LP	Stateside	(S)SL10192	1966	£15	£6	
Rain Rain Go Away	7"	Stateside	SS593	1967	£4	£1.50	
Ride Your Pony	7"	Stateside	SS441	1965	£5	£2	
Ride Your Pony	7" EP	Stateside	SE1038	1966	£12	£6	
Work Work Work	7"	Stateside	SS465	1965	£5	£2	
Working In A Coalmine	7"	Stateside	SS528	1966	£4	£1.50	
Ya Ya	7"	Sue	WI367	1965	£10	£5	
Ya Ya	LP	Fury	1002	1962	£30	£15	*US*
You're Breaking Me Up	7" EP	Stateside	SE1043	1966	£12	£6	

DORSEY, TOMMY

Dixieland Jazz Vol. 1	10" LP	Brunswick	LA8524	1951	£15	£6	
Ecstasy	10" LP	Brunswick	LA8669	1954	£10	£4	
Tenderly	10" LP	Brunswick	LA8640	1954	£10	£4	
Tommy Dorsey	10" LP	Brunswick	LA8610	1953	£10	£4	
Tommy Dorsey And His Orchestra	7" EP	HMV	7EG8004	1954	£5	£2	*with Frank Sinatra*
Tommy Dorsey No. 1	7" EP	RCA	RCX1002	1958	£5	£2	

DORSEY BROTHERS

Dixieland Jazz 1934–5	LP	Brunswick	LAT8256	1958	£10	£4	

DOT, JOHNNY & THE DASHERS

I Love An Angel	7"	Salvo	SLO1805	1962	£10	£5	

DOTTIE & BONNIE

Bunch Of Roses	7"	Island	WI161	1964	£10	£5	*Don Drummond B side*
Dearest	7"	Island	WI148	1964	£10	£5	
I'll Know	7"	Ska Beat	JB274	1967	£10	£5	
I'm So Glad	7"	Rio	R43	1964	£10	£5	*Douglas Brothers B side*
Sun Rises	7"	Island	WI149	1964	£10	£5	*Don Drummond B side*
Your Kisses	7"	Island	WI143	1964	£10	£5	

DOUBLE FEATURE

Baby Get Your Head Screwed On	7"	Deram	DM115	1967	£15	£7.50	
Handbags And Gladrags	7"	Deram	DM165	1967	£6	£2.50	
Tide Turned	LP	Marathon		1987	£20	£8	*Dutch*

DOUBLES

Hey Girl	7"	HMV	POP613	1959	£60	£30	

DOUCET, SUZANNE

Swan Song	7"	Liberty	LBF15150	1968	£5	£2	

DOUGHNUT RING

Dance Around Julie	7"	Deram	DM215	1968	£15	£7.50	

DOUGHTY, JOHNNY

Round Rye Bay For More	LP	Topic	12TS324	1977	£12	£5	

DOUGLAS, CARL

Crazy Feeling	7"	Go	AJ11401	1966	£6	£2.50	*Peter Perry B side*
Let The Birds Sing	7"	Go	AJ11408	1967	£8	£4	
Nobody Cries	7"	United Artists	UP1206	1967	£60	£30	
Sell My Soul To The Devil	7"	United Artists	UP2227	1968	£5	£2	

DOUGLAS, CRAIG

Are You Really Mine	7"	Decca	F11075	1958	£8	£4	
Bandwagon Ball	LP	Top Rank	35103	1961	£25	£10	
Come Closer	7"	Fontana	TF475	1964	£5	£2	
Come Softly To Me	7"	Top Rank	JAR110	1959	£4	£1.50	
Craig	7" EP	Decca	DFE6633	1960	£12	£6	
Craig Douglas	LP	Top Rank	BUY049	1960	£30	£15	
Craig Sings For Roxy	7" EP	Top Rank	JKR8033	1959	£12	£6	
Craig's Movie Songs	7" EP	Columbia	SEG8219	1963	£15	£7.50	
Cuddle Up With Craig	7" EP	Decca	DFE8509	1962	£10	£5	
Hundred Pounds Of Clay	7"	Top Rank	JAR555	1961	£6	£2.50	
Hundred Pounds Of Clay (Censored Version)	7"	Top Rank	JAR556	1961	£12	£6	*picture sleeve*

Hundred Pounds Of Clay (Censored Version)	7"	Top Rank	JAR556	1961	**£4**	**£1.50**	
Only Sixteen	7"	Top Rank	JAR159	1959	**£4**	**£1.50**	
Our Favourite Melodies	7"	Columbia	DB4854	1962	**£4**	**£1.50**	
Our Favourite Melodies	LP	Columbia	33SX1468	1962	**£60**	**£30**	
Sitting In A Tree House	7"	Decca	F11055	1958	**£8**	**£4**	
Teenager In Love	7"	Top Rank	JAR133	1959	**£4**	**£1.50**	

DOUGLAS, KIRK & THE MELLOMEN

Whale Of A Tale	7"	Brunswick	05408	1955	**£6**	**£2.50**	

DOUGLAS, MARK

It Matters Not	7"	Ember	EMBS166	1962	**£40**	**£20**	

DOUGLAS, NORMA

Be It Resolved	7"	London	HLZ8475	1957	**£15**	**£7.50**	

DOUGLAS BROTHERS

Down And Out	7"	Rio	R63	1965	**£10**	**£5**	*Ronald Wilson B side*
Valley Of Tears	7"	Rio	R57	1965	**£10**	**£5**	*Charmers B side*

DOVE, RONNIE

Ronnie Dove	LP	Stateside	SL10149	1965	**£15**	**£6**	

DOVELLS

All The Hits Of The Teen Groups	LP	Parkway	P7010	1962	**£25**	**£10**	*US*
Betty In Bermudas	7"	Cameo					
		Parkway	P882	1963	**£4**	**£1.50**	
Biggest Hits	LP	Wyncote	(SW)9114	1965	**£12**	**£5**	*US*
Bristol Stomp	7"	Columbia	DB4718	1961	**£8**	**£4**	
Bristol Stomp	LP	Parkway	P7006	1961	**£30**	**£15**	*US*
Bristol Twistin' Annie	7"	Columbia	DB4877	1962	**£6**	**£2.50**	
Discotheque	LP	Wyncote	(S)W9052	1965	**£12**	**£5**	*US*
Doin' The New Continental	7"	Columbia	DB4810	1962	**£6**	**£2.50**	
Don't Knock The Twist	LP	Parkway	P7011	1962	**£25**	**£10**	*US*
Dragster On The Prowl	7"	Cameo					
		Parkway	P901	1963	**£6**	**£2.50**	
For Your Hully Gully Party	LP	Parkway	P7021	1963	**£25**	**£10**	*US*
Hully Gully Baby	7"	Cameo					
		Parkway	P845	1962	**£4**	**£1.50**	
You Can't Run Away From Yourself	7"	Cameo					
		Parkway	P861	1963	**£4**	**£1.50**	
You Can't Sit Down	7"	Cameo					
		Parkway	P867	1963	**£4**	**£1.50**	

DOW, NICK

Burd Margaret	LP	Dingle	DIN306	1978	**£10**	**£4**	

DOWE, BRENT

Knock Three Times	7"	Summit	SUM8521	1971	**£4**	**£1.50**	

DOWELL, JOE

Wooden Heart	LP	Smash	SRS67000	1961	**£20**	**£8**	*US*

DOWLANDS

All My Loving	7"	Oriole	CB1897	1964	**£8**	**£4**	
Breakups	7"	Oriole	CB1815	1963	**£30**	**£15**	
Don't Ever Change	7"	Oriole	CB1781	1962	**£100**	**£50**	
Don't Make Me Over	7"	Columbia	DB7547	1965	**£30**	**£15**	
I Walk The Line	7"	Oriole	CB1926	1964	**£30**	**£15**	
Julie	7"	Oriole	CB1748	1962	**£30**	**£15**	
Lucky Johnny	7"	Oriole	CB1892	1963	**£400**	**£250**	*best auctioned*
Wishing And Hoping	7"	Oriole	CB1947	1964	**£60**	**£30**	

DOWNBEATS

Thinking Of You	7"	Starlite	ST45051	1961	**£10**	**£5**	

DOWNBEATS (2)

Chantent En Français	7" EP	Philips	434932	196–	**£6**	**£2.50**	*French*
Dans La Rue	7" EP	Philips	434990	196–	**£6**	**£2.50**	*French*

DOWNES, BOB

Bob Downes was an averagely talented flautist who attempted to haul himself into the first division by surrounding himself with the best British jazz musicians of the time and adopting a suitably 'progressive' image. So far, so good, but he also frequently insisted on opening his mouth to sing. Bob Downes has a terrible voice!

Deep Down Heavy	LP	MFP	MFP1412	1970	**£10**	**£4**	
Diversions	LP	Ophenian	BDOM001	1973	**£10**	**£4**	
Electric City	LP	Vertigo	6360005	1970	**£25**	**£10**	*spiral label*
Episodes At 4 a.m.	LP	Ophenian	BDOM002	1974	**£10**	**£4**	
Hell's Angels	LP	Ophenian	BDOM003	1975	**£10**	**£4**	
Open Music – Dream Journey	LP	Philips	SBL7922	1970	**£60**	**£30**	
Solo	LP	Ophenian	BDOM004	1976	**£10**	**£4**	

DOWNES, JULIA

Let Sleeping Dogs Lie	LP	Naive	NAVL2	1982	**£40**	**£20**	

DOWNES, PAUL & PHIL BEER

Title	Format	Label	Cat. No.	Year	Mint	Good	Notes
Dance Without Music	LP	Sweet Folk And Count	SFA046	1976	**£10**	**£4**	

DOWNING, AL

Title	Format	Label	Cat. No.	Year	Mint	Good	Notes
Yes I'm Loving You	7"	Sue	WI341	1964	**£12**	**£6**	

DOWNLINERS SECT

The Downliners Sect's brand of R&B failed to make the group stars in the sixties despite a large number of record releases. One suspects that the lack of cool typified by singer Don Crane's trademark deerstalker hat, and by the group's foray into country music for one album, did not help. In recent years Crane has sung with members of the Yardbirds and the Nashville Teens in the optimistically titled British Invasion All Stars.

Title	Format	Label	Cat. No.	Year	Mint	Good	Notes
All Night Worker	7"	Columbia	DB7817	1966	**£15**	**£7.50**	
Baby What's Wrong	7"	Columbia	DB7300	1964	**£15**	**£7.50**	
Bad Storm Coming	7"	Columbia	DB7712	1965	**£15**	**£7.50**	
Cost Of Living	7"	Columbia	DB8008	1966	**£15**	**£7.50**	
Country Sect	LP	Columbia	33SX1745	1965	**£40**	**£20**	
Downliners Sect	LP	HMV	SGLP534	1964	**£100**	**£50**	*Swedish*
Find Out What's Happening	7"	Columbia	DB7415	1964	**£15**	**£7.50**	
Glendora	7"	Columbia	DB7939	1966	**£20**	**£10**	
I Got Mine	7"	Columbia	DB7597	1965	**£15**	**£7.50**	
Little Egypt	7"	Columbia	DB7347	1964	**£15**	**£7.50**	
Nite In Great Newport Street	7" EP	Contrast	RBCSP001	1964	**£200**	**£100**	
Rock Sect's In	LP	Columbia	SX/SCX6028	1966	**£50**	**£25**	
Sect	LP	Columbia	33SX1658	1964	**£50**	**£25**	
Sect Sing Sick Songs	7" EP	Columbia	SEG8438	1965	**£60**	**£30**	
Wreck Of The Old '97	7"	Columbia	DB7509	1965	**£15**	**£7.50**	

DOWNTOWN ALL STARS

Title	Format	Label	Cat. No.	Year	Mint	Good	Notes
Downtown Jump	7"	Downtown	DT426	1969	**£4**	**£1.50**	

DOYLE, DANNY

Title	Format	Label	Cat. No.	Year	Mint	Good	Notes
Highwaymen	LP	Granvaile	GRLP001	1981	**£10**	**£4**	*Irish*

DR CALCULUS

Title	Format	Label	Cat. No.	Year	Mint	Good	Notes
Designer Beatnik	CD	Ten	DIXCD45	1986	**£30**	**£15**	

DR FEELGOOD & THE INTERNS

Title	Format	Label	Cat. No.	Year	Mint	Good	Notes
Blang Dong	7"	Columbia	DB7228	1964	**£8**	**£4**	
Doctor Feelgood	LP	OKeh	M12/S14101	1962	**£30**	**£15**	*US*
Don't Tell Me No Dirty	7"	CBS	202099	1966	**£10**	**£5**	
Dr Feelgood	7"	Columbia	DB4838	1962	**£8**	**£4**	
Dr Feelgood & The Interns	7" EP	Columbia	SEG8310	1964	**£40**	**£20**	
Sugar Bee	7"	Capitol	CL15569	1968	**£10**	**£5**	

DR HOOK

Title	Format	Label	Cat. No.	Year	Mint	Good	Notes
Cover Of Radio Times	7"	CBS	1037	1973	**£40**	**£20**	*1 sided promo*

DR JOHN

Mac Rebennack achieved early notoriety as the only white musician to break into the tough New Orleans R&B session world. With the advent of flower power, he reinvented himself as the voodoo magician Dr John, and recorded the weirdly mystical *Gris Gris* album. Three other LPs followed in similar style, before Rebennack reverted to R&B, while still retaining the Dr John pseudonym. He continues to be a prolific maker of records, both his own and other people's, for which he is an in-demand session pianist.

Title	Format	Label	Cat. No.	Year	Mint	Good	Notes
Babylon	LP	Atlantic	228018	1969	**£20**	**£8**	
Gris Gris	LP	Atlantic	587147	1968	**£20**	**£8**	
Gris Gris	LP	Atlantic	K40168	1972	**£12**	**£5**	
Gumbo	LP	Atlantic	K40384	1972	**£15**	**£6**	
In The Right Place	LP	Atlantic	K50017	1973	**£10**	**£4**	
Remedies	LP	Atlantic	2400015	1970	**£20**	**£8**	
Sun, Moon, & Herbs	LP	Atlantic	2400161	1971	**£20**	**£8**	
Sun, Moon, & Herbs	LP	Atlantic	K40250	1971	**£12**	**£5**	

DR K'S BLUES BAND

Title	Format	Label	Cat. No.	Year	Mint	Good	Notes
Dr K's Blues Band	LP	Spark	UK101	1968	**£40**	**£20**	

DR MARIGOLD'S PRESCRIPTION

Title	Format	Label	Cat. No.	Year	Mint	Good	Notes
Pictures Of Life	LP	Marble Arch	MALS1222	1969	**£12**	**£5**	

DR STRANGELY STRANGE

Dr. Strangely Strange attempted to play the same kind of eccentrically pitched folk music as the Incredible String Band, but found that the market was only big enough for one. *Kip Of The Serenes* is one of the rarest rock releases on the Island label, although one track is well known to the many people who bought the *Nice Enough To Eat* sampler LP.

Title	Format	Label	Cat. No.	Year	Mint	Good	Notes
Heavy Petting	LP	Vertigo	6360009	1970	**£60**	**£30**	*spiral label*
Kip Of The Serenes	LP	Island	ILPS9106	1969	**£75**	**£37.50**	*pink label*

DR TECHNICAL & THE MACHINES

Title	Format	Label	Cat. No.	Year	Mint	Good	Notes
Zones	7"	Hawkfan	HWFB1	1983	**£8**	**£4**	*1 sided*

DR WEST'S MEDICINE SHOW & JUNK BAND

Title	Format	Label	Cat. No.	Year	Mint	Good	Notes
Bullets La Verne	7"	Page One	POF23061	1968	**£15**	**£7.50**	
Eggplant That Ate Chicago	LP	Page One	POLS17	1968	**£30**	**£15**	

DR WHO

Title	Format	Label	Cat. No.	Year	Mint	VG	Notes
Dr Who And The Pescatons	LP	Argo	ZSW564	1976	**£10**	**£4**	

DR Z

The rarest album on the Vertigo 'spiral' label is the work of a typical keyboard trio from the period and is housed in an elaborate opening-out sleeve. Legend suggests that only eighty copies of the record were sold, and it is certainly scarce enough today for this to be true.

Title	Format	Label	Cat. No.	Year	Mint	VG	Notes
Lady Ladybird	7"	Fontana	6007023	1970	**£20**	**£10**	
Three Parts To My Soul	LP	Vertigo	6360048	1971	**£250**	**£150**	*spiral label*

DRAG SET

Title	Format	Label	Cat. No.	Year	Mint	VG	Notes
Day And Night	7"	Go	AJ11405	1966	**£125**	**£62.50**	

DRAGON

Title	Format	Label	Cat. No.	Year	Mint	VG	Notes
Dragon	LP	Acorn	CF268	1976	**£40**	**£20**	
Scented Gardens For The Blind	LP	Vertigo	6360903	1974	**£60**	**£30**	*French*
Universal Radio	LP	Vertigo	6360902	1971	**£60**	**£30**	*New Zealand*

DRAGONFLY

Title	Format	Label	Cat. No.	Year	Mint	VG	Notes
Almost Abandoned	LP	Retreat	6002	1974	**£10**	**£4**	

DRAGONFLY (2)

Title	Format	Label	Cat. No.	Year	Mint	VG	Notes
Dragonfly	LP	Megaphone	1202	1970	**£200**	**£100**	*US*

DRAGONWYCK

Title	Format	Label	Cat. No.	Year	Mint	VG	Notes
Dragonwyck	LP	private		1972	**£2000**	**£1400**	*US acetate*
Dragonwyck	LP	private		1970	**£1000**	**£700**	*US*

DRAKE, CHARLIE

Title	Format	Label	Cat. No.	Year	Mint	VG	Notes
Hello My Darlings	7" EP	Parlophone	GEP8720	1958	**£8**	**£4**	
Hits From The Man In The Moon	7" EP	Parlophone	GEP8903	1964	**£8**	**£4**	
Naughty	7" EP	Parlophone	GEP8812	1960	**£8**	**£4**	
Sea Cruise	7"	Parlophone	R4552	1959	**£4**	**£1.50**	
Splish Splash	7"	Parlophone	R4461	1958	**£4**	**£1.50**	
You Never Know	7"	Charisma	CB270	1975	**£5**	**£2**	*with Peter Gabriel*

DRAKE, NICK

Nick Drake's shyly melodic music has had a considerable cult following for some time. The three original albums that he recorded before his death of a drug overdose have long remained collectable, despite the ready availability of reissue copies on vinyl and CD. When producer Joe Boyd sold his Witchseason company, which included the rights to Drake's records, to Island, he made it a condition of sale that Nick Drake's music should never become unavailable. Listening to the late-night beauty of the *Five Leaves Left* arrangements, to the sparkling playing by the likes of Richard Thompson, John Cale, and Chris McGregor on *Bryter Layter*, to the stark introspection of *Pink Moon*, and to the musical and lyrical poetry throughout, it is easy to understand Boyd's enthusiasm.

Title	Format	Label	Cat. No.	Year	Mint	VG	Notes
Bryter Layter	LP	Island	ILPS9134	1970	**£50**	**£25**	
Bryter Layter	LP	Island	ILPS9134	1989	**£10**	**£4**	*blue label*
Five Leaves Left	LP	Island	ILPS9105	1969	**£75**	**£37.50**	*pink label*
Five Leaves Left	LP	Island	ILPS9105	1970	**£20**	**£8**	*pink rim label*
Five Leaves Left	LP	Island	ILPS9105	1989	**£10**	**£4**	*blue label*
Fruit Tree	CD	Hannibal	HNCD5402	1996	**£40**	**£20**	*4 CD boxed set*
Fruit Tree	LP	Island	NDSP100	1979	**£50**	**£25**	*triple, boxed*
Fruit Tree	LP	Hannibal	HNBX5302	1986	**£50**	**£25**	*4 LP boxed set*
Heaven In A Wild Flower	LP	Island	ILPS9826	1985	**£12**	**£5**	
Introduction	7"	Island	RSS7	1983	**£25**	**£12.50**	*promo*
Island LP Sampler	LP	Island	RSS7	1979	**£25**	**£10**	*promo*
Pink Moon	LP	Island	ILPS9184	1972	**£50**	**£25**	
Pink Moon	LP	Island	ILPS9184	1989	**£10**	**£4**	*blue label*
Time Of No Reply	LP	Hannibal	HNBL1318	1987	**£10**	**£4**	

DRAMA

Title	Format	Label	Cat. No.	Year	Mint	VG	Notes
Drama	LP	Philips	6413021	1971	**£125**	**£62.50**	*Dutch*

DRAMATICS

Title	Format	Label	Cat. No.	Year	Mint	VG	Notes
Whatcha See Is Whatcha Get	LP	Stax	2362025	1972	**£10**	**£4**	

DRANSFIELD, BARRY

Title	Format	Label	Cat. No.	Year	Mint	VG	Notes
Barry Dransfield	LP	Polydor	2383160	1972	**£250**	**£150**	
Bowin' And Scrapin'	LP	Topic	12TS386	1978	**£25**	**£10**	

DRANSFIELD, ROBIN

Title	Format	Label	Cat. No.	Year	Mint	VG	Notes
Tidewave	LP	Topic	12TS414	1980	**£10**	**£4**	

DRANSFIELD, ROBIN & BARRY

Title	Format	Label	Cat. No.	Year	Mint	VG	Notes
Fiddler's Dream	LP	Transatlantic	TRA322	1976	**£25**	**£10**	*credited to Dransfield*
Lord Of All I Behold	LP	Trailer	LER2026	1971	**£40**	**£20**	
Popular To Contrary Belief	LP	Free Reed	FRR018	1977	**£12**	**£5**	
Rout Of The Blues	LP	Trailer	LER2011	1970	**£40**	**£20**	

DRAPER, RUSTY

Title	Format	Label	Cat. No.	Year	Mint	VG	Notes
Chicken Picking Hawk	7"	Mercury	7MT229	1958	**£6**	**£2.50**	
Folsom Prison Blues	7"	London	HLU9989	1965	**£5**	**£2**	
Gambling Gal	7"	Mercury	7MT211	1958	**£6**	**£2.50**	
Hits That Sold A Million	LP	Mercury	MMC14040	1960	**£20**	**£8**	
Mule Skinner Blues	7"	Mercury	AMT1101	1960	**£5**	**£2**	
Mule Skinner Blues	7" EP	Mercury	ZEP10095	1960	**£10**	**£5**	

Presenting Rusty Draper	7" EP	Mercury	MEP9506	1956	**£15**	**£7.50**	
Rock And Roll Ruby	78	Mercury	MT113	1956	**£6**	**£2.50**	
Rusty Draper	7" EP	Mercury	ZEP10016	1959	**£10**	**£5**	
Rusty Draper No. 1	7" EP	London	REU1431	1964	**£15**	**£7.50**	
Rusty Draper No. 2	7" EP	London	REU1432	1964	**£15**	**£7.50**	
Rusty In Gambling Mood	7" EP	Mercury	ZEP10059	1960	**£10**	**£5**	
Shopping Around	7"	Mercury	AMT1019	1959	**£10**	**£5**	
Sun Will Always Shine	7"	Mercury	AMT1033	1959	**£4**	**£1.50**	
That's Why I Love You Like I Do	7"	London	HLU9786	1963	**£8**	**£4**	

DREAM

Guitarist with Dream was Terje Rypdal, later to make many highly acclaimed albums for the ECM label.

Dream	LP	Karussell	2915068	1976	**£50**	**£25**	*German*
Get Dreamy	LP	Polydor	SLPHM184099	1967	**£100**	**£50**	*German*

DREAM (2)

Reality From Dream	LP	private	CP109	1975	**£15**	**£6**	

DREAM POLICE

The Dream Police achieved little success in their own right, but managed to provide members for a much more successful group – the Average White Band.

I've Got No Choice	7"	Decca	F13105	1970	**£4**	**£1.50**	
Living Is Easy	7"	Decca	F12998	1970	**£5**	**£2**	
Our Song	7"	Decca	F13078	1970	**£4**	**£1.50**	

DREAMERS

Maybe Song	7"	Columbia	DB8340	1968	**£4**	**£1.50**	

DREAMERS (2)

Dear Love	7"	Downtown	DT408	1969	**£4**	**£1.50**	
Sweet Chariot	7"	Downtown	DT407	1969	**£4**	**£1.50**	

DREAMIES

Auralgraphic Entertainment	LP	Stone Theatre	DM68481	1968	**£150**	**£75**	*US*

DREAMLETS

Really Now	7"	Ska Beat	JB182	1965	**£10**	**£5**	*Skatalites B side*

DREAMLOVERS

Bird	LP	Columbia	CL2020/CS8820	1963	**£20**	**£8**	*US*
When We Get Married	7"	Columbia	DB4711	1961	**£75**	**£37.50**	

DREAMS

Best Of Dreams	LP	Dolphin	DOLB7002	1969	**£15**	**£6**	*Irish*

DREAMS DIE FIRST?

Dare To Dream	LP	Serial		1986	**£15**	**£6**	*Dutch*

DREAMTIMERS

Dancin' Lady	7"	London	HLU9368	1961	**£8**	**£4**	

DREAMWEAVERS

It's Almost Tomorrow	7"	Brunswick	05515	1956	**£25**	**£12.50**	
Little Love Can Go A Long Long Way	7"	Brunswick	05568	1956	**£12**	**£6**	
You're Mine	7"	Brunswick	05607	1956	**£6**	**£2.50**	

DREGS

Dregs	7"	Disturbing	DRO1	1979	**£20**	**£10**	

DRESSLAR, LEN

Chain Gang	7"	Mercury	7MT3	1956	**£6**	**£2.50**	*export*

DREVAR, JOHN EXPRESSION

Closer She Gets	7"	MGM	MGM1367	1967	**£40**	**£20**	

DREW, KENNY

Kenny Drew Trio	LP	Riverside	RLP12224	196–	**£15**	**£6**	

DREW, PATTI

Workin' On A Groovy Thing	7"	Capitol	CL15557	1968	**£4**	**£1.50**	

DRIFTERS

At The Club	7"	Atlantic	AT4019	1965	**£4**	**£1.50**	
Baby What I Mean	7"	Atlantic	584065	1967	**£4**	**£1.50**	
Clyde McPhatter & The Drifters	LP	Atlantic	8003	1956	**£150**	**£75**	*US*
Come On Over To My Place	7"	Atlantic	AT4023	1965	**£4**	**£1.50**	
Dance With Me	7"	London	HLE8988	1959	**£10**	**£5**	
Drifters	7" EP	London	REK1355	1963	**£25**	**£12.50**	
Drifters	LP	Clarion	(SD)608	1964	**£15**	**£6**	*US*
Drifting	7" EP	London	REK1385	1963	**£25**	**£12.50**	
Drifting Vol. 2	7" EP	Atlantic	AET6003	1964	**£15**	**£7.50**	
Follow Me	7"	Atlantic	AT4034	1965	**£6**	**£2.50**	
Good Gravy	LP	Atlantic	587144	1968	**£20**	**£8**	
Good Life	LP	Atlantic	ATL5023	1965	**£15**	**£6**	
Greatest Hits	LP	London	HAK2318	1960	**£30**	**£15**	

Title	Format	Label	Cat. No.	Year	Price	Price	Notes
I Count The Tears	7"	London	HLK9287	1961	**£4**	**£1.50**	
I Count The Tears	7"	London	HLK7115	1961	**£10**	**£5**	*export*
I'll Take You Home	7"	London	HLK9785	1963	**£4**	**£1.50**	
I'll Take You Where The Music's Playing	7"	Atlantic	584152	1968	**£4**	**£1.50**	
I'll Take You Where The Music's Playing	7"	Atlantic	AT4040	1965	**£4**	**£1.50**	
I'll Take You Where The Music's Playing	LP	Atlantic	587061	1967	**£10**	**£4**	
I'll Take You Where The Music's Playing	LP	Atlantic	ATL/STL5039	1966	**£15**	**£6**	
I've Got Sand In My Shoes	7"	Atlantic	AT4008	1964	**£4**	**£1.50**	
In The Land Of Make Believe	7"	London	HLK9848	1964	**£4**	**£1.50**	
Lonely Winds	7"	London	HLK9145	1960	**£6**	**£2.50**	
Memories Are Made Of This	7"	Atlantic	AT4084	1966	**£4**	**£1.50**	
Moonlight Bay	7"	London	HLE8686	1958	**£100**	**£50**	
On Broadway	7"	London	HLK9699	1963	**£5**	**£2**	
One Way Love	7"	London	HLK9886	1964	**£4**	**£1.50**	
Our Biggest Hits	LP	Atlantic	ATL5015	1965	**£12**	**£5**	
Our Biggest Hits	LP	Atlantic	587038	1966	**£10**	**£4**	
Please Stay	7"	London	HLK9382	1961	**£5**	**£2**	
Rat Race	7"	London	HLK9750	1963	**£5**	**£2**	
Rockin' And Driftin'	LP	Atlantic	8022	1958	**£150**	**£75**	*US*
Rockin' And Driftin'	LP	Atlantic	587123	1968	**£15**	**£6**	
Room Full Of Tears	7"	London	HLK9500	1962	**£5**	**£2**	
Saturday Night At The Movies	7"	Atlantic	AT4012	1964	**£4**	**£1.50**	
Save The Last Dance For Me	7"	London	HLK9201	1960	**£4**	**£1.50**	
Save The Last Dance For Me	7"	London	HLK7114	1961	**£10**	**£5**	*export*
Save The Last Dance For Me	7" EP	London	REK1282	1961	**£25**	**£12.50**	
Save The Last Dance For Me	LP	London	HAK2450	1962	**£30**	**£15**	
Save The Last Dance For Me	LP	Atlantic	587063	1967	**£10**	**£4**	
Soldier Of Fortune	7"	London	HLE8344	1956	**£750**	**£500**	*best auctioned*
Some Kind Of Wonderful	7"	London	HLK9326	1961	**£6**	**£2.50**	
Souvenirs	LP	Atlantic	590010	1966	**£12**	**£5**	
Stranger On The Shore	7"	London	HLK9554	1962	**£4**	**£1.50**	
Sweets For My Sweet	7"	London	HLK9427	1961	**£5**	**£2**	
There Goes My Baby	7"	London	HLE8892	1959	**£12**	**£6**	
This Magic Moment	7"	London	HLE9081	1960	**£6**	**£2.50**	
Tonight	7" EP	Atlantic	AET6012	1965	**£15**	**£7.50**	
Under The Boardwalk	7"	Atlantic	AT4001	1964	**£4**	**£1.50**	
Under The Boardwalk	LP	Atlantic	(SD)8099	1964	**£25**	**£10**	*US*
Up On The Roof	7"	London	HLK9626	1962	**£4**	**£1.50**	
Up On The Roof	LP	Atlantic	(SD)8073	1963	**£25**	**£10**	*US*
Up On The Roof	LP	Atlantic	587/588160	1969	**£10**	**£4**	
We Gotta Sing	7"	Atlantic	AT4062	1966	**£6**	**£2.50**	
When My Little Girl Is Smiling	7"	London	HLK9522	1962	**£4**	**£1.50**	

DRIFTERS (2)

Cliff Richard's backing group was originally called the Drifters, and they released two singles under that name in their own right, before changing name to the Shadows, in order to avoid confusion with the more famous American Drifters. In America, a change was made for them for the single 'Jet Black' (the B side of the UK 'Drifting' single), as this was credited to the Four Jets.

Title	Format	Label	Cat. No.	Year	Price	Price	Notes
Drifting	7"	Columbia	DB4325	1959	**£30**	**£15**	
Feeling Fine	7"	Columbia	DB4263	1959	**£50**	**£25**	

DRIFTING SLIM

Title	Format	Label	Cat. No.	Year	Price	Price	Notes
Good Morning Baby	7"	Blue Horizon	451005	1966	**£100**	**£50**	

DRIFTWOOD

Title	Format	Label	Cat. No.	Year	Price	Price	Notes
Driftwood	LP	Decca	SKL5069	1970	**£30**	**£15**	

DRIFTWOOD, JIMMY

Title	Format	Label	Cat. No.	Year	Price	Price	Notes
Country Guitar Vol. 13	7" EP	RCA	RCX191	1960	**£5**	**£2**	
Songs Of Billy Yank And Johnny Reb	LP	RCA	RD27226	1961	**£10**	**£4**	
Tall Tales In Song Vol. 1	7" EP	RCA	RCX193	1960	**£6**	**£2.50**	
Tall Tales In Song Vol. 2	7" EP	RCA	RCX195	1960	**£6**	**£2.50**	
Tall Tales In Song Vol. 3	7" EP	RCA	RCX198	1960	**£6**	**£2.50**	

DRISCOLL, JULIE

As far as the general public is concerned, Julie Driscoll is something of a one-hit wonder, having topped the charts with a superb version of Bob Dylan's 'This Wheel's On Fire' and then having apparently dropped from sight. In fact, she married jazz pianist Keith Tippett, and as Julie Tippetts has appeared on a number of jazz records by her husband and by others. 'This Wheel's On Fire' was the most visible product of a profitable association with the Brian Auger Trinity, documented by the various Marmalade recordings credited to one or both of them, and going back, through their membership of Steampacket, to the single 'Don't Do It No More'.

Title	Format	Label	Cat. No.	Year	Price	Price	Notes
1969	LP	Polydor	2480074	1971	**£15**	**£6**	
1969	LP	Polydor	2383077	1971	**£12**	**£5**	
Don't Do It No More	7"	Parlophone	R5296	1965	**£12**	**£6**	
I Didn't Want To Have To Do It	7"	Parlophone	R5444	1966	**£6**	**£2.50**	
I Know You Love Me Not	7"	Parlophone	R5588	1967	**£6**	**£2.50**	
Take Me By The Hand	7"	Columbia	DB7118	1963	**£12**	**£6**	

DRISCOLL, JULIE & BRIAN AUGER

Title	Format	Label	Cat. No.	Year	Price	Price	Notes
Julie Driscoll And Brian Auger	LP	MFP	MFP1265	1968	**£10**	**£4**	
Open	LP	Marmalade	607/608002	1967	**£20**	**£8**	
Save Me	7"	Marmalade	598004	1967	**£4**	**£1.50**	
Streetnoise	LP	Marmalade	608005/6	1968	**£25**	**£10**	*double*

Streetnoise Part 1	LP	Marmalade	608014	1969	**£10**	**£4**	
Streetnoise Part 2	LP	Marmalade	608015	1969	**£10**	**£4**	
This Wheel's On Fire	7"	Marmalade	598006	1968	**£4**	**£1.50**	

DRIVE

No Girls	7"	First Strike	FST007	1990	**£8**	**£4**	

DRIVE (2)

Jerkin'	7"	NRG	NE467	1978	**£15**	**£7.50**	

DRIVE (3)

Lead vocals on 'Curfew' are handled by Melanie Blatt (then calling herself Melanie Guillaume), famous later as the 'French one' in All Saints.

Curfew	12"	Ninja Tune	DRIVE1	1993	**£15**	**£7.50**	
Curfew	CD-s	Ninja Tune	DRIVECD1	1993	**£25**	**£12.50**	

DRNWYN

Gypsies In The Mist	LP	Wilderland	31778	1978	**£60**	**£30**	*US*

D-ROK

Get Out Of My Way	12"	Warhammer	DROK08722	1991	**£6**	**£2.50**	
Get Out Of My Way	CD-s	Warhammer	DROK08724	1991	**£8**	**£4**	

D'RONE, FRANK

Band Rocked On	7" EP	Mercury	ZEP10116	1959	**£15**	**£7.50**	
Strawberry Blonde	7"	Mercury	AMT1123	1960	**£5**	**£2**	

DRONES

Be My Baby	12"	Valer	VRSP1	1977	**£30**	**£15**	*test pressing*
Bone Idol	7"	Valer	VRS1	1977	**£5**	**£2**	
Can't See	7"	Fabulous	JC4	1980	**£4**	**£1.50**	
Further Temptations	LP	Valer	VRLP1	1977	**£20**	**£8**	
Temptations Of A White Collar Worker	7"	Ohms	GOODMIX1	1977	**£5**	**£2**	*picture sleeve, plastic bag*

DROSSELBART

Drosselbart	LP	Polydor	2371126	1970	**£25**	**£10**	*German*

DRUG ADDIX

Make A Record	7"	Chiswick	SW39	1978	**£6**	**£2.50**	

DRUGSTORE

Alive	7"	Honey	HON1	1993	**£6**	**£2.50**	
Drugstore	CD	Honey	8286170	1995	**£12**	**£5**	*with CD single (8500662)*
Injection	7"	Honey	HON8	1995	**£4**	**£1.50**	*clear vinyl*
Injection	CD-s	Honey	HONCD8	1995	**£5**	**£2**	
Xmas At The Drugstore	7"	Honey	DXMAS95	1995	**£8**	**£4**	*1 sided freebie*

DRUID

Fluid Druid	LP	EMI	EMC3128	1976	**£10**	**£4**	
Towards The Sun	LP	EMI	EMC3081	1975	**£10**	**£4**	

DRUID CHASE

Take Me In Your Garden	7"	CBS	3053	1967	**£10**	**£5**	

DRUIDS

It's Just A Little Bit Too Late	7"	Parlophone	R5134	1964	**£8**	**£4**	
Long Tall Texan	7"	Parlophone	R5097	1964	**£6**	**£2.50**	

DRUIDS (2)

Burnt Offering	LP	Argo	ZFB22	1970	**£100**	**£50**	
Pastime With Good Company	LP	Argo	ZFB39	1972	**£75**	**£37.50**	

DRUIDS OF STONEHENGE

Creation	LP	Uni	(7)3004	1968	**£60**	**£30**	*US*

DRUMBAGO

Dulcimania	7"	Trojan	TR638	1968	**£5**	**£2**	*Clancy Eccles B side*
I Am Drunk	7"	Island	WI085	1963	**£10**	**£5**	
I'm Not Worthy	7"	Blue Beat	BB51	1961	**£12**	**£6**	*Magic Notes B side*
Reggae Jeggae	7"	Blue Cat	BS145	1968	**£6**	**£2.50**	*Tyrone Taylor B side*

DRUMMOND, DON

Allepon	7"	Ska Beat	JB187	1965	**£10**	**£5**	*Justin Hinds B side*
Best Of Don Drummond	LP	Studio One	SOL9008	1968	**£100**	**£50**	
Cool Smoke	7"	Island	WI231	1965	**£10**	**£5**	*Techniques B side*
Coolie Boy	7"	Island	WI204	1965	**£10**	**£5**	*Lord Antics B side*
Doctor Dekker	7"	Ska Beat	JB189	1965	**£10**	**£5**	*Owen & Leon B side*
Don De Lion	7"	Ska Beat	JB191	1965	**£10**	**£5**	*Movers B side*
Far East	7"	Blue Beat	BB179	1963	**£12**	**£6**	
Heavenless	7"	Studio One	SO2078	1969	**£12**	**£6**	*Glen Brown B side*
Looking Through The Window	7"	Island	WI294	1966	**£10**	**£5**	*Soul Brothers B side*
Man In The Street	7"	Island	WI208	1965	**£10**	**£5**	*Rita & Bunny B side*
Memorial Album	LP	Trojan	TTL23	1969	**£25**	**£10**	

Memory Of Don	7"	Trojan	TR678	1969	**£6**	**£2.50**	*John Holt B side*
Musical Storeroom	7"	Island	WI153	1964	**£10**	**£5**	*Stranger Cole B side*
Scandal	7"	Island	WI094	1963	**£10**	**£5**	*W. Sparks B side*
Schooling The Duke	7"	Island	WI021	1962	**£10**	**£5**	
Scrap Iron	7"	Black Swan	WI406	1963	**£10**	**£5**	
Shock	7"	R&B	JB105	1963	**£10**	**£5**	*Tonettes B side*
Ska Town	7"	Blue Beat	BB298	1965	**£12**	**£6**	*Eric Morris B side*
Stampede	7"	Island	WI192	1965	**£10**	**£5**	*Justin Hinds B side*
Treasure Island	7"	Island	WI195	1965	**£10**	**£5**	*Riots B side*
University Goes Ska	7"	Island	WI242	1965	**£10**	**£5**	*Derrick Morgan B side*

DRUMMOND, DON JR

Memory Of Don Drummond	7"	Jackpot	JP710	1970	**£5**	**£2**	

DRUSKY, ROY

Just About That Time	7"	Brunswick	05785	1959	**£5**	**£2**	

DRY ICE

Running To The Convent	7"	B&C	CB115	1970	**£10**	**£5**	

DRY RIB

Dry Season	7"	Clockwork	COR001	1979	**£20**	**£10**	

DSCHINN

Dschinn	LP	Bacillus	BLPS19120	1972	**£20**	**£8**	*German*

D'SILVA, AMANCIO

Integration	LP	Columbia	SX/SCX6322	1969	**£50**	**£25**	
Reflections	LP	Columbia	SCX6465	1970	**£50**	**£25**	

DUALS

Stick Shift	7"	London	HL9450	1961	**£20**	**£10**	
Stick Shift	LP	Sue	LP2002	1961	**£60**	**£30**	*US*

DUBLINERS

At Home With The Dubliners	LP	Columbia	SCX6380	1969	**£15**	**£6**	
At It Again	LP	Major Minor	SMLP34	1968	**£10**	**£4**	
Drop Of The Dubliners	LP	Major Minor	(S)MCP5024	1969	**£10**	**£4**	
Drop Of The Hard Stuff	LP	Major Minor	MMLP3	1967	**£12**	**£5**	
Dubliners	LP	Major Minor	GOL200	1968	**£10**	**£4**	
Dubliners Now	LP	Polydor	2383329	1975	**£10**	**£4**	
Dubliners With Luke Kelly	LP	Transatlantic	TRA116	1964	**£15**	**£6**	
Fifteen Years On	LP	Polydor	2683070	1977	**£12**	**£5**	*double*
Finnegan Wakes	LP	Hallmark	CHM695	1966	**£10**	**£4**	
Finnegan Wakes	LP	Transatlantic	TRA139	1966	**£15**	**£6**	
In Concert	LP	Transatlantic	TRA124	1965	**£15**	**£6**	
In Person	7" EP	Transatlantic	TRAEP121	1965	**£5**	**£2**	
Live At The Albert Hall London	LP	Major Minor	SMLP44	1969	**£10**	**£4**	
More Of The Hard Stuff	LP	Major Minor	MMLP/SMLP5	1967	**£12**	**£5**	
Plain And Simple	LP	Polydor	2383235	1973	**£10**	**£4**	
Revolution	LP	Columbia	SCX6423	1970	**£15**	**£6**	

DUBS

Could This Be Magic	7"	London	HLU8526	1957	**£150**	**£75**	
Dubs Meet The Shells	LP	Josie	JM/JSS4001	195–	**£60**	**£30**	*US*
Gonna Make A Change	7"	London	HL8684	1958	**£250**	**£150**	*best auctioned*

DUCKS DELUXE

Ducks Deluxe was one of the better 'pub rock' bands to emerge during the seventies. The group included Martin Belmont, Sean Tyla and Andy McMaster, all of whom found a little success in subsequent years (Belmont with Graham Parker's Rumour, Tyler as a solo artist, McMaster with the Motors).

Last Night Of A Pub Rock Band	LP	Blue Moon	BMLP001	1982	**£12**	**£5**	*double*

DUDLEY

El Pizza	7"	Vogue	V9171	1960	**£8**	**£4**	

DUFFAS, SHENLEY

Bet You Don't Know	7"	Upsetter	US380	1972	**£8**	**£4**	
Big Mouth	7"	R&B	JB146	1964	**£10**	**£5**	*Frankie Anderson B side*
Christopher Columbus	7"	R&B	JB152	1964	**£10**	**£5**	*Carl Bryan B side*
Digging A Ditch	7"	Black Swan	WI440	1964	**£10**	**£5**	
Easy Squeal	7"	Island	WI125	1963	**£10**	**£5**	
Fret Man Fret	7"	Island	WI063	1963	**£10**	**£5**	
Gather Them In	7"	Black Swan	WI443	1964	**£10**	**£5**	
Give To Get	7"	Island	WI036	1962	**£10**	**£5**	
I Will Be Glad	7"	Rio	R41	1964	**£10**	**£5**	
Know The Lord	7"	Island	WI115	1963	**£10**	**£5**	*Tommy McCook B side*
La La La La	7"	Island	WI182	1965	**£10**	**£5**	*Upcoming Willows B side*
Mother-In-Law	7"	R&B	JB154	1964	**£10**	**£5**	*Don Drummond B side*
No More Wedding Bells	7"	R&B	JB134	1963	**£10**	**£5**	
Rukembine	7"	Island	WI186	1965	**£10**	**£5**	

What A Disaster	7"	Island	WI093	1963	£10	£5	
You Are Mine	7"	Island	WI184	1965	£10	£5	*Upcoming Willows B side*

DUFFY

Joker	7"	Chapter One	CH184	1973	£8	£4	
Just In Case You're Interested	LP	Ariola	85846	1975	£15	£6	*German*
Scruffy Duffy	LP	Chapter One	CHSR814	1970	£75	£37.50	

DUFFY, STEPHEN TIN TIN

Because We Love You	CD	10	DIXCD29	1986	£20	£8	
I Love You	12"	10	TIN9112	1986	£10	£5	
Icing On The Cake	12"	10	TING313	1985	£10	£5	
Kiss Me	12"	WEA	TIN1T	1982	£6	£2.50	
Kiss Me	7"	WEA	TIN1	1982	£4	£1.50	

DUFFY'S NUCLEUS

Hound Dog	7"	Decca	F22547	1967	£10	£5	
Hound Dog	7" EP	Decca	457142	1967	£40	£20	*French*

DUKE, BILLY

Ain't She Pretty	7"	Ember	EMBS160	1962	£4	£1.50	
Walking Cane	7"	Ember	EMBS153	1962	£4	£1.50	

DUKE, DENVER & JEFFREY NULL BLUEGRASS BOYS

Denver Duke & Jeffrey Null Bluegrass Boys	7" EP	Starlite	STEP33	1963	£10	£5	

DUKE, DORIS

I'm A Loser	LP	Mojo	2916001	1971	£10	£4	
Legend In Her Own Time	LP	Mojo	2916006	1971	£10	£4	
Woman	LP	Contempo	CLP519	1975	£10	£4	

DUKE, GEORGE

Aura Will Prevail	LP	BASF	BAP5064	1974	£10	£4	*German*
Brazilian Love Affair	LP	Epic	EPC84311	1980	£10	£4	
Feel	LP	MPS	23124	1974	£10	£4	*German*
I Love The Blues, She Heard My Cry	LP	BASF	BAP5071	1975	£10	£4	*German*
Live In Los Angeles	LP	Sunset	SLS50232	1971	£12	£5	*US*

DUKE ALL STARS

Letter To Mummy And Daddy	7"	Blue Cat	BS111	1968	£8	£4	

DUKE & DUCHESS

Get Ready For Love	7"	London	HLU8206	1955	£15	£7.50	

DUKES, AGGIE

John John	7"	Vogue	V9090	1957	£300	£180	*best auctioned*

DUKES OF STRATOSPHEAR

As is well known, the Dukes are actually XTC, using the alias to produce one and a half albums' worth of material that would be hailed as true masterpieces of sixties psychedelia, if only they had actually been recorded in the sixties!

Psonic Psunspot	LP	Virgin	VP2440	1987	£10	£4	*multi-coloured vinyl*
You're A Good Man Albert Brown	7"	Virgin	VSY982	1987	£4	£1.50	*multi-coloured vinyl*

DULCIMER

And I Turned As I Had Turned As A Boy	LP	Nepentha	6437003	1971	£50	£25	
Land Fit For Heroes	LP	Happy Face	MMLP1021	1980	£12	£5	

DUMB ANGELS

Love And Mercy	7"	Fierce	FRIGHT033	1988	£6	£2.50	

DUMBELLS (ROXY MUSIC)

Giddy Up	7"	Editions EG	EGO3	1976	£6	£2.50	
Giddy Up	7"	Polydor	POSP209	1981	£5	£2	

DUMMER, JOHN

Blue	LP	Vertigo	6360055	1972	£60	£30	*spiral label*
Cabal	LP	Mercury	SMCL20136	1969	£50	£25	
Famous Music Band	LP	Fontana	6309008	1970	£50	£25	
John Dummer's Blues Band	LP	Mercury	SMCL20167	1969	£75	£37.50	
Medicine Weasel	7"	Philips	6006176	1971	£4	£1.50	
Nine By Nine	7"	Philips	6006111	1970	£5	£2	
Oobleedooblee Jubilee	7"	Vertigo	6059074	1972	£4	£1.50	
Oobleedooblee Jubilee	LP	Vertigo	6360083	1973	£30	£15	*spiral label*
This Is John Dummer	LP	Philips	6382039	1972	£30	£15	
Travelling Man	7"	Mercury	MF1040	1968	£5	£2	
Try Me One More Time	7"	Mercury	MF1119	1969	£5	£2	
Try Me One More Time	LP	Philips	6382040	1973	£30	£15	

DUMMIES

Desperate for some more chart success, Slade tried the stratagem of issuing singles under the name of the Dummies. They hoped that radio programmers who responded with disinterest to the name of Slade would hear the music of the Dummies with unprejudiced ears. They may have done just that, but unfortunately they still did not appear to like what they heard.

Didn't You Used To Be You?	7"	Cheapskate	CHEAP003	1980	£5	£2	
Maybe Tonite	7"	Cheapskate	CHEAP14	1981	£8	£4	
When The Lights Are Out	7"	Pye	7P163	1980	£5	£2	
When The Lights Are Out	7"	Cheapskate	FWL001	1979	£5	£2	

DUMPY'S RUSTY NUTS

Just For Kicks	7"	Cool King	CNK006	1981	£6	£2.50	

DUNBAR, AYNSLEY

Frank Zappa once described Aynsley Dunbar as the only drummer capable of playing the complicated rhythms that some of his pieces contained. A graduate of the John Mayall blues school, Dunbar tried for a couple of years to make his own group a success, before accepting that he could do very well playing drums for other people (Zappa, Jefferson Starship and Journey). The Aynsley Dunbar Retaliation was a fairly routine blues group, but Blue Whale was a more ambitious affair, being a big band with an open, improvisational approach.

Aynsley Dunbar Retaliation	LP	Liberty	LBL/LBS83154	1968	£30	£15	
Blue Whale	LP	Warner Bros	K46062	1971	£12	£5	
Blue Whale	LP	Warner Bros	WS3010	1971	£15	£6	
Doctor Dunbar's Prescription	LP	Liberty	LBL/LBS83177	1968	£30	£15	
Remains To Be Heard	LP	Liberty	LBS83316	1970	£20	£8	
To Mum From Aynsley & The Boys	LP	Liberty	LBS83223	1969	£25	£10	
Warning	7"	Blue Horizon	453109	1967	£12	£6	
Warning	7"	Blue Horizon	453109	1967	£30	£15	*picture sleeve*
Watch 'n' Chain	7"	Liberty	LBF15132	1968	£4	£1.50	

DUNBAR, SCOTT

From Lake Mary	LP	Ahura Mazda	AMSSDS1	1971	£20	£8	

DUNBAR, SLY

Sly Wicked And Slick	LP	Virgin	FL1042	1979	£10	£4	

DUNCAN, JOHNNY

All Of The Monkeys Ain't In The Zoo	7"	Columbia	DB4167	1958	£5	£2	
Any Time	7"	Columbia	DB4415	1960	£4	£1.50	
Ballad Of Jed Clampett	7"	Columbia	DB7164	1963	£5	£2	
Beyond The Sunset	LP	Columbia	33SX1328	1961	£20	£8	
Blue Blue Heartaches	7"	Columbia	DB3996	1957	£5	£2	
Dang Me	7"	Columbia	DB7334	1964	£4	£1.50	
Footprints In The Snow	7"	Columbia	DB4029	1957	£5	£2	
Footprints In The Snow	7" EP	Columbia	SEG7753	1958	£12	£6	
Goodnight Irene	7"	Columbia	DB4074	1958	£10	£5	
Itching For My Baby	7"	Columbia	DB4118	1958	£8	£4	
Johnny Duncan & His Blue Grass Boys	7" EP	Columbia	SEG7708	1957	£12	£6	
Johnny Duncan & His Blue Grass Boys No. 2	7" EP	Columbia	SEG7733	1957	£12	£6	
Kansas City	7"	Columbia	DB4311	1959	£6	£2.50	
Kawliga	7"	Columbia	DB3925	1957	£12	£6	
Last Train To San Fernando	7"	Columbia	DB3959	1957	£8	£4	
Legend Of Gunga Din	7"	Pye	7N15380	1961	£5	£2	
Long Time Gone	7"	Pye	7N15420	1962	£5	£2	
My Lucky Love	7"	Columbia	DB4179	1958	£4	£1.50	
Rosalie	7"	Columbia	DB4282	1959	£5	£2	
Salute To Hank Williams	LP	Encore	ENC190	1959	£15	£6	
Salutes Hank Williams	10" LP	Columbia	33S1129	1958	£30	£15	
Tennessee Sing Song	7" EP	Columbia	SEG7850	1958	£10	£5	
Tennessee Song Bag	10" LP	Columbia	33S1122	1957	£30	£15	
Tobacco Road	7"	Pye	7N15358	1961	£5	£2	

DUNCAN, LESLEY

Despite making several fine records in the late sixties and early seventies, Ms Duncan's most collectable recording, a charity remake of her 'Sing Children Sing', is sought after primarily because Kate Bush is one of the singers participating in the ensemble – despite the fact that her voice cannot actually be distinguished!

Hey Boy	7"	Mercury	MF939	1965	£4	£1.50	
I Want A Steady Guy	7"	Parlophone	R5034	1963	£4	£1.50	
Just For The Boy	7"	Mercury	MF847	1965	£4	£1.50	
Lullaby	7"	RCA	RCA1746	1968	£4	£1.50	
Road To Nowhere	7"	RCA	RCA1783	1969	£4	£1.50	
Run To Love	7"	Mercury	MF876	1965	£4	£1.50	
Sing Children Sing	7"	CBS	8061	1979	£15	£7.50	*picture sleeve*
Sing Children Sing	LP	CBS	64202	1971	£10	£4	
Tell Him	7"	Parlophone	R5106	1964	£4	£1.50	
When My Baby Cries	7"	Mercury	MF830	1964	£4	£1.50	

DUNCAN, TOMMY

Dance Dance Dance	7"	Sue	WI4002	1966	£15	£7.50	

DUNGEON FOLK

Country Meets Folk	LP	Crown Folk	REC365		£25	£10	

DUNKLEY, ERROL

Black Cinderella	7"	Camel	CA87	1972	£4	£1.50	
Deep Meditation	7"	Big	BG324	1971	£5	£2	
Having A Party	7"	Jackpot	JP702	1969	£6	£2.50	
I Am Not Your Man	7"	Island	WI3150	1968	£10	£5	
I Am Not Your Man	7"	Amalgamated	AMG805	1968	£12	£6	
I Spy	7"	Amalgamated	AMG820	1968	£8	£4	
I'll Take You In My Arms	7"	Fab	FAB117	1969	£4	£1.50	*King Cannon B side*

Title	Format	Label	Cat. No.	Year	Mint	VG	Notes
Love Me Forever	7"	Rio	R109	1966	£12	£6	*Vietnam Allstars B side*
O Lord	7"	Explosion	EX2053	1971	£4	£1.50	
Please Stop Your Lying	7"	Amalgamated	AMG800	1968	£12	£6	
Satisfaction	7"	Banana	BA302	1970	£5	£2	
Scorcher	7"	Amalgamated	AMG807	1968	£12	£6	
Why Did You Do It	7"	Grape	GR3039	1973	£5	£2	
You Never Know	7"	Attack	ATLP1003	197–	£10	£4	
You're Gonna Need Me	7"	Rio	R131	1967	£12	£6	

DUNN, BLIND WILLIE

Title	Format	Label	Cat. No.	Year	Mint	VG	Notes
Jet Black Blues	7"	Columbia	SCM5100	1954	£10	£5	

DUNN, GEORGE

Title	Format	Label	Cat. No.	Year	Mint	VG	Notes
George Dunn	LP	Leader	LEE4042	1973	£25	£10	

DUNNE, PECKER

Title	Format	Label	Cat. No.	Year	Mint	VG	Notes
Introducing The Pecker	LP	Emerald	GES1152	1976	£10	£4	

DUNNING, TONY

Title	Format	Label	Cat. No.	Year	Mint	VG	Notes
Pretend	7"	Palette	PG9018	1961	£5	£2	
Seventeen Tomorrow	7"	Palette	PG9006	1960	£5	£2	
Under Moscow Skies	7"	Palette	PG9027	1961	£5	£2	

DUPREE, CHAMPION JACK

Title	Format	Label	Cat. No.	Year	Mint	VG	Notes
Ba' La Fouche	7"	Blue Horizon	573152	1969	£10	£5	
Barrelhouse Woman	7"	Decca	F12611	1967	£10	£5	
Blues Anthology Vol. 1	7" EP	Storyville	SEP381	1961	£20	£10	
Blues From The Gutter	LP	London	LTZK15171	1959	£60	£30	
Cabbage Greens	LP	XTRA	XTRA1028	1965	£15	£6	
Champion Jack Dupree	7" EP	XX	MIN716	196–	£12	£6	
Champion Jack Dupree	LP	Storyville	SLP107	1964	£10	£4	
Champion Jack Dupree	LP	Storyville	670194	1967	£25	£10	
Champion Jack Dupree And His Blues Band	LP	Decca	SKL4871	1967	£60	£30	
Champion Of The Blues	LP	Atlantic	(SD)8056	1961	£20	£8	US
Fisherman's Blues	78	Jazz Parade	B16	1951	£8	£3	
From New Orleans To Chicago	LP	Decca	LK/SKL4747	1966	£75	£37.50	
Get Your Head Happy	7"	Blue Horizon	451007	1966	£100	£50	*with T. S. McPhee*
I Haven't Done No One No Harm	7"	Blue Horizon	573140	1968	£10	£5	
I Want To Be A Hippy	7"	Blue Horizon	573158	1968	£10	£5	
Jack Dupree	7" EP	Ember	EMBEP4564	1965	£12	£6	
London Special	7" EP	Decca	DFE8586	1964	£30	£15	
Natural And Soulful Blues	LP	London	LTZK15217/ SAHK6151	1961	£40	£20	
Portraits In Blues	LP	Storyville	SLP161	1964	£20	£8	
Rhythm And Blues Vol. 1	7" EP	RCA	RCX7137	1964	£12	£6	
Scooby Dooby Doo	LP	Blue Horizon	763214	1969	£50	£25	
Sings The Blues	LP	King	735	1961	£30	£15	US
Trouble Trouble	LP	Storyville	SLP145	1964	£20	£8	
Two Shades Of Blue	LP	Ember	CJS800	1962	£20	£8	*with Jimmy Rushing*
When You Feel The Feeling You Was Feeling	LP	Blue Horizon	763206	1968	£50	£25	
Whiskey Head Woman	7"	Storyville	A45051	1962	£12	£6	
Women Blues	LP	Folkways	FS3825	1961	£20	£8	US

DUPREE, SIMON & THE BIG SOUND

Title	Format	Label	Cat. No.	Year	Mint	VG	Notes
Broken Hearted Pirates	7"	Parlophone	R5757	1969	£4	£1.50	
Day Time, Night Time	7"	Parlophone	R5594	1967	£4	£1.50	
Eagle Flies Tonight	7"	Parlophone	R5816	1969	£4	£1.50	
I See The Light	7"	Parlophone	R5542	1966	£5	£2	
Part Of My Past	7"	Parlophone	R5697	1968	£4	£1.50	
Reservations	7"	Parlophone	R5574	1967	£4	£1.50	
Thinking About My Life	7"	Parlophone	R5727	1968	£4	£1.50	
Thinking About My Life	7" EP	Odeon	FO135	1968	£20	£10	*French*
Without Reservations	LP	Parlophone	PMC/PCS7029	1967	£30	£15	
Without Reservations	LP	Parlophone	PCS7029	1969	£10	£4	*black & white label*

DUPREES

Title	Format	Label	Cat. No.	Year	Mint	VG	Notes
Around The Corner	7"	CBS	201803	1965	£4	£1.50	
Gone With the Wind	7"	London	HLU9709	1963	£8	£4	
Have You Heard	7"	London	HLU9813	1963	£8	£4	
Have You Heard	7" EP	London	RE10157	1964	£20	£10	*French*
Have You Heard	LP	Coed	LPC906	1963	£40	£20	US
I'd Rather Be Here In Your Arms	7"	London	HLU9678	1963	£10	£5	
It's No Sin	7"	London	HLU9843	1964	£8	£4	
My Own True Love	7"	Stateside	SS143	1962	£8	£4	
She Waits For Him	7"	CBS	202028	1966	£4	£1.50	
Why Don't You Believe Me	7"	London	HLU9774	1963	£8	£4	
You Belong To Me	7"	HMV	POP1073	1962	£15	£7.50	
You Belong To Me	LP	Coed	LPC905	1962	£40	£20	US

DURAN DURAN

Title	Format	Label	Cat. No.	Year	Mint	VG	Notes
All She Wants Is	12"	Parlophone	12DDDJ11	1988	£12	£6	*promo*
All She Wants Is	CD-s	EMI	CDDD11	1988	£15	£7.50	*3" single*
Big Thing	7"	EMI		1988	£8	£4	*promo*
Big Thing	CD	Parlophone	CDDDB33	1988	£50	£25	*promo box set with cassette, badge, booklet*

Burning The Ground ... CD-s ... EMI ... CDDD13 ... 1989 **£40** ... **£20**
Careless Memories ... 12" ... EMI ... 12EMI5168 ... 1981 **£6** ... **£2.50**
Come Undone ... CD-s ... EMI ... CDDD17 ... 1993 **£8** ... **£4**
Come Undone ... CD-s ... Parlophone ... CDDDS17 ... 1993 **£5** ... **£2**
Decade ... CD ... Capitol ... DPRO79607 ... 1993 **£20** ... **£8** ... *US promo with 4 versions of Ordinary World*
Do You Believe In Shame? ... 10" ... Parlophone ... 10DD12 ... 1989 **£6** ... **£2.50** ... *numbered sleeve*
Do You Believe In Shame? ... 7" ... Parlophone ... DDA/B/C12 ... 1989 **£15** ... **£7.50** ... *triple*
Do You Believe In Shame? ... CD-s ... Parlophone ... CDDD12 ... 1989 **£15** ... **£7.50** ... *3" single*
I Don't Want Your Love ... 12" ... Parlophone ... 12YOURS1 ... 1988 **£6** ... **£2.50** ... *1 side etched*
I Don't Want Your Love ... CD-s ... EMI ... CDYOUR1 ... 1988 **£8** ... **£4**
Liberty ... CD ... Parlophone ... CDPCSD112 ... 1990 **£50** ... **£25** ... *promo box set with cassette, biog, photo*
Master Mixes ... LP ... EMI ... [illegible] ... 1987 **£[illegible]** ... **£[illegible]** ... *double*
Meet El Presidente ... 7" ... Parlophone ... TOUR1 ... 1987 **£5** ... **£2**
My Own Way (3 versions) ... 12" ... EMI ... ... 1982 **£8** ... **£4** ... *promo*
Notorious (Latin Rascals Mix) ... 12" ... EMI ... 12DDN45 ... 1986 **£8** ... **£4**
Ordinary World ... CD-s ... Parlophone ... CDDDS16 ... 1992 **£12** ... **£6**
Ordinary World ... CD-s ... EMI ... CDDDPD16 ... 1993 **£5** ... **£2** ... *picture disc*
Perfect Day ... CD-s ... EMI ... ... 1995 **£25** ... **£12.50** ... *'choc ice' promo*
Presidential Suite ... CD-s ... Parlophone ... CDTOUR1 ... 1987 **£8** ... **£4**
Reflex ... 12" ... EMI ... 12DURANP2 ... 1984 **£8** ... **£4** ... *picture disc*
Reflex ... 7" ... EMI ... DURANP2 ... 1984 **£4** ... **£1.50** ... *poster sleeve*
Serious ... CD-s ... EMI ... CDDD15 ... 1990 **£10** ... **£5**
Sing Blue Silver ... Video ... PMI ... MVP9910632 ... 1984 **£20** ... **£10**
Skin Trade ... 7" ... Parlophone ... TRADE1 ... 1987 **£20** ... **£10** ... *bum picture sleeve*
Skin Trade ... 7" ... Parlophone ... TRADEX1 ... 1987 **£8** ... **£4** ... *poster sleeve*
Sound Of Thunder ... 12" ... EMI ... PSLP344 ... 1981 **£20** ... **£10** ... *promo sampler*
Tour Sampler ... CD ... Capitol ... DPRO79786 ... 1993 **£20** ... **£8** ... *US promo*
Violence Of Summer ... CD-s ... Parlophone ... CDD14 ... 1990 **£5** ... **£2**
White Lines ... 12" ... Parlophone ... 12DDDJ007 ... 1995 **£15** ... **£7.50** ... *pearl vinyl, promo*

DURANTE, JIMMY

Club Durante ... LP ... Brunswick ... LAT8216 ... 1957 **£10** ... **£4**
In Person ... 10" LP ... MGM ... MGMD102 ... 1952 **£15** ... **£6**
It's Bigger Than Both Of Us ... 7" ... Brunswick ... 05445 ... 1955 **£4** ... **£1.50**
Jimmy Durante ... 7" EP ... MGM ... MGMEP508 ... 1954 **£8** ... **£4**
Jimmy Durante Sings ... 10" LP ... Brunswick ... LA8582 ... 1953 **£15** ... **£6**
Pupalina ... 7" ... Brunswick ... 05395 ... 1955 **£4** ... **£1.50**
Schnozzles ... 7" EP ... MGM ... MGMEP597 ... 1957 **£6** ... **£2.50**
Swingin' With Rhythm And Blues ... 7" ... Brunswick ... 05495 ... 1955 **£4** ... **£1.50**

DURBIN, ALLISON

I Have Loved Me A Man ... LP ... Decca ... LKR/SKLR4996 ... 1969 **£25** ... **£10**

DURHAM, JUDITH

Again And Again ... 7" ... Columbia ... DB8290 ... 1967 **£4** ... **£1.50**
Climb Every Mountain ... LP ... A&M ... AMLS2011 ... 1971 **£10** ... **£4**
For Christmas With Love ... LP ... Columbia ... SCX6374 ... 1969 **£10** ... **£4**
Gift Of Song ... LP ... A&M ... AMLS967 ... 1970 **£10** ... **£4**

DURHAM, TERRY

Crystal Telephone ... LP ... Deram ... DML/SML1042 ... 1969 **£12** ... **£5**

DURUTTI COLUMN

Enigma ... 7" ... Sordide Sentimentale ... SS45005 ... 1981 **£15** ... **£7.50** ... *French*
For Patti ... 7" ... Factory Benelux ... FBN100 ... 1982 **£20** ... **£10**
Live At The Venue London ... LP ... VU ... VINI1 ... 1983 **£10** ... **£4**
Return Of The Durutti Column ... LP ... Factory ... FACT14 ... 1980 **£15** ... **£6** ... *sandpaper sleeve, with flexi (FACT14C)*

DURYER, ANDREW

Ballads Of A Wanderer ... LP ... Real ... RR2003 ... 1975 **£20** ... **£8**

DUSHON, JEAN

Make Way For Jean Dushon ... LP ... Chess ... CRL4000 ... 1965 **£12** ... **£5**

DUSSELDORF

La Dusseldorf ... 7" ... Radar ... ADA5 ... 1978 **£15** ... **£7.50** ... *promo*

DUST

Dust ... LP ... Kama Sutra ... 2319014 ... 1971 **£15** ... **£6**

DUST BROTHERS

Early records by the Chemical Brothers were released under the duo's original name – which they were forced to change under threat of court action from an American production team who had a prior claim to it.

Fourteenth Century Sky ... 12" ... Boys Own ... COLLECT004 ... 1994 **£15** ... **£7.50**
My Mercury Mouth ... 12" ... Junior Boys Own ... JBO20 ... 1994 **£15** ... **£7.50**
Song To The Siren ... 12" ... Junior Boys Own ... JBO10 ... 1993 **£25** ... **£12.50**
Song To The Siren ... 12" ... Dust Brothers ... DB333 ... 1993 **£50** ... **£25**

DUSTY, SLIM

Singsong	LP	Decca	LK4551	1963	**£12**	**£5**	
Slim Dusty And His Country Rockers	7" EP	Columbia	SEG8009	1960	**£8**	**£4**	

DUTCH SWING COLLEGE

Dutch Swing College	10" LP	Philips	BBR8021	1954	**£15**	**£6**	
Dutch Swing College	LP	Philips	BBL7099	1956	**£10**	**£4**	
Gems Of Jazz Vol. 1	10" LP	Philips	BBR8018	1954	**£15**	**£6**	

DUTRONC, JACQUES

Et Moi, Et Moi, Et Moi	7"	Vogue	VRS7015	1966	**£4**	**£1.50**	
Jacques Dutronc	LP	Vogue	VRL3029	1967	**£15**	**£6**	
L'Idole	7"	Vogue	VRS7024	1966	**£4**	**£1.50**	
Le Plus Difficile	7"	Vogue	VRS7027	1967	**£4**	**£1.50**	
Les Cactus	7"	Vogue	VRS7021	1966	**£4**	**£1.50**	

DUTY CYCLE

Nero	LP	Mirasound	MS5030	1976	**£75**	**£37.50**	*Dutch*

DUVAL, JOSE

Message Of Love	7"	London	HLR8458	1957	**£10**	**£5**	

DUVEEN, BOEING & THE BEAUTIFUL SOUP

The psychedelic single by Boeing Duveen, which sets two Lewis Carroll poems to music, is actually the work of Dr Sam Hutt. Hutt, who specialized in helping people overcome drug addictions (notably at many of the rock festivals, starting at the Isle of Wight in 1969), was one of the many lesser names with a significant role in the sixties and early-seventies counter-culture. During the eighties and nineties, while continuing to work as a doctor, Hutt has also worked extensively as a country singer – music that he is inclined to tackle for its comic potential – using the name Hank Wangford.

Jabberwock	7"	Parlophone	R5696	1968	**£50**	**£25**	
Jabberwock	7"	Parlophone	R5696	1968	**£100**	**£50**	*picture sleeve*

DWAYNE, MARK

Remember Me Huh	7"	Oriole	CB1712	1962	**£4**	**£1.50**	
Today's Teardrops	7"	Oriole	CB1744	1962	**£4**	**£1.50**	

DWYER, FINBARR

Irish Traditional Accordionist	LP	Outlet	OLP1004	1970	**£10**	**£4**	*Irish*

DYKE & THE BLAZERS

Funky Broadway	7"	Pye	7N25413	1967	**£10**	**£5**	
Funky Broadway	LP	Original Sound	LP(S)8876	1967	**£30**	**£15**	*US*
Greatest Hits	LP	Original Sound	LPS8877	1969	**£30**	**£15**	*US*

DYLAN, BOB

Bob Dylan has recorded so prolifically over the years that collecting him consists to a large extent of trying to obtain some of the large number of bootleg LPs that have been issued. Apart from documenting some crucially important live performances, such as the famous Albert Hall concert with the Band (which was only issued by Columbia thirty years after the event), these also allow Dylan's many studio out-takes to be heard. Many of these are, arguably, better than the tracks that were released – as the small selection made available on the official *Bootleg Series* box set makes clear. A few out-takes are also officially available on scarce promotional releases and on the very first US issue of *Freewheelin'*, which included four songs that are not on any of the subsequent releases of the record. These are 'Rocks And Gravel' (called 'Solid Gravel' on some pressings), 'Let Me Die In My Footsteps', 'Gamblin' Willie's Dead Man's Hand', and 'Talkin' John Birch Society Blues'. It should be stressed that only copies playing these tracks, which are not actually listed on the sleeve, are worth the large sums of money quoted below.

All I Really Want To Do	7" EP	CBS	5923	1964	**£40**	**£20**	*French*
Another Side Of Bob Dylan	LP	CBS	(S)BPG62429	1964	**£15**	**£6**	
Blonde On Blonde	LP	CBS	66012	1966	**£30**	**£15**	*double, mono*
Blonde On Blonde	LP	CBS	66012	1966	**£25**	**£10**	*double, stereo*
Blood On The Tracks	LP	Columbia	PC33235	1974	**£2500**	**£1750**	*test pressing with different versions of 5 tracks*
Blowin' In The Wind	7"	Columbia	42856	1963	**£150**	**£75**	*US*
Blowin' In The Wind	7" EP	CBS	5688	1964	**£40**	**£20**	*French*
Blowing In The Wind	7" EP	Fontana	TFE18010	1965	**£40**	**£20**	*with other artists*
Bob Dylan	7" EP	CBS	EP6051	1965	**£15**	**£7.50**	
Bob Dylan	LP	CBS	(S)BPG62022	1962	**£15**	**£6**	
Bob Dylan	LP	Columbia	CL1779	1962	**£75**	**£37.50**	*US mono, 6 eye logos on label*
Bob Dylan	LP	Columbia	CS8579	1962	**£100**	**£50**	*US stereo, 6 eye logos on label*
Bob Dylan And The Grateful Dead	CD	Columbia	CSK1435	1989	**£15**	**£6**	*US promo picture disc*
Bob Dylan In Concerto	12"	Gong	5A/6B	1976	**£50**	**£25**	*Italian*
Bringing It All Back Home	LP	CBS	(S)BPG62515	1965	**£15**	**£6**	
Can You Please Crawl Out Your Window	7"	CBS	201900	1965	**£5**	**£2**	
Can You Please Crawl Out Your Window	7" EP	CBS	6265	1965	**£40**	**£20**	*French*
Desire	LP	CBS	Q86003	1976	**£15**	**£6**	*quad*
Everything Is Broken	CD-s	CBS	6553582	1989	**£8**	**£4**	
Everything Is Broken	CD-s	CBS	6553583	1989	**£5**	**£2**	*3" single*
Forever Young	CD	Columbia	CSK1157	1988	**£25**	**£10**	*US 18 track promo sampler*

Title	Format	Label	Number	Year	Price		Notes
Forever Young	CD	CBS	XPCD116	1990	**£20**	**£8**	*13 track promo sampler*
Four Songs From Renaldo And Clara	12″	Columbia	AS422	1978	**£40**	**£20**	*US promo*
Freewheelin'	LP	Columbia	CS8786	1963	**£12000**	**£10000**	*US stereo, 4 different tracks*
Freewheelin'	LP	CBS	(S)BPG62193	1963	**£15**	**£6**	
Freewheelin'	LP	Columbia	CL1986	1963	**£5000**	**£3500**	*US mono, 4 different tracks*
George Jackson	7″	CBS	7688	1971	**£5**	**£2**	
Greatest Hits	LP	CBS	BPG62847	1967	**£10**	**£4**	*mono*
Highway 61 Revisited	CD	DCC	GZS1021	1992	**£15**	**£6**	*US audiophile*
Highway 61 Revisited	LP	CBS	(S)BPG62572	1965	**£15**	**£6**	
Highway 61 Revisited	LP	CBS	BPG62572	1965	**£12**	**£5**	*stereo*
Highway 61 Revisited	LP	Columbia	CS9189	1965	**£100**	**£50**	*US, alternate take of 'From A Buick 6'*
Hurricane	7″	CBS	3878	1976	**£5**	**£2**	*picture sleeve*
I Want You	7″	CBS	202258	1966	**£5**	**£2**	
I Want You	7″ EP	CBS	5769	1966	**£30**	**£15**	*French*
It's Unbelievable	CD-s	CBS	6563042	1990	**£8**	**£4**	
John Wesley Harding	LP	CBS	BPG63252	1968	**£15**	**£6**	*mono*
John Wesley Harding	LP	CBS	SBPG63252	1968	**£10**	**£4**	*stereo*
Just Like Tom Thumb's Blues	7″ EP	CBS	6270	1966	**£40**	**£20**	*French*
Leopard-Skin Pill-Box Hat	7″ EP	CBS	6345	1967	**£40**	**£20**	*French*
Leopardskin Pillbox Hat	7″	CBS	2700	1967	**£40**	**£20**	*picture sleeve*
Leopardskin Pillbox Hat	7″	CBS	2700	1967	**£4**	**£1.50**	
Like A Rolling Stone	7″	CBS	201811	1965	**£4**	**£1.50**	
Like A Rolling Stone	7″ EP	CBS	6107	1965	**£40**	**£20**	*French*
Like A Rolling Stone (Parts 1 & 2)	7″	CBS	201811	1965	**£50**	**£25**	*demo*
Maggie's Farm	7″	CBS	201781	1965	**£5**	**£2**	
Million Dollar Bash	7″	CBS	3665	1975	**£4**	**£1.50**	
Mixed Up Confusion	7″	CBS	2476	196–	**£25**	**£12.50**	*Dutch, picture sleeve*
Mixed Up Confusion	7″	Columbia	442656	1963	**£200**	**£100**	*US, best auctioned*
Mr Tambourine Man	7″ EP	CBS	EP6078	1966	**£20**	**£10**	
Nashville Skyline	LP	CBS	63601	1969	**£15**	**£6**	*mono*
Nashville Skyline	LP	CBS	CQ32872	1974	**£20**	**£8**	*US quad*
Nashville Skyline	LP	Columbia	HC49825	1981	**£20**	**£8**	*US audiophile*
Nine Song Publisher's Sampler	LP	Warner Bros	XTD221567	1963	**£600**	**£400**	*US promo*
On A Night Like This	7″	Island	WIP6168	1974	**£4**	**£1.50**	
One Of Us Must Know	7″	CBS	202053	1966	**£4**	**£1.50**	
One Too Many Mornings	7″ EP	CBS	EP6070	1966	**£20**	**£10**	
Planet Waves	LP	Ashes And Sands	7E501	1973	**£75**	**£37.50**	*US own label*
Planet Waves	LP	Asylum	EQ1003	1974	**£25**	**£10**	*US quad*
Political World	CD-s	CBS	6556435	1990	**£8**	**£4**	
Political World	CD-s	CBS	6556432	1990	**£5**	**£2**	
Positively Fourth Street	7″	CBS	201824	1965	**£4**	**£1.50**	
Positively Fourth Street	7″	Columbia	43389	1965	**£100**	**£50**	*US mispress, plays alternate 'Crawl Out Your Window'*
Positively Fourth Street	7″ EP	CBS	6210	1965	**£40**	**£20**	*French*
Rainy Day Women	7″	CBS	202307	1966	**£4**	**£1.50**	
Rainy Day Women Nos. 12 & 35	7″ EP	CBS	5660	1966	**£40**	**£20**	*French*
Rita May	7″	CBS	4859	1977	**£5**	**£2**	*picture sleeve*
Subterranean Homesick Blues	7″	CBS	201753	1965	**£6**	**£2.50**	
Subterranean Homesick Blues	7″ EP	CBS	6096	1965	**£40**	**£20**	*French*
Tangled Up In Blue	7″	CBS	3160	1975	**£4**	**£1.50**	
Thirtieth Anniversary Concert	CD	Columbia	XPCD308	1993	**£20**	**£8**	*US promo sampler*
Times They Are A-Changin'	7″	CBS	201751	1965	**£6**	**£2.50**	
Times They Are A-Changin'	LP	Mobile Fidelity	MFSL1114	1984	**£12**	**£5**	*US audiophile*
Times They Are A-Changin'	LP	CBS	(S)BPG62251	1964	**£15**	**£6**	
Vs A. J. Weberman	LP	Folkways	FB5322	1971	**£100**	**£50**	*US*
Watching The River Flow	7″	CBS	7329	1971	**£4**	**£1.50**	
Wigwam	7″	CBS	5122	1970	**£4**	**£1.50**	
With God On Our Side	7″ EP	Fontana	TFE18009	1965	**£40**	**£20**	*with other artists*
With God On Our Side	7″ EP	CBS	6266	1965	**£40**	**£20**	*French*
World Of Folk Music	LP	Warner Bros	XGPB508	1964	**£200**	**£100**	*US promo, with other artists*
Ye Playboys And Playgirls	7″ EP	Fontana	TFE18011	1965	**£40**	**£20**	*with other artists*

DYMON, FRANKIE

Title	Format	Label	Number	Year	Price		Notes
Let It Out	LP	BASF	20212416	1971	**£15**	**£6**	*German*

DYNAMICS

Title	Format	Label	Number	Year	Price		Notes
Ice Cream Song	7″	Atlantic	584270	1969	**£4**	**£1.50**	
Misery	7″	London	HLX9809	1963	**£20**	**£10**	
So In Love With Me	7″	King	KG1007	1964	**£8**	**£4**	

DYNAMICS *(2)*

Title	Format	Label	Number	Year	Price		Notes
Dynamics With Jimmy Hannah	LP	Bolo	BLP8001	1962	**£20**	**£8**	*US*

DYNAMICS *(3)*

Title	Format	Label	Number	Year	Price		Notes
My Friends	7″	Blue Cat	BS104	1968	**£8**	**£4**	*Neville Irons B side*

DYNAMITES

Title	Format	Label	Number	Year	Price		Notes
Fire Corner	LP	Trojan	TTL21	1969	**£15**	**£6**	
John Public	7″	Duke	DU30	1969	**£4**	**£1.50**	

Title	Format	Label	Cat. No.	Year	Mint	VG	Notes
Mr Midnight	7"	Clandisc	CLA200	1969	£4	£1.50	*King Stitt B side*
Rahtid	7"	Trojan	TR647	1969	£4	£1.50	*Clancy Eccles B side*
Sha La La La	7"	Clandisc	CLA219	1970	£4	£1.50	

DYNAMITES (2)

Title	Format	Label	Cat. No.	Year	Mint	VG	Notes
Someone Like Me	7" EP	Columbia	ESRF1729	1965	£10	£5	*French*

DYNATONES

Title	Format	Label	Cat. No.	Year	Mint	VG	Notes
Fife Piper	7"	Pye	7N25389	1966	£40	£20	
Steel Guitar Rag	7"	Top Rank	JAR149	1959	£5	£2	

DYSON, ALAN

Title	Format	Label	Cat. No.	Year	Mint	VG	Notes
Still Small Voice Of Alan Dyson	LP	Pye	NPL18212	1968	£20	£8	

DYSON, RONNIE

Title	Format	Label	Cat. No.	Year	Mint	VG	Notes
We Can Make It Last Forever	7"	CBS	2430	1974	£5	£2	

DZYAN

Title	Format	Label	Cat. No.	Year	Mint	VG	Notes
Dzyan	LP	Aronda	10006	1972	£12	£5	*German*
Electric Silence	LP	Bacillus	19202	1975	£10	£4	*German*
Time Machine	LP	Bacillus	BLPS19161	1973	£15	£6	*German*

e

E. F. BAND

Title	Format	Label	Cat. No.	Year	Value	Value	Notes
Another Day Gone	7"	Rok	ROKXI/XII	1980	£15	£7.50	*B side by Synchromesh*
Deep Cut	LP	Bullet	CULP2	1983	£10	£4	
Devil's Eye	7"	Redball	RR036	1980	£10	£5	
Night Angel	7"	Aerco	EF1	1980	£10	£5	
Self Made Suicide	7"	Redball	RR026	1980	£10	£5	

EAGER, VINCE

Title	Format	Label	Cat. No.	Year	Value	Value	Notes
Five Days Five Days	7"	Parlophone	R4482	1958	£15	£7.50	
Lonely Blue Boy	7"	Top Rank	JAR307	1960	£5	£2	
Makin' Love	7"	Top Rank	JAR191	1959	£4	£1.50	
No Other Arms, No Other Lips	7"	Parlophone	R4550	1959	£10	£5	
Plays Tribute To Elvis Presley	LP	Avenue	AVE093	1971	£10	£4	
Tread Softly Stranger	7"	Decca	F11023	1958	£30	£15	*2 x 1 sided demos only*
Vince Eager & The Vagabonds No. 1	7" EP	Decca	DFE6504	1958	£50	£25	
When's Your Birthday Baby	7"	Parlophone	R4531	1959	£10	£5	
Why	7"	Top Rank	JAR275	1960	£4	£1.50	

EAGLE

Title	Format	Label	Cat. No.	Year	Value	Value	Notes
Come Under Mrs Nancy's Tent	LP	Pye	NSPL28138	1969	£20	£8	
Kickin' It Back To You	7"	Pye	7N25530	1970	£4	£1.50	

EAGLES

Title	Format	Label	Cat. No.	Year	Value	Value	Notes
1994 Tour Collection Airplay Sampler	CD	Elektra	PRCD89832	1994	£15	£6	*US promo*
Common Thread – The Songs Of The Eagles	CD	Giant	CTDX93	1993	£25	£10	*Canadian promo double – one disc covers, one disc originals*
Hotel California	CD	Asylum	C8815	1988	£15	£6	*HMV boxed set*
Hotel California	CD	DCC	GZS1024	1992	£15	£6	*US audiophile*
Hotel California	CD-s	Elektra	EKR10CD	1988	£5	£2	*3" single*
Hotel California	LP	Mobile Fidelity	MFSL1126	1981	£10	£4	*US audiophile*
On The Border	LP	Asylum	EQ1004	1975	£10	£4	*US quad*
One Of These Nights	LP	Asylum	EQ1039	1975	£10	£4	*US quad*
Take It Easy	7"	Asylum	AYM505	1972	£4	£1.50	*promo, picture sleeve*
Take It Easy	CD-s	Asylum	9693412	1989	£5	£2	*3" single*

EAGLES (2)

Title	Format	Label	Cat. No.	Year	Value	Value	Notes
Andorra	7"	Pye	7N15613	1964	£4	£1.50	
Bristol Express	7"	Pye	7N15451	1962	£4	£1.50	
Come On Baby	7"	Pye	7N15550	1963	£4	£1.50	
Desperadoes	7"	Pye	7N15503	1962	£4	£1.50	
Eagles Nest	7"	Pye	7N15571	1963	£4	£1.50	
Exodus	7"	Pye	7N15473	1962	£4	£1.50	
New Sound TV Themes	7" EP	Pye	NEP24166	1962	£10	£5	
Smash Hits	LP	Pye	NPL18084	1963	£25	£10	
Wishing And Hoping	7"	Pye	7N15650	1964	£6	£2.50	

EAGLES (3)

Title	Format	Label	Cat. No.	Year	Value	Value	Notes
Rudam Bam	7"	Songbird	SB1006	1969	£4	£1.50	

EAGLIN, SNOOKS

Title	Format	Label	Cat. No.	Year	Value	Value	Notes
Blues Anthology Vol. 6	7" EP	Storyville	SEP386	1963	£8	£4	
Country Boy	7"	Storyville	A45056	196–	£8	£4	
Message From New Orleans	LP	Heritage	HLP1002	1961	£20	£8	
New Orleans Street Singer	LP	Folkways	FA2476	1961	£20	£8	
New Orleans Street Singer	LP	Storyville	SLP119	1964	£10	£4	
Portraits In Blues Vol. 1	LP	Storyville	SLP146	1964	£10	£4	
Vol. 2 – Blues From New Orleans	LP	Storyville	SLP140	1964	£10	£4	

EANES, JIM

Title	Format	Label	Cat. No.	Year	Value	Value	Notes
Christmas Doll	7"	Melodisc	1530	1959	£8	£4	

EARDLEY, JOHN

Title	Format	Label	Cat. No.	Year	Value	Value	Notes
Down East	LP	Esquire	32040	1958	£30	£15	

EARL, ROBERT

Title	Format	Label	Cat. No.	Year	Price	Price	Notes
Robert Earl	7" EP	Philips	BBE12032	1958	**£5**	**£2**	
Showcase	LP	Philips	BBL7394	1960	**£10**	**£4**	
Wonderful Secret Of Love	7" EP	Philips	BBE12240	1959	**£5**	**£2**	

EARLAND, CHARLES

Title	Format	Label	Cat. No.	Year	Price	Price	Notes
Intensity	LP	Prestige	PR10041	197–	**£10**	**£4**	
Odyssey	LP	Mercury	SRM11049	1976	**£10**	**£4**	

EARLS

Title	Format	Label	Cat. No.	Year	Price	Price	Notes
Never	7"	London	HL9702	1963	**£25**	**£12.50**	
Remember Me Baby	LP	Old Town	LP104	1963	**£75**	**£37.50**	*US*
Remember Then	7"	Stateside	SS153	1963	**£20**	**£10**	

EARTH

Title	Format	Label	Cat. No.	Year	Price	Price	Notes
Resurrection City	7"	CBS	4671	1969	**£20**	**£10**	
Stranger Of Fortune	7"	Decca	F22908	1969	**£6**	**£2.50**	

EARTH, WIND & FIRE

Title	Format	Label	Cat. No.	Year	Price	Price	Notes
Earth, Wind And Fire	LP	Warner Bros	WS1905	1971	**£25**	**£10**	
Head To The Sky	LP	Columbia	CQ32194	1974	**£10**	**£4**	*US quad*
Last Days And Time	LP	CBS	65208	1973	**£10**	**£4**	
Open Our Eyes	LP	Columbia	CQ32712	1974	**£10**	**£4**	*US quad*

EARTH & FIRE

Title	Format	Label	Cat. No.	Year	Price	Price	Notes
Atlantis	LP	Polydor	2925013	1973	**£12**	**£5**	*Dutch*
Best Of Earth And Fire	LP	Polydor	2491004	1975	**£10**	**£4**	*Dutch*
Earth And Fire	LP	Nepentha	6437004	1971	**£150**	**£75**	
Earth And Fire	LP	Polydor	2441011	1971	**£75**	**£37.50**	*Dutch*
Invitation	7"	Nepentha	6129001	1971	**£20**	**£10**	
Seasons	7"	Polydor	56790	1970	**£6**	**£2.50**	
Song Of Marching Children	LP	Polydor	2925003	1971	**£20**	**£8**	*Dutch*
To The World A Future	LP	Polydor	2925033	1975	**£10**	**£4**	*Dutch*

EARTH BOYS

Title	Format	Label	Cat. No.	Year	Price	Price	Notes
Space Girl	7"	Capitol	CL14979	1959	**£5**	**£2**	

EARTH OPERA

Title	Format	Label	Cat. No.	Year	Price	Price	Notes
Earth Opera	LP	Elektra	EKS74016	1968	**£15**	**£6**	
Great American Eagle Tragedy	LP	Elektra	EKS74038	1969	**£10**	**£4**	

EARTHBOUND (PRODIGY)

Title	Format	Label	Cat. No.	Year	Price	Price	Notes
One Love	12"	XL	EB1	1993	**£20**	**£10**	*white label*
One Love (Remix)	12"	XL	EB2	1993	**£20**	**£10**	*white label*

EARTHLINGS

Title	Format	Label	Cat. No.	Year	Price	Price	Notes
Landing Of The Daleks	7"	Parlophone	R5242	1965	**£25**	**£12.50**	

EARTHQUAKE

Title	Format	Label	Cat. No.	Year	Price	Price	Notes
Live	LP	United Artists	UAS29853	1975	**£10**	**£4**	

EARTHQUAKERS

Title	Format	Label	Cat. No.	Year	Price	Price	Notes
Whistling In The Sunshine	7"	Stateside	SS2050	1967	**£4**	**£1.50**	

EARTHQUAKES

Title	Format	Label	Cat. No.	Year	Price	Price	Notes
Brother Moses	7"	Duke	DU55	1969	**£4**	**£1.50**	
Earth Quake	7"	Duke	DU56	1969	**£4**	**£1.50**	
I Can't Stop Loving You	7"	Duke	DU54	1969	**£4**	**£1.50**	

EASLEY, TIM

Title	Format	Label	Cat. No.	Year	Price	Price	Notes
Susie Q	7"	Bell	BLL1036	1968	**£4**	**£1.50**	

EAST OF EDEN

East Of Eden were virtually two separate groups, with only violinist Dave Arbus being a member of both. The Harvest recordings, made after the group gained a chart hit with the atypical 'Jig A Jig', are routine seventies rock. The Deram LPs, on the other hand, contain fiercely experimental music in which Don Drummond rubs shoulders with Charles Mingus, and saxophones, flutes and violins jostle with each other for supremacy.

Title	Format	Label	Cat. No.	Year	Price	Price	Notes
Boogie Woogie Flu	7"	Harvest	HAR5055	1972	**£4**	**£1.50**	
East Of Eden	LP	Harvest	SHVL792	1971	**£15**	**£6**	
King Of Siam	7"	Atlantic	584198	1968	**£10**	**£5**	
Mercator Projected	LP	Deram	SML1038	1969	**£20**	**£8**	
Mercator Projected	LP	Deram	DML1038	1969	**£30**	**£15**	*mono*
New Leaf	LP	Harvest	SHVL796	1971	**£10**	**£4**	
Northern Hemisphere	7"	Deram	DM242	1969	**£10**	**£5**	
Ramadhan	7"	Deram	DM338	1971	**£4**	**£1.50**	
Snafu	LP	Deram	SML1050	1970	**£15**	**£6**	

EAST VILLAGE OTHER

Title	Format	Label	Cat. No.	Year	Price	Price	Notes
Electric Newspaper	LP	ESP-Disk	1034	1966	**£50**	**£25**	*US*

EASTERHOUSE

Title	Format	Label	Cat. No.	Year	Price	Price	Notes
In Our Own Hands	12"	Easterhouse	EIREX1	1985	**£6**	**£2.50**	*hand-stencilled picture sleeve*

EASTON, SHEENA

101	CD-s	MCA	DMCA(X)1348	1989	**£5**	**£2**	*3" single, 2 versions*
For Your Eyes Only	7"	EMI	PSR460	1981	**£10**	**£5**	*promo*

EASTWOOD, CLINT

Cowboy Favorites	LP	Cameo Parkway	C(S)1056	1963	**£20**	**£8**	*US*
Rowdy	7"	Cameo Parkway	C240	1962	**£5**	**£2**	
Rowdy	7"	Cameo Parkway	C240	1962	**£10**	**£5**	*picture sleeve*

EASY RIDERS

Remember The Alamo	LP	London	HAR2323/SAHR6126	1960	**£12**	**£5**	

EASY STREET

Easy Street	LP	Polydor	2383415	1976	**£10**	**£4**	
Person To Person	7"	Muscle	AP591	197–	**£20**	**£10**	
Under The Glass	LP	Polydor	2383444	1977	**£10**	**£4**	

EASYBEATS

The Easybeats were responsible for one of the classic beat singles, 'Friday On My Mind'. Originally from Australia, the group gained considerable success there, but were unable to find a satisfactory follow-up to their big hit single in the UK. Guitarists Harry Vanda and George Young (brother of AC/DC's Angus and Malcolm) managed to maintain successful careers as songwriters and producers, however, and recorded further albums in the eighties as members of the group Flash and the Pan.

Best Of The Easybeats	LP	Parlophone	PMEO9958	1967	**£50**	**£25**	*Australian*
Come And See Her	7"	United Artists	UP1144	1966	**£6**	**£2.50**	
Falling Off The Edge Of The World	LP	United Artists	UAS6667	1968	**£30**	**£15**	*US*
Friday On My Mind	7"	United Artists	UP1157	1966	**£4**	**£1.50**	
Friday On My Mind	7" EP	United Artists	36106	1966	**£30**	**£15**	*French*
Friday On My Mind	LP	United Artists	UAL3/UAS6588	1967	**£40**	**£20**	*US*
Friends	7"	Polydor	2001028	1970	**£4**	**£1.50**	
Friends	LP	Polydor	2482010	1970	**£30**	**£15**	
Good Friday	LP	United Artists	(S)ULP1167	1967	**£60**	**£30**	
Good Times	7"	United Artists	UP2243	1969	**£4**	**£1.50**	
Heaven & Hell	7" EP	United Artists	36117	1967	**£30**	**£15**	*French*
Heaven And Hell	7"	United Artists	UP1183	1967	**£4**	**£1.50**	
Hello How Are You	7"	United Artists	UP2209	1968	**£4**	**£1.50**	
I Love Marie	7"	Polydor	56357	1969	**£4**	**£1.50**	
Land Of Make Believe	7"	United Artists	UP2219	1968	**£4**	**£1.50**	
Music Goes Round My Head	7"	United Artists	UP1201	1967	**£4**	**£1.50**	
St Louis	7"	Polydor	56335	1969	**£4**	**£1.50**	
Vigil	LP	United Artists	(S)ULP1193	1968	**£30**	**£15**	
Volume Three	LP	Parlophone	PMCO7537	1966	**£50**	**£25**	*Australian*
Who'll Be The One	7"	United Artists	UP1175	1966	**£4**	**£1.50**	
Who'll Be The One	7" EP	United Artists	36112	1966	**£30**	**£15**	*French*

EAT

Autogift	CD-s	Fiction	WANCD100	1989	**£5**	**£2**	
Plastic Bag	CD-s	Fiction	CIFCD1	1989	**£5**	**£2**	
Psycho Couch	CD-s	Non Fiction	YESCD3	1990	**£5**	**£2**	
Sell Me A God	CD-s	Fiction	8389442	1989	**£5**	**£2**	
Summer In The City	CD-s	Fiction	CIFCD2	1989	**£5**	**£2**	

EAT STATIC

Almost Human	12"	Alien	ARO2	1992	**£6**	**£2.50**	
Inanna	12"	Static Music	AR1	1992	**£6**	**£2.50**	
Monkey Man	12"	Static Music	HAB1	1992	**£6**	**£2.50**	

EATER

Album	LP	The Label	TLRLP001	1978	**£15**	**£6**	

EBONIES

Never Gonna Break Your Heart Again	7"	Philips	BF1648	1968	**£5**	**£2**	

EBSTEIN, KATJA

No More Love For Me	7"	Liberty	LBF15317	1970	**£8**	**£4**	

ECCENTRICS

What You Got	7"	Pye	7N15850	1965	**£25**	**£12.50**	

ECCLES, CLANCY

Africa	7"	Clandisc	CLA214	1970	**£5**	**£2**	
Auntie Lulu	7"	Duke	DU9	1969	**£4**	**£1.50**	*Slickers B side*
Beat Dance	7"	Clandisc	CLA206	1969	**£4**	**£1.50**	*King Stitt B side*
Black Beret	7"	Clandisc	CLA212	1970	**£5**	**£2**	
C.N. Express	7"	Pama	PM722	1968	**£6**	**£2.50**	
Constantinople	7"	Trojan	TR648	1969	**£4**	**£1.50**	
Credit Squeeze	7"	Clandisc	CLA227	1970	**£5**	**£2**	
Fattie Fattie	7"	Trojan	TR658	1969	**£4**	**£1.50**	*Silverstars B side*
Feel The Rhythm	7"	Doctor Bird	DB1156	1968	**£10**	**£5**	
Festival '68	7"	Nu Beat	NB006	1968	**£6**	**£2.50**	
Fight	7"	Pama	PM712	1968	**£6**	**£2.50**	
Freedom	7"	Blue Beat	BB67	1961	**£12**	**£6**	

Freedom	LP	Trojan	TTL22	1969	**£15**	**£6**	
Glory Hallelujah	7"	Island	WI098	1963	**£10**	**£5**	
John Crow Skank	7"	Clandisc	CLA235	1971	**£4**	**£1.50**	
Judgement	7"	Island	WI044	1963	**£10**	**£5**	
Miss Ida	7"	Ska Beat	JB198	1965	**£10**	**£5**	*King Rocky B side*
Mother's Advice	7"	Pama	PM703	1967	**£6**	**£2.50**	
Open Up	7"	Clandisc	CLA209	1969	**£4**	**£1.50**	*Higgs & Wilson B side*
Phantom	7"	Clandisc	CLA213	1970	**£5**	**£2**	
Power For The People	7"	Clandisc	CLA236	1971	**£4**	**£1.50**	
Promises	7"	Clandisc	CLA211	1970	**£5**	**£2**	
River Jordan	7"	Blue Beat	BB34	1961	**£12**	**£6**	
Rod Of Correction	7"	Clandisc	CLA232	1971	**£4**	**£1.50**	
Sammy No Dead	7"	Ska Beat	JB194	1965	**£10**	**£5**	
Shu Be Do	7"	Duke	DU31	1969	**£4**	**£1.50**	
Sweet Africa	7"	Trojan	TR639	1968	**£6**	**£2.50**	
Sweet Jamaica	7"	Clandisc	CLA231	1971	**£4**	**£1.50**	
Unite Tonight	7"	Clandisc	CLA221	1970	**£5**	**£2**	
What Will Your Mama Say	7"	Pama	PM701	1967	**£6**	**£2.50**	
World Needs Loving	7"	Clandisc	CLA201	1969	**£4**	**£1.50**	

ECHO & THE BUNNYMEN

Bring On The Dancing Horses	7"	Korova	KOW43	1988	**£5**	**£2**	*shaped picture disc*
Crocodiles	7"	Korova	ECHO1	1981	**£4**	**£1.50**	*promo*
Cutter	12"	Korova	KOW26T	1983	**£6**	**£2.50**	*with cassette and poster*
Echo And The Bunnymen	CD	WEA	2421372	1987	**£40**	**£20**	*promo canvas hold-all, with cassette and video*
Peel Sessions	CD-s	Strange Fruit	SFPSCD060	1989	**£5**	**£2**	
Pictures On My Wall	CD-s	Document	DC003	1991	**£5**	**£2**	
Songs To Learn And Sing	LP	Korova	KODE13	1985	**£25**	**£10**	*with 7", autographed*

ECHO BASE

Soul band Echo Base had Oscar Harrison as their drummer – afterwards to be found behind the kit with Ocean Colour Scene.

Out Of My Reach	7"	DEP International	DEP14	1984	**£8**	**£4**	
Puppet At The Go Go	7"	DEP International	DEP19	1985	**£8**	**£4**	

ECHOBELLY

Bellyache	CD-s	Pandemonium	PANNCD001	1993	**£5**	**£2**	*fold-out cover*

ECHOES

Baby Blue	7"	Top Rank	JAR553	1961	**£10**	**£5**	
Born To Be With You	7"	Top Rank	JAR399	1960	**£10**	**£5**	

ECHOES (2)

Searchin' For You Baby	7"	Philips	BF1683	1968	**£6**	**£2.50**	

ECHOES (3)

Are You Mine	7"	Blue Beat	BB89	1962	**£12**	**£6**	

ECKSTINE, BILLY

At Basin Street East	LP	Mercury	MMC14100/ CMS18066	1962	**£10**	**£4**	*with Quincy Jones*
Basie–Eckstine Incorporated	7" EP	Columbia	SEG8043/ ESG7827	1960	**£5**	**£2**	
Best Of Mister B No. 1	7" EP	Mercury	ZEP10005	1959	**£5**	**£2**	
Best Of Mister B No. 2	7" EP	Emarcy	YEP9509	1959	**£5**	**£2**	
Billy Eckstine	7" EP	MGM	MGMEP511	1954	**£5**	**£2**	
Billy Eckstine's Imagination	LP	Mercury	MMB12002	1959	**£10**	**£4**	
Billy's Best	LP	Mercury	MMC14043	1960	**£10**	**£4**	
Cashmere Voice	7" EP	MGM	MGMEP523	1955	**£5**	**£2**	
Count Basie And Billy Eckstine	LP	Columbia	33SX1202/ SCX3290	1960	**£10**	**£4**	*with Count Basie*
Date With Rhythm	7" EP	Parlophone	GEP8672	1957	**£5**	**£2**	
Enchantment No. 1	7" EP	MGM	MGMEP545	1956	**£5**	**£2**	
Four Great Standards	7" EP	MGM	MGMEP598	1957	**£5**	**£2**	
Gentle On My Mind	LP	Tamla Motown	(S)TML11101	1969	**£20**	**£8**	
Golden Saxophones	LP	London	HAD2241/ SAHD6070	1960	**£10**	**£4**	
Had You Been Around	7"	Tamla Motown	TMG533	1965	**£40**	**£20**	
Kiss Of Fire	7"	MGM	SP1011	1953	**£8**	**£4**	
Love Me Or Leave Me	7"	MGM	SP1136	1955	**£4**	**£1.50**	
My Way	LP	Tamla Motown	(S)TML11046	1967	**£30**	**£15**	
No Cover, No Minimum	LP	Columbia	33SX1327/ SCX3381	1961	**£10**	**£4**	
No One But You	7"	MGM	SP1101	1954	**£6**	**£2.50**	
Once More With Feeling	LP	Columbia	33SX1249/ SCX3322	1960	**£10**	**£4**	
Prime Of My Life	LP	Tamla Motown	TML11025	1966	**£40**	**£20**	

Title	Format	Label	Cat. No.	Year			
Tenderly	10" LP	MGM	MGMD126	1954	**£12**	**£5**	
That Old Feeling	10" LP	MGM	MGMD138	1956	**£12**	**£5**	
Weaver Of Dreams	10" LP	MGM	MGMD151	1958	**£12**	**£5**	

ECKSTINE, BILLY & SARAH VAUGHAN

Title	Format	Label	Cat. No.	Year			
Best Of Berlin	7" EP	Mercury	SEZ19016	1961	**£6**	**£2.50**	*stereo*
Best Of Berlin Vol. 1	7" EP	Mercury	ZEP10108	1961	**£5**	**£2**	
Best Of Irving Berlin	LP	Mercury	MPL6530	1958	**£10**	**£4**	
Billy Eckstine And Sarah Vaughan	7" EP	MGM	MGMEP690	1959	**£5**	**£2**	
Dedicated To You	7" EP	MGM	MGMEP561	1956	**£5**	**£2**	
More Of Irving Berlin	7" EP	Mercury	SEZ19023	1962	**£6**	**£2.50**	*stereo*
Passing Strangers	7"	Mercury	AMT1071	1959	**£4**	**£1.50**	
Passing Strangers	7" EP	Mercury	10025MCE	1965	**£5**	**£2**	
Together Again	7" EP	Mercury	10027MCE	1960	**£5**	**£2**	

ECLECTION

Eclection had a very similar sound to the early Fairport Convention and two of its members – Trevor Lucas and Gerry Conway – played with the more famous group in later years. When singer Kerilee Male left in October 1968, the group took the unusual step of re-recording their current single with Male's replacement, Dorris Henderson. Despite this, however, neither version sold particularly well.

Title	Format	Label	Cat. No.	Year			
Another Time Another Place	7"	Elektra	EKSN45040	1968	**£4**	**£1.50**	
Eclection	LP	Elektra	EKS74023	1968	**£40**	**£20**	
Eclection	LP	Elektra	EKL4023	1968	**£50**	**£25**	*mono*
Nevertheless	7"	Elektra	EKSN45033	1968	**£4**	**£1.50**	
Please	7"	Elektra	EKSN45042	1968	**£4**	**£1.50**	
Please (Mark II)	7"	Elektra	EKSN45046	1968	**£4**	**£1.50**	

EDDIE, JASON

Even a Joe Meek production (on 'Singing The Blues') could not give Al Wycherley the kind of success enjoyed by his elder brother, Ron – who used the stage name Billy Fury.

Title	Format	Label	Cat. No.	Year			
Heart And Soul	7"	Tangerine	DP0010	1969	**£4**	**£1.50**	
Singing The Blues	7"	Parlophone	R5473	1966	**£100**	**£50**	
Whatcha Gonna Do Baby	7"	Parlophone	R5388	1965	**£75**	**£37.50**	

EDDIE AND THE HOT RODS

Title	Format	Label	Cat. No.	Year			
Writing On The Wall	7"	Island	WIP6270	1976	**£10**	**£5**	*picture sleeve*

EDDIE'S CROWD

Title	Format	Label	Cat. No.	Year			
Baby Don't Look Down	7"	CBS	202078	1966	**£25**	**£12.50**	

EDDY, DUANE

Title	Format	Label	Cat. No.	Year			
1,000,000 Dollars Of Twang	LP	London	HAW2325	1961	**£10**	**£4**	
1,000,000 Dollars Of Twang Vol. 2	LP	London	HAW2435	1964	**£10**	**£4**	
Because They're Young	7"	London	HL7096	1960	**£4**	**£1.50**	*export*
Because They're Young	7" EP	London	REW1252	1960	**£8**	**£3**	
Biggest Twang Of All	LP	Reprise	R(S)LP6218	1967	**£10**	**£4**	
Bonnie Come Back	7"	London	HL7090	1960	**£15**	**£7.50**	*export*
Break My Mind	7"	CBS	3962	1969	**£8**	**£4**	
Cannonball	7"	London	HL8764	1958	**£5**	**£2**	*tri-centre*
Caravan	7"	Parlophone	R4826	1961	**£4**	**£1.50**	
Cottonmouth	7" EP	Colpix	PXE304	1965	**£25**	**£12.50**	
Country Twang	7" EP	RCA	RCX7115	1963	**£12**	**£6**	
Dance With The Guitar Man	7"	RCA	RCA1701	1968	**£8**	**£4**	*Sam Cooke B side*
Dance With The Guitar Man	LP	RCA	RD7545	1963	**£10**	**£4**	
Dance With The Guitar Man	LP	RCA	SF7545	1963	**£15**	**£6**	*stereo*
Daydream	7"	Reprise	RS20504	1966	**£6**	**£2.50**	
Duane A Go Go	LP	Colpix	PXL490	1965	**£10**	**£4**	
Duane Does Dylan	LP	Golden Guinea	GGL10337	1968	**£10**	**£4**	
Duane Does Dylan	LP	Golden Guinea	GGSL10337	1968	**£15**	**£6**	*stereo*
Duane Does Dylan	LP	Colpix	PXL494	1965	**£15**	**£6**	
Especially For You	LP	London	HAW2191	1959	**£10**	**£4**	
Especially For You	LP	London	SAHW6045	1959	**£12**	**£5**	*stereo*
Forty Miles Of Bad Road	7"	London	HL7080	1959	**£6**	**£2.50**	*export*
Girls Girls Girls	LP	London	SAHW6173	1961	**£12**	**£5**	*stereo*
Girls Girls Girls	LP	London	HAW2373	1961	**£10**	**£4**	
Have Twangy Guitar Will Travel	LP	London	HAW2160	1958	**£12**	**£5**	
House Of The Rising Sun	7"	Colpix	PX788	1964	**£4**	**£1.50**	
Lonely Guitar	LP	RCA	RD/SF7621	1964	**£15**	**£6**	
Lonely One	7"	London	HLW8821	1959	**£5**	**£2**	*tri-centre*
Lonely One	7"	London	HL7072	1959	**£6**	**£2.50**	*export*
Lonely One	7" EP	London	REW1216	1959	**£8**	**£3**	
Love Confusion	7"	Target	101	1975	**£5**	**£2**	
Mister Twang	7" EP	RCA	RCX7129	1963	**£15**	**£7.50**	
Monsoon	7"	Reprise	RS20557	1967	**£6**	**£2.50**	
Movie Themes	7" EP	London	REW1303	1961	**£8**	**£3**	
Niki Hoeky	7"	Reprise	RS20690	1968	**£6**	**£2.50**	
Pepe	7" EP	London	REW1287	1961	**£8**	**£3**	
Peter Gunn	7"	London	SLW4001	1959	**£40**	**£20**	*stereo*
Ramrod	7"	London	HL8723	1958	**£5**	**£2**	*tri-centre*
Ramrod	7"	Ford	500	1957	**£150**	**£75**	*US*
Ramrod	7"	London	HL7057	1958	**£6**	**£2.50**	*export*
Rebel Rouser	7"	London	HL8669	1958	**£6**	**£2.50**	*tri-centre*
Rebel Rouser	7" EP	London	RE1175	1958	**£10**	**£5**	
Roarin' Twangies	LP	Reprise	R(S)LP6240	1967	**£20**	**£8**	

Songs Of Our Heritage	LP	London	SAHW6119	1960	**£12**	**£5**	*stereo*
Songs Of Our Heritage	LP	London	HAW2285	1960	**£10**	**£4**	
Trash	7"	Colpix	PX779	1964	**£4**	**£1.50**	
Twang's The Thang	LP	London	HAW2236	1960	**£10**	**£4**	
Twang's The Thang	LP	London	SAHW6068	1960	**£12**	**£5**	*stereo*
Twangin' Golden Hits	LP	RCA	RD7689	1964	**£10**	**£4**	
Twangin' Golden Hits	LP	RCA	SF7689	1965	**£15**	**£6**	*stereo*
Twangin' Up A Small Storm	7" EP	RCA	RCX7146	1964	**£20**	**£10**	
Twangin' Up A Storm	LP	RCA	RD7568	1963	**£10**	**£4**	
Twangin' Up A Storm	LP	RCA	SF7568	1963	**£15**	**£6**	*stereo*
Twangs A Country Song	LP	RCA	RD7560	1963	**£10**	**£4**	
Twangs A Country Song	LP	RCA	SF7560	1963	**£15**	**£6**	*stereo*
Twangsville	LP	RCA	SF7754	1965	**£20**	**£8**	*stereo*
Twangsville	LP	RCA	RD7754	1965	**£15**	**£6**	
Twangy	7" EP	London	REW1257	1960	**£8**	**£3**	
Twangy Guitar Silky Strings	LP	RCA	RD7510	1962	**£10**	**£4**	
Twangy Guitar Silky Strings	LP	RCA	SF7510	1962	**£15**	**£6**	*stereo*
Twangy No. 2	7" EP	London	REW1341	1961	**£10**	**£5**	
Twistin' And Twangin'	LP	RCA	RD27264	1962	**£10**	**£4**	
Twistin' And Twangin'	LP	RCA	SF5134	1962	**£15**	**£6**	*stereo*
Water Skiing	LP	RCA	RD7656	1964	**£15**	**£6**	
Water Skiing	LP	RCA	SF7656	1964	**£20**	**£8**	*stereo*
Yep	7" EP	London	REW1217	1959	**£8**	**£3**	
Yep!	7"	London	HL7076	1959	**£15**	**£7.50**	*export*

EDDY, PEARL

That's What A Heart Is For	7"	HMV	7M262	1954	**£5**	**£2**	

EDDY & TEDDY

Bye Bye Butterfly	7"	London	HLU9367	1961	**£5**	**£2**	

EDEN

Eden	LP	Total	22009	1975	**£15**	**£6**	*Canadian*

EDEN, TONI

Grown Up Dreams	7"	Columbia	DB4458	1960	**£6**	**£2.50**	
Send Me	7"	Decca	F11342	1961	**£4**	**£1.50**	
Teen Street	7"	Columbia	DB4409	1960	**£8**	**£4**	
Will I Ever	7"	Columbia	DB4527	1960	**£5**	**£2**	

EDEN ROSE

On The Way To Eden	LP	Katema	KA33507	1970	**£200**	**£100**	*French*

EDEN STREET SKIFFLE GROUP

Skiffle Album No. 1	78	Headquarters & General Stores	no number	1957	**£100**	**£50**	*set of 10 78 rpm flexis*

EDEN'S CHILDREN

Eden's Children	LP	Stateside	(S)SL10235	1968	**£30**	**£15**	
Sure Looks Real	LP	ABC	S652	1969	**£25**	**£10**	*US*

EDGE

Edge	LP	Nose	NRS48003	1970	**£30**	**£15**	*US*

EDISON, HARRY

Gee Baby Ain't I Good To You	LP	HMV	CLP1350	1960	**£20**	**£8**	
Harry Edison Quartet	10" LP	Vogue	LDE118	1955	**£40**	**£20**	
Sweets	LP	Columbia	33CX10087	1957	**£20**	**£8**	
Swinger	LP	HMV	CLP1277	1959	**£20**	**£8**	
Swings Buck Clayton	LP	HMV	CLP1321	1960	**£20**	**£8**	

EDMUNDS, DAVE

Blue Monday	7"	Regal Zonophone	RZ3037	1971	**£5**	**£2**	
College Radio Network Presents Dave Edmunds	LP	Swansong	PR320	1978	**£15**	**£6**	*US promo*
Down, Down, Down	7"	Regal Zonophone	RZ3059	1972	**£5**	**£2**	
I'm A-Comin' Home	7"	Regal Zonophone	RZ3032	1971	**£5**	**£2**	
Information	12"	Columbia	AS991725	1983	**£20**	**£10**	*US promo picture disc*
Rockpile	LP	Regal Zonophone	SLRZ1026	1971	**£25**	**£10**	

EDSELS

Rama Lama Ding Dong	7"	Pye	7N25086	1961	**£60**	**£30**	

EDWARD BEAR

Bearings	LP	Capitol	ST426	1969	**£10**	**£4**	
Eclipse	LP	Capitol	SKAO6349	1970	**£10**	**£4**	*US*

EDWARD H. DAFIS

Ffordd Newydd Eingl-Americanaidd Gret O Fyw	LP	Sain	1034M	1975	**£25**	**£10**	
Hen Ffordd Gymreig O Fyw	LP	Sain	1016M	1974	**£30**	**£15**	
Plant Y Fflam	LP	Sain	1196M	1980	**£12**	**£5**	
Sneb Yn Becso Dam	LP	Sain	1053M	1976	**£20**	**£8**	

Title	Format	Label	Cat. No.	Year	Price	Price	Notes
Yn Erbyn Y Ffactore	LP	Sain	1144M	1979	£12	£5	

EDWARDS, BOBBY

Title	Format	Label	Cat. No.	Year	Price	Price	Notes
You're The Reason	7"	Top Rank	JAR584	1961	£6	£2.50	

EDWARDS, BRENT

Title	Format	Label	Cat. No.	Year	Price	Price	Notes
Pride	7"	Pye	7N25197	1963	£4	£1.50	

EDWARDS, CHUCK

Title	Format	Label	Cat. No.	Year	Price	Price	Notes
Downtown Soulville	7"	Soul City	SC104	1968	£6	£2.50	

EDWARDS, GARY

Title	Format	Label	Cat. No.	Year	Price	Price	Notes
Africa	7"	Oriole	CB1733	1962	£5	£2	
Hopscotch	7"	Oriole	CB1759	1962	£12	£6	
Method	7"	Oriole	CB1717	1962	£4	£1.50	
Twist Or Bust	7"	Oriole	CB1700	1962	£5	£2	

EDWARDS, JACKIE

Title	Format	Label	Cat. No.	Year	Price	Price	Notes
All My Days	7"	Island	WI008	1962	£10	£5	
Best Of Jackie Edwards	LP	Island	ILP936	1966	£50	£25	
By Demand	LP	Island	ILP940	1966	£50	£25	
By Demand	LP	Trojan	TTL46	1970	£15	£6	
Come Back Girl	7"	Island	WIP6008	1967	£4	£1.50	
Come On Home	LP	Trojan	TTL45	1970	£15	£6	
Come On Home	LP	Island	ILP931	1966	£50	£25	
He'll Have To Go	7"	Aladdin	WI601	1965	£5	£2	
Heaven Just Knows	7"	Starlite	ST45046	1961	£10	£5	
Hush	7"	Aladdin	WI605	1965	£5	£2	
Hush	7" EP	Island	IEP708	1966	£20	£10	
I Feel So Bad	7"	Island	WI3006	1966	£40	£20	
Julie On My Mind	7"	Island	WIP6026	1968	£4	£1.50	
L-O-V-E	7"	Island	WI274	1966	£10	£5	
Let It Be Me	LP	Direction	863977	1969	£10	£4	
Lonely Game	7"	Decca	F11547	1962	£4	£1.50	
More Than Words Can Say	7"	Starlite	ST45062	1961	£10	£5	
Most Of Wilfred Jackie Edwards	LP	Trojan	TTL40	1970	£15	£6	
Most Of Wilfred Jackie Edwards	LP	Island	ILP906	1964	£50	£25	
One More Week	7"	Island	WI019	1962	£10	£5	
Only A Fool Breaks His Own Heart	7"	Island	WI3030	1967	£10	£5	
Premature Golden Sands	LP	Trojan	TTL57	1970	£15	£6	
Premature Golden Sands	LP	Island	ILP960/ILPS9060	1967	£40	£20	*pink label*
Put Your Tears Away	LP	Island	IWPS4	1969	£25	£10	
Royal Telephone	7"	Island	WI3018	1966	£10	£5	
Sacred Songs Vol. 1	7" EP	Island	IEP701	1966	£10	£5	*no picture sleeve*
Sacred Songs Vol. 2	7" EP	Island	IEP702	1966	£10	£5	*no picture sleeve*
Same One	7"	Aladdin	WI611	1965	£5	£2	
Sea Cruise	7"	Fontana	TF465	1964	£10	£5	
Sometimes	7"	Island	WI270	1966	£10	£5	
Stagger Lee	7"	Sue	WI329	1964	£10	£5	
Stand Up For Jesus	LP	Island	ILP912	1964	£40	£20	
Things You Do	7"	Black Swan	WI416	1964	£10	£5	
Think Twice	7"	Island	WI287	1966	£10	£5	
White Christmas	7"	Island	WI255	1965	£10	£5	
Why Make Believe	7"	Black Swan	WI404	1963	£10	£5	
You're My Girl	7"	Island	WIP6042	1968	£4	£1.50	
You're My Girl	7"	Island	WI3157	1968	£10	£5	

EDWARDS, JACKIE & JIMMY CLIFF

Title	Format	Label	Cat. No.	Year	Price	Price	Notes
Set Me Free	7"	Island	WIP6036	1968	£4	£1.50	

EDWARDS, JACKIE & MILLIE

Title	Format	Label	Cat. No.	Year	Price	Price	Notes
Best Of Jackie & Millie Vol. 2	LP	Island	ILP963	1968	£60	£30	*pink label*
Best Of Jackie & Millie Vol. 2	LP	Trojan	TTL52	1970	£15	£6	
Best Of Jackie And Millie Vol. 2	LP	Trojan	TTL52	1970	£12	£5	
In A Dream	7"	Island	WIP6012	1967	£6	£2.50	
Jackie And Millie	LP	Trojan	TBL155	1970	£15	£6	
My Desire	7"	Island	WI265	1966	£10	£5	
Pledging My Love	LP	Island	ILP941	1966	£60	£30	
This Is My Story	7"	Island	WI253	1965	£10	£5	*Sound System B side*

EDWARDS, JIMMY

Title	Format	Label	Cat. No.	Year	Price	Price	Notes
Love Bug Crawl	7"	Mercury	7MT193	1958	£300	£180	*best auctioned*

EDWARDS, NOKIE

Title	Format	Label	Cat. No.	Year	Price	Price	Notes
Again	LP	Cream	ISP80546	1972	£20	£8	*Japanese*
King Of Guitars	LP	Stateside	80859	1973	£20	£8	*Japanese*
Nokie	LP	Cream	CR9006	1971	£15	£6	*US*
Nokie Edwards	LP	Stateside	97019	1974	£20	£8	*Japanese*

EDWARDS, PAUL

Title	Format	Label	Cat. No.	Year	Price	Price	Notes
Longstone Farm	LP	Cottage	COT301	1976	£25	£10	

EDWARDS, RUPIE

Title	Format	Label	Cat. No.	Year	Price	Price	Notes
Black Man	7"	Nu Beat	NB082	1971	£4	£1.50	
Christmas Parade	7"	Big	BG337	1972	£4	£1.50	
Full Moon	7"	Explosion	EX2030	1970	£4	£1.50	
Guilty Convict	7"	Blue Beat	BB90	1962	£12	£6	
I Can't Forget	7"	Doctor Bird	DB1163	1968	£10	£5	

I'm Gonna Live Some Life	7"	Bullet	BU494	1971	**£4**	**£1.50**	
Jimmy As Job Card	7"	Big	BG335	1972	**£4**	**£1.50**	
Long Lost Love	7"	Crab	CRAB35	1969	**£4**	**£1.50**	
Love At First Sight	7"	Explosion	EX2031	1970	**£4**	**£1.50**	
Press Along	7"	Big	BG333	1972	**£4**	**£1.50**	
Sharp Pan Ya Machete	7"	Crab	CRAB41	1970	**£4**	**£1.50**	
Soulful Stew	7"	Big	BG320	1971	**£4**	**£1.50**	

EDWARDS, SAMUEL

Israel	7"	Blue Cat	BS159	1969	**£4**	**£1.50**	

EDWARDS, TOMMY

Baby Let Me Take You Dreaming	7"	MGM	SP1168	1956	**£8**	**£4**	
Fool Such As I	7"	MGM	SP1030	1953	**£8**	**£4**	
For Young Lovers	LP	MGM	C791	1959	**£25**	**£10**	
I've Been There	7" EP	MGM	MGMEP707	1959	**£20**	**£10**	
It's All In The Game	LP	MGM	C734	1959	**£25**	**£10**	
Tommy Edwards	LP	Lion	70120	195–	**£25**	**£10**	*US*
Tommy Edwards Sings	LP	Regent	MG6096	195–	**£25**	**£10**	*US*
Ways Of Love	7" EP	MGM	MGMEP712	1960	**£20**	**£10**	
You Started Me Dreaming	LP	MGM	C824	1960	**£25**	**£10**	

EDWARDS, VINCE

County Durham Dream	7"	United Artists	UP2230	1968	**£4**	**£1.50**	
I Can't Turn Back Time	7"	United Artists	UP1179	1967	**£5**	**£2**	

EDWARDS, VINCE (2)

No Not Much	7"	Colpix	PX771	1964	**£4**	**£1.50**	

EDWARDS, WILFRED & THE CARIBS

Little Bitty Girl	7"	Starlite	ST45076	1962	**£10**	**£5**	
Tell Me Darling	7"	Starlite	ST45026	1960	**£10**	**£5**	
We're Gonna Love	7"	Starlite	ST45016	1960	**£10**	**£5**	

EDWARD'S GROUP

Dear Hearts	7"	Island	WI040	1963	**£10**	**£5**	*Osbourne Graham B side*
He Gave You To Me	7"	Island	WI082	1963	**£10**	**£5**	
Hey Girl	7"	Island	WI087	1963	**£10**	**£5**	
Russian Roulette	7"	Island	WI047	1963	**£10**	**£5**	

EDWARDS HAND

Edwards Hand	LP	GRT	10005	1969	**£15**	**£6**	*US*
Rainshine	LP	Regal Zonophone	SRZA8513	1973	**£60**	**£30**	*demo only*
Stranded	LP	RCA	SF8154	1971	**£10**	**£4**	

EDWICK RUMBOLD

Shades Of Grey	7"	Parlophone	R5622	1967	**£50**	**£25**	
Specially When	7"	CBS	202393	1966	**£50**	**£25**	

EELA CRAIG

Eela Craig	LP	Pro Disc	208711	1971	**£75**	**£37.50**	*Austrian*
Hats Of Glass	LP	Vertigo	6360638	1977	**£25**	**£10**	*German*
Missa Universalis	LP	Vertigo	6360639	1978	**£25**	**£10**	*German*
One Nighter	LP	Vertigo	6360635	1976	**£25**	**£10**	*German*

EFENDI'S GARDEN

Efendi's Garden	LP	Babylon	80004	1979	**£25**	**£10**	*German*

EGANS, WILLIE

Willie Egans	7" EP	XX	MIN714	196–	**£10**	**£5**	

EGG

The records made by Egg contain the most impressive music of any made by those groups whose dominant voice is that of the keyboards. Organist Dave Stewart has been making records ever since, with Hatfield and the North and other related groups (he's even been in the charts a few times, but not as a member of the Eurythmics!), but he has arguably never bettered the youthful enthusiasm of his work with Egg. The group's music is difficult in places, but only in the same way that Soft Machine's music is. It utilizes awkward time signatures and convoluted melody lines, but never forgets its essential function of communicating with an audience.

Civil Surface	LP	Caroline	C1510	1974	**£10**	**£4**	
Egg	LP	Nova	SDN14	1970	**£15**	**£6**	
Polite Force	LP	Deram	SML1074	1970	**£15**	**£6**	
Seven Is A Jolly Good Time	7"	Deram	DM269	1969	**£10**	**£5**	

EGGY

You're Still Mine	7"	Spark	SRL1024	1970	**£10**	**£5**	

EIFFEL TOWER

Eiffel Tower	LP	Chappell	LPC1032	1969	**£60**	**£30**	

EIGHT-EYED SPY

Diddy Wah Diddy	7"	Fetish	FE19	1982	**£6**	**£2.50**	
Eight-Eyed Spy	LP	Fetish	FR2003	1981	**£10**	**£4**	

EIGHTH WONDER

Baby Baby	CD-s	CBS	BABECD1	1988	**£5**	**£2**	

Cross My Heart	CD-s	CBS	6515522	1988	£5	£2	
I'm Not Scared	10″	CBS	SCAREY1	1988	£10	£4	
I'm Not Scared	7″	CBS	SCAREQ1	1988	£4	£1.50	*poster sleeve*
I'm Not Scared	CD-s	CBS	SCAREC1	1988	£15	£7.50	

EIGHT-O-EIGHT STATE

Cubik Olympic	CD-s	ZTT	ZANG5CD	1990	£5	£2	
Extended Pleasures Of Dance	CD-s	ZTT	ZANG2CD	1989	£30	£15	
In Yer Face	CD-s	ZTT	ZANG14CD	1991	£5	£2	
Let Yourself Go	12″	Creed	STATE003	1988	£6	£2.50	
Lift	CD-s	ZTT	ZANG20CD	1991	£5	£2	
Newbuild	LP	Creed	STATE002	1988	£12	£5	
Ooops	CD-s	ZTT	ZANG19CD	1991	£6	£2.50	*with Björk*
Pacific 202	CD-s	ZTT	ZANG1CD	1989	£8	£4	*3″ single*
Pacific 202	12″	ZTT	ZANG1TX	1989	£8	£4	

EIGHTIES LADIES

Turned On To You	12″	Music Of Life	MOLIF6	1986	£6	£2.50	

EIH, DAMIN, A.L.K. AND BROTHER CLARK

Never Mind	LP	Demelot	NS7310	1973	£100	£50	*US*

EILIFF

Eiliff	LP	Philips	6305103	1971	£50	£25	*German*
Girlrls	LP	Philips	6305145	1972	£20	£8	*German*

EIRE APPARENT

Follow Me	7″	Track	604019	1967	£6	£2.50	
Rock'n'Roll Band	7″	Buddah	201039	1969	£5	£2	
Sunrise	LP	Buddah	203021	1969	£25	£10	

EKLAND, BRITT

Do It To Me	7″	Jet	JETP161	1979	£6	£2.50	*picture disc*

EKSEN TRICK BRICK BAND

Sky Story	LP	Aerco	AERL17	1978	£25	£10	

EKSEPTION

3	LP	Philips	6423005	1971	£12	£5	*Dutch*
4	LP	Philips	6423019	1972	£12	£5	*Dutch*
5	LP	Philips	6423042	1972	£12	£5	*Dutch*
Beggar Julia's Time Trip	LP	Philips	6314001	1969	£12	£5	
Ekseption	LP	Philips	6314005	1970	£12	£5	
Trinity	LP	Philips	6423056	1973	£10	£4	*Dutch*

EL PASO

Mosquito One	7″	Punch	PH61	1971	£5	£2	
Out De Light Baby	7″	Big Shot	BI572	1971	£5	£2	

EL SHALOM

Frost	LP	Attacca	27625	1976	£30	£15	*German*

ELAINE

I Never Wonder Where My Baby Goes	7″	Columbia	DB7091	1963	£5	£2	

ELASTIC BAND

Do Unto Others	7″	Decca	F12815	1968	£20	£10	
Expansions On Life	LP	Nova	DN/SND6	1969	£30	£15	
Think Of You Baby	7″	Decca	F12763	1968	£20	£10	

ELASTICA

Line Up	7″	Deceptive	BLUFF004	1994	£5	£2	
Stutter	7″	Deceptive	BLUFF003	1993	£12	£6	

ELASTICK BAND

Spazz	7″	Stateside	SS2056	1967	£200	£100	*demo*

ELBERT, DONNIE

In Between The Heartaches	7″	Polydor	56234	1968	£6	£2.50	
Let's Do The Stroll	7″	Parlophone	R4403	1958	£75	£37.50	
Little Piece Of Leather	7″	Sue	WI377	1965	£12	£6	
Sensational Donnie Elbert Sings	LP	King	629	1959	£75	£37.50	*US*
This Old Heart Of Mine	7″	Polydor	56265	1968	£4	£1.50	
You Can Push It Or Pull It	7″	Sue	WI396	1965	£12	£6	

ELCORT

Tammy	7″	Parlophone	R5447	1966	£6	£2.50	

ELDERBERRY JAK

Elderberry Jak	LP	Forest	AW14019	1968	£75	£37.50	*US*
Long Overdue	LP	Electric Fox	LP555	1975	£30	£15	*US*

ELDORADOS

Crazy Little Mama	LP	Vee Jay	VJLP1001	1959	£200	£100	*US*

ELDORADOS (2)

Eldorados	7″ EP	Decca	DFE8543	1963	£60	£30	

ELDRIDGE, ROY

Title	Format	Label	Cat. No.	Year	Mint	VG	Notes
Roy And Diz No. 2	LP	Columbia	33CX10084	1957	£30	£15	with Dizzy Gillespie
Roy Eldridge	10" LP	Columbia	33C9031	1957	£30	£15	
Roy Eldridge And Dizzy Gillespie	LP	Columbia	33CX10025	1956	£40	£20	
Roy Eldridge Quintet	10" LP	Columbia	33C9005	1955	£40	£20	

ELECAMPANE

Title	Format	Label	Cat. No.	Year	Mint	VG	Notes
Further Adventures Of Mr Punch	LP	Dame Jane	ODJ2	1978	£30	£15	
When God's On The Water	LP	Dame Jane	ODJ1	1975	£60	£30	

ELECTRAS

Title	Format	Label	Cat. No.	Year	Mint	VG	Notes
Electras	LP	private		196–	£300	£180	US

ELECTRIC BANANA

The library records credited to Electric Banana, and intended for use as background film and TV music, are actually the work of the Pretty Things.

Title	Format	Label	Cat. No.	Year	Mint	VG	Notes
Electric Banana	10" LP	De Wolfe	DWLP3040	1967	£60	£30	
Electric Banana	LP	De Wolfe	DWSLP3040	1967	£20	£8	
Even More Electric Banana	LP	De Wolfe	DWSLP3282	1969	£25	£10	
Hot Licks	LP	De Wolfe	DWSLP3284	1973	£10	£4	
More Electric Banana	LP	De Wolfe	DWSLP3069	1968	£25	£10	
Return Of The Electric Banana	LP	De Wolfe	DWSLP3381	1979	£12	£5	

ELECTRIC BLUES

Title	Format	Label	Cat. No.	Year	Mint	VG	Notes
Still Going Strong	LP	private		1979	£100	£50	Dutch

ELECTRIC CRAYONS

Title	Format	Label	Cat. No.	Year	Mint	VG	Notes
Hip Shake Junkie	7"	Emergency	MIV3	1989	£8	£4	

ELECTRIC FLAG

At its best, Mike Bloomfield's big band sounds marvellous – the driving 'Killing Floor' or the long, crafted 'Another Country' (both on *A Long Time Comin'*) – but the Electric Flag's music was extremely uneven. Calling itself An American Music Band, the Electric Flag really wanted to play everything. It would probably have been better, however, if it had not tried to cast its net so wide. As it is, the band seems to lack focus. *Electric Flag* was recorded after many of the original members, including Bloomfield, had left. *The Trip* is a film soundtrack and contains a large number of very short tracks – frustrating.

Title	Format	Label	Cat. No.	Year	Mint	VG	Notes
Electric Flag	LP	CBS	63462	1969	£10	£4	
Groovin' Is Easy	7"	CBS	3584	1968	£4	£1.50	
Long Time Comin'	LP	CBS	63294	1968	£15	£6	
Sunny	7"	CBS	4066	1969	£4	£1.50	
Trip	LP	Sidewalk	(S)T5908	1967	£25	£10	US

ELECTRIC JOHNNY

Title	Format	Label	Cat. No.	Year	Mint	VG	Notes
Black Eyes Rock	7"	London	HLU9384	1961	£20	£10	

ELECTRIC JUNKYARD

Title	Format	Label	Cat. No.	Year	Mint	VG	Notes
Electric Junkyard	LP	RCA	LSP4158	1969	£15	£6	US

ELECTRIC LIGHT ORCHESTRA

Title	Format	Label	Cat. No.	Year	Mint	VG	Notes
All Over The World	10"	Jet	JET10195	1980	£10	£5	blue vinyl
Calling America	12"	Epic	QTA6844	1986	£6	£2.50	
Can't Get It Out Of My Head	7"	Jet	ELO1JB	1977	£5	£2	jukebox issue
Discovery	LP	Jet	HZ45769	1981	£12	£5	US audiophile
Eldorado	LP	Jet		1981	£12	£5	US audiophile
Electric Light Orchestra	LP	Harvest	Q4SHVL797	1974	£75	£37.50	quad
Electric Light Orchestra	LP	Harvest	SHVL797	1971	£10	£4	
Four Little Diamonds	12"	Jet	TA3869	1983	£6	£2.50	
Getting To The Point	12"	Epic	QTA7317	1986	£6	£2.50	
Greatest Hits	LP	Jet	HZ46310	1981	£12	£5	US audiophile
Livin' Thing	7"	United Artists	UP36184	1976	£5	£2	blue vinyl
Mr Blue Sky	7"	Jet	ELO2	1981	£20	£10	
Night The Light Went Out In Long Beach	LP	Warner Bros	WBK56058	1974	£10	£4	German
Olé ELO	LP	Jet/United Artists	SP123	1976	£15	£6	US promo, gold vinyl
Olé ELO	LP	Jet	JETLP19	1976	£10	£4	
On The Third Day	LP	Jet	UAG30091	1977	£10	£4	
Out Of The Blue	LP	Jet	JETDP400	1978	£12	£5	blue vinyl double
Roll Over Beethoven	12"	Harvest	PSLP213	1977	£8	£4	promo
Roll Over Beethoven/Manhattan Rumble	7"	Harvest	HAR5063	1973	£8	£4	
Secret Messages	7"	Jet	PA3720	1983	£6	£2.50	picture disc
Secret Messages	LP	Jet	HZ48490	1983	£12	£5	US audiophile
Shine A Little Love	12"	Jet	SJET12144	1979	£12	£6	
Showdown	12"	Harvest	HAR125121	1977	£6	£2.50	
Showdown	7"	Harvest	HAR5077	1973	£5	£2	
So Serious	12"	Epic	QTA7090	1986	£6	£2.50	
Strange Magic	7"	Jet	ELO2JB	1977	£5	£2	jukebox issue
Sweet Talking Woman	12"	Jet	SJET12121	1978	£6	£2.50	mauve vinyl
Ticket To The Moon	12"	Jet	JET127018	1981	£10	£5	picture disc
Time	LP	Jet	HZ47371	1981	£12	£5	US audiophile
Wild West Hero	12"	Jet	SJET12109	1978	£6	£2.50	yellow vinyl
Xanadu	10"	MCA	2315	1980	£150	£75	US promo picture disc

ELECTRIC PRUNES

The Electric Prunes were two groups, in both style and personnel, for sometime during the recording of *Mass In F Minor* there was a complete change in membership. The 1966–7 releases contain many prime examples of psychedelia, most notably the quartet of singles, which go a long way towards defining the genre. *Mass In F Minor*, on the other hand, is exactly what it says it is – a rock mass. The album is an interesting and reasonably successful experiment, albeit one that is ultimately the responsibility of composer David Axelrod; however, it is very short on playing time.

Everybody Knows	7"	Reprise	RS20652	1968	**£15**	**£7.50**	
Get Me To The World On Time	7"	Reprise	RS20564	1967	**£6**	**£2.50**	
Great Banana Hoax	7"	Reprise	RS20607	1967	**£6**	**£2.50**	
I Had Too Much To Dream	7"	Reprise	RS20532	1966	**£6**	**£2.50**	
I Had Too Much To Dream	7" EP	Reprise	RVEP60098	1966	**£50**	**£25**	*French*
I Had Too Much To Dream	LP	Reprise	R(S)6248	1967	**£50**	**£25**	*US*
Just Good Old Rock'n'Roll	LP	Reprise	RS6342	1969	**£20**	**£8**	*US*
Long Day's Flight	7"	Reprise	RS23212	1967	**£8**	**£4**	
Long Day's Flight	7" EP	Reprise	RVEP60110	1967	**£50**	**£25**	*French*
Long Day's Flight	CD	Edsel	EDCD179	1989	**£12**	**£5**	
Mass In F Minor	LP	Reprise	R(S)LP6275	1968	**£20**	**£8**	
Mass In F Minor	LP	Reprise	K34003	1973	**£10**	**£4**	
Release Of An Oath	LP	Reprise	R(S)LP6316	1968	**£20**	**£8**	
Underground	LP	Reprise	R(S)6262	1967	**£60**	**£30**	*US*

ELECTRIC SANDWICH

Electric Sandwich	LP	Brain	1018	1972	**£25**	**£10**	*German*

ELECTRIC TOILET

In The Hands Of Karma	LP	Nasco	9004	1970	**£100**	**£50**	*US*
In The Hands Of Karma	LP	Psycho	PSYCHO8	1983	**£15**	**£6**	

ELECTRONIC

Disappointed	CD-s	Parlophone	CDR6311	1993	**£5**	**£2**	
Feel Every Beat	CD-s	Factory	FAC328C	1991	**£5**	**£2**	
Get The Message	CD-s	Factory	FAC287C	1991	**£5**	**£2**	
Getting Away With It	CD-s	Factory	FACD257	1989	**£5**	**£2**	

ELECTROPHON

Zygoat	LP	Polydor	2383270	1974	**£10**	**£4**	

ELEGANTS

Little Star	7"	HMV	POP520	1958	**£15**	**£7.50**	
Please Believe Me	7"	HMV	POP551	1958	**£30**	**£15**	

ELENA

Evening Time	7"	Columbia	DB7598	1965	**£4**	**£1.50**	

ELEPHANT BAND

Stone Penguin	7"	Mojo	2092036	1972	**£5**	**£2**	

ELEPHANT'S MEMORY

Elephant's Memory	LP	Apple	SAPCOR22	1972	**£10**	**£4**	

ELERI, JANET & DIANE

Answer	LP	Fanfare	FR2196	197–	**£75**	**£37.50**	

ELEVEN FIFTY-NINE

This Is Our Sacrifice Of Praise	LP	Dovetail	DOVE4	1974	**£100**	**£50**	

ELF

Carolina Country Ball	LP	Purple	TPSA3506	1974	**£20**	**£8**	
Elf	LP	Epic	KE31789	1972	**£20**	**£8**	*US*
L.A. 59	7"	Purple	PUR118	1974	**£6**	**£2.50**	
Trying To Burn The Sun	LP	MGM	M3G4994	1975	**£12**	**£5**	*US*

ELFENBEIN

Made In Rock	LP	MDM	011246	1977	**£15**	**£6**	*German*

ELGINS

Darling Baby	LP	Tamla Motown	(S)TML11081	1968	**£40**	**£20**	
Heaven Must Have Sent You	7"	Tamla Motown	TMG583	1966	**£20**	**£10**	
It's Been A Long Time	7"	Tamla Motown	TMG615	1967	**£15**	**£7.50**	
Put Yourself In My Place	7"	Tamla Motown	TMG642	1968	**£8**	**£4**	
Put Yourself In My Place	7"	Tamla Motown	TMG551	1966	**£30**	**£15**	

ELIAS & HIS ZIG ZAG JIVE FLUTES

Tom Hark	7"	Columbia	DB4109	1958	**£4**	**£1.50**	

ELIAS HULK

Unchained	LP	Youngblood	SSYB8	1970	**£150**	**£75**	

ELIGIBLES

Along The Trail	LP	Capitol	(S)T1310	1960	**£10**	**£4**	

Faker Faker	7"	Capitol	CL15067	1959	**£5**	**£2**	
Little Engine	7"	Capitol	CL15098	1959	**£5**	**£2**	
Love Is A Gamble	LP	Capitol	(S)T1411	1961	**£10**	**£4**	
Young Is My Lover	7"	Capitol	CL15203	1960	**£4**	**£1.50**	

ELIMINATORS

Guitars And Percussion	LP	Pye	NPL18160	1966	**£10**	**£4**	

ELIXIR

Son Of Odin	LP	Elixir	ELIXIR2	1986	**£30**	**£15**	
Treachery	7"	Elixir	ELIXIR1	1985	**£50**	**£25**	

ELIZABETH

Elizabeth	LP	Vanguard	SVRL19010	1968	**£60**	**£30**	

ELKI & OWEN

Groovy Kinda Love	7"	Revolution	REV004	1969	**£4**	**£1.50**	

ELLEDGE, JIMMY

Funny How Time Slips Away	7" EP	RCA	RCX7132	1964	**£20**	**£10**	
Pink Dally Rue	7"	Hickory	451363	1965	**£4**	**£1.50**	
Swanee River Rocket	7"	RCA	RCA1274	1962	**£6**	**£2.50**	

ELLIE POP

Ellie Pop	LP	Mainstream	S6115	1968	**£60**	**£30**	*US*

ELLINGTON, DUKE

Anatomy Of A Murder	LP	Philips	BBL7338	1959	**£15**	**£6**	
Anatomy Of A Murder	LP	Philips	SBBL514	1960	**£15**	**£6**	
At His Very Best	LP	RCA	RD27133	1959	**£15**	**£6**	
At Newport	LP	Philips	BBL7133	1957	**£15**	**£6**	
At The Bal Masqué	LP	Philips	BBL7315/ SBBL543	1960	**£12**	**£5**	
Back To Back	LP	HMV	CLP1316	1959	**£15**	**£6**	*with Johnny Hodges*
Black, Brown And Beige	LP	Philips	BBL7251/ SBBL506	1958	**£10**	**£4**	
Blues In Orbit	LP	Philips	BBL7381/ SBBL567	1960	**£12**	**£5**	
Blues Serenade	10" LP	HMV	DLP1172	1958	**£15**	**£6**	
Caravan	7" EP	RCA	RCX1022	1959	**£5**	**£2**	
Cosmic Scene	LP	Philips	BBL7287	1959	**£20**	**£8**	
Dance To The Duke	7" EP	Capitol	EAP1637	1956	**£5**	**£2**	
Dance To The Duke	7" EP	Capitol	EAP1004	1957	**£5**	**£2**	
Dance To The Duke No. 2	7" EP	Capitol	EAP2637	1956	**£5**	**£2**	
Dance To The Duke No. 3	7" EP	Capitol	EAP3637	1956	**£5**	**£2**	
Drum Is A Woman	LP	Philips	BBL7179	1957	**£15**	**£6**	
Duke – 1926	10" LP	London	AL3551	1956	**£20**	**£8**	
Duke Ellington	10" LP	Philips	BBR8060	1955	**£25**	**£10**	
Duke Ellington	7" EP	RCA	RCX1006	1958	**£5**	**£2**	
Duke Ellington And Al Hibbler	7" EP	HMV	7EG8158	1955	**£5**	**£2**	
Duke Ellington And His Orchestra	7" EP	Philips	BBE12002	1955	**£5**	**£2**	
Duke Ellington And His Orchestra	7" EP	HMV	7EG8033	1954	**£5**	**£2**	
Duke Ellington And His Orchestra Vol. 1	10" LP	Vogue Coral	LRA10027	1955	**£20**	**£8**	
Duke Ellington And His Orchestra Vol. 2	10" LP	Vogue Coral	LRA10028	1955	**£20**	**£8**	
Duke Ellington And Jimmy Blanton	7" EP	HMV	7EG8189	1956	**£5**	**£2**	
Duke Ellington And The Coronets	10" LP	Vogue	LDE035	1953	**£20**	**£8**	
Duke Ellington And The Coronets	7" EP	Vogue	EPV1060	1955	**£5**	**£2**	
Duke Ellington Orchestra	10" LP	Philips	BBR8086	1956	**£25**	**£10**	
Duke Ellington Presents	LP	Parlophone	PMC1136	1961	**£12**	**£5**	
Duke Ellington Presents	LP	London	LTZN15078	1957	**£15**	**£6**	
Duke Ellington Presents Ivie Anderson	7" EP	HMV	7EG8209	1957	**£5**	**£2**	
Duke Ellington–Billy Strayhorn	7" EP	Vogue	EPV1051	1955	**£5**	**£2**	
Duke In London	7" EP	Decca	DFE6376	1957	**£5**	**£2**	
Duke Plays Ellington	10" LP	Capitol	LC6670	1954	**£20**	**£8**	
Duke Plays Ellington	7" EP	Capitol	EAP1477	1954	**£5**	**£2**	
Duke Plays Ellington Part 2	7" EP	Capitol	EAP2477	1954	**£5**	**£2**	
Ellington '55	LP	Capitol	LCT6008	1955	**£15**	**£6**	
Ellington '55 Part 1	7" EP	Capitol	EAP1521	1955	**£5**	**£2**	
Ellington '55 Part 2	7" EP	Capitol	EAP2521	1955	**£5**	**£2**	
Ellington '55 Part 3	7" EP	Capitol	EAP3521	1955	**£5**	**£2**	
Ellington Highlights, 1940	10" LP	HMV	DLP1034	1954	**£20**	**£8**	
Ellington Jazz Party	LP	Philips	BBL7324/ SBBL516	1959	**£10**	**£4**	
Ellington Showcase	LP	Capitol	T679	1956	**£15**	**£6**	
Ellington Sidemen	LP	Philips	BBL7163	1957	**£15**	**£6**	
Ellington Uptown	LP	Philips	BBL7443	1961	**£12**	**£5**	
Ellington Uptown	LP	Philips	BBL7003	1954	**£15**	**£6**	
Ellington's Greatest	10" LP	HMV	DLP1007	1953	**£20**	**£8**	
Festival Session	LP	Philips	BBL7355/ SBBL556	1960	**£12**	**£5**	
Great Ellington Soloists	10" LP	HMV	DLP1025	1954	**£20**	**£8**	
Harlem Twist	7" EP	Fontana	TFE17117	1959	**£5**	**£2**	
Historically Speaking	LP	Parlophone	PMC1116	1960	**£10**	**£4**	
Historically Speaking – The Duke	LP	London	LTZN15029	1957	**£15**	**£6**	
In A Mellotone	LP	RCA	RD27134	1959	**£15**	**£6**	
Jazz Cocktail	10" LP	Columbia	33S1044	1954	**£20**	**£8**	

Masterpieces By Ellington	LP	Columbia	33SX1022	1954	**£25**	**£10**	
Mood Ellington	10" LP	Philips	BBR8044	1955	**£20**	**£8**	
Newport 1958	LP	Philips	BBL7279	1959	**£10**	**£4**	
Newport Jazz Festival	LP	Philips	BBL7152	1957	**£15**	**£6**	*Side 2 by Buck Clayton*
Nutcracker Suite	LP	Philips	BBL7418/ SBBL594	1961	**£15**	**£6**	
Perfume Suite/Black Brown And Beige	10" LP	HMV	DLP1070	1955	**£20**	**£8**	
Piano In The Background	LP	Philips	BBL7460	1961	**£12**	**£5**	
Premiered By Ellington	10" LP	Capitol	LC6616	1953	**£20**	**£8**	
Saturday Night Function	10" LP	HMV	DLP1094	1955	**£20**	**£8**	
Side By Side	LP	HMV	CLP1374	1961	**£15**	**£6**	*with Johnny Hodges*
Solitude	LP	Philips	BBL7229	1958	**£15**	**£6**	
Such Sweet Thunder	LP	Realm	RM52421	1967	**£12**	**£5**	
Such Sweet Thunder	LP	Philips	BBL7203	1958	**£15**	**£6**	
Ultra Deluxe	7" EP	Capitol	EAP120114	1961	**£5**	**£2**	

ELLINGTON, MARC

Marc Ellington	LP	Philips	SBL7883	1969	**£25**	**£10**	
Marc Time	LP	Xtra	XTRA1154	1972	**£20**	**£8**	
Question Of Roads	LP	Philips	6308120	1972	**£15**	**£6**	
Rains/Reins Of Change	LP	B&C	CAS193	1971	**£15**	**£6**	
Restoration	LP	Philips	6308143	1972	**£15**	**£6**	

ELLINGTON, RAY

ABC Boogie	7"	Columbia	SCM5147	1954	**£10**	**£5**	
All's Going Well	7"	Columbia	SCM5088	1954	**£4**	**£1.50**	
Charlie Brown	7"	Pye	7N15189	1959	**£5**	**£2**	
Cloudburst	7"	Columbia	SCM5199	1955	**£4**	**£1.50**	
Giddy-Up A Ding Dong	7"	Columbia	DB3838	1956	**£12**	**£6**	
Keep That Coffee Hot	7"	Columbia	SCM5274	1956	**£4**	**£1.50**	
Ko Ko Mo	7"	Columbia	SCM5177	1955	**£8**	**£4**	
Little Red Monkey	7"	Columbia	SCM5050	1953	**£4**	**£1.50**	
Long Black Nylons	7"	Columbia	DB4057	1958	**£10**	**£5**	
Madison	7"	Ember	EMBS102	1960	**£5**	**£2**	
Owl Song	7"	Columbia	SCM5104	1954	**£4**	**£1.50**	
Play It Boy Play	7"	Columbia	SCM5187	1955	**£4**	**£1.50**	
Stranded In The Jungle	7"	Columbia	DB3821	1956	**£12**	**£6**	
That Rock'n'Rollin' Man	7"	Columbia	DB3905	1957	**£12**	**£6**	
Who's Got The Money?	7"	Columbia	SCM5250	1956	**£4**	**£1.50**	

ELLIOT, DEREK & DOROTHY

Derek And Dorothy Elliot	LP	Trailer	LER2023	1972	**£10**	**£4**	
Yorkshire Relish	LP	Tradition	TSR025	1976	**£10**	**£4**	

ELLIOT, JACK

Jack Elliot Of Birtley	LP	Leader	LEA4001	1969	**£15**	**£6**	

ELLIOT, MAMA CASS

Bubblegum, Lemonade And Something For Mama	LP	Stateside	(S)SL5014	1969	**£10**	**£4**	
Dream A Little Dream	LP	Stateside	(S)SL5004	1968	**£10**	**£4**	

ELLIOTT, BERN

Bern Elliott & The Fenmen Play	7" EP	Decca	DFE8561	1964	**£15**	**£7.50**	*with the Fenmen*
Good Times	7"	Decca	F11970	1964	**£4**	**£1.50**	*with the Clan*
Guess Who	7"	Decca	F12051	1965	**£4**	**£1.50**	
Money	7"	Decca	F11770	1963	**£4**	**£1.50**	*with the Fenmen*
New Orleans	7"	Decca	F11852	1964	**£4**	**£1.50**	*with the Fenmen*
Voodoo Woman	7"	Decca	F12171	1965	**£4**	**£1.50**	

ELLIOTT, BILL & ELASTIC OZ BAND

God Save Us	7"	Apple	36	1971	**£6**	**£2.50**	
God Save Us	7"	Apple	36	1971	**£15**	**£7.50**	*picture sleeve*

ELLIOTT, DON

Don Elliott	10" LP	London	LZN14037	1957	**£10**	**£4**	
Don Elliott And His Choir	LP	Brunswick	LAT8263	1958	**£10**	**£4**	
Musical Offering	LP	HMV	CLP1186	1958	**£10**	**£4**	
Six Valves	10" LP	London	LZU14034	1956	**£30**	**£15**	*with Rusty Dedrick*

ELLIOTT, MARI

Silly Billy	7"	GTO	GT58	1976	**£10**	**£5**	

ELLIOTT, MIKE

Milk And Honey	7"	Ackee	ACK151	1972	**£5**	**£2**	

ELLIOTT, PETER

Devotion	7"	Parlophone	R4457	1958	**£4**	**£1.50**	
To The Aisle	7"	Parlophone	R4355	1957	**£5**	**£2**	

ELLIOTT, RAMBLING JACK

Blues And Country	7" EP	Collector	JEA6	1964	**£10**	**£5**	
Bull Durham Sacks And Railroad Tracks	LP	Reprise	RSLP6387	1970	**£10**	**£4**	
Country Style	LP	Stateside	SL10143	1965	**£10**	**£4**	
In London	LP	Encore	ENC194	196–	**£15**	**£6**	
In London	LP	Columbia	33SX1166	1959	**£25**	**£10**	
Jack Elliott	LP	Fontana	TFL6044	1965	**£10**	**£4**	

Title	Format	Label	Cat. No.	Year	Mint	VG	Notes
Jack Takes The Floor	10" LP	Topic	10T15	1958	£25	£10	
Kids Stuff	7" EP	Columbia	SEG8046	1960	£8	£4	
More Pretty Girls	7"	Fontana	TF575	1965	£4	£1.50	
Muleskinner	LP	Topic	12T106	1964	£15	£6	
Rambling Boys	10" LP	Topic	10T14	1958	£25	£10	*with Derroll Adams*
Rambling Jack Elliott	7" EP	Collector	JEA5	1963	£10	£5	
Rambling Jack Elliott	LP	Vanguard		1964	£10	£4	*US*
Roll On Buddy	LP	Topic	12T105	1964	£15	£6	*with Derroll Adams*
Rusty Jigs And Sandy Sam	7"	Columbia	DB7593	1965	£4	£1.50	
Sings	LP	Columbia	33SX1291	1961	£15	£6	
Sings The Songs Of Woody Guthrie	LP	Stateside	SL10167	1966	£10	£4	
Talking Woody Guthrie	LP	Topic	12T93	1963	£15	£6	
Woody Guthrie's Blues	8" LP	Topic	T5	1955	£25	£10	

ELLIOTT, RON

Title	Format	Label	Cat. No.	Year	Mint	VG	Notes
Candlestick Maker	LP	Warner Bros	WS1833	1969	£15	£6	*US*

ELLIOTT, SHAWN

Title	Format	Label	Cat. No.	Year	Mint	VG	Notes
My Girl	7"	Columbia	DB7418	1964	£4	£1.50	
Shame And Scandal In The Family	7"	Rio	R51	1964	£6	£2.50	

ELLIOTS OF BIRTLEY

Title	Format	Label	Cat. No.	Year	Mint	VG	Notes
Elliots Of Birtley	LP	Folkways	FG3565	1961	£25	£10	*US*
Musical Portrait Of A Durham Mining Family	LP	XTRA	XTRA1091	1969	£12	£5	

ELLIOTT'S SUNSHINE

Title	Format	Label	Cat. No.	Year	Mint	VG	Notes
It Is Too Late	7"	Philips	BF1649	1968	£4	£1.50	

ELLIS, ALTON

Title	Format	Label	Cat. No.	Year	Mint	VG	Notes
Ain't That Loving You	7"	Trojan	TR004	1967	£10	£5	*Tommy McCook B side*
Ain't That Loving You	7"	Treasure Isle	TI7016	1967	£10	£5	*Tommy McCook B side*
All That We Need Is Love	7"	Spur	SP3	1972	£5	£2	
Alton's Official Daughter	7"	Ackee	ACK511	1973	£5	£2	
Back To Africa	7"	Gas	GAS164	1971	£4	£1.50	
Bam Bye	7"	Banana	BA330	1971	£4	£1.50	
Better Example	7"	Bamboo	BAM2	1969	£4	£1.50	*Duke Morgan B side*
Big Bad Boy	7"	Grape	GR3029	1972	£4	£1.50	
Black Man's Pride	7"	Bullet	BU466	1971	£5	£2	
Blessings Of Love	7"	Doctor Bird	DB1044	1966	£10	£5	
Breaking Up	7"	Trojan	TR642	1968	£8	£4	
Bye Bye Love	7"	Nu Beat	NB013	1968	£6	£2.50	*Monty Morris B side*
Change Of Plans	7"	Studio One	SO2084	1969	£12	£6	*Cables B side*
Cry Tough	7"	Island	WI3046	1967	£12	£6	*Tommy McCook B side*
Dance Crasher	7"	Island	WI239	1965	£12	£6	*Baba Brooks B side*
Deliver Us	7"	Gas	GAS161	1970	£4	£1.50	
Diana	7"	Duke	DU14	1969	£4	£1.50	
Diana	7"	Gas	GAS105	1969	£4	£1.50	
Don't Care	7"	Bullet	BU485	1971	£4	£1.50	
Don't Gamble With Love	7"	Island	WI230	1965	£12	£6	
Duke Of Earl	7"	Treasure Isle	TI7010	1967	£10	£5	
Easy Squeeze	7"	Studio One	SO2003	1967	£12	£6	*Mr Foundation B side*
Fool	7"	Coxsone	CS7071	1968	£10	£5	*Soul Vendors B side*
Girl I've Got A Date	7"	Doctor Bird	DB1059	1966	£10	£5	*Lyn Taitt & Tommy McCook B side*
Good Good Loving	7"	Fab	FAB165	1971	£5	£2	
Greatest Hits	LP	Count Shelly	SSLO02	1973	£25	£10	
Hey World	7"	Banana	BA347	1971	£4	£1.50	
I Am Just A Guy	7"	Studio One	SO2028	1967	£12	£6	*Soul Vendors B side*
I Am Still In Love	7"	Studio One	SO2020	1967	£12	£6	*Roy Richards B side*
I Can't Stand It	7"	Trojan	TR630	1968	£8	£4	
I Can't Stand It	7"	Nu Beat	NB010	1968	£6	£2.50	
I'll Be There	7"	Smash	SMA2320	1971	£4	£1.50	
I'll Be Waiting	7"	Technique	TE905	1970	£4	£1.50	
It's Your Thing	7"	Technique	TE903	1970	£4	£1.50	
La-La Means I Love You	7"	Nu Beat	NB014	1968	£6	£2.50	
Laba Laba Reggae	7"	Trojan	TR634	1968	£8	£4	
Let's Stay Together	7"	Ackee	ACK148	1972	£5	£2	
Little Loving	7"	Smash	SMA2319	1971	£4	£1.50	
Live And Learn	7"	Studio One	SO2037	1968	£12	£6	*Heptones B side*
Message	7"	Pama	PM707	1968	£6	£2.50	
Mr Soul Of Jamaica	LP	Treasure Isle	013	196–	£100	£50	
My Time Is The Right Time	7"	Pama	PM717	1968	£6	£2.50	*Johnny Moore B side*
Oowee Baby	7"	Treasure Isle	TI7030	1968	£10	£5	
Oppression	7"	Ackee	ACK145	1972	£4	£1.50	
Play It Cool	7"	Jackpot	JP796	1972	£4	£1.50	
Preacher	7"	Doctor Bird	DB1049	1966	£10	£5	*Lyn Taitt B side*
Remember That Sunday	7"	Duke	DU72	1970	£4	£1.50	
Rock Steady	7"	Treasure Isle	TI7004	1967	£10	£5	*Tommy McCook B side*
Shake It	7"	Doctor Bird	DB1055	1966	£10	£5	*Silvertones B side*
Sings Rock And Soul	LP	Coxsone	CSL8008	1967	£100	£50	
Sunday Coming	7"	Banana	BA318	1971	£4	£1.50	
Sunday Coming	LP	Bamboo	BDLPS214	1971	£40	£20	

Suzie	7"	Gas	GAS151	1970	**£4**	**£1.50**	
Too Late To Turn Back Now	7"	Ackee	ACK502	1972	**£4**	**£1.50**	
Tumbling Tears	7"	Bamboo	BAM29	1970	**£4**	**£1.50**	
What Does It Take	7"	Duke Reid	DR2501	1970	**£4**	**£1.50**	*Tommy McCook B side*
Willow Tree	7"	Treasure Isle	TI7044	1968	**£10**	**£5**	
Wise Birds Follow Spring	7"	Trojan	TR009	1967	**£10**	**£5**	*Tommy McCook B side*
Wonderful World	7"	Camel	CA94	1972	**£4**	**£1.50**	
Working On A Groovy Thing	7"	Pama	PS361	1972	**£4**	**£1.50**	
You Made Me So Very Happy	7"	Duke Reid	DR2512	1970	**£4**	**£1.50**	*Tommy McCook B side*

ELLIS, BOBBY

Dollar A Head	7"	Island	WI3130	1968	**£10**	**£5**	*Rudy Mills B side*
Emperor	7"	Island	WI3089	1967	**£10**	**£5**	*Derrick Harriott B side*
Feeling Peckish	7"	Island	WI3091	1967	**£10**	**£5**	*Keith & Tex B side*
Now We Know	7"	Island	WI3092	1967	**£10**	**£5**	*Rudy Mills B side*
Shuntin'	7"	Island	WI3135	1968	**£10**	**£5**	*Derrick Harriott B side*

ELLIS, DON

Don Ellis's updating of the big band sound won many fans from the progressive rock genre, who could readily appreciate Ellis's musical games with unusual time signatures as well the electronics he introduced via his specially built four-valve amplified trumpet. *Autumn* was produced by Al Kooper, who must have realized that his own big band experiments with Blood, Sweat and Tears were made to sound a little ordinary by comparison. Drummer Ralph Humphrey went from Don Ellis to the only other band that could possibly provide him with the same rhythmic challenge – that of Frank Zappa.

At Fillmore	LP	CBS	66261	1969	**£20**	**£8**	*double*
Autumn	LP	CBS	63503	1968	**£15**	**£6**	
Don Ellis Orchestra Live	LP	Liberty	LBL/LBS83060	1968	**£20**	**£8**	
Electric Bath	LP	CBS	63230	1968	**£15**	**£6**	
Goes Underground	LP	CBS	63680	1969	**£12**	**£5**	
Haiku	LP	BASF	MC25341	1974	**£15**	**£6**	*German*
Live At Monterey	LP	Fontana	(S)TL5426	1967	**£20**	**£8**	
Shock Treatment	LP	CBS	63356	1968	**£15**	**£6**	
Soaring	LP	BASF	21251233	1973	**£15**	**£6**	*German*
Tears Of Joy	LP	Columbia	CG30927	1971	**£15**	**£6**	*US*

ELLIS, HERB

Herb Ellis	LP	Columbia	33CX10066	1957	**£15**	**£6**	
Meets Jimmy Giuffre	LP	HMV	CLP1337	1960	**£12**	**£5**	
Nothing But The Blues	LP	Columbia	33CX10139	1959	**£15**	**£6**	

ELLIS, HORTENSE

Groovy Kind Of Love	7"	Coxsone	CS7033	1968	**£10**	**£5**	*Three Tops B side*
I'll Come Softly	7"	R&B	JB101	1963	**£10**	**£5**	
I've Been A Fool	7"	Blue Beat	BB295	1965	**£12**	**£6**	
Midnight Train	7"	Blue Beat	BB119	1962	**£12**	**£6**	*Duke Reid B side*

ELLIS, JIMMY

Ellis Sings Elvis By Request	LP	Boblo	78829		**£20**	**£8**	*US*

ELLIS, JO-JO

Fly	7"	Fury	FY302	1972	**£10**	**£5**	

ELLIS, LARRY

Nothing You Can Do	7"	Felsted	AF110	1958	**£8**	**£4**	

ELLIS, MATTHEW

Am I	LP	Regal Zonophone	SRZA8505	1971	**£20**	**£8**	
Matthew Ellis	LP	Regal Zonophone	SRZA8501	1971	**£10**	**£4**	

ELLIS, SHIRLEY

Clapping Song	7"	London	HLR9961	1965	**£4**	**£1.50**	
Ever See A Diver Kiss His Wife	7"	London	HLR10021	1966	**£4**	**£1.50**	
In Action	LP	Congress	CGL/CGS3002	1964	**£20**	**£8**	*US*
Name Game	7"	London	HLR9946	1965	**£4**	**£1.50**	
Name Game	LP	Congress	CGL/CGS3003	1965	**£20**	**£8**	*US*
Nitty Gritty	7"	London	HLR9824	1963	**£4**	**£1.50**	
Puzzle Song	7"	London	HLR9973	1965	**£4**	**£1.50**	
Soul Time	7"	CBS	202606	1967	**£8**	**£4**	
Soul Time	LP	CBS	(S)BPG63044	1967	**£20**	**£8**	
Sugar Let's Shing A Ling	7"	CBS	2817	1967	**£6**	**£2.50**	
Sugar, Let's Shing A Ling	LP	Columbia	CL2679/CS9479	1967	**£20**	**£8**	*US*

ELLIS, STEVE & THE STARFIRES

Steve Ellis Songbook	LP	IGL	105	1967	**£1000**	**£700**	*US*

ELLIS, WAYGOOD

I Like What I'm Trying To Do	7"	Polydor	56729	1967	**£8**	**£4**	

ELLISON, ANDY

Been A Long Time	7"	Track	604018	1967	**£40**	**£20**	*John's Children B side*

Fool From Upper Eden	7"	CBS	3357	1968	£40	£20	
You Can't Do That	7"	SNB	553308	1968	£40	£20	*2 different B sides*

ELLISON, LORRAINE

Call Me Any Time You Need Some Lovin'	7"	Mercury	6052073	1971	£5	£2	
Stay With Me	7"	Warner Bros	WB5850	1966	£5	£2	
Stay With Me	LP	Warner Bros	WB1821	1970	£12	£5	
Try A Little Bit Harder	7"	Warner Bros	WB2094	1968	£4	£1.50	

ELLUFFANT

The most sought-after of the privately pressed albums issued in the Netherlands contains improvised music, recorded live on behalf of the drug-help organization Release. The keyboard/percussion duo played on equipment they had built themselves, which helped to give them a very individual sound.

Release Concert	LP	Disko Thiel		1972	£1000	£500	*Dutch*

ELMER GANTRY'S VELVET OPERA

Lead singer Dave Terry was reported in the press at the time as being the only man in the country legally allowed to smoke marijuana – having been prescribed it as a calming aid for an occasionally violent personality. The group's song 'Mary Jane' is by way of being a tribute to this state of affairs, but their finest three minutes is undoubtedly the driving 'Flames', which by rights should have been an enormous chart hit. The group's second album was recorded as just Velvet Opera, with Terry replaced by Paul Brett. Subsequently, the rhythm section of John Ford and Richard Hudson joined the Strawbs and later formed a successful band of their own, Hudson-Ford.

Elmer Gantry's Velvet Opera	LP	Direction	863300	1968	£40	£20	
Flames	7"	Direction	583083	1967	£6	£2.50	
Mary Jane	7"	Direction	583481	1968	£4	£1.50	
Volcano	7"	Direction	583924	1969	£4	£1.50	

ELOY

Eloy	LP	Philips	6305089	1971	£100	£50	*bin cover*
Inside	LP	Electrola	1C06429479	1973	£15	£6	*German*
Planets	LP	Heavy Metal	HMIPD1	1982	£10	£4	*picture disc*
Time To Turn	LP	Heavy Metal	HMIPD3	1982	£10	£4	*picture disc*

ELROY, JEFF & THE BLUE BOYS

Honey Machine	7"	Philips	BF1533	1966	£12	£6	

ELVES

Amber Velvet	7"	MCA	MU1114	1970	£25	£12.50	

ELVIN, LEE & JAY

So The Story Goes	7"	Fontana	H191	1959	£8	£4	

EMANON

Raging Pain	7"	Clubland	SJP777	1977	£20	£10	

EMBERS

Chelsea Boots	7"	Decca	F11625	1963	£8	£4	

EMBERS (2)

Rock And Roll Eleven	LP	JCP Recording	2006		£75	£37.50	*US*

EMBRACE

All You Good People	7"	Fierce Panda	NING29	1996	£15	£7.50	

EMBRYO

Apo Calypso	LP	April	0010	1977	£12	£5	*German*
Bad Heads And Bad Cats	LP	April	005	1976	£12	£5	*German*
Embryos Rache	LP	United Artists	UAS29239	1971	£25	£10	*German*
Father, Son And Holy Ghosts	LP	United Artists	UAS29344	1972	£20	£8	*German*
Live	LP	April	003	1976	£12	£5	*German*
Opal	LP	Ohr	OMM56003	1970	£30	£15	*German*
Rocksession	LP	Brain	1036	1973	£15	£6	*German*
Rocksession	LP	Brain	201109	1975	£12	£5	*German*
Steig aus	LP	Brain	1023	1973	£15	£6	*German*
Surfin'	LP	BASF	223853	1975	£12	£5	*German*
We Keep On	LP	BASF	20218653	1974	£15	£6	*German*

EMERALD WEB

Dragon Wings And Wizard Tales	LP	Stargate	AR4230	1979	£20	£8	*US*

EMERALDS

King Lonely The Blue	7"	Decca	F12304	1965	£20	£10	

EMERGENCY

Emergency	LP	CBS	64381	1971	£12	£5	*German*
Entrance	LP	CBS	64928	1972	£10	£4	*German*
Get To The Country	LP	Brain	1037	1973	£10	£4	*German*
Gold Rock	LP	Brain	201104	1973	£10	£4	*German*
No Compromise	LP	Brain	1052	1974	£10	£4	*German*

EMERSON, KEITH

Christmas Album	CD	Priority	KEITHCD1	1988	£12	£5	

EMERSON, LAKE & PALMER

Emerson, Lake & Palmer	LP	Island	ILPS9132	1970	**£15**	**£6**	*pink label*
Fanfare For The Common Man	12"	Atlantic	K10946T	1977	**£10**	**£5**	
Jerusalem	7"	Manticore	K13503	1974	**£6**	**£2.50**	*picture sleeve*
Pictures At An Exhibition	LP	Mobile Fidelity	MFSL1031	1979	**£12**	**£5**	*US audiophile*
Tarkus	CD	Mobile Fidelity	UDCD598	1994	**£15**	**£6**	*US audiophile*
Trilogy	CD	Mobile Fidelity	UDCD621	1995	**£15**	**£6**	*US audiophile*
Works Volume One	LP	Atlantic		1976	**£10**	**£4**	*promo*

EMILY

Old Stone Bridge	7"	Sha La La	007	1987	**£4**	**£1.50**	*flexi, B side by Remember Fun*
Old Stone Bridge	7"	Big Fun	001	1987	**£4**	**£1.50**	*flexi*

EMJAYS

All My Love All My Life	7"	Top Rank	JAR145	1959	**£20**	**£10**	

EMLYN, ENDAF

Hiraeth	LP	Wren	WRL537	1972	**£40**	**£20**	
Salem	LP	Sain	1012M	1974	**£20**	**£8**	
Syrffio (Mewn Cariad)	LP	Sain	1051M	1976	**£15**	**£6**	

EMMET SPICELAND

Emmet Spiceland	LP	Page One	POLS011	1968	**£50**	**£25**	
Emmet Spiceland Album	LP	Hawk	HALP166	1977	**£40**	**£20**	*Irish*
Lowlands	7"	Page One	POF089	1968	**£4**	**£1.50**	
So Long Marianne	7"	Page One	POF143	1969	**£4**	**£1.50**	

EMOTIONS

Come Dance Baby	7"	London	HLR9640	1962	**£20**	**£10**	
Love	7"	London	HLR9701	1963	**£20**	**£10**	
Story Untold	7"	Stateside	SS237	1963	**£10**	**£5**	

EMOTIONS (2)

Careless Hands	7"	Caltone	TONE120	1968	**£8**	**£4**	
Rainbow	7"	Caltone	TONE100	1967	**£8**	**£4**	
Rudeboy Confession	7"	Ska Beat	JB263	1966	**£10**	**£5**	
Rumbay	7"	High Note	HS026	1969	**£4**	**£1.50**	
Soulful Music	7"	Caltone	TONE118	1968	**£8**	**£4**	
Storm	7"	High Note	HS018	1969	**£4**	**£1.50**	

EMOTIONS (3)

So I Can Love You	LP	Stax	SXATS1030	1970	**£10**	**£4**	
Somebody New	7"	Deep Soul	DS9104	1970	**£10**	**£5**	

EMPERORS

Karate	7"	Stateside	SS565	1966	**£6**	**£2.50**	
Karate	7"	Pama	PM786	1969	**£4**	**£1.50**	

EMTIDI

Emtidi	LP	Thorofon	ATH109	1970	**£60**	**£30**	*German*
Saat	LP	Pilz	20290778	1972	**£40**	**£20**	*German*

ENCHANTED FOREST

You're Never Gonna Get My Lovin'	7"	Stateside	SS2080	1968	**£4**	**£1.50**	

ENCHANTERS

We Got Love	7"	Warner Bros	WB2054	1967	**£5**	**£2**	

END

I Can't Get Any Joy	7"	Philips	BF1444	1965	**£8**	**£4**	
Introspection	LP	Decca	LK/SKL5015	1969	**£75**	**£37.50**	
Shades Of Orange	7"	Decca	F12750	1968	**£15**	**£7.50**	

ENDLE ST CLOUD

Thank You All Very Much	LP	International Artist	IALP12	1970	**£40**	**£20**	*US*

ENDRIGO, SERGIO

Marianne	7"	Pye	7N25502	1968	**£5**	**£2**	

ENDSLEY, MELVIN

I Got A Feeling	7"	RCA	RCA1051	1958	**£20**	**£10**	
I Like Your Kind Of Love	7"	RCA	RCA1004	1957	**£25**	**£12.50**	

ENERGY

Energy	LP	Harvest	34893	1974	**£25**	**£10**	*Spanish*

ENEVOLDSEN, BOB

Bob Enevoldsen Quintet	10" LP	London	LZU14035	1956	**£40**	**£20**	

ENFORCERS

Musical Fever	7"	Blue Cat	BS120	1968	**£8**	**£4**	*Ed Nangle B side*

ENGEL, SCOTT

Charlie Bop	7"	Vogue	V9150	1959	**£250**	**£150**	*best auctioned*
Living End	7"	Vogue	V9145	1959	**£300**	**£180**	*best auctioned*
Paper Doll	7"	Vogue	V9125	1958	**£250**	**£150**	*best auctioned*
Scott Engel	7" EP	Liberty	LEP2261	1966	**£20**	**£10**	

ENGEL, SCOTT & JOHN STEWART

I Only Came To Dance With You	7"	Capitol	CL15440	1966	**£10**	**£5**	
I Only Came To Dance With You	LP	Tower	ST5026	1965	**£30**	**£15**	*US*

ENGLAND

England	LP	Deroy	DER1356	1976	**£250**	**£150**	
Garden Shed	LP	Arista	ARTY153	1977	**£30**	**£15**	
Garden Shed	LP	Arista	ARTY153	1977	**£75**	**£37.50**	*with booklet*

ENGLAND SISTERS

Heartbeat	7"	HMV	POP710	1960	**£25**	**£12.50**	

ENGLAND'S GLORY

England's Glory	LP	Venus	VEN105	1973	**£300**	**£180**	*pink label*

ENGLEBERG, FRED

Songs Of Fred Engleberg	LP	Elektra	EKL247	1964	**£12**	**£5**	*US*

ENGLISH, ERROL

I Don't Want To Love You	7"	Big Shot	BI547	1970	**£4**	**£1.50**	
Once In My Life	7"	Big Shot	BI548	1970	**£4**	**£1.50**	
Open The Door To Your Heart	7"	Torpedo	TOR8	1970	**£4**	**£1.50**	
Sad Girl	7"	Torpedo	TOR16	1970	**£4**	**£1.50**	
Sha La La La Lee	7"	Torpedo	TOR22	1970	**£10**	**£5**	
Sometimes	7"	Duke	DU99	1971	**£4**	**£1.50**	
Where You Lead Me	7"	Torpedo	TOR9	1970	**£4**	**£1.50**	

ENID

Masterminded by keyboard player Robert John Godfrey, the Enid have produced a succession of elaborately arranged progressive rock albums, in defiance of the prevailing fashions, for over twenty years. Noted for his refusal to compromise, Godfrey has devoted everything to his art, issuing albums himself and selling them by mail order when unable to find a regular record company. He was also the arranger on Barclay James Harvest's best album, *Once Again*, recently winning a protracted court case to gain belated recognition of his writing contribution to the album. Though uncredited, the Enid were the backing group on the earliest recordings by Kim Wilde – a very rare foray into the world of unashamedly commercial music.

Aerie Fairie Nonsense	LP	Honeybee	INS3012	1977	**£10**	**£4**	
And Then There Were None	12"	EMI	12EMI5505	1984	**£6**	**£2.50**	
Dambusters March	7"	Pye	7P106	1979	**£6**	**£2.50**	
Fand	LP	Enid	ENID9	1985	**£10**	**£4**	
Fool	7"	Pye	7P187	1980	**£6**	**£2.50**	
Golden Earrings	7"	EMI	INTS540	1977	**£6**	**£2.50**	
Golden Earrings	7"	EMI	EMI5109	1980	**£8**	**£4**	
Heigh Ho	7"	Bronze	BRO134	1981	**£5**	**£2**	
In The Region Of The Summer Stars	LP	Buk	BULP2014	1976	**£15**	**£6**	*white label*
In The Region Of The Summer Stars	LP	Honeybee	INS3005	1977	**£10**	**£4**	*with poster*
In The Region Of The Summer Stars	LP	Buk	BULP2014	1977	**£10**	**£4**	*black label*
Itchycoo Park	12"	Sedition	EDITL3314	1986	**£6**	**£2.50**	
Jubilee	7"	EMI	INT534	1977	**£4**	**£1.50**	
Live At Hammersmith Vol. 1	LP	Enid	ENID1	1984	**£10**	**£4**	
Live At Hammersmith Vol. 2	LP	Enid	ENID2	1984	**£10**	**£4**	
Liverpool Album	LP	The Stand	LE1	1984	**£10**	**£4**	
Lovers	7"	Buk	BUK3002	1976	**£10**	**£5**	
Lovers And Fools	LP	Dojo	DOJOLP24	1987	**£12**	**£5**	*double*
Salome	CD-s	Wonderful Music Co.	ENID2999	1990	**£5**	**£2**	
Salome	LP	Enid	ENID10	1986	**£10**	**£4**	
Six Pieces	LP	Pye	NH116	1979	**£10**	**£4**	
Six Pieces	LP	Enid	ENID4	1984	**£10**	**£4**	
Spell	LP	Enid	ENID8	1984	**£10**	**£4**	*2 x 45 rpm discs*
The Stand	LP	The Stand	THESTAND1	1983	**£25**	**£10**	
The Stand 2	LP	The Stand	STAND2	1985	**£25**	**£10**	
Then There Were None	7"	Rak	RAK349	1982	**£4**	**£1.50**	
Touch Me	LP	Enid	ENID5	1984	**£10**	**£4**	
Touch Me	LP	Pye	NSPH18593	1979	**£10**	**£4**	
When You Wish Upon A Star	7"	Bronze	BRO127	1981	**£4**	**£1.50**	

ENNIS, RAY & THE BLUE JEANS

What Have They Done To Hazel	7"	Columbia	DB8431	1968	**£15**	**£7.50**	

ENNIS, SEAMUS

Bonnie Bunch Of Roses	LP	Tradition	TLP1013	1959	**£25**	**£10**	
Feidlim Tonn Ri's Castle	LP	Claddagh	CC19	1977	**£12**	**£5**	*Irish*
Forty Years Of Irish Piping	LP	Free Reed	FRRD001/2	1976	**£20**	**£8**	*double*
Fox Chase	LP	Tara	1009	1977	**£12**	**£5**	*Irish*
Irish Pipe And Tin Whistle Songs	LP	Olympic	ALTLAS6129	1976	**£12**	**£5**	*US*
Masters Of Irish Music	LP	Leader	LEA2003	1969	**£15**	**£6**	
Pure Drop	LP	Tara	1002	1973	**£12**	**£5**	*Irish*
Wandering Minstrel	LP	Topic	12TS250	1974	**£12**	**£5**	

ENO, BRIAN

When, as a member of Roxy Music, his task was to make some sense of the controls of a distinctly non-user-friendly synthesizer, Brian Eno always used to describe himself as a non-musician. If this was in any way an accurate description, then the lack of preconceptions has clearly been an advantage for Eno, for his solo career has been distinguished by some very interesting ideas. The novelty of his approach is typified by his experiments with creative musak – what he calls 'ambient' music – where the listener is not intended to listen at all closely. Eno's career has thrown up one ultra-rarity: an early, alternative version of his *Music For Films* LP, which was limited to around a hundred copies. These days his music can be heard in millions of households around the world, even if those listening are likely to be unaware of the fact: the fragment of music that plays when Microsoft software starts up on a home computer was created by Eno.

Another Green World	CD-s	Virgin	CDT41	1989	**£5**	**£2**	*3" single*
Before And After Science	LP	Polydor	2302071	1977	**£10**	**£4**	*with 4 prints*
Discreet Music	LP	Obscure	OBS3	1975	**£10**	**£4**	
Lion Sleeps Tonight	7"	Island	WIP6233	1975	**£5**	**£2**	
Music For Films	LP	Editions EG	EGM1	1976	**£150**	**£75**	*different tracks to '78 issue*
My Squelchy Life	CD	Opal		1990	**£30**	**£15**	*demo only*
One Word	CD-s	Land	LANDH04	1990	**£5**	**£2**	*with John Cale*
Seven Deadly Finns	7"	Island	WIP6178	1974	**£5**	**£2**	

ENOS & SHEILA

La La Bamba	7"	Blue Cat	BS135	1968	**£8**	**£4**	
Tonight You're Mine	7"	Blue Cat	BS138	1968	**£8**	**£4**	

ENOUGH'S ENOUGH

Please Remember	7"	Tattoo	TT101	1968	**£100**	**£50**	

ENTICERS

Calling For Your Love	7"	Atlantic	2091136	1971	**£6**	**£2.50**	

ENTWISTLE, JOHN

Backtrack 14 (The Ox)	LP	Track	2407014	1971	**£12**	**£5**	
I Believe In Everything	7"	Track	2094008	1971	**£5**	**£2**	
Mad Dog	7"	Decca	FR13567	1975	**£5**	**£2**	
Mad Dog	LP	Decca	TXS114	1975	**£10**	**£4**	
Rigor Mortis Sets In	LP	Track	2406106	1973	**£12**	**£5**	
Smash Your Head Against The Wall	LP	Track	2406005	1971	**£10**	**£4**	
Too Late The Hero	7"	WEA	K79249P	1981	**£5**	**£2**	*autographed picture disc*
Whistle Rymes	LP	Track	2406104	1972	**£10**	**£4**	

ENYA

Book Of Days	CD-s	WEA	YZ640CDX	1992	**£10**	**£5**	*boxed with 4 prints*
Caribbean Blue	CD-s	WEA	YZ604CD	1991	**£6**	**£2.50**	
Celts	CD	BBC	BBCCD605	1987	**£30**	**£15**	
Celts	CD-s	WEA	YZ705CDX	1992	**£8**	**£4**	*with 4 prints*
Enya	LP	BBC	REB605	1987	**£15**	**£6**	
Evening Falls	CD-s	WEA	YZ356CD	1988	**£10**	**£5**	*3" single*
Exile	CD-s	WEA	YZ580CD	1991	**£8**	**£4**	
How Can I Keep From Singing	CD-s	WEA	YZ635CD	1991	**£5**	**£2**	
I Want Tomorrow	7"	BBC	RESL201	1987	**£6**	**£2.50**	
I Want Tomorrow	CD-s	BBC	CDRSL201	1987	**£30**	**£15**	
Orinoco Flow	CD-s	WEA	YZ312CD	1988	**£10**	**£5**	*3" single*
Storms In Africa	CD-s	WEA	YZ368CD	1989	**£10**	**£5**	*3" single*
Storms In Africa	CD-s	WEA	YZ368CDX	1989	**£15**	**£7.50**	*picture disc*
Watermark	Minidisc	WEA	2292438758	1993	**£25**	**£10**	

EPICS

Henry Long	7"	CBS	3564	1968	**£4**	**£1.50**	
How Wrong Can You Be	7"	Pye	7N17053	1966	**£4**	**£1.50**	
There's No Pleasing You	7"	Pye	7N15829	1965	**£4**	**£1.50**	

EPIDAURUS

Earthly Paradise	LP	private	E1004	1977	**£100**	**£50**	*German*

EPIDERMIS

Genius Of Original Force	LP	Kerston	FK65063	1977	**£25**	**£10**	*German*

EPILEPTICS

1970s Have Been Made In Hong Kong	7"	Stortbeat	BEAT8	1979	**£4**	**£1.50**	

EPISODE SIX

Episode Six's pleasant but undistinguished harmony music would be very much less collectable were it not for the fact that the group's vocalist was Ian Gillan (and the bass player was Roger Glover), although the likes of 'Here There And Everywhere' are light years away from the dynamism of Deep Purple's 'Sweet Child In Time' and 'Speed King'.

Episode Six	7" EP			196–	**£200**	**£100**	*Portuguese, best auctioned*
Here There And Everywhere	7" EP	Pye	PNV24175	1966	**£200**	**£100**	*French*
Here, There, And Everywhere	7"	Pye	7N17147	1966	**£15**	**£7.50**	
I Can See Through You	7"	Pye	7N17376	1967	**£15**	**£7.50**	
I Can See Through You	LP	Pye	260404	1969	**£20**	**£8**	*US*
I Hear Trumpets Blow	7"	Pye	7N17110	1966	**£15**	**£7.50**	
I Will Warm Your Heart	7"	Pye	7N17194	1966	**£25**	**£12.50**	*with Sheila Carter*
Little One	7"	MGM	MGM1409	1968	**£25**	**£12.50**	*credited to Episode*
Love, Hate, Revenge	7"	Pye	7N17244	1967	**£15**	**£7.50**	
Lucky Sunday	7"	Chapter One	CH103	1968	**£10**	**£5**	

Title	Format	Label	Cat. No.	Year	Mint	VG	Notes
Morning Dew	7"	Pye	7N17330	1967	**£15**	**£7.50**	
Mozart Versus The Rest	7"	Chapter One	CH104	1969	**£10**	**£5**	
Put Yourself In My Place	7"	Pye	7N17018	1966	**£15**	**£7.50**	

EPITAPH

Title	Format	Label	Cat. No.	Year	Mint	VG	Notes
Epitaph	LP	Polydor	2371225	1971	**£15**	**£6**	*German*
Outside The Law	LP	Membran	221311	1974	**£12**	**£5**	*German*
Stop, Look And Listen	LP	Polydor	2371274	1972	**£12**	**£5**	*German*

EPPERSON, MINNIE

Title	Format	Label	Cat. No.	Year	Mint	VG	Notes
Grab Your Clothes	7"	Action	ACT4503	1968	**£6**	**£2.50**	

EPPS, PRESTON

Title	Format	Label	Cat. No.	Year	Mint	VG	Notes
Bongo Bongo Bongo	7"	Top Rank	JAR413	1960	**£5**	**£2**	
Bongo Bongo Bongo	LP	Original Sound	(S)8851	1960	**£15**	**£6**	*US*
Bongo Boogie	7"	Top Rank	JAR345	1960	**£6**	**£2.50**	
Bongo Rock	7"	Top Rank	JAR140	1959	**£8**	**£4**	
Surfin' Bongos	LP	Original Sound	(S)8872	1963	**£12**	**£5**	*US*

EPSILON

Title	Format	Label	Cat. No.	Year	Mint	VG	Notes
Epsilon	LP	Bacillus	BLPS19070	1971	**£10**	**£4**	*German*
Move On	LP	Bacillus	BLPS19078	1972	**£12**	**£5**	*German*
Off	LP	Philips	6305216	1974	**£10**	**£4**	*German*

EQUALS

'Baby Come Back' is a genuine sixties classic, although this number one hit for the Equals sold too well for copies of the single to have become particularly collectable. The record launched the career of Eddie Grant in fine style, setting him firmly on the road to becoming the West Indies' second most successful musical ambassador.

Title	Format	Label	Cat. No.	Year	Mint	VG	Notes
At The Top	LP	President	PTLS1058	1970	**£10**	**£4**	
Baby Come Back	7" EP	President	PTE1	1968	**£10**	**£5**	
Best Of The Equals	LP	President	PTLS1050	1969	**£10**	**£4**	
Born Ya!	LP	Mercury	9109601	1976	**£15**	**£6**	
Equals	7" EP	President	PTE2	1969	**£5**	**£2**	
Equals Explosion	LP	President	PTL1015	1968	**£10**	**£4**	
I Can See But You Don't Know	7"	President	PT303	1970	**£8**	**£4**	
Sensational Equals	LP	President	PTL(S)1020	1968	**£10**	**£4**	
Strike Again	LP	President	PTLS1030	1969	**£10**	**£4**	
Supreme	LP	President	PTL(S)1025	1968	**£10**	**£4**	
Unequalled	LP	President	PTL1006	1967	**£10**	**£4**	

EQUINOX

Title	Format	Label	Cat. No.	Year	Mint	VG	Notes
Hard Rock	LP	Boulevard	4118	1973	**£15**	**£6**	

EQUIPE 84

Title	Format	Label	Cat. No.	Year	Mint	VG	Notes
Auschwitz	7"	Major Minor	MM517	1967	**£10**	**£5**	
Dr Jekyll And Mr Hyde	LP	Ariston	ARLP12107	1973	**£20**	**£8**	*Italian*

ERASURE

Title	Format	Label	Cat. No.	Year	Mint	VG	Notes
Abbaesque (Club Mixes)	12"	Mute	ERAS4	1992	**£15**	**£7.50**	*promo*
Am I Right	CD-s	Mute	CDMUTE134	1991	**£5**	**£2**	
Blue Savannah	CD-s	Mute	LCDMUTE109	1990	**£5**	**£2**	
Blue Savannah (Der Deutsche Mixes)	12"	Mute	XL12MUTE109	1990	**£8**	**£4**	
Chains Of Love	CD-s	Mute	CDMUTE83	1988	**£5**	**£2**	
Chains Of Love (Marx Brothers & Foghorn Mixes)	12"	Mute	D12MUTE83	1988	**£6**	**£2.50**	*promo*
Chorus	12"	Mute	P12MUTE125	1991	**£10**	**£5**	*promo*
Chorus	CD	Mute	STUMM95	1991	**£12**	**£5**	*box set with prints*
Chorus	CD-s	Mute	CDMUTE125	1991	**£5**	**£2**	
Chorus Software Installation Guide User Manual	CD	Sire		1991	**£75**	**£37.50**	*US promo 'hardback book' holding CD and cassette*
Circus (Two Ring Edition)	12"	Mute	LSTUMM35	1987	**£15**	**£7.50**	*double promo sampler*
Cowboy	CD	Mute	ERASSAY3	1996	**£40**	**£20**	*interview promo*
Crackers International	CD-s	Mute	CDMUTE93	1988	**£5**	**£2**	
Crackers International Part II: Stop (Remix)	CD-s	Mute	LCDMUTE93	1988	**£15**	**£7.50**	*with card & gift label, 6" x 3" sleeve*
Don't Say Your Love Is Killing Me	12"	Mute	P12MUTE195	1996	**£60**	**£30**	*test pressing with press release*
Drama	CD-s	Mute	CDMUTE89	1989	**£5**	**£2**	
Erasure	CD	Mute	ERASSAY2	1996	**£40**	**£20**	*interview promo*
Ghost	12"	Mute	PL12MUTE166	1994	**£12**	**£6**	*1 sided promo*
Heavenly Action	12"	Mute	D12MUTE42	1985	**£30**	**£15**	*double*
Heavenly Action (Yellow Brick Mix)	12"	Mute	L12MUTE42	1985	**£50**	**£25**	
I Love Saturday	7"	Mute	MUTE166	1994	**£30**	**£15**	
I Say I Say I Say	CD	Mute	ERASSAY1	1994	**£40**	**£20**	*promo*
It Doesn't Have To Be This Way	CD-s	Mute	CDMUTE56	1987	**£10**	**£5**	
Little Respect	CD-s	Mute	LCDMUTE85	1988	**£6**	**£2.50**	
Little Respect (Big Train Mix)	12"	Mute	L12MUTE85	1988	**£6**	**£2.50**	
Love To Hate You	CD-s	Mute	CDMUTE131	1991	**£5**	**£2**	
Oh L'Amour	12"	Mute	P12MUTE45	1986	**£20**	**£10**	*blue vinyl promo*
Oh L'Amour	CD-s	Intercord	INT826840	1988	**£5**	**£2**	
Oh L'Amour (Funky Sisters Mix)	12"	Mute	L12MUTE45	1986	**£10**	**£5**	

Title	Format	Label	Cat. No.	Year	Mint	VG	Notes
Oh L'Amour (Remix)	12"	Mute	12MUTE45	1986	**£10**	**£5**	*Thomas The Tank Engine picture sleeve*
Pop	CD	Mute	ERAS5CD		**£40**	**£20**	*promo compilation*
Pop	CD	Mute	ERASINT1	1992	**£40**	**£20**	*interview promo*
Push Me Shove Me (Moonbeam Mix)	12"	Mute	ERAS1	1990	**£15**	**£7.50**	*promo*
Rain	12"	Mute	PL12MUTE208	1997	**£8**	**£4**	*promo*
Rain	12"	Mute	P12MUTE208	1997	**£8**	**£4**	*promo*
Ship Of Fools	CD-s	Mute	CDMUTE74	1988	**£5**	**£2**	*3" single*
Ship Of Fools (Orbital Mix)	12"	Mute	ERAS2	1990	**£15**	**£7.50**	*promo*
Ship Of Fools (Stephen Hague Remix)	12"	Mute	D12MUTE74	1988	**£6**	**£2.50**	*promo*
Sometimes	7"	Mute	DMUTE51	1986	**£6**	**£2.50**	*double*
Sometimes	CD-s	Intercord	INT826854	1988	**£5**	**£2**	
Sometimes (Danny Rampling Mix)	12"	Mute	ERAS3	1990	**£15**	**£7.50**	*promo*
Star	CD-s	Mute	CDMUTE111	1990	**£5**	**£2**	
Supernature (Daniel Miller & Phil Legg Mix)	12"	Mute	XL12MUTE99	1990	**£8**	**£4**	*with outer envelope*
Who Needs Love Like That (Mexican Mix)	12"	Mute	L12MUTE40	1985	**£25**	**£12.50**	
Wild	CD	Mute	STUMM75	1989	**£75**	**£37.50**	*promo box set, with LP, cassette, inserts*
You Surround Me	CD-s	Mute	LCDMUTE99	1989	**£6**	**£2.50**	*3" single*

ERGO SUM

Title	Format	Label	Cat. No.	Year	Mint	VG	Notes
Mexico	LP	Theleme	6332500	1972	**£75**	**£37.50**	*French*

ERICA

Title	Format	Label	Cat. No.	Year	Mint	VG	Notes
You Used To Think	LP	ESP-Disk	1099	1968	**£30**	**£15**	*US*

ERICKSON, ROKY

Title	Format	Label	Cat. No.	Year	Mint	VG	Notes
Beauty And The Beast	LP	One Big Guitar	OBG9003	1987	**£20**	**£8**	*test pressing only*

ERICSON, ROLF

Title	Format	Label	Cat. No.	Year	Mint	VG	Notes
Transatlantic Wail	LP	Nixa	NJL5	1957	**£15**	**£6**	

EROC

Title	Format	Label	Cat. No.	Year	Mint	VG	Notes
Eroc	LP	Brain	1069	1975	**£12**	**£5**	*German*
Zwei	LP	Brain	0060007	1976	**£12**	**£5**	*German*

ERROL & HIS GROUP

Title	Format	Label	Cat. No.	Year	Mint	VG	Notes
Gypsy	7"	Blue Beat	BB284	1965	**£12**	**£6**	

ERVIN, BOOKER

Title	Format	Label	Cat. No.	Year	Mint	VG	Notes
In Between	LP	Blue Note	BST84283	1969	**£25**	**£10**	

ERWIN, BLUEGRASS

Title	Format	Label	Cat. No.	Year	Mint	VG	Notes
I Won't Cry Alone	7"	Top Rank	JAR252	1959	**£4**	**£1.50**	

ERWIN, PEE WEE

Title	Format	Label	Cat. No.	Year	Mint	VG	Notes
Oh Play That Thing!	LP	London	LTZT15153/ SAH6011	1959	**£10**	**£4**	

ESCALATORS

Title	Format	Label	Cat. No.	Year	Mint	VG	Notes
Something's Missing	7"	Big Beat	NS86	1983	**£5**	**£2**	

ESCORTS

Title	Format	Label	Cat. No.	Year	Mint	VG	Notes
C'mon Home Baby	7"	Fontana	TF570	1965	**£10**	**£5**	
Dizzie Miss Lizzie	7"	Fontana	TF453	1964	**£10**	**£5**	
From Head To Toe	7"	Columbia	DB8061	1966	**£15**	**£7.50**	
I Can Tell	7"	Lyntone	LYN509	1964	**£20**	**£10**	*flexi, Lance Harvey B side*
I Don't Want To Go On Without You	7"	Fontana	TF516	1964	**£8**	**£4**	
Let It Be Me	7"	Fontana	TF651	1966	**£10**	**£5**	
One To Cry	7"	Fontana	TF474	1964	**£10**	**£5**	

ESCORTS (2)

Title	Format	Label	Cat. No.	Year	Mint	VG	Notes
Submarine Race Watching	7"	Coral	Q72458	1963	**£5**	**£2**	

ESPERANTO ROCK ORCHESTRA

Title	Format	Label	Cat. No.	Year	Mint	VG	Notes
Danse Macabre	LP	A&M	AMLH63624	1974	**£10**	**£4**	
Esperanto Rock Orchestra	LP	A&M	AMLH68175	1973	**£10**	**£4**	
Last Tango	LP	A&M	AMLH68294	1975	**£10**	**£4**	

ESPRIT DE CORPS

Title	Format	Label	Cat. No.	Year	Mint	VG	Notes
If (Would It Turn Out Wrong)	7"	Jam	JAM24	1972	**£10**	**£5**	
Lonely	7"	Jam	JAM32	1973	**£6**	**£2.50**	

ESQUEIXADA SNIFF

Title	Format	Label	Cat. No.	Year	Mint	VG	Notes
En Concert	LP	Edigsa	UM2055	1979	**£10**	**£4**	*Spanish*
Ocells	LP	Edigsa	CM456	1979	**£10**	**£4**	*Spanish*

ESQUERITA

Title	Format	Label	Cat. No.	Year	Mint	VG	Notes
Esquerita	LP	Capitol	T1186	1959	**£300**	**£180**	*US*
Rocking The Joint	7"	Capitol	CL14938	1958	**£60**	**£30**	
Wildcat Shakeout	LP	Speciality	SPE6603	1972	**£20**	**£8**	

ESQUIRES

Title	Format	Label	Cat. No.	Year	Mint	VG	Notes
And Get Away	7"	Stateside	SS2077	1968	**£5**	**£2**	

Title	Format	Label	Number	Year	Mint	VG+	Notes
Get On Up	7"	Stateside	SS2048	1967	£6	£2.50	
Get On Up And Get Away	LP	London	HAQ/SHQ8356	1968	£10	£4	

ESSEX

Title	Format	Label	Number	Year	Mint	VG+	Notes
Easier Said Than Done	7"	Columbia	DB7077	1963	£6	£2.50	
Easier Said Than Done	LP	Columbia	33SX1593	1963	£20	£8	
She's Got Everything	7"	Columbia	DB7178	1963	£5	£2	
Walkin' Miracle	7"	Columbia	DB7122	1963	£6	£2.50	
Walkin' Miracle	LP	Columbia	33SX1613	1964	£20	£8	
Young And Lively	LP	Roulette	(S)R25246	1964	£20	£8	*US*

ESSEX, DAVID

Title	Format	Label	Number	Year	Mint	VG+	Notes
And The Tears Came Tumbling Down	7"	Fontana	TF559	1965	£25	£12.50	
Can't Nobody Love You	7"	Fontana	TF620	1965	£25	£12.50	
Day The Earth Stood Still	7"	Decca	F12967	1969	£15	£7.50	
Hello It's Me	7"	Sound For Industry	SFI200	1975	£10	£5	*flexi*
Just For Tonight	7"	Pye	7N17621	1968	£8	£4	
Love Story	7"	Uni	UN502	1968	£8	£4	
Myfanwy	CD-s	Arista	RISCD11	1987	£6	£2.50	
Rock On	CD-s	CBS	6549482	1989	£5	£2	
Special Promotion	7"	CBS	DJ3B1	1974	£10	£5	*promo*
Sun Ain't Gonna	CD-s	Lamplight	CDLAMP6	1989	£5	£2	
That Takes Me Back	7"	Decca	F12935	1969	£15	£7.50	
Thigh High	7"	Fontana	TF733	1966	£20	£10	
This Little Girl Of Mine	7"	Fontana	TF680	1966	£25	£12.50	

ESTABLISHMENT

Title	Format	Label	Number	Year	Mint	VG+	Notes
Bad Catholics	LP	Phaeton	SPIN992	1981	£20	£8	
Unfree Child	LP	EMI	SPLEAF7018	1977	£50	£25	

ESTEFAN, GLORIA

Title	Format	Label	Number	Year	Mint	VG+	Notes
1-2-3	7"	Epic	6529580	1988	£4	£1.50	*poster sleeve*
1-2-3	CD-s	Epic	6529582	1988	£5	£2	
Anything For You	CD-s	Epic	6516732	1988	£5	£2	
Betcha Say That	12"	Epic	6511259	1987	£6	£2.50	
Can't Stay Away From You	12"	Epic	6514449	1988	£6	£2.50	
Can't Stay Away From You	7"	Epic	6531957	1989	£5	£2	*shaped picture disc*
Can't Stay Away From You	7"	Epic	6514440	1988	£10	£5	*poster sleeve*
Can't Stay Away From You	CD-s	Epic	6514442	1988	£6	£2.50	*3" single*
Can't Stay Away From You	CD-s	Epic	6514442	1988	£5	£2	
Don't Wanna Lose You	CD-s	Epic	6550543	1989	£5	£2	*3" single*
Eyes Of Innocence	CD	Epic	EPC26167	1984	£20	£8	
Falling In Love	7"	Epic	TA6956	1986	£5	£2	
Get On Your Feet	12"	Epic	6554508	1989	£8	£4	
Get On Your Feet	CD-s	Epic	6554502	1989	£5	£2	
Gloria Estefan & Miami Sound Machine	CD	Epic	ESK1336	1988	£15	£6	*US promo sampler*
Here We Are	7"	Epic	6557287	1990	£5	£2	*envelope pack with print*
Hold Me, Thrill Me, Ask Me	CD	Epic		1994	£15	£6	*US interview promo*
Into The Light	CD	Epic		1991	£25	£10	*Australian, with bonus Love Songs CD*
Into The Light	CD	Epic	ESK3028	1991	£15	£6	*US promo with bonus track*
Let It Loose	CD	Epic	4509102	1987	£20	£8	
Let It Loose	LP	Epic	4509101	1987	£10	£4	
Oye Mi Canto	CD-s	Epic	6552875	1989	£12	£6	*picture disc*
Primitive Love	CD	Epic	EPC26491	1985	£20	£8	
Rhythm Is Gonna Get You	12"	Epic	6508059	1988	£10	£5	
Rhythm Is Gonna Get You	7"	Epic	6545147	1988	£5	£2	*with badge*
Rhythm Is Gonna Get You	7"	Epic	6545149	1988	£5	£2	*poster picture sleeve*
Rhythm Is Gonna Get You	7"	Epic	6545140	1988	£4	£1.50	*calendar picture sleeve*
Rhythm Is Gonna Get You	7"	Epic	6508057	1988	£5	£2	
Rhythm Is Gonna Get You	CD-s	Epic	6545142	1988	£5	£2	
Solid Gold	CD-s	Epic	6548543	1989	£5	£2	*3" single*

ESTES, SLEEPY JOHN

Title	Format	Label	Number	Year	Mint	VG+	Notes
1929–1940	LP	Folkways	RF8	1967	£10	£4	
Broke And Hungry	LP	Delmark	DL608	1964	£15	£6	
Brownsville Blues	LP	Delmark	DL613	1965	£15	£6	
Electric Sleep	LP	Delmark	DL619	1966	£10	£4	
In Europe	LP	Delmark	DL611	1965	£10	£4	
Legend	LP	Delmark	DL603	1961	£15	£6	
Legend Of Sleepy John Estes	LP	Esquire	32195	1963	£30	£15	
Old Original Tennessee Blues	LP	Revival	RVS1008	1971	£10	£4	*with Furry Lewis and Will Shade*
Portraits In Blues Vol. 10	LP	Storyville	SLP172	1965	£15	£6	
Sleepy John's Got The Blues	7" EP	Delmark	DJB3	1966	£6	£2.50	
Tennessee Jug Busters	LP	77	LA1227	1964	£20	£8	

ESTICK, JACKIE

Title	Format	Label	Number	Year	Mint	VG+	Notes
Boss Girl	7"	Blue Beat	BB64	1961	£12	£6	*Count Ossie B side*
Since You've Been Gone	7"	Island	WI042	1963	£10	£5	
Ska	7"	Ska Beat	JB256	1966	£10	£5	

ESTUS, DEON

Title	Format	Label	Number	Year	Mint	VG+	Notes
Heaven Help Me	CD-s	Mika	MIKCD2	1989	£8	£4	

ETCETERAS

Little Lady	7"	Oriole	CB1973	1964	**£10**	**£5**	
Where Is My Love	7"	Oriole	CB1950	1964	**£6**	**£2.50**	

ETERNAL

Angel Of Mine	12"	EMI	12EMDJ493	1997	**£6**	**£2.50**	*promo*
Crazy	7"	EMI	EM364	1994	**£25**	**£12.50**	
Don't You Love Me	12"	EMI	12EMDJ465	1997	**£8**	**£4**	*promo double*
Good Thing – The House Mixes	12"	EMI	12EMDJD419	1996	**£8**	**£4**	*promo double*
I Wanna Be The Only One	12"	EMI	12EMDJX472	1997	**£6**	**£2.50**	*promo*
I Wanna Be The Only One	12"	EMI	12EMDJ472	1997	**£6**	**£2.50**	*promo*
I Wanna Be The Only One	12"	EMI	12EMDJD472	1997	**£8**	**£4**	*promo double*
I Wanna Be The Only One	CD-s	EMI	CDEMDJX472	1997	**£5**	**£2**	*promo*
Megamix	12"	EMI	12DJHITS001	1997	**£8**	**£4**	*1 sided promo*
Megamix	CD-s	EMI	CDDJHITS001	1997	**£8**	**£4**	*promo*
Oh Baby I	CD-s	EMI	CDEM353	1994	**£5**	**£2**	
Power Of A Woman	12"	EMI	12EMDJX396	1995	**£8**	**£4**	*promo double*
Power Of A Woman	CD-s	EMI	CDEMDDJ1090	1996	**£6**	**£2.50**	*promo*
Stay	CD-s	EMI	CDEM283	1993	**£5**	**£2**	

ETERNALS

Rocking In The Jungle	7"	London	HL8995	1959	**£75**	**£37.50**	*tri-centre*

ETERNALS (2)

Christmas Joy	7"	Moodisc	MU3506	1970	**£5**	**£2**	
Keep On Dancing	7"	Moodisc	MU3508	1971	**£5**	**£2**	
Push Me In The Corner	7"	Moodisc	MU3507	1971	**£5**	**£2**	
Queen Of The Minstrels	7"	Coxsone	CS7091	1969	**£10**	**£5**	

ETERNITY'S CHILDREN

Eternity's Children	LP	Tower	ST5123	1968	**£15**	**£6**	*US*
Timeless	LP	Tower	ST5144	1968	**£15**	**£6**	*US*

ETHEL THE FROG

Eleanor Rigby	7"	EMI	EMI5041	1980	**£8**	**£4**	
Ethel The Frog	LP	EMI	EMC3329	1980	**£15**	**£6**	

ETHERIDGE, MELISSA

Angels	CD-s	Island	CID440	1989	**£5**	**£2**	
Bring Me Some Water	CD-s	Island	CID393	1989	**£5**	**£2**	
Don't You Need	CD-s	Island	CID376	1988	**£5**	**£2**	
No Souvenirs	CD-s	Island	CID431	1989	**£5**	**£2**	
Nowhere To Go	CD-s	Island	CID642	1996	**£5**	**£2**	
Similar Features	CD-s	Island	CID356	1988	**£5**	**£2**	

ETHIOPIANS

Best Of Five	7"	Songbird	SB1064	1971	**£4**	**£1.50**	
Buss Your Mouth	7"	Nu Beat	NB038	1969	**£4**	**£1.50**	*Reggae Boys B side*
Come On Now	7"	Doctor Bird	DB1141	1968	**£10**	**£5**	
Do It Sweet	7"	Doctor Bird	DB1092	1967	**£10**	**£5**	
Drop Him	7"	Duke	DU102	1971	**£4**	**£1.50**	
Engine 54	7"	Doctor Bird	DB1147	1968	**£10**	**£5**	
Everyday Talking	7"	Doctor Bird	DB1199	1969	**£10**	**£5**	
Everything Crash	7"	Doctor Bird	DB1169	1968	**£10**	**£5**	
Fire A Muss Muss Tail	7"	Crab	CRAB2	1968	**£6**	**£2.50**	
For You	7"	Island	WI3036	1967	**£10**	**£5**	*Soul Brothers B side*
Go Rock Steady	LP	Doctor Bird	DLM5011	1968	**£100**	**£50**	
Good Ambition	7"	Songbird	SB1047	1970	**£4**	**£1.50**	
He's Not A Rebel	7"	Big Shot	BI569	1971	**£5**	**£2**	
Hong Kong Flu	7"	Doctor Bird	DB1185	1969	**£10**	**£5**	
Hong Kong Flu	7"	J.J.	JJ3303	1970	**£4**	**£1.50**	
I Am Free	7"	Island	WI3015	1966	**£10**	**£5**	*Soul Brothers B side*
I'm A King	7"	Crab	CRAB7	1969	**£6**	**£2.50**	
I'm Gonna Take Over Now	7"	Rio	R114	1967	**£8**	**£4**	*Jackie Mittoo B side*
Israel Want To Be Free	7"	G.G.	GG4533	1972	**£4**	**£1.50**	
Leave Me Business Alone	7"	Studio One	SO2035	1967	**£12**	**£6**	*Soul Vendors B side*
Let's Get Together	7"	Coxsone	CS7022	1967	**£10**	**£5**	*Hamlins B side*
Live Good	7"	Ska Beat	JB260	1966	**£10**	**£5**	*Soul Brothers B side*
Lot's Wife	7"	Songbird	SB1062	1971	**£4**	**£1.50**	
Love Bug	7"	G.G.	GG4519	1971	**£4**	**£1.50**	
Love Bug	7"	Supreme	SUP221	1971	**£4**	**£1.50**	
Mi Want Girl	7"	Randys	RAN509	1971	**£4**	**£1.50**	
Monkey Money	7"	Fab	FAB180	1971	**£4**	**£1.50**	
Mother's Tender Care	7"	Duke Reid	DR2507	1970	**£4**	**£1.50**	*Tommy McCook B side*
Mr Tom	7"	Randys	RAN512	1969	**£4**	**£1.50**	
My Testimony	7"	Nu Beat	NB031	1969	**£4**	**£1.50**	*J. J. Allstars B side*
No Baptism	7"	Songbird	SB1040	1970	**£4**	**£1.50**	
Not Me	7"	Doctor Bird	DB1172	1969	**£10**	**£5**	
Owe Me No Pay Me	7"	Rio	R110	1966	**£8**	**£4**	
Pirate	7"	Treasure Isle	TI7067	1971	**£4**	**£1.50**	*Tommy McCook B side*
Praise For I	7"	High Note	HS042	1970	**£5**	**£2**	
Promises	7"	Technique	TE919	1972	**£4**	**£1.50**	
Reggae Hit The Town	7"	Crab	CRAB4	1968	**£6**	**£2.50**	
Reggae Power	LP	Trojan	TTL10	1969	**£20**	**£8**	
Rim Bim Bam	7"	Duke	DU108	1971	**£4**	**£1.50**	

Satan Girl	7"	Gas	GAS142	1970	£4	£1.50	
Selah	7"	Big Shot	BI574	1971	£4	£1.50	
Solid As A Rock	7"	Big	SUP226	1971	£4	£1.50	
Solid As A Rock	7"	Punch	PH96	1971	£4	£1.50	
Starvation	7"	Explosion	EX2050	1971	£4	£1.50	
Starvation	7"	Supreme	SUP226	1971	£4	£1.50	
Stay In My Lonely Arms	7"	Rio	R126	1967	£8	£4	
Train To Glory	7"	Doctor Bird	DB1148	1968	£10	£5	
Train To Skaville	7"	Rio	R130	1967	£8	£4	
True Man	7"	Randys	RAN510	1969	£4	£1.50	*Randy's Allstars B side*
Walkie Talkie	7"	Bamboo	BAM26	1970	£4	£1.50	*Sound Dimension B side*
Well Red	7"	Trojan	TR697	1969	£4	£1.50	*J. J. Allstars B side*
What A Fire	7"	Doctor Bird	DB1186	1969	£10	£5	
What A Pain	7"	Songbird	SB1059	1971	£4	£1.50	
What To Do	7"	Rio	R123	1967	£8	£4	*Jackie Mittoo B side*
Whip	7"	Doctor Bird	DB1096	1967	£10	£5	
Woman Capture Man	7"	Trojan	TR666	1969	£4	£1.50	
Woman Capture Man	LP	Trojan	TBL112	1970	£30	£15	
World Goes Ska	7"	Doctor Bird	DB1103	1967	£10	£5	
Wreck It Up	7"	J.J.	JJ3302	1970	£5	£2	
You Are For Me	7"	Prince Buster	PB38	1972	£4	£1.50	
You'll Want To Come Back	7"	Bamboo	BAM38	1970	£4	£1.50	*Jackie Mittoo B side*

ETIVES

An Gaol A Thug Mi Og	LP	Ayrespin	AYRC015	1984	£15	£6	

ETNA

Etna	LP	Catoca	CTL1002	1975	£25	£10	*Italian*

ETRON FOU LELOUBLAN

Batelages	LP	Gratte-Ciel	CIEL2001	1976	£10	£4	*French*
En direct	LP	Celluloid	CEL6572	1979	£10	£4	
Les Trois Fous Perdegagnent	LP	L'Orchestra	OLPS55002	1979	£10	£4	*Italian*

ETTA & HARVEY

If I Can't Have You	7"	London	HLM9180	1960	£30	£15	

EUBANKS, JACK

Searchin'	7"	London	HLU9501	1962	£4	£1.50	
What'd I Say	7"	London	HLU9312	1961	£4	£1.50	

EULENSPYGEL

2	LP	Spiegelei	287607	1971	£20	£8	*German*
Ausschuss	LP	Spiegelei	287807	1972	£25	£10	*German*

EUPHONIOUS WAIL

Euphonious Wail	LP	Kapp	KS3668	1973	£20	£8	*US*

EUPHORIA

Euphoria	LP	Heritage	HTS35005	1969	£25	£10	*US*

EUPHORIA (2)

Gift From Euphoria	LP	Capitol	SKAO363	1969	£75	£37.50	*US*

EUPHORIA (3)

Lost In Trance	LP	Rainbow	1003	1973	£100	£50	*US*

EUREKA BRASS BAND

Jazz At Preservation Hall Vol. 1	LP	London	HAK/SHK8162	1964	£12	£5	
New Orleans Parade	LP	Melodisc	MLP12101	1955	£12	£5	

EUROPE

Let The Good Times Rock	CD-s	Epic	CDEUR5	1988	£5	£2	
Open Your Heart	CD-s	Epic	CDEUR4	1988	£5	£2	
Solid Gold	CD-s	Epic	654564	1988	£5	£2	*3" single*
Superstitious	CD-s	Epic	CDEUR3	1988	£5	£2	

EURYTHMICS

Angel	CD-s	RCA	DACD21	1990	£5	£2	
Angel (Remix)	12"	RCA	DAT25	1990	£6	£2.50	
Beethoven	7"	RCA	DA11P	1987	£6	£2.50	*poster sleeve*
Beethoven	CD-s	RCA	DA11CD	1987	£5	£2	
Belinda	7"	RCA	RCA115	1981	£10	£5	
Christmas Message	7"	Lyntone	LYN13916	1983	£6	£2.50	*flexi*
Dave And Annie's Christmas Message '87	7"	Lyntone	no number	1987	£6	£2.50	*flexi*
Dave And Annie's Christmas Message '89	7"	Flexi	FLX880	1989	£6	£2.50	*flexi*
Dave And Annie's Christmas Message '90	7"	Flexi	FLX1000	1990	£6	£2.50	*flexi*
Don't Ask Me Why	CD-s	RCA	DACD20	1989	£5	£2	*black box, poster*
Don't Ask Me Why	CD-s	RCA	DACD19	1989	£5	£2	
I Love You Like A Ball And Chain	7"	RCA	BYTI100	1985	£5	£2	*promo*
I Need A Man (Live)	CD-s	RCA	DA15CD	1988	£5	£2	*metal tin*
I'm Never Gonna Cry Again	12"	RCA	RCAT68	1981	£20	£10	
I'm Never Gonna Cry Again	7"	RCA	RCA68	1981	£5	£2	

Intro Speech	7"	RCA	EUC001	1983	£20	£10	
It's Alright	12"	RCA	PB40376	1985	£6	£2.50	*double*
It's Alright	7"	RCA	PB40375	1985	£8	£4	*double*
Julia	7"	Virgin	VSY734	1985	£4	£1.50	*picture disc*
King And Queen Of America	CD-s	RCA	DACD23	1990	£5	£2	*in wooden box*
King And Queen Of America	CD-s	RCA	DACD24	1990	£8	£4	*in wooden box*
Love Is A Stranger	7"	RCA	DAP1	1982	£4	£1.50	*picture disc*
Miracle Of Love	7"	RCA	DA9P	1986	£6	£2.50	*shaped picture disc*
Revival	CD-s	RCA	DACD17	1989	£5	£2	
Right By Your Side	7"	RCA	DA4	1983	£20	£10	*with 4 track cassette*
Right By Your Side	7"	RCA	DAP4	1983	£4	£1.50	*picture disc*
Rough And Tough	CD	RCA	CP353016	1987	£50	£25	*US live promo*
Sexcrime (1984)	12"	Virgin	VSY72812	1984	£6	£2.50	*picture disc*
Sexcrime (1984)	CD-s	Virgin	VVCS2	1988	£5	£2	
Sexcrime (1984)	CD-s	Virgin	CDT22	1988	£5	£2	*3" single*
Sexcrime (1984)	CD-s	Virgin	CDF22	1988	£5	£2	
Shame	CD-s	RCA	DA14CD	1987	£6	£2.50	
Sweet Dreams	7"	RCA	DAP2	1983	£4	£1.50	*picture disc*
Sweet Dreams	LP	RCA	RCALP6063	1983	£10	£4	*picture disc*
Sweet Dreams Are Made Of This	CD-s	RCA	PD42651	1989	£5	£2	
This Is The House	12"	RCA	RCAT199	1982	£25	£12.50	
This Is The House	7"	RCA	RCA199	1982	£8	£4	
Thorn In My Side	7"	RCA	DA8	1986	£5	£2	*with badge*
Touch	LP	RCA	PL70109	1983	£10	£4	*picture disc*
Walk	12"	RCA	RCAT230	1982	£30	£15	
Walk	7"	RCA	RCA230	1982	£8	£4	
We Two Are One	CD	RCA	PD74251	1989	£40	£20	*promo box set, with video and interview cassette*
We Two Are One Two	CD	BMG	780349	1991	£25	£10	*laser disc*
Who's That Girl	7"	RCA	DAP3	1983	£4	£1.50	*picture disc*
You Have Placed A Chill In My Heart	CD-s	RCA	DA16CD	1988	£6	£2.50	*black metal tin*
Yuletide Message To All Our Pals	7"	Lyntone	LYN15292	1984	£6	£2.50	*flexi*

EVANS, BARBARA

Souvenirs	7"	RCA	RCA1122	1959	£15	£7.50	

EVANS, BILL

Alone	LP	Verve	SVLP9251	1970	£10	£4	
At The Montreux Jazz Festival	LP	Verve	(S)VLP9243	1969	£12	£5	
Conversations With Myself	LP	Verve	VLP9054	1963	£15	£6	
Dig It	LP	Fontana	FJL104	1964	£10	£4	
Everybody Digs Bill Evans	LP	Riverside	RLP12291	1958	£15	£6	
Explorations	LP	Riverside	RLP351	1961	£15	£6	
Further Conversations With Myself	LP	Verve	(S)VLP9198	1968	£12	£5	
Montreux II	LP	CTI	CTL4	1972	£10	£4	
New Piano Jazz Conceptions	LP	Riverside	RLP12223	196–	£15	£6	
Portrait In Jazz	LP	Riverside	RLP12315/1162	1959	£15	£6	
Waltz For Debby	LP	Riverside	RLP(9)399	1961	£15	£6	

EVANS, CHRISTINE

Somewhere There's Love	7"	Philips	BF1496	1966	£6	£2.50	

EVANS, DAVE

Elephantasia	LP	Village Thing	VTS14	1972	£10	£4	
Words In Between	LP	Village Thing	VTS6	1971	£10	£4	

EVANS, GIL

Although technically an arranger, Gil Evans produced jazz that was so individual that it effectively amounted to recomposition. At his best when creating music around a star soloist (*New Bottle Old Wine* featured Cannonball Adderley; *Miles Ahead*, *Porgy And Bess* and *Sketches Of Spain* featured Miles Davis and are listed under his name), Evans was ready to record an album with Jimi Hendrix, when the guitarist's untimely end aborted the project. Evans went on to record many of Hendrix's tunes anyway, but although these work very well as modern jazz pieces, they offer no more than a tantalizing glimpse of what might have been.

Gil Evans And Ten	LP	Esquire	32070	1959	£20	£8	
Great Jazz Standards	7" EP	Vogue	EPV1266	1960	£5	£2	
Great Jazz Standards	LP	Vogue	LAE12234	1960	£20	£8	
Great Jazz Standards	LP	Fontana	688000ZL	1965	£12	£5	
New Bottle, Old Wine	LP	Vogue	LAE12173	1959	£20	£8	
Out Of The Cool	LP	HMV	CLP1456	1961	£15	£6	
Plays The Music Of Jimi Hendrix	LP	RCA	LSA3197	1974	£12	£5	*US*
Roots (New Bottle, Old Wine)	LP	Fontana	688003ZL	1965	£12	£5	
Svengali	LP	Atlantic	AD1643	1974	£12	£5	*US*

EVANS, LARRY

Crazy About My Baby	7"	London	HLU8269	1956	£400	£250	*best auctioned*

EVANS, MAUREEN

All The Angels Sang	7"	CBS	201773	1965	£4	£1.50	
Like I Do	LP	Oriole	PS40046	1963	£30	£15	
Melancholy Me	7" EP	Oriole	EP7076	1963	£25	£12.50	
Never Let Him Go	7"	CBS	201752	1965	£4	£1.50	
Oliver	7" EP	Oriole	EP7039	1961	£5	£2	*with David Kossoff*
Somewhere There's Love	7"	CBS	202621	1967	£5	£2	

EVANS, PAUL

21 Years In A Tennessee Jail	LP	Kapp	KL1346/KS3346	1964	£25	£10	*US*
Another Town, Another Jail	LP	Kapp	KL1475/KS3475	1966	£20	£8	*US*

Title	Format	Label	Cat. No.	Year	Mint	VG	Notes
Brigade Of Broken Hearts	7"	London	HLL9183	1960	£5	£2	
Even Tan	7"	London	HLR9770	1963	£6	£2.50	
Folk Songs Of Many Lands	LP	Carlton	(STLP)130	1961	£25	£10	US
Happy Go Lucky Me	7"	London	HLL9129	1960	£5	£2	
Hear Paul Evans In Your Home Tonight	LP	Carlton	(STLP)129	1961	£25	£10	US
Hushabye Little Guitar	7"	London	HLL9239	1960	£8	£4	
Midnight Special	7"	London	HLL9045	1960	£8	£4	
Paul Evans	7" EP	London	RER1349	1962	£50	£25	
Seven Little Girls Sitting In The Back Seat	7"	London	HLL8968	1959	£6	£2.50	
Sings The Fabulous Teens	LP	London	HAL2248	1960	£60	£30	

EVANS, RUSSELL & THE NITEHAWKS

Title	Format	Label	Cat. No.	Year	Mint	VG	Notes
Send Me Some Cornbread	7"	Atlantic	584010	1966	£5	£2	

EVEN DOZEN JUG BAND

The Even Dozen Jug Band, while in itself having little to distinguish it from the many other folk groups playing in America during the early sixties, was nevertheless a remarkably effective training school for some later well-known musicians. Playing in the group were John Sebastian (soon to form the Lovin' Spoonful), Maria D'Amato (famous later under her married name, Maria Muldaur), Steve Katz (guitarist with the Blues Project and Blood, Sweat and Tears), guitarist Stefan Grossman, and Joshua Rifkin (later responsible for bringing the works of Scott Joplin to public notice).

Title	Format	Label	Cat. No.	Year	Mint	VG	Notes
Even Dozen Jug Band	LP	Elektra	EKS7246	1964	£20	£8	US
Even Dozen Jug Band	LP	Bounty	BY6023	1966	£15	£6	
Jug Band Songs Of The Southern Mountains	LP	Legacy	LEG119	1965	£15	£6	US

EVERETT, BETTY

Title	Format	Label	Cat. No.	Year	Mint	VG	Notes
Getting Mighty Crowded	7"	Fontana	TF520	1964	£4	£1.50	
I Can't Hear You	7"	Stateside	SS321	1964	£6	£2.50	
I've Got A Claim On You	7"	Sue	WI352	1965	£15	£7.50	
It's In His Kiss	7"	Stateside	SS280	1964	£5	£2	
It's In His Kiss	LP	Fontana	TL5136	1965	£30	£15	
It's In His Kiss	LP	Joy	JOYS106	1968	£10	£4	
There'll Come A Time	LP	Uni	UNLS109	1969	£12	£5	
Very Best Of Betty Everett	LP	Vee Jay	VJLP/VJS1122	1965	£25	£10	US
You're No Good	7"	Stateside	SS259	1964	£6	£2.50	
Your Loving Arms	7"	King	KG1002	1964	£4	£1.50	

EVERETT, BETTY & JERRY BUTLER

Title	Format	Label	Cat. No.	Year	Mint	VG	Notes
Delicious Together	LP	Fontana	TL5237	1965	£15	£6	
Delicious Together	LP	Joy	JOYS123	1968	£10	£4	
Let It Be Me	7"	Stateside	SS339	1964	£5	£2	
Smile	7"	Fontana	TF528	1965	£5	£2	

EVERETT, VINCE

Title	Format	Label	Cat. No.	Year	Mint	VG	Notes
Every Now And Then	7"	Fontana	TF915	1968	£10	£5	

EVERGREEN BLUES

Title	Format	Label	Cat. No.	Year	Mint	VG	Notes
Laura	7"	Mercury	MF1025	1968	£4	£1.50	
Midnight Confessions	7"	Mercury	MF1012	1967	£4	£1.50	
Seven Do Eleven	LP	Mercury	SMCL20122	1968	£10	£4	

EVERGREEN BLUESHOES

Title	Format	Label	Cat. No.	Year	Mint	VG	Notes
Ballad Of Evergreen Blueshoes	LP	London	HAU/SHU8399	1969	£10	£4	

EVERLY, DON

Title	Format	Label	Cat. No.	Year	Mint	VG	Notes
Don Everly	LP	A&M	AMLH2007	1971	£12	£5	
Sunset Towers	LP	Ode	77023	1974	£12	£5	US

EVERLY, PHIL

Title	Format	Label	Cat. No.	Year	Mint	VG	Notes
Ich Bin Dein	7"	Elektra	ELK12381	1977	£5	£2	sung in German
Mystic Line	LP	Pye	NSPL18473	1975	£10	£4	
Nothing's Too Good For My Baby	LP	Pye	NSPL18448	1974	£10	£4	
Star Spangled Springer	LP	RCA	SF8370	1973	£15	£6	

EVERLY BROTHERS

Title	Format	Label	Cat. No.	Year	Mint	VG	Notes
Ain't That Lovin' You Baby	7"	Warner Bros	WB129	1964	£4	£1.50	
All I Have To Do Is Dream	7"	London	HLA8618	1958	£5	£2	tri-centre
Beat 'n' Soul	LP	Warner Bros	W(S)1605	1965	£15	£6	
Bird Dog	7"	London	HLA8685	1958	£5	£2	tri-centre
Both Sides Of An Evening	LP	Warner Bros	WM4052	1961	£20	£8	
Both Sides Of An Evening	LP	Warner Bros	WS8052	1961	£25	£10	stereo
Both Sides Of An Evening Vol. 1	7" EP	Warner Bros	WEP6115	1963	£25	£12.50	
Both Sides Of An Evening Vol. 1	7" EP	Warner Bros	WSE6115	1963	£50	£25	stereo
Both Sides Of An Evening Vol. 2	7" EP	Warner Bros	WEP6117	1964	£25	£12.50	
Both Sides Of An Evening Vol. 2	7" EP	Warner Bros	WSE6117	1964	£50	£25	stereo
Both Sides Of An Evening Vol. 3	7" EP	Warner Bros	WEP6138	1965	£25	£12.50	
Bowling Green	7"	Warner Bros	WB7020	1967	£6	£2.50	
Bye Bye Love	7"	London	HLA8440	1957	£15	£7.50	
Cathy's Clown	7"	Warner Bros	WB1	1960	£4	£1.50	
Christmas With The Everly Brothers	LP	Warner Bros	WS8116	1962	£30	£15	stereo
Christmas With The Everly Brothers	LP	Warner Bros	WM8116	1962	£25	£12.50	
Crying In The Rain	7"	Warner Bros	WB56	1962	£4	£1.50	
Date With The Everly Brothers	LP	Warner Bros	WM4028	1960	£20	£8	
Date With The Everly Brothers	LP	Warner Bros	WS8028	1960	£30	£15	stereo
Date With The Everly Brothers Vol. 1	7" EP	Warner Bros	WSE6107	1963	£50	£25	stereo
Date With The Everly Brothers Vol. 1	7" EP	Warner Bros	WEP6107	1963	£25	£12.50	

Title	Format	Label	Cat. No.	Year	Mint	VG	Notes
Date With The Everly Brothers Vol. 2	7" EP	Warner Bros	WSE6109	1963	**£50**	**£25**	*stereo*
Date With The Everly Brothers Vol. 2	7" EP	Warner Bros	WEP6109	1963	**£25**	**£12.50**	
Especially For You	7" EP	Warner Bros	WSEP2034	1961	**£30**	**£15**	*stereo*
Especially For You	7" EP	Warner Bros	WEP6034	1961	**£15**	**£7.50**	
Everly Brothers	7" EP	London	REA1113	1958	**£15**	**£7.50**	
Everly Brothers	LP	London	HAA2081	1958	**£40**	**£20**	
Everly Brothers	LP	Cadence	CLP3003	1958	**£50**	**£25**	*US*
Everly Brothers' Best	LP	Cadence	CLP3025	1959	**£50**	**£25**	*US*
Everly Brothers No. 2	7" EP	London	REA1148	1958	**£15**	**£7.50**	
Everly Brothers No. 3	7" EP	London	REA1149	1958	**£20**	**£10**	
Everly Brothers No. 4	7" EP	London	REA1174	1959	**£20**	**£10**	
Everly Brothers No. 5	7" EP	London	REA1229	1960	**£25**	**£12.50**	
Everly Brothers No. 6	7" EP	London	REA1311	1961	**£25**	**£12.50**	
Everly Brothers Show	LP	Warner Bros	WS1858	1970	**£12**	**£5**	*double*
Everly Brothers Sing	LP	Warner Bros	W1708	1967	**£15**	**£6**	
Everly Brothers Sing	LP	Warner Bros	WS1708	1967	**£20**	**£8**	*stereo*
Everly Brothers Single Set	7"	Lightning	SET1	1980	**£20**	**£10**	*15 x 7", boxed plus book*
Fabulous Style Of The Everly Brothers	LP	London	HAA2266	1960	**£25**	**£10**	
Fabulous Style Of The Everly Brothers	LP	Cadence	CLP3040/25040	1960	**£40**	**£20**	*US*
Ferris Wheel	7"	Warner Bros	WB135	1964	**£4**	**£1.50**	
Fifteen Everly Hits Fifteen	LP	Cadence	CLP3062/25062	1963	**£30**	**£15**	*US*
Folk Songs Of The Everly Brothers	LP	Cadence	CLP3059/25059	1962	**£40**	**£20**	*US*
Foreverly Yours	7" EP	Warner Bros	WSEP2049	1962	**£40**	**£20**	*stereo*
Foreverly Yours	7" EP	Warner Bros	WEP6049	1962	**£15**	**£7.50**	
Girl Sang The Blues	7"	Warner Bros	WB109	1963	**£4**	**£1.50**	
Golden Hits	LP	Warner Bros	WM/WS8108	1962	**£10**	**£4**	
Gone Gone Gone	7"	Warner Bros	WB146	1964	**£4**	**£1.50**	
Gone Gone Gone	LP	Warner Bros	WS8169	1965	**£20**	**£8**	*stereo*
Gone Gone Gone	LP	Warner Bros	WM8169	1965	**£15**	**£6**	
Hit Sound Of The Everly Brothers	LP	Warner Bros	W1676	1967	**£15**	**£6**	
Hit Sound Of The Everly Brothers	LP	Warner Bros	WS1676	1967	**£25**	**£10**	*stereo*
How Can I Meet Her	7"	Warner Bros	WB67	1962	**£4**	**£1.50**	
I'll Never Get Over You	7"	Warner Bros	WB5639	1965	**£4**	**£1.50**	
I've Been Wrong Before	7"	Warner Bros	WB5754	1966	**£6**	**£2.50**	
In Our Image	LP	Warner Bros	W1620	1965	**£15**	**£6**	*mono*
In Our Image	LP	Warner Bros	WS1620	1965	**£25**	**£10**	*stereo*
Instant Party	7" EP	Warner Bros	WEP6111	1963	**£25**	**£12.50**	
Instant Party	7" EP	Warner Bros	WSE6111	1963	**£50**	**£25**	*stereo*
Instant Party	LP	Warner Bros	WM4061	1962	**£20**	**£8**	
Instant Party	LP	Warner Bros	WS8061	1962	**£25**	**£10**	*stereo*
Instant Party Vol. 2	7" EP	Warner Bros	WSE6113	1963	**£50**	**£25**	*stereo*
Instant Party Vol. 2	7" EP	Warner Bros	WEP6113	1963	**£25**	**£12.50**	
It's Been Nice	7"	Warner Bros	WB99	1963	**£4**	**£1.50**	
It's Everly Time	7" EP	Warner Bros	WSEP2056	1962	**£40**	**£20**	*stereo*
It's Everly Time	7" EP	Warner Bros	WEP6056	1962	**£20**	**£10**	
It's Everly Time	LP	Warner Bros	WM4012	1960	**£20**	**£8**	
It's Everly Time	LP	Warner Bros	WS8012	1960	**£30**	**£15**	*stereo*
It's My Time	7"	Warner Bros	WB7192	1968	**£5**	**£2**	
Leave My Girl Alone	7" EP	Warner Bros	WEP622	1967	**£30**	**£15**	
Let It Be Me	7"	London	HLA9039	1960	**£10**	**£5**	*tri-centre*
Lightning Express	7"	London		1962	**£60**	**£30**	*test pressing*
Like Strangers	7"	London	HLA9250	1960	**£5**	**£2**	
Love Is Strange	7"	Warner Bros	WB5649	1965	**£4**	**£1.50**	
Love Is Strange	7" EP	Warner Bros	WEP610	1966	**£25**	**£12.50**	
Love Of The Common People	7"	Warner Bros	WB7088	1967	**£6**	**£2.50**	
Mary Jane	7"	Warner Bros	WB7062	1967	**£6**	**£2.50**	
Milk Train	7"	Warner Bros	WB7226	1968	**£6**	**£2.50**	
Muskrat	7"	Warner Bros	WB50	1961	**£4**	**£1.50**	
No One Can Make My Sunshine Smile	7"	Warner Bros	WB79	1962	**£4**	**£1.50**	
Oh Boy	7"	Warner Bros	WB6074	1967	**£6**	**£2.50**	
Pass The Chicken And Listen	LP	RCA	SF8332	1973	**£10**	**£4**	
People Get Ready	7" EP	Warner Bros	WEP612	1966	**£20**	**£10**	
Poor Jenny	7"	London	HLA8863	1959	**£6**	**£2.50**	*tri-centre*
Power Of Love	7"	Warner Bros	WB5743	1966	**£5**	**£2**	
Price Of Love	7"	Warner Bros	WB5628	1965	**£4**	**£1.50**	
Price Of Love	7"	Warner Bros	WB161	1965	**£4**	**£1.50**	
Price Of Love	7" EP	Warner Bros	WEP604	1965	**£15**	**£7.50**	
Problems	7"	London	HLA8781	1958	**£5**	**£2**	*tri-centre*
Ridin' High	7"	RCA	RCA2232	1972	**£5**	**£2**	
Rock 'n' Soul	7" EP	Warner Bros	WEP608	1965	**£15**	**£7.50**	
Rock 'n' Soul	LP	Warner Bros	WM8171	1965	**£15**	**£6**	
Rock 'n' Soul	LP	Warner Bros	WS8171	1965	**£25**	**£10**	*stereo*
Rock 'n' Soul	LP	Warner Bros	W(S)1578	1965	**£15**	**£6**	
Rock 'n' Soul Vol. 2	7" EP	Warner Bros	WEP609	1965	**£15**	**£7.50**	
Roots	LP	Warner Bros	W(S)1752	1968	**£15**	**£6**	
See See Rider	7" EP	Warner Bros	WEP618	1966	**£30**	**£15**	
Sing Great Country Hits	LP	Warner Bros	WM/WS8138	1963	**£15**	**£6**	
Sing Great Country Hits Vol. 1	7" EP	Warner Bros	WEP6128	1964	**£25**	**£12.50**	
Sing Great Country Hits Vol. 2	7" EP	Warner Bros	WEP6131	1964	**£25**	**£12.50**	
Sing Great Country Hits Vol. 3	7" EP	Warner Bros	WEP6132	1964	**£25**	**£12.50**	
So It Will Always Be	7"	Warner Bros	WB94	1963	**£4**	**£1.50**	
So Sad	7"	Warner Bros	WB19	1960	**£4**	**£1.50**	
Somebody Help Me	7" EP	Warner Bros	WEP623	1967	**£20**	**£10**	
Songs Our Daddy Taught Us	LP	London	HAA2150	1958	**£40**	**£20**	
Songs Our Daddy Taught Us Part 1	7" EP	London	REA1195	1959	**£30**	**£15**	
Songs Our Daddy Taught Us Part 2	7" EP	London	REA1196	1959	**£30**	**£15**	
Songs Our Daddy Taught Us Part 3	7" EP	London	REA1197	1959	**£30**	**£15**	

Title	Format	Label	Number	Year	Mint	VG+	Notes
Stories We Could Tell	LP	RCA	SF8270	1972	**£10**	**£4**	
Sun Keeps Shining	7"	Columbia	21496	1956	**£250**	**£150**	*US, best auctioned*
Temptation	7"	Warner Bros	WB42	1961	**£4**	**£1.50**	
That'll Be The Day	7"	Warner Bros	WB158	1965	**£5**	**£2**	
This Little Girl Of Mine	7"	London	HLA8554	1958	**£15**	**£7.50**	
Till I Kissed You	7"	London	HLA8934	1959	**£6**	**£2.50**	*tri-centre*
Two Yanks In England	LP	Warner Bros	W1646	1965	**£15**	**£6**	*with the Hollies*
Two Yanks In England	LP	Warner Bros	WS1646	1965	**£25**	**£10**	*stereo*
Very Best Of The Everly Brothers	LP	Warner Bros	WM/WS8163	1964	**£10**	**£4**	
Very Best Of The Everly Brothers	LP	St Michael	IMP111	1980	**£20**	**£8**	
Wake Up Little Susie	7" EP	Warner Bros	K16407	1974	**£5**	**£2**	
Wake Up Little Suzie	7"	London	HLA8498	1957	**£6**	**£2.50**	
Walk Right Back	7"	Warner Bros	WB33	1961	**£4**	**£1.50**	
When Will I Be Loved	7"	London	HLA9157	1960	**£5**	**£2**	
You're My Girl	7"	Warner Bros	WB154	1965	**£4**	**£1.50**	
You're The One I Love	7"	Warner Bros	WB143	1964	**£8**	**£4**	
Yves	7"	Warner Bros	WB7425	1970	**£6**	**£2.50**	

EVERPRESENT FULLNESS

Title	Format	Label	Number	Year	Mint	VG+	Notes
Everpresent Fullness	LP	White Whale	7132	1970	**£20**	**£8**	*US*

EVERY MOTHER'S SON

Title	Format	Label	Number	Year	Mint	VG+	Notes
Come And Take A Ride In My Boat	7"	MGM	MGM1341	1967	**£10**	**£5**	
Every Mother's Son	LP	MGM	C(S)8044	1967	**£10**	**£4**	*US*
Every Mother's Son Back	LP	MGM	C(S)8061	1968	**£10**	**£4**	
Pony With The Golden Mane	7"	MGM	MGM1372	1967	**£5**	**£2**	
Put Your Mind At Ease	7"	MGM	MGM1350	1967	**£5**	**£2**	

EVERYONE

Title	Format	Label	Number	Year	Mint	VG+	Notes
Everyone	LP	B&C	CAS1028	1971	**£10**	**£4**	

EVERYONE INVOLVED

Title	Format	Label	Number	Year	Mint	VG+	Notes
Circus Keeps On Turning	7"	Arcturus	ARC3	1972	**£20**	**£10**	
Either Or	LP	Arcturus	ARC4	1972	**£350**	**£210**	

EVERYTHING BUT THE GIRL

Title	Format	Label	Number	Year	Mint	VG+	Notes
Driving	CD-s	Blanco Y Negro	NEG40CD	1989	**£5**	**£2**	
I Always Was Your Girl	CD-s	Blanco Y Negro	NEG33CD	1988	**£8**	**£4**	
I Don't Want To Talk About It	CD-s	Blanco Y Negro	NEG34CD	1988	**£5**	**£2**	*3" single*
Love Is Here Where I Live	CD-s	Blanco Y Negro	NEG37CD	1988	**£5**	**£2**	*3" single*
Native Land	12"	Blanco Y Negro	NEG6T	1984	**£6**	**£2.50**	
Night And Day	CD-s	Cherry Red	CDCHERRY37	1989	**£5**	**£2**	
Old Friends	CD-s	Blanco Y Negro	NEG51CD	1991	**£5**	**£2**	
Take Me	CD-s	Blanco Y Negro	NEG44CD	1990	**£5**	**£2**	
These Early Days	CD-s	Blanco Y Negro	NEG39CD	1988	**£5**	**£2**	*3" single*
These Early Days	CD-s	Blanco Y Negro	NEG30CD	1988	**£8**	**£4**	*3" single*
Twin Cities	CD-s	Blanco Y Negro	NEG53CD	1991	**£5**	**£2**	

EVERYTHING IS EVERYTHING

Title	Format	Label	Number	Year	Mint	VG+	Notes
Everything Is Everything	LP	Vanguard	SVRL19036	1968	**£10**	**£4**	

EWAN & DENVER

Title	Format	Label	Number	Year	Mint	VG+	Notes
I Want You So Bad	7"	Giant	GN17	1967	**£5**	**£2**	

EWAN & GERRY

Title	Format	Label	Number	Year	Mint	VG+	Notes
Oh Babe	7"	Blue Beat	BB385	1967	**£12**	**£6**	
Right Track	7"	Giant	GN4	1967	**£6**	**£2.50**	
Rock Steady Train	7"	Giant	GN9	1967	**£6**	**£2.50**	
Tennessee Waltz	7"	Giant	GN14	1967	**£6**	**£2.50**	

EWELL, DON

Title	Format	Label	Number	Year	Mint	VG+	Notes
Piano Solos Of King Oliver Tunes	LP	Tempo	TAP7	1957	**£25**	**£10**	

EXCALIBUR

Title	Format	Label	Number	Year	Mint	VG+	Notes
First Album	LP	Reprise	REP44163	1972	**£100**	**£50**	*German*

EXCALIBUR (2)

Title	Format	Label	Number	Year	Mint	VG+	Notes
Sceptre	LP	Yarmouth	01	1970	**£300**	**£180**	

EXCELSIOR SPRING

Title	Format	Label	Number	Year	Mint	VG+	Notes
Happy Miranda	7"	Instant	IN002	1968	**£8**	**£4**	

EXCEPTIONS

Dave Pegg, the bass player with Fairport Convention and Jethro Tull, was a member of the Exceptions, while his colleague Roger Hill has also played for Fairport.

Title	Format	Label	Number	Year	Mint	VG+	Notes
Eagle Flies On Sunday	7"	CBS	202632	1967	**£10**	**£5**	
Exceptional Exceptions	LP	President	PTLS1026	1969	**£15**	**£6**	

Gaberdine Saturday Night	7"	CBS	2830	1967	£10	£5	

EXCEPTIONS (2)

What More Do You Want	7"	Decca	F12100	1965	£8	£4	

EXCHECKERS

Drummer with this third-division Merseybeat group was Aynsley Dunbar, whose subsequent career included stints with John Mayall, Frank Zappa, Journey and Jefferson Starship.

All The World Is Mine	7"	Decca	F11871	1964	£6	£2.50	

EXCITERS

Do Wah Diddy	7"	United Artists	UP2274	1969	£4	£1.50	
Doo Wah Diddy Diddy	7"	United Artists	UP1041	1964	£8	£4	
Doo Wah Diddy Diddy	7" EP	United Artists	UEP1005	1965	£40	£20	
Exciters	LP	United Artists	ULP1032	1964	£50	£25	
Exciters	LP	Roulette	(S)R25326	1966	£30	£15	US
He's Got The Power	7"	United Artists	UP1017	1963	£4	£1.50	
I Want You To Be My Boy	7"	Columbia	DB7479	1965	£4	£1.50	
It's So Exciting	7"	United Artists	UP1026	1963	£4	£1.50	
Just Not Ready	7"	Columbia	DB7544	1965	£5	£2	
Little Bit Of Soap	7"	London	HLZ10018	1966	£5	£2	
Run Mascara	7"	Columbia	DB7606	1965	£6	£2.50	
Tell Him	7"	United Artists	UP1011	1963	£5	£2	
Tell Him	LP	United Artists	UAL3264/UAS6264	1963	£50	£25	US
Weddings Make Me Cry	7"	London	HLZ10038	1966	£10	£5	

EXCURSION

Night Train	LP	Gemini	GMX5029	1970	£20	£8	

EXECUTIVES

It's Been So Long	7"	Columbia	DB7573	1965	£4	£1.50	
Lock Your Door	7"	Columbia	DB7919	1966	£4	£1.50	
March Of The Mods	7"	Columbia	DB7323	1964	£4	£1.50	
Return Of The Mods	7"	Columbia	DB7770	1965	£5	£2	
Strictly For The Beat	7"	Columbia	DB7393	1964	£4	£1.50	

EXECUTIVES (2)

Gaza Strip	7"	CBS	3067	1967	£4	£1.50	
I Ain't Got Nobody	7"	CBS	4013	1969	£4	£1.50	
Smokey Atmosphere	7"	CBS	202652	1967	£4	£1.50	
Tracy Took A Trip	7"	CBS	3431	1968	£6	£2.50	
Tracy Took A Trip	7"	CBS	3431	1968	£20	£10	demo, picture sleeve

EXILE

Don't Tax Me	7"	Boring	BO1	1977	£20	£10	
Real People	7"	Charly	CYS1033	1978	£12	£6	

EXILES

Freedom, Come All Ye	LP	Topic	12T143	1966	£20	£8	
Hale And The Hanged	LP	Topic	12T164	1967	£20	£8	

EXIT

Exit	LP	Better Daze	XPL1008	1969	£20	£8	US

EXITS

Yodelling	7"	Way Out	WOO1	1978	£30	£15	

EXITS (2)

Fashion Plague	7"	Lightning	GIL519	1978	£10	£5	

EXMAGMA

Exmagma	LP	Neusi	B204	1973	£20	£8	German
Goldball	LP	Disjuncta	0009	1973	£15	£6	French

EXORDIUM

Trouble With Adam	LP	Face To Face	FTF1001	197–	£40	£20	

EXPEDITION

Live	LP	Cegep	1653	1972	£15	£6	Canadian

EXPERIMENTS WITH ICE

Experiments With Ice	LP	United Dairies	EX001	1981	£15	£6	

EXPLOSIVE

Cities Make The Country Colder	7"	President	PT244	1969	£5	£2	
Who Planted Thorns In Alice's Garden	7"	President	PT262	1969	£5	£2	

EXPORT

Export	LP	His Master's Vice	VICE1	1980	£10	£4	
Wheeler Dealer	7"	His Master's Vice	VICE2	1981	£6	£2.50	

EXPOZER

Rock Japan	7"	Hard	HARD1	1980	**£8**	**£4**	

EXTREEM

On The Beach	7"	Strike	JH326	1966	**£6**	**£2.50**	

EXTREME

Holehearted	CD-s	A&M	AMCD839	1991	**£5**	**£2**	
More Than Words	CD-s	A&M	AMCD792	1991	**£6**	**£2.50**	
Song For Love	CD-s	A&M	AMCD698	1992	**£5**	**£2**	

EXTREME NOISE TERROR

Ear Slaughter – Radioactive	LP	Manic Ears	ACHE01	1986	**£10**	**£4**	*with Chaos UK*

EXUMA

Exuma	LP	Mercury	6338018	1970	**£10**	**£4**	
Exuma II	LP	Mercury	SR61314	1971	**£10**	**£4**	*US*
Snake	LP	Kama Sutra	KSBS2052	1972	**£10**	**£4**	*US*

EYE FULL TOWER

How About Me	7"	Polydor	56734	1967	**£4**	**£1.50**	

EYELESS IN GAZA

Kodak Ghosts Run Amok	7"	Ambivalent Scale	ASR002	1980	**£10**	**£5**	

EYES

Mod band the Eyes owed everything to the Who – even going so far as to record a Who sound-alike under the title 'My Degeneration'. Their handful of singles, and the EP which comprises the tracks from the first two singles, are now extremely collectable as prime examples of the freakbeat genre. The group also recorded an album, but this was a quickly and cheaply recorded exploitation affair, issued under the thin disguise of a pseudonym – *Tribute To The Rolling Stones* by the Pupils.

Arrival Of The Eyes	7" EP	Mercury	MCE10035	1966	**£400**	**£250**	
Blink	LP	Bam Caruso	KIRI028	1984	**£12**	**£5**	*2 sleeves*
Good Day Sunshine	7"	Mercury	MF934	1966	**£75**	**£37.50**	
Man With Money	7"	Mercury	MF910	1966	**£150**	**£75**	
My Immediate Pleasure	7"	Mercury	MF897	1966	**£100**	**£50**	
When The Night Falls	7"	Mercury	MF881	1965	**£100**	**£50**	

EYES OF BLUE

Crossroads Of Time	LP	Mercury	SMCL20134	1968	**£30**	**£15**	
In Fields Of Ardath	LP	Mercury	SMCL20164	1969	**£30**	**£15**	
Largo	7"	Mercury	MF1049	1968	**£5**	**£2**	
Supermarket Full Of Cans	7"	Deram	DM114	1967	**£15**	**£7.50**	
Up And Down	7"	Deram	DM106	1966	**£15**	**£7.50**	

EYNESBURY GIANT

From The Cask	LP	Ultimate	URL602	1978	**£15**	**£6**	

E-ZEE POSSEE

Everything Starts With An E	CD-s	More Protein	PROCD1	1989	**£6**	**£2.50**	

EZELL, WILL

Chicago Piano	LP	Gannet	12002	1973	**£10**	**£4**	
Gin Mill Jazz	10" LP	London	AL3539	1955	**£20**	**£8**	

FABARES, SHELLEY

Title	Format	Label	Cat. No.	Year	Mint	VG	Notes
Johnny Angel	7"	Pye	7N25132	1962	£5	£2	
Johnny Loves Me	7"	Pye	7N25151	1962	£4	£1.50	
My Prayer	7"	Fontana	TF592	1965	£5	£2	
Shelley	LP	Colpix	CLP/CST426	1962	£25	£10	US
Things We Did Last Summer	LP	Colpix	CLP/CST431	1962	£25	£10	US

FABIAN

Title	Format	Label	Cat. No.	Year	Mint	VG	Notes
Fabulous Fabian	LP	HMV	CLP1345	1960	£30	£15	
Good Old Summertime	LP	Chancellor	CHL(S)5012	1960	£30	£15	US
Got The Feeling	7"	HMV	POP659	1959	£8	£4	
Grapevine	7"	HMV	POP869	1961	£4	£1.50	
High Time	LP	RCA	LPM/LSP2314	1960	£30	£15	US
Hold That Tiger	LP	HMV	CLP1301	1959	£40	£20	
Hound Dog Man	7"	HMV	POP695	1960	£8	£4	
I'm A Man	7"	HMV	POP587	1959	£20	£10	
I'm Gonna Sit Right Down And Write Myself A Letter	7"	HMV	POP778	1960	£4	£1.50	
Kissin' And Twistin'	7"	HMV	POP810	1960	£4	£1.50	
Rockin' Hot	LP	Chancellor	CHL5019	1961	£40	£20	US
Sixteen Fabulous Hits	LP	Chancellor	CHL5024	1962	£30	£15	US
String Along	7"	HMV	POP724	1960	£4	£1.50	
Tiger	7"	HMV	POP643	1959	£10	£5	
Tomorrow	7"	HMV	POP800	1960	£4	£1.50	
Turn Me Loose	7"	HMV	POP612	1959	£15	£7.50	
You Know You Belong To Somebody Else	7"	HMV	POP829	1961	£4	£1.50	
You're Only Young Once	7"	HMV	POP934	1961	£4	£1.50	
Young And Wonderful	LP	HMV	CLP1433/ CSD1352	1961	£30	£15	

FABIAN & FRANKIE AVALON

Title	Format	Label	Cat. No.	Year	Mint	VG	Notes
Hit Makers	LP	Chancellor	CHL5009	1960	£30	£15	US

FABULOUS DIALS

Title	Format	Label	Cat. No.	Year	Mint	VG	Notes
Bossa Nova Stomp	7"	Pye	7N25200	1963	£15	£7.50	

FACE TO FACE

Title	Format	Label	Cat. No.	Year	Mint	VG	Notes
Turning To You	LP	Acorn	AC001	1978	£75	£37.50	

FACES

Title	Format	Label	Cat. No.	Year	Mint	VG	Notes
Borstal Boys	7"	Warner Bros	K16281	1973	£10	£5	
First Step	LP	Warner Bros	WS3000	1970	£12	£5	
First Step	LP	Warner Bros	K46053	1970	£10	£4	*green label*
Flying	7"	Warner Bros	WB8005	1970	£4	£1.50	
Had Me A Real Good Time	7"	Warner Bros	WB8018	1970	£4	£1.50	
Long Player	LP	Warner Bros	W3011	1971	£12	£5	
Long Player	LP	Warner Bros	K46064	1971	£10	£4	
Nod's As Good As A Wink	LP	Warner Bros	K56006	1971	£10	£4	*green label*
Nod's As Good As A Wink	LP	Warner Bros	K56006	1971	£12	£5	*with poster*
Ooh La La	LP	Warner Bros	K56011	1973	£10	£4	*green label*

FACTORY

Title	Format	Label	Cat. No.	Year	Mint	VG	Notes
Path Through the Forest	7"	MGM	MGM1444	1968	£200	£100	*best auctioned*
Try A Little Sunshine	7"	CBS	4540	1969	£200	£100	*best auctioned*

FACTORY (2)

Title	Format	Label	Cat. No.	Year	Mint	VG	Notes
Time Machine	7"	Oak	RGJ718	1970	£150	£75	

FACTORY (3)

Title	Format	Label	Cat. No.	Year	Mint	VG	Notes
You Are The Music	7"	Future Earth	FER011	1982	£8	£4	

FACTOTUMS

Title	Format	Label	Cat. No.	Year	Mint	VG	Notes
Cloudy	7"	Pye	7N17402	1967	£5	£2	
Here Today	7"	Piccadilly	7N35333	1966	£6	£2.50	
I Can't Give You Anything	7"	Piccadilly	7N35355	1966	£6	£2.50	
In My Lonely Room	7"	Immediate	IM009	1965	£12	£6	
Mr And Mrs Regards	7"	CBS	4140	1969	£4	£1.50	
You're So Good To Be	7"	Immediate	IM022	1965	£12	£6	

FADING COLOURS

Title	Format	Label	Cat. No.	Year	Mint	VG	Notes
Be With Me	7"	Ember	EMBS237	1967	£4	£1.50	
Just Like Romeo And Juliet	7"	Ember	EMBS229	1966	£20	£10	

FAGEN, DONALD

Title	Format	Label	Cat. No.	Year	Mint	VG	Notes
Century's End	CD-s	Warner Bros	W7972CD	1988	£5	£2	*3" single*
Kamakiriad	CD	Reprise	245230DJ	1993	£25	£10	*US gold promo, autographed*
Words And Music	CD	Reprise	PROCD6161	1993	£20	£8	*US promo*

FAHEY, BRIAN

Title	Format	Label	Cat. No.	Year	Mint	VG	Notes
Gidian's Way	7"	Parlophone	R5262	1965	£6	£2.50	
Time For TV	LP	Columbia	TWO175	1967	£10	£4	

FAHEY, BRIAN ORCHESTRA

'At The Sign Of The Swinging Cymbal' is the theme tune of radio's *Pick Of The Pops*, although it inevitably sounds incomplete without Alan Freeman's perfectly timed interjections.

Title	Format	Label	Cat. No.	Year	Mint	VG	Notes
At The Sign Of The Swinging Cymbal	7"	Parlophone	R4686	1960	£6	£2.50	
At The Sign Of The Swinging Cymbal	7"	Parlophone	R4909	1962	£4	£1.50	
Twang	7"	United Artists	UP1115	1965	£4	£1.50	

FAHEY, JOHN

Title	Format	Label	Cat. No.	Year	Mint	VG	Notes
Blind Joe Death	LP	Takoma	C1002	1967	£15	£6	*US*
Dance Of Death	LP	Takoma	1004	1967	£15	£6	*US*
Days Have Gone By	LP	Takoma	1014	1967	£15	£6	*US*
Death Chants, Breakdowns & Military Waltzes	LP	Sonet	SNTF608	1969	£10	£4	
Death Chants, Breakdowns And Military Waltzes	LP	Takoma	C1003	1967	£15	£6	*US*
Essential John Fahey	LP	Vanguard	VSD55/56	1974	£12	£5	*double*
Great San Bernadino Birthday Party (Guitar Vol. 4)	LP	Takoma	1008	1967	£15	£6	*US*
New Possibility	LP	Takoma	1020	1968	£15	£6	*US*
Requia	LP	Vanguard	SVRL19055	1968	£12	£5	
Transfiguration Of Blind Joe Death	LP	Transatlantic	TRA173	1967	£20	£8	*with booklet*
Transfiguration Of Blind Joe Death	LP	Sonet	SNTF607	1969	£12	£5	
Transfiguration Of Blind Joe Death	LP	Transatlantic	TRA173	1967	£12	£5	
Voice Of The Turtle	LP	Takoma	1019	1968	£15	£6	*US*
Yellow Princess	LP	Vanguard	SVRL19033	1968	£12	£5	

FAINE JADE

Title	Format	Label	Cat. No.	Year	Mint	VG	Notes
Introspection: A Faine Jade Recital	LP	R.S.V.P.	8002	1968	£400	£250	*US*

FAIR, JAD

Title	Format	Label	Cat. No.	Year	Mint	VG	Notes
Zombies Of Mora-Tau	7"	Armageddon	AEP003	1980	£10	£5	

FAIR, YVONNE

Title	Format	Label	Cat. No.	Year	Mint	VG	Notes
Bitch Is Black	LP	Tamla Motown	STML12008	1975	£10	£4	

FAIR SET

Title	Format	Label	Cat. No.	Year	Mint	VG	Notes
Honey And Wine	7"	Decca	F12168	1965	£6	£2.50	

FAIRBURN, WERLY

Title	Format	Label	Cat. No.	Year	Mint	VG	Notes
All The Time	7"	London	HLC8349	1956	£750	£500	*best auctioned*

FAIRE, JOHNNY

Title	Format	Label	Cat. No.	Year	Mint	VG	Notes
Bertha Lou	7"	London	HLU8569	1958	£300	£180	*best auctioned*

FAIRFIELD PARLOUR

From Home To Home is the third LP by the English Kaleidoscope. The change of name to Fairfield Parlour brought no more than a marginal improvement to the group's fortunes, however, and the record today is almost as scarce as the first two.

Title	Format	Label	Cat. No.	Year	Mint	VG	Notes
Bordeaux Rose	7"	Prism	PRI1	1976	£5	£2	
Bordeaux Rose	7"	Vertigo	6059003	1970	£4	£1.50	
From Home To Home	LP	Vertigo	6360001	1970	£60	£30	*spiral label*
Just Another Day	7"	Vertigo	6059008	1970	£10	£5	

FAIRGROUND ATTRACTION

Title	Format	Label	Cat. No.	Year	Mint	VG	Notes
Clare	CD-s	RCA	PD42608	1989	£5	£2	
Find My Love	CD-s	RCA	PD42080	1988	£5	£2	
Perfect	CD-s	RCA	PD41846	1988	£5	£2	
Perfect	CD-s	RCA	PD42649	1988	£5	£2	
Smile In A Whisper	CD-s	RCA	PD42250	1988	£5	£2	
Walking After Midnight	CD-s	RCA	PD43654	1990	£5	£2	

FAIRIES

Title	Format	Label	Cat. No.	Year	Mint	VG	Notes
Don't Mind	7"	HMV	POP1445	1965	£60	£30	
Don't Think Twice It's Alright	7"	Decca	F11943	1964	£60	£30	
Get Yourself Home	7"	HMV	POP1404	1965	£100	£50	

FAIRPORT CONVENTION

On their first LP Fairport Convention sound like an English Jefferson Airplane. The folk music influence begins to be felt on *What We Did On Our Holidays* and takes over altogether on *Liege and Lief*. Thus over the course of four LPs, recorded in a period of not much more than a year, it is possible to hear the genesis of a new kind of rock music. The personnel changes in the group became rather complicated after this, but the various editions of Fairport Convention – and indeed the many groups derived from it – were able to explore the possibilities of the folk-rock fusion in many fruitful ways. The success of Fairport Convention's annual 'reunion' at Copredy testifies to the tremendous loyalty of their considerable number of both fans and past members! Virtually all of the group's records are now collectable to a greater or lesser extent. It should be noted that, unlike many late sixties albums, the mono version of the Polydor LP does not appear to contain any different mixes to the stereo version, but it does somehow manage to deliver a crisper, more dynamic sound, which justifies its higher value.

Airing Cupboard Tapes	cass	Woodworm	no number	1981	**£15**	**£6**	
Angel Delight	LP	Island	ILPS9162	1971	**£12**	**£5**	
AT2	LP	Woodworm	WR1	1984	**£12**	**£5**	
Babbacombe Lee	LP	Island	ILPS9176	1971	**£12**	**£5**	
Bonny Bunch Of Roses	LP	Vertigo	9102015	1977	**£12**	**£5**	
Boot	cass	Woodworm	no number	1984	**£15**	**£6**	*double*
Expletive Delighted	LP	Woodworm	WR009	1986	**£12**	**£5**	
Fairport Convention	LP	Polydor	583035	1968	**£50**	**£25**	
Fairport Convention	LP	Polydor	582035	1968	**£60**	**£30**	*mono*
Farewell Farewell	LP	Woodworm	BEAR22	1979	**£15**	**£6**	
Farewell Farewell	LP	Simons	GAMA1	1979	**£12**	**£5**	
Full House	LP	Island	ILPS9130	1970	**£15**	**£6**	*pink label*
Full House	LP	Island	ILPS9130	1970	**£250**	**£150**	*test pressing with 'Poor Will & The Jolly Hangman'*
Gladys Leap	CD	Woodworm	WRCD007	1985	**£12**	**£5**	
Gottle O'Geer	LP	Island	ILPS9389	1976	**£15**	**£6**	
History Of Fairport Convention	LP	Island	ICD4	1972	**£15**	**£6**	*double*
If (Stomp)	7"	Polydor	2058014	1970	**£8**	**£4**	
If I Had A Ribbon Bow	7"	Track	604020	1968	**£20**	**£10**	
In Real Time	LP	Island	ILPS9883	1987	**£12**	**£5**	
James O'Donnell's Jig	7"	Hawk	HASP423	1978	**£6**	**£2.50**	*Irish*
John Lee	7"	Island	WIP6128	1971	**£8**	**£4**	*picture sleeve*
Liege And Lief	CD	Island	CID9115	1986	**£12**	**£5**	
Liege And Lief	LP	Island	ILPS9115	1969	**£15**	**£6**	*pink label*
Live – A Movable Feast	LP	Island	ILPS9285	1974	**£12**	**£5**	
Live At Broughton Castle	LP	Stony Plain	SP51052	1985	**£12**	**£5**	
Live At L.A. Troubadour	LP	Island	HELP28	1976	**£25**	**£10**	
Meet On The Ledge	12"	Island	12IF324	1987	**£6**	**£2.50**	*with poster*
Meet On The Ledge	7"	Island	WIP6047	1968	**£8**	**£4**	
Moat On The Ledge	LP	Woodworm	WR001	1982	**£12**	**£5**	
Nine	LP	Island	ILPS9246	1973	**£12**	**£5**	
Now Be Thankful	7"	Island	WIP6089	1970	**£5**	**£2**	
Other Boot	cass	Woodworm	no number	1987	**£15**	**£6**	*double*
Red And Gold	CD	New Routes	RUECD002	1989	**£12**	**£5**	
Rising For The Moon	LP	Island	ILPS9313	1975	**£12**	**£5**	
Rosie	LP	Island	ILPS9208	1973	**£12**	**£5**	
Rubber Band	7"	Simons	PMW1	1979	**£5**	**£2**	
Si Tu Dois Partir	7"	Island	WIP6064	1969	**£4**	**£1.50**	
Third Leg	cass	Woodworm	no number	1988	**£15**	**£6**	*double*
Tippler's Tales	LP	Vertigo	9102022	1978	**£12**	**£5**	
Tour Sampler	LP	Island	ISS2	1975	**£100**	**£50**	
Unhalfbricking	LP	Island	ILPS9102	1969	**£20**	**£8**	*pink label*
What We Did On Our Holidays	LP	Island	ILPS9092	1968	**£20**	**£8**	*pink label*
White Dress	7"	Island	WIP6241	1975	**£8**	**£4**	*picture sleeve*

FAIRWAYS

Yoko Ono	7"	Mercury	MF1116	1969	**£5**	**£2**	

FAIRWEATHER

Named after lead singer Andy Fairweather-Low, Fairweather were essentially a slimmed down version of Amen Corner. Seeing the way that rock music was going, the group attempted to put their pop past behind it by signing to RCA's new progressive label, Neon. They blew it, however, by gaining a hit single!

Beginning From An End	LP	Neon	NE1	1971	**£10**	**£4**	

FAIRWEATHER, AL

Al And Sandy	LP	Columbia	33SX1159	1959	**£15**	**£6**	*with Sandy Brown*
Al's Pals	LP	Columbia	33SX1221	1960	**£15**	**£6**	
Doctor McJazz	LP	Columbia	33SX1306/ SCX3367	1961	**£15**	**£6**	
Fairweather Friends	10" LP	Nixa	NJT511	1958	**£12**	**£5**	
Incredible McJazz	LP	Columbia	33SX1509	1963	**£20**	**£8**	

FAIRY TALE

Once Upon A Time	LP	Blossom	17001	1969	**£20**	**£8**	*Dutch*

FAIRY'S MOKE

Fairy's Moke	LP	Deroy	DER1175	1975	**£100**	**£50**	

FAIRYTALE

Guess I Was Dreaming	7"	Decca	F12644	1967	**£50**	**£25**	
Lovely People	7"	Decca	F12665	1967	**£50**	**£25**	

FAITH, ADAM

Adam Faith has remained a public figure ever since his first forays into the charts – though not in general as a singer, but rather as an actor and a financial commentator. His first recordings took the soft pop-and-strings sound of Buddy Holly's 'It Doesn't Matter Any More' as their starting point – the weakness of using as the basis for an entire style what Holly undoubtedly viewed as a limited novelty being emphasized by the rather low collectors' values reached by Faith's records today. It was to his credit, however, that with the arrival of

British beat, Faith's response was to find a beat backing group, the Roulettes, for himself. On records like 'The First Time', the results were quite successful, although collectors are more interested in the records made by the Roulettes without their employer.

Title	Format	Label	Cat. No.	Year			Notes
Adam	7" EP	Parlophone	GEP8824	1960	**£8**	**£4**	
Adam	7" EP	Parlophone	SGE2014	1960	**£12**	**£6**	*stereo*
Adam	LP	Parlophone	PMC1128	1960	**£10**	**£4**	*mono*
Adam	LP	Regal	(S)REG1033	1960	**£10**	**£4**	*export*
Adam	LP	Parlophone	PCS3010	1960	**£15**	**£6**	*stereo*
Adam Faith	7" EP	Parlophone	GEP8851	1961	**£8**	**£4**	
Adam Faith	LP	Parlophone	PCS3025	1961	**£15**	**£6**	*stereo*
Adam Faith	LP	Parlophone	PMC1162	1961	**£10**	**£4**	*mono*
Adam Faith	LP	Amy	8005	1965	**£20**	**£8**	*US*
Adam Faith No. 2	7" EP	Parlophone	GEP8852	1961	**£8**	**£4**	
Adam Faith No. 3	7" EP	Parlophone	GEP8854	1961	**£8**	**£4**	
Adam No. 2	7" EP	Parlophone	SGE2015	1960	**£12**	**£6**	*stereo*
Adam No. 2	7" EP	Parlophone	GEP8826	1960	**£8**	**£4**	
Adam No. 3	7" EP	Parlophone	GEP8831	1960	**£8**	**£4**	
Adam No. 3	7" EP	Parlophone	SGE2018	1960	**£12**	**£6**	*stereo*
Adam's Hit Parade	7" EP	Parlophone	GEP8811	1960	**£6**	**£2.50**	
Adam's Hit Parade Vol. 2	7" EP	Parlophone	GEP8841	1961	**£6**	**£2.50**	
Adam's Hit Parade Vol. 3	7" EP	Parlophone	GEP8862	1962	**£8**	**£4**	
Adam's Latest Hits	7" EP	Parlophone	GEP8877	1963	**£8**	**£4**	
Beat Girl	7" EP	Columbia	SEG8138	1962	**£25**	**£12.50**	*with John Barry*
Beat Girl	LP	Columbia	33SX1225	1960	**£30**	**£15**	*with John Barry*
Cheryl's Going Home	7"	Parlophone	R5516	1966	**£4**	**£1.50**	
Daddy What'll Happen To Me	7"	Parlophone	R5635	1967	**£4**	**£1.50**	
England's Top Singer	LP	MGM	(S)E3591	1961	**£20**	**£8**	*US*
Faith Alive	LP	Parlophone	PMC1249	1965	**£50**	**£25**	
For You	LP	Parlophone	PMC1213	1963	**£12**	**£5**	
For You – Adam	7" EP	Parlophone	GEP8904	1964	**£8**	**£4**	
From Adam With Love	LP	Parlophone	PCS3038	1962	**£15**	**£6**	*stereo*
From Adam With Love	LP	Parlophone	PMC1192	1962	**£10**	**£4**	*mono*
Heartsick Feeling	7"	HMV	POP438	1958	**£75**	**£37.50**	
Hey Little Lovin' Girl	7"	Parlophone	R5673	1968	**£4**	**£1.50**	
High School Confidential	7"	HMV	POP557	1958	**£60**	**£30**	
Message To Martha – From Adam	7" EP	Parlophone	GEP8929	1965	**£8**	**£4**	
On The Move	LP	Parlophone	PMC1228	1964	**£25**	**£10**	
Poor Me	78	Parlophone	R4623	1960	**£20**	**£10**	
Runk Bunk	7"	Top Rank	JAR126	1959	**£15**	**£7.50**	
Songs And Things	7" EP	Parlophone	GEP8939	1965	**£10**	**£5**	
To Hell With Love	7"	Parlophone	R5649	1967	**£4**	**£1.50**	
Top Of The Pops	7" EP	Parlophone	GEP8893	1964	**£10**	**£5**	
What Do You Want?	78	Parlophone	R4591	1959	**£20**	**£10**	
What More Can Anyone Do	7"	Parlophone	R5556	1967	**£4**	**£1.50**	

FAITH, GEORGE

Title	Format	Label	Cat. No.	Year			Notes
To Be A Lover	LP	Island	ILPS9504	1977	**£10**	**£4**	

FAITH NO MORE

Title	Format	Label	Cat. No.	Year			Notes
Anne's Song	12"	Slash	LASHX18	1988	**£8**	**£4**	
Anne's Song	7"	Slash	LASHP18	1988	**£6**	**£2.50**	*picture disc*
Epic	7"	Slash	LASPD21	1990	**£5**	**£2**	*shaped picture disc*
Epic	CD-s	Slash	LASCD21	1990	**£5**	**£2**	
Epic	CD-s	Slash	LASCD26	1990	**£5**	**£2**	
From Out Of Nowhere	CD-s	Slash	LASCD24	1990	**£5**	**£2**	
King For A Day	CD	Slash		199–	**£15**	**£6**	*Australian with bonus 6 track CD of B sides and alternate versions*

FAITHFUL, AUSTIN

Title	Format	Label	Cat. No.	Year			Notes
Ain't That Peculiar	7"	Pyramid	PYR6042	1968	**£8**	**£4**	
Eternal Love	7"	Pyramid	PYR6028	1968	**£8**	**£4**	*Roland Alphonso B side*
Uncle Joe	7"	Blue Cat	BS140	1968	**£6**	**£2.50**	

FAITHFULL, MARIANNE

Marianne Faithfull's current acclaim as a convincing Kurt Weill interpreter, together with the worldly wise aura she projects as a successful media personality, has ensured that interest in the recordings of her youth remains high – with the two Rolling Stones songs 'As Tears Go By' and 'Sister Morphine' acting as brackets.

Title	Format	Label	Cat. No.	Year			Notes
A Bientôt Nous Deux	7" EP	Decca	457094	1965	**£20**	**£10**	*French*
As Tears Go By	7"	Decca	F11923	1964	**£4**	**£1.50**	
Blowing In The Wind	7"	Decca	F12007	1964	**£5**	**£2**	
Come And Stay With Me	7"	Decca	F12075	1965	**£4**	**£1.50**	
Come And Stay With Me	7" EP	Decca	457068	1965	**£15**	**£7.50**	*French*
Come My Way	LP	Decca	LK4688	1965	**£25**	**£10**	
Conversation With Marianne Faithfull	CD	Island	MFCCD1	1987	**£20**	**£8**	*promo*
Coquillages	7" EP	Decca	457119	1966	**£20**	**£10**	*French*
Counting	7"	Decca	F12443	1966	**£4**	**£1.50**	
Counting	7" EP	Decca	457125	1966	**£15**	**£7.50**	*French*
Faithful Forever	LP	London	LL3/PS482	1966	**£25**	**£10**	*US*
Go Away From My World	LP	London	LL3/PS452	1965	**£25**	**£10**	*US*
Greensleeves	7" EP	Decca	457049	1964	**£25**	**£12.50**	*French*
Hier Ou Demain	7" EP	Decca	457139	1967	**£20**	**£10**	*French*
Is This What I Get For Loving You	7"	Decca	F12524	1966	**£4**	**£1.50**	
Love In A Mist	LP	Decca	LK/SKL4854	1967	**£30**	**£15**	

Marianne Faithfull	7" EP	Decca	DFE8624	1965	£12	£6	
Marianne Faithfull	LP	Decca	LK4689	1965	£30	£15	
North Country Maid	LP	Decca	LK4778	1966	£30	£15	
Sister Morphine	7"	Decca	F12889	1969	£25	£12.50	
Summer Nights	7"	Decca	F12193	1965	£4	£1.50	
Summer Nights	7" EP	Decca	457085	1965	£15	£7.50	*French*
This Little Bird	7"	Decca	F12162	1965	£4	£1.50	
Tomorrow's Calling	7"	Decca	F12408	1966	£4	£1.50	
Yesterday	7"	Decca	F12268	1965	£4	£1.50	
Yesterday	7" EP	Decca	457097	1965	£15	£7.50	*French*

FAITHFUL BREATH

Fading Beauty	LP	Fb	AA6963233	1973	£30	£15	*German*

FALCONS

Billy The Kid	7"	London	HLU10146	1967	£5	£2	
I Found A Love	7"	London	HLK9565	1962	£30	£15	
You're So Fine	7"	London	HLT8876	1959	£60	£30	

FALCONS (2)

Stampede	7"	Philips	BF1297	1964	£6	£2.50	

FALCONS (3)

Fever	LP	Ariola	85067	1970	£15	£6	*German*

FALL

Bingo Masters Breakout	7"	Step Forward	SF7	1978	£5	£2	
Fall In A Hole	LP	Flying Nun	MARK1/2	1983	£30	£15	*New Zealand, with 12"*
Fiery Jack	7"	Step Forward	SF13	1980	£5	£2	*2 picture sleeves*
Grotesque	LP	Rough Trade	ROUGH18	1980	£10	£4	
It's The New Thing	7"	Step Forward	SF9	1978	£4	£1.50	
Jerusalem	CD-s	Beggars Banquet	FALL2CD	1988	£6	£2.50	*3" single*
Kicker Conspiracy	7"	Rough Trade	RT143	1983	£6	£2.50	*double picture sleeve*
Marquis Cha Cha	7"	Kamera	ERA014	1982	£15	£7.50	
Popcorn Double Feature	CD-s	Cog Sinister	SINCD5	1990	£5	£2	
Rowche Rumble	7"	Step Forward	SF11	1979	£4	£1.50	
Selections From The Infotainment Scan	CD	Matador	PRCD5094	1993	£20	£8	*with new live track*
Slates	10"	Rough Trade	RT071	1981	£6	£2.50	
Telephone Thing	CD-s	Cog Sinister	SINCD4	1990	£5	£2	
Totale's Turns	LP	Rough Trade	ROUGH10	1980	£10	£4	
White Lightning	CD-s	Cog Sinister	SINCD6	1990	£5	£2	

FALLEN ANGELS

Fallen Angels	LP	London	HAZ/SHZ8359	1968	£30	£15	
It's A Long Way Down	LP	Roulette	SR42011	1968	£100	£50	*US*

FALLIN, JOHNNY

Party Kiss	7"	Capitol	CL15043	1959	£15	£7.50	
Wild Streak	7"	Capitol	CL15091	1959	£25	£12.50	

FALLING LEAVES

Beggar's Parade	7"	Decca	F12420	1966	£10	£5	
She Loves To Be Loved	7"	Parlophone	R5233	1965	£30	£15	

FALTSKOG, AGNETHA

The blonde singer from Abba was an established solo artist in Sweden before becoming a member of the successful group, and for a time reverted to her solo career after Abba disbanded, until deciding to withdraw completely from public life.

Agnetha	LP	Cupol	CLPL1002	197–	£12	£5	*Swedish*
Agnetha	LP	Cupol	CLP64	1968	£25	£10	*Swedish*
Agnetha	LP	Embassy	EMB31094	1974	£40	£20	
Agnetha Faltskog	LP	Cupol		1972	£12	£5	*Swedish*
Agnetha Vol. 2	LP	Cupol	CLP80	1969	£20	£8	*Swedish*
Agnetha Vol. 2	LP	Cupol	CLPL1003	197–	£12	£5	*Swedish*
Basta	LP	Cupol	CLPL1023	1973	£30	£15	*Swedish*
Can't Shake Loose	7"	Epic	WA3812	1983	£12	£6	*picture disc*
Can't Shake Loose	7"	Epic	EPCA3812	1983	£8	£4	*poster picture sleeve*
Elva Kvinnor I Ett Hus	LP	Cupol	CLPS351	1975	£12	£5	*Swedish*
Heat Is On	7"	Epic	WA3436	1983	£15	£7.50	*picture disc*
Nar En Vacker Tanke Blir En Sang	LP	Cupol	CLPN348	1971	£30	£15	*Swedish*
Som Jag Ar	LP	Cupol	CLPL1016	197–	£12	£5	*Swedish*
Som Jag Ar	LP	Cupol	CLPN345	1970	£25	£10	*Swedish*
Tio Ar Med	LP	Cupol	CLPS352	1979	£12	£5	*Swedish*

FAME, GEORGIE

Georgie Fame's lengthy and still-flourishing career (his earliest recordings are as a member of Billy Fury's backing group) has produced few real collectors' items. Of his series of distinctive, jazz-inflected albums, only the first is in the same price league as his contemporaries – the others sold well when new, but are clearly considered by modern collectors to be too polished and too far removed from how British R&B should sound. Two scarce early singles were credited to the Blue Flames, with no mention of Georgie Fame's name. They are listed in this guide under the Blue Flames.

Bend A Little	7"	Columbia	DB7328	1964	£4	£1.50	
Do Re Mi	7"	Columbia	DB7255	1964	£5	£2	
Do The Dog	7" EP	Columbia	ESRF1516	1964	£15	£7.50	*French*
Fame At Last	7" EP	Columbia	SEG8393	1964	£10	£5	

Fame At Last	LP	Columbia	33SX1638	1964	£20	£8	
Fats For Fame	7" EP	Columbia	SEG8406	1965	£12	£6	
Georgie Does His Own Thing With Strings	LP	CBS	(S)63650	1969	£12	£5	
Get Away	7"	208 Luxembourg		1964	£8	£4	*1 sided promo*
Get Away	7" EP	Columbia	SEG8518	1966	£10	£5	
Get Away	7" EP	Columbia	ESRF1796	1966	£10	£5	*French*
Get Away	LP	Imperial	LP9331/12331	1966	£15	£6	*US*
Getaway	7"	Columbia	DB7946	1966	£4	£1.50	
Hall Of Fame	LP	Columbia	SX6120	1967	£12	£5	
In The Meantime	7"	Columbia	DB7494	1965	£4	£1.50	
In The Meantime	7" EP	Columbia	ESRF1645	1964	£15	£7.50	*French*
Knock On Wood	7" EP	CBS	EP6363	1967	£8	£4	
Like We Used To Be	7"	Columbia	DB7633	1965	£4	£1.50	
Like We Used To Be	7" EP	Columbia	ESRF1706	1965	£10	£5	*French*
Move It On Over	7" EP	Columbia	SEG8454	1965	£12	£6	
R&B At The Flamingo	7" EP	Columbia	SEG8382	1964	£12	£6	
R&B At The Flamingo	LP	Columbia	SX1599	1964	£30	£15	
Rhythm And Blue Beat	7" EP	Columbia	SEG8334	1964	£15	£7.50	
Seventh Son	LP	CBS	63786	1969	£10	£4	
Shop Around	7"	Columbia	DB7193	1964	£6	£2.50	
Shorty	LP	Epic	BN26563	1968	£30	£15	*German*
Sitting In The Park	7"	Columbia	DB8096	1966	£4	£1.50	
Sitting In The Park	7" EP	Columbia	ESRF1848	1967	£10	£5	*French*
Somebody Stole My Thunder	7"	CBS	5035	1970	£10	£5	
Something	7"	Columbia	DB7727	1965	£4	£1.50	
Something	7" EP	Columbia	ESRF1751	1966	£10	£5	*French*
Sound Venture	LP	Columbia	SX6076	1966	£15	£6	
Sunny	7"	Columbia	DB8015	1966	£4	£1.50	
Sweet Things	LP	Columbia	SX6043	1966	£20	£8	
Third Face Of Fame	LP	CBS	(S)63293	1968	£12	£5	
Two Faces Of Fame	LP	CBS	63018	1967	£10	£4	
Yeh Yeh	7"	Columbia	DB7428	1964	£50	£25	*promo, picture sleeve*
Yeh Yeh	7" EP	Columbia	ESRF1618	1964	£12	£6	*French*
Yeh Yeh	LP	Imperial	LP9282/12282	1965	£15	£6	*US*

FAMILY

Family's first single, 'Scene Thru The Eye Of A Lens', is something of a psychedelic classic, but has only very recently been reissued on a CD album. All the members of Traffic were also involved in the making of the record, with Stevie Winwood playing the vital mellotron part. *Music In A Doll's House* continued the Traffic connection, being to some extent taken over by Dave Mason, who produced the record and played on it. It is a wonderful LP, however, and proof that the real sixties gems have already been discovered, and do not cost a fortune. Subsequent Family records are increasingly ordinary, although each undoubtedly has its moments, and they are all highlighted by the extraordinary Roger Chapman voice.

Family Entertainment	LP	Reprise	RSLP6340	1969	£15	£6	*with poster, stereo*
Family Entertainment	LP	Reprise	RLP6340	1969	£30	£15	*with poster, mono*
Larf And Sing	7"	Reprise	SAM1	1971	£8	£4	*promo*
Me My Friend	7"	Reprise	RS23270	1968	£4	£1.50	
Music In A Doll's House	LP	Reprise	RSLP6312	1968	£20	£8	*with poster, stereo*
Music In A Doll's House	LP	Reprise	RLP6312	1968	£50	£25	*with poster, mono*
No Mule's Fool	7"	Reprise	RS27001	1969	£5	£2	*picture sleeve*
Scene Thru The Eye Of A Lens	7"	Liberty	LBF15031	1967	£100	£50	
Second Generation Woman	7"	Reprise	RS23315	1968	£4	£1.50	
Song For Me	LP	Reprise	RSLP9001	1970	£10	£4	
Today	7"	Reprise	RS27005	1970	£5	£2	*picture sleeve*

FAMILY CIRCLE

Phoenix Reggae	7"	Attack	AT8001	1969	£5	£2	

FAMILY DOGG

Family Dogg	7"	MGM	MGM1360	1967	£4	£1.50	
Way Of Life	LP	Bell	SBLL122	1969	£15	£6	

FAMILY OF APOSTOLIC

Family Of Apostolic	LP	Vanguard	SDVL1	1969	£20	£8	*double*

FAMOUS JUG BAND

Chameleon	LP	Liberty	LBS83355	1970	£15	£6	
Only Friend I Own	7"	Liberty	LBF15224	1969	£4	£1.50	
Sunshine Possibilities	LP	Liberty	LBS83263	1969	£25	£10	

FAMOUS WARD SINGERS

Famous Ward Singers	10" LP	London	LZC14013	1955	£10	£4	
Famous Ward Singers Vol. 1	7" EP	London	EZC19024	1958	£12	£6	
Famous Ward Singers Vol. 2	7" EP	London	EZC19033	1958	£8	£4	
Famous Ward Singers Vol. 3	7" EP	London	EZC19034	1958	£10	£5	

FAN CLUB

Avenue	7"	M&S	SJP791	1978	£8	£4	

FANATICS

Despite an obvious Velvet Underground fixation, the Fanatics actually comprised three quarters of the membership of the future Ocean Colour Scene.

Suburban Love Songs	12"	Chapter 22	12CHAP38	1989	£20	£10	

FANKHAUSER, MERRELL

Title	Format	Label	Cat. No.	Year	Price	Price	Notes
Merrell Fankhauser	LP	Maui	101	1976	**£20**	**£8**	*US*
Merrell Fankhauser & His HMS Bounty	LP	Shamley	SS701	1968	**£25**	**£10**	*US*

FANSHAWE, DAVID

Title	Format	Label	Cat. No.	Year	Price	Price	Notes
Sound Odyssey	LP	KPM	KPM1152	1975	**£15**	**£6**	

FANTASTIC BAGGYS

Title	Format	Label	Cat. No.	Year	Price	Price	Notes
Summer Means Fun	7"	United Artists	UP36142	1976	**£4**	**£1.50**	*Jan And Dean B side*
Tell 'Em I'm Surfin'	LP	Imperial	LP9270/12270	1964	**£75**	**£37.50**	*US*

FANTASTIC DEE-JAYS

Title	Format	Label	Cat. No.	Year	Price	Price	Notes
Fantastic Dee Jays	LP	Stone		1966	**£400**	**£250**	*US*

FANTASTIC FOUR

Title	Format	Label	Cat. No.	Year	Price	Price	Notes
Fantastic Four	LP	Tamla Motown	(S)TML11105	1969	**£20**	**£8**	
I Love You Madly	7"	Tamla Motown	TMG678	1968	**£10**	**£5**	

FANTASTICS

Title	Format	Label	Cat. No.	Year	Price	Price	Notes
Baby Make Your Own Sweet Music	7"	MGM	MGM1434	1968	**£4**	**£1.50**	

FANTASY

Title	Format	Label	Cat. No.	Year	Price	Price	Notes
Paint A Picture	LP	Polydor	2383246	1973	**£200**	**£100**	
Politely Insane	7"	Polydor	2058405	1973	**£20**	**£10**	

FANTONI, BARRY

Title	Format	Label	Cat. No.	Year	Price	Price	Notes
Little Man In A Little Box	7"	Fontana	TF707	1966	**£15**	**£7.50**	

FAPARDOKLY

Title	Format	Label	Cat. No.	Year	Price	Price	Notes
Fapardokly	LP	V.I.P.	250	1966	**£1000**	**£700**	*US*
Fapardokly	LP	Psycho	PSYCHO5	1983	**£10**	**£4**	

FAR CRY

Title	Format	Label	Cat. No.	Year	Price	Price	Notes
Far Cry	LP	Vanguard	SVRL19041	1969	**£30**	**£15**	

FAR EAST FAMILY BAND

Title	Format	Label	Cat. No.	Year	Price	Price	Notes
Cave Down To Earth	LP	Muland	CD7139M	1975	**£25**	**£10**	*Japanese*
Far Out	LP	Denon	5047	1975	**£25**	**£10**	*Japanese*
Nipponjin	LP	Vertigo	6370850	1975	**£25**	**£10**	
Parallel World	LP	Muland	LQ7002M	1976	**£25**	**£10**	*Japanese*
Tenkeyin	LP	All Ears	114797	1977	**£20**	**£8**	*US*
Torn Hatano	LP	Muland	7024	1977	**£25**	**£10**	*Japanese*

FAR OUT

Title	Format	Label	Cat. No.	Year	Price	Price	Notes
Far Out	LP	Denon		1972	**£200**	**£100**	*Japanese*

FARAWAY FOLK

Title	Format	Label	Cat. No.	Year	Price	Price	Notes
Introducing The Faraway Folk	7" EP	RA	EP7001	197–	**£15**	**£7.50**	
Live At Bolton	LP	RA	RALP6006ST	1970	**£60**	**£30**	
On The Radio	LP	RA	RALP6019	1974	**£30**	**£15**	
Only Authorised Employees To Break Bottles	LP	RA	RALP6022	1974	**£25**	**£10**	
Seasonal Man	LP	Ra	RALP6029	1975	**£150**	**£75**	
Shadow Of A Pie	7"	Tabitha	TAB3	197–	**£5**	**£2**	
Time And Tide	LP	RA	RALP6012ST	1972	**£75**	**£37.50**	

FARDON, DON

Title	Format	Label	Cat. No.	Year	Price	Price	Notes
Indian Reservation	7"	Pye	7N25437	1967	**£4**	**£1.50**	
Lament Of The Cherokee Indian Reservation	LP	GNP	2044	1968	**£10**	**£4**	*US*
Letter	7" EP	Vogue	EPL8583	1967	**£15**	**£7.50**	*French*

FARINA, RICHARD & ERIC VON SCHMIDT

Title	Format	Label	Cat. No.	Year	Price	Price	Notes
Dick Farina & Eric Von Schmidt	LP	Folklore	FLEUT7	1963	**£50**	**£25**	

FARINA, RICHARD & MIMI

Richard and Mimi Farina were a folk duo typical of the many folk acts that were a dominant strain within the American music of the early sixties. Most managed to come up with a significant song or two – the Farinas' included 'Pack Up All Your Sorrows' and 'Hard Lovin' Loser', which were recorded by Judy Collins. Richard Farina was killed in a motor-cycle accident in 1966, but his wife Mimi, who is Joan Baez's sister, has managed to follow a reasonably successful career since as a musician and actress.

Title	Format	Label	Cat. No.	Year	Price	Price	Notes
Best Of Richard And Mimi Farina	LP	Vanguard	VSD21/22	1973	**£12**	**£5**	*double*
Celebrations For A Grey Day	LP	Fontana	(S)TFL6060	1965	**£12**	**£5**	
Memories	LP	Vanguard	VSD79263	1968	**£10**	**£4**	*US*
Refelections In A Crystal Wind	LP	Fontana	(S)TFL6075	1965	**£12**	**£5**	
Richard & Mimi Farina	LP	Vanguard	VSD79174	1965	**£12**	**£5**	*US*
Richard Farina	LP	Vanguard	VSD79281	1968	**£10**	**£4**	*US*

FARINAS

The Farinas were a blues and soul group from Leicester, but as soon as they began to write their own material, they changed their name – to Family.

Title	Format	Label	Cat. No.	Year	Mint	VG	Notes
Bye Bye Johnny	7"	Victor Buckland Sound Studio		1964	£500	£330	
I Like It Like That	7"	Fontana	TF493	1964	£60	£30	

FARLOW, TAL

Title	Format	Label	Cat. No.	Year	Mint	VG	Notes
Interpretations	LP	Columbia	33CX10029	1956	£30	£15	
Swinging Guitar	LP	Columbia	33CX10132	1959	£15	£6	
Tal Farlow	10" LP	Columbia	33C9041	1957	£25	£10	
Tal Farlow	10" LP	Columbia	33C9052	1957	£15	£6	

FARLOWE, CHRIS

Title	Format	Label	Cat. No.	Year	Mint	VG	Notes
14 Things To Think About	LP	Immediate	IMLP005	1966	£30	£15	
Air Travel	7"	Decca	F11536	1962	£20	£10	
Art Of Chris Farlowe	LP	Immediate	IMLP006	1966	£30	£15	
Best Of Chris Farlowe Vol. 1	LP	Immediate	IMLP/IMCP010	1968	£20	£8	
Buzz With The Fuzz	7"	Columbia	DB7614	1965	£125	£62.50	
Chris Farlowe	7" EP	Decca	DFE8665	1965	£40	£20	
Chris Farlowe	LP	Regal	REG2025	1968	£15	£6	export
Chris Farlowe And The Thunderbirds	LP	Columbia	SX/SCX6034	1966	£40	£20	
Dawn	7"	Immediate	IM074	1969	£4	£1.50	
Fool	7"	Immediate	IM016	1965	£5	£2	
From Here To Mama Rosa	LP	Polydor	2425029	1970	£10	£4	
Girl Trouble	7"	Columbia	DB7237	1964	£8	£4	
Handbags And Gladrags	7"	Immediate	IM065	1967	£4	£1.50	
Hits	7" EP	Immediate	IMEP004	1966	£15	£7.50	
Hound Dog	7"	Columbia	DB7379	1964	£8	£4	
I Remember	7"	Columbia	DB7120	1963	£8	£4	
In The Midnight Hour	7" EP	Immediate	IMEP001	1965	£25	£12.50	
Just A Dream	7"	Columbia	DB7311	1964	£8	£4	
Just A Dream	7"	Columbia	DB7983	1966	£6	£2.50	
Last Goodbye	LP	Immediate	IMLP021	1969	£40	£20	
Moanin'	7"	Immediate	IM056	1967	£4	£1.50	
My Way Of Giving	7"	Immediate	IM041	1967	£6	£2.50	
Out Of Time	7"	Immediate	IM035	1966	£4	£1.50	
Out Of Time	7" EP	Columbia	ESRF1806	1966	£20	£10	French
Paint It Black	7"	Immediate	IM071	1968	£5	£2	
Paperman Fly In The Sky	7"	Immediate	IM066	1968	£5	£2	
Ride On Baby	7"	Immediate	IM038	1966	£4	£1.50	
Ride On Baby	7" EP	Columbia	ESRF1837	1966	£20	£10	French
Stormy Monday	7" EP	Island	IEP709	1966	£60	£30	
Stormy Monday	LP	MFP	MFP1186	1967	£10	£4	
Think	7"	Immediate	IM023	1966	£5	£2	
Yesterday's Paper	7" EP	Columbia	ESRF1875	1967	£20	£10	French
Yesterday's Papers	7"	Immediate	IM049	1967	£4	£1.50	

FARM

Title	Format	Label	Cat. No.	Year	Mint	VG	Notes
Hearts And Minds	12"	Skysaw	END1	1984	£6	£2.50	

FARM BAND

Title	Format	Label	Cat. No.	Year	Mint	VG	Notes
Farm Band	LP	Mescalero	S334	1972	£30	£15	US double

FARMER, ART

Title	Format	Label	Cat. No.	Year	Mint	VG	Notes
Art Farmer	7" EP	Vogue	EPV1045	1955	£5	£2	
Art Farmer Quintet	10" LP	Esquire	20087	1957	£40	£20	
Art Farmer Quintet	10" LP	Esquire	20057	1956	£50	£25	
Aztec Suite	LP	London	LTZT15198	1960	£20	£8	
Brass Shout	LP	London	LTZT15184	1960	£20	£8	
Charts	LP	Esquire	32042	1958	£20	£8	
Early Art	LP	Esquire	32120	1961	£20	£8	
Interaction	LP	London	HAK/SHK8135	1964	£15	£6	
Modern Art	LP	London	LTZT15167/SAHT6028	1959	£20	£8	
Music For That Wild Party	LP	Esquire	32037	1958	£25	£10	
Plays The Great Jazz Hits	LP	CBS	(S)BPG63113	1968	£12	£5	
Portrait	LP	Contemporary	LAC12197	1959	£20	£8	
Work Of Art	10" LP	Esquire	20033	1954	£40	£20	

FARMER, JULES

Title	Format	Label	Cat. No.	Year	Mint	VG	Notes
Love Me Now	7"	London	HLP8967	1959	£5	£2	

FARMER, MYLENE

Title	Format	Label	Cat. No.	Year	Mint	VG	Notes
Ainsi Sois-Je	CD	Polydor	8355642	1990	£20	£8	
Ainsi Sois-Je	CD-s	Polydor	0803602	1989	£30	£15	CD video

FARMLIFE

Title	Format	Label	Cat. No.	Year	Mint	VG	Notes
Big Country	7"	Whaam!	WHAAM13	1983	£30	£15	test pressing

FARNER, MARK & DON BREWER

Title	Format	Label	Cat. No.	Year	Mint	VG	Notes
Monumental Funk	LP	Quadico	Q7401	1974	£20	£8	US picture disc

FARNON, ROBERT

Title	Format	Label	Cat. No.	Year	Mint	VG	Notes
Canadian Impressions	LP	Decca	LK4119	1955	£15	£6	
Captain Horatio Hornblower	LP	Delyse	ECB3157/DS6057	1960	£50	£25	
Pop Makes Progress	LP	Chapter One	CHS804	1970	£30	£15	with Tony Coe

FARO, WAYNE SCHMALTZ BAND

Title	Format	Label	Cat. No.	Year	Mint	VG	Notes
There's Still Time	7"	Deram	DM222	1969	£5	£2	

FARON'S FLAMINGOES

See If She Cares	7"	Oriole	CB1834	1963	**£8**	**£4**	
Shake Sherry	7"	Oriole	CB1867	1963	**£10**	**£5**	

FARR, GARY

Addressed To The Censors Of Love	LP	Atco	SD7034	1973	**£20**	**£8**	*US*
Dem Bones Dem Bones Dem T-Bones	7" EP	Columbia	SEG8414	1965	**£100**	**£50**	*with the T-Bones*
Everyday	7"	Marmalade	598007	1968	**£4**	**£1.50**	*with Kevin Westlake*
Give All She's Got	7"	Columbia	DB7608	1965	**£25**	**£12.50**	*with the T-Bones*
Hey Daddy	7"	Marmalade	598017	1969	**£5**	**£2**	
Strange Fruit	LP	CBS	64138	1971	**£25**	**£10**	
Take Something With You	LP	Marmalade	608013	1969	**£30**	**£15**	

FARRELL, DO & DENA

Young Magic	7"	HMV	POP427	1957	**£6**	**£2.50**	

FARRELL, JOE

Joe Farrell Quartet	LP	Philips	6308046	1970	**£10**	**£4**	

FARREN, MICK

Carnivorous Circus (Mona)	LP	Transatlantic	TRA212	1970	**£40**	**£20**	
Vampires Stole My Lunch Money	LP	Logo	LOGO2010	1978	**£10**	**£4**	

FARRIERS

Farriers	LP	Broadside	BRO112	1969	**£15**	**£6**	

FARRIERS & KEMPION

Brummagem Ballads	LP	Broadside	BRO119	1976	**£12**	**£5**	

FASCINATIONS

Girls Are Out To Get You	7"	Sue	WI4049	1968	**£15**	**£7.50**	
Girls Are Out To Get You	7"	Stateside	SS594	1967	**£40**	**£20**	
Girls Are Out To Get You	7"	Mojo	2092004	1971	**£4**	**£1.50**	

FASCINATORS

Chapel Bells	7"	Capitol	CL14942	1958	**£200**	**£100**	*best auctioned*
Oh Rose Marie	7"	Capitol	CL15062	1959	**£50**	**£25**	

FASHIONS

I.O.U.	7"	Stateside	SS2115	1968	**£5**	**£2**	
I.O.U.	7"	Evolution	E2444	1969	**£4**	**£1.50**	

FAST BREEDER & THE RADIO ACTORS

Nuclear Waste	7"	Virgin	NONUKE235	1978	**£6**	**£2.50**	
Nuclear Waste	7"	Virgin	NONUKE235	1978	**£15**	**£7.50**	*picture sleeve*

FAST CARS

Kids Just Wanna Dance	7"	Streets Ahead	SA3	1979	**£40**	**£20**	

FAST EDDIE

My Babe	7"	Well Suspect	BLAM001	1982	**£5**	**£2**	

FAST SET

Junction One	7"	Axis	AXIS1	1980	**£10**	**£5**	

FAT

Fat	LP	RCA	LPS4368	1970	**£15**	**£6**	

FAT MATTRESS

Even while still a member of the Jimi Hendrix Experience, bassist Noel Redding began playing with his own group in order to switch back to the guitar he had always really preferred. Fat Mattress inevitably attracted attention simply because of Redding's presence, but the sad fact was that the most interesting aspect of the group was the cover of the first LP, which opens out into a two-foot-square sheet of card.

Fat Mattress	LP	Polydor	583056	1969	**£12**	**£5**	
Fat Mattress 2	LP	Polydor	2383025	1970	**£10**	**£4**	
Highway	7"	Polydor	2058053	1970	**£5**	**£2**	
Magic Forest	7"	Polydor	56367	1969	**£5**	**£2**	
Naturally	7"	Polydor	56352	1969	**£4**	**£1.50**	

FATBACK BAND

Keep On Steppin'	LP	Polydor	2391143	1975	**£10**	**£4**	
Yum Yum	LP	Polydor	2391184	1975	**£10**	**£4**	

FATHERS ANGELS

Bok To Bach	7"	MGM	MGM1459	1968	**£75**	**£37.50**	

FATS & THE CHESSMEN

Big Ben Twist	7"	Pye	7N25122	1962	**£4**	**£1.50**	

FAUN

Faun	LP	Gregar	GG70000	1969	**£40**	**£20**	*US*

FAUST

The first record issued by the German group, Faust, was a clear vinyl disc, housed in a clear plastic sleeve printed with the X-ray photograph of a hand, and with a clear plastic insert containing red printed sleeve notes, mostly in German, and having no obvious connection with the music. With expectations raised for the record's contents to be somewhat on the weird side, the music does not disappoint. Constructed as a collage, the music places an emphasis on interesting sounds rather than obvious melodies or rhythms, shifting rapidly through a succession of different short segments. Almost before the listener has time to work out what is going on at any one time, Faust have shifted on to something else. A similar approach has been followed by artists like Henry Cow and John Zorn, both of whom have actually been rather better at it, but then they were not playing in 1971. Faust are becoming increasingly collectable, with even the once ubiquitous *Faust Tapes* (originally sold for the price of a single) now qualifying for inclusion in this guide.

Extracts From Faust Party 3	7"	Recommended	RR1.5	1980	£**8**	£**4**	
Faust	LP	Recommended	RRONE	1979	£**15**	£**6**	*clear vinyl*
Faust	LP	Polydor	2310142	1971	£**30**	£**15**	*clear vinyl*
Faust	LP	Polydor	2310142	1971	£**20**	£**8**	
Faust IV	LP	Virgin	V2004	1973	£**20**	£**8**	
Faust Party 3 Extracts 2	7"	Recommended	RR6.5	1981	£**8**	£**4**	
Faust Tapes	LP	Recommended	RRSIX	1980	£**12**	£**5**	*in plastic bag*
Faust Tapes	LP	Virgin	VC501	1973	£**10**	£**4**	
Last LP	LP	Recommended	ReR36	1988	£**25**	£**10**	
Last LP	LP	Recommended	ReR36	1988	£**40**	£**20**	*with print*
Munich & Elsewhere	LP	Recommended	RR25	1986	£**25**	£**10**	*white vinyl*
So Far	7"	Polydor	2001299	1972	£**5**	£**2**	
So Far	LP	Polydor	2310196	1972	£**50**	£**25**	*with 10 prints*
So Far	LP	Recommended	RR2	1979	£**20**	£**8**	*with 10 prints*

FAVOURITE SONS

That Driving Beat	7"	Mercury	MF911	1965	£**60**	£**30**	

FAWKES, WALLY

Fawkes On Holiday	10" LP	Decca	LF1312	1958	£**15**	£**6**	

FAWKES, WALLY & BRUCE TURNER

Fawkes–Turner Sextet	10" LP	Decca	LF1214	1956	£**25**	£**10**	

FAY, BILL

Bill Fay	LP	Nova	SDN12	1970	£**25**	£**10**	
Some Good Advice	7"	Deram	DM143	1967	£**30**	£**15**	
Time Of Last Persecution	LP	Deram	SML1079	1971	£**50**	£**25**	

FAYE, FRANCIS

Frenesi	7"	HMV	POP898	1961	£**4**	£**1.50**	
I Wish I Could Shimmy Like My Sister Kate	7"	Vogue	V9186	1961	£**6**	£**2.50**	

FEAR OF FALLING

Like A Lion	7"	Excellent	XL7	1983	£**15**	£**7.50**	

FEARNS BRASS FOUNDRY

Don't Change It	7"	Decca	F12721	1968	£**8**	£**4**	
Love, Sink And Drown	7"	Decca	F12835	1968	£**5**	£**2**	

FEATHER, LEONARD

Hi Fi Suite	LP	MGM	C762	1957	£**10**	£**4**	*with Dick Hyman*
One World Jazz	LP	Philips	BBL7361	1960	£**10**	£**4**	
Winter Sequence	10" LP	MGM	D135	1955	£**40**	£**20**	

FEATHERS, CHARLIE & MAC CURTIS

Rockabilly Kings	LP	Polydor	2310293	1974	£**10**	£**4**	

FEDERAL DUCK

Federal Duck	LP	Musicor	MS3162	1968	£**20**	£**8**	*US*

FEDERALS

Boot Hill	7"	Parlophone	R5013	1963	£**5**	£**2**	
Brazil	7"	Parlophone	R4988	1963	£**5**	£**2**	
Bucket Full Of Love	7"	Parlophone	R5320	1965	£**6**	£**2.50**	
Climb	7"	Parlophone	R5100	1964	£**5**	£**2**	
Marlena	7"	Parlophone	R5139	1964	£**5**	£**2**	
Twilight Time	7"	Parlophone	R5193	1964	£**5**	£**2**	

FEDERALS (2)

Federals	LP	Electrocord	EDE0202	1966	£**50**	£**25**	*Romanian*
I've Passed This Way Before	7"	Island	WI3126	1967	£**10**	£**5**	
In This World	7"	Camel	CA40	1970	£**4**	£**1.50**	
Shocking Love	7"	Island	WI3152	1968	£**10**	£**5**	
Wailing Festival	7"	High Note	HS024	1969	£**4**	£**1.50**	

FELDER'S ORIOLES

Backstreet	7"	Piccadilly	7N35332	1966	£**10**	£**5**	
Down Home Girl	7"	Piccadilly	7N35247	1965	£**10**	£**5**	
I Know You Don't Love Me No More	7"	Piccadilly	7N35311	1966	£**10**	£**5**	
Sweet Tasting Wine	7"	Piccadilly	7N35269	1965	£**10**	£**5**	

FELDMAN, MARTY

At Last The 1948 Show	LP	Pye	NPL18198	1967	£**10**	£**4**	*with John Cleese and others*
I Feel A Song Going Off	LP	Decca	LK/SKL4983	1969	£**10**	£**4**	
Marty	LP	Pye	NPL18258	1968	£**10**	£**4**	

FELDMAN, VICTOR

Arrival Of Victor Feldman	LP	Contemporary	LAC12172	1959	£20	£8	
Big Band	7" EP	Tempo	EXA29	1956	£15	£7.50	
Encore	7" EP	Esquire	EP114	1956	£15	£7.50	
In London Vol. 1	LP	Tempo	TAP8	1957	£75	£37.50	
In London Vol. 2	LP	Tempo	TAP12	1957	£50	£25	
Jimmy Deuchar–Victor Feldman Quintet	7" EP	Tempo	EXA88	1958	£15	£6	
Modern Jazz Quartet	7" EP	Esquire	EP43	1955	£15	£7.50	
Modern Jazz Quartet	7" EP	Esquire	EP54	1955	£15	£7.50	
Modern Jazz Quartet	7" EP	Esquire	EP104	1956	£15	£7.50	
Modern Jazz Quartet	7" EP	Esquire	EP35	1955	£15	£6	
Modern Jazz Quintet/Sextet	7" EP	Esquire	EP84	1956	£15	£7.50	
Modern Jazz Quintet/Sextet	7" EP	Esquire	EP64	1955	£15	£7.50	
Multi-Recording Session	10" LP	Esquire	20046	1955	£40	£20	
Quartet Vol. 1	7" EP	Tempo	EXA57	1957	£15	£6	
Transatlantic Alliance	LP	Tempo	TAP19	1958	£100	£50	
Vibes To The Power Of Three	LP	Top Rank	30007	1960	£20	£8	*with Terry Gibbs & Larry Bunker*
Victor Feldman Modern Jazz Quartet	10" LP	Tempo	LAP6	1956	£50	£25	
Victor Feldman Ninetet	7" EP	Tempo	EXA67	1957	£15	£6	
Victor Feldman's Sextet	10" LP	Tempo	LAP5	1955	£75	£37.50	
Victor Feldman–Dizzy Reece	7" EP	Tempo	EXA85	1957	£15	£6	
With Kenny Graham	10" LP	Esquire	20064	1956	£25	£10	
With Mallets Aforethought	7" EP	Top Rank	JKP2046	1960	£15	£6	

FELICE, DEE TRIO

In The Heat	LP	Bethlehem	B1000	1969	£20	£8	US

FELIUS ANDROMEDA

Meditations	7"	Decca	F12694	1967	£30	£15	

FELIX, JULIE

Changes	LP	Fontana	(S)TL5368	1966	£10	£4	
Flowers	LP	Fontana	(S)TL5437	1967	£10	£4	
Julie Felix	LP	Decca	LK4626	1964	£10	£4	
Julie Felix In Concert	LP	World Record Club	ST842	1968	£10	£4	
Second Album	LP	Decca	LK4724	1965	£10	£4	
Sings Dylan & Guthrie	LP	Decca	LK4683	1965	£10	£4	
Third Album	LP	Decca	LK4820	1966	£10	£4	
This World Goes Round And Round	LP	Fontana	(S)TL5473	1968	£10	£4	

FELIX, LENNIE

Cat Meets Mice	LP	Columbia	33SX1298	1961	£10	£4	
Cat On A Hot Tin Piano	10" LP	Columbia	33S1144	1959	£10	£4	
Let's Put Out The Cat	LP	Top Rank	35034	1960	£10	£4	
That Cat Felix	10" LP	Nixa	NJT514	1958	£15	£6	

FELIX & HIS GUITAR

Chili Beans	7"	London	HLU8875	1959	£6	£2.50	

FELT

Index	7"	Shanghai	CUS321	1979	£30	£15	
My Face Is On Fire	7"	Cherry Red	CHERRY45	1982	£5	£2	
Primitive Painters	CD-s	Cherry Red	CDCHERRY89	1988	£5	£2	
Something Sends Me To Sleep	7"	Cherry Red	CHERRY26	1981	£6	£2.50	

FELT (2)

Felt	LP	Nasco	9006	1971	£150	£75	US

FENCE

The lone single release by the Fence is collected by fans of the Levellers, due to the fact that the latter's drummer Charlie Heather and bass player Jeremy Cunningham made their recording debut here.

Frozen Water	7"	Hag	HAG1	1987	£20	£10	

FENDA, JAYMES & THE VULCANS

Mistletoe Love	7"	Parlophone	R5210	1964	£6	£2.50	

FENDER, JAN

Holly Holy Version	7"	Fab	FAB166	1971	£5	£2	
Sea Of Love	7"	Prince Buster	PB5	1971	£5	£2	

FENDER, JAN & BUSTER

Sweet Pea	7"	Fab	FAB164	1971	£4	£1.50	

FENDERMEN

Don't You Just Know It	7"	Top Rank	JAR513	1960	£6	£2.50	
Mule Skinner Blues	7"	Top Rank	JAR395	1960	£5	£2	
Mule Skinner Blues	LP	Soma	MG1240	1960	£400	£250	US

FENMEN

Be My Girl	7"	Decca	F11955	1964	£8	£4	
California Dreamin'	7"	CBS	202075	1966	£4	£1.50	

I've Got Everything You Need	7"	Decca	F12269	1965	£4	£1.50	
Rejected	7"	CBS	202236	1966	£15	£7.50	

FENTON, SHANE & THE FENTONES

Bernard Jewry has had two separate singing careers. Best known as Alvin Stardust in the seventies, he was also Shane Fenton in the early sixties, achieving a few minor successes in a style which owed everything to Cliff Richard and Billy Fury.

Don't Do That	7"	Parlophone	R5047	1963	£4	£1.50	
Eastern Seaboard	7"	Fury	FY305	1972	£10	£5	
Fool's Paradise	7"	Parlophone	R5020	1963	£4	£1.50	
Good Rocking Tonight	LP	Contour	2870409	1974	£10	£4	
Hey Lulu	7"	Parlophone	R5131	1964	£4	£1.50	
I Ain't Got Nobody	7"	Parlophone	R4982	1963	£4	£1.50	
I'm A Moody Guy	7"	Parlophone	R4827	1961	£4	£1.50	
It's All Over Now	7"	Parlophone	R4883	1962	£5	£2	
It's Gonna Take Magic	7"	Parlophone	R4921	1962	£4	£1.50	
Too Young For Sad Memories	7"	Parlophone	R4951	1962	£4	£1.50	
Walk Away	7"	Parlophone	R4866	1962	£5	£2	

FENTONES

Breeze And I	7"	Parlophone	R4937	1962	£4	£1.50	
Mexican	7"	Parlophone	R4899	1962	£5	£2	

FENWAYS

Walk	7"	Liberty	LIB66082	1965	£6	£2.50	

FENWICK, RAY

Keep America Beautiful	LP	Decca	SKL5090	1971	£25	£10	

FENWYCK

Many Sides Of Jerry Raye Featuring Fenwyck	LP	De Ville	LP101	1967	£300	£180	*US, red vinyl*

FERGUSON, H-BOMB

Feel Like I Do	78	Esquire	10372	1954	£15	£7.50	

FERGUSON, HELENA

Where Is The Party	7"	London	HLZ10164	1967	£20	£10	

FERGUSON, JOHNNY

Angela Jones	7"	MGM	MGM1059	1960	£4	£1.50	

FERGUSON, MAYNARD

Around The Horn	LP	Emarcy	EJL1275	1958	£15	£6	
Boy With Lots Of Brass	LP	Mercury	MMC14050/ CMS18034	1960	£12	£5	
Dimensions	LP	Emarcy	EJL1287	1958	£20	£8	
Jam Session	LP	Emarcy	EJL1270	1958	£15	£6	
Jazz For Dancing	LP	Columbia	33SX1270/ SCX3338	1960	£12	£5	
M.F. Horn 2	LP	CBS	65027	1972	£10	£4	
Message From Birdland	LP	Columbia	33SX1210/ SCX3245	1960	£15	£6	
Message From Newport	LP	Columbia	33SX1146	1959	£15	£6	
Newport Suite	LP	Columbia	33SX1301/ SCX3363	1961	£12	£5	
Swingin' My Way Through College	LP	Columbia	33SX1173	1959	£12	£5	

FERKO STRING BAND

Alabama Jubilee	7"	London	HL8140	1955	£12	£6	
Ferko String Band Vol. 1	10" LP	London	HBC1064	1957	£12	£5	
Happy Days Are Here Again	7"	London	HL7052	1958	£6	£2.50	export
Happy Days Are Here Again	7"	London	HLF8215	1955	£10	£5	
Ma She's Making Eyes At Me	7"	London	HLF8183	1955	£10	£5	
Philadelphia Mummers Parade Vol. 1	7" EP	London	REF1041	1956	£6	£2.50	
Philadelphia Mummers Parade Vol. 2	7" EP	London	REF1052	1956	£6	£2.50	

FERLINGHETTI, LAWRENCE

Impeachment Of President Eisenhower	LP	Fantasy	7004	1958	£40	£20	*US, red vinyl*
Poetry Readings In The Cellar	LP	Fantasy	7002	1957	£40	£20	*US, red vinyl*

FERNANDO, PHIL

Make Ready For Love	7"	Pye	7N15142	1958	£4	£1.50	

FERNBACH, ANDY

If You Miss Your Connection	LP	Liberty	LBS83233	1969	£75	£37.50	

FERNICK, MAJA

Give Me Your Love Again	7"	Philips	6006196	1972	£5	£2	

FERRER, JOE DEVILS BOYS

Rocking Crickets	7"	Oriole	CB1629	1961	£8	£4	

FERRER, NINO

Metronomie	LP	Riviera	XCED421082U	1972	£15	£6	*French*

FERRIS, EUGENE

There Was A Smile In Your Eyes	7"	Planet	PLF112	1966	£8	£4	

FERRIS WHEEL

Can't Break The Habit	LP	Pye	NPL18203	1967	£15	£6	
Can't Stop Now	7"	Polydor	56366	1969	£4	£1.50	
Ferris Wheel	LP	Polydor	583086	1970	£10	£4	
Let It Be Me	7"	Pye	7N17538	1968	£4	£1.50	
Na Na Song	7"	Pye	7N17631	1968	£4	£1.50	
Number One Guy	7"	Pye	7N17387	1967	£8	£4	

FERRY, BRYAN

Bête Noire	CD	Virgin	CDVP2474	1988	£12	£5	*picture disc*
Bride Stripped Bare	LP	Polydor	POLD5003	1978	£100	£50	*test pressing with 2 different tracks*
Bride Stripped Bare	LP	Polydor	POLD5003	1978	£200	£100	*test pressing with 2 different tracks, proof sleeve*
Bryan Ferry Box Set	CD	Editions EG	EGBC5	1989	£25	£10	*3 disc set*
Don't Stop The Dance	12"	Editions EG	FERPX2	1985	£6	£2.50	*picture disc*
He'll Have To Go	CD-s	Editions EG	EGOCD48	1989	£6	£2.50	*3" single*
Hold On I'm Coming	12"	Polydor	PPSP10	1978	£10	£5	*promo*
In Crowd	7"	Island	WIP6196	1974	£5	£2	*picture sleeve*
Interview	CD	Virgin	DPRO12699	1994	£15	£6	*US promo*
Kiss And Tell	CD-s	Virgin	CDEP19	1988	£5	£2	
Let's Stick Together	CD-s	Virgin	CDT10	1988	£6	£2.50	*3" single*
Let's Stick Together (Remix)	CD-s	Editions EG	EGOCD44	1988	£6	£2.50	
Limbo (Latin Mix)	CD-s	Virgin	VSCD1066	1988	£6	£2.50	
Price Of Love	CD-s	Editions EG	EGOCD46	1989	£6	£2.50	
Right Stuff	CD-s	Virgin	CDEP8	1988	£6	£2.50	
These Foolish Things	CD	Polydor	8230212	1984	£12	£5	

FERRY, CATHERINE

One Two Three	7"	Barclay	BAR42	1976	£8	£4	

FERRY AID

Let It Be	12"	Sun	AIDT1	1987	£6	£2.50	

FEVER TREE

Fever Tree were one of the many San Francisco groups who got to make a few records, but never managed to consolidate them into a long-term career. The group was responsible for a terrific single, 'San Francisco Girls', which was something of a Haight-Ashbury response to the Beach Boys, with gritty vocals and a keening guitar reclaiming the California girls as their own. In general, however, Fever Tree did not feature the guitar playing enough, preferring a pseudo-classical approach which squandered the group's real strengths without replacing them with anything that was not done better by others.

Another Time Another Place	LP	MCA	MUPS374	1968	£20	£8	
Creation	LP	Uni	73067	1969	£20	£8	*US*
Fever Tree	LP	Uni	UNLS102	1968	£20	£8	
Fever Tree	LP	Uni	UNL102	1968	£25	£10	*mono*
For Sale	LP	Ampex	A10113	1970	£20	£8	*US*
San Francisco Girls	7"	MCA	MU1043	1968	£6	£2.50	

FEZA, MONGEZI

Music For Xaba	LP	Sonet	SNTF642	1975	£12	£5	

FICHTE, HUBERT

Beat And Prosa Im Star Club Hamburg	LP	Philips	843933	1964	£75	£37.50	*German, with Ian & The Zodiacs*

FICKLE FINGER

Fickle Lizzie-Anne	7"	Page One	POF150	1969	£6	£2.50	

FICKLE PICKLE

American Pie	7"	B&C	CB177	1972	£4	£1.50	
California Calling	7"	B&C	CB178	1972	£4	£1.50	
Millionaire	7"	Fontana	TF1069	1970	£5	£2	
Sinful Skinful	LP	Negram	EQ20049	1970	£50	£25	*Dutch*

FIDDLER'S DRAM

Fiddler's Dram	LP	Dingles	DID711	1980	£10	£4	
To See The Play	LP	Dingles	DIN304	1978	£12	£5	

FI-DELS

Try A Little Harder	7"	Jay Boy	BOY69	1973	£4	£1.50	

FIELD, KEITH

Day That War Broke Out	7"	Polydor	56278	1968	£6	£2.50	

FIELD MICE

Emma's House	7"	Sarah	SARAH012	1988	£5	£2	
I Can See Myself	7"	Caff	CAFF2	1990	£15	£7.50	

FIELDING, ALAN

How Many Nights, How Many Days	7"	Decca	F11404	1962	£4	£1.50	

Too Late To Worry, Too Blue To Cry	7"	Decca	F11518	1962	£4	£1.50	

FIELDING, JERRY ORCHESTRA

Dance Date Vol. 1	7" EP	London	REP1026	1955	£8	£4	
Faintly Reminiscent	10" LP	London	HAPB1022	1954	£10	£4	
Faintly Reminiscent	7"	London	HL7001	1955	£8	£4	*export*
Gypsy In My Soul	7"	Brunswick	05399	1955	£6	£2.50	
I'm In Love	7"	London	HL7004	1955	£8	£4	*export*
Peanut Vendor	7"	London	HL7002	1955	£8	£4	*export*
Plays A Dance Concert	10" LP	London	HAPB1027	1954	£10	£4	
Tea For Two	7"	London	HL7003	1955	£8	£4	*export*
When I Grow Too Old To Dream	7"	London	HL8017	1954	£15	£7.50	

FIELDS

Fields	LP	CBS	69009	1971	£25	£10	*with poster*

FIELDS (2)

Fields	LP	Uni	UNLS104	1969	£10	£4	

FIELDS, ERNIE

Chattanooga Choo Choo	7"	London	HL9100	1960	£5	£2	
In The Mood	7"	London	HL8985	1959	£4	£1.50	
In The Mood	LP	London	HA2263	1960	£25	£12.50	
Raunchy	7"	London	HL9227	1960	£4	£1.50	
Saxy	7" EP	London	RE1260	1960	£25	£12.50	

FIELDS, IRVING

Mr Piano Play	7"	Parlophone	CMSP9	1954	£5	£2	*export*

FIELDS, KANSAS & MILTON SEALEY

Kansas Fields & Milton Sealey	7" EP	Ducretet	DEP95017	1956	£6	£2.50	

FIELDS OF THE NEPHILIM

Blue Water	12"	Situation 2	SIT48T	1987	£10	£5	*with poster*
Blue Water	7"	Situation 2	SIT48	1987	£8	£4	
Burning The Fields	12"	Tower	N1	1985	£10	£5	*green sleeve, label with band photos*
Burning The Fields	12"	Tower	N1	1984	£40	£20	*red sleeve*
Burning The Fields	12"	Tower	N1	1985	£6	£2.50	*coloured vinyl*
Chord Of Souls	12"	Situation 2		1988	£12	£6	*promo*
For Her Light	CD-s	Beggars Banquet	BEG244CD	1990	£5	£2	
Power	7"	Situation 2	SIT42	1986	£25	£12.50	*promo*
Preacher Man	7"	Situation 2	SIT46	1987	£12	£6	
Psychonaut Lib III	CD-s	Situation 2	SIT057CD	1989	£5	£2	
Summerland (Dreamed)	CD-s	Beggars Banquet	BEG250CD	1990	£5	£2	

FIESTA MOBILE

Diario	LP	RCA	DPSL10605	1973	£50	£25	*Italian*

FIESTAS

So Fine	7"	London	HL8870	1959	£20	£10	

FIFTEENTH

Andelain	12"	Tanz	TANZ3	1986	£6	£2.50	
Andelain	12"	Tanz	TANZ3	1986	£6	£2.50	

FIFTH AVENUE

Bells Of Rhymney	7"	Immediate	IM002	1965	£15	£7.50	

FIFTH COLUMN

Gerry Rafferty and Joe Egan later formed Stealer's Wheel.

Benjamin Day	7"	Columbia	DB8068	1966	£10	£5	

FIFTH DIMENSION

Go Where You Wanna Go	7"	Liberty	LIB12051	1967	£8	£4	
I'll Be Loving You For Ever	7"	Liberty	LBF15356	1970	£8	£4	

FIFTH ESTATE

Ding Dong The Witch Is Dead	LP	Jubilee	JGM/JGS8005	1967	£25	£10	*US*

FIFTY FANTASTICS

God's Got Religion	7"	South Circular	SGS108	1979	£6	£2.50	*B side by Steppes*
God's Got Religion	7"	Dining Out	TUX5	1980	£5	£2	

FIFTY FOOT HOSE

Along with the group the United States of America, the Fifty Foot Hose were early pioneers in the use of electronics within a general rock group sound. The results are undoubtedly dated to modern ears, and the album *Cauldron* is apparently a mere blueprint compared to the sonic experiments that the group performed live. *Cauldron* is nevertheless a vital sixties artefact with far more to offer than some of the more celebrated rarities from the period.

Cauldron	LP	Mercury	SLML4030	1969	£75	£37.50	

FIFTY YEAR VOID (SAINT ETIENNE)

Blade's Love Machine	12"	Blade	BLADE1	1992	**£25**	**£12.50**	*promo only*

FIGGY DUFF

After The Tempest	LP	Celtic	CM023	1985	**£100**	**£50**	

FILBY, PAULINE

I'm Hungry	7"	Church Missionary Society	LIVSP81	196–	**£25**	**£12.50**	*Nadia Cattouse B side*
My World	7" EP	Herald	ELR1081	1968	**£75**	**£37.50**	
Show Me A Rainbow	LP	Herald	LLR567	1969	**£300**	**£180**	

FILET OF SOUL

Freedom	LP	Monoquid Squid	ST4857	1968	**£60**	**£30**	US

FILTHY RICH

She's Seventeen	7"	JM	TR102	1987	**£8**	**£4**	

FINCHLEY BOYS

Everlasting Tribute	LP	Golden Throat	20019	1972	**£100**	**£50**	US

FINDERS KEEPERS

Bass player Glen Hughes was later a member of Deep Purple.

Light	7"	CBS	202249	1966	**£6**	**£2.50**	
Light/Power Of Love	7"	CBS	202249	1966	**£50**	**£25**	*demo only*
On The Beach	7"	Fontana	TF892	1967	**£15**	**£7.50**	
Sadie The Cleaning Lady	7"	Fontana	TF938	1968	**£6**	**£2.50**	

FINE WINE

Fine Wine	LP	Polydor	2310438	1976	**£12**	**£5**	*German*

FINE YOUNG CANNIBALS

Don't Look Back	CD-s	London	LONCD220	1989	**£5**	**£2**	
Ever Fallen In Love	CD-s	London	LONCD121	1987	**£5**	**£2**	
Good Thing	CD-s	London	LONCD218	1989	**£5**	**£2**	
I'm Not Satisfied	CD-s	London	LONCD252	1990	**£5**	**£2**	
I'm Not The Man I Used To Be	CD-s	London	LONCD244	1989	**£5**	**£2**	
She Drives Me Crazy	CD-s	London	LONCD199	1988	**£5**	**£2**	
She Drives Me Crazy	CD-s	London	8863612	1989	**£5**	**£2**	
Suspicious Minds	CD-s	Polygram	0804882	1988	**£8**	**£4**	*CD video*

FINGERS

All Kinds Of People	7"	Columbia	DB8112	1967	**£15**	**£7.50**	
I'll Take You Where The Music's Playing	7"	Columbia	DB8026	1966	**£4**	**£1.50**	

FINI TRIBE

Curling And Stretching	12"	Finiflex	LT1001	1984	**£6**	**£2.50**	
Destimony	12"	Finiflex	FT002	1988	**£6**	**£2.50**	

FINN, LEE & THE RHYTHM MEN

High Class Feeling	7"	Starlite	ST45103	1963	**£175**	**£87.50**	

FINN, MICKEY & THE BLUE MEN

Pills	7"	Oriole	CB1927	1964	**£40**	**£20**	
Reeling And Rocking	7"	Oriole	CB1940	1964	**£40**	**£20**	
Tom Hark	7"	Blue Beat	BB203	1964	**£30**	**£15**	

FINN, SIMON

Pass The Distance	LP	Mushroom	100MR2	1970	**£60**	**£30**	

FINN, TIM

How'm I Gonna Sleep	CD-s	Capitol	CDCL542	1989	**£5**	**£2**	
Live At The Borderline	CD	Capitol	FINN1	1993	**£25**	**£10**	*promo*

FINN MACCUILL

Sink Ye – Swim Ye	LP	private	REL460	1978	**£200**	**£100**	

FINNEGAN, LARRY

Dear One	7"	HMV	POP1022	1962	**£6**	**£2.50**	
It's Walking Talking Time	7"	London	HLU9613	1962	**£6**	**£2.50**	
Larry Finnegan	LP	MFP	50136	1966	**£25**	**£10**	*Swedish*
Other Ringo	7"	Ember	EMBS207	1965	**£8**	**£4**	*picture sleeve*

FINNEGAN, MIKE

Just One Minute More	7"	CBS	6656	1978	**£5**	**£2**	

FIRE

Father's Name Is Dad	7"	Decca	F12753	1968	**£100**	**£50**	
Magic Shoemaker	LP	Pye	NSPL18343	1970	**£200**	**£100**	

Round The Gum Tree	7"	Decca	F12856	1968	**£20**	**£10**	

FIRE (2)

Could You Understand Me	LP	Killroy		1973	**£250**	**£150**	*Dutch*

FIRE ESCAPE

Love Special Delivery	7" EP	Vogue	INT18117	1966	**£25**	**£12.50**	*French*
Psychotic Reaction	LP	GNP Crescendo	2034	1966	**£30**	**£15**	*US*

FIRE EXIT

Timewall	7"	Time Bomb Explosion	1	1979	**£5**	**£2**	

FIRE ISLAND

In Your Bones	12"	Boy's Own	BOIX11	1992	**£10**	**£5**	

FIREBALLS

Bottle Of Wine	LP	Stateside	(S)SL10237	1968	**£15**	**£6**	
Bulldog	7"	Top Rank	JAR276	1960	**£6**	**£2.50**	
Come On, React!	LP	London	HA/SH8396	1969	**£10**	**£4**	
Fireballs	LP	Top Rank	RM324	1960	**£30**	**£15**	*US*
Foot Patter	7"	Top Rank	JAR354	1960	**£5**	**£2**	
Here Are The Fireballs	LP	Warwick	W2042	1961	**£25**	**£10**	*US*
Quite A Party	7"	Pye	7N25092	1961	**£4**	**£1.50**	
Torquay	7"	Top Rank	JAR218	1959	**£6**	**£2.50**	
Vaquero	7"	Top Rank	JAR507	1960	**£5**	**£2**	
Vaquero	LP	Top Rank	25105	1961	**£30**	**£15**	

FIREBIRDS

Light My Fire	LP	Crown	CST589	1968	**£50**	**£25**	*US*

FIRECLOWN

Fireclown	10"	Fireclown	FC1001	1983	**£25**	**£12.50**	

FIREFLIES

I Can't Say Goodbye	7"	London	HLU9057	1960	**£8**	**£4**	
You Were Mine	7"	Top Rank	JAR198	1959	**£8**	**£4**	
You Were Mine	LP	Taurus	(S)1002	1961	**£50**	**£25**	*US*

FIREHOUSE FIVE PLUS TWO

Crashes A Party	LP	Good Time Jazz	LAG12236/ SGA5012	1960	**£10**	**£4**	
Firehouse Five Plus Two	10" LP	Vogue	LDE183	1956	**£10**	**£4**	
Firehouse Five Plus Two	LP	Good Time Jazz	LAG12079	1958	**£10**	**£4**	
Firehouse Five Plus Two Vol. 2	LP	Good Time Jazz	LAG12089	1958	**£10**	**£4**	
Firehouse Five Story Vol. 3	LP	Good Time Jazz	LAG12099	1958	**£10**	**£4**	
For Lovers	LP	Good Time Jazz	LAG12074	1958	**£10**	**£4**	
Goes South	LP	Good Time Jazz	LAG12087	1958	**£10**	**£4**	
Goes South Vol. 1	10" LP	Good Time Jazz	LDG036	1954	**£12**	**£5**	
Goes South Vol. 2	10" LP	Good Time Jazz	LDG079	1954	**£12**	**£5**	
Goes South Vol. 3	10" LP	Good Time Jazz	LDG094	1954	**£12**	**£5**	
Goes South Vol. 4	10" LP	Good Time Jazz	LDG169	1955	**£12**	**£5**	
Goes To Sea	LP	Good Time Jazz	LAG12150/ SGA5003	1958	**£10**	**£4**	

FIREMAN

One of the more surprising album releases of 1993 was one whose origin would be guessed by few casual listeners. For the ambient work credited to the Fireman is actually the work of none other than Paul McCartney, working in collaboration with Youth, the producer who has, of course, worked with the Orb. The LP version of *Strawberries . . .* was issued on clear vinyl only for a very limited period. By the time that most McCartney collectors had realized the involvement of their hero, the record had already been deleted.

Strawberries Oceans Ships Forest	LP	Parlophone	PCSD145	1993	**£30**	**£15**	*clear vinyl double, white sleeve*

FIRESIGN THEATRE

Dear Friends	LP	CBS	31099	1972	**£12**	**£5**	*US, double*
Don't Crush That Dwarf	LP	CBS	30102	1970	**£12**	**£5**	*US*
Everything You Know Is Wrong	LP	CBS	33141	1974	**£10**	**£4**	*US*
How Can You Be In Two Places At Once	LP	CBS	65130	1968	**£15**	**£6**	
I Think We're All Bozos On This Bus	LP	CBS	30737	1971	**£12**	**£5**	*US*
In The Next World	LP	CBS	31383	1972	**£10**	**£4**	*US*
Not Insane Or Anything You Want	LP	CBS	31585	1972	**£10**	**£4**	*US*
Tale Of The Giant Rat	LP	CBS	32370	1974	**£10**	**£4**	*US*
TV Or Not TV	LP	CBS	32199	1973	**£10**	**£4**	*US*
Waiting For The Electrician Or Someone Like Him	LP	CBS	65129	1968	**£15**	**£6**	

FIRING SQUAD

Title	Format	Label	Cat. No.	Year	Mint	VG	Notes
Little Bit More	7"	Parlophone	R5152	1964	£15	£7.50	

FIRKIN THE FOX

Title	Format	Label	Cat. No.	Year	Mint	VG	Notes
Behind Bars	LP	Woodworm	WR005	1984	£50	£25	

FIRM

Title	Format	Label	Cat. No.	Year	Mint	VG	Notes
Firm	CD	Atlantic	7812392	1985	£12	£5	
Firm Mean Business	CD	Atlantic	7816282	1986	£12	£5	
Radioactive	7"	Atlantic	A9586P	1985	£6	£2.50	shaped picture disc

FIRST AID

Title	Format	Label	Cat. No.	Year	Mint	VG	Notes
Nostradamus	LP	Decca	TXS117	1977	£15	£6	

FIRST CHOICE

Title	Format	Label	Cat. No.	Year	Mint	VG	Notes
This Is The House Where Love Died	7"	Pye	7N25613	1973	£100	£50	*demo only*

FIRST GEAR

Title	Format	Label	Cat. No.	Year	Mint	VG	Notes
In Crowd	7"	Pye	7N15763	1965	£20	£10	
Leave My Kitten Alone	7"	Pye	7N15703	1964	£100	£50	

FIRST IMPRESSIONS

Title	Format	Label	Cat. No.	Year	Mint	VG	Notes
I'm Coming Home	7"	Pye	7N15797	1965	£5	£2	

FIRST MODERN PIANO QUARTET

Title	Format	Label	Cat. No.	Year	Mint	VG	Notes
Gallery Of Gershwin	LP	Coral	LVA9110/ SVL3002	1959	£12	£5	

FIRST MYSTERIOUS APPEARANCE

Title	Format	Label	Cat. No.	Year	Mint	VG	Notes
First Mysterious Appearance	LP	Impossible		1983	£25	£10	*Dutch*

FIRST STEPS

Title	Format	Label	Cat. No.	Year	Mint	VG	Notes
Anywhere Else But Here	7"	English Rose	ER3	1981	£10	£5	
Beat Is Back	7"	English Rose	ER1	1980	£10	£5	

FISCHER, WILD MAN

Title	Format	Label	Cat. No.	Year	Mint	VG	Notes
Evening With Wild Man Fischer	LP	Reprise	RSLP6332	1970	£30	£15	
Wildmania	LP	Rhino	RNLP001	1977	£10	£4	*US*

FISCHER & EPSTEIN

Title	Format	Label	Cat. No.	Year	Mint	VG	Notes
It's A Beatle World	LP	Swan	514	1964	£15	£6	*US*

FISCHERMAN'S FRIEND

Title	Format	Label	Cat. No.	Year	Mint	VG	Notes
Money	12"	EG	OP51	1991	£8	£4	

FISH

Title	Format	Label	Cat. No.	Year	Mint	VG	Notes
Big Wedge	CD-s	EMI	CDEM125	1990	£5	£2	
Company	CD-s	EMI		1990	£10	£5	*German*
Funny Farm Interview	CD	Dick Brothers	DDICK15CD	1995	£20	£8	*promo*
Gentleman's Excuse Me	12"	EMI	12EMPD135	1990	£6	£2.50	*picture disc*
Gentleman's Excuse Me	CD-s	EMI	CDEM135	1990	£5	£2	
Internal Exile	CD-s	EMI	FISCD1	1991	£5	£2	
State Of Mind	12"	EMI	12EMPD109	1989	£6	£2.50	*picture disc*
State Of Mind	CD-s	EMI	CDEM109	1989	£5	£2	
Vigil In The Wilderness Of Mirrors	LP	EMI	EMDPD1015	1990	£12	£5	*picture disc*

FISHER, ARCHIE

Title	Format	Label	Cat. No.	Year	Mint	VG	Notes
Archie Fisher	LP	XTRA	XTRA1070	1968	£25	£10	
Man With A Rhyme	LP	Folk Legacy	FSS61	1976	£25	£10	*US*
Orfeo	LP	Decca	SKL5057	1970	£25	£10	

FISHER, CHIP

Title	Format	Label	Cat. No.	Year	Mint	VG	Notes
At The Sugar Bowl	7" EP	RCA	RCX143	1959	£40	£20	
Poor Me	7"	Parlophone	R4604	1959	£8	£4	

FISHER, CILLA & ARTIE TREZISE

Title	Format	Label	Cat. No.	Year	Mint	VG	Notes
Balcanquhal	LP	Trailer	LER2100	1976	£25	£10	
For Foul Day And Fair	LP	Kettle	KAC1	1979	£10	£4	

FISHER, EDDIE

Title	Format	Label	Cat. No.	Year	Mint	VG	Notes
April Showers	7" EP	HMV	7EG8046	1954	£6	£2.50	
Bundle Of Joy	7" EP	HMV	7EG8207	1957	£5	£2	
Cindy Oh Cindy	7"	HMV	POP273	1956	£10	£5	
Count Your Blessings Instead Of Sheep	7"	HMV	7M266	1954	£6	£2.50	
Downhearted	7"	HMV	7M126	1953	£8	£4	
Dungaree Doll	7"	HMV	7M374	1956	£10	£5	
Even Now	7"	HMV	7M125	1953	£8	£4	
Everything I Have Is Yours	7"	HMV	7M115	1953	£10	£5	
Girl, A Girl	7"	HMV	7M212	1954	£6	£2.50	
Green Years	7"	HMV	7M257	1954	£5	£2	
How Deep Is The Ocean	7"	HMV	7M185	1954	£5	£2	
How Deep Is The Ocean	7" EP	HMV	7EG8146	1955	£6	£2.50	
How Do You Speak To An Angel?	7"	HMV	7M242	1954	£6	£2.50	
I Need You Now	7"	HMV	7M251	1954	£6	£2.50	
I'm Walking Behind You	7"	HMV	7M133	1953	£8	£4	
I'm Yours	7"	HMV	7M101	1953	£10	£5	
Just Another Polka	7"	HMV	7M146	1953	£6	£2.50	

Just To Be With You	7"	HMV	7M201	1954	£5	£2	
Kari Waits For Me	7"	RCA	RCA1061	1958	£4	£1.50	
Magic Fingers	7"	HMV	7M353	1956	£5	£2	
Many Times	7"	HMV	7M168	1953	£6	£2.50	
My Friend	7"	HMV	7M235	1954	£6	£2.50	
My Serenade Is You	10" LP	HMV	DLP1074	1955	£15	£6	
Night And Day	7" EP	HMV	7EG8026	1954	£6	£2.50	
No Other One	7"	HMV	7M402	1956	£5	£2	
Oh My Papa	7"	HMV	7M172	1953	£8	£4	
Outside Of Heaven	7"	HMV	7M117	1953	£10	£5	
Sayonara	7"	RCA	RCA1030	1958	£4	£1.50	
Sings Academy Award Winning Songs	LP	HMV	CLP1095	1956	£10	£4	
Some Day Soon	7"	HMV	POP296	1957	£4	£1.50	
Sweet Heartaches	7"	HMV	7M421	1956	£5	£2	
Take My Love	7" EP	HMV	7EG8156	1955	£6	£2.50	
Time For Romance	10" LP	HMV	DLP1040	1954	£15	£6	
Tonight My Heart She Is Crying	7"	HMV	POP342	1957	£4	£1.50	
Trust In Me	7"	HMV	7M116	1953	£8	£4	
Wedding Bells	7"	HMV	7M294	1955	£6	£2.50	
Wish You Were Here	7"	HMV	7M159	1953	£8	£4	

FISHER, RAY

Bonny Birdy	LP	Trailer	LER2038	1972	£25	£10	

FISHER, RAY & ARCHIE

Far Over The Forth	7" EP	Topic	TOP67	1961	£30	£15	

FISHER, TONI

Big Hurt	7"	Top Rank	JAR261	1960	£4	£1.50	

FISHER FAMILY

Fisher Family	LP	Topic	12T137	1965	£25	£10	

FISHERS

Hide In The Rock	LP	Sharing	SC008	1978	£20	£8	

FISK JUBILEE SINGERS

Fisk Jubilee Singers	LP	Topic	12T39	1959	£15	£6	

FIST

Back With A Vengeance	LP	Neat	NEAT1003	1985	£25	£10	*yellow vinyl*
Back With A Vengeance	LP	Neat	NEAT1003	1985	£10	£4	
Collision Course	7"	MCA	MCA663	1981	£8	£4	
Collision Course	7"	MCA	MCA663	1981	£50	£25	*picture sleeve*
Forever Amber	7"	MCA	MCA640	1980	£5	£2	
Name, Rank And Serial Number	7"	MCA	MCA615	1980	£10	£5	
Turn The Hell On	LP	MCA	MCF3082	1980	£10	£4	

FITCH, JOHN & ASSOCIATES

Stoned Out Of It	7"	Beacon	BEA118	1971	£10	£5	

FITZ & COOZERS

Cover Me	7"	Nu Beat	NB003	1968	£6	£2.50	

FITZGERALD, ELLA

At Newport	LP	Columbia	33CX10100	1958	£15	£6	*side 2 by Billie Holiday*
At The Opera House	LP	Columbia	33CX10126	1958	£20	£8	*with Oscar Peterson*
Cole Porter Songbook Vol. 1	LP	HMV	CLP1083	1956	£20	£8	
Cole Porter Songbook Vol. 2	LP	HMV	CLP1084	1956	£20	£8	
Duke Ellington Songbook Vol. 1	LP	HMV	CLP1213/4	1958	£30	£15	*double*
Duke Ellington Songbook Vol. 2	LP	HMV	CLP1227/8	1958	£30	£15	*double*
Ella And Her Fellas	LP	Brunswick	LAT8223	1957	£15	£6	
Ella And Louis	LP	HMV	CLP1098	1956	£15	£6	*with Louis Armstrong*
Ella And Louis Again No. 1	LP	HMV	CLP1146	1957	£15	£6	*with Louis Armstrong*
Ella And Louis Again No. 2	LP	HMV	CLP1147	1957	£15	£6	*with Louis Armstrong*
Ella At Juan-Les-Pins	LP	Verve	VLP9083	1965	£10	£4	
Ella Sings Gershwin	10" LP	Brunswick	LA8648	1954	£30	£15	
Ella Swings Brightly With Nelson	LP	Verve	(S)VLP9001	1962	£12	£5	
Ella Swings Gently With Nelson	LP	Verve	VLP9028	1962	£10	£4	*with Nelson Riddle*
Ella Swings Lightly	LP	HMV	CLP1267	1959	£20	£8	
Ella Wishes You A Swinging Christmas	LP	HMV	CLP1397	1960	£20	£8	
First Lady Of Song	LP	Brunswick	LAT8264	1958	£15	£6	
Get Ready	7"	Reprise	R20850	1969	£4	£1.50	
Hello Love	LP	HMV	CLP1383/ CSD1315	1960	£20	£8	
Irving Berlin Songbook Vol. 1	LP	HMV	CLP1183	1958	£20	£8	
Irving Berlin Songbook Vol. 2	LP	HMV	CLP1184	1958	£20	£8	
Let No Man Write My Epitaph	LP	HMV	CLP1396	1960	£20	£8	
Like Someone In Love	LP	HMV	CLP1166	1958	£20	£8	
Lullabies Of Birdland	LP	Brunswick	LAT8115	1956	£20	£8	
Mack The Knife	LP	HMV	CLP1391	1960	£20	£8	
Porgy And Bess Vol. 1	LP	HMV	CLP1245	1959	£15	£6	*with Louis Armstrong*

Porgy And Bess Vol. 2	LP	HMV	CLP1246	1959	**£15**	**£6**	*with Louis Armstrong*
Rhythm Is My Business	LP	Verve	VLP9020	1963	**£12**	**£5**	
Rodgers And Hart Songbook Vol. 1	LP	HMV	CLP1116	1957	**£20**	**£8**	
Rodgers And Hart Songbook Vol. 2	LP	HMV	CLP1117	1957	**£20**	**£8**	
Sings Gershwin Vol. 1	LP	HMV	CLP1338/CSD1292	1959	**£20**	**£8**	
Sings Gershwin Vol. 2	LP	HMV	CLP1339/CSD1293	1959	**£20**	**£8**	
Sings Gershwin Vol. 3	LP	HMV	CLP1347/CSD1299	1960	**£20**	**£8**	
Sings Gershwin Vol. 4	LP	HMV	CLP1348/CSD1300	1960	**£20**	**£8**	
Sings Gershwin Vol. 5	LP	HMV	CLP1353/CSD1304	1960	**£20**	**£8**	
Sings The Harold Arlen Song Book Vol. 1	LP	HMV	CSD1389	1961	**£20**	**£8**	
Sings The Harold Arlen Song Book Vol. 2	LP	HMV	CSD1390	1961	**£20**	**£8**	
Songs In A Mellow Mood	LP	Brunswick	LAT8056	1955	**£20**	**£8**	
Souvenir Album	10" LP	Brunswick	LA8665	1954	**£20**	**£8**	
Souvenir Album	10" LP	Brunswick	LA8581	1953	**£30**	**£15**	
Sweet And Hot	LP	Brunswick	LAT8091	1956	**£20**	**£8**	
Sweet Songs For Swingers	LP	HMV	CLP1322/CSD1287	1960	**£20**	**£8**	

FITZGERALD, G. F.

Mouseproof	LP	Uni	UNLS115	1970	**£40**	**£20**	

FIVE A.M. EVENT

Hungry	7"	Pye	7N17154	1966	**£125**	**£62.50**	

FIVE AMERICANS

Evol, Not Love	7"	Pye	7N25373	1966	**£20**	**£10**	
I See The Light	7"	Pye	7N25354	1966	**£10**	**£5**	
I See The Light	7" EP	Vogue	INT18087	1966	**£15**	**£7.50**	*French*
I See The Light	LP	Hanna Barbera	LP8503/ST9503	1966	**£30**	**£15**	*US*
Now And Then	LP	Abnak	ABST2071	1968	**£15**	**£6**	*US*
Progressions	LP	Abnak	AB(ST)2069	1967	**£15**	**£6**	*US*
Sound Of Love	7" EP	Stateside	FSE1007	1967	**£15**	**£7.50**	*French*
Western Union	7" EP	Stateside	FSE102	1967	**£12**	**£6**	*French*
Western Union	LP	Abnak	AB(ST)2067	1967	**£20**	**£8**	*US*

FIVE & A PENNY

You Don't Know Where Your Interest Lies	7"	Polydor	56282	1968	**£15**	**£7.50**	

FIVE BLIND BOYS

Five Blind Boys	7" EP	Vocalion	EPVP1282	1964	**£10**	**£5**	
Negro Spirituals	7" EP	Vocalion	EPVP1276	1964	**£10**	**£4**	

FIVE BLOBS

Blob	7"	Philips	PB881	1958	**£10**	**£5**	

FIVE BY FIVE

Fire	7"	Pye	7N25477	1968	**£15**	**£7.50**	
Next Exit	LP	Paula	LPS2202	1968	**£15**	**£6**	*US*

FIVE CARD STUD

Beg Me	7"	Philips	BF1567	1967	**£6**	**£2.50**	

FIVE CHESTERNUTS

The Five Chesternuts were together for less than four months, but managed to make one (now rare) single during that time. Hank Marvin and Bruce Welch, who subsequently formed the Shadows, were both members.

Jean Dorothy	7"	Columbia	DB4165	1958	**£100**	**£50**	

FIVE COUNTS

Watermelon Walk	7"	Oriole	CBA1769	1962	**£4**	**£1.50**	

FIVE CRESTAS

How Sweet It Is	7"	Excel	ESSP288/9	1966	**£50**	**£25**	

FIVE DALLAS BOYS

Big Man	7"	Columbia	DB4154	1958	**£4**	**£1.50**	
Fatty Patty	7"	Columbia	DB4231	1958	**£5**	**£2**	
Five Dallas Boys	7" EP	Columbia	SEG8035	1960	**£8**	**£4**	

FIVE DAY RAIN

Five Day Rain	LP	private		1993	**£50**	**£25**	
Five Day Rain	LP	private		1970	**£750**	**£500**	*no sleeve*

FIVE DAY WEEK STRAW PEOPLE

Five Day Week Straw People	LP	Saga	FID2123	1968	**£60**	**£30**	

FIVE DU-TONES

Title	Format	Label	Cat. No.	Year	Price	Price	Notes
Shake A Tail Feather	7"	Stateside	SS206	1963	**£12**	**£6**	
Shake A Tail Feather	7"	President	PT134	1968	**£4**	**£1.50**	

FIVE EMPREES

Title	Format	Label	Cat. No.	Year	Price	Price	Notes
Five Empress	LP	Freeport	FR3001/FRS4001	1965	**£30**	**£15**	*US*
Little Miss Sad	7"	Stateside	SS470	1965	**£4**	**£1.50**	
Little Miss Sad	LP	Freeport	FR3002/FRS4002	1966	**£20**	**£8**	*US*

FIVE FLEETS

Title	Format	Label	Cat. No.	Year	Price	Price	Notes
Oh What A Feeling	7"	Felsted	AF103	1958	**£200**	**£100**	*best auctioned*

FIVE HAND REEL

Title	Format	Label	Cat. No.	Year	Price	Price	Notes
Five Hand Reel	LP	Rubber	RUB019	1976	**£10**	**£4**	

FIVE KEYS

Title	Format	Label	Cat. No.	Year	Price	Price	Notes
Best Of The Five Keys	LP	Aladdin	806	1956	**£500**	**£330**	*US*
Blues Don't Care	7"	Capitol	CL14756	1957	**£60**	**£30**	
Cos You're My Love	7"	Capitol	CL14545	1956	**£200**	**£100**	*best auctioned*
Doggone It	7"	Capitol	CL14325	1955	**£400**	**£250**	*best auctioned*
Fantastic Five Keys	LP	Capitol	T1769	1962	**£150**	**£75**	*US*
Five Keys	LP	King	688	1960	**£200**	**£100**	*US*
Five Keys On Stage	LP	Capitol	T828	1957	**£200**	**£100**	*US*
Five Keys On The Town	LP	Score	LP4003	1957	**£400**	**£250**	*US*
Four Walls	7"	Capitol	CL14736	1957	**£60**	**£30**	
From Me To You	7"	Capitol	CL14829	1958	**£75**	**£37.50**	
Ling Ting Tong	78	Capitol	CL14184	1954	**£50**	**£25**	
Really O Truly Oh	7"	Capitol	CL14967	1958	**£75**	**£37.50**	
Rhythm And Blues Hits Past And Present	LP	King	692	1960	**£200**	**£100**	*US*
She's The Most	7"	Capitol	CL14582	1956	**£200**	**£100**	*best auctioned*
That's Right	7"	Capitol	CL14639	1956	**£100**	**£50**	
Verdict	7"	Capitol	CL14313	1955	**£500**	**£330**	*best auctioned*
Wisdom Of A Fool	7"	Capitol	CL14686	1957	**£100**	**£50**	

FIVE LIVERPOOLS

Title	Format	Label	Cat. No.	Year	Price	Price	Notes
Tokio International	LP	CBS	62460	1965	**£250**	**£150**	*German*

FIVE MAN ELECTRICAL BAND

Title	Format	Label	Cat. No.	Year	Price	Price	Notes
Five Man Electrical Band	LP	Capitol	ST165	1969	**£15**	**£6**	*US*

FIVE OF DIAMONDS

Title	Format	Label	Cat. No.	Year	Price	Price	Notes
Five Of Diamonds	7" EP	Oak	RGJ150FD	1965	**£300**	**£180**	*best auctioned*

FIVE ROYALES

Within Greil Marcus's collection of rock essays, *Stranded*, Ed Ward writes an account of the recording career of the Five Royales. It is a moving story, a piece of great rock writing that immediately makes the reader want to seek out the group's records – and as Ward admits at the end, it is completely made up. The music that inspired Ward, however, is likely to inspire any fan of the period. The Five Royales perform superior doo-wop with the added distinction of fiery blues guitar, courtesy of Lowman Pauling, who also managed to write two classic songs – 'Think', covered by James Brown, and 'Dedicated To The One I Love', made into a big hit by the Mamas and the Papas.

Title	Format	Label	Cat. No.	Year	Price	Price	Notes
Dedicated To The One I Love	7"	Ember	EMBS124	1960	**£75**	**£37.50**	
Dedicated To You	LP	King	580	1957	**£200**	**£100**	*US*
Five Royales	LP	King	678	1960	**£150**	**£75**	*US*
Five Royales Sing For You	LP	King	616	1959	**£175**	**£87.50**	*US*
Rockin' Five Royales	LP	Apollo	LP488	1956	**£400**	**£200**	*US*
Twenty-Four All Time Hits	LP	King	955	1966	**£25**	**£10**	*US*

FIVE SATINS

Title	Format	Label	Cat. No.	Year	Price	Price	Notes
Encore	LP	Ember	ELP401	1960	**£40**	**£20**	*US*
Five Satins Sing	LP	Ember	ELP100	1957	**£200**	**£100**	*US*
Five Satins Sing	LP	Ember	ELP100	1957	**£500**	**£330**	*US, blue vinyl*
Five Satins Sing	LP	Mount Vernon	108	196–	**£25**	**£10**	*US*
Shadows	7"	Top Rank	JAR239	1959	**£20**	**£10**	
To The Aisle	7"	London	HL8501	1957	**£500**	**£330**	*best auctioned*
Wonderful Girl	7"	Top Rank	JAR199	1959	**£20**	**£10**	
Your Memory	7"	MGM	MGM1087	1960	**£50**	**£25**	

FIVE SMITH BROTHERS

Title	Format	Label	Cat. No.	Year	Price	Price	Notes
ABC Boogie	7"	Decca	F10403	1954	**£6**	**£2.50**	
I'm In Favour Of Friendship	7"	Decca	F10527	1955	**£8**	**£4**	
You're As Sweet Today	7"	Decca	F10507	1955	**£4**	**£1.50**	

FIVE STAIRSTEPS & CUBIE

Title	Format	Label	Cat. No.	Year	Price	Price	Notes
Million To One	7"	Pye	7N25448	1968	**£5**	**£2**	
We Must Be In Love	7"	Buddah	201070	1969	**£5**	**£2**	

FIVE STEPS BEYOND

Title	Format	Label	Cat. No.	Year	Price	Price	Notes
Not So Young Today	7"	CBS	202490	1967	**£6**	**£2.50**	

FIVE THIRTY

Title	Format	Label	Cat. No.	Year	Price	Price	Notes
Abstain	CD-s	East West	YZ530CD	1990	**£5**	**£2**	
Air Conditioned Nightmare	CD-s	East West	YZ543CD	1990	**£5**	**£2**	
Bed	LP	East West		1985	**£20**	**£8**	
Catcher In The Rye	12"	Other	12OTH2	1985	**£20**	**£10**	

Supernova	CD-s	East West	YZ594CD	1991	**£5**	**£2**	
You EP	CD-s	East West	YZ624CD	1991	**£5**	**£2**	

FIVE'S COMPANY

Ballad Of Fred The Pixie	LP	Saga	FID2151	1969	**£10**	**£4**	
Session Man	7"	Pye	7N17199	1966	**£10**	**£5**	
Some Girls	7"	Pye	7N17162	1966	**£4**	**£1.50**	
Sunday For Seven Days	7"	Pye	7N17118	1966	**£5**	**£2**	

FIZZBOMBS

Sign On The Line	7"	Narodnik	NRK003	1987	**£5**	**£2**	

FLACK, ROBERTA

First Take	LP	Atlantic	588204	1969	**£10**	**£4**	

FLACK, ROBERTA & DONNY HATHAWAY

Roberta Flack And Donny Hathaway	LP	Atlantic	K40380	1972	**£10**	**£4**	

FLAIRS

Flairs	LP	Crown	CLP5356	1963	**£40**	**£20**	*US*
Swing Pretty Mama	7"	Oriole	CB1392	1957	**£350**	**£210**	*best auctioned*

FLAKY PASTRY

Ingredients	LP	Flaky Pastry	FALP001	1976	**£15**	**£6**	

FLAME

The one album made by Flame has been described, with some degree of accuracy, as the best album that the Beatles never made. Beach Boy Carl Wilson was a member, taking advantage of a lull in his main group's schedule, and subsequently recruited two of his Flame colleagues, Ricky Fataar and Blondie Chaplin, for the Beach Boys. Later still, Fataar re-established his interest in the Beatles when he took on the Ringo Starr role within Neil Innes's parody group, the Rutles.

Flame	LP	Stateside	SSL10312	1971	**£25**	**£10**	
See The Light	7"	Stateside	SS2183	1970	**£4**	**£1.50**	

FLAMES

Broadway Jungle	7"	Island	WI139	1964	**£12**	**£6**	
He's The Greatest	7"	Island	WI130	1964	**£12**	**£6**	
Helena Darling	7"	Blue Beat	BB205	1964	**£12**	**£6**	
It Takes Time	7"	Blue Beat	BB300	1965	**£12**	**£6**	*Liges B side*
Little Flea	7"	Island	WI136	1964	**£12**	**£6**	
Mini Really Fit Dem	7"	Nu Beat	NB020	1968	**£5**	**£2**	
When I Get Home	7"	Island	WI138	1964	**£12**	**£6**	
You've Lost Your Date	7"	Nu Beat	NB028	1969	**£6**	**£2.50**	

FLAMES (2)

Burning Soul	LP	Page One	FOR(S)009	1968	**£20**	**£8**	
Streamliner	7"	Flame	FAN1011	1968	**£10**	**£5**	*picture sleeve*

FLAMIN' GROOVIES

Feel A Whole Lot Better	7"	Sire	6078619	1978	**£4**	**£1.50**	*picture sleeve*
Flamin' Groovies	LP	Kama Sutra	2683003	1971	**£12**	**£5**	*double*
Flamingo	LP	Kama Sutra	KSBS2021	1971	**£12**	**£5**	*US*
Married Woman	7"	United Artists	UP35464	1972	**£5**	**£2**	
Shake Some Action	LP	Sire	9103251	1977	**£10**	**£4**	
Slow Death	7"	United Artists	REM406	1976	**£5**	**£2**	
Slow Death	7"	United Artists	UP35392	1972	**£4**	**£1.50**	
Slow Death	7"	United Artists	UP35392	1972	**£20**	**£10**	*promo picture sleeve*
Sneekers	10" LP	Snazz	R2371	1969	**£20**	**£8**	*US*
Supersnazz	LP	Epic	BN26487	1969	**£15**	**£6**	*US*
Teenage Head	7"	Kama Sutra	2013031	1971	**£5**	**£2**	
Teenage Head	LP	Kama Sutra	KSBS2031	1971	**£12**	**£5**	*US*

FLAMING LIPS

This Here Giraffe	CD-s	Warner Bros	W0335CDX	1996	**£5**	**£2**	*shaped picture disc*

FLAMING YOUTH

Flaming Youth's *Ark II* was a *Melody Maker* album of the month, but its remarkable lack of commercial success probably goes to show that the music press is very much less influential than it would like to believe. The group's drummer, however, has done very well subsequently – he is Phil Collins, albeit almost unrecognizable from the picture on the LP cover.

Ark 2	LP	Fontana	STL5533	1969	**£25**	**£10**	
From Now On	7"	Fontana	6001003	1970	**£10**	**£5**	
Guide Me Orion	7"	Fontana	TF1057	1969	**£15**	**£7.50**	*picture sleeve*
Man, Woman And Child	7"	Fontana	6001002	1970	**£10**	**£5**	

FLAMINGO, JOHNNY

My Teenage Girl	7"	Vogue	V9089	1957	**£75**	**£37.50**	
So Long	7"	Vogue	V9100	1958	**£60**	**£30**	

FLAMINGOS

John Peel once presented a radio programme in which he outlined the history of the falsetto male vocal within black pop music. His choice of 'I Only Have Eyes For You' by the Flamingos as an early milestone in this history was confirmed as a wise one by the memorable inclusion of the song at a key point within the film, *American Graffiti*. It is a doo-wop performance of remarkable power and beauty – a fact that was further acknowledged by Art Garfunkel's hit cover of the song, using an identical arrangement. The Flamingos were actually unusually long-lived for a doo-wop group, and their biggest hit is just one high point within an extensive catalogue.

At Night	7"	Top Rank	JAR519	1960	**£15**	**£7.50**	

Title	Format	Label	Cat. No.	Year	Mint	VG	Notes
Boogaloo Party	7"	Philips	BF1786	1969	**£6**	**£2.50**	*picture sleeve*
Boogaloo Party	7"	Philips	BF1483	1966	**£8**	**£4**	
Favorites	LP	End	LP(S)307	1960	**£50**	**£25**	US
Flamingos	LP	Checker	LP1433/LPS3005	1959	**£150**	**£75**	US
Flamingos	LP	Constellation	CS3	1964	**£25**	**£10**	US
Flamingos Meet The Moonglows	LP	Vee Jay	LP1052	1962	**£40**	**£20**	US
Hits Now And Then	LP	Philips	SBL7906	1969	**£10**	**£4**	
I Only Have Eyes For You	7"	Top Rank	JAR263	1960	**£75**	**£37.50**	
Just For A Kick	7"	London	HLN8373	1957	**£400**	**£250**	*best auctioned*
Ladder Of Love	7"	Brunswick	05696	1957	**£350**	**£210**	*best auctioned*
Love Walked In	7"	Top Rank	JAR213	1959	**£20**	**£10**	
Nobody Loves Me Like You	7"	Top Rank	JAR367	1960	**£20**	**£10**	
Requestfully Yours	LP	End	LP(S)308	1960	**£50**	**£25**	US
Serenade	LP	End	LP(S)304	1959	**£60**	**£30**	US
Sound Of The Flamingos	LP	End	LP(S)316	1962	**£50**	**£25**	US
Their Hits – Then And Now	LP	Philips	2/PHS600206	1966	**£20**	**£8**	US

FLAMMA–SHERMAN

Title	Format	Label	Cat. No.	Year	Mint	VG	Notes
Move Me	7"	SNB	554142	1969	**£15**	**£7.50**	

FLANAGAN, TOMMY

Title	Format	Label	Cat. No.	Year	Mint	VG	Notes
Jazz . . . It's Magic!	LP	Pye	NPL28009	1960	**£20**	**£8**	

FLANAGAN BROTHERS

Title	Format	Label	Cat. No.	Year	Mint	VG	Notes
Salton City	7"	Coral	Q72342	1958	**£8**	**£4**	

FLANAGAN BROTHERS (2)

Title	Format	Label	Cat. No.	Year	Mint	VG	Notes
Irish Delight	LP	Topic	12T365	1979	**£10**	**£4**	

FLANDERS, TOMMY

Title	Format	Label	Cat. No.	Year	Mint	VG	Notes
Moonstone	LP	Verve	SVLP6020	1969	**£12**	**£5**	

FLARES

Title	Format	Label	Cat. No.	Year	Mint	VG	Notes
Foot Stompin' Hits	LP	London	HAU8034	1963	**£30**	**£15**	
Foot Stomping	7"	London	HLU9441	1961	**£15**	**£7.50**	

FLASH

Title	Format	Label	Cat. No.	Year	Mint	VG	Notes
Flash	LP	Sovereign	SVNA7251	1972	**£12**	**£5**	
Flash In The Can	LP	Sovereign	SVNA7255	1972	**£12**	**£5**	
Flash In The Can	LP	Sovereign	SVNA7255	1972	**£20**	**£8**	*sleeve showing band in studio*
Out Of Our Hands	LP	Sovereign	SVNA7260	1973	**£12**	**£5**	

FLASH & THE BOARD OF DIRECTORS

Title	Format	Label	Cat. No.	Year	Mint	VG	Notes
Busy Signal	7"	Bell	BLL1007	1968	**£4**	**£1.50**	

FLASKET BRINNER

Title	Format	Label	Cat. No.	Year	Mint	VG	Notes
Flasket Brinner	LP	Silence	SRS4606	1971	**£30**	**£15**	*Swedish*

FLAT EARTH SOCIETY

Title	Format	Label	Cat. No.	Year	Mint	VG	Notes
Waleeco	LP	Fleetwood	3027	1968	**£100**	**£50**	US
Waleeco	LP	Psycho	PSYCHO17	1983	**£10**	**£4**	

FLATT & SCRUGGS

Title	Format	Label	Cat. No.	Year	Mint	VG	Notes
At Carnegie Hall	LP	CBS	BPG62259	1963	**£10**	**£4**	
Ballad Of Jed Clampett	7"	CBS	201793	1965	**£4**	**£1.50**	
Country & Western Aces	7" EP	Mercury	10010MCE	1964	**£6**	**£2.50**	
Country & Western Trailblazers No. 4	7" EP	Mercury	ZEP10106	1961	**£6**	**£2.50**	
Folk Songs Of Our Land	LP	CBS	BPG62095	1963	**£10**	**£4**	
Songs Of The Famous Carter Family	LP	Philips	BBL7516	1962	**£10**	**£4**	

FLAVOUR

Title	Format	Label	Cat. No.	Year	Mint	VG	Notes
Sally Had A Party	7"	Direction	583597	1968	**£4**	**£1.50**	

FLAX

Title	Format	Label	Cat. No.	Year	Mint	VG	Notes
One	LP	Vertigo		1976	**£150**	**£75**	

FLEE REKKERS

Title	Format	Label	Cat. No.	Year	Mint	VG	Notes
Blue Tango	7"	Pye	7N15326	1960	**£6**	**£2.50**	
Fabulous Flee Rekkers	7" EP	Pye	NEP24141	1961	**£40**	**£20**	
Fireball	7"	Piccadilly	7N35109	1963	**£8**	**£4**	
Green Jeans	7"	Triumph	RGM1008	1960	**£15**	**£7.50**	
Green Jeans	7"	Top Rank	JAR431	1960	**£30**	**£15**	
Lone Rider	7"	Piccadilly	7N35006	1961	**£8**	**£4**	
Stage To Cimmaron	7"	Piccadilly	7N35048	1962	**£8**	**£4**	
Sunburst	7"	Piccadilly	7N35081	1962	**£8**	**£4**	
Sunday Date	7"	Pye	7N15288	1960	**£6**	**£2.50**	

FLEETWOOD MAC

Most of the collectable Fleetwood Mac records come from the first part of the group's career, when its sound was very different to the commercial pop style that later became its forte. The Blue Horizon recordings – and especially the eponymous first LP – are probably the most authentic blues recordings to have been made by white, English musicians. Remarkably, that first LP climbed to number four in the album charts, although mint copies of the record have become surprisingly scarce these days.

Title	Format	Label	Cat. No.	Year	Mint	VG	Notes
Albatross	7"	Blue Horizon	573145	1968	**£4**	**£1.50**	
Albatross	CD-s	CBS	6546133	1989	**£5**	**£2**	
Albatross	CD-s	CBS	6551713	1989	**£5**	**£2**	*3" single*

Title	Format	Label	Cat. No.	Year	Mint	VG	Notes
As Long As You Follow	CD-s	Warner Bros	W7644CD	1988	**£5**	**£2**	*3" single*
Behind The Mask	CD	Warner Bros	9267602DJ	1990	**£20**	**£8**	*US promo picture disc*
Behind The Mask	LP	Warner Bros	7599262062	1990	**£15**	**£6**	*picture disc box set*
Big Love	12"	Warner Bros	W8398TP	1987	**£6**	**£2.50**	*picture disc*
Black Magic Woman	7"	Blue Horizon	573138	1968	**£5**	**£2**	
Blues Jam At Chess	LP	Blue Horizon	766227	1969	**£40**	**£20**	*double, with other artists*
Can't Go Back	12"	Warner Bros	W9848T	1983	**£6**	**£2.50**	
Everywhere	CD-s	Warner Bros	W8143CD	1988	**£5**	**£2**	*3" single*
Family Man	7"	Warner Bros	W8114B	1988	**£4**	**£1.50**	*boxed, with 2 prints*
Farmer's Daughter	7"	Warner Bros	K17746	1981	**£4**	**£1.50**	
Fleetwood Mac	LP	Blue Horizon	763200	1968	**£30**	**£15**	*mono*
Fleetwood Mac	LP	Blue Horizon	763200	1968	**£25**	**£10**	
Fleetwood Mac	LP	Mobile Fidelity	MFSL1012	1978	**£12**	**£5**	*US audiophile*
Fleetwood Mac	LP	Reprise	K54043	1975	**£12**	**£5**	*white vinyl*
Go Your Own Way	7"	Warner Bros	K16872	1977	**£15**	**£7.50**	*picture sleeve*
Green Manalishi	7"	Reprise	RS27007	1970	**£20**	**£10**	*picture sleeve*
Green Manalishi	7"	Reprise	RS27007	1970	**£4**	**£1.50**	
Hold Me	CD-s	Warner Bros	W7528CD	1989	**£5**	**£2**	*3" single*
I Believe My Time Ain't Long	7"	Blue Horizon	573051	1967	**£6**	**£2.50**	
I Believe My Time Ain't Long	7"	Blue Horizon	573051	1967	**£40**	**£20**	*picture sleeve*
In The Back Of My Mind	CD-s	Warner Bros	W9739CDX	1990	**£5**	**£2**	*foldout sleeve*
Isn't It Midnight	CD-s	Warner Bros	W7860CD	1988	**£5**	**£2**	*3" single*
Kiln House	LP	Reprise	RSLP9004	1970	**£10**	**£4**	
Little Lies	12"	Warner Bros	W8291TP	1987	**£6**	**£2.50**	*picture disc*
Man Of The World	7"	Immediate	IM080	1969	**£4**	**£1.50**	
Mirage	LP	Mobile Fidelity	MFSL1119	1984	**£10**	**£4**	*US audiophile*
Mr Wonderful	LP	Blue Horizon	763205	1968	**£25**	**£10**	
Need Your Love So Bad	7"	Blue Horizon	573139	1968	**£4**	**£1.50**	
Need Your Love So Bad	7"	Blue Horizon	573157	1969	**£4**	**£1.50**	
Oh Diane	7"	Warner Bros	FLEET1P	1982	**£6**	**£2.50**	*picture disc*
Oh Well	7"	Reprise	RS27000	1969	**£4**	**£1.50**	
Original Fleetwood Mac	LP	Blue Horizon	763875	1971	**£10**	**£4**	
Pious Bird Of Good Omen	LP	Blue Horizon	763215	1969	**£15**	**£6**	
Rhiannon	7"	Reprise	K14430	1976	**£8**	**£4**	*picture sleeve*
Rumours	CD	Reprise		1988	**£15**	**£6**	*HMV box set*
Rumours	LP	Warner Bros	K56344	1977	**£12**	**£5**	*white vinyl*
Rumours	LP	Nautilus	NR 8	1981	**£12**	**£5**	*US audiophile*
Save Me	CD-s	Warner Bros	W9866CDX	1990	**£5**	**£2**	*foldout sleeve*
Selections From 25 Years – The Chain	CD	Warner Bros	PROCD5905	1992	**£20**	**£8**	
Seven Wonders	12"	Warner Bros	W8317TP	1987	**£6**	**£2.50**	*picture disc*
Sky's The Limit	CD-s	WEA	W9740CD	1990	**£5**	**£2**	
Then Play On	LP	Reprise	K44103	1970	**£15**	**£6**	*with uncredited 'Oh Well' parts 1 & 2*
Then Play On	LP	Reprise	RSLP9000	1969	**£15**	**£6**	
Tusk	LP	Warner Bros	PROA866	1979	**£10**	**£4**	*US promo sampler*
Warm Ways	7"	Reprise	K14403	1975	**£6**	**£2.50**	*picture sleeve*

FLEETWOODS

Title	Format	Label	Cat. No.	Year	Mint	VG	Notes
Almost There	7"	Liberty	LIB10191	1965	**£6**	**£2.50**	
Before And After	LP	Dolton	BLP2/BST8030	1965	**£25**	**£10**	*US*
Best Of The Oldies	LP	Dolton	BLP2/BST8011	1962	**£30**	**£15**	*US*
Come Softly To Me	7"	London	HLU8841	1959	**£8**	**£4**	
Come Softly To Me	7"	London	SLU4003	1959	**£30**	**£15**	*stereo*
Deep In A Dream	LP	London	HAG2419	1961	**£30**	**£15**	
Fleetwoods	LP	Dolton	BLP2/BST8002	1960	**£40**	**£20**	*US*
Fleetwoods Sing For Lovers By Night	LP	Dolton	BLP2/BST8020	1963	**£30**	**£15**	*US*
Folk Rock	LP	Dolton	BLP2/BST8039	1965	**£25**	**£10**	*US*
Goodnight My Love	7"	Liberty	LIB75	1964	**£4**	**£1.50**	
Goodnight My Love	LP	Dolton	BLP2/BST8025	1963	**£30**	**£15**	*US*
Graduation's Here	7"	London	HLU8895	1959	**£8**	**£4**	
Greatest Hits	LP	Dolton	BLP2/BST8018	1962	**£30**	**£15**	*US*
He's The Great Imposter	7"	London	HLG9426	1961	**£6**	**£2.50**	
Mr Blue	7"	Top Rank	JAR202	1959	**£6**	**£2.50**	
Mr Blue	LP	Top Rank	BUY028	1960	**£25**	**£10**	
Outside My Window	7"	Top Rank	JAR294	1960	**£4**	**£1.50**	
Outside My Window	7"	Top Rank	JAR294	1960	**£10**	**£5**	*picture sleeve*
Ruby Red Baby Blue	7"	Liberty	LIB93	1964	**£4**	**£1.50**	
Runaround	7"	Top Rank	JAR383	1960	**£5**	**£2**	
Softly	LP	London	SAHG6188	1961	**£40**	**£20**	*stereo*
Softly	LP	London	HAG2388	1961	**£30**	**£15**	
They Tell Me It's Summer	7"	Liberty	LIB62	1964	**£4**	**£1.50**	
Tragedy	7"	London	HLG9341	1961	**£6**	**£2.50**	

FLEMING, HELEN

Title	Format	Label	Cat. No.	Year	Mint	VG	Notes
Eve's Ten Commandments	7"	Blue Beat	BB341	1966	**£12**	**£6**	

FLEMONS, WADE

Title	Format	Label	Cat. No.	Year	Mint	VG	Notes
Easy Loving	7"	Top Rank	JAR371	1960	**£4**	**£1.50**	
Slow Motion	7"	Top Rank	JAR206	1959	**£4**	**£1.50**	
Wade Flemons	LP	Vee Jay	LP1011	1959	**£40**	**£20**	*US*
What's Happening	7"	Top Rank	JAR327	1960	**£4**	**£1.50**	

FLESH VOLCANO

Title	Format	Label	Cat. No.	Year	Mint	VG	Notes
Slut	12"	Some Bizzare	SLUT1	1987	**£10**	**£5**	

FLETCHER, DARROW

Title	Format	Label	Cat. No.	Year	Mint	VG	Notes
Pain Gets A Little Deeper	7"	London	HLU10024	1966	**£40**	**£20**	

FLETCHER, DON

Title	Format	Label	Cat. No.	Year	Mint	VG	Notes
Two Wrongs Don't Make A Right	7"	Vocalion	VP9271	1966	**£8**	**£4**	

FLEUR DE LYS

A legendary psychedelic group, the Fleur De Lys recorded both under their own name and as backing group to singer Sharon Tandy. They produced a number of striking singles, but with little commercial impact. Frequent personnel changes produced a large number of ex-members. Of these, Gordon Haskell made a number of solo recordings in the early seventies and was a member of King Crimson for a while. Bryn Haworth began a solo career during the seventies, and still performs as a born-again Christian singer-songwriter, while Pete Sears ended up as a member of Jefferson Starship.

Title	Format	Label	Cat. No.	Year	Mint	VG	Notes
Circles	7"	Immediate	IM032	1966	**£150**	**£75**	
Dong With A Luminous Nose	7"	Polydor	56251	1968	**£50**	**£25**	
I Can See A Light	7"	Polydor	56200	1967	**£40**	**£20**	
Moondreams	7"	Immediate	IM020	1965	**£100**	**£50**	
Mud In Your Eye	7"	Polydor	56124	1966	**£250**	**£150**	*best auctioned*
Stop Crossing The Bridge	7"	Atlantic	584193	1968	**£40**	**£20**	
You're Just A Liar	7"	Atlantic	584243	1969	**£50**	**£25**	

FLICK, VIC SOUND

Title	Format	Label	Cat. No.	Year	Mint	VG	Notes
Hang On	7"	Chapter One	CH136	1970	**£8**	**£4**	

FLIED EGG

Title	Format	Label	Cat. No.	Year	Mint	VG	Notes
Dr Siegel's Fried Egg Shooting Machine	LP	Philips		1971	**£100**	**£50**	*Japanese*
Goodbye	LP	Philips	55504	1972	**£150**	**£75**	*Japanese*

FLIES

Title	Format	Label	Cat. No.	Year	Mint	VG	Notes
House Of Love	7"	Decca	F12594	1967	**£30**	**£15**	
I'm Not Your Stepping Stone	7"	Decca	F12533	1966	**£50**	**£25**	
Magic Train	7"	RCA	RCA1757	1968	**£20**	**£10**	

FLINGELS

Title	Format	Label	Cat. No.	Year	Mint	VG	Notes
Ireland Awake	LP	Saga	EROS8095	1969	**£15**	**£6**	

FLINT, SHELBY

Title	Format	Label	Cat. No.	Year	Mint	VG	Notes
Angel On My Shoulder	7"	Warner Bros	WB30	1961	**£4**	**£1.50**	

FLINTLOCK

Title	Format	Label	Cat. No.	Year	Mint	VG	Notes
Hot From The Lock	LP	Pinnacle	PLP8309	1976	**£12**	**£5**	
On The Way	LP	Pinnacle	PLP8307	1975	**£12**	**£5**	
Tears 'n' Cheers	LP	Pinnacle	PLP8310	1977	**£12**	**£5**	

FLINTSTONES

Title	Format	Label	Cat. No.	Year	Mint	VG	Notes
Workout	7"	HMV	POP1266	1964	**£10**	**£5**	

FLIP, BUNNY

Title	Format	Label	Cat. No.	Year	Mint	VG	Notes
Shanky Dog	7"	Pressure Beat	PB5510	1972	**£5**	**£2**	

FLIP & THE DATELINERS

Title	Format	Label	Cat. No.	Year	Mint	VG	Notes
My Johnny Doesn't Come Around Anymore	7"	HMV	POP1359	1964	**£30**	**£15**	

FLIPS

Title	Format	Label	Cat. No.	Year	Mint	VG	Notes
Rockin' Twist	7"	London	HLU9490	1962	**£6**	**£2.50**	

FLIRTATIONS

Title	Format	Label	Cat. No.	Year	Mint	VG	Notes
Nothing But A Heartache	7"	Deram	DM216	1968	**£5**	**£2**	
Sounds Like The Flirtations	LP	Deram	DML/SML1046	1969	**£10**	**£4**	

FLO & EDDIE

Title	Format	Label	Cat. No.	Year	Mint	VG	Notes
Flo And Eddie	LP	Reprise	K44234	1973	**£10**	**£4**	
Phlorescent Leech And Eddie	LP	Reprise	K44201	1972	**£10**	**£4**	

FLOATING BRIDGE

Title	Format	Label	Cat. No.	Year	Mint	VG	Notes
Floating Bridge	LP	Liberty	LBS83271	1969	**£15**	**£6**	

FLOCK

The Flock were one of the crop of rock big bands to emerge at the end of the sixties. They were made distinctive by the presence of a violin as a lead instrument; its wielder, Jerry Goodman, later found a context in which he could shine even brighter, as a member of John McLaughlin's Mahavishnu Orchestra.

Title	Format	Label	Cat. No.	Year	Mint	VG	Notes
Dinosaur Swamps	LP	CBS	64055	1970	**£10**	**£4**	
Flock	LP	CBS	63733	1969	**£12**	**£5**	

FLOCK OF SEAGULLS

Title	Format	Label	Cat. No.	Year	Mint	VG	Notes
It's Not Me Talking	7"	Cocteau	COQ3	1981	**£4**	**£1.50**	

FLOH DE COLOGNE

Title	Format	Label	Cat. No.	Year	Mint	VG	Notes
Fliessbandbabys Beat Show	LP	Ohr	OMM556000	1970	**£20**	**£8**	*German*
Geler Symphonie	LP	Ohr	OMM556033	1973	**£15**	**£6**	*German*
Lucky Streik	LP	Ohr	OMM556029	1973	**£20**	**£8**	*German double*
Munien	LP	Plane	99201	1974	**£12**	**£5**	*German*
Profitgier	LP	Ohr	OMM556010	1971	**£25**	**£10**	*German, red vinyl*
Rotkäppchen	LP	Plane	20905	1977	**£12**	**£5**	*German*

Tilt	LP	Plane	99202	1975	£12	£5	German
Vietnam	LP	Plane	33101	1968	£25	£10	German

FLOOD, DICK

Three Bells	7"	Felsted	AF125	1959	£4	£1.50	

FLOOR

First Floor	LP	Philips	XPY855701	1967	£40	£20	Dutch

FLORIAN GEYER

Beggars' Pride	LP	private	6621284	1976	£175	£87.50	German

FLORIBUNDA ROSE

One Way Street	7"	Piccadilly	7N35408	1967	£10	£5	

FLOWER TRAVELLING BAND

Anywhere	LP	Philips	8507	1970	£150	£75	Japanese
Made In Japan	LP	Atlantic	S8187	1972	£100	£50	Japanese
Make Up	LP	Atlantic	5073/4	1973	£150	£75	Japanese double
Satori	7"	Atlantic	2091128	1971	£15	£7.50	
Satori	LP	Atlantic	S8056	1971	£100	£50	Japanese

FLOWER, PHIL

Every Day I Have To Cry	7"	A&M	AMS784	1970	£15	£7.50	

FLOWERPOT MEN

Man Without A Woman	7"	Deram	DM183	1968	£4	£1.50	
Walk In The Sky	7"	Deram	DM160	1967	£4	£1.50	

FLOWERS

Challenge	LP	CBS	10063	1969	£100	£50	Japanese

FLOWERS, LLOYD

Lovers Town	7"	Blue Beat	BB88	1962	£12	£6	

FLOWERS AND FROLICS

Bees On Horseback	LP	Free Reed	FRR016	1977	£12	£5	

FLOYD, EDDIE

Big Bird	7"	Stax	601035	1968	£4	£1.50	
Bye Bye Baby	7"	Speciality	SPE1001	1967	£8	£4	
California Girl	LP	Stax	SXATS1036	1970	£10	£4	
I've Never Found A Girl	LP	Stax	SXATS1003	1968	£10	£4	
Knock On Wood	7"	Atlantic	584041	1966	£4	£1.50	
Knock On Wood	LP	Atco	228014	1969	£10	£4	
Knock On Wood	LP	Stax	589006	1967	£12	£5	
On A Saturday Night	7"	Stax	601024	1967	£4	£1.50	
Raise Your Hand	7"	Stax	601001	1967	£4	£1.50	
Set My Soul On Fire	7"	London	HL10129	1967	£4	£1.50	
Things Get Better	7"	Stax	601016	1967	£4	£1.50	

FLOYD, PRETTY BOY & THE GEMS

Hold Tight	12"	Montreco	EPMRC3005	1978	£10	£5	
Look At Her Dancin'	7"	Heavenly Sound	HSP4	1981	£8	£4	
Sharon	7"	Rip Off	RIP10	1979	£8	£4	
Spread The Word Around	7"	Rip Off	RIPOFF1	1979	£8	£4	

FLUTE & VOICE

Imaginations Of Light	LP	Pilz	20210882	1971	£40	£20	German

FLUX

Grand Result	LP	Rosegarden		1982	£50	£25	Dutch

FLY ON THE WALL

Devon Dumb	7"	Next Wave	NEXT1	1979	£12	£6	

FLYING BURRITO BROTHERS

Burrito Deluxe	LP	A&M	AMLS983	1970	£10	£4	
Flying Burrito Brothers	LP	A&M	AMLS64295	1971	£10	£4	
Gilded Palace Of Sin	LP	A&M	AMLS931	1969	£12	£5	
Last Of The Red Hot Burritos	LP	A&M	AMLS64343	1971	£10	£4	
Live In Amsterdam	LP	Bumble	GEXD301	1973	£12	£5	double
Train Song	7"	A&M	AMS756	1969	£4	£1.50	
Tried So Hard	7"	A&M	AMS816	1970	£4	£1.50	

FLYING CIRCUS

Prepared In Peace	LP	Harvest	SHSP4010	1970	£10	£4	

FLYING COLUMN

Folk Music Time In Ireland	LP	Emerald	GES1035	1970	£10	£4	
Four Green Fields	LP	Emerald	GES1059	1971	£10	£4	

FLYING MACHINE

Down To Earth	LP	Pye	NSPL18328	1970	£10	£4	
Hanging On The Edge Of Sadness	7"	Pye	7N17914	1970	£4	£1.50	
Send My Baby Home Again	7"	Pye	7N17811	1969	£4	£1.50	
Smile A Little Smile For Me	7"	Pye	7N17722	1969	£4	£1.50	2 different B sides

FLYING SAUCER ATTACK

Flying Saucer Attack	LP	Heartbeat	FSA62	1994	£15	£6	
Land Beyond The Sun	7"	Domino	RUG23	1994	£8	£4	
Soaring High	7"	Heartbeat	FSA6	1993	£30	£15	*3 different sleeves*
Wish	7"	Heartbeat	FSA61	1993	£20	£10	

FLYNN, STEVE

Mr Rainbow	7"	Parlophone	R5625	1967	£15	£7.50	
Your Life And My Life	7"	Parlophone	R5689	1968	£4	£1.50	

FLYS

Bunch Of Five	7"	Zama	ZA10	1977	£10	£5	

FLYTE

Dawn Dancer	LP	Don Quixote		1979	£25	£10	*Dutch*

FOCAL POINT

Love You Forever	7"	Deram	DM186	1968	£20	£10	

FOCUS

Hocus Pocus	7"	Blue Horizon	2096004	1971	£5	£2	
Moving Waves	LP	Blue Horizon	2931002	1971	£10	£4	*with poster*
Tommy	7"	Blue Horizon	2096008	1972	£6	£2.50	

FOCUS & P. J. PROBY

Focus Con Proby	LP	EMI	5C06425713	1977	£15	£6	*European*

FOCUS THREE

Ten Thousand Years Behind My Mind	7"	Columbia	DB8279	1967	£30	£15	

FOETUS

The aggressively avant-garde rock songs made by Jim Thirlwell (or Clint Ruin, as he sometimes likes to be known) are credited to a bewildering variety of names, of which the common denominator is 'Foetus'. For the sake of imposing some kind of order on the chaos that Thirlwell loves, records originally issued under such diverse descriptions as Foetus Corruptus, Foetus Over Frisco, Foetus Under Glass, Philip And His Foetus Vibrations, and You've Got Foetus On Your Breath are all listed here. Other records have been released using still further variations of the Foetus idea.

Ache	LP	Self Immolation	WOMBOYBL2	1982	£60	£30	
Butterfly Potion	CD-s	Big Cat	ABBCD16	1990	£5	£2	*as Foetus Inc.*
Custom Built For Capitalism	12"	Self Immolation	WOMBWSUSC125	1982	£25	£12.50	
Deaf	LP	Self Immolation	WOMBOYBL1	1981	£60	£30	
OKFM	7"	Self Immolation	WOMBS201	1981	£20	£10	
Rife	LP	Rifle	RIFLE1	198–	£15	£6	*double*
Tell Me, What Is The Bane Of Your Life	7"	Self Immolation	WOMBKX07	1982	£20	£10	
Wash It All Off	7"	Self Immolation	WOMBALL007	1981	£20	£10	

FOGCUTTERS

Cry Cry Cry	7"	Liberty	LIB55793	1964	£6	£2.50	

FOGERTY, TOM & THE BLUE VELVETS

Come On, Baby	7"	Orchestra	617	1961	£40	£20	US
Have You Ever Been Lonely?	7"	Orchestra	1010	1961	£40	£20	US
Yes You Did	7"	Orchestra		1962	£40	£20	US

FOGGY

How Come The Sun	7"	York	SYK534	1972	£4	£1.50	
Kitty Starr	7"	York	SYK542	1972	£4	£1.50	
Patchwork Album	LP	Canon	CNN5957	1976	£25	£10	
Simple Gifts	LP	York	FYK411	1972	£40	£20	

FOGGY DEW-O

Born To Take The Highway	LP	Decca	LK/SKL5035	1969	£15	£6	
Foggy Dew-O	LP	Eclipse	ECS2118	1968	£10	£4	
Foggy Dew-O	LP	Decca	LK/SKL4940	1968	£25	£10	
Reflections	7"	Decca	F12776	1968	£4	£1.50	

FOLEY, RED

Beyond The Sunset	LP	Decca	DL8296	1958	£15	£6	US
Company's Comin'	LP	Decca	DL(7)4140	1961	£12	£5	US
Country Double Date	7" EP	Brunswick	OE9148	1955	£8	£4	*with Ernest Tubb*
Dear Hearts And Gentle People	LP	Decca	DL(7)4290	1962	£12	£5	US
Golden Favorites	LP	Decca	DL4107	1961	£12	£5	US
He Walks With Thee	LP	Decca	DL8767	1958	£15	£6	US
Hearts Of Stone	7"	Brunswick	05363	1955	£10	£5	
Let's All Sing To Him	LP	Decca	DL(7)8903	1959	£12	£5	US
Let's All Sing With Red Foley	LP	Decca	DL(7)8847	1959	£15	£6	US
Lift Up Your Voice	10" LP	Decca	DL5338	1954	£30	£15	US
My Keepsake Album	LP	Decca	DL8806	1958	£15	£6	US
Night Watch	7"	Brunswick	05508	1955	£10	£5	
Red And Ernie	LP	Brunswick	LAT8206	1957	£15	£6	*with Ernest Tubb*

Title	Format	Label	Cat. No.	Year	Mint	Good	Notes
Sing Along	LP	Brunswick	LAT8343/ STA3034	1960	£15	£6	
Skinnie Minnie Fishtail	7"	Brunswick	05321	1954	£8	£4	
Songs Of Devotion	LP	Decca	DL(7)4198	1961	£12	£5	US
Souvenir Album	10" LP	Decca	DL5303	1951	£30	£15	US
Souvenir Album	LP	Decca	DL8294	1958	£20	£8	US

FOLEY, SIMON

Title	Format	Label	Cat. No.	Year	Mint	Good	Notes
To Strive With Princes	LP	Look	LKLP6324	1977	£15	£6	

FOLK BLUES INC.

Title	Format	Label	Cat. No.	Year	Mint	Good	Notes
Don't Hide	7"	Eyemark	EMS1006	1966	£5	£2	
F.B.I.	LP	Good Earth	GDS802	1977	£40	£20	

FOLK SONG CLUB

Title	Format	Label	Cat. No.	Year	Mint	Good	Notes
Imperial College	LP	private	no number	1965	£150	£75	

FOLK STOW

Title	Format	Label	Cat. No.	Year	Mint	Good	Notes
Folk Stow	LP	Stoof	MU7456	1978	£50	£25	

FOLKAL POINT

Title	Format	Label	Cat. No.	Year	Mint	Good	Notes
Folkal Point	LP	Midas	MR003	1972	£250	£150	

FOLKCORN

Title	Format	Label	Cat. No.	Year	Mint	Good	Notes
Goedenavond Spielman	LP	Spoof		1978	£30	£15	

FOLKES, CALVIN

Title	Format	Label	Cat. No.	Year	Mint	Good	Notes
Hello Everybody	7"	Port-O-Jam	PJ4118	1964	£10	£5	*Irving Six B side*
My Bonnie	7"	Port-O-Jam	PJ4117	1964	£10	£5	
Someone	7"	Rio	R5	1963	£10	£5	
You'll Never Know	7"	Rio	R8	1963	£10	£5	

FOLKLANDERS

Title	Format	Label	Cat. No.	Year	Mint	Good	Notes
Two Little Fishes	7" EP	Urban	PB001	196–	£5	£2	

FOLKLORDS

Title	Format	Label	Cat. No.	Year	Mint	Good	Notes
Release The Sunshine	LP	Allied	11	1969	£60	£30	*Canadian*

FOLKLORE

Title	Format	Label	Cat. No.	Year	Mint	Good	Notes
First Of Folklore	LP	Homespun	HPL104	1975	£40	£20	*Irish*
Room For Company	LP	Tank	BSS210	1977	£60	£30	

FOLKS BROTHERS

Title	Format	Label	Cat. No.	Year	Mint	Good	Notes
Carolina	7"	Blue Beat	BB30	1961	£12	£6	*Eric Morris B side*

FOLKWAYS

Title	Format	Label	Cat. No.	Year	Mint	Good	Notes
No Other Name	LP	Folk Heritage		1972	£10	£4	

FOLLY'S FOOL

Title	Format	Label	Cat. No.	Year	Mint	Good	Notes
Folly's Fool	LP	Century		1975	£75	£37.50	US

FOLQUE

Title	Format	Label	Cat. No.	Year	Mint	Good	Notes
Folque	LP	Phonogram		1974	£150	£75	*Norwegian*

FONTAINE, EDDIE

Title	Format	Label	Cat. No.	Year	Mint	Good	Notes
Cool It Baby	7"	Brunswick	05624	1956	£100	£50	
Nothing Shaking	7"	London	HLM8711	1958	£20	£10	
Rock Love	7"	HMV	7M304	1955	£250	£150	*best auctioned*

FONTANA, ARLENE

Title	Format	Label	Cat. No.	Year	Mint	Good	Notes
I'm In Love	7"	Pye	7N25010	1959	£5	£2	

FONTANA, WAYNE

Title	Format	Label	Cat. No.	Year	Mint	Good	Notes
Charlie Cass/Linda	7"	Fontana	TF1054	1969	£10	£5	
Come On Home	7" EP	Fontana	465307	1966	£20	£10	*French*
Give Me Just A Little More Time	7"	Philips	6006035	1970	£30	£15	
Wayne One	LP	Fontana	(S)TL5351	1966	£10	£4	

FONTANA, WAYNE & THE MINDBENDERS

Title	Format	Label	Cat. No.	Year	Mint	Good	Notes
Eric, Rick, Wayne, & Bob	LP	Fontana	TL5257	1966	£50	£25	
For You For You	7"	Fontana	TF418	1963	£4	£1.50	
Game Of Love	7" EP	Fontana	TE17449	1965	£10	£5	
Game Of Love	7" EP	Fontana	465272	1965	£20	£10	*French*
Hello Josephine	7"	Fontana	TF404	1963	£6	£2.50	
Just A Little Bit Too Late	7"	Fontana	TF579	1965	£4	£1.50	
Little Darling	7"	Fontana	TF436	1964	£5	£2	
Road Runner	7" EP	Fontana	TE17421	1964	£30	£15	
She Needs Love	7"	Fontana	TF611	1965	£4	£1.50	
She Needs Love	7" EP	Fontana	465295	1965	£20	£10	*French*
Stop Look And Listen	7"	Fontana	TF451	1964	£4	£1.50	
Um Um Um Um Um	7" EP	Fontana	TE17435	1964	£10	£5	
Walking On Air	7" EP	Fontana	TE17453	1965	£30	£15	
Wayne Fontana & The Mindbenders	LP	Fontana	TL5230	1965	£30	£15	
Wayne Fontana & The Mindbenders	LP	Wing	WL1166	1967	£15	£6	
Wayne Fontana & The Mindbenders	LP	Fontana	SFL13106	1969	£10	£4	

FONTANE SISTERS

Title	Format	Label	Cat. No.	Year	Mint	Good	Notes
Adorable	7"	London	HLD8225	1956	£40	£20	

Banana Boat Song	7"	London	HLD8378	1957	£15	£7.50	
Billy Boy	7"	London	HLD8861	1959	£8	£4	
Chanson D'Amour	7"	London	HLD8621	1958	£8	£4	
Eddie My Love	7"	London	HL7009	1956	£25	£12.50	*export*
Eddie My Love	7"	London	HLD8265	1956	£40	£20	
Fontane Sisters	LP	Dot	DLP3004	1956	£60	£30	*US*
Fontane Sisters No. 1	7" EP	London	RED1029	1955	£50	£25	
Fontane Sisters No. 2	7" EP	London	RED1037	1955	£40	£20	
Fontanes Sing	LP	London	HAD2053	1957	£75	£37.50	
Fool Around	7"	London	HLD8488	1957	£12	£6	
Happy Days And Lonely Nights	7"	London	HL8099	1954	£60	£30	
Hearts Of Stone	7"	London	HL8113	1955	£75	£37.50	
I'm In Love Again	7"	London	HLD8289	1956	£25	£12.50	
Listen To Your Heart	7"	London	HLD9037	1960	£5	£2	
Please Don't Leave Me	7"	London	HLD8415	1957	£15	£7.50	
Rock Love	7"	London	HL8126	1955	£75	£37.50	
Rolling Stone	7"	London	HLD8211	1955	£60	£30	
Seventeen	7"	London	HLD8177	1955	£60	£30	
Silver Bells	7"	London	HLD8343	1956	£15	£7.50	
Theme From A Summer Place	7"	London	HLD9078	1960	£5	£2	
Tips Of My Fingers	LP	Dot	DLP3531/25531	1963	£25	£10	*US*
Voices	7"	London	HLD8318	1956	£20	£10	*with Pat Boone*

FOOD

Forever Is A Dream	LP	Capitol	ST304	1969	£30	£15	*US*

FOOD BRAIN

Social Gathering	LP	Polydor	2310072	1970	£75	£37.50	*German*

FOOL

Simon and Marijke of the Fool were a design team (the Beatles' shop mural; Eric Clapton's guitar; the Incredible String Band's second LP cover), rather than musicians, but they nevertheless recorded two interesting and eclectic LPs (the second was credited to 'Simon and Marijke'), the first being produced by the Hollies' Graham Nash.

Fool	LP	Mercury	SMCL20138	1969	£40	£20	

FOOLS DANCE

Fools Dance	LP	Top Hat	TH22	1986	£10	£4	
Fools Dance	LP	Top Hole Turn	TURN19	1985	£15	£6	
They'll Never Know	12"	Lambs To The Slaught	LTS22T	1987	£10	£5	
They'll Never Know	7"	Lambs To The Slaught	LTS22	1987	£6	£2.50	

FOOT IN COLD WATER

Foot In Cold Water	LP	Elektra	K52011	1974	£15	£6	
Second Foot	LP	Daffodil	16028	1973	£20	£8	*Canadian*

FOOTE, CHUCK

You're Running Out Of Kisses	7"	London	HLU9495	1962	£5	£2	

FORBES

Beatles	7"	Power Exchange	PX253	1977	£4	£1.50	

FORBES, BILL

Once More	7"	Columbia	DB4269	1959	£5	£2	
You're Sixteen	7"	Columbia	DB4566	1961	£4	£1.50	

FORCE, ROBERT & ALBERT D'OSSCHE

Cross Over	LP	Sonet	SNKF168	1980	£10	£4	

FORCE FIVE

Baby Don't Care	7"	United Artists	UP1102	1965	£20	£10	
Don't Know Which Way To Turn	7"	United Artists	UP1141	1966	£15	£7.50	
Don't Make My Baby Blue	7"	United Artists	UP1051	1964	£8	£4	
I Want You Babe	7"	United Artists	UP1118	1965	£15	£7.50	
Yeah I'm Waiting	7"	United Artists	UP1089	1965	£15	£7.50	

FORCE WEST

All The Children Sleep	7"	Columbia	DB8174	1967	£6	£2.50	
Gotta Find Another Baby	7"	Columbia	DB7908	1966	£6	£2.50	
I Can't Give What I Haven't Got	7"	Decca	F12223	1965	£5	£2	
I'll Be Moving On	7"	CBS	3798	1968	£4	£1.50	
I'll Walk In The Rain	7"	CBS	3632	1968	£4	£1.50	
Sherry	7"	CBS	4385	1969	£5	£2	
When the Sun Comes Out	7"	Columbia	DB7963	1966	£5	£2	

FORD, CLINTON

Dandy	7" EP	Piccadilly	NEP34057	1966	£6	£2.50	
Old Shep	7"	Oriole	CB1500	1959	£4	£1.50	

FORD, DEAN & THE GAYLORDS

Mr Heartbreak's Here Instead	7"	Columbia	DB7402	1964	£10	£5	
Name Game	7"	Columbia	DB7610	1965	£10	£5	
Twenty Miles	7"	Columbia	DB7264	1964	£10	£5	

FORD, DEE DEE

Title	Format	Label	Cat. No.	Year	Mint	VG	Notes
Good Morning Blues	7"	London	HLU9245	1960	£30	£15	

FORD, EMILE

Title	Format	Label	Cat. No.	Year	Mint	VG	Notes
Emile	7" EP	Pye	NEP24119	1959	£6	£2.50	
Emile	LP	Piccadilly	NPL38001	1961	£15	£6	
Emile Ford Hit Parade	7" EP	Pye	NEP24124	1960	£8	£4	
Emile Ford Hit Parade Vol. 2	7" EP	Pye	NEP24133	1960	£10	£5	
New Tracks With Emile	LP	Pye	NPL18049	1959	£15	£6	
You'll Never Know What You're Missin'	7"	Pye	7N15268	1960	£5	£2	

FORD, FRANKIE

Title	Format	Label	Cat. No.	Year	Mint	VG	Notes
Alimony	7"	Top Rank	JAR186	1959	£8	£4	
Cheating Woman	7"	Top Rank	JAR282	1960	£15	£7.50	*Huey Piano Smith B side*
Let's Take A Sea Cruise	LP	Ace	LP1005	1959	£200	£100	*US*
Sea Cruise	7"	Sue	WI366	1965	£8	£4	
Sea Cruise	7"	London	HL8850	1959	£40	£20	
Time After Time	7"	Top Rank	JAR299	1960	£5	£2	
What's Going On	7"	Sue	WI369	1965	£15	£7.50	
You Talk Too Much	7"	London	HLP9222	1960	£15	£7.50	

FORD, JON

Title	Format	Label	Cat. No.	Year	Mint	VG	Notes
Two's Company, Three's A Crowd	7"	Philips	BF1690	1968	£4	£1.50	
You Got Me Where You Want Me	7"	Philips	6006030	1970	£40	£20	

FORD, NEAL & THE FANATICS

Title	Format	Label	Cat. No.	Year	Mint	VG	Notes
Neal Ford And The Fanatics	LP	Hickory	LPS141	1967	£40	£20	*US*

FORD, PERRY

Title	Format	Label	Cat. No.	Year	Mint	VG	Notes
Prince Of Fools	7"	Decca	F11497	1962	£4	£1.50	

FORD, ROCKY

Title	Format	Label	Cat. No.	Year	Mint	VG	Notes
New Singing Star	LP	Audio Lab	AL1561	1960	£25	£10	*US*

FORD, TENNESSEE ERNIE

Title	Format	Label	Cat. No.	Year	Mint	VG	Notes
Anticipation Blues	7" EP	Capitol	EAP120067	1961	£15	£7.50	
Ballad Of Davy Crockett	7"	Capitol	CL14506	1956	£10	£5	
Blackeyed Susie	7"	Capitol	CL15010	1959	£4	£1.50	
Capitol Presents	10" LP	Capitol	LC6573	1952	£30	£15	
Catfish Boogie	7"	Capitol	CL14006	1953	£20	£10	
Gather Round	7" EP	Capitol	EAP11227	1960	£10	£5	
Give Me Your Word	7"	Capitol	CL14005	1953	£15	£7.50	
His Hands	7"	Capitol	CL14261	1955	£6	£2.50	
In The Middle Of An Island	7"	Capitol	CL14759	1957	£4	£1.50	
Little Red Rocking Hood	7"	Capitol	CL15210	1961	£6	£2.50	
Ol' Rockin' Ern	LP	Capitol	T888	1958	£25	£10	
Sixteen Tons	7"	Capitol	CL14500	1956	£10	£5	
Sixteen Tons	7" EP	Capitol	EAP1014	1956	£10	£5	
Sixteen Tons	LP	Capitol	T1380	1960	£20	£8	
Star Carol	7" EP	Capitol	SEP11071	1961	£5	£2	*stereo*
Sunday Barbecue	7"	Capitol	CL14896	1958	£4	£1.50	
Tennessee Ernie Ford	7" EP	Capitol	EAP1639	1956	£8	£4	
That's All	7"	Capitol	CL14557	1956	£5	£2	
There Is Beauty In Everything	7"	Capitol	CL14273	1955	£6	£2.50	
This Lusty Land	10" LP	Capitol	LC6825	1956	£15	£6	
This Must Be The Place	7"	Capitol	CL14133	1954	£8	£4	*with Betty Hutton*
Who Will Shoe Your Pretty Little Foot	7"	Capitol	CL14616	1956	£4	£1.50	

FORD THEATRE

Title	Format	Label	Cat. No.	Year	Mint	VG	Notes
Time Changes	LP	Stateside	SSL10288	1969	£10	£4	
Trilogy For The Masses	LP	ABC	ABCS658	1968	£30	£15	*US*

FOREHAND, EDDIE BUSTER

Title	Format	Label	Cat. No.	Year	Mint	VG	Notes
Young Boy Blues	7"	Action	ACT4519	1969	£5	£2	

FOREIGNER

Title	Format	Label	Cat. No.	Year	Mint	VG	Notes
Double Vision	LP	Mobile Fidelity	MFSL1052	1982	£12	£5	*US audiophile*
I Don't Want To Live Without You	CD-s	Atlantic	A9101CD	1988	£5	£2	
Inside Information	CD	Atlantic	7818082	1987	£40	£20	*promo box set, with cassette, single, press kit*
Profiled!	CD	Atlantic	PRCD4007	1991	£20	£8	*US promo*

FORELAND

Title	Format	Label	Cat. No.	Year	Mint	VG	Notes
Foreland	LP	private	GL1	1975	£100	£50	

FORERUNNERS

Title	Format	Label	Cat. No.	Year	Mint	VG	Notes
Bony Moronie	7"	Solar	SRP100	1964	£30	£15	

FOREST

Title	Format	Label	Cat. No.	Year	Mint	VG	Notes
Forest	LP	Harvest	SHVL760	1969	£60	£30	
Full Circle	LP	Harvest	SHVL784	1970	£75	£37.50	
Searching For Shadows	7"	Harvest	HAR5007	1969	£15	£7.50	

FORESTERS

Title	Format	Label	Number	Year	Mint	Good	Notes
Broken Hearted Clown	7"	Polydor	56038	1965	£4	£1.50	
Early Morning Hours	7"	Polydor	56104	1966	£4	£1.50	
How Can I Tell Her	7"	Polydor	56057	1965	£4	£1.50	
Sometimes When You're Lonely	7"	Columbia	DB8040	1966	£4	£1.50	

FOREVER AMBER

Title	Format	Label	Number	Year	Mint	Good	Notes
Love Cycle	LP	Advance	no number	1969	£1250	£875	

FOREVER MORE

Title	Format	Label	Number	Year	Mint	Good	Notes
Words On Black Plastic	LP	RCA	3015	1971	£10	£4	
Yours Forever More	LP	RCA	SF8016	1969	£10	£4	

FORK IN THE ROAD

Title	Format	Label	Number	Year	Mint	Good	Notes
Can't Turn Around	7"	Ember	EMBS131	1961	£125	£62.50	

FORMAT

Title	Format	Label	Number	Year	Mint	Good	Notes
Maxwell's Silver Hammer	7"	CBS	4600	1969	£4	£1.50	

FORMATIONS

Title	Format	Label	Number	Year	Mint	Good	Notes
At The Top Of The Stairs	7"	MGM	MGM1399	1968	£60	£30	

FORMERLY FAT HARRY

Title	Format	Label	Number	Year	Mint	Good	Notes
Formerly Fat Harry	LP	Harvest	SHSP4016	1971	£12	£5	

FORMINX

The writing credit to 'Papathanassiou' reveals the presence of a very young Vangelis in this obscure group. Anyone, however, expecting to find an early indication of the melodic keyboard gifts to be found flowering on the likes of 'Chariots Of Fire' will be sadly disappointed by this novelty beat item.

Title	Format	Label	Number	Year	Mint	Good	Notes
Jenka Beat	7"	Vocalion	V9235	1965	£15	£7.50	

FORMULA ONE

Title	Format	Label	Number	Year	Mint	Good	Notes
I Just Can't Go To Sleep	7"	Warner Bros	WB155	1965	£10	£5	

FORRAY, ANDY

Title	Format	Label	Number	Year	Mint	Good	Notes
Dream With Me	7"	Decca	F12733	1968	£25	£12.50	
Proud One	7"	Parlophone	R5729	1968	£4	£1.50	
Sarah Jane	7"	Parlophone	R5715	1968	£4	£1.50	

FORRESTER, SHARON

Title	Format	Label	Number	Year	Mint	Good	Notes
Silly Wasn't I?	7"	Ashanti	ASH403	1973	£5	£2	

FORSYTH, BRUCE

Title	Format	Label	Number	Year	Mint	Good	Notes
I'm In Charge	7" EP	Parlophone	GEP8807	1960	£5	£2	
Mr Entertainment	LP	Parlophone	PMC1132/ PCS3031	1960	£10	£4	

FORT MUDGE MEMORIAL DUMP

Title	Format	Label	Number	Year	Mint	Good	Notes
Fort Mudge Memorial Dump	LP	Mercury	61256	1970	£30	£15	US

FORTES MENTUM

Title	Format	Label	Number	Year	Mint	Good	Notes
Gotta Go	7"	Parlophone	R5768	1969	£5	£2	
I Can't Go On	7"	Parlophone	R5726	1968	£5	£2	
Saga Of A Wrinkled Man	7"	Parlophone	R5684	1968	£15	£7.50	

FORTUNA

Title	Format	Label	Number	Year	Mint	Good	Notes
From The Edinburgh Festival Fringe 1976	LP	Sweet Folk And Count	SFA058	1976	£10	£4	

FORTUNE, JOHNNY

Title	Format	Label	Number	Year	Mint	Good	Notes
Soul Surfer	LP	Park Avenue	401	1963	£25	£10	US

FORTUNE, LANCE

Title	Format	Label	Number	Year	Mint	Good	Notes
Be Mine	7"	Pye	7N15240	1960	£4	£1.50	
I Wonder	7"	Pye	7N15297	1960	£4	£1.50	
This Love I Have For You	7"	Pye	7N15260	1960	£4	£1.50	
Who's Gonna Tell Me?	7"	Pye	7N15347	1961	£4	£1.50	

FORTUNE, SONNY

Title	Format	Label	Number	Year	Mint	Good	Notes
Awakening	LP	Horizon	SP704	1975	£15	£6	US

FORTUNES

Title	Format	Label	Number	Year	Mint	Good	Notes
Caroline	7"	Decca	F11809	1964	£15	£7.50	
Fortunes	LP	Decca	LK4736	1965	£25	£10	
Fortunes	LP	Capitol	ST21891	1972	£10	£4	
Fortunes	LP	Decca	SKL4736	1965	£40	£20	*stereo*
Freedom	LP	Capitol	ST647	1971	£12	£5	US
Here Comes That Rainy Day Feeling Again	LP	Capitol	ST809	1971	£12	£5	US
Here It Comes Again	7"	Decca	F12243	1965	£4	£1.50	
I Like The Look Of You	7"	Decca	F11912	1964	£5	£2	
Idol	7" EP	United Artists	36119	1967	£20	£10	*French*
Is It Really Worth Your While	7"	Decca	F12485	1966	£5	£2	
Look Homeward Angel	7"	Decca	F11985	1964	£5	£2	
Our Love Has Gone	7"	Decca	F12612	1967	£5	£2	
Silent Street	7"	Decca	F12429	1966	£4	£1.50	

Summertime Summertime	7"	Decca	F11718	1963	**£8**	**£4**	
Summertime Summertime	7"	Decca	F11718	1963	**£25**	**£12.50**	*picture sleeve*
That Same Old Feeling	LP	World Pacific	WPS21904	1970	**£12**	**£5**	*US*
This Golden Ring	7"	Decca	F12321	1966	**£4**	**£1.50**	
This Golden Ring	7" EP	Decca	457105	1966	**£20**	**£10**	*French*
You've Got Your Troubles	7" EP	Decca	457089	1965	**£20**	**£10**	*French*

FORTY-FIVES

Couldn't Believe A Word	7"	Chopper	CHEAP5	1979	**£4**	**£1.50**	

FORTY-NINTH PARALLEL

Forty-Ninth Parallel	LP	Maverick	MAS7001	1969	**£125**	**£62.50**	*US*

FORWOOD, SHIRLEY

Two H[illegible]	7"	London	HLD8402	1957	**£20**	**£8**	

FOSTER, FRANK

Frank Foster Quartet	10" LP	Vogue	LDE112	1955	**£100**	**£50**	
Frank Foster With Elmo Hope	LP	Esquire	32033	1957	**£40**	**£20**	
Manhattan Fever	LP	Blue Note	BST84278	1968	**£25**	**£10**	

FOSTER, JACKIE

Oh Leona	7"	Planetone	RC13	1963	**£6**	**£2.50**	

FOSTER, JOHN

John Foster Sings	LP	Island	ILP939	1966	**£25**	**£10**	

FOSTER, LES

Do It Nice	7"	Big Shot	BI529	1969	**£4**	**£1.50**	

FOSTERCHILD

Fosterchild	LP	Columbia	PES90382	1977	**£30**	**£15**	*Canadian*
Troubled Child	LP	Columbia	PCC80003	1978	**£30**	**£15**	*Canadian*

FOTHERINGAY

The group formed by Sandy Denny after leaving Fairport Convention for the first time operated in very much the same folk-rock area, but included some of Denny's most winning material on its only album. Sadly the group came apart during sessions for a second album, leaving the members to join the Fairport team pool.

Fotheringay	LP	Island	ILPS9125	1970	**£20**	**£8**	*pink label*
Peace In The End	7"	Island	WIP6085	1970	**£6**	**£2.50**	

FOUNDATIONS

Baby Now That I've Found You	7" EP	Pye	PNV24199	1967	**£8**	**£4**	*French*
Digging The Foundations	LP	Pye	NPL18290	1969	**£10**	**£4**	
From The Foundations	LP	Pye	NPL18206	1967	**£10**	**£4**	
It's All Right	7" EP	Pye	NEP24297	1968	**£10**	**£5**	
Rocking The Foundations	LP	Pye	NPL18227	1968	**£10**	**£4**	

FOUNTAIN, PETE

Mr New Orleans Jazz Meets Mr Honky-Tonk	LP	Coral	LVA9141	1960	**£10**	**£4**	*with Big Tiny Little*
Salutes The Great Clarinettists	LP	Coral	LVA9132	1960	**£10**	**£4**	

FOUR

It's Alright	7"	Decca	F11999	1964	**£5**	**£2**	

FOUR ACES

Bahama Mama	7"	Brunswick	05663	1957	**£4**	**£1.50**	
Beyond The Blue Horizon	LP	Decca	DL(7)8944	1959	**£12**	**£5**	*US*
Four Aces	10" LP	Decca	DL5429	195–	**£20**	**£8**	*US*
Four Aces	7" EP	Brunswick	OE9458	1959	**£5**	**£2**	
Friendly Persuasion	7"	Brunswick	05623	1956	**£4**	**£1.50**	
Gal With The Yaller Shoes	7"	Brunswick	05566	1956	**£4**	**£1.50**	
Gang That Sang	7"	Brunswick	05256	1954	**£4**	**£1.50**	
Golden Hits	LP	Decca	DL(7)4013	1960	**£12**	**£5**	*US*
Hanging Up A Horseshoe	7"	Brunswick	05758	1958	**£4**	**£1.50**	
Heart	7"	Brunswick	05651	1957	**£4**	**£1.50**	
Heart And Soul	LP	Decca	DL8228	1956	**£15**	**£6**	*US*
Hits From Broadway	LP	Decca	DL(7)8855	1959	**£12**	**£5**	*US*
Hits From Hollywood	LP	Brunswick	LAT8249	1958	**£12**	**£5**	
I'm Yours	7"	Decca	A73010	195–	**£6**	**£2.50**	*export*
If You Can Dream	7"	Brunswick	05573	1956	**£4**	**£1.50**	
It Shall Come To Pass	7"	Brunswick	05322	1954	**£4**	**£1.50**	
It's A Woman's World	7"	Brunswick	05348	1954	**£5**	**£2**	
Just Squeeze Me	10" LP	Brunswick	LA8614	1953	**£15**	**£6**	
Love Is A Many Splendoured Thing	7"	Brunswick	05480	1955	**£8**	**£4**	
Melody Of Love	7"	Brunswick	05379	1955	**£5**	**£2**	
Mood For Love	LP	Decca	DL8122	1956	**£15**	**£6**	*US*
Mood For Love Vol. 1	7" EP	Brunswick	OE9157	1955	**£5**	**£2**	
Mood For Love Vol. 2	7" EP	Brunswick	OE9192	1955	**£5**	**£2**	
Mr Sandman	7"	Brunswick	05355	1954	**£12**	**£6**	
Presenting	7" EP	Brunswick	OE9090	1955	**£6**	**£2.50**	
Rock and Roll Rhapsody	7"	Brunswick	05743	1958	**£4**	**£1.50**	
Sentimental Souvenirs	LP	Decca	DL8191	1956	**£15**	**£6**	*US*
She Sees All The Hollywood Hits	LP	Decca	DL8312	1957	**£15**	**£6**	*US*
Shuffling Along	LP	Brunswick	LAT8221	1957	**£12**	**£5**	

Title	Format	Label	Cat. No.	Year	Mint	VG	Notes
Sing Film Titles	7" EP	Brunswick	OE9324	1957	£6	£2.50	
Slewfoot	7"	Brunswick	05429	1955	£4	£1.50	
Stranger In Paradise	7"	Brunswick	05418	1955	£8	£4	
Swingin' Aces	LP	Brunswick	STA3014	1958	£15	£6	
There Goes My Heart	7"	Brunswick	05401	1955	£4	£1.50	
Three Coins In The Fountain	7"	Brunswick	05308	1954	£10	£5	
To Love Again	7"	Brunswick	05562	1956	£4	£1.50	
Woman In Love	7"	Brunswick	05589	1956	£5	£2	
World Outside	7"	Brunswick	05767	1958	£4	£1.50	
Written On The Wind	LP	Decca	DL8424	1957	£15	£6	US

FOUR ACES (2)

Title	Format	Label	Cat. No.	Year	Mint	VG	Notes
River Bank Coberley Again	7"	Island	WI178	1965	£10	£5	
Sweet Chariot	7"	Island	WI179	1965	£10	£5	

FOUR ACES (3)

Title	Format	Label	Cat. No.	Year	Mint	VG	Notes
Why Do You	7"	Anton	EAG178/9	196–	£200	£100	

FOUR COINS

Title	Format	Label	Cat. No.	Year	Mint	VG	Notes
World Outside	7"	Fontana	H168	1958	£4	£1.50	

FOUR DEGREES

Title	Format	Label	Cat. No.	Year	Mint	VG	Notes
Four Degrees	LP	Oak	RGJ187	1965	£300	£180	1 sided, no sleeve

FOUR DOLLS

Title	Format	Label	Cat. No.	Year	Mint	VG	Notes
Three On A Date	7"	Capitol	CL14778	1957	£4	£1.50	
Whoop-A-Lala	7"	Capitol	CL14845	1958	£4	£1.50	

FOUR ESCORTS

Title	Format	Label	Cat. No.	Year	Mint	VG	Notes
Loop De Loop Mambo	7"	HMV	7M277	1954	£6	£2.50	

FOUR ESQUIRES

Title	Format	Label	Cat. No.	Year	Mint	VG	Notes
Act Your Age	7"	Pye	7N25027	1959	£4	£1.50	
Adorable	7"	London	HLA8224	1956	£25	£12.50	
Always And Forever	7"	London	HLO8579	1958	£6	£2.50	
Hideaway	7"	London	HL8746	1958	£5	£2	
Look Homeward Angel	7"	London	HL8376	1957	£30	£15	demo
Love Me Forever	7"	London	HLO8533	1958	£10	£5	
Sphinx Won't Tell	7"	London	HL8152	1955	£25	£12.50	
Wouldn't It Be Wonderful	7"	Pye	7N25049	1960	£4	£1.50	

FOUR FOLK

Title	Format	Label	Cat. No.	Year	Mint	VG	Notes
Hard Cases	LP	Reality	RY1003	1966	£50	£25	

FOUR FRESHMEN

Title	Format	Label	Cat. No.	Year	Mint	VG	Notes
Four Freshmen And Five Guitars	7" EP	Capitol	SEP11255	1961	£5	£2	stereo
Four Freshmen And Five Guitars Pt 2	7" EP	Capitol	SEP21255	1961	£5	£2	stereo
Four Freshmen And Five Guitars Pt 3	7" EP	Capitol	SEP31255	1961	£5	£2	stereo
Four Freshmen And Five Saxes	LP	Capitol	T844	1957	£10	£4	
Four Freshmen And Five Trombones	LP	Capitol	LC6812	1956	£10	£4	
Four Freshmen And Five Trumpets	LP	Capitol	T763	1957	£10	£4	
Freshmen Favorites	LP	Capitol	T743	1956	£10	£4	US
Voices In Latin	LP	Capitol	T992	1958	£10	£4	US
Voices In Modern	10" LP	Capitol	LC6685	1954	£10	£4	
Voices In Modern	LP	Capitol	T522	1955	£10	£4	US

FOUR GIBSON GIRLS

Title	Format	Label	Cat. No.	Year	Mint	VG	Notes
June, July And August	7"	Oriole	CB1447	1958	£6	£2.50	
Safety Sue	7"	Oriole	CB1453	1958	£5	£2	

FOUR GUYS

Title	Format	Label	Cat. No.	Year	Mint	VG	Notes
Mine	7"	Vogue Coral	Q72054	1955	£6	£2.50	

FOUR JACKS

Title	Format	Label	Cat. No.	Year	Mint	VG	Notes
Hey Baby	7"	Decca	F10984	1958	£5	£2	
Hey Baby	7" EP	Decca	DFE6460	1958	£20	£10	

FOUR JONES BOYS

Title	Format	Label	Cat. No.	Year	Mint	VG	Notes
Certain Smile	7"	Columbia	DB4170	1958	£4	£1.50	
Day The Rains Came	7"	Columbia	DB4217	1958	£4	£1.50	
Rock-A-Hula Baby	7"	Columbia	DB4046	1957	£4	£1.50	
Tutti Frutti	7"	Decca	F10717	1956	£6	£2.50	

FOUR JUST MEN

Title	Format	Label	Cat. No.	Year	Mint	VG	Notes
That's My Baby	7"	Parlophone	R5186	1964	£60	£30	

FOUR KENTS

Title	Format	Label	Cat. No.	Year	Mint	VG	Notes
Moving Finger Writes	7"	RCA	RCA1705	1968	£4	£1.50	

FOUR KINSMEN

Title	Format	Label	Cat. No.	Year	Mint	VG	Notes
It Looks Like The Daybreak	7"	Decca	F22671	1967	£4	£1.50	

FOUR KNIGHTS

Title	Format	Label	Cat. No.	Year	Mint	VG	Notes
Foolish Tears	7"	Coral	Q72355	1959	£6	£2.50	
Foolishly Yours	7"	Capitol	CL14290	1955	£6	£2.50	
Four Knights	7" EP	Capitol	EAP1506	1955	£30	£15	
Four Knights	LP	Coral	CRL52221	195–	£20	£8	US
Honey Bunch	7"	Capitol	CL14244	1955	£20	£10	

In The Chapel In The Moonlight	7"	Capitol	CL14154	1954	£**10**	£**5**	
Million Dollar Baby	LP	Coral	CRL(7)57309	1960	£**15**	£**6**	*US*
Saw Your Eyes	7"	Capitol	CL14204	1954	£**8**	£**4**	
Spotlight Songs	10" LP	Capitol	LC6604	1953	£**30**	£**15**	
Spotlight Songs	10" LP	Capitol	H345	1953	£**75**	£**37.50**	*US*
Spotlight Songs	LP	Capitol	T345	1953	£**30**	£**15**	*US*
Till Then	7"	Capitol	CL14076	1954	£**15**	£**7.50**	
You	7"	Capitol	CL14516	1956	£**5**	£**2**	

FOUR LADS

Dixieland Doin's	LP	London	HAR2413/ SAHR6213	1962	£**10**	£**4**	
Four Hits	7" EP	London	RER1289	1961	£**8**	£**4**	
Four Lads	LP	Philips	BBL7256	1958	£**10**	£**4**	
Golly	7"	Philips	JK1021	1957	£**8**	£**4**	
Moments To Remember	7" EP	Philips	BBE12044	1956	£**6**	£**2.50**	
Standing On The Corner	7"	Philips	PB1000	1960	£**4**	£**1.50**	

FOUR LEAVED CLOVER

Why	7"	Oak	RGJ207	1965	£**250**	£**150**	*best auctioned*

FOUR LOVERS

These were the earliest recordings made by the group that later became the Four Seasons.

Joyride	LP	RCA	LPM1317	1956	£**500**	£**330**	*US, best auctioned*
My Life For Your Love	7"	Epic	9255	1957	£**400**	£**250**	*US, best auctioned*
Shake A Hand	7"	RCA	476812	1957	£**25**	£**12.50**	*US*

FOUR MATADORS

Man's Gotta Stand Tall	7"	Columbia	DB7806	1966	£**40**	£**20**	

FOUR PALMS

Jeannie, Joanie, Shirley & Tony	7"	Vogue	V9116	1958	£**250**	£**150**	*best auctioned*

FOUR PENNIES

Black Girl	7"	Philips	BF1366	1964	£**4**	£**1.50**	
Do You Want Me To	7"	Philips	BF1296	1964	£**4**	£**1.50**	
Four Pennies	7" EP	Philips	BE12561	1964	£**8**	£**4**	
Juliet	LP	Wing	WL1146	1967	£**15**	£**6**	
Keep The Freeway Open	7"	Philips	BF1491	1966	£**4**	£**1.50**	
Mixed Bag	LP	Philips	BL7734	1966	£**75**	£**37.50**	
No Sad Songs For Me	7"	Philips	BF1519	1966	£**4**	£**1.50**	
Smooth Side Of The Four Pennies	7" EP	Philips	BE12571	1964	£**6**	£**2.50**	
Spin With The Four Pennies	7" EP	Philips	BE12562	1964	£**10**	£**5**	
Swinging Side Of The Four Pennies	7" EP	Philips	BE12570	1964	£**10**	£**5**	
Two Sides Of The Four Pennies	LP	Philips	BL7642	1964	£**30**	£**15**	

FOUR PENNIES (2)

My Block	7"	Stateside	SS198	1963	£**12**	£**6**	
When The Boys Are Happy	7"	Stateside	SS244	1963	£**10**	£**5**	

FOUR PLUS ONE

The group that issued its first single under the name Four Plus One, issued its second as the In Crowd, and eventually, after a few changes in personnel, got round to making an LP – as Tomorrow.

Time Is On My Side	7"	Parlophone	R5221	1965	£**40**	£**20**	

FOUR PREPS

Big Man	7" EP	Capitol	EAP11064	1959	£**6**	£**2.50**	
Campus Encores	7" EP	Capitol	EAP11647	1961	£**5**	£**2**	
Dreamy Eyes	7" EP	Capitol	EAP1862	1957	£**6**	£**2.50**	
Four Preps	LP	Capitol	T994	1958	£**10**	£**4**	*US*
Lazy Summer Nights	7" EP	Capitol	EAP11139	1959	£**5**	£**2**	
Things We Did Last Summer	LP	Capitol	T1090	1958	£**10**	£**4**	
Twenty Six Miles	7"	Capitol	CL14815	1957	£**4**	£**1.50**	
Twenty Six Miles	7" EP	Capitol	EAP11015	1958	£**6**	£**2.50**	

FOUR SAXOPHONES

Four Saxophones In Twelve Tones	10" LP	Vogue	LDE170	1956	£**12**	£**5**	

FOUR SEASONS

Ain't That A Shame	7"	Stateside	SS194	1963	£**4**	£**1.50**	
Ain't That A Shame	LP	Stateside	SL10042	1963	£**20**	£**8**	
All The Song Hits	LP	Philips	2/600150	1964	£**10**	£**4**	*US*
Alone	7"	Stateside	SS315	1964	£**5**	£**2**	
Big Girls Don't Cry	7"	Stateside	SS145	1963	£**4**	£**1.50**	
Big Girls Don't Cry	LP	Vee Jay	LP/SR1056	1963	£**15**	£**6**	*US*
Born To Wander	LP	Philips	BL7611	1964	£**12**	£**5**	
Bye Bye Baby	7"	Philips	BF1395	1965	£**4**	£**1.50**	
C'mon Marianne	7"	Philips	BF1584	1967	£**4**	£**1.50**	
Candy Girl	7"	Stateside	SS216	1963	£**5**	£**2**	
Christmas Album	LP	Philips	(S)BL7753	1966	£**15**	£**6**	
Dawn	7"	Philips	BF1317	1964	£**4**	£**1.50**	
Dawn	LP	Philips	BL7621	1964	£**12**	£**5**	
Don't Think Twice	7" EP	Philips	452049	1965	£**15**	£**7.50**	*French*
Electric Stories	7"	Philips	BF1743	1969	£**6**	£**2.50**	
Entertain You	LP	Philips	BL7663	1965	£**12**	£**5**	

Four Seasons Sing	7" EP	Stateside	SE1011	1964	£20	£10	
Gold Vault Of Hits	LP	Philips	(S)BL7719	1966	£10	£4	
Golden Hits	LP	Vee Jay	LP/SR1065	1963	£12	£5	*US*
Greetings	LP	Stateside	SL10051	1963	£20	£8	
Hits Of The Four Seasons	cass-s	Philips	MCP1000	1968	£6	£2.50	
I've Got You Under My Skin	7"	Philips	BF1511	1966	£4	£1.50	
I've Got You Under My Skin	7" EP	Philips	452060	1966	£15	£7.50	*French*
Let's Hang On	7"	Philips	BF1439	1965	£4	£1.50	
Looking Back	LP	Philips	(S)BL7752	1966	£10	£4	
More Golden Hits	LP	Vee Jay	LP/SR1088	1964	£12	£5	*US*
More Great Hits Of 1964	LP	Vee Jay	LP/SR1136	1965	£12	£5	*US*
Opus 17	7"	Philips	BF1493	1966	£4	£1.50	
Peanuts	7"	Stateside	SS262	1964	£5	£2	
Rag Doll	7"	Philips	BF1347	1964	£4	£1.50	
Rag Doll	7"	Philips	BF1763	1969	£4	£1.50	*picture sleeve*
Rag Doll	7" EP	Philips	452030	1964	£15	£7.50	*French*
Rag Doll	LP	Philips	BL7643	1964	£10	£4	
Recorded Live On Stage	LP	Vee Jay	LP/SR1154	1965	£15	£6	*US*
Ronnie	7"	Philips	BF1334	1964	£4	£1.50	
Santa Claus Is Coming To Town	7"	Stateside	SS241	1963	£6	£2.50	
Seasoned Hits	LP	Fontana	SFJL952	1968	£10	£4	
Second Vault Of Golden Hits	LP	Philips	(S)BL7751	1967	£10	£4	
Sherry	7"	Stateside	SS122	1962	£4	£1.50	
Sherry	7" EP	Pathe	EMF332	1962	£15	£7.50	*French*
Sherry	LP	Stateside	SL10033	1963	£20	£8	
Since I Don't Have You	7"	Stateside	SS343	1964	£5	£2	
Sing Big Hits	LP	Philips	(S)BL7687	1965	£10	£4	
Stay	LP	Vee Jay	LP/SR1082	1964	£15	£6	*US*
Walk Like a Man	7"	Stateside	SS169	1963	£4	£1.50	
Watch The Flowers Grow	7"	Philips	BF1621	1967	£4	£1.50	
We Love Girls	LP	Vee Jay	LP/SR1121	1965	£15	£6	*US*
Whatever You Say	7"	Warner Bros	K16107	1971	£15	£7.50	
Working My Way Back To You	7"	Philips	BF1474	1966	£4	£1.50	
Working My Way Back To You	LP	Philips	BL7699	1965	£10	£4	

FOUR SIGHTS

But I Can Tell	7"	Columbia	DB7227	1964	£5	£2	

FOUR SKINS

Fistful Of 4 Skins	LP	Syndicate	SYN1	1983	£10	£4	
From Chaos To 1984	LP	Syndicate	SYNLP5	1984	£15	£6	
Good, The Bad And The 4 Skins	LP	Secret	SEC4	1982	£10	£4	
Lowlife	7"	Secret	SHH141	1982	£6	£2.50	
One Law For Them	7"	Clockwork Fun	CF101	1981	£8	£4	
Yesterday's Heroes	7"	Secret	SHH125	1981	£5	£2	

FOUR SPICES

Fire Engine Boogie	7"	MGM	MGM944	1957	£20	£10	

FOUR SQUARES

Four Squares	7" EP	Hollick & Taylor	HT1009	1964	£50	£25	

FOUR TONES

Voom Ba Voom	7"	Decca	F11074	1958	£8	£4	

FOUR TOPHATTERS

Go Baby Go	7"	London	HLA8163	1955	£200	£100	*best auctioned*
Wild Rosie	7"	London	HLA8198	1955	£200	£100	*best auctioned*

FOUR TOPS

7 Rooms Of Gloom	7"	Tamla Motown	TMG612	1967	£5	£2	
Ask The Lonely	7"	Tamla Motown	TMG507	1965	£25	£12.50	
Baby I Need Your Loving	7"	Stateside	SS336	1964	£20	£10	
Baby I Need Your Loving	CD-s	Motown	ZD41947	1989	£5	£2	
Do What You Gotta Do	7"	Tamla Motown	TMG710	1969	£4	£1.50	
Four Tops	7" EP	Tamla Motown	TME2012	1966	£10	£5	
Four Tops	LP	Tamla Motown	TML11010	1965	£30	£15	
Four Tops Hits	7" EP	Tamla Motown	TME2018	1967	£8	£4	
I Can't Help Myself	7"	Tamla Motown	TMG515	1965	£6	£2.50	
I'm In A Different World	7"	Tamla Motown	TMG675	1968	£4	£1.50	
It's The Same Old Song	7"	Tamla Motown	TMG528	1965	£8	£4	
Jazz Impressions	LP	Workshop	217	1962	£400	£250	*US*
Live	LP	Tamla Motown	(S)TML11041	1967	£10	£4	
Loving You Is Sweeter Than Ever	7"	Tamla Motown	TMG568	1966	£5	£2	

Title	Format	Label	Number	Year	Value		Notes
On Broadway	LP	Motown	(MS)657	1967	**£15**	**£6**	*US*
On Top	LP	Tamla Motown	(S)TML11037	1966	**£12**	**£5**	
Reach Out	LP	Tamla Motown	(S)TML11056	1967	**£10**	**£4**	
Reach Out & I'll Be There	7"	Tamla Motown	TMG579	1966	**£4**	**£1.50**	
Second Album	LP	Tamla Motown	TML11021	1966	**£25**	**£10**	
Shaft In Africa	LP	Probe	SPB1077	1973	**£15**	**£6**	
Shake Me Wake Me	7"	Tamla Motown	TMG553	1966	**£15**	**£7.50**	
Something About You	7"	Tamla Motown	TMG542	1965	**£8**	**£4**	
Standing In The Shadows Of Love	7"	Tamla Motown	TMG589	1967	**£4**	**£1.50**	
Without The One You Love	7"	Stateside	SS371	1965	**£25**	**£12.50**	
You Keep Running Away	7"	Tamla Motown	TMG623	1967	**£4**	**£1.50**	

FOUR TUNES

Title	Format	Label	Number	Year	Value		Notes
12 x 4	LP	Jubilee	LP1039	195–	**£75**	**£37.50**	*US*
I Gambled With Love	78	London	L1231	1954	**£20**	**£10**	
I Sold My Heart To The Junkman	7"	London	HL8151	1955	**£75**	**£37.50**	
Tired Of Waiting	7"	London	HLJ8164	1955	**£30**	**£15**	

FOUR WINDS

Title	Format	Label	Number	Year	Value		Notes
Short Shorts	7"	London	HLU8556	1958	**£25**	**£12.50**	

FOURMOST

Title	Format	Label	Number	Year	Value		Notes
Apples, Peaches, Pumpkin Pie	7"	CBS	3814	1968	**£5**	**£2**	
Auntie Maggie's Remedy	7"	Parlophone	R5528	1966	**£6**	**£2.50**	
Baby I Need Your Lovin'	7"	Parlophone	R5194	1964	**£4**	**£1.50**	
Easy Squeezy	7"	CBS	4461	1969	**£8**	**£4**	
Everything In The Garden	7"	Parlophone	R5304	1965	**£4**	**£1.50**	
First And Fourmost	LP	Parlophone	PMC1259	1965	**£60**	**£30**	
Fourmost Sound	7" EP	Parlophone	GEP8892	1964	**£30**	**£15**	
Girls Girls Girls	7"	Parlophone	R5379	1965	**£4**	**£1.50**	
Hello Little Girl	7" EP	Odeon	SOE3748	1963	**£50**	**£25**	*French*
Here There And Everywhere	7"	Parlophone	R5491	1966	**£5**	**£2**	
How Can I Tell Her	7"	Parlophone	R5157	1964	**£4**	**£1.50**	
How Can I Tell Her	7" EP	Parlophone	GEP8917	1964	**£40**	**£20**	
Rosetta	7"	CBS	4041	1969	**£10**	**£5**	

FOURMYULA

Title	Format	Label	Number	Year	Value		Notes
Honey Chile	7"	Columbia	DB8549	1969	**£4**	**£1.50**	

FOURTEEN

Title	Format	Label	Number	Year	Value		Notes
Easy To Fool	7"	Olga	S051	1968	**£5**	**£2**	
Through My Door	7"	Olga	OLE002	1968	**£5**	**£2**	
Umbrella	7"	Olga	OLE006	1968	**£6**	**£2.50**	

FOURTEEN ICED BEARS

Title	Format	Label	Number	Year	Value		Notes
Balloon Song	7"	Penetration		1987	**£5**	**£2**	*flexi*
Come Get Me	7"	Sarah	SARAH5	1988	**£8**	**£4**	
Falling Backwards	7"	Thunderball Surfacer	002	198–	**£5**	**£2**	*B side by Crocodile Ride*
Inside	12"	Frank	COPPOLA1	1986	**£8**	**£5**	
Like A Dolphin	12"	Frank	CAPRA202	1987	**£6**	**£2.50**	
Mother Sleep	7"	Thunderball	7TBL2	1989	**£20**	**£10**	*test pressing*

FOURTH CEKCION

Title	Format	Label	Number	Year	Value		Notes
Fourth Cekcion	LP	Solar	110	1970	**£50**	**£25**	*US*

FOURTH WAY

Title	Format	Label	Number	Year	Value		Notes
Fourth Way	LP	Capitol	ST317	1970	**£10**	**£4**	*US*
Sun And Moon Have Come Together	LP	Harvest	SKAO423	1970	**£10**	**£4**	*US*
Werewolf	LP	Harvest	ST666	1971	**£10**	**£4**	*US*

FOURUM

Title	Format	Label	Number	Year	Value		Notes
Fourum	LP	Sirius		197–	**£50**	**£25**	
Gunnerside Gill Remembered	LP	Guardian	GRF54	1980	**£20**	**£8**	

FOWLEY, KIM

Title	Format	Label	Number	Year	Value		Notes
Born To Be Wild	LP	Imperial	LP12413	1968	**£15**	**£6**	*US*
Day The Earth Stood Still	LP	Silence	MNWLP7P	1970	**£75**	**£37.50**	*Swedish*
Good Clean Fun	LP	Imperial	LP12443	1969	**£15**	**£6**	*US*
I'm Bad	LP	Capitol	ST11075	1972	**£20**	**£8**	*US*
International Heroes	LP	Capitol	ST11159	1973	**£12**	**£5**	*US*
Lights	7"	Parlophone	R5521	1966	**£10**	**£5**	
Lights The Blind Can See	7"	CBS	202338	1966	**£6**	**£2.50**	
Lijud Fran Waholm	LP	Silence	MNW14P	1970	**£20**	**£8**	*Swedish*
Love Is Alive And Well	LP	Tower	(S)T5080	1967	**£30**	**£15**	*US*
Outrageous	LP	Imperial	LP12423	1969	**£20**	**£8**	*US*
They're Coming To Take Me Away	7"	CBS	202243	1966	**£5**	**£2**	
Trip	7"	Island	WI278	1966	**£6**	**£2.50**	

Title	Format	Label	Cat. No.	Year	Price	Price	Notes
Trip	7" EP	Vogue	INT18086	1966	£60	£30	French
Underground All Stars	LP	Dot	25964	1969	£25	£10	US

FOX

Title	Format	Label	Cat. No.	Year	Price	Price	Notes
Mr Carpenter	7"	CBS	3381	1968	£30	£15	

FOX (2)

Title	Format	Label	Cat. No.	Year	Price	Price	Notes
For Fox Sake	LP	Fontana	6309007	1970	£60	£30	
Second Hand Love	7"	Fontana	6007016	1970	£15	£7.50	

FOX, DON

Title	Format	Label	Cat. No.	Year	Price	Price	Notes
Be My Girl	7"	Decca	F10927	1957	£4	£1.50	
Party Time	7"	Decca	F10955	1957	£4	£1.50	
Pretend You Don't See Her	7"	Decca	F10983	1958	£4	£1.50	
She Was Only Seventeen	7"	Decca	F11057	1958	£4	£1.50	
T'Ain't What You Do	7"	Triumph	RGM1022	1960	£25	£12.50	
Three Swinging Clicks	7"	Honey Hit	TB125	196–	£5	£2	picture sleeve

FOX, SAMANTHA

Title	Format	Label	Cat. No.	Year	Price	Price	Notes
Aim To Win	12"	Lamborghini	LMG10	1984	£8	£4	picture disc
I Only Wanna Be With You	CD-s	Jive	FOXYCD11	1989	£6	£2.50	in tin
I Wanna Have Some Fun	CD-s	Jive	FOXYCD12	1989	£6	£2.50	in tin
Naughty Girls	CD-s	Jive	FOXYCD9	1988	£6	£2.50	
Touch Me	LP	Jive	HIPR39	1988	£10	£4	picture disc
True Devotion	CD-s	Jive	FOXYCD8	1987	£6	£2.50	

FOXX, INEZ

Title	Format	Label	Cat. No.	Year	Price	Price	Notes
You Hurt Me For The Last Time	7"	Stax	2025151	1973	£5	£2	

FOXX, INEZ & CHARLIE

Title	Format	Label	Cat. No.	Year	Price	Price	Notes
Baby Give It To Me	7"	Direction	584042	1969	£4	£1.50	
Come By Here	LP	Direction	863085	1968	£10	£4	
Come On In	7"	Direction	583816	1968	£4	£1.50	
Count The Days	7"	Direction	583192	1967	£4	£1.50	
Greatest Hits	LP	Direction	863281	1968	£10	£4	
Here We Go Round	7"	Sue	WI307	1964	£12	£6	
Hi Diddle Diddle	7"	Sue	WI314	1964	£12	£6	
Hummingbird	7"	London	HLC10009	1965	£4	£1.50	
Hurt By Love	7"	Sue	WI323	1964	£10	£5	
I Ain't Going For That	7"	Direction	582712	1967	£4	£1.50	
Inez & Charles Foxx	LP	London	SHA8241	1965	£25	£10	
Jaybirds	7"	Sue	WI304	1964	£12	£6	
La De Da I Love You	7"	United Artists	UP35013	1970	£4	£1.50	
La De Dah I Love You	7"	Sue	WI356	1964	£12	£6	
Mockingbird	7"	Sue	WI301	1963	£12	£6	
Mockingbird	7"	United Artists	UP2269	1969	£4	£1.50	
Mockingbird	LP	Sue	ILP911	1964	£40	£20	
My Momma Told Me	7"	London	HLC9971	1965	£5	£2	
No Stranger To Love	7"	Stateside	SS556	1966	£8	£4	
Tightrope	7"	Pye	7N25561	1971	£4	£1.50	
Tightrope	7"	Stateside	SS586	1967	£10	£5	

FOYER DES ARTS

Title	Format	Label	Cat. No.	Year	Price	Price	Notes
Su Seltsame Sekretärin	10" LP	Aronda	002	1980	£25	£10	German

FRABJOY & THE RUNCIBLE SPOON

The tracks credited to Graham Gouldman and Kevin Godley on the Marmalade label sampler LP were actually by Frabjoy and the Runcible Spoon. The group also included Lol Creme in its line-up and can be viewed, therefore, as a first dry-run for 10cc. An album was apparently recorded, but was lost when the Marmalade label folded.

Title	Format	Label	Cat. No.	Year	Price	Price	Notes
I'm Beside Myself	7"	Marmalade	598019	1969	£10	£5	

FRACTION

Title	Format	Label	Cat. No.	Year	Price	Price	Notes
Moon Blood	LP	Angelus	571	1971	£1000	£700	

FRAGILE

Title	Format	Label	Cat. No.	Year	Price	Price	Notes
Fragile	LP	private		1976	£250	£150	Dutch

FRAME

Title	Format	Label	Cat. No.	Year	Price	Price	Notes
Doctor Doctor	7"	RCA	RCA1571	1967	£40	£20	
My Feet Don't Fit His Shoes	7"	RCA	RCA1556	1966	£6	£2.50	

FRAME (2)

Title	Format	Label	Cat. No.	Year	Price	Price	Notes
Frame Of Mind	LP	Bellaphon	BLPS19107	1972	£25	£10	German

FRAMPTON, PETER

Title	Format	Label	Cat. No.	Year	Price	Price	Notes
Frampton Comes Alive (Edited)	LP	A&M	PR3703	1978	£10	£4	US picture disc

FRANC, PETER

Title	Format	Label	Cat. No.	Year	Price	Price	Notes
En Route	LP	Dawn	DNLS3051	1973	£10	£4	
Profile	LP	Dawn	DNLS3043	1972	£10	£4	

FRANCIS, BOBBY

Title	Format	Label	Cat. No.	Year	Price	Price	Notes
Chain Gang	7"	Doctor Bird	DB1153	1968	£10	£5	
Judy Drowned	7"	Ska Beat	JB193	1965	£10	£5	

FRANCIS, CONNIE

Title	Format	Label	Cat. No.	Year	Mint	VG	Notes
All Time International Hits	LP	MGM	C1012	1965	**£10**	**£4**	
All Time International Hits	LP	MGM	CS6083	1965	**£15**	**£6**	*stereo*
Another Page	7"	MGM	MGM1334	1967	**£4**	**£1.50**	
At The Copa	LP	MGM	C861	1961	**£10**	**£4**	
At The Copa	LP	MGM	CS6035	1961	**£15**	**£6**	*stereo*
Award-Winning Motion Picture Hits	LP	MGM	C940	1963	**£10**	**£4**	
Award-Winning Motion Picture Hits	LP	MGM	CS6070	1963	**£15**	**£6**	*stereo*
Be Anything	7"	MGM	MGM1236	1963	**£4**	**£1.50**	
Best Of Connie Francis	LP	Readers Digest	GBCFA106	1981	**£25**	**£10**	*4 LP set*
Best Of Connie Francis	LP	MGM	C8041	1967	**£10**	**£4**	
Blue Winter	7"	MGM	MGM1221	1963	**£4**	**£1.50**	
Christmas With Connie	LP	MGM	C797	1959	**£25**	**£10**	
Connie And Clyde	LP	MGM	C(S)8086	1968	**£15**	**£6**	
Connie Francis	7" EP	MGM	MGMEP686	1958	**£15**	**£7.50**	
Connie Francis	7" EP	MGM	MGMEP792	1965	**£15**	**£7.50**	
Connie Francis Favourites	7" EP	MGM	MGMEP759	1961	**£15**	**£7.50**	
Connie Sings For Mama	7" EP	MGM	MGMEP789	1964	**£15**	**£7.50**	
Connie's American Hits	7" EP	MGM	MGMEP769	1963	**£15**	**£7.50**	
Connie's Greatest Hits	LP	MGM	C831	1960	**£10**	**£4**	
Country And Western Golden Hits	LP	MGM	C812	1960	**£25**	**£10**	
Country Music Connie Style	LP	MGM	CS6062	1962	**£20**	**£8**	*stereo*
Country Music Connie Style	LP	MGM	C916	1962	**£15**	**£6**	
Do The Twist	LP	MGM	C879	1961	**£25**	**£10**	
Don't Break The Heart That Loves You	7"	MGM	MGM1157	1962	**£4**	**£1.50**	
Don't Ever Leave Me	7"	MGM	MGM1253	1964	**£4**	**£1.50**	
Drowning My Sorrows	7"	MGM	MGM1207	1963	**£4**	**£1.50**	
Exciting Connie Francis	LP	MGM	C786	1959	**£15**	**£6**	
Faded Orchid	7"	MGM	MGM962	1957	**£30**	**£15**	
First Lady Of Record	7" EP	MGM	MGMEP742	1960	**£12**	**£6**	
Folk Song Favourites	LP	MGM	C883	1962	**£10**	**£4**	
Folk Song Favourites	LP	MGM	CS6054	1962	**£15**	**£6**	*stereo*
Follow The Boys	7"	MGM	MGM1193	1962	**£4**	**£1.50**	
Follow The Boys	LP	MGM	C931	1963	**£10**	**£4**	
Follow The Boys	LP	MGM	CS6068	1963	**£15**	**£6**	*stereo*
For Mama	LP	MGM	C1006/CS6082	1965	**£15**	**£6**	
Forget Domani	7"	MGM	MGM1265	1965	**£8**	**£4**	
From Italy With Love	7" EP	MGM	MGMEP783	1963	**£15**	**£7.50**	
Fun Songs For Children	LP	MGM	C819	1960	**£50**	**£25**	
Girl In Love	7" EP	MGM	MGMEP658	1956	**£15**	**£7.50**	
Great American Waltzes	LP	MGM	C958	1964	**£10**	**£4**	
Great American Waltzes	LP	MGM	CS6075	1964	**£15**	**£6**	*stereo*
Great Country Hits Vol. 2	LP	MGM	ACB00167	1975	**£10**	**£4**	
Hawaii Connie	LP	MGM	C(S)8110	1969	**£25**	**£10**	
Heartaches	7" EP	MGM	MGMEP677	1958	**£12**	**£6**	
Hey Ring A Ding	7" EP	MGM	MGMEP773	1963	**£15**	**£7.50**	
I Never Had A Sweetheart	7"	MGM	MGM945	1957	**£30**	**£15**	
I Was Such A Fool	7"	MGM	MGM1171	1962	**£4**	**£1.50**	
I'll Get By	7"	MGM	MGM993	1958	**£4**	**£1.50**	
I'm Gonna Be Warm This Winter	7"	MGM	MGM1185	1962	**£4**	**£1.50**	
If I Didn't Care	7" EP	MGM	MGMEP697	1959	**£15**	**£7.50**	
If My Pillow Could Talk	7"	MGM	MGM1202	1963	**£4**	**£1.50**	
Irish Favourites	LP	MGM	C898	1962	**£20**	**£8**	
Irish Favourites	LP	MGM	CS6056	1962	**£25**	**£10**	*stereo*
Italian Favourites	7" EP	MGM	MGMEP760	1961	**£15**	**£7.50**	
Italian Favourites	LP	MGM	C821/CS6002	1960	**£15**	**£6**	
Jealous Heart	7"	MGM	MGM1293	1966	**£4**	**£1.50**	
Jealous Heart	LP	MGM	C(S)8009	1966	**£15**	**£6**	
Jewish Favourites	LP	MGM	CS6021	1961	**£15**	**£6**	*stereo*
Jewish Favourites	LP	MGM	C845	1961	**£10**	**£4**	
Live At Sahara In Las Vegas	LP	MGM	C(S)8036	1967	**£15**	**£6**	
Looking For Love	LP	MGM	C983/CS6079	1965	**£15**	**£6**	
Love Is Me, Love Is You	7"	MGM	MGM1305	1966	**£4**	**£1.50**	
Love Italian Style	LP	MGM	C(S)8050	1968	**£10**	**£4**	
Majesty Of Love	7"	MGM	MGM969	1957	**£20**	**£10**	*with Marvin Rainwater*
Mala Femmena	7" EP	MGM	MGMEP780	1963	**£15**	**£7.50**	
Mama	7"	MGM	MGM1070	1960	**£30**	**£15**	
More Italian Favourites	LP	MGM	CS6029	1961	**£15**	**£6**	*stereo*
More Italian Favourites	LP	MGM	C854	1961	**£10**	**£4**	
More Italian Hits	LP	MGM	CS6067	1963	**£15**	**£6**	*stereo*
More Italian Hits	LP	MGM	C930	1963	**£10**	**£4**	
Movie Greats Of The Sixties	LP	MGM	C(S)8027	1966	**£15**	**£6**	
Mr Love	7"	MGM	MGM1493	1969	**£4**	**£1.50**	
Mr Twister	7"	MGM	MGM1151	1962	**£4**	**£1.50**	
My Child	7"	MGM	MGM1271	1965	**£4**	**£1.50**	
My First Real Love	7"	MGM	SP1169	1956	**£100**	**£50**	
My Heart Cries For You	7"	MGM	MGM1347	1967	**£4**	**£1.50**	
My Heart Cries For You	LP	MGM	C(S)8054	1968	**£10**	**£4**	
My Sailor Boy	7"	MGM	MGM932	1956	**£60**	**£30**	
My Thanks To You	LP	MGM	C782	1959	**£20**	**£8**	
My Thanks To You	LP	World Record Club	TP618	1966	**£10**	**£4**	
My World Is Slipping Away	7"	MGM	MGM1381	1968	**£4**	**£1.50**	
Never On Sunday	LP	MGM	C875	1961	**£10**	**£4**	
Never On Sunday	LP	MGM	CS6047	1961	**£15**	**£6**	*stereo*

New Kind Of Connie	LP	MGM	C998/CS6080	1965	£10	£4	
Phoenix Love Theme	7"	MGM	MGM1295	1966	£4	£1.50	
Plenty Good Lovin'	7"	MGM	MGM1036	1959	£4	£1.50	
Rock And Roll Million Sellers	7" EP	MGM	MGMEP717	1960	£20	£10	
Rock And Roll Million Sellers	LP	MGM	C804	1960	£25	£10	
Rock And Roll Million Sellers No. 2	7" EP	MGM	MGMEP720	1960	£20	£10	
Rock And Roll Million Sellers No. 3	7" EP	MGM	MGMEP731	1960	£15	£7.50	
Roundabout	7"	MGM	MGM1282	1965	£4	£1.50	
Sings Great Country Favourites	LP	MGM	C1003/CS6081	1965	£15	£6	*with Hank Williams Jr*
Sixteen Of Connie's Greatest Hits	LP	MGM	C970	1964	£10	£4	
Somebody Else Is Takin' My Place	7"	MGM	MGM1446	1968	£4	£1.50	
Somewhere My Love	7"	MGM	MGM1320	1966	£4	£1.50	
Songs Of Les Reed	LP	MGM	CS8117	1969	£15	£6	
Songs To A Swinging Band	LP	MGM	C870	1961	£10	£4	
Songs To A Swinging Band	LP	MGM	CS6044	1961	£15	£6	*stereo*
Spanish And Latin American Favourites	LP	MGM	C836	1960	£10	£4	
Spanish And Latin American Favourites	LP	MGM	CS6012	1960	£15	£6	*stereo*
Spanish Nights And You	7"	MGM	MGM1327	1966	£4	£1.50	
Summer Of His Years	7"	MGM	MGM1220	1963	£4	£1.50	
Time Alone Will Tell	7"	MGM	MGM1336	1967	£4	£1.50	
Toward The End Of The Day	7"	MGM	MGM1012	1959	£4	£1.50	
Vacation	7"	MGM	MGM1165	1962	£4	£1.50	
Valentino	7"	MGM	MGM1060	1960	£4	£1.50	
Wedding Cake	7"	MGM	MGM1471	1969	£4	£1.50	
What Kind Of Fool Am I	7" EP	MGM	MGMEP775	1963	£15	£7.50	
Whatever Happened To Rosemary	7"	MGM	MGM1212	1963	£4	£1.50	
When The Boys Meet The Girls	LP	MGM	C(S)8006	1966	£10	£4	
Where The Boys Are	7" EP	MGM	MGMEP756	1961	£15	£7.50	
Who's Happy Now?	LP	United Artists	ULP30182	1978	£100	£50	*withdrawn sleeve*
Who's Sorry Now	10" LP	MGM	MGMD153	1958	£50	£25	
Why Say Goodbye	7"	MGM	MGM1407	1968	£4	£1.50	
You Always Hurt The One You Love	7"	MGM	MGM998	1958	£4	£1.50	
You're My Everything	7" EP	MGM	MGMEP711	1960	£15	£7.50	

FRANCIS, JOE 'KING'

Have Me Baby	7"	Rio	R90	1966	£6	£2.50	
I Don't Want You No More	7"	Ska Beat	JB184	1965	£10	£5	
I Got A Ska	7"	Ska Beat	JB262	1966	£10	£5	
Pull It Out	7"	Rainbow	RAI114	1967	£6	£2.50	
Wicked Woman	7"	Blue Beat	BB323	1965	£12	£6	

FRANCIS, LITTLE WILLIE

I'm Ashamed	7"	Blue Beat	BB151	1963	£12	£6	

FRANCIS, NAT

Just To Keep You	7"	Blue Beat	BB361	1966	£12	£6	
Mama Kiss Him Goodnight	7"	Blue Beat	BB346	1966	£12	£6	
Three Nights Of Love	7"	Blue Beat	BB376	1967	£12	£6	

FRANCIS, PANAMA BLUES BAND

Tough Talk	LP	Stateside	SL10070	1964	£12	£5	

FRANCIS, RITCHIE

Songbird	LP	Pegasus	PEG11	1971	£12	£5	

FRANCIS, WILBERT

Memories Of You	7"	Ska Beat	JB267	1966	£10	£5	

FRANCIS, WINSTON

California Dreaming	LP	Bamboo	BDLPS216	1971	£25	£10	
Games People Play	7"	Studio One	SO2086	1969	£12	£6	*Albert Griffiths B side*
If Your Heart Be Lonely	7"	Coxsone	CS7087	1969	£10	£5	
Mr Fix It	7"	Fab	FAB271	1973	£4	£1.50	
Mr Fix It	LP	Bamboo	BDLP207	1970	£30	£15	
Reggae And Cry	7"	Coxsone	CS7089	1969	£10	£5	*Freedom Singers B side*
Same Old Song	7"	Bamboo	BAM10	1969	£4	£1.50	*Sound Dimension B side*
Too Experienced	7"	Punch	PH5	1969	£4	£1.50	*Jackie Mittoo B side*
Turn Back The Hands Of Time	7"	Bamboo	BAM46	1970	£4	£1.50	

FRANCIS & THE SWINGERS

Warn The People	7"	Blue Beat	BB379	1967	£12	£6	

FRANCISCO

Cosmic Beam Experience	LP	Cosmic Beam	001	1976	£60	£30	US

FRANK, JACKSON C.

The album made by the otherwise obscure Mr Frank is collectable as a rare outside production by Paul Simon. One track also features the young Al Stewart.

Again	LP	B&C	BCLP4	1978	£75	£37.50	
Blues Run The Game	7"	Columbia	DB7795	1965	£15	£7.50	
Jackson C. Frank	LP	Columbia	33SX1788	1965	£200	£100	

FRANKIE & JOHNNY

'Frankie' was singer Maggie Bell, who was later the vocalist with Stone the Crows.

Climb Every Mountain	7"	Parlophone	R5518	1966	**£6**	**£2.50**	
I'll Hold You	7"	Decca	F22376	1966	**£100**	**£50**	

FRANKIE & THE CLASSICALS

I Only Have Eyes For You	7"	Philips	BF1586	1967	**£75**	**£37.50**	

FRANKIE GOES TO HOLLYWOOD

As record companies became aware of the collectors' market during the eighties, they realized that it was possible to create instant collectors' items by issuing various limited-edition versions of each potential hit record. Arguably, the most thorough exploration of the possibilities of this tactic was carried out by ZTT records and Frankie Goes To Hollywood. Each single by the group comes in a bewildering variety of alternative mixes, and different shaped picture discs, with a correspondingly wide range of values. In fact, due to Trevor Horn's skill as a producer, the different mixes make sense on musical grounds, but this is very much a happy accident.

Pleasurefix/Starfix	12"	ZTT	FGTH1	1985	**£10**	**£5**	*pink label promo*
Power Of Love	12"	ZTT	12XZTAS5	1984	**£6**	**£2.50**	*gatefold sleeve, 5 photos*
Rage Hard	CD-s	ZTT	ZCID22	1986	**£12**	**£6**	
Relax	7"	ZTT	PZTAS1	1983	**£4**	**£1.50**	*picture disc*
Relax	cass-s	ZTT	CTIS102	1984	**£6**	**£2.50**	
Relax (Live Version)	cass	Ocean	no number	1985	**£15**	**£6**	*with FGTH computer game*
Relax (Original Mix)	12"	ZTT	12ZTAS1	1984	**£12**	**£6**	
Relax (Remixes)	12"	ZTT	SAM1231	1993	**£10**	**£5**	*double promo*
Relax (Sex Mix)	12"	ZTT	12ZTAS1 (1A2U)	1983	**£10**	**£5**	
Relax (Sex Mix)	12"	ZTT	12PZTAS1	1983	**£6**	**£2.50**	*picture disc*
Relax (The Last Seven Inches)	7"	ZTT	ZTAS1DJ	1983	**£5**	**£2**	*promo*
Relax (The Last Seven Inches)	7"	ZTT	ZTAS1DJ	1983	**£6**	**£2.50**	*promo, mispressed B side – plays 'Ferry(Go)'*
Relax (US Mix)/Two Tribes (Carnage)	12"	ZTT	XZTAS3DJ	1984	**£8**	**£4**	*promo, grey ZTT sleeve*
Relax (Warp Mix)	7"	ZTT	ZTAS1	1983	**£8**	**£4**	*white label promo*
Two Tribes	12"	ZTT	SAM1301	1993	**£10**	**£5**	*double promo*
Two Tribes	7"	ZTT	PZTAS3	1984	**£4**	**£1.50**	*picture disc*
Two Tribes (Hibakusha)	12"	ZTT	XZIP1	1984	**£15**	**£7.50**	*ZTT sleeve*
Warriors	CD-s	ZTT	ZCID25	1986	**£10**	**£5**	
Warriors (Attack Mix)	12"	ZTT	12ZTAK25	1986	**£8**	**£4**	*white label promo*
Watching The Wildlife (Die Letzten . . . Mix)	12"	ZTT	ZTE26	1987	**£6**	**£2.50**	
Welcome To The Pleasure Dome	7"	ZTT	ZTAS7 (7A7U)	1985	**£8**	**£4**	*blue label*
Welcome To The Pleasure Dome	7"	ZTT	PZTAS7	1985	**£5**	**£2**	*shaped picture disc*
Welcome To The Pleasure Dome	CD	ZTT	CID101	1984	**£25**	**£10**	*with San José, not Happy Hi*
Welcome To The Pleasure Dome	LP	ZTT	NEAT1	1984	**£15**	**£6**	*double picture disc*
Welcome To The Pleasure Dome (Tribal/Urban Mix)	12"	ZTT	12ZTAJ7	1985	**£15**	**£7.50**	*promo*
Welcome To The Pleasuredome (Remixes)	12"	ZTT	SAM1275	1993	**£10**	**£5**	*double promo*

FRANKLIN, ALAN EXPLOSION

Blues Climax	LP	Horne		1970	**£100**	**£50**	*US*

FRANKLIN, ARETHA

Few of Aretha Franklin's earliest recordings are particularly valuable, despite the fact that they seldom appear on the market. There is a staggering lack of direction on the CBS recordings, as for six years neither Miss Franklin herself nor the record company seemed to have any idea as to the most effective setting for that extraordinary voice. Signing with Atlantic at the end of 1966, Aretha Franklin immediately struck gold with the powerful Southern soul sound of 'I Never Loved A Man', a sound that seemed to have been waiting for Aretha Franklin as much as she had been waiting for the sound.

Amazing Grace	LP	Atlantic	K60023	1972	**£15**	**£6**	*double*
Aretha	LP	Fontana	TFL5173	1961	**£20**	**£8**	
Aretha Arrives	LP	Atlantic	587/588085	1967	**£15**	**£6**	
Aretha Franklin Now/Lady Soul	CD	Mobile Fidelity	UDCD623	1995	**£15**	**£6**	*US audiophile*
Aretha Gold	LP	Atlantic	588192	1969	**£10**	**£4**	
Aretha Now	LP	Atlantic	587/588114	1968	**£10**	**£4**	
Baby I Love You	7"	Atlantic	584127	1967	**£4**	**£1.50**	
Best Of Aretha Franklin	LP	Atlantic	QD8295	1971	**£10**	**£4**	*US quad*
Can't You See Me	7"	CBS	201732	1965	**£4**	**£1.50**	
Don't Play That Song	LP	Atlantic	2400021	1970	**£10**	**£4**	
Electrifying Aretha Franklin	LP	Columbia	CL1761/CS8561	1962	**£15**	**£5**	*US*
Freeway Of Love	7"	Arista	ARIST22624	1986	**£5**	**£2**	*pink vinyl*
I Never Loved A Man	7"	Atlantic	584084	1967	**£4**	**£1.50**	
I Never Loved A Man	CD	Mobile Fidelity	UDCD574	1992	**£15**	**£6**	*US audiophile*
I Never Loved A Man	LP	Atlantic	587/588066	1967	**£15**	**£6**	
I Say A Little Prayer	7"	Atlantic	584206	1968	**£4**	**£1.50**	
I Say A Little Prayer	LP	Atlantic	2464007	1970	**£10**	**£4**	
Lady Soul	LP	Atlantic	587/588099	1968	**£10**	**£4**	
Laughing On The Outside	LP	Columbia	CL2079/CS8879	1963	**£15**	**£6**	*US*
Lee Cross	7"	CBS	3059	1967	**£4**	**£1.50**	

Title	Format	Label	Cat. No.	Year	Mint	VG	Notes
Lee Cross	LP	CBS	63160	1967	**£10**	**£4**	
Live At Paris Olympia	LP	Atlantic	587/588149	1968	**£15**	**£6**	
Live At The Fillmore West	LP	Atlantic	2400136	1971	**£10**	**£4**	
Live At The Fillmore West	LP	Atlantic	QD7205	1971	**£12**	**£5**	*US quad*
Love Is The Only Thing	7"	Fontana	H271	1961	**£8**	**£4**	
Natural Woman	7"	Atlantic	584141	1967	**£4**	**£1.50**	
Operation Heartbreak	7"	Fontana	H343	1961	**£6**	**£2.50**	
Queen Of Soul	CD	Atlantic	PRO290126	1992	**£15**	**£6**	*US promo sampler*
Respect	7"	Atlantic	584115	1967	**£4**	**£1.50**	
Runnin' Out Of Fools	LP	Columbia	CL2281/CS9081	1964	**£15**	**£6**	*US*
Satisfaction/Chain Of Fools	7"	Atlantic	584157	1967	**£4**	**£1.50**	
Satisfaction/Night Life	7"	Atlantic	584157	1967	**£6**	**£2.50**	
Since You've Been Gone	7"	Atlantic	584172	1968	**£4**	**£1.50**	
Songs Of Faith	LP	Chess	CRL(S)54550	1967	**£10**	**£4**	
Soul '69	LP	Atlantic	588163	1969	**£10**	**£4**	
Soul Sister	LP	CBS	(S)BPG62744	1966	**£10**	**£4**	
Take A Look	LP	CBS	63269	1967	**£10**	**£4**	
Take It Like You Give It	LP	CBS	(S)BPG62969	1967	**£10**	**£4**	
Tender . . . Swinging Aretha Franklin	LP	Columbia	CL1876/CS8676	1962	**£15**	**£6**	*US*
Think	7"	Atlantic	584186	1968	**£4**	**£1.50**	
This Girl's In Love With You	LP	Atlantic	2400004	1969	**£10**	**£4**	
Through The Storm	CD-s	Arista	162185	1989	**£5**	**£2**	*3" single*
Today I Sing The Blues	7" EP	Fontana	TE467217	1962	**£15**	**£7.50**	
Unforgettable	LP	Columbia	CL2163/CS8963	1964	**£15**	**£6**	*US*
Yeah/In Person	LP	CBS	(S)BPG62556	1965	**£10**	**£4**	
Young, Gifted And Black	LP	Atlantic	2400188	1971	**£10**	**£4**	

FRANKLIN, CAROLYN

Title	Format	Label	Cat. No.	Year	Mint	VG	Notes
Baby Dynamite!	LP	RCA	RD/SF8035	1969	**£10**	**£4**	
Boxer	7"	RCA	RCA1851	1969	**£4**	**£1.50**	

FRANKLIN, ERMA

Title	Format	Label	Cat. No.	Year	Mint	VG	Notes
Gotta Find Me A Lover	7"	MCA	MU1073	1969	**£4**	**£1.50**	
Her Name Is Erma	LP	Epic	LN3824/BN619	1962	**£20**	**£8**	*US*
Open Up Your Soul	7"	London	HLZ10201	1968	**£5**	**£2**	
Piece Of My Heart	7"	London	HLZ10170	1967	**£6**	**£2.50**	
Right To Cry	7"	London	HLZ10220	1968	**£5**	**£2**	
Soul Sister	LP	MCA	MUPS394	1970	**£15**	**£6**	
Time After Time	7"	Soul City	SC118	1969	**£4**	**£1.50**	

FRANKLIN, MARIE

Title	Format	Label	Cat. No.	Year	Mint	VG	Notes
You Ain't Changed	7"	MGM	MGM1455	1968	**£5**	**£2**	

FRANKS, JOHNNY

Title	Format	Label	Cat. No.	Year	Mint	VG	Notes
Good Old Country Music	7"	Melodisc	1459	1958	**£4**	**£1.50**	
Tweedle Dee	78	Melodisc	P230	1955	**£8**	**£3**	

FRANKSON, BONNIE

Title	Format	Label	Cat. No.	Year	Mint	VG	Notes
Dearest	7"	Jolly	JY021	1968	**£5**	**£2**	
Dearest	7"	Columbia	DB114	1969	**£5**	**£2**	
Lovin' You	7"	Jolly	JY014	1968	**£5**	**£2**	

FRANTIC

Title	Format	Label	Cat. No.	Year	Mint	VG	Notes
Conception	LP	Lizard	20103	1971	**£20**	**£8**	*US*

FRANTIC ELEVATORS

Mick Hucknall was the leader of the Frantic Elevators, who began as a punk group, but who had anticipated the smooth soul sound of Hucknall's Simply Red by the end of their career. The song 'Holding Back The Years' was, in fact, recorded by both groups.

Title	Format	Label	Cat. No.	Year	Mint	VG	Notes
Early Years	LP	Receiver	KNOB2	1988	**£12**	**£5**	*with interview disc*
Early Years	LP	TJM	TJM101	1987	**£20**	**£8**	
Holding Back The Years	7"	No Waiting	WAIT1	1982	**£20**	**£10**	
Hunchback Of Notre Dame	7"	TJM	TJM6	1980	**£100**	**£50**	*demo*
Searching For The Only One	7"	Crackin' Up	CRACK1	1980	**£15**	**£7.50**	
Voice In The Dark	7"	TJM	TJM5	1979	**£15**	**£7.50**	
You Know What You Told Me	7"	Erics	006	1980	**£15**	**£7.50**	

FRANZ K

Title	Format	Label	Cat. No.	Year	Mint	VG	Notes
Rock In Deutsch	LP	Zebra	2949014	1973	**£15**	**£6**	*German*
Sensemann	LP	Ruhr	007	1972	**£50**	**£25**	*German*
Sensemann	LP	Philips	6305127	1972	**£40**	**£20**	*German*

FRASER, JOHN

Title	Format	Label	Cat. No.	Year	Mint	VG	Notes
Presenting	7" EP	Pye	NEP24068	1958	**£8**	**£4**	

FRASER, NORMA

Title	Format	Label	Cat. No.	Year	Mint	VG	Notes
Everybody Loves A Lover	7"	Ska Beat	JB223	1965	**£10**	**£5**	
First Cut Is The Deepest	7"	Coxsone	CS7017	1967	**£10**	**£5**	*Bumps Oakley B side*
Heartaches	7"	Doctor Bird	DB1032	1966	**£10**	**£5**	*Tommy McCook B side*
Heartaches	7"	Coxsone	CS7049	1968	**£10**	**£5**	*Righteous Flames B side*
Respect	7"	Coxsone	CS7060	1968	**£10**	**£5**	
Telling Me Lies	7"	Studio One	SO2025	1967	**£12**	**£6**	*Viceroys B side*

FRATERNITY OF MAN

The group's 'Don't Bogart Me' was included in the soundtrack of the film *Easy Rider*, although their records are otherwise little known. Guitarist Elliot Ingber had previously played with Frank Zappa's Mothers of Invention, while drummer Richard Hayward subsequently joined Little Feat.

Title	Format	Label	Cat. No.	Year	Mint	VG	Notes
Don't Bogart Me	7"	Stateside	SS2166	1970	**£4**	**£1.50**	
Fraternity Of Man	LP	ABC	S647	1968	**£20**	**£8**	*US*
Get It On	LP	Dot	DLP25955	1969	**£20**	**£8**	*US*

FRAYS

Singer Mike Patto was a member of this collectable group.

Title	Format	Label	Cat. No.	Year	Mint	VG	Notes
For Your Precious Love	7"	Decca	F12229	1965	**£25**	**£12.50**	
Walk On	7"	Decca	F12153	1965	**£150**	**£75**	

FRAZIER CHORUS

Title	Format	Label	Cat. No.	Year	Mint	VG	Notes
Sloppy Heart	7"	4AD	AD708	1987	**£5**	**£2**	*promo*

FREAK SCENE

Title	Format	Label	Cat. No.	Year	Mint	VG	Notes
Psychedelic Psoul	LP	Columbia	CL2556/CS9356	1967	**£75**	**£37.50**	*US*

FREAKS OF NATURE

The rare Island single credited to the Freaks of Nature actually features members of Them (after Van Morrison had left the group), backed by the Soft Machine, at a time when Daevid Allen contributions on guitar made the band into a four-piece. Production was by the maverick Kim Fowley.

Title	Format	Label	Cat. No.	Year	Mint	VG	Notes
People Let's Freak Out	7"	Island	WI3017	1966	**£40**	**£20**	

FREBERG, STAN

Title	Format	Label	Cat. No.	Year	Mint	VG	Notes
Any Requests	7" EP	Capitol	EAP1496	1955	**£6**	**£2.50**	
Banana Boat Song	7"	Capitol	CL14712	1957	**£6**	**£2.50**	
Best Of Stan Freberg	LP	Capitol	T2020	1964	**£10**	**£4**	
Best Of The Stan Freberg Show	LP	Capitol	WBO1035	1958	**£12**	**£5**	*US*
Child's Garden Of Freberg	LP	Capitol	T777	1957	**£15**	**£6**	
Comedy Caravan	LP	Capitol	T732	1956	**£15**	**£6**	*US*
Face The Funnies	LP	Capitol	T1694	1962	**£12**	**£5**	*US*
Freberg Again	7" EP	Capitol	EAP120115	1961	**£6**	**£2.50**	
Great Pretender	7"	Capitol	CL14571	1956	**£8**	**£4**	
Great Pretender	7" EP	Capitol	EAP120050	1961	**£8**	**£4**	
Green Christmas	7"	Capitol	CL14966	1958	**£5**	**£2**	
Heartbreak Hotel	7"	Capitol	CL14608	1956	**£12**	**£6**	
Lone Psychiatrist	7"	Capitol	CL14316	1955	**£10**	**£5**	
Madison Avenue Werewolf	LP	Capitol	T1816	1962	**£12**	**£5**	*US*
Mickey Mouse's Birthday Party	LP	Capitol	J3264	1963	**£12**	**£5**	*US*
Old Payola Roll Blues	7"	Capitol	CL15122	1960	**£8**	**£4**	
Omaha	7" EP	Capitol	EAP11101	1959	**£6**	**£2.50**	
Real Saint George	7" EP	Capitol	EAP1628	1956	**£8**	**£4**	
Sh'boom	7"	Capitol	CL14187	1954	**£12**	**£6**	
Stan Freberg	LP	Capitol	LCT6170/1	1959	**£20**	**£8**	*double*
Stan Freberg With The Original Cast	LP	Capitol	T1242	1959	**£12**	**£5**	*US*
Underground Show Number One	LP	Capitol	(S)T2551	1966	**£10**	**£4**	*US*
United States Of America	LP	Capitol	(S)W1573	1961	**£12**	**£5**	*US*
Yellow Rose Of Texas	7"	Capitol	CL14509	1956	**£8**	**£4**	

FRED, JOHN & HIS PLAYBOY BAND

Title	Format	Label	Cat. No.	Year	Mint	VG	Notes
34:40 Of John Fred	LP	Paula	LP(S)2193	1967	**£12**	**£5**	*US*
Agnes English	LP	Pye	NPL28111	1967	**£10**	**£4**	
John Fred & His Playboys	LP	Paula	LP(S)2191	1966	**£12**	**£5**	*US*
Judy In Disguise	LP	Paula	LPS2197	1968	**£12**	**£5**	*US*
Permanently Stated	LP	Paula	LPS2201	1968	**£10**	**£4**	*US*
Shirley	7"	CBS	3475	1968	**£5**	**£2**	

FREDDIE & THE DREAMERS

Title	Format	Label	Cat. No.	Year	Mint	VG	Notes
Brown And Porter's	7"	Columbia	DB8200	1967	**£4**	**£1.50**	
Do The Freddie	LP	Mercury	MG2/SR61026	1965	**£10**	**£4**	*US*
Frantic Freddie	LP	Mercury	MG2/SR61053	1965	**£10**	**£4**	*US*
Freddie And The Dreamers	7" EP	Columbia	SEG8457	1965	**£10**	**£5**	
Freddie And The Dreamers	7" EP	Columbia	SEG8323	1964	**£6**	**£2.50**	
Freddie And The Dreamers	LP	Columbia	33SX1577	1963	**£10**	**£4**	
Freddie And The Dreamers	LP	Mercury	MG2/SR61017	1965	**£10**	**£4**	*US*
Freddie Sings Just For You	7" EP	Columbia	SEG8349	1964	**£6**	**£2.50**	
Fun Lovin' Freddie	LP	Mercury	MG2/SR61061	1966	**£10**	**£4**	*US*
Gabardine Mac	7"	Columbia	DB8517	1968	**£4**	**£1.50**	
Get Around Downtown Girl	7"	Columbia	DB8606	1969	**£4**	**£1.50**	
I'm Tellin' You Now	7" EP	Columbia	ESRF1654	1964	**£12**	**£6**	*French*
I'm Telling You Now	LP	Tower	(D)T5003	1965	**£10**	**£4**	*US*
If You Gotta Make A Fool Of Somebody	7" EP	Columbia	SEG8275	1963	**£6**	**£2.50**	
In Disneyland	LP	Columbia	SX/SCX6069	1966	**£10**	**£4**	
Just For You	7" EP	Columbia	SEG8337	1964	**£8**	**£4**	*2 tracks by Peter & Gordon*
King Freddie & Dreaming Knights	LP	Columbia	SX6177	1967	**£10**	**£4**	
Little Big Time	7"	Columbia	DB8496	1968	**£4**	**£1.50**	
Ready Freddie Go	7" EP	Columbia	SEG8403	1965	**£10**	**£5**	
Seaside Swingers	LP	Mercury	MG2/SR61031	1965	**£15**	**£6**	*US, with John Leyton and Mike Sarne*

Sing Along Party	LP	Columbia	SX1785	1965	**£10**	**£4**	
Some Other Guy	7" EP	Columbia	ESRF1486	1963	**£12**	**£6**	*French*
Songs From What A Crazy World	7" EP	Columbia	SEG8287	1963	**£8**	**£4**	
Windmill In Old Amsterdam	7"	Columbia	DC763	1965	**£6**	**£2.50**	*export*
You Were Made For Me	LP	Columbia	33SX1663	1964	**£10**	**£4**	
You Were Made For Me	7" EP	Columbia	SEG8302	1964	**£6**	**£2.50**	

FREDDY & FITZY

Do Good	7"	Doctor Bird	DB1033	1966	**£10**	**£5**	

FREDERICKS, BILL

Almost	7"	Polydor	2059035	1978	**£4**	**£1.50**	

FREDERICKS, DOLORES

Cha Cha Joe	7"	Brunswick	05540	1956	**£15**	**£7.50**	

FREDERICKS, DOTTY

Just Wait	7"	Top Rank	JAR106	1959	**£5**	**£2**	

FREDERICKS, MARC

Mystic Midnight	7"	London	HLD8281	1956	**£12**	**£6**	

FREDERICKS, TOMMY

Prince Of Players	7"	London	HLU8555	1958	**£30**	**£15**	

FREDRIC

Phases And Faces	LP	Forte	80461	1968	**£500**	**£330**	*US*

FREE

With an average age of around eighteen, the members of the newly formed Free had amazingly still managed to acquire some professional experience – most notably in the case of Andy Fraser, who had played bass (albeit briefly) with John Mayall. They could have been enormous (and the classic 'All Right Now' – included in extended form on *Fire And Water* – was indeed a considerable hit), but dissipated their momentum in a welter of petty disputes, leading to members leaving and returning in a quite bewildering manner. The most collectable record remaining from all this is *Kossoff, Kirke, Tetsu And Rabbit*, which is prevented from being a Free LP only by the absence of singer Paul Rodgers.

All Right Now	7"	Island	WIP6082	1970	**£4**	**£1.50**	
All Right Now	CD-s	Island	CID486	1991	**£5**	**£2**	
Broad Daylight	7"	Island	WIP6054	1969	**£25**	**£12.50**	
Fire And Water	LP	Island	ILPS9120	1970	**£20**	**£8**	*pink label*
Free	LP	Island	ILPS9104	1969	**£25**	**£10**	*pink label*
Free EP	12"	Island	PIEP6	1982	**£6**	**£2.50**	*picture disc*
Free Story	LP	Island	ISLD4	1973	**£15**	**£6**	*double*
Highway	LP	Island	ILPS9138	1970	**£10**	**£4**	
I'll Be Creeping	7"	Island	WIP6062	1969	**£25**	**£12.50**	
I'll Be Creeping	7"	Island	WIP6062	1969	**£100**	**£50**	*picture sleeve*
Live	LP	Island	ILPS9160	1971	**£10**	**£4**	
My Brother Jake	CD-s	Island	CID495	1991	**£5**	**£2**	
Stealer	7"	Island	WIP6093	1970	**£4**	**£1.50**	
Tons Of Sobs	LP	Island	ILPS9089	1969	**£25**	**£10**	*pink label*
Travellin' In Style	7"	Island	WIP6160	1973	**£4**	**£1.50**	

FREE (2)

Keep In Touch	7"	Philips	BF1754	1969	**£20**	**£10**	

FREE AGENTS

Free Agents	LP	Groovy	STP1	1980	**£15**	**£6**	

FREE DESIGN

Heaven/Earth	LP	Project	3	1969	**£10**	**£4**	

FREE FERRY

Mary What Have You Become	7"	CBS	4456	1969	**£5**	**£2**	

FREE 'N' EASY

Free 'n' Easy	LP	Oak	RGJ628	1968	**£100**	**£50**	

FREE SOULS

I Want To Be Free	7"	Blue Beat	BB264	1964	**£12**	**£6**	

FREE SPIRITS

Out Of Sight And Sound	LP	ABC	(S)593	1967	**£10**	**£4**	*US*

FREEBORNE

Peak Impression	LP	Monitor	MPS607	1967	**£75**	**£37.50**	*US*

FREED, ALAN

Presents The King's Henchmen	LP	Coral	CRL57216	195–	**£50**	**£25**	*US*
Right Now Right Now	7"	Vogue Coral	Q72219	1957	**£60**	**£30**	
Rock Around The Block	LP	Coral	CRL57213	195–	**£50**	**£25**	*US*
Rock'n'Roll Boogie	7"	Vogue Coral	Q72230	1957	**£60**	**£30**	
Rock'n'Roll Dance Party	LP	Vogue Coral	LVA9033	1957	**£40**	**£20**	
Rock'n'Roll Dance Party Vol. 2	LP	Vogue Coral	LVA9066	1957	**£50**	**£25**	
Rock'n'Roll Show	LP	Brunswick	BL54043	1958	**£50**	**£25**	*US*
TV Record Hop	LP	Coral	CRL57177	195–	**£50**	**£25**	*US*

FREEDOM

Title	Format	Label	Cat. No.	Year	Value	Value	Notes
At Last	LP	Metronome	MLP15371	1970	**£25**	**£10**	
Escape While You Can	7"	Plexium	PXM3	1968	**£5**	**£2**	
Freedom	LP	Probe	SPBA6252	1970	**£20**	**£8**	
Is More Than A Word	LP	Vertigo	6360072	1972	**£60**	**£30**	*spiral label*
Through The Years	LP	Vertigo	6360049	1971	**£40**	**£20**	*spiral label*
Where Will You Be Tonight	7"	Mercury	MF1033	1968	**£10**	**£5**	
Where Will You Be Tonight	7"	Mercury	MF1033	1968	**£20**	**£10**	*picture sleeve*

FREEDOM CRY

Title	Format	Label	Cat. No.	Year	Value	Value	Notes
In Disneyland	LP	Columbia	SCX6069	1966	**£30**	**£15**	

FREEDOM SINGERS

Title	Format	Label	Cat. No.	Year	Value	Value	Notes
I Want Money	7"	Coxsone	CS7016	1967	**£10**	**£5**	*Slim Smith B side*
Work Crazy	7"	Studio One	SO2011	1967	**£12**	**£6**	

FREEDOM SOUNDS

Title	Format	Label	Cat. No.	Year	Value	Value	Notes
People Get Ready	LP	Atlantic	SD1492	1968	**£15**	**£6**	

FREEDOM'S CHILDREN

Title	Format	Label	Cat. No.	Year	Value	Value	Notes
Astra	LP	Parlophone	PCSJ12066	1970	**£200**	**£100**	*South African*

FREEMAN, ART

Title	Format	Label	Cat. No.	Year	Value	Value	Notes
Slipping Around	7"	Atlantic	584053	1966	**£75**	**£37.50**	

FREEMAN, BOBBY

Title	Format	Label	Cat. No.	Year	Value	Value	Notes
Betty Lou Got A New Pair Of Shoes	7"	London	HLJ8721	1958	**£25**	**£12.50**	
C'mon And Swim	7"	Pye	7N25260	1964	**£10**	**£5**	
C'Mon And Swim	LP	Autumn	LP102	1964	**£30**	**£15**	*US*
Do You Wanna Dance	7"	London	HLJ8644	1958	**£20**	**£10**	
Do You Wanna Dance	LP	Jubilee	(SD)JLP1086	1959	**£40**	**£20**	*US*
Duck	7"	Pye	7N25347	1966	**£8**	**£4**	*2 B sides*
Ebb Tide	7"	London	HLJ9031	1960	**£6**	**£2.50**	
Get In The Swim	LP	Josie	JM/JGS4007	1965	**£25**	**£10**	*US*
Lovable Style Of Bobby Freeman	LP	King	930	1965	**£30**	**£15**	*US*
Mary Ann Thomas	7"	London	HLJ8898	1959	**£15**	**£7.50**	
Need Your Love	7"	London	HLJ8782	1959	**£20**	**£10**	
Shimmy Shimmy	7"	Parlophone	R4684	1960	**£5**	**£2**	
Swim	7"	Pye	7N25280	1964	**£10**	**£5**	
Twist With Bobby Freeman	LP	Jubilee	JGM5010	1962	**£30**	**£15**	*US*

FREEMAN, BUD

Title	Format	Label	Cat. No.	Year	Value	Value	Notes
Bud Freeman	LP	London	LTZN15030	1957	**£15**	**£6**	
Chicago Style	7" EP	Fontana	TFE17082	1958	**£5**	**£2**	
Classics In Jazz	10" LP	Capitol	LC6706	1955	**£20**	**£8**	
Comes Jazz	10" LP	Columbia	33S1016	1954	**£25**	**£10**	
Jazz For Sale	7" EP	Top Rank	JKR8021	1959	**£5**	**£2**	
Jazz Scene	7" EP	Parlophone	GEP8783	1959	**£5**	**£2**	
Midnight At Eddie Condon's	LP	Emarcy	EJL1257	1957	**£15**	**£6**	
Wolverine Jazz	10" LP	Brunswick	LA8526	1951	**£20**	**£8**	

FREEMAN, CAROL

Title	Format	Label	Cat. No.	Year	Value	Value	Notes
Rolling Sea	7"	CBS	202579	1967	**£6**	**£2.50**	

FREEMAN, ERNIE

Title	Format	Label	Cat. No.	Year	Value	Value	Notes
Big River	7"	London	HLP9041	1960	**£4**	**£1.50**	
Dumplin's	7"	London	HL7029	1957	**£6**	**£2.50**	*export*
Dumplin's	7"	London	HLP8558	1958	**£6**	**£2.50**	
Ernie Freeman & His Rhythm Guitar	7" EP	London	REU1059	1956	**£30**	**£15**	
Ernie Freeman Vol. 2	7" EP	London	REP1210	1959	**£20**	**£10**	
Indian Love Call	7"	London	HLP8660	1958	**£5**	**£2**	
Raunchy	7"	London	HLP8523	1957	**£8**	**£4**	
Raunchy '65	7"	London	HLA9944	1965	**£5**	**£2**	

FREEMAN, GEORGE

Title	Format	Label	Cat. No.	Year	Value	Value	Notes
I'm Like A Fish	7"	Jay Boy	BOY54	1971	**£5**	**£2**	

FREEMAN, MARGARET

Title	Format	Label	Cat. No.	Year	Value	Value	Notes
Mister Ting-a-Ling	7"	Starlite	ST45040	1961	**£5**	**£2**	

FREEMAN, RUSS & CHET BAKER

Title	Format	Label	Cat. No.	Year	Value	Value	Notes
Freeman/Baker Quartet	LP	Vogue	LAE12119	1959	**£20**	**£8**	

FREEMAN, STAN

Title	Format	Label	Cat. No.	Year	Value	Value	Notes
Piano Moods	10" LP	Columbia	33S1056	1955	**£12**	**£5**	

FREEMEN

Title	Format	Label	Cat. No.	Year	Value	Value	Notes
Lark In The Morning	LP	Emerald	GES1063	1971	**£10**	**£4**	
On The One Road	LP	Emerald	GES1050	1970	**£10**	**£4**	

FREEWHEELERS

Title	Format	Label	Cat. No.	Year	Value	Value	Notes
Why Do You Treat Me Like A Fool	7"	HMV	POP1406	1965	**£4**	**£1.50**	

FRENCH, DON

Title	Format	Label	Cat. No.	Year	Value	Value	Notes
Goldilocks	7"	London	HLW8884	1959	**£100**	**£50**	
Little Blonde Girl	7"	London	HLW8989	1959	**£75**	**£37.50**	

FRENCH, RAY

Title	Format	Label	Cat. No.	Year	Mint	VG	Notes
Since I Lost My Baby	7"	Pye	7N17215	1966	**£5**	**£2**	

FRENCH IMPRESSIONISTS

Title	Format	Label	Cat. No.	Year	Mint	VG	Notes
Santa Baby	7"	Operation Twilight	OPT20	1982	**£4**	**£1.50**	

FRENCH REVOLUTION

Title	Format	Label	Cat. No.	Year	Mint	VG	Notes
Nine Till Five	7"	Decca	F22898	1969	**£60**	**£30**	

FRENZY

Title	Format	Label	Cat. No.	Year	Mint	VG	Notes
Robot Riot	12"	Nervous	12NEP002	1984	**£6**	**£2.50**	*blue vinyl*
This Is The Last Time	7"	Frenzy	FRENZY1	1981	**£5**	**£2**	
Without You	7"	Frenzy	FRENZY3	1981	**£5**	**£2**	

FRESH

Title	Format	Label	Cat. No.	Year	Mint	VG	Notes
Fresh Out Of Borstal	LP	RCA	SF8122	1970	**£10**	**£4**	
Fresh Today	LP	RCA	LSA3027	1971	**£10**	**£4**	

FRESH AIR

Title	Format	Label	Cat. No.	Year	Mint	VG	Notes
Running Wild	7"	Pye	7N17736	1969	**£60**	**£30**	

FRESH MAGGOTS

Title	Format	Label	Cat. No.	Year	Mint	VG	Notes
Car Song	7"	RCA	RCA2150	1971	**£10**	**£5**	
Fresh Maggots	LP	RCA	SF8205	1971	**£125**	**£62.50**	

FRESH WINDOWS

Title	Format	Label	Cat. No.	Year	Mint	VG	Notes
Fashion Conscious	7"	Fontana	TF839	1967	**£75**	**£37.50**	

FRESHIES

Title	Format	Label	Cat. No.	Year	Mint	VG	Notes
Baiser	7"	Razz	RAZZXEP1	1978	**£8**	**£4**	*Chris Sievey B side*
I'm In Love With The Girl . . .	7"	Razz	RAZZ12	1980	**£6**	**£2.50**	*promo*
Men From Banana Island . . .	7"	Razz	RAZZ3	1979	**£4**	**£1.50**	
Straight In At No. 2	7"	Razz	RAZZEP2	1979	**£6**	**£2.50**	

FRESHMEN

Title	Format	Label	Cat. No.	Year	Mint	VG	Notes
Go Granny Go	7"	Pye	7N17592	1968	**£4**	**£1.50**	
Just To See You Smile	7"	Pye	7N17689	1969	**£4**	**£1.50**	
Movin' On	LP	Pye	N(S)PL18263	1968	**£40**	**£20**	
Papa Oom Mow Mow	7"	Pye	7N17432	1967	**£4**	**£1.50**	
Peace On Earth	LP	CBS	64099	1970	**£30**	**£15**	
She Sang Hymns Out Of Tune	7"	Pye	7N17757	1969	**£4**	**£1.50**	

FREUR

It seems incredible that a bunch of Goth meets New Romantic posers, who initially could think of no better name for themselves than an unpronouncable squiggle, should eventually metamorphose into the respected dance music innovators, Underworld. Mind you, when one does know this to be the case, then 'Doot Doot', the group's big hit everywhere except in the UK, does indeed sound like a very early dry run for the likes of 'Born Slippy' and 'Push Upstairs'.

Title	Format	Label	Cat. No.	Year	Mint	VG	Notes
Doot Doot	12"	CBS	A123141	1983	**£6**	**£2.50**	
Doot Doot	7"	CBS	WA3141	1983	**£5**	**£2**	*picture disc*

FRIAR TUCK

Title	Format	Label	Cat. No.	Year	Mint	VG	Notes
And His Psychedelic Guitar	LP	Mercury	MG21111/ SR61111	1968	**£20**	**£8**	*US*

FRIDAY, CAROL

Title	Format	Label	Cat. No.	Year	Mint	VG	Notes
Everybody I Know	7"	Parlophone	R5369	1965	**£10**	**£5**	

FRIEDHOF

Title	Format	Label	Cat. No.	Year	Mint	VG	Notes
Friedhof	LP	Sound-Star-Ton	0103	1971	**£125**	**£62.50**	*German*

FRIEDMAN, PERRY

Title	Format	Label	Cat. No.	Year	Mint	VG	Notes
Vive La Canadienne	7" EP	Topic	TOP56	1961	**£5**	**£2**	

FRIEND, TERRY

Title	Format	Label	Cat. No.	Year	Mint	VG	Notes
Come The Day	LP	Tramp	no number	1977	**£30**	**£15**	

FRIENDS

Title	Format	Label	Cat. No.	Year	Mint	VG	Notes
Night Walker	7"	Rock Shop	RSR002	1983	**£15**	**£7.50**	
Piccolo Man	7"	Deram	DM198	1968	**£15**	**£7.50**	

FRIENDS *(2)*

Title	Format	Label	Cat. No.	Year	Mint	VG	Notes
Friends To Friends	LP	TVO		1980	**£25**	**£10**	*Dutch*

FRIENDS AGAIN

Title	Format	Label	Cat. No.	Year	Mint	VG	Notes
Honey At The Core	7"	Moonboot	MOON1	1983	**£5**	**£2**	

FRIENDS BY FEATHER

Title	Format	Label	Cat. No.	Year	Mint	VG	Notes
Friends By Feather	LP	Columbia	CS30137	1969	**£15**	**£6**	*US*

FRIENDS O'MINE

Title	Format	Label	Cat. No.	Year	Mint	VG	Notes
Friends O'Mine	LP	Westwood		1972	**£250**	**£150**	

FRIENDSOUND

Title	Format	Label	Cat. No.	Year	Mint	VG	Notes
Joyride	LP	RCA	SF8027	1969	**£75**	**£37.50**	

FRIJID PINK

Title	Format	Label	Cat. No.	Year	Mint	VG	Notes
All Pink Inside	LP	Fantasy	9464	1975	**£15**	**£6**	US
Defrosted	LP	Deram	SML1077	1970	**£20**	**£8**	
Earth Omen	LP	Lionel	1004	1973	**£15**	**£6**	US
Frijid Pink	LP	Deram	SML1062	1970	**£20**	**£8**	

FRISCO, JACKIE

Title	Format	Label	Cat. No.	Year	Mint	VG	Notes
Sugar Baby	7"	Decca	F11566	1963	**£4**	**£1.50**	

FRITCHIE, VONNIE

Title	Format	Label	Cat. No.	Year	Mint	VG	Notes
Sugar Booger Avenue	7"	London	HLU8178	1955	**£25**	**£12.50**	

FRITH, FRED

Title	Format	Label	Cat. No.	Year	Mint	VG	Notes
Gravity	LP	Ralph	FF8057L	1980	**£10**	**£4**	US
Guitar Solos	LP	Caroline	C1508	1974	**£10**	**£4**	
Guitar Solos 2	LP	Caroline	C1518	1976	**£10**	**£4**	*with G. F. Fitzgerald, Hans Reichel, Derek Bailey*
Live In Japan	LP	Recommended	RRJ003/004	1982	**£30**	**£15**	*Japanese double, mailing envelope cover, 2 posters, 2 booklets*
Speechless	LP	Ralph	FF8106	1981	**£10**	**£4**	US

FRITZ, MIKE & MO

Title	Format	Label	Cat. No.	Year	Mint	VG	Notes
Somebody Stole The Sun	7"	Philips	BF1427	1965	**£4**	**£1.50**	
What Colour Is A Man?	7"	Philips	BF1441	1965	**£4**	**£1.50**	

FRIZZELL, LEFTY

Title	Format	Label	Cat. No.	Year	Mint	VG	Notes
Greatest Hits	LP	Columbia	CL2488/CS9288	1966	**£12**	**£5**	US
Listen To Lefty	10" LP	Columbia	HL9021	1952	**£30**	**£15**	US
One And Only	LP	Columbia	CL1342	1959	**£25**	**£10**	US
One And Only Lefty Frizzell	LP	CBS	BPG62188	1963	**£12**	**£5**	
Puttin' On	LP	Columbia	CL2772/CS9572	1967	**£12**	**£5**	US
Sad Side Of Love	LP	Columbia	BPG62595	1965	**£12**	**£5**	
Saginaw, Michigan	LP	Columbia	CL2169/CS8969	1964	**£12**	**£5**	US
Songs Of Jimmie Rodgers	10" LP	Columbia	HL9019	1951	**£30**	**£15**	US

FRIZZLE, REV. DWIGHT

Title	Format	Label	Cat. No.	Year	Mint	VG	Notes
Beyond The Black Crack	LP				**£40**	**£20**	US

FROBOESS, CORNELIA

Title	Format	Label	Cat. No.	Year	Mint	VG	Notes
German Teenagers	LP	HMV	1671	1962	**£40**	**£20**	*with Rex Gildo*

FROEBA, FRANK

Title	Format	Label	Cat. No.	Year	Mint	VG	Notes
Back Room Piano	10" LP	Brunswick	LA8547	1952	**£12**	**£5**	
Moonlight Playing Time	10" LP	Brunswick	LA8611	1953	**£12**	**£5**	
Parlor Piano	10" LP	Brunswick	LA8555	1953	**£12**	**£5**	

FROG, WYNDER K.

Title	Format	Label	Cat. No.	Year	Mint	VG	Notes
Green Door	7"	Island	WIP6006	1967	**£6**	**£2.50**	
Green Door	7" EP	Fontana	460221	1967	**£20**	**£10**	*French*
I Am A Man	7"	Island	WIP6014	1967	**£5**	**£2**	
Into The Fire	LP	United Artists	6740	1970	**£25**	**£10**	US
Jumping Jack Flash	7"	Island	WIP6044	1968	**£5**	**£2**	
Out Of The Frying Pan	LP	Island	ILP982/ILPS9082	1968	**£30**	**£15**	*pink label*
Sunshine Super Frog	LP	Island	ILP944/ILPS9044	1967	**£30**	**£15**	
Sunshine Superman	7"	Island	WI3011	1966	**£6**	**£2.50**	
Turn On Your Lovelight	7"	Island	WI280	1966	**£6**	**£2.50**	

FROGGATT, RAYMOND

Title	Format	Label	Cat. No.	Year	Mint	VG	Notes
Bleach	LP	Bell	BELLS207	1972	**£15**	**£6**	
Rogues And Thieves	LP	Reprise	K44257	1974	**£10**	**£4**	
Voice And Writing Of Raymond Froggatt	LP	Polydor	583044	1969	**£15**	**£6**	

FROGGIE BEAVER

Title	Format	Label	Cat. No.	Year	Mint	VG	Notes
From The Pond	LP	Froggie Beaver	7301	1973	**£75**	**£37.50**	US

FROGMEN

Title	Format	Label	Cat. No.	Year	Mint	VG	Notes
Underwater	7"	Oriole	CB1617	1961	**£25**	**£12.50**	

FROGMORTON

Title	Format	Label	Cat. No.	Year	Mint	VG	Notes
At Last	LP	Philips	6308261	1976	**£15**	**£6**	

FROHMADER, PETER

Title	Format	Label	Cat. No.	Year	Mint	VG	Notes
Nekropolis 2	LP	Hasch Platten	KIF002	1982	**£60**	**£30**	*German*

FROLK HEAVEN

The obscure progressive album by the extraordinarily named Frolk Heaven derives much of its value from the fact that Stewart Copeland, who was later with Curved Air and the Police, is the drummer.

Title	Format	Label	Cat. No.	Year	Mint	VG	Notes
At The Apex Of High	LP	LRS	RT6032	197–	**£300**	**£180**	US

FROMAN, JANE

Title	Format	Label	Cat. No.	Year	Mint	VG	Notes
Finger Of Suspicion Points At You	7"	Capitol	CL14209	1954	**£8**	**£4**	
I Wonder	7"	Capitol	CL14254	1955	**£8**	**£4**	

Jane Froman	7" EP	Capitol	EAP1600	1956	**£5**	**£2**	
Song From Desiree	7"	Capitol	CL14208	1954	**£4**	**£1.50**	
Songs At Sunset Pt 1	7" EP	Capitol	EAP1889	1957	**£5**	**£2**	
Songs At Sunset Pt 2	7" EP	Capitol	EAP2889	1957	**£5**	**£2**	
Songs At Sunset Pt 3	7" EP	Capitol	EAP3889	1957	**£5**	**£2**	
With A Song In My Heart	10" LP	Capitol	LC6554	1952	**£10**	**£4**	
Yours Alone	10" LP	Capitol	LC6605	1953	**£10**	**£4**	

FRONT

System	7"	The Label	TLR005	1977	**£5**	**£2**	

FRONT LINE

Got Love	7"	Atlantic	AT4057	1965	**£25**	**£12.50**	

FRONTIERE, DOM

Jet Rink Ballad	7"	London	HLU8385	1957	**£20**	**£10**	

FROST

Frost Music	LP	Vanguard	VSD6520	1969	**£12**	**£5**	*US*
Rock and Roll Music	LP	Vanguard	SVRL19056	1969	**£12**	**£5**	
Through The Eyes Of Love	LP	Vanguard	VSD6556	1970	**£12**	**£5**	*US*

FROST, DAVID

Deck Of Cards	7"	Parlophone	R5441	1966	**£4**	**£1.50**	
Frost Report On Britain	LP	Parlophone	PMC7005	1966	**£10**	**£4**	
Frost Report On Everything	LP	Pye	NPL18199	1967	**£10**	**£4**	

FROST, DAVID & OTHERS

That Was The Week That Was	LP	Parlophone	PMC1197/ PCS3040	1963	**£10**	**£4**	

FROST, FRANK & THE NIGHTHAWKS

Hey Boss Man!	LP	Philips	1975	1961	**£400**	**£250**	*US*

FROST, MAX & THE TROOPERS

Shape Of Things To Come	7"	Capitol	CL15565	1968	**£15**	**£7.50**	
Shape Of Things To Come	LP	Tower	ST5147	1968	**£30**	**£15**	*US*

FROST LANE

Frost Lane	LP	Cutty Wren	no number	1971	**£60**	**£30**	

FRUIT EATING BEARS

Chevie Heavy	7"	Lightning		1978	**£12**	**£6**	
Door In My Face	7"	DJM	DJS857	1978	**£20**	**£10**	

FRUIT MACHINE

Follow Me	7"	Spark	SRL1003	1969	**£25**	**£12.50**	
I'm Alone Today	7"	Spark	SRL1027	1970	**£60**	**£30**	
I'm Alone Today	7"	Saprk	SRL1027	1969	**£100**	**£50**	*picture sleeve*

FRUMIOUS BANDERSNATCH

Limited Edition	7" EP	Muggles Gramophone Works		196–	**£300**	**£180**	*US*

FRUMMOX

Here To There	LP	Probe	SPB1007	1969	**£12**	**£5**	

FRUMPY

All Will Be Changed	LP	Philips	6305067	1971	**£15**	**£6**	
By The Way	LP	Vertigo	6360604	1972	**£12**	**£5**	*German*
Frumpy 2	LP	Philips	6305098	1972	**£20**	**£8**	*blue & black vinyl*
In And Out Of Studios	LP	Fontana	643401	1972	**£12**	**£5**	*German*
Live	LP	Philips	6623022	1972	**£15**	**£6**	*German double*

FRUSCELLA, TONY

Tony Fruscella	LP	London	LTZK15044	1957	**£25**	**£10**	

FRUUPP

Future Legends	LP	Dawn	DNLS3053	1973	**£25**	**£10**	
Modern Masquerades	LP	Dawn	DNLS3070	1975	**£25**	**£10**	
Prince Of Heaven	7"	Dawn	DNS1087	1974	**£4**	**£1.50**	
Prince Of Heaven's Eyes	LP	Dawn	DNLH2	1974	**£25**	**£10**	*with booklet*
Seven Secrets	LP	Dawn	DNLS3058	1974	**£25**	**£10**	

FUCHS, PAUL & LIMPE (ANIMA SOUND)

Anima	LP	Pilz	20290972	1972	**£20**	**£8**	*German*
Anima Sound (Echolette)	LP	Melocord	STLPNB0027	1971	**£40**	**£20**	*German*
Sturmischer Himmel	LP	Ohr	OMM56011	1974	**£20**	**£8**	*German*

FUCHSIA

Fuchsia	LP	Pegasus	PEG8	1971	**£40**	**£20**	

FUD CHRISTIAN ALL STARS

Never Fall In Love	7"	Big Shot	BI571	1971	**£5**	**£2**	

FUGI

Red Moon	7"	Blue Horizon	2096005	1971	**£12**	**£6**	

FUGITIVES

Fugitive ... 7" ... Vogue ... V9176 ... 1961 **£15** ... **£7.50** ...

FUGITIVES *(2)*

Musical Pressure ... 7" ... Doctor Bird ... DB1082 ... 1967 **£10** ... **£5** ...
Real Gone Loser ... 7" ... Doctor Bird ... DB1116 ... 1967 **£10** ... **£5** ...

FUGITIVES *(3)*

The Fugitives who made the extremely rare album, *Fugitives At Dave's Hideout*, evolved into the important psychedelic band, SRC.

Friday At The Café A GoGo (Long Hot Summer) ... LP ... Westchester ... 1005 ... 1965 **£250** ... **£150** ... *US, with other artists*
Fugitives At Dave's Hideout ... LP ... Hideout ... 1001 ... 1965 **£1000** ... **£700** ... *US*

FUGITIVES *(4)*

On The Run ... LP ... Justice ... 141 ... **£150** ... **£75** ... *US*

FUGS

Ballads Of Contemporary Protest ... LP ... Broadside ... 304 ... 1966 **£30** ... **£15** ... *US*
Belle Of Avenue A ... LP ... Reprise ... RS6359 ... 1969 **£15** ... **£6** ... *US*
Crystal Liaison ... 7" ... Transatlantic ... BIG115 ... 1968 **£4** ... **£1.50** ...
First Album ... LP ... Fontana ... (S)TL5513 ... 1968 **£20** ... **£8** ...
Fugs 4 Rounders Score ... LP ... ESP-Disk ... 2018 ... 1967 **£15** ... **£6** ... *US*
Fugs II ... LP ... Fontana ... (S)TL5524 ... 1968 **£20** ... **£8** ...
Golden Filth ... LP ... Reprise ... RS6396 ... 1970 **£12** ... **£5** ... *US*
It Crawled Into My Hand Honest ... LP ... Transatlantic ... TRA181 ... 1968 **£12** ... **£5** ...
Tenderness Junction ... LP ... Transatlantic ... TRA180 ... 1968 **£20** ... **£8** ... *with poster*
Virgin Fugs ... LP ... Fontana ... (S)TL5501 ... 1967 **£15** ... **£6** ...

FULHAM FURIES

These Boots Are Made For Walking ... 7" ... GM ... GMS9050 ... 1978 **£20** ... **£10** ...

FULL MOON

Moon Fools ... LP ... Amor Sound ... FM001 ... 1977 **£75** ... **£37.50** ... *Dutch*
Nothing Ventured, Nothing Gained ... LP ... Amor Sound ... ... 197– **£75** ... **£37.50** ... *Dutch*
What's Going On ... LP ... Amor Sound ... ... 197– **£50** ... **£25** ... *Dutch*

FULLER, BLIND BOY

1935–40 ... LP ... Philips ... BBL7510 ... 1962 **£30** ... **£15** ...
On Down Vol. 1 ... LP ... Saydisc ... SDR143 ... 1968 **£12** ... **£5** ...
On Down Vol. 2 ... LP ... Saydisc ... SDR168 ... 1969 **£12** ... **£5** ...

FULLER, BOBBY

I Fought The Law ... 7" ... London ... HLU10030 ... 1966 **£15** ... **£7.50** ...
I Fought The Law ... LP ... Mustang ... M(S)901 ... 1966 **£40** ... **£20** ... *US*
KRLA King Of The Wheels ... LP ... Mustang ... M(S)900 ... 1966 **£50** ... **£25** ... *US*
Love's Made A Fool Of You ... 7" ... London ... HLU10041 ... 1966 **£6** ... **£2.50** ...
Love's Made A Fool Of You ... 7" EP ... London ... RE10179 ... 1966 **£60** ... **£30** ... *French*
Memorial Album ... LP ... President ... PTL1003 ... 1967 **£15** ... **£6** ...

FULLER, GIL

Man From Monterey ... LP ... Fontana ... 688147ZL ... 1966 **£12** ... **£5** ... *with Dizzy Gillespie*

FULLER, JERRY

Guilty Of Loving You ... 7" ... London ... HLN9439 ... 1961 **£4** ... **£1.50** ...
Mother Goose At The Bandstand ... 7" ... Salvo ... SLO1802 ... 1962 **£8** ... **£4** ...
Teenage Love ... LP ... Lin ... LP100 ... 1960 **£20** ... **£8** ... *US*
Tennessee Waltz ... 7" ... London ... HLH8982 ... 1959 **£5** ... **£2** ...

FULLER, JESSE

Favourites ... LP ... Stateside ... SL10154 ... 1965 **£10** ... **£4** ...
Frisco Bound ... 10" LP ... Cavalier ... 5006 ... 195– **£40** ... **£20** ... *US*
Frisco Bound ... LP ... Cavalier ... 6009 ... 195– **£30** ... **£15** ... *US*
Going Back To My Old Used To Be ... 7" ... Fontana ... TF821 ... 1967 **£8** ... **£4** ...
Jesse Fuller ... LP ... Good Time Jazz ... LAG12159 ... 1958 **£12** ... **£5** ...
Lone Cat ... LP ... Good Time Jazz ... LAG12279 ... 1960 **£12** ... **£5** ...
Move On Down The Line ... LP ... Topic ... 12T134 ... 1965 **£20** ... **£8** ...
Runnin' Wild ... 7" ... Good Time Jazz ... GV2427 ... 1967 **£4** ... **£1.50** ...
San Francisco Bay Blues ... 7" ... Good Time Jazz ... GV2426 ... 1965 **£4** ... **£1.50** ...
San Francisco Bay Blues ... LP ... Vocalion ... VRLP574 ... 196– **£10** ... **£4** ...
San Francisco Bay Blues ... LP ... Good Time Jazz ... LAG574 ... 1963 **£12** ... **£5** ...
San Francisco Bay Blues ... LP ... Stateside ... SL10166 ... 1966 **£10** ... **£4** ...
Session ... LP ... Fontana ... TL5313 ... 1966 **£10** ... **£4** ...
Working On The Railroad ... 10" LP ... Topic ... 10T59 ... 1960 **£20** ... **£8** ...

FULLER, RANDY

It's Love Come What May ... 7" ... President ... PTL111 ... 1967 **£5** ... **£2** ...

FULSON, LOWELL

Black Nights ... 7" ... Polydor ... 56515 ... 1970 **£8** ... **£4** ...
Hung Down Head ... LP ... Chess ... 408 ... 196– **£20** ... **£8** ... *US*

Title	Format	Label	Cat. No.	Year	Mint	VG	Notes
I Love My Baby	78	London	L1199	1953	**£20**	**£10**	
In A Heavy Bag	LP	Polydor	2384038	1969	**£10**	**£4**	
Lowell Fulson	LP	Kent	KLP5016	1965	**£20**	**£8**	*US*
Lowell Fulson Now	LP	Kent	KST531	1969	**£12**	**£5**	*US*
San Francisco Blues	LP	Fontana	SFJL920	1969	**£15**	**£6**	
Stop And Think	7"	Outasite	45502	1966	**£50**	**£25**	*with Leon Blue*
Talking Woman	7"	Sue	WI4023	1966	**£20**	**£10**	
Too Many Drivers	7"	Sue	WI375	1965	**£12**	**£6**	
Tramp	7"	Fontana	TF795	1967	**£15**	**£7.50**	
Tramp	LP	Kent	KLP/KST520	1967	**£20**	**£8**	*US*

FUMBLE

Title	Format	Label	Cat. No.	Year	Mint	VG	Notes
Fumble	LP	Sovereign	SVNA7254	1972	**£12**	**£5**	
Poetry In Lotion	LP	RCA	SF8403	1974	**£10**	**£4**	

FUN FOUR

Title	Format	Label	Cat. No.	Year	Mint	VG	Notes
Singing In The Showers	7"	NMC	NMC010	1980	**£15**	**£7.50**	

FUNGUS

Title	Format	Label	Cat. No.	Year	Mint	VG	Notes
Fungus	LP	Negram	NR102	1974	**£30**	**£15**	*Dutch*
Lief Ende Leid	LP	Negram	NR115	1975	**£30**	**£15**	*Dutch*
Premonitions	7"	Fungus	FUN1	1973	**£200**	**£100**	
Van De Kiel Naar Vlaring	LP	Negram	NK211	1976	**£30**	**£15**	*Dutch*

FUNHOUSE

Title	Format	Label	Cat. No.	Year	Mint	VG	Notes
Out Of Control	12"	Ensign	ENY22	1982	**£10**	**£5**	
Out Of Control	7"	Ensign	ENY22	1982	**£8**	**£4**	

FUNKADELIC

The records made by Funkadelic represent one of the main branches of George Clinton's P-Funk organization – other records being listed under the Parliament name.

Title	Format	Label	Cat. No.	Year	Mint	VG	Notes
America Eats Its Young	LP	Westbound	2WB2020	1972	**£30**	**£15**	*US*
Can You Get To That	7"	Janus	6146001	1971	**£4**	**£1.50**	
Can You Get To That	7"	Janus	6146001	1974	**£4**	**£1.50**	
Cosmic Slop	LP	Westbound	WB2022	1973	**£20**	**£8**	*US*
Electric Spanking Of War Babies	LP	Warner Bros	K56874	1981	**£12**	**£5**	
Free Your Mind & Your Ass Will Follow	LP	Pye	NSPL28144	1971	**£30**	**£15**	
Funkadelic	LP	Pye	NSPL28137	1970	**£30**	**£15**	
Greatest Hits	LP	Westbound	1004	1975	**£15**	**£6**	*US*
Hardcore Jollies	LP	Warner Bros	K56299	1978	**£15**	**£6**	
I Got A Thing, You Got A Thing . . .	7"	Pye	7N25519	1970	**£6**	**£2.50**	
Let's Take It To The Stage	LP	20th Century	W215	1975	**£15**	**£6**	
Maggot Brain	LP	Westbound	6310201	1971	**£25**	**£10**	
One Nation Under A Groove	LP	Warner Bros	K56359	1978	**£12**	**£5**	*with 12"*
Standing On The Verge Of Getting It On	LP	Westbound	1001	1974	**£25**	**£10**	*US*
Tales Of Kidd Funkadelic	LP	Westbound	227	1976	**£20**	**£8**	*US*
Uncle Jam Wants You	LP	Warner Bros	K56712	1979	**£15**	**£6**	
You And Your Folks, Me And Mine	7"	Pye	7N25548	1971	**£6**	**£2.50**	

FUREKAABEN

Title	Format	Label	Cat. No.	Year	Mint	VG	Notes
Prinsesse Vaerelset	LP	Spectator	1017	1970	**£60**	**£30**	*Danish*

FUREY, FINBAR

Title	Format	Label	Cat. No.	Year	Mint	VG	Notes
Prince Of Pipers	LP	Polydor	2908023	1974	**£15**	**£6**	*Irish*
Traditional Irish Pipe Music	LP	XTRA	XTRA1077	1969	**£25**	**£10**	

FUREY, FINBAR & BOB STEWART

Title	Format	Label	Cat. No.	Year	Mint	VG	Notes
Tomorrow We Part	LP	Broadside	BRO133	1979	**£10**	**£4**	

FUREY, FINBAR & EDDIE

Title	Format	Label	Cat. No.	Year	Mint	VG	Notes
Dawning Of The Day	LP	Dawn	DNLS3037	1972	**£25**	**£10**	
Dream In My Hand	LP	Interchord	264291U	1974	**£12**	**£5**	*German*
Finbar And Eddie Furey	LP	Transatlantic	TRA168	1968	**£20**	**£8**	
Four Green Fields	LP	Plane	S12F200	1972	**£12**	**£5**	*German*
Lonesome Boatman	LP	Transatlantic	TRA191	1969	**£15**	**£6**	
Town Is Not Their Own	LP	Harp	HPE613	1969	**£12**	**£5**	*Irish*

FUREY, TED

Title	Format	Label	Cat. No.	Year	Mint	VG	Notes
Traditional Fiddle	LP	Outlet	OLP1020	1973	**£25**	**£10**	*Irish*

FURNITURE

Title	Format	Label	Cat. No.	Year	Mint	VG	Notes
Shaking Story	7"	Guy From Paraguay	PARA1	1980	**£6**	**£2.50**	

FURTADO, TOMMY

Title	Format	Label	Cat. No.	Year	Mint	VG	Notes
Sun Tan Sam	7"	London	HLA8418	1957	**£20**	**£10**	

FURY, BILLY

Billy Fury is held in high regard as one of the most convincing British rock'n'rollers and yet the proportion of rock to ballads in his output is far too small for the reputation to be sustained by deep enquiry. *The Sound Of Fury* is certainly a competent slice of rockabilly, and Fury wrote much of the material himself, but to release an album in this style in 1960 was to indulge in a piece of historical re-creation rather than to be part of the development of something new. Cliff Richard's exploration of the Buddy Holly style was much more to the point, and it is significant that he survived the onslaught of the Beatles, whereas Billy Fury did not.

Title	Format	Label	Cat. No.	Year	Mint	VG	Notes
All The Way To The USA	7"	Parlophone	R5819	1969	£15	£7.50	
Am I Blue	7" EP	Decca	DFE8558	1963	£30	£15	
Angel Face	7"	Decca	F11158	1959	£25	£12.50	*tri-centre*
Angel Face	78	Decca	F11158	1959	£100	£50	
Best Of Billy Fury	LP	Ace Of Clubs	ACL1229	1967	£20	£8	
Beyond The Shadow Of A Doubt	7"	Parlophone	R5658	1967	£10	£5	
Billy	LP	Decca	LK4533	1963	£30	£15	
Billy Fury	7" EP	Decca	DFE6694	1961	£40	£20	
Billy Fury	LP	Ace Of Clubs	ACL1047	1960	£25	£10	
Billy Fury And The Gamblers	7" EP	Decca	DFE8641	1965	£60	£30	
Billy Fury And The Tornadoes	7" EP	Decca	DFE8525	1963	£25	£12.50	
Billy Fury Hits	7" EP	Decca	DFE8505	1962	£20	£10	
Billy Fury No. 2	7" EP	Decca	DFE6699	1962	£40	£20	
Colette	7"	Decca	F11200	1960	£30	£15	[illegible]
Devil Or Angel	7"	Polydor	POSP528	1982	£8	£4	*microphone sleeve*
Don't Let A Little Pride	7"	Decca	F12409	1966	£6	£2.50	
Don't Worry	7"	Decca	F11334	1961	£5	£2	
Forget Him	7"	Polydor	POSP558	1983	£4	£1.50	
Give Me Your Word	7"	Decca	F12459	1966	£6	£2.50	
Halfway To Paradise	7"	Decca	F11349	1961	£4	£1.50	
Halfway To Paradise	7"	NEMS	NES018	1976	£6	£2.50	
Halfway To Paradise	LP	Ace Of Clubs	ACL1083	1961	£25	£10	
Hippy Hippy Shake	7"	Decca	F40719	1964	£30	£15	*export*
Hippy Hippy Shake	7"	Decca	F40719	1964	£60	£30	*export, picture sleeve*
Hurtin' Is Lovin'	7"	Parlophone	R5560	1967	£10	£5	
I Call For My Rose	7"	Parlophone	R5788	1969	£10	£5	
I Will	7"	Decca	F11888	1964	£4	£1.50	
I'll Be Your Sweetheart	7"	Warner Bros	K16402	1974	£4	£1.50	
I'll Never Quite Get Over You	7"	Decca	F12325	1966	£4	£1.50	
I've Got A Horse	LP	Decca	LK4677	1965	£40	£20	
Interview With Stuart Colman	10" LP	Polydor		1982	£20	£8	*promo*
Lady	7"	Parlophone	R5747	1968	£10	£5	
Let Me Go Lover	7"	Polydor	POSP558	1983	£15	£7.50	
Letter Full Of Tears	7"	Decca	F11437	1962	£4	£1.50	
Long Live Rock	7" EP	Ronco	MREP001	1973	£10	£5	*with other artists, no picture sleeve*
Loving You	7"	Parlophone	R5605	1967	£10	£5	
Margo	7"	Decca	F11128	1959	£20	£10	*tri-centre*
Margo	78	Decca	F11128	1959	£75	£37.50	
Maybe Tomorrow	7"	Decca	F11102	1959	£20	£10	*tri-centre*
Maybe Tomorrow	7" EP	Decca	DFE6597	1959	£60	£30	*tri-centre*
Maybe Tomorrow	78	Decca	F11102	1959	£50	£25	
My Christmas Prayer	7"	Decca	F11189	1959	£50	£25	*tri-centre*
My Christmas Prayer	7" EP	Decca	DFE8686	1983	£6	£2.50	
My Christmas Prayer	78	Decca	F11189	1959	£150	£75	
Once Upon A Dream	7"	Decca	F11485	1962	£4	£1.50	
Paradise Alley	7"	Parlophone	R5874	1970	£20	£10	
Phone Box	7"	Parlophone	R5723	1968	£12	£6	
Play It Cool	7" EP	Decca	DFE6708	1962	£100	£50	*export, blue/green sleeve*
Play It Cool	7" EP	Decca	DFE6708	1962	£20	£10	
Silly Boy Blue	7"	Parlophone	R5681	1968	£20	£10	
Somebody Else's Girl	7"	Decca	F11744	1963	£4	£1.50	
Sound Of Fury	10" LP	Decca	LF1329	1960	£50	£25	
Suzanne In The Mirror	7"	Parlophone	R5634	1967	£10	£5	
Telstar '74	7"	Warner Bros	K16442	1974	£4	£1.50	
That's Love	7"	Decca	F11237	1960	£8	£4	
Thousand Stars	7"	Decca	F11311	1960	£6	£2.50	
We Want Billy	LP	Decca	SKL4548	1963	£40	£20	*with the Tornados, stereo*
We Want Billy	LP	Decca	LK4548	1963	£30	£15	*with the Tornados*
Why Are You Leaving	7"	Parlophone	R5845	1970	£15	£7.50	
Will The Real Man Stand Up	7"	Fury	FY301	1972	£10	£5	
Wondrous Place	7"	Decca	F11267	1960	£8	£4	
World Of Billy Fury	LP	Decca	SPA188	1972	£10	£4	

FURYS

Title	Format	Label	Cat. No.	Year	Mint	VG	Notes
Never More	7" EP	Columbia	ESDF1488	1963	£10	£5	*French*

FUSE

This hard rock band included guitarist Rick Nielsen (who did not, however, have the lead guitar role) and bassist Tom Peterson, who subsequently enjoyed considerable success as members of Cheap Trick.

Title	Format	Label	Cat. No.	Year	Mint	VG	Notes
Fuse	LP	Epic	26502	1968	£30	£15	*US*

FUSION

The private pressing issued by the group Fusion is much rarer than its modest value would suggest. The guitarist was Nik Kershaw, and his later solo single, 'Human Racing', appears here in a very similar version.

Title	Format	Label	Cat. No.	Year	Mint	VG	Notes
Till I Hear from You	LP	Telephone	TEL101	1980	£15	£6	*blue vinyl*

FUSION ORCHESTRA

Title	Format	Label	Cat. No.	Year	Mint	VG	Notes
Skeleton In Armour	LP	EMI	EMA758	1973	£50	£25	
When My Mama's Not At Home	7"	EMI	EMI2056	1973	£4	£1.50	

FUT

Desperate to believe in the existence of rare Beatles out-takes, collectors seized on 'Have You Heard The Word' as one. Unless, of course, it was the Bee Gees and the Beatles singing together. The latest rumour suggests that it is members of the Bee Gees and the Marbles, which is a less exciting but more likely possibility, given that the Marbles' singer, Graham Bonnet, is a cousin of the Gibb brothers.

Have You Heard The Word	7"	Beacon	BEA160	1971	£40	£20	

FUTURE SOUND OF LONDON

Accelerator	LP	Jumpin' & Pumpin'	LPTOT2	1992	£12	£5	*double*
Bring On The Pulse	12"	Jumpin' & Pumpin'	12TOT11	1991	£10	£5	
Cascade	CD-s	Virgin	VSCDT1478	1993	£5	£2	
Far Out Son Of Lung	12"	Virgin	VST1540P	1994	£20	£10	*white vinyl promo*
I'm Not Gonna Let You Do It	12"	Jumpin' & Pumpin'	12TOT25	1992	£8	£4	
ISDN	CD	Virgin	CDV2755	1994	£20	£8	*Black card cover*
ISDN	LP	Virgin	V2755	1994	£20	£8	*embossed black sleeve*
ISDN Show	CD	Virgin	ISDNSHOW1	1997	£20	£8	*promo*
Metropolis	12"	Union City	UCRT11	1992	£8	£4	
My Kingdom	CD-s	Virgin	VSD1605	1996	£6	£2.50	*promo*
Papua New Guinea	12"	Jumpin' & Pumpin'	12TOT17	1991	£8	£4	
Papua New Guinea	CD-s	Jumpin' & Pumpin'	CDSTOT17	1992	£6	£2.50	
Semtex (Part One)	12"	Virgin	SEMTEXDJ1	1995	£15	£7.50	*promo*
Slider	7"	Virgin	PROMO500	1994	£20	£10	*promo double*
Smart Systems	12"	Jumpin' & Pumpin'	12TOT18	1991	£6	£2.50	
Tingler	12"	Jumpin' & Pumpin'	12TOT16	1991	£8	£4	
We Have Explosive Mantronix Plastik Formula	12"	Virgin	VSTDJ1616	1997	£6	£2.50	*promo*

FUTURES

You Better Be Certain	7"	Buddah	BDS430	1975	£6	£2.50	

FUZZ

Fuzz	LP	Mojo	2916010	1971	£10	£4	

FUZZY DUCK

Big Brass Band	7"	Mam	MAM51	1971	£10	£5	
Double Time Woman	7"	Mam	MAM37	1971	£10	£5	
Fuzzy Duck	LP	Mam	MAM1005	1971	£150	£75	
Fuzzy Duck	LP	Reflection	MM05	1990	£15	£6	*with 7"*

FYNN McCOOL

Fynn McCool	LP	RCA	SF8112	1970	£40	£20	
US Thumbstyle	7"	RCA	RCA1956	1970	£4	£1.50	

g

G, TOMMY & THE CHARMS

I Know What I Want	7"	London	HLB10107	1967	**£6**	**£2.50**	

G, WINSTON

Cloud Nine	7"	Decca	F12444	1966	**£6**	**£2.50**	
Like A Baby	7"	Parlophone	R5266	1965	**£8**	**£4**	
Mother Ferguson's Love Dust	7"	Decca	F12559	1967	**£10**	**£5**	
Riding With The Milkman	7"	Decca	F12623	1967	**£10**	**£5**	
Until You Were Gone	7"	Parlophone	R5330	1966	**£5**	**£2**	*with the Wicked*

G. G. ALLSTARS

African Melody	7"	Explosion	EX2024	1970	**£4**	**£1.50**	
Barabus	7"	Explosion	EX2014	1970	**£4**	**£1.50**	
Ganja Plane	7"	Explosion	EX2025	1970	**£4**	**£1.50**	
Man From Carolina	7"	Explosion	EX2023	1970	**£4**	**£1.50**	
Man From Carolina	LP	Trojan	TBL129	1970	**£12**	**£5**	

GABBIDON, BASIL

Ena Mena	7"	Blue Beat	BB155	1963	**£12**	**£6**	
I Bet You Don't Know	7"	Island	WI076	1963	**£10**	**£5**	
I Found My Baby	7"	Island	WI033	1962	**£10**	**£5**	
I Was Wrong	7"	Blue Beat	BB69	1961	**£12**	**£6**	
I'll Find Love	7"	Blue Beat	BB161	1963	**£12**	**£6**	*Mellow Larks B side*
Independence Blues	7"	Blue Beat	BB124	1962	**£12**	**£6**	
Iverene	7"	Blue Beat	BB111	1962	**£12**	**£6**	
No More Wedding	7"	Blue Beat	BB38	1961	**£12**	**£6**	
Our Melody	7"	Blue Beat	BB129	1962	**£12**	**£6**	
St Louis Woman	7"	Island	WI089	1963	**£10**	**£5**	
Tic Toc	7"	Blue Beat	BB288	1965	**£12**	**£6**	

GABERLUNZIE

Freedom's Sword	LP	Revival	RVS1010	1974	**£15**	**£6**	
Wind And Water Time And Tide	LP	Music World Scotland	MWSL5507	1976	**£15**	**£6**	

GABRIEL, PETER

Before Us – A Brief History	CD	Geffen	PROCD4412	1992	**£20**	**£8**	*US promo sampler*
Big Time	CD-s	Virgin	GAIL312	1987	**£8**	**£4**	
Big Time	CD-s	Virgin	VVD241	1988	**£15**	**£6**	*CD video*
Biko (Live)	CD-s	Virgin	CDPGS612	1987	**£5**	**£2**	
Blood Of Eden	CD-s	Virgin	PGSDX9	1992	**£6**	**£2.50**	
D.I.Y. (Remix)	7"	Charisma	CB319	1978	**£25**	**£12.50**	
Deutsches Album	LP	Charisma	6302221	1982	**£10**	**£4**	*4th LP in German*
Digging In The Dirt	CD-s	Virgin	PGSDG7	1992	**£5**	**£2**	
Don't Give Up	7"	Virgin	PGSP2	1986	**£10**	**£5**	*with Kate Bush*
Ein Deutsches Album	LP	Charisma	6302035	1980	**£10**	**£4**	*3rd LP in German*
Games Without Frontiers (Live)	12"	Virgin	GAB122	1983	**£8**	**£4**	*double*
Kiss That Frog	CD-s	Virgin	PGSDX10	1992	**£5**	**£2**	
Live – Secret World Tour	CD	Virgin		1994	**£40**	**£20**	*Japanese double CD*
Modern Love	7"	Charisma	CB302	1977	**£60**	**£30**	*picture label*
Peter Gabriel 4	LP	Charisma		1982	**£12**	**£5**	*audiophile*
Peter Gabriel Plays Live	LP	Charisma	PGDL1	1983	**£50**	**£25**	*double, test pressing, original mixes*
Schock Den Affen	7"	Charisma	60000876	1982	**£8**	**£4**	*German*
Shaking The Tree	CD-s	Virgin	VSCD1167	1989	**£5**	**£2**	*with Youssou N'Dour*
Shock The Monkey	12"	Charisma	SHOCK350	1982	**£15**	**£7.50**	
Shock The Monkey	7"	Charisma	SHOCK122	1982	**£6**	**£2.50**	*picture disc*
Shock The Monkey/instrumental	7"	Charisma	SHOCK1	1982	**£20**	**£10**	
Sledgehammer	CD-s	Virgin	CDT4	1988	**£5**	**£2**	*3" single*
Solsbury Hill	7"	Charisma	CB301	1977	**£6**	**£2.50**	*picture sleeve*
Solsbury Hill	7"	Sound For Industry	SFI381	1978	**£4**	**£1.50**	*flexi*
Solsbury Hill	CD-s	Virgin	CDT33	1988	**£8**	**£4**	*3" single*
Solsbury Hill	CD-s	Virgin	VSCDT1322	1990	**£5**	**£2**	
Spiel Ohne Grenzen	7"	Charisma	6000448	1980	**£8**	**£4**	*German*
Steam	CD-s	Virgin	PGSDX8	1992	**£8**	**£4**	*house-shaped box*
Us	CD	Real World	PGCD7	1992	**£40**	**£20**	*promo box set, with prints, press sheet, photo*

GABRIEL & THE ANGELS

Don't Wanna Twist No More	7"	Stateside	SS150	1963	£5	£2	

GABRIELLI BRASS

Canterbury Tales Theme	7"	Polydor	56252	1968	£4	£1.50	
Ride Your Pony	7"	Polydor	56047	1965	£4	£1.50	

GADGETS

The Gadgets performed improvised industrial music which was released on three limited-edition albums. (The third is the *Blue Album* from 1983.) One of the trio was Matt Johnson, subsequently the central pillar of The The.

Gadgetree	LP	Final Solution	FSLP001	1979	£15	£6	*blue or brown cover design/insert*
Love, Curiosity, Freckles, & Doubt	LP	Final Solution	FSLP002	1980	£15	£6	

GADSON, MEL

Comin' Down With Love	7"	London	HLX9105	1960	£4	£1.50	

GAGALACTYCA

Gagalactyca	LP	Holyground	HG1135	1990	£15	£6	

GAGARIN, MAJOR YURI

Conquest Of Space	7" EP	Britone	MK100	1961	£20	£10	

GAGS

Death In Buzzard's Gulch	LP	Look	LKLP6312	1979	£50	£25	

GAILLARD, SLIM

Central Avenue Boogie	78	Vogue	V2044	1951	£4	£1.50	
Jam Man	78	Parlophone	R3291	1950	£10	£5	
Musical Aggregations	7" EP	Columbia	SEB10046	1957	£15	£7.50	
Slim Gaillard No. 1	7" EP	Parlophone	GEP8595	1957	£12	£6	
Slim Gaillard Rides Again	7" EP	London	RED1251	1960	£15	£7.50	
Voot Boogie	78	Vogue	V2029	1951	£4	£1.50	

GAINORS

Secret	7"	London	HLU8734	1958	£100	£50	

GALACTIC FEDERATION

March Of The Sky People	7"	Polydor	56093	1966	£15	£7.50	

GALACTIC SUPERMARKET

Galactic Supermarket	LP	Komische	KM58010	1974	£20	£8	*German*

GALACTUS

Cosmic Force Field	LP	Airship		1971	£25	£10	*US*

GALADRIEL

Galadriel	LP	Polydor	2480059	1970	£175	£87.50	*German*

GALAHADS

Galahads	LP	Liberty	LRP3371/ LST7371	1964	£15	£6	*US*

GALAXIE 500

Blue Thunder	7"	Rough Trade	G5SFI	1990	£5	£2	*promo*
Rain	7"	Caff	CAFF9	1988	£15	£7.50	

GALAXY

Day Without The Sun	LP	Sky Queen	SQR1677	1976	£250	£150	*US*

GALAXY-LIN

G	LP	Polydor	2925037	1975	£12	£5	*Dutch*
Galaxy-Lin	LP	Polydor	2480259	1974	£12	£5	*German*

GALBRAITH, BARRY

Guitar And The Wind	LP	Brunswick	LAT8273	1959	£15	£6	

GALE, EDDIE

Black Rhythm Happening	LP	Blue Note	BST84320	1969	£15	£6	
Ghetto Music	LP	Blue Note	BST84294	1968	£15	£6	

GALE, SUNNY

C'est La Vie	7"	HMV	7M344	1955	£5	£2	
Certain Smile	7"	Brunswick	05753	1958	£5	£2	
Come Go With Me	7"	Brunswick	05661	1957	£5	£2	
Goodnight, Well It's Time To Go	7"	HMV	7M243	1954	£6	£2.50	
Send My Baby Back To Me	7"	HMV	7M147	1953	£6	£2.50	
Sunny And Blue	LP	RCA	LPM1277	1956	£20	£8	*US*
Two Hearts	7"	Brunswick	05659	1957	£4	£1.50	

GALENS

Baby I Do Love You	7"	London	HLH9804	1963	£5	£2	

GALL, FRANCE

1968	LP	Philips	844706	1968	£30	£15	*Canadian*
Ella Elle L'a	CD-s	WEA	YZ316CD	1988	£10	£5	

Et Des Baisers	7" EP	Philips	437095	1964	£30	£15	French
Poupée De Cire	LP	Barclay	77728L	1965	£25	£10	French
Poupée De Cire Poupée De Son	7"	Philips	BF1408	1965	£4	£1.50	

GALLAGHER, RORY

Rory Gallagher's brand of tough blues-rock continues to have a significant following despite the fairly low profile that the man himself adopted at the end of his career. His earliest recordings with Taste scrape into the collectors' price bracket, and since his death they have been joined by many of his solo albums from the seventies.

Blueprint	LP	Polydor	2383189	1973	£15	£6	
Deuce	LP	Polydor	2383076	1971	£15	£6	
In The Beginning	LP	Emerald	GES1110	1974	£15	£6	
Irish Tour '74	LP	Polydor	2659031	1974	£12	£5	double
Live In Europe	LP	Polydor	2383112	1972	£15	£6	
Rory Gallagher	LP	Polydor	2383044	1971	£20	£8	
Tattoo	LP	Polydor	2383230	1973	£10	£4	

GALLAGHER & LYLE

Trees	7"	Polydor	56170	1967	£5	£2	

GALLAHADS

Ooh-Ah	7"	Capitol	CL14282	1955	£4	£1.50	

GALLANTS

Man From UNCLE Theme	7"	Capitol	CL15408	1965	£8	£4	

GALLERY

Barley	LP			197–	£250	£150	

GALLEY

Smiling Morn	LP			197–	£100	£50	

GALLIARD

I Wrapped Her In Ribbons	7"	Deram	DM306	1970	£4	£1.50	
New Dawn	LP	Deram	SML1075	1970	£60	£30	
Strange Pleasures	LP	Nova	SDN4	1969	£20	£8	

GALLION, BOB

Froggy Went A Courtin'	7"	MGM	MGM1057	1960	£5	£2	
Two Country Greats	7" EP	Hickory	LPE1508	1965	£5	£2	with Ramsey Kearney
You Take The Table	7"	MGM	MGM1028	1959	£4	£1.50	

GALT, JAMES

Comes The Dawn	7"	Pye	7N15936	1965	£5	£2	
With My Baby	7"	Pye	7N17021	1965	£20	£10	

GAMBLERS

Cry Me A River	7"	Parlophone	R5557	1967	£12	£6	
Dr Goldfoot	7"	Decca	F12399	1966	£10	£5	
Nobody But Me	7"	Decca	F11872	1964	£8	£4	
Now I'm All Alone	7"	Decca	F12060	1965	£10	£5	
You've Really Got A Hold On Me	7"	Decca	F11780	1963	£6	£2.50	

GAMBRELL, FREDDIE

Freddie Gambrell	LP	Vogue	LAE12205	1960	£12	£5	

GAME

The inclusion of the Game's 'Addicted Man' on the programme caused a section of television's *Juke Box Jury* to be edited out, second thoughts deciding that it was not appropriate to publicize a song about drug taking. Parlophone was persuaded to withdraw the single, which is now understandably rare. All four of the group's Who-influenced singles have become very collectable. Lead singer Tony Bird, who was only fifteen at the time of the 'Addicted Man' debacle, recorded as a solo artist for CBS in the late seventies – the resulting albums are listed under his name.

Addicted Man	7"	Parlophone	R5553	1967	£400	£250	best auctioned
But I Do	7"	Pye	7N15889	1965	£75	£37.50	
Gonna Get Me Someone	7"	Decca	F12469	1966	£75	£37.50	
It's Shocking What They Call Me	7"	Parlophone	R5569	1967	£250	£150	

GAMMA

Alpha	LP	GA		1973	£50	£25	Dutch
Darts	LP	GA		1974	£25	£10	Dutch

GAMMA GOOCHEE

Gamma Goochee	7" EP	Colpix	8007	1966	£8	£4	French, B side by Nooney Rickett

GAMMER & HIS FAMILIARS

Rocket Ticket	LP	Gammer	EJ9851	1981	£10	£4	
Will The New Baby	12"	Gammer	GAMMER5	1984	£6	£2.50	
Won't Look Out	LP	Gammer	EJ9699	1981	£10	£4	

GANDALF

Gandalf	LP	Capitol	ST121	1969	£75	£37.50	US

GANDALF THE GREY

Title	Format	Label	Cat. No.	Year	Mint	VG	Notes
Grey Wizard Am I	LP	Grey Wizard Records	7	1972	**£400**	**£250**	US

GANDERTON, RON WARREN

Title	Format	Label	Cat. No.	Year	Mint	VG	Notes
Guitar Star	LP	Celestial Sound	LPRWG1	1973	**£15**	**£6**	
Precious As England	LP	Celestial Sound	LPRWG3	1981	**£15**	**£6**	
Sound Ceremony	LP	Celestial Sound	LPRWG2	1974	**£15**	**£6**	

GANDY, LITTLE JIMMY

Title	Format	Label	Cat. No.	Year	Mint	VG	Notes
Cool Thirteen	7"	Roulette	RO510	1969	**£5**	**£2**	

GANIM'S ASIA MINORS

Title	Format	Label	Cat. No.	Year	Mint	VG	Notes
Daddy Lolo	7"	London	HLE8637	1958	**£5**	**£2**	

GANT, CECIL

Title	Format	Label	Cat. No.	Year	Mint	VG	Notes
Cecil Gant	LP	King	671	1960	**£40**	**£20**	US
Incomparable Cecil Gant	LP	Sound	601	1957	**£40**	**£20**	US
Rock Little Baby	LP	Flyright	LP4710	1974	**£10**	**£4**	

GANT, DON

Title	Format	Label	Cat. No.	Year	Mint	VG	Notes
Early In The Morning	7"	Hickory	451297	1965	**£6**	**£2.50**	

GANTS

Title	Format	Label	Cat. No.	Year	Mint	VG	Notes
Gants Again	LP	Liberty	LRP3473/ LSP7473	1966	**£20**	**£8**	US
Gants Galore	LP	Liberty	LRP3455/ LST7455	1966	**£20**	**£8**	US
Greener Days	7"	Liberty	LIB55940	1967	**£4**	**£1.50**	
Road Runner	7"	Liberty	LIB55829	1965	**£15**	**£7.50**	
Road Runner	LP	Liberty	LRP3432/ LST7432	1965	**£30**	**£15**	US

GARBAGE

When premier league producer Butch Vig (Nirvana, the Smashing Pumpkins, Sonic Youth) decided to form his own group, it should have come as no surprise to anyone that he managed to find considerable extra mileage in the grunge formula. Some specially packaged items have helped to boost the group's collectability, but, in any case, the strength of the music would have been enough. Vocalist Shirley Manson was previously a member of the Scottish group Goodbye Mr MacKenzie, though not as the lead singer.

Title	Format	Label	Cat. No.	Year	Mint	VG	Notes
Garbage	7"	Mushroom	LX31450	1995	**£20**	**£10**	*album on boxed set of 6 singles*
Garbage	LP	Mushroom	LX31450	1995	**£12**	**£5**	*boxed set of 6 x 7" records*
Goldie Milk	12"	Mushroom	DJMILK2	1996	**£10**	**£5**	
Massive Attack Milk	12"	Mushroom	DJMILK3	1996	**£10**	**£5**	
Milk	CD-s	Mushroom	MILKCDP	1996	**£10**	**£5**	*promo*
Only Happy When It Rains	7"	Mushroom	SX1199	1995	**£6**	**£2.50**	
Push It	CD-s	Mushroom	MUSH28CDSX	1998	**£5**	**£2**	*3" single*
Push It	CD-s	Mushroom	TRASH17	1998	**£15**	**£7.50**	*promo in foil bag*
Queer	7"	Mushroom	SX1237	1995	**£8**	**£4**	*with pink carrier bag*
Rabbit In The Moon Milk	12"	Mushroom	DJMILK1	1996	**£10**	**£5**	
Stupid Girl	12"	Mushroom	TRASH09/010	1996	**£8**	**£4**	*promo*
Stupid Girl	7"	Mushroom	SX1271	1996	**£5**	**£2**	*red cloth sleeve*
Stupid Girl	7"	Mushroom	SX1271	1996	**£5**	**£2**	*jukebox issue*
Stupid Girl	7"	Mushroom	SX1271	1996	**£8**	**£4**	*blue cloth sleeve*
Stupid Girl	CD-s	Mushroom	TRASH16	1998	**£15**	**£7.50**	*promo in foil bag*
Stupid Girl Remixes	CD-s	Mushroom	TRASH011	1996	**£20**	**£10**	*promo*
Subhuman	7"	Mushroom	SX1138	1995	**£25**	**£12.50**	*rubber sleeve*
Subhuman	7"	Mushroom	S1138	1995	**£10**	**£5**	
Subhuman	CD-s	Mushroom	D1138	1995	**£12**	**£5**	
Version 2.0	CD	Mushroom	TRASH19	1998	**£20**	**£8**	*promo with CD-ROM tracks*
Vow	7"	Discordant	CORD001	1995	**£50**	**£25**	*metal case*
Vow	7"	Discordant	CORD001	1995	**£15**	**£7.50**	
Vow	CD-s	Mushroom	TRASH02	1995	**£50**	**£25**	*promo, rubber sleeve*

GARBAREK, JAN

Title	Format	Label	Cat. No.	Year	Mint	VG	Notes
Afric Pepperbird	LP	ECM	ECM1007ST	1971	**£20**	**£8**	
Dansere	LP	ECM	ECM1075ST	1976	**£10**	**£4**	*with Bobo Stenson*
Dis	LP	ECM	ECM1093T	1977	**£10**	**£4**	
Esoteric Circle	LP	Freedom	147300	1976	**£25**	**£10**	*German, with Terje Rypdal*
Red Lanta	LP	ECM	ECM1038ST	1974	**£12**	**£5**	*with Art Lande*
Sart	LP	ECM	ECM1015ST	1972	**£12**	**£5**	
Til Vigris	LP	NJF	LP1	1967	**£75**	**£37.50**	*Norwegian*
Triptykon	LP	ECM	ECM1029ST	1973	**£20**	**£8**	
Walking Muza	LP	Polydor	XLP0342	1966	**£75**	**£37.50**	*Norwegian*
Witchi-Tai-To	LP	ECM	ECM1041ST	1974	**£12**	**£5**	*with Bobo Stenson*

GARBUTT, VIN

Title	Format	Label	Cat. No.	Year	Mint	VG	Notes
Valley Of Tees	LP	Trailer	LER2078	1972	**£12**	**£5**	
Young Tin Whistle Pest	LP	Trailer	LER2081	1975	**£10**	**£4**	

GARCIA, JERRY

Garcia	LP	Warner Bros	K46139	1972	£10	£4	
Hooteroll?	LP	Douglas	DGL69013	1971	£10	£4	

GARDEN ODYSSEY ENTERPRISE

Sad And Lonely	7"	Deram	DM267	1969	£10	£5	

GARDINER, PAUL

The collectability of Paul Gardiner's promotional issue of 'Stormtrooper In Drag' derives from the identity of the lead singer on the track, who is Gardiner's friend, Gary Numan.

Stormtrooper In Drag	12"	Beggars Banquet	BEG61T	1981	£150	£75	*promo*

GARDNER, BORIS

Elizabethan Reggae	7"	Doctor Bird	DB1205	1969	£6	£2.50	
Hooked On A Feeling	7"	Treasure Isle	TI7056	1969	£6	£2.50	
Lucky Is The Boy	7"	High Note	HS010	1968	£8	£4	
Never My Love	7"	Duke	DU21	1969	£4	£1.50	
Reggae Happening	LP	Trojan	TBL121	1970	£10	£4	

GARDNER, DAVE

All By Myself	7"	Brunswick	05740	1958	£20	£10	

GARDNER, DON & DEE DEE FORD

Don't You Worry	7"	Stateside	SS130	1962	£6	£2.50	
Don't You Worry	7"	Soul City	SC101	1968	£5	£2	
I Need Your Loving	7"	Stateside	SS114	1962	£5	£2	
In Sweden	LP	Sue	LP1044	1965	£25	£10	*US*
Need Your Lovin'	LP	Fire	LP105	1962	£50	£25	*US*

GARFIELD

Out There Tonight	LP	Capricorn	CPO193	1977	£12	£5	*US*
Strange Streets	LP	Mercury	SRM11082	1976	£12	£5	*US*

GARFIELD, JOHNNY

Stranger In Paradise	7"	Pye	7N15758	1965	£20	£10	

GARLAND, HANK

Three-Four The Blues	LP	CBS Realm	52573	196–	£10	£4	*with Gary Burton*

GARLAND, JUDY

Alone	LP	Capitol	LCT6136	1957	£10	£4	
At The Grove	LP	Capitol	ST1118	1959	£10	£4	*stereo*
Born In A Trunk	7" EP	Philips	BBE12012	1955	£5	£2	
Born To Sing	10" LP	MGM	MGMD1334	1955	£10	£4	
Couple Of Swells	7"	MGM	SP1001	1953	£4	£1.50	*with Fred Astaire*
Garland For Judy	7" EP	Capitol	EAP120051	1961	£5	£2	
Judy	LP	Capitol	LCT6121	1957	£10	£4	
Judy At Carnegie Hall Pt 1	7" EP	Capitol	EAP71569	1961	£5	£2	
Judy At Carnegie Hall Pt 2	7" EP	Capitol	EAP81569	1961	£5	£2	
Judy At The Palace	10" LP	Brunswick	LA8725	1955	£15	£6	
Judy In Love	LP	Capitol	ST1036	1959	£10	£4	*stereo*
Judy In Love Pt 1	7" EP	Capitol	EAP11036	1959	£5	£2	
Judy In Love Pt 2	7" EP	Capitol	EAP21036	1959	£5	£2	
Judy In Love Pt 3	7" EP	Capitol	EAP31036	1959	£5	£2	
Letter	LP	Capitol	ST1188	1959	£10	£4	*stereo*
Look For The Silver Lining	7"	MGM	SP1157	1956	£4	£1.50	
Miss Show Business	LP	Capitol	LCT6103	1956	£10	£4	
Star Is Born	LP	Philips	BBL7007	1955	£10	£4	

GARLAND, RED

All Morning Long	LP	Esquire	32099	1960	£20	£8	*with John Coltrane & Donald Byrd*
At The Prelude	LP	Esquire	32126	1961	£12	£5	
Groovy	LP	Esquire	32056	1958	£20	£8	
Manteca	LP	Esquire	32096	1960	£15	£6	*with Ray Barreto*
Red In Bluesville	LP	Esquire	32116	1961	£15	£6	

GARNER, ERROLL

Afternoon Of An Elf	LP	Mercury	MPL6539	1958	£15	£6	
At The Piano	LP	Philips	BBL7078	1956	£15	£6	
At The Piano	LP	Mercury	MPL6507	1957	£15	£6	
Concert By The Sea	LP	Philips	BBL7106	1957	£12	£5	
Erroll	LP	Mercury	MMB12010	1959	£12	£5	
Erroll Garner	10" LP	Felsted	L87002	195–	£20	£8	
Erroll Garner	LP	London	LTZC15126	1958	£12	£5	
Erroll Garner Trio	LP	Vogue	LAE12209	1960	£12	£5	
Erroll Garner Trio Vol. 1	10" LP	Vogue	LDE034	1953	£20	£8	
Garner Touch	LP	Philips	BBL7193	1957	£12	£5	
Giant Jazz Gallery	LP	Philips	BBL7448	1961	£10	£4	
Gone Garner Gonest	LP	Philips	BBL7034	1955	£12	£5	
Gone With Garner	10" LP	Oriole	MG26042	1955	£20	£8	
Mambo Moves Garner	LP	Mercury	MPL6501	1956	£20	£8	
Margie	10" LP	Felsted	EDL87002	1954	£20	£8	
Most Happy Piano	LP	Philips	BBL7282	1958	£12	£5	
Music Maestro Please	LP	Philips	BBL7426	1961	£10	£4	

Other Voices	LP	Philips	BBL7204	1958	£12	£5	
Paris Impressions Vol. 1	LP	Philips	BBL7313	1959	£10	£4	
Paris Impressions Vol. 2	LP	Philips	BBL7314	1959	£10	£4	
Passport To Fame	10" LP	Felsted	EDL87015	1955	£20	£8	
Penthouse Serenade	LP	London	LTZC15125	1958	£12	£5	
Piano Gems	10" LP	Columbia	33S1059	1955	£20	£8	
Piano Moods	10" LP	Columbia	33S1050	1955	£20	£8	
Piano Wizardry	7" EP	London	REU1066	1956	£5	£2	
Plays For Dancing	10" LP	Philips	BBR8002	1954	£20	£8	
Soliloquy	LP	Philips	BBL7226	1958	£12	£5	
Solo Flight	10" LP	Philips	BBR8045	1955	£20	£8	
Undecided	7" EP	CBS	REP4006	196–	£5	£2	

GARNETT, COL

With A Girl Like You	7"	Page One	POF002	1966	£5	£2	

GARNETT, GALE

I'll Cry Alone	7"	RCA	RCA1451	1965	£15	£7.50	
My Kind Of Folk Songs	LP	RCA	RD7726	1965	£12	£5	
We'll Sing In The Sunshine	7"	RCA	RCA1418	1964	£6	£2.50	

GARON, JESSE & DESPERADOS

Splashing Along	7"	Narodnik	NRK001	1986	£4	£1.50	

GARR, ARTIE

This was the name first used by Art Garfunkel.

Dream Alone	7"	Warwick	515	1959	£25	£12.50	*US*
Private World	7"	Octavia	8002	1960	£20	£10	*US*

GARRETT, VERNON

If I Could Turn Back The Hands Of Time	7"	Stateside	SS2006	1967	£10	£5	
Shine It On	7"	Action	ACT4508	1968	£4	£1.50	
Shine It On	7"	Stateside	SS2026	1967	£6	£2.50	

GARRICK, DAVID

A Boy Called David	LP	Piccadilly	NPL38024	1967	£10	£4	
David	7" EP	Piccadilly	NEP34056	1966	£30	£15	
Dear Mrs Applebee	7" EP	Pye	PNV24182	1966	£10	£5	*French*
Don't Go Out Into The Rain Sugar	LP	Piccadilly	N(S)PL38035	1968	£10	£4	
I've Found A Love	7" EP	Pye	PNV24187	1967	£10	£5	*French*
Lady Jane	7"	Piccadilly	7N35317	1966	£4	£1.50	

GARRICK, MICHAEL

Garrick is a British jazz pianist who recorded prolifically for the Don Rendell-Ian Carr group and under his own name, but despite the considerable efforts of Argo records on his behalf – including frequent full-page adverts in relevant publications like *Jazz Journal* – his record sales were rather poor. His rare albums are actually well worth seeking out, as they are consistently inventive and thought-provoking. His albums integrating poetry with jazz broke new ground, while later extravaganzas like *Mr Smith's Apocalypse* transcend the jazz category altogether, emerging as more like particularly fine pieces of early-seventies progressive music.

Anthem	7" EP	Argo	EAF/ZFA92	1965	£75	£37.50	
Before Night/Day	7" EP	Argo	EAF115	1966	£40	£20	
Black Marigolds	LP	Argo	(Z)DA88	1968	£50	£25	
Case Of Jazz	LP	Airborne		1963	£75	£37.50	
Cold Mountain	LP	Argo	ZDA153	1972	£50	£25	
Epiphany	7"	Argo	AFW105	1971	£5	£2	
Heart Is A Lotus	LP	Argo	ZDA135	1970	£50	£25	*with Norma Winstone*
Home Stretch Blues	LP	Argo	ZDA154	1972	£75	£37.50	
Illumination	LP	Impulse	AS49	1973	£25	£10	
Jazz Praises At St Pauls	LP	Airborne	NBP0021	1968	£50	£25	
Kronos	LP	Hep	2013	1982	£25	£10	
Moonscape	LP	Airborne		1964	£75	£37.50	
Mr Smith's Apocalypse	LP	Argo	ZAGF1	1971	£60	£30	
October Woman	LP	Argo	(Z)DA33	1965	£50	£25	
Poetry And Jazz In Concert	LP	Argo	(Z)DA26/27	1964	£75	£37.50	*double, with Adrian Mitchell*
Poetry And Jazz In Concert 250	LP	Argo	ZPR264/5	1969	£60	£30	*double*
Promises	LP	Argo	(Z)DA36	1965	£50	£25	
Troppo	LP	Argo	ZDA163	1974	£40	£20	
You've Changed	LP	Hep	2011	1978	£25	£10	

GARRIE, NICK

Nightmare Of J. B. Stanislas	LP	A-Z	STECLP107	1970	£15	£6	*French*

GARRITY, FREDDIE

Little Red Donkey	7"	Columbia	DB8348	1968	£4	£1.50	
Oliver In The Overworld	LP	Starline	SRS5019	1970	£10	£4	

GARSIDE, ROBIN & PAUL GOUGH

Sea Songs	LP	Northern Sound	NSR01	1977	£25	£10	

GARVIN, REX

I Gotta Go Now	7"	Atlantic	584097	1967	£5	£2	
Sock It To Them JB	7"	Atlantic	584028	1966	£5	£2	

GARY & STU

Harlan Fare	LP	Carnaby	6302012	1971	£40	£20	
Sweet White Dove	7"	Carnaby	6151003	1972	£5	£2	

GARY & THE ARIELS

Say You Love Me	7"	Fontana	TF476	1964	£4	£1.50	

GARYBALDI

Astrolabio	LP	Fonit	LPQ09075	1973	£125	£62.50	*Italian*
Nuda	LP	CGD	FGL5113	1972	£75	£37.50	*Italian*

GAS

Cradle To The Grave	LP	Good Vibrations	GASLP1	198–	£25	£10	
Emotional Warfare	LP	Polydor	POLE1052	1981	£20	£8	

GAS WORKS

Gas Works	LP	Regal Zonophone	SLRZ1036	1973	£15	£6	

GASH

Young Man's Gash	LP	Brain	1014	1972	£25	£10	*German*

GASKIN

End Of The World	LP	Rondelet	ABOUT4	1981	£15	£6	
I'm No Fool	7"	Rondelet	ROUND7	1981	£6	£2.50	
Mony Mony	7"	Rondelet	ROUND21	1982	£6	£2.50	

GASLIGHT CHOIR

This double LP was produced privately by Taunton School to commemorate a visit by Princess Anne to the school in May 1970. The choir part of the title means exactly what it says, for one of the LPs comprises a selection of mainly classical songs performed by the school choir. The other LP, however, contains folk songs – a mixture of traditional and contemporary – sung and played competently enough by a school group called Gaslight.

Gaslight Choir	LP	private	SDE32732	1970	£100	£50	*double*

GASOLIN

Gasolin	LP	CBS	80470	1974	£75	£37.50	*German*

GASS

Catch My Soul	LP	Polydor	2383035	1971	£10	£4	
Juju	LP	Polydor	2383022	1970	£25	£10	
New Breed	7"	Parlophone	R5456	1966	£15	£7.50	
One Of These Days	7"	Parlophone	R5344	1965	£6	£2.50	

GASS COMPANY

Everybody Needs Love	7"	President	PT170	1968	£20	£10	

GATES, DAVID

Happiest Man Alive	7"	Top Rank	JAR504	1960	£10	£5	

GATES OF EDEN

In Your Love	7"	Pye	7N17252	1967	£6	£2.50	
Mini Shirts	7" EP	Pye	PNV24181	1966	£20	£10	*French*
One To Seven	7"	Pye	7N17278	1967	£10	£5	
Too Much On My Mind	7"	Pye	7N17195	1966	£8	£4	

GATHERERS

Words Of My Mouth	7"	Duke	DU153	1973	£8	£4	

GATOR CREEK

Gator Creek	LP	Mercury	6338035	1970	£10	£4	

GATORS

In Concert	LP	Bulletin		1967	£15	£6	*US*

GAUCHOS

Gauchos Featuring Jim Doval	LP	ABC	(S)506	1965	£15	£6	*US*

GAUGERS

Beware Of The Aberdonian	LP	Topic	12TS284	1976	£15	£6	

GAUGHAN, DICK

Coppers And Brass	LP	Topic	12TS315	1977	£10	£4	
Gaughan	LP	Topic	12TS384	1978	£10	£4	
Kist O'Gold	LP	Trailer	LER2103	1977	£10	£4	
No More Forever	LP	Trailer	LER2072	1972	£12	£5	

GAUGHAN, DICK & ANDY IRVINE

Parallel Lines	LP	Folk Freak	FF4007	1982	£10	£4	*German*

GAVARENTZ, GEORGE

Title	Format	Label	Cat. No.	Year	Mint	VG	Notes
They Came To Rob Las Vegas	LP	Philips	SBL7898	1969	£40	£20	

GAVIN, FRANKIE & ALEC FINN

Title	Format	Label	Cat. No.	Year	Mint	VG	Notes
Frankie Gavin And Alec Finn	LP	Shanachie	29008	1977	£10	£4	US

GAVIN, JIMMY

Title	Format	Label	Cat. No.	Year	Mint	VG	Notes
I Sit In My Window	7"	London	HLU8478	1957	£50	£25	

GAYDEN, MAC

Title	Format	Label	Cat. No.	Year	Mint	VG	Notes
McGavock Gayden	LP	EMI	EMA760	1973	£20	£8	

GAYE, MARVIN

Title	Format	Label	Cat. No.	Year	Mint	VG	Notes
Abraham, Martin And John	7"	Tamla Motown	TMG734	1970	£4	£1.50	
Ain't That Peculiar	7"	Tamla Motown	TMG539	1965	£10	£5	
Can I Get A Witness	7"	Stateside	SS243	1963	£30	£15	
Chained	7"	Tamla Motown	TMG676	1968	£6	£2.50	
Come Get To This	7"	Tamla Motown	TMG882	1973	£6	£2.50	
Greatest Hits	LP	Tamla Motown	(S)TML11065	1968	£10	£4	
Hello Broadway	LP	Tamla Motown	TML11015	1965	£60	£30	
How Sweet It Is	7"	Stateside	SS360	1964	£20	£10	
How Sweet It Is	LP	Tamla Motown	TML11004	1965	£40	£20	
I Heard It Through The Grapevine	7"	Tamla Motown	TMG686	1969	£4	£1.50	
I'll Be Doggone	7"	Tamla Motown	TMG510	1965	£25	£12.50	
In The Groove	LP	Tamla Motown	(S)TML11091	1969	£20	£8	
Let's Get It On	7"	Tamla Motown	TMG868	1973	£12	£6	*demo, picture sleeve*
Little Darling	7"	Tamla Motown	TMG574	1966	£10	£5	
Marvin Gaye	7" EP	Tamla Motown	TME2016	1966	£25	£12.50	
Marvin Gaye	LP	Stateside	SL10100	1964	£100	£50	
Marvin Gaye & His Girls	LP	Tamla Motown	(S)TML11123	1969	£15	£6	
Moods Of Marvin Gaye	LP	Tamla Motown	(S)TML11033	1966	£30	£15	
MPG	LP	Tamla Motown	(S)TML11119	1969	£15	£6	
On Stage Recorded Live	LP	Tamla	242	1963	£60	£30	US
One More Heartache	7"	Tamla Motown	TMG552	1966	£10	£5	
Originals From Marvin Gaye	7" EP	Tamla Motown	TME2019	1967	£20	£10	
Pretty Little Baby	7"	Tamla Motown	TMG524	1965	£15	£7.50	
Pride And Joy	7"	Oriole	CBA1846	1963	£50	£25	
Soulful Moods Of Marvin Gaye	LP	Tamla	221	1961	£100	£50	US
Stubborn Kind Of Fellow	7"	Oriole	CBA1803	1963	£60	£30	
Take This Heart Of Mine	7"	Tamla Motown	TMG563	1966	£10	£5	
That Stubborn Kind Of Fella	LP	Tamla	239	1963	£75	£37.50	US
That's The Way Love Is	7"	Tamla Motown	TMG718	1969	£4	£1.50	
That's The Way Love Is	LP	Tamla Motown	(S)TML11136	1970	£15	£6	
Too Busy Thinking About My Baby	7"	Tamla Motown	TMG705	1969	£4	£1.50	
Tribute To The Great Nat King Cole	LP	Tamla Motown	TML11022	1966	£50	£25	*mono*
Tribute To The Great Nat King Cole	LP	Tamla Motown	STML11022	1966	£60	£30	*stereo*
Trouble Man	LP	Tamla Motown	STML11225	1973	£10	£4	
Try It Baby	7"	Stateside	SS326	1964	£20	£10	
What's Going On	CD	Motown	C8818	1988	£15	£6	*HMV box set*
What's Going On	LP	Tamla Motown	STML11190	1971	£10	£4	
What's Going On	LP	Tamla Motown	STML11190	1971	£12	£5	*with lyric sheet*
When I'm Alone I Cry	LP	Tamla	251	1964	£50	£25	US
You	7"	Tamla Motown	TMG640	1968	£6	£2.50	
You're A Wonderful One	7"	Stateside	SS284	1964	£20	£10	
Your Unchanged Love	7"	Tamla Motown	TMG618	1967	£8	£4	

GAYE, MARVIN & KIM WESTON

Title	Format	Label	Number	Year	Mint	VG	Notes
It Takes Two	7"	Tamla Motown	TMG590	1967	£6	£2.50	
Take Two	LP	Tamla Motown	(S)TML11049	1967	£20	£8	
What Good Am I Without You	7"	Stateside	SS363	1964	£20	£10	

GAYE, MARVIN & MARY WELLS

Title	Format	Label	Number	Year	Mint	VG	Notes
Once Upon A Time	7"	Stateside	SS316	1964	£15	£7.50	
Together	LP	Stateside	SL10097	1964	£60	£30	

GAYE, MARVIN & TAMMI TERRELL

Title	Format	Label	Number	Year	Mint	VG	Notes
Ain't No Mountain High Enough	7"	Tamla Motown	TMG611	1967	£6	£2.50	
Ain't Nothing Like The Real Thing	7"	Tamla Motown	TMG655	1968	£4	£1.50	
Easy	LP	Tamla Motown	(S)TML11132	1970	£12	£5	
Good Lovin' Ain't Easy To Come By	7"	Tamla Motown	TMG697	1969	£4	£1.50	
Greatest Hits	LP	Tamla Motown	(S)TML11153	1970	£10	£4	
If I Could Build My Whole World Around You	7"	Tamla Motown	TMG635	1967	£4	£1.50	
Onion Song	7"	Tamla Motown	TMG715	1969	£4	£1.50	
United	LP	Tamla Motown	(S)TML11062	1968	£20	£8	
You Ain't Livin' Till You're Lovin'	7"	Tamla Motown	TMG681	1969	£4	£1.50	
You're All I Need To Get By	7"	Tamla Motown	TMG668	1968	£4	£1.50	
You're All I Need To Get By	LP	Tamla Motown	(S)TML11084	1968	£15	£6	
Your Precious Love	7"	Tamla Motown	TMG625	1967	£5	£2	

GAYLADS

Title	Format	Label	Number	Year	Mint	VG	Notes
Fire And Rain	7"	Trojan	TR7799	1970	£4	£1.50	
Go Away	7"	Blue Cat	BS110	1968	£8	£4	*Soul Vendors B side*
Goodbye Daddy	7"	Island	WI281	1966	£10	£5	
I'm Free	7"	Studio One	SO2038	1968	£12	£6	*Soul Vendors B side*
It's All In The Game	7"	Trojan	TR7782	1970	£5	£2	
It's Hard To Confess	7"	Doctor Bird	DB1124	1968	£10	£5	
Lady With The Red Dress On	7"	Doctor Bird	DB1014	1966	£10	£5	
Looking For A Girl	7"	Fab	FAB62	1968	£8	£4	
Love Me With All Your Heart	7"	Studio One	SO2017	1967	£12	£6	
No Good Girl	7"	Island	WI3025	1967	£10	£5	
Put On Your Style	7"	Rio	R125	1967	£8	£4	*Soul Brothers B side*
Rock Steady	LP	Coxsone	CSL8005	1967	£100	£50	
Same Things	7"	Upsetter	US323	1969	£4	£1.50	
She Want It	7"	Doctor Bird	DB1145	1968	£10	£5	
Soul Sister	7"	Trojan	TR7771	1970	£5	£2	
Stop Making Love	7"	Island	WI3002	1966	£10	£5	
Sunshine Golden 18	LP	Coxsone	CSL8006	1967	£60	£30	
Tears From My Eyes	7"	Studio One	SO2002	1967	£12	£6	
Tell The Children The Truth	7"	Trojan	TR7763	1970	£4	£1.50	
That's What Love Will Do	7"	Trojan	TR7738	1970	£5	£2	
There'll Come A Day	7"	R&B	JB159	1964	£10	£5	*Billy Cooke B side*
There's A Fire	7"	Trojan	TR7703	1970	£4	£1.50	
Whap Whap	7"	R&B	JB165	1964	£10	£5	
You Had Your Chance	7"	Trojan	TR688	1969	£4	£1.50	
You Should Never Do That	7"	Doctor Bird	DB1031	1966	£10	£5	*Winston Stewart B side*
You'll Never Leave Him	7"	Island	WI291	1966	£10	£5	
Young, Gifted And Black	7"	Trojan	TR7743	1970	£5	£2	

GAYLETTS

Title	Format	Label	Number	Year	Mint	VG	Notes
I Like Your World	7"	Island	WI3141	1968	£10	£5	
If You Can't Be Good	7"	Big Shot	BI502	1968	£5	£2	
Silent River Runs Deep	7"	Island	WI3129	1968	£10	£5	
Son Of A Preacher Man	7"	London	HLJ10302	1970	£4	£1.50	
Son Of A Preacher Man	7"	Big Shot	BI516	1969	£4	£1.50	

GAYLORDS

Title	Format	Label	Number	Year	Mint	VG	Notes
He's A Good Face	7"	Columbia	DB7805	1966	£10	£5	

GAYLORDS (2)

Title	Format	Label	Number	Year	Mint	VG	Notes
Chipmunk Ska	7"	Island	WI269	1966	£10	£5	

GAYNAIR, WILTON

Title	Format	Label	Number	Year	Mint	VG	Notes
Blue Bogey	LP	Tempo	TAP25	1960	£40	£20	
Blue Bogey Vol. 1	7" EP	Tempo	EXA103	1960	£20	£10	

GAYNOR, ROSEMARY

Title	Format	Label	Number	Year	Mint	VG	Notes
Ain't That A Shame	7"	Columbia	SCM5196	1955	£4	£1.50	

GAYTEN, PAUL

Title	Format	Label	Number	Year	Mint	VG	Notes
Hunch	7"	London	HLM8998	1959	**£100**	**£50**	

GAYTONES

Title	Format	Label	Number	Year	Mint	VG	Notes
Black Man Kingdom Come	7"	Smash	SMA2330	1973	**£8**	**£4**	
Jamaican Hilite	7"	Green Door	GD4016	1971	**£4**	**£1.50**	
Target	7"	High Note	HS037	1970	**£4**	**£1.50**	

G-CLEFS

Title	Format	Label	Number	Year	Mint	VG	Notes
Girl Has To Know	7"	London	HLU9530	1962	**£8**	**£4**	
I Understand	7"	London	HLU9433	1961	**£4**	**£1.50**	
Ka Ding Dong	7"	Columbia	DB3851	1956	**£300**	**£180**	*best auctioned*
Make Up Your Mind	7"	London	HLU9563	1962	**£8**	**£4**	

GEDDES AXE

Title	Format	Label	Number	Year	Mint	VG	Notes
Return Of The Gods	7"	ACS	ACS1	1981	**£8**	**£4**	
Sharpen Your Wits	7"	Steel City	AXE1	1982	**£5**	**£2**	

GEE, MATTHEW

Title	Format	Label	Number	Year	Mint	VG	Notes
Jazz By Gee	LP	London	LTZU15075	1957	**£25**	**£10**	
Jazz By Gee!	LP	Riverside	RLP12221	196–	**£15**	**£6**	

GEE, ROY

Title	Format	Label	Number	Year	Mint	VG	Notes
Consider Me	7"	J-Dan	JDN4412	1970	**£4**	**£1.50**	
Try To Understand	7"	J-Dan	JDN4413	1970	**£4**	**£1.50**	

GEESIN, RON

Title	Format	Label	Number	Year	Mint	VG	Notes
As He Stands	LP	Ron	RON28	1973	**£12**	**£5**	
Atmospheres	LP	KPM	KPM1201	1977	**£15**	**£6**	
Body	LP	Harvest	SHSP4008	1970	**£12**	**£5**	*with Roger Waters*
Electrosound	LP	KPM	KPM1102	1972	**£15**	**£6**	
Electrosound (Vol. 2)	LP	KPM	KPM1154	1975	**£12**	**£5**	
Mr Mayor Stamp Your Foot	7" EP	private	RRG319/320	1965	**£50**	**£25**	
Patruns	LP	Ron	RON31	1975	**£12**	**£5**	
Raise Of The Eyebrows	LP	Transatlantic	TRA161	1967	**£25**	**£10**	
Right Through	LP	Ron	RON323	1977	**£12**	**£5**	

GEISLER, LADI

Title	Format	Label	Number	Year	Mint	VG	Notes
Alte Kameraden Beaten Zum Tanz	LP	Ariola	72643	1965	**£40**	**£20**	*German*
Gitarrenmethode	LP	Polydor	004525	1965	**£20**	**£8**	*German, with booklet*
Guitar A La Carte	LP	Polydor	249292	1967	**£15**	**£6**	*German*
Happy Guitar	LP	Ariola	72157IU	1964	**£15**	**£6**	*German*
Mister Guitar	LP	Polydor	237117	1962	**£30**	**£15**	*German, stereo*
Mister Guitar	LP	Polydor	46617	1962	**£15**	**£6**	*German, mono*

GELLER, HERB

Title	Format	Label	Number	Year	Mint	VG	Notes
Fire In The West	LP	Stateside	(S)SL10249	1963	**£10**	**£4**	
Herb Geller	LP	Emarcy	EJL1268	1958	**£20**	**£8**	

GEMINI

Title	Format	Label	Number	Year	Mint	VG	Notes
Space Walk	7"	Columbia	DB7638	1965	**£25**	**£12.50**	

GENE

Title	Format	Label	Number	Year	Mint	VG	Notes
Be My Light, Be My Guide	7"	Costermonger	COST2	1994	**£8**	**£4**	
Be My Light, Be My Guide	CD-s	Costermonger	COST2CD	1994	**£12**	**£6**	
For The Dead	7"	Costermonger	COST1	1994	**£25**	**£12.50**	
For The Dead	CD-s	Costermonger	COST1CD	1994	**£40**	**£20**	
Sleep Well Tonight	CD-s	Costermonger	COST3CD	1994	**£8**	**£4**	

GENE & DEBBE

Title	Format	Label	Number	Year	Mint	VG	Notes
Go With Me	7"	London	HLE10165	1967	**£4**	**£1.50**	
Lovin' Season	7"	London	HLE10203	1968	**£4**	**£1.50**	
Playboy	7"	London	HLE10179	1968	**£5**	**£2**	

GENE & EUNICE

Title	Format	Label	Number	Year	Mint	VG	Notes
Bom Bom Lulu	7"	Vogue	V9136	1959	**£40**	**£20**	
Doodle Doodle Do	7"	Vogue	V9083	1957	**£100**	**£50**	
I Gotta Go Home	7"	Vogue	V9062	1956	**£100**	**£50**	
I Mean Love	7"	Vogue	V9106	1958	**£100**	**£50**	
Let's Get Together	7"	Vogue	V9071	1957	**£100**	**£50**	
Poco Loco	7"	London	HL8956	1959	**£25**	**£12.50**	
This Is My Story	7"	Vogue	V9066	1957	**£100**	**£50**	
Vow	7"	Vogue	V9126	1958	**£30**	**£15**	

GENE LOVES JEZEBEL

Title	Format	Label	Number	Year	Mint	VG	Notes
Gorgeous	CD-s	Beggars Banquet	BEG202CD	1987	**£5**	**£2**	
Immigrants	CD	Beggars Banquet	BEG14CD	1988	**£15**	**£6**	
Shaving My Neck	12"	Situation 2	SIT18T	1982	**£12**	**£6**	

GENERAL HAVOC

Title	Format	Label	Number	Year	Mint	VG	Notes
Fast Jaspal EP	7"	Chapati Heat	BIRD1	1991	**£10**	**£5**	

GENERAL HUMBERT

Title	Format	Label	Number	Year	Mint	VG	Notes
General Humbert	LP	Dolphin	DOLM5015	1976	**£20**	**£8**	*Irish*

General Humbert II	LP	Gael Linn	CEF095	1982	**£10**	**£4**	*Irish*

GENERATION X

Day By Day	7"	Generation X	GX1	1977	**£25**	**£12.50**	*test pressing*
Wild Youth	7"	Chrysalis	CHS2189	1977	**£15**	**£7.50**	*mispressed B-side, plays 'No No No'*

GENESIS

Genesis's first LP was produced by Jonathan King – an unlikely choice for a determinedly progressive group, except that King and Genesis were all ex-pupils of Charterhouse. The record has been reissued several times – the first being as early as 1973 – but the original *From Genesis To Revelation* is quite scarce. Even more so are the early singles, of which 'Happy The Man', 'I Know What I Like' and 'The Carpet Crawlers' all have non-album B sides. The albums *Trespass* and *Nursery Cryme* remained in the catalogue for years, of course, but their inclusion here refers to the original pressings with their deep pink Charisma labels.

3 x 3	7" EP	Charisma	GEN1	1982	**£5**	**£2**	*picture disc*
Carpet Crawlers	7"	Charisma	CB251	1975	**£15**	**£7.50**	
Counting Out Time	7"	Charisma	CB238	1974	**£8**	**£4**	
Domino	CD-s	Virgin	VVD359	1989	**£15**	**£7.50**	*3" single*
Firth Of Fifth	7"	Genesis Information	GI01	1983	**£5**	**£2**	*flexi*
Foxtrot/Selling England By The Pound	LP	Charisma	CGS103	1975	**£75**	**£37.50**	*boxed, poster*
From Genesis To Revelation	LP	Decca	LK4990	1969	**£150**	**£75**	*mono*
From Genesis To Revelation	LP	Decca	SKL4990	1969	**£50**	**£25**	*stereo, no box round Decca logo*
Happy The Man	7"	Charisma	CB181	1972	**£50**	**£25**	
Happy The Man	7"	Charisma	CB181	1972	**£250**	**£150**	*picture sleeve*
Hold On My Heart	CD-s	Virgin	GENDG8	1992	**£6**	**£2.50**	*with 4 cards*
I Can't Dance	CD-s	Virgin	GENDG7	1991	**£5**	**£2**	
I Know What I Like	7"	Charisma	CB224	1973	**£5**	**£2**	
Illegal Alien	7"	Charisma	ALS1	1984	**£12**	**£6**	*shaped picture disc*
In The Beginning	LP	Decca	SKL4990	1974	**£15**	**£6**	
Invisible Touch	CD	Virgin	GENPCD2	1986	**£12**	**£5**	*picture disc*
Invisible Touch (Live)	CD-s	Virgin	GENDX10	1992	**£6**	**£2.50**	*boxed*
Jesus He Knows Me	CD-s	Virgin	GENDX9	1992	**£6**	**£2.50**	*boxed with space for other CDs*
Knife	7"	Charisma	CB152	1971	**£250**	**£150**	*picture sleeve*
Knife	7"	Charisma	CB152	1971	**£50**	**£25**	
Land Of Confusion	CD-s	Virgin	SNEG312	1986	**£5**	**£2**	
Looking For Someone	7"	Charisma	GS1	1970	**£300**	**£180**	*promo*
Mama	CD-s	Virgin	CDT5	1988	**£5**	**£2**	*3" single*
Man On The Corner	7"	Charisma	CB393	1982	**£50**	**£25**	*picture sleeve*
Nursery Cryme	LP	Charisma	CAS1052	1972	**£30**	**£15**	*with tour label*
Nursery Cryme	LP	Charisma	CAS1052	1971	**£15**	**£6**	*dark pink label*
Paperlate	7"	Charisma	JBGEN1	1982	**£4**	**£1.50**	*jukebox issue*
Silent Sun	7"	Decca	F12735	1968	**£200**	**£100**	
Spot The Pigeon EP	CD-s	Virgin	CDF40	1988	**£5**	**£2**	*export*
Spot The Pigeon EP	CD-s	Virgin	CDT40	1988	**£6**	**£2.50**	*3" single*
That's All	7"	Charisma/ Virgin	TATA1	1983	**£12**	**£6**	*picture disc*
Tonight Tonight Tonight	CD-s	Virgin	CDEP1	1987	**£30**	**£15**	*with Invisible Touch*
Tonight Tonight Tonight	CD-s	Virgin	DRAW412	1987	**£6**	**£2.50**	
Trespass	LP	Charisma	CAS1020	1970	**£15**	**£6**	*dark pink label*
Trespass/Nursery Cryme	LP	Charisma	CGS102	1975	**£75**	**£37.50**	*boxed, poster*
Trick Of The Tail	7"	Charisma	CB277	1976	**£4**	**£1.50**	*jukebox issue, purple label*
Trick Of The Tail	LP	Mobile Fidelity	MFSL1062	1981	**£20**	**£8**	*US audiophile*
Twilight Alehouse	7"	Charisma	no number	1975	**£15**	**£7.50**	*flexi*
We Can't Dance	CD	Virgin	DJGCD1	1991	**£40**	**£20**	*promo box set, with cassette and prints*
We Can't Dance	CD	Virgin	DJGCD1	1991	**£15**	**£6**	*promo with card cover*
When The Sour Turns To Sweet	LP	Metal Masters	MACHMP4	1986	**£10**	**£4**	*picture disc*
Where The Sour Turns To Sweet	7"	Decca	F12949	1969	**£200**	**£100**	
Winter's Tale	7"	Decca	F12775	1968	**£200**	**£100**	

GENESIS (2)

In The Beginning	LP	Mercury	SR61175	1968	**£20**	**£8**	*US*

GENEVA

Nature's Whore	CD-s	Nude	PNUD22CD	1996	**£15**	**£7.50**	*promo*
No One Speaks	7"	Nude	NUD22S	1996	**£5**	**£2**	

GENEVEVE

Once	7"	CBS	202061	1966	**£5**	**£2**	*picture sleeve*

GENGHIS KHAN

Love You	7"	Wabbit	WAB61/63	1983	**£20**	**£10**	*double*

GENOCIDE

Images Of Delusion	7"	Safari	SAP2	1979	**£5**	**£2**	

GENTILES

Goodbye Baby	7"	Pye	7N17530	1968	**£5**	**£2**	

GENTLE, JOHNNY

Gentle Touch	7" EP	Philips	BBE12345	1959	**£30**	**£15**	

GENTLE, TIM & THE GENTLEMEN

Title	Format	Label	Number	Year	Mint	VG	Notes
Without You	7"	Oriole	CB1988	1965	£8	£4	

GENTLE GIANT

Gentle Giant's intricately constructed and faultlessly performed music seems to epitomize what the Vertigo label was all about. The album *Octopus*, in particular, stands as something of a landmark within the progressive rock genre. One can hear the band, on successive albums, learning how to create music that requires a high degree of skill for its execution and an even higher degree of inventiveness for its original creation. At the same time, the music is perfectly accessible, if a little hard to dance to! Gentle Giant's ancestor, by the way, was Simon Dupree and the Big Sound, both groups revolving around the Shulman brothers, although they have little in common musically.

Title	Format	Label	Number	Year	Mint	VG	Notes
Acquiring The Taste	LP	Vertigo	6360041	1971	£15	£6	*spiral label*
Gentle Giant	LP	Vertigo	6360020	1970	£15	£6	*spiral label*
In A Glass House	LP	WWA	WWA002	1973	£20	£8	
Octopus	LP	Vertigo	6360080	1972	£15	£6	*spiral label*
Power And The Glory	LP	WWA	WWA010	1974	£12	£5	
Three Friends	LP	Vertigo	6360070	1972	£15	£6	*spiral label*

GENTLE INFLUENCE

Title	Format	Label	Number	Year	Mint	VG	Notes
Always Be A Part Of My Living	7"	Pye	7N17743	1969	£5	£2	
Never Trust In Tomorrow	7"	Pye	7N17666	1969	£5	£2	

GENTLE PEOPLE

Title	Format	Label	Number	Year	Mint	VG	Notes
It's Too Late	7"	Columbia	DB8276	1967	£5	£2	

GENTLE REIGN

Title	Format	Label	Number	Year	Mint	VG	Notes
Gentle Reign	LP	Vanguard		1968	£12	£5	*US*

GENTRYS

Title	Format	Label	Number	Year	Mint	VG	Notes
Brown Paper Sack	7"	MGM	MGM1296	1966	£10	£5	
Everyday I Have To Cry	7"	MGM	MGM1312	1966	£4	£1.50	
Gentrys	LP	Sun	117	1970	£20	£8	*US*
Gentrys	LP	MGM	GAS127	1966	£25	£10	*US*
Keep On Dancing	7"	MGM	MGM1284	1965	£4	£1.50	
Keep On Dancing	7" EP	MGM	63628	1965	£15	£7.50	*French*
Keep On Dancing	LP	MGM	(S)E4336	1965	£30	£15	*US*
Time	LP	MGM	(S)E4346	1966	£30	£15	*US*

GENTS

Title	Format	Label	Number	Year	Mint	VG	Notes
Faker	7"	Posh	POSH001	1981	£4	£1.50	

GEOFFREY

Title	Format	Label	Number	Year	Mint	VG	Notes
ABH	7"	Music Bank	BECK694	1978	£10	£5	

GEORDIE

Title	Format	Label	Number	Year	Mint	VG	Notes
Don't Be Fooled By The Name	LP	EMI	EMA764	1974	£10	£4	
Save The World	LP	EMI	EMC3134	1976	£15	£6	

GEORGE, BARBARA

Title	Format	Label	Number	Year	Mint	VG	Notes
I Know	7"	London	HL9513	1962	£8	£4	
I Know You Don't Love Me Anymore	LP	A.F.O.	5001	1962	£75	£37.50	*US*
Send For Me	7"	Sue	WI316	1964	£12	£6	

GEORGE, LLOYD

Title	Format	Label	Number	Year	Mint	VG	Notes
Sing Real Loud	7"	London	HLP9562	1962	£25	£12.50	

GEORGE, RENE

Title	Format	Label	Number	Year	Mint	VG	Notes
Messengers Of Autumn	LP	RCS		1981	£40	£20	*Dutch*

GEORGE & BEN

Title	Format	Label	Number	Year	Mint	VG	Notes
Boa Constrictions Natural Vine	LP	Vanguard		1968	£12	£5	

GEORGE & CAROLE

Title	Format	Label	Number	Year	Mint	VG	Notes
At Pythingdean	LP	Decca	LK4999	1969	£20	£8	

GEORGETTES

Title	Format	Label	Number	Year	Mint	VG	Notes
Down By The River	7"	Pye	7N25058	1960	£5	£2	
Love Like A Fool	7"	London	HL8548	1958	£25	£12.50	

GEORGIA TOM

Title	Format	Label	Number	Year	Mint	VG	Notes
Georgia Tom And Friends	LP	Riverside	RLP8803	1967	£15	£6	

GEORGIE & THE MONARCHS

The rare single by Georgie and the Monarchs features the recording debut of Van Morrison, who played saxophone for the band.

Title	Format	Label	Number	Year	Mint	VG	Notes
Boo-Zooh	7"	CBS	1307	1963	£30	£15	*picture sleeve, German or Dutch*

GERDES, GEORGE

Title	Format	Label	Number	Year	Mint	VG	Notes
Obituary	LP	United Artists	UAS5549	1972	£12	£5	*US*
Son Of Obituary	LP	United Artists	UAS5593	1972	£12	£5	*US*

GERMAN BLUE FLAMES

Title	Format	Label	Number	Year	Mint	VG	Notes
German Blue Flames	LP	Ariola	72256IT	1965	£100	£50	*German*

GERMAN OAK

Title	Format	Label	Number	Year	Mint	VG	Notes
German Oak	LP	Bunker	BU172	1972	£40	£20	*German*

GERMS

Forming	7"	What	WHAT01	1977	£**10**	£**5**	

GERMS, WESLEY

Whiplash	7"	Upsetter	US390	1972	£**6**	£**2.50**	

GERONIMO BLACK

Geronimo Black	LP	MCA	MCF2683	1974	£**15**	£**6**	

GERRARD, DENNY

Sinister Morning	LP	Nova	SDN10	1970	£**30**	£**15**	*with High Tide*

GERRY & THE HOLOGRAMS

Here is a record to file next to the Sun album *The Wit And Wisdom Of Ronald Reagan*, an LP that is completely silent. It is impossible to tell what, if anything, is recorded on the single by Gerry and the Holograms. For the record is painted and glued into its sleeve, rendering it completely unplayable. As concepts go, this one has a kind of anarchic brilliance about it!

Emperor's New Music	7"	Absurd	A5	1979	£**8**	£**4**	*unplayable record*

GERRY & THE PACEMAKERS

Don't Let The Sun Catch You Crying	7" EP	Columbia	SEG8346	1964	£**12**	£**6**	
Don't Let The Sun Catch You Crying	7" EP	Columbia	ESRF1549	1964	£**15**	£**7.50**	*French*
Don't Let The Sun Catch You Crying	LP	Laurie	LLP/SLP2024	1964	£**20**	£**8**	*US*
Ferry Cross The Mersey	7" EP	Columbia	ESRF1637	1964	£**15**	£**7.50**	*French*
Ferry Cross The Mersey	LP	Columbia	33SX1693	1965	£**20**	£**8**	*mono*
Ferry Cross The Mersey	LP	Columbia	SCX3544	1965	£**30**	£**15**	*stereo*
Gerry In California	7" EP	Columbia	SEG8388	1965	£**20**	£**10**	
Girl On A Swing	LP	Laurie	LLP/SLP2037	1965	£**20**	£**8**	*US*
Girl On The Swing	7"	Columbia	DB8044	1966	£**4**	£**1.50**	
Greatest Hits	LP	Laurie	LLP/SLP2031	1965	£**15**	£**6**	*US*
Hits From Ferry Cross The Mersey	7" EP	Columbia	SEG8397	1965	£**15**	£**7.50**	
How Do You Do It	7" EP	Columbia	SEG8257	1963	£**10**	£**5**	
How Do You Do It	7" EP	Columbia	ESDF1490	1963	£**15**	£**7.50**	*French*
How Do You Like It	LP	Columbia	33SX1546	1963	£**15**	£**6**	*mono*
How Do You Like It	LP	Columbia	SCX3492	1963	£**25**	£**10**	*stereo*
I'll Be There	LP	Laurie	LLP/SLP2030	1964	£**20**	£**8**	*US*
I'm The One	7" EP	Columbia	SEG8311	1964	£**10**	£**5**	
It's Gonna Be Alright	7" EP	Columbia	SEG8367	1964	£**15**	£**7.50**	
Remember	7"	DJM	DJS298	1974	£**4**	£**1.50**	
Rip It Up	7" EP	Columbia	SEG8426	1965	£**25**	£**12.50**	
Second Album	LP	Laurie	LLP/SLP2027	1964	£**20**	£**8**	*US*
You'll Never Walk Alone	7" EP	Columbia	ESRF1446	1963	£**15**	£**7.50**	*French*
You'll Never Walk Alone	7" EP	Columbia	SEG8295	1963	£**10**	£**5**	
You'll Never Walk Alone	LP	Regal	SREG1070	1967	£**20**	£**8**	*export*

GERVASE

Pepper Grinder	7"	Decca	F12822	1968	£**6**	£**2.50**	

GESTURES

Run Run Run	7"	Stateside	SS379	1965	£**10**	£**5**	

GETZ, STAN

At Storyville	10" LP	Vogue	LDE089	1954	£**40**	£**20**	
At Storyville Vol. 1	LP	Vogue	LAE12158	1959	£**20**	£**8**	
At Storyville Vol. 2	LP	Vogue	LAE12199	1959	£**20**	£**8**	
At The Opera House	LP	Columbia	33CX10127	1958	£**20**	£**8**	*with J. J. Johnson*
At The Shrine No. 1	LP	Columbia	33CX10000	1955	£**30**	£**15**	
At The Shrine No. 2	LP	Columbia	33CX10001	1955	£**30**	£**15**	
Big Band Bossa Nova	LP	Verve	VLP9024	1963	£**10**	£**4**	*with Gary McFarland*
Captain Marvel	LP	Verve	2304225	1975	£**12**	£**5**	*with Chick Corea*
Crazy Rhythm	LP	Verve	VLP9139	1966	£**12**	£**5**	
Didn't We	LP	Verve	SVLP9081	1970	£**12**	£**5**	
Dynasty	LP	Verve	V688022	1972	£**20**	£**8**	*double*
Focus	LP	HMV	CLP1577	1962	£**15**	£**6**	
Getz Age	LP	Columbia	33SX1707	1965	£**12**	£**5**	
Getz Au Go Go	LP	Verve	VLP9081	1964	£**15**	£**6**	
Getz/Gilberto	LP	Verve	2317009	1971	£**10**	£**4**	*with Joao Gilberto*
Getz/Gilberto	LP	Verve	VLP9065	1964	£**12**	£**5**	
Getz/Gilberto No. 2	LP	Verve	VLP9132	1965	£**12**	£**5**	
Girl From Ipanema	7"	Verve	VS520	1964	£**4**	£**1.50**	*with Astrud & Joao Gilberto*
Greatest Hits	LP	Stateside	SL10161	1966	£**10**	£**4**	
Imported From Europe	LP	HMV	CLP1351	1960	£**15**	£**6**	
Interpretations	LP	Columbia	33CX10057	1956	£**40**	£**20**	
Jazz Samba	LP	Verve	(S)VLP9013	1962	£**15**	£**6**	*with Charlie Byrd*
Jazz Samba	LP	Verve	2317006	1971	£**10**	£**4**	*with Charlie Byrd*
Jazz Samba Encore	LP	Verve	(S)VLP9038	1963	£**12**	£**5**	
Jazz Samba Encore	LP	Verve	(S)VLP9038	1963	£**15**	£**6**	*with Luiz Bonfa*
Jazz Samba Encore!	LP	Verve	2317008	1971	£**10**	£**4**	*with Luiz Bonfa*
Mickey One	LP	MGM	C(S)8001	1965	£**15**	£**6**	
Modern World Of Getz	LP	Columbia	33SX1686	1964	£**12**	£**5**	
Reflections	LP	Verve	VLP9069	1964	£**12**	£**5**	
Soft Swing	LP	HMV	CLP1320	1960	£**15**	£**6**	
Stan Getz	LP	Columbia	33CX10082	1957	£**20**	£**8**	
Stan Getz Plays	10" LP	Esquire	20007	1953	£**40**	£**20**	
Stan Getz Quartet	10" LP	Vogue	LDE147	1955	£**30**	£**15**	

Stan Getz Quartet	LP	Esquire	32011	1956	£30	£15	
Stan Meets Chet	LP	HMV	CLP1292	1959	£25	£10	*with Chet Baker*
Steamer	LP	HMV	CLP1276	1959	£20	£8	
The Steamer	LP	World Record Club	T341	196–	£10	£4	
What The World Needs Now	LP	Verve	(S)VLP9232	1969	£12	£5	

G-FORCE

G-Force	LP	Jet	JETPD229	1980	£10	£4	*picture disc*
Hot Gossip	7"	Jet	JET183	1980	£6	£2.50	
White Knuckles	7"	Jet	JET7005	1980	£6	£2.50	

GHOST

I've Got To Get To Know You	7"	Gemini	GMS014	1970	£10	£5	
When You're Dead	7"	Gemini	GMS007	1969	£15	£7.50	
When You're Dead – One Second	LP	Gemini	GME1004	1970	£150	£75	

GHOST DANCE

Celebrate	CD-s	Chrysalis	CHSCD3402	1989	£5	£2	
Grip Of Love	12"	Karbon	KAR604T	1986	£6	£2.50	
Grip Of Love	7"	Karbon	KAR604	1986	£5	£2	
Heart Full Of Soul	7"	Karbon	KAR606	1986	£6	£2.50	*promo*
River Of No Return	12"	Karbon	KAR602T	1986	£6	£2.50	
Stop The World	CD-s	Chrysalis	CCD1706	1989	£5	£2	
When I Call	7"	Karbon	KAR608	1987	£6	£2.50	*promo*

GHOULS

Dracula's Deuce	LP	Capitol	(S)T2215	1965	£15	£6	*US*

GIANT, BILL

Better Let Her Go	7"	MGM	MGM1135	1961	£6	£2.50	

GIANT CRAB

Cool It Helios	LP	Uni	73057	1969	£15	£6	*US*
Giant Crab Comes Forth	LP	Uni	73037	1968	£15	£6	*US*

GIANT SUNFLOWER

Big Apple	7"	CBS	2805	1967	£5	£2	
Mark Twain	7"	CBS	3033	1967	£4	£1.50	

GIANTS

Live	LP	Polydor	LPHM46426/ SLPHM237626	1964	£40	£20	*German*

GIANTS (2)

Giants	LP	International	ZO201V	1976	£50	£25	*French*

GIBB, MAURICE

Sing A Rude Song	LP	Polydor	2383018	1970	£20	£8	

GIBB, ROBIN

Robin's Reign	LP	Polydor	583085	1970	£12	£5	
Saved By The Bell/Alexandria Good Time	7"	Polydor	BM56337	1969	£10	£5	

GIBBONS, STEVE

Alright Now	7"	Wizard	WIZ102	1971	£4	£1.50	
Short Stories	LP	Wizard	SWZA5501	1971	£50	£25	

GIBBS, CARLTON

Ghost Walk	7"	Amalgamated	AMG872	1971	£6	£2.50	
Seeing Is Believing	7"	Amalgamated	AMG870	1971	£8	£4	

GIBBS, GEORGIA

Arrivederci Roma	7"	Mercury	7MT210	1958	£8	£4	
Balling The Jack	7"	Vogue Coral	Q72088	1955	£10	£5	
Great Balls Of Fire	7"	RCA	RCA1029	1958	£15	£7.50	
Her Nibbs Miss Gibbs	10" LP	Mercury	MPT7511	1957	£25	£10	
Hucklebuck	7"	Columbia	DB4259	1959	£5	£2	
Hula Hoop Song	7"	Columbia	DB4201	1958	£4	£1.50	
I'll Be Seeing You	7" EP	Mercury	EP13265	1955	£6	£2.50	
I'll Know	7"	Vogue Coral	Q72182	1956	£6	£2.50	
Sings The Oldies	10" LP	Mercury	MPT7500	1956	£25	£10	
Stroll That Stole My Heart	7"	London	HLP9098	1960	£4	£1.50	
Sugar Candy	7"	RCA	RCA1011	1957	£6	£2.50	
Sweet Georgia Gibbs	7" EP	Mercury	MEP9505	1956	£6	£2.50	
Sweet Georgia Gibbs Vol. 2	7" EP	Mercury	MEP9516	1957	£10	£5	
Swinging With Her Nibbs	LP	Mercury	MPL6508	1957	£15	£6	

GIBBS, JOE

African Dub Chapter One	LP	Lightning	LIP10	1978	£15	£6	
African Dub Chapter Three	LP	Lightning	LIP12	1979	£15	£6	
African Dub Chapter Two	LP	Lightning	LIP11	1979	£15	£6	
Franco Nero	7"	Amalgamated	AMG858	1970	£5	£2	
Gift Of God	7"	Amalgamated	AMG868	1970	£5	£2	
Hijacked	7"	Amalgamated	AMG865	1970	£4	£1.50	
Let It Be	7"	Amalgamated	AMG860	1970	£4	£1.50	
Majestic Dub	LP	Laser	LASL3	1979	£12	£5	

Movements	7"	Amalgamated	AMG867	1970	**£5**	**£2**	
Nevada Joe	7"	Amalgamated	AMG855	1970	**£5**	**£2**	
News Flash	7"	Pressure Beat	PR5504	1970	**£5**	**£2**	
Ration	7"	Jackpot	JP811	1973	**£4**	**£1.50**	
Rock The Clock	7"	Amalgamated	AMG859	1970	**£5**	**£2**	

GIBBS, MICHAEL

Michael Gibbs is a jazz composer and arranger of major importance. Unfortunately, he is not at all prolific and of what he has recorded, much is hard to find. The vital early albums are listed below – other Gibbs creations can be found scattered through various records by Gary Burton, while his arranging skills have been employed by such diverse artists as John McLaughlin and Joni Mitchell.

Just Ahead	LP	Polydor	2683011	1972	**£30**	**£15**	*double*
Michael Gibbs	LP	Deram	SML1063	1970	**£50**	**£25**	
Tanglewood '63	LP	Deram	SML1087	1971	**£30**	**£15**	

GIBBS, SIR

People Grudgeful	7"	Amalgamated	AMG822	1968	**£8**	**£4**	

GIBBS, TERRY

Exciting Terry Gibbs Big Band	LP	Verve	CLP1560/ CSD1439	1961	**£12**	**£5**	
Launching A New Sound In Music	LP	Mercury	MMC14018	1959	**£12**	**£5**	
Swing Is Here	LP	HMV	CLP1394/ CSD1324	1960	**£12**	**£5**	
Swingin' With Terry Gibbs	LP	Emarcy	EJL1263	1957	**£15**	**£6**	
Terry Gibbs	10" LP	Vogue Coral	LRA10035	1955	**£30**	**£15**	
Terry Gibbs	LP	Vogue Coral	LVA9013	1956	**£15**	**£6**	
Terry Gibbs	LP	Emarcy	EJT752	1957	**£15**	**£6**	
Terry Gibbs	LP	Emarcy	EJL1269	1958	**£15**	**£6**	

GIBSON, BOB

Where I'm Bound	LP	Bounty	BY6006	1966	**£25**	**£10**	

GIBSON, DEBBIE

Anything Is Possible	CD-s	East West	A7735CD	1991	**£5**	**£2**	
Electric Youth	CD-s	WEA	A8919CDP	1989	**£5**	**£2**	*picture disc*
Electric Youth	LP	WEA	WX231Y	1988	**£15**	**£6**	*yellow vinyl, poster*
Foolish Beat	CD-s	WEA	A9059CD	1988	**£6**	**£2.50**	
Lost In Your Eyes	CD-s	Atlantic	A8970CD	1989	**£5**	**£2**	
Only In My Dreams	12"	Atlantic	A9322TP	1987	**£15**	**£7.50**	*picture disc*
Only In My Dreams	12"	WEA	A9322T	1987	**£15**	**£7.50**	
Out Of The Blue	CD-s	Atlantic	A9091CD	1988	**£8**	**£4**	
Staying Together	7"	Atlantic	A9020V	1988	**£6**	**£2.50**	
Staying Together	CD-s	WEA	A9020CD	1988	**£8**	**£4**	
We Could Be Together	CD-s	Atlantic	A8896CD	1989	**£5**	**£2**	
We Could Be Together	CD-s	Atlantic	7567887	1989	**£5**	**£2**	

GIBSON, DON

Big Hearted Me	7"	RCA	RCA1158	1959	**£4**	**£1.50**	
Blue And Lonesome	7" EP	RCA	RCX1050	1960	**£8**	**£4**	
Blue Blue Day	7"	RCA	RCA1073	1958	**£4**	**£1.50**	
Don't Tell Me Your Trouble	7"	RCA	RCA1150	1959	**£4**	**£1.50**	
Give Myself A Party	7"	RCA	RCA1098	1958	**£4**	**£1.50**	
God Walks These Hills	LP	RCA	RD7641	1964	**£10**	**£4**	
I Wrote A Song	LP	RCA	RD/SF7576	1963	**£10**	**£4**	
Look Who's Blue	7" EP	RCA	RCX213	1962	**£8**	**£4**	
Look Who's Blue	LP	RCA	LPM/LSP2184	1960	**£15**	**£6**	*US*
May You Never Be Alone	7" EP	RCA	RCX7122	1963	**£8**	**£4**	
No One Stands Alone	LP	RCA	LPM/LSP1918	1959	**£15**	**£6**	*US*
Oh Lonesome Me	7"	RCA	RCA1056	1958	**£4**	**£1.50**	
Oh Lonesome Me	LP	RCA	LPM1743	1958	**£20**	**£8**	*US*
Sea Of Heartbreak	7"	RCA	RCA1243	1961	**£4**	**£1.50**	
Some Favourites Of Mine	LP	RCA	RD/SF7506	1962	**£10**	**£4**	
Songs By Don Gibson	LP	Lion	70069	1958	**£30**	**£15**	*US*
Sweet Dreams	7"	MGM	SP1177	1956	**£100**	**£50**	
Sweet Dreams	LP	RCA	LPM/LSP2269	1960	**£15**	**£6**	*US*
That Gibson Boy	7" EP	RCA	RCX214	1962	**£8**	**£4**	
That Gibson Boy	LP	RCA	RD27158	1960	**£12**	**£5**	

GIBSON, HENRY

Grass Menagerie	LP	Epic	15120	1969	**£15**	**£6**	*US*

GIBSON, JODY & THE MULESKINNERS

Kissin' Time	7"	Parlophone	R4579	1959	**£4**	**£1.50**	
So You Think You've Got Troubles	7"	Parlophone	R4645	1960	**£4**	**£1.50**	

GIBSON, STEVE & THE RED CAPS

Silhouettes	7"	HMV	POP417	1957	**£100**	**£50**	
Steve Gibson & The Red Caps	10" LP	Mercury	MG25116	195–	**£150**	**£75**	*US*

GIBSON, WAYNE

Come On Let's Go	7"	Decca	F11800	1964	**£6**	**£2.50**	
Ding Dong The Witch Is Dead	7"	Parlophone	R5357	1965	**£15**	**£7.50**	
For No One	7"	Columbia	DB7998	1966	**£4**	**£1.50**	
Kelly	7"	Pye	7N15680	1964	**£4**	**£1.50**	
Linda Lu	7"	Decca	F11713	1963	**£6**	**£2.50**	
One Little Smile	7"	Columbia	DB7683	1965	**£20**	**£10**	

Portland Town	7"	Pye	7N15798	1965	£4	£1.50	
Under My Thumb	7"	Columbia	DB7911	1966	£12	£6	

GIDIAN

Feeling	7"	Columbia	DB8041	1966	£4	£1.50	
Fight For Your Love	7"	Columbia	DB7916	1966	£4	£1.50	
Try Me Out	7"	Columbia	DB7826	1966	£10	£5	

GIFT

Blue Apple	LP	Nova	SDL8002	1974	£60	£30	*German*
Gift	LP	Telefunken	SLE14680	1972	£20	£8	*German*

GIFTED CHILDREN

Painting By Numbers	7"	Whaam!	WHAAM001	1981	£20	£10	

GIGGETTY

Black Country Time	LP	Bridge	GE103	1980	£10	£4	
Black Country Time	LP	Revolver	REVLP1	1980	£10	£4	
Dawn To Dusk In The Black Country	LP	private	GE100	1975	£75	£37.50	

GIGUERE, RUSS

Hexagram II	LP	Warner Bros	WS1910	1971	£12	£5	*US*

GIGYMEN

Gigymen	LP	Spaceward	3S3/EDENLP76	1975	£15	£6	

GIL, GILBERTO

Gilberto Gil	LP	Famous	SFM1001	1971	£15	£6	

GILA

Bury My Heart At Wounded Knee	LP	Warner Bros	46234	1973	£25	£10	*German*
Gila	LP	BASF	20211096	1971	£100	£50	*German*

GILBERT

These singles are early efforts by Gilbert O'Sullivan, who found considerable chart success during the first half of the seventies. During 1999 he attempted to make a come-back, although it has to be admitted that his hit albums and singles are hard even to give away these days.

Disappear	7"	CBS	3089	1967	£8	£4	
Mister Moody's Garden	7"	Major Minor	MM613	1969	£10	£5	
What Can I Do	7"	CBS	3399	1968	£8	£4	

GILBERT, GEORGE

Medway Flows Softly	LP	Mime	LPMS7041	1974	£40	£20	

GILBERT & LEWIS

Ends With The Sea	7"	4AD	AD106	1981	£4	£1.50	

GILBERTO, ASTRUD

And Roses And Roses	7" EP	Verve	VEP5019	1966	£5	£2	
Astrud Gilberto Album	LP	Verve	SVLP9087	1969	£10	£4	
Beach Samba	LP	Verve	SVLP9187	1968	£10	£4	
Gilberto And Turrentine	LP	CTI	CTL1	1972	£10	£4	*with Stanley Turrentine*
I Haven't Got Anything Better To Do	LP	Verve	SVLP9242	1969	£10	£4	
Shadow Of Your Smile	LP	Verve	SVLP9107	1970	£10	£4	
Windy	LP	Verve	SVLP9233	1969	£10	£4	

GILDED CAGE

Long Long Road	7"	Tepee	TPR1003	1969	£4	£1.50	

GILES, GILES & FRIPP

Although this is the group that evolved into King Crimson, little of the music on *Cheerful Insanity* sounds much like that produced by any King Crimson line-up. Instead, much of it is of the novelty-song variety, with flat English vocals conveying lyrics that aim to be whimsical, but which mostly sound embarrassing. The record is certainly distinctive, however, and in places Robert Fripp does reveal himself to be a highly talented guitarist, even if conveying no hint that he would ever become a major influence within seventies rock and beyond.

Cheerful Insanity Of Giles, Giles And Fripp	LP	Deram	SPA423	1970	£30	£15	
Cheerful Insanity Of Giles, Giles And Fripp	LP	Deram	DML/SML1022	1968	£50	£25	
One In A Million	7"	Deram	DM188	1968	£75	£37.50	
Thursday Morning	7"	Deram	DM210	1968	£75	£37.50	

GILES FARNABY'S DREAM BAND

Giles Farnaby was an English composer of madrigals and dance tunes who lived from about 1563 until 1640. Clearly, therefore, his Dream Band was not one that he had any hand in assembling personally. With much 'traditional' material actually dating from Farnaby's era, the folk-rock interpretations of his music on this album fall in naturally alongside recordings by Ashley Hutchings and the Albion Band. Some well-known British jazz musicians make up the rhythm section, playing behind an amalgamation of medieval music specialists St George's Canzona and folk group Trevor Crozier's Broken Consort, with singing group the Druids making an occasional appearance.

Giles Farnaby's Dream Band	LP	Argo	ZDA158	1973	£75	£37.50	
Newcastle Brown	7"	Argo	AFW112	1973	£5	£2	

GILFELLON, TOM

In The Middle Of The Tune	LP	Topic	12TS282	1976	£15	£6	
Loving Mad Tom	LP	Trailer	LER2079	1972	£12	£5	

GILGAMESH

Title	Format	Label	Number	Year	Mint	VG	Notes
Gilgamesh	LP	Caroline	CA2007	1975	**£12**	**£5**	

GILKYSON, TERRY & THE EASYRIDERS

Title	Format	Label	Number	Year	Mint	VG	Notes
Golden Minutes Of Folk Music	10" LP	Brunswick	LA8618	1953	**£15**	**£6**	
Lonesome Rider	7" EP	Fontana	TFE17327	1960	**£6**	**£2.50**	
Marianne	7"	Philips	JK1007	1958	**£10**	**£5**	
Remember The Alamo	LP	London	HAR2323	1961	**£10**	**£4**	
Rolling	7" EP	London	RER1333	1961	**£8**	**£4**	
Rolling	LP	London	HAR2301/ SAHR6111	1961	**£10**	**£4**	
Strolling Blues	7" EP	Fontana	TFE17326	1960	**£6**	**£2.50**	

GILL, COLIN & DESMOND

Title	Format	Label	Number	Year	Mint	VG	Notes
History Of Lore	LP	Profile	GMOR142	1977	**£50**	**£25**	

GILLAN, IAN

Title	Format	Label	Number	Year	Mint	VG	Notes
Child In Time	LP	Polydor	ACBR261	1976	**£10**	**£4**	
Higher And Higher	7"	Lyntone	LYN10599	1981	**£25**	**£12.50**	*hard vinyl test pressing*
Ian Gillan Band Sampler	LP	Island	ILPS9511DJ	1977	**£15**	**£6**	*1 sided promo*
Living For The City	7"	Virgin	VSY519	1982	**£5**	**£2**	*picture disc*
Mad Elaine	7"	Island	WIP6423	1978	**£5**	**£2**	
No Good Luck	CD-s	East West	YZ513CD	1990	**£5**	**£2**	
She Tears Me Down	12"	Acrobat	BAT1212	1979	**£8**	**£4**	*promo*
Twin Exhausted	12"	Island	R553B	1978	**£12**	**£6**	*promo, Illusion B side*

GILLES ZEITSCHIFF

Title	Format	Label	Number	Year	Mint	VG	Notes
Gilles Zeitschiff	LP	Kosmische	KM58012	1974	**£15**	**£6**	*German*

GILLESPIE, DANA

Title	Format	Label	Number	Year	Mint	VG	Notes
Andy Warhol	7"	RCA	RCA2446	1974	**£5**	**£2**	
Box Of Surprises	LP	Decca	LK5012	1969	**£60**	**£30**	*mono*
Box Of Surprises	LP	Decca	SKL5012	1969	**£40**	**£20**	
Donna Donna	7"	Pye	7N15872	1965	**£5**	**£2**	
Pay You Back With Interest	7"	Pye	7N17280	1967	**£4**	**£1.50**	
Thank You Boy	7"	Pye	7N15962	1965	**£4**	**£1.50**	
Weren't Born A Man	LP	RCA	APL10354	1973	**£10**	**£4**	

GILLESPIE, DARLENE

Title	Format	Label	Number	Year	Mint	VG	Notes
Darlene Of The Teens	LP	Disneyland	WDL3010		**£25**	**£10**	*US*

GILLESPIE DIZZY

Title	Format	Label	Number	Year	Mint	VG	Notes
Always	7" EP	Verve	VRE5022	1966	**£5**	**£2**	
Be Bop	7" EP	Philips	BE12552	1964	**£5**	**£2**	
Birks Works	7" EP	Columbia	SEB10096	1957	**£5**	**£2**	
Champ	7" EP	Vogue	EPV1094	1956	**£5**	**£2**	
Concert In Paris	LP	Columbia	33SX1574	1963	**£15**	**£6**	
Diz 'n' Bird In Concert	LP	Vogue	LAE12252	1961	**£10**	**£4**	*with Charlie Parker*
Diz And Don	7" EP	MGM	MGMEP579	1957	**£5**	**£2**	*2 tracks by Don Byas*
Dizzy Atmosphere	LP	London	LTZU15121	1958	**£20**	**£8**	
Dizzy Gillespie	10" LP	Columbia	33C9030	1957	**£40**	**£20**	
Dizzy Gillespie	7" EP	Vogue	EPV1022	1955	**£5**	**£2**	
Dizzy Gillespie	7" EP	Vogue	EPV1078	1956	**£5**	**£2**	
Dizzy Gillespie	LP	RCA	RD7827	1965	**£10**	**£4**	
Dizzy Gillespie And His Orchestra	10" LP	HMV	DLP1047	1954	**£40**	**£20**	
Dizzy Gillespie And His Orchestra	10" LP	Vogue	LDE135	1955	**£40**	**£20**	
Dizzy Gillespie And His Orchestra	10" LP	Vogue	LDE076	1954	**£40**	**£20**	
Dizzy Gillespie And His Orchestra	7" EP	Vogue	EPV1157	1956	**£5**	**£2**	
Dizzy Gillespie And His Orchestra	7" EP	Vogue	EPV1158	1956	**£5**	**£2**	
Dizzy Gillespie And His Orchestra	LP	Columbia	33CX10002	1955	**£30**	**£15**	
Dizzy Gillespie And Stuff Smith	LP	HMV	CLP1291	1959	**£20**	**£8**	
Dizzy Gillespie Plays	10" LP	Vogue	LDE017	1953	**£40**	**£20**	
Dizzy Gillespie Plays – Johnny Richards Conducts	10" LP	Vogue	LDE033	1953	**£40**	**£20**	
Dizzy Gillespie With Strings	7" EP	Vogue	EPV1049	1955	**£5**	**£2**	
Dizzy Gillespie/Stan Getz Sextet	10" LP	Columbia	33C9009	1955	**£40**	**£20**	
Dizzy Gillespie/Stan Getz Sextet	7" EP	HMV	7EG8596	1960	**£5**	**£2**	
Dizzy Gillespie–Stan Getz Sextet	10" LP	Columbia	33C9027	1956	**£75**	**£37.50**	
Dizzy In Greece	LP	Columbia	33CX10144	1959	**£20**	**£8**	
Dizzy With Strings	7" EP	Esquire	EP193	1958	**£5**	**£2**	
Duets	LP	Columbia	33CX10121	1958	**£30**	**£15**	*with Sonny Rollins & Sonny Stitt*
Film Themes	7" EP	Philips	BE12583	1965	**£5**	**£2**	
For Musicians Only	LP	Columbia	33CX10095	1958	**£20**	**£8**	*with Stan Getz and Sonny Stitt*
Gillespiana	LP	HMV	CLP1484/ CSD1392	1962	**£20**	**£8**	
Greatest	LP	RCA	RD27242	1961	**£10**	**£4**	
Greatest Trumpet Of Them All	LP	HMV	CLP1381	1960	**£20**	**£8**	
Have Trumpet, Will Excite	LP	HMV	CLP1318	1959	**£20**	**£8**	
Mellow Sounds	7" EP	HMV	7EG8577	1960	**£5**	**£2**	
More Mellow Sounds	7" EP	HMV	7EG8646	1961	**£5**	**£2**	
New Sound In Jazz	7" EP	Philips	430793BE	1963	**£5**	**£2**	
Newport Jazz Festival 1957	LP	Columbia	33CX10111	1958	**£15**	**£6**	*Side 2 by Count Basie*

Title	Format	Label	Cat. No.	Year	Mint	VG	Notes
One More Time	7" EP	Columbia	SEB10087	1957	£5	£2	with Charlie Parker
Operatic Strings	10" LP	Esquire	20003	1953	£40	£20	
Operatic Strings	LP	Fontana	TL5343	1967	£10	£4	
Operatic Strings – Jealousy	10" LP	Felsted	EDL87006	1954	£40	£20	
Paris Concert	10" LP	Vogue	LDE039	1954	£40	£20	
Pile Driver	7" EP	Columbia	SEB10075	1957	£5	£2	
Portrait Of Duke Ellington	LP	HMV	CLP1431	1961	£20	£8	
Two By Two	7" EP	MGM	MGMEP681	1958	£5	£2	2 tracks by Kai Winding

GILLEY, MICKEY

Title	Format	Label	Cat. No.	Year	Mint	VG	Notes
Lonely Wine	LP	Astro	101	1964	£200	£100	US

GILLUM, JAZZ

Title	Format	Label	Cat. No.	Year	Mint	VG	Notes
1938–47	LP	RCA	RD7816	1968	£15	£6	
Jazz Gillum	LP	Folkways	FS3826	1961	£20	£8	

GILMER, JIMMY

Title	Format	Label	Cat. No.	Year	Mint	VG	Notes
Ain't Gonna Tell Nobody	7"	London	HLD9872	1964	£4	£1.50	
Buddy's Buddy	LP	Dot	DLP3577	1964	£25	£10	
Campusology	LP	Dot	DLP3709/25709	1966	£25	£10	US
Daisy Petal Picking	7"	London	HLD9827	1964	£4	£1.50	
Firewater	LP	Dot	DLP25856	1968	£15	£6	US
Folkbeat	LP	Dot	DLP3668/25668	1965	£25	£10	US
I'm Gonna Go Walkin'	7"	London	HLD9632	1962	£5	£2	
Look At Me	7"	London	HLD9898	1964	£5	£2	
Lucky 'Leven	LP	Dot	DLP3643/25643	1965	£25	£10	US
She Belongs To Me	7"	Stateside	SS472	1965	£4	£1.50	
Sugar Shack	7"	London	HLD9789	1963	£5	£2	
Sugar Shack	7" EP	London	RE10154	1964	£20	£10	French, B side by the Surfaris
Sugar Shack	LP	London	HAD/SHD8150	1964	£30	£15	
Thunder 'n' Lightnin'	7"	Stateside	SS418	1965	£5	£2	
Torquay	LP	Dot	DLP3512/25512	1963	£25	£10	US

GILMOUR, DAVE

Title	Format	Label	Cat. No.	Year	Mint	VG	Notes
Blue Light	12"	Harvest	12HAR5226	1984	£6	£2.50	
Love On The Air	7"	Harvest	HARP5229	1984	£8	£4	shaped picture disc
There's No Way Out Of Here	7"	Harvest	HAR5167	1978	£4	£1.50	

GILREATH, JAMES

Title	Format	Label	Cat. No.	Year	Mint	VG	Notes
Little Band Of Gold	7"	Pye	7N25190	1963	£5	£2	
Lollipops, Lace And Lipstick	7"	Pye	7N25213	1963	£4	£1.50	

GILTRAP, GORDON

Title	Format	Label	Cat. No.	Year	Mint	VG	Notes
Giltrap	LP	Philips	6308175	1973	£20	£8	
Gordon Giltrap	LP	Transatlantic	TRA175	1968	£25	£10	
In At The Deep End	LP	KPM	KPM1330	1982	£10	£4	
No Way Of Knowing	7"	Philips	6006344	1973	£10	£5	
Portrait	LP	Transatlantic	TRA202	1969	£20	£8	
Soundwaves	LP	KPM	KPM1292	1982	£10	£4	
Testament Of Time	LP	MCA	MKPS2020	1971	£20	£8	
Themes	LP	Themes International		1981	£10	£4	

GIN BOTTLE SEVEN

Title	Format	Label	Cat. No.	Year	Mint	VG	Notes
Gin Bottle Jazz	LP	London	LTZU15115	1958	£15	£6	

GINGER & THE SNAPS

This is an alternative name used by the Honeys and, like those records, these are keenly sought by Beach Boys completists.

Title	Format	Label	Cat. No.	Year	Mint	VG	Notes
Love Me The Way That I Love You	7"	Tore	1008	1961	£30	£15	US
Seven Days In September	7"	MGM	13413	1965	£60	£30	US

GINGER JUG BAND

Title	Format	Label	Cat. No.	Year	Mint	VG	Notes
Ginger Jug Band	LP	private	GJB001	197–	£50	£25	

GINGER SNAPS

Title	Format	Label	Cat. No.	Year	Mint	VG	Notes
Sh Down Down Song	7"	RCA	RCA1483	1965	£5	£2	

GINHOUSE

Title	Format	Label	Cat. No.	Year	Mint	VG	Notes
Ginhouse	LP	B&C	CAS1031	1971	£40	£20	

GINKS

Title	Format	Label	Cat. No.	Year	Mint	VG	Notes
Tribute To The Beatles	LP	Summit	ATL4176	1965	£10	£4	

GINNY & GALLIONS

Title	Format	Label	Cat. No.	Year	Mint	VG	Notes
Two Sides	LP	Downey	DS1003	1964	£20	£8	US

GINO & GINA

Title	Format	Label	Cat. No.	Year	Mint	VG	Notes
Pretty Baby	7"	Mercury	7MT230	1958	£25	£12.50	

GINSBERG, ALLEN

Title	Format	Label	Cat. No.	Year	Mint	VG	Notes
Allen Ginsberg Reads Kaddish	LP	Atlantic	4001	1966	£25	£10	US
At The ICA	LP	Saga	PSY3002	1967	£20	£8	
Ginsberg Thing	LP	Transatlantic	TRA192	1968	£25	£10	

Title	Format	Label	Number	Year	Mint	Value	Notes
Howl And Other Poems	LP	Fantasy	7006	1959	£50	£25	*US, red vinyl*
Reading At Better Books	LP	Better Books	no number	1965	£75	£37.50	
Reading At The Architectural Association	LP	Love Books	LB0001	1965	£75	£37.50	*with other poets*
Songs Of Innocence And Experience	LP	Forecast	FVS3083	1969	£25	£10	*US*
Wales: A Visitation	7"	Cape Goliard		196–	£20	£10	*with book*

GIORDANO, LOU

This very rare single was co-produced by Buddy Holly and Phil Everly, who can also be heard on both sides of the record.

Title	Format	Label	Number	Year	Mint	Value	Notes
Stay Close To Me	7"	Brunswick	955115	1959	£500	£330	*US, best auctioned*

GIORGIO

Title	Format	Label	Number	Year	Mint	Value	Notes
Baby I Need You	7"	Electratone	EP1003	1968	£40	£20	
Bla Bla Diddley	7"	Page One	POF028	1967	£4	£1.50	
Bla Bla Diddly	7" EP	DiscAZ	1093	1967	£15	£6	*French*
Full Stop	7"	Page One	POF003	1966	£4	£1.50	
Girl Without A Heart	7"	Polydor	56101	1966	£4	£1.50	

GIPSY LOVE

Title	Format	Label	Number	Year	Mint	Value	Notes
Gipsy Love	LP	BASF	BAP5026	1972	£15	£6	

GIRARD, GEORGE

Title	Format	Label	Number	Year	Mint	Value	Notes
Stompin' At The Famous Door	LP	HMV	CLP1123	1957	£15	£6	

GIRL

Title	Format	Label	Number	Year	Mint	Value	Notes
Hollywood Tease	7"	Jet	JET176	1980	£4	£1.50	*poster sleeve*
Love Is A Game	7"	Jet	JET191	1980	£4	£1.50	*white vinyl*
Thru The Twilite	7"	Jet	JETP7014	1981	£4	£1.50	*picture disc*

GIRL SATCHMO

Title	Format	Label	Number	Year	Mint	Value	Notes
Blue Beat Chariot	7"	Blue Beat	BB227	1964	£12	£6	
Don't Be Sad	7"	Blue Beat	BB156	1963	£12	£6	
Mash Potato	7"	Blue Beat	BB45	1961	£12	£6	
Take You For A Ride	7"	Fab	FAB111	1969	£4	£1.50	
Twist Around The Town	7"	Blue Beat	BB79	1962	£12	£6	

GIRL WONDER

Title	Format	Label	Number	Year	Mint	Value	Notes
Mommy Out Of The Light	7"	Doctor Bird	DB1015	1966	£10	£5	

GIRLFRIENDS

Title	Format	Label	Number	Year	Mint	Value	Notes
Jimmy Boy	7"	Colpix	PX712	1963	£10	£5	

GIRLIE

Title	Format	Label	Number	Year	Mint	Value	Notes
African Meeting	7"	Duke	DU42	1969	£4	£1.50	
Boss Cocky	7"	Treasure Isle	TI7053	1969	£5	£2	*Love Shocks B side*
Madame Straggae	7"	Bullet	BU400	1969	£4	£1.50	*Laurel Aitken B side*
Small Change	7"	Joe	JRS7	1970	£4	£1.50	

GIRLS TOGETHER OUTRAGEOUSLY

Title	Format	Label	Number	Year	Mint	Value	Notes
Permanent Damage	LP	Straight	STS1059	1969	£40	£20	

GISLASON, BJORGVIN

Title	Format	Label	Number	Year	Mint	Value	Notes
Orugglega	LP	Steinar	065	1983	£30	£15	*Icelandic*

GITTE

Title	Format	Label	Number	Year	Mint	Value	Notes
Favoriter	LP	HMV	KELP117	1968	£20	£8	*Danish*
Gitte	LP	Capitol	ST10424	1965	£20	£8	*German*
Gitte Haenning	LP	HMV	KELP102	1964	£20	£8	*Danish*
Greatest Hits	LP	Odeon	BOKS20	1965	£75	£37.50	*Danish*
Red Mantle	LP	RCA	LSP4815	1972	£40	£20	*US*

GIUFFRE, JIMMY

Title	Format	Label	Number	Year	Mint	Value	Notes
Easy Way	LP	HMV	CLP1344	1960	£15	£6	
Jimmy Giuffre	10" LP	Capitol	LC6699	1955	£30	£15	
Jimmy Giuffre Clarinet	LP	London	LTZK15059	1957	£15	£6	
Jimmy Giuffre Three	LP	London	LTZK15130	1958	£15	£6	
Music Man	LP	London	LTZK15216	1961	£15	£6	
Train And The River	LP	Atlantic	590011	1968	£15	£6	
Trav'lin' Light	LP	London	LTZK15137	1958	£15	£6	

GIZMO

Title	Format	Label	Number	Year	Mint	Value	Notes
Just Like Master Bates	LP	Ace	ACE001	1979	£30	£15	*white vinyl*
Just Like Master Bates/Victims	LP	Gizmo		198–	£50	£25	*autographed double*
Psychedelic Rock And Roll	7"	MCM	4	197–	£6	£2.50	
Victims	LP	Sleep'N'Eat		1979	£30	£15	

GLACIERS

Title	Format	Label	Number	Year	Mint	Value	Notes
From Sea To Sky	LP	Mercury	MG2/SR60895	1964	£20	£8	*US*

GLACKIN, PADDY & PADDY KEENAN

Title	Format	Label	Number	Year	Mint	Value	Notes
Doublin	LP	Tara	2007	1979	£10	£4	*Irish*

GLACKIN, PADDY, MICK GAVIN, MICHAEL O'BRIEN

Title	Format	Label	Number	Year	Mint	Value	Notes
Flags Of Dublin	LP	Topic	12TS383	1978	£10	£4	

GLADIATORS

Bleak House	7"	HMV	POP1134	1963	**£10**	**£5**	

GLADIATORS (2)

Girl Don't Make Me Wait	7"	Direction	583854	1968	**£4**	**£1.50**	
Gladiators	LP	Virgin	V2161	1980	**£10**	**£4**	
My Girl	7"	Duke	DU58	1970	**£4**	**£1.50**	
Naturality	LP	Front Line	FL1035	1978	**£12**	**£5**	
Proverbial Reggae	LP	Front Line	FL1002	1978	**£12**	**£5**	
Sonia	7"	Ackee	ACK149	1972	**£4**	**£1.50**	
Sweet So Till	LP	Front Line	FL1048	1979	**£12**	**£5**	
Train Is Coming	7"	Doctor Bird	DB1114	1967	**£10**	**£5**	
Trenchtown Mix Up	LP	Virgin	V2062	1976	**£12**	**£5**	
Waiting On The Shores Of Nowhere	7"	Direction	584308	1969	**£4**	**£1.50**	

GLADIOLAS

Little Darling	7"	London	HLO8435	1957	**£200**	**£150**	

GLANS OVER SJO OCH STRAND

First	LP	Silence	MNW13P	1970	**£30**	**£15**	*Swedish*
Second	LP	Silence	MNW22P	1971	**£40**	**£20**	*Swedish*

GLASEL, JOHNNY

Jazz Session	10" LP	HMV	DLP1198	1958	**£20**	**£8**	

GLASER, TOMPALL

Land – Folk Songs	LP	Decca	DL(7)4041	1960	**£20**	**£8**	*US*
Through The Eyes Of Love	LP	MGM	C8082	1968	**£20**	**£8**	

GLASS, PHILIP

Philip Glass is one of the pioneering minimalist composers, whose knack of finding easily attractive riffs for development has made his career prosper to the point where he has become probably the best-known modern composer. Some of his work overlaps with rock – he produced the album by Polyrock (listed under their name) and set lyrics by the likes of Paul Simon and David Byrne, using the warm tones of Linda Ronstadt to deliver them, on his album *Songs From Liquid Days*. His success must be particularly gratifying given that his earliest works were considered so *outré* by the classical establishment, that Glass was forced to issue them on his own Chatham Square label.

Music In Fifths/Music In Similar Motion	LP	Chatham Square	LP1003	1973	**£30**	**£15**	*US*
Music With Changing Parts	LP	Chatham Square	LP1001/2	197–	**£40**	**£20**	*US double*
Solo Music	LP	Shandar	SHAN83515	1978	**£12**	**£5**	*French*
Two Pages	LP	Folkways	FTS33902	197–	**£15**	**£6**	*US*

GLASS FAMILY

Electric Band	LP	Warner Bros	WS1776	1968	**£25**	**£10**	*US*

GLASS HARP

Glass Harp	LP	MCA	MUPS431	1971	**£15**	**£6**	
Synergy	LP	MCA	MUPS449	1972	**£15**	**£6**	

GLASS MENAGERIE

Do My Thing Myself	7"	Polydor	56341	1969	**£4**	**£1.50**	
Frederick Jordan	7"	Pye	7N17615	1968	**£30**	**£15**	
Have You Forgotten Who You Are	7"	Polydor	56318	1969	**£4**	**£1.50**	
She's A Rainbow	7"	Pye	7N17518	1968	**£5**	**£2**	
You Didn't Have To Be So Nice	7"	Pye	7N17568	1968	**£4**	**£1.50**	

GLASS OPENING

Silver Bells And Cockle Shells	7"	Plexium	P1236	1968	**£200**	**£100**	

GLASS PRISM

On Joy And Sorrow	LP	RCA	LSP4270	1970	**£15**	**£6**	*US*
Poe Through The Glass Prism	LP	RCA	LSP4201	1969	**£15**	**£6**	*US*

GLEASON, JACKIE

Rain	7"	Capitol	CL14289	1955	**£4**	**£1.50**	
Riff Jazz	LP	Capitol	LCT6169	1958	**£10**	**£4**	
What Is A Boy?	7"	Brunswick	04775	1960	**£4**	**£1.50**	

GLEEMEN

Gleemen	LP	CGD	FGS5073	1970	**£100**	**£50**	*Italian*

GLEN & LLOYD

Feel Good Now	7"	Doctor Bird	DB1099	1967	**£10**	**£5**	
Live And Let Others Live	7"	Ska Beat	JB250	1966	**£10**	**£5**	

GLENCOE

Glencoe	LP	Epic	EPC65207	1972	**£10**	**£4**	
Spirit Of Glencoe	LP	Epic	EPC65717	1973	**£10**	**£4**	

GLENN, GERRY

Music For James Bond	7" EP	Embassy	WEP1120	1964	**£8**	**£4**	

GLENN, LLOYD

Chica Boo	LP	Aladdin	808	1956	**£125**	**£62.50**	*US, red vinyl*
Chica Boo	LP	Aladdin	808	1956	**£40**	**£20**	*US*

GLENN, TYREE

At The Embers	LP	Esquire	32061	1958	**£12**	**£5**	

GLICKIN, PADDY, MICK GAVIN, MICHAEL O'BRIEN

Flags Of Dublin	LP	Topic	12TS383	1979	**£10**	**£4**	

GLITTER, GARY

Records by the man who was christened Paul Gadd can also be found listed in the *Guide* under the names Paul Raven, Paul Monday and Rubber Bucket.

Boys Will Be Boys	CD	Arista	8225712	1984	**£12**	**£5**	
When I'm On I'm On	7"	Eagle	ERS009	1981	**£5**	**£2**	

GLITTERHOUSE

Barbarella	7"	Stateside	SS2129	1968	**£5**	**£2**	*2 different B sides*

GLOBAL VILLAGE TRUCKING CO.

Global Village Trucking Co.	LP	Caroline	C1516	1976	**£10**	**£4**	

GLOBE TROTTERS

At Sundown	7"	Parlophone	CMSP18	1954	**£10**	**£5**	

GLOOMYS

Daybreak	7"	Columbia	DB8391	1968	**£5**	**£2**	
Daybreak	LP	Columbia	SMC74360	1967	**£15**	**£6**	*German*
II	LP	Columbia	1C05228406	1969	**£12**	**£5**	*German*

GLORIES

I Love You But Give Me My Freedom	7"	Direction	583084	1967	**£5**	**£2**	
I Stand Accused	7"	CBS	2736	1967	**£10**	**£5**	

GLORY

Meat Music Sampler	LP	Texas Revolution	TRR69	1969	**£60**	**£30**	*US*

GLOVE

Blue Sunshine	LP	Wonderland	SHELP2	1983	**£15**	**£6**	*double-printed sleeve*
Like An Animal	12"	Wonderland	SHEX3	1983	**£6**	**£2.50**	
Like An Animal	7"	Wonderland	SHE3	1983	**£4**	**£1.50**	
Punish Me With Kisses	7"	Wonderland	SHE5	1983	**£5**	**£2**	

GLOVER, ROGER

Butterfly Ball	LP	Purple	TPSA7514	1974	**£10**	**£4**	
Love Is All	7"	Purple	PUR125	1974	**£4**	**£1.50**	

GMT

One By One	12"	Mausoleum	BONE1283102	1991	**£6**	**£2.50**	

GNASHER

Medina Road	7"	Purple	PUR119	1974	**£5**	**£2**	

GNIDROLOG

Gnidrolog played an idiosyncratic form of progressive rock, characterized by abrupt tempo and key changes that gave their music an interestingly fractured feel. The group's extraordinary name was actually an imperfect anagram of the surname of the Goldring brothers, who were the front men.

In Spite Of Harry's Toenail	LP	RCA	SF8261	1971	**£25**	**£10**	
Lady Lake	LP	RCA	SF8322	1972	**£75**	**£37.50**	

GNOMES OF ZURICH

Hang On Baby	7"	CBS	202556	1967	**£15**	**£7.50**	
High Hopes	7"	CBS	2694	1967	**£15**	**£7.50**	
Please Mr Sun	7"	Planet	PLF121	1966	**£20**	**£10**	
Second Fiddle	7"	RCA	RCA1606	1967	**£10**	**£5**	

G-NOTES

Ronnie	7"	Oriole	CB1456	1958	**£8**	**£4**	

GOBBLEDEGOOKS

Where Have You Been	7"	Decca	F12023	1964	**£5**	**£2**	

GO-BETWEENS

I Need Two Heads	7"	Postcard	80-4	1980	**£10**	**£5**	*cream or brown sleeves*
Peel Sessions	CD-s	Strange Fruit	SFPSCD074	1989	**£5**	**£2**	
Streets Of Your Town	CD-s	Beggars Banquet	BEG218CD	1988	**£5**	**£2**	
Was There Anything I Could Do	CD-s	Beggars Banquet	BEG219CD	1988	**£5**	**£2**	

GOBLIN

Suspiria	LP	EMI	EMC3222	1977	**£20**	**£8**	

GOD'S GIFT

These Days	7"	Newmarket		1979	**£6**	**£2.50**	

GODARD, VIC

Title	Format	Label	Cat. No.	Year	Mint	VG	Notes
Holiday Hymn	12"	El Benelux	EL4T	1985	£6	£2.50	
Holiday Hymn	LP	MCA	El01	1985	£25	£10	*test pressing*

GODCHAUX, KEITH & DONNA

Title	Format	Label	Cat. No.	Year	Mint	VG	Notes
Keith & Donna Godchaux	LP	Round	RX104	1975	£12	£5	

GODDARD, GEOFF

Title	Format	Label	Cat. No.	Year	Mint	VG	Notes
Girl Bride	7"	HMV	POP938	1961	£30	£15	
My Little Girl's Come Home	7"	HMV	POP1068	1962	£40	£20	
Saturday Dance	7"	HMV	POP1160	1963	£30	£15	
Sky Man	7"	HMV	POP1213	1963	£75	£37.50	

GODDING, BRIAN

For those of us who waited years for guitarist Brian Godding's solo LP (after admiring his playing in Blossom Toes and the Mike Westbrook band), it is rather distressing to find the record becoming unavailable only months after its release. Reckless Records is not the first collectors' shop to try its hand at running its own record label and neither is it the first to find that the problems of distribution and achieving actual sales can be enormous.

Title	Format	Label	Cat. No.	Year	Mint	VG	Notes
Slaughter On Shaftesbury Avenue	LP	Reckless	RECK16	1989	£10	£4	

GODFATHERS

Title	Format	Label	Cat. No.	Year	Mint	VG	Notes
Cause I Said So	CD-s	Epic	CDGFT2	1988	£5	£2	
I'm Lost And Then I'm Found	CD-s	Epic	GFTC5	1990	£5	£2	
Love Is Dead	CD-s	Epic	CDGFT3	1988	£5	£2	
Night Tracks	CD-s	Strange Fruit	SFNTCD019	1989	£5	£2	
She Gives Me Love	CD-s	Epic	CDGFT4	1989	£5	£2	

GODFREY & STEWART

Title	Format	Label	Cat. No.	Year	Mint	VG	Notes
Joined By The Heart	LP	The Stand	HEARTLP	198–	£15	£6	
Seed And The Sower	LP	Enid	ENID11	1986	£10	£4	

GODFREY, HUGH

Title	Format	Label	Cat. No.	Year	Mint	VG	Notes
A Dey Pon Dem	7"	Coxsone	CS7001	1967	£10	£5	*Soul Brothers B side*
Go Tell Him	7"	Studio One	SO2015	1967	£12	£6	

GODFREY, ROBERT JOHN

To all intents and purposes, Robert John Godfrey is the Enid. His solo album is effectively the first Enid album, therefore, and the hardest to find of the fully released series as it was not reissued on vinyl.

Title	Format	Label	Cat. No.	Year	Mint	VG	Notes
Fall Of Hyperion	LP	Charisma	CAS1084	1974	£25	£10	

GODLEY & CREME

Title	Format	Label	Cat. No.	Year	Mint	VG	Notes
Consequences	LP	Mercury	CONS017	1977	£20	£8	*triple, boxed*
Consequences – Edited Highlights	LP	Mercury	LKP001	1977	£12	£5	*promo*
Cry	CD-s	Polydor	0801012	1985	£12	£6	*CD video*
Five O'Clock	7"	Mercury	SAMP017	1979	£8	£4	*promo double*
Under Your Thumb	7"	Polydor	POSP322	1981	£4	£1.50	

GODS

Ken Hensley, the leader of Uriah Heep, began his career as a member of the Gods. The original line-up also included guitarist Mick Taylor, who can be heard playing on the Polydor single.

Title	Format	Label	Cat. No.	Year	Mint	VG	Notes
Baby's Rich	7"	Columbia	DB8486	1968	£15	£7.50	
Come On Down To My Boat Baby	7"	Polydor	56168	1967	£100	£50	
Genesis	LP	Columbia	SX/SCX6286	1968	£100	£50	
Gods	LP	Harvest	SHSM2011	1976	£10	£4	
Hey Bulldog	7"	Columbia	DB8544	1969	£15	£7.50	
Maria	7"	Columbia	DB8572	1969	£15	£7.50	
To Samuel A Son	LP	Columbia	SCX6372	1970	£75	£37.50	

GODZ

Title	Format	Label	Cat. No.	Year	Mint	VG	Notes
Contact High	LP	Fontana	STL5500	1967	£15	£6	
Godz 2	LP	Fontana	STL5512	1969	£15	£6	
Godzundheit	LP	ESP-Disk	2017	1970	£20	£8	*US*
Third Testament	LP	ESP-Disk	1077	1969	£20	£8	*US*

GOGMAGOG

Title	Format	Label	Cat. No.	Year	Mint	VG	Notes
I Will Be There	12"	Food For Thought	YUMT109	1985	£20	£10	

GO-GOs

Title	Format	Label	Cat. No.	Year	Mint	VG	Notes
Automatic	7"	Initial	IRS101	1981	£4	£1.50	*picture disc*
Cool Jerk	CD-s	A&M	AMCD712	1990	£5	£2	
Our Lips Are Sealed	7"	IRS	PFP1007	1981	£5	£2	*pink vinyl*
Return To The Valley Of The Go-Go's	CD	IRS		199–	£30	£15	*US with bonus CD*

GO-GOs (2)

Title	Format	Label	Cat. No.	Year	Mint	VG	Notes
I'm Gonna Spend My Christmas With A Dalek	7"	Oriole	CB1982	1964	£20	£10	
I'm Gonna Spend My Christmas With A Dalek	7"	Oriole	CB1982	1964	£30	£15	*picture sleeve*
Swim	LP	RCA	LPM/LSP2930	1964	£25	£10	*US*

GOING RED

Title	Format	Label	Cat. No.	Year	Mint	VG	Notes
Some Boys	7"	Razz	CLEAN1	1981	£5	£2	

Some Boys	7"	MCA	MCA673	1981	£4	£1.50	

GOINS, HERBIE & NIGHT-TIMERS

Incredible Miss Brown	7"	Parlophone	R5533	1966	£20	£10	
Incredible Miss Brown	7" EP	Odeon	MEO133	1966	£30	£15	*French*
Number One in Your Heart	7"	Parlophone	R5478	1966	£50	£25	
Number One In Your Heart	LP	Parlophone	PMC7026	1967	£75	£37.50	

GOLDBERG, BARRY

Another Day	7"	Pye	7N25465	1968	£4	£1.50	
Blowing My Mind	LP	Epic	LN24/BN26199	1966	£20	£8	*US*
Reunion	LP	Pye	NSPL28116	1968	£12	£5	
Two Jews Blues	LP	Buddah	203020	1969	£10	£4	

GOLDEN APPLES OF THE SUN

Monkey Time	7"	Immediate	IM010	1965	£20	£10	
Monkey Time	7"	Decca	F12194	1965	£30	£15	*demo*

GOLDEN CRUSADERS

Hey Good Looking	7"	Columbia	DB7357	1964	£8	£4	
I Don't Care	7"	Columbia	DB7485	1965	£8	£4	
I'm In Love With You	7"	Columbia	DB7232	1964	£8	£4	

GOLDEN DAWN

Power Plant	LP	International Artist	IA4	1967	£75	£37.50	*US*

GOLDEN DAWN (2)

My Secret World	7"	Sarah	009	1988	£4	£1.50	*with poster*

GOLDEN EARRING

Golden Earring are best known in the UK for their powerful hit single, 'Radar Love', but in their native Holland they are a star group with a long and successful career. The list of collectables below is just a small part of a huge discography extending over thirty years.

Another Forty-Five Miles	7"	Major Minor	MM679	1970	£4	£1.50	
Back Home	7"	Polydor	2001073	1970	£4	£1.50	
Dong Dong Di Ki Di Gi Dong	7"	Capitol	CL15567	1968	£5	£2	
Eight Miles High	LP	Major Minor	SMLP65	1969	£20	£8	
Eight Miles High	LP	Polydor	656019	1969	£15	£6	
I've Just Lost Somebody	7"	Capitol	CL15552	1968	£5	£2	
It's Alright But It Could Be Better	7"	Major Minor	MM633	1969	£4	£1.50	
Just A Little Bit Of Peace	7"	Major Minor	MM601	1969	£4	£1.50	
Just Earring	LP	Polydor	736007	1964	£25	£10	*Dutch*
Miracle Mirror	LP	Polydor	1236283	1968	£20	£8	*Dutch*
On The Double	LP	Polydor	2653001	1969	£30	£15	*Dutch double*
Seven Tears	LP	Polydor	2310135	1971	£12	£5	
That Day	7"	Polydor	56514	1970	£8	£4	
Together	LP	Polydor	2310210	1972	£10	£4	
Winter Harvest	LP	Polydor	736068	1967	£25	£10	*Dutch*
It's Alright But It Could Be Better	7"	Major Minor	MM633	1969	£4	£1.50	
Just A Little Bit Of Peace	7"	Major Minor	MM601	1969	£4	£1.50	
Just Earring	LP	Polydor	736007	1964	£25	£10	*Dutch*
Miracle Mirror	LP	Polydor	1236283	1968	£20	£8	*Dutch*
On The Double	LP	Polydor	2653001	1969	£30	£15	*Dutch double*
Seven Tears	LP	Polydor	2310135	1971	£12	£5	
That Day	7"	Polydor	56514	1970	£8	£4	
Together	LP	Polydor	2310210	1972	£10	£4	
Winter Harvest	LP	Polydor	736068	1967	£25	£10	*Dutch*

GOLDEN GATE QUARTET

Get On Board	LP	Columbia	33SX1370	1961	£10	£4	
Shout For Joy!	LP	Columbia	33SX1172	1959	£10	£4	
Sings Great Spirituals	7" EP	Columbia	SEG7700	1957	£5	£2	
That Golden Chariot	10" LP	Fontana	TFR6009	1958	£10	£4	

GOLDEN GATE STRINGS

Mr Tambourine Man	7"	Columbia	DB7634	1965	£4	£1.50	

GOLDEN RING

Gathering Of Friends For Making Music	LP	D.T.S.	LFX5	1966	£25	£10	

GOLDENROD

Goldenrod	LP	Chartmaker	CSG1101	1967	£150	£75	*US*

GOLDIE

Can't You Hear My Heartbeat	7"	Decca	F12070	1965	£5	£2	*with the Gingerbreads*
Can't You Hear My Heartbeat	7" EP	Decca	457072	1965	£25	£12.50	*French, with the Gingerbreads*
Going Back	7"	Immediate	IM026	1966	£15	£7.50	
I Do	7"	Fontana	TF693	1966	£6	£2.50	
Sailor Boy	7"	Decca	F12199	1965	£4	£1.50	*with the Gingerbreads*
That's Why I Love You	7"	Decca	F12126	1965	£4	£1.50	*with the Gingerbreads*

GOLDING, JOHN

Discarded Verse	LP	Cottage	101S	1974	£10	£4	

GOLDSBORO, BOBBY

Autumn Of My Life	7"	United Artists	UP2223	1968	£4	£1.50	
Bobby Goldsboro Album	LP	United Artists	UAL3/UAS6358	1964	£15	£6	US
Honey	LP	United Artists	(S)ULP1195	1968	£10	£4	
I Can't Stop Loving You	LP	United Artists	UAL3/UAS6381	1964	£15	£6	US
It's Too Late	7"	United Artists	UP1128	1966	£5	£2	
It's Too Late	LP	United Artists	(S)ULP1135	1966	£15	£6	
Little Things	7"	United Artists	UP1079	1965	£5	£2	
Little Things	7" EP	United Artists	UEP1006	1965	£20	£10	
Little Things	LP	United Artists	UAL3/UAS6425	1965	£15	£6	US
Runaround	7"	Stateside	SS193	1963	£6	£2.50	
Solid Goldsboro	LP	United Artists	(S)ULP1163	1967	£12	£5	
Take Your Love	7"	United Artists	UP1146	1966	£6	£2.50	
Talented Bobby Goldsboro	7" EP	United Artists	UEP1016	1966	£20	£10	
Too Many People	7"	United Artists	UP1177	1967	£20	£10	

GOLDSMITH

Life Is Killing Me	7"	Bedlam	BLM001	1983	£15	£7.50	

GOLDTONES

Goldtones Featuring Randy Seol	LP	LaBrea	L8011	1966	£15	£6	US

GOLEM

Golem	LP	Delta	251281	1974	£25	£10	German

GOLIARD

Fortune My Foe	LP	Broadside	BRO127	1976	£15	£6	

GOLIATH

Goliath	LP	CBS	64229	1970	£40	£20	
Port And Lemon Lady	7"	CBS	5312	1971	£4	£1.50	

GOLLIWOGS

The Golliwogs were the same group that later found considerable success as Creedence Clearwater Revival.

Brown-Eyed Girl	7"	Vocalion	VF9266	1966	£25	£12.50	
Don't Tell Me No Lies	7"	Fantasy	590	1964	£20	£10	US
Fight Fire	7"	Vocalion	VF9283	1967	£25	£12.50	
Walking On The Water	7"	Scorpio	408	1966	£20	£10	US
You Came Walking	7"	Fantasy	597	1965	£20	£10	US
You Got Nothin' On Me	7"	Fantasy	599	1965	£20	£10	US

GOLOWIN, SERGIUS

Lord Krishna Von Goloka	LP	Kosmische	KM58002	1973	£20	£8	German

GOLSON, BENNY

Benny Golson And The Philadelphians	LP	London	LTZK15176/ SAHT6061	1960	£20	£8	
Groovin' With Golson	LP	Esquire	32105	1960	£20	£8	
Modern Touch	LP	Riverside	RLP12256	196–	£15	£6	
Stockholm Sojourn	LP	Stateside	SL10150	1965	£10	£4	with Art Farmer

GOMORRHA

Gomorrha	LP	Cornet	15038	1970	£25	£10	German
I Turned To See Whose Voice It Was	LP	Brain	1003	1971	£20	£8	German
Trauma	LP	BASF	20204138	1972	£15	£6	German

GONADS

Pure Punk For Now People	7"	Secret	SHH131	1982	£5	£2	

GONDOLIERS

God's Green Acres	7"	Starlite	ST45001	1958	£4	£1.50	

GONELLA, NAT

Salute To Satchmo	10" LP	Columbia	33S1146	1959	£12	£5	

GONG

Gong's eccentric blend of hippy humour and electric jazz is very early seventies, yet is becoming of increasing interest to modern listeners, who appreciate the influence that the band has had on groups like Ozric Tentacles and Porcupine Tree. All the collectable early albums are masterminded by Daevid Allen (an original member of Soft Machine), although the group's creative peak was arguably reached on later albums like *You* and *Shamal*. Allen had departed by the time of the latter album, although in more recent times he has reclaimed the Gong name as his own.

Angel's Egg	LP	Virgin	V2007	1973	£30	£15	*with book*
Camembert Electrique	LP	Byg	529353	1971	£20	£8	*French, with insert*
Continental Circus	LP	Philips	6332033	1972	£15	£6	*French, no Polygram credit*
Flying Teapot	LP	Virgin	V2002	1973	£10	£4	*black and white label*
Gazeuse	LP	Virgin	V2074	1977	£10	£4	
Live Etc.	LP	Virgin	VGD3501	1977	£12	£5	*double*
Magick Brother	LP	Byg	529305	1970	£25	£10	*French*
Magick Brother	LP	Byg	529029	1970	£30	£15	*French*
Opium For The People	7"	Affinity	AF5101	1977	£5	£2	*as Planet Gong*

Shamal	LP	Virgin	V2046	1976	**£10**	**£4**	
You	LP	Virgin	V2019	1974	**£10**	**£4**	

GONKS

That's All Right Mama	7"	Decca	F11984	1964	**£10**	**£5**	

GONSALVES, PAUL

Boom Jackie Boom Chick	LP	Vocalion	LAE587	1964	**£75**	**£37.50**	
Hummingbird	LP	Deram	SML1064	1970	**£20**	**£8**	

GONZALEZ

Gonzalez	LP	EMI	EMC3046	1974	**£25**	**£10**	
Our Only Weapon Is Our Music	LP	EMI	EMC3100	1975	**£12**	**£5**	

GONZALEZ, BELLE

Belle	LP	Columbia	SCX6484	1971	**£60**	**£30**	
Bottles	7"	Columbia	DB8852	1972	**£4**	**£1.50**	
Contemporary Poets Set In Jazz	7" EP	Jupiter	JEPOC39	1966	**£10**	**£5**	
Poets Set In Jazz	7" EP	Jupiter	JEPOC37	1965	**£10**	**£5**	

GOOD, JACK FAT NOISE

Fat Noise	7"	Decca	F11233	1960	**£5**	**£2**	

GOOD EARTH

It's Hard Rock & All That	LP	Saga	FID2112	1968	**£12**	**£5**	

GOOD SHIP LOLLIPOP

Maxwell's Silver Hammer	7"	Ember	EMBS276	1969	**£6**	**£2.50**	*picture sleeve*
Maxwell's Silver Hammer	7"	Ember	EMBS276	1970	**£4**	**£1.50**	

GOODBYE MR MACKENZIE

Blacker Than Black	CD-s	Parlophone	CDR6257	1990	**£5**	**£2**	
Death Of A Salesman	7"	Scruples	YTS1	1984	**£10**	**£5**	
Goodbye Mr Mackenzie	CD-s	Capitol	CDCL501	1988	**£5**	**£2**	
Goodwill City	CD-s	Capitol	CDCL538	1989	**£5**	**£2**	
Love Child	CD-s	Parlophone	CDR6247	1990	**£5**	**£2**	
Open Your Arms	CD-s	Capitol	CDCL513	1988	**£5**	**£2**	
Rattler	CD-s	Capitol	CDCL522	1989	**£5**	**£2**	

GOODEES

Condition Red	7"	Stax	STAX113	1969	**£8**	**£4**	

GOODHAND-TAIT, PHILIP

I'm Gonna Put Some Hurt On You	7"	Parlophone	R5448	1966	**£6**	**£2.50**	
Love Has Got A Hold On Me	7"	Decca	F12868	1969	**£4**	**£1.50**	
No Problem	7"	Parlophone	R5498	1966	**£5**	**£2**	
You Can't Take Love	7"	Parlophone	R5547	1966	**£6**	**£2.50**	

GOODISON, JOHNNY

Little Understanding	7"	Deram	DM319	1970	**£4**	**£1.50**	

GOODMAN, BENNY

1937–1938 Jazz Concert No. 2 Vol. 1	LP	Philips	BBL7009	1955	**£20**	**£8**	
1937–1938 Jazz Concert No. 2 Vol. 2	LP	Philips	BBL7010	1955	**£20**	**£8**	
After Hours	10" LP	Capitol	LC6565	1952	**£20**	**£8**	
Benny Goodman Band	10" LP	Capitol	LC6831	1956	**£15**	**£6**	
Benny Goodman Orchestra	10" LP	HMV	DLP1116	1956	**£15**	**£6**	
Benny Goodman Orchestra	10" LP	HMV	DLP1112	1956	**£20**	**£8**	
Benny Goodman Orchestra	LP	Capitol	LCT6012	1955	**£20**	**£8**	
Benny Goodman Orchestra And Quartet	LP	Capitol	LCT6104	1956	**£15**	**£6**	
Benny Goodman Quartet	10" LP	HMV	DLPC6	1955	**£20**	**£8**	
Benny Goodman Sextet	10" LP	Fontana	TFR6006	1958	**£15**	**£6**	
Benny Goodman Sextet	LP	Philips	BBL7021	1955	**£12**	**£5**	
Benny Goodman Small Groups	10" LP	Capitol	LC6810	1956	**£15**	**£6**	
Benny Goodman Story Vol. 1	LP	Brunswick	LAT8102	1956	**£15**	**£6**	
Benny Goodman Story Vol. 2	LP	Brunswick	LAT8103	1956	**£15**	**£6**	
Benny Goodman Trio	10" LP	Fontana	TFR6022	1959	**£12**	**£5**	
Benny Goodman Trio	10" LP	HMV	DLPC11	1956	**£15**	**£6**	
Benny In Brussels	LP	Philips	BBL7299	1959	**£10**	**£4**	
Benny In Brussels	LP	Philips	BBL7300	1959	**£10**	**£4**	
Benny Rides Again	LP	Columbia	33SX1038	1955	**£15**	**£6**	
Carnegie Hall Jazz Concert Vol. 1	LP	Philips	BBL7000	1954	**£20**	**£8**	
Carnegie Hall Jazz Concert Vol. 2	LP	Philips	BBL7001	1954	**£20**	**£8**	
Classics In Jazz	10" LP	Capitol	LC6680	1954	**£20**	**£8**	
Dizzy Fingers	10" LP	Capitol	LC6601	1953	**£20**	**£8**	
Easy Does It	10" LP	Capitol	LC6557	1952	**£20**	**£8**	
Goodman Touch	10" LP	Capitol	LC6620	1953	**£20**	**£8**	
Happy Session	LP	Philips	BBL7318	1959	**£10**	**£4**	
Let's Hear The Melody	10" LP	Philips	BBR8064	1955	**£15**	**£6**	
Makes History	LP	Philips	BBL7073	1956	**£15**	**£6**	
Plays For Fletcher Henderson Fund	LP	Columbia	33SX1020	1954	**£20**	**£8**	
Presents Eddie Sauter Arrangements	LP	Philips	BBL7043	1955	**£15**	**£6**	
Session For Sextet	10" LP	Columbia	33S1048	1954	**£20**	**£8**	
Session For Sextet No. 2	LP	Columbia	33SX1035	1955	**£15**	**£6**	
Session For Six	10" LP	Capitol	LC6526	1951	**£20**	**£8**	

GOODMAN, DAVE

Justifiable Homicide	7"	The Label	TLR008	1978	**£30**	**£15**	*Steve Jones & Paul Cook named on sleeve*

GOODTHUNDER

Goodthunder	LP	Elektra	K42123	1972	£15	£6	

GOODWIN, RON

And His Concert Orchestra	7" EP	Parlophone	GEP8555	1955	£6	£2.50	
Decline And Fall Of A Birdwatcher	LP	Stateside	(S)SL10259	1968	£75	£37.50	
Escape From The Dark	LP	EMI	EMC3148	1976	£20	£8	
Limelight	7"	Parlophone	MSP6035	1953	£4	£1.50	
Monte Carlo Or Bust!	LP	Paramount	SPFL255	1969	£30	£15	
Out Of This World	LP	Parlophone	PCS3006	1958	£20	£8	

GOOFERS

Dipsy Doodle	7"	Vogue Coral	Q72289	1957	£15	£7.50	
Flip Flop And Fly	7"	Vogue Coral	Q72074	1955	£40	£20	
Goofie Dry Bones	7"	Vogue Coral	Q72094	1955	£15	£7.50	
Hearts Of Stone	7"	Vogue Coral	Q72051	1955	£40	£20	
Push Push Push Cart	7"	Vogue Coral	Q72267	1957	£15	£7.50	
Sick Sick Sick	7"	Vogue Coral	Q72124	1956	£15	£7.50	
Tennessee Rock And Roll	7"	Vogue Coral	Q72171	1956	£25	£12.50	

GOONS

Best Of The Goon Shows	LP	Parlophone	PMC1108	1959	£10	£4	
Best Of The Goon Shows No. 2	LP	Parlophone	PMC1129	1960	£10	£4	
Eeh Ah Oh Oooh	7"	Decca	F10885	1957	£4	£1.50	
Goons	7" EP	Decca	DFE6396	1956	£6	£2.50	
I'm Walking Backwards For Christmas	7"	Decca	F10756	1956	£6	£2.50	
My September Love	7"	Parlophone	R4251	1956	£5	£2	
Russian Love Song	7"	Decca	F10945	1957	£4	£1.50	
Unchained Melodies	10" LP	Decca	LF1332	1964	£15	£6	
Ying Tong Song	7"	Decca	F10780	1956	£5	£2	

GOPAL, SAM

Sam Gopal is a percussionist whose work can be found on several albums by the likes of Daevid Allen, G. F. Fitzgerald, and Isaac Guillory. The demand for his solo album, however, derives primarily from the fact that it is Lemmy, of future Motorhead fame, who plays guitar on the album.

Escalator	7"	Stable	SLE8001	1969	£25	£12.50	*promo sampler*
Escalator	LP	Stable	SLE8001	1969	£75	£37.50	
Horse	7"	Stable	STA5602	1969	£25	£12.50	

GORDON, BARRY

Rock Around Mother Goose	7"	MGM	MGM935	1956	£8	£4	

GORDON, DEXTER

Daddy Plays The Horn	LP	London	LTZN15098	1957	£40	£20	
Dexter Calling	LP	Blue Note	BLP/BST84083	1961	£25	£10	
Dexter Rides Again	LP	Realm	RM191	1964	£10	£4	
Doin' Alright	LP	Blue Note	BLP/BST84077	1961	£30	£15	
Gettin' Around	LP	Blue Note	BLP/BST84204	1965	£25	£10	
Go!	LP	Blue Note	BLP/BST84112	1962	£25	£10	
Master Swingers	LP	Fontana	FJL907	1967	£10	£4	*with Wardell Gray*
One Flight Up	LP	Blue Note	BLP/BST84176	1964	£25	£10	
Our Man In Paris	LP	Blue Note	BLP/BST84146	1963	£25	£10	
Swingin' Affair	LP	Blue Note	BLP/BST84133	1963	£25	£10	

GORDON, JOE FOLK FOUR

Gay Gordons	LP	HMV	CLP1379/ CSD1314	1960	£10	£4	
Johnnie Lad	7" EP	HMV	7EG8454	1960	£5	£2	

GORDON, PHIL

Down The Road Apiece	7"	Brunswick	05545	1956	£5	£2	

GORDON, RABBI JOSEPH

Competition	7"	Bam Caruso	NRIC030	1985	£8	£4	*no picture sleeve*

GORDON, RONNIE

Coming Home	7"	R&B	JB127	1963	£15	£7.50	

GORDON, ROSCOE

Just A Little Bit	7"	Top Rank	JAR332	1960	£15	£7.50	
Just A Little Bit	7"	Stateside	SS204	1963	£15	£7.50	
Keep On Doggin'	7"	Vocalion	VP9245	1965	£15	£7.50	
No More Doggin'	7"	Island	WI272	1966	£15	£7.50	
Surely I Love You	7"	Island	WI256	1965	£10	£5	

GORDON, VINCENT

Everybody Bawlin'	7"	Duke	DU37	1969	£4	£1.50	*Silvertones B side*
Soul Trombone	7"	Coxsone	CS7085	1969	£10	£5	*Larry & Alvin B side*

GORE, CHARLIE

I Didn't Know	7"	Parlophone	CMSP30	1954	£15	£7.50	*export*
I'll Find Somebody	7"	Parlophone	CMSP19	1954	£15	£7.50	*export*
Two Of A Kind	7"	Parlophone	CMSP26	1954	£15	£7.50	*export*

GORE, LESLEY

The girl who first sung 'It's My Party' made a remarkably large number of other records, although she tends only to be remembered for that original hit. She was, in fact, discovered by Quincy Jones and his production work on her records marked his first ventures outside the world of jazz.

All About Love	LP	Mercury	20076MCL	1965	**£15**	**£6**	
Boys Boys Boys	LP	Mercury	20020MCL	1964	**£15**	**£6**	
California Nights	LP	Mercury	MG2/SR61120	1967	**£15**	**£6**	*US*
Girl Talk	LP	Wing	WL1183	1967	**£10**	**£4**	
Girl Talk	LP	Mercury	20033MCL	1964	**£15**	**£6**	
Golden Hits	LP	Mercury	MG2/SR61024	1965	**£15**	**£6**	*US*
Golden Hits Vol. 2	LP	Mercury	SR61185	1968	**£15**	**£6**	*US*
I Won't Love You Any More	7"	Mercury	MF889	1965	**£4**	**£1.50**	
I'll Cry If I Want To	LP	Mercury	MMC14127	1963	**£20**	**£8**	
I'm Fallin' Down	7"	Mercury	MF984	1966	**£5**	**£2**	
It's My Party	7"	Mercury	AMT1205	1963	**£4**	**£1.50**	
Lesley Gore	7" EP	Mercury	10017MCE	1964	**£15**	**£7.50**	
Maybe I Know	7"	Mercury	MF829	1964	**£4**	**£1.50**	
My Town, My Guy And Me	LP	Mercury	20071MCL	1965	**£15**	**£6**	
My Town, My Guy, And Me	7"	Mercury	MF872	1965	**£4**	**£1.50**	
Sings Of Mixed-Up Hearts	LP	Mercury	20001MCL	1963	**£15**	**£6**	
You Don't Own Me	7"	Mercury	MF803	1964	**£4**	**£1.50**	

GORKY'S ZYGOTIC MYNCI

Patio	10"	Ankst	ANKST040	1993	**£10**	**£5**	

GORME, EYDIE

Climb Up The Wall	7"	Vogue Coral	Q2014	1954	**£6**	**£2.50**	
Cozy	LP	HMV	CLP1463	1962	**£10**	**£4**	*with Steve Lawrence*
Don't Try To Fight It Baby	7"	CBS	AAG149	1963	**£5**	**£2**	
Everybody Go Home	7"	CBS	AAG170	1963	**£4**	**£1.50**	
Eydie Gorme	LP	HMV	CLP1156	1958	**£10**	**£4**	
Eydie Gorme's Delight	LP	Coral	LVA9086	1958	**£10**	**£4**	
Eydie In Love	LP	HMV	CLP1250	1959	**£10**	**£4**	
Eydie Swings The Blues	LP	HMV	CLP1170	1958	**£10**	**£4**	
Facts Of Life	7"	London	HLT9290	1961	**£5**	**£2**	*with Steve Lawrence*
Give A Fool A Chance	7"	Vogue Coral	Q72092	1955	**£5**	**£2**	
Golden Hits	LP	HMV	CLP1404/ CSD1329	1961	**£10**	**£4**	*with Steve Lawrence*
Gorme Sings Showstoppers	LP	HMV	CLP1257	1959	**£10**	**£4**	
I Want To Stay Here	7"	CBS	AAG163	1963	**£5**	**£2**	*with Steve Lawrence, picture sleeve*
I'll Remember April	7" EP	HMV	GES5795	1959	**£6**	**£2.50**	*stereo*
Kiss In Your Eyes	7"	HMV	POP400	1957	**£4**	**£1.50**	
Love Is A Season	7" EP	HMV	GES5789	1959	**£6**	**£2.50**	*stereo*
Love Is A Season	LP	HMV	CLP1290	1959	**£10**	**£4**	
Love Me Forever	7"	HMV	POP432	1958	**£5**	**£2**	
Make Yourself Comfortable	7"	Vogue Coral	Q72044	1955	**£5**	**£2**	*with Steve Lawrence*
Sincerely Yours	7"	London	HL8227	1956	**£10**	**£5**	
Soldier Boy	7"	Vogue Coral	Q72103	1955	**£5**	**£2**	
Steve And Eydie	7" EP	CBS	AGG20035	1963	**£5**	**£2**	*with Steve Lawrence*
Steve Lawrence And Eydie Gorme	7" EP	Coral	FEP2017	1959	**£8**	**£4**	*with Steve Lawrence*
Sure	7"	Vogue Coral	Q2027	1954	**£5**	**£2**	
Take A Deep Breath	7"	Vogue Coral	Q72085	1955	**£5**	**£2**	*with Steve Lawrence*
Vamps The Roaring Twenties	LP	HMV	CLP1201	1958	**£10**	**£4**	
We Got Us	LP	HMV	CLP1372/ CSD1310	1960	**£10**	**£4**	*with Steve Lawrence*
Yes My Darling Daughter	7"	CBS	AAG105	1962	**£4**	**£1.50**	

GORSHIN, FRANK

Riddler	7"	Pye	7N25402	1966	**£15**	**£7.50**	
Riddler	7"	Pye	7N25402	1966	**£50**	**£25**	*picture sleeve*

GOSPEL CLASSICS

More Love That's What We Need	7"	Chess	CRS8080	1968	**£20**	**£10**	

GOSPEL GARDEN

Finders Keepers	7"	Camp	602006	1968	**£6**	**£2.50**	

GOSPEL OAK

Gospel Oak	LP	Uni	UNLS113	1970	**£25**	**£10**	

GOSPELFOLK

Prodigal	LP	Emblem	7DR324	1969	**£200**	**£100**	

GOTHIC HORIZON

Girl With Guitar	7"	Argo	AFW108	1972	**£8**	**£4**	
If You Can Smile	7"	Argo	AFW107	1973	**£8**	**£4**	
Jason Lodge Poetry Book	7"	Argo	AFW102	1970	**£8**	**£4**	
Jason Lodge Poetry Book	LP	Argo	ZFB26	1970	**£100**	**£50**	
Marjorie	7"	Argo	AFW104	1971	**£8**	**£4**	
Tomorrow Is Another Day	LP	Argo	ZDA150	1972	**£75**	**£37.50**	

GOULDER, DAVE

January Man	LP	Argo	ZFB10	1970	**£20**	**£8**	*with Liz Dyer*
Raven And The Crow	LP	Argo	ZFB30	1971	**£20**	**£8**	*with Liz Dyer*

Requiem For Steam	LP	Big Ben	BB004	1973	**£10**	**£4**	

GOULDMAN, GRAHAM

Graham Gouldman Thing	LP	RCA	LPM/LSP3954	1968	**£40**	**£20**	*US*
Nowhere To Go	7"	CBS	7739	1972	**£4**	**£1.50**	
Stop Stop Stop	7"	Decca	F12334	1966	**£25**	**£12.50**	
Upstairs Downstairs	7"	RCA	RCA1667	1968	**£10**	**£5**	
Windmills Of Your Mind	7"	Spark	SRL1026	1969	**£6**	**£2.50**	

GOVE

Dead Letter Blues	7"	London	HLE10295	1969	**£6**	**£2.50**	

GOWEN, ALAN

Before A Word Is Said	LP	Europa	JF2007	1981	**£10**	**£4**	*French*
Two Rainbows Daily	LP	Red	ROUGE1	1980	**£10**	**£4**	

GRAAS, JOHN

French Horn Vol. 1	7" EP	London	REP1003	1954	**£8**	**£4**	
Jazz Studio 2	LP	Brunswick	LAT8046	1954	**£20**	**£8**	*with Herb Geller*
Jazz Studio 3	LP	Brunswick	LAT8069	1955	**£20**	**£8**	*with Gerry Mulligan*

GRABHAM, MICK

Mick The Lad	LP	United Artists	UAS29341	1972	**£10**	**£4**	

GRACE

Billy Boy	7"	MCA	MCA667	1981	**£5**	**£2**	
Fire Of London	7"	MCA	MCA628	1980	**£8**	**£4**	

GRACIE, CHARLIE

Angel Of Love	7"	Coral	Q72373	1959	**£10**	**£5**	
Butterfly	7"	Parlophone	R4290	1957	**£30**	**£15**	*gold label*
Cameo Parkway Sessions	LP	London	HAU8513	1978	**£10**	**£4**	
Cool Baby	7"	London	HLU8521	1957	**£20**	**£10**	
Crazy Girl	7"	London	HLU8596	1958	**£25**	**£12.50**	
Doodlebug	7"	Coral	Q72362	1959	**£10**	**£5**	
Fabulous	7"	Parlophone	R4313	1957	**£30**	**£15**	*gold label*
Fabulous	7"	London	HLU10563	1978	**£8**	**£4**	*tri-centre!*
Fabulous Charlie Gracie	7" EP	Parlophone	GEP8630	1957	**£30**	**£15**	
He'll Never Love You Like I Do	7"	Stateside	SS402	1965	**£30**	**£15**	
Night And Day USA	7"	London	HLU9603	1962	**£10**	**£5**	
Oh Well-A	7"	Coral	Q72381	1959	**£10**	**£5**	
Race	7"	Columbia	DB4477	1960	**£10**	**£5**	
Wandering Eyes	7"	London	HL8467	1957	**£15**	**£7.50**	

GRACIOUS

Beautiful	7"	Polydor	56333	1968	**£15**	**£7.50**	
Gracious	LP	Vertigo	6360002	1970	**£50**	**£25**	*spiral label*
Once On A Windy Day	7"	Vertigo	6059009	1970	**£5**	**£2**	
This Is Gracious	LP	Philips	6382004	1972	**£60**	**£30**	

GRADUATE

Rock musicians whose respected careers start from shaky beginnings have difficulty forgetting the fact when they are unwise enough to commit them to vinyl. Two of the grinning mod revivalists on the cover of the Graduate LP are Roland Orzabel and Curt Smith, later of Tears For Fears. The extraordinary perfectionism applied to the recording of the *Seeds Of Love* album shows how these two like to be taken seriously. With Graduate's forgettable music in their past, however, it is hard.

Acting My Age	LP	Precision	PART001	1980	**£10**	**£4**	
Ambition	7"	Precision	PAR111	1980	**£5**	**£2**	
Elvis Should Play Ska	7"	Precision	PAR100	1980	**£4**	**£1.50**	
Ever Met A Day	7"	Precision	PAR104	1980	**£5**	**£2**	
Made One	7"	Blue Hat	5BHR	198–	**£8**	**£4**	

GRAHAM, BOBBY

Interest in the two singles released by drummer Bobby Graham is due primarily to the fact that they were co-recordings with guitarist Jimmy Page.

Skin Deep	7"	Fontana	TF521	1965	**£10**	**£5**	
Teensville	7"	Fontana	TF667	1966	**£10**	**£5**	

GRAHAM, CHICK & THE COASTERS

Dance Baby Dance	7"	Decca	F11932	1964	**£4**	**£1.50**	
Education	7"	Decca	F11859	1964	**£4**	**£1.50**	

GRAHAM, DAVEY

The number of recordings made by innovative folk-blues guitarist Davey Graham has been limited by his belief that acts of creativity are inevitably balanced by acts of destruction elsewhere in the world. His playing was nevertheless a major influence on the likes of Bert Jansch and John Renbourn, with his difficult instrumental 'Angie' being a required test piece for acoustic guitarists in the sixties (his own version can be found on the *3/4 AD* EP).

3/4 AD	7" EP	Topic	TOP70	1962	**£50**	**£25**	*with Alexis Korner*
All That Moody	LP	Eron	007	1976	**£125**	**£62.50**	
Both Sides Now	7"	Decca	F12841	1968	**£5**	**£2**	
Complete Guitarist	LP	Kicking Mule	SNKF138	1978	**£10**	**£4**	
Dance For Two People	LP	Kicking Mule	SNKF158	1979	**£10**	**£4**	
Folk Blues & Beyond	LP	Decca	LK4649	1964	**£60**	**£30**	
Folk Roots New Routes	LP	Decca	LK4652	1964	**£100**	**£50**	*with Shirley Collins*
Folk Roots New Routes	LP	Righteous	GDC001	1980	**£15**	**£6**	*with Shirley Collins*

Title	Format	Label	Cat. No.	Year	Mint	VG	Notes
From A London Hootenanny	7" EP	Decca	DFE8538	1963	£15	£7.50	2 tracks by the Thamesiders
Godington Boundary	LP	President	PTLS1039	1970	£30	£15	
Guitar Player	LP	Golden Guinea	GGL0224	1962	£30	£15	
Hat	LP	Decca	SKL5011	1969	£50	£25	
Holly Kaleidoscope	LP	Decca	SKL5056	1970	£50	£25	
Large As Life & Twice As Natural	LP	Decca	SKL4969	1968	£50	£25	
Midnight Man	LP	Decca	LK4780	1966	£60	£30	

GRAHAM, ERNIE

Title	Format	Label	Cat. No.	Year	Mint	VG	Notes
Afro-Cubists	10" LP	Esquire	20012	1953	£50	£25	
Ernie Graham	LP	Liberty	LBS83485	1971	£25	£10	

GRAHAM, KENNY

Title	Format	Label	Cat. No.	Year	Mint	VG	Notes
Afro-Cubists	10" LP	Esquire	20023	1953	£30	£15	
Kenny Graham And His Satellites	LP	MGM	C764	1958	£30	£15	
Kenny Graham's Afro Cubists	LP	Nixa	NJL12	1957	£40	£20	
Presenting Kenny Graham Part 1	7" EP	Pye	NJE1053	1957	£15	£7.50	

GRAHAM, LEN

Title	Format	Label	Cat. No.	Year	Mint	VG	Notes
Wind And Water	LP	Topic	12TS334	1977	£10	£4	

GRAHAM, LOU

Title	Format	Label	Cat. No.	Year	Mint	VG	Notes
Wee Willie Brown	7"	Coral	Q72322	1958	£300	£180	best auctioned

GRAHAM, LYNDA

Title	Format	Label	Cat. No.	Year	Mint	VG	Notes
As Long As The River Flows	7"	Philips	326552BF	1962	£4	£1.50	
Without Your Love	7"	Philips	BF1249	1963	£4	£1.50	
You'd Better Believe It	7"	Philips	BF1308	1964	£4	£1.50	

GRAIL

Title	Format	Label	Cat. No.	Year	Mint	VG	Notes
Grail	LP	Metronome	15393	1971	£100	£50	German

GRAINER, RON

Title	Format	Label	Cat. No.	Year	Mint	VG	Notes
Maigret	LP	Ace Of Clubs	ACL1135	1963	£10	£4	
Paul Temple Theme	7"	RCA	RCA1898	1969	£6	£2.50	

GRAINER, RON ORCHESTRA

Title	Format	Label	Cat. No.	Year	Mint	VG	Notes
Man In A Suitcase	7"	Pye	7N17383	1967	£10	£5	
Prisoner	7"	RCA	RCA1635	1967	£40	£20	
Prisoner Arrival	7" EP	Six Of One	6OF1	1979	£10	£5	
That Was The Week That Was	7"	Decca	F11597	1963	£4	£1.50	
Theme Music From Inspector Maigret	7" EP	Warner Bros	WEP6012	1960	£6	£2.50	

GRAINGER, GLENDA

Title	Format	Label	Cat. No.	Year	Mint	VG	Notes
Mr Kiss Kiss Bang Bang	7"	Audio Fidelity	AFSP007	196–	£5	£2	

GRAMMER, BILLY

Title	Format	Label	Cat. No.	Year	Mint	VG	Notes
Billy Grammer Hits	7" EP	Felsted	GEP1005	1959	£40	£20	
Gotta Travel On	7"	London	HLU8752	1958	£8	£4	
Kissing Tree	7"	Felsted	AF121	1959	£6	£2.50	
Rainbow Round My Shoulder	7"	Brunswick	05851	1961	£5	£2	
Travellin' On	LP	Monument	MLP/SLP14000	1961	£20	£8	US
Willy, Quit Your Playing	7"	Felsted	AF128	1959	£6	£2.50	

GRANAHAN, GERRY

Title	Format	Label	Cat. No.	Year	Mint	VG	Notes
It Hurts	7"	Top Rank	JAR262	1960	£8	£4	Richie Robin, B side
No Chemise Please	7"	London	HL8668	1958	£20	£10	

GRAND FUNK RAILROAD

Title	Format	Label	Cat. No.	Year	Mint	VG	Notes
Closer To Home	LP	Capitol	EST471	1970	£10	£4	
E Pluribus Funk	LP	Capitol	EAS853	1972	£10	£4	
Grand Funk	LP	Capitol	EST406	1970	£10	£4	
Live	LP	Capitol	EST633	1971	£12	£5	double
Mark, Don, & Mel 1969–71	LP	Capitol	ESTSP10	1972	£12	£5	double
On Time	LP	Capitol	EST307	1969	£10	£4	
Survival	LP	Capitol	ESW764	1971	£10	£4	
We're An American Band	LP	Capitol	SMAS11207	1973	£10	£4	US, yellow vinyl

GRAND PRIX

Title	Format	Label	Cat. No.	Year	Mint	VG	Notes
Thinking Of You	7"	RCA	RCA7	1980	£5	£2	

GRANDISONS

Title	Format	Label	Cat. No.	Year	Mint	VG	Notes
All Right	7"	RCA	RCA1339	1963	£4	£1.50	

GRANDMA'S ROCKERS

Title	Format	Label	Cat. No.	Year	Mint	VG	Notes
Homemade Apple Pie	LP	Fredlo	6727	1967	£250	£150	US

GRANFALLOON

Title	Format	Label	Cat. No.	Year	Mint	VG	Notes
Laser Pace	LP	Takoma	9021	1973	£40	£20	US

GRANGER, GERRI

Title	Format	Label	Cat. No.	Year	Mint	VG	Notes
Just Tell Him Jane Said Hello	7"	London	HLX9759	1963	£4	£1.50	

GRANICUS

Title	Format	Label	Cat. No.	Year	Mint	VG	Notes
Granicus	LP	RCA	AFL10321	1973	£25	£10	US

GRANNIE

Grannie	LP	SRT	SRT71138	1971	**£500**	**£330**	

GRANNY'S INTENTIONS

Hilda The Builder	7"	Deram	DM214	1968	**£4**	**£1.50**	
Honest Injun	LP	Deram	SML1060	1970	**£30**	**£15**	
Julie Don't Love Me Anymore	7"	Deram	DM184	1968	**£4**	**£1.50**	
Story Of David	7"	Deram	DM158	1967	**£5**	**£2**	
Take Me Back	7"	Deram	DM293	1970	**£4**	**£1.50**	

GRANT, EARL

Earl Grant	7" EP	Brunswick	OE9460	1960	**£6**	**£2.50**	
End	7"	Brunswick	05762	1958	**£4**	**£1.50**	
End	LP	Brunswick	LAT8297	1959	**£10**	**£4**	
House Of Bamboo	7"	Brunswick	05824	1960	**£8**	**£4**	
Nothin' But The Blues	LP	Brunswick	LAT8332	1960	**£10**	**£4**	
Swinging Gently	7" EP	Brunswick	OE9493	1963	**£5**	**£2**	

GRANT, ERKEY & THE EARWIGS

I'm A Hog For You	7"	Pye	7N15521	1963	**£20**	**£10**	

GRANT, GOGI

Both Ends Of The Candle	LP	RCA	RD27054	1958	**£10**	**£4**	
Gigi	LP	RCA	RD27097	1959	**£10**	**£4**	*with Tony Martin*
Goin' Home	7"	London	HLG9185	1960	**£4**	**£1.50**	
Golden Ladder	7"	London	HLB8550	1958	**£6**	**£2.50**	
If You Want To Get To Heaven – Shout!	LP	London	HAG2242/ SAHG6072	1960	**£10**	**£4**	
Kiss Me, Honey Honey, Kiss Me	7"	RCA	RCA1105	1959	**£4**	**£1.50**	
Suddenly There's A Valley	7"	London	HLB8192	1955	**£12**	**£6**	
Suddenly There's Gogi Grant	LP	London	HAB2032	1957	**£15**	**£6**	
Wayward Wind	7"	London	HLB8282	1956	**£10**	**£5**	
We Believe In Love	7"	London	HLB8257	1956	**£10**	**£5**	
You're In Love	7"	London	HLB8364	1957	**£8**	**£4**	

GRANT, JULIE

Baby Baby	7"	Pye	7N15756	1965	**£4**	**£1.50**	
Count On Me	7"	Pye	7N15508	1963	**£4**	**£1.50**	
This Is Julie Grant	7" EP	Pye	NEP24171	1962	**£10**	**£5**	

GRANT, LEE & THE CAPITOLS

Breaking Point	7"	Parlophone	R5531	1966	**£12**	**£6**	

GRANT, TOP

Money Money Money	7"	Island	WI074	1963	**£6**	**£2.50**	
Riverbank Cobberley	7"	Island	WI072	1963	**£6**	**£2.50**	
Searching	7"	Island	WI034	1962	**£6**	**£2.50**	
Suzie	7"	Island	WI052	1962	**£6**	**£2.50**	
War In Africa	7"	Island	WI077	1963	**£6**	**£2.50**	

GRANTCHESTER MEADOW

Candlelight	7"	Amber	ABR004	1971	**£20**	**£10**	

GRANZ, NORMAN

Norman Granz was a major force within fifties jazz without playing a note himself. His Clef label (issued in the UK on the Columbia 33CX100 series) was an important showcase for a large number of artists. All the records on the label are now sought after by jazz collectors. Alongside this, Granz organized a series of concerts in which he encouraged various well-known musicians from different areas of jazz to play together. The recorded evidence of these concerts is listed in this *Guide* under the heading Jazz at the Philharmonic.

GRAPE

Baby In A Plastic Bag	7"	Pencil Toast	PENT001	1992	**£20**	**£10**	

GRAPEFRUIT

Around Grapefruit	LP	Stateside	(S)SL5008	1969	**£20**	**£8**	
C'mon Marianne	7"	RCA	RCA1716	1968	**£4**	**£1.50**	
Dear Delilah	7"	RCA	RCA1656	1968	**£4**	**£1.50**	
Deep Water	7"	RCA	RCA1855	1969	**£4**	**£1.50**	
Deep Water	LP	RCA	SF8030	1969	**£15**	**£6**	
Elevator	7"	RCA	RCA1677	1968	**£4**	**£1.50**	
Lady Godiva	7"	RCA	RCA1907	1969	**£4**	**£1.50**	
Round Going Round	7"	Stateside	SS8011	1969	**£4**	**£1.50**	
Someday Soon	7"	Stateside	SS8005	1968	**£4**	**£1.50**	

GRAPPELLY, STEPHANE

Stephane Grappelly	10" LP	Felsted	SDL86048	1956	**£20**	**£8**	
Stephane Grappelly And His Quintet	LP	Felsted	PDL85027	1957	**£20**	**£8**	

GRASS ROOTS

Golden Grass	LP	Dunhill	(S)SL5005	1969	**£10**	**£4**	
Leaving It Behind	LP	Stateside	SSL5012	1969	**£10**	**£4**	
Let's Live For Today	7"	Pye	7N25422	1967	**£6**	**£2.50**	
Let's Live For Today	LP	Dunhill	D(S)50020	1967	**£10**	**£4**	US
Midnight Confessions	7"	RCA	RCA1737	1968	**£4**	**£1.50**	
Things I Should Have Said	7"	Pye	7N25431	1967	**£4**	**£1.50**	
Where Were You When I Needed You	7" EP	RCA	86906	1966	**£15**	**£7.50**	*French*
Where Were You When I Needed You	LP	Dunhill	D(S)50011	1966	**£10**	**£4**	US

GRATEFUL DEAD

It used to be maintained that the Grateful Dead found it difficult to transfer the sparkle and uplift of their best live performances on to vinyl. This is hardly surprising, since, supremely amongst the groups evolving out of the late sixties period of rock experimentation, the Grateful Dead took risks. (The past tense has to be sadly appropriate, since with the death of guitarist Jerry Garcia the rest of the band will not be the Grateful Dead even if they decide to perform together.) During their long live shows, the Dead would use much of their studio material as skeletons around which to fashion long improvisations. In so far as they got better at it as they went along, the best Grateful Dead showcase is probably the late live album *Without A Net*. The group's style changed very little over the years and *Anthem Of The Sun*, which is mostly live, is almost as good (albeit strangely underrated when first released). Especially recommended too, as a very fine example of the Dead aiming high in the studio, is the scarce single 'Born Cross-Eyed'. This is different to the version on *Anthem Of The Sun* and has a non-album B side, a studio recording of 'Dark Star'. Both songs can also be found on the anthology *What A Long Strange Trip It's Been*. Records of interest to Grateful Dead collectors can also be found listed under the names of Mickey Hart, Ned Lagin and Ken Kesey.

Title	Format	Label	Cat. No.	Year	Mint	Good	Notes
American Beauty	LP	Warner Bros	WS1893	1971	**£10**	**£4**	
American Beauty	LP	Mobile Fidelity	MFSL1014	1978	**£15**	**£6**	*US audiophile*
Ante Up	CD	Arista	ASCD9921	1989	**£20**	**£8**	*US interview promo*
Anthem Of The Sun	LP	Warner Bros	WS1749	1968	**£25**	**£10**	
Aoxomoxoa	LP	Warner Bros	WS1790	1969	**£20**	**£8**	
Blues For Allah	CD	Grateful Dead	GDPD4001	1990	**£15**	**£6**	*picture disc*
Born Cross-Eyed	7"	Warner Bros	WB7186	1967	**£30**	**£15**	
Built To Last	CD	Arista	ADP8575	1989	**£20**	**£8**	*US promo picture disc, playing cards*
Dark Star	7"	Warner Bros	SAM79	1977	**£10**	**£5**	
Dead Zone	CD	Arista		1986	**£100**	**£50**	*6 discs, booklet, poster*
Europe '72	LP	Warner Bros	K66019	1972	**£15**	**£6**	*triple*
From The Mars Hotel	LP	Mobile Fidelity	MFSL1172	1980	**£15**	**£6**	*US audiophile*
Grateful Dead	LP	Warner Bros	WS1689	1967	**£25**	**£10**	
Grateful Dead	LP	Warner Bros	W1689	1967	**£50**	**£25**	*mono*
Grateful Dead Live	LP	Warner Bros	K66009	1971	**£15**	**£6**	*double*
Greetings From The Mars Hotel	CD	Mobile Fidelity	MFCD830	1985	**£15**	**£6**	*US audiophile*
Greetings From The Mars Hotel	CD	Grateful Dead	GDPD4007	1990	**£15**	**£6**	*picture disc*
Historic Dead	LP	Polydor	2310171	1972	**£20**	**£8**	
Historic Dead	LP	Sunflower	SNF5004	1971	**£30**	**£15**	*US*
History Of The Grateful Dead	LP	Pride	PRD0016	1972	**£25**	**£15**	*US*
History Of The Grateful Dead (Bear's Choice)	LP	Warner Bros	K46246	1973	**£10**	**£4**	
Let Me Sing Your Blues Away	7"	Warner Bros	K19301	1973	**£4**	**£1.50**	
Live Dead	LP	Warner Bros	WS1830	1970	**£25**	**£10**	*double*
Live Dead	LP	Warner Bros	K66002	1971	**£12**	**£5**	*green label, double*
One More Saturday Night	7"	Warner Bros	K16167	1972	**£4**	**£1.50**	
Steal Your Face	CD	Grateful Dead	GDPD4006	1990	**£15**	**£6**	*picture disc*
Steal Your Face	LP	United Artists	UAD60131/2	1976	**£20**	**£8**	*double plus bonus LP*
Stealin'	7"	Scorpio	201	1966	**£250**	**£150**	*US*
Terrapin Station	LP	Direct Disk	SD16619	1979	**£30**	**£15**	*US audiophile*
U.S. Blues	7"	United Artists	UP36030	1974	**£4**	**£1.50**	
Uncle John's Band	7"	Warner Bros	WB7410	1970	**£5**	**£2**	
Vintage Dead	LP	Polydor	2310172	1972	**£20**	**£8**	
Vintage Dead	LP	Sunflower	SNF5001	1970	**£30**	**£15**	*US*
Wake Of The Flood	CD	Grateful Dead	GDPD4002	1990	**£15**	**£6**	*picture disc*
Workingman's Dead	LP	Warner Bros	WS1869	1970	**£10**	**£4**	

GRAVENITES, NICK

Title	Format	Label	Cat. No.	Year	Mint	Good	Notes
My Labours	LP	CBS	63818	1969	**£12**	**£5**	
Steelyard Blues	LP	Liberty	352662	1973	**£10**	**£4**	*US*

GRAVES, CONLEY

Title	Format	Label	Cat. No.	Year	Mint	Good	Notes
Genius At Work	LP	Brunswick	LAT8116	1956	**£12**	**£5**	

GRAVESTONE

Title	Format	Label	Cat. No.	Year	Mint	Good	Notes
Doomsday	LP	AVC	793102	1979	**£30**	**£15**	*German*
War	LP	AVC	80020	1972	**£30**	**£15**	*German*

GRAVY TRAIN

Title	Format	Label	Cat. No.	Year	Mint	Good	Notes
Ballad Of A Peaceful Man	LP	Vertigo	6360051	1971	**£150**	**£75**	*spiral label*
Climb Aboard The Gravy Train	7"	Dawn	DNS1115	1975	**£4**	**£1.50**	
Gravy Train	LP	Vertigo	6360023	1970	**£30**	**£15**	*spiral label*
Second Birth	LP	Dawn	DNLS3046	1973	**£30**	**£15**	
Staircase To The Day	LP	Dawn	DNLH1	1974	**£30**	**£15**	
Starbright Starlight	7"	Dawn	DNS1058	1974	**£4**	**£1.50**	
Strength Of A Dream	7"	Dawn	DNS1036	1973	**£4**	**£1.50**	

GRAY, BARRY

Title	Format	Label	Cat. No.	Year	Mint	Good	Notes
Adventures Of Twizzle	7" EP	HMV	7EG8339	1957	**£10**	**£5**	
Captain Scarlet	7"	Pye	7N17391	1967	**£15**	**£7.50**	*picture sleeve*
Captain Scarlet	7"	Pye	7N17391	1967	**£8**	**£4**	
Fireball XL5	7"	Melodisc	1591	1964	**£6**	**£2.50**	
Fireball XL5	7"	Melodisc	1591	1964	**£30**	**£15**	*picture sleeve*
Joe 90	7"	Pye	7N17625	1968	**£25**	**£12.50**	*picture sleeve*
Joe 90	7"	Pye	7N17625	1969	**£10**	**£5**	
Robot Man	7"	Philips	326587BF	1963	**£8**	**£4**	*with Mary Jane*
Robot Man	7"	Philips	326587BF	1963	**£25**	**£12.50**	*picture sleeve, with Mary Jane*
Supercar Club	7"	National	LYN250	1962	**£12**	**£6**	

Title	Format	Label	Cat. No.	Year	Mint	VG	Notes
Supercar: Flight Of Fancy	LP	Golden Guinea	GGL0106	1961	**£30**	**£15**	
Thunderbirds Are Go!	LP	United Artists	SULP1159	1967	**£75**	**£37.50**	*stereo*
Thunderbirds Are Go!	LP	United Artists	ULP1159	1966	**£60**	**£30**	*mono*
Thunderbirds Theme	7"	Pye	7N17016	1965	**£20**	**£10**	*picture sleeve*
Thunderbirds Theme	7"	Pye	7N17016	1965	**£8**	**£4**	
Twizzle: Stories And Songs	7" EP	HMV	7EG8417	1957	**£10**	**£5**	

GRAY, CLAUDE

Title	Format	Label	Cat. No.	Year	Mint	VG	Notes
Country And Western Aces	7" EP	Mercury	10012MCE	1964	**£8**	**£4**	

GRAY, DOBIE

Title	Format	Label	Cat. No.	Year	Mint	VG	Notes
Dobie Gray Sings For In Crowders	LP	Charger	CHRM/ CHRS2002	1965	**£25**	**£10**	*US*
In Crowd	7"	London	HL9953	1965	**£5**	**£2**	
See You At The Go-Go	7"	Pye	7N25307	1965	**£12**	**£6**	

GRAY, DOLORES

Title	Format	Label	Cat. No.	Year	Mint	VG	Notes
After You Get What You Want	7"	Brunswick	05382	1955	**£4**	**£1.50**	
Rock Love	7"	Brunswick	05407	1955	**£10**	**£5**	
There'll Be Some Changes Made	7"	Capitol	CL14732	1957	**£4**	**£1.50**	

GRAY, GLENN

Title	Format	Label	Cat. No.	Year	Mint	VG	Notes
Glenn Gray And The Casa Loma Orchestra	LP	Capitol	LCT6128	1957	**£10**	**£4**	

GRAY, HERBIE

Title	Format	Label	Cat. No.	Year	Mint	VG	Notes
We're Staying Here	7"	Giant	GN38	1968	**£5**	**£2**	

GRAY, JERRY

Title	Format	Label	Cat. No.	Year	Mint	VG	Notes
Jerry Gray And His Orchestra	LP	Brunswick	LAT8164	1957	**£12**	**£5**	

GRAY, JOHNNIE

Title	Format	Label	Cat. No.	Year	Mint	VG	Notes
Apache	7"	Fontana	H134	1958	**£8**	**£4**	
Tequila	7"	Fontana	H123	1958	**£8**	**£4**	

GRAY, OWEN

Title	Format	Label	Cat. No.	Year	Mint	VG	Notes
Am Satisfy	7"	Collins Downbeat	CR007	1968	**£8**	**£4**	*Sir Collins B side*
Ay Ay Ay	7"	Fab	FAB96	1969	**£4**	**£1.50**	
Best Twist	7"	Blue Beat	BB113	1962	**£12**	**£6**	
Big Mabel	7"	Blue Beat	BB147	1963	**£12**	**£6**	
Call Me My Pet	7"	Blue Beat	BB188	1963	**£12**	**£6**	
Collins Greetings	7"	Collins Downbeat	CR003	1967	**£8**	**£4**	
Come On Baby	7"	Chek	TD101	1962	**£8**	**£4**	
Cupid	LP	Melodisc	MLP12153	1963	**£15**	**£6**	
Cutest Little Woman	7"	Blue Beat	BB8	1960	**£12**	**£6**	
Days I'm Living	7"	Blue Beat	BB365	1966	**£12**	**£6**	
Do You Want To Jump	7"	Blue Beat	BB108	1962	**£12**	**£6**	
Dolly Baby	7"	Island	WI020	1962	**£10**	**£5**	
Don't Take Your Love Away	7"	Camel	CA34	1969	**£4**	**£1.50**	
Draw Me Nearer	7"	Blue Beat	BB217	1964	**£12**	**£6**	
Every Beat Of My Heart	7"	Camel	CA37	1969	**£4**	**£1.50**	
Experienced	7"	Trojan	TR670	1969	**£4**	**£1.50**	
Get Drunk	7"	Blue Beat	BB43	1961	**£12**	**£6**	
Girl What You Doing To Me	7"	Camel	CA25	1969	**£4**	**£1.50**	
Give It To Me	7"	Coxsone	CS7053	1968	**£10**	**£5**	
Give Me A Little Sign	7"	Coxsone	CS7047	1968	**£10**	**£5**	
Groovin'	7"	Downtown	DT423	1969	**£4**	**£1.50**	*Herbie Gray B side*
Help Me	7"	Island	WIP6000	1967	**£10**	**£5**	
I Can Feel It	7"	Bamboo	BAM47	1970	**£4**	**£1.50**	
I Can't Stop Loving You	7"	Blue Cat	BS156	1969	**£6**	**£2.50**	
I Can't Stop Loving You	7"	Trojan	TR650	1969	**£4**	**£1.50**	
I Feel Good	7"	Starlite	ST45078	1962	**£8**	**£4**	
I'm Gonna Take You Back	7"	Collins Downbeat	CR010	1968	**£8**	**£4**	*Glen Adams B side*
I'm So Lonely	7"	Collins Downbeat	CR004	1967	**£8**	**£4**	*Sir Collins B side*
I'm Still Waiting	7"	Island	WI048	1962	**£10**	**£5**	
In My Dreams	7"	Starlite	ST45088	1962	**£8**	**£4**	
It's Gonna Work Out Fine	7"	Aladdin	WI603	1965	**£6**	**£2.50**	
Jenny Lee	7"	Starlite	ST45019	1960	**£10**	**£5**	
Linda Lu	7"	Island	WI607	1965	**£6**	**£2.50**	
Lovey Dovey	7"	Downtown	DT428	1969	**£4**	**£1.50**	*Herbie Gray B side*
Lovey Dovey	7"	Trojan	TR632	1968	**£4**	**£1.50**	
Mash It	7"	Starlite	ST45032	1961	**£8**	**£4**	
Midnight Track	7"	Island	WI030	1962	**£10**	**£5**	
No Good Woman	7"	Blue Beat	BB103	1962	**£12**	**£6**	
On The Beach	7"	Dice	CC3	1962	**£10**	**£5**	
Paradise	7"	Island	WI267	1966	**£10**	**£5**	
Please Let Me Go	7"	Starlite	ST45015	1960	**£10**	**£5**	
Pretty Girl	7"	Blue Beat	BB127	1962	**£12**	**£6**	
Reggae Dance	7"	Duke	DU12	1969	**£4**	**£1.50**	
Reggae With Soul	LP	Trojan	TTL24	1969	**£10**	**£4**	
Rocking In My Feet	7"	Blue Beat	BB75	1962	**£12**	**£6**	
Seven Lonely Days	7"	Duke	DU33	1969	**£4**	**£1.50**	
She's Gone To Napoli	7"	Blue Beat	BB149	1963	**£12**	**£6**	*with Laurel Aitken*

Shook Shimmy And Shake	7"	Island	WI252	1965	**£10**	**£5**	
Sings	LP	Starlite	STLP5	1961	**£100**	**£50**	
Snow Falling	7"	Blue Beat	BB201	1963	**£12**	**£6**	
Sugar Dumpling	7"	Pama	PM810	1970	**£4**	**£1.50**	
Swing Low	7"	Fab	FAB126	1969	**£4**	**£1.50**	
These Foolish Things	7"	Blue Cat	BS123	1968	**£6**	**£2.50**	
They Got To Move	7"	Blue Beat	BB136	1962	**£12**	**£6**	
Three Coins In The Fountain	7"	Fab	FAB90	1969	**£4**	**£1.50**	
Tree In The Meadow	7"	Blue Beat	BB139	1962	**£12**	**£6**	
Twist Baby	7"	Island	WI002	1962	**£10**	**£5**	
Understand My Love	7"	Fab	FAB120	1969	**£4**	**£1.50**	
You Don't Know Like I Know	7"	Island	WI258	1965	**£10**	**£5**	

GRAY, WARDELL

Chase And Steeplechase	10" LP	Brunswick	LA8646	1954	**£60**	**£30**	*with Dexter Gordon*
Memorial Album Vol. 1	LP	Stateside	SL10144	1965	**£10**	**£4**	
Memorial Album Vol. 2	LP	Stateside	SL10145	1965	**£10**	**£4**	
Memorial Vol. 1	LP	Esquire	32016	1956	**£30**	**£15**	
Memorial Vol. 2	LP	Esquire	32023	1957	**£30**	**£15**	

GRAY BROTHERS

Always	7"	Blue Cat	BS124	1968	**£6**	**£2.50**	

GRAYZELL, RUDY

Looking At The Moon	7"	London	HL8094	1954	**£150**	**£75**	

GRAZINA

Be My Baby	7"	HMV	POP1212	1963	**£6**	**£2.50**	
Don't Be Shy	7"	HMV	POP1149	1963	**£6**	**£2.50**	
Lover Please Believe Me	7"	HMV	POP1094	1962	**£6**	**£2.50**	

GREASE BAND

Grease Band	LP	Harvest	SHVL790	1971	**£10**	**£4**	

GREAT, JOHNNY B

School Is In	7"	Decca	F11740	1963	**£4**	**£1.50**	
You'll Never Leave Me	7"	Decca	F11804	1964	**£4**	**£1.50**	

GREAT AWAKENING

The instrumental version of 'Amazing Grace' credited to the Great Awakening starts with a single electric guitar, then rapidly adds further guitars until a whole choir of them are wailing away at the traditional theme. Then the guitars are stripped away until the solo guitar is left to finish the piece. It is extraordinarily effective – and the 'Cohen' arranging credit has led many observers, including disc jockey John Peel when playing the record at the time of its first release and the present author, to assume that this must be David Cohen from Country Joe and the Fish. Further research by Q magazine, however, revealed that this is actually an altogether less celebrated David Cohen, who worked as a session musician in the late sixties.

Amazing Grace	7"	London	HLU10284	1969	**£4**	**£1.50**	

GREAT DJELI

Great Djeli	LP	Gawsounds Production		1981	**£50**	**£25**	*Dutch*

GREAT LEAP FORWARD

Controlling The Edges Of Tone	7"	Ron Johnson	ZRON20	1987	**£4**	**£1.50**	

GREAT SATURDAY NIGHT SWINDLE

Great Saturday Night Swindle	LP	CBS	82044	1977	**£30**	**£15**	*Irish*

GREAT SOCIETY

The Great Society was one of the first and best known locally of the San Francisco bands, but its career was halted when singer Grace Slick was invited to join the rival Jefferson Airplane. During its short life, the band only recorded the one single, but a good live recording produced enough material for the two posthumous albums listed. These reveal the group to be a tight, efficient unit that would undoubtedly have sounded very impressive indeed had a studio album ever been recorded. Particularly interesting are the early versions of two songs that Jefferson Airplane made their own – 'White Rabbit' and 'Somebody To Love'.

Conspicuous Only In Its Absence	LP	CBS	63476	1968	**£15**	**£6**	
How It Was	LP	CBS	CS9702	1968	**£20**	**£8**	*US*
Someone To Love	7"	North Beach	1001	1966	**£50**	**£25**	*US*

GREATEST SHOW ON EARTH

Going's Easy	LP	Harvest	SHVL783	1970	**£25**	**£10**	
Greatest Show On Earth	LP	Harvest	SHSM2004	1975	**£15**	**£6**	*double*
Horizons	LP	Harvest	SHVL769	1970	**£25**	**£10**	

GRECO, BUDDY

At Mister Kelly's	LP	Vogue Coral	LVA9021	1956	**£12**	**£5**	
I've Grown Accustomed To Her Face	7"	London	HLR8613	1958	**£4**	**£1.50**	
My Buddy	LP	Fontana	TFL5098	1960	**£10**	**£4**	
Songs For Swinging Losers	LP	Fontana	TFL5125/ STFL552	1961	**£10**	**£4**	
With All My Heart	7"	London	HLR8452	1957	**£10**	**£5**	

GRECO, JULIETTE

Juliette Greco Sings	10" LP	Philips	BBR8023	1954	**£12**	**£5**	

GREEK FOUNTAIN RIVER FRONT BAND

Takes Requests	LP	Montel	LLP110	1965	**£50**	**£25**	*US*

GREEN, AL

Al Green Gets Next To You	LP	London	SHU8424	1971	£10	£4	
Back Up Train	7"	Bell	BLL1188	1971	£4	£1.50	
Back Up Train	7"	Stateside	SS2079	1968	£8	£4	
Back Up Train	LP	Action	ACLP6008	1969	£20	£8	
Call Me	LP	London	SHU8457	1973	£10	£4	
Don't Hurt Me No More	7"	Action	ACT4540	1969	£4	£1.50	
Full Of Fire (Extended)	7"	London	HLU10511	1975	£5	£2	*promo only*
I'm Still In Love With You	LP	London	SHU8443	1972	£10	£4	
Let's Stay Together	LP	London	SHU8430	1972	£10	£4	

GREEN, BRIAN

Brian Green Display	LP	Fontana	SFJL912	1968	£25	£10	

GREEN, GRANT

Alive	LP	Blue Note	BST84360	1970	£12	£5	
Am I Blue	LP	Blue Note	BLP/BST84139	1965	£30	£15	
Carryin' On	LP	Blue Note	BST84327	1969	£15	£6	
Feelin' The Spirit	LP	Blue Note	BLP/BST84132	1963	£30	£15	
Goin' West	LP	Blue Note	BST84310	1969	£15	£6	
Grant's First Stand	LP	Blue Note	BLP/BST84064	1961	£40	£20	
Grantstand	LP	Blue Note	BLP/BST84086	196–	£30	£15	
Green Is Beautiful	LP	Blue Note	BST84342	1970	£12	£5	
Green Street	LP	Blue Note	BLP/BST84071	1962	£30	£15	
I Want To Hold Your Hand	LP	Blue Note	BLP/BST84202	1966	£30	£15	
Idle Moments	LP	Blue Note	BLP/BST84154	1964	£30	£15	
Latin Bit	LP	Blue Note	BLP/BST84111	1963	£30	£15	
Shades Of Green	LP	Blue Note	BST84413	1970	£12	£5	
Street Of Dreams	LP	Blue Note	BLP/BST84253	1968	£20	£8	
Sunday Mornin'	LP	Blue Note	BLP/BST84099	1962	£40	£20	
Talkin' About!	LP	Blue Note	BLP/BST84183	1964	£40	£20	
Visions	LP	Blue Note	BST84373	1970	£12	£5	

GREEN, IAN

Last Pink Rose	7"	Polydor	56194	1967	£4	£1.50	
Revelation	LP	CBS	63840	1970	£10	£4	

GREEN, KATHE

If I Thought You'd Ever Change Your Mind	7"	Deram	DM279	1969	£4	£1.50	
Run The Length Of Your Wildness	LP	Deram	SML1039	1969	£30	£15	

GREEN, PETER

Like B. B. King before him, Peter Green discovered the knack of playing a single note on the guitar with real soul. Performances like 'The Supernatural', with John Mayall, or 'I Loved Another Woman' and 'Love That Burns' with Fleetwood Mac, are testimony and tribute to an outstanding blues guitar voice. *The End Of The Game* is a different kind of guitar playing. In place of soul and beauty, there is anger and anguish burning out of every twisted note of these largely improvised instrumentals. It is no wonder that Green's next act was to quit the music business, give away all his money and embark on a life of withdrawn paranoia. He has managed the occasional foray back into the recording studio, however, and has happily been touring extensively during the last couple of years. While he is clearly not the musician he once was, there are occasional flashes of the old brilliance – enough to make one glad that he is back.

Apostle	7"	PVK	PV16	1978	£5	£2	
Beast Of Burden	7"	Reprise	K14141	1972	£6	£2.50	
Blue Guitar	LP	Creole	CRX5	1981	£10	£4	*blue vinyl*
End Of The Game	LP	Reprise	K44106	1972	£10	£4	
End Of The Game	LP	Reprise	RSLP9006	1970	£15	£6	
Give Me Back My Freedom	7"	PVK	PV103	1981	£4	£1.50	
Heavy Heart	7"	Reprise	RS27012	1971	£4	£1.50	
Heavy Heart	7"	Reprise	K14092	1971	£6	£2.50	
In The Skies	7"	PVK	PV24	1979	£4	£1.50	*picture sleeve*
In The Skies	LP	PVK	PVLS101	1979	£10	£4	*green vinyl*
Loser Two Times	7"	PVK	PV41	1980	£4	£1.50	
Promised Land	7"	PVK	PV112	1981	£4	£1.50	
Walking In The Road	7"	PVK	PV36	1980	£4	£1.50	

GREEN, TOM

Rock Springs Railroad Station	7"	Action	ACT4621	1974	£10	£5	

GREEN, URBIE

All About Urbie Green	LP	HMV	CLP1158	1958	£15	£6	
Urbie Green Orchestra	LP	London	LTZN15002	1956	£20	£8	

GREEN ANGELS

Let It Happen	7"	Parlophone	R5390	1965	£4	£1.50	

GREEN BULLFROG

Green Bullfrog	LP	MCA	MKPS2021	1972	£30	£15	

GREEN DAY

Welcome To Paradise	CD-s	WEA	W0269CDX	1995	£5	£2	*green case*

GREEN GINGER TREE

From The Land Of Green Ginger	7" EP	Decca	DFE8623	1965	£75	£37.50	

GREEN MAN

What Ails Thee?	LP	private		1975	£200	£100	

GREEN ON RED

Title	Format	Label	Number	Year	Mint	VG	Notes
Two Bibles	LP	private		1981	**£20**	**£8**	*US*

GREEN RIVER BOYS

Title	Format	Label	Number	Year	Mint	VG	Notes
Big Bluegrass Special	LP	Capitol	(S)T1810	1962	**£25**	**£10**	*US*

GREENBAUM, NORMAN

Title	Format	Label	Number	Year	Mint	VG	Notes
Spirit In The Sky	LP	Reprise	RS6365	1969	**£15**	**£6**	*US*

GREENBEATS

Title	Format	Label	Number	Year	Mint	VG	Notes
Pretty Woman	7"	Spin	SP2007	1967	**£4**	**£1.50**	

GREENE, BERNIE & HIS STEREO MAD-MEN

Title	Format	Label	Number	Year	Mint	VG	Notes
Musically Mad	LP	RCA	LPM/LSP1929	1958	**£20**	**£8**	*US*

GREENE, CLAUDE 'FATS'

Title	Format	Label	Number	Year	Mint	VG	Notes
Fats Shake 'Em Up	7"	Island	WI290	1966	**£5**	**£2**	

GREENE, DODO

Title	Format	Label	Number	Year	Mint	VG	Notes
My Hour Of Need	LP	Blue Note	BLP/BST9001	1962	**£40**	**£20**	

GREENE, LORNE

Title	Format	Label	Number	Year	Mint	VG	Notes
Man	LP	RCA	RD7709	1965	**£10**	**£4**	
Young At Heart	LP	RCA	RD7566	1963	**£10**	**£4**	

GREENGAGE

Title	Format	Label	Number	Year	Mint	VG	Notes
Greengage	LP	Look	LKLP6414	1979	**£15**	**£6**	

GREENSLADE

Title	Format	Label	Number	Year	Mint	VG	Notes
Bedside Manners Are Extra	LP	Warner Bros	K46259	1973	**£10**	**£4**	
Greenslade	LP	Warner Bros	K46207	1973	**£10**	**£4**	
Spyglass Guest	LP	Warner Bros	K56055	1974	**£10**	**£4**	
Time And Tide	LP	Warner Bros	K56126	1975	**£10**	**£4**	

GREENSLADE, ARTHUR

Title	Format	Label	Number	Year	Mint	VG	Notes
Cask Of The Amontillado	7" EP	Brunswick	OE9171	1955	**£5**	**£2**	
Rockin' Susannah	7"	Decca	F11363	1961	**£4**	**£1.50**	

GREENSLADE, DAVE

The Pentateuch is not so much a double LP that includes a book, as a book that just happens to have a couple of records tucked into pockets in its cover. The illustrations, packed with a wealth of often disturbing detail, are the essence of *The Pentateuch* – Dave Greenslade's rather simple keyboard music just cannot match their impact. Now if only Patrick Woodruffe, or some other talented illustrator, would get together with Vangelis, or, better still, Tomita . . .

Title	Format	Label	Number	Year	Mint	VG	Notes
Pentateuch	LP	EMI	EMC3321/2	1979	**£25**	**£10**	*double with book*

GREENWICH, ELLIE

Title	Format	Label	Number	Year	Mint	VG	Notes
Composes, Produces And Sings	LP	United Artists	UAS6648	1968	**£12**	**£5**	*US*
I Want You To Be My Baby	7"	United Artists	UP1180	1967	**£6**	**£2.50**	
Let It Be Written, Let It Be Sung	LP	MGM	2315243	1973	**£10**	**£4**	
Sunshine After The Rain	7"	United Artists	UP2214	1968	**£6**	**£2.50**	

GREENWOOD, NICK

Although Vincent Crane was perfectly capable of supplying a bass line with his organ pedals, Arthur Brown's management insisted on adding a bass player to the Crazy World. This was Nick Greenwood – later a member of Khan. Kingdom records issued his solo LP in 1972, which is now extremely scarce.

Title	Format	Label	Number	Year	Mint	VG	Notes
Cold Cuts	LP	Kingdom	KVLP9002	1972	**£300**	**£180**	

GREENWOOD, STOCKER & FRIENDS

Title	Format	Label	Number	Year	Mint	VG	Notes
Billy And Nine	LP	Changes		1979	**£50**	**£25**	

GREGG, BOBBY & FRIENDS

Title	Format	Label	Number	Year	Mint	VG	Notes
Jam	7"	Columbia	DB4825	1962	**£5**	**£2**	

GREGORY, IAN

Title	Format	Label	Number	Year	Mint	VG	Notes
Can't You Hear The Beat	7"	Pye	7N15397	1961	**£20**	**£10**	
How Many Times	7"	Columbia	DB7085	1963	**£6**	**£2.50**	
Mr Lovebug	7"	Pye	7N15435	1962	**£20**	**£10**	
Time Will Tell	7"	Pye	7N15295	1960	**£20**	**£10**	

GREGORY, JOHNNY ORCHESTRA

Title	Format	Label	Number	Year	Mint	VG	Notes
Bonanza	7"	Fontana	H286	1960	**£5**	**£2**	
Bonanza	7" EP	Fontana	TFE17331	1960	**£8**	**£4**	
Channel Thrill: The TV Thriller Themes	LP	Fontana	STFL585	1962	**£10**	**£4**	*stereo*
Maverick	7" EP	Fontana	TFE17325	1960	**£8**	**£4**	
Route 66	7"	Fontana	H341	1961	**£5**	**£2**	
Route Sixty-Six	7" EP	Fontana	TFE17382	1962	**£8**	**£4**	
Spies And Dolls	LP	Philips	6308111	1972	**£15**	**£6**	
TV Thrillers	7" EP	Fontana	TFE17389	1962	**£10**	**£5**	
Wagon Train	7"	Fontana	H288	1961	**£5**	**£2**	

GREGORY, TONY

Title	Format	Label	Number	Year	Mint	VG	Notes
Baby Come On Home	7"	Doctor Bird	DB1007	1966	**£10**	**£5**	
Get Out Of My Life	7"	Island	WI3029	1967	**£10**	**£5**	*Soul Brothers B side*
Give Me One More Chance	7"	Doctor Bird	DB1016	1966	**£10**	**£5**	
Only A Fool	7"	Coxsone	CS7013	1967	**£10**	**£5**	

Sings	LP	Coxsone	CSL8011	1967	**£50**	**£25**	

GREMLINS

Coming Generation	7"	Mercury	MF981	1966	**£10**	**£5**	
You Gotta Believe It	7"	Mercury	MF1004	1967	**£10**	**£5**	

GRENFELL, JOYCE

At Home	7" EP	HMV	7EG8787	1958	**£5**	**£2**	
Requests The Pleasure	LP	Philips	BBL7004	1954	**£10**	**£4**	

GREY, JOEL

Be My Next	7"	Capitol	CL14832	1958	**£10**	**£5**	
Last Night In The Back Porch	7"	MGM	SPC1	1954	**£5**	**£2**	*export*

GREY, RONNIE & THE JETS

Run Manny Run	7"	Capitol	CL14329	1955	**£20**	**£10**	

GREYHOUND

Black And White	LP	Trojan	TRLS27	1971	**£10**	**£4**	

GRID

Beat Called Love	CD-s	East West	YZ498CD	1990	**£5**	**£2**	
Boom!	12"	Virgin	VST1369	1991	**£10**	**£5**	
Floatation	12"	East West	YZ475T	1990	**£6**	**£2.50**	
Floatation	CD-s	East West	YZ475CD	1990	**£8**	**£4**	
Heartbeat	CD-s	Virgin	VSCDT1427	1993	**£5**	**£2**	
Intergalactica	12"	Grid	GRID001	1989	**£20**	**£10**	*white label*
On The Grid	12"	Grid	GRID002	1989	**£20**	**£10**	*white label*
Texas Cowboys	12"	Deconstruction	CORBY3	1994	**£10**	**£5**	*promo*

GRIER, ROOSEVELT

C'mon Cupid	7"	Pama	PM784	1969	**£4**	**£1.50**	
People Make The World	7"	Action	ACT4515	1968	**£4**	**£1.50**	
Who's Got The Ball Y'All	7"	Pama	PM774	1969	**£4**	**£1.50**	

GRIFFIN

I Am The Noise In Your Head	7"	Bell	BLL1075	1969	**£20**	**£10**	
In The Darkness	7"	MGM	2006088	1972	**£5**	**£2**	

GRIFFIN, JAMES

Summer Holiday	LP	Reprise	R(9)6091	1963	**£12**	**£5**	*US*

GRIFFIN, JOHNNY

Big Soul-Band	LP	Riverside	RLP12331	1960	**£15**	**£6**	
Big Soul-Band	LP	Riverside	RLP331/1179	1960	**£15**	**£6**	
Change Of Pace	LP	Riverside	RLP368	1961	**£15**	**£6**	
Lookin' At Monk	LP	Jazzland	JLP39	1961	**£20**	**£8**	*with Eddie 'Lockjaw' Davis*
Man I Love	LP	Polydor	583734	1969	**£20**	**£8**	
Tough Tenors	LP	Jazzland	JLP31	1960	**£20**	**£8**	*with Eddie 'Lockjaw' Davis*

GRIFFIN, SYLVIA

Love's A State Of Mind	CD-s	Rocket	BLACD7	1988	**£6**	**£2.50**	

GRIFFITH, ANDY

Andy Griffith	7" EP	Capitol	EAP1630	1956	**£6**	**£2.50**	
Ko Ko Mo	7"	Capitol	CL14263	1955	**£6**	**£2.50**	
Mama Guitar	7"	Capitol	CL14766	1957	**£5**	**£2**	
Midnight Special	7"	Capitol	CL14936	1958	**£4**	**£1.50**	
No Time For Sergeants	7"	Capitol	CL14619	1956	**£4**	**£1.50**	

GRIFFITH, MARI

Welsh Folk	LP	Rediffusion	ZS131	1973	**£30**	**£15**	

GRIFFITH, NANCI

From A Distance	CD-s	MCA	DMCA1282	1988	**£5**	**£2**	
It's A Hard Life	CD-s	MCA	DMCAT1358	1989	**£5**	**£2**	
Portrait Of An Artist	CD	MCA	CD451693	1989	**£20**	**£8**	*US promo sampler*
Present Echoes	CD	Elektra		1993	**£20**	**£8**	*US promo, 6 Other Voices tracks with 6 original versions*

GRIFFITHS, MARCIA

Don't Let Me Down	7"	Escort	ES808	1969	**£4**	**£1.50**	*Reggaeites B side*
Feel Like Jumping	7"	Coxsone	CS7055	1968	**£10**	**£5**	*Horace Taylor B side*
Funny	7"	Island	WI285	1966	**£15**	**£7.50**	*King Sparrow B side*
Hound Dog	7"	Studio One	SO2008	1967	**£12**	**£6**	*Hugh Godfrey B side*
Mojo Girl	7"	Coxsone	CS7035	1968	**£10**	**£5**	*Hamlins B side*
Mr Everything	7"	Rio	R121	1966	**£8**	**£4**	*Soul Brothers B side*
Naturally	LP	Sky Note	SKYLP9	1978	**£10**	**£4**	
Put A Little Love In Your Heart	7"	Trojan	TR693	1969	**£4**	**£1.50**	*J Boys B side*
Shimmering	7"	Bamboo	BAM59	1970	**£5**	**£2**	
Talk	7"	High Note	HS029	1969	**£6**	**£2.50**	
Tell Me Now	7"	Gas	GAS111	1969	**£6**	**£2.50**	*Stan Hope B side*
Truly	7"	Studio One	SO2059	1968	**£12**	**£6**	*Simms & Robinson B side*
Words	7"	Studio One	SO2047	1968	**£12**	**£6**	*Sharks B side*

You Keep Me On The Move	7"	Studio One	SO2069	1968	**£12**	**£6**	*Mr Foundation B side*

GRIGNARD, FERRE

Hash Bamboo Shuffle	7" EP	Philips	434337	196–	**£6**	**£2.50**	*French*
La Si Do 25	7" EP	Barclay	71199	1968	**£8**	**£4**	*French*
Ring Ring I've Got To Sing	7" EP	Philips	434330	196–	**£6**	**£2.50**	*French*

GRIM REAPER

Fear No Evil	LP	Ebony	EBON32	1985	**£12**	**£5**	
Rock You To Hell	LP	RCA	PL86250	1987	**£10**	**£4**	
See You In Hell	LP	Ebony	EBON16	1983	**£15**	**£6**	

GRIMES, CAROL

Fools Meeting	LP	B&C	CAS1023	1970	**£40**	**£20**	*with Delivery*
Warm Blood	LP	Caroline	CA2001	1974	**£10**	**£4**	

GRIMES, TINY

Callin' The Blues	LP	Esquire	32092	1960	**£15**	**£6**	

GRIMMS

Grimms	LP	Island	HELP11	1973	**£10**	**£4**	
Rocking Duck	LP	Island	ILPS9248	1973	**£10**	**£4**	

GRIN

All Out	LP	Epic	EPC65166	1973	**£12**	**£5**	
Grin	LP	Epic	64272	1971	**£12**	**£5**	
One Plus One	LP	Epic	64652	1972	**£12**	**£5**	

GRIN (2)

View From The Valley	LP	Hasznee		1985	**£25**	**£10**	*Dutch*

GRINGO

Gringo	LP	MCA	MKPS2017	1971	**£12**	**£5**	

GRINNE, JOE

Mr Editor	7"	Coxsone	CS7098	1969	**£10**	**£5**	

GRISBY DYKE

Adventures Of Miss Rosemary La Page	7"	Deram	DM232	1969	**£4**	**£1.50**	

GROBSCHNITT

Ballermann	LP	Brain	21050	1974	**£20**	**£8**	*German double*
Grobschnitt	LP	Brain	1008	1972	**£25**	**£10**	*German*
Jumbo	LP	Brain	0001076	1975	**£15**	**£6**	*German; English lyrics*
Jumbo	LP	Brain	0001081	1975	**£15**	**£6**	*German; German lyrics*

GRODECK WHIPPERJENNY

Grodeck Whipperjenny	LP	People	3000	1970	**£75**	**£37.50**	*US*

GROOM, DEWEY

Butane Blues	7"	Starlite	ST45085	1962	**£8**	**£4**	
Heartaches For Sale	7"	Starlite	ST45105	1963	**£5**	**£2**	
Walking Papers	7"	Starlite	ST45095	1963	**£6**	**£2.50**	

GROOP

Lovin' Tree	7"	CBS	3351	1968	**£4**	**£1.50**	

GROOVE

Wind	7"	Parlophone	R5783	1969	**£6**	**£2.50**	

GROOVE (2)

Heart Complaint	7"	Trendy	WHIP1	1980	**£10**	**£5**	

GROOVE FARM

Baby Blue Marine	7"	Lyntone	LYN18632	1988	**£10**	**£5**	*flexi, B side by Sea Urchins, picture sleeve*
Baby Blue Marine	7"	Lyntone	LYN18632	1988	**£8**	**£4**	*flexi, B side by Sea Urchins, no picture sleeve*
Driving In Your New Car	7"	Subway Organisation	SUBWAY22N	1988	**£12**	**£6**	*promo*
Only The Most Ignorant . . .	7"	Raving Pop Blast	RPBGF2	1989	**£5**	**£2**	
Sore Heads And Happy Hearts	7"	Raving Pop Blast	RPBGF1	1987	**£6**	**£2.50**	

GROOVERS

You've Got To Cry	7"	Island	WI3080	1967	**£10**	**£5**	*Alva Lewis B side*

GROOVEY, WINSTON

Free The People	LP	Pama	PMP2011	1969	**£10**	**£4**	
Funky Chicken	7"	Jackpot	JP708	1969	**£4**	**£1.50**	*Cimarrons B side*
Funny	7"	Jackpot	JP709	1969	**£4**	**£1.50**	*Cimarrons B side*
Island In The Sun	7"	Nu Beat	NB041	1969	**£4**	**£1.50**	

Josephine	7"	Nu Beat	NB042	1969	**£4**	**£1.50**	
You Can't Turn Your Back On Me	7"	Attack	ATT8019	1969	**£4**	**£1.50**	*Pama Dice B side*

GROOV-U

On Campus	LP	Gateway	GLP3010		**£15**	**£6**	*US*

GROSSETT, G. G.

Greater Sounds	7"	Crab	CRAB33	1969	**£4**	**£1.50**	
Run Girl Run	7"	Crab	CRAB10	1969	**£4**	**£1.50**	*Dennis Walks B side*

GROSSMAN, STEFAN

Aunt Molly's Murray Farm	LP	Fontana	(S)TL5463	1968	**£15**	**£6**	
Gramercy Park Sheik	LP	Fontana	STLS485	1969	**£15**	**£6**	
Ragtime Cowboy Jew	LP	Transatlantic	TRA223	1970	**£15**	**£6**	*double*
Yazoo Basin Boogie	LP	Transatlantic	TRA217	1970	**£10**	**£4**	

GROSSMAN, STEVE

Some Shapes To Come	LP	P.M.Records	PMR002	1975	**£12**	**£5**	*US*

GROSVENOR, LUTHER

Under Open Skies	LP	Island	ILPS9168	1971	**£10**	**£4**	

GROSZMANN, CARL

Face Of A Permanent Stranger	7"	Ring O'	2017107	1977	**£4**	**£1.50**	
Face Of A Permanent Stranger	7"	Ring O'	2017107	1977	**£8**	**£4**	*promo picture sleeve*
I've Had It	7"	Ring O'	2017103	1975	**£6**	**£2.50**	

GROUNDHOGS

Tony McPhee is a guitarist with a particularly good understanding of the blues, as his numerous session appearances on records by people like John Lee Hooker and Champion Jack Dupree testify. He is also one of the first musicians involved in the British blues boom of the late sixties to realize that it would not be possible to keep recycling the same twelve-bar repertoire indefinitely without the public losing interest. *Blues Obituary* announced the end of an era with music that, while obviously inspired by a love of the blues, nevertheless ranged very much more widely. Subsequently, McPhee became a little too convinced that he could play like Jimi Hendrix; however, each Groundhogs LP still has its moments, with *Split* being something of a minor classic. Tony McPhee is still a familiar figure on the pub and club circuit, with or without a line-up of the Groundhogs.

BDD	7"	Liberty	LBF15263	1969	**£6**	**£2.50**	
Best Of 1969–72	LP	United Artists	600063/4	1974	**£10**	**£4**	*double*
Blues Obituary	LP	Liberty	LBS83253	1969	**£30**	**£15**	
Eccentric Man	7"	Liberty	LBF15346	1970	**£6**	**£2.50**	
Hoggin' The Stage	LP	Psycho	PSYCHO24	1984	**£20**	**£8**	*double with EP*
Hogwash	LP	United Artists	UAG29419	1972	**£10**	**£4**	
I'll Never Fall In Love Again	7"	Planet	PLF104	1966	**£40**	**£20**	*credited to John Lee's Groundhogs*
Live At Leeds	LP	Liberty		1971	**£200**	**£100**	*promo*
Scratching The Surface	LP	Liberty	LBL/LBS83199	1968	**£40**	**£20**	
Solid	LP	WWA	WWA004	1974	**£10**	**£4**	
Split	LP	Liberty	LBS83401	1971	**£10**	**£4**	
Thank Christ For The Bomb	LP	Liberty	LBS83295	1970	**£10**	**£4**	
Who Will Save The World	LP	United Artists	UAG29237	1972	**£10**	**£4**	
You Don't Love Me	7"	Liberty	LBF15174	1968	**£6**	**£2.50**	

GROUP 1850

Agemo's Trip To Mother Earth	LP	Philips	SBL7884	1968	**£75**	**£37.50**	
Live	LP	Orange	OP1	1975	**£15**	**£6**	*Dutch*
Live 2	LP	Rubber	RR1852	1974	**£25**	**£10**	*Dutch*
Live On Tour	LP	Rubber	ME5	1973	**£25**	**£10**	*Dutch*
Paradise Now	LP	Discofoon	VD7063	1969	**£50**	**£25**	*Dutch*
Polyandri	LP	Rubber	RR1851	1974	**£25**	**£10**	*Dutch*

GROUP 5

En Direct De Liverpool	LP	Barclay	80230	1964	**£100**	**£50**	*French*

GROUP B

I Know Your Name Girl	7"	Vocalion	VF9284	1967	**£10**	**£5**	

GROUP IMAGE

Mouth In The Clouds	LP	Stable	SLE8005	1969	**£20**	**£8**	

GROUP ONE

Chanson D'Amour	7"	HMV	POP492	1958	**£4**	**£1.50**	
She's Neat	7"	HMV	POP463	1958	**£10**	**£5**	

GROUP SIX

Rock A Boogie	7"	Oriole	CB1488	1959	**£12**	**£6**	

GROUP THERAPY

You're In Need Of Group Therapy	LP	Philips	SBL7883	1969	**£10**	**£4**	

GROUP X

Roti Calliope	7"	Fontana	TF417	1963	**£6**	**£2.50**	
There Are 8 Million Cossack Melodies	7"	Fontana	267274TF	1963	**£5**	**£2**	
There Are 8 Million Cossack Melodies	7"	Fontana	267274TF	1963	**£10**	**£5**	*picture sleeve*

GROVE, BOBBY

It Was For You	LP	King	831	1963	**£15**	**£6**	*US*

GROWING CONCERN

Growing Concern .... LP .... Mainstream..... S6108 .... 1968 **£60**..........**£30** .... US

GRUMBLE

The single credited to Grumble was actually made by 10cc.

Da Doo Ron Ron .... 7" .... RCA.............. RCA2384 .... 1973 **£4**........ **£1.50** ....

GRUNBLATT, GEORGES

K-Priss .... LP .... Polydor .... 2473911 .... 1980 **£15**..........**£6** .... *French*

GRUNSKY, JACK

Toronto .... LP .... Kuckuck.......... 2375002 .... 1970 **£10**..........**£4** .... *German*

GRUNT FUTTOCK

Rock'n'Roll Christian .... 7" .... Regal Zonophone ..... RZ3042 .... 1972 **£20**..........**£10** ....

GRUPO SINTESIS

Aqui Estamos .... LP .... Egrem .... LD3951 .... 1981 **£30**..........**£15** .... *Cuban*

GRYCE, GIGI

Gigi Gryce Octet .... 10" LP Vogue .... LDE113 .... 1955 **£40**..........**£20** ....
Gigi Gryce Orchestra .... 10" LP Vogue .... LDE070 .... 1954 **£40**..........**£20** ....
Jazz Time Paris Vol. 2 .... 10" LP Vogue .... LDE048 .... 1954 **£40**..........**£20** ... *with Clifford Brown*

GRYPHON

The growing influence of folk music during the early seventies led a few groups to try the integration of medieval instruments into a folk-rock setting. The most successful of these was Gryphon, whose *Midnight Mushrumps* in particular is something of a landmark. Later albums found the group retreating to a more ordinary rock sound, but Richard Harvey subsequently made much use of his love for medieval music in his solo career.

Gryphon .... LP .... Transatlantic .... TRA262 .... 1973 **£10**..........**£4** ....
Midnight Mushrumps .... LP .... Transatlantic .... TRA282 .... 1974 **£10**..........**£4** ....
Raindance .... LP .... Transatlantic .... TRA302 .... 1975 **£10**..........**£4** ....
Red Queen To Gryphon Three .... LP .... Transatlantic .... TRA287 .... 1974 **£10**..........**£4** ....

GRYPHON (2)

Gryphon .... LP .... NR .... 12497 .... 197– **£60**..........**£30** .... US

G.T.O.s

She Rides With Me .... 7" .... Polydor .... 56721 .... 1967 **£6**........ **£2.50** ....

GTR

When The Heart Rules The Mind .... 7" .... Arista.............. GTRSD1 .... 1986 **£5**..........**£2** .... *picture disc*

GUARDIOLA, JOSE & ROSE MARY

Algo Prodigioso .... 7" .... HMV .... POP1147 .... 1963 **£10**..........**£5** ....

GUARNIERI, JOHNNY

Songs Of Will Hudson And Eddie De Lange .... LP .... Vogue Coral.... LVA9049 .... 1957 **£15**..........**£6** ....

GUDIBRALLAN

Gudibrallan .... LP .... Silence.......... SRS4612 .... 1971 **£30**..........**£15** .... *Swedish*

GUESS WHO

Hey Ho What You Do To Me .... 7" EP .. Vogue .... INT18038 .... 1965 **£15**...... **£7.50** .... *French*
His Girl .... 7" .... King.............. KG1044 .... 1966 **£15**...... **£7.50** ....
Miss Felicity Grey .... 7" .... Fontana .... TF861 .... 1967 **£5**..........**£2** ....
Shakin' All Over .... 7" .... Pye.............. 7N25305 .... 1965 **£8**..........**£4** ....
This Time Long Ago .... 7" .... Fontana .... TF831 .... 1967 **£6**........ **£2.50** ....

GUEST, EARL

Foxy .... 7" .... Columbia .... DB7212 .... 1964 **£5**..........**£2** ....
Winkle Picker Stomp .... 7" .... Columbia .... DB4707 .... 1962 **£4**........ **£1.50** ....

GUEST, REG SYNDICATE

Reg Guest Trio .... 7" EP .. NFS .... 68CFH1002 .... 1968 **£50**..........**£25** ....
Underworld .... 7" .... Mercury .... MF927 .... 1965 **£50**..........**£25** ....
Underworld .... LP .... Mercury .... 20089MCL .... 1966 **£25**..........**£10** ....

GUGGENHEIM

Guggenheim .... LP .... Indigo .... GOLP7001 .... 1972 **£75**.... **£37.50** ....

GUILLOTEENS

I Don't Believe .... 7" .... Pye.............. 7N25324 .... 1965 **£25**.... **£12.50** ....

GUITAR, BONNIE

Dark Moon .... LP .... Dot .... DLP3335/25335 ..... 1962 **£12**..........**£5** .... US
Moonlight And Shadows .... LP .... London .... HAD2122 .... 1958 **£12**..........**£5** ....
Very Precious Love .... 7" .... London .... HLD8591 .... 1958 **£8**..........**£4** ....
Whispering Hope .... LP .... Dot .... DLP3151/DLP25151 .... 1959 **£12**..........**£5** .... US

GUITAR CRUSHER WITH JIMMY SPRUILL

Since My Baby Hit The Numbers .... 7″........ Blue Horizon... 573149.................. 1969 £15...... £7.50 ....

GUITAR JUNIOR

Pick Me Up On Your Way Down .... LP .... Goldband .... 1085 .... 1960 £15.......... £6 .... US

GUITAR NUBBIT

Georgia Chain Gang .... 7″........ Bootleg .... 501 .... 1964 £20.......... £10 ....

GUITAR RED

Just You And I .... 7″........ Pye.................. 7N25219................ 1963 £8.............. £4 ....

GUITAR SHORTY

Carolina Slide Guitar .... LP .... Flyright .... LP500 .... 1972 £10.......... £4 ....

GUITAR SLIM

Things That I Used To Do .... LP .... Speciality .... 2120 .... 1964 £25.......... £10 .... US

GULDA, FRIEDRICH

At Birdland .... LP .... Decca............... LK4188.................. 1958 £20.......... £8 ....
Man Of Letters .... LP .... Decca............... LK4189.................. 1958 £20.......... £8 ....

GULLIN, LARS

Holiday For Piano .... 10″ LP Esquire .... 20015 .... 1953 £50.......... £25 ....
Lars Gullin Compositions .... 10″ LP Esquire .... 20019 .... 1953 £50.......... £25 ....
New Sounds From Europe Vol. 3 .... 10″ LP Vogue .... LDE052.................. 1954 £50.......... £25 ....

GULLIVER

Gulliver .... LP .... Elektra............. 2410006.................. 1970 £10.......... £4 ....

GULLIVER'S TRAVELS

Gulliver's Travels .... LP .... Instant .... INLP003.................. 1968 £40.......... £20 ....

GUN

The Gun were a guitar trio fronted by Adrian Gurvitz, who has popped up periodically ever since. 'Race With The Devil' was the Gun's calling card, a classic piece of hard rock, powered by one of those simple guitar riffs that seems to have been waiting around for ever for someone to just come along and play it. Not much of the rest of the Gun's material is in the same class, unfortunately.

Drives You Mad .... 7″........ CBS................. 4052 .... 1969 £4........ £1.50 ....
Gun .... LP .... CBS................. 63552 .... 1968 £15.......... £6 ....
Gunsight .... LP .... CBS................. 63683 .... 1969 £25.......... £10 ....
Hobo/Long Hair Wild Man .... 7″........ CBS................. 4443 .... 1969 £5.............. £2 ....
Race With The Devil .... 7″........ CBS................. 3764 .... 1968 £4........ £1.50 ...... *2 different B sides*
Running Wild .... 7″........ CBS................. 4952 .... 1970 £4........ £1.50 ....

GUN (2)

Better Days .... CD-s ... A&M .... CDEE505................ 1989 £5.............. £2 ....
Higher Ground .... CD-s ... A&M .... AMCD869.............. 1991 £5.............. £2 ....
Inside Out .... CD-s ... A&M .... CDEE531................ 1989 £5.............. £2 ....
Money (Everybody Loves Her) .... CD-s ... A&M .... CDEE520................ 1989 £5.............. £2 ....
Shame On You .... CD-s ... A&M .... AMCD573.............. 1990 £5.............. £2 ....
Steal Your Fire .... CD-s ... A&M .... AMCD851.............. 1992 £6........ £2.50 ....
Taking On The World .... CD-s ... A&M .... CDEE541................ 1990 £5.............. £2 ....

GUNN, JON

I've Just Made My Mind Up .... 7″........ Deram.............. DM133.................... 1967 £5.............. £2 ....

GUNNER, JIM

Desperado .... 7″........ Fontana .... H313 .... 1961 £6........ £2.50 ....
Hoolee Jump .... 7″........ Decca............... F11276 .... 1960 £6........ £2.50 ....

GUNNER, TONY

Rough Road .... 7″........ London .... HLU9492.................. 1962 £8.............. £4 ....

GUNS 'N' ROSES

With a raunchy image and music to match, Guns 'n' Roses have slipped effortlessly into the niche left vacant by the semi-retired Rolling Stones. The fact that the group is too young to have a particularly extensive back catalogue is no problem for collectors. The record company is only too willing to provide instant collectors' items in the form of limited-edition releases of one sort or another. (The US promotional doormat – definitely an item for the collector who must have everything – was selling for £60 when first produced!)

Civil War .... 12″...... WEA................ SAM694 .... 1991 £15...... £7.50 .... *promo*
Don't Cry .... CD-s ... Geffen.............. GFSTD9.................. 1991 £8.............. £4 ....
Guns 'n' Radio .... CD ...... Geffen.............. PROCD4340........... 1991 £25.......... £10 .... *US promo*
It's So Easy .... 12″...... Geffen.............. GEF22TP .... 1987 £25..... £12.50 .... *picture disc*
It's So Easy .... 12″...... Geffen.............. GEF22T .... 1987 £10.......... £4 ....
It's So Easy .... 7″........ Geffen.............. GEF22.................... 1987 £6........ £2.50 ....
Live ?!*@ Like A Suicide .... LP .... Uzi Suicide...... USR001 .... 1986 £100........ £50 .... US
Live And Let Die .... CD-s ... Geffen.............. GFSTD17................ 1991 £6........ £2.50 ....
Night Train .... CD-s ... Geffen.............. GEF60CD .... 1989 £6........ £2.50 .... *3″ single*
Nightrain .... 7″........ Geffen.............. GEF60P................... 1989 £6........ £2.50 ...... *shaped picture disc*
November Rain .... CD-s ... Geffen.............. GFSTD18................ 1992 £8.............. £4 .... *picture disc*
On Tour Now! .... CD ...... Geffen.............. PROCD4441........... 1993 £20.......... £8 .... *US promo*
Paradise City .... 7″........ Geffen.............. GEF50X .... 1989 £5.............. £2 .... *holster pack*
Paradise City .... 7″........ Geffen.............. GEF50P................... 1989 £6........ £2.50 ...... *shaped picture disc, clear background*
Paradise City .... 7″........ Geffen.............. GEF50P................... 1989 £10.......... £5 ...... *shaped picture disc, white background*

Title	Format	Label	Cat. No.	Year	Mint	VG	Notes
Paradise City	CD-s	Geffen	GEF50CD	1989	**£8**	**£4**	
Patience	CD-s	Geffen	GEF56CD	1989	**£8**	**£4**	*3″ single*
Sample Your Illusion	CD	Geffen		1991	**£20**	**£8**	*promo sampler*
Since I Don't Have You	CD-s	Geffen	GFSXD70	1993	**£8**	**£4**	*in tin*
Spaghetti Incident	CD	Geffen		1993	**£25**	**£10**	*US promo in spaghetti tin*
Sweet Child O' Mine	CD-s	Geffen	GEF55CD	1989	**£8**	**£4**	*3″ single*
Sweet Child Of Mine	10″	Geffen	GEF43TE	1988	**£15**	**£7.50**	*revolving sleeve*
Sweet Child Of Mine	12″	Geffen	GEF43TV	1988	**£8**	**£4**	*metallic sleeve*
Sweet Child Of Mine	7″	Geffen	GEF55P	1989	**£8**	**£4**	*shaped picture disc*
Use Your Illusion World Tour I	CD	Geffen	GEI39521	1993	**£25**	**£10**	*Laser disc*
Use Your Illusion World Tour II	CD	Geffen	GEI39522	1993	**£25**	**£10**	*Laser disc*
Welcome To The Jungle	12″	Geffen	GEF47TP	1988	**£8**	**£4**	*picture disc*
Welcome To The Jungle	12″	Geffen	GEF47T	1988	**£8**	**£4**	*with patch*
Welcome To The Jungle	10″	Geffen	GEF30T	1987	**£20**	**£10**	
Welcome To The Jungle	12″	Geffen	GEF30TW	1987	**£8**	**£4**	*poster sleeve*
Welcome To The Jungle	12″	Geffen	GEF30TP	1987	**£30**	**£15**	*picture disc*
Welcome To The Jungle	7″	Geffen	GEF30	1987	**£5**	**£2**	
Welcome To The Jungle	CD-s	Geffen	GEF47CD	1988	**£12**	**£6**	*3″ single*
You Could Be Mine	CD-s	Geffen	GFSTD6	1991	**£8**	**£4**	*card sleeve*

GUNTER, ARTHUR

Title	Format	Label	Cat. No.	Year	Mint	VG	Notes
Black And Blues	LP	Excello	8017	1970	**£75**	**£37.50**	*US*
Blues After Hours	LP	Blue Horizon	2431012	1971	**£40**	**£20**	

GUNTHER, HARDROCK

Title	Format	Label	Cat. No.	Year	Mint	VG	Notes
Mountain Music	7″ EP	Brunswick	OE9167	1955	**£15**	**£7.50**	

GURU GURU

Title	Format	Label	Cat. No.	Year	Mint	VG	Notes
Dance Of The Flames	LP	Atlantic	K50044	1974	**£15**	**£6**	
Der Elektrolurch	LP	Brain	21057	1974	**£20**	**£8**	*German double*
Don't Call Us We'll Call You	LP	Atlantic	K50022	1973	**£15**	**£6**	
Guru Guru	LP	Brain	1025	1973	**£20**	**£8**	*German*
Hinten	LP	Ohr	556017	1971	**£30**	**£15**	*German*
Kan Guru	LP	Brain	1007	1972	**£20**	**£8**	*German*
This Is Guru Guru	LP	Brain	200145	1973	**£15**	**£6**	*German*
UFO	LP	Ohr	556005	1970	**£40**	**£20**	*German*

GURUS

Title	Format	Label	Cat. No.	Year	Mint	VG	Notes
Blue Snow Night	7″	United Artists	UP1160	1966	**£12**	**£6**	

GUSTAFSON, JOHNNY

Title	Format	Label	Cat. No.	Year	Mint	VG	Notes
Just To Be With You	7″	Polydor	56022	1965	**£5**	**£2**	
Take Me For A Little While	7″	Polydor	56043	1965	**£8**	**£4**	

GUTHRIE, ARLO

Title	Format	Label	Cat. No.	Year	Mint	VG	Notes
Alice's Restaurant	LP	Reprise	RLP6267	1967	**£10**	**£4**	
Alice's Restaurant Soundtrack	LP	United Artists	UAS29061	1969	**£10**	**£4**	
Arlo	LP	Reprise	RSLP6299	1968	**£10**	**£4**	
Motorcycle Song	7″	Reprise	RS20644	1967	**£5**	**£2**	
Valley Of Pray	7″	Reprise	RS20951	1970	**£4**	**£1.50**	*demo*

GUTHRIE, WOODY

Title	Format	Label	Cat. No.	Year	Mint	VG	Notes
Blind Sonny Terry And Woody Guthrie	LP	Ember	CW136	1969	**£10**	**£4**	
Bound For Glory	LP	Topic	12T21	1958	**£25**	**£10**	
Cisco Houston And Woody Guthrie	LP	Ember	CW135	1969	**£10**	**£4**	
Dust Bowl Ballads	LP	RCA	RD7642	1964	**£20**	**£8**	
Greatest Songs of Woody Guthrie	LP	Vanguard	VSD35/36	1972	**£12**	**£5**	*US double, with other artists*
Guthrie's Story	LP	Topic	12T31	1958	**£25**	**£10**	
Hard It Ain't Hard	7″ EP	Melodisc	EPM784	1958	**£8**	**£4**	
Hey Lolly Lolly	7″ EP	Melodisc	EPM791	1959	**£8**	**£4**	
More Songs By Guthrie	LP	Melodisc	MLP12106	1955	**£25**	**£10**	
Poor Boy	LP	XTRA	XTRA1065	1968	**£10**	**£4**	
Songs To Grow On Vol. 1	LP	XTRA	XTRA1067	1968	**£10**	**£4**	
Woody Guthrie	LP	XTRA	XTRA1064	1966	**£10**	**£4**	
Woody Guthrie	LP	Ember	CW129	1968	**£10**	**£4**	
Woody Guthrie	LP	XTRA	XTRA1012	1965	**£10**	**£4**	
Worried Man Blues	7″ EP	Melodisc	EPM785	1958	**£8**	**£4**	

GUVNERS

Title	Format	Label	Cat. No.	Year	Mint	VG	Notes
Let's Make A Habit Of This	7″	Piccadilly	7N35117	1963	**£5**	**£2**	

GUY, BARRY

Title	Format	Label	Cat. No.	Year	Mint	VG	Notes
Ode	LP	Incus	INCUS6/7	197–	**£25**	**£10**	*double*
Statement V-XI	LP	Incus	INCUS22	1977	**£12**	**£5**	

GUY, BOB

'Dear Jeepers' is an early Frank Zappa composition.

Title	Format	Label	Cat. No.	Year	Mint	VG	Notes
Dear Jeepers	7″	Donna	1380	1963	**£150**	**£75**	*US*

GUY, BUDDY

Title	Format	Label	Cat. No.	Year	Mint	VG	Notes
Blues Today	LP	Vanguard	SVRL19004	1968	**£15**	**£6**	
Buddy And The Juniors	LP	Harvest	SHSP4006	1970	**£15**	**£6**	
Buddy Guy & Junior Wells Play The Blues	LP	Atlantic	K40240	1972	**£10**	**£4**	

Coming At You	LP	Vanguard	SVRL19001	1968	**£15**	**£6**	
Crazy Music	7" EP	Chess	CRE6004	1965	**£12**	**£6**	
First Time I Met The Blues	LP	Python	KM2	1969	**£20**	**£8**	
Hold That Plane	LP	Vanguard	VSD79323	1972	**£10**	**£4**	
Hot And Cool	LP	Vanguard	SVRL79290	1969	**£10**	**£4**	
I Was Walking Through The Woods	LP	Chess	LP409	196–	**£20**	**£8**	*US*
Left My Blues In San Francisco	LP	Chess	CRL(S)4546	1969	**£12**	**£5**	
Let Me Love You Baby	7"	Chess	CRS8004	1965	**£6**	**£2.50**	
Man And His Blues	LP	Vanguard	SVRL19002	1968	**£15**	**£6**	
Mary Had A Little Lamb	7"	Fontana	TF951	1968	**£6**	**£2.50**	
This Is Buddy Guy	LP	Vanguard	SVRL19008	1969	**£15**	**£6**	

GUY CALLED GERALD

Voodoo Ray	12"	Rham	RX8804	1988	**£8**	**£4**	

GUYS

You Go Your Way	7"	Tepee	TPRSP1001	1969	**£5**	**£2**	

GYGAFO

Legend Of The Kingfisher	LP	Holyground	HG1155	1989	**£50**	**£25**	*1973 LP with 1989 cover*

GYPSIES

Jerk It	7"	CBS	2785	1967	**£15**	**£7.50**	

GYPSY

Brenda And The Rattlesnake	LP	United Artists	UAS29420	1972	**£10**	**£4**	
Gypsy	LP	United Artists	UAS29155	1971	**£10**	**£4**	

H. P. LOVECRAFT

H. P. Lovecraft was a writer of gothic fiction and not responsible for the music of the group that borrowed his name. In fact, the two albums made by the original line-up are highly inventive collections of songs, which graft some of the psychedelic pop trappings of UK groups like the Blossom Toes or Family on to the West Coast group sound of the late sixties, complete with a vocal sound that owes much to the power harmonies of Jefferson Airplane. The albums are much less celebrated than those of people like Country Joe and the Fish and Quicksilver Messenger Service, but are well worth investigation. A third album was made by a revised version of the group, and is listed in this guide under the name Lovecraft, but sadly this is a very disappointing affair.

Title	Format	Label	Cat. No.	Year	Mint	Half	Notes
H. P. Lovecraft	LP	Philips	(S)BL7830	1967	**£40**	**£20**	
H. P. Lovecraft 2	LP	Philips	SBL7872	1968	**£25**	**£10**	
This Is H. P. Lovecraft – Sailing On The White Ship	LP	Philips	6336210	1970	**£15**	**£6**	
This Is H. P. Lovecraft Vol. 2 – Spin Spin Spin	LP	Philips	6336213	1970	**£15**	**£6**	
Wayfarin' Stranger	7"	Philips	BF1620	1967	**£4**	**£1.50**	
White Ship	7"	Philips	BF1639	1968	**£4**	**£1.50**	

HAACK, BRUCE

Title	Format	Label	Cat. No.	Year	Mint	Half	Notes
Electric Luzifer	LP	Columbia	9991	1970	**£20**	**£8**	*US*

HABIBIYYA

Title	Format	Label	Cat. No.	Year	Mint	Half	Notes
If Man But Knew	LP	Island	HELP7	1972	**£12**	**£5**	

HABITS

The drummer with the Nice, Brian Davidson, was previously a member of the Habits.

Title	Format	Label	Cat. No.	Year	Mint	Half	Notes
Elbow Baby	7"	Decca	F12348	1966	**£15**	**£7.50**	

HACKENSACK

Title	Format	Label	Cat. No.	Year	Mint	Half	Notes
Here Comes The Judge	LP	Zel	UZ003	197–	**£150**	**£75**	
Moving On	7"	Island	WIP6149	1972	**£8**	**£4**	
Up The Hardway	LP	Polydor	2383263	1974	**£60**	**£30**	

HACKETT, BOBBY

Title	Format	Label	Cat. No.	Year	Mint	Half	Notes
At The Embers	LP	Capitol	T1077	1959	**£10**	**£4**	
Bobby Hackett Jazz Band	10" LP	Capitol	LC6824	1956	**£12**	**£5**	
Bobby, Billy And Brazil	LP	Verve	(S)VLP9212	1968	**£10**	**£4**	*with Billy Butterfield*
Gotham Jazz Scene	LP	Capitol	T857	1958	**£10**	**£4**	
Jazz Session	10" LP	Columbia	33S1053	1955	**£15**	**£6**	
Rendezvous	LP	Capitol	T719	1956	**£10**	**£4**	
Trumpet Solos	10" LP	Brunswick	LA8587	1953	**£15**	**£6**	

HACKETT, STEVE

Title	Format	Label	Cat. No.	Year	Mint	Half	Notes
Cell 151	12"	Charisma	CELL12/13	1983	**£10**	**£5**	*double*
Picture Postcard	7"	Charisma	CB390	1981	**£6**	**£2.50**	*with postcard*

HADDOCK

Title	Format	Label	Cat. No.	Year	Mint	Half	Notes
Dockside	LP	Seagull		1981	**£25**	**£10**	*Dutch*
Still Alive	LP	Seagull		1986	**£25**	**£10**	*Dutch*

HADEN, CHARLIE

Title	Format	Label	Cat. No.	Year	Mint	Half	Notes
Closeness Duets	LP	Horizon	SP710	1976	**£12**	**£5**	*US*
Liberation Music Orchestra	LP	Probe	SPB1037	1969	**£20**	**£8**	

HADLEY, TONY

Title	Format	Label	Cat. No.	Year	Mint	Half	Notes
For Your Blue Eyes Only	CD-s	EMI	CDEM234	1992	**£5**	**£2**	
Game Of Love	CD-s	EMI	CDEM254	1992	**£5**	**£2**	
Lost In Your Love	CD-s	EMI	CDEM222	1992	**£5**	**£2**	
State Of Play	CD	EMI	CDEMC3619	1992	**£30**	**£15**	

HAFLER TRIO

Title	Format	Label	Cat. No.	Year	Mint	Half	Notes
Bang! – An Open Letter	LP	Doublevision	DVR4	1984	**£10**	**£4**	
Sea Org	10" LP	Touch	T05	1986	**£10**	**£4**	
Three Ways Of Saying Two	LP	Charrm	3	1986	**£10**	**£4**	

HAGAR, SAMMY

Title	Format	Label	Cat. No.	Year	Mint	Half	Notes
Sammy Hagar	LP	Capitol	EST11599	1977	**£10**	**£4**	*red vinyl*
Sammy Hagar Returns	CD	Geffen		1988	**£20**	**£8**	*US promo*

HAGER, JOAN

Happy Is A Girl Named Me	7"	Brunswick	05650	1957	£6	£2.50	

HAGGARD, MERLE

I'm A Lonesome Fugitive	LP	Capitol	(S)T2702	1967	£10	£4	
Just Between The Two Of Us	LP	Capitol	(S)T2453	1966	£10	£4	with Bonnie Owens
Legend Of Bonnie And Clyde	LP	Capitol	(S)T2912	1968	£10	£4	
Mama Tried	LP	Capitol	(S)T2972	1969	£10	£4	
To All The Girls I've Loved Before	LP	Premier	PMP1003	1987	£15	£6	

HAGGIS

Live	LP	Univers		1977	£200	£100	Dutch

HAHN, JERRY BROTHERHOOD

Jerry Hahn Brotherhood	LP	Columbia	CS1044	1970	£15	£6	US

HAHN, JOYCE

Gonna Find Me A Bluebird	7"	London	HLA8453	1957	£8	£4	

HAIG, AL

Al Haig Trio	10" LP	Vogue	LDE092	1954	£40	£20	
Jazz Will O' The Wisp	LP	XTRA	XTRA1125	1971	£10	£4	

HAIKARA

Iso Iintu	LP	Satril	SATLP1016	1975	£75	£37.50	Finnish

HAINES, NORMAN

Daffodil	7"	Parlophone	R5871	1970	£20	£10	
Den Of Iniquity	7"	Parlophone	SPSR338	1971	£25	£12.50	promo only
Den Of Iniquity	LP	Parlophone	PCS7130	1971	£400	£250	
Give To You Girl	7"	Parlophone	R5960	1972	£20	£10	

HAIR

Hair Piece	LP	Columbia	SCX6452	1970	£100	£50	

HAIR (2)

Rave Up	LP	Pye	NSPL18314	1969	£50	£25	

HAIRBAND

Band On The Wagon	LP	Bell	SBLL69	1969	£30	£15	
Big Louis	7"	Bell	BLL1076	1969	£6	£2.50	

HAIRCUT 100

Blue Hat For A Blue Day	LP	Arista	HCC101	1982	£40	£20	test pressing only

HAIRY CHAPTER

Can't Get Through	LP	Bacillus	6494002	1971	£20	£8	German
Can't Get Through	LP	Bacillus	BLPS19074	1971	£15	£6	German
Eyes	LP	Opp	521	1970	£20	£8	German

HAIRY ONES

Get Off My Cloud	7" EP	Barclay	70898	1965	£10	£5	French

HAL HOPPERS

Baby I've Had It	7"	London	HL8129	1955	£12	£6	
Do Nothing Blues	7"	London	HL8107	1954	£15	£7.50	

HALE & THE HUSHABYES

The group name disguises the combined forces of Jackie DeShannon, Sonny and Cher, the Blossoms, and Brian Wilson.

Yes Sir, That's My Baby	7"	Apogee	104	1964	£100	£50	US
Yes Sir, That's My Baby	7"	Reprise	0299	1964	£40	£20	US

HALEY, BILL

Bill Haley & His Comets	7" EP	Brunswick	OE9459	1959	£30	£15	tri-centre
Bill Haley And His Comets	7" EP	Warner Bros	WEP6001	1960	£12	£6	
Bill Haley And The Comets	LP	Warner Bros	W(S)1738	1960	£25	£10	US
Bill Haley And The Comets	LP	Valiant	VS103	1970	£10	£4	
Bill Haley And The Comets	LP	XTRA	XTRA1027	1965	£15	£6	
Bill Haley Vol. 1	7" EP	Warner Bros	WEP6133	1964	£20	£10	
Bill Haley Vol. 2	7" EP	Warner Bros	WEP6136	1964	£20	£10	
Bill Haley's Chicks	LP	Brunswick	LAT8295	1959	£40	£20	
Bill Haley's Chicks	LP	Brunswick	STA3011	1959	£50	£25	stereo
Bill Haley's Chicks	LP	Ace Of Hearts	AH66	1964	£10	£4	
Bill Haley's Chicks	LP	Decca	DL(7)8821	1959	£50	£25	US
Bill Haley's Juke Box	7" EP	Warner Bros	WEP6025	1961	£15	£7.50	
Bill Haley's Juke Box	7" EP	Warner Bros	WSEP2025	1961	£25	£12.50	stereo
Bill Haley's Juke Box	LP	Warner Bros	W1391	1960	£25	£10	
Billy Goat	7"	Brunswick	05688	1957	£10	£5	
Birth Of The Boogie	7"	Brunswick	05910	1964	£8	£4	
Caldonia	7"	Brunswick	05805	1959	£12	£6	
Candy Kisses	7"	Warner Bros	WB6	1960	£5	£2	
Crazy Man Crazy	78	London	L1190	1953	£20	£10	
Crazy Man, Crazy	7"	Pye	7N25455	1968	£10	£5	
Dim Dim The Lights	7"	Brunswick	05373	1955	£40	£20	gold label
Dim Dim The Lights	7" EP	Brunswick	OE9129	1955	£20	£10	gold label

Title	Format	Label	Number	Year	Mint	VG	Notes
Dipsy Doodle	7"	Brunswick	05719	1957	**£15**	**£7.50**	
Don't Knock The Rock	7"	Brunswick	05640	1957	**£15**	**£7.50**	
Farewell So Long Goodbye	7"	London	HLF8161	1955	**£100**	**£50**	*gold label*
Forty Cups Of Coffee	7"	Brunswick	05658	1957	**£15**	**£7.50**	
Goofing Around	7"	Brunswick	05641	1957	**£15**	**£7.50**	
Green Door	7"	Brunswick	05917	1964	**£8**	**£4**	
Greentree Boogie	7"	London	HL8142	1955	**£100**	**£50**	*gold label*
He Digs Rock And Roll	LP	Decca	DL8315	1956	**£100**	**£50**	*US*
I Got A Woman	7"	Brunswick	05788	1959	**£10**	**£5**	
I'm Gonna Dry Every Little Tear	78	Melodisc	1376	1956	**£15**	**£7.50**	
Lean Jean	7"	Brunswick	05752	1958	**£10**	**£5**	
Live It Up	10" LP	London	HAPB1042	1955	**£100**	**£50**	*gold label*
Live It Up Pt 1	7" EP	London	REF1049	1956	**£30**	**£15**	
Live It Up Pt 2	7" EP	London	REF1050	1956	**£30**	**£15**	
Live It Up Pt 3	7" EP	London	REF1058	1956	**£25**	**£12.50**	
Mambo Rock	7"	Brunswick	05405	1955	**£40**	**£20**	*gold label*
Mary Mary Lou	7"	Brunswick	05735	1958	**£10**	**£5**	
Ooh Looka There Ain't She Pretty	7"	Brunswick	05810	1959	**£12**	**£6**	
Pat-A-Cake	78	London	L1216	1953	**£20**	**£10**	
Razzle Dazzle	7"	Brunswick	05453	1955	**£30**	**£15**	*gold label*
Rip It Up	7"	Decca	BM31171	1956	**£25**	**£12.50**	*export*
Rip It Up	7"	Brunswick	05615	1956	**£15**	**£7.50**	
Rock Around The Clock	7"	Brunswick	05317	1954	**£50**	**£25**	*gold label, tri centre*
Rock Around The Clock	7"	Decca	AD1010	1968	**£5**	**£2**	*export*
Rock Around The Clock	7"	Warner Bros	WB133	1964	**£6**	**£2.50**	
Rock Around The Clock	7" EP	Brunswick	OE9250	1956	**£15**	**£7.50**	*2 covers*
Rock Around The Clock	LP	Decca	DL8225	1955	**£125**	**£62.50**	*US*
Rock Around The Clock	LP	Brunswick	LAT8117	1956	**£30**	**£15**	
Rock Around The Clock	LP	Ace Of Hearts	AH13	1961	**£12**	**£5**	
Rock The Joint	7"	London	HLF8371	1957	**£100**	**£50**	*gold label*
Rock The Joint	LP	Golden Guinea	GGL0282	1963	**£10**	**£4**	
Rock The Joint	LP	London	HAF2037	1957	**£50**	**£25**	
Rock With Bill Haley & The Comets	LP	Somerset	P4600	1956	**£30**	**£15**	*US*
Rock With Bill Haley & The Comets	LP	Essex	LP202	1956	**£125**	**£62.50**	*US*
Rock With Bill Haley And The Comets	LP	Trans World	202	1956	**£50**	**£25**	*US*
Rock'n'Roll	7" EP	Brunswick	OE9214	1956	**£15**	**£7.50**	
Rock'n'Roll	7" EP	London	REF1031	1955	**£40**	**£20**	
Rock'n'Roll Stage Show	LP	Brunswick	LAT8139	1956	**£25**	**£10**	
Rock'n'Roll Stage Show	LP	Decca	DL8345	1956	**£100**	**£50**	*US*
Rock'n'Roll Stage Show Pt 1	7" EP	Brunswick	OE9278	1956	**£15**	**£7.50**	
Rock'n'Roll Stage Show Pt 2	7" EP	Brunswick	OE9279	1956	**£15**	**£7.50**	
Rock'n'Roll Stage Show Pt 3	7" EP	Brunswick	OE9280	1956	**£15**	**£7.50**	
Rock-A-Beatin' Boogie	7"	Brunswick	05509	1955	**£30**	**£15**	*gold label*
Rockin' Around The World	7" EP	Brunswick	OE9446	1959	**£30**	**£15**	
Rockin' Around The World	LP	Decca	DL8692	1957	**£50**	**£25**	*US*
Rockin' Chair On The Moon	7"	London	HLF8194	1955	**£125**	**£62.50**	*gold label*
Rockin' The Joint	LP	Brunswick	LAT8268	1957	**£40**	**£20**	
Rockin' The Joint	LP	Decca	DL8775	1958	**£50**	**£25**	*US*
Rockin' The Oldies	LP	Brunswick	LAT8219	1957	**£40**	**£20**	
Rockin' The Oldies	LP	Ace Of Hearts	AH35	1962	**£10**	**£4**	
Rockin' The Oldies	LP	Decca	DL8569	1957	**£50**	**£25**	*US*
Rockin' The Oldies Pt 1	7" EP	Brunswick	OE9349	1958	**£20**	**£10**	
Rockin' The Oldies Pt 2	7" EP	Brunswick	OE9350	1958	**£20**	**£10**	
Rockin' The Oldies Pt 3	7" EP	Brunswick	OE9351	1958	**£20**	**£10**	
Rockin' Through The Rye	7"	Brunswick	05582	1956	**£15**	**£7.50**	
Rudy's Rock	7"	Brunswick	05616	1956	**£15**	**£7.50**	
Saints Rock'n'Roll	7"	Brunswick	05565	1956	**£15**	**£7.50**	
See You Later Alligator	7"	Brunswick	05530	1956	**£30**	**£15**	*gold label*
Shake, Rattle And Roll	10" LP	Decca	DL5560	1954	**£350**	**£210**	*US*
Shake, Rattle And Roll	7"	Brunswick	05338	1954	**£40**	**£20**	*gold label*
Skinnie Minnie	7"	Brunswick	05742	1958	**£12**	**£6**	
Skokiaan	7"	Brunswick	05818	1960	**£6**	**£2.50**	
Spanish Twist	7"	London	HLU9471	1961	**£8**	**£4**	
Strictly Instrumental	LP	Decca	DL(7)8964	1959	**£50**	**£25**	*US*
Strictly Instrumental	LP	Brunswick	LAT8326	1960	**£30**	**£15**	
Tenor Man	7"	Stateside	SS196	1963	**£4**	**£1.50**	
They Sold A Million No. 15	7" EP	Brunswick	OE9431	1959	**£10**	**£5**	*2 tracks by the Four Aces*
Twisting Knights At The Round Table	LP	Columbia	33SX1460	1962	**£20**	**£8**	
Whoa Mabel	7"	Brunswick	05766	1958	**£12**	**£6**	

HALF NELSON

Half Nelson was the name originally used by Sparks. The one LP made under this name was reissued as *Sparks* a year later.

Title	Format	Label	Number	Year	Mint	VG	Notes
Half Nelson	LP	Bearsville	BV2048	1972	**£20**	**£8**	*US*

HALF TRIBE

Title	Format	Label	Number	Year	Mint	VG	Notes
Only Starting	LP	private		1965	**£500**	**£330**	*US*

HALL, CONNIE & JAMES O'GWYNN

Title	Format	Label	Number	Year	Mint	VG	Notes
Country And Western Trailblazers No. 3	7" EP	Mercury	ZEP10080	1960	**£5**	**£2**	

HALL, DARYL & JOHN OATES

Title	Format	Label	Number	Year	Mint	VG	Notes
Downtown Life	CD-s	Arista	661730	1988	**£5**	**£2**	
Maneater	CD-s	RCA	PD49465	1989	**£5**	**£2**	*3" single*
Voices	CD	Mobile Fidelity	UDCD830	1990	**£15**	**£6**	*US audiophile*

HALL, DEREK & MIKE COOPER

Out Of The Shades	7" EP	Kennet	KRS766	196–	£25	£12.50	

HALL, DICKSON

All Time Country And western Hits	LP	Fontana	Z4011	1960	£10	£4	
Fabulous Country Hits No. 1	7" EP	London	RER1158	1958	£8	£4	
Fabulous Country Hits No. 2	7" EP	London	RER1159	1958	£8	£4	
Fabulous Country Hits No. 3	7" EP	London	RER1160	1958	£8	£4	
Fabulous Country Hits Way Out West	LP	Kapp	KL1067	1957	£10	£4	US
Outlaws Of The Old West	10" LP	MGM	E329	1954	£15	£6	US
Outlaws Of The Old West	7" EP	MGM	MGMEP626	1957	£10	£5	
Outlaws Of The Old West	LP	MGM	E3263	1956	£12	£5	US
Twenty-Five All-Time Country & Western Hits	LP	Epic	LN3427	1958	£10	£4	US

HALL, EDMOND

Celestial Express	LP	Blue Note	B6505	1969	£12	£5	
Petite Fleur	LP	London	LTZT15166	1959	£10	£4	
Rumpus On Rampart Street	LP	Top Rank	35050	1960	£10	£4	

HALL, EDMUND

Edmund Hall All Stars	10" LP	London	LZC14005	1955	£15	£6	

HALL, GERRI

Who Can I Run To	7"	Sue	WI4026	1966	£50	£25	demo

HALL, JIM

Jazz Guitar	LP	Vogue	LAE12072	1958	£20	£8	

HALL, JIMMY GRAY

Be That Way	7"	Epic	EPC2312	1974	£8	£4	

HALL, JUANITA

Sings The Blues	LP	Storyville	SLP113	1964	£15	£6	
Storyville Blues Anthology Vol. 2	7" EP	Storyville	SEP382	1962	£6	£2.50	

HALL, LANI

Sundown Lady	LP	A&M	AMLS64359	1974	£10	£4	

HALL, LARRY

Ladder Of Love	7"	Salvo	SLO1811	1962	£8	£4	
Sandy	7"	Parlophone	R4625	1960	£4	£1.50	

HALL, RENE

Twitchy	7"	London	HLU8581	1958	£30	£15	

HALL, ROBIN

Bonnie Lass O' Fyvie	7" EP	Collector	JES6	1960	£5	£2	
Football Crazy	7"	Decca	F11266	1960	£4	£1.50	picture sleeve, with Jimmie MacGregor
Glasgow Street Songs Vol. 3	7" EP	Collector	JES9	1961	£5	£2	
Last Leaves Of Traditional Ballads	10" LP	Collector	JFS4002	1961	£12	£5	
MacPherson's Rant	7" EP	Collector	JES7	1960	£5	£2	
Robin Hall	7" EP	Collector	JES12	1964	£5	£2	
Robin Hall Sings Again	7" EP	Collector	JES13	1964	£5	£2	
Scottish Choice	LP	Ace Of Clubs	ACL1065	1961	£10	£4	with Jimmie MacGregor

HALL, RONNIE

I'll Stand Aside	7"	Fontana	TF569	1965	£8	£4	

HALL, ROY

Blue Suede Shoes	7"	Brunswick	05555	1956	£300	£180	best auctioned
See You Later Alligator	7"	Brunswick	05531	1956	£500	£330	best auctioned
Three Alley Cats	7"	Brunswick	05627	1956	£300	£180	best auctioned

HALL, TERRY

Lenny The Lion	7" EP	Decca	DFE/STO8554	1963	£5	£2	

HALL, TERRY *(2)*

Missing	CD-s	Chrysalis	CHSCD3381	1989	£5	£2	

HALL, TONY

Fieldvole Music	LP	Free Reed	FRR012	1977	£20	£8	

HALLADAY, CHANCE

John Henry	7"	Vogue	V9203	1962	£6	£2.50	

HALLBERG, BENGT

New Sounds From Sweden	10" LP	Esquire	20014	1953	£50	£25	

HALLELUJAH

Hallelujah Babe	LP	Metronome	LMLP15805	1971	£25	£10	German

HALLELUJAH SKIFFLE GROUP

I Saw The Light	7"	Oriole	CB1429	1958	£10	£5	

HALLIARD

The Halliard were a folk trio led by Nic Jones, whose later solo work consists of particularly fine traditional interpretations. Tragically, Jones's career was cut short by a serious car accident, which left him unable to play the guitar.

Halliard And Jon Raven	LP	Broadside	BRO106	1968	**£75**	**£37.50**	
It's The Irish In Me	LP	Saga	SOC1058	1967	**£50**	**£25**	

HALLIWELL, GERI

Interview	CD	EMI	CDIN122	1999	**£20**	**£8**	*promo*

HALLYDAY, JOHNNY

America's Rockin' Hits	LP	Philips	BBL7556	1961	**£75**	**£37.50**	
Chante	LP	Philips	77746L	1965	**£40**	**£20**	*French*
Disque d'or	LP	Pye Golden Guinea	GGL0311	1964	**£25**	**£10**	
Hey Little Girl	7"	Philips	373012BF	1963	**£5**	**£2**	
Johnny Hallyday	7" EP	Vogue	VRE5013	1966	**£75**	**£37.50**	
L'Idole des jeunes	LP	Mode	MDINT9095	1964	**£20**	**£8**	*French*
La Génération perdue	LP	Philips	840586	1967	**£25**	**£10**	*French, stereo*
La Génération perdue	LP	Philips	70381L	1967	**£20**	**£8**	*French, mono*
Le Disque d'or	LP	Vogue	16009	1973	**£30**	**£15**	*French*
Olympia '64	LP	Philips	B77987L	1964	**£30**	**£15**	*French*
Pour moi tu es la seule	7"	Philips	BF1449	1965	**£6**	**£2.50**	
Rocking	7" EP	Philips	432813BE	1962	**£100**	**£50**	
Shake The Hand Of A Fool	7"	Philips	PB1238	1962	**£5**	**£2**	
Twistin' The Rock	LP	Vogue	MDINT9059	1962	**£25**	**£10**	*French*

HALOS

Halos	LP	Warwick	W2046	1962	**£60**	**£30**	*US*
Nag	7"	London	HLU9424	1961	**£20**	**£10**	

HAMBLEN, STUART

Go On By	7"	HMV	7MC30	1955	**£8**	**£4**	*export*
Hell Train	7"	HMV	7M394	1956	**£6**	**£2.50**	
This Ole House	7"	HMV	7MC20	1954	**£12**	**£6**	*export*

HAMBRO, LENNY

Lenny Hambro And Eddie Bert	10" LP	London	LZC14025	1956	**£20**	**£8**	
Message From Hambro	LP	Philips	BBL7161	1957	**£15**	**£6**	

HAMEL, PETER MICHAEL

Buddhist Meditation East West	LP	Harmonia Mundi	29222926	1975	**£12**	**£5**	*German double*
Hamel	LP	Vertigo	67641055	1972	**£20**	**£8**	*German double*
Voice Of Silence	LP	Vertigo	6360613	1973	**£12**	**£5**	*German*

HAMFATS, HARLEM

Harlem Hamfats	LP	Ace Of Hearts	AH27	1962	**£10**	**£4**	

HAMILL, CLAIRE

Abracadabra	LP	Konk	KONK104	1975	**£10**	**£4**	
October	LP	Island	ILPS9225	1973	**£10**	**£4**	
One House Left Standing	LP	Island	ILPS9182	1971	**£10**	**£4**	
Stage Door Johnnies	LP	Konk	KONK101	1974	**£10**	**£4**	

HAMILTON, CHICO

Chico Hamilton Quintet	LP	Vogue	LAE12039	1957	**£20**	**£8**	
Chico Hamilton Quintet	LP	Vogue	LAE12045	1957	**£20**	**£8**	
Chico Hamilton Trio	LP	Vogue	LAE12077	1958	**£20**	**£8**	
Chico Hamnilton Quintet	LP	Vogue	LAE12085	1958	**£15**	**£6**	
Ellington Suite	LP	Vogue	LAE12210	1960	**£15**	**£6**	
Gamut	LP	Solid State	USS7010	1968	**£12**	**£5**	
Introducing Freddie Gambrell	LP	Vogue	LAE12160	1959	**£15**	**£6**	
Original	LP	Vogue	LAE12239	1961	**£12**	**£5**	

HAMILTON, GAVIN

It Won't Be The Same	7"	King	KG1067	1967	**£15**	**£7.50**	

HAMILTON IV, GEORGE

Before This Day Ends	7"	HMV	POP813	1960	**£4**	**£1.50**	
I Know Where I'm Going	7"	HMV	POP505	1958	**£4**	**£1.50**	
On Campus	LP	HMV	CLP1202	1958	**£12**	**£5**	
Rose And A Candy Bar	7"	London	HL8361	1957	**£100**	**£50**	*gold label*
Sing Me A Sad Song	LP	HMV	CLP1263	1959	**£12**	**£5**	
Why Don't They Understand	7"	HMV	POP429	1957	**£6**	**£2.50**	
Your Cheatin' Heart	7"	HMV	POP534	1958	**£4**	**£1.50**	

HAMILTON, GUY

Lifetime Of Loneliness	7"	HMV	POP1418	1965	**£5**	**£2**	

HAMILTON, M.

Something Gotta Ring	7"	Ska Beat	JB265	1967	**£10**	**£5**	

HAMILTON, ROY

And I Love Her	7"	RCA	RCA1500	1966	**£5**	**£2**	
Come Out Swinging	7" EP	Fontana	TFE17170	1959	**£8**	**£4**	
Crazy Feeling	7"	Fontana	H143	1958	**£8**	**£4**	

Title	Format	Label	Cat. No.	Year	Mint	VG	Notes
Dark End Of The Street	7"	Deep Soul	DS9106	1970	£8	£4	
Don't Let Go	7"	Fontana	H113	1958	£12	£6	
I Need Your Loving	7"	Fontana	H193	1959	£6	£2.50	
Mood Moves	7" EP	Fontana	TFE17163	1959	£8	£4	
Pledging My Love	7"	Fontana	H180	1959	£8	£4	
Theme From The VIPs	7"	MGM	MGM1210	1963	£6	£2.50	
There She Is	7"	MGM	MGM1251	1964	£100	£50	
Thousand Years Ago	7"	MGM	MGM1268	1965	£6	£2.50	
Warm Soul	LP	MGM	C960	1964	£15	£6	
Why Fight The Feeling	7" EP	Fontana	TFE17160	1959	£8	£4	
You Can Have Her	7"	Fontana	H298	1961	£10	£5	
You're Gonna Need Magic	7"	Fontana	H320	1961	£6	£2.50	

HAMILTON, RUSS

Title	Format	Label	Cat. No.	Year	Mint	VG	Notes
It's A Sin To Tell A Lie	7"	Oriole	CB1531	1960	£4	£1.50	
My Unbreakable Heart	7"	Oriole	CB1506	1959	£4	£1.50	
Rainbow	LP	Kapp	KL1076	1957	£40	£20	US
Russ Hamilton	7" EP	Oriole	EP7005	1958	£10	£5	
Smile Smile Smile	7"	Oriole	CB1508	1959	£4	£1.50	
Things No Money Can Buy	7"	Oriole	CB1527	1960	£4	£1.50	
We Will Make Love	LP	Oriole	MG20031	1958	£30	£15	

HAMILTON, SARA

Title	Format	Label	Cat. No.	Year	Mint	VG	Notes
Someone Ought To Care	LP	Polydor	2310261	1973	£20	£8	

HAMILTON & THE MOVEMENT

Title	Format	Label	Cat. No.	Year	Mint	VG	Notes
I'm Not the Marrying Kind	7"	CBS	202573	1967	£60	£30	
Really Saying Something	7"	Polydor	BM56026	1965	£60	£30	

HAMLINS

Title	Format	Label	Cat. No.	Year	Mint	VG	Notes
Everyone Got To Be There	7"	Studio One	SO2036	1967	£12	£6	*Minstrels B side*
Sentimental Reasons	7"	Coxsone	CS7048	1968	£10	£5	*Soul Vendors B side*
Sugar And Spice	7"	Blue Cat	BS115	1968	£8	£4	*Soul Vendors B side*

HAMMER, JACK

Title	Format	Label	Cat. No.	Year	Mint	VG	Notes
Brave New World	LP	Polydor	582001	1966	£30	£15	
Crazy Twist	7"	Oriole	CB1728	1962	£5	£2	
Kissing Twist	7"	Oriole	CB1645	1961	£4	£1.50	
Number 2539	7"	Oriole	CB1753	1962	£5	£2	
Thanks	7"	Polydor	56091	1966	£5	£2	
What Greater Love	7"	United Artists	UP35029	1969	£20	£10	
Young Only Once	7"	Oriole	CB1634	1961	£5	£2	

HAMMER, JAN

Title	Format	Label	Cat. No.	Year	Mint	VG	Notes
First Seven Days	LP	Atlantic	K50184	1975	£10	£4	
Like Children	LP	Atlantic	K50092	1974	£10	£4	

HAMMERSMITH

Title	Format	Label	Cat. No.	Year	Mint	VG	Notes
Hammersmith	LP	Mercury	SRM11040	1975	£12	£5	US
It's For You	LP	Mercury	SRM11102	1976	£10	£4	US

HAMMERSMITH GORILLAS

Title	Format	Label	Cat. No.	Year	Mint	VG	Notes
You Really Got Me	7"	Penny Farthing	PEN849	1974	£6	£2.50	

HAMMILL, PETER

Title	Format	Label	Cat. No.	Year	Mint	VG	Notes
Birthday Special	7"	Charisma	CB245	1975	£5	£2	
Chameleon In The Shadow Of The Night	LP	Charisma	CAS1067	1973	£12	£5	
Crying Wolf	7"	Charisma	PH001	1978	£20	£10	*promo*
Fool's Mate	LP	Charisma	CAS1037	1971	£15	£6	
Future Now	LP	Charisma	CAS1137	1978	£10	£4	
In Camera	LP	Charisma	CAS1089	1974	£10	£4	
Nadir's Last Chance	LP	Charisma	CAS1099	1975	£10	£4	
Over	LP	Charisma	CAS1125	1977	£10	£4	
PH7	LP	Charisma	CAS1146	1979	£10	£4	
Polaroid	7"	Charisma	CB339	1979	£6	£2.50	*credited to Rikki Nadir*
Silent Corner And The Empty Stage	LP	Charisma	CAS1083	1974	£12	£5	
Vision	LP	GIR	92111016	1978	£10	£4	*US compilation*

HAMMOND, JOHN

Title	Format	Label	Cat. No.	Year	Mint	VG	Notes
Best Of (Southern Fried)	LP	Vanguard	VSD11/12	1974	£12	£5	*double*
Big City Blues	LP	Fontana	TFL6046	1964	£25	£10	
Brown Eyed Handsome Man	7"	Atlantic	584190	1968	£5	£2	
Country Blues	LP	Vanguard	VRS/VSD79198	1965	£20	£8	US
I Can Tell	LP	Atlantic	SD8152	1968	£20	£8	US
I Live The Life I Love	7"	Fontana	TF560	1965	£8	£4	
I'm Satisfied	LP	CBS	65051	1972	£15	£6	
John Hammond	LP	Vanguard	VRS9132	1963	£20	£8	US
Little Big Man	LP	CBS	30545	1971	£15	£6	US
Mirrors	LP	Vanguard	VRS/VSD79245	1968	£20	£8	US
So Many Roads	LP	Fontana	TFL6059	1965	£20	£8	
Sooner Or Later	LP	Atlantic	SD8206	1968	£20	£8	US
Source Point	LP	CBS	64365	1971	£15	£6	
Southern Fried	LP	Atlantic	SD8251	1970	£15	£6	US
When I Need	LP	CBS	30549	1971	£15	£6	US

HAMNER, CURLEY

Twistin' And Turnin'	7"	Felsted	SD80061	1959	£5	£2	

HAMPSHIRE, SUSAN

When Love Is True	7"	Decca	F12185	1965	£4	£1.50	

HAMPTON, LIONEL

All American Award Concert	LP	Brunswick	LAT8086	1956	£15	£6	
Apollo Hall Concert 1954	LP	Philips	BBL7015	1955	£15	£6	
At The Pasadena Auditorium	7" EP	Vogue	EPV1161	1957	£5	£2	
At The Pasadena Auditorium	LP	Vogue	LAE12014	1956	£15	£6	
Hamp 1956	LP	Oriole	MG20012	1956	£15	£6	
Hamp's Big Band	LP	Audio Fidelity	AFLP1913/ AFSD5913	1960	£12	£5	
Hamp's Boogie Woogie	10" LP	Brunswick	LA8527	1951	£25	£10	
Hamp's Boogie Woogie	7"	Vogue	V2406	1957	£12	£6	
Hamp's Boogie Woogie	7" EP	Columbia	SEB10108	1959	£5	£2	
Hampton And The Old World	LP	Philips	BBL7119	1957	£15	£6	
High And The Mighty	LP	Columbia	33CX10146	1959	£15	£6	
Hot Mallets	LP	HMV	CLP1023	1955	£15	£6	
In Paris Vol. 1	10" LP	Felsted	EDL87007	1954	£25	£10	
In Paris Vol. 2	10" LP	Felsted	EDL87008	1954	£25	£10	
Jazz Flamenco	LP	RCA	RD27006	1957	£15	£6	
Jazz Time Paris Vol. 1	10" LP	Vogue	LDE043	1954	£25	£10	
Jivin' The Vibes	LP	Camden	CDN129	1959	£10	£4	
Lionel Hampton	LP	Felsted	PDL85006	1956	£20	£8	
Lionel Hampton And His All Stars	LP	Columbia	33CX10086	1957	£20	£8	
Lionel Hampton And His Orchestra	7" EP	MGM	MGMEP552	1956	£5	£2	
Lionel Hampton And Stan Getz	LP	Columbia	33CX10041	1956	£30	£15	
Lionel Hampton Group	LP	Vogue	LAE12034	1957	£15	£6	
Lionel Hampton Orchestra	7" EP	Oriole	EP7046	1962	£5	£2	
Lionel Hampton Plays Love Songs	LP	HMV	CLP1136	1957	£15	£6	
Lionel Hampton Quartet	10" LP	Columbia	33C9011	1955	£25	£10	
Lionel Hampton Quartet	LP	Columbia	33CX10006	1955	£25	£10	
Lionel Hampton Vol. 3	10" LP	Vogue	LDE063	1954	£25	£10	
Lionel Hampton–Art Tatum–Buddy Rich Trio	LP	Columbia	33CX10045	1956	£20	£8	
Many Splendored Vibes	LP	Columbia	33SX1500	1962	£10	£4	
Moonglow	10" LP	Brunswick	LA8551	1952	£25	£10	
New French Sound Vol. 1	LP	Felsted	PDL85002	1955	£15	£6	
New Sounds From Europe Vol. 2	10" LP	Vogue	LDE051	1954	£25	£10	
One And Only Lionel Hampton	LP	Fontana	Z4053	1961	£10	£4	
Open House	LP	Camden	CDN138	1960	£10	£4	
Perdido	7"	Vogue	V2405	1957	£10	£5	

HAMPTON, SLIDE

Jazz With A Twist	LP	London	HAK/SHK8008	1962	£12	£5	

HANCOCK, HERBIE

Jazz pianist Herbie Hancock has tried his hand at a particularly wide range of styles over the years, from straightforward modern jazz to hiphop. The trilogy of early-seventies recordings, *Mwandishi*, *Crossings* and *Sextant* finds him entering the composed electric jazz world defined by Weather Report. Typically, they are amongst the most impressive jazz recordings of the period, and arguably they are Hancock's personal best. *Crossings* is especially fine. *Treasure Chest* is an anthology of music taken from these electric jazz recordings and from Hancock's sixties work. It also includes a short track whose music is taken from *Crossings*, but in a remixed form not otherwise available.

Blind Man, Blind Man	7"	Blue Note	451887	1963	£6	£2.50	
Blow-Up	LP	MGM	C8039	1967	£60	£30	*with the Yardbirds*
Crossings	LP	Warner Bros	K46164	1972	£12	£5	
Death Wish	LP	CBS	80546	1974	£12	£5	
Direct Steps	LP	CBS Sony	30AP1032	1979	£25	£10	*Japanese*
Empyrean Isles	LP	Blue Note	BLP/BST84175	1965	£25	£10	
Fat Albert Rotunda	LP	Warner Bros	K46039	1974	£15	£6	
Fat Albert Rotunda	LP	Warner Bros	WS1834	1971	£20	£8	
Fat Mama	7"	Warner Bros	WB7358	1970	£4	£1.50	
Head Hunters	LP	CBS	65928	1973	£10	£4	
Inventions And Dimensions	LP	Blue Note	BLP/BST84147	1964	£25	£10	
Live In Japan	LP	CBS Sony	98/99	1975	£30	£15	*Japanese double*
Live Under The Sky	LP	CBS Sony	1037875	1976	£20	£8	*Japanese*
Maiden Voyage	LP	Blue Note	BLP/BST84195	1966	£25	£10	
Man Child	LP	CBS	69185	1975	£10	£4	
Mwandishi	LP	Warner Bros	K46077	1971	£12	£5	
My Point Of View	LP	Blue Note	BLP/BST84126	1964	£25	£10	
Prisoner	LP	Blue Note	BST84321	1969	£15	£6	
Sextant	LP	CBS	65582	1972	£12	£5	
Speak Like A Child	LP	Blue Note	BST84279	1968	£15	£6	
Takin' Off	LP	Blue Note	BLP/BST84109	1964	£30	£15	
Thrust	LP	CBS	80193	1974	£10	£4	
Treasure Chest	LP	Warner Bros	2WS2807	1974	£20	£8	*US double*

HANCOCK, SHEILA

Putting Out The Dustbin	LP	Transatlantic	TRA106	1962	£12	£5	

HANCOCK, TONY

Blood Donor	7" EP	Pye	NEP24175	1963	£5	£2	
Blood Donor & Radio Ham	LP	Pye	NPL18068	1961	£10	£4	
Face To Face	LP	Piccadilly	FTF38500	1963	£50	£25	
It's Hancock	LP	Decca	LK4740	1965	£10	£4	

Title	Format	Label	Cat. No.	Year	Mint	VG	Notes
Little Pieces Of Hancock	7" EP	Pye	NEP24146	1961	£5	£2	
Little Pieces Of Hancock Vol. 2	7" EP	Pye	NEP24161	1962	£5	£2	
Pieces Of Hancock	LP	Pye	NPL18054	1960	£10	£4	
Publicity Photograph	7" EP	Pye	NEP24170	1963	£5	£2	
This Is Hancock	LP	Pye	NPL18045	1960	£10	£4	

HAND, OWEN

Title	Format	Label	Cat. No.	Year	Mint	VG	Notes
Something New	LP	Transatlantic	TRA127	1966	£75	£37.50	

HANDLE, JOHNNY

Title	Format	Label	Cat. No.	Year	Mint	VG	Notes
Collier Lad	LP	Topic	12TS270	1975	£10	£4	
Stottin' Doon The Waall	7" EP	Topic	TOP78	1962	£10	£5	

HANDSOME BEASTS

Title	Format	Label	Cat. No.	Year	Mint	VG	Notes
All Riot Now	7"	Heavy Metal	HEAVY1	1981	£4	£1.50	
Breaker	7"	Heavy Metal	HEAVY2	1981	£4	£1.50	
Sweeties	7"	Heavy Metal	HEAVY11	1982	£4	£1.50	

HANDY, JOHN

Title	Format	Label	Cat. No.	Year	Mint	VG	Notes
Concert Ensemble	LP	CBS	63387	1968	£12	£5	

HANDY, WAYNE

Title	Format	Label	Cat. No.	Year	Mint	VG	Notes
Say Yeah	7"	London	HL8547	1958	£400	£250	*best auctioned*

HANFORD, PAUL

Title	Format	Label	Cat. No.	Year	Mint	VG	Notes
Minute You're Gone	7"	Oriole	CB1866	1963	£5	£2	

HANGMEN

Title	Format	Label	Cat. No.	Year	Mint	VG	Notes
Bitter Sweet	LP	Monument	SLP18077	1966	£15	£6	*US*

HANK & THE MELLOWMEN

Title	Format	Label	Cat. No.	Year	Mint	VG	Notes
Santa Anno	7"	Lyntone	LYN153/4	196–	£4	£1.50	*flexi*
So In Love With You	7"	Lyntone	LYN201	196–	£4	£1.50	*flexi*

HANLY, MICHAEL

Title	Format	Label	Cat. No.	Year	Mint	VG	Notes
As I Went Over Blackwater	LP	Mulligan	LUN040	1980	£10	£4	*Irish*
Celtic Folkweave	LP	Polydor	2908013	1974	£40	£20	*Irish, with Michael O'Donnel*
Kiss In The Morning Early	LP	Mulligan	LUN005	1976	£10	£4	*Irish*

HANNA, BOBBY

Title	Format	Label	Cat. No.	Year	Mint	VG	Notes
Blame It On Me	7"	Decca	F12695	1967	£5	£2	
Written On The Wind	7"	Decca	F12783	1968	£5	£2	

HANNA, GEORGE & SARAH ANNE O'NEILL

Title	Format	Label	Cat. No.	Year	Mint	VG	Notes
On The Shores Of Lough Neagh	LP	Topic	12TS372	1978	£12	£5	

HANNA, JOSH

Title	Format	Label	Cat. No.	Year	Mint	VG	Notes
Shut Your Mouth	7"	Decca	F12532	1966	£8	£4	

HANNA, KEN

Title	Format	Label	Cat. No.	Year	Mint	VG	Notes
Ken Hanna Orchestra	10" LP	London	HAPB1031	1954	£10	£4	

HANNA BARBERA

Title	Format	Label	Cat. No.	Year	Mint	VG	Notes
Flintstones – Goldilocks & The Bearosauruses	7" EP	Hanna Barbera	HBE3	1966	£5	£2	
Flintstones – Hansel And Gretel	7" EP	Hanna Barbera	HBE1	1966	£5	£2	
Flintstones – Mary Poppins	7" EP	Hanna Barbera	HBE6	1966	£5	£2	
Flintstones – Three Little Pigs	7" EP	Hanna Barbera	HBE9	1966	£5	£2	
Snagglepuss Tales – Wizard Of Oz	7" EP	Hanna Barbera	HBE4	1966	£5	£2	
Top Cat – Robin Hood	7" EP	Hanna Barbera	HBE7	1966	£5	£2	
Uncle Remus – Brer Rabbit & The Tar Baby	7" EP	Hanna Barbera	HBE2	1966	£5	£2	
Yogi Bear & Boo Boo – Jack & The Beanstalk	7" EP	Hanna Barbera	HBE5	1966	£5	£2	
Yogi Bear & Boo Boo – Little Red Riding Hood	7" EP	Hanna Barbera	HBE8	1966	£5	£2	

HANNIBAL

Hannibal's only album is definitely a neglected gem from the progressive era. Occasionally let down a little by the lyrics, the music is nevertheless sparkling and inventive, these qualities being enhanced by fluent jazz-rock playing from all concerned. The keyboard player turned up on a few Roy Wood records, but remarkably none of the members of Hannibal was able to sustain a career in music.

Title	Format	Label	Cat. No.	Year	Mint	VG	Notes
Hannibal	LP	B&C	CAS1022	1970	£30	£15	
Winds Of Change	7"	B&C	HB1	1974	£4	£1.50	

HANNIBAL, LANCE

Title	Format	Label	Cat. No.	Year	Mint	VG	Notes
Read The News	7"	Blue Cat	BS148	1968	£4	£1.50	*Rico B side*

HANOI ROCKS

Title	Format	Label	Cat. No.	Year	Mint	VG	Notes
Back To The Mystery City	LP	Lick	LICLP1	1983	£10	£4	*white vinyl*
Best Of Hanoi Rocks	CD	Lick	LICCD8	1988	£12	£5	

Don't You Ever Leave Me	12"	CBS	WA4885	1984	**£10**	**£4**	*picture disc*
Don't You Ever Leave Me	12"	CBS	TA4885	1984	**£8**	**£4**	
Malibu Beach	7"	Lick	LIXPD1	1983	**£8**	**£4**	*picture disc*
Self Destruction Blues	LP	Lick	LICLPPD4	1986	**£10**	**£4**	*picture disc*
Underwater World	12"	CBS	WA4732	1984	**£10**	**£5**	*picture disc*
Underwater World	12"	CBS	TA4732	1984	**£6**	**£2.50**	
Up Around The Bend	12"	CBS	TA4513	1984	**£6**	**£2.50**	*with transfer*
Up Around The Bend	7"	CBS	A4513	1984	**£5**	**£2**	*withy transfer*
Up Around The Bend	7"	CBS	DA4513	1984	**£10**	**£5**	*double*

HANSON

Mmm Bop	CD-s	Mercury	5745012	1997	**£8**	**£4**	

HANSSON & KARLSSON

Man At The Moon	LP	Polydor	46265	1969	**£15**	**£6**	*Swedish*
Monument	LP	Polydor	46260	1969	**£12**	**£5**	
Rex	LP	Polydor	46264	1968	**£15**	**£6**	*Swedish*
Swedish Underground	LP	Polydor	184196	1967	**£15**	**£6**	

HANUMAN

Hanuman	LP	Kuckuck	2375012	1972	**£15**	**£6**	*German*

HA'PENNYS

Love Is Not The Same	LP	Fersch	1110	1968	**£150**	**£75**	*US*

HAPPENINGS

Go Away Little Girl	7"	Fontana	TF766	1966	**£4**	**£1.50**	
Go Away Little Girl	7" EP	Vogue	INT18100	1966	**£6**	**£2.50**	*French*
Golden Hits	LP	B.T.Puppy	BTLPS1004	1968	**£12**	**£5**	*US*
Greatest Hits	LP	Jubilee	JGS8030	1969	**£12**	**£5**	*US*
Happenings	LP	B.T.Puppy	(S)1001	1966	**£15**	**£6**	*US*
I Got Rhythm	7" EP	B.T.Puppy	701	1967	**£6**	**£2.50**	*French*
Piece Of Mind	LP	Jubilee	JGS8028	1969	**£12**	**£5**	*US*
Psycle	LP	B.T.Puppy	(S)1003	1967	**£15**	**£6**	*US*
See You In September	7"	Fontana	TF735	1966	**£4**	**£1.50**	
See You In September	7" EP	Vogue	INT18090	1966	**£6**	**£2.50**	*French, B side by Jimmy Mays & Soul Breed*
See You In September	LP	Fontana	TL5383	1967	**£12**	**£5**	

HAPPENINGS & TOKENS

Back To Back	LP	B.T.Puppy	(S)1002	1967	**£15**	**£6**	*US*

HAPPY DRAGON BAND

Happy Dragon Band	LP	Fiddlers Music Compa		1978	**£60**	**£30**	*US*

HAPPY FAMILY

Puritans	7"	4AD	AD204	1982	**£5**	**£2**	

HAPPY MAGAZINE

Satisfied Street	7"	Polydor	56233	1968	**£5**	**£2**	
Who Belongs To You	7"	Polydor	56307	1968	**£4**	**£1.50**	

HAPPY MONDAYS

It would be offending the sensibilities of no one – least of all the man himself – to suggest that Shaun Ryder's success as a lead singer has never depended on his ablity to carry a tune. With his out-of-key rants, masquerading as melodies, and with support provided by a bunch of musicians who considered having a good time to be far more important than merely making music, it might seem surprising that Ryder has proved to be one of the more influential rock figures of the last fifteen years. All those who infer from Ryder's frequently loutish behaviour that he and his cohorts are no more than talentless oafs have to reckon with the fact that the Happy Mondays have managed to produce several recordings under Ryder's leadership that are fast approaching the status of classics.

Judge Fudge	CD-s	Factory	FACD332	1991	**£5**	**£2**	
Kinky Afro	CD-s	Factory	FACD302	1990	**£5**	**£2**	
Loose Fit	CD-s	Factory	FACD312	1991	**£5**	**£2**	
Madchester, Rave On	CD-s	Factory	FACD242	1989	**£5**	**£2**	
Peel Sessions	CD-s	Strange Fruit	SFPSCD077	1990	**£5**	**£2**	
Peel Sessions 2	CD-s	Strange Fruit	SFPSCD084	1991	**£5**	**£2**	
Squirrel And G Man . . .	LP	Factory	FACT170	1987	**£10**	**£4**	*plastic sleeve, with 'Desmond'*
Step On	CD-s	Factory	FACD272	1990	**£5**	**£2**	
Step On (Melon Mix)	12"	Factory	FAC272	1990	**£10**	**£5**	*1 sided promo*
Sunshine And Love EP	CD-s	Factory	FACD372	1992	**£5**	**£2**	
Wrote For Luck	CD-s	Factory	FACD232	1989	**£5**	**£2**	
Yes Please	CD-s	Factory	FACD420D	1992	**£5**	**£2**	

HAPSHASH & THE COLOURED COAT

Colinda	7"	Liberty	LBF15188	1969	**£10**	**£5**	
Human Host And The Heavy Metal Kids	LP	Minit	MLL/MLS40001E	1967	**£60**	**£30**	*red vinyl*
Human Host And The Heavy Metal Kids	LP	Liberty	MLS40001E	1967	**£40**	**£20**	
Western Flyer	LP	Liberty	LBL/LBS83212	1969	**£20**	**£8**	

HARBOUR LITES

I Would Give All	7"	HMV	POP1465	1965	**£4**	**£1.50**	
Run For Your Life	7"	Fontana	TF682	1966	**£5**	**£2**	

HARD CORPS

Title	Format	Label	Cat. No.	Year	Value	Value	Notes
Dirty	12"	Hard Corps	HC01	1984	**£30**	**£15**	
Dirty	12"	Survival	SUR12026	1984	**£8**	**£4**	
Dirty	7"	Survival	SUR026	1984	**£6**	**£2.50**	
Je suis passée	12"	Polydor	HARDA1	1985	**£20**	**£10**	*plastic sleeve, poster*
Je suis passée	12"	Immaculate	12IMMAC2	1985	**£8**	**£4**	
Metal And Flesh	CD	Concrete Productions	CPPRODCD011	1990	**£20**	**£8**	
Metal And Flesh	LP	Concrete Productions	CPPRODLP011	1990	**£15**	**£6**	*clear vinyl*
To Breathe	12"	Polydor	HARDX2	1985	**£30**	**£15**	
To Breathe	7"	Polydor	HARD2	1985	**£25**	**£12.50**	

HARD MEAT

Title	Format	Label	Cat. No.	Year	Value	Value	Notes
Hard Meat	LP	Warner Bros	WS1852	1970	**£12**	**£5**	
Rain	7"	Island	WIP6066	1969	**£6**	**£2.50**	
Through A Window	LP	Warner Bros	WS1879	1970	**£25**	**£10**	

HARD ROAD

Title	Format	Label	Cat. No.	Year	Value	Value	Notes
No Problem	LP	Goodstuff	LP1002	1979	**£20**	**£8**	

HARD STUFF

Title	Format	Label	Cat. No.	Year	Value	Value	Notes
Bolex Dementia	LP	Purple	TPSA7507	1973	**£20**	**£8**	
Bullet Proof	LP	Purple	TPSA7505	1972	**£20**	**£8**	
Inside Your Life	7"	Purple	PUR116	1973	**£5**	**£2**	
Jay Time	7"	Purple	PUR103	1972	**£5**	**£2**	

HARD TIMES

Title	Format	Label	Cat. No.	Year	Value	Value	Notes
Blew Mind	LP	World Pacific	WPS21867	1968	**£15**	**£6**	*US*

HARD TRAVELLIN'

Title	Format	Label	Cat. No.	Year	Value	Value	Notes
Hard Travellin'	LP	Flams Ltd	PR1065	1971	**£100**	**£50**	

HARD WATER

Title	Format	Label	Cat. No.	Year	Value	Value	Notes
Hard Water	LP	Capitol	ST2954	1968	**£20**	**£8**	*US*

HARDCAKE SPECIAL

Title	Format	Label	Cat. No.	Year	Value	Value	Notes
Hardcake Special	LP	Brain	1060	1974	**£10**	**£4**	*German*

HARDEN, WILBUR

Title	Format	Label	Cat. No.	Year	Value	Value	Notes
Mainstream 1958	LP	London	LTZC15159	1959	**£20**	**£8**	*with John Coltrane*

HARDIN, EDDIE

Title	Format	Label	Cat. No.	Year	Value	Value	Notes
Home Is Where You Find It	LP	Decca	TXS106	1972	**£10**	**£4**	

HARDIN, TIM

Tim Hardin's fragile voice made his own interpretations of his best material the most moving versions of all – and he wrote some classic songs; 'Hang On To A Dream', 'If I Were A Carpenter' and 'Reason To Believe' among them. Particularly moving is his 'Suite For Susan Moore and Damian', which is a kind of stream-of-consciousness tribute to his wife and child. It was a real tragedy when this precious talent succumbed to heroin addiction in 1980.

Title	Format	Label	Cat. No.	Year	Value	Value	Notes
Bird On A Wire	LP	CBS	64335	1970	**£10**	**£4**	
Hang On To a Dream	7"	Verve	VS1504	1966	**£4**	**£1.50**	
Live In Concert	LP	Verve	(S)VLP6010	1968	**£15**	**£6**	
Suite For Susan Moore & Damian	LP	CBS	63571	1970	**£25**	**£10**	
This Is Tim Hardin	LP	Atco	587/588082	1967	**£20**	**£8**	
Tim Hardin 1	LP	Verve	(S)VLP5018	1966	**£20**	**£8**	
Tim Hardin 1/Tim Hardin 2	LP	Verve	2683048	1974	**£15**	**£6**	*double*
Tim Hardin 2	LP	Verve	(S)VLP6002	1967	**£20**	**£8**	
Tim Hardin 4	LP	Verve	(S)VLP6016	1969	**£15**	**£6**	

HARDIN & YORK

Title	Format	Label	Cat. No.	Year	Value	Value	Notes
For The World	LP	Decca	SKL5095	1971	**£10**	**£4**	
Tomorrow Today	LP	Bell	SBLL125	1969	**£10**	**£4**	
World's Smallest Big Band	LP	Bell	SBLL136	1970	**£10**	**£4**	

HARDING, RICHARD

Title	Format	Label	Cat. No.	Year	Value	Value	Notes
Jezebel	7"	HMV	POP887	1961	**£15**	**£7.50**	

HARDMAN, ROSEMARY

Title	Format	Label	Cat. No.	Year	Value	Value	Notes
Eagle Over Blue Mountain	LP	Plant Life	PLR014	1978	**£12**	**£5**	
Firebird	LP	Trailer	LER2075	1972	**£20**	**£8**	
Jerseyburger	LP	Alida Star Cottage	ASC7754	1975	**£150**	**£75**	
Queen Of Hearts	LP	Folk Heritage	FHR002M	1969	**£125**	**£62.50**	
Second Season Came	LP	Trailer	LER3018	1971	**£20**	**£8**	*with Bob Axford*
Stopped In My Tracks	LP	Plant Life	PLR023	1980	**£12**	**£5**	
Weakness Of Eve	LP	Plant Life	PLR053	1983	**£12**	**£5**	

HARDY, DAVE

Title	Format	Label	Cat. No.	Year	Value	Value	Notes
Leaving The Dales	LP	Red Rag	RRR008	1976	**£30**	**£15**	

HARDY, FRANÇOISE

As one of France's top sixties pop-music stars, Françoise Hardy also gained a considerable following in Britain. The EPs *C'est fab* and *C'est Françoise* in particular sold well enough to enter the lower reaches of the charts – a rare feat for records sung in a language other than English.

After some years of retirement from the music business, Françoise Hardy was persuaded to add vocals to a version of Blur's 'To The End', the success of which encouraged her to record a whole new album – the excellent *Le Danger.*

All Because Of You	7"	United Artists	UP35070	1969	£4	**£1.50**	
All Over The World	7"	Pye	7N15802	1965	£4	**£1.50**	
Autumn Rendezvous	7"	Vogue	VRS7014	1966	£4	**£1.50**	
Autumn Rendezvous	7" EP	Vogue	VRE5018	1967	£5	**£2**	
C'est Fab	7" EP	Pye	NEP24188	1964	£6	**£2.50**	
C'est Françoise	7" EP	Pye	NEP24193	1964	£6	**£2.50**	
Catch A Falling Star	7"	Pye	7N15612	1964	£4	**£1.50**	
Chante En Allemand	7" EP	Vogue	VRE5012	1966	£5	**£2**	
Comment Te Dire Adieu	7"	United Artists	UP35011	1969	£4	**£1.50**	
Dis Lui Non	7" EP	Vogue	VRE5003	1965	£5	**£2**	
En Anglais	LP	United Artists	ULP1207	1968	£15	**£6**	
Et Même	7"	Pye	7N15740	1964	£4	**£1.50**	
Françoise	7" EP	Vogue	VRE5000	1965	£5	**£2**	
Françoise	LP	Vogue	VRL3028	1967	£12	**£5**	
Françoise Hardy	7" EP	Vogue	VRE5001	1965	£5	**£2**	
Françoise Hardy	LP	Vogue	VRL3000	1965	£12	**£5**	
Françoise Hardy	LP	Vogue	VRL3021	1966	£15	**£6**	
Françoise Hardy	LP	Pye	NPL18094	1964	£12	**£5**	
Françoise Sings In English	7" EP	Pye	NEP24192	1964	£6	**£2.50**	
Françoise Hardy Sings In English	LP	Vogue	VRL3025	1966	£12	**£5**	
In Vogue	LP	Pye	NPL18099	1964	£12	**£5**	
Just Call And I'll Be There	7"	Vogue	VRS7001	1966	£4	**£1.50**	
L'Amitié	7" EP	Vogue	VRE5015	1966	£5	**£2**	
La Maison Où J'ai Grandi	7"	Vogue	VRS7011	1966	£4	**£1.50**	
Le Meilleur de Françoise Hardy	LP	Vogue	VRL3023	1966	£12	**£5**	
Le Temps Des Souvenirs	7" EP	Vogue	VRE5008	1965	£5	**£2**	
Mon Amie La Rose	7" EP	Vogue	VRE5017	1967	£5	**£2**	
Now You Want To Be Loved	7"	United Artists	UP1208	1968	£4	**£1.50**	
On Se Quitte Toujours	7"	Vogue	VRS7026	1967	£4	**£1.50**	
One-Nine-Seven-Zero	LP	United Artists	UAS29046	1970	£12	**£5**	
Pourtant Tu M'aimes	7"	Pye	7N15696	1964	£4	**£1.50**	
Si C'est Ça	7"	Vogue	VRS7020	1966	£4	**£1.50**	
So Many Friends	7"	Vogue	VRS7004	1966	£4	**£1.50**	
Soon Is Slipping Away	7"	United Artists	UP35105	1970	£4	**£1.50**	
This Little Heart	7"	Vogue	VRS7010	1966	£4	**£1.50**	
Tous Les Garçons Et Les Filles	7"	Pye	7N15653	1964	£4	**£1.50**	
Voilà	7"	Vogue	VRS7025	1966	£4	**£1.50**	
Voilà!	LP	Vogue	VRL3031	1967	£12	**£5**	
Will You Love Me Tomorrow	7"	United Artists	UP2253	1968	£4	**£1.50**	

HARE, COLIN

Colin Hare was the second guitarist with the Honeybus, whose best material was written by the first, Pete Dello. Sadly, Hare's solo album rather shows why this was.

Didn't I Tell You	7"	Warner Bros	K16203	1972	£4	**£1.50**	
Grannie Grannie	7"	Penny Farthing	PEN736	1970	£4	**£1.50**	
March Hare	LP	Penny Farthing	PELS516	1971	£30	**£15**	
Underground Girl	7"	Penny Farthing	PEN750	1971	£4	**£1.50**	

HARGRAVE, RON

Latch On	7"	MGM	MGM956	1957	£2000	**£1400**	*best auctioned*

HARLEY, STEVE

Big Big Deal	7"	EMI	EMI2233	1974	£10	**£5**	
Lighthouse	CD-s	Food For Thought	no number	1993	£6	**£2.50**	*promo only*

HARLOWE, RAY & GYP FOX

First Rays	LP	Water Wheel	WR711	1978	£40	**£20**	*US*

HARMONIA

De Luxe	LP	Brain	1073	1975	£15	**£6**	*German*
Harmonia	LP	Brain	1044	1974	£15	**£6**	*German*

HARMONIANS

Music Street	7"	Ackee	ACK107	1970	£4	**£1.50**	

HARMONICA FATS

Tore Up	7"	Stateside	SS184	1963	£10	**£5**	
Tore Up	7"	Action	ACT4507	1968	£8	**£4**	

HARMONICA FRANK

In the pages of *Mystery Train*, the acclaimed sociological study of American themes as revealed in the work of various rock musicians, Greil Marcus chooses the almost forgotten figure of white bluesman Frank Floyd to illustrate his thesis. As it happens, the single that Harmonica Frank recorded for Sun is one of the rarest releases on a particularly collectable label – anyone in possession of a copy can virtually name their own price.

Rockin' Chair Daddy	7"	Sun	205	1954	£1500	**£1000**	*US, best auctioned*

HARMONISERS

Mother Hen	7"	Duke	DU32	1969	£5	£2	Winston Sinclair B side

HARMONIZING FOUR

Who Knows	7"	Rymska	RA102	1966	£5	£2	

HARMONY

Harmony	LP	Breakthrough		1972	£40	£20	

HARMONY FLAMES

USA Hit Parade No. 1	7" EP	Fontana	TFE17152	1959	£5	£2	

HARMONY GRASS

This Is Us	LP	RCA	SF8034	1970	£10	£4	

HARNELL, JOE

Dance The Bossa Nova	7" EP	London	RER1344	1962	£6	£2.50	

HARNER, BILLY

Trigger Finger	LP	Blue Horizon	2431013	1972	£12	£5	
What About The Music	7"	Kama Sutra	2013029	1971	£4	£1.50	
What About The Music	7"	Kama Sutra	2013029	1971	£250	£150	with instrumental version

HARPER, BUD

Mr Soul	7"	Vocalion	VP9252	1965	£15	£7.50	

HARPER, DON

Dr Who Theme	7"	Columbia	DB9023	1973	£15	£7.50	
Homo Electronicus	LP	Columbia	SCX6559	1974	£20	£8	

HARPER, HERBIE

Herbie Harper Octet	10" LP	London	LZN14031	1956	£25	£10	

HARPER, JOE 'HARMONICA'

Lazy Train	7"	MGM	MGM983	1958	£4	£1.50	

HARPER, MIKE

You've Got Too Much Going For You	7"	Concord	CON026	1970	£10	£5	

HARPER, ROY

Born In Captivity	LP	Hardup	PUB5002	1984	£25	£10	
Bullinamingvase	LP	Harvest	SHSP4060	1977	£12	£5	with 'Watford Gap'
Bullinamingvase	LP	Harvest	SHSP4060	1977	£20	£8	with 7" (PSR407)
Come Out Fighting Ghengis Smith	LP	CBS	(S)BPG63184	1967	£20	£8	
Commercial Break	LP	Harvest	SHSP4077	1977	£200	£100	test pressing
Descendants Of Smith	CD	EMI	CDEMC3524	1988	£12	£5	
Flashes From The Archives Of Oblivion	LP	Harvest	SHDW405	1974	£20	£8	double
Flat Baroque And Beserk	LP	Harvest	SHVL776	1970	£10	£4	
Flat Baroque And Beserk	CD	Hard Up	HUCD003	1993	£12	£5	boxed, with 40 page booklet & poster, signed
Folkjokeopus	LP	Liberty	LBS83231	1969	£20	£8	
Introducing Roy Harper	LP	Chrysalis	PRO620	1977	£30	£15	US promo
Life Goes By	7"	CBS	3371	1968	£10	£5	
Lifemask	LP	Harvest	SHVL808	1973	£10	£4	
Midspring Dithering	7"	CBS	203001	1967	£15	£7.50	
Mrs Space	7"	Harvest	PSR408	1977	£4	£1.50	promo
Playing Games	7"	Harvest	HAR5203	1980	£4	£1.50	
Return Of The Sophisticated Beggar	LP	Youngblood	SYB7	1970	£20	£8	
Return Of The Sophisticated Beggar	LP	Birth	RAB3	1972	£15	£6	
Sail Away	7"	Harvest	HAR5140	1977	£4	£1.50	
Sophisticated Beggar	LP	Strike	JHL105	1967	£200	£100	
Stormcock	LP	Harvest	SHVL789	1971	£10	£4	
Take Me In Your Eyes	7"	Strike	JH304	1966	£25	£12.50	picture sleeve
Valentine	LP	Harvest	SHSP4027	1974	£12	£5	lyric booklet
Work Of Heart	LP	Awareness	AWL1002	1988	£10	£4	with 2 singles

HARPERS BIZARRE

59th Street Bridge Song	7"	Warner Bros	WB5890	1967	£4	£1.50	
59th Street Bridge Song	7" EP	Warner Bros	WEP1454	1967	£20	£10	French
Anything Goes	7"	Warner Bros	WB7388	1970	£4	£1.50	
Anything Goes	7"	Warner Bros	WB7063	1967	£4	£1.50	
Anything Goes	LP	Warner Bros	WS1716	1967	£15	£6	US
Battle Of New Orleans	7"	Warner Bros	WB7223	1968	£4	£1.50	
Best Of Harpers Bizarre	LP	Warner Bros	K56044	1974	£10	£4	
Come To The Sunshine	7"	Warner Bros	WB7528	1967	£4	£1.50	
Cotton Candy Sandman	7"	Warner Bros	WB7172	1968	£4	£1.50	
Feelin' Groovy	LP	Warner Bros	WS1693	1967	£15	£6	US
Harpers Bizarre 4	LP	Warner Bros	WS1784	1969	£15	£6	US
I Love You Alice B. Toklas	7"	Warner Bros	WB7238	1969	£4	£1.50	
Secret Life Of Harpers Bizarre	LP	Warner Bros	W(S)1739	1968	£12	£5	

HARPO, SLIM

Baby Scratch My Back	7"	Stateside	SS491	1966	£8	£4	
Baby Scratch My Back	LP	Excello	LP8005	1966	£25	£10	US

Title	Format	Label	Number	Year	Mint	Good	Notes
Best Of Slim Harpo	LP	Excello	LP8010	1969	**£12**	**£5**	*US*
Blues Hangover	LP	Flyright	LP520	1976	**£10**	**£4**	
Folsom Prison Blues	7"	Blue Horizon	573175	1970	**£15**	**£7.50**	
He Knew The Blues	LP	Sonet	SNTF769	1978	**£10**	**£4**	
He Knew The Blues	LP	Blue Horizon	763854	1970	**£50**	**£25**	
I'm A King Bee	7"	Stateside	SS557	1966	**£12**	**£6**	
I'm Gonna Keep What I've Got	7"	President	PT164	1968	**£4**	**£1.50**	
I'm Your Breadmaker Baby	7"	Stateside	SS581	1967	**£10**	**£5**	
Long Drink Of The Blues	LP	Stateside	SL10135	1965	**£40**	**£20**	*with Lightnin' Slim*
Raining In My Heart	7"	Pye	7N25098	1961	**£6**	**£2.50**	
Raining In My Heart	7"	Pye	7N25220	1963	**£8**	**£4**	
Raining In My Heart	LP	Excello	LP8003	1961	**£40**	**£20**	*US*
Shake Your Hips	7"	Stateside	SS527	1966	**£15**	**£7.50**	
Slim Harpo Knew The Blues	LP	Excello	LP8013	1970	**£12**	**£5**	*US*
Something Inside Me	7"	Liberty	LBF15170	1968	**£8**	**£4**	*Papa Lightfoot B side*
Tip On In	7"	President	PT187	1968	**£4**	**£1.50**	
Tip On In	LP	President	PTL1017	1968	**£15**	**£6**	
Trigger Finger	LP	Blue Horizon	2431013	1971	**£60**	**£30**	

HARRIER

Title	Format	Label	Number	Year	Mint	Good	Notes
Out On The Street	12"	Black Horse	HARR1T	1984	**£8**	**£4**	

HARRIOTT, DERRICK

Title	Format	Label	Number	Year	Mint	Good	Notes
Another Lonely Night	7"	Big Shot	BI511	1969	**£4**	**£1.50**	
Be True	7"	Blue Beat	BB178	1963	**£12**	**£6**	
Best Of Derrick Harriott	LP	Trojan	TTL43	1970	**£20**	**£8**	
Best Of Derrick Harriott	LP	Island	ILP928	1965	**£100**	**£50**	
Best Of Derrick Harriott Vol. 2	LP	Island	ILP983	1968	**£75**	**£37.50**	*pink label*
Best Of Vol. 2	LP	Trojan	TTL55	1970	**£20**	**£8**	
Born To Love You	7"	Island	WI3147	1968	**£10**	**£5**	*Ike & Crystalites B side*
Derrick	7"	Ska Beat	JB199	1965	**£10**	**£5**	
Groovy Situation	7"	Songbird	SB1042	1970	**£4**	**£1.50**	
Happy Times	7"	Island	WI3064	1967	**£10**	**£5**	
Have Faith In Me	7"	Blue Beat	BB131	1962	**£12**	**£6**	
I'm Only Human	7"	Island	WI170	1965	**£10**	**£5**	
John Tom	7"	Doctor Bird	DB1002	1966	**£10**	**£5**	*Audrey Williams B side*
Let Me Down Easy	7"	Explosion	EX2071	1973	**£5**	**£2**	
Loser	7"	Island	WI3063	1967	**£10**	**£5**	
Message From A Black Man	7"	Song Bird	SB1028	1970	**£4**	**£1.50**	
My Three Loves	7"	Island	WI237	1965	**£10**	**£5**	
No Man Is An Island	7"	Songbird	SB1033	1970	**£4**	**£1.50**	
Psychedelic Train	7"	Songbird	SB1029	1970	**£4**	**£1.50**	
Psychedelic Train	LP	Trojan	TBL141	1970	**£15**	**£6**	
Reggae HIts	LP	Trojan	TBL116	1970	**£15**	**£6**	
Riding For A Fall	7"	Songbird	SB1013	1969	**£4**	**£1.50**	
Rock Steady Party	LP	Island	ILP955	1967	**£100**	**£50**	*pink label*
Rocksteady Party	LP	Trojan	TTL50	1970	**£30**	**£15**	
Sings Jamaica Reggae	LP	Pama	SECO13	1969	**£40**	**£20**	
Sitting On Top	7"	Songbird	SB1014	1969	**£4**	**£1.50**	
Standing In	7"	Big Shot	BI505	1968	**£6**	**£2.50**	
Together	7"	Island	WI245	1965	**£10**	**£5**	
Undertaker	LP	Trojan	TBL114	1970	**£15**	**£6**	
Walk The Streets	7"	Island	WI3077	1967	**£10**	**£5**	*Bobby Ellis B side*
What Can I Do	7"	Island	WI157	1964	**£10**	**£5**	

HARRIOTT, JOE

Jamaican saxophonist Joe Harriott was perhaps the first jazz player working in Britain to break free from the prevailing trad/mainstream orthodoxy. His *Free Form* album pioneered an approach to free improvisation – had Harriott been an American he would undoubtedly have received as much acclaim as fellow adventurers John Coltrane and Ornette Coleman. Later, he linked up with violinist John Mayer for a series of equally ground-breaking experiments in fusing jazz with Indian music (*Indo-Jazz Suite* is listed here – other albums appear under Mayer's name). Most sought after of all, however, is the last album made by Harriott before his death from cancer in 1973, *Hum Dono* containing uplifting music made in collaboration with guitarist Amancio D'Silva. Fans of television cookery may or may not be interested to know that Ainsley Harriott is the saxophonist's son.

Title	Format	Label	Number	Year	Mint	Good	Notes
Abstract	LP	Columbia	33SX1477	1963	**£100**	**£50**	
Blue Harriott	7" EP	Columbia	SEG7939	1959	**£15**	**£7.50**	
Cool Jazz With Joe	7" EP	Melodisc	EPM7117	195–	**£15**	**£7.50**	
Free Form	LP	Jazzland	JLP49	1961	**£50**	**£25**	
Guy Called Joe	7" EP	Columbia	SEG8070	1961	**£15**	**£7.50**	
High Spirits	LP	Columbia	33SX1692	1964	**£100**	**£50**	
Hum-Dono	LP	Columbia	SCX6354	1969	**£100**	**£50**	
Indo-Jazz Suite	LP	Columbia	SX/SCX6025	1966	**£50**	**£25**	*with John Mayer*
Joe Harriott	7" EP	Polygon	JTE106	195–	**£15**	**£7.50**	
Joe Harriott Quartet	7" EP	Columbia	SEG7665	1957	**£15**	**£7.50**	
Memorial	LP	One Up	OU2011	1973	**£40**	**£20**	
Movement	LP	Columbia	33SX1627	1963	**£100**	**£50**	
No Strings	7" EP	Pye	NJE1003	1956	**£15**	**£7.50**	
Personal Portrait	LP	Columbia	SX/SCX6249	1968	**£50**	**£25**	
Southern Horizons	LP	Jazzland	JLP37	1961	**£50**	**£25**	
Swings High	LP	Melodisc	SLP12150	1967	**£75**	**£37.50**	
Tony Kinsey Trio With Joe Harriott	7" EP	Esquire	EP36	1955	**£15**	**£7.50**	
Tony Kinsey Trio With Joe Harriott	7" EP	Esquire	EP82	1956	**£15**	**£7.50**	
Tony Kinsey Trio With Joe Harriott	7" EP	Esquire	EP52	1955	**£15**	**£7.50**	

HARRIS, ANITA

Anita Harris	7" EP	Pye	NEP24288	1967	**£5**	**£2**	
Playground	7"	CBS	2991	1967	**£4**	**£1.50**	
Something Must Be Done	7"	Pye	7N17069	1966	**£4**	**£1.50**	
Willingly	7"	Decca	F12082	1965	**£4**	**£1.50**	

HARRIS, BARRY

Preminado	LP	Riverside	RLP354	1961	**£15**	**£6**	

HARRIS, BETTY

Cry To Me	7"	London	HL9796	1963	**£6**	**£2.50**	
Nearer To You	7"	Stateside	SS2045	1967	**£10**	**£5**	
Ride Your Pony	7"	Action	ACT4535	1969	**£6**	**£2.50**	
Soul Perfection	LP	Action	ACLP6007	1969	**£20**	**£8**	
What A Sad Feeling	7"	Stateside	SS475	1965	**£8**	**£4**	

HARRIS, BILL

Bill Harris	LP	Emarcy	EJL1267	1958	**£12**	**£5**	

HARRIS, BRENDA JO

I Can Remember	7"	Roulette	RO503	1968	**£4**	**£1.50**	

HARRIS, DON 'SUGARCANE'

Cupful Of Dreams	LP	BASF	MPS68030	1973	**£10**	**£4**	
Don 'Sugarcane' Harris	LP	Epic	26286	1970	**£10**	**£4**	*US*
Fiddler On The Rock	LP	BASF	MPS68028	1970	**£10**	**£4**	
Got The Blues	LP	BASF	MPS68029	1972	**£10**	**£4**	
Keep On Driving	LP	BASF	MPS68027	1970	**£10**	**£4**	
Sugarcane	LP	Epic	30027	1971	**£10**	**£4**	

HARRIS, EDDIE

Breakfast At Tiffany's	LP	Stateside	SL10009	1962	**£12**	**£5**	
Electrifying Eddie Harris	LP	Atlantic	K40220	1973	**£10**	**£4**	
Electrifying Eddie Harris	LP	Atlantic	781985	1968	**£12**	**£5**	
Free Speech	LP	Atlantic	2466013	1971	**£12**	**£5**	
Goes To The Movies	LP	Stateside	SL10049	1963	**£12**	**£5**	
I Need Some Money	LP	Atlantic	K50127	1975	**£10**	**£4**	
In Sound	LP	Atlantic	SD1448	1966	**£12**	**£5**	*US*
Is It In?	LP	Atlantic	K50084	1974	**£10**	**£4**	
Mean Greens	LP	Atlantic	SD1453	1966	**£12**	**£5**	*US*
Mighty Like A Rose	LP	Stateside	SL10018	1963	**£12**	**£5**	
Plug Me In	LP	Atlantic	K40123	1973	**£10**	**£4**	
Plug Me In	LP	Atlantic	SD1506	1969	**£12**	**£5**	*US*
Silver Cycles	LP	Atlantic	K40416	1973	**£10**	**£4**	
Silver Cycles	LP	Atlantic	588177	1969	**£10**	**£4**	
Sings The Blues	LP	Atlantic	K40482	1973	**£10**	**£4**	
Tender Storm	LP	Atlantic	SD1478	1967	**£12**	**£5**	*US*

HARRIS, EMMYLOU

Gliding Bird	LP	Jubilee	JGS8031	1969	**£50**	**£25**	*US, colour cover*
Quarter Moon In A Ten Cent Town	LP	Mobile Fidelity	MFSL1015	1978	**£10**	**£4**	*US audiophile*

HARRIS, JET

Anniversary Album	LP	Q	LPMM1038	197–	**£15**	**£6**	
Besame Mucho	7"	Decca	F11466	1962	**£4**	**£1.50**	
Big Bad Bass	7"	Decca	F11841	1964	**£5**	**£2**	
Inside Jet Harris	LP	Ellie Jay	EJSP8622	1978	**£15**	**£6**	
Jet Harris	7" EP	Decca	DFE8502	1962	**£15**	**£7.50**	
Main Title Theme	7"	Decca	F11488	1962	**£4**	**£1.50**	
My Lady	7"	Fontana	TF849	1967	**£8**	**£4**	
Theme For A Fallen Idol	7"	SRT	SRTS75355	1975	**£4**	**£1.50**	

HARRIS, JET & TONY MEEHAN

Applejack	7"	Decca	F11710	1963	**£4**	**£1.50**	
Diamonds	7" EP	Decca	DFE7099	1963	**£60**	**£30**	*export*
Jet And Tony	7" EP	Decca	DFE8528	1963	**£12**	**£6**	

HARRIS, JOHNNY

Fragment Of Fear	7"	Warner Bros	WB8016	1970	**£6**	**£2.50**	
Movements	LP	Warner Bros	K46054	1972	**£20**	**£8**	

HARRIS, JUNE

Over And Over Again	7"	CBS	201774	1965	**£6**	**£2.50**	

HARRIS, PAT

Hippy Hippy Shake	7"	Pye	7N15567	1963	**£6**	**£2.50**	

HARRIS, PEPPERMINT

Peppermint Harris	LP	Time	5	1962	**£15**	**£6**	*US*

HARRIS, PHIL

I Guess I'll Have To Change My Plan	7"	HMV	7M231	1954	**£4**	**£1.50**	
I Wouldn't Touch You With A Ten Foot Pole	7"	HMV	7M289	1955	**£4**	**£1.50**	
Take Your Girlie To The Movies	7"	HMV	7M199	1954	**£4**	**£1.50**	

HARRIS, RICHARD

Title	Format	Label	Cat. No.	Year	Mint		Notes
Tramp Shining	LP	Stateside	SSL5019	1969	**£10**	**£4**	
Tramp Shining	LP	RCA	RD/SF7947	1968	**£12**	**£5**	
Yard Went On Forever	LP	Stateside	SSL5001	1968	**£12**	**£5**	

HARRIS, ROLF

Title	Format	Label	Cat. No.	Year	Mint		Notes
Favourites	7" EP	Columbia	SEG8531	1967	**£5**	**£2**	
Jake The Peg	7" EP	Columbia	SEG8516	1966	**£5**	**£2**	
Sun Arise	7"	Columbia	DB4888	1962	**£4**	**£1.50**	
Tie Me Kangaroo Down Sport	7"	Columbia	DB4483	1960	**£4**	**£1.50**	

HARRIS, RONNIE

Title	Format	Label	Cat. No.	Year	Mint		Notes
Cabaret	7"	Columbia	SCM5206	1955	**£4**	**£1.50**	
Cry Upon My Shoulder	7"	Columbia	DB3814	1956	**£4**	**£1.50**	
Don't Go To Strangers	7"	Columbia	SCM5159	1955	**£4**	**£1.50**	
Hello Mrs Jones	7"	Columbia	SCM5178	1955	**£4**	**£1.50**	
Hold My Hand	7"	Columbia	SCM5138	1954	**£4**	**£1.50**	
I Love Paris	7"	Columbia	SCM5139	1954	**£4**	**£1.50**	
I've Changed My Mind A Thousand Times	7"	Columbia	SCM5242	1956	**£4**	**£1.50**	
On The Way To Your Heart	7"	Columbia	SCM5189	1955	**£4**	**£1.50**	
Stranger In Paradise	7"	Columbia	SCM5176	1955	**£5**	**£2**	
That's Right	7"	Columbia	DB3836	1956	**£5**	**£2**	
What Is The Reason?	7"	Columbia	SCM5266	1956	**£4**	**£1.50**	

HARRIS, ROY

Title	Format	Label	Cat. No.	Year	Mint		Notes
Bitter And The Sweet	LP	Topic	12TS217	1972	**£10**	**£4**	
Champions Of Folly	LP	Topic	12TS256	1975	**£10**	**£4**	

HARRIS, SHAKEY JAKE

Title	Format	Label	Cat. No.	Year	Mint		Notes
Devil's Harmonica	LP	Polydor	2391015	1972	**£15**	**£6**	
Further On Up The Road	LP	Liberty	83217	1969	**£15**	**£6**	

HARRIS, SUE

Title	Format	Label	Cat. No.	Year	Mint		Notes
Hammers And Tongues	LP	Free Reed	FRR020	1978	**£12**	**£5**	

HARRIS, THURSTON

Title	Format	Label	Cat. No.	Year	Mint		Notes
Be Baba Leba	7"	Vogue	V9108	1958	**£200**	**£100**	*best auctioned*
Do What You Did	7"	Vogue	V9098	1958	**£200**	**£100**	*best auctioned*
Hey Little Girl	7"	Vogue	V9146	1959	**£75**	**£37.50**	
In The Bottom Of My Heart	7"	Vogue	V9144	1959	**£60**	**£30**	
Little Bitty Pretty One	7"	Vogue	V9092	1957	**£60**	**£30**	
Little Bitty Pretty One	7"	Sue	WI4016	1966	**£12**	**£6**	
Purple Stew	7"	Vogue	V9139	1959	**£60**	**£30**	
Runk Bunk	7"	Vogue	V9149	1959	**£100**	**£50**	
Slip Slop	7"	Vogue	V9151	1959	**£100**	**£50**	
Smokey Joes	7"	Vogue	V9122	1958	**£75**	**£37.50**	
Tears From My Heart	7"	Vogue	V9127	1958	**£60**	**£30**	

HARRIS, WEE WILLIE

Title	Format	Label	Cat. No.	Year	Mint		Notes
Listen To The River Roll Along	7"	Polydor	56140	1966	**£6**	**£2.50**	
Love Bug Crawl	7"	Decca	F10980	1958	**£30**	**£15**	
No Chemise Please	7"	Decca	F11044	1958	**£25**	**£12.50**	
Rocking At The Two I's	7"	Decca	F10970	1957	**£25**	**£12.50**	
Rocking With Wee Willie	7" EP	Decca	DFE6465	1958	**£100**	**£50**	
Someone's In The Kitchen With Diana	7"	Parlophone	R5504	1966	**£6**	**£2.50**	
Wild One	7"	Decca	F11217	1960	**£10**	**£5**	
You Must Be Joking	7"	HMV	POP1198	1963	**£6**	**£2.50**	

HARRIS, WYNONIE

Title	Format	Label	Cat. No.	Year	Mint		Notes
Adam Come And Get Your Rib	78	Vogue	V2166	1953	**£10**	**£5**	
Battle Of The Blues	7" EP	Bluebeat	BBEP301	1961	**£60**	**£30**	
Bloodshot Eyes	7"	Vogue	V2127	1956	**£75**	**£37.50**	*tri-centre*
Bloodshot Eyes	78	Vogue	V2127	1952	**£10**	**£5**	
Do It Again Please	78	Vogue	V2133	1952	**£10**	**£5**	
Drinkin' Wine Spo Dee O Dee	78	Vogue	V2006	1951	**£10**	**£5**	
Good Morning Judge	78	Vogue	V2128	1952	**£10**	**£5**	
Good Rockin' Blues	LP	King	KS1086	1970	**£15**	**£6**	*US*
Lovin' Machine	78	Vogue	V2111	1952	**£10**	**£5**	
Put It Back	78	Vogue	V2134	1952	**£10**	**£5**	
Teardrops From My Eyes	78	Vogue	V2144	1952	**£10**	**£5**	
Wynonie Mister Blues Harris	7" EP	Vogue	EPV1103	1956	**£150**	**£75**	

HARRIS, WYNONIE, AMOS MILBURN & PRINCE WATERFORD

Title	Format	Label	Cat. No.	Year	Mint		Notes
Party After Hours	10" LP	Aladdin	703	1956	**£200**	**£100**	*US*
Party After Hours	10" LP	Aladdin	703	1956	**£300**	**£180**	*US, red vinyl*

HARRIS SISTERS

Title	Format	Label	Cat. No.	Year	Mint		Notes
Kissing Bug	7"	Capitol	CL14232	1955	**£8**	**£4**	

HARRISON, DANNY

Title	Format	Label	Cat. No.	Year	Mint		Notes
I'm A Rolling Stone	7"	Coral	Q72479	1965	**£6**	**£2.50**	
Introducing Danny Harrison	7" EP	Starlite	STEP23	1962	**£6**	**£2.50**	

HARRISON, EARL

Title	Format	Label	Cat. No.	Year	Mint		Notes
Humphrey Stomp	7"	London	HL10121	1967	**£25**	**£12.50**	

HARRISON, GEORGE

Songs By George Harrison consists of three out-takes from *Somewhere In England* together with a live version of 'For You Blue'. It is available as either a CD or a vinyl single, but in either case only as a bonus within a deluxe, partly hand-made, edition of a book of George Harrison's lyrics. £250 was the new selling price of the last sets to be available in 1992 and they were produced as a limited edition of 2,500 copies. (A few promotional copies extra to the main edition were also made available.) The value of the set may well not rise any further, since it is likely that all collectors interested in the set will already have acquired one during the lengthy period of time it took for the edition to sell out.

Title	Format	Label	Cat. No.	Year	Mint	Ex	Notes
All Things Must Pass	LP	Apple	STCH639	1971	**£15**	**£6**	*3 LP box, poster*
Bangla Desh	7"	Apple	R5912	1971	**£50**	**£25**	*picture sleeve*
Best Of Dark Horse	CD	Dark Horse	257262DJ	1987	**£20**	**£8**	*US promo picture disc*
Cheer Down	12"	Dark Horse	W2696T	1989	**£6**	**£2.50**	
Cheer Down	CD-s	Dark Horse	W2696CD	1989	**£10**	**£5**	*3" single*
Cloud Nine	CD	Dark Horse	256432	1987	**£20**	**£8**	*US promo picture disc*
Concert For Bangla Desh	LP	Apple	STCX3385	1972	**£15**	**£6**	*3 LPs, booklet, boxed, with other artists*
Dark Horse	7"	Apple	R6001	1975	**£6**	**£2.50**	*picture sleeve*
Dark Horse Radio Special	LP	Dark Horse	SP22002	1974	**£200**	**£100**	*US promo*
Electronic Sound	LP	Apple	ZAPPLE2	1969	**£50**	**£25**	
Faster	7"	Dark Horse	K17423P	1979	**£15**	**£7.50**	*picture disc*
Gone Troppo	LP	Dark Horse	9237341	1982	**£15**	**£6**	*US audiophile promo*
Got My Mind Set On You	12"	Dark Horse	W8178TP	1987	**£10**	**£5**	*picture disc*
Got My Mind Set On You	12"	Dark Horse	W8178T	1987	**£6**	**£2.50**	*with poster*
Got My Mind Set On You	7"	Dark Horse	W8178	1987	**£6**	**£2.50**	*green label*
Is This Love	CD-s	Dark Horse	W7913CD	1988	**£5**	**£2**	*3" single*
My Sweet Lord	7"	Apple	R5884	1976	**£8**	**£4**	*black and white picture sleeve*
My Sweet Lord	7"	Apple	R5884	1971	**£5**	**£2**	*picture sleeve, colour head shot of George*
Shanghai Surprise	7"	Ganga Publishing	SHANGHAI1	1986	**£300**	**£180**	*promo only, with Vicki Brown*
Somewhere In England	LP	Dark Horse	DHK3472	1980	**£30**	**£15**	*US original issue with 4 different tracks*
Songs By George Harrison	7"	Genesis publications	SGH777	1988	**£250**	**£150**	*issued with limited-edition book*
Songs By George Harrison	CD	Genesis publications	SGHCD777	1988	**£250**	**£150**	*issued with limited-edition book*
Songs By George Harrison Vol. 2	7"	Genesis	SGH778	1992	**£250**	**£150**	*with limited-edition book*
Songs By George Harrison Vol. 2	CD	Genesis publications	SGHCD778	1992	**£250**	**£150**	*issued with limited-edition book*
Teardrops	7"	Dark Horse	K17837DJ	1981	**£10**	**£5**	*promo*
Thirty-Three And A Third Dialogue Album	LP	Dark Horse	PRO649	1976	**£30**	**£15**	*US promo*
This Guitar	7"	Apple	R6012	1976	**£8**	**£4**	
This Song	7"	Dark Horse	K16856	1976	**£4**	**£1.50**	*with US picture sleeve*
When We Was Fab	12"	Dark Horse	W8131TP	1988	**£8**	**£4**	*picture disc*
When We Was Fab	CD-s	Dark Horse	W8131CD	1988	**£5**	**£2**	*3" single*
Wonderwall	LP	Apple	SAPCOR1	1968	**£25**	**£10**	*stereo*
Wonderwall	LP	Apple	APCOR1	1968	**£60**	**£30**	*mono*
You	7"	Apple	R6007	1975	**£6**	**£2.50**	*picture sleeve*

HARRISON, MIKE

Title	Format	Label	Cat. No.	Year	Mint	Ex	Notes
Mike Harrison	LP	Island	ILPS9170	1971	**£10**	**£4**	
Smokestack Lightning	LP	Island	ILPS9209	1972	**£10**	**£4**	

HARRISON, NOEL

Title	Format	Label	Cat. No.	Year	Mint	Ex	Notes
At The Blue Angel	LP	Philips	BBL7399	1960	**£10**	**£4**	
Great Electric Experiment Is Over	LP	Reprise	RSLP6321	1969	**£12**	**£5**	
Noel Harrison	7" EP	Decca	DFE8616	1965	**£5**	**£2**	
Noel Harrison	7" EP	HMV	7EG8383	1957	**£6**	**£2.50**	
To Ramona	7" EP	Decca	DFE8639	1965	**£5**	**£2**	
Windmills Of Your Mind	7"	Reprise	RS20758	1969	**£4**	**£1.50**	

HARRISON, WILBERT

Title	Format	Label	Cat. No.	Year	Mint	Ex	Notes
Battle Of The Giants	LP	Joy	JOYS191	1971	**£10**	**£4**	*with Baby Washington*
I'm Broke	7"	Island	WI031	1962	**£10**	**£5**	
Kansas City	7"	Top Rank	JAR132	1959	**£8**	**£4**	
Kansas City	LP	Sphere Sound	(S)SR7000	1964	**£30**	**£15**	*US*
Let's Stick Together	7"	Sue	WI363	1965	**£10**	**£5**	
Let's Work Together	7"	London	HL10307	1970	**£5**	**£2**	
Let's Work Together	LP	London	HA/SH8415	1969	**£20**	**£8**	

HARRISON, YVONNE

Title	Format	Label	Cat. No.	Year	Mint	Ex	Notes
Chase	7"	Caltone	TONE102	1967	**£8**	**£4**	

HARRY, DEBBIE

Title	Format	Label	Cat. No.	Year	Mint	Ex	Notes
Brite Side	CD-s	Chrysalis	CHSCD3452	1989	**£5**	**£2**	
Brite Side (Remix)	CD-s	Chrysalis	CHSCCD3452	1989	**£5**	**£2**	
Def Dumb And Blonde	CD	Reprise	259382	1989	**£20**	**£8**	*US promo, 3D insert*
I Want That Man	CD-s	Chrysalis	CHSCD3369	1989	**£5**	**£2**	

HARSH REALITY

Guitarist and bass player Mark Griffiths made his first solo album in 1996, having long been associated with both Ian Matthews and Cliff Richard. His recording debut is here, as a member of obscure underground band, Harsh Reality.

Heaven And Hell	7"	Philips	BF1769	1969	£6	£2.50	
Heaven And Hell	LP	Philips	SBL7891	1969	£75	£37.50	
Tobacco Ash Sunday	7"	Philips	BF1710	1968	£5	£2	

HART, BOB, PERCY WEBB, ERNEST AUSTIN

Flash Company	LP	Topic	12TS243	1974	£10	£4	

HART, CAJUN

Got To Find A Way	7"	Warner Bros	WB7258	1969	£100	£50	

HART, DERRY & THE HARTBEATS

Come On Baby	7"	Decca	F11138	1959	£10	£5	

HART, MICKEY

Rolling Thunder	LP	Warner Bros	K46182	1972	£12	£5	

HART, MIKE

Basher, Chalky, Pongo, & Me	LP	Polydor	2310211	1972	£20	£8	
Mike Hart Bleeds	LP	Dandelion	63756	1970	£15	£6	

HART, TIM

Tim Hart	LP	Chrysalis	CHR1218	1979	£12	£5	

HART, TIM & MADDY PRIOR

Folk Songs Of Olde England 1	LP	Tepee	ARPS3	1968	£25	£10	
Folk Songs Of Olde England 2	LP	Tepee	ARPS4	1969	£25	£10	
Summer Solstice	LP	Mooncrest	CREST12	1976	£10	£4	*gatefold sleeve*
Summer Solstice	LP	B&C	CAS1035	1971	£15	£6	

HARTE, FRANK

Daybreak And A Candle-End	LP	Spin	995	1987	£10	£4	*Irish*
Dublin Street Songs	LP	Topic	12T172	1967	£20	£8	
Through Dublin City	LP	Topic	12T218	1973	£10	£4	

HARTFORD, JOHN

Earthwords And Music	LP	RCA	LSP3796	1967	£12	£5	*US*
Gentle On My Mind	LP	RCA	LSP4068	1968	£12	£5	*US*
Housing Project	LP	RCA	LSP3998	1968	£12	£5	*US*
Iron Mountain Depot	LP	RCA	LSP4337	1970	£12	£5	*US*
John Hartford	LP	RCA	LSP4156	1969	£12	£5	*US*
Looks At Life	LP	RCA	LSP3687	1967	£12	£5	*US*
Love Album	LP	RCA	LSP3884	1968	£12	£5	*US*

HARTH, ALFRED

Just Music	LP	ECM	ECM1002ST	1970	£20	£8	

HARTLEY, KEEF

The Keef Hartley Band was one of the many groups to emerge from the John Mayall school of blues, and one of the best. They favoured a tough, riff-based approach to blues-rock, and by gradually adding brass instruments the group became a key element within the growth of jazz-rock. The first two albums are the best – after that Miller Anderson, who was both the lead singer and the lead guitarist, became a little too fond of writing sensitive, reflective material, which did not really suit the band. *Little Big Band*, however, which presents the group's most exciting music re-arranged for a much bigger unit, is a splendid return to form.

Battle Of North West Six	LP	Deram	DML1054	1969	£20	£8	*mono*
Battle Of North West Six	LP	Deram	SML1054	1969	£15	£6	
Best Of The Keef Hartley Band	LP	Deram	DPA3011/2	1974	£12	£5	*double*
Halfbreed	LP	Deram	SML1037	1969	£15	£6	
Lancashire Hustler	LP	Deram	SDL13	1973	£12	£5	
Leave It Till The Morning	7"	Deram	DM250	1969	£4	£1.50	
Little Big Band	LP	Deram	SDL4	1971	£15	£6	
Overdog	LP	Deram	SDL2	1971	£15	£6	
Seventy Second Brave	LP	Deram	SDL9	1972	£12	£5	
Time Is Near	LP	Deram	SML1071	1970	£15	£6	
Time Is Near	LP	Deram	DML1037	1969	£20	£8	*mono*
Waiting Around	7"	Deram	DM273	1969	£4	£1.50	

HARUMI

Harumi	LP	Verve	FT30302	1968	£25	£10	*US double*

HARVEST OF DREAMS

Harvest Of Dreams	LP	private		1982	£100	£50	*US*

HARVESTERS

Twelve Years On	LP	SRT	SRTZ78CUS135	1978	£25	£10	

HARVEY, ALEX

Agent OO Soul	7"	Fontana	TF610	1965	£30	£15	
Ain't That Just Too Bad	7"	Polydor	56017	1965	£60	£30	
Alex Harvey And His Soul Band	LP	Polydor	LPHM46424	1964	£100	£50	
Blues	LP	Polydor	LPHM46441	1964	£100	£50	
Framed	LP	Vertigo	6360081	1972	£40	£20	*spiral label*
Got My Mojo Working	7"	Polydor	NH52907	1964	£50	£25	
I Just Wanna Make Love To You	7"	Polydor	NH52264	1964	£30	£15	

Maybe Someday	7"	Decca	F12660	1967	£30	£15	
Midnight Moses	7"	Fontana	TF1063	1969	£30	£15	
Next	LP	Vertigo	6360103	1974	£10	£4	
Presents The Loch Ness Monster	LP	K-Tel	NE984	1977	£30	£15	
Roman Wall Blues	LP	Fontana	(S)TL5534	1969	£150	£75	
Sunday Song	7"	Decca	F12640	1967	£30	£15	
Work Song	7"	Fontana	TF764	1966	£30	£15	

HARVEY, ALEX (2)

Alex Harvey	LP	Capitol	EST789	1971	£10	£4	
Souvenirs	LP	Capitol	EST11128	1972	£10	£4	

HARVEY, JANCIS

Distance Of Doors	LP	Pilgrim King	KLP5	1973	£75	£37.50	
From The Darkness Came Light	LP	Westwood	WRS144	1979	£25	£10	
Portrait Of Jancis Harvey	LP	Westwood	WRS107	1976	£30	£15	
Time Was Now	LP	Westwood	WR5054	1975	£40	£20	

HARVEY, P. J.

Dress	CD-s	Too Pure	PURECD5	1992	£10	£5	
Dry	CD	Too Pure	PURECDD10	1992	£30	£15	*with demos CD*
Dry	LP	Too Pure	PURED10	1992	£25	£10	*with demos LP*
Interview	CD	Island	PJICD1	1995	£20	£8	*promo*
Sheela Na Gig	CD-s	Too Pure	PURECD8	1992	£20	£10	
Sheela-Na-Gig	7"	Too Pure	PURES8	1992	£12	£6	

HARVEY, PETER

Rainin' In My Heart	7"	Columbia	DB4873	1962	£4	£1.50	

HARVEY, PHIL

The name of Phil Harvey covers the identity of Phil Spector.

Bumbershoot	7"	Imperial	5583	1959	£50	£25	*US*

HARVEY, RICHARD

Richard Harvey was the dominant influence within Gryphon and his interest in, knowledge of and skill with medieval instruments has kept him busy as a session musician and soundtrack composer ever since. *A New Way Of Seeing* was produced specially for a new equipment launch by the computer company ICL and has never been issued commercially, although the considerable number of copies that have found their way on to the collectors' market since attention was drawn to the record in the first edition of this *Price Guide* have had the effect of depressing the record's value.

Black Birds Of Brittany	7"	Streetsong	No.1	1978	£10	£5	*Shirley Collins B side*
Brass At La Sauve-Majeure	LP	ASV	ALH926	1983	£15	£6	
Divisions On A Ground	LP	Transatlantic	TRA292	1975	£50	£25	
New Way Of Seeing	LP	ICL	ICL001	1979	£25	£10	

HARVEY & THE MOONGLOWS

Ten Commandments Of Love	7"	London	HLM8730	1958	£200	£100	*best auctioned*

HARVEY BOYS

Nothing Is Too Good For You	7"	London	HLA8397	1957	£20	£10	

HARVEY'S FOLK

Songs Of Sister	LP	Galliard			£40	£20	

HARVEY'S PEOPLE

Loving And Living	LP	Galliard	GAL4001	1969	£40	£20	

HARWOOD, CHRIS

Nice To Meet Miss Christine	LP	Birth	RAB1	1970	£50	£25	

HASKELL, GORDON

Boat Trip	7"	CBS	4509	1969	£8	£4	
It Is And It Isn't	LP	Atlantic	K40311	1972	£15	£6	
Oo-La-Di-Doo-Da-Day	7"	CBS	4795	1970	£8	£4	
Sail In My Boat	LP	CBS	63741	1969	£125	£62.50	
Serve At Room Temperature	LP	RCA		1973	£150	£75	

HASKELL, JACK

Around The World	7"	London	HL8426	1957	£10	£5	

HASLAM, MICHAEL

There Goes The Forgotten Man	7"	Parlophone	R5267	1965	£5	£2	

HASSLES

The first recordings by Billy Joel (apart from a little unspecified session work) were with the Hassles, whose only claim to fame this is.

Hassles	CD	EMI		1992	£20	£8	*US*
Hassles	LP	United Artists	UAS6631	1968	£20	£8	*US*
Hour Of The Wolf	LP	United Artists	UAS6699	1969	£20	£8	*US*
You Got Me Humming	7"	United Artists	UP1199	1967	£8	£4	

HAT & TIE

Bread To Spend	7"	President	PT122	1967	£50	£25	
Chance For Romance	7"	President	PT105	1966	£50	£25	

HATCH, TONY ORCHESTRA

Crossroads	7"	Pye	7N15754	1965	**£5**	**£2**	*picture sleeve*
Crossroads Theme	7"	Pye	7N17169	1966	**£4**	**£1.50**	*picture sleeve*
Out Of This World Theme	7"	Pye	7N15460	1962	**£5**	**£2**	*picture sleeve*
Sweeney 2	7"	EMI	EMI2780	1978	**£6**	**£2.50**	
Theme From Who-Dun-It	7"	Pye	7N17814	1969	**£20**	**£10**	

HATCHER, GEORGE BAND

Black Moon Rising	7"	United Artists	UP36233	1977	**£4**	**£1.50**	
Have Band Will Travel	10"	United Artists	EXP100	1977	**£6**	**£2.50**	

HATE

Hate Kills	LP	Famous	SFMA5752	1970	**£40**	**£20**	

HATFIELD & THE NORTH

Afters	LP	Virgin	VR5	1980	**£25**	**£10**	
Hatfield & The North	LP	Virgin	V2008	1974	**£10**	**£4**	
Rotters Club	LP	Virgin	V2030	1975	**£10**	**£4**	

HATHAWAY, DONNY

Donny Hathaway	LP	Atlantic	2400143	1971	**£15**	**£6**	
Donny Hathaway	LP	Atlantic	K40241	1970	**£12**	**£5**	
Everything Is Everything	LP	Atlantic	2465019	1971	**£15**	**£6**	
Everything Is Everything	LP	Atlantic	K40063	1970	**£12**	**£5**	
Extension Of A Man	LP	Atlantic	K40487	1973	**£12**	**£5**	
Ghetto	7"	Atco	226010	1970	**£4**	**£1.50**	
Live	LP	Atlantic	K40369	1972	**£12**	**£5**	

HAVEN, ALAN

Images	7"	Fontana	TF542	1965	**£4**	**£1.50**	
Knack	7"	Fontana	TF590	1965	**£6**	**£2.50**	
Theme From A Jolly Bad Fellow	7"	United Artists	UP1057	1964	**£6**	**£2.50**	
Through 'Til Two	LP	Fontana	TL5400	1967	**£10**	**£4**	*with Tony Crombie*

HAVENS, RICHIE

1983	LP	Verve	2610001	1969	**£15**	**£6**	*double*
Alarm Clock	LP	Polydor	2310080	1971	**£10**	**£4**	
Electric Havens	LP	Transatlantic	TRA187	1966	**£12**	**£5**	
Great Blind Degree	LP	Polydor	2480049	1972	**£10**	**£4**	
Lady Madonna	7"	Verve	VS1519	1969	**£4**	**£1.50**	
Live On Stage	LP	Polydor	2659015	1972	**£12**	**£5**	*double*
Mixed Bag	LP	Verve	(S)VLP6008	1967	**£12**	**£5**	
Mixed Bag 2	LP	Polydor	2310356	1974	**£10**	**£4**	
Portfolio	LP	Polydor	2480166	1973	**£10**	**£4**	
Richie Havens' Record	LP	Transatlantic	TRA199	1965	**£12**	**£5**	
Something Else Again	LP	Verve	(S)VLP6005	1968	**£12**	**£5**	
State Of Mind	LP	Verve	2304050	1971	**£10**	**£4**	
Stonehenge	LP	Verve	(S)VLP6021	1968	**£12**	**£5**	

HAVENSTREET

End Of The Line	LP	private		1976	**£100**	**£50**	

HAWES, HAMPTON

All Night Session Vol. 1	LP	Contemporary	LAC12161	1959	**£15**	**£6**	
All Night Session Vol. 2	LP	Contemporary	LAC12162	1959	**£15**	**£6**	
All Night Session Vol. 3	LP	Contemporary	LAC12163	1959	**£15**	**£6**	
Everybody Likes Hampton Hawes	LP	Contemporary	LAC12091	1958	**£15**	**£6**	
Hampton Hawes Quartet	10" LP	Esquire	20079	1956	**£25**	**£10**	
Here And Now	LP	Contemporary	LAC602	1966	**£10**	**£4**	
This Is Hampton Hawes	LP	Contemporary	LAC12081	1958	**£20**	**£8**	
Trio Vol. 1	LP	Vogue	LAE12059	1957	**£20**	**£8**	
Vol. 1 – The Trio	LP	Contemporary	LAC12056	1957	**£20**	**£8**	

HAWK

African Day	LP	Parlophone	PCSJ12080	1971	**£20**	**£8**	*South African*

HAWKE, TOMMY

Good Gravy	7"	Top Rank	JAR348	1960	**£6**	**£2.50**	

HAWKES, CHIP

Nashville Album	LP	RCA	PL25044	1977	**£30**	**£15**	

HAWKINS, BUDDY BOY & WILLIAM MOORE

Buddy Boy Hawkins/William Moore	7" EP	Heritage	RE102	195–	**£12**	**£6**	

HAWKINS, COLEMAN

Alive At The Village Gate	LP	Verve	VLP9044	1963	**£12**	**£5**	
Back In Bean's Bag	LP	CBS	BPG62157	1964	**£10**	**£4**	
Bean And The Boys	7" EP	Esquire	EP192	1958	**£5**	**£2**	
Blue Saxophones	LP	Columbia	33CX10143	1959	**£20**	**£8**	*with Ben Webster*
Capitol Presents Coleman Hawkins & Sonny Greer	10" LP	Capitol	LC6650	1954	**£40**	**£20**	
Cattin'	LP	Fontana	SJL131	1966	**£10**	**£4**	
Classics In Jazz	10" LP	Capitol	LC6580	1953	**£40**	**£20**	
Coleman Hawkins	7" EP	Vogue	EPV1021	1955	**£5**	**£2**	
Coleman Hawkins	LP	Moodsville	MV7	1961	**£15**	**£6**	
Coleman Hawkins All Stars	LP	Swingsville	SV2005	1962	**£15**	**£6**	

Title	Format	Label	Cat. No.	Year	Mint	VG	Notes
Coleman Hawkins Group	7" EP	Mercury	EP16029	195–	£5	£2	
Coleman Hawkins Group	LP	London	LTZC15048	1957	£20	£8	
Coleman Hawkins Sextet	7" EP	Esquire	EP235	1961	£5	£2	
Desafinado	LP	HMV	CLP1630/ CSD1484	1963	£12	£5	
Genius Of Coleman Hawkins	LP	HMV	CLP1293	1959	£20	£8	
Gilded Hawk	LP	Capitol	T819	1957	£20	£8	
Hawk Eyes	LP	Esquire	32102	1960	£20	£8	
Hawk Flies High	LP	London	LTZU15117	1958	£20	£8	
Hawk Returns	7" EP	London	EZC19020	1958	£5	£2	
Hawk Talks	7" EP	Brunswick	OE9166	1955	£5	£2	
Hawk Talks	LP	Brunswick	LAT8242	1958	£25	£10	
High And Mighty Hawk	LP	Felsted	FAJ7005/SJA2005	1959	£30	£15	
Lucky Duck	7"	Brunswick	05459	1955	£6	£2.50	
Meditations	LP	Fontana	TL5273	1965	£10	£4	
Newport Jazz Festival 1957	LP	Columbia	33CX10103	1958	£15	£6	*with Roy Eldridge*
Soul	LP	Esquire	32095	1960	£20	£8	
Stasch	LP	Swingsville	SVLP2013	1962	£15	£6	
Swing!	LP	Fontana	FJL102	1964	£10	£4	
Ten Coleman Hawkins Specials	10" LP	HMV	DLP1055	1954	£40	£20	
Today And Now	LP	HMV	CLP1689	1964	£12	£5	
With The Red Garland Trio	LP	Swingsville	SV2001	1962	£15	£6	

HAWKINS, DALE

Title	Format	Label	Cat. No.	Year	Mint	VG	Notes
Hot Dog	7"	London	HLM9060	1960	£25	£12.50	
La Do Da Da	7"	London	HLM8728	1958	£30	£15	
LA, Memphis & Tyler, Texas	LP	Bell	SBLL127	1970	£12	£5	
Let's All Twist	LP	Roulette	(S)R25175	1962	£50	£25	*US*
Liza Jane	7"	London	HLM9016	1959	£25	£12.50	
Susie Q	7"	London	HL8482	1957	£300	£180	*best auctioned*
Susie Q	7"	Janus	no number	1971	£20	£10	*promo, plus 3 tracks by other artists*
Suzie-Q	LP	Chess	1429	1958	£300	£180	*US*
Yea Yea Classcutter	7"	London	HLM8842	1959	£30	£15	

HAWKINS, ERSKINE

Title	Format	Label	Cat. No.	Year	Mint	VG	Notes
Hawk Blows At Midnight	LP	Brunswick	LAT8374/ STA3042	1960	£12	£5	

HAWKINS, HAWKSHAW

Title	Format	Label	Cat. No.	Year	Mint	VG	Notes
All New Hawkshaw Hawkins	LP	London	HA8181	1964	£12	£5	
Betty Lorraine	7"	Parlophone	CMSP1	1954	£20	£10	*export, Charlie Gore B side*
Country And Western	7" EP	Parlophone	GEP8742	1958	£15	£7.50	
Grand Ole Opry Favorites	LP	King	592	1958	£25	£10	*US*
Hawkshaw Hawkins	LP	King	599	1959	£25	£10	*US*
Hawkshaw Hawkins	LP	King	587	1958	£25	£10	*US*
Hawkshaw Hawkins – Country And Western	7" EP	Vogue	VE170117	1958	£25	£12.50	
Lonesome 7-7203	7"	London	HL9737	1963	£5	£2	
Taken From Our Vaults Vol. 1	LP	King	(S)858	1963	£12	£5	*US*
Taken From Our Vaults Vol. 2	LP	King	(S)870	1963	£12	£5	*US*
Taken From Our Vaults Vol. 3	LP	King	(S)873	1963	£12	£5	*US*

HAWKINS, RONNIE

Title	Format	Label	Cat. No.	Year	Mint	VG	Notes
Arkansas Rockpile	LP	Roulette	RCP1003	1970	£15	£6	
Best Of Ronnie Hawkins & His Band	LP	Roulette	SR42045	1970	£15	£6	*US*
Clara	7"	Columbia	DB4442	1960	£25	£12.50	
Folk Ballads	LP	Columbia	33SX1295	1960	£30	£13	*mono*
Folk Ballads	LP	Columbia	SCX3358	1960	£50	£25	*stereo*
Forty Days	7"	Columbia	DB4319	1959	£40	£20	
Hawk	LP	Cotillion	SD9039	1971	£15	£6	*US*
Hey, Bo Diddley	7"	Quality	6128	1959	£100	£50	*Canadian*
Mary Lou	7"	Columbia	DB4345	1959	£20	£10	
Mojo Man	LP	Roulette	R25390	1964	£30	£15	*US*
Mr Dynamo	LP	Columbia	33SX1238	1960	£50	£25	*mono*
Mr Dynamo	LP	Roulette	SR25102	1960	£150	£75	*US, red vinyl*
Mr Dynamo	LP	Columbia	SCX3315	1960	£75	£37.50	*stereo*
Rock'n'Roll Resurrection	LP	Monument	MNT65122	1972	£10	£4	
Rocking With Ronnie	7" EP	Columbia	SEG7983	1960	£60	£30	
Rocking With Ronnie	7" EP	Columbia	ESG7792	1960	£75	£37.50	*stereo*
Rocking With Ronnie No. 2	7" EP	Columbia	SEG7988	1960	£60	£30	
Rocking With Ronnie No. 2	7" EP	Columbia	ESG7795	1960	£75	£37.50	*stereo*
Ronnie Hawkins	LP	Roulette	SR25078	1959	£150	£75	*US, red vinyl*
Ronnie Hawkins	LP	Yorkville	YVS33002	1968	£20	£8	*US*
Ronnie Hawkins	LP	Atlantic	2400009	1970	£15	£6	
Ronnie Hawkins	LP	Roulette	(S)R25078	1959	£75	£37.50	*US*
Rrrracket Time	LP	WLW	WLW101	1965	£20	£8	*Canadian*
Songs Of Hank Williams	LP	Roulette	(S)R25137	1960	£30	£15	*US*
Southern Love	7"	Columbia	DB4412	1960	£10	£5	
Who Do You Love	7"	Columbia	DB7036	1963	£12	£6	

HAWKINS, SCREAMING JAY

Title	Format	Label	Cat. No.	Year	Mint	VG	Notes
At Home	LP	Epic	LN3448	1956	£500	£330	*US*
I Hear Voices	7"	Sue	WI379	1965	£15	£7.50	
I Put A Spell On You	7"	Direction	584097	1969	£8	£4	
I Put A Spell On You	78	Fontana	H107	1958	£60	£30	
I Put A Spell On You	LP	Direction	863481	1969	£20	£8	

I Put A Spell On You	LP	Epic	LN3457	1957	**£200**	**£100**	*US*
Night And Day	LP	Planet	PLL1001	1966	**£60**	**£30**	
Night At Forbidden City	LP	Sounds Of Hawaii	5015	196–	**£30**	**£15**	*US*
Screaming Jay Hawkins	LP	Philips	PHS600336	1970	**£15**	**£6**	*US*
Whammy	7"	Columbia	DB7460	1965	**£10**	**£5**	
What That Is	LP	Mercury	SMCL20178	1969	**£10**	**£4**	

HAWKS

Grissle	7"	Stateside	SS2147	1968	**£5**	**£2**	*B side by the Sheep*

HAWKS (2)

Words Of Hope	7"	Five Believers	FB001	1981	**£6**	**£2.50**	

HAWKSHAW, ALAN

27 Top TV Themes And Commercials	LP	Columbia	TWO391	1972	**£15**	**£6**	
Big Beat	LP	KPM	KPM1044	1969	**£40**	**£20**	
Flute For Moderns	LP	KPM	KPM1080	1972	**£20**	**£8**	
Music For A Young Generation	LP	KPM	KPM1086	1971	**£25**	**£10**	
Soul Organ	LP	KPM	KPM1027	1967	**£25**	**£10**	

HAWKSWORTH, JOHNNY ORCHESTRA

Lunar Walk	7"	Pye	7N15969	1965	**£6**	**£2.50**	

HAWKWIND

By overlaying simple riff music with electronic noise Hawkwind succeeded in creating the perfect backdrop for Michael Moorcock's science fiction and sword-and-sorcery novels. The link was cemented by Moorcock himself contributing to many of the group's records; by Hawkwind returning the favour in supplying the music for Moorcock's own *New World's Fair* LP; and by Moorcock inspiring the creation of a science fiction novel in which the members of Hawkwind were the main characters. Here is the origin of the close interrelation between fantasy and heavy metal music. The perfect artefact to summarize all this is the Hawkwind LP *Warrior On The Edge Of Time*, whose cover, showing a mounted hero waiting on the edge of a precipice, opens out into a cardboard shield.

Angels Of Death	LP	RCA	NL71150	1986	**£20**	**£8**	
Approved History Of Hawkwind	LP	Samurai	SAMR046	1986	**£30**	**£15**	*set of 3 picture discs*
Business Trip	LP	Emergency Broadcast	EBS111	1994	**£12**	**£5**	*clear vinyl double*
Choose Your Masques	LP	RCA	RCALP6055	1982	**£15**	**£6**	
Chronicle Of The Black Sword	CD	Flicknife	SHARP033CD	1985	**£12**	**£5**	*with 3 extra tracks*
Church Of Hawkwind	LP	RCA	RCALP9004	1982	**£20**	**£8**	*with booklet*
Decide Your Future	12"	4 Real	4R2	1993	**£6**	**£2.50**	
Doremi Fasolatido	LP	United Artists	UAG29364	1972	**£15**	**£6**	*with poster*
Early Years Live	12"	Receiver	REPLAY3014	1990	**£6**	**£2.50**	*blue vinyl*
Electric Tepee	CD	Dojo	DOJOCD244	1995	**£15**	**£6**	
Electric Tepee	LP	Castle	ESD181	1992	**£12**	**£5**	*double*
Hall Of The Mountain Grill	LP	United Artists	UAG29672	1974	**£10**	**£4**	
Hawkfan 12	LP	Hawkfan	HWFB2	1986	**£50**	**£25**	*with poster, insert, bag*
Hawkwind	LP	Liberty	LBS83348	1970	**£25**	**£10**	*blue label*
Hawkwind	LP	Liberty	SLSP1972921	1984	**£10**	**£4**	*picture disc*
Hawkwind	LP	Liberty	LBS83348	1970	**£15**	**£6**	*black label*
Hurry On Hawkwind	7" EP	United Artists	USEP1	1973	**£50**	**£25**	
Hurry On Sundown	7"	Liberty	LBF15382	1970	**£75**	**£37.50**	
In Search Of Space	LP	United Artists	UAG29202	1971	**£15**	**£6**	*with booklet*
Kings Of Speed	7"	United Artists	UP35808	1975	**£25**	**£12.50**	*picture sleeve*
Levitation	LP	Bronze	BRON530	1980	**£15**	**£6**	*blue vinyl*
Official Picture Log Book	LP	Flicknife	HWBOX01	1987	**£40**	**£20**	*3 picture discs, interview LP, boxed*
PSI Power	7"	Charisma	CB323	1978	**£4**	**£1.50**	*as Hawklords*
PXR5	LP	Charisma	CDS4016	1979	**£15**	**£6**	*with poster*
Quark, Strangeness And Charm	12"	Emergency Broadcast	EBS110	1994	**£8**	**£4**	*clear vinyl*
Repeat Performance	LP	Charisma	BG2	1980	**£10**	**£4**	
Roadhawks	LP	United Artists	UAK29919	1976	**£10**	**£4**	*with poster*
Silver Machine	7"	United Artists	UPP35381	1983	**£5**	**£2**	*picture disc*
Silver Machine	7"	Samurai	HW001	1986	**£6**	**£2.50**	*shaped picture disc*
Silver Machine	7"	RCA	RCAP267	1982	**£6**	**£2.50**	*picture disc*
Silver Machine	7"	United Artists	UPP35381	1982	**£10**	**£5**	*mispress – B side plays Beatles 'Ask Me Why'*
Silver Machine	7"	United Artists	UP35381	1972	**£6**	**£2.50**	*silver & blue picture sleeve*
Sonic Attack	7"	United Artists	WD3637	1973	**£200**	**£100**	*1 sided promo, cloth sleeve*
Sonic Attack	LP	RCA	RCALP6004	1981	**£15**	**£6**	*with insert*
Space Ritual	LP	United Artists	UAD60037/8	1973	**£20**	**£8**	*double*
Spirit Of The Age	12"	4 Real	4R1	1993	**£10**	**£5**	
Stonehenge: This Is Hawkwind Do Not Panic	LP	Flicknife	SHARP022	1984	**£15**	**£6**	*double*
Twenty-Five Years	12"	Charisma	CB33212	1979	**£6**	**£2.50**	*as Hawklords, black vinyl*
Twenty-Five Years On	LP	Charisma	CDS4014	1978	**£12**	**£5**	*as Hawklords, with tour book*
Urban Guerilla	7"	United Artists	UP35566	1973	**£6**	**£2.50**	
Warrior On The Edge Of Time	LP	United Artists	UAG29766	1975	**£15**	**£6**	*shield cover*
Who's Gonna Win The War	7"	Bronze	BRO109	1980	**£6**	**£2.50**	*cream label*
Zones	LP	Flicknife	PSHARP014	1984	**£10**	**£4**	*picture disc*

HAX CEL

Zwai Life	LP	Dizzy	DS726	1972	**£15**	**£6**	*German*

HAY, BARRY

Only Parrots, Frogs And Angels	LP	Polydor	2925006	1972	**£30**	**£15**	*Dutch*

HAYDOCK'S ROCKHOUSE

Cupid	7"	Columbia	DB8050	1966	**£20**	**£10**	
Lovin' You	7"	Columbia	DB8135	1967	**£20**	**£10**	

HAYES, BILL

Ballad Of Davy Crockett	7"	London	HLA8220	1956	**£25**	**£12.50**	
Berry Tree	7"	London	HL8149	1955	**£15**	**£7.50**	
Das Ist Musik	7"	London	HLA8300	1956	**£10**	**£5**	
Donkey Song	7"	MGM	SP1036	1953	**£12**	**£6**	
Great Pioneers Of The West	7" EP	London	REA1051	1956	**£25**	**£12.50**	
Kwela Kwela	7"	London	HLA8239	1956	**£12**	**£6**	
Legend Of Wyatt Earp	7"	London	HLA8325	1956	**£20**	**£10**	
Sings The Best Of Disney	7" EP	HMV	7EG8355	1957	**£5**	**£2**	
Wimoweh	7"	London	HLR8833	1959	**£6**	**£2.50**	
Wringle Wrangle	7"	London	HL8430	1957	**£8**	**£4**	

HAYES, ISAAC

Black Moses	LP	Stax	2628004	1972	**£12**	**£5**	*double*
Blue Hayes	LP	Stax	2465016	1971	**£12**	**£5**	
Chocolate Chip	LP	ABC	ABCL5129	1975	**£10**	**£4**	
Groove-A-Thon	LP	ABC	ABCL5155	1975	**£10**	**£4**	
Hot Buttered Soul	LP	Stax	SXATS1028	1969	**£15**	**£6**	
Hot Buttered Soul	LP	Stax	2325011	1971	**£12**	**£5**	
I Stand Accused	7"	Stax	STAX154	1970	**£4**	**£1.50**	
Isaac Hayes Movement	LP	Stax	SXATS1032	1970	**£15**	**£6**	
Isaac Hayes Movement	LP	Stax	2325014	1971	**£12**	**£5**	
Joy	LP	Stax	2325111	1974	**£10**	**£4**	
Live At The Sahara Tahoe	LP	Stax	2659026	1973	**£12**	**£5**	*double*
Presenting Isaac Hayes	LP	Stax		1967	**£20**	**£8**	
Shaft	LP	Stax	2659007	1971	**£12**	**£5**	*double*
To Be Continued	LP	Stax	2325026	1971	**£12**	**£5**	
Tough Guys	LP	Stax	STXH5001	1974	**£10**	**£4**	
Truck Turner	LP	Stax	STXD4001/2	1974	**£12**	**£5**	*double*
Use Me	LP	Stax	STX1043	1975	**£10**	**£4**	
Walk On By	7"	Stax	STAX133	1969	**£4**	**£1.50**	

HAYES, LINDA & THE PLATTERS

Please Have Mercy	7"	Parlophone	MSP6174	1955	**£200**	**£100**	

HAYES, PETER LIND

Life Gets Teejus Don't It	7"	Brunswick	05821	1960	**£4**	**£1.50**	

HAYES, TUBBY

The increasing value of the records made by Tubby Hayes (which include those listed under the name of his group, the Jazz Couriers), reflects the growing affection felt for one of Britain's greatest saxophonists, who died during heart surgery in 1973 at the age of just thirty-eight.

100% Proof	LP	Fontana	(S)TL5410	1966	**£75**	**£37.50**	
100% Proof	LP	Philips	6382041	1973	**£30**	**£15**	
Change Of Setting	LP	World Record Club	T631	196–	**£50**	**£25**	*with Paul Gonsalves*
Down In The Village	LP	Fontana	680998TL/ 886163TY	1963	**£150**	**£75**	
Eighth Wonder	7" EP	Tempo	EXA82	1958	**£50**	**£25**	
Equation In Rhythm	LP	Fontana	TFL5190/ STFL598	1962	**£40**	**£20**	*with Jack Costanzo*
Jazz Date	LP	Wing	WL1088	1965	**£20**	**£8**	*one side by Cleo Laine*
Jazz Tête-à-Tête	LP	77	ELEU1221	1966	**£75**	**£37.50**	
Just Friends	LP	Columbia	SX6003	196–	**£75**	**£37.50**	*with Paul Gonsalves*
Late Spot At Scott's	LP	Fontana	TL5200	1964	**£250**	**£150**	
Mexican Green	LP	Fontana	SFJL911	1969	**£125**	**£62.50**	
Modern Jazz Scene	7" EP	Tempo	EXA36	1956	**£30**	**£15**	
Ode To Ernie	7"	Tempo	A148	1957	**£10**	**£5**	
Palladium Jazz Date	LP	Fontana	TFL5151/ STFL570	1961	**£75**	**£37.50**	*one side by Cleo Laine*
Return Visit	LP	Fontana	(S)TL5195	1964	**£100**	**£50**	
Sally	7"	Fontana	H397	1962	**£6**	**£2.50**	
Tubbs	LP	Fontana	TFL5142/ STFL562	1961	**£100**	**£50**	
Tubbs In New York	LP	Wing	WL1162	1967	**£20**	**£8**	
Tubbs In New York	LP	Fontana	TFL5183/ STFL595	1961	**£75**	**£37.50**	
Tubby Hayes And His Orchestra	7" EP	Tempo	EXA17	1955	**£40**	**£20**	
Tubby Hayes And His Orchestra	7" EP	Tempo	EXA14	1955	**£40**	**£20**	
Tubby Hayes Orchestra	LP	Fontana	6309002	1970	**£60**	**£30**	
Tubby Hayes Quartet	7" EP	Tempo	EXA28	1956	**£50**	**£25**	
Tubby Hayes Quartet	7" EP	Tempo	EXA27	1956	**£50**	**£25**	
Tubby Hayes Quintet	7" EP	Tempo	EXA55	1957	**£30**	**£15**	
Tubby Hayes Quintet	LP	Tempo	TAP6	1956	**£150**	**£75**	

Title	Format	Label	Cat. No.	Year	Mint	VG	Notes
Tubby Tours	LP	Fontana	(S)TL5221	1966	**£75**	**£37.50**	
Tubby's Groove	LP	Tempo	TAP29	1961	**£250**	**£150**	

HAYMARKET SQUARE

Title	Format	Label	Cat. No.	Year	Mint	VG	Notes
Magic Lantern	LP	Chaparral	CRM201	1968	**£1000**	**£700**	*US*

HAYNES, ROY

Title	Format	Label	Cat. No.	Year	Mint	VG	Notes
Roy Haynes Band	10" LP	Vogue	LDE130	1955	**£40**	**£20**	
We Three	LP	Esquire	32103	1960	**£30**	**£15**	*with Phineas Newborn & Paul Chambers*

HAYNES, STEVE

Title	Format	Label	Cat. No.	Year	Mint	VG	Notes
Save Me Save Me	7"	Black Bear	BLA2008	1978	**£8**	**£4**	

HAYSTACKS BALBOA

Title	Format	Label	Cat. No.	Year	Mint	VG	Notes
Haystacks Balboa	LP	Polydor	2489002	1970	**£100**	**£50**	

HAYWARD, JUSTIN

Title	Format	Label	Cat. No.	Year	Mint	VG	Notes
I Can't Face The World Without You	7"	Parlophone	R5496	1966	**£75**	**£37.50**	
London Is Behind Me	7"	Pye	7N17014	1965	**£60**	**£30**	
Moving Mountains	CD	Towerbell	TOWCD15	1985	**£25**	**£10**	

HAYWARD, RICK

Title	Format	Label	Cat. No.	Year	Mint	VG	Notes
Rick Hayward	LP	Blue Horizon	2431006	1971	**£60**	**£30**	

HAYWARD, SUSAN

Title	Format	Label	Cat. No.	Year	Mint	VG	Notes
I'll Cry Tomorrow	7" EP	MGM	MGMEP555	1956	**£5**	**£2**	

HAYWOOD, JOE

Title	Format	Label	Cat. No.	Year	Mint	VG	Notes
Warm And Tender Love	7"	Island	WI218	1965	**£5**	**£2**	

HAYWOOD, LEON

Title	Format	Label	Cat. No.	Year	Mint	VG	Notes
Ain't No Use	7"	Vocalion	VP9280	1966	**£6**	**£2.50**	
Ever Since You Were Sweet Sixteen	7"	Vocalion	VP9288	1967	**£10**	**£5**	
Soul Cargo	LP	Vocalion	VAL8064	1967	**£15**	**£6**	

HAZE

Title	Format	Label	Cat. No.	Year	Mint	VG	Notes
Hazecolor Dia	LP	Bacillus	6494007	1971	**£10**	**£4**	*German*

HAZEL & THE JOLLY BOYS

Title	Format	Label	Cat. No.	Year	Mint	VG	Notes
Stop Them	7"	Doctor Bird	DB1063	1966	**£10**	**£5**	

HAZLEWOOD, LEE

Title	Format	Label	Cat. No.	Year	Mint	VG	Notes
Friday's Child	LP	Reprise	RS6163	1964	**£25**	**£10**	*US*
Love And Other Crimes	LP	Reprise	RSLP6297	1968	**£15**	**£6**	
My Baby Cried All Night Long	7"	MGM	MGM1348	1967	**£5**	**£2**	
Ode To Billie Joe	7"	Reprise	RS20613	1967	**£4**	**£1.50**	
Poet, Fool Or Bum	LP	Stateside	SSL10315	1974	**£15**	**£6**	
Rainbow Woman	7"	Reprise	RS20667	1968	**£4**	**£1.50**	
Requiem For An Almost Lady	LP	Reprise	K44161	1972	**£10**	**£4**	
Sand	7"	MGM	MGM1310	1966	**£4**	**£1.50**	
These Boots Are Made For Walkin'	LP	MGM	2354036	197–	**£12**	**£5**	
Trouble Is A Lonesome Town	LP	London	HAN/SHN8398	1970	**£15**	**£6**	
Very Special World Of Lee Hazlewood	LP	MGM	CS8014	1966	**£15**	**£6**	
Words Mean Nothing	7"	London	HLW9223	1960	**£8**	**£4**	

HEAD

Title	Format	Label	Cat. No.	Year	Mint	VG	Notes
G.T.F.	LP	SRT	72254	1973	**£25**	**£10**	

HEAD, MURRAY

Title	Format	Label	Cat. No.	Year	Mint	VG	Notes
Nigel Lived	LP	CBS	65503	1973	**£12**	**£5**	
She Was Perfection	7"	Immediate	IM053	1967	**£30**	**£15**	
Superstar	7"	MCA	MK5019	1969	**£4**	**£1.50**	*picture sleeve*

HEAD, ROY

Title	Format	Label	Cat. No.	Year	Mint	VG	Notes
Apple Of My Eye	7"	Vocalion	VP9254	1966	**£4**	**£1.50**	
Just A Little Bit	7"	Pye	7N25340	1965	**£6**	**£2.50**	
Just A Little Bit Of Roy Head	7" EP	Pye	NEP44053	1966	**£12**	**£6**	
Most Wanted Woman In Town	7"	London	HLD10487	1975	**£5**	**£2**	
Roy Head And The Traits	LP	TNT	101	1965	**£50**	**£25**	*US*
To Make A Big Man Cry	7"	London	HLZ10097	1966	**£4**	**£1.50**	
Treat Her Right	7"	Vocalion	VP9248	1965	**£4**	**£1.50**	
Treat Me Right	LP	Scepter	(S)S532	1965	**£20**	**£8**	*US*

HEAD MACHINE

Title	Format	Label	Cat. No.	Year	Mint	VG	Notes
Orgasm	LP	Major Minor	SMLP79	1970	**£125**	**£62.50**	

HEAD SHOP

Title	Format	Label	Cat. No.	Year	Mint	VG	Notes
Head Shop	LP	Epic	BN26476	1969	**£25**	**£10**	*US*

HEADACHE

Title	Format	Label	Cat. No.	Year	Mint	VG	Notes
Can't Stand Still	7"	Lout	001	1977	**£15**	**£7.50**	

HEADBAND

Title	Format	Label	Cat. No.	Year	Mint	VG	Notes
Song For Tooley	LP	Polydor	2907008	1971	**£75**	**£37.50**	*Australian*

HEADHUNTERS

Title	Format	Label	Cat. No.	Year	Mint	VG	Notes
Straight From The Gate	LP	Arista	SPART1046	1977	**£15**	**£6**	

Title	Format	Label	Cat. No.	Year	Mint	VG	Notes
Survival Of The Fittest	LP	Arista	ARTY116	1975	**£25**	**£10**	

HEADS, HANDS & FEET

Title	Format	Label	Cat. No.	Year	Mint	VG	Notes
Heads, Hands & Feet	LP	Island	ILPS9149	1971	**£15**	**£6**	
Tracks	LP	Island	ILPS9185	1972	**£12**	**£5**	

HEADSTONE

Title	Format	Label	Cat. No.	Year	Mint	VG	Notes
Still Looking	LP	Starr	SLP1056	1971	**£200**	**£100**	*US*

HEALY, PAT

Title	Format	Label	Cat. No.	Year	Mint	VG	Notes
Just Before Dawn	LP	Vogue	VA160131	1959	**£15**	**£6**	

HEANEY, JOE

Title	Format	Label	Cat. No.	Year	Mint	VG	Notes
Bonny Bunch Of Roses	7" EP	Collector	JEI7	1961	**£5**	**£2**	
Irish Traditional Songs In Gaelic And English	LP	Topic	12T91	1963	**£12**	**£5**	
Morrissey And The Russian Sailor	7" EP	Collector	JEI5	1960	**£5**	**£2**	
O Mo Dhuchas	LP	Gael-Linn	CEF051	1976	**£10**	**£4**	*Irish*

HEART

Title	Format	Label	Cat. No.	Year	Mint	VG	Notes
All I Wanna Do Is Make Love To You	CD-s	Capitol	CDCL569	1990	**£5**	**£2**	
Brigade	CD	Capitol	DPRO79967	1990	**£15**	**£6**	*US promo picture disc*
Dreamboat Annie	LP	Nautilus	NR 3	1979	**£12**	**£5**	*US audiophile*
Dreamboat Annie	LP	Mushroom	MRS5005	1976	**£20**	**£8**	*US picture disc*
Heart Box Set	CD	Capitol	CDHGIFT1	1990	**£25**	**£10**	*3 CDs boxed*
Heart Box Set	LP	Capitol	HGIFT1	1990	**£20**	**£8**	*3 LPs, boxed, booklet*
Heartless	7"	Arista	ARISTA140	1977	**£4**	**£1.50**	
I Didn't Want To Need You	CD-s	Capitol	CDCL580	1990	**£5**	**£2**	
Little Queen	LP	Portrait	HR44799	1981	**£12**	**£5**	*US audiophile*
Magazine	LP	Arista	SPART1024	1977	**£15**	**£6**	*1st version, without 1978 recordings*
Magazine	LP	Mushroom	MRS1SP	1978	**£12**	**£5**	*US picture disc*
Never	CD-s	Capitol	CDCL482	1988	**£5**	**£2**	
Nothin' At All	7"	Capitol	CL406	1986	**£4**	**£1.50**	*heart-shaped picture disc*
Nothin' At All	CD-s	Capitol	CDCL507	1988	**£5**	**£2**	
Radio Star Audio Cue Card	CD	Capitol		1987	**£15**	**£6**	*US interview promo*
Secret	CD-s	Capitol	CDCL603	1991	**£5**	**£2**	
Stranded	CD-s	Capitol	CDCL595	1990	**£5**	**£2**	
There's The Girl	CD-s	Capitol	CDCL473	1987	**£5**	**£2**	
These Dreams	CD-s	Capitol	CDCL477	1988	**£5**	**£2**	
What About Love?	CD-s	Capitol	CDCL487	1988	**£5**	**£2**	
Who Will You Run To?	7"	Capitol	CLP457	1987	**£6**	**£2.50**	*picture disc*
With Love From Heart	CD	Capitol	CDLOVE2	1988	**£20**	**£8**	*2 CDs boxed*
With Love From Heart	LP	Capitol	LOVE2	1988	**£15**	**£6**	*2 LPs, boxed, inserts*
You're The Voice	CD-s	Capitol	CDCL624	1991	**£5**	**£2**	

HEARTBEATS

Title	Format	Label	Cat. No.	Year	Mint	VG	Notes
Go	7"	Nothing Shaking	SHAD1	1981	**£10**	**£5**	*blue vinyl*
Thousand Miles Away	LP	Roulette	(S)R25107	1960	**£75**	**£37.50**	*US*

HEARTBREAKERS

Title	Format	Label	Cat. No.	Year	Mint	VG	Notes
Chinese Rocks	12"	Track	2094135T	1977	**£8**	**£4**	
Chinese Rocks	7"	Track	2094135	1977	**£5**	**£2**	
It's Not Enough	7"	Track	2094142	1977	**£50**	**£25**	*picture sleeve*
One Track Mind	7"	Track	2094137	1977	**£6**	**£2.50**	

HEARTBREAKERS (2)

Frank Zappa plays guitar on 'Every Time I See You'.

Title	Format	Label	Cat. No.	Year	Mint	VG	Notes
Every Time I See You	7"	Donna	1381	1964	**£150**	**£75**	*US*

HEARTS

Title	Format	Label	Cat. No.	Year	Mint	VG	Notes
Dear Abby	7"	Stateside	SS268	1964	**£5**	**£2**	

HEARTS (2)

Title	Format	Label	Cat. No.	Year	Mint	VG	Notes
Young Woman	7"	Parlophone	R5147	1964	**£20**	**£10**	

HEARTS & FLOWERS

Title	Format	Label	Cat. No.	Year	Mint	VG	Notes
Now Is The Time	LP	Capitol	(S)T2762	1967	**£50**	**£25**	*US*
Of Horses, Kids, & Forgotten Women	LP	Capitol	ST2868	1968	**£50**	**£25**	*US*
Rock'n'Roll Gypsies	7"	Capitol	CL15492	1967	**£5**	**£2**	
She Sang Hymns Out Of Tune	7"	Capitol	CL15549	1968	**£4**	**£1.50**	

HEARTS OF SOUL

Title	Format	Label	Cat. No.	Year	Mint	VG	Notes
Waterman	7"	Columbia	DB8670	1970	**£8**	**£4**	

HEATERS

Title	Format	Label	Cat. No.	Year	Mint	VG	Notes
Melting Pot	7"	Upsetter	US329	1970	**£5**	**£2**	

HEATH, GORDON & LEE PAYANT

Title	Format	Label	Cat. No.	Year	Mint	VG	Notes
Evening At L'Abbaye	LP	Elektra	EKL119	1954	**£15**	**£6**	*US*

HEATH, JIMMY

Title	Format	Label	Cat. No.	Year			Notes
Really Big	LP	Riverside	RLP333	1960	**£15**	**£6**	
Thumper	LP	Riverside	RLP12314/1160	1960	**£15**	**£6**	
Triple Threat	LP	Riverside	RLP400	1962	**£15**	**£6**	

HEATH, TED

Title	Format	Label	Cat. No.	Year			Notes
Al Jolson Classics No. 1	7" EP	Decca	DFE6510	1958	**£5**	**£2**	
All Time Top Twelve	LP	Decca	SKL4054	1959	**£15**	**£6**	*stereo*
At Carnegie Hall	LP	Decca	LK4165	1957	**£10**	**£4**	
At The London Palladium	LP	Decca	LK4062	1953	**£10**	**£4**	
At The London Palladium Vol. 3	LP	Decca	LK4097	1955	**£10**	**£4**	
At The London Palladium Vol. 4	LP	Decca	LK4134	1956	**£10**	**£4**	
Australian Suite	7" EP	Decca	DFE6300	1956	**£8**	**£4**	
Beaulieu Festival Suite	7" EP	Decca	STO135	1960	**£8**	**£4**	*stereo*
Beaulieu Festival Suite	7" EP	Decca	DFE6625	1960	**£5**	**£2**	
Big Band Dixie Sound	LP	Decca	SKL4076	1960	**£15**	**£6**	*stereo*
Big Band Percussion	LP	Decca	PFS34004	1962	**£15**	**£6**	*stereo*
Big Ones	LP	Decca	PFS4182	1969	**£10**	**£4**	
Creep	7"	Decca	F10222	1954	**£4**	**£1.50**	
Fats Waller Album	7" EP	Decca	DFE6159	1955	**£8**	**£4**	
Fats Waller Album	LP	Decca	LK4074	1954	**£10**	**£4**	
Fats Waller Album No. 2	7" EP	Decca	DFE6160	1955	**£5**	**£2**	
First American Tour	LP	Decca	LK4167	1957	**£10**	**£4**	
Four Classics	7" EP	Decca	DFE6323	1956	**£5**	**£2**	
Four Hits From The All Time Top Twelve	7" EP	Decca	STO122	1959	**£6**	**£2.50**	*stereo*
Four Hits From The All Time Top Twelve	7" EP	Decca	DFE6579	1959	**£5**	**£2**	
Gershwin For Moderns	LP	Decca	LK4098	1955	**£10**	**£4**	
Gershwin For Moderns No. 1	7" EP	Decca	DFE6290	1956	**£5**	**£2**	
Gershwin For Moderns No. 2	7" EP	Decca	DFE6354	1956	**£5**	**£2**	
Goes Latin	LP	Decca	SKL4389	1961	**£15**	**£6**	*stereo*
Great Film Hits	7" EP	Decca	STO155	1961	**£5**	**£2**	*stereo*
Hits I Missed	7" EP	Decca	STO103	1958	**£5**	**£2**	*stereo*
Hits I Missed	LP	Decca	SKL4003	1958	**£10**	**£4**	*stereo*
Hits I Missed	LP	Decca	LK4275	1958	**£10**	**£4**	
Hits I Missed No. 1	7" EP	Decca	DFE6509	1958	**£5**	**£2**	
Hundredth London Palladium Sunday Concert	LP	Decca	LK4075	1954	**£10**	**£4**	
Hundredth London Palladium Sunday Concert Vol. 1	7" EP	Decca	DFE6189	1955	**£5**	**£2**	
Hundredth London Palladium Sunday Concert Vol. 2	7" EP	Decca	DFE6190	1955	**£5**	**£2**	
Hundredth London Palladium Sunday Concert Vol. 3	7" EP	Decca	DFE6191	1955	**£5**	**£2**	
In Concert	LP	Decca	SKL4079	1960	**£15**	**£6**	*stereo*
Instruments Of The Dance Orchestra	LP	Decca	SKL4117	1961	**£15**	**£6**	*stereo*
Kern For Moderns	LP	Decca	LK4121	1956	**£10**	**£4**	
Kern For Moderns No. 1	7" EP	Decca	DFE6304	1956	**£5**	**£2**	
Kern For Moderns No. 2	7" EP	Decca	DFE6305	1956	**£5**	**£2**	
Kern For Moderns No. 3	7" EP	Decca	DFE6306	1956	**£5**	**£2**	
Listen To My Music	10" LP	Decca	LF1060	1952	**£10**	**£4**	
London Palladium Highlights	7" EP	Decca	DFE6120	1955	**£5**	**£2**	
London Palladium Highlights No. 2	7" EP	Decca	DFE6317	1956	**£5**	**£2**	
London Palladium Highlights No. 3	7" EP	Decca	DFE6346	1956	**£5**	**£2**	
London Palladium Highlights No. 4	7" EP	Decca	DFE6373	1956	**£5**	**£2**	
Moments At Montreux	7" EP	Decca	STO8532	1963	**£5**	**£2**	*stereo*
My Very Good Friends The Band Leaders	LP	Decca	SKL4090	1960	**£15**	**£6**	*stereo*
My Very Good Friends The Bandleaders	7" EP	Decca	DFE6642	1960	**£5**	**£2**	
Old English No. 1	7" EP	Decca	DFE6511	1958	**£5**	**£2**	
Olde Englyshe	LP	Decca	LK4280	1958	**£10**	**£4**	
Our Kind Of Jazz	7" EP	Decca	DFE6500	1958	**£5**	**£2**	
Plays The Blues	LP	Decca	SKL4074	1960	**£15**	**£6**	*stereo*
Plays The Great Film Hits	LP	Decca	SKL4055	1959	**£15**	**£6**	*stereo*
Recalls The Fabulous Dorseys No. 1	7" EP	Decca	DFE6451	1957	**£5**	**£2**	
Rodgers For Moderns	LP	Decca	LK4148	1956	**£10**	**£4**	
Selection	10" LP	Decca	LF1064	1952	**£10**	**£4**	
Seven Eleven	7"	Decca	F10200	1954	**£4**	**£1.50**	
Shall We Dance	LP	Decca	SKL4046	1959	**£10**	**£4**	
Skin Deep	7"	Decca	F10246	1954	**£4**	**£1.50**	
Spotlight On Sidemen	LP	Decca	LK4204	1957	**£10**	**£4**	
Strike Up The Band	LP	Decca	LK4064	1953	**£10**	**£4**	
Swing Session	7" EP	Decca	STO109	1959	**£8**	**£4**	*stereo*
Swing Session	LP	Decca	SKL4030	1959	**£10**	**£4**	*stereo*
Swings In Hi Stereo	7" EP	Decca	STO113	1959	**£5**	**£2**	*stereo*
Swings In Hi-Stereo	LP	Decca	SKL4023	1958	**£10**	**£4**	
Ted Heath And His Music	7" EP	Decca	DFE6025	1955	**£8**	**£4**	
Ted Heath And His Music No. 2	7" EP	Decca	DFE6027	1955	**£8**	**£4**	
Ted Heath And His Music No. 3	7" EP	Decca	DFE6403	1957	**£5**	**£2**	
Ted Heath And His Music No. 4	7" EP	Decca	DFE6432	1957	**£5**	**£2**	
Ted Heath And His Music No. 5	7" EP	Decca	DFE6487	1958	**£5**	**£2**	
Tempo For Dancers	10" LP	Decca	LF1037	1951	**£15**	**£6**	

HEATHCOTE, GEORGE & SHARON PEOPLE

Title	Format	Label	Cat. No.	Year			Notes
Freely Freely	LP	Genesis	GENESIS1	1975	**£100**	**£50**	

HEATHER BLACK

Title	Format	Label	Number	Year	Mint	VG	Notes
Heather Black	LP	American Playboy	1001	196–	£50	£25	US

HEAVEN

Title	Format	Label	Number	Year	Mint	VG	Notes
Brass Rock	LP	CBS	66293	1971	£15	£6	*double*

HEAVEN 17

Title	Format	Label	Number	Year	Mint	VG	Notes
Ballad Of Go Go Brown	CD-s	Virgin	VSCD1113	1988	£5	£2	
Height Of The Fighting	7"	Virgin	VS483	1982	£10	£5	
Temptation	CD-s	Virgin	CDT19	1988	£5	£2	*3" single*
Train Of Love In Motion	CD-s	Virgin	VSCD1134	1988	£5	£2	*3" single*
We Don't Need This Fascist Groove Thang	CD-s	Virgin	CDT21	1988	£5	£2	*3" single*

HEAVY BALLOON

Title	Format	Label	Number	Year	Mint	VG	Notes
32000 Pound	LP	Elephant	EVS104	1968	£60	£30	US

HEAVY JELLY

A joke review of an imaginary band called 'Heavy Jelly' in one of the rock weeklies led to the formation of two separate bands, adopting the name in an attempt to make the joke real. The first of these became familiar to many people through a track included on the Island sampler album *Nice Enough To Eat*. Also released as a single, 'I Keep Singing The Same Old Song' was actually the work of the group Skip Bifferty, who never seriously intended to use the new name for subsequent work. As it happens, the single is rather good. A second Heavy Jelly, in which John Mayall's departing bass player Steve Thompson joined singer Jackie Lomax and members of Aynsley Dunbar's Retaliation, did actually gig for a short while, and issued the single 'Chewn In' on the Head label together with an album that failed to be given a full release.

Title	Format	Label	Number	Year	Mint	VG	Notes
I Keep Singing The Same Old Song	7"	Island	WIP6049	1968	£10	£5	

HEAVY JELLY (2)

Title	Format	Label	Number	Year	Mint	VG	Notes
Chewn In	7"	Head	HDS4001	1969	£8	£4	
Take Me Down To The Water	LP	Head		1969	£100	£50	*demo*

HEBB, BOBBY

Title	Format	Label	Number	Year	Mint	VG	Notes
I Love Everything About You	7"	Philips	BF1570	1967	£4	£1.50	
Love Me	7"	Philips	BF1541	1967	£5	£2	
Satisfied Mind	7"	Philips	BF1522	1966	£4	£1.50	
Sunny	7" EP	Philips	452056	1966	£10	£5	*French*
Sunny	LP	Philips	BL7740	1966	£12	£5	
You Want To Change Me	7"	Philips	BF1702	1968	£15	£7.50	

HEBBERT, MICHAEL

Title	Format	Label	Number	Year	Mint	VG	Notes
Rampin' Cat	LP	Free Reed	FRR009	1977	£10	£4	

HECKSTALL-SMITH, DICK

Colosseum broke apart during the extensive rehearsals of the difficult 'Pirate's Dream', but the piece was rescued for Dick Heckstall-Smith's solo LP. This is close enough to the sound of Colosseum to make it the legitimate follow-up to *Colosseum Live* and is something of an odd record for a saxophonist to have made, as Heckstall-Smith's own contributions do not exactly dominate the centre stage. The record is, however, a fine addition to the small body of adventurous songwriting otherwise largely occupied by the works of Jack Bruce. Meanwhile the very scarce Heckstall-Smith EP provides a kind of glimpse of an alternative world; the start of the career of a straight-ahead jazz saxophonist, that actually proceeded on rather different lines. (Although, in the nineties, Heckstall-Smith has unexpectedly decided to reclaim his jazz career – his *Woza Nasu* album in particular is rather fine.)

Title	Format	Label	Number	Year	Mint	VG	Notes
Jazz Gumbo Vol. 2	LP	Nixa	NJT510	1958	£100	£50	*side 2 by Wally Fawkes & Bruce Turner*
Story Ended	LP	Bronze	ILPS9196	1972	£15	£6	
Very Special Old Jazz	7" EP	Pye	NJE1037	1957	£100	£50	

HEDAYAT, DASHIELL (DAEVID ALLEN)

Title	Format	Label	Number	Year	Mint	VG	Notes
Melmoth La Devanture . . .	LP	Arion	30T079	1969	£40	£20	*French*
Obsolete	LP	Shandar	SR83512	1971	£25	£10	*French*

HEDGEHOG PIE

Title	Format	Label	Number	Year	Mint	VG	Notes
Green Lady	LP	Rubber	RUB014	1975	£25	£10	
Hedgehog Pie	LP	Rubber	RUB009	1975	£15	£6	
His Round	LP	Rubber	RUB002	1972	£15	£6	
Just Act Normal	LP	Rubber	RUB024	1978	£20	£8	
Lambton Worm	7" EP	Rubber	TUB12	1976	£20	£10	

HEDLUND, SVEN

Title	Format	Label	Number	Year	Mint	VG	Notes
Sings Elvis	LP	Olga	005	1973	£15	£6	*Swedish*

HEFTI, NEIL

Title	Format	Label	Number	Year	Mint	VG	Notes
Barefoot In The Park	LP	London	HAD8337	1967	£20	£8	
Batman	LP	RCA	LPM/LSP3573	1966	£30	£15	US
Batman Theme	7"	RCA	RCA1521	1966	£8	£4	
Boeing Boeing	LP	RCA	RD7795	1966	£15	£6	
Duel At Diablo	LP	United Artists	(S)ULP1141	1966	£10	£4	
Harlow	LP	Warner Bros	W1599	1965	£15	£6	
How To Murder Your Wife	LP	United Artists	(S)ULP1098	1965	£20	£8	
Odd Couple	LP	Dot	(S)LPD514	1968	£20	£8	

HEIGHT, DONALD

Title	Format	Label	Number	Year	Mint	VG	Notes
365 Days	7"	London	HLZ10116	1967	£20	£10	
Rags To Riches	7"	Avco	6105005	1971	£6	£2.50	

Title	Format	Label	Cat. No.	Year	Mint	VG	Notes
Talk Of The Grapevine	7"	London	HLZ10062	1966	**£40**	**£20**	

HEIGHT, RONNIE

Title	Format	Label	Cat. No.	Year	Mint	VG	Notes
Come Softly To Me	7"	Decca	F11126	1958	**£10**	**£5**	

HEINZ

Heinz Burt's good looks and spiky dyed blond hair ensured his promotion from bass player with the Tornados, but after a good start with the top five single, 'Just Like Eddie', his career fizzled out. Although Heinz mimed the Eddie Cochran guitar style on television, it was actually the future Deep Purple star, Ritchie Blackmore, who played the lead breaks on the record.

Title	Format	Label	Cat. No.	Year	Mint	VG	Notes
Country Boy	7"	Decca	F11768	1963	**£4**	**£1.50**	
Diggin' My Potatoes	7"	Columbia	DB7482	1965	**£12**	**£6**	
Don't Think Twice It's Alright	7"	Columbia	DB7559	1965	**£10**	**£5**	
Dreams Do Come True	7"	Decca	F11652	1963	**£10**	**£5**	
End Of The World	7"	Columbia	DB7656	1965	**£15**	**£7.50**	
Heart Full Of Sorrow	7"	Columbia	DB7779	1965	**£15**	**£7.50**	
Heinz	7" EP	Decca	DFE8545	1963	**£30**	**£15**	
Live It Up	7" EP	Decca	DFE8559	1963	**£30**	**£15**	
Movin' In	7"	Columbia	DB7942	1966	**£20**	**£10**	
Please Little Girl	7"	Decca	F11920	1964	**£8**	**£4**	
Questions I Can't Answer	7"	Columbia	DB7374	1964	**£10**	**£5**	
Tribute To Eddie	LP	Decca	LK4599	1964	**£50**	**£25**	
You Were There	7"	Decca	F11831	1964	**£6**	**£2.50**	

HELDEN

Title	Format	Label	Cat. No.	Year	Mint	VG	Notes
Holding On	12"	Zica	12ZICA01	1983	**£10**	**£5**	
Holding On	7"	Zica	ZICA01	1983	**£5**	**£2**	

HELDON

Title	Format	Label	Cat. No.	Year	Mint	VG	Notes
Agneta Nilsson (IV)	LP	Urus	000011	1976	**£12**	**£5**	*French*
Allez Teja	LP	Disjuncta	000002	1975	**£12**	**£5**	*French*
Guerilla électronique	LP	Disjuncta	000001	1974	**£12**	**£5**	*French*
Interface	LP	Cobra	37013	1976	**£12**	**£5**	*French*
It's Always Rock And Roll	LP	Disjuncta	000006/7	1975	**£15**	**£6**	*French double*
Stand By	LP	Egg	900578	1979	**£10**	**£4**	*French*
Un rêve sans conséquence spéciale	LP	Cobra	37002	1976	**£12**	**£5**	*French*

HELL, RICHARD

It was the American Richard Hell who invented the punk style. The ripped clothing comes from him, as does the nihilist attitude – Richard Hell's theme song is 'Blank Generation'. He was originally the bass player for Television, which is presumably why that group tend to be classed as punk/new wave, despite a fascination with long guitar solos.

Title	Format	Label	Cat. No.	Year	Mint	VG	Notes
Blank Generation	12"	Sire	6078608	1977	**£6**	**£2.50**	
Blank Generation	7"	Sire	6078608	1977	**£6**	**£2.50**	
Blank Generation	7"	Ork	81976	1976	**£10**	**£5**	*US*
Blank Generation	LP	Sire	SR6037	1977	**£12**	**£5**	*with inner sleeve*
I Could Live With You In Another World	7"	Stiff	BUY7	1976	**£5**	**£2**	
Kid With The Replaceable Head	7"	Radar	ADA30	1979	**£4**	**£1.50**	

HELL PREACHERS INC.

Title	Format	Label	Cat. No.	Year	Mint	VG	Notes
Supreme Psychedelic Underground	LP	Marble Arch	MALS1169	1969	**£25**	**£10**	

HELLHAMMER

Title	Format	Label	Cat. No.	Year	Mint	VG	Notes
Apocalyptic Raids	12"	Noise	N008	1984	**£10**	**£5**	

HELLING, DAVE

Title	Format	Label	Cat. No.	Year	Mint	VG	Notes
Christine	7"	Planet	PLF101	1966	**£10**	**£5**	
It Ain't Me Babe	7"	Stateside	SS409	1965	**£4**	**£1.50**	

HELLIONS

Three singles, but all of them unsuccessful, for a group that included two future members of Traffic (Dave Mason and Jim Capaldi) and one future member of Spooky Tooth and Mott the Hoople (Luther Grosvenor/Ariel Bender).

Title	Format	Label	Cat. No.	Year	Mint	VG	Notes
Daydreaming Of You	7"	Piccadilly	7N35213	1965	**£12**	**£6**	
Little Lovin'	7"	Piccadilly	7N35265	1965	**£12**	**£6**	
Tomorrow Never Comes	7"	Piccadilly	7N35232	1965	**£12**	**£6**	

HELLO

Title	Format	Label	Cat. No.	Year	Mint	VG	Notes
Another School Day	7"	Bell	BLL1333	1973	**£10**	**£5**	
You Move Me	7"	Bell	BLL1238	1972	**£10**	**£5**	

HELMS, BOBBY

Title	Format	Label	Cat. No.	Year	Mint	VG	Notes
Best Of Bobby Helms	LP	Columbia	CL2060/CS8860	1963	**£25**	**£10**	*US*
Bobby Helms	7" EP	Brunswick	OE9461	1960	**£30**	**£15**	
Fraulein	7"	Brunswick	05711	1957	**£4**	**£1.50**	
Jacqueline	7"	Brunswick	05748	1958	**£6**	**£2.50**	
Jingle Bell Rock	7"	Brunswick	05765	1958	**£10**	**£5**	
Love My Lady	7"	Brunswick	05741	1958	**£5**	**£2**	
My Special Agent	7"	Brunswick	05721	1957	**£8**	**£4**	
New River Train	7"	Brunswick	05786	1959	**£4**	**£1.50**	
No Other Baby	7"	Brunswick	05730	1958	**£6**	**£2.50**	
Schoolboy Crush	7"	Brunswick	05754	1958	**£8**	**£4**	
To My Special Angel	LP	Brunswick	LAT8250	1957	**£50**	**£25**	

HELP

Title	Format	Label	Cat. No.	Year	Mint	VG	Notes
Help	LP	Decca	DL75257	1971	**£30**	**£15**	*US*

Title	Format	Label	Cat. No.	Year	Mint	VG	Notes
Second Coming	LP	Decca	DL75304	1971	**£30**	**£15**	*US*

HELP YOURSELF

Title	Format	Label	Cat. No.	Year	Mint	VG	Notes
Beware Of The Shadow	LP	United Artists	UAS29413	1972	**£10**	**£4**	
Help Yourself	LP	Liberty	LIBS83484	1971	**£30**	**£15**	
Return Of Ken Whaley/Happy Days	LP	United Artists	UDG4001	1973	**£25**	**£10**	*double*
Running Down Deep	7"	Liberty	LBF15459	1971	**£4**	**£1.50**	
Strange Affair	LP	United Artists	UAS29287	1972	**£10**	**£4**	

HEMLOCK

Title	Format	Label	Cat. No.	Year	Mint	VG	Notes
Hemlock	LP	Deram	SML1102	1973	**£30**	**£15**	
Mr Horizontal	7"	Deram	DM379	1973	**£4**	**£1.50**	

HEMMINGS, DAVID

Title	Format	Label	Cat. No.	Year	Mint	VG	Notes
Happens	LP	MGM	4490	1968	**£20**	**£8**	*US, with the Byrds*

HENDERSON, BERTHA & ROSA HENDERSON

Title	Format	Label	Cat. No.	Year	Mint	VG	Notes
Female Blues Vol. 2	7" EP	Collector	JEL14	1961	**£10**	**£5**	

HENDERSON, BILL

Title	Format	Label	Cat. No.	Year	Mint	VG	Notes
Bill Henderson	LP	Stateside	SL10019	1963	**£12**	**£5**	
Sweet Pumpkin	7"	Top Rank	JAR412	1960	**£8**	**£4**	

HENDERSON, BOBBY

Title	Format	Label	Cat. No.	Year	Mint	VG	Notes
Handful Of Keys	LP	Vanguard	PPL11007	1957	**£15**	**£6**	

HENDERSON, BRIAN

Title	Format	Label	Cat. No.	Year	Mint	VG	Notes
Folk's In A Hurry	7"	Columbia	DB8006	1966	**£4**	**£1.50**	

HENDERSON, DORRIS

Dorris Henderson was the second female lead singer to be employed by folk-rock pioneers, the Eclection. She had earlier made two very scarce folk LPs on which she is backed by John Renbourn and Danny Thompson.

Title	Format	Label	Cat. No.	Year	Mint	VG	Notes
Hangman	7"	Columbia	DB7567	1965	**£8**	**£4**	
Message To Pretty	7"	Fontana	TF811	1967	**£8**	**£4**	
There You Go	LP	Columbia	SX6001	1965	**£150**	**£75**	
Watch The Stars	LP	Fontana	(S)TL5385	1967	**£150**	**£75**	

HENDERSON, FLETCHER

Title	Format	Label	Cat. No.	Year	Mint	VG	Notes
At Connie's Inn	10" LP	HMV	DLP1066	1955	**£25**	**£10**	
Big Band Story Vol. 1	7" EP	Collector	JE115	1959	**£5**	**£2**	
Birth Of Big Band Jazz	10" LP	London	AL3547	1955	**£25**	**£10**	
Fletcher Henderson	10" LP	Audubon	AAF-AAK	195–	**£100**	**£50**	*6 LP set*
Fletcher Henderson Jazz Group	7" EP	Collector	JE111	1959	**£5**	**£2**	

HENDERSON, JOE

Title	Format	Label	Cat. No.	Year	Mint	VG	Notes
In 'n Out	LP	Blue Note	BLP/BST84166	1964	**£20**	**£8**	
Inner Urge	LP	Blue Note	BLP/BST84189	1965	**£20**	**£8**	
Joe Henderson	7" EP	London	REU1376	1963	**£6**	**£2.50**	
Kicker	LP	Milestone	MSP9008	1971	**£12**	**£5**	
Mode For Joe	LP	Blue Note	BLP/BST84227	1966	**£20**	**£8**	
Our Thing	LP	Blue Note	BLP/BST84152	1963	**£25**	**£10**	
Page One	LP	Blue Note	BLP/BST84140	1963	**£20**	**£8**	
Power To The People	LP	CBS	64068	1970	**£12**	**£5**	

HENDERSON, LORNA

Title	Format	Label	Cat. No.	Year	Mint	VG	Notes
Lollipops To Lipstick	7"	Oriole	CB1549	1960	**£4**	**£1.50**	

HENDRICKS, BOBBY

Title	Format	Label	Cat. No.	Year	Mint	VG	Notes
I'm Coming Home	7"	Mercury	AMT1163	1961	**£4**	**£1.50**	
Itchy Twitchy Feeling	7"	London	HL8714	1958	**£40**	**£20**	
Itchy Twitchy Feeling	7"	Sue	WI315	1964	**£8**	**£4**	
Little John Green	7"	Top Rank	JAR193	1959	**£5**	**£2**	

HENDRICKS, HUGH

Title	Format	Label	Cat. No.	Year	Mint	VG	Notes
Land Of Kinks	7"	Spinning Wheel	SW103	1970	**£5**	**£2**	*O'Neil Hall B side*

HENDRICKS, JON

Title	Format	Label	Cat. No.	Year	Mint	VG	Notes
Four Brothers	7"	Brunswick	05521	1956	**£4**	**£1.50**	
Good Git-Together	7" EP	Vogue	EPV1268	1961	**£6**	**£2.50**	
Good Git-Together	LP	Vogue	LAE12231	1960	**£10**	**£4**	

HENDRIK, TONY FIVE

Title	Format	Label	Cat. No.	Year	Mint	VG	Notes
Nightflight	LP	Columbia	SMC74255	1966	**£15**	**£6**	*German*

HENDRIX, JIMI

Collecting Jimi Hendrix begins with a copy of *Electric Ladyland*, which is as good a demonstration of the power and potential of rock music as one is likely to find anywhere. There are any number of examples of Hendrix's genius as a guitarist to be found among the double album's tracks: for those who still believe that Hendrix was all about noise and bombast, there is '1983 . . . A Merman I Should Turn To Be', an extended composition in which the resources of the recording studio are tested to the limit, yet to a largely gentle and subtle effect. With regard to actual collectors' items, there is the original 'puppet' cover for *Band Of Gypsies*; the first pressing of *Axis: Bold As Love* with its rare poster; the scarce red vinyl edition of *The Cry Of Love*; and the even scarcer record club compilation *Electric Hendrix*. None, however, can give the excitement and emotional impact of an hour and a half spent in *Electric Ladyland*. (Many collectors deny the existence of a mono version of the album, although at least one copy would appear to have been spotted.)

Title	Format	Label	Cat. No.	Year	Mint	VG	Notes
6 Singles Pack	7"	Polydor	2608001	1980	**£15**	**£7.50**	*6 x 7"*

All Along The Watchtower	7"	Track	604025	1968	**£4**	**£1.50**	
All Along The Watchtower	CD-s	Polydor	PZCD100	1990	**£8**	**£4**	
All I Want	7" EP	Visadisc	348	1967	**£15**	**£7.50**	*French*
And A Happy New Year	7"	Reprise	PRO595	196–	**£50**	**£25**	*US promo*
Angel	7"	Track	2094007	1971	**£4**	**£1.50**	
Are You Experienced	LP	Track	612001	1967	**£50**	**£25**	*mono*
Are You Experienced	LP	Track	613001	1967	**£40**	**£20**	*stereo*
Are You Experienced?	CD	Polydor	C88CD111	1988	**£15**	**£6**	*HMV boxed set*
Axis: Bold As Love	LP	Reprise	R6281	1968	**£150**	**£75**	*US mono*
Axis: Bold As Love	LP	Track	612003	1967	**£50**	**£25**	*mono*
Axis: Bold As Love	LP	Track	613003	1967	**£40**	**£20**	*stereo*
Axis: Bold As Love	LP	Track	612003	1967	**£75**	**£37.50**	*with lyric sheet*
Backtrack 10	LP	Track	2407010	1970	**£10**	**£4**	
Backtrack 11	LP	Track	2407011	1970	**£10**	**£4**	
Band Of Gypsys	CD	Track	8219932	1984	**£15**	**£6**	
Band Of Gypsys	LP	Track	2406002	1970	**£10**	**£4**	*single sleeve*
Band Of Gypsys	LP	Track	2406002	1970	**£20**	**£8**	*kaftan g-fold*
Band Of Gypsys	LP	Track	2406002	1970	**£50**	**£25**	*puppet cover*
Between The Lines	CD	Reprise	PROCD4541	1990	**£25**	**£10**	*US promo sampler*
Burning Of The Midnight Lamp	7"	Track	604007	1967	**£4**	**£1.50**	
Calling Long Distance	CD	Univibes	UV001	1992	**£25**	**£10**	*Irish*
Cornerstones	CD	Polydor	8472312	1990	**£60**	**£30**	*promo box set with video*
Crash Landing	LP	Polydor	2310398	1975	**£10**	**£4**	
Crosstown Traffic	7"	Track	604029	1969	**£5**	**£2**	
Cry Of Love	LP	Track	2408101	1971	**£1000**	**£700**	*red vinyl*
Cry Of Love	LP	Track	2408101	1971	**£15**	**£6**	
Electric Hendrix	LP	Track	2856002	1968	**£500**	**£330**	
Electric Ladyland	LP	Polydor	2657012	1973	**£20**	**£8**	*double*
Electric Ladyland	LP	Track	613008/9	1968	**£50**	**£25**	*double*
Electric Ladyland	LP	Track	612008/9	1968	**£1000**	**£700**	*mono double*
Electric Ladyland Part 1	LP	Polydor	2310271	1973	**£10**	**£4**	
Electric Ladyland Part 1	LP	Track	613010	1968	**£20**	**£8**	
Electric Ladyland Part 2	LP	Polydor	2310272	1973	**£10**	**£4**	
Electric Ladyland Part 2	LP	Track	613017	1968	**£20**	**£8**	
Exp Over Sweden	CD	Univibes	UV002	1994	**£25**	**£10**	*Irish*
Fire	7"	Track	604033	1969	**£5**	**£2**	
Gloria	7"	Polydor	JIMI1	1978	**£5**	**£2**	*1 sided*
Gypsy Eyes	7"	Track	2094010	1971	**£10**	**£5**	*picture sleeve*
Hear My Train A-Comin'	7"	Reprise	K14286	1973	**£4**	**£1.50**	
Hey Joe	7"	Polydor	56139	1966	**£5**	**£2**	
Hey Joe	7" EP	Barclay	071111	1967	**£40**	**£20**	*French*
In The West	CD	Polydor	8313122	1989	**£15**	**£6**	
Isle Of Wight	LP	Polydor	2302016	1971	**£10**	**£4**	
Jimi Hendrix	LP	Polydor	2625038	1980	**£75**	**£37.50**	*German, 12 LP boxed set*
Jimi Hendrix	LP	St Michael	2891139	1978	**£50**	**£25**	
Jimi In Denmark	CD	Univibes	UV003	1995	**£25**	**£10**	*Irish*
Jimi Plays Berkeley	CD-s	BMG	791168	1992	**£5**	**£2**	
Johnny B. Goode	7"	Polydor	2001277	1972	**£4**	**£1.50**	
Little Drummer Boy	12"	Reprise	PROA840	1979	**£40**	**£20**	*US promo*
Live And Unreleased – The Radio Show	CD	Castle Communication	HBCD100	1989	**£30**	**£15**	*3 CD set*
Live And Unreleased – The Radio Show	LP	Castle	HBLP100	1989	**£30**	**£15**	*5 LP set*
Live At Winterland	LP	Polydor	8330041	1987	**£12**	**£5**	*double*
Loose Ends	CD	Polydor	8375742	1989	**£15**	**£6**	
Loose Ends	LP	Polydor	2310301	1973	**£12**	**£5**	
Midnight Lightning	LP	Polydor	2310415	1975	**£10**	**£4**	
Nine To The Universe	LP	Polydor	2344155	1980	**£12**	**£5**	
Peel Sessions	CD-s	Strange Fruit	SFPSCD065	1988	**£5**	**£2**	
Purple Haze	7"	Track	604001	1967	**£4**	**£1.50**	
Purple Haze	7"	Track	604001	1967	**£6**	**£2.50**	*white Track label*
Purple Haze	CD-s	Polydor	PZCD33	1989	**£5**	**£2**	
Radio One	CD	Ryko		1989	**£40**	**£20**	*US promo picture disc, alternate Drivin' South*
Radio One	CD	Castle Communication	CCSCP212	1989	**£20**	**£8**	*promo picture disc*
Rainbow Bridge	LP	Reprise	K44159	1971	**£10**	**£4**	
Smash Hits	LP	Track	612004	1968	**£40**	**£20**	*mono*
Smash Hits	LP	Track	613004	1968	**£20**	**£8**	*stereo*
Smash Hits	LP	Reprise	MS2025	1969	**£40**	**£20**	*US, with poster*
Stages 1967–1970	CD	Reprise	PROCD5194	1991	**£25**	**£10**	*US promo sampler*
Ultimate Experience	CD	Polydor	5172352	1992	**£12**	**£5**	*picture disc*
Voodoo Chile	7"	Track	2095001	1970	**£5**	**£2**	*picture sleeve*
War Heroes	LP	Polydor	2302020	1972	**£10**	**£4**	
Wind Cries Mary	7"	Track	604004	1967	**£4**	**£1.50**	
Wind Cries Mary	7" EP	Barclay	071157	1967	**£40**	**£20**	*French*

HENDRIX, JIMI & CURTIS KNIGHT

Ballad Of Jimi	7"	London	HL7126	1970	**£20**	**£10**	*export*
Ballad Of Jimi	7"	London	HL10321	1970	**£4**	**£1.50**	
Get That Feeling	LP	London	HAU/SHU8349	1968	**£12**	**£5**	
How Would You Feel	7"	Track	604009	1967	**£5**	**£2**	
Hush Now	7"	London	HL10160	1967	**£25**	**£12.50**	*export picture sleeve*
Hush Now	7"	London	HL10160	1967	**£5**	**£2**	
No Such Animal	7"	RCA	RCA2033	1970	**£10**	**£5**	*picture sleeve*
Strange Things	LP	London	HAU/SHU8369	1968	**£12**	**£5**	

HENDRIX, MARGIE

I Call You Lover . . .	7"	Mercury	MF976	1966	£4	£1.50	
Restless	7"	Mercury	MF1001	1967	£8	£4	

HENKE, MEL

Mel Henke	LP	Contemporary	LAC12112	1958	£20	£8	

HENLEY, LARRY

My Reasons For Living	7"	Hickory	451272	1964	£6	£2.50	

HENNESSYS

Road And The Miles	LP	Cambrian	CLP593	1969	£60	£30	

HENNIG, SONNY

Tränengas	LP	Kuckuck	2375008	1971	£30	£15	*German*

HENRI, ADRIAN

Adrian Henri	LP	Charivari		196–	£30	£15	
Adrian Henri And Hugo Williams	LP	Argo	PLP1194	196–	£30	£15	

HENRY, BOB

I Need Someone	7"	Philips	BF1450	1965	£6	£2.50	

HENRY, CLARENCE 'FROGMAN'

Ain't Got No Home	7"	London	HLN8389	1957	£150	£75	
Ain't Got No Home	7"	London	HLU10025	1966	£4	£1.50	
Alive And Well And Living In New Orleans	LP	Roulette	SR42039	1969	£15	£6	*US*
But I Do	7"	Pye	7N25078	1961	£4	£1.50	
Clarence Henry Hit Parade	7" EP	Pye	NEP44007	1961	£40	£20	
Dream Myself A Sweetheart	7"	Pye	7N25141	1962	£4	£1.50	
Jealous Kind	7"	Pye	7N25169	1962	£4	£1.50	
Little Green Frog	7"	London	HLU9936	1964	£4	£1.50	
Little Too Much	7"	Pye	7N25123	1962	£4	£1.50	
Lonely Street	7"	Pye	7N25108	1961	£4	£1.50	
Standing In The Need Of Love	7"	Pye	7N25115	1961	£4	£1.50	
You Always Hurt The One You Love	7"	Pye	7N25089	1961	£4	£1.50	
You Always Hurt The One You Love	LP	Pye	NPL28017	1961	£40	£20	

HENRY, ERNIE

Presenting Ernie Henry	LP	Riverside	RLP12222	196–	£15	£6	

HENRY, PIERRE

Messe de Liverpool	LP	Philips	6510001	1970	£15	£6	*French*
Messe pour le temps présent	LP	Philips	836893	1967	£25	£10	*French, with Michel Colombier*

HENRY, ROBERT

Walk Away Like A Winner	7"	Philips	BF1476	1966	£25	£12.50	

HENRY III

I'll Reach The End	7"	Island	WI3081	1967	£10	£5	*Don Tony Lee B side*
Out Of Time	7"	Dynamic	DYN402	1970	£4	£1.50	*Viceroys B side*
So Much Love	7"	RCA	RCA1568	1967	£6	£2.50	
Thank You Girl	7"	Island	WI3078	1967	£10	£5	

HENRY COW

Of all the groups that followed in the wake of Soft Machine, Henry Cow presented the most avant-garde approach. The music on *Legend* and its companions was marketed as rock for want of an alternative category, but in truth the distance between it and *Johnny B. Goode* is about as far as one can get. In essence, the group achieved the difficult feat of creating an extensively improvised music that sounds very little like jazz, partly through the use of unusual timbres – bassoon as a leading voice, for instance – and partly through the use of spiky melody lines and lop-sided rhythms. (Drummer Chris Cutler refers to the album as *Leg End*, incidentally, which is why the cover design features a sock!) Henry Cow's musicians, who include Cutler, guitarist Fred Frith and reed player Lindsay Cooper, have been extraordinarily prolific ever since – to the extent that an entire rock music genre has developed around them – much of it being released through the label that Cutler co-founded, Recommended Records.

Concerts	LP	Caroline	CAD3002	1976	£12	£5	*double*
In Praise Of Learning	LP	Virgin	V2027	1975	£10	£4	*with Slapp Happy*
Legend	LP	Virgin	V2005	1973	£10	£4	
Unrest	LP	Virgin	V2011	1974	£10	£4	
Western Culture	LP	Broadcast	BC1	1978	£10	£4	

HENRY TREE

Electric Holy Man	LP	Mainstream	S6129	1970	£60	£30	*US*

HENSKE, JUDY

Death Defying	LP	Reprise	RS6203	1965	£15	£6	
High Flying Bird	LP	Elektra	EKL/EKS7241	1964	£15	£6	*US*
Judy Henske	LP	Elektra	EKL/EKS7231	1963	£15	£6	*US*
Little Bit Of Sunshine	LP	Mercury	MG2/SR61010	1965	£15	£6	*US*

HENSKE, JUDY & JERRY YESTER

Farewell Aldebaran	LP	Straight	STS1052	1969	£25	£10	
Road To Nowhere	7"	Reprise	RS20485	1966	£4	£1.50	

Rosebud	LP	Reprise	RS6426	1971	£15	£6	US

HENSLEY, ROBERT HENRY

You're Gonna See Me Cry	7"	Polydor	56295	1968	£5	£2	

HENSON, NICKY

Till I See You Cry	7"	Parlophone	R4976	1963	£4	£1.50	

HEP STARS

This Swedish group had future Abba star Benny Andersson as keyboard player and songwriter.

Hep Stars	LP	Olga	LP004	1966	£25	£10	*Swedish*
It's Been A Long Long Time	LP	Cupol	CLPNS342	1968	£15	£6	*Swedish*
Jul Med	LP	Olga	LP006	1966	£15	£6	*Swedish*
Let It Be Me	7"	Olga	OLE13	1968	£40	£20	
Malaika	7"	Olga	OLE14	1968	£40	£20	*picture sleeve*
Malaika	7"	Olga	OLE14	1968	£20	£10	
Pa Svenska	LP	Olga	LP011	196–	£20	£8	*Swedish*
Songs We Sang	LP	Olga	LP007	196–	£20	£8	*Swedish*
Sunny Girl	7"	Decca	F22446	1966	£20	£10	
Wedding	7"	Olga	OLE001	1967	£10	£5	

HEPTONES

Be A Man	7"	Banana	BA311	1970	£6	£2.50	*U Roy B side*
Better Days	LP	Third World	TDWD1	1978	£10	£4	
Change Is Gonna Come	7"	Studio One	SO2005	1967	£12	£6	
Cool Rasta	LP	Trojan	TRLS128	1976	£12	£5	
Cry Baby Cry	7"	Studio One	SO2049	1968	£12	£6	
Dock Of The Bay	7"	Studio One	SO2052	1968	£12	£6	*King Rocky B side*
Equal Rights	7"	Coxsone	CS7068	1968	£10	£5	
Fat Girl	7"	Studio One	SO2014	1967	£12	£6	*Delroy Wilson B side*
Freedom Line	7"	Banana	BA349	1971	£5	£2	*Sound Dimension B side*
Good Life	LP	Greensleeves	GREL6	1979	£10	£4	
Gunmen Coming To Town	7"	Rio	R104	1966	£8	£4	*Tommy McCook B side*
Heptones	LP	Studio One	SOL9002	1967	£100	£50	
Heptones	LP	Studio One	SOL0016	196–	£100	£50	
Heptones And Friends	LP	Trojan	TBL183	1972	£20	£8	
Heptones And Friends Vol. 2	LP	Attack	ATLP1001	1975	£15	£6	
Hurry Up	7"	Upsetter	US339	1970	£5	£2	
Hypocrite	7"	Green Door	GD4020	1972	£6	£2.50	*Johnny Lover B side*
I Shall Be Released	7"	Bamboo	BAM11	1969	£6	£2.50	
I Shall Be Released	7"	Studio One	SO2083	1969	£12	£6	
I'm In The Mood For Love	7"	Ashanti	ASH411	1972	£5	£2	*Tommy McCook B side*
If I Knew	7"	Studio One	SO2021	1967	£12	£6	
Love Won't Come Easy	7"	Coxsone	CS7052	1968	£10	£5	
Message From A Blackman	7"	Bamboo	BAM43	1970	£6	£2.50	*Sound Dimension B side*
Nightfood	LP	Island	ILPS9381	1976	£12	£5	
On Top	LP	Studio One	SOL9010	1968	£100	£50	
Only Sixteen	7"	Studio One	SO2033	1967	£12	£6	
Our Day Will Come	7"	Prince Buster	PB37	1972	£6	£2.50	*Prince Buster B side*
Party Time	7"	Studio One	SO2055	1968	£12	£6	
Party Time	LP	Island	ILPS9456	1977	£12	£5	
Schoolgirls	7"	Caltone	TONE105	1967	£8	£4	
Soul Power	7"	Coxsone	CS7082	1968	£10	£5	
Suspicious Minds	7"	Banana	BA325	1971	£6	£2.50	
Sweet Talking	7"	Coxsone	CS7092	1969	£10	£5	
We've Got Love	7"	Ska Beat	JB266	1967	£10	£5	
Why Did You Leave	7"	Studio One	SO2026	1967	£12	£6	*Gaylads B side*
Why Must I	7"	Studio One	SO2027	1967	£12	£6	*Slim Smith B side*
Young Generation	7"	Bamboo	BAM39	1970	£6	£2.50	
Young, Gifted And Black	7"	Bamboo	BAM28	1970	£6	£2.50	*Sound Dimension B side*

HERB & KAY

Coffee Blues	7"	Parlophone	CMSP31	1955	£10	£5	*export*
This Ole House	7"	Parlophone	CMSP23	1954	£10	£5	*export*
This Ole House	7"	Parlophone	MSP6127	1954	£10	£5	

HERBAL MIXTURE

Blues guitarist Tony McPhee led this psychedelic pop band, which also included fellow member of the Groundhogs, bass player Pete Cruickshank.

Love That's Died	7"	Columbia	DB8021	1966	£75	£37.50	
Machines	7"	Columbia	DB8083	1966	£75	£37.50	

HERBIE & THE ROYALISTS

Soul Of The Matter	LP	Saga	FID2121	1968	£15	£6	

HERBIE'S PEOPLE

One Little Smile	7"	CBS	202058	1966	£5	£2	
Residential Area	7"	CBS	202584	1967	£5	£2	
Sweet And Tender Romance	7"	CBS	202005	1965	£15	£7.50	

HERD

Game	7"	Fontana	TF1011	1969	£4	£1.50	
Goodbye Baby Goodbye	7"	Parlophone	R5284	1965	£15	£7.50	
I Can Fly	7"	Fontana	TF819	1967	£4	£1.50	
Lookin' Thru You	LP	Fontana	SRF67579	1968	£25	£10	*US*
Nostalgia	LP	Bumble	GEMP5001	1972	£12	£5	
Paradise Lost	7"	Fontana	TF887	1967	£8	£4	*picture sleeve*
Paradise Lost	LP	Fontana	(S)TL5458	1968	£30	£15	
She Was Really Saying Something	7"	Parlophone	R5353	1965	£25	£12.50	
So Much In Love	7"	Parlophone	R5413	1966	£25	£12.50	
Sunshine Cottage	7"	Fontana	TF975	1968	£4	£1.50	

HERDSMEN

Blow In Paris	10" LP	Vogue	LDE058	1954	£12	£5	
Blow In Paris Vol. 2	10" LP	Vogue	LDE091	1954	£12	£5	

HERETIC

Burnt At The Stake	12"	Thunderbolt	THBE1004	1984	£10	£5	

HERETICS

Evening With The Heretics	LP	Heritage	101	1975	£20	£8	

HERITAGE

Remorse Code	LP	Rondelet	ABOUT12	1982	£12	£5	
Strange Place To Be	7"	Rondelet	ROUND8	1981	£10	£5	

HERMAN

El Fishy	7"	Big Shot	BI573	1971	£4	£1.50	
New Love	7"	Big Shot	BI578	1971	£6	£2.50	*Augustus Pablo B side*
Tar Baby	7"	Big Shot	BI577	1971	£4	£1.50	*Tommy McCook B side*

HERMAN, BONGO

True Grit	7"	Song Bird	SB1018	1970	£4	£1.50	

HERMAN, WOODY

At Carnegie Hall Vol. 1	10" LP	MGM	D108	1952	£20	£8	
At Carnegie Hall Vol. 2	10" LP	MGM	D110	1953	£20	£8	
At The Monterey Jazz Festival	LP	London	LTZK15200/ SAHK6100	1960	£12	£5	
Blues Groove	LP	Capitol	T784	1957	£15	£6	
Classics In Jazz	10" LP	Capitol	LC6560	1952	£20	£8	
Fancy Woman	7"	London	HL8031	1954	£15	£7.50	
Fourth Herd	LP	Jazzland	JLP17	1960	£12	£5	
Girl Upstairs	7"	Capitol	CL14333	1955	£4	£1.50	
Great Big Bands Vol. 2	LP	Capitol	T20809	1965	£10	£4	
Herd From Mars Vol. 1	7" EP	London	REP1001	1954	£5	£2	
Herd From Mars Vol. 2	7" EP	London	REP1002	1955	£5	£2	
Herd Rides Again	LP	Top Rank	35038	1959	£12	£5	
Here's Herman	10" LP	Columbia	33S1060	1955	£20	£8	
Hush	7"	Chess	CRS8095	1969	£4	£1.50	
Jackpot!	LP	Capitol	T748	1956	£15	£6	
Jazz – The Utmost!	LP	Columbia	33CX10129	1959	£20	£8	
Men From Mars	10" LP	London	HAPB1018	1954	£20	£8	
Mexican Hat Trick	7"	Capitol	CL14231	1955	£4	£1.50	
Moody Woody	LP	Top Rank	BUY009	1960	£12	£5	
Music For Tired Lovers	LP	Philips	BBL7056	1955	£15	£6	*with Erroll Garner*
Muskrat Ramble	7"	Capitol	CL14183	1954	£6	£2.50	
Sequence In Jazz	10" LP	Columbia	33S1068	1955	£20	£8	
Sorry 'Bout The Whole Darned Thing	7"	London	HL8122	1955	£12	£6	
Stomping At The Savoy	10" LP	London	HAPB1014	1953	£20	£8	
Summer Sequence	10" LP	Fontana	TFR6015	1958	£15	£6	
Three Herds	LP	Philips	BBL7123	1958	£15	£6	
Thundering Herds Vol. 1	LP	CBS	BPG62158	1964	£10	£4	
Thundering Herds Vol. 2	LP	CBS	BPG62159	1964	£10	£4	
Thundering Herds Vol. 3	LP	CBS	BPG62160	1964	£10	£4	
Twelve Shades Of Blue	LP	Philips	BBL7124	1957	£15	£6	
Woodchopper's Ball	LP	Brunswick	LAT8092	1956	£15	£6	
Woody Herman	LP	HMV	CLP1130	1957	£15	£6	
Woody Herman Band	10" LP	Capitol	LCT6014	1955	£20	£8	
Woody Herman Sextet	LP	World Record Club	T323	196–	£10	£4	
Wooftie	7"	London	HL8013	1954	£15	£7.50	

HERMAN'S HERMITS

Best Of Herman's Hermits	LP	Columbia	SCXC27	196–	£15	£6	*export*
Best Of Herman's Hermits Vol. 2	LP	Columbia	SCXC32	1966	£15	£6	*export*
Blaze	LP	Columbia	SCXC35	196–	£20	£8	*export*
Both Sides Of Herman's Hermits	LP	Columbia	SX6084	1966	£12	£5	
Dandy	7" EP	Columbia	SEG8520	1967	£10	£5	
Herman's Hermits	LP	Columbia	33SX1727	1965	£12	£5	
Herman's Hermits	LP	Regal	SREG1117	196–	£15	£6	*export*
Herman's Hermits' Hits	7" EP	Columbia	SEG8442	1965	£8	£4	
Hermania	7" EP	Columbia	SEG8380	1965	£10	£5	
Hold On – Soundtrack Songs	7" EP	Columbia	SEG8503	1966	£10	£5	
I'm Henry VIII, I Am	7" EP	Columbia	ESRF1707	1965	£10	£5	*French*

I'm Into Something Good	7" EP	Columbia	ESRF1615	1964	**£10**	**£5**	*French*
Je Suis Anglais	7" EP	Columbia	ESRF1750	1966	**£15**	**£7.50**	*French*
London Look	7" EP	Yardley	SLE15	1967	**£15**	**£7.50**	*French, promo*
Mrs Brown You've Got A Lovely Daughter	7" EP	Columbia	ESRF1663	1965	**£10**	**£5**	*French*
Mrs Brown You've Got A Lovely Daughter	7" EP	Columbia	SEG8440	1965	**£8**	**£4**	
Mrs Brown You've Got A Lovely Daughter	LP	Columbia	SCX6303	1968	**£12**	**£5**	
Museum	7" EP	Columbia	ESRF1865	1967	**£10**	**£5**	*French*
Must To Avoid	7" EP	Columbia	SEG8477	1966	**£8**	**£4**	
There's A Kind Of Hush	7" EP	Columbia	ESRF1846	1967	**£10**	**£5**	*French*
There's A Kind Of Hush	LP	Columbia	SX/SCX6174	1967	**£12**	**£5**	
There's A Kind Of Hush	LP	Columbia	SCXC34	196–	**£20**	**£8**	[illegible]
Train	7"	Buddah	BDS700	1974	**£20**	**£10**	

HERO

Hero	LP	Ariola	87304	1973	**£60**	**£30**	*German*

HEROLD, TED

I Don't Know Why	7"	Polydor	NH66817	1960	**£20**	**£10**	
Ted Herold	LP	Polydor	46754	1961	**£75**	**£37.50**	*German*

HERON

Bye And Bye	7"	Dawn	DNX2509	1971	**£5**	**£2**	*picture sleeve*
Heron	LP	Dawn	DNLS3010	1970	**£40**	**£20**	
Take Me Back Home	7"	Dawn	DNS1015	1970	**£4**	**£1.50**	
Twice As Nice	LP	Dawn	DNLS3025	1972	**£40**	**£20**	*double*

HERON, MIKE

Diamond Of Dream	LP	Bronze	ILPS9460	1977	**£10**	**£4**	
Mike Heron	LP	Casablanca	NBLP7186	1980	**£12**	**£5**	*US*
Mike Heron's Reputation	LP	Neighborhood	NBH80637	1975	**£10**	**£4**	
Smiling Men With Bad Reputations	LP	Island	ILPS9146	1971	**£10**	**£4**	

HERSH, KRISTIN

Hips And Makers	CD	4AD	CADD4002CD	1994	**£15**	**£6**	*with cards*
Velvet Days	7"	4AD	KH2	1993	**£6**	**£2.50**	*promo*

HERVEY, PAT & ART SNIDER

Can't Get You Out Of My Mind	7"	President	PT110	1967	**£4**	**£1.50**	

HESITATIONS

Born Free	7"	London	HLR10180	1968	**£6**	**£2.50**	
Impossible Dream	7"	London	HLR10198	1968	**£5**	**£2**	
New Born Free	LP	London	HAR/SHR8360	1968	**£10**	**£4**	

HESTER, CAROLYN

At Town Hall	LP	Dot	DLP3649	1966	**£10**	**£4**	
Carolyn Hester	LP	Columbia	CL1796/CS8596	1962	**£15**	**£6**	*US*
Carolyn Hester	LP	CBS	(S)BPG62033	1966	**£10**	**£4**	
Carolyn Hester Coalition	LP	Pye	NSPL28121	1969	**£10**	**£4**	
That's My Song	LP	Dot	DLP3604/25604	1964	**£12**	**£5**	*US*
This Is My Living	LP	Columbia	CL2031/CS8831	1963	**£12**	**£5**	*US*
This Life I'm Living	LP	Realm	RM2338	1967	**£10**	**£4**	

HEWETT SISTERS

Baby-O	7"	HMV	POP567	1959	**£10**	**£5**	

HEWITT, BEN

Break It Up	7" EP	Mercury	ZEP10035	1959	**£100**	**£50**	
For Quite A While	7"	Mercury	AMT1055	1959	**£12**	**£6**	
I Want A Girl	7"	Mercury	AMT1084	1960	**£25**	**£12.50**	
You Break Me Up	7"	Mercury	AMT1041	1959	**£40**	**£20**	

HEYWARD, NICK

North Of A Miracle	CD	Arista	1610102	1984	**£20**	**£8**	

HEYWOOD, ANNE

I'd Rather Have Roses	7"	Top Rank	JAR130	1959	**£4**	**£1.50**	

HEYWOOD, EDDIE

Soft Summer Breeze	7"	Mercury	7MT131	1957	**£4**	**£1.50**	

HI FI FOUR

Davy You Upset My Life	7"	Parlophone	MSP6210	1956	**£100**	**£50**	

HI FIs

Baby's In Black	7"	Pye	7N15788	1965	**£6**	**£2.50**	
I Keep Forgettin'	7"	Pye	7N15710	1964	**£15**	**£7.50**	
It's Gonna Be Morning	7"	Alp	595010	1966	**£25**	**£12.50**	
Snakes And Hi Fi's	LP	Star Club	STY158035	1967	**£50**	**£25**	*German*
Snakes And Hifi's	LP	Starclub	158035STY	1967	**£50**	**£25**	*German*
Take Me Or Leave Me	7"	Piccadilly	7N35130	1963	**£4**	**£1.50**	
Will Ya Won't Ya	7"	Pye	7N15635	1964	**£4**	**£1.50**	

HI LITERS

Dance Me To Death	7"	Mercury	AMT1011	1958	**£75**	**£37.50**	

HIATT, JOHN

Title	Format	Label	Cat. No.	Year	Mint	Ex	Notes
Hanging Round The Observatory	LP	Epic	KE32688	1974	**£12**	**£5**	*US*
Overcoats	LP	Epic	33190	1975	**£10**	**£4**	*US*

HIBBERT, LENNIE

Title	Format	Label	Cat. No.	Year	Mint	Ex	Notes
Creation	LP	Studio One	SOL0015	196–	**£100**	**£50**	

HIBBLER, AL

Title	Format	Label	Cat. No.	Year	Mint	Ex	Notes
After The Lights Go Down Low	7"	Brunswick	05552	1956	**£4**	**£1.50**	
Al Hibbler Sings Love Songs	7" EP	HMV	7EG8326	1957	**£5**	**£2**	
Around The Corner From The Blues	7"	Brunswick	05703	1957	**£4**	**£1.50**	
Danny Boy	7"	London	HL7086	1959	**£4**	**£1.50**	*export*
Duke Ellington And Al Hibbler	7" EP	HMV	7EG8158	1955	**£5**	**£2**	
Eleventh Hour Melody	7"	Brunswick	05523	1956	**£4**	**£1.50**	
He	7"	Brunswick	05492	1955	**£4**	**£1.50**	
Here's Hibbler Part 1	7" EP	Brunswick	OE9331	1957	**£5**	**£2**	
Here's Hibbler Part 2	7" EP	Brunswick	OE9332	1957	**£5**	**£2**	
Here's Hibbler Part 3	7" EP	Brunswick	OE9333	1957	**£5**	**£2**	
Now I Lay Me Down To Dream	7"	London	HL8184	1955	**£10**	**£5**	
Starring Al Hibbler	LP	Brunswick	LAT8140	1956	**£12**	**£5**	
They Say You're Laughing At Me	7"	Brunswick	05454	1955	**£6**	**£2.50**	
Unchained Melody	7"	Brunswick	05420	1955	**£15**	**£7.50**	

HICKEY, EDDIE

Title	Format	Label	Cat. No.	Year	Mint	Ex	Notes
Another Sleepless Night	7"	Decca	F11241	1960	**£4**	**£1.50**	

HICKEY, ERSEL

Title	Format	Label	Cat. No.	Year	Mint	Ex	Notes
Don't Be Afraid Of Love	7"	Fontana	H198	1959	**£40**	**£20**	

HICKMAN, DWAYNE

Title	Format	Label	Cat. No.	Year	Mint	Ex	Notes
I'm A Lover Not A Fighter	7"	Capitol	CL15164	1960	**£5**	**£2**	

HICKORY

Title	Format	Label	Cat. No.	Year	Mint	Ex	Notes
Green Light	7"	CBS	3963	1969	**£20**	**£10**	

HICKORY STIX

Title	Format	Label	Cat. No.	Year	Mint	Ex	Notes
Hello My Darling	7"	Oak	RGJ149	1964	**£100**	**£50**	

HICKORY WIND

Title	Format	Label	Cat. No.	Year	Mint	Ex	Notes
Hickory Wind	LP	Gigantic		1969	**£1000**	**£700**	*US*

HICKS, COLIN & THE CABIN BOYS

Title	Format	Label	Cat. No.	Year	Mint	Ex	Notes
La Dee Dah	7"	Pye	7N15125	1958	**£6**	**£2.50**	
Little Boy Blue	7"	Pye	7N15163	1958	**£8**	**£4**	
Wild Eyes And Tender Lips	7"	Pye	7N15114	1957	**£12**	**£6**	

HICKS, JIMMY

Title	Format	Label	Cat. No.	Year	Mint	Ex	Notes
I'm Mr Big Stuff	7"	London	HLU10396	1972	**£6**	**£2.50**	

HIDEAWAYS

Title	Format	Label	Cat. No.	Year	Mint	Ex	Notes
Hideout	7"	Action	ACT4544	1969	**£4**	**£1.50**	

HI-FI

Title	Format	Label	Cat. No.	Year	Mint	Ex	Notes
Demonstration Record	12"	Butt	FUNEP3	1982	**£6**	**£2.50**	
Moods For Mallards	LP	Shanghai	HAI102	1983	**£10**	**£4**	

HIGGINS, CHUCK

Title	Format	Label	Cat. No.	Year	Mint	Ex	Notes
Pachuko Hop	LP	Combo	LP300	1960	**£40**	**£20**	*US, Higgins cover*
Pachuko Hop	LP	Combo	LP300	1960	**£100**	**£50**	*US, nude cover*

HIGGINS, GARY

Title	Format	Label	Cat. No.	Year	Mint	Ex	Notes
Red Hash	LP	Nufusmoon	WM13673	1973	**£20**	**£8**	

HIGGINS, LIZZIE

Title	Format	Label	Cat. No.	Year	Mint	Ex	Notes
Up And Awa Wi The Laverock	LP	Topic	12TS260	1975	**£10**	**£4**	

HIGGS, JOE

Title	Format	Label	Cat. No.	Year	Mint	Ex	Notes
I Am The Song	7"	Island	WI3026	1967	**£10**	**£5**	
Life Of Contradiction	LP	Grounation	GROL508	1975	**£15**	**£6**	
Neighbour Neighbour	7"	Coxsone	CS7004	1967	**£10**	**£5**	*Melodians B side*
Unity Is Power	LP	Island	ILPS9535	1979	**£12**	**£5**	
You Hurt My Soul	7"	Island	WI3131	1968	**£10**	**£5**	*Lyn Taitt B side*

HIGGS & WILSON

Title	Format	Label	Cat. No.	Year	Mint	Ex	Notes
Come On Home	7"	Starlite	ST45042	1961	**£10**	**£5**	
How Can I Be Sure	7"	Blue Beat	BB95	1962	**£12**	**£6**	
If You Want Pardon	7"	Blue Beat	BB190	1963	**£12**	**£6**	*Baba Brooks B side*
It Is The Day	7"	Starlite	ST45036	1961	**£10**	**£5**	
Lazy Saturday Night	7"	Island	WI081	1963	**£10**	**£5**	*Prince Buster B side*
Let Me Know	7"	R&B	JB109	1963	**£10**	**£5**	
Love Is Not For Me	7"	Rio	R29	1964	**£10**	**£5**	
Pretty Baby	7"	Starlite	ST45035	1961	**£10**	**£5**	
Sha Ba Ba	7"	Starlite	ST45053	1961	**£10**	**£5**	
When You Tell Me	7"	Blue Beat	BB3	1960	**£12**	**£6**	

HIGH

Title	Format	Label	Cat. No.	Year	Mint	Ex	Notes
Long Live The High	7"	CBS	4164	1969	**£5**	**£2**	

HIGH & MIGHTY

Tryin' To Stop Cryin'	7"	HMV	POP1548	1966	£20	£10	

HIGH BROOM

Dancing In The Moonlight	7"	Columbia	DB8969	1973	£4	£1.50	
Dancing In The Moonlight	7"	Island	WIP6088	1970	£10	£5	

HIGH KEYS

Qué será será	7"	London	HLK9768	1963	£10	£5	

HIGH LEVEL RANTERS

Bonny Pit Laddie	LP	Topic	212TS271/2	1975	£12	£5	*Double*
English Sporting Ballads	LP	Broadside	BRO128	1977	£25	£10	*with tracks by Martin Wyndham-Read*
Four In A Bar	LP	Topic	12TS388	1979	£10	£4	
High Level	LP	Trailer	LER2030	1971	£10	£4	
Keep Your Feet Still Geordie Hinnie	LP	Trailer	LER2020	1970	£10	£4	
Lads Of Northumbria	LP	Trailer	LER2007	1969	£10	£4	
Mile To Ride	LP	Trailer	LER2037	1972	£10	£4	
Northumberland For Ever	LP	Topic	12TS186	1968	£12	£5	
Northumberland For Ever	LP	Topic	12TS186	197–	£10	£4	*reissue with different cover*

HIGH NUMBERS

'I'm The Face' is one of the most celebrated single rarities. The High Numbers was, of course, the original name of the Who. The group also recorded a version of 'The Kids Are Alright' before the name change, but this was only ever available as an acetate.

I'm The Face	7"	Back Door	DOOR4	1980	£10	£5	*picture sleeve*
I'm The Face	7"	Fontana	TF480	1964	£400	£250	*best auctioned*

HIGH SOCIETY

Graham Gouldman was the leader of High Society, which changed its name to the Manchester Mob for the next release.

People Passing By	7"	Fontana	TF771	1966	£10	£5	

HIGH STREET EAST

Newcastle Brown	7"	Rubber	RUBBERONE	1970	£10	£5	

HIGH TIDE

High Tide were a heavy group from the time when the heavy metal style was not so rigidly set as to preclude a more experimental approach like this. A heavily distorted guitar is here partnered by an electric violin (courtesy of Simon House, who was later to join Hawkwind) and the two instruments manage to create an extraordinary maelstrom of sound. The singer, meanwhile, is a Jim Morrison sound-alike, the slightly doom-laden voice sounding very effective in this context.

High Tide	LP	Liberty	LBS83294	1970	£50	£25	
High Tide	LP	Psycho	PSYCHO27	1984	£10	£4	
Sea Shanties	LP	Liberty	LBS83264	1969	£60	£30	
Sea Shanties	LP	Psycho	PSYCHO26	1984	£10	£4	

HIGH TIDE (2)

Baby Dancing	7"	Sunday Morning	no number	1981	£6	£2.50	*no picture sleeve*

HIGH TREASON

High Treason	LP	Abbott	ABS1209	1968	£60	£30	*US*

HIGH TREASON (2)

Saturday Night Special	7"	Burlington	BURLS001	1980	£20	£10	

HIGHLY LIKELY

Whatever Happened To You?	7"	BBC	RESL10	1973	£4	£1.50	

HIGHTOWER, DEAN

Twangy – With A Beat	LP	HMV	CLP1360	1960	£25	£10	

HIGHTOWER, DONNA

Take One	LP	Capitol	T1133	1959	£12	£5	

HIGHTOWER, ROSETTA

Hightower	LP	CBS	64201	1971	£10	£4	
Rosetta Hightower	LP	Rediffusion	ZS88	1971	£12	£5	

HIGHWAYMEN

Highwaymen	LP	HMV	CLP1510	1961	£10	£4	

HIGNEY, KENNETH

Attic Demonstration	LP	Kebrutney		1976	£60	£30	*US*

HILARY HILARY

How Come You're So Dumb	7"	Modern	STP2	1980	£50	£25	

HILDEBRAND, DIANE

Early Morning Blues And Greens	LP	Elektra	EKS74031	1969	£12	£5	
Jan's Blues	7"	Elektra	EKSN45055	1969	£4	£1.50	

HI-LITES

Title	Format	Label	Catalogue No.	Year	Mint	VG	Notes
For Your Precious Love	LP	Dandee	DLP206	195–	£20	£8	US

HILL, ANDREW

Title	Format	Label	Catalogue No.	Year	Mint	VG	Notes
Andrew!!!	LP	Blue Note	BLP/BST84203	1965	£25	£10	
Black Fire	LP	Blue Note	BLP/BST84151	1963	£25	£10	
Compulsion	LP	Blue Note	BLP/BST84217	1965	£20	£8	
Grass Roots	LP	Blue Note	BST84303	1968	£12	£5	
Judgement	LP	Blue Note	BLP/BST84159	1964	£20	£8	
Lift Every Voice	LP	Blue Note	BST84330	1969	£12	£5	
Point Of Departure	LP	Blue Note	BLP/BST84167	1964	£25	£10	
Smoke Stack	LP	Blue Note	BLP/BST84160	1964	£25	£10	

HILL, BENNY

Title	Format	Label	Catalogue No.	Year	Mint	VG	Notes
I Can't Tell A Waltz From A Tango	7"	Decca	F10442	1955	£5	£2	
Sings?	LP	Pye	NPL18133	1966	£10	£4	
Who Done It	7"	Columbia	SCM5238	1956	£4	£1.50	

HILL, BUNKER

Title	Format	Label	Catalogue No.	Year	Mint	VG	Notes
Hide And Go Seek	7"	Stateside	SS135	1962	£6	£2.50	

HILL, DAVID

Title	Format	Label	Catalogue No.	Year	Mint	VG	Notes
All Shook Up	7"	Vogue	V9076	1957	£125	£62.50	
That's Love	7"	RCA	RCA1041	1958	£175	£87.50	

HILL, JESSE

Title	Format	Label	Catalogue No.	Year	Mint	VG	Notes
Ooh Poo Pah Doo	7"	London	HLU9117	1960	£10	£5	

HILL, VINCE

Title	Format	Label	Catalogue No.	Year	Mint	VG	Notes
Four Sides Of Vince Hill	7" EP	Columbia	SEG8509	1966	£5	£2	

HILL, Z. Z.

Title	Format	Label	Catalogue No.	Year	Mint	VG	Notes
Brand New Z. Z. Hill	LP	Mojo	2916013	1972	£10	£4	
Gimme Gimme	7" EP	Sue	IEP711	1966	£100	£50	
I Keep On Loving You	7"	United Artists	UP35727	1975	£4	£1.50	
Make Me Yours	7"	Action	ACT4532	1969	£10	£5	
Someone To Love	7"	R&B	MRB5005	1965	£15	£7.50	
Whole Lot Of Soul	LP	Action	ACLP6004	1969	£20	£8	

HILLAGE, STEVE

Title	Format	Label	Catalogue No.	Year	Mint	VG	Notes
Rainbow Dome Musick	LP	Virgin	VR1	1979	£10	£4	*clear vinyl*
Six Pack	7"	Virgin	SIXPACK2	1979	£5	£2	*picture disc*

HILLER BROTHERS

Title	Format	Label	Catalogue No.	Year	Mint	VG	Notes
Little Darlin'	7"	Honey Hit	TB124	196–	£4	£1.50	*picture sleeve*

HILLERY, JANE

Title	Format	Label	Catalogue No.	Year	Mint	VG	Notes
You've Got A Hold On Me	7"	Columbia	DB7918	1966	£10	£5	

HILLMEN

Title	Format	Label	Catalogue No.	Year	Mint	VG	Notes
Hillmen	LP	Together	STT1012	1970	£20	£8	US

HILLOW HAMMET

Title	Format	Label	Catalogue No.	Year	Mint	VG	Notes
Hammer	LP	House Of Fox	LP2	1968	£100	£50	US

HILLS, GILLIAN

Title	Format	Label	Catalogue No.	Year	Mint	VG	Notes
Tomorrow Is Another Day	7"	Vogue	VRS7005	1965	£6	£2.50	

HILLSIDERS

Title	Format	Label	Catalogue No.	Year	Mint	VG	Notes
Our Country	LP	Polydor	2460203	1973	£15	£6	

HILLTOPPERS

Title	Format	Label	Catalogue No.	Year	Mint	VG	Notes
Alone	7"	London	HLD9038	1960	£5	£2	
Do The Bop	7"	London	HLD8278	1956	£50	£25	
Fallen Star	7"	London	HLD8455	1957	£12	£6	
From The Vine Came The Grape	7"	London	HL8026	1954	£30	£15	
Hilltoppers	LP	Dot	DLP3073	1958	£30	£15	US
Hilltoppers Vol. 2	7" EP	London	RED1030	1955	£20	£10	
Hilltoppers Vol. 3	7" EP	London	RED1099	1957	£20	£10	
I'm Serious	7"	London	HLD8441	1957	£12	£6	
If I Didn't Care	7"	London	HL8092	1954	£30	£15	
Joker	7"	London	HLD8528	1957	£15	£7.50	
Kentuckian Song	7"	London	HLD8168	1955	£30	£15	
Marianne	7"	London	HLD8381	1957	£10	£5	
My Treasure	7"	London	HLD8255	1956	£20	£10	
Only You	7"	London	HLD8221	1956	£10	£5	
Poor Butterfly	7"	London	HL8070	1954	£30	£15	
Presenting The Hilltoppers	7" EP	London	RED1012	1955	£20	£10	
Searching	7"	London	HLD8208	1955	£40	£20	
So Tired	7"	London	HLD8333	1956	£15	£7.50	
Tops In Pops	LP	London	HAD2071	1957	£25	£10	
Towering Hilltoppers	LP	London	HAD2029	1957	£25	£10	
Tryin'	7"	London	HLD8298	1956	£15	£7.50	
Will You Remember	7"	London	HL8081	1954	£30	£15	
You Sure Look Good To Me	7"	London	HLD8603	1958	£8	£4	
You Try Somebody Else	7"	London	HL8116	1955	£30	£15	

HI-LOs

All Over The Place	LP	Philips	BBL7411/ SBBL589	1960	**£10**	**£4**	
All Over The Place	LP	Philips	SBBL589	1960	**£10**	**£4**	*stereo*
All That Jazz	LP	Columbia	CL1259/CS8077	1959	**£12**	**£5**	*US*
And All That Jazz	LP	Philips	BBL7288	1959	**£10**	**£4**	
Broadway Playbill	LP	Columbia	CL1416/CS8213	1959	**£12**	**£5**	*US*
Here Are The Hi-Lo's	7" EP	Philips	BBE12425	1960	**£5**	**£2**	
Here Are The Hi-Lo's	7" EP	Philips	BBE12127	1957	**£5**	**£2**	
Here Are The Hi-Lo's	7" EP	Philips	SBBE9035	195–	**£6**	**£2.50**	*stereo*
Hi-Lo's	LP	Kapp	KL1027	195–	**£12**	**£5**	*US*
Hi-Lo's, I Presume	LP	Starlite	7007	195–	**£12**	**£5**	*US*
In Stereo	LP	Omega	XSD11	195–	**£12**	**£5**	*US*
Listen To The Hi-Lo's	LP	Starlite	7006	195–	**£12**	**£5**	*US*
Love Nest	LP	Philips	BBL7235	1958	**£10**	**£4**	
Now Hear This	LP	Philips	BBL7177	1957	**£10**	**£4**	
On Hand	LP	Kapp	KL1194	195–	**£12**	**£5**	*US*
On Hand	LP	Starlite	7008	195–	**£12**	**£5**	*US*
Suddenly It's The Hi-Lo's	LP	Philips	BBL7154	1957	**£10**	**£4**	
They Didn't Believe Me	7" EP	London	REU1110	1958	**£8**	**£5**	
This Time It's Love	LP	Philips	BBL7534	1961	**£10**	**£4**	
Under Glass	7" EP	London	REU1077	1957	**£8**	**£4**	
Under Glass	LP	London	HAU2026	1957	**£12**	**£5**	

HILTON, RONNIE

Always	7" EP	HMV	7EG8121	1955	**£6**	**£2.50**	
Blossom Fell	7"	HMV	7M285	1955	**£10**	**£5**	
By The Fireside	10" LP	HMV	DLP1109	1955	**£15**	**£6**	
For Those In Love	7" EP	HMV	7EG8198	1957	**£5**	**£2**	
For Those In Love No. 2	7" EP	HMV	7EG8202	1957	**£5**	**£2**	
For Those In Love No. 3	7" EP	HMV	7EG8270	1957	**£5**	**£2**	
He	7"	HMV	7M336	1955	**£5**	**£2**	
Here Comes My Love	7"	HMV	7M382	1956	**£4**	**£1.50**	
Hey There	7" EP	HMV	7EG8149	1955	**£5**	**£2**	
Hit Parade	7" EP	HMV	7EG8446	1957	**£5**	**£2**	
I'm Beginning To See The Light	LP	HMV	CLP1295	1959	**£10**	**£4**	
My Loving Hands	7"	HMV	7M303	1955	**£5**	**£2**	
No Other Love	7"	HMV	7M390	1956	**£20**	**£10**	
Song For You	7" EP	HMV	7EG8375	1957	**£5**	**£2**	
Two Different Worlds	7"	HMV	POP274	1956	**£8**	**£4**	
Who Are We	7"	HMV	7M413	1956	**£8**	**£4**	
Windmill In Old Amsterdam	7" EP	HMV	7EG8937	1966	**£5**	**£2**	
Wisdom Of A Fool	7"	HMV	POP291	1957	**£6**	**£2.50**	
Woman In Love	7"	HMV	POP248	1956	**£8**	**£4**	
Wonderful Wonderful	7"	HMV	POP364	1957	**£5**	**£2**	
Young And Foolish	7"	HMV	7M358	1956	**£8**	**£4**	

HILTONAIRES

Best Of The Hiltonaires	LP	Coxsone	CSL8004	1967	**£100**	**£50**	

HIM & OTHERS

I Mean It	7"	Parlophone	R5510	1966	**£400**	**£250**	*best auctioned*

HINCHCLIFFE, PAULINE & CLAIRE ROSS

All In The Morning	LP	Keepoint	MF12101	1965	**£25**	**£10**	

HINDS, JUSTIN

Botheration	7"	Island	WI171	1965	**£10**	**£5**	
Botheration	7"	Treasure Isle	TI7063	1971	**£4**	**£1.50**	*Vincent Hinds B side*
Carry Go Bring Come	7"	Treasure Isle	TI7005	1967	**£10**	**£5**	
Drink Milk	7"	Duke	DU67	1970	**£5**	**£2**	
Here I Stand	7"	Treasure Isle	TI7002	1967	**£10**	**£5**	
Higher The Monkey Climbs	7"	Doctor Bird	DB1048	1966	**£10**	**£5**	
Jordan River	7"	Ska Beat	JB176	1964	**£10**	**£5**	
Jump Out Of Frying Pan	7"	Island	WI174	1965	**£10**	**£5**	
Mighty Redeemer	7"	Treasure Isle	TI7068	1971	**£4**	**£1.50**	
Never Too Young	7"	Island	WI244	1965	**£10**	**£5**	*Skatalites B side*
On A Saturday Night	7"	Treasure Isle	TI7014	1967	**£10**	**£5**	
On A Saturday Night	7"	Island	WI3048	1967	**£10**	**£5**	
Once A Man	7"	Treasure Isle	TI7017	1967	**£10**	**£5**	*Tommy McCook B side*
Peace And Love	7"	Island	WI236	1965	**£10**	**£5**	*Skatalites B side*
Rub Up, Push Up	7"	Island	WI194	1965	**£10**	**£5**	
Say Me Say	7"	Duke Reid	DR2511	1970	**£4**	**£1.50**	
Turn Them Back	7"	Island	WI232	1965	**£10**	**£5**	*Tommy McCook B side*
You Should've Known Better	7"	Trojan	TR652	1969	**£4**	**£1.50**	*Tommy McCook B side*

HINDS, NEVILLE

Black Man's Time	7"	Upsetter	US384	1971	**£4**	**£1.50**	*Upsetters B side*
Sunday Gravy	7"	Duke Reid	DR2503	1970	**£4**	**£1.50**	*John Holt B side*

HINE, RUPERT

Pick Up A Bone	LP	Purple	TPSA7502	1971	**£30**	**£15**	
Unfinished Picture	LP	Purple	TPSA7509	1973	**£10**	**£4**	

HINES, EARL

Title	Format	Label	Cat. No.	Year	Mint	VG	Notes
Blues In Thirds	LP	Fontana	SFJL902	1967	£10	£4	
Earl 'Father' Hines	LP	Philips	BBL7185	1957	£20	£8	
Earl Hines And His All Stars	10" LP	Mercury	MG25018	1954	£50	£25	
Earl Hines And His Orchestra	7" EP	HMV	7EG8114	1955	£5	£2	
Earl's Backroom And Cozy's Caravan	LP	Felsted	FAJ7002	1958	£15	£6	*with Cozy Cole*
Earl's Pearls	LP	MGM	C833	1960	£12	£5	
Fatha Plays Fats	LP	Vogue	LAE12067	1957	£12	£5	
Fats Waller Songs	10" LP	Vogue Coral	LRA10031	1955	£40	£20	
Grand Terrace Swing	10" LP	HMV	DLP1132	1957	£30	£15	
Jazz Means Hines	LP	Fontana	TL5378	1967	£10	£4	
Midnight In New Orleans	7" EP	MGM	MGMEP573	1956	£5	£2	
Paris One Night Stand	LP	Philips	BBL7222	1958	£15	£6	
Piano Moods	10" LP	Columbia	33S1063	1955	£40	£20	
Spontaneous Explorations	LP	Stateside	SL10116	1965	£12	£5	

HINES, FRAZER

Title	Format	Label	Cat. No.	Year	Mint	VG	Notes
Who Is Dr Who	7"	Major Minor	MM579	1968	£25	£12.50	

HINES, SONNY

Title	Format	Label	Cat. No.	Year	Mint	VG	Notes
Anytime, Any Day, Anywhere	7"	King	KG1009	1965	£6	£2.50	

HINGE

Title	Format	Label	Cat. No.	Year	Mint	VG	Notes
Village Postman	7"	RCA	RCA1721	1968	£12	£6	

HINTON, JOE

Title	Format	Label	Cat. No.	Year	Mint	VG	Notes
Funny How Time Slips Away	7"	Vocalion	VP9224	1964	£10	£5	
Funny How Time Slips Away	LP	Vocalion	VAP8043	1966	£30	£15	
Just A Kid Named Joe	7"	Vocalion	VP9258	1966	£5	£2	

HINTON, MILT

Title	Format	Label	Cat. No.	Year	Mint	VG	Notes
Milt Hinton Band	LP	London	LTZN15001	1956	£20	£8	

HI-NUMBERS

Title	Format	Label	Cat. No.	Year	Mint	VG	Notes
Heart Of Stone	7"	Decca	F12233	1965	£25	£12.50	

HIPPIES

Title	Format	Label	Cat. No.	Year	Mint	VG	Notes
Memory Lane	7"	Cameo Parkway	P863	1963	£10	£5	*Reggie Harrison B side*

HIPPY BOYS

Title	Format	Label	Cat. No.	Year	Mint	VG	Notes
Cloud Burst	7"	Duke	DU92	1970	£4	£1.50	*Lloyd Charmers B side*
Doctor No Go	7"	High Note	HS021	1969	£4	£1.50	
Love	7"	Trojan	TR668	1969	£4	£1.50	
Michael Row The Boat Ashore	7"	Trojan	TR669	1969	£4	£1.50	
Piccadilly Hop	7"	High Note	HS038	1970	£5	£2	
Reggae Pressure	7"	High Note	HS035	1969	£4	£1.50	
Reggae With The Hippy Boys	LP	Big Shot	BSLP5005	1969	£25	£10	

HIPSTER IMAGE

Title	Format	Label	Cat. No.	Year	Mint	VG	Notes
Can't Let You Go	7"	Decca	F12137	1965	£50	£25	

HIRT, AL

Title	Format	Label	Cat. No.	Year	Mint	VG	Notes
Swingin' Dixie	LP	Audio Fidelity	AFLP1877/ AFSD5877	1960	£15	£6	

HIS NAME IS ALIVE

Title	Format	Label	Cat. No.	Year	Mint	VG	Notes
Extracts From Mouth To Mouth	CD-s	4AD	HNIA2	1993	£8	£4	*promo*
How Ghosts Affect Relationships	7"	4AD	HNIA1	1990	£5	£2	*promo*

HI-SPOTS

Title	Format	Label	Cat. No.	Year	Mint	VG	Notes
Lend Me Your Comb	7"	Melodisc	1457	1958	£10	£5	
Secretly	7"	Melodisc	1473	1958	£6	£2.50	

HIT PACK

Title	Format	Label	Cat. No.	Year	Mint	VG	Notes
Never Say No To Your Baby	7"	Tamla Motown	TMG513	1965	£50	£25	

HIT PARADE

Title	Format	Label	Cat. No.	Year	Mint	VG	Notes
Forever	7"	JSH	JSH1	1984	£5	£2	
My Favourite Girl	7"	JSH	JSH2	1984	£4	£1.50	

HIT SQUAD

Title	Format	Label	Cat. No.	Year	Mint	VG	Notes
Wax On The Melt	12"	Eastern Bloc	EASTERN01	1988	£50	£25	*promo*

HITCHCOCK, ALFRED

Title	Format	Label	Cat. No.	Year	Mint	VG	Notes
Music To Be Murdered By	LP	London	SHP6012	1959	£30	£15	*stereo*
Music To Be Murdered By	LP	London	HAP2130	1958	£25	£10	

HITCHCOCK, ROBYN

Title	Format	Label	Cat. No.	Year	Mint	VG	Notes
America	7"	Albion	ION103	1982	£5	£2	
Bells Of Rhymney	12"	Midnight Music	DONG8	1984	£6	£2.50	
Eaten By Her Own Dinner	12"	Midnight Music	DONG2	1982	£8	£4	

Title	Format	Label	Number	Year	Mint	Value	Notes
Eaten By Her Own Dinner	7"	Midnight Music	DING2	1982	**£8**	**£4**	
Heaven	12"	Midnight Music	DONG12	1985	**£6**	**£2.50**	
Man Who Invented Himself	7"	Armageddon	AS008	1981	**£4**	**£1.50**	
Man Who Invented Himself	7"	Armageddon	AS008	1981	**£8**	**£4**	*with flexi (4SPURT1)*
Nightride To Trinidad	12"	Albion	12ION1036	1983	**£10**	**£5**	

HI-TENSION

Title	Format	Label	Number	Year	Mint	Value	Notes
There's A Reason	12"	Island	12WIP6493	1979	**£6**	**£2.50**	

HI-TONES

Title	Format	Label	Number	Year	Mint	Value	Notes
Ten Virgins	7"	Island	WI086	1963	**£10**	**£5**	
You Hold The Key	7"	R&B	JB123	1963	**£10**	**£5**	*Don Drummond B side*

HITTERS

The group playing a version of the reggae song 'Hypocrite' was actually Brinsley Schwarz, and the track was included on that group's compilation LP *Original Golden Greats*.

Title	Format	Label	Number	Year	Mint	Value	Notes
Hypocrite	7"	United Artists	UP35530	1973	**£15**	**£7.50**	

H.M.S. BOUNTY

Title	Format	Label	Number	Year	Mint	Value	Notes
Things	LP	Time Stood Still	TSSLP2	1985	**£12**	**£5**	*US*
Things	LP	Shamley	SS701	1968	**£75**	**£37.50**	*US*

HOAX

Title	Format	Label	Number	Year	Mint	Value	Notes
Only The Blind Can See In The Dark	7"	Hologram	HOAX1	1980	**£6**	**£2.50**	
Quiet In The Sixpennys	7"	Hologram	HOAX4	1982	**£6**	**£2.50**	
So What	12"	Hologram	HOAX3	1981	**£10**	**£5**	

HOBBIT

Title	Format	Label	Number	Year	Mint	Value	Notes
First And Last	LP	Deroy		197–	**£75**	**£37.50**	

HOBBITS

Title	Format	Label	Number	Year	Mint	Value	Notes
Back From Middle Earth	LP	Perception	PLP10	1969	**£20**	**£8**	*US*
Daffodil Days	7"	Decca	AD1004	1968	**£5**	**£2**	*export*
Down To Middle Earth	LP	MCA	MUP301	1967	**£15**	**£6**	
Men And Doors	LP	Decca	DL75009	1968	**£20**	**£8**	*US*

HOBBS, CHRISTOPHER, JOHN ADAMS & GAVIN BRYARS

Title	Format	Label	Number	Year	Mint	Value	Notes
Ensemble Pieces	LP	Obscure	OBS2	1975	**£10**	**£4**	

HOBBY HORSE

Title	Format	Label	Number	Year	Mint	Value	Notes
Summertime Summertime	7"	Bell	BELL1248	1972	**£6**	**£2.50**	

HOBOKEN

Title	Format	Label	Number	Year	Mint	Value	Notes
Hoboken	LP	Oak	no number	1973	**£500**	**£330**	

HODES, ART

Title	Format	Label	Number	Year	Mint	Value	Notes
Funky Piano	LP	Blue Note	B6502	1969	**£10**	**£4**	
Sittin' In Vol. 1	LP	Blue Note	B6508	1969	**£10**	**£4**	

HODGE, CHRIS

Title	Format	Label	Number	Year	Mint	Value	Notes
We're On Our Way	7"	Apple	43	1972	**£15**	**£7.50**	*picture sleeve*

HODGES, CHARLES

Title	Format	Label	Number	Year	Mint	Value	Notes
Try A Little Love	7"	Major Minor	MM654	1969	**£10**	**£5**	

HODGES, EDDIE

Title	Format	Label	Number	Year	Mint	Value	Notes
Bandit Of My Dreams	7"	London	HLA9305	1962	**£8**	**£4**	
Eddie Hodges	7" EP	London	REA1353	1963	**£30**	**£15**	
I'm Gonna Knock On Your Door	7"	London	HLA9369	1961	**£6**	**£2.50**	
Love Minus Zero: No Limit	7"	Stateside	SS469	1965	**£5**	**£2**	
Made To Love	7"	London	HLA9576	1962	**£4**	**£1.50**	

HODGES, JOHNNY

Title	Format	Label	Number	Year	Mint	Value	Notes
Big Sound	LP	Columbia	33CX10136	1959	**£20**	**£8**	
Blues-A-Plenty	LP	HMV	CLP1430	1961	**£15**	**£6**	
Ellingtonia '56	LP	Columbia	33CX10055	1956	**£20**	**£8**	
In A Tender Mood	LP	Columbia	33C9051	1957	**£30**	**£15**	
Johnny Hodges With The Ellington All Stars	LP	Columbia	33CX10098	1958	**£15**	**£6**	
Memories Of Ellington	LP	Columbia	33CX10013	1955	**£40**	**£20**	
Wings And Things	LP	Verve	(S)VLP9117	1965	**£10**	**£4**	*with Wild Bill Davis*
With The Ellingtonians	10" LP	Vogue	LDE011	1952	**£40**	**£20**	

HOELDERLIN

Title	Format	Label	Number	Year	Mint	Value	Notes
Clown And Clouds	LP	Spiegelei	266056U	1976	**£20**	**£8**	*German*
Hoelderlin	LP	Spiegelei	160601	1975	**£20**	**£8**	*German*
Hoelderlin Träum	LP	Pilz	20213145	1972	**£75**	**£37.50**	*German*
Live Träumstadt	LP	Spiegelei	180602	1978	**£15**	**£6**	*German double*
Rare Birds	LP	Spiegelei	160608	1977	**£12**	**£5**	*German*

HOFFNUNG, GERARD

At The Oxford Union	10" LP	Decca	LF1330	1960	£12	£5	

HOGAN, ANNIE

Plays Kickabye	12"	Doublevision	DVR9	1985	£10	£5	

HOGAN, SILAS

Trouble At Home	LP	Blue Horizon	2431008	1971	£50	£25	

HOGARTH

Suzie's Getting Married	7"	Liberty	LBF15156	1968	£6	£2.50	

HOGG, SMOKEY

I'm So Lonely	LP	Realm	RM197	1964	£20	£8	
Sings The Blues	LP	Ember	EMB3405	1968	£12	£5	
Smokey Hogg	LP	Time	6	1962	£25	£10	US

HOGS

'Blues Theme' is collectable on two counts – the B side is a Frank Zappa production, while the Hogs afterwards changed their name to the Chocolate Watch Band.

Blues Theme	7"	HBR	511	1966	£150	£75	US

HOKUS POKE

Earth Harmony	LP	Vertigo	6360064	1972	£50	£25	*spiral label*

HOLDE FEE

Malaga	LP	private	1383001	1975	£10	£4	*German*

HOLDEN, RANDY

Population II	LP	Hobbit	HB5002	1969	£100	£50	US

HOLDEN, RON

I Love You So	LP	Donna	DLP(S)2111	1960	£30	£15	US
Love You So	7"	London	HLU9116	1960	£30	£15	

HOLDER, FRANK

Bechuanaland	7"	Parlophone	R4459	1958	£5	£2	

HOLDER, RAM BROTHERS

Ram Blues	7"	Parlophone	R5471	1966	£10	£5	

HOLDER, RAM JOHN

Black London Blues	LP	Beacon	BEAS2	1974	£30	£15	
Bootleg Blues	LP	Beacon	BEAS17	1974	£30	£15	
Ram Blues Gospel And Soul	LP	Melodisc	MLP12133	1963	£30	£15	
You Simply Are	LP	Fresh Air	9299470	1975	£12	£5	

HOLDSWORTH, ALLAN

If a candidate is needed for the most technically skilled guitarist of all, there is really no need to look any further than Allan Holdsworth. Whether playing jazz or rock or something in between, the speed of his fingers on the fretboard is seldom less than jaw-dropping. Not that Velvet Darkness is the best demonstration of this – doubters are better referred to one of the more recent recordings, such as the excellent *Metal Fatigue*. Meanwhile, collectors will need the man's recordings with Tony Williams' Lifetime, Soft Machine and Igginbottom, all listed within this guide.

Velvet Darkness	LP	CTI	6068	1977	£25	£10	

HOLE

Pretty On The Inside	LP	City Slang	SLANG012	1991	£10	£4	*red vinyl*

HOLE IN THE WALL

Hole In The Wall	LP	Sonet	SLP1420	1972	£60	£30	*Norwegian*

HOLIDAY, BILLIE

An Evening With Billie Holiday	7" EP	Columbia	SEB10035	1956	£5	£2	
At Jazz At The Philharmonic	10" LP	Columbia	33C9023	1956	£50	£25	
Billie Holiday	10" LP	Columbia	33S1034	1954	£50	£25	
Billie Holiday	7" EP	Columbia	SEB10009	1955	£5	£2	
Billie Holiday	7" EP	Vogue	EPV1128	1956	£5	£2	
Billie Holiday	LP	MGM	C792	1959	£15	£6	
Billie Holiday	LP	Fontana	TL5287	1966	£12	£5	
Billie Holiday	LP	Stateside	SL10007	1962	£15	£6	
Billie Holiday Memorial	LP	Fontana	TFL5106	1960	£15	£6	
Billie Holiday Sings	7" EP	Columbia	SEB10048	1956	£5	£2	
Blue	7" EP	Fontana	TFE17026	1960	£5	£2	
Detour Ahead	7"	Vogue	V2408	1956	£4	£1.50	
Don't Worry 'Bout Me	7"	MGM	MGM1033	1959	£4	£1.50	
Embraceable You	7" EP	Melodisc	EPM7125	195–	£5	£2	
Favourites	10" LP	Philips	BBR8032	1955	£40	£20	
Lady Day	7" EP	Fontana	TFE17010	1959	£5	£2	
Lady Day Vol. 1	7" EP	Brunswick	OE9172	1955	£5	£2	
Lady Day Vol. 2	7" EP	Brunswick	OE9199	1956	£5	£2	
Lady Day Vol. 3	7" EP	Brunswick	OE9251	1956	£5	£2	
Lady In Satin	LP	Fontana	TFL5032	1959	£20	£8	
Lady Sings The Blues	LP	Columbia	33CX10092	1957	£30	£15	
Last Live Recording	LP	Island	ILP929	1966	£15	£6	

Lover Man	10″ LP	Brunswick	LA8676	1954	£40	£20	
Music For Torching	LP	Columbia	33CX10019	1956	£40	£20	
Once Upon A Time	LP	Fontana	TL5262	1965	£12	£5	
Solitude	LP	Columbia	33CX10076	1957	£30	£15	
Songs For Distingué Lovers	LP	Columbia	33CX10145	1959	£20	£8	
Unforgettable Lady Day	LP	HMV	CLP1414	1960	£15	£6	
Velvet Moods	LP	Columbia	33CX10064	1957	£30	£15	

HOLIDAY, CHICO

Chico Holiday	7″ EP	RCA	RCX171	1959	£20	£10	
God, Country And My Baby	7″	Coral	Q72443	1961	£5	£2	
Young Ideas	7″	RCA	RCA1117	1959	£5	£2	

HOLIDAY, JIMMY

Baby I Love You	7″	Liberty	LIB12040	1966	£8	£4	
Everybody Needs Help	7″	Liberty	LIB12053	1967	£5	£2	
Give Me Your Love	7″	Minit	MLF11008	1968	£5	£2	
Give Me Your Love	7″	Liberty	LIB12048	1967	£8	£4	
How Can I Forget	7″	Vocalion	V9206	1963	£15	£7.50	
I Lied	7″	London	HLY9868	1964	£8	£4	

HOLIDAY, JIMMY & CLYDIE KING

Oh Darling How I Miss You	7″	Polydor	56035	1965	£8	£4	
One Man In My Life	7″	Polydor	56166	1967	£8	£4	
Ready Willing And Able	7″	Liberty	LIB12058	1967	£15	£7.50	

HOLIDAY, JOE

Joe Holiday Rhythm	10″ LP	Esquire	20027	1954	£40	£20	

HOLIDAY, JOHNNY

Holiday For Romance	7″ EP	London	RED1227	1959	£5	£2	
Sentimental Holiday	7″ EP	London	RED1226	1959	£5	£2	

HOLIDAYS

I'll Love You Forever	7″	Polydor	56720	1966	£60	£30	

HOLIEN, DANNY

Danny Holien	LP	Tumbleweed	TW3503	1972	£15	£6	

HOLLAND, BRIAN

I'm So Glad	7″	Invictus	INV2553	1974	£5	£2	

HOLLAND, DAVE

Conference Of The Birds	LP	ECM	ECM1027ST	1973	£12	£5	
Music From Two Basses	LP	ECM	ECM1011ST	1971	£20	£8	

HOLLAND, EDDIE

Eddie Holland	LP	Motown	604	1963	£60	£30	*US*
If It's Love	7″	Oriole	CBA1808	1963	£300	£180	*best auctioned*
Jamie	7″	Fontana	H387	1962	£250	£150	*best auctioned*

HOLLAND, LYNN

And The Angels Sing	7″	Ember	EMBS198	1964	£5	£2	*picture sleeve*

HOLLAND, TONY

Sidewalk	7″	HMV	POP1135	1963	£25	£12.50	

HOLLAND–DOZIER

Why Can't We Be Lovers	7″	Invictus	INV525	1972	£5	£2	

HOLLIDAY, BRENDA

Hurt A Little Everyday	7″	Tamla Motown	TMG581	1966	£75	£37.50	*demo only*

HOLLIDAY, MICHAEL

All Of You	7″	Columbia	DB3973	1957	£6	£2.50	
All Time Favourites	7″ EP	Columbia	SEG7761	1958	£5	£2	
Best Of Michael Holliday	LP	Columbia	33SX1586	1964	£10	£4	
Four Feather Falls	7″ EP	Columbia	SEG7986/ ESG7793	1960	£15	£7.50	
Gal With The Yaller Shoes	7″	Columbia	SCM5273	1956	£8	£4	
Happy Holliday	7″ EP	Columbia	SEG8161	1962	£6	£2.50	
Happy Holliday	LP	Columbia	33SX1354	1961	£10	£4	
Hi!	10″ LP	Columbia	33S1114	1958	£20	£8	
Holliday Mixture	LP	Columbia	33SX1262/ SCX3331	1960	£10	£4	
In A Sentimental Mood	7″ EP	Columbia	ESG7864	1961	£6	£2.50	*stereo*
In A Sentimental Mood	7″ EP	Columbia	SEG8115	1961	£5	£2	
Melody Mike	7″ EP	Columbia	SEG7818	1958	£6	£2.50	
Memories Of Mike	7″ EP	Columbia	SEG8373	1964	£6	£2.50	
Mike	LP	Columbia	33SX1170	1959	£12	£5	
Mike And The Other Fella	7″ EP	Columbia	SEG7892	1959	£6	£2.50	
Mike No. 1	7″ EP	Columbia	SEG7972	1960	£5	£2	
Mike No. 1	7″ EP	Columbia	ESG7784	1960	£6	£2.50	*stereo*
Mike No. 2	7″ EP	Columbia	ESG7803	1960	£6	£2.50	*stereo*
Mike No. 2	7″ EP	Columbia	SEG7996	1960	£5	£2	
Mike No. 3	7″ EP	Columbia	ESG7842	1961	£6	£2.50	*stereo*
Mike No. 3	7″ EP	Columbia	SEG8074	1961	£5	£2	

Title	Format	Label	Cat. No.	Year	Mint	VG	Notes
Mike Sings Country And Western Style	7" EP	Columbia	SEG8242	1963	£6	£2.50	
Mike Sings Ragtime	7" EP	Columbia	ESG7856	1961	£6	£2.50	stereo
Mike Sings Ragtime	7" EP	Columbia	SEG8101	1961	£5	£2	
More Happy Holliday	7" EP	Columbia	SEG8186	1962	£6	£2.50	
Music With Mike	7" EP	Columbia	SEG7683	1957	£6	£2.50	
My Guitar And Me	7" EP	Columbia	SEG7638	1956	£6	£2.50	
My House Is Your House	7"	Columbia	DB3919	1957	£5	£2	
Nothin' To Do	7"	Columbia	SCM5252	1956	£8	£4	
Old Cape Cod	7"	Columbia	DB3992	1957	£4	£1.50	
Relax With Mike	7" EP	Columbia	SEG7752	1958	£5	£2	
Runaway Train	7"	Columbia	DB3813	1956	£12	£6	
Sentimental Journey	7" EP	Columbia	SEG7836	1958	£5	£2	
Sixteen Tons	7"	Columbia	SCM5221	1956	£8	£4	
Story Of My Life	7"	Columbia	DB4058	1958	£4	£1.50	
To Bing From Mike	LP	Columbia	33SX1425/ SCX3441	1962	£10	£4	
Wringle Wrangle	7"	Columbia	DB3948	1957	£5	£2	
Yaller Yaller Gold	7"	Columbia	DB3871	1957	£5	£2	

HOLLIDAY, SUSAN

Title	Format	Label	Cat. No.	Year	Mint	VG	Notes
Any Day Now	7"	Columbia	DB7403	1964	£6	£2.50	
Dark Despair	7"	Columbia	DB7363	1964	£6	£2.50	
I Wanna Say Hello	LP	Columbia	SX6067	1966	£75	£37.50	
Nevertheless	7"	Columbia	DB7709	1965	£6	£2.50	
Sometimes	7"	Columbia	DB7616	1965	£6	£2.50	

HOLLIER, TIM

Title	Format	Label	Cat. No.	Year	Mint	VG	Notes
Message To A Harlequin	LP	United Artists	(S)ULP1211	1968	£15	£6	
Sky Sail	LP	Philips	6308044	1971	£12	£5	
Story Of Mill Reef – Something To Brighten The Morning	LP	York	YR503	1974	£50	£25	with Vicki Hodge & Albert Finney

HOLLIES

The Hollies were easily one of the most successful of the first wave of British beat groups to emerge in the sixties and yet they seldom seem to receive much credit for the fact. Inevitably they tended to labour in the shadow of the Beatles and their records show a similar pattern of development. *Butterfly* is a kind of Lance-Corporal Pepper – it uses the same kind of inventive arranging and is one of the more interesting albums of the period. One is inclined to believe that it is actually much more of a psychedelic classic than celebrated rarities like those of Kaleidoscope.

Title	Format	Label	Cat. No.	Year	Mint	VG	Notes
After The Fox	7"	United Artists	UP1152	1966	£20	£10	with Peter Sellers
Ain't That Just Like Me	7"	Parlophone	R5030	1963	£10	£5	
Air That I Breathe	CD-s	EMI	CDEM80	1988	£5	£2	
Another Night	LP	Polydor	2442128	1975	£10	£4	
Bus Stop	7" EP	Odeon	MEO125	1966	£25	£12.50	French, sleeve with titles only
Bus Stop	7" EP	Odeon	MEO125	1966	£75	£37.50	French, sleeve with group picture
Bus Stop	LP	Imperial	LP9330/12330	1966	£25	£10	US
Butterfly	LP	Parlophone	PCS7039	1967	£25	£10	stereo
Butterfly	LP	Parlophone	PMC7039	1967	£30	£10	mono
Carrie Anne	7" EP	Fontana	460211	1967	£25	£12.50	French
Confessions Of The Mind	LP	Parlophone	PCS7116	1970	£12	£5	
Days	LP	Odeon	SMO74315	1965	£60	£30	German
Distant Light	LP	Parlophone	PAS10005	1971	£10	£4	
Everything You Wanted To Hear	LP	Epic	AS138	1972	£25	£10	US promo
Evolution	LP	Parlophone	PMC/PCS7022	1967	£25	£10	
For Certain Because	LP	Parlophone	PMC/PCS7011	1966	£20	£8	
He Ain't Heavy He's My Brother	CD-s	EMI	CDEM74	1988	£5	£2	
Hear! Here!	LP	Imperial	LP9299/12299	1965	£30	£15	US
Heartbeat	7"	Polydor	POSP175	1980	£5	£2	
Here I Go Again	7" EP	Parlophone	GEP8915	1964	£30	£15	
Here I Go Again	LP	Imperial	LP9265/12265	1964	£40	£20	US
Hollies	7" EP	Parlophone	GEP8909	1964	£25	£12.50	
Hollies	LP	Polydor	2383262	1974	£10	£4	
Hollies	LP	Regal	SREG2024	1967	£25	£10	export
Hollies	LP	Parlophone	PMC1261	1965	£20	£8	
Hollies – Beat Group	LP	Imperial	LP9312/12312	1966	£25	£10	US
Hollies Greatest	LP	Parlophone	PMC/PCS7057	1968	£12	£5	
I Can't Let Go	7" EP	Parlophone	GEP8951	1966	£30	£15	
I'm Alive	7" EP	Parlophone	GEP8942	1965	£30	£15	
I'm Alive	7" EP	Odeon	SOE3770	1965	£40	£20	French
If I Needed Someone	7" EP	Odeon	MEO101	1965	£40	£20	French
In The Hollies Style	7" EP	Parlophone	GEP8934	1965	£30	£15	
In The Hollies Style	LP	Parlophone	PMC1235	1965	£30	£15	
Jesus Was A Crossmaker	7"	Epic	510989	1973	£8	£4	US
Just One Look	7" EP	Parlophone	GEP8911	1964	£30	£15	
Kill Me Quick	7"	Parlophon	QMSP16410	1967	£30	£15	Italian
King Midas In Reverse	7"	Parlophone	R5637	1967	£4	£1.50	
Legendary Top Tens 1963–1988	CD	Fast Forward	FFCD822	1994	£20	£8	
Like Every Time Before	7"	Hansa	14093	1968	£10	£5	German
Look Through Any Window	7" EP	Odeon	SOE3773	1965	£40	£20	French
Maker – Would You Believe	7" EP	Fontana	460249	1968	£30	£15	French
Music For 5 a.m.	7"	Mercury	YARD002	196–	£10	£5	with other artists
Non Prego Per Me	7"	Parlophon	QMSP16402	1967	£30	£15	Italian
On A Carousel	7" EP	Fontana	460201	1967	£30	£15	French
Other Side Of The Hollies	LP	Parlophone	PMC7176	1978	£12	£5	
Out On The Road	LP	Hansa	87119	1973	£25	£10	German

Title	Format	Label	Cat. No.	Year	Value		Notes
Romany	LP	Polydor	2383144	1972	**£10**	**£4**	
Russian Roulette	LP	Polydor	2383421	1976	**£10**	**£4**	
Searchin'	7"	Parlophone	R5052	1963	**£6**	**£2.50**	
Sing Dylan	LP	Parlophone	PMC/PCS7078	1969	**£15**	**£6**	
Sing Hollies	LP	Parlophone	PCS7092	1969	**£15**	**£6**	
Soldier's Song	7"	Polydor	2059246	1980	**£6**	**£2.50**	
Something To Live For	12"	Polydor	POSPX35	1979	**£8**	**£4**	
Stay	7"	Parlophone	R5077	1963	**£4**	**£1.50**	
Stay	7" EP	Odeon	SOE3749	1963	**£40**	**£20**	*French*
Stay With The Hollies	LP	Parlophone	PMC1220	1964	**£25**	**£10**	
Stay With The Hollies	LP	World Records	ST1035	1968	**£25**	**£10**	
Stay With The Hollies	LP	Parlophone	PCS3054	1964	**£40**	**£20**	*stereo*
Stop Stop Stop	LP	Imperial	LP9339/12339	1967	**£25**	**£10**	*US*
Tell Me To My Face	7" EP	Odeon	MEO144	1967	**£40**	**£20**	*French*
Twenty Golden Hits	CD	Mobile Fidelity	UDCD521	1989	**£15**	**£6**	*US audiophile*
Up Front	LP	St Michael	21020101	1978	**£30**	**£15**	
Vintage Hollies	LP	World Records	ST979	1967	**£25**	**£10**	
We're Through	7" EP	Parlophone	GEP8927	1964	**£30**	**£15**	
Would You Believe	LP	Parlophone	PCS7008	1966	**£25**	**£10**	*stereo*
Would You Believe	LP	Parlophone	PMC7008	1966	**£15**	**£6**	
Write On	LP	Polydor	2442141	1976	**£10**	**£4**	

HOLLOW MEN

Title	Format	Label	Cat. No.	Year	Value		Notes
Circa	CD-s	Arista	260978	1990	**£5**	**£2**	
Drowning Man	12"	Blind Eye	BE007	1989	**£8**	**£4**	*with promo booklet*
Drowning Man	12"	Blind Eye	BE007	1989	**£6**	**£2.50**	*fully autographed*
Gold And Ivory	12"	Evensong	EVE212	1987	**£40**	**£20**	*test pressing in proof sleeve*
Gold And Ivory	12"	Evensong	EVE212	1987	**£6**	**£2.50**	*with postcard*
Late Flowering Lust	7"	Evensong	EVE107	1985	**£8**	**£4**	
Man Who Would Be King	CD	Dead Man's Curve	VIVIDONE	1988	**£12**	**£5**	
Moon's A Balloon	CD-s	Arista	663508	1990	**£5**	**£2**	
Pink Panther	CD-s	Arista	664026	1991	**£5**	**£2**	
Thanks To The Rolling Sea	CD-s	Arista	663167	1990	**£5**	**£2**	
White Train	7"	Gigantic	GI101	1988	**£6**	**£2.50**	*promo*
White Train	CD-s	Arista	662695	1989	**£5**	**£2**	

HOLLOWAY, BRENDA

Title	Format	Label	Cat. No.	Year	Value		Notes
Artistry Of Brenda Holloway	LP	Tamla Motown	(S)TML11083	1968	**£75**	**£37.50**	
Every Little Bit Hurts	7"	Stateside	SS307	1964	**£30**	**£15**	
Every Little Bit Hurts	LP	Tamla	257	1965	**£60**	**£30**	*US*
Hurt A Little Everyday	7"	Tamla Motown	TMG581	1966	**£25**	**£12.50**	
Just Look What I've Done	7"	Tamla Motown	TMG608	1967	**£15**	**£7.50**	
Just Look What You've Done	7"	Tamla Motown	TMG700	1969	**£5**	**£2**	
Operator	7"	Tamla Motown	TMG519	1965	**£40**	**£20**	
Together Till The End Of Time	7"	Tamla Motown	TMG556	1966	**£30**	**£15**	
When I'm Gone	7"	Tamla Motown	TMG508	1965	**£60**	**£30**	
You've Made Me So Very Happy	7"	Tamla Motown	TMG622	1967	**£15**	**£7.50**	

HOLLOWAY, PATRICE

Title	Format	Label	Cat. No.	Year	Value		Notes
Love And Desire	7"	Capitol	CL15484	1966	**£60**	**£30**	

HOLLOWAY, STANLEY

Title	Format	Label	Cat. No.	Year	Value		Notes
'Ere's 'Olloway	LP	Philips	BBL7237	1958	**£10**	**£4**	
Famous Adventures With Old Sam And The Ramsbottoms	10" LP	Columbia	33S1093	1956	**£10**	**£4**	
Hi-De-Hi	7"	HMV	JH13	1952	**£6**	**£2.50**	

HOLLY

Title	Format	Label	Cat. No.	Year	Value		Notes
Hobo Joe	7"	Erics	ERICS007	1979	**£10**	**£5**	
Yankee Rose	7"	Erics	ERICS003	1979	**£10**	**£5**	

HOLLY, BUDDY

There is a strong case for viewing Buddy Holly as the true father of the music we call rock. It was Buddy Holly and the Crickets who set the pattern for the line-up that is still considered as the classic one for a rock group – lead and rhythm guitars, bass guitar and drums. His songs too, based on blues chord progressions but with bright, major tonalities, defined a style that has been revisited by songwriters from Lennon and McCartney to Costello to Gallagher and all points in between. It should be noted, incidentally, that while most of Holly's records were credited to him by name, a few were credited merely to the Crickets. All, however, are listed here.

Title	Format	Label	Cat. No.	Year	Value		Notes
Baby I Don't Care	7"	Coral	Q72432	1961	**£4**	**£1.50**	
Best Of Buddy Holly	LP	Coral	CX(S)B8	1966	**£20**	**£8**	*US*
Blue Days Black Nights	7"	Brunswick	05581	1956	**£500**	**£330**	*best auctioned*
Bo Diddley	7"	Coral	Q72463	1963	**£4**	**£1.50**	
Brown Eyed Handsome Man	7"	Coral	Q72459	1963	**£4**	**£1.50**	
Brown-Eyed Handsome Man	LP	MCA	MUP(S)314	1968	**£10**	**£4**	

Title	Format	Label	Number	Year	Mint	VG	Notes
Buddy By Request	7" EP	Coral	FEP2065	1964	£30	£15	
Buddy Holly	7" EP	Coral	FEP2032	1959	£30	£15	*tri-centre*
Buddy Holly	LP	Coral	CRL57210	1958	£200	£100	*US*
Buddy Holly	LP	Vogue Coral	LVA9085	1958	£60	£30	
Buddy Holly	LP	Coral	LVA9085	1958	£25	£10	
Buddy Holly And The Crickets	LP	Coral	CRL(7)57405	1962	£40	£20	*US*
Buddy Holly No. 1	7" EP	Brunswick	OE9456	1959	£50	£25	*tri-centre*
Buddy Holly No. 2	7" EP	Brunswick	OE9457	1959	£50	£25	*tri-centre*
Buddy Holly Sings	7" EP	Coral	FEP2070	1965	£50	£25	
Buddy Holly Story	LP	Coral	LVA9105	1959	£15	£6	
Buddy Holly Story	LP	World Records	SM301-5	1975	£25	£10	*5 LPs, boxed*
Buddy Holly Story	LP	Coral	CRL57279	1959	£75	£37.50	*US*
Buddy Holly Story 2	LP	Coral	LVA9127	1960	£15	£6	
Buddy Holly Story Vol. 2	LP	Coral	CRL57326	1959	£60	£30	*US*
Chirping Crickets	LP	Coral	LVA9081	1958	£30	£15	
Chirping Crickets	LP	Brunswick	BL54038	1957	£250	£150	*US*
Chirping Crickets	LP	Vogue Coral	LVA9081	1958	£50	£25	
Complete Buddy Holly	LP	MCA	CDSP807	1978	£30	£15	*6 LPs, book, boxed*
Early In The Morning	7"	Coral	Q72333	1958	£8	£4	
Early In The Morning	78	Coral	Q72333	1958	£20	£10	
Four More	7" EP	Coral	FEP2060	1960	£20	£10	
Giant	LP	MCA	MUPS371	1969	£10	£4	
Good Rockin'	LP	Vocalion	VL73923	1971	£50	£25	*US*
Great Buddy Holly	LP	Vocalion	VL(7)3811	1967	£20	£8	*US*
Greatest Hits	LP	Coral	CRL(7)57492	1967	£20	£8	*US*
He's The One	LP	MCA	MUP(S)315	1968	£10	£4	
Heartbeat	7"	Coral	Q72346	1958	£6	£2.50	
Heartbeat	7" EP	Coral	FEP2015	1959	£30	£15	
Heartbeat	78	Coral	Q72346	1958	£20	£10	
Heartbeat	78	Coral	Q72392	1960	£200	£100	
Heartbeat	LP	Marks & Spencer	IMP114	1978	£40	£20	
Holly In The Hills	LP	Coral	LVA9227	1965	£50	£25	*with 'Wishing'*
Holly In The Hills	LP	Coral	LVA9227	1965	£30	£15	*with 'Reminiscing'*
Holly In The Hills	LP	Coral	CRL(7)57463	1965	£30	£15	*US*
It Doesn't Matter Anymore	7"	Coral	Q72360	1958	£4	£1.50	
It Doesn't Matter Anymore	78	Coral	Q72360	1958	£20	£10	
It's So Easy	7"	Coral	Q72343	1958	£8	£4	
It's So Easy	7" EP	Coral	FEP2014	1959	£30	£15	
It's So Easy	78	Coral	Q72343	1958	£20	£10	
Late Great Buddy Holly	7" EP	Coral	FEP2044	1960	£20	£10	*round centre*
Late Great Buddy Holly	7" EP	Coral	FEP2044	1960	£50	£25	*tri-centre*
Learning The Game	7"	Coral	Q72411	1960	£5	£2	
Listen To Me	7"	Coral	Q72449	1962	£6	£2.50	
Listen To Me	7"	Coral	Q72288	1958	£8	£4	
Listen To Me	7" EP	Coral	FEP2002	1958	£30	£15	
Listen To Me	7" EP	Coral	FEP2002	1958	£250	£150	*no glasses cover*
Listen To Me	78	Coral	Q72288	1958	£12	£6	
Listen To Me	LP	MCA	MUP(S)312	1968	£10	£4	
Look At Me	7"	Coral	Q72445	1961	£6	£2.50	
Love's Made A Fool Of You	7"	Coral	Q72475	1964	£6	£2.50	
Maybe Baby	7"	Coral	Q72307	1958	£8	£4	
Maybe Baby	7"	Coral	Q72483	1966	£15	£6	
Maybe Baby	78	Coral	Q72307	1958	£12	£6	
Midnight Shift	7"	Brunswick	05800	1959	£30	£15	
Midnight Shift	78	Brunswick	05800	1959	£100	£50	
Oh Boy	7"	Decca	AD1012	1968	£25	£12.50	*export*
Oh Boy	7"	Coral	Q72298	1957	£8	£4	
Oh Boy	78	Coral	Q72298	1957	£10	£5	
Oh Boy	CD-s	MCA	DMCAT1368	1989	£10	£5	
Peggy Sue	7"	Vogue Coral	Q72293	1957	£30	£15	
Peggy Sue	7"	Coral	Q72293	1958	£10	£5	
Peggy Sue	78	Vogue Coral	Q72293	1957	£75	£37.50	
Peggy Sue	CD-s	Old Gold	OG6154	1990	£10	£5	
Peggy Sue Got Married	7"	Coral	Q72376	1959	£10	£5	
Peggy Sue Got Married	78	Coral	Q72376	1959	£100	£50	
Rave On	7"	Coral	Q72325	1958	£8	£4	
Rave On	7"	Decca	AD1009	1968	£25	£12.50	*export*
Rave On	7" EP	Coral	FEP2005	1958	£30	£15	
Rave On	78	Coral	Q72325	1958	£12	£6	
Rave On	LP	MCA	MUP(S)313	1968	£10	£4	
Reminiscing	7"	Coral	Q72455	1962	£4	£1.50	
Reminiscing	LP	Coral	LVA9212	1963	£15	£6	
Rock & Roll Collection	LP	Decca	DXSE7207	1972	£10	£4	*US*
Showcase	LP	Coral	LVA9222	1964	£20	£8	
Showcase Vol. 1	7" EP	Coral	FEP2068	1964	£50	£25	
Showcase Vol. 2	7" EP	Coral	FEP2069	1964	£50	£25	
Something Special	LP	Rollercoaster	ROLL2013	1986	£10	£4	
Sound Of The Crickets	7" EP	Coral	FEP2003	1958	£20	£10	
That Tex Mex Sound	7" EP	Coral	FEP2066	1964	£50	£25	
That'll Be The Day	7"	MCA	BHB1	1984	£30	£15	*10 single boxed set*
That'll Be The Day	7"	Coral	Q72279	1957	£10	£5	
That'll Be The Day	7"	Vogue Coral	Q72279	1957	£15	£7.50	
That'll Be The Day	7" EP	Coral	FEP2062	1960	£20	£10	
That'll Be The Day	78	Vogue Coral	Q72279	1957	£10	£5	
That'll Be The Day	CD-s	Old Gold	OG6147	1989	£10	£5	
That'll Be The Day	LP	Ace Of Hearts	AH3	1961	£12	£5	

That'll Be The Day	LP	Decca	DL8707	1958	**£400**	**£250**	*US*
Think It Over	7"	Coral	Q72329	1958	**£8**	**£4**	
Think It Over	78	Coral	Q72329	1958	**£20**	**£10**	
True Love Ways	7"	Coral	Q72397	1960	**£6**	**£2.50**	
True Love Ways	CD-s	MCA	DMCA1302	1988	**£10**	**£5**	
True Love Ways	LP	MCA	MUP(S)319	1968	**£10**	**£4**	
What To Do	7"	Coral	Q72419	1961	**£6**	**£2.50**	
What To Do	7"	Coral	Q72469	1963	**£8**	**£4**	
Wishing	7"	Coral	Q72466	1963	**£5**	**£2**	
Wishing	7" EP	Coral	FEP2067	1964	**£40**	**£20**	
Wishing	LP	MCA	MUP320	1968	**£12**	**£5**	
You've Got Love	7"	Coral	Q72472	1964	**£8**	**£4**	

HOLLY, STEVE

Strange World	7"	Planet	PLF107	1966	**£10**	**£5**	

HOLLY & JOEY

I Got You Babe	7"	Virgin	VS478	1982	**£5**	**£2**	

HOLLYWOOD, KENNY

'Magic Star' is a considerable novelty, being nothing other than the Tornados' huge hit 'Telstar' with added vocals.

Magic Star	7"	Decca	F11546	1962	**£15**	**£7.50**	

HOLLYWOOD ARGYLES

Alley Oop	7"	London	HLU9146	1960	**£20**	**£10**	
Alley Oop	LP	Lute	L9001	1960	**£200**	**£100**	*US*
Gun Totin' Critter Called Jack	7"	Top Rank	JAR530	1960	**£6**	**£2.50**	

HOLLYWOOD FLAMES

Buzz Buzz Buzz	7"	London	HL8545	1958	**£40**	**£20**	
Buzz Buzz Buzz	7"	London	HL7030	1957	**£25**	**£12.50**	*export*
If I Thought You Needed Me	7"	London	HLE9071	1960	**£15**	**£7.50**	
Much Too Much	7"	London	HLW8955	1959	**£40**	**£20**	

HOLLYWOOD PERSUADERS

The B side of 'Tijuana' was written by Frank Zappa, who also played guitar on the song.

Tijuana	7"	Original Sound	39	1963	**£150**	**£75**	*US*

HOLLYWOOD VINES

When Johnny Comes Sliding Home	7"	Capitol	CL15191	1961	**£5**	**£2**	

HOLMAN, BILL

Bill Holman Octet	10" LP	Capitol	KPL101	1954	**£30**	**£15**	
Fabulous Bill Holman	LP	Coral	LVA9088	1958	**£25**	**£10**	
In A Jazz Orbit	LP	HMV	CLP1289	1959	**£15**	**£6**	

HOLMAN, EDDIE

Hey There Lonely Girl	7"	Stateside	SS2159	1970	**£5**	**£2**	
I Surrender	7"	Action	ACT4547	1969	**£25**	**£12.50**	
Since I Don't Have You	7"	Stateside	SS2170	1970	**£6**	**£2.50**	
This Can't Be True	7"	Cameo Parkway	P960	1965	**£25**	**£12.50**	
This Could Be A Night To Remember	7"	Salsoul	SZ2026	1977	**£4**	**£1.50**	

HOLMES, JAKE

Above Ground Sound	LP	Tower	ST5079	1967	**£12**	**£5**	*US*
How Much Time	LP	CBS	64905	1972	**£15**	**£6**	
Jake Holmes	LP	Polydor	583579	1970	**£20**	**£8**	
So Close So Very Far To Go	LP	Polydor	2425036	1970	**£15**	**£6**	

HOLMES, JOE & LEN GRAHAM

After Dawning	LP	Topic	12TS401	1979	**£10**	**£4**	
Chaste Muses, Bards And Sages	LP	Free Reed	FRR007	1976	**£12**	**£5**	

HOLMES, RICHARD 'GROOVE'

Comin' On Home	LP	Blue Note	BST84372	1970	**£12**	**£5**	
Soul Message	LP	Transatlantic	PR7435	1968	**£15**	**£6**	
Spicy	LP	Transatlantic	PR7493	1968	**£15**	**£6**	
Welcome Home	LP	Liberty	LBL/LBS83197	1969	**£12**	**£5**	

HOLOCAUST

Comin' Through	12"	Phoenix	12PSP4	1982	**£6**	**£2.50**	
Heavy Metal Mania	12"	Phoenix	12PSP1	1980	**£15**	**£7.50**	
Heavy Metal Mania	7"	Phoenix	PSP1	1980	**£15**	**£7.50**	
Live (Hot Curry And Wine)	LP	Phoenix	PSPLP4	1983	**£20**	**£8**	
Lovin' Feelin' Danger	7"	Phoenix	PSP3	1981	**£10**	**£5**	
Nightcomers	LP	Phoenix	PSLP1	1981	**£12**	**£5**	
No Man's Land	LP	Phoenix	PSPLP5	1984	**£10**	**£4**	
Smokin' Valves	12"	Phoenix	12PSP2	1980	**£10**	**£5**	
Smokin' Valves	7"	Phoenix	PSP2	1980	**£6**	**£2.50**	

HOLT, JOHN

Ali Baba	7"	Trojan	TR661	1969	**£4**	**£1.50**	

Title	Format	Label	Cat. No.	Year	Mint	VG+	Notes
Build Our Dreams	7"	Banana	BA345	1971	£5	£2	*Leroy Sibbles B side*
Close To Me	7"	Prince Buster	PB40	1972	£4	£1.50	
Come Out Of My Bed	7"	Duke Reid	DR2506	1970	£4	£1.50	*Winston Wright B side*
Dusty Roads	LP	Trojan	TRLS85	1974	£10	£4	
First Time	7"	Prince Buster	PB43	1972	£4	£1.50	
For Your Love	7"	Prince Buster	PB49	1972	£4	£1.50	
Further You Look	LP	Trojan	TRLS55	1973	£10	£4	
Get Ready	7"	Prince Buster	PB41	1972	£4	£1.50	
Greatest Hits	LP	Melodisc	MLP12170	197–	£25	£10	
Have Sympathy	7"	Trojan	TR694	1969	£4	£1.50	*Harry J B side*
Holly Holy	7"	Bamboo	BAM62	1970	£5	£2	
Holt	LP	Trojan	TRL(S)43	1972	£10	£4	
I Cried A Tear	7"	Island	WI041	1963	£10	£5	
John Holt And Friends	LP	Melodisc	MLP12191	197–	£25	£10	
Let's Build Our Dreams	7"	Treasure Isle	TI7061	1971	£5	£2	*Tommy McCook B side*
Let's Go Dancing	7"	Fab	FAB224	1973	£4	£1.50	
Little Happiness	7"	Fab	FAB18	1972	£4	£1.50	*Delroy Wilson B side*
Little Tear	7"	Jackpot	JP735	1970	£4	£1.50	*Jeff Barns B side*
Love I Can Feel	7"	Bamboo	BAM44	1970	£5	£2	*Johnny Last B side*
Love I Can Feel	LP	Attack	ATLP1001	1973	£10	£4	
Love I Can Feel	LP	Bamboo	BDLPS210	1970	£30	£15	
OK Fred	7"	Banana	BA340	1971	£5	£2	
OK Fred	LP	Melodisc	MLP12180	197–	£25	£10	
One Thousand Volts Of Holt	LP	Trojan	TRLS75	1973	£10	£4	
Paragons Medley	7"	Treasure Isle	TI7066	1971	£5	£2	*Tommy McCook B side*
Pledging My Love	LP	Trojan	TBL184	1972	£12	£5	
Rain From The Skies	7"	Prince Buster	PB42	1972	£4	£1.50	
Sea Cruise	7"	Unity	UN549	1970	£4	£1.50	
Share My Rest	7"	Supreme	SUP212	1970	£5	£2	*Al Brown B side*
Sister Big Stuff	7"	Treasure Isle	TI7065	1971	£5	£2	*Tommy McCook B side*
Stealing Stealing	7"	Duke	DU73	1970	£5	£2	*Winston Wright B side*
Still In Chains	LP	Trojan	TRL(S)37	1972	£10	£4	
Strange Things	7"	Punch	PH60	1971	£5	£2	*Winston Wright B side*
Thousand Volts Of Holt	LP	Trojan	TRLS75	1974	£10	£4	
Time Is The Master	LP	Cactus	CTLP109	1974	£10	£4	
Tonight	7"	Trojan	TR643	1968	£8	£4	
What You Gonna Do Now	7"	Trojan	TR674	1969	£4	£1.50	
Why Can't I Touch You	7"	Banana	BA314	1970	£5	£2	*Sound Dimension B side*
Wooden Heart	7"	Trojan	TR7702	1969	£4	£1.50	

HOLTS, ROOSEVELT

Title	Format	Label	Cat. No.	Year	Mint	VG+	Notes
Presenting The Country Blues	LP	Blue Horizon	763201	1968	£40	£20	

HOLY GHOST RECEPTION COMMITTEE

Title	Format	Label	Cat. No.	Year	Mint	VG+	Notes
Songs For Liturgical Worship	LP	Paulist		1968	£100	£50	*US*
Torchbearers	LP	Paulist	P04436	1969	£100	£50	*US*

HOLY MACKEREL

Title	Format	Label	Cat. No.	Year	Mint	VG+	Notes
Holy Mackerel	LP	CBS	65297	1972	£15	£6	

HOLY MODAL ROUNDERS

Title	Format	Label	Cat. No.	Year	Mint	VG+	Notes
Alleged In Their Own Time	LP	Rounder	3004	1975	£15	£6	*US*
Good Taste Is Timeless	LP	Metromedia	MD1039	1971	£15	£6	*US*
Holy Modal Rounders	LP	Transatlantic	TRA7451	1970	£15	£6	
Holy Modal Rounders	LP	Prestige	PR7410	1965	£20	£8	*US*
Holy Modal Rounders 2	LP	Prestige	PRS7451	1967	£20	£8	*US*
Indian War Whoop	LP	ESP-Disk	1068	1967	£30	£15	*US*
Last Round	LP	Adelphi	AD1030	1978	£15	£6	*US*
Moray Eels Eat The Holy Modal Rounders	LP	Elektra	EKL4026	1968	£15	£6	
Peter Stampfel & Steve Weber	LP	Rounder		1981	£15	£6	*US*
Stampfel And Weber	LP	Fantasy	F24711	1972	£20	£8	*US double*

HOMBRES

Title	Format	Label	Cat. No.	Year	Mint	VG+	Notes
Let It All Hang Out	7"	Verve	VS1510	1967	£8	£4	
Let It Out	LP	Verve	FT(S)3036	1967	£12	£5	*US*

HOME

Title	Format	Label	Cat. No.	Year	Mint	VG+	Notes
Alchemist	LP	CBS	65550	1973	£10	£4	
Home	LP	CBS	64752	1972	£20	£8	
Pause For A Hoarse Horse	LP	CBS	64365	1971	£40	£20	
unreleased album	LP	CBS		197–	£100	£50	*test pressing*

HOME SERVICE

Title	Format	Label	Cat. No.	Year	Mint	VG+	Notes
Alright Jack	LP	Making Waves	SPIN119	1986	£10	£4	
Mysteries	LP	Coda	NAT001	1984	£12	£5	

HOMER

Title	Format	Label	Cat. No.	Year	Mint	VG	Notes
Grown In The USA	LP	United Recording Art	URA101	1970	**£150**	**£75**	*US*

HOMER & JETHRO

Title	Format	Label	Cat. No.	Year	Mint	VG	Notes
Barefoot Ballads	LP	RCA	LPM1412	1957	**£15**	**£6**	*US*
Don't Let Your Sweet Love Die	7"	Parlophone	CMSP2	1954	**£8**	**£4**	*export*
Homer & Jethro Fracture Frank Loesser	10" LP	RCA	LPM3112	1953	**£25**	**£10**	*US*
Life Can Be Miserable	LP	RCA	LPM/LSP1880	1958	**£12**	**£5**	*US*
Musical Madness	LP	Audio Lab	AL1513	1958	**£25**	**£10**	*US*
Swappin' Partners	7"	HMV	7M211	1954	**£6**	**£2.50**	
They Sure Are Corny	LP	King	639	1959	**£15**	**£6**	*US*
Wanted For Murder Of The Standards	7" EP	Parlophone	GEP8791	1959	**£10**	**£5**	
Worst Of Homer And Jethro	LP	RCA	LPM1560	1957	**£15**	**£6**	*US*

HOMOSEXUALS

Title	Format	Label	Cat. No.	Year	Mint	VG	Notes
Bigger Than The Number Yet Missing The Dot	7"	Black Noise	BN1	1981	**£5**	**£2**	
Divorce Proceedings	12"	Black Noise	F12No.2	1979	**£6**	**£2.50**	
Hearts In Exile	7"	L'Orelei	PF151	1979	**£5**	**£2**	

HONDA, MINAKO

Title	Format	Label	Cat. No.	Year	Mint	VG	Notes
Cancel	LP	Eastworld	WTP90433	1986	**£20**	**£8**	*Japanese, with Brian May*
Golden Days	7"	Columbia	DB9153	1987	**£20**	**£10**	*with Brian May*

HONDELLS

Title	Format	Label	Cat. No.	Year	Mint	VG	Notes
Cheryl's Going Home	7"	Mercury	MF967	1967	**£6**	**£2.50**	
Go Little Honda	LP	Mercury	MG2/SR60940	1964	**£40**	**£20**	*US*
Hondells	LP	Mercury	MG2/SR60982	1965	**£40**	**£20**	*US*
Little Honda	7"	Mercury	MF834	1964	**£8**	**£4**	
Younger Girl	7"	Mercury	MF925	1965	**£5**	**£2**	

HONEST MEN

Title	Format	Label	Cat. No.	Year	Mint	VG	Notes
Cherie	7"	Tamla Motown	TMG706	1969	**£10**	**£5**	

HONEY CONE

Title	Format	Label	Cat. No.	Year	Mint	VG	Notes
Honey Cone	LP	Hot Wax	SHW5002	1969	**£10**	**£4**	

HONEY DREAMERS

Title	Format	Label	Cat. No.	Year	Mint	VG	Notes
Sing Gershwin	7" EP	Vogue	VE170124	1958	**£5**	**£2**	

HONEYBUS

Readers of small print on record labels will see the songwriting credit Dello on the B sides of the first two singles by the Applejacks and will be instantly transported to a field where a girl and her packet of Nimble bread hang suspended from a balloon. It was Pete Dello, who as leader of the Honeybus, wrote and sang the memorable 'I Can't Let Maggie Go', a song which provided the group's only hit and was later used in the well-known bread advert on television. The Honeybus gave up trying in mid 1969, following Pete Dello's decision to leave. These days, Dello owns a string of garages, bought, no doubt, out of the proceeds from the one classic hit.

Title	Format	Label	Cat. No.	Year	Mint	VG	Notes
Delighted To See You	7"	Deram	DM131	1967	**£5**	**£2**	
Do I Still Figure In Your Life	7"	Deram	DM152	1967	**£5**	**£2**	
For You	7"	Warner Bros	K16250	1973	**£5**	**£2**	
Girl Of Independent Means	7"	Deram	DM207	1968	**£4**	**£1.50**	
Recital	LP	Warner Bros	K46248	1973	**£150**	**£75**	
She Sold Blackpool Rock	7"	Deram	DM254	1969	**£5**	**£2**	
Story	7"	Deram	DM289	1970	**£4**	**£1.50**	
Story	LP	Deram	SML1056	1970	**£50**	**£25**	

HONEYCOMBS

Title	Format	Label	Cat. No.	Year	Mint	VG	Notes
All Systems Go	LP	Pye	NPL18132	1965	**£75**	**£37.50**	
Colour Slide	7" EP	Pye	PNV24126	1964	**£30**	**£15**	*French*
Don't Love You No More	7"	Pye	7N15781	1965	**£75**	**£37.50**	
Eyes	7"	Pye	7N15736	1964	**£4**	**£1.50**	
Have I The Right	7" EP	Pye	PNV24122	1964	**£30**	**£15**	*French, B side by the Kinks*
Honeycombs	LP	Pye	NPL18097	1964	**£40**	**£20**	
Honeycombs	LP	Golden Guinea	GGL0350	1965	**£15**	**£6**	
In Tokyo	LP	Pye	PS1277Y	1965	**£150**	**£75**	*Japanese*
It's So Hard	7"	Pye	7N17138	1966	**£5**	**£2**	
Something Better Beginning	7"	Pye	7N15827	1965	**£5**	**£2**	
That Loving Feeling	7"	Pye	7N17173	1966	**£8**	**£4**	
That's The Way	7" EP	Pye	NEP24230	1965	**£25**	**£12.50**	
This Year Next Year	7"	Pye	7N15979	1965	**£4**	**£1.50**	
Who Is Sylvia	7"	Pye	7N17059	1966	**£5**	**£2**	

HONEYCRACK

Honeycrack's rediscovery of the delights of tightly harmonized, high-tension power pop was one of the many highlights of a period that proved to be a new golden age in the history of rock – the mid-nineties. In addition to their own sparkling material, the group also turned in a definitive rendering of a forgotten Beatles song, 'Hey Bulldog'. Honeycrack's one rarity, however, is a single pressed as a benefit for fans at the early gigs.

Title	Format	Label	Cat. No.	Year	Mint	VG	Notes
King Of Misery	7"	Sony	PPP1	1995	**£10**	**£5**	
King Of Misery	CD-s	Sony	PPPCD1	1995	**£10**	**£5**	

HONEYDEW

Title	Format	Label	Cat. No.	Year	Mint	VG	Notes
Honeydew	LP	Argo	ZFB15	1971	**£10**	**£4**	

HONEYS

The Honeys consisted of Brian Wilson's wife Marilyn, her sister Diane Rovell, and their cousin Ginger Blake. Their records were produced by Brian Wilson, who applied the same imagination and innovation as he did on his own records with the Beach Boys.

Title	Format	Label	Cat. No.	Year	Mint	VG	Notes
He's A Doll	7"	Warner Bros	5430	1964	**£150**	**£75**	US
One You Can't Have	7"	Capitol	5093	1963	**£75**	**£37.50**	US
Pray For Surf	7"	Capitol	5034	1963	**£75**	**£37.50**	US
Shoot The Curl	7"	Capitol	4952	1963	**£50**	**£25**	US
Surfing Down The Swanee River	7"	Capitol	CL15299	1963	**£30**	**£15**	
Tonight You Belong To Me	7"	Capitol	2454	1969	**£30**	**£15**	US

HONEYTONES

Title	Format	Label	Cat. No.	Year	Mint	VG	Notes
Don't Look Now But	7"	London	HLX8671	1958	**£40**	**£20**	

HONEYTREE

Title	Format	Label	Cat. No.	Year	Mint	VG	Notes
Marantha Marathon	LP	Myrrh	MYR1086	1979	**£15**	**£6**	
Way I Feel	LP	Myrrh	MYR1018	1974	**£30**	**£15**	

HOOD, ROBBIN

Title	Format	Label	Cat. No.	Year	Mint	VG	Notes
Rock-A-Bye Blues	7"	MGM	SP1178	1956	**£5**	**£2**	

HOOK

Title	Format	Label	Cat. No.	Year	Mint	VG	Notes
Hooked	LP	Uni	73038	1968	**£30**	**£15**	US
Show You The Way	7"	Uni	UN507	1969	**£5**	**£2**	
Will Grab You	LP	Uni	73023	1968	**£30**	**£15**	US

HOOKER, EARL

Title	Format	Label	Cat. No.	Year	Mint	VG	Notes
Boogie Don't Blot	7"	Blue Horizon	573166	1969	**£15**	**£7.50**	
Don't Have To Worry	LP	Stateside	SSL10298	1969	**£25**	**£10**	
Sweet Black Angel	LP	Blue Horizon	763850	1970	**£75**	**£37.50**	

HOOKER, JOHN LEE

Title	Format	Label	Cat. No.	Year	Mint	VG	Notes
Alone	LP	Speciality	SNTF5005	1972	**£10**	**£4**	
Best Of John Lee Hooker	LP	Joy	JOYS156	1970	**£10**	**£4**	
Big Maceo Merriweather & John Lee Hooker	LP	Fortune	3002	196–	**£20**	**£8**	US
Big Soul Of John Lee Hooker	LP	Joy	JOYS147	1969	**£10**	**£4**	
Blue!	LP	Fontana	FJL119	1965	**£20**	**£8**	
Blues Of John Lee Hooker	7" EP	Stateside	SE1019	1964	**£10**	**£5**	
Boom Boom	7"	Stateside	SS203	1963	**£8**	**£4**	
Burnin'	LP	Joy	JOY(S)124	1968	**£10**	**£4**	
Burning Hell	LP	Riverside	RLP008	1965	**£20**	**£8**	
Coast To Coast Blues Band	LP	United Artists	UAS29235	1971	**£15**	**£6**	
Concert At Newport	LP	Joy	JOYS142	1969	**£10**	**£4**	
Democrat Man	7" EP	Riverside	REP3207	1960	**£10**	**£5**	
Dimples	7"	Stateside	SS297	1964	**£5**	**£2**	
Don't Turn Me From Your Door	LP	London	HAK8097	1963	**£30**	**£15**	
Down At The Landing	7" EP	Chess	CRE6000	1965	**£15**	**£7.50**	
Driftin' Blues	LP	Atlantic	590003	1967	**£10**	**£4**	
Driftin' Through The Blues	LP	Ember	(ST)EMB3371	1966	**£15**	**£6**	
Endless Boogie	LP	Probe	SPB1034	1971	**£10**	**£4**	
Folk Blues	LP	Fontana	688700ZL	1964	**£20**	**£8**	
Folk Blues	LP	Riverside	RLP12838	1962	**£25**	**£10**	
Folklore Of John Lee Hooker	LP	Joy	JOYS133	1969	**£10**	**£4**	
Folklore Of John Lee Hooker	LP	Stateside	SL10014	1962	**£20**	**£8**	
Healer	CD-s	Silvertone	ORECD10	1989	**£5**	**£2**	3" single
High Priced Woman	7"	Pye	7N25255	1964	**£4**	**£1.50**	
Hooker Hopkins Hogg	LP	Sonet	SNTF5013	1973	**£10**	**£4**	*with Lightnin' Hopkins & Smokey Hogg*
House Of The Blues	LP	Pye	NPL28042	1964	**£25**	**£10**	
I Love You Honey	7"	Stateside	SS341	1964	**£6**	**£2.50**	
I Want To Shout The Blues	LP	Stateside	SL10074	1964	**£15**	**£6**	
I'm In The Mood	7"	Sue	WI361	1965	**£15**	**£7.50**	
I'm John Lee Hooker	7" EP	Stateside	SE1023	1964	**£10**	**£5**	
I'm John Lee Hooker	LP	Joy	JOY(S)101	1968	**£10**	**£4**	
I'm John Lee Hooker	LP	Vee Jay	LP1007	1959	**£30**	**£15**	US
If You Miss 'Im . . . I Got 'Im	LP	Probe	SPB1016	1971	**£10**	**£4**	*with Earl Hooker*
In Person	LP	Joy	JOYS152	1969	**£10**	**£4**	
It Serves You Right To Suffer	LP	HMV	CLP5032/CSD3542	1966	**£25**	**£10**	
John Lee Hooker	7" EP	Atlantic	AET6010	1965	**£12**	**£6**	
John Lee Hooker	LP	XTRA	XTRA114	1971	**£10**	**£4**	
John Lee Hooker And His Guitar	LP	Advent	LP2801	196–	**£25**	**£10**	
John Lee Hooker Sings The Blues	LP	King	727	1961	**£30**	**£15**	US
Johnny Lee	LP	Green Bottle	GN4002	1973	**£10**	**£4**	
Journey	7" EP	Chess	CRE6014	1966	**£15**	**£7.50**	
Let's Go Out Tonight	7"	Chess	CRS8039	1966	**£6**	**£2.50**	
Live At Café Au Go-Go	LP	HMV	CLP/CSD3612	1966	**£15**	**£6**	
Love Blues	7" EP	Pye	NEP44034	1964	**£15**	**£7.50**	
Mad Man Blues	LP	Checker	6467305	1973	**£10**	**£4**	
Mai Lee	7"	Planet	PLF114	1966	**£15**	**£7.50**	
Need Somebody	78	London	HL8037	1954	**£20**	**£10**	
Never Get Out Of These Blues Alive	LP	Probe	SPB1057	1972	**£10**	**£4**	

On Campus	LP	Vee Jay	LP/SR1066	1963	£15	£6	US
Plays And Sings The Blues	LP	Chess	CRL4500	1965	£15	£6	
Preachin' The Blues	LP	Stateside	SL10053	1964	£20	£8	
Real Folk Blues	LP	Chess	CRL4527	1966	£15	£6	
Real Folk Blues Vol. 3	7" EP	Chess	CRE6021	1966	£15	£7.50	
Rhythm And Blues	7" EP	Stateside	SE1008	1962	£10	£5	with Jimmy Reed
Serves You Right To Suffer	7" EP	Impulse	9103	1973	£6	£2.50	
Shake It Baby	7"	Polydor	NH52930	1964	£6	£2.50	
Simply The Truth	LP	Stateside	(S)SL10280	1969	£12	£5	
Sings The Blues	LP	Ember	EMB3356	1965	£15	£6	
That's Where It's At	LP	Stax	2362017	1971	£10	£4	
That's Where It's At	LP	Stax	SXATS1025	1970	£10	£4	
Thinking Blues	7" EP	Ember	EMBEP4561	1964	£20	£10	
Travelin'	LP	Joy	JOYS129	1969	£10	£4	
Tupelo Blues	LP	Storyville	673020	1970	£10	£4	
Urban Blues	LP	Stateside	(S)SL10246	1968	£15	£6	
Walking The Boogie	7" EP	Chess	CRE6007	1966	£15	£7.50	
Wednesday Evening	7" EP	Riverside	REP3202	1960	£10	£5	
Whistlin' And Moanin' Blues	78	Vogue	V2102	1952	£20	£10	
You're Leavin' Me Baby	LP	Storyville	673005	1970	£10	£4	

HOOKER, JOHN LEE & CANNED HEAT

Hooker And Heat	LP	Liberty	LPS103/4	1971	£25	£10	double

HOOKFOOT

Hookfoot	LP	DJM	DJLPS413	1971	£10	£4	

HOOKS, MARSHALL & CO.

I Want The Same Thing Tomorrow	7"	Blue Horizon	2096002	1971	£8	£4	
Marshall Hooks & Co.	LP	Blue Horizon	2431003	1971	£40	£20	

HOOTCH

Hootch	LP	Progress	PRS4844	1974	£300	£180	US

HOOTENANNY SINGERS

This Swedish group had the future Abba star, Björn Ulvaeus, as singer and songwriter.

Basta	LP	Polar	POLL101	1967	£15	£6	Swedish
Bellman Pa Vart Satt	LP	Polar	POLS214	196–	£15	£6	Swedish
Civila	LP	Polar	POLS211	196–	£15	£6	Swedish
Dan Andersson Pa Vart Satt	LP	Polar	POLS249	197–	£15	£6	Swedish
De Basta Med . . . & Bjorn Ulvaeus	LP	Polar	POLL103	196–	£15	£6	Swedish
Evert Taube	LP	Polar	POLS204	196–	£15	£6	Swedish
Evert Taube Pa Vart Satt	LP	Polar	POLS260	1974	£15	£6	Swedish
Frogg	7" EP	Pathe	EGF794	1964	£20	£10	French
Gabriella	7"	United Artists	UP1082	1965	£15	£7.50	
Hootenanny Singers	LP	Polar	POLS201	196–	£15	£6	Swedish
International	LP	Polar	POLP206	1965	£15	£6	Swedish
Manga Ansikten	LP	Polar	POLP209	196–	£15	£6	Swedish
No Time	7" EP	Pathe	EGF880	1965	£20	£10	French
Skillingtryck	LP	Polar	POLS225	1970	£15	£6	Swedish
Vara Backraste Visor	LP	Polar	POLS229	197–	£15	£6	Swedish
Vara Backraste Visor 2	LP	Polar	POLS236	197–	£15	£6	Swedish

HOPE, BOB

Paris Holiday	7"	London	HLU8593	1958	£6	£2.50	with Bing Crosby

HOPE, ELMO

Informal Jazz	LP	Esquire	32039	1958	£40	£20	
With Frank Butler And James Bond	LP	Vocalion	LAEH590	1966	£12	£5	

HOPE, LYNN

Blue Moon	7"	Vogue	V9081	1957	£25	£12.50	
Eleven Till Two	7"	Vogue	V9082	1957	£25	£12.50	
Lynn Hope	LP	Aladdin	820	195–	£60	£30	US
Lynn Hope & His Tenor Sax	7" EP	Vogue	VE170146	1960	£50	£25	
Lynn Hope & His Tenor Sax	7" EP	Vogue	VE170103	1957	£50	£25	
Lynn Hope And His Tenor Sax	10" LP	Aladdin	707	195–	£100	£50	US
Shocking	7"	Blue Beat	BB21	1960	£12	£6	
Temptation	7"	Vogue	V9115	1958	£10	£5	
Tenderly	LP	Score	LP4015	1957	£40	£20	US

HOPKIN, MARY

Aderyn Llwyd	7"	Cambrian	CSP703	1969	£10	£5	picture sleeve
Earth Song/Ocean Song	LP	Apple	SAPCOR21	1971	£15	£6	
Let My Name Be Sorrow	7"	Apple	34	1971	£8	£4	picture sleeve
Llais Swynol Mary Hopkin	7" EP	Cambrian	CEP414	1968	£8	£4	
Lontana Dagli Occhi	7"	Apple	7	1969	£6	£2.50	European
Mary Ac Edward	7" EP	Cambrian	CEP420	1969	£8	£4	
Pleserau Serch	7"	Cambrian	CSP712	1970	£10	£5	picture sleeve
Postcard	LP	Apple	SAPCOR5	1969	£10	£4	
Postcard	LP	Apple	APCOR5	1969	£12	£5	mono
Prince En Avignon	7"	Apple	9	1969	£6	£2.50	European
Qué será será	7"	Apple	27	1970	£6	£2.50	European
Think About Your Children	7"	Apple	30	1970	£4	£1.50	picture sleeve
Those Were The Days	LP	Apple	SAPCOR23	1972	£60	£30	
Water, Paper And Clay	7"	Apple	39	1971	£12	£6	picture sleeve

Welsh World Of Mary Hopkin	LP	Decca	SPA546	1977	£15	£6	
Wrap Me In Your Arms	7"	Good Earth	GD11	1977	£5	£2	

HOPKINS, LIGHTNIN'

Autobiography In Blues	LP	Tradition	TLP1040	1960	£25	£10	US
Blue Bird Blues	LP	Fontana	688803ZL	1966	£20	£8	
Blues	LP	Ace Of Hearts	(Z)AHT183	1970	£10	£4	
Blues	LP	Fontana	TL5264	1965	£20	£8	
Blues From East Texas	LP	Heritage	H1000	1960	£60	£30	*with Joel Hopkins*
Blues Hoot	LP	Stateside	SL10076	1964	£25	£10	*with Sonny Terry & Brownie McGhee*
Blues In The Bottle	LP	XTRA	XTRA5036	1968	£12	£5	
Blues/Folk	LP	Time	1	1962	£15	£6	US
Blues/Folk Vol. 2	LP	Time	3	1962	£15	£6	US
Burnin' In L.A.	LP	Fontana	688801ZL	1965	£20	£8	
California Mudslide And Earthquake	LP	Liberty	LBS83293	1970	£15	£6	
Country Blues	LP	Tradition	TLP1035	1960	£25	£10	US
Dirty Blues	LP	Mainstream	MSL1001	1973	£10	£4	
Dirty House Blues	LP	Realm	RM171	1964	£20	£8	
Down Home Blues	LP	Stateside	SL10155	1965	£20	£8	
Earth Blues	LP	Minit	MLL/MLS40006	1968	£15	£6	
Fast Life Woman	LP	Verve	V8453	1962	£20	£8	US
Free Form Patterns	LP	International Artist	6	1968	£75	£37.50	US
Goin' Away	LP	Bluesville	BV1073	1964	£15	£6	US
Got To Move Your Baby	LP	XTRA	XTRA5044	1968	£10	£4	
His Greatest Hits	LP	Bluesville	BV1084	1964	£15	£6	US
Hootin' The Blues	LP	Stateside	SL10110	1965	£20	£8	
I've Been Buked And Scorned	LP	Ember	EMB3423	1968	£20	£8	
King Of Dowling Street	LP	Liberty	LBL83254	1969	£15	£6	
Last Night Blues	LP	Bluesville	BV1029	1961	£20	£8	US
Last Night Blues	LP	Fontana	688301ZL	1964	£20	£8	
Last Of The Great Blues Singers	LP	Time	70004	1960	£20	£8	US
Let's Work Awhile	LP	Blue Horizon	2431005	1971	£60	£30	
Lightnin'	LP	Bluesville	BV1019	1961	£30	£15	US
Lightnin'	LP	Poppy	60002	1969	£10	£4	US
Lightnin' And The Blues	LP	Herald	1012	1960	£150	£75	US
Lightnin' Hopkins	LP	Boulevard	BLVD4001	1971	£10	£4	
Lightnin' Hopkins	LP	Fontana	688807ZL	1966	£20	£8	
Lightnin' Hopkins	LP	Folkways	FS3822	1961	£20	£8	
Lightnin' Hopkins	LP	77	LA121	1960	£30	£15	
Lightnin' Hopkins	LP	Vee Jay	LP1044	1962	£25	£10	US
Lightnin' Hopkins And John Lee Hooker	LP	Storyville	SLP174	1965	£25	£10	*with John Lee Hooker*
Lightnin' Hopkins And The Blues	LP	Imperial	LP9211/12211	1962	£20	£8	US
Lightnin' Hopkins On Stage	LP	Imperial	LP9180	1962	£20	£8	US
Lightnin' Hopkins Strums The Blues	LP	Score	4022	1960	£75	£37.50	US
Lightnin' Strikes	LP	Joy	JOY(S)115	1969	£10	£4	
Lightnin' Strikes	LP	A&M	AMLB40001/2	1971	£12	£5	*double*
Lightnin' Strikes	LP	Stateside	SL10031	1963	£20	£8	
Lightnin' Strikes	LP	Verve	(S)VLP5014	1966	£12	£5	
Lightnin' Vol. 1	LP	Poppy	PYS11000	1970	£10	£4	
Lightnin' Vol. 2	LP	Poppy	PYS11002	1970	£10	£4	
Live At The Bird Lounge	LP	Ember	EMB3416	1968	£20	£8	
Lonesome Lightnin'	LP	Polydor	2941005	1972	£10	£4	
Low Down Dirty Blues	LP	Mainstream	MSL1031	1975	£10	£4	
Mojo Hand	LP	Fire	104	1962	£50	£25	US
My Life In The Blues	LP	Prestige	PR7370	1965	£15	£6	US
Nothin' But The Blues	LP	Mount Vernon	104	196–	£15	£6	US
Roots Of Hopkins	LP	Verve	(S)VLP5003	1966	£20	£8	
Roots Of Lightnin' Hopkins	LP	XTRA	XTRA1127	1971	£15	£6	
Sings The Blues	LP	Realm	RM128	1963	£20	£8	
Smokes Like Lightnin'	LP	Bluesville	BV1070	1963	£15	£6	US
Something Blue	LP	Verve	FV(S)3013	1967	£15	£6	US
Soul Blues	LP	Prestige	PR(S)7377	1966	£15	£6	US
That's My Story	LP	Polydor	545019	1969	£10	£4	
There's Good Rockin' Tonight	LP	Storyville	616001	1970	£25	£10	*with John Lee Hooker*
Time For Blues	LP	Ember	EMB3389	1967	£20	£8	
Walkin' This Road By Myself	LP	Bluesville	BV1057	1961	£20	£8	US

HOPKINS, LINDA

I Diddle Dum Dum	7"	Coral	Q72423	1961	£15	£7.50	
Mama's Doing The Twist	7"	Coral	Q72448	1962	£10	£5	

HOPKINS, NICKY

Mr Big	7"	CBS	202055	1966	£8	£4	
Mr Pleasant	7"	Polydor	56175	1967	£8	£4	
Revolutionary Piano	LP	CBS	62679	1966	£20	£8	
Tin Man Was A Dreamer	LP	CBS	65416	1973	£10	£4	

HOPPER, HUGH

Although Hugh Hopper's fuzz bass guitar lines seemed like the element most rooted to rock in Soft Machine's rapid espousal of a jazz approach, it is Hopper who has actually continued to work mostly in a jazz context, while his former colleagues Mike Ratledge and Karl Jenkins have opted for a more commercial approach.

1984	LP	CBS	65466	1973	£10	£4	
Cruel But Fair	LP	Compendium	FIDARDO4	1976	£10	£4	
Hopper Tunity Box	LP	Compendium	FIDARDO7	1977	£10	£4	
Monster Band	LP	Atmosphere	IRI5003	1979	£10	£4	
Rogue Element	LP	Ogun	OG527	1978	£12	£5	*with Elton Dean, Alan Gowen, Dave Sheen*

HOPSCOTCH

Long Black Veil	7"	United Artists	UP35022	1969	£4	£1.50	
Look At The Lights Go Up	7"	United Artists	UP2231	1969	£20	£10	

HORACE & THE IMPERIALS

Young Love	7"	Nu Beat	NB012	1968	£6	£2.50	

HORDE CATALYTIQUE POUR LA FIN

Gestation Sonore	LP	Futura	SON003	1971	£12	£5	*French*

HORDEN RAIKES

Horden Raikes	LP	Folk Heritage	FHR026	1972	£15	£6	
King Cotton	LP	Folk Heritage	FHR042	1972	£12	£5	

HORIZON

Stage Struck	7"	SRT	SRTS81432	1981	£6	£2.50	

HORN, PAUL

Cosmic Consciousness	LP	Liberty	LBL83084E	1968	£15	£6	
In Kashmir	LP	Liberty	LBL83084	1968	£12	£5	
Inside	LP	Epic	EPC65201	1969	£12	£5	
Inside Two	LP	Epic	31600	1973	£10	£4	*US*
Special Edition	LP	Island	ISLD6	1974	£12	£5	*double*
Visions	LP	Epic	32837	1974	£10	£4	*US*

HORNE, KENNETH & OTHERS

Beyond Our Ken	LP	Parlophone	PMC1238	1964	£15	£6	

HORNE, LENA

At The Waldorf Astoria	LP	RCA	RD27021/SF5007	1957	£10	£4	
Give The Lady What She Wants	LP	RCA	RD27098/SF5019	1959	£10	£4	
If You Can Dream	7"	HMV	7M423	1956	£4	£1.50	
It's All Right With Me	7"	HMV	7M319	1955	£5	£2	
It's Love	LP	RCA	LPM1148	1955	£20	£8	*US*
Lena Horne	7" EP	MGM	MGMEP503	1954	£5	£2	
Let's Put Out The Lights	7" EP	RCA	SRC7012	1959	£5	£2	*stereo*
Love Me Or Leave Me	7"	HMV	7M309	1955	£5	£2	
Maybe I'm Amazed	7"	Buddah	2011078	1971	£8	£4	
Stormy Weather	LP	RCA	LPM1375	1956	£20	£8	*US*

HORNETS

Motorcycles USA	LP	Liberty	LST7348	1964	£20	£8	*US*

HORNSBY, BRUCE

Defenders Of THe Flag	CD-s	RCA	PD49512	1988	£5	£2	
Look Out Any Window	CD-s	RCA	PD49534	1988	£5	£2	
Valley Road	CD-s	RCA	PD49562	1988	£5	£2	

HORNSEY AT WAR

Dead Beat Revival	7"	War	WAR001	197–	£5	£2	

HORRORCOMIC

I Don't Mind	7"	Lightning	GIL512	1978	£10	£5	
I'm All Hung Up On Pierrepoint	7"	Lightning	BVZ0007	1977	£10	£5	
Jesus Christ	7"	B&C	BCS18	1979	£10	£5	

HORSE

Horse	LP	RCA	SF8109	1970	£125	£62.50	

HORSES

Album No. 1	LP	White Whale	WW7121	1969	£25	£10	*US*

HORSLIPS

Horslips were employing traditional musical elements from their native Ireland long before the Pogues and the Waterboys made it fashionable. Their first LP, *Happy To Meet*, comes within an intricate package that is designed to look like a concertina and which is not often found in mint condition.

Drive The Cold Winter Away	LP	Oats	MOO9	1976	£10	£4	
Happy To Meet Sorry To Part	LP	Oats	MOO3	1972	£20	£8	*octagonal cover with booklet*
Live	LP	Oats	MOO10	1976	£15	£6	*Irish double*
Tain	LP	Oats	MOO5	1973	£10	£4	

HORTON, JOHNNY

All Grown Up	7"	CBS	AAG132	1963	£5	£2	
Battle Of New Orleans	7"	Philips	PB932	1959	£4	£1.50	
Country And Western Aces	7" EP	Mercury	10008MCE	1964	£25	£12.50	
Done Rovin'	LP	London	HAU8096	1963	£30	£15	
Done Rovin'	LP	Briar	104	195–	£75	£37.50	*US*

Fantastic	LP	Mercury	MG20478	1959	**£40**	**£20**	US
Fantastic Johnny Horton	7" EP	Mercury	ZEP10074	1960	**£30**	**£15**	
Free And Easy Songs	LP	SESAC	1201	1959	**£75**	**£37.50**	US
Greatest Hits	LP	Columbia	CL1596/CS8396	1961	**£20**	**£8**	US
Honky Tonk Man	LP	Philips	BBL7536	1961	**£25**	**£10**	
I Can't Forget You	LP	Columbia	CL2299/CS9099	1965	**£20**	**£8**	US
Johnny Horton	LP	Dot	DLP3221	1962	**£25**	**£10**	US
Johnny Horton Makes History	LP	Columbia	CL1478/CS8269	1960	**£20**	**£8**	US
Johnny Reb	7"	Philips	PB951	1959	**£5**	**£2**	
Mr Moonlight	7"	Philips	PB1130	1961	**£4**	**£1.50**	
North to Alaska	7"	Philips	PB1062	1960	**£4**	**£1.50**	
Ole Slew Foot	7"	Philips	PB1170	1961	**£5**	**£2**	
Sink The Bismarck	7"	Philips	PB995	1960	**£5**	**£2**	
Sleepy Eyed John	7"	Philips	PB1132	1961	**£5**	**£2**	
Spectacular Johnny Horton	LP	Philips	BBL7464	1960	**£25**	**£10**	
Take Me Like I Am	7"	Philips	PB976	1959	**£4**	**£1.50**	
Voice Of Johnny Horton	LP	Fontana	FJL306	1965	**£10**	**£4**	
Words	7"	Philips	PB1226	1962	**£5**	**£2**	

HORTON, SHAKEY

Soul Of Blues Harmonica	LP	Argo	4037	1964	**£40**	**£20**	US
Southern Comfort	LP	London	HAK/SHK8405	1970	**£60**	**£30**	
Walter Shakey Horton With Hot Cottage	LP	XTRA	XTRA1135	1974	**£10**	**£4**	

HOST

Pa Sterke Vinger	LP	Philips	6317601	1974	**£100**	**£50**	*Norwegian*

HOT BUTTER

More Hot Butter	LP	Pye	NSPL28181	1973	**£10**	**£4**	
Popcorn	LP	Pye	NSPL28169	1973	**£10**	**£4**	

HOT CHOCOLATE

Give Peace A Chance	7"	Apple	18	1969	**£20**	**£10**	
Love Is Life	7"	RAK	RAK346	1970	**£5**	**£2**	*with promo picture sleeve*

HOT CLUB

Dirt That She Walks In Is Sacred Ground To Me	7"	RAK	RAK346	1982	**£6**	**£2.50**	

HOT DOGGERS

Surfin' USA	LP	Epic	LN24/BN26054	1963	**£30**	**£15**	US

HOT POOP

Does Their Own Stuff	LP	Hot Poop	HPS3072	1967	**£60**	**£30**	US

HOT POTATO

Hot Potato	LP	private	PMTB1	1973	**£75**	**£37.50**	

HOT ROD ALL STARS

Control Your Doggy	7"	Torpedo	TOR14	1970	**£4**	**£1.50**	
Judge	7"	Joe's	DU41	1969	**£4**	**£1.50**	*Ron B side*
Lick A Pop	7"	Duke	DU59	1969	**£4**	**£1.50**	
Moonhop In London	7"	Torpedo	TOR10	1970	**£10**	**£5**	
Paint Your Wagon	7"	Duke	DU65	1970	**£4**	**£1.50**	
Pussy Got Nine Life	7"	Torpedo	TOR1	1970	**£4**	**£1.50**	*Boss Sounds B side*
Return Of The Bad Man	7"	Duke	DU66	1970	**£4**	**£1.50**	
Skinhead Speaks His Mind	7"	Hot Rod	HR104	1970	**£10**	**£5**	*Carl Levey B side*
Skinheads Don't Fear	7"	Torpedo	TOR5	1970	**£10**	**£5**	
Strong Man	7"	Trojan	TR7732	1970	**£4**	**£1.50**	
Virgin Soldier	7"	Trojan	TR7733	1970	**£4**	**£1.50**	

HOT SOUP

Openers	LP	Rama Rama	RR78	1969	**£20**	**£8**	US

HOT SPRINGS

It's All Right	7"	Columbia	DB7821	1966	**£8**	**£4**	

HOT TODDYS

Shakin' And Stompin'	7"	Pye	7N25020	1959	**£12**	**£6**	

HOT TUNA

America's Choice	LP	Grunt	BFD10820	1975	**£10**	**£4**	US quad
Electric Live	LP	RCA	LSP4550	1971	**£10**	**£4**	
Yellow Fever	LP	Grunt	BFD11238	1975	**£10**	**£4**	US quad

HOT VULTURES

Carrion On	LP	Red Rag	RRR005	1976	**£12**	**£5**	
East Street Shakes	LP	Red Rag	RRR015	1978	**£10**	**£4**	

HOTHOUSE FLOWERS

Don't Go	CD-s	Polygram	0804822	1988	**£10**	**£5**	CD video
Don't Go	CD-s	London	LONCD174	1988	**£5**	**£2**	
Easier In The Morning	CD-s	London	LONCD186	1988	**£5**	**£2**	
Home	CD	London	8281972	1990	**£40**	**£20**	*promo box set, with cassette and video*
I'm Sorry	CD-s	London	LONCD187	1988	**£5**	**£2**	

HOTLEGS

Hotlegs were not the one-hit wonders they might appear to be. The group who scored with a novelty recording, 'Neanderthal Man', were only waiting for successful songwriter Graham Gouldman to join them before starting to make records as 10cc.

Title	Format	Label	Cat. No.	Year	Mint	VG	Notes
Lady Sadie	7"	Philips	6006140	1971	**£5**	**£2**	
Songs	LP	Philips	6308080	1971	**£15**	**£6**	
Thinks School Stinks	LP	Philips	6308057	1971	**£12**	**£5**	

HOTRODS

Title	Format	Label	Cat. No.	Year	Mint	VG	Notes
I Don't Love You No More	7"	Columbia	DB7693	1965	**£30**	**£15**	

HOTZENPLOTZ

Title	Format	Label	Cat. No.	Year	Mint	VG	Notes
Songs Aus Der Schau	LP	Ho	1001	1972	**£20**	**£8**	*German*

HOU-LOPS

Title	Format	Label	Cat. No.	Year	Mint	VG	Notes
69	LP	Canusa	33110	1969	**£20**	**£8**	*Canadian*
Off	LP	Apex	APL1591	1967	**£25**	**£10**	*Canadian*
Palamares	LP	Trans-Canadian	916	1968	**£50**	**£25**	*Canadian*

HOUND DOGS

Title	Format	Label	Cat. No.	Year	Mint	VG	Notes
Respect	LP	Profi	LP3	1966	**£50**	**£25**	*German*
Twist Festival 1964	LP	Philips	48063	1964	**£60**	**£30**	*German*

HOUNDHEAD HENRY & FRANKIE JAXON

Title	Format	Label	Cat. No.	Year	Mint	VG	Notes
Male Blues Vol. 6	7" EP	Collector	JEL10	1960	**£10**	**£5**	

HOUNDS

Title	Format	Label	Cat. No.	Year	Mint	VG	Notes
Lion Sleeps Tonight	LP	Gazell	GMG1207	1967	**£20**	**£8**	*Swedish*
My World Fell Down	7" EP	Pathe	EGF983	1966	**£10**	**£5**	*French*

HOURGLASS

Title	Format	Label	Cat. No.	Year	Mint	VG	Notes
Hourglass	LP	Liberty	LBL/LBS83219	1968	**£15**	**£6**	
Hourglass	LP	United Artists	USD303/4	1973	**£12**	**£5**	*double*
Power Of Love	LP	Liberty	LST7555	1968	**£15**	**£6**	*US*

HOUSE OF LORDS

Title	Format	Label	Cat. No.	Year	Mint	VG	Notes
In The Land Of Dreams	7"	B&C	CB112	1969	**£10**	**£5**	

HOUSE OF LOVE

Title	Format	Label	Cat. No.	Year	Mint	VG	Notes
Beatles And The Stones	CD-s	Fontana	HOLCD422	1990	**£5**	**£2**	
Christine	CD-s	Creation	CRESCD53	1991	**£5**	**£2**	
Destroy The Heart	CD-s	Creation	CRESCD57	1990	**£5**	**£2**	
House Of Love	CD	Fontana		1989	**£15**	**£6**	*US promo black disc*
House Of Love	LP	Creation	CRELP034	1988	**£10**	**£4**	*with 7" (CREFRE01)*
I Don't Know Why I Love You	CD-s	Fontana	HOLCD2	1989	**£5**	**£2**	
Live Cabaret Metro, Chicago 2-6-90	CD	Fontana	SACD189	1990	**£15**	**£6**	*US promo*
Never	CD-s	Fontana	HOLCD1	1989	**£5**	**£2**	
Real Animal	12"	Creation	CRE044T	1987	**£8**	**£4**	
Shine On	12"	Creation	CRE043T	1987	**£8**	**£4**	
Shine On	CD-s	Fontana	HOLCD3	1990	**£5**	**£2**	

HOUSE, SON

Title	Format	Label	Cat. No.	Year	Mint	VG	Notes
Father Of The Folk Blues	LP	CBS	(S)BPG62604	1966	**£25**	**£10**	
John The Revelator	LP	Liberty	LBS83391	1970	**£30**	**£15**	
Son House And J. D. Short	LP	XTRA	XTRA1080	1969	**£25**	**£10**	*with J. D. Short*
Vocal Intensity	LP	Saydisc	SL504	196–	**£25**	**£10**	

HOUSEHOLD

Title	Format	Label	Cat. No.	Year	Mint	VG	Notes
Guess I'll Learn How To Fly	7"	United Artists	UP1190	1967	**£4**	**£1.50**	
Twenty-First Summer	7"	United Artists	UP2210	1968	**£4**	**£1.50**	

HOUSEMARTINS

Title	Format	Label	Cat. No.	Year	Mint	VG	Notes
Christmas Box Set	7"	Go! Discs	GODB16	1986	**£25**	**£12.50**	*4 single set, autographed*
Christmas Box Set	7"	Go! Discs	GODB16	1986	**£10**	**£5**	*4 single set*
Housemartins From Outer Space	cass	private		1984	**£15**	**£6**	
Themes From The Well-Dressed Man	cass	private		1984	**£15**	**£6**	
There Is Always Something There To Remind Me	CD-s	Go! Discs	GODCD22	1988	**£5**	**£2**	

HOUSTON, BOBBI

Title	Format	Label	Cat. No.	Year	Mint	VG	Notes
I Want To Make It With You	7"	Action	ACT4622	1974	**£5**	**£2**	

HOUSTON, CISCO

Title	Format	Label	Cat. No.	Year	Mint	VG	Notes
Cisco Houston	LP	XTRA	XTRA1002	1965	**£12**	**£5**	
Cisco Special	LP	Top Rank	30028	1960	**£50**	**£25**	
I Ain't Got No Home	LP	Fontana	FJL412	1968	**£10**	**£4**	

HOUSTON, CISSY

Title	Format	Label	Cat. No.	Year	Mint	VG	Notes
Cissy Houston	LP	Janus	6310205	1971	**£10**	**£4**	
I Just Don't Know What To Do With Myself	7"	Pye	7N25537	1970	**£10**	**£5**	
Long And Winding Road	LP	Pye	NSPL28146	1971	**£10**	**£4**	
Presenting Cissy Houston	LP	Major Minor	SMLP80	1970	**£10**	**£4**	

HOUSTON, DAVID

Title	Format	Label	Cat. No.	Year	Mint	Good	Notes
Blue Prelude	7"	London	HL8147	1955	£20	£10	

HOUSTON, JOE

Title	Format	Label	Cat. No.	Year	Mint	Good	Notes
Joe Houston Blows All Night Long	LP	Modern	LMP1206	1956	£25	£10	*US*
Rockin' At The Drive-In	LP	Combo	LP400	1960	£50	£25	*US*
Where Is Joe?	LP	Combo	LP100	1960	£50	£25	*US*

HOUSTON, SAM

Title	Format	Label	Cat. No.	Year	Mint	Good	Notes
My Mother's Eyes	7"	Island	WI172	1965	£6	£2.50	

HOUSTON, THELMA

Title	Format	Label	Cat. No.	Year	Mint	Good	Notes
Black California	7"	Mowest	MW3004	1973	£6	£2.50	*demo only*
I've Got The Music In Me	LP	Sheffield Lab	2	1974	£10	£4	*US audiophile*
Sunshower	LP	Stateside	SSL5010	1969	£12	£5	
Sunshower	LP	Probe	SPB1053	1972	£10	£4	
Thelma Houston	LP	Mowest	MWS7003	1973	£10	£4	

HOUSTON, WHITNEY

Title	Format	Label	Cat. No.	Year	Mint	Good	Notes
All At Once	7"	Arista	ARIST640	1985	£6	£2.50	*promo*
Didn't We Almost Have It All	CD-s	Arista	RISCD31	1987	£6	£2.50	
I Wanna Dance With Somebody	CD-s	Arista	RISCD1	1987	£6	£2.50	
It Isn't, It Wasn't, It Ain't Never Gonna Be	CD-s	Arista	662545	1989	£5	£2	*with Aretha Franklin*
Love Will Save The Day	CD-s	Arista	661516	1988	£10	£5	*picture disc*
One Moment In Time	CD-s	Arista	661613	1988	£5	£2	
So Emotional	CD-s	Arista	RISCD43	1987	£5	£2	
Whitney Houston	LP	Arista	WHIT1	1986	£10	£4	*with cards,book,calendar, boxed*

HOWARD, BRIAN & THE SILHOUETTES

Title	Format	Label	Cat. No.	Year	Mint	Good	Notes
Back In The USA	7"	Fontana	TF464	1964	£8	£4	
Somebody Help Me	7"	Columbia	DB4914	1962	£10	£5	
Worrying Kind	7"	Columbia	DB7067	1963	£10	£5	

HOWARD, HARLAN

Title	Format	Label	Cat. No.	Year	Mint	Good	Notes
All-Time Favorite Country Songwriter	LP	Monument	MLP/SLP18038	1965	£12	£5	*US*
Harlan Howard Sings Harlan Howard	LP	Capitol	(S)T1631	1961	£12	£5	*US*

HOWARD, JAN

Title	Format	Label	Cat. No.	Year	Mint	Good	Notes
One You Slip Around With	7"	London	HL7088	1960	£12	£6	*export*

HOWARD, ROLAND S. & LYDIA LUNCH

Title	Format	Label	Cat. No.	Year	Mint	Good	Notes
Some Velvet Morning	12"	4AD	BAD210	1986	£8	£4	*with card*

HOWE, CATHERINE

Title	Format	Label	Cat. No.	Year	Mint	Good	Notes
Nothing More Than Strangers	7"	Reflection	HRS11	1971	£12	£6	
What A Beautiful Place	LP	Reflection	REFL11	1971	£200	£100	

HOWELL, EDDIE

Title	Format	Label	Cat. No.	Year	Mint	Good	Notes
Man From Manhattan	7"	Warner Bros	K16701	1976	£25	£12.50	*with Queen*

HOWERD, FRANKIE

Title	Format	Label	Cat. No.	Year	Mint	Good	Notes
At The Establishment	LP	Decca	LK4556	1963	£10	£4	
Funny Thing Happened On The Way To The Forum	LP	Pye		196–	£10	£4	
It's All Right With Me	7"	Columbia	DB4230	1958	£4	£1.50	
Kiddy Geddin	7"	Decca	F10420	1954	£6	£2.50	

HOWLAND, CHRIS

Title	Format	Label	Cat. No.	Year	Mint	Good	Notes
Ma He's Making Eyes At Me	7"	Columbia	DB4114	1958	£4	£1.50	
Susie Darlin'	7"	Columbia	DB4194	1959	£4	£1.50	

HOWLIN' WOLF

Title	Format	Label	Cat. No.	Year	Mint	Good	Notes
AKA Chester Burnett	LP	Chess	60016	1972	£12	£5	*US double*
Back Door Wolf	LP	Chess	CH50045	1974	£12	£5	*US*
Big City Blues	LP	Ember	EMB3370	1966	£15	£6	
Blues For Mr Crump	LP	Polydor	2383257	1974	£15	£7.50	*with Junior Parker and Bobby Bland*
Down In The Bottom	7"	Pye	7N25101	1961	£8	£4	
Evil	7"	Chess	CRS8097	1969	£5	£2	
Evil	LP	Chess	LP1540	1969	£30	£15	*US*
Going Back Home	LP	Syndicate Chapter	SC003	1971	£10	£4	
Howlin' Wolf	LP	Chess	LP1469	1962	£40	£20	*US*
Howlin' Wolf	LP	Python	PLP13	1971	£30	£15	
Howlin' Wolf Album	LP	Chess	CRLS4543	1969	£40	£20	
Just Like I Treat You	7"	Pye	7N25192	1963	£8	£4	
Killing Floor	7"	Chess	CRS8010	1965	£6	£2.50	
Little Girl	7"	Pye	7N25269	1964	£8	£4	
London Sessions	LP	Rolling Stones	COC49101	1971	£10	£4	
Love Me Darling	7"	Pye	7N25283	1964	£8	£4	
Message To The Young	LP	Chess	6310108	1971	£10	£4	
Moanin' In The Moonlight	LP	Chess	LP1434	1958	£50	£25	*US*
Moaning In The Moonlight	LP	Chess	CRL4006	1964	£20	£8	

More Real Folk Blues	LP	Chess	LP1512	1966	£20	£8	US
Ooh Baby	7"	Chess	CRS8016	1965	£6	£2.50	
Poor Boy	LP	Chess	CRL4508	1965	£15	£6	
Real Folk Blues	LP	Chess	LP1502	1966	£20	£8	US
Real Folk Blues Vol. 1	7" EP	Chess	CRE6017	1966	£15	£7.50	
Rhythm & Blues With Howlin' Wolf	7" EP	London	REU1072	1956	£75	£37.50	
Smokestack Lightning	7"	Pye	7N25244	1964	£5	£2	
Smokestack Lightning	7" EP	Pye	NEP44015	1963	£15	£7.50	
Tell Me	7" EP	Pye	NEP44032	1964	£15	£7.50	

HOYLE, LINDA

Linda Hoyle was the singer with Affinity and her jazz-inflected tones on that group's album suggested that she could make a good jazz record. Her solo LP, recorded with members of Nucleus, is exactly that.

Pieces Of Me	LP	Vertigo	6360060	1971	£125	£62.50	spiral label

HU & THE HILLTOPS

I'll Follow You	LP	Polydor	736033	1966	£20	£8	Dutch

HUBBARD, FREDDIE

Backlash	LP	Atlantic	SD1477	1967	£15	£6	US
Black Angel	LP	Atlantic	SD1549	1970	£15	£6	US
Blue Spirits	LP	Blue Note	BLP/BST84196	1965	£20	£8	
Breaking Point	LP	Blue Note	BLP/BST84172	1964	£20	£8	
Goin' Up	LP	Blue Note	BLP/BST84056	1960	£25	£10	
Groovy!	LP	Fontana	FJL136	1968	£12	£5	
High Blues Pressure	LP	Atlantic	SD1501	1969	£15	£6	US
High Energy	LP	CBS	80478	1975	£10	£4	
Hub Cap	LP	Blue Note	BLP/BST84073	1961	£30	£15	
Hub-Tones	LP	Blue Note	BLP/BST84115	1962	£20	£8	
Night Of The Cookers Vol. 1	LP	Blue Note	BLP/BST84207	1965	£20	£8	
Night Of The Cookers Vol. 2	LP	Blue Note	BLP/BST84208	1965	£20	£8	
Open Sesame	LP	Blue Note	BLP/BST84040	1960	£30	£15	
Polar AC	LP	CTI	CTI6056	1975	£10	£4	
Ready For Freddie	LP	Blue Note	BLP/BST84085	1961	£20	£8	
Sing Me A Song Of Songmy	LP	Atlantic	SD1576	1971	£12	£5	US
Sky Dive	LP	CTI	CTL11	1973	£10	£4	
Straight Life	LP	CTI	CTL5	1972	£10	£4	

HUCKNALL, MICK

Early Years	LP	TJM	TJM101	1987	£15	£6	

HUDSON, JACK

Summer Days And You	LP	Folk Heritage	FHR041	1972	£20	£8	

HUDSON, JOHNNY

Makin' Up Is So Much Fun	7"	Decca	F11679	1963	£5	£2	

HUDSON, KEITH

Darkest Night On A Wet Looking Road	7"	Spur	SP1	1972	£5	£2	
Don't Get Me Confused	7"	Smash	SMA2311	1970	£5	£2	D. Smith B side
Flesh Of My Skin	LP	Mamba	001	1974	£15	£6	
Light Of Day	7"	Smash	SMA2526	1971	£4	£1.50	
Melody Maker	7"	Summit	SUM8541	1973	£5	£2	
Rasta Communication	LP	Greensleeves	GREL5	1979	£12	£5	
Satan Side	7"	Duke	DU145	1972	£5	£2	Don T. Junior B side
Silver Platter	7"	Randys	RAN534	1973	£5	£2	with I Roy
Tambourine Man	7"	Big Shot	BI528	1969	£10	£5	
Too Expensive	LP	Virgin	V2056	1976	£12	£5	
Torch Of Freedom	LP	Atra	1001	1975	£15	£6	

HUDSON, ROCK

Rock Gently	LP	Stanyan	10014	1971	£12	£5	US

HUDSON-FORD

Repertoire	LP	Arnakata	ARN5001	1977	£15	£6	

HUDSON PEOPLE

Trip To Your Mind	12"	Hithouse	HIT1	1978	£15	£7.50	

HUE & CRY

Here Come Everybody	12"	Stampede	STAMP2	1986	£12	£6	
I Refuse	CD-s	Circa	YRCD8	1988	£5	£2	
Looking For Linda	CD-s	Circa	YRCD24	1989	£5	£2	
Ordinary Angel	CD-s	Circa	YRCD18	1988	£5	£2	
Peaceful Face	CD-s	Circa	YRCD41	1989	£5	£2	
Sweet Invisibility	CD-s	Circa	YRCD37	1989	£5	£2	
Violently	CD-s	Circa	YRCD29	1989	£5	£2	

HUEYS

Coo Coo Over You	7"	London	HLU10264	1969	£5	£2	

HUGG, MIKE

Somewhere	LP	Polydor	2383140	1972	£10	£4	
Stress And Strain	LP	Polydor	2383213	1973	£10	£4	

HUGGETT FAMILY

Title	Format	Label	Number	Year	Mint	VG	Notes
Huggett Family	LP	Pye	NSPL18407	1973	£50	£25	

HUGHES, CAROL

Title	Format	Label	Number	Year	Mint	VG	Notes
Lend Me Your Comb	7"	Columbia	DB4094	1958	£4	£1.50	

HUGHES, DANNY

Title	Format	Label	Number	Year	Mint	VG	Notes
Hi Ho Silver Lining	7"	Pye	7N17750	1969	£5	£2	

HUGHES, FRED

Title	Format	Label	Number	Year	Mint	VG	Notes
Oo Wee Baby I Love You	7"	Fontana	TF583	1965	£15	£7.50	
Send My Baby Back	LP	Wand	WD(S)664	1965	£20	£8	US

HUGHES, GLENN

Title	Format	Label	Number	Year	Mint	VG	Notes
Play Me Out	LP	Safari	LONG2	1977	£10	£4	with inner

HUGHES, JIMMY

Title	Format	Label	Number	Year	Mint	VG	Notes
Chains Of Love	7"	Stax	STAX126	1969	£6	£2.50	
Goodbye My Love	7"	Sue	WI4006	1966	£12	£6	
Hi Heel Sneakers	7"	Atlantic	584135	1967	£5	£2	
I'm Qualified	7"	London	HL9680	1963	£10	£5	
Neighbour Neighbour	7"	Atlantic	584017	1966	£5	£2	
Something Special	LP	Stax	SXATS1010	1969	£10	£4	
Steal Away	7"	Pye	7N25254	1964	£5	£2	
Steal Away	LP	Vee Jay	(SR)1102	1965	£20	£8	US
Sweet Things You Do	7"	Stax	STAX117	1969	£4	£1.50	
Why Not Tonight	LP	Atlantic	587068	1967	£25	£10	

HUGO & LUIGI

Title	Format	Label	Number	Year	Mint	VG	Notes
Hugo And Luigi	7" EP	Columbia	SEG7862	1958	£6	£2.50	
La Plume De Ma Tante	7"	RCA	RCA1127	1959	£4	£1.50	
Shenandoah Rose	7"	Columbia	DB3978	1957	£6	£2.50	
Twilight In Tennessee	7"	Columbia	DB4156	1958	£4	£1.50	

HULL, ALAN

Title	Format	Label	Number	Year	Mint	VG	Notes
Pipedream	LP	Charisma	CAS1069	1973	£10	£4	
We Can Sing Together	7"	Transatlantic	BIG129	1970	£6	£2.50	

HULLABALOOS

Title	Format	Label	Number	Year	Mint	VG	Notes
Did You Ever	7" EP	Roulette	VREX65033	1965	£30	£15	French
Don't Stop	7"	Columbia	DB7626	1965	£4	£1.50	
England's Newest Singing Sensations	LP	Roulette	(S)R25297	1965	£20	£8	US
Hullabaloos On Hullabaloo	LP	Roulette	(S)R25310	1965	£20	£8	US
I'll Show You How To Love	7"	Columbia	DB7558	1965	£4	£1.50	
I'm Gonna Love You Too	7"	Columbia	DB7392	1964	£4	£1.50	
I'm Gonna Love You Too	7" EP	Roulette	VREX65024	1964	£30	£15	French

HULTGREEN, GEORG

Title	Format	Label	Number	Year	Mint	VG	Notes
Say Hello	7"	Warner Bros	WB8017	1970	£4	£1.50	

HUMAN BEANS

Title	Format	Label	Number	Year	Mint	VG	Notes
Morning Dew	7"	Columbia	DB8230	1967	£40	£20	

HUMAN BEAST

Title	Format	Label	Number	Year	Mint	VG	Notes
Human Beast Vol. 1	LP	Decca	SKL5053	1970	£125	£62.50	

HUMAN BEINZ

Title	Format	Label	Number	Year	Mint	VG	Notes
Evolution	LP	Capitol	ST2926	1968	£50	£25	US
Human Beinz/Mammals	LP	Gateway	GLP3012	1968	£40	£20	US
Nobody But Me	7"	Capitol	CL15529	1968	£20	£10	
Nobody But Me	LP	Capitol	ST2906	1968	£30	£15	US
Turn On Your Lovelight	7"	Capitol	CL15542	1968	£12	£6	

HUMAN INSTINCT

Title	Format	Label	Number	Year	Mint	VG	Notes
Burning Up Years	LP			1969	£300	£180	New Zealand
Can't Stop Loving You	7"	Mercury	MF951	1965	£20	£10	
Day In My Mind's Mind	7"	Deram	DM167	1967	£25	£12.50	
Go Go	7"	Mercury	MF990	1966	£20	£10	
Pins In It	LP	Pye		1971	£300	£180	New Zealand
Renaissance Fair	7"	Deram	DM177	1968	£25	£12.50	
Rich Man	7"	Mercury	MF972	1966	£25	£12.50	
Stoned Guitars	LP	Allied	ARBS107	1970	£350	£210	New Zealand

HUMAN LEAGUE

Title	Format	Label	Number	Year	Mint	VG	Notes
Being Boiled	7"	Fast Product	FAST4	1978	£5	£2	
Dignity Of Labour	12"	Fast Product	FAST10	1979	£6	£2.50	with flexi
Empire State Human	12"	Virgin	VS35112	1980	£8	£4	
Empire State Human	7"	Virgin	VS351	1980	£15	£7.50	double
Greatest Hits	CD	Virgin	CDHLP1	1988	£12	£5	picture disc
Hard Times/Love Action	CD-s	Virgin	CDT6	1988	£6	£2.50	3" single
Heart Like A Wheel	CD-s	Virgin	VSCDX1262	1990	£8	£4	
Heart Like A Wheel	CD-s	Virgin	VSCDT1262	1990	£5	£2	
Holiday '80	12"	Virgin	SV105	1981	£25	£12.50	
Holiday '80	7"	Virgin	SV105	1980	£5	£2	double, purple & blue label
Holiday '80	7"	Virgin	SV105	1981	£4	£1.50	double
Human League Interview	CD	East West	PRCD91852	1995	£15	£6	US interview promo

Keep Feeling Fascination	CD-s	Virgin	CDT24	1988	£6	£2.50	*3" single*
Love Is All That Matters	CD-s	Virgin	VSCD1025	1988	£8	£4	
Only After Dark	7"	Virgin	VS351	1980	£5	£2	
Soundtrack To A Generation	CD-s	Virgin	VSCDX1303	1990	£10	£5	
Soundtrack To A Generation	CD-s	Virgin	VSCDT1303	1990	£6	£2.50	

HUMAN ZOO

Human Zoo	LP	Accent	ACS5055	1969	£25	£10	*US*

HUMBLE PIE

As Safe As Yesterday Is	LP	Immediate	IMSP025	1969	£15	£6	
Eat It	LP	A&M	AMLS6004	1973	£12	£5	*double*
Humble Pie	LP	A&M	AMLS986	1970	£10	£4	
Performance: Rockin' The Fillmore	LP	A&M	AMLH63506	1971	£12	£5	*double*
Rock On	LP	A&M	AMLS2013	1971	£10	£4	
Smokin'	LP	A&M	AMLS64342	1972	£10	£4	
Street Rats	LP	A&M	AMLS68282	1975	£10	£4	
Thunderbox	LP	A&M	AMLH63611	1974	£12	£5	*double*
Town And Country	LP	Immediate	IMSP027	1969	£15	£6	

HUMBLEBUMS

'He's humble . . . ,' Billy Connolly used to quip when explaining the origin of his group's name. Originally a folk duo featuring Connolly and fellow Glaswegian Tam Harvey, the Humblebums broadened their appeal a little when Harvey was replaced by singer-songwriter Gerry Rafferty. Some of Rafferty's songs with the group are amongst the best that Paul McCartney never wrote, although both Rafferty and Connolly have become rather more famous since.

Complete	LP	Transatlantic	TRAT288	1974	£20	£8	*3 LP set*
First Collection	LP	Transatlantic	TRA186	1969	£10	£4	
Humblebums	LP	Transatlantic	TRA201	1969	£10	£4	
Open Up The Door	LP	Transatlantic	TRA218	1970	£10	£4	

HUMES, HELEN

Helen Humes And The Benny Carter All Stars	LP	Contemporary	LAC12245	1961	£12	£5	
If I Could Be With You	7"	Vogue	V2048	1956	£5	£2	
When The Saints Come Marching In	7"	Contemporary	CV2415	1959	£4	£1.50	

HUMPHREY, BOBBI

Fancy Dancer	LP	Blue Note	UAG20003	1976	£10	£4	
Flute-In	LP	Blue Note	BST84379	1970	£10	£4	

HUMPHREY, DELLA

Don't Make The Good Girls So Bad	7"	Action	ACT4525	1969	£4	£1.50	

HUMPY BONG

Don't You Be Too Long	7"	Parlophone	R5859	1970	£20	£10	

HUNGER

Strickly From Hunger	LP	Public	1006	1969	£400	£250	*US*
Strickly From Hunger	LP	Psycho	PSYCHO14	1984	£15	£6	

HUNGRY WOLF

Hungry Wolf	LP	Philips	6308009	1970	£60	£30	

HUNT, GERALDINE

Never Never Leave Me	7"	Roulette	RO515	1969	£5	£2	

HUNT, MARSHA

Desdemona	7"	Track	604034	1969	£6	£2.50	
Walk On Gilded Splinters	7"	Track	604030	1969	£4	£1.50	
Woman Child	LP	Track	2410101	1971	£20	£8	

HUNT, MICHAEL

Waters Of The Tyne	LP	Decca	LK4902	1967	£30	£15	

HUNT, PEE WEE

Dixieland Detour	10" LP	Capitol	LC6608	1953	£20	£8	
It's Never Too Late To Fall In Love	7"	Capitol	CL14225	1955	£5	£2	
Save Your Love For Me	7"	Capitol	CL14286	1955	£5	£2	
Swingin' Around	10" LP	Capitol	LC6671	1954	£20	£8	

HUNT, TOMMY

Greatest Hits	LP	Dynamo	8001	1967	£15	£6	*US*
I Just Don't Know What To Do With Myself	LP	Scepter	(S)S506	1962	£15	£6	*US*
I'm Wondering	7"	Top Rank	JAR605	1962	£6	£2.50	

HUNT, WILLIE AMOS

Would You Believe	7"	Camp	602003	1967	£25	£12.50	

HUNT & TURNER

Magic Landscape	LP	Village Thing	VTS11	1972	£15	£6	

HUNTER

Some Time For Thinking	7"	RCA	RCA1995	1970	£8	£4	

HUNTER, CAROL

Title	Format	Label	Number	Year	Mint	VG	Notes
Look Out Cleveland	7"	Purple	PUR115	1973	£4	£1.50	

HUNTER, DANNY

Title	Format	Label	Number	Year	Mint	VG	Notes
Lost Weekend	7"	Fontana	H300	1961	£5	£2	
Make It Up	7"	HMV	POP722	1960	£8	£4	
Who's Gonna Walk Ya Home?	7"	HMV	POP775	1960	£8	£4	

HUNTER, DAVE

Title	Format	Label	Number	Year	Mint	VG	Notes
She's A Heartbreaker	7"	RCA	RCA1766	1968	£5	£2	

HUNTER, GREG

Title	Format	Label	Number	Year	Mint	VG	Notes
Five O'Clock World	7"	Parlophone	R5483	1966	£4	£1.50	

HUNTER, IAN

Title	Format	Label	Number	Year	Mint	VG	Notes
American Music	CD-s	Mercury	MERCD315	1990	£5	£2	*with Mick Ronson*
You Nearly Did Me In	7"	CBS	4479	1976	£10	£5	
You're Never Alone With A Schizophrenic	CD	Chrysalis	CD25CR03	1994	£12	£5	*Chrysalis 25 pack*

HUNTER, IVORY JOE

Title	Format	Label	Number	Year	Mint	VG	Notes
Fabulous Ivory Joe Hunter	LP	Goldisc	403	1961	£30	£15	*US*
Golden Hits	LP	Smash	MGS2/SRS67037	1963	£20	£8	*US*
I Almost Lost My Mind	78	MGM	MGM271	1950	£12	£6	
I Get That Lonesome Feeling	LP	MGM	E3488	1957	£75	£37.50	*US*
I'm Hooked	7"	Capitol	CL15220	1961	£10	£5	
Ivory Joe Hunter	LP	Sage	603	1959	£50	£25	*US*
Ivory Joe Hunter	LP	Atlantic	8008	1958	£75	£37.50	*US*
Ivory Joe Hunter	LP	Sound	603	1957	£75	£37.50	*US*
Love's A Hurting Game	7"	London	HLE8486	1957	£100	£50	
May The Best Man Win	7"	Capitol	CL15226	1961	£10	£5	
Since I Met You Baby	7"	Columbia	DB3872	1957	£125	£62.50	
Sings The Old And The New	LP	Atlantic	8015	1958	£75	£37.50	*US*
Sixteen Of His Greatest Hits	LP	King	605	1958	£100	£50	*US*
Tear Fell	7"	London	HLE8261	1956	£250	£150	*best auctioned*
This Is Ivory Joe Hunter	LP	Dot	DLP3569/25569	1964	£20	£8	*US*

HUNTER, ROBERT

Title	Format	Label	Number	Year	Mint	VG	Notes
Amagamalin Street	LP	Relix	RRLP2003	1984	£15	£6	*US double*
Jack O'Roses	LP	Dark Star	DSLP8001	1980	£10	£4	
Tales Of Great Rum Runners	LP	Round	RX101	1974	£15	£6	*US*
Tiger Rose	LP	Round	RX105	1975	£10	£4	

HUNTER, TAB

Title	Format	Label	Number	Year	Mint	VG	Notes
Don't Let It Get Around	7"	London	HLD8535	1958	£10	£5	
I Can't Stop Loving You	7"	London	HLD9559	1962	£5	£2	
My Only Love	7"	Warner Bros	WB8	1960	£4	£1.50	
Ninety-Nine Ways	7"	London	HLD8410	1957	£8	£4	
R.F.D. Tab Hunter	LP	Warner Bros	W(S)1367	1960	£25	£10	*US*
Tab Hunter	7" EP	Warner Bros	WEP6023	1961	£12	£6	
Tab Hunter	7" EP	Warner Bros	WSEP2023	1961	£15	£7.50	*stereo*
Tab Hunter	LP	Warner Bros	WS8008	1960	£25	£10	*stereo*
Tab Hunter	LP	Warner Bros	WM4008	1960	£20	£8	*mono*
Waitin' For The Fall	7"	Warner Bros	WB20	1960	£4	£1.50	
When I Fall In Love	LP	Warner Bros	W(S)1292	1959	£30	£15	*US*
Wild Side Of Life	7"	London	HLD9381	1961	£6	£2.50	
Young Love	7"	London	HLD8380	1957	£15	£7.50	
Young Love	7" EP	London	RED1134	1958	£20	£10	
Young Love	LP	London	HAD2401	1961	£30	£15	
Young Love	LP	London	SAHG6201	1961	£40	£20	*stereo*

HUNTER MUSKETT

Title	Format	Label	Number	Year	Mint	VG	Notes
Every Time You Move	LP	Nova	SDN20	1970	£100	£50	
Hunter Muskett	LP	Bradley	BRADL1003	1973	£20	£8	

HUNTERS

Title	Format	Label	Number	Year	Mint	VG	Notes
Golden Earrings	7"	Fontana	H303	1961	£5	£2	
Hits From The Hunters	LP	Fontana	TFL5175	1962	£30	£15	
Hits From The Hunters	LP	Fontana	STFL572	1962	£40	£20	*stereo*
Storm	7"	Fontana	H323	1961	£5	£2	
Teen Scene	7"	Fontana	H276	1960	£6	£2.50	
Teen Scene	7"	Fontana	TF514	1964	£6	£2.50	
Teen Scene	LP	Fontana	TFL5140	1961	£30	£15	
Teen Scene	LP	Fontana	STFL561	1961	£40	£20	*stereo*

HUNTERS (2)

Title	Format	Label	Number	Year	Mint	VG	Notes
Russian Spy And I	7"	RCA	RCA1541	1966	£8	£4	

HURDY GURDY

Title	Format	Label	Number	Year	Mint	VG	Notes
Hurdy Gurdy	LP	CBS	64781	1971	£150	£75	*Danish*

HURRICANE STRINGS

Title	Format	Label	Number	Year	Mint	VG	Notes
Venus	7"	Columbia	DB7027	1963	£5	£2	

HURRICANES

Title	Format	Label	Number	Year	Mint	VG	Notes
Got To Be Mine	7"	Upsetter	US363	1971	£6	£2.50	*Upsetters B side*

HURT, MISSISSIPPI JOHN

Immortal	LP	Vanguard	VRS/VSD79248	1967	**£12**	**£5**	*US*
Last Sessions	LP	Vanguard	VSD79327	1973	**£10**	**£4**	
Mississippi John Hurt	LP	Fontana	TFL6079	1967	**£15**	**£6**	
Mississippi John Hurt	LP	Vanguard	VSD19/20	1973	**£12**	**£5**	*double*
Original 1928 Recordings	LP	Spookane	SPL1001	1971	**£40**	**£20**	
Today	LP	Vanguard	VRS/VSD79220	1966	**£15**	**£6**	*US*

HURVITZ, SANDY

Sandy's Album Is Here	LP	Bizarre	5064	1968	**£20**	**£8**	*US*

HUSH

Grey	7"	Fontana	TF944	1968	**£150**	**£75**	

HUSKER DÜ

Amusement	7"	Reflex	38285	1980	**£40**	**£20**	*US*
Could You Be The One	12"	Warner Bros	W8456T	1987	**£6**	**£2.50**	
Do You Remember	CD	Warner Bros	PROCD6853	1993	**£25**	**£10**	*US promo compilation*
Don't Want To Know If You're Lonely	12"	Warner Bros	W8746T	1986	**£6**	**£2.50**	
Eight Miles HIgh	CD-s	SST	SST025CD	1988	**£5**	**£2**	
Everything Falls Apart	LP	Reflex	REFLEXD	1982	**£25**	**£10**	*US*
Ice Cold Ice	12"	Warner Bros	W8276T	1987	**£6**	**£2.50**	
In A Free Land	7"	New Alliance	NAR010	1982	**£40**	**£20**	*US*
Makes No Sense At All	CD-s	SST	SST051CD	1988	**£5**	**£2**	
Sorry Somehow	12"	Warner Bros	W8612T	1986	**£6**	**£2.50**	
Sorry Somehow	7"	WEA	W8612F	1986	**£6**	**£2.50**	*double*

HUSKY, FERLIN

Born To Lose	LP	Capitol	T1204	1959	**£15**	**£6**	*US*
Boulevard Of Broken Dreams	LP	Capitol	T880	1957	**£15**	**£6**	*US*
Country Music Holiday	7" EP	Capitol	EAP1921	1957	**£8**	**£4**	
Country Round Up	7" EP	Parlophone	GEP8795	1959	**£20**	**£10**	
Country Tunes Sung From The Heart	LP	King	647	1959	**£15**	**£6**	*US*
Easy Livin'	LP	King	728	1960	**£15**	**£6**	*US*
Fallen Star	7"	Capitol	CL14753	1957	**£12**	**£6**	
Ferlin Husky Hits	7" EP	Capitol	EAP1837	1957	**£8**	**£4**	
Ferlin's Favorites	LP	Capitol	T1280	1960	**£15**	**£6**	*US*
Ferlin's Favourites Part 1	7" EP	Capitol	EAP11280	1960	**£8**	**£4**	
Ferlin's Favourites Part 2	7" EP	Capitol	EAP21280	1960	**£8**	**£4**	
Ferlin's Favourites Part 3	7" EP	Capitol	EAP31280	1960	**£8**	**£4**	
Gone	7"	Capitol	CL14702	1957	**£8**	**£4**	
Gone	LP	Capitol	T1383	1960	**£15**	**£6**	*US*
I Feel That Old Heartache Again	7"	Capitol	CL14916	1958	**£5**	**£2**	
Kingdom Of Love	7"	Capitol	CL14922	1958	**£4**	**£1.50**	
Make Me Live Again	7"	Capitol	CL14785	1957	**£4**	**£1.50**	
Ole Opry Favourites	LP	Fontana	FJL304	1965	**£10**	**£4**	
Sittin' On A Rainbow	LP	Capitol	T976	1959	**£15**	**£6**	*US*
Slow Down Brother	7"	Capitol	CL14883	1958	**£10**	**£5**	
Songs Of The Home And Heart	7" EP	Capitol	EAP1718	1957	**£8**	**£4**	
Songs Of The Home And Heart	LP	Capitol	T718	1956	**£20**	**£8**	*US*
Wang Dang Do	7"	Capitol	CL14824	1958	**£15**	**£7.50**	

HUSTIN, JACQUES

Fleur de liberté	7"	EMI	EMI2143	1974	**£10**	**£5**	

HUSTLER

High Street	LP	A&M	AMLS68276	1974	**£10**	**£4**	
Play Loud	LP	A&M	AMLH33001	1975	**£10**	**£4**	

HUSTLERS

Gimme What I Want	7"	Philips	BF1275	1963	**£4**	**£1.50**	
Sick Of Giving	7"	Mercury	MF817	1964	**£10**	**£5**	
You Can't Sit Down	7"	Mercury	MF807	1964	**£4**	**£1.50**	

HUTCH, WILLIE

Foxy Brown	LP	Tamla Motown	STML11269	1974	**£12**	**£5**	
Mack	LP	Tamla Motown	STMA8003	1973	**£12**	**£5**	
Ode To My Lady	LP	Tamla Motown	STML12015	1975	**£15**	**£6**	

HUTCHERSON, BOBBY

Components	LP	Blue Note	BLP/BST84213	1965	**£15**	**£6**	
Dialogue	LP	Blue Note	BLP/BST84198	1965	**£15**	**£6**	
Happenings	LP	Blue Note	BLP/BST84231	1966	**£12**	**£5**	
Head On	LP	Blue Note	BST84376	1970	**£10**	**£4**	
Now	LP	Blue Note	BST84333	1969	**£10**	**£4**	
San Francisco	LP	Blue Note	BST84362	1970	**£10**	**£4**	
Stick-Up	LP	Blue Note	BLP/BST84244	1966	**£12**	**£5**	
Total Eclipse	LP	Blue Note	BST84291	1968	**£10**	**£4**	

HUTCHINGS, ASHLEY

Compleat Dancing Master	LP	Island	HELP17	1974	**£10**	**£4**	
Hour With Cecil Sharp And Ashley Hutchings	LP	Dambusters	DAM014	1986	**£20**	**£8**	

Kickin' Up The Sawdust	LP	Harvest	SHSP4073	1977	**£40**	**£20**	
Morris On	LP	Island	HELP5	1972	**£10**	**£4**	
Rattlebone & Ploughjack	LP	Island	HELP24	1976	**£25**	**£10**	
Son Of Morris On	LP	Harvest	SHSM2012	1976	**£10**	**£4**	

HUTCHINS, HUTCH

Feels Like Rain	LP	Goodwood	GM12324	1977	**£50**	**£25**	

HUTCHINS, SAM

Dang Me	7"	Bell	BLL1044	1969	**£4**	**£1.50**	

HUTSON, LEROY

All Because Of You	7"	Warner Bros	K16536	1975	**£4**	**£1.50**	
Leroy Hutson	LP	Warner Bros	K56139	1975	**£40**	**£20**	
Man	LP	Buddah	BDLP4013	1974	**£10**	**£4**	

HUTTO, J. B.

Hawk Squat	LP	Delmark	DS617	1970	**£10**	**£4**	

HUTTON, BETTY

Capitol Presents	10" LP	Capitol	LC6639	1954	**£10**	**£4**	
Somebody Loves Me	7"	HMV	7M103	1953	**£6**	**£2.50**	

HUTTON SISTERS

Ko Ko Mo	7"	Capitol	CL14250	1955	**£15**	**£7.50**	

HYATT, CHARLIE

Kiss Me Neck	LP	Island	ILP932	1966	**£30**	**£15**	
Kiss Me Neck	LP	Trojan	TTl44	1970	**£15**	**£6**	
Rass!	7" EP	Island	IEP707	1966	**£12**	**£6**	*with Bam*

HYGRADES

She Cared	7"	Columbia	DB7734	1965	**£4**	**£1.50**	

HYLAND, BRIAN

Bashful Blonde	LP	London	HAR2289	1961	**£60**	**£30**	
Country Meets Folk	LP	HMV	CLP1759	1963	**£30**	**£15**	
Four Little Heels	7"	London	HLR9203	1960	**£4**	**£1.50**	
Get The Message	7"	Philips	BF1601	1967	**£4**	**£1.50**	
Here's To Our Love	LP	Philips	PHM2/PHS600136	1964	**£20**	**£8**	US
I Gotta Go	7"	London	HLR9262	1961	**£4**	**£1.50**	
Itsy Bitsy Teeny Weeny . . .	7"	London	HLR9161	1960	**£4**	**£1.50**	
Joker Went Wild	7"	Philips	BF1508	1966	**£4**	**£1.50**	
Joker Went Wild	LP	Philips	BL7762	1966	**£20**	**£8**	
Let Me Belong To You	LP	HMV	CLP1553	1962	**£50**	**£25**	
Rockin' Folk	LP	Philips	PHM2/PHS600158	1965	**£20**	**£8**	US
Rosemary	7"	London	HLR9113	1960	**£10**	**£5**	
Sealed With A Kiss	7" EP	HMV	7EG8780	1962	**£25**	**£12.50**	
Sealed With A Kiss	LP	ABC-Paramount	(S)431	1962	**£25**	**£10**	US

HYMAN, C.

Ska Is Movin' On	7"	Ska Beat	JB200	1965	**£10**	**£5**	

HYMAN, DICK

Age Of Electronicus	LP	Command	SCMD946	1970	**£30**	**£15**	
Electrics	LP	Command	9383	1968	**£40**	**£20**	US
Moog	LP	Command	SCMD508	1969	**£20**	**£8**	
Swings	7" EP	MGM	MGMEP646	1958	**£5**	**£2**	
Threepenny Opera Theme	7"	MGM	SP1164	1956	**£4**	**£1.50**	

i

I D COMPANY

I D Company	LP	Hör Zu	SHZE801BL	1970	**£15**	**£6**	*German*

I DRIVE

I Drive	LP	Metronome	15420	1972	**£40**	**£20**	*German*

I JAH MAN

Haile I Hymn	LP	Island	ILPS9521	1978	**£10**	**£4**	
Jah Heavy Load	7"	Lucky	LY6016	1976	**£6**	**£2.50**	

I LIFE

Kiss You Gave	7"	R&B	JB140	1964	**£10**	**£5**	

I LUV WIGHT

Let The World Wash In	7"	Philips	6006043	1970	**£60**	**£30**	*picture sleeve*
Let The World Wash In	7"	Philips	6006043	1970	**£15**	**£7.50**	

IAN, JANIS

For All The Seasons Of Your Mind	LP	Verve	(S)VLP6003	1968	**£10**	**£4**	
Janis Ian	LP	Verve	(S)VLP6001	1967	**£12**	**£5**	
Secret Life Of Eddie Fink	LP	Verve	FTS3048	1968	**£10**	**£4**	*US*
Society's Child	7"	Verve	VS1506	1967	**£4**	**£1.50**	
Society's Child	7"	Verve	VS1503	1967	**£6**	**£2.50**	
Sunflakes Fall, Snowrays Call	7"	Verve	VS1513	1968	**£5**	**£2**	
Who Really Cares	LP	Verve	FTS3063	1969	**£10**	**£4**	*US*

IAN & BELINDA

Who Wants To Live Forever	12"	Odeon	12ODO112	1989	**£15**	**£7.50**	*with Brian May*
Who Wants To Live Forever	7"	Odeon	ODO112	1989	**£5**	**£2**	*with Brian May*

IAN & SYLVIA

Best Of Ian And Sylvia	LP	Vanguard	SVRL19004	1968	**£10**	**£4**	
Early Morning Rain	LP	Fontana	TF6053	1965	**£12**	**£5**	
Four Strong Winds	LP	Vanguard	VSD2149	1964	**£12**	**£5**	*US*
Ian And Sylvia	LP	Vanguard	VSD2113	1962	**£12**	**£5**	*US*
Northern Journey	LP	Vanguard	VSD79154	1964	**£12**	**£5**	*US*
Play One More	LP	Vanguard	VSD79215	1966	**£12**	**£5**	*US*

IAN & THE ZODIACS

Beechwood 45789	7"	Oriole	CB1849	1963	**£25**	**£12.50**	
Gear Again – 12 Hits	LP	Wing	WL1074	1965	**£30**	**£15**	
Ian And The Zodiacs	LP	Philips	PHM200176/ PHS600176	1966	**£50**	**£25**	*US*
Just Listen To	LP	Starclub	158020STY	1966	**£100**	**£50**	*German*
Just The Little Things I Like	7"	Fontana	TF548	1965	**£15**	**£7.50**	
Locomotive!	LP	Starclub	158029STY	1966	**£100**	**£50**	*German*
No Money, No Honey	7"	Fontana	TF708	1966	**£12**	**£6**	
Starclub Show 7	LP	Starclub	158007STY	1965	**£75**	**£37.50**	*German*
Wade In The Water	7"	Fontana	TF753	1966	**£25**	**£12.50**	

IBIS

Ibis	LP	Polydor	2448036	1975	**£30**	**£15**	*Italian*

IBLISS

Supernova	LP	Spiegelei	285015U	1972	**£15**	**£6**	*German*

ICARUS

Devil Rides Out	7"	Spark	SRL1012	1969	**£10**	**£5**	
Marvel World	LP	Pye	NSPL28161	1971	**£100**	**£50**	

ICE

Anniversary Of Love	7"	Decca	F12680	1967	**£40**	**£20**	
Ice Man	7"	Decca	F12749	1968	**£40**	**£20**	

ICE (2)

Saga Of The Ice King	LP	Storm	SR3307	1979	**£100**	**£50**	*with blue booklet*

ICECROSS

First	LP	Icecross	IC534753	1973	**£125**	**£62.50**	*Icelandic*

ICEHOUSE

Title	Format	Label	Cat. No.	Year	Mint	VG	Notes
Crazy	CD-s	Chrysalis	CHSCD3156	1988	£5	£2	
Electric Blue	CD-s	Chrysalis	CHSCD3239	1988	£5	£2	
Full Circle	CD	Chrysalis			£25	£10	*import double CD set*
Touch The Fire	CD-s	Chrysalis	CHSCD3472	1989	£5	£2	

ICICLE WORKS

Title	Format	Label	Cat. No.	Year	Mint	VG	Notes
Ascending	cass	private		198–	£15	£6	
I Still Want You	CD-s	Epic	WORKSC102	1990	£5	£2	
Kiss Off	CD-s	Beggars Banquet	IW1CD	1988	£5	£2	
Little Girl Lost	CD-s	Beggars Banquet	BEG215CD	1988	£10	£5	*picture disc*
Melanie Still Hurts	CD-s	Epic	WORKSC101	1990	£5	£2	
Motorcycle Rider	CD-s	Epic	WORKSC100	1990	£5	£2	
Nirvana	7"	Troll Kitchen	WORKS1	1983	£6	£2.50	

ICONS OF FILTH

Title	Format	Label	Cat. No.	Year	Mint	VG	Notes
Braindeath	7"	Mortarhate	MORT10	1985	£5	£2	
Used Abused Unamused	7"	Corpus Christi	CHRISTITS7	1983	£5	£2	

ID

Title	Format	Label	Cat. No.	Year	Mint	VG	Notes
Inner Sounds Of The Id	LP	RCA	LPM/LSP3805	1967	£40	£20	*US*

ID (2)

Title	Format	Label	Cat. No.	Year	Mint	VG	Notes
Where Are We Going	LP	Aurora	AR1000	1975	£60	£30	*US*

IDEALS

Title	Format	Label	Cat. No.	Year	Mint	VG	Notes
Knee Socks	7"	Pye	7N25103	1961	£25	£12.50	

IDEM DITO

Title	Format	Label	Cat. No.	Year	Mint	VG	Notes
Facing Aquarius	LP	Audio Art		1985	£20	£8	*Dutch*

IDES OF MARCH

Title	Format	Label	Cat. No.	Year	Mint	VG	Notes
Hole In My Soul	7"	London	HLU10183	1968	£4	£1.50	
Ides Of March	LP	Warner Bros	WS1863	1970	£10	£4	
You Wouldn't Listen	7"	London	HLU10058	1966	£4	£1.50	

IDLE FLOWERS

Title	Format	Label	Cat. No.	Year	Mint	VG	Notes
All I Want Is You	7"	Miles Ahead	AHEAD1	1984	£10	£5	

IDLE RACE

The Idle Race produced intelligent pop music with occasional touches of psychedelia (most notably in the single 'Imposters Of Life's Magazine'). The group's records displayed a degree of production skill and craftsmanship unusual in a little-known pop act of the time, but then the group's leader was Jeff Lynne.

Title	Format	Label	Cat. No.	Year	Mint	VG	Notes
Birthday Party	LP	Liberty	LBL/LBS83132	1968	£30	£15	
Birthday Party	LP	Sunset	SLS50381	1976	£10	£4	
Come With Me	7"	Liberty	LBF15242	1969	£15	£7.50	
Dancing Flower	7"	Regal Zonophone	RZ3036	1971	£15	£7.50	
Days Of Broken Arrows	7"	Liberty	LBF15218	1969	£15	£7.50	
End Of The Road	7"	Liberty	LBF15101	1968	£15	£7.50	
I Like My Toys	7"	Liberty	LBF15129	1968	£30	£15	*demo*
Idle Race	LP	Liberty	LBS83211	1969	£50	£25	
Imposters Of Life's Magazine	7"	Liberty	LBF15026	1967	£25	£12.50	
On With The Show	LP	Sunset	SLS50354	1973	£10	£4	
Skeleton And The Roundabout	7"	Liberty	LBF15054	1968	£15	£7.50	
Time Is	LP	Regal Zonophone	SLRZ1017	1971	£75	£37.50	

IDOL, BILLY

Title	Format	Label	Cat. No.	Year	Mint	VG	Notes
Catch My Fall	CD-s	Chrysalis	IDOLCD13	1988	£5	£2	
Cradle Of Love	CD-s	Chrysalis	IDOLCD14	1990	£5	£2	
Hot In The City	CD-s	Chrysalis	IDOLCD12	1987	£5	£2	
L.A. Woman	CD-s	Chrysalis	IDOLCD15	1990	£5	£2	
Prodigal Blues	CD-s	Chrysalis	IDOLCD16	1990	£5	£2	

IDOLS

Title	Format	Label	Cat. No.	Year	Mint	VG	Notes
Don't Walk Away	7"	Mercury	MF840	1965	£5	£2	

IF

If was a jazz-rock group formed by the previously mainstream jazz players Dick Morrissey and Terry Smith (saxophone and guitar respectively). It was interesting as a group formed from the jazz side of the jazz-rock divide, but was ultimately less convincing than the likes of Colosseum or Manfred Mann Chapter Three. Morrissey reappeared later as co-leader of the successful fusion group, Morrissey-Mullen.

Title	Format	Label	Cat. No.	Year	Mint	VG	Notes
Double Diamond	LP	Brain	201035	1973	£20	£8	*German*
Goldenrock	LP	Brain	201103	1974	£20	£8	*German*
If	LP	Island	ILPS9129	1970	£25	£10	*pink label*
If 2	LP	Island	ILPS9137	1970	£25	£10	
If 3	LP	United Artists	UAG29158	1971	£20	£8	
If 4	LP	United Artists	UAG29315	1972	£20	£8	
Raise The Level Of Your Conscious Mind	7"	Island	WIP6083	1970	£4	£1.50	

This Is If	LP	Brain	201005	1973	£15	£6	German

IFE, KRIS

Hush	7"	MGM	MGM1369	1967	£5	£2	
Imagination	7"	Parlophone	R5741	1968	£5	£2	

IFIELD, FRANK

Give Him My Regards	7" EP	Columbia	SEG8495	1965	£5	£2	
Hong Kong Blues	7" EP	Columbia	SEG8456	1965	£5	£2	
I'll Remember You	LP	Columbia	SCX3460	1962	£10	£4	
Just One More Chance	7" EP	Columbia	ESG7897	1963	£6	£2.50	stereo

IGGINBOTTOM

The LP by Igginbottom marks the recording debut of the guitarists' guitarist, Allan Holdsworth, in a surprisingly understated context.

Igginbottom's Wrench	LP	Deram	SML1051	1969	£100	£50	
Igginbottom's Wrench	LP	Deram	DML1051	1969	£125	£62.50	mono

IGLESIAS, JULIO

Gwendolyne	7"	Decca	F23005	1970	£8	£4	

IGNERANTS

Radio Interference	7"	Rundown	ACE008	1979	£15	£7.50	

IGUANA

Iguana	LP	Polydor	2383108	1972	£12	£5	

IGUANAS

This Is What I Was Made For	7"	RCA	RCA1484	1965	£12	£6	

IHRE KINDER

2375004	LP	Kuckuck	2375004	1970	£20	£8	German
Anfang Ohne Ende	LP	Kuckuck	2375016	1972	£20	£8	German
Empty Hands	LP	Kuckuck	2371165	1971	£20	£8	German
Ihre Kinder	LP	Philips	844393	1969	£30	£15	German
Leere Hande	LP	Kuckuck	2375001	1970	£30	£15	German
Werdohl	LP	Kuckuck	2375013	1971	£20	£8	German

IKARUS

Ikarus	LP	Plus	4	1971	£15	£6	German

IKETTES

Fine Fine Fine	7"	Stateside	SS434	1965	£6	£2.50	
Fine Fine Fine	7" EP	Stateside	SE1033	1965	£50	£25	
I'm Blue	7"	London	HLK9508	1962	£8	£4	
I'm So Thankful	7"	Polydor	56506	1970	£5	£2	
Never More Lonely For You	7"	Polydor	56516	1970	£5	£2	
Peaches 'n' Cream	7"	Stateside	SS407	1965	£8	£4	
Prisoner Of Love	7"	Sue	WI389	1965	£15	£7.50	
Soul Hits	LP	Modern	M(ST)102	1965	£30	£15	US
Whatcha Gonna Do	7"	London	HLU10081	1966	£6	£2.50	

ILANIT

I'm No One	7"	Pye	7N25739	1977	£6	£2.50	

ILL WIND

Flashes	LP	ABC	S641	1968	£75	£37.50	US

ILLINOIS SPEED PRESS

James William Guercio, who guided the early careers of Blood Sweat And Tears and Chicago, had less success with the Illinois Speed Press. The group's fluent blues guitar playing, offset by imaginative song structures and the occasional touch of country, was perfect for the times and its commercial failure can only really be explained by the fact that the Allman Brothers were doing something similar, but with even more dramatic effect. Guitarist Paul Cotton wandered further down the country road when he replaced Jim Messina in Poco, with whom he stayed until that group's demise in the mid-eighties.

Duet	LP	CBS	CS9976	1970	£20	£8	US
Illinois Speed Press	LP	CBS	CS9792	1969	£25	£10	US

ILLSLEY, JOHN

I Want To See The Moon	CD-s	Vertigo	VERCD39	1988	£5	£2	

ILLUSION

Did You See Her Eyes	7"	Dot	122	1969	£4	£1.50	
If It's So	LP	Paramount	SPFL264	1970	£12	£5	
Illusion	LP	Dot	(S)LPD531	1969	£12	£5	
Together (As A Way Of Life)	LP	Dot	SLPD537	1970	£12	£5	

ILLUSIVE DREAM

Electric Garden	7"	RCA	RCA1791	1969	£15	£7.50	

ILLUSTRATION

Illustration	LP	Janus	JLS3010	1969	£25	£10	US

ILMO SMOKEHOUSE

Ilmo Smokehouse	LP	Beautiful Sound	3002	1971	£15	£6	US

ILORI, SOLOMON

Title	Format	Label	Cat. No.	Year	Mint	VG+	Notes
African High Life	LP	Blue Note	BLP/BST84136	1963	£30	£15	
Yabe E	7"	Blue Note	451899	1963	£6	£2.50	

IM & DAVID

Title	Format	Label	Cat. No.	Year	Mint	VG+	Notes
Candid Eye	7"	Bamboo	BAM57	1970	£8	£4	*Sound Dimension B side*

IMAGE

Guitarist with the Image was Dave Edmunds, who subsequently achieved considerable success in his own right.

Title	Format	Label	Cat. No.	Year	Mint	VG+	Notes
Come To The Party	7"	Parlophone	R5281	1965	£25	£12.50	
Home Is Anywhere	7"	Parlophone	R5352	1965	£25	£12.50	
I Can't Stop Myself	7"	Parlophone	R5442	1966	£25	£12.50	

IMAGES

Title	Format	Label	Cat. No.	Year	Mint	VG+	Notes
I Only Have Myself To Blame	7"	Polydor	BM56011	1965	£15	£7.50	

IMAN CALIFATO INDEPENDIENTE

Title	Format	Label	Cat. No.	Year	Mint	VG+	Notes
Camuno Del Aguila	LP	CBS	84277	1978	£20	£8	*Spanish*

IMBRUGLIA, NATALIE

With her excellent 'Torn', and indeed the whole of the album from which the song is taken, Natalie Imbruglia has proved that it is quite possible to make the transition from soap star to rock star while pleasing both fans and critics alike – always providing, of course, that the star can demonstrate the creative talent that she has!

Title	Format	Label	Cat. No.	Year	Mint	VG+	Notes
Torn	CD-s	RCA	74321527992	1998	£15	£7.50	

IMLACH, HAMISH

Title	Format	Label	Cat. No.	Year	Mint	VG+	Notes
Ballads Of Booze	LP	XTRA	XTRA1094	1970	£10	£4	
Before And After	LP	XTRA	XTRA1059	1967	£10	£4	
Fine Old English Tory Times	LP	XTRA	XTRA1128	1972	£10	£4	
Murdered Ballads	LP	XTRA	XTRA1131	1973	£10	£4	
Old Rarity	LP	XTRA	XTRA1121	1971	£10	£4	
Two Sides Of Hamish Imlach	LP	XTRA	XTRA1069	1968	£10	£4	

IMMORTALS

Title	Format	Label	Cat. No.	Year	Mint	VG+	Notes
No Turning Back	12"	MCA	MCAT1057	1986	£30	£15	
No Turning Back	7"	MCA	MCA1057	1986	£25	£12.50	

IMORTALS

Title	Format	Label	Cat. No.	Year	Mint	VG+	Notes
Ultimate Warlord	12"	Excaliber	EXC517	1982	£25	£12.50	
Ultimate Warlord	7"	Excaliber	EXC517	1982	£20	£10	

IMPAC

Title	Format	Label	Cat. No.	Year	Mint	VG+	Notes
Too Far Out	7"	CBS	202402	1966	£50	£25	

IMPACS

Title	Format	Label	Cat. No.	Year	Mint	VG+	Notes
Impact!	LP	King	(KS)886	1964	£20	£8	*US*
Weekend With The Impacs	LP	King	(KS)916	1964	£20	£8	*US*

IMP-ACTS

Title	Format	Label	Cat. No.	Year	Mint	VG+	Notes
Dum Dum Song	7" EP	Pye	PNV24152	1965	£10	£5	*French, B side by Kenny Bernard*

IMPACTS

Title	Format	Label	Cat. No.	Year	Mint	VG+	Notes
Wipe Out	LP	Del-Fi	DFLP/DFS1234	1963	£20	£8	*US*

IMPALA SYNDROME

Title	Format	Label	Cat. No.	Year	Mint	VG+	Notes
Impala Syndrome	LP	Parallax	P4002	1969	£30	£15	*US*

IMPALAS

Title	Format	Label	Cat. No.	Year	Mint	VG+	Notes
Oh What A Fool	7"	MGM	MGM1031	1959	£8	£4	
Peggy Darling	7"	MGM	MGM1068	1960	£6	£2.50	
Sorry	7"	MGM	MGM1015	1959	£12	£6	
Sorry	7" EP	MGM	MGMEP696	1959	£200	£100	
Sorry I Ran All The Way Home	LP	Cub	(S)8003	1959	£125	£62.50	*US*

IMPERIALS

Title	Format	Label	Cat. No.	Year	Mint	VG+	Notes
Follow The Man With The Music	LP	Key	KL025	1974	£10	£4	
Time To Get It Together	LP	Key	KL012	1972	£10	£4	

IMPERSONATORS

Title	Format	Label	Cat. No.	Year	Mint	VG+	Notes
Make It Easy On Yourself	7"	Big Shot	BI524	1969	£5	£2	

IMPOSSIBLE DREAMERS

Title	Format	Label	Cat. No.	Year	Mint	VG+	Notes
Books Books Books	7"	Merciful Release	MR1	1980	£8	£4	
Life On Earth	12"	One Hundred Things	MR5	1982	£6	£2.50	

IMPOSTERS

Title	Format	Label	Cat. No.	Year	Mint	VG+	Notes
Apache '69	7"	Mercury	MF1080	1969	£8	£4	

IMPRESSIONS

Title	Format	Label	Cat. No.	Year	Mint	VG+	Notes
Amen	7"	HMV	POP1492	1965	£4	£1.50	
Amen	LP	Buddah	2359009	1970	£10	£4	

Big 16	LP	HMV	CLP1935/ CSD1642	1965	**£20**	**£8**	
Big 16 Vol. 2	LP	Stateside	(S)SL10279	1969	**£10**	**£4**	
Can't Satisfy	7"	Stateside	SS2139	1969	**£4**	**£1.50**	
Can't Satisfy	7"	HMV	POP1545	1966	**£10**	**£5**	
Check Out Your Mind	LP	Buddah	2318017	1971	**£10**	**£4**	
Fabulous Impressions	LP	HMV	CLP/CSD3631	1967	**£15**	**£6**	
Gypsy Woman	7"	HMV	POP961	1961	**£20**	**£10**	
I Need You	7"	HMV	POP1472	1965	**£6**	**£2.50**	
I'm So Proud	7"	HMV	POP1295	1964	**£5**	**£2**	
I'm The One Who Loves You	7"	HMV	POP1129	1963	**£8**	**£4**	
Impressions	LP	ABC	(S)450	1963	**£25**	**£10**	*US*
It's All Right	7"	HMV	POP1226	1963	**£6**	**£2.50**	
It's All Right	7" EP	HMV	7EG8896	1965	**£25**	**£12.50**	
Keep On Pushing	7"	HMV	POP1317	1964	**£5**	**£2**	
Keep On Pushing	LP	ABC	(S)493	1964	**£20**	**£8**	*US*
Meeting Over Yonder	7"	HMV	POP1446	1965	**£5**	**£2**	
Mighty Mighty Spade And Whitey	7"	Buddah	201062	1969	**£4**	**£1.50**	
Never Ending Impressions	LP	HMV	CLP1743	1964	**£25**	**£10**	
One By One	LP	ABC	(S)523	1965	**£20**	**£8**	*US*
People Get Ready	7"	HMV	POP1408	1965	**£6**	**£2.50**	
People Get Ready	LP	ABC	(S)505	1965	**£20**	**£8**	*US*
Ridin' High	LP	HMV	CLP/CSD3548	1966	**£15**	**£6**	
Since I Lost The One I Love	7"	HMV	POP1516	1966	**£5**	**£2**	
Soulfully	7" EP	HMV	7EG8954	1966	**£25**	**£12.50**	
Talking About My Baby	7"	HMV	POP1262	1964	**£8**	**£4**	
This Is My Country	LP	Buddah	203012	1969	**£10**	**£4**	
Too Slow	7"	HMV	POP1526	1966	**£5**	**£2**	
We're A Winner	7"	Stateside	SS2083	1968	**£5**	**£2**	
We're A Winner	LP	Stateside	(S)SL10239	1968	**£10**	**£4**	
Woman's Got Soul	7"	HMV	POP1429	1965	**£6**	**£2.50**	
You Always Hurt Me	7"	HMV	POP1581	1967	**£8**	**£4**	
You Must Believe Me	7"	HMV	POP1343	1964	**£5**	**£2**	
You've Been Cheating	7"	HMV	POP1498	1966	**£8**	**£4**	
Young Mod's Forgotten Story	LP	Buddah	2359003	1970	**£10**	**£4**	

IMPROVED SOUND LIMITED

Improved Sound Limited	LP	Liberty	LBS83505/6	1971	**£20**	**£8**	*German double*

IMPROVISORS' SYMPOSIUM

Pisa 1980	LP	Incus	INCUS37	1981	**£12**	**£5**	

IMPS

Dim Dumb Blonde	7"	Parlophone	R4398	1958	**£8**	**£4**	

IN BETWEENS

The In Betweens' sole single, a version of the Young Rascals' American hit, 'You Better Run', was produced by the legendary Kim Fowley. Success did not come to the group until a few years later, however, when it had changed its name to Slade.

Take A Heart	7" EP	Barclay	2017	1966	**£300**	**£180**	*French, best auctioned*
Take A Heart	7" EP	Barclay	70907	1965	**£300**	**£180**	*French, best auctioned*
You Better Run	7"	Columbia	DB8080	1966	**£300**	**£180**	*best auctioned*

IN CROWD

The soul singles of the In Crowd gave no indication that the group would ever evolve into that cornerstone of psychedelia, Tomorrow. 'That's How Strong My Love Is' was recorded before Steve Howe joined the group, but the other singles all feature his guitar playing, in behind Keith West's singing.

Stop! Wait A Minute	7"	Parlophone	R5328	1965	**£40**	**£20**	
That's How Strong My Love Is	7"	Parlophone	R5276	1965	**£75**	**£37.50**	
Why Must They Criticise	7"	Parlophone	R5364	1965	**£40**	**£20**	

IN CROWD (2)

Where In The World	7"	Deram	DM272	1969	**£8**	**£4**	

IN THE NURSERY

Sonority – A Strength	12"	New European	BADVC55	1985	**£8**	**£4**	
When Cherished Dreams Come True	LP	Paragon	VIRTUE2	1983	**£15**	**£6**	
Witness To A Scream	7"	Paragon	VIRTUE5	1984	**£12**	**£6**	

IN TWO A CIRCLE

Rise	12"	Arcadia	ARC001	1986	**£8**	**£4**	

INADEQUATES

Audie	7"	Capitol	CL15051	1959	**£4**	**£1.50**	

INCA

Satya Sai – Maitreya Kali	LP	private			**£1000**	**£700**	*US*

INCAS

I'll Keep Holding On	7"	Parlophone	R5551	1966	**£20**	**£10**	
Keele Rag Record	7" EP	Lyntone	LYN765/6	1965	**£30**	**£15**	*with other artists*

INCAS (2)

Title	Format	Label	Catalogue no.	Year	Mint	VG	Notes
X Certificate	LP	Tank	BSS112	1975	£10	£4	

INCOGNITO

Title	Format	Label	Catalogue no.	Year	Mint	VG	Notes
Parisienne Girl	12"	Ensign	ENY4412	1980	£6	£2.50	

INCREDIBLE BONGO BAND

Title	Format	Label	Catalogue no.	Year	Mint	VG	Notes
Bongo Rock	LP	MGM	2315255	1972	£15	£6	
Bongo Rock	LP	DJM	20452	1976	£12	£5	

INCREDIBLE HOG

Title	Format	Label	Catalogue no.	Year	Mint	VG	Notes
Lame	7"	Dart	ART2026	1973	£8	£4	
Volume One	LP	Dart	65372	1973	£100	£50	

INCREDIBLE STRING BAND

Title	Format	Label	Catalogue no.	Year	Mint	VG	Notes
5000 Spirits Or The Layers Of The Onion	LP	Elektra	EKS7257	1968	£15	£6	
5000 Spirits Or The Layers Of The Onion	LP	Elektra	EUK/EUKS7257	1967	£20	£8	
Be Glad For The Song Has No Ending	LP	Island	ILPS9140	1970	£10	£4	
Big Huge	LP	Elektra	EKL/EKS74037	1968	£15	£6	
Big Ted	7"	Elektra	EKSN45074	1969	£4	£1.50	
Changing Horses	LP	Elektra	EKS74057	1969	£15	£6	
Earthspan	LP	Island	ILPS9211	1972	£10	£4	
Hangman's Beautiful Daughter	LP	Elektra	EUK/EUKS7258	1968	£20	£8	
Hangman's Beautiful Daughter	LP	Elektra	EKL/EKS74021	1968	£15	£6	
Hard Rope & Silken Twine	LP	Island	ILPS9270	1974	£10	£4	
I Looked Up	LP	Elektra	2469002	1970	£12	£5	
I Looked Up	LP	Elektra	EKS74061	1970	£15	£6	
Incredible String Band	LP	Elektra	EKL322	1966	£40	£20	
Incredible String Band	LP	Elektra	EUK254	1966	£40	£20	
Incredible String Band	LP	Elektra	EUK254	1966	£75	£37.50	*white Elektra label*
Liquid Acrobat As Regards The Air	LP	Island	ILPS9172	1971	£10	£4	
No Ruinous Feud	LP	Island	ILPS9229	1973	£10	£4	
Painting Box	7"	Elektra	EKSN45028	1967	£4	£1.50	
Seasons They Change	LP	Island	ISLD9	1976	£12	£5	*double*
This Moment	7"	Elektra	2101003	1970	£4	£1.50	
U	LP	Elektra	2665001	1970	£15	£6	*double*
Wee Tam	LP	Elektra	EKL/EKS74036	1968	£15	£6	
Wee Tam/The Big Huge	LP	Elektra	EKL/EKS74036/7	1968	£40	£20	*double*

INCREDIBLES

Title	Format	Label	Catalogue no.	Year	Mint	VG	Notes
There's Nothing Else To Say	7"	Stateside	SS2053	1967	£75	£37.50	

INCROWD

Title	Format	Label	Catalogue no.	Year	Mint	VG	Notes
I'll Be Free	LP	Polydor	736042	1966	£20	£8	*Dutch*

INCUBUS

Title	Format	Label	Catalogue no.	Year	Mint	VG	Notes
To The Devil A Daughter	LP	Guardian	GRC2165	1984	£10	£4	

IND, PETER

Title	Format	Label	Catalogue no.	Year	Mint	VG	Notes
Improvisation	LP	Wave	LP3	1970	£15	£6	
Jazz At The 1969 Richmond Festival	LP	Wave	LP5	1970	£15	£6	
Looking Out	LP	Esquire	32159	1962	£20	£8	
Looking Out	LP	Wave	LP1	1970	£15	£6	
Time For Improvisation	LP	Wave	LP4	1970	£15	£6	

INDEPENDENT FOLK

Title	Format	Label	Catalogue no.	Year	Mint	VG	Notes
Independent Folk	LP	Great Western	DM015	1977	£100	£50	

INDEX

Title	Format	Label	Catalogue no.	Year	Mint	VG	Notes
Index	LP	private		1967	£1000	£700	*US*

INDIAN SUMMER

Title	Format	Label	Catalogue no.	Year	Mint	VG	Notes
Indian Summer	LP	Neon	NE3	1971	£30	£15	

INDIGO GIRLS

Like Richard Thompson and precious few other rock artists, the duo of Emily Saliers and Amy Ray, who perform as the Indigo Girls, just get better and better. Popular in the USA, they have still to break beyond the bounds of a cult following in Britain, which explains the tiny list of collectables here. For once, however, the US is wiser, for the Indigo Girls' 'Joni Mitchell meets Chrissie Hynde in a Texas bar' take on singer-songwriting is very special.

Title	Format	Label	Catalogue no.	Year	Mint	VG	Notes
Closer To Fine	CD-s	Epic	6551352	1989	£5	£2	
Closer To Fine	CD-s	Epic	6549072	1989	£5	£2	

INDO JAZZMEN

Title	Format	Label	Catalogue no.	Year	Mint	VG	Notes
Ragas + Reflections	LP	Saga	EROS2145	1968	£25	£10	

INDO-BRITISH ENSEMBLE

Title	Format	Label	Catalogue no.	Year	Mint	VG	Notes
Curried Jazz	LP	MFP	1307	197–	£10	£4	

INFA RIOT

Title	Format	Label	Catalogue no.	Year	Mint	VG	Notes
Kids Of The Eighties	7"	Secret	SHH117	1981	£5	£2	
Sound And Fury	7"	Panache	PAN101	1984	£5	£2	*as the Infas*
Still Out Of Order	LP	Secret	SEC7	1982	£10	£4	

Winner	7"	Secret	SHH133	1982	£5	£2	

INFANTES JUBILATE

Exploding Galaxy	7"	Music Factory	CUB5	1968	**£30**	**£15**	

INFESTED

Flies	7"	Dead City		197–	**£100**	**£50**	*existence doubtful*
No But I've Got A Dark Brown Overcoat	7"	Great Disaster		197–	**£100**	**£50**	*existence doubtful*

INFLUENCE

I Want To Live	7"	Orange	OAS201	1969	**£6**	**£2.50**	
Influence	LP	ABC	ABCS630	1968	**£30**	**£15**	*US*

INFORMATION

Face To The Sun	7"	Evolution	E24615	1970	**£8**	**£4**	
Orphan	7"	Beacon	BEA3121	1968	**£5**	**£2**	

INGHAM, NICK

Terminator	LP	Columbia	TWOX1045	1975	**£10**	**£4**	

INGLE, RED

Cigareets, Whuskey, & Wild Wild Women	7" EP	Capitol	EAP20052	1959	**£12**	**£6**	

INGMANN, JORGEN

Apache	LP	Atco	(SD)33130	1961	**£25**	**£10**	*US*
Drina	7" EP	Columbia	SEG8340	1964	**£10**	**£5**	
Many Guitars Of Jorgen Ingmann	LP	Atco	(SD)33139	1962	**£20**	**£8**	*US*
Swinging Guitar	LP	Mercury	MG20200	1956	**£25**	**£10**	*US*

INGOES

Although the only record made by the Ingoes is this rather uninspiring and obscure French EP, the group is, in fact, an early version of the Blossom Toes, featuring both guitarists and the bass player.

Dansez Le Monkiss	7" EP	Riviera	231141	1966	**£25**	**£12.50**	*French*

INGRAM, LUTHER

Home Don't Seem Like A Home	7"	Stax	STAX148	1970	**£4**	**£1.50**	
My Honey And Me	7"	Stax	STAX142	1970	**£4**	**£1.50**	

INITIALS

School Days	7"	London	HLR9860	1964	**£6**	**£2.50**	

INJAROC

Halen Y Ddaer!	LP	Sain	1094M	1977	**£20**	**£8**	

IN-KEEPERS

In-Keepers	LP	Morgan	MR109P	1968	**£15**	**£6**	

INKER, DAVE

Profile	LP	Ariola	27297	1976	**£25**	**£10**	*German*

INKSPOTS

Charlie Fuqua's Inkspots	7" EP	HMV	7EG8410	1957	**£6**	**£2.50**	
Ebb Tide	7"	Parlophone	MSP6074	1954	**£10**	**£5**	
Here In My Lonely Room	7"	Parlophone	MSP6063	1954	**£10**	**£5**	
Inkspots	10" LP	Britone	LP1003	195–	**£15**	**£6**	
Melody Of Love	7"	Parlophone	MSP6152	1955	**£8**	**£4**	
Souvenir	10" LP	Brunswick	LA8590	1953	**£15**	**£6**	
Street Of Dreams	10" LP	Brunswick	LA8710	1955	**£15**	**£6**	
Swing High Swing Low Vol. 1	7" EP	Brunswick	OE9158	1955	**£6**	**£2.50**	
Yesterdays	7"	Parlophone	MSP6126	1954	**£10**	**£5**	
Yesterdays	7" EP	Parlophone	GEP8673	1957	**£6**	**£2.50**	

INMAN, AUTREY

American Country Jubilee No. 1	7" EP	Decca	DFE8571	1963	**£6**	**£2.50**	

INN KEEPERS

Duppy Serenade	7"	Banana	BA328	1971	**£5**	**£2**	

INNER CITY UNIT

Paradise Beach	7"	Riddle	RID003	1979	**£5**	**£2**	
Solitary Ashtray	7"	Riddle	RID001	1979	**£5**	**£2**	

INNES, NEIL

How Sweet To Be An Idiot	LP	United Artists	UAG29492	1973	**£12**	**£5**	
Off The Record	LP	MMC	MMC001	1982	**£12**	**£5**	*double*
Rutland Times	LP	BBC	REB233	1976	**£10**	**£4**	

INNOCENCE

Mairzy Doats	7" EP	Kama Sutra	617107	1967	**£8**	**£4**	*French*

INNOCENCE MISSION

Black Sheep Wall	CD-s	A&M	AMCD563	1990	**£5**	**£2**	
Wonder Of Birds	CD-s	A&M	AMCD543	1990	**£5**	**£2**	

INNOCENTS

Gee Whiz	7"	Top Rank	JAR541	1961	**£12**	**£6**	
Honest I Do	7"	Top Rank	JAR508	1960	**£12**	**£6**	

INNOCENTS (2)

Fine Fine Bird	7"	Columbia	DB7173	1963	**£4**	**£1.50**	
Medley	7"	Regal Zonophone	RZ502	1964	**£5**	**£2**	*with the Leroys*
Stepping Stones	7"	Columbia	DB7098	1963	**£4**	**£1.50**	
Stick With Me Baby	7"	Columbia	DB7314	1964	**£4**	**£1.50**	

INNOCENTS (3)

One Way Love	7"	Kingdom	KV8010	1980	**£6**	**£2.50**	

IN-SECT

Introducing	LP	Camden	CAL909	1965	**£20**	**£8**	*US*

INSECT TRUST

At a time when rock was blossoming with new approaches and unusual instruments, the Insect Trust still managed to sound unique. They are like a folk group, with a strong female lead singer, into which a couple of avant-garde jazz saxophonists have unaccountably wandered. The combination still sounds fresh today.

Hoboken Saturday Night	LP	Atco	SD33313	1970	**£30**	**£15**	*US*
Insect Trust	LP	Capitol	EST109	1968	**£50**	**£25**	

INSIDE OUT

Bringing It All Back	LP	Fredlo	6834	1968	**£100**	**£50**	*US*

INSPIRAL CARPETS

Butterfly	7"	Playtime	AMUSE4	1988	**£5**	**£2**	*promo only*
Find Out Why	CD-s	Cow	DUNG5CD	1989	**£5**	**£2**	
Keep The Circle Around	12"	Playtime	AMUSE2T	1988	**£10**	**£5**	
Keep The Circle Around	7"	Playtime	AMUSE2	1988	**£10**	**£5**	
Move	CD-s	Cow	DUNG6CD	1989	**£5**	**£2**	
Peel Sessions	CD-s	Strange Fruit	SFPSCD072	1989	**£5**	**£2**	
Train Surfing	12"	Playtime	AMUSE4T	1988	**£10**	**£5**	*promo*

INSPIRATIONS

Touch Me, Hold Me, Kiss Me	7"	Polydor	56730	1967	**£60**	**£30**	

INSPIRATIONS (2)

Down In The Park	7"	Camel	CA11	1969	**£4**	**£1.50**	
La La	7"	Amalgamated	AMG861	1970	**£5**	**£2**	
Reggae Fever	LP	Trojan	TTL27	1970	**£15**	**£6**	
Take Back Your Duck	7"	Amalgamated	AMG857	1970	**£5**	**£2**	
Train Is Coming	7"	Amalgamated	AMG862	1970	**£5**	**£2**	
Wonder Of Love	7"	Camel	CA21	1969	**£4**	**£1.50**	

INSTANT SUNSHINE

Here We Go Again	7"	Page One	POF085	1968	**£4**	**£1.50**	
Live At Tiddy Dols	LP	Page One	POL007	1968	**£25**	**£10**	

INTERCONTINENTAL EXPRESS

London	LP	Compendium	FIDARDO8	1976	**£10**	**£4**	

INTERLUDE

Dunskey Castle	LP	Seagull		1982	**£25**	**£10**	*Dutch*
Interlude	LP	VR		1979	**£25**	**£10**	*Dutch*

INTERNATIONAL SUBMARINE BAND

The International Submarine Band, led by Gram Parsons, is often credited with making the first country-rock LP, for *Safe At Home* pre-dates the Byrds' *Sweetheart Of The Rodeo*, in which Parsons was also involved.

Safe At Home	LP	Shiloh	RI4088	1979	**£12**	**£5**	*US*
Safe At Home	LP	LHI	LHI12001	1968	**£75**	**£37.50**	*US, coloured label*

INTERNS

Cry To Me	7"	Philips	BF1345	1964	**£8**	**£4**	
Don't You Dare	7"	Philips	BF1320	1964	**£6**	**£2.50**	
Is It Really What You Want	7"	Parlophone	R5479	1966	**£20**	**£10**	
Please Say Something Nice	7"	Parlophone	R5586	1967	**£4**	**£1.50**	

INTERWEAVE

Interweave	LP	Silver Dragon		1986	**£75**	**£37.50**	*Dutch*

INTRA VEIN

Speed Of The City	7"	Bum	FP001	1979	**£25**	**£12.50**	*PVC sleeve*

INTRIGUES

In A Moment	7"	London	HL10293	1969	**£6**	**£2.50**	
In A Moment	LP	Yew	YS777	1970	**£15**	**£6**	*US*

INTRUDERS

Cowboys To Girls	LP	Gamble	KZ5004	1968	**£25**	**£10**	*US*
Intruders Are Together	LP	Gamble	(KZ)5001	1967	**£25**	**£10**	*US*
Slow Drag	7"	Action	ACT4523	1969	**£8**	**£4**	
United	7"	London	HL10069	1966	**£20**	**£10**	

INVADERS

Limbo Girl	7"	Columbia	DB105	1967	£5	£2	
Soulful Music	7"	Studio One	SO2044	1968	£12	£6	*Soul Vendors B side*
Stop Teasing	7"	Columbia	DB109	1968	£5	£2	

INVADERS (2)

On The Right Track	LP	Justice	JLP125	1967	£150	£75	*US*

INVICTAS

A Go-Go	LP	Sahara	101	1965	£75	£37.50	*US*

INVITATIONS

Hallelujah	7"	Stateside	SS453	1965	£6	£2.50	
Let's Love And Find Together	7"	Polydor	2066366	1974	£6	£2.50	
What's Wrong With Me Baby	7"	Stateside	SS478	1965	£40	£20	

INXS

Bitter Tears	CD-s	Mercury	INXCD17	1991	£5	£2	
By My Side	CD-s	Mercury	INXCD16	1991	£5	£2	
Devil Inside	CD-s	Mercury	INXCD10	1988	£8	£4	
Disappear	CD-s	Mercury	INXCD15	1990	£5	£2	
Don't Change	12"	Mercury	INXS121	1983	£12	£6	
Don't Change	7"	Mercury	INXS1	1983	£6	£2.50	
Gift	CD-s	Mercury	INXCD25	1993	£5	£2	*with tour pass*
Good Times	CD-s	East West	A7751CD	1991	£5	£2	*with Jimmy Barnes*
Greatest Hits	CD	Mercury	5262292	1994	£15	£6	*double*
Inxs	CD	Atlantic	PR34162	1990	£20	£8	*US promo compilation*
Just Keep Walking	7"	RCA	RCA89	1981	£25	£12.50	*picture sleeve*
Kick	LP	Mercury	MERHP114	1987	£10	£4	*picture disc*
Listen Like Thieves	7"	Mercury	INXSP6	1986	£5	£2	*shaped picture disc*
Listen Like Thieves	LP	Mercury	MERH82	1986	£12	£5	*with LP The Swing*
Mystify	CD-s	Mercury	0808762	1989	£20	£10	*CD video*
Mystify	CD-s	Mercury	INXCD13	1989	£5	£2	
Need You Tonight	12"	Mercury	INXS812	1987	£6	£2.50	
Need You Tonight	CD-s	Mercury	0803942	1988	£20	£10	*CD video*
Need You Tonight	CD-s	Mercury	INXCD8	1987	£6	£2.50	
Never Tear Us Apart	CD-s	Mercury	INXCD11	1988	£5	£2	
Never Tear Us Apart	CD-s	Mercury	0803962	1988	£20	£10	*CD video*
New Sensation	CD	Atlantic	PR2575	1989	£30	£15	*US promo double*
New Sensation	CD-s	Mercury	INXCD9	1987	£5	£2	
One Thing	12"	Mercury	INXS212	1983	£12	£6	*2 tracks*
One Thing	12"	Mercury	INXS222	1983	£10	£5	*3 tracks*
One Thing	7"	Mercury	INXS2	1983	£5	£2	
Original Sin	12"	Mercury	INXS312	1984	£12	£6	
Original Sin	7"	Mercury	INXS3	1984	£8	£4	
Profiled!	CD	Atlantic	PRCD36752	1991	£20	£8	*US promo*
Searchin'	CD-s	Mercury	INXCD30	1997	£12	£6	*3 different singles*
Shining Star	CD-s	Mercury	INXCD18	1991	£5	£2	
Suicide Blonde	CD-s	Mercury	INXCD14	1990	£5	£2	
This Time	7"	Mercury	INXSD4	1986	£5	£2	*double*
What You Need	12"	Mercury	INXSD512	1986	£8	£4	*double*

IONA

Cuckoo	LP	Silverscales	KOO13913	1978	£50	£25	
Iona	LP	Celtic Music	CM001	1978	£30	£15	

IPSISSIMUS

Hold On	7"	Parlophone	R5774	1969	£30	£15	

IQ

Awake And Nervous	12"	Jim White	IQPROMO101	1984	£30	£15	
Barbell Is In	12"	Sahara	IQ121002	1984	£10	£5	
Barbell Is In	7"	Sahara	IQ1002	1984	£6	£2.50	
Beef In A Box	7"	Lyntone	LYN12028/9	1982	£5	£2	*with other artists*
Corners	12"	Sahara	IQ121003	1985	£10	£5	
Corners	7"	Sahara	IQ1003	1985	£6	£2.50	
Different Magic Roundabout	7"	fan club	ONEMOREBOXER1	1988	£10	£5	
Fascination	7"	fan club	ANOTHERBOXER	1987	£15	£7.50	
Hollow Afternoon	7"	IQ	IQFREEB1	1984	£30	£15	
It All Stops Here	7"	Samurai	IQSD1	1986	£15	£7.50	*shaped picture disc*
Living Proof	CD	Samurai	SAMRCD045	1986	£20	£8	
Nine In A Pond Is Here	LP	fan club	BOXER1	1985	£30	£15	*double*
Nomzamo	7"	fan club	OTHERBOXER1	1986	£15	£7.50	
Promises	12"	Squawk	VERX34	1987	£8	£4	
Sold On You	CD-s	Squawk	VERCD42	1989	£6	£2.50	
Tales From The Lush Attic	CD	Samurai	SAMRCD1001	1986	£12	£5	
Tales From The Lush Attic	LP	COSL	MAJ1001	1984	£10	£4	*brown sleeve*
Tales From The Lush Attic	LP	MJL	MAJ1001	1983	£15	£6	*blue sleeve*
Wake	CD	Samurai	SAMRCD136	1986	£12	£5	
Wake	LP	Sahara	SAH136	1985	£10	£4	

IRELAND, TONY

Johny O'Cockley's Well	LP	Peak	3581	1983	£10	£4	*German*

IRISH COFFEE

Irish Coffee	LP	Triangle	BE920321	1971	£350	£210	*Belgian*

IRISH FOLK GROUP

Right Of A Man To Be Free	LP	Derry	SDBL513	1979	£10	£4	

IRISH RAMBLERS

Patriot Game	LP	Golden Guinea	GGL0269	1963	£10	£4	

IRISH ROVERS

First Of The Irish Rovers	LP	Brunswick	STA8679	1967	£10	£4	
Life Of The Rover	LP	MCA	MUPS406	1970	£10	£4	
Liverpool Lou	LP	MCA	MUPS353	1969	£10	£4	
Tales To Warm Your Mind	LP	MCA	MUPS389	1969	£10	£4	
Unicorn	LP	MCA	MUPS310	1968	£10	£4	

IROLT KATTEKWAN

Irolt Kattekwan	LP	Philips		1977	£30	£15	*Dutch*

IRON BUTTERFLY

Ball	LP	Atlantic	228011	1969	£15	£6	
Heavy	LP	Atco	2465015	1970	£15	£6	
In-A-Gadda-Da-Vida	LP	Atco	588166	1968	£15	£6	
Live	LP	Atlantic	2400014	1970	£12	£5	
Metamorphosis	LP	Atlantic	2401003	1970	£12	£5	

IRON MAIDEN

Iron Maiden's striking death mascot has found particularly effective use as a recurring theme on the group's record covers and picture discs. Many of these are now very collectable, as befits a group that is probably the most successful of the New Wave of British Heavy Metal (though Def Leppard might argue the point).

Aces High	12″	EMI	12EMIP5502	1984	£10	£5	*picture disc*
Best Of The Beast	CD	EMI	BEST001	1996	£100	£50	*promo box set with interview CD & video*
Bring Your Daughter To The Slaughter	CD-s	EMI	CDEM171	1990	£5	£2	
Bring Your Daughter To The Slaughter	7″	EMI	EMPD171	1990	£4	£1.50	*picture disc*
Can I Play With Madness	7″	EMI	EMP49	1988	£4	£1.50	*shaped picture disc*
Can I Play With Madness	CD-s	EMI	CDEM49	1988	£5	£2	
Can I Play With Madness/The Evil That Men Do	CD-s	EMI	CDIRN9	1990	£5	£2	
Clairvoyant	7″	EMI	EMP79	1988	£5	£2	*shaped picture disc*
Clairvoyant	CD-s	EMI	CDEM79	1988	£5	£2	
Clairvoyant/Infinite Dreams	CD-s	EMI	CDIRN10	1990	£5	£2	
Evil That Men Do	7″	EMI	EMP64	1988	£4	£1.50	*shaped picture disc*
Evil That Men Do	CD-s	EMI	CDEM64	1988	£5	£2	
Fear Of The Dark	7″	EMI	EMPD263	1992	£4	£1.50	*shaped picture disc, B side plays Tailgunner*
First Ten Years	12″	EMI	IRN1-10	1990	£50	£25	*10 double records, boxed*
First Ten Years	CD-s	EMI	CDIRN1-10	1990	£50	£25	*10 CDs, boxed*
Flight Of Icarus	12″	EMI	12EMIP5378	1983	£10	£5	*picture disc*
Flight Of Icarus	cass-s	EMI	TCIM4	1983	£6	£2.50	
Flight Of Icarus/The Trooper	CD-s	EMI	CDIRN5	1990	£5	£2	
Holy Smoke	CD-s	EMI	CDEM153	1990	£5	£2	
Infinite Dreams	7″	EMI	EMPD117	1989	£4	£1.50	*shaped picture disc*
Infinite Dreams	CD-s	EMI	CDEM117	1989	£5	£2	
Killers	LP	EMI	EMC3357	1981	£40	£20	*cover over-printed with Boom Town Rats cover design!*
Maiden England	CD	EMI		1994	£60	£30	*box set with video*
Maiden Japan	12″	EMI	12EMI5219	1981	£8	£4	
No Prayer 1991 Tour CD	CD	Epic	ESK73695	1991	£25	£10	*US promo*
No Prayer For The Dying	10″	EMI		1990	£40	£20	*boxed promo*
No Prayer For The Dying	CD	EMI		1990	£60	£30	*promo pack*
No Prayer For The Dying	LP	EMI	EMDPD1017	1990	£15	£6	*picture disc*
Number Of The Beast	7″	EMI	EMI5287	1982	£5	£2	*red vinyl*
Number Of The Beast	LP	EMI	EMCP3400	1982	£20	£8	*picture disc*
Piece Of Mind	LP	Capitol		1983	£30	£15	*US picture disc*
Powerslave	LP	EMI	POWERP1	1984	£25	£10	*picture disc*
Purgatory	7″	EMI	EMI5184	1981	£20	£10	
Purgatory/Maiden Japan	CD-s	EMI	CDIRN3	1990	£5	£2	
Run To The Hills	12″	EMI	12EMIP5542	1985	£6	£2.50	*picture disc*
Run To The Hills	7″	EMI	EMIP5263	1982	£40	£20	*picture disc, band photo on both sides*
Run To The Hills	7″	EMI	EMI5263	1982	£4	£1.50	
Run To The Hills	7″	EMI	EMIP5263	1982	£6	£2.50	*picture disc*
Run To The Hills (Live)	7″	EMI	EMI5542	1985	£5	£2	*with Christmas card*
Run To The Hills/The Number Of The Beast	CD-s	EMI	CDIRN4	1990	£5	£2	
Running Free	12″	EMI	12EMIP5532	1985	£6	£2.50	*picture disc*
Running Free	7″	EMI	EMI5032	1980	£12	£6	
Running Free	7″	EMI	EMI5532	1985	£5	£2	*poster sleeve*
Running Free/Run To The Hills	CD-s	EMI	CDIRN7	1990	£5	£2	
Running Free/Sanctuary	CD-s	EMI	CDIRN1	1990	£5	£2	
Sanctuary	7″	EMI	EMI5065	1980	£8	£4	*censored picture sleeve*
Sanctuary	7″	EMI	EMI5065	1980	£15	£7.50	*uncensored picture sleeve*
Seventh Son Of A Seventh Son	LP	EMI	EMDP1006	1988	£10	£4	*picture disc, banner*

Title	Format	Label	Number	Year	Mint	VG	Notes
Soundhouse Tapes	7" EP	Rock Hard	ROK1	1979	£50	£25	
Stranger In A Strange Land	12"	EMI	12EMIP5589	1986	£8	£4	*picture disc*
Stranger In A Strange Land	7"	EMI	EMI5589	1986	£4	£1.50	*poster sleeve*
Trooper	7"	EMI	EMIP5397	1983	£12	£6	*shaped picture disc*
Twilight Zone	7"	EMI	EMI5145	1981	£20	£10	*red or clear vinyl*
Twilight Zone	7"	EMI	EMI5145	1981	£8	£4	
Twilight Zone	7"	EMI	EMI5145	1981	£100	£50	*brown vinyl mispress*
Two Minutes To Midnight	12"	EMI	12EMIP5489	1984	£6	£2.50	*picture disc*
Two Minutes To Midnight/Aces High	CD-s	EMI	CDIRN6	1990	£5	£2	
Wasted Years	7"	EMI	EMIP5583	1986	£10	£5	*shaped picture disc*
Wasted Years/Stranger In A Strange Land	CD-s	EMI	CDIRN8	1990	£5	£2	
Women In Uniform	12"	EMI	12EMI5105	1980	£6	£2.50	
Women In Uniform	7"	EMI	EMI5105	1980	£8	£4	
Women In Uniform/Twilight Zone	CD-s	EMI	CDIRN2	1990	£5	£2	

IRON MAIDEN (2)

Title	Format	Label	Number	Year	Mint	VG	Notes
Falling	7"	Gemini	GMS006	1971	£10	£5	

IRVINE, ANDY & PAUL BRADY

Title	Format	Label	Number	Year	Mint	VG	Notes
Andy Irvine And Paul Brady	LP	Mulligan	LUN008	1976	£10	£4	*Irish*

IRVINE, WELDON

Title	Format	Label	Number	Year	Mint	VG	Notes
In Harmony	LP	Strata East	SES19749	1975	£10	£4	

IRVING, LONNIE

Title	Format	Label	Number	Year	Mint	VG	Notes
Pinball Machine	7"	Melodisc	1546	1960	£10	£5	

IRWIN, BIG DEE

Title	Format	Label	Number	Year	Mint	VG	Notes
Donkey Walk	7"	Stateside	SS261	1964	£5	£2	
I Can't Stand The Pain	7"	Minit	MLF11013	1969	£4	£1.50	
Swinging On A Star	7" EP	Colpix	PXE301	1963	£10	£5	*with Little Eva*
Swinging On A Star	LP	Golden Guinea	GSGL10497	1965	£10	£4	*with Little Eva*
You Satisfy My Needs	7"	Stateside	SS450	1965	£40	£20	

IRWIN, PEE WEE

Title	Format	Label	Number	Year	Mint	VG	Notes
Dixieland Band	LP	London	HAA2009	1956	£10	£4	

ISAACS, DAVID

Title	Format	Label	Number	Year	Mint	VG	Notes
Good Father	7"	Upsetter	US302	1969	£5	£2	*Slim Smith B side*
He'll Have To Go	7"	Upsetter	US311	1969	£5	£2	
I Can't Take It Anymore	7"	Punch	PH6	1969	£4	£1.50	*Lloyd Douglas B side*
I'd Rather Be Lonely	7"	Island	WI261	1966	£8	£4	
I've Got Memories	7"	Upsetter	US305	1969	£5	£2	
Just Enough	7"	Bullet	BU459	1971	£4	£1.50	*Roy Patin B side*
Place In The Sun	7"	Trojan	TR616	1968	£6	£2.50	*Upsetters B side*
Stranger On The Shore	7"	Upsetter	US400	1973	£6	£2.50	*Dillinger B side*
Who To Tell	7"	Upsetter	US319	1969	£5	£2	*Busty Brown B side*
You'll Be Sorry	7"	Punch	PH84	1971	£4	£1.50	

ISAACS, GREGORY

Title	Format	Label	Number	Year	Mint	VG	Notes
All I Have Is Love	LP	Trojan	TRLS121	1976	£12	£5	
Cool Ruler	LP	Front Line	FL1020	1978	£12	£5	
Extra Classic	LP	Conflict	COLP2002	1978	£12	£5	
In Person	LP	Trojan	TRLS102	1975	£12	£5	
Mr Issacs	LP	Deb	DEBLP04	1978	£12	£5	
Soon Forward	LP	Front Line	FL1044	1979	£10	£4	

ISAAK, CHRIS

Title	Format	Label	Number	Year	Mint	VG	Notes
San Francisco Days	CD	Reprise	45116DJ	1993	£15	£6	*US promo picture disc*

ISAIAH

Title	Format	Label	Number	Year	Mint	VG	Notes
Isaiah	LP	CBS	80843	1975	£40	£20	*Austrian*

ISCA FAYRE

Title	Format	Label	Number	Year	Mint	VG	Notes
Then Around Me Young And Old	LP	Candle	CAN761	1976	£50	£25	

ISHERWOOD, JOHN

Title	Format	Label	Number	Year	Mint	VG	Notes
Laughing Cry	LP	Decca	LK/SKL5051	1970	£30	£15	

ISKRA 1903

Title	Format	Label	Number	Year	Mint	VG	Notes
Free Improvisation	LP	Deutsche Grammophon	2563298/299/300	1974	£50	£25	*3 LP set – with New Phonic Art & Wired*
Iskra 1903	LP	Incus	INCUS3/4	1972	£30	£15	*double*

ISLAND BOYS

Title	Format	Label	Number	Year	Mint	VG	Notes
Go Calypso No. 1	7" EP	London	RER1122	1958	£5	£2	
Go Calypso No. 2	7" EP	London	RER1123	1958	£5	£2	
Go Calypso No. 3	7" EP	London	RER1124	1958	£5	£2	

ISLE, JIMMY

Title	Format	Label	Number	Year	Mint	VG	Notes
Billy Boy	7"	Top Rank	JAR274	1960	£5	£2	
Diamond Ring	7"	London	HLS8832	1959	£50	£25	

ISLEY BROTHERS

Title	Format	Label	Cat. No.	Year	Mint	VG	Notes
Behind A Painted Smile	7"	Tamla Motown	TMG693	1969	£4	£1.50	
Behind A Painted Smile	LP	Tamla Motown	(S)TML11112	1969	£15	£6	
Brothers Isley	LP	Stateside	SSL10300	1970	£12	£5	
Got To Have You Back	7"	Tamla Motown	TMG606	1967	£6	£2.50	
How Deep Is The Ocean	7"	RCA	RCA1190	1960	£8	£4	
I Guess I'll Always Love You	7"	Tamla Motown	TMG572	1966	£10	£5	
I Guess I'll Always Love You	7"	Tamla Motown	TMG683	1969	£4	£1.50	
Isley Brothers	7" EP	RCA	RCX7149	1964	£40	£20	
It's Our Thing	LP	Major Minor	SMLP59	1969	£12	£5	
It's Your Thing	7"	Major Minor	MM621	1969	£4	£1.50	
Last Lost Girl	7"	Atlantic	AT4010	1964	£8	£4	
Nobody But Me	7"	Stateside	SS218	1963	£6	£2.50	
Respectable	7"	RCA	RCA1172	1960	£10	£5	
Shake It With Me Baby	7"	United Artists	UP1050	1964	£5	£2	
Shout	7"	RCA	RCA1149	1959	£10	£5	
Shout	LP	RCA	RD27165/SF7055	1960	£30	£15	
Soul On The Rocks	LP	Tamla Motown	(S)TML11066	1968	£25	£10	
Take Me In Your Arms	7"	Tamla Motown	TMG652	1968	£8	£4	
Take Some Time Out	LP	Scepter	SC(S)552	1966	£20	£8	US
Take Some Time Out For Love	7"	Tamla Motown	TMG566	1966	£10	£5	
Tango	7"	United Artists	UP1034	1963	£5	£2	
Tell Me Who	7"	RCA	RCA1213	1960	£8	£4	
This Old Heart Of Mine	7"	Tamla Motown	TMG555	1966	£4	£1.50	
This Old Heart Of Mine	LP	Tamla Motown	STML11034	1966	£15	£6	
Twist And Shout	7"	Stateside	SS112	1962	£6	£2.50	
Twist And Shout	LP	Wand	WD(S)653	1962	£25	£10	US
Twisting And Shouting	LP	United Artists	ULP1064	1964	£25	£10	
Twisting With Linda	7"	Stateside	SS132	1962	£5	£2	
Warpath	7"	Stateside	SS2188	1971	£4	£1.50	

ISLEY, TEX & GRAY CRAIG

Title	Format	Label	Cat. No.	Year	Mint	VG	Notes
North Carolina Boys	LP	Leader	LEA4040	1972	£12	£5	

ISOLATION

Title	Format	Label	Cat. No.	Year	Mint	VG	Notes
Isolation	LP	Riverside	HASLP2083	1973	£750	£500	

ISRAEL VIBRATION

Title	Format	Label	Cat. No.	Year	Mint	VG	Notes
Same Song	LP	Harvest	SHSP4099	1979	£10	£4	

ISRAELITES

Title	Format	Label	Cat. No.	Year	Mint	VG	Notes
Can't Help From Crying	7"	J-Dan	JDN4410	1970	£4	£1.50	

IT BITES

Title	Format	Label	Cat. No.	Year	Mint	VG	Notes
Calling All The Heroes	7"	Virgin	VSP872	1986	£5	£2	*picture disc*
Eat Me In St Louis	CD	Virgin	CDVX2591	1989	£12	£5	*with bonus 3" CD*
Kiss Like Judas	CD-s	Virgin	CDEP21	1988	£5	£2	
Midnight	CD-s	Virgin	VSCD1065	1988	£5	£2	
Old Man And The Angel	CD-s	Virgin	MIKE94112	1987	£5	£2	
Sister Sarah	CD-s	Virgin	VSCD1202	1989	£5	£2	
Still Too Young To Remember	CD-s	Virgin	VSCD1184	1989	£5	£2	*3 versions*
Underneath Your Pillow	CD-s	Virgin	VSCD1215	1989	£5	£2	*3" single*

ITALS

Title	Format	Label	Cat. No.	Year	Mint	VG	Notes
Don't Throw It Away	7"	Giant	GN12	1967	£5	£2	*Caribbeats B side*
New Loving	7"	Giant	GN8	1967	£5	£2	*Soul Brothers B side*

ITHACA

Title	Format	Label	Cat. No.	Year	Mint	VG	Notes
Game For All Who Know	LP	Merlin	HF6	1972	£600	£400	

IT'S A BEAUTIFUL DAY

The reputation of this American progressive band relies not on their scarce risqué album cover, but on one classic recording – the attractive, violin-centred 'White Bird'. Several years later, David Laflamme, the violinist in question, was still playing the piece as a cornerstone of his solo set. One of the other tracks on the group's debut album uses exactly the same riff pattern as Deep Purple's slightly later 'Sweet Child In Time', although no plagiarism case has ever been brought.

Title	Format	Label	Cat. No.	Year	Mint	VG	Notes
Choice Quality Stuff	LP	CBS	64314	1971	£10	£4	
It's A Beautiful Day	LP	CBS	63722	1969	£15	£6	
It's A Beautiful Day	LP	San Francisco Sound	11790	1985	£12	£5	*US audiophile*
It's A Beautiful Day	LP	Columbia	CS9768	1969	£60	£30	*US, topless girl on cover*
Live At Carnegie Hall	LP	CBS	64929	1972	£10	£4	
Marrying Maiden	LP	CBS	64065	1970	£10	£4	
White Bird	7"	CBS	4457	1969	£5	£2	

IT'S ALL MEAT

It's All Meat	LP	Columbia	ELS374	1970	**£60**	**£30**	*Canadian*

IVAN

The rare single by Ivan is a Buddy Holly collectable, as the label credit actually masks the identity of Crickets drummer Jerry Allison and Holly himself.

Real Wild Child	7"	Coral	Q72341	1958	**£200**	**£100**	*best auctioned*

IVAN'S MEADS

Sins Of A Family	7"	Parlophone	R5342	1965	**£10**	**£5**	
We'll Talk About It Tomorrow	7"	Parlophone	R5503	1966	**£10**	**£5**	

IVES, BURL

Australian Folk Songs	10" LP	Brunswick	LA8739	1956	**£10**	**£4**	
Ballads And Folk Songs Vol. 1	10" LP	Brunswick	LA8583	1953	**£10**	**£4**	
Big Daddy Hits	7" EP	Brunswick	OE9489	1962	**£5**	**£2**	
Burl Ives	10" LP	Brunswick	LA8552	1953	**£10**	**£4**	
Down To The Sea In Ships	LP	Brunswick	LAT8142	1956	**£10**	**£4**	
Dying Stockman	7"	Brunswick	05551	1956	**£4**	**£1.50**	
Folk Songs – Dramatic And Humorous	10" LP	Brunswick	LA8633	1954	**£10**	**£4**	
Goober Peas	7"	Brunswick	05510	1956	**£5**	**£2**	
Marianne	7"	Decca	BM31183	1956	**£6**	**£2.50**	*export*
Mister In-Between	7" EP	Brunswick	OE9491	1962	**£5**	**£2**	
Songs For And About Men	7" EP	Brunswick	OE9200	1956	**£5**	**£2**	
Songs For And About Men Vol. 2	7" EP	Brunswick	OE9201	1956	**£5**	**£2**	
Songs For And About Men Vol. 3	7" EP	Brunswick	OE9202	1956	**£5**	**£2**	
Women	10" LP	Brunswick	LA8641	1954	**£10**	**£4**	

IVEYS

The Iveys was the original name for the group Badfinger. The album *Maybe Tomorrow* received a limited release in Europe, but the British and American issues were cancelled. (A UK cover for the album, however, was sold at auction in 1988.) Counterfeits of the European issue exist, but they do not have the Apple labels of the originals.

Dear Angie	7"	Apple	14	1969	**£150**	**£75**	*European*
Maybe Tomorrow	7"	Apple	5	1968	**£25**	**£12.50**	
Maybe Tomorrow	LP	Apple	SAPCOR8	1969	**£250**	**£150**	*European*

IVOR & SHEILA

Changing Times	LP	Eron	027	1981	**£20**	**£8**	

IVORY, JACK

Hi Heeled Sneakers	7"	Atlantic	AT4075	1966	**£6**	**£2.50**	
Soul Discovery	LP	Atco	(SD)33178	1965	**£20**	**£8**	*US*

IVY LEAGUE

Funny How Love Can Be	7" EP	Piccadilly	NEP34038	1965	**£10**	**£5**	
Holly And The Ivy League	7" EP	Piccadilly	NEP34046	1965	**£15**	**£7.50**	
Our Love Is Slipping Away	7" EP	Piccadilly	NEP34048	1966	**£20**	**£10**	
Sounds Of The Ivy League	LP	Marble Arch	MAL741	1967	**£10**	**£4**	
That's Why I'm Crying	7" EP	Pye	PNV24143	1965	**£15**	**£7.50**	*French*
This Is The Ivy League	LP	Piccadilly	NPL38015	1965	**£25**	**£10**	
Tomorrow Is Another Day	LP	Marble Arch	MAL821	1968	**£10**	**£4**	
Tossing And Turning	7" EP	Piccadilly	NEP34042	1965	**£10**	**£5**	
What More Do You Want	7"	Piccadilly	7N35200	1964	**£4**	**£1.50**	

IVY THREE

Yogi	7"	London	HLW9178	1960	**£6**	**£2.50**	

IWAN, DAFYDD

Myn Duw, Mi A Wn Y Daw!	7" EP	Sain	SAIN2	1969	**£8**	**£4**	
Pam Fod Eira Yn Wyn?	7" EP	Sain	SAIN18	1971	**£6**	**£2.50**	

j

J, HARRY ALL STARS

Liquidator	7"	Trojan	TR675	1969	£4	£1.50	
Liquidator	LP	Trojan	TBL104	1970	£10	£4	
Reach For The Sky	7"	Harry J	HJ6608	1970	£4	£1.50	

J & B

Wow Wow Wow	7"	Polydor	56095	1966	£5	£2	

J.D. (THE ROC)

Superbad	7"	Sioux	SI008	1972	£6	£2.50	*Montego Melon B side*

J.J. ALL STARS

Collecting Coins	7"	Duke	DU94	1970	£4	£1.50	
Memphis Underground	7"	Trojan	TR691	1969	£4	£1.50	
This Land	7"	Duke	DU95	1970	£5	£2	

JABULA

Jabula	LP	Caroline	CA2004	1975	£10	£4	
Thunder Into Our Hearts	LP	Caroline	CA2009	1976	£10	£4	

JACK

Kid Stardust	7"	Too Pure	PURE49	1995	£15	£7.50	

JACK & THE BEANSTALKS

Work It Up	7"	Supreme	SUP203	1969	£5	£2	

JACKAL

Awake	LP	Periwinkle	PER7309	1973	£60	£30	*Canadian*
Underneath The Arches	12"	Criminal Damage	CRI12134	1986	£6	£2.50	

JACKIE & BRIDIE

Folk World Of Jackie And Bridie	LP	Concord	CONS1002	1970	£25	£10	
Hold Back The Dawn	LP	Fontana	TL5212	1964	£25	£10	
Next Time Around	LP	Galliard	GAL4019		£40	£20	
Perfect Round	LP	Galliard	GAL4009	1971	£25	£10	

JACKIE & DOREEN

Adorable You	7"	Ska Beat	JB209	1965	£10	£5	

JACKIE & ROY

Jackie And Roy	7" EP	Vogue	VE170131	1959	£75	£37.50	
Jackie And Roy	LP	Vogue	VA160111	1958	£75	£37.50	
You Smell So Good	7"	Vogue	V9101	1958	£75	£37.50	

JACKPOTS

Jack In The Box	LP	Sonet	SLP68	1968	£20	£8	

JACKS

Jacks	LP	Crown	CLP5021	1957	£30	£15	*US*
Jumpin' With The Jacks	LP	RPM	LRP3006	195–	£100	£50	*US*

JACK'S ANGELS

Our Fantasy's Kingdom	LP	Amadeo	9224	1968	£20	£8	*Austrian*

JACKSON, ALEXANDER & THE TURNKEYS

Whip	7"	Sue	WI386	1965	£20	£10	

JACKSON, BO WEEVIL

Some Scream High Yellow	7"	Jazz Collector	JDL81	1959	£6	£2.50	

JACKSON, BULL MOOSE

Bull Moose Jackson	LP	Audio Lab	AL1524	1959	£50	£25	*US*
Nosey Joe	78	Vogue	V2129	1952	£8	£3	

JACKSON, CALVIN

Calvin Jackson Quartet	LP	Philips	BBL7084	1956	£10	£4	
Rave Notice	LP	Philips	BBL7107	1958	£10	£4	

JACKSON, CHRIS

I'll Never Forget You	7"	Soul City	SC112	1969	£15	£7.50	
Since There's No Doubt	7"	Soul City	SC120	1969	£50	£25	*test pressing*

JACKSON, CHUCK

Any Day Now	7"	Stateside	SS102	1962	£10	£5	
Any Day Now	7"	Pye	7N25276	1964	£8	£4	
Any Day Now	LP	Wand	LP/WDS654	1962	£25	£10	*US*
Beg Me	7"	Pye	7N25247	1964	£8	£4	
Breaking Point	7"	Top Rank	JAR607	1962	£15	£7.50	
Chains Of Love	7"	Pye	7N25384	1966	£25	£12.50	
Chuck Jackson Arrives	LP	Tamla Motown	(S)TML11071	1968	£30	£15	
Dedicated To The King	LP	Wand	LP/WDS680	1966	£25	£10	*US*
Encore	LP	Wand	LP/WDS655	1963	£25	£10	*US*
Girls Girls Girls	7"	Tamla Motown	TMG651	1968	£8	£4	
Goin' Back To Chuck Jackson	LP	Tamla Motown	(S)TML11117	1969	£20	£8	
Greatest Hits	LP	Wand	LP/WDS683	1967	£20	£8	*US*
Hand It Over	7"	Kent	TOWN104	1985	£6	£2.50	*Candy & the Kisses B side*
Honey Come Back	7"	Tamla Motown	TMG729	1970	£5	£2	
I Don't Want To Cry	7"	Top Rank	JAR564	1961	£20	£10	
I Don't Want To Cry	LP	Wand	LP/WDS650	1961	£25	£10	*US*
I Keep Forgettin'	7"	Stateside	SS127	1962	£8	£4	
I Need You	7"	Pye	7N25301	1965	£6	£2.50	
If I Didn't Love You	7"	Pye	7N25321	1965	£6	£2.50	
Mr Everything	LP	Wand	LP/WDS667	1965	£25	£10	*US*
On Tour	LP	Wand	LP/WDS658	1964	£25	£10	*US*
Shame On Me	7"	Pye	7N25439	1967	£6	£2.50	
Since I Don't Have You	7"	Pye	7N25287	1965	£25	£12.50	
Tell Him I'm Not Home	7"	Stateside	SS171	1963	£8	£4	
Through All Times	LP	Probe	SPB1084	1972	£10	£4	
Tribute To Rhythm And Blues	LP	Pye	NPL28082	1967	£20	£8	
Tribute To Rhythm And Blues Vol. 2	LP	Wand	LP/WDS676	1966	£25	£10	*US*

JACKSON, CHUCK & MAXINE BROWN

Hold On, We're Coming	LP	Wand	LP/WDS678	1966	£20	£8	*US*
Saying Something	LP	Pye	NPL28091	1967	£20	£8	
Something You Got	7"	Pye	7N25308	1965	£8	£4	

JACKSON, CHUCK & TAMMI TERRELL

Early Show	LP	Wand	LP/WDS682	1967	£20	£8	*US*

JACKSON, DEON

Love Makes The World Go Around	7"	Atlantic	AT4070	1966	£10	£5	
Love Makes The World Go Round	LP	Atco	(SD)33188	1966	£20	£8	*US*
Love Takes A Long Time Growing	7"	Atlantic	584012	1966	£8	£4	
Ooh Baby	7"	Atlantic	584159	1968	£6	£2.50	

JACKSON, FRED

Hootin' 'n' Tootin'	LP	Blue Note	BLP/BST84094	1962	£40	£20	

JACKSON, GEORGE

Find 'Em, Fool 'Em And Forget 'Em	7"	Capitol	CL15605	1969	£5	£2	
Let 'Em Know You Care	7"	London	HLU10413	1973	£4	£1.50	

JACKSON, GORDON

Me And My Zoo	7"	Marmalade	598010	1969	£4	£1.50	
Song For Freedom	7"	Marmalade	598021	1969	£4	£1.50	
Thinking Back	LP	Marmalade	608012	1969	£40	£20	

JACKSON, HAROLD & THE TORNADOES

Move It On Down The Line	7"	Vogue	V9105	1958	£50	£25	

JACKSON, J. J.

Although he called his group The Greatest Little Soul Band, the music that J. J. Jackson played was actually jazz-rock. Indeed, the soul band description was probably a marketing mistake. Fans of Colosseum and Manfred Mann Chapter Three would have loved this, but they looked no further than the cover. More precise is the comparison with the group If, whose leaders Dick Morrissey and Terry Smith both played with Jackson. The sleeve notes to the MCA album end with the words: 'go and see the band and you'll realise that if they aren't the biggest thing in the country in six months, there's no justice'. Sadly, there was none.

And Proud Of It	LP	Perception	PLP12		£20	£8	*US*
But It's Alright	LP	Calla	C(S)1101	1967	£20	£8	*US*
Come See Me	7"	Strike	JH329	1967	£5	£2	
Do The Boogaloo	7"	Polydor	56718	1966	£5	£2	
Great J. J. Jackson	LP	Warner Bros	WS1797	1969	£20	£8	*US*
Greatest Little Soul Band	LP	MCA	SKA100	1969	£15	£6	
J. J. Jackson's Dilemma	LP	RCA	SF8093	1970	£15	£6	
Sho Nuff	7"	Warner Bros	WB2082	1967	£4	£1.50	
With The Greatest Little Soul Band	LP	Strike	JHL104	1967	£15	£6	

JACKSON, JANET

Alright	7"	Breakout	USASD693	1990	£5	£2	*shaped picture disc*

Come Back To Me	CD-s	Breakout	USACD681	1990	£6	£2.50	
Come Give Your Love To Me	12"	A&M	AMSX8303	1983	£8	£4	
Come Give Your Love To Me	7"	A&M	AMS8303	1983	£5	£2	
Control	7"	A&M	AMS359	1986	£6	£2.50	*with cassette*
Design Of A Decade 1986/1996	CD	A&M	5404222	1995	£15	£6	*double*
Don't Mess Up This Good Thing	12"	A&M	AMX112	1983	£8	£4	
Don't Mess Up This Good Thing	7"	A&M	AM112	1983	£5	£2	
Janet	CD	Virgin	CDVX2720	1993	£15	£6	*with bonus remix CD*
Let's Wait A While	7"	Breakout	USAD601	1987	£6	£2.50	*clear vinyl & picture disc set*
Miss You Much	CD-s	Breakout	USACD663	1989	£6	£2.50	
Rhythm Nation	CD	A&M	AMAD3920	1989	£12	£5	*picture disc, numbered sleeve, poster*
Rhythm Nation	CD-s	Breakout	USACD673	1989	£6	£2.50	
Two To The Power Of Love	12"	A&M	AMX210	1984	£15	£7.50	*with Cliff Richard*
Two To The Power Of Love	7"	A&M	AM210	1984	£10	£5	*with Cliff Richard*
When I Think Of You	7"	A&M	AMS337	1986	£8	£4	*clear vinyl & picture disc set*

JACKSON, JERMAINE

Tell Me I'm Not Dreamin'	7"	Epic	JMJDJ1	1984	£25	£12.50	*promo*

JACKSON, JERRY

Gypsy Eyes	7"	London	HLR9689	1963	£10	£5	
It's Rough Out There	7"	Cameo Parkway	P100	1962	£100	£50	

JACKSON, JIM

RCA Victor Race Series Vol. 7	7" EP	RCA	RCX7182	1966	£10	£5	

JACKSON, JIMMY

Country And Blues	7" EP	Columbia	SEG7768	1958	£30	£15	
I Shall Not Be Moved	7"	Columbia	DB3898	1957	£10	£5	
Love A Love A Love A	7"	Columbia	DB4085	1958	£5	£2	
River Line	7"	Columbia	DB3957	1957	£8	£4	
Rock 'n' Skiffle	7" EP	Columbia	SEG7750	1958	£30	£15	
Sitting In The Balcony	7"	Columbia	DB3937	1957	£20	£10	
This Little Light Of Mine	7"	Columbia	DB4153	1958	£5	£2	
White Silver Sands	7"	Columbia	DB3988	1957	£5	£2	

JACKSON, JOE

I'm The Man	7"	A&M	SP1800	1980	£10	£5	*US 5 x 7", poster, boxed*
Night And Day	CD	Mobile Fidelity	UDCD539	1991	£15	£6	*US audiophile*
Will Power	CD	Mobile Fidelity	UDCD503	1988	£15	£6	*US audiophile*

JACKSON, LEVI

This pseudonym hides the identity of burly MOR singer Solomon King, best known for his hit single, 'She Wears My Ring'. The uptempo rhythm of 'This Beautiful Day' has turned the single into a substantial Northern Soul collectable, although for anyone who is not a fan of that particular genre, King/Jackson's rather unsoulful singing and the off-Broadway arrangement conspire to make the song sound like a rejected out-take from the musical, *Hair*.

This Beautiful Day	7"	Columbia	DB8807	1971	£40	£20	

JACKSON, LIL' SON

Rockin' And Rollin'	LP	Imperial	9142	1961	£75	£37.50	*US*

JACKSON, MAHALIA

Great Gettin' Up Morning	LP	Philips	BBL7362	1960	£10	£4	
I Believe	LP	Philips	BBL7456/ SBBL610	1961	£10	£4	
Just As I Am	LP	Top Rank	30006	1960	£10	£4	
Mahalia Jackson	10" LP	Vogue	LDE005	1952	£15	£6	
Newport 1958	LP	Philips	BBL7289/ SBBL547	1959	£12	£5	
Power And The Glory	LP	Philips	BBL7391/ SBBL576	1960	£10	£4	

JACKSON, MICHAEL

Michael Jackson has made the two biggest-selling albums ever, and has in the process acquired a legion of fans keen to collect anything they can find. Within the collectors' market, Jackson has joined the select few stars for whom there are dealers specializing exclusively in his music. The *Dangerous* picture disc is a distinct oddity, in that it does not actually play Michael Jackson's music at all. Copies were produced for promo and test purposes before it was realized that the vinyl release was going to be a double. A commercial picture disc was never produced in consequence (although double-album picture discs, such as Frankie Goes To Hollywood's *Welcome To The Pleasure Dome*, have been issued in the past). The Michael Jackson Megamix 12" was withdrawn and half the original thousand copies were destroyed. Counterfeits exist of the remainder, but these are identifiable by the fact that they play at 33 rpm, whereas the real thing plays at 45 rpm (despite the label stating that it is actually 33 rpm).

Ain't No Sunshine	LP	Pickwick	TMS3511	1982	£10	£4	
Another Part Of Me	7"	Epic	6528449	1988	£10	£5	*with backstage pass*
Another Part Of Me	7"	Epic	6528440	1988	£8	£4	*poster picture sleeve*
Another Part Of Me	7"	Epic	4528449	1988	£6	£2.50	*with tour pass*
Another Part Of Me	CD-s	Epic	6528443	1988	£12	£6	*3" single*
Another Part Of Me	CD-s	Epic	6528442	1988	£12	£6	

Title	Format	Label	Cat. No.	Year	Price	Price	Notes
Another Part Of Me	CD-s	Epic	6530042	1988	£25	£12.50	*picture disc*
Bad	12"	Epic	6511006	1987	£15	£7.50	*red vinyl*
Bad	7"	Epic	MJ5	1988	£40	£20	*5 picture discs*
Bad	cass	Epic	450290	1987	£15	£6	*with note pad, pen, calendar*
Bad	CD	Epic	EPC4502909	1987	£20	£8	*picture disc*
Bad	LP	Epic	4502900	1987	£10	£4	*picture disc*
Bad Mixes	CD	Epic	ESK1215MC	1988	£200	£100	*US promo*
Billie Jean (Meanjean Mix)	CD-s	Epic		198–	£40	£20	
Black Or White	CD-s	Epic	6575982	1991	£5	£2	
Black Or White (Clivilles & Cole Remixes)	CD-s	Epic	6577312	1992	£5	£2	
Blood On The Dancefloor	12"	Epic	XPR3125	1997	£6	£2.50	*promo*
Blood On The Dancefloor	12"	Epic	XPR3136	1997	£6	£2.50	*promo*
Dangerous	CD	Epic		1992	£25	£10	*Australian double, with remix disc*
Dangerous	CD	Epic	4658029	1992	£25	£10	*10"-square pop-up pack*
Dangerous	LP	Epic		1991	£1000	£700	*US sample picture disc – plays Richard Clayderman!*
Dirty Diana	12"	Epic	6528646	1988	£15	£7.50	*poster picture sleeve*
Dirty Diana	7"	Epic	6515467	1988	£5	£2	*with cardboard figure*
Dirty Diana	CD-s	Epic	6515462	1988	£10	£5	*3" single*
Dirty Diana	CD-s	Epic	6515469	1988	£15	£7.50	
DMC Megamix	12"	Epic	XPR2266	1995	£12	£6	*promo*
Don't Stop 'Til You Get Enough	12"	Epic	XPR3033	1996	£6	£2.50	*promo*
Don't Stop 'Til You Get Enough	12"	Epic	12EPC7763	1979	£8	£4	*no picture sleeve*
Earthsong	12"	Epic	XPR2271	1995	£15	£7.50	*promo*
Epic Hits	LP	Epic	SXPR1207	1979	£15	£6	*promo*
ET	cass	MCA	CAC70000	1982	£15	£6	*with book & poster, boxed*
ET	LP	MCA	MCA70000	1982	£75	£37.50	*with book and poster, boxed*
Farewell My Summer Love	12"	Motown	TMGT1342	1984	£6	£2.50	
Girl Is Mine	7"	Epic	EPCA112729	1982	£20	£10	*picture disc, with Paul McCartney*
Girl You're So Together	12"	Motown	TMGT1345	1984	£6	£2.50	
Got To Be There	CD-s	Motown	ZD41951	1989	£6	£2.50	*3" single*
Greatest Original Hits	7" EP	Epic	EPC2906	1983	£15	£7.50	
Happy	7"	Tamla Motown	TMG986	1983	£8	£4	*poster picture sleeve*
Happy	7"	Tamla Motown	TMG986	1983	£10	£5	*picture disc*
Heal The World	CD-s	Epic	6584885	1992	£6	£2.50	*picture disc*
HIStory	12"	Epic	XPR3169	1997	£6	£2.50	*promo*
HIStory	12"	Epic	XPR3159	1997	£6	£2.50	*promo*
HIStory	12"	Epic	XPR3149	1997	£6	£2.50	*promo*
HIStory	7"	Epic	664796	1997	£6	£2.50	*jukebox issue*
HIStory	CD-s	Epic	XPCD2176	1997	£10	£5	*promo*
History Begins	CD	Epic	XPCD656	1995	£40	£20	*promo*
History Of Motown	LP	Motown	PR84	1981	£25	£10	*4 LP box set, with Jacksons*
I Just Can't Stop Loving You	12"	Epic	6502026	1987	£10	£5	*with poster*
I Just Can't Stop Loving You	7"	Epic	6502020	1987	£10	£5	*poster picture sleeve*
In The Closet	12"	Epic	E2S4467	1992	£15	£7.50	*US promo double*
Is It Scary	12"	Epic	XPR3168	1997	£25	£12.50	*promo*
Is It Scary	12"	Epic	XPR3196	1997	£25	£12.50	*promo*
Jam	12"	Epic	XPR1814	1992	£25	£12.50	*promo double*
Jam	12"	Epic	E2S4581	1992	£20	£10	*US promo double*
Jam	7"	Epic	6583607	1992	£5	£2	*with 2 prints*
Jam	CD-s	Epic	6583602	1992	£6	£2.50	
Leave Me Alone	7"	Epic	6546720	1989	£25	£12.50	*pop-up sleeve*
Leave Me Alone	CD-s	Epic	6546723	1989	£12	£6	*3" single*
Leave Me Alone	CD-s	Epic	6546722	1989	£10	£5	
Liberian Girl	7"	Epic	6549479	1989	£15	£7.50	*mobile pack*
Liberian Girl	CD-s	Epic	6549473	1989	£12	£6	*3" single*
Liberian Girl	CD-s	Epic	6549472	1989	£10	£5	
Man In The Mirror	7"	Epic	EPC6513889	1988	£10	£5	*shaped picture disc*
Man In The Mirror	CD-s	Epic	6513882	1988	£12	£6	*3" single*
Man In The Mirror	CD-s	Epic	6513882	1988	£15	£7.50	
Megamix	12"	Epic	XPR1242	1984	£60	£30	
MJ Club Megamix	12"	Epic	XPR2207	1996	£12	£6	*promo*
Off The Wall	LP	Epic	HE47545	1980	£12	£5	*US audiophile*
Off The Wall	LP	Epic	EPC83458	1980	£25	£10	*with 7" picture disc*
P.Y.T.	7"	Epic	A3910	1984	£5	£2	
Remember The Time	12"	Epic	XPR1733	1992	£6	£2.50	*promo*
Remember The Time	12"	Epic		1992	£20	£10	*US promo double*
Rock With You	12"	Epic	XPR2229	1995	£10	£5	*promo*
Rock With You	12"	Epic	12EPC8206	1979	£8	£4	*no picture sleeve*
Rock With You	CD-s	Epic	XPCD7222	1995	£15	£7.50	*promo*
Scream	12"	Epic	XPR2184	1995	£25	£12.50	*promo double*
Singles Pack	7"	Epic	MJ1	1983	£40	£20	*9 x red vinyl*
Smile	CD-s	Epic		1997	£400	£200	
Smooth Criminal	12"	Epic	6530261	1987	£20	£10	*with advent calendar*
Smooth Criminal	7"	Epic	6530260	1987	£15	£7.50	*boxed with postcards*
Smooth Criminal	CD-s	Epic	6530263	1987	£12	£6	
Smooth Criminal (Funkin' Smooth Mix)	12"	Epic		1988	£30	£15	

Title	Format	Label	Cat. No.	Year	Mint	Ex	Notes
Smooth Criminal (Smokin' Gun Mix)	12"	Epic		1988	£40	£20	
Smooth Criminal (Vancouver Feetbeat)	12"	Epic		1988	£30	£15	
Stranger In Moscow	12"	Epic	XPR3076	1996	£8	£4	*promo*
Stranger In Moscow	12"	Epic	XPR3057	1996	£8	£4	*promo*
Stranger In Moscow	12"	Epic	XPR3073	1996	£8	£4	*promo*
Stranger In Moscow	7"	Epic	663787	1997	£6	£2.50	*jukebox issue*
They Don't Care About Us	12"	Epic	XPR3030	1996	£8	£4	*promo*
They Don't Care About Us	12"	Epic	XPR3020	1996	£8	£4	*promo*
They Don't Care About Us	7"	Epic	662950	1996	£6	£2.50	*jukebox issue*
This Time Around	CD-s	Epic	SAMPCD3598	1996	£50	£25	*promo*
Thriller	12"	Epic	TA3643	1983	£60	£30	*calendar sleeve*
Thriller	7"	Epic	EPCA3643	1983	£8	£4	*poster sleeve*
Thriller	LP	Epic	HE48112	1982	£15	£6	*US audiophile*
Thriller	LP	Epic	EPC1185930	1982	£30	£15	*picture disc*
Tour Souvenir Pack	CD-s	Epic	65828114(MJ4)	1992	£30	£15	*4 picture disc box set*
Wanna Be Startin' Something	12"	Epic	XPR2265	1995	£12	£6	*promo*
Way You Make Me Feel	12"	Epic	6512753	1987	£20	£10	*double groove*
Way You Make Me Feel	CD-s	Epic	6512759	1987	£10	£5	
Who Is It	12"	Epic	XPR1797	1992	£8	£4	*promo*
Who Is It	12"	Epic		1993	£20	£10	*US promo double*
Who Is It	7"	Epic	6581797	1992	£5	£2	*with cardboard Michael Jackson*
You Can't Win	12"	Epic	12EPC7135	1979	£8	£4	*no picture sleeve*
You Can't Win	7"	Epic	EPC7135	1979	£10	£5	*picture disc*
You Can't Win	CD-s	Epic	6516613	1988	£5	£2	

JACKSON, MILLIE

Title	Format	Label	Cat. No.	Year	Mint	Ex	Notes
It Hurts So Good	LP	Polydor	2391091	1972	£10	£4	
Millie	LP	Spring	6701	1973	£12	£5	*US*
Millie Jackson	LP	Polydor	2391025	1972	£10	£4	

JACKSON, MILT

Title	Format	Label	Cat. No.	Year	Mint	Ex	Notes
At The Museum Of Modern Art	LP	Mercury	LML/SML4016	1965	£10	£4	
Bags And Flutes	LP	London	LTZK15177	1960	£12	£5	
Bags Meets Wes	LP	Riverside	RLP(9)407	1962	£12	£5	*with Wes Montgomery*
Bags' Opus	LP	London	LTZK15172/ SAHT6049	1959	£12	£5	
Ballad Artistry	7" EP	London	REK1315	1962	£5	£2	
Ballad Artistry	LP	London	LTZK15220/ SAHK6163	1961	£12	£5	
Ballads And Blues	LP	London	LTZK15064	1957	£20	£8	
Bean Bags	LP	London	LTZK15196/ SAHK6095	1960	£12	£5	*with Coleman Hawkins*
Born Free	LP	Mercury	LML/SML4028	1966	£10	£4	
Cherry	LP	CTI	CTL8	1973	£10	£4	
Goodbye	LP	CTI	CTH1002	1974	£10	£4	
In A New Setting	LP	Mercury	LML/SML4008	1965	£10	£4	
Jackson's-Ville	LP	London	LTZK15091	1957	£20	£8	
Jackson's-Ville	LP	London	LTZC15091	1957	£20	£8	
Jazz Skyline	LP	London	LTZC15074	1957	£20	£8	
Milt Jackson	LP	Philips	BBL7459	1961	£12	£5	
Milt Jackson	LP	Blue Note	BLP/BST81509	1962	£25	£10	*with Thelonious Monk*
Milt Jackson And His New Group	10" LP	Vogue	LDE044	1954	£50	£25	
Milt Jackson Quartet	10" LP	London	LZC14006	1955	£30	£15	
Milt Jackson Quartet	LP	Esquire	32009	1955	£25	£10	
Milt Jackson Quartet	LP	Realm	RM119	1963	£12	£5	
Milt Jackson Quintet	10" LP	Esquire	20042	1955	£40	£20	
Milt Jackson Septet	7" EP	London	EZC19004	1956	£5	£2	
Modern Jazz Quartet/Quintet	LP	Esquire	32134	1962	£12	£5	
Olinga	LP	CTI	CTH1004	1975	£10	£4	
Opus De Jazz	LP	London	LTZC15026	1957	£25	£10	
Plenty, Plenty Soul	LP	London	LTZK15141	1959	£15	£6	
Statements	LP	HMV	CLP1589/ CSD1455	1963	£12	£5	
Sunflower	LP	CTI	CTL15	1973	£10	£4	
Vibrations	LP	Atlantic	ATL/SAL5012	1964	£12	£5	
Wizard Of The Vibes	LP	Vogue	LAE12046	1957	£15	£6	

JACKSON, PAPA CHARLIE

Title	Format	Label	Cat. No.	Year	Mint	Ex	Notes
Long Gone Lost John	78	Tempo	R30	1950	£6	£2.50	
Papa Charlie Jackson	7" EP	Heritage	R100	1960	£15	£7.50	
Papa Charlie Jackson	LP	Heritage	HLP1011	1960	£40	£20	

JACKSON, PYTHON LEE

Title	Format	Label	Cat. No.	Year	Mint	Ex	Notes
In A Broken Dream	7"	Young Blood	YEP89	1980	£6	£2.50	
In A Broken Dream	7" EP	Young Blood	YEP89	1985	£6	£2.50	*promo*

JACKSON, SHIRLEY

Title	Format	Label	Cat. No.	Year	Mint	Ex	Notes
Broken Home	7"	Decca	F11788	1963	£5	£2	

JACKSON, SHOVELVILLE K.

Title	Format	Label	Cat. No.	Year	Mint	Ex	Notes
Be Careful Of Stones That You Throw	7"	Melodisc	1683	196–	£6	£2.50	

JACKSON, SIMONE

Title	Format	Label	Cat. No.	Year	Mint	Ex	Notes
Doing What You Know Is Wrong	7" EP	Pye	PNV24111	1963	£6	£2.50	*French*

JACKSON, STONEWALL

Title	Format	Label	Cat. No.	Year	Mint	VG	Notes
Dynamic Stonewall Jackson	LP	Columbia	CL1391/CS8186	1959	**£15**	**£6**	*US*
Greatest Hits	LP	CBS	BPG62587	1965	**£10**	**£4**	
I'm Gonna Find You	7"	Philips	PB1073	1960	**£4**	**£1.50**	
Sadness In A Song	LP	Columbia	CL1770/CS8570	1962	**£15**	**£6**	*US*
Waterloo	7"	Philips	PB941	1959	**£6**	**£2.50**	

JACKSON, TONY

It must have seemed a good idea to Tony Jackson, as the lead singer of the Searchers, to strike out on his own. Unfortunately, it turned out that his personal following was only a fraction of the following enjoyed by the Searchers as a group. None of Tony Jackson's singles got anywhere at all, while the remaining Searchers enjoyed a further two-year run of chart success.

Title	Format	Label	Cat. No.	Year	Mint	VG	Notes
Anything Else You Want	7"	CBS	202408	1966	**£20**	**£10**	
Bye Bye Baby	7"	Pye	7N15685	1964	**£10**	**£5**	
Follow Me	7"	CBS	202297	1966	**£30**	**£15**	
Love Potion No. 9	7"	Pye	7N15766	1965	**£25**	**£12.50**	
Never Leave Your Baby's Side	7"	CBS	202069	1966	**£20**	**£10**	
Stage Door	7"	Pye	7N15876	1965	**£12**	**£6**	
This Little Girl Of Mine	7"	Pye	7N15745	1964	**£15**	**£7.50**	
Tony Jackson Group	7" EP	Estudio		1967	**£200**	**£100**	*Portuguese, best auctioned*
You're My Number One	7"	CBS	202039	1966	**£20**	**£10**	
You're My Number One	7" EP	CBS	5726	1966	**£150**	**£75**	*French*

JACKSON, WALTER

Title	Format	Label	Cat. No.	Year	Mint	VG	Notes
Corner In The Sun	7"	Columbia	DB8054	1966	**£8**	**£4**	
It's An Uphill Climb To The Bottom	7"	Columbia	DB7949	1966	**£15**	**£7.50**	
Speak Her Name	7"	Columbia	DB8154	1967	**£8**	**£4**	
Welcome Home	7"	Columbia	DB7620	1965	**£8**	**£4**	

JACKSON, WANDA

Wanda Jackson was one of the best female rock 'n' roll singers, although her competition was rather limited. Adopting the same rasping tones as Brenda Lee on her up-tempo material, Wanda Jackson's older voice had a greater depth and hence rather more power. In common with most of the American singers of her generation, she took the country route once the initial rock 'n' roll years were over.

Title	Format	Label	Cat. No.	Year	Mint	VG	Notes
Blues In My Heart	LP	Capitol	(S)T2306	1964	**£12**	**£5**	
If I Cried Every Time You Hurt Me	7"	Capitol	CL15249	1962	**£6**	**£2.50**	
In The Middle Of A Heartache	7"	Capitol	CL15234	1962	**£6**	**£2.50**	
Let's Have A Party	7"	Capitol	CL15147	1960	**£12**	**£6**	
Let's Have A Party	7" EP	Capitol	EAP11041	1959	**£60**	**£30**	
Little Bitty Tear	7" EP	Capitol	EAP120353	1962	**£30**	**£15**	
Love Me Forever	LP	Capitol	(S)T1911	1963	**£15**	**£6**	*US*
Lovin' Country Style	LP	Decca	DL4224	1962	**£25**	**£10**	*US*
Mean Mean Man	7"	Capitol	CL15176	1961	**£12**	**£6**	
Reaching	7"	Capitol	CL15090	1959	**£10**	**£5**	
Right Or Wrong	7"	Capitol	CL15223	1961	**£5**	**£2**	
Right Or Wrong	LP	Capitol	T1596	1961	**£40**	**£20**	
Rockin' With Wanda	LP	Capitol	T1384	1960	**£75**	**£37.50**	
Salutes The Country Music Hall Of Fame	LP	Capitol	(S)T2606	1967	**£10**	**£4**	
Sings Country Songs	LP	Capitol	(S)T2438	1966	**£10**	**£4**	
There's A Party Goin' On	LP	Capitol	T1511	1961	**£60**	**£30**	
There's A Party Goin' On	LP	Capitol	ST1511	1961	**£75**	**£37.50**	*stereo*
Two Sides Of Wanda Jackson	LP	Capitol	(S)T2030	1964	**£20**	**£8**	
Wanda Jackson	LP	Capitol	T1041	1958	**£100**	**£50**	
Wonderful Wanda	LP	Capitol	T1776	1962	**£25**	**£10**	
You're The One For Me	7"	Capitol	CL15033	1959	**£10**	**£5**	

JACKSON & SMITH

Title	Format	Label	Cat. No.	Year	Mint	VG	Notes
Ain't That Loving You Baby	7"	Polydor	BM56051	1965	**£6**	**£2.50**	
Party '66	7"	Polydor	BM56086	1966	**£5**	**£2**	

JACKSON BROTHERS

Title	Format	Label	Cat. No.	Year	Mint	VG	Notes
Tell Him No	7"	London	HLX8845	1959	**£15**	**£7.50**	

JACKSON FIVE

Title	Format	Label	Cat. No.	Year	Mint	VG	Notes
ABC	7"	Tamla Motown	TMB738	1970	**£50**	**£25**	*demo, picture sleeve*
ABC	LP	Tamla Motown	(S)TML11156	1970	**£10**	**£4**	
Anthology	LP	Tamla Motown	TMSP6004	1977	**£12**	**£5**	*double*
Christmas Album	LP	Tamla Motown	STML11168	1970	**£10**	**£4**	
Dancing Machine	LP	Tamla Motown	STML11275	1974	**£10**	**£4**	
Diana Ross Presents The Jackson Five	LP	Tamla Motown	(S)TML11142	1970	**£10**	**£4**	
Get It Together	LP	Tamla Motown	STML11243	1973	**£12**	**£5**	*with photo*
Jackson Five	LP	Pickwick	TMS3505	1982	**£10**	**£4**	
Looking Through The Windows	7"	Tamla Motown	TMG833	1972	**£12**	**£6**	*demo, picture sleeve*
Mama's Pearl	7"	Tamla Motown	TMG769	1971	**£40**	**£20**	*promo picture sleeve*

Title	Format	Label	Cat. No.	Year	Mint	VG	Notes
Maybe Tomorrow	LP	Tamla Motown	STML11188	1971	**£10**	**£4**	
Motown 20th Anniversary Singles Box	7"	Motown	SPTMG2	1980	**£25**	**£12.50**	*15 single box set*
Motown Special	LP	Motown	STMX6006	1977	**£10**	**£4**	
Moving Violations	LP	Tamla Motown	STML11290	1975	**£10**	**£4**	
Moving Violations	LP	Tamla Motown	STML11290	1975	**£10**	**£4**	
Skywriter	7"	Tamla Motown	TMG865	1973	**£10**	**£5**	*demo, picture sleeve*
Sugar Daddy (and others)	7"	Rice Krispies	no number	1975	**£25**	**£12.50**	*6 different card discs*
Talk And Sing To Valentine Readers	7"	Lyntone	LYN2639	1974	**£5**	**£2**	*flexi*
Third Album	LP	Tamla Motown	STML11174	1971	**£10**	**£4**	
Vintage Gold	CD-s	Motown	ZD41949	1989	**£6**	**£2.50**	*3" single*
You Can Cry On My Shoulder	CD-s	Motown	8000	1986	**£6**	**£2.50**	
Zip-A-Dee-Doo-Dah	LP	MFP	MFP50418	1979	**£10**	**£4**	

JACKSON HEIGHTS

Title	Format	Label	Cat. No.	Year	Mint	VG	Notes
Bump And Grind	LP	Vertigo	6360092	1973	**£12**	**£5**	
Fifth Avenue Bus	LP	Vertigo	6360067	1972	**£20**	**£8**	*spiral label*
King Progress	LP	Charisma	CAS1018	1970	**£10**	**£4**	
Ragamuffin's Fool	LP	Vertigo	6360077	1973	**£20**	**£8**	*spiral label*

JACKSON SISTERS

Title	Format	Label	Cat. No.	Year	Mint	VG	Notes
I Believe In Miracles	12"	Urban	URBX4	1987	**£6**	**£2.50**	
I Believe In Miracles	7"	Mums	MUM1829	1973	**£15**	**£7.50**	
I Believe In Miracles	7"	Urban	URB4	1987	**£4**	**£1.50**	

JACKSONS

Title	Format	Label	Cat. No.	Year	Mint	VG	Notes
2300 Jackson Street	CD-s	Epic	6552062	1989	**£5**	**£2**	
Blame It On The Boogie	12"	Epic	E126983	1979	**£6**	**£2.50**	
Blame It On The Boogie	12"	Epic	EPC127876	1979	**£6**	**£2.50**	
Blame It On The Boogie	12"	Epic	SEPC126683	1978	**£6**	**£2.50**	
Destiny	12"	Epic	SEPC126983	1978	**£6**	**£2.50**	
Enjoy Yourself	12"	Epic	SEPC5063	1977	**£10**	**£5**	
Goin' Places	LP	Epic	PAL348351G	1978	**£10**	**£4**	*US picture disc*
Heartbreak Hotel	12"	Epic	EPC129391	1980	**£10**	**£5**	
Jacksons	LP	CBS	AL34229	1977	**£10**	**£4**	*US picture disc*
Nothing	CD-s	Epic	6548082	1989	**£5**	**£2**	
Shake Your Body	12"	Epic	EPC127181	1979	**£6**	**£2.50**	
Solid Gold	CD-s	Epic	6545703	1989	**£6**	**£2.50**	*3" single*
State Of Shock	7"	Epic	EPCA4431	1984	**£8**	**£4**	*picture disc*
Taste Of Victory	LP	Epic	SAI7561	1985	**£40**	**£20**	*picture disc*
Victory	LP	Epic	EPC86303	1984	**£25**	**£10**	*picture disc*
Walk Right Now	7"	Epic	EPCA1294	1981	**£6**	**£2.50**	*picture disc*

JACKY

Title	Format	Label	Cat. No.	Year	Mint	VG	Notes
White Horses	LP	Philips	SBL7851	1968	**£10**	**£4**	

JACOB, DIRK

Title	Format	Label	Cat. No.	Year	Mint	VG	Notes
Yes Till Death	LP	Blowin' Brains	VSATL112	1969	**£100**	**£50**	*US*

JACOBS, DICK

Title	Format	Label	Cat. No.	Year	Mint	VG	Notes
Big Beat	7"	Vogue Coral	Q72245	1957	**£6**	**£2.50**	
Man With The Golden Arm Theme	7"	Vogue Coral	Q72154	1956	**£5**	**£2**	
Rock-A-Billy Gal	7"	Vogue Coral	Q72260	1957	**£5**	**£2**	
Skiffle Sound	LP	Coral	LVA9076	1957	**£25**	**£10**	
Themes From Horror Films	LP	Coral	LVA9102	1959	**£10**	**£4**	

JACOBS, HANK

Title	Format	Label	Cat. No.	Year	Mint	VG	Notes
Monkey Hips And Rice	7"	Sue	WI313	1964	**£15**	**£7.50**	
So Far Away	LP	Sue	1023	1964	**£25**	**£10**	*US*

JACOBS, JIMMY & THE NITESPOTS

Title	Format	Label	Cat. No.	Year	Mint	VG	Notes
Swingin' Soho	LP	Gargoyle	ADV305011	196–	**£10**	**£4**	

JACOBS CREEK

Title	Format	Label	Cat. No.	Year	Mint	VG	Notes
Jacobs Creek	LP	CBS	63730	1968	**£15**	**£6**	*German*

JACQUES, BRIAN & BRIGANTINE

Title	Format	Label	Cat. No.	Year	Mint	VG	Notes
Gig Wid Brig	LP	Sweet Folk & Country	SFAO11	1974	**£10**	**£4**	

JACQUES, HATTIE

Title	Format	Label	Cat. No.	Year	Mint	VG	Notes
Bungles Of Bojun	7" EP	Avenue	NUE143	1971	**£5**	**£2**	

JACQUET, ILLINOIS

Title	Format	Label	Cat. No.	Year	Mint	VG	Notes
Blow Illinois Blow	7"	Vogue	V2387	1956	**£4**	**£1.50**	
Groovin' With Jacquet	LP	Columbia	33CX10085	1957	**£40**	**£20**	
Illinois Jacquet	10" LP	Columbia	33C9018	1956	**£40**	**£20**	
Illinois Jacquet	10" LP	Vogue	LDE026	1953	**£50**	**£25**	
Jazz At The Philharmonic	LP	Melodisc	MLP12301	195–	**£40**	**£20**	

JADE

Title	Format	Label	Cat. No.	Year	Mint	VG	Notes
Fly On Strange Wings	LP	DJM	DJLPS407	1970	**£30**	**£15**	

JADE (2)

Title	Format	Label	Cat. No.	Year	Mint	VG	Notes
Faces Of Jade	LP	General American Rec	GAR11311	1968	**£60**	**£30**	*US*

JADE WARRIOR

Jade Warrior was essentially a duo – Tony Duhig and Jon Field – whose music is perfectly described by the album covers. Mostly instrumental, with a hint of the Orient and an emphasis on a gentle textural beauty, Jade Warrior's music laid down the ground rules for much of what is defined as 'new age'.

Title	Format	Label	Cat. No.	Year	Mint	VG	Notes
Demon Trucker	7"	Vertigo	6059069	1972	**£5**	**£2**	
Eclipse	LP	Vertigo		1973	**£200**	**£100**	*promo only*
Floating World	LP	Island	ILPS9290	1974	**£10**	**£4**	
Jade Warrior	LP	Vertigo	6360033	1971	**£30**	**£15**	*spiral label*
Kites	LP	Island	ILPS9393	1976	**£10**	**£4**	
Last Autumn's Dream	LP	Vertigo	6360079	1972	**£30**	**£15**	*spiral label*
Reflections	LP	Butt	BUTT001	1979	**£10**	**£4**	
Released	LP	Vertigo	6360062	1971	**£40**	**£20**	*spiral label*
Waves	LP	Island	ILPS9318	1975	**£10**	**£4**	
Way Of The Sun	LP	Island	ILPS9552	1978	**£10**	**£4**	

JADES

Both sides of the rare single by the Jades were written by a sixteen-year-old Lou Reed, who also played rhythm guitar. This is his recording debut.

Title	Format	Label	Cat. No.	Year	Mint	VG	Notes
Leave Her For Me	7"	Time	1002	1957	**£200**	**£100**	*US*

JAFFRAY

Title	Format	Label	Cat. No.	Year	Mint	VG	Notes
Seven Sided Dice	LP	private		1978	**£250**	**£150**	

JAGGER, MICK

Title	Format	Label	Cat. No.	Year	Mint	VG	Notes
Let's Work	7"	CBS	6510280	1987	**£5**	**£2**	*poster sleeve*
Memo From Turner	7"	Decca	F13067	1970	**£4**	**£1.50**	
Memo From Turner	7"	Decca	F13067	1970	**£30**	**£15**	*export, picture sleeve*
Ned Kelly	LP	United Artists	UAS29108	1970	**£15**	**£6**	*with other artists*
Performance	LP	Warner Bros	WS2554	1970	**£15**	**£6**	*with other artists*
Throwaway	7"	CBS	THROWP1	1987	**£6**	**£2.50**	*picture disc*
Throwaway	CD-s	CBS	THROWC1	1987	**£10**	**£5**	
Wandering Spirit	CD	Atlantic	PRCD5002	1993	**£40**	**£20**	*US interview promo*

JAGS

Title	Format	Label	Cat. No.	Year	Mint	VG	Notes
Cry Wolf	7"	Decca	F11397	1961	**£4**	**£1.50**	

JAGUAR

Title	Format	Label	Cat. No.	Year	Mint	VG	Notes
Axe Crazy	7"	Neat	NEAT16	1982	**£8**	**£4**	
Back Street Woman	7"	Heavy Metal	HEAVY10	1981	**£8**	**£4**	
Power Games	LP	Neat	NEAT1007	1983	**£25**	**£10**	*purple vinyl*
Power Games	LP	Neat	NEAT1007	1983	**£10**	**£4**	

JAGUARS

Title	Format	Label	Cat. No.	Year	Mint	VG	Notes
Opus To Spring	7"	Impression	IMP101	1963	**£15**	**£7.50**	
We'll Live On Happily	7"	Contest	RGJ152	1965	**£150**	**£75**	

JAH LION

Title	Format	Label	Cat. No.	Year	Mint	VG	Notes
Colombia Colly	LP	Island	ILPS9386	1976	**£12**	**£5**	

JAH WOOSH

Title	Format	Label	Cat. No.	Year	Mint	VG	Notes
Dreadlocks Affair	LP	Trojan	TRLS113	1976	**£12**	**£5**	
Jah Jah Dey Dey	LP	Cactus	CTLP116	1976	**£12**	**£5**	
Jah Woosh	LP	Cactus	CTLP103	1974	**£15**	**£6**	
Lick Him With The Dustbin	LP	Kab		1977	**£12**	**£5**	
Psalms Of Wisdom	LP	Blackwax	2	1977	**£12**	**£5**	
Religious Dread	LP	Trojan	TRLS157	1978	**£10**	**£4**	
World Marijuana Tour	LP	Carib Gems		1977	**£15**	**£6**	

JAIM

Title	Format	Label	Cat. No.	Year	Mint	VG	Notes
Prophesy Fulfilled	LP	Ethereal	1001	1970	**£20**	**£8**	*US*

JAKLIN

Title	Format	Label	Cat. No.	Year	Mint	VG	Notes
Jaklin	LP	Stable	SLE8003	1969	**£200**	**£100**	

JAM

Title	Format	Label	Cat. No.	Year	Mint	VG	Notes
Beat Surrender	12"	Polydor	POSP540X	1982	**£20**	**£10**	*mispressed B side*
Beat Surrender	7"	Polydor	PODJ540	1982	**£6**	**£2.50**	*promo, censored version*
Beat Surrender	7"	Polydor	PODJ540	1982	**£125**	**£62.50**	*autographed double, handwritten lyrics*
Compact Snap!	CD	Polydor	8217122	1983	**£12**	**£5**	
Funeral Pyre	7"	Fan Club		1982	**£15**	**£7.50**	*flexi*
Going Underground	7"	Polydor	POSPJ113/ 2816024	1980	**£5**	**£2**	*double*
In The City	7"	Polydor	2058266	1997	**£25**	**£12.50**	*1 sided promo*
In The City	7"	Polydor	2058866	1977	**£4**	**£1.50**	
Live At The Roxy	LP	Receiver		1991	**£150**	**£75**	*test pressing*
News Of The World	7"	Polydor	2058995	1978	**£20**	**£10**	*mispress with 2 B sides*
Peel Sessions	CD-s	Strange Fruit	SFPSCD080	1990	**£5**	**£2**	

Pop Art Poem	7"	Lyntone	LYN9048	1980	**£25**	**£12.50**	*hard vinyl test pressing*
Snap!	LP	Polydor	SNAP1	1983	**£12**	**£5**	*double, with 7" (SNAP45)*
Snap! Medley	7"	Polydor	LEE1	1983	**£15**	**£7.50**	*promo*
Tales From The Riverbank	7"	Fan Club	no number	1982	**£15**	**£7.50**	*flexi*
That's Entertainment	CD-s	Polydor	PZCD155	1991	**£5**	**£2**	
When You're Young	7"	Polydor	POSP69	1979	**£20**	**£10**	*mispress with 2 B sides*
When You're Young	7"	Fan Club	no number	1981	**£15**	**£7.50**	*flexi*

JAM (2)

From The Road	LP	private		1976	**£500**	**£330**	*Dutch*

JAMAICAN SHADOWS

Dirty Dozen	7"	Upsetter	US320	1969	**£6**	**£2.50**	
Have Mercy	7"	Coxsone	CS7005	1967	**£10**	**£5**	

JAMAICANS

Bab Boom	7"	Treasure Isle	TI7012	1967	**£10**	**£5**	*Tommy McCook B side*
Cool Night	7"	Doctor Bird	DB1109	1967	**£10**	**£5**	
Dedicated To You	7"	Trojan	TR007	1967	**£10**	**£5**	
Early In The Morning	7"	Escort	ES806	1969	**£4**	**£1.50**	
Peace And Love	7"	Treasure Isle	TI7037	1968	**£10**	**£5**	
Things You Say You Love	7"	Treasure Isle	TI7007	1967	**£10**	**£5**	

JAMAL, AHMAD

Ahmad Jamal	LP	London	LTZM15170	1959	**£20**	**£8**	
Alhambra	LP	Pye	NJL38	1962	**£15**	**£6**	
At The Top	LP	Impulse	SIPL521	1970	**£12**	**£5**	
But Not For Me	LP	London	LTZM15162	1959	**£20**	**£8**	
Cry Young	LP	Chess	CRL4532	1968	**£12**	**£5**	
Macanudo	LP	Pye	NJL50	1963	**£15**	**£6**	
Naked City Theme	LP	Chess	CRL4001	1964	**£15**	**£6**	
Roar Of The Grease Paint	LP	Chess	CRL4509	1967	**£15**	**£6**	
Standard-Eyes	LP	Chess	CRL4530	1968	**£12**	**£5**	

JAMES

Chain Mail	12"	Blanco Y Negro	JIM3T	1986	**£10**	**£4**	
Chain Mail	7"	Blanco Y Negro	JIM3	1986	**£5**	**£2**	
Come Home	CD-s	Fontana	JIMCD6	1990	**£5**	**£2**	
Come Home	CD-s	Rough Trade	RTT245CD	1989	**£6**	**£2.50**	
How Was It For You	CD-s	Fontana	JIMCD5	1990	**£5**	**£2**	
James II	7"	Factory	FAC119	1985	**£6**	**£2.50**	
Jimone	7"	Factory	FAC78	1984	**£6**	**£2.50**	
Lose Control	CD-s	Fontana	JIMCD7	1990	**£5**	**£2**	
One Man Clapping	CD-s	Rough Trade	ONEMAN001CD	1989	**£5**	**£2**	
Sit Down	12"	Rough Trade	RTT225	1989	**£6**	**£2.50**	*with postcard*
Sit Down	7"	Rough Trade	RT225	1989	**£4**	**£1.50**	
Sit Down	CD-s	Rough Trade	RTT225CD	1989	**£8**	**£4**	*3" single*
Sit Down	CD-s	Fontana	JIMCD8	1991	**£5**	**£2**	
So Many Ways	12"	Blanco Y Negro	JIM4T	1986	**£10**	**£4**	
So Many Ways	7"	Blanco Y Negro	JIM4	1986	**£5**	**£2**	
Sound	CD-s	Fontana	JIMCD9	1991	**£5**	**£2**	
What For	12"	Blanco Y Negro	NEG31T	1988	**£8**	**£4**	
Yaho	12"	Blanco Y Negro	NEG26T	1988	**£8**	**£4**	

JAMES, B. B.

Consider Me	7"	Upsetter	US328	1970	**£5**	**£2**	

JAMES, BOB

One	LP	CTI	CTL6043	1975	**£10**	**£4**	
Two	LP	CTI	CTL6057	1975	**£10**	**£4**	

JAMES, BOBBY & DAVE BARKER

You Said It	7"	Smash	SMA2314	1971	**£4**	**£1.50**	

JAMES, CALVIN

Some Things You Never Get Used To	7"	Columbia	DB7516	1965	**£6**	**£2.50**	

JAMES, COL

Doesn't Anybody Make Short Movies	7"	Oriole	CB1736	1962	**£5**	**£2**	

JAMES, DICK

Garden Of Eden	7"	Parlophone	R4255	1957	**£6**	**£2.50**	
He	7"	Parlophone	MSP6190	1955	**£5**	**£2**	
I Only Know I Love You	7"	Parlophone	R4220	1956	**£4**	**£1.50**	
Joker	7"	Parlophone	MSP6047	1953	**£4**	**£1.50**	
Mother Nature And Father Time	7"	Parlophone	MSP6039	1953	**£5**	**£2**	
Robin Hood	7"	Parlophone	MSP6199	1956	**£15**	**£7.50**	
Skiffling Sing Song	7"	Parlophone	R4375	1957	**£4**	**£1.50**	

Unchained Melody	7"	Parlophone	MSP6170	1955	**£6**	**£2.50**	
Westward Ho The Wagons	7"	Parlophone	R4314	1957	**£4**	**£1.50**	

JAMES, ELMORE

As one of the major influences on the British blues boom, Elmore James both defined electric blues slide guitar playing and created the style's test piece, 'Dust My Blues' (a.k.a. 'Dust My Broom'). The high stabbing chord, with the slide chattering at the twelfth, octave fret, that sets the pattern for the song was re-worked for numerous other songs by James, who knew a good thing when he heard it, and also by his many followers. Fleetwood Mac's Jeremy Spencer, for example, based his entire blues career on being an Elmore James sound-alike and reworked the slide guitar figure for several of his contributions to the group's Blue Horizon albums. The slide guitar solo that James created for the original song, moreover, became so quickly assimilated into the blues vocabulary that Jesse Davis was able to quote it directly, and thereby sound traditional, on Taj Mahal's triumphant reclaiming of the blues for black America, 'Statesboro' Blues'.

Anthology Of The Blues Legend	LP	Kent	KLP9001	196–	**£15**	**£6**	*US*
Best Of Elmore James	LP	Sue	ILP918	1965	**£30**	**£15**	
Blues After Hours	LP	Crown	CLP5168	1961	**£30**	**£15**	*US*
Calling The Blues	7"	Sue	WI392	1965	**£60**	**£30**	
Dust My Blues	7"	Sue	WI335	1964	**£12**	**£6**	
I Need You	7"	Sue	WI4007	1966	**£12**	**£6**	
I Need You	LP	Sphere Sound	7008	1964	**£20**	**£8**	*US*
It Hurts Me Too	7"	Sue	WI383	1965	**£12**	**£6**	
Late Fantastically Great Elmore James	LP	Ember	EMB3397	1968	**£10**	**£4**	
Legend Of Elmore James	LP	United Artists	UAS29109	1970	**£15**	**£6**	
Memorial Album	LP	Sue	ILP927	1965	**£30**	**£15**	
Original Folk Blues	LP	Kent	KLP5022	1964	**£25**	**£10**	*US*
Resurrection Of Elmore James	LP	Kent	KLP9010	196–	**£15**	**£6**	*US*
Sky Is Crying	LP	Sphere Sound	7002	1964	**£20**	**£8**	*US*
Something Inside Of Me	LP	Bell	MBLL/SBLL104	1968	**£20**	**£8**	
To Know A Man	LP	Blue Horizon	766230	1969	**£50**	**£25**	*double*
Tough	LP	Blue Horizon	763204	1968	**£30**	**£15**	*with John Brim*
Whose Muddy Shoes	LP	Chess	1537	1969	**£15**	**£6**	*US*

JAMES, ETTA

All I Could Do Was Cry	7"	London	HLM9139	1960	**£15**	**£7.50**	
Anything To Say You're Mine	7"	Pye	7N25080	1961	**£6**	**£2.50**	
At Last	7"	Pye	7N25079	1961	**£6**	**£2.50**	
At Last	LP	Argo	(S)4003	1961	**£25**	**£10**	*US*
At Last	LP	Chess	CRL4524	1967	**£15**	**£6**	
Etta James	LP	Argo	(S)4013	1962	**£20**	**£8**	*US*
Etta James Sings For Lovers	LP	Argo	(S)4018	1962	**£20**	**£8**	*US*
Fool That I Am	7"	Pye	7N25113	1961	**£6**	**£2.50**	
I Got You Babe	7"	Chess	CRS8076	1968	**£5**	**£2**	
I Prefer You	7"	Chess	CRS8052	1967	**£6**	**£2.50**	
Miss Etta James	LP	Kent	3002	196–	**£25**	**£10**	*US, red vinyl*
Miss Etta James	LP	Kent	3002	196–	**£20**	**£8**	*US*
My Dearest Darling	7"	London	HLM9234	1960	**£12**	**£6**	
Pushover	7"	Pye	7N25205	1963	**£6**	**£2.50**	
Queen Of Soul	LP	Argo	(S)4040	1965	**£20**	**£8**	*US*
Rock With Me Henry	7"	Sue	WI359	1965	**£12**	**£6**	
Rocks The House	LP	Chess	CRL4502	1963	**£20**	**£8**	
Second Time Around	LP	Argo	(S)4011	1961	**£20**	**£8**	*US*
Security	7"	Chess	CRS8069	1967	**£5**	**£2**	
Something's Got A Hold Of Me	7"	Pye	7N25131	1962	**£6**	**£2.50**	
Soul Of Etta James	LP	Ember	EMB3390	1968	**£10**	**£4**	
Stop The Wedding	7"	Pye	7N25162	1962	**£6**	**£2.50**	
Tell Mama	7"	Chess	CRS8063	1967	**£6**	**£2.50**	
Tell Mama	LP	Chess	CRL4536	1968	**£15**	**£6**	
Top Ten	LP	Argo	(S)4025	1963	**£20**	**£8**	*US*
You Got It	7"	Chess	CRS8082	1968	**£4**	**£1.50**	

JAMES, ETTA & SUGAR PIE DESANTO

Do I Make Myself Clear	7"	Chess	CRS8025	1965	**£8**	**£4**	

JAMES, HARRY

All Time Favourites	10" LP	Columbia	33S1014	1954	**£15**	**£6**	
Harry James In Hi-Fi	10" LP	Capitol	LC6800	1956	**£15**	**£6**	
Harry James Orchestra	LP	Philips	BBL7036	1955	**£15**	**£6**	
More Harry James In Hi-Fi	LP	Capitol	LCT6107	1956	**£12**	**£5**	
Rhythm Session	10" LP	Columbia	33S1031	1954	**£15**	**£6**	
Soft Lights, Sweet Trumpet	10" LP	Philips	BBR8010	1954	**£15**	**£6**	
Trumpet Time	10" LP	Columbia	33S1052	1955	**£15**	**£6**	
Wild About Harry	LP	Capitol	LCT6146	1957	**£12**	**£5**	

JAMES, HOMESICK

Crossroads	7"	Sue	WI319	1964	**£12**	**£6**	
Set A Date	7"	Sue	WI330	1965	**£15**	**£7.50**	

JAMES, HOMESICK & SNOOKY PRIOR

Homesick James And Snooky Prior	LP	Caroline	C1502	1974	**£12**	**£5**	

JAMES, JASON

Miss Pilkington's Maid	7"	CBS	2705	1967	**£10**	**£5**	

JAMES, JERRY & THE BANDITS

Sweet Little Sixteen	7"	Solar	SRP101	1964	**£5**	**£2**	

JAMES, JESSE

Lonesome Day Blues	78	Vocalion	V1037	1954	**£8**	**£3**	

JAMES, JIMMY

Ain't Love Good Ain't Love Proud	7" EP	Pye	PNV24183	1966	**£20**	**£10**	*French*
Ain't Love Good, Ain't Love Proud	7"	Piccadilly	7N35349	1966	**£6**	**£2.50**	
Bewildered And Blue	7"	Dice	CC4	1962	**£10**	**£5**	
Help Yourself	7"	Trojan	TR7806	1970	**£8**	**£4**	
Hey Girl	7"	Pye	7N45472	1975	**£6**	**£2.50**	
Hi Diddley Dee Dum Dum	7"	Piccadilly	7N35320	1966	**£5**	**£2**	
I Can't Get Back Home To My Baby	7"	Piccadilly	7N35360	1967	**£6**	**£2.50**	
I Feel Alright	7"	Piccadilly	7N35298	1966	**£5**	**£2**	
Jimmy James & The Vagabonds	7" EP	Piccadilly	NEP34053	1966	**£25**	**£12.50**	
Jump Children	7"	R&B	JB112	1963	**£8**	**£4**	
New Religion	7" EP	Pye	PNV24188	1967	**£20**	**£10**	*French*
New Religion	LP	Piccadilly	NPL38027	1966	**£20**	**£8**	
No Good To Cry	7"	Piccadilly	7N35374	1967	**£5**	**£2**	
No Good To Cry	7" EP	Pye	PNV24193	1967	**£20**	**£10**	*French*
Open Up Your Soul	LP	Pye	N(S)PL18231	1968	**£15**	**£6**	
Shoo Be Doo You're Mine	7"	Columbia	DB7653	1965	**£6**	**£2.50**	
Thinking Of You	7"	Black Swan	WI437	1964	**£10**	**£5**	
This Heart Of Mine	7"	Piccadilly	7N35331	1966	**£6**	**£2.50**	
You Don't Stand A Chance	LP	Pye	NSPL18457	1975	**£10**	**£4**	
Your Love	7"	Ska Beat	JB242	1966	**£8**	**£4**	

JAMES, JOHN

Acoustica Eclectica	LP	Stoptime	STOP101	1984	**£10**	**£4**	
Descriptive Guitar Instrumentals	LP	Kicking Mule	SNKF128	1976	**£10**	**£4**	
Head In The Clouds	LP	Transatlantic	TRA305	1975	**£12**	**£5**	
John James	LP	Transatlantic	TRA242	1971	**£12**	**£5**	
Live In Concert	LP	Kicking Mule	SNKF136	1978	**£10**	**£4**	
Morning Brings The Light	LP	Transatlantic	TRA219	1970	**£12**	**£5**	
Sky In My Pie	LP	Transatlantic	TRA250	1971	**£12**	**£5**	*with Pete Berryman*

JAMES, JONI

After Hours	LP	MGM	C933	1963	**£10**	**£4**	
Almost Always	7"	MGM	SP1041	1953	**£8**	**£4**	
Am I In Love	7"	MGM	SP1089	1954	**£6**	**£2.50**	
At Carnegie Hall	LP	MGM	(S)E3800	1959	**£10**	**£4**	*US*
Award Winning Album	10" LP	MGM	E234	195–	**£20**	**£8**	*US*
Award Winning Album	LP	MGM	E3346	1956	**£15**	**£6**	*US*
Country Girl Style	LP	MGM	(S)E4101	1962	**£10**	**£4**	*US*
Give Us This Day	7"	MGM	MGM918	1957	**£4**	**£1.50**	
Give Us This Day	LP	MGM	E3528	1958	**£15**	**£6**	*US*
Have You Heart	7"	MGM	SP1025	1953	**£6**	**£2.50**	
How Important Can It Be	7"	MGM	SP1125	1955	**£5**	**£2**	
Hundred Strings And Joni In Hollywood	LP	MGM	C839/CS6015	1961	**£10**	**£4**	
I Feel A Song Comin' On	LP	MGM	(S)E4053	1962	**£10**	**£4**	*US*
I Love You	7" EP	MGM	MGMEP651	1958	**£5**	**£2**	
I Need You Now	7"	MGM	SP1081	1954	**£5**	**£2**	
I'll Never Stand In Your Way	7"	MGM	SP1064	1954	**£8**	**£4**	
I'm Your Girl	LP	MGM	(S)E4054	1962	**£10**	**£4**	*US*
In A Garden Of Roses	7"	MGM	SP1100	1954	**£5**	**£2**	
In The Still Of The Night	LP	MGM	E3328	1956	**£15**	**£6**	*US*
Is This The End Of The Line	7"	MGM	SP1135	1955	**£5**	**£2**	
Joni James	7" EP	MGM	MGMEP504	1954	**£8**	**£4**	
Joni James Sings To You	7" EP	MGM	MGMEP518	1955	**£8**	**£4**	
Let There Be Love	10" LP	MGM	D127	1954	**£20**	**£8**	
Little Girl Blue	7" EP	MGM	MGMEP530	1956	**£8**	**£4**	
Love Letters	7" EP	MGM	MGMEP558	1956	**£5**	**£2**	
Mama Don't Cry At My Wedding	7"	MGM	SP1105	1954	**£5**	**£2**	
Merry Christmas From Joni	LP	MGM	E3468	1957	**£15**	**£6**	*US*
Mood Is Blue	LP	MGM	(S)E3991	1961	**£10**	**£4**	*US*
Mood Is Romance	LP	MGM	(S)E3990	1961	**£10**	**£4**	*US*
Mood Is Swinging	LP	MGM	(S)E3987	1961	**£10**	**£4**	*US*
One Hundred Strings And Joni	LP	MGM	C777	1959	**£12**	**£5**	
Only Trust Your Heart	7"	MGM	MGM954	1957	**£4**	**£1.50**	
Sings Irish Favourites	LP	MGM	C823/CS6005	1960	**£10**	**£4**	
Songs Of Hank Williams	7" EP	MGM	ES3501	1960	**£10**	**£5**	*stereo*
Songs Of Hank Williams	7" EP	MGM	MGMEP728	1960	**£8**	**£4**	
Songs Of Hank Williams	LP	MGM	C785	1959	**£10**	**£4**	
Stage Songs	7" EP	MGM	MGMEP595	1957	**£5**	**£2**	
Swings Sweet	LP	MGM	C825	1960	**£10**	**£4**	
There Must Be A Way	7"	MGM	MGM1002	1959	**£4**	**£1.50**	
Ti Voglio Bene	LP	MGM	C809	1960	**£12**	**£5**	
Why Don't You Believe Me?	7"	MGM	SP1013	1953	**£10**	**£5**	
You Are My Love	7"	MGM	SP1149	1956	**£5**	**£2**	
You're My Everything	7"	MGM	SP1094	1954	**£5**	**£2**	
Your Cheatin' Heart	7"	MGM	SP1026	1953	**£8**	**£4**	

JAMES, LEONARD

Boppin' And A-Strollin'	LP	Decca	DL8772	1958	**£20**	**£8**	*US*

JAMES, NICKY

Stagger Lee	7"	Columbia	DB7747	1965	**£10**	**£5**	
Would You Believe	7"	Philips	BF1635	1968	**£5**	**£2**	

JAMES, RICKY

Knee Deep In The Blues	7"	HMV	POP306	1957	**£15**	**£7.50**	
Party Doll	7"	HMV	POP334	1957	**£20**	**£10**	

JAMES, ROGER FOUR

Title	Format	Label	Number	Year	Mint	VG	Notes
Better Than Here	7"	Columbia	DB7829	1966	£5	£2	
Better Than Here	7"	Columbia	DB7813	1966	£6	£2.50	

JAMES, RUBY

Title	Format	Label	Number	Year	Mint	VG	Notes
Getting Mighty Crowded	7"	Fontana	TF1051	1969	£5	£2	

JAMES, SID

Title	Format	Label	Number	Year	Mint	VG	Notes
Kids	7"	HMV	POP886	1961	£4	£1.50	*with Dean Rogers*
Ooter Song	7"	Decca	F11328	1961	£6	£2.50	*with Liz Fraser*
Our House	7"	Pye	7N4528	1973	£6	£2.50	*picture sleeve*

JAMES, SKIP

Title	Format	Label	Number	Year	Mint	VG	Notes
Devil Got My Woman	LP	Vanguard	VSD79273	1968	£12	£5	
Greatest Of The Delta Blues Singers	LP	Storyville	670185	1967	£12	£5	
Original 1930–31 Recordings	LP	Spokane	SPL1003	1970	£30	£15	
Skip James Today	LP	Vanguard	VSD79219	1965	£12	£5	

JAMES, SONNY

Title	Format	Label	Number	Year	Mint	VG	Notes
Are You Mine	7"	Capitol	CL14879	1958	£4	£1.50	
Cat Came Back	7"	Capitol	CL14635	1956	£10	£5	
Dear Love	7"	Capitol	CL14742	1957	£5	£2	
First Date, First Kiss, First Love	7"	Capitol	CL14708	1957	£6	£2.50	
Honey	LP	Capitol	T988	1958	£20	£8	
I Can See It In Your Eyes	7"	Capitol	CL14915	1958	£4	£1.50	
Jenny Lou	7"	London	HL9132	1960	£5	£2	
Kathleen	7"	Capitol	CL14848	1958	£5	£2	
Mighty Lovable Man	7"	Capitol	CL14788	1957	£10	£5	
Sonny	LP	Capitol	T867	1957	£25	£10	
Southern Gentleman	LP	Capitol	T779	1957	£25	£10	
This Is Sonny James	LP	Capitol	T1178	1959	£20	£8	*US*
Twenty Feet Of Muddy Water	7"	Capitol	CL14664	1956	£8	£4	
Uh Uh Umm	7"	Capitol	CL14814	1957	£10	£5	
Yo-Yo	7"	Capitol	CL14991	1959	£6	£2.50	
You're The Only World I Know	7" EP	Capitol	EAP120654	1964	£10	£5	
Young Love	7"	Capitol	CL14683	1957	£8	£4	
Young Love	7" EP	Capitol	EAP1827	1957	£20	£10	
Young Love	LP	London	HAD8049	1963	£50	£25	

JAMES, TOMMY & THE SHONDELLS

Tommy James and the Shondells produced a kind of basic guitar pop whose closest British equivalent was perhaps the Troggs. Records like 'Hanky Panky', 'Mony Mony' and 'I Think We're Alone Now' were enormous American hits and have proved to be a considerable influence on the kind of straightforward teenage rock typified by the likes of the Ramones and the Runaways.

Title	Format	Label	Number	Year	Mint	VG	Notes
Best Of Tommy James And The Shondelles	LP	Roulette	SR42040	1970	£10	£4	*US*
Cellophane Symphony	LP	Roulette	R/SRLP3	1969	£12	£5	
Crimson And Clover	7"	Roulette	RO502	1968	£4	£1.50	
Crimson And Clover	LP	Roulette	R/SRLP2	1968	£15	£6	
Getting Together	LP	Roulette	SR25357	1968	£15	£6	*US*
Hanky Panky	7"	Roulette	RK7000	1966	£5	£2	
Hanky Panky	7" EP	Roulette	VREX65044	1966	£15	£7.50	*French, B side by Dave Baby Cortez*
Hanky Panky	LP	Roulette	(S)R25336	1966	£15	£6	*US*
I Think We're Alone Now	7"	Major Minor	MM511	1967	£4	£1.50	
I Think We're Alone Now	7" EP	Roulette	VREX65049	1967	£15	£7.50	*French*
I Think We're Alone Now	LP	Roulette	(S)R25353	1967	£15	£6	*US*
It's Only Love	7"	Pye	7N25398	1966	£4	£1.50	
It's Only Love	7" EP	Roulette	VREX65048	1966	£15	£7.50	*French*
It's Only Love	LP	Roulette	(S)R25344	1967	£15	£6	*US*
Mirage	7" EP	Roulette	VREX65051	1967	£15	£7.50	*French*
Mony Mony	7"	Major Minor	MM567	1968	£4	£1.50	
Mony Mony	LP	Roulette	R/SRLP1	1968	£15	£6	
Say I Am	7" EP	Roulette	VREX65045	1966	£15	£7.50	*French*
Something Special	LP	Major Minor	M/SMLP27	1968	£15	£6	
Wish It Were You	7"	Major Minor	MM558	1968	£4	£1.50	

JAMES BOYS

Title	Format	Label	Number	Year	Mint	VG	Notes
Mule	7"	Direction	583721	1968	£4	£1.50	

JAMES BROTHERS

Title	Format	Label	Number	Year	Mint	VG	Notes
Does It Have To Be Me	7"	Page One	POF088	1968	£4	£1.50	
I Forgot To Give You Love	7"	Page One	POF077	1968	£4	£1.50	

JAMES GANG

Title	Format	Label	Number	Year	Mint	VG	Notes
Miami	LP	Atco	QD36102	1974	£10	£4	*US quad*
Rides Again	LP	Probe	SPB6253	1970	£10	£4	
Stop	7"	Stateside	SS2173	1970	£6	£2.50	
Thirds	LP	Probe	SPB1038	1971	£10	£4	
Yer Album	LP	Stateside	SSL10295	1969	£12	£5	

JAMESON, BOBBY

Title	Format	Label	Number	Year	Mint	VG	Notes
All I Want Is My Baby	7"	Decca	F12032	1964	£12	£6	
Rum-Pum	7"	Brit	WI1001	1965	£8	£4	

JAMESON, BOBBY (2)

'Gotta Find My Roogalator' was arranged by Frank Zappa.

Title	Format	Label	Cat. No.	Year	Mint	VG	Notes
Gotta Find My Roogalator	7"	Penthouse	503	1962	**£150**	**£75**	*US*
I Wanna Love You	7"	London	HL9921	1964	**£15**	**£7.50**	

JAMESON, STEPHEN

Title	Format	Label	Cat. No.	Year	Mint	VG	Notes
Stephen Jameson	LP	Dawn	DNLS3044	1973	**£10**	**£4**	

JAMESON RAID

Title	Format	Label	Cat. No.	Year	Mint	VG	Notes
Hypnotist	7"	Blackbird	BRAID001	1980	**£30**	**£15**	
Seven Days Of Splendour	7"	GBH	GRC1	1979	**£12**	**£6**	

JAMIES

Title	Format	Label	Cat. No.	Year	Mint	VG	Notes
Summertime Summertime	7"	Columbia	DB4885	1962	**£10**	**£5**	
Summertime Summertime	7"	Fontana	H153	1958	**£20**	**£10**	

JAMIE'S AGENT ORANGE

Title	Format	Label	Cat. No.	Year	Mint	VG	Notes
Losing My Way	7"	Emma	EC002	1990	**£5**	**£2**	

JAMME

Title	Format	Label	Cat. No.	Year	Mint	VG	Notes
Jamme	LP	Stateside	SSL5024	1970	**£10**	**£4**	

JAMMER, JOE

Title	Format	Label	Cat. No.	Year	Mint	VG	Notes
Bad News	LP	Regal Zonophone	SRZA8515	1973	**£15**	**£6**	

JAN & ARNIE

Title	Format	Label	Cat. No.	Year	Mint	VG	Notes
Jennie Lee	7"	London	HL8653	1958	**£30**	**£15**	

JAN & DEAN

Title	Format	Label	Cat. No.	Year	Mint	VG	Notes
Baby Talk	7"	London	HLN8936	1959	**£15**	**£7.50**	
Batman	7"	Liberty	LIB55860	1966	**£8**	**£4**	
Clementine	7"	London	HLU9063	1960	**£10**	**£5**	
Command Performance	LP	Liberty	LRP3403/ LST7403	1965	**£20**	**£8**	*US*
Dead Man's Curve	7"	Liberty	LIB55672	1964	**£5**	**£2**	
Dead Man's Curve/New Girl In School	LP	Liberty	LBY1220	1964	**£20**	**£8**	
Drag City	7"	Liberty	LIB55641	1964	**£4**	**£1.50**	
Drag City	7" EP	Liberty	LEP2155	1964	**£15**	**£7.50**	*French*
Drag City	LP	Liberty	LRP3339/ LST7339	1963	**£20**	**£8**	*US*
Filet Of Soul	LP	Liberty	LBY1339	1966	**£15**	**£6**	
Folk And Roll	LP	Liberty	LBY1304	1965	**£15**	**£6**	
From All Over The World	7"	Liberty	LIB55766	1965	**£5**	**£2**	
Golden Hits	LP	Liberty	LBY1279	1962	**£15**	**£6**	
Golden Hits	LP	Liberty	LBL/LBS83016	1967	**£10**	**£4**	
Golden Hits Vol. 2	LP	Liberty	LRP3417/ LST7417	1965	**£12**	**£5**	*US*
Golden Hits Vol. 3	LP	Liberty	LRP3460/ LST7460	1966	**£12**	**£5**	*US*
Heart And Soul	7"	London	HLH9395	1961	**£10**	**£5**	
Honolulu Lulu	7"	Liberty	LIB55613	1963	**£5**	**£2**	
I Found A Girl	7"	Liberty	LIB55833	1965	**£5**	**£2**	
Jan & Dean	LP	Dore	101	1960	**£75**	**£37.50**	*US with photo*
Linda	7"	Liberty	LIB55531	1963	**£4**	**£1.50**	
Little Old Lady From Pasadena	7"	Liberty	LIB55704	1964	**£5**	**£2**	
Little Old Lady From Pasadena	7" EP	Liberty	LEP2189	1964	**£15**	**£7.50**	*French*
Little Old Lady From Pasadena	LP	Liberty	LRP3377/ LST7377	1964	**£20**	**£8**	*US*
Meet Batman	LP	Liberty	LBY1309	1966	**£20**	**£8**	
New Girl In School	7"	Liberty	LIB55923	1966	**£5**	**£2**	
Norwegian Wood	7"	Liberty	LIB10225	1966	**£10**	**£5**	
Pop Symphony No. 1	LP	Liberty	LRP3414/ LST7414	1965	**£20**	**£8**	*US*
Popsicle	7"	Liberty	LIB10244	1966	**£6**	**£2.50**	
Popsicle	LP	Liberty	LRP3458/ LST7458	1966	**£20**	**£8**	*US*
Remember Jan & Dean	7" EP	United Artists	REM402	1976	**£8**	**£4**	
Ride The Wild Surf	7"	Liberty	LIB55724	1964	**£5**	**£2**	
Ride The Wild Surf	LP	Liberty	LBY1229	1964	**£20**	**£8**	
Save For A Rainy Day	LP	J&D	101	1967	**£75**	**£37.50**	*US*
Sidewalk Surfin'	7"	Liberty	LIB55727	1965	**£5**	**£2**	
Sunday Kind Of Love	7"	Liberty	LIB55397	1962	**£5**	**£2**	
Surf 'n' Drag Hits	7" EP	Liberty	LEP2213	1965	**£20**	**£10**	
Surf City	7"	Liberty	LIB55580	1963	**£4**	**£1.50**	
Surf City	7" EP	Liberty	LEP2112	1963	**£15**	**£7.50**	*French*
Surf City	LP	Liberty	LBY1163	1963	**£20**	**£8**	
Take Linda Surfing	LP	Liberty	LRP3294/ LST7294	1963	**£25**	**£10**	*US, with Beach Boys*
Tennessee	7"	Liberty	LIB10252	1966	**£8**	**£4**	
There's A Girl	7"	London	HLU8990	1959	**£15**	**£7.50**	
Titanic Twosome	7" EP	Liberty	LEP2258	1966	**£20**	**£10**	
Yellow Balloon	7"	CBS	202630	1967	**£6**	**£2.50**	
You Really Know How To Hurt A Guy	7"	Liberty	LIB55792	1964	**£5**	**£2**	

JAN & KELLY

Title	Format	Label	Number	Year	Price	Price	Notes
And Then He Kicked Me	7"	Philips	BF1323	1964	£4	£1.50	
Time For A Laugh	7" EP	Philips	BE12536	1963	£6	£2.50	

JAN & KJELD

Title	Format	Label	Number	Year	Price	Price	Notes
Goldener Lowe Fur	LP	Ariola	70586IT	1964	£25	£10	*German*
Jan Und Kjeld	LP	Ariola	31023	1964	£20	£8	*German*
Kids From Copenhagen	LP	Ember	EMB3312	1960	£15	£6	
Les Banjo Boys A Paris	10" LP	Vogue	KV26	1960	£20	£8	*French*
With A Banjo On My Knee	LP	Ariola	31231	1965	£20	£8	*German*

JAN & LORRAINE

Title	Format	Label	Number	Year	Price	Price	Notes
Gypsy People	LP	ABC	ABCS691	1969	£20	£8	*US*

JAN DUKES DE GREY

Title	Format	Label	Number	Year	Price	Price	Notes
Mice & Rats In The Loft	LP	Transatlantic	TRA234	1971	£50	£25	
Sorcerers	LP	Nova	SDN8	1970	£25	£10	

JANAWAY, BRUCE

Title	Format	Label	Number	Year	Price	Price	Notes
Puritanical Odes	LP	Deep Range	SRTCUS216	1978	£30	£15	

JANE

Title	Format	Label	Number	Year	Price	Price	Notes
Fire, Water, Earth And Air	LP	Brain	1084	1975	£20	£8	*German*
Here We Are	LP	Brain	1032	1973	£20	£8	*German*
Lady	LP	Brain	1066	1975	£20	£8	*German*
Three	LP	Brain	1048	1974	£20	£8	*German*
Together	LP	Brain	1002	1972	£25	£10	*German*

JANES, PETER

Title	Format	Label	Number	Year	Price	Price	Notes
Do You Believe	7"	CBS	3299	1968	£5	£2	
Emperors And Armies	7"	CBS	3004	1967	£4	£1.50	*picture sleeve*

JANE'S ADDICTION

Title	Format	Label	Number	Year	Price	Price	Notes
Been Caught Stealing	CD-s	WEA	W0011CD	1991	£5	£2	
Classic Girl	CD-s	WEA	W0031CD	1991	£5	£2	
Three Days	CD-s	WEA	W9584CD	1990	£5	£2	

JANIE

Title	Format	Label	Number	Year	Price	Price	Notes
You Better Not Do That	7"	Capitol	CL15180	1961	£4	£1.50	

JANIS, CONRAD

Title	Format	Label	Number	Year	Price	Price	Notes
Dixieland Jam Session	LP	London	LTZU15095	1957	£12	£5	

JANIS, JOHNNY

Title	Format	Label	Number	Year	Price	Price	Notes
Better To Love You	7"	London	HLU8650	1958	£8	£4	
For The First Time	LP	ABC-Paramount	LP140	1957	£30	£15	*US*
Once In A Blue Moon	LP	London	HAU8270	1966	£15	£6	

JANSCH, BERT

With Davy Graham maintaining a deliberately low profile, it was left to Bert Jansch to define the sound and style of folk guitar playing in the sixties. His serviceable folk-singer's voice gives added interest to his records, but the guitar is the real focus – beginning with a faultless version of Graham's difficult 'Angie' and moving onwards from there.

Title	Format	Label	Number	Year	Price	Price	Notes
Avocet	LP	Charisma	CLASS6	1979	£10	£4	
Bert Jansch	7" EP	Transatlantic	TRAEP145	1966	£15	£7.50	
Bert Jansch	LP	Transatlantic	TRA125	1965	£15	£6	
Birthday Blues	LP	Transatlantic	TRA179	1968	£15	£6	
Black Birds Of Brittany	7"	Streetsong	1	1978	£5	£2	*picture sleeve, with Richard Harvey*
From The Outside	LP	Konexion	KOMA788006	1985	£10	£4	
Heartbreak	LP	Logo	LOGO1035	1982	£10	£4	
It Don't Bother Me	LP	Transatlantic	TRA132	1965	£15	£6	
Jack Orion	LP	Transatlantic	TRA143	1966	£15	£6	
L.A. Turnaround	LP	Charisma	CAS1090	1974	£10	£4	
Life Depends On Love	7"	Transatlantic	BIG102	1968	£5	£2	
Live At La Foret	LP	Columbia	YX7273AK	1980	£15	£6	*Japanese*
Lucky Thirteen	LP	Vanguard	VSD79212	1966	£15	£6	*US*
Moonshine	LP	Reprise	K44225	1973	£10	£4	
Nicola	LP	Transatlantic	TRA157	1967	£15	£6	
Rare Conundrum	LP	Charisma	CAS1127	1977	£10	£4	
Rosemary Lane	LP	Transatlantic	TRA235	1971	£12	£5	
Thirteen Down	LP	Sonet	SNKF162	1980	£10	£4	

JANSCH, BERT & JOHN RENBOURN

Title	Format	Label	Number	Year	Price	Price	Notes
Bert & John	LP	Transatlantic	TRA144	1966	£15	£6	
Stepping Stones	LP	Vanguard	VSD6506	1969	£12	£5	*US (As 'Bert & John' with 2 extra tracks)*

JANUS

Title	Format	Label	Number	Year	Price	Price	Notes
Gravedigger	LP	Harvest	IC06229433	1972	£75	£37.50	*German*

JAPAN

The pretty-boy posing of Japan was an unlikely environment for intelligent, questing music to be produced, and yet with each record release, the group became more and more of a vital force. Peaking with the refreshingly innovative *Ghosts*, it was perhaps inevitable that David Sylvian would then wish to continue the quest on his own.

Don't Rain On My Parade	7"	Ariola	AHA510	1978	£10	£5	
Gentlemen Take Polaroids	CD-s	Virgin	CDT32	1988	£6	£2.50	3" single
Ghosts	7"	Virgin	VSY472	1982	£4	£1.50	picture disc
Ghosts	CD-s	Virgin	CDT11	1988	£6	£2.50	3" single
I Second That Emotion	7"	Ariola	AHA559	1980	£5	£2	red vinyl
Interview Album	LP	Ariola		1979	£12	£5	US promo
Life In Tokyo	12"	Ariola	AHAD540	1979	£10	£5	red vinyl
Life In Tokyo	7"	Ariola	AHA540	1979	£5	£2	red vinyl
Sometimes I Feel So Low	7"	Ariola	AHA529	1978	£5	£2	
Sometimes I Feel So Low	7"	Ariola	AHA529	1978	£8	£4	blue vinyl
Unconventional	7"	Ariola	AHA525	1978	£12	£6	picture sleeve

JARMAN, JOSEPH

As If It Were Seasons	LP	Delmark	DS417	1969	£12	£5	
Song For	LP	Delmark	DL410/DS9410	1967	£12	£5	
Together Alone	LP	Delmark	DS428	1974	£12	£5	with Anthony Braxton

JARMELS

Little Bit Of Soap	7"	Top Rank	JAR580	1961	£25	£12.50	
She Loves To Dance	7"	Top Rank	JAR560	1961	£10	£5	

JARR, COOK E.

Pledging My Love	LP	RCA	LSP4159	1969	£15	£6	US

JARRE, JEAN-MICHEL

There is no rarer record than Jean-Michel Jarre's *Music For Supermarkets* – the LP was issued in a limited edition of just one copy and auctioned for charity in 1983, when it fetched a sum of the order of £10,000. Meanwhile, there are a couple of other rare Jarre albums which the keen collector does stand a reasonable chance of obtaining, although at a considerable price none the less, for the early soundtracks have never had a UK issue and are scarce even in their countries of origin.

Calypso	CD-s	Polydor	PZCD84	1990	£20	£10	
Calypso	12"	Polydor	PZ84	1990	£8	£4	
Cartolina	7"	Labrador	LA4050	1973	£30	£15	French
Chronologie 4	7"	Dreyfus	JMJ0693	1993	£20	£10	French
Deserted Palace	LP	Sam Fox	SF1029	1972	£500	£330	US promo
Equinoxe 4	7"	Polydor	2001896	1979	£5	£2	
Equinoxe 4 (remix)	12"	Polydor	JM1	1979	£12	£6	promo
Equinoxe 5	7"	Polydor	POSP20	1978	£6	£2.50	etched autograph
Equinoxe 7 (live)	7"	Polydor	2001968	1980	£8	£4	
Hong Kong	CD-s	Dreyfus	FDM37521	1994	£50	£25	French
Hypnose	7"	Motors	MT4043	1973	£75	£37.50	French
La Cage	7"	Pathe	C00611739	1971	£300	£180	French, best auctioned
Les Granges Brûlées	7"	Eden Roc	ER62002	1973	£60	£30	French
Les Granges Brûlées	LP	Eden Roc	ER62502	1973	£200	£100	French
Les Granges Brûlées	LP	Gamma	GS177	1973	£200	£100	French
London Kid	CD-s	Polydor	PZCD32	1988	£20	£10	
Magnetic Fields 2	7"	Polydor	POSP292	1981	£4	£1.50	
Magnetic Fields 4 (remix)	7"	Polydor	POSP363	1981	£8	£4	
Orient Express	12"	Polydor	POSPX430DJ	1982	£25	£12.50	promo
Orient Express	7"	Polydor	POSP430	1982	£6	£2.50	
Oxygène	CD	Polydor	C8813	1988	£25	£10	HMV box set
Oxygène	CD	Mobile Fidelity	UDCD613	1994	£15	£6	US audiophile
Oxygène	LP	Polydor	C8813	1988	£20	£8	HMV box set
Oxygène 4	CD-s	Polydor	PZCD55	1989	£15	£7.50	
Oxygène/Equinox	LP	Polydor	2683077	1980	£15	£6	double
Pop Corn	7"	Motors	MT4028	1971	£75	£37.50	French
Rendezvous 4 (remix)	12"	Polydor	POSPX788	1986	£20	£10	2 different sleeves
Revolutions	12"	Polydor	PZ25	1988	£6	£2.50	
Revolutions	CD-s	Polydor	PZCD25	1988	£20	£10	
Tenth Anniversary	CD	Polydor	8337372	1987	£40	£20	boxed set
Une Alarme Qui Swingue	7"	Dreyfus	JMJ1001	1991	£30	£15	French
Zig Zag	7"	Motors	MT4032	1973	£20	£10	French
Zoolook (remix)	12"	Polydor	POSPX718	1984	£15	£7.50	
Zoolookologie	7"	Polydor	POSP740	1985	£6	£2.50	
Zoolookologie (remix)	12"	Polydor	POSPX740	1985	£15	£7.50	
Zoolookologie (remix)	7"	Polydor	POSPG740	1985	£12	£6	double

JARRE, MAURICE

Professionals	LP	RCA	RD/SF7876	1967	£15	£6	
Villa Rides	LP	Dot	(S)LPD515	1968	£10	£4	

JARRETT, KEITH

Arbour Zena	LP	ECM	ECM1070ST	1975	£12	£5	
Backhand	LP	Impulse	AS9305	1975	£15	£6	US
Belonging	LP	ECM	ECM1050ST	1974	£12	£5	
Birth	LP	Atlantic	SD1612	197–	£15	£6	US
Byablue	LP	Impulse	AS9331	1976	£12	£5	US
Death And The Flower	LP	Impulse	IMPL8006	1975	£15	£6	
El Juicio	LP	Atlantic	SD1673	1975	£15	£6	US
Facing You	LP	ECM	ECM1017ST	1971	£12	£5	
Fort Yawuh	LP	Impulse	AS9240	1973	£15	£6	US
Hymns/Spheres	LP	ECM	ECM1086/7ST	1976	£15	£6	double
In The Light	LP	ECM	ECM1033/4ST	1973	£15	£6	double
Köln Concert	LP	ECM	ECM1064/5ST	1975	£15	£6	double

Luminessence	LP	ECM	ECM1049ST	1974	**£12**	**£5**	
Mourning Of A Star	LP	Atlantic	K40309	1972	**£15**	**£6**	
Mysteries	LP	Impulse	AS9315	1976	**£12**	**£5**	*US*
Ruta And Daitya	LP	ECM	ECM1021ST	1972	**£12**	**£5**	*with Jack DeJohnette*
Shades	LP	Impulse	ASD9322	1976	**£12**	**£5**	*US*
Solo Concerts – Bremen/Lausanne	LP	ECM	ECM1035/6/7ST	1973	**£25**	**£10**	*triple*
Staircase	LP	ECM	ECM1090/1ST	1976	**£15**	**£6**	*double*
Sun Bear Concerts	LP	ECM	ECM1100ST	1976	**£100**	**£50**	*10 LP set*
Survivors' Suite	LP	ECM	ECM1085ST	1976	**£10**	**£4**	
Treasure Island	LP	Impulse	AS9274	1974	**£15**	**£6**	*US*

JARVIS STREET REVUE

Mr Oil Man	LP	Columbia	90020	1970	**£125**	**£62.50**	*Canadian*

JASMIN T

Some Other Guy	7"	Tangerine	DP0013	1969	**£5**	**£2**	

JASMINE MINKS

Think	7"	Creation	CRE004	1984	**£6**	**£2.50**	
Where The Traffic Goes	7"	Creation	CRE008	1984	**£4**	**£1.50**	

JASON CREST

Black Mass	7"	Philips	BF1809	1969	**£100**	**£50**	
Juliano The Bull	7"	Philips	BF1650	1968	**£25**	**£12.50**	
Lemon Tree	7"	Philips	BF1687	1968	**£30**	**£15**	
Turquoise Tandem Cycle	7"	Philips	BF1633	1968	**£50**	**£25**	*export picture sleeve*
Turquoise Tandem Cycle	7"	Philips	BF1633	1968	**£30**	**£15**	
Waterloo Road	7"	Philips	BF1752	1969	**£25**	**£12.50**	

JASON'S GENERATION

It's Up To You	7"	Polydor	56042	1966	**£40**	**£20**	

JASPAR, BOBBY

Bobby Jaspar	LP	London	LTZU15128	1958	**£25**	**£10**	
Bobby Jaspar And His All Stars	LP	Felsted	PDL85017	1956	**£25**	**£10**	
New Jazz Group	10" LP	Vogue	LDE167	1956	**£25**	**£10**	
New Jazz Vol. 1	10" LP	Vogue	LDE125	1955	**£40**	**£20**	
New Sounds From Europe Vol. 4	10" LP	Vogue	LDE041	1954	**£40**	**£20**	

JASPER

Liberation	LP	Spark	SRLP103	1969	**£250**	**£150**	

JASPER WRATH

Jasper Wrath	LP	Sunflower	SNF5003	1971	**£60**	**£30**	*US*

JAVALINS

For Twen	LP	Columbia	SMC83880	1984	**£25**	**£10**	*German*

JAWBONE

Gotta Go	7"	B&C	CB190	1972	**£4**	**£1.50**	
How's Ya Pa	7"	Carnaby	CNS4007	1970	**£6**	**£2.50**	
Jawbone	LP	Carnaby	CNLS6004	1970	**£60**	**£30**	
Way Way Down	7"	Carnaby	CNS4020	1971	**£6**	**£2.50**	

JAXON, BOB

Ali Baba	7"	London	HL8156	1955	**£20**	**£10**	
Beach Party	7"	RCA	RCA1019	1957	**£50**	**£25**	

JAY

I Rise, I Fall	7"	Coral	Q72471	1964	**£10**	**£5**	

JAY, DAVID & RENE HALKETT

Nothing	7"	4AD	AD112	1981	**£5**	**£2**	*with lyric sheet*

JAY, LAURIE COMBO

Song Called Soul	7"	Decca	F12083	1965	**£15**	**£7.50**	
Teenage Idol	7"	HMV	POP1234	1963	**£5**	**£2**	

JAY, PETER & THE BLUEMEN

Just Too Late	7"	Triumph	RGM1000	1960	**£20**	**£10**	
Paradise Garden	7"	Pye	7N15290	1960	**£25**	**£12.50**	

JAY, PETER & THE JAYWALKERS

Before The Beginning	7"	Piccadilly	7N35325	1966	**£6**	**£2.50**	
Can Can '62	7"	Decca	F11531	1962	**£4**	**£1.50**	
Parade Of Tin Soldiers	7"	Decca	F11757	1963	**£4**	**£1.50**	
Parchman Farm	7"	Piccadilly	7N35220	1965	**£8**	**£4**	
Poet And Peasant	7"	Decca	F11659	1963	**£4**	**£1.50**	
Tonight You're Gonna Fall	7"	Piccadilly	7N35212	1964	**£4**	**£1.50**	
Totem Pole	7"	Decca	F11593	1963	**£4**	**£1.50**	
Where Did Our Love Go	7"	Piccadilly	7N35199	1964	**£5**	**£2**	
You Girl	7"	Decca	F11840	1964	**£4**	**£1.50**	

JAY & JOYA

I'll Be Lonely	7"	Trojan	TR633	1968	**£5**	**£2**	*Supersonics B side*

JAY & THE AMERICANS

At The Café Wha	LP	United Artists	UAL3300/ UAS6300	1963	£20	£8	US
Blockbusters	LP	United Artists	UAL3417/ UAS6417	1965	£20	£8	US
Cara Mia	7"	United Artists	UP1094	1965	£4	£1.50	
Come A Little Bit Closer	7" EP	United Artists	UEP1003	1965	£25	£12.50	
Come A Little Bit Closer	7" EP	United Artists	36054	1964	£15	£7.50	French
Come A Little Bit Closer	LP	United Artists	UAL3407/ UAS6407	1964	£20	£8	US
Come A Little Closer	7"	United Artists	UP1069	1964	£4	£1.50	
Come Dance With Me	7"	United Artists	UP1039	1964	£4	£1.50	
Crying	7"	United Artists	UP1132	1966	£4	£1.50	
En Français	7" EP	United Artists	36102	1966	£20	£10	French
Got Hung Up Along The Way	7"	United Artists	UP1191	1967	£25	£12.50	
Greatest Hits	LP	United Artists	UAL3453/ UAS6453	1965	£15	£6	US
Greatest Hits Vol. 2	LP	United Artists	UAL3555/ UAS6555	1966	£15	£6	US
Jay And The Americans	LP	United Artists	(S)ULP1117	1966	£20	£8	
Kansas City	7" EP	United Artists	36027	1963	£15	£7.50	French
Let's Lock The Door	7"	United Artists	UP1075	1965	£4	£1.50	
Livin' Above Your Head	LP	United Artists	(S)ULP1150	1967	£20	£8	
Living Above Your Head	7"	United Artists	UP1142	1966	£12	£6	
Living With Jay & The Americans	7" EP	United Artists	UEP1017	1966	£25	£12.50	
Raining In My Sunshine	7"	United Artists	UP1162	1966	£4	£1.50	
Sand Of Time	LP	United Artists	UAS6671	1969	£15	£6	US
She Cried	7"	HMV	POP1009	1962	£8	£4	
She Cried	LP	United Artists	UAL3222/ UAS6222	1962	£20	£8	US
Some Enchanted Evening	7"	United Artists	UP1108	1965	£4	£1.50	
Some Enchanted Evening	7" EP	United Artists	36065	1965	£15	£7.50	French
Strangers Tomorrow	7"	United Artists	UP1018	1963	£4	£1.50	
Sunday And Me	7"	United Artists	UP1119	1966	£4	£1.50	
Sunday And Me	7" EP	United Artists	36074	1965	£15	£7.50	French
Sunday And Me	LP	United Artists	(S)ULP1128	1966	£20	£8	
Think Of The Good Times	7"	United Artists	UP1088	1965	£4	£1.50	
This Is It	7"	United Artists	UP1002	1964	£4	£1.50	
Tonight	7" EP	United Artists	36018	1962	£15	£7.50	French
Try Some Of This	LP	United Artists	(S)ULP1164	1967	£20	£8	
Wax Museum Vol. 1	LP	United Artists	UAS6719	1970	£12	£5	US
Wax Museum Vol. 2	LP	United Artists	UAS6751	1970	£12	£5	US
Why Can't You Bring Me Home	7"	United Artists	UP1129	1966	£4	£1.50	

JAY & THE TECHNIQUES

Apples, Peaches, Pumpkin Pie	7"	Philips	BF1597	1967	£5	£2	
Apples, Peaches, Pumpkin Pie	LP	Philips	(S)BL7834	1967	£10	£4	
Baby Make Your Own Sweet Music	7"	Mercury	MF1034	1968	£5	£2	
Keep The Ball Rolling	7"	Philips	BF1618	1967	£4	£1.50	
Strawberry Shortcake	7"	Philips	BF1644	1968	£4	£1.50	

JAY BEE FOUR

Lucille	7" EP	Barclay	70751	1965	£8	£4	French

JAY BOYS

Dog	7"	Harry J	HJ6602	1970	£4	£1.50	
Jack The Ripper	7"	Harry J	HJ6607	1970	£4	£1.50	
Jay Moon Walk	7"	Harry J	HJ6609	1970	£4	£1.50	
Je T'aime	7"	Harry J	HJ6610	1970	£4	£1.50	
Splendour Splash	7"	Trojan	TR665	1969	£5	£2	Trevor Shield B side

JAY JAYS

Jay Jays	LP	Philips	625819	1966	£150	£75	Dutch

JAYBIRDS

Although these singles conform to the Embassy label's policy of issuing sound-alike versions of current chart hits, the fact that the Jaybirds later became Ten Years After gives them a modest collectability. (It should be noted, however, that Alvin Lee has denied his involvement with the Embassy group.)

All Day And All Of The Night	7"	Embassy	WB663	1964	£5	£2	

JAYBIRDS (2)

Somebody Help Me	7"	Sue	WI4013	1966	£12	£6	

JAYE, JERRY

My Girl Josephine	7"	London	HLU10128	1967	£20	£10	

JAYE SISTERS

Sure Fire Love	7"	London	HLT9011	1959	£30	£15	

JAYHAWKS

Stranded In The Jungle	7"	Parlophone	R4228	1956	£300	£180	best auctioned

JAYNETTS

Sally Go Round The Roses	7"	Stateside	SS227	1963	£5	£2	
Sally Go Round The Roses	LP	Tuff	LP13	1963	£60	£30	US

JAYS

Shock A Boom	7"	Parlophone	R4764	1963	**£4**	**£1.50**	

JAZZ AT THE PHILHARMONIC

1955 Vol. 1	LP	Columbia	33CX10078	1957	**£15**	**£6**	
1955 Vol. 2	LP	Columbia	33CX10079	1957	**£15**	**£6**	
Jam Concert No. 1	LP	Columbia	33CX10059	1956	**£15**	**£6**	
Jam Session	LP	Columbia	33CX10030	1956	**£15**	**£6**	
Jam Session	LP	Emarcy	EJL103	1956	**£15**	**£6**	
Jam Session Group	LP	Columbia	33CX10043	1956	**£15**	**£6**	
Jam Session No. 2	LP	Columbia	33CX10021	1956	**£15**	**£6**	
Jam Session No. 5	LP	Columbia	33CX10067	1957	**£15**	**£6**	
Midnight Jazz At Carnegie Hall	LP	Columbia	33CX10020	1956	**£20**	**£8**	
New Vol. 1	LP	Columbia	33CX10032	1956	**£15**	**£6**	
New Vol. 2	LP	Columbia	33CX10033	1956	**£15**	**£6**	
New Vol. 3	LP	Columbia	33CX10034	1956	**£15**	**£6**	
New Vol. 4	LP	Columbia	33CX10035	1956	**£15**	**£6**	
New Vol. 5	LP	Columbia	33CX10036	1956	**£15**	**£6**	
New Vol. 7	LP	Columbia	33CX10037	1956	**£15**	**£6**	
Volume 1	LP	Columbia	33CX10009	1955	**£20**	**£8**	
Volume 2	LP	Columbia	33CX10010	1955	**£20**	**£8**	
Volume 3	LP	Columbia	33CX10011	1955	**£20**	**£8**	

JAZZ BUTCHER

Christmas With The Pygmies	7"	Glass	HMMM001	1986	**£6**	**£2.50**	*promo*
Girl Go	CD-s	Creation	CRE77CD	1990	**£5**	**£2**	

JAZZ CITY WORKSHOP

Jazz City Workshop	LP	London	LTZN15037	1957	**£12**	**£5**	

JAZZ COURIERS

Couriers Of Jazz	LP	London	LTZL15188	1960	**£100**	**£50**	
In Concert	LP	Tempo	TAP22	1958	**£100**	**£50**	
In Concert	LP	MFP	MFP1072	1966	**£15**	**£6**	
Jazz Couriers	7" EP	Tempo	EXA75	1957	**£20**	**£10**	
Jazz Couriers	7" EP	Tempo	EXA87	1958	**£20**	**£10**	
Jazz Couriers	LP	Tempo	TAP15	1957	**£200**	**£100**	
Last Word	LP	Tempo	TAP26	1959	**£200**	**£100**	

JAZZ CRUSADERS

Thing	LP	Fontana	688149ZL	1966	**£12**	**£5**	

JAZZ GIANTS

Jazz Giants	10" LP	Emarcy	EJT751	1957	**£15**	**£6**	

JAZZ HIP TRIO

Jazz In Relief	LP	Major Minor	MMLP8	1967	**£40**	**£20**	

JAZZ IN A STABLE GROUP

Jazz In A Stable	LP	Esquire	32018	1956	**£15**	**£6**	

JAZZ MESSAGE GROUP

Jazz Message	LP	London	LTZC15028	1957	**£12**	**£5**	

JAZZ MODES

Jazz Modes	LP	London	LTZK15203/ SAHK6117	1961	**£25**	**£10**	
Most Happy Fella	LP	London	LTZK15191	1960	**£25**	**£10**	

JAZZ ROCK EXPERIENCE

Jazz Rock Experience	LP	Nova	SDN19	1970	**£15**	**£6**	

JAZZ STUDIO FOUR GROUP

Jazz Studio Four	LP	Brunswick	LAT8098	1956	**£12**	**£5**	

JAZZ TODAY UNIT

Jam Session	10" LP	Polygon	JTL1	1955	**£12**	**£5**	

JAZZ WAVE LTD

On Tour	LP	Blue Note	BST89905	1970	**£10**	**£4**	

JBs

Breakin' Bread	LP	Polydor	2391161	1975	**£25**	**£10**	
Damn Right I Am Somebody	LP	Polydor	2391125	1974	**£30**	**£15**	
Doing It To Death	7"	Polydor	2066322	1973	**£4**	**£1.50**	
Doing It To Death	LP	Polydor	2391087	1974	**£40**	**£20**	
Food For Thought	LP	Polydor	2391034	1972	**£30**	**£15**	
Gimme Some More	7"	Mojo	2093007	1974	**£5**	**£2**	
Givin' Up Food For Funk	7"	Mojo	2093021	1974	**£5**	**£2**	
Giving Up Food For Funk	LP	Polydor	2391204	1976	**£30**	**£15**	
Grunt	7"	Mojo	2027002	1971	**£5**	**£2**	
Hot Pants Road	7"	Mojo	2093016	1974	**£5**	**£2**	
Hustle With Speed	LP	Polydor	2391194	1975	**£25**	**£10**	
JB Shout	7"	Mojo	2093025	1974	**£4**	**£1.50**	
Pass The Peas	LP	Polydor	2918004	1972	**£30**	**£15**	
These Are The JB's	7"	Polydor	2001115	1971	**£5**	**£2**	

JEAN, CATHY & THE ROOMATES

Title	Format	Label	Cat. No.	Year			Notes
Please Love Me	7"	Parlophone	R4764	1961	**£30**	**£15**	

JEAN, EARL

Title	Format	Label	Cat. No.	Year			Notes
I'm Into Something Good	7"	Colpix	PX729	1964	**£10**	**£5**	
Randy	7"	Colpix	PX748	1964	**£10**	**£5**	

JEAN, LANA

Title	Format	Label	Cat. No.	Year			Notes
It Hurts To be Sixteen	7"	Pye	7N25214	1963	**£8**	**£4**	

JEAN & THE STATESIDES

Title	Format	Label	Cat. No.	Year			Notes
Mama Didn't Lie	7"	Columbia	DB7651	1965	**£6**	**£2.50**	
Putty In Your Hands	7"	Columbia	DB7287	1964	**£6**	**£2.50**	
You Won't Forget Me	7"	Columbia	DB7439	1965	**£6**	**£2.50**	

JEANNIE

Title	Format	Label	Cat. No.	Year			Notes
Don't Lie To Me	7"	Piccadilly	7N35147	1963	**£5**	**£2**	
I Love Him	7"	Parlophone	R5343	1965	**£4**	**£1.50**	
I Want You	7"	Piccadilly	7N35164	1964	**£5**	**£2**	

JEANS, AUDREY

Title	Format	Label	Cat. No.	Year			Notes
Ticky Ticky Tick	7"	Decca	F10768	1956	**£6**	**£2.50**	

JEDDAH

Title	Format	Label	Cat. No.	Year			Notes
Eleanor Rigby	7"	Death	RIP2001	1983	**£12**	**£6**	*with poster, no picture sleeve*

JEEPS

Title	Format	Label	Cat. No.	Year			Notes
He Saw Eesaw	7"	Strike	JH308	1966	**£4**	**£1.50**	

JEFFERSON

Title	Format	Label	Cat. No.	Year			Notes
Colour Of My Love	LP	Pye	NSPL18316	1969	**£10**	**£4**	

JEFFERSON, BLIND LEMON

Title	Format	Label	Cat. No.	Year			Notes
Blind Lemon	LP	Riverside	126		**£20**	**£8**	*US*
Blind Lemon Jefferson	10" LP	Poydras	99	195–	**£25**	**£10**	
Blind Lemon Jefferson & Rambling Thomas	LP	Heritage	HLP1007	195–	**£50**	**£25**	
Blind Lemon Jefferson/Willard 'Ramblin' Thomas	LP	Collector's Classics	CC5	196–	**£12**	**£5**	
Folk Blues	10" LP	London	AL3508	1953	**£30**	**£15**	
Folk Blues Classics	LP	Riverside	125		**£20**	**£8**	*US*
Gone Dead On You Blues	78	Jazz Collecor	L126	1954	**£10**	**£5**	
Gone Dead On You Blues	78	Tempo	R54	1952	**£10**	**£5**	
Immortal	LP	CBS	63738	1969	**£12**	**£5**	
Jack O'Diamonds Blues	78	Jazz Collecor	L103	1953	**£10**	**£5**	
Lock Step Blues	78	Tempo	R39	1950	**£10**	**£5**	
Male Blues Vol. 5	7" EP	Collector	JEL8	1960	**£8**	**£4**	*with Buddy Boy Hawkins*
Male Blues Vol. 8	7" EP	Collector	JEL24	1964	**£8**	**£4**	*with Leadbelly*
Masters Of The Blues Vol. 1	LP	Collector's Classics	CC22	196–	**£12**	**£5**	
Penitentiary Blues	10" LP	London	AL3546	1955	**£30**	**£15**	
Shuckin' Sugar Blues	78	Jazz Collecor	L91	1953	**£10**	**£5**	
Shuckin' Sugar Blues	78	Tempo	R46	1951	**£10**	**£5**	
Sings The Blues	10" LP	London	AL3564	1957	**£30**	**£15**	
Weary Dog Blues	78	Tempo	R38	1950	**£10**	**£5**	

JEFFERSON, BLIND LEMON & ED BELL

Title	Format	Label	Cat. No.	Year			Notes
Male Blues Vol. 7	7" EP	Collector	JEL13	1961	**£6**	**£2.50**	

JEFFERSON, EDDIE

Title	Format	Label	Cat. No.	Year			Notes
Some Other Time	7"	Stateside	SS591	1967	**£5**	**£2**	

JEFFERSON, GEORGE PAUL

Title	Format	Label	Cat. No.	Year			Notes
Looking For My Mind	7"	Fontana	TF923	1968	**£8**	**£4**	

JEFFERSON AIRPLANE

Jefferson Airplane were the premier Californian group, and the records they made in the sixties are the most impressive and essential of the West Coast genre – a fact that the inferior records made by various later editions of Jefferson Airplane and Jefferson Starship should never be allowed to obscure. The group was not well served by RCA in Britain, however. The UK version of *Surrealistic Pillow* is actually a compilation drawn from the first two American LPs and manages to leave out two of the most powerful and essential tracks – 'White Rabbit' and 'Plastic Fantastic Lover'. Original copies of the first US album, *Takes Off*, included the B side of the group's debut American single, 'Runnin' Round This World', but this was withdrawn due to a drug reference.

Title	Format	Label	Cat. No.	Year			Notes
After Bathing At Baxters	LP	RCA	RD/SF7926	1967	**£20**	**£8**	*black label*
Ballad Of You And Me And Pooneil	7"	RCA	RCA1647	1967	**£4**	**£1.50**	
Bless Its Pointed Little Head	LP	RCA	RD/SF8019	1969	**£15**	**£6**	
Bless Its Pointed Little Head	LP	RCA		1969	**£30**	**£15**	*US interview promo*
Crown Of Creation	CD	Mobile Fidelity	UDCD523	1989	**£15**	**£6**	*US audiophile*
Crown Of Creation	LP	RCA	RD/SF7976	1968	**£15**	**£6**	*black label*
Greasy Heart	7"	RCA	RCA1711	1968	**£4**	**£1.50**	
If You Feel Like China Breaking	7"	RCA	RCA1736	1968	**£4**	**£1.50**	
Jefferson Airplane Love You	CD	RCA	RDJ661132	1992	**£20**	**£8**	*US promo sampler*
Long John Silver	LP	Grunt	FTR1007	1972	**£10**	**£4**	*cigar box cover*
Somebody To Love	7"	RCA	RCA1594	1967	**£4**	**£1.50**	
Surrealistic Pillow	7" EP	RCA	86560	1967	**£25**	**£12.50**	*French*

Surrealistic Pillow	LP	RCA	LPM/LSP3766	1967	**£25**	**£10**	*US*
Surrealistic Pillow	LP	RCA	RD/SF7889	1967	**£20**	**£8**	*black label*
Takes Off	LP	RCA	INT1476	1974	**£12**	**£5**	
Takes Off	LP	RCA	SF8195	1971	**£20**	**£8**	
Takes Off	LP	RCA	LPM/LSP3584	1966	**£30**	**£15**	*US*
Takes Off	LP	RCA	LPM/LSP3584	1966	**£250**	**£150**	*US with 'Runnin' Round This World'*
Volunteers	7"	RCA	RCA1933	1970	**£4**	**£1.50**	
Volunteers	LP	RCA	SF8076	1969	**£15**	**£6**	
Volunteers	LP	RCA	APDI0320	1973	**£30**	**£15**	*US quad*
White Rabbit	7"	RCA	RCA1964	1970	**£4**	**£1.50**	
White Rabbit	7"	RCA	RCA1631	1967	**£5**	**£2**	
White Rabbit	CD-s	RCA	PD46463	1989	**£5**	**£2**	

JEFFERSON STARSHIP

Dragonfly	LP	Grunt	BFD10717	1974	**£10**	**£4**	*US quad*
Gold	LP	Grunt	DJL13363	1978	**£12**	**£5**	*US promo picture disc*
Nothing's Gonna Stop Us Now	CD-s	RCA	PD49451	1989	**£5**	**£2**	
Red Octopus	LP	Grunt	BFD10999	1975	**£10**	**£4**	*US quad*
Spitfire	LP	Grunt	BFD11557	1976	**£10**	**£4**	*US quad*

JELLY BEAN BANDITS

Jelly Bean Bandits	LP	Mainstream	S6103	1967	**£75**	**£37.50**	*US*

JELLY BEANS

Baby Be Mine	7"	Red Bird	RB10011	1964	**£10**	**£5**	
I Wanna Love Him So Bad	7"	Pye	7N25252	1964	**£10**	**£5**	
You Don't Mean Me No Good	7"	Right On	R102	1975	**£4**	**£1.50**	

JELLYBREAD

Jellybread have the distinction of being perhaps the least collectable of the Blue Horizon roster. Pete Wingfield, pianist and leader of the band, would suggest that the reason for this lies in the records not being very good! In fact, the group's blend of soul and blues has worn remarkably well. The lack of guitar histrionics no doubt makes the group sound unexciting to fans of their British blues contemporaries, but it also helps to give Jellybread a distinctive sound that makes their music much less tied to its era. A scarce privately pressed album (theoretically limited to 99 copies, but actually more in the region of 500) predates the Blue Horizon material and is the most vital music recorded by the group.

65 Parkway	LP	Blue Horizon	2431002	1970	**£20**	**£8**	
65 Parkway	LP	Blue Horizon	763866	1970	**£25**	**£10**	
Back To Begin Again	LP	Blue Horizon	2931004	1972	**£60**	**£30**	
Chairman Mao's Boogaloo	7"	Blue Horizon	573162	1969	**£5**	**£2**	
Comment	7"	Blue Horizon	573169	1970	**£5**	**£2**	
Creeepin' And Crawlin'	7"	Blue Horizon	2096001	1971	**£5**	**£2**	
Down Along The Cove	7"	Blue Horizon	2096006	1971	**£6**	**£2.50**	
First Slice	LP	Blue Horizon	763853	1969	**£25**	**£10**	
Jellybread	LP	Liphook	IBC/LP/3627	1969	**£125**	**£62.50**	
Old Man Hank	7"	Blue Horizon	573180	1970	**£5**	**£2**	
Rockin' Pneumonia & The Boogie Woogie Flu	7"	Blue Horizon	573174	1970	**£5**	**£2**	

JELLYFISH

Belly Button	CD	Charisma		1991	**£20**	**£8**	*US promo with pop-up cover*

JELLYROLL

Jellyroll	LP	MCA	MUPS420	1970	**£12**	**£5**	

JENGHIZ KHAN

Well Cut	LP	Barclay	920313T	1971	**£60**	**£30**	*French*

JENKINS, JOHNNY

Ton Ton Macoute	LP	Atlantic	2400033	1970	**£10**	**£4**	

JENKINS, KARL & MIKE RATLEDGE

Push Button	LP	De Wolfe	DWSLP3414	1979	**£15**	**£6**	

JENKINS, MARTIN

Carry Your Smile	LP	Oblivion	OBL002	1984	**£12**	**£5**	

JENNIFERS

Gaz Coombes, front-man for Supergrass, had his first single released while still in his last year at school. The Jennifers included drummer Danny Goffrey as well, who also became a member of Supergrass.

Just Got Back Today	12"	Nude	NUD2T	1992	**£10**	**£5**	
Just Got Back Today	CD-s	Nude	NUD2CD	1992	**£10**	**£5**	

JENNINGS, WAYLON

Waylon Jennings is one of the best known of country artists and as a pioneer of the 'outlaw' sound, reflecting a deliberate move away from the showbiz concerns of the Grand Ole Opry, he has been enormously influential on the modern breed of rock-inflected country singers. The reason for the inclusion here of the American single, 'Jole Blon', however, lies in the identity of the song's producer and guitarist. This is Buddy Holly, in whose group at the time Jennings played bass.

At JD's	LP	Sounds	1001	1964	**£75**	**£37.50**	*US*
Folk Country	LP	RCA	LPM/LSP3523	1966	**£12**	**£5**	*US*
Hangin' On	LP	RCA	LSP3918	1968	**£10**	**£4**	*US*
Jole Blon	7"	Brunswick	955130	1959	**£100**	**£50**	*US*

Leavin' Town	LP	RCA	LPM/LSP3620	1966	**£12**	**£5**	*US*
Love Of The Common People	LP	RCA	LPM/LSP3825	1967	**£10**	**£4**	*US*
Only The Greatest	LP	RCA	SF8003	1968	**£10**	**£4**	
Waylon Sings Ol' Harlan	LP	RCA	LPM/LSP3660	1967	**£12**	**£5**	*US*

JENSEN, KRIS

Claudette	7"	Fontana	267267TF	1963	**£6**	**£2.50**	
Come Back To Me	7"	Hickory	451256	1964	**£4**	**£1.50**	
Donna Donna	7"	Hickory	451224	1964	**£6**	**£2.50**	
Introducing Kris Jensen And Sue Thompson	7" EP	Hickory	LPE1507	1965	**£10**	**£5**	*2 tracks by Sue Thompson*
Looking For Love	7"	Hickory	451243	1964	**£4**	**£1.50**	
Somebody's Smiling	7"	Hickory	451285	1965	**£5**	**£2**	
That's A Whole Lotta Love	7"	Hickory	451311	1965	**£5**	**£2**	
Torture	7"	Fontana	267241TF	1962	**£6**	**£2.50**	
Torture	LP	Hickory	MH110	1962	**£20**	**£8**	*US*

JENSENS

Deep Thinking	7"	Philips	BF1686	1968	**£6**	**£2.50**	

JEREMY & THE SATYRS

Jeremy and the Satyrs, led by flautist Jeremy Steig, were one of the first American groups to bring jazz skills and sounds to rock. This was fledgling jazz-rock, with the two halves meeting on equal terms (unlike Blood, Sweat and Tears, for example, where the jazz content was no more than superficial). The Satyrs' experiment only lasted for one album, but each member has been a familiar session name ever since – Eddie Gomez, Donald McDonald, Warren Bernhardt and Adrian Guillory.

Jeremy & The Satyrs	LP	Reprise	RS6282	1968	**£25**	**£10**	*US*

JERICHO

Don't You Let Me Down	7"	A&M	AMS883	1972	**£15**	**£7.50**	
Hey Man	7"	A&M	AMS70--	1972	**£15**	**£7.50**	
Jericho	LP	A&M	AMLS68079	1972	**£60**	**£30**	
Junkies, Monkeys, & Donkeys	LP	A&M	AMLH68050	1971	**£75**	**£37.50**	*credited to Jericho Jones*
Mama's Gonna Take You Home	7"	A&M	AMS7037	1972	**£12**	**£6**	
Time is Now	7"	A&M	AMS833	1971	**£15**	**£7.50**	

JERKS

Come Back Bogart	7"	Laser	LAS25	1980	**£6**	**£2.50**	
Cool	7"	Lightning	GIL549	1978	**£10**	**£5**	
Get Your Woofing Dog Off Me	7"	Underground	URA1	1978	**£12**	**£6**	

JERMZ

Power Cut	7"	One Way	EFP1	1985	**£25**	**£12.50**	

JERONIMO

Cosmic Blues	LP	Bellaphon	BI1530	1970	**£25**	**£10**	*German*
Jeronimo	LP	Bellaphon	BLPS19044	1971	**£125**	**£62.50**	*German*
Time Ride	LP	Bellaphon	BLPS19095	1972	**£20**	**£8**	*German*

JERRY & THE FREEDOM SINGERS

It's All In The Game	7"	Banana	BA308	1970	**£5**	**£2**	

JERUSALEM

Jerusalem	LP	Deram	SDL6	1972	**£60**	**£30**	
Kamakazi Moth	7"	Deram	DMS358	1972	**£5**	**£2**	

JESS & JAMES

Something For Nothing	7"	MGM	MGM1420	1968	**£4**	**£1.50**	

JESTERS

Casa Pedro	7"	R&L	RL15/16	1962	**£6**	**£2.50**	

JESUS & MARY CHAIN

Automatic	CD	Blanco Y Negro	SAM589	1989	**£15**	**£6**	*promo picture disc*
Blues From A Gun	10"	Blanco Y Negro	NEG41TE	1989	**£8**	**£4**	
Blues From A Gun	CD-s	Blanco Y Negro	NEG41CD	1989	**£5**	**£2**	
Darklands	CD-s	Blanco Y Negro	NEGCD29	1987	**£5**	**£2**	
Happy When It Rains	7"	Blanco Y Negro	NEGB025	1987	**£4**	**£1.50**	*boxed, cards*
Head On	7"	Blanco Y Negro	NEG42	1989	**£10**	**£5**	*4 x 7" boxed set*
Head On	CD-s	Blanco Y Negro	NEG42CD	1989	**£5**	**£2**	
Just Like Honey	7"	Blanco Y Negro	NEGF017	1985	**£5**	**£2**	*double*
Riot	7"	Fierce	FRIGHT004	1985	**£10**	**£5**	*2 different sleeves*
Rollercoaster EP	CD-s	Blanco Y Negro	NEG45CD	1990	**£5**	**£2**	
Sidewalking	CD-s	Blanco Y Negro	NRG32CD	1988	**£5**	**£2**	*3" single*
Some Candy Talking	12"	Blanco Y Negro	NEG19T	1986	**£6**	**£2.50**	*with poster*

Title	Format	Label	Cat. No.	Year	Price	Price	Notes
Ten Smash Hits	CD	Def American	PROCD5336	1992	£**20**	£**8**	*US promo*
Upside Down	12"	Creation	CRE012T	1984	£**30**	£**15**	*demo only*
Upside Down	7"	Creation	CRE012	1984	£**8**	£**4**	*black, red & white picture sleeve*
Upside Down	7"	Creation	CRE012	1984	£**5**	£**2**	*pink, blue, or yellow picture sleeve*

JESUS JONES

A prediction – Jesus Jones' *Liquidiser* album will, in years to come, be seen as one of the major rock music milestones. Its sophisticated blend of high energy guitar rock with modern sampling technology works so well and so seamlessly that it is easy to pass over what has been achieved here. But when, in addition, the songs themselves are so well crafted and memorable, the result is so obviously a masterpiece that it becomes astonishing that the group is not more highly rated than it seems to be!

Title	Format	Label	Cat. No.	Year	Price	Price	Notes
Bring It On Down	CD-s	Food	CDFOOD22	1989	£**5**	£[illegible]	
Info Freako	CD-s	Food	CDFOOD18	1989	£**6**	£**2.50**	
Never Enough	CD-s	Food	CDFOOD21	1989	£**5**	£**2**	

JESUS LOVES YOU

Title	Format	Label	Cat. No.	Year	Price	Price	Notes
After The Love	12"	More Protein	PRTX12	1989	£**6**	£**2.50**	
After The Love	12"	More Protein	PROT1312DJ	1991	£**12**	£**6**	*promo*
After The Love	CD-s	More Protein	PROCD2	1990	£**6**	£**2.50**	*3" single*
After The Love	CD-s	More Protein	PROCD13	1991	£**5**	£**2**	
Generations Of Love	CD-s	More Protein	PROCD5	1990	£**5**	£**2**	
One On One	12"	More Protein	JLY1	1990	£**20**	£**10**	*promo, as JLY Posse*
One On One	12"	More Protein	PROT712	1990	£**15**	£**7.50**	*promo*
One On One	CD-s	More Protein	PROCD7	1990	£**5**	£**2**	
Sweet Toxic Love	CD-s	Virgin	VSCDX1449	1992	£**10**	£**5**	

JET SET

Title	Format	Label	Cat. No.	Year	Price	Price	Notes
VC10	7"	Delta	DW5001	1962	£**6**	£**2.50**	*picture sleeve*
You Got Me Hooked	7"	Parlophone	R5199	1964	£**5**	£**2**	

JETHRO TULL

The first record made by Jethro Tull, the MGM single 'Sunshine Day', was mistakenly credited to 'Jethro Toe'. Both sides of the record – less bluesy than the music on *This Was*, but easily recognizable as the same group – were subsequently made available on the Polydor compilation *Rare Tracks*, but the single itself hardly sold at all and is extremely scarce. Copies that correct the spelling of the group's name on the label are counterfeits, this being emphasized by their having American-style large centre holes on what is supposed to be a UK release.

Title	Format	Label	Cat. No.	Year	Price	Price	Notes
1982 Tour Sampler	LP	Chrysalis	47PDJ	1982	£**15**	£**6**	*US promo*
Another Christmas Song	CD-s	Chrysalis	TULLCD5	1989	£**6**	£**2.50**	
Aqualung	CD	Chrysalis	CD25CR08	1994	£**12**	£**5**	*Chrysalis 25 pack*
Aqualung	LP	Chrysalis	CH41044	1973	£**25**	£**10**	*US quad*
Aqualung	LP	Chrysalis	CHR1044/ ILPS9145	1971	£**10**	£**4**	
Aqualung	LP	Island	ILPS9145		£**10**	£**4**	*pink rim label*
Aqualung	LP	Mobile Fidelity	MFSL1061	1980	£**30**	£**15**	*US audiophile*
Benefit	LP	Chrysalis	ILPS9123	1970	£**10**	£**4**	
Benefit	LP	Island	ILPS9123	1970	£**25**	£**10**	*pink label*
Benefit	LP	Island	6339009	1970	£**15**	£**6**	*German, gatefold sleeve, poster*
Broadsword	7"	Chrysalis	CHSP2619	1982	£**8**	£**4**	*picture disc*
Broadsword & The Beast	LP	Mobile Fidelity	MFSL1092	1982	£**12**	£**5**	*US audiophile*
Coronach	12"	Chrysalis	TULLX2	1986	£**15**	£**7.50**	
Coronach	7"	Chrysalis	TULL2	1986	£**4**	£**1.50**	
Home	7"	Chrysalis	CHS2394	1979	£**8**	£**4**	
Inside	7"	Chrysalis	WIP6081	1970	£**6**	£**2.50**	
Jethro Tull Radio Show	LP	Chrysalis	PRO622	1976	£**20**	£**8**	*US promo*
Life Is A Long Song	7"	Chrysalis	WIP6106	1971	£**5**	£**2**	
Living In The (Slightly More Recent) Past	CD-s	Chrysalis	23970/1	1993	£**6**	£**2.50**	*2 CD set*
Living In The Past	7"	Island	WIP6056	1969	£**4**	£**1.50**	
Living In The Past	LP	Chrysalis	CJT1	1972	£**15**	£**6**	*hard cover double*
Living In The Past	LP	Chrysalis	CJT1	1972	£**200**	£**100**	*double, leather cover*
Love Story	7"	Island	WIP6048	1968	£**4**	£**1.50**	
Love Story	7"	Island	WIP6048	1968	£**6**	£**2.50**	*'Henderson' song-writing credit*
Moths	7"	Chrysalis	CHS2214	1978	£**6**	£**2.50**	
Moths/Beltane	7"	Chrysalis	CHS2214	1978	£**20**	£**10**	
North Sea Oil	7"	Chrysalis	CHS2378	1979	£**6**	£**2.50**	
Part Of The Machine	CD-s	Chrysalis	TULLPCD1	1988	£**10**	£**5**	*picture disc*
Passion Play	7"	Chrysalis	CHS2012	1973	£**50**	£**25**	
Ring Out Solstice Bells	7"	Chrysalis	CXP2275	1976	£**5**	£**2**	*picture sleeve*
Ring Out Solstice Bells	7"	Chrysalis	CHS2443	1979	£**4**	£**1.50**	
Rocks On The Road	12"	Chrysalis	TULLX7	1992	£**6**	£**2.50**	*picture disc*
Rocks On The Road	CD-s	Chrysalis	TULLCD7	1992	£**6**	£**2.50**	*boxed double*
Said She Was A Dancer	7"	Chrysalis	TULLP4	1988	£**6**	£**2.50**	*shaped picture disc*
Said She Was A Dancer	CD-s	Chrysalis	TULLCD4	1987	£**8**	£**4**	
Song For Jeffrey	7"	Island	WIP6043	1968	£**15**	£**7.50**	
Stand Up	CD	Mobile Fidelity	UDCD524	1989	£**15**	£**6**	*US audiophile*
Stand Up	LP	Island	ILPS9103	1969	£**15**	£**6**	*pink label*
Steel Monkey	7"	Chrysalis	TULLP3	1987	£**5**	£**2**	*picture disc*
Stitch In Time	7"	Chrysalis	CHS2260	1978	£**5**	£**2**	
Sunshine Day	7"	MGM	MGM1384	1968	£**150**	£**75**	*credited to Jethro Toe*

Title	Format	Label	Cat. No.	Year	Mint	VG	Notes
Thick As A Brick	CD	Mobile Fidelity	UDCD510	1988	£15	£6	*US audiophile*
Thick As A Brick	LP	Chrysalis	CHR1003	1972	£12	£5	*newspaper sleeve*
This Is Not Love	CD-s	Chrysalis	TULLCD6	1991	£5	£2	
This Was	LP	Island	ILPS9085	1968	£25	£10	*pink label*
This Was	LP	Island	ILP985	1968	£30	£15	*mono, pink label*
Under Wraps	LP	Chrysalis	CDLP1461	1984	£10	£4	*picture disc*
War Child	LP	Chrysalis	CH41067	1974	£20	£8	*US quad*
Whistler	7"	Chrysalis	CHS2135	1977	£4	£1.50	
Witch's Promise	7"	Chrysalis	WIP6077	1970	£8	£4	*picture sleeve*
Working John, Working Joe	7"	Chrysalis	CHS2468	1979	£5	£2	

JETSTREAMS

Title	Format	Label	Cat. No.	Year	Mint	VG	Notes
Bongo Rock	7"	Decca	F11149	1959	£15	£7.50	

JETT, JOAN

Title	Format	Label	Cat. No.	Year	Mint	VG	Notes
I Hate Myself For Loving You	CD-s	London	LONCD195	1988	£5	£2	

JEWELS

Title	Format	Label	Cat. No.	Year	Mint	VG	Notes
But I Do	7"	Colpix	PX11048	1965	£8	£4	
Opportunity	7"	Colpix	PX11034	1964	£8	£4	

JIGILO JUG BAND

Title	Format	Label	Cat. No.	Year	Mint	VG	Notes
Live At The Limping Whippet	12"	Performance	PERF1	1980	£8	£4	

JIGSAW

Title	Format	Label	Cat. No.	Year	Mint	VG	Notes
Aurora Borealis	LP	Philips	6308072	1971	£30	£15	
Broken Hearted	LP	BASF	BAG22291065	1973	£12	£5	
I've Seen The Film	LP	BASF	BAP5051	1974	£12	£5	
Jesu Joy Of Man's Desiring	7"	Philips	6006131	1971	£4	£1.50	
Keeping My Head Above Water	7"	Philips	6006182	1971	£4	£1.50	
Let Me Go Home	7"	Music Factory	CUB6	1968	£40	£20	
Letherslade Farm	LP	Philips	6309033	1970	£50	£25	
Lollipop And Goody Man	7"	Fontana	6007017	1970	£8	£4	
One Way Street	7"	Philips	6006112	1970	£6	£2.50	

JILL & THE BOULEVARDS

Title	Format	Label	Cat. No.	Year	Mint	VG	Notes
Eugene	7"	Columbia	DB4823	1962	£8	£4	

JILL & THE Y'VERNS

Title	Format	Label	Cat. No.	Year	Mint	VG	Notes
My Soulful Dress	7"	Oak	RGJ503	196–	£40	£20	

JILTED JOHN

Title	Format	Label	Cat. No.	Year	Mint	VG	Notes
Jilted John	7"	Rabid	TOSH105	1978	£5	£2	*picture sleeve*

JIM & JEAN

Title	Format	Label	Cat. No.	Year	Mint	VG	Notes
Changes	7" EP	Verve	519901	1967	£8	£4	*French*

JIM & JOE

Title	Format	Label	Cat. No.	Year	Mint	VG	Notes
Fireball Mail	7"	London	HL9831	1964	£8	£4	

JIM & MONICA

Title	Format	Label	Cat. No.	Year	Mint	VG	Notes
Slippin' And Slidin'	7"	Stateside	SS266	1964	£10	£5	

JIMBILIN

Title	Format	Label	Cat. No.	Year	Mint	VG	Notes
Human Race	7"	Bamboo	BAM68	1971	£5	£2	

JIMMIE & THE NIGHT HOPPERS

Title	Format	Label	Cat. No.	Year	Mint	VG	Notes
Night Hop	7"	London	HLP8830	1959	£15	£7.50	

JIMMY & THE RACKETS

Title	Format	Label	Cat. No.	Year	Mint	VG	Notes
Jimmy And The Rackets	LP	Elite	SOLP30039	1965	£30	£15	*German*

JIV-A-TONES

Title	Format	Label	Cat. No.	Year	Mint	VG	Notes
Flirty Gertie	7"	Felsted	AF101	1958	£150	£75	

JIVE FIVE

Title	Format	Label	Cat. No.	Year	Mint	VG	Notes
I'm A Happy Man	7"	United Artists	UP1106	1965	£10	£5	
Jive Five	LP	United Artists	UAL3455/ UAS6455	1965	£25	£10	*US*
My True Story	7"	Parlophone	R4822	1961	£100	£50	
What Time Is It	7"	Stateside	SS133	1962	£40	£20	

JIVERS

Title	Format	Label	Cat. No.	Year	Mint	VG	Notes
Little Mama	7"	Vogue	V9060	1956	£400	£250	*best auctioned*
Ray Pearl	7"	Vogue	V9068	1957	£400	£250	*best auctioned*

JIVERS (2)

Title	Format	Label	Cat. No.	Year	Mint	VG	Notes
Wear My Crown	7"	Trojan	TR604	1968	£4	£1.50	

JIVING JUNIORS

Title	Format	Label	Cat. No.	Year	Mint	VG	Notes
Don't Leave Me	7"	Island	WI027	1962	£12	£6	
Lollipop Girl	7"	Blue Beat	BB4	1960	£15	£7.50	
My Heart's Desire	7"	Blue Beat	BB5	1960	£15	£7.50	
Over The River	7"	Blue Beat	BB36	1961	£15	£7.50	
Slop And Mash	7"	Starlite	ST45049	1961	£12	£6	
Sugar Dandy	7"	Island	WI003	1962	£12	£6	
Sugar Dandy	7"	Island	WI129	1963	£10	£5	

Tu Woo Up Tu Woo	7"	Starlite	ST45028	1960	£12	£6	

JO, DAMITA

I'd Do It Again	7"	HMV	7MC2	1954	£6	£2.50	*export*
I'll Save The Last Dance For You	7" EP	Mercury	ZEP10118	1961	£8	£4	
Midnight Session	LP	Columbia	SX/SCX6094	1966	£10	£4	

JO JO GUNNE

Beggin' You Baby	7"	Decca	F12906	1969	£4	£1.50	
Every Story Has An End	7"	Decca	F12807	1968	£4	£1.50	

JOBIM, ANTONIO CARLOS

Stone Flower	LP	CTI	CTL3	1972	£10	£4	

JODIMARS

Cloud Ninety-nine	7"	Capitol	CL14700	1957	£30	£15	
Dance To The Bop	7"	Capitol	CL14642	1956	£30	£15	
Lotsa Love	7"	Capitol	CL14627	1956	£30	£15	
Midnight	7"	Capitol	CL14663	1956	£30	£15	
Rattle Shaking Daddy	7"	Capitol	CL14641	1956	£30	£15	
Well Now Dig This	7"	Capitol	CL14518	1956	£40	£20	
Well Now Dig This	LP	Speciality	SPE6608	196–	£15	£6	

JODOROWSKY, ALEXANDRO

El Topo	LP	Apple	SWAO3388	1971	£15	£6	*US*

JODY GRIND

Far Canal	LP	Transatlantic	TRA221	1970	£30	£15	
One Step On	LP	Transatlantic	TRA210	1969	£50	£25	

JOE, AL T.

Fatso	7"	Blue Beat	BB169	1963	£12	£6	
Goodbye Dreamboat	7"	Blue Beat	BB166	1963	£12	£6	
I'm On My Own	7"	Dice	CC9	1962	£10	£5	
Jacqueline	7"	Blue Beat	BB368	1966	£12	£6	
You Cheated On Me	7"	Blue Beat	BB126	1962	£12	£6	

JOE & ANN

Gee Baby	7"	Black Swan	WI468	1965	£10	£5	

JOE & EDDIE

Joe And Eddie	LP	Vocalion	VAN8036	1964	£15	£6	
Walkin' Down The Line	7"	Vocalion	VP9250	1965	£6	£2.50	

JOE SOAP

Keep It Clean	LP	Polydor	2383233	1973	£10	£4	

JOE THE BOSS

If Life Was A Thing	7"	Joe	JRS10	1970	£4	£1.50	*Lloyd Kingpin B side*
Son Of Al Capone	7"	Joe	JRS6	1970	£5	£2	

JOEL, BILLY

52nd Street	LP	Columbia	HC45609	1981	£10	£4	*US audiophile*
Ballad Of Billy The Kid	7"	Philips	6078018	1973	£20	£10	
Billy Joel	LP	Columbia	ABS1	1978	£75	£37.50	*US promo, 5 LPs, boxed*
Cold Spring Harbour	LP	Philips	6369150	1972	£10	£4	*recorded too fast*
Entertainer	7"	Philips		1973	£25	£12.50	
Honesty	7"	CBS	7150	1979	£15	£7.50	
Interchords	LP	Columbia	AS402	1976	£12	£5	*US interview promo*
Leningrad	CD-s	CBS	JOELC3	1989	£5	£2	*3" single*
Now Playing	LP	CBS	BJ1	1978	£12	£5	*promo*
Piano Man	LP	Philips	6369160	1973	£25	£10	
Piano Man	LP	Columbia	CQ32544	1974	£10	£4	*US quad*
She's Got A Way	7"	Philips	6078001	1972	£4	£1.50	
Songs From The Attic	LP	Columbia	AS1343	1981	£15	£6	*US sampler & interview promo*
Souvenir	LP	Columbia	AS326	1974	£15	£6	*US 1 sided live promo*
Stranger	LP	Columbia	HC34987	1980	£10	£4	*US audiophile*
Streetlife Serenade	LP	Columbia	PCQ33146	1974	£10	£4	*US quad*
That's Not Her Style – The Storm Front Tour CD	CD	Columbia		1990	£20	£8	*US promo*
Turnstiles	LP	Columbia	PCQ33848	1976	£10	£4	*US quad*
We Didn't Start The Fire	CD-s	CBS	JOELC1	1989	£5	£2	

JOE'S ALLSTARS

Battle Cry Of Biafra	7"	Joe	DU28	1969	£4	£1.50	
Hey Jude	7"	Joe	DU24	1969	£4	£1.50	
Tony B's Theme	7"	Joe	JRS9	1970	£5	£2	

JOEY & THE CONTINENTALS

She Rides With Me	7"	Polydor	56520	1970	£6	£2.50	

JOEY & THE GENTLEMEN

Like I Love You	7"	Fontana	TF444	1964	£5	£2	

JOHANNES

First Album	LP	Pallas	HF100	1971	**£75**	**£37.50**	*German*

JOHN, ANDREW

Machine Stops	LP	CBS	64835	1971	**£15**	**£6**	

JOHN, DAVID & THE MOOD

Bring It To Jerome	7"	Parlophone	R5255	1965	**£150**	**£75**	
Diggin' For Gold	7"	Parlophone	R5301	1965	**£175**	**£87.50**	
Pretty Thing	7"	Vocalion	V9220	1964	**£200**	**£100**	

JOHN, ELTON

Act Of War	12"	Rocket	EJSR812	1985	**£10**	**£5**	
Act Of War	7"	Rocket	EJS8	1985	**£4**	**£1.50**	*with Millie Jackson*
Aida Press Kit	CD	Mercury	ADV19991	1999	**£50**	**£25**	*box set with 2 CDs, booklet, cards, candle*
All Quiet On The Western Front	7"	Rocket	XPRES88	1982	**£4**	**£1.50**	
All Quiet On The Western Front	7"	Rocket	XPRPO88	1982	**£10**	**£5**	*poster sleeve*
Blessed	CD-s	Rocket	EJSDD38	1995	**£15**	**£7.50**	
Blessed	CD-s	Rocket	EJSCD38	1995	**£15**	**£7.50**	
Border Song	7"	DJM	DJS217	1970	**£15**	**£7.50**	
Candle In The Wind	CD-s	Rocket	EJSCD15	1987	**£8**	**£4**	
Candle In The Wind	LP	St Michael	20940102	1978	**£25**	**£10**	
Candle In The Wind (live)	7"	Rocket	EJSP15	1988	**£6**	**£2.50**	*picture disc*
Captain Fantastic	LP	DJM	DJV2300	1978	**£15**	**£6**	*picture disc*
Captain Fantastic	LP	DJM	DJLPX1	1975	**£75**	**£37.50**	*brown vinyl, autographed cover*
Captain Fantastic	LP	DJM	DJLPX1	1975	**£40**	**£20**	*brown vinyl*
Celebrating Elton John's 50th Birthday	CD	Rocket	ELTON50	1997	**£50**	**£25**	*promo*
Club At The End Of The Street	12"	Rocket	EJS2112	1990	**£400**	**£250**	*best auctioned*
Club At The End Of The Street	7"	Rocket	EJS21	1990	**£400**	**£250**	*best auctioned*
Club At The End Of The Street	CD-s	Rocket	EJSCD21	1990	**£25**	**£12.50**	*with 'Give Peace A Chance'*
Club At The End Of The Street	CD-s	Rocket	EJSCD23	1990	**£5**	**£2**	
Dear God	7"	Rocket	XPRES45	1980	**£20**	**£10**	*no picture sleeve*
Dear God	7"	Rocket	ELTON1	1980	**£6**	**£2.50**	*double*
Don't Let The Sun Go Down On Me	CD-s	Rocket	EJSCD26	1991	**£5**	**£2**	
Duets	CD	Rocket		1993	**£75**	**£37.50**	*promo box set of 16 CD singles*
Duets	CD	Rocket	DUINT1	1994	**£20**	**£8**	*interview promo*
Easier To Walk Away	CD-s	Rocket	EJSCD25	1990	**£5**	**£2**	
Elton John	LP	DJM	DJM14512	1978	**£25**	**£10**	*5 LPs, boxed*
Elton John And Bernie Taupin Collection	CD	Polygram	PIPCD002	1990	**£50**	**£25**	*US promo double compilation*
Empty Garden	7"	Rocket	XPPIC77	1982	**£5**	**£2**	*picture disc*
Empty Sky	LP	DJM	DJLPM403	1969	**£60**	**£30**	*mono*
Excerpts From To Be Continued	CD	MCA		1990	**£20**	**£8**	*Canadian promo sampler*
Fishing Trip	CD	Happenstance	HAPP002	1993	**£500**	**£330**	*4 CD set, private pressing*
Four From Four Eyes	7" EP	DJM	DJR18001	1977	**£5**	**£2**	
Friends	7"	DJM	DJS244	1971	**£5**	**£2**	
Funeral For A Friend	12"	DJM	DJT15000	1978	**£6**	**£2.50**	
Games	LP	Viking	105	1970	**£75**	**£37.50**	*US, with other artists*
Gli Opera	7"	Rocket		1977	**£8**	**£4**	*sung in Italian*
Goaldigger Song	7"	Rocket	GOALD1	1977	**£200**	**£100**	*autographed*
Goodbye Yellow Brick Road	CD	Mobile Fidelity	UDCD526	1990	**£15**	**£6**	*US audiophile*
Goodbye Yellow Brick Road	LP	Superdisk	SD216614	1982	**£15**	**£6**	*audiophile*
Goodbye Yellow Brick Road	LP	DJM	DJE29001	1976	**£12**	**£5**	*yellow vinyl double*
Goodbye Yellow Brick Road	LP	Nautilus	10003	1980	**£25**	**£10**	*US audiophile*
Greatest Hits	CD	DCC	GZS1071	1994	**£15**	**£6**	*US audiophile*
Greatest Hits Volume One	LP	Nautilus		1981	**£10**	**£4**	*US audiophile*
Healing Hands	CD-s	Rocket	EJSCD19	1989	**£5**	**£2**	
Honky Chateau	CD	Mobile Fidelity	UDCD536	1990	**£15**	**£6**	*US audiophile*
I Don't Wanna Go On With You Like That	12"	Rocket	EJS1612	1988	**£60**	**£30**	*blue vinyl, no picture sleeve*
I Don't Want To Go On With You Like That	CD-s	Rocket	EJSCD16	1988	**£6**	**£2.50**	
I Don't Want To Go On With You Like That	CD-s	Polygram	0805242	1988	**£10**	**£5**	*CD video*
I Saw Her Standing There	7"	DJM	DJS354	1975	**£5**	**£2**	*picture sleeve, with John Lennon*
I Saw Her Standing There	7"	DJM	DJS10965	1981	**£4**	**£1.50**	*with John Lennon*
I'm Still Standing	7"	Rocket	EJPIC1	1983	**£10**	**£5**	*shaped picture disc*
I've Been Loving You	7"	Philips	BF1643	1968	**£250**	**£150**	*best auctioned*
It's Me That You Need	7"	DJM	DJS205	1969	**£60**	**£30**	*picture sleeve*
It's Me That You Need	7"	DJM	DJS205	1969	**£25**	**£12.50**	
Je Veux De La Tendresse	7"	Rocket	6000675	1980	**£6**	**£2.50**	*sung in French*
Lady Samantha	7"	Philips	BF1739	1969	**£25**	**£12.50**	
Last Song	CD-s	Rocket	EJSCD30	1992	**£5**	**£2**	
Les Areuse	12"			1981	**£6**	**£2.50**	*sung in French, with France Gall*

Title	Format	Label	Cat. No.	Year	Mint	VG	Notes
Les Areuse	7"			1981	**£4**	**£1.50**	*sung in French, with France Gall*
Live In Australia	CD	Rocket	0805161	1988	**£15**	**£6**	*CD video*
Live In Australia With The Melbourne S.O.	LP	Rocket	EJBXL1	1987	**£15**	**£6**	*boxed set double*
Live In Australia With The Melbourne Symphony Orchestra	CD	Rocket	EJBXD1	1987	**£40**	**£20**	*gold double boxed set*
Madman Across The Water	CD	Mobile Fidelity	UDCD516	1989	**£15**	**£6**	*US audiophile*
Mama Can't Buy You Love	7"	Rocket	XPRES20	1979	**£200**	**£100**	
Nikita	7"	Rocket	EJSD9	1985	**£10**	**£5**	*double, pop-up picture sleeve*
Nikita	CD-s	Polygram	0802722	1988	**£10**	**£5**	*CD video*
One	CD-s	Rocket	EJSCD28	1992	**£5**	**£2**	
Plays The Siran	CD	Happenstance	HAPP001	1993	**£500**	**£330**	*private pressing*
Rock And Roll Madonna	7"	DJM	DJS222	1970	**£15**	**£7.50**	
Rocket Man	7"	DJM	DJX501	1972	**£12**	**£6**	*gatefold picture sleeve*
Sacrifice	CD-s	Rocket	EJSCD22	1990	**£5**	**£2**	
Sacrifice	CD-s	Rocket	EJSCD20	1989	**£5**	**£2**	
Sad Songs	7"	Rocket	PHPIC7	1984	**£5**	**£2**	*shaped picture disc*
Single Man	LP	MCA	MCAP14591	1979	**£10**	**£4**	*US picture disc*
Slow Rivers	12"	Rocket	EJS1312	1986	**£6**	**£2.50**	*with Cliff Richard*
Slow Rivers	7"	Rocket	EJSP13	1986	**£8**	**£4**	*picture disc, with Cliff Richard*
Something About The Way You Look Tonight	CD-s	Rocket	EJSCX41	1997	**£20**	**£10**	
Something About The Way You Look Tonight	CD-s	Rocket	EJSCD41	1997	**£20**	**£10**	
Special 12 Record Pack	7"	DJM	EJ12	1978	**£40**	**£20**	*12 singles, boxed*
Superior Sound Of Elton John	CD	DJM	8100622	1983	**£20**	**£8**	*remix compilation*
That's Why They Call It The Blues	7"	Rocket	XPPRES91	1983	**£8**	**£4**	*title without 'I Guess'*
Town Of Plenty	7"	Rocket	EJSLB17	1988	**£4**	**£1.50**	*boxed with 4 photos*
Town Of Plenty	CD-s	Rocket	EJSCD17	1988	**£5**	**£2**	
Tumbleweed Connection	CD	Mobile Fidelity	UDCD543	1991	**£15**	**£6**	*US audiophile*
Twenty-Five Years On	CD	Rocket	DJMDJ1	1995	**£25**	**£10**	*promo compilation*
Two Rooms – The Interview	CD	Mercury		1991	**£20**	**£8**	*promo*
Warlock Sampler	LP	Warlock Music	WMM101/2	1970	**£1000**	**£700**	*demo only, with Linda Peters (Thompson), best auctioned*
Word In Spanish	CD-s	Rocket	EJSCD18	1988	**£8**	**£4**	
World	CD	Rocket	EJCD89	1989	**£20**	**£8**	*promo sampler*
Wrap Her Up	12"	Rocket	EJS1012	1985	**£8**	**£4**	*double*
Wrap Her Up	7"	Rocket	EJPIC10	1985	**£8**	**£4**	*shaped picture disc, with George Michael*
Wrap Her Up	7"	Rocket	EJSC10	1985	**£5**	**£2**	*cube bag sleeve, with George Michael*
Wrap Her Up	7"	Rocket	EJSP10	1985	**£15**	**£7.50**	*with George Michael, shaped picture disc*
You Gotta Love Someone	CD-s	Rocket	EJSCD24	1990	**£5**	**£2**	

JOHN, LITTLE WILLIE

Title	Format	Label	Cat. No.	Year	Mint	VG	Notes
Action	LP	King	691	1960	**£60**	**£30**	*US*
Come On And Join Little Willie John	LP	London	HA8126	1964	**£40**	**£20**	
Fever	7"	Parlophone	R4209	1956	**£60**	**£30**	
Fever	LP	King	395564	1956	**£100**	**£50**	*US*
Free At Last	LP	King	KS1081	1970	**£25**	**£10**	*US*
Heartbreak	7"	Parlophone	R4674	1960	**£15**	**£7.50**	
Leave My Kitten Alone	7"	Parlophone	R4571	1959	**£20**	**£10**	
Let's Rock While The Rocking's Good	7"	Parlophone	R4472	1958	**£30**	**£15**	
Little Willie Sings All Originals	LP	King	K(S)949	1966	**£30**	**£15**	*US*
Mr Little Willie John	LP	King	603	1958	**£75**	**£37.50**	*US*
Sleep	7"	Parlophone	R4699	1960	**£15**	**£7.50**	
Sure Things	LP	Parlophone	PMC1163	1959	**£75**	**£37.50**	
Sweet, The Hot, The Teenage Beat	LP	King	767	1961	**£40**	**£20**	*US*
Talk To Me	7"	Parlophone	R4432	1958	**£20**	**£10**	
Talk To Me	LP	King	395596	1958	**£75**	**£37.50**	*US*
These Are My Favorite Songs	LP	King	895	1964	**£40**	**£20**	*US*
Uh Uh Baby	7"	Parlophone	R4396	1958	**£20**	**£10**	

JOHN, MABLE

Title	Format	Label	Cat. No.	Year	Mint	VG	Notes
Able Mable	7"	Stax	601034	1968	**£4**	**£1.50**	
It's Catching	7"	Atlantic	584022	1966	**£5**	**£2**	
Same Time Same Place	7"	Stax	601010	1967	**£6**	**£2.50**	

JOHN, ROBERT

Title	Format	Label	Cat. No.	Year	Mint	VG	Notes
Raindrops, Love And Sunshine	7"	A&M	AMS835	1968	**£5**	**£2**	

JOHN & PAUL

Title	Format	Label	Cat. No.	Year	Mint	VG	Notes
People Say	7"	London	HLU9997	1965	**£6**	**£2.50**	

JOHN & SANDRA

Title	Format	Label	Cat. No.	Year	Mint	VG	Notes
John And Sandra	LP	Argo	ZFB2	1970	**£10**	**£4**	

JOHN BULL BREED

I'm A Man	7"	Polydor	56065	1966	£150	£75	

JOHN THE POSTMAN

Psychedelic Rock'n'Roll 5 Skinners	12"	Bent	BIGBENT4	1978	£8	£4	
Puerile	12"	Bent	BIGBENT2	1978	£8	£4	

JOHN THE REVELATOR

Wild Blues	LP	Decca	6419002	1970	£30	£15	*Dutch*

JOHNNIE & JOE

Over the Mountain Across The Sea	7"	London	HLM8682	1958	£200	£100	*best auctioned*

JOHNNY & CHAS & THE GUNNERS

Bobby	7"	Decca	F11365	1961	£15	£7.50	

JOHNNY & JACK

Hits	LP	RCA	LPM2017	1959	£12	£5	*US*
Honey I Need You	7"	HMV	7MC21	1954	£10	£5	*export*
Tennessee Mountain Boys	LP	RCA	LPM1587	1957	£12	£5	*US*

JOHNNY & JOHN

Bumper To Bumper	7"	Polydor	BM56087	1966	£8	£4	

JOHNNY & JUDY

Bother Me Baby	7"	Vogue	V9128	1959	£300	£180	*best auctioned*

JOHNNY & THE ATTRACTIONS

Young Wings Can Fly	7"	Doctor Bird	DB1118	1967	£10	£5	*Dudley Williamson B side*

JOHNNY & THE BLUEBEATS

Shame	7"	Blue Beat	BB229	1964	£12	£6	

JOHNNY & THE COPYCATS

I'm A Hog For You Baby	7"	Narco	AB102	1964	£40	£20	

JOHNNY & THE HURRICANES

Beatnik Fly	7"	London	HLI9072	1959	£4	£1.50	
Big Sound	LP	London	HAX2322	1960	£25	£10	
Crossfire	7"	London	HL8899	1959	£15	£7.50	*tri-centre*
Down Yonder	7"	London	HLX9134	1960	£4	£1.50	
Greens And Jeans	7"	London	HLX9660	1963	£4	£1.50	
Hep Canary	7"	London	HL7099	1960	£30	£15	*export*
Johnny & The Hurricanes	7" EP	London	REX1347	1962	£15	£7.50	
Johnny & The Hurricanes	LP	Warwick	W(ST)2007	1959	£50	£25	*US*
Johnny & The Hurricanes Vol. 2	7" EP	London	REX1414	1964	£20	£10	
Live At The Star Club	LP	Atila	1030	1962	£40	£20	*US*
Minnesota Fats	7"	London	HLX9617	1962	£4	£1.50	
Money Honey	7"	Stateside	SS347	1964	£5	£2	
Red River Rock	7"	London	HL8948	1959	£5	£2	*tri-centre*
Red River Rock	LP	London	HA2227	1960	£30	£15	*plum label*
Red River Rock	LP	London	HA2227	196–	£12	£5	*black label*
Reveille Rock	7"	London	HL9017	1959	£6	£2.50	*tri-centre*
Rocking Goose	7" EP	London	REX1284	1961	£20	£10	
Salvation	7"	London	HLX9536	1962	£5	£2	
Stormsville	LP	London	HAI2269	1960	£25	£10	
Traffic Jam	7"	London	HLX9491	1962	£4	£1.50	
You Are My Sunshine	7"	London	HLX7116	1962	£20	£10	*export*

JOHNNY & THE SELF ABUSERS

It is unlikely that Johnny and the Self Abusers would have become international stars if they had retained that name. Fortunately they decided to change it to Simple Minds . . .

Saints And Sinners	7"	Chiswick	NS22	1977	£10	£5	*picture sleeve*

JOHNNY & THE VIBRATIONS

Bird Stompin'	7"	Warner Bros	WB107	1963	£4	£1.50	

JOHNNY'S BOYS

Sleepwalk	7"	Decca	F11156	1959	£5	£2	

JOHNNY'S JAZZ

R.J. Boogie	7"	Decca	FJ10663	1956	£4	£1.50	

JOHNS, GLYN

I'll Follow The Sun	7"	Pye	7N15818	1965	£4	£1.50	
January Blues	7"	Decca	F11478	1962	£4	£1.50	
Mary Anne	7"	Immediate	IM013	1965	£10	£5	
Today You're Gone	7"	Lyntone	LYN827/8	196–	£4	£1.50	

JOHNS, GLYNIS

I Can't Resist Men	7"	Columbia	SCM5149	1954	£4	£1.50	

JOHN'S CHILDREN

The collectability of John's Children derives mainly from the fact that Marc Bolan played with the group for a short time. 'Desdemona' is a Bolan song, as is the withdrawn and extremely scarce 'Midsummer Night's Scene'. (Other unreleased Marc Bolan contributions were included on his LP *Beginning Of Doves*.) Many of the other John's Children recordings were actually made by session musicians (including Jeff Beck on the B side of 'Just What You Want'), as the group were too incompetent to do the job themselves.

Come And Play With Me In The Garden	7"	Track	604005	1967	**£30**	**£15**	
Come And Play With Me In The Garden	7"	Track	604005	1967	**£100**	**£50**	*picture sleeve*
Desdemona	7"	Track	604003	1967	**£30**	**£15**	
Desdemona	7"	Track	604003	1967	**£100**	**£50**	*picture sleeve*
Go Go Girl	7"	Track	604010	1967	**£40**	**£20**	
Just What You Want	7"	Columbia	DB8124	1967	**£75**	**£37.50**	
Love I Thought I'd Found	7"	Columbia	DB8030	1966	**£200**	**£100**	*picture sleeve, best auctioned*
Love I Thought I'd Found	7"	Columbia	DB8030	1966	**£75**	**£37.50**	
Midsummer Night's Scene	7"	Track	604005	1967	**£1500**	**£1000**	*test pressing, best auctioned*
Midsummer Night's Scene	LP	Bam Caruso	KIRI095	1987	**£15**	**£6**	
Orgasm	LP	White Whale	WW7128	1967	**£100**	**£50**	*US*

JOHNSON, BETTY

1492	7"	London	HLU8432	1957	**£25**	**£12.50**	
Betty Johnson	LP	Atlantic	8017	1958	**£40**	**£20**	*US*
Does Your Heart Beat For Me	7"	London	HLE8839	1959	**£20**	**£10**	
Dream	7"	London	HLE8678	1958	**£12**	**£6**	
Dream	7" EP	London	REE1221	1959	**£50**	**£25**	
Honky Tonk Rock	7"	London	HLU8326	1956	**£100**	**£50**	
Hoopa Hula	7"	London	HLE8725	1958	**£25**	**£12.50**	
I Dreamed	7"	London	HLU8365	1957	**£30**	**£15**	
I'll Wait	7"	London	HLU8307	1956	**£30**	**£15**	
Little Blue Man	7"	London	HLE8557	1958	**£25**	**£12.50**	
Songs You Heard When You Fell In Love	LP	London	HAE2163	1959	**£30**	**£15**	
There's Never Been A Night	7"	London	HLE8701	1958	**£30**	**£15**	

JOHNSON, BLIND WILLIE

Blind Willie Johnson	LP	Folkways	10	1965	**£12**	**£5**	*US*
Blind Willie Johnson	LP	XTRA	XTRA1098	1970	**£10**	**£4**	
Blues	LP	Folkways	3585	1957	**£20**	**£8**	*US*
Treasures Of North American Negro Music No. 2	7" EP	Fontana	TFE17052	1958	**£8**	**£4**	

JOHNSON, BOB & PETE KNIGHT

King Of Elfland's Daughter	LP	Chrysalis	CHR1137	1977	**£10**	**£4**	

JOHNSON, BOBBY & THE ATOMS

Do It Again A Little Bit Slower	7"	Ember	EMBS245	1967	**£8**	**£4**	*picture sleeve*
Do It Again A Little Bit Slower	7"	Ember	EMBS245	1967	**£4**	**£1.50**	

JOHNSON, BRYAN

Looking High	7" EP	Decca	DFE6664	1961	**£8**	**£4**	

JOHNSON, BUBBER

Come Home	LP	King	395569	1957	**£40**	**£20**	*US*
Confidential	7"	Parlophone	R4259	1957	**£20**	**£10**	
Sings Sweet Love Songs	LP	King	624	1959	**£30**	**£15**	*US*

JOHNSON, BUDD

Blues A La Mode	LP	Felsted	FAJ7007/SJA2007	1959	**£25**	**£10**	

JOHNSON, BUDDY & ELLA

Buddy Johnson Wails	7" EP	Mercury	ZEP10009	1959	**£50**	**£25**	
Buddy Johnson Wails	LP	Mercury	MG20072	1958	**£40**	**£20**	*US*
Go Ahead And Rock And Roll	LP	Roulette	(S)R25085	1959	**£40**	**£20**	*US*
Rock And Roll	10" LP	Mercury	MPT7515	1957	**£100**	**£50**	
Rock'n'Roll	LP	Mercury	MG20209	1956	**£40**	**£20**	*US*
Rock'n'Roll Stage Show	LP	Wing	MGW12005	1956	**£40**	**£20**	*US*
Swing Me	LP	Mercury	MG20347	1958	**£40**	**£20**	*US*
Walkin'	LP	Mercury	MG20322	1958	**£40**	**£20**	*US*

JOHNSON, BUNK

Bunk And Lu	LP	Good Time Jazz	LAG12121	1958	**£12**	**£5**	*with Lu Watters*
Bunk Johnson And His New Orleans Band	LP	Columbia	33SX1015	1954	**£15**	**£6**	
Bunk Johnson And His Superior Jazz Band	LP	Good Time Jazz	LAG545	1963	**£12**	**£5**	
Bunk Johnson And The Yerba Buena Jazz Band	10" LP	Good Time Jazz	LDG110	1955	**£20**	**£8**	
Bunk Johnson's Band 1944	LP	Storyville	SLP152	1964	**£12**	**£5**	
One You Love	7" EP	Melodisc	EPM752	1955	**£5**	**£2**	

JOHNSON, DANIEL

Come On My People	7"	Island	WI250	1965	**£10**	**£5**	

JOHNSON, DICK

Dick Johnson Quartet .... LP .... Emarcy .... EJT753 .... 1957 £25 .... £10 ....

JOHNSON, DOMINO

Summertime .... 7" .... Green Door ..... GD4045 .... 1972 £5 .... £2 .... *Swans B side*

JOHNSON, DON

Heartbeat .... 7" .... Epic .... EPCA6500648 .... 1986 £5 .... £2 ...... *face-shaped picture disc*

JOHNSON, DUNCAN

Big Architect .... 7" .... Spark .... SLR1022 .... 1969 £4 .... £1.50 ....

JOHNSON, HOLLY

Love Train .... CD-s ... MCA .... DMCA1306 .... 1989 £6 .... £2.50 ....
Love Train .... CD-s ... MCA .... DMCAT1306 .... 1989 £6 .... £2.50 .... *3" single*

JOHNSON, J. J.

Across 110th Street .... LP .... United Artists .. UAS29451 .... 1973 £12 .... £5 .. *with Bobby Womack*
Blue Trombone .... LP .... Fontana .... TFL5137 .... 1961 £12 .... £5 ....
Boneology .... LP .... Realm .... RM195 .... 1964 £12 .... £5 ....
Dial JJ5 .... LP .... Fontana .... TFL5021 .... 1958 £12 .... £5 ....
First Place .... LP .... Fontana .... TFL5005 .... 1958 £12 .... £5 ....
J Is For Jazz .... LP .... Philips .... BBL7143 .... 1957 £20 .... £8 ....
J. J. Johnson Quintet .... 10" LP Vogue .... LDE162 .... 1955 £50 .... £25 ....
J. J. Johnson Sextet .... 10" LP Vogue .... LDE124 .... 1955 £50 .... £25 ....
J.J. In Person .... LP .... Fontana .... TFL5041/ STFL512 .... 1960 £12 .... £5 ....
J.J.! .... LP .... RCA .... RD/SF7721 .... 1965 £10 .... £4 ....
Jay & Kai Plus Six .... LP .... Fontana .... TFL5022 .... 1958 £12 .... £5 .... *with Kai Winding*
Jay Jay Johnson Vol. 1 .... LP .... Blue Note .... BLP/BST81505 ...... 196– £25 .... £10 ....
Jay Jay Johnson Vol. 2 .... LP .... Blue Note .... BLP/BST81506 ...... 196– £25 .... £10 ....
Reflections .... LP .... Realm .... RM167 .... 1963 £12 .... £5 .... *with Kai Winding*

JOHNSON, JAMES P.

Daddy Of The Piano .... 10" LP Brunswick .... LA8548 .... 1952 £10 .... £4 ....
Early Harlem Piano .... 10" LP London .... AL3511 .... 1954 £20 .... £8 ....
Fats Waller Favourites .... 10" LP Brunswick .... LA8622 .... 1953 £20 .... £8 ....
Feeling Blue .... 7" .... Columbia .... SCM5127 .... 1954 £5 .... £2 ....
Harlem Party Piano .... 10" LP London .... HBU1057 .... 1956 £20 .... £8 .... *B side by Luckey Roberts*
James P. Johnson .... 10" LP London .... AL3540 .... 1955 £20 .... £8 ....
James P. Johnson .... 7" EP .. HMV .... 7EG8164 .... 1956 £6 .... £2.50 ....
James P. Johnson .... 7" EP .. Tempo .... EXA65 .... 1957 £6 .... £2.50 ....
Jimmy Johnson And Joe Sullivan .... 7" EP .. Fontana .... TFE17246 .... 1960 £5 .... £2 ....
Louisiana Sugar Babies .... 7" EP .. HMV .... 7EG8215 .... 1957 £10 .... £5 .... *with Fats Waller*

JOHNSON, JIMMY

Don't Answer The Door .... 7" .... Sue .... WI387 .... 1965 £12 .... £6 ....

JOHNSON, JOHNNY & THE BANDWAGON

Breaking Down The Walls Of Heartache .... 7" .... Direction .... 583670 .... 1968 £4 .... £1.50 ....
Honey Bee .... 7" .... Stateside .... SS2207 .... 1972 £5 .... £2 ....
Johnny Johnson And The Bandwagon .... LP .... Direction .... 863500 .... 1968 £10 .... £4 ....
Let's Hang On .... 7" .... Direction .... 584180 .... 1969 £6 .... £2.50 ....
Soul Survivor .... LP .... Bell .... SBLL138 .... 1970 £10 .... £4 ....

JOHNSON, JUDI

How Many Times .... 7" .... HMV .... POP1399 .... 1965 £6 .... £2.50 ....
My Baby's Face .... 7" .... HMV .... POP1371 .... 1964 £6 .... £2.50 ....

JOHNSON, KENNY & NORTHWIND

Lakeside Highway .... LP .... NWG .... 76103 .... 1976 £15 .... £6 ....

JOHNSON, LARRY

Presenting The Country Blues .... LP .... Blue Horizon ... 763851 .... 1970 £40 .... £20 ....

JOHNSON, LAURIE

Avengers .... 7" .... Pye .... 7N17015 .... 1965 £25 .... £12.50 .... *picture sleeve*
Avengers .... 7" .... Pye .... 7N17015 .... 1965 £6 .... £2.50 ....
Avengers .... LP .... Marble Arch .... MAL695 .... 1967 £20 .... £8 ....
Avengers .... LP .... HBR .... 8/9506 .... 1966 £30 .... £15 .... *US*
Belstone Fox .... LP .... Ronco .... RR2006 .... 1973 £10 .... £4 ....
Brass Band Swinging .... LP .... Columbia .... 33SX1231 .... 1960 £12 .... £5 ....
Buttercup .... 7" .... HMV .... 7MC47 .... 1956 £4 .... £1.50 .... *export*
Jason King Theme .... 7" .... Columbia .... DB8826 .... 1971 £15 ...... £7.50 ....
Music From The Avengers, New Avengers & The Professionals .... LP .... Unicorn .... KPM7009 .... 1980 £15 .... £6 ....
New Avengers Theme .... 7" .... EMI .... EMI2562 .... 1976 £6 .... £2.50 .... *picture sleeve*
Synthesis .... LP .... Columbia .... SCX6412 .... 1970 £40 .... £20 ....
Themes And . . . . LP .... MGM .... CS8104 .... 1969 £10 .... £4 ....

JOHNSON, LINTON KWESI

Dread Beat And Blood .... LP .... Front Line .... FL1017 .... 1978 £12 .... £5 .... *credited to Poet & The Roots*
Forces Of Victory .... LP .... Island .... ILPS9566 .... 1979 £10 .... £4 ....

JOHNSON, LONNIE

Title	Format	Label	Cat. No.	Year	Mint	Near Mint	Notes
Another Night To Cry	LP	Bluesville	BV1062	1963	£15	£6	US
Blues And Ballads	LP	Bluesville	BV1011	1960	£20	£8	US
Blues By Lonnie Johnson	LP	Bluesville	BV1007	1960	£20	£8	US
Blues For Everybody	78	Melodisc	1186	1951	£8	£3	
Idle Hours	LP	Bluesville	BV1044	1961	£20	£8	US
Jelly Roll Baker	78	Vogue	V2015	1951	£8	£3	
Keep What You Got	78	Melodisc	1221	1952	£8	£3	
Little Rockin' Chair	78	Vogue	V2079	1951	£8	£3	
Lonesome Road	7" EP	Parlophone	GEP8635	1957	£25	£12.50	
Lonesome Road	LP	King	395520	195–	£60	£30	US
Lonnie Johnson	LP	Storyville	616010	1969	£10	£4	
Lonnie Johnson	LP	XTRA	XTRA1037	1966	£15	£6	
Lonnie's Blues	7" EP	Parlophone	GEP8663	1957	£25	£12.50	
Lonnie's Blues No. 2	7" EP	Parlophone	GEP8693	1958	£25	£12.50	
Losing Game	LP	Bluesville	BV1024	1961	£20	£8	US
Masters Of The Blues Vol. 6	LP	Collector's Classics	CC30	196–	£12	£5	
Portraits In Blues Vol. 6	LP	Storyville	SLP162	1964	£10	£4	
Sings 24 Twelve Bar Blues	LP	King	K(S)958	1966	£12	£5	US
Solid Blues	78	Melodisc	1138	1951	£8	£3	
Woman Blues	LP	Bluesville	BV1054	1963	£15	£6	US

JOHNSON, LOU

Title	Format	Label	Cat. No.	Year	Mint	Near Mint	Notes
Always Something There To Remind Me	7"	London	HLX9917	1964	£15	£7.50	
Always Something There To Remind Me	7"	London	HLX10269	1969	£4	£1.50	
Magic Potion	7"	London	HLX9805	1963	£15	£7.50	
Magic Potion Of Lou Johnson	7" EP	London	REX1438	1964	£50	£25	
Message To Martha	7"	London	HLX9929	1964	£6	£2.50	
Please Stop The Wedding	7"	London	HLX9965	1965	£5	£2	
Unsatisfied	7"	London	HLX9994	1965	£30	£15	

JOHNSON, LUTHER

Title	Format	Label	Cat. No.	Year	Mint	Near Mint	Notes
With The Muddy Waters Blues Band	LP	Transatlantic	TRA188	1968	£10	£4	

JOHNSON, MARV

Title	Format	Label	Cat. No.	Year	Mint	Near Mint	Notes
Ain't Gonna Be That Way	7"	London	HLT9165	1960	£12	£6	
Come To Me	7"	London	HLT8856	1959	£75	£37.50	
Happy Days	7"	London	HLT9265	1961	£12	£6	
I Believe	LP	United Artists	UAL3187/ UAS6187	1962	£50	£25	US
I Love The Way You Love Me	7"	London	HL7095	1960	£10	£5	export
I Love The Way You Love Me	7"	London	HLT9109	1960	£12	£6	
I'll Pick A Rose For My Rose	7"	Tamla Motown	TMG680	1969	£4	£1.50	
I'll Pick A Rose For My Rose	LP	Tamla Motown	(S)TML11111	1969	£15	£6	
Marvellous Marv	LP	London	HAT2271	1960	£60	£30	
Merry-Go-Round	7"	London	HLT9311	1961	£20	£10	
More Marv Johnson	LP	United Artists	UAL3118/ UAS6118	1960	£60	£30	US
Move Two Mountains	7"	London	HLT9187	1960	£10	£5	
Why Do You Want To Let Me Go	7"	Tamla Motown	TMG525	1965	£50	£25	
You Got What It Takes	7"	London	HLT9013	1959	£6	£2.50	

JOHNSON, MATT

Title	Format	Label	Cat. No.	Year	Mint	Near Mint	Notes
Burning Blue Soul	LP	4AD	CAD113	1981	£12	£5	psychedelic eye sleeve

JOHNSON, MIRRIAM

Title	Format	Label	Cat. No.	Year	Mint	Near Mint	Notes
Lonesome Road	7"	London	HLW9337	1961	£6	£2.50	

JOHNSON, NORMAN

Title	Format	Label	Cat. No.	Year	Mint	Near Mint	Notes
Take It Baby	7"	Action	ACT4545	1969	£15	£7.50	
You're Everything	7"	Action	ACT4601	1971	£6	£2.50	
You're Everything	7"	Action	ACT4529	1969	£10	£5	

JOHNSON, PAUL

Title	Format	Label	Cat. No.	Year	Mint	Near Mint	Notes
Paul Johnson	LP	CBS	4506401	1988	£10	£4	

JOHNSON, PETE

Title	Format	Label	Cat. No.	Year	Mint	Near Mint	Notes
Boogie Woogie Mood	LP	Vogue Coral	LRA10016	1955	£15	£6	
Eight To The Bar	10" LP	HMV	DLP1011	1953	£30	£15	with Albert Ammons
J.J. Boogie	7"	Vogue	V2007	1956	£25	£12.50	
Pete Johnson	10" LP	London	AL3549	1955	£30	£15	
Pete Johnson	7" EP	Vogue	EPV1039	1955	£20	£10	
Pete's Blues	LP	Savoy	MG14018	195–	£25	£10	US
Roll Em Boy	7" EP	Top Rank	JKR8009	1959	£10	£5	
Swanee River Boogie	7"	Vogue	V2008	1956	£25	£12.50	

JOHNSON, PLAS

Title	Format	Label	Cat. No.	Year	Mint	Near Mint	Notes
Big Twist	7"	Capitol	CL14772	1957	£8	£4	
Bop Me Daddy	10" LP	London	HBU1078	1957	£25	£10	
Dinah	7"	Capitol	CL14903	1958	£8	£4	
Popcorn	7"	Capitol	CL14836	1958	£6	£2.50	

Title	Format	Label	Number	Year	Mint	VG+	Notes
Robbins Nest Cha Cha	7"	Capitol	CL14973	1959	£4	£1.50	
You Send Me	7"	Capitol	CL14816	1957	£8	£4	

JOHNSON, PROFESSOR GOSPEL SINGERS

Title	Format	Label	Number	Year	Mint	VG+	Notes
Where Shall I Be	7" EP	Brunswick	OE9352	1958	£8	£4	

JOHNSON, RAY

Title	Format	Label	Number	Year	Mint	VG+	Notes
Calypso Blues	7"	Vogue	V9093	1958	£30	£15	
If You Don't Want Me Baby	7"	Vogue	V9073	1957	£30	£15	

JOHNSON, ROBERT

According to legend, bluesman Robert Johnson met the devil at the crossroads and sold his soul in exchange for prowess on the guitar. In any event, the twenty-nine songs that Johnson recorded in 1936 and 1937 have come to be regarded as the finest and most influential country blues recordings of all. The majority of Johnson's songs have been covered by blues performers in later years, and the British blues boom of the late sixties would have been almost impossible without Johnson's work to draw on. Not that this does Johnson himself any good at all, for he was murdered by a jealous husband just one year after his last recording session.

Title	Format	Label	Number	Year	Mint	VG+	Notes
Blues Legend 1936–7	LP	Smokestack	SSLP1	196–	£30	£15	
King Of The Delta Blues Singers	LP	CBS	BPG62456	1963	£25	£10	
King Of The Delta Blues Singers Vol. 2	LP	CBS	64102	1970	£15	£6	
Robert Johnson	LP	Philips	BBL7539	1962	£50	£25	
Robert Johnson	LP	Kokomo	K1000	1967	£40	£20	

JOHNSON, ROY LEE

Title	Format	Label	Number	Year	Mint	VG+	Notes
So Anna Just Love Me	7"	Action	ACT4518	1969	£5	£2	

JOHNSON, RUBY

Title	Format	Label	Number	Year	Mint	VG+	Notes
If I Ever Needed Love	7"	Stax	601020	1967	£6	£2.50	

JOHNSON, TEDDY & PEARL CARR

Title	Format	Label	Number	Year	Mint	VG+	Notes
Meet Teddy And Pearl	7" EP	Pye	NEP24112	1959	£6	£2.50	

JOHNSON, THEO

Title	Format	Label	Number	Year	Mint	VG+	Notes
Masters Of War	7"	Island	WI604	1965	£5	£2	

JOHNSON, TOMMY

Title	Format	Label	Number	Year	Mint	VG+	Notes
Legacy Of Tommy Johnson	LP	Saydisc	SDM224	196–	£15	£6	

JOHNSTON, ADRIENNE

Title	Format	Label	Number	Year	Mint	VG+	Notes
Adrienne Of The Johnstons	LP	RCA	SF8416	1975	£10	£4	

JOHNSTON, BRUCE

Title	Format	Label	Number	Year	Mint	VG+	Notes
Original Surfer Stomp	7"	London	HL9780	1963	£20	£10	
Surfer's Pajama Party	LP	Del-Fi	DFLP/DFST1228	1963	£50	£25	US
Surfin' Round The World	LP	Columbia	CL2057/CS8857	1963	£60	£30	US

JOHNSTON BROTHERS

Title	Format	Label	Number	Year	Mint	VG+	Notes
Bandit	7"	Decca	F10302	1954	£5	£2	
Chee Chee-oo Chee	7"	Decca	F10513	1955	£4	£1.50	
Creep	7"	Decca	F10234	1954	£6	£2.50	
Dreamboat	7"	Decca	F10526	1955	£4	£1.50	
Easy No. 1	7" EP	Decca	DFE6503	1958	£5	£2	
Give Her My Love	7"	Decca	F10828	1956	£5	£2	
Heart	7"	Decca	F10860	1957	£4	£1.50	
Hernando's Hideaway	7"	Decca	F10608	1955	£8	£4	
How Little We Know	7"	Decca	F10747	1956	£4	£1.50	
I Get So Lonely	7"	Decca	F10286	1954	£5	£2	
I Like Music – You Like Music	7"	Decca	F10939	1957	£4	£1.50	
In The Middle Of The House	7"	Decca	F10781	1956	£8	£4	
Join In And Sing	7"	Decca	F10414	1954	£4	£1.50	
Join In And Sing	7" EP	Decca	DFE6311	1956	£5	£2	
Join In And Sing Again	7"	Decca	F10636	1955	£5	£2	
Join In And Sing Again	7" EP	Decca	DFE6458	1957	£5	£2	
Join In And Sing No. 3	7"	Decca	F10814	1956	£5	£2	
Join The Johnston Brothers	7" EP	Decca	DFE6249	1956	£5	£2	
Majorca	7"	Decca	F10451	1955	£4	£1.50	
Mambo In The Moonlight	7"	Decca	F10401	1954	£4	£1.50	
No Other Love	7"	Decca	F10721	1956	£5	£2	
Right To Be Wrong	7"	Decca	F10490	1955	£4	£1.50	
Sh'boom	7"	Decca	F10364	1954	£8	£4	

JOHNSTONS

Title	Format	Label	Number	Year	Mint	VG+	Notes
Barley Corn	LP	Transatlantic	TRA185	1969	£15	£6	
Bitter Green	LP	Transatlantic	TRA211	1969	£15	£6	
Colours Of The Dawn	LP	Transatlantic	TRA231	1971	£12	£5	
Give A Damn	LP	Transatlantic	TRA184	1968	£15	£6	
If I Sang My Song	LP	Transatlantic	TRA251	1972	£12	£5	
Johnstons	LP	Transatlantic	TRA169	1968	£25	£10	
Johnstons Sampler	LP	Transatlantic	TRASAM16	1970	£10	£4	
Travelling People	LP	Marble Arch	MAL808	1968	£20	£8	
Travelling People	LP	Hallmark	HMA237	1968	£20	£8	

JOINER, ARKANSAS, JUNIOR HIGH SCHOOL BAND

Title	Format	Label	Number	Year	Mint	VG+	Notes
National City	7"	London	HLG9147	1960	£4	£1.50	

JOINT EFFORT

Cannabis	LP	Amphion Seahorse	AS8100	1972	£60	£30	US

JOKERS

Dogfight	7"	Salvo	SLO1806	1962	£15	£7.50	

JOKERS WILD

The ultra-collectability of the Jokers Wild's privately pressed record derives not so much from the fact that the drummer, Willie Wilson, was later in Quiver, nor from the fact that the bassist, Ricky Wills, was later in Cochise and the re-formed Small Faces, but from the presence of the lead guitarist, who is David Gilmour – subsequently to be found playing within the ranks of Pink Floyd.

Don't Ask Me Why	7"	Regent Sound	RSR0031	1966	£500	£330	best auctioned
Jokers Wild	LP	Regent Sound	RSLP007	1966	£1000	£700	1 sided

JOLLIVER ARKANSAW

Home	LP	Bell	SBLL119	1969	£25	£10	

JOLLY BOYS

On The Water	7"	Moodisc	MU3504	1970	£5	£2	Mudies All Stars B side

JOLSON, AL

Al Jolson	7" EP	Fontana	TFE17024	1958	£5	£2	
Jolson Memories	10" LP	Brunswick	LA8512	1951	£10	£4	
Jolson Sings Again	10" LP	Brunswick	LA8502	1950	£10	£4	
Souvenir	10" LP	Brunswick	LA8509	1951	£10	£4	
They Sold A Million No. 2	7" EP	Brunswick	OE9418	1959	£5	£2	
They Sold A Million No. 3	7" EP	Brunswick	OE9419	1959	£5	£2	

JON

Is It Love	7"	Columbia	DB8249	1967	£30	£15	
So Much For Mary	7"	Parlophone	R5604	1967	£6	£2.50	
So Much For Mary	7"	Parlophone	R5604	1967	£20	£10	picture sleeve

JON & ALUN

Relax Your Mind	LP	Decca	LK/SKL4547	1963	£30	£15	

JON & ROBIN & THE IN CROWD

Do It Again A Little Bit Slower	7"	Stateside	SS2027	1967	£4	£1.50	
Do It Again A Little Bit Slower	7" EP	Barclay	071178	1967	£8	£4	French

JON & VANGELIS

Friends Of Mr Cairo	LP	Polydor	POLD5039	1981	£20	£8	promo with black & white sleeve
State Of Independence	12"	Polydor	POSPX323	1981	£25	£12.50	promo in blue film cannister
Wisdom Chain	CD-s	Arista	664063	1991	£6	£2.50	with Irene Papas

JONAS PALM

Ze Wormnest	LP	Piglet	PR1002	1980	£15	£6	German

JONATHAN & CHARLES

Another Week To Go	LP	Herald	LLR566	1969	£250	£150	

JONES, AL

Mad Mad World	7"	HMV	POP451	1958	£150	£75	

JONES, ALUN

Alun Ashworth Jones	LP	Parlophone	PMC/PCS7081	1969	£20	£8	
Jonesville	LP	Village Thing	VTS19	1972	£15	£6	

JONES, BEVERLY

Boy I Saw With You	7"	HMV	POP1109	1963	£5	£2	
Heatwave	7"	Parlophone	R5189	1964	£6	£2.50	
Wait Until My Bobby Gets Home	7"	HMV	POP1201	1963	£5	£2	
Why Do Lovers Break Each Others' Hearts	7"	HMV	POP1140	1963	£6	£2.50	

JONES, BRIAN

The one record credited to Brian Jones comes from the brief period between his leaving the Rolling Stones and his death, but it actually does not feature him at all. His decision to sponsor an ethnic band, however, is entirely symptomatic of his questing, open-minded approach at the time – the same approach that made the Stones' *Their Satanic Majesties Request* into one of the high points of sixties psychedelia, whatever the contrary views of modern critics may say. The Joujouka pipers, incidentally, turn up again in an intriguing meeting with saxophonist Ornette Coleman, on his album *Dancing In Your Head.*

Pipes Of Pan At Joujouka	LP	Rolling Stones	COC49100	1971	£75	£37.50	*'Brian Jones Plays With'*
Pipes Of Pan At Joujouka	LP	Rolling Stones	COC49100	1971	£50	£25	*'Brian Jones Presents'*

JONES, CAROL

Boys With Eyes Of Blue	7"	Triumph	RGM1012	1960	£75	£37.50	

JONES, CASEY & THE ENGINEERS

One Way Ticket	7"	Columbia	DB7083	1963	£20	£10	

JONES, CASEY & THE GOVERNORS

Beat Hits Vol. 2	LP	Bellaphon	BWS305	1965	£50	£25	*German*
Casey Jones And The Governors	LP	Golden	12LP108	1965	£50	£25	*German*
Don't Ha Ha	7" EP	Riviera	231087	1965	£40	£20	*French*
Don't Ha Ha	7" EP	President	425	1964	£60	£30	*French*
Don't Ha Ha	LP	Golden	12LP106	1964	£60	£30	*German*

JONES, CURTIS

In London	LP	Decca	LK4587	1964	£40	£20	
Now Resident In Europe	LP	Blue Horizon	763207	1968	£40	£20	
RCA Victor Race series Vol. 9	7" EP	RCA	RCX7184	1966	£10	£5	

JONES, DAVY

The Davy Jones whose records are listed here is the actor who became a member of the Monkees. Just to confuse matters, another Davy Jones also had records issued on the Pye label, but from 1960 to 1962. He has no connection with the Monkees whatsoever. A third Davy Jones made records with the Lower Third and the King Bees on the Vocalion and Parlophone labels. These are rare, but are listed in the guide under the name used by Jones later on – David Bowie. A David Jones who made one single for Philips in 1965 does not appear to have any connection with either the Monkees or David Bowie.

Davy Jones	LP	Pye	NPL18178	1967	£15	£6	
Davy Jones	LP	Bell	6067	1971	£10	£4	*US*
Do It In The Name Of Love	7"	Bell	BLL986	1971	£10	£5	*with Micky Dolenz*
Happy Birthday Mickey Mouse	7"	Warner Bros	K17161	1978	£5	£2	
I'll Love You Forever	7"	J.J.	2001	1983	£8	£4	
It Ain't Me Babe	7"	Pye	7N17302	1967	£4	£1.50	
It Ain't Me Babe	7"	Pye	7N17302	1967	£8	£4	*picture sleeve*
It Ain't Me Babe	7" EP	Pye	PNV24189	1967	£20	£10	*French*
Life Line	7"	MCA	MCA348	1977	£5	£2	*picture sleeve*
Rainy Jane	7"	Bell	BLL1163	1971	£5	£2	
Theme For A New Love	7"	Pye	7N17380	1967	£4	£1.50	
Theme For A New Love	7"	Pye	7N25432	1967	£4	£1.50	
Theme For A New Love	7"	Pye	7N17380	1967	£8	£4	*picture sleeve*
What Are We Going To Do	7"	Colpix	PX784	1965	£4	£1.50	

JONES, DAVY (2)

Amapola	7"	Pye	7N15254	1960	£4	£1.50	
Model Girl	7"	Pye	7N25072	1961	£5	£2	

JONES, DILL

Jones The Jazz	LP	Columbia	33SX1336	1961	£60	£30	
Piano Moods Vol. 2	7" EP	Polygon	JTE104	1956	£8	£4	
Piano Moods Vol. 5	7" EP	Pye	NJE1024	1956	£12	£6	

JONES, DOROTHY

Takin' That Long Walk Home	7"	Philips	322794BF	1961	£5	£2	

JONES, ELVIN

Coalition	LP	Blue Note	BST84361	1970	£10	£4	
Elvin Jones	LP	Blue Note	BST84414	1970	£10	£4	
Genesis	LP	Blue Note	BST84369	1970	£10	£4	
Heavy Sounds	LP	Impulse	MIPL/SIPL513	1969	£12	£5	
Live	LP	P.M.Records	PMR004	1975	£12	£5	*US*
Live At The Lighthouse	LP	Blue Note	BNLA015	1973	£15	£6	*double*
Midnight Walk	LP	Atlantic	1485	1968	£12	£5	
On The Mountain	LP	P.M.Records	PMR005	1975	£12	£5	*US*
Poly-Currents	LP	Blue Note	BST84331	1969	£12	£5	
Puttin' It Together	LP	Blue Note	BST84282	1968	£12	£5	
Ultimate	LP	Blue Note	BST84305	1968	£12	£5	

JONES, ETTA

Don't Go To Strangers	LP	Prestige	PRLP7186	1960	£12	£5	*US*
From The Heart	LP	Prestige	PRLP7214	1962	£12	£5	*US*
Holler	LP	Prestige	PRLP7284	1963	£12	£5	*US*
Lonely And Blue	LP	Prestige	PRLP7241	1962	£12	£5	*US*
Love Shout	LP	Prestige	PRLP7272	1963	£12	£5	*US*
Sings	LP	King	544	1958	£25	£10	*US*
Sings	LP	King	707	1961	£20	£8	*US*
So Warm	LP	Prestige	PRLP7204	1961	£12	£5	*US*
Something Nice	LP	Prestige	PRLP7194	1961	£12	£5	*US*

JONES, GEORGE

Accidentally On Purpose	7"	Mercury	AMT1100	1960	£6	£2.50	
Ballad Side Of George Jones	LP	Mercury	MG2/SR60836	1963	£12	£5	*US*
Best Of American Country Music Vol. 4	7" EP	Ember	EMBEP4548	1964	£5	£2	

Big Harlen Taylor	7"	Mercury	AMT1078	1959	**£6**	**£2.50**	
Blue And Lonesome	LP	Mercury	MG2/SR60906	1964	**£12**	**£5**	*US*
Blue Grass Hootenanny	LP	United Artists	ULP1077	1965	**£10**	**£4**	*with Melba Montgomery*
Blue Moon Of Kentucky	LP	United Artists	(S)ULP1137	1966	**£10**	**£4**	*with Melba Montgomery*
C&W Aces	7" EP	Mercury	10009MCE	1964	**£10**	**£5**	
Candy Hearts	7"	Mercury	AMT1124	1961	**£6**	**£2.50**	
Country & Western 1 Male Singer	LP	Mercury	MG2/SR60937	1964	**£12**	**£5**	*US*
Country And Western	7" EP	Mercury	ZEP10012	1959	**£25**	**£12.50**	*with Jimmie Skinner*
Country And Western Hits	LP	Mercury	MG2/SR60624	1961	**£12**	**£5**	*US*
Country And Western Winners	LP	Mercury	SMWL21003	1968	**£10**	**£4**	
Country Church Time	LP	Mercury	MG20462	1959	**£20**	**£8**	*US*
Country Heart	LP	Musicor	M2(S)5094	1966	**£10**	**£4**	*US*
Country Song Hits	7" EP	Melodisc	EPM7109	195–	**£25**	**£12.50**	
Crown Prince Of Country Music	LP	Starday	SLP125	1960	**£15**	**£6**	*US*
Crown Prince Of Country Music	LP	Ember	CW101	1963	**£10**	**£4**	
Duets Country Style	LP	Mercury	MG2/SR60747	1962	**£12**	**£5**	*US, with Margie Singleton*
Fabulous Country Music Sound	LP	Starday	SLP151	1962	**£15**	**£6**	*US*
Fabulous Country Music Sound	LP	Ember	CW109	1964	**£10**	**£4**	
Fourteen Country Favourites	LP	Mercury	MG20306	1958	**£20**	**£8**	*US*
From The Heart	LP	Mercury	MG2/SR60694	1962	**£12**	**£5**	*US*
George Jones	7" EP	Mercury	ZEP10036	1959	**£60**	**£30**	
George Jones	LP	London	HAB8259	1966	**£15**	**£6**	
George Jones And Gene Pitney	LP	Stateside	SL10147	1965	**£10**	**£4**	*with Gene Pitney*
George Jones Salutes Hank Williams	LP	Mercury	MG20257/ SR60257	1958	**£12**	**£5**	*US*
George Jones Song Book	LP	London	HAB8340	1967	**£15**	**£6**	
George Jones Story	LP	Starday	SLP366	1966	**£15**	**£6**	*US*
Grand Ole Opry's New Star	LP	Starday	SLP101	1958	**£50**	**£25**	*US*
Great George Jones	LP	United Artists	(S)ULP1136	1966	**£10**	**£4**	
Greatest Hits	LP	London	HAB8125	1964	**£15**	**£6**	
Greatest Hits	LP	Mercury	SMCL20107	1967	**£10**	**£4**	
Heartaches And Tears	LP	Mercury	MG2/SR60990	1965	**£12**	**£5**	*US*
Hits Of His Country Cousins	LP	United Artists	ULP1037	1963	**£10**	**£4**	
I Get Lonely In A Hurry	LP	United Artists	ULP1091	1965	**£10**	**£4**	
I Saw Me	7"	United Artists	UP1015	1963	**£5**	**£2**	
I Wish Tonight Would Never End	LP	United Artists	ULP1050	1964	**£10**	**£4**	
If My Heart Had Windows	7"	Stateside	SS2145	1969	**£4**	**£1.50**	
It's Country Time Again	LP	Stateside	SL10173	1966	**£10**	**£4**	*with Gene Pitney*
Love Bug	LP	Stateside	(S)SL10184	1966	**£10**	**£4**	
More New Favourites	LP	United Artists	ULP1074	1964	**£10**	**£4**	
Mr Country And Western Music	LP	Stateside	SL10157	1965	**£10**	**£4**	
Musical Loves, Life And Sorrows . . .	LP	Musicor	MS3159	1968	**£10**	**£4**	*US*
My Favourites Of Hank Williams	LP	United Artists	ULP1014	1963	**£10**	**£4**	
New Favourites	LP	United Artists	ULP1007	1962	**£10**	**£4**	
Novelty Side Of George Jones	LP	Mercury	MG2/SR60793	1963	**£15**	**£6**	*US*
Race Is On	7"	United Artists	UP1080	1965	**£6**	**£2.50**	
She Thinks I Still Care	7"	HMV	POP1037	1962	**£6**	**£2.50**	
Singing The Blues	LP	Mercury	MG2/SR61029	1965	**£12**	**£5**	*US*
Sings Like The Dickens	LP	United Artists	ULP1082	1965	**£10**	**£4**	
Sings The Songs Of Dallas Frazier	LP	Stateside	(S)SL10236	1968	**£10**	**£4**	
Song Book And Picture Album	LP	Starday	SLP401	1967	**£15**	**£6**	*US*
Treasure Of Love	7"	Mercury	AMT1021	1959	**£10**	**£5**	
Trouble In Mind	LP	United Artists	ULP1101	1965	**£10**	**£4**	
Variety Is The Spice	LP	Stateside	(S)SL10215	1967	**£10**	**£4**	
We Found Heaven Right Here On Earth	LP	Stateside	(S)SL10195	1967	**£10**	**£4**	
What's In Our Hearts	LP	United Artists	ULP1070	1964	**£10**	**£4**	*with Melba Montgomery*
White Lightning	7"	Mercury	AMT1036	1959	**£30**	**£15**	
White Lightning And Other Favorites	LP	Mercury	MG20477	1959	**£20**	**£8**	*US*
Who Shot Sam	7"	Mercury	AMT1058	1959	**£12**	**£6**	
Your Heart Turned Left	7"	United Artists	UP1044	1964	**£5**	**£2**	

JONES, GLORIA

Finders Keepers	7"	Stateside	SS555	1966	**£20**	**£10**	
Heartbeat	7"	Capitol	CL15429	1966	**£10**	**£5**	

JONES, GRACE

La Vie En Rose	12"	Island	IPR2004	1986	**£6**	**£2.50**	*promo*

JONES, GRANDPA

Country And Western	7" EP	Parlophone	GEP8766	1958	**£15**	**£7.50**	
Country Round Up	7" EP	Parlophone	GEP8781	1959	**£12**	**£6**	
Dark As A Dungeon	7"	Brunswick	05676	1957	**£20**	**£10**	
Do You Remember?	LP	King	845	1963	**£20**	**£8**	*US*
Evening With Grandpa Jones	LP	Decca	DL4364	1963	**£20**	**£8**	*US*
Grandpa Sings Jimmie Rodgers	7" EP	London	REU1417	1964	**£20**	**£10**	
Greatest Hits	LP	King	554	1958	**£20**	**£8**	*US*
Make The Rafters Ring	LP	London	HAU/SHU8010	1962	**£25**	**£10**	
Meet Grandpa Jones	7" EP	Parlophone	GEP8666	1957	**£12**	**£6**	
Mountain Music Vol. 3	7" EP	Brunswick	OE9455	1959	**£12**	**£6**	
Other Side Of Grandpa Jones	LP	King	888	1964	**£20**	**£8**	*US*
Rollin' Along	LP	King	809	1963	**£20**	**£8**	*US*
Sixteen Sacred Gospel Songs	LP	King	822	1963	**£20**	**£8**	*US*
Strictly Country Tunes	LP	King	625	1959	**£20**	**£8**	*US*

Yodelling Hits	LP	London	HAU/SHU8119	1964	£25	£10	

JONES, HANK

Hank Jones Quartet	LP	London	LTZC15118	1958	£20	£8	
Hank Jones Quartet/Quintet	LP	London	LTZC15014	1956	£25	£10	
Have You Met Hank Jones?	LP	London	LTZC15079	1958	£25	£10	

JONES, HEATHER

Jiawl!	LP	Sain	1047M	1976	£20	£8	
Mae'r Olwyn Yn Troi	LP	Sain	1008M	1973	£25	£10	

JONES, HOWARD

All I Want	7"	WEA	HOW10G	1986	£5	£2	*double*
Everlasting Love	CD-s	WEA	HOW13CDX	1989	£6	£2.50	*3" single*
Everlasting Love	CD-s	WEA	HOW13CD	1989	£5	£2	*3" single*
Look Mama	12"	WEA	HOW7TE	1985	£8	£4	
Prisoner	CD-s	WEA	HOW14CD	1989	£5	£2	*3" single*
Tears To Tell	CD-s	WEA	HOW17CD	1992	£15	£7.50	
Things Can Only Get Better	7"	WEA	HOW6P	1985	£8	£4	*green shaped picture disc*
What Is Love?	12"	WEA	HOW2	1983	£8	£4	*with 7" SAM183*
Working In The Backroom	CD	D-Tox	D-TOXCD1	199–	£25	£10	

JONES, HUW

Dwr	7"	Sain	SAIN1	1969	£10	£5	*picture sleeve*

JONES, JANET

Sing To Me Lady	LP	Midas	MR005	1974	£250	£150	

JONES, JANIE

Back On My Feet Again	7"	President	PT309	1970	£4	£1.50	
Charlie Smith	7"	Pye	7N17550	1968	£4	£1.50	
Girl's Song	7"	Major Minor	MM577	1968	£4	£1.50	
Gunning For You	7"	HMV	POP1514	1966	£8	£4	
House Of The Ju-Ju Queen	7"	Big Beat	NS91	1983	£4	£1.50	
Tickle Me Tootsie Wootsies	7"	Columbia	DB8173	1967	£4	£1.50	
Witches Brew	7"	HMV	POP1495	1965	£10	£5	

JONES, JERRY

Live At The Kingston Hotel, Jamaica	LP	Bamboo	BALPS213	1971	£25	£10	
Still Waters	7"	Bamboo	BAM65	1971	£5	£2	*Sound Dimension B side*
Still Waters	7"	Banana	BA316	1970	£5	£2	*Sound Dimension B side*

JONES, JIMMY

39-21-46	7"	Stateside	SS2041	1967	£5	£2	
Good Timin'	LP	MGM	C832	1960	£50	£25	
I Just Go For You	7"	MGM	MGM1091	1960	£4	£1.50	
I Say Love	7"	MGM	MGM1133	1961	£4	£1.50	
I Told You So	7"	MGM	MGM1123	1961	£4	£1.50	
Jimmy Handyman Jones	7" EP	MGM	MGMEP745	1960	£30	£15	
Mister Music Man	7"	MGM	MGM1146	1961	£4	£1.50	
Original Hits	7" EP	MGM	MGMEP787	1961	£25	£12.50	
Ready For Love	7"	MGM	MGM1103	1960	£4	£1.50	
Walkin'	7"	Columbia	DB7592	1965	£20	£8	
You're Much Too Young	7"	MGM	MGM1168	1962	£4	£1.50	

JONES, JO

Jo Jones	LP	Top Rank	25039	1959	£10	£4	
Jo Jones Special	LP	Vanguard	PPL11002	1956	£15	£6	
Jo Jones Trio	LP	Top Rank	35039	1960	£10	£4	

JONES, JOE

You Talk Too Much	7"	Columbia	DB4533	1960	£8	£4	
You Talk Too Much	LP	Roulette	(S)R25143	1961	£20	£8	*US*

JONES, JOHN PAUL

Baja	7"	Pye	7N15637	1964	£50	£25	

JONES, JONAH

I Dig Chicks	LP	Capitol	T1193	1959	£10	£4	
Jonah Jones–Alix Combelle Sextet	10" LP	Vogue	LDE145	1955	£20	£8	
Jonah Jones Sextet	10" LP	London	LZN14003	1955	£20	£8	
Jumpin' With Jonah	LP	Capitol	(S)T1039	1959	£10	£4	
On The Sunny Side Of The Street	LP	Brunswick	LAT8633	1965	£10	£4	
Swinging At The Cinema	LP	Capitol	T1083	1959	£10	£4	

JONES, JUSTIN

Dance By Yourself	7"	London	HLU9463	1961	£30	£15	

JONES, LINDA

Hypnotised	7"	Warner Bros	WB2070	1967	£25	£12.50	
Hypnotised	LP	Loma	5907	1967	£30	£15	*US*
I Just Can't Live My Life	7"	Warner Bros	K16621	1975	£5	£2	
Your Precious Love	LP	Turbo	7007	1973	£15	£6	*US*

JONES, MAGGIE

Columbia Recordings In Chronological Order Vol. 1	LP	VJM	VLP23	1970	**£10**	**£4**	
Columbia Recordings In Chronological Order Vol. 2	LP	VJM	VLP25	1970	**£10**	**£4**	

JONES, NIC

Ballads And Songs	LP	Trailer	LER2014	1970	**£25**	**£10**	
From The Devil To A Stranger	LP	Transatlantic	TRA507	1978	**£15**	**£6**	
Nic Jones	LP	Trailer	LER2027	1971	**£20**	**£8**	
Noah's Ark Trap	LP	Trailer	LER2091	1977	**£25**	**£10**	

JONES, NIGEL MAZLYN

Breaking Cover	LP	Isle Of Light	IOL0230	1982	**£15**	**£6**	
Sentinel	LP	Avada	AVA105	1978	**£25**	**£10**	
Ship To Shore	LP	Isle Of Light	IOL666/1	1976	**£40**	**£20**	

JONES, PALMER

Great Magic Of Love	7"	Direction	583603	1968	**£4**	**£1.50**	

JONES, PAUL

And The Sun Will Shine	7"	Columbia	DB8379	1968	**£12**	**£6**	
Come Into My Music Box	LP	Columbia	SCX6347	1969	**£20**	**£8**	
Crucifix In A Horseshoe	LP	Vertigo	6360059	1971	**£25**	**£10**	*spiral label*
High Time	7"	HMV	POP1554	1966	**£4**	**£1.50**	
High Time	7" EP	Pathe	EGF952	1966	**£12**	**£6**	*French*
I've Been A Bad Bad Boy	7"	HMV	POP1576	1967	**£4**	**£1.50**	
I've Been A Bad Bad Boy	7" EP	Pathe	EGF965	1966	**£12**	**£6**	*French*
Love Me Love My Friends	LP	HMV	CLP/CSD3602	1967	**£15**	**£6**	
My Way	LP	HMV	CLP/CSD3586	1966	**£15**	**£6**	
Privilege	7" EP	HMV	7EG8974	1966	**£10**	**£5**	
Privilege	7" EP	Pathe	EGF982	1966	**£12**	**£6**	*French*
Privilege	LP	HMV	CLP3523	1966	**£15**	**£6**	
When I Was Six Years Old	7"	Columbia	DB8417	1968	**£4**	**£1.50**	

JONES, QUINCY

A few statistics tell their own story. Quincy Jones is the producer of the biggest-selling album of all time, Michael Jackson's *Thriller*, and of one of the biggest-selling singles, the various artists USA For Africa record, *We Are The World*. He has received the largest number of Grammy nominations of any artist – 76 of them to date – and is second only to conductor Sir Georg Solti in the number he has actually been given – 26. Through his work as a film soundtrack composer, he has had seven Oscar nominations, as well as receiving an Emmy Award for his score for the *Roots* television series. He has a number of international arts awards, including the French Legion d'Honneur, and has been granted honorary doctorates from seven American universities and from the prestigious Berklee College of Music. He runs his own highly successful label, Qwest Records; he is the owner of the black culture showcase *Vibe* magazine; and he has spearheaded the formation of Qwest Broadcasting, already established as one of the largest independently owned broadcasting companies in the USA.

Adventurers	LP	Symbolic	001	1969	**£25**	**£10**	
Around The World	LP	Mercury	MMC14098/ CMS18064	1962	**£10**	**£4**	
Big Band Bash	7" EP	Mercury	ZEP10047	1960	**£8**	**£4**	
Big Band Bossa Nova	LP	Mercury	MMC14125/ CMS18080	1963	**£15**	**£6**	
Birth Of A Band	7" EP	Mercury	ZEP10109/ SEZ19017	1961	**£5**	**£2**	
Birth Of A Band	LP	Mercury	MMC14038/ CMS18026	1960	**£15**	**£6**	
Birth Of A Band Part 2	7" EP	Mercury	ZEP10119/ SEZ19021	1961	**£5**	**£2**	
Double Six Meet Quincy Jones	7" EP	Columbia	SEG8088	1961	**£5**	**£2**	
Explores The Music Of Henry Mancini	LP	Mercury	(S)MCL20016	1964	**£12**	**£5**	
Fab!	LP	Fontana	FJL127	1966	**£12**	**£5**	
Go West, Man	LP	HMV	CLP1157	1958	**£15**	**£6**	
Golden Boy	LP	Mercury	20047MCL	1965	**£12**	**£5**	
Great Wide World Of Quincy Jones	LP	Mercury	MMC14046/ CMS18031	1960	**£15**	**£6**	
Gula Matira	LP	A&M	AMLS992	1971	**£10**	**£4**	
Heist	LP	WEA	K44168	1972	**£10**	**£4**	
How To Steal A Diamond	LP	Atlantic	K40371	1972	**£10**	**£4**	
I Dig Dancers	LP	Mercury	MMC14080/ CMS18055	1961	**£10**	**£4**	
In Cold Blood	LP	RCA	RD/SF7931	1968	**£20**	**£8**	
In The Heat Of The Night	LP	United Artists	(S)ULP1181	1968	**£20**	**£8**	
Ironside	LP	A&M	AMLP8005	1975	**£10**	**£4**	
Italian Job	LP	Paramount	SPFL256	1969	**£60**	**£30**	
Lost Man	LP	Uni	UNLS103	1969	**£12**	**£5**	
MacKenna's Gold	LP	RCA	SF8017	1969	**£10**	**£4**	
Mellow Madness	LP	A&M	AMLH64526	1975	**£10**	**£4**	
Mirage	LP	Mercury	20072(S)MCL	1966	**£12**	**£5**	
Pawnbroker	LP	Mercury	20063SML	1965	**£15**	**£6**	
Plays For Pussycats	LP	Mercury	20073(S)MCL	1966	**£12**	**£5**	
Plays Hip Hits	LP	Mercury	MMC14128	1963	**£10**	**£4**	
Quincy's Got A Brand New Bag	LP	Mercury	20078(S)MCL	1966	**£15**	**£6**	
Quincy's Home Again	LP	Columbia	33SX1637	1965	**£12**	**£5**	
Quintessence	LP	HMV	CLP1581/ CSD1452	1962	**£12**	**£5**	
Smackwater Jack	LP	A&M	AMLS63037	1971	**£12**	**£5**	
Soul Bossa Nova	7"	Mercury	AMT1195	1962	**£8**	**£4**	

They Call Me Mister Tibbs	LP	United Artists	UAS29128	1970	**£40**	**£20**	
This Is How I Feel About Jazz	LP	HMV	CLP1162	1958	**£15**	**£6**	
Travellin' On The Quincy Jones Bandwagon	LP	Mercury	SMWL30003	1967	**£10**	**£4**	
Walking In Space	LP	A&M	AMLS961	1969	**£10**	**£4**	
You've Got It Bad Girl	LP	A&M	AMLS63041	1973	**£10**	**£4**	

JONES, RICK

Hiya Maya	LP	Argo	ZDA156	1973	**£12**	**£5**	
Twixt You And Me	LP	Argo	ZFB27	1971	**£10**	**£4**	

JONES, RONNIE

Anyone Who Knows What Love Is	7"	Decca	F12146	1965	**£6**	**£2.50**	
I Need Your Loving	7"	Decca	F12012	1964	**£6**	**£2.50**	
I'm So Clean	7"	Parlophone	R5326	1965	**£20**	**£10**	
In My Love Mind	7"	Polydor	56222	1967	**£5**	**£2**	
Little Bitty Pretty One	7"	CBS	3304	1968	**£4**	**£1.50**	
Little Bitty Pretty One	7"	CBS	2699	1967	**£4**	**£1.50**	
My Love	7"	Decca	F12066	1965	**£8**	**£4**	

JONES, SALENA

Live And Let Die	7"	Indigo	GOPOP	1973	**£6**	**£2.50**	*picture sleeve*

JONES, SAMANTHA

And Suddenly	7"	United Artists	UP2258	1968	**£8**	**£4**	
Don't Come Any Closer	7"	United Artists	UP1087	1965	**£4**	**£1.50**	
Ford Leads The Way	7"	Ford		1968	**£10**	**£5**	*picture sleeve*
It's All Because Of You	7"	United Artists	UP1072	1965	**£4**	**£1.50**	
Surrounded By A Ray Of Sunshine	7"	United Artists	UP1185	1967	**£25**	**£12.50**	

JONES, SANDIE

Music Of Love	7"	Polydor	2058223	1972	**£10**	**£5**	

JONES, SPIKE

Deep Purple	7"	HMV	7MC3	1954	**£6**	**£2.50**	*export*
Fun In Hi Fi	7" EP	HMV	7EG8286	1957	**£6**	**£2.50**	
Hot Lips	7"	HMV	7M121	1953	**£8**	**£4**	
I Saw Mommy Kissing Santa Claus	7"	HMV	7M160	1953	**£8**	**£4**	
I Wanna Go Back To West Virginia	7"	HMV	7MC17	1954	**£6**	**£2.50**	*export*
Omnibust TV Schedule	LP	London	HAG2270/ SHG6090	1960	**£10**	**£4**	
Secret Love	7"	HMV	7M324	1955	**£6**	**£2.50**	
Sixty Years Of Music America Hates Best	LP	London	HAG2298/ SHG6109	1961	**£10**	**£4**	
Spike Jones In Hi Fi	7" EP	Warner Bros	WEP6044	1961	**£6**	**£2.50**	
Spike Jones In Hi-Fi	LP	Warner Bros	WM4004/ WS8004	1959	**£12**	**£5**	
Spike Jones In Stereo	7" EP	Warner Bros	WSEP2044	1961	**£8**	**£4**	
Spike Jones No. 1	7" EP	RCA	RCX1030	1959	**£6**	**£2.50**	
Spike Jones No. 2	7" EP	RCA	RCX1037	1959	**£6**	**£2.50**	
Thank You, Music Lovers	LP	RCA	RD7724	1965	**£10**	**£4**	

JONES, STAN

Creakin' Leather	LP	Pye	DPL39000	1958	**£15**	**£6**	

JONES, STEVE

Live	CD	MCA	CD4518179	1990	**£12**	**£5**	*promo only*

JONES, THAD

Leonard Feather Presents Mad Thad	LP	Nixa	NJL13	1957	**£40**	**£20**	
Thad Jones	LP	Vogue	LDE172	1956	**£40**	**£20**	

JONES, THAD & MEL LEWIS JAZZ ORCHESTRA

Central Park North	LP	United Artists	UAS29058	1969	**£10**	**£4**	
Consummation	LP	Blue Note	BST84346	1970	**£10**	**£4**	
Live At The Village Vanguard	LP	United Artists	USS7008	1967	**£12**	**£5**	
Monday Night	LP	United Artists	UAS29016	1968	**£12**	**£5**	
Presenting Thad Jones–Mel Lewis & The Jazz Orchestra	LP	United Artists	SULP1169	1967	**£12**	**£5**	

JONES, THELMA

House That Jack Built	7"	Soul City	SC110	1969	**£10**	**£5**	
Stranger	7"	Sue	WI4047	1968	**£10**	**£5**	

JONES, TOM

Bama Lama Bama Loo	7" EP	Decca	457078	1965	**£10**	**£5**	*French*
Carrying A Torch	CD-s	Dover	ROJCD12	1991	**£5**	**£2**	*with Van Morrison*
Chills And Fever	7"	Decca	F11966	1964	**£20**	**£10**	
Detroit City	7"	Decca	F22563	1967	**£6**	**£2.50**	*export*
Detroit City	7" EP	Decca	457141	1967	**£8**	**£4**	*French*
Green Green Grass Of Home	7"	Decca	F12516	1966	**£6**	**£2.50**	*export*
Green Green Grass Of Home	7" EP	Decca	457134	1967	**£8**	**£4**	*French*
It's Not Unusual	7" EP	Decca	457065	1965	**£8**	**£4**	*French*
Little Lonely One	7"	Columbia	DB7566	1965	**£15**	**£7.50**	
Little Lonely One	7" EP	Columbia	ESRF1684	1965	**£10**	**£5**	*French, B side by Beau Brummell*
Lonely Joe	7"	Columbia	DB7733	1965	**£15**	**£7.50**	
Not Responsible	7" EP	Decca	457118	1966	**£8**	**£4**	*French*

Title	Format	Label	Cat. No.	Year	Mint	Avg	Notes
On Stage	7" EP	Decca	DFE8617	1965	£8	£4	
Stop Breaking My Heart	7"	Decca	F12349	1966	£5	£2	
Stop Breaking My Heart	7" EP	Decca	457107	1966	£8	£4	*French*
Thunderball	7"	Decca	F12292	1966	£4	£1.50	
Till	7"	Decca	FR13237	1971	£6	£2.50	*export*
To Make A Big Man Cry	7"	Decca	F12315	1966	£6	£2.50	*export*
Tom Jones	7" EP	Columbia	SEG8464	1965	£25	£12.50	
What A Party	7" EP	Decca	457127	1966	£8	£4	*French*
What A Party	7" EP	Decca	DFE8668	1965	£8	£4	
What's New Pussycat	7" EP	Decca	457088	1965	£8	£4	*French*
With These Hands	7" EP	Decca	457082	1965	£8	£4	*French*

JONES, WIZZ

Title	Format	Label	Cat. No.	Year	Mint	Avg	Notes
Ballad Of Hollis Brown	7"	Columbia	DB7776	1965	£8	£4	*with Pete Stanley*
Legendary Me	LP	Village Thing	VTS4	1970	£25	£10	
Magical Flight	LP	Plant Life	PLR009	1977	£10	£4	
Right Now	LP	CBS	64809	1971	£40	£20	
Roll On River	LP	Folk Freak	FF4006	1981	£12	£5	*German, with Werner Lammerhirt*
Sixteen Tons Of Bluegrass	LP	Columbia	SX6083	1966	£125	£62.50	*with Pete Stanley*
Solo Flight	LP	Autogram	FLLP507	1973	£30	£15	*with EP, German*
When I Leave Berlin	LP	Village Thing	VTS24	1974	£15	£6	
Wizz Jones	LP	United Artists	(S)ULP1209	1969	£125	£62.50	

JONES BOYS

Title	Format	Label	Cat. No.	Year	Mint	Avg	Notes
Cool Baby	7"	Columbia	DB4046	1957	£5	£2	

JONESY

Alan Bown's R&B band was a significant part of the sixties rock scene in Britain, even if it never managed to break through into the first division. Part of the problem was no doubt due to the difficulty Bown himself faced in finding a strong image when he was neither a singer nor a guitarist, but a trumpet player. Within Jonesy, Bown finally dealt with the problem by relegating himself to the status of band member rather than leader, but it is his trumpet playing that gives the band's slant on jazz-rock such a distinctive edge. If the electric-period Miles Davis had ever decided to play within a song-based band, it might have sounded something like this.

Title	Format	Label	Cat. No.	Year	Mint	Avg	Notes
Growing	LP	Dawn	DNLS3055	1973	£15	£6	
Keeping Up	LP	Dawn	DNLS3048	1973	£15	£6	
No Alternative	LP	Dawn	DNLS3042	1972	£25	£10	

JONNS, HARLEM RESHUFFLE

Title	Format	Label	Cat. No.	Year	Mint	Avg	Notes
Everything Under The Sun	7"	Fontana	TF1004	1969	£4	£1.50	
Harlem Jonns Reshuffle	LP	Fontana	STL5509	1969	£10	£4	
You Are The One I Love	7"	Fontana	TF970	1968	£5	£2	

JONSTON McPHILBRY

Title	Format	Label	Cat. No.	Year	Mint	Avg	Notes
She's Gone	7"	Fontana	TF663	1966	£75	£37.50	

JOPLIN, JANIS

Title	Format	Label	Cat. No.	Year	Mint	Avg	Notes
Cheap Thrills	CD	CBS	CD63392	1984	£12	£5	*with Big Brother & The Holding Co.*
I Got Dem Ol' Kozmic Blues Again	LP	CBS	63546	1969	£10	£4	
In Concert	LP	CBS	67241	1972	£12	£5	*double*
Janis	LP	CBS	88115	1974	£12	£5	*double*
Move Over	7"	CBS	9136	1971	£4	£1.50	
Pearl	LP	CBS	Q64188	1974	£15	£6	*quad*
Pearl	LP	CBS	64188	1971	£10	£4	
Turtle Blues	7"	CBS	3683	1969	£25	£12.50	

JORDAN, CHRISTOPHER

Title	Format	Label	Cat. No.	Year	Mint	Avg	Notes
Knack	7" EP	United Artists	36075	1965	£8	£4	*French*

JORDAN, DANNY

Title	Format	Label	Cat. No.	Year	Mint	Avg	Notes
Jeannie	7"	Mercury	AMT1159	1961	£4	£1.50	

JORDAN, DICK

Title	Format	Label	Cat. No.	Year	Mint	Avg	Notes
Angel On My Shoulder	7"	Oriole	CB1591	1960	£5	£2	
Hallelujah I Love Her So	7"	Oriole	CB1534	1960	£6	£2.50	
Little Christine	7"	Oriole	CB1548	1960	£6	£2.50	

JORDAN, DUKE

Title	Format	Label	Cat. No.	Year	Mint	Avg	Notes
Duke Jordan	10" LP	Vogue	LDE099	1954	£40	£20	
Flight To Jordan	LP	Blue Note	BLP/BST84046	196–	£50	£25	

JORDAN, FRED

Title	Format	Label	Cat. No.	Year	Mint	Avg	Notes
Songs Of A Shropshire Farm Worker	LP	Topic	12T150	1966	£12	£5	
When The Frost Is On The Pumpkin	LP	Topic	12TS233	1974	£10	£4	

JORDAN, LOUIS

Title	Format	Label	Cat. No.	Year	Mint	Avg	Notes
Dad Gum Ya Hide Boy	78	Melodisc	1031	1954	£8	£3	
Go Blow Your Horn	LP	Score	4007	195–	£60	£30	*US*
Greatest Hits	LP	Decca	DL5035	1967	£10	£4	*US*
Hallelujah, Louis Jordan Is Back	LP	HMV	CLP1809	1964	£20	£8	
Is You Is Or Is You Ain't My Baby	7"	Melodisc	1616	196–	£6	£2.50	*with Chris Barber*
Let The Good Times Roll	LP	Ace Of Hearts	AH85	1965	£12	£5	
Let The Good Times Roll	LP	Decca	DL8551	1958	£30	£15	*US*
Let The Good Times Roll	LP	Coral	CP59	1970	£10	£4	
Louis Jordan	7" EP	Melodisc	EPM766	1956	£60	£30	
Man, We're Wailin'	LP	Mercury	MPL6541	1958	£30	£15	

Messy Bessy 78 Melodisc 1349 1956 £8 £3
Ooo Wee 7" Downbeat CHA3 1960 £12 £6
Saturday Night Fish Fry 78 Brunswick 04402 1950 £6 £2.50
Somebody Up There Digs Me 10" LP Mercury MPT7521 1957 £40 £20
Somebody Up There Digs Me LP Mercury MG20242 1957 £40 £20 *US*

JORDAN, SHEILA

Portrait LP Blue Note BLP/BST89002 1962 £40 £20

JORDAN BROTHERS

Never Never 7" London HLW8908 1959 £20 £10
No Wings On My Angel 7" London HLW9308 1961 £5 £2
Things I Didn't Say 7" London HLW9235 1960 £8 £4

JORDANAIRES

Beautiful City 10" LP RCA LPM3081 1953 £30 £15 *US*
Don't Be Cruel 7" Capitol CL15281 1963 £8 £4
Gloryland LP Capitol T1167 1959 £30 £15 *US*
Heavenly Spirit LP Capitol T1011 1958 £30 £15 *US*
Little Miss Ruby 7" Capitol CL14921 1958 £10 £5
Peace In The Valley LP Decca DL8681 1957 £30 £15 *US*
Spotlight On The Jordanaires LP Capitol T1742 1962 £30 £15
Sugaree 7" Capitol CL14687 1957 £40 £20
Summer Vacation 7" Capitol CL14773 1957 £8 £4

JOSEF K

Chance Meeting 7" Absolute ABS1 1980 £20 £10
Chance Meeting 7" Postcard 81-5 1981 £5 £2 *with postcard*
It's Kinda Funny 7" Postcard 80-5 1980 £8 £4 *colour insert in bag*
It's Kinda Funny 7" Postcard 80-5 1980 £4 £1.50
Only Fun In Town LP Postcard 81-7 1981 £12 £5
Radio Drill Time 7" Postcard 80-3 1980 £10 £5 *with poster*
Radio Drill Time 7" Postcard 80-3 1980 £5 £2
Sorry For laughing 7" Postcard 81-4 1981 £5 £2
Sorry For Laughing LP Postcard 81-1 1981 £200 £100 *test pressing with proof sleeve*
Sorry For Laughing LP Postcard 81-1 1981 £100 £50 *test pressing*

JOSEFUS

Dead Man LP Hookah 330 1970 £150 £75 *US*
Josefus LP Mainstream 6127 1970 £75 £37.50 *US*

JOSEPH, MARGIE

Makes A New Impression LP Stax 2362008 1972 £10 £4
Margie Joseph LP Atlantic K40462 1973 £10 £4

JOSHUA

Joshua LP Key KL014 1973 £75 £37.50

JOSHUA FOX

Joshua Fox LP Tetragrammaton 125 1968 £30 £15 *US*

JOSIE, MARVA

Crazy Stockings 7" Polydor 56711 1966 £5 £2

JOURNEY

Departure LP Columbia HC46339 1981 £10 £4 *US audiophile*
Dream After Dream LP Columbia HC47998 1982 £10 £4 *US audiophile*
Escape LP Columbia HC47408 1981 £10 £4 *US audiophile*
Escape LP Mobile Fidelity MFSL1144 1981 £15 £6 *US audiophile*
Infinity LP Columbia HC4912 1981 £10 £4 *US audiophile*
Who's Crying Now CD-s CBS 6545412 1989 £5 £2

JOURNEYMEN

Introducing The Journeymen LP Ember EMB3382 1966 £12 £5
Journeymen LP Capitol (S)T1629 1961 £15 £6 *US*
Live LP Capitol 1770 1962 £25 £10 *US*
New Directions In Folk Music LP Capitol (S)T1951 1963 £15 £6 *US*

JOY, CARL & THE JOYBOYS

Be My Girl 7" Top Rank JAR529 1961 £5 £2
Bye Bye Baby Goodbye 7" Brunswick 05806 1959 £5 £2

JOY, RODDIE

Come Back Baby 7" Red Bird RB021 1965 £25 £12.50

JOY & DAVID

Joe's Been A Gitting There 7" Parlophone R4855 1961 £20 £10
Let's Go See Grandma 7" Triumph RGM1002 1960 £25 £12.50
My Very Good Friend The Milkman 7" Decca F11291 1960 £20 £10
Rocking Away The Blues 7" Decca F11123 1959 £25 £12.50
Whoopee 7" Parlophone R4477 1958 £25 £12.50

JOY DIVISION

Atmosphere 7" Sordide Sentimentale SS33002 1980 £40 £20 *A4 folder*

Atmosphere ... CD-s ... Factory ... FACD213 ... 1988 **£5** ... **£2**
Earcom 2 ... 12" ... Fast Products ... FAST9 ... 1979 **£12** ... **£6** ... *with other artists*
Factory Sample ... 7" EP .. Factory ... FAC2 ... 1979 **£30** ... **£15** ... *double, 5 stickers, with other artists*
Ideal Beginning ... 7" ... Enigma ... PSS138 ... 1981 **£10** ... **£5**
Ideal For Living ... 12" ... Anonymous ... ANON1 ... 1978 **£50** ... **£25**
Ideal For Living ... 7" ... Enigma ... PSS139 ... 1978 **£75** ... **£37.50** ... *picture sleeve*
Peel Sessions ... CD-s ... Strange Fruit ... SFPSCD013 ... 1988 **£5** ... **£2**
Peel Sessions II ... CD-s ... Strange Fruit ... SFPSCD033 ... 1988 **£5** ... **£2**
Still ... LP ... Factory ... FACT40 ... 1981 **£15** ... **£6** ... *double, hard cloth cover*

JOY UNLIMITED

Mimic ... LP ... BASF ... 1222331 ... 1975 **£12** ... **£5** ... German
Overground ... LP ... Polydor ... 2371050 ... 1970 **£20** ... **£8** ... German
Reflections ... LP ... BASF ... 20216861 ... 1973 **£15** ... **£6** ... German
Schmetterlinge ... LP ... Pilz ... 2021090/1 ... 1971 **£25** ... **£10** ... German
Turbulence ... LP ... Page One ... POLS028 ... 1970 **£25** ... **£10**

JOYCE, JOHNNY

Joyce's Choice Mixture ... LP ... Freedom ... FLP99003 ... 1976 **£15** ... **£6**

JOYRIDE

Friend Sound ... LP ... RCA ... SF8027 ... 1969 **£40** ... **£20**

J.S.D. BAND

Country Of The Blind ... LP ... Regal Zonophone ... SLRZ1018 ... 1971 **£30** ... **£15**
J.S.D. Band ... LP ... Fly ... HIFLY11 ... 1972 **£10** ... **£4**
Story So Far ... 7" ... Regal Zonophone ... JSD1 ... 1971 **£10** ... **£5** ... *promo with release sheet & photo*

JUAN & JUNIOR

To Girls ... 7" ... CBS ... 3223 ... 1968 **£5** ... **£2**

JUBALAIRES

King's Highway ... 7" EP .. Brunswick ... OE9198 ... 1955 **£5** ... **£2**

JUDAS JUMP

Run For Your Life ... 7" ... Parlophone ... R5828 ... 1969 **£4** ... **£1.50**
Scorch ... LP ... Parlophone ... PAS10001 ... 1970 **£15** ... **£6**
This Feelin' We Feel ... 7" ... Parlophone ... R5838 ... 1970 **£4** ... **£1.50**

JUDAS PRIEST

Johnny B. Goode ... CD-s ... Atlantic ... A9114CD ... 1988 **£5** ... **£2** ... *3" single*
Painkiller ... CD-s ... CBS ... 6562732 ... 1990 **£5** ... **£2**
Touch Of Evil ... 7" ... Columbia ... 6565890 ... 1991 **£4** ... **£1.50** ... *shaped disc*
Touch Of Evil ... CD-s ... CBS ... 6565892 ... 1991 **£5** ... **£2**
Tyrant ... 12" ... Gull ... GULS7612 ... 1983 **£8** ... **£4** ... *white vinyl*

JUDD

Judd ... LP ... Penny Farthing ... PELS504 ... 1970 **£25** ... **£10**

JUDGE, TERRY & THE BARRISTERS

Come With Me And Love Me ... 7" ... Fontana ... TF599 ... 1965 **£5** ... **£2**
Hey Look At Her ... 7" ... Oriole ... CB1896 ... 1963 **£6** ... **£2.50**
I Don't Care ... 7" ... Oriole ... CB1938 ... 1964 **£6** ... **£2.50**

JUDGE HAPPINESS

Hey Judge ... 7" ... Mynah ... SCS8501 ... 1985 **£10** ... **£5**
Hey Judge ... 7" ... Mynah ... SCS8501 ... 1985 **£25** ... **£12.50** ... *picture sleeve*

JUG TRUST

Cat And Mouse ... 7" ... Parlophone ... R5825 ... 1970 **£4** ... **£1.50**

JUGGERNAUTS

Come Throw Yourself ... 7" ... Supreme ... 842 ... 1984 **£5** ... **£2**

JUICY LUCY

Get A Whiff Of This ... LP ... Bronze ... ILPS9157 ... 1971 **£10** ... **£4**
Juicy Lucy ... LP ... Vertigo ... VO2 ... 1969 **£20** ... **£8** ... *spiral label*
Lie Back & Enjoy It ... LP ... Vertigo ... 6360014 ... 1970 **£20** ... **£8** ... *spiral label*
Who Do You Love ... 7" ... Vertigo ... V1 ... 1970 **£4** ... **£1.50**

JULIAN

Sue Saturday ... 7" ... Pye ... 7N15236 ... 1959 **£15** ... **£7.50**

JULIAN, DON

Greatest Oldies ... LP ... Amazon ... 1009 ... 1963 **£25** ... **£10** ... US

JULIAN'S TREATMENT

Phantom City ... 7" ... Youngblood ... YB1009 ... 1972 **£5** ... **£2**
Time Before This ... LP ... Youngblood ... SYB2 ... 1972 **£75** ... **£37.50** ... *double*

JULY

The LP by July is a typical piece of psychedelia from 1968 – full of interesting ideas and sounds, but definitely a formative record for the musicians involved. These include Tony Duhig and Jon Field, who went on to form Jade Warrior, and Tom Newman, later a solo artist and also studio engineer for Virgin records.

Dandelion Seeds	LP	Bam Caruso	KIRI097	1987	**£10**	**£4**	
Hello Who's There	7"	Major Minor	MM580	1968	**£50**	**£25**	
July	LP	Major Minor	MMLP/SMLP29	1968	**£300**	**£180**	
July	LP	Epic	BN26416	1969	**£100**	**£50**	*US*
My Clown	7"	Major Minor	MM568	1968	**£60**	**£30**	

JUMBLE LANE

Jumble Lane	LP	Holyground	HG115	1971	**£400**	**£250**	

JUMP SQUAD

Lord Of The Dance	7"	101	UR2	1981	**£5**	**£2**	

JUMPIN' JACKS

Tried And Tested	7"	HMV	POP440	1958	**£12**	**£6**	

JUMPLEADS

Stag Must Die	LP	Ock	OC001	1982	**£40**	**£20**	*with stag's head cut-out*

JUNCO PARTNERS

As Long As I Have You	7"	Columbia	DB7665	1965	**£50**	**£25**	
Junco Partners	LP	Philips	6308032	1971	**£30**	**£15**	

JUNCTION 32

Junction 32	LP	Holyground	HG119	1975	**£300**	**£180**	

JUNE, ROSANNE

Charge Of The Light Brigade	7"	London	HLU8352	1956	**£12**	**£6**	

JUNE, ROSEMARY

I'll Always Be In Love With You	7"	Fontana	H141	1958	**£5**	**£2**	
I'll Be With You In Apple Blossom Time	7"	Pye	7N25005	1959	**£4**	**£1.50**	

JUNE BRIDES

Every Conversation	7"	Pink	PINKY2	1984	**£4**	**£1.50**	
In The Rain	7"	Pink	PINKY1	1984	**£10**	**£5**	

JUNIORS

Both guitarist Mick Taylor and bass-player John Glascock (later with Jethro Tull) were members of the Juniors – an appropriate name indeed for Taylor, as he was barely fifteen when he made his recording debut on the band's single.

There's A Pretty Girl	7"	Columbia	DB7339	1964	**£25**	**£12.50**	

JUNIORS, IVAN D.

On My Mind	7"	Oriole	CB1874	1963	**£6**	**£2.50**	

JUNIOR'S EYES

The group's album is rather fine – boosted perhaps by the experience of backing David Bowie on his first album. Guitarist Tim Renwick subsequently helped to form Quiver, before embarking on a career as a busy session musician, leavened by on-stage work with Pink Floyd.

Battersea Power Station	LP	Regal Zonophone	SLRZ1008	1969	**£30**	**£15**	
Mr Golden Trumpet Player	7"	Regal Zonophone	RZ3009	1968	**£10**	**£5**	
Star Child	7"	Regal Zonophone	RZ3023	1969	**£8**	**£4**	
Woman Love	7"	Regal Zonophone	RZ3018	1969	**£6**	**£2.50**	
Woman Love/White Light Part 2	7"	Regal Zonophone	RZ3018	1969	**£15**	**£7.50**	

JUNIPHER GREEN

Dreams In The Sky	7"	Columbia	DB8809	1971	**£20**	**£10**	
Friendship	LP	Sonet	SLP1413/4	1971	**£150**	**£75**	*Norwegian double*

JUNOFF, LENA

Yesterday Has Gone	7"	Olga	008	1968	**£10**	**£5**	

JUPP, ERIC ORCHESTRA

Eric Jupp & His Orchestra	7" EP	Columbia	SEG7589	1955	**£8**	**£4**	
Perfect Combination	7" EP	Columbia	SEG7621	1956	**£5**	**£2**	
Rhythm And Blues	7" EP	Columbia	SEG7603	1956	**£8**	**£4**	

JUST FOUR MEN

Don't Come Any Closer	7"	Parlophone	R5241	1965	**£50**	**£25**	
That's My Baby	7"	Parlophone	R5208	1964	**£50**	**£25**	

JUST PLAIN JONES

Crazy Crazy	7"	CBS	7480	1971	**£4**	**£1.50**	

JUST PLAIN SMITH

Title	Format	Label	Cat. No.	Year	Mint	Half	Notes
February's Child	7"	Sunshine	SUN7702	1969	**£125**	**£62.50**	

JUST US

Title	Format	Label	Cat. No.	Year	Mint	Half	Notes
What Are We Gonna Do	7" EP	Kapp	KEV13036	1966	**£10**	**£5**	*French*

JUST WILLIAM

Title	Format	Label	Cat. No.	Year	Mint	Half	Notes
I Don't Care	7"	Spark	SRL1018	1970	**£10**	**£5**	

JUSTE, SAMANTHA

Title	Format	Label	Cat. No.	Year	Mint	Half	Notes
No One Needs My Love Today	7"	Go	AJ11402	1966	**£6**	**£2.50**	

JUSTICE, JIMMY

Title	Format	Label	Cat. No.	Year	Mint	Half	Notes
Ain't That Funny	7"	Pye	7N15443	1962	**£6**	**£2.50**	*picture sleeve*
I Understand Just How You Feel	7"	Pye	7N15301	1960	**£10**	**£5**	
I'm Past Forgetting	7"	RCA	RCA1681	1968	**£15**	**£7.50**	
Jimmy Justice Hit Parade	7" EP	Pye	NEP24159	1962	**£20**	**£10**	
Little Bit Of Soap	7"	Pye	7N15376	1961	**£6**	**£2.50**	
Little Cracked Bell	7"	Pye	7N15509	1963	**£4**	**£1.50**	
Smash Hits	LP	Pye	NPL18085	1962	**£25**	**£10**	
Teacher	7"	Pye	7N15351	1961	**£8**	**£4**	
Two Sides Of Jimmy Justice	LP	Pye	NPL18080	1962	**£25**	**£10**	

JUSTICE, KAY & THE ESCORTS

Title	Format	Label	Cat. No.	Year	Mint	Half	Notes
If You Took Your Love From Me	7"	Columbia	SCM5132	1954	**£5**	**£2**	

JUSTIFIED ANCIENTS OF MU MU

1987 is an entirely brilliant example of the art of disc-jockey-as-producer, consisting of a kaleidoscope of bits of other people's records welded together into an inspired whole. Unfortunately, some of these other people – Benny Andersson and Björn Ulvaeus of Abba to be precise – took exception to their music being used in this way and obtained a court order for the recall of all remaining copies of the record. In a way, the JAMM were able to have the last laugh, for they later successfully advertised 'the last remaining five copies' of the record at £1000 each. Collectors do not have to pay as much as this, however – £60 is enough to acquire one of the copies that appears on the market from time to time.

Title	Format	Label	Cat. No.	Year	Mint	Half	Notes
1987	cass	KLF	JAMSCLP1	1987	**£20**	**£8**	
1987	LP	KLF	JAMSLP1	1987	**£60**	**£30**	
1987 – The 45 Edits	12"	KLF	JAMS25T	1987	**£10**	**£5**	
All You Need Is Love	12"	KLF	JAMS23T	1987	**£15**	**£7.50**	
All You Need Is Love	12"	KLF	JAMS23	1987	**£30**	**£15**	*1 sided promo*
All You Need Is Love	7"	KLF	JAMS23	1987	**£10**	**£5**	
Burn The Beat	12"	KLF	JAMS26T	1988	**£12**	**£6**	
Deep Shit	7"	KLF	JAMSDS1	1987	**£200**	**£100**	*flexi*
Down Town	12"	KLF	JAMS27	1987	**£12**	**£6**	*1 sided promo*
Down Town	12"	KLF	JAMS27T	1987	**£10**	**£5**	
Down Town	7"	KLF	JAMS27	1987	**£4**	**£1.50**	*no picture sleeve*
It's Grim Up North	12"	KLF	JAMS28T	1988	**£60**	**£30**	*1 sided, grey vinyl*
Made In Wales (Who Killed The Jams)	LP	KLF	JAMSLP2	1988	**£10**	**£4**	
Shag Times	CD	KLF	JAMSCD3	1989	**£30**	**£15**	
Shag Times	LP	KLF	JAMSDLP3	1989	**£15**	**£6**	*double*
Whitney Joins The J.A.M.s	12"	KLF	JAMS24T	1987	**£12**	**£6**	

JUSTIN, JAY

Title	Format	Label	Cat. No.	Year	Mint	Half	Notes
I Sell Summertime	7"	Columbia	DB8439	1968	**£4**	**£1.50**	

JUSTIN & KARLSSON

Title	Format	Label	Cat. No.	Year	Mint	Half	Notes
Somewhere They Can't Find Me	7"	Piccadilly	7N35295	1966	**£10**	**£5**	

JUSTINE

Title	Format	Label	Cat. No.	Year	Mint	Half	Notes
Justine	LP	Uni	UNLS111	1970	**£10**	**£4**	

JUSTIS, BILL

Title	Format	Label	Cat. No.	Year	Mint	Half	Notes
Cloud Nine	LP	Philips	1950	1959	**£100**	**£50**	*US*
College Man	7"	London	HLS8614	1958	**£10**	**£5**	
I'm Gonna Learn To Dance	7"	Mercury	AMT1201	1963	**£4**	**£1.50**	
Raunchy	7"	London	HLS8517	1957	**£10**	**£5**	

JUVENILES

Title	Format	Label	Cat. No.	Year	Mint	Half	Notes
Bo Diddley	7"	Pye	7N25349	1966	**£60**	**£30**	

JYNX

Title	Format	Label	Cat. No.	Year	Mint	Half	Notes
How	7"	Columbia	DB7304	1964	**£25**	**£12.50**	

K, CAROLINE

Now Wait For Last Year	LP	Earthly Delights	EARTH1	1987	**£10**	**£4**	

K, JOHNNY & THE SINGIN' SWINGIN' EIGHT

Lemonade	7"	Fontana	H408	1963	**£5**	**£2**	

K, MOSES & THE PROPHETS

I Went Out With My Baby Tonight	7"	Decca	F12244	1965	**£8**	**£4**	

K9s

K9 Hassle	7"	Dog Breath	WOOF1	1985	**£8**	**£4**	

KAEMPFERT, BERT

Man Could Get Killed	LP	Brunswick	LAT/STA8651	1966	**£10**	**£4**	

KAIPA

Inget Nytt Unders Solen	LP	Decca	SKL5260	1976	**£30**	**£15**	*Swedish*
Kaipa	LP	Decca	SKL5221	1975	**£30**	**£15**	*Swedish*
Solo	LP	Decca	SKL5293	1978	**£25**	**£10**	*Swedish*

KAK

Kak	LP	Epic	BN26429	1969	**£100**	**£50**	*US*

KALA

Kala	LP	Bradley	BRADL1002	1973	**£15**	**£6**	

KALACAKRA

Crawling To Lhasa	LP	private		1974	**£60**	**£30**	*German*

KALAMARIS

Staldfroes	LP	Scanfolk	3	1974	**£40**	**£20**	*Danish*

KALASANDRO

Chi Chi	7"	Warner Bros	WB13	1960	**£6**	**£2.50**	

KALB, DANNY & STEFAN GROSSMAN

Crosscurrents	LP	Cotillion	SD9007	1969	**£15**	**£6**	*US*

KALEIDOSCOPE

The two LPs made by Kaleidoscope were among the first of the more obscure psychedelic records to attract the attention of collectors. Accordingly, they reached the £100 mark some time before other similar records, but then stayed there while more recent discoveries leap-frogged ahead. In truth, the records are interesting, but lack the finesse of the established classics of the period (like *Music From A Doll's House* or *Dear Mr Fantasy*). They have the kudos of rarity, but, as is usually the case, their lack of renown is not without reason.

Balloon	7"	Fontana	TF1048	1969	**£75**	**£37.50**	
Do It Again For Jeffrey	7"	Fontana	TF1002	1969	**£25**	**£12.50**	
Dream For Julie	7"	Fontana	TF895	1968	**£30**	**£15**	
Faintly Blowing	LP	5 Hours Back	TOCK006	1987	**£15**	**£6**	
Faintly Blowing	LP	Fontana	STL5491	1969	**£150**	**£75**	
Flight From Ashiya	7"	Fontana	TF863	1967	**£60**	**£30**	*picture sleeve*
Flight From Ashiya	7"	Fontana	TF863	1967	**£25**	**£12.50**	
Jenny Artichoke	7"	Fontana	TF964	1968	**£25**	**£12.50**	
Tangerine Dream	LP	Fontana	(S)TL5448	1967	**£150**	**£75**	
Tangerine Dream	LP	5 Hours Back	TOCK005	1987	**£15**	**£6**	

KALEIDOSCOPE (2)

The American Kaleidoscope had a sound like no other group of the time. Over the course of three LPs (a fourth, *Bernice*, is an unfortunate fall from grace; *When Scopes Collide* is a later attempt at a reunion) and culminating with the magnificent *Incredible*, which entirely lives up to its name, the group maintained a questing, innovative approach. A key factor was their fascination with Middle Eastern music, which gives some of Kaleidoscope's material a world music flavour very much ahead of its time. Both Chris Darrow and David Lindley have recorded much music since Kaleidoscope's demise, although little of it has been in the same league. The cover of the group's first album, incidentally, makes it clear that a youthful Mr Bean was a member of the band – his chosen stage name, Fenrus Epp, also being a bit of a giveaway!

Beacon From Mars	LP	Epic	LN24/BN26333	1968	**£60**	**£30**	*US*
Bernice	LP	CBS	64005	1970	**£10**	**£4**	
Incredible	LP	Epic	BN26467	1969	**£30**	**£15**	*US*
Side Trips	LP	Epic	LN24/BN26305	1967	**£50**	**£25**	*US*
When Scopes Collide	LP	Island	ILPS9462	1976	**£10**	**£4**	

KALEIDOSKOP

Kaleidoskop	LP	Lava	TCH0002	1974	**£20**	**£8**	*German*

KALIN TWINS

Chicken Thief	7"	Brunswick	05826	1960	**£6**	**£2.50**	
Cool	7"	Brunswick	05797	1959	**£4**	**£1.50**	
Forget Me Not	7"	Brunswick	05759	1958	**£4**	**£1.50**	
Kalin Twins	7" EP	Brunswick	OE9449	1959	**£30**	**£15**	
Kalin Twins	LP	Decca	DL8812	1958	**£40**	**£20**	*US*
Meaning Of The Blues	7"	Brunswick	05814	1959	**£4**	**£1.50**	
Momma Poppa	7"	Brunswick	05848	1961	**£4**	**£1.50**	
Oh My Goodness	7"	Brunswick	05775	1959	**£5**	**£2**	
One More Time	7"	Brunswick	05862	1961	**£4**	**£1.50**	
Sweet Sugar Lips	7"	Brunswick	05803	1959	**£4**	**£1.50**	
When	7" EP	Brunswick	OE9383	1958	**£30**	**£15**	
Zing Went The Strings Of My Heart	7"	Brunswick	05844	1960	**£4**	**£1.50**	

KALLABASH CORP

Kallabash Corp	LP	Uncle Bill	311	1970	**£60**	**£30**	*US*

KALLEN, KITTY

Forgive Me	7"	Brunswick	05447	1955	**£4**	**£1.50**	
Go On With The Wedding	7"	Brunswick	05536	1956	**£5**	**£2**	
How Lonely Can I Get	7"	Brunswick	05494	1955	**£4**	**£1.50**	
I'm A Lonely Little Petunia	7"	Brunswick	05402	1955	**£4**	**£1.50**	
In The Chapel In The Moonlight	7"	Brunswick	05261	1954	**£8**	**£4**	
It's A Lonesome Old Town	LP	Decca	DL8397	1958	**£15**	**£6**	*US*
Kiddy Geddin	7"	Brunswick	05359	1954	**£6**	**£2.50**	
Kitty Who?	7"	Brunswick	05431	1955	**£4**	**£1.50**	
Let's Make The Most Of Tonight	7"	Brunswick	05475	1955	**£4**	**£1.50**	
Little Lie	7"	Brunswick	05394	1955	**£5**	**£2**	
Little Things Mean A Lot	7"	Brunswick	05287	1954	**£40**	**£20**	
Little Things Mean A Lot	LP	Vocalion	VL3679	1959	**£15**	**£6**	*US*
Long Lonely Nights	7"	Brunswick	05705	1957	**£4**	**£1.50**	
Pretty Kitty Kallen Sings	10" LP	Mercury	MG25206	195–	**£20**	**£8**	*US*
Spirit Of Christmas	7"	Brunswick	05357	1954	**£10**	**£5**	
True Love	7"	Brunswick	05612	1956	**£4**	**£1.50**	

KALLMAN, DICK

Born To Be Loved	7"	Vogue	V9162	1960	**£5**	**£2**	

KALPANA IMPROVISATIONS

Instrumental And Dance Music Of India	LP	Polydor	184172	1968	**£10**	**£4**	

KANE, AMORY

Just To Be There	LP	CBS	63849	1970	**£20**	**£8**	
Memories Of Time Unwound	LP	MCA	MUP(S)348	1968	**£25**	**£10**	

KANE, EDEN

Come Back	7"	Fontana	TF413	1963	**£4**	**£1.50**	
Eden Kane	LP	Ace Of Clubs	ACL1133	1962	**£25**	**£10**	
Eden Kane Hits	7" EP	Decca	DFE8503	1962	**£15**	**£7.50**	
Hot Chocolate Crazy	7"	Pye	7N15284	1960	**£15**	**£7.50**	
It's Eden	7" EP	Fontana	TFE17424	1964	**£12**	**£6**	
It's Eden	LP	Fontana	TL5211	1964	**£30**	**£15**	
Magic Town	7"	Decca	F12342	1966	**£8**	**£4**	
Six Great New Swingers	7" EP	Decca	DFE8567	1964	**£20**	**£10**	
Smoke Gets In Your Eyes	LP	Wing	WL1218	1966	**£15**	**£6**	
Tomorrow Night	7"	Fontana	TF398	1963	**£5**	**£2**	*picture sleeve*
Well I Ask You	7" EP	Decca	DFE6696	1962	**£15**	**£7.50**	

KANE, JACK

Bow Before Me, Son Of God	LP	Rex Mundi	REX23	1973	**£75**	**£37.50**	

KANE, LEE

Around And Around	7"	Capitol	CL14328	1955	**£4**	**£1.50**	
Every Day	7"	Capitol	CL14297	1955	**£4**	**£1.50**	

KANE, PAUL

Paul Kane was one of the names tried by Paul Simon during the early years of his career.

He Was My Brother	7"	Tribute	128	196–	**£50**	**£25**	*US*

KANE'S COUSINS

Undergum Bubbleground	LP	Shove Love	ST9827	1968	**£12**	**£5**	*US*

KANGAROO

Kangaroo	LP	MGM	SE4586	1968	**£30**	**£15**	*US*

KANSAS

Strange how all the groups called after place names seem to have the same sound. Regardless of the musical content, however, the LP *Point Of Know Return* by Kansas has a particularly striking cover, showing a galleon in full sail, just about to fall over the edge of the world. The record is available as a picture disc, which shows off the artwork even more dramatically, but this was unfortunately issued as an American promotional release only and is scarce.

Leftoverture	LP	Kirshner	HZ44224	1981	**£12**	**£5**	*US audiophile*
Point Of Know Return	LP	Kirshner	HZ44929	1981	**£12**	**£5**	*US audiophile*

Point Of Know Return	LP	Kirshner	JZ34929	1977	**£25**	**£10**	*US promo picture disc*
Vinyl Confessions	LP	Kirshner	HZ48002	1982	**£12**	**£5**	*US audiophile*

KANSAS CITY MELROSE & CASINO SIMPSON

Kansas City Melrose And Casino Simpson	LP	Chicago Piano	12001	1972	**£10**	**£4**	

KANTNER, PAUL

Blows Against The Empire	LP	RCA	LSP4448	1970	**£60**	**£30**	*US clear vinyl*
Blows Against The Empire	LP	RCA	SF8163	1970	**£10**	**£4**	*with booklet*
Sunfighter	LP	Grunt	FTR1002	1971	**£10**	**£4**	*with booklet*

KAPUTTER HAMSTER

Kaputter Hamster	LP	e-Pa Records	102009	1974	**£150**	**£75**	*German*

KARAS, ANTON

Harry Lime Theme	7"	Decca	F9235	1960	**£5**	**£2**	

KARAT

Karat	LP	Amiga	855573	1977	**£10**	**£4**	*East German*

KARINA

Tomorrow I'm Coming Your Way	7"	United Artists	UP35205	1971	**£6**	**£2.50**	

KARLOFF, BORIS

Evening With Boris Karloff And Friends	LP	Brunswick	LAT8678	1967	**£15**	**£6**	
Hans Christian Andersen	LP	Caedmon	CAL1021	1960	**£12**	**£5**	
How The Grinch Stole Christmas	LP	MGM	(S)E901	1966	**£15**	**£6**	*US*
Tales Of The Frightened Vol. 1	LP	MGM	MG2/SR60815	1963	**£20**	**£8**	*US*
Tales Of The Frightened Vol. 2	LP	MGM	MG2/SR60816	1963	**£20**	**£8**	*US*

KAROO

Mama's Out Of Town	7"	Oak	RGJ193	1965	**£100**	**£50**	

KARTHAGO

Karthago	LP	BASF	20211851	1971	**£12**	**£5**	*German*

KASENATZ-KATZ SINGING ORCHESTRAL CIRCUS

Kasenatz-Katz Singing Orchestral Circus	LP	Pye	NSPL28119	1968	**£10**	**£4**	

KASHMIR

Stay Calm	LP	private		1986	**£25**	**£10**	

KATCH 22

100,000 Years	7"	Fontana	TF984	1968	**£5**	**£2**	
Major Catastrophe	7"	Fontana	TF768	1966	**£20**	**£10**	
Makin' Up My Mind	7"	Fontana	TF874	1967	**£5**	**£2**	
Out Of My Life	7"	Fontana	TF1005	1969	**£5**	**£2**	
World's Getting Smaller	7"	Fontana	TF930	1968	**£5**	**£2**	

KATE

The third single by Kate featured the original drummer with the Pretty Things, Viv Prince, but he is not involved in the first two. His presence does help to improve the quality rating, but it did nothing for the group's success.

Hold Me Now	7"	CBS	3815	1968	**£15**	**£7.50**	
Shout It	7"	CBS	4123	1969	**£15**	**£7.50**	
Strange Girl	7"	CBS	3631	1968	**£15**	**£7.50**	

KATMANDU

Katmandu	LP	Mainstream	S6131	1971	**£60**	**£0**	*US*

KATTONG

Gitarre Vor'm Bauch	LP	Schwann	AMS515	1971	**£25**	**£10**	*German*
Stiehl Dem Volk Die Geduld	LP	Schwann	AMS519	1972	**£25**	**£10**	*German*

KATZ

Live At The Rum Runner	7" EP	Tetlour	TET118	196–	**£60**	**£30**	

KATZ, DICK

Kool For Katz	10" LP	Pye	NPT19033	1959	**£12**	**£5**	

KATZ, MICKEY

David Crockett	7"	Capitol	CL14579	1956	**£4**	**£1.50**	
Poiple Kishke Eater	7"	Capitol	CL14926	1958	**£4**	**£1.50**	

KAUFMANN, BOB

Trip Through A Blown Mind	LP	LHI	12002	1967	**£25**	**£10**	*US*

KAY, ARTHUR ORIGINALS

Ska Wars	7"	Red Admiral	NYMPH1	1980	**£4**	**£1.50**	
Sooty Is A Rudie	7"	Red Admiral	NYMPH2	1980	**£6**	**£2.50**	

KAY, BARBARA

Yes I'm Ready	7"	Pye	7N15914	1965	**£4**	**£1.50**	

KAY, JOHN

Title	Format	Label	Cat. No.	Year	Mint	VG	Notes
Forgotten Songs And Unsung Heroes	LP	Probe	SPB1054	1972	£10	£4	
John Kay And The Sparrows	LP	Columbia	CS9758	1970	£15	£6	US
My Sportin' Life	LP	Probe	SPBA6274	1973	£10	£4	

KAY, KATHIE

Title	Format	Label	Cat. No.	Year	Mint	VG	Notes
House With Love In It	7"	HMV	POP265	1956	£4	£1.50	
Jimmy Unknown	7"	HMV	7M363	1956	£6	£2.50	
Suddenly There's A Valley	7"	HMV	7M335	1955	£6	£2.50	
We Will Make Love	7"	HMV	POP352	1957	£4	£1.50	

KAYAK

Title	Format	Label	Cat. No.	Year	Mint	VG	Notes
Kayak	LP	Harvest	SHSP4036	1974	£10	£4	
Phantom Of The Night	LP	Janus	JXS7039	1978	£20	£8	US picture disc
Royal Bed Bouncer	LP	Vertigo	6360530	1975	£10	£4	
See See The Sun	LP	Harvest	SHSP4033	1973	£10	£4	

KAYE, DANNY

Title	Format	Label	Cat. No.	Year	Mint	VG	Notes
At The Palace	10" LP	Brunswick	LA8660	1954	£10	£4	
Best Things Happen While You're Dancing	7"	Brunswick	05344	1954	£4	£1.50	
Children's Favourites	7" EP	Brunswick	OE9022	1954	£5	£2	
Danny Kaye	10" LP	Brunswick	LA8507	1951	£10	£4	
Five Pennies	7"	London	HL7091	1960	£4	£1.50	export
Hans Christian Andersen	10" LP	Brunswick	LA8572	1953	£10	£4	
Knock On Wood	10" LP	Brunswick	LA8668	1954	£10	£4	
Knock On Wood	7"	Brunswick	05296	1954	£4	£1.50	
Pure Delight	10" LP	Fontana	TFR6008	1958	£10	£4	
Wonderful Copenhagen	7"	Decca	A73013	1952	£20	£10	export
Wonderful Copenhagen	7"	Brunswick	05023	1959	£6	£2.50	tri-centre

KAYE, DAVE

Title	Format	Label	Cat. No.	Year	Mint	VG	Notes
Fool Such As I	7"	Decca	F11866	1964	£20	£10	
In My Way	7"	Decca	F12073	1965	£20	£10	
Yesterday When I Was Young	7"	Major Minor	MM641	1969	£6	£2.50	

KAYE, LINDA

Title	Format	Label	Cat. No.	Year	Mint	VG	Notes
I Can't Stop Thinking About You	7"	Columbia	DB7915	1966	£12	£6	

KAYE, PETER

Title	Format	Label	Cat. No.	Year	Mint	VG	Notes
Do Me A Favour	7"	Aral	PS116	1964	£5	£2	picture sleeve

KAYE, SHIRLEY

Title	Format	Label	Cat. No.	Year	Mint	VG	Notes
Make Me Yours	7"	Trojan	TR015	1968	£10	£5	

KAYE SISTERS

Title	Format	Label	Cat. No.	Year	Mint	VG	Notes
Are You Ready Freddy?	7"	Philips	PB806	1958	£6	£2.50	
At The Colony	7" EP	Philips	BBE12256	1959	£10	£5	
Come To Me	7"	Philips	PB1088	1960	£4	£1.50	picture sleeve
Favourites	7" EP	Philips	BBE12392	1960	£10	£5	
Ivory Tower	7"	HMV	7M401	1956	£15	£7.50	
Kaye Sisters	7" EP	Philips	BBE12166	1957	£8	£4	
Lay Down Your Arms	7"	HMV	POP251	1956	£10	£5	
Paper Roses	7"	Philips	PB1024	1960	£4	£1.50	picture sleeve
Stroll Me	7"	Philips	PB832	1958	£4	£1.50	

KEANE, DOLORES

Title	Format	Label	Cat. No.	Year	Mint	VG	Notes
Broken Hearted I'll Wander	LP	Mulligan	LUN033	1979	£10	£4	Irish, with John Faulkner
There Was A Maid	LP	Claddagh	CC23	1978	£10	£4	Irish

KEANE, SHAKE

Title	Format	Label	Cat. No.	Year	Mint	VG	Notes
Dig It	LP	Decca	PFS4154	1969	£30	£15	
In The Chapel In The Moonlight	7"	HMV	7MC23	1955	£4	£1.50	export
That's The Voice	LP	Ace Of Clubs	ACL1219	1967	£10	£4	
With The Keating Sound	LP	Decca	SKL4720	1965	£12	£5	

KEATING, JOHNNY

Title	Format	Label	Cat. No.	Year	Mint	VG	Notes
Keating Sound	LP	Decca	PFS4060	1964	£12	£5	
Space Experience	LP	Columbia	TWO393	1972	£12	£5	stereo or quadrophonic
Space Experience 2	LP	Columbia	TWOX1044	1975	£12	£5	
Swinging Scots	LP	London	LTZD15122	1958	£15	£6	
Z Cars	7" EP	Piccadilly	NEP34011	1962	£5	£2	

KEBNEKAISE

Title	Format	Label	Cat. No.	Year	Mint	VG	Notes
III	LP	Silence	SRS4629	1975	£10	£4	Swedish
Kebnekaise	LP	Silence	SRS4618	1973	£15	£6	Swedish
Resa Mot Okant Mal	LP	Silence	SRS4605	1971	£15	£6	Swedish

KEENAN, PADDY

Title	Format	Label	Cat. No.	Year	Mint	VG	Notes
Paddy Keenan	LP	Gael Linn	CEF045	1975	£12	£5	Irish

KEENE, REX

Title	Format	Label	Cat. No.	Year	Mint	VG	Notes
Happy Texas Ranger	7"	Columbia	DB3831	1956	£5	£2	

KEFFORD, ACE STAND

For Your Love	7"	Atlantic	584260	1969	£20	£10	

KEITH

98.6	7"	Mercury	MF955	1967	£4	£1.50	
98.6	LP	Mercury	20103MCL	1967	£15	£6	
Daylight Saving Time	7"	Mercury	MF989	1966	£4	£1.50	
Tell It To My Face	7" EP	Mercury	126220	1967	£10	£5	*French*

KEITH, BRIAN

When The First Tear Shows	7"	Page One	POF103	1968	£4	£1.50	

KEITH, BRYAN

Mean Mama	7"	London	HLU9707	1963	£6	£2.50	

KEITH, RON

Party Music	7"	A&M	AMS7217	1976	£40	£20	

KEITH & ENID

Just A Closer Walk	7"	Dice	CC20	1963	£10	£5	
Keith And Enid Sing	LP	Island	ILP901	1963	£50	£25	
Lost My Love	7"	Island	WI429	1964	£10	£5	
Never Leave My Throne	7"	Starlite	ST45047	1961	£10	£5	
Sacred Vow	7"	Dice	CC14	1963	£10	£5	
Send Me	7"	Blue Beat	BB11	1960	£12	£6	*Trenton Spence B side*
Sing	LP	Trojan	TBL154	1970	£10	£4	
Sing	LP	Trojan	TTL37	1970	£12	£5	
When It's Spring	7"	Blue Beat	BB125	1962	£12	£6	
Worried Over You	7"	Blue Beat	BB6	1960	£12	£6	
You're Gonna Break My Heart	7"	Starlite	ST45067	1961	£10	£5	

KEITH & KEN

You'll Love Jamaica	LP	London	HAR/SHR8229	1965	£20	£8	

KEITH & TEX

Hypnotizing Eyes	7"	Island	WI3137	1968	£10	£5	
Tighten Up Your Gird	7"	Explosion	EX2008	1969	£5	£2	
Tonight	7"	Island	WI3085	1967	£10	£5	*Lyn Taitt B side*

KELLER, JERRY

Here Comes Jerry Keller	LP	London	HAR2261/ SAHR6083	1960	£30	£15	
Here Comes Summer	7"	London	HLR8890	1959	£4	£1.50	*tri-centre*
If I Had A Girl	7"	London	HLR8980	1959	£4	£1.50	
Now Now Now	7"	London	HLR9106	1960	£4	£1.50	

KELLEY, PETER

Path Of The Wave	LP	London	SHK8402	1969	£20	£8	

KELLUM, MURRAY

Long Tall Texan	7"	London	HLU9830	1964	£10	£5	*Glen Sutton B side*

KELLY

Mary Mary	7"	Deram	DM277	1969	£8	£4	

KELLY, CHARLIE

So Nice Like Rice	7"	Island	WI3155	1968	£10	£5	*Stranger Cole B side*

KELLY, DAVE

Blues guitarist Dave Kelly was a significant figure within the British blues boom. In addition to the collectable solo albums listed below, he also recorded with Tramp and the John Dummer Blues Band. Later he was a founder member of the Blues Band with Paul Jones, the success of which has kept his career alive through into the nineties, without him ever having to compromise his love of the blues.

Black Blue Kelly	LP	Mercury	6310001	1971	£125	£62.50	
Keeps It In The Family	LP	Mercury	SMCL20151	1969	£75	£37.50	

KELLY, FRANK & THE HUNTERS

I Saw Linda Yesterday	7"	Fontana	267261TF	1963	£4	£1.50	
Send Me The Pillow That You Dream On	7"	Fontana	267242TF	1962	£4	£1.50	
Some Other Time	7"	Fontana	TF454	1964	£4	£1.50	
What Do You Wanna Do	7"	Fontana	267277TF	1963	£4	£1.50	

KELLY, GENE

'S Wonderful	10" LP	MGM	D133	1955	£10	£4	
'S Wonderful	7"	MGM	SP1015	1953	£4	£1.50	
Singin' In The Rain	7"	MGM	SP1012	1953	£8	£4	
Song And Dance Man	10" LP	MGM	D117	1953	£10	£4	

KELLY, JO-ANN

Jo-Ann Kelly had a voice to rival that of blues power-house Bessie Smith, although she was English, white, and at the time of her debut EP, just twenty years old. In addition to the collectable records listed, she also appeared on the various artists EP, *New Sounds In Folk*, and on records by her brother Dave Kelly, Tony McPhee, John Dummer, the Brunning Hall Sunflower Blues Band, Tramp, and Chilli Willi and the Red Hot Peppers. She last performed live in 1990, but died that year of a brain tumour.

Blues And Gospel	7" EP	GW	EP1	1964	£100	£50	
Do It	LP	Red Rag	RRR006	1976	£30	£15	*with Peter Emery*
Jo-Ann Kelly	LP	CBS	63841	1969	£100	£50	
Jo-Ann Kelly Meets Dick Wellstood	LP	BBC Radioplay	TSRP7726	197–	£200	£100	
Same Thing On Their Minds	LP	Sunset	SLS50209	1971	£30	£15	*with Tony McPhee*
With Fahey, Mann, & Miller	LP	Blue Goose	2009	1972	£40	£20	*US*

KELLY, JOHN

Fiddle And Concertina Player	LP	Free Reed	FRS504	1975	£10	£4	

KELLY, JONATHAN

Don't You Believe It	7"	Parlophone	R5851	1970	£4	£1.50	
Jonathan Kelly	LP	Parlophone	PCS7114	1970	£20	£8	

KELLY, KEITH

Cold White And Beautiful	7"	Parlophone	R4797	1961	£4	£1.50	
Listen Little Girl	7"	Parlophone	R4676	1960	£5	£2	
Save Your Love For Me	7"	CBS	201794	1965	£4	£1.50	
Tease Me	7"	Parlophone	R4640	1960	£6	£2.50	
With You	7"	Parlophone	R4713	1960	£4	£1.50	

KELLY, PAT

Cool Breezing	LP	Pama	PMLP2013	1971	£30	£15	
How Long Will It Take	7"	Gas	GAS115	1969	£4	£1.50	
I Just Don't Know What To Do With Myself	7"	Jackpot	JP734	1970	£8	£4	
I Just Don't Know What To Do With Myself	7"	Gas	GAS157	1970	£8	£4	
Little Boy Blue	7"	Giant	GN37	1968	£8	£4	
Sings	LP	Pama	PMLP12	1969	£25	£10	
Somebody's Baby	7"	Island	WI3121	1968	£10	£5	*Beverley Simmons B side*
Workman Song	7"	Gas	GAS110	1969	£4	£1.50	

KELLY, PAUL

Chills And Fever	7"	Atlantic	AT4053	1965	£15	£7.50	
Sweet Sweet Lovin'	7"	Philips	BF1591	1967	£6	£2.50	

KELLY, PETE SOULUTION

Midnight Confessions	7"	Decca	F12755	1968	£8	£4	

KELLY, SALLY

Little Cutie	7"	Decca	F11175	1959	£4	£1.50	

KELLY, STAN

Ballad Of Armagh Jail	7"	Transatlantic	TRASP21	1968	£4	£1.50	
Liverpool Packet	7" EP	Topic	TOP27	1960	£5	£2	
Songs For Swinging Landlords	7" EP	Topic	TOP60	1961	£5	£2	

KELLY, WYNTON

Kelly Great	LP	Top Rank	35107	1961	£15	£6	
Undiluted	LP	Verve	VLP9103	1965	£10	£4	
Wynton Kelly	LP	Riverside	RLP12254	196–	£15	£6	

KELLY BROTHERS

Falling In Love Again	7"	Sue	WI4034	1967	£30	£15	
Sweet Soul	LP	President	PTL1019	1968	£15	£6	
That's What You Mean To Me	7"	Blue Horizon	573177	1970	£15	£7.50	
You Put Your Touch On Me	7"	President	PT143	1968	£5	£2	

KELSEY, REV. SAMUEL

Rev. Kelsey	7" EP	Brunswick	OE9256	1956	£10	£5	
Wedding Ceremony Of Sister R. Tharpe	78	Vocalion	V1014	1952	£8	£3	

KEMP, LINDSAY

Reality From Dream	LP	private			£150	£75	*with the Grimsby Folk Group*

KEMP, WAYNE

Little Home Wrecker	7"	Atlantic	584006	1966	£30	£15	

KEMPION

Cam Ye O'er Frae France	LP	Sweet Folk & Country	SFA044	1977	£15	£6	
Kempion	LP	Broadside	BRO123	1977	£10	£4	

KENDALL, JOHNNY & THE HERALDS

On The Move	LP	RCA	CAL10041	1965	£50	£25	*German*
St James Infirmary	7"	RCA	RCA1416	1964	£10	£5	

KENDALL SISTERS

Won't You Be My Baby	7"	London	HLM8622	1958	£40	£20	

KENDRICK, GRAHAM

Bright Side Up	LP	Key	KL016	1973	£15	£6	
Footsteps On The Sea	LP	Key	KL011	1973	£15	£6	
Paid On The Nail	LP	Key	KL024	1974	£10	£4	*with Peter Roe*

KENDRICK, LINDA

Title	Format	Label	Cat. No.	Year	Mint	VG	Notes
Friend Of Mine	7"	Polydor	56146	1966	£4	£1.50	
It's The Little Things	7"	Polydor	56076	1966	£15	£7.50	
Linda Kendrick	LP	Philips	SBL7921	1970	£15	£6	

KENDRICK, NAT & THE SWANS

Title	Format	Label	Cat. No.	Year	Mint	VG	Notes
Dish Rag	7"	Top Rank	JAR387	1960	£8	£4	
Mashed Potato	7"	Top Rank	JAR351	1960	£8	£4	

KENICKIE

Title	Format	Label	Cat. No.	Year	Mint	VG	Notes
Catsuit City	7"	Slampt	SLAMPT1	1995	£25	£12.50	
Punka	CD-s	EMI	CDDISC001	1996	£5	£2	
Skillex	CD-s	Fierce Panda	NING16CD	1996	£5	£2	

KENNEDY, JERRY

Title	Format	Label	Cat. No.	Year	Mint	VG	Notes
Dancing Guitars Rock Elvis' Hits	LP	Smash	MGS2/SRS67004	1962	£15	£6	*US*

KENNEDY, NORMAN

Title	Format	Label	Cat. No.	Year	Mint	VG	Notes
Scots Songs And Ballads	LP	Topic	12T178	1968	£15	£6	

KENNER, CHRIS

Title	Format	Label	Cat. No.	Year	Mint	VG	Notes
I Like It Like That	7"	London	HLU9410	1961	£8	£4	
Land Of A Thousand Dances	7"	Sue	WI351	1965	£15	£7.50	
Land Of A Thousand Dances	LP	Atlantic	587008	1966	£15	£6	

KENNY & CASH

Title	Format	Label	Cat. No.	Year	Mint	VG	Notes
Knees	7"	Decca	F12283	1965	£6	£2.50	

KENNY & CORKY

Title	Format	Label	Cat. No.	Year	Mint	VG	Notes
Nuttin' For Christmas	7"	London	HLX9002	1959	£4	£1.50	

KENNY & DENY

Title	Format	Label	Cat. No.	Year	Mint	VG	Notes
Try To Forget Me	7"	Decca	F12138	1965	£25	£12.50	

KENNY & THE CADETS

The single by Kenny and the Cadets is an early spin-off from the Beach Boys, as the record features both Brian and Carl Wilson (together with their mother).

Title	Format	Label	Cat. No.	Year	Mint	VG	Notes
Barbie	7"	Randy	422	1962	£125	£62.50	*US*

KENNY & THE KASUALS

Title	Format	Label	Cat. No.	Year	Mint	VG	Notes
Garage Kings	LP	Mark	7000	1969	£40	£20	*US*
Live At The Studio Club	LP	Mark	5000	1966	£300	£180	*US*
Teen Dreams	LP	Mark	6000	1968	£150	£75	*US, red vinyl*

KENNY & THE WRANGLERS

Title	Format	Label	Cat. No.	Year	Mint	VG	Notes
Doobie Doo	7"	Parlophone	R5275	1965	£6	£2.50	
Somebody Help Me	7"	Parlophone	R5224	1964	£6	£2.50	

KENSINGTON MARKET

Title	Format	Label	Cat. No.	Year	Mint	VG	Notes
Aardvark	LP	Warner Bros	WS1780	1969	£12	£5	*US*
Avenue Road	LP	Warner Bros	WS1754	1968	£12	£5	*US*

KENT, AL

Title	Format	Label	Cat. No.	Year	Mint	VG	Notes
You Gotta Pay The Price	7"	Track	604016	1967	£25	£12.50	
You Gotta Pay The Price	7"	Mojo	2092015	1971	£8	£4	*demo only*

KENT, ENOCH

Title	Format	Label	Cat. No.	Year	Mint	VG	Notes
Sings The Butcher Boy And Other Ballads	7" EP	Topic	TOP81	1962	£5	£2	

KENT, PAUL

Title	Format	Label	Cat. No.	Year	Mint	VG	Notes
P. C. Kent	LP	RCA	SF8083	1970	£20	£8	
Paul Kent	LP	B&C	CAS1044	1971	£15	£6	

KENT, RICHARD STYLE

Title	Format	Label	Cat. No.	Year	Mint	VG	Notes
Crocodile Tears	7"	MCA	MU1032	1968	£20	£10	
Little Bit O' Soul	7"	Mercury	MF1090	1969	£20	£10	
Marching Off To War	7"	Columbia	DB8182	1967	£30	£15	
No Matter What You Do	7"	Columbia	DB7964	1966	£75	£37.50	
You Can't Put Me Down	7"	Columbia	DB8051	1966	£30	£15	

KENT, SHIRLEY

Title	Format	Label	Cat. No.	Year	Mint	VG	Notes
Sings For Charec 67	7"	Keele University	103	1966	£15	£7.50	*with the Master Singers*

KENT & DIMPLE

Title	Format	Label	Cat. No.	Year	Mint	VG	Notes
Day Is Done	7"	Island	WI046	1963	£10	£5	

KENT & JEANIE

Title	Format	Label	Cat. No.	Year	Mint	VG	Notes
Daddy	7"	Blue Beat	BB98	1962	£12	£6	

KENTIGERN

Title	Format	Label	Cat. No.	Year	Mint	VG	Notes
Kentigern	LP	Topic	12TS394	1979	£10	£4	

KENTON, STAN

Title	Format	Label	Cat. No.	Year	Price	Price	Note
A-Ting-A-Ling	7"	Capitol	CL14259	1955	£4	£1.50	
Adventures In Jazz	LP	Capitol	(S)T1796	1962	£10	£4	
Adventures In Time	LP	Capitol	(S)T1844	1963	£10	£4	
Artistry In Rhythm	10" LP	Capitol	LC6545	1952	£25	£10	
Back To Balboa	LP	Capitol	T995	1958	£15	£6	
Ballad Style	LP	Capitol	(S)T1068	1959	£12	£5	
City Of Glass	10" LP	Capitol	LC6577	1953	£25	£10	
Classics	10" LP	Capitol	LC6676	1954	£25	£10	
Concert In Progressive Jazz	10" LP	Capitol	LC6546	1952	£25	£10	
Cuban Fire	LP	Capitol	LCT6118	1956	£20	£8	
Encores	10" LP	Capitol	LC6523	1951	£25	£10	
[illegible]	LP	Brunswick	LAT8122	1956	£15	£6	
In Hi-Fi	LP	Capitol	LCT6109	1956	£15	£6	
Innovations In Modern Music	LP	Capitol	LCT6006	1954	£25	£10	
Kenton Era Vol. 1	LP	Capitol	LCT6157	1958	£15	£6	
Kenton Era Vol. 2	LP	Capitol	LCT6158	1958	£15	£6	
Kenton Era Vol. 3	LP	Capitol	LCT6159	1958	£15	£6	
Kenton Era Vol. 4	LP	Capitol	LCT6160	1958	£15	£6	
Kenton Showcase	LP	Capitol	LCT6009	1955	£20	£8	
Kenton Sidemen	LP	Vogue	LAE12028	1957	£15	£6	
Kenton With Voices	LP	Capitol	LCT6138	1957	£15	£6	
Lush Interlude	LP	Capitol	T1130	1959	£12	£5	
Milestones	10" LP	Capitol	LC6517	1951	£25	£10	
New Concepts Of Artistry In Rhythm	10" LP	Capitol	LC6595	1953	£25	£10	
Portraits On Standards	10" LP	Capitol	LC6697	1955	£25	£10	
Presents	10" LP	Capitol	LC6548	1952	£25	£10	
Rendezvous With Kenton	LP	Capitol	(S)T932	1958	£15	£6	
Road Show Vol. 1	LP	Capitol	(S)T11327	1961	£10	£4	
Road Show Vol. 2	LP	Capitol	(S)T21327	1961	£10	£4	
Sketches On Standards	10" LP	Capitol	LC6602	1953	£25	£10	
Stage Door Swings	LP	Capitol	(S)T1166	1959	£12	£5	
Standards In Silhouette	LP	Capitol	(S)T1394	1961	£10	£4	
This Modern World	10" LP	Capitol	LC6667	1954	£25	£10	
West Side Story	LP	Capitol	(S)T1609	1961	£10	£4	

KEN-TONES

Title	Format	Label	Cat. No.	Year	Price	Price	Note
Get With It	7"	Parlophone	MSP6229	1956	£4	£1.50	
I Saw Esau	7"	Parlophone	R4257	1957	£4	£1.50	

KENTUCKY BOYS

Title	Format	Label	Cat. No.	Year	Price	Price	Note
Don't Fetch It	7"	HMV	7M312	1955	£4	£1.50	

KENTUCKY COLONELS

Title	Format	Label	Cat. No.	Year	Price	Price	Note
Appalachian Swing	LP	World Pacific	(S)T1821	1964	£20	£8	US
Kentucky Colonels	LP	United Artists	UAS29514	1974	£10	£4	
New Sound Of Bluegrass	LP	Briar	M109	1963	£20	£8	US

KENWRIGHT, BILL

Title	Format	Label	Cat. No.	Year	Price	Price	Note
I Want To Go Back There Again	7"	Columbia	DB8239	1967	£4	£1.50	

KENYATTA, ROBIN

Title	Format	Label	Cat. No.	Year	Price	Price	Note
Girl From Martinique	LP	ECM	ECM1008ST	1971	£20	£8	

KERN, WOODY

Title	Format	Label	Cat. No.	Year	Price	Price	Note
Awful Disclosures Of Maria Monk	LP	Pye	NSPL18273	1967	£25	£10	
Biography	7"	Pye	7N17672	1969	£4	£1.50	

KERNOCHAN, SARAH

Title	Format	Label	Cat. No.	Year	Price	Price	Note
House Of Pain	LP	RCA	0598	1974	£15	£6	

KEROUAC, JACK

Title	Format	Label	Cat. No.	Year	Price	Price	Note
Blues And Haikus	LP	Hanover	HML5006	1959	£75	£37.50	US
Poetry For The Beat Generation	LP	Hanover	HML5000	1959	£75	£37.50	US
Poetry For The Beat Generation	LP	Dot	DLP3154	1959	£100	£50	US
Readings On The Beat Generation	LP	Verve	MGV15005	1959	£75	£37.50	US

KERR, ANITA QUARTET

Title	Format	Label	Cat. No.	Year	Price	Price	Note
Anita Kerr Quartet	7" EP	RCA	RCX7164	1964	£5	£2	

KERR, MOIRA

Title	Format	Label	Cat. No.	Year	Price	Price	Note
Folk Warm And Gentle	LP	Beltona	SBE102	1969	£50	£25	

KERR, PATRICK

Title	Format	Label	Cat. No.	Year	Price	Price	Note
Magic Potion	7"	Decca	F12069	1965	£5	£2	

KERR, RICHARD

Title	Format	Label	Cat. No.	Year	Price	Price	Note
From Now Until Then	LP	Warner Bros	K46206	1972	£12	£5	

KERRIES

Title	Format	Label	Cat. No.	Year	Price	Price	Note
Kerries	LP	Major Minor	MMLP/SMLP9	1967	£15	£6	

KERRY, CHRIS

Title	Format	Label	Cat. No.	Year	Price	Price	Note
Seven Deadly Sins	7"	Mercury	MF957	1965	£8	£4	
Watermelon Man	7"	Mercury	MF985	1966	£8	£4	

KERSHAW, NIK
Radio Musicola	CD	MCA	DMCG6016	1986	£20	£8	

KESEY, KEN & THE GRATEFUL DEAD
Acid Test	LP	Sound City	EX27690	1967	£150	£75	*US*
Acid Test	LP	Psycho	PSYCHO4	1983	£25	£10	

KESSEL, BARNEY
Barney Kessel	10" LP	Vogue	LDE085	1954	£30	£15	
Barney Kessel Vol. 2	10" LP	Contemporary	LDC153	1955	£30	£15	
Easy Like	LP	Contemporary	LAC12082	1958	£25	£10	
Music To Listen To Barney Kessel By	LP	Contemporary	LAC12068/ SCA5002	1958	£15	£6	
Plays Carmen	LP	Contemporary	LAC12214	1960	£12	£5	
Plays Standards	LP	Contemporary	LAC12098	1959	£12	£5	
Poll Winners	LP	Contemporary	LAC12122	1959	£15	£6	
Poll Winners Ride Again	LP	Vogue	LAC12186	1959	£12	£5	*with Ray Brown & Shelly Manne*
Poll Winners Three	LP	Contemporary	LAC12237	1960	£10	£4	*with Ray Brown & Shelly Manne*
Slow Burn	LP	Phil Spector	2307011	1977	£10	£4	
Some Like It Hot	LP	Contemporary	LAC12206	1960	£12	£5	
To Swing Or Not To Swing	LP	Contemporary	LAC12058	1958	£15	£6	

KESTREL
Kestrel	LP	Cube	HIFLY19	1975	£125	£62.50	

KESTRELS
I Can't Say Goodbye	7"	Pye	7N15248	1960	£4	£1.50	
Kestrels	LP	Donegall	MAU500	1958	£20	£8	
Smash Hits	LP	Piccadilly	NPL38009	1963	£25	£10	
There Comes A Time	7"	Pye	7N15234	1959	£4	£1.50	

KESTY
Only Fools And Fiddles	LP	private		1979	£20	£8	

KETTELS
Overflight	LP	Karussell	635081	1968	£15	£6	*German*

KEY LARGO
Key Largo	LP	Blue Horizon	763859	1970	£20	£8	
Voodoo Rhythm	7"	Blue Horizon	573178	1971	£8	£4	

KEYES, EBONY
Sitting In The Ring	7"	Piccadilly	7N35358	1966	£25	£12.50	

KEYES, KAROL
Can't You Hear The Music	7"	Fontana	TF846	1967	£4	£1.50	
Fool In Love	7"	Columbia	DB7899	1966	£4	£1.50	
One In A Million	7"	Columbia	DB8001	1966	£25	£12.50	
You Beat Me To The Punch	7"	Fontana	TF517	1964	£5	£2	

KEYES, TROY
Love Explosions	7"	Stateside	SS2087	1968	£5	£2	

KEYMEN
Gazackstahagen	7"	HMV	POP584	1959	£5	£2	

KEYNOTES
Dime And A Dollar	7"	Decca	F10302	1954	£4	£1.50	*Johnston Brothers B side*
Steam Heat	7"	Decca	F10643	1955	£6	£2.50	

KHALSA STRING BAND
Khalsa String Band	LP	private	NR4108	1973	£50	£25	

KHAN
Space Shanty	LP	Deram	SDLR11	1972	£20	£8	

KHAN, ASHISH
Ashish Khan	LP	Liberty	LBL83083E	1968	£10	£4	

KHAN, USTAD ALI AKBAR
Dhun Palas Kafi	LP	Transatlantic	TRA183	1969	£10	£4	
Music From India No. 5	LP	HMV	ASD2367	1969	£10	£4	
Peaceful Music	LP	Mushroom	100MR14	1971	£40	£20	

KHAN, USTAD VILAYAT
Duets	LP	HMV	ALP/ASD2295	1967	£10	£4	
Guru	LP	RCA	SF8025	1969	£10	£4	
Music Of India	LP	HMV	ALP1946/ASD498	1962	£12	£5	
Raga Tilakkamod	LP	Transatlantic	TRA239	1970	£10	£4	
Ustad Vilayat Khan	LP	Track		1971	£10	£4	

KHANDARS
Don't Dig A Hole For Me	7"	Blue Beat	BB332	1965	£12	£6	*Buster's Allstars B side*

KHANS

New Orleans 2am	7"	London	HLU9555	1962	£5	£2	

KHARTOMB

Swahili Lullaby	7"	Whaam!	WHAAM14	1983	£4	£1.50	

KHAZAD DOOM

Level Six And A Half	LP	LPL	LPL892	1970	£1000	£700	US

KICKSTANDS

Black Boots And Bikes	LP	Capitol	(S)T2078	1964	£15	£6	US

KIDD, JOHNNY & THE PIRATES

The group's 'Shakin' All Over' got to number one in the UK charts and was a thoroughly deserved success as just about the only rock'n'roll classic to have originated in Britain. Frequent personnel changes prevented the group from ever managing to fully consolidate their early success and Kidd himself was killed in a car crash in 1966. Towards the end of the seventies, the best-known line-up of the Pirates, with Mick Green on guitar, established itself as a hard-working live favourite, easily competing with punk bands half their age.

Always And Ever	7"	HMV	POP1269	1964	£4	£1.50	
Birds And The Bees	7"	HMV	POP1397	1965	£4	£1.50	
Hungry For Love	7"	HMV	POP1228	1963	£4	£1.50	
Hurry On Back To Love	7"	HMV	POP978	1962	£5	£2	
I'll Never Get Over You	7"	HMV	POP1173	1963	£4	£1.50	
If You Were The Only Girl	7"	HMV	POP674	1959	£8	£4	
It's Got To Be You	7"	HMV	POP1520	1965	£8	£4	
Jealous Girl	7"	HMV	POP1309	1964	£4	£1.50	
Johnny Kidd & The Pirates	7" EP	HMV	7EG8834	1964	£30	£15	
Linda Lu	7"	HMV	POP853	1961	£6	£2.50	
Please Don't Bring Me Down	7"	HMV	POP919	1961	£6	£2.50	
Please Don't Touch	7"	HMV	POP615	1959	£8	£4	
Restless	7"	HMV	POP790	1960	£5	£2	
Send For That Girl	7"	HMV	POP1559	1966	£8	£4	
Shakin' All Over	7" EP	HMV	7EG8628	1960	£30	£15	
Shakin' All Over	7" EP	Pathe	EGF813	1965	£60	£30	French
Shakin' All Over	LP	Starline	SRS5100	1971	£10	£4	
Shaking All Over	7"	HMV	POP753	1960	£8	£4	
Shaking All Over '65	7"	HMV	POP1424	1965	£5	£2	
Shot Of Rhythm And Blues	7"	HMV	POP1088	1962	£4	£1.50	
Whole Lotta Woman	7"	HMV	POP1353	1964	£4	£1.50	
You Got What It Takes	7"	HMV	POP698	1960	£5	£2	

KIDS NEXT DOOR

Inky Dinky Spider	7"	London	HLR9993	1965	£4	£1.50	

KIDZ NEXT DOOR (2)

What's It All About?	7"	Warner Bros	K17492	1979	£12	£6	

KIESEWETTER, KNUT

That's Me	LP	Starclub	158033STY	1967	£50	£25	German

KILDAIRE, ROY

What About It	7"	Blue Beat	BB226	1964	£12	£6	

KILEEN, JUDY

Just Walking In The Rain	7"	London	HLU8328	1956	£20	£10	

KILFENORA CEILI BAND

Kilfenora Ceili Band	LP	Transatlantic	TRS108	1974	£12	£5	

KILGORE, MERLE

Dear Mama	7"	Melodisc	1545	1960	£8	£4	
Ernie	7"	London	HLP8392	1957	£200	£100	
Forty Two In Chicago	7"	Mercury	AMT1193	1962	£6	£2.50	
It Can't Rain All The Time	7"	London	HL8103	1954	£100	£50	

KILGORE, THEOLA

I'll Keep Trying	7"	Sue	WI4035	1967	£10	£5	

KILLEN, LOU & SALLY

Bright Shining Morning	LP	Front Hall	FHR06	1975	£20	£8	US

KILLEN, LOUIS

Along The Coaly Tyne	LP	Topic	12T189	1969	£20	£8	*with Johnny Handle & Colin Ross*
Ballads And Broadsides	LP	Topic	12T126	1965	£20	£8	
Collier's Rant	7" EP	Topic	TOP74	1962	£15	£7.50	*with Johnny Handle*
Northumbrian Garland	7" EP	Topic	TOP75	1962	£15	£7.50	
Tommy Armstrong Of Tyneside	LP	Topic	12T122	1965	£12	£5	*with Tom Gilfellon, Johnny Handle, & Colin Ross*

KILLERMETERS

Twisted Wheel	7"	Gem	GEMS22	1980	£10	£5	
Why Should It Happen To Me	7"	Psycho	P2620	1979	£50	£25	*picture sleeve*
Why Should It Happen To Me	7"	Psycho	P2620	1979	£15	£7.50	*no picture sleeve*

KILLERS

Title	Format	Label	Cat. No.	Year	Mint	VG	Notes
Killer	LP	Ariola	ARL5003	1977	**£10**	**£4**	

KILLIGREW, JOHN

Title	Format	Label	Cat. No.	Year	Mint	VG	Notes
John Killigrew	LP	Penny Farthing	PELS513	1971	**£10**	**£4**	

KILLING FLOOR

Title	Format	Label	Cat. No.	Year	Mint	VG	Notes
Call For The Politicians	7"	Penny Farthing	PEN745	1970	**£10**	**£5**	
Killing Floor	LP	Spark	SRLP102	1970	**£150**	**£75**	
Original Killing Floor	LP	Spark	SRLM2004	1973	**£50**	**£25**	
Out Of Uranus	LP	Penny Farthing	PELS511	1970	**£100**	**£50**	

KILLING JOKE

Title	Format	Label	Cat. No.	Year	Mint	VG	Notes
America	CD-s	Editions EG	EGOCD40	1988	**£5**	**£2**	
Kings And Queens	12"	Editions EG	EGOY21	1985	**£6**	**£2.50**	
Love Like Blood	12"	Editions EG	EGOY20	1985	**£6**	**£2.50**	
Me Or You	12"	Editions EG	EGOXD14	1983	**£10**	**£5**	*double*
Money Is Not Our God	CD-s	Noise	AG0543	1990	**£5**	**£2**	
Nervous System	10"	Malicious Damage	MD410	1979	**£10**	**£4**	*with 5 inserts*
Nervous System	12"	Island	WIP6550	1981	**£6**	**£2.50**	
Requiem	12"	Malicious Damage	EGMDX100	1980	**£6**	**£2.50**	
Revelations	CD	Editions EG	EGCD59	1987	**£12**	**£5**	
Sanity	7"	Editions EG	EGO30	1986	**£8**	**£4**	*with Wardance cassette*
Wardance	7"	Malicious Damage	MD540	1980	**£4**	**£1.50**	*with insert*

KILLJOYS

Title	Format	Label	Cat. No.	Year	Mint	VG	Notes
Johnny Won't Get To Heaven	7"	Raw	RAW3	1977	**£6**	**£2.50**	

KILOWATTS

Title	Format	Label	Cat. No.	Year	Mint	VG	Notes
Bring It On Home	7"	Doctor Bird	DB1140	1968	**£10**	**£5**	

KILTIES

Title	Format	Label	Cat. No.	Year	Mint	VG	Notes
Teach You To Rock	7"	Beltona	BL2666	1956	**£8**	**£4**	

KIM & THE KINETICS

Title	Format	Label	Cat. No.	Year	Mint	VG	Notes
Wee Wee Hours	7"	Mortonsound	3036/3	196–	**£30**	**£15**	
Without A Song	7"	Mortonsound	3032/3	196–	**£30**	**£15**	

KIMBER, BILL & THE COURIERS

Title	Format	Label	Cat. No.	Year	Mint	VG	Notes
Shakin' Up A Storm	LP	Renown	NLP248	1965	**£100**	**£50**	*South African*
Swinging Fashion	LP	Renown	NLP262	1965	**£100**	**£50**	*South African*

KIMBER, WILLIAM

Title	Format	Label	Cat. No.	Year	Mint	VG	Notes
Art Of William Kimber	LP	Topic	12T249	1974	**£10**	**£4**	
William Kimber	LP	EFSDS	LP1001	197–	**£12**	**£5**	

KIMBER, WILLIAM E.

Title	Format	Label	Cat. No.	Year	Mint	VG	Notes
Kilburn Towers	7"	Parlophone	R5735	1968	**£4**	**£1.50**	

KIMBLE, STEVIE

Title	Format	Label	Cat. No.	Year	Mint	VG	Notes
Some Things Take A Little Time	7"	Decca	F12378	1966	**£10**	**£5**	

KIMMEL, JOHN J.

Title	Format	Label	Cat. No.	Year	Mint	VG	Notes
Early Recordings Of Irish Traditional Dance Music	LP	Leader	LEO2060	1977	**£12**	**£5**	

KIN PING MEH

Title	Format	Label	Cat. No.	Year	Mint	VG	Notes
Concrete	LP	Nova	628370	1975	**£15**	**£6**	*German*
Kin Ping Meh	LP	Polydor	2371259	1971	**£100**	**£50**	*German*
Kin Ping Meh 2	LP	Zebra	2949005	1972	**£20**	**£8**	*German*
Kin Ping Meh 3	LP	Zebra	2949011	1973	**£20**	**£8**	*German*
Kin Ping Meh 6	LP	Bacillus	BAC2046	1977	**£15**	**£6**	*German*
Virtues And Sins	LP	Nova	622015	1974	**£15**	**£6**	*German*

KINESPHERE

Title	Format	Label	Cat. No.	Year	Mint	VG	Notes
All Around You	LP	Kinesphere	KIN5001	1976	**£75**	**£37.50**	

KINETIC

Title	Format	Label	Cat. No.	Year	Mint	VG	Notes
Live Your Life	7" EP	Vogue	EPL8544	1967	**£20**	**£10**	*French*
Live Your Life	LP	Vogue	CLVLX148	1966	**£100**	**£50**	*French*
Suddenly Tomorrow	7" EP	Vogue	EPL8520	1967	**£20**	**£10**	*French*

KING

Title	Format	Label	Cat. No.	Year	Mint	VG	Notes
Bittersweet	CD	CBS	86320	1985	**£25**	**£10**	

KING, AL

Title	Format	Label	Cat. No.	Year	Mint	VG	Notes
Think Twice Before You Speak	7"	Sue	WI4045	1968	**£15**	**£7.50**	

KING, ALBERT

Title	Format	Label	Cat. No.	Year	Mint	VG	Notes
Big Blues	LP	King	852	1962	**£40**	**£20**	*US*

Title	Format	Label	Cat. No.	Year	Mint	VG	Notes
Born Under A Bad Sign	7"	Stax	601015	1967	£4	£1.50	
Born Under A Bad Sign	LP	Stax	723	1967	£15	£6	US
Cold Feet	7"	Stax	601029	1968	£4	£1.50	
Crosscut Saw	7"	Atlantic	584099	1967	£6	£2.50	
Does The King's Things	LP	Stax	SXATS1017	1968	£12	£5	
Door To Door	LP	Chess	1538	1969	£12	£5	US, with Otis Rush
King Of The Blues Guitar	LP	Atlantic	588173	1969	£12	£5	
Live Wire Blues Power	LP	Stax	(S)XATS1002	1968	£12	£5	
Lucy	7"	Stax	601042	1968	£4	£1.50	
Travelling To California	LP	Polydor	2343026	1967	£12	£5	
Years Gone By	LP	Stax	SXATS1022	1970	£10	£4	

KING, ANNA

Title	Format	Label	Cat. No.	Year	Mint	VG	Notes
Baby Baby Baby	7"	Philips	BF1402	1965	£5	£2	with Bobby Byrd
Back To Soul	7" EP	Philips	BE12584	1965	£15	£7.50	
Back To Soul	LP	Philips	(S)BL7655	1965	£40	£20	

KING, ANTHONY

Title	Format	Label	Cat. No.	Year	Mint	VG	Notes
Electrical Bazaar – Synthesizers Unlimited	LP	Peer International		197–	£20	£8	

KING, B. B.

Title	Format	Label	Cat. No.	Year	Mint	VG	Notes
Ain't Nobody Home	7"	Probe	PRO546	1971	£4	£1.50	
B. B. King	LP	Crown	CLP5359	1963	£15	£6	US
B. B. King Sings Spirituals	LP	Crown	CLP5119/CST152	1960	£15	£6	US
B. B. King Sings Spirituals	LP	Crown	CST152	1960	£20	£8	US, red vinyl
B. B. King Story Vol. 1	LP	Blue Horizon	763216	1968	£40	£20	
B. B. King Story Vol. 2	LP	Blue Horizon	763226	1969	£40	£20	
B. B. King Wails	LP	Crown	CST147	1960	£20	£8	US, red vinyl
B. B. King Wails	LP	Crown	CLP5115/CST147	1960	£15	£6	US
Best Of B. B. King	LP	Galaxy	202	1963	£15	£6	US
Blues	LP	Crown	CLP5063	1960	£15	£6	US
Blues In My Heart	LP	Crown	CLP5309	1962	£15	£6	US
Blues Is King	LP	HMV	CLP3608	1967	£20	£8	
Blues On Top Of Blues	LP	Stateside	(S)SL10238	1968	£15	£6	
Completely Well	LP	Stateside	SSL10299	1970	£15	£6	
Confessin' The Blues	LP	HMV	CLP3514	1966	£20	£8	
Don't Answer The Door	7"	HMV	POP1568	1966	£5	£2	
Don't Waste My Time	7"	Stateside	SS2141	1969	£4	£1.50	
Easy Listening Blues	LP	Crown	CLP5286	1962	£15	£6	US
Electric B. B. King	LP	Stateside	SSL10284	1969	£15	£6	
Every Day I Have The Blues	7"	Blue Horizon	573161	1969	£8	£4	
Great B. B. King	LP	Crown	CLP5143	1961	£15	£6	US
Hummingbird	7"	Stateside	SS2176	1970	£4	£1.50	
In London	LP	Probe	SPB1041	1971	£10	£4	
Indianola Mississippi Seeds	LP	Probe	SPBA6255	1970	£10	£4	
Jungle	7"	Polydor	56735	1967	£4	£1.50	
King Of The Blues	LP	Crown	CST195	1961	£20	£8	US, red vinyl
King Of The Blues	LP	Crown	CLP5167/CST195	1961	£15	£6	US
Live And Well	LP	Stateside	SSL10297	1970	£15	£6	
Live At Cook County Jail	LP	Probe	SPB1032	1971	£10	£4	
Live At The Regal	LP	HMV	CLP1870	1965	£20	£8	
Lucille	LP	Stateside	(S)SL10272	1969	£15	£6	
Mr Blues	LP	ABC	(S)456	1963	£15	£6	US
My Kind Of Blues	LP	Crown	CLP5188	1961	£15	£6	US
Night Life	7"	HMV	POP1580	1967	£4	£1.50	
Paying The Cost To Be The Boss	7"	Stateside	SS2112	1968	£4	£1.50	
R&B And Soul	LP	Ember	EMB3379	1967	£10	£4	
Rock Me Baby	LP	Ember	EMBS196	1964	£8	£4	
So Excited	7"	Stateside	SS2169	1970	£4	£1.50	
Take A Swing With Me	LP	Blue Horizon	2431004	1970	£40	£20	
Think It Over	7"	HMV	POP1594	1967	£4	£1.50	
Thrill Is Gone	7"	Stateside	SS2161	1970	£4	£1.50	
Tomorrow Night	7"	HMV	POP1101	1962	£8	£4	
Twist With B. B. King	LP	Crown	CLP5248	1962	£15	£6	US
Woman I Love	7"	Blue Horizon	573144	1968	£8	£4	
You Never Know	7"	Sue	WI358	1965	£8	£4	

KING, B. B. & BOBBY BLAND

Title	Format	Label	Cat. No.	Year	Mint	VG	Notes
Together For The First Time	LP	ABC	ABCD605	1974	£12	£5	double

KING, BEN E.

Title	Format	Label	Cat. No.	Year	Mint	VG	Notes
Amor Amor	7"	London	HLK9416	1961	£4	£1.50	
Cry No More	7"	Atlantic	AT4043	1965	£10	£5	
Don't Play That Song	7"	London	HLK9544	1962	£4	£1.50	
Don't Play That Song	LP	London	HAK8012	1962	£25	£10	
Don't Take Your Love From Me	7"	Atlantic	584184	1968	£10	£5	
Goodnight My Love, Pleasant Dreams	7"	Atlantic	AT4065	1966	£200	£100	demo with 'News' B side
Goodnight My Love, Pleasant Dreams	7"	Atlantic	AT4065	1966	£4	£1.50	
Greatest Hits	LP	Atco	SD33165	1964	£15	£6	US
Grooving	7"	London	HLK9840	1964	£4	£1.50	
Here Comes The Night	7"	London	HLK9457	1961	£5	£2	
How Can I Forget	7"	London	HLK9691	1963	£4	£1.50	
How Can I Forget	7" EP	London	REK1361	1963	£25	£12.50	
I (Who Have Nothing)	7"	London	HLK9778	1963	£4	£1.50	
I Could Have Danced All Night	7"	London	HLK9819	1963	£4	£1.50	
I'm Standing By	7"	London	HLK9631	1962	£6	£2.50	

I'm Standing By	7" EP	London	REK1386	1963	£25	£12.50	
Let The Water Run Down	7"	Atlantic	AT4007	1964	£4	£1.50	
Record	7"	Atlantic	AT4025	1965	£6	£2.50	
Seven Letters	7"	Atlantic	584149	1968	£4	£1.50	
Seven Letters	7"	Atlantic	AT4018	1965	£5	£2	
Seven Letters	LP	Atlantic	588125	1968	£10	£4	
Songs For Soulful Lovers	LP	London	HAK/SHK8026	1963	£25	£10	
Songs For Soulful Lovers	LP	Atlantic	587/588055	1966	£10	£4	
Spanish Harlem	7"	London	HLK9258	1961	£6	£2.50	
Spanish Harlem	LP	London	HAK2395/ SAHK6195	1961	£25	£10	
Spanish Harlem	LP	Atlantic	590001	1967	£10	£4	
Stand By Me	7"	London	HLK9358	1961	£6	£2.50	
Tears, Tears, Tears	7"	Atlantic	584106	1967	£5	£2	
Too Bad	7"	London	HLK9586	1962	£4	£1.50	
What Is Soul?	7"	Atlantic	584069	1967	£4	£1.50	
What Is Soul?	LP	Atlantic	587072	1967	£15	£6	
What Now My Love	7" EP	Atlantic	AET6004	1964	£20	£10	
Yes	7"	London	HLK9517	1962	£4	£1.50	

KING, BOB

Hey Honey	7"	Oriole	CB1497	1959	£60	£30	

KING, BUZZY

Schoolboy Blues	7"	Top Rank	JAR278	1960	£10	£5	

KING, CARL

Out Of My Depth	7"	CBS	202407	1966	£6	£2.50	

KING, CAROLE

It Might As Well Rain Until September	7"	London	HLU9591	1962	£4	£1.50	
Music	LP	Ode	SQ88013	1971	£10	£4	*US quad*
Road To Nowhere	7"	London	HLU10036	1966	£4	£1.50	
Tapestry	LP	Epic/Ode	HE44946	1980	£12	£5	*US audiophile*

KING, CLAUDE

Burning Of Atlanta	7"	CBS	AAG119	1962	£4	£1.50	
Commancheros	7"	Philips	BF1199	1961	£4	£1.50	
Meet Claude King	LP	CBS	BPG62114	1962	£20	£8	
Sweet Loving	7"	Philips	BF1173	1961	£4	£1.50	
Tiger Woman	7" EP	CBS	EP6067	1965	£15	£7.50	
Wolverton Mountain	7"	CBS	AAG108	1962	£6	£2.50	

KING, CLYDIE

One Part Two Part	7"	Minit	MLF11014	1969	£5	£2	

KING, DANNY & MAYFAIR SET

Amen	7"	Columbia	DB7792	1965	£10	£5	
Pretty Things	7"	Columbia	DB7456	1965	£20	£10	
Tossing And Turning	7"	Columbia	DB7276	1964	£15	£7.50	

KING, DAVE

Birds And The Bees	7"	Decca	F10741	1956	£4	£1.50	
Christmas And You	7"	Decca	F10791	1956	£6	£2.50	
Memories Are Made Of This	7"	Decca	F10684	1956	£6	£2.50	
No. 2	7" EP	Decca	DFE6514	1958	£10	£5	
Selection	7" EP	Decca	DFE6385	1956	£8	£4	
Shake Me I Rattle	7"	Decca	F10947	1957	£4	£1.50	
Story Of My Life	7"	Decca	F10973	1958	£5	£2	
You Can't Be True To Two	7"	Decca	F10720	1956	£5	£2	

KING, DEE

Sally Go Round The Roses	7"	Piccadilly	7N35316	1966	£4	£1.50	

KING, DENNIS

Regan's Theme From The Sweeney	7"	EMI	EMI2578	1977	£8	£4	

KING, FREDDIE

Bonanza Of Instrumentals	LP	King	(S)928	1965	£20	£8	*US*
Bossa Nova And Blues	LP	King	821	1962	£30	£15	*US*
Boy-Girl-Boy	LP	King	777	1962	£30	£15	*US*
Driving Sideways	7"	Sue	WI349	1965	£15	£7.50	
Freddie King Goes Surfin'	LP	King	(S)856	1963	£25	£10	*US*
Freddie King Is A Blues Master	LP	Atlantic	588186	1969	£20	£8	
Freddie King Sings The Blues	LP	King	762	1961	£40	£20	*US*
Getting Ready	LP	A&M	AMLS65004	1971	£12	£5	
Hide Away	LP	King	KS1059	1969	£15	£6	*US*
Hideaway	7"	Parlophone	R4777	1961	£15	£7.50	
His Early Years	LP	Polydor	2343047	1971	£10	£4	
King Of R&B Vol. 2	LP	Polydor	2343009	1969	£12	£5	
Let's Hide Away And Dance Away	LP	King	773	1961	£40	£20	*US*
Live Performances Vol. 1	LP	Black Bear	904	1972	£15	£6	
Live Performances Vol. 2	LP	Black Bear	905	1972	£15	£6	
Play It Cool	7"	Atlantic	584235	1969	£4	£1.50	
Texas Cannonball	LP	A&M	AMLS68113	1972	£10	£4	
Twenty-Four Vocals And Instrumentals	LP	King	964	1966	£20	£8	*US*
Volume 1	LP	Python	KM5	1969	£25	£10	
Volume 2	LP	Python	KM7	1969	£25	£10	

Title	Format	Label	Cat. No.	Year	Mint	VG	Notes
Volume 3	LP	Python	PLPKM11	1969	**£25**	**£10**	

KING, HAMILTON

Title	Format	Label	Cat. No.	Year	Mint	VG	Notes
Ain't It Time	7"	HMV	POP1356	1964	**£8**	**£4**	
Bird Without Wings	7"	HMV	POP1425	1965	**£8**	**£4**	
Not Until	7"	HMV	POP1289	1964	**£5**	**£2**	

KING, HANK

Title	Format	Label	Cat. No.	Year	Mint	VG	Notes
Country And Western	7" EP	Starlite	STEP41	1963	**£12**	**£6**	
Country And Western	7" EP	Starlite	GRK510	1966	**£6**	**£2.50**	

KING, JAY W.

Title	Format	Label	Cat. No.	Year	Mint	VG	Notes
I'm So Afraid	7"	Stateside	SS505	1966	**£10**	**£5**	

KING, JONATHAN

Title	Format	Label	Cat. No.	Year	Mint	VG	Notes
Everyone's Gone To The Moon	7" EP	Decca	457090	1965	**£10**	**£5**	*French*
Or Then Again	LP	Decca	LK/SKL4908	1967	**£10**	**£4**	

KING, MARK

Title	Format	Label	Cat. No.	Year	Mint	VG	Notes
Clocks Go Forward	12"	Polydor	MKX2DJ	1984	**£10**	**£5**	*promo*

KING, MARTIN LUTHER

Title	Format	Label	Cat. No.	Year	Mint	VG	Notes
Great March To Freedom	LP	Tamla Motown	TML11076	1968	**£100**	**£50**	
I Have A Dream	7"	Pama	PM732	1968	**£6**	**£2.50**	
In The Struggle For Freedom	LP	Hallmark	CHM631	1968	**£12**	**£5**	

KING, PAUL

Title	Format	Label	Cat. No.	Year	Mint	VG	Notes
Been In The Pen Too Long	LP	Dawn	DNLS3035	1972	**£12**	**£5**	
Hey Rosalyn	7"	Red Bus	RBUS79	1983	**£5**	**£2**	*as P. King*
Look At Me Now	7"	Dawn	DNS1031	1973	**£6**	**£2.50**	*as P. Rufus King*
Whoa Buck	7"	Dawn	DNS1023	1972	**£6**	**£2.50**	

KING, PEE WEE

Title	Format	Label	Cat. No.	Year	Mint	VG	Notes
Bimbo	7"	HMV	7MC14	1954	**£5**	**£2**	*export*

KING, RAMONA

Title	Format	Label	Cat. No.	Year	Mint	VG	Notes
It's In His Kiss	7"	Warner Bros	WB125	1964	**£4**	**£1.50**	

KING, REG

Title	Format	Label	Cat. No.	Year	Mint	VG	Notes
Reg King	LP	United Artists	UAS29157	1971	**£50**	**£25**	

KING, SAMMY

Title	Format	Label	Cat. No.	Year	Mint	VG	Notes
Great Balls Of Fire	7"	HMV	POP1285	1964	**£4**	**£1.50**	

KING, SID & THE FIVE STRINGS

Title	Format	Label	Cat. No.	Year	Mint	VG	Notes
Booger Red	78	Philips	PB589	1956	**£15**	**£7.50**	

KING, SOLOMON

Title	Format	Label	Cat. No.	Year	Mint	VG	Notes
She Wears My Ring	7"	Columbia	DB8306	1967	**£5**	**£2**	
She Wears My Ring	LP	Columbia	SX/SCX6250	1968	**£10**	**£4**	
This Beautiful Day	7"	Columbia	DB8676	1970	**£30**	**£15**	

KING, SONNY

Title	Format	Label	Cat. No.	Year	Mint	VG	Notes
For Losers Only	LP	Pye	NPL28001	1960	**£15**	**£6**	

KING, TEDDI

Title	Format	Label	Cat. No.	Year	Mint	VG	Notes
Miss Teddi King With Ruby Braff	10" LP	Vogue	LDE142	1955	**£50**	**£25**	
Now In Vogue	LP	Vogue	VA160109	1957	**£40**	**£20**	

KING, TEDDY

Title	Format	Label	Cat. No.	Year	Mint	VG	Notes
Mexican Divorce	7"	Fab	FAB27	1967	**£8**	**£4**	*Soul Tops B side*

KING, TONY

Title	Format	Label	Cat. No.	Year	Mint	VG	Notes
Proud Mary	7"	Trojan	TR667	1969	**£5**	**£2**	

KING, WENDY

Title	Format	Label	Cat. No.	Year	Mint	VG	Notes
Wendy Experience	LP	Look	LKLP6355	1979	**£15**	**£6**	

KING BEES

Title	Format	Label	Cat. No.	Year	Mint	VG	Notes
On Your Way Down The Drain	7" EP	RCA	86521	1966	**£15**	**£7.50**	*French*

KING BEES (2)

The rare single 'Liza Jane' is listed in the *Guide* under the name later used by the group's lead singer – David Bowie.

KING BISCUIT BOY

Title	Format	Label	Cat. No.	Year	Mint	VG	Notes
Gooduns	LP	Paramount	SPFA7001	1971	**£15**	**£6**	
Official Music	LP	Paramount	SPFL270	1971	**£15**	**£6**	

KING BROTHERS

Title	Format	Label	Cat. No.	Year	Mint	VG	Notes
Harmony Kings	7" EP	Parlophone	GEP8638	1957	**£6**	**£2.50**	
Hop, Skip And Jump	7"	Parlophone	R4554	1959	**£5**	**£2**	
In The Middle Of An Island	7"	Parlophone	R4338	1957	**£4**	**£1.50**	
King Brothers	LP	Parlophone	PMC1060	1958	**£10**	**£4**	
King Size Hits	7" EP	Parlophone	GEP8838	1961	**£5**	**£2**	
Kings Of Song	7" EP	Parlophone	GEP8760	1958	**£6**	**£2.50**	
Little By Little	7"	Parlophone	R4288	1957	**£5**	**£2**	

Lullabies Of Broadway	7" EP	Parlophone	GEP8665	1957	**£5**	**£2**	
Put A Light In The Window	7"	Parlophone	R4389	1958	**£4**	**£1.50**	
Sing Al Jolson	7" EP	Parlophone	GEP8651	1957	**£5**	**£2**	
Six Five Jive	7"	Parlophone	R4410	1958	**£5**	**£2**	
That's Entertainment	7" EP	Parlophone	GEP8726	1958	**£5**	**£2**	
Torero	7"	Parlophone	R4438	1958	**£4**	**£1.50**	
Wake Up Little Susie	7"	Parlophone	R4367	1957	**£4**	**£1.50**	
White Sports Coat	7"	Parlophone	R4310	1957	**£4**	**£1.50**	

KING CANNON

Soul Pipe	7"	Duke	DU13	1969	**£4**	**£1.50**	
Soul Scorcher	7"	Trojan	TR663	1969	**£4**	**£1.50**	
Thunderstorm	7"	Trojan	TR636	1968	**£4**	**£1.50**	*Burt Walters B side*

KING CRIMSON

It is difficult today to convey the sense of excitement of the new that was apparent at King Crimson's early concerts. The one LP that exists of the original line-up is a frustrating affair in so far as it fails to display all the facets of a remarkable group. *In The Court Of The Crimson King* is, nevertheless, the progressive rock textbook, its vital place in the music being finally recognized by a noticeable rise in the value of original copies. The novel eccentricity apparent in the subsequent 'Cat Food' single gives a hint of what might have followed. Unfortunately, the original line-up came apart after an American tour. Both *In The Wake Of Poseidon* and *McDonald And Giles* contain material that had been destined for the real, unheard second King Crimson album. With later King Crimson albums being essentially the work of Robert Fripp, rather than the co-operative unit that was there at the start, it is rather as though the Beatles had gone their separate ways immediately after making *Revolver*.

Cat Food	7"	Island	WIP6080	1970	**£20**	**£10**	*picture sleeve*
Court Of The Crimson King	7"	Island	WIP6071	1969	**£8**	**£4**	
Earthbound	LP	Island	HELP6	1972	**£15**	**£6**	
In The Court Of The Crimson King	CD	Polydor	8000302	1983	**£12**	**£5**	
In The Court Of The Crimson King	LP	Island	ILPS9111	1969	**£30**	**£15**	*pink label*
In The Court Of The Crimson King	LP	Mobile Fidelity	MFSL1075	1980	**£25**	**£10**	*US audiophile*
In The Wake Of Poseidon	CD	Editions EG	EGCD2	1987	**£12**	**£5**	
In The Wake Of Poseidon	LP	Island	ILPS9127	1970	**£20**	**£8**	*pink label*
Islands	CD	Editions EG	EGCD5	1987	**£12**	**£5**	
Islands	LP	Island	ILPS9175	1971	**£15**	**£6**	
Larks' Tongues In Aspic	CD	Editions EG	EGCD7	1987	**£12**	**£5**	
Lizard	LP	Island	ILPS9141	1970	**£15**	**£6**	
Return Of King Crimson	LP	Editions EG		1981	**£15**	**£6**	*interview promo*
Thela Hun Ginjeet	12"	Editions EG	KCX001	1981	**£6**	**£2.50**	*promo*
Three Of A Perfect Pair	CD	Editions EG	8178822	1984	**£12**	**£5**	
Twenty-First Century Schizoid Man	7"	Island	WIP6274	1976	**£4**	**£1.50**	
Twenty-First Century Schizoid Man	7"	Island	WIP6274	1976	**£15**	**£7.50**	*picture sleeve*

KING CRY CRY

I Had A Talk	7"	Banana	BA356	1971	**£8**	**£4**	*Burning Spear B side*

KING EARL BOOGIE BAND

Plastic Jesus	7"	Dawn	DNS1024	1972	**£5**	**£2**	
Starlight	7"	Dawn	DNS1028	1972	**£5**	**£2**	
Trouble At Mill	LP	Dawn	DNLS3040	1972	**£10**	**£4**	

KING FIGHTER

People Will Talk	7"	Jump Up	JU518	1967	**£4**	**£1.50**	

KING GEORGE

I'm Gonna Be Somebody	7"	RCA	RCA1573	1967	**£8**	**£4**	

KING HORROR

Cutting Blade	7"	Grape	GR3003	1969	**£5**	**£2**	
Dracula Prince Of Darkness	7"	Duke	DU34	1969	**£5**	**£2**	*Joe's All Stars B side*
Frankenstein	7"	Nu Beat	NB051	1970	**£5**	**£2**	*Winston Groovy B side*
Hole	7"	Grape	GR3006	1969	**£5**	**£2**	*Winston Groovy B side*
Lochness Monster	7"	Grape	GR3007	1969	**£5**	**£2**	*Visions B side*
Police	7"	Jackpot	JP714	1969	**£5**	**£2**	*Pama Dice B side*
Wood In The Fire	7"	Jackpot	JP713	1969	**£5**	**£2**	

KING KURT

America	7"	Polydor	KURTP1	1986	**£4**	**£1.50**	*shaped picture disc*
Banana Banana	7"	Stiff	BUY206	1984	**£5**	**£2**	*shaped picture disc*
Destination Zululand	7"	Stiff	BUY189	1983	**£6**	**£2.50**	*shaped picture disc*
Mack The Knife	7"	Stiff	PBUY199	1984	**£5**	**£2**	*shaped picture disc*
Mack The Knife	7"	Stiff	BUY199	1984	**£4**	**£1.50**	*picture disc*
Zulu Beat	7"	Thin Sliced	TSR2	1982	**£6**	**£2.50**	*60-plus coloured vinyl/ sleeve combinations!*

KING OF MONTEGO BAY

Burn	7"	Blue Beat	BB322	1965	**£12**	**£6**	

KING ROCKY

King Is Back	7"	Studio One	SO2045	1968	**£12**	**£6**	*Three Tops B side*

KING SPORTY

D.J. Special	7"	Banana	BA323	1970	**£6**	**£2.50**	*Richard & Mad B side*

Title	Format	Label	Cat. No.	Year	Mint	VG	Notes
For Our Desire	7″	Punch	PH44	1970	£5	£2	*Winston Wright B side*
Inspiration	7″	Banana	BA321	1970	£6	£2.50	
Lover's Version	7″	Banana	BA322	1970	£6	£2.50	*Dudley Sibley B side*

KING STITT

Title	Format	Label	Cat. No.	Year	Mint	VG	Notes
Back Out Version	7″	Banana	BA332	1971	£4	£1.50	*Vegetables B side*
Herbsman Shuffle	7″	Clandisc	CLA207	1969	£4	£1.50	*Higgs & Wilson B side*
King Of Kings	7″	Clandisc	CLA223	1970	£4	£1.50	*Dynamites B side*
On The Street	7″	Clandisc	CLA203	1969	£4	£1.50	*Cynthia Richards B side*
Rhyming Time	7″	Banana	BA334	1971	£4	£1.50	
[illegible]	7″	Clandisc	[illegible]	1969	[illegible]	[illegible]	

KING TRUMAN

Title	Format	Label	Cat. No.	Year	Mint	VG	Notes
Like A Gun	12″	Acid Jazz	JAZID9T	1989	£6	£2.50	

KINGBEES

Title	Format	Label	Cat. No.	Year	Mint	VG	Notes
I'm A Kingbee	7″	Tempo	TPO103	1966	£200	£100	*picture sleeve*

KINGDOM

Title	Format	Label	Cat. No.	Year	Mint	VG	Notes
Kingdom	LP	Speciality	SPS2135	1970	£75	£37.50	*US*

KINGDOM COME

Title	Format	Label	Cat. No.	Year	Mint	VG	Notes
Galactic Zoo Dossier	LP	Polydor	2310130	1972	£30	£15	*with poster*
Galactic Zoo Dossier	LP	Polydor	2310130	1971	£20	£8	
Journey	LP	Polydor	2310254	1973	£15	£6	
Kingdom Come	LP	Polydor	2310178	1973	£15	£6	
Lost Ears	LP	Gull	GUD2003/4	1977	£20	£8	*double*

KINGDOMS

The record credited to Kingdoms marks the recording debut of Guy Chadwick, who was later to find much more success with his band the House Of Love.

Title	Format	Label	Cat. No.	Year	Mint	VG	Notes
Heartland	12″	Regard	RG114	1984	£8	£4	
Heartland	7″	Regard	RG114	1984	£5	£2	

KINGLY BAND

Title	Format	Label	Cat. No.	Year	Mint	VG	Notes
Bitter And The Sweet	7″	Decca	F12926	1969	£4	£1.50	

KINGMAKER

Title	Format	Label	Cat. No.	Year	Mint	VG	Notes
Celebrated Working Man	7″	Sacred Heart	NONE1	1991	£10	£5	*promo*

KINGPINS

Title	Format	Label	Cat. No.	Year	Mint	VG	Notes
It Won't Be This Way Always	LP	King	865	1963	£20	£8	*US*
Ungaua	7″	London	HLU8658	1958	£10	£5	

KINGPINS (2)

Title	Format	Label	Cat. No.	Year	Mint	VG	Notes
Two Right Feet	7″	Oriole	CB1986	1965	£12	£6	

KINGS IV

Title	Format	Label	Cat. No.	Year	Mint	VG	Notes
Some Like It Hot	7″	London	HLT8914	1959	£8	£4	

KING'S GALLIARD

Title	Format	Label	Cat. No.	Year	Mint	VG	Notes
Morning Dew	LP	Dolphin	DOLM5014	1976	£10	£4	*Irish*

KING'S HENCHMEN

Title	Format	Label	Cat. No.	Year	Mint	VG	Notes
Alan Freed Presents Vol. 1	7″ EP	Coral	FEP2025	1959	£100	£50	

KINGSLEY, CHARLES CREATION

Title	Format	Label	Cat. No.	Year	Mint	VG	Notes
Summer Without Sun	7″	Columbia	DB7758	1965	£50	£25	

KINGSMEN

Title	Format	Label	Cat. No.	Year	Mint	VG	Notes
15 Great Hits	LP	Wand	WD(S)674	1966	£15	£6	*US*
Annie Fanny	7″	Pye	7N25322	1965	£4	£1.50	
Climb	7″	Pye	7N25311	1965	£4	£1.50	
Climb	7″ EP	Vogue	INT18015	1965	£15	£7.50	*French*
Daytime Shadows	7″	Pye	7N25406	1967	£5	£2	
Death Of An Angel	7″	Pye	7N25273	1964	£5	£2	
Fever	7″ EP	Pye	NEP44063	1966	£12	£6	
Gamma Goochee	7″ EP	Vogue	INT18065	1966	£15	£7.50	*French*
Greatest Hits	LP	Marble Arch	MAL829	1968	£10	£4	
How To Stuff A Wild Bikini	7″ EP	Vogue	INT18025	1965	£15	£7.50	*French*
In Person	LP	Pye	NPL28050	1964	£15	£6	
Jolly Green Giant	7″	Pye	7N25292	1965	£5	£2	
Killer Joe	7″	Pye	7N25370	1966	£6	£2.50	
Kingsmen	7″ EP	Pye	NEP44023	1964	£15	£7.50	
Little Latin Lupe Lu	7″	Pye	7N25262	1964	£4	£1.50	
Little Latin Lupe Lu	7″ EP	Vogue	EPL8273	1964	£15	£7.50	*French*
Louie Louie	7″	Pye	7N25366	1966	£4	£1.50	
Louie Louie	7″	Pye	7N25231	1963	£8	£4	
Louie Louie	7″ EP	Vogue	EPL8172	1963	£15	£7.50	*French, B side by Jocko Henderson*
Mojo Workout	7″ EP	Pye	NEP44040	1965	£15	£7.50	
Money	7″ EP	Vogue	EPL8209	1964	£15	£7.50	*French*
On Campus	LP	Pye	NPL28068	1965	£15	£6	

Volume II	LP	Pye	NPL28054	1964	£15	£6	
Volume III	LP	Wand	WD(S)662	1965	£15	£6	US

KINGSMEN (2)

Better Believe It	7"	London	HLE8735	1958	£15	£7.50	
Conga Rock	7"	London	HLE8812	1959	£20	£10	
Weekend	7" EP	London	REE1211	1959	£60	£30	

KINGSTON, JOE

Time Is On My Friends	7"	Blue Beat	BB253	1964	£12	£6	

KINGSTON PETE

Little Boy Blue	7"	Blue Beat	BB403	1967	£12	£6	

KINGSTON TRIO

The Kingston Trio were enormously popular in America, their harmonized approach to folk music inspiring many future rock stars to begin their careers in music. The line of influence leads from the Kingston Trio to Haight-Ashbury, to the music of Jefferson Airplane and the Grateful Dead, and from there to the entire sound of modern AOR. John Stewart was a member of the Kingston Trio on the later releases.

Aspen Gold	LP	Nautilus	NR2	1979	£12	£5	*US audiophile*
Encores	LP	Capitol	(S)T1612	1961	£10	£4	
Folk Era	LP	Capitol	(S)T2180	1964	£10	£4	
From The Hungry i	LP	Capitol	T1107	1959	£10	£4	
Goin' Places	LP	Capitol	(S)T1564	1961	£10	£4	
Greenback Dollar	7"	Capitol	CL15287	1963	£4	£1.50	
Greenback Dollar	7" EP	Capitol	EAP120460	1963	£5	£2	
Here We Go Again Part 1	7" EP	Capitol	EAP11258	1960	£5	£2	
Here We Go Again Part 1	7" EP	Capitol	SEP11258	1960	£8	£4	*stereo*
Here We Go Again Part 2	7" EP	Capitol	EAP21258	1960	£5	£2	
Here We Go Again Part 2	7" EP	Capitol	SEP21258	1960	£8	£4	*stereo*
Here We Go Again Part 3	7" EP	Capitol	EAP31258	1960	£5	£2	
Here We Go Again Part 3	7" EP	Capitol	SEP31258	1960	£8	£4	*stereo*
Kingston Trio	7" EP	Brunswick	OE9511	1965	£6	£2.50	
Kingston Trio	LP	Capitol	T996	1958	£12	£5	
Lemon Tree	7" EP	Capitol	EAP120655	1964	£5	£2	
M.T.A.	7" EP	Capitol	EAP11119	1959	£6	£2.50	
Make Way!	LP	Capitol	(S)T1474	1961	£10	£4	
Raspberries Strawberries	7" EP	Capitol	EAP11182	1959	£5	£2	
Scarlet Ribbons	7"	Capitol	CL14918	1958	£4	£1.50	
Stereo Concert	LP	Capitol	ST1183	1959	£12	£5	
String Along	LP	Capitol	(S)T1397	1960	£10	£4	
Time To Think	7" EP	Capitol	EAP42011	1962	£5	£2	
Tom Dooley	7"	Capitol	CL14951	1958	£4	£1.50	
Tom Dooley	7" EP	Capitol	EAP11136	1959	£5	£2	
Worried Man	7" EP	Capitol	EAP11322	1960	£5	£2	

KINGSTONIANS

Clip	7"	Songbird	SB1011	1969	£4	£1.50	*Bruce Anthony B side*
Fun Galore	7"	Doctor Bird	DB1126	1968	£10	£5	
Hold Down	7"	Crab	CRAB19	1969	£4	£1.50	*Barry York B side*
I Am Just A Minstrel	7"	Bullet	BU409	1969	£4	£1.50	
I Need You	7"	Trojan	TR770	1969	£4	£1.50	
Lion's Den	7"	Duke	DU126	1972	£4	£1.50	
Mix It Up	7"	Trojan	TR627	1968	£4	£1.50	
Mother Miserable	7"	Coxsone	CS7066	1968	£10	£5	
Mummy And Daddy	7"	Doctor Bird	DB1123	1968	£10	£5	
Nice Nice	7"	Big Shot	BI526	1969	£4	£1.50	
Out There	7"	Songbird	SB1045	1970	£4	£1.50	*Crystalites B side*
Put Down Your Fire	7"	Doctor Bird	DB1120	1968	£10	£5	
Rumble Rumble	7"	Songbird	SB1041	1970	£4	£1.50	*Crystalites B side*
Singer Man	7"	Songbird	SB1019	1970	£4	£1.50	*Crystalites B side*
Sufferer	7"	Big Shot	BI508	1968	£6	£2.50	
Sufferer	LP	Trojan	TBL113	1970	£10	£4	
Winey Winey	7"	Rio	R140	1967	£8	£4	
You Can't Wine	7"	Duke	DU88	1970	£4	£1.50	*Rupie Edwards B side*

KINKS

The Kinks' long career is shot through with many collectors' items, although the majority of these come from the early, hit-making years. All the original Pye albums are becoming increasingly scarce, although their value is held down by the Kinks being seemingly irredeemably out of fashion. The original pressing of *Village Green Preservation Society* was withdrawn and replaced with a version containing more tracks, but the shorter album does contain one or two different mixes. The American compilations, *Kink Kronikles* and *The Great Lost Kinks Album*, are highly sought-after in the UK as they contain many tracks that are not otherwise available. Meanwhile, no Kinks records have sold as few copies as the first two singles, 'Long Tall Sally' and 'You Still Want Me' – most copies appearing on the market are likely, therefore, to be demos.

All Day And All Of The Night	7"	Pye	7N15714	1964	£60	£30	*export, picture sleeve*
All Day And All Of The Night	7" EP	Pye	PNV24127	1964	£25	£12.50	*French*
All The Good Times	LP	Pye	IIPP100	1973	£40	£20	*4 LPs, boxed*
Apeman	7"	Pye	7N45016	1970	£4	£1.50	
Arthur	LP	Pye	NPL18317	1969	£25	£10	*mono*
Arthur	LP	Pye	NSPL18317	1969	£15	£6	
Autumn Almanac/David Watts	7"	Pye	7N17405	1967	£40	£20	*export*
Celluloid Heroes	LP	RCA	RS1059	1976	£10	£4	
Dandy	7" EP	Pye	PNV24177	1966	£20	£10	*French*

Dead End Street	7" EP	Pye	PNV24184	1966	**£20**	**£10**	*French*
Dedicated Follower Of Fashion	7"	PRT	PYS7	1988	**£10**	**£5**	*picture disc*
Dedicated Follower Of Fashion	7" EP	Pye	PNV24167	1966	**£20**	**£10**	*French*
Dedicated Kinks	7" EP	Pye	NEP24258	1966	**£40**	**£20**	
Did Ya	CD-s	Columbia	COL6575932	1991	**£5**	**£2**	
Down All The Days	CD-s	London	LONCD239	1989	**£5**	**£2**	
Drivin'	7"	Pye	7N17776	1969	**£4**	**£1.50**	
Everybody's In Showbiz	LP	RCA	DPS2035	1972	**£12**	**£5**	*double*
Face To Face	LP	Pye	NSPL18149	1966	**£50**	**£25**	*stereo*
Face To Face	LP	Pye	NPL18149	1966	**£20**	**£8**	
Give The People What They Want	LP	Arista	SPART1171	1981	**£20**	**£8**	*test pressing, US mix*
Give The People What They Want	LP	Arista	AL9567	1981	**£10**	**£4**	*US, different mixes*
God Save The Kinks	CD	Essential	KINKS1/2/3	1998	**£15**	**£6**	*3 different samplers*
God's Children	7"	Pye	7N8001	1971	**£25**	**£12.50**	*export, picture sleeve*
God's Children	7"	Pye	7N8001	1971	**£10**	**£5**	*export*
Got Love If You Want It	7" EP	Pye	PNV24131	1964	**£60**	**£30**	*French*
Great Lost Kinks Album	LP	Reprise	MS2172	1973	**£40**	**£20**	*US*
Greatest Hits	CD	PRT	KINKCD7251	1984	**£15**	**£6**	*misplaced cue codes*
Greatest Hits	LP	PRT	KINK1	1983	**£12**	**£5**	*with bonus 10"*
Greatest Hits	LP	Reprise	R(S)6217	1966	**£15**	**£6**	*US*
Greatest Hits	LP	PRT	KINK1	1983	**£12**	**£5**	*with 10" LP (Dead End Street)*
How Are You	7"	Music Week		1986	**£4**	**£1.50**	*promo*
How Do I Get Close	CD-s	London	LONCD250	1990	**£5**	**£2**	
In Germany	LP	Vogue	LDVS17077	1965	**£100**	**£50**	*German*
Kinda Kinks	LP	Pye	NPL18112	1965	**£20**	**£8**	
Kinda Kinks	LP	Pye	NSPL18112	1965	**£75**	**£37.50**	*stereo, export*
Kink Kontroversy	LP	Pye	NPL18131	1966	**£20**	**£8**	
Kink Kontroversy	LP	Pye	NSPL18131	1966	**£75**	**£37.50**	*stereo, export*
Kink Kronikles	LP	Reprise	RS6454	1972	**£30**	**£15**	*US*
Kinks	7" EP	Pye	AMEP1001	1975	**£10**	**£5**	*export, red or blue vinyl*
Kinks	7" EP	Pye	NEP5039	1964	**£500**	**£250**	*export, best auctioned*
Kinks	LP	Pye	NPL18326	1970	**£15**	**£6**	*double*
Kinks	LP	Pye	NPL18096	1964	**£20**	**£8**	
Kinks	LP	Pye	NSPL83021	1964	**£100**	**£50**	*stereo, export*
Kinks	LP	Golden Guinea	GSGL10357	1967	**£20**	**£8**	*stereo*
Kinks	LP	Pye	NSPL15096	196–	**£75**	**£37.50**	*export, stereo*
Kinks' Kinkdom	LP	Reprise	R(S)6185	1965	**£20**	**£8**	*US*
Kinksize	LP	Reprise	R(S)6158	1965	**£20**	**£8**	*US*
Kinksize Hits	7" EP	Pye	NEP24203	1964	**£10**	**£5**	
Kinksize Session	7" EP	Pye	NEP24200	1964	**£10**	**£5**	
Kwyet Kinks	7" EP	Pye	NEP24221	1965	**£15**	**£7.50**	
Live At Kelvin Hall	LP	Pye	NPL18191	1967	**£20**	**£8**	
Live At Kelvin Hall	LP	Pye	NSPL18191	1967	**£40**	**£20**	*stereo*
Lola (live)	7"	Arista	ARIST404	1980	**£4**	**£1.50**	*export*
Lola Vs Powerman & The Money-Go-Round	LP	Pye	NSPL18359	1970	**£10**	**£4**	
Long Tall Sally	7"	Pye	7N15611	1964	**£40**	**£20**	
Low Budget Interview	LP	Arista	SP69	1979	**£15**	**£6**	*US promo*
Mister Pleasant	7" EP	Pye	PNV24191	1967	**£20**	**£10**	*French*
Mr Pleasant	7"	Pye	7N17314	1967	**£40**	**£20**	*export*
Muswell Hillbillies	LP	RCA	SF8423	1971	**£10**	**£4**	
No More Looking Back	7"	RCA	RCM1	1976	**£4**	**£1.50**	
Percy	7"	Pye	7NX8001	1971	**£8**	**£4**	*picture sleeve*
Percy	LP	Pye	NSPL18365	1971	**£10**	**£4**	
Plastic Man	7"	Pye	7N17724	1969	**£4**	**£1.50**	
Predictable	7"	Arista	ARIPD426	1981	**£4**	**£1.50**	*picture disc*
Preservation Act 1	LP	RCA	SF8392	1973	**£10**	**£4**	
Preservation Act 2	LP	RCA	LPL25040	1974	**£12**	**£5**	*double*
Schoolboys In Disgrace	LP	RCA	RS1028	1975	**£10**	**£4**	
Shangri-La	7"	Pye	7N17812	1969	**£4**	**£1.50**	
Shangri-La/Last Of The Steam Powered Trains	7"	Pye	7N17812	1969	**£75**	**£37.50**	*demo*
Soap Opera	LP	RCA	SF8411	1975	**£10**	**£4**	
Something Else	7" EP	Pye	NEP24296	1968	**£250**	**£150**	*with 'David Watts'*
Something Else	LP	Pye	NPL18193	1967	**£25**	**£10**	
Something Else	LP	Pye	NSPL18193	1967	**£40**	**£20**	*stereo*
Sunny Afternoon	7"	PRT	PYS2	1987	**£10**	**£5**	*picture disc*
Sunny Afternoon	7" EP	Pye	PNV24173	1966	**£25**	**£12.50**	*French, R. Davies, Quaife facing right on sleeve*
Sunny Afternoon	7" EP	Pye	PNV24173	1966	**£20**	**£10**	*French, R. Davies, Quaife facing left on sleeve*
Then, Now And In Between	LP	Reprise	PRO328	1969	**£200**	**£100**	*US, boxed with various items of memorabilia*
Till The End Of The Day	7"	Pye	7N15981	1965	**£60**	**£30**	*export, picture sleeve*
Till The End Of The Day	7" EP	Pye	PNV24160	1965	**£20**	**£10**	*French*
Tired Of Waiting For You	7" EP	Pye	PNV24132	1965	**£30**	**£15**	*French*
Ultimate Collection	CD	Castle	CTVCD001	1990	**£20**	**£8**	*promo with leather pouch*
Victoria	7"	Pye	7N17865	1969	**£4**	**£1.50**	
Village Green Preservation Society	LP	Pye	NSPL18233	1968	**£20**	**£8**	*stereo*
Village Green Preservation Society	LP	Pye	N(S)PL18233	1967	**£500**	**£330**	*12 track test pressing*
Village Green Preservation Society	LP	Pye	NPL18233	1968	**£25**	**£10**	*mono*

Title	Format	Label	Cat. No.	Year	Mint	VG	Notes
Vol. 5	7" EP	Pye	PNV24140	1965	**£25**	**£12.50**	*French*
Waterloo Sunset	7" EP	Pye	PNV24194	1967	**£20**	**£10**	*French*
Waterloo Sunset '94	CD-s	Konk	KNKD2	1994	**£5**	**£2**	
Well Respected Man	7"	Pye	7N17100	1966	**£60**	**£30**	*export*
Well Respected Man	7" EP	Pye	PNV24151	1965	**£20**	**£10**	*French*
Where Have All The Good Times Gone	7"	Pye	7N45313	1973	**£15**	**£7.50**	*picture sleeve only*
You Really Got Me	LP	Reprise	R(S)6143	1965	**£20**	**£8**	*US*
You Still Want Me	7"	Pye	7N15636	1964	**£60**	**£30**	

KINSEY, TONY

Title	Format	Label	Cat. No.	Year	Mint	VG	Notes
Construction In Jazz	LP	KPM	KPM1094	1971	**£15**	**£6**	*other side by Johnny Pearson*
Evening With Mr Percussion	LP	Ember	EMB3337	1961	**£100**	**£50**	*with Tubby Hayes*
Foursome	7" EP	Parlophone	SGE2008	1959	**£6**	**£2.50**	
How To Succeed	LP	Decca	LK4534	1963	**£20**	**£8**	
Jazz At The Flamingo Session	LP	Decca	LK4207	1957	**£30**	**£15**	
Presenting The Tony Kinsey Quartet No. 1	7" EP	Decca	DFE6282	1956	**£5**	**£2**	
Presenting The Tony Kinsey Quartet No. 2	7" EP	Decca	DFE6283	1956	**£5**	**£2**	
Red Bird – Jazz And Poetry	7" EP	Parlophone	SGE2004	1959	**£6**	**£2.50**	
Red Bird Jazz And Poetry	7" EP	Parlophone	GEP8765	1958	**£6**	**£2.50**	*with Christopher Logue*
Time Gentlemen Please	LP	Decca	LK4274	1959	**£60**	**£30**	
Tony Kinsey Quintet	LP	Decca	LK4186	1957	**£60**	**£30**	

KINSMEN

Title	Format	Label	Cat. No.	Year	Mint	VG	Notes
Glasshouse Green Splinter Red	7"	Decca	F22724	1968	**£8**	**£4**	
It's Good To See You	7"	Decca	F22777	1968	**£6**	**£2.50**	

KIPPINGTON LODGE

The career of Nick Lowe begins here, as singer and bass player for the group that was later renamed after the guitarist, Brinsley Schwarz.

Title	Format	Label	Cat. No.	Year	Mint	VG	Notes
In My Life	7"	Parlophone	R5776	1969	**£20**	**£10**	
Kippington Lodge	7" EP	EMI	NUT2894	1978	**£5**	**£2**	
Rumours	7"	Parlophone	R5677	1968	**£20**	**£10**	
Shy Boy	7"	Parlophone	R5645	1967	**£15**	**£7.50**	
Tell Me A Story	7"	Parlophone	R5717	1968	**£20**	**£10**	
Tomorrow Today	7"	Parlophone	R5750	1968	**£20**	**£10**	

KIRBY

Title	Format	Label	Cat. No.	Year	Mint	VG	Notes
Bottom Line	7"	Hot Wax	WAX1	1978	**£6**	**£2.50**	
Composition	LP	Hot Wax	HW2	1978	**£60**	**£30**	
Love Letters	7"	Anchor	ANC1031	1976	**£8**	**£4**	

KIRBY, KATHY

Title	Format	Label	Cat. No.	Year	Mint	VG	Notes
Adam Adamant Theme	7"	Decca	F12432	1966	**£10**	**£5**	
Best Of Kathy Kirby	LP	Ace Of Clubs	ACL1235	1968	**£10**	**£4**	
Come Back Here With My Heart	7"	Columbia	DB8521	1969	**£4**	**£1.50**	
Danny	7"	Pye	7N15342	1961	**£8**	**£4**	
Do You Really Have A Heart	7"	Columbia	DB8910	1972	**£5**	**£2**	
I Almost Called Your Name	7"	Columbia	DB8400	1968	**£4**	**£1.50**	
I'll Catch The Sun	7"	Columbia	DB8559	1969	**£4**	**£1.50**	
In All The World	7"	Columbia	DB8192	1967	**£4**	**£1.50**	
Is That All There Is?	7"	Columbia	DB8634	1969	**£4**	**£1.50**	
Kathy Kirby	7" EP	Decca	DFE8547	1963	**£6**	**£2.50**	
Kathy Kirby Vol. 2	7" EP	Decca	DFE8596	1965	**£6**	**£2.50**	
Little Song For You	7"	Columbia	DB8965	1973	**£5**	**£2**	
Love Can Be	7"	Pye	7N15313	1960	**£10**	**£5**	
Make Someone Happy	LP	Decca	LK4746	1966	**£12**	**£5**	
My Thanks To You	LP	Columbia	SX/SCX6259	1968	**£75**	**£37.50**	
My Way	7"	Columbia	DB8721	1970	**£5**	**£2**	
No One's Gonna Hurt You Any More	7"	Columbia	DB8139	1967	**£4**	**£1.50**	
Singer With The Band	7"	Orange	OAS216	1973	**£20**	**£10**	
Sings Sixteen Hits From Stars And Garters	LP	Decca	LK4575	1963	**£10**	**£4**	
So Here I Go	7"	Columbia	DB8795	1971	**£5**	**£2**	
Song For Europe	7" EP	Decca	DFE8611	1965	**£8**	**£4**	
Turn Around	7"	Columbia	DB8302	1967	**£4**	**£1.50**	
Wheel Of Fortune	7"	Columbia	DB8682	1969	**£4**	**£1.50**	

KIRCHIN, BASIL

Title	Format	Label	Cat. No.	Year	Mint	VG	Notes
World Within Worlds (Parts 1 & 2)	LP	Columbia	SCX6463	1971	**£12**	**£5**	
World Within Worlds (Parts 3 & 4)	LP	Island	HELP18	1974	**£10**	**£4**	

KIRCHIN BAND

Title	Format	Label	Cat. No.	Year	Mint	VG	Notes
Ivor & Basil Kirchin Band	7" EP	Parlophone	GEP8569	1956	**£6**	**£2.50**	
Kirchin Bandbox	7" EP	Parlophone	GEP8531	1955	**£5**	**£2**	
Mambo Macoco	7"	Parlophone	MSP6144	1954	**£4**	**£1.50**	
Mother Goose Jumps	7"	Decca	F10434	1955	**£8**	**£4**	
Rock Around The World	7"	Parlophone	R4266	1957	**£5**	**£2**	
Rockin' And Rollin'	7"	Parlophone	R4237	1956	**£6**	**£2.50**	
Roller	7"	Parlophone	R4222	1956	**£4**	**£1.50**	

KIRK, DEE

Title	Format	Label	Cat. No.	Year	Mint	VG	Notes
I'll Cry	7"	Salvo	SLO1809	1962	**£10**	**£5**	

KIRK, ROLAND

Blacknuss	LP	Atlantic	K40358	1972	£15	£6	
Bright Moments	LP	Atlantic	K60077	1973	£15	£6	
Case Of The Three Sided Dream In Audio Colour	LP	Atlantic	SD1674	1975	£15	£6	US double (3 sides)
Domino	LP	Mercury	MCL20045	1965	£20	£8	
Gifts And Messages	LP	Mercury	SMWL21020	1969	£15	£6	
Here Comes The Whistleman	LP	Atlantic	SD3007	1968	£15	£6	US
Hip!	LP	Fontana	FJL114	1965	£15	£6	
I Talk With The Spirits	LP	Mercury	(S)LML4005	1966	£20	£8	
Inflated Tear	LP	Atlantic	SD1502	1969	£20	£8	US
Kirk In Copenhagen	LP	Mercury	MCL20021	1964	£20	£8	
Kirk's Work	LP	Esquire	32161	1962	£20	£8	with Jack McDuff
Left And Right	LP	Atlantic	588178	1969	£15	£6	
Meeting Of The Times	LP	Atlantic	K40457	1973	£15	£6	with Al Hibbler
Meets The Benny Golson Orchestra	7" EP	Mercury	10015MCE	1964	£5	£2	
Meets The Benny Golson Orchestra	LP	Mercury	20002MCL	1964	£20	£8	
Natural Black Inventions: Root Strata	LP	Atlantic	2400164	1971	£15	£6	
Now Please Don't You Cry, Beautiful Edith	LP	Verve	(S)VLP9193	1968	£20	£8	
Other Folk's Music	LP	Atlantic	SD1686	1976	£12	£5	US
Prepare Thyself To Deal	LP	Atlantic	SD1640	197–	£15	£6	US
Rahsaan Rahsaan	LP	Atlantic	2400110	1971	£15	£6	
Rip, Rig And Panic	LP	Mercury	(S)LML4015	1965	£20	£8	
Roland Speaks	7" EP	Mercury	10016MCE	1965	£5	£2	
Slightly Latin	LP	Mercury	(S)LML4019	1967	£15	£6	
Volunteered Slavery	LP	Atlantic	588207	1970	£15	£6	
We Free Kings	LP	Mercury	MMC14126	1963	£20	£8	
We Free Kings	LP	Mercury	MCL20037	1965	£15	£6	

KIRKBYS

It's A Crime	7"	RCA	RCA1542	1966	£50	£25	

KIRKPATRICK, JOHN

Among The Attractions	LP	Topic	12TS295	1976	£10	£4	with Sue Harris
Jump At The Sun	LP	Trailer	LER2033	1972	£15	£6	with Sue Harris
Plain Capers	LP	Free Reed	FRR010	1976	£10	£4	
Rose Of Britain's Isle	LP	Topic	12TS247	1974	£10	£4	with Sue Harris

KIRSCH, JULIAN

Clever Little Man	7"	Columbia	DB8541	1969	£8	£4	

KISS

Kiss's cartoon approach to heavy metal – turning the music into an affectionate parody of itself – is made into a perfect piece of pop art by their adoption of over-the-top stage costumes and elaborate character-defining make-up. The group's decision to abandon the grease-paint in the eighties had the effect of turning them into just another hard rock group; the reunion tour in 1996 of the original line-up, with the original stage clothes and faces, was a belated, though none the less gratifying acknowledgement of the fact. For this reason, the most essential Kiss records are those that play games with the image: the solo singles with their cardboard cut-out masks; the album *Unmasked*, with its cartoon story cover; or any of the many picture disc releases.

2000 Man	12"	Casablanca	NBL1001	1980	£8	£4	no picture sleeve
2000 Man	7"	Casablanca	NB1001	1980	£10	£5	
Alive	LP	Casablanca	CBC4011/2	1976	£12	£5	double
Alive	LP	Casablanca	CALD5001	1977	£40	£20	red vinyl double
Alive Vol. II	LP	Casablanca	CALD5004	1977	£40	£20	red vinyl double
Alive Vol. II	LP	Casablanca	CALD5004	1977	£12	£5	double
Alive Vol. II	LP	Casablanca	CALD5004	1977	£15	£6	double, with booklet
Animalize	LP	Phonogram	PIC8224951	1984	£10	£4	picture disc
Asylum	LP	Mercury	PIC8260991	1989	£10	£4	picture disc
Beth	7"	Casablanca	CBX519	1976	£12	£6	
Crazy Crazy Nights	CD-s	Polygram	0802322	1988	£20	£10	gold CD video
Creatures Of The Night	12"	Casablanca	KISS412	1982	£10	£5	
Creatures Of The Night	12"	Casablanca	KISSD4	1982	£15	£7.50	1 sided, double groove, etched autographs
Creatures Of The Night	7"	Casablanca	KISS4	1983	£4	£1.50	
Creatures Of The Night	LP	Casablanca	PIC6302219	1982	£10	£4	picture disc
Destroyer	LP	Casablanca	CBC4008	1976	£10	£4	
Destroyer	LP	Casablanca	CAL2009	1977	£30	£15	red vinyl
Destroyer	LP	Casablanca	PIC6399064	1982	£10	£4	picture disc
Double Platinum	LP	Casablanca	CALD5005	1978	£12	£5	double
Dressed To Kill	LP	Casablanca	CAL2008	1977	£30	£15	red vinyl
Dressed To Kill	LP	Casablanca	CBC4004	1975	£10	£4	
Dynasty	LP	Casablanca	PIC9128024	1982	£10	£4	picture disc
Dynasty	LP	Casablanca	CALH2051	1979	£40	£20	red vinyl
Elder	LP	Casablanca	PIC6302163	1981	£10	£4	picture disc
Forever (remix)	CD-s	Vertigo	KISCD11	1990	£5	£2	
God Gave Rock'n'Roll To You II	CD-s	East West	88696CD	1991	£5	£2	
Hard Luck Woman	7"	Casablanca	CAN102	1977	£12	£6	picture sleeve
Hide Your Heart	CD-s	Vertigo	KISCD10	1989	£5	£2	
Hotter Than Hell	LP	Casablanca	PIC6399058	1982	£10	£4	picture disc
Hotter Than Hell	LP	Casablanca	CAL2007	1977	£30	£15	red vinyl
I Was Made For Lovin' You	12"	Casablanca	CANL152	1979	£12	£6	
I Was Made For Lovin' You	7"	Casablanca	CAN152	1979	£4	£1.50	
Killer	12"	Casablanca	KISS312	1982	£12	£6	
Killer	7"	Casablanca	KISS3	1982	£5	£2	
Killers	LP	Casablanca	PIC6302193	1982	£10	£4	picture disc

Kiss	LP	Casablanca	CAL2006	1977	**£30**	**£15**	*red vinyl*
Kiss	LP	Casablanca	CBC4003	1975	**£10**	**£4**	
Kiss	LP	Casablanca	PIC6399057	1982	**£10**	**£4**	*picture disc*
Let's Put The X In Sex	12"	Vertigo	KIZZA2	1988	**£6**	**£2.50**	*promo*
Lick It Up	7"	Vertigo	KISSP5	1983	**£6**	**£2.50**	*poster sleeve*
Lick It Up	7"	Vertigo	KPIC5	1983	**£20**	**£10**	*shaped picture disc*
Lick It Up	LP	Mercury	PIC8142971	1989	**£10**	**£4**	*picture disc*
Love Gun	LP	Casablanca	PIC6399063	1982	**£10**	**£4**	*picture disc*
Love Gun	LP	Casablanca	CALH2017	1977	**£30**	**£15**	*red vinyl*
Love Gun	LP	Casablanca	CALH2017	1977	**£10**	**£4**	*with card gun and inner sleeve*
Nothin' To Lose	7"	Casablanca	CBX503	1975	**£15**	**£7.50**	
Originals	LP	Casablanca	NBLP7032	1976	**£50**	**£25**	*US, 3 LP set with inserts*
Reason To Live	CD-s	Vertigo	KISCD8	1987	**£5**	**£2**	
Rock And Roll All Nite	7"	Casablanca	CAN126	1978	**£12**	**£6**	*picture sleeve*
Rock And Roll All Nite	7"	Casablanca	CBX510	1975	**£12**	**£6**	
Rock And Roll Over	LP	Casablanca	CALH2001	1977	**£30**	**£15**	*red vinyl*
Rock And Roll Over	LP	Casablanca	PIC6399060	1982	**£10**	**£4**	*picture disc*
Rocket Ride	12"	Casablanca	CANL117	1977	**£6**	**£2.50**	
Rocket Ride	7"	Casablanca	CAN117	1978	**£5**	**£2**	
Shout It Out Loud	7"	Casablanca	CBX516	1976	**£8**	**£4**	
Smashes, Thrashes And Hits	LP	Mercury	8368871	1988	**£10**	**£4**	*US picture disc, gatefold sleeve*
Talk To Me	7"	Mercury	MER19	1980	**£6**	**£2.50**	
Tears Are Falling	CD-s	Polygram	0800582	1989	**£15**	**£7.50**	*CD video*
Then She Kissed Me	12"	Casablanca	CANL110	1977	**£8**	**£4**	
Then She Kissed Me	7"	Casablanca	CAN110	1977	**£8**	**£4**	
Turn On The Night	CD-s	Vertigo	KISCD9	1988	**£5**	**£2**	
Unholy	CD-s	Vertigo	KISCD12	1992	**£5**	**£2**	
Unmasked	LP	Mercury	PIC6302032	1980	**£10**	**£4**	*picture disc*
What Makes The World Go Round	7"	Mercury	KISS1	1980	**£6**	**£2.50**	
World Without Heroes	7"	Casablanca	KISSP2	1982	**£6**	**£2.50**	*picture disc*

KISS–ACE FREHLEY

Ace Frehley	LP	Casablanca	NBLP7121	1978	**£15**	**£6**	*US with poster & paper*
Ace Frehley	LP	Casablanca	NBPIX7121	1978	**£20**	**£8**	*picture disc*
New York Groove	7"	Casablanca	CAN135	1979	**£8**	**£4**	
New York Groove	7"	Casablanca	CAN135	1979	**£25**	**£12.50**	*with mask, blue vinyl*

KISS–GENE SIMMONS

Gene Simmons	LP	Casablanca	NBLP7120	1978	**£15**	**£6**	*US with poster & paper*
Radioactive	7"	Casablanca	CAN134	1979	**£8**	**£4**	
Radioactive	7"	Casablanca	CAN134	1979	**£15**	**£7.50**	*with mask, red vinyl*
To Ace, Paul & Peter	LP	Casablanca	NBPIX7120	1978	**£20**	**£8**	*picture disc*

KISS–PAUL STANLEY

Hold Me Touch Me	7"	Casablanca	CAN140	1979	**£8**	**£4**	
Hold Me, Touch Me	7"	Casablanca	CAN140	1979	**£15**	**£7.50**	*with mask, purple vinyl*
Paul Stanley	LP	Casablanca	NBLP7123	1978	**£15**	**£6**	*US with poster & paper*
To Ace, Gene & Peter	LP	Casablanca	NBPIX7123	1978	**£20**	**£8**	*picture disc*

KISS–PETER CRISS

Peter Criss	LP	Casablanca	NBLP7122	1978	**£15**	**£6**	*US with poster & paper*
To Ace, Paul & Gene	LP	Casablanca	NBPIX7122	1978	**£20**	**£8**	*picture disc*
You Matter To Me	7"	Casablanca	CAN139	1979	**£10**	**£5**	
You Matter To Me	7"	Casablanca	CAN139	1979	**£15**	**£7.50**	*with mask, green vinyl*

KISSOON, MAC

Wear It On Your Face	7"	Boulevard	no number	196–	**£4**	**£1.50**	

KIT KATS

Do Their Thing Live	LP	Jamie	LPM/LPS3032	1967	**£15**	**£6**	*US*
It's Just A Matter Of Time	LP	Jamie	LPM/LPS3029	1966	**£15**	**£6**	*US*
That's The Way	7"	London	HLW10075	1966	**£4**	**£1.50**	

KITCHEN CINQ

Everything But	LP	LHI	12000	1967	**£40**	**£20**	*US*

KITCHENS OF DISTINCTION

Last Gasp Death Shuffle	7"	Gold Rush	GRR3	1987	**£4**	**£1.50**	

KITT, EARTHA

Bad But Beautiful	LP	MGM	C878	1962	**£10**	**£4**	
Bad But Beautiful No. 1	7" EP	MGM	MGMEP772	1963	**£5**	**£2**	
Bad But Beautiful No. 2	7" EP	MGM	MGMEP774	1963	**£5**	**£2**	
Bad But Beautiful No. 3	7" EP	MGM	MGMEP777	1963	**£5**	**£2**	
C'est Si Bon	7"	HMV	7M288	1955	**£6**	**£2.50**	
Down To Eartha	10" LP	HMV	DLP1087	1955	**£12**	**£5**	
Down To Eartha	LP	RCA	RD27084	1958	**£10**	**£4**	
Eartha Kitt	7" EP	HMV	7EG8079	1955	**£6**	**£2.50**	
Eartha Kitt	7" EP	HMV	7EG8258	1957	**£6**	**£2.50**	

Eartha Kitt Revisited	7" EP	London	RER1266	1960	£6	£2.50	
Easy Does It	7"	HMV	7M246	1954	£6	£2.50	
Fabulous	LP	London	HAR2207/ SHR6058	1960	£10	£4	
Honolulu Rock-A-Roll-a	7"	HMV	7M422	1956	£12	£6	
I Want To Be Evil	7"	RCA	RCA1093	1958	£4	£1.50	
Just An Old Fashioned Girl	7"	HMV	POP309	1957	£6	£2.50	
Just An Old Fashioned Girl	7"	RCA	RCA1087	1958	£4	£1.50	
Let's Do It	7"	HMV	7M234	1954	£6	£2.50	
Love Is A Gamble	7"	London	HLR8969	1959	£4	£1.50	
Monotonous	7"	HMV	7M282	1955	£6	£2.50	
Revisited	LP	London	HAR2296/ SHR6107	1960	£10	£4	
Saint Louis Blues	7" EP	RCA	SRC7009	1959	£8	£4	
Somebody Bad Stole De Wedding Bell	7"	HMV	7M198	1954	£6	£2.50	
St Louis Blues	LP	RCA	RD27076	1958	£10	£4	
That Bad Eartha	10" LP	HMV	DLP1067	1955	£12	£5	
That Bad Eartha	LP	RCA	RD27067	1958	£10	£4	
That Blue Eartha	7" EP	RCA	SRC7015	1959	£8	£4	
That's The Way	7"	London	HL7119	1963	£8	£4	*export*
There Is No Cure For L'Amour	7"	HMV	POP346	1957	£4	£1.50	
Thursday's Child	LP	HMV	CLP1104	1957	£12	£5	
Thursday's Child	LP	RCA	RD27099	1959	£10	£4	
Under The Bridges Of Paris	7"	HMV	7M191	1954	£8	£4	

KITTENS

Round About Way	7"	Decca	F12036	1964	£4	£1.50	

KLAN

Fify The Fly	7" EP	Palette	22029	1967	£10	£5	*French*
Stop Little Girl	7" EP	Palette	22024	1967	£10	£5	*French*

KLEE, SUSIE

Mr Zero	7"	Polydor	BM56082	1966	£4	£1.50	

KLEIN, ALAN

Striped Purple Shirt	7"	Oriole	CB1719	1962	£15	£7.50	
Three Coins In The Sewer	7"	Oriole	CB1737	1962	£15	£7.50	
Well At Least It's British	LP	Decca	LK4621	1964	£10	£4	

KLEINOW, SNEAKY PETE

Sneaky Pete	LP	Shiloh	SLP4086	1970	£15	£6	*US*

KLEMMER, JOHN

Barefoot Ballet	LP	ABC	D950	1976	£12	£5	*US*
Intensity	LP	Impulse	AS9244	1973	£15	£6	*US*
Waterfalls	LP	Impulse	AS9220	1973	£15	£6	*US*

KLEPTOMANIA

Elephants Lost	LP	Flame	FLP03	1979	£30	£15	*Dutch*

KLF

3 a.m. Eternal	CD-s	KLF	KLF005CD	1991	£5	£2	
3 a.m. Eternal (Live At The S.S.L.)	12"	KLF	KLF005S	1991	£6	£2.50	*white label*
3 a.m. Eternal (Xmas Top Of The Pops Version)	12"	KLF	KLF005TOTP	1992	£40	£20	
America	7"	KLF	PUB1	1991	£15	£7.50	*promo*
America: What Time Is January	12"	KLF	92PROMO2	1992	£40	£20	*1 sided white label*
Burn The Beat	7"	KLF	KLF002	1988	£6	£2.50	
Burn The Beat II	12"	KLF	KLF002T	1988	£12	£6	
Chill Out	CD	KLF	JAMSCD5	1989	£25	£10	
Chill Out	LP	KLF	JAMSLP5	1989	£15	£6	
Justified And Ancient	12"	KLF	USA4X	1992	£40	£20	*picture disc*
Justified And Ancient	CD-s	KLF	KLF99CD	1991	£5	£2	*with Tammy Wynette*
Justified And Ancient (All Bound For Mu Mu Land)	12"	KLF	CHOCICE1	1991	£10	£5	*white label*
Justified And Ancient (Anti-Acapella Version)	12"	KLF	CHOCICE3	1991	£40	£20	*1 sided white label*
Justified And Ancient (Stand By The JAMS)	12"	KLF	CHOCICE2	1991	£10	£5	*white label*
Kylie In A Trance	12"	KLF	KLF010RR	1989	£30	£15	
Kylie Said To Jason	12"	KLF	KLF010T	1989	£6	£2.50	
Kylie Said To Jason	12"	KLF	KLF010P	1989	£8	£4	*with poster*
Kylie Said To Jason	12"	KLF	PROMO2	1989	£15	£7.50	*promo with release sheet*
Kylie Said To Jason	CD-s	KLF	KLF010CD	1989	£30	£15	
Kylie Said To Jason (Trance Kylie Express)	12"	KLF	KLF010R	1989	£15	£7.50	
Last Train To Trancentral (Remixes)	12"	KLF	KLF008R	1989	£50	£25	
Madrugada Eterna	12"	KLF	KLF011T	1990	£100	£50	
Make It Rain	12"	KLF	LPPROMO1	1988	£12	£6	*promo*
What Time Is Love ('89 Primal Remix)	12"	KLF	KLF004R	1989	£12	£6	
What Time Is Love (Live At Trancentral)	12"	KLF	KLF004P	1989	£30	£15	*promo*
What Time Is Love (Trance Mix)	12"	KLF	KLF004T	1989	£10	£5	
What Time Is Love Story	CD	KLF	JAMSCD4	1989	£30	£15	
What Time Is Love Story	LP	KLF	JAMSLP4	1989	£30	£15	

What Time Is Love?	12"	KLF	92PROMO3	1992	£100	£50	*1 sided promo*
What Time Is Love?	CD-s	KLF	KLF004CD	1990	£6	£2.50	
What Time Is Love? (Live At Trancentral)	12"	KLF	KLF004X	1990	£15	£7.50	
White Room	CD	KLF	JAMSCD6	1989	£15	£6	
White Room	LP	KLF	JAMSLP6	1989	£40	£20	*promo*

KLINGER, TONY & MICHAEL LYONS

Extreems	LP	Deram	SML1095	1971	£15	£6	

KLINT, PETER

Walkin' Proud	7"	Mercury	MF997	1966	£8	£4	

KLOCKWERK ORANGE

Abracadabra	LP	CBS	81119	1975	£125	£62.50	*Austrian*

KLOOGER, ANNETTE

Magic Touch	7"	Decca	F10733	1956	£5	£2	
Mama Teach Me To Dance	7"	Decca	F10776	1956	£4	£1.50	
Rock And Roll Waltz	7"	Decca	F10701	1956	£6	£2.50	
Why Do Fools Fall In Love	7"	Decca	F10738	1956	£6	£2.50	
Wisdom Of A Fool	7"	Decca	F10844	1957	£4	£1.50	

KNACK

Did You Ever Have To Make Up Your Mind	7"	Piccadilly	7N35315	1966	£5	£2	
I'm Aware	7" EP	Capitol	EAP120923	1966	£10	£5	*French*
It's Love Baby	7"	Decca	F12278	1965	£20	£10	
Marriage Guidance And Advice Bureau	7"	Piccadilly	7N35367	1967	£5	£2	
Save All My Love For Joey	7"	Piccadilly	7N35347	1966	£5	£2	
Stop!	7"	Piccadilly	7N35322	1966	£5	£2	
Who'll Be The Next In Line	7"	Decca	F12234	1965	£20	£10	

KNACKS

Baby	7" EP	Barclay	70857	1965	£10	£5	*French*

KNEES

Day Tripper	7"	United Artists	UP35773	1974	£15	£7.50	

KNEF, HILDEGARD

Das Mädchen Aus Hamburg	7" EP	Fontana	460592	1958	£100	£50	*German*
From Here On It Gets Rough	LP	London	PS596	1966	£20	£8	*US*
Grand Gala	LP	Decca	6376101	1969	£25	£10	*Dutch*
Love For Sale	LP	Decca	SKL4992	1969	£15	£6	
Man I Love	LP	Decca	25090	1964	£60	£30	*German*
Worum Geht's Hier	LP	Decca	25160	1965	£100	£50	*German*

KNICKERBOCKERS

The Knickerbockers' 'Lies' is a near-perfect copy of the Beatles, let down only by a guitar solo much weaker than anything George Harrison might have produced. The single was a top twenty hit in America and is really the only recording for which the group is much remembered, although the other material listed below is actually well worth seeking out.

Can You Help Me	7"	London	HLH10102	1967	£8	£4	
Fabulous Knickerbockers	LP	London	HA8294	1966	£60	£30	
High On Love	7"	London	HLH10061	1966	£8	£4	
Jerk & Twine Time	LP	Challenge	LP621	1965	£100	£50	*US*
Lies	7"	London	HLH10013	1966	£8	£4	
Lies	7" EP	London	RE10178	1966	£60	£30	*French*
Lloyd Thaxton Presents	LP	Challenge	LP1264	1965	£100	£50	*US*
One Track Mind	7"	London	HLH10035	1966	£8	£4	
Rumours, Gossip, Words Untrue	7"	London	HLH10093	1966	£8	£4	

KNIGHT, BAKER

Would You Believe It	7"	Reprise	RS20465	1966	£5	£2	

KNIGHT, CURTIS

Fancy Meeting You Here	7"	RCA	RCA1888	1969	£5	£2	
Zeus, The Second Coming	LP	Dawn	DNLS3060	1974	£10	£4	

KNIGHT, GLADYS & THE PIPS

End Of Our Road	7"	Tamla Motown	TMG645	1968	£4	£1.50	
Everybody Needs Love	7"	Tamla Motown	TMG619	1967	£5	£2	
Everybody Needs Love	LP	Tamla Motown	(S)TML11058	1968	£15	£6	
Everybody Needs Love/ Stepping Closer To Your Heart	7"	Tamla Motown	TMG619	1967	£50	£25	*demo*
Feelin' Bluesy	LP	Tamla Motown	(S)TML11080	1968	£15	£6	
Giving Up	7"	Stateside	SS318	1964	£10	£5	
Gladys Knight & The Pips	LP	Maxx	3000	1964	£25	£10	*US*
Gladys Knight & The Pips	LP	Sphere Sound	7006	1964	£25	£10	*US*
I Heard It Through The Grapevine	7"	Tamla Motown	TMG629	1967	£6	£2.50	

Title	Format	Label	Number	Year	Price	Price	Notes
I Wish It Would Rain	7"	Tamla Motown	TMG674	1968	£4	**£1.50**	
It Should Have Been Me	7"	Tamla Motown	TMG660	1968	£5	**£2**	
Just Walk In My Shoes	7"	Tamla Motown	TMG576	1966	£25	**£12.50**	
Letter Full Of Tears	7"	Sue	WI394	1965	£12	**£6**	
Letter Full Of Tears	LP	Fury	1003	1962	£60	**£30**	*US*
License To Kill	CD-s	MCA	DMCA1339	1989	£6	**£2.50**	*3" single, with Michael Kamen tracks*
Lovers Always Forgive	7"	Stateside	SS352	1964	£10	**£5**	
Nitty Gritty	LP	Tamla Motown	TML11135	1970	£10	**£4**	*mono*
Silk 'n' Soul	LP	Tamla Motown	(S)TML11100	1969	£15	**£6**	
Take Me In Your Arms And Love Me	7"	Tamla Motown	TMG604	1967	£5	**£2**	
Take Me In Your Arms And Love Me	7"	Tamla Motown	TMG864	1973	£20	**£10**	
Tastiest Hits	LP	Bell	MBLL103	1968	£10	**£4**	

KNIGHT, JASON

Title	Format	Label	Number	Year	Price	Price	Notes
Our Love Is Getting Stronger	7"	Pye	7N17399	1967	£40	**£20**	

KNIGHT, JEAN

Title	Format	Label	Number	Year	Price	Price	Notes
Mr Big Stuff	LP	Stax	2362022	1972	£10	**£4**	

KNIGHT, MARIE

Title	Format	Label	Number	Year	Price	Price	Notes
Come Tomorrow	7"	Fontana	H354	1962	£6	**£2.50**	
Cry Me A River	7"	Stateside	SS419	1965	£6	**£2.50**	
Gospel Songs Vol. 1	7" EP	Brunswick	OE9283	1957	£6	**£2.50**	
Songs Of The Gospel	7" EP	Mercury	10034MCE	1964	£6	**£2.50**	
Songs Of The Gospel	LP	Mercury	MPL6546	1958	£12	**£5**	
Storm Is Passing Over	7" EP	Mercury	10001MCE	1964	£6	**£2.50**	

KNIGHT, ROBERT

Title	Format	Label	Number	Year	Price	Price	Notes
Everlasting Love	7"	Monument	MON1008	1968	£4	**£1.50**	
Everlasting Love	LP	Monument	(S)LMO5015	1968	£10	**£4**	
Free Me	7"	London	HLD9496	1962	£6	**£2.50**	
Love On A Mountain Top	7"	Monument	MON1017	1968	£4	**£1.50**	
Love On A Mountain Top	LP	Monument	MNT65956	1971	£10	**£4**	

KNIGHT, SONNY

Title	Format	Label	Number	Year	Price	Price	Notes
But Officer	7"	Vogue	V9134	1959	£100	**£50**	
Confidential	7"	London	HLD8362	1957	£250	**£150**	*gold label, best auctioned*
Confidential	7"	London	HL7016	1957	£75	**£37.50**	*export*
If You Want This Love	LP	Aura	AR/AS3001	1964	£15	**£6**	*US*

KNIGHT, TERRY & THE PACK

This group contains the roots of the popular heavy-metal-by-numbers seventies band, Grand Funk Railroad. Knight (real name Terry Knapp) was the more famous group's non-playing mastermind, while Pack members Don Brewer and Mark Farner were responsible for whatever funk the group could muster.

Title	Format	Label	Number	Year	Price	Price	Notes
I (Who Have Nothing)	7"	Cameo Parkway	C102	1966	£50	**£25**	
Reflections	LP	Cameo	C2007	1967	£30	**£15**	*US*
Terry Knight & The Pack	LP	Lucky Eleven	(S)8000	1966	£50	**£25**	*US*

KNIGHT, TONY

Tony Knight's Chessmen included saxophonist Lol Coxhill in their line-up, a man happy to play music in any company, even if his best preference is for free improvisation.

Title	Format	Label	Number	Year	Price	Price	Notes
Did You Ever Hear The Sound	7"	Decca	F11989	1964	£15	**£7.50**	
How Sweet	7"	Decca	F12109	1965	£15	**£7.50**	

KNIGHT BROTHERS

Title	Format	Label	Number	Year	Price	Price	Notes
Temptation 'Bout To Get Me	7"	Chess	CRS8015	1965	£10	**£5**	
That'll Get It	7"	Chess	CRS8046	1966	£8	**£4**	

KNIGHTRIDER

Title	Format	Label	Number	Year	Price	Price	Notes
Shout Out Loud	7"	Omega	KS1299	1987	£10	**£5**	*no picture sleeve*

KNIGHTS

Title	Format	Label	Number	Year	Price	Price	Notes
Hot Rod High	LP	Capitol	(S)T2189	1964	£30	**£15**	*US*

KNIGHTS (2)

Title	Format	Label	Number	Year	Price	Price	Notes
Across The Board	LP	Ace	MG200854	1966	£400	**£250**	*US*
Cold Days Hot Nights	LP	Ace Recording	4763	196–	£400	**£250**	*US*
Knights 1967	LP	Ace	MG201303	1967	£400	**£250**	*US*
Off Campus	LP	Co	1269	1965	£400	**£250**	*US*

KNOCKER JUNGLE

Title	Format	Label	Number	Year	Price	Price	Notes
I Don't Know Why	7"	Ember	EMBS293	1970	£5	**£2**	
Knocker Jungle	LP	Ember	NR5052	1970	£40	**£20**	

KNOCKOUTS

Darling Lorraine	7"	Top Rank	JAR279	1960	**£15**	**£7.50**	
Go Ape With The Knockouts	LP	Tribute	1202	1964	**£30**	**£15**	*US*

KNOPFLER, DAVID

Soul Kissing	7"	Peach River	BBPR7	1983	**£5**	**£2**	

KNOPFLER, MARK

Arguably, the instantly memorable theme that he wrote for the film *Local Hero* is the best piece of music that Mark Knopfler has ever produced.

Comfort And Joy	12"	Vertigo	MARK1	1984	**£25**	**£12.50**	*1 sided promo*
Going Home	12"	Vertigo	DSFM4	1983	**£8**	**£4**	*promo*
Joy	12"	Vertigo	DSTR712	1984	**£20**	**£10**	
Joy	7"	Vertigo	DSDJ7	1984	**£15**	**£7.50**	*promo only*
Poor Boy Blues	CD-s	CBS	656373	1990	**£6**	**£2.50**	*with Chet Atkins*
Storybook Love	CD-s	Vertigo	VERCD37	1988	**£10**	**£5**	

KNOX, BUDDY

All Time Loser	7"	Liberty	LIB55694	1964	**£4**	**£1.50**	
Buddy Knox	LP	Roulette	R25003	1957	**£100**	**£50**	*US*
Buddy Knox And Jimmy Bowen	LP	Roulette	R25048	1957	**£150**	**£75**	*US, with Jimmy Bowen*
C'mon Baby	7"	Columbia	DB4180	1958	**£15**	**£7.50**	
Chi-Hua-Hua	7"	Liberty	LIB55411	1962	**£5**	**£2**	
Devil Woman	7"	Columbia	DB4014	1957	**£20**	**£10**	
God Knows I Love You	7"	United Artists	UP35019	1969	**£5**	**£2**	
Golden Hits	LP	Liberty	LBY1114	1962	**£25**	**£10**	
Gypsy Man	LP	United Artists	UAS6689	1969	**£20**	**£8**	*US*
I Think I'm Gonna Kill Myself	7"	Columbia	DB4302	1959	**£15**	**£7.50**	
Ling Ting Tong	7"	London	HLG9331	1961	**£6**	**£2.50**	
Lovey Dovey	7"	London	HLG9268	1961	**£10**	**£5**	
Party Doll	7"	Columbia	DB3914	1957	**£100**	**£50**	*gold label*
Rock A Buddy Knox	7" EP	Columbia	SEG7732	1957	**£75**	**£37.50**	
Rock Reflections	LP	Sunset	SLS50206	1971	**£10**	**£4**	
Rock Your Little Baby To Sleep	7"	Columbia	DB3952	1957	**£40**	**£20**	*gold label*
Shadaroom	7"	Liberty	LIB55592	1963	**£4**	**£1.50**	
She's Gone	7"	Liberty	LIB55473	1962	**£5**	**£2**	
Swinging Daddy	7"	Columbia	DB4077	1958	**£20**	**£10**	
Three Eyed Man	7"	London	HLG9472	1961	**£6**	**£2.50**	

KOALA

Koala	LP	Capitol	176	1969	**£15**	**£6**	*US*

KOCH, MARIZA

Arabas	LP	Minos		1972	**£75**	**£37.50**	*Greek*

KODAKS

Kodaks Vs The Starlites	LP	Sphere Sound	LP7005	1964	**£50**	**£25**	*US*

KODIAKS

Tell Me Rhonda	7"	Decca	F12942	1969	**£5**	**£2**	

KOERNER, RAY & GLOVER

Blues, Rags And Hollers	LP	Audiophile	AP78	1963	**£25**	**£10**	*US*
Lots More Blues, Rags And Hollers	LP	Elektra	EKL/EKS7267	1964	**£25**	**£10**	*US*
Return Of Koerner, Ray And Glover	LP	Elektra	EKL/EKS7305	1966	**£20**	**£8**	*US*

KOERNER, SPIDER JOHN

Friends And Lovers	7"	Elektra	EKSN45063	1969	**£5**	**£2**	*with Willie Murphy*
Running Jumping Standing Still	LP	Elektra	EKL/EKS74041	1968	**£25**	**£10**	*with Willie Murphy*
Running Jumping Standing Still	LP	Elektra	K42026	1971	**£15**	**£6**	*with Willie Murphy*
Spider Blues	LP	Elektra	EKL/EKS7290	1965	**£25**	**£10**	*US*
Won't You Give Me Some Love	7"	Elektra	EKSN45005	1967	**£5**	**£2**	

KOFFMAN, MOE

Little Pixie	7"	London	HLJ8633	1958	**£5**	**£2**	
Little Pixie	7" EP	London	REJ1163	1958	**£10**	**£5**	
Mighty Peculiar	7"	CBS	3544	1968	**£4**	**£1.50**	
Shepherd's Cha-Cha	7"	London	HLJ8813	1959	**£5**	**£2**	
Swingin' Shepherd Blues	7"	London	HLJ8549	1958	**£6**	**£2.50**	

KOLETTES

Who's That Guy	7"	Pye	7N25278	1964	**£10**	**£5**	

KOLINDA

1514	LP	Hexagone	883017	1978	**£20**	**£8**	*French*
Kolinda	LP	Hexagone	883006	1975	**£20**	**£8**	*French*

KOLLEKTIV

Kollektiv	LP	Brain	1034	1973	**£15**	**£6**	*German*

KOLOC, BONNIE

After All This Time	LP	London	SHO8432	1972	**£15**	**£6**	
Hold On To Me	LP	London	SHO8440	1972	**£10**	**£4**	

KOMACK, JIMMIE

Title	Format	Label	Cat. No.	Year	Mint	Good	Notes
Cold Summer Blues	7"	Vogue Coral	Q2031	1954	£6	£2.50	
Rock-A-Bye Your Baby With A Dixie Melody	7"	Vogue Coral	Q72087	1955	£4	£1.50	
Wabash 47473	7"	Vogue Coral	Q72061	1955	£5	£2	

KOMKOL

Title	Format	Label	Cat. No.	Year	Mint	Good	Notes
Index	LP	Kanal	LEUB25	1972	£15	£6	German

KONGOS, JOHN

Title	Format	Label	Cat. No.	Year	Mint	Good	Notes
Confusions About Goldfish	LP	Dawn	DNLS3002	1969	£10	£4	
He's Gonna Step On You Again	7"	Fly	BUG8	1971	£4	£1.50	picture sleeve
I Love Mary	7"	Piccadilly	7N35341	1966	£4	£1.50	

KONITZ, LEE

Title	Format	Label	Cat. No.	Year	Mint	Good	Notes
Abstraction	LP	Atlantic	590020	1968	£12	£5	
Inside Hi-Fi	LP	Atlantic	590027	1969	£12	£5	
Inside Hi-Fi	LP	London	LTZK15092	1957	£20	£8	
Lee Konitz	10" LP	Vogue	LDE060	1954	£50	£25	
Lee Konitz	10" LP	Vogue	LDE154	1955	£50	£25	
Lee Konitz	10" LP	Vogue	LDE129	1955	£50	£25	
Lee Konitz Collates	LP	Esquire		195–	£20	£8	
Lee Konitz With The Gerry Mulligan Quartet	LP	Vogue	LAE12181	1959	£20	£8	
Lee Konitz With Warne Marsh	LP	London	LTZK15025	1957	£25	£10	
Real Lee Konitz	LP	London	LTZK15147	1959	£20	£8	
Subconscious-Lee	LP	XTRA	XTRA5049	1968	£12	£5	with Lennie Tristano
Very Cool	LP	Columbia	33CX10119	1958	£20	£8	
You And Lee	LP	HMV	CLP1406/ CSD1331	1960	£15	£6	

KONRADS

Title	Format	Label	Cat. No.	Year	Mint	Good	Notes
Baby It's Too Late Now	7"	CBS	201812	1965	£4	£1.50	

KONSTRUKTIVITS

Title	Format	Label	Cat. No.	Year	Mint	Good	Notes
Glenacaul	LP	Sterile	SR10	1986	£15	£6	
Psyko Genetika	LP	Third Mind	TM02	198–	£15	£6	

KOOBAS

Title	Format	Label	Cat. No.	Year	Mint	Good	Notes
Barricades	LP	Bam Caruso	KIRI047	1988	£12	£5	
First Cut Is The Deepest	7"	Columbia	DB8419	1968	£30	£15	
Gypsy Fred	7"	Columbia	DB8187	1967	£30	£15	
Koobas	LP	Columbia	SX/SCX6271	1969	£400	£250	
Sally	7"	Columbia	DB8103	1967	£30	£15	
Sweet Music	7"	Columbia	DB7988	1966	£30	£15	
Take Me For A Little While	7"	Pye	7N17012	1965	£30	£15	
You'd Better Make Up Your Mind	7"	Pye	7N17087	1966	£30	£15	

KOOL

Title	Format	Label	Cat. No.	Year	Mint	Good	Notes
Step Out Of Your Mind	7"	CBS	2865	1969	£4	£1.50	

KOOL & THE GANG

Title	Format	Label	Cat. No.	Year	Mint	Good	Notes
Best Of Kool And The Gang	LP	Polydor	2347002	1974	£40	£20	
Funky Man	7"	Mojo	2027005	1971	£4	£1.50	
Kool And The Gang	7"	London	HLZ10308	1970	£4	£1.50	
Light Of Worlds	LP	Polydor	2310357	1974	£10	£4	
Live At P.J.'s	LP	Polydor	2347001	1974	£50	£25	
Live At The Sex Machine	LP	Polydor	2347003	1974	£15	£6	
Live At The Sex Machine	LP	Polydor	2343083	1976	£10	£4	
Love The Life You Live	7"	Mojo	2027006	1972	£4	£1.50	
Music Is The Message	LP	Polydor	2347004	1974	£20	£8	
Spirit Of The Boogie	LP	Polydor	2310416	1975	£10	£4	
Wild And Peaceful	LP	Polydor	2310299	1974	£10	£4	

KOOPER, AL

Title	Format	Label	Cat. No.	Year	Mint	Good	Notes
Easy Does It	LP	CBS	66252	1970	£12	£5	double
Hey Western Union Man	7"	CBS	4160	1969	£5	£2	
Kooper Session	LP	CBS	63797	1970	£12	£5	with Shuggie Otis
Parchman Farm	7"	Mercury	MF885	1965	£6	£2.50	
Season Of The Witch	7"	CBS	3770	1968	£4	£1.50	with Steve Stills
Super Session	LP	CBS	63396	1968	£15	£6	with Mike Bloomfield & Steve Stills
Super Session	LP	CBS	Q63396	1973	£20	£8	quad, with Mike Bloomfield & Steve Stills
Super Session	LP	Mobile Fidelity	MFSL1178	1984	£10	£4	US audiophile, with Mike Bloomfield & Steve Stills
You Never Know Who Your Friends Are	7"	CBS	4011	1969	£4	£1.50	

KOOYMANS, GEORGE

Title	Format	Label	Cat. No.	Year	Mint	Good	Notes
Jo Jo	LP	Polydor	2925004	1971	£25	£10	Dutch

KOPPEL, ANDERS

Aftenlandet	LP	Demos	38	1977	£20	£8	Danish

KOPPYCATS (IAN & THE ZODIACS)

Beatles Best	LP	Fontana	SFL13052-3	1968	£25	£10	double
Beatles Best	LP	Fontana	700153	1966	£25	£10	Dutch stereo
Beatles Best	LP	Fontana	200153WGL	1966	£20	£8	Dutch mono
More Beatles Best	LP	Fontana	701543	1967	£25	£10	Dutch stereo
More Beatles Best	LP	Fontana	701543WPY	1967	£20	£8	Dutch mono

KORAN, TAMARA & PERCEPTION

Veils Of Morning Lace	7"	Domain	D7	1968	£10	£5	

KÖRBERG, TOMMY

Dear Mrs Jones	7"	Sonet	SON2005	1969	£5	£2	

KORDA, PAUL

Go On Home	7"	Columbia	DB7994	1966	£10	£5	
Passing Strangers	LP	MAM	MAM1003	1971	£12	£5	

KORNER, ALEXIS

Somewhat like John Mayall, Alexis Korner's importance within the development of rock music had more to do with the musicians he managed to discover than with what he actually played himself. *R&B From The Marquee*, viewed as being of crucial significance at the time, today sounds rather thin and ineffectual, and an unlikely base from which to begin a rock revolution. In truth, musicians like Charlie Watts, Jack Bruce and Robert Plant achieved far more after they left Korner than they ever did with him. Nevertheless, Alexis Korner was an important catalyst – a position best demonstrated on the double LP *Bootleg Him*, which provides a useful survey of his career via a well-chosen selection of out-takes and otherwise unreleased tracks.

Accidentally Born In New Orleans	LP	Transatlantic	TRA269	1973	£20	£8	
Alexis Korner	LP	Polydor	2374109	1974	£15	£6	German
Alexis Korner	LP	RAK	SRAK501	1971	£20	£8	
Alexis Korner Blues Incorporated	7" EP	Tempo	EXA102	1958	£100	£50	
All Stars Blues Inc	LP	Transatlantic	TRASAM7	1969	£12	£5	
At The Cavern	LP	Oriole	PS40058	1964	£100	£50	
Blues At The Roundhouse	LP	77		1957	£200	£100	
Blues From The Roundhouse Vol. 1	7" EP	Tempo	EXA76	1957	£75	£37.50	
Blues Incorporated	LP	Ace Of Clubs	ACL1187	1965	£50	£25	
Blues Incorporated	LP	Polydor	236206	1967	£50	£25	
Bootleg Him	LP	RAK	SRAKSP51	1972	£25	£10	double
Both Sides	LP	Metronome	MLP15364	1969	£30	£15	German
C.C. Rider	7"	King	KG1017	1965	£20	£10	
County Jail	7"	Tempo	A166	1957	£50	£25	
Get Off My Cloud	LP	CBS	69155	1975	£15	£6	
I Need Your Loving	7"	Parlophone	R5206	1963	£10	£5	
I Wonder Who	LP	Fontana	STL5381	1967	£60	£30	
Just Easy	LP	Intercord	INT60099	1978	£12	£5	German
Little Baby	7"	Parlophone	R5247	1965	£12	£6	
Me	LP	Jeton	1003305	1979	£25	£10	German
Mr Blues	LP	Mushroom	35434	1974	£20	£8	German
New Church	LP	Metronome		1970	£30	£15	German
New Generation Of Blues	LP	Liberty	LBL/LBS83147	1968	£30	£15	
Party LP	LP	Intercord	170000	1980	£15	£6	German double
R&B At The Marquee	LP	Ace Of Clubs	ACL1130	1962	£40	£20	
Red Hot From Alex	LP	Transatlantic	TRA117	1964	£100	£50	
River's Invitation	7"	Fontana	TF706	1966	£10	£5	
Rosie	7"	Fontana	TF817	1967	£12	£6	
Sky High	LP	Spot	JW551	1965	£500	£330	
Snape Live On Tour	LP	Brain	21039	1974	£20	£8	German double
Up-Town	7"	Lyntone	LYN299	196-	£40	£20	flexi
What's That Sound I Hear	LP	Sunset	SLS50245	1971	£10	£4	

KORNFELD, ARTIE TREE

Time To Remember	LP	Probe	SPB1022	1970	£10	£4	

KOSMIC KOMMANDO

Cat 007	12"	Rephlex	CAT007EP	1994	£10	£5	clear vinyl

KOSSOFF, KIRKE, TETSU & RABBIT

Kossoff, Kirke, Tetsu & Rabbit	LP	Island	ILPS9188	1971	£25	£10	

KOSSOFF, PAUL

Back Street Crawler	LP	Island	ILPS9264	1973	£10	£4	
Blue Soul	LP	Island	PKSP100	1986	£12	£5	double
Croydon, June 15th, 1975	LP	Street Tones	STLP1002	1983	£15	£6	double
Koss	LP	DJM	DJE29002	1977	£12	£5	double
Mr Big/Blue Soul	LP	Street Tones	SDLP0012PD	1983	£12	£5	picture disc

KOTHARI, CHIM

Sitar And Spice	7"	Deram	DM108	1966	£6	£2.50	
Sound Of The Sitar	LP	Deram	DML1002	1966	£30	£15	

KOTTKE, LEO

Circle Around The Sun	LP	Symposium	2001	1970	£15	£6	US
Live At The Scholar Coffee House	LP	Oblivion	S1A	1969	£20	£8	US

KOVAC, ROLAND SET

Title	Format	Label	Cat. No.	Year	Price	Price	Notes
Roland Kovac Set	LP	private			£300	£180	

KRAAN

Title	Format	Label	Cat. No.	Year	Price	Price	Notes
Kraan	LP	Speigelei	28778/9	1973	£20	£8	*German*
Winthrup	LP	Speigelei	28523/9	1972	£20	£8	*German*

KRACKER

Title	Format	Label	Cat. No.	Year	Price	Price	Notes
Kracker Brand	LP	Rolling Stones	COC49102	1973	£12	£5	*test pressing only*

KRACO

Title	Format	Label	Cat. No.	Year	Price	Price	Notes
Circumvision	LP	Unidentified Artist	UAP1	1978	£75	£37.50	*Dutch*

KRAFTWERK

Title	Format	Label	Cat. No.	Year	Price	Price	Notes
Autobahn	LP	Vertigo	6360620	1975	£12	£5	*embossed sleeve*
Comet Melody 2	7"	Vertigo	6147015	1975	£8	£4	
Computer Love	12"	EMI	12EMI5207	1981	£10	£5	*'The Model' as B side*
Computer Welt	LP	Kling Klang	06264311	1981	£10	£4	*sung in German*
Das Model	12"	Kling Klang	06245176	1978	£8	£4	*sung in German*
Die Mensch Maschine	LP	Kling Klang	05832843	1978	£10	£4	*sung in German*
Die Mensch Maschine	LP	Kling Klang	05832843	1978	£150	£75	*German, red vinyl*
Electric Café	CD	EMI	CDP7464162	1986	£12	£5	
Elektrokinetik	LP	Vertigo	6449006	1981	£20	£8	
Exceller Eight	LP	Vertigo	6360629	1975	£15	£6	
Kometenmelodie	7"	Vertigo	VER3	1984	£8	£4	
Kraftwerk	12"	EMI	KLANGBOX101	1997	£400	£250	*promo box set, 4 x 12", T-shirt*
Kraftwerk	LP	Vertigo	6641077	1973	£20	£8	*double*
Kraftwerk	LP	Vertigo	6641077	1973	£75	£37.50	*spiral label double*
Kraftwerk 1	LP	Philips	6305058	1971	£60	£30	*German*
Kraftwerk 2	LP	Philips	6305117	1972	£60	£30	*German*
Mix	LP	EMI	EM1408	1991	£12	£5	*double*
Musique Non Stop	12"	EMI	12EMI5588	1986	£10	£5	
Neon Lights	12"	Capitol	CL15998	1978	£10	£5	*luminous vinyl*
Neon Lights	7"	Capitol	CL15998	1978	£6	£2.50	*picture sleeve*
Pocket Calculator	12"	EMI	12EMI5175	1981	£8	£4	
Pocket Calculator	7"	EMI		1981	£4	£1.50	*promo, English/German versions*
Pocket Calculator	cass-s	EMI	TCEMI5175	1981	£10	£4	
Radioactivity	7"	Capitol	CL15853	1976	£8	£4	*picture sleeve*
Radioactivity	CD	EMI	CDP7464742	1987	£12	£5	
Radioactivity	CD-s	EMI	CDEM201	1991	£12	£6	
Radioactivity	LP	Capitol	EST11457	1976	£12	£5	*with insert*
Radioaktivitat	LP	Kling Klang	06282087	1975	£10	£4	*sung in German*
Ralf And Florian	LP	Vertigo	6360616	1973	£25	£10	
Ralf And Florian	LP	Vertigo	6360616	1973	£75	£37.50	*spiral label*
Robotronik	CD-s	EMI	CDEM192	1991	£15	£7.50	
Robots	7"	Capitol	CL15981	1978	£12	£6	*picture sleeve*
Showroom Dummies	12"	EMI	12EMI5272	1982	£8	£4	
Showroom Dummies	12"	Capitol	CL16098	1979	£10	£5	
Showroom Dummies	12"	Capitol	CLX104	1977	£10	£5	
Technopop	LP	EMI	EMC3407	1983	£500	£330	
Telephone Call	12"	EMI	12EMI5602	1987	£15	£7.50	
Tour De France	12"	EMI	12EMI5413	1984	£12	£6	
Tour De France	7"	EMI	EMI5413	1984	£5	£2	
Trans Europa Express	LP	Kling Klang	06482306	1977	£10	£4	*sung in German*
Trans-Europe Express	CD	EMI	CDP7464732	1987	£12	£5	

KRAMER, BILLY J.

Title	Format	Label	Cat. No.	Year	Price	Price	Notes
Colour Of My Love	7"	MGM	MGM1474	1969	£4	£1.50	
Sorry	7"	Parlophone	R5552	1967	£4	£1.50	
Town Of Tuxley Toymaker	7"	Reaction	591014	1967	£15	£7.50	

KRAMER, BILLY J. & THE DAKOTAS

Title	Format	Label	Cat. No.	Year	Price	Price	Notes
Bad To Me	7" EP	Odeon	SOE3743	1963	£20	£10	*French, B side by the Dakotas*
Billy J Plays The States	7" EP	Parlophone	GEP8928	1965	£25	£12.50	
Billy J. Kramer	LP	Regal	REG1057	196–	£12	£5	*export*
Do You Want To Know A Secret	CD-s	EMI	CDEM174	1991	£5	£2	
From A Window	7" EP	Parlophone	GEP8921	1964	£25	£12.50	
I'll Keep You Satisfied	7" EP	Parlophone	GEP8895	1964	£12	£6	
I'll Keep You Satisfied	LP	Imperial	LP9273/12273	1964	£20	£8	*US*
Kramer Hits	7" EP	Parlophone	GEP8885	1963	£12	£6	
Listen	LP	Parlophone	PMC1209	1963	£15	£6	
Listen	LP	Parlophone	PCS3047	1963	£25	£10	*stereo*
Little Children	7" EP	Parlophone	GEP8907	1964	£15	£7.50	
Little Children	7" EP	Odeon	SOE3753	1964	£20	£10	*French*
Little Children	LP	Imperial	LP9267/12267	1964	£20	£8	*US*
Neon City	7"	Parlophone	R5362	1965	£4	£1.50	
Trains And Boats And Planes	LP	Imperial	LP9291/12291	1965	£20	£8	*US*
We're Doing Fine	7"	Parlophone	R5408	1966	£6	£2.50	
You Make Me Feel Like Someone	7"	Parlophone	R5482	1966	£4	£1.50	

KRAUS, PETER

Title	Format	Label	Number	Year	Mint	VG+	Notes
Bella Italia	LP	Polydor	46753/237253	1961	£40	£20	German
Bossa Nova	LP	Polydor	46630	1961	£75	£37.50	German mono
Bossa Nova	LP	Polydor	237130	1961	£40	£20	German stereo
Das Haben Die Mädchen Gerne	LP	Polydor	46812	1963	£25	£10	German
Liebelei	7" EP	Polydor	20330	1958	£15	£6	German
Peter Kraus	10" LP	Polydor	45197LPH	1958	£60	£30	German
Seine Grossen Erfolge	LP	Polydor	46770	1962	£30	£15	German
Singt Evergreens	LP	Polydor	46535/237035	1961	£40	£20	German
Teenager Evergreens	LP	Polydor	46857	1964	£30	£15	German

KRAUT

Title	Format	Label	Number	Year	Mint	VG+	Notes
Unemployed	7"	Cabbage	K0002	1982	£15	£7.50	

KRAVETZ, JEAN-JACQUES

Title	Format	Label	Number	Year	Mint	VG+	Notes
Kravetz	LP	Vertigo	6360605	1972	£20	£8	German

KRAVITZ, LENNY

Title	Format	Label	Number	Year	Mint	VG+	Notes
Always On The Run	CD-s	Virgin	VUSCD34	1991	£5	£2	
I Build This Garden For Us	CD-s	Virgin	VUSCD17	1990	£12	£6	
It Ain't Over 'Til It's Over	CD-s	Virgin	VUSCD43	1991	£5	£2	
Let Love Rule	CD-s	Virgin	VUSCD10	1989	£8	£4	3" single
Let Love Rule	CD-s	Virgin	VUSCD26	1990	£8	£3	
Live In Amsterdam	LP	Virgin	LENNY1	1990	£30	£15	promo
Mr Cabdriver	CD-s	Virgin	VUSCD20	1990	£5	£2	
Stand By My Woman	CD-s	Virgin	VUSCX45	1991	£8	£4	

KRAY CHERUBS

Title	Format	Label	Number	Year	Mint	VG+	Notes
No	7"	Fierce	FRIGHT014	1988	£10	£5	1 sided
Riot In Hell Mom	7"	Snakeskin	SS002	1989	£8	£4	Saucerman B side

KRAZY KATS

Title	Format	Label	Number	Year	Mint	VG+	Notes
Movin' Out	LP	Damon	12478		£15	£6	US

KREED

Title	Format	Label	Number	Year	Mint	VG+	Notes
Kreed!	LP	Visions Of Sound	7156	1971	£1000	£700	US

KRENZ, BILL RAGTIMERS

Title	Format	Label	Number	Year	Mint	VG+	Notes
Goofus	7"	London	HLU8258	1956	£15	£7.50	

KREW

Title	Format	Label	Number	Year	Mint	VG+	Notes
Everything Is Alright	7" EP	Riviera	231214	1966	£10	£5	French

KREW KATS

Title	Format	Label	Number	Year	Mint	VG+	Notes
Samovar	7"	HMV	POP894	1961	£10	£5	
Trambone	7"	HMV	POP840	1961	£6	£2.50	

KRIEGEL, VOLKER

Title	Format	Label	Number	Year	Mint	VG+	Notes
Lift	LP	MPS	21217531	1973	£10	£4	German
Mild Maniac	LP	MPS	21220206	1974	£10	£4	German
Missing Link	LP	MPS	33214311	1972	£12	£5	German double
Spectrum	LP	MPS	2120874	1971	£12	£5	German

KRISTINA, SONJA

Title	Format	Label	Number	Year	Mint	VG+	Notes
Let The Sunshine In	7"	Polydor	56299	1968	£10	£5	
Sonja Kristina	LP	Chopper	CHOPE5	1980	£30	£15	
St Tropez	7"	Chopper	CHOP101	1980	£6	£2.50	

KRISTYL

Title	Format	Label	Number	Year	Mint	VG+	Notes
Kristyl	LP	private		1975	£200	£100	US

KROG, KARIN

Title	Format	Label	Number	Year	Mint	VG+	Notes
By Myself	LP	Philips	838054PY	1964	£20	£8	
Gershwin With Karin Krog	LP	Polydor	2382045	1974	£15	£6	German
Jazz Moments	LP	Sonet	SLPS1404	1966	£20	£8	
Joy	LP	Sonet	SLPS1405	1968	£20	£8	

KROKODIL

Title	Format	Label	Number	Year	Mint	VG+	Notes
Getting Up For The Morning	LP	Bellaphon	BLPS19117	1972	£25	£10	German
Invisible World Revealed	LP	United Artists	UAS29250	1971	£25	£10	German
Krokodil	LP	Liberty	LBS83306	1969	£25	£10	
Musik	LP	United Artists	UAS293971	1971	£25	£10	German
Swamp	LP	Liberty	LBS83417	1970	£25	£10	
Sweat And Swim	LP	Bellaphon	7502	1973	£30	£15	German double

KRUG, MANFRED

Title	Format	Label	Number	Year	Mint	VG+	Notes
And Modern Jazz Big Band '65	LP	Amiga	850057	1965	£25	£10	East German

KRUGER, JEFF

Title	Format	Label	Number	Year	Mint	VG+	Notes
Jazz At The Flamingo	LP	Tempo	TAP5	1956	£30	£15	

KRUPA, GENE

Title	Format	Label	Number	Year	Mint	VG+	Notes
Burnin' Beat	LP	Verve	SVLP9014	1962	£12	£5	with Buddy Rich
Collates	10" LP	Columbia	33C9000	1955	£20	£8	
Drummin' Man	10" LP	Columbia	33S1051	1955	£20	£8	
Gene Krupa And Buddy Rich	LP	Columbia	33CX10040	1956	£15	£6	

Gene Krupa Orchestra	LP	HMV	CLP1087	1956	**£15**	**£6**	
Great Performances Of Gene Krupa	LP	CBS	BPG62289/90	1963	**£15**	**£6**	*double*
Jazz At The Philharmonic	LP	Columbia	33CX10015	1955	**£25**	**£10**	
Krupa Rocks	LP	Columbia	33CX10133	1959	**£15**	**£6**	
Plays Gerry Mulligan Arrangements	LP	HMV	CLP1281	1959	**£15**	**£6**	
Rhythm Parade	10" LP	Columbia	33S1064	1955	**£20**	**£8**	
Rockin' Mr Krupa	10" LP	Columbia	33C9032	1957	**£20**	**£8**	
Selections From The Benny Goodman Story	LP	Columbia	33CX10027	1956	**£20**	**£8**	*with Lionel Hampton & Teddy Wilson*

KRYSIA

Krysia	LP	RCA	LPL15052	1974	**£10**	**£4**	

KRYSTAL GENERATION

Wanted Dead Or Alive	7"	Mercury	6052120	1972	**£4**	**£1.50**	

KRYSTALS

Krystals	LP	Fourmost	8943	1967	**£30**	**£15**	*Canadian*

KUBAN, BOB & THE IN MEN

Cheater	7"	Bell	BLL1027	1968	**£4**	**£1.50**	
Cheater	7"	Stateside	SS488	1966	**£20**	**£10**	
Cheater	7" EP	Columbia	ESRF1761	1966	**£20**	**£10**	*French*
Look Out For The Cheater	LP	Musicland	(SLP)3500	1966	**£25**	**£10**	*US*
Teaser	7"	Stateside	SS514	1966	**£8**	**£4**	

KUBAS

I Love Her	7"	Columbia	DB7451	1965	**£30**	**£15**	

KUBINEC, DAVE

Schopi	7"	Parlophone	R5762	1969	**£4**	**£1.50**	

KUFF LINX

So Tough	7"	London	HLU8583	1958	**£125**	**£62.50**	

KUHN, ROLF

Streamline	LP	Vanguard	PPL11009	1958	**£10**	**£4**	

KUHN, STEVE

Ecstasy	LP	ECM	ECM1058ST	1975	**£12**	**£5**	
Trance	LP	ECM	ECM1052ST	1975	**£15**	**£6**	

KUHR, LENNY

Troubadour	7"	Philips	BF1777	1969	**£10**	**£5**	

KUKL

The Icelandic group Kukl emerged in the early eighties as a kind of super-group, drawing members from each of three bands. Björk was one of the members and her presence is responsible for the rapidly increasing values of the group's two albums.

Eye	LP	Crass	19841	1984	**£40**	**£20**	
Holidays In Europe	LP	Crass	No.4	1985	**£40**	**£20**	

KULA SHAKER

Kula Shaker's recasting of hippy psychedelia for the nineties pushed the group rapidly to the top in 1996, media interest being happily kindled by the fact that photogenic lead singer Crispian Mills is the son of actress Hayley Mills. 'Grateful When You're Dead' is, of course, a tribute to Jerry Garcia, the late-lamented lead guitarist with the Grateful Dead.

Govinda	12"	Columbia	XPR2324	1996	**£10**	**£5**	*promo*
Govinda	7"	Columbia	KULA75	1996	**£15**	**£7.50**	
Grateful When You're Dead/Jerry Was There	CD-s	Columbia	KULACD2	1996	**£8**	**£4**	
K	CD	Columbia	SHAKER1CDK	1996	**£15**	**£6**	*digipak*
Tattva	CD-s	Columbia	KULACD3	1996	**£5**	**£2**	*with poster*
Tattva (Lucky 13 Mix)	7"	Columbia	KULA71	1995	**£25**	**£12.50**	
Tattva (Lucky 13 Mix)	CD-s	Columbia	KULACD1	1995	**£30**	**£15**	

KULT

No Home Today	7"	CBS	4276	1969	**£75**	**£37.50**	

KUPFERBERG, TULI

No Deposit No Return	LP	ESP-Disk	1035	1966	**£15**	**£6**	*US*
No Deposit No Return	LP	ESP-Disk	1035	1966	**£20**	**£8**	*US, gold vinyl*

KURASS

Stampede	7"	Escort	ES825	1970	**£6**	**£2.50**	*King Stitt B side*

KUSTOM KINGS

Kustom City, USA	LP	Smash	MGS2/SRS67051	1964	**£25**	**£10**	*US*

KUTI, FELA RANSOME

Afrodisiac	LP	Regal Zonophone	SLRZ1034	1973	**£20**	**£8**	
Black President	LP	Arista	SPART1167	1981	**£10**	**£4**	
Everything Scatter	LP	Creole	CRLP509	1979	**£12**	**£5**	
Gentlemen	LP	Creole	CRLP502	1979	**£12**	**£5**	

Title	Format	Label	Number	Year	Mint	VG	Notes
Shakara	LP	Creole	CRLP501	1975	**£15**	**£6**	
With Ginger Baker Live	LP	Regal Zonophone	SLRZ1023	1972	**£15**	**£6**	
Yellow Fever	LP	Decca	PFS4412	1978	**£12**	**£5**	
Zombie	LP	Creole	CRLP511	1977	**£12**	**£5**	

KWESKIN, JIM JUG BAND

Title	Format	Label	Number	Year	Mint	VG	Notes
American Aviator	LP	Reprise	6353	1969	**£12**	**£5**	*US*
Garden Of Joy	LP	Reprise	R(S)6266	1967	**£12**	**£5**	*US*
Greatest Hits	LP	Vanguard	VSD13/14	1973	**£15**	**£6**	*US double*
Jim Kweskin Jug Band	LP	Fontana	TFL6036	1964	**£12**	**£5**	
Jug Band Music	LP	Vanguard	VRS/VSD79163	1966	**£12**	**£5**	*US*
Jump For Joy	LP	Vanguard	VSD79243	1967	**£12**	**£5**	*US*
Relax Your Mind	LP	Vanguard	VSD79188	1966	**£15**	**£6**	*US*
See Reverse Side For Title	LP	Fontana	(S)TFL6080	1967	**£12**	**£5**	
Unblushing Brassiness	LP	Vanguard	VSD2158	1963	**£20**	**£8**	*US*
Whatever Happened To Those Good Old Days	LP	Vanguard	SVRL19046	1968	**£12**	**£5**	

KYNARD, CHARLES

Title	Format	Label	Number	Year	Mint	VG	Notes
Woga	LP	Mainstream	MSL1009	1973	**£10**	**£4**	
Your Mama Won't Dance	LP	Mainstream	MSL1017	1973	**£10**	**£4**	

KYTES

Title	Format	Label	Number	Year	Mint	VG	Notes
Blessed	7"	Pye	7N17136	1966	**£4**	**£1.50**	
Frosted Panes	7"	Pye	7N17179	1966	**£10**	**£5**	
Running In The Water	7"	Island	WI6027	1968	**£25**	**£12.50**	

KYTTOCK KYND

Title	Format	Label	Number	Year	Mint	VG	Notes
Kyttock Kynd	LP	Decca	SKL4782	1970	**£50**	**£25**	

L

L7

Title	Format	Label	Number	Year	Mint	VG	Notes
Hungry For Stink	CD	Slash		1994	**£12**	**£5**	*Australian with bonus 4 track live CD*

LA BAMBOCHE

Title	Format	Label	Number	Year	Mint	VG	Notes
La Bamboche	LP	Hexagone	883003	1974	**£20**	**£8**	*French*
La Saison Des Amours	LP	Ballon Noir	13007	197–	**£20**	**£8**	*French*
Née De La Lune	LP	Hexagone	883037	1980	**£20**	**£8**	*French*
Quitte Paris	LP	Hexagone	883012	1976	**£20**	**£8**	*French*

LA CHIFONNIE

Title	Format	Label	Number	Year	Mint	VG	Notes
Au Dessus Du Pont	LP	Hexagone	883022	1979	**£25**	**£10**	*French*
La Chiffonie	LP	Hexagone	883008	1976	**£25**	**£10**	*French*

LA DE DA BAND

Title	Format	Label	Number	Year	Mint	VG	Notes
Come Together	7"	Parlophone	R5810	1969	**£4**	**£1.50**	

LA DE DAS

Title	Format	Label	Number	Year	Mint	VG	Notes
Happy Prince	LP	Columbia	SCXM7899	1969	**£60**	**£30**	*New Zealand*
Legend	LP	EMI	EMA309	1975	**£15**	**£6**	*Australian*
Rock And Roll Sandwich	LP	EMI	EMC2504	1973	**£40**	**£20**	*Australian*

LA DUSSELDORF

Title	Format	Label	Number	Year	Mint	VG	Notes
La Düsseldorf	7"	Radar	ADA5	1978	**£10**	**£5**	*promo only*

LA PERVERSITA

Title	Format	Label	Number	Year	Mint	VG	Notes
La Perversita	LP	Invisible	10005	1979	**£10**	**£4**	*French*

LA PESTE

Title	Format	Label	Number	Year	Mint	VG	Notes
Better Off Dead	7"	Backlash	CB711	1978	**£10**	**£5**	

LA ROCA, PETE

Title	Format	Label	Number	Year	Mint	VG	Notes
Basra	LP	Blue Note	BLP/BST84205	1965	**£30**	**£15**	

LA ROSA, JULIUS

Title	Format	Label	Number	Year	Mint	VG	Notes
Domani	7"	London	HLA8170	1955	**£15**	**£7.50**	
Jingle Bells	7"	London	HLA8353	1956	**£8**	**£4**	
Julius La Rosa	LP	London	HAA2031	1957	**£30**	**£15**	
Julius La Rosa Sings	7" EP	London	REP1005	1954	**£20**	**£10**	
Lipstick And Candy And Rubber Sole Shoe	7"	HMV	7M384	1956	**£5**	**£2**	
Mobile	7"	London	HL8154	1955	**£20**	**£10**	
No Other Love	7"	London	HLA8272	1956	**£12**	**£6**	
Suddenly There's A Valley	7"	London	HLA8193	1955	**£20**	**£10**	
Torero	7"	RCA	RCA1063	1958	**£4**	**£1.50**	

LABELLE, PATTI & THE BLUEBELLES

Title	Format	Label	Number	Year	Mint	VG	Notes
All Or Nothing	7"	Atlantic	AT4055	1965	**£8**	**£4**	
Apollo Presents The Bluebelles	LP	Newtown	631	1963	**£30**	**£15**	*US*
Danny Boy	7"	Cameo Parkway	P935	1965	**£6**	**£2.50**	
Down The Aisle	7"	Sue	WI324	1964	**£12**	**£6**	
Dreamer	LP	Atlantic	(SD)8101	1965	**£20**	**£8**	*US*
I Sold My Heart To The Junkman	7"	HMV	POP1029	1962	**£12**	**£6**	
On Stage	LP	Parkway	7043	1965	**£25**	**£10**	*US*
Over The Rainbow	7"	Atlantic	AT4064	1966	**£4**	**£1.50**	
Over The Rainbow	LP	Atlantic	587001	1966	**£15**	**£6**	
Patti's Prayer	7"	Atlantic	584007	1966	**£4**	**£1.50**	
Sleigh Bells, Jingle Bells And Bluebelles	LP	Newtown	632	1963	**£25**	**£10**	*US*
Take Me For A Little While	7"	Atlantic	584072	1967	**£4**	**£1.50**	

LACE

Title	Format	Label	Number	Year	Mint	VG	Notes
I'm A Gambler	7"	Page One	POF135	1969	**£4**	**£1.50**	
People People	7"	Columbia	DB8499	1968	**£10**	**£5**	

LACEWING

Title	Format	Label	Number	Year	Mint	VG	Notes
Lacewing	LP	Mainstream	S6132	1970	**£60**	**£30**	*US*

LACEY, DAVE & THE CORVETTES

Title	Format	Label	Number	Year	Mint	VG	Notes
That's What They All Say	7"	Philips	BF1419	1965	**£4**	**£1.50**	

LACKEY & SWEENEY

Junk Store Songs For Sale	LP	Village Thing	VTS23	1973	£15	£6	

LACY, STEVE

Crust	LP	Emanem	304	1975	£15	£6	
Forest And The Zoo	LP	Fontana	SFJL932	1970	£20	£8	
Gap	LP	America	30AM6125	1973	£15	£6	
Scraps	LP	Saravah	SH10049	1974	£15	£6	
Solo – In Concert At Théâtre Du Chêne Noir	LP	Emanem	301	1974	£15	£6	

LADDERS

Gotta See Jane	12"	Statik	TAK212	1983	£6	£2.50	

LADD'S BLACK ACES

Ladd's Black Aces	10" LP	London	AL3556	1956	£10	£4	

LADNIER, TOMMY

Blues And Stomps Vol. 1	10" LP	London	AL3524	1954	£20	£8	
Plays The Blues With Ma Rainey & Edmonia Henderson	10" LP	London	AL3548	1955	£20	£8	

LADY

Lady	LP	Vertigo	6360636	1976	£12	£5	*German*

LADY JUNE

Linguistic Leprosy	LP	Caroline	C1509	1974	£15	£6	

LADY LAKE

No Pictures	LP	Q Records	BW1001	1978	£25	£10	*Dutch*

LADYBIRDS

I Wanna Fly	7"	Columbia	DB7523	1965	£4	£1.50	
Lady Bird	7"	Columbia	DB7197	1964	£4	£1.50	
Memories	7"	Columbia	DB7351	1964	£4	£1.50	
White Cliffs Of Dover	7"	Columbia	DB7250	1964	£4	£1.50	

LAFAYETTES

Caravan Of Lonely Men	7"	RCA	RCA1308	1962	£6	£2.50	
Nobody But You	7"	RCA	RCA1299	1962	£4	£1.50	
Nobody But You	7" EP	RCA	75724	1962	£10	£5	*French*

LAGGAN

I Am The Common Man	LP	S.T.U.C.		1978	£40	£20	
I Am The Common Man	LP	Klub	KLP16	1980	£15	£6	
Scottish Folk Songs	LP	Arfolk		1975	£60	£30	

LAGIN, NED

Despite bearing a list of musician credits featuring many of the stars of West Coast rock, *Seastones* is actually an electronic work having more in common with the classical avant-garde than rock music of any kind. The record label (though not the cover) has a co-credit to Phil Lesh – and the record is often misleadingly listed under his name. The Grateful Dead have actually been frequent sponsors of modern classical works, *Seastones* merely being the first of these.

Seastones	LP	Round	RX106	1975	£25	£10	*US*

LAGRIMA

Lagrima	LP	Hexagone		1978	£30	£15	*French*

LAI, FRANCIS

I'll Never Forget Whatsisname	LP	Brunswick	LAT/STA8689	1967	£15	£6	

LAIBACH

Across The Universe	CD-s	Mute	CDMUTE91	1988	£5	£2	*3" single*
Die Liebe	CD-s	Cherry Red	CDCHERRY91	1985	£5	£2	
Panorama	12"	East West	12EWS3	1984	£6	£2.50	
Sympathy For The Devil	CD-s	Mute	MUTE80CD	1988	£5	£2	

LAINE, CLEO

All About Me	LP	Fontana	680992TL/ 886159TY	1962	£10	£4	
April Age	7" EP	Pye	NJE1026	1957	£5	£2	
Cleo	7" EP	Fontana	TFE17404	1964	£5	£2	
Cleo Laine	10" LP	Esquire	15007	1955	£15	£6	
Cleo Laine	7" EP	Esquire	EP102	1956	£5	£2	
Cleo Laine	7" EP	Esquire	EP122	1957	£5	£2	
Cleo Laine	7" EP	Pye	NJE1010	1956	£5	£2	
Cleo Sings Elizabethan	7" EP	Columbia	SEG7938	1959	£5	£2	
Cleo's Choice	10" LP	Pye	NPT19024	1958	£12	£5	
Fabulous Cleo	7" EP	Fontana	TFE17381	1961	£5	£2	
I Got Rhythm	7" EP	Parlophone	GEP8613	1957	£5	£2	
Shakespeare And All That Jazz	LP	Fontana	STL5209	1964	£10	£4	
She's The Tops	LP	MGM	C765	1958	£10	£4	
Woman Talk	LP	Fontana	(S)TL5316	1966	£10	£4	

LAINE, DENNY

The singles released by Denny Laine on the Deram label represented a bold experiment by the former Moody Blue and future Wing. Abandoning the usual rock group line-up, Laine surrounded himself with a small group of amplified violins and cellos – the Electric String

Band – and thereby anticipated some of what was later achieved by the Electric Light Orchestra. Sadly, Laine's innovations found little public support and he never again attempted anything similar.

Say You Don't Mind	7"	Deram	DM122	1967	£4	£1.50	
Too Much In Love	7"	Deram	DM171	1968	£6	£2.50	

LAINE, FRANKIE

All Of Me	7" EP	Mercury	MEP9500	1956	£10	£5	
All Time Hits	7" EP	Mercury	ZEP10062	1960	£8	£4	
Annabel Lee	7"	Philips	PB797	1958	£4	£1.50	
Autumn Leaves	7" EP	Philips	BBE12216	1958	£10	£5	
Balladeer	LP	Philips	BBL7357	1960	£10	£4	
Call Of The Wild	LP	CBS	(S)BPG62082	1962	£10	£4	
Command Performance	LP	Columbia	CL625	1956	£20	£8	*US*
Concert Date	LP	Mercury	MG20085	1955	£20	£8	*US*
Cry Of The Wild Goose	10" LP	Mercury	MPT7007	1956	£20	£8	
Deuces Wild	LP	Philips	BBL7535/ SBBL663	1962	£10	£4	
Deuces Wild No. 1	7" EP	CBS	AGG20003	1962	£8	£4	
Deuces Wild No. 2	7" EP	CBS	AGG20007	1962	£8	£4	
Deuces Wild No. 3	7" EP	CBS	AGG20011	1962	£8	£4	
Favorites	10" LP	Mercury	MG25007	195–	£25	£10	*US*
Foreign Affair	LP	Philips	BBL7238	1958	£12	£5	
Frankie And Johnnie	7" EP	Philips	BBE12153	1957	£10	£5	*with Johnnie Ray*
Frankie Laine	7" EP	Columbia	SEG7505	1954	£10	£5	
Frankie Laine Songs	10" LP	Mercury	MG10002	1952	£30	£15	
Georgia On My Mind	7" EP	Mercury	MEP9000	1956	£10	£5	
Golden Hits	LP	Mercury	MG20587	1960	£12	£5	*US*
Good Evening Friends	7"	Philips	JK1026	1957	£15	£7.50	*with Johnnie Ray*
Greater Sin	7"	Philips	JK1032	1957	£12	£6	
Greatest Hits	LP	Columbia	CL1231	1959	£15	£6	*US*
Guys And Dolls	10" LP	Columbia	CL2567	195–	£25	£10	*US*
Hell Bent For Leather	LP	Philips	BBL7468/ SBBL616	1961	£10	£4	
I Believe	7" EP	Philips	BBE12005	1955	£10	£5	
I'd Give My Life	7"	Columbia	SCM5085	1954	£12	£6	
I'm Just A Poor Bachelor	7"	Columbia	SCM5031	1953	£20	£10	
Jazz Spectacular	LP	Philips	BBL7080	1956	£12	£5	
Jealousy	7"	Columbia	SCM5017	1953	£25	£12.50	
Juba Juba Jubilee	7" EP	Philips	BBE12103	1956	£8	£4	
Juba Juba Jubilee	LP	Philips	BBL7111	1957	£15	£6	
Love Is A Golden Ring	7"	Philips	JK1009	1957	£10	£5	
Lover's Laine	10" LP	Columbia	CL2504	195–	£25	£10	*US*
Lovin' Up A Storm	7"	Philips	PB836	1958	£4	£1.50	
Moby Dick	7" EP	Philips	BBE12087	1956	£10	£5	
Moonlight Gambler	7"	Philips	JK1000	1956	£10	£5	
Moonlight Gambler	7" EP	Philips	BBE12130	1957	£10	£5	
Mr Rhythm	10" LP	Philips	BBR8068	1955	£20	£8	
Mr Rhythm Sings	10" LP	Mercury	MG25097	1954	£25	£10	
Mr Rhythm Sings	10" LP	Mercury	MG10001	1952	£30	£15	
My Gal And A Prayer	7"	Philips	PB821	1958	£4	£1.50	
One For My Baby	10" LP	Columbia	CL2548	195–	£25	£10	*US*
Rawhide	7"	Philips	PB965	1959	£4	£1.50	
Reunion In Rhythm	LP	Philips	BBL7294/ SBBL541	1959	£12	£5	
Rockin'	LP	Philips	BBL7155	1957	£15	£6	
Ruby And The Pearl	7"	Columbia	SCM5016	1953	£20	£10	
September In The Rain	7"	Columbia	SCM5064	1953	£15	£7.50	
Showcase Of Hits	LP	Philips	BBL7263	1958	£15	£6	
Sings	10" LP	Columbia	33S1047	1954	£25	£10	
Sings For Us	LP	Mercury	MG20083	1955	£20	£8	*US*
Song Of The Open Road	7" EP	CBS	AGG20036	1963	£8	£4	
Songs By Frankie Laine	10" LP	Mercury	MG25098	1954	£25	£10	
Songs By Frankie Laine	LP	Mercury	MG20069	1955	£20	£8	*US*
Stay As Sweet As You Are	7" EP	Mercury	MEP9520	1957	£10	£5	
Swan Song	7"	Columbia	SCM5073	1953	£15	£7.50	
That's My Desire	10" LP	Mercury	MPT7513	1957	£20	£8	
That's My Desire	LP	Mercury	MG20080	1955	£20	£8	*US*
Torching	LP	Philips	BBL7260	1958	£12	£5	
Voice Of Your Choice	10" LP	Philips	BBR8014	1954	£25	£10	
Wanderlust	LP	CBS	(S)BPG62126	1963	£10	£4	
Western Favourites	7" EP	Philips	BBE12447	1960	£10	£5	
With All My Heart	LP	Mercury	MG20105	1955	£20	£8	*US*
Without Him	7"	Philips	JK1017	1957	£10	£5	

LAINE, LINDA & THE SINNERS

Don't Say It Baby	7"	Columbia	DB7549	1965	£6	£2.50	
Doncha Know	7"	Columbia	DB7204	1964	£5	£2	
Low Grades And High Fever	7"	Columbia	DB7370	1964	£5	£2	

LAINE, SCOTT

Tearaway Johnnie	7"	Windsor	WB114	1963	£5	£2	

LAING, DENZIL

Medicine Stick	7"	Songbird	SB1054	1971	£5	£2	*Crystalites B side*

LAITY, PETE

Rash Adventure	LP	Oblivion	OBL004	1984	**£10**	**£4**	
True Dare Kiss Or Promise	LP	Accolade	OBL006	1986	**£10**	**£4**	

LAKE, ALAN

Good Times	7"	Ember	EMBS278	1970	**£10**	**£5**	*picture sleeve*

LAKE, BONNIE & HER BEAUX

Miracle Of Love	7"	Brunswick	05622	1956	**£10**	**£5**	

LAMAR, LEE

Sophia	7"	London	HLB8508	1957	**£40**	**£20**	

LAMB, KEVIN

Sailing Down The Years	LP	Arista	AB4166	1978	**£12**	**£5**	
Who Is The Hero	LP	Birth	RAB4	1971	**£20**	**£8**	

LAMBE, JEANNIE

Day After Day After Day	7"	CBS	2731	1967	**£4**	**£1.50**	
Miss Disc	7"	CBS	202636	1967	**£8**	**£4**	

LAMBERT, HENDRICKS & ROSS

Hottest New Group In Jazz	LP	Philips	BBL7368/ SBBL562	1960	**£12**	**£5**	
Sing A Song Of Basie	LP	HMV	CLP1203	1958	**£20**	**£8**	
Swingers	LP	Vogue	LAE12219	1960	**£20**	**£8**	

LAMBRETTAS

Go Steady	7"	Rocket	XPRES23	1979	**£4**	**£1.50**	
Page Three	7"	Rocket	XPRES36	1980	**£50**	**£25**	
Page Three	7"	Rocket	XPRES36	1980	**£75**	**£37.50**	*picture sleeve*

LAMEGO, DANNY & HIS JUMPIN' JACKS

Big Weekend	LP	Forget-Me-Not	105A	1964	**£20**	**£8**	US

LAMERS, JOHN

Crazy Love	LP	CNR	5050	1962	**£25**	**£10**	Dutch

LAMOND, TONI

Silent Voices	7"	Philips	BF1722	1968	**£8**	**£4**	

LAMP SISTERS

Woman With The Blues	7"	Sue	WI4048	1968	**£20**	**£10**	

LANA SISTERS

The Lana Sisters were not actually related to each other, but did include the young Mary O'Brien, who had yet to assume her better-known stage name of Dusty Springfield.

Buzzin'	7"	Fontana	H176	1959	**£10**	**£5**	
Mister Dee-Jay	7"	Fontana	H190	1959	**£10**	**£5**	
Ring-a My Phone	7"	Fontana	H148	1958	**£15**	**£7.50**	
Sitting In The Back Seat	7"	Fontana	H221	1959	**£6**	**£2.50**	
Someone Loves You, Joe	7"	Fontana	H252	1960	**£4**	**£1.50**	
Twosome	7"	Fontana	H283	1960	**£4**	**£1.50**	
You've Got What It Takes	7"	Fontana	H235	1960	**£5**	**£2**	

LANAGAN, CYNTHIA

Body And Soul	7"	Columbia	SCMC6	1954	**£4**	**£1.50**	*export*
I'm Available	7"	Parlophone	R4383	1957	**£4**	**£1.50**	
Jamie Boy	7"	Parlophone	R4316	1957	**£4**	**£1.50**	

LANCASHIRE FAYRE

Not Easily Forgotten	LP	Fellside	FE045	1985	**£10**	**£4**	

LANCASTER, PETER

Rhythm 'n' Blues Show	LP	Polydor	249105	1967	**£30**	**£15**	German

LANCASTRIANS

Let's Lock The Door	7"	Pye	7N15791	1965	**£4**	**£1.50**	
Lonely Man	7"	Pye	7N15927	1965	**£4**	**£1.50**	
There'll Be No More Goodbyes	7"	Pye	7N15846	1965	**£4**	**£1.50**	
This World Keeps Going Round	7"	Pye	7N17043	1966	**£10**	**£5**	
We'll Sing In The Sunshine	7"	Pye	7N15732	1964	**£5**	**£2**	

LANCE, MAJOR

Ain't No Soul	7"	Columbia	DB8122	1967	**£25**	**£12.50**	
Beat	7"	Soul City	SC114	1969	**£6**	**£2.50**	
Best Of Major Lance	LP	Epic	EPC81519	1976	**£12**	**£5**	
Come See	7"	Columbia	DB7527	1965	**£10**	**£5**	
Everybody Loves A Good Time	7"	Columbia	DB7787	1965	**£8**	**£4**	
Follow That Leader	7"	Atlantic	584277	1969	**£4**	**£1.50**	
Greatest Hits	LP	OKeh	OKM12110/ OKS14110	1965	**£40**	**£20**	US
Hey Little Girl	7"	Columbia	DB7168	1963	**£8**	**£4**	
I Wanna Make Up	7"	Stax	2025124	1973	**£4**	**£1.50**	

I'm So Lost	7"	Columbia	DB7463	1965	£6	£2.50	
Investigate	7"	Columbia	DB7967	1966	£25	£12.50	
Live At The Torch	LP	Contempo	COLP1001	1973	£15	£6	
Matador	7"	Columbia	DB7271	1964	£10	£5	
Monkey Time	7"	Columbia	DB7099	1963	£20	£10	
Monkey Time	LP	OKeh	OKM12105/ OKS14105	1963	£75	£37.50	US
Pride And Joy	7"	Columbia	DB7609	1965	£15	£7.50	
Rhythm	7"	Columbia	DB7365	1964	£10	£5	
Rhythm Of Major Lance	LP	Columbia	33SX1728	1965	£75	£37.50	
Sweeter As The Days Go By	7"	Atlantic	584302	1969	£4	£1.50	
Too Hot To Hold	7"	Columbia	DB7688	1965	£10	£5	
Um Um Um Um Um Um	7"	Columbia	DB7205	1964	£6	£2.50	
Um Um Um Um Um Um	7" EP	Columbia	SEG8318	1964	£50	£25	
Um Um Um Um Um Um	LP	OKeh	OKM12106/ OKS14106	1964	£75	£37.50	US

LANCELOT, RICK & THE SEVEN KNIGHTS

Say Girl	7"	RCA	RCA1502	1966	£4	£1.50	

LANCERS

Alphabet Rock	7"	Vogue Coral	Q72128	1956	£20	£10	
First Travelling Saleslady	7"	Vogue Coral	Q72183	1956	£5	£2	
Get Out Of The Car	7"	Vogue Coral	Q72081	1955	£10	£5	
Jo-Ann	7"	Vogue Coral	Q72100	1955	£6	£2.50	
Man Is As Good As His Word	7"	Vogue Coral	Q72157	1956	£5	£2	
Mister Sandman	7"	Vogue Coral	Q2038	1954	£12	£6	
Never Leave Me	7"	Vogue Coral	Q72220	1957	£5	£2	
Oh Sweet Mama	10" LP	London	HAPB1029	1954	£25	£10	
Presenting The Lancers	7" EP	London	REP1027	1955	£20	£10	
So High So Low So Wide	7"	London	HL8079	1954	£30	£15	
Stop Chasing Me Baby	7"	London	HL8027	1954	£30	£15	
Stroll	7"	Coral	Q72300	1958	£5	£2	
Timberjack	7"	Vogue Coral	Q72062	1955	£8	£4	

LAND, HAROLD

Fox	LP	Vogue	LAE12269	1961	£20	£8	
Harold In The Land Of Jazz	LP	Contemporary	LAC12178	1959	£20	£8	

LANDER, BOB & THE SPOTNICKS

Midnight Special	7"	Oriole	CB1784	1962	£6	£2.50	
My Old Kentucky Home	7"	Oriole	CB1756	1962	£12	£6	

LANDIS, BILL & BRETT

Baby Talk	7"	Parlophone	R4570	1959	£5	£2	
By You, By You	7"	Parlophone	R4551	1959	£4	£1.50	
Since You've Gone	7"	Parlophone	R4516	1959	£4	£1.50	

LANDIS, JERRY

Jerry Landis was one of the many pseudonyms adopted by Paul Simon in the years before he discovered folk music. In America, the 'He Was My Brother' single was issued under the name Paul Kane.

Anna Belle	7"	MGM	12822	1959	£20	£10	US
He Was My Brother	7"	Oriole	CB1390	1962	£40	£20	
I'm Lonely	7"	Canadian American	130	1961	£20	£10	US
Just A Boy	7"	Warwick	552	1960	£20	£10	US
Just A Boy	7"	Warwick	588	1960	£20	£10	US
Lisa	7"	Amy	875	1962	£25	£12.50	US
Play Me A Sad Song	7"	Warwick	616	1961	£20	£10	US

LANDIS, JOYA

Kansas City	7"	Trojan	TR620	1968	£8	£4	
Moonlight Lover	7"	Trojan	TR641	1968	£8	£4	

LANDS, HOAGY

I'm Yours	7"	Stateside	SS2085	1968	£6	£2.50	
Next In Line	7"	Stateside	SS2030	1967	£100	£50	
Why Didn't You Let Me Know	7"	Action	ACT4605	1972	£4	£1.50	

LANDSCAPE

European Man	12"	RCA	EDMT1	1980	£8	£4	

LANDSLIDE

Two Sided Fantasy	LP	Capitol	ST11006	1972	£40	£20	US

LANE, DES

Moonbird	7"	Top Rank	JAR203	1959	£4	£1.50	
Penny-Whistle Rock	7"	Decca	F10821	1956	£5	£2	
Rock Mister Piper	7"	Decca	F10847	1957	£6	£2.50	

LANE, GARY & THE GARRISONS

I'm A Lucky Boy	7"	Fontana	267221TF	1962	£5	£2	
Start Walking Boy	7"	Fontana	H338	1961	£6	£2.50	

LANE, MICKEY LEE

Hey Sah-lo-ney	7"	Stateside	SS456	1965	£20	£10	

Shaggy Dog	7"	Stateside	SS354	1964	£4	£1.50	

LANE, RONNIE

Anymore For Anymore	LP	GM	GMS1024	1974	£10	£4	
Mahoney's Last Stand	LP	Atlantic	K50308	1976	£10	£4	*with Ron Wood*
One For The Road	LP	Island	ILPS9366	1975	£10	£4	
Ronnie Lane And Slim Chance	LP	Island	ILPS9321	1975	£10	£4	

LANE, TONY & THE DELTONES

It's Great	7"	Sabre	SA455	1964	£5	£2	

LANE BROTHERS

Mimi	7"	London	HLR9150	1960	£10	£5	

LANE SISTERS

Peek A Boo Moon	7"	Columbia	DB4671	1961	£5	£2	

LANG, DON

Come Go With Me	7"	HMV	POP335	1957	£15	£7.50	
Don't Open That Door	7"	HMV	POP805	1960	£4	£1.50	
Four Brothers	7"	HMV	7M354	1956	£15	£7.50	
Hand Jive	10" LP	HMV	DLP1179	1958	£100	£50	
Hey Daddy	7"	HMV	POP510	1958	£4	£1.50	
Hoot And A Holler	7"	HMV	POP649	1959	£4	£1.50	
Percy Green	7"	HMV	POP623	1959	£5	£2	
Queen Of The Hop	7"	HMV	POP547	1958	£6	£2.50	
Red Planet Rock	7"	HMV	POP414	1957	£15	£7.50	
Reveille Rock	7"	HMV	POP682	1959	£4	£1.50	
Rock And Roll Blues	7"	HMV	7M416	1956	£15	£7.50	
Rock Around The Islands	7"	HMV	7M381	1956	£15	£7.50	
Rock Mister Piper	7"	HMV	POP289	1957	£15	£7.50	
Rock'n'Roll	7" EP	HMV	7EG8208	1957	£60	£30	
Sink The Bismarck	7"	HMV	POP714	1960	£10	£5	
Six Five Hand Jive	7"	HMV	POP434	1958	£12	£6	
Six Five Special	7"	HMV	POP350	1957	£12	£6	
Skiffle Special	10" LP	HMV	DLP1151	1957	£75	£37.50	
Sweet Sue	7"	HMV	POP260	1956	£8	£4	
Tequila	7"	HMV	POP465	1958	£8	£4	
Twenty Top Twenty Twists	LP	Ace Of Clubs	ACL1111	1962	£15	£6	
White Silver Sands	7"	HMV	POP382	1957	£6	£2.50	
Wicked Women	7"	Decca	F11483	1962	£4	£1.50	
Wiggle Wiggle	7"	HMV	POP585	1959	£4	£1.50	
Witch Doctor	7"	HMV	POP488	1958	£5	£2	

LANG, EDDIE & LONNIE JOHNSON

Blue Guitars	LP	Parlophone	PMC7019	1967	£30	£15	
Blue Guitars Vol. 2	LP	Parlophone	PMC7106	1970	£30	£15	

LANG, K. D.

Constant Craving	CD-s	Sire	W0157CD	1993	£5	£2	
Constant Craving	CD-s	Sire	W0100CD	1992	£10	£5	
Constant Craving (live)	CD-s	Sire	W0157CDX	1993	£6	£2.50	
Damned Old Dog	7"	Bumstead		1983	£100	£50	*Canadian*
Making Of Shadowland	CD	Sire	PROCD3120	1988	£20	£8	*US promo*
Miss Chatelaine	12"	Sire	W0135TW	1992	£8	£4	*with poster*
Miss Chatelaine	CD-s	Sire	W0135CD	1992	£5	£2	
Miss Chatelaine	CD-s	Sire	W0181CDX	1993	£5	£2	*with 3 cards*
Our Day Will Come	7"	Sire	W7697	1988	£15	£7.50	
Our Day Will Come	12"	Sire	W7697T	1988	£50	£25	
Ridin' The Rails	7"	Warner Bros	W9535	1990	£10	£5	*Darlene Love B side*
Sugar Moon	12"	Sire	W7841T	1988	£40	£20	
Sugar Moon	7"	Sire	W7841	1988	£15	£7.50	

LANG, RAY

Last Train	7"	Brunswick	05683	1957	£4	£1.50	

LANGE, STEVIE

Remember My Name	7"	RCA	RCA152	1981	£8	£4	
Remember My Name	7"	RCA	LIM1	1981	£5	£2	
Remember My Name	7"	Jive	JIVE23	1983	£5	£2	*no picture sleeve*

LANGFORDS

Send Me An Angel	7"	Torino	TSP341	196–	£4	£1.50	*picture sleeve*

LANGHORN, GORDON

Give A Fool A Chance	7"	Decca	F10591	1955	£6	£2.50	

LANGLEY, PERPETUAL

So Sad	7"	Planet	PLF110	1966	£8	£4	
Surrender	7"	Planet	PLF115	1966	£8	£4	

LANG'SYNE

Lang'Syne	LP	Dusselton	TS2737	1976	£750	£500	*German*

LANGTON, LLOYD

Outside The Law	LP	Flicknife	SHARP015	1983	£10	£4	*with 7" FREE001*

LANGTON, PHIL TRIO

Phil Langton Trio	LP	Holyground		196–	**£15**	**£6**	

LANSON, SNOOKY

It's Almost Tomorrow	7"	London	HLD8223	1956	**£75**	**£37.50**	
Last Minute Love	7"	London	HLD8236	1956	**£125**	**£62.50**	
Seven Days	7"	London	HLD8249	1956	**£125**	**£62.50**	
Seven Days	7"	London	HL7005	1956	**£40**	**£20**	*export*

LANZA, MARIO

Great Caruso	LP	HMV	ALP1071	1953	**£10**	**£4**	
On Broadway	10" LP	HMV	BLP1091	1957	**£10**	**£4**	
Operatic Arias	LP	HMV	ALP1202	1954	**£10**	**£4**	
Seven Hills Of Rome	10" LP	RCA	RA13001	1958	**£10**	**£4**	
Songs Of Romance	10" LP	HMV	BLP1071	1955	**£10**	**£4**	
Touch Of Your Hand	10" LP	HMV	BLP1094	1957	**£10**	**£4**	

LANZON & HUSBAND

Nostalgia	LP	Bradleys	BRADL1007	1974	**£75**	**£37.50**	

LAPERA

L'Acqua Purificatrice	LP	Durium	MSA77360	1975	**£20**	**£8**	*Italian*

LARD FREE

I'm Around About Midnight	LP	Vamp	VP59502	1975	**£15**	**£6**	*French*
Lard Free	LP	Vamp	VP59500	1973	**£25**	**£10**	*French*
Lard Free	LP	Cobra	37007	1977	**£12**	**£5**	*French*

LARKINS, ELLIS

Manhattan At Midnight	LP	Brunswick	LAT8189	1957	**£15**	**£6**	
Melodies Of Harold Arlen	10" LP	Brunswick	LA8694	1955	**£20**	**£8**	

LARKS

Jerk	7"	Pye	7N25284	1964	**£12**	**£6**	
Jerk	LP	Money	LP1102	1965	**£30**	**£15**	*US*
Soul Kaleidoscope	LP	Money	LP/MS1107	1966	**£20**	**£8**	*US*
Superslick	LP	Money	MY/MS1110	1967	**£20**	**£8**	*US*

LARNER, SAM

Garland For Sam	LP	Topic	12T244	1974	**£10**	**£4**	
Now Is The Time For Fishing	LP	Folkways	FG3507	1961	**£15**	**£6**	

LARRY & ALVIN

Can't You Understand	7"	Studio One	SO2067	1968	**£12**	**£6**	
Lonely Room	7"	Studio One	SO2080	1969	**£12**	**£6**	
Love Got Me	7"	Coxsone	CS7081	1968	**£10**	**£5**	*Bob Andy B side*

LARRY & JOHNNY

An attempt on the part of Larry Williams and Johnny Guitar Watson to cash in on the success of the Beatles produced considerably less income than did the fact that the Beatles themselves covered some of Williams's songs: 'Slow Down', 'Bad Boy' and 'Dizzy Miss Lizzy'.

Beatle Time	7"	Outasite	45501	1965	**£50**	**£25**	

LARRY & TOMMY

You've Gotta Bend A Little	7"	Polydor	56741	1968	**£5**	**£2**	

LARSON, JACK

I Love The Way She Laughs	7"	Top Rank	JAR573	1961	**£4**	**£1.50**	

LAs

Feelin'	7"	Go! Discs	GOLAB6	1991	**£6**	**£2.50**	*boxed set with badge & 3 stickers*
Feelin'	CD-s	Go! Discs	LASCD6	1991	**£6**	**£2.50**	
La's	LP	Go! Discs	8282021	1990	**£25**	**£10**	
Sound Sampler	CD	Go! Discs	LASCD1	1990	**£15**	**£6**	*promo*
There She Goes	12"	Go! Discs	GOLAS212	1988	**£15**	**£7.50**	
There She Goes	7"	Go! Discs	GOLAB5	1990	**£6**	**£2.50**	*boxed set with badge & 3 stickers*
There She Goes	7"	Go! Discs	GOLAR2	1988	**£8**	**£4**	
There She Goes	7"	Go! Discs	GOLAS2	1988	**£8**	**£4**	
There She Goes	CD-s	Go! Discs	LASCD5	1990	**£6**	**£2.50**	
There She Goes	CD-s	Go! Discs	LASCD2	1988	**£15**	**£7.50**	
Timeless Melody	12"	Go! Discs	LASDJ312	1989	**£40**	**£20**	*promo*
Timeless Melody	7"	Go! Discs	GOLAS3	1989	**£75**	**£37.50**	*test pressing*
Way Out	12"	Go! Discs	GOLAS112	1987	**£15**	**£7.50**	
Way Out	12"	Go! Discs	GOLAR112	1987	**£20**	**£10**	
Way Out	7"	Go! Discs	GOLAS1	1987	**£10**	**£5**	

LASSIES

Sleepy Head	7"	Brunswick	05571	1956	**£4**	**£1.50**	

LAST, JAMES

Voodoo Party	LP	Polydor	2371235	1972	**£10**	**£4**	

LAST CHANT

Run Of The Dove	7"	Chicken Jazz	JAZZ4	1981	**£5**	**£2**	

LAST EXIT

Last Exit was a rock group formed from within the ranks of the Newcastle Big Band and, like its parent organization, played in pubs and clubs around Newcastle. The singer/bass player was Gordon Sumner – better known as Sting – and it is he that can be heard on the group's locally produced single. (The Last Exit that recorded in the eighties has nothing to do with Sting, although, as it happens, the group's music is rather fine – an exhilarating brand of improvised noise-funk that makes virtually any other music sound tame.)

| Whispering Voices | 7" | Wudwink | WUD01 | 1975 | **£25** | **£12.50** | |

LAST FLIGHT

| Dance To The Music | 7" | Heavy Metal | HEAVY5 | 1981 | **£5** | **£2** | |

LAST POETS

The sound of Black Power. The Last Poets deliver their angry, razor-sharp rants over a percussion backing – and if that sounds like a description of rap music, then that is exactly what it is. The rhythms are 1971 rhythms (no drum machines), but the style and the stance is the same.

Chastisement	LP	Blue Thumb	539	1972	**£15**	**£6**	*US*
Last Poets	LP	Douglas	Z30811	1971	**£15**	**£6**	*US*
Right On	LP	Juggernaut	8802	1971	**£15**	**£6**	*US*
This Is Madness	LP	Douglas	DGL69012	1971	**£15**	**£6**	

LAST RESORT

| Having Fun? | 7" | Red Meat | RMRS01 | 1978 | **£10** | **£5** | |

LAST WORDS

| Animal World | 7" | Rough Trade | RT022 | 1979 | **£5** | **£2** | |

LATCHES

| Long Tall Sally | LP | Northern Productions | | 1973 | **£25** | **£10** | *Dutch* |

LATEEF, YUSEF

Autophysiopsychic	LP	CTI	CTI7082	1978	**£10**	**£4**	
Before Dawn	LP	Columbia	33CX10124	1958	**£25**	**£10**	
Blue Lateef	LP	Atlantic	SD1508	1969	**£15**	**£6**	*US*
Club Date	LP	Impulse	IMPL8013	1976	**£10**	**£4**	
Cry! Tender	LP	XTRA	XTRA5040	1968	**£15**	**£6**	
Cry! Tender	LP	Esquire		1961	**£20**	**£8**	
Eastern Sounds	LP	Fontana	688202ZL	1964	**£20**	**£8**	
Gentle Giant	LP	Atlantic	K50051	1973	**£15**	**£6**	
Golden Flute	LP	Impulse	IMPL8036	1976	**£10**	**£4**	
Hush 'n' Thunder	LP	Atlantic	SD1635	1973	**£15**	**£6**	*US*
Live At Pep's	LP	HMV	CLP3547	1964	**£20**	**£8**	
Many Faces Of Yusef Lateef	LP	Milestone	ML47009	1974	**£10**	**£4**	
Part Of The Search	LP	Atlantic	K50041	1974	**£10**	**£4**	
Sax Masters	LP	Vogue	VJD512	1976	**£10**	**£4**	
Sounds Of Yusef	LP	Esquire	32069	1958	**£25**	**£10**	
Suite Sixteen	LP	Atlantic	SD1563	197–	**£15**	**£6**	*US*
Ten Years Hence	LP	Atlantic	K60102	1975	**£10**	**£4**	
Yusef Lateef	LP	Prestige	PR24007	1973	**£10**	**£4**	
Yusef Lateef–Donald Byrd	LP	Delmark	DL407	1967	**£15**	**£6**	

LATTER, GENE

Always	7"	CBS	202655	1967	**£4**	**£1.50**	
Little Piece Of Leather	7"	CBS	2843	1967	**£6**	**£2.50**	
Mother's Little Helper	7"	Decca	F12397	1966	**£6**	**£2.50**	
Sign On The Dotted Line	7"	Spark	SRL1022	1970	**£5**	**£2**	
With A Child's Heart	7"	CBS	2986	1967	**£4**	**£1.50**	

LAUDAN, STANLEY

| Two Guitars | 7" | Oriole | CB1434 | 1958 | **£4** | **£1.50** | |

LAUER, MARTIN

| Wenn Ich Ein Cowboy War | LP | Polydor | 46777/237277 | 1963 | **£20** | **£8** | *German* |

LAUGHING APPLE

Ha-Ha He-He	7"	Autonomy	AUT001	1981	**£5**	**£2**	
Precious Feeling	7"	Essential	ESS001	1982	**£5**	**£2**	

LAUGHING GRAVY

This Beach Boys cover was actually co-produced by Brian Wilson and features Dean Torrence of Jan and Dean on vocals.

| Vegetables | 7" | White Whale | 261 | 1967 | **£60** | **£30** | *US* |

LAUGHING WIND

| Laughing Wind | LP | Tower | | 1967 | **£30** | **£15** | *US* |

LAUPER, CYNDI

Change Of Heart	7"	Portrait	CYNDI1P	1986	**£5**	**£2**	*picture disc*
Heading West	CD-s	Epic	CDCYN6	1989	**£5**	**£2**	
Heading West	CD-s	Epic	CYNC6	1989	**£5**	**£2**	*picture disc*
Hole In My Heart	CD-s	Epic	CYNC3	1988	**£5**	**£2**	
I Drove All Night	CD-s	Epic	CYNC4/ CDCYN4	1989	**£5**	**£2**	*2 versions*
Money Changes Everything	12"	Portrait	TA6009	1985	**£6**	**£2.50**	
My First Night Without You	CD-s	Epic	CDCYN5	1989	**£5**	**£2**	
My First Night Without You	CD-s	Epic	CYNC5	1989	**£8**	**£4**	

My First Night Without You	CD-s	Epic	6550911	1989	£5	£2	3" single
She Bop	7"	Portrait	WA4620	1984	£6	£2.50	picture disc
Time After Time	7"	Portrait	WA4290	1984	£5	£2	picture disc
What's Going On	7"	Portrait	CYNP1	1987	£4	£1.50	picture disc

LAURENCE, ZACK

Beatle Concerto	7" EP	HMV	7EG8968	1966	£5	£2	

LAURENZ, JOHN

Goodbye Stranger Goodbye	7"	London	HL8138	1955	£20	£10	

LAURIE

I Love Onions	7"	Decca	F12424	1966	£4	£1.50	

LAURIE, CY

Cy Laurie Jazz Band	10" LP	Esquire	20037	1955	£15	£6	
Cy Laurie Jazz Band	LP	Esquire	32008	1955	£15	£6	

LAURIE, LINDA

All Winter Long	7"	Top Rank	JAR277	1960	£4	£1.50	
Ambrose	7"	London	HL8807	1959	£6	£2.50	

LAVA

Tears Are Going Home	LP	Brain	1031	1973	£15	£6	German

LAVERN, ROGER & THE MICRONS

Christmas Stocking	7"	Decca	F11791	1963	£25	£12.50	

LAVETTE, BETTY

Doin' The Best I Can	7"	Atlantic	K11198	1978	£4	£1.50	
He Made A Woman Out Of Me	7"	Polydor	56786	1969	£5	£2	
I Feel Good All Over	7"	Pama	PM748	1968	£8	£4	
I Feel Good All Over	7"	Stateside	SS2015	1967	£15	£7.50	
Let Me Down Easy	7"	Mojo	2092030	1972	£4	£1.50	
Your Turn To Cry	7"	Atlantic	K10299	1973	£6	£2.50	

LAWRENCE, AZAR

Bridge Into The New Age	LP	Prestige	P10086	1975	£12	£5	US
Summer Solstice	LP	Prestige	P10097	1976	£12	£5	US

LAWRENCE, AZIE

Jamaica Blues	7"	Melodisc	1563	1960	£4	£1.50	
Love In Every Land	7"	Mezzotone	ME7004	1959	£4	£1.50	
No Dice	7"	Starlite	ST45041	1961	£4	£1.50	
Palms Of Victory	7"	Blue Beat	BB71	1961	£12	£6	
Pempelem	7"	Blue Beat	BB222	1964	£12	£6	
West Indians In England	7"	Starlite	ST45022	1960	£4	£1.50	
West Indians In England	7"	Mezzotone	ME7001/2	1959	£4	£1.50	
You Didn't Want To Know	7"	Melodisc	1572	1960	£4	£1.50	

LAWRENCE, DIANE

I Won't Hang Around Like A Hound Dog	7"	Doctor Bird	DB1075	1967	£10	£5	
Treat Me Nice	7"	Jolly	JY005	1968	£4	£1.50	

LAWRENCE, ELLIOT

Gerry Mulligan Arrangements	LP	Vogue	LAE12057	1957	£10	£4	
Plays Tiny Kahn & Johnny Mandel Arrangements	LP	Vogue	LAE12101	1958	£10	£4	
Swinging At The Steel Pier	LP	Vogue	LAE12071	1958	£10	£4	

LAWRENCE, LARRY

Goofin' Off	7"	Pye	7N25042	1959	£4	£1.50	
Jug-A-Roo	7"	Ember	EMBS106	1960	£4	£1.50	
Squad Car Theme	7"	Ember	EMBS106	1960	£8	£4	picture sleeve

LAWRENCE, LEE

Beyond The Stars	7"	Columbia	SCM5175	1955	£4	£1.50	
By You By You By You	7"	Columbia	DB3885	1957	£4	£1.50	
Chapel Of The Roses	7"	Columbia	DB3922	1957	£4	£1.50	
Don't Tell Me Not To Love You	7"	Columbia	SCM5228	1956	£4	£1.50	
High Upon A Mountain	7"	Columbia	DB3830	1956	£6	£2.50	
Lee Lawrence	7" EP	Columbia	SEG7780	1958	£10	£5	
Lights Of Paris	7"	Decca	F10438	1955	£4	£1.50	
Little Mustard Seed	7"	Decca	F10285	1954	£5	£2	
Lonely Ballerina	7"	Columbia	DB3981	1957	£4	£1.50	
More Than A Millionaire	7"	Columbia	SCM5190	1955	£4	£1.50	
My Own True Love	7"	Decca	F10422	1955	£4	£1.50	
My World Stood Still	7"	Columbia	SCM5181	1955	£4	£1.50	
Presenting Lee Lawrence	10" LP	Decca	LF1132	1953	£15	£6	
Rock'n'Roll Opera	7"	Columbia	DB3855	1956	£12	£6	
Story Of Tina	7"	Decca	F10367	1954	£5	£2	
Suddenly There's A Valley	7"	Columbia	SCM5201	1955	£8	£4	
Things I Didn't Do	7"	Decca	F10408	1954	£4	£1.50	
Valley Valparaiso	7"	Columbia	SCM5283	1956	£4	£1.50	
We Believe In Love	7"	Columbia	SCM5254	1956	£4	£1.50	
Will You Be Mine Alone?	7"	Decca	F10485	1955	£4	£1.50	

LAWRENCE, STEVE

Banana Boat Song	7"	Vogue Coral	Q72228	1957	£5	£2	
Fabulous	7"	Vogue Coral	Q72264	1957	£6	£2.50	
Footsteps	7"	HMV	POP726	1960	£4	£1.50	
Fraulein	7"	Vogue Coral	Q72281	1957	£5	£2	
Here's Steve Lawrence No. 1	7" EP	Coral	FEP2010	1959	£8	£4	
Here's Steve Lawrence No. 2	7" EP	Coral	FEP2012	1959	£8	£4	
Never Mind	7"	Vogue Coral	Q72286	1957	£5	£2	
Open Up The Gates Of Mercy	7"	Vogue Coral	Q72114	1955	£5	£2	
Party Doll	7"	Vogue Coral	Q72243	1957	£6	£2.50	
Portrait Of My Love	LP	HMV	CLP1504/ CSD1404	1962	£10	£4	
Pretty Blue Eyes	7"	HMV	POP689	1960	£4	£1.50	
Songs Everybody Knows	LP	Coral	LVA9219	1964	£10	£4	
Speedo	7"	Vogue Coral	Q72133	1956	£10	£5	
Steve Lawrence	LP	Top Rank	BUY033	1960	£10	£4	
Steve Lawrence Sound	LP	HMV	CLP1462/ CSD1374	1961	£10	£4	
Swing Softly With Me	LP	HMV	CLP1326	1960	£10	£4	
This Night	7"	Parlophone	MSP6038	1953	£8	£4	
Too Little Time	7"	Parlophone	MSP6080	1954	£8	£4	
You Can't Hold A Memory In Your Arms	7"	Parlophone	MSP6106	1954	£8	£4	

LAWRIE, BILLY

Roll Over Beethoven	7"	Polydor	56363	1969	£20	£10	

LAWS, HUBERT

Afro Classic	LP	CTI	CTL7	1972	£10	£4	
Morning Star	LP	CTI	CTL14	1973	£10	£4	

LAWS, RONNIE

Fever	LP	Blue Note	UAG20007	1976	£10	£4	
Flame	LP	Blue Note	UAG30204	1978	£10	£4	
Friends And Strangers	LP	Blue Note	UAG30079	1977	£10	£4	
Pressure Sensitive	LP	Blue Note	BNLA452	1975	£12	£5	
Pressure Sensitive	LP	Blue Note	UAG20002	1976	£10	£4	

LAWSON, JULIET

Boo	LP	Sovereign	SVNA7257	1972	£25	£10	

LAWSON, SHIRLEY

Star	7"	Soul City	SC108	1969	£25	£12.50	

LAWSON-HAGGART JAZZ BAND

Blues On The River	10" LP	Brunswick	LA8580	1953	£12	£5	
Jelly Roll's Jazz	10" LP	Brunswick	LA8576	1953	£12	£5	
King Oliver's Jazz	10" LP	Brunswick	LA8593	1953	£12	£5	
Louis' Hot 5's And 7's	10" LP	Brunswick	LA8698	1955	£12	£5	
Ragtime Jamboree	10" LP	Brunswick	LA8635	1954	£12	£5	
South Of The Mason–Dixon Line	10" LP	Brunswick	LA8703	1955	£12	£5	
Windy City Jazz	10" LP	Brunswick	LA8639	1954	£12	£5	

LAWSON-HAGGART ROCKIN' BAND

Boppin' At The Hop	7" EP	Brunswick	OE9451	1959	£30	£15	
Boppin' At The Hop	LP	Brunswick	LAT8288/ STA3010	1959	£30	£15	

LAWTON, LOU

Doin' The Philly Dog	7"	Ember	EMBS232	1967	£15	£7.50	
I'm Just A Fool	7"	Speciality	SPE1005	1967	£12	£6	

LAY, SAM

In Bluesland	LP	Blue Thumb	BTS8814	1969	£15	£6	*US*

LAYNE, OSSIE

Come Back	7"	R&B	MRB5006	1965	£6	£2.50	

LAYTON, EDDIE

Doodles	7"	Mercury	AMT1064	1959	£4	£1.50	

LAZARUS, KEN

Reggae Greatest Hits Vol. 1	LP	London	ZGJ107	1970	£12	£5	
Reggae Greatest Hits Vol. 2	LP	London	ZGJ108	1970	£12	£5	
Reggae Scorcher	LP	London	LGJ/ZGJ102	1970	£15	£6	

LAZY LESTER

I'm A Lover Not A Fighter	7"	Stateside	SS277	1964	£10	£5	
Made Up My Mind	LP	Blue Horizon	2431007	1971	£60	£30	

LAZY SMOKE

Corridor Of Faces	LP	Onyx	ES6903	1967	£1000	£700	*US*

LE BON, SIMON

Grey Lady Of The Sea	CD-s	Parlophone	DT0001	1988	£60	£30	*promo*

LE CHEILE

Title	Format	Label	Number	Year	Mint	VG	Notes
Airis	LP	Inchecronin	INC7423	1978	**£12**	**£5**	
Lord Mayo	LP	Inchecronin	INC7424	1978	**£12**	**£5**	

LE FORGE, JACK

Title	Format	Label	Number	Year	Mint	VG	Notes
Our Crazy Affair	7"	Stateside	SS444	1965	**£4**	**£1.50**	

LE GRIFFE

Title	Format	Label	Number	Year	Mint	VG	Notes
Breaking Strain	LP	Bullet	BULP2	1984	**£15**	**£6**	
Fast Bikes	12"	Bullet	BOLT1	1983	**£10**	**£5**	
Fast Bikes	7"	Bullet	BOL1	1983	**£5**	**£2**	
You're Killing Me	12"	Bullet	BOLT7	1983	**£12**	**£6**	
You're Killing Me	7"	Bullet	BOL7	1983	**£5**	**£2**	

LE MAT

Title	Format	Label	Number	Year	Mint	VG	Notes
Waltz Of The Fool	7"	Whaam!	WHAAM8	1982	**£4**	**£1.50**	

LE ORME

Title	Format	Label	Number	Year	Mint	VG	Notes
Collage	LP	Philips	6323007	1971	**£15**	**£6**	*Italian*
Contrappunti	LP	Philips	6323035	1974	**£12**	**£5**	*Italian*
Felona And Serona	LP	Charisma	CAS1072	1973	**£15**	**£6**	
Florian	LP	Philips	6323086	1979	**£10**	**£4**	*Italian*
In Concert	LP	Philips	6323028	1974	**£15**	**£6**	*Italian*
Piccola Rapsodie Dell Ape	LP	Philips	6323102	1980	**£10**	**£4**	*Italian*
Smogmagica	LP	Philips	6323041	1975	**£12**	**£5**	*Italian*
Storia O Legganda	LP	Philips	6323052	1977	**£10**	**£4**	*Italian*
Uomo Di Pezza	LP	Philips	6323013	1972	**£15**	**£6**	*Italian*
Venerdi	LP	Polydor	2393341	1982	**£10**	**£4**	*Italian*
Verita Nascoste	LP	Philips	6323045	1976	**£12**	**£5**	*Italian*

LE REVE DU DIABLE

Title	Format	Label	Number	Year	Mint	VG	Notes
Le Rêve Du Diable	LP	Escargot	ESC352	1977	**£20**	**£8**	*French*

LE RITZ

Title	Format	Label	Number	Year	Mint	VG	Notes
Punker	7"	Breaker	BS2001	1977	**£20**	**£10**	

LE SAGE, BILL

Title	Format	Label	Number	Year	Mint	VG	Notes
Bill's Recipes	LP	Saga	STM6019	1959	**£12**	**£5**	
Presenting The Bill Le Sage/Ronnie Ross Quartet	LP	World		196–	**£15**	**£6**	

LEA, BARBARA

Title	Format	Label	Number	Year	Mint	VG	Notes
In Love	LP	Esquire	32063	1957	**£10**	**£4**	
Nobody Else But Me	LP	Esquire	32043	1956	**£10**	**£4**	
Woman In Love	10" LP	London	HBU1058	1956	**£10**	**£4**	

LEA, JIMMY

Title	Format	Label	Number	Year	Mint	VG	Notes
Citizen Kane	7"	Trojan	KANE001	1985	**£10**	**£5**	

LEA VALLEY SKIFFLE GROUP

Title	Format	Label	Number	Year	Mint	VG	Notes
Lea Valley Skiffle Group	7" EP	Esquire	EP163	1958	**£40**	**£20**	

LEADBELLY

Title	Format	Label	Number	Year	Mint	VG	Notes
Alabama Bound	7"	HMV	MH190	1955	**£10**	**£5**	*with Golden Gate Quartet*
Backwater Blues	78	Capitol	CL13282	1950	**£8**	**£3**	
Classics In Jazz	10" LP	Capitol	LC6597	1953	**£20**	**£8**	
Demon Of A Man	LP	Storyville	SLP124	1964	**£10**	**£4**	
From The Last Sessions	LP	Folkways	3019	1967	**£10**	**£4**	*US*
Good Morning Blues	LP	RCA	RD7567	1963	**£10**	**£4**	
His Guitar, His Voice, His Piano	LP	Capitol	T1821	1963	**£10**	**£4**	
How Long Blues	7" EP	Melodisc	EPM763	1956	**£12**	**£6**	
Huddie Ledbetter	10" LP	Folkways	2013	1960	**£20**	**£8**	*US*
Keep Your Hands Off Her	LP	Verve	(S)VLP5011	1967	**£10**	**£4**	
Last Sessions Vol. 1	LP	Melodisc	MLP12113	1959	**£15**	**£6**	
Last Sessions Vol. 2	LP	Melodisc	MLP12114	1959	**£15**	**£6**	
Leadbelly	10" LP	Folkways	4	1960	**£12**	**£5**	*US*
Leadbelly	10" LP	Folkways	24	1960	**£12**	**£5**	*US*
Leadbelly	10" LP	Folkways	43	1960	**£12**	**£5**	*US*
Leadbelly	10" LP	Folkways	14	1960	**£12**	**£5**	*US*
Leadbelly	10" LP	Capitol	H369	195–	**£75**	**£37.50**	*US*
Leadbelly	7" EP	Capitol	EAP120111	1961	**£8**	**£4**	
Leadbelly	7" EP	Melodisc	EPM777	1958	**£12**	**£6**	
Leadbelly	7" EP	Storyville	SEP337	196–	**£8**	**£4**	
Leadbelly 2	LP	Storyville	SLP139	1964	**£10**	**£4**	
Leadbelly Box	LP	XTRA	XTRA1017	1965	**£15**	**£6**	*double*
Leadbelly Vol. 1	10" LP	Melodisc	MLP511	1957	**£15**	**£6**	
Leadbelly Vol. 2	10" LP	Melodisc	MLP512	1957	**£15**	**£6**	
Leadbelly Vol. 3	10" LP	Melodisc	MLP515	1958	**£15**	**£6**	
Ledbetter's Best	7" EP	Capitol	EAP41821	1961	**£8**	**£4**	
Ledbetter's Best	7" EP	Capitol	EAP11821	1961	**£8**	**£4**	
Library Of Congress Recordings	LP	Elektra	EKL301/2	1966	**£25**	**£10**	*3 LPs, boxed*
Memorial Vol. 3	LP	Stinson	SLP48	1962	**£15**	**£6**	*US, red vinyl*
Midnight Special	LP	RCA	LPV505	1964	**£10**	**£4**	*US*
Party Plays And Songs	7" EP	Melodisc	EPM787	1959	**£10**	**£5**	
Plays Party Songs	10" LP	Melodisc	MLP517	1958	**£15**	**£6**	
Rock Island Line	10" LP	Folkways	2014	1960	**£20**	**£8**	*US*

Rock Island Line	7" EP	RCA	RCX146	1959	**£8**	**£4**	
Saga Of Leadbelly	LP	Melodisc	MLP12107	1958	**£15**	**£6**	
See See Rider	7" EP	Melodisc	EPM782	1958	**£12**	**£6**	
Shout On	LP	XTRA	XTRA1126	1971	**£15**	**£6**	
Sinful Songs	10" LP	Allegro	4027	195–	**£30**	**£15**	*US*
Sings And Plays	LP	Society	SOC994	1965	**£10**	**£4**	
Sings Folk Songs	LP	XTRA	XTRA1046	1966	**£15**	**£6**	
Storyville Blues Anthology Vol. 7	7" EP	Storyville	SEP387	1963	**£8**	**£4**	
Take This Hammer	LP	Verve	(S)VLP5002	1965	**£10**	**£4**	

LEADERBEATS

Dance, Dance Dance	7"	Top Rank	JAR405	1960	**£4**	**£1.50**	

LEADERS

Night People	7"	Fontana	TF602	1965	**£5**	**£2**	

LEADERS (2)

Tit For Tat	7"	Amalgamated	AMG804	1968	**£10**	**£5**	*Marvetts B side*

LEADING FIGURES

Oscillation '67	LP	Deram	DML/SML1006	1967	**£15**	**£6**	
Sound And Movement	LP	Ace Of Clubs	SCL1225	1967	**£30**	**£15**	

LEAFHOUND

Some records gain a reputation within the collectors' market out of all proportion to their musical worth. The Leafhound LP is very much a case in point – the cover and its title imply some kind of psychedelic masterpiece, whereas the music is actually rather ordinary hard rock, with a singer who would love to be Robert Plant, but who sadly is not. The singer, Pete French, actually managed to sustain a surprisingly lengthy rock career, including stints with Brunning Hall Sunflower Blues Band and Black Cat Bones (a group that effectively evolved directly into Leafhound) before making *Growers Of Mushrooms*, and with Big Bertha, Atomic Rooster, Cactus and Randy Pie afterwards.

Growers Of Mushrooms	LP	Decca	SKLR5094	1971	**£600**	**£400**	
Growers Of Mushrooms	LP	Discwasher	TP396	1978	**£50**	**£25**	*US, with poster*
Leafhound	LP	Telefunken	SLE14604	1970	**£75**	**£37.50**	*German*

LEAGUE OF GENTLEMEN

Each Little Falling Tear	7"	Columbia	DB7666	1965	**£30**	**£15**	
How Can You Tell	7"	Planet	PLF109	1966	**£30**	**£15**	

LEAPER, BOB

High Wire	7"	Pye	7N15700	1965	**£20**	**£10**	

LEAPERS CREEPERS SLEEPERS

Ba Boo	7"	Island	WI275	1966	**£6**	**£2.50**	

LEAR, KEVIN 'KING'

Count Me Out	7"	Polydor	BM56203	1967	**£10**	**£5**	
Cry Me A River	7"	Page One	POF109	1968	**£8**	**£4**	
Power Of Love	7"	Page One	POF087	1968	**£4**	**£1.50**	
Snake	7"	Page One	POF132	1969	**£6**	**£2.50**	

LEARY, TIMOTHY

L.S.D.	LP	Pixie	CA1069	1966	**£100**	**£50**	*US*
Origins Of Dance	12"	Evolution	EVO1	1990	**£6**	**£2.50**	*with The Grid*
Turn On, Tune In, Drop Out	LP	ESP-Disk	1027	1966	**£40**	**£20**	*US*
Turn On, Tune In, Drop Out	LP	Mercury	MG2/SR61131	1967	**£30**	**£15**	*US*
You Can Be Anyone This Time Around	LP	Douglas	1	196–	**£50**	**£25**	*US*

LEATHER COATED MINDS

The album by the Leather Coated Minds contains the recording debut of J. J. Cale, although those seeking the roots of his inimitable sleepy guitar and singing style will be disappointed. Instead the music is exactly the kind of fare that bad sixties films included in their soundtracks whenever a party was shown. As is often the case in the record collectors' market, a high price tag is no guarantee of musical quality.

Trip Down Sunset Strip	LP	Fontana	(S)TL5412	1967	**£40**	**£20**	

LEATHER NUN

Slow Death	7"	Industrial	IR0006	1979	**£8**	**£4**	

LEAVES

All The Good That's Happening	LP	Capitol	(S)T2638	1967	**£75**	**£37.50**	*US*
Hey Joe	7"	Fontana	TF713	1966	**£20**	**£10**	
Hey Joe	LP	Mira	LP(S)3005	1966	**£50**	**£25**	*US*

LEAVILL, OTIS

There's Nothing Better	7"	Atlantic	2091160	1971	**£5**	**£2**	

LED ZEPPELIN

Original pressings of the Led Zeppelin LPs I–IV are easily identified by their purple and red Atlantic labels and pre-Kinney catalogue numbers, but for the very first LP, it is possible to identify which copies were issued during the few weeks following its release. These all have covers on which the title and company name are printed in turquoise, instead of the orange which has been used on every copy since. Similarly, the very first copies of the third LP are identifiable by the message 'Do what thou wilt' scratched in the vinyl, although there are many more copies like this than some collectors imagine. The rarest Led Zeppelin records are the early UK singles, which exist in demonstration form only due to the group's constant refusal to allow their full commercial release.

Black Dog	7"	Atlantic	2849	1971	**£5**	**£2**	*US*
Collector's Item	CD-s	Atlantic	PRCD27	1995	**£50**	**£25**	*4 track German promo*
Communication Breakdown	7"	Atlantic	584269	1969	**£400**	**£250**	*demo, best auctioned*

D'yer Maker	7"	Atlantic	2986	1973	£5	£2	US
D'yer Maker	7"	Atlantic	K10296	1973	£125	£62.50	demo
Dazed And Confused	7" EP	Atlantic	1019	1969	£250	£150	US
Good Times Bad Times	7"	Atlantic	2613	1969	£10	£5	US
Houses Of The Holy	7" EP	Atlantic	PR213	1973	£75	£37.50	US promo
Immigrant Song	7"	Atlantic	2777	1970	£8	£4	US
In Through The Out Door	LP	Swansong	SSK59410	1979	£75	£37.50	set of 6 LPs in different sleeves A-F
Led Zeppelin	7" EP	Atlantic	171	1970	£100	£50	US
Led Zeppelin	LP	Atlantic	588171	1969	£75	£37.50	turquoise lettering on cover
Led Zeppelin	LP	Atlantic	588171	1969	£20	£8	
Led Zeppelin 2	LP	Atlantic	588198	1969	£15	£6	
Led Zeppelin 2	LP	Mobile Fidelity	MFSL1065	1980	£25	£10	US audiophile
Led Zeppelin 3	LP	Atlantic	2401012	1970	£150	£75	test pressing with alternate mixes
Led Zeppelin 3	LP	Atlantic	SD7201	1971	£50	£25	US mono promo
Led Zeppelin 3	LP	Atlantic	2401002	1970	£15	£6	
Led Zeppelin 4	LP	Atlantic	2401012	1971	£15	£6	
Led Zeppelin 4	LP	Atlantic	K50008/C8814	1988	£15	£6	HMV boxed set
Led Zeppelin 4	LP	Atlantic	K50008	1978	£30	£15	lilac vinyl
Led Zeppelin IV	CD	Atlantic	K50008/C8814	1988	£20	£8	HMV boxed set
Over The Hills And Far Away	7"	Atlantic	2970	1973	£5	£2	US
Profiled!	CD	Atlantic	PRCD36292	1990	£40	£20	US promo
Remasters	10"	Atlantic	LZ2	1990	£20	£10	4 track promo
Remasters	CD-s	Atlantic	CDLZ1	1990	£25	£12.50	4 track promo
Rock And Roll	7"	Atlantic	2865	1972	£5	£2	US
Stairway To Heaven	7"	Atlantic	LZ3	1990	£50	£25	promo with letter
Stairway To Heaven	7"	Atlantic	LZ3LC	1990	£12	£6	jukebox issue
Stairway To Heaven	7" EP	Atlantic	PR175	1973	£100	£50	US promo, picture sleeve
Stairway To Heaven	7" EP	Atlantic	PR269	1973	£40	£20	US promo
Trampled Underfoot	7"	Swan Song	DC1	1979	£10	£5	custom sleeve
Whole Lotta Love	7"	Atlantic	584309	1969	£400	£250	demo, best auctioned
Whole Lotta Love	7"	Atlantic	2690	1969	£5	£2	US

LED ZEPPELIN & DUSTY SPRINGFIELD

Climb Aboard Led Zeppelin/Dusty In Memphis	LP	Atlantic	TLST135	1969	£50	£25	US promo

LEE, ARTHUR

Ninth Wave	7"	Capitol	4980	1964	£30	£15	US
Vindicator	LP	A&M	AMLS64356	1972	£12	£5	

LEE, BENNY

Love Plays The Strings Of My Banjo	7"	Parlophone	MSP6214	1956	£4	£1.50	
Rock'n'Rollin' Santa Claus	7"	Parlophone	R4245	1956	£15	£7.50	
Sweet Heartaches	7"	Parlophone	MSP6252	1956	£4	£1.50	

LEE, BRENDA

Ain't Gonna Cry No More	7"	Brunswick	05963	1966	£4	£1.50	
Ain't That Love	7"	Brunswick	05720	1957	£75	£37.50	
All Alone Am I	7" EP	Brunswick	OE9492	1963	£25	£12.50	
All Alone Am I	LP	Brunswick	LAT/STA8530	1962	£15	£6	
All The Way	LP	Brunswick	LAT8383/ STA3048	1961	£15	£6	
Bill Bailey	7"	Brunswick	05780	1959	£10	£5	tri-centre
By Request	LP	Brunswick	LAT/STA8576	1964	£15	£6	
Bye Bye Blues	LP	Brunswick	LAT/STA8649	1966	£15	£6	
Call Me	LP	MCA	MUP(S)321	1968	£10	£4	
Christmas Will Be Just Another Lonely Day	7"	Brunswick	05921	1964	£4	£1.50	
Coming On Strong	7"	Brunswick	05967	1966	£4	£1.50	
Coming On Strong	LP	Brunswick	LAT/STA8672	1967	£15	£6	
Dum Dum	7"	Brunswick	05854	1961	£4	£1.50	
Emotions	LP	Brunswick	LAT8376/ STA3044	1961	£15	£6	
Fairyland	7"	Decca	BM31186	1958	£40	£20	export
For The First Time	LP	MCA	MUP(S)332	1968	£10	£4	with Pete Fountain
Four From Sixty Four	7" EP	Brunswick	OE9510	1965	£25	£12.50	
Good Life	LP	MCA	MUP(S)322	1968	£10	£4	
Grandma What Great Songs	LP	Brunswick	LAT8319	1958	£40	£20	
I Want To Be Wanted	7"	Brunswick	05839	1960	£4	£1.50	
I'm Gonna Lassoo Santa Claus	7"	Brunswick	05628	1956	£125	£62.50	
I'm Sorry	7"	Brunswick	05833	1960	£5	£2	
Is It True	7"	Brunswick	05915	1964	£4	£1.50	
Johnny One Time	LP	MCA	MUP(S)396	1970	£10	£4	
Let Me Sing	LP	Brunswick	LAT/STA8548	1963	£15	£6	
Let's Jump The Broomstick	7"	Brunswick	05823	1960	£4	£1.50	
Love You	LP	Ace Of Hearts	AH59	1963	£20	£8	
Love You Till I Die	7"	Brunswick	05685	1957	£100	£50	
Merry Christmas	LP	MCA	MUP(S)330	1968	£10	£4	
Merry Christmas From Brenda	LP	Brunswick	LAT/STA8590	1964	£15	£6	
Miss Dynamite	LP	Brunswick	LAT8347	1959	£30	£15	
Pretend	7" EP	Brunswick	OE9482	1962	£30	£15	
Reflections In Blue	LP	MCA	MUP(S)306	1968	£10	£4	

Title	Format	Label	Cat. No.	Year	Mint	VG	Notes
Ring-A My Phone	7"	Brunswick	05755	1958	£100	£50	
Rock The Bop	7" EP	Brunswick	OE9462	1959	£50	£25	*tri-centre*
Rockin' Around The Christmas Tree	7"	Brunswick	05880	1962	£4	£1.50	
Show For Christmas Seals	LP	Decca	MG(7)9226	1962	£15	£6	*US*
Sincerely	LP	Brunswick	LAT8396/ STA3056	1961	£15	£6	
Speak To Me Pretty	7" EP	Brunswick	OE9488	1962	£25	£12.50	
Sweet Nothings	7"	Brunswick	05819	1960	£15	£7.50	*tri-centre*
Ten Golden Years	LP	Decca	DL(7)4757	1966	£12	£5	*US, gatefold*
That's All	LP	Brunswick	LAT/STA8516	1962	£15	£6	
That's All Right	7"	Decca	AD1003	1968	£8	£4	*export*
This Is Brenda Lee	LP	Brunswick	LAT8360	1960	£25	£10	
Too Many Rivers	LP	Brunswick	LAT/STA8622	1965	£15	£6	
Top Teen Hits	LP	Brunswick	LAT/STA8603	1965	£15	£6	
Tribute To Al Jolson	7" EP	Brunswick	OE9499	1964	£25	£12.50	
Versatile Brenda Lee	LP	Brunswick	LAT8614	1965	£15	£6	
Where's The Melody	7"	Brunswick	05976	1967	£4	£1.50	

LEE, BUNNY ALL STARS

Title	Format	Label	Cat. No.	Year	Mint	VG	Notes
Leaping With Mr Lee	LP	Island	ILP986	1968	£100	£50	*pink label*
Stanley	7"	Smash	SMA2304	1971	£4	£1.50	

LEE, BYRON

Title	Format	Label	Cat. No.	Year	Mint	VG	Notes
Byron Lee & The Dragonaires	LP	Major Minor	SMLP53	1969	£10	£4	
Caribbean Jungle	LP	Island	ILP905	1964	£40	£20	
Dumplings	7"	Blue Beat	BB2	1960	£12	£6	*Buddy Davidson B side*
Every Day Will Be Like A Holiday	7"	Major Minor	MM615	1969	£4	£1.50	
Jamaica Ska	7"	Parlophone	R5182	1964	£5	£2	
Joy Ride	7"	Starlite	ST45045	1961	£5	£2	
Mash Mr Lee	7"	Blue Beat	BB28	1961	£12	£6	*Keith Lynn B side*
Mr Walker	7"	Trojan	TR631	1968	£4	£1.50	
My Sweet Lord	7"	Dynamic	DYN409	1971	£4	£1.50	
Night Train From Jamaica	7"	MGM	MGM1256	1964	£5	£2	
Reggae	LP	Trojan	TRLS18	1972	£10	£4	
Reggae Blast Off	LP	Trojan	TBL110	1970	£10	£4	
Reggae Hot Cool Easy	LP	Trojan	TRLS40	1972	£10	£4	
Reggae Splash Down	LP	Trojan	TRLS28	1972	£10	£4	
River Bank	7"	Parlophone	R5124	1964	£5	£2	
Rocksteady Explosion	LP	Trojan	TTL5	1969	£10	£4	
Say Bye Bye	7"	Parlophone	R5140	1964	£5	£2	
Ska Time	7" EP	Atlantic	AET6014	1965	£50	£25	
Sloopy	7"	Doctor Bird	DB1003	1966	£10	£5	
Sloopy	7"	Pyramid	PYR6015	1967	£4	£1.50	
Soul Limbo	7"	Trojan	TR624	1968	£4	£1.50	
Soul Serenade	7"	Duke	DU39	1969	£4	£1.50	
Sound Of Jamaica	LP	Tower Hall	LP006	1970	£25	£10	*US*
Sour Apples	7"	Parlophone	R5125	1964	£5	£2	
Too Late	7"	Parlophone	R5177	1964	£5	£2	
Walk Like A Dragon	7"	Island	WI220	1965	£10	£5	*Ken Lazarus B side*
Way Back Home	7"	Dynamic	DYN414	1971	£4	£1.50	

LEE, CHRISTOPHER

Title	Format	Label	Cat. No.	Year	Mint	VG	Notes
Hammer Presents Dracula	LP	Columbia	TWOQ45001	1974	£10	£4	*quad*

LEE, CURTIS

Title	Format	Label	Cat. No.	Year	Mint	VG	Notes
Get My Bag	7"	CBS	2717	1967	£15	£7.50	
Night At Daddy Gees	7"	London	HLX9533	1962	£10	£5	
Pledge Of Love	7"	London	HLX9313	1961	£12	£6	
Pretty Little Angel Eyes	7"	London	HLX9397	1961	£10	£5	
Under The Moon Of Love	7"	London	HLX9445	1961	£10	£5	
With All My Heart	7"	Top Rank	JAR317	1960	£25	£12.50	

LEE, DAVE

Title	Format	Label	Cat. No.	Year	Mint	VG	Notes
Adam Adamant	7"	Fontana	TF723	1966	£4	£1.50	
Our Man Crichton	LP	Colpix	PXL550	196–	£20	£8	
Take Four	7"	Decca	F11600	1963	£4	£1.50	

LEE, DEREK

Title	Format	Label	Cat. No.	Year	Mint	VG	Notes
Girl	7"	Parlophone	R5468	1966	£5	£2	

LEE, DICKIE

Title	Format	Label	Cat. No.	Year	Mint	VG	Notes
I Saw Linda Yesterday	7"	Mercury	AMT1196	1962	£5	£2	
Patches	7"	Mercury	AMT1190	1962	£4	£1.50	
Penny A Kiss, A Penny A Hug	7"	MGM	MGM1013	1959	£20	£10	

LEE, DINAH

Title	Format	Label	Cat. No.	Year	Mint	VG	Notes
I Can't Believe What You Say	7"	Aladdin	WI608	1965	£8	£4	
I'll Forgive You Then Forget You	7"	Aladdin	WI606	1965	£6	£2.50	

LEE, DON TONY

Title	Format	Label	Cat. No.	Year	Mint	VG	Notes
It's Reggae Time	7"	Big Shot	BI504	1968	£6	£2.50	*Errol Dunkley B side*
It's Reggae Time	7"	Island	WI3160	1968	£10	£5	*Errol Dunkley B side*
Lee's Special	7"	Doctor Bird	DB1106	1967	£10	£5	*Lloyd & The Groovers B side*

LEE, FREDDIE FINGERS

Pianist Lee recorded these three singles in his own name, together with a fourth as At Last The 1958 Rock'n' Roll Show. Ian Hunter, known by his real name of Ian Patterson at the time, played bass in the band.

Title	Format	Label	Cat. No.	Year	Mint	VG	Notes
Bossy Boss	7"	Columbia	DB8002	1966	£5	£2	
Friendly Undertaker	7"	Fontana	TF619	1965	£10	£5	
I'm Gonna Buy Me A Dog	7"	Fontana	TF655	1966	£8	£4	

LEE, JACKIE

Title	Format	Label	Cat. No.	Year	Mint	VG	Notes
Duck	7"	Fontana	TF646	1965	£10	£5	
Duck	7"	London	HLM10233	1968	£4	£1.50	
Duck	LP	Mirwood	SW7000	1966	£20	£8	US
Duck	LP	London	HAM8336	1967	£12	£5	
Whether It's Right Or Wrong	7"	B&C	CB105	1969	£4	£1.50	*with Delores Hall*

LEE, JACKIE (2)

Title	Format	Label	Cat. No.	Year	Mint	VG	Notes
Down Our Street	7"	Philips	BF1283	1963	£4	£1.50	*with the Raindrops*
End Of The World	7"	Oriole	CB1800	1963	£4	£1.50	*with the Raindrops*
Here I Go Again	7"	Philips	BF1328	1963	£4	£1.50	*with the Raindrops*
I Was The Last One To Know	7"	Oriole	CB1702	1962	£4	£1.50	*with the Raindrops*
Lonely Clown	7"	Columbia	DB7685	1965	£4	£1.50	
Party Lights	7"	Oriole	CB1757	1962	£4	£1.50	*with the Raindrops*
There Goes The Lucky One	7"	Oriole	CB1727	1962	£4	£1.50	*with the Raindrops*
Town I Live In	7"	Columbia	DB8052	1966	£5	£2	

LEE, JAMIE & THE ATLANTICS

Title	Format	Label	Cat. No.	Year	Mint	VG	Notes
In The Night	7"	Decca	F11571	1963	£25	£12.50	

LEE, JIMMY

Title	Format	Label	Cat. No.	Year	Mint	VG	Notes
All My Life	7"	Starlite	ST45059	1961	£12	£6	

LEE, JOHNNIE

Title	Format	Label	Cat. No.	Year	Mint	VG	Notes
Echo	7"	Pye	7N15201	1959	£4	£1.50	
I'm Finally Free	7"	Pye	7N15233	1959	£4	£1.50	
Kiss Tomorrow Goodbye	7"	CBS	202591	1967	£4	£1.50	

LEE, JULIA

Title	Format	Label	Cat. No.	Year	Mint	VG	Notes
Party Time	10" LP	Capitol	LC6535	1952	£40	£20	
Party Time	LP	Capitol	T228	1955	£30	£15	US

LEE, LADY

Title	Format	Label	Cat. No.	Year	Mint	VG	Notes
My Whole World	7"	Columbia	DB7121	1965	£5	£2	
When Love Comes Along	7"	Decca	F11961	1964	£4	£1.50	

LEE, LAURA

Title	Format	Label	Cat. No.	Year	Mint	VG	Notes
As Long As I Got You	7"	Chess	CRS8070	1968	£4	£1.50	
Dirty Man	7"	Chess	CRS8062	1967	£4	£1.50	
Two Sides Of Laura Lee	LP	Hot Wax	SHW5009	1972	£12	£5	
Woman's Love Rights	LP	Hot Wax	SHW5006	1972	£12	£5	

LEE, LAURA (2)

Title	Format	Label	Cat. No.	Year	Mint	VG	Notes
Brand New Heartbeat	7"	Decca	F11513	1962	£5	£2	
Love In Every Room	7"	Columbia	DB8495	1968	£4	£1.50	
Tell Tommy I Miss Him	7"	Triumph	RGM1030	1960	£20	£10	

LEE, LEAPY

Although comedian Lee Graham made a large number of singles and scored a top five hit with one of them ('Little Arrows'), his sole collectors' item is sought after because Ray Davies wrote and produced the A side, using members of the Kinks to provide the musical backing.

Title	Format	Label	Cat. No.	Year	Mint	VG	Notes
King Of The Whole Wide World	7"	Decca	F12369	1966	£20	£10	

LEE, MICKEY

Title	Format	Label	Cat. No.	Year	Mint	VG	Notes
Hello My Little Queen	7"	Smash	SMA2332	1973	£8	£4	*Augustus Pablo B side*

LEE, NICKIE

Title	Format	Label	Cat. No.	Year	Mint	VG	Notes
And Black Is Beautiful	7"	Deep Soul	DS9103	1970	£4	£1.50	

LEE, PEGGY

Title	Format	Label	Cat. No.	Year	Mint	VG	Notes
All Aglow Again	LP	Capitol	T1366	1961	£10	£4	
Alright Okay You Win	7" EP	Capitol	EAP11213	1959	£5	£2	
Basin Street East Presents	LP	Capitol	(S)T1520	1962	£10	£4	
Baubles, Bangles And Beads	7"	Brunswick	05421	1955	£4	£1.50	
Beauty And The Beat	LP	Capitol	(S)T1219	1960	£10	£4	*with George Shearing*
Beauty And The Beat Pt 1	7" EP	Capitol	EAP71219	1960	£5	£2	*with George Shearing*
Beauty And The Beat Pt 2	7" EP	Capitol	EAP81219	1960	£5	£2	*with George Shearing*
Beauty And The Beat Pt 3	7" EP	Capitol	EAP91219	1960	£5	£2	*with George Shearing*
Bella Notte	7"	Brunswick	05483	1955	£4	£1.50	
Black Coffee	10" LP	Brunswick	LA8629	1953	£15	£6	
Black Coffee	LP	Decca	DL8358	1956	£15	£6	US
Black Coffee	LP	Ace Of Hearts	AH5	1961	£10	£4	
Blues Cross Country	LP	Capitol	(S)T1671	1962	£10	£4	
Capitol Presents Peggy Lee	10" LP	Capitol	LC6584	1953	£15	£6	
Christmas Carousel	LP	Capitol	(S)T1423	1961	£10	£4	
Dream Street	LP	Brunswick	LAT8171	1957	£12	£5	

Title	Format	Label	Number	Year	Price		Notes
Favourites	7" EP	Capitol	EAP120074	1961	£5	£2	
Fever	7"	Capitol	CL14902	1958	£4	£1.50	
Fever	7" EP	Capitol	EAP11052	1959	£6	£2.50	
He Needs Me	7"	Brunswick	05472	1955	£4	£1.50	
He's A Tramp	7"	Brunswick	05482	1955	£6	£2.50	
I Belong To You	7"	Brunswick	05435	1955	£4	£1.50	
I Go To Sleep	7"	Capitol	CL15413	1965	£4	£1.50	
I Like Men	LP	Capitol	(S)T1131	1959	£10	£4	
I'm A Woman	7" EP	Capitol	EAP41857	1961	£5	£2	
If You Go	LP	Capitol	(S)T1630	1962	£10	£4	
In The Name Of Love	7" EP	Capitol	EAP42096	1963	£5	£2	
Is That All There Is?	LP	Capitol	T386	1956	£12	£5	*US*
Johnny Guitar	7"	Brunswick	05286	1954	£6	£2.50	
Jump For Joy	7" EP	Capitol	EAP1979	1958	£5	£2	
Jump For Joy	LP	Capitol	(S)T979	1957	£10	£4	
Lady And The Tramp	10" LP	Brunswick	LA8731	1956	£15	£6	
Latin A La Lee	LP	Capitol	(S)T1290	1960	£10	£4	
Latin A La Lee Pt 1	7" EP	Capitol	SEP51290	1961	£5	£2	*stereo*
Latin A La Lee Pt 2	7" EP	Capitol	SEP61290	1961	£5	£2	*stereo*
Latin A La Lee Pt 3	7" EP	Capitol	SEP71290	1961	£5	£2	*stereo*
Let Me Go Lover	7"	Brunswick	05360	1955	£6	£2.50	
Man I Love	LP	Capitol	T864	1956	£10	£4	
Mink Jazz	LP	Capitol	(S)T1850	1964	£10	£4	
Miss Wonderful	LP	Brunswick	LAT8287	1959	£10	£4	
Mr Wonderful	7"	Brunswick	05671	1957	£4	£1.50	
My Best To You	10" LP	Capitol	H204	1952	£20	£8	*US*
My Best To You	10" LP	Capitol	LC6817	1956	£15	£6	
Olé A La Lee	LP	Capitol	(S)T1475	1966	£10	£4	
Olé A La Lee Pt 1	7" EP	Capitol	SEP11475	1961	£5	£2	*stereo*
Olé A La Lee Pt 2	7" EP	Capitol	SEP21475	1961	£5	£2	*stereo*
Ooh That Kiss	7"	Brunswick	05461	1955	£4	£1.50	
Peggy With Benny	7" EP	Philips	BBE12172	1958	£5	£2	*with Benny Goodman*
Pete Kelly's Blues	LP	Brunswick	LAT8078	1955	£12	£5	
Pete Kelly's Blues No. 1	7" EP	Brunswick	OE9153	1955	£6	£2.50	
Pete Kelly's Blues No. 2	7" EP	Brunswick	OE9154	1955	£6	£2.50	
Presenting Peggy Lee	7" EP	Brunswick	OE9282	1956	£6	£2.50	
Pretty Eyes	LP	Capitol	(S)T1401	1960	£10	£4	
Rendezvous	10" LP	Capitol	H155	1952	£20	£8	*US*
Sea Shells	LP	Brunswick	LAT8266	1958	£12	£5	
Sea Shells Part 1	7" EP	Brunswick	OE9400	1958	£6	£2.50	
Sea Shells Part 2	7" EP	Brunswick	OE9401	1958	£6	£2.50	
Sisters	7"	Brunswick	05345	1954	£5	£2	
Songs In An Intimate Style	10" LP	Brunswick	LA8717	1955	£15	£6	
Songs In Intimate Style	10" LP	Decca	DL5539	1953	£20	£8	*US*
Straight Ahead	7"	Brunswick	05368	1955	£5	£2	
Sugar	7"	Brunswick	05471	1955	£4	£1.50	
Sugar And Spice	7" EP	Capitol	EAP11772	1961	£5	£2	
Things Are Swingin'	7" EP	Capitol	EAP11049	1959	£5	£2	
Things Are Swingin'	LP	Capitol	T1049	1959	£10	£4	
Three Cheers For Mister Magoo	7"	Brunswick	05549	1956	£4	£1.50	

LEE, ROBERTA

Title	Format	Label	Number	Year	Price		Notes
Ridin' To Tennessee	7"	Brunswick	05388	1955	£5	£2	
True Love And Tender Care	7"	HMV	7M261	1954	£4	£1.50	

LEE, ROBIN

Title	Format	Label	Number	Year	Price		Notes
Gamblin' Man	7"	Reprise	R20068	1962	£6	£2.50	

LEE, VINNY & THE RIDERS

Title	Format	Label	Number	Year	Price		Notes
Gamblers Guitar	7"	HMV	POP856	1961	£5	£2	

LEE, WARREN

Title	Format	Label	Number	Year	Price		Notes
Underdog Backstreet	7"	Pama	PM762	1969	£4	£1.50	

LEE & JIMMY

Title	Format	Label	Number	Year	Price		Notes
Rasta Train	7"	Dip	DL5075	1975	£5	£2	

LEE KINGS

Title	Format	Label	Number	Year	Price		Notes
Bingo	LP	RCA	10106	1966	£30	£15	*Swedish*

LEEMAN, MARK FIVE

A popular live act, the Mark Leeman Five had their first single produced by Manfred Mann. When vocalist Leeman was killed in a car crash after recording the second single, the group decided to keep the name, although without him their music lacked a crucial ingredient. Drummer Brian Davison subsequently joined the Nice.

Title	Format	Label	Number	Year	Price		Notes
Blow My Blues Away	7"	Columbia	DB7648	1965	£15	£7.50	
Follow Me	7"	Columbia	DB7955	1966	£10	£5	
Forbidden Fruit	7"	Columbia	DB7812	1966	£10	£5	
Portland Town	7"	Columbia	DB7452	1965	£10	£5	

LEER, THOMAS

Title	Format	Label	Number	Year	Price		Notes
Bridge	LP	Industrial	IR0007	1979	£10	£4	*with Robert Rental*
Private Plane	7"	Oblique	ER101	1978	£6	£2.50	

LEES, JOHN

Title	Format	Label	Number	Year	Price		Notes
Best Of My Love	7"	Polydor	2058513	1974	£10	£5	

LEESIDERS

Title	Format	Label	Cat. No.	Year	Mint	Good	Notes
Leesiders	LP	Ash	ALP105S	1970	£50	£25	

LEFEVRE, RAYMOND

Title	Format	Label	Cat. No.	Year	Mint	Good	Notes
Soul Coaxing	7"	Major Minor	MM559	1968	£4	£1.50	

LEFT BANKE

The delicate chamber and pop music made by the Left Banke is one of the overlooked delights of the sixties. Songs like 'Walk Away Renee' (covered by the Four Tops), 'Pretty Ballerina' and 'Desiree' are distinctive – beautiful even – and they were hits in America, but not Britain. The group's creative centre was pianist Michael Brown, but he rather squandered his talents by continual indecision as to whether he actually wanted to be in a group. The Left Banke duly floundered and Brown's attempts to relaunch himself via the groups Montage, Stories and the Beckies were not at all successful.

Title	Format	Label	Cat. No.	Year	Mint	Good	Notes
Desiree	7"	Philips	BF1614	1967	£5	£2	
Desiree	7"	Philips	BF1614	1967	£8	£4	*picture sleeve*
Ivy Ivy	7"	Philips	BF1575	1967	£5	£2	
Pretty Ballerina	7"	Philips	BF1540	1967	£5	£2	
Too	LP	Smash	SRS67113	1968	£50	£25	*US*
Walk Away Renee	7"	Philips	BF1517	1966	£5	£2	
Walk Away Renee	LP	Philips	(S)BL7773	1967	£40	£20	

LEFT END

Title	Format	Label	Cat. No.	Year	Mint	Good	Notes
Spoiled Rotten	LP	Polydor	PD6022	1975	£20	£8	*US*

LEFT HANDED MARRIAGE

Brian May, the guitarist with Queen, was briefly a member of the Left Handed Marriage, but he does not play on the group's ultra-rare private pressing.

Title	Format	Label	Cat. No.	Year	Mint	Good	Notes
On The Right Side Of The Left Handed Marriage	LP	private		1967	£600	£400	

LEFTFIELD

Occupying a position in the spectrum of adventurous dance music roughly half way between the Orb and the Prodigy, between Underworld and the Chemical Brothers, Leftfield's music effectively defines the genre. Should anyone require one album to summarize the vibrant state of popular music in the nineties and to demonstrate the music's astonishing ability to keep reinventing itself for each new generation, then Leftfield's *Leftism* may well be the one.

Title	Format	Label	Cat. No.	Year	Mint	Good	Notes
Afro-Left	12"	Hard Hands	AFROEP	1995	£10	£5	*promo double*
Leftism	12"	Hard Hands	LEFTEP1	1994	£6	£2.50	*promo sampler*
More Than I Know	12"	Outer Rhythm	FOOT9R	1990	£6	£2.50	
More Than I Know	12"	Outer Rhythm	FOOT009	1991	£15	£7.50	
Original	12"	Hard Hands	LEFTEP2	1995	£6	£2.50	*promo double, with Toni Halliday*
Release The Dubs	12"	Hard Hands	HAND001R	1992	£8	£4	
Release The Pressure	12"	Hard Hands	HAND29P	1995	£6	£2.50	*promo double*
Song Of Life	12"	Hard Hands	HAND002R	1992	£8	£4	
Song Of Life	12"	Hard Hands	HAND002T	1992	£6	£2.50	

LEGAY

Title	Format	Label	Cat. No.	Year	Mint	Good	Notes
No One	7"	Fontana	TF904	1969	£75	£37.50	

LEGEND

Title	Format	Label	Cat. No.	Year	Mint	Good	Notes
Don't You Know	7"	Vertigo	6059036	1971	£5	£2	
Georgia George	7"	Bell	BLL1082	1970	£5	£2	
Legend	LP	Bell	MBLL/SBLL115	1969	£50	£25	
Life	7"	Vertigo	6059021	1971	£5	£2	
Moonshine	LP	Vertigo	6360063	1972	£50	£25	*spiral label*
National Gas	7"	Bell	BLL1048	1969	£6	£2.50	
Red Boot Album	LP	Vertigo	6360019	1971	£50	£25	*spiral label*

LEGEND (2)

Title	Format	Label	Cat. No.	Year	Mint	Good	Notes
Destroys The Blues	7"	Creation	CRE010	1984	£4	£1.50	

LEGEND (3)

Title	Format	Label	Cat. No.	Year	Mint	Good	Notes
Death In The Nursey	LP	Workshop	WR3477	1982	£10	£4	
Frontline	12"	Workshop	WR3478	1982	£20	£10	
Legend	LP	Workshop	WR2007	1980	£40	£20	

LEGEND (4)

Title	Format	Label	Cat. No.	Year	Mint	Good	Notes
Legend	LP	Megaphone	101	1968	£60	£30	*US*

LEGEND (5)

Title	Format	Label	Cat. No.	Year	Mint	Good	Notes
Hideaway	7"	Legend	LEG1	1981	£40	£20	

LEGENDARY MASKED SURFERS

Title	Format	Label	Cat. No.	Year	Mint	Good	Notes
Gonna Hustle You	7"	United Artists	UP35542	1973	£5	£2	

LEGENDS

Title	Format	Label	Cat. No.	Year	Mint	Good	Notes
I've Found Her	7"	Pye	7N15904	1965	£5	£2	
Tomorrows's Gonna Be Another Day	7"	Parlophone	R5581	1967	£15	£7.50	
Under The Sky	7"	Parlophone	R5613	1967	£8	£4	

LEGENDS (2)

Title	Format	Label	Cat. No.	Year	Mint	Good	Notes
Let Loose	LP	Ermine	101	1963	£30	£15	*US*
Let Loose	LP	Capitol	(S)T1925	1963	£20	£8	*US*

LEGRAND, MICHEL

Title	Format	Label	Number	Year	Mint	VG+	Notes
Happy Ending	LP	United Artists	UAS29084	1970	£10	£4	
Legrand Jazz	LP	Philips	BBL7328/ SBBL510	1959	£12	£5	
Legrand Piano	LP	Philips	BBL7378/ SBBL572	1960	£12	£5	
Les Parapluies De Cherbourg	LP	Philips	BL7631	1963	£10	£4	
Love Theme From Lady Sings The Blues	7"	Tamla Motown	TMG848	1973	£10	£5	*demo, picture sleeve, with Gil Askey*
Never Say Never Again	LP	Seven Seas	K28P4122	1983	£50	£25	*Japanese*
Thomas Crown Affair	LP	United Artists	SULP1218	1968	£20	£8	
Young Girls Of Rochefort	LP	Philips	(S)BL7792	1966	£10	£4	

LEGS DIAMOND

Title	Format	Label	Number	Year	Mint	VG+	Notes
Diamond Is A Hard Rock	LP	Mercury	SRM11191	1979	£15	£6	*US*
Legs Diamond	LP	Mercury	SRM11136	1978	£15	£6	*US*

LEHRER, TOM

Title	Format	Label	Number	Year	Mint	VG+	Notes
Evening Wasted	LP	Decca	LK4332/SKL4097	1960	£10	£4	
More Of Tom Lehrer	10" LP	Decca	LF1323	1959	£10	£4	
Poisoning Pigeons In The Park	7"	Decca	F11243	1960	£4	£1.50	*picture sleeve*
Songs By Tom Lehrer	10" LP	Decca	LF1311	1958	£10	£4	
Tom Lehrer Revisited	LP	Decca	LK4375	1960	£10	£4	

LEIBER STOLLER ORCHESTRA

Title	Format	Label	Number	Year	Mint	VG+	Notes
Blue Baion	7"	HMV	POP1050	1962	£8	£4	
Yakety Yak	LP	Atlantic	(SD)847	1960	£25	£10	*US*

LEIBER, JERRY

Title	Format	Label	Number	Year	Mint	VG+	Notes
Scooby-Doo	LP	Kapp	KL1127	1959	£25	£10	*US*

LEIBSTANDARTE SS

Title	Format	Label	Number	Year	Mint	VG+	Notes
Triumph Of The Will	LP	Come Organisation		1981	£50	£25	
Weltanschauung	LP	Come Organisation		198–	£30	£15	

LEIGH, ANDY

Title	Format	Label	Number	Year	Mint	VG+	Notes
Magician	LP	Polydor	2343034	1970	£10	£4	

LEIGHTON, BERNIE

Title	Format	Label	Number	Year	Mint	VG+	Notes
Lawrence Of Arabia Theme	7"	Pye	7N25177	1963	£4	£1.50	*picture sleeve*

LELAND

Title	Format	Label	Number	Year	Mint	VG+	Notes
This Is My World	LP	Contempt	R2954	1978	£20	£8	*US*

LEMEL, GARY

Title	Format	Label	Number	Year	Mint	VG+	Notes
Beautiful People	7"	London	HLM7124	1967	£6	£2.50	*export*

LEMER, PETE

Title	Format	Label	Number	Year	Mint	VG+	Notes
Local Colour	LP	ESP-Disk	1057	1968	£50	£25	*US*

LEMMINGS

Title	Format	Label	Number	Year	Mint	VG+	Notes
Out Of My Mind	7"	Pye	7N15837	1965	£6	£2.50	
You Can't Blame Me For Trying	7"	Pye	7N15899	1965	£6	£2.50	

LEMON DIPS

Title	Format	Label	Number	Year	Mint	VG+	Notes
Who's Gonna Buy?	LP	De Wolfe	DWLP3114	1969	£75	£37.50	

LEMON INTERRUPT

The two singles issued by Lemon Interrupt were the first recordings by the electronic dance music trio that subsequently preferred to be known as Underworld.

Title	Format	Label	Number	Year	Mint	VG+	Notes
Dirty	12"	Junior Boys Own	JBO712	1993	£25	£12.50	
Eclipse	12"	Junior Boys Own	JBO12002	1993	£25	£12.50	

LEMON KITTENS

Title	Format	Label	Number	Year	Mint	VG+	Notes
Big Dentist	LP	Illuminated	JAMS131	1982	£25	£10	
Cake Beast	12"	United Dairies	UD07	1981	£15	£7.50	
Spoonfed And Writhing	7"	Step Forward	SF10	1979	£8	£4	
We Buy A Hammer For Daddy	LP	United Dairies	UD02	1980	£30	£15	

LEMON PIPERS

Title	Format	Label	Number	Year	Mint	VG+	Notes
Green Tambourine	LP	Pye	NPL28112	1968	£12	£5	
Green Tambourine	LP	Buddah	2349006	1970	£10	£4	
Jelly Jungle	7"	Pye	7N25464	1968	£5	£2	
Jungle Marmalade	LP	Pye	NSPL28118	1969	£10	£4	
Presenting	7" EP	Pye	NEP44091	1968	£6	£2.50	*side 2 by 1910 Fruitgum Company*

LEMON TREE

Title	Format	Label	Number	Year	Mint	VG+	Notes
It's So Nice To Come Home	7"	Parlophone	R5739	1968	£6	£2.50	
William Chalker's Time Machine	7"	Parlophone	R5671	1968	£15	£7.50	

LEMONHEADS

Car Button Cloth	CD	Atlantic	PROP214	1996	**£25**	**£12.50**	*promo with extra track*
Different Drum	CD-s	Roughneck	HYPE3CD	1990	**£5**	**£2**	
Hate Your Friends	LP	Taang!	T15	1987	**£12**	**£5**	*US, yellow label, sleeve lettering, vinyl*
Hate Your Friends	LP	Taang!	T15	1987	**£15**	**£6**	*US, yellow label and sleeve lettering*
Laughing All The Way To The Cleaners	7"	Armory Arms	1/2/Huh-Bag1	1986	**£75**	**£37.50**	*US*
Luka	CD-s	World Service	SERVS010CD	1989	**£5**	**£2**	

LENNON, FREDDIE

John Lennon's father was one of the many people who tried to divert a little piece of Beatlemania in his own direction, but with no more success than most of the others.

That's My Life	7"	Piccadilly	7N35290	1966	**£30**	**£15**	
That's My Life	7" EP	Pye	PNV24172	1966	**£50**	**£25**	*French, B side by Brian Diamond & The Cutters*

LENNON, JIMMY & THE ATLANTICS

I Learned To Yodel	7"	Decca	F11825	1964	**£25**	**£12.50**	

LENNON, JOHN

The expensive albums recorded by John Lennon and Yoko Ono together are rare because, at the height of the Beatles' influence and popularity, even John Lennon could not sell records of a foetal heartbeat, inconsequential chatter, ambient noises and the like. Later Lennon–Ono collaborations include some excellent, and underrated, pieces of rock avant garde, such as the superbly cathartic 'Open Your Box', but the early records are strictly for the completist. The American *Roots* album is not a bootleg (although bootleg copies of the Adam VIII original do exist. These are distinguishable from the original records by the letters 't' and 'e' being joined together in the word 'stereo' on the front of the cover, where they are separate in the original.) The owner of the label claimed that Lennon had assigned the album to him and began an intensive TV advertising campaign for it. Lennon disagreed, however, and won a court injunction for the record's withdrawal. *Roots* is of particular interest to collectors because it consists of the original version of the LP that became *Rock'n'Roll* – all the tracks are Phil Spector productions and the selection of songs is slightly different. The rare version of the 'Cold Turkey' single picture sleeve differs from the regular commercial UK issue in having the X-ray skulls together on the front, rather than one on each side. A French issue duplicates the rare design, but with a green and black sleeve, and it is rather more common (selling for £30).

Cold Turkey	7"	Apple	1001	1969	**£10**	**£5**	*picture sleeve*
Cold Turkey	7"	Apple	1001	1969	**£200**	**£100**	*2 skulls (on one side) picture sleeve, Dutch or promo*
Double Fantasy	CD	Geffen	299131	1983	**£12**	**£5**	*with Yoko Ono*
Double Fantasy	CD	Mobile Fidelity	UDCD600	1991	**£15**	**£6**	*US audiophile, with Yoko Ono*
Double Fantasy	LP	Nautilus	NR47	1980	**£25**	**£10**	*US audiophile, poster, with Yoko Ono*
Give Peace A Chance	7"	Apple	13	1969	**£6**	**£2.50**	*picture sleeve*
Give Peace A Chance	7"	Apple	R5795	1969	**£15**	**£7.50**	
Happy First Birthday Capital Radio	7"	Warner Bros	SAM20	1974	**£30**	**£15**	*promo*
Happy Xmas (War Is Over)	7"	Apple	R5970	1972	**£5**	**£2**	*picture sleeve, green vinyl, with Yoko Ono*
Imagine	7"	Apple	R6009	1975	**£6**	**£2.50**	*picture sleeve*
Imagine	7"	Parlophone	RP6199	1988	**£4**	**£1.50**	*picture disc*
Imagine	CD-s	Parlophone	CDR6199	1988	**£5**	**£2**	
Imagine	LP	Apple	PAS10004	1971	**£10**	**£4**	*inner, postcard*
Imagine	LP	Apple	Q4PAS10004	1974	**£100**	**£50**	*quad*
Imagine	LP	Mobile Fidelity	MFSL1153	1984	**£15**	**£6**	*US audiophile*
Instant Karma	7"	Apple	1003	1970	**£6**	**£2.50**	*picture sleeve*
John Lennon	LP	Parlophone	JLB8	1981	**£60**	**£30**	*8 LP boxed set*
John Lennon Collection	CD	Parlophone	CDEMTV37	1989	**£15**	**£6**	*with promo edit of Number Nine Dream*
John Lennon Collection	LP	Geffen	LS2023	1982	**£15**	**£6**	*US audiophile promo*
John Lennon On Ronnie Hawkins	7"	Cotillion	PR105	1970	**£30**	**£15**	*US promo*
John Lennon On Ronnie Hawkins	7"	Atlantic	PRO104	1970	**£50**	**£25**	*US promo*
KYA Peace Talk	LP	Capitol	KYA1969	1969	**£50**	**£25**	*US promo, with Yoko Ono*
Live Peace In Toronto	CD	Parlophone	CDP7904282	1989	**£12**	**£5**	*with Yoko Ono*
Live Peace In Toronto	LP	Apple	CORE2001	1969	**£50**	**£25**	*with calendar, with Yoko Ono*
Milk And Honey	CD	Polydor	8171602	1990	**£12**	**£5**	*with Yoko Ono*
Milk And Honey	LP	Polydor	POLHP5	1984	**£20**	**£8**	*picture disc, thick*
Mind Games	7"	Apple	R5994	1973	**£5**	**£2**	*picture sleeve*
Number Nine Dream (2 versions)	7"	Apple	R6003DJ	1974	**£30**	**£15**	*promo*
Power To The People	7"	Apple	R5892	1971	**£8**	**£4**	*picture sleeve*
Roots	LP	Adam VIII	LP8018	1975	**£250**	**£150**	*US*
Some Time In New York City	LP	Apple	PCSP716	1972	**£12**	**£5**	*double with inner sleeves & postcard*
Sometime In New York City	CD	Parlophone	CDS7467828	1987	**£25**	**£10**	*double, with Yoko Ono*
Unfinished Music No. 1: Two Virgins	LP	Apple	SAPCOR2	1968	**£200**	**£100**	*stereo, with Yoko Ono*
Unfinished Music No. 1: Two Virgins	LP	Apple	APCOR2	1968	**£750**	**£500**	*mono, with Yoko Ono*
Unfinished Music No. 2: Life With The Lions	LP	Apple	ZAPPLE1	1969	**£60**	**£30**	*with Yoko Ono*
Unfinished Music No. 2: Life With The Lions	LP	Apple	ZAPPLE1	1969	**£75**	**£37.50**	*card insert, with Yoko Ono*

Wedding Album	LP	Apple	SAPCOR11	1969	**£150**	**£75**	*boxed, inserts, with Yoko Ono*
Whatever Gets You Thru The Night	7"	EMI	PSR369	1974	**£200**	**£100**	*interview promo*
Woman Is The Nigger Of The World	7"	Apple	R5953	1972	**£350**	**£210**	*demo only, best auctioned*
You Know My Name	7"	Apple	1002	1969	**£1500**	**£1000**	*test pressing, best auctioned*

LENNON, JOHN & THE BLEECHERS

Ram You Hard	7"	Punch	PH23	1970	**£5**	**£2**	*Upsetters B side*

LENNON, JULIAN

Now You're In Heaven	CD-s	Virgin	VSCD1154	1989	**£5**	**£2**	*3" single*
Too Late For Goodbyes	7"	Charisma	JLY1	1984	**£5**	**£2**	*picture disc*
Valotte	7"	Charisma	JLS2	1984	**£6**	**£2.50**	*shaped picture disc*
You're The One	CD-s	Virgin	VSCD1182	1989	**£5**	**£2**	*3" single*

LENNON, SEAN

Sean Lennon	CD	Grand Royal	SEAN001	1998	**£15**	**£6**	*promo*

LENNON SISTERS

Graduation Day	7"	Vogue Coral	Q72176	1956	**£5**	**£2**	
Great Folk Songs	LP	London	HAD/SHD8154	1964	**£12**	**£5**	
Sad Movies	7"	London	HLD9417	1961	**£5**	**£2**	
Shake Me I Rattle	7"	Vogue Coral	Q72285	1957	**£6**	**£2.50**	
Today	LP	Mercury	20120SMCL	1968	**£10**	**£4**	
Young And In Love	7"	Vogue Coral	Q72259	1957	**£5**	**£2**	

LENNOX, ANNIE

Diva	CD	Arista		1992	**£25**	**£10**	*US promo with bonus interview disc*
Put A Little Love In Your Heart	CD-s	A&M	CDEE484	1988	**£5**	**£2**	*with Al Green, 3" single*

LENNY THE LION

I Wish That I Could Be Father Christmas	7"	Parlophone	R4609	1959	**£5**	**£2**	

LENOIR, J. B.

Alabama Blues	LP	CBS	62593	1966	**£25**	**£10**	
Crusade	LP	Polydor	2482014	1970	**£15**	**£6**	
I Sing The Way I Feel	7"	Sue	WI339	1965	**£15**	**£7.50**	
J. B. Lenoir	LP	Python	PLP25	1972	**£30**	**£15**	
J. B. Lenoir	LP	Rarity	LP2	1975	**£15**	**£6**	
Man Watch Your Woman	7"	Bootleg	503	1965	**£30**	**£15**	
Mojo Boogie	7"	Blue Horizon	451004	1966	**£100**	**£50**	
Natural Man	LP	Chess	1410	1963	**£25**	**£10**	*US*

LENT, ROBIN

Scarecrow's Journey	LP	Nepentha	6437002	1971	**£30**	**£15**	

LENTILMAS

The Lentilmas flexi-disc was a promotional release given away to journalists as a 1977 Christmas present. The record is supposed to include Christmas carols sung by the Sex Pistols.

Lentilmas	7"	Virgin	no number	1977	**£125**	**£62.50**	*flexi*

LENTON, VAL

You Don't Care	7"	Immediate	IM008	1965	**£15**	**£7.50**	

LEONARD, DEKE

Nothing Is Happening	7"	United Artists	UP35556	1973	**£5**	**£2**	*demo*

LEONETTI, TOMMY

Dream Lover	7"	RCA	RCA1107	1959	**£4**	**£1.50**	
Ever Since You Went Away	7"	Capitol	CL14272	1955	**£4**	**£1.50**	
That's What You Made Me	7"	Capitol	CL14199	1954	**£4**	**£1.50**	

LEO'S SUNSHIPP

Give Me The Sunshine	12"	Grapevine	REDC3	1979	**£10**	**£5**	

LEROY & ROCKY

Love Me Girl	7"	Studio One	SO2042	1968	**£12**	**£6**	*Wrigglers B side*

LEROYS

Chills	7"	HMV	POP1312	1964	**£6**	**£2.50**	
Don't Cry Baby	7"	HMV	POP1274	1964	**£4**	**£1.50**	
I Come Smiling On Through	7"	HMV	POP1368	1964	**£4**	**£1.50**	
Money	7"	Lyntone	LYN504	1963	**£4**	**£1.50**	*flexi*

LES COMPAGNONS DE LA CHANSON

Galley Slave	7"	Columbia	SCM5056	1953	**£8**	**£4**	
Song Successes In English	7" EP	Columbia	SEG7829	1958	**£5**	**£2**	
Three Bells	7"	Columbia	SCM5005	1953	**£10**	**£5**	

LES COPAINS

Les Croulants	LP	Symco	100	1963	**£25**	**£10**	*French*

LES CRUCHES

Title	Format	Label	Number	Year	Mint	VG	Notes
Live	LP	CBS	52499	1968	**£25**	**£10**	*Dutch*

LES FLAMBEAUX

Title	Format	Label	Number	Year	Mint	VG	Notes
Les Flambeaux	LP	Mushroom	100MR13	1971	**£30**	**£15**	

LES GOSSES

Title	Format	Label	Number	Year	Mint	VG	Notes
1 April 1963–31 Mei 1971	LP	private		1971	**£750**	**£500**	*Dutch*

LES HABITS JAUNES

Title	Format	Label	Number	Year	Mint	VG	Notes
Canada Beat!	LP	Laval	4202	1964	**£20**	**£8**	*Canadian*

LES HOBEAUX

Title	Format	Label	Number	Year	Mint	VG	Notes
Dynamo	7"	HMV	POP444	1958	**£10**	**£5**	
Mama Don't Allow	7"	HMV	POP403	1957	**£10**	**£5**	
Oh Mary Don't You Weep	7"	HMV	POP377	1957	**£10**	**£5**	
Soho Skiffle	7" EP	HMV	7EG8297	1957	**£25**	**£12.50**	

LES MISSILES

Title	Format	Label	Number	Year	Mint	VG	Notes
Les Missiles De France	7" EP	Columbia	SEG8371	1964	**£5**	**£2**	

LES NAPOLEONS

Title	Format	Label	Number	Year	Mint	VG	Notes
A Go Go	LP	Passe Temps	17	1965	**£60**	**£30**	*Canadian*

LES PLAYERS

Title	Format	Label	Number	Year	Mint	VG	Notes
Les Players	7" EP	Polydor	EPH27129	1965	**£5**	**£2**	

LES RITA MITSOUKO

Title	Format	Label	Number	Year	Mint	VG	Notes
Singing In The Shower	CD-s	Virgin	VSCD1163	1989	**£10**	**£5**	

LES ZARJAZ

Title	Format	Label	Number	Year	Mint	VG	Notes
One Charming Nyte	7"	Creation	CRE013	1985	**£5**	**£2**	

LESLEY, LORNE

Title	Format	Label	Number	Year	Mint	VG	Notes
So High So Low	7"	Parlophone	R4581	1959	**£4**	**£1.50**	
Somebody's Gonna Be Sorry	7"	Philips	BF1487	1966	**£4**	**£1.50**	
We're Gonna Dance	7"	Polydor	NH66956	1960	**£5**	**£2**	

LESLEY, MICHAEL

Title	Format	Label	Number	Year	Mint	VG	Notes
Make Up Or Break Up	7"	Pye	7N15959	1965	**£6**	**£2.50**	

LESLIE, JOHN & CHRIS

Title	Format	Label	Number	Year	Mint	VG	Notes
Ship Of Time	LP	Cottage	COT901	1976	**£15**	**£6**	

LESTER, KETTY

Title	Format	Label	Number	Year	Mint	VG	Notes
Ketty Lester	7" EP	London	REN1348	1962	**£20**	**£10**	
Love Letters	7"	London	HLN9527	1962	**£4**	**£1.50**	
Love Letters	LP	London	HAN2455	1963	**£25**	**£10**	
Roses Grow With Thorns	7"	RCA	RCA1403	1964	**£15**	**£7.50**	
Some Things Are Better Left Unsaid	7"	RCA	RCA1394	1964	**£40**	**£20**	
Soul Of Me	LP	RCA	RD7669	1964	**£12**	**£5**	
West Coast	7"	Capitol	CL15427	1965	**£10**	**£5**	
Where Is Love	LP	RCA	RD7712	1965	**£12**	**£5**	

LETHE

Title	Format	Label	Number	Year	Mint	VG	Notes
Lethe	LP	M.M.P.		1981	**£100**	**£50**	*Dutch*

LETTERMEN

Title	Format	Label	Number	Year	Mint	VG	Notes
Lettermen	7" EP	Capitol	EAP41669	1961	**£5**	**£2**	

LETTERMEN (2)

Title	Format	Label	Number	Year	Mint	VG	Notes
First Class	LP	Stag	SG10075	1974	**£175**	**£87.50**	

LETTERS

Title	Format	Label	Number	Year	Mint	VG	Notes
Nobody Loves Me	7"	Heartbeat	PULSE9	1979	**£12**	**£6**	

LETTS, DON & JAH WOBBLE

Title	Format	Label	Number	Year	Mint	VG	Notes
Steel Leg: Stratetime And The Wide Man	12"	Virgin	VS23912	1979	**£10**	**£5**	
Steel Leg: Stratetime And The Wide Man	7"	Virgin	VS239	1979	**£6**	**£2.50**	

LEVEE BREAKERS

Title	Format	Label	Number	Year	Mint	VG	Notes
Baby I'm Leaving You	7"	Parlophone	R5291	1965	**£15**	**£7.50**	

LEVEE CAMP MOAN

Title	Format	Label	Number	Year	Mint	VG	Notes
Levee Camp Moan	LP	County	no number	1969	**£500**	**£330**	
Peacock Farm	LP	County	no number	1969	**£500**	**£330**	

LEVEL 42

Title	Format	Label	Number	Year	Mint	VG	Notes
Children Say (Extended Remix)	CD-s	Polydor	POCD911	1987	**£5**	**£2**	*card sleeve*
Chinese Way	12"	Polydor	POSPX538	1983	**£10**	**£5**	*yellow vinyl*
Chinese Way	12"	Polydor	POSPPX538	1983	**£8**	**£4**	*double*
Family Of Five	CD-s	Polygram	0802769	1988	**£10**	**£5**	*CD video*
Guaranteed	CD	RCA	PD75005	1991	**£25**	**£10**	*promo box set with cassette*
Guaranteed	CD-s	RCA	PD44746	1991	**£5**	**£2**	

Title	Format	Label	Cat. No.	Year	Mint	VG+	Notes
Heaven In My Hands	CD-s	Polydor	PZCD14	1988	£5	£2	
Heaven In My Hands	CD-s	Polygram	0805022	1988	£10	£5	CD video
Hot Water	12"	Polydor	POSPA697	1986	£20	£10	
It's Over	CD-s	Polygram	0801562	1989	£10	£5	CD video
Leaving Me Now	10"	Polydor	POSPT776	1985	£6	£2.50	
Leaving Me Now	CD-s	Polygram	0802182	1988	£10	£5	CD video
Lessons In Love	CD-s	Polygram	0800042	1988	£10	£5	CD video
Love Meeting Love	12"	Elite	DAZZ5	1980	£25	£12.50	no picture sleeve
Micro-Kid	12"	Polydor	POSPX643	1983	£15	£7.50	double
Out Of Sight Out Of Mind	12"	Polydor	POSPP570	1984	£6	£2.50	picture disc
Overtime	CD-s	RCA	PD44998	1991	£5	£2	
Running In The Family	CD-s	Polygram	0800002	1988	£10	£5	CD video
Running In The Family (Platinum Edition)	CD	Polydor	8836892	1987	£12	£5	with extra remixes
Sandstorm	12"	Elite	DAZZ4	1980	£60	£30	promo
Something About You	10"	Polydor	POSPT759	1985	£6	£2.50	
Strategy	LP	Elite	LEVLP1	1981	£400	£250	test pressing only
Take A Look	CD-s	Polygram	0805762	1989	£10	£5	CD video
Take A Look	CD-s	Polydor	PZCD24	1988	£5	£2	
Take Care Of Yourself	CD-s	Polydor	PZCD58	1989	£5	£2	
Tracie	CD-s	Polydor	PZCD34	1989	£5	£2	
Wings Of Love	12"	Polydor	POSPX200	1980	£8	£4	no picture sleeve
You Can't Blame Louis	12"	Polydor	POSPX500	1982	£20	£10	test pressing, no picture sleeve

LEVELLERS

Title	Format	Label	Cat. No.	Year	Mint	VG+	Notes
Big Friday	CD-s	Probe Plus	PP25CD	1990	£5	£2	
Carry Me	12"	Hag	HAG005	1989	£10	£5	Brighton address on sleeve
Far From Home	CD-s	China	WOKCD2010	1991	£5	£2	
Live 1992	LP	On The Fiddle	OTFLP2	1992	£15	£6	
One Way	CD-s	China	WOKCD2008	1991	£5	£2	
Outside Inside	7"	Hag	HAG006	1989	£5	£2	promo only
Peel Sessions	CD-s	Strange Fruit	SFPSCD083	1991	£5	£2	
Police On My Back	12"	On The Fiddle	OTFEP1	1991	£10	£5	

LEVENE, GERRY & THE AVENGERS

Title	Format	Label	Cat. No.	Year	Mint	VG+	Notes
Doctor Feelgood	7"	Decca	F11815	1964	£25	£12.50	

LEVEY, STAN

Title	Format	Label	Cat. No.	Year	Mint	VG+	Notes
Grand Stan	LP	London	LTZN15100	1957	£15	£6	
This Time The Drum's On Me	LP	Parlophone	PMC1086	1959	£15	£6	

LEVIATHAN

Title	Format	Label	Cat. No.	Year	Mint	VG+	Notes
Flames	7"	Elektra	EKSN45075	1969	£30	£15	
Leviathan	LP	Elektra	EKS74046	1969	£300	£180	test pressing
Remember The Times	7"	Elektra	EKSN45052/7	1968	£60	£30	promo double in folder
Remember The Times	7"	Elektra	EKSN45052	1968	£30	£15	
War Machine	7"	Elektra	EKSN45057	1969	£30	£15	

LEVINE, HANK

Title	Format	Label	Cat. No.	Year	Mint	VG+	Notes
Image	7"	HMV	POP947	1961	£6	£2.50	

LEVITATION

Title	Format	Label	Cat. No.	Year	Mint	VG+	Notes
Need For Not	LP	Rough Trade	R2861	1992	£10	£4	with 7" (LEV001) and etching

LEVON & THE HAWKS

Title	Format	Label	Cat. No.	Year	Mint	VG+	Notes
Go Go, Lisa Jane	7"	Atco	6625	1968	£20	£10	US
Stones I Throw	7"	Atlantic	AT4054	1965	£25	£12.50	

LEVY, BEN

Title	Format	Label	Cat. No.	Year	Mint	VG+	Notes
Doren	7"	Ska Beat	JB245	1966	£10	£5	
I'll Make You Glad	7"	Ska Beat	JB255	1966	£10	£5	

LEVY, CARL & THE CIMARRONS

Title	Format	Label	Cat. No.	Year	Mint	VG+	Notes
Remember Easter Monday	7"	Hot Rod	HR101	1970	£5	£2	Peggy & Jimmy B side
Walk The Hot Street	7"	Hot Rod	HR100	1970	£5	£2	Peggy & The Cimarrons B side

LEVY, KEN & THE PHANTOMS

Title	Format	Label	Cat. No.	Year	Mint	VG+	Notes
Ken Levy And The Phantoms	LP	Nashville	NSLP30102	1965	£75	£37.50	Swedish
Wow!	LP	Nashville	NSLP30101	1964	£100	£50	Swedish

LEWIE, JONAH

Title	Format	Label	Cat. No.	Year	Mint	VG+	Notes
On The Other Hand There's A Fist	LP	Stiff	SEEZ8	1978	£10	£4	yellow vinyl
On The Other Hand There's A Fist	LP	Stiff	SEEZP8	1978	£10	£4	picture disc

LEWIS, ALVA

Title	Format	Label	Cat. No.	Year	Mint	VG+	Notes
Return Home	7"	Caltone	TONE111	1967	£10	£5	King Rock B side

LEWIS, BARBARA

Title	Format	Label	Cat. No.	Year	Mint	VG+	Notes
Baby I'm Yours	7"	Atlantic	AT4031	1965	£6	£2.50	
Baby I'm Yours	LP	Atlantic	ATL5042	1966	£20	£8	

Title	Format	Label	Cat. No.	Year	Mint	VG	Notes
Baby What Do You Want Me To Do	7″	Atlantic	584061	1967	£15	£7.50	
Don't Forget About Me	7″	Atlantic	AT4068	1966	£6	£2.50	
Hello Stranger	7″	Atlantic	584153	1968	£4	£1.50	
Hello Stranger	7″	London	HLK9724	1963	£10	£5	
Hello Stranger	LP	Atlantic	(SD)8086	1963	£30	£15	US
It's Magic	LP	Atlantic	587002	1966	£20	£8	
Make Me Belong To You	7″	Atlantic	584037	1966	£4	£1.50	
Make Me Your Baby	7″	Atlantic	AT4041	1965	£6	£2.50	
Many Grooves Of Barbara Lewis	LP	Stax	SXATS1035	1970	£12	£5	
Pushing A Good Thing Too Far	7″	Atlantic	AT4013	1964	£6	£2.50	
Sho-Nuff	7″	Atlantic	584174	1968	£5	£2	
Snap Your Fingers	7″	London	HLK9832	1964	£8	£4	
Snap Your Fingers	7″ EP	Atlantic	AET6015	1965	£30	£15	
Snap Your Fingers	LP	Atlantic	(SD)8090	1964	£30	£15	US
Some Day We're Gonna Love Again	7″	Atlantic	2091143	1971	£4	£1.50	
Straighten Up Your Heart	7″	London	HLK9779	1963	£10	£5	
Workin' On A Groovy Thing	LP	Atlantic	SD8173	1968	£20	£8	US

LEWIS, BOBBY

Title	Format	Label	Cat. No.	Year	Mint	VG	Notes
I'm Tossing And Turning Again	7″	Stateside	SS126	1962	£8	£4	
One Track Mind	7″	Parlophone	R4831	1961	£8	£4	
Tossing And Turning	7″	Parlophone	R4794	1961	£10	£5	
Tossing And Turning	LP	Beltone	4000	1961	£60	£30	US

LEWIS, DAVE

Title	Format	Label	Cat. No.	Year	Mint	VG	Notes
Giving Gas	7″ EP	Pye	NEP44057	1966	£10	£5	

LEWIS, DAVID

Title	Format	Label	Cat. No.	Year	Mint	VG	Notes
Songs Of David Lewis	LP	private	AX1	1970	£350	£210	

LEWIS, FURRY

Title	Format	Label	Cat. No.	Year	Mint	VG	Notes
Back On My Feet Again	LP	Bluesville	BV(S)1036	1961	£25	£10	US
Early Years 1927–9	LP	Spookane	SPL1004	1971	£40	£20	
Furry Lewis	LP	Xtra	XTRA116	1971	£12	£5	
Furry Lewis	LP	Folkways	FS3823	1961	£25	£10	
In Memphis	LP	Saydisc	SDR190	1970	£20	£8	
Presenting The Country Blues	LP	Blue Horizon	763228	1969	£50	£25	

LEWIS, GARY & THE PLAYBOYS

Title	Format	Label	Cat. No.	Year	Mint	VG	Notes
Count Me In	7″	Liberty	LIB55778	1965	£6	£2.50	
Count Me In	7″ EP	Liberty	LEP2236	1965	£15	£7.50	French
Everybody Loves A Clown	7″ EP	Liberty	LEP2241	1965	£15	£7.50	French
Everybody Loves A Clown	LP	Liberty	LRP3428/ LST7428	1965	£15	£6	US
Golden Greats	LP	Liberty	LRP3468/ LST7468	1966	£15	£6	US
Green Grass	7″	Liberty	LIB55880	1966	£4	£1.50	
Hits Again	LP	Liberty	LRP3452/ LST7452	1966	£15	£6	US
Jill	7″	Liberty	LBF15025	1967	£5	£2	
Just Our Style	LP	Liberty	LBY1322	1966	£12	£5	
Listen	LP	Liberty	LRP3524/ LST7524	1967	£12	£5	US
My Heart's Symphony	7″	Liberty	LIB55898	1966	£5	£2	
New Directions	LP	Liberty	LRP3519/ LST7519	1967	£12	£5	US
Paint Me A Picture	7″	Liberty	LIB55914	1966	£4	£1.50	
Session With Gary Lewis	LP	Liberty	LRP3419/ LST7419	1965	£15	£6	US
She's Just My Style	LP	Liberty	LRP3435/ LST7435	1966	£15	£6	US
Sure Gonna Miss Her	7″	Liberty	LIB55865	1966	£4	£1.50	
This Diamond Ring	7″	Liberty	LIB10187	1965	£4	£1.50	
This Diamond Ring	7″ EP	Liberty	LEP2216	1965	£15	£7.50	French
This Diamond Ring	LP	Liberty	LBY1259	1965	£20	£8	
Where Will The Words Come From	7″ EP	Liberty	LEP2270	1967	£15	£7.50	French
You Don't Have To Paint Me A Picture	LP	Liberty	LRP3487/ LST7487	1967	£12	£5	US

LEWIS, GEORGE

Title	Format	Label	Cat. No.	Year	Mint	VG	Notes
Blues From The Bayou	LP	HMV	CLP1371/ CSD1309	1960	£15	£6	
Concert	LP	Blue Note	BLP/BST81208	196–	£20	£8	
Dallas Blues	7″ EP	Storyville	SEP504	196–	£5	£2	
Doctor Jazz	LP	HMV	CLP1413/ CSD1337	1961	£15	£6	
George Lewis	7″ EP	Tempo	EXA66	1957	£5	£2	
George Lewis	7″ EP	Tempo	EXA62	1957	£5	£2	
George Lewis	7″ EP	Tempo	EXA97	1958	£5	£2	
George Lewis	7″ EP	Tempo	EXA101	1959	£5	£2	
George Lewis And His New Orleans Allstars	10″ LP	Vogue	LDE012	1952	£20	£8	
George Lewis And His New Orleans Ragtime Band	10″ LP	Esquire	20086	1957	£15	£6	
George Lewis And His New Orleans Stompers	7″ EP	Vogue	EPV1081	1956	£5	£2	
George Lewis And His New Orleans Stompers	7″ EP	Tempo	EXA15	1956	£5	£2	

Title	Format	Label	Number	Year	Mint	VG	Notes
George Lewis And His New Orleans Stompers	7" EP	Vogue	EPV1066	1955	£5	£2	
George Lewis And His New Orleans Stompers	LP	Vogue	LAE12005	1955	£20	£8	
George Lewis In Hi Fi	7" EP	Vogue	EPV1252	1959	£5	£2	
George Lewis In Hi Fi	7" EP	Vogue	EPV1220	1959	£5	£2	
George Lewis Jam Session	10" LP	Vogue	LDE082	1954	£20	£8	
George Lewis Ragtime Band	10" LP	Esquire	20073	1956	£20	£8	
George Lewis Ragtime Band	10" LP	Esquire	20067	1956	£20	£8	
George Lewis Ragtime Band	LP	Tempo	TAP13	1957	£25	£10	
George Lewis Vol. 1	LP	Blue Note	BLP/BST81205	196–	£20	£8	
George Lewis Vol. 2	LP	Blue Note	BLP/BST81206	196–	£20	£8	
George Lewis' Ragtime Band	7" EP	Tempo	EXA70	1957	£5	£2	
High Society	7" EP	Storyville	SEP503	196–	£5	£2	
Ice Cream	7" EP	Storyville	SEP315	195–	£5	£2	
Isle Of Capri	7" EP	Storyville	SEP365	1961	£5	£2	
Jazz At Preservation Hall Vol. 4	LP	London	HAK/SHK8165	1964	£15	£6	
Jazz At Vespers	LP	London	LTZU15112	1958	£15	£6	
Jazz From New Orleans	7" EP	Storyville	SEP349	1960	£5	£2	
Louisiana	7" EP	Storyville	SEP322	195–	£5	£2	
Muskrat Ramble	7" EP	Storyville	SEP369	1961	£5	£2	
New Orleans Jazz Concert	10" LP	Brunswick	LA8627	1953	£20	£8	*with Freddie Kohlman*
New Orleans Music	7" EP	Good Time Jazz	EPG1182	195–	£5	£2	
New Orleans Ragtime Band Vol. 1	7" EP	Esquire	EP125	1957	£5	£2	
New Orleans Ragtime Band Vol. 2	7" EP	Esquire	EP135	1957	£5	£2	
New Orleans Ragtime Band Vol. 3	7" EP	Esquire	EP155	1957	£5	£2	
New Orleans Ragtime Band Vol. 4	7" EP	Esquire	EP175	1958	£5	£2	
New Orleans Ragtime Band Vol. 5	7" EP	Esquire	EP209	1959	£5	£2	
New Orleans Ragtime Band Vol. 6	7" EP	Esquire	EP211	1959	£5	£2	
New Orleans Ragtime Band Vol. 7	7" EP	Esquire	EP215	1959	£5	£2	
New Orleans Ragtime Band Vol. 8	7" EP	Esquire	EP219	1959	£5	£2	
New Orleans Ragtime Band Vol. 9	7" EP	Esquire	EP225	1960	£5	£2	
Newport Jazz Festival 1957	LP	Columbia	33CX10099	1958	£15	£6	*side 2 by Turk Murphy*
Panama	7" EP	Storyville	SEP321	195–	£5	£2	
Perennial George Lewis	LP	Columbia	33CX10131	1959	£15	£6	
Raggin' And Stompin'	10" LP	Columbia	33C9042	1959	£15	£6	
Smile Darn Ya Smile	LP	77	LA1228	1964	£15	£6	
Sounds Of New Orleans	7" EP	HMV	7EG8540	1960	£5	£2	
Till We Meet Again	7" EP	Storyville	SEP361	1961	£5	£2	
Vol. 1 Jazz Band	10" LP	London	HAPB1041	1955	£20	£8	
Vol. 2 All Stars	10" LP	London	HBU1045	1956	£20	£8	
Willie The Weeper	7" EP	Storyville	SEP325	195–	£5	£2	

LEWIS, HOPETON

Title	Format	Label	Number	Year	Mint	VG	Notes
Boom Shacka Lacka	7"	Duke Reid	DR2505	1970	£5	£2	*Tommy McCook B side*
Everybody Rocking	7"	Island	WI3076	1968	£10	£5	
Grooving Out On Life	LP	Trojan	TRL36	1971	£10	£4	
Judgement Day	7"	Treasure Isle	TI7071	1972	£5	£2	*Earl Lindo B side*
Let Me Come On Home	7"	Island	WI3056	1967	£10	£5	
Let The Little Girl Dance	7"	Island	WI3059	1967	£10	£5	
Rock A Shacka	7"	Island	WI3068	1967	£10	£5	
Rock Steady	7"	Island	WI3054	1967	£10	£5	
Run Down	7"	Island	WI3057	1967	£10	£5	
Skinny Leg Girl	7"	Fab	FAB43	1968	£10	£5	
Take It Easy	LP	Island	ILP957	1967	£100	£50	*pink label*
Testify	7"	Duke Reid	DR2516	1970	£5	£2	*Tommy McCook B side*
To The Other Man	7"	Treasure Isle	TI7060	1971	£5	£2	*Tommy McCook B side*

LEWIS, HUGH X.

Title	Format	Label	Number	Year	Mint	VG	Notes
Hugh X Album	LP	London	HAR8293	1966	£10	£4	
Just Before Dawn	LP	London	HAR8303	1967	£10	£4	

LEWIS, JENNIFER & ANGELA STRANGE

Title	Format	Label	Number	Year	Mint	VG	Notes
Bring It To Me	7"	Columbia	DB7662	1965	£5	£2	
I've Heard It All Before	7"	Columbia	DB7814	1966	£6	£2.50	

LEWIS, JERRY

Title	Format	Label	Number	Year	Mint	VG	Notes
Capitol Presents Jerry Lewis	10" LP	Capitol	LC6591	1953	£10	£4	
Rock-A-Bye Your Baby With A Dixie Melody	7"	Brunswick	05636	1957	£5	£2	

LEWIS, JERRY LEE

Title	Format	Label	Number	Year	Mint	VG	Notes
Another Place, Another Time	7"	Mercury	MF1020	1968	£4	£1.50	
Another Time, Another Place	LP	Mercury	SMWL21011	1969	£10	£4	
Baby Baby Bye Bye	7"	London	HLS9131	1960	£8	£4	
Baby Hold Me Close	7"	Philips	BF1407	1965	£4	£1.50	
Break Up	7"	London	HLS8700	1958	£6	£2.50	
Breathless	7"	London	HLS8592	1958	£6	£2.50	
Breathless	LP	London	HAS8323	1966	£30	£15	

Title	Format	Label	Cat. No.	Year	Mint	VG	Notes
By Request – More Greatest Live Show On Earth	LP	Philips	(S)BL7746	1967	£10	£4	
Carry Me Back To Old Virginia	7"	London	HLS9980	1965	£5	£2	
Country Songs For City Folks	LP	Philips	BL7688	1965	£10	£4	
Country Style	7" EP	Philips	BE12599	1966	£15	£7.50	
Fabulous Jerry Lee Lewis Vol. 1	7" EP	Sun	JLLEP001	197–	£8	£4	
Fabulous Jerry Lee Lewis Vol. 2	7" EP	Sun	JLLEP002	197–	£8	£4	
Four More From Jerry Lee Lewis	7" EP	London	RES1378	1963	£25	£12.50	
Golden Hits	LP	Philips	BL7622	1964	£10	£4	
Good Golly Miss Molly	7"	London	HLS9688	1963	£4	£1.50	
Good Golly Miss Molly	7"	London	HL7120	1963	£10	£5	*export*
Got You On My Mind	LP	Fontana	SFJL964	1968	£10	£4	
Great Balls Of Fire	7"	London	HLS8529	1957	£10	£5	
Great Balls Of Fire	7"	Mercury	MF1110	1969	£4	£1.50	
Great Balls Of Fire	7"	Mercury	MF1110	1969	£6	£2.50	*picture sleeve*
Greatest Live Show On Earth	LP	Philips	(S)BL7650	1964	£10	£4	
Hang Up My Rock & Roll Shoes	7"	London	HLS9202	1960	£5	£2	
High School Confidential	7"	London	HLS8780	1959	£12	£6	
High School Confidential	7"	London	HL7050	1958	£12	£6	*export*
Hit The Road Jack	7"	Mercury	AMT1216	1963	£4	£1.50	
I'll Sail My Ship Alone	7"	London	HLS9083	1960	£5	£2	
I'm On Fire	7"	Philips	BF1324	1964	£5	£2	
I'm On Fire	LP	Mercury	SMCL20156	1969	£10	£4	
In The Mood	7"	London	HL7123	1963	£25	£12.50	*export*
It Won't Happen With Me	7"	London	HLS9414	1961	£4	£1.50	
It's A Hang Up Baby	7"	Philips	BF1594	1967	£4	£1.50	
Jerry Lee Lewis	LP	London	HAS2138	1959	£50	£25	
Jerry Lee Lewis	LP	Sun	SLP1230	1958	£75	£37.50	*US*
Jerry Lee Lewis No. 1	7" EP	London	RES1140	1958	£30	£15	*tri-centre*
Jerry Lee Lewis No. 2	7" EP	London	RES1186	1959	£40	£20	*tri-centre*
Jerry Lee Lewis No. 3	7" EP	London	RES1187	1959	£40	£20	*tri-centre*
Jerry Lee Lewis No. 4	7" EP	London	RES1296	1961	£25	£12.50	
Jerry Lee Lewis No. 5	7" EP	London	RES1336	1962	£20	£10	
Jerry Lee Lewis No. 6	7" EP	London	RES1351	1963	£20	£10	
Jerry Lee Lewis Vol. 2	LP	London	HAS2440	1962	£40	£20	
Jerry Lee's Greatest	LP	Sun	SLP1265	1961	£75	£37.50	*US*
Let's Talk About Us	7"	London	HLS8941	1959	£6	£2.50	*tri-centre*
Lewis Boogie	7"	London	HLS9867	1964	£6	£2.50	
Little Queenie	7"	London	HLS8993	1959	£8	£4	*tri-centre*
Live At The Star Club Hamburg	LP	Philips	BL7646	1965	£12	£5	*with the Nashville Teens*
Long Tall Sally	7"	Mercury	MF1105	1969	£4	£1.50	
Long Tall Sally	7"	Mercury	MF1105	1969	£6	£2.50	*picture sleeve*
Loving Up A Storm	7"	London	HLS8840	1959	£10	£5	
Memphis Beat	7"	Philips	BF1521	1966	£4	£1.50	
Memphis Beat	LP	Philips	(S)BL7706	1967	£10	£4	
Rambling Rose	7"	London	HLS9526	1962	£4	£1.50	
Return Of Rock	LP	Philips	(S)BL7668	1967	£10	£4	
Rocking Pneumonia	7"	Philips	BF1425	1965	£4	£1.50	
Save The Last Dance For Me	7"	London	HL7117	1962	£25	£12.50	*export*
She Still Comes Around	LP	Mercury	SMCL21047	1969	£10	£4	
Shotgun Man	7"	Philips	BF1615	1967	£4	£1.50	
Soul My Way	LP	Mercury	20117MCL	1968	£10	£4	
Sunstroke	LP	Ember	NR5038	1966	£10	£4	*with Carl Perkins*
Sweet Little Sixteen	7"	London	HLS9584	1962	£4	£1.50	
Teenage Letter	7"	London	HLS9722	1963	£5	£2	
Together	LP	Mercury	SMCL20172	1970	£10	£4	*with Linda Gail Lewis*
When I Get Paid	7"	London	HLS9446	1961	£4	£1.50	
Whole Lotta Shaking Goin' On	LP	London	HAS8251	1965	£25	£10	
Whole Lotta Shaking Goin' On	7"	London	HLS8457	1957	£15	£7.50	
You Win Again	7"	London	HLS8559	1958	£15	£7.50	

LEWIS, JIMMY

Title	Format	Label	Cat. No.	Year	Mint	VG	Notes
Girls From Texas	7"	Minit	MLF11002	1968	£15	£7.50	

LEWIS, JOHN

Title	Format	Label	Cat. No.	Year	Mint	VG	Notes
Afternoon In Paris	LP	Oriole	MG20036	1960	£12	£5	*with Sacha Distel*
Cool!	LP	Fontana	FJL106	1964	£10	£4	
Golden Striker	LP	London	LTZK15218	1961	£15	£6	
Grand Encounter	LP	Vogue	LAE12065	1958	£25	£10	*with Bill Perkins*
Improvised Meditations And Excursions	LP	London	LTZK15186	1960	£15	£6	
Odds Against Tomorrow	LP	London	HAT2220	1960	£15	£6	
Wonderful World Of Jazz	LP	London	LTZK15237	1961	£15	£6	

LEWIS, LEW

Title	Format	Label	Cat. No.	Year	Mint	VG	Notes
Lucky Seven	7"	Lew Lewis	LEW1	1978	£5	£2	

LEWIS, LINDA

Title	Format	Label	Cat. No.	Year	Mint	VG	Notes
Lark	LP	Reprise	K44208	1972	£10	£4	
You Turn My Bitter Into Sweet	7"	Polydor	56173	1967	£40	£20	

LEWIS, MARGARET

Title	Format	Label	Cat. No.	Year	Mint	VG	Notes
Something's Wrong Baby	7"	Starlite	ST45081	1962	£8	£4	

LEWIS, MEADE LUX

Title	Format	Label	Cat. No.	Year	Mint	VG	Notes
Barrel House Piano	LP	Tops	L1533		£20	£8	*US*
Blues Piano Artistry	LP	Riverside	9402		£20	£8	*US*

Boogie Woogie And Blues	7" EP	Melodisc	EPM7107	1956	£25	£12.50	
Boogie Woogie Piano And Drums No. 1	7" EP	Columbia	SEB10030	1956	£10	£5	
Boogie Woogie Piano And Drums No. 2	7" EP	Columbia	SEB10052	1957	£10	£5	
House Party	LP	Philips	652014BL	1962	£15	£6	
Jazz At The Philharmonic	10" LP	Columbia	33C9021	1956	£15	£6	*with Slim Gaillard*
Meade Lux Lewis	7" EP	Vogue	EPV1065	1955	£25	£12.50	
Out Of The Roaring Twenties	10" LP	HMV	DLP1176	1958	£15	£6	
Yancey's Last Ride	LP	Columbia	33CX10094	1957	£20	£8	

LEWIS, MIA

It's Goodbye Now	7"	Decca	F12240	1965	£4	£1.50	
Nothing Lasts Forever	7"	Parlophone	R5526	1966	£8	£4	
Wish I Didn't Love Him	7"	Decca	F12117	1965	£4	£1.50	

LEWIS, NEIL

Profile	LP	Swamp	WAM680	1980	£20	£8	

LEWIS, PATTI

Earthbound	7"	Columbia	DB3825	1956	£4	£1.50	

LEWIS, PETER

Sing Life Sing Lore	LP	Quest	QLP539	1974	£20	£8	

LEWIS, PHILLIPPA

Just Like In The Movies	7"	Decca	F12152	1965	£6	£2.50	

LEWIS, RAMSEY

At The Bohemian Caverns	LP	Pye	NJL55	1965	£10	£4	
Choice!	LP	Chess	CRL4518	1965	£12	£5	
Dancin' In The Street	LP	Chess	CRL(S)4533	1968	£10	£4	
Day Tripper	7"	Chess	CRS8051	1967	£6	£2.50	
Down To Earth	LP	Fontana	SFJL962	1960	£15	£6	
Function At The Junction	7"	Chess	CRS8058	1967	£4	£1.50	
Girl Talk	7"	Chess	CRS8061	1967	£4	£1.50	
Hang On Ramsey	LP	Chess	CRL4517	1966	£10	£4	
Hang On Sloopy	7"	Chess	CRS8024	1965	£4	£1.50	
Hard Day's Night	7"	Chess	CRS8029	1966	£4	£1.50	
Hard Day's Night	7" EP	Chess	CRE6019	1966	£10	£5	
Hi Heel Sneakers	7"	Chess	CRS8031	1966	£4	£1.50	
Hour With	LP	Cadet	645	1959	£10	£4	*US*
In Crowd	7"	Chess	CRS8020	1965	£4	£1.50	
In Crowd	LP	Chess	CRL4511	1965	£10	£4	
More Music From Soul	LP	Cadet	680	1962	£10	£4	*US*
Movie Album	LP	Chess	CRL4531	1967	£10	£4	
Never On Sunday	LP	Cadet	686	1962	£10	£4	*US*
Stretchin' Out	LP	Cadet	665	1962	£10	£4	*US*
Uptight	7"	Chess	CRS8044	1966	£4	£1.50	
Wade In The Water	7"	Chess	CRS8041	1966	£6	£2.50	
Wade In The Water	LP	Chess	CRL4522	1966	£10	£4	

LEWIS, REGGIE

Natty Natty	7"	Upsetter	US391	1972	£4	£1.50	*Upsetters B side*

LEWIS, RICHARD

Hey Little Girl	7"	Downbeat	CHA1	1960	£20	£10	

LEWIS, SMILEY

Big Mamou	78	London	L1189	1953	£50	£25	
Don't Be That Way	7"	London	HLU8337	1956	£600	£400	*best auctioned*
I Hear You Knocking	7"	Liberty	LBF15337	1970	£4	£1.50	
I Hear You Knocking	LP	Imperial	LP9141	1961	£150	£75	*US*
One Night	7"	London	HLU8312	1956	£600	£400	*best auctioned*
Shame Shame Shame	7"	London	HLP8367	1957	£500	£330	*best auctioned*
Shame, Shame, Shame	LP	Liberty	LBS83308	1970	£12	£5	

LEWIS, STEVIE

Take Me For A Little While	7"	Mercury	MF871	1965	£8	£4	

LEWIS, TINY

Too Much Rocking	7"	Parlophone	R4617	1959	£75	£37.50	

LEWIS SISTERS

You Need Me	7"	Tamla Motown	TMG536	1965	£50	£25	

LEWRY, DAVE

All I Want To Do Is Play Guitar	LP	Westwood	WRS019	1972	£30	£15	

LEYTON, JOHN

All I Want Is You	7"	HMV	POP1374	1964	£5	£2	*with Mike Sarne & Grazina Frame*
Always Yours	LP	HMV	CLP1664	1962	£50	£25	
Beautiful Dreamer	7"	HMV	POP1230	1963	£4	£1.50	
Beautiful Dreamer	7" EP	HMV	7EG8843	1964	£30	£15	
Cupboard Love	7"	HMV	POP1122	1963	£4	£1.50	
Dancing In The Graveyard	7"	York	SYK551	1973	£5	£2	
Don't Let Her Go Away	7"	HMV	POP1338	1964	£6	£2.50	
Down The River Nile	7"	HMV	POP1054	1962	£4	£1.50	

Title	Format	Label	Cat. No.	Year	Price	Price	Notes
Girl On The Floor Above	7"	HMV	POP798	1960	£60	£30	
I'll Cut Your Tail Off	7"	HMV	POP1175	1963	£4	£1.50	
John Leyton	7" EP	Top Rank	JKP3016	1962	£30	£15	
John Leyton	LP	York	FYK416	1973	£20	£8	
John Leyton Hit Parade	7" EP	HMV	7EG8747	1962	£25	£12.50	
Lone Rider	7"	HMV	POP992	1962	£10	£5	
Lonely City	7"	HMV	POP1014	1962	£4	£1.50	
Lonely Johnny	7"	HMV	POP1076	1962	£5	£2	
Make Love To Me	7"	HMV	POP1264	1964	£4	£1.50	
On Lovers' Hill	7"	HMV	POP1204	1963	£5	£2	
Rock'n'Roll	7"	York	YR210	1974	£5	£2	
Son This Is She	7"	HMV	POP956	1961	£4	£1.50	
Tell Laura I Love Her	7"	Top Rank	JAR426	1960	£40	£20	
Tell Laura I Love Her	7" EP	HMV	7EG8854	1964	£30	£15	
Two Sides Of John Leyton	LP	HMV	CLP1497	1961	£30	£15	
Wild Wind	7"	Top Rank	JAR585	1961	£4	£1.50	

L.F.O.

Title	Format	Label	Cat. No.	Year	Price	Price	Notes
L.F.O.	12"	Warp	WAP5	1990	£8	£4	

LIAISON

Title	Format	Label	Cat. No.	Year	Price	Price	Notes
Play It With A Passion	7"	Catweazle	CR001	1982	£30	£15	*picture sleeve*
Play It With A Passion	7"	Catweazle	CR001	1982	£8	£4	

LIBERATION SUITE

Title	Format	Label	Cat. No.	Year	Price	Price	Notes
Liberation Suite	LP	Myrrh	MYR1027	1975	£10	£4	

LIBERMAN, JEFFREY

Title	Format	Label	Cat. No.	Year	Price	Price	Notes
Jeffrey Liberman	LP	Librah	1545	1975	£150	£75	*US*
Solitude Within	LP	Librah	6969	1975	£150	£75	*US*
Synergy	LP	Librah	12157	1978	£100	£50	*US*

LICKS

Title	Format	Label	Cat. No.	Year	Price	Price	Notes
1970s Have Been Made In Hong Kong	7"	Stortbeat	BEAT8	1979	£8	£4	

LIEBMAN, DAVE

Title	Format	Label	Cat. No.	Year	Price	Price	Notes
Drum Ode	LP	ECM	ECM1046ST	1975	£20	£8	
Lookout Farm	LP	ECM	ECM1039ST	1974	£20	£8	
Sweet Hands	LP	Horizon	SP702	1975	£12	£5	*US*

LIED DES TEUFELS

Title	Format	Label	Cat. No.	Year	Price	Price	Notes
Lied Des Teufels	LP	Kuckuck	2375019	1973	£10	£4	*German*

LIEUTENANT PIGEON

Title	Format	Label	Cat. No.	Year	Price	Price	Notes
Pigeon Party	LP	Decca	SKL5196	1974	£10	£4	
Pigeon Pie	LP	Decca	SKL5174	1974	£10	£4	
World Of Lieutenant Pigeon	LP	Decca	SPA414	1976	£12	£5	*test pressing only*

LIFE

Title	Format	Label	Cat. No.	Year	Price	Price	Notes
Hands Of The Clock	7"	Polydor	56778	1969	£4	£1.50	
Life	LP	Columbia	C06234264	1970	£100	£50	*Swedish*
Life After Death	LP	Polydor	2383295	1974	£30	£15	

LIFE (2)

Title	Format	Label	Cat. No.	Year	Price	Price	Notes
Cats' Eyes	7"	Philips	6006280	1973	£4	£1.50	*blue paper label*

LIFE AFTER LIFE

Title	Format	Label	Cat. No.	Year	Price	Price	Notes
Life After Life	LP	Time Track	SRTSKL453	1985	£200	£100	

LIFE 'N' SOUL

Title	Format	Label	Cat. No.	Year	Price	Price	Notes
Here Comes Yesterday Again	7"	Decca	F12851	1968	£4	£1.50	
Peacefully Asleep	7"	Decca	F12659	1967	£10	£5	

LIGGINS, JOE & THE HONEYDRIPPERS

Title	Format	Label	Cat. No.	Year	Price	Price	Notes
I've Got A Right To Cry	78	Parlophone	R3309	1950	£8	£4	

LIGHT

Title	Format	Label	Cat. No.	Year	Price	Price	Notes
Story Of Moses	LP	Brain	1013	1972	£15	£6	*German*

LIGHT (2)

Title	Format	Label	Cat. No.	Year	Price	Price	Notes
Light	LP	Mint	MINT11	1978	£25	£10	*Irish*

LIGHT, ENOCH

Title	Format	Label	Cat. No.	Year	Price	Price	Notes
Permissive Polyphonics	LP	PROJECT	3	1970	£10	£4	
Spaced Out	LP	Columbia	TWO312	1969	£20	£8	

LIGHT FANTASIC

Title	Format	Label	Cat. No.	Year	Price	Price	Notes
Jeanie	7"	RCA	RCA2331	1973	£15	£7.50	

LIGHT OF DARKNESS

Title	Format	Label	Cat. No.	Year	Price	Price	Notes
Light Of Darkness	LP	Philips	6305062	1970	£100	£50	*German*

LIGHT OF THE WORLD

Title	Format	Label	Cat. No.	Year	Price	Price	Notes
Check Us Out	LP	EMI	EMC3410	1982	£10	£4	

LIGHTCRUST DOUGHBOYS

Title	Format	Label	Cat. No.	Year	Price	Price	Notes
Lightcrust Doughboys	LP	Audio Lab	AL1525	1959	£30	£15	*US*

LIGHTBEARERS

Going Dutch	LP	Dovetail	DOVE22	1975	**£25**	**£10**	

LIGHTFOOT, GORDON

Back Here On Earth	LP	United Artists	SULP1239	1969	**£10**	**£4**	
Day Before Yesterday	7"	Fontana	TF405	1963	**£10**	**£5**	
Did She Mention My Name	LP	United Artists	SULP1199	1968	**£12**	**£5**	
Early Lightfoot	LP	United Artists	UAS29012	1969	**£25**	**£10**	
I'm The One	7"	Decca	F11527	1962	**£10**	**£5**	
Just Like Tom Thumb's Blues	7"	United Artists	UP1109	1965	**£8**	**£4**	
Lightfoot	LP	United Artists	UAL3487/ UAS6487	1965	**£25**	**£10**	*US*
Negotiations	7"	Fontana	267275	1963	**£10**	**£5**	
Sunday Concert	LP	United Artists	UAS29040	1969	**£12**	**£5**	
Two Tones At The Village Corner	LP	Canatal	CTLP4026	1962	**£400**	**£250**	*Canadian, with Terry Whelan*
Way I Feel	LP	United Artists	UAL3587/ UAS6587	1967	**£25**	**£10**	*US*

LIGHTFOOT, PAPA GEORGE

More Down Home Blues	7" EP	Jan & Dil	JR451	196–	**£10**	**£5**	
Natchez Trace	LP	Liberty	LBS83353	1969	**£12**	**£5**	

LIGHTFOOT, TERRY

Alleycat	LP	Columbia	33SX1721	1965	**£10**	**£4**	
Jazz Gumbo Vol. 1	10" LP	Nixa	NJT503	1956	**£12**	**£5**	
Lightfoot At Lansdowne	LP	Columbia	33SX1449	1962	**£10**	**£4**	
Terry Lightfoot's Jazzmen	7" EP	Nixa	NJE1027	1956	**£8**	**£4**	
Trad Parade	LP	Columbia	33SX1290/ SCX3354	1961	**£12**	**£5**	
Tradition In Colour	LP	Columbia	33SX1073	1958	**£12**	**£5**	
World Of Trad	LP	Columbia	33SX1353	1961	**£15**	**£6**	

LIGHTHOUSE

Eight Miles High	7"	RCA	RCA1884	1969	**£4**	**£1.50**	
Lighthouse	LP	RCA	LSP4173	1969	**£15**	**£6**	*US*
One Fine Morning	LP	Vertigo	6342010	1971	**£20**	**£8**	*spiral label*
Peacing It All Together	LP	RCA	SF8121	1970	**£12**	**£5**	
Suite Feeling	LP	RCA	SF8103	1970	**£12**	**£5**	
Thoughts Of Moving On	LP	Vertigo	6342011	1971	**£20**	**£8**	*spiral label*

LIGHTNIN' ROD

Hustler's Convention	LP	United Artists	UALA156F	1973	**£15**	**£6**	*US*

LIGHTNIN' ROD & JIMI HENDRIX

'Doriella Du Fontane' is one of the more overlooked records involving Jimi Hendrix. Although released in 1984, and featuring Hendrix in the unaccustomed role of providing rhythmic support to a rapper, the record is not the result of an eighties remixing project. Lightnin' Rod was a member of the Last Poets, whose blend of street poetry and percussion anticipates the work of artists like Public Enemy by some years. His collaboration with Jimi Hendrix was recorded during the guitarist's lifetime and represents an important reminder of Hendrix's occasional wish to reaffirm his blackness.

Doriella Du Fontane	12"	Celluloid	CRT332	1984	**£10**	**£5**	

LIGHTNIN' SLIM

Bell Ringer	LP	Excello	(S)8004	1965	**£20**	**£8**	*US*
Downhome Blues Part 1	LP	Python	PLP8	1969	**£30**	**£15**	
Just A Little Bit	7"	Blue Horizon	2096013	1972	**£15**	**£7.50**	
London Gumbo	LP	Blue Horizon	2931005	1972	**£50**	**£25**	
Rooster Blues	LP	Blue Horizon	763863	1970	**£50**	**£25**	
Rooster Blues	LP	Excello	8000	1960	**£30**	**£15**	*US*

LIGHTNING

Lightning	LP	P.I.P.	PP6807	1969	**£30**	**£15**	*US*

LIGHTNING RAIDERS

Criminal World	7"	Revenge	REVS200	1981	**£10**	**£5**	
Lightning Raiders	12"	Revenge		198–	**£20**	**£10**	*promo sampler*
Psychedlik Musik	7"	Arista	ARIST341	1980	**£15**	**£7.50**	
Sweet Revenge	12"	Revenge	RSS39	1981	**£8**	**£4**	*promo*

LIGHTNING SEEDS

All I Want	CD-s	Ghetto	CDGTG9	1990	**£5**	**£2**	
Jollification	CD	Epic	4772379	1994	**£12**	**£5**	*strawberry scented packaging, pic disc*
Joy	CD-s	Ghetto	CDGTG6	1989	**£5**	**£2**	
Life Of Riley	CD-s	Virgin	VSCDG1402	1992	**£5**	**£2**	
Pure	CD-s	Ghetto	CDGTG4	1989	**£6**	**£2.50**	
Sense	CD-s	Virgin	VSCDT1414	1992	**£5**	**£2**	
Sweet Dreams	CD-s	Ghetto	CDGTG8	1990	**£5**	**£2**	
Upside Down	CD-s	Ghetto	CDGTG7	1989	**£5**	**£2**	

LIGHTSHINE

Feeling	LP	Trefiton	HS1049ST	1973	**£100**	**£50**	*German*

LIKE A SONG

Like A Song	LP	De Wolfe	DWLP3273	1973	**£10**	**£4**	

LILAC ANGELS

I'm Not Afraid To Say Yes .... LP .... Dingerland....... 09490211 .... 1973 £**10** .... £**4** .... *German*

LILAC TIME

All For Love And Love For All .... CD-s ... Fontana .... LILCD8 .... 1990 £**5** .... £**2**
American Eyes .... CD-s ... Fontana .... LILCD5 .... 1989 £**5** .... £**2**
And Love For All .... CD ...... Fontana .... 8461902 .... 1990 £**12** .... £**5**
Black Velvet .... CD-s ... Fontana .... LILCD4 .... 1988 £**5** .... £**2**
Days Of The Week .... CD-s ... Fontana .... LILCD6 .... 1989 £**5** .... £**2**
Girl Who Waves At Trains .... CD-s ... Fontana .... LILCD7 .... 1989 £**5** .... £**2**
It'll End In Tears .... CD-s ... Fontana .... LILCD10 .... 1990 £**5** .... £**2**
Laundry .... CD-s ... Fontana .... LILCD9 .... 1990 £**5** .... £**2**
Lilac Time .... CD ...... Swordfish .... SWFCD6 .... 1988 £**25** .... £**10**
Lilac Time .... CD ...... Fontana .... 8348352 .... 1988 £**15** .... £**6**
Lilac Time .... LP .... Swordfish .... SWFLP6 .... 1988 £**10** .... £**4**
Madresfield .... 7" .... Caff .... CAFF12 .... 1990 £**15** .... £**7.50**
Paradise Circus .... CD ...... Fontana .... 8386412 .... 1989 £**15** .... £**6**
Return To Yesterday .... 12" ...... Swordfish .... 12LILAC1 .... 1988 £**10** .... £**5**
Return To Yesterday .... 7" .... Swordfish .... LILAC1 .... 1988 £**5** .... £**2** .... *no picture sleeve*
Return To Yesterday .... CD-s ... Fontana .... LILCD2 .... 1988 £**6** .... £**2.50**
Return To Yesterday .... CD-s ... Polygram .... 0804602 .... 1988 £**10** .... £**5** .... *CD video*
You've Got To Love .... CD-s ... Fontana .... LILCD3 .... 1988 £**6** .... £**2.50**

LIMBUS

Cosmic Music Experience .... LP .... CPM .... LPS001 .... 1969 £**150** .... £**75** .... *German*
Mandalas .... LP .... Ohr .... OMM56001 .... 1970 £**20** .... £**8** .... *German*
New Atlantis .... LP .... private .... 1976 £**125** .. £**62.50** .... *German*

LIMELIGHT

Ashes To Ashes .... 7" .... Future Earth .... FER010 .... 1982 £**5** .... £**2**
Limelight .... LP .... Future Earth .... FER008 .... 1980 £**25** .... £**10**
Limelight .... LP .... Avatar .... AALP5005 .... 1981 £**25** .... £**10** .... *with 7"*
Metal Man .... 7" .... Future Earth .... FER006 .... 1980 £**6** .... £**2.50**

LIMELIGHT (BRINSLEY SCHWARZ)

I Should Have Known Better .... 7" .... United Artists .. UP35779 .... 1975 £**8** .... £**4**

LIMELITERS

Four Folk Songs .... 7" EP .. RCA .... RCX7151 .... 1964 £**5** .... £**2**
Fun And Folk .... 7" EP .. RCA .... RCX7126 .... 1963 £**5** .... £**2**
Limeliters .... LP .... Elektra .... EKL180 .... 1961 £**12** .... £**5** .... *US*

LIMERICK, ALISON

Where Love Lives .... 12" ...... Arista .... 613509 .... 1990 £**6** .... £**2.50**

LIMEYS

Cara Lin .... 7" .... Decca .... F12382 .... 1966 £**20** .... £**10**
I Can't Find My Way Through .... 7" .... Pye .... 7N15820 .... 1965 £**4** .... £**1.50**
Mountain's High .... 7" .... Decca .... F12466 .... 1966 £**4** .... £**1.50**
Some Tears Fall Dry .... 7" .... Pye .... 7N15909 .... 1965 £**4** .... £**1.50**

LINCOLN, ABBEY

That's Him .... LP .... Riverside .... RLP12251 .... 196– £**15** .... £**6**

LINCOLN, PETER

In The Day Of My Youth .... 7" .... Major Minor ... MM520 .... 1967 £**5** .... £**2**

LINCOLN, PHILAMORE

North Wind Blew South .... LP .... Epic .... BN26497 .... 1967 £**12** .... £**5** .... *US*
Running By The River .... 7" .... Nems .... 563711 .... 1968 £**5** .... £**2**

LINCOLN STREET EXIT

Drive It .... LP .... London .... SHAU122 .... 1970 £**125** .. £**62.50** .... *German*

LINCOLN X

Heartaches And Happiness .... 7" .... Oriole .... CB1823 .... 1963 £**4** .... £**1.50**

LINCOLNS

Tribute To Elvis .... LP .... Attic .... TCA70 .... 1977 £**25** .... £**10** .... *Canadian*

LIND, BOB

Don't Be Concerned .... LP .... Fontana .... (S)TL5340 .... 1966 £**15** .... £**6**
Elusive Bob Lind .... LP .... Verve .... (S)VLP5015 .... 1966 £**10** .... £**4**
Photographs Of Feelings .... LP .... Fontana .... (S)TL5395 .... 1967 £**10** .... £**4**

LINDBERG, DADDY

Shirl .... 7" .... Columbia .... DB8138 .... 1967 £**5** .... £**2**

LINDEN, KATHY

Billy .... 7" .... Felsted .... AF102 .... 1958 £**5** .... £**2**
Goodbye Jimmy Goodbye .... 7" .... Felsted .... AF122 .... 1959 £**4** .... £**1.50**
Kathy .... 7" EP .. Felsted .... GEP1001 .... 1959 £**15** .... £**7.50**
Kathy In Love Vol. 1 .... 7" EP .. Felsted .... GEP1002 .... 1959 £**15** .... £**7.50**
Kathy In Love Vol. 2 .... 7" EP .. Felsted .... GEP1004 .... 1959 £**15** .... £**7.50**
Kissin' Conversation .... 7" .... Felsted .... AF111 .... 1958 £**5** .... £**2**
Mary Lou Wilson And Johnny Brown .... 7" .... Felsted .... AF130 .... 1960 £**5** .... £**2**
Oh Johnny Oh Johnny Oh .... 7" .... Felsted .... AF108 .... 1958 £**4** .... £**1.50**

That Certain Boy	LP	Felsted	7501	195–	**£25**	**£10**	*US*
You Don't Know Girls	7"	Felsted	AF124	1959	**£5**	**£2**	
You'd Be Surprised	7"	Felsted	AF105	1958	**£5**	**£2**	

LINDENBERG, UDO

Daumen Im Wind	LP	Telefunken	SLE14679	1972	**£10**	**£4**	*German*
Lindenberg	LP	Telefunken	SLE14637	1971	**£10**	**£4**	*German*

LINDH, BJORN J:SON

Cous Cous	LP	Metronome	MLP15450	1972	**£10**	**£4**	*Swedish*
Fran Storsted Till Grodspad	LP	SR	RELP1135	1971	**£12**	**£5**	*Swedish*

LINDISFARNE

Lindisfarne became quite popular in their day, achieving the remarkable feat, for a group marketed as being 'progressive', of gaining a pair of top ten single hits. Today, their cheery, sing-along folk-rock is not highly regarded and even the fact that their earliest albums are on the collectable Charisma pink label does not appear to be enough to give them a collectors' value.

Clear White Light	7"	Charisma	CB137	1970	**£6**	**£2.50**	
Lady Eleanor	7"	Charisma	CB153	1971	**£4**	**£1.50**	*picture sleeve*
Lady Eleanor 88	CD-s	Virgin	LADYD1	1988	**£5**	**£2**	*3" single*
Peel Sessions	CD-s	Strange Fruit	SFPSCD059	1988	**£5**	**£2**	

LINDYS

Boy With The Eyes Of Blue	7"	Decca	F11272	1960	**£10**	**£5**	
Train Of Love	7"	Decca	F11253	1960	**£8**	**£4**	

LINK

Link EP	12"	Evolution	EVO05	1992	**£15**	**£7.50**	
Link EP	12"	Symbiotic	SYM001	1993	**£15**	**£7.50**	

LINN, ELMO

Sam Houston	7"	Starlite	ST45101	1963	**£6**	**£2.50**	

LINN COUNTY

Fever Shot	LP	Mercury	SMCL20165	1969	**£10**	**£4**	
Proud Flesh Soothseer	LP	Mercury	SMCL20142	1968	**£10**	**£4**	
Till The Break Of Dawn	LP	Philips	SBL7923	1970	**£10**	**£4**	

LINUS & THE LITTLE PEOPLE

Lovin' La La	7"	Evolution		1970	**£5**	**£2**	

LION, JOHNNY

Johnny Lion And The Jumping Jewels	LP	Philips	12902	1963	**£25**	**£10**	*Dutch*

LION TAMERS

Speak Your Mind	7"	Polydor	56283	1968	**£4**	**£1.50**	

LIONROCK

Dub Plate No. 1	12"	Distort & Cavort		1993	**£8**	**£4**	
Lionrock – The Remixes	12"	DeConstruction	74321124381	1992	**£8**	**£4**	
Packet Of Peace	12"	DeConstruction	74321144372	1993	**£25**	**£12.50**	*promo*
Roots 'n' Culture	12"	M.E.R.C.	002	1992	**£8**	**£4**	

LIONS OF JUDAH

Our Love's A Growin' Thing	7"	Fontana	TF1016	1969	**£5**	**£2**	

LIP MOVES

Guest	7"	Tichonderoga	HP1	1979	**£5**	**£2**	

LIPSCOMB, MANCE

Trouble In Mind	LP	Reprise	R(9)2012	1961	**£12**	**£5**	*US*

LIQUID SMOKE

Liquid Smoke	LP	Avco	33005	1969	**£50**	**£25**	*US*

LISTEN

The lead singer of Listen was Robert Plant and he is, in fact, the only member of the group to appear on the single credited to them.

You Better Run	7"	CBS	202456	1965	**£150**	**£75**	

LISTENING

Listening	LP	Vanguard	VSD6504	1969	**£60**	**£30**	*US*

LITA FORD & OZZY OSBOURNE

Close My Eyes Forever	CD-s	Dreamland	PA49396	1989	**£6**	**£2.50**	*3" single*

LITE STORM

Warning	LP	Beverly Hills	BHS1135	1973	**£60**	**£30**	*US*

LITTER

$100 Fine	LP	Hexagon	HX681	1969	**£250**	**£150**	*US*
Distortions	LP	Warick	671	1968	**£300**	**£180**	*US*
Emerge	LP	Probe	CLPS4504	1969	**£25**	**£10**	

LITTLE, BIG TINY

Honky Tonk Piano Vol. 1	7" EP	Coral	FEP2058	1960	**£6**	**£2.50**	

Title	Format	Label	Cat. No.	Year	Mint	VG	Notes
Honky Tonk Piano Vol. 2	7" EP	Coral	FEP2059	1960	£6	£2.50	
School Day	7"	Vogue Coral	Q72263	1957	£25	£12.50	

LITTLE, MARIE

Title	Format	Label	Cat. No.	Year	Mint	VG	Notes
Factory Girl	LP	Argo	ZFB19	1971	£100	£50	
Marie Little	LP	Trailer	LER2084	1973	£60	£30	

LITTLE ANGELS

Title	Format	Label	Cat. No.	Year	Mint	VG	Notes
'87 EP	12"	Song Management	LAN001	1987	£25	£12.50	
Big Bad EP	CD-s	Polydor	LTLCD2	1989	£6	£2.50	
Do You Wanna Riot	CD-s	Polydor	LTLCD3	1989	£5	£2	
Don't Pray For Me	CD-s	Polydor	LTLCD4	1989	£5	£2	
I Ain't Gonna Cry	CD-s	Polydor	LTLCD11	1991	£5	£2	
Kicking Up Dust	CD-s	Polydor	LTLCD5	1990	£5	£2	
Ninety Degrees In The Shade	7"	Polydor	LTLD1	1988	£4	£1.50	*poster sleeve*
Product Of The Working Class	CD-s	Polydor	LTCDB9	1991	£8	£4	*CD set*
Too Posh To Mosh	LP	Powerstation	AMP14	1987	£15	£6	
Young Gods	CD-s	Polydor	LTLCD10	1991	£10	£5	*with booklet*

LITTLE ANTHONY & THE IMPERIALS

Title	Format	Label	Cat. No.	Year	Mint	VG	Notes
Bayou Bayou Baby	7"	Top Rank	JAR366	1960	£10	£5	
Best Of Little Anthony And The Imperials	LP	DCP	DC3809/DS6809	1966	£25	£10	*US*
Better Use Your Head	7"	United Artists	UP1137	1966	£25	£12.50	
Goin' Out Of My Head	7"	United Artists	UP1073	1964	£6	£2.50	
Goin' Out Of My Head	LP	United Artists	ULP1100	1966	£30	£15	
Gonna Fix You Good	7"	United Artists	UP1151	1966	£25	£12.50	
Hurt	7"	United Artists	UP1126	1966	£5	£2	
Hurt So Bad	7"	United Artists	UP1083	1965	£8	£4	
I Miss You So	7"	United Artists	UP1112	1965	£4	£1.50	
I'm On The Outside Lookin' In	LP	United Artists	ULP1089	1964	£60	£30	
I'm On The Outside Looking In	7"	United Artists	UP1065	1964	£5	£2	
Little Anthony And The Imperials	7" EP	United Artists	UEP1004	1965	£50	£25	
Oh Yeah	7"	London	HL8848	1959	£20	£10	
Shades Of The 40s	LP	End	311	1960	£50	£25	*US*
Shimmy Shimmy Ko Ko Bop	7"	Top Rank	JAR256	1959	£10	£5	
Take Me Back	7"	United Artists	UP1098	1965	£4	£1.50	
Tears On My Pillow	7"	London	HLH8704	1958	£40	£20	
We Are Little Anthony & The Imperials	LP	End	303	1960	£75	£37.50	*US*

LITTLE BEVERLEY

Title	Format	Label	Cat. No.	Year	Mint	VG	Notes
What A Guy	7"	Pama	PM731	1968	£4	£1.50	

LITTLE BILL & THE BLUENOTES

Title	Format	Label	Cat. No.	Year	Mint	VG	Notes
I Love An Angel	7"	Top Rank	JAR176	1959	£8	£4	

LITTLE BOY BLUE

Title	Format	Label	Cat. No.	Year	Mint	VG	Notes
Dark End Of The Street	7"	Jackpot	JP701	1969	£4	£1.50	
Since You Are Gone	7"	Jackpot	JP705	1969	£4	£1.50	

LITTLE BOY BLUES

Title	Format	Label	Cat. No.	Year	Mint	VG	Notes
In The Woodland Of Weir	LP	Fontana	MGF2/SRF67578	1967	£20	£8	*US*

LITTLE CAESAR & THE ROMANS

Title	Format	Label	Cat. No.	Year	Mint	VG	Notes
Memories Of Those Oldies But Goodies	LP	Del-Fi	DFLP1218	1961	£25	£10	*US*

LITTLE DARLINGS

Title	Format	Label	Cat. No.	Year	Mint	VG	Notes
Little Bit Of Soul	7"	Fontana	TF539	1965	£50	£25	

LITTLE DIPPERS

Title	Format	Label	Cat. No.	Year	Mint	VG	Notes
Forever	7"	Pye	7N25051	1960	£4	£1.50	
Lonely	7"	London	HLG9269	1961	£8	£4	

LITTLE EVA

Title	Format	Label	Cat. No.	Year	Mint	VG	Notes
Keep Your Hands Off My Baby	7"	London	HLU9633	1962	£4	£1.50	
Let's Turkey Trot	7"	London	HLU9687	1963	£4	£1.50	
Locomotion	LP	London	HAU8036	1963	£25	£10	
Please Hurt Me	7"	Colpix	PX11119	1963	£4	£1.50	
Run To Her	7"	Colpix	PX11035	1964	£4	£1.50	
Stand By Me	7"	Stateside	SS477	1965	£8	£4	
Trouble With Boys	7"	Colpix	PX11013	1963	£5	£2	

LITTLE FEAT

Title	Format	Label	Cat. No.	Year	Mint	VG	Notes
Feats Don't Fail Me Now	LP	Warner Bros	K56030	198–	£10	£4	*Nimbus supercut*
Waiting For Columbus	LP	Mobile Fidelity	MFSL2013	1978	£15	£6	*US audiophile double*

LITTLE FOLK

Title	Format	Label	Cat. No.	Year	Mint	VG	Notes
Leave Them A Flower	LP	Studio Republic	CR1001	1971	£15	£6	

LITTLE FRANKIE

Title	Format	Label	Cat. No.	Year	Mint	VG	Notes
It Doesn't Matter Any More	7"	Columbia	DB7681	1965	£6	£2.50	
Kind Of Boy You Can't Forget	7"	Columbia	DB7490	1965	£5	£2	
Make-A-Love	7"	Columbia	DB7578	1965	£8	£4	

LITTLE FREE ROCK

Little Free Rock	LP	Transatlantic	TRA608	1969	£60	£30	

LITTLE GEORGE

Mary Anne	7"	Rio	R45	1964	£10	£5	*Edward's Allstars B side*

LITTLE HANK

Mr Bang Bang Man	7"	London	HLU10090	1966	£30	£15	
Mr Bang Bang Man	7"	Monument	MON1045	1970	£5	£2	

LITTLE JOE

Peanuts	7"	Reprise	R20142	1963	£6	£2.50	
Stay	7"	Fontana	H281	1960	£10	£5	

LITTLE JOEY & THE FLIPS

Bongo Stomp	7"	Pye	7N25152	1962	£5	£2	

LITTLE JOHN

Little John	LP	Epic	64421	1971	£15	£6	

LITTLE JOHNNY & THE THREE TEENAGERS

Baby Lover	7"	Decca	F10990	1958	£8	£4	

LITTLE LUMAN

Hurry Harry	7"	Rio	R44	1964	£10	£5	*Roland Alphonso B side*

LITTLE LUTHER

Eenie Meenie Minie Mo	7"	Pye	7N25266	1964	£30	£15	

LITTLE MAC & THE BOSS SOUNDS

In The Midnight Hour	7"	Atlantic	584031	1966	£4	£1.50	

LITTLE MILTON

Little Milton is a fine blues singer and an even finer blues guitarist – very much in the manner of B. B. King on both counts – but most of his releases are soul records, where he is rather more ordinary. The *Grits Ain't Groceries* LP provides a reasonable balance between the styles, with the outstanding track being a smouldering version of 'I Can't Quit You Baby' (also the B side of the 'Grits Ain't Groceries' single).

Blindman	7"	Pye	7N25289	1965	£6	£2.50	
Early In The Morning	7"	Sue	WI4021	1966	£15	£7.50	
Grits Ain't Groceries	7"	Chess	CRS8087	1969	£6	£2.50	
Grits Ain't Groceries	LP	Chess	CRLS4552	1969	£15	£6	
Let's Get Together	7"	Chess	CRS8101	1969	£6	£2.50	
Little Milton Sings Big Blues	LP	Checker	3002	1966	£20	£8	*US*
We're Gonna Make It	7"	Chess	CRS8013	1965	£6	£2.50	
We're Gonna Make It	LP	Checker	2995	1965	£30	£15	*US*
Who's Cheating Who	7"	Chess	CRS8018	1965	£8	£4	

LITTLE MR LEE & THE CHEROKEES

Young Lover	7"	Vocalion	VP9268	1966	£15	£7.50	

LITTLE NORMA

Ten Commandments Of Woman	7"	Dice	CC26	1964	£10	£5	

LITTLE RAY

'I Been Trying' is an early example of Arthur Lee's songwriting, although Lee (later the leader of the group Love) does not appear to be otherwise involved in the record.

I Been Trying	7"	Donna	1404	1964	£50	£25	*US*

LITTLE RICHARD

Baby Face	7"	London	HL7056	1958	£10	£5	*export*
Baby Face	7"	London	HLU8770	1958	£4	£1.50	
Baby What You Want Me To Do	7"	Action	ACT4528	1969	£5	£2	
Bama Lama Bama Loo	7"	London	HL9896	1964	£5	£2	
Blueberry Hill	7"	Fontana	TF519	1964	£5	£2	
By The Light Of The Silvery Moon	7"	London	HLU8831	1959	£4	£1.50	
By The Light Of The Silvery Moon	7"	London	HL7079	1959	£12	£6	*export*
Coming Home	LP	Coral	LVA9220	1964	£15	£6	
Crying In The Chapel	7"	London	HLK9708	1963	£5	£2	
Do You Feel It	7" EP	Stateside	SE1042	1966	£15	£7.50	
Explosive Little Richard	LP	Columbia	SX/SCX6136	1967	£15	£6	
Fabulous Little Richard	LP	London	HAU2193	1959	£30	£15	
Four Dynamic Numbers	7" EP	Summit	LSE2049	1963	£8	£4	*with Brock Peters*
Get Down And Get With It	7"	Columbia	DB8116	1967	£8	£4	
Girl Can't Help It	7"	London	HLO8382	1957	£75	£37.50	*gold label*
Good Golly Miss Molly	7"	London	HLU8560	1958	£15	£7.50	
Great Hits	LP	Fontana	TL5314	1966	£10	£4	
He Got What He Wanted	7"	Mercury	AMT1189	1962	£6	£2.50	
He's Back	7" EP	London	REK1400	1963	£15	£7.50	
Here's Little Richard	LP	London	HAO2055	1957	£25	£10	
Here's Little Richard	LP	Speciality	100	1957	£150	£75	*US*
Here's Little Richard	LP	London	HAO2055	1957	£40	£20	*glossy red rear sleeve*
Holy Mackrel	7"	Stateside	SS508	1966	£5	£2	
I Don't Know What You've Got	7"	Fontana	TF652	1966	£8	£4	

I Don't Wanna Discuss It	7"	Columbia	DB8263	1967	£15	£7.50	
I Got It	7"	London	HLU9065	1960	£10	£5	
I Need Love	7"	Columbia	DB8058	1966	£6	£2.50	
It Ain't What You Do	7"	Sue	WI4015	1966	£15	£7.50	
It's Real	LP	Mercury	MG2/SR60656	1961	£20	£8	*US*
It's Real	LP	Mercury	MCL20036	1965	£12	£5	
Jenny Jenny	7"	London	HLO8470	1957	£15	£7.50	
Jenny Jenny	7"	London	HL7022	1957	£12	£6	*export*
Joy Joy Joy	7"	Mercury	AMT1165	1961	£4	£1.50	
Kansas City	7"	London	HLU8868	1959	£6	£2.50	
Keep A Knocking	7"	London	HLO8509	1957	£15	£7.50	
Little Bit Of Something	7"	Columbia	DB8240	1967	£15	£7.50	
Little Richard	LP	Camden	CDN125	1959	£15	£6	*some tracks by Buck Ram Orchestra*
Little Richard	LP	Camden	CAL420	1956	£50	£25	*US*
Little Richard	LP	Speciality	SP2103	1957	£30	£15	*US*
Little Richard & His Band Vol. 1	7" EP	London	REO1071	1957	£20	£10	*gold label*
Little Richard & His Band Vol. 2	7" EP	London	REO1074	1957	£20	£10	*gold label*
Little Richard & His Band Vol. 3	7" EP	London	REO1103	1957	£20	£10	
Little Richard & His Band Vol. 4	7" EP	London	REO1106	1957	£20	£10	
Little Richard & His Band Vol. 5	7" EP	London	REU1208	1959	£20	£10	
Little Richard & His Band Vol. 6	7" EP	London	REU1234	1960	£20	£10	
Little Richard & His Band Vol. 7	7" EP	London	REU1235	1960	£20	£10	
Little Richard Is Back	LP	Fontana	TL5235	1965	£12	£5	
Little Richard Sings Freedom Songs	LP	Egmont	EGM9207	1963	£10	£4	
Little Richard Vol. 2	LP	London	HAU2126	1958	£30	£15	
Little Richard/Memphis Slim	7" EP	Vocalion	VEP170155	1964	£40	£20	*with Memphis Slim*
Long Tall Sally	7"	London	HLO8366	1957	£75	£37.50	*gold label*
Lucille	7"	London	HLO8446	1957	£15	£7.50	
Ooh My Soul	7"	London	HLO8647	1958	£8	£4	
Ooh My Soul	7"	London	HL7049	1958	£10	£5	*export*
Poor Dog	7"	Columbia	DB7974	1966	£8	£4	
Pray Along With Little Richard	LP	Egmont	EGM9270	1963	£10	£4	
Pray Along With Little Richard Vol. 1	LP	Top Rank	25025	1960	£40	£20	*plain white sleeve*
Pray Along With Little Richard Vol. 2	LP	Top Rank	25026	1960	£75	£37.50	*plain white sleeve*
Rip It Up	7"	London	HLO8336	1956	£75	£37.50	*gold label*
She Knows How To Rock	7"	London	HL7074	1959	£15	£7.50	*export*
She's Together	7"	Decca	AD1006	1968	£20	£10	*export*
She's Together	7"	MCA	MU1006	1968	£4	£1.50	
Sings Gospel	LP	Stateside	SL10054	1964	£15	£6	
Travelling Shoes	7"	London	HLK9756	1963	£5	£2	
Whole Lotta Shakin' Goin' On	7"	London	HL7085	1959	£40	£20	*export*
Whole Lotta Shakin' Goin' On	7"	Stateside	SS340	1964	£5	£2	
Without Love	7"	Sue	WI4001	1966	£15	£7.50	
You Can't Keep A Good Man Down	LP	Union Pacific	UP003	1970	£15	£6	

LITTLE ROYS

Bongonyah	7"	Camel	CA36	1969	£4	£1.50	
Gold Digger	7"	Camel	CA42	1970	£4	£1.50	*Matadors B side*
Selassie Want Us Back	7"	Camel	CA57	1970	£4	£1.50	*Roy And Joy B side*

LITTLE TONY & HIS BROTHERS

Four And Twenty Thousand Kisses	7"	Durium	DC16657	1961	£6	£2.50	
Hippy Hippy Shake	7"	Decca	F11169	1959	£6	£2.50	
I Can't Help It	7"	Decca	F11164	1959	£5	£2	
I Love You	7"	Decca	F21218	1960	£4	£1.50	
Let Her Go	7"	Durium	DRS54008	1958	£5	£2	
Let Her Go	LP	Durium	DRL50020	1966	£20	£8	
Little Tony	LP	Durium	DRL50006	1965	£25	£10	
Long Is The Lonely Night	7"	Durium	DRS54012	1967	£5	£2	
Non E Normale	7" EP	Durium	DRE52012	1966	£15	£7.50	
Presenting Little Tony	7" EP	Durium	U20058	1958	£30	£15	
Princess	7"	Decca	F21223	1960	£4	£1.50	
Teddy Girl	7"	Decca	F21247	1960	£6	£2.50	
Too Good	7"	Decca	F11190	1959	£5	£2	
Who's That Knocking	7"	Durium	DC16639	1959	£10	£5	

LITTLE WALTER

Best Of Little Walter	LP	Chess	LP1428	1958	£30	£15	*US*
Little Walter	LP	Pye	NPL28043	1964	£20	£8	
Little Walter & His Jukes	7" EP	London	REU1061	1956	£75	£37.50	
Little Walter And His Dukes	LP	Python	PLPKM20	1969	£25	£10	
My Babe	7"	London	HLM9175	1960	£15	£7.50	
My Babe	7"	Pye	7N25263	1964	£6	£2.50	
Thunderbird	LP	Syndicate Chapter	SC004	1971	£10	£4	

LITTLE WILBUR

Records credited to Little Wilbur are listed in this *Guide* under the name Wilbur Whitfield.

LIVELY ONES

Great Surf Hits	LP	Del-Fi	DFLP/DFST1238	1963	£25	£10	*US*
Surf Drums	LP	London	HA8082	1963	£30	£15	
Surf Rider	LP	London	HA8107	1963	£25	£10	
Surfin' South Of The Border	LP	Del-Fi	DFLP0DFST1240	1964	£25	£10	*US*
This Is Surf City	LP	Del-Fi	DFLP/DFST1237	1963	£25	£10	*US*

LIVERBIRDS

More Of	LP	Starclub	158020STY	1966	**£100**	**£50**	*German*
Star Club Show 4	LP	Starclub	148003STL/ 158003STY	1965	**£75**	**£37.50**	*German*

LIVERPOOL BEATS

New Merseyside Sound	LP	Rondo	2026	1964	**£50**	**£25**	*US*
This Is Liverpool	LP	Vogue	17005	1964	**£50**	**£25**	*German*

LIVERPOOL FISHERMEN

Swallow The Anchor	LP	Mushroom	150MR9	1971	**£100**	**£50**	

LIVERPOOL FIVE

Arrive	LP	RCA	LPM/LSP3583	1966	**£20**	**£8**	*US*
Heart	7" EP	RCA	86493	1965	**£15**	**£7.50**	*French*
Out Of Sight	LP	RCA	LPM/LSP3682	1967	**£20**	**£8**	*US*

LIVERPOOL KIDS

Beatle Mash	LP	Palace	777	1964	**£20**	**£8**	*US*

LIVERPOOL SCENE

The first Liverpool Scene consisted of the three poets Roger McGough, Brian Patten and Adrian Henri, with music supplied by guitarist Andy Roberts. The group that performs on the RCA records is more of a regular rock group, although it is still one that tends to act as an umbrella for the individual talents beneath – Henri and Roberts as before, with poet/saxophonist Mike Evans and singer/guitarist Mike Hart also making telling contributions. Each LP is tremendously varied, encompassing rock, jazz and folk; poetry, comedy and drama – a real pot-pourri, in fact, but it worked.

Amazing Adventures Of	LP	RCA	SF7995	1968	**£15**	**£6**	
Bread On The Night	LP	RCA	SF8057	1969	**£15**	**£6**	
Heirloon	LP	RCA	SF8134	1970	**£12**	**£5**	
Incredible New Liverpool Scene	LP	CBS	63045	1967	**£30**	**£15**	
St Adrian Co. Broadway & 3rd	LP	RCA	SF8100	1970	**£15**	**£6**	

LIVERPOOLS

Beatle-Mania In The USA	LP	Wyncote	9001	1964	**£15**	**£6**	*US*
Hit Sounds From England	LP	Wyncote	9061	1965	**£15**	**£6**	*US*

LIVID, RICKY & THE TONE DEAFS

Tomorrow	7"	Parlophone	R5136	1964	**£5**	**£2**	

LIVIN' BLUES

Bamboozle	LP	Philips	6413024	1971	**£12**	**£5**	*Dutch*
Dutch Treat	LP	Dwarf	2003	1971	**£12**	**£5**	*US*
Hell's Session	LP	Philips	6440315	1969	**£12**	**£5**	*Dutch*
Rockin' At The Tweedmill	LP	Philips	6423052	1972	**£12**	**£5**	*German*
Wang Dang Doodle	LP	Philips	6440125	1970	**£12**	**£5**	*Dutch*

LIVING COLOUR

Cult Of Personality	CD-s	Epic	CDLCL3	1988	**£8**	**£4**	
Cult Of Personality	CD-s	Epic	CDLCL5	1989	**£5**	**£2**	
Glamour Boys	CD-s	Epic	CDLCL2	1988	**£5**	**£2**	
Glamour Boys (remix)	CD-s	Epic	CDLCL6	1989	**£5**	**£2**	
Love Rears Its Ugly Head	CD-s	Epic	6565935	1991	**£5**	**£2**	*picture disc*
Middle Man	CD-s	Epic	CDLCL1	1988	**£5**	**£2**	
Open Letter (To A Landlord)	CD-s	Epic	CDLCL4	1989	**£5**	**£2**	
Solace Of You	CD-s	Epic	6569089	1991	**£5**	**£2**	
Type	CD-s	Epic	CDLCL7	1990	**£5**	**£2**	

LIVING DAYLIGHTS

Always With Him	7"	Philips	BF1613	1967	**£20**	**£10**	
Let's Live For Today	7"	Philips	BF1561	1967	**£12**	**£6**	
Let's Live For Today	7" EP	Fontana	460234	1967	**£25**	**£12.50**	*French*

LIVING IN TEXAS

And David Cried	7"	Rhythmic	RMNS2	1983	**£5**	**£2**	

LIVINGSTONES

In Concert	LP	Waverley	(S)ZLP2105	1968	**£15**	**£6**	

LIZA & THE JET SET

How Can I Know?	7"	Parlophone	R5248	1965	**£6**	**£2.50**	

LIZZY & THE PARAGONS

On The Beach	7"	Ackee	ACK118	1971	**£5**	**£2**	*Dave Barker B side*

LLAN

Realise	7"	CBS	202405	1966	**£20**	**£10**	

LLEWELLYN, BARRY

Meaning Of Life	7"	Downtown	DT515	1975	**£5**	**£2**	*Morwell Esquire B side*

LLOYD, A. L.

All For Me Grog	7" EP	Topic	TOP66	1961	**£15**	**£7.50**	
Australian Bush Songs	LP	Riverside	RLP12606	196–	**£20**	**£8**	*US*
Best Of A. L. Lloyd	LP	XTRA	XTRA5023	1966	**£25**	**£10**	
Bird In The Bush	LP	Topic	12T135	1965	**£60**	**£30**	*with Anne Briggs & Frankie Armstrong*

Title	Format	Label	Cat. No.	Year	Mint	VG	Notes
England And Her Folk Songs	7" EP	Collector	JEB8	1962	**£20**	**£10**	
English And Scottish Folk Ballads	LP	Topic	12T103	1964	**£25**	**£10**	*with Ewan MacColl*
English Drinking Songs	LP	Riverside	RLP12618	196–	**£20**	**£8**	*US*
English Street Songs	LP	Riverside	RLP12614	196–	**£20**	**£8**	*US*
First Person	LP	Topic	12T118	1965	**£25**	**£10**	
Great Australian Legend	LP	Topic	12TS203	1971	**£75**	**£37.50**	*with Trevor Lucas*
Leviathan!	LP	Topic	12T174	1967	**£25**	**£10**	
Outback Ballads	LP	Topic	12T51	1960	**£25**	**£10**	
Selection From The Penguin Book Of English Folk Songs	LP	Collector	JGB5001	1961	**£40**	**£20**	

LLOYD, A. L., EWAN MACCOLL & HARRY H. CORBETT

Title	Format	Label	Cat. No.	Year	Mint	VG	Notes
Blood Red Roses	7" EP	Topic	TOP99	1963	**£15**	**£7.50**	
Blow The Man Down	7" EP	Topic	TOP98	1963	**£15**	**£7.50**	
Santy Anna	7" EP	Topic	TOP100	1963	**£15**	**£7.50**	

LLOYD, CHARLES

In tune with the questing spirit of the times, jazz saxophonist Charles Lloyd's group in the late sixties was marketed as though it was a rock band, with appearances at venues like the Fillmore, album titles like *Love-In*, and stage dress that included kaftans and beads. Such tactics undoubtedly gave Lloyd's music more prominence than it would otherwise have achieved, but the group did also contain two musicians who subsequently played with Miles Davis, before embarking on highly successful solo careers – drummer Jack DeJohnette and pianist Keith Jarrett.

Title	Format	Label	Cat. No.	Year	Mint	VG	Notes
Dream Weaver	LP	Atlantic	587025	1966	**£20**	**£8**	
Flowering Of The Original Charles Lloyd Quartet	LP	Atlantic	2400165	1971	**£15**	**£6**	
Forest Flower	LP	Atlantic	SD1473	1967	**£20**	**£8**	*US*
In Europe	LP	Atlantic	588108	1968	**£20**	**£8**	
In The Soviet Union	LP	Atlantic	2400108	1971	**£15**	**£6**	
Journey Within	LP	Atlantic	587/588101	1968	**£20**	**£8**	
Love-In	LP	Atlantic	587/588077	1967	**£20**	**£8**	
Soundtrack	LP	Atlantic	SD1519	1969	**£15**	**£6**	*US*
Waves	LP	A&M	SP3044	1972	**£15**	**£6**	*US*

LLOYD, JIMMY

Title	Format	Label	Cat. No.	Year	Mint	VG	Notes
Call On Me	7"	Philips	326568BF	1963	**£4**	**£1.50**	
Focus On Jimmy Lloyd	7" EP	Philips	BBE12186	1959	**£8**	**£4**	
Prince Of Players	7"	Philips	PB795	1958	**£4**	**£1.50**	
Teenage Sonata	7"	Philips	PB1010	1960	**£4**	**£1.50**	
Witch Doctor	7"	Philips	PB827	1958	**£5**	**£2**	
You Are My Sunshine	7" EP	Philips	BBE12509	1962	**£6**	**£2.50**	

LLOYD, PEGGY

Title	Format	Label	Cat. No.	Year	Mint	VG	Notes
Dixieland Honky Tonk	7" EP	London	REP1017	1955	**£8**	**£4**	

LLOYD, RUE

Title	Format	Label	Cat. No.	Year	Mint	VG	Notes
Cheer Up	7"	Green Door	GD4036	1972	**£5**	**£2**	
Loving You	7"	Green Door	GD4033	1972	**£5**	**£2**	

LLOYD & CECIL

Title	Format	Label	Cat. No.	Year	Mint	VG	Notes
Come Over Here	7"	Blue Beat	BB49	1961	**£12**	**£6**	*C. Byrd B side*

LLOYD & DEVON

Title	Format	Label	Cat. No.	Year	Mint	VG	Notes
Love Is The Key	7"	Punch	PH14	1967	**£5**	**£2**	*Virtues B side*
Out Of The Fire	7"	Blue Cat	BS151	1968	**£6**	**£2.50**	

LLOYD & GLEN

Title	Format	Label	Cat. No.	Year	Mint	VG	Notes
Keep On Pushing	7"	Doctor Bird	DB1071	1967	**£10**	**£5**	*Bobby Aitken B side*
That Girl	7"	Coxsone	CS7011	1967	**£10**	**£5**	

LLOYD & JOHNNY

Title	Format	Label	Cat. No.	Year	Mint	VG	Notes
My Argument	7"	Island	WI3158	1968	**£10**	**£5**	*George Dekker B side*

LLOYD & JOY

Title	Format	Label	Cat. No.	Year	Mint	VG	Notes
Back To Africa	7"	Explosion	EX2047	1971	**£5**	**£2**	

LLOYD & THE GROOVERS

Title	Format	Label	Cat. No.	Year	Mint	VG	Notes
Do It To Me Baby	7"	Caltone	TONE108	1967	**£8**	**£4**	*Diplomats B side*
Listen To The Music	7"	Caltone	TONE112	1968	**£8**	**£4**	*Diplomats B side*
My Heart My Soul	7"	Caltone	TONE109	1967	**£8**	**£4**	*Diplomats B side*

LLOYDIE & THE LOWBITES

Title	Format	Label	Cat. No.	Year	Mint	VG	Notes
Censored	LP	Lowbite	LOW1	1971	**£15**	**£6**	

LLOYD'S ALLSTARS

Title	Format	Label	Cat. No.	Year	Mint	VG	Notes
Love Kiss Blue	7"	Doctor Bird	DB1178	1969	**£10**	**£5**	*Uniques B side*

LLYGOD FFYRNIG

Title	Format	Label	Cat. No.	Year	Mint	VG	Notes
N.C.B.	7"	Pwdwr	PWDWR1	1978	**£50**	**£25**	

LOADER, DICKIE

Title	Format	Label	Cat. No.	Year	Mint	VG	Notes
Heatwave	7"	Palette	PG9015	1961	**£10**	**£5**	

LOADER, RUSS

Title	Format	Label	Cat. No.	Year	Mint	VG	Notes
Count The Stars	7"	Columbia	DB7696	1965	**£4**	**£1.50**	
When Your Heart Is Broken	7"	Columbia	DB7522	1965	**£4**	**£1.50**	

LOADING ZONE

Title	Format	Label	Cat. No.	Year	Mint	VG	Notes
Loading Zone	LP	RCA	LSP3959	1968	**£25**	**£10**	*US*

One For All LP Umbrella US101 1968 **£40** **£20** *US*

LOADSTONE

Loadstone LP Barnaby 21235004 1969 **£20** **£8** *US*

LOCHLIN, HANK

Best Of Hank Lochlin LP King 672 1961 **£15** **£6** *US*
Country Guitar Vol. 3 7" EP RCA RCX115 1958 **£8** **£4**
Encores 7" EP Parlophone GEP8875 1963 **£10** **£5**
Encores LP King 738 1961 **£15** **£6** *US*
Foreign Love LP RCA LPM1673 1958 **£15** **£6** *US*
Happy Journey LP RCA LPM/LSP2464 1962 **£12** **£5** *US*
Irish Songs Country Style 7" EP RCA RCX7150 1964 **£6** **£2.50**
Irish Songs Country Style LP RCA RD7623 1964 **£10** **£4**
Please Help Me, I'm Falling LP RCA RD27201 1961 **£15** **£6**
Seven Days 7" EP RCA RCX217 1962 **£8** **£4**
Tribute To Roy Acuff LP RCA LPM/LSP2597 1962 **£12** **£5** *US*
Waltz Of The Wind 7" EP RCA RCX7116 1963 **£8** **£4**
Ways Of Love LP RCA LPM/LSP2680 1963 **£12** **£5** *US*

LOCKE, JOSEF

Hear My Song, Violetta 7" Columbia SCM5009 1953 **£5** **£2**
My Heart And I 7" Columbia SCM5008 1953 **£5** **£2**

LOCKETS

Doncha Know 7" Pye 7N25232 1963 **£6** **£2.50**

LOCKJAW

Journalist Jive 7" Raw RAW19 1978 **£10** **£5**
Radio Call Sign 7" Raw RAW8 1977 **£6** **£2.50**

LOCKRAN, GERRY

Blues At Sunrise LP Saga FID2165 1969 **£10** **£4**
Blues Vendetta LP Waverley ZLP2091 1968 **£25** **£10**
Essential LP Spark SRLP104 1969 **£12** **£5**
Hold On I'm Coming LP Planet PLL1002 1967 **£50** **£25**

LOCKYER, MALCOLM

Eccentric Dr Who 7" Columbia DB7663 1965 **£25** **£12.50**

LOCOMOTIVE

Mr Armageddon 7" Parlophone R5758 1969 **£5** **£2**
Mr Armageddon 7" Parlophone R5758 1969 **£20** **£10** *promo in picture sleeve*
Roll Over Mary 7" Parlophone R5835 1970 **£5** **£2**
Rudi's In Love 7" Parlophone R5718 1968 **£4** **£1.50**
Rudi's In Love 7" Parlophone R5915 1971 **£4** **£1.50**
Rudy A Message To You 7" Direction 583114 1967 **£4** **£1.50**
We Are Everything You See LP Parlophone PCS7093 1969 **£125** **£62.50**
You Must Be Joking 7" Parlophone R5801 1969 **£6** **£2.50**

LODGE, JOHN

Natural Avenue CD London 8204642 1987 **£12** **£5**

LOFGREN, NILS

Back It Up LP A&M SP8362 1975 **£12** **£5** *US promo*

LOFT

Up The Hill And Down The Slope 7" Creation CRE015 1985 **£4** **£1.50**
Why Does The Rain Fall 7" Creation CRE009 1984 **£6** **£2.50**

LOFTON, CRIPPLE CLARENCE

Blues Pianist 10" LP Vogue LDE122 1955 **£25** **£10**
Cripple Clarence Lofton 7" EP Vogue EPV1209 1959 **£25** **£12.50**
Lost Recording Date 10" LP London AL3531 1954 **£25** **£10**

LOLLIPOP SHOPPE

Just Colour LP Uni 73019 1968 **£75** **£37.50** *US*

LOMAN, LAURIE

Whither Thou Goest 7" London HL8101 1954 **£20** **£10**

LOMAX, ALAN

Alan Lomax Sings 7" EP Pye NJE1055 1957 **£10** **£5**
Blues In The Mississippi Night LP Pye NJL8 1957 **£10** **£4**
Dirty Old Town 7" Decca F10787 1956 **£5** **£2**
Great American Ballads LP HMV CLP1192 1958 **£10** **£4**
Oh Lula 7" EP Decca DFE6367 1956 **£6** **£2.50**
Presents American Song Train LP Pye NPL18013 1958 **£10** **£4**
Songs From Texas 7" EP Melodisc EPM788 1959 **£8** **£4**
Sounds Of The South LP Atlantic 590033 1969 **£10** **£4**

LOMAX, JACKIE

Genuine Imitation Life 7" CBS 2554 1968 **£4** **£1.50**
How The Web Was Woven 7" Apple 23 1970 **£8** **£4** *picture sleeve*
Interview With Jackie Lomax LP Warner Bros PRO520 1972 **£15** **£6** *US promo*
Is This What You Want LP Apple APCOR6 1969 **£30** **£15** *mono*
Is This What You Want LP Apple SAPCOR6 1969 **£15** **£6** *stereo*
New Day 7" Apple 11 1969 **£8** **£4**

Sour Milk Sea 7" Apple 3 1968 **£5** **£2**

LOMAX ALLIANCE

Try As You May 7" CBS 2729 1967 **£5** **£2**

LOMBARDO, GUY

Cherry Pink And Apple Blossom White 7" Brunswick 05443 1955 **£4** **£1.50**

LOMBARDY, AL

Blues 7" London HL8076 1954 **£25** **£12.50**
In A Little Spanish Town 7" London HL8127 1955 **£25** **£12.50**

LONDON

Animal Games LP MCA MCF2823 1978 **£10** **£4**
Summer Of Love 12" MCA 12MCA319 1977 **£6** **£2.50**

LONDON, FRANCO ORCHESTRA

Theme From Robinson Crusoe 7" Philips BF1470 1966 **£10** **£5**

LONDON, JIMMY

Bridge Over Troubled Waters LP Trojan TRL39 1972 **£12** **£5**

LONDON, JOE

It Might Have Been 7" London HLW9008 1959 **£5** **£2**

LONDON, JULIE

About The Blues LP London HAU2091 1958 **£20** **£8**
All Through The Night 7" EP Liberty LEP2260 1966 **£8** **£4**
All Through The Night LP Liberty (S)LBY1300 1966 **£10** **£4**
Around Midnight LP London HAG2299 1961 **£15** **£6**
Baby Baby All The Time 7" London HLU8279 1956 **£15** **£7.50** *gold label*
Best Of Julie London LP Liberty LBY1023 1962 **£10** **£4**
Boy On A Dolphin 7" London HLU8414 1957 **£6** **£2.50**
Calendar Girl LP London HAU2038 1957 **£20** **£8**
Cry Me A River 7" London HLU8240 1956 **£30** **£15** *gold label*
Desafinado 7" EP Liberty LEP2103 1963 **£8** **£4**
End Of The World LP Liberty LRP3300/LST7300 1963 **£10** **£4** *US*
Feeling Good LP Liberty (S)LBY1281 1966 **£10** **£4**
For The Night People LP Liberty (S)LBY1334 1967 **£10** **£4**
Great Performances LP Liberty LBL/LBS83049 1968 **£10** **£4**
I'm Coming Back To You 7" Liberty LIB55605 1963 **£5** **£2**
In Person At The Americana LP Liberty LBY1222 1965 **£10** **£4**
Julie LP London HAU2112 1958 **£20** **£8**
Julie At Home LP London HAG2280/SAHG6097 1960 **£15** **£6**
Julie Is Her Name LP Liberty LST7027 1957 **£40** **£20** *US, blue vinyl*
Julie Is Her Name LP London HAU2005 1956 **£25** **£10**
Julie Is Her Name Vol. 2 LP London HAU2186/SAHU6042 1959 **£20** **£8**
Julie London LP Liberty LRP3342/LST7342 1964 **£10** **£4** *US*
Julie Part 1 7" EP London REU1180 1959 **£10** **£5**
Julie Part 2 7" EP London REU1181 1959 **£10** **£5**
Julie Part 3 7" EP London REU1182 1959 **£10** **£5**
Latin In A Satin Mood LP Liberty (S)LBY1136 1963 **£10** **£4**
London By Night LP London HAU2171 1959 **£15** **£6**
London's Girl Friends Vol. 1 7" EP London REN1092 1957 **£12** **£6**
Lonely Girl LP Liberty LRP3012 1956 **£25** **£10** *US*
Love Letters LP Liberty (S)LBY1083 1962 **£10** **£4**
Love On The Rocks LP Liberty (S)LBY1113 1963 **£10** **£4**
Make Love To Me LP London HAU2083 1958 **£20** **£8**
Make Love To Me Part 1 7" EP London REU1151 1958 **£10** **£5**
Make Love To Me Part 2 7" EP London REU1152 1958 **£10** **£5**
Make Love To Me Part 3 7" EP London REU1153 1958 **£10** **£5**
Man Of The West 7" London HLU8769 1958 **£6** **£2.50**
Meaning Of The Blues 7" London HLU8394 1957 **£10** **£5** *gold label*
Must Be Catchin' 7" London HLU8891 1959 **£8** **£4**
My Strange Affair 7" London HLU8657 1958 **£6** **£2.50**
Nice Girls Don't Stay For Breakfast LP Liberty (S)LBY1364 1967 **£10** **£4**
Our Fair Lady LP Liberty (S)LBY1251 1965 **£10** **£4**
Saddle The Wind 7" London HLU8602 1958 **£6** **£2.50**
Sanctuary 7" London HLG9360 1961 **£4** **£1.50**
Send For Me LP London HAG2353/SAHG6154 1961 **£15** **£6**
Sings Film Songs 7" EP London REU1076 1957 **£12** **£6** *gold label*
Sings Latin In A Satin Mood LP Liberty (S)LBY1136 1963 **£10** **£4**
Sophisticated Lady LP Liberty LRP3203/LST7203 1962 **£10** **£4** *US*
Swing Me An Old Song LP London HAW2225 1960 **£15** **£6**
Whatever Julie Wants LP London HAG2405/SAHG6205 1962 **£15** **£6**
Wonderful World Of Julie London LP Liberty (S)LBY1185 1964 **£10** **£4**
Your Number Please LP London HAW2229 1960 **£15** **£6**
Yummy Yummy Yummy LP Liberty LBL/LBS83183 1969 **£10** **£4**

LONDON, LAURIE

Gospel Train 7" Parlophone R4408 1958 **£4** **£1.50**

Title	Format	Label	Number	Year	Mint	VG	Notes
He's Got The Whole World In His Hands	7"	Parlophone	R4359	1957	**£4**	**£1.50**	
Laurie London	7" EP	Parlophone	GEP8664	1957	**£20**	**£10**	
Laurie London	LP	Capitol	T1016	1958	**£25**	**£10**	*US*
Little Laurie London No. 2	7" EP	Parlophone	GEP8689	1958	**£20**	**£10**	
Pretty-Eyed Baby	7"	Parlophone	R4557	1959	**£5**	**£2**	

LONDON, MARK

Title	Format	Label	Number	Year	Mint	VG	Notes
Stranger In The World	7"	Pye	7N15825	1965	**£6**	**£2.50**	

LONDON, PETER

Title	Format	Label	Number	Year	Mint	VG	Notes
Bless You	7"	Pye	7N15957	1965	**£25**	**£12.50**	

LONDON & BRIDGES

Title	Format	Label	Number	Year	Mint	VG	Notes
It Just Ain't Right	7"	CBS	202056	1966	**£20**	**£10**	

LONDON BALALAIKA ENSEMBLE

Title	Format	Label	Number	Year	Mint	VG	Notes
London Balalaika Ensemble	LP	Deram	D/SML712	1968	**£10**	**£4**	

LONDON BEATS

Title	Format	Label	Number	Year	Mint	VG	Notes
London Beats	LP	Pronit	XL0278	1964	**£50**	**£25**	*Polish*

LONDON JAZZ CHAMBER GROUP

Title	Format	Label	Number	Year	Mint	VG	Notes
Adam's Rib Suite	LP	Ember	CJS823	1972	**£15**	**£6**	

LONDON JAZZ FOUR

Title	Format	Label	Number	Year	Mint	VG	Notes
It Strikes A Chord	7"	Polydor	56214	1967	**£4**	**£1.50**	
Norwegian Wood	7"	Polydor	BM56092	1966	**£5**	**£2**	
Take A New Look At The Beatles	LP	Polydor	582005	1967	**£40**	**£20**	

LONDON JAZZ QUARTET

Title	Format	Label	Number	Year	Mint	VG	Notes
London Jazz Quartet	LP	Tempo	TAP28	1960	**£300**	**£180**	

LONDON PX

Title	Format	Label	Number	Year	Mint	VG	Notes
Arnold Layne	7"	Terrapyn	SYD1	1982	**£8**	**£4**	*flexi*
Orders	7"	New Puritan	NP1	1982	**£12**	**£6**	

LONDON STUDIO GROUP

Title	Format	Label	Number	Year	Mint	VG	Notes
Wild One	10" LP	De Wolfe	DWLP2974	1966	**£20**	**£8**	

LONDON WAITS

Title	Format	Label	Number	Year	Mint	VG	Notes
Serenadio	7"	Immediate	IM030	1966	**£10**	**£5**	

LONDON'S GENTLEMEN OF JAZZ

Although there are no musician credits on the album, this is actually the work of the Phil Seamen Trio. Rated by many as Britain's best jazz drummer (and Ginger Baker named him as a major influence), Seamen made few records. This one is not one of his best, but is nevertheless an essential purchase for his fans.

Title	Format	Label	Number	Year	Mint	VG	Notes
Fiddler On The Roof–Sweet Charity	LP	Ace Of Clubs	ACL/SCL1254	1969	**£20**	**£8**	

LONE RANGER

Title	Format	Label	Number	Year	Mint	VG	Notes
Adventures Of The Lone Ranger	LP	Decca	DL8578		**£25**	**£10**	*US*
Lone Ranger No. 1	7" EP	Brunswick	OE9394	1959	**£5**	**£2**	
Lone Ranger No. 2	7" EP	Brunswick	OE9395	1959	**£5**	**£2**	
Lone Ranger No. 3	7" EP	Brunswick	OE9396	1959	**£5**	**£2**	

LONESOME, JOHNNY

Title	Format	Label	Number	Year	Mint	VG	Notes
Marie Marie	7"	HMV	POP837	1961	**£4**	**£1.50**	

LONESOME PINE FIDDLERS

Title	Format	Label	Number	Year	Mint	VG	Notes
More Bluegrass	LP	London	HAB8143	1964	**£10**	**£4**	

LONESOME STONE

Title	Format	Label	Number	Year	Mint	VG	Notes
Lonesome Stone	LP	Reflection	RL306	1973	**£25**	**£10**	

LONESOME SUNDOWN

Title	Format	Label	Number	Year	Mint	VG	Notes
Lonesome Lonely Blues	LP	Blue Horizon	763864	1970	**£50**	**£25**	

LONESOME TRAVELLERS

Title	Format	Label	Number	Year	Mint	VG	Notes
Lonesome Travellers	LP	Tradition	TSR004	1970	**£25**	**£10**	
Lost Children	LP	Nebula	NEB100	1971	**£30**	**£15**	

LONG, SHORTY

Title	Format	Label	Number	Year	Mint	VG	Notes
Chantilly Lace	7"	Tamla Motown	TMG600	1967	**£6**	**£2.50**	
Function At The Junction	7"	Tamla Motown	TMG573	1966	**£12**	**£6**	
Here Comes The Judge	7"	Tamla Motown	TMG663	1968	**£4**	**£1.50**	
Here Comes The Judge	LP	Tamla Motown	(S)TML11086	1968	**£20**	**£8**	
Night Fo' Last	7"	Tamla Motown	TMG644	1968	**£6**	**£2.50**	
Out To Get You	7"	Tamla Motown	TMG512	1965	**£50**	**£25**	
Prime Of Shorty Long	LP	Tamla Motown	(S)TML11144	1970	**£15**	**£6**	

LONG & THE SHORT

Choc Ice	7"	Decca	F12043	1964	£10	£5	
Letter	7"	Decca	F11964	1964	£10	£5	

LONG TALL SHORTY

By Your Love	7"	Warner Bros	K17491	1979	£20	£10	
If I Was You	7"	Dr.Creation	LYN9904	1981	£4	£1.50	*flexi*
On The Streets Again	7"	Diamond	DIA002	1985	£8	£4	*with poster*
What's Going On	7"	Diamond	DIA005	1986	£5	£2	
Win Or Lose	7"	Ramkup	CAC007	1981	£25	£12.50	

LONGBOATMEN

Take Her Any Time	7"	Polydor	56115	1966	£300	£180	*best auctioned*

LONGBRANCH PENNYWHISTLE

Longbranch Pennywhistle was a duo comprising J. D. Souther and Glenn Frey, both of whom have been familiar faces within the American country-rock scene ever since – Frey being a member of the Eagles.

Longbranch Pennywhistle	LP	Amos	AAS7007	1969	£20	£8	*US*

LONGET, CLAUDINE

Colours	LP	A&M	AMLS929	1968	£10	£4	*with Randy Newman*

LONGMAN, BRENDA & IAN

No Royalties	LP	Private	PLP1081	1977	£30	£15	

LONGPIGS

She Said	12"	Elektra		1993	£40	£20	*promo only*

LOOP

Arc-Lite	CD-s	Situation 2	SIT64CD	1989	£5	£2	
Fade Out	LP	Chapter 22	CHAPLLP34	1988	£10	£4	*2 × 45 rpm discs, signed*

LOOSE ENDS

Send The People Away	7"	Decca	F12437	1966	£10	£5	
Taxman	7"	Decca	F12476	1966	£10	£5	

LOOSE TUBES

Open Letter	CD	Editions EG	EEGCD55	1988	£12	£5	

LOOT

Baby Come Closer	7"	Page One	POF013	1966	£10	£5	
Baby Come Closer	7" EP	Fontana	460206	1967	£50	£25	*French*
Don't Turn Around	7"	CBS	3231	1968	£10	£5	
I've Just Gotta Love You	7"	Page One	POF026	1967	£15	£7.50	
She's A Winner	7"	Page One	POF095	1968	£40	£20	*2 different B sides*
Try To Keep It Secret	7"	Page One	POF115	1969	£40	£20	
Whenever You're Ready	7"	CBS	2938	1967	£15	£7.50	
Whenever You're Ready	7" EP	Palette	22021	1967	£50	£25	*French*

LOPEZ, TRINI

Jean Marie	7"	London	HL9808	1963	£4	£1.50	
More Of Trini Lopez	LP	London	HA8160	1964	£12	£5	
Teenage Love Songs	LP	London	HA8132	1964	£15	£6	

LOR, DENISE

Every Day Of My Life	7"	Parlophone	MSP6148	1955	£4	£1.50	
If I Give My Heart To You	7"	Parlophone	MSP6120	1954	£5	£2	

LORAN, KENNY

Mama's Little Baby	7"	Capitol	CL15081	1959	£25	£12.50	

L'ORANGE MECHANIK

Symphony	7"	Artpop	POP44	1985	£5	£2	

LORD, BRIAN & THE MIDNIGHTERS

The Brian Lord single features both Frank Zappa and his colleague in the Mothers of Invention, Ray Collins.

Big Surfer	7"	Capitol	4981	1963	£100	£50	*US*
Big Surfer	7"	Vigah	001	1963	£200	£100	*US*

LORD, JON

Bouree	7"	Purple	PUR131	1976	£4	£1.50	

LORD, TONY

World's Champion	7"	Planet	PLF102	1966	£10	£5	

LORD BEGINNER

Victory Test Match	7"	Melodisc	CAL1	1963	£4	£1.50	

LORD BRISCO

Jonah	7"	Island	WI187	1965	£10	£5	
My Love Has Come	7"	Black Swan	WI450	1964	£10	£5	*Baba Brooks B side*

Spiritual Mambo	7"	Black Swan	WI447	1964	£10	£5	Baba Brooks B side
Trojan	7"	Black Swan	WI454	1964	£10	£5	

LORD BRYNNER

Congo War	7"	Island	WI266	1966	£10	£5	

LORD BUCKLEY

Bad Rapping The Marquis De Sade	LP	World Pacific	WPS21889	1969	£20	£8	US
Best Of Lord Buckley	LP	Crestview	CRV(7)801	1963	£20	£8	US
Best Of Lord Buckley	LP	Elektra	EKS74047	1969	£15	£6	US
Blowing His Mind And Yours Too	LP	Fontana	TL5396	1960	£15	£6	
Buckley's Best	LP	Liberty	LBS83191	1968	£15	£6	
Hipsters, Flipsters, & Finger Poppin' Daddies	10" LP	RCA	LPM3246	195–	£50	£25	US
In Concert	LP	Fontana	688010ZL	1965	£15	£6	
Lord Buckley	LP	Bizarre	RS6389	1970	£15	£6	US
Most Immaculately Hip Autocrat	LP	Straight	STS1054	1970	£15	£6	US
Way Out Humor Of Lord Buckley	LP	World Pacific	WP1279	1959	£20	£8	US

LORD BURGESS & HIS SUN ISLANDERS

Calypso Au Go-Go	LP	Pye	NPL28109	1968	£10	£4	

LORD CHARLES & HIS BAND

Jamaican Bits And Pieces	7"	Sound Of Jamaica	JA1	197–	£12	£6	

LORD CREATOR

Big Bamboo	7"	Jump Up	JU524	1967	£4	£1.50	
Drive With Care	7"	National Calypso	NC2001	1964	£4	£1.50	
Evening News	7"	Blue Beat	BB292	1965	£12	£6	
Independent Jamaica	7"	Island	WI001	1962	£12	£6	
Jamaica Jump Up	7"	Jump Up	JU503	1967	£4	£1.50	
Jamaica's Anniversary	7"	Port-O-Jam	PJ4119	1964	£10	£5	
Obeah Wedding	7"	Doctor Bird	DB1029	1966	£10	£5	Bertram Ennis B side
Peeping Tom	7"	Kalypso	XX24	1963	£4	£1.50	
Rhythm Of The Blues	7"	Port-O-Jam	PJ4005	1964	£10	£5	
We Will Be Lovers	7"	Island	WI105	1963	£10	£5	
Wicked Lady	7"	Black Swan	WI463	1965	£10	£5	Maytals B side

LORD CRISTO

Dumb Boy And The Parrot	7"	Jump Up	JU515	1967	£4	£1.50	
Election War Zone	7"	Jump Up	JU517	1967	£4	£1.50	

LORD INVADER

Kings Of Calypso Vol. 2	7" EP	Pye	NEP24038	1957	£5	£2	

LORD IVANHOE

Kings Of Calypso Vol. 6	7" EP	Pye	NEP24087	1958	£5	£2	

LORD KITCHENER

Black Pudding	7"	Melodisc	1498	1959	£4	£1.50	
Calypsos Too Hot To Handle	LP	Melodisc	12129	196–	£15	£6	
Calypsos Too Hot To Handle	LP	Melodisc	12199	196–	£15	£6	extra tracks
Calypsos Too Hot To Handle Vol. 2	LP	Melodisc	12130	196–	£15	£6	
Calypsos Too Hot To Handle Vol. 2	LP	Melodisc	12200	196–	£15	£6	extra tracks
Dr Kitch	7"	Aladdin	WI612	1965	£5	£2	
If You're Brown	7"	Melodisc	1531	1959	£4	£1.50	
Jamaica Turkey	7"	Melodisc	1577	1960	£4	£1.50	
King Of Calypso Vol. 2	10" LP	Melodisc	MLP510	1957	£15	£6	
Kitch – King Of Calypso	10" LP	Melodisc	MLP500	1955	£15	£6	

LORD LEBBY

Caledonia	7"	Starlite	ST45018	1960	£40	£20	
Sweet Jamaica	7"	Kalypso	XX05	1960	£8	£4	

LORD NELSON

I Got An Itch	7"	Stateside	SS189	1963	£5	£2	
It's Delinquency	7"	Stateside	SS281	1964	£5	£2	
Proud West Indian	7" EP	Stateside	SE1024	1964	£12	£6	

LORD NELSON & HIS CREW

Return Of Rock	LP	Metronome	HLP10213	1968	£20	£8	German

LORD POWER

Temptation	7"	Coxsone	CS7079	1968	£10	£5	Al & Vibrators B side

LORD ROCKINGHAM'S XI

Oh Boy	7" EP	Decca	DFE6555	1958	£25	£12.50	
Ra Ra Rockingham	7"	Decca	F11139	1959	£4	£1.50	
Return Of Lord Rockingham's XI	LP	Columbia	SCX6291	1968	£20	£8	
Rockingham Twist	7"	Decca	F11426	1962	£4	£1.50	
Squelch	7"	Decca	F11024	1958	£5	£2	
Wee Tom	7"	Decca	F11104	1959	£5	£2	

LORD SITAR

Suggestions that the name Lord Sitar hides the identity of George Harrison have given the album whatever collectability it has. It is actually extremely unlikely that Harrison would ever have considered recording a set of cover versions like this – even more so that he could then have kept the matter quiet for thirty years.

Lord Sitar	LP	Columbia	SCX6256	1968	**£30**	**£15**	

LORD TANAMO

Come Down	7"	Island	WI108	1963	**£10**	**£5**	
I Had A Dream	7"	Rio	R21	1964	**£10**	**£5**	*Osbourne Graham B side*
I Love You Truly	7"	Caribou	CRC3	196–	**£8**	**£4**	
I'm In The Mood For Ska	7"	Ska Beat	JB224	1965	**£10**	**£5**	
Keep On Moving	7"	Banana	BA319	1971	**£5**	**£2**	*Jackie Mittoo B side*
Mothers Love	7"	Ska Beat	JB243	1966	**£10**	**£5**	
Sweet Dreaming	7"	Kalypso	XX20	1960	**£6**	**£2.50**	

LORDAN, JERRY

All My Own Work	LP	Parlophone	PCS3014	1961	**£75**	**£37.50**	*stereo*
All My Own Work	LP	Parlophone	PMC1133	1961	**£60**	**£30**	*mono*
I'll Stay Single	7"	Parlophone	R4588	1959	**£4**	**£1.50**	
Let's Try Again	7"	Parlophone	R4748	1961	**£4**	**£1.50**	
Old Man And The Sea	7"	CBS	5057	1970	**£8**	**£4**	
One Good Solid 24 Carat Reason	7"	Parlophone	R4903	1962	**£5**	**£2**	
Ring, Write, Or Call	7"	Parlophone	R4695	1960	**£4**	**£1.50**	
Sing Like An Angel	7"	Parlophone	R4653	1960	**£4**	**£1.50**	
Who Could Be Bluer	7"	Parlophone	R4627	1960	**£4**	**£1.50**	

LORDS

Best Of The Lords	LP	Columbia	29783	1971	**£15**	**£6**	*German*
Don't Mince Matters	7"	Columbia	DB8121	1967	**£50**	**£25**	
Gloryland	7"	Columbia	DB8367	1968	**£6**	**£2.50**	
Good Side Of June	LP	Columbia	74244	1968	**£25**	**£10**	*German*
Hey Baby	7" EP	Columbia	ESRF1656	1965	**£40**	**£20**	*French*
In Black And White	LP	Columbia	83859	1965	**£40**	**£20**	*German*
Inside Out	LP	Columbia	1C06228887	1971	**£15**	**£6**	*German*
Lords	LP	Columbia	31972	1974	**£10**	**£4**	*German*
Lords 2	LP	Columbia	84013	1966	**£30**	**£15**	*German*
Shakin' All Over '70	LP	Columbia	1C06228478	1970	**£15**	**£6**	*German*
Some Folks	LP	Hör Zu	SHZT174	1967	**£30**	**£15**	*German*
Ulleogamaxbe	LP	Columbia	SMC74343	1969	**£30**	**£15**	*German*

LOREN, SOPHIA

In Rome	LP	Columbia	OL6310/OS2710	1964	**£30**	**£15**	*US, with John Barry*

LORRIE, MYRNA

Life's Changing Scene	7"	London	HLU8294	1956	**£40**	**£20**	
Underway	7"	London	HLU8187	1955	**£25**	**£12.50**	

LORY, DICK

Cool It Baby	7"	London	HLD8348	1956	**£400**	**£250**	*best auctioned*
I Got Over You	7"	Liberty	LIB55529	1963	**£4**	**£1.50**	
My Last Date	7"	London	HLG9284	1961	**£15**	**£7.50**	
Pain Is Here	7"	Liberty	LIB55415	1962	**£4**	**£1.50**	

LOS BRAVOS

Black Is Black	7" EP	Barclay	071050	1966	**£12**	**£6**	*French*
Black Is Black	LP	Decca	LK4822	1966	**£20**	**£8**	
Going Nowhere	7" EP	Barclay	071091	1966	**£10**	**£5**	*French, 2 different sleeves*
Los Bravos	LP	Decca	LK/SKL4905	1968	**£15**	**£6**	
Los Bravos	LP	Eclipse	ECJR2026	1970	**£10**	**£4**	

LOS BRINCOS

Lola	7"	Page One	POF023	1967	**£30**	**£15**	*picture sleeve*
Nobody Wants You Now	7"	Page One	POF031	1967	**£6**	**£2.50**	

LOS CANARIOS

Get On Your Knees	7"	Major Minor	MM532	1967	**£5**	**£2**	

LOS LOBOS

Just Another Band From East LA	LP	New Vista	1001	1978	**£75**	**£37.50**	*US*
Si Se Puede!	LP	Pan American	101	1976	**£50**	**£25**	*US*

LOSS, JOE

Thunderbirds	7"	HMV	POP1500	1966	**£10**	**£5**	

LOST & FOUND

Everybody's Here	LP	International Artist	IALP3	1967	**£40**	**£20**	*US*

LOST JOCKEY

Professor Slack	7"	Operation Twilight	OPT11	1982	**£5**	**£2**	

LOST NATION

Title	Format	Label	Cat. No.	Year	Mint	Good	Notes
Paradise Lost	LP	Rare Earth	RS518	1970	£50	£25	US

LOTHAR AND THE HAND PEOPLE

Lothar was a theremin, the electronic instrument best known for its crucial role in the Beach Boys 'Good Vibrations', and it was supported by a couple of early synthesizers wielded by the Hand People, alongside their more usual group instruments. Much of the material on the group's two albums manages to sound unusual, in an era that specialized in unusual sounds.

Title	Format	Label	Cat. No.	Year	Mint	Good	Notes
Presenting	LP	Capitol	ST2997	1968	£50	£25	US
Sdrawkcab	7"	Capitol	CL15610	1969	£8	£4	
Space Hymn	LP	Capitol	ST247	1969	£50	£25	US

LOTIS, DENNIS

Title	Format	Label	Cat. No.	Year	Mint	Good	Notes
Bidin' My Time	LP	Columbia	33SX1089	1958	£12	£5	
Chain Reaction	7"	Decca	F10471	1955	£5	£2	
Face Of An Angel, Heart Of A Devil	7"	Decca	F10469	1955	£5	£2	
Hallelujah It's Dennis Lotis	7" EP	Columbia	SEG7955	1959	£5	£2	
Honey Love	7"	Decca	F10392	1954	£6	£2.50	
How About You	7" EP	Pye	NEP24046	1957	£8	£4	
How About You	LP	Pye	NPL18002	1957	£20	£8	
How About You Part 2	7" EP	Pye	NEP24053	1957	£8	£4	
How About You Part 3	7" EP	Pye	NEP24055	1957	£8	£4	
Let's Be Happy	7" EP	Pye	NEP24043	1957	£5	£2	
Presenting Dennis Lotis	7" EP	Pye	NEP24017	1956	£5	£2	
Such A Night	7"	Decca	F10287	1954	£8	£4	

LOTIS, PETER

Title	Format	Label	Cat. No.	Year	Mint	Good	Notes
Doo-Dah	7"	Ember	EMBS110	1960	£4	£1.50	picture sleeve

LOTUS

Title	Format	Label	Cat. No.	Year	Mint	Good	Notes
Lotus	LP		SMA1	1974	£50	£25	Swedish
Second	LP		SMA16	1975	£50	£25	Swedish

LOTUS EATERS

Title	Format	Label	Cat. No.	Year	Mint	Good	Notes
No Sense Of Sin	LP	Sylvan	206263	1984	£15	£6	

LOU, BONNIE

Title	Format	Label	Cat. No.	Year	Mint	Good	Notes
Barnyard Hop	7"	Parlophone	MSP6178	1955	£10	£5	
Blue Tennessee Rain	7"	Parlophone	MSP6117	1954	£12	£6	
Bo Weevil	7"	Parlophone	MSP6234	1956	£20	£10	
Dancin' In My Socks	7"	Parlophone	MSP6188	1955	£20	£10	
Don't Stop Kissing Me Goodnight	7"	Parlophone	MSP6095	1954	£12	£6	
Drop Me A Line	7"	Parlophone	MSP6173	1955	£10	£5	
Hand-Me-Down Heart	7"	Parlophone	MSP6036	1953	£25	£12.50	
Huckleberry Pie	7"	Parlophone	MSP6108	1954	£12	£6	
I'm Available	7"	Parlophone	DP545	195–	£15	£7.50	export
La Dee Dah	7"	Parlophone	R4409	1958	£50	£25	with Rusty York
Lonesome Lover	7"	Parlophone	MSP6253	1956	£15	£7.50	
Miss The Love	7"	Parlophone	MSP6223	1956	£8	£4	
No Rock'n'Roll Tonight	7"	Parlophone	R4215	1956	£10	£5	
Papaya Mama	7"	Parlophone	MSP6051	1953	£20	£10	
Runnin' Away	7"	Parlophone	R4350	1957	£10	£5	
Seven Lonely Days	7"	Parlophone	MSP6021	1953	£25	£12.50	
Tennessee Mambo	7"	Parlophone	MSP6151	1955	£15	£7.50	
Tennessee Wig Walk	7"	Parlophone	MSP6048	1953	£30	£15	
Texas Polka	7"	Parlophone	MSP6072	1954	£12	£6	
Tweedle Dee	7"	Parlophone	MSP6157	1955	£20	£10	
Two Step Side Step	7"	Parlophone	MSP6132	1954	£12	£6	

LOUDERMILK, JOHN D.

Title	Format	Label	Cat. No.	Year	Mint	Good	Notes
Angela Jones	7"	RCA	RCA1323	1962	£5	£2	
Language Of Love	LP	RCA	RD27248/SF5123	1962	£15	£6	
Sidewalks	7"	RCA	RCA1761	1968	£4	£1.50	
Sings A Bizarre Collection	LP	RCA	RD/SF7890	1967	£10	£4	
Suburban Attitudes In Country Verse	LP	RCA	LPM/LSP3807	1967	£10	£4	US
Twelve Sides Of John D. Loudermilk	LP	RCA	RD/SF7515	1962	£15	£6	

LOUDEST WHISPER

Title	Format	Label	Cat. No.	Year	Mint	Good	Notes
Children Of Lir	LP	Polydor		1975	£400	£250	Irish
Hard Times	LP	Fiona	011	1983	£125	£62.50	Irish
Loudest Whisper	LP	Polydor	2908043	1981	£125	£62.50	Irish
Name Of The Game	7"	Polydor	2078113	1980	£20	£10	Irish

LOUIS, JOE HILL

Title	Format	Label	Cat. No.	Year	Mint	Good	Notes
Blues In The Morning	LP	Polydor	2383214	1974	£10	£4	
Heartache Baby	7"	Bootleg	502	1965	£25	£12.50	
Memphis Blues And Breakdowns	LP	Advent	LP2803	196–	£30	£15	

LOUISE

Title	Format	Label	Cat. No.	Year	Mint	Good	Notes
All That Matters	12"	EMI	12EMDJD506	1998	£10	£5	promo double
Arms Around The World	12"	EMI	12EMDJ490	1997	£6	£2.50	promo
Arms Around The World	12"	EMI	12EMDJD490	1997	£8	£4	promo double
Let's Go Round Again	12"	EMI	12EMDJ500	1997	£6	£2.50	promo
Let's Go Round Again	12"	EMI	12EMDJD500	1997	£10	£5	promo double
Light Of My Life	CD-s	EMI	CDEM454	1996	£5	£2	with 3 prints
Soft And Gentle	CD-s	EMI	LOUPREM101	1997	£8	£4	promo

LOUISIANA RED

Title	Format	Label	Cat. No.	Year	Mint	VG	Notes
I Done Woke Up	7"	Sue	WI337	1964	**£15**	**£7.50**	
Keep Your Hands Off My Woman	7"	Columbia	DB7270	1964	**£10**	**£5**	
Lowdown Back Porch Blues	LP	Columbia	33SX1612	1964	**£25**	**£10**	
Seventh Son	LP	Polydor	2941002	1972	**£15**	**£6**	
Sings The Blues	LP	Atlantic	K40436	1972	**£12**	**£5**	

LOUNGE LIZARDS

Title	Format	Label	Cat. No.	Year	Mint	VG	Notes
No Pain For Cakes	CD	Antilles	ANCD8714	1987	**£12**	**£5**	

LOUSSIER, JACQUES

Title	Format	Label	Cat. No.	Year	Mint	VG	Notes
Air On A G String	7"	Decca	F22383	1966	**£4**	**£1.50**	
Play Bach	LP	London	GLB1002	1962	**£10**	**£4**	
Play Bach No. 2	LP	London	GLB1004	1963	**£10**	**£4**	

LOUVIN, CHARLIE

Title	Format	Label	Cat. No.	Year	Mint	VG	Notes
I Forgot To Cry	LP	Capitol	(S)T2787	1967	**£12**	**£5**	*US*
I'll Remember Always	LP	Capitol	(S)T2689	1967	**£12**	**£5**	*US*
Less And Less	LP	Capitol	(S)T2208	1965	**£12**	**£5**	*US*
Lonesome Is Me	LP	Capitol	(S)T2482	1966	**£12**	**£5**	*US*
Many Moods Of Charlie Louvin	LP	Capitol	(S)T2437	1966	**£15**	**£6**	*US*
Will You Visit Me On Sundays	LP	Capitol	ST2958	1968	**£12**	**£5**	*US*

LOUVIN, IRA

Title	Format	Label	Cat. No.	Year	Mint	VG	Notes
Unforgettable Ira Louvin	LP	Capitol	(S)T2413	1965	**£12**	**£5**	*US*

LOUVIN BROTHERS

Title	Format	Label	Cat. No.	Year	Mint	VG	Notes
Country Christmas	LP	Capitol	(S)T1616	1961	**£15**	**£6**	*US*
Country Love Ballads	7" EP	Capitol	EAP11106	1959	**£8**	**£4**	
Country Love Ballads	LP	Capitol	T1106	1959	**£25**	**£10**	*US*
Encore	LP	Capitol	T1547	1961	**£15**	**£6**	*US*
Family Who Prays	LP	Capitol	T1061	1958	**£25**	**£10**	*US*
Ira And Charlie	7" EP	Capitol	EAP1910	1957	**£10**	**£5**	
Ira And Charlie	LP	Capitol	T910	1958	**£40**	**£20**	*US*
Keep Your Eyes On Jesus	LP	Capitol	(S)T1834	1963	**£15**	**£6**	*US*
Knoxville Girl	7"	Capitol	CL14989	1959	**£4**	**£1.50**	
Louvin Brothers	LP	MGM	E3426	1956	**£100**	**£50**	*US*
My Baby's Gone	LP	Capitol	T1385	1960	**£25**	**£10**	*US*
Nearer My God To Thee	LP	Capitol	T825	1957	**£40**	**£20**	*US*
Satan Is Real	LP	Capitol	T1277	1960	**£25**	**£10**	*US*
Sing And Play Their Current Hits	LP	Capitol	(S)T2091	1964	**£15**	**£6**	*US*
Tragic Songs Of Life	7" EP	Capitol	EAP1769	1957	**£10**	**£5**	
Tragic Songs Of Life	LP	Capitol	T769	1957	**£50**	**£25**	*US*
Tribute To The Delmore Brothers	LP	Capitol	T1449	1960	**£20**	**£8**	*US*
Weapon Of Prayer	LP	Capitol	(S)T1721	1962	**£15**	**£6**	*US*
You're Learning	7"	Capitol	CL15078	1959	**£4**	**£1.50**	

LOVABLES

Title	Format	Label	Cat. No.	Year	Mint	VG	Notes
You're The Cause Of It	7"	Stateside	SS2108	1968	**£8**	**£4**	

LOVE

The personnel of Love varies from album to album, but the group always revolves around the singing and writing talents of Arthur Lee. His is an inconsistent talent, but at his best he is little short of brilliant. All of Love's albums (except perhaps the first, on which the group have barely emerged from their garage punk beginnings) contain moments of pure magic, although none is entirely flawless. The critics' favourite is *Forever Changes*, whose largely gentle sound is enhanced by modest orchestration, but the heavier, guitar-centred *Four Sail* actually has songs of greater distinction. It is a very fine, and very underrated record. The first side of *Da Capo* has some excellent songs too, but the album as a whole is let down by the extended jam on side two, which does not really work. *Out Here* and *False Start* are similar in sound to *Four Sail*, though overall neither is in the same league. Each contains one masterpiece, however – 'The Everlasting First' is a collaboration with Jimi Hendrix, who makes a typically fine contribution to an unusually structured song; while 'Love Is More Than Words' is dominated by a long, highly charged guitar solo that turns the track into one of the classic pieces of rock improvisation.

Title	Format	Label	Cat. No.	Year	Mint	VG	Notes
Alone Again Or	7"	Elektra	EKSN45024	1968	**£4**	**£1.50**	
Andmoreagain	7"	Elektra	EKSN45026	1968	**£6**	**£2.50**	
Da Capo	LP	Elektra	EKL4005/ EKS74005	1967	**£30**	**£15**	
Do The Merlin	7"	LSD	1009	1966	**£250**	**£150**	*US, best auctioned*
Everlasting First	7"	Harvest	HAR5030	1970	**£5**	**£2**	*with Jimi Hendrix*
False Start	LP	Harvest	SHVL787	1971	**£20**	**£8**	
Forever Changes	LP	Elektra	EKS74013	1967	**£30**	**£15**	
Forever Changes	LP	Elektra	EKS74013	1970	**£15**	**£7.50**	*red label*
Forever Changes	LP	Elektra	EKL4013	1967	**£40**	**£20**	*mono*
Four Sail	LP	Elektra	EKS74049	1969	**£20**	**£8**	
Four Sail	LP	Elektra	K42030	1976	**£10**	**£4**	
I'm With You	7"	Elektra	EKSN45086	1970	**£4**	**£1.50**	
Laughing Stock	7"	Elektra	EKSN45038	1968	**£8**	**£4**	
Love	LP	Elektra	EKL/EKS74001	1966	**£30**	**£15**	
Love	LP	Elektra	K42068	1972	**£10**	**£4**	
Love Revisited	LP	Elektra	2469009	1970	**£10**	**£4**	
My Little Red Book	7"	London	HLZ10053	1966	**£10**	**£5**	
My Little Red Book	7" EP	Vogue	INT18072	1966	**£75**	**£37.50**	*French*
Out Here	LP	Harvest	SHDW3/4	1970	**£20**	**£8**	*double*
Reel To Real	LP	RSO	2394145	1974	**£10**	**£4**	
Seven And Seven Is	7"	London	HLZ10073	1966	**£10**	**£5**	
Seven And Seven Is	7" EP	Vogue	INT18095	1966	**£100**	**£50**	*French*
She Comes In Colours	7"	Elektra	EKSN45010	1967	**£8**	**£4**	
Softly To Me	7"	Elektra	EKSN45016	1967	**£6**	**£2.50**	

Stand Out	7"	Harvest	HAR5014	1970	£4	£1.50	

LOVE (2)

Welsh Girl	7"	Fierce	FRIGHT036	1990	£15	£7.50	1 sided

LOVE, CHRISTOPHER

Curse Goes On	7"	London	HLU10263	1969	£5	£2	

LOVE, DARLENE

Boy I'm Gonna Marry	7"	London	HLU9725	1963	£15	£7.50	
Fine Fine Boy	7"	London	HLU9815	1963	£15	£7.50	
Lord If You're A Woman	12"	Phil Spector	2010019	1977	£10	£5	
Wait Till My Bobby Gets Home	7"	London	HLU9765	1963	£15	£7.50	
Wait Till My Bobby Gets Home	7"	London	HLU10244	1969	£8	£4	
Wait Till My Bobby Gets Home	7" EP	London	REU1411	1964	£100	£50	

LOVE, GARFIELD & JIMMY SPRUILL

Next Time You See Me	7"	Blue Horizon	573150	1969	£15	£7.50	

LOVE, GEOFF ORCHESTRA

Coronation Street Theme	7"	Columbia	DB4627	1961	£5	£2	

LOVE, MARY

Hurt is Just Beginning	7"	Stateside	SS2135	1969	£10	£5	
Lay This Burden Down	7"	Stateside	SS2009	1967	£25	£12.50	
You Turned My Bitter Into Sweet	7"	King	KG1024	1965	£50	£25	

LOVE, RONNIE

Chills And Fever	7"	London	HLD9272	1961	£15	£7.50	

LOVE, WILLIE & WILLIE NIX

Two Willies From Memphis	LP	Highway 51	H700	1966	£60	£30	

LOVE AFFAIR

Everlasting Love Affair	LP	CBS	63416	1969	£15	£6	
Help	7"	Parlophone	R5918	1971	£6	£2.50	
Let Me Dance	7"	Pye	7N45218	1970	£5	£2	
New Day	LP	CBS	64109	1970	£12	£5	
Rainbow Valley	7"	CBS	3366	1968	£6	£2.50	picture sleeve
She Smiled Sweetly	7"	Decca	F12558	1967	£30	£15	
Wake Me I Am Dreaming	7"	Parlophone	R5887	1971	£6	£2.50	

LOVE & TEARS

Love And Tears	LP	Polydor	2371334	1972	£15	£6	German

LOVE CHILDREN

Paper Chase	7"	Deram	DM303	1970	£4	£1.50	

LOVE GENERATION

She Touched Me	7"	Liberty	LBF15018	1967	£4	£1.50	

LOVE SCULPTURE

Love Sculpture evolved from the Human Beans as a blues group and showcase for the flashy guitar playing of Dave Edmunds. The success of their version of Khachaturian's 'Sabre Dance' led them to try another classical reworking, but due to copyright problems, 'Mars' was only made available on the US version of *Forms And Feelings* and has not been reissued since.

Blues Helping	LP	Parlophone	PCS7059	1968	£25	£10	
Blues Helping	LP	Parlophone	PMC7059	1968	£30	£15	mono
Forms And Feelings	LP	Parlophone	PCS7090	1969	£25	£10	
Forms And Feelings	LP	Parrot	PAS71035	1969	£30	£15	US
In The Land Of The Few	7"	Parlophone	R5831	1970	£6	£2.50	
River To Another Day	7"	Parlophone	R5664	1968	£15	£7.50	
Seagull	7"	Parlophone	R5807	1969	£6	£2.50	
Wang Dang Doodle	7"	Parlophone	R5731	1968	£10	£5	

LOVECRAFT

Valley Of The Moon	LP	Reprise	RS6419	1970	£10	£4	US

LOVECUT D. B.

Heartspin	12"	Suburbs Of Hell	SOH009EP	1991	£6	£2.50	

LOVED ONES

Loved One	7" EP	Festival	1528	196–	£10	£5	French
Magic Box	LP	Astor	WG5127	1967	£25	£10	US

LOVER, JOHNNY

Pumpkin Eater	7"	Amalgamated	AMG871	1970	£6	£2.50	
Two Edged Sword	7"	Amalgamated	AMG873	1970	£6	£2.50	

LOVERS

Let's Elope	7"	Vogue	V9111	1958	£350	£210	best auctioned

LOVETTE, EDDIE

Too Experienced	LP	London	LGJ/ZGJ103	1970	£10	£4	

LOVICH, LENE

Title	Format	Label	Cat. No.	Year	Mint	VG	Notes
I Saw Mommy Kissing Santa Claus	7"	Polydor	2058812	1976	**£10**	**£5**	
I Think We're Alone Now (Japanese)	7"	Stiff	BUYJ32	1978	**£6**	**£2.50**	

LOVIN'

Title	Format	Label	Cat. No.	Year	Mint	VG	Notes
All You've Got	7"	Page One	POF041	1967	**£30**	**£15**	
Keep On Believing	7"	Page One	POF035	1967	**£20**	**£10**	

LOVIN' SPOONFUL

Title	Format	Label	Cat. No.	Year	Mint	VG	Notes
Almost Grown	7" EP	Vogue	INT18032	1965	**£12**	**£6**	*French*
Darling Be Home Soon	7" EP	Kama Sutra	617108	1967	**£10**	**£5**	*French*
Day Blues	7" EP	Kama Sutra	KEP303	1967	**£10**	**£5**	
Daydream	7" EP	Kama Sutra	617102	1966	**£10**	**£5**	*French*
Daydream	LP	Pye	NPL28078	1966	**£10**	**£4**	
Did You Ever Have To Make Up Your Mind	7" EP	Kama Sutra	KEP300	1966	**£8**	**£4**	
Do You Believe In Magic	7"	Pye	7N25327	1965	**£4**	**£1.50**	
Do You Believe In Magic	7" EP	Kama Sutra	KEP306	1967	**£10**	**£5**	
Do You Believe In Magic	7" EP	Kama Sutra	617101	1965	**£10**	**£5**	*French*
Do You Believe In Magic	LP	Pye	NPL28069	1965	**£10**	**£4**	
Everything Playing	LP	Kama Sutra	KLP404	1968	**£10**	**£4**	
Hums Of The Lovin' Spoonful	LP	Kama Sutra	KLP401	1967	**£10**	**£4**	
Jug Band Music	7" EP	Kama Sutra	KEP301	1966	**£10**	**£5**	
Loving You	7" EP	Kama Sutra	KEP305	1967	**£10**	**£5**	
Nashville Cats	7" EP	Kama Sutra	KEP304	1967	**£10**	**£5**	
Nashville Cats	7" EP	Kama Sutra	617106	1967	**£10**	**£5**	*French*
Never Going Back	7"	Kama Sutra	KAS213	1967	**£4**	**£1.50**	
Rain On The Roof	7" EP	Kama Sutra	617105	1966	**£10**	**£5**	*French*
Revelation Revolution '69	LP	Kama Sutra	KLP406	1969	**£10**	**£4**	
Six O'Clock	7" EP	Kama Sutra	617110	1967	**£10**	**£5**	*French*
Summer In The City	7" EP	Kama Sutra	KEP302	1966	**£10**	**£5**	
Summer In The City	7" EP	Kama Sutra	617103	1966	**£10**	**£5**	*French*
Summer In The City	CD-s	Special Edition	CD311	1988	**£5**	**£2**	*3" single*
You Didn't Have To Be So Nice	7"	Pye	7N25344	1966	**£4**	**£1.50**	
You're A Big Boy Now	LP	Kama Sutra	KLP402	1967	**£10**	**£4**	

LOVING KIND

Title	Format	Label	Cat. No.	Year	Mint	VG	Notes
Accidental Love	7"	Piccadilly	7N35299	1966	**£6**	**£2.50**	
Ain't That Peculiar	7"	Piccadilly	7N35342	1966	**£10**	**£5**	
I Love The Things You Do	7"	Piccadilly	7N35318	1966	**£8**	**£4**	

LOW, BRUCE

Title	Format	Label	Cat. No.	Year	Mint	VG	Notes
Just Walking In The Rain	7"	HMV	JO464	1956	**£10**	**£5**	*export*

LOW NOISE

Title	Format	Label	Cat. No.	Year	Mint	VG	Notes
Jungle Line	12"	Happy Birthday	UR5	1981	**£6**	**£2.50**	

LOW NUMBERS

Title	Format	Label	Cat. No.	Year	Mint	VG	Notes
Keep In Touch	7"	Warner Bros	K17493	1979	**£5**	**£2**	

LOWE, DENNIS

Title	Format	Label	Cat. No.	Year	Mint	VG	Notes
Stand Up For The Sound	7"	Downtown	DT468	1970	**£4**	**£1.50**	*Owen & Dennis B side*
What's Your Name	7"	Downtown	DT465	1970	**£4**	**£1.50**	*Music Doctors B side*

LOWE, JEZ

Title	Format	Label	Cat. No.	Year	Mint	VG	Notes
Galloways	LP	Fellside	FE049	1985	**£10**	**£4**	
Jez Lowe	LP	Fellside	FE023	1980	**£10**	**£4**	
Old Durham Road	LP	Fellside	FE034	1983	**£10**	**£4**	

LOWE, JIM

Title	Format	Label	Cat. No.	Year	Mint	VG	Notes
Blue Suede Shoes	7"	London	HLD8276	1956	**£60**	**£30**	
By You By You By You	7"	London	HLD8368	1957	**£20**	**£10**	*gold label*
Close The Door	7"	London	HLD8171	1955	**£30**	**£15**	*gold label*
Door Of Fame	LP	Mercury	MG20246	1957	**£30**	**£15**	*US*
Four Walls	7"	London	HLD8431	1957	**£15**	**£7.50**	
Green Door	7"	London	HLD8317	1956	**£30**	**£15**	*gold label*
He'll Have To Go	7"	London	HLD9043	1960	**£8**	**£4**	
Love Is A $64, 000 Question	7"	London	HLD8288	1956	**£40**	**£20**	*gold label*
Rock A Chicka	7"	London	HLD8538	1958	**£75**	**£37.50**	
Songs They Sing Behind The Green Door	LP	London	HAD2108	1958	**£30**	**£15**	
Wicked Women	LP	London	HAD2146	1959	**£20**	**£8**	

LOWE, MUNDELL

Title	Format	Label	Cat. No.	Year	Mint	VG	Notes
Mundell Lowe Quartet	LP	London	LTZU15020	1957	**£20**	**£8**	
Mundell Lowe Quintet	10" LP	HMV	DLP1084	1955	**£20**	**£8**	

LOWE, NICK

Nick Lowe's response to David Bowie releasing an album called *Low*, was to make a record called *Bowi*, although this was unfortunately only a four-track single, rather than an album. The humour of the concept is enough to make one listen fondly to the music regardless (actually the songs are quite memorable), but not quite enough to make the record into a collectors' item.

Title	Format	Label	Cat. No.	Year	Mint	VG	Notes
Bowi	12"	Stiff	Last1	1977	**£10**	**£8**	*promo*

Live At The El Mocambo	7"	Columbia		1978	£8	£4	*Canadian promo*

LOWE, PETER

Banana Boat Song	7"	Parlophone	R4270	1957	**£4**	**£1.50**	

LOWE, SAMMY

Hey Lawdy Lawdy Mary	7"	RCA	RCA1239	1961	**£6**	**£2.50**	

LOWLIFE

Demos	LP	private	LOLIFDEMO1	1988	**£20**	**£8**	

LOWTHER, HENRY

Henry Lowther is a classically trained violinist who took up the trumpet in order to play jazz and plays both instruments as a session musician on numerous LP releases. He played on the fringes of jazz as a member of Manfred Mann, John Mayall's Bluesbreakers, and the Keef Hartley Band, and he is featured on several of the British jazz albums to be made during the late sixties and early seventies. His own moment came with the LP *Child Song*, which is as fresh and sparkling as British jazz gets. The record is also, unfortunately, as rare as British jazz gets, and commands a correspondingly high price.

Child Song	LP	Deram	SML1070	1970	**£75**	**£37.50**	

LOYD, MARK

Everybody Tries	7"	Parlophone	R5332	1965	**£5**	**£2**	
When Evening Falls	7"	Parlophone	R5423	1966	**£100**	**£50**	

LUCAS, BUDDY

I Want To Know	7"	Pye	7N25045	1960	**£8**	**£4**	

LUCAS, TREVOR

Singer/guitarist Trevor Lucas became well known as a member of Fairport Convention, following stints with the Eclection and Fotheringay – he was also the partner of singer Sandy Denny. Originally from Australia, Lucas recorded a folk album there, but *Overlander* is extremely hard to find now.

Overlander	LP	Reality	RY1002	1966	**£300**	**£180**	
Waltzing Matilda	7"	Reality	RE505	1966	**£20**	**£10**	

LUCAS & THE MIKE COTTON SOUND

I Saw Pity In The Face Of A Friend	7"	Polydor	56114	1966	**£5**	**£2**	
Mother In Law	7"	MGM	MGM1427	1968	**£5**	**£2**	
Step Out Of Line	7"	Pye	7N17313	1967	**£15**	**£7.50**	
We Got A Thing Going Baby	7"	MGM	MGM1398	1968	**£10**	**£5**	

LUCIEN, JON

Premonition	LP	Columbia	PC34255	1976	**£25**	**£10**	*US*
Rashida	LP	RCA	AYL13820	197–	**£30**	**£15**	*US*
Rashida	LP	RCA	AFL10161	1973	**£40**	**£20**	*US*
Song For My Lady	LP	Columbia		1975	**£25**	**£10**	*US*

LUCIFER

Big Gun	LP	private	LLP1	1972	**£60**	**£30**	
Don't Care	7"	private	L001/002	1971	**£5**	**£2**	
Exit	LP	private	LLP2	1972	**£60**	**£30**	
Fuck You	7"	private	L003/004	1972	**£5**	**£2**	
Prick	7"	Lucifer	L005/6/3/4	1972	**£25**	**£12.50**	*boxed double*
Prick	7"	Lucifer	L005/006	1972	**£5**	**£2**	

LUCIFER'S FRIEND

Lucifer's Friend	LP	Philips	6305068	1971	**£12**	**£5**	*German*
Where The Groupies Killed The Blues	LP	Vertigo	6360602	1973	**£10**	**£4**	*German*

LUCY

Never Never	7"	Lightning	GIL516	1977	**£15**	**£7.50**	
Really Got Me Goin'	7"	B&C	BCS8	1978	**£6**	**£2.50**	

LUDLOWS

Wind And The Sea	LP	Pye	NPL18150	1966	**£10**	**£4**	

LUDUS

Seduction	12"	New Hormones	ORG16	1981	**£8**	**£4**	*double*

LUIGI ANA DA BOYS

Feeling The Ceiling	LP	Criminal	CR0001	1978	**£50**	**£25**	

LUKE, ROBIN

Chicka Chicka Honey	7"	London	HLD8771	1958	**£10**	**£5**	
Robin Luke	7" EP	London	RED1222	1959	**£60**	**£30**	
Susie Darling	7"	London	HLD8676	1958	**£6**	**£2.50**	

LULU

Boom Bang-A-Bang	7" EP	Columbia		1969	**£8**	**£4**	*French*
Can't Hear You No More	7"	Decca	F11965	1964	**£5**	**£2**	
Chocolate Ice	7" EP	Decca	457099	1966	**£10**	**£5**	*French*
Let's Pretend	7"	Columbia	DB8221	1967	**£4**	**£1.50**	
Love Loves To Love Lulu	LP	Columbia	SX/SCX6201	1968	**£10**	**£4**	
Lulu	7" EP	Decca	DFE8597	1965	**£20**	**£10**	
Lulu	LP	Ace Of Clubs	ACL1232	1967	**£10**	**£4**	
Lulu's Album	LP	Columbia	SX/SCX6365	1969	**£10**	**£4**	

Man With The Golden Gun	7"	Chelsea	2005015	1974	£5	£2	
Satisfied	7"	Decca	F12128	1965	£4	£1.50	
Satisfied	7" EP	Decca	457084	1965	£10	£5	*French*
Shout	7"	Decca	F11884	1964	£4	£1.50	
Shout	7" EP	Decca	457045	1964	£15	£7.50	*French*
Something To Shout About	LP	Decca	LK4719	1965	£25	£10	
That's Really Some Good	7" EP	Decca	457052	1964	£10	£5	*French*
To Sir With Love	LP	Fontana	STL5446	1967	£30	£15	*with the Mindbenders*
What A Wonderful Feeling	7" EP	Decca	457132	1966	£10	£5	*French*

LUMAN, BOB

Ain't Got Time To Be Unhappy	7"	CBS	3602	1968	£8	£4	
Bad Bad Day	7"	Hickory	451289	1965	£5	£2	
Bigger Men Than I	7"	Hickory	451238	1964	£4	£1.50	
Can't Take The Country From The Boys	LP	Hickory	LPM121	1964	£10	£4	*side 2 by Bobby Lord*
Come On And Sing	7"	Hickory	451410	1965	£4	£1.50	
Dreamy Doll	7"	Warner Bros	WB12	1960	£4	£1.50	
Great Snowman	7"	Warner Bros	WB37	1961	£4	£1.50	
Hey Joe	7"	Warner Bros	WB75	1962	£4	£1.50	
Hickory Showcase Vol. 2	7" EP	Hickory	LPE1501	1964	£10	£5	*side 2 by Bobby Lord*
Hickory Showcase Vol. 3	7" EP	Hickory	LPE1504	1964	£10	£5	*side 2 by Bobby Lord*
I Like Your Kind Of Love	7"	Hickory	451221	1964	£4	£1.50	
Let's Think About Living	7" EP	Warner Bros	WSEP2046	1961	£40	£20	*stereo*
Let's Think About Living	7" EP	Warner Bros	WEP6046	1961	£25	£12.50	
Let's Think About Living	LP	Warner Bros	WM4025	1960	£40	£20	
Let's Think About Living	LP	Warner Bros	WS8025	1960	£50	£25	*stereo*
Let's Think About Living No. 2	7" EP	Warner Bros	WSEP2055	1962	£40	£20	*stereo*
Let's Think About Living No. 2	7" EP	Warner Bros	WEP6055	1962	£25	£12.50	
Let's Think About Living No. 3	7" EP	Warner Bros	WSE6102	1962	£40	£20	*stereo*
Let's Think About Living No. 3	7" EP	Warner Bros	WEP6102	1962	£25	£12.50	
Livin' Lovin' Sounds	LP	Hickory	LPM124	1964	£15	£6	
Old George Dickie	7"	Hickory	451277	1964	£4	£1.50	
Private Eye	7"	Warner Bros	WB49	1961	£4	£1.50	
Why Why Bye Bye	7"	Warner Bros	WB28	1960	£4	£1.50	

LUMBLE

Overdose	LP	Radnor	R2003	1970	£60	£30	*US*

LUMLEY, RUFUS

I'm Standing	7"	Stateside	SS516	1966	£60	£30	

LUNAR TWO

Get It, Take It	7"	Spot	JWS551	196–	£4	£1.50	

LUNCEFORD, JIMMIE

For Dancers Only	10" LP	Brunswick	LA8738	1956	£20	£8	
Jimmie Lunceford Orchestra	LP	Brunswick	LAT8027	1954	£15	£6	
Lunceford Special	LP	Philips	BBL7037	1955	£15	£6	

LUNCH, LYDIA

Stinkfist	CD-s	Widowspeak	WSP020	1989	£5	£2	*with Jim Thirwell*
Unearthly Delights	7"	Clawfist	XPIG19	1993	£5	£2	

LUND, ART

This Is Art	LP	Vogue Coral	LVA9056	1957	£10	£4	

LUND, GARRETT

Almost Grown	LP	private	5113	1975	£500	£330	*US*

LUREX, LARRY

Larry Lurex is Freddie Mercury, and his single, issued just before the start of Queen's career is sought-after in both its UK and US incarnations. The latter, however, turns up suspiciously often and it is likely that many copies are actually counterfeits.

I Can Hear Music	7"	Anthem	104	1973	£50	£25	*US*
I Can Hear Music	7"	EMI	EMI2030	1973	£150	£75	

LURKERS

Fulham Fallout	LP	Beggars Banquet	BEGA2	1978	£10	£4	*with picture disc flexi*
Shadow	7"	Beggars Banquet	BEG1	1978	£5	£2	*red, blue, or white vinyl*

LUSH

Black Spring	CD-s	4AD	ADBAD1016	1991	£5	£2	
Mad Love	CD-s	4AD	BAD0003CD	1990	£5	£2	
Scar	CD-s	4AD	JAD911CD	1989	£5	£2	
Sweetness And Light	CD-s	4AD	BAD0013CD	1990	£5	£2	

LUSHER, DON

Rock'n'Roll	7"	Decca	F10560	1955	£5	£2	

LUSTMORD

Lustmord	LP	Sterile	SR3	1982	£40	£20	

LUTCHER, NELLIE

Blues In The Night	7"	Brunswick	05352	1954	£8	£4	

It's Been Said	7"	Brunswick	05437	1955	£10	£5	
Nellie Lutcher	7" EP	Philips	BBE12045	1956	£20	£10	
Our New Nellie	LP	London	HAU2036	1957	£25	£10	
Real Gone	10" LP	Capitol	LC6506	1951	£40	£20	
Real Gone	7" EP	Capitol	EAP20066	1960	£30	£15	
Real Gone	LP	Capitol	T232	195–	£25	£10	US
Real Gone	LP	Music For Pleasure	MFP1038	1966	£10	£4	
Whee! Nellie	10" LP	Epic	1108	195–	£40	£20	US
Whose Honey Are You	7"	Brunswick	05497	1955	£5	£2	

LUTHA

	LP				£200	£100	*New Zealand*

LUTHER

It's Good For The Soul	7"	Atlantic	K10781	1976	£10	£5	

LUTHER, FRANK

While few people will be familiar with the name of Frank Luther, everyone who ever listened to *Children's Favourites* with Uncle Mac will know Luther's classic children's song. Now, after me, 'I'm a troll, foll-de-roll!'

Three Billygoats Gruff	7"	Decca	F9051	1954	£10	£4	

LUTHER & LITTLE EVA

Ain't Got No Home	7"	Parlophone	R4292	1957	£300	£180	*best auctioned*

LUV BUG

You Can Count On Me	7"	Roxy-Ritz	TEASE2	1986	£4	£1.50	

LUV MACHINE

Luv Machine	LP	Polydor	2460102	1971	£100	£50	
Witches Wand	7"	Polydor	2058080	1971	£8	£4	

LUVVERS

Lulu's backing group recorded one unsuccessful single without her. Guitarist James Dewar was later the singer and bass player in the Robin Trower band.

House On The Hill	7"	Parlophone	R5459	1966	£20	£10	

LUVZIT, MICK

Long Time Between Lovers	7"	Decca	F12421	1966	£4	£1.50	

LUZIFER

Black Mass	LP	RCA	UNI73111	1971	£20	£8	US

L-VOAG

Move	7"	Sesame Songs	MOVE1	1979	£8	£4	
Way Out	LP	Axis	No.9	1979	£10	£4	

LYMAN, ARTHUR GROUP

Bahia	LP	Vogue	VA160166	1960	£12	£5	
Greatest Hits Vol. 1	7" EP	Vogue	VEH70166	1959	£6	£2.50	
Greatest Hits Vol. 2	7" EP	Vogue	VEH70167	1959	£6	£2.50	
Greatest Hits Vol. 3	7" EP	Vogue	VEH70168	1959	£6	£2.50	
Hawaiian Sunset	LP	Vogue	VA160171	1961	£12	£5	
Love For Sale	LP	Vogue	SAVH8030	1963	£12	£5	
More Exotic Sounds	LP	Vogue	VA160149	1959	£12	£5	
Taboo Vol. 1	LP	Vogue	VA160142/ SAV8002	1959	£12	£5	
Taboo Vol. 2	LP	Vogue	VA160174/ SAV8003	1961	£12	£5	

LYMON, FRANKIE & THE TEENAGERS

ABC's In Love	7"	Columbia	DB3858	1956	£25	£12.50	
At The London Palladium	10" LP	Columbia	33S1127	1958	£100	£50	
Frankie Lymon & The Teenagers	7" EP	Columbia	SEG7734	1957	£50	£25	
Goody Goody	7"	Columbia	DB3983	1957	£10	£5	
I Promise To Remember	7"	Columbia	DB3819	1956	£25	£12.50	
I Want You To Be My Girl	7"	Columbia	SCM5285	1956	£30	£15	
I'm Not A Juvenile Delinquent	7"	Columbia	DB3878	1957	£20	£10	
I'm Not A Juvenile Delinquent	7" EP	Columbia	SEG7694	1957	£40	£20	
Jerry Blavatt Presents The Teenagers	LP	Roulette	R25250	1964	£75	£37.50	US
Little Bitty Pretty One	7"	Columbia	DB4499	1960	£20	£10	
Mama Don't Allow It	7"	Columbia	DB4134	1958	£10	£5	
My Girl	7"	Columbia	DB4028	1957	£15	£7.50	
No Matter What You've Done	7"	Columbia	DB4295	1959	£12	£6	
Only Way To Love	7"	Columbia	DB4245	1959	£10	£5	
Out In The Cold Again	7"	Columbia	DB3942	1957	£25	£12.50	
Rock And Roll	LP	Roulette	R25036	1958	£150	£75	US
Rockin' With Frankie	10" LP	Columbia	33S1134	1957	£400	£250	
Teenage Love	7"	Columbia	DB3910	1957	£25	£12.50	
Teenage Rock	7" EP	Columbia	SEG7662	1957	£40	£20	
Teenagers	LP	Gee	GLP701	1961	£75	£37.50	*US grey label*
Teenagers	LP	Gee	GLP701	1957	£250	£150	*US red label*
Teenagers At The London Palladium	LP	Roulette	R25013	1958	£150	£75	US
Thumb Thumb	7"	Columbia	DB4073	1958	£12	£6	
Why Do Fools Fall In Love?	7"	Columbia	SCM5265	1956	£30	£15	

Why Do Fools Fall In Love?	7"	King	KG1043	1966	**£5**	**£2**	

LYMON, LEWIS

Too Young	7"	Oriole	CB1419	1958	**£300**	**£180**	*best auctioned*

LYNCH, DERMOTT

Adults Only	7"	Doctor Bird	DB1115	1967	**£10**	**£5**	
Hot Shot	7"	Blue Cat	BS101	1968	**£8**	**£4**	
I Got Everything	7"	Blue Cat	BS122	1968	**£8**	**£4**	
Something Is Worrying Me	7"	Blue Cat	BS129	1968	**£8**	**£4**	*Trevor B side*
You Went Away	7"	Blue Cat	BS130	1968	**£8**	**£4**	*Trevor B side*

LYNCH, KENNY

Along Comes Love	7"	Columbia	DB8498	1968	**£5**	**£2**	
Drifter	7"	Columbia	DB8599	1969	**£6**	**£2.50**	
For You	7"	HMV	POP1229	1963	**£4**	**£1.50**	
Hey Girl	7" EP	HMV	7EG8820	1963	**£20**	**£10**	
It Would Take A Miracle	7"	HMV	POP1005	1962	**£4**	**£1.50**	
It's Too Late	7"	HMV	POP1577	1967	**£4**	**£1.50**	
Kenny Lynch	7" EP	HMV	7EG8855	1964	**£20**	**£10**	
Loving You Is Sweeter Than Ever	7"	Columbia	DB8703	1970	**£5**	**£2**	
Misery	7"	HMV	POP1136	1963	**£4**	**£1.50**	
Mister Moonlight	7"	Columbia	DB8329	1968	**£5**	**£2**	
Mountain Of Love	7"	HMV	POP751	1960	**£6**	**£2.50**	
Movin' Away	7"	HMV	POP1604	1967	**£15**	**£7.50**	
My Own Two Feet	7"	HMV	POP1367	1964	**£6**	**£2.50**	
Puff	7"	HMV	POP1057	1962	**£4**	**£1.50**	
Up On The Roof	LP	HMV	CLP1635	1963	**£25**	**£10**	*mono*
Up On The Roof	LP	HMV	CSD1489	1963	**£40**	**£20**	*stereo*
We Like Kenny	LP	MFP	MFP1022	1966	**£10**	**£4**	
What Am I To You	7" EP	HMV	7EG8881	1965	**£20**	**£10**	

LYNCH, LEE

Joe Poor Loves Daphne Elizabeth Rich	7"	Ember	EMBS282	1970	**£5**	**£2**	*picture sleeve*
Stay Awhile	7"	Ember	EMBS262	1969	**£5**	**£2**	*picture sleeve*
Sweet Woman	7"	Ember	EMBS271	1970	**£5**	**£2**	*picture sleeve*
You Won't See Me	7"	Decca	F12375	1966	**£4**	**£1.50**	

LYNDELL, LINDA

Bring Your Love Back To Me	7"	Stax	601041	1968	**£15**	**£7.50**	

LYNGSTAD, ANNI-FRID

Anni-Frid Lyngstad has achieved some success as a solo artist (some of the records are credited to 'Frida') both before and after being a member of Abba.

Anni-Frid Lyngstad	LP	Columbia	04851017	197N	**£15**	**£6**	*Swedish*
Frida	LP	Columbia	E05434549	1971	**£12**	**£5**	*Swedish*
Frida	LP	Columbia	06234380	1971	**£50**	**£25**	*Swedish*
Frida Ensam	LP	Polar	POLS265	1976	**£12**	**£5**	*Swedish*
Heart Of The Country	12"	Epic	TA4886	1984	**£8**	**£4**	
Something's Going On	CD	CBS	CDCBS85966	1988	**£12**	**£5**	

LYNN, BARBARA

Barbara Lynn Story	LP	Sue	ILP949	1967	**£60**	**£30**	
Here Is Barbara Lynn	LP	Atlantic	SD8171	1968	**£30**	**£15**	*US*
Letter To Mommy And Daddy	7"	Sue	WI4028	1967	**£15**	**£7.50**	
Oh Baby	7"	London	HLW9918	1964	**£10**	**£5**	
Sister Of Soul	LP	Jamie	JLP(S)3026	1964	**£30**	**£15**	*US*
Until Then I Suffer	7"	Atlantic	2091133	1971	**£5**	**£2**	
You Can't Buy Me Love	7"	Immediate	IM011	1965	**£15**	**£7.50**	
You Left The Water Running	7"	London	HLU10094	1966	**£10**	**£5**	
You'll Lose A Good Thing	7"	Sue	WI4038	1967	**£15**	**£7.50**	
You'll Lose A Good Thing	LP	Jamie	JLP(S70)3023	1962	**£30**	**£15**	*US*

LYNN, BOBBY

Earthquake	7"	Stateside	SS2088	1968	**£20**	**£10**	

LYNN, KARI

Lonesome And Sorry	7"	Oriole	CB1644	1961	**£5**	**£2**	
Yo Yo	7"	Oriole	CB1632	1961	**£5**	**£2**	

LYNN, LORETTA

Before I'm Over You	LP	Decca	DL(7)4541	1964	**£15**	**£6**	*US*
Blue Kentucky Girl	LP	Decca	DL(7)4665	1965	**£15**	**£6**	*US*
Country Christmas	LP	Decca	DL(7)4817	1966	**£12**	**£5**	*US*
Hymns	LP	Decca	DL(7)4695	1965	**£12**	**£5**	*US*
I Like 'Em Country	LP	Decca	DL(7)4744	1966	**£12**	**£5**	*US*
Loretta Lynn Sings	LP	Decca	DL(7)4457	1963	**£20**	**£8**	*US*
Mr & Mrs Used To Be	LP	Decca	DL(7)4639	1965	**£12**	**£5**	*US, with Ernest Tubb*
Songs From My Heart	LP	Decca	DL(7)4620	1965	**£15**	**£6**	*US*
You Ain't Woman Enough	LP	Decca	DL(7)4783	1966	**£12**	**£5**	*US*

LYNN, PATTI

I See It All Now	7"	Fontana	H370	1962	**£5**	**£2**	
Johnny Angel	7"	Fontana	H391	1962	**£5**	**£2**	
Patti	7" EP	Fontana	TFE17392	1962	**£30**	**£15**	

Tell Me Telstar	7"	Fontana	267247TF	1962	**£6**	**£2.50**	

LYNN, TAMMI

I'm Gonna Run Away From You	7"	Atlantic	AT4071	1966	**£25**	**£12.50**	
Love Is Here And Now You're Gone	LP	Mojo	2916007	1971	**£12**	**£5**	

LYNN, VERA

Auf Wiederseh'n Sweetheart	7"	Decca	F9927	1959	**£4**	**£1.50**	
Faithful Hussar	7"	Decca	F10846	1957	**£4**	**£1.50**	
House With Love In It	7"	Decca	F10799	1956	**£4**	**£1.50**	
My Son My Son	7"	Decca	F10372	1954	**£15**	**£7.50**	
Travellin' Home	7"	Decca	F10903	1957	**£4**	**£1.50**	
Who Are We?	7"	Decca	F10715	1956	**£4**	**£1.50**	

LYNNE, GLORIA

At The Las Vegas Thunderbird	LP	London	HAY8112	1964	**£10**	**£4**	
Lonely And Sentimental	LP	Top Rank	BUY031	1960	**£10**	**£4**	

LYNNE, SUE

Baby Baby Baby	7"	RCA	RCA1874	1969	**£4**	**£1.50**	
Don't Pity Me	7"	RCA	RCA1822	1969	**£100**	**£50**	
Reach For The Moon	7"	RCA	RCA1724	1968	**£5**	**£2**	

LYNOTT, PHIL

Solo In Soho	LP	Vertigo	PHIL1	1980	**£10**	**£4**	*picture disc*

LYNTON, JACKIE

The backing group on the A side of 'All Of Me' is called the Jury. The bass player is Pat Donaldson – kept busy on a variety of sessions following his stints with Zoot Money and with Fotheringay – while the guitarist is Albert Lee, here making his first recording.

All Of Me	7"	Piccadilly	7N35064	1962	**£5**	**£2**	
Answer Me	7"	Columbia	DB8224	1967	**£4**	**£1.50**	
Decision	7"	Columbia	DB8180	1967	**£4**	**£1.50**	
He'll Have To Go	7"	Columbia	DB8097	1967	**£4**	**£1.50**	
Jackie Lynton Album	LP	WWA	WWA012	1974	**£12**	**£5**	

LYNYRD SKYNYRD

Down South Jukin'	7" EP	MCA	MCEP101	1978	**£4**	**£1.50**	
Free Bird	12"	MCA	MCATP251	1982	**£6**	**£2.50**	*picture disc*
Free Bird	7"	MCA	MCA251	1976	**£5**	**£2**	*picture sleeve*
Free Bird	7"	MCA	MCA275	1976	**£5**	**£2**	*picture sleeve*
Free Bird	CD-s	MCA	DMCA1315	1989	**£5**	**£2**	
Ten From The Swamp	CD	MCA	CD332033	1991	**£20**	**£8**	*US promo sampler*
Travis Tritt Interviews Lynyrd Skynyrd	CD	Atlantic	PRCD50782	1993	**£15**	**£6**	*US promo*

LYON, BARBARA

Band Of Gold	7"	Columbia	SCM5232	1956	**£5**	**£2**	
Birds And The Bees	7"	Columbia	SCM5276	1956	**£5**	**£2**	
It's Better In The Dark	7"	Columbia	DB3826	1956	**£4**	**£1.50**	
Letter To A Soldier	7"	Columbia	DB3865	1956	**£8**	**£4**	
My Charlie	7"	Triumph	RGM1027	1960	**£25**	**£12.50**	
My Four Friends	7" EP	Columbia	SEG7640	1956	**£10**	**£5**	
Whisper	7"	Columbia	SCM5207	1955	**£5**	**£2**	
Yes You Are	7"	Columbia	SCM5186	1955	**£5**	**£2**	

LYON, PATTI

I See It All Now	7"	Fontana	H370	1962	**£5**	**£2**	

LYONESSE

Cantrique	LP	PDU	PLDA6029	1975	**£75**	**£37.50**	*Italian*
Lyonesse	LP	PDU	PLDA5093	1974	**£75**	**£37.50**	*Italian*

LYONS, JOHN

May Morning Dew	LP	Topic	12TS248	1974	**£12**	**£5**	

LYONS, TIM

Easter Snow	LP	Innisfree	SIF1014	1978	**£10**	**£4**	*US*
Green Linnet	LP	Trailer	LER3036	1972	**£10**	**£4**	

LYRICS

A Get It	7"	Coxsone	CS7003	1967	**£10**	**£5**	*Ken Parker B side*
Give Thanks	7"	Randys	RAN511	1971	**£4**	**£1.50**	*Randy's All Stars B side*
Give Thanks And Praises	7"	Randys	RAN504	1970	**£4**	**£1.50**	*Tommy McCook B side*
Music Like Dirt	7"	Coxsone	CS7067	1968	**£10**	**£5**	

LYTELL, JIMMY

Hot Cargo	7"	London	HL8873	1959	**£5**	**£2**	

LYTLE, JOHNNY

Blue Vibes	LP	Jazzland	JLP22	1960	**£10**	**£4**	
Gonna Get That Boat	7"	Minit	MLF11006	1968	**£5**	**£2**	

LYTTELTON, HUMPHREY

And His Band	LP	Society	SOC1003	1965	**£10**	**£4**	
Baby Doll	7"	Parlophone	R4277	1957	**£4**	**£1.50**	

Title	Format	Label	Cat. No.	Year	Mint	VG	Notes
Bad Penny Blues	7"	Parlophone	CMSP41	1958	**£20**	**£10**	*export*
Best Of Humph 1949–56	LP	Parlophone	PMC7147	1971	**£10**	**£4**	
Big H	7" EP	Columbia	SEG8130	1961	**£8**	**£4**	
Blues In The Night	LP	Columbia	33SX1239/ SCX3316	1960	**£20**	**£8**	
Duke Ellington Classics	LP	Polydor	2460140	1969	**£30**	**£15**	
East Coast Trot	7"	Parlophone	MSP6076	1954	**£4**	**£1.50**	
Here's Humph	10" LP	Parlophone	PMD1049	1957	**£15**	**£6**	
Humph At The Conway	LP	Parlophone	PMC1012	1954	**£15**	**£6**	
Humph In Perspective	LP	Parlophone	PMC1070	1958	**£25**	**£10**	
Humph Meets Cab	LP	Columbia	33SX1364	1960	**£40**	**£20**	
Humph Plays Standards	LP	Columbia	33SX1305	1960	**£25**	**£10**	
Humph Returns To The Conway	LP	Columbia	33SX1382	1961	**£20**	**£8**	
Humph Swings Out	10" LP	Parlophone	PMD1044	1956	**£25**	**£10**	
Humph's Blues No. 2	7" EP	Parlophone	GEP8645	1957	**£6**	**£2.50**	
Humphrey Lyttelton And His Band	LP	Esquire	32007	1955	**£15**	**£6**	
I Play As I Please	LP	Decca	LK4276	1958	**£15**	**£6**	
It's Mardi Gras	7"	Parlophone	R4262	1957	**£4**	**£1.50**	
Jazz At The Royal Festival Hall	10" LP	Parlophone	PMD1032	1955	**£30**	**£15**	
Jazz Concert	10" LP	Parlophone	PMD1006	1953	**£15**	**£6**	
Jazz Session With Humph	10" LP	Parlophone	PMD1035	1956	**£15**	**£6**	
Just Once For All Time	7"	Parlophone	MSP6093	1954	**£4**	**£1.50**	
Kater Street Rag	7"	Parlophone	MSP6045	1953	**£4**	**£1.50**	
Kath Meets Humph	10" LP	Parlophone	PMD1052	1958	**£20**	**£8**	*with Kathy Stobart*
La Paloma	7"	Decca	F11058	1958	**£4**	**£1.50**	
Late Night Final	LP	Columbia	33SX1484	1962	**£20**	**£8**	
Love Love Love	7"	Parlophone	R4212	1956	**£4**	**£1.50**	
Mainly Traditional	7"	Parlophone	MSP6097	1954	**£4**	**£1.50**	
Martiniquen Song	7"	Parlophone	MSP6061	1953	**£4**	**£1.50**	
Maryland My Maryland	7"	Parlophone	MSP6033	1953	**£4**	**£1.50**	
Mezzy's Tune	7"	Parlophone	MSP6128	1954	**£4**	**£1.50**	
Muskrat Ramble	7"	Parlophone	MSP6023	1953	**£4**	**£1.50**	
Once In A While	LP	Black Lion	BLP12149	1974	**£10**	**£4**	
One Day I Met An African	LP	Black Lion	BLP12199	1980	**£10**	**£4**	
Out Of The Gallion	7"	Parlophone	MSP6001	1953	**£4**	**£1.50**	
Shake It And Break It	7"	Parlophone	MSP6034	1953	**£4**	**£1.50**	
Sir Humph's Delight	LP	Black Lion	BLP12188	1979	**£10**	**£4**	
South Bank Swing Session	LP	Polydor	2460233	1973	**£15**	**£6**	
Spreadin' Joy	LP	Black Lion	BLP12173	1978	**£10**	**£4**	
Triple Exposure	LP	Parlophone	PMC1110	1959	**£50**	**£25**	
When The Saints Go Marching In	7"	Tempo	A10	1956	**£4**	**£1.50**	

M

Title	Format	Label	Cat. No.	Year	Mint	Good	Notes
Pop Musik (1989 remix)	CD-s	Freestyle	FRSCD1	1989	£5	£2	

MAAJUN

Title	Format	Label	Cat. No.	Year	Mint	Good	Notes
Vivre La Mort Du Vieux Monde	LP	Vogue	SLVX545	1971	£50	£25	*French*

MABLE JOY

Title	Format	Label	Cat. No.	Year	Mint	Good	Notes
Mable Joy	LP	Real	RR2004	1975	£30	£15	

MABON, WILLIE

Title	Format	Label	Cat. No.	Year	Mint	Good	Notes
Got To Have Some	7"	Sue	WI320	1964	£12	£6	
I'm The Fixer	7"	Sue	WI382	1965	£12	£6	
Just Got Some	7"	Sue	WI331	1965	£12	£6	
Willie Mabon	LP	Chess	1439	195–	£50	£25	*US*

MACARI, GLO

Title	Format	Label	Cat. No.	Year	Mint	Good	Notes
He Knows I Love Him Too Much	7"	Piccadilly	7N35218	1965	£6	£2.50	

MACARTHUR PARK

Title	Format	Label	Cat. No.	Year	Mint	Good	Notes
Taffeta Rose	7"	Columbia	DB8683	1970	£6	£2.50	

MACCOLL, EWAN

Title	Format	Label	Cat. No.	Year	Mint	Good	Notes
As We Were A-Sailing	LP	Argo	ZDA137	1970	£15	£6	*with other artists*
Bad Lads And Hard Cases	LP	Riverside	RLP12632	196–	£20	£8	*US*
Barrack Room Ballads	10" LP	Topic	10T26	1958	£30	£15	
Best Of Ewan MacColl	LP	PRE	13004	1961	£25	£10	
Blow Boys Blow	LP	XTRA	XTRA1052	1967	£12	£5	*with A. L. Lloyd*
Bundook Ballads	LP	Topic	12T130	1965	£25	£10	
English And Scottish Popular Ballads	LP	Folkways	FG3509	1961	£15	£6	*US*
English And Scottish Popular Ballads Vol. 1	LP	Riverside	RLP12621/2	196–	£30	£15	*US double, with A. L. Lloyd*
English And Scottish Popular Ballads Vol. 2	LP	Riverside	RLP12623/4	196–	£30	£15	*US double, with A. L. Lloyd*
English And Scottish Popular Ballads Vol. 2	LP	Folkways	FG3510	1961	£15	£6	*US*
English And Scottish Popular Ballads Vol. 3	LP	Riverside	RLP12625/6	196–	£30	£15	*US double, with A. L. Lloyd*
English And Scottish Popular Ballads Vol. 4	LP	Riverside	RLP12627/8	196–	£30	£15	*US double, with A. L. Lloyd*
English And Scottish Popular Ballads Vol. 5	LP	Riverside	RLP12629	196–	£20	£8	*US, with A. L. Lloyd*
Popular Scottish Songs	LP	Folkways	FW8757	1960	£15	£6	*US*
Scots Drinking Songs	LP	Riverside	RLP12605	196–	£20	£8	*US*
Scots Folk Songs	LP	Riverside	RLP12609	196–	£20	£8	*US*
Scots Street Songs	LP	Riverside	RLP12612	196–	£20	£8	*US*
Second Shift	10" LP	Topic	10T25	1958	£30	£15	
Shuttle And Cage	10" LP	Topic	10T13	1958	£30	£15	
Solo Flight	LP	Argo	ZFB12	1972	£15	£6	
Songs Of Robert Burns	LP	Folkways	FW8758	1959	£20	£8	*US*
Still I Love Him	10" LP	Topic	10T50	1960	£40	£20	*with Isla Cameron*
Streets Of Song	LP	Topic	12T41	1960	£25	£10	*with Dominic Behan*
Thar She Blows!	LP	Riverside	RLP12635	196–	£20	£8	*US, with A. L. Lloyd*

MACCOLL, EWAN & PEGGY SEEGER

Title	Format	Label	Cat. No.	Year	Mint	Good	Notes
Amorous Muse	LP	Argo	ZFB66	1972	£15	£6	
Amorous Muse	LP	Argo	(Z)DA84	1968	£15	£6	
Angry Muse	LP	Argo	ZFB65	1972	£15	£6	
Angry Muse	LP	Argo	(Z)DA83	1968	£15	£6	
At The Present Moment	LP	Rounder	4003	1973	£15	£6	*US*
Ballad Of John Axon	LP	Argo	DA139	1971	£25	£10	*with Charles Parker*
Ballad Of John Axon	LP	Argo	RG474	1965	£25	£10	*with Charles Parker*
Big Hewer	LP	Argo	RG538	1968	£25	£10	*with Charles Parker*
Big Hewer	LP	Argo	DA140	1971	£20	£8	*with Charles Parker*
Bothy Ballads Of Scotland	LP	Folkways	FW8759	1961	£15	£6	*US*
Chorus From The Gallows	LP	Topic	12T16	1960	£30	£15	
Fight Game	LP	Argo	DA141	1971	£15	£6	*with Charles Parker*
Fight Game	LP	Argo	RG539	1968	£25	£10	*with Charles Parker*
Folkways Record Of Contemporary Songs	LP	Folkways	FW8736	1973	£12	£5	*US*
Jacobite Rebellions	LP	Topic	12T79	1962	£25	£10	

Long Harvest Vol. 1	LP	Argo	(Z)DA66	1967	**£15**	£6	
Long Harvest Vol. 2	LP	Argo	(Z)DA67	1967	**£15**	£6	
Long Harvest Vol. 3	LP	Argo	(Z)DA68	1967	**£15**	£6	
Long Harvest Vol. 4	LP	Argo	(Z)DA69	1967	**£15**	£6	
Long Harvest Vol. 5	LP	Argo	(Z)DA70	1967	**£15**	£6	
Long Harvest Vol. 6	LP	Argo	(Z)DA71	1967	**£15**	£6	
Long Harvest Vol. 7	LP	Argo	(Z)DA72	1967	**£15**	£6	
Long Harvest Vol. 8	LP	Argo	(Z)DA73	1967	**£15**	£6	
Long Harvest Vol. 9	LP	Argo	(Z)DA74	1967	**£15**	£6	
Long Harvest Vol. 10	LP	Argo	(Z)DA75	1967	**£15**	£6	
Manchester Angel	LP	Topic	12T147	1966	**£20**	£8	
New Briton Gazette	LP	Folkways	FW8734	1973	**£15**	£6	*US*
On The Edge	LP	Argo	RG-	196–	**£25**	£10	*with Charles Parker*
On The Edge	LP	Argo	DA136	1971	**£15**	£6	*with Charles Parker*
Paper Stage Vol. 1	LP	Argo	(Z)DA98	1969	**£15**	£6	
Paper Stage Vol. 2	LP	Argo	(Z)DA99	1969	**£15**	£6	
Singing The Fishing	LP	Argo	RG502	196–	**£25**	£10	*with Charles Parker*
Singing The Fishing	LP	Argo	DA142	1971	**£15**	£6	*with Charles Parker*
Songs Of Two Rebellions	LP	Folkways	FW8756	1960	**£15**	£6	*US*
Steam Whistle Ballads	LP	Topic	12T104	1964	**£20**	£8	
Traditional Songs And Ballads	LP	Folways	FW8760	1964	**£15**	£6	*US*
Travelling People	LP	Argo	DA133	1970	**£30**	£15	*with Charles Parker*
Two Way Trip	LP	Folkways	FW8755	1961	**£15**	£6	*US*
Wanton Muse	LP	Argo	ZFB67	1972	**£15**	£6	
Wanton Muse	LP	Argo	(Z)DA85	1968	**£15**	£6	
We Are The Engineers	7"	AUEW	AUEW1	196–	**£4**	£1.50	
World Of Ewan MacColl And Peggy Seeger	LP	Argo	SPA102	1970	**£12**	£5	
World Of Ewan MacColl And Peggy Seeger Vol. 2	LP	Argo	SPA216	1972	**£10**	£4	

MACCOLL, KIRSTY

The daughter of traditional folk master Ewan MacColl is one of our most underrated singer-songwriters. She scored an early success with the witty 'There's A Guy Works Down The Chip Shop Swears He's Elvis', but she is otherwise best known for her cover versions of Billy Bragg's 'New England' and Ray Davies's 'Days'. Despite her relative lack of success, however, she continues to deliver classy collections of her clever and imaginative material. Her recording debut was as a young teenager with the family – Peggy Seeger's 'Penelope Isn't Waiting Any More'.

Days	CD-s	Virgin	KMACDX2	1989	**£5**	£2	*3" single*
Free World	CD-s	Virgin	KMACD1	1989	**£5**	£2	*3" single*
Innocence	CD-s	Virgin	KMACD3	1989	**£5**	£2	*3" single*
You Caught Me Out	7"	Stiff	BUY57	1979	**£4**	£2	*demo*

MACEO & ALL THE KING'S MEN

It is extraordinary how the same musicians that formed James Brown's band in the late sixties lack a significant percentage of their drive and rhythmic power when Brown is not there. Here is the proof that James Brown is indeed the master of his own music.

Funky Music Machine	LP	Mojo	2916017	1972	**£50**	£25	
Funky Music Machine	LP	Contempo	CRM114	1975	**£25**	£10	
Got To Get 'Cha	7"	Pye	7N25571	1972	**£5**	£2	

MACEO & THE MACKS

Cross The Tracks	12"	Urban	URBX1	1987	**£8**	£4	
Us	LP	Polydor	2391122	1974	**£25**	£10	
Us	LP	Urban	URBLP8	1988	**£10**	£4	

MACERO, TEO

The CBS staff producer who is perhaps best known as the man who worked on Miles Davis's ground-breaking albums on the label is also a talented alto saxophonist and composer in his own right – which is probably why he is such an effective producer.

Teo	LP	Esquire	32113	1961	**£25**	£10	

MACGREGOR, MARY

Torn Between Two Lovers	LP	Eurodisc	913119	1980	**£10**	£4	

MACHINE

Machine	LP	Polydor	2441020	1980	**£20**	£8	*Dutch*

MACHINE (2)

Stupidity	7"	Granta	GR7STD	1967	**£15**	£7.50	

MACHINES

True Life	7"	Wax	EAR1	1978	**£40**	£20	

MACHITO

Kenya	LP	Columbia	33SX1103	1958	**£20**	£8	

MACK, JOHNNY

Reggae All Night Long	7"	Columbia	DB116	1970	**£4**	£1.50	

MACK, LONNIE

For Collectors Only	LP	Elektra	2410007	1970	**£12**	£5	
Glad I'm In The Band	LP	Elektra	EKL/EKS74040	1969	**£10**	£4	
Hills Of Indiana	LP	Elektra	K42097	1972	**£10**	£4	
Lonnie On The Move	7"	Stateside	SS312	1964	**£5**	£2	
Memphis	7"	Stateside	SS207	1963	**£6**	£2.50	
Memphis	7"	Elektra	EKSN45044	1969	**£4**	£1.50	

Title	Format	Label	Number	Year	Price	Price	Notes
Sa-Ba-Hoola	7"	Stateside	SS393	1965	**£8**	**£4**	
Save Your Money	7"	President	PT142	1967	**£4**	**£1.50**	
Save Your Money	7"	Elektra	EKSN45060	1969	**£4**	**£1.50**	
Soul Express	7"	President	PT198	1968	**£4**	**£1.50**	
Wham	7"	Stateside	SS226	1963	**£6**	**£2.50**	
Wham Of The Memphis Man	LP	President	PTL1004	1967	**£20**	**£8**	
Whatever's Right	LP	Elektra	EKS74050	1969	**£10**	**£4**	
Where There's A Will	7"	President	PT127	1967	**£4**	**£1.50**	

MACK, WARNER

Title	Format	Label	Number	Year	Price	Price	Notes
Country Touch	LP	Brunswick	LAT8658	1966	**£12**	**£5**	
Drifting Apart	LP	Brunswick	LAT8684	1967	**£10**	**£4**	
Golden Country Hits	LP	London	HAR/SHR8002	1962	**£15**	**£6**	
Golden Country Hits Vol. 2	LP	London	HAR/SHR8025	1963	**£15**	**£6**	
Rock A Chicka	7"	Brunswick	05728	1958	**£100**	**£50**	

MACK SISTERS

Title	Format	Label	Number	Year	Price	Price	Notes
Long Range Love	7"	London	HLU8331	1956	**£25**	**£12.50**	

MACKAY, ANDY

Title	Format	Label	Number	Year	Price	Price	Notes
Wild Weekend	7"	Island	WIP6243	1975	**£6**	**£2.50**	*promo in picture sleeve*

MACKAY, MAHNA

Title	Format	Label	Number	Year	Price	Price	Notes
Mah Na Mah Na	7"	Parlophone	R5808	1969	**£4**	**£1.50**	

MACKENZIE, PIBROCH

Title	Format	Label	Number	Year	Price	Price	Notes
Highland Fiddle Music	LP	Waverley	ZLP2077	1968	**£12**	**£5**	
Mull Fiddler	LP	Waverley	(S)ZLP2115	1969	**£12**	**£5**	

MACKENZIE JET COMBO

Title	Format	Label	Number	Year	Price	Price	Notes
Milkman's Theme	7"	Torpedo	TOR18	1970	**£4**	**£1.50**	

MACKENZIE THEORY

Title	Format	Label	Number	Year	Price	Price	Notes
Out Of The Blue	LP	Mushroom	L34925	1973	**£15**	**£6**	*Australian*

MACKINTOSH, KEN

Title	Format	Label	Number	Year	Price	Price	Notes
Applejack	7"	HMV	POP300	1957	**£8**	**£4**	
Big Guitar	7"	HMV	POP464	1958	**£4**	**£1.50**	
Dancing To The Roaring Twenties	7" EP	HMV	7EG8468	1958	**£5**	**£2**	
Keep It Moving	7"	HMV	POP358	1957	**£4**	**£1.50**	
Ken Mackintosh	10" LP	HMV	DLP1093	1955	**£12**	**£5**	
One Night Stand	10" LP	HMV	DLP1178	1958	**£12**	**£5**	
Raunchy	7"	HMV	POP426	1957	**£4**	**£1.50**	
Regimental Rock	7"	HMV	POP287	1957	**£5**	**£2**	
Rock Man Rock	7"	HMV	POP327	1957	**£8**	**£4**	
Six Five Blues	7"	HMV	POP396	1957	**£4**	**£1.50**	
Swinging Shepherd Blues	7"	HMV	POP441	1958	**£4**	**£1.50**	
Teenager's Special	7" EP	HMV	7EG8170	1956	**£10**	**£5**	

MACLAINE, PETE & CLAN

Title	Format	Label	Number	Year	Price	Price	Notes
U.S. Mail	7"	Decca	F11699	1963	**£6**	**£2.50**	

MACLEAN, DOUGIE

Title	Format	Label	Number	Year	Price	Price	Notes
Snaigow	LP	Plant Life	PLR022	1980	**£12**	**£5**	

MACLENNAN, DOLINA & ROBIN GRAY

Title	Format	Label	Number	Year	Price	Price	Notes
By Mormond Braes	7" EP	Topic	TOP68	1964	**£5**	**£2**	

MACLEOD, JOHN FIRST XI

Title	Format	Label	Number	Year	Price	Price	Notes
Don't Shoot The Ref	7"	Fontana	TF696	1966	**£4**	**£1.50**	

MACLISE, ANGUS

Title	Format	Label	Number	Year	Price	Price	Notes
Trance	7"	Fierce	FRIGHT010	1987	**£6**	**£2.50**	

MACMAHON, DOLLY

Title	Format	Label	Number	Year	Price	Price	Notes
Dolly	LP	Claddagh	CC3	1966	**£10**	**£4**	*Irish*

MACON, UNCLE DAVE

Title	Format	Label	Number	Year	Price	Price	Notes
Uncle Dave Macon	LP	Ace Of Hearts	AH135	1966	**£10**	**£4**	
Uncle Dave Macon No. 1	7" EP	RCA	RCX7112	1963	**£10**	**£5**	
Uncle Dave Macon No. 2	7" EP	RCA	RCX7113	1963	**£10**	**£5**	

MACRAE, GORDON

Title	Format	Label	Number	Year	Price	Price	Notes
Bella Notte	7"	Capitol	CL14361	1955	**£5**	**£2**	
C'est Magnifique	7"	Capitol	CL14168	1954	**£5**	**£2**	
Count Your Blessings Instead Of Sheep	7"	Capitol	CL14193	1954	**£5**	**£2**	
Jim Bowie	7"	Capitol	CL14334	1955	**£5**	**£2**	
Stranger In Paradise	7"	Capitol	CL14276	1955	**£5**	**£2**	

MACRAE, JOSH

Title	Format	Label	Number	Year	Price	Price	Notes
Josh MacRae	7" EP	Top Rank	JKP2061	1960	**£8**	**£4**	
Josh MacRae	LP	Transatlantic	TRA150	1966	**£10**	**£4**	
Messing About On The River	7"	Pye	7N15319	1960	**£4**	**£1.50**	
Talking Army Blues	7"	Top Rank	JAR290	1960	**£5**	**£2**	
Walking Talking Singing	7" EP	Pye	NEP24131	1960	**£10**	**£5**	
Wild Side Of Life	7"	Pye	7N15308	1960	**£4**	**£1.50**	

MACREEL

Title	Format	Label	Cat. No.	Year	Mint	VG	Notes
Step It Out	LP	JMR		1984	**£100**	**£50**	*Dutch*

MAD DOG

Title	Format	Label	Cat. No.	Year	Mint	VG	Notes
Pop Sounds	LP	Chappell	LPC1053	1974	**£20**	**£8**	

MAD LADS

Title	Format	Label	Cat. No.	Year	Mint	VG	Notes
Don't Have To Shop Around	7"	Atlantic	AT4051	1965	**£6**	**£2.50**	
I Want Someone	7"	Atlantic	AT4083	1966	**£6**	**£2.50**	
Mad Lads In Action	LP	Volt	414	1966	**£25**	**£10**	*US*
Sugar Sugar	7"	Atlantic	584038	1966	**£5**	**£2**	

MAD LADS (2)

Title	Format	Label	Cat. No.	Year	Mint	VG	Notes
Losing You	7"	Coxsone	CS7099	1969	**£10**	**£5**	*Winston Jarrett*

MAD MAGAZINE

Title	Format	Label	Cat. No.	Year	Mint	VG	Notes
Fink Along With Mad	LP	Big Top	1206	196–	**£20**	**£8**	*US*
Mad Twists Rock'n'Roll	LP	Big Top	1305	1963	**£20**	**£8**	*US*

MAD RIVER

The first album made by Mad River is a superior example of West Coast rock in the same style, and at least as impressive as the early albums by the Grateful Dead and Quicksilver Messenger Service. As it happens, the album was cut at the wrong speed, so that the music on the original pressings is higher and faster than it should be. The eighties reissue of the album on Edsel corrects this fault. *Paradise Bar And Grill* has more of a country-rock emphasis and is rather less remarkable. A very rare EP predates both albums and includes early versions of two of the first album songs.

Title	Format	Label	Cat. No.	Year	Mint	VG	Notes
Mad River	LP	Capitol	ST2985	1968	**£40**	**£20**	*US*
Paradise Bar And Grill	LP	Capitol	ST185	1969	**£40**	**£20**	*US*
Wind Chimes	7" EP	Wee	10021	1967	**£300**	**£180**	*US, best auctioned*

MAD ROY

Title	Format	Label	Cat. No.	Year	Mint	VG	Notes
Home Version	7"	Banana	BA326	1971	**£5**	**£2**	
Nannie Goat Version	7"	Banana	BA324	1970	**£5**	**£2**	
Universal Love	7"	Banana	BA327	1971	**£5**	**£2**	*Roland Alphonso B side*

MADARA, JOHNNY

Title	Format	Label	Cat. No.	Year	Mint	VG	Notes
Be My Girl	7"	HMV	POP389	1957	**£4**	**£1.50**	

MADDEN, TOM & FRANK WARREN

Title	Format	Label	Cat. No.	Year	Mint	VG	Notes
Little Thatched Cabin	LP	Inchecronin	INC7727	1977	**£15**	**£6**	

MADDER LAKE

Title	Format	Label	Cat. No.	Year	Mint	VG	Notes
Still Point	LP	Mushroom	L34915	1973	**£25**	**£10**	*Australian*

MADDOX, JOHNNY

Title	Format	Label	Cat. No.	Year	Mint	VG	Notes
Crazy Otto Medley	7"	London	HL8134	1955	**£10**	**£5**	
Dixieland Band	7"	London	HLD8347	1956	**£6**	**£2.50**	
Dixieland Blues	LP	London	HAD2175/ SHD6022	1959	**£10**	**£4**	
Do Do Do	7"	London	HLD8203	1955	**£10**	**£5**	
Hands Off	7"	London	HLD8277	1956	**£20**	**£10**	
Honky Tonk Jazz	7" EP	London	RED1150	1958	**£6**	**£2.50**	
Hurdy Gurdy Song	7"	London	HLD8826	1959	**£4**	**£1.50**	
My Old Flames	LP	London	HAD2101	1958	**£10**	**£4**	
Nickelodeon Tango	7"	London	MSD1503/4	1955	**£60**	**£30**	*demo*
Old Fashioned Love	7" EP	London	RED1270	1961	**£6**	**£2.50**	
Plays	10" LP	London	HBD1060	1956	**£10**	**£4**	
Presenting Johnny Maddox	7" EP	London	REP1020	1955	**£8**	**£4**	
Presenting Johnny Maddox No. 2	7" EP	London	REP1040	1955	**£8**	**£4**	
Yellow Dog Blues	7"	London	HLD8540	1958	**£6**	**£2.50**	

MADDOX, ROSE

Title	Format	Label	Cat. No.	Year	Mint	VG	Notes
Alone With You	LP	Capitol	(S)T1993	1963	**£12**	**£5**	*US*
Big Bouquet Of Roses	LP	Capitol	(S)T1548	1961	**£12**	**£5**	*US*
Gambler's Love	7"	Capitol	CL15023	1959	**£4**	**£1.50**	
Glorybound Train	LP	Capitol	(S)T1437	1960	**£12**	**£5**	*US*
One Rose	LP	Capitol	(S)T1312	1960	**£12**	**£5**	*US*
Precious Memories	LP	Columbia	CL1159	1958	**£20**	**£8**	*US*
Rose Maddox Sings Bluegrass	LP	Capitol	(S)T1779	1962	**£12**	**£5**	*US*

MADDOX BROTHERS & ROSE

Title	Format	Label	Cat. No.	Year	Mint	VG	Notes
Collection Of Standard Sacred Songs	LP	King	669	1960	**£30**	**£15**	*US*
I'll Write Your Name In The Sand	LP	King	752	1961	**£25**	**£10**	*US*
Maddox Brothers And Rose	LP	King	677	1961	**£25**	**£10**	*US*

MADE IN SHEFFIELD

Title	Format	Label	Cat. No.	Year	Mint	VG	Notes
Amelia Jane	7"	Fontana	TF871	1967	**£12**	**£6**	

MADE IN SWEDEN

Title	Format	Label	Cat. No.	Year	Mint	VG	Notes
Live At The Golden Circle	LP	Sonet	SLP2506	1970	**£10**	**£4**	
Mad River	LP	Sonet	SNTF621	1971	**£10**	**£4**	
Made In England	LP	Sonet	SLP2512	1970	**£10**	**£4**	
Made In Sweden	LP	Sonet	SLP71	1969	**£10**	**£4**	
Snakes In A Hole	LP	Sonet	SLP2504	1969	**£10**	**£4**	

MADIGAN, BETTY

Jerome Kern Songbook Vol. 1	7" EP	Coral	FEP2009	1958	**£5**	**£2**	
Jerome Kern Songbook Vol. 2	7" EP	Coral	FEP2011	1959	**£5**	**£2**	

MADISON DYKE

Zeitmaschine	LP	Racket Records	RRK15001	1977	**£15**	**£6**	*German*

MADNESS

Absolutely	LP	Stiff	STIFF29	1980	**£25**	**£10**	*different cover pose*
Carols On 45	7"	Lyntone	LYN10719	1982	**£4**	**£1.50**	*flexi*
Grey Day	12"	Stiff	BUYIT112	1981	**£15**	**£7.50**	
I Pronounce You	CD-s	Virgin	VSCD1054	1988	**£5**	**£2**	
It Must Be Love	12"	Stiff	BUYIT134	1982	**£6**	**£2.50**	
Keep Moving	LP	Stiff	PSEEZ53	1984	**£10**	**£4**	*picture disc*
Madness Pack	7"	Stiff	GRAB1	1982	**£20**	**£10**	*6 × 7" in plastic wallet*
One Step Beyond	12"	Stiff	BUYIT56	1979	**£6**	**£2.50**	
Peel Sessions	CD-s	Strange Fruit	SFPSCD007	1988	**£5**	**£2**	
Prince	7"	2-Tone	TT3	1979	**£5**	**£2**	*paper labels, no picture sleeve*
Return Of The Los Palmas 7	12"	Stiff	BUYIT108	1981	**£6**	**£2.50**	*with comic*
Swan Lake	12"	Stiff	MAD1	1979	**£15**	**£7.50**	*promo*
Take It Or Leave It	7"	Lyntone	LYN10208	1982	**£5**	**£2**	*flexi*
Uno Paso Adalante	7"	Stiff	MO1922	1980	**£6**	**£2.50**	*sung in Spanish*

MADONNA

Astute marketing has kept Madonna at the top for far longer than seemed likely when her pictures first started to appear on teenagers' bedroom walls. That and the fact that she does actually have a considerable musical talent – as her remarkable album, *Ray Of Light*, makes very clear. Virtually everything she has released is now a collectors' item of some kind, with particular interest being generated by the series of picture disc releases. The value of many of these is much higher than can be explained merely by their rarity, although the early 'Crazy For You' is reckoned to be one of the scarcest commercially released picture discs of all. More valuable still, by quite a long way, is the withdrawn picture disc release of 'Erotica'.

Angel	7"	Sire	W8881P	1985	**£12**	**£6**	*shaped picture disc*
Angel	7"	Sire	W8881P	1985	**£20**	**£10**	*shaped picture disc, plinth*
Bedtime Stories	CD	Maverick	9457672	1994	**£40**	**£20**	*US promo velvet digipak*
Bedtime Story	CD-s	Maverick	W0285CDX	1995	**£6**	**£2.50**	
Borderline	7"	Sire	W9260F	1984	**£60**	**£30**	*double*
Borderline	7"	Sire	W9260P	1986	**£30**	**£15**	*shaped picture disc*
Causing A Commotion	7"	Sire	W8224	1987	**£30**	**£15**	*with badge*
Causing A Commotion (Silver Screen Mix)	12"	Sire	W8224TP	1987	**£15**	**£7.50**	*picture disc*
Cherish	12"	Sire	W2883TP	1989	**£10**	**£5**	*picture disc*
Cherish	CD-s	Sire	W2883CD	1989	**£5**	**£2**	*3" single*
Crazy For You	7"	Geffen	WA6323	1985	**£50**	**£25**	*shaped picture disc*
Crazy For You	CD-s	Sire	W0008CD	1991	**£5**	**£2**	*picture disc*
Crazy For You (Remix)	7"	Sire	W0008P	1991	**£5**	**£2**	*shaped picture disc, plinth*
Dear Jessie	12"	Sire	W2668TP	1989	**£6**	**£2.50**	*picture disc*
Dear Jessie	12"	Sire	W2668T	1989	**£6**	**£2.50**	*poster sleeve*
Dear Jessie	CD-s	Sire	W2668CD	1989	**£5**	**£2**	
Dear Jessie	CD-s	Sire	W2668CD	1989	**£40**	**£20**	*picture disc*
Deeper And Deeper	12"	Maverick	W0146TP	1992	**£6**	**£2.50**	*picture disc*
Dress You Up	7"	Sire	W8848P	1985	**£20**	**£10**	*shaped picture disc*
Dress You Up (Formal Mix)	12"	Sire	W8848T	1985	**£15**	**£7.50**	*poster sleeve*
Erotica	12"	Maverick	W0138TP	1992	**£500**	**£330**	*picture disc, gold insert*
Erotica	CD	Sire		1992	**£30**	**£15**	*Australian, fold-out cover*
Everybody	12"	Sire	W9899T	1982	**£75**	**£37.50**	*no picture sleeve*
Everybody	7"	Sire	W9899	1982	**£100**	**£50**	
Express Yourself	7"	Sire	W2948W	1989	**£15**	**£7.50**	*zipper sleeve*
Express Yourself	7"	Sire	W2948X	1989	**£12**	**£6**	*poster sleeve*
Express Yourself	CD-s	Sire	W2948CD	1989	**£5**	**£2**	*3" single*
Express Yourself (Non-Stop Express Mix)	12"	Sire	W2948TP	1989	**£20**	**£10**	*picture disc*
Fever	7"	Maverick	W0168P	1993	**£6**	**£2.50**	*picture disc*
Frozen	12"	Sire	SAM3173	1998	**£25**	**£12.50**	*promo*
Gambler	12"	Geffen	A6585TA	1985	**£10**	**£5**	
Gambler	7"	Geffen	QA6585	1985	**£12**	**£6**	*poster sleeve*
Hanky Panky	12"	Sire	W9789TP	1990	**£12**	**£6**	*picture disc*
Hanky Panky	CD-s	Sire	W9789CD	1990	**£5**	**£2**	
Holiday	12"	Sire	W0037TP	1991	**£6**	**£2.50**	*picture disc, insert*
Holiday (Edit)	7"	Sire	W9405	1983	**£4**	**£1.50**	*train picture sleeve*
Holiday (Full Length Version)	12"	Sire	W9405T	1983	**£10**	**£5**	*train picture sleeve*
Holiday (Full Length Version)	12"	Sire	W9405P	1985	**£20**	**£10**	*picture disc*
Holiday Collection	CD-s	Sire	W0037CD	1991	**£5**	**£2**	
I'm Breathless	CD	Sire	7599262092	1990	**£50**	**£25**	*promo box set with video*
I'm Breathless	CD	Sire	2620942DJ	1990	**£25**	**£10**	*US promo picture disc*
Into The Groove	12"	Sire	W8934T	1985	**£10**	**£5**	*with poster*
Into The Groove	7"	Sire	W8934P	1985	**£20**	**£10**	*shaped picture disc*

Justify My Love	12"	Sire	W9000TP	1990	**£6**	**£2.50**	*picture disc, insert*
Justify My Love	CD-s	Sire	W9000CD	1990	**£5**	**£2**	
Keep It Together	12"	Sire	SAM641	1989	**£25**	**£12.50**	*promo*
La Isla Bonita (Extended Remix)	12"	Sire	W8378TP	1987	**£15**	**£7.50**	*picture disc*
Like A Prayer	CD	Sire	K9258442	1989	**£200**	**£100**	*promo box set with cassette, slides, badge, photos, biog*
Like A Prayer	CD	Sire		1989	**£25**	**£10**	*US promo gold picture disc*
Like A Prayer	CD-s	Sire	W7539CD	1989	**£5**	**£2**	*3" single*
Like A Prayer (3 mixes)	12"	Sire	W7539TX	1989	**£8**	**£4**	
Like A Prayer (Extended Remix)	12"	Sire	W7539TP	1989	**£8**	**£4**	*picture disc*
Like A Virgin	LP	Sire		1984	**£50**	**£25**	*US, white vinyl*
Like A Virgin	LP	Sire	WX20P	1985	**£30**	**£15**	*picture disc*
Like A Virgin (US Dance Remix)	12"	Sire	W9210T	1984	**£15**	**£7.50**	*with poster*
Live To Tell	12"	Sire	W8717T	1986	**£10**	**£5**	*with poster*
Look Of Love	12"	Sire	W8115TP	1987	**£15**	**£7.50**	*picture disc*
Love Don't Live Here Anymore	12"	Warner Bros	SAM1880	1996	**£30**	**£15**	*promo only*
Lucky Star	7"	Sire	W9522	1983	**£125**	**£62.50**	*sunglasses picture sleeve*
Lucky Star (Full Length Version)	12"	Sire	W9522T	1983	**£30**	**£15**	*sunglasses picture sleeve*
Lucky Star (Full Length Version)	12"	Sire	W9522T	1983	**£10**	**£5**	*TV screen picture sleeve*
Lucky Star (Full Length Version)	12"	Sire	W9522T	1983	**£25**	**£12.50**	*TV screen picture sleeve, poster*
Lucky Star (US Remix)	12"	Sire	W9522TV	1983	**£40**	**£20**	*plain sleeve*
Material Girl	7"	Sire	W9083	1985	**£100**	**£50**	*poster sleeve*
Material Girl (Jellybean Dance Remix)	12"	Sire	W9083T	1985	**£15**	**£7.50**	*with poster*
Open Your Heart (Extended Version)	12"	Sire	W8480TP	1986	**£15**	**£7.50**	*picture disc*
Papa Don't Preach	CD-s	Sire	9256812	1989	**£40**	**£20**	*CD video*
Papa Don't Preach (Extended Remix)	12"	Sire	W8636TP	1986	**£20**	**£10**	*picture disc*
Papa Don't Preach (Extended Version)	12"	Sire	W8636T	1986	**£10**	**£5**	*with poster*
Rain	12"	Sire	WO190TP	1993	**£5**	**£2**	*picture disc*
Rescue Me	CD-s	Sire	W0024CD	1991	**£5**	**£2**	
Royal Box (Immaculate Collection)	CD	Sire	7599264642	1990	**£60**	**£30**	*CD, video, poster,cards – boxed*
Secret	7"	Maverick	W0268P	1994	**£8**	**£4**	*picture disc, insert*
True Blue	LP	Sire	WX54	1986	**£40**	**£20**	*clear vinyl*
True Blue	LP	Sire	WX54	1986	**£40**	**£20**	*blue vinyl, poster*
True Blue	LP	Sire		1986	**£40**	**£20**	*US picture disc*
True Blue (Extended Dance Version)	12"	Sire	W8550TP	1986	**£15**	**£7.50**	*picture disc*
Vogue	12"	Sire	W9851TP	1990	**£10**	**£5**	*picture disc*
Vogue	12"	Sire	W9851TX	1990	**£6**	**£2.50**	*with poster*
Vogue	7"	Sire	W9851P	1990	**£4**	**£1.50**	*picture disc*
Vogue	CD-s	Sire	W9851CD	1990	**£5**	**£2**	
Who's That Girl (Extended Version)	12"	Sire	W8341TP	1987	**£30**	**£15**	*picture disc*
You Can Dance	LP	Sire	PROMAD1	1987	**£60**	**£30**	*promo picture disc*
You Can Dance – Radio Edits	CD	Sire	PROCD2892	1987	**£25**	**£10**	*US promo*

MADRIGAL

Beneath The Greenwood Tree	LP	private	MAD100	1973	**£75**	**£37.50**	

MADURA

Madura	LP	CBS	67222	1971	**£20**	**£8**	*Italian double*

MAESTRO, JOHNNY

Before I Loved Her	7"	United Artists	UP1004	1964	**£10**	**£5**	
Johnny Maestro Story	LP	Buddah	BDS5091	1971	**£15**	**£6**	*US*
Mr Happiness	7"	HMV	POP909	1961	**£25**	**£12.50**	
What A Surprise	7"	HMV	POP875	1961	**£25**	**£12.50**	

MAGENTA

Canterbury Moon	LP	Cottage	COT821	1978	**£60**	**£30**	
Recollections	LP	Little Stan	LSP811	1980	**£100**	**£50**	*double*
Wot's Next Then?	LP	Little Stan	LSP831	1983	**£100**	**£50**	

MAGI

Win Or Lose	LP	Uncle Dirty's	6102N13	1972	**£300**	**£180**	*US*

MAGIC

Enclosed	LP	Armadillo	8031	1969	**£400**	**£250**	*US*

MAGIC CARPET

The Magic Carpet album is a delightful period piece, mixing oriental sonorities with contemporary folk music to create a sound that epitomizes the interests of the hippy movement. Sitar player Clem Alford made three albums subsequently (one under the name Sagram), while singer Alisha Sufit waited until the nineties before recording her own solo album. She has often been found at record fairs, selling copies of this and also reissues of the Magic Carpet album.

Magic Carpet	LP	Mushroom	200MR20	1972	**£100**	**£50**	

MAGIC CHRISTIANS

If You Want It	7"	Major Minor	MM673	1970	**£5**	**£2**	
Magic Christians	LP	Major Minor	SMLP71	1970	**£25**	**£10**	

MAGIC LANTERNS

Auntie Grizelda	7"	CBS	202637	1967	**£4**	**£1.50**	

Excuse Me Baby	7" EP	CBS	5798	1966	£20	£10	French
Haymarket Square	LP	Chaparral	CRM201	1966	£50	£25	US
Lit Up With The Magic Lanterns	LP	CBS	62935	1969	£20	£8	
Rumplestiltskin	7"	CBS	202250	1966	£20	£10	
Shame Shame	LP	Atlantic	SD8217	1969	£15	£6	US

MAGIC MIXTURE

This Is Magic Mixture	LP	Saga	FID2125	1968	£50	£25	

MAGIC MUSHROOM BAND

Bomshamkar	LP	Aftermath	AFT3	1987	£20	£8	
Politics Of Ecstasy	LP	Pagan	PM003	1986	£50	£25	*with poster*
Process Of Illumination	LP	Fungus	FUN003	1990	£15	£6	*with comic*
Spaced Out	LP	Fungus	FUN005	1991	£15	£6	*with booklet*

MAGIC NOTES

Album Of Memory	7"	Blue Beat	BB9	1960	£12	£6	

MAGIC SAM

Black Magic	LP	Delmark	DS620	1971	£12	£5	
Magic Sam 1937–69	LP	Blue Horizon	763223	1969	£50	£25	
Mean Mistreater	7" EP	Rooster	707	1969	£8	£4	
Twenty-One Days In Jail	7"	Python	PEN701	1969	£25	£12.50	
West Side Soul	LP	Delmark	DS615	1970	£12	£5	

MAGIC VALLEY

Taking The Heart Out Of Love	7"	Penny Farthing	PEN701	1969	£5	£2	

MAGICAL RING

Light Flight	LP	Chicago	2000900152	1977	£50	£25	French

MAGICIANS

Liars	7"	Decca	F12374	1966	£4	£1.50	
Tarzan March	7"	Decca	F12602	1967	£4	£1.50	

MAGISTRATES

After The Fox	7"	MGM	MGM1437	1968	£4	£1.50	
Here Comes The Judge	7"	MGM	MGM1425	1968	£4	£1.50	

MAGMA

French group Magma acquired a certain notoriety in recent times when snooker player Steve Davis – himself something of an avid record collector – decided to indulge his love of their music and organized a tour for them. Magma have always been the brainchild of drummer Christian Vander, whose distinctive music combines science fiction imagery, jazz-rock solos (virtuoso violinist Didier Lockwood was a member for a time) and operatic vocals, within an overall progressive rock framework. Uniquely, Vander's chosen language for the songs is a Germanic tongue of his own invention. As these elements will suggest, Magma's music is not quite like that of any other group, although values of original album issues have been kept low by the frequent availability of reissue copies.

1001 Centigrade	LP	Philips	6397031	1971	£15	£6	
Inedits	LP	Tapioca	TP10001	1977	£12	£5	French
Kohntarkosz	LP	A&M	AMLH68260	1974	£12	£5	
Live	LP	Utopia	DUTS001	1975	£15	£6	double
Magma	LP	Philips	635951/2	1970	£15	£6	double
Mekanik Destruktiw Kommandoh	LP	A&M	AMLH64397	1973	£10	£4	
Mekanik Machine	7"	A&M	AMS7119	1974	£5	£2	

MAGNA CARTA

In Concert	LP	Vertigo	6360068	1972	£10	£4	*spiral label*
Lord Of The Ages	LP	Vertigo	6360093	1973	£10	£4	
Magna Carta	LP	Mercury	SMCL20166	1969	£30	£15	
Mid Winter	7"	Mercury	MF1096	1969	£5	£2	
Romeo Jack	7"	Fontana	TF1060	1969	£5	£2	
Seasons	LP	Vertigo	6360003	1970	£12	£5	*spiral label*
Songs From Wasties Orchard	LP	Vertigo	6360040	1971	£15	£6	*spiral label*

MAGNIFICENT MEN

Peace Of Mind	7"	Capitol	CL15462	1966	£15	£7.50	
Save The Country	7"	Capitol	CL15570	1968	£4	£1.50	

MAGNUM

Black Nights	7"	Jet	JET7007	1981	£8	£4	
Changes	7"	Jet	JET155	1979	£4	£1.50	*with patch*
Days Of No Trust	7"	Polydor	POSPP910	1988	£4	£1.50	*with patch*
Days Of No Trust	CD-s	Polydor	POCD910	1988	£5	£2	
Heartbroke And Busted	CD-s	Polydor	PZCDT94	1990	£5	£2	*in tin*
It Must Have Been Love	CD-s	Polydor	POCD930	1988	£5	£2	
Kingdom Of Madness	LP	Jet	JETLP210	1978	£12	£5	*'king' sleeve*
Magnum	CD-s	Special Edition	CD37	1988	£5	£2	*3" single*
Marauder	CD	Castle	CLACD124	1986	£12	£5	
Midnight	12"	Polydor	POSPP833	1986	£6	£2.50	*picture disc*
On The Wings Of Heaven	CD-s	Polygram	0803881	1988	£10	£5	*CD video*
Rockin' Chair	CD-s	Polydor	PZCD88	1990	£5	£2	
Start Talking Love	CD-s	Polygram	0804062	1988	£10	£5	*CD video*
Start Talking Love	CD-s	Polydor	POCD920	1988	£10	£5	*card sleeve*
Sweets For My Sweet	7"	CBS	2959	1975	£25	£12.50	

MAGPIES

Title	Format	Label	Cat. No.	Year	Price	Price	Notes
Blue Boy	7"	Doctor Bird	DB1132	1968	**£10**	**£5**	
Lulu	7"	Doctor Bird	DB1129	1968	**£10**	**£5**	

MAGUIRE, JOHN

Title	Format	Label	Cat. No.	Year	Price	Price	Notes
Come Day, Go Day, God Send Sunday	LP	Leader	LEE4062	1973	**£10**	**£4**	

MAGUS

Title	Format	Label	Cat. No.	Year	Price	Price	Notes
Breezin' Away	LP	Northern Sound	NSR200	1980	**£100**	**£50**	

MAHAL, TAJ

Taj Mahal is in many ways the black equivalent of Ry Cooder. He has an archivist's approach to his musical culture, rediscovering old songs and presenting them as fresh pieces of music in order to encourage his audience to delve further. His earliest records are exclusively concerned with the blues, but he has ranged more widely since. In fact, Ry Cooder and Taj Mahal were both members of the cult sixties group the Rising Sons and Cooder is also a member of the band on the first Taj Mahal LP.

Title	Format	Label	Cat. No.	Year	Price	Price	Notes
Giant Step/De Ole Folks	LP	CBS	66226	1969	**£15**	**£6**	*double*
Natch'l Blues	LP	Direction	863397	1968	**£12**	**£5**	
Real Thing	LP	CBS	66288	1971	**£12**	**£5**	*double*
Taj Mahal	LP	Direction	863279	1967	**£15**	**£6**	

MAHAVISHNU ORCHESTRA

Title	Format	Label	Cat. No.	Year	Price	Price	Notes
Birds Of Fire	LP	CBS	CQ31996	1974	**£12**	**£5**	*quad*

MAHJUN

Title	Format	Label	Cat. No.	Year	Price	Price	Notes
Happy French Band	LP	Gratte-Ciel	ZL37049	1977	**£10**	**£4**	*French*
Mahjun	LP	Saravah	SH10047	1974	**£20**	**£8**	*French*
Mahjun	LP	Saravah	SH10040	1973	**£20**	**£8**	*French*

MAHOGANY RUSH

Title	Format	Label	Cat. No.	Year	Price	Price	Notes
Child Of The Novelty	LP	20th Century	S451	1973	**£12**	**£5**	*US*
Maxoom	LP	Nine	936	1972	**£25**	**£10**	*US*
Maxoom	LP	20th Century	S463	1975	**£12**	**£5**	*US*

MAHONEY, SKIP & THE CASUALS

Title	Format	Label	Cat. No.	Year	Price	Price	Notes
Land Of Love	LP	Contempo	CLP539	1976	**£12**	**£5**	

MAIN ATTRACTION

Title	Format	Label	Cat. No.	Year	Price	Price	Notes
And Now	LP	Tower	ST5117	1968	**£12**	**£5**	*US*

MAIN INGREDIENT

Title	Format	Label	Cat. No.	Year	Price	Price	Notes
Tasteful Soul	LP	RCA	LSA3020	1971	**£10**	**£4**	

MAINEEAXE

Title	Format	Label	Cat. No.	Year	Price	Price	Notes
Gonna Make You Rock	7"	Powerstation	OHM6	1984	**£4**	**£1.50**	

MAINHORSE

Title	Format	Label	Cat. No.	Year	Price	Price	Notes
Mainhorse	LP	Polydor	2383049	1971	**£12**	**£5**	

MAINLAND

Title	Format	Label	Cat. No.	Year	Price	Price	Notes
Exposure	LP	Christy	ACML0200	1979	**£12**	**£5**	

MAINLINE

Title	Format	Label	Cat. No.	Year	Price	Price	Notes
Canada Our Home	LP	GRT	92301011	1971	**£15**	**£6**	*Canada*

MAIRS, JULIE & CHRIS STOWELL

Title	Format	Label	Cat. No.	Year	Price	Price	Notes
Soft Sea Blue	LP	Cottage	COT211	1977	**£15**	**£6**	

MAJAMOOD

Title	Format	Label	Cat. No.	Year	Price	Price	Notes
Two Hundred Million Red Ants	7"	Doctor Bird	DB1052	1966	**£12**	**£6**	

MAJIC SHIP

Title	Format	Label	Cat. No.	Year	Price	Price	Notes
Majic Ship	LP	Bel Ami	BA711	1968	**£500**	**£330**	*US*

MAJOR ACCIDENT

Title	Format	Label	Cat. No.	Year	Price	Price	Notes
Warboots	7"	Massacred Melodies	MAME1001	1982	**£25**	**£12.50**	*test pressing*

MAJOR SURGERY

Title	Format	Label	Cat. No.	Year	Price	Price	Notes
First Cut	LP	Next	NEXT1	1977	**£15**	**£6**	

MAJORETTES

Title	Format	Label	Cat. No.	Year	Price	Price	Notes
White Levis	7"	Lyntone	LYN982	1963	**£6**	**£2.50**	*flexi*

MAJORITY

Title	Format	Label	Cat. No.	Year	Price	Price	Notes
Little Bit Of Sunlight	7"	Decca	F12271	1965	**£5**	**£2**	
Running Away With My Baby	7"	Decca	F12638	1967	**£15**	**£7.50**	
Simplified	7"	Decca	F12453	1966	**£20**	**£10**	

MAJORS

Title	Format	Label	Cat. No.	Year	Price	Price	Notes
Meet The Majors	7" EP	London	REP1358	1963	**£75**	**£37.50**	
Meet The Majors	LP	London	HAP8068	1963	**£100**	**£50**	
Ooh Wee Baby	7"	Liberty	LIB66009	1964	**£15**	**£7.50**	
She's A Troublemaker	7"	London	HLP9627	1962	**£10**	**£5**	
What In The World	7"	London	HLP9693	1963	**£8**	**£4**	
Wonderful Dream	7"	London	HLP9602	1962	**£8**	**£4**	

MAKADOPOULOS & HIS GREEK SERENADERS

Never On Sunday	7"	Palette	PG9005	1961	**£5**	**£2**	*picture sleeve*

MAKEBA, MIRIAM

Click Song	7"	London	HL9747	1963	**£4**	**£1.50**	
In Concert	LP	Reprise	RLP6253	1967	**£10**	**£4**	
Keep Me In Mind	LP	Reprise	RSLP6381	1970	**£10**	**£4**	
Makeba!	LP	Reprise	R(S)LP6310	1968	**£10**	**£4**	
Miriam Makeba	LP	London	HA2332	1961	**£10**	**£4**	

MAKEM, SARAH

Ulster Ballad Singer	LP	Topic	12T185	1969	**£12**	**£5**	

MAKEM, TOMMY

Bard Of Armagh	LP	CBS	64001	1970	**£10**	**£4**	
Ever The Winds	LP	Polydor	2383328	1975	**£10**	**£4**	
In The Dark Green Woods	LP	Polydor	2383280	1974	**£10**	**£4**	
It's Tommy Makem	LP	Emerald	MLD20	1967	**£12**	**£5**	
Sings Tommy Makem	LP	CBS	63112	1967	**£12**	**£5**	

MAKEM, TOMMY & LIAM CLANCY

Makem And Clancy Concert	LP	CBS	88302	1977	**£12**	**£5**	*double*
Tommy Makem And Liam Clancy	LP	Epic	EPC82081	1976	**£10**	**£4**	

MAKIN' TIME

No Lumps Of Fat Or Gristle Guaranteed	LP	Ready To Eat	READY1	1986	**£10**	**£4**	
Rhythm'n'Soul	LP	Countdown	DOWN1	1985	**£10**	**£4**	
Time, Trouble And Money	LP	Re-Elect The President	ELECT1	1987	**£10**	**£4**	

MAL & THE PRIMITIVES

Every Minute Of Every Day	7"	Pye	7N15915	1965	**£60**	**£30**	
Mal Dei Primitives	LP	RCA	PSL10442	1967	**£50**	**£25**	*Italian*
Sua Eccelenza	LP	RCA	PSL10439	1967	**£75**	**£37.50**	*Italian*

MALCOLM, CARLOS

Bonanza Ska	7"	Island	WI173	1965	**£10**	**£5**	

MALCOLM, GEORGE

Bach Goes To Town	7"	Parlophone	MSP6058	1953	**£4**	**£1.50**	

MALCOLM, HUGH

Good Time Rock	7"	Amalgamated	AMG827	1968	**£8**	**£4**	*Lyn Taitt B side*

MALCOLM & ALWYN

Fool's Wisdom	LP	Pye	NSPL18404	1973	**£12**	**£5**	
Wildwall	LP	Key	K1022	1974	**£25**	**£10**	

MALDOON

Maldoon	LP	Purple	TPS3502	1972	**£10**	**£4**	

MALDOON, CURTISS

Curtiss Maldoon	LP	Purple	TPS3501	1971	**£10**	**£4**	
One Way Ticket	7"	Purple	PUR106	1972	**£4**	**£1.50**	

MALE

Zensur Zensur	LP	Modell Music	ROCKON1	1978	**£15**	**£6**	*German*

MALICORNE

Almanach	LP	Hexagone	883007	1976	**£15**	**£6**	*French*
En Public	LP	Ballon Noire	BAL13010	1978	**£10**	**£4**	*French*
L'Extraordinaire	LP	Ballon Noire	BAL13006	1978	**£10**	**£4**	*French*
Le Bestiaire	LP	Ballon Noire	BAL13012	1979	**£10**	**£4**	*French*
Malicorne	LP	Hexagone	883004	1974	**£15**	**£6**	*French*
Malicorne II	LP	Hexagone	883005	1975	**£15**	**£6**	*French*
Malicorne IV	LP	Hexagone	883015	1976	**£15**	**£6**	*French*
Quintessence	LP	Hexagone	883018	1979	**£15**	**£6**	*French*

MALLARD

Mallard was the group formed by members of Captain Beefheart's original Magic Band and its music has much of the same flavour as albums like *Strictly Personal.*

In A Different Climate	LP	Virgin	V2077	1977	**£10**	**£4**	
Mallard	LP	Virgin	V2045	1976	**£10**	**£4**	

MALON

Rebellion	LP	Philips	6397032	1971	**£15**	**£6**	*French*

MALONE, WIL

Wil Malone	LP	Fontana	STL5541	1970	**£50**	**£25**	

MALONE, WILSON VOICEBAND

Funny Sad Music	LP	Morgan	MR112P	1968	**£15**	**£6**	

MALTBY, RICHARD

Man With The Golden Arm Theme	7"	HMV	7M393	1956	**£5**	**£2**	
Rat Race	7"	Columbia	DB4606	1961	**£5**	**£2**	

MAMAS & PAPAS

Title	Format	Label	Number	Year	Mint	VG+	Notes
California Dreamin'	7" EP	RCA	86902	1966	£12	£6	*French*
California Dreamin'	LP	St Michael	MO101225	1979	£10	£4	
California Dreamin'	7"	RCA	RCA1503	1966	£4	£1.50	
Cass, John, Michelle, & Denny	LP	RCA	RD/SF7834	1966	£10	£4	
Dedicated To The One I Love	7" EP	RCA	86911	1967	£10	£5	*French*
Deliver	LP	RCA	RD/SF7880	1967	£10	£4	
Gathering Of Flowers	LP	Probe	SPB1003/4	1970	£12	£5	*double*
I Saw Her Again	7" EP	RCA	86907	1966	£10	£5	*French*
If You Can Believe Your Eyes And Ears	LP	RCA	RD7803	1966	£12	£5	
Look Through My Window	7" EP	RCA	86910	1966	£10	£5	*French*
Monday Monday	7" EP	RCA	86905	1966	£10	£5	*French*
Monterey Pop Festival	LP	Dunhill	DS50100	1971	£12	£5	*US*
Papas And Mamas	LP	RCA	RD/SF7960	1968	£10	£4	
You've Got To Hide Your Love Away	7"	RCA	RCA1525	1966	£6	£2.50	*Barry McGuire B side*

MAMA'S BOYS

Title	Format	Label	Number	Year	Mint	VG+	Notes
Belfast City Blues	7"	Scoff	DT015	1982	£10	£5	
Higher Ground	CD-s	Jive	MBOYCD1	1987	£5	£2	
Plug It In	LP	Pussy	PU010	1982	£20	£8	
Silence Is Out Of Fashion	7"	Pussy		1981	£6	£2.50	
Turn It Up/Too Little Of You To Love	LP	Spartan	SPLP001	1983	£12	£5	*double*

MAMMOTH

Title	Format	Label	Number	Year	Mint	VG+	Notes
All The Days	12"	Jive	MOTHX4	1989	£8	£4	*picture disc*

MAMMUT

Title	Format	Label	Number	Year	Mint	VG+	Notes
Mammut	LP	Mouse	TTM5022	1971	£300	£180	*German*

MAN

Title	Format	Label	Number	Year	Mint	VG+	Notes
2oz Of Plastic With A Hole In The Middle	LP	Dawn	DNLS3003	1969	£15	£6	*orange label*
Bananas	7" EP	United Artists	REM408	1976	£5	£2	
Be Good To Yourself	LP	United Artists	UAG29417	1972	£10	£4	*map of Wales cover*
Christmas At The Patti	10" LP	United Artists	UDX205/6	1973	£15	£6	*double*
Daughter Of The Fireplace	7"	Liberty	LBF15448	1971	£6	£2.50	
Do You Like It Here	LP	United Artists	UAG29236	1971	£10	£4	
Don't Go Away	7"	United Artists	UP35643	1974	£12	£6	
Live At The Padget Rooms	LP	United Artists	USP100	1972	£20	£8	
Man	LP	Liberty	LBS83464	1970	£10	£4	
Revelation	LP	Pye	N(S)PL18275	1969	£15	£6	
Sudden Life	7"	Pye	7N17684	1969	£8	£4	

MAN FRIDAY & JIVE JUNIOR

Title	Format	Label	Number	Year	Mint	VG+	Notes
Picking Up Sounds	12"	Malaco	MAL1211	1983	£40	£20	
Picking Up Sounds	7"	Malaco	MAL011	1983	£15	£7.50	

MAN FROM DELMONTE

Title	Format	Label	Number	Year	Mint	VG+	Notes
Drive Drive Drive	7"	Ugly Man	UGLY3	1987	£5	£2	
Water In My Eyes	12"	Ugly Man	UGLY5T	1987	£8	£4	
Water In My Eyes	7"	Ugly Man	UGLY5	1987	£4	£1.50	

MAN FROM U.N.C.L.E.

Music associated with the sixties cult TV series, *The Man From U.N.C.L.E.*, can be found in the *Guide* under the names of Hugo Montenegro (who was responsible for the main theme), the Challengers and the Gallants – with a late entry from 1982 by Moskow. Meanwhile, David McCallum, who starred as agent Illya Kuryakin in the programmes, took the opportunity to record a pair of moderately collectable albums.

MANASSAS

Manassas was the group formed by Steve Stills in the wake of the first disbanding of Crosby, Stills and Nash. It was something of a supergroup itself, with various ex-members of the CSN rhythm section and of the Flying Burrito Brothers being involved. Steve Stills, however, remains firmly in control and the Manassas album is very much a showcase for his talents. It includes some of Stills' best songs.

Title	Format	Label	Number	Year	Mint	VG+	Notes
Manassas	LP	Atlantic	K60021	1972	£12	£5	*double*

MANASSEH

Title	Format	Label	Number	Year	Mint	VG+	Notes
Manasseh	LP	Genesis	12	1977	£25	£10	

MANCE, JUNIOR

Title	Format	Label	Number	Year	Mint	VG+	Notes
At The Village Vanguard	LP	Jazzland	JLP41	1961	£15	£6	
Big Chief	LP	Jazzland	JLP(9)53	1961	£15	£6	
Harlem Lullaby	LP	Atlantic	1479	1968	£12	£5	
Junior Mance And His Swinging Piano	LP	HMV	CLP1342	1959	£15	£6	
Soulful Piano	LP	Jazzland	JLP30	1960	£15	£6	
With A Lotta Help From My Friends	LP	Atlantic	2400028	1971	£10	£4	

MANCHESTER MEKON

Title	Format	Label	Number	Year	Mint	VG+	Notes
No Forgetting	7"	Newmarket	NEW102	1979	£8	£4	

MANCHESTER MOB

Although future 10cc star, Graham Gouldman, was successful at creating hits for the likes of the Hollies, the Yardbirds and Herman's Hermits, he had no luck with any of the groups that he fronted during the sixties – the Manchester Mob being one.

Title	Format	Label	Number	Year	Mint	VG+	Notes
Bony Maronie At The Hop	7"	Parlophone	R5552	1967	£40	£20	

MANCHESTER PLAYBOYS

I Feel So Good	7"	Fontana	TF745	1966	£30	£15	
Wooly Bully	7" EP	Barclay	70852	1965	£50	£25	*French*

MANCHESTERS

Tribute To The Beatles	LP	Ember	FA2029	1966	£15	£6	

MANCINI, HENRY

Arabesque	LP	RCA	RD7817	1966	£10	£4	
Great Race	LP	RCA	RD7759	1965	£25	£10	
Gunn	LP	RCA	RD/SF7899	1967	£10	£4	
Hatari!	7" EP	RCA	RCX7107	1962	£6	£2.50	
Peter Gunn	LP	RCA	RD27123/SF5033	1959	£10	£4	
Peter Gunn Theme	7"	RCA	RCA1134	1959	£4	£1.50	
Pink Panther	7" EP	RCA	RCX7136	1964	£10	£5	
Two For The Road	LP	RCA	RD/SF7891	1967	£10	£4	
Victor, Victoria	LP	MGM	2315437	1982	£15	£6	
What Did You Do In The War Daddy?	LP	RCA	SF7818	1966	£10	£4	

MANCUSO, GUS

Introducing Gus Mancuso	LP	Vogue	LAE12069	1958	£12	£5	

MANDEL, HARVEY

Baby Batter	LP	Dawn	DNLS3015	1971	£10	£4	
Cristo Redentor	CD	Editions EG	EEGCD62	1989	£12	£5	
Cristo Redentor	LP	Philips	SBL7873	1968	£12	£5	
Games Guitars Play	LP	Philips	SBL7915	1970	£10	£4	
Righteous	LP	Philips	SBL7904	1969	£10	£4	

MANDELA, NELSON

Why I'm Ready To Die	LP	Ember	CEL905	1964	£20	£8	

MANDINGO

Fever Pitch	7"	EMI	EMI2062	1973	£4	£1.50	
Medicine Man	7"	EMI	EMI2014	1973	£6	£2.50	
Primeval Rythm Of Life	LP	Columbia	Q4TWO400	1973	£25	£10	*quad*
Primeval Rythm Of Life	LP	Columbia	TWO400	1973	£20	£8	
Sacrifice	LP	EMI	EMC3010	1973	£10	£4	
Savage Rite	LP	EMI	EMC3217	1977	£10	£4	
Story Of Survival	LP	EMI	EMC3038	1975	£10	£4	

MANDRAGORA

Over The Moon	LP	SAB	01	1986	£20	£8	

MANDRAKE

Mandrake	7"	Philips	PB1093	1960	£5	£2	

MANDRAKE MEMORIAL

Mandrake Memorial	LP	Poppy	PYS40002	1968	£50	£25	*US*
Medium	LP	RCA	SF8028	1969	£40	£20	
Puzzle	LP	Poppy	PYS11003	1970	£50	£25	*US*

MANDRAKE PADDLE STEAMER

Strange Walking Man	7"	Parlophone	R5780	1969	£50	£25	

MANDRILL

Composite Truth	LP	Polydor	2391061	1973	£12	£5	
Just Outside Of Town	LP	Polydor	2391092	1973	£12	£5	
Mandrill	LP	Polydor	2489028	1970	£12	£5	
Mandrill Is	LP	Polydor	2391030	1972	£12	£5	

MANEATERS

Nine To Five	7"	Editions EG	EGO8	1982	£75	£37.50	*Adam & Toyah picture sleeve*

MANGIONE BROTHERS

Jazz Brothers	LP	Riverside	RLP(9)335	1961	£15	£6	

MANHATTAN JAZZ SEPTET

Manhattan Jazz Septet	LP	Vogue Coral	LVA9053	1957	£25	£10	

MANHATTANS

Baby I Need You	7"	Carnival	CAR100	1966	£6	£2.50	
I Wanna Be Your Everything	7"	Sue	WI384	1965	£15	£7.50	
Million To One	LP	London	SHB8449	1973	£10	£4	
That New Girl	7"	Carnival	CAR101	1966	£6	£2.50	

MANIACS

Chelsea 1977	7"	United Artists	UP36327	1977	£4	£1.50	

MANIAX

Out Of Reach	7"	White Label	WLR101/2	1966	£6	£2.50	

MANIC STREET PREACHERS

The group's ascendancy to the position of one of the key groups of the late nineties was achieved in the face of much controversy and setback, including the disappearance of founder member Richey James. It is rather encouraging, however, that the album responsible for pushing the Manic Street Preachers into the premier league, *Everything Must Go*, is a collection of particularly fine songs, thoughtfully and powerfully performed and produced. One result has been an enormous rise in the value of the group's earliest, and rarest, material.

Australia	12"	Columbia	XPR3094	1996	£50	£25	*1 sided promo*
Australia	7"	Columbia	664044	1996	£5	£2	*jukebox issue*
Design For Life	12"	Columbia	XPR3043	1996	£15	£7.50	*promo*
Design For Life	7"	Columbia	663070	1996	£5	£2	*jukebox issue*
Everything Must Go	7"	Columbia	663468	1996	£5	£2	*jukebox issue*
Faster	CD-s	Columbia	6604472	1994	£10	£5	
Feminine Is Beautiful	7"	Caff	15	1991	£100	£50	
From Despair To Where	CD-s	Columbia	6597277	1993	£12	£6	
Generation Terrorists	CD	Columbia	4710600	1992	£30	£15	*picture disc*
Generation Terrorists	CD-s	Columbia	XPCD171	1992	£10	£5	*promo sampler*
Generation Terrorists	LP	Columbia	4710601	1992	£12	£5	*double*
Generation Terrorists	LP	Columbia	4710609	1992	£25	£10	*double picture disc*
Gold Against The Soul	CD	Columbia	47406492	1993	£15	£6	*gold CD*
Gold Against The Soul	CD-s	Columbia	XPCD285	1993	£15	£7.50	*promo sampler*
Gold Against The Soul	LP	Columbia	47406491	1993	£12	£5	*with carrier bag*
Holy Bible	CD	Epic	4774212	1994	£15	£6	*picture disc*
Holy Bible	LP	Epic	4774219	1994	£15	£6	*picture disc*
Kevin Carter	12"	Columbia	XPR3049	1996	£25	£12.50	*1 sided promo*
La Tristessa Durera	CD-s	Columbia	6594772	1993	£10	£5	
Life Becoming A Landslide	CD-s	Columbia	6600702	1994	£10	£5	
Little Baby Nothing	CD-s	Columbia	6587965	1994	£6	£2.50	
Little Baby Nothing	CD-s	Columbia	6587967	1994	£5	£2	
Love's Sweet Exile	CD-s	CBS	6575822	1991	£6	£2.50	
Motorcycle Emptiness	12"	Columbia	6580838	1992	£10	£5	*picture disc*
Motorcycle Emptiness	CD-s	Columbia	XPCD185	1992	£12	£6	*promo*
Motorcycle Emptiness	CD-s	Columbia	6580832	1992	£8	£4	
Motown Junk	12"	Heavenly	HVN812	1991	£30	£15	
Motown Junk	CD-s	Heavenly	HVN8CD	1991	£60	£30	
New Art Riot	CD-s	Damaged Goods	YUBB4CD	1992	£6	£2.50	*picture disc*
New Art Riot EP	12"	Damaged Goods	YUBB004	1990	£8	£4	
New Art Riot EP	12"	Damaged Goods	YUBB004	1990	£10	£5	*yellow label*
New Art Riot EP	12"	Damaged Goods	YUBB004	1990	£25	£12.50	*white label*
New Art Riot EP	12"	Damaged Goods	YUBB004	1990	£15	£7.50	*black & white label*
New Art Riot EP	12"	Damaged Goods	YUBB004P	1990	£20	£10	*pink vinyl*
Repeat	12"	Columbia	6575828	1991	£8	£4	*gatefold sleeve*
Revol	CD-s	Columbia	6606862	1994	£6	£2.50	
Revol	CD-s	Columbia	6606865	1994	£10	£5	
Roses In The Hospital	CD-s	Columbia	6597272	1993	£10	£5	
Six Singles From Generation Terrorists	CD-s	Columbia	MANIC1-6CD	1997	£75	£37.50	
Slash 'n' Burn	12"	Columbia	6578736	1992	£6	£2.50	*with print*
Slash 'n' Burn	CD-s	Columbia	6578732	1992	£10	£5	*gold CD*
Stay Beautiful	12"	Columbia	6573378	1991	£10	£5	*poster sleeve*
Stay Beautiful	12"	Columbia	6573376	1991	£6	£2.50	
Stay Beautiful	CD-s	CBS	6573372	1991	£6	£2.50	
Suicide Alley	7"	SBS	002	1989	£400	£250	*picture sleeve*
Suicide Alley	7"	SBS	002	1989	£100	£50	*no picture sleeve*
Suicide Alley	7"	SBS	SBS002	1988	£500	£330	*hand made sleeve*
Symphony Of Tourette	7"	Columbia	XPS272	1993	£50	£25	*1 sided promo*
Theme From M*A*S*H	12"	Columbia	6583826	1992	£6	£2.50	*Fatima Mansions B side*
Theme From M*A*S*H	CD-s	Columbia	6583822	1992	£15	£7.50	*Fatima Mansions B side*
UK Channel Boredom	7"	Hopelessly Devoted		1990	£40	£20	*flexi*
You Love Us	12"	Columbia	6577246	1992	£6	£2.50	*gatefold sleeve*
You Love Us	12"	Heavenly	HVN1012	1991	£10	£5	
You Love Us	7"	Heavenly	HVN10P	1991	£25	£12.50	*1 sided promo*
You Love Us	7"	Heavenly	HVN10	1991	£10	£5	
You Love Us	CD-s	Columbia	6577242	1992	£6	£2.50	
You Love Us	CD-s	Heavenly	HVN10CD	1991	£30	£15	

MANILOW, BARRY

Greatest Hits	LP	Arista	A2L8601	1978	£12	£5	*2 shaped picture discs*
I Write The Songs	7"	Arista	ARIST40	1976	£10	£5	*picture sleeve*

MANISH BOYS

The rare single by the Manish Boys, 'I Pity The Fool', is listed in the guide under the name later used by the group's lead singer – David Bowie.

MANN, BARRY

Angelica	7"	Capitol	CL15463	1966	£4	£1.50	
Bless You	7"	HMV	POP1108	1963	£6	£2.50	
Hey Baby I'm Dancing	7"	HMV	POP1084	1962	£6	£2.50	

Little Miss USA	7"	HMV	POP949	1961	£6	£2.50	
Talk To Me Baby	7"	Colpix	PX776	1964	£5	£2	
Who Put The Bomp	7"	HMV	POP911	1961	£12	£6	
Who Put The Bomp	LP	HMV	CLP1559	1963	£125	£62.50	
Young Electric Psychedelic Hippy . . .	7"	Capitol	CL15538	1968	£4	£1.50	

MANN, CARL

Like Mann	LP	London	HAS2277	1960	£125	£62.50	
Like Mann	LP	Philips	1960	1960	£300	£180	US
Mona Lisa	7"	London	HLS8935	1959	£15	£7.50	
Pretend	7"	London	HLS9006	1959	£15	£7.50	
South Of The Border	7"	London	HLS9170	1960	£12	£6	

MANN, GLORIA

It Happened Again	7"	Brunswick	05610	1956	£5	£2	
Why Do Fools Fall In Love	7"	Brunswick	05569	1956	£8	£4	

MANN, HERBIE

Afro-Jazziac	LP	SRCP	3002	1969	£12	£5	
At Newport	LP	Atlantic	ATL5008	1964	£15	£6	
At The Village Gate	LP	Atlantic	587/588054	1967	£15	£6	
Concerto Grosso In D Blues	LP	Polydor	2465005	1970	£12	£5	
Discotheque	LP	Atlantic	K50128	1975	£10	£4	
East Coast Jazz No. 4 Part 1	7" EP	London	EZN19006	1956	£5	£2	
Evolution Of Mann	LP	Atlantic	K60020	1972	£15	£6	*double*
Flute Fraternity	10" LP	Top Rank	25015	1960	£15	£6	*with Buddy Colette*
Free For All	LP	Atlantic	590013	1968	£12	£5	
Glory Of Love	LP	A&M	AMLS944	1969	£10	£4	
Herbie Mann	7" EP	Fontana	TFE17113	1958	£5	£2	
Herbie Mann–Sam Most Quintet	LP	London	LTZN15049	1957	£20	£8	
Hold On I'm Comin'	LP	Atlantic	K40467	1973	£12	£5	
Impressions Of The Middle East	LP	Atlantic	1475	1968	£12	£5	US
Inspiration I Feel	LP	Atlantic	588156	1969	£12	£5	
Latin Mann	LP	CBS	(S)BPG62585	1966	£12	£5	
Live At Newport	LP	Atlantic	SD1413	1965	£15	£6	US
London Underground	LP	Atlantic	K50032	1974	£10	£4	
Magic Flute Of Herbie Mann	7" EP	Columbia	SEB10102	1959	£5	£2	
Memphis Two-Step	LP	Atlantic	2400121	1971	£10	£4	
Memphis Underground	LP	Atlantic	588200	1969	£12	£5	
Mississippi Gambler	LP	Atlantic	K40385	1972	£12	£5	
Monday Night At The Village Gate	LP	Atlantic	587/588003	1966	£15	£6	
Muscle Shoals Nitty Gritty	LP	Atlantic	K40096	1970	£12	£5	
New Mann At Newport	LP	Atlantic	1471	1967	£12	£5	US
Nirvana	LP	Atlantic	587/588028	1966	£15	£6	*with Bill Evans*
Philly Dog	7"	Atlantic	584052	1966	£6	£2.50	*Dave Pike B side*
Push Push	LP	Atco	2400191	1972	£12	£5	
Reggae	LP	Atlantic	K50053	1975	£10	£4	
Returns To The Village Gate	LP	Atlantic	SD1407	1963	£15	£6	US
Right Now	LP	London	HAK/SHK8043	1963	£15	£6	
Roar Of The Grease Paint	LP	Atlantic	ATL/SAL5035	1965	£12	£5	
Salute To The Flute	LP	Fontana	TFL5013	1958	£15	£6	
St Thomas	LP	Solid State	USS7007	1969	£12	£5	
Standing Ovation At Newport	LP	Atlantic	ATL/SAL5038	1966	£15	£6	
Stone Flute	LP	Atlantic	2465088	1970	£12	£5	
String Album	LP	Atlantic	1490	1968	£12	£5	US
Turtle Bay	LP	Atlantic	K50020	1974	£10	£4	
Water Bed	LP	Atlantic	K50174	1975	£10	£4	

MANN, JOHNNY SINGERS

Ballads Of The King	7" EP	London	REG1325	1961	£5	£2	

MANN, MANFRED

When Manfred Mann decided to call a halt to his pop career, the result was one of the best albums of all to emerge from the interface between jazz and rock. Essentially the work of a big band, *Manfred Mann Chapter Three* showcased some fine playing – most notably from saxophonist Bernie Living, formerly with the Mike Westbrook band – and also demonstrated the excellence of the Mann–Hugg writing team. 'Travelling Lady' was an update of 'A B Side' – to be found on the reverse of the single 'Ragamuffin Man' and itself the same piece of music as that used in a TV advert. The powerful brass riff that drives 'Time', meanwhile, was adopted as the theme tune for a radio jazz programme. Manfred Mann had earlier indicated that he might have something like this up his sleeve when he released the *Instrumental Asylum* EP (whose tracks are also to be found on the LP *Soul Of Mann*). Paul Jones had just left the group, so the others took advantage of their singerless condition to make a record of sparkling jazz versions of a few well-known rock tunes. The presence of Jack Bruce on bass, together with trumpeter Henry Lowther and saxophonist Lyn Dobson, was a distinct bonus. *Instrumental Assassination* attempted to repeat the formula, somewhat less successfully, as new member Klaus Voorman was no substitute, in this kind of music, for the three jazzers he replaced. In recent years, the group has been touring as the Manfreds, without Manfred Mann himself (who prefers to persevere with his Earth Band) but with both of the original singers, Paul Jones and Mike D'Abo. With an enviable roster of hit records with which to tickle their audience's feelings of nostalgia, and with their performance skills finely honed, the group delivers what is arguably the finest show of its kind.

5-4-3-2-1	7"	HMV	POP1252	1964	£4	£1.50	
As Is	LP	Fontana	(S)TL5377	1966	£15	£6	
As Is	LP	Fontana	(S)TL5377	1966	£100	£50	*train cover*
As Was	7" EP	HMV	7EG8962	1966	£12	£6	
Cock A Hoop	7"	HMV	POP1225	1963	£8	£4	
Come Tomorrow	7"	Electrola	E22892	1965	£12	£6	*sung in German*
Do Wah Diddy Diddy	7" EP	Pathe	EGF747	1964	£15	£7.50	*French*
Five Faces Of Manfred Mann	LP	HMV	CLP1731	1964	£20	£8	
Greatest Hits	LP	United Artists	UAL3551/ UAS6551	1966	£12	£5	US

Grooving With Manfred Mann	7" EP	HMV	7EG8876	1965	£8	£4	
Ha Ha Said The Clown	7"	Fontana	TF812	1967	£5	£2	*picture sleeve*
Ha Ha Said The Clown	7" EP	Fontana	465376	1966	£15	£7.50	*French*
Hits Of Manfred Mann	cass-s	Philips	MCF5002	1968	£10	£4	
Hits Of Manfred Mann & DDDBM & T	cass-s	Philips	MCF5005	1968	£10	£4	
Hubble Bubble	7"	HMV	POP1282	1964	£4	£1.50	
If You Gotta Go, Go Now	7" EP	Pathe	EGF853	1965	£15	£7.50	*French*
Instrumental Assassination	7" EP	Fontana	TE17483	1966	£5	£2	
Instrumental Asylum	7" EP	HMV	7EG8949	1966	£10	£5	
Just Like A Woman	7" EP	Fontana	465320	1966	£15	£7.50	*French*
Machines	7" EP	HMV	7EG8942	1966	£10	£5	
Manfred Mann	7" EP	HMV	7EG8848	1964	£12	£6	
Manfred Mann Album	LP	Ascot	ALM13015/ ALS16015	1964	£20	£8	*US*
Mann Made	LP	HMV	CLP1911/ CSD1628	1964	£20	£8	
Mann Made	LP	Electrola	SME84039	1965	£75	£37.50	*German, white and gold label*
Mann Made Hits	LP	HMV	CLP3559	1966	£20	£8	
Maxwell House Shake	7"	Lyntone	LYN1981	1970	£4	£1.50	*flexi*
Michelin Theme	7"	Michelin	MIC1	1971	£8	£4	*gatefold sleeve*
Mighty Garvey	LP	Fontana	(S)TL5470	1968	£12	£5	
Mighty Quinn	LP	Mercury	SR61168	1968	£12	£5	*US*
My Little Red Book Of Winners	LP	Ascot	ALM13021/ ALS16021	1965	£30	£15	*US*
No Living Without Loving	7" EP	HMV	7EG8922	1965	£8	£4	
One In The Middle	7" EP	HMV	7EG8908	1965	£8	£4	
Pretty Flamingo	7" EP	Pathe	EGF901	1966	£15	£7.50	*French*
Pretty Flamingo	LP	United Artists	UAL3549/ UAS6549	1966	£15	£6	*US*
Ragamuffin Man	7"	Fontana	TF1013	1969	£4	£1.50	
Semi-Detached, Suburban Mr James	7" EP	Fontana	465341	1966	£15	£7.50	*French*
Sha La La	7" EP	Pathe	EGF781	1964	£15	£7.50	*French*
Ski 'Full-Of-Fitness' Theme	7"	Ski	SKI01	1971	£10	£5	*picture sleeve*
Ski 'Full-Of-Fitness' Theme	7"	Ski	SKI01	1971	£4	£1.50	
So Long Dad	7"	Fontana	TF862	1967	£4	£1.50	
Soul Of Mann	LP	HMV	CLP/CSD3594	1967	£20	£8	
Sweet Pea	7"	Fontana	TF828	1967	£4	£1.50	
There's No Living Without Your Loving	7"	HMV	7XEA22017/8	1965	£15	£7.50	*promo*
Up The Junction	7"	Fontana	TF908	1968	£6	£2.50	*picture sleeve*
Up The Junction	LP	Fontana	6852005	1970	£12	£5	
Up The Junction	LP	Fontana	(S)TL5460	1968	£20	£8	
What A Man	LP	Fontana	SFL13003	1968	£12	£5	
Why Should We Not	7"	HMV	POP1189	1963	£10	£5	
You Gave Me Somebody To Love	7"	HMV	POP1541	1966	£5	£2	

MANN, MANFRED CHAPTER THREE

Happy Being Me	7"	Vertigo	6059012	1970	£4	£1.50	
Manfred Mann Chapter Three	LP	Vertigo	VO3	1969	£20	£8	*spiral label*
Manfred Mann Chapter Three Vol. 2	LP	Vertigo	6360012	1970	£25	£10	*spiral label*

MANN, SHADOW

Come Live With Me	7"	Roulette	RO504	1968	£8	£4	
Shadow Mann	LP	Tomorrow Productions		1968	£20	£8	*US*

MANNE, SHELLY

2, 3, 4	LP	HMV	CLP1625	1962	£12	£5	
At The Black Hawk Vol. 1	LP	Contemporary	LAC12250/ SCA5015	1961	£12	£5	
At The Black Hawk Vol. 2	LP	Contemporary	LAC12255/ SCA5016	1961	£12	£5	
At The Black Hawk Vol. 3	LP	Contemporary	LAC12260/ SCA5017	1961	£12	£5	
At The Black Hawk Vol. 4	LP	Contemporary	LAC12265/ SCA5018	1961	£12	£5	
Bells Are Ringing	LP	Contemporary	LAC12212	1960	£10	£4	
Daktari	7"	Atlantic	584180	1968	£5	£2	
My Fair Lady	LP	Contemporary	LAC12100	1958	£12	£5	
Peter Gunne	LP	Contemporary	LAC12193	1959	£12	£5	
Proper Time	LP	Contemporary	LAC12293	1961	£12	£5	
Shelly Manne	10" LP	London	LZC14019	1955	£40	£20	
Shelly Manne And Co.	LP	Stateside	SL10125	1965	£10	£4	
Shelly Manne And His Friends	LP	Contemporary	LAC12075	1958	£15	£6	
Shelly Manne And His Men Vol. 1	10" LP	Vogue	LDE072	1954	£40	£20	
Shelly Manne And His Men Vol. 1	LP	Contemporary	LAC12138	1959	£15	£6	
Shelly Manne And His Men Vol. 2	10" LP	Contemporary	LDC143	1955	£40	£20	
Shelly Manne And His Men Vol. 2	LP	Contemporary	LAC12148	1959	£15	£6	
Shelly Manne And Russ Freeman	10" LP	Contemporary	LDC192	1956	£40	£20	
Son Of Gunn	LP	Contemporary	LAC12220	1960	£12	£5	
Songs Fom Li'l Abner	LP	Contemporary	LAC12130	1958	£12	£5	
Three	10" LP	Contemporary	LDC190	1956	£40	£20	*with Shorty Rogers and Jimmy Giuffre*
Three And The Two	LP	Contemporary	LAC12276	1961	£12	£5	
Vol. 4	LP	Contemporary	LAC12062	1957	£15	£6	
Vol. 7 – The Gambit	LP	Vogue	LAC12241	1961	£12	£5	
Volume 6	LP	Contemporary	LAC12232	1960	£10	£4	

MANNIN FOLK

King Of The Sea	LP	Kelly	MAN2	1976	£40	£20	

MANNING, BOB

It's All Right With Me	7"	Capitol	CL14190	1954	£4	£1.50	
Majorca	7"	Capitol	CL14256	1955	£4	£1.50	
Mission San Michel	7"	Capitol	CL14288	1955	£4	£1.50	
My Love Song To You	7"	Capitol	CL14234	1955	£4	£1.50	
Very Thought Of You	7"	Capitol	CL14220	1955	£4	£1.50	
What A Wonderful Way To Die	7"	Capitol	CL14318	1955	£4	£1.50	

MANNING, MARTY & THE CHEETAHS

Tarzan March	7"	CBS	2721	1967	£4	£1.50	

MANNION, EDDIE

Just Driftin'	7"	HMV	POP804	1960	£4	£1.50	

MANONE, WINGY

Go-Group	LP	London	HBU1063	1956	£15	£6	
Party Doll	7"	Brunswick	05655	1957	£8	£4	
Trumpet On The Wing	LP	Brunswick	LAT8236	1958	£15	£6	

MANOWAR

All Men Play On Ten	12"	10	TEN3012	1984	£8	£4	*gatefold sleeve*
Blow Your Speakers	12"	Atlantic	BT9463	1987	£6	£2.50	*with poster*
Defender	12"	Music For Nations	12KUT102	1983	£10	£5	

MANSANO, JOE

Life On Reggae Planet	7"	Blue Cat	BS150	1968	£8	£4	*Rico B side*

MANSFIELD, JAYNE

As Clouds Drift By	7"	London	HL10147	1967	£15	£7.50	*Jimi Hendrix plays on B side*
Busts Up Las Vegas	LP	20th Century			£25	£10	*US*
Shakespeare, Tchaikovsky And Me	LP	MGM	(S)E4204	1964	£20	£8	*US*

MANSFIELD, KEITH

All You Need Is Keith Mansfield	LP	CBS	63426	1968	£15	£6	
Loot	LP	CBS	70073	1970	£15	£6	

MANSON, CHARLES

It's Comin' Down Fast	7"	Fierce	FRIGHT012	1988	£10	£5	
Lie	LP	Awareness	22145	1970	£75	£37.50	*US*
Love And Terror Cult	LP	Fierce	FRIGHT001	1986	£25	£10	
Rise	7"	Fierce	FRIGHT006	1986	£10	£5	

MANSON, JEANE

I've Already Seen It In Your Eyes	7"	CBS	7222	1979	£8	£4	

MANSUN

Stripper Vicar	CD-s	Parlophone	CDRS6447	1996	£8	£4	
Take It Easy Chicken	7"	Sci Fi Hi Fi	MANSON1	1995	£20	£10	
Wide Open Space	CD-s	Parlophone	CDR6453	1996	£8	£4	
Wide Open Space	CD-s	Parlophone	CDRS6453	1996	£6	£2.50	*with poster*

MANTELL, JOHN

Remember Child	7"	CBS	201783	1965	£15	£7.50	

MANTLER, MIKE

Jazz Composers' Orchestra	LP	Virgin	JD3001	1974	£15	£6	*double*

MANTON, BOB

No Trees In Brixton Prison	7"	Mainstreet	MS101	1981	£5	£2	

MANUEL, IAN

Frosty Ploughshare	LP	Topic	12TS220	1972	£10	£4	

MANUELA & DRAFI

Im Duett	LP	Hör Zu	SHZE536	1966	£40	£20	*German*

MAPHIA

Hans Im Gluck	LP	Alco	ALC80541	1974	£15	£6	*German*

MAPHIS, JOE

Fire On The Strings	LP	Columbia	CL1005	1957	£25	£10	*US*

MAPHIS, JOE & ROSE LEE

Mr And Mrs Country Music	LP	Starday	SLP286	1964	£10	£4	*US*
With The Blue Ridge Mountain Boys	LP	Capitol	(S)T1778	1962	£12	£5	*US*

MAPLE OAK

Bass player Peter Quaife joined this group after leaving the Kinks, which was not the best career move he could have made. He had left by the time the album was recorded – this has a reputation as the most incompetent progressive rock record ever made.

Maple Oak	LP	Decca	SKL5085	1971	£200	£100	

Son Of A Gun	7"	Decca	F13008	1970	**£10**	**£5**	

MAPP, LUCILLE

I'm Available	7"	Columbia	DB4040	1957	**£4**	**£1.50**	
Lucille Mapp	7" EP	Columbia	SEG7773	1957	**£6**	**£2.50**	
Mangos	7"	Columbia	DB3916	1957	**£4**	**£1.50**	
Street Of Dreams	7" EP	Columbia	SEG7726	1957	**£6**	**£2.50**	

MAQUINA

Why	LP	White Diablo	1003	1971	**£100**	**£50**	*Spanish*

MARA, TOMMY

Pledging My Love	7"	MGM	SP1128	1955	**£4**	**£1.50**	
Presenting Tommy Mara	7" EP	Felsted	GEP1003	1958	**£10**	**£5**	
Where The Blues Of The Night	7"	Felsted	AF109	1958	**£4**	**£1.50**	

MARAKESH

Marakesh	LP	Mirasound		1976	**£100**	**£50**	*Dutch*

MARATHONS

Peanut Butter	7"	Vogue	V9185	1961	**£12**	**£6**	
Peanut Butter	7"	Pye	7N25088	1961	**£8**	**£4**	
Peanut Butter	LP	Arvee	A428	1961	**£60**	**£30**	*US*

MARAUDERS

Baby	7"	Fontana	TF609	1965	**£4**	**£1.50**	
Check In	LP	no label		196–	**£50**	**£25**	*US*
Heart Full Of Tears	7"	Decca	F11748	1963	**£4**	**£1.50**	
Little Egypt	7"	Decca	F11836	1964	**£5**	**£2**	
That's What I Want	7"	Decca	F11695	1963	**£5**	**£2**	

MARBLE PHROGG

Marble Phrogg	LP	Derrick	8868	1968	**£1000**	**£700**	*US*
Marble Phrogg	LP	Derrick	8868	1992	**£15**	**£6**	*US*

MARBLES

Discovered by the Bee Gees, the Marbles scored an immediate hit with a Bee Gees composed single, 'Only One Woman', on which they sounded remarkably like the better-known group. Singer Graham Bonnet later moved into rather different territory when he became the lead vocalist with Ritchie Blackmore's Rainbow.

Marbles	LP	Cotillion	SD9029	1970	**£15**	**£6**	*US*
Only One Woman	7"	Polydor	56272	1968	**£4**	**£1.50**	

MARC & THE MAMBAS

Bite Black And Blues	LP	Gutterheart	GH1	1984	**£20**	**£8**	*fan club only*
Sleaze	12"	Some Bizarre	BZS512	1982	**£15**	**£7.50**	*fan club*
Torment	12"	Some Bizarre	BZS2112	1983	**£6**	**£2.50**	
Torment	7"	Some Bizarre	BZSDJ21	1983	**£10**	**£5**	*promo*

MARCEL

Dream Consumed	LP	BASF	20210944	1971	**£12**	**£5**	*German*

MARCELLE, LYDIA

Another Kind Of Fellow	7"	Sue	WI4025	1966	**£20**	**£10**	

MARCELLINO, MUZZY

Mary Lou	7"	London	HLU8355	1956	**£15**	**£7.50**	*Mr Ford & Mr Goon-Bones B side*

MARCELS

Blue Moon	7"	Pye	7N25073	1961	**£4**	**£1.50**	
Blue Moon	LP	Pye	NPL28016	1961	**£75**	**£37.50**	
Heartaches	7"	Pye	7N25114	1961	**£6**	**£2.50**	
I Wanna Be The Leader	7"	Pye	7N25201	1963	**£4**	**£1.50**	
My Melancholy Baby	7"	Pye	7N25124	1962	**£5**	**£2**	
Summertime	7"	Pye	7N25083	1961	**£4**	**£1.50**	
You Are My Sunshine	7"	Pye	7N25105	1961	**£5**	**£2**	

MARCH, GLORIA

Baby Of Mine	7"	London	HLB8568	1958	**£10**	**£5**	

MARCH, HAL

Hear Me Good	7"	London	HLD8534	1958	**£12**	**£6**	

MARCH, JO

Dormi, Dormi, Dormi	7"	London	HLR8696	1958	**£4**	**£1.50**	
Virgin Mary Had One Son	7"	London	HLR8763	1958	**£4**	**£1.50**	

MARCH, PEGGY

I Will Follow Him	LP	RCA	LPM/LSP2732	1963	**£15**	**£6**	*US*
If You Loved Me	7"	RCA	RCA1687	1968	**£15**	**£7.50**	
In Our Fashion	LP	RCA	LPM/LSP3408	1965	**£15**	**£6**	*US*
Let Her Go	7"	RCA	RCA1472	1965	**£4**	**£1.50**	
No Foolin'	LP	RCA	LSP3883	1968	**£12**	**£5**	*US*
Watch What You Do With My Baby	7"	RCA	RCA1426	1964	**£4**	**£1.50**	

MARCH HARE

The two singles made by March Hare both feature Peter Skellern as lead singer.

Cry My Heart	7"	Chapter One	CH101	1968	£4	£1.50	
I Could Make It There With You	7"	Deram	DM258	1969	£4	£1.50	

MARCH VIOLETS

Grooving In Green	7"	Merciful Release	MR017	1982	£8	£4	
Religious As Hell	7"	Merciful Release	MR013	1982	£8	£4	

MARCHAN, BOBBY

Ain't No Reason For Girls To Be Lonely	7"	Action	ACT4533	1969	£5	£2	
There's Something On Your Mind	LP	Sphere Sound	SSR7004	1964	£30	£15	US

MARCLAY, CHRISTIAN

Christian Marclay is a scratch-mixer, a virtuoso player of record turntables, yet he chooses not to work in the dance music field. A frequent contributor to the records of John Zorn and other members of the contemporary New York avant-garde, Marclay has also found time for a couple of records of his own. *More Encores* is made up entirely of extracts from other people's records, teased and manipulated by Marclay until they begin to take on meanings entirely different from those intended by the original artists. Just as extraordinary is *Record Without A Cover*, a description intended to be taken entirely literally – any resultant scratches fitting naturally into the collage of clicks and scratch sounds already present in the grooves.

More Encores	10" LP	No Man's Land	NML8816	1989	£25	£10	German
Record Without A Cover	LP	Recycled	no number	1985	£50	£25	US

MARCUS

Marcus	LP	United Artists	UAS30000	1976	£15	£6	

MARDEN, JANIE

Make The Night A Little Longer	7"	Piccadilly	7N35128	1963	£5	£2	
Soldier Boy	7"	Decca	F10600	1955	£4	£1.50	
They Long To Be Close To You	7"	Decca	F12101	1965	£5	£2	
You Are My Love	7"	Decca	F10673	1955	£4	£1.50	

MARESCA, ERNIE

Love Express	7"	London	HLU9720	1963	£6	£2.50	
Mary Jane	7"	London	HLU9579	1962	£8	£4	
Rockin' Boulevard Street	7"	Stateside	SS560	1966	£6	£2.50	
Rovin' Kind	7"	London	HLU9834	1964	£5	£2	
Shout Shout	7"	London	HLU9531	1962	£8	£4	
Shout! Shout! Knock Yourself Out	LP	Seville	SV7/87001	1962	£30	£15	US

MARGO & THE MARVETTES

Cherry Pie	7"	Parlophone	R5154	1964	£6	£2.50	
Copper Kettle	7"	Parlophone	R5227	1964	£5	£2	
Seven Letters	7"	Piccadilly	7N35387	1967	£5	£2	
When Love Slips Away	7"	Pye	7N17423	1967	£15	£7.50	

MARGRET, ANN

And Here She Is	LP	RCA	RD27239/SF5116	1962	£15	£6	
Anne Margaret	LP	RCA	RD/SF7691	1964	£15	£6	
Bachelors' Paradise	LP	RCA	RD/SF7649	1964	£15	£6	
Beauty And The Beard	LP	RCA	RD/SF7632	1964	£15	£6	with Al Hirt
Bye Bye Birdie	LP	RCA	RD/SF7580	1963	£15	£6	
On The Way Up	LP	RCA	RD/SF7503	1962	£15	£6	
Vivacious One	7" EP	RCA	RCX7148	1964	£25	£12.50	

MARGUERITA

Woman Come	7"	Black Swan	WI431	1964	£10	£5	Eric Morris B side

MARGULIS, CHARLIE

Gigi	7"	London	HLL8774	1959	£5	£2	

MARIANI

Perpetuum Mobile	LP	Sonobeat	1004	197–	£1,500	£1000	US

MARIANNE

You Know My Name	7"	Columbia	DB8420	1968	£4	£1.50	

MARIANO, CHARLIE

Beauties Of 1918	LP	Vogue	LAE12166	1959	£15	£6	with Jerry Dodgion
Charlie Mariano Quartet/Septet	LP	Parlophone	PMC1094	1959	£15	£6	
Charlie Mariano Sextet	10" LP	London	LZN14032	1956	£50	£25	
Charlie Mariano Sextet	LP	London	LTZN15031	1957	£30	£15	

MARIE, ANNE

Runaround	7"	Fontana	TF523	1965	£4	£1.50	

MARIE CELESTE

And Then Perhaps	LP	private		1971	£300	£180	

MARILLION

The considerable success of an 'old-fashioned' progressive group was one of the more surprising aspects of rock music in the eighties. Marillion achieved this, however, by gigging hard up and down the country and building a sizeable following before making any records at all. In common with other stars of the eighties, Marillion's recording career has been highlighted by a succession of picture disc releases, and it is these that now form the central axis of a Marillion collection.

Title	Format	Label	Cat. No.	Year	Mint	VG	Notes
Assassing	12"	EMI	12MARILP2	1984	£**10**	£**5**	*picture disc*
Clutching At Straws	LP	EMI	EMDP1002	1987	£**10**	£**4**	*picture disc*
Cover My Eyes	CD-s	EMI	CDMARIL13	1991	£**5**	£**2**	
Dry Land	CD-s	EMI	CDMARIL15	1991	£**5**	£**2**	
Easter	CD-s	EMI	CDMARIL12	1990	£**5**	£**2**	
Freaks	7"	EMI	MARILP9	1988	£**6**	£**2.50**	*shaped picture disc*
Freaks Live	CD-s	EMI	CDMARIL9	1988	£**5**	£**2**	
Fugazi	LP	EMI	MRLP1	1984	£**15**	£**6**	*picture disc*
Garden Party	12"	EMI	12EMIS5393	1983	£**8**	£**4**	*with poster*
Garden Party	7"	EMI	EMIP5393	1983	£**10**	£**5**	*shaped picture disc*
Heart Of Lothian	12"	EMI	12MARILP5	1985	£**6**	£**2.50**	*picture disc*
Hooks In You	CD-s	EMI	CDMARIL10	1989	£**5**	£**2**	
Incommunicado	CD-s	EMI	CDMARIL6	1987	£**8**	£**4**	
Kayleigh	12"	EMI	12MARILP3	1985	£**8**	£**4**	*picture disc*
Kayleigh	7"	EMI	MARILP3	1985	£**6**	£**2.50**	*picture disc*
Lavender Blue	12"	EMI	12MARILP4	1985	£**6**	£**2.50**	*picture disc*
Market Square Heroes	12"	EMI	12EMIP5351	1983	£**30**	£**15**	*picture disc*
Misplaced Childhood	LP	EMI	MRLP2	1985	£**10**	£**4**	*picture disc*
No One Can	CD-s	EMI	CDMARIL14	1991	£**5**	£**2**	
Punch And Judy	12"	EMI	12MARILP1	1984	£**10**	£**5**	*picture disc*
Real To Reel	LP	EMI	JESTP1	1984	£**10**	£**4**	*picture disc*
Script For A Jester's Tear	LP	EMI	EMCP3429	1984	£**20**	£**8**	*picture disc*
Sugar Mice	12"	EMI	12MARILP7	1987	£**8**	£**4**	*picture disc*
Sugar Mice	7"	EMI	MARILP7	1987	£**5**	£**2**	*picture disc with poster*
Sugar Mice	CD-s	EMI	CDMARIL7	1987	£**8**	£**4**	
Uninvited Guest	CD-s	EMI	CDMARIL11	1989	£**5**	£**2**	
Warm Wet Circles	12"	EMI	12MARILP8	1987	£**6**	£**2.50**	*picture disc*
Warm Wet Circles	CD-s	EMI	CDMARIL8	1987	£**5**	£**2**	

MARINE GIRLS

Title	Format	Label	Cat. No.	Year	Mint	VG	Notes
Beach Party	LP	Whaam!	COD1	1981	£**15**	£**6**	
On My Mind	7"	Cherry Red	CHERRY40	1982	£**4**	£**1.50**	
On My Mind	7"	In Phaze	COD2	1982	£**10**	£**5**	

MARINERS

Title	Format	Label	Cat. No.	Year	Mint	VG	Notes
I Love You Fair Dinkum	7"	London	HLA8201	1955	£**12**	£**6**	
Spirituals	LP	London	HAA2007	1956	£**10**	£**4**	

MARINI, MARINO

Title	Format	Label	Cat. No.	Year	Mint	VG	Notes
Ciao Ciao Bambina	7"	Durium	DC16636	1959	£**4**	£**1.50**	
Come Prima	7"	Durium	DC16632	1958	£**4**	£**1.50**	
Guitar Boogie	7"	Durium	DC16631	1958	£**4**	£**1.50**	
Marino At San Remo	7" EP	Durium	U20047	1958	£**5**	£**2**	
Stella Stella	7"	Durium	DC16635	1958	£**4**	£**1.50**	
That Crazy Quartet	7" EP	Durium	U20030	1958	£**5**	£**2**	

MARION

Title	Format	Label	Cat. No.	Year	Mint	VG	Notes
Sleep	CD-s	London	LONCD360	1995	£**5**	£**2**	
Toys For Boys	10"	London	LON10366	1995	£**10**	£**5**	*export*
Toys For Boys	CD-s	London	LONCD366	1995	£**5**	£**2**	
Violent Men	7"	Rough Trade	RT3193	1994	£**10**	£**5**	
Violent Men	CD-s	Rough Trade	RT3193	1994	£**10**	£**5**	

MARION (2)

Title	Format	Label	Cat. No.	Year	Mint	VG	Notes
Tom Tom Tom	7"	Columbia	DB8987	1973	£**10**	£**5**	

MARIONETTES

Title	Format	Label	Cat. No.	Year	Mint	VG	Notes
Like A Man	7"	Parlophone	R5416	1966	£**4**	£**1.50**	
Raining It's Pouring	7"	Parlophone	R5356	1965	£**6**	£**2.50**	

MARK ALMOND

Title	Format	Label	Cat. No.	Year	Mint	VG	Notes
Mark Almond	LP	Harvest	SHSP4011	1971	£**10**	£**4**	

MARK FIVE

Title	Format	Label	Cat. No.	Year	Mint	VG	Notes
Baby What's Wrong	7"	Fontana	TF513	1964	£**30**	£**15**	

MARK FOUR

The Mark Four who recorded singles for Decca and Fontana were an early line-up of the Creation. The bass player was John Dalton, later a member of the Kinks.

Title	Format	Label	Cat. No.	Year	Mint	VG	Notes
Crazy Country Hop	7"	Mercury	MF825	1964	£**20**	£**10**	
Hurt Me If You Will	7"	Decca	F12204	1965	£**40**	£**20**	
Live At The Beat Scene Club	7"	Bam Caruso	OPRA037	1985	£**6**	£**2.50**	
Live At The Beat Scene Club	7" EP	Bam Caruso	OPRA037	1985	£**6**	£**2.50**	
Rock Around The Clock	7"	Mercury	MF815	1964	£**20**	£**10**	
Work All Day	7"	Fontana	TF664	1966	£**60**	£**30**	

MARK II

Title	Format	Label	Cat. No.	Year	Mint	VG	Notes
Night Theme	7"	Columbia	DB4549	1960	£**4**	£**1.50**	

MARK IV

I Got A Wife	7"	Mercury	AMT1025	1959	**£6**	**£2.50**	
Move Over Rover	7"	Mercury	AMT1045	1959	**£5**	**£2**	
Ring Ring Ring Those Bells	7"	Mercury	AMT1060	1959	**£4**	**£1.50**	

MARKETTS

Balbao Blue	7"	Liberty	LIB55443	1962	**£4**	**£1.50**	
Batman	LP	Warner Bros	W1642	1966	**£30**	**£15**	
Batman Theme	7"	Warner Bros	WB5696	1966	**£25**	**£12.50**	*picture sleeve*
Batman Theme	7"	Warner Bros	WB5696	1966	**£6**	**£2.50**	
Out Of Limits	7"	Warner Bros	WB120	1964	**£6**	**£2.50**	
Out Of Limits	LP	Warner Bros	(S)T1537	1964	**£20**	**£8**	*US*
Surfer Stomp	7"	Liberty	LIB55401	1962	**£5**	**£2**	
Surfer Stomp	LP	Liberty	LRP3226/ LST7226	1962	**£25**	**£10**	*US*
Surfing Scene	LP	Liberty	LRP3326/ LST7326	1963	**£25**	**£10**	*US*
Take To Wheels	LP	Warner Bros	WM8140	1963	**£20**	**£8**	
Tarzan's March	7"	Warner Bros	WB5847	1967	**£25**	**£12.50**	

MARKEYS

Damifiknow	LP	Stax	SXATS1021	1969	**£10**	**£4**	
Do The Pop-Eye	LP	London	HAK8011	1962	**£30**	**£15**	
Foxy	7"	London	HLK9510	1962	**£4**	**£1.50**	
Great Memphis Sound	LP	Atlantic	587/588024	1966	**£12**	**£5**	
Last Night	7"	Atlantic	584074	1967	**£4**	**£1.50**	
Last Night	7"	London	HLK9399	1961	**£5**	**£2**	
Last Night	LP	Atlantic	(SD)8055	1961	**£30**	**£15**	*US*
Mellow Jelly	LP	Atlantic	587/588135	1968	**£12**	**£5**	
Morning After	7"	London	HLK9449	1961	**£4**	**£1.50**	
Philly Dog	7"	Atlantic	AT4079	1966	**£5**	**£2**	

MARKHAM, PIGMEAT

Pigmeat Markham was a black American comedian who might well be described as the James Brown of comedy for the way in which he kept his art in the ghetto, even when he himself had moved out of it. Markham invented the 'Here Comes The Judge' by-line which featured on the TV show *Rowan And Martin's Laugh-In*, although the song built around it was commandeered by Shorty Long for Tamla Motown.

Here Come The Judge	LP	Chess	LPS1523	1968	**£20**	**£8**	*US*
Here Comes The Judge	7"	Chess	CRS8077	1968	**£4**	**£1.50**	

MARKLEY

Markley: A Group	LP	Forward	STF1007	1969	**£30**	**£15**	*US*

MARKSMEN

Smersh	7"	Parlophone	R5075	1963	**£8**	**£4**	

MARLEY, BOB

During the late sixties and early seventies, reggae music was considered to be virtually worthless by a majority of rock fans – an opinion that was hardly ameliorated by the fact that most reggae albums of the time seemed to be bargain priced compilations with tacky covers. Bob Marley put an end to all that. The influential rock magazine *Let It Rock* ran a feature on Marley's music at the time of the release of the first Island LP, *Catch A Fire*. Every reader thereby encouraged to give the record a listen found music that was as exciting as it was sophisticated, producer Chris Blackwell having consciously enhanced its appeal for the rock audience in the UK by remixing the Jamaican version of the music with additional keyboard and lead guitar parts (as well as issuing the record in an attractive cover made with a hinged top like a giant cigarette lighter). When Eric Clapton decided to record a version of 'I Shot The Sheriff' and when Marley himself managed to produce a performance as magnificent as the live 'No Woman No Cry', his rise to the position of reggae's first international star seemed inevitable. Marley's recording career stretched back as far as the beginning of the sixties, some of the records listed below being credited to the Wailers.

African Herbsman	7"	Upsetter	US392	1972	**£15**	**£7.50**	
African Herbsman	LP	Trojan	TRLS62	1973	**£25**	**£10**	
And I Love Her	7"	Ska Beat	JB230	1966	**£50**	**£25**	
Baby Baby We've Got A Date	7"	Blue Mountain	BM1021	1973	**£10**	**£5**	
Babylon By Bus	LP	Island	ISLD11	1978	**£15**	**£6**	*with 12" (IPR2026)*
Bend Down Low	7"	Island	WI3043	1967	**£50**	**£25**	
Burial	7"	Fab	FAB41	1968	**£75**	**£37.50**	*test pressing*
Burnin'	LP	Island	ILPS9256	1973	**£15**	**£7.50**	
Catch A Fire	LP	Island	ILPS9241	1972	**£25**	**£10**	*lighter cover*
Concrete Jungle	7"	Island	WIP6164	1973	**£10**	**£5**	
Confrontation	CD	Mango	CID9760	1988	**£12**	**£5**	
Confrontation	LP	Island	PILPS9760	1983	**£20**	**£8**	*picture disc*
Could You Be Loved	7"	Island	ISP210	1984	**£4**	**£1.50**	*picture disc*
Dancing Shoes	7"	Rio	R116	1967	**£40**	**£20**	
Do You Remermber	7"	Island	WI211	1965	**£50**	**£25**	
Donna	7"	Island	WI216	1965	**£50**	**£25**	
Down Presser	7"	Punch	PH77	1971	**£30**	**£15**	*Junior Byles B side*
Dreamland	7"	Upsetter	US371	1971	**£20**	**£10**	*Upsetters B side*
Duppy Conqueror	7"	Unity	UN562	1972	**£40**	**£20**	*Upsetters B side*
Duppy Conqueror	7"	Upsetter	US348	1971	**£12**	**£6**	*Upsetters B side*
Exodus	CD	Mobile Fidelity		1995	**£15**	**£6**	*US audiophile*
Exodus	LP	Island	ILPS9498	1977	**£10**	**£4**	
Freedom Train	7"	Summit	SUM8530	1971	**£10**	**£5**	
Get Up Stand Up	12"	Island	12BMRM1	198–	**£6**	**£2.50**	*promo*
Get Up Stand Up	7"	Island	WIP6167	1973	**£10**	**£5**	

Title	Format	Label	Cat. No.	Year	Price		Notes
Get Up Stand Up	7"	Island	BMRM1	1975	**£5**	**£2**	*1 sided promo*
Good Good Rudie	7"	Doctor Bird	DB1021	1966	**£40**	**£20**	*City Slickers B side*
Guava Jelly	7"	Green Door	GD4025	1972	**£15**	**£7.50**	
Have Faith In The Lord	7"	Studio One	SO2010	1967	**£40**	**£20**	*Joe Higgs B side*
He Who Feels It Knows It	7"	Island	WI3001	1966	**£50**	**£25**	
Hooligan	7"	Island	WI212	1965	**£50**	**£25**	
I Am The Toughest	7"	Island	WI3042	1967	**£50**	**£25**	*Marcia Griffiths B side*
I Like It Like This	7"	Supreme	SUP216	1973	**£30**	**£15**	
I Made A Mistake	7"	Ska Beat	JB226	1965	**£50**	**£25**	*Soul Brothers B side*
I Need You	7"	Island	WI3035	1967	**£50**	**£25**	*Ken Boothe B side*
I Shot The Sheriff	7"	Island	IDJ2	1974	**£8**	**£4**	*promo*
I Stand Predominant	7"	Studio One	SO2024	1967	**£50**	**£25**	*Norma Frazer B side*
It Hurts To Be Alone	7"	Island	WI188	1965	**£50**	**£25**	
Jah Live	7"	Island	WIP6265	1974	**£4**	**£1.50**	
Jailhouse	7"	Bamboo	BAM55	1970	**£40**	**£20**	*John Holt B side*
Jamming	7"	Island	WIP6410	1977	**£4**	**£1.50**	*picture sleeve*
Johnny Was	7"	Island	WIP6296	1975	**£4**	**£1.50**	
Judge Not	7"	Island	WI088	1963	**£200**	**£100**	
Jumbie Jamboree	7"	Island	WI260	1966	**£50**	**£25**	*Skatalites B side*
Kaya	7"	Upsetter	US356	1971	**£20**	**£10**	*Upsetters B side*
Legend	LP	Island	PBMW1	1984	**£10**	**£4**	*picture disc*
Let Him Go	7"	Island	WI3009	1966	**£50**	**£25**	*2 different B sides*
Lick Samba	7"	Bullet	BU493	1971	**£15**	**£7.50**	
Live	LP	Island	ILPS9376	1975	**£12**	**£5**	*with poster*
Lively Up Yourself	7"	Green Door	GD4002	1971	**£12**	**£6**	*Tommy McCook B side*
Lively Up Yourself	7"	Punch	PH102	1973	**£15**	**£7.50**	*Tommy McCook B side*
Lonesome Feelings	7"	Ska Beat	JB211	1965	**£50**	**£25**	
Lonesome Track	7"	Ska Beat	JB249	1966	**£50**	**£25**	
Love And Affection	7"	Ska Beat	JB228	1965	**£50**	**£25**	
More Axe	7"	Upsetter	US372	1971	**£20**	**£10**	*Upsetters B side*
More Axe	7"	Upsetter	US369	1971	**£20**	**£10**	*Upsetters B side*
Mr Brown	7"	Upsetter	US354	1971	**£20**	**£10**	*Upsetters B side*
Mr Brown	7"	Trojan	TR7926	1974	**£4**	**£1.50**	
Mr Brown	7"	Trojan	TR7979	1976	**£4**	**£1.50**	
Mr Chatterbox	7"	Jackpot	JP730	1970	**£20**	**£10**	*Doreen Shaeffer B side*
My Cup	7"	Upsetter	US340	1970	**£20**	**£10**	*Lee Perry B side*
Natty Dread	7"	Island	WIP6212	1974	**£4**	**£1.50**	
Natty Dread	LP	Island	ILPS9281	1975	**£10**	**£4**	
Natural Mystic	12"	Daddy Kool	DK12102	1984	**£6**	**£2.50**	
Nice Time	7"	Doctor Bird	DB1091	1967	**£40**	**£20**	
Nice Time	7"	Fab	FAB37	1968	**£75**	**£37.50**	*test pressing*
No Woman No Cry	12"	Island	12WIP6244	1974	**£6**	**£2.50**	*picture sleeve*
No Woman No Cry	7"	Island	WIP6244	1974	**£4**	**£1.50**	*picture sleeve*
Oh My Darling	7"	Coxsone	CS7021	1967	**£40**	**£20**	*Hamlins B side*
One Cup Of Coffee	7"	Island	WI128	1963	**£175**	**£87.50**	*Ernest Ranglin B side*
One Love	12"	Island	12ISPX169	1984	**£6**	**£2.50**	
One Love	12"	Island	12ISPP169	1984	**£8**	**£4**	*picture disc*
One Love – People Get Ready	CD-s	Tuff Gong	TGXCD1	1991	**£5**	**£2**	
Picture On The Wall	7"	Upsetter	US368	1971	**£15**	**£7.50**	*Upsetters B side*
Playboy	7"	Island	WI206	1965	**£50**	**£25**	
Pound Get A Blow	7"	Fab	FAB34	1968	**£75**	**£37.50**	*test pressing*
Put It On	7"	Island	WI268	1966	**£50**	**£25**	
Radio Sampler	LP	Island	ISS3	1975	**£30**	**£15**	*promo pack*
Rainbow Country	12"	Daddy Kool	DK12101	1984	**£6**	**£2.50**	*Pablo & The Upsetters B side*
Rasta Put It On	7"	Doctor Bird	DB1039	1966	**£40**	**£20**	*Roland Alphonso B side*
Rasta Revolution	LP	Trojan	TRLS89	1974	**£15**	**£6**	
Rastaman Vibration	LP	Island	ILPS9383	1976	**£10**	**£4**	
Record Shop Sampler	LP	Island	RSS1	197–	**£25**	**£10**	*promo, side 2 by Robert Palmer*
Reggae On Broadway	7"	CBS	8144	1972	**£10**	**£5**	
Roots Rock Reggae	7"	Island	WIP6309	1976	**£4**	**£1.50**	
Rude Boy	7"	Doctor Bird	DB1013	1966	**£40**	**£20**	*Roland Alphonso B side*
Run For Cover	7"	Escort	ERT842	1970	**£50**	**£25**	
Screw Face	7"	Punch	PH101	1973	**£15**	**£7.50**	
Shame And Scandal	7"	Island	WI215	1965	**£50**	**£25**	
Simmer Down	7"	Ska Beat	JB186	1965	**£50**	**£25**	
Small Axe	7"	Punch	PH69	1971	**£20**	**£10**	*Dave Barker B side*
Small Axe	7"	Upsetter	US357	1971	**£20**	**£10**	
Soul Rebel	LP	Trojan	TBL126	1971	**£30**	**£15**	
Soul Shake Down Party	7"	Trojan	TR7911	1974	**£4**	**£1.50**	
Soul Shake Down Party	7"	Trojan	TR7759	1970	**£12**	**£6**	*Beverly Allstars B side*
Soultown	7"	Bullet	BU464	1971	**£25**	**£12.50**	
Stir It Up	7"	Trojan	TR617	1968	**£40**	**£20**	
Stir It Up	7"	Island	WIP6478	1976	**£12**	**£6**	*demo*
Stop The Train	7"	Summit	SUM8526	1972	**£25**	**£12.50**	
Thank You Lord	7"	Fab	FAB36	1968	**£75**	**£37.50**	*test pressing*
Trenchtown Rock	7"	Green Door	GD4005	1971	**£15**	**£7.50**	
Trenchtown Rock	7"	Island	IDJ7	1974	**£5**	**£2**	*promo*
Version Of Cup	7"	Upsetter	US342	1970	**£25**	**£12.50**	*Upsetters B side*

Waiting In Vain	7"	Island	ISP180	1983	£4	**£1.50**	*picture disc*
War	12"	Island	IPR2026	1977	£6	**£2.50**	
What's New Pussycat	7"	Island	WI254	1965	£50	**£25**	

MARLEY, RITA

Come To Me	7"	Island	WI3052	1967	£12	**£6**	*Soul Boys B side*
Pied Piper	7"	Rio	R108	1966	£40	**£20**	
You Lied	7"	Rio	R118	1966	£30	**£15**	*Soul Brothers B side*

MARLO, MICKI

Prize Of Gold	7"	Capitol	CL14271	1955	£6	**£2.50**	
That's Right	7"	London	HL8481	1957	£15	**£7.50**	*B side with Paul Anka*

MARLON

Let's Go To The Disco	7"	Purple	PUR120	1974	£4	**£1.50**	

MARLOWE, MARION

Hands Of Time	7"	London	HLA8306	1956	£50	**£25**	

MARMALADE

The Marmalade were frequent visitors to the charts at the end of the sixties, but their good-humoured harmony pop is not the kind of thing to appeal to many collectors today. Nevertheless, the group's early single, 'I See The Rain' is well worth hearing for the combination of harmony singing with a much heavier guitar sound than was the group's normal practice.

I See The Rain	7"	CBS	2948	1967	£6	**£2.50**	
There's A Lot Of It About	LP	CBS	63414	1968	£12	**£5**	

MARQUIS OF KENSINGTON

Changing Of The Guards	7"	Immediate	IM052	1967	£10	**£5**	

MARR, HANK

Tonk Game	7"	Blue Beat	BB26	1960	£12	**£6**	

MARRIOT, MIKE

Buskin'	LP	Top Line	TOP1LP	1982	£20	**£8**	

MARRIOTT, STEVE

The lead singer with the Small Faces made a solo single two years before the group was formed, when he was only sixteen. Perhaps surprisingly, he performs without any discernible R&B influence but in a style that owes everything to Buddy Holly.

Give Her My Regards	7"	Decca	F11619	1963	£75	**£37.50**	
Marriott	LP	A&M	AMLH64572	1976	£10	**£4**	

M/A/R/R/S

Pump Up The Volume	CD-s	4AD	CAD707R	1987	£10	**£5**	

MARS, BETTY

Come-Comedie	7"	Columbia	DB8879	1972	£4	**£1.50**	

MARS, JOHNNY

Blues From Mars	LP	Polydor	2460168	1972	£10	**£4**	

MARSDEN, BERYL

I Know	7"	Decca	F11707	1963	£6	**£2.50**	
Music Talk	7"	Columbia	DB7797	1965	£6	**£2.50**	
What's She Got	7"	Columbia	DB7888	1966	£6	**£2.50**	
When The Lovelight Starts	7"	Decca	F11819	1964	£6	**£2.50**	
Who You Gonna Hurt	7"	Columbia	DB7718	1965	£6	**£2.50**	

MARSDEN, GERRY

In addition to the hunks of raw rock 'n' roll, 'You'll Never Walk Alone' and 'Ferry Cross The Mersey', that he recorded with Gerry and the Pacemakers, the man who saw fit to lampoon Cliff Richard for his lack of rock 'n' roll credibility (his filmed comments are included in the *Compleat Beatles* video) was also responsible for such roots classics as 'I've Got My Ukelele' (not included here) and the B side of 'Liverpool', which features a collaboration with that rock music giant Derek Nimmo.

Ferry Cross The Mersey	CD-s	PWL	PWCD41	1989	£5	**£2**	*with Paul McCartney*
Gilbert Green	7"	CBS	2946	1967	£5	**£2**	
Liverpool	7"	CBS	3575	1968	£5	**£2**	*B side with Derek Nimmo*
Please Let Them Be	7"	CBS	2784	1967	£5	**£2**	

MARSEILLE

French Way	7"	Mountain	BON1	1978	£6	**£2.50**	

MARSH, STEVE

Girl In Love	7"	Decca	F11244	1960	£4	**£1.50**	
I Shouldn't Be Kissing You	7"	Ember	EMBS139	1962	£4	**£1.50**	
You Don't Have To Tell Me	7"	Decca	F11209	1960	£4	**£1.50**	

MARSH, STEVIE

If You Were The Only Boy In The World	7"	Decca	F11181	1959	£4	**£1.50**	

MARSH, WARNE

Jazz Of Two Cities	LP	London	LTZP15080	1957	£30	**£15**	

Warne Marsh	LP	Wave	LP6	1970	£15	£6	

MARSHALL, GARY

One Twitchy Baby	7"	Parlophone	R4758	1961	£6	£2.50	

MARSHALL, JACK

Eighteenth Century Jazz	LP	Capitol	T1108	1959	£10	£4	
Soundsville	LP	Capitol	(S)T1194	1961	£10	£4	
Thunder Road Chase	7"	Capitol	CL14888	1958	£6	£2.50	

MARSHALL, LARRY

Girl Of My Dreams	7"	Bamboo	BAM22	1970	£5	£2	*Sound Dimension B side*
Maga Dog	7"	Banana	BA364	1971	£5	£2	*Ossie Robinson B side*
Man From Galilee	7"	Bamboo	BAM52	1970	£5	£2	
Move Your Feet	7"	Blue Beat	BB374	1967	£12	£6	
No One To Give Me Love	7"	Caltone	TONE126	1968	£8	£4	*Phil Pratt B side*
Stay A Little Longer	7"	Banana	BA300	1970	£5	£2	*Maytals B side*
Suspicion	7"	Blue Beat	BB380	1967	£12	£6	

MARSHALL, LOIS

British Folk Songs	LP	HMV	ALP1671	1959	£10	£4	

MARSHMALLOW WAY

Marshmallow Way	LP	United Artists	UAS6708	1970	£15	£6	US

MARSON, STUART

Night Falls On The Orchestra	LP	Sweet Folk And Count	SFA012	1974	£10	£4	

MARSUPILAMI

Arena	LP	Transatlantic	TRA230	1971	£30	£15	
Marsupilami	LP	Transatlantic	TRA213	1970	£40	£20	

MARTELL, PIERA

My Ship Of Love	7"	CBS	2293	1974	£6	£2.50	

MARTELL, RAY

She Caught The Train	7"	Joe	JRS3	1970	£5	£2	*Pama Dice B side*
This Little Light	7"	Doctor Bird	DB1503	1970	£4	£1.50	

MARTELLS

Time To Say Goodnight	7"	Decca	F12463	1966	£4	£1.50	

MARTERIE, RALPH

Big Band Sound	7" EP	Mercury	ZEP10024	1959	£5	£2	*with tracks by Quincy Jones*
Music For A Private Eye	7" EP	Mercury	ZEP10068	1960	£6	£2.50	
Presenting	7" EP	Mercury	MEP9517	1957	£12	£6	
Swinging Sound	7" EP	Mercury	ZEP10040	1959	£6	£2.50	

MARTHA & THE VANDELLAS

Come And Get These Memories	7"	Oriole	CBA1819	1963	£125	£62.50	
Come And Get These Memories	LP	Oriole	PS40052	1963	£150	£75	
Dance Party	LP	Tamla Motown	TML11013	1965	£50	£25	
Dancing In The Street	7"	Stateside	SS345	1964	£10	£5	
Dancing In The Street	LP	Tamla Motown	(S)TML11099	1969	£10	£4	
Greatest Hits	LP	Tamla Motown	(S)TML11040	1967	£15	£6	
Heat Wave	7"	Stateside	SS228	1963	£30	£15	
Heatwave	LP	Tamla Motown	TML11005	1965	£30	£15	
Hitting	7" EP	Tamla Motown	TME2017	1966	£60	£30	
Honey Chile	7"	Tamla Motown	TMG636	1968	£6	£2.50	
I Can't Dance To The Music You're Playing	7"	Tamla Motown	TMG669	1968	£5	£2	
I Promise To Wait My Love	7"	Tamla Motown	TMG657	1968	£4	£1.50	
I'll Have To Let Him Go	7"	Oriole	CBA1814	1963	£300	£180	*best auctioned*
I'm Ready For Love	7"	Tamla Motown	TMG582	1966	£4	£1.50	
In My Lonely Room	7"	Stateside	SS305	1964	£30	£15	
Jimmy Mack	7"	Tamla Motown	TMG599	1967	£4	£1.50	
Live	LP	Gordy	(GS)925	1967	£20	£8	US
Live Wire	7"	Stateside	SS272	1964	£25	£12.50	
Love Bug Leave My Heart Alone	7"	Tamla Motown	TMG621	1967	£5	£2	
Martha & The Vandellas	7" EP	Tamla Motown	TME2009	1965	£75	£37.50	
My Baby Loves Me	7"	Tamla Motown	TMG549	1966	£10	£5	

Title	Format	Label	Cat. No.	Year	Mint	VG	Notes
Natural Resources	LP	Tamla Motown	STML11166	1970	£10	£4	
Nowhere to Run	7"	Tamla Motown	TMG502	1965	£8	£4	
Quicksand	7"	Stateside	SS250	1964	£25	£12.50	
Ridin' High	LP	Tamla Motown	(S)TML11078	1968	£15	£6	
Sugar 'n' Spice	LP	Tamla Motown	(S)TML11134	1970	£10	£4	
Watch Out	LP	Tamla Motown	(S)TML11051	1967	£20	£8	
What Am I Going To Do	7"	Tamla Motown	TMG567	1966	£8	£4	
Wild One	7"	Stateside	SS383	1965	£20	£10	
You've Been In Love Too Long	7"	Tamla Motown	TMG530	1965	£12	£6	

MARTIN, ALAN

Title	Format	Label	Cat. No.	Year	Mint	VG	Notes
Days Are Lonely	7"	Rio	R94	1966	£6	£2.50	
Mother Brother	7"	Rio	R10	1963	£10	£5	
Must Know I Love You	7"	Rio	R66	1965	£10	£5	*Vic Brown B side*
Party	7"	Rio	R3	1963	£10	£5	
Rome Wasn't Built In A Day	7"	Rio	R96	1966	£6	£2.50	
Secretly	7"	Rio	R9	1963	£10	£5	
Since I Married Dorothy	7"	Rio	R74	1965	£10	£5	
Sweet Rosemarie	7"	Rio	R67	1965	£10	£5	*Honey Duckers B side*
Why Must I Cry	7"	Rio	R68	1965	£10	£5	
You Came Late	7"	Rio	R6	1963	£10	£5	

MARTIN, DAVE

Title	Format	Label	Cat. No.	Year	Mint	VG	Notes
All My Dreams	7"	Port-O-Jam	PJ4115	1964	£10	£5	
Let Them Fight	7"	Port-O-Jam	PJ4112	1964	£10	£5	

MARTIN, DEAN

Title	Format	Label	Cat. No.	Year	Mint	VG	Notes
Ain't Gonna Lead This Life	7"	Capitol	CL15064	1959	£5	£2	
All In A Night's Work	7"	Capitol	CL15198	1961	£5	£2	
Angel Baby	7"	Capitol	CL14890	1958	£5	£2	
Bamboozled	7"	Capitol	CL14714	1957	£5	£2	
Beau James	7"	Capitol	CL14758	1957	£5	£2	
Belle From Barcelona	7"	Capitol	CL14253	1955	£10	£5	
Bumming Around	7"	Reprise	RS23259	1968	£5	£2	
Capitol Presents	10" LP	Capitol	LC6590	1953	£40	£20	
Career	7"	Capitol	CL15102	1959	£5	£2	
Cha Cha D'Amor	7" EP	Capitol	EAP71702	1961	£5	£2	
Cha Cha De Amor	LP	Capitol	(S)T1702	1963	£12	£5	
Chee Chhe-oo Chee	7"	Capitol	CL14311	1955	£10	£5	
Come On Down	7"	Reprise	R20893	1970	£5	£2	
Country Star	LP	Reprise	R6061	1963	£10	£4	
Dame Su Amor	7"	Reprise	R20082	1962	£5	£2	
Dean Goes Dixie	LP	Encore	ENC103	1962	£12	£5	
Dean Martin	7" EP	Capitol	EAP19123	1955	£15	£7.50	
Dean Martin And Jerry Lewis	7" EP	Capitol	EAP1033	1956	£10	£5	*with Jerry Lewis*
Dean Martin Sings, Nicolini Lucchesi Plays	10" LP	Britone	LP1002	1956	£50	£25	
Dino	LP	Capitol	(S)T1659	1962	£15	£6	
Dino Latino	7" EP	Reprise	R20031	1964	£10	£5	
Dino Latino	LP	Reprise	R6054	1963	£10	£4	
Dream With Dean	LP	Reprise	R6123	1964	£10	£4	
Everybody Loves Somebody	7" EP	Reprise	R30034	1964	£5	£2	
French Style	7" EP	Reprise	R30005	1963	£10	£5	
French Style	LP	Reprise	R(9)6021	1962	£10	£4	
From The Bottom Of My Heart	7"	Reprise	R20116	1963	£5	£2	
Gentle On My Mind	7"	Reprise	RS23343	1969	£5	£2	
Giuggiola	7"	Capitol	CL15209	1961	£5	£2	
Give Me A Sign	7"	Capitol	CL14656	1956	£5	£2	
Good Mornin' Life	7"	Capitol	CL14813	1957	£5	£2	
Hey Brother Pour The Wine	7"	Capitol	CL14123	1954	£20	£10	
Hollywood Or Bust	7" EP	Capitol	EAP1806	1957	£10	£5	
How Do You Speak To An Angel?	7"	Capitol	CL14150	1954	£10	£5	
I'll Be Seeing You	7" EP	Reprise	R30044	1965	£8	£4	
I'm Not The Marrying Kind	7"	Pye	DMA1	1967	£8	£4	*1 sided promo*
I'm Yours	7" EP	Capitol	EAP120152	1961	£8	£4	
If I Could Sing Like Bing	7"	Capitol	CL14180	1954	£8	£4	
In Movieland	7" EP	Capitol	EAP120124	1961	£10	£5	
In Napoli	7"	Capitol	CL14370	1955	£10	£5	
Innamorata	7"	Capitol	CL14507	1956	£10	£5	
It Takes So Long	7"	Capitol	CL14990	1959	£5	£2	
Let Me Go Lover	7"	Capitol	CL14226	1955	£15	£7.50	
Line And Dino	7" EP	Capitol	EAP120060	1961	£5	£2	*with Line Renaud*
Look	7"	Capitol	CL14801	1957	£4	£1.50	
Love Is A Career	LP	Stateside	(S)SL10201	1967	£10	£4	
Love Love Love	7" EP	Reprise	R30074	1966	£6	£2.50	
Mambo Italiano	7"	Capitol	CL14227	1955	£15	£7.50	
Man Who Plays The Mandolino	7"	Capitol	CL14690	1957	£6	£2.50	
Me 'n' You 'n' The Moon	7"	Capitol	CL14625	1956	£5	£2	
Memories Are Made Of This	7"	Capitol	CL14523	1956	£8	£4	
Mr Happiness	7" EP	Reprise	R30084	1967	£6	£2.50	

Title	Format	Label	Cat. No.	Year	Mint	VG	Notes
Once Upon A Time	7"	Capitol	CL14943	1958	**£5**	**£2**	
Open Up The Doghouse	7"	Capitol	CL14215	1955	**£12**	**£6**	
Pardners	7"	Capitol	CL14626	1956	**£5**	**£2**	*with Jerry Lewis*
Peddler Man	7"	Capitol	CL14170	1954	**£10**	**£5**	
Pretty Baby	LP	Capitol	T849	1957	**£15**	**£6**	
Relax-ay-voo	7"	Capitol	CL14356	1955	**£10**	**£5**	
Relaxing With Dean Martin	7" EP	Capitol	EAP120072	1961	**£8**	**£4**	
Return To Me	7"	Capitol	CL14844	1958	**£5**	**£2**	
Return To Me	7" EP	Capitol	EAP1939	1957	**£6**	**£2.50**	
Rides Again	LP	Reprise	R6085	1964	**£10**	**£4**	
Rio Bravo	7"	Capitol	CL15015	1959	**£12**	**£6**	
Robin And The Seven Hoods	7" EP	Reprise	R30039	1965	**£10**	**£5**	
Sam's Song	7"	Reprise	R20128	1963	**£5**	**£2**	*with Sammy Davis Jr*
Send Me Some Loving	7" EP	Reprise	R30051	1965	**£6**	**£2.50**	
Simpatico	7"	Capitol	CL14367	1955	**£10**	**£5**	
Sings Songs From The Silencers	7" EP	Reprise	R30078	1967	**£10**	**£5**	
Sings Songs From The Silencers	LP	Reprise	R6211	1966	**£10**	**£4**	
Sleep Warm	LP	Capitol	(S)T1150	1959	**£12**	**£5**	
Sogni D'Oro	7"	Capitol	CL15172	1960	**£5**	**£2**	
Somebody Loves You	7" EP	Capitol	EAP61702	1961	**£6**	**£2.50**	
Sparklin' Eyes	7"	Capitol	CL15188	1961	**£5**	**£2**	
Sunny Italy	7" EP	Capitol	EAP1481	1955	**£15**	**£7.50**	
Sway	7"	Capitol	CL14138	1954	**£20**	**£10**	
Swinging Down Yonder No. 1	7" EP	Capitol	EAP1007	1956	**£8**	**£4**	
Swinging Down Yonder No. 2	7" EP	Capitol	EAP1022	1956	**£8**	**£4**	
Swinging Down Yonder No. 3	7" EP	Capitol	EAP1037	1956	**£8**	**£4**	
Ten Thousand Bedrooms	7" EP	Capitol	EAP1840	1957	**£15**	**£7.50**	
Test Of Time	7"	Capitol	CL14624	1956	**£5**	**£2**	
This Is Dean Martin	LP	Capitol	T1047	1958	**£15**	**£6**	
This Time I'm Swingin'	LP	Capitol	(S)T1442	1961	**£15**	**£6**	
Tik A Tee, Tik A Tay	7"	Reprise	R20058	1962	**£5**	**£2**	
Triche Trache	7"	Capitol	CL14782	1957	**£5**	**£2**	
Under The Bridges Of Paris	7"	Capitol	CL14255	1955	**£15**	**£7.50**	
Via Veneto	7"	Reprise	R20215	1963	**£5**	**£2**	
Volare	7"	Capitol	CL14910	1958	**£5**	**£2**	
Volare	7" EP	Capitol	EAP11027	1958	**£5**	**£2**	
Watching The World Go By	7"	Capitol	CL14586	1956	**£6**	**£2.50**	
We'll Sing In The Sunshine	7" EP	Reprise	R30036	1965	**£6**	**£2.50**	
When You Pretend	7"	Capitol	CL14505	1956	**£6**	**£2.50**	
Who Was That Lady?	7"	Capitol	CL15127	1960	**£5**	**£2**	
Winter Romance Pt 1	7" EP	Capitol	EAP11285	1960	**£6**	**£2.50**	
Winter Romance Pt 2	7" EP	Capitol	EAP21285	1960	**£6**	**£2.50**	
Winter Romance Pt 3	7" EP	Capitol	EAP31285	1960	**£6**	**£2.50**	
Young And Foolish	7"	Capitol	CL14519	1956	**£10**	**£5**	

MARTIN, DEREK

Title	Format	Label	Cat. No.	Year	Mint	VG	Notes
Daddy Rolling Stone	7"	Sue	WI308	1964	**£15**	**£7.50**	*credited to Derak Martin*
Soul Power	7"	Stax	601039	1968	**£10**	**£5**	
You Better Go	7"	Columbia	DB7694	1965	**£15**	**£7.50**	

MARTIN, DEWEY

Martin had already flexed his gruff vocal chords while drumming with Buffalo Springfield, so he had no problem in fronting a solo album after the group split up. Only the first track is written by Martin himself, and this is pretty good, but the rest of the album tries for a country approach, for which Martin's hard rocking voice is not very suitable.

Title	Format	Label	Cat. No.	Year	Mint	VG	Notes
Dewey Martin And Medicine Ball	LP	Uni	73088	1970	**£20**	**£8**	*US*

MARTIN, DON & DANDY

Title	Format	Label	Cat. No.	Year	Mint	VG	Notes
Got A Feelin'	7"	Giant	GN6	1967	**£4**	**£1.50**	
Keep On Fighting	7"	Giant	GN24	1968	**£4**	**£1.50**	

MARTIN, GEORGE

Title	Format	Label	Cat. No.	Year	Mint	VG	Notes
All My Loving	7"	Parlophone	R5135	1964	**£4**	**£1.50**	
All Quiet On The Mersey Front	7"	Parlophone	R5222	1965	**£4**	**£1.50**	
And I Love Her	LP	Studio Two	TWO141	1966	**£12**	**£5**	
Beatles – George Martin Interview	CD	EMI	RNB1	1993	**£20**	**£8**	*promo*
Beatles To Bond And Bach	LP	St Michael	IMP105	1978	**£15**	**£6**	
British Maid	LP	United Artists	(S)ULP1196	1968	**£10**	**£4**	
By George! It's The David Frost Theme	7"	United Artists	UP1154	1966	**£5**	**£2**	
I Feel Fine	7"	Parlophone	R5256	1965	**£4**	**£1.50**	
In My Life	CD	Echo	ECHPR20	1998	**£25**	**£10**	*promo double*
Instrumentally Salutes Beatles Girls	LP	United Artists	(S)ULP1157	1966	**£15**	**£6**	
Live And Let Die	LP	United Artists	UAS29475	1973	**£10**	**£4**	
Love In The Open Air	7"	United Artists	UP1165	1966	**£12**	**£6**	
Music From A Hard Day's Night	7" EP	Parlophone	GEP8930	1965	**£15**	**£7.50**	
Off The Beatles Track	LP	Parlophone	PMC1227/ PCS3057	1964	**£20**	**£8**	
Plays Help	LP	Columbia	SX1775/TWO102	1965	**£12**	**£5**	
Ringo's Theme	7"	Parlophone	R5166	1964	**£5**	**£2**	
Theme One	7"	United Artists	UP1194	1967	**£6**	**£2.50**	
World's No. 1 Producer	CD	EMI	GMCD001	1998	**£50**	**£25**	*promo*
Yesterday	7"	Parlophone	R5375	1965	**£6**	**£2.50**	

MARTIN, GRADY SLEW FOOT FIVE

Title	Format	Label	Cat. No.	Year	Mint	VG	Notes
Nashville	7"	Brunswick	05535	1956	**£10**	**£5**	

MARTIN, JANIS

Here Today & Gone Tomorrow Love	7"	Palette	PG9000	1960	**£20**	**£10**	

MARTIN, JEAN

Ain't Gonna Kiss Ya	7"	Decca	F11751	1963	**£5**	**£2**	
Will You Still Love Me Tomorrow	7"	Decca	F11897	1964	**£5**	**£2**	

MARTIN, JERRY

Shake-a Take-a	7"	London	HLU9692	1963	**£5**	**£2**	

MARTIN, KERRY

Stroll Me	7"	Parlophone	R4449	1958	**£5**	**£2**	

MARTIN, LUCIA

Big Jim	7"	Parlophone	R4915	1962	**£6**	**£2.50**	

MARTIN, MARK

Extraordinary Girl	7"	Page One	POF020	1967	**£4**	**£1.50**	

MARTIN, MILES FOLK GROUP

Miles Martin Folk Group	LP	Amber		1971	**£100**	**£50**	

MARTIN, PAUL

Snake In The Grass	7"	Sue	WI4041	1967	**£15**	**£7.50**	

MARTIN, RAY

It's Great To Be Young	7" EP	Columbia	SEG7639	1956	**£5**	**£2**	
Sound Of Sight	LP	Decca	PFS4043	1964	**£10**	**£4**	

MARTIN, RICKY & THE TYME MACHINE

Something Else	7"	Olga	OLE4	1968	**£6**	**£2.50**	

MARTIN, RODGE

When She Touches Me	7"	Polydor	56725	1967	**£5**	**£2**	

MARTIN, RON

Give Your Love To Me	7"	Doctor Bird	DB1151	1968	**£10**	**£5**	

MARTIN, SETH

Another Day Goes By	7"	Page One	POF073	1968	**£4**	**£1.50**	

MARTIN, SHANE

You're So Young	7"	CBS	3894	1969	**£100**	**£50**	

MARTIN, STEVE

Only You	7"	Columbia	SCM5212	1956	**£4**	**£1.50**	

MARTIN, TONY

All Of You	7"	HMV	POP282	1957	**£4**	**£1.50**	
Bigger Your Heart Is	7"	Tamla Motown	TMG537	1965	**£50**	**£25**	
Dream Music	10" LP	Mercury	MPT7516	1957	**£15**	**£6**	
Favourites	10" LP	Mercury	MPT7005	1956	**£15**	**£6**	
Golden Years	7"	HMV	7M136	1953	**£6**	**£2.50**	
Greatest Hits	LP	London	HAD2341	1961	**£10**	**£4**	
I Could Write A Book	7"	HMV	7M203	1954	**£4**	**£1.50**	
I Love Paris	7"	HMV	7M258	1954	**£4**	**£1.50**	
It's Better In The Dark	7"	HMV	POP257	1956	**£4**	**£1.50**	
Love You Funny Thing	7"	HMV	7M376	1956	**£4**	**£1.50**	
My Bambina	7"	HMV	7M283	1955	**£4**	**£1.50**	
Please Please	7"	HMV	7M137	1953	**£5**	**£2**	
Sorta On The Border	7"	HMV	7M158	1953	**£5**	**£2**	
Speak To Me Of Love	10" LP	HMV	DLP1137	1957	**£10**	**£4**	
Stranger In Paradise	7"	HMV	7M302	1955	**£8**	**£4**	
Talkin' To Your Picture	7"	Stateside	SS394	1965	**£60**	**£30**	
Tenement Symphony	7"	HMV	7M105	1953	**£4**	**£1.50**	
Tenement Symphony	7" EP	HMV	7EG8124	1955	**£5**	**£2**	
That's What A Rainy Day Is For	7"	HMV	7M210	1954	**£4**	**£1.50**	
Tony Martin	7" EP	HMV	7EG8006	1954	**£5**	**£2**	
Tony Martin Sings Vol. 1	10" LP	Brunswick	LA8713	1955	**£15**	**£6**	
Uno	7"	HMV	7M254	1954	**£4**	**£1.50**	
Walk Hand In Hand	7"	HMV	7M414	1956	**£5**	**£2**	
Walk Hand In Hand	7"	HMV	7MC41	1956	**£6**	**£2.50**	*export*
What's The Time In Nicaragua	7"	HMV	7M320	1955	**£4**	**£1.50**	

MARTIN, TRADE

Hula Hula Dancin' Doll	7"	London	HL9662	1963	**£5**	**£2**	

MARTIN, VINCE

Cindy Oh Cindy	7"	London	HLN8340	1956	**£20**	**£10**	*with the Tarriers*
Old Grey Goose	7"	HMV	POP594	1959	**£5**	**£2**	

MARTIN & FINLEY

It's Another Sunday	7"	Tamla Motown	TMG867	1973	**£50**	**£25**	*demo*

MARTIN & THE BROWNSHIRTS

Taxi Driver	7"	Lightning	GIL507	1978	**£12**	**£6**	

MARTINDALE, WINK

Black Land Farmer	7"	London	HLD9419	1961	**£4**	**£1.50**	
Deck Of Cards	7"	London	HLD8962	1959	**£4**	**£1.50**	
Deck Of Cards	7" EP	London	RED1370	1963	**£12**	**£6**	
Deck Of Cards	7" EP	Dot	DEP20000	1965	**£5**	**£2**	
Deck Of Cards	LP	Golden Guinea	GGL0288	1964	**£10**	**£4**	
Life Gets Teejus Don't It?	7"	London	HLD9042	1960	**£4**	**£1.50**	
Wink Martindale	LP	London	HAD2240	1960	**£20**	**£8**	

MARTINO, AL

Al Martino	LP	Top Rank	BUY030	1960	**£10**	**£4**	
Al Martino Sings	7" EP	Capitol	EAP1405	1955	**£12**	**£6**	
Come Close To Me	7"	Capitol	CL14379	1955	**£6**	**£2.50**	
Darling I Love You	7"	Top Rank	JAR187	1959	**£5**	**£2**	
Darling I Love You	7" EP	Ember	EMBEP4528	1963	**£6**	**£2.50**	
Don't Go To Strangers	7"	Capitol	CL14224	1955	**£10**	**£5**	
Girl I Left In Rome	7"	Capitol	CL14614	1956	**£4**	**£1.50**	
Give Me Something To Go On With	7"	Capitol	CL14148	1954	**£12**	**£6**	
I Can't Get You Out Of My Heart	7"	Top Rank	JAR108	1959	**£5**	**£2**	
I Still Believe	7"	Capitol	CL14192	1954	**£10**	**£5**	
I'm Sorry	7"	Capitol	CL14680	1957	**£4**	**£1.50**	
Journey's End	7"	Capitol	CL14550	1956	**£4**	**£1.50**	
Losing You	7" EP	Capitol	EAP120590	1964	**£5**	**£2**	
Mama	7"	Top Rank	JAR337	1960	**£4**	**£1.50**	
Man From Laramie	7"	Capitol	CL14343	1955	**£15**	**£7.50**	
Not As A Stranger	7"	Capitol	CL14202	1954	**£10**	**£5**	
Sings Of Love	7" EP	Capitol	EAP42107	1963	**£5**	**£2**	
Snowy Snowy Mountains	7"	Capitol	CL14284	1955	**£8**	**£4**	
Story Of Tina	7"	Capitol	CL14163	1954	**£15**	**£7.50**	
Summertime	7"	Top Rank	JAR312	1960	**£4**	**£1.50**	
Swing Along With Al Martino	LP	Top Rank	25025	1960	**£10**	**£4**	
To Please My Lady	7" EP	Capitol	EAP120153	1961	**£6**	**£2.50**	
Wanted	7"	Capitol	CL14128	1954	**£15**	**£7.50**	

MARTIN'S MAGIC SOUNDS

Martin's Magic Sounds	LP	Deram	DML/SML1014	1968	**£10**	**£4**	*credited to Irving Martin*

MARTYN, JOHN

John Martyn's first two albums are fairly conventional folk affairs, but his marriage to singer Beverley seemed to make him decide to experiment a little. The two LPs recorded by John and Beverley together are wonderful pieces of folk-rock with the strongly melodic, distinctive songs being enhanced by sympathetic playing from some well-known session names. Thereafter, John Martyn began to explore the sonic possibilities of the amplified guitar, coaxing a range of exciting and unusual sounds from his effects pedals, but without ever abandoning his love of melody. In live performance he was particularly impressive, as a dense wash of echoplexed sound would fill the hall – emanating from a man apparently playing nothing more than an acoustic guitar! This is brilliantly captured on the mock-bootleg *Live At Leeds*, which was available in some European record shops, but could only be obtained by mail order from John Martyn himself in the UK.

Bless The Weather	LP	Island	ILPS9167	1971	**£10**	**£4**	
Classic John Martyn	CD-s	Island	CID265	1986	**£15**	**£7.50**	
Johnny Too Bad	12"	Island	IPR2046	1981	**£6**	**£2.50**	
Live At Leeds	LP	Island	ILPS9343	1975	**£30**	**£15**	*autographed*
Live At Leeds	LP	Island	ILPS9343	1975	**£20**	**£8**	
London Conversation	LP	Island	ILP952	1967	**£40**	**£20**	*pink label*
May You Never	7"	Island	WIP6116	1971	**£4**	**£1.50**	
Philentropy	LP	Body Swerve	JMLP001	1983	**£10**	**£4**	
Tumbler	LP	Island	ILP991/ILPS9091	1968	**£40**	**£20**	*pink label*

MARTYN, JOHN & BEVERLEY

John The Baptist	7"	Island	WIP6076	1969	**£4**	**£1.50**	
Road To Ruin	LP	Island	ILPS9133	1970	**£20**	**£8**	*pink label*
Road To Ruin	LP	Island	ILPS9133	1970	**£12**	**£5**	
Stormbringer	LP	Island	ILPS9113	1970	**£40**	**£20**	*pink label*

MARTYN, KID

In New Orleans With Kid Sheik's Band	LP	77	LA1220	1962	**£12**	**£5**	

MARVELETTES

As Long As I Know He's Mine	7"	Stateside	SS251	1964	**£30**	**£15**	
Beechwood 45789	7"	Oriole	CBA1764	1962	**£60**	**£30**	
Danger Heartbreak Dead Ahead	7"	Tamla Motown	TMG535	1965	**£15**	**£7.50**	
Don't Mess With Bill	7"	Tamla Motown	TMG546	1966	**£20**	**£10**	
Finders Keepers, Losers Weepers	7"	Tamla Motown	TMG1000	1975	**£20**	**£10**	*Kim Weston B side*
He's A Good Guy	7"	Stateside	SS273	1964	**£30**	**£15**	
Here I Am Baby	7"	Tamla Motown	TMG659	1968	**£8**	**£4**	
Hunter Gets Captured By The Game	7"	Tamla Motown	TMG594	1967	**£10**	**£5**	
I'll Keep Holding On	7"	Tamla Motown	TMG518	1965	**£25**	**£12.50**	

Title	Format	Label	Cat. No.	Year	Value		Notes
In Full Bloom	LP	Tamla Motown	(S)TML11145	1970	£20	£8	
Locking Up My Heart	7"	Oriole	CBA1817	1963	£300	£180	best auctioned
Marvelettes	7" EP	Tamla Motown	TME2003	1965	£60	£30	
Marvelettes	LP	Tamla Motown	(S)TML11052	1967	£25	£10	
Marvellous Marvelettes	LP	Tamla Motown	TML11008	1965	£125	£62.50	
My Baby Must Be A Magician	7"	Tamla Motown	TMG639	1968	£8	£4	
Please Mr Postman	7"	Fontana	H355	1961	£30	£15	
Reaching For Something I Can't Have	7"	Tamla Motown	TMG701	1969	£5	£2	
Reaching For Something I Can't Have/ Magician	7"	Tamla Motown	TMG860	1973	£25	£12.50	demo
Sophisticated Soul	LP	Tamla Motown	(S)TML11090	1969	£20	£8	
Too Many Fish In The Sea	7"	Stateside	SS369	1965	£20	£10	
Twisting Postman	7"	Fontana	H386	1962	£40	£20	
When You're Young And In Love	7"	Tamla Motown	TMG609	1967	£5	£2	
You're My Remedy	7"	Stateside	SS334	1964	£25	£12.50	
You're The One	7"	Tamla Motown	TMG562	1966	£15	£7.50	

MARVELOWS

Title	Format	Label	Cat. No.	Year	Value		Notes
I Do	7"	HMV	POP1433	1965	£10	£5	

MARVELS

Title	Format	Label	Cat. No.	Year	Value		Notes
Keep On Searching	7"	Columbia	DB8341	1968	£6	£2.50	

MARVELS (2)

Title	Format	Label	Cat. No.	Year	Value		Notes
Angelo	7"	Dice	CC8	1962	£10	£5	
Don't Cry My Love	7"	Dice	CC17	1963	£10	£5	
Don't Let Him Take Your Love From Me	7"	Pama	PM817	1970	£4	£1.50	
Love One Another	7"	Pama	PM813	1970	£4	£1.50	
Sonia	7"	Blue Beat	BB191	1963	£12	£6	

MARVETTES

Title	Format	Label	Cat. No.	Year	Value		Notes
I Want A Revival	7"	Tabernacle	TS1001	1968	£4	£1.50	
It's Revival Time	LP	Coxsone	TLP1002	196–	£100	£50	
Sweet Jesus	7"	Tabernacle	TS1003	1968	£4	£1.50	

MARVIN, BRETT & THE THUNDERBOLTS

Title	Format	Label	Cat. No.	Year	Value		Notes
Brett Marvin & The Thunderbolts	LP	Sonet	SNTF616	1970	£10	£4	

MARVIN, HANK

Title	Format	Label	Cat. No.	Year	Value		Notes
Break Another Dawn	7"	Columbia	DB8693	1970	£6	£2.50	
Break Another Dawn/Would You Believe It?	7"	Columbia	DB8693	1970	£100	£50	demo
Goodnight Dick	7"	Columbia	DB8552	1969	£5	£2	
Hank Marvin	LP	Columbia	SCX6352	1969	£12	£5	
Hank Marvin	LP	Columbia	SX6352	1969	£15	£6	mono
London's Not Too Far	7"	Columbia	DB8326	1968	£5	£2	Shadows B side
Midnight Cowboy	7"	Columbia	DB8628	1969	£8	£4	Shadows B side
Sacha	7"	Columbia	DB8601	1969	£5	£2	

MARVIN, JOEL

Title	Format	Label	Cat. No.	Year	Value		Notes
Too Late	7"	Explosion	EX2028	1970	£5	£2	

MARVIN, WELCH & FARRAR

Title	Format	Label	Cat. No.	Year	Value		Notes
Faithful	7"	Regal Zonophone	RZ3030	1971	£4	£1.50	
Lady Of The Morning	7"	Regal Zonophone	RZ3035	1971	£4	£1.50	
Marmaduke	7"	Regal Zonophone	RZ3048	1972	£6	£2.50	
Marvin, Welch & Farrar	LP	Regal Zonophone	SRZA8502	1971	£12	£5	
Second Opinion	LP	Regal Zonophone	4SRZA8504	1971	£20	£8	quad
Second Opinion	LP	Regal Zonophone	SRZA8504	1971	£15	£6	

MARVIN & FARRAR

Title	Format	Label	Cat. No.	Year	Value		Notes
Marvin & Farrar	LP	EMI	EMA755	1973	£10	£4	
Music Makes My Day	7"	EMI	EMI2044	1973	£5	£2	
Small And Lonely Light	7"	EMI	EMI2335	1975	£4	£1.50	

MARVIN & JOHNNY

Title	Format	Label	Cat. No.	Year	Value		Notes
Cherry Pie	7"	Black Swan	WI467	1965	£12	£6	
Smack Smack	7"	Vogue	V9099	1958	£250	£150	
Yak Yak	7"	Vogue	V9074	1957	£300	£180	best auctioned

MARX, ANDY

Title	Format	Label	Cat. No.	Year	Value		Notes
Circle	LP	Spiegelei	285171U	1973	£15	£6	German

MARX, GROUCHO

Evening With Groucho Marx	LP	A&M	PR3515	1972	£25	£10	US picture disc
Hooray For Captain Spaulding	LP	Decca	DL5405	1968	£30	£15	US

MARY BUTTERWORTH

Mary Butterworth	LP	Custom Fidelity	CFS2092	1969	£400	£250	US

MARZ, RAINER

Drean Is Over	LP	Bacillus	BLPS19094	1972	£12	£5	German

MARZ & EPERJESSY

Marz And Eperjessy	LP	Bacillus	6494009	1971	£10	£4	German

MASAI

Across The Tracks	7"	Contempo	CS2007	1974	£6	£2.50	
Stranger To Myself	7"	Turbo	TURB01	1982	£8	£4	

MASCOTS

Hey Little Angel	7"	Pye	7N25189	1963	£6	£2.50	

MASEKELA, HUGH

Alive And Well At The Whiskey	LP	Uni	UNL(S)101	1968	£10	£4	
And The Union Of South Africa	LP	Rare Earth	SRE3002	1971	£10	£4	
Home Is Where The Music Is	LP	Blue Thumb	ICD3	1972	£10	£4	
Hugh Masekela	LP	Fontana	SFL13056	1969	£10	£4	

MASKED MARAUDERS

By 1969, if rock music was supposed to have matured into an art form, and its exponents were to be taken as serious musicians, then it went with the territory that the members of various star groups should, in the manner of jazz musicians, start playing on each other's albums. Al Kooper had shown the way by inviting Mike Bloomfield and Steve Stills to participate in the making of his *Super Session* album; Bloomfield had jammed on record with Moby Grape; and groups like Blind Faith and Crosby, Stills and Nash had been set up as a meeting-place for star performers. It was against this background that *Rolling Stone* magazine printed a review of an album by the 'Masked Marauders', a title that was apparently a thinly disguised cover for a collaboration between the Beatles, Mick Jagger and Bob Dylan. The album really exists, too. Whether a joke on *Rolling Stone*'s part inspired someone to actually make the record, or whether the magazine was simply happy to go along with a record company joke, is no longer clear. The album, however, is an interesting novelty, even if it becomes obvious fairly quickly that it is the work of impersonators. Despite this, the concept of such a stellar gathering being directed, amongst other tellingly inappropriate choices, towards the production of a version of 'I Am The Japanese Sandman' is so delicious, that the record becomes an essential purchase despite itself!

Masked Marauders	LP	Reprise	RS6378	1969	£15	£6	US

MASKERS

Beat Meets Rhythm & Blues	LP	Artone	PDR552	1966	£30	£15	Dutch
Sensations In Sound	LP	Artone	PDS510	1966	£20	£8	Dutch

MASON

Mason	LP	Dawn	DNLS3050	1974	£10	£4	

MASON (2)

Harbour	LP	Eleventh Hour	1001	1971	£75	£37.50	US

MASON, BARBARA

Love's The Thing	LP	Buddah	BDLP4032	1975	£10	£4	
Oh How It Hurts	7"	Direction	583382	1968	£8	£4	
Oh How It Hurts	LP	Action	ACLP6002	1969	£25	£10	
Slipping Away	7"	Action	ACT4542	1969	£8	£4	
Transition	LP	Buddah	BDLP4027	1975	£10	£4	
Yes I'm Ready	7"	London	HL9977	1965	£15	£7.50	

MASON, BARRY

Over The Hills & Far Away	7"	Deram	DM104	1966	£30	£15	

MASON, BONNIE JO

Cher recorded her tribute to Ringo Starr under this pseudonym.

Ringo, I Love You	7"	Annette	1000	1964	£60	£30	US

MASON, DAVE

Alone Together	CD	Mobile Fidelity	UDCD573	1992	£15	£6	US audiophile
Alone Together	LP	Blue Thumb	BTS19	1970	£15	£6	US, marbled vinyl
Alone Together	LP	Harvest	SHTC251	1970	£12	£5	
Head Keeper	LP	Blue Thumb	ILPS9203	1972	£12	£5	
Little Woman	7"	Island	WIP6032	1968	£8	£4	
Only You Know And I Know	7"	Harvest	HAR5024	1970	£4	£1.50	
Scrapbook	LP	Island	ICD5	1972	£12	£5	double
World In Changes	7"	Harvest	HAR5017	1970	£4	£1.50	

MASON, GLEN

Battle Of New Orleans	7"	Parlophone	R4562	1959	£4	£1.50	
Don't Forbid Me	7"	Parlophone	R4271	1957	£4	£1.50	
Glendora	7"	Parlophone	R4203	1956	£10	£5	
Green Door	7"	Parlophone	R4244	1956	£10	£5	
Hot Diggity	7"	Parlophone	MSP6240	1956	£6	£2.50	

I May Never Pass This Way Again	7"	Parlophone	R4415	1958	£4	£1.50	
You Got What It Takes	7"	Parlophone	R4626	1960	£4	£1.50	

MASON, JAMES

Tell Tale Heart	7" EP	Brunswick	OE9444	1959	£5	£2	

MASON, MARLIN

Don't Throw My Love Away	7"	Vogue Coral	Q72168	1956	£4	£1.50	

MASON, SPENCER

Flugel In Carnaby Street	7"	Parlophone	R5555	1967	£4	£1.50	

MASON PROFFIT

Moving Towards Happiness	LP	Happy Tiger	1019	1970	£12	£5	*US*
Wanted	LP	Happy Tiger	1009	1969	£12	£5	*US*

MASS

Labour Of Love	LP	4AD	CAD107	1981	£10	£4	*with inner sleeve*
You And I	7"	4AD	AD14	1980	£8	£4	*with poster*

MASSED ALBERTS

Goodbye Dolly	7"	Parlophone	R5159	1964	£4	£1.50	

MASSIVE ATTACK

Daydreaming	CD-s	Wild Bunch	WBRX1	1990	£5	£2	
Safe From Harm	CD-s	Wild Bunch	WBRX3	1991	£5	£2	
Unfinished Sympathy	12"	Wild Bunch	WBRR2	1991	£10	£5	
Unfinished Symphony	CD-s	Wild Bunch	WBRX2	1991	£5	£2	

MASTERBOY

Shake It Up And Dance	CD-s	Polydor	CIOCD2	1991	£5	£2	

MASTERFLEET

High On The Sea	LP	Sussex	LPSX5	1973	£12	£5	

MASTERMINDS

She Belongs To Me	7"	Immediate	IM005	1965	£10	£5	

MASTERPLAN

Love Crazy	7"	Satril	SAT136	1978	£6	£2.50	

MASTERS

'Breaktime' was co-written by Frank Zappa.

Breaktime	7"	Emmy	10082	1962	£150	£75	*US*

MASTERS, SAMMY

Big Man Cried	7"	London	HLR9949	1965	£6	£2.50	
Rocking Red Wing	7"	Warner Bros	WB10	1960	£20	£10	

MASTERS, VALERIE

Christmas Calling	7"	Columbia	DB7426	1964	£50	£25	
Cow Cow Boogie	7"	Fontana	H253	1960	£4	£1.50	
Ding-Dong	7"	Fontana	H145	1958	£4	£1.50	
Jack O'Diamonds	7"	Fontana	H195	1959	£4	£1.50	
Sharing	7"	Fontana	H132	1958	£4	£1.50	

MASTER'S APPRENTICES

Best Of	LP	EMI	EMC2517	1972	£40	£20	*Australian*
Choice Cuts	LP	Columbia	SCX07903	1971	£75	£37.50	*Australian*
I'm Your Satisfier	7"	Regal Zonophone	RZ3031	1971	£12	£6	
Master's Apprentices	LP	Regal Zonophone	SLRZ1016	1970	£100	£50	
Masterpiece	LP	Columbia	SCX07915	1972	£75	£37.50	*Australian*
Nickelodeon	LP	Columbia	7992	1972	£150	£75	*Australian*
Toast To Panama Red	LP	Regal Zonophone	SLRZ1022	1971	£100	£50	

MASTERS OF DECEIT

Hensley's Electric Jazz Band And Synthetic Symphonette	LP	Vanguard	6522	1969	£30	£15	*US*

MASTERSOUNDS

Ballads And Blues	LP	Vogue	LAE12223	1960	£10	£4	
In Concert	LP	Vogue	LAE12226	1960	£10	£4	

MATADORS

I'm Sorry	7"	Green Door	GD4017	1971	£5	£2	*Rhythm Rulers B side*

MATALON, ZACK

Stranger In Town	LP	Nixa	NPL18006	1957	£10	£4	

MATATA

Good Good Understanding	7"	President	PT438	1975	£4	£1.50	
I Feel Funky	7"	President	PT406	1973	£6	£2.50	

Title	Format	Label	Cat. No.	Year	Price	Price	Notes
I Wanna Do My Thing	7"	President	PT380	1972	£4	**£1.50**	
Independence	LP	President	PTLS1057	1975	£40	**£20**	
Matata	LP	President	PTLS1052	1974	£15	**£6**	

MATCHING MOLE

Title	Format	Label	Cat. No.	Year	Price	Price	Notes
Little Red Record	LP	CBS	65260	1973	£10	**£4**	
Matching Mole	LP	CBS	64850	1972	£10	**£4**	
O Caroline	7"	CBS	8101	1972	£4	**£1.50**	

MATHETAI

Title	Format	Label	Cat. No.	Year	Price	Price	Notes
Knowing	LP	Cavs	CAV017	1977	£125	**£62.50**	

MATHEWS, WILSON, DOONAN

Title	Format	Label	Cat. No.	Year	Price	Price	Notes
Mathews, Wilson, Doonan	LP	Rola	R009	1981	£10	**£4**	

MATHIEU, MIREILLE

Title	Format	Label	Cat. No.	Year	Price	Price	Notes
Mireille Mathieu	LP	Fontana	TL5363	1966	£10	**£4**	
Mireille Mathieu's Christmas	LP	Columbia	SCX6369	1968	£10	**£4**	

MATHIS, COUNTRY JOHNNY

Title	Format	Label	Cat. No.	Year	Price	Price	Notes
Country And Western Express No. 5	7" EP	Top Rank	JKP2064	1960	£15	**£7.50**	

MATHIS, JOHNNY

Title	Format	Label	Cat. No.	Year	Price	Price	Notes
Ave Maria	7" EP	Fontana	TFE17064	1958	£5	**£2**	
Away From Home	LP	HMV	CSD1638	1966	£30	**£15**	*stereo*
Certain Smile	7"	Fontana	H142	1958	£4	**£1.50**	
Certain Smile	LP	Columbia	CL1194	1958	£20	**£8**	*US*
Chances Are	7"	Philips	JK1029	1957	£10	**£5**	
Christmas With Johnny Mathis	7" EP	Fontana	TFE17162	1958	£5	**£2**	
Come To Me	7" EP	Fontana	TFE17039	1958	£5	**£2**	
Eli Eli	7" EP	Fontana	TFE17282	1960	£5	**£2**	
Faithfully	LP	Fontana	TFL5084	1960	£10	**£4**	
Faithfully	LP	Fontana	STFL522	1960	£15	**£6**	*stereo*
Four Hits	7" EP	Fontana	TFE17275	1960	£5	**£2**	
Gina	7"	CBS	AAG117	1962	£4	**£1.50**	*picture insert*
Good Night Dear Lord	LP	Columbia	CL1119	1958	£20	**£8**	*US*
Greatest Hits	LP	Fontana	TFL5058	1959	£10	**£4**	
Handful Of Stars	7" EP	Fontana	TFE17091	1958	£5	**£2**	
Heavenly	LP	Fontana	TFL5023	1958	£12	**£5**	
I'll Be Seeing You	7" EP	Fontana	TFE17283	1960	£5	**£2**	
I'll Buy You A Star	LP	Fontana	TFL5134/ STFL557	1961	£10	**£4**	
It's De Lovely	7" EP	Fontana	TFE17194	1959	£5	**£2**	
It's De Lovely	7" EP	Fontana	STFE8001	1960	£8	**£4**	*stereo*
Johnny Mathis	7" EP	Philips	BBE12156	1957	£6	**£2.50**	
Johnny Mathis	7" EP	Fontana	TFE17011	1958	£5	**£2**	
Johnny Mathis	LP	Fontana	TFL5011	1957	£15	**£6**	
Johnny's Moods	LP	Fontana	TFL5117/ STFL545	1961	£10	**£4**	
Let Me Love You	7" EP	Fontana	TFE17025	1958	£5	**£2**	
Like Someone In Love	7" EP	Fontana	STFE8018	1960	£8	**£4**	*stereo*
Like Someone In Love	7" EP	Fontana	TFE17285	1960	£5	**£2**	
Love Is Everything	LP	HMV	CLP/CSD3522	1966	£10	**£4**	
Meet Mister Mathis	7" EP	Fontana	TFE17177	1959	£5	**£2**	
Merry Christmas	LP	Fontana	TFL5031/ STFL506	1958	£12	**£5**	
More Greatest Hits	LP	Fontana	STFL517	1960	£15	**£6**	*stereo*
More Greatest Hits	LP	Fontana	TFL5083	1960	£10	**£4**	
My Love For You	7"	Fontana	H267	1960	£4	**£1.50**	*picture sleeve*
Olé	LP	HMV	CSD1578	1965	£40	**£20**	*stereo*
Open Fire, Two Guitars	LP	Fontana	TFL5050/ STFL515	1959	£12	**£5**	
Portrait Of Johnny	LP	Fontana	TFL5153/ STFL571	1961	£10	**£4**	
Rhythms And Ballads Of Broadway	LP	Fontana	SET(S)101	1960	£15	**£6**	*double*
Ride On A Rainbow	LP	Fontana	TFL5061	1960	£10	**£4**	
Ride On A Rainbow	LP	Fontana	STFL516	1960	£15	**£6**	*stereo*
Shadow Of Your Smile	LP	HMV	CLP/CSD3556	1966	£10	**£4**	
So Nice	7" EP	Fontana	STFE8000	1960	£8	**£4**	*stereo*
So Nice	7" EP	Fontana	TFE17215	1960	£5	**£2**	
Swing Low	7" EP	Fontana	TFE17089	1958	£5	**£2**	
Swing Softly	LP	Fontana	TFL5039/ STFL500	1959	£12	**£5**	
Teacher Teacher	7"	Fontana	H130	1958	£4	**£1.50**	
Tender Is The Night	LP	HMV	CSD1535	1964	£10	**£4**	*stereo*
Tenderly	7" EP	Fontana	TFE17281	1960	£5	**£2**	
There Goes My Heart	7" EP	Fontana	TFE17088	1958	£5	**£2**	
This Is Love	LP	HMV	CSD1600	1965	£15	**£6**	*stereo*
Twelfth Of Never	7" EP	Fontana	TFE17056	1958	£5	**£2**	
Warm	LP	Fontana	TFL5015/ STFL510	1958	£12	**£5**	
While We're Young	7" EP	Fontana	TFE17047	1958	£5	**£2**	
Wild Is The Wind	7"	Fontana	H103	1957	£4	**£1.50**	
Wild Is The Wind	LP	Columbia	CL1090	1957	£30	**£15**	*US*
Wonderful Wonderful	LP	Fontana	TFL5003	1957	£15	**£6**	
Wonderful World Of Make Believe	LP	HMV	CSD1553	1965	£20	**£8**	*stereo*
Your Teenage Dreams	7"	HMV	POP1217	1963	£6	**£2.50**	*export, picture sleeve*

MATOS, TONY

Cha Cha .... LP .... Salvo .... SLO5520LP .... 1962 £10 .... £4 ....

MATTHEWS, IAN

If You Saw Through My Eyes .... LP .... Vertigo .... 6360034 .... 1971 £12 .... £5 .... *spiral label*
Matthews Southern Comfort .... LP .... Uni .... UNLS108 .... 1970 £12 .... £5 ....
Some Days You Eat The Bear .... LP .... Elektra .... K42160 .... 1974 £10 .... £4 ....
Tigers Will Survive .... LP .... Vertigo .... 6360056 .... 1972 £12 .... £5 .... *spiral label*
Valley Hi .... LP .... Elektra .... K42144 .... 1973 £10 .... £4 ....

MATTHEWS, JOE

Sorry Ain't Good Enough .... 7" .... Sue .... WI4046 .... 1968 £25 .... £12.50 ....

MATTHEWS, WINSTON

Sun Is Shining .... 7" .... Banana .... BA329 .... 1971 £4 .... £1.50 ..... *Inn Keepers B side*

MATTHEW'S SOUTHERN COMFORT

Second Spring .... LP .... Uni .... UNLS112 .... 1970 £10 .... £4 ....
Woodstock .... CD-s ... MCA .... 2574542 .... 1989 £5 .... £2 ....

MATUMBI

Seven Seals .... LP .... Harvest .... SHSP4090 .... 1978 £10 .... £4 ....

MATUSOW, HARVEY JEWS HARP BAND

Afghan Red .... 7" .... Head .... HEAD4004 .... 1969 £4 .... £1.50 ....
War Between The Fats And The Thins ..... LP .... Head .... HDLS6001 .... 1969 £25 .... £10 ....

MAUDS

Hold On .... 7" .... Mercury .... MF1000 .... 1967 £5 .... £2 ....
Hold On .... LP .... Mercury .... MG2/SR61135 .... 1967 £15 .... £6 .... US
Soul Drippin' .... 7" .... Mercury .... MF1062 .... 1968 £4 .... £1.50 ....

MAUGH, BUGSY

Bugsy .... LP .... Dot .... DLP25917 .... 1969 £15 .... £6 .... US

MAUGHAN, SUSAN

Bobby's Girl .... LP .... Wing .... WL1105 .... 1967 £10 .... £4 ....
Effervescent Miss Maughan .... 7" EP .. Philips .... 433621BE .... 1962 £12 .... £6 ....
Four Beaux And A Belle .... 7" EP .. Philips .... BE12549 .... 1963 £15 ..... £7.50 ....
Hey Look Me Over .... LP .... Fontana .... SFL13135 .... 1969 £10 .... £4 ....
Hi I'm Susan Maughan & I Sing .... 7" EP .. Philips .... BBE12525 .... 1962 £12 .... £6 ....
I Can't Make You Love Me .... 7" .... Spark .... SRL1049 .... 1971 £4 .... £1.50 ....
I Didn't Mean What I Said .... 7" .... Philips .... 326533BF .... 1962 £4 .... £1.50 ....
I Wanna Be Bobby's Girl But . . . . LP .... Philips .... 632300BL .... 1963 £30 .... £15 ....
Make Him Mine .... 7" .... Philips .... BF1382 .... 1964 £4 .... £1.50 ....
Mama Do The Twist .... 7" .... Philips .... BF1216 .... 1961 £5 .... £2 ....
More Of Susan Maughan .... 7" EP .. Philips .... 433641BE .... 1963 £15 ..... £7.50 ....
Sentimental Susan .... LP .... Philips .... BL7637 .... 1965 £15 .... £6 ....
Some Of These Days .... 7" .... Philips .... BF1236 .... 1961 £5 .... £2 ....
Swingin' Susan .... LP .... Philips .... BL7577 .... 1964 £15 .... £6 ....
That Other Place .... 7" .... Philips .... BF1363 .... 1964 £5 .... £2 ....

MAUPIN, BENNIE

Jewel In The Lotus .... LP .... ECM .... ECM1043ST .... 1974 £20 .... £8 ....

MAUREENY WISHFUL

Maureeny Wishful .... LP .... Moonshine ...... WO2388 .... 1968 £100 .... £50 ....

MAURICE & MAC

Why Don't You Try Me .... 7" .... Chess .... CRS8081 .... 1968 £6 .... £2.50 ....
You Left The Water Running .... 7" .... Chess .... CRS8074 .... 1968 £5 .... £2 ....

MAX GROUP

Abraham Vision .... 7" .... Fab .... FAB110 .... 1969 £4 .... £1.50 ....

MAXEDON, SMILEY

Crazy To Care .... 7" .... Columbia .... SCMC3 .... 1954 £10 .... £5 .... *export*

MAXEY, JOE S.

Sign Of The Crab .... 7" .... Action .... ACT4607 .... 1973 £5 .... £2 ....

MAXI

Do I Dream .... 7" .... Decca .... F13394 .... 1973 £5 .... £2 ....

MAXIE & GLEN

Jordan River .... 7" .... G.G. .... GG4520 .... 1971 £4 .... £1.50 .... *Glen Adams B side*

MAXIMILIAN

Snake .... 7" .... London .... HLX9356 .... 1961 £25 .... £12.50 ....

MAXIMILIAN (2)

Maximilian .... LP .... ABC .... ABCS696 .... 1969 £60 .... £30 .... US

MAXIM'S TRASH

Disco Girls .... 7" .... Gimp .... GIMP1 .... 1979 £30 .... £15 ....

MAXIMUM BAND

Cupid	7"	Fab	FAB51	1968	**£4**	**£1.50**	

MAXWELL, DIANE

Almost Seventeen	LP	Challenge	CHL607/ CHS2501	1959	**£15**	**£6**	US

MAY, BILLY

Arthur Murray Cha Cha Mambos Pt 1	7" EP	Capitol	EAP1578	1955	**£5**	**£2**	
Arthur Murray Cha Cha Mambos Pt 2	7" EP	Capitol	EAP2578	1955	**£5**	**£2**	
Dixieland Band	7" EP	Tempo	EXA4	1955	**£5**	**£2**	
It's Billy May Time	7" EP	Capitol	EAP1613	1956	**£5**	**£2**	
Making Whoopee	7" EP	Capitol	EAP20064	1960	**£5**	**£2**	
Man With The Golden Arm	7"	Capitol	CL14551	1956	**£6**	**£2.50**	
More May	7" EP	Capitol	EAP1536	1955	**£5**	**£2**	
Nightmare	7"	Capitol	CL14609	1956	**£5**	**£2**	
Sorta Dixie No. 1	7" EP	Capitol	EAP1677	1957	**£5**	**£2**	
Sorta Dixie No. 2	7" EP	Capitol	EAP2677	1957	**£5**	**£2**	
Sorta Dixie No. 3	7" EP	Capitol	EAP3677	1957	**£5**	**£2**	
Sorta May Pt 1	7" EP	Capitol	EAP1562	1955	**£5**	**£2**	
Sorta May Pt 2	7" EP	Capitol	EAP2562	1955	**£5**	**£2**	
Sorta May Pt 3	7" EP	Capitol	EAP3562	1955	**£5**	**£2**	

MAY, BRIAN

Back To The Light	7"	Parlophone	RDJ6329	1992	**£10**	**£5**	*promo*
Back To The Light	CD	Parlophone	CDPCSDX123	1993	**£15**	**£6**	*gold CD*
Back To The Light	CD-s	Parlophone	CDR(X)6329	1992	**£5**	**£2**	*2 versions*
Back To The Light	LP	Parlophone	077778040019	1993	**£15**	**£6**	*textured sleeve*
Driven By You	7"	Parlophone	RDJ6304	1991	**£50**	**£25**	*promo*
Driven By You	CD-s	Parlophone	CDRDJ6304	1991	**£40**	**£20**	*4 track promo*
Driven By You	CD-s	Parlophone	CRD6304	1991	**£6**	**£2.50**	
Last Horizon	CD-s	Parlophone	CDRS6371	1993	**£5**	**£2**	
Resurrection	CD-s	Parlophone	CDR6351	1993	**£8**	**£4**	
Resurrection	CD-s	Parlophone	CDRS6351	1993	**£8**	**£4**	
Starfleet	7"	EMI	EMI5436	1983	**£10**	**£5**	
Starfleet	CD	Collectors' Pipeline		1992	**£25**	**£10**	US
Starfleet Project	LP	EMI	SFLT1078061	1983	**£10**	**£4**	
Too Much Love Will Kill You	CD-s	Parlophone	CDRS6320	1992	**£6**	**£2.50**	*round card sleeve*
Too Much Love Will Kill You	CD-s	Parlophone	MAYDJ1	1992	**£12**	**£6**	*promo sampler*

MAY, PHIL

Phil May & The Fallen Angels	LP	Philips	6410969	1978	**£12**	**£5**	Dutch

MAY BLITZ

May Blitz	LP	Vertigo	6360007	1970	**£30**	**£15**	*spiral label*
Second Of May	LP	Vertigo	6360037	1971	**£60**	**£30**	*spiral label*

MAYALL, JOHN

The various editions of the Bluesbreakers that John Mayall led during the sixties were an extraordinary training-ground for many of the more influential musicians of that time. Cream, Fleetwood Mac, the Aynsley Dunbar Retaliation, the Keef Hartley Band, Colosseum, Free, Mark-Almond, Stone the Crows and even the Rolling Stones were all staffed by Mayall alumni. By placing a premium on instrumental prowess, but at the same time managing to place many of his albums among the best-sellers, John Mayall was of crucial importance in the growing maturity of rock music generally. He was never really a singles artist, however, and his original 45 rpm releases have become quite scarce. All the songs are actually available on LP, but it should be noted that the version of 'Double Trouble' included on the stereo pressing of *Looking Back* lacks the echo that helps to make the lead guitar part on the single into one of Peter Green's finest performances. (The mono *Looking Back* retains the echo in all its glory.)

Back To The Roots	LP	Polydor	2657005	1971	**£20**	**£8**	*double*
Banquet In Blues	LP	ABC	ABCL5187	1976	**£12**	**£5**	
Bare Wires	LP	Decca	LK/SKL4945	1968	**£20**	**£8**	
Bear	7"	Decca	F12846	1968	**£4**	**£1.50**	
Beyond The Turning Point	LP	Polydor	2483016	1971	**£10**	**£4**	
Blues Alone	LP	Ace Of Clubs	ACL/SCL1243	1967	**£10**	**£4**	
Blues From Laurel Canyon	LP	Decca	LK/SKL4972	1969	**£20**	**£8**	
Bluesbreakers	LP	Teldec	HZ630122	1981	**£75**	**£37.50**	*German, 12 LP box set*
Bluesbreakers With Eric Clapton	CD	Mobile Fidelity	UDCD616	1994	**£15**	**£6**	*US audiophile*
Bluesbreakers With Eric Clapton	LP	Decca	LK4804	1966	**£25**	**£10**	
Bluesbreakers With Eric Clapton	LP	Decca	SKL4804	1969	**£30**	**£15**	*stereo, unboxed Decca logo*
Bluesbreakers With Eric Clapton	LP	Decca	SKL4804	197–	**£10**	**£4**	*boxed logo*
Crawling Up A Hill	7"	Decca	F11900	1964	**£25**	**£12.50**	
Crocodile Walk	7"	Decca	F12120	1965	**£20**	**£10**	
Crusade	LP	Decca	LK/SKL4890	1967	**£20**	**£8**	
Diary Of A Band Vol. 1	LP	Decca	LK/SKL4918	1968	**£20**	**£8**	
Diary Of A Band Vol. 2	LP	Decca	LK/SKL4919	1968	**£20**	**£8**	
Don't Waste My Time	7"	Polydor	56544	1970	**£5**	**£2**	
Double Trouble	7"	Decca	F12621	1967	**£5**	**£2**	
Empty Rooms	LP	Polydor	583580	1970	**£15**	**£6**	
Hard Road	LP	Decca	LK/SKL4853	1967	**£20**	**£8**	
I'm Your Witchdoctor	7"	Immediate	IM012	1965	**£20**	**£10**	
I'm Your Witchdoctor	7"	Immediate	IM051	1967	**£15**	**£7.50**	
Jazz Blues Fusion	LP	Polydor	2425103	1972	**£15**	**£6**	
Jenny	7"	Decca	F12732	1968	**£5**	**£2**	

John Mayall Plays John Mayall	LP	Decca	LK4680	1965	£30	£15	
John Mayall's Bluesbreakers With Paul Butterfield	7" EP	Decca	DFER8673	1967	£25	£12.50	
Latest Edition	LP	Polydor	2391141	1975	£10	£4	
Lonely Years	7"	Purdah	453502	1966	£75	£37.50	
Looking Back	7"	Decca	F12506	1966	£5	£2	
Looking Back	7" EP	Decca	457030	1964	£25	£12.50	*French*
Looking Back	LP	Decca	LK/SKL5010	1970	£15	£6	
Memories	LP	Polydor	2425085	1971	£15	£6	
Moving On	LP	Polydor	2391047	1973	£10	£4	
New Year, New Band, New Company	LP	ABC	ABCL5115	1975	£10	£4	
No Reply	7"	Decca	F12792	1968	£4	£1.50	
Parchman Farm	7"	Decca	F12490	1966	£10	£5	
Sitting In The Rain	7"	Decca	F12545	1967	£5	£2	
So Many Roads	LP	Decca	SLK16590P	1970	£20	£8	*German*
Suspicions	7"	Decca	F12684	1967	£5	£2	
Ten Years Are Gone	LP	Polydor	2683036	1973	£12	£5	*double*
Thinking Of My Woman	7"	Polydor	2066021	1971	£5	£2	
Through The Years	LP	Decca	SKL5086	1971	£15	£6	
Turning Point	LP	Polydor	583571	1970	£15	£6	
USA Union	LP	Polydor	2425020	1970	£15	£6	

MAYDAY

Day After Day	7"	Reddingtons	DAN2	1980	£6	£2.50	

MAYER, JOHN

Acka Raga	7"	Columbia	DB8037	1966	£4	£1.50	
Etudes	LP	Sonet	SNTF603	1969	£20	£8	
Indo-Jazz Fusions	LP	Double-Up	DUO123	197–	£15	£6	*double*
Indo-Jazz Fusions	LP	Columbia	SX/SCX6122	1967	£40	£20	*with Joe Harriott*
Indo-Jazz Fusions II	LP	Columbia	SX/SCX6215	1968	£40	£20	*with Joe Harriott*
Music For People Who Go Your Own Way	7"	National Petrol	W1	196–	£10	£5	*picture sleeve*
Radha Krishna	LP	Columbia	SCX6462	1971	£40	£20	

MAYER, NATHANIEL

Going Back To The Village Of Love	LP	Fortune	8014	1964	£20	£8	*US*
Village Of Love	7"	HMV	POP1041	1962	£25	£12.50	

MAYFIELD, CURTIS

Back To The World	LP	Buddah	2318085	1973	£10	£4	
Claudine	LP	Buddah	BDLP4010	1974	£10	£4	
Curtis	LP	Buddah	BDLH5005	1974	£10	£4	
Curtis	LP	Buddah	2318015	1971	£15	£6	
Curtis Live	LP	Buddah	2659005	1971	£15	£6	*double*
Curtis Live	LP	Buddah	BDLP2001	1974	£12	£5	*double*
Give Get Take And Have	LP	Buddah	BDLP4042	1976	£10	£4	
Got To Find A Way	LP	Buddah	BDLP4029	1974	£10	£4	
Move On Up	LP	Buddah	BDLP4015	1974	£10	£4	
Roots	LP	Buddah	BDLH5006	1974	£10	£4	
Roots	LP	Buddah	2318045	1972	£10	£4	
Superfly	LP	Buddah	2318065	1972	£10	£4	
Sweet Exorcist	LP	Buddah	BDLH5001	1974	£10	£4	
Sweet Exorcist	LP	Buddah	2318099	1974	£10	£4	
There's No Place Like America Today	LP	Buddah	BDLP4033	1975	£10	£4	

MAYFIELD, PERCY

Bought Blues	LP	Tangerine	TRC1510	1969	£10	£4	
My Jug And I	LP	HMV	CLP/CSD3572	1967	£10	£4	
Percy Mayfield	LP	Tangerine	TRC1505	1969	£10	£4	
River's Invitation	7"	HMV	POP1185	1963	£4	£1.50	

MAYFIELD'S MULE

Mayfield's Mule included Andy Scott who was later a member of Sweet.

Double Dealing Woman	7"	Parlophone	R5817	1969	£10	£5	
Double Dealing Woman	7"	Parlophone	R5817	1969	£15	£7.50	*picture sleeve*
I See A River	7"	Parlophone	R5843	1970	£10	£5	
We Go Rollin'	7"	Parlophone	R5858	1970	£6	£2.50	

MAYHEM

Bloodrush	12"	Vigilante	VIG1T	1985	£6	£2.50	

MAYL, GENE

Dixieland Rhythm Kings	10" LP	London	HAPB1037	1955	£15	£6	
Dixieland Rhythm Kings	LP	London	LTZU15069	1957	£15	£6	

MAYPOLE

Maypole	LP	Colossus	CS1007	1970	£60	£30	*US*

MAYTALS

54-46 Was My Number	7"	Pyramid	PYR6030	1968	£8	£4	*Roland Alphonso B side*
54-46, That's My Number	7"	Trojan	TR7726	1969	£4	£1.50	
Aldina	7"	Pyramid	PYR6070	1969	£5	£2	
Another Chance	7"	R&B	JB141	1964	£10	£5	*Frankie Anderson B side*

Title	Format	Label	Cat. No.	Year	Mint	VG+	Notes
Bam Bam	7"	Doctor Bird	DB1038	1966	£10	£5	
Bim Today Bam Tomorrow	7"	Pyramid	PYR6050	1968	£8	£4	
Bla Bla Bla	7"	Trojan	TR7741	1970	£4	£1.50	
Christmas Feelings	7"	Ska Beat	JB174	1964	£10	£5	
Country Road	7"	Dragon	DRA1013	1973	£4	£1.50	
Do The Reggay	7"	Pyramid	PYR6057	1968	£8	£4	*Beverley's Allstars B side*
Dog War	7"	Blue Beat	BB231	1964	£12	£6	*Rico B side*
Don't Trouble Trouble	7"	Pyramid	PYR6066	1969	£8	£4	*Beverley's Allstars B side*
Everytime	7"	Island	WI102	1963	£10	£5	*Tommy McCook B side*
Fever	7"	Dragon	DRA1021	1974	£4	£1.50	
From The Roots	LP	Trojan	TRLS65	1973	£15	£6	
Funky Kingston	LP	Dragon	DRLS5002	1973	£12	£5	
Funky Kingston	LP	Island	ILPS9186	1973	£12	£5	
Give Me Your Love	7"	R&B	JB153	1964	£10	£5	
Hallelujah	7"	Blue Beat	BB176	1963	£12	£6	
He Is Real	7"	Blue Beat	BB215	1964	£12	£6	
Hurry Up	7"	R&B	JB130	1963	£10	£5	
I've Got A Pain	7"	Blue Beat	BB220	1964	£12	£6	*Buster's Allstars B side*
In The Dark	7"	Dragon	DRA1016	1973	£4	£1.50	
In The Dark	LP	Island	ILPS9231	1974	£12	£5	
In The Dark	LP	Dragon	DRLS5004	1974	£12	£5	
John And James	7"	Black Swan	WI464	1965	£8	£4	*Theo Beckford B side*
Joy And Jean	7"	Ska Beat	JB202	1965	£10	£5	
Judgement Day	7"	Blue Beat	BB255	1964	£12	£6	
Just Tell Me	7"	Pyramid	PYR6048	1968	£8	£4	
Light Of The World	7"	Blue Beat	BB299	1965	£12	£6	
Little Flea	7"	Blue Beat	BB245	1964	£12	£6	
Looking Down The Street	7"	Blue Beat	BB281	1965	£12	£6	*Buster's Allstars B side*
Louie Louie	7"	Trojan	TR7865	1972	£4	£1.50	
Man Who Knows	7"	R&B	JB161	1964	£10	£5	
Marching On	7"	R&B	JB150	1964	£10	£5	*Lester Sterling B side*
Marching On	7"	Banana	BA340	1971	£4	£1.50	*Roland Alphonso B side*
Matthew Mark	7"	R&B	JB103	1963	£10	£5	*Don Drummond B side*
Millie	7"	Blue Beat	BB221	1964	£12	£6	
Monkey Man	7"	Trojan	TR7711	1969	£4	£1.50	
Monkey Man	LP	Trojan	TBL107	1970	£25	£10	
My Darling	7"	Ska Beat	JB237	1966	£10	£5	*Charmers B side*
My New Name	7"	Island	WI213	1965	£10	£5	
Never Grow Old	LP	R&B	JBL1113	1964	£100	£50	
Never You Change	7"	Island	WI200	1965	£10	£5	
Original Golden Oldies Vol. 3	LP	Prince Buster	PB11	1974	£20	£8	
Pass The Pipe	LP	Island	ILPS9534	1979	£10	£4	
Peeping Tom	7"	Summit	SUM8510	1970	£4	£1.50	*Beverley's Allstars B side*
Pressure Drop	7"	Pyramid	PYR6073	1969	£5	£2	*Beverley's Allstars B Side*
Pressure Drop	7"	Trojan	TR7709	1969	£4	£1.50	*Beverley's Allstars B side*
Redemption Song	7"	Dynamic	DYN438	1972	£4	£1.50	
Sailing On	7"	Dragon	DRA1026	1974	£4	£1.50	
Scare Him	7"	Pyramid	PYR6064	1969	£6	£2.50	
Schooldays	7"	Pyramid	PYR6055	1968	£8	£4	
Sensational Maytals	LP	Doctor Bird	DLM5003	1966	£100	£50	
She's My Scorcher	7"	Trojan	TR7757	1970	£4	£1.50	
Shining Light	7"	R&B	JB155	1964	£10	£5	*Lester Sterling B side*
Sit Right Down	7"	Dragon	DRA1007	1973	£4	£1.50	
Ska War	7"	Blue Beat	BB306	1965	£12	£6	*Skatalites B side*
Struggle	7"	Pyramid	PYR6043	1968	£8	£4	*Roland Alphonso B side*
Sun, Moon And Stars	7"	Trojan	TR7768	1970	£4	£1.50	
Sweet And Dandy	7"	Pyramid	PYR6074	1969	£5	£2	
Tell Me The Reason	7"	Island	WI219	1965	£10	£5	*Philip James B side*
Time Tough	7"	Dragon	DRA1024	1974	£4	£1.50	
We Shall Overcome	7"	Pyramid	PYR6052	1968	£8	£4	*Desmond Dekker B side*
You Got Me Spinning	7"	Blue Beat	BB270	1964	£12	£6	

MAYTONES

Title	Format	Label	Cat. No.	Year	Mint	VG+	Notes
Babylon A Fall	7"	Duke	DU116	1971	£4	£1.50	*Tony King B side*
Barrabus	7"	Explosion	EX2014	1970	£4	£1.50	*G.G. All Stars B side*
Billy Goat	7"	Blue Cat	BS149	1968	£6	£2.50	
Botheration	7"	Blue Cat	BS165	1969	£6	£2.50	*G.G. Rhythm Section B side*
Copper Girl	7"	Blue Cat	BS166	1969	£6	£2.50	
Funny Man	7"	Explosion	EX2012	1970	£4	£1.50	*G.G. All Stars B side*
Hands And Feet	7"	Attack	ATT8029	1972	£4	£1.50	*Lloyd & Carey B side*
I've Been Loving You	7"	Songbird	SB1009	1969	£5	£2	
Loving Reggae	7"	Blue Cat	BS152	1969	£6	£2.50	
Mi Nah Tek You Lick	7"	Blue Cat	BS173	1969	£6	£2.50	

Sentimental Reason	7"	Explosion	EX2013	1970	**£4**	**£1.50**	

MAZE

Ian Paice and Roger Evans of Maze were soon to experience a considerable change of fortune (albeit short-lived in the case of Evans), as they were recruited by Ritchie Blackmore as founder members of Deep Purple.

Catari Catari	7"	MGM	MGM1368	1967	**£40**	**£20**	
Hello Stranger	7"	Reaction	591009	1966	**£75**	**£37.50**	
In Special Danse Discotheque	7" EP	Vogue	INT18136	1967	**£300**	**£180**	*French, best auctioned*

MAZE (2)

Armageddon	LP	MTA	MTS5012	1969	**£100**	**£50**	*US*

MC SPY-D & FRIENDS

Amazing Spider-Man	12"	Parlophone	12RDJ6404	1995	**£20**	**£10**	*promo*

MC5

The revolutionary political stance of the MC5 (for Motor City 5) was backed up by the fact that the group's manager was John Sinclair, the leader of the White Panthers and hero of a John Lennon song, and by the music, which on the crucial first LP was aggressive and rowdy to an extent unprecedented in 1969. The group were the centre of controversy almost immediately – the live introduction to the music on the first album has singer Rob Tyner swearing at the audience, with the result that at least one US record shop chain refused to stock the record. In retaliation, the MC5 took out a press advertisement in which they encouraged fans to boycott the shops – and included an Elektra logo to suggest that the record company was behind the action. The MC5 were promptly dropped from the label and the album withdrawn – to be replaced by a version including the more acceptable replacement line, 'Kick out the jams, brothers and sisters!' Guitarists Wayne Kramer and the late Fred 'Sonic' Smith (husband of Patti Smith) have been frequent guests on a variety of albums since, their status as major influences on late seventies punk undisputed.

Back In The USA	LP	Atlantic	2400016	1970	**£20**	**£8**	
Back In The USA	LP	Atlantic	K50346	1977	**£10**	**£4**	
High Time	LP	Atlantic	2400135	1971	**£15**	**£6**	
High Time	LP	Atlantic	K40223	1971	**£12**	**£5**	
I Can Only Give You Everything	7"	AMG	1001	1966	**£30**	**£15**	*US*
Kick Out The Jams	7"	Elektra	EKSN45056	1968	**£15**	**£7.50**	
Kick Out The Jams	LP	Elektra	EKS74042	1969	**£30**	**£15**	
Kick Out The Jams	LP	Elektra	EKS74042	1969	**£75**	**£37.50**	*US, uncensored intro*
Kick Out The Jams	LP	Elektra	K42027	1977	**£10**	**£4**	
Kick Out The Jams	LP	Elektra	EKL74042	1969	**£40**	**£20**	*mono*
Looking At You	7"	A-Square	333	1967	**£30**	**£15**	*US*
Ramblin' Rose	7"	Elektra	EKSN45067	1969	**£10**	**£5**	

McALOON, SEAN & JOHN REA

Drops Of Brandy	LP	Topic	12TS287	1976	**£10**	**£4**	

McARTHUR, NEIL

Immediately after the demise of the Zombies, lead singer Colin Blunstone adopted a new stage name, Neil McArthur, and recorded a new version of the Zombies' best-known song, 'She's Not There'. The new interpretation is dramatically different from the original, even while keeping the same tempo. Few people were fooled by the name change, however, for Blunstone's breathy singing voice is very distinctive. Before long he was back using his own name.

Don't Try To Explain	7"	Deram	DM262	1969	**£5**	**£2**	
It's Not Easy	7"	Deram	DM275	1969	**£5**	**£2**	
She's Not There	7"	Deram	DM225	1969	**£5**	**£2**	

McAULEY, JACKIE

Jackie McAuley	LP	Dawn	DNLS3023	1971	**£40**	**£20**	
Rocking Shoes	7"	Dawn	DNS1020	1971	**£4**	**£1.50**	
Turning Green	7"	Dawn	DNS1011	1971	**£4**	**£1.50**	

McAULEY SCHENKER GROUP

Anytime	CD-s	EMI	CDEM127	1990	**£5**	**£2**	

McAULIFF, LEON

Cozy Inn	LP	ABC	(S)394	1961	**£15**	**£6**	*US*
Take Off	LP	Dot	DLP3139	1958	**£15**	**£6**	*US*

McAVOY, GERRY

Street Talk	7"	Bridgehouse	BHS004	1979	**£6**	**£2.50**	

McBEATH, JIMMY

Come A'Ye Tramps And Hawkers	7" EP	Collector	JES10	1961	**£5**	**£2**	
Wild Rover No More	LP	Topic	12T173	1967	**£10**	**£4**	

McBRAIN, NICKO

Rhythm Of The Beast	7"	EMI	NICKOPD1	1991	**£5**	**£2**	*shaped picture disc, plinth*

McBRIDE, OWEN

Owen McBride	LP	Philo	1005	1973	**£12**	**£5**	*US*

McCAIN, JERRY

Homogenised Love	7"	Python	P02	1969	**£25**	**£12.50**	

McCALL, CASH

Anytime	7"	Ember	EMBS173	1963	**£6**	**£2.50**	
It's Wonderful	7"	Chess	CRS8056	1967	**£5**	**£2**	
Many Are The Words	7"	Ember	EMBS204	1965	**£6**	**£2.50**	

McCALL, DARRELL

My Kind Of Lovin'	7"	Capitol	CL15196	1961	£4	£1.50	

McCALL, TOUSSAINT

Nothing Takes The Place Of You	7"	Pye	7N25420	1967	£8	£4	

McCALLUM, DAVID

Communication	7"	Capitol	CL15439	1966	£4	£1.50	
Music . . . A Bit More Of Me	LP	Capitol	(S)T2498	1966	£10	£4	
Music . . . A Part Of Me	LP	Capitol	(S)T2432	1966	£10	£4	

McCALMANS

Audience With The McCalmans	LP	RCA	LSA3179	1973	£10	£4	
McCalmans Folk	LP	One Up	OU2161	1968	£10	£4	
Turn Again	LP	CBS	64145	1970	£12	£5	

McCALMON, IAN FOLK GROUP

All In One Hand	LP	Waverley	(S)ZLP2103	1968	£15	£6	

McCANN, JIM

McCanned!	LP	Polydor	2489053	1973	£40	£20	

McCANN, LES

Bucket O'Grease	7"	Mercury	MF973	1966	£5	£2	
Comment	LP	Atlantic	SD1547	1970	£15	£6	US
Invitation To Openness	LP	Atlantic	SD1603	1972	£15	£6	US
Live At Montreux	LP	Atlantic	SD2312	197–	£15	£6	US double
Much Les	LP	Atlantic	588176	1969	£15	£6	
Talk To The People	LP	Atlantic	SD1619	1973	£15	£6	US
Truth	LP	Vogue	LAE12238	1960	£15	£6	
Wailers	LP	Fontana	688150ZL	1966	£15	£6	

McCARTHY

In Purgatory	7"	Wall Of Salmon	MAC001	1986	£12	£6	

McCARTHY, KEITH

Everybody Rude Now	7"	Coxsone	CS7014	1967	£10	£5	

McCARTHY, LYN & GRAHAM

I Think It's Going To Rain	7"	Columbia	DB8422	1968	£4	£1.50	

McCARTNEY, CECIL

Om	LP	Columbia	SX/SCX6283	1968	£25	£10	

McCARTNEY, PAUL

Some of Paul McCartney's more unusual records have been released under pseudonyms – The Country Hams, Suzy and the Redstripes, Percy 'Thrills' Thrillington, and the Fireman. Rarities issued under his own name include a series of lavish packages promoting various of his album releases. Most collectable of these is the picture disc version of *Back To The Egg*, which has acquired legendary status. (The regular issue of the album is, of course, quite common and not at all collectable.) The rare version of the Apple single R5999, it should be mentioned, has 'Sally G' as the A side; there is nothing special about copies with 'Junior's Farm' on the A side. The first edition of the *Price Guide* included the LP *CHOBA B CCCP* in its McCartney section. This was a collection of rock 'n' roll cover versions that Paul McCartney decided to issue in Russia only. The first copies to be seen in the UK were eagerly snapped up by collectors at a much higher price than they were worth. Over the succeeding months more and more copies turned up and the prices took a nose-dive – today one can hardly give copies of the record away. The album has now been issued in the UK, but on CD only.

All My Trials	CD-s	Parlophone	CDRX6278	1990	£5	£2	
All The Best	7"	Parlophone	PMBOX11-19	1988	£60	£30	boxed set, print with facsimile autograph
All The Best	7"	Parlophone	PMBOX11-19	1988	£175	£87.50	boxed set, print with real autograph
Back To The Egg	LP	Parlophone	PCTCP257	1979	£1000	£700	promo picture disc
Back To The Egg	LP	Parlophone	PCTC257	1979	£200	£100	promo, boxed
Band On The Run	7"	Apple	R5997	1974	£30	£15	demo with long/short versions
Band On The Run	LP	Columbia	HC36482	1981	£20	£8	US audiophile
Band On The Run	LP	Capitol	SEAX11901	1978	£30	£15	US picture disc
Band On The Run	LP	Apple		197–	£25	£10	yellow vinyl
Band On The Run Interview Album	LP	Apple	SPRO2955/6	1974	£40	£20	US promo
Biker Like An Icon	CD-s	Parlophone	CDRDJ6347	1993	£30	£15	promo only
Birthday	CD-s	Parlophone	CDR6271	1990	£5	£2	
Boxed Set Of 9 Promo Singles	7"	Parlophone	PMBOX1	1986	£150	£75	numbered and signed
Brung To Ewe By Ram	LP	Apple	SPRO6210	1971	£30	£15	US 1 sided interview promo
C'mon People	CD-s	Parlophone	CDRDJ6338	1993	£15	£7.50	promo only
Deliverance	12"	Parlophone	12DELIVDJ1	1993	£10	£5	demo
Ebony And Ivory	12"	Parlophone	12R6054	1982	£75	£37.50	sepia picture sleeve
Ebony And Ivory	7"	Parlophone	R6054	1982	£40	£20	sepia picture sleeve
Family Way	LP	Decca	LK/SKL4847	1966	£100	£50	with George Martin
Figure Of Eight	7"	Parlophone	RDJ6235	1989	£15	£7.50	demo
Figure Of Eight	CD-s	Parlophone	CD3R6235	1989	£5	£2	3" single, card sleeve
Figure Of Eight	CD-s	Parlophone	CDRS6235	1989	£5	£2	card sleeve
Flowers In The Dirt	CD	Parlophone	CDPCSDX106	1989	£40	£20	with 3" CD, postcards, poster
Flowers In The Dirt	CD	Parlophone	CDPCSD106	1989	£40	£20	promo in A4 box
Getting Closer	7"	Parlophone	R6027	1979	£6	£2.50	picture sleeve
Give Ireland Back To The Irish	7"	Apple	R5936	1972	£6	£2.50	shamrock sleeve

Title	Format	Label	Cat. No.	Year	Mint	Half	Notes
Good Sign	12"	Parlophone	GOOD1	1989	**£40**	**£20**	*promo*
I've Had Enough	7"	Parlophone	R6020	1978	**£6**	**£2.50**	*picture sleeve*
Junior's Farm	7"	Apple	R5999	1974	**£25**	**£12.50**	*demo with long/short versions*
Let 'Em In	7"	Parlophone	R6015	1976	**£20**	**£10**	*demo with long/short versions*
Love Is Strange	7"	Apple	R5932	1972	**£350**	**£210**	*test pressing, best auctioned*
Mary Had A Little Lamb	7"	Apple	R5949	1972	**£5**	**£2**	*picture sleeve*
McCartney	CD	DCC	GZS1029	1992	**£15**	**£6**	*US audiophile*
McCartney	LP	Apple	PCS7102	1970	**£40**	**£20**	*promo with interview sheets*
McCartney	r-reel	Apple	TDPCS7102	1970	**£40**	**£20**	*stereo*
McCartney	r-reel	Apple	TAPMC7102	1970	**£60**	**£30**	*mono*
McCartney Interview	LP	Columbia	A2S821	1980	**£100**	**£50**	*US promo double with book*
McCartney Rocks	CD	Capitol	DPRO79987	1990	**£50**	**£25**	*US promo*
MPL Presents	LP	Capitol		1979	**£500**	**£330**	*promo 6 LP boxed set*
Mull Of Kintyre	7"	Capitol	R6018	1977	**£20**	**£10**	*blue vinyl test pressing*
My Brave Face	CD-s	Parlophone	CDR6213	1989	**£5**	**£2**	
My Love	7"	Apple	R5985	1973	**£10**	**£5**	*credited to 'McCartney's Wings'*
No More Lonely Nights	12"	Parlophone	12PR6080	1984	**£6**	**£2.50**	*picture disc*
No More Lonely Nights (Arthur Baker Remix)	12"	Parlophone	12RA6080	1984	**£25**	**£10**	
No More Lonely Nights (Mole Mix)	12"	Parlophone	12R6080DJ	1984	**£100**	**£50**	*1 sided promo*
Off The Ground	CD	Parlophone	CDPCSD125	1992	**£40**	**£20**	*promo box set, with cassette and press kit*
Off The Ground Complete Works	CD	EMI		1993	**£25**	**£10**	*German double CD*
Old Siam, Sir	7"	Parlophone	R6026	1979	**£6**	**£2.50**	*picture sleeve*
Once Upon A Long Ago	CD-s	Parlophone		1987	**£60**	**£30**	*promo, different sleeve*
One Upon A Long Ago	CD-s	Parlophone	CDR6170	1987	**£8**	**£4**	
One Upon A Long Ago (Extended Version)	12"	Parlophone	12RX6170	1987	**£6**	**£2.50**	
Où Est Le Soleil?	12"	Parlophone	12SOL1	1990	**£10**	**£5**	*demo*
Party	12"	Parlophone	12RDJ6238	1989	**£30**	**£15**	*promo*
Paul Is Live	CD	Parlophone	PMLIVE1	1993	**£25**	**£12.50**	*5 track sampler, promo only*
Paul McCartney & Bob Harris Talk About Buddy Holly	LP	MCA	BH1	1983	**£25**	**£10**	*US promo*
Paul McCartney Collection	CD	Parlophone	CDPMCOLDJ1	1993	**£25**	**£10**	*18 track sampler, promo only*
Press	10"	Parlophone	10R6133	1986	**£8**	**£3**	
Put It There	CD-s	Parlophone	CDR6246	1990	**£5**	**£2**	
Sally G	7"	Apple	R5999	1975	**£100**	**£50**	*demo, Junior's Farm on B side*
Silly Love Songs	7"	Parlophone	R6014	1976	**£20**	**£10**	*demo with long/short versions*
Spies Like Us	12"	Parlophone	12RP6118	1985	**£6**	**£2.50**	*picture disc*
Spies Like Us	7"	Parlophone	RP6118	1985	**£10**	**£5**	*shaped picture disc*
Spies Like Us	7"	Parlophone	RDJ6118	1985	**£15**	**£7.50**	*demo*
Temporary Secretary	12"	Parlophone	12R6039	1980	**£15**	**£7.50**	
Temporary Secretary	7"	Parlophone	R6039	1980	**£30**	**£15**	*demo only*
This One	12"	Parlophone	12RLOVE6223	1989	**£20**	**£10**	*1 sided demo*
This One	7"	Parlophone	RX6223	1989	**£5**	**£2**	*envelope pack with 6 cards*
This One	CD-s	Parlophone	CDR6223	1989	**£5**	**£2**	
Tripping The Live Fantastic	CD	Parlophone		1990	**£30**	**£15**	*French double with bonus Birthday CD single*
Tug Of War	LP	Parlophone	PCTC259	1982	**£100**	**£50**	*promo, press pack, cassette interview*
Venus And Mars	CD	DCC	GZS1067	1994	**£15**	**£6**	*US audiophile*
Waterfalls	7"	Parlophone	R6037DJ	1980	**£20**	**£10**	*demo*
We All Stand Together	7"	Parlophone	RP6086	1984	**£8**	**£4**	*shaped picture disc*
Wings Over America	LP	Capitol	SWCO11593	1977	**£60**	**£30**	*US promo, red, white and blue vinyl*
With A Little Luck	7"	Parlophone	R6019	1978	**£20**	**£10**	*demo*
Wonderful Christmastime	7"	Parlophone	R6029	1979	**£6**	**£2.50**	*picture sleeve*

McCHURCH SOUNDROOM

Title	Format	Label	Cat. No.	Year	Mint	Half	Notes
Delusion	LP	Pilz	20211037	1971	**£30**	**£15**	*German*

McCLAREN, DAVE

Title	Format	Label	Cat. No.	Year	Mint	Half	Notes
Love Is What I Bring	7"	Big	BG323	1971	**£8**	**£4**	*Rupie Edwards B side*

McCLENNAN, TOMMY

Title	Format	Label	Cat. No.	Year	Mint	Half	Notes
Travelin' Highway Man	LP	Flyright	LP112	1975	**£15**	**£6**	

McCLINTON, DELBERT

Title	Format	Label	Cat. No.	Year	Mint	Half	Notes
Hully Gully	7"	Decca	F11541	1962	**£5**	**£2**	

McCLURE, BOBBY

Title	Format	Label	Cat. No.	Year	Mint	Half	Notes
Peak Of Love	7"	Chess	CRS8048	1966	**£20**	**£10**	

You Bring Out The Love In Me	7"	Island	USA006	1975	£6	£2.50	*Survival Kit B side*

McCLURE, CHRIS

Hazy People	7"	Polydor	56227	1968	£5	£2	

McCONNELL, CATHAL

Irish Jubilee	LP	Topic	12TS290	1976	£10	£4	*with Robin Morton*
On Lough Ernie's Shore	LP	Topic	12TS377	1978	£10	£4	

McCOOK, TOMMY

Avengers	7"	Unity	UN506	1969	£4	£1.50	*Laurel Aitken B side*
Black Coffee	7"	Trojan	TR7706	1969	£4	£1.50	*Vic Taylor B side*
Bridge View	7"	R&B	JB163	1964	£10	£5	*Naomi & Co B side*
Buck And The Preacher	7"	Pyramid	PYR7002	1973	£4	£1.50	
Crying Every Night	7"	Spinning Wheel	SW109	1971	£5	£2	*Herman Marquis B side*
Dream Boat	7"	Unity	UN534	1969	£5	£2	
Exodus	7"	Port-O-Jam	PJ4001	1964	£10	£5	*Lee Perry B side*
Indian Love Call	7"	Doctor Bird	DB1053	1966	£10	£5	*Owen & Leon B side*
Jam Session	7"	Doctor Bird	DB1058	1966	£10	£5	*Lloyd & Glen B side*
Jerk Time	7"	Rio	R100	1966	£8	£4	*Uniques B side*
Junior Jive	7"	Island	WI124	1963	£10	£5	*Horace Seaton B side*
Key To The City	7"	Duke	DU78	1970	£5	£2	*Dorothy Reid B side*
Last Flight To Reggae City	7"	Unity	UN501	1968	£6	£2.50	*with Stranger Cole, Junior Smith B side*
Lock Jaw	7"	Trojan	TR7717	1969	£4	£1.50	*Yardbrooms B side*
Love Is A Treasure	7"	Duke	DU161	1973	£4	£1.50	
Moving	7"	Treasure Isle	TI7042	1968	£10	£5	*Silvertones B side*
Music Is My Occupation	7"	Ska Beat	JB179	1965	£10	£5	*Mellodites B side*
My Business	7"	Ska Beat	JB178	1965	£10	£5	*Don Drummond B side*
One Two Three	7"	Island	WI3047	1967	£10	£5	*Treasure Isle Boys B side*
Open Jaw	7"	Duke	DU77	1970	£5	£2	*John Holt B side*
Our Man Flint	7"	Treasure Isle	TI7039	1968	£10	£5	*Silvertones B side*
Out Of Space	7"	Rio	R101	1966	£8	£4	*Uniques B side*
Peanut Vendor	7"	Unity	UN535	1969	£5	£2	
Psalm Nine To Keep In Mind	7"	Big Shot	BI585	1971	£5	£2	
Rooster	7"	Duke	DU76	1970	£5	£2	*Phyllis Dillon B side*
Rub It Down	7"	Technique	TE927	1973	£4	£1.50	
Saboo	7"	Island	WI3049	1967	£10	£5	*Movin Brothers B side*
Saboo	7"	Treasure Isle	TI7018	1967	£10	£5	*Movin Brothers B side*
Saints	7"	Trojan	TR657	1969	£4	£1.50	*Soul Ofrous B side*
Sampson	7"	R&B	JB139	1964	£10	£5	*Roy & Annette B side*
Ska Jam	7"	Rio	R103	1966	£8	£4	
Stupid Doctor	7"	Spinning Wheel	SW110	1971	£5	£2	*Rob Walker B side*
Two For One	7"	Black Swan	WI422	1964	£10	£5	*Lascelles Perkins B side*
Venus	7"	Treasure Isle	TI7032	1968	£10	£5	

McCORMICK, GAYLE

Flesh And Blood	LP	MCA	MUPS482	1972	£15	£6	

McCORMICK, GEORGE

Don't Fix Up The Doghouse	7"	MGM	SPC6	1955	£6	£2.50	*export*

McCORMICK BROTHERS

Authentic Bluegrass Hits	7" EP	Hickory	LPE1509	1966	£10	£5	
Red Hen Boogie	7"	Polydor	NH66986	1963	£30	£15	

McCOY, BUDD

Hiawatha	7"	RCA	RCA1106	1959	£4	£1.50	

McCOY, CLYDE

Dancing To The Blues	7" EP	Mercury	MEP9513	1957	£8	£4	

McCOY, JOE

One In A Hundred	7"	Collector	JDL81	1959	£20	£10	

McCOY, VIOLA

1923–1927	10" LP	Ristic	LP27	195–	£40	£20	

McCOYS

Beat The Clock	7" EP	Bang	770005	1966	£20	£10	*French*
Don't Worry Mother	7"	Immediate	IM028	1966	£4	£1.50	
Fever	7"	Immediate	IM021	1965	£4	£1.50	
Fever	7" EP	Atlantic	750007	1965	£20	£10	*French*
Hang On Sloopy	7"	Immediate	IM001	1965	£4	£1.50	
Hang On Sloopy	7" EP	Barclay	70864	1965	£30	£15	*French, embossed sleeve, B side by Strangeloves*
Hang On Sloopy	7" EP	Barclay	70864	1965	£25	£12.50	*French, B side by Strangeloves*
Hang On Sloopy	LP	Immediate	IMLP001	1965	£40	£20	

Human Ball	LP	Mercury	SR61207	1969	£15	£6	US
I Got To Go Back	7"	Immediate	IM046	1967	£5	£2	
Infinite McCoys	LP	Mercury	(S)MCL20128	1968	£20	£8	
Jesse Brady	7"	Mercury	MF1067	1968	£4	£1.50	
McCoys Vol. 1	7" EP	Immediate	IMEP002	1966	£25	£12.50	
McCoys Vol. 2	7" EP	Immediate	IMEP003	1966	£25	£12.50	
Runaway	7"	Immediate	IM034	1966	£4	£1.50	
Say Those Magic Words	7"	London	HLZ10154	1967	£12	£6	
So Good	7"	Immediate	IM037	1966	£4	£1.50	
Up And Down	7"	Immediate	IM029	1966	£4	£1.50	
You Make Me Feel So Good	LP	Bang	BLP(S)213	1966	£40	£20	US

McCRACKLIN, JIMMY

Christmas Time	7"	Outasite	45120	1966	£30	£15	
Every Night Every Day	7"	Liberty	LIB66094	1965	£4	£1.50	
Every Night, Every Day	LP	Imperial	LP9285/12285	1965	£15	£6	US
How Do You Like Your Love	7"	Minit	MLF11003	1968	£5	£2	
I Got Eyes For You	7"	R&B	MRB5001	1965	£15	£7.50	
I Just Gotta Know	LP	Stax	8506	1963	£25	£10	US
Jimmy McCracklin	7" EP	Vocalion	VEP170160	1965	£75	£37.50	
Jimmy McCracklin Sings	LP	Chess	1464	1961	£30	£15	US
Just Got To Know	7"	Top Rank	JAR617	1962	£10	£5	
My Answer	LP	Imperial	LP9306/12306	1966	£15	£6	US
New Soul	LP	Imperial	LP9316/12316	1966	£15	£6	US
Piece Of Jimmy McCracklin	LP	Minit	MLL/S40003	1968	£15	£6	
Pretty Little Sweet Thing	7"	Minit	MLF11009	1968	£5	£2	
Think	7"	Liberty	LIB66129	1966	£4	£1.50	
Think	LP	Imperial	LP9297/12297	1965	£15	£6	US
Walk	7"	London	HLM8598	1958	£30	£15	
Walk	7"	London	HL7035	1958	£20	£10	export

McCULLOCH, DANNY

Wings Of A Man	LP	Capitol	E(S)T174	1969	£10	£4	

McCULLOCH, GORDEANNA & THE CLUTHA

Sheath And Knife	LP	Topic	12TS370	1978	£10	£4	

McCULLOCH, IAN

Faith And Healing	CD-s	WEA	YZ436CD	1989	£5	£2	3" single
Proud To Fall	CD-s	WEA	YZ417CD	1989	£5	£2	3" single
Unravelled	CD	Sire		1992	£20	£8	US promo compilation

McCULLOCH, IAN (2)

Come On Home	7"	Decca	F11855	1964	£6	£2.50	

McCURDY, ED

Box Of Dalliance	LP	Transatlantic	XTRA1048	1966	£25	£10	2 LP boxed set
When Dalliance Was In Flower	LP	Transatlantic	TRA115	1964	£15	£6	

McCURN, GEORGE

I'm Just A Country Boy	7"	London	HLH9705	1963	£5	£2	

McCUTCHEON, JOHN

Wind That Shakes The Barley	LP	June Appal	JA014	1977	£10	£4	US

McDANIEL, LUKE

Automobile Song	7"	Parlophone	CMSP29	1955	£15	£7.50	export

McDANIEL, MAISIE

Country Style	7" EP	Fontana	TFE17398	1962	£6	£2.50	
Meet Maisie McDaniel	7" EP	Fontana	TE17397	1963	£8	£4	

McDANIELS, EUGENE

Outlaw	LP	Atlantic	2465022	1971	£15	£6	

McDANIELS, GENE

Change Of Mood	7" EP	Liberty	LEP2054	1962	£25	£12.50	
Chip Chip	7"	Liberty	LIB55405	1962	£4	£1.50	
Facts Of Life	LP	Sunset	SLS50017E	1968	£10	£4	
Forgotten Man	7"	Liberty	LIB55752	1965	£6	£2.50	
Gene McDaniels	7" EP	London	REG1298	1961	£30	£15	
Gene McDaniels Sings Movie Memories	LP	Liberty	LRP3204/ LST7204	1962	£25	£10	US
Hit After Hit	LP	Liberty	LRP3258/ LST7258	1962	£30	£15	US
Hundred Pounds Of Clay	7"	London	HLG9319	1961	£5	£2	
Hundred Pounds Of Clay	LP	London	HAG2384/ SAHG6184	1961	£30	£15	
In Times Like These	7"	Liberty	LIB55723	1964	£5	£2	
In Times Like These	LP	Liberty	LRP3146/ LST7146	1960	£30	£15	US
It's A Lonely Town	7"	Liberty	LIB55597	1963	£5	£2	
Point Of No Return	7"	Liberty	LIB55480	1962	£5	£2	
Sometimes I'm Happy	LP	Liberty	LBY1003	1962	£25	£10	
Spanish Lace	LP	Liberty	(S)LBY1128	1963	£25	£10	
Tear	7"	London	HLG9396	1961	£5	£2	
Tower Of Strength	7"	London	HLG9448	1961	£5	£2	
Tower Of Strength	LP	Liberty	LBY1021	1962	£25	£10	

Walk With A Winner .... 7" .... Liberty .... LIB55805 .... 1965 £50 .... £25 ....
Wonderful World Of Gene McDaniels ..... LP .... Liberty .... LRP3311/ LST7311 .... 1963 £20 .... £8 .... *US*

McDAVID, BILL

Kiss Me For Christmas .... 7" .... Starlite .... ST4563 .... 1961 £4 .... £1.50 ....

McDEVITT, CHAS

Across The Bridge .... 7" .... Oriole .... CB1405 .... 1958 £6 .... £2.50 .. *with Shirley Douglas*
Chas And Nancy .... 7" EP .. Oriole .... EP7002 .... 1957 £15 .... £7.50 .. *with Nancy Whiskey*
Face In The Rain .... 7" .... Oriole .... CB1386 .... 1957 £6 .... £2.50 .. *with Nancy Whiskey*
Forever .... 7" .... Top Rank .... JAR338 .... 1960 £4 .... £1.50 .. *with Shirley Douglas*
Freight Train .... 7" .... Oriole .... CB1352 .... 1957 £8 .... £4 .. *with Nancy Whiskey*
Greenback Dollar .... 7" .... Oriole .... CB1371 .... 1957 £8 .... £4 .. *with Nancy Whiskey*
It Takes A Worried Man .... 7" .... Oriole .... CB1357 .... 1957 £8 .... £4 ....
Johnny O .... 7" .... Oriole .... CB1403 .... 1958 £6 .... £2.50 .. *with Nancy Whiskey*
Juke Box Jumble .... 7" .... Oriole .... CB1457 .... 1958 £6 .... £2.50 .. *with Shirley Douglas*
Naughty But Nice .... 7" EP .. Columbia .... SEG8471 .... 1965 £5 .... £2 ....
Sing Sing Sing .... 7" .... Oriole .... CB1395 .... 1957 £6 .... £2.50 ....
Six Big Folk Hits .... 7" EP .. Columbia .... SEG8468 .... 1965 £5 .... £2 ....
Teenage Letter .... 7" .... Oriole .... CB1511 .... 1959 £4 .... £1.50 .. *with Shirley Douglas B side*

McDONALD, ALISTAIR

Battle Ballads .... LP .... Major Minor ... MMLP51 .... 1969 £10 .... £4 ....

McDONALD, COUNTRY JOE

Joe McDonald .... LP .... Custom Fidelity .... 1965 £1000 .... £700 .. *US, plain sleeve, best auctioned*

McDONALD, GAVIN

Lines .... LP .... Regal Zonophone ..... SLRZ1027 .... 1972 £10 .... £4 ....

McDONALD, SHELAGH

Shelagh McDonald .... LP .... B&C .... CAS1019 .... 1970 £20 .... £8 ....
Stargazer .... LP .... B&C .... CAS1043 .... 1971 £25 .... £10 ....

McDONALD, SKEETS

Country's Best .... LP .... Capitol .... T1179 .... 1959 £20 .... £8 .... *US*
Fallen Angel .... 7" .... Capitol .... CL14566 .... 1956 £20 .... £10 ....
Going Steady With The Blues .... 7" EP .. Capitol .... EAP11040 .... 1959 £40 .... £20 ....
Going Steady With The Blues .... LP .... Capitol .... T1040 .... 1958 £30 .... £15 .... *US*

McDONALD & GILES

McDonald & Giles .... LP .... Island .... ILPS9126 .... 1970 £20 .... £8 .... *pink label*

McDOWELL, MISSISSIPPI FRED

1904–72 .... LP .... Xtra .... XTRA1136 .... 1974 £10 .... £4 ....
Eight Years Ramblin' .... LP .... Revival .... RVS1001 .... 1971 £10 .... £4 .... *with Johnny Woods*
Going Down South .... LP .... Polydor .... 236278 .... 1969 £10 .... £4 ....
I Do Not Play No Rock'n'Roll .... LP .... Capitol .... EST409 .... 1970 £12 .... £5 ....
Long Way From Home .... LP .... CBS .... 63735 .... 1970 £12 .... £5 ....
Mississippi Delta Blues .... LP .... Fontana .... 688806ZL .... 1966 £12 .... £5 ....
My Home Is In The Delta .... LP .... Bounty .... BY6022 .... 1966 £12 .... £5 ....

McDUFF, BROTHER JACK

Carpetbaggers .... 7" .... Stateside .... SS328 .... 1964 £4 .... £1.50 ....
Change Is Gonna Come .... LP .... Atlantic .... 587030 .... 1966 £15 .... £6 ....
Concert McDuff .... LP .... Stateside .... SL10165 .... 1966 £15 .... £6 ....
Double Barrelled Soul .... LP .... Atlantic .... SD1498 .... 1968 £15 .... £6 .... *US, with David Newman*
Down Home Style .... LP .... Blue Note .... BST84322 .... 1969 £12 .... £5 ....
Dynamic! .... LP .... Stateside .... SL10101 .... 1964 £15 .... £6 ....
If The Cap Fits, Wear It .... LP .... York .... FYK407 .... 1972 £10 .... £4 ....
Live At The Jazz Workshop .... LP .... Stateside .... SL10121 .... 1965 £15 .... £6 ....
Live At The Jazz Workshop .... LP .... Transatlantic .... PR7286 .... 1968 £12 .... £5 ....
Live! .... LP .... Stateside .... SL10060 .... 1964 £15 .... £6 ....
Moon Rappin' .... LP .... Blue Note .... BST84334 .... 1969 £12 .... £5 ....
Prelude .... LP .... Stateside .... SL10142 .... 1965 £15 .... £6 ....
Rock Candy .... 7" .... Stateside .... SS302 .... 1964 £4 .... £1.50 ....
Rock Candy .... LP .... Prestige .... PR24013 .... 1972 £10 .... £4 ....
Sanctified Samba .... 7" .... Stateside .... SS275 .... 1964 £4 .... £1.50 ....
Screamin' .... LP .... Transatlantic .... PR7259 .... 1967 £15 .... £6 ....
Silk And Soul .... LP .... Transatlantic .... PR7404 .... 1967 £15 .... £6 ....
To Seek A New Home .... LP .... Blue Note .... BST84348 .... 1970 £10 .... £4 ....
Walk On By .... LP .... Transatlantic .... PR7476 .... 1967 £15 .... £6 ....
Who Knows What Tomorrow Brings .... LP .... Blue Note .... BST84358 .... 1970 £10 .... £4 ....

McELROY, WILLIE

Fair Of Enniskillen .... LP .... Outlet .... OAS3001 .... 1977 £12 .... £5 .... *Irish*

McENROE & CASH

Rock'n'Roll .... 12" .... Music For Nations .... 12KUT141 .... 1991 £6 .... £2.50 ....

McEVOY, JOHNNY

Johnny McEvoy .... LP .... Hawk .... HALPX112 .... 1973 £10 .... £4 ....

Sounds Like Johnny McEvoy	LP	Halpix	117	1974	£15	£6	

McEWEN, RORY & ALEX & ISLA CAMERON

Folksong Jubilee	LP	HMV	CLP1220	1958	£60	£30	

McEWEN, RORY & ALEX, WITH CAROLYNE & DICK FARINA

Four For Fun	7" EP	Waverley	ELP113	1963	£20	£10	

McFADDEN, BOB

Beat Generation	7"	Coral	Q72378	1959	£8	£4	

McGARRITY, LOU

Salute To Louis	10" LP	Parlophone	PMD1063	1958	£10	£4	

McGEAR, MIKE

After various jokey performances as a member of the Scaffold and of Grimms, the solo recordings by Mike McGear find him in a relatively serious singer-songwriter mode. *McGear* is of considerable interest to Paul McCartney collectors as the album is virtually a Wings album with Mike McGear as guest star. McGear and McCartney are, of course, brothers.

All The Whales In The Ocean	7"	Carrere	CAR144	1980	£10	£5	*picture sleeve*
All The Whales In The Ocean	7"	Carrere	CAR144	1980	£5	£2	
McGear	LP	Warner Bros	K56051	1974	£10	£4	
McGear	LP	Centre Labs		198–	£25	£10	*6 tracks, numbered & autographed*
McGear's Limited Edition	LP	Warner Bros	KMG1	1974	£25	£10	*promo sampler with press kit*
No Lardidar	7"	Conn	SRTS81CUS1112	1981	£10	£5	
Woman	LP	Island	ILPS9191	1972	£10	£4	

McGEEGAN, PAT

Chance Of A Lifetime	7"	Emerald	MD1096	1968	£4	£1.50	

McGHEE, BROWNIE

At The Bunkhouse	LP	Smash	MGS27067	1965	£12	£5	*US*
Black Country Blues	LP	London	LTZC15144	1958	£25	£10	
Blues	10" LP	Folkways	2030	1955	£15	£6	*US*
Bluest	7" EP	Pye	NJE1060	1957	£8	£4	*with Dave Lee*
Brownie McGhee	LP	XTRA	XTRA1021	1965	£10	£4	
Brownie McGhee	LP	Sharp	2003		£25	£10	*US*
Me And My Dog	78	Melodisc	1127	1951	£8	£3	

McGHEE, HOWARD

Howard McGhee And Milt Jackson	LP	London	LTZC15062	1957	£25	£10	
Howard McGhee Sextet	10" LP	Vogue	LDE008	1952	£75	£37.50	
Jazz Concert West Coast	LP	London	LTZC15045	1957	£20	£8	
Last Word	LP	Realm	RM187	1964	£10	£4	
Maggie's Back In Town	LP	Contemporary	LAC12303	1961	£12	£5	
Return Of Howard McGhee	LP	London	LTZN15011	1956	£30	£15	
Sharp Edge	LP	Fontana	FJL906	1967	£10	£4	
Together Again!	LP	Contemporary	LAC12291	1961	£15	£6	*with Teddy Edwards*
With The Frank Hunter Orchestra	LP	London	HAN2033	1957	£30	£15	

McGHEE, STICKS & JOHN LEE HOOKER

Highway Of Blues	LP	Audio Lab	AL1520	1959	£40	£20	*US*

McGINN, MATT

Little Ticks Of Time	LP	XTRA	XTRA1078	1969	£10	£4	
Matt McGinn Again	LP	XTRA	XTRA1057	1968	£12	£5	

McGLYNN, ARTY

McGlynn's Fancy	LP	Mint Julep	JULEP16	1980	£25	£10	

McGOUGH, ROGER

British Poets Of Our Time	LP	Argo	ZPL1190	1975	£20	£8	*B side by Brian Patten*
Summer With Monika	LP	Island	ILPS9551	1978	£10	£4	

McGOUGH & McGEAR

It would be pleasing to imagine that the high value of the album recorded by two-thirds of the Scaffold was in some way a tribute to the songwriting of Mike McGear or the inimitable poetic talents of Roger McGough. Sadly, the value has more to do with the cast of supporting musicians used on this poor-selling album, which includes Jimi Hendrix.

McGough & McGear	CD	Parlophone	CDP7918772	1990	£12	£5	
McGough & McGear	LP	Parlophone	PCS7047	1968	£200	£100	
McGough & McGear	LP	Parlophone	PMC7047	1968	£250	£150	*mono*

McGRATH, BAT

Introducing	LP	Epic	26499	1969	£12	£5	*US*

McGREGOR, CHRIS

The rare *South African Cold Castle Jazz Festival* is the earliest recording to feature the musicians who came to Britain with pianist Chris McGregor, but playing in different groups. After the festival McGregor invited them to join his own Blue Notes. The music played by these South African exiles (who were unable to function as a mixed-race group in their home country) is an exciting blend of modern jazz and kwela. It is heard to best effect on the big band Brotherhood of Breath recordings, but much of the distinctive sound is intact on the small group records. In addition to those listed below, there are also listings of collectable records by other members of McGregor's Blue Notes – Dudu Pukwana, Mongezi Feza, and Louis Moholo.

African Sound	LP	Gallotone		1963	**£150**	**£75**	*South African*
Brotherhood	LP	RCA	SF8269	1972	**£30**	**£15**	
Brotherhood Of Breath	LP	Neon	NE2	1971	**£40**	**£20**	
Cold Castle National Jazz Festival	LP	Gallotone	NSL1010	1963	**£150**	**£75**	*South African, with other artists*
In His Good Time	LP	Ogun	OG521	1979	**£12**	**£5**	
Kwela	LP	77		1968	**£100**	**£50**	
Live At Willisau	LP	Ogun	OG100	1974	**£15**	**£6**	
Up To Earth	LP	Polydor	583072	1968	**£200**	**£100**	*test pressing*
Very Urgent	LP	Polydor	184137	1968	**£50**	**£25**	

McGREGOR, FREDDIE

Wise Words	7"	Fab	FAB261	1973	**£5**	**£2**	*New Establishment B side*

McGRIFF, EDNA

Edna McGriff's The Name	7" EP	Gala	45XP1014	196–	**£6**	**£2.50**	

McGRIFF, JIMMY

All About My Girl	7"	Sue	WI303	1963	**£15**	**£7.50**	
At The Apollo	LP	London	HAC8242	1966	**£30**	**£15**	
Bag Full Of Soul	LP	United Artists	(S)ULP1158	1966	**£12**	**£5**	
Big Band	LP	United Artists	(S)ULP1170	1968	**£12**	**£5**	
Black Pearl	LP	Blue Note	BST84374	1970	**£10**	**£4**	
Blues For Mr Jimmy	LP	London	HAC8247	1966	**£30**	**£15**	
Electric Funk	LP	Blue Note	BST84350	1970	**£15**	**£6**	
Fly Dude	LP	People	PLEO14	1974	**£12**	**£5**	
Good Things Don't Happen Every Day	LP	Groove Merchant	GM2205	1973	**£12**	**£5**	*with Junior Parker*
Gospel Time	LP	Sue	ILP908	1964	**£40**	**£20**	
Greatest Organ Hits	LP	United Artists	UAS29010	1969	**£12**	**£5**	
Groove Grease	LP	Groove Merchant	GM503	1972	**£12**	**£5**	
I've Got A New Woman	LP	Solid State	USS7012	1969	**£12**	**£5**	
I've Got A Woman	7"	Sue	WI317	1964	**£12**	**£6**	
I've Got A Woman	LP	Sue	ILP907	1964	**£40**	**£20**	
If You're Ready Come Go With Me	LP	Groove Merchant	GM529	1972	**£10**	**£4**	*US*
Last Minute	7"	Sue	WI310	1964	**£12**	**£6**	
Let's Stay Together	LP	People	PLEO19	1974	**£12**	**£5**	
Round Midnight	7"	Sue	WI333	1964	**£10**	**£5**	
See See Rider	7"	United Artists	UP1170	1966	**£4**	**£1.50**	
Something To Listen To	LP	Blue Note	BST84364	1970	**£10**	**£4**	
Stump Juice	LP	Groove Merchant	GM3309	1975	**£10**	**£4**	*US*
Worm	7"	United Artists	UP35025	1969	**£5**	**£2**	
Worm	LP	United Artists	UAS29004	1968	**£12**	**£5**	

McGUFFIE, BILL

Bill McGuffie Big Band	LP	Rediffusion	ZS130	1972	**£15**	**£6**	
Concerto For Boogie	7"	Parlophone	MSP6040	1953	**£4**	**£1.50**	
Fugue For Thought (Daleks: Invasion Earth)	7"	Philips	BF1550	1967	**£25**	**£12.50**	
Latin Overtones	LP	Philips	LPS16001	1968	**£25**	**£10**	

McGUINN, ROGER

Airplay Anthology	LP	Columbia	AS353	1975	**£15**	**£6**	*US promo*

McGUINNESS FLINT

McGuinness Flint	LP	Capitol	EAST22625	1970	**£10**	**£4**	

McGUIRE, BARRY

Eve Of Destruction	7"	RCA	RCA1469	1965	**£4**	**£1.50**	
Eve Of Destruction	7" EP	RCA	86900	1965	**£12**	**£6**	*French*
Eve Of Destruction	LP	RCA	RD7751	1965	**£15**	**£6**	
Eve Of Destruction Man	LP	Ember	EMB3362	1966	**£10**	**£4**	
Masters Of War	7"	RCA	RCA1638	1967	**£4**	**£1.50**	
This Precious Time	7" EP	RCA	86904	1966	**£8**	**£4**	*French*
This Precious Time	LP	Dunhill	D50005	1966	**£15**	**£6**	*US, with Mamas & Papas*
World's Last Private Citizen	LP	Dunhill	D50033	1968	**£10**	**£4**	*US*

McGUIRE SISTERS

Beginning To Miss You	7"	Vogue Coral	Q72265	1957	**£4**	**£1.50**	
By Request	10" LP	Coral	CRL56123	1955	**£20**	**£8**	*US*
Children's Holiday	LP	Vogue Coral	LVA9072	1957	**£15**	**£6**	
Delilah Jones	7"	Vogue Coral	Q72161	1956	**£8**	**£4**	
Ding Dong	7"	Vogue Coral	Q72327	1958	**£4**	**£1.50**	
Do You Remember When?	LP	Vogue Coral	LVA9024	1956	**£15**	**£6**	
Endless	7"	Vogue Coral	Q72201	1956	**£4**	**£1.50**	
Forgive Me	7"	Vogue Coral	Q72296	1957	**£4**	**£1.50**	
Goodnight My Love, Pleasant Dreams	7"	Vogue Coral	Q72216	1957	**£4**	**£1.50**	
Greetings	LP	Coral	CRL57225	1958	**£15**	**£6**	*US*
He	7"	Vogue Coral	Q72108	1955	**£8**	**£4**	
He	LP	Coral	CRL57033	195–	**£15**	**£6**	*US*
Heart	7"	Vogue Coral	Q72238	1957	**£4**	**£1.50**	
His And Hers	LP	Coral	LVA9140	1961	**£15**	**£6**	

In The Alps	7"	Vogue Coral	Q72188	1956	£4	**£1.50**	
Interlude	7"	Vogue Coral	Q72272	1957	£4	**£1.50**	
Lonesome Polecat	7"	Vogue Coral	Q2028	1954	£6	**£2.50**	
May You Always	7" EP	Coral	FEP2033	1959	£10	**£5**	
May You Always	LP	Coral	LVA9115	1959	£15	**£6**	
McGuire Sisters	7" EP	Coral	FEP2001	1958	£10	**£5**	
Melody Of Love	7"	Vogue Coral	Q72052	1955	£5	**£2**	
Missing	7"	Vogue Coral	Q72145	1956	£5	**£2**	
Musical Magic	LP	Coral	CRL57180	1957	£15	**£6**	*US*
No More	7"	Vogue Coral	Q72050	1955	£15	**£7.50**	
Our Golden Favorites	LP	Coral	LVA9133	1960	£10	**£4**	
Sincerely	LP	Coral	CRL57052	195–	£15	**£6**	*US*
Something's Gotta Give	7"	Vogue Coral	Q72082	1955	£5	**£2**	
Sugartime	7"	Coral	Q72305	1958	£5	**£2**	
Sugartime	LP	Coral	CRL57217	1958	£15	**£6**	*US*
Teenage Party	LP	Coral	LVA9073	1957	£15	**£6**	
Tip Toe Through The Tulips	7"	Vogue Coral	Q72209	1956	£4	**£1.50**	
Volare	7" EP	Coral	FEP2006	1958	£10	**£5**	
When The Lights Are Low	LP	Coral	LVA9082	1958	£10	**£4**	
Without Him	7"	Vogue Coral	Q72249	1957	£4	**£1.50**	
Young And Foolish	7"	Vogue Coral	Q72117	1956	£5	**£2**	

McKAY, FREDDIE

Lonely Man	LP	Dragon	DRLS5005	1974	£12	**£5**	
Our Rendezvous	7"	Grape	GR3060	1973	£5	**£2**	*Soul Dynamites B side*
Our Rendezvous	7"	Dragon	DRA1012	1973	£5	**£2**	
Picture On The Wall	7"	Banana	BA348	1971	£5	**£2**	*Sound Dimension B side*
Picture On The Wall	LP	Attack	ATLP1013	1973	£15	**£6**	
Picture On The Wall	LP	Banana	BALPS01	1971	£40	**£20**	
Sweet You, Sour You	7"	Banana	BA358	1971	£5	**£2**	

McKAY, SCOTT

Cold Cold Heart	7"	London	HLU9885	1964	£4	**£1.50**	
I Can't Make Your Way	7"	Columbia	DB8147	1967	£20	**£10**	

McKAY, TONY

Nobody's Perfect	7"	Polydor	BM56513	1966	£25	**£12.50**	

McKENNA, MAE

Mae McKenna	LP	Transatlantic	TRA297	1975	£10	**£4**	

McKENNA, VAL

Baby Do It	7"	Piccadilly	7N35237	1965	£4	**£1.50**	
I Can't Believe What You Say	7"	Piccadilly	7N35286	1966	£4	**£1.50**	
Mixed Up Shook Up Girl	7"	Piccadilly	7N35256	1965	£5	**£2**	

McKENNA MENDELSON MAINLINE

Better Watch Out	7"	Liberty	LBF15235	1969	£4	**£1.50**	
Blues	LP	Paragon	No.15	1968	£50	**£25**	*Canadian*
Stink	LP	Liberty	LBS83251	1969	£25	**£10**	

McKENZIE, DOUG & BOB

Take Off	7"	Mercury	HOSER1	1982	£12	**£6**	

McKENZIE, JUDY

Judy	LP	Key	KL005	1970	£15	**£6**	
Peace And Love And Freedom	LP	Key	KL009	1971	£15	**£6**	

McKENZIE, MARLENE

Left Me For Another	7"	Double D	DD106	1968	£6	**£2.50**	*Bobby Aitken B side*

McKENZIE, SCOTT

Voice Of Scott McKenzie	LP	CBS	(S)BPG63157	1967	£10	**£4**	

McKINLEY, RAY & JOE MARSALA

Dixieland Jazz Battle	10" LP	Brunswick	LA8545	1952	£12	**£5**	

McKINLEYS

Give Him My Love	7"	Columbia	DB7583	1965	£8	**£4**	
Someone Cares For Me	7"	Columbia	DB7230	1964	£8	**£4**	
Sweet And Tender Romance	7"	Parlophone	R5211	1964	£6	**£2.50**	
When He Comes Along	7"	Columbia	DB7310	1964	£5	**£2**	

McKUEN, ROD

Happy Is A Boy Named Me	7"	London	HLU8390	1957	£25	**£12.50**	
Summer Love	LP	Decca	DL8714	1958	£20	**£8**	*US*
Two Brothers	7"	Brunswick	05828	1960	£8	**£4**	

McKUSICK, HAL

East Coast Jazz	LP	London	LTZN15006	1956	£40	**£20**	
Hal McKusick Quartet	LP	Parlophone	PMC1093	1959	£20	**£8**	
Hal McKusick Quintet	LP	Vogue Coral	LVA9062	1957	£25	**£10**	
Jazz At The Academy	LP	Vogue Coral	LVA9054	1957	£25	**£10**	

McLACHLAN, SARAH

Fumbling Towards Ecstacy	CD	Arista	SARAH1	1994	£15	**£6**	*promo sampler*

McLAIN, TOMMY

Title	Format	Label	Cat. No.	Year	Mint	VG	Notes
Sweet Dreams	7"	London	HL10065	1966	£6	£2.50	
Think It Over	7"	London	HL10091	1966	£5	£2	

McLAREN, MALCOLM

Title	Format	Label	Cat. No.	Year	Mint	VG	Notes
Madame Butterfly	CD-s	Virgin	CDT30	1988	£5	£2	*3" single*

McLAUGHLIN, DINNY

Title	Format	Label	Cat. No.	Year	Mint	VG	Notes
Rake O'Reels And A Clatter Of Jigs	LP	Robin	ROBALM027	1971	£20	£8	*Irish*

McLAUGHLIN, JOHN

John McLaughlin apparently spent much of the sixties driving a van for an amplification company, while playing his guitar wherever and whenever he could. He was given the chance to make an album for the Marmalade label, but while *Extrapolation* is an above-average British jazz record of the period, it was almost immediately eclipsed by McLaughlin's good fortune in being invited to play with Miles Davis. As a player on the key albums to start electric jazz, it was therefore John McLaughlin who made highly amplified guitar respectable in jazz (although he had to work up to it – the tone on both *In A Silent Way* and *Bitches Brew* is quite mild).

Title	Format	Label	Cat. No.	Year	Mint	VG	Notes
Devotion	LP	Douglas	DGL65075	1972	£10	£4	
Extrapolation	LP	Marmalade	608007	1969	£15	£6	
Extrapolation	LP	Polydor	2343012	1970	£10	£4	
Love, Devotion & Surrender	LP	CBS	Q69037	1974	£15	£6	*quad, with Carlos Santana*
My Goal's Beyond	LP	Douglas	DGL69014	1972	£10	£4	
Where Fortune Smiles	LP	Dawn	DNLS3018	1971	£30	£15	*with John Surman and others*

McLEAN, DON

Title	Format	Label	Cat. No.	Year	Mint	VG	Notes
American Pie	CD-s	Liberty	CDEMCT3	1991	£5	£2	

McLEAN, JACKIE

Title	Format	Label	Cat. No.	Year	Mint	VG	Notes
'Bout Soul	LP	Blue Note	BST84284	1968	£15	£6	
Action Action Action	LP	Blue Note	BLP/BST84218	1965	£30	£15	
Bluesnik	LP	Blue Note	BLP/BST84067	196–	£25	£10	
Capuchin Swing	LP	Blue Note	BLP/BST84038	196–	£25	£10	
Demon's Dance	LP	Blue Note	BST84345	1969	£15	£6	
Destination Out	LP	Blue Note	BLP/BST84165	1964	£25	£10	
Fickle Sonance	LP	Blue Note	BLP/BST84089	1961	£40	£20	
It's Time!	LP	Blue Note	BLP/BST84179	1964	£30	£15	
Jackie's Bag	LP	Blue Note	BLP/BST84051	196–	£40	£20	
Jackie's Pal	LP	Esquire	32111	1960	£25	£10	
Let Freedom Ring	LP	Blue Note	BLP/BST84106	1962	£25	£10	
Lights Out	LP	Esquire	32041	1958	£30	£15	
New And Old Gospel	LP	Blue Note	BLP/BST84262	1967	£25	£10	
One Step Beyond	LP	Blue Note	BLP/BST84137	1963	£25	£10	
Right Now!	LP	Blue Note	BLP/BST84215	1965	£30	£15	

McLEAN, NANA

Title	Format	Label	Cat. No.	Year	Mint	VG	Notes
Little Love	7"	Banana	BA355	1971	£5	£2	*Sound Dimension B side*

McLEAN, PHIL

Title	Format	Label	Cat. No.	Year	Mint	VG	Notes
Big Mouth Bill	7"	Top Rank	JAR613	1962	£5	£2	
Small Sad Sam	7"	Top Rank	JAR597	1961	£5	£2	

McLEASH, GERALD

Title	Format	Label	Cat. No.	Year	Mint	VG	Notes
False Reaper	7"	G.G.	GG4516	1971	£4	£1.50	*G.G. All Stars B side*

McLOLLIE, OSCAR HONEYJUMPERS

Title	Format	Label	Cat. No.	Year	Mint	VG	Notes
Love Me Tonight	7"	London	HL8130	1955	£150	£75	

McLUHAN, MARSHALL

Title	Format	Label	Cat. No.	Year	Mint	VG	Notes
Medium Is The Message	LP	Columbia	CL2701/CS9501	1967	£25	£10	*US*

McLYNNS

Title	Format	Label	Cat. No.	Year	Mint	VG	Notes
Old Market Street	LP	CBS	63836	1970	£75	£37.50	

McMANUS, ROSS

The front-man with the Joe Loss Orchestra is likely to be best remembered as the singer of the 'secret lemonade drinker' TV advertisement. His son – then known by his given name of Declan – sang backing vocals on the same song, before choosing the stage name of Elvis Costello in order to launch his solo career.

Title	Format	Label	Cat. No.	Year	Mint	VG	Notes
Sings Elvis Presley's Golden Hits	LP	Golden Guinea		196–	£10	£4	

McMILLAN, RODDY

Title	Format	Label	Cat. No.	Year	Mint	VG	Notes
McPherson's Rant	7" EP	Beltona	SEP83	1960	£5	£2	

McNABB, IAN

Title	Format	Label	Cat. No.	Year	Mint	VG	Notes
Great Dreams Of Heaven	CD-s	WayCool	14CD	1991	£5	£2	
Merseybeast	CD	Island	5242402	1996	£15	£6	*double*
These Are The Days	CD-s	Fat Cat	FC001CD	1991	£5	£2	

McNAIR, BARBARA

Title	Format	Label	Cat. No.	Year	Mint	VG	Notes
Here I Am	LP	Motown	(S)644	1966	£30	£15	*US*
I Enjoy Being A Girl	7" EP	Warner Bros	WEP6129	1964	£25	£12.50	

I Enjoy Being A Girl	LP	Warner Bros	W(S)1541	1964	**£20**	**£8**	US
Livin' End	LP	Warner Bros	W(S)1570	1964	**£20**	**£8**	US
Real Barbara McNair	LP	Motown	S680	1969	**£25**	**£10**	US
You're Gonna Love My Baby	7"	Tamla Motown	TMG544	1966	**£200**	**£100**	

McNAIR, HAROLD

Affectionate Fink	LP	Island	ILP926	1965	**£60**	**£30**	
Fence	LP	B&C	CAS1016	1970	**£40**	**£20**	
Flute And Nut	LP	RCA	INTS1096	1970	**£40**	**£20**	
Harold McNair	LP	RCA	SF7969	1968	**£40**	**£20**	
Harold McNair	LP	B&C	CAS1045	1971	**£40**	**£20**	
Hipster	7"	RCA	RCA1742	1968	**£6**	**£2.50**	

McNEELY, BIG JAY

Big Jay McNeely	10" LP	Federal	29596	1954	**£150**	**£75**	US
Big Jay McNeely	LP	Warner Bros	W(S)1523	1963	**£20**	**£8**	US
Big Jay McNeely In 3-D	LP	King	650	1959	**£50**	**£25**	US
Big Jay McNeely In 3-D	LP	Federal	395530	1956	**£100**	**£50**	US
Big Jay's Party	LP	Warner Bros	WM8143	1964	**£15**	**£6**	
Rhythm And Blues Concert	10" LP	Savoy	MG15045	1955	**£100**	**£50**	US
Something On Your Mind	7"	Top Rank	JAR169	1959	**£8**	**£4**	
Something On Your Mind	7"	Sue	WI373	1965	**£15**	**£7.50**	

McNEIL, DAVID

Don't Let Your Chance Go By	7"	President	PT212	1968	**£8**	**£4**	

McNEIL, PAUL

Contemporary Folk	LP	Decca	LK4699	1965	**£25**	**£10**	
Traditionally At The Troubadour	LP	Decca	LK4803	1966	**£40**	**£20**	
You Ain't Goin' Nowhere	7"	MGM	MGM1408	1968	**£6**	**£2.50**	*with Linda Peters*

McOIL

All Our Hopes	LP	private	2066	1979	**£100**	**£50**	German

McPARTLAND, JIMMY

Dixieland At Carnegie Hall	LP	Columbia	33SX1122	1959	**£12**	**£5**	
Shades Of Bix	10" LP	Vogue Coral	LRA10006	1954	**£15**	**£6**	

McPARTLAND, MARIAN

Marian McPartland	10" LP	Capitol	LC6828	1956	**£15**	**£6**	
Marian McPartland	LP	Capitol	LCT6017	1955	**£12**	**£5**	
Marian McPartland Trio	LP	Capitol	T785	1957	**£12**	**£5**	
With You In Mind	LP	Capitol	T895	1958	**£12**	**£5**	

McPEAKE FAMILY

At Home With The McPeakes	LP	Fontana	(S)TL5258	1965	**£25**	**£10**	
Delightful McPeakes	LP	Philips	6856017	1967	**£25**	**£10**	
Irish Folk!	LP	Fontana	TL5214	1964	**£25**	**£10**	
Irish To Be Sure	LP	Windmill	WMD151	1972	**£25**	**£10**	
McPeake	LP	Evolution	Z1002	1969	**£60**	**£30**	
McPeake Family	LP	Topic	12T87	1963	**£40**	**£20**	
McPeake Family Of Belfast	LP	Transatlantic	XTRA5012	1966	**£15**	**£6**	
Pleasant And Delightful	LP	Fontana	(S)TL5433	1967	**£25**	**£10**	

McPHATTER, CLYDE

Best Of Clyde McPhatter	LP	Atlantic	ATL5001	1964	**£50**	**£25**	
Clyde	LP	Atlantic	8031	1959	**£125**	**£62.50**	US
Clyde McPhatter	7" EP	London	REE1202	1959	**£200**	**£100**	best auctioned
Come What May	7"	London	HLE8707	1958	**£40**	**£20**	
Everybody's Somebody's Fool	7"	Stateside	SS487	1966	**£4**	**£1.50**	
Golden Blues Hits	LP	Mercury	MG2/SR60655	1962	**£30**	**£15**	US
Greatest Hits	LP	Mercury	MG2/SR60783	1963	**£25**	**£10**	US
Greatest Hits	LP	MGM	(S)E3866	1960	**£30**	**£15**	US
Just Give Me A Ring	7"	London	HLE9079	1960	**£30**	**£15**	
Just To Hold Your Hand	7"	London	HLE8462	1957	**£100**	**£50**	
Lavender Lace	7"	Stateside	SS592	1967	**£4**	**£1.50**	
Let's Start Over Again	LP	MGM	(S)E3775	1959	**£40**	**£20**	US
Let's Try Again	7"	MGM	MGM1048	1959	**£10**	**£5**	
Little Bitty Pretty One	7"	Mercury	AMT1181	1962	**£8**	**£4**	
Live At The Apollo	LP	Mercury	MG2/SR60915	1964	**£30**	**£15**	US
Long Lonely Nights	7"	London	HLE8476	1957	**£75**	**£37.50**	
Love Ballads	LP	Atlantic	8024	1958	**£150**	**£75**	US
Lover Please	7"	Mercury	AMT1174	1962	**£10**	**£5**	
Lover Please	LP	Mercury	MMC14120	1963	**£60**	**£30**	
Lover's Question	7"	London	HLE8755	1958	**£25**	**£12.50**	
Lovey Dovey	7"	London	HLE8878	1959	**£25**	**£12.50**	
Masquerade Is Over	7"	MGM	MGM1014	1959	**£10**	**£5**	
McPhatter & Wilson Meet the Dominoes	LP	Ember	NR5001	1962	**£100**	**£50**	*with Jackie Wilson*
Rhythm And Soul	LP	Mercury	MG2/SR60750	1962	**£40**	**£20**	US
Rock And Cry	7"	London	HLE8525	1957	**£60**	**£30**	
Seven Days	7"	London	HLE8250	1956	**£300**	**£180**	best auctioned
Seven Days	7"	London	HL7006	1956	**£75**	**£37.50**	export
Shot Of Rhythm & Blues	7"	Stateside	SS567	1966	**£5**	**£2**	
Shot Of Rhythm & Blues	7"	Pama	PM775	1969	**£4**	**£1.50**	
Since You've Been Gone	7"	London	HLE8906	1959	**£25**	**£12.50**	
Songs Of The Big City	LP	Mercury	MG2/SR60902	1964	**£30**	**£15**	US

Ta Ta	7"	Mercury	AMT1108	1960	£6	£2.50	
Ta Ta	LP	Mercury	MG2/SR60597	1960	£40	£20	US
Think Me A Kiss	7"	MGM	MGM1061	1960	£8	£4	
This Is Not Goodbye	7" EP	MGM	MGMEP739	1960	£100	£50	
Tomorrow Is A-Comin'	7"	Mercury	AMT1136	1961	£6	£2.50	
Treasure Of Love	7"	London	HLE8293	1956	£175	£87.50	
Tribute	LP	Atlantic	K30033	1973	£10	£4	
Twice As Nice	7"	MGM	MGM1040	1959	£10	£5	
Twice As Nice	7" EP	MGM	MGMEP705	1959	£100	£50	
You Went Back On Your Word	7"	London	HLE9000	1959	£30	£15	
You're For Me	7"	Mercury	AMT1120	1960	£6	£2.50	

McPHEE, TONY

The lead guitarist of the Groundhogs has also made a number of solo recordings. He continued to play live until his death in 1999, though without issuing any more records.

I Asked For Water . . . But She Gave Me Gasoline	LP	Liberty	LBS83252	1969	£60	£30	with other artists
Me & The Devil	LP	Liberty	LBL/LBS83190	1968	£60	£30	
Someone To Love Me	7"	Purdah	453501	1966	£100	£50	
Time Of Action	7"	Tony McPhee	TS001	198–	£6	£2.50	
Two Sides Of Tony McPhee	LP	WWA	WWA001	1973	£15	£6	

McPHERSON, CHARLES

Bebop Revisited	LP	Stateside	SL10151	1965	£12	£5	
Siku Ya Bibi	LP	Mainstream	MSL1004	1973	£10	£4	

McPHERSON, GILLIAN

Poets And Painters And Performers Of Blues	LP	RCA	SF8220	1971	£20	£8	

McQUAID, JOHN

Stations In The Sky	LP	Royalty	RR101085201	1985	£10	£4	US

McRAE, CARMEN

Afterglow	LP	Brunswick	LAT8257	1958	£10	£4	
Blue Moon	LP	Brunswick	LAT8147	1956	£10	£4	
Book Of Ballads	LP	London	HAR2185	1959	£12	£5	
By Special Request	LP	Brunswick	LAT8104	1956	£12	£5	
London's Girl Friends No. 3	7" EP	London	REN1094	1957	£10	£5	
Love Is Here To Stay	7"	Brunswick	05502	1955	£4	£1.50	
Play For Keeps	7"	London	HLR8837	1959	£5	£2	
So Much	7" EP	Mercury	ZEP10132	1962	£5	£2	
Take Five	7"	Fontana	H379	1962	£5	£2	with Dave Brubeck
Torchy	LP	Brunswick	LAT8133	1956	£10	£4	
Whatever Lola Wants	7"	Brunswick	05652	1957	£4	£1.50	

McSHANN, JAY

Kansas City Memories	10" LP	Brunswick	LA8735	1956	£40	£20	

McTELL, BLIND WILLIE

Atlanta Twelve String Guitar	LP	Atlantic	K40400	1973	£10	£4	
Blind Willie McTell	LP	Storyville	670186	1967	£12	£5	
Blind Willie McTell 1927–35	LP	Roots	RL324	196–	£10	£4	
Last Session	LP	Transatlantic	PR1040	1966	£10	£4	

McTELL, RALPH

8 Frames A Second	LP	Transatlantic	TRA165	1968	£10	£4	
My Side Of Your Window	LP	Transatlantic	TRA209	1969	£10	£4	
Spiral Staircase	LP	Transatlantic	TRA177	1969	£10	£4	
You, Well Meaning, Brought Me Here	LP	Famous	SFMA5753	1971	£10	£4	

McVAY, RAY

Genesis	7"	Parlophone	R5460	1966	£4	£1.50	
Kinda Kinky	7"	Pye	7N15816	1965	£12	£6	
Revenge	7"	Pye	7N15777	1965	£20	£10	
They Call Me Mr Tibbs	7"	Philips	6006083	1971	£8	£4	

McVIE, CHRISTINE

Christine McVie	CD	WEA	9250592	1984	£12	£5	
Got A Hold On Me	12"	Warner Bros	W9372PT	1984	£6	£2.50	picture disc

McVOY, CARL

Tootsie	7"	London	HLU8617	1958	£150	£75	

McWILLIAMS, DAVID

'The Days Of Pearly Spencer' by David McWilliams, with its megaphone vocals and fountaining strings, was heavily promoted by the pirate radio stations and is, in consequence, particularly redolent of that era. The song is something of an oddity within McWilliams's recordings, however, as none of his other folky material makes any attempt to match the inventiveness of Pearly Spencer's arrangement. Everyone remembers the single as having been a hit, but in fact it was only when Marc Almond covered the song in an identical arrangement some twenty-four years later that it climbed into the top five.

David McWilliams Vol. 2	LP	Major Minor	S/MMLP10	1967	£12	£5	
David McWilliams Vol. 3	LP	Major Minor	S/MMLP11	1968	£12	£5	
Days Of David McWilliams	LP	Major Minor	MCP5026	1969	£12	£5	
Days Of Pearly Spencer	7"	Major Minor	MM533	1968	£6	£2.50	
Days Of Pearly Spencer	7"	Parlophone	R5886	1971	£4	£1.50	
God And My Country	7"	CBS	202348	1966	£4	£1.50	
Lord Offaly	LP	Dawn	DNLS3039	1972	£10	£4	

Singing Songs By David McWilliams	LP	Major Minor	S/MMLP2	1967	**£15**	**£6**	
Stranger	7"	Major Minor	MM592	1969	**£4**	**£1.50**	

ME & THEM

Everything I Do Is Wrong	7"	Pye	7N15631	1964	**£5**	**£2**	
Feel So Good	7"	Pye	7N15596	1964	**£6**	**£2.50**	
Getaway	7"	Pye	7N15683	1964	**£5**	**£2**	

MEAN STREET DEALERS

Bent Needles	LP	Graduate	GRADLP1	1979	**£12**	**£5**	
Bent Needles	LP	Mean Street Dealers	MSD001	1979	**£25**	**£10**	
Japanese Motorbikes	7"	Graduate	GRAD5	1980	**£5**	**£2**	

MEANIES

Waiting For You	7"	Vendetta	VD002	1979	**£50**	**£25**	

MEASLES

Casting My Spell	7"	Columbia	DB7531	1965	**£20**	**£10**	
Kicks	7"	Columbia	DB7875	1966	**£15**	**£7.50**	
Night People	7"	Columbia	DB7673	1965	**£12**	**£6**	
Walking In	7"	Columbia	DB8029	1966	**£12**	**£6**	

MEAT LOAF

Bat Out Of Hell	12"	Epic	SEPC127018	1979	**£10**	**£5**	*red vinyl*
Bat Out Of Hell	LP	Epic	EPC82419	1982	**£15**	**£6**	*audiophile*
Bat Out Of Hell	LP	Epic	EPC1182419	1982	**£20**	**£8**	*picture disc*
Clap Your Hands, Stamp Your Feet	7"	Ode	ODS66304	1975	**£40**	**£20**	
Dead Ringer For Love	7"	Epic	EPCA111697	1981	**£4**	**£1.50**	*picture disc*
Dead Ringer For Love	CD-s	Epic	6569822	1991	**£5**	**£2**	
Deadringer	LP	Epic	EPC1183645	1985	**£10**	**£4**	*picture disc*
Getting Away With Murder	10"	Arista	ARIST10683	1986	**£6**	**£2.50**	*round sleeve*
Getting Away With Murder	7"	Arista	ARIST683P	1986	**£5**	**£2**	*shaped picture disc*
If You Really Want To	12"	Epic	EPCAWA3357	1983	**£6**	**£2.50**	*picture disc*
In Europe '82	12"	Epic	EPCA122251	1982	**£8**	**£4**	
In Europe '82	12"	Epic	EPCA122251	1982	**£12**	**£6**	*clear vinyl*
Live At Father's Place	LP	Epic	AS409	1978	**£15**	**£6**	*US promo*
Live At The El Mocambo	LP	CBS	CDN9	1978	**£15**	**£6**	*Canadian promo*
Meatloaf (Featuring Stoney And Meatloaf)	LP	Prodigal	PDL2010	1979	**£10**	**£4**	*with Stoney*
Midnight At The Lost And Found	7"	Epic	EPCAWA3748	1983	**£5**	**£2**	*picture disc*
Midnight At The Lost And Found	7"	Epic	EPCADA3748	1983	**£10**	**£5**	*signed double*
Midnight At The Lost And Found	7"	Epic	EPCADA3748	1983	**£5**	**£2**	*double*
Modern Girl	12"	Arista	ARIPD12585	1984	**£6**	**£2.50**	*picture disc*
Modern Girl	7"	Arista	ARISDP585	1984	**£8**	**£4**	*shaped picture disc, poster, plinth*
Modern Girl	7"	Arista	ARISDP585	1984	**£5**	**£2**	*shaped picture disc*
More Than You Deserve	7"	RSO	RS407	1974	**£20**	**£10**	*US*
Nowhere Fast	7"	Arista	ARISG600	1985	**£5**	**£2**	*signed*
Nowhere Fast	7"	Arista	ARISD600	1985	**£5**	**£2**	*shaped picture disc*
Piece Of The Action	12"	Arista	ARIST12603	1985	**£6**	**£2.50**	*with poster*
Piece Of The Action	7"	Arista	ARISD603	1985	**£6**	**£2.50**	*shaped picture disc*
Razor's Edge	7"	Epic	EPCAWA3511	1983	**£4**	**£1.50**	*picture disc*
Read 'Em And Weep	12"	Epic	EPCA122012	1982	**£6**	**£2.50**	
Special Girl	CD-s	Arista	RISCD14	1987	**£6**	**£2.50**	
Stand By Me	7"	Ode	ODS66304	1975	**£30**	**£15**	
Stoney & Meatloaf	LP	Rare Earth	SRE3005	1972	**£15**	**£6**	*with Stoney*
Time For Heroes	12"	Orpheum	012387	1987	**£40**	**£20**	*US, with Brian May, Tangerine Dream B side*
Time For Heroes	7"	Orpheum	060187	1987	**£40**	**£20**	*US, with Brian May, Tangerine Dream B side*
Time For Heroes	CD-s	Orpheum	060187D	1987	**£40**	**£20**	*US, with Brian May, Tangerine Dream B side*
What You See Is What You Get	7"	Prodigal	PROD10	1979	**£5**	**£2**	*with Stoney*
What You See Is What You Get	7"	Rare Earth	RES103	1971	**£8**	**£4**	*Stoney And Meatloaf credit*

MEAT PUPPETS

In A Car	CD-s	SST	SST044CD	1988	**£5**	**£2**	

MEAT WHIPLASH

Don't Slip Up	7"	Creation	CRE020	1985	**£6**	**£2.50**	*sleeve photo of band by fence*

MEATBEAT MANIFESTO

I Got The Fear	12"	Sweatbox	SOX023R	1988	**£6**	**£2.50**	
Suck Hard	12"	Sweatbox	SOX023	1987	**£8**	**£4**	

MEC OP SINGERS

Dies Irae	7" EP	DiscAZ	1071	1967	**£8**	**£4**	*French*

MECKI MARK MEN

Marathon	LP	Sonet	SLP2521	1971	**£12**	**£5**	*Swedish*
Mecki Mark Band	LP	Limelight	86054	1968	**£15**	**£6**	*US*
Running In The Summernight	LP	Limelight	86068	1969	**£15**	**£6**	*US*

MEDDY EVILS

Title	Format	Label	Cat. No.	Year	Price	Price	Notes
Find Somebody To Love	7"	Pye	7N15941	1965	£75	£37.50	
Ma's Place	7"	Pye	7N17091	1966	£75	£37.50	

MEDIA

Title	Format	Label	Cat. No.	Year	Price	Price	Notes
Back On The Beach Again	7"	Brain Booster Music	4	1980	£5	£2	

MEDICINE HEAD

Title	Format	Label	Cat. No.	Year	Price	Price	Notes
Coast To Coast	7"	Dandelion	5075	1970	£6	£2.50	
Dark Side Of The Moon	LP	Polydor	2310166	1971	£15	£6	
Heavy On The Drum	LP	Dandelion	DAN8005	1971	£20	£8	
His Guiding Hand	7"	Dandelion	4661	1970	£10	£5	
New Bottles Old Medicine	LP	Dandelion	63757	1970	£20	£8	
Pictures In The Sky	7"	Dandelion	DAN7003	1971	£5	£2	*picture sleeve*

MEDITATIONS

Title	Format	Label	Cat. No.	Year	Price	Price	Notes
Transcendental Meditation	7"	Liberty	LBF15045	1968	£4	£1.50	

MEDITATORS

Title	Format	Label	Cat. No.	Year	Price	Price	Notes
When You Go To A Party	7"	Big	BG302	1970	£4	£1.50	

MEDIUM

Title	Format	Label	Cat. No.	Year	Price	Price	Notes
Edward Never Lies	7"	CBS	3404	1968	£15	£7.50	
Medium	LP	Gamma	GS503	1969	£20	£8	*US*

MEDLEY, BILL

Title	Format	Label	Cat. No.	Year	Price	Price	Notes
Peace Brother Peace	7"	MGM	MGM1456	1968	£4	£1.50	

MEDLIN, JOE

Title	Format	Label	Cat. No.	Year	Price	Price	Notes
I Kneel At Your Throne	7"	Mercury	AMT1032	1959	£4	£1.50	

MEDWIN, MICHAEL & OTHERS

Title	Format	Label	Cat. No.	Year	Price	Price	Notes
Army Game	7"	HMV	POP490	1958	£4	£1.50	

MEEHAN, KEITH

Title	Format	Label	Cat. No.	Year	Price	Price	Notes
Darkness Of My Life	7"	Marmalade	598016	1969	£8	£4	*Tony Meehan B side*

MEEHAN, TONY

Title	Format	Label	Cat. No.	Year	Price	Price	Notes
Song Of Mexico	7"	Decca	F11801	1964	£5	£2	

MEEK, JOE ORCHESTRA

Title	Format	Label	Cat. No.	Year	Price	Price	Notes
Kennedy March	7"	Decca	F11796	1963	£25	£12.50	

MEGADETH

Title	Format	Label	Cat. No.	Year	Price	Price	Notes
Anarchy In The UK	7"	Capitol	CLP480	1988	£6	£2.50	*shaped picture disc*
Hangar 18	7"	Capitol	CLPD604	1991	£5	£2	*shaped picture disc*
Hangar 18	CD-s	Capitol	CDCL604	1991	£5	£2	
Holy Wars . . . The Punishment Due	CD-s	Capitol	CDCL588	1990	£5	£2	
Killing Is My Business	LP	Music For Nations	MFN46DM	1988	£12	£5	*double with poster*
Mary Jane	7"	Capitol	CLP489	1988	£5	£2	*picture disc*
No More Mr Nice Guy	7"	SBK	SBKPD4	1990	£5	£2	*shaped picture disc*
No More Mr Nice Guy	CD-s	SBK	CDSBK4	1989	£6	£2.50	
Peace Sells . . . But Who's Buying?	LP	Capitol	ESTP2022	1986	£10	£4	*picture disc*
Skin O' My Teeth	CD-s	Capitol	CDCL669	1992	£5	£2	*picture disc*
Sweating Bullets	CD-s	Capitol	CDCLX682	1993	£5	£2	*in collectors' box*
Symphony For Destruction	CD-s	Capitol	CDCL662	1992	£5	£2	
Wake Up Dead	12"	Capitol	12CL476	1987	£6	£2.50	
Wake Up Dead	12"	Capitol	12CL476	1987	£8	£4	*with certificate*
Wake Up Dead	7"	Capitol	CL476	1987	£4	£1.50	
Wake Up Dead	7"	Capitol	CLP476	1987	£8	£4	*shaped picture disc*
Youthanasia/Hidden Treasures	CD	Capitol	724383273928	1996	£30	£15	*double*

MEGAS

Title	Format	Label	Cat. No.	Year	Price	Price	Notes
Hofudlausnir	LP	Gramm	GRAMM36	1988	£20	£8	*Icelandic*
Loftmynd	LP	Gramm	GRAMM34	1987	£20	£8	*Icelandic*

MEGATON

Title	Format	Label	Cat. No.	Year	Price	Price	Notes
Megaton	LP	Deram	SMLR1086	1971	£250	£150	
Megaton	LP	Decca	SLK16690P	1971	£75	£37.50	*German*
Out Of Your Own Little World	7"	Deram	DM331	1971	£20	£10	

MEGATON (2)

Title	Format	Label	Cat. No.	Year	Price	Price	Notes
Aluminium Lady	7"	Hot Metal	HMM69	1981	£25	£12.50	

MEGATONS

Title	Format	Label	Cat. No.	Year	Price	Price	Notes
Shimmy Shimmy Walk	7"	Sue	WI325	1965	£15	£7.50	

MEGATRONS

Title	Format	Label	Cat. No.	Year	Price	Price	Notes
Velvet Waters	7"	Top Rank	JAR146	1959	£4	£1.50	
Whispering Winds	7"	Top Rank	JAR236	1959	£4	£1.50	

MEHEGAN, JOHN

Title	Format	Label	Cat. No.	Year	Price	Price	Notes
First Mehegan Vol. 1	7" EP	London	EZC19005	1956	£5	£2	
First Mehegan Vol. 2	7" EP	London	EZC19015	1956	£5	£2	

MEID, LOTHAR

Mensch Dieser Klaus	LP	Philips	6305283	1975	£12	£5	German

MEIGHAN, BOB

Dancer	LP	Capitol	ST11555	1976	£15	£6	US
Me'hun	LP	Capitol	ST11686	1977	£15	£6	US

MEINERT, CARSTEN

Musictrain	LP	Spectator	SL1007	1970	£15	£6	Danish
To You	LP	Spectator	SL1001	1969	£40	£20	Danish

MEISENFLOO

Meisenfloo	LP	Lagua	60723	1972	£50	£25	German

MEKONS

Dream And Lie Of . . . (Amnesia)	CD-s	Blast First	BFFP53CD	1989	£5	£2	
Never Been In A Riot	7"	Fast Product	FAST1	1978	£6	£2.50	

MEL & DAVE

Spinning Wheel	7"	Upsetter	US330	1970	£5	£2	

MEL & TIM

Starting All Over Again	LP	Stax	2325090	1973	£10	£4	

MELANIE

Affectionately	LP	Buddah	203028	1969	£10	£4	
All The Right Noises	LP	Buddah	2318034	1971	£10	£4	
Born To Be	LP	Buddah	203019	1969	£10	£4	
Candles In The Rain	LP	Buddah	2318009	1970	£10	£4	
Four Sides Of Melanie	LP	Buddah	26590013	1974	£12	£5	double
Garden In The City	LP	Buddah	2318054	1972	£10	£4	scratch & sniff sleeve
Gather Me	LP	Buddah	2322002	1971	£10	£4	
Good Book	LP	Buddah	2322001	1971	£10	£4	
Leftover Wine	LP	Buddah	2318011	1970	£10	£4	
Ruby Tuesday	CD-s	Silvertone	CDYUM117	1989	£5	£2	
Stoneground Words	LP	Neighborhood	NHTC251	1972	£10	£4	
Tuning My Guitar	7"	Buddah	201063	1969	£8	£4	

MELLE, GIL

Gil Melle Quintet	10" LP	Vogue	LDE141	1955	£50	£25	

MELLEN, SUSAN

Mellen Bird	LP	Mam	MAMAS1014	1975	£20	£8	

MELLENCAMP, JOHN

Mr Happy Go Lucky	CD	Mercury	3145328962	1996	£75	£37.50	US promo pack, with interview CD & book

MELLENCAMP, JOHN COUGAR

Check It Out	CD-s	Mercury	JCMCD10	1988	£5	£2	
Cherry Bomb	CD-s	Mercury	JCMCD9	1987	£5	£2	
Paper In Fire	CD-s	Mercury	0802122	1989	£10	£5	CD video
Pop Singer	CD-s	Mercury	0802002	1989	£10	£5	CD video
Pop Singer	CD-s	Mercury	JCMCD12	1989	£5	£2	
Rooty Toot Toot	CD-s	Mercury	JCMCD11	1988	£5	£2	

MELLOKINGS

Tonight Tonight	LP	Herald	H1013	1960	£100	£50	US

MELLO-LARKS

Just For A Lark	LP	Camden	CAL530	1959	£25	£10	US

MELLOTONES

Facts Of Life	7"	Camel	CA18	1969	£4	£1.50	Termites B side
Fat Girl In Red	7"	Amalgamated	AMG812	1968	£8	£4	Versatiles B side
Feel Good	7"	Amalgamated	AMG817	1968	£8	£4	
Let's Join Together	7"	Pyramid	PYR6060	1969	£6	£2.50	Beverley's Allstars B side
None Such	7"	Doctor Bird	DB1136	1968	£10	£5	Val Bennett B side
Uncle Charlie	7"	Trojan	TR612	1968	£8	£4	

MELLOW CANDLE

The rarest album on the Deram label contains folk-rock with two good female singers and is certainly strong enough to have sold very much better than it did. Several band members turned up on later albums by a range of artists including Mike Oldfield, Jade Warrior, Amazing Blondel, Paul Kossoff and Gary Moore, but for Mellow Candle themselves, sadly one failure was all they were allowed to have.

Dan The Wing	7"	Deram	DM357	1972	£40	£20	
Feeling High	7"	SNB	553645	1968	£40	£20	
Swaddling Songs	LP	Deram	SDL7	1972	£500	£330	

MELLOW CATS

Another Moses	7"	Blue Beat	BB54	1961	£12	£6	
Rock A Man Soul	7"	Blue Beat	BB68	1961	£12	£6	Monto & The Cyclones B side

MELLOW FRUITFULNESS

Meditation	LP	Columbia	SX6242	1967	£15	£6	

MELLOW LARKS

Love You Baby .... 7" .... Blue Beat .... BB16 .... 1960 **£12** .... **£6** ....

MELLY, GEORGE

Abdul Abulbul Amir .... 7" EP .. Decca .... DFE6557 .... 1958 **£5** .... **£2** ....
Black Bottom .... 7" .... Decca .... FJ10840 .... 1957 **£4** .... **£1.50** ....
Cemetery Blues .... 7" .... Tempo .... A147 .... 1956 **£4** .... **£1.50** ....
Frankie And Johnny .... 7" .... Decca .... F10457 .... 1955 **£4** .... **£1.50** ....
George Melly .... 7" EP .. Tempo .... EXA47 .... 1957 **£6** .... **£2.50** ....
Heebie Jeebies .... 7" .... Decca .... FJ10806 .... 1956 **£4** .... **£1.50** ....
Jenny's Ball .... 7" .... Tempo .... A144 .... 1956 **£4** .... **£1.50** ....
Kingdom Come .... 7" .... Decca .... F10763 .... 1956 **£4** .... **£1.50** ....
Michigan Water Blues .... 7" EP .. Decca .... DFE6552 .... 1958 **£5** .... **£2** ....
Nuts .... LP .... Warner Bros .... K46188 .... 1972 **£10** .... **£4** ....
Psychological Significance . . . . 7" EP .. Columbia .... SEG8093 .... 1961 **£5** .... **£2** ....
Waiting For A Train .... 7" .... Decca .... FJ10779 .... 1956 **£4** .... **£1.50** ....
With Mick Mulligan's Jazz Band .... 7" EP .. Tempo .... EXA41 .... 1957 **£6** .... **£2.50** ....

MELODIANS

Come Ethiopians, Come .... 7" .... Summit .... SUM8522 .... 1971 **£4** .... **£1.50** .... *Beverley's All Stars B side*
Come On Little Girl .... 7" .... Treasure Isle .... TI7028 .... 1968 **£10** .... **£5** .... *Tommy McCook B side*
Everbody Bawlin' .... 7" .... Trojan .... TR660 .... 1969 **£4** .... **£1.50** .... *Tommy McCook B side*
It Took A Miracle .... 7" .... Summit .... SUM8512 .... 1971 **£4** .... **£1.50** .... *Beverley's All Stars B side*
Last Train To Expo '67 .... 7" .... Treasure Isle .... TI7023 .... 1967 **£10** .... **£5** .... *Tommy McCook B side*
Lay It On .... 7" .... Island .... WI3014 .... 1966 **£10** .... **£5** ....
Let's Join Together .... 7" .... Studio One .... SO2013 .... 1967 **£12** .... **£6** .... *Gaylads B side*
Little Nut Tree .... 7" .... Doctor Bird .... DB1125 .... 1968 **£10** .... **£5** ....
Personally Speaking .... 7" .... Gas .... GAS116 .... 1969 **£4** .... **£1.50** .... *Lloyd Robinson B side*
Ring Of Gold .... 7" .... Gas .... GAS108 .... 1969 **£4** .... **£1.50** ....
Rivers Of Babylon .... 7" .... Summit .... SUM8508 .... 1970 **£4** .... **£1.50** ....
Say Darling say .... 7" .... Trojan .... TR7764 .... 1970 **£5** .... **£2** ....
Sweet Rose .... 7" .... Fab .... FAB61 .... 1968 **£8** .... **£4** ....
Sweet Sensation .... 7" .... Trojan .... TR695 .... 1969 **£4** .... **£1.50** ....
Sweet Sensation .... LP .... Trojan .... 1970 **£12** .... **£5** ....
Swing And Dine .... 7" .... Doctor Bird .... DB1139 .... 1968 **£10** .... **£5** ....
Walking In The Rain .... 7" .... Summit .... SUM8505 .... 1970 **£4** .... **£1.50** ....
When There Is You .... 7" .... Crab .... CRAB15 .... 1969 **£4** .... **£1.50** .... *Uniques B side*
You Don't Need Me .... 7" .... Treasure Isle .... TI7006 .... 1967 **£10** .... **£5** ....
You Have Caught Me .... 7" .... Treasure Isle .... TI7022 .... 1967 **£10** .... **£5** ....

MELODY ENCHANTERS

Blueberry Hill .... 7" .... R&B .... JB117 .... 1963 **£10** .... **£5** ....
Enchanter's Ball .... 7" .... Island .... WI049 .... 1963 **£10** .... **£5** ....

MELODY FAIR

Something Happened To Me .... 7" .... Decca .... F12801 .... 1968 **£4** .... **£1.50** ....

MELODY MAKER ALL STARS

Melody Maker All Stars .... 10" LP Esquire .... 20001 .... 1952 **£30** .... **£15** ....
Melody Maker All Stars .... 10" LP Esquire .... 20031 .... 1954 **£30** .... **£15** ....
Melody Maker All Stars .... 10" LP Esquire .... 20008 .... 1953 **£30** .... **£15** ....

MELODY MAKER JAZZ POLL WINNERS

All The Winners .... 10" LP Pye .... NJT518 .... 1959 **£15** .... **£6** ....

MELODY MAKER MODERN GROUP

Melody Maker Modern Group .... 10" LP Esquire .... 20030 .... 1954 **£30** .... **£15** ....

MELROSE, KANSAS CITY

Kansas City Melrose & Casino Simpson .... LP .... Chicago Piano .... 12001 .... 1972 **£12** .... **£5** ....

MELSEN, MONIQUE

Love Beat .... 7" .... Decca .... F23170 .... 1971 **£8** .... **£4** ....

MELSON, JOE

Hey Mister Cupid .... 7" .... Polydor .... NH66961 .... 1961 **£30** .... **£15** ....
Oh Yeah .... 7" .... Polydor .... NH66959 .... 1961 **£30** .... **£15** ....

MELTON, BARRY

We Are Like The Ocean .... LP .... Music Is Medicine .... MIM9007 .... 1977 **£20** .... **£8** .... US

MELTON CONSTABLE

Melton Constable .... LP .... SIS .... 197– **£300** .... **£180** ....

MELTZER, TINA & DAVID

Poet Song .... LP .... Vanguard .... 6519 .... 1968 **£75** .... **£37.50** .... US

MELVIN, HAROLD

Harold Melvin & The Blue Notes .... LP .... CBS .... 65350 .... 1973 **£10** .... **£4** ....

MEMBERS

Fear On The Streets	7"	XS		1977	£6	£2.50	
Offshore Banking Business	7"	Stiff	OFF3	1978	£4	£1.50	

MEMOS

My Type Of Girl	7"	Parlophone	R4616	1959	£60	£30	

MEMPHIS BEND

Ubangi Stomp	7"	United Artists	UP36132	1976	£5	£2	

MEMPHIS HORNS

Memphis Horns	LP	Mojo	2466010	1971	£12	£5	

MEMPHIS JUG BAND

Memphis Jug Band	7" EP	HMV	7EG8073	1955	£50	£25	
Memphis Jug Band	LP	Saydisc	RL33	1970	£12	£5	
Memphis Jug Band Vol. 2	LP	Saydisc	RL337	1971	£12	£5	

MEMPHIS MINNIE

1934–1936	LP	Limited Edition	no number	1969	£20	£8	
1936–1941	LP	Limited Edition	no number	1969	£20	£8	
1941–1949	LP	Sunflower	ET1400	1969	£20	£8	
Memphis Minnie	7" EP	Heritage	H103	1964	£20	£10	

MEMPHIS SLIM

All Kinds Of Blues	LP	Bluesville	BV(S)1053	1963	£12	£5	US
All Kinds Of Blues	LP	XTRA	XTRA5063	1970	£10	£4	
Alone With My Friends	LP	Battle	BM6118	1963	£12	£5	US
And The Real Honky Tonk	LP	Folkways	FG3535	1961	£15	£6	US
At The Gate Of Horn	LP	Vee Jay	VJLP1012	1959	£30	£15	US
Big City Girl	7"	Storyville	A45055	1962	£8	£4	
Blue Memphis	LP	Barclay	920214	1972	£50	£25	*with Peter Green*
Blues In Europe	LP	Storyville	SLP188	1966	£10	£4	
Bluesingly Yours	LP	Polydor	623263	1968	£10	£4	
Boogie Woogie & The Blues	7" EP	Storyville	SEP385	1962	£10	£5	
Boogie Woogie Piano	LP	CBS	63470	1961	£15	£6	
Broken Soul Blues	LP	United Artists	ULP1042	1963	£15	£6	
Chicago Blues	LP	Folkways	FG3536	1961	£15	£6	US
Chicago Blues	LP	XTRA	XTRA1085	1969	£10	£4	
Clap Your Hands	LP	Fontana	TL5254	1965	£10	£4	
Frisco Bay Blues	LP	Fontana	688315ZL	1964	£15	£6	
Going To Kansas City	7" EP	Collector	JEN5	1961	£10	£5	
Just Blues	LP	Bluesville	BV(S)1018	1961	£15	£6	US
Memphis Slim	LP	Collector	JGN1004	1961	£15	£6	
Memphis Slim	LP	King	LP885	1964	£15	£6	US
Memphis Slim	LP	Chess	LP1455	1961	£25	£10	US
Memphis Slim	LP	World Record Club	T394	1962	£10	£4	
Memphis Slim	LP	XTRA	XTRA1008	1965	£12	£5	
Memphis Slim Vol. 2	LP	Collector	JGN1005	1961	£15	£6	
Memphis Slim, USA	LP	Candid	9024	1962	£20	£8	US
No Strain	LP	Fontana	688302ZL	1964	£15	£6	
Old Times, New Times	LP	Barclay	920332/3	1972	£12	£5	*double*
Pinetop Blues	7"	Collector	JDN102	1960	£5	£2	
Pinetop's Blues	LP	Polydor	623211	1967	£10	£4	
Real Folk Blues	LP	Chess	1510	1966	£20	£8	US
Self Portrait	LP	Scepter	SM535	1966	£12	£5	US
Steady Rollin' Blues	LP	Bluesville	BV(S)1075	1964	£15	£6	US
Travellin' With The Blues	LP	Storyville	SLP118	1964	£10	£4	
Tribute To Big Bill Broonzy	LP	Candid	9023	1961	£20	£8	US
World's Foremost Blues Singer	7" EP	Summit	LSE2041	1963	£6	£2.50	

MEN

One of the Men was thinking of growing his hair long on one side only; the others were still working out how to get the best out of their new synthesizers. This was, in fact, the Human League.

I Don't Depend On You	12"	Virgin	VS26912	1979	£10	£5	
I Don't Depend On You	7"	Virgin	VS269	1979	£6	£2.50	

MEN AT WORK

Down Under	7"	Epic	EPCA1980	1983	£4	£1.50	*shaped picture disc*

MEN WITHOUT HATS

Pop Goes The World	CD-s	Mercury	MERCD257	1987	£5	£2	

MENACE

G.L.C.	7"	Small Wonder	SMALL5	1977	£4	£1.50	
I Need Nothing	7"	Illegal	IL008	1978	£4	£1.50	
Last Year's Youth	7"	Small Wonder	SMALL16	1979	£4	£1.50	
Screwed Up	12"	Illegal	IL004	1977	£6	£2.50	
Screwed Up	7"	Illegal	IL004	1977	£4	£1.50	
Young Ones	7"	Fresh	FRESH14	1978	£4	£1.50	

MENDES, CARLOS

Shadows	7"	Pye	7N25581	1972	£5	£2	

MENDES, SERGIO & BRASIL '66

Title	Format	Label	Cat. No.	Year	Mint	VG	Notes
Live At Expo 70	LP	A&M	AMLS989	1970	£20	£8	
Stillness	LP	A&M	AMLS2000	1970	£15	£6	

MENDES PREY

Title	Format	Label	Cat. No.	Year	Mint	VG	Notes
On To The Borderline	7"	Mendes Prey	AM076	1983	£40	£20	
Wonderland	12"	Wag	12WAG2	1986	£15	£7.50	
Wonderland	7"	Wag	WAG2	1986	£15	£7.50	

MENSWEAR

Title	Format	Label	Cat. No.	Year	Mint	VG	Notes
Day Dreamer	10"	Laurel	LAUXDJ5	1995	£8	£4	*promo*
I'll Manage Somehow	7"	Laurel	LAU4	1995	£8	£4	
I'll Manage Somehow	CD-s	Laurel	LAU4	1995	£10	£5	

MENZIES, IAN

Title	Format	Label	Cat. No.	Year	Mint	VG	Notes
Have Tartan, Will Trad	LP	Pye	NJL23	1960	£10	£4	
Melody Maker All Stars	7" EP	Pye	NJE1049	1958	£5	£2	

MERCER, MARY MAE

Title	Format	Label	Cat. No.	Year	Mint	VG	Notes
Mary Mae Mercer	7" EP	Decca	DFE8599	1965	£40	£20	

MERCHANT, NATALIE

Title	Format	Label	Cat. No.	Year	Mint	VG	Notes
Companion To Tigerlily	CD	East West	NATPRO1	1996	£20	£8	*US promo picture disc*

MERCHANTS OF DREAM

Title	Format	Label	Cat. No.	Year	Mint	VG	Notes
Strange Night Voyage	LP	A&M	SP4199	1967	£20	£8	*US*

MERCURY, FREDDIE

Title	Format	Label	Cat. No.	Year	Mint	VG	Notes
Barcelona	12"	Polydor	POSPP887	1987	£40	£20	*with Montserrat Caballe, picture disc*
Barcelona	12"	Polydor	POSPX887	1987	£10	£5	*with Montserrat Caballe, gatefold sleeve*
Barcelona	7"	Polydor	POSP887	1987	£4	£1.50	*with Montserrat Caballe*
Barcelona	CD-s	Polygram	0805482	1989	£50	£25	*CD video*
Barcelona	CD-s	Polydor	POCD887	1987	£100	£50	*signed*
Barcelona	CD-s	Polydor	POCD887	1987	£15	£7.50	
Fallen Priest	CD-s	Polydor	08055802	1989	£50	£25	*CD video*
Freddie Mercury Album	CD	EMI	CDPCSDX124	1992	£12	£5	*boxed with 5 photos*
Golden Boy	12"	Polydor	POSPX23	1988	£10	£5	*with Montserrat Caballe*
Golden Boy	7"	Polydor	PO23	1988	£4	£1.50	*with Montserrat Caballe*
Golden Boy	CD-s	Polydor	POCD23	1988	£25	£12.50	
Great Pretender	10"	Parlophone	10R6151	1987	£40	£20	*promo*
Great Pretender	12"	Parlophone	12R6151	1987	£6	£2.50	
Great Pretender	7"	Parlophone	R6151	1987	£4	£1.50	
Great Pretender	7"	Parlophone	RP6151	1987	£50	£25	*shaped picture disc & plinth*
Great Pretender	CD-s	EMI	CDR6336	1993	£5	£2	
How Can I Go On	12"	Polydor	POSPX29	1989	£10	£5	*with Montserrat Caballe*
How Can I Go On	7"	Polydor	POSX29	1988	£40	£20	*with Montserrat Caballe, picture disc*
How Can I Go On	CD-s	Polydor	PZCD29	1989	£20	£10	*with Montserrat Caballe*
How Can I Go On	CD-s	Polydor	PZCD234	1992	£6	£2.50	
I Was Born To Love You	12"	CBS	TA6019	1985	£10	£5	
I Was Born To Love You	7"	CBS	DA6019	1985	£25	£12.50	*double*
I Was Born To Love You	7"	CBS	A6019	1985	£4	£1.50	
In My Defence	CD-s	EMI	CDR6331	1992	£5	£2	*2 versions*
Living On My Own	12"	CBS	GTA6555	1985	£20	£10	*gatefold sleeve*
Living On My Own	12"	CBS	TA6555	1985	£8	£4	
Living On My Own	7"	CBS	A6555	1985	£4	£1.50	
Living On My Own	CD-s	EMI	CDR6355	1993	£5	£2	
Love Kills	12"	CBS	TA4735	1984	£12	£6	*Giorgio Moroder B side*
Love Kills	7"	CBS	A4735	1984	£5	£2	*Giorgio Moroder B side*
Love Kills	7"	CBS	WA4735	1984	£40	£20	*Giorgio Moroder B side, picture disc*
Love Me Like There's No Tomorrow	12"	CBS	TA6725	1985	£30	£15	
Made In Heaven	12"	CBS	TA6413	1985	£12	£6	
Made In Heaven	7"	CBS	WA6413	1985	£40	£20	*shaped picture disc*
Made In Heaven	7"	CBS	A6413	1985	£5	£2	
Mr Bad Guy	CD	CBS	CD86312	1985	£15	£6	
Mr Bad Guy	CD	CBS	CD86312	1985	£150	£75	*14 tracks*
Mr Bad Guy	LP	CBS	86312	1985	£10	£4	
Time	12"	EMI	12EMI5559	1986	£10	£5	
Zabou	CD	EMI	5647466092	1986	£60	£30	*German, with other artists*
Zabou	LP	EMI	1C06642407281	1986	£50	£25	*German, with other artists*

MERCURY REV

Yerself Is Steam/Lego My Ego	CD	Beggars Banquet	BBQCD125	1995	£15	£6	*double*

MERION

I Go To Sleep	7"	Page One	POF041	1967	£4	£1.50	

MERKIN

Music From Merkin Manor	LP	Windi	1005	1969	£250	£150	*US*

MERMAN, ETHEL

Call Me Madam	10" LP	Brunswick	LA8539	1952	£10	£4	
Duet From Ford 50th Anniversary TV Show	10" LP	Brunswick	LA8638	1954	£10	£4	
Husband A Wife	7"	Brunswick	05346	1954	£4	£1.50	
Songs From Call Me Madam	LP	Brunswick	LAT8016	1952	£10	£4	
Songs She Has Made Famous	10" LP	Brunswick	LA8636	1954	£12	£5	
There's No Business Like Show Business	7"	Brunswick	05381	1955	£5	£2	

MERRELL, RAY

This Irish country singer is still recording today. Needless to say, however, his £150 single is not in Merrell's usual style – instead its brass riffing and pounding rhythm make it a Northern soul favourite, despite the rather unconvincing vocals.

Battle Of Waterloo	7"	Aral	PS115	1964	£6	£2.50	*picture sleeve*
Tears Of Joy	7"	Jayboy	BOY22	1970	£150	£75	

MERRICK, TONY

Lady Jane	7"	Columbia	DB7913	1966	£4	£1.50	

MERRILL, BOB

Nairobi	7"	Columbia	DB4086	1958	£4	£1.50	

MERRILL, BUDDY

Sweet September	7"	Vocalion	VN9261	1966	£6	£2.50	

MERRILL, HELEN

Date With The Blues	7" EP	MGM	MGMEP699	1959	£5	£2	
Nearness Of You	LP	Mercury	MMB12000	1959	£15	£6	

MERRY-GO-ROUND

Merry-Go-Round	LP	A&M	(SP)4132	1967	£15	£6	*US*

MERRYMEN

Big Bamboo	7"	Doctor Bird	DB1004	1966	£10	£5	
Caribbean Treasure Chest	LP	Island	ILP984	1968	£30	£15	*pink label*
Caribbean Treasure Chest	LP	Trojan	TTL56	1970	£15	£6	

MERRYWEATHER, BIG MACEO

Big Maceo Merryweather And John Lee Hooker	LP	Fortune	3002		£25	£10	*US*

MERRYWEATHER, NEIL

Word Of Mouth	LP	Capitol	STBB278	1969	£20	£8	*US double*

MERSEYBEATS

Don't Let It Happen To Us	7"	Fontana	TF568	1965	£4	£1.50	
England's Best Sellers	LP	ARC International	834	1964	£40	£20	*US*
I Love You, Yes I Do	7"	Fontana	TF607	1965	£4	£1.50	
I Stand Accused	7"	Fontana	TF645	1965	£4	£1.50	
I Think Of You	7" EP	Fontana	TE17423	1964	£20	£10	
I Think Of You	7" EP	Fontana	465328	1966	£25	£12.50	*French*
It's Love That Really Counts	7"	Fontana	TF412	1963	£4	£1.50	
Last Night	7"	Fontana	TF504	1964	£4	£1.50	
Merseybeats	LP	Fontana	TL5210	1964	£60	£30	
Merseybeats	LP	Wing	WL1163	1965	£20	£8	
Merseybeats On Stage	7" EP	Fontana	TE17422	1964	£20	£10	
Wishin' And Hopin'	7" EP	Fontana	TE17432	1964	£15	£7.50	

MERSEYBOYS

Fifteen Greatest Songs Of The Beatles	LP	Ace Of Clubs	ACL1169	1964	£10	£4	

MERSEYS

Cat	7"	Fontana	TF845	1967	£4	£1.50	
Lovely Loretta	7"	Fontana	TF955	1968	£4	£1.50	
Penny In My Pocket	7"	Fontana	TF916	1968	£4	£1.50	
Rhythm Of Love	7"	Fontana	TF776	1966	£4	£1.50	
Rhythm Of Love	7" EP	Fontana	465356	1966	£25	£12.50	*French*
So Sad About Us	7"	Fontana	TF732	1966	£4	£1.50	
Sorrow	7"	Fontana	TF694	1966	£4	£1.50	

MERSEYSIPPI JAZZ BAND

All The Girls	10" LP	Esquire	20083	1957	£15	£6	
Any Old Rags	10" LP	Esquire	20093	1958	£15	£6	
Mersey Tunnel Jazz	10" LP	Esquire	20088	1957	£15	£6	
Merseysippi Jazz Band	7" EP	Esquire	EP90	1956	£8	£4	
Merseysippi Jazz Band	7" EP	Esquire	EP60	1955	£8	£4	

Title	Format	Label	Cat. No.	Year	Mint	VG	Notes
Merseysippi Jazz Band	7" EP	Esquire	EP130	1957	**£8**	**£4**	
Merseysippi Jazz Band	7" EP	Esquire	EP30	1955	**£8**	**£4**	
Merseysippi Jazz Band	7" EP	Esquire	EP118	1956	**£8**	**£4**	
West Coast Shout	10" LP	Esquire	20063	1956	**£15**	**£6**	

MERTON PARKAS

Title	Format	Label	Cat. No.	Year	Mint	VG	Notes
Flat Nineteen	7"	Well Suspect	BLAM002	1983	**£5**	**£2**	
You Need Wheels	7"	Beggars Banquet	BEG22	1979	**£5**	**£2**	*with patch*

MESMERIZING EYE

Title	Format	Label	Cat. No.	Year	Mint	VG	Notes
Psychedelia	LP	Smash	MGS27090	1967	**£25**	**£10**	*US*

MESSAGE

Title	Format	Label	Cat. No.	Year	Mint	VG	Notes
Dawn Anew Is Coming	LP	Bacillus	BLPS19081	1972	**£12**	**£5**	*German*

MESSENGER

Title	Format	Label	Cat. No.	Year	Mint	VG	Notes
Oy I Value Elation	7"	Anagram	A001	1967	**£10**	**£5**	

MESSINA, JIM

Title	Format	Label	Cat. No.	Year	Mint	VG	Notes
Dragsters	LP	Audio Fidelity	DF(S)7037	1964	**£40**	**£20**	*US*
Jim Messina And The Jesters	LP	Thimble	3	196–	**£30**	**£15**	*US*

METABOLIST

Title	Format	Label	Cat. No.	Year	Mint	VG	Notes
Dromm	7"	Dromm	DRO1	1979	**£6**	**£2.50**	
Identity	7"	Dromm	DRO3	1979	**£5**	**£2**	

METAL GURUS

Title	Format	Label	Cat. No.	Year	Mint	VG	Notes
Merry Xmas Everybody	CD-s	Phonogram	GURCD1	1990	**£5**	**£2**	

METALLICA

Title	Format	Label	Cat. No.	Year	Mint	VG	Notes
Creeping Death	12"	Music For Nations	12KUT112	1984	**£6**	**£2.50**	*beige label*
Creeping Death	12"	Music For Nations	GV12KUT112	1987	**£25**	**£12.50**	*gold vinyl*
Creeping Death	12"	Music For Nations	P12KUT112	1984	**£20**	**£10**	*picture disc*
Creeping Death	12"	Music For Nations	CV12KUT112	1987	**£25**	**£12.50**	*blue vinyl*
Creeping Death	12"	Music For Nations	GV12KUT112	1987	**£40**	**£20**	*1 side gold vinyl, 1 side black vinyl*
Creeping Death	12"	Vertigo	METAL412	1989	**£6**	**£2.50**	
Creeping Death	CD-s	Vertigo	8422192	1989	**£40**	**£20**	
Creeping Death	CD-s	Music For Nations	CD12KUT112	1984	**£40**	**£20**	
Enter Sandman	12"	Vertigo	METBX712	1991	**£20**	**£10**	*boxed with 4 prints*
Enter Sandman	7"	Vertigo	METAL7	1991	**£6**	**£2.50**	*picture disc*
Enter Sandman	7"	Vertigo	METDJ7	1991	**£5**	**£2**	*promo*
Enter Sandman	CD-s	Vertigo	METCD7	1991	**£30**	**£15**	*boxed set*
Enter Sandman	CD-s	Vertigo	METCD7	1991	**£5**	**£2**	
Eye Of The Beholder	12"	Vertigo		1988	**£20**	**£10**	*promo*
Fifteen Pieces Of Live Shit	CD	Elektra	PRCD88792	1993	**£40**	**£20**	*US double promo*
Garage Days Revisited	12"	Vertigo	METAL112	1987	**£15**	**£7.50**	
Good, The Bad And The Live	12"	Vertigo	8754871	1990	**£50**	**£25**	*6 × 12" plus EP*
Harvester Of Sorrow	12"	Vertigo	METAL212	1988	**£8**	**£4**	
Harvester Of Sorrow	7"	Vertigo	METAL2	1988	**£20**	**£10**	*promo, special sleeve*
Harvester Of Sorrow	7"	Vertigo	METDJ2	1988	**£50**	**£25**	*promo*
Harvester Of Sorrow	CD-s	Vertigo	METCD2	1988	**£20**	**£10**	
Hero Of The Day	7"	Vertigo	METJB13	1996	**£5**	**£2**	*jukebox issue*
Hero Of The Day	CD-s	Vertigo	METCX13	1996	**£5**	**£2**	
Hero Of The Day	CD-s	Vertigo	METCY13	1996	**£6**	**£2.50**	*with poster*
Jump In The Fire	12"	Music For Nations	12KUT105	1984	**£6**	**£2.50**	*beige label*
Jump In The Fire	12"	Music For Nations	12KUT105XP	1984	**£20**	**£10**	*with patch*
Jump In The Fire	12"	Music For Nations	CV12KUT105	1984	**£15**	**£7.50**	*red vinyl*
Jump in The Fire	7"	Music For Nations	PKUT105	1986	**£15**	**£7.50**	*shaped picture disc*
Kill 'Em All	CD	Music For Nations	MFNCD7	1984	**£25**	**£10**	
Kill 'Em All	LP	Music For Nations	MFN7P	1986	**£15**	**£6**	*picture disc*
Kill 'Em All	LP	Music For Nations	MFN7DM	1987	**£15**	**£6**	*double*
Kill 'Em All	LP	Music For Nations	MFN7	1983	**£10**	**£4**	*beige label*
Live Shit, Binge & Purge	CD	Vertigo	5187250	1993	**£60**	**£30**	*3 CD & video box set with book*
Load – The Interview	CD	Vertigo	METINT1	1996	**£40**	**£20**	*promo*
Mandatory Metallica	CD	Elektra	PRCD8020	1988	**£25**	**£10**	*US promo*
Mandatory Metallica	CD	Vertigo	MMCJ1	1996	**£30**	**£15**	*promo sampler*
Mandatory Metallica 2	CD	Vertigo	MMCJ2	1997	**£40**	**£20**	*promo sample double*
Master Of Puppets	CD	Music For Nations	MFNCD60	1986	**£20**	**£8**	
Master Of Puppets	LP	Music For Nations	MFN60P	1986	**£15**	**£6**	*picture disc*

Title	Format	Label	Cat. No.	Year	Mint	VG	Notes
Master Of Puppets	LP	Music For Nations	MFN60DM	1987	**£15**	**£6**	*double*
Master Of Puppets	LP	Music For Nations	MFN60	1986	**£10**	**£4**	
Metallican	CD	Vertigo	MECAN1	1991	**£60**	**£30**	*in can with video & T-shirt*
Nothing Else Matters	CD-s	Vertigo	METCD10	1992	**£5**	**£2**	
Nothing Else Matters – Live	CD-s	Vertigo	METCL10	1992	**£15**	**£7.50**	
One	10"	Vertigo	METPD510	1989	**£20**	**£10**	*picture disc*
One	12"	Vertigo	METAL512	1989	**£6**	**£2.50**	*white labels*
One	12"	Vertigo	METDJ512	1989	**£40**	**£20**	*promo*
One	7"	Vertigo	METAL5	1989	**£4**	**£1.50**	
One	7"	Vertigo	METDJ5	1989	**£50**	**£25**	*promo*
One	7"	Vertigo	METAP5	1989	**£10**	**£5**	*with poster*
One	CD-s	Vertigo	METCD5	1989	**£15**	**£7.50**	
One (Demo Version)	12"	Vertigo	METALG512	1989	**£15**	**£7.50**	*gatefold picture sleeve*
Ride The Lightning	CD	Music For Nations	MFN27P	1984	**£25**	**£10**	
Ride The Lightning	LP	Music For Nations	MFN27	1984	**£60**	**£30**	*green or blue vinyl*
Ride The Lightning	LP	Music For Nations	MFN27P	1986	**£15**	**£6**	*picture disc*
Ride The Lightning	LP	Music For Nations	MFN27	1984	**£10**	**£4**	*beige label*
Ride The Lightning	LP	Music For Nations	MFN27DM	1987	**£15**	**£6**	*double*
Sad But True	12"	Vertigo	METAL1112	1993	**£20**	**£10**	*picture disc*
Sad But True	CD-s	Vertigo	METCH11	1993	**£8**	**£4**	*picture disc*
Sad But True	CD-s	Vertigo	METCD11	1993	**£5**	**£2**	
Unforgiven	12"	Vertigo	METAL812	1991	**£6**	**£2.50**	
Unforgiven	12"	Vertigo	METAP812	1991	**£6**	**£2.50**	*picture disc*
Unforgiven	CD-s	Vertigo	METCD8	1991	**£8**	**£4**	
Until It Sleeps	7"	Vertigo	METJB12	1996	**£5**	**£2**	*jukebox issue*
Until It Sleeps	CD-s	Vertigo	METCX12	1996	**£6**	**£2.50**	
Wherever I May Roam	12"	Vertigo	METAL912	1992	**£6**	**£2.50**	
Wherever I May Roam	CD-s	Vertigo	METCD9	1992	**£8**	**£4**	*picture disc*
Wherever I May Roam	CD-s	Vertigo	METCB9	1992	**£8**	**£4**	
Whiplash	12"	Megaforce	MRS04P	1987	**£20**	**£10**	*picture disc*
Whiplash Sampler	CD-s	Vertigo	METCD100	1988	**£40**	**£20**	*promo*

METEORS

Title	Format	Label	Cat. No.	Year	Mint	VG	Notes
Crazed	7"	Lost Soul	LOST101	1981	**£6**	**£2.50**	
In Heaven	LP	Lost Soul	LOSTLP3001	1981	**£15**	**£6**	
Johnny Remember Me	7"	ID	EYE1P	1983	**£4**	**£1.50**	*picture disc*
Meteor Madness	10"	Ace	SWT65	1981	**£50**	**£25**	*test pressing*
Meteor Madness	7"	Ace	SW65	1981	**£10**	**£5**	*blue vinyl*
Meteor Madness	7"	Ace	SW65	1981	**£6**	**£2.50**	
Mutant Rock	12"	I.D.	EYET10	1986	**£8**	**£4**	*green or blue vinyl*
Mutant Rock	7"	WXYZ	ABCD5	1982	**£5**	**£2**	
Mutant Rock	7"	I.D.	EYE10	1986	**£5**	**£2**	*green vinyl*
Radioactive Kid	7"	Chiswick	CHIS147	1981	**£6**	**£2.50**	
Radioactive Kid	7"	Ace	NS74	1981	**£6**	**£2.50**	*clear vinyl*
Surf City	12"	Anagram	12ANA31	1986	**£6**	**£2.50**	

METERS

Title	Format	Label	Cat. No.	Year	Mint	VG	Notes
Best Of The Meters	LP	Reprise	K54076	1976	**£10**	**£4**	
Cabbage Alley	LP	Reprise	K33242	1972	**£15**	**£6**	
Cissy Strut	LP	Island	ILPS9250	1974	**£15**	**£6**	
Fire On The Bayou	LP	Reprise	K54044	1975	**£15**	**£6**	
Good Old Funky Music	LP	Pye	PKL5578	1979	**£10**	**£4**	
Look A Py-Py	7"	Direction	584751	1970	**£4**	**£1.50**	
Look-ka Py Py	LP	Josie	JOS4011	1970	**£20**	**£8**	*US*
Meters	LP	Josie	JOS4010	1969	**£20**	**£8**	*US*
New Directions	LP	Reprise	K56378	1977	**£10**	**£4**	
Rejuvenation	LP	Reprise	K54027	1974	**£15**	**£6**	
Sophisticated Cissy	7"	Stateside	SS2140	1969	**£5**	**£2**	
Struttin'	LP	Josie	JOS4012	1970	**£20**	**£8**	*US*
Trick Bag	LP	Reprise	K54078	1976	**£15**	**£6**	

METHENY, PAT

Title	Format	Label	Cat. No.	Year	Mint	VG	Notes
Bright Size Life	LP	ECM	ECM1073ST	1975	**£12**	**£5**	
Watercolors	LP	ECM	ECM1097T	1976	**£10**	**£4**	

METHUSELAH

Methuselah made one of the more obscure albums for Elektra, although it is an interesting one that deserved to do better. John Gladwin and Terry Wincott subsequently formed Amazing Blondel.

Title	Format	Label	Cat. No.	Year	Mint	VG	Notes
Matthew, Mark, Luke, & John	LP	Elektra	EKS74052	1969	**£50**	**£25**	*US*

METIS, FRANK

Title	Format	Label	Cat. No.	Year	Mint	VG	Notes
Show Business	7" EP	London	REN1048	1956	**£6**	**£2.50**	

METROPHASE

Title	Format	Label	Cat. No.	Year	Mint	VG	Notes
In Black	7"	Neo London	MS01	1979	**£5**	**£2**	
New Age	7"	Neo London	MS02	1979	**£5**	**£2**	

METROTONES

Title	Format	Label	Number	Year	Mint	VG	Notes
Tops In Rock And Roll	10″ LP	Columbia	6341	1955	**£150**	**£75**	US

MEZA, LEE

Title	Format	Label	Number	Year	Mint	VG	Notes
If It Happens	7″	Stateside	SS589	1967	**£20**	**£10**	

MEZZROW, MEZZ

Title	Format	Label	Number	Year	Mint	VG	Notes
At The Schola Cantorum, Paris	LP	Ducretet-Thomson	TKL93092	1956	**£20**	**£8**	
King Jazz Story	7″ EP	Storyville	SEP394	1962	**£5**	**£2**	
Mezzrow–Bechet Quintet	LP	Vogue	LAE12017	1956	**£15**	**£6**	
Pleyel Concert	LP	Vogue	LAE12007	1955	**£15**	**£6**	

MGM STUDIO ORCHESTRA

Title	Format	Label	Number	Year	Mint	VG	Notes
Rock Around The Clock	7″	MGM	SP1144	1955	**£4**	**£1.50**	

M.I. FIVE

Deep Purple's drummer, Ian Paice, first appeared on record with M.I. Five, as did the original singer with the more famous group, Rod Evans.

Title	Format	Label	Number	Year	Mint	VG	Notes
You'll Never Stop Me Loving You	7″	Parlophone	R5486	1966	**£40**	**£20**	

MICHAEL, GEORGE

In deciding to title one of his albums *Listen Without Prejudice*, George Michael was attempting to counter the obvious unfairness of the critical attitude that his glitzy, frothy image with Wham! implied a lack of real talent. He is justifiably proud of his songwriting ability and, indeed, his skill at turning a song idea into an effective recording through his own talents on playing and production. He is also the possessor of a sublimely beautiful singing voice. If anyone should be looking for a successor to Smokey Robinson, a singer whose ability to break hearts through the sheer tonal majesty of his voice is legendary, then there is really no need to look any further. As the title of one of his Wham! hits suggested, George Michael is indeed our man.

Title	Format	Label	Number	Year	Mint	VG	Notes
Careless Whisper	12″	Epic	QTA4603	1984	**£25**	**£12.50**	
Careless Whisper	12″	Epic	WA4603	1984	**£25**	**£12.50**	*picture disc*
Careless Whisper	7″	Epic	A4603	1984	**£20**	**£10**	*poster picture sleeve*
Cowboys And Angels	CD-s	Epic	6567742	1991	**£8**	**£4**	
Don't Let The Sun Go Down On Me	CD-s	Epic	6576462	1991	**£5**	**£2**	*with Elton John*
Faith	12″	Epic	EMUP3	1987	**£15**	**£7.50**	*picture disc*
Faith	CD	Epic	4600009	1987	**£30**	**£15**	*picture disc*
Faith	CD	Columbia	CSK2850	1987	**£20**	**£8**	*US promo, hologram cover*
Faith	CD-s	Epic	CDEMU3	1987	**£10**	**£5**	
Faith	LP	Epic		1987	**£30**	**£15**	*Australian picture disc*
Father Figure	7″	Epic	EMU4	1987	**£5**	**£2**	*with calendar*
Father Figure	7″	Epic	EMUP4	1988	**£10**	**£5**	*shaped picture disc*
Father Figure	CD-s	Epic	CDEMU4	1988	**£10**	**£5**	
Freedom	CD-s	Epic	GEOC3	1990	**£6**	**£2.50**	
Heal The Pain	CD-s	Epic	6566475	1991	**£6**	**£2.50**	
I Want Your Sex	12″	Epic	QT1	1987	**£6**	**£2.50**	
I Want Your Sex	CD-s	Epic	6546013	1989	**£5**	**£2**	*3″ single*
I Want Your Sex	CD-s	Epic	CDLUST1	1987	**£6**	**£2.50**	
Jesus To A Child	7″	Virgin	VSLH1571	1996	**£5**	**£2**	*jukebox issue*
Kissing A Fool	CD-s	Epic	CDEMU7	1988	**£5**	**£2**	
Listen Without Prejudice	CD	Epic	4672959	1990	**£30**	**£15**	*picture disc*
Listen Without Prejudice	LP	Epic		1990	**£40**	**£20**	*Brazilian picture disc*
Listen Without Prejudice – An Interview	CD	Columbia	CSK72226	1990	**£20**	**£8**	*US promo*
Monkey	7″	Epic	EMUG6	1988	**£4**	**£1.50**	*with photo*
Monkey	CD-s	Epic	CDEMU6	1988	**£8**	**£4**	
Older	CD	Virgin	CDV2802	1996	**£40**	**£20**	*press pack with CD and cassette*
One More Try	7″	Epic	EMUB5	1988	**£8**	**£4**	*with badge*
One More Try	CD-s	Epic	EPC6515322		**£8**	**£4**	*3″ single*
One More Try	CD-s	Epic	CPEMU5	1988	**£10**	**£5**	*picture disc*
Praying For Time	CD-s	Epic	GEOC1	1990	**£6**	**£2.50**	
Star People '97	7″	Virgin	VSLH1641	1997	**£4**	**£1.50**	*jukebox issue*
Too Funky	CD-s	Epic	6580582	1992	**£6**	**£2.50**	
Waiting For That Day	CD-s	Epic	GEOC2	1990	**£5**	**£2**	
Waiting For That Day	CD-s	Epic	CDGEO2	1990	**£5**	**£2**	
Wembley	cass	Epic	XPC4060	1991	**£15**	**£6**	

MICHAELS, MARILYN

Title	Format	Label	Number	Year	Mint	VG	Notes
Tell Tommy I Miss Him	7″	RCA	RCA1208	1960	**£5**	**£2**	

MICHIGAN RAG

Title	Format	Label	Number	Year	Mint	VG	Notes
Don't Run Away	7″	Blue Horizon	2096009	1972	**£10**	**£5**	

MICHIGANS

Title	Format	Label	Number	Year	Mint	VG	Notes
Intermission Riff	7″	Vogue	V9207	1963	**£5**	**£2**	

MICKEY & KITTY

Title	Format	Label	Number	Year	Mint	VG	Notes
Buttercup	7″	London	HLE9054	1960	**£15**	**£7.50**	

MICKEY & SYLVIA

Title	Format	Label	Number	Year	Mint	VG	Notes
Bewildered	7″	RCA	RCA1064	1958	**£20**	**£10**	
Love Is Strange	7″	HMV	POP331	1957	**£200**	**£100**	
Love Is Strange	7″	RCA	RCA1487	1965	**£15**	**£7.50**	
Love Is Strange	LP	RCA	CDN5133	1965	**£75**	**£37.50**	

New Sounds	LP	Vik	LX1102	1958	£125	£62.50	US
Sweeter As The Day Goes By	7"	RCA	RCA1206	1960	£10	£5	

MICKEY FINN

Garden Of My Mind	7"	Direction	583086	1967	£75	£37.50	
If I Had You Baby	7"	Polydor	56719	1966	£75	£37.50	
Sporting Life	7"	Columbia	DB7510	1965	£75	£37.50	

MIDDLETON, TONY

Don't Ever Leave Me	7"	Polydor	56704	1966	£250	£150	best auctioned
My Little Red Book	7"	London	HLR9983	1965	£12	£6	with Burt Bacharach

MIDKNIGHTS

Midknights	7" EP	E.R.S.	MN1/MEP101	1963	£100	£50	

MIDNIGHT AT NIXA GROUP

Midnight At Nixa	LP	Nixa	NJL3		£10	£4	

MIDNIGHT CIRCUS

Midnight Circus	LP	Bellaphon		1972	£100	£50	

MIDNIGHT CRUISER

Rich Bitch	7"	It	IT2	1977	£6	£2.50	

MIDNIGHT OIL

Beds Are Burning	CD-s	CBS	CDOIL1	1988	£5	£2	
Beds Are Burning	CD-s	CBS	CDOIL3	1989	£5	£2	
Blue Sky Mining	CD-s	CBS	CDOIL5	1990	£5	£2	
Dead Heart	CD-s	CBS	CDOIL2	1988	£5	£2	
Dead Heart	CD-s	CBS	CDOIL4	1989	£5	£2	
Earth And Sun And Moon	CD	CBS	4736052	1993	£25	£10	embossed green fold-out envelope
Forgotten Years	CD-s	CBS	CDOIL6	1990	£5	£2	

MIDNIGHT RAGS

Cars That Ate New York	7"	Velvet Moon	VM1	1980	£5	£2	
Public Enemy	7"	Ace	ACE005	1980	£5	£2	

MIDNIGHT SHIFT

'Saturday Jump' was the theme for the long-running *Saturday Club* programme on BBC radio.

Saturday Jump	7"	Decca	F12487	1966	£8	£4	

MIDNIGHT SUN

Dansk Beat	LP	Sonet	SLP2411	1975	£15	£6	Danish
Midnight Dream	LP	Sonet	SLPS1547	1973	£12	£5	Danish
Midnight Sun	LP	MCA	MKPS2019	1972	£15	£6	
Midnight Sun	LP	MCA	MCF2687	1973	£10	£4	
Rainbow Band	LP	Sonet	SLPS1523	1970	£50	£25	
Rainbow Band	LP	Sonet	SLPS1523A	1971	£15	£6	different vocals
Walking Circles	LP	Sonet	SLPS1536	1972	£15	£6	
Walking Circles	LP	MCA	MKPS2024	1972	£15	£6	
Walking Circles	LP	MCA	MCF2691	1973	£10	£4	

MIDNIGHTS

Show Me Around	7"	Ember	EMBS220	1966	£5	£2	

MIGHT OF COINCIDENCE

Why Couldn't People Wait	LP	Entropia	BM0001	1972	£60	£30	

MIGHTY AVENGERS

Blue Turns To Grey	7"	Decca	F12085	1965	£10	£5	
Hide Your Pride	7"	Decca	F11891	1964	£6	£2.50	
Sleepy City	7"	Decca	F12198	1965	£15	£7.50	
So Much In Love	7"	Decca	F11962	1964	£6	£2.50	

MIGHTY AVENGERS (2)

Scatter Shot	7"	Rymska	RA101	1966	£10	£5	Byron Lee B side

MIGHTY BABY

The group evolved out of the Action, but their music sounded little like that of the earlier group. With late arrivals Martin Stone (playing impressive lead guitar) and Ian Whiteman (keyboards and woodwinds) dominating the proceedings, Mighty Baby produced a floating, melodic kind of progressive rock that is amongst the most memorable of the genre. Remarkably, the best songs of all remained as forgotten out-takes until issued by Castle in 1985 (*Action Speaks Louder Than . . .*). Although credited to the Action, these five songs are actually the work of Mighty Baby and, despite their somewhat unsophisticated production, they emerge as classic recordings. (These tracks are also included on the CD reissue of the *Mighty Baby* album.)

Devil's Whisper	7"	Blue Horizon	2096003	1971	£40	£20	
Egyptian Tomb	LP	Psycho	PSYCHO31	1985	£10	£4	
Jug Of Love	LP	Blue Horizon	2931001	1971	£75	£37.50	
Mighty Baby	LP	Head	HDLS6002	1969	£75	£37.50	

MIGHTY DIAMONDS

Deeper Roots	LP	Front Line	FL8001	1979	£12	£5	
Ice In Fire	LP	Virgin	V2078	1977	£12	£5	
Planet Earth	LP	Virgin	V2102	1978	£12	£5	
Right Time	LP	Virgin	V2052	1976	£12	£5	

MIGHTY FLEA & MICKEY BAKER

Let The Good Times Roll	LP	Polydor	2460185	1973	**£12**	**£5**	

MIGHTY FLYERS

Low Flying Angels	LP	Myrrh	MYR1016	1974	**£30**	**£15**	

MIGHTY LEMON DROPS

Fall Down	7"	fan club		1989	**£5**	**£2**	

MIGHTY MEN

No Way Out	7"	Salvo	SLO1804	1962	**£20**	**£10**	

MIGHTY SAM

Fannie Mae	7"	Stateside	SS544	1966	**£5**	**£2**	
Mighty Soul	LP	Soul City	SCM004	1970	**£30**	**£15**	
Papa True Love	7"	Soul City	SC115	1969	**£6**	**£2.50**	
Sweet Dreams	7"	Stateside	SS534	1966	**£5**	**£2**	
When She Touches Me	7"	Stateside	SS2076	1968	**£5**	**£2**	

MIGHTY TERROR

Kings Of Calypso No. 1	7" EP	Pye	NEP24009	1956	**£5**	**£2**	
Kings Of Calypso No. 5	7" EP	Pye	NEP24086	1958	**£5**	**£2**	

MIGHTY VIKINGS

Do Re Mi	7"	Island	WI3060	1967	**£8**	**£4**	
Rockitty Fockitty	7"	Island	WI3074	1967	**£8**	**£4**	

MIGIL FIVE

Meet The Migil Five	7" EP	Pye	NEP24191	1964	**£12**	**£6**	
Mockingbird Hill	LP	Pye	NPL18093	1964	**£25**	**£10**	
Together	7"	Columbia	DB8196	1967	**£10**	**£5**	

MIGIL FOUR

Maybe	7"	Pye	7N15572	1963	**£4**	**£1.50**	

MIKE & THE MECHANICS

All I Need Is A Miracle	12"	WEA	U8765TP	1985	**£6**	**£2.50**	*picture disc*
Everybody Gets A Second Chance	CD-s	Virgin	VSCDX1396	1992	**£5**	**£2**	*with sheet music*
Get Up	CD-s	Virgin	VSCDG1359	1991	**£6**	**£2.50**	
Living Years	CD-s	WEA	U7717CD	1988	**£5**	**£2**	*3" single*
Nobody Knows	CD-s	WEA	U7602CD	1989	**£5**	**£2**	
Nobody's Perfect	CD-s	WEA	U7789CD	1988	**£5**	**£2**	*3" single*
Silent Running	7"	WEA	U8908P	1985	**£5**	**£2**	*shaped picture disc*
Time And Place	CD-s	Virgin	VSCDX1351	1991	**£5**	**£2**	*with 5 prints*
Word Of Mouth	CD-s	Virgin	VSCD1345	1991	**£5**	**£2**	
Word Of Mouth	CD-s	Virgin	VSCDX1345	1991	**£6**	**£2.50**	*numbered picture disc*

MIKE & THE MODIFIERS

I Found Myself A Brand New Baby	7"	Oriole	CB1775	1962	**£600**	**£400**	*best auctioned*

MIKLAGARD

Miklagard	LP	Edge	791	1979	**£25**	**£10**	*Swedish*

MILAN

Since leaving the cast of TV's *EastEnders*, Martine McCutcheon's emergence as a chart-topping recording artist is actually something of a return to her roots. Before finding fame as Tiffany, Martine was a member of a vocal trio called Milan, whose solitary single release was sadly not very successful.

Lead Me On	12"	Polydor	PZ312	1994	**£10**	**£5**	

MILANO, BOBBY

If Tears Could Bring You Back	7"	Capitol	CL14309	1955	**£4**	**£1.50**	
King Or A Slave	7"	Capitol	CL14252	1955	**£4**	**£1.50**	

MILBURN, AMOS

Blues Boss	LP	Motown	608	1963	**£150**	**£75**	*US*
Every Day Of The Week	7"	Vogue	V9064	1957	**£100**	**£50**	*tri-centre*
Let's Have A Party	LP	Score	LP4012	1957	**£150**	**£75**	*US*
Million Sellers	LP	Imperial	A9176	1962	**£60**	**£30**	*US*
One Scotch One Bourbon One Beer	7"	Vogue	V9163	1960	**£75**	**£37.50**	
Rock And Roll	7" EP	Vogue	VE170102	1957	**£200**	**£100**	
Rockin' The Boogie	10" LP	Aladdin	704	1956	**£200**	**£100**	*US*
Rockin' The Boogie	10" LP	Aladdin	704	1956	**£250**	**£150**	*US, red vinyl*
Rockin' The Boogie	LP	Aladdin	810	1958	**£150**	**£75**	*US*
Rum And Coca Cola	7"	Vogue	V9069	1957	**£100**	**£50**	
Thinking Of You Baby	7"	Vogue	V9080	1957	**£100**	**£50**	

MILBURN, AMOS JR

Gloria	7"	London	HLU9795	1963	**£10**	**£5**	

MILEM, PERCY

Crying Baby, Baby, Baby	7"	Stateside	SS566	1966	**£10**	**£5**	

MILES, BARRY

Miles Of Genius	LP	Egmont	AJS14	1960	**£12**	**£5**	

MILES, BUDDY

Expressway To Your Skull is exciting and dynamic big-band jazz-rock and it deserves to be very much more widely appreciated than it seems to be. This is the music that the Electric Flag were trying to create, without ever quite getting there – here Buddy Miles manages it without guitarist Mike Bloomfield's help. The sleeve notes to the album are by Jimi Hendrix, who knew a good thing when he heard it, although he does not play on the record. It is possible that he does play on the follow-up, *Electric Church*, but in a surprisingly understated manner, if it is he.

Title	Format	Label	Cat. No.	Year	Mint	VG	Notes
Electric Church	LP	Mercury	SMCL20163	1969	**£10**	**£4**	
Expressway To Your Skull	LP	Mercury	SMCL20137	1968	**£15**	**£6**	
Them Changes	LP	Mercury	6338016	1970	**£10**	**£4**	
Train	7"	Mercury	MF1065	1968	**£4**	**£1.50**	
With Carlos Santana	LP	Columbia	CQ31308	1974	**£10**	**£4**	*US quad*

MILES, DICK

Title	Format	Label	Cat. No.	Year	Mint	VG	Notes
Cheating The Tide	LP	Greenwich Village	GVR227	1984	**£10**	**£4**	

MILES, GARRY

Title	Format	Label	Cat. No.	Year	Mint	VG	Notes
Look For A Star	7"	London	HLG9155	1960	**£6**	**£2.50**	
Looking For A Star	7" EP	London	REG1264	1960	**£40**	**£20**	

MILES, JOSIE

Title	Format	Label	Cat. No.	Year	Mint	VG	Notes
Josie Miles	7" EP	Poydras	103	196–	**£5**	**£2**	

MILES, LENNY

Title	Format	Label	Cat. No.	Year	Mint	VG	Notes
Don't Believe Him Donna	7"	Top Rank	JAR546	1961	**£6**	**£2.50**	

MILES, LIZZIE

Title	Format	Label	Cat. No.	Year	Mint	VG	Notes
Blues They Sang	7" EP	HMV	7EG8178	1956	**£15**	**£7.50**	*side 2 by Billy Young*
Clambake On Bourbon Street	LP	Cook	1185	1957	**£15**	**£6**	*US*
Hot Songs	LP	Cook	1183	1956	**£15**	**£6**	*US*
Jazz	10" LP	Nixa	SLPY150	1954	**£15**	**£6**	
Lizzie Miles New Orleans Boys	7" EP	Melodisc	EPM755	1955	**£12**	**£6**	
Moans And Blues	LP	Cook	1182	1956	**£15**	**£6**	*US*
Night In New Orleans	LP	Capitol	T792	1957	**£15**	**£6**	
Scintillating Lizzie	7" EP	Columbia	SEB10088	1959	**£6**	**£2.50**	
Torchy Lullabies	LP	Cook	1184	1956	**£15**	**£6**	*US*

MILESTONES

Title	Format	Label	Cat. No.	Year	Mint	VG	Notes
Milestones	LP	Bellaphon	3311	1971	**£15**	**£6**	*German*

MILKSHAKES

Title	Format	Label	Cat. No.	Year	Mint	VG	Notes
Please Don't Tell My Baby	7"	Bilko	BILK0	1982	**£5**	**£2**	

MILKWOOD

Many of the groups to emerge as 'new wave' at the end of the seventies were not as new as all that. The Cars evolved from a group called Milkwood, who released a typically countryish mainstream rock LP as early as 1972.

Title	Format	Label	Cat. No.	Year	Mint	VG	Notes
How's The Weather	LP	Paramount	PAS6046	1972	**£25**	**£10**	*US*

MILKWOOD TAPESTRY

Title	Format	Label	Cat. No.	Year	Mint	VG	Notes
Milkwood Tapestry	LP	Metromedia	MD1007	1969	**£30**	**£15**	*US*

MILLENNIUM

Title	Format	Label	Cat. No.	Year	Mint	VG	Notes
Begin	LP	Columbia	CS9663	1968	**£12**	**£5**	*US*

MILLER

Title	Format	Label	Cat. No.	Year	Mint	VG	Notes
Baby I Got News For You	7"	Columbia	DB7735	1965	**£125**	**£62.50**	
Baby I Got News For You	7"	Oak	RGJ190	1965	**£200**	**£100**	

MILLER, BOB & THE MILLERMEN

Title	Format	Label	Cat. No.	Year	Mint	VG	Notes
Uptown And Downtown	7"	Mercury	MF947	1965	**£4**	**£1.50**	

MILLER, BOBBIE

Title	Format	Label	Cat. No.	Year	Mint	VG	Notes
Every Beat Of My Heart	7"	Decca	F12252	1965	**£4**	**£1.50**	
Everywhere I Go	7"	Decca	F12354	1966	**£60**	**£30**	*Ian Stewart B side*
What A Guy	7"	Decca	F12064	1965	**£25**	**£12.50**	

MILLER, CHUCK

Title	Format	Label	Cat. No.	Year	Mint	VG	Notes
Auctioneer	7"	Mercury	AMT1026	1959	**£6**	**£2.50**	
Auctioneer	7"	Mercury	7MT153	1958	**£15**	**£7.50**	
Down The Road Apiece	7"	Mercury	7MT215	1958	**£50**	**£25**	
Going Going Gone	7" EP	Mercury	ZEP10058	1960	**£40**	**£20**	
No Baby Like You	7"	Capitol	CL14543	1956	**£8**	**£4**	

MILLER, FRANKIE

Title	Format	Label	Cat. No.	Year	Mint	VG	Notes
Country Music	7" EP	Top Rank	JKP3013	1962	**£20**	**£10**	
Popping Johnnie	7"	Melodisc	1529	1959	**£5**	**£2**	
Rain Rain	7"	Melodisc	1552	1960	**£5**	**£2**	
True Blue	7"	Melodisc	1519	1959	**£8**	**£4**	
True Country Style Of Frankie Miller	LP	Ember	CW107	1964	**£15**	**£6**	

MILLER, GARY

Title	Format	Label	Cat. No.	Year	Mint	VG	Notes
Flower Drum Song	7" EP	Pye	NEP24123	1960	£5	£2	
Gary Miller Hit Parade Vol. 1	7" EP	Pye	NEP24047	1957	£12	£6	
Gary Miller Hit Parade Vol. 2	7" EP	Pye	NEP24072	1958	£10	£5	
Gary On The Ball	LP	Pye	NPL18059	1961	£12	£5	
Lollipop	7"	Pye	7N15136	1958	£4	£1.50	
Meet Mister Miller Pt 1	7" EP	Pye	NEP24057	1957	£10	£5	
Meet Mister Miller Pt 2	7" EP	Pye	NEP24058	1957	£10	£5	
Meet Mister Miller Pt 3	7" EP	Pye	NEP24059	1957	£10	£5	
Meet Mr Miller	LP	Pye	NPL18008	1957	£20	£8	
Stingray	7"	Pye	7N15698	1964	£8	£4	
Story Of My Life	7"	Pye	7N15120	1958	£4	£1.50	
Yellow Rose Of Texas	7" EP	Pye	NEP24013	1956	£20	£10	*2 different sleeves*

MILLER, GLEN

Title	Format	Label	Cat. No.	Year	Mint	VG	Notes
Rocksteady Party	7"	Doctor Bird	DB1128	1968	£10	£5	
Where Is The Love	7"	Doctor Bird	DB1089	1967	£10	£5	

MILLER, GLENN

Title	Format	Label	Cat. No.	Year	Mint	VG	Notes
Army Airforce Band	LP	HMV	RLS637	1956	£50	£25	*5 LP set*
Concert Vol. 1	10" LP	HMV	DLP1012	1953	£15	£6	
Concert Vol. 2	10" LP	HMV	DLP1013	1953	£15	£6	
Concert Vol. 3	10" LP	HMV	DLP1021	1953	£15	£6	
Concert Vol. 4	10" LP	HMV	DLP1081	1955	£10	£4	
Glenn Miller	10" LP	Philips	BBR8092	1956	£10	£4	
Glenn Miller	10" LP	Philips	BBR8072	1955	£10	£4	
Glenn Miller Story	10" LP	HMV	DLP1024	1954	£10	£4	
I Got Rhythm	7"	Columbia	SCM5086	1954	£5	£2	
Limited Edition	LP	HMV	RLS598	1954	£50	£25	*5 LP set*
Limited Edition Vol. 2	LP	HMV	RLS599	1956	£50	£25	*5 LP set*
Little Brown Jug	7"	HMV	7M195	1954	£8	£4	
Miller Magic	10" LP	HMV	DLP1122	1956	£10	£4	
Orchestra Wives	10" LP	HMV	DLP1059	1954	£10	£4	
Polka Dots And Moonbeams	10" LP	HMV	DLP1145	1957	£10	£4	
Sun Valley Serenade	10" LP	HMV	DLP1104	1955	£10	£4	
Sunrise Serenade	10" LP	HMV	DLP1062	1955	£10	£4	
Time For Melody	10" LP	HMV	DLP1049	1954	£10	£4	

MILLER, HARRY

Title	Format	Label	Cat. No.	Year	Mint	VG	Notes
Berlin Bones	LP	FMP	SAJ930	1981	£12	£5	*German*
Bracknell Breakdown	LP	Ogun	OG320	1978	£12	£5	
Children At Play	LP	Ogun	OG200	1974	£15	£6	
Down South	LP	Vera Jazz	4213	1984	£12	£5	
Family Affair	LP	Ogun	OG310	1977	£12	£5	
In Conference	LP	Ogun	OG523	1978	£12	£5	
Opened But Hardly Touched	LP	FMP	SAJ848/50	1980	£20	£8	*German double*
Sweeter The Meat	LP	FMP	SAJ690	1979	£12	£5	*German*
Zweckngal	LP	FMP	SAJ34	1980	£12	£5	*German*

MILLER, JIMMY & BARBECUES

Title	Format	Label	Cat. No.	Year	Mint	VG	Notes
Jelly Baby	7"	Columbia	DB4081	1958	£40	£20	
Sizzling Hot	7"	Columbia	DB4006	1957	£60	£30	

MILLER, JODY

Title	Format	Label	Cat. No.	Year	Mint	VG	Notes
Home Of The Brave	7"	Capitol	CL15415	1965	£4	£1.50	
If You Were A Carpenter	7"	Capitol	CL15482	1966	£4	£1.50	

MILLER, KENNY

Title	Format	Label	Cat. No.	Year	Mint	VG	Notes
Take My Tip	7"	Stateside	SS405	1965	£20	£10	

MILLER, MANDY

Title	Format	Label	Cat. No.	Year	Mint	VG	Notes
Children's Choice	7" EP	Parlophone	GEP8776	1958	£5	£2	
Nellie The Elephant	7"	Parlophone	R4219	1956	£5	£2	

MILLER, MAX

Title	Format	Label	Cat. No.	Year	Mint	VG	Notes
Cheeky Chappie	7" EP	HMV	7EG8558	1959	£5	£2	
Max At The Met	10" LP	Pye	NPT19026	1958	£10	£4	
Max At The Met	7" EP	Pye	NEP24154	1961	£5	£2	
Max At The Met Vol. 2	7" EP	Pye	NEP24162	1962	£5	£2	

MILLER, MITCH

Title	Format	Label	Cat. No.	Year	Mint	VG	Notes
Lisbon Antigua	7" EP	Philips	BBE12043	1956	£5	£2	

MILLER, NED

Title	Format	Label	Cat. No.	Year	Mint	VG	Notes
Best Of Ned Miller	LP	Capitol	T2414	1966	£25	£10	
Do What You Do Do Well	7"	London	HL9937	1964	£4	£1.50	
From A Jack To A King	LP	London	HA8072	1963	£20	£8	
From A Jack To A King	LP	Fabor	FLP1001	1963	£40	£20	*US, coloured vinyl*
Go On Back, You Fool	7"	Capitol	CL15301	1963	£4	£1.50	
In The Name Of Love	LP	Capitol	ST2914	1969	£20	£8	
Ned Miller	7" EP	Capitol	EAP120492	1963	£12	£6	
Ned Miller	7" EP	London	RE1382	1963	£15	£7.50	

MILLER, ROGER

Title	Format	Label	Cat. No.	Year	Mint	VG	Notes
King Of The Road	7" EP	Philips	BE12578	1965	£5	£2	

MILLER, RUSS

I Sit In My Window	7"	HMV	POP391	1957	**£30**	**£15**	

MILLER, STEVE BAND

Steve Miller could never quite decide whether he wanted to lead a progressive rock outfit or a blues band – so for much of the time the group's early records are both. Boz Scaggs was a member long enough to appear on the first two albums, while 'My Dark Hour' features a rare guest appearance from Paul McCartney, on bass, drums, and backing vocals, at a time when he was still technically a member of the Beatles.

Anthology	LP	Capitol	ESTSP12	1972	**£12**	**£5**	*double*
Brave New World	LP	Capitol	EST184	1970	**£10**	**£4**	
Children Of The Future	LP	Capitol	(S)T2920	1968	**£15**	**£6**	
Fly Like An Eagle	LP	Mobile Fidelity	MFSL1021	1978	**£12**	**£5**	*US audiophile*
Going To The Country	7"	Capitol	CL15656	1970	**£4**	**£1.50**	
Joker	CD-s	Capitol	CDCL583	1990	**£5**	**£2**	
Little Girl	7"	Capitol	CL15618	1969	**£4**	**£1.50**	
Living In The USA	7"	Capitol	CL15564	1968	**£5**	**£2**	
My Dark Hour	7"	Capitol	CL15604	1969	**£5**	**£2**	
Revolution	LP	United Artists	ULP1226	1968	**£15**	**£6**	*with other artists*
Sailor	LP	Capitol	(S)T2984	1969	**£15**	**£6**	
Sittin' In Circles	7"	Capitol	CL15539	1968	**£5**	**£2**	

MILLER, SUZI

Ay Ay Senores	7"	Decca	F10677	1956	**£4**	**£1.50**	
Banjo's Back In Town	7"	Decca	F10593	1955	**£4**	**£1.50**	
Dance With Me Henry	7"	Decca	F10512	1955	**£6**	**£2.50**	
Get Up Get Up	7"	Decca	F10722	1956	**£4**	**£1.50**	
Happy Days And Lonely Nights	7"	Decca	F10389	1954	**£15**	**£7.50**	*with the Johnston Brothers*
I Love My Baby	7"	Decca	F10848	1957	**£4**	**£1.50**	
Tweedle Dee	7"	Decca	F10475	1955	**£8**	**£4**	
Two Step Side Step	7"	Decca	F10423	1954	**£6**	**£2.50**	*with the Johnston Brothers*

MILLERS THUMB

Sitting On The Right Side	LP	Tradition	TSC3	1976	**£100**	**£50**	

MILLIE

Best Of Millie Small	LP	Trojan	TTL49	1970	**£15**	**£6**	
Best Of Millie Small	LP	Island	ILP953	1967	**£40**	**£20**	*pink label*
Bloodshot Eyes	7"	Fontana	TF617	1965	**£8**	**£4**	
Bournvita Song	7"	Cadbury's	BNVT01	1964	**£15**	**£7.50**	*picture sleeve*
Chicken Feed	7"	Fontana	TF796	1967	**£4**	**£1.50**	
Don't You Know	7"	Fontana	TF425	1963	**£4**	**£1.50**	
How Can I Be Sure	7"	Blue Beat	BB96	1962	**£12**	**£6**	*with Owen Gray*
I Love The Way You Love	7"	Fontana	TF502	1964	**£4**	**£1.50**	
I've Fallen In Love With A Snowman	7"	Fontana	TF515	1965	**£4**	**£1.50**	
Killer Joe	7"	Fontana	TF740	1966	**£4**	**£1.50**	
Millie	7" EP	Bluebeat	BBEP302	1961	**£75**	**£37.50**	
Millie & Her Boyfriends	LP	Trojan	TTL17	1969	**£15**	**£6**	
Millie And Her Boyfriends	7" EP	Island	IEP705	1966	**£30**	**£15**	
Millie Sings Fats Domino	LP	Fontana	TL5276	1965	**£30**	**£15**	
More Millie	LP	Fontana	(S)TL5220	1964	**£25**	**£10**	
My Boy Lollipop	7"	Fontana	TF449	1964	**£4**	**£1.50**	
My Boy Lollipop	7" EP	Fontana	TE17425	1964	**£15**	**£7.50**	
My Boy Lollipop	LP	Smash	MGS27055	1964	**£30**	**£15**	*US*
My Love And I	7"	Pyramid	PYR6080	1970	**£4**	**£1.50**	
My Street	7"	Brit	WI1002	1965	**£10**	**£5**	
My Street	7"	Fontana	TF591	1965	**£4**	**£1.50**	
Pledging My Love	LP	Trojan	TTL47	1970	**£15**	**£6**	*with Jackie Edwards*
Readin' Writin' Arithmetic	7"	Decca	F12948	1969	**£5**	**£2**	
See You Later Alligator	7"	Fontana	TF529	1965	**£4**	**£1.50**	
Sugar Plum	7"	Island	WI014	1962	**£10**	**£5**	*with Owen Gray*
Sweet William	7"	Fontana	TF479	1964	**£4**	**£1.50**	
This World	7"	Island	WI050	1962	**£10**	**£5**	*with Roy Panton*
Time Will Tell	LP	Trojan	TBL108	1970	**£15**	**£6**	
When I Dance With You	7"	Fontana	TF948	1968	**£4**	**£1.50**	
You Better Forget	7"	Island	WIP6021	1967	**£4**	**£1.50**	

MILLIGAN, SPIKE

I'm Walking Out With A Mountain	7"	Parlophone	R4839	1961	**£5**	**£2**	
Milligan Preserved	LP	Parlophone	PMC1148	1961	**£10**	**£4**	
Muses With Milligan	LP	Decca	LK4701	1965	**£10**	**£4**	
Olympic Team	7"	Pye	7N15720	1964	**£4**	**£1.50**	
Purple Aeroplane	7"	Parlophone	R5513	1966	**£4**	**£1.50**	
Q5 Piano Tune	7"	Parlophone	R5771	1969	**£4**	**£1.50**	
Tower Bridge	7"	Parlophone	R5543	1966	**£4**	**£1.50**	
Wish I Knew	7"	Parlophone	R4406	1958	**£5**	**£2**	
World Of Beachcomber	LP	Pye	NPL18271	1969	**£10**	**£4**	
Wormwood Scrubs Tango	7"	Parlophone	R4891	1962	**£5**	**£2**	

MILLINDER, LUCKY

Grape Vine	78	Vogue	V9021	1951	**£8**	**£3**	
I'm Waiting Just For You	78	Vogue	V9007	1951	**£8**	**£3**	

Ram Bunk Shush	78	Vogue	V2138	1952	£8	£3	

MILLINS, PAUL

Paul Millins	LP	Fresh Air	6370505	1975	£30	£15	*with Jo-Ann Kelly*

MILLIONAIRES

Chatterbox	7"	Decca	F12468	1966	£30	£15	

MILLIONAIRES (2)

Never For Me	7"	Mercury	6052301	1973	£4	£1.50	*black label*

MILLS, BARBARA

Queen Of Fools	7"	Hickory	451323	1965	£75	£37.50	
Queen Of Fools	7"	London	HLE10491	1975	£5	£2	
Try	7"	Hickory	451392	1965	£8	£4	

MILLS, FREDDIE

One For The Road Medley	7"	Parlophone	R4374		£20	£10	

MILLS, GARRY

Running Bear	7"	Top Rank	JAR301	1960	£4	£1.50	
Who's Gonna Take You Home Tonight?	7"	Top Rank	JAR542	1961	£4	£1.50	

MILLS, GARY

Bless You	7"	Decca	F11383	1961	£4	£1.50	
Comin' Down With Love	7"	Top Rank	JAR393	1960	£4	£1.50	
Hey Baby	7"	Top Rank	JAR119	1959	£10	£5	
I'll Step Down	7"	Decca	F11358	1961	£4	£1.50	
Look For A Star	7"	Top Rank	JAR336	1960	£4	£1.50	
Looking For A Star	7" EP	Top Rank	JKP3001	1961	£30	£15	
Sad Little Girl	7"	Decca	F11415	1961	£4	£1.50	
Save A Dream For Me	7"	Decca	F11471	1962	£4	£1.50	
Top Teen Baby	7"	Top Rank	JAR500	1960	£6	£2.50	*picture sleeve*
Top Teen Baby	7"	Top Rank	JAR500	1960	£4	£1.50	

MILLS, HAYLEY

Gypsy Girl	LP	Mainstream	6090	1966	£15	£6	*US stereo*
In Search Of The Castaways	LP	Disneyland	ST3916	1962	£15	£6	*US stereo*
Let's Get Together	7"	Decca	F21396	1961	£4	£1.50	
Let's Get Together	LP	Buena Vista	STER3311	1962	£15	£6	*US stereo*
Let's Get Together	LP	Decca	LKR4426	1962	£20	£8	
Parent Trap	LP	Buena Vista	STER3309	1961	£15	£6	*US stereo*
Pollyanna	LP	Disneyland	ST1960	1960	£15	£6	*US*
Summer Magic	LP	MGM	(S)E4025	1963	£15	£6	*US*

MILLS, MAUDE

Maude Mills	7" EP	Vintage Jazz	VEP34	196–	£8	£4	

MILLS, RUDY

Heavy Load	7"	Crab	CRAB24	1969	£4	£1.50	
John Jones	7"	Big Shot	BI509	1968	£6	£2.50	
Lemi Li	7"	Explosion	EX2007	1969	£5	£2	
Reggae Hits	LP	Pama	SECO12	1969	£25	£10	
Tears On My Pillow	7"	Crab	CRAB20	1969	£4	£1.50	

MILLS, STEPHANIE

For The First Time	LP	Tamla Motown	STML12017	1976	£10	£4	
This Empty Place/I See You For The First Time	7"	Tamla Motown	TMG1020	1976	£20	£10	*demo*

MILLS BROTHERS

Barber Shop Harmony	LP	Decca	DL8890	195–	£12	£5	*US*
Best Of The Mills Brothers	LP	Decca	DXB193/DXSB7193	195–	£12	£5	*US*
Dream Of You	7"	Brunswick	05550	1956	£4	£1.50	
End Of The World	LP	London	HAD/SAHD8092	1963	£10	£4	
Four Boys And A Guitar	10" LP	Brunswick	LA8702	1955	£10	£4	
Get A Job	7"	London	HLD8553	1958	£15	£7.50	
Glow	LP	Decca	DL8827	195–	£12	£5	*US*
Greatest Hits	LP	London	HAD2319	1961	£10	£4	
Greatest Hits	LP	London	HAD2192/SHD6046	1959	£10	£4	
Gum Drop	7"	Brunswick	05487	1955	£12	£6	
Harmonizin'	LP	Decca	DL8892	195–	£12	£5	*US*
How Blue?	7"	Brunswick	05325	1954	£6	£2.50	
I've Changed My Mind A Thousand Times	7"	Brunswick	05522	1956	£5	£2	
In Hi-Fi	LP	Decca	DL8664	195–	£12	£5	*US*
Louis Armstrong And The Mills Brothers	10" LP	Brunswick	LA8681	1954	£12	£5	
Meet The Mills Brothers	10" LP	Brunswick	LA8664	1954	£15	£6	
Memory Lane	LP	Decca	DL8219	195–	£12	£5	*US*
Mills Brothers	7" EP	London	RED1215	1959	£10	£5	
Mills Brothers No. 2	7" EP	Brunswick	OE9060	1955	£5	£2	
Ninety-Eight Cents	7"	Brunswick	05600	1956	£4	£1.50	

One Dozen Roses	LP	Decca	DL8491	195–	£12	£5	US
Paper Valentine	7"	Brunswick	05390	1955	£5	£2	
Presenting	7" EP	Brunswick	OE9014	1954	£8	£4	
San Antonio Rose	LP	London	HAD2383/ SAHD6183	1961	£10	£4	
Sing	LP	London	HAD2250/ SHD6074	1960	£10	£4	
Singin' And Swingin'	LP	Decca	DL8209	195–	£12	£5	US
Singing And Swinging Pt 1	7" EP	Brunswick	OE9239	1956	£5	£2	
Smack Dab In The Middle	7"	Brunswick	05439	1955	£8	£4	
Souvenir Album	10" LP	Decca	DL5102	195–	£20	£8	US
Souvenir Album	LP	Decca	DL8148	195–	£12	£5	US
Suddenly There's A Valley	7"	Brunswick	05488	1955	£5	£2	
That's Right	7"	Brunswick	05606	1956	£5	£2	
Wonderful Words	10" LP	Decca	DL5337	195–	£20	£8	US
Yes You Are	7"	Brunswick	05452	1955	£5	£2	

MILLSTONE GRIT

Millstone Grit	LP	Box	488	1980	£12	£5	

MILLTOWN BROTHERS

Applegreen	CD-s	A&M	AMCD704	1990	£5	£2	
Coming From The Mill	12"	Big Round	BIGR101T	1989	£10	£5	
Coming From The Mill	CD-s	Big Round	BIGR101CD	1989	£10	£5	
Roses	7"	Big Round	BIGR101	1989	£6	£2.50	
Which Way Should I Jump	12"	Big Round	BIGR104T	1989	£6	£2.50	

MILSAP, RONNIE

Ain't No Sole Left In These Ole Shoes	7"	Pye	7N25392	1966	£15	£7.50	
Soul Sensations	7" EP	Pye	NEP44078	1966	£10	£5	*with Roscoe Robinson*

MILTON, JOHNNY & THE CONDORS

Somethin' Else	7"	Decca	F11862	1964	£4	£1.50	

MILTON, ROY

Great Roy Milton	LP	Kent	554	1963	£30	£15	US
Rock'n'Roll Versus Rhythm And Blues	LP	Dooto	DL223	1959	£60	£30	*US, with Chuck Higgins*

MIMMS, GARNETT

All About Love	7"	United Artists	UP1172	1966	£6	£2.50	
As Long As I Have You	LP	United Artists	UAL3396/ UAS6396	1965	£30	£15	US
As Long As I Love You	7"	United Artists	UP1186	1967	£5	£2	
Cry Baby	7"	United Artists	UP1033	1963	£6	£2.50	
Cry Baby	LP	United Artists	ULP1067	1963	£50	£25	
For Your Precious Love	7"	United Artists	UP1038	1963	£6	£2.50	
I Can Hear My Baby Crying	7"	Verve	VS569	1968	£5	£2	
I'll Take Good Care Of You	7"	United Artists	UP1130	1966	£50	£25	
I'll Take Good Care Of You	LP	United Artists	UAL3498/ UAS6498	1965	£30	£15	US
It Was Easier To Hurt Her	7"	United Artists	UP1090	1965	£10	£5	
It's Been Such A Long Way Home	7"	United Artists	UP1147	1966	£6	£2.50	
Live	LP	United Artists	(S)ULP1174	1967	£30	£15	
My Baby	7"	United Artists	UP1153	1966	£5	£2	
Roll With The Punches	7"	United Artists	UP1181	1967	£6	£2.50	
Tell Me Baby	7"	United Artists	UP1048	1964	£6	£2.50	
Warm And Soulful	LP	United Artists	(S)ULP1145	1966	£40	£20	
We Can Find That Love	7"	Verve	VS574	1968	£5	£2	

MIND EXPANDERS

What's Happening	LP	Dot	DLP25773	1967	£30	£15	*US, stereo*
What's Happening	LP	Dot	DLP3773	1967	£60	£30	*US, mono*

MINDBENDERS

Ashes To Ashes	7"	Fontana	TF731	1966	£4	£1.50	
Ashes To Ashes	7" EP	Fontana	465322	1966	£15	£7.50	*French*
Blessed Are The Lonely	7"	Fontana	TF910	1968	£4	£1.50	
Can't Live With You	7"	Fontana	TF697	1966	£4	£1.50	
Groovy Kind Of Love	LP	Fontana	MGF2/SRF67554	1966	£30	£15	US
I Want Her, She Wants Me	7"	Fontana	TF780	1966	£4	£1.50	
Letter	7"	Fontana	TF869	1967	£4	£1.50	
Mindbenders	LP	Fontana	(S)TL5324	1966	£50	£25	
Mindbenders	LP	Fontana	SFL13045	1968	£15	£6	
Schoolgirl	7"	Fontana	TF877	1967	£4	£1.50	
Uncle Joe The Ice Cream Man	7"	Fontana	TF961	1968	£4	£1.50	
We'll Talk About It Tomorrow	7"	Fontana	TF806	1967	£4	£1.50	
We'll Talk About It Tomorrow	7" EP	Fontana	465378	1967	£15	£7.50	*French*
With Woman In Mind	LP	Fontana	(S)TL5403	1967	£50	£25	

MINEO, SAL

Aladdin	LP	Columbia	CL1117	1958	£50	£25	US
Cutting In	7"	Fontana	H118	1958	£30	£15	
Sal	LP	Fontana	TFL5004	1958	£50	£25	

Seven Steps To Love	7"	Fontana	H135	1958	£15	£7.50	
Start Moving	7"	Philips	JK1024	1958	£20	£10	

MINGUS, CHARLES

Although he was an impressive player of the double bass, Charles Mingus is increasingly remembered as the leader of some particularly inspiring line-ups and as the finest jazz composer since Duke Ellington. In the sixties, Mingus's music was the first port of call for rock fans wishing to develop an interest in jazz. His pieces were recorded by groups as diverse as the Pentangle, East of Eden, and Alexis Korner. Mingus returned the favour to the rock world when he collaborated with Joni Mitchell on her exploration of the man's music on the album *Mingus*. Of Mingus's own albums, *Mingus Ah Um*, *Oh Yeah*, *The Black Saint And The Sinner Lady* and all the recordings featuring saxophonist Eric Dolphy are rightly regarded as classics of modern jazz.

Black Saint And The Sinner Lady	LP	HMV	CLP1694	1963	£20	£8	
Blues And Roots	LP	London	LTZK15194/ SAHK6087	1960	£25	£10	
Charles Mingus	7" EP	Philips	BBE12399	1960	£5	£2	
Charles Mingus Presents Charles Mingus	LP	Atlantic	SD8005	1962	£20	£8	
Charlie Mingus	LP	Atlantic	ATL/SAL5019	1965	£20	£8	
Charlie Mingus Quintet With Max Roach	LP	Vocalion	LAEF/SEAF591	1965	£20	£8	
Chazz	LP	Vocalion	LAE543	1963	£20	£8	
Clown	LP	London	LTZK15164	1959	£25	£10	
Duke's Choice	LP	Atlantic	545111	1970	£15	£6	
East Coasting	LP	Parlophone	PMC1092	1959	£25	£10	
East Coasting	LP	Polydor	623215	1968	£15	£6	
Great Concert Of Charles Mingus	LP	America	30AM003/4/5	1971	£25	£10	*French triple*
Jazz Composers Workshop	LP	Realm	RM211	1966	£20	£8	
Jazz Experiments	LP	London	LTZN15087	1957	£25	£10	
Jazz Makers	7" EP	Mercury	10021MCE	1965	£5	£2	
Jazz Portraits	LP	United Artists	ULP1004	1962	£20	£8	
Jazz Workshop Vol. 2	10" LP	Vogue	LDE178	1956	£40	£20	
Let My Children Hear Music	LP	CBS	64715	1972	£12	£5	
Mingus Ah Um	LP	Philips	BBL7352	1960	£20	£8	
Mingus Ah Um	LP	CBS	52346	1969	£15	£6	
Mingus At Monterey	LP	Liberty	LDS84002	1969	£20	£8	*double*
Mingus Dynasty	7" EP	Philips	BBE12451/ SBBE9050	1961	£5	£2	
Mingus Dynasty	LP	CBS	(S)BPG62261	1966	£20	£8	
Mingus Mingus Mingus	LP	HMV	CLP1742/ CSD1545	1965	£20	£8	
Mingus Plays Piano	LP	HMV	CLP1796	1964	£20	£8	
Mingus Revisited	LP	Mercury	SMWL21056	1969	£15	£6	
My Favourite Quintet	LP	Liberty	LBS83346	1970	£15	£6	
Oh Yeah	LP	London	HAK/SHK8007	1962	£20	£8	
Pithecanthropus Erectus	LP	London	LTZK15052	1957	£25	£10	
Pithecanthropus Erectus	LP	Atlantic	587131	1968	£15	£6	
Reincarnation Of A Lovebird	LP	Atlantic	587166	1969	£15	£6	
Scenes In The City	7" EP	Parlophone	GEP8786	1963	£5	£2	
Things Ain't What They Used To Be	7" EP	Philips	BBE12453/ SBBE9052	1961	£5	£2	
Tijuana Moods	LP	RCA	RD/SF7514	1962	£20	£8	
Tonight At Noon	LP	Atlantic	SD1416	196–	£20	£8	*US*
Town Hall Concert	LP	United Artists	ULP1068	1965	£20	£8	
Trio	LP	London	LTZJ15129	1958	£25	£10	

MINIM

Wrapped In A Union Jack	LP	Polydor	582011	1967	£60	£30	

MINISTRY

Cold Life	12"	Situation 2	SIT17T	1982	£6	£2.50	
Work For Love	7"	Arista	ARIST510	1983	£4	£1.50	*with cassette*

MINISTRY OF SOUND

This totally obscure sixties beat group has no connection with the dance music club responsible for sponsoring a number of highly regarded DJ mix albums in the nineties!

White Collar Worker	7"	Decca	F12449	1966	£8	£4	

MINNELLI, LIZA

Don't Drop Bombs	12"	Epic	ZEE2	1989	£6	£2.50	
Don't Drop Bombs	CD-s	Epic	ZEEC2	1989	£8	£4	
Losing My Mind	CD-s	Epic	ZEEC1	1989	£8	£4	
Love Pains	CD-s	Epic	CDZEE4	1990	£8	£4	
Middle Of The Street	7"	Capitol	CL15483	1966	£4	£1.50	
So Sorry, I Said	CD-s	Epic	ZEEC3/CDZEE3	1989	£8	£4	*2 versions*

MINOGUE, DANNII

All I Wanna Do	12"	Warner Bros	SAM3022	1997	£15	£7.50	*promo double*
All I Wanna Do	12"	Warner Bros	SAM3009	1997	£10	£5	*promo double*
Everything I Wanted	10"	Warner Bros	SAM3106	1997	£10	£5	*promo*
Everything I Wanted	12"	Warner Bros	SAM3105	1997	£10	£5	*promo double*
Everything I Wanted	12"	Warner Bros	SAM3108	1997	£8	£4	*promo*
Love And Kisses	7"	MCA	MCSR1529	1991	£20	£10	*signed poster sleeve*

MINOGUE, KYLIE

The former soap star's appearances on TV chat shows like that hosted by Clive James have revealed her to have considerable intelligence – which might have come as a surprise to all those whose view of the lady was prejudiced by seeing her cavorting around chanting 'lucky

lucky lucky'. As it happens, Kylie's records have become more impressive artistically as they have declined in popularity, and her eponymous album from March 1998 is recommended to anyone who likes well-crafted modern pop. This album was actually first issued the previous year, but was withdrawn because its original title, *Impossible Princess*, was felt to be unfortunately timed with the death of Princess Diana.

Better The Devil You Know	CD-s	PWL	PWCD56	1990	**£12**	**£6**	
Celebration	12"	PWL	PWLT257	1992	**£15**	**£7.50**	
Confide In Me	7"	DeConstruction	2784827	1994	**£8**	**£4**	*jukebox issue*
Confide In Me	7"	DeConstruction	21227477JB	1994	**£8**	**£4**	*jukebox issue*
Confide In Me	CD-s	DeConstruction	2784820	1994	**£5**	**£2**	
Especially For You	CD-s	PWL	PWCD24	1988	**£20**	**£10**	
Got To Be Certain	CD-s	PWL	PWCD12	1988	**£15**	**£7.50**	
Got To Be Certain (Extra Beat Boys Mix)	12"	PWL	PWLT12R	1988	**£12**	**£6**	
Hand On Your Heart	CD-s	PWL	PWCD35	1989	**£10**	**£5**	
Hand On Your Heart (Heartache Mix)	12"	PWL	PWLT35R	1989	**£30**	**£15**	
I Should Be So Lucky	CD-s	PWL			**£40**	**£20**	*German or Dutch*
I Should Be So Lucky (Bicentennial Mix)	12"	PWL	PWLT8R	1988	**£12**	**£6**	
If You Were With Me Now	CD-s	PWL	PWCD208	1991	**£5**	**£2**	*with Keith Washington*
Impossible Princess	CD	Deconstruction	KYLIE1	1997	**£75**	**£37.50**	*promo only*
Je Ne Sais Pas Pourquoi	CD-s	PWL	PWCD21	1988	**£20**	**£10**	
Je Ne Sais Pas Pourquoi	12"	PWL	PWLT21R	1988	**£12**	**£6**	
Je Ne Sais Pas Pourquoi	7"	PWL	PWLP21	1988	**£20**	**£10**	*poster picture sleeve*
Keep On Pumpin' It	CD-s	PWL	PWCD207	1991	**£15**	**£7.50**	
Kylie Minogue	CD	Deconstruction	KM001	1994	**£30**	**£15**	*promo in fold-out sleeve*
Locomotion (Sankie Mix)	12"	PWL	PWLT14R	1988	**£12**	**£6**	
Never Too Late	CD-s	PWL	PWCD45	1989	**£10**	**£5**	
Rhythm Of Love	CD	PWL	HFCDL18	1990	**£20**	**£8**	*with 3 bonus tracks*
Rhythm Of Love	LP	PWL	HFL18	1990	**£100**	**£50**	*gold leaf sleeve*
Shocked	7"	PWL	PWLP81	1991	**£8**	**£4**	*picture disc*
Shocked	CD-s	PWL	PWCD81	1991	**£12**	**£6**	
Step Back In Time	CD-s	PWL	PWCD64	1990	**£15**	**£7.50**	
Tears On My Pillow	CD-s	PWL	PWCD47	1989	**£15**	**£7.50**	
What Do I Have To Do	12"	PWL	PWLT72R	1991	**£60**	**£30**	
What Do I Have To Do	CD-s	PWL	PWCD72	1991	**£12**	**£6**	
Where Is The Feeling	12"	RCA	FEEL2	1994	**£20**	**£10**	*promo*
Where Is The Feeling	12"	RCA	FEEL1	1994	**£8**	**£4**	*promo*
Where Is The Feeling	12"	RCA	FEEL3	1994	**£75**	**£37.50**	*promo*
Where Is The Feeling	12"	RCA	FEEL4	1994	**£15**	**£7.50**	*promo*
Word Is Out	12"	PWL	PWLT204R	1991	**£10**	**£5**	*1 sided*
Word Is Out	CD-s	PWL	PWCD204	1991	**£12**	**£6**	
Wouldn't Change A Thing	CD-s	PWL	PWCD42	1989	**£12**	**£6**	
Wouldn't Change A Thing (Espagna Mix)	12"	PWL	PWLT42R	1989	**£12**	**£6**	

MINOR THREAT

Out Of Step	LP	Discord		198–	**£25**	**£10**	*US*

MINORBOPS

Need You Tonight	7"	Vogue	V9110	1958	**£400**	**£250**	*best auctioned*

MINOTAURUS

Fly Away	LP	private	1010	1971	**£50**	**£25**	*German*
Rain Over Thessalia	LP	Thorofon	ATH112	1970	**£50**	**£25**	*German*

MINSTRELS

Miss Highty Tighty	7"	Studio One	SO2050	1968	**£12**	**£6**	*Westmorelites B side*

MINT

Luv	7"	Tangerine	DP14	1969	**£4**	**£1.50**	

MINUTE MEN

Yankee Diddle	7"	Capitol	CL15206	1961	**£4**	**£1.50**	

MINUTEMEN (2)

Buzz Or Howl Under The Influence Of The Heat	12"	SST	SST016	1984	**£6**	**£2.50**	
Paranoid Time	7"	SST	SST002	1983	**£6**	**£2.50**	

MIRACLES

Ain't It Baby	7"	London	HL9366	1961	**£60**	**£30**	
Away We A Go Go	LP	Tamla Motown	(S)TML11044	1967	**£25**	**£10**	
Christmas With The Miracles	LP	Tamla	236	1963	**£100**	**£50**	*US*
Come On Do The Jerk	7"	Stateside	SS377	1965	**£20**	**£10**	
Cookin' With The Miracles	LP	Tamla	223	1962	**£100**	**£50**	*US*
Doin' Mickey's Monkey	LP	Tamla	T2245	1963	**£100**	**£50**	*US, stereo*
Doin' Mickey's Monkey	LP	Tamla	245	1963	**£60**	**£30**	*US, mono*
Fabulous Miracles	LP	Stateside	SL10099	1964	**£100**	**£50**	
From The Beginning	LP	Tamla Motown	(S)TML11031	1966	**£30**	**£15**	
Going To A Go Go	LP	Tamla Motown	TML11024	1966	**£30**	**£15**	

Title	Format	Label	Cat. No.	Year	Mint	VG	Notes
Going To A Go-Go	7"	Tamla Motown	TMG547	1966	£6	£2.50	
Hi We're The Miracles	LP	Tamla	220	1961	£125	£62.50	US
Hi We're The Miracles	LP	Oriole	PS40044	1963	£125	£62.50	
I Gotta Dance To Keep From Crying	7"	Stateside	SS263	1964	£30	£15	
I Like It Like That	7"	Stateside	SS324	1964	£20	£10	
I Like It Like That	LP	Tamla Motown	TML11003	1965	£40	£20	
I'll Try Something New	LP	Tamla	230	1962	£100	£50	US
I'm The One You Need	7"	Tamla Motown	TMG584	1966	£6	£2.50	
Man In You	7"	Stateside	SS282	1964	£20	£10	
Mickey's Monkey	7"	Oriole	CBA1863	1963	£40	£20	
My Girl Has Gone	7"	Tamla Motown	TMG540	1965	£12	£6	
Nothing But A Man	LP	Motown	MT/S630	1965	£25	£10	US, with other artists
On Stage	LP	Tamla	241	1963	£60	£30	US
Ooh Baby Baby	7"	Tamla Motown	TMG503	1965	£20	£10	
Shop Around	7"	London	HL9276	1961	£40	£20	
Shop Around	7" EP	London	RE1295	1961	£100	£50	
Shop Around	LP	Tamla	224	1962	£100	£50	US
That's What Love Is Made Of	7"	Stateside	SS353	1964	£20	£10	
Tracks Of My Tears	7"	Tamla Motown	TMG522	1965	£25	£12.50	
What's So Good About Goodbye	7"	Fontana	H384	1962	£100	£50	
Whole Lotta Shakin' In My Heart	7"	Tamla Motown	TMG569	1966	£12	£6	
You've Really Got A Hold On Me	7"	Oriole	CBA1795	1963	£60	£30	

MIRAGE

Title	Format	Label	Cat. No.	Year	Mint	VG	Notes
Carolyn	7"	Page One	POF111	1969	£5	£2	
Go Away	7"	CBS	202007	1965	£10	£5	
Hold On	7"	Philips	BF1554	1967	£6	£2.50	
It's In Her Kiss	7"	CBS	201772	1965	£10	£5	
Mystery Lady	7"	Page One	POF078	1968	£5	£2	
Tomorrow Never Knows	7"	Philips	BF1534	1966	£20	£10	
Wedding Of Ramona Blair	7"	Philips	BF1571	1967	£40	£20	

MIRETTES

Title	Format	Label	Cat. No.	Year	Mint	VG	Notes
In The Midnight Hour	LP	MCA	MUP(S)344	1969	£10	£4	

MIRK

Title	Format	Label	Cat. No.	Year	Mint	VG	Notes
Moddans Bower	LP	Mother Earth	MUM1205	1979	£50	£25	
Tak A Dram	LP	Spring Thyme	SPR1009	1982	£20	£8	

MIRKWOOD

Title	Format	Label	Cat. No.	Year	Mint	VG	Notes
Mirkwood	LP	Flams Ltd	PR1067	1973	£500	£330	

MIRROR

Title	Format	Label	Cat. No.	Year	Mint	VG	Notes
Gingerbread Man	7"	Philips	BF1666	1968	£40	£20	

MIRROR (2)

Title	Format	Label	Cat. No.	Year	Mint	VG	Notes
Daybreak	LP	TLP	TLP7623	1976	£100	£50	Dutch

MIRRORS

Title	Format	Label	Cat. No.	Year	Mint	VG	Notes
Cure For Cancer	7"	Lightning	GIL503	1978	£10	£5	
Dark Glasses	7"	Lightning	GIL540	1979	£10	£5	

MISFITS

Title	Format	Label	Cat. No.	Year	Mint	VG	Notes
Beware	12"	Cherry Red	PLP9	1981	£50	£25	
Horror Business	7"	Plan 9	PL1009	198–	£50	£25	
Night Of The Living Dead	7"	Plan 9		1980	£50	£25	

MISFITS (2)

Title	Format	Label	Cat. No.	Year	Mint	VG	Notes
You Won't See Me	7"	Aberdeen Students	PRI101	1966	£6	£2.50	

MISS JANE

Title	Format	Label	Cat. No.	Year	Mint	VG	Notes
Bad Mind People	7"	Pama	PM704	1968	£5	£2	

MISS LAVELL

Title	Format	Label	Cat. No.	Year	Mint	VG	Notes
Everybody's Got Somebody	7"	Vocalion	VP9236	1965	£10	£5	

MISS X

Title	Format	Label	Cat. No.	Year	Mint	VG	Notes
Christine	7"	Ember	EMBS175	1963	£6	£2.50	

MISSING LINK

Title	Format	Label	Cat. No.	Year	Mint	VG	Notes
Nevergreen	LP	United Artists	UAS29439	1972	£20	£8	German

MISSING SCIENTISTS

Title	Format	Label	Cat. No.	Year	Mint	VG	Notes
Big City Bright Lights	7"	Rough Trade	RT057	1980	£6	£2.50	

MISSION

Title	Format	Label	Cat. No.	Year	Mint	VG	Notes
Beyond The Pale (Armageddon Mix)	CD-s	Mercury	MTHCD6	1988	£5	£2	
Butterfly On A Wheel	CD-s	Mercury	MYCDB8	1990	£5	£2	12" box

Title	Format	Label	Cat. No.	Year	Mint	Good	Notes
Carved In Sand	CD	Mercury	8422512	1990	**£40**	**£20**	*promo box set, with sampler CD and cassette, video, single, biog*
Deliverance	CD-s	Mercury	MTHCD9	1990	**£5**	**£2**	*2 versions*
Deliverance Tour 1990 Sampler	CD	Mercury	SACD166	1990	**£20**	**£8**	*US promo, with the Wonderstuff*
Garden Of Delight	12"	Chapter 22		1986	**£8**	**£4**	*promo*
Hands Across The Ocean	CD-s	Mercury	MTHCD11	1990	**£5**	**£2**	
Into The Blue	CD-s	Mercury	MTHCD10	1990	**£5**	**£2**	
Kingdom Come	12"	Mercury	MYTHX7	1988	**£8**	**£4**	*promo*
Like A Hurricane	12"	Chapter 22	L12CHAP7	1986	**£6**	**£2.50**	*autographed*
Stay With Me	7"	Mercury	MYSG1	1986	**£4**	**£1.50**	*autographed, gatefold picture sleeve*
Tower Of Strength	CD-s	Polygram	0805262	1988	**£8**	**£4**	*CD video*
Tower Of Strength	CD-s	Mercury	MTHCD4	1988	**£5**	**£2**	
Wasteland	7"	Mercury	MYTHB2	1987	**£5**	**£2**	*2 singles, 5 photos, boxed*
Wasteland	CD-s	Polygram	0801202	1988	**£8**	**£4**	*CD video*
Words Upon The Sand	CD	Mercury	CDP169	1990	**£20**	**£8**	*US promo*

MISSION BELLES

Title	Format	Label	Cat. No.	Year	Mint	Good	Notes
Sincerely	7"	Decca	F12154	1965	**£4**	**£1.50**	

MISSISSIPPI

Title	Format	Label	Cat. No.	Year	Mint	Good	Notes
Mr Union Railway Man	7"	Fox	FOX1	1970	**£6**	**£2.50**	

MISSOURI

Title	Format	Label	Cat. No.	Year	Mint	Good	Notes
Missouri	LP	Panama	PRS1022	1978	**£25**	**£10**	*US*

MISSUS BEASTLY

Title	Format	Label	Cat. No.	Year	Mint	Good	Notes
Dr Aftershave And The Mixed Pickles	LP	April	001	1976	**£10**	**£4**	*German*
Missus Beastly	LP	Nova	622030	1974	**£15**	**£6**	*German*
Nara Asst Incense	LP	Opp	532	1970	**£30**	**£15**	*German*

MISTURA

Title	Format	Label	Cat. No.	Year	Mint	Good	Notes
Flasher	7"	Route	RT30	1976	**£4**	**£1.50**	

MISTY

Title	Format	Label	Cat. No.	Year	Mint	Good	Notes
Misty	LP	Cottage	COT511	1977	**£30**	**£15**	

MISUNDERSTOOD

The Misunderstood were essentially two groups, with Glenn Campbell, the Jimi Hendrix of the pedal steel guitar, as the only common link. The first line-up, which also included guitarist Tony Hill, later with High Tide, recorded two of the most remarkable singles of the era – for all that they somehow managed to avoid the charts – 'I Can Take You To The Sun' and 'Children Of The Sun'. Sponsored by John Peel, the group seemed destined for greatness, but problems with work permits and the draft (all but Hill were American) caused it to fall apart. Campbell tried again a couple of years later, with some good musicians, including guitarists David O'List (the Nice), Neil Hubbard (the Grease Band) and saxophonist Chris Mercer (John Mayall), but the line-up never quite managed to catch fire. Campbell, Hubbard and Mercer re-grouped as Juicy Lucy, while bass player Nic Potter and drummer Guy Evans joined Van Der Graaf Generator.

Title	Format	Label	Cat. No.	Year	Mint	Good	Notes
Children Of The Sun	7"	Fontana	TF998	1969	**£30**	**£15**	
I Can Take You To The Sun	7"	Fontana	TF777	1966	**£30**	**£15**	
Never Had A Girl Like You	7"	Fontana	TF1041	1969	**£25**	**£12.50**	
You're Tuff Enough	7"	Fontana	TF1028	1969	**£15**	**£7.50**	
You're Tuff Enough	7"	Fontana	TF1028	1969	**£30**	**£15**	*picture sleeve*

MITCHELL, BLUE

Title	Format	Label	Cat. No.	Year	Mint	Good	Notes
Bantu Village	LP	Blue Note	BST84324	1969	**£15**	**£6**	
Big Six	LP	Riverside	RLP12273	196–	**£15**	**£6**	
Blue Soul	LP	Riverside	RLP12309/1155	1960	**£15**	**£6**	
Blue's Blues	LP	Mainstream	MRL374	1973	**£10**	**£4**	*US*
Boss Horn	LP	Blue Note	BLP/BST84257	1967	**£25**	**£10**	
Bring It Home To Me	LP	Blue Note	BLP/BST84228	1966	**£25**	**£10**	
Collision In Black	LP	Blue Note	BST84300	1968	**£15**	**£6**	
Down With It	LP	Blue Note	BLP/BST84214	1965	**£25**	**£10**	
Heads Up!	LP	Blue Note	BST84272	1968	**£25**	**£10**	
Smooth As The Wind	LP	Riverside	RLP367	1961	**£15**	**£6**	
Thing To Do	LP	Blue Note	BLP/BST84178	1964	**£15**	**£6**	

MITCHELL, CHAD TRIO

Title	Format	Label	Cat. No.	Year	Mint	Good	Notes
Dona Dona Dona	7" EP	Kapp	KEV13015	1965	**£10**	**£5**	*French*
Paddy	7" EP	Colpix	CPS855	1965	**£8**	**£4**	*French, no picture sleeve*

MITCHELL, GROVER

Title	Format	Label	Cat. No.	Year	Mint	Good	Notes
What Hurts	7"	Vanguard	VS5003	1976	**£20**	**£10**	

MITCHELL, GUY

Title	Format	Label	Cat. No.	Year	Mint	Good	Notes
Best Of Guy Mitchell	LP	Realm	RM52336	1966	**£10**	**£4**	
C'mon Let's Go	7"	Philips	PB766	1958	**£5**	**£2**	
Call Rosie On The Phone	7"	Philips	JK1027	1957	**£15**	**£7.50**	
Feet Up	7"	Columbia	SCM5018	1952	**£25**	**£12.50**	
Guy In Love	LP	Philips	BBL7246	1958	**£20**	**£8**	
Guy Mitchell	7" EP	Columbia	SEG7513	1954	**£8**	**£4**	
Guy Mitchell Sings	10" LP	Columbia	33S1028	1954	**£30**	**£15**	
Hangin' Around	7"	Philips	PB830	1958	**£4**	**£1.50**	
Knee Deep In The Blues	7"	Philips	JK1005	1957	**£25**	**£12.50**	

Title	Format	Label	Cat. No.	Year	Mint	VG	Notes
Let It Shine, Let It Shine	7"	Philips	PB858	1958	**£4**	**£1.50**	
My Heart Cries For You	7"	Philips	PB885	1958	**£4**	**£1.50**	
My Shoes Keep Walking Back To You	7"	Philips	PB1050	1960	**£4**	**£1.50**	
Pennies From Heaven	7" EP	Philips	BBE12215	1958	**£10**	**£5**	
Pretty Little Black Eyed Susie	7"	Columbia	SCM5037	1953	**£20**	**£10**	
Pride O' Dixie	7"	Philips	PB915	1959	**£4**	**£1.50**	
Rock-A-Billy	7"	Philips	JK1015	1957	**£20**	**£10**	
She Wears Red Feathers	7"	Columbia	SCM5032	1953	**£25**	**£12.50**	
Showcase Of Hits	LP	Philips	BBL7265	1958	**£20**	**£8**	
Singing The Blues	7"	CBS	202238	1966	**£8**	**£4**	
Singing The Blues	7"	Philips	JK1001	1956	**£40**	**£20**	
Singing The Blues	7" EP	Philips	BBE12112	1957	**£10**	**£5**	
Sings No. 1	7" EP	Philips	BBE12008	1955	**£8**	**£4**	
Sings No. 2	7" EP	Philips	BBE12093	1956	**£10**	**£5**	
Successes	7" EP	Columbia	SEG7598	1955	**£8**	**£4**	
Sunshine Guitar	LP	Philips	BBL7465	1961	**£20**	**£8**	
Sweet Stuff	7"	Philips	JK1023	1957	**£15**	**£7.50**	
Train Of Love	7"	Columbia	SCM5022	1953	**£20**	**£10**	*with Mindy Carsom*
Travelling Shoes	LP	London	HAB/SHB8364	1968	**£10**	**£4**	
Voice Of Your Choice	10" LP	Philips	BBR8031	1955	**£25**	**£10**	
Wonderful Guy	7" EP	Columbia	SEG7581	1955	**£8**	**£4**	
Wonderin' And Worryin'	7"	Philips	PB798	1958	**£4**	**£1.50**	

MITCHELL, JONI

Joni Mitchell's way with words, combined with an ear for an unusual melody, a love of musical change and adventure, and above all, a beautiful voice, has made her into one of the world's dozen or so truly essential rock artists. This guide persists in listing her first LP as *Song To A Seagull*, since although the label has only the more prosaic *Joni Mitchell*, the cover has the more interesting title spelled out by seagulls, painted, as the majority of her album sleeves are, by Joni Mitchell herself.

Title	Format	Label	Cat. No.	Year	Mint	VG	Notes
Blue	CD	Reprise	CD8811	1988	**£15**	**£6**	*box set*
Blue	LP	Reprise	K44128	1971	**£10**	**£4**	*blue inner sleeve*
Chalk Mark In A Rain Storm – Inside Information	CD	Geffen		1988	**£40**	**£20**	*promo box set, with cassette, photo, biog*
Chelsea Morning	7"	Reprise	RS23402	1969	**£4**	**£1.50**	
Chinese Café	7"	Geffen	DA3122	1983	**£4**	**£1.50**	*with interview 7"*
Clouds	LP	Reprise	RSLP6341	1969	**£15**	**£6**	
Clouds	LP	Reprise	RSLP6341	1969	**£15**	**£6**	*with US gatefold sleeve*
Come In From The Cold	CD-s	Geffen	GFSTD4	1991	**£5**	**£2**	
Conversation With Joni Mitchell	CD	Geffen	PROCD3076	1988	**£25**	**£10**	*US promo*
Court And Spark	LP	Nautilus	NR11	1981	**£12**	**£5**	*US audiophile*
Court And Spark	LP	Asylum	EQ10001	1974	**£15**	**£6**	*US quad*
Hissing Of Summer Lawns	LP	Nimbus/ Asylum	K53018	1982	**£12**	**£5**	*audiophile*
Hissing Of Summer Lawns	LP	Asylum	EQ1051	1975	**£15**	**£6**	*US quad*
Ladies Of The Canyon	LP	Reprise	RSLP6376	1970	**£15**	**£6**	
Miles Of Aisles	LP	Asylum	SYSP902	1975	**£12**	**£5**	*double*
My Secret Place	CD-s	Geffen	GEF37CD	1988	**£5**	**£2**	*3" single*
Night In The City	7"	Reprise	RS20694	1968	**£4**	**£1.50**	
Night Ride Home	CD-s	Geffen	GFSTD2	1991	**£5**	**£2**	
Night Ride Home Radio Program	CD	Geffen	GEFD9143	1991	**£40**	**£20**	*US promo*
Shadows And Light	LP	Asylum	K62030	1980	**£12**	**£5**	*double*
Song To A Seagull	LP	Reprise	RSLP6293	1968	**£15**	**£6**	
Wild Things Run Fast	LP	Geffen	GHS2019	1982	**£25**	**£10**	*US audiophile promo*
You Turn Me On I'm A Radio	7"	Asylum	AYM511	1972	**£4**	**£1.50**	

MITCHELL, KEVIN

Title	Format	Label	Cat. No.	Year	Mint	VG	Notes
Free And Easy	LP	Topic	12TS314	1977	**£12**	**£5**	

MITCHELL, PAT

Title	Format	Label	Cat. No.	Year	Mint	VG	Notes
Uillean Pipes	LP	Topic	12TS294	1976	**£10**	**£4**	

MITCHELL, RED

Title	Format	Label	Cat. No.	Year	Mint	VG	Notes
Presenting Red Mitchell	LP	Contemporary	LAC12155	1959	**£20**	**£8**	
Red Mitchell	LP	London	LTZN15041	1957	**£20**	**£8**	

MITCHELL, RONNIE

Title	Format	Label	Cat. No.	Year	Mint	VG	Notes
How Many Times	7"	London	HLU9220	1960	**£4**	**£1.50**	

MITCHELL, ROSCOE

Title	Format	Label	Cat. No.	Year	Mint	VG	Notes
Sound	LP	Delmark	DL408/DS9408	1967	**£12**	**£5**	

MITCHELL, SINX

Title	Format	Label	Cat. No.	Year	Mint	VG	Notes
Weird Sensation	7"	Hickory	451248	1964	**£8**	**£4**	

MITCHELL, VALERIE

Title	Format	Label	Cat. No.	Year	Mint	VG	Notes
There Goes My Heart Again	7"	Oak	RGJ160	1965	**£30**	**£15**	*picture sleeve*

MITCHELL, WARREN

Title	Format	Label	Cat. No.	Year	Mint	VG	Notes
Alf Garnett – Sex And Other Thoughts	LP	Pye	NPL18192	1968	**£10**	**£4**	
Till Death Us Do Part	LP	Pye	NPL18154	1966	**£10**	**£4**	*with other artists*

MITCHELL, WILLIE

Title	Format	Label	Cat. No.	Year	Mint	VG	Notes
20–75	7"	London	HLU9926	1964	**£4**	**£1.50**	
Bad Eye	7"	London	HLU10039	1966	**£4**	**£1.50**	

Everything Is Gonna Be Alright	7"	London	HLU10004	1965	**£8**	**£4**	
Hit Sound Of Willie Mitchell	LP	London	HAU8319	1967	**£10**	**£4**	
Live	LP	London	HAU/SHU8368	1968	**£10**	**£4**	
Mercy	7"	London	HLU10085	1966	**£4**	**£1.50**	
On Top	LP	London	HAU/SHU8388	1969	**£10**	**£4**	
Solid Soul	LP	London	HAU/SHU8372	1969	**£10**	**£4**	
Soul Bag	LP	London	HAU/SHU8408	1970	**£10**	**£4**	
Soul Serenade	LP	London	HAU/SHU8365	1968	**£10**	**£4**	
Sunrise Serenade	LP	Hi	(S)HL32010	1963	**£12**	**£5**	*US*

MITCHELL/COE MYSTERIES

Exiled	LP	RCA	PL25297	1980	**£10**	**£4**	

MITCHELLS

Get Those Elephants Outa Here	LP	MGM	C803	1960	**£20**	**£8**	

MITCHUM, ROBERT

Ballad Of Thunder Road	7"	Capitol	CL15251	1962	**£6**	**£2.50**	
Calypso Is Like So	LP	Capitol	T853		**£25**	**£10**	*US*
Rachel And The Stranger	7" EP	Brunswick	OE9197	1955	**£10**	**£5**	
That Man	LP	Monument	LMO5011	1967	**£10**	**£4**	
What Is This Generation Coming To?	7"	Capitol	CL14701	1957	**£10**	**£5**	

MITHRANDIR

For You The Old Women	LP	private		1976	**£40**	**£20**	*US*

MITHRANDIR (2)

Dreamers Of Fortune	7"	New Leaf	SVC570	1982	**£30**	**£15**	
Magick EP	7"	New Leaf	SVC01	1982	**£50**	**£25**	

MITTOO, JACKIE

Ba Ba Boom	7"	Coxsone	CS7009	1967	**£10**	**£5**	*Slim Smith B side*
Can I Change My Mind	7"	Bamboo	BAM31	1970	**£4**	**£1.50**	*Brentford Allstars B side*
Clean Up	7"	Bamboo	BAM15	1969	**£4**	**£1.50**	
Dancing Groove	7"	Bamboo	BAM51	1970	**£4**	**£1.50**	*Black & George B side*
Dark Of The Moon	7"	Bamboo	BAM17	1970	**£4**	**£1.50**	
Dark Of The Sun	7"	Doctor Bird	DB1177	1969	**£10**	**£5**	*Matador Allstars B side*
Evening Time	LP	Coxsone	CSL8014	1968	**£100**	**£50**	
Gold Dust	7"	Bamboo	BAM20	1970	**£4**	**£1.50**	*Supertones B side*
Holly Holy	7"	Banana	BA315	1970	**£5**	**£2**	*Larry Marshall B side*
In London	LP	Coxsone	CSL8009	1967	**£100**	**£50**	
Keep On Dancing	LP	Coxsone	CSL8020	1969	**£100**	**£50**	
Killer Diller	7"	Island	WI293	1966	**£10**	**£5**	*Patrick Hytton B side*
Man Pon Spot	7"	Coxsone	CS7046	1968	**£10**	**£5**	*Bop & The Beltones B side*
Mission Impossible	7"	Coxsone	CS7075	1968	**£10**	**£5**	*Heptones B side*
Napoleon Solo	7"	Coxsone	CS7050	1968	**£10**	**£5**	*Cannonball Bryan B side*
Norwegian Wood	7"	Coxsone	CS7040	1968	**£10**	**£5**	*Gaylads B side*
Now	LP	Bamboo	BDLPS209	1970	**£30**	**£15**	
Our Thing	7"	Bamboo	BAM6	1969	**£4**	**£1.50**	*C. Marshall B side*
Peenie Wallie	7"	Banana	BA320	1971	**£5**	**£2**	*Roy Richards B side*
Put It On	7"	Studio One	SO2043	1968	**£12**	**£6**	*Soul Vendors B side*
Ram Jam	7"	Coxsone	CS7019	1967	**£10**	**£5**	*Summertaires B side*
Somebody Help Me	7"	Coxsone	CS7002	1967	**£10**	**£5**	*Gaylads B side*
Somethin' Stupid	7"	Coxsone	CS7026	1967	**£10**	**£5**	*Lyrics B side*
Songbird	7"	Coxsone	CS7070	1968	**£10**	**£5**	
Sure Shot	7"	Coxsone	CS7042	1968	**£10**	**£5**	*Octaves B side*
Wishbone	LP	London	SHU8436	1972	**£12**	**£5**	

MIX BLOOD

Last Train To Skaville	7"	Creole	CR201	1980	**£6**	**£2.50**	

MIXTURES

Stompin' At The Rainbow	LP	Linda	3301	1962	**£20**	**£8**	*US*

MIZAROLLI, JOHN

Message From The Fifth Stone	LP	Carrere	CAL142	1982	**£12**	**£5**	

MIZZY, VIC

Addams Family Main Theme	7"	RCA	RCA1440	1965	**£15**	**£7.50**	

MNEMONISTS

Gyromancy	LP	Dys	DYS10	1985	**£12**	**£5**	*US*
Mnemonist Orchestra	7"	Recommended	REX84	1984	**£8**	**£4**	

MO & CO

You've Got A Friend	LP	Cottage	COT131	1979	**£12**	**£5**	

MO & STEVE

Oh What A Day It's Going To Be	7"	Pye	7N17175	1966	**£4**	**£1.50**	

MOB

Title	Format	Label	Cat. No.	Year	Mint	VG	Notes
Send Me To Coventry	7"	Kalida	AKB1/2	1980	**£10**	**£5**	

MOBLEY, HANK

Title	Format	Label	Cat. No.	Year	Mint	VG	Notes
All Stars	LP	Blue Note	BLP/BST81544	196–	**£30**	**£15**	
Caddy For Daddy	LP	Blue Note	BLP/BST84230	1966	**£20**	**£8**	
Dippin'	LP	Blue Note	BLP/BST84209	1965	**£30**	**£15**	
Flip	LP	Blue Note	BST84329	1969	**£12**	**£5**	
Hi Voltage	LP	Blue Note	BST84273	1968	**£20**	**£8**	
Jazz Message No. 2	LP	London	LTZC15099	1957	**£30**	**£15**	
Mobley's Message	LP	Esquire	32029	1957	**£30**	**£15**	
No Room For Squares	LP	Blue Note	BLP/BST84149	1963	**£25**	**£10**	
Reach Out!	LP	Blue Note	BST84288	1968	**£15**	**£6**	
Roll Call	LP	Blue Note	BLP/BST84058	1961	**£30**	**£15**	
Soul Station	LP	Blue Note	BLP/BST84031	196–	**£40**	**£20**	
Turnaround!	LP	Blue Note	BLP/BST84186	1964	**£30**	**£15**	
Workout	LP	Blue Note	BLP/BST84080	1961	**£30**	**£15**	

MOBY

Title	Format	Label	Cat. No.	Year	Mint	VG	Notes
Everything Is Wrong	CD	Mute	CDSTUMM130	1995	**£15**	**£6**	*double*
Go	CD-s	Outer Rhythm	FOOT015CD	1991	**£5**	**£2**	

MOBY DICK

Title	Format	Label	Cat. No.	Year	Mint	VG	Notes
Nothing To Fear	7"	Ebony	EBON5	1982	**£8**	**£4**	

MOBY GRAPE

When Columbia records in America decided to try the marketing device of simultaneously releasing every track from Moby Grape's first LP on five singles, this was certainly recognition of the fact that every track is distinctive enough to withstand the treatment. The LP is frequently held up as San Francisco's best, an assessment that is not far from the truth. Thereafter, Moby Grape's career was one of decline, although *Wow* has its moments. The *Grape Jam* record that accompanied the US release is a wasted opportunity, however. Acquiring the services of a master guitarist like Mike Bloomfield and then sitting him in front of a piano is simply daft.

Title	Format	Label	Cat. No.	Year	Mint	VG	Notes
Can't Be So Bad	7"	CBS	3555	1968	**£4**	**£1.50**	
Moby Grape	LP	CBS	(S)BPG63090	1967	**£15**	**£6**	
Moby Grape	LP	San Francisco Sound	04805	1983	**£10**	**£4**	*US audiophile*
Moby Grape '69	LP	CBS	63430	1969	**£10**	**£4**	
Omaha	7"	CBS	2935	1967	**£6**	**£2.50**	
Trucking Man	7"	CBS	3945	1969	**£4**	**£1.50**	
Truly Fine Citizen	LP	CBS	63698	1970	**£10**	**£4**	
Wow	LP	CBS	63271	1968	**£15**	**£6**	
Wow/Grape Jam	LP	Columbia	CS9613	1968	**£25**	**£10**	*US double*
Wow/Grape Jam	LP	San Francisco Sound	04801	1983	**£20**	**£8**	*US audiophile double*

MOCK TURTLES

Title	Format	Label	Cat. No.	Year	Mint	VG	Notes
And Then She Smiles	12"	Mirage	015	1989	**£6**	**£2.50**	
Pomona	12"	Mirage	003	1987	**£12**	**£6**	
Wicker Man	12"	Mirage	009	1989	**£8**	**£4**	

MOCKINGBIRDS

Kevin Godley and Graham Gouldman of 10cc were both members of the Mockingbirds, while the Immediate single also featured Julie Driscoll on backing vocals.

Title	Format	Label	Cat. No.	Year	Mint	VG	Notes
How To Find A Lover	7"	Decca	F12510	1966	**£40**	**£20**	
I Can Feel We're Parting	7"	Columbia	DB7565	1965	**£50**	**£25**	
One By One	7"	Decca	F12434	1966	**£40**	**£20**	
That's How It's Gonna Stay	7"	Columbia	DB7480	1965	**£50**	**£25**	
You Stole My Love	7"	Immediate	IM015	1965	**£125**	**£62.50**	

M.O.D.

Title	Format	Label	Cat. No.	Year	Mint	VG	Notes
M.O.D.	7"	Vertigo	6059233	1979	**£5**	**£2**	

MODE

Title	Format	Label	Cat. No.	Year	Mint	VG	Notes
Mode	7" EP	private		1967	**£200**	**£100**	*best auctioned*

MODELS

Title	Format	Label	Cat. No.	Year	Mint	VG	Notes
Freeze	7"	Skip Forward	SF3	1977	**£5**	**£2**	

MODERN ART

Title	Format	Label	Cat. No.	Year	Mint	VG	Notes
Dreams To Live	7"	Color Disc	COLORS1	1985	**£20**	**£10**	
Penny Valentine	7"	Color Disc	COLORS5	1986	**£8**	**£4**	
Stereoland	LP	Color Disc	COLOR3	1987	**£40**	**£20**	

MODERN ENGLISH

Title	Format	Label	Cat. No.	Year	Mint	VG	Notes
Drowning Man	7"	Limp	LMP2	1979	**£10**	**£5**	
Swans On Glass	7"	4AD	AD6	1980	**£4**	**£1.50**	

MODERN EON

Title	Format	Label	Cat. No.	Year	Mint	VG	Notes
Euthenics	7"	Inevitable	INEV003	1981	**£5**	**£2**	
Pieces	7"	Modern Eon	EON001	1980	**£12**	**£6**	

MODERN FOLK QUARTET

Title	Format	Label	Cat. No.	Year	Mint	VG	Notes
Changes	LP	Warner Bros	WM8157	1964	**£10**	**£4**	
Modern Folk Quartet	LP	Warner Bros	WM/WS8135	1963	**£10**	**£4**	

Title	Format	Label	Cat. No.	Year	Mint	VG	Notes
Night Time Girl	7"	RCA	RCA1514	1966	£8	£4	
Palm Springs Weekend	LP	Warner Bros	W(S)1519	1963	£12	£5	*US, with Connie Stevens*

MODERN JAZZ QUARTET

Title	Format	Label	Cat. No.	Year	Mint	VG	Notes
All Of You	7" EP	Fontana	469204TE	195–	£5	£2	
At Music Inn	7" EP	London	REK1320	1961	£5	£2	
At Music Inn	LP	London	LTZK15085	1957	£15	£6	
At Music Inn Volume 2	LP	London	LTZK15173/ SAHK6050	1959	£15	£6	*with Sonny Rollins*
At The Opera House	LP	Columbia	33CX10128	1958	£20	£8	*with Oscar Peterson*
Best Of The Modern Jazz Quartet	LP	Stateside	SL10141	1965	£12	£5	
Blues At Carnegie Hall	LP	Atlantic	SD1468	1967	£12	£5	*US*
Collaboration	LP	Atlantic	SD1429	1966	£12	£5	*US*
Comedy Suite	LP	London	HAK/SHK8046	1963	£12	£5	
Concorde	10" LP	Esquire	20069	1956	£40	£20	
Concorde	LP	Transatlantic	PR7005	196–	£10	£4	
European Concert	7" EP	London	REK1319	1961	£5	£2	
Five Ways Of Playing La Ronde	7" EP	Esquire	EP166	1958	£5	£2	
Fontessa	LP	London	LTZK15022/ SAHK6031	1957	£15	£6	
Gershwin Ballad Medley	7" EP	Esquire	EP116	1956	£5	£2	
Jazz Dialogue	LP	Atlantic	SD1449	1966	£12	£5	*US*
Legendary Profile	LP	Atlantic	K40421	1973	£10	£4	
Live At The Lighthouse	LP	Atlantic	SD1486	1967	£12	£5	*US*
Lonely Woman	LP	London	HAK/SHK8016	1963	£12	£5	
Looking Back	LP	Esquire	32124	1961	£15	£6	
Modern Jazz Quartet	10" LP	Esquire	20038	1955	£40	£20	
Modern Jazz Quartet	7" EP	London	REK1314	1961	£5	£2	
Modern Jazz Quartet	7" EP	London	EZK19047	1959	£5	£2	
Modern Jazz Quartet	7" EP	Esquire	EP109	1956	£5	£2	
Modern Jazz Quartet	7" EP	Esquire	EP106	1956	£5	£2	
Modern Jazz Quartet	LP	London	LTZK15136	1958	£15	£6	
Modern Jazz Quartet And Orchestra	LP	Atlantic	SD1359	1961	£15	£6	*US*
No Sun In Venice	LP	Atlantic	SD1284	1958	£15	£6	*US*
Odds Against Tomorrow	LP	London	LTZT15181	1960	£15	£6	
One Never Knows	7" EP	London	EZK19046	1959	£5	£2	
One Never Knows	LP	London	LTZK15140/ SAHK6029	1958	£15	£6	
Plastic Dreams	LP	Atlantic	K40318	1972	£10	£4	
Porgy And Bess	LP	Philips	BL7692	1965	£12	£5	
Pyramid	LP	London	LTZK15193/ SAHK6086	1960	£15	£6	
Quartet	7" EP	London	EZC19019	1957	£5	£2	
Quartet Is A Quartet Is A Quartet	LP	Atlantic	587044	1966	£12	£5	
Sheriff	LP	London	HAK/SHK8161	1964	£12	£5	
Space	LP	Apple	SAPCOR10	1969	£30	£15	*single or gatefold sleeve*
Stockholm Concert	LP	Atlantic	590012	1968	£12	£5	
Sun Dance	LP	Atlantic	588126	1968	£12	£5	
Third Stream Music	LP	London	LTZK15207/ SAHK6124	1961	£15	£6	
Under The Jasmine Tree	LP	Apple	SAPCOR4	1968	£30	£15	*stereo*
Under The Jasmine Tree	LP	Apple	APCOR4	1968	£40	£20	*mono*

MODERN JAZZ SEXTET

Title	Format	Label	Cat. No.	Year	Mint	VG	Notes
Modern Jazz Sextet	LP	Columbia	33CX10048	1956	£40	£20	

MODERN JAZZ SOCIETY

Title	Format	Label	Cat. No.	Year	Mint	VG	Notes
Concert Of Contemporary Music	LP	Columbia	33CX10038	1956	£40	£20	

MODERNAIRES

Title	Format	Label	Cat. No.	Year	Mint	VG	Notes
At My Front Door	7"	Vogue Coral	Q72112	1955	£6	£2.50	
Birds And Puppies And Tropical Fish	7"	Vogue Coral	Q72069	1955	£5	£2	
Go On With The Wedding	7"	Vogue Coral	Q72158	1956	£4	£1.50	
Here Comes The Modernaires	LP	Coral	LVA9080	1958	£10	£4	
Let's Dance	7"	Vogue Coral	Q72135	1956	£4	£1.50	
Mood Indigo	7"	Vogue Coral	Q2024	1954	£5	£2	
New Juke Box Saturday Night	7"	Vogue Coral	Q2035	1954	£5	£2	
Sluefoot	7"	Vogue Coral	Q72084	1955	£5	£2	
Stop, Look And Listen	10" LP	Vogue Coral	LVC10012	1955	£15	£6	

MODS

Title	Format	Label	Cat. No.	Year	Mint	VG	Notes
Lost Touch	LP	Bootlegged	007	1980	£20	£8	
Something On My Mind	7"	RCA	RCA1399	1964	£4	£1.50	

MOFFAT ALLSTARS

Title	Format	Label	Cat. No.	Year	Mint	VG	Notes
Riot	7"	Jackpot	JP719	1969	£5	£2	*Impersonators B side*

MOGUL THRASH

Title	Format	Label	Cat. No.	Year	Mint	VG	Notes
Mogul Thrash	LP	RCA	SF8156	1971	£20	£8	
Sleeping In The Kitchen	7"	RCA	RCA2030	1970	£4	£1.50	

MOGWAI

Title	Format	Label	Cat. No.	Year	Mint	VG	Notes
4 Track 3 Band Tour EP	7"	Che	CHE59	1996	£12	£6	*with Urusei Yatsura & Blackwater*
Angels Vs The Aliens	7"	Che	CHE61	1996	£8	£4	*green vinyl*

Stereo Dee	7"	Flotsam & Jetsam	SHAG1304	1997	**£20**	**£10**	*with PH Family*
Summer	7"	Love Train	PUBE014	1996	**£10**	**£5**	
Tuner	7"	Rock Action	RAR01	1996	**£25**	**£12.50**	

MOHAWK, ESSRA

Essra	LP	Private Stock	PVLP1016	1977	**£10**	**£4**	
Essra Mohawk	LP	Mooncrest	CREST24	1975	**£10**	**£4**	

MOHAWKS

Baby Hold On	7"	Pama	PM739	1968	**£5**	**£2**	
Champ	7"	Pama	PM719	1968	**£8**	**£4**	
Champ	LP	Pama	PMLP5	1968	**£50**	**£25**	
Mony Mony	7"	Pama	PM757	1968	**£5**	**£2**	
Ride Your Pony	7"	Pama	PM758	1968	**£5**	**£2**	
Sweet Soul Music	7"	Pama	PM751	1968	**£5**	**£2**	

MOHOLO, LOUIS

Spirits Rejoice!	LP	Ogun	OG520	1978	**£15**	**£6**	

MOJO BLUESBAND

Hey Bartender	LP	Ex Libris	12387	1970	**£30**	**£15**	*Swiss*

MOJO HANNAH

Six Days On The Road	LP	Kingdom	KVL9001	1972	**£15**	**£6**	

MOJO MEN

Dance With Me	7"	Pye	7N25336	1965	**£5**	**£2**	
Dance With Me	7" EP	Vogue	INT18050	1965	**£60**	**£30**	*French*
Hanky Panky	7"	Reprise	RS20486	1966	**£20**	**£10**	
Me About You	7"	Reprise	RS20580	1967	**£6**	**£2.50**	
Sit Down I Think I Love You	7"	Reprise	RS20539	1967	**£5**	**£2**	

MOJOS

Comin' On To Cry	7"	Decca	F12127	1965	**£5**	**£2**	
Everything's Alright	7"	Decca	F11853	1964	**£5**	**£2**	
Forever	7"	Decca	F11732	1963	**£5**	**£2**	
Goodbye Dolly Gray	7"	Decca	F12557	1967	**£6**	**£2.50**	
Mojos	7" EP	Decca	DFE8591	1964	**£40**	**£20**	
Until My Baby Comes Home	7"	Liberty	LBF15097	1968	**£25**	**£12.50**	
Wait A Minute	7"	Decca	F12231	1965	**£10**	**£5**	*Stu James credit*

MOLES

Noting that the Moles' single was on the Parlophone label, and that it had moreover been produced by George Martin, many observers concluded that it must be a Beatles performance. In fact, 'the Moles' was indeed a pseudonym, but for the rather less exciting Simon Dupree and the Big Sound.

We Are The Moles	7"	Parlophone	R5743	1968	**£20**	**£10**	

MOLLOY, MATT

Heathery Breeze	LP	Polydor	2904018	1981	**£10**	**£4**	*Irish*
Matt Molloy	LP	Mulligan	LUN004	1976	**£10**	**£4**	*Irish*
Matt Molloy, Paul Brady, Tommy Peoples	LP	Mulligan	LUN017	1978	**£10**	**£4**	*Irish*

MOLLY HATCHET

Beatin' The Odds	LP	Epic	AS99844	1980	**£25**	**£10**	*US promo picture disc*
Flirtin' With Disaster	LP	CBS	AL36110	1979	**£25**	**£10**	*US picture disc*
Molly Hatchet	LP	Epic	35347	1978	**£25**	**£10**	*US picture disc*
Take No Prisoners	LP	Epic	AS991320	1981	**£25**	**£10**	*US promo picture disc*

MOLOCH

Moloch	LP	Enterprise	ENS1002	1972	**£20**	**£8**	*US*

MOLONEY, MICK

We Have Met Together	LP	Transatlantic	TRA263	1973	**£12**	**£5**	

MOLONEY, PADDY & SEAN POTTS

Tin Whistles	LP	Claddagh	CC15	1974	**£12**	**£5**	*Irish*

MOMENTS

Walk Right In	7"	London	HLN9656	1963	**£5**	**£2**	

MOMUS

Hippopotamomus	CD-s	Creation	CRECD097	1991	**£20**	**£10**	*with 'Michelin Man'*

MON DYH

Murderer	LP	Elgenprod	6622192	1981	**£10**	**£4**	*German*

MONARCHS

Look Homeward Angel	7"	London	HLU9862	1964	**£20**	**£10**	

MONCUR III, GRACHAN

Evolution	LP	Blue Note	BLP/BST84153	1963	**£20**	**£8**	
Some Other Stuff	LP	Blue Note	BLP/BST84177	1964	**£20**	**£8**	

MONDAY, PAUL

Paul Monday was one of several names used by the man who found success as Gary Glitter.

Title	Format	Label	Cat. No.	Year	Mint	VG	Notes
Here Comes The Sun	7"	MCA	MK5008	1969	**£10**	**£5**	
Musical Man	7"	MCA	MU1024	1968	**£10**	**£5**	

MONEY

Title	Format	Label	Cat. No.	Year	Mint	VG	Notes
Aren't We All Searching	7"	Gull	GULL64	1979	**£5**	**£2**	
Fast World	7"	Hobo	HOS011	1980	**£30**	**£15**	

MONEY, ZOOT

Title	Format	Label	Cat. No.	Year	Mint	VG	Notes
Big Time Operator	7"	Columbia	DB7975	1966	**£15**	**£7.50**	
Big Time Operator	7" EP	Columbia	SEG8519	1966	**£125**	**£62.50**	
Big Time Operator	7" EP	Columbia	ESRF1801	1966	**£100**	**£50**	*French*
Good	7"	Columbia	DB7518	1965	**£15**	**£7.50**	
It Should Have Been Me	LP	Columbia	SX1734	1965	**£60**	**£30**	
Let's Run For Cover	7"	Columbia	DB7876	1966	**£15**	**£7.50**	
Mr Money	LP	Magic Moon	LUNE1	1980	**£10**	**£4**	
Nick Knack	7" EP	Columbia	ESRF1874	1967	**£100**	**£50**	*French*
Nick Knack	7"	Columbia	DB8172	1967	**£15**	**£7.50**	
No One But You	7"	Polydor	2058020	1970	**£15**	**£7.50**	
Please Stay	7"	Columbia	DB7600	1965	**£15**	**£7.50**	
Please Stay	7" EP	Columbia	ESRF1766	1966	**£100**	**£50**	*French*
Something Is Worrying Me	7"	Columbia	DB7697	1965	**£15**	**£7.50**	
Star Of the Show	7"	Columbia	DB8090	1966	**£15**	**£7.50**	
Transition	LP	Direction	863231	1968	**£25**	**£10**	
Two Of Us	7"	Magic Moon	MACH6	1980	**£5**	**£2**	
Uncle Willie	7"	Decca	F11954	1964	**£25**	**£12.50**	
Welcome To My Head	LP	Capitol	318	1969	**£25**	**£10**	*US*
Your Feet's Too Big	7"	Magic Moon	MACH3	1980	**£4**	**£1.50**	
Zoot	LP	Columbia	SX/SCX6075	1966	**£30**	**£15**	
Zoot Money	LP	Polydor	2482019	1970	**£15**	**£6**	

MONGREL

Title	Format	Label	Cat. No.	Year	Mint	VG	Notes
Get Your Teeth Into This	LP	Polydor	2383182	1973	**£15**	**£6**	

MONGRELS

Title	Format	Label	Cat. No.	Year	Mint	VG	Notes
I Long To Hear	7"	Decca	F12003	1964	**£20**	**£10**	
My Love For You	7"	Decca	F12086	1965	**£20**	**£10**	

MONITORS

Title	Format	Label	Cat. No.	Year	Mint	VG	Notes
Greetings We're The Monitors	LP	Tamla Motown	(S)TML11108	1969	**£40**	**£20**	

MONK, THELONIOUS

Title	Format	Label	Cat. No.	Year	Mint	VG	Notes
Alone In San Francisco	LP	Riverside	RLP312	1965	**£12**	**£5**	
Blue Monk	7" EP	Esquire	EP246	1962	**£5**	**£2**	
Brilliant Corners	LP	London	LTZU15097	1957	**£25**	**£10**	
Brilliant Corners	LP	Riverside	RLP12226	1961	**£20**	**£8**	
Criss-Cross	LP	CBS	(S)BPG62173	1964	**£12**	**£5**	
Five By Monk By Five	LP	Riverside	RLP305	1965	**£12**	**£5**	
Genius Of Modern Music Vol. 1	LP	Blue Note	BLP/BST81510	1964	**£25**	**£10**	
Genius Of Modern Music Vol. 2	LP	Blue Note	BLP/BST81511	1964	**£25**	**£10**	
Golden Monk	LP	Stateside	SL10152	1965	**£12**	**£5**	
In Concert	LP	Storyville	673022	1969	**£10**	**£4**	
In Europe Vol. 1	LP	Riverside	RLP002	1964	**£12**	**£5**	
In Europe Vol. 2	LP	Riverside	RLP003	1965	**£12**	**£5**	
In Europe Vol. 3	LP	Riverside	RLP004	1966	**£12**	**£5**	
It's Monk's Time	LP	CBS	(S)BPG62391	1965	**£12**	**£5**	
Man I Love	LP	Black Lion	2460197	1973	**£10**	**£4**	
Misterioso	LP	CBS	(S)BPG62620	1966	**£12**	**£5**	
Misterioso	LP	Riverside	RLP279	1964	**£12**	**£5**	
Monk	LP	CBS	(S)BPG62497	1965	**£12**	**£5**	
Monk's Blues	LP	CBS	63609	1969	**£10**	**£4**	
Monk's Dream	LP	CBS	(S)BPG62135	1963	**£12**	**£5**	
Monk's Moods	LP	Transatlantic	PR7159	1967	**£10**	**£4**	
Monk's Moods	LP	Esquire	32119	1961	**£25**	**£10**	
Monk's Music	LP	Riverside	RLP12242	1962	**£15**	**£6**	
Nica's Tempo	LP	Realm	RM52223	1965	**£10**	**£4**	
Nutty	7" EP	Riverside	REP3214	196–	**£5**	**£2**	*with John Coltrane*
Nutty Monk	7" EP	Esquire	EP236	1961	**£5**	**£2**	
Plays Duke	LP	Storyville	673014	1969	**£10**	**£4**	
Pure Monk	LP	DJM	DJSLM2017	1975	**£10**	**£4**	
Quartet Plus Two At The Black Hawk	LP	Riverside	RLP12323/1171	1962	**£15**	**£6**	
Ruby My Dear	7" EP	Riverside	REP3217	196–	**£5**	**£2**	*with John Coltrane*
Solo	LP	CBS	(S)BPG62549	1965	**£12**	**£5**	
Something In Blue	LP	Black Lion	2460152	1972	**£10**	**£4**	
Straight, No Chaser	LP	CBS	(S)BPG63009	1967	**£12**	**£5**	
The Thelonious Monk	LP	Storyville	673024	1970	**£10**	**£4**	
Thelonious Himself	LP	London	LTZU15120	1958	**£25**	**£10**	
Thelonious Himself	LP	Riverside	RLP12235	1963	**£15**	**£6**	
Thelonious In Action	LP	Riverside	RLP12262	1961	**£15**	**£6**	
Thelonious Monk	10" LP	Esquire	20049	1955	**£50**	**£25**	
Thelonious Monk	7" EP	Vogue	EPV1115	1956	**£5**	**£2**	
Thelonious Monk	LP	CBS	(S)BPG62248	1964	**£12**	**£5**	
Thelonious Monk	LP	Prestige	PR24006	1972	**£12**	**£5**	*double*

Thelonious Monk Orchestra At Town Hall	LP	Riverside	RLP12300	1962	£15	£6	
Thelonious Monk Plays	10" LP	Esquire	20075	1956	£50	£25	
Thelonious Monk Plays Duke Ellington	LP	Riverside	RLP12201	1961	£20	£8	
Thelonious Monk Plays Duke Ellington	LP	London	LTZU15019	1957	£25	£10	
Thelonious Monk Quintet	10" LP	Esquire	20039	1955	£50	£25	
Thelonious Monk Quintets	LP	Esquire	32109	1960	£25	£10	
Thelonious Monk Trio	7" EP	Esquire	EP75	1955	£5	£2	
Thelonious Monk Vol. 1	LP	Philips	BBL1510	1961	£15	£6	
Thelonious Monk Vol. 2	LP	Philips	BBL1511	1962	£15	£6	
Thelonious Monk With John Coltrane	LP	Riverside	JLP(9)46	1963	£12	£5	
Unique	LP	Riverside	RLP12209	196–	£15	£6	
Unique Thelonious	LP	London	LTXU15071	1957	£25	£10	
Way Out!	LP	Fontana	FJL113	1965	£10	£4	
Who's Afraid Of The Big Bad Monk?	LP	CBS	88034	1975	£10	£4	
Work	LP	Transatlantic	PR7169	1967	£12	£5	
Work	LP	Esquire	32115	1961	£25	£10	

MONKEES

Just because the Monkees were a manufactured group, put together by businessmen keen to create a facsimile of the Beatles' *A Hard Day's Night* and *Help* films to turn into a TV series, it does not follow automatically that the group's music was worthless. In fact, some real craftsman-songwriters were drafted in to write the songs (Neil Diamond, John Stewart and Carole King among them) and a set of crack session musicians were employed to do the actual playing. All the Monkees had to do on the records was sing. The result, in 'I'm A Believer', 'A Little Bit Me, A Little Bit You' and the rest, was some of the decade's most sparkling pop singles. When the Monkees had become sufficiently entrenched in the pop market place to be able to start dictating their own terms, the result was some worthy self-produced material, but an inevitable decline in sales. These later Monkees releases are now the most sought after (the early albums are still very common, though they are not often found in excellent condition). Most desirable is the soundtrack album, *Head*, to the film that is either an extraordinary psychedelic masterpiece or a self-indulgent mess, depending on the critic's point of view. One song from it, however, 'Porpoise Song', is rightly acclaimed for its aching beauty and its floating ambience as a period classic.

Alternate Title	7" EP	RCA	86956	1967	£15	£7.50	*French*
Barrel Full Of Monkees	LP	Colgems	SCOS1001	1971	£20	£8	*US*
Best Of The Monkees	CD	Arista	EMD018	1993	£20	£8	
Birds, The Bees And The Monkees	LP	RCA	RD/SF7948	1968	£10	£4	
Changes	LP	Colgems	COS119	1970	£25	£10	*US*
D. W. Washburn	7"	RCA	RCA1706	1968	£4	£1.50	
Daydream Believer	7"	RCA	RCA1645	1967	£4	£1.50	
Daydream Believer	CD-s	Arista	662157	1989	£8	£4	
Golden Hits	LP	RCA	PRS329	1972	£20	£8	*US*
Good Clean Fun	7"	RCA	RCA1887	1969	£4	£1.50	
Greatest Hits	LP	Colgems	COS115	1969	£15	£6	*US*
Head	LP	RCA	RD/SF8051	1969	£40	£20	
Headquarters	LP	Colgems	COM/COS103	1967	£15	£6	*US, photo of 2 bearded Monkees*
Headquarters	LP	RCA	RD/SF7886	1967	£10	£4	
Hey Hey It's The Monkees – 20 Smash Hits	CD	Platinum	PLATCD05	1988	£12	£5	
I'm A Believer	7" EP	Arista	ARIST487	1982	£6	£2.50	
I'm A Believer	7" EP	RCA	86952	1966	£15	£7.50	*French*
Instant Replay	LP	RCA	RD/SF8016	1969	£15	£6	
Last Train To Clarksville	7"	RCA	RCA1547	1966	£4	£1.50	
Last Train To Clarksville	7" EP	RCA	86950	1966	£15	£7.50	*French*
Last Train To Clarksville	CD-s	Arista	162053	1989	£6	£2.50	*3" single*
Last Train To Clarksville	CD-s	Arista	662158	1989	£8	£4	
Listen To The Band	7"	RCA	RCA1824	1969	£4	£1.50	
Little Bit Me, A Little Bit You	7" EP	RCA	86955	1967	£15	£7.50	*French*
Monkees	10"	Arista	112157	1989	£15	£7.50	*promo*
Monkees	7" EP	Arista	112157	1989	£8	£4	*boxed with booklet & patch*
Monkees	7" EP	Arista	ARIST326	1980	£5	£2	
Monkees	CD-s	Arista	112157	1989	£6	£2.50	
Monkees	LP	RCA	RD/SF7844	1967	£10	£4	
Monkees Present	LP	Colgems	COS117	1969	£25	£10	*US*
Monkees Theme	7"	Bell	BLL1354	1974	£5	£2	
Monkees Vol. 2	10"	Arista	112158	1989	£15	£7.50	*promo*
Monkees Vol. 2	7" EP	Arista	ARIST402	1981	£5	£2	
Monkees Vol. 2	CD-s	Arista	112158	1989	£8	£4	
More Of The Monkees	LP	RCA	RD/SF7868	1967	£10	£4	
Oh My My	7"	RCA	RCA1958	1970	£5	£2	
Pisces, Aquarius, Capricorn And Jones Ltd	LP	RCA	RD/SF7912	1967	£10	£4	
Porpoise Song	7"	RCA	RCA1862	1969	£5	£2	
Re-Focus	LP	Bell	6081	1973	£30	£15	*US*
Six Track Hits	7" EP	Scoop	7SR5035	1984	£6	£2.50	
Teardrop City	7"	RCA	RCA1802	1969	£4	£1.50	
Tema Dei Monkees	7"	RCA	1546	1967	£12	£6	*sung in Italian*
That Was Then, This Is Now	12"	Arista	ARIST12673	1986	£6	£2.50	
That Was Then, This Is Now	7"	Arista	ARIST2673	1986	£5	£2	*picture disc*
That Was Then, This Is Now	7"	Arista	ARIST4673	1986	£6	£2.50	*picture disc*
That Was Then, This Is Now	7"	Arista	ARIST3673	1986	£5	£2	*picture disc*
That Was Then, This Is Now	7"	Arista	ARIST1673	1986	£5	£2	*picture disc*

MONKS

It's Black Monk Time	LP	Polydor	249900	1966	£100	£50	*German*

MONOGRAMS

Juke Box Cha Cha	7"	Parlophone	R4515	1959	£4	£1.50	

MONOPOLY

House Of Lords	7"	Polydor	56164	1967	£4	£1.50	
We Belong Together	7"	Pye	7N17940	1970	£4	£1.50	
We're All Going To The Seaside	7"	Polydor	56188	1967	£4	£1.50	

MONOTONES

Book Of Love	7"	London	HLM8625	1958	£40	£20	

MONOTONES (2)

What Would I Do	7"	Pye	7N15608	1964	£4	£1.50	

MONRO, MATT

Blue And Sentimental	10" LP	Decca	LF1276	1957	£30	£15	
Everybody Falls In Love With Someone	7"	Decca	F10816	1956	£10	£5	
From Russia With Love	7" EP	Parlophone	GEP8889	1963	£10	£5	
Garden Of Eden	7"	Decca	F10845	1957	£10	£5	
Ghost Of Your Past	7"	Ember	EMBS120	1961	£6	£2.50	
My House Is Your House	7"	Decca	F10870	1957	£10	£5	
Prisoner Of Love	7"	Fontana	H167	1958	£8	£4	
Story Of Ireland	7"	Fontana	H122	1958	£8	£4	

MONROE, BARRY

Never Again	7"	Polydor	56088	1966	£4	£1.50	

MONROE, BILL

Bluegrass Ramble	LP	Brunswick	LAT/STA8511	1963	£10	£4	
Bluegrass Special	LP	Brunswick	LAT/STA8579	1965	£10	£4	
Country Date	7" EP	Brunswick	OE9160	1955	£10	£5	
Country Waltz	7" EP	Brunswick	OE9195	1955	£10	£5	
Early Bluegrass	LP	Camden	CAL774	1963	£10	£4	US
Father Of Bluegrass Music	LP	Camden	CAL719	1962	£10	£4	US
Four Walls	7"	Brunswick	05681	1957	£6	£2.50	
Gotta Travel On	7"	Brunswick	05776	1959	£5	£2	
Great Bill Monroe	LP	Harmony	HL7290	1961	£10	£4	US
I Saw The Light	LP	Decca	DL(7)8769	1959	£15	£6	US
I Saw The Light	LP	Brunswick	LAT8338	1961	£10	£4	
Knee Deep In Bluegrass	LP	Decca	DL(7)8731	1958	£15	£6	US
Mr Bluegrass	LP	Decca	DL(7)4080	1960	£15	£6	US
My All Time Country Favorites	LP	Decca	DL(7)4327	1962	£10	£4	US
New John Henry Blues	7"	Brunswick	05567	1956	£8	£4	

MONROE, MARILYN

Gentlemen Prefer Blondes	10" LP	MGM	D116	1953	£60	£30	
Gentlemen Prefer Blondes	LP	MGM	E3231	1955	£50	£25	US
Heat Wave	78	HMV	B10847	1955	£12	£6	
I Wanna Be Loved By You	7"	London	HLT8862	1959	£15	£7.50	
I'm Gonna File My Claim	7"	HMV	7M232	1954	£20	£10	
Let's Make Love	7" EP	Philips	SBBE9031	1961	£20	£10	*stereo*
Let's Make Love	7" EP	Philips	BBE12414	1960	£12	£6	
Let's Make Love	LP	Philips	BBL7414	1960	£25	£10	
Let's Make Love	LP	Philips	SBBL592	1960	£40	£20	*stereo*
Marilyn	LP	20th Century	FXG/SXG5000	1959	£60	£30	*US, with poster*
Marilyn	LP	Stateside	(S)SL10048	1963	£25	£10	
Marilyn Monroe	LP	Ascot	ALM13008/ ALS16008	1964	£30	£15	US
Some Like It Hot	7" EP	London	RET1231	1960	£50	£25	*tri-centre*
Some Like It Hot	LP	London	HAT2176	1959	£40	£20	
Some Like It Hot	LP	London	SAHT6040	1959	£60	£30	*stereo*
There's No Business Like Show Business	7" EP	HMV	7EG8090	1955	£25	£12.50	
Unforgettable	LP	Movietone	72016	1967	£20	£8	US

MONROE, VAUGHN

Black Denim Trousers And Motorcycle Boots	7"	HMV	7M332	1955	£12	£6	
Greatest Hits	7" EP	RCA	RCX1043	1959	£8	£4	
Less Than Tomorrow	7"	HMV	7M144	1953	£4	£1.50	
They Were Doin' The Mambo	7"	HMV	7M247	1954	£4	£1.50	

MONROE BROTHERS

Country Guitar Vol. 14	7" EP	RCA	RCX7103	1963	£8	£4	
Country Guitar Vol. 15	7" EP	RCA	RCX7104	1963	£8	£4	
Country Guitar Vol. 16	7" EP	RCA	RCX7105	1963	£6	£2.50	*with Bill Monroe*

MONSOON

Ever So Lonely	7"	Indipop	IND1	1981	£6	£2.50	

MONSTERAS BLUESBAND

Mixture	LP	Frog Music	LFK03	1978	£40	£20	*Swedish*

MONTANA SLIM

Dynamite Trail	LP	Decca	DL4092	1960	£20	£8	US
I'm Ragged But I'm Right	LP	Decca	DL8917	1959	£20	£8	US
Wilf Carter As Montana Slim	LP	Starday	SLP300	1964	£12	£5	US
Wilf Carter/Montana Slim	LP	Camden	CAL527	1959	£15	£6	US

MONTANAS

All That Is Mine Can Be Yours	7"	Piccadilly	7N35262	1965	£5	£2	

Ciao Baby 7" Pye 7N17282 1967 £4 **£1.50**
Roundabout 7" Pye 7N17697 1969 £5 **£2**
Step In The Right Direction 7" Pye 7N17499 1968 £5 **£2**
Take My Hand 7" Pye 7N17338 1967 £5 **£2**
That's When Happiness Began 7" Pye 7N17183 1966 £25 **£12.50**
That's When Happiness Began 7" EP Pye PNV24179 1966 £100 **£50** *French*
You're Making A Big Mistake 7" Pye 7N17597 1968 £5 **£2**
You've Got To Be Loved 7" Pye 7N17394 1967 £5 **£2**

MONTCLAIRS

Hung Up On Your Love 7" Contempo CS2036 1975 £5 **£2**

MONTE, LOU

Darktown Strutters' Ball 7" HMV 7M190 1954 £4 **£1.50**

MONTE, VINNIE

Joannie Don't Be Angry 7" Stateside SS156 1963 £4 **£1.50**
Summer Spree 7" London HL8947 1959 £6 **£2.50**

MONTENEGRO, HUGO

Get Off The Moon 7" Oriole CBA1792 1963 £10 **£5**
Hurry Sundown LP RCA RD/SF7877 1967 £15 **£6**
Lady In Cement LP Stateside (S)SL10267 1969 £25 **£10**
Man From UNCLE LP RCA RD7758 1966 £30 **£15**
Moog Power LP RCA SF8053 1969 £25 **£10**
More Music From The Man From UNCLE LP RCA RD7832 1966 £30 **£15**

MONTEZ, CHRIS

Chris Montez 7" EP Pye NEP44080 1966 £8 **£4**
Let's Dance 7" EP London REU1392 1963 £25 **£12.50**
Let's Dance LP CBS 65408 1972 £10 **£4**
Let's Dance And Have Some Kinda Fun LP London HAU8079 1963 £25 **£10**
More I See You 7" EP Pye NEP44071 1966 £10 **£5**
More I See You LP Pye NPL23080 1966 £10 **£4**
Time After Time LP Pye N(S)PL28187 1967 £10 **£4**

MONTGOMERY, JACK

Dearly Beloved 7" Kent TOWN102 1985 £6 **£2.50** *Marie Knight B side*

MONTGOMERY, LITTLE BROTHER

1930–1969 LP Saydisc SDR213 1971 £10 **£4**
Chicago Blues Session LP 77 LA1221 1963 £15 **£6** *with Sunnyland Slim*
Faro Street Jive LP XTRA XTRA1115 1971 £10 **£4**
Home Again LP Saydisc SDM223 1972 £10 **£4**
Little Brother Montgomery LP XTRA XTRA1018 1966 £10 **£4**
Little Brother Montgomery LP Columbia 33SX1289 1960 £15 **£6**
Little Brother Montgomery LP Decca LK4664 1965 £12 **£5**
Pinetop's Boogie Woogie 7" Columbia DB4595 1961 £8 **£4**
Southside Blues LP Riverside 403 1960 £15 **£6** *US*

MONTGOMERY, MARIAN

Love Makes Two People Sing 7" Reaction 591018 1967 £5 **£2**

MONTGOMERY, STUART

Certain Sea Words LP private 1969 £15 **£6**

MONTGOMERY, WES

Full House LP Riverside RLP434 1962 £10 **£4**
Go! LP Fontana FJL109 1965 £10 **£4**
Groove Yard LP Riverside RLP12362 1961 £12 **£5** *with Buddy & Monk Montgomery*
Incredible Jazz Guitar LP Riverside RLP12320/1169 1960 £12 **£5**
Movin' Along LP Riverside RLP12342 1960 £10 **£4**
Wes Montgomery Trio LP Riverside RLP12310 1959 £12 **£5**

MONTGOMERY BROTHERS

Montgomery Brothers Plus Five Others LP Vogue LAE12137 1959 £20 **£8**
Montgomeryland LP Vogue LAE12246 1961 £12 **£5**

MONTROSE, JACK

Blues And Vanilla LP RCA RD27023 1958 £15 **£6**
Jack Montrose Sextet LP Vogue LAE12042 1957 £25 **£10**
Jack Montrose With Bob Gordon LP London LTZK15043 1957 £25 **£10**

MONTY & ROY

Tra La La Boogie 7" Blue Beat BB61 1961 £12 **£6**

MONTY PYTHON

Always Look On The Bright Side Of Life CD-s Virgin PYTHD1 1991 £5 **£2**
Brian 7" Warner Bros K17495PRO 1980 £4 **£1.50** *bleeped promo*
Live At The City Center, April 1976 LP Arista AL4073 1976 £12 **£5** *US*
Python On Song 7" Charisma MP001 1975 £5 **£2** *double*

MONUMENT

First Monument LP Beacon BEAS15 1971 £50 **£25**

MOOCHE

Hot Smoke And Sasafrass	7"	Pye	7N17735	1969	£15	£7.50	

MOOD MOSAIC

Chinese Chequers	7"	Columbia	DB8149	1967	£6	£2.50	
Mood Mosaic	LP	Columbia	SX6153/TWO160	1967	£25	£10	
Touch Of Velvet, A Sting Of Brass	7"	Columbia	DB7801	1966	£8	£4	
Touch Of Velvet, A Sting Of Brass	7"	Columbia	DB8618	1969	£5	£2	
Yellow Spotted Capricorn	7"	Parlophone	R5716	1968	£5	£2	*Elmer Hockett B side*

MOOD OF HAMILTON

Why Can't There Be More Love?	7"	Columbia	DB8304	1967	£10	£5	

MOOD REACTION

Live At The Cumberland	LP	Pama	PSP1007	1970	£15	£6	

MOOD SIX

She's Too Far	7"	EMI	EMI5336	1982	£20	£10	*test pressing*

MOODIE, AMEIL

Mello Reggae	7"	Blue Cat	BS143	1968	£6	£2.50	
Ratchet Knife	7"	Blue Cat	BS164	1969	£6	£2.50	

MOODS

Duckwalk	7"	Starlite	ST45098	1963	£12	£6	

MOODY, CLYDE

Best Of Clyde Moody	LP	King	891	1964	£20	£8	*US*
I Need The Prayers	7"	Parlophone	CMSP11	1954	£6	£2.50	*export*

MOODY, JAMES

James Moody	10" LP	Esquire	20035	1955	£50	£25	
James Moody	10" LP	Esquire	20077	1956	£40	£20	
James Moody	10" LP	Esquire	20071	1956	£40	£20	
James Moody	10" LP	Esquire	20036	1955	£50	£25	
Moody's Workshop	LP	XTRA	XTRA5017	1966	£15	£6	

MOODY, JAMES & GEORGE WALLINGTON

Beginning And End Of Bop	LP	Blue Note	B6503	1969	£20	£8	

MOODY BLUES

Boulevard De La Madeleine	7"	Decca	F12498	1966	£4	£1.50	
Boulevard De La Madeleine	7" EP	Decca	457117	1966	£15	£7.50	*French*
Bye Bye Bird	7" EP	Decca	457098	1966	£15	£7.50	*French*
Days Of Future Passed	CD	Mobile Fidelity	UDCD512	1988	£15	£6	*US audiophile*
Days Of Future Passed	LP	Mobile Fidelity	MFSL1042	1980	£10	£4	*US audiophile*
Days Of Future Passed	LP	Deram	DML707	1968	£10	£4	*mono*
Every Good Boy Deserves Favour	CD	Mobile Fidelity		1995	£15	£6	*US audiophile*
Everyday	7"	Decca	F12266	1965	£4	£1.50	
Fly Me High	7"	Decca	F12607	1967	£6	£2.50	
Go Now	7" EP	Decca	457057	1964	£15	£7.50	*French*
I Know You're Out There Somewhere	CD-s	Polydor	POCD921	1988	£5	£2	
In Search Of The Lost Chord	LP	Deram	DML717	1968	£12	£5	*mono*
Isn't Life Strange	7"	Threshold	TH9	1972	£4	£1.50	*picture sleeve*
Life's Not Life	7"	Decca	F12543	1967	£30	£15	
Lose Your Money	7"	Decca	F11971	1964	£20	£10	
Love And Beauty	7"	Decca	F12670	1967	£6	£2.50	
Magnificent Moodies	LP	Decca	LK4711	1966	£10	£4	
Miracle	CD-s	Polydor	0804092	1988	£10	£5	*CD video*
Moody Blues	7" EP	Decca	DFE8622	1965	£10	£5	
Moody Blues	7" EP	Decca	DFE8622	1968	£5	£2	*boxed Decca logo*
Octave	CD	Decca	8203292	1986	£12	£5	
Octave	LP	Decca	TXS129	1978	£10	£4	*blue vinyl*
On The Threshold Of A Dream	CD	Mobile Fidelity	UDCD612	1994	£15	£6	*US audiophile*
On The Threshold Of A Dream	LP	Deram	DML1035	1968	£12	£5	*mono*
On The Threshold Of A Dream	LP	Nautilus	NR21	1981	£15	£6	*US audiophile*
Question Of Balance	CD	Decca	8202112	1986	£12	£5	
Ride My See-Saw	7"	Deram	DM213	1968	£4	£1.50	
Say It With Love	CD-s	Polydor	PZCD153	1991	£5	£2	
Seventh Sojourn	LP	Mobile Fidelity	MFSL1151	1984	£10	£4	*US audiophile*
Talking Out Of Turn	7"	Threshold	THPD29	1981	£5	£2	*picture disc*
To Our Children's Children's Children	LP	Threshold	THM1	1969	£15	£6	*mono*
Watching And Waiting	7"	Threshold	TH1	1969	£4	£1.50	
Your Wildest Dreams	CD-s	Polydor	0800222	1988	£10	£5	*CD video*

MOOLAH

Woe Ye Demons	LP	Annuit Coeptis	M1	1969	£125	£62.50	*US*

MOON

Pirate	7"	Liberty	LBF15333	1970	£5	£2	
Someday Girl	7"	Liberty	LBF15076	1968	£5	£2	

Title	Format	Label	Number	Year	Mint	VG	Notes
Without Earth	LP	Liberty	LBL/LBS83146	1968	£**15**	£**6**	

MOON, KEITH

Title	Format	Label	Number	Year	Mint	VG	Notes
Don't Worry Baby	7"	Polydor	2058584	1975	£**5**	£**2**	
Two Sides Of The Moon	LP	Polydor	2442134	1975	£**15**	£**6**	

MOON, LARRY

Title	Format	Label	Number	Year	Mint	VG	Notes
Tia Juana Ball	7"	Ember	EMB171	1963	£**10**	£**5**	

MOON, PERRY

Title	Format	Label	Number	Year	Mint	VG	Notes
Nine Five Baby	7"	Sway	SW002	1963	£**6**	£**2.50**	*Planets B side*

MOON, TERRY

Title	Format	Label	Number	Year	Mint	VG	Notes
Moon Man	7"	Planetone	RC11	1963	£**6**	£**2.50**	*Mike Elliot B side*

MOONDOG

Louis T. Hardin was a New York street musician and composer, who never let the fact that he was blind get in the way of his full-time career as an eccentric. His infrequent recordings contain idiosyncratic instrumental works, which blend a classical approach with elements of jazz and rock. He successfully sued DJ Alan Freed in the fifties, forcing him to change the name of his programme, *Moondog's Rock and Roll Party*.

Title	Format	Label	Number	Year	Mint	VG	Notes
H'art Songs	LP	Kopf	RRF33016	1978	£**15**	£**6**	*German*
Moondog	LP	Esquire	32055	1958	£**40**	£**20**	
Moondog	LP	CBS	63906	1969	£**20**	£**8**	
Moondog 2	LP	CBS	30897	1971	£**25**	£**10**	*US*
Moondog In Europe	LP	Kopf	RRF33014	1978	£**20**	£**8**	*German*
On The Streets Of New York	7" EP	London	REP1010	1954	£**30**	£**15**	

MOONEY, ART

Title	Format	Label	Number	Year	Mint	VG	Notes
Giant	7"	MGM	MGM943	1957	£**6**	£**2.50**	
Rebel Without A Cause Theme	7"	MGM	MGM923	1957	£**6**	£**2.50**	
Rock And Roll Tumbleweed	7"	MGM	MGM951	1957	£**12**	£**6**	

MOONGLOWS

Title	Format	Label	Number	Year	Mint	VG	Notes
Best Of Bobby Lester & The Moonglows	LP	Chess	LP1471	1962	£**75**	£**37.50**	*US*
Collectors Showcase	LP	Constellation	CS2	1964	£**20**	£**8**	*US*
I Knew From The Start	7"	London	HLN8374	1957	£**400**	£**250**	*best auctioned*
Look It's The Moonglows	LP	Chess	LP1430	1958	£**150**	£**75**	*US*

MOONGOONERS

This is a name used by Scott Walker in two of his many attempts to find success in the days before the Walker Brothers – this time in a duo with his fellow 'brother', John Maus.

Title	Format	Label	Number	Year	Mint	VG	Notes
Moongoon Stomp	7"	Candix	335	1962	£**20**	£**10**	*US*
Moongoon Twist	7"	Essar	1007	1962	£**20**	£**10**	*US*
Moongoon Twist	7"	Donna	1373	1962	£**15**	£**7.50**	*US*

MOONKYTE

Title	Format	Label	Number	Year	Mint	VG	Notes
Count Me Out	LP	Mother	SMOT1	1971	£**100**	£**50**	

MOONLIGHTERS

Title	Format	Label	Number	Year	Mint	VG	Notes
Going Out	7"	Island	WI043	1963	£**10**	£**5**	

MOONRAKERS

Title	Format	Label	Number	Year	Mint	VG	Notes
Together With Him	LP	Shamley	SS704	1968	£**20**	£**8**	*US*

MOON'S TRAIN

Title	Format	Label	Number	Year	Mint	VG	Notes
Deed I Do	7"	MGM	MGM1333	1967	£**8**	£**4**	

MOONSHINE, MICKEY

Title	Format	Label	Number	Year	Mint	VG	Notes
Baby Blue	7"	Decca	F13555	1974	£**4**	£**1.50**	

MOONSHINERS

Title	Format	Label	Number	Year	Mint	VG	Notes
Breakout	LP	Stateside	SL10137	1965	£**10**	£**4**	
Hold Up	LP	Page One	POLS004	1967	£**15**	£**6**	

MOONTREKKERS

Title	Format	Label	Number	Year	Mint	VG	Notes
Moondust	7"	Decca	F11714	1963	£**10**	£**5**	
Night Of The Vampire	7"	Parlophone	R4814	1961	£**15**	£**7.50**	
There's Something At The Bottom	7"	Parlophone	R4888	1962	£**20**	£**10**	

MOORCOCK, MICHAEL

Title	Format	Label	Number	Year	Mint	VG	Notes
Brothel In Rosenstrasse	7"	Flicknife	EJSP9831	1982	£**25**	£**12.50**	*with lyric sheet*
Dodgem Dude	7"	Flicknife	FLEP200	1980	£**5**	£**2**	
New World's Fair	LP	United Artists	UAG29732	1975	£**40**	£**20**	*with Deep Fix*

MOORE, ALAN & DAVID J

Title	Format	Label	Number	Year	Mint	VG	Notes
V For Vendetta	12"	Glass	12032	1984	£**6**	£**2.50**	*cartoon strip insert*

MOORE, ALEXANDER

Title	Format	Label	Number	Year	Mint	VG	Notes
Whistling Alex Moore	LP	77	77LA127	1960	£**10**	£**4**	

MOORE, ANTHONY

Title	Format	Label	Number	Year	Mint	VG	Notes
Flying Doesn't Help	LP	Quango	HMG98	1979	£**10**	£**4**	

Pieces From The Cloudland Ballroom	LP	Polydor	2310162	1971	£**30**	£**15**	
Secrets Of The Blue Bag	LP	Polydor	2310179	1972	£**30**	£**15**	

MOORE, BARRY

Treaty Stone	LP	Mulligan	LUN022	1978	£**20**	£**8**	*Irish*

MOORE, BOB

Viva	LP	Hickory	131	1968	£**50**	£**25**	*US*

MOORE, BOBBY

Searching For My Love	7"	Chess	CRS8033	1966	£**5**	£**2**	
Searching For My Love	LP	Chess	CRL4521	1966	£**20**	£**8**	

MOORE, BREW

Quartet And Quintet	LP	Vocalion	LAE564	1964	£**12**	£**5**	

MOORE, BUTCH

Walking The Streets In The Rain	7"	Pye	7N15832	1965	£**4**	£**1.50**	

MOORE, CHRISTY

Anti Nuclear	12"	Alt	101	1978	£**20**	£**10**	*with Barry Moore & The Early Grave Band*
Christy Moore	LP	Polydor	2383426	1976	£**12**	£**5**	
Iron Behind The Velvet	LP	Tara	2002	1978	£**10**	£**4**	*Irish*
Live In Dublin	LP	Tara	2005	1978	£**10**	£**4**	*Irish, with Donal Lunny & Jimmy Faulkner*
Paddy On The Road	LP	Mercury	20170SMCL	1969	£**200**	£**100**	
Prosperous	LP	Trailer	LER3035	1972	£**25**	£**10**	
Whatever Tickles Your Fancy	LP	Polydor	2383344	1975	£**20**	£**8**	

MOORE, DUDLEY

Bedazzled	LP	Decca	LK/SKL4923	1968	£**50**	£**25**	
Dudley Moore Trio	LP	Decca	LK/SKL4976	1969	£**20**	£**8**	
Genuine Dud	LP	Decca	LK4788	1966	£**15**	£**6**	
Music Of Dudley Moore	LP	Decca	LK/SKL4980	1969	£**12**	£**5**	
Other Side Of Dudley Moore	LP	Decca	LK4732	1965	£**15**	£**6**	
Today	LP	Atlantic	K40397	1972	£**10**	£**4**	
World Of Dudley Moore	LP	Decca	SPA106	1970	£**12**	£**5**	

MOORE, GARY

After The War	CD-s	Virgin	VSCD1153	1988	£**5**	£**2**	
After The War	CD-s	Virgin	GMSCD1	1989	£**6**	£**2.50**	*3" single in tin*
Always Gonna Love You	7"	Virgin	VSY528	1982	£**4**	£**1.50**	*picture disc*
Back On The Streets	7"	MCA	MCA386	1978	£**20**	£**10**	*picture sleeve*
Empty Rooms	CD-s	Virgin	CDT35	1988	£**5**	£**2**	*3" single*
Falling In Love With You	7"	Virgin	VSY564	1983	£**4**	£**1.50**	*picture disc*
Friday On My Mind	CD-s	10	KERRY164	1987	£**8**	£**4**	
Gary Moore EP	CD-s	Special Edition	CD34	1988	£**5**	£**2**	*3" single*
Grinding Stone	LP	Columbia	65527	1973	£**10**	£**4**	
Hold On To Your Love	7"	10	TENS13	1984	£**6**	£**2.50**	*shaped picture disc*
Military Man	12"	10	TENC4912	1985	£**8**	£**4**	*1 sided promo, with Phil Lynott*
Oh Pretty Woman	CD-s	Virgin	VSCDT1233	1990	£**5**	£**2**	
Out In The Fields	7"	10	TENS49	1985	£**10**	£**5**	*shaped picture disc (2 different), with Phil Lynott*
Out In The Fields	7"	10	TEND49	1985	£**4**	£**1.50**	*double, with Phil Lynott*
Over The Hills And Far Away	7"	10	TENS134	1986	£**6**	£**2.50**	*shaped picture disc*
Over The Hills And Far Away	CD-s	Virgin	CDT16	1988	£**5**	£**2**	*3" single*
Over The Hills And Far Away	CD-s	10	TENCD134	1988	£**5**	£**2**	
Parisienne Walkways	7"	MCA	MCA419	1979	£**5**	£**2**	*picture sleeve*
Ready For Love	CD-s	Virgin	GMSCD2/CDX2	1989	£**5**	£**2**	*2 versions*
Separate Ways	CD-s	Virgin	VSCDX1437	1992	£**8**	£**4**	*boxed with booklet*
Shapes Of Things	7"	10	TENS19	1984	£**8**	£**4**	*shaped picture disc*
Spanish Guitar	7"	MCA	MCA534	1979	£**8**	£**4**	*picture sleeve*
Still Got The Blues	CD-s	Virgin	VSCDT1267	1990	£**5**	£**2**	*2 versions*
Too Tired	CD-s	Virgin	VSCD1306	1990	£**5**	£**2**	*2 versions*
Walking By Myself	CD-s	Virgin	VSCDT1281	1990	£**5**	£**2**	
Wild Frontier	CD-s	10	KERRY159	1987	£**8**	£**4**	

MOORE, GATEMOUTH

I'm A Fool To Care	LP	King	684	1960	£**300**	£**180**	*US*

MOORE, JOHNNY

Big Big Boss	7"	Doctor Bird	DB1180	1969	£**10**	£**5**	*Carl Bryan B side*

MOORE, LATTIE

Best Of Lattie Moore	LP	Audio Lab	AL1555	1960	£**25**	£**10**	*US*
Country Side	LP	Audio Lab	AL1573	1962	£**25**	£**10**	*US*

MOORE, MERRILL

Bellyfull Of Blue Thunder	LP	Ember	EMB3392	1967	£**10**	£**4**	
Down The Road A-Piece	7"	Ember	EMBS253	1968	£**8**	£**4**	

Hard Top Race ... 7" ... Capitol ... CL14369 ... 1955 £**100** ... £**50**
Rough House 88 ... LP ... Ember ... EMB3394 ... 1968 £**10** ... £**4**
Sweet Mama ... 7" ... B&C ... CB100 ... 1969 £**4** ... £**1.50**

MOORE, NICKY

Year Of The Lie ... 7" ... Street Tunes ... STS006 ... 1981 £**5** ... £**2**

MOORE, OSCAR

Oscar Moore Trio ... 10" LP ... London ... HAPB1035 ... 1955 £**25** ... £**10**

MOORE, PETE

Solid Rockin' Brass ... LP ... Gold Star ... 1500009 ... 1974 £**10** ... £**4**

MOORE, PHIL

Moore's Tour – An American In England ... LP ... MGM ... C790 ... 1959 £**12** ... £**5**

MOORE, R. STEVIE

R. Stevie Moore is one of rock music's eccentrics, preferring to issue his records through his own mail order scheme than to tangle with record companies who would doubtless attempt to compromise Moore's quirky approach. The original issue of his first album, *Phonography*, was produced in an edition of just ninety-nine copies and long ago sold out. The Zappa household has one, and so did UK collector, the late Michael Gerzon, whose copy is likely to be the only one in the country.

Delicate Tension ... LP ... HP Music ... HPS30735 ... 1979 £**20** ... £**8** ... *US*
Phonography ... LP ... Vital ... VS0001 ... 1976 £**100** ... £**50** ... *US*
Phonography ... LP ... HP Music ... HPS30734 ... 1978 £**20** ... £**8** ... *US*

MOORE, ROGER

Where Does Love Go ... 7" ... CBS ... 202014 ... 1965 £**4** ... £**1.50** ... *picture sleeve*

MOORE, SCOTTY

Guitar That Changed The World ... LP ... Columbia ... 33SX1680 ... 1964 £**40** ... £**20**

MOORE, THURSTON, KIM GORDON, EPIC SOUNDTRACKS

Sitting On A Barbed Wire Fence ... 7" ... Imaginary ... FREE003 ... 1992 £**5** ... £**2** ... *promo*

MOORE, WHISTLING ALEX

Whistling Alex Moore ... LP ... 77 ... LA126 ... 1961 £**20** ... £**8**

MOORS MURDERERS

The Moors Murderers, a punk group of which Steve Strange and Chrissie Hynde were both members, were supposed to have released a single called 'Free Myra Hindley'. Although acetates have turned up, it seems unlikely that regular vinyl copies exist.

Free Myra Hindley ... 7" ... Pop Corn ... ... 1978 £**1000** ... £**700** ... *existence doubtful*

MOOSKNUKKL GROOVBAND

Moosknukkl Groovband ... LP ... Spiegelei ... 285163V ... 1972 £**50** ... £**25** ... *German*

MOPED, JOHNNY

Basically The Original Johnny Moped Tape ... 7" ... Chiswick ... PROMO3 ... 1976 £**8** ... £**4** ... *promo*

MOPEDS

Whiskey And Soda ... 7" ... Columbia ... DB108 ... 1968 £**4** ... £**1.50**

MOQUETTES

Right String But Wrong Yo Yo ... 7" ... Columbia ... DB7315 ... 1964 £**25** ... £**12.50**

MORE

Trickster ... 7" ... Atlantic ... K11744 ... 1982 £**10** ... £**5**
Warhead ... LP ... Atlantic ... K50775 ... 1981 £**10** ... £**4**
We Are The Band ... 7" ... Atlantic ... K11561 ... 1980 £**5** ... £**2** ... *picture sleeve*

MORECAMBE & WISE

Boom Oo Yatta-Ta-Ta ... 7" ... HMV ... POP1240 ... 1963 £**4** ... £**1.50**
Evening With Morecambe And Wise ... LP ... Philips ... BL7750 ... 1966 £**10** ... £**4**
Mr Morecambe Meets Mr Wise ... LP ... HMV ... CLP1682/CSD1522 ... 1964 £**10** ... £**4**

MOREL, TERRY

Songs Of A Woman In Love ... LP ... Bethlehem ... 47 ... 1955 £**20** ... £**8** ... *US*

MORELLO, JOE

Another Step Forward ... LP ... London ... ZGO117 ... 1972 £**10** ... £**4**

MORGAN

Nova Solis ... LP ... RCA ... SF8321 ... 1972 £**25** ... £**10**

MORGAN, AL

Jealous Heart ... 10" LP ... London ... HAPB1001 ... 1951 £**12** ... £**5**
Jealous Heart ... 7" ... London ... HLU8741 ... 1958 £**5** ... £**2**
Little Red Book ... 10" LP ... London ... HAPB1003 ... 1951 £**12** ... £**5**

MORGAN, DAVY

Tomorrow I'll Be Gone ... 7" ... Columbia ... DB7624 ... 1965 £**25** ... £**12.50**
True To Life ... 7" ... Parlophone ... R5692 ... 1968 £**6** ... £**2.50**

MORGAN, DERRICK

Title	Format	Label	Cat. No.	Year	Mint	VG	Notes
Amelita	7"	Island	WI289	1966	£10	£5	
Angel With Blue Eyes	7"	Island	WI080	1963	£10	£5	
Are You Going To Marry Me?	7"	Blue Beat	BB110	1962	£12	£6	*with Patsy Todd*
Around The Corner	7"	Ska Beat	JB188	1965	£10	£5	
Baby Please Don't Leave Me	7"	Blue Beat	BB65	1961	£12	£6	*with Patsy Todd*
Balzing Fire	7"	Rio	R1	1963	£10	£5	
Be Still	7"	Blue Beat	BB76	1962	£12	£6	
Ben Johnson Day	7"	Pyramid	PYR6056	1968	£8	£4	*Maytals B side*
Best Of Derrick Morgan	LP	Doctor Bird	DLMB5014	1969	£100	£50	
Blazing Fire	7"	Island	WI051	1962	£10	£5	
Call My Name	7"	Blue Beat	BB171	1963	£12	£6	*with Patsy Todd*
Cherry Home	7"	Island	WI013	1962	£10	£5	
Cherry Pie	7"	Black Swan	WI425	1964	£10	£5	
Come Back My Love	7"	Blue Beat	BB121	1962	£12	£6	
Come On	7"	Island	WI024	1962	£10	£5	*Monty & Cyclones B side*
Come On Over	7"	Blue Beat	BB85	1962	£12	£6	
Conquering Ruler	7"	Island	WI3094	1967	£10	£5	*Lloyd & Devon B side*
Conquering Ruler	7"	Unity	UN569	1970	£4	£1.50	
Contented Wife	7"	Blue Beat	BB261	1964	£12	£6	
Cool Off Rudies	7"	Rio	R122	1966	£8	£4	
Copy Cat	7"	Bullet	BU419	1969	£4	£1.50	
Court Dismiss	7"	Pyramid	PYR6014	1967	£8	£4	*Frederick McLean B side*
Derrick Morgan And His Friends	LP	Island	ILP990	1969	£60	£30	*pink label*
Derrick Top The Pop	7"	Unity	UN540	1969	£4	£1.50	
Do The Beng Beng	7"	Pyramid	PYR6025	1968	£8	£4	
Don't Cry	7"	Blue Beat	BB12	1960	£12	£6	
Don't Say	7"	Pyramid	PYR6063	1969	£6	£2.50	
Don't You Know Little Girl	7"	Blue Beat	BB82	1962	£12	£6	*Basil Gabbidon B side*
Eternity	7"	Blue Beat	BB318	1965	£12	£6	*with Patsy Todd*
Fat Man	7"	Blue Beat	BB7	1960	£12	£6	
Feel So Fine	7"	Blue Beat	BB57	1961	£12	£6	*with Patsy Todd, Roland Alphonso B side*
Forward March	LP	Island	ILP903	1963	£100	£50	
Forward March	LP	Trojan	TTL38	1970	£15	£6	
Gather Together	7"	Island	WI3010	1966	£10	£5	
Gimme Back	7"	Island	WI3101	1967	£10	£5	*Viceroys B side*
Give You My Love	7"	Nu Beat	NB027	1969	£5	£2	
Greedy Gal	7"	Pyramid	PYR6013	1967	£8	£4	*Soul Brothers B side*
Heart Of Stone	7"	Ska Beat	JB185	1965	£10	£5	*with Naomi Campbell*
Hey Boy, Hey Girl	7"	Nu Beat	NB008	1968	£6	£2.50	*with Patsy Todd*
Hold You Jack	7"	Island	WI3159	1968	£10	£5	
Hop	7"	Island	WI006	1962	£10	£5	
Housewive's Choice	7"	Island	WI018	1962	£10	£5	*with Patsy Todd*
I Am The Ruler	7"	Pyramid	PYR6029	1968	£8	£4	
I Found A Queen	7"	Island	WI288	1966	£10	£5	
I Love You	7"	Nu Beat	NB016	1968	£4	£1.50	*Junior Smith B side*
I Want A Lover	7"	Island	WI193	1965	£10	£5	*with Naomi Campbell*
I'm Sending This Message	7"	Island	WI091	1963	£10	£5	*Larry Lawrence B side*
In London	LP	Pama	ECO10	1969	£30	£15	
In My Heart	7"	Blue Beat	BB100	1962	£12	£6	*Bell's Group B side*
In The Mood	LP	Magnet	MGT004	197–	£15	£6	
It's Alright	7"	Island	WI277	1966	£10	£5	
Jezebel	7"	Blue Beat	BB148	1963	£12	£6	
Johnny Grove	7"	Blue Beat	BB283	1965	£12	£6	*Buster's Allstars B side*
Joybells	7"	Blue Beat	BB141	1962	£12	£6	
Judge Dread In Court	7"	Pyramid	PYR6019	1967	£8	£4	
Katy Katy	7"	Blue Beat	BB268	1964	£12	£6	
Kill Me Dead	7"	Pyramid	PYR6021	1967	£8	£4	
King For Tonight	7"	Pyramid	PYR6046	1968	£8	£4	
Leave Earth	7"	Blue Beat	BB35	1961	£12	£6	
Leave Her Alone	7"	Island	WI037	1962	£10	£5	
Let Them Talk	7"	Blue Beat	BB233	1964	£12	£6	
Little Brown Girl	7"	Blue Beat	BB152	1963	£12	£6	*with Patsy Todd*
Look Before You Leap	7"	Island	WI055	1962	£10	£5	*with Patsy Todd*
Love And Leave Me	7"	Blue Beat	BB135	1962	£12	£6	*with Lloyd Clarke*
Love Not To Brag	7"	Blue Beat	BB97	1962	£12	£6	*Drumbago B side*
Lover Boy	7"	Blue Beat	BB207	1964	£12	£6	*with Patsy Todd*
Lover Boy	7"	Blue Beat	BB18	1960	£12	£6	
Me Naw Give Up	7"	Pyramid	PYR6053	1968	£8	£4	*Beverley's Allstars B side*
Meekly Wait	7"	Blue Beat	BB94	1962	£12	£6	*with Yvonne Harrison*
Millie Girl	7"	Blue Beat	BB91	1962	£12	£6	
Miss Lulu	7"	Blue Beat	BB239	1964	£12	£6	*with Patsy Todd*
Moon Hop	7"	Crab	CRAB21	1970	£4	£1.50	
Moon Hop	LP	Pama	PSP1006	1969	£30	£15	
National Dance	7"	Island	WI224	1965	£10	£5	*with Patsy Todd, Desmond Dekker B side*

Never Give Up	7"	Smash	SMA2339	1973	£4	£1.50	
No Dice	7"	Pyramid	PYR6024	1968	£8	£4	
No Raise, No Praise	7"	Island	WI053	1962	£10	£5	
Now We Know	7"	Blue Beat	BB31	1961	£12	£6	
Oh My Love	7"	Blue Beat	BB123	1962	£12	£6	*with Patsy Todd*
Oh Shirley	7"	Blue Beat	BB106	1962	£12	£6	*with Patsy Todd*
Patricia My Dear	7"	Blue Beat	BB177	1963	£12	£6	
Please Don't Talk About Me (with Eric Morris)	7"	Island	WI011	1962	£10	£5	
Return Of Jack Slade	7"	Unity	UN546	1970	£4	£1.50	
River To The Bank	7"	Crab	CRAB3	1968	£5	£2	*Peter King B side*
Send Me Some Loving	7"	Crab	CRAB23	1970	£4	£1.50	
[illegible]	7"	Jackpot	JP700	1969	£4	£1.50	
Seven Letters	7"	Crab	CRAB8	[illegible]	£4	£1.50	*[illegible] B side*
Seven Letters	LP	Trojan	TTL5	1969	£20	£8	
Shake A Leg	7"	Blue Beat	BB62	1961	£12	£6	*with Drumbago*
Should Be Ashamed	7"	Blue Beat	BB130	1962	£12	£6	
Shower Of Rain	7"	Big Shot	BI506	1968	£6	£2.50	*Val Bennett B side*
Someone	7"	Island	WI3079	1967	£10	£5	
Starvation	7"	Island	WI225	1965	£10	£5	
Steal Away	7"	Blue Beat	BB224	1964	£12	£6	*with Patsy Todd*
Stir The Pot	7"	Blue Beat	BB280	1965	£12	£6	
Street Girl	7"	Black Swan	WI402	1964	£10	£5	
Sweeter Than Honey	7"	Blue Beat	BB329	1965	£12	£6	
Tears On My Pillow	7"	Blue Beat	BB187	1963	£12	£6	
Telephone	7"	Blue Beat	BB196	1963	£12	£6	
Throw Them Away	7"	Blue Beat	BB311	1965	£12	£6	
Times Are Going	7"	Blue Beat	BB48	1961	£12	£6	
Tougher Than Tough	7"	Pyramid	PYR6010	1967	£8	£4	*Roland Alphonso B side*
Travel On	7"	Island	WI004	1962	£10	£5	
Troubles	7"	Blue Beat	BB247	1964	£12	£6	*with Patsy Todd*
Try Me	7"	Pyramid	PYR6045	1968	£8	£4	
Trying To Make You Mine	7"	Blue Beat	BB160	1963	£12	£6	
Want More	7"	Pyramid	PYR6040	1968	£8	£4	*Roland Alphonso B side*
Weep No More	7"	Blue Beat	BB276	1965	£12	£6	
Woman A Grumble	7"	Pyramid	PYR6039	1968	£8	£4	
You I Love	7"	Blue Beat	BB291	1965	£12	£6	*with Patsy Todd*
You Never Miss Your Water	7"	Pyramid	PYR6027	1968	£8	£4	

MORGAN, FRANK

Frank Morgan	LP	Vogue	LAE12012	1956	£30	£15	

MORGAN, FREDDY

Side Saddle	7"	London	HL7077	1959	£10	£5	*export*

MORGAN, GEORGE

Country And Western Spectacular	7" EP	Philips	BBE12149	1957	£8	£4	
Morgan, By George	LP	Columbia	CL1044	1957	£15	£6	*US*

MORGAN, JANE

All The Way	LP	London	HAR2110	1958	£15	£6	
All The Way Part 1	7" EP	London	RER1161	1958	£10	£5	
All The Way Part 2	7" EP	London	RER1162	1958	£10	£5	
Around The World	7"	London	HLR8436	1957	£10	£5	
At The Coconut Grove	LP	London	HAR2430/SAHR6226	1962	£12	£5	
Ballads Of Lady Jane	LP	London	HAR2316	1960	£12	£5	
Day The Rains Came	7"	London	HL7064	1958	£6	£2.50	*export*
Day The Rains Came	7" EP	London	RER1204	1959	£10	£5	
Day The Rains Came	LP	London	HAR2158	1959	£15	£6	
Enchanted Island	7"	London	HLR8649	1958	£5	£2	
Fascination	7"	London	HLR8468	1957	£8	£4	
Fascination	LP	London	HAR2086	1957	£15	£6	
From The First Hello	7"	London	HLR8395	1957	£15	£7.50	
Great Songs From The Great Shows Vol. 1	LP	London	HAR2136	1959	£12	£5	
Great Songs From The Great Shows Vol. 2	LP	London	HAR2137	1959	£12	£5	
I'm New At The Game Of Romance	7"	London	HLR8539	1958	£6	£2.50	
I've Got Bells On My Heart	7"	London	HLR8611	1958	£6	£2.50	
In My Style	LP	Columbia	SX6010	1965	£10	£4	
Jane In Spain	LP	London	HAR2244	1960	£12	£5	
Jane Morgan	7" EP	London	RER1331	1961	£12	£6	
Jane Morgan	LP	Kapp	KL1023	195–	£15	£6	*US*
Jane Morgan	LP	Kapp	KL1098	1958	£15	£6	*US*
Jane Morgan Time	LP	London	HAR2371	1961	£12	£5	
Love Makes The World Go Around	LP	London	HAR/SHR8069	1963	£12	£5	
Second Time Around	LP	London	HAR2377/SAHR6177	1961	£12	£5	
Serenades The Victors	LP	Colpix	PXL460	1963	£10	£4	
Something Old, Something New	LP	London	HAR2133	1958	£15	£6	
What Now My Love	LP	London	HAR/SHR8042	1962	£12	£5	
Why Oh Why	7"	London	HL8148	1955	£20	£10	

MORGAN, JAYE P.

Are You Lonesome Tonight?	7"	MGM	MGM1005	1959	£4	£1.50	

Have You Ever Been Lonely	7"	Brunswick	05519	1956	£5	£2	
Jaye P Sings	7" EP	London	REP1013	1954	£12	£6	
Longest Walk	7"	HMV	7M327	1955	£5	£2	
Not One Goodbye	7"	HMV	7M365	1956	£4	£1.50	
Pepper Hot Baby	7"	HMV	7M348	1955	£10	£5	

MORGAN, JOHN

Records credited in the name of pianist John Morgan are listed in this guide along with those by his group, Spirit of John Morgan.

MORGAN, LEE

Another Monday Night At Birdland	LP	Columbia	33SX1181	1959	£15	£6	*all star band*
Birdland Story Vol. 1	LP	Columbia	33SX1399	1961	£15	£6	
Capra Black	LP	Blue Note	BST84901	1973	£12	£5	
Caramba	LP	Blue Note	BST84289	1968	£12	£5	
Charisma	LP	Blue Note	BST84312	1969	£12	£5	
Cooker	LP	Blue Note	BLP/BST81578	196–	£25	£10	
Cornbread	LP	Blue Note	BLP/BST84222	1965	£20	£8	
Delightfulee Morgan	LP	Blue Note	BLP/BST84243	1966	£25	£10	
Expoobident	LP	Stateside	SL10016	1962	£15	£6	
Gigolo	LP	Blue Note	BLP/BST84212	1965	£20	£8	
Introducing Lee Morgan	LP	London	LTZC15101	1958	£40	£20	
Lee Morgan	LP	Blue Note	BST84381	1970	£12	£5	
Leeway	LP	Blue Note	BLP/BST84034	1965	£30	£15	
Live At The Lighthouse	LP	Blue Note	BST89906	1970	£12	£5	
Monday Night At Birdland	LP	Columbia	33SX1160	1959	£15	£6	*all star band*
Rumproller	LP	Blue Note	BLP/BST84199	1966	£25	£10	
Search For The New Land	LP	Blue Note	BLP/BST84169	1966	£25	£10	
Sidewinder	LP	Blue Note	BLP/BST84157	1965	£25	£10	
Sixth Sense	LP	Blue Note	BST84335	1969	£12	£5	

MORGAN, MACE THUNDERBIRDS

Shake And Swing	7" EP	Starlite	STEP36	1963	£15	£7.50	

MORGAN, MARY

From The Candy Store On The Corner	7"	Parlophone	R4227	1956	£4	£1.50	
Jimmy Unknown	7"	Parlophone	MSP6204	1956	£4	£1.50	

MORGAN, PC ALEXANDER

Sussex By The Sea	7"	Columbia	DB8095	1966	£6	£2.50	

MORGAN, RUSS

Moonlight Music	7" EP	Brunswick	OE9068	1955	£5	£2	

MORGAN & MARK SEVEN

I'm Gonna Turn My Life Around	7"	Polydor	BM56083	1966	£4	£1.50	

MORGAN BROTHERS

Kissin' On The Red Light	7"	MGM	MGM1026	1959	£4	£1.50	
Nola	7"	MGM	MGM1007	1959	£5	£2	

MORGAN TWINS

Let's Get Going	7"	RCA	RCA1083	1958	£75	£37.50	

MORGEN, STEVE

Morgen	LP	Probe	CPLP4507	1969	£75	£37.50	*US*

MORIN & WILSON

Peaceful Company	LP	Sovereign	SVNA7252	1972	£20	£8	

MORISETTE, JOHNNY

Meet Me At The Twisting Place	7"	Stateside	SS107	1962	£4	£1.50	

MORISSETTE, ALANIS

She is inclined to play down the fact, but *Jagged Little Pill* was actually Alanis Morissette's third album. Her first two are dramatically different in approach, for they present the singer as a new Kylie Minogue, as she was in her Stock–Aitken–Waterman days. Given that Alanis is co-writer of the material, she was, presumably, not particularly unhappy about the fact at the time, although it is undoubtedly true that her mature style is much more likely to stand the test of time.

Alanis	CD	MCA	MCBBD10253	1991	£30	£15	*Canadian*
Alanis	CD	MCA	MCAD10253	1991	£40	£20	*Canadian*
All I Really Want	CD-s	Maverick	W0330CDDJ	1996	£20	£10	*promo*
Fate Stay With Me	7"	Lamor		1985	£100	£50	*Canadian, best auctioned*
Now Is The Time	CD	MCA	MCAD10731	1992	£40	£20	*Canadian*

MORLY GREY

Only Truth	LP	Starshine		1969	£40	£20	*US*

MORMOS

Ça Doit Etre Bien	LP	CBS	64558	1973	£40	£20	*French*
Great Wall Of China	LP	CBS	64430	1971	£75	£37.50	*German*
Magic Spell Of Mother's Wrath	LP	CBS	64979	1972	£100	£50	*French*

MORNING

Title	Format	Label	Cat. No.	Year	Mint	VG	Notes
Morning	LP	Liberty	LBS83463	1970	**£10**	**£4**	

MORNING AFTER

Title	Format	Label	Cat. No.	Year	Mint	VG	Notes
Blue Blood	LP	Sky	SKYLP71014	1971	**£60**	**£30**	

MORNING DEW

Title	Format	Label	Cat. No.	Year	Mint	VG	Notes
Morning Dew	LP	Roulette	R(S)41045	1967	**£75**	**£37.50**	*US*

MORNING GLORY

Title	Format	Label	Cat. No.	Year	Mint	VG	Notes
Morning Glory	LP	Island	ILPS9237	1973	**£12**	**£5**	

MORPHEUS

Title	Format	Label	Cat. No.	Year	Mint	VG	Notes
Rabenteuer	LP	private	34705	1976	**£30**	**£15**	*German*

MORRICONE, ENNIO

Title	Format	Label	Cat. No.	Year	Mint	VG	Notes
Big Gundown	LP	United Artists	SULP1228	1969	**£10**	**£4**	
Burglars	LP	Bell	BELLS209	1972	**£10**	**£4**	
Fistful Of Dollars	LP	RCA	SF7875	1967	**£15**	**£6**	
Love Circle	LP	CBS	70067	1970	**£25**	**£10**	
Sicilian Claw	LP	Stateside	SSL10307	1970	**£10**	**£4**	
Two Mules For Sister Sara	LP	MCA	MKPS2013	1970	**£10**	**£4**	

MORRIS, DERRICK

Title	Format	Label	Cat. No.	Year	Mint	VG	Notes
What's Your Grouse	7"	Pyramid	PYR6061	1969	**£4**	**£1.50**	*Beverley's Allstars*

MORRIS, ERIC

Title	Format	Label	Cat. No.	Year	Mint	VG	Notes
By The Sea	7"	Rio	R72	1965	**£10**	**£5**	
Children Of Today	7"	Island	WI234	1965	**£10**	**£5**	*Baba Brooks B side*
Country Girl	7"	Blue Beat	BB184	1963	**£12**	**£6**	
Fast Mouth	7"	Island	WI199	1965	**£10**	**£5**	
G.I. Lady	7"	Blue Beat	BB115	1962	**£12**	**£6**	
Home Sweet Home	7"	Black Swan	WI445	1965	**£10**	**£5**	*Lester Sterling B side*
Humpty Dumpty	7"	Blue Beat	BB53	1961	**£12**	**£6**	
If I Didn't Love You	7"	Doctor Bird	DB1056	1966	**£10**	**£5**	*Tommy McCook B side*
Little District	7"	Rio	R39	1964	**£10**	**£5**	
Live As A Man	7"	Rio	R48	1964	**£10**	**£5**	
Lonely Blue Boy	7"	Blue Beat	BB153	1963	**£12**	**£6**	*Prince Buster B side*
Love Can Break A Man	7"	Blue Beat	BB218	1964	**£12**	**£6**	
Love Can Make A Mansion	7"	Island	WI183	1965	**£10**	**£5**	
Mama No Fret	7"	Island	WI147	1964	**£10**	**£5**	*Frankie Anderson B side*
Miss Peggy's Grandmother	7"	Blue Beat	BB137	1962	**£12**	**£6**	*Buster's Allstars B side*
Money Can't Buy Life	7"	Blue Beat	BB83	1962	**£12**	**£6**	*Alton Ellis B side*
My Forty-Five	7"	Blue Beat	BB74	1962	**£12**	**£6**	
Oh My Dear	7"	Port-O-Jam	PJ4006	1964	**£10**	**£5**	
Over The Hills	7"	Blue Beat	BB128	1962	**£12**	**£6**	
Pack Up Your Troubles	7"	Blue Beat	BB105	1962	**£12**	**£6**	
Penny Reel	7"	Island	WI142	1964	**£10**	**£5**	*Dotty & Bonnie B side*
River Come Down	7"	Black Swan	WI439	1964	**£10**	**£5**	
Search The World	7"	Starlite	ST45052	1961	**£10**	**£5**	*Buster's Group B side*
Seven Long Years	7"	Blue Beat	BB140	1962	**£12**	**£6**	
Sinners Repent And Pray	7"	Blue Beat	BB81	1962	**£12**	**£6**	*Alton Ellis B side*
So You Shot Reds	7"	Blue Beat	BB193	1963	**£12**	**£6**	
Solomon Grundie	7"	Black Swan	WI414	1964	**£10**	**£5**	*Baba Brooks B side*
Stitch In Time	7"	Blue Beat	BB273	1964	**£12**	**£6**	
Suddenly	7"	Island	WI185	1965	**£10**	**£5**	
Supper In The Gutter	7"	Black Swan	WI433	1964	**£10**	**£5**	
What A Man Doeth	7"	Island	WI151	1964	**£10**	**£5**	*Duke Reid B side*

MORRIS, HEMSLEY

Title	Format	Label	Cat. No.	Year	Mint	VG	Notes
Love Is Strange	7"	Caltone	TONE104	1967	**£10**	**£5**	*Don Drummond Jr B side*

MORRIS, JOE

Title	Format	Label	Cat. No.	Year	Mint	VG	Notes
Just Your Way Baby	78	London	HL8088	1954	**£30**	**£15**	
Travelin' Man	78	London	HL8098	1954	**£8**	**£3**	

MORRIS, LIBBY

Title	Format	Label	Cat. No.	Year	Mint	VG	Notes
When Liberace Winked At Me	7"	Parlophone	R4225	1956	**£4**	**£1.50**	

MORRIS, MILTON

Title	Format	Label	Cat. No.	Year	Mint	VG	Notes
No Bread And Butter	7"	Upsetter	US318	1969	**£4**	**£1.50**	*Upsetters B side*

MORRIS, MONTY

Title	Format	Label	Cat. No.	Year	Mint	VG	Notes
Can't Get No Peace	7"	Camel	CA12	1969	**£4**	**£1.50**	*Upsetters B side*
Deportation	7"	Big Shot	BI513	1969	**£4**	**£1.50**	
Last Laugh	7"	Doctor Bird	DB1162	1968	**£10**	**£5**	
Same Face	7"	Doctor Bird	DB1176	1969	**£10**	**£5**	
Say What You're Saying	7"	Pama	PM721	1968	**£4**	**£1.50**	

MORRIS, ROGER

Title	Format	Label	Cat. No.	Year	Mint	VG	Notes
First Album	LP	Regal Zonophone	SRZA8509	1972	**£20**	**£8**	

MORRIS, RUSSELL

Title	Format	Label	Cat. No.	Year	Mint	VG	Notes
Real Thing	7"	Decca	F22964	1969	**£30**	**£15**	

MORRIS, VICTOR

Title	Format	Label	Cat. No.	Year	Mint	VG	Notes
Now I'm Alone	7"	Amalgamated	AMG813	1968	**£5**	**£2**	

MORRIS & MITCH

Title	Format	Label	Cat. No.	Year	Mint	VG	Notes
Cumberland Gap	7"	Decca	F10900	1957	**£5**	**£2**	
Highway Patrol	7"	Decca	F11086	1958	**£5**	**£2**	
Six Five Nothing Special	7" EP	Decca	DFE6486	1958	**£15**	**£7.50**	
What Is A Skiffler?	7"	Decca	F10929	1957	**£5**	**£2**	

MORRIS & THE MINORS

Title	Format	Label	Cat. No.	Year	Mint	VG	Notes
State The Obvious	7"	Round	MOR1	1980	**£5**	**£2**	

MORRISEY, PAT

Title	Format	Label	Cat. No.	Year	Mint	VG	Notes
I'm Pat Morrisey, I Sing	LP	Mercury	MG20197	1956	**£20**	**£8**	*US*

MORRISON, CURLEY JIM

Title	Format	Label	Cat. No.	Year	Mint	VG	Notes
Air Force Blues	7"	Starlite	ST45065	1961	**£100**	**£50**	

MORRISON, JAMES

Title	Format	Label	Cat. No.	Year	Mint	VG	Notes
James Morrison And Tom Ennis	LP	Topic	12T390	1980	**£10**	**£4**	*with Tom Ennis*
Pure Genius Of James Morrison	LP	Shanachie	33004	1978	**£10**	**£4**	*US*

MORRISON, TOM

Title	Format	Label	Cat. No.	Year	Mint	VG	Notes
Adventures Of Mighty Mouse & His Pals	7" EP	MGM	MGMEP709	1960	**£5**	**£2**	

MORRISON, VAN

Title	Format	Label	Cat. No.	Year	Mint	VG	Notes
Astral Weeks	LP	Warner Bros	WS1768	1968	**£10**	**£4**	
Avalon Sunset	CD	Polydor	AST1	1989	**£50**	**£25**	*promo box set, with cassette, biog, photo, slides, pen*
Blowin' Your Mind	LP	London	HAZ8346	1967	**£25**	**£10**	
Brown-Eyed Girl	7"	London	HLZ10150	1967	**£20**	**£10**	
Brown-Eyed Girl	7"	London	HLM10453	1974	**£5**	**£2**	
Brown-Eyed Girl	7"	President	PT328	1970	**£6**	**£2.50**	
Caldonia	7"	Warner Bros	K16392	1974	**£4**	**£1.50**	
Coney Island	CD-s	Polydor	VANCD4	1990	**£5**	**£2**	
Enlightenment	CD-s	Polydor	VANCD8	1991	**£5**	**£2**	
Excerpts From Van	CD	Polydor	VANCD001	1990	**£20**	**£8**	*promo*
Gloria	CD-s	Polydor	VANCD5	1990	**£5**	**£2**	
Have I Told You Lately	CD-s	Polydor	VANCD1	1989	**£5**	**£2**	
His Band And Street Choir	LP	Warner Bros	WS1884	1970	**£10**	**£4**	
I Can't Stop Loving You	CD-s	Polydor	VANCD9	1991	**£5**	**£2**	*with the Chieftains*
I'll Tell Me Ma	CD-s	Mercury	MERCD262	1988	**£5**	**£2**	*with the Chieftains*
In The Days Before Rock'n'Roll	CD-s	Polydor	VANCD7	1990	**£5**	**£2**	
Jackie Wilson Said	7"	Warner Bros	K16210	1972	**£4**	**£1.50**	
Joyous Sound	7"	Warner Bros	K16986	1977	**£4**	**£1.50**	
Live At The Roxy	LP	Warner Bros	WBMS102	1978	**£30**	**£15**	*US promo*
Moondance	CD	Warner Bros	C88110	1988	**£15**	**£6**	*box set*
Moondance	LP	Warner Bros	WS1835	1970	**£10**	**£4**	
Moondance	LP	Nautilus	SD110	1981	**£12**	**£5**	*US audiophile*
Orangefield	CD-s	Polydor	VANCD3	1989	**£5**	**£2**	
Real Real Gone	CD-s	Polydor	VANCD6	1990	**£5**	**£2**	
Sense Of Wonder	LP	Mercury	MERH54	1985	**£30**	**£15**	*test pressing with 'Crazy Jane On God'*
Tupelo Honey	LP	Warner Bros	WS1950	1971	**£10**	**£4**	
Whenever God Shines His Light	CD-s	Polydor	VANCD2	1989	**£5**	**£2**	*with Cliff Richard*
Why Must I Always Explain?	CD-s	Polydor	VANCD10	1991	**£5**	**£2**	

MORRISSEY

Title	Format	Label	Cat. No.	Year	Mint	VG	Notes
Boxers	CD-s	Parlophone	CDRDJX6400	1995	**£15**	**£7.50**	*promo*
Certain People I Know	CD-s	HMV	CDPOP1631	1992	**£8**	**£4**	
Education In Reverse	LP	HMV		1988	**£15**	**£6**	*Australian*
Every Day Is Like Sunday	12"	HMV	12POP1619	1988	**£6**	**£2.50**	
Every Day Is Like Sunday	CD-s	HMV	CDPOP1619	1988	**£12**	**£6**	
Have-A-Go Merchant	7"	Parlophone	RDJ6400	1995	**£8**	**£4**	*promo*
Have-A-Go Merchant	CD-s	Parlophone	CDRDJ6400	1995	**£15**	**£7.50**	*promo*
Hold On To Your Friends	CD-s	Parlophone	CDRDJ6383	1994	**£5**	**£2**	*promo*
Interesting Drug	12"	HMV	12POPS1621	1989	**£8**	**£4**	*1 side etched*
Interesting Drug	CD-s	HMV	CDPOP1621	1989	**£10**	**£5**	
Jack The Ripper	7"	HMV	POPDJ1632	1993	**£6**	**£2.50**	*promo*
Jack The Ripper (live)	CD-s	HMV	POPDJ1632	1993	**£8**	**£4**	*promo only*
Last Of The Famous International Playboys	12"	HMV	12POP1620	1989	**£6**	**£2.50**	
Last Of The Famous International Playboys	CD-s	HMV	CDPOP1620	1989	**£12**	**£6**	
More You Ignore Me, The Closer I Get	7"	Parlophone	RDJ6372	1994	**£5**	**£2**	*promo*
More You Ignore Me, The Closer I Get	CD-s	Parlophone	CDRDJ6372	1994	**£5**	**£2**	*promo*
More You Ignore Me, The Closer I Get	CD-s	Parlophone	CDRDJ6372	1994	**£15**	**£7.50**	*promo with 45 rpm logo on disc*
My Love Life	CD-s	HMV	CDPOP1628	1991	**£8**	**£4**	

Title	Format	Label	Cat. No.	Year	Mint	VG+	Notes
November Spawned A Monster	CD-s	HMV	CDPOP1623	1990	£10	£5	
Now My Heart Is Full	CD	Sire	PROCD6778	1994	£25	£10	*US promo compilation*
Ouija Board, Ouija Board	CD-s	HMV	CDPOP1622	1989	£10	£5	
Our Frank	CD-s	HMV	CDPOP1625	1991	£10	£5	
Piccadilly Palare	CD-s	HMV	CDPOP1624	1990	£10	£5	
Pregnant For The Last Time	CD-s	HMV	CDPOP1627	1991	£10	£5	
Sing Your Life	CD-s	HMV	CDPOP1626	1991	£10	£5	
Suedehead	12"	HMV	12POP1618	1988	£6	£2.50	
Suedehead	CD-s	HMV	CDPOP1618	1988	£12	£6	
Sunny	CD-s	Parlophone	CDRDJ6243	1993	£5	£2	*promo*
Viva Hate!	CD	HMV	CDCSD3787	1988	£30	£15	*promo boxed set*
We Hate It When Our Friends Become Successful	10"	HMV	POPDJ1629	1992	£15	£7.50	*promo*
You're The One For Me, Fatty	10"	HMV	POPDJ1630	1992	£15	£7.50	*promo*
You're The One For Me, Fatty	CD-s	HMV	CDPOP1630	1992	£8	£4	

MORRISSEY, DICK

Title	Format	Label	Cat. No.	Year	Mint	VG+	Notes
Have You Heard	LP	77	LEU128	1961	£100	£50	
Here And Now And Sounding Good	LP	Mercury	20093MCL	1967	£100	£50	
It's Morrissey, Man	LP	Fontana	TFL5149	1961	£100	£50	
Storm Warning	LP	Mercury	20077MCL	1967	£60	£30	

MORROW, BUDDY

Title	Format	Label	Cat. No.	Year	Mint	VG+	Notes
Buddy Morrow And His Orchestra	7" EP	HMV	7EG8076	1955	£5	£2	
Dragnet	7"	HMV	7M162	1953	£4	£1.50	
Impact	7" EP	RCA	RCX174	1959	£5	£2	
Knock On Wood	7"	HMV	7M216	1954	£4	£1.50	
Staccato's Theme	7"	RCA	RCA1167	1960	£4	£1.50	

MORSE, ELLA MAE

Title	Format	Label	Cat. No.	Year	Mint	VG+	Notes
Barrelhouse Boogie And The Blues	10" LP	Capitol	LC6687	1954	£60	£30	
Barrelhouse Boogie And The Blues	7" EP	Capitol	EAP1513	1955	£40	£20	
Barrelhouse Boogie And The Blues	LP	Capitol	T513	1956	£30	£15	*US*
Birmingham	7"	Capitol	CL14376	1955	£25	£12.50	
Bring Back My Baby To Me	7"	Capitol	CL14223	1955	£40	£20	
Down In Mexico	7"	Capitol	CL14572	1956	£20	£10	
Heart Full Of Hope	7"	Capitol	CL14332	1955	£25	£12.50	
Hits Of Ella Mae Morse & Freddie Slack	LP	Capitol	T1802	1962	£20	£8	*US*
I'm Gone	7"	Capitol	CL14760	1957	£10	£5	
Morse Code	LP	Capitol	T898	1957	£25	£10	*US*
Razzle Dazzle	7"	Capitol	CL14341	1955	£75	£37.50	
Rockin' Brew	LP	Ember	SPE6605	1967	£12	£5	*with Freddie Slack*
Seventeen	7"	Capitol	CL14362	1955	£60	£30	
Smack Dab In The Middle	7"	Capitol	CL14303	1955	£30	£15	
What Good'll It Do Me	7"	Capitol	CL14726	1957	£10	£5	
When Boy Kiss Girl	7"	Capitol	CL14508	1956	£12	£6	

MORTIFEE, ANN

Title	Format	Label	Cat. No.	Year	Mint	VG+	Notes
Baptism	LP	EMI	EMC3094	1975	£25	£10	

MORTIMER, AZIE

Title	Format	Label	Cat. No.	Year	Mint	VG+	Notes
Lips	7"	London	HLX9237	1960	£8	£4	

MORTON, JELLY ROLL

Title	Format	Label	Cat. No.	Year	Mint	VG+	Notes
Burnin' The Iceberg	7"	HMV	7M256	1954	£5	£2	
Classic Jazz Piano Vol. 1	10" LP	London	AL3534	1954	£25	£10	
Classic Jazz Piano Vol. 2	10" LP	London	AL3559	1956	£25	£10	
Classic Piano Solos	LP	Riverside	RLP12111	1962	£15	£6	
Fat Frances	7"	HMV	7M178	1954	£5	£2	
Jazz Originators Vol. 3	7" EP	Collector	JE120	1959	£5	£2	
Jelly Roll Morton	7" EP	Vogue	EPV1126	1956	£5	£2	
Jelly Roll Morton	7" EP	RCA	RCX168	1955	£5	£2	
Jelly Roll Morton	7" EP	Storyville	SEP379	1961	£5	£2	
Jelly Roll Morton	LP	Fontana	TL5261	1965	£10	£4	
Jelly Roll Morton & His Red Hot Peppers	10" LP	HMV	DLP1016	1953	£25	£10	
Jelly Roll Morton No. 2	7" EP	RCA	RCX207	1960	£5	£2	
Jungle Blues	7"	HMV	7M207	1954	£5	£2	
King Of New Orleans Jazz	LP	RCA	RD27113	1959	£20	£8	
King Of New Orleans Jazz Vol. 2	LP	RCA	RD27184	1961	£20	£8	
Kings Of Jazz	10" LP	London	AL3520	1954	£25	£10	
Morton Sixes And Sevens	LP	Fontana	TL5415	1967	£10	£4	
Morton's Red Hot Peppers	10" LP	HMV	DLP1044	1954	£25	£10	
Morton's Red Hot Peppers No. 3	10" LP	HMV	DLP1071	1955	£25	£10	
Mr Jelly Lord	LP	Riverside	RLP12132	1961	£15	£6	
New Orleans Memories	10" LP	Vogue	LDE080	1954	£25	£10	
Smoke House Blues	7"	HMV	7M187	1954	£5	£2	
Solos	10" LP	London	AL3519	1954	£25	£10	
Tank Town Bump	7"	HMV	7M132	1953	£5	£2	
Treasures Of North American Negro Music Vol. 4	7" EP	Fontana	TFE17263	1960	£5	£2	

MORTON, MANDY

Title	Format	Label	Cat. No.	Year	Mint	VG+	Notes
Ghost Of Christmas Past	7"	Polydor	2382101	1980	£4	£1.50	
Magic Lady	LP	Banshee	BAN1011	1978	£200	£100	*with Spriguns*
Magic Lady	LP	Banshee	BAN1011	1978	£300	£180	*blue vinyl*
Sea Of Storms	LP	Polydor	2382101	1980	£15	£6	*German*

Title	Format	Label	Cat. No.	Year	Mint	VG	Notes
Song For Me (Music Prince)	7"	Banshee	BANS791	1979	£10	£5	with Spriguns
Valley Of Light	LP	Banshee		1983	£50	£25	

MORTON, ROBIN & CATHAL McCONNEL

Title	Format	Label	Cat. No.	Year	Mint	VG	Notes
Irish Jubilee	LP	Mercier	IRL10	1970	£25	£10	Irish

MOSAICS

Title	Format	Label	Cat. No.	Year	Mint	VG	Notes
Let's Go Drag Racing	7"	Columbia	DB7990	1966	£8	£4	

MOSCA, SAL

Title	Format	Label	Cat. No.	Year	Mint	VG	Notes
At The Den	LP	Wave	LP2	1970	£15	£6	with Peter Ind
At The Piano	LP	Wave	LP8	1970	£15	£6	

MOSELEY, REVEREND AND OTHERS

Title	Format	Label	Cat. No.	Year	Mint	VG	Notes
Treasures Of North American Negro Music Vol. 6	7" EP	Fontana	TFE17265	1960	£10	£5	

MOSES

Title	Format	Label	Cat. No.	Year	Mint	VG	Notes
Changes	LP	Spectator	2037	1971	£100	£50	Danish

MOSES & JOSHUA

Title	Format	Label	Cat. No.	Year	Mint	VG	Notes
Get Out Of My Heart	7"	Bell	BLL1018	1968	£4	£1.50	

MOSKOW

Title	Format	Label	Cat. No.	Year	Mint	VG	Notes
Man From UNCLE	7"	Moskow	SRS2103	1982	£5	£2	

MOSS, BUDDY

Title	Format	Label	Cat. No.	Year	Mint	VG	Notes
Georgia Blues Vol. 2	LP	Kokomo	K1003	196–	£40	£20	

MOSS, GENE & THE MONSTERS

Title	Format	Label	Cat. No.	Year	Mint	VG	Notes
Dracula's Greatest Hits	LP	RCA	LSP2977	1964	£25	£10	US

MOSS, JENNY

Title	Format	Label	Cat. No.	Year	Mint	VG	Notes
Hobbies	7"	Columbia	DB7061	1963	£40	£20	

MOST

Title	Format	Label	Cat. No.	Year	Mint	VG	Notes
Carefree	7"	SRT	STSCUS570	1979	£5	£2	

MOST, ABE OCTET

Title	Format	Label	Cat. No.	Year	Mint	VG	Notes
Presenting The Abe Most Octet	7" EP	London	REP1028	1955	£8	£4	

MOST, MICKIE

Title	Format	Label	Cat. No.	Year	Mint	VG	Notes
Big Beat Ball	LP	Rave	RMG1157	1963	£100	£50	South African
Feminine Look	7"	Columbia	DB7117	1963	£8	£4	
Hear The Most	LP	Rave	RMG1139	1962	£100	£50	South African
Mickie Most	LP	Rave	RMG1151	1962	£100	£50	South African
Money Honey	7"	Columbia	DB7245	1964	£10	£5	
Sea Cruise	7"	Columbia	DB7180	1963	£10	£5	
That's Alright	7" EP	Columbia	ESRF1588	1964	£25	£12.50	French
Yes Indeed I Do	7"	Decca	F11664	1963	£10	£5	

MOST, SAM

Title	Format	Label	Cat. No.	Year	Mint	VG	Notes
Plays Bird, Bud, Monk And Miles	LP	Parlophone	PMC1087	1959	£20	£8	
Sam Most	LP	London	LTZN15063	1957	£20	£8	
Sam Most Sextet	10" LP	Vanguard	PPT12009	1956	£20	£8	

MOST BROTHERS

Title	Format	Label	Cat. No.	Year	Mint	VG	Notes
Dottie	7"	Decca	F11040	1958	£6	£2.50	
Teen Angel	7"	Decca	F10998	1958	£8	£4	
Whistle Bait	7"	Decca	F10968	1957	£8	£4	

MOTEN, BENNY

Title	Format	Label	Cat. No.	Year	Mint	VG	Notes
Plays Kay-Cee Jazz	10" LP	HMV	DLP1057	1954	£20	£8	

MOTHER EARTH

Title	Format	Label	Cat. No.	Year	Mint	VG	Notes
Bring Me Home	LP	Reprise	K44133	1971	£10	£4	
I Did My Part	7"	Mercury	MF1081	1969	£5	£2	
Living With The Animals	LP	Mercury	SMCL20143	1968	£12	£5	
Make A Joyful Noise	LP	Mercury	SMCL20173	1969	£12	£5	
Satisfied	LP	Mercury	6338023	1970	£12	£5	
Tracy Nelson Country	LP	Mercury	SMCL20179	1969	£12	£5	

MOTHER MALLARD'S PORTABLE MASTERPIECE COMPANY

Title	Format	Label	Cat. No.	Year	Mint	VG	Notes
Like A Duck To Water	LP	Earthquack	0002	1973	£25	£10	US
Mother Mallard's Portable Masterpiece Company	LP	Earthquack	0001	1973	£25	£10	US

MOTHER TUCKER'S YELLOW DUCK

Title	Format	Label	Cat. No.	Year	Mint	VG	Notes
Home Grown Stuff	LP	Capitol		1969	£40	£20	Canadian
Starting A New Day	LP	Capitol		197–	£40	£20	Canadian

MOTHER YOD

Title	Format	Label	Cat. No.	Year	Mint	VG	Notes
Mother Yod	LP	Prescription	DRUG1	1997	£20	£8	

MOTHERHOOD

Title	Format	Label	Cat. No.	Year	Mint	VG	Notes
I Feel So Free	LP	United Artists	UAS69173	1969	£15	£6	German

MOTHERLIGHT

Title	Format	Label	Number	Year	Mint	VG	Notes
Bobak, Jons, Malone	LP	Morgan Blue Town	BT5003	1969	**£100**	**£50**	

MOTHER'S LOVE

Title	Format	Label	Number	Year	Mint	VG	Notes
Take One	LP	Havoc	IHLP3A	1967	**£75**	**£37.50**	*Dutch*

MOTHER'S RUIN

Title	Format	Label	Number	Year	Mint	VG	Notes
Say It's Not True	7"	Spectra	SPC7	1982	**£20**	**£10**	
Street Lights	7"	Spectra	SPC6	1982	**£12**	**£6**	
Streetfighters	7"	Spectra	SPC1	1981	**£10**	**£5**	

MOTHMEN

Title	Format	Label	Number	Year	Mint	VG	Notes
Show Me Your House And Car	12"	Do It	DUNIT12	1981	**£6**	**£2.50**	
Show Me Your House And Car	7"	Do It	DUN12	1981	**£5**	**£2**	

MOTHS

Title	Format	Label	Number	Year	Mint	VG	Notes
Moths	LP	Deroy	no number	1969	**£400**	**£250**	

MOTIAN, PAUL

Title	Format	Label	Number	Year	Mint	VG	Notes
Conception Vessel	LP	ECM	ECM1028ST	1974	**£10**	**£4**	
Tribute	LP	ECM	ECM1048ST	1975	**£10**	**£4**	

MOTIFFE

Title	Format	Label	Number	Year	Mint	VG	Notes
Motiffe	LP	Deroy	777	1972	**£250**	**£150**	

MOTIONS

Title	Format	Label	Number	Year	Mint	VG	Notes
Electric Baby	LP	Philips	PHS600317	1970	**£20**	**£8**	*US*
Every Step I Take	7" EP	Vogue	INT18097	1966	**£10**	**£5**	*French*
I've Waited So Long	7" EP	Vogue	INT18017	1965	**£10**	**£5**	*French*
Impressions Of Wonderful	LP	Negram	CD1103	1968	**£20**	**£8**	*US*
Introducing	LP	Negram	NJH2	1965	**£40**	**£20**	*Dutch*
Live	LP	Marble Arch	MALH201	1968	**£15**	**£6**	*US*
Song Book	LP	Teenbeat	APLP101	1967	**£20**	**£8**	*Dutch*
Stop Your Crying	7"	Pye	7N25390	1966	**£4**	**£1.50**	
Their Own Way	LP	Negram	IHLP2	1968	**£20**	**£8**	*Dutch*
Wasted Words	7" EP	Vogue	INT18069	1966	**£10**	**£5**	*French*

MOTIVATION

Title	Format	Label	Number	Year	Mint	VG	Notes
Come On Down	7"	Direction	583248	1968	**£20**	**£10**	

MOTLEY CRUE

Title	Format	Label	Number	Year	Mint	VG	Notes
Dr Feelgood	7"	Elektra	EKR97P	1989	**£5**	**£2**	*shaped picture disc*
Dr Feelgood	CD-s	Elektra	EKR97CD	1989	**£5**	**£2**	*3" single*
Girls Girls Girls	12"	Elektra	EKR59TP	1987	**£8**	**£4**	*picture disc*
Girls Girls Girls	12"	Elektra	EKR59TB	1987	**£8**	**£4**	*with patch, boxed*
Girls Girls Girls	7"	Elektra	EKR59	1987	**£5**	**£2**	*X-rated picture sleeve*
Girls Girls Girls	7"	Elektra	EKR59P	1987	**£5**	**£2**	*poster sleeve*
Helter Skelter	12"	Elektra		198–	**£20**	**£10**	*US promo picture disc, poster*
Looks That Kill	12"	Elektra	E9756T	1984	**£8**	**£4**	*with transfer*
Looks That Kill	12"	Elektra	E9756TP	1984	**£15**	**£7.50**	*picture disc*
Looks That Kill	7"	Elektra	E9756	1984	**£6**	**£2.50**	
Primal Scream	CD-s	Elektra	EKR133CD	1991	**£5**	**£2**	
Shout At The Devil	LP	Elektra	9602891	1983	**£15**	**£6**	*picture disc, poster*
Smokin' In The Boys' Room	12"	Elektra	EKR33T	1986	**£8**	**£4**	*with patch & poster*
Smokin' In The Boys' Room	7"	Elektra	EKR16TP	1986	**£12**	**£6**	*mask shaped picture disc*
Smokin' In The Boys' Room	7"	Elektra	EKR33PA/PB	1986	**£25**	**£12.50**	*2 interlocking shaped picture discs*
Too Fast For Love	LP	Leathur	LR123	1981	**£60**	**£30**	*US*
Too Young To Fall In Love	12"	Elektra	E9732T	1984	**£8**	**£4**	*with poster*
Too Young To Fall In Love	7"	Elektra	E9732	1984	**£6**	**£2.50**	
You're All I Need	12"	Elektra	EKR65TB	1988	**£6**	**£2.50**	*with patch & poster, boxed*
You're All I Need	12"	Elektra	EKR65TP	1988	**£6**	**£2.50**	*picture disc*

MOTORHEAD

When Lemmy left Hawkwind, he covered over the psychedelic designs on his equipment with black paint and thereby defined the image for his new group. Motorhead managed to become popular among fans of punk at a time when heavy metal was distinctly out of fashion. Of course, the group's approach to heavy metal was a bit different – short pieces played very fast, the emphasis being on energy rather than on displays of virtuosity – and they very much anticipated the thrash metal style of the late eighties. The first edition of this guide gave the information that only ten copies of the 'Motorhead' single on white vinyl exist – information that has since been repeated elsewhere. In fact, it turns out that the single was not at all limited – and the author was inundated with phone calls from collectors telling him so!

Title	Format	Label	Number	Year	Mint	VG	Notes
1916	CD	Epic	4674819	1991	**£12**	**£5**	*picture disc*
Ace Of Spades	12"	Bronze	BROX106	1980	**£6**	**£2.50**	
Ace Of Spades	7"	GWR	GWR15	1988	**£10**	**£5**	
Ace Of Spades	LP	Bronze	BRON531	1980	**£10**	**£4**	*gold vinyl*
Beerdrinkers And Hellraisers	12"	Big Beat	SWT61	1980	**£6**	**£2.50**	*orange vinyl*
Bomber	7"	Bronze	BRO85	1979	**£5**	**£2**	*blue vinyl*
Bomber	LP	Bronze	BRON523	1979	**£10**	**£4**	*blue vinyl*
Iron Fist	7"	Bronze	BRO146	1982	**£5**	**£2**	*blue vinyl*
Killed By Death	7"	Bronze	BROP185	1984	**£10**	**£5**	*shaped picture disc*
Motorhead	12"	Chiswick	S13	1977	**£6**	**£2.50**	
Motorhead	7"	Big Beat	NSP13	1980	**£5**	**£2**	*picture disc (2 versions)*

Motorhead	CD-s	Castle Communication	CD310	1988	£5	£2	
Motorhead	LP	Chiswick	WIK2	1977	£40	£20	silver sleeve
Motorhead (Live)	7"	Bronze	BROP124	1981	£6	£2.50	picture disc
No Remorse	CD	Castle Communication	CLACD121	1986	£12	£5	leather sleeve
No Remorse	LP	Bronze	PROLP5	1984	£12	£5	double, 'leather' sleeve
No Sleep Till Hammersmith	LP	Bronze	BRON535	1981	£10	£4	gold vinyl
One To Sing The Blues	CD-s	Epic	6565782	1990	£5	£2	
Orgasmatron	CD	GWR	GWCD1	1986	£50	£25	mispressing – plays the Beatles' Please Please Me
Overkill	12"	Bronze	12BRO67	1979	£6	£2.50	
Overkill	7"	Bronze	BRO67	1979	£4	£1.50	with badge
Overkill	LP	Bronze	BRON515	1979	£10	£4	green vinyl
St Valentine's Massacre EP	10"	Bronze	BROX116	1981	£6	£2.50	with Girlschool
White Line Fever	7"	Stiff	BUY9	1977	£10	£5	picture sleeve

MOTORWAY

All I Wanna Be Is Your Romeo	7"	Neat	NEAT01	1980	£6	£2.50	

MOTOWNS

Si, Proprio I Motowns!	LP	RCA	S14	1967	£50	£25	Italian

MOTT THE HOOPLE

All The Young Dudes	CD-s	CBS	6581772	1992	£5	£2	
Brain Capers	LP	Island	ILPS9178	1971	£30	£15	with mask
Brain Capers	LP	Island	ILPS9178	1971	£10	£4	
Downtown	7"	Island	WIP6112	1971	£5	£2	
Mad Shadows	LP	Island	ILPS9119	1970	£10	£4	pink label
Midnight Lady	7"	Island	WIP6105	1971	£5	£2	picture sleeve
Mott The Hoople	LP	Island	ILPS9108	1969	£15	£6	pink label
Mott The Hoople	LP	Island	ILPS9108	1969	£30	£15	with 'Road To Birmingham', pink label
Rock And Roll Queen	7"	Island	WIP6072	1969	£8	£4	
The Hoople	LP	Columbia	PCQ32871	1974	£10	£4	US quad
Wild Life	LP	Island	ILPS9144	1971	£10	£4	

MOULD, BOB

See A Little Light	CD-s	Virgin	VUSCD2	1989	£5	£2	
Workbook	CD	Virgin	PRCDBOB	1989	£20	£8	US promo picture disc, cloth cover

MOULE, KEN

Jazz At Toad Hall	LP	Decca	LK4261/SKL4042	1958	£20	£8	
Ken Moule	LP	Decca	LK4192	1957	£25	£10	
Mae West	7"	Ember	EMS275	1970	£5	£2	
Mae West	7"	Ember	EMS275	1970	£10	£5	picture sleeve

MOULTRIE, MATTIE

That's How Strong My Love Is	7"	CBS	202547	1967	£5	£2	

MOUND CITY BLUE BLOWERS

Blues Blowing Jazz Vol. 1	7" EP	Collector	JEL1	1959	£5	£2	
Mound City Blue Blowers	7" EP	HMV	7EG8096	1955	£5	£2	

MOUNT RUSHMORE

Stone Free	7"	Dot	115	1968	£4	£1.50	

MOUNTAIN

Mountain was formed by Felix Pappalardi in a deliberate attempt to capture some of the market that had been opened up by Cream. Pappalardi had, of course, worked with Cream on both *Disraeli Gears* and *Wheels Of Fire*. Guitarist Leslie West was not in Eric Clapton's league, but Mountain nevertheless had its moments – most notably on *Nantucket Sleighride*, a section of which was made familiar to Sunday TV viewers in the London area as the theme tune to *Weekend World*.

Avalanche	LP	Columbia	CQ33088	1974	£10	£4	US quad
Best Of Mountain	LP	Columbia	CQ32079	1973	£10	£4	US quad
Dreams Of Milk And Honey	7"	Bell	BLL1078	1970	£5	£2	
Flowers Of Evil	LP	Island	ILPS9179	1971	£10	£4	
Mountain Climbing	LP	Bell	SBLL133	1970	£15	£6	
Nantucket Sleighride	LP	Island	ILPS9148	1971	£12	£5	
Road Goes Ever On	LP	Island	ILPS9199	1972	£10	£4	
Twin Peaks	LP	CBS	88095	1974	£12	£5	double

MOUNTAIN, VALERIE

Go It Alone	7"	Columbia	DB4660	1961	£4	£1.50	
Some People	7" EP	Pye	NEP24158	1962	£6	£2.50	with the Eagles

MOUNTAIN ASH

Hermit	LP	Witches Bane	LKLP6036	1975	£150	£75	

MOUNTAIN BUS

Sundance	LP	Good	101	1971	£75	£37.50	US

MOURNING PHASE

Title	Format	Label	Cat. No.	Year	Mint	VG	Notes
Eden (Mourning Phase)	LP	Eden	EDEN1	1991	**£15**	**£6**	
Mourning Phase	LP	private		1971	**£500**	**£330**	

MOUSE

Title	Format	Label	Cat. No.	Year	Mint	VG	Notes
All The Fallen Teen Angels	7"	Sovereign	SOV127	1974	**£10**	**£5**	
Lady Killer	LP	Sovereign	SVNA7262	1974	**£125**	**£62.50**	
We Can Make It	7"	Sovereign	SOV122	1973	**£10**	**£5**	

MOUSE & THE TRAPS

Title	Format	Label	Cat. No.	Year	Mint	VG	Notes
L.O.V.E.	7"	President	PT174	1968	**£10**	**£5**	
Sometimes You Just Can't Win	7"	President	PT210	1968	[illegible]	[illegible]	

MOUSEFOLK

Title	Format	Label	Cat. No.	Year	Mint	VG	Notes
Don't Let It Slip Away	7"	Tea Time Surf's Up	01	1988	**£4**	**£1.50**	*flexi, picture sleeve*

MOUSKOURI, NANA

Title	Format	Label	Cat. No.	Year	Mint	VG	Notes
One That Got Away	7"	Fontana	261365TF	1963	**£6**	**£2.50**	

MOUZON, ALPHONSE

Title	Format	Label	Cat. No.	Year	Mint	VG	Notes
Man Incognito	LP	United Artists	UAG20005	1976	**£10**	**£4**	

MOVE

The Move could never quite decide whether they wished to become part of the burgeoning progressive rock scene or whether they just wanted to be a pop group. In the event, much of the group's music is an uneasy compromise between the two, with the series of hit singles receiving the most care and invention in their construction. The most interesting Move release is possibly the live EP *Something Else*, where the group powers its way through an assortment of dynamic cover versions. They turn Spooky Tooth's 'Sunshine Help Me' into something of a showcase for Roy Wood's squally lead guitar, but the fact that the melodic bass playing is given at least as much prominence in the mix makes the music sound remarkably fresh.

Title	Format	Label	Cat. No.	Year	Mint	VG	Notes
Blackberry Way	7"	Regal Zonophone	RZ3015	1969	**£4**	**£1.50**	
Brontosaurus	7"	Regal Zonophone	RZ3026	1970	**£4**	**£1.50**	
Cherry Blossom Clinic	7"	Regal Zonophone		1968	**£50**	**£25**	*test pressing*
Curly	7"	Regal Zonophone	RZ3021	1969	**£4**	**£1.50**	
Fire Brigade	7"	MagniFly	ECHO104	1972	**£4**	**£1.50**	*picture sleeve*
Fire Brigade	7"	Regal Zonophone	RZ3005	1968	**£4**	**£1.50**	
Flowers In The Rain	7"	Regal Zonophone	RZ3001	1967	**£4**	**£1.50**	
I Can Hear The Grass Grow	7"	Deram	DM117	1967	**£4**	**£1.50**	
I Can Hear The Grass Grow	7" EP	Deram	15002	1967	**£25**	**£12.50**	*French*
Looking On	LP	Fly	FLY1	1971	**£10**	**£4**	
Message From The Country	LP	Harvest	SHSP4013	1971	**£10**	**£4**	
Move	LP	Regal Zonophone	LRZ1002	1968	**£40**	**£20**	*mono*
Move	LP	Regal Zonophone	SLRZ1002	1968	**£25**	**£10**	*stereo*
Move/Shazam	LP	Fly	TOOFA5/6	1972	**£12**	**£5**	*double*
Night Of Fear	7"	Deram	DM109	1966	**£4**	**£1.50**	
Shazam	LP	Regal Zonophone	SLRZ1012	1970	**£20**	**£8**	
Something Else	7" EP	Regal Zonophone	TRZ2001	1968	**£30**	**£15**	
Something Else From The Move	7"	EMI	PSRS315	1968	**£25**	**£12.50**	*1 sided promo sampler*
Wild Tiger Woman	7"	Regal Zonophone	RZ3012	1968	**£5**	**£2**	

MOVEMENT

Title	Format	Label	Cat. No.	Year	Mint	VG	Notes
Head For The Sun	7"	Transatlantic	BIG112	1968	**£75**	**£37.50**	
Something You've Got	7"	Pye	7N17443	1968	**£75**	**£37.50**	

MOVING FINGER

Title	Format	Label	Cat. No.	Year	Mint	VG	Notes
Higher And Higher	7"	Mercury	MF1077	1969	**£4**	**£1.50**	
Jeremy The Lamp	7"	Mercury	MF1051	1968	**£15**	**£7.50**	
So Many People	7"	Decca	F13406	1973	**£4**	**£1.50**	

MOVING GELATINE PLATES

Title	Format	Label	Cat. No.	Year	Mint	VG	Notes
Moving Gelatine Plates	LP	CBS	64399	1971	**£75**	**£37.50**	*French*
World Of Genius Hans	LP	CBS	64146	1972	**£75**	**£37.50**	*French*

MOVING HEARTS

Title	Format	Label	Cat. No.	Year	Mint	VG	Notes
Live Hearts	LP	WEA	IR0203	1983	**£10**	**£4**	
Moving Hearts	LP	WEA	K583387	1981	**£10**	**£4**	

MOVING SIDEWALKS

Title	Format	Label	Cat. No.	Year	Mint	VG	Notes
Flash	LP	Tantara	TYS6919	1968	**£200**	**£100**	*US*

MOWREY JNR & WATSON

Title	Format	Label	Cat. No.	Year	Mint	VG	Notes
Busker	LP	Riverdale	RRL1000	1976	**£50**	**£25**	

MOYET, ALISON

Love Letters	CD-s	CBS	MOYETC5	1987	£5	£2	

MOZART, MICKEY

Little Dipper	7"	Columbia	DB4308	1959	£4	£1.50	

M-PEOPLE

Open Up Your Heart	12"	DeConstruction	OPEN4	1994	£8	£4	*promo*

MR BEAN

Elected	CD-s	London	LONCD319	1992	£5	£2	*with Bruce Dickinson*

MR BIG

Drill Song	CD-s	Atlantic	A7712CD	1991	£5	£2	
Green Tinted Sixties Mind	CD-s	Atlantic	A7702CD	1991	£5	£2	
Just Take My Heart	CD-s	East West	A7490CD	1992	£5	£2	
To Be With You	CD-s	Atlantic	A7514CD	1992	£5	£2	

MR BROWN

Mellan Tre Ogon	LP	Fly Khan	0177	1977	£30	£15	*Swedish*

MR CLEAN

Both sides of the Mr Clean single are the work of Frank Zappa, who wrote and produced the songs and played guitar on them.

Mr Clean	7"	Original Sound	40	1964	£150	£75	*US*

MR DYNAMITE

Sh'mon	7"	Sue	WI4027	1967	£20	£10	

MR FLOOD'S PARTY

Compared To What	7"	Ember	EMBS312	1970	£6	£2.50	
Mr Flood's Party	LP	Cotillion	9003	1969	£20	£8	*US*

MR FOUNDATION

Time To Pray	7"	Supreme	SUP201	1969	£5	£2	
Time-oh	7"	Studio One	SO2061	1968	£12	£6	*Dudley Sibley & Peter Austin B side*

MR FOX

Complete Mr Fox	LP	Transatlantic	TRA303	1975	£25	£10	*double*
Gypsy	LP	Transatlantic	TRA236	1971	£40	£20	
Little Woman	7"	Transatlantic	BIG135	1970	£4	£1.50	
Mr Fox	LP	Transatlantic	TRA226	1970	£30	£15	

MR GASSER & THE WEIRDOS

Hot Rod Hootenanny	LP	Capitol	(S)T2010	1963	£25	£10	*US*
Rods 'n' Ratfinks	LP	Capitol	(S)T2057	1963	£25	£10	*US*
Surfink!	LP	Capitol	(S)T2114	1964	£30	£15	*US*

MR MISTER

Broken Wings	CD-s	RCA	PD49449	1989	£5	£2	

MR MO'S MESSENGERS

Feelin' Good	7"	Columbia	DB8133	1967	£5	£2	

MTUME UMOJA ENSEMBLE

Alkebu-Lan is an uncompromising celebration of black culture, mixing avant-garde and modal jazz with poetry and chanting in a heady brew. Much of the music is similar to that of pianist McCoy Tyner and in fact some of the musicians here did also play with Tyner. Mtume himself was percussionist in Miles Davis's seventies band, but later moved into considerably more commercial areas, scoring a sizeable US hit with 'Juicy Fruit' and producing several tracks for Madonna.

Alkebu-Lan	LP	Strata-East	SES19724	1972	£30	£15	*US double*

MU

Last Album	LP	Appaloosa	AP017	1981	£15	£6	*Italian*
Lemurian Music	LP	United Artists	UAG29709	1975	£30	£15	
Mu	LP	RTV	300	1971	£300	£180	*US*

M.U. (MENTALLY UNFIT)

Motion In Tune	LP	Backstreet/ Backlash	BBR010	1981	£60	£30	*Dutch*

MUCKRAM WAKES

Map Of Derbyshire	LP	Trailer	LER2085	1973	£20	£8	
Muckram Wakes	LP	Trailer	LER2093	1976	£12	£5	
Warbles, Jangles And Reeds	LP	Highway	SHY7009	1980	£12	£5	

MUD

Flower Power	7"	CBS	203002	1967	£25	£12.50	*picture sleeve*
Flower Power	7"	CBS	203002	1967	£15	£7.50	
Jumping Jehosaphat	7"	Philips	6006022	1970	£5	£2	
Lonely This Christmas	7"	RAK	RAK187	1974	£4	£1.50	*picture sleeve*
Secrets That You Keep	7"	RAK	RAK194	1975	£4	£1.50	*picture sleeve*
Shangri-La	7"	Philips	BF1775	1969	£8	£4	
Up The Airy Mountain	7"	CBS	3355	1968	£8	£4	

MUDCRUTCH

The songs issued by Mudcrutch are the earliest recordings to feature Tom Petty.

Depot Street	7"	Shelter	40357	1975	**£15**	**£7.50**	*US*
Up In Mississippi	7"	Pepper	9449	1971	**£200**	**£100**	*US, best auctioned*

MUDLARKS

Book Of Love	7"	Columbia	DB4133	1958	**£5**	**£2**	
Lollipop	7"	Columbia	DB4099	1958	**£5**	**£2**	
Love Game	7"	Columbia	DB4250	1959	**£4**	**£1.50**	
Mudlarks	7" EP	Columbia	SEG7854	1958	**£20**	**£10**	
New Love	7"	Columbia	DB4064	1958	**£4**	**£1.50**	
There's Never Been A Night	7"	Columbia	DB4190	1958	**£4**	**£1.50**	
Which Witch Doctor	7"	Columbia	DB4210	1958	**£4**	**£1.50**	

MUGWUMPS

I Don't Wanna Know	7"	Warner Bros	WB144	1964	**£5**	**£2**	
Mugwumps	LP	Warner Bros	W1697	1967	**£15**	**£6**	

MUIR, BOBBY

Baby What You Done Me Wrong	7"	Blue Beat	BB20	1960	**£12**	**£6**	
Spanish Town Twist	7"	Blue Beat	BB77	1962	**£12**	**£6**	
That's My Girl	7"	Blue Beat	BB44	1961	**£12**	**£6**	

MULCAYS

Harbour Lights	7"	London	HLF8188	1955	**£15**	**£7.50**	
Harmonics By The Mulcays	7" EP	London	REF1046	1956	**£12**	**£6**	
Merry Christmas	7" EP	London	REP1016	1954	**£12**	**£6**	

MULDAUR, GEOFF

Geoff Muldaur	LP	Prestige	14004	1964	**£15**	**£6**	*US*
Sleepy Man Blues	LP	Prestige	7727	1965	**£15**	**£6**	*US*

MULDAUR, GEOFF & MARIA

Pottery Pie	LP	Reprise	RS6350	1970	**£10**	**£4**	*US*
Sweet Potatoes	LP	Warner Bros	MS2073	1972	**£10**	**£4**	*US*

MULDOONS

I'm Lost Without You	7"	Decca	F12164	1965	**£20**	**£10**	

MULESKINNERS

Back Door Man	7"	Fontana	TF527	1965	**£75**	**£37.50**	
Muleskinners	7" EP	Keepoint	KEEEP7104	196–	**£600**	**£400**	*best auctioned*

MULLICAN, MOON

Cherokee Boogie	78	Vogue	V9013	1951	**£12**	**£6**	
Country Round Up	7" EP	Parlophone	GEP8794	1959	**£40**	**£20**	
His All-Time Greatest Hits	LP	King	555	1958	**£60**	**£30**	*US*
I'll Sail My Ship Alone	LP	Sterling	ST601	196–	**£30**	**£15**	*US*
Instrumentals	LP	Audio Lab	AL1568	1962	**£50**	**£25**	*US*
Many Moods Of Moon Mullican	LP	King	681	1960	**£60**	**£30**	*US*
Moon Over Mullican	LP	Coral	CRL57235	1958	**£150**	**£75**	*US*
Mr Piano Man	LP	Starday	SLP267	1964	**£20**	**£8**	*US*
Piano Breakdown	7" EP	Parlophone	CGEP15	195–	**£30**	**£15**	*export*
Seven Nights To Rock	7"	Parlophone	MSP6254	1956	**£350**	**£210**	*with Boyd Bennett, best auctioned*
Sixteen Of His Favorite Tunes	LP	King	628	1959	**£60**	**£30**	*US*
Twenty-Four Of His Favorite Tunes	LP	KIng	937	1965	**£15**	**£6**	*US*
Unforgettable Moon Mullican	LP	Starday	SLP398	1967	**£15**	**£6**	*US*

MULLIGAN, GERRY

At The Village Vanguard	LP	HMV	CLP1488/ CSD1396	1962	**£15**	**£6**	
California Concerts	LP	Vogue	LAE12006	1956	**£25**	**£10**	
Collaborations	LP	Verve	VLP9116	1966	**£10**	**£4**	
Concert In Jazz	LP	HMV	CLP1549/ CSD1432	1962	**£12**	**£5**	
Concert Jazz Band	LP	Verve	VLP9037	1963	**£12**	**£5**	
Concert Jazz Band	LP	HMV	CLP1432/ CSD1351	1961	**£15**	**£6**	
Genius Of Gerry Mulligan	LP	Vocalion	LAE12268	1960	**£15**	**£6**	
Gerry Mulligan Allstars	10" LP	Esquire	20032	1954	**£50**	**£25**	
Gerry Mulligan Allstars	LP	Esquire	32014	1956	**£25**	**£10**	
Gerry Mulligan And Paul Desmond Quartet	LP	Columbia	33CX10113	1958	**£15**	**£6**	
Gerry Mulligan Meets Ben Webster	LP	HMV	CLP1373	1960	**£15**	**£6**	
Gerry Mulligan Meets Johnny Hodges	LP	HMV	CLP1465/ CSD1372	1962	**£15**	**£6**	
Gerry Mulligan Quartet	10" LP	Vogue	LDE075	1954	**£50**	**£25**	
Gerry Mulligan Quartet	LP	Vogue	LAE12050	1957	**£20**	**£8**	
Gerry Mulligan Quartet	LP	Vogue	LAE12080	1958	**£20**	**£8**	
Gerry Mulligan Quartet	LP	Vogue	LAE12015	1956	**£25**	**£10**	
Gerry Mulligan Quartet Vol. 1	10" LP	Vogue	LDE029	1953	**£50**	**£25**	
Gerry Mulligan Quartet Vol. 2	10" LP	Vogue	LDE030	1953	**£50**	**£25**	
Gerry Mulligan Quartet Vol. 3	10" LP	Vogue	LDE031	1953	**£50**	**£25**	
Gerry Mulligan Quartet Vol. 4	10" LP	Vogue	LDE083	1954	**£50**	**£25**	

Title	Format	Label	Cat. No.	Year	Mint	VG	Notes
Gerry Mulligan Quartet With Lee Konitz	10″ LP	Vogue	LDE156	1955	**£50**	**£25**	
Gerry Mulligan Tentette	10″ LP	Capitol	LC6621	1953	**£50**	**£25**	
Getz Meets Mulligan In Hi-Fi	LP	Columbia	33CX10120	1958	**£15**	**£6**	*with Stan Getz*
I Want To Live	LP	London	LTZT15161/ SAHT6023	1959	**£15**	**£6**	*with Shelly Manne*
Mainstream Of Jazz	LP	Emarcy	EJL1259	1957	**£25**	**£10**	
Mainstream Vol. 1	7″ EP	Emarcy	ERE1574	1958	**£5**	**£2**	
Mainstream Vol. 2	7″ EP	Emarcy	ERE1575	1958	**£5**	**£2**	
Mulligan Mania	7″ EP	Mercury	ZEP10071	1960	**£5**	**£2**	
Mulligan Meets Monk	LP	London	LTZU15127	1958	**£20**	**£8**	*with Thelonious Monk*
Mulligan Meets Monk	LP	Riverside	RLP12247	1962	**£15**	**£6**	
On Tour	LP	HMV	CLP1585	1962	**£12**	**£5**	*with Zoot Sims*
Phil Sunkel's Jazz Concerto Grosso	LP	HMV	CLP1204	1958	**£20**	**£8**	*with Bob Brookmeyer*
Presenting Gerry Mulligan & His Tentette	7″ EP	Capitol	EAP1439	1955	**£5**	**£2**	
Presenting Gerry Mulligan & His Tentette	7″ EP	Capitol	EAP2439	1955	**£5**	**£2**	
Presenting The Gerry Mulligan Sextet	7″ EP	Emarcy	ERE1553	1958	**£5**	**£2**	
Presenting The Gerry Mulligan Sextet	LP	Emarcy	EJL101	1956	**£25**	**£10**	
Presenting The Gerry Mulligan Sextet Vol. 2	7″ EP	Emarcy	ERE1556	1958	**£5**	**£2**	
Presenting The Gerry Mulligan Sextet Vol. 3	7″ EP	Emarcy	ERE1560	1958	**£5**	**£2**	
Relax	LP	Fontana	FJL105	1964	**£10**	**£4**	
Reunion With Chet Baker	LP	Vogue	LAE12185/ SEA5007	1959	**£20**	**£8**	
Saxy	LP	Fontana	FJL133	1966	**£10**	**£4**	
Songbook Vol. 1	LP	Vogue	LAE12128/ SEA5006	1959	**£25**	**£10**	
What Is There To Say?	LP	Philips	BBL7320	1959	**£10**	**£4**	
What Is There To Say?	LP	Philips	SBBL552	1959	**£12**	**£5**	

MULLIGAN, MICK

Title	Format	Label	Cat. No.	Year	Mint	VG	Notes
Jazz At The Railway Arms	LP	Tempo	TAP14	1957	**£25**	**£10**	*with George Melly*
Meet Mick Mulligan	LP	Pye	NJL21	1959	**£12**	**£5**	
Mick Mulligan's Jazz Band	7″ EP	Tempo	EXA25	1955	**£6**	**£2.50**	
Saints Meet The Sinners	LP	Parlophone	PMC1103/ PCS3005	1959	**£12**	**£5**	*with George Melly*

MUMFORD, GENE

Title	Format	Label	Cat. No.	Year	Mint	VG	Notes
More Than You Know	7″	Philips	PB862	1958	**£4**	**£1.50**	

MUMPS

Title	Format	Label	Cat. No.	Year	Mint	VG	Notes
Matter Of Taste	LP	MPS	0068169	1977	**£15**	**£6**	*German*

MUNGO JERRY

Title	Format	Label	Cat. No.	Year	Mint	VG	Notes
Baby Jump	7″	Dawn	DNX2505	1971	**£4**	**£1.50**	*picture sleeve*
In The Summertime	12″	Pye	BD114	1977	**£6**	**£2.50**	
In The Summertime	7″	Pye	7N2502	1970	**£8**	**£4**	*jukebox issue*
Lady Rose	7″	Dawn	DNX2510	1971	**£5**	**£2**	*picture sleeve*
Mungo Jerry	LP	Dawn	DNLS3008	1970	**£10**	**£4**	*with 3D glasses*
Open Up	7″	Dawn	DNX2514	1972	**£4**	**£1.50**	*picture sleeve*
You Don't Have To Be In The Army	7″	Dawn	DNX2513	1971	**£5**	**£2**	*picture sleeve*

MUNNINGS, RAY

Title	Format	Label	Cat. No.	Year	Mint	VG	Notes
Funky Nassau	7″	Tammi	TAM103	1979	**£5**	**£2**	
It Could Happen To You	7″	Tammi	TAM102	1979	**£5**	**£2**	

MUNRO, CAROLINE

Title	Format	Label	Cat. No.	Year	Mint	VG	Notes
Tar And Cement	7″	Columbia	DB8189	1967	**£5**	**£2**	

MUNRO, CAROLINE (2)

Title	Format	Label	Cat. No.	Year	Mint	VG	Notes
Pump Me Up	12″	Numa	NUM5	1985	**£8**	**£4**	
Pump Me Up	7″	Numa	NU5	1985	**£5**	**£2**	

MUNRO, HAL

Title	Format	Label	Cat. No.	Year	Mint	VG	Notes
Breathless	7″	Embassy	WB284	1958	**£4**	**£1.50**	
C'mon Everybody	7″	Embassy	WB336	1959	**£4**	**£1.50**	

MUNRO, JANET & SEAN CONNERY

Title	Format	Label	Cat. No.	Year	Mint	VG	Notes
Pretty Irish Girl	7″	Top Rank	JAR163	1959	**£4**	**£1.50**	

MUNSON, STEPHAN

Title	Format	Label	Cat. No.	Year	Mint	VG	Notes
And David Cried	7″	Rhythmic	RMNS2	1982	**£4**	**£1.50**	

MUNSTERS

Title	Format	Label	Cat. No.	Year	Mint	VG	Notes
Munsters	LP	Decca	DL4588	1964	**£20**	**£8**	*US*

MURAD, JERRY HARMONICATS

Title	Format	Label	Cat. No.	Year	Mint	VG	Notes
It's Cha Cha Time	7″ EP	Mercury	ZEP10001	1959	**£5**	**£2**	

MURDER INC.

Title	Format	Label	Cat. No.	Year	Mint	VG	Notes
Sounds So False	7″	MIL	MIL1	1980	**£5**	**£2**	

MURE, BILLY

Title	Format	Label	Cat. No.	Year	Mint	VG	Notes
Supersonic Guitars Vol. 2	LP	MGM	CS5011	1960	**£10**	**£4**	*stereo*

Supersonics In Flight	7" EP	RCA	RCX158	1959	£8	£4	
Supersonics In Flight	7" EP	RCA	SRC7032	1959	£15	£7.50	*stereo*
Versatile Billy Mure	7" EP	Felsted	GEP1006	1959	£5	£2	

MURGATROYD BAND

Magpie	7"	Decca	F13256	1972	£4	£1.50	

MURMAIDS

Popsicles And Icicles	7"	Stateside	SS247	1963	£5	£2	
Popsicles And Icicles	7" EP	Columbia	ESRF1487	1964	£8	£4	*French*

MURPHEY, MICHAEL

Geronimo's Cadillac	LP	Regal Zonophone	SRZA8512	1972	£10	£4	

MURPHY, DENIS & JULIA CLIFFORD

Star Above The Garter	LP	Claddagh	CC5	1969	£10	£4	*Irish*

MURPHY, MARK

Hit Parade	LP	Capitol	(S)T5011	1960	£10	£4	
Mark Time!	LP	Fontana	(S)TL5217	1964	£10	£4	
Meet Mark Murphy	LP	Brunswick	LAT8172	1957	£10	£4	
This Could Be The Start Of Something	LP	Capitol	T1177	1959	£10	£4	
Who Can I Turn To	LP	Immediate	IMLP/IMSP004	1966	£50	£25	

MURPHY, NOEL

Another Round	LP	Fontana	STL5496	1969	£10	£4	
Murf	LP	Village Thing	VTS25	1973	£10	£4	
Nya-a-a-a-h!	LP	Fontana	(S)TL5450	1967	£12	£5	

MURPHY, ROSE

Songs By Rose Murphy	10" LP	Mercury	MG10004	1953	£10	£4	

MURPHY, TURK

Music Of Jelly Roll Morton	LP	Philips	BBL7051	1955	£12	£5	
New Orleans Shuffle	LP	Philips	BBL7145	1957	£10	£4	
Turk Murphy Jazz Band	10" LP	Good Time Jazz	LDG037	1954	£12	£5	
Turk Murphy Jazz Band	10" LP	Good Time Jazz	LDG078	1954	£12	£5	
Turk Murphy Jazz Band	10" LP	Good Time Jazz	LDG180	1956	£12	£5	
Turk Murphy Jazz Band	10" LP	Good Time Jazz	LDG186	1956	£12	£5	
Turk Murphy Jazz Band	LP	Philips	BBL7095	1956	£12	£5	
Turk Murphy Jazz Band	LP	Philips	BBL7088	1956	£12	£5	

MURPHY BLEND

First Loss	LP	Kuckuck	2375005	1970	£100	£50	*German*

MURRAY, ALEX

Teen Angel	7"	Decca	F11203	1960	£4	£1.50	

MURRAY, LARRY

Sweet Country Suite	LP	Verve	FTS3090	1969	£30	£15	*US*

MURRAY, MARTIN

I Know What I Want	7"	Pye	7N17070	1966	£4	£1.50	

MURRAY, MISTER

Down Came The Rain	7"	Fontana	TF623	1965	£4	£1.50	

MURRAY, MITCH CLAN

Skyliner	7"	Clan	597001	1966	£6	£2.50	

MURRAY, PETE/PASCAL FRUITS

TV Themes	7" EP	ATV	ATV1	1969	£6	£2.50	

MURRAY, RUBY

Ain't That A Grand And Glorious Feeling	7"	Columbia	DB4042	1957	£4	£1.50	
Endearing Young Charms	10" LP	Columbia	33S1135	1958	£20	£8	
Endearing Young Charms	7" EP	Columbia	SEG7952	1959	£6	£2.50	
Evermore	7"	Columbia	SCM5180	1955	£8	£4	
Everybody's Sweetheart No. 1	7" EP	Columbia	SEG7620	1956	£6	£2.50	
Everybody's Sweetheart No. 2	7" EP	Columbia	SEG7631	1956	£6	£2.50	
Everybody's Sweetheart No. 3	7" EP	Columbia	SEG7636	1956	£6	£2.50	
Forgive Me My Darling	7"	Columbia	DB4075	1958	£4	£1.50	
From The First Hello	7"	Columbia	DB3911	1957	£5	£2	
Goodbye Jimmy Goodbye	7"	Columbia	DB4305	1959	£4	£1.50	
If Anyone Finds This, I Love You	7"	Columbia	SCM5169	1955	£8	£4	
In Love	7"	Columbia	DB3852	1956	£5	£2	
In My Life	7"	Columbia	DB4108	1958	£4	£1.50	
It Only Hurts For A Little While	7"	Columbia	DB3810	1956	£6	£2.50	
Little White Lies	7"	Columbia	DB3994	1957	£4	£1.50	
Love's Old Sweet Song	7" EP	Columbia	ESG7830	1960	£10	£5	*stereo*

Love's Old Sweet Song	7" EP	Columbia	SEG8052	1960	**£6**	**£2.50**	
Mr Wonderful	7"	Columbia	DB3933	1957	**£5**	**£2**	
Mucushla Mine	7" EP	Columbia	SEG7748	1957	**£6**	**£2.50**	
Oh Please Make Him Jealous	7"	Columbia	SCM5225	1956	**£6**	**£2.50**	
Real Love	7"	Columbia	DB4192	1958	**£4**	**£1.50**	
Ruby	LP	Columbia	33SX1201/ SCX3289	1960	**£15**	**£6**	
Ruby Is A Gem	7" EP	Columbia	SEG7588	1955	**£10**	**£5**	
Scarlet Ribbons	7"	Columbia	DB3955	1957	**£5**	**£2**	
Softly Softly	7"	Columbia	SCM5162	1955	**£12**	**£6**	
Spring, Spring, Spring	7"	Columbia	SCM5165	1955	**£5**	**£2**	
True Love	7"	Columbia	DB3849	1956	**£6**	**£2.50**	
When Irish Eyes Are Smiling	10" LP	Columbia	33S1079	1955	**£15**	**£6**	

MURROUGH, MAC

Mac Murrough	LP	Polydor	2908014	1974	**£200**	**£100**	
Merry And Fine	LP	Polydor	2908030	1977	**£100**	**£50**	

MURTAUGH, JOHN

Blues Current	LP	Polydor	2482015	1970	**£15**	**£6**	

MUSHROOM

Devil Amongst The Tailors	7"	Hawk	HASP320	1973	**£20**	**£10**	
Early One Morning	LP	Hawk	HALPX116	1973	**£350**	**£210**	*with poster*
Early One Morning	LP	Hawk	HALPX116	1973	**£250**	**£150**	
Kings And Queens	7"	Hawk	HASP340	1974	**£20**	**£10**	

MUSHROOM SOUP

In the first (1991) edition of this guide, an album was listed by a group called Mushroom Soup. For long a feature within the wants lists of a few dealers, the record's details were so delightful (*Mushroom Soup: And Other Recipes* on the Roll and Butter label, catalogue number PAT1) that one longed for it to be real, despite the almost certain knowledge that it was not! (As was said in the first edition.) Of course, the record was a fiction – but as such, it joins a fairly long catalogue of imaginary records, some of which have had collectors scouring the specialist shops and record fairs far and wide in an increasingly frantic and fruitless quest. One collectors' shop always used to head its wants list with an intriguing reference to an album called *Where's Mutley?*; others are more mischievous, slipping in a tantalizing reference to a twelve-inch version of a record one was certain only existed as a seven-inch, or else advertising a previously undiscovered picture disc (such records have always 'just been sold', of course). It was Greil Marcus who started a tradition of joke references within otherwise sensible discographies, with the 'Zurvans: *Close The Book* (End)' entry at the end of his desert island anthology, *Stranded*. It is not Marcus's fault if his quiet wit has been worn a little thin in the work of other authors who have repeated the joke to the point of exhaustion (Dodo Resurrection indeed!!). From time to time, the rock press has put its own slant on the process by reviewing records of its own invention – some of which have subsequently turned out to be real after all. Examples can be found in this guide under the headings 'Heavy Jelly' and 'Masked Marauders'. As for Mushroom Soup, their discography has miraculously expanded of late, if we are to believe the entry in a limited edition *Rare Record Guide* published in 1994. An imaginary band that has managed to produce nine separate collectors' items (including three made by some kind of spin-off unit) is clearly a force to be reckoned with. Perhaps the band could be persuaded to re-form for some kind of imaginary tour – the support slot to the Beatles reunion is still vacant, so far as we know!

MUSIC BOX

Songs Of Sunshine	LP	Westwood	MRS013	1972	**£125**	**£62.50**	

MUSIC DOCTORS

Reggae In The Summertime	LP	Trojan	TBL117	1970	**£10**	**£4**	

MUSIC EMPORIUM

Music Emporium	LP	Sentinel	100	1969	**£2000**	**£1400**	*US*
Music Emporium	LP	Psycho	PSYCHO11	1983	**£10**	**£4**	

MUSIC EXPLOSION

Little Bit O'Soul	7"	Stateside	SS2028	1967	**£8**	**£4**	
Little Bit O'Soul	7" EP	Vogue	INT18140	1967	**£20**	**£10**	*French*
Little Bit O'Soul	LP	London	HAP/SHP8352	1967	**£12**	**£5**	
Little Black Egg	7"	Philips	BF1547	1967	**£4**	**£1.50**	

MUSIC IMPROVISATION COMPANY

1968–70	LP	Incus	INCUS17	1976	**£12**	**£5**	
Packaged Eel	LP	ECM	ECM1005ST	1971	**£20**	**£8**	

MUSIC MACHINE

Bonniwell Music Machine	LP	Warner Bros	WS1732	1967	**£30**	**£15**	*US*
People In Me	7"	Pye	7N25414	1967	**£20**	**£10**	*demo*
Talk Talk	7"	Pye	7N25407	1967	**£20**	**£10**	
Talk Talk	7" EP	Vogue	INT18121	1967	**£150**	**£75**	*French*
Turn On The Music Machine	LP	Original Sound	5015/8875	1966	**£40**	**£20**	*US*

MUSICA ELETTRONICA VIVA

Although based in Rome, the members of MEV were American. Using the most advanced technology available to them at the time, MEV performed free electronic improvisations. Only AMM was working in anything like the same area, so it was appropriate that one LP release devoted a side to each group (it is listed under AMM in this guide). Alvin Curran, Frederic Rzewski, and Richard Teitelbaum have all composed and recorded electronic works since, while Teitelbaum has also worked as an improvisor with saxophonist Anthony Braxton.

Leave The City	LP	Byg	529335	1970	**£25**	**£10**	*French*
Musica Elettronica Viva	LP	Polydor	583769	1969	**£25**	**£10**	

MUSICA URBANA

Musica Urbana	LP	Edigsa	UM2033	1976	**£15**	**£6**	*Spanish*

MUSKETEER GRIPWEED

The single credited to Musketeer Gripweed is taken from the soundtrack of the film *How I Won The War* and is an often overlooked rarity from the oeuvre of the man who played the character in the film – John Lennon. As it happens, Lennon's contribution to the record is fairly minimal. His role in the film was not a singing one and on the record he merely contributes a fragment of speech to a basically instrumental piece.

How I Won The War	7"	United Artists	UP1196	1966	**£60**	**£30**	

MUSSELWHITE, CHARLIE

Charlie Musselwhite	LP	Vanguard	VSD79287	1968	**£12**	**£5**	*US*
Stand Back, Here Comes Charlie Musslewhite	LP	Vanguard	VSD79232	1967	**£12**	**£5**	*US*
Stone Blues	LP	Vanguard	SVRL19012	1968	**£12**	**£5**	
Tennessee Woman	LP	Vanguard	VSD6528	1969	**£12**	**£5**	*US*

MUSSULLI, BOOTS

Diga Diga Doo	7"	Capitol	KC65002	1954	**£4**	**£1.50**	
Kenton Presents Jazz	10" LP	Capitol	KPL106	1955	**£25**	**£10**	

MUSTANG

Why	7"	Parlophone	R5579	1967	**£15**	**£7.50**	

MUSTANGS

Dartell Stomp	LP	Providence	PLP001	1963	**£30**	**£15**	*US*
Liverpool Beat	LP	Ariola	72251	1966	**£30**	**£15**	*German*
Mustangs	LP	Ariola	71741IT	1965	**£50**	**£25**	*German*

MUSTWANGS

Rock Lomond	7"	Mercury	AMT1140	1961	**£5**	**£2**	

MUTANTES

A Divina Comedia Ou Ando Meio Desligado	LP	Polydor		1970	**£40**	**£20**	*Brazilian*
Ao Vivo	LP	Som Livre	4036097	1976	**£15**	**£6**	*Brazilian*
E Seus Cometas No Pais Do Baurets	LP	Polydor		1972	**£30**	**£15**	*Brazilian*
Jardim Eletrico	LP	Polydor		1971	**£40**	**£20**	*Brazilian*
Mutantes	LP	Polydor	2451002	1969	**£40**	**£20**	*Brazilian*
Os Mutantes	LP	Polydor		1968	**£50**	**£25**	*Brazilian*
Tudo Foi Feito Pelo Sol	LP	Polydor		1975	**£15**	**£6**	*Brazilian*

MUTE DRIVERS

Mute Drivers	LP	Mute Drivers	MD001	198–	**£10**	**£4**	

MUTT 'N' JEFF

Don't Nag Me Ma	7"	Decca	F12335	1966	**£5**	**£2**	

MUTZIE

Light Of Your Shadow	LP	Sussex	7001	1970	**£30**	**£15**	*US*

MY BLOODY VALENTINE

After a shaky start (as represented by many of their early collectable records), My Bloody Valentine achieved greatness with the release of their *Isn't Anything* album. Decades after the invention of the electric guitar, they managed to find entirely new ways of making it sound – and added this to a melodic strength in a combination that is frequently exhilarating.

Ecstasy	LP	Lazy	LAZY08	1987	**£25**	**£10**	
Ecstasy And Wine	CD	Lazy	LAZY12CD	1989	**£30**	**£15**	
Ecstasy And Wine	LP	Lazy	LAZY12	1989	**£15**	**£6**	
Feed Me With Your Kiss	12"	Creation	CRE061T	1988	**£6**	**£2.50**	
Feed Me With Your Kiss	7"	Creation	CRE061	1988	**£4**	**£1.50**	
Feed Me With Your Kiss	CD-s	Creation	CRE061CD	1990	**£5**	**£2**	
Geek!	12"	Fever	FEV5	1986	**£15**	**£7.50**	
Glider EP	CD-s	Creation	CRECD73	1990	**£5**	**£2**	
Isn't Anything	LP	Creation	CRELP040	1988	**£12**	**£5**	*with 7" (CREFRE4)*
New Record By My Bloody Valentine	12"	Kaleidoscope Sound	KS101	1986	**£30**	**£15**	
No Place To Go	7"	Fever	FEV5X	1986	**£10**	**£5**	
Strawberry Wine	12"	Lazy	LAZY07T	1987	**£25**	**£12.50**	
Sunny Sundae Smile	12"	Lazy	LAZY04T	1987	**£30**	**£15**	
Sunny Sundae Smile	7"	Lazy	LAZY04	1987	**£15**	**£7.50**	
This Is Your Bloody Valentine	mini LP	Tycoon	ST7501	1985	**£50**	**£25**	*German*
Tremolo	CD-s	Creation	CRESCD085	1991	**£5**	**£2**	
You Made Me Realise	12"	Creation	CRE055T	1988	**£6**	**£2.50**	
You Made Me Realise	7"	Creation	CRE055	1988	**£4**	**£1.50**	
You Made Me Realise	CD-s	Creation	CRECD055	1990	**£5**	**£2**	

MY CAPTAINS

History	7"	4AD	AD103	1981	**£5**	**£2**	

MY DEAR WATSON

Elusive Face	7"	Parlophone	R5687	1968	**£15**	**£7.50**	
Have You Seen Your Saviour	7"	DJM	DJS224	1970	**£5**	**£2**	
Stop Stop I'll Be There	7"	Parlophone	R5737	1968	**£15**	**£7.50**	

MY LIFE STORY

Title	Format	Label	Cat. No.	Year	Mint	VG	Notes
17 Reasons Why	12"	Parlophone		1996	**£20**	**£10**	*promo*
Duchess	12"	Parlophone	12RDJ6474	1997	**£10**	**£5**	*promo*
Funny Ha Ha	12"	Mother Tongue	MOTHER3T	1994	**£8**	**£4**	
Funny Ha Ha	7"	Mother Tongue	MOTHER3S	1994	**£4**	**£1.50**	
Funny Ha Ha	CD-s	Mother Tongue	MOTHER3CD	1994	**£10**	**£5**	
Girl A, Girl B, Boy C	12"	Mother Tongue	MOTHER212	1993	**£10**	**£5**	
Girl A, Girl B, Boy C	7"	Mother Tongue	MOTHER27	1993	**£5**	**£2**	
Girl A, Girl B, Boy C	CD-s	Mother Tongue	MOTHER2CD	1993	**£12**	**£6**	
Home Sweet Zoo	7"	Think Tank	CHAPTER1	1986	**£60**	**£30**	
Mornington Crescent	CD	Mother Tongue	MOTHERCD1	1995	**£20**	**£8**	
Mornington Crescent	LP	Mother Tongue	MOTHERLP1	1995	**£15**	**£6**	
Mornington Crescent Companion	CD-s	Mother Tongue	MOTHER5CD	1994	**£15**	**£7.50**	
You Can't Uneat The Apple	CD-s	Parlophone	CDRDJ6485	1997	**£6**	**£2.50**	*promo*
You Don't Sparkle	12"	Mother Tongue	MOTHER4T	1994	**£8**	**£4**	
You Don't Sparkle	7"	Mother Tongue	MOTHER4S	1994	**£4**	**£1.50**	
You Don't Sparkle	CD-s	Mother Tongue	MOTHER4CD	1994	**£10**	**£5**	

MY LORDE SHERIFFE'S COMPLAINTE

Title	Format	Label	Cat. No.	Year	Mint	VG	Notes
My Lorde Sheriffe's Complainte	LP	Frog	FROG1	1979	**£25**	**£10**	

MY SOLID GROUND

Title	Format	Label	Cat. No.	Year	Mint	VG	Notes
My Solid Ground	LP	Bacillus	6494008	1971	**£100**	**£50**	*German*

MYERS, DAVE

Title	Format	Label	Cat. No.	Year	Mint	VG	Notes
Greatest Racing Themes	LP	Carole	CAR(S)8002	1967	**£12**	**£5**	*US*
Hangin' Twenty	LP	Del-Fi	DFLP/DFST1239	1963	**£15**	**£6**	*US*

MYLES, BILLY

Title	Format	Label	Cat. No.	Year	Mint	VG	Notes
Joker	7"	HMV	POP423	1957	**£15**	**£7.50**	

MYNEDIAD AM DDIM

Title	Format	Label	Cat. No.	Year	Mint	VG	Notes
Mae'r Grwp Yn Talu	LP	Sain	1064M	1976	**£15**	**£6**	
Mynediad Am Ddim	LP	Sain	1021M	1975	**£25**	**£10**	
Rhwng Saith Stol	LP	Sain	1083M	1977	**£15**	**£6**	
Torth O Fara	LP	Sain	1137M	1978	**£12**	**£5**	

MYRES, ROWLAND

Title	Format	Label	Cat. No.	Year	Mint	VG	Notes
Just For The Record	LP	Deroy	DER1063	1974	**£100**	**£50**	

MYRTELLES

Title	Format	Label	Cat. No.	Year	Mint	VG	Notes
Don't Wanna Cry Again	7"	Oriole	CB1805	1963	**£10**	**£5**	

MYRTH

Title	Format	Label	Cat. No.	Year	Mint	VG	Notes
Myrth	LP	RCA	LSP4210	1969	**£12**	**£5**	*US*

MYSTERIES

Title	Format	Label	Cat. No.	Year	Mint	VG	Notes
Give Me Rhythm And Blues	7"	Decca	F11919	1964	**£15**	**£7.50**	

MYSTERY MAKER

Title	Format	Label	Cat. No.	Year	Mint	VG	Notes
Mystery Maker	LP	Caves	UHC3	1977	**£100**	**£50**	

MYSTIC ASTROLOGICAL CRYSTAL BAND

Title	Format	Label	Cat. No.	Year	Mint	VG	Notes
Clip Out, Put On Book	LP	Carole	S8003	1968	**£30**	**£15**	*US*
Mystic Astrological Crystal Band	LP	Carole	(S)8001	1967	**£30**	**£15**	*US*

MYSTIC INSTITUTE

Title	Format	Label	Cat. No.	Year	Mint	VG	Notes
Cyberdon	12"	Evolution	EVO06	1992	**£15**	**£7.50**	

MYSTIC MOODS ORCHESTRA

Title	Format	Label	Cat. No.	Year	Mint	VG	Notes
Cosmic Force	LP	Mobile Fidelity	1002	1981	**£15**	**£6**	*US audiophile*
Emotions	LP	Mobile Fidelity	1001	1981	**£15**	**£6**	*US audiophile*
Stormy Weekend	LP	Mobile Fidelity	1003	1981	**£15**	**£6**	*US audiophile*

MYSTIC SIVA

Title	Format	Label	Cat. No.	Year	Mint	VG	Notes
Mystic Siva	LP	Vo	19713	1972	**£500**	**£330**	*US*

MYSTICS

Title	Format	Label	Cat. No.	Year	Mint	VG	Notes
Adam And Eve	7"	HMV	POP646	1959	**£50**	**£25**	
Don't Take The Stars	7"	Top Rank	JAR243	1959	**£20**	**£10**	

MYTHOS

Dreamlab	LP	Kosmische	KM58016	1975	**£20**	**£8**	*German*
Mythos	LP	Ohr	OMM556019	1972	**£30**	**£15**	*German*
Strange Guys	LP	Venus	MYF1003	1977	**£15**	**£6**	*German*

MYTHRA

Death And Destiny	7"	Guardian	GRMA16	1979	**£6**	**£2.50**	*no picture sleeve*
Death And Destiny	7"	Streetbeat	LAMP2	1980	**£6**	**£2.50**	
Death Or Destiny	12"	Streetbeat	12LAMP2	1980	**£60**	**£30**	*picture sleeve*
Death Or Destiny	7"	Streetbeat	LAMP2	1980	**£50**	**£25**	*picture sleeve*
Killer	12"	Streetbeat	LAMP2T	1980	**£15**	**£7.50**	

NA FILI

Title	Format	Label	Cat. No.	Year			Notes
Chanter's Tune	LP	Transatlantic	TRA353	1977	£10	£4	
Farewell To Connacht	LP	Outlet	SOLP1010	1971	£12	£5	*Irish*
Kindly Welcome	LP	Dolphin	DOL1008	1974	£10	£4	*Irish*
Na Fili 3	LP	Outlet	SOLP1017	1973	£12	£5	*Irish*
One Day For Recreation (with Sean O Se)	LP	Circa	003	1980	£10	£4	*Irish*

NADIR, RIKKI

The records credited to Rikki Nadir are actually by Peter Hammill, in a back-to-basic rock 'n' roll mood, and are listed in this guide along with his other solo work.

NAMYSLOWSKI, ZBIGNIEW

Title	Format	Label	Cat. No.	Year			Notes
Lola	LP	Decca	LK4644	1964	£12	£5	

NANETTE

Title	Format	Label	Cat. No.	Year			Notes
Nanette	LP	Columbia	SCX6398	1970	£15	£6	

NANGLE, ED

Title	Format	Label	Cat. No.	Year			Notes
Whipping The Prince	7"	Coxsone	CS7038	1968	£10	£5	*Heptones B side*

NANTOS, NICK & THE FIREBALLERS

Title	Format	Label	Cat. No.	Year			Notes
Guitars On Fire	7" EP	Summit	LSE2042	1963	£5	£2	

NAPALM DEATH

Title	Format	Label	Cat. No.	Year			Notes
Mentally Murdered	CD-s	Earache	MOSH14CD	1989	£5	£2	
Peel Sessions	CD-s	Strange Fruit	SFPDCD049	1989	£5	£2	
Suffer The Children	CD-s	Earache	MOSH24CD	1990	£5	£2	

NAPOLEON, MARTY

Title	Format	Label	Cat. No.	Year			Notes
Sings And Swings	7" EP	London	EZN19001	1956	£5	£2	

NAPOLEON XIV

This was a pseudonym adopted by recording engineer Jerry Samuels for his zany novelty hit 'They're Coming To Take Me Away Ha Ha'. The record was hardly a suitable basis for a lengthy rock career, however, especially when Samuels allowed Richard Stern to take his place in public appearances and when rock maverick Kim Fowley also tried to cast himself in the role.

Title	Format	Label	Cat. No.	Year			Notes
I'm In Love With My Little Red Tricycle	7"	Warner Bros	WB5853	1966	£6	£2.50	
They're Coming To Take Me Away	7" EP	Warner Bros	WB108	1966	£20	£10	*French*
They're Coming To Take Me Away	LP	Warner Bros	W(S)1661	1966	£50	£25	*US*
They're Coming To Take Me Away Ha Ha	7"	Warner Bros	WB5831	1966	£4	£1.50	

NARDINI, PETER

Title	Format	Label	Cat. No.	Year			Notes
I Think You're Great	7"	Kettle	KS701	198–	£4	£1.50	
I Think You're Great	7"	Kettle	KS701	198–	£10	£5	*picture sleeve*

NARNIA

Title	Format	Label	Cat. No.	Year			Notes
Narnia	LP	Myrrh	MYR1007	1974	£100	£50	

NASCIMBENE, MARIO

Title	Format	Label	Cat. No.	Year			Notes
Solomon And Sheba	LP	London	HAT2221	1960	£30	£15	

NASH, GENE

Title	Format	Label	Cat. No.	Year			Notes
Ja Ja Ja	7"	Capitol	CL15042	1959	£10	£5	

NASH, JOHNNY

Title	Format	Label	Cat. No.	Year			Notes
Glad You're My Baby	7"	MGM	MGM1480	1969	£6	£2.50	
I Got Rhythm	LP	HMV	CLP1325/ CSD1288	1960	£15	£6	
Johnny Nash	LP	HMV	CLP1251	1959	£20	£8	
Johnny Nash And Kim Weston	LP	Major Minor	MMLP/SMLP54	1969	£10	£4	
Ladder Of Love	7"	HMV	POP402	1957	£4	£1.50	
Love Ain't Nothing	7"	Pye	7N25250	1964	£10	£5	
Presenting Johnny Nash	7" EP	RCA	RCX7163	1964	£50	£25	
Prince Of Peace	LP	Major Minor	M/SMLP63	1969	£12	£5	
Quiet Hour	LP	HMV	CLP1299	1959	£15	£6	
Soul Folk	LP	Major Minor	M/SMLP56	1969	£12	£5	
Strange Feeling	7"	Chess	CRS8005	1965	£6	£2.50	

You Got Soul	LP	Major Minor	M/SMLP47	1969	£12	£5	

NASHVILLE FIVE

Like Nashville	7" EP	Decca	DFE6706	1962	£15	£7.50	

NASHVILLE TEENS

All Along The Watchtower	7"	Decca	F12754	1968	£4	£1.50	
Biggest Night Of Her Life	7"	Decca	F12657	1967	£4	£1.50	
Ella James	7"	Parlophone	R5925	1971	£5	£2	
Find My Way Back Home	7"	Decca	F12089	1965	£4	£1.50	
Find My Way Back Home	7" EP	Decca	457074	1965	£60	£30	*French*
Forbidden Fruit	7"	Decca	F12458	1966	£6	£2.50	
Google Eye	7"	Decca	F12000	1964	£4	£1.50	
Hard Way	7"	Decca	F12316	1966	£5	£2	
I'm Coming Home	7"	Decca	F12580	1967	£4	£1.50	
Lament Of The Cherokee Reservation Indian	7"	Major Minor	MM599	1969	£5	£2	
Nashville Teens	7" EP	Decca	DFE8600	1965	£30	£15	
Nashville Teens	LP	New World	NW6002	1975	£25	£10	
That's My Woman	7"	Decca	F12542	1966	£6	£2.50	
Tobacco Road	7" EP	Decca	457047	1964	£40	£20	*French*
Tobacco Road	LP	London	LL3407/PS407	1964	£50	£25	*US*

NASTY MEDIA

Spiked Copy	7"	Lightning	GIL542	1978	£6	£2.50	

NATIONAL HEAD BAND

Albert One	LP	Warner Bros	K46094	1971	£10	£4	

NATIONAL PINION POLE

Make Your Mark Little Mark	7"	Planet	PLF111	1966	£10	£5	

NATURAL ACOUSTIC BAND

Branching In	LP	RCA	SF8314	1972	£10	£4	
Learning To Live	LP	RCA	SF8272	1972	£10	£4	

NATURALS

Blue Roses	7"	Parlophone	R5257	1965	£5	£2	
Daisy Chain	7"	Parlophone	R5116	1964	£4	£1.50	
I Should Have Known Better	7"	Parlophone	R5165	1964	£4	£1.50	
It Was You	7"	Parlophone	R5202	1964	£5	£2	

NAURA, MICHAEL

Vanessa	LP	ECM	ECM1053ST	1975	£12	£5	

NAVARRO, FATS

Featured With The Tadd Dameron Quintet	LP	Jazzland	JLP50	1962	£15	£6	
Memorial	10" LP	London	LZC14015	1955	£50	£25	
Memorial Vol. 1	LP	CBS Realm	52192	1965	£10	£4	
Memorial Vol. 2	LP	CBS Realm	52208	1965	£10	£4	
Trumpet Giants	LP	Stateside	SL10103	1964	£10	£4	*with tracks by Miles Davis & Dizzy Gillespie*

NAYLOR, JERRY

Stop Your Crying	7"	Top Rank	JAR591	1961	£10	£5	

NAYLOR, SHEL

The collectability of 'One Fine Day' derives not so much from Naylor's vocal performance, but rather from the fine Jimmy Page guitar solo, together with the fact that the song is a Dave Davies composition never recorded by the Kinks themselves. Naylor, whose real name was Robert Woodward, later achieved a number one hit as a member and prime mover of the novelty group Lieutenant Pigeon.

How Deep Is The Ocean	7"	Decca	F11776	1963	£8	£4	
One Fine Day	7"	Decca	F11856	1964	£100	£50	

NAZARETH

Bad Bad Boy	7"	Mooncrest	MOON9	1973	£5	£2	*picture sleeve*
Dear John	7"	Pegasus	PGS2	1972	£12	£6	
Exercises	LP	Pegasus	PEG14	1972	£15	£6	
Fool About You	7"	Charisma	BCP8	1972	£40	£20	*test pressing*
If You See My Baby	7"	Pegasus	PGS5	1972	£12	£6	
Morning Dew	7"	Pegasus	PGS4	1972	£12	£6	
Nazareth	LP	Pegasus	PEG10	1971	£15	£6	
Nazareth EP	CD-s	Special Edition	CD317	1988	£5	£2	
Sound Elixir	LP	Sahara	SAH130	1985	£10	£4	
Whatever You Want Babe	7"	Mountain	NAZ4	1979	£6	£2.50	*purple vinyl, picture sleeve*

NAZZ

The Nazz were responsible for a classic psychedelic single, 'Open My Eyes' (included on the first album), that by some miraculous means entirely failed to become a hit. Leader of the group was Todd Rundgren, who has managed to maintain a successful solo career ever since.

Hello It's Me	7"	Screen Gems	SGC219002	1969	£6	£2.50	
Nazz	LP	Screen Gems	SGC22001	1968	£40	£20	
Nazz 3	LP	Screen Gems	SGC5004	1969	£40	£20	*US*

Title	Format	Label	Number	Year	Mint	VG+	Notes
Nazz 3	LP	Screen Gems	SGC5004	1969	£50	£25	US, green vinyl
Nazz Nazz	LP	Screen Gems	SGC5002	1969	£75	£37.50	US
Nazz Nazz	LP	Screen Gems	SGC5002	1969	£75	£37.50	US, red vinyl
Not Wrong Long	7"	Screen Gems	SGC219003	1969	£6	£2.50	
Open My Eyes	7"	Atlantic	584224	1968	£40	£20	demo
Open My Eyes	7"	Screen Gems	SGC219001	1968	£6	£2.50	

NAZZ (2)

Presumably to avoid confusion with Todd Rundgren's slightly more successful group, this Nazz subsequently changed its name to Alice Cooper.

Lay Down And Die, Goodbye	7"	Very	001	1967	£500	£330	US, best auctioned

N'DOUR, YOUSSOU

Lion	CD-s	Virgin	VSCD1207	1989	£5	£2	3" single, with Peter Gabriel

NEAL, JOHNNY & THE STARLINERS

And I Will Love You	7"	Pye	7N15388	1961	£50	£25	

NEAL, TOMMY

Goin' To A Happening	7"	Vocalion	VP9290	1968	£10	£5	

NEAT CHANGE

Guitarist with this group was Peter Banks, who became part of the first line-up of Yes.

I Lied To Auntie May	7"	Decca	F12809	1968	£25	£12.50	picture sleeve
I Lied To Auntie May	7"	Decca	F12809	1968	£10	£5	

NECROMANDUS

Quicksand Dream	LP	Reflection	MM09	1990	£10	£4	

NECROMONICON

Tips Zum Selbstmord	LP	Best Prehodi	F60634	1972	£500	£330	German

NED & NELDA

This typically irreverent parody was the work of Frank Zappa and Ray Collins.

Hey Nelda	7"	Vigah	002	1963	£150	£75	US

NEE, BERNIE

Medal Of Honour	7"	Philips	PB794	1958	£10	£5	

NEEFS, LOUIS

Jennifer Jennings	7"	Columbia	DB8561	1969	£12	£6	

NEELY, ELGIN

Four Walls	7"	Vogue	V9240	1965	£4	£1.50	

NEGATIVES

Scene Of The Crime	7"	Aardvark	STEAL3	1981	£5	£2	

NEIGHB'RHOOD CHILDR'N

Neighb'rhood Childr'n	LP	Acta	38005	1968	£75	£37.50	US

NEIL, FRED

Bleecker & MacDonald	LP	Elektra	EKL/EKS7293	1965	£40	£20	US
Candy Man	7"	Elektra	EKSN45036	1968	£4	£1.50	
Everybody's Talkin'	7"	Capitol	CL15616	1969	£4	£1.50	
Everybody's Talkin'	LP	Capitol	ST2665	1969	£15	£6	US
Hootenanny Live At The Bitter End	LP	FM	FM309	1964	£20	£8	US
Little Bit Of Rain	LP	Elektra	EKS74073	1970	£15	£6	US
Other Side Of This Life	LP	Capitol	ST657	1971	£25	£10	US
Sessions	LP	Capitol	ST2862	1971	£15	£6	US
Tear Down The Walls	LP	Elektra	EKL/EKS7248	1964	£20	£8	US
World Of Folk Music	LP	FM	FM319	1964	£20	£8	US

NEIL & JACK

Neil Diamond began his recording career here.

I'm Afraid	7"	Duel	517	1961	£150	£75	US
You Are My Love At Last	7"	Duel	508	1960	£150	£75	US

NEKROPOLIS

Suite Til Sommeren	LP	private		1976	£150	£75	

NEKTAR

Down To Earth	LP	United Artists	UAG29680	1974	£10	£4	
Journey To The Centre Of The Eye	LP	Bellaphon	BLPS19064	1972	£10	£4	German
Live At The Roundhouse	LP	Bellaphon	BLPS19182	1974	£10	£4	German
Nektar	LP	Bellaphon	BLPS19224	1976	£10	£4	German
Remember The Future	LP	United Artists	UAS29545	1973	£10	£4	
Sounds Like This	LP	United Artists	UAD60041/2	1973	£12	£5	double
Tab In The Ocean	LP	United Artists	UAS29499	1972	£10	£4	

NELLIE

I Who Have Nothing	7"	Gas	GAS126	1969	£4	£1.50	

NELSON, BILL

Title	Format	Label	Cat. No.	Year	Mint	VG	Notes
Northern Dream	LP	Smile	LAF2182	1971	**£25**	**£10**	*with booklet*

NELSON, DAVID

Title	Format	Label	Cat. No.	Year	Mint	VG	Notes
Somebody Loves Me	7"	Philips	BF1321	1964	**£5**	**£2**	

NELSON, EARL

Title	Format	Label	Cat. No.	Year	Mint	VG	Notes
No Time To Cry	7"	London	HLW8950	1959	**£8**	**£4**	

NELSON, OLIVER

Title	Format	Label	Cat. No.	Year	Mint	VG	Notes
Blues And The Abstract Truth	LP	HMV	CLP1528	1961	**£20**	**£8**	
Live From Los Angeles	LP	Impulse	MIPL/SIPL510	1960	**£12**	**£5**	
More Blues And The Abstract Truth	LP	HMV	CLP1868/ CSD1604	1965	**£15**	**£6**	

NELSON, OZZIE & HARRIET

Title	Format	Label	Cat. No.	Year	Mint	VG	Notes
Ozzie And Harriet Nelson	LP	London	HAP2145	1959	**£25**	**£10**	

NELSON, RICK

Title	Format	Label	Cat. No.	Year	Mint	VG	Notes
Album Seven	LP	London	HAP2445	1962	**£25**	**£10**	*mono*
Album Seven	LP	London	SAHP6236	1962	**£30**	**£15**	*stereo*
Another Side Of Rick	LP	MCA	MUP(S)302	1968	**£10**	**£4**	
Be Bop Baby	7"	London	HLP8499	1957	**£20**	**£10**	
Believe What You Say	7"	London	HLP8594	1958	**£10**	**£5**	
Best Always	LP	Brunswick	LAT/STA8615	1965	**£25**	**£10**	
Bright Lights, Country Music	LP	Brunswick	LAT/STA8657	1966	**£25**	**£10**	
Come Out Dancin'	7"	Brunswick	05939	1965	**£5**	**£2**	
Country Fever	LP	Brunswick	LAT/STA8680	1967	**£25**	**£10**	
Everlovin'	7"	London	HLP9440	1961	**£4**	**£1.50**	
Fools Rush In	7"	Brunswick	05895	1963	**£4**	**£1.50**	
For You	7"	Brunswick	05900	1964	**£4**	**£1.50**	
For Your Sweet Love	LP	Brunswick	LAT8545	1963	**£25**	**£10**	*mono*
For Your Sweet Love	LP	Brunswick	STA8545	1963	**£30**	**£15**	*stereo*
Happy Guy	7"	Brunswick	05924	1964	**£4**	**£1.50**	
Happy Guy	7" EP	Brunswick	OE9512	1965	**£25**	**£12.50**	
Hello Mary Lou	7"	London	HLP9347	1961	**£4**	**£1.50**	
I Got A Feeling	7" EP	London	REP1238	1960	**£25**	**£12.50**	
I Got A Woman	7"	Brunswick	05885	1963	**£4**	**£1.50**	
I Wanna Be Loved	7"	London	HLP9021	1960	**£4**	**£1.50**	
I'm In Love Again	7" EP	Liberty	LEP4028	1965	**£30**	**£15**	
I'm Walking	7"	HMV	POP355	1957	**£100**	**£50**	*gold label*
In Concert	LP	MCA	MUPS409	1970	**£10**	**£4**	
It's A Young World	7" EP	London	REP1339	1962	**£20**	**£10**	
It's Up To You	7"	London	HLP9648	1963	**£4**	**£1.50**	
It's Up To You	7" EP	London	REP1362	1963	**£20**	**£10**	
It's Up To You	LP	London	HAP8066	1963	**£25**	**£10**	
Just A Little Too Much	7"	London	HL7081	1959	**£6**	**£2.50**	*export*
Just A Little Too Much	7"	London	HLP8927	1959	**£6**	**£2.50**	
Lonely Corner	7"	Brunswick	05918	1964	**£4**	**£1.50**	
Long Vacation	LP	Imperial	LP9244/12244	1963	**£25**	**£10**	*US*
Love And Kisses	LP	Brunswick	LAT/STA8630	1965	**£25**	**£10**	
Milkcow Blues	7"	London	HLP9260	1961	**£6**	**£2.50**	
Million Sellers	LP	Liberty	LBY3027	1963	**£20**	**£8**	
More Songs By Ricky	LP	London	SAHP6102	1960	**£40**	**£20**	*stereo*
More Songs By Ricky	LP	London	HAP2290	1960	**£30**	**£15**	*mono*
More Songs By Ricky	LP	Imperial	LP12059	1960	**£150**	**£75**	*US, blue vinyl*
My Babe	7"	London	HLP8738	1958	**£6**	**£2.50**	
Never Be Anyone Else But You	7"	London	HLP8817	1959	**£5**	**£2**	
On The Flip Side	LP	Decca	DL(7)4836	1967	**£20**	**£8**	*US, with Joanie Sommers*
One Boy Too Late	7" EP	Brunswick	OE9502	1963	**£25**	**£12.50**	
Perspective	LP	Decca	DL75014	1968	**£15**	**£6**	*US*
Poor Little Fool	7"	London	HLP8670	1958	**£4**	**£1.50**	
Rick Is 21	LP	London	SAHP6179	1961	**£40**	**£20**	*stereo*
Rick Is 21	LP	London	HAP2379	1961	**£30**	**£15**	*mono*
Rick Nelson Country	LP	MCA	24004	1973	**£10**	**£4**	*US*
Ricky	LP	London	HAP2080	1957	**£40**	**£20**	
Ricky Nelson	LP	London	HAP2119	1958	**£40**	**£20**	
Ricky Nelson No. 1	7" EP	London	REP1168	1959	**£25**	**£12.50**	
Ricky Nelson No. 2	7" EP	London	REP1169	1959	**£25**	**£12.50**	
Ricky Nelson No. 3	7" EP	London	REP1170	1959	**£25**	**£12.50**	
Ricky Nelson No. 4	7" EP	London	REP1300	1961	**£25**	**£12.50**	
Ricky No. 1	7" EP	London	REP1141	1958	**£25**	**£12.50**	
Ricky No. 2	7" EP	London	REP1142	1958	**£25**	**£12.50**	
Ricky No. 3	7" EP	London	REP1143	1958	**£25**	**£12.50**	
Ricky No. 4	7" EP	London	REP1144	1958	**£25**	**£12.50**	
Ricky Sings Again	LP	London	HAP2159	1959	**£30**	**£15**	
Ricky Sings Again Pt 1	7" EP	London	REP1200	1959	**£25**	**£12.50**	
Ricky Sings Again Pt 2	7" EP	London	REP1201	1959	**£25**	**£12.50**	
Ricky Sings Spirituals	7" EP	London	REP1249	1960	**£25**	**£12.50**	
Sings For You	7" EP	Liberty	LEP4001	1964	**£25**	**£12.50**	
Sings For You	LP	Brunswick	LAT8562	1964	**£25**	**£10**	*mono*
Sings For You	LP	Brunswick	STA8562	1964	**£30**	**£15**	*stereo*
Someday	7"	London	HLP8732	1958	**£4**	**£1.50**	
Songs By Ricky	LP	London	HAP2206	1959	**£30**	**£15**	
Spotlight On Rick	LP	Brunswick	LAT/STA8596	1964	**£25**	**£10**	
Stood Up	7"	London	HLP8542	1958	**£12**	**£6**	

String Along	7"	Brunswick	05889	1963	£5	£2	
Teen Time	LP	Verve	V2083	1957	£150	£75	US
Teenage Idol	7"	London	HLP9583	1962	£4	£1.50	
That's All	7" EP	Liberty	LEP4019	1964	£25	£12.50	
Today's Teardrops	7"	Liberty	LIB66004	1964	£5	£2	
Very Thought Of You	7"	Brunswick	05908	1964	£4	£1.50	
Very Thought Of You	LP	Brunswick	LAT/STA8581	1964	£25	£10	
Yes Sir That's My Baby	7"	London	HLP9188	1960	£4	£1.50	
You Are My One And Only Love	7"	HMV	POP390	1957	£75	£37.50	Barney Kessel B side
You Can't Just Quit	7"	Brunswick	05964	1966	£6	£2.50	
Young Emotions	7"	London	HLP9121	1960	£4	£1.50	
Young World	7"	London	HLP9524	1962	£4	£1.50	

NELSON, SANDY

And Then There Were Drums	7"	London	HLP9612	1962	£4	£1.50	
Bouncy	7"	London	HLP9214	1960	£4	£1.50	
Compelling Percussion	LP	London	HAP/SHP8029	1963	£12	£5	
Drum Party	7"	London	HLP9015	1959	£5	£2	
Drummin' Up A Storm	7"	London	HLP9558	1962	£4	£1.50	
Drummin' Up A Storm	LP	London	HAP/SHP8009	1962	£15	£6	
Drums A Go-go	LP	Liberty	LBY3061	1965	£10	£4	
Drums Are My Beat	LP	London	HAP2446/ SAHP6237	1962	£15	£6	
Get With It	7"	London	HLP9377	1961	£4	£1.50	
In The Mood	7" EP	London	REP1371	1963	£10	£5	
Let There Be Drums	7" EP	London	REP1337	1962	£10	£5	
Let There Be Drums	LP	London	HAP2425/ SAHP6221	1961	£15	£6	
Live In Las Vegas	LP	Liberty	LBY3035	1965	£10	£4	
Ooh Poo Pah Doo	7"	London	HLP9717	1963	£4	£1.50	
Rushing For Percussion	7" EP	Top Rank	JKP2060	1960	£15	£7.50	2 tracks by Preston Epps
Sandy Nelson Plays	7" EP	Liberty	LEP4033	1965	£10	£5	
Sandy Nelson Plays	LP	Liberty	LBY3007	1964	£10	£4	
Superdrums	LP	Liberty	(S)LBY3080	1967	£10	£4	
Teen Beat	7"	Top Rank	JAR197	1959	£4	£1.50	
Teen Beat	LP	London	HAP2260/ SAHP6082	1960	£15	£6	
Teenage House Party	LP	London	HAP/SHP8051	1963	£15	£6	

NELSON, TERRY

Bulldog Push	7"	Dice	CC25	1964	£10	£5	
Love On Saturday Night	7"	Dice	CC22	1963	£10	£5	
My Blue Eyed Baby	7"	Dice	CC27	1964	£10	£5	
Run Baby Run	7"	Dice	CC23	1963	£10	£5	

NELSON, WILLIE

And Then I Wrote	LP	Liberty	LRP3238/ LST7238	1962	£15	£6	US
And Then I Wrote	LP	Liberty	(S)LBY1240	1966	£12	£5	
Country Willie	LP	RCA	RD7749	1965	£12	£5	
Half A Man	7"	Liberty	LIB55532	1963	£4	£1.50	
Here's Willie Nelson	LP	Liberty	LRP3308/ LST7308	1963	£15	£6	US
River Boy	7"	Liberty	LIB55697	1964	£4	£1.50	
Texas In My Soul	LP	RCA	RD7997	1969	£10	£4	

NELSON TRIO

All In Good Time	7"	London	HLL9019	1960	£5	£2	

NENA

It's All In The Game	LP	Sony	303P686	1985	£75	£37.50	Japanese picture disc

NEO MAYA

I Won't Hurt You	7"	Pye	7N17371	1967	£30	£15	

NEOGY, CHIITRA

Perfumed Garden	LP	Morgan	M1003L	1968	£15	£6	
Perfumed Garden	LP	Gemini	GMX5030	1970	£10	£4	

NEON HEARTS

Regulations	7"	Neon Hearts	NEON1	1977	£12	£6	

NEON ROSE

Dream Of Glory And Pride	LP	Vertigo	6316250	1974	£20	£8	Swedish
Reload	LP	Vertigo	6316252	1975	£20	£8	Swedish
Two	LP	Vertigo	6316251	1974	£20	£8	Swedish

NEP-TUNES

Surfer's Holiday	LP	Family	(S)FLP552	1963	£20	£8	US

NEPTUNE'S EMPIRE

Neptune's Empire	LP	Polymax	PXX01	1971	£75	£37.50	

NERO & THE GLADIATORS

Czardas	7"	Decca	F11413	1961	£8	£4	
Entry Of The Gladiators	7"	Decca	F11329	1961	£6	£2.50	
In The Hall Of The Mountain King	7"	Decca	F11367	1961	£6	£2.50	

NERVE

Title	Format	Label	Cat. No.	Year	Mint	VG	Notes
It Is	7"	Page One	POF081	1968	**£8**	**£4**	
Magic Spectacles	7"	Page One	POF055	1968	**£8**	**£4**	
Piece By Piece	7"	Page One	POF097	1968	**£5**	**£2**	
Ten Downing Street	7"	Page One	POF019	1967	**£4**	**£1.50**	

NERVES

Title	Format	Label	Cat. No.	Year	Mint	VG	Notes
TV Adverts	7"	Lightning	GIL520	1978	**£10**	**£5**	

NERVOUS NORVUS

Title	Format	Label	Cat. No.	Year	Mint	VG	Notes
Ape Call	7"	London	HLD8338	1956	**£50**	**£25**	*gold label*
Bullfrog Hop	7"	London	HLD8383	1957	**£75**	**£37.50**	*gold label*
Does A Chinese Chicken Have A Pigtail	7"	Salvo	SLO1812	1962	**£20**	**£10**	*Rod Barton B side*

NESBIT, JIM

Title	Format	Label	Cat. No.	Year	Mint	VG	Notes
Tiger In My Tank	7"	Vocalion	V9241	1965	**£15**	**£7.50**	

NESMITH, MICHAEL

Title	Format	Label	Cat. No.	Year	Mint	VG	Notes
And The First National Band	7" EP	Island	IEP4	1976	**£5**	**£2**	
And The Hits Just Keep On Coming	LP	RCA	LSP4695	1972	**£10**	**£4**	*US*
I Fall To Pieces	7"	Island	IEP4	1976	**£5**	**£2**	*picture sleeve*
Joanne	7"	RCA	RCA2001	1970	**£5**	**£2**	
Just A Little Love	7"	Edan	1001	197–	**£50**	**£25**	*US*
Loose Salute	LP	RCA	LSP4415	1970	**£10**	**£4**	*US*
Magnetic South	LP	RCA	SF8136	1970	**£10**	**£4**	
Mike Nesmith Radio Special	LP	Pacific Arts	PAC71300	1976	**£15**	**£6**	*US promo*
Navajo Trail	7"	Island	WIP6398	1978	**£4**	**£1.50**	
Nevada Fighter	7"	RCA	RCA2086	1971	**£5**	**£2**	
Nevada Fighter	LP	RCA	SF8209	1971	**£10**	**£4**	
Pretty Much Your Standard Ranch Stash	LP	RCA	APL10164	1973	**£10**	**£4**	*US*
Prison	LP	Pacific Arts	PAC7101	1975	**£15**	**£6**	*US, boxed with booklet*
Silver Moon	7"	RCA	RCA2053	1971	**£5**	**£2**	
Tantamount To Treason	LP	RCA	SF8276	1972	**£10**	**£4**	
Wichita Train Whistle Sings	LP	Dot	(S)LDP516	1968	**£20**	**£8**	

NEU

The increasingly collectable work of the German electronic group Neu is closely related to that of Kraftwerk. Klaus Dinger and Thomas Homann were members of the parent group on the first album, *Kraftwerk 1*, before deciding that they could achieve more on their own.

Title	Format	Label	Cat. No.	Year	Mint	VG	Notes
Isi	7"	United Artists	UP35874	1975	**£4**	**£1.50**	
Neu	LP	United Artists	UAS29396	1972	**£30**	**£15**	
Neu '75	LP	United Artists	UAS29782	1975	**£25**	**£10**	
Neu 2	LP	United Artists	UAS29500	1973	**£25**	**£10**	
Super	7"	United Artists	UP35485	1973	**£4**	**£1.50**	
Two Originals Of Neu	LP	Brain	800142	1978	**£15**	**£6**	*German double*

NEURONIUM

Title	Format	Label	Cat. No.	Year	Mint	VG	Notes
Quasar 2C361	LP	Harvest	21442	1977	**£10**	**£4**	*Spanish*
Vuelo Quinico	LP	Harvest	21523	1978	**£10**	**£4**	*Spanish*

NEUTRONS

Title	Format	Label	Cat. No.	Year	Mint	VG	Notes
Black Hole Star	LP	United Artists	UAG29652	1974	**£10**	**£4**	
Tales From The Blue Cocoons	LP	United Artists	UAG29726	1975	**£10**	**£4**	

NEVILLE, AARON

Title	Format	Label	Cat. No.	Year	Mint	VG	Notes
Here 'Tis	LP	Liberty	LBY3089	1967	**£20**	**£8**	
Tell It Like It Is	7"	Stateside	SS584	1967	**£8**	**£4**	
Tell It Like It Is	7"	B&C	CB107	1969	**£4**	**£1.50**	
Tell It Like It Is	LP	Par-Lo	LP1	1967	**£25**	**£10**	*US*

NEW AGE STEPPERS

Title	Format	Label	Cat. No.	Year	Mint	VG	Notes
Fade Away	7"	ONU Sound	ONU1	1980	**£4**	**£1.50**	*B side by the London Underground*

NEW BREED

Title	Format	Label	Cat. No.	Year	Mint	VG	Notes
Friends And Lovers Forever	7"	Decca	F12295	1965	**£20**	**£10**	

NEW CHRISTY MINSTRELS

Title	Format	Label	Cat. No.	Year	Mint	VG	Notes
Green Green	7"	CBS	AAG160	1963	**£4**	**£1.50**	
Ramblin'	LP	CBS	BPG62269	1963	**£10**	**£4**	
Sing And Play Cowboys And Indians	LP	CBS	BPG62492	1965	**£10**	**£4**	
Tell Tall Tales	LP	CBS	BPG62268	1963	**£10**	**£4**	
Three Wheels On My Wagon	7"	CBS	201328	1965	**£4**	**£1.50**	
Three Wheels On My Wagon	7" EP	CBS	EP6057	1965	**£5**	**£2**	

NEW COLONY SIX

Title	Format	Label	Cat. No.	Year	Mint	VG	Notes
At The River's Edge	7"	Stateside	SS522	1966	**£50**	**£25**	
Attacking A Strawman	LP	Mercury	SR61228	1970	**£20**	**£8**	*US*
Breakthrough	LP	Sentar	LP101	1966	**£250**	**£150**	*US*
Colonization	LP	Sentar	(S)ST3001	1967	**£50**	**£25**	*US*
I Confess	7"	London	HLZ10033	1966	**£25**	**£12.50**	
I Will Always	7"	Mercury	MF1030	1968	**£4**	**£1.50**	
Revelations	LP	Mercury	SR61165	1969	**£20**	**£8**	*US*
Things I'd Like To Say	7"	Mercury	MF1086	1969	**£4**	**£1.50**	

NEW DAWN

There's A New Dawn	LP	Hoot/Garland	704569	1970	£400	£250	US

NEW DAWN (2)

Mainline	LP	private		1969	£100	£50	

NEW DEAL STRING BAND

Down In The Willow	LP	Argo	ZDA104	1969	£20	£8	

NEW DIMENSIONS

Deuces And Eights	LP	Sutton	(SSU)331	1963	£12	£5	US
Soul Surf	LP	Sutton	(SSU)336	1964	£12	£5	US
Surf 'n' Bongos	LP	Sutton	(SSU)332	1963	£12	£5	US

NEW FORESTERS

Travel	7"	Lyntone	LYN932/3	1965	£25	£12.50	Lizards B side

NEW FORMULA

Stay Indoors	7"	Pye	7N17818	1969	£15	£7.50	

NEW GENERATION

This was the first version of the Sutherland Brothers, who made several records in the seventies, both on their own and with the group Quiver. Gavin Sutherland had the good fortune to see one of his songs turned into a major hit by Rod Stewart – 'Sailing'.

Smokey Blues Away	7"	Spark	SRL1007	1969	£5	£2	

NEW HEARTS

Just Another Teenage Anthem*	7"	CBS	5800	1977	£4	£1.50	
Plain Jane	7"	CBS	6381	1978	£4	£1.50	

NEW HEAVENLY BLUE

Educated Homegrown	LP	RCA	SF8189	1971	£10	£4	
New Heavenly Blue	LP	Atlantic	SD7247	1972	£12	£5	US

NEW HERITAGE

All Manner Of Things	LP	Westwood	WRS028	1973	£30	£15	

NEW JAZZ ORCHESTRA

The LPs credited to the New Jazz Orchestra are listed under the name of the orchestra's leader, Neil Ardley.

NEW LORDS

New Lords	LP	Columbia	1C06229429	1971	£10	£4	German

NEW LOST CITY RAMBLERS

New Lost City Ramblers	LP	XTRA	XTRA1001	1965	£10	£4	

NEW MODEL

Chilean Warning	7"	Mr Clean	MRC1	1983	£5	£2	in folder

NEW MODEL ARMY

Aries Enterprises	cass	private		1981	£20	£8	with other artists
Bittersweet	7"	Quiet!	QS002	1983	£6	£2.50	with flexi
Great Expectations	7"	Abstract	ABS0020	1983	£5	£2	
Green And Grey	CD-s	EMI	CDNMA9	1989	£5	£2	
Poison Street	7"	EMI	NMA5	1987	£8	£4	red vinyl

NEW MONITORS

Fence Around Your Heart	7"	Buddah	2011118	1972	£5	£2	

NEW ORDER

Best Of New Order	CD and cass	London	8285802	1995	£40	£20	promo boxed set
Blue Monday	12"	Factory	FAC73RD	1988	£6	£2.50	promo
Blue Monday	CD-s	Factory	FACD73R	1988	£5	£2	
Blue Monday	CD-s	Factory	FACDV73R	1988	£40	£20	CD video
Brotherhood	CD	Factory	FACD150SP	1987	£12	£5	with 'State Of The Nation'
Brotherhood	CD	Factory	FACD150SP	1987	£15	£6	metallic box
Confusion	7"	Factory	FAC93	1983	£8	£4	promo
Gatefold Substance	LP	Factory	FACT200S	1987	£20	£8	numbered g/f sleeve
Hacienda Christmas Flexi	7"	Factory	FAC51B	1982	£6	£2.50	flexi
Peel Sessions	CD-s	Strange Fruit	SFPSCD001	1988	£5	£2	
Peel Sessions II	CD-s	Strange Fruit	SFPSCD039	1988	£5	£2	
Power, Corruption And Lies	LP	Factory		1983	£75	£37.50	German, multi-coloured vinyl
Round And Round	CD-s	Factory	FACD263R	1989	£5	£2	3" single
Round And Round (Ben Grosse remix)	12"	Factory	FAC263DJ	1989	£6	£2.50	promo
Run 2	12"	Factory	FAC273	1989	£8	£4	
Run 2	7"	Factory	FAC2737	1989	£10	£5	promo
Substance	cass	Factory	FACT200C	1987	£15	£6	box set
Thieves Like Us	7"	Factory	FAC103	1984	£6	£2.50	promo
Touched By The Hand Of God	CD-s	Factory	FACD187	1987	£6	£2.50	
Touched By The Hand Of God	CD-s	Factory	FACD193	1989	£15	£7.50	gatefold card sleeve
True Faith	CD-s	Factory	FACDV183	1989	£10	£5	CD video

NEW ORDER (2)

Title	Format	Label	Cat. No.	Year	Price		Notes
Bradford Red Light District	LP	Come	CARA12	1981	**£15**	£6	

NEW ORDER (3)

Title	Format	Label	Cat. No.	Year	Price		Notes
You've Got Me High	7" EP	Warner Bros	WB113	1966	**£12**	£6	*French*

NEW ORLEANS ALL STAR JAZZ BAND

Title	Format	Label	Cat. No.	Year	Price		Notes
New Orleans All Star Jazz Band	LP	Vogue	LAE12013	1956	**£12**	£5	
Struttin' With Some Barbecue	7"	Vogue	V2380	1956	**£5**	£2	

NEW ORLEANS BOOTBLACKS

Title	Format	Label	Cat. No.	Year	Price		Notes
Flat Foot	7"	Columbia	SCM5090	1954	**£4**	£1.50	

NEW ORLEANS RHYTHM KINGS

Title	Format	Label	Cat. No.	Year	Price		Notes
New Orleans Rhythm Kings	10" LP	London	AL3552	1956	**£15**	£6	

NEW RELIGION

Title	Format	Label	Cat. No.	Year	Price		Notes
In The Black Caribbean	7"	Bamboo	BAM70	1972	**£5**	£2	

NEW TROLLS

Title	Format	Label	Cat. No.	Year	Price		Notes
Concerto Grosso	LP	Fonit Cetra	LPX8	1972	**£10**	£4	*Italian*
Searching For A Land	LP	Fonit Cetra	DPU70	1973	**£12**	£5	*Italian double*
Senza Oravio Senza Bandiera	LP	Fonit Cetra	LPX3	1971	**£10**	£4	*Italian*
Ut	LP	Fonit Cetra	LPX20	1972	**£10**	£4	*Italian*

NEW TWEEDY BROTHERS

Title	Format	Label	Cat. No.	Year	Price		Notes
New Tweedy Brothers	LP	Ridon	234	1966	**£1000**	£700	*US*
New Tweedy Brothers	LP	private		1992	**£15**	£6	*US*

NEW VAUDEVILLE BAND

Title	Format	Label	Cat. No.	Year	Price		Notes
Bonnie And Clyde	7"	Fontana	TF909	1968	**£4**	£1.50	*picture sleeve*
Finchley Central	7"	Fontana	TF824	1967	**£4**	£1.50	*picture sleeve*
Finchley Central	7" EP	Fontana	465381	1967	**£6**	£2.50	*French*
Finchley Central	LP	Fontana	(S)TL5430	1967	**£10**	£4	
New Vaudeville Band	7" EP	Fontana	TFE17497	1968	**£5**	£2	
Peek-A-Boo	7" EP	Fontana	465362	1966	**£6**	£2.50	*French*
Winchester Cathedral	7" EP	Fontana	465342	1966	**£6**	£2.50	*French*
Winchester Cathedral	LP	Fontana	886408TY	1966	**£10**	£4	

NEW VICTORY BAND

Title	Format	Label	Cat. No.	Year	Price		Notes
One More Dance And Then	LP	Topic	12TS382	1978	**£12**	£5	

NEW YORK ART QUARTET

Title	Format	Label	Cat. No.	Year	Price		Notes
Mohawk	LP	Fontana	681009ZL	1967	**£20**	£8	
New York Art Quartet	LP	ESP-Disk	1004	1965	**£25**	£10	*US*

NEW YORK BLONDES

The 'Madam X' featured on the New York Blondes' single is Debbie Harry, who was highly annoyed at the record's release. She had in fact recorded her vocal part purely as a demo for US DJ Rodney Bigenheimer to follow when making his own record (and the single's B side is indeed by him).

Title	Format	Label	Cat. No.	Year	Price		Notes
Little GTO	7"	London	HL10574	1979	**£5**	£2	*picture sleeve*

NEW YORK DOLLS

Title	Format	Label	Cat. No.	Year	Price		Notes
Jet Boy	7"	Mercury	6052402	1973	**£4**	£1.50	
New York Dolls	CD-s	Counterpoint	CDEP14C	1988	**£5**	£2	
New York Dolls	LP	Mercury	6338270	1973	**£10**	£4	
Personality Crisis	CD-s	See For Miles	SEACD3	1990	**£5**	£2	
Stranded In The Jungle	7"	Mercury	6052615	1974	**£4**	£1.50	
Too Much Too Soon	LP	Mercury	6338498	1974	**£10**	£4	

NEW YORK PUBLIC LIBRARY

Title	Format	Label	Cat. No.	Year	Price		Notes
Got To Get Away	7"	MCA	MU1025	1968	**£5**	£2	
I Ain't Gonna Eat Out My Heart Anymore	7"	Columbia	DB7948	1966	**£15**	£7.50	
Love Me Two Times	7"	MCA	MU1045	1968	**£5**	£2	

NEW YORK ROCK & ROLL ENSEMBLE

Title	Format	Label	Cat. No.	Year	Price		Notes
Faithful Friends	LP	Atco	228032	1969	**£10**	£4	
New York Rock & Roll Ensemble	LP	Atco	33240	1968	**£12**	£5	*US*
Reflections	LP	Atco	33312	1970	**£10**	£4	*US*

NEWBEATS

Title	Format	Label	Cat. No.	Year	Price		Notes
Ain't That Lovin' You Baby	7" EP	Hickory	LPE1506	1965	**£12**	£6	
Big Beat Sounds	LP	Hickory	LP(S)122	1965	**£20**	£8	*US*
Birds Are For The Bees	7" EP	CBS	6095	1965	**£10**	£5	*French*
Bread And Butter	7" EP	CBS	5916	1964	**£10**	£5	*French*
Bread And Butter	LP	Hickory	LPM120	1965	**£20**	£8	
Crying My Heart Out	7"	Hickory	451387	1965	**£6**	£2.50	
My Yesterday Love	7"	Hickory	451422	1965	**£4**	£1.50	
Newbeats	7" EP	Hickory	LPE1503	1964	**£10**	£5	
Oh Girls Girls	7" EP	Hickory	LPE1510	1966	**£15**	£7.50	
Run Baby Run	7"	Hickory	451332	1965	**£4**	£1.50	
Run Baby Run	7" EP	CBS	6209	1965	**£10**	£5	*French*
Run Baby Run	LP	Hickory	LP(S)128	1965	**£20**	£8	*US*
Too Sweet To Be Forgotten	7"	Hickory	451366	1965	**£5**	£2	

NEWBORN, PHINEAS

Title	Format	Label	Cat. No.	Year	Mint	VG	Notes
I Love A Piano	LP	Columbia	33SX1311/ SCX3370	1961	£**12**	£**5**	
Phineas Newborn	LP	London	LTZK15057	1957	£**20**	£**8**	

NEWCASTLE BIG BAND

The Newcastle Big Band was a semi-professional sixteen-piece jazz band whose privately produced LP would mean little to anyone who had not actually seen the band live, were it not for the fact that the bass player just happened to go by the name of Sting.

Title	Format	Label	Cat. No.	Year	Mint	VG	Notes
Newcastle Big Band	LP	Impulse	ISSNBB106	1972	£**300**	£**180**	

NEWLEY, ANTHONY

Title	Format	Label	Cat. No.	Year	Mint	VG	Notes
Can Heironymus Merkin Ever Forget Mercy Humppe . . .	LP	MCA	MUPS380	1969	£**10**	£**4**	
I've Waited So Long	7"	Decca	F11127	1959	£**4**	£**1.50**	
Idle On Parade	7"	Decca	F11137	1959	£**5**	£**2**	
Idle On Parade	7" EP	Decca	DFE6566	1959	£**8**	£**4**	
In My Solitude	LP	Decca	LK4600	1964	£**10**	£**4**	
Love Is A Now And Then Thing	LP	Decca	LK4343	1960	£**10**	£**4**	
More Hits From Tony	7" EP	Decca	DFE6655	1960	£**5**	£**2**	
Newley Delivered	LP	Decca	LK4654	1965	£**10**	£**4**	
Newley Recorded	LP	RCA	RD/SF7837	1967	£**10**	£**4**	
Personality	7"	Decca	F11142	1959	£**4**	£**1.50**	
Stop The World – I Want To Get Off	LP	Decca	LK4408	1961	£**10**	£**4**	
This Time The Dream's On Me	7" EP	Decca	DFE6687	1961	£**5**	£**2**	
Tony	LP	Decca	LK4406	1961	£**10**	£**4**	
Tony's Hits	7" EP	Decca	DFE6629	1960	£**5**	£**2**	
Tribute	7"	Decca	F11818	1964	£**5**	£**2**	
Who Can I Turn To	LP	RCA	RD/SF7737	1966	£**10**	£**4**	

NEWLEY, ANTHONY, PETER SELLERS & JOAN COLLINS

Title	Format	Label	Cat. No.	Year	Mint	VG	Notes
Fool Britannia	7" EP	Ember	EMBEP4530	1963	£**5**	£**2**	

NEWMAN, ANDY

Title	Format	Label	Cat. No.	Year	Mint	VG	Notes
Rainbow	LP	Track	2406103	1971	£**10**	£**4**	

NEWMAN, BRAD

Title	Format	Label	Cat. No.	Year	Mint	VG	Notes
Somebody To Love	7"	Fontana	H357	1962	£**4**	£**1.50**	

NEWMAN, CHRIS

Title	Format	Label	Cat. No.	Year	Mint	VG	Notes
Chris Newman	LP	Coast	COASTAL3	1981	£**10**	£**4**	

NEWMAN, COLIN

Title	Format	Label	Cat. No.	Year	Mint	VG	Notes
Not To	CD-s	4AD	CN1	1988	£**5**	£**2**	
We Means We Starts	7"	4AD	AD209	1982	£**4**	£**1.50**	

NEWMAN, DEL SOUND

Title	Format	Label	Cat. No.	Year	Mint	VG	Notes
Flower Garden	LP	Columbia	SCX6181	1967	£**20**	£**8**	

NEWMAN, JIMMY

Title	Format	Label	Cat. No.	Year	Mint	VG	Notes
Fallen Star	7"	London	HLD8460	1957	£**15**	£**7.50**	
Grin And Bear It	7"	MGM	MGM1037	1959	£**5**	£**2**	
Grin And Bear It	7" EP	MGM	MGMEP706	1959	£**25**	£**12.50**	
What About Me	7"	MGM	MGM1085	1960	£**4**	£**1.50**	
Whatcha Gonna Do	7"	MGM	MGM1009	1959	£**6**	£**2.50**	

NEWMAN, JOE

Title	Format	Label	Cat. No.	Year	Mint	VG	Notes
I Feel Like A Newman	LP	Vogue	LAE12049	1957	£**30**	£**15**	
Joe Newman And His Band	10" LP	Vanguard	PPT12001	1955	£**40**	£**20**	
Joe Newman And The Boys In The Band	10" LP	Vogue	LDE126	1955	£**40**	£**20**	
Joe Newman Octet	10" LP	HMV	DLP1114	1956	£**30**	£**15**	
Joe Newman Sextet	LP	Vogue Coral	LVA9052	1957	£**20**	£**8**	
Locking Horns	LP	Columbia	33SX1064	1957	£**15**	£**6**	*with Zoot Sims*
Soft Swingin' Jazz	LP	Coral	LVA9106	1959	£**20**	£**8**	*with Shirley Scott*
With Woodwinds	LP	Columbia	33SX1143	1959	£**15**	£**6**	

NEWMAN, LIONEL ORCHESTRA

Title	Format	Label	Cat. No.	Year	Mint	VG	Notes
Hey Eula	7"	Columbia	DB4150	1958	£**4**	£**1.50**	

NEWMAN, PAUL

Title	Format	Label	Cat. No.	Year	Mint	VG	Notes
Ain't You Got A Heart	7"	Mercury	MF969	1966	£**10**	£**5**	

NEWMAN, RANDY

Title	Format	Label	Cat. No.	Year	Mint	VG	Notes
12 Songs	LP	Reprise	RSLP6373	1970	£**10**	£**4**	
Creates Something New Under The Sun	LP	Reprise	R(S)LP6286	1968	£**12**	£**5**	
Falling In Love	CD-s	Warner Bros	W7578CD	1988	£**5**	£**2**	*3" single*
Good Old Boys	LP	Reprise	MS42193	1974	£**10**	£**4**	*US quad*
I Love L.A.	CD-s	Warner Bros	9256802	1989	£**10**	£**5**	*CD video*
I Think It's Gonna Rain Today	78	Reprise	0284	1968	£**10**	£**5**	*US promo*
It's Money That Matters	CD-s	Warner Bros	W7709CD	1988	£**5**	£**2**	*3" single*

NEWMAN, TOM

Title	Format	Label	Cat. No.	Year	Mint	VG	Notes
Faerie Symphony	LP	Decca	TXS123	1977	£**15**	£**6**	
Fine Old Tom	LP	Virgin	V2022	1975	£**10**	£**4**	
Live At The Argonaut	LP	Virgin	V2042	1975	£**75**	£**37.50**	*test pressing only*
Ozymandias	LP	Oceandsic		1988	£**25**	£**10**	*test pressing*

NEWMAN, TONY

Soul Thing	7"	Decca	F13041	1970	£4	£1.50	
Soul Thing	7"	Decca	F12795	1968	£5	£2	

NEWPORT ALL-STARS

That Newport Jazz	LP	CBS	BPG62395	1964	£12	£5	

NEWPORT JAZZ FESTIVAL ALL STARS

Newport Jazz Festival All Stars	LP	London	LTZK15202	1961	£10	£4	

NEWPORTERS

Having achieved little success as the Moongooners, Scott Engel and John Maus next tried the name Newporters.

Adventures In Paradise	7"	Scotchtown	500	1963	£30	£15	*US*

NEWS

Entertainer	7"	Decca	F12356	1966	£4	£1.50	
This Is The Moment	7"	Decca	F12477	1966	£10	£5	

NEWTON, WAYNE

Comin' On Too Strong	7"	Capitol	CL15380	1965	£5	£2	

NEWTON-JOHN, OLIVIA

If Not For You	LP	Polydor	2310136	1976	£12	£5	*German*
If Not For You	LP	Uni	UNLS73117	1971	£25	£10	*US*
Magic	7"	Jet	P196	1980	£6	£2.50	*picture disc*
Olivia Newton-John	LP	Pye	NSPL28155	1971	£10	£4	
Physical	LP	MCA	MCA16011	1981	£10	£4	*audiophile*
Rumour	CD-s	Mercury	MERCD272	1988	£6	£2.50	
Till You Say You'll Be Mine	7"	Decca	F12396	1966	£100	£50	
Totally Hot	LP	EMI	EMAP789	1978	£15	£6	*picture disc*
When You Wish Upon A Star	CD-s	Mercury	MERCD313	1989	£10	£5	
Xanadu	10"	Jet	10185	1980	£15	£6	*pink vinyl, with E.L.O.*

NEWTOWN NEUROTICS

Hypocrite	7"	No Wonder	SRTS79CUS363	1979	£15	£7.50	
Kick Out The Tories	7"	No Wonder	NOW56	1982	£4	£1.50	
Licensing Hours	7"	CNT	CNT010	1982	£4	£1.50	
When The Oil Runs Out	7"	No Wonder	NOW4	1980	£8	£4	*with insert*

NI DHOMHNAILL, MAIREAD

Mairead Ni Dhomhnaill	LP	Gael-Linn	CEF055	1976	£10	£4	*Irish*

NI DHOMHNAILL, TRIONA

Triona	LP	Gael-Linn	CEF043	1975	£10	£4	*Irish*

NI GHUAIRIM, SORCHA

Sings Traditional Irish Songs	LP	Folkways	FW6861	1966	£12	£5	*US*

NI RIAIN, NOIRIN

Caoineadh Na Maighdine	LP	Gael-Linn	CEF084	1980	£12	£5	*Irish*
Seinn Aililiu	LP	Gael-Linn	CEF067	1978	£12	£5	*Irish*

NIADEM'S GHOST

In Sheltered Winds	LP	Hibination	HIDE001	1986	£20	£8	
Thirst	cass	Hibination	HIDE002	1987	£10	£5	

NIAGARA

Niagara	LP	United Artists	UAS29232	1971	£10	£4	*German*
S.U.B.	LP	United Artists	UAS29343	1972	£10	£4	*German*

NICE

America	7"	Immediate	IM068	1968	£8	£4	*picture sleeve*
Ars Longa Vita Brevis	LP	Immediate	IMSP020	1968	£12	£5	
Elegy	LP	Charisma	CAS1030	1971	£10	£4	*pink label*
Five Bridges Suite	LP	Charisma	CAS1014	1970	£10	£4	*pink label*
Nice	LP	Immediate	IMSP026	1969	£10	£4	
She Belongs To Me	7"	Immediate	AS4	1969	£15	£7.50	*promo*
Thoughts Of Emerlist Davjack	7"	Immediate	AS2	1967	£25	£12.50	*promo with John Peel interview*
Thoughts Of Emerlist Davjack	7"	Immediate	IM059	1967	£4	£1.50	
Thoughts Of Emerlist Davjack	LP	Immediate	IMLP/IMSP016	1967	£15	£6	

NICELY, NICK

DCT Dreams	7"	Voxette	VOX1001	1980	£5	£2	
Hillyfields (1892)	7"	EMI	EMI5256	1982	£5	£2	

NICHOLLS, BILLY

Forever's No Time At All	7"	Track	2094109	1973	£8	£4	*with Pete Townshend*
Would You Believe	7"	Immediate	IM063	1968	£25	£12.50	*with the Small Faces*
Would You Believe	LP	Immediate	IMLP009	1967	£750	£500	

NICHOLLS, JANICE

Janice Nicholls was a regular member of the teenage panel called upon every week to mark selected new singles out of five on TV's *Thank*

Your Lucky Stars. In those innocent days, a Birmingham accent was considered a novelty on TV, and Ms Nicholls's cry of 'Oi'll give it foive' was greeted with enthusiastic applause.

Oi'll Give It Five	7"	Decca	F11586	1963	£6	**£2.50**	

NICHOLLS, SUE

Sue Nicholls achieved a minor hit with her first single release, but she is much better known these days for her role in TV's *Coronation Street*, as Audrey Roberts.

All The Way To Heaven	7"	Pye	7N17674	1969	£4	**£1.50**	
Where Will You Be	7"	Pye	7N17565	1968	£4	**£1.50**	

NICHOLS, MIKE & ELAINE MAY

Best Of Mike Nichols And Elaine May	LP	Mercury	20031MCL	1965	£10	**£4**	

NICHOLS, RED

Jazz Time	10" LP	Capitol	LC6534	1951	£20	**£8**	

NICHOLSON, LEA

Concertina Record	LP	Kicking Mule	SNKF165	1980	£10	**£4**	
Horsemusic	LP	Trailer	LER3010	1971	£20	**£8**	

NICHOLSON, ROGER

Gentle Sound Of The Dulcimer	LP	Argo	ZDA204	1974	£10	**£4**	
Times And Traditions For Dulcimer	LP	Trailer	LER2094	1976	£10	**£4**	*with Jake Walton & Andrew Cronshaw*

NICKS, STEVIE

Bella Donna	LP	Mobile Fidelity	MFSL1121	1982	£10	**£4**	*US audiophile*
Has Anyone Ever Written Anything For You?	12"	EMI	12EMI5574	1986	£8	**£4**	
I Can't Wait	12"	Parlophone	12R6110	1986	£6	**£2.50**	
I Can't Wait	CD-s	EMI	CDEM214	1991	£5	**£2**	
Leather And Lace	7"	WEA	K79265	1981	£4	**£1.50**	
Long Way To Go	12"	EMI	12EMG97	1989	£6	**£2.50**	*gatefold sleeve*
Long Way To Go	CD-s	EMI	CDEM97	1989	£5	**£2**	*3" single*
Nightbird	7"	WEA	U9690	1984	£12	**£6**	
Other Side Of The Mirror	CD	EMI	CDEMC1008	1989	£15	**£6**	*hologram cover*
Other Side Of The Mirror	LP	EMI	EMD1008	1989	£10	**£4**	*hologram sleeve*
Reflections: The Other Side Of The Mirror	CD	Modern	PR2881	1989	£20	**£8**	*US interview promo*
Rock A Little	CD	Parlophone	CZ80	1986	£12	**£5**	
Rooms On Fire	12"	EMI	12EMP90	1989	£6	**£2.50**	*poster sleeve*
Rooms On Fire (Extended)	CD-s	EMI	CDEM90	1989	£5	**£2**	
Sometimes It's A Bitch	CD-s	EMI	CDEM203	1991	£5	**£2**	
Stand Back	12"	WEA	U9870T	1983	£8	**£4**	
Talk To Me	12"	Parlophone	12R6124	1986	£6	**£2.50**	
Whole Lotta Trouble	12"	EMI	12EMP114	1989	£6	**£2.50**	*with poster*
Whole Lotta Trouble	CD-s	EMI	CDEM114	1989	£5	**£2**	

NICO

Chelsea Girl	LP	MGM	2353025	1971	£15	**£6**	
Desert Shore	LP	Reprise	RSLP6424	1971	£15	**£6**	
End	LP	Island	ILPS9311	1974	£10	**£4**	
I'm Not Saying	7"	Immediate	IM003	1965	£25	**£12.50**	
Marble Index	LP	Elektra	EKL/EKS74029	1968	£25	**£10**	
Peel Sessions	CD-s	Strange Fruit	SFPSCD064	1988	£5	**£2**	
Vegas	7"	Flicknife	FLS206	1981	£5	**£2**	

NICODEMUS

Back Street Orange	LP	Zedikiah	1070	1978	£30	**£15**	*US*

NICOL, JIMMY

Drummer Jimmy Nicol was briefly a member of the Beatles when he deputized for a sick Ringo Starr during the group's world tour in 1964. In a recent interview he declared the experience to have been the worst in his life, although this would seem to be more a reaction to the confounding of his subsequent expectations than to anything that actually happened on the tour. For, sadly, Nicol's fame was short-lived and none of the records he made afterwards was at all successful.

Baby Please Don't Go	7"	Pye	7N15699	1964	£20	**£10**	
Clementine	7"	Decca	F12107	1965	£6	**£2.50**	
Humpty Dumpty	7"	Pye	7N15623	1964	£8	**£4**	
Husky	7"	Pye	7N15666	1964	£6	**£2.50**	

NICOLL, WATT

Nice To Be Nice	LP	XTRA	XTRA1122	1971	£10	**£4**	

NICRA

Listen/Hear	LP	Ogun	OG010	1977	£15	**£6**	

NIEHAUS, LENNIE

Lennie Niehaus	10" LP	Contemporary	LDC150	1955	£40	**£20**	
Lennie Niehaus Quintet	LP	Contemporary	LDC120	1955	£40	**£20**	
Vol. 1 The Quintet	LP	Vogue	LAC12167	1960	£20	**£8**	
Vol. 3 – The Octet No. 2	LP	Contemporary	LAC12054	1957	£25	**£10**	
Vol. 5 The Sextet	LP	Contemporary	LAC12151	1959	£20	**£8**	
Zounds!	LP	Contemporary	LAC12222	1960	£20	**£8**	

NIGHT OWLS

Twisting The Oldies ... LP ... Valmor ... 79 ... 1962 £**20** ... £**8** ... *US*

NIGHT SUN

Mournin' ... LP ... Zebra ... 2949004 ... 1972 £**15** ... £**6** ... *German*

NIGHT-TIMERS

Music Played On ... 7" ... Parlophone ... R5355 ... 1965 £**15** ... £**7.50**

NIGHTBIRDS

Cat On A Hot Tin Roof ... 7" ... Oriole ... CB1490 ... 1959 £**5** ... £**2**

NIGHTBLOOMS

Crystal Eyes ... 7" ... Fierce ... FRIGHT041 ... 1990 £**6** ... £**2.50**

NIGHTCAPS

Wine Wine Wine ... LP ... Vandan ... VRLP8124 ... 1961 £**40** ... £**20** ... *US*

NIGHTCRAWLERS

Little Black Egg ... 7" ... London ... HLR10109 ... 1967 £**20** ... £**10**
Little Black Egg ... LP ... Kapp ... KL1520/KS3520 ... 1967 £**60** ... £**30** ... *US*

NIGHTHAWK, ROBERT

Robert Nighthawk ... 7" EP .. XX ... MIN718 ... 196– £**6** ... £**2.50**

NIGHTHAWKS

Rock And Roll ... LP ... Aladdin ... 101 ... 195– £**75** ... £**37.50** ... *US*

NIGHTINGALE, MAXINE

Don't Push Me Baby ... 7" ... Pye ... 7N17798 ... 1969 £**4** ... £**1.50**

NIGHTINGALES

This Package ... 12" ... Vindaloo ... VILP2X ... 1985 £**8** ... £**4**

NIGHTMARES IN WAX

Birth Of A Nation ... 7" ... Inevitable ... INEV002 ... 1979 £**12** ... £**6**
Black Leather ... 12" ... KY ... KY91/2 ... 1985 £**10** ... £**5** ... *3 tracks*
Black Leather ... 12" ... KY ... KY9 ... 1984 £**10** ... £**5** ... *2 tracks*

NIGHTRIDERS

It's Only The Dog ... 7" ... Polydor ... 56116 ... 1966 £**75** ... £**37.50**
Love Me Right Now ... 7" ... Polydor ... ... 1966 £**75** ... £**37.50** ... *demo*

NIGHTRIDERS (2)

I Saw Her With Another Guy ... 7" ... Stardust ... STR1001 ... 1979 £**10** ... £**5**

NIGHTROCKERS

Dance To The Rock ... 7" EP .. Golf Drouot ... 71014 ... 1967 £**8** ... £**4** ... *French*
I Can Tell ... 7" EP .. Golf Drouot ... 71013 ... 1967 £**8** ... £**4** ... *French*

NIGHTSHADOWS

Invasion Of The Acid Eaters ... LP ... Hottrax ... ... 1982 £**15** ... £**6** ... *US*
Live At The Spot ... LP ... Hottrax ... ST1430 ... 1981 £**15** ... £**6** ... *US*
Square Root Of Two ... LP ... Spectrum Sounds ... ... 1968 £**1000** ... £**700** ... *US*
Square Root Of Two ... LP ... Hottrax ... ST1414 ... 1978 £**30** ... £**15** ... *US*

NIGHTSHIFT

Corrine Corrina ... 7" ... Piccadilly ... 7N35243 ... 1965 £**8** ... £**4**
That's My Story ... 7" ... Piccadilly ... 7N35264 ... 1965 £**10** ... £**5**

NIGHTSHIFT (2)

Nightshift ... LP ... private ... ... 1980 £**50** ... £**25** ... *Dutch*

NIGHTTIME FLYER

Out With A Vengeance ... 7" ... Red Eye ... EYE2 ... 1981 £**12** ... £**6**

NIGHTWING

Barrel Of Pain ... 7" ... Ovation ... OVS1209 ... 1980 £**10** ... £**5**
Night Of Mystery ... 12" ... Gull ... GULS7712 ... 1984 £**6** ... £**2.50**
Night Of Mystery ... 7" ... Gull ... GULS77 ... 1984 £**4** ... £**1.50**
Something In The Air ... LP ... Ovation ... OV1757 ... 1979 £**10** ... £**4**
Stand Up And Be Counted ... LP ... Gull ... PGULP1038 ... 1983 £**10** ... £**4** ... *picture disc*

NIGHTWINGS

Grande Randonnee ... LP ... Crossroad ... ... 1981 £**100** ... £**50** ... *Dutch*

NIHILIST SPASM BAND

IX – X = X ... LP ... United Dairies ... UD016 ... 1985 £**10** ... £**4**

NILES, JOHN JACOB

Folk Balladeer ... LP ... RCA ... RD7729 ... 1965 £**12** ... £**5**

NILLY, WILLY

On The Spur Of The Moment ... 7" ... Ad Hoc ... AH1 ... 1984 £**25** ... £**12.50**

NILSSON, HARRY

Nilsson Sampler	LP	RCA	HNS1	197–	**£12**	**£5**	*promo*
Nilsson Schmilsson	CD	Mobile Fidelity	UDCD541	1990	**£15**	**£6**	*US audiophile*
Point	LP	RCA	SF8166	1971	**£10**	**£4**	
Scatalogue	LP	RCA	SP33567	1974	**£12**	**£5**	*US promo compilation*
Skidoo	LP	RCA	SF8010	1969	**£10**	**£4**	
Spotlight On Nilsson	LP	Tower	(D)T5095	1967	**£12**	**£5**	*US*

NILSSON, HARRY & JOHN LENNON

Pussy Cats	LP	RCA	APD10570	1974	**£10**	**£4**	*US quad*

NIMOY, LEONARD

Mr Spock's Music From Outer Space	LP	Dot	(S)LPD511	1967	**£25**	**£10**	
Music From Outer Space	LP	Rediffusion	ZS156	1972	**£15**	**£6**	
New World Of Leonard Nimoy	LP	Dot	DLP25966	1969	**£20**	**£8**	*US*
Outer Space/Inner Mind	LP	Paramount	1030	197–	**£25**	**£10**	*US*
Touch Of Leonard Nimoy	LP	Dot	DLP25910	1969	**£20**	**£8**	*US*
Two Sides Of Leonard Nimoy	LP	Dot	DLP25835	1968	**£20**	**£8**	*US*
Way I Feel	LP	Dot	DLP25883	1968	**£20**	**£8**	*US*

NINA

Do You Know How Christmas Trees Are Grown?	7"	CBS	4681	1970	**£8**	**£4**	

NINE DAYS WONDER

Nine Days Wonder	LP	Harvest	SHSP4014	1971	**£25**	**£10**	
Only The Dancers	LP	Bacillus	BLPS19200	1975	**£12**	**£5**	*German*
Sonnet To Billy Frost	LP	Bacillus	BLPS19234	1975	**£12**	**£5**	*German*
We Never Lost Control	LP	Bacillus	BLPS19163	1973	**£15**	**£6**	*German*

NINE INCH NAILS

Down In It	CD-s	Island	CID482	1990	**£10**	**£5**	*6 tracks*
Sin	9"	Island	9IS508	1991	**£6**	**£2.50**	

NINE NINE NINE

I'm Alive	7"	Labritian	LAB999	1977	**£5**	**£2**	
Nasty Nasty	78	United Artists	FREE7	1977	**£20**	**£10**	*promo*

NINE SENSE

Oh! For The Edge	LP	Ogun	OG900	1976	**£12**	**£5**	

NINE-THIRTY FLY

Nine-Thirty Fly	LP	Ember	NR5062	1972	**£100**	**£50**	

NINETEEN EIGHTY-FOUR

Got To Have Your Love	7"	Transatlantic	BIG120	1969	**£4**	**£1.50**	
Little Girl	7"	Decca	F23159	1971	**£4**	**£1.50**	
This Little Boy	7"	Transatlantic	BIG117	1969	**£4**	**£1.50**	

NINETEEN-TEN FRUITGUM CO.

Goody Goody Gumdrops	LP	Buddah	203014	1969	**£10**	**£4**	
Hard Ride	LP	Buddah	2359006	1970	**£10**	**£4**	
Simon Says	LP	Pye	N(S)PL28115	1968	**£10**	**£4**	

NINEY

Blood And Fire	7"	Big Shot	BI568	1971	**£4**	**£1.50**	
Honey No Money	7"	Pressure Beat	PR5501	1970	**£5**	**£2**	*Inspirations B side*
Niney Special	7"	Amalgamated	AMG856	1970	**£5**	**£2**	
You Must Believe	7"	Big	BG317	1971	**£5**	**£2**	

NING

Machine	7"	Decca	F23114	1971	**£4**	**£1.50**	

NINO & THE EBBTIDES

Those Oldies But Goodies	7"	Top Rank	JAR572	1961	**£25**	**£12.50**	

NINTH CREATION

Bubble Gum	LP	Rite Track	RKA01M	1969	**£20**	**£8**	*US*

NIPPLE ERECTORS

The Pogues' Shane MacGowan began his recording career with the punk Nipple Erectors, later abbreviated to the less controversial Nips.

King Of The Bop	7"	Soho	SH1	1978	**£8**	**£4**	*matt picture sleeve*
King Of The Bop	7"	Soho	SH1	1978	**£15**	**£7.50**	*glossy picture sleeve*

NIPS

All The Time In The World	7"	Soho	SH4	1978	**£15**	**£7.50**	
Gabrielle	7"	Soho	SH9	1979	**£5**	**£2**	
Gabrielle	7"	Soho	SH9	1980	**£20**	**£10**	*'licensed to cool' stamp*
Gabrielle	7"	Chiswick	CHIS119	1979	**£6**	**£2.50**	
Happy Song	7"	Burning Rome	TP5	1981	**£10**	**£5**	
Only At The End Of The Beginning	LP	Soho	HOHO1	1980	**£20**	**£8**	

NIRVANA

The original Nirvana had long since ceased recording when Kurt Cobain arrived on the scene with a band of the same name, but it was clearly very much in Patrick Campbell-Lyons's interest to claim copyright infringement. He received an out-of-court financial settlement, although there is little possibility of confusion between the adventurous psychedelic pop of Campbell-Lyons's band and the agonized guitar mayhem of the American newcomers.

Title	Format	Label	Number	Year	Mint	VG	Notes
All Of Us	7"	Island	WIP6045	1968	£6	£2.50	
All Of Us	LP	Island	ILP987/ILPS9087	1968	£40	£20	pink label
Dedicated To Markos III	LP	Pye	NSPL28132	1970	£50	£25	
Girl In The Park	7"	Island	WIP6038	1968	£6	£2.50	
Local Anaesthetic	LP	Vertigo	6360031	1971	£30	£15	spiral label
Nirvana	LP	Metromedia	1018	1970	£30	£15	US
Oh! What A Performance	7"	Island	WIP6057	1969	£6	£2.50	
Pentecost Hotel	7"	Island	WIP6020	1967	£6	£2.50	
Pentecost Hotel	7"	Philips	6006127	1971	£4	£1.50	
Pentecost Hotel	7" EP	Fontana	460236	1967	£20	£10	French
Rainbow Chaser	7"	Philips	6006129	1972	£4	£1.50	
Rainbow Chaser	7"	Island	WIP6029	1968	£6	£2.50	
Saddest Day Of My Life	7"	Vertigo	6059035	1970	£6	£2.50	
Songs Of Love And Praise	LP	Philips	6308089	1972	£40	£20	
Stadium	7"	Philips	6006166	1972	£4	£1.50	
The Story Of Simon Simopath	LP	Island	ILP959/ILPS9059	1967	£40	£20	pink label
Tiny Goddess	7"	Island	WIP6016	1967	£8	£4	
Wings Of Love	7"	Island	WIP6052	1968	£6	£2.50	
World Is Cold Without You	7"	Pye	7N25525	1970	£8	£4	

NIRVANA (2)

Although his approach to music was not very similar, Kurt Cobain became a Jimi Hendrix for the nineties rock generation when he chose the ultimate escape from the unwelcome pressures of stardom. It may well be the case that Nirvana had already passed their best – but sadly, we shall never know. It remains the case, however, that *Nevermind* seems more like one of the all-time classic rock albums with every month that passes.

Title	Format	Label	Number	Year	Mint	VG	Notes
Bleach	CD	Tupelo	TUPCD6	1989	£15	£6	with Love Buzz & Downer
Bleach	LP	Tupelo	TUPLP6	1989	£200	£100	white vinyl
Bleach	LP	Sub Pop	SP34	1989	£40	£20	US, white vinyl
Bleach	LP	Sub Pop	SP34	1989	£15	£6	US, with poster
Bleach	LP	Tupelo	TUPLP6	1989	£60	£30	green vinyl
Blew	12"	Tupelo	TUPEP8	1989	£30	£15	
Blew	CD-s	Tupelo	TUPCD8	1989	£30	£15	
Come As You Are	12"	Geffen	DGCTP7	1992	£12	£6	picture disc
Come As You Are	CD-s	MCA	DGCTD7	1992	£5	£2	
Grunge Is Dead	CD-s	Geffen		199–	£75	£37.50	12" boxed set – 6 CD singles, T-shirt, poster, photo
Hormoaning	LP	Geffen	GEF21711	1991	£20	£8	burgundy vinyl
In Bloom	12"	Geffen	GFSTP34	1992	£10	£5	picture disc
In Bloom	CD-s	BMG	GFSTD34	1992	£5	£2	
In Utero	LP	Geffen	GEF24536	1993	£15	£6	clear vinyl
Lithium	12"	Geffen	DGCTP9	1992	£10	£5	picture disc
Love Buzz	7"	Sub Pop	SP23	1988	£100	£50	US, 'Guitars' matrix message
Molly's Lips	7"	Sub Pop	SP97	1991	£20	£10	US, black vinyl
Molly's Lips	7"	Sub Pop	SP97	1991	£30	£15	US, green vinyl
Nevermind It's An Interview	CD	DGC	PROCD4382	1991	£25	£10	US promo
Oh, The Guilt	CD-s	Touch & Go	TG83CD	1993	£10	£5	with track by Jesus Lizard
Oh, The Guilt	7"	Touch & Go	TG83	1993	£6	£2.50	blue vinyl
Oh, The Guilt	7"	Touch & Go	TG83	1993	£12	£6	blue vinyl, with poster
Penny Royal Tea	7"	Geffen	no number	1994	£750	£500	test pressing, best auctioned
Penny Royal Tea	CD-s	Geffen	no number	1994	£750	£500	promo, best auctioned
Sliver	12"	Tupelo	TUPEP25	1991	£25	£12.50	blue vinyl
Sliver	12"	Tupelo	TUPEP25	1991	£8	£4	
Sliver	7"	Sub Pop	SP73	1990	£15	£7.50	US, blue vinyl, foldover picture sleeve
Sliver	7"	Tupelo	TUP25	1991	£15	£7.50	green vinyl
Sliver	CD-s	Tupelo	TUPCD25	1991	£5	£2	
Smells Like Teen Spirit	12"	Geffen	DGCTP5	1991	£12	£6	picture disc
Smells Like Teen Spirit	CD-s	Geffen	DGCTD5	1991	£6	£2.50	

NITE-LITERS

Title	Format	Label	Number	Year	Mint	VG	Notes
Instrumental Directions	LP	RCA	SF8282	1972	£10	£4	

NITE PEOPLE

Title	Format	Label	Number	Year	Mint	VG	Notes
Is This A Dream	7"	Page One	POF159	1969	£5	£2	
Love, Love, Love	7"	Page One	POF149	1969	£8	£4	with insert
Morning Sun	7"	Fontana	TF919	1968	£8	£4	
P.M.	LP	Page One	POLS025	1969	£200	£100	
Season Of The Rain	7"	Page One	POF174	1970	£5	£2	
Summertime Blues	7"	Fontana	TF885	1967	£25	£12.50	
Sweet Tasting Wine	7"	Fontana	TF747	1966	£6	£2.50	
Trying To Find Another Man	7"	Fontana	TF808	1967	£5	£2	

NITE ROCKERS

Title	Format	Label	Number	Year	Mint	VG	Notes
Ooh Baby	7"	RCA	RCA1079	1958	£60	£30	

NITESHADES

Title	Format	Label	Cat. No.	Year	Mint	VG	Notes
Be My Guest	7"	CBS	201763	1965	£4	£1.50	
Fell So Fast	7"	CBS	201817	1965	£4	£1.50	

NITTY GRITTY DIRT BAND

Title	Format	Label	Cat. No.	Year	Mint	VG	Notes
Alive	LP	Liberty	LST7615	1969	£12	£5	*US*
Buy For My The Rain	7" EP	Liberty	LEP2279	1967	£15	£7.50	*French*
Dead And Alive	LP	Liberty	LBS83286	1969	£12	£5	
Nitty Gritty Dirt Band	LP	Liberty	LRP3501/ LST7501	1967	£12	£5	*US*
Pure Dirt	LP	Liberty	LBL/LBS83122	1968	£12	£5	
Rare Junk	LP	Liberty	LST7611	1967	£12	£5	*US*
Ricochet	LP	Liberty	LRP3516/ LST7516	1967	£12	£5	*US*
Will The Circle Be Unbroken	LP	United Artists	UAS9801	1973	£25	£10	*US triple*

NITZER EBB

Title	Format	Label	Cat. No.	Year	Mint	VG	Notes
Isn't It Funny How Your Body Works	12"	Power Of Voice	NEP1	1985	£6	£2.50	
Warsaw Ghetto	12"	Power Of Voice Communications	NEP/NEBX2	1986	£10	£4	*double*

NITZSCHE, JACK

Jack Nitzsche was Phil Spector's arranger during the sixties and, hence, due to as much credit as Spector himself for the invention of the 'wall of sound' that is so characteristic of Spector's productions. Nitzsche made a number of instrumental records in a series of attempts to take advantage of contemporary music fads, but his masterpiece is *St Giles Cripplegate*, recorded in 1972. This is a suite of short pieces scored for a small group of strings and is essentially a classical work made contemporary by its use of acid harmonies.

Title	Format	Label	Cat. No.	Year	Mint	VG	Notes
Chopin '66	LP	Reprise	R(S)6200	1966	£15	£6	*US*
Hits Of The Beatles	LP	Reprise	R(S)6115	1964	£20	£8	*US*
Lonely Surfer	7"	Reprise	R20202	1963	£6	£2.50	
Lonely Surfer	7" EP	Reprise	RVEP60036	1963	£20	£10	*French*
Lonely Surfer	LP	Reprise	R(S)6101	1963	£25	£10	*US*
Night Walker	7"	Reprise	R20337	1964	£4	£1.50	
St Giles Cripplegate	LP	Reprise	K41211	1972	£12	£5	

NIVENS

Title	Format	Label	Cat. No.	Year	Mint	VG	Notes
Let Loose Of My Knee	7"	Woosh	WOOSH1	1988	£5	£2	*flexi, B side by Holidaymakers*

NIX NOMADS

Title	Format	Label	Cat. No.	Year	Mint	VG	Notes
You're Nobody Till Somebody Loves You	7"	HMV	POP1354	1964	£60	£30	

N-JOI

Title	Format	Label	Cat. No.	Year	Mint	VG	Notes
Anthem	12"	DeConstruction	PT44042	1990	£10	£5	

NO DOUBT

Title	Format	Label	Cat. No.	Year	Mint	VG	Notes
Don't Speak	7"	Interscope	INSJB95515	1997	£5	£2	*jukebox issue*
Just A Girl	7"	Interscope	INSJB95539	1997	£5	£2	*jukebox issue*

NO INTRODUCTION

Title	Format	Label	Cat. No.	Year	Mint	VG	Notes
No Introduction	LP	Spark		1968	£20	£8	

NO MAN

Title	Format	Label	Cat. No.	Year	Mint	VG	Notes
Colours	12"	Probe Plus	PP27T	1990	£8	£4	
Colours	7"	Hidden Art	HA4	1990	£8	£4	
Girl From Missouri	12"	Plastic Head	PLASS012	1989	£6	£2.50	

NO OTHER NAME

Title	Format	Label	Cat. No.	Year	Mint	VG	Notes
Death Into Life	LP	Daylight	LD500	1979	£20	£8	

NO QUARTER

Title	Format	Label	Cat. No.	Year	Mint	VG	Notes
Survivors	12"	Reel	REEL1	1983	£25	£12.50	

NO RIGHT TURN

Title	Format	Label	Cat. No.	Year	Mint	VG	Notes
No	LP	Chelful	CHL001	1983	£20	£8	

NOAKES, RAB

Title	Format	Label	Cat. No.	Year	Mint	VG	Notes
Do You See The Light	LP	Decca	SKL5061	1970	£15	£6	
Never Too Late	LP	Warner Bros	K56114	1975	£10	£4	
Rab Noakes	LP	A&M	AMLS68119	1972	£10	£4	
Red Pump Special	LP	Warner Bros	K46284	1974	£10	£4	
Restless	LP	Ring O	2339201	1978	£10	£4	
Waiting Here For You	7"	Ring O	2017115	1978	£5	£2	*picture sleeve*

NOBLE, PATSY ANN

Title	Format	Label	Cat. No.	Year	Mint	VG	Notes
Accidents Will Happen	7"	Columbia	DB7088	1963	£6	£2.50	
Don't You Ever Change Your Mind	7"	Columbia	DB4956	1963	£4	£1.50	
Good Looking Boy	7"	HMV	POP980	1961	£6	£2.50	
He Who Rides A Tiger	7"	Polydor	BM56054	1965	£6	£2.50	
Heartbreak Avenue	7"	Columbia	DB7008	1963	£4	£1.50	
I Did Nothing Wrong	7"	Columbia	DB7258	1964	£4	£1.50	
I Was Only Foolin' Myself	7"	Columbia	DB7060	1963	£4	£1.50	
It's Better To Cry Today	7"	Columbia	DB7148	1963	£4	£1.50	
Private Property	7"	Columbia	DB7318	1964	£4	£1.50	

Then You Can Tell Me Goodbye	7"	Columbia	DB7472	1965	£4	£1.50	
Tied Up With Mary	7"	Columbia	DB7386	1964	£4	£1.50	

NOBLE, STEVE & ALEX MAGUIRE

Live At Oscar's	LP	Incus	INCUS52	1986	£12	£5	

NOBLE, TRISHA

Live For Life	7"	MGM	MGM1371	1967	£4	£1.50	

NOBLEMEN

Thunder Wagon	7"	Top Rank	JAR155	1959	£8	£4	

NOBLES, CLIFF

Horse	LP	Direction	863477	1969	£10	£4	

NOCTURNAL EMISSIONS

Befehlsnotstand	LP	Sterile	SR5	1984	£40	£20	
Beyond Logic	LP	Earthly Delights	EARTH05	1989	£10	£4	
Chaos – Live At The Ritzy	LP	CFC	LP2	1984	£40	£20	
Drowning In A Sea Of Bliss	LP	Sterile	SR4	1984	£50	£25	
Fruiting Body	LP	Sterile	ION2	1984	£40	£20	
Mouth Of The Babes	LP	Earthly Delights	EARTH06	1990	£10	£4	
No Sacrifice	12"	Sterile	SR6	1984	£10	£5	
Shake Those Chains, Rattle Those Cages	LP	Sterile	SR9	1986	£10	£4	
Songs Of Love And Revolution	LP	Sterile	SR7	1985	£15	£6	
Spiritflesh	LP	Earthly Delights	EARTH04	1988	£20	£8	
Tissue Of Lies	LP	Sterile	EMISS001	1984	£60	£30	*numbered*
Tissue Of Lies	LP	Sterile	EMISS001	1984	£30	£15	
Viral Shedding	LP	Illuminated	JAMSLP33	1984	£15	£6	
World Is My Womb	LP	Earthly Delights	EARTH02	1987	£15	£6	

NOCTURNES

Troilka	7"	Solar	SRP102	1964	£10	£5	

NOCTURNES (2)

Nocturnes	LP	Columbia	SX/SCX6223	1968	£10	£4	
Wanted Alive	LP	Columbia	SX/SCX6315	1968	£12	£5	

NOCTURNS

Carrying On	7"	Decca	F12002	1964	£4	£1.50	

NOEL, DICK

Birds And The Bees	7"	London	HLH8295	1956	£15	£7.50	

NOIR

We Had To Let You Have It	LP	Dawn	DNLS3029	1971	£15	£6	

NOLAN SISTERS

Blackpool	7"	Nevis	NEVS007	1972	£10	£5	
But I Do	7"	EMI	EMI2209	1974	£8	£4	
Medley	7"	Target	SAM84	1978	£5	£2	*promo*
Nolan Sisters	LP	Hanover Grand	HG19751	1977	£25	£10	
Silent Night	7" EP	Nevis	NEVEP005	1972	£5	£2	
Singing Nolans	LP	Nevis	NEVR009	1972	£15	£6	

NOLAND, TERRY

Oh Baby Look At Me	7"	Coral	Q72311	1958	£100	£50	
Terry Noland	LP	Brunswick	BL54041	1958	£150	£75	*US*

NOMADI

Interpretano	LP	Columbia	06417990	1974	£10	£4	*Italian*

NON

Mode Of Infection	7"	Non	MR00	1978	£60	£30	*any speed, 2 holes!*

NOONE, JIMMY

Jimmy Noone Orchestra	10" LP	Vogue Coral	LRA10026	1955	£12	£5	

NORDINE, KEN

Classic Collection	LP	Dot	DLP25880	1968	£15	£6	*US*
Colors	LP	Philips	2/600224	196–	£15	£6	*US*
Concert In The Sky	LP	Decca	DL8550	1957	£25	£10	*US*
Ken Nordine Reads	7" EP	London	RED1091	1957	£20	£10	
Love Words	LP	Dot	DLP3115/ DLP25115	1958	£15	£6	*US*
My Baby	LP	Dot	DLP3142/ DLP25142	1958	£15	£6	*US*
Next!	LP	Dot	DLP3196/ DLP25196	1959	£15	£6	*US*
Shifting Whispering Sands	7"	London	HLD8205	1955	£10	£5	*gold label*
Ship That Never Sailed	7"	London	HLD8417	1957	£4	£1.50	
Son Of Word Jazz	LP	London	LTZD15145	1959	£20	£8	
Twink	LP	Philips	2/600258	196–	£15	£6	*US*

Word Jazz	7" EP	London	EZD19040	1959	£12	£6	
Word Jazz	LP	London	LTZD15131	1958	£25	£10	
Word Jazz Vol. 2	LP	Dot	DLP3301/25301	1960	£20	£8	US

NORFOLK & JOY

Scotsounds	LP	Dara	MPA031	1979	£25	£10	

NORMAN, LARRY

So Long Ago/The Garden	LP	MGM	SE4942	1973	£12	£5	US
Upon This Rock	LP	Key	DOVE6	1969	£10	£4	

NORMAN, MONTY

Dr No	7" EP	United Artists	UEP1010	1965	£15	£7.50	
Dr No	LP	United Artists	SULP1097	1965	£15	£6	
Dr No	LP	United Artists	ULP1097	1965	£12	£5	*mono*
Garden Of Eden	7"	HMV	POP281	1957	£5	£2	

NORMAN, OLIVER

Down In The Basement	7"	Polydor	56176	1967	£6	£2.50	

NORMAN & THE HOOLIGANS

I'm A Punk	7"	President	PT461	1977	£8	£4	

NORMAN & THE INVADERS

Night Train To Surbiton	7"	United Artists	UP1077	1965	£8	£4	
Stacey	7"	United Artists	UP1031	1964	£4	£1.50	

NORMAN CONQUEST

Two People	7"	MGM	MGM1376	1968	£50	£25	

NORTH, FREDDIE

Friend	LP	Mojo	2916012	1972	£10	£4	

NORTH, ROY

Blues In Three	7"	Oak	RGJ107	1963	£25	£12.50	

NORTH STARS

She's So Far Out She's In	7"	Fontana	TF726	1966	£8	£4	

NORTHERN LIGHTS

The singles credited to Northern Lights were actually by the Hootenanny Singers and are therefore of considerable interest to Abba collectors.

No Time	7"	United Artists	UP1123	1966	£20	£10	
Through Darkness Light	7"	United Artists	UP1161	1966	£20	£10	

NORTHWIND

Sister Brother Lover	LP	Regal Zonophone	SLRZ1020	1971	£150	£75	

NORVO, RED

Ad Lib	LP	London	LTZD15116	1958	£12	£5	
Hi-Five	LP	RCA	RD27013	1957	£12	£5	
Move!	LP	Realm	RM158	1963	£12	£5	
Red Norvo	10" LP	London	LZU14039	1957	£25	£10	
Red Norvo All Stars	LP	Philips	BBL7077	1956	£20	£8	
Red Norvo Nine	10" LP	Vogue	LDE061	1954	£40	£20	
Red Norvo Trio	10" LP	Brunswick	LA8718	1955	£40	£20	
Red Norvo Trio	10" LP	Vogue	LDE115	1955	£40	£20	
Windjammer City Style	LP	London	HAD2134	1958	£10	£4	

NOSEY PARKER

Nosey Parker	LP	private		1975	£200	£100	US

NOSFERATU

Nosferatu	LP	Vogue	LDVS17178	1970	£200	£100	*German*

NOSMO

Goodbye (Nothing To Say)	7"	Pye	7N45383	1974	£5	£2	

NOSTRADAMUS

Nostradamus	LP	Zodiac		1972	£200	£100	*Greek*

NOTATIONS

Need Your Love	7"	Chapter One	SCH174	1974	£20	£10	

NOTATIONS (2)

Notations	LP	Curtom	K56212	1976	£20	£8	

NOTES, FREDDIE & THE RUDIES

Montego Bay	7"	Trojan	TR7791	1970	£4	£1.50	
Montego Bay	LP	Trojan	TBL152	1970	£15	£6	
Unity	LP	Trojan	TBL109	1970	£15	£6	

NOTHINGS

At Times Like This	7"	CBS	201779	1965	£4	£1.50	

NOTSENSIBLES

Death To Disco ...... 7" ...... Bent ...... SMALLBENT5 ...... 1980 £4 ...... £1.50
Instant Classics ...... LP ...... Bent/Snotty Snail ...... SSLP1 ...... 1980 £12 ...... £5
Margaret Thatcher ...... 7" ...... Redball ...... RR021 ...... 1979 £5 ...... £2

NOTTING HILLBILLIES

Feel Like Going Home ...... CD-s ... Vertigo ...... NHBCD2 ...... 1990 £5 ...... £2
Will You Miss Me ...... CD-s ... Vertigo ...... NHBCD3 ...... 1990 £5 ...... £2
Your Own Sweet Way ...... CD-s ... Vertigo ...... NHBCD1 ...... 1990 £5 ...... £2

NOTTS ALLIANCE

Cheerful 'Orn ...... LP ...... Tradition ...... TSR011 ...... 1972 £10 ...... £4

NOVA LOCAL

Nova 1 ...... LP ...... MCA ...... MUPS377 ...... 1968 £30 ...... £15

NOVAC

Novac ...... LP ...... Hör Zu ...... SHZE804 ...... 1970 £20 ...... £8 ...... *German*

NOVAK

Silver Seas ...... 7" ...... Enraptured ...... WORM2 ...... 1997 £20 ...... £10 ...... *cloth sleeve*

NOVALIS

Banished Bridge ...... LP ...... Brain ...... 1029 ...... 1973 £15 ...... £6 ...... *German*
Novalis ...... LP ...... Brain ...... 1070 ...... 1975 £12 ...... £5 ...... *German*
Sommerabend ...... LP ...... Brain ...... 1087 ...... 1976 £12 ...... £5 ...... *German*

NOVAS

Push A Little Harder ...... 7" ...... RCA ...... RCA1360 ...... 1963 £5 ...... £2

NOVAS (2)

Crusher ...... 7" ...... London ...... HLU9940 ...... 1965 £20 ...... £10

NOVELLS

Happening (That Did It) ...... LP ...... Mothers ...... MRS73 ...... 1968 £30 ...... £15 ...... *US*

NOVEMBER

16 E November ...... LP ...... Sonet ...... SLP2530 ...... 1972 £15 ...... £6 ...... *Swedish*
En Hy Tid Ar Nar ...... LP ...... Sonet ...... SLP2509 ...... 1970 £15 ...... £6 ...... *Swedish*
Zia ...... LP ...... Sonet ...... SLP2520 ...... 1971 £30 ...... £15 ...... *Swedish*

NOW

Development Corporations ...... 7" ...... Ultimate ...... ULT401 ...... 1978 £20 ...... £10 ...... *blue vinyl, picture sleeve*
Development Corporations ...... 7" ...... Ultimate ...... ULT401 ...... 1978 £12 ...... £6
Into The 1980's ...... 7" ...... Raw ...... RAW31 ...... 1979 £20 ...... £10

NOW (2)

Marcia ...... 7" ...... NEMS ...... 564125 ...... 1969 £5 ...... £2

NOWY, RALF

Escalation ...... LP ...... Atlantic ...... K40556 ...... 1974 £10 ...... £4 ...... *German*
Lucifer's Dream ...... LP ...... Intercord ...... 260158 ...... 1973 £12 ...... £5 ...... *German*
Nowy 2 ...... LP ...... Atlantic ...... ATL50205 ...... 1975 £10 ...... £4 ...... *German*

NOYES BROTHERS

Sheep From Goats ...... LP ...... Object Music ... OBJ009/10 ...... 1980 £15 ...... £6

NOYS OF US

He's Alright Jill ...... 7" ...... KRS ...... KRS502 ...... 196– £25 .... £12.50

NRBQ

NRBQ ...... LP ...... CBS ...... 63653 ...... 1969 £10 ...... £4

NSU

Turn On Or Turn Me Down ...... LP ...... Stable ...... SLE8002 ...... 1969 £100 ...... £50

NU NOTES

Hall Of Mirrors ...... 7" ...... HMV ...... POP1232 ...... 1963 £25 .... £12.50
Kathy ...... 7" ...... HMV ...... POP1311 ...... 1964 £6 ...... £2.50

NU TORNADOS

Philadelphia USA ...... 7" ...... London ...... HLU8756 ...... 1958 £10 ...... £5

NUBBIT, GUITAR

Georgia Chain Gang ...... 7" ...... Bootleg ...... 501 ...... 1964 £25 .... £12.50
Guitar Nubbit ...... 7" EP .. XX ...... MIN705 ...... 196– £6 ...... £2.50

NUCLEAR SOCKETTS

Honour Before Glory ...... 7" ...... Subversive ...... SUB001 ...... 1981 £5 ...... £2
Play Loud ...... 7" ...... Subversive ...... SUB002 ...... 1981 £5 ...... £2

NUCLEUS

Alley Cat ...... LP ...... Vertigo ...... 6360 124 ...... 1977 £12 ...... £5
Awakening ...... LP ...... Mood ...... 24000 ...... 1980 £20 ...... £8
Belladonna ...... LP ...... Vertigo ...... 6360076 ...... 1972 £40 ...... £20 ...... *spiral label*

Title	Format	Label	Cat. No.	Year	Mint	VG	Notes
Belladonna	LP	Vertigo	6360076	1973	£12	£5	
Elastic Rock	LP	Vertigo	6360008	1970	£25	£10	spiral label
Elastic Rock	LP	Vertigo	6360008	1973	£10	£4	
Labyrinth	LP	Vertigo	6360091	1973	£12	£5	
Roots	LP	Vertigo	6360100	1973	£12	£5	
Snake Hips Etcetera	LP	Vertigo	6360119	1975	£12	£5	
Solar Plexus	LP	Vertigo	6360039	1971	£25	£10	spiral label
Solar Plexus	LP	Vertigo	6360039	1973	£10	£4	
Under The Sun	LP	Vertigo	6360 110	1974	£12	£5	
We'll Talk About It Later	LP	Vertigo	6360027	1970	£30	£15	spiral label
We'll Talk About It Later	LP	Vertigo	6360027	1973	£10	£4	

NUCLEUS (2)

Title	Format	Label	Cat. No.	Year	Mint	VG	Notes
Nucleus	LP	Mainstream	6120	1967	£60	£30	US

NUGENT, TED

Title	Format	Label	Cat. No.	Year	Mint	VG	Notes
State Of Shock	LP	Epic	AS99607	1979	£10	£4	US picture disc

NUGGETS

Title	Format	Label	Cat. No.	Year	Mint	VG	Notes
Quirl Up In My Arms	7"	Capitol	CL14216	1955	£12	£6	
Shtiggy Boom	7"	Capitol	CL14267	1955	£10	£5	

NUMAN, GARY

Title	Format	Label	Cat. No.	Year	Mint	VG	Notes
America	7"	IRS	ILPD1004	1988	£15	£7.50	picture disc, Gary on both sides
America	CD-s	IRS	ILSCD1004	1988	£8	£4	
Berserker	CD	Numa	NUMACD1001	1991	£25	£10	fan club issue
Cars	12"	Intercord	INT126502	1979	£12	£6	German
Cars	12"	Beggars Banquet	BEG264T	1993	£8	£4	promo
Cars	7"	Beggars Banquet	BEG23	1979	£5	£2	dark red vinyl
Cars ('93 Sprint)	7"	Beggars Banquet	BEG264L	1993	£6	£2.50	shaped picture disc
Cars ('93 Sprint)	CD-s	Beggars Banquet	BEG264CD	1993	£8	£4	
Cars (E Reg Model)	7"	Beggars Banquet	BEG199P	1987	£4	£1.50	picture disc
Emotion	CD-s	Numa	NUCD22	1991	£5	£2	
Fury	CD	Numa	CDNUMA1003	1986	£30	£15	
Fury	LP	Numa	NUMAP1003	1986	£25	£10	picture disc, Your Fascination picture
Ghost	LP	Numa	NUMAD1007	1987	£15	£6	double
Heart	CD-s	IRS	NUMANCD1	1991	£5	£2	
I Can't Stop	7"	Numa	NUP17	1986	£5	£2	shaped picture disc
I Die, You Die	7"	Beggars Banquet	BEG46	1980	£5	£2	dark red vinyl
I Die, You Die	7"	Beggars Banquet	BEG46A1	1980	£15	£7.50	test pressing, different mix
Images Five And Six	LP	Fan Club	GNFCDA3	1987	£15	£6	double
Images Nine And Ten	LP	Fan Club	GNFCDA5	1989	£15	£6	double
Images One And Two	LP	Fan Club	GNFCDA1	1986	£20	£8	double
Images Seven And Eight	LP	Fan Club	GNFCDA4	1987	£15	£6	double
Images Three And Four	LP	Fan Club	GNFCDA2	1987	£20	£8	double
Live EP	12"	Numa	NUM7	1985	£50	£25	multicoloured vinyl
Live EP	7"	Numa	NU7	1985	£6	£2.50	blue or white vinyl
Machine And Soul	7"	Numa	NU24DJ	1992	£4	£1.50	fan club issue
Machine And Soul	CD	Numa	NUMACDX1009	1993	£15	£6	9 tracks
Metal Rhythm	CD	IRS	EIRSACD1021	1989	£25	£10	
Metal Rhythm	CD	IRS	ILPCD035	1988	£25	£10	
Metal Rhythm	LP	IRS	ILPX035	1988	£10	£4	picture disc
New Anger	CD-s	IRS	ILSCD1003	1988	£10	£5	
Peel Sessions	CD-s	Strange Fruit	SFPMACD202	1989	£5	£2	
Photograph	LP	Intercord	INT146606	1981	£60	£30	German
Plan	LP	Beggars Banquet	BEGA55P	1985	£10	£4	picture disc
Question Of Faith	7"	Numa	NU26	1992	£10	£5	fan club issue
Remember I Was Vapour	12"	Intercord	INT126600	1980	£10	£5	German
Selection	CD-s	Beggars Banquet	BBP5CD	1989	£5	£2	
Skin Mechanic – Live	CD	IRS	EIRSACD1019	1989	£15	£6	
Strange Charm	CD	Numa	CDNUMA1005	1986	£30	£15	
Telekon	LP	Beggars Banquet	BEGA19	1980	£12	£5	green vinyl
Telekon	LP	Beggars Banquet	BEGA19	1980	£20	£8	red, yellow, blue, or orange vinyl
Telekon	LP	Beggars Banquet	BEGA19	1980	£40	£20	clear or white vinyl
This Is Love	12"	Numa	NUMX16	1986	£8	£4	double
This Is My Life	7"	Beggars Banquet	TUB1	1984	£40	£20	test pressing
Warriors	7"	Beggars Banquet	BEG95P	1983	£15	£7.50	shaped picture disc
We Are Glass	7"	Beggars Banquet	BEG35	1980	£5	£2	dark red vinyl
Your Fascination	12"	Numa	NUMP9	1985	£6	£2.50	picture disc

Your Fascination	7"	Numa	NUP9	1985	**£4**	**£1.50**	*picture disc*

NUMBER NINE BREAD STREET

Number Nine Bread Street	LP	Holyground	HG112	1967	**£350**	**£210**	

NURSE WITH WOUND

150 Murderous Passions	CD	United Dairies	UD09CD	1991	**£20**	**£8**	
150 Murderous Passions	LP	United Dairies	UD09	1991	**£15**	**£6**	
Alas The Madonna Does Not Function	12"	United Dairies	UD027	1986	**£15**	**£7.50**	
Alien	7"	World Serpent	WS7004	1993	**£15**	**£7.50**	
Automating Vol. 1	LP	United Dairies	UD019	1986	**£15**	**£6**	
Automating Vol. 2	LP	United Dairies	UD030	1989	**£15**	**£6**	
Burial Of The Stoned Sardine	7"	Harbinger	001	1990	**£8**	**£4**	*Current 93 B side*
Chance Meeting On A Dissecting Table . . .	LP	United Dairies	UD1	1979	**£75**	**£37.50**	
Cooloorta Moon	12"	Idle Hole	MIRROR003	1988	**£12**	**£6**	
Crank	7"	Wisewound	WW01	1987	**£15**	**£7.50**	*B side by Termite Queen*
Creakiness	LP	United Dairies	UD038	1991	**£15**	**£6**	
Drunk With The Old Man Of The Mountains	LP	United Dairies	UD025	1987	**£60**	**£30**	
Faith's Favourites	12"	Yankhi	YANKHI02	1988	**£15**	**£7.50**	*B side by Current 93*
Homotopy To Marie	LP	United Dairies	UD013	1985	**£25**	**£10**	
Insect And Individual Silenced	LP	United Dairies	UD08	1981	**£40**	**£20**	
Merzbild Schwet	LP	United Dairies	UD04	1980	**£60**	**£30**	
Missing Sense	LP	United Dairies	UD020	1986	**£15**	**£6**	*B side by Organum*
Ostranenie 1913	LP	Third Mind	YMR03	1984	**£25**	**£10**	
Presents The Sisters Of Pataphysics	LP	Idle Hole	MIRRORTWO	1989	**£15**	**£6**	
Sinister Senile	7"	Shock	SX004	1990	**£15**	**£7.50**	
Soliloquy For Lilith	LP	Idle Hole	MIRRORONE	1988	**£40**	**£20**	*3 LPs, boxed*
Soliloquy For Lilith Parts 5–6	LP	Idle Hole	MIRROR1C	1988	**£15**	**£6**	
Soresucker	12"	United Dairies	UD031	1990	**£10**	**£5**	
Soresucker	CD-s	United Dairies	UD031CD	1990	**£5**	**£2**	
Spiral Insana	LP	Torso	33016	1986	**£10**	**£4**	*Dutch*
Steel Dream March Of The Metal Men	7"	Clawfist	12	1992	**£8**	**£4**	
Sucked Orange	LP	United Dairies	UD032	1989	**£15**	**£6**	*colour insert*
To The Quiet Man From A Tiny Girl	LP	United Dairies	UD03	1980	**£60**	**£30**	

NUTHIN' FANCY

Looking For A Good Time	7"	Dynamic Cat	DC1001	198–	**£100**	**£50**	

NUTRONS

Very Best Things	7"	Melodisc	1593	1964	**£10**	**£5**	

NUTTER, MAY'F

Head Shrinker	7"	Vocalion	VP9282	1966	**£5**	**£2**	

NUTTY SQUIRRELS

Uh! Oh!	7"	Pye	7N25044	1959	**£4**	**£1.50**	

NYAH EARTH

Dual Heat	7"	Attack	ATT8017	1970	**£5**	**£2**	
Nyah Bingy	7"	Attack	ATT8016	1970	**£5**	**£2**	

NYL

Nyl	LP	Urus	000013	1976	**£12**	**£5**	*French*

NYMAN, MICHAEL

Decay Music	LP	Obscure	OBS6	1976	**£12**	**£5**	

NYRO, LAURA

Laura Nyro was a singer-songwriter with soul – and it is that quality that makes her records so distinctive. The trilogy begun by *Eli And The Thirteenth Confession* represents her best work, with *Eli* perhaps having the edge. Any album that can take the listener from the bleakest despair ('Poverty Train'), through the wistfully romantic ('Emmie'), to uplifting joy ('Eli's Comin' ') can only be described as special.

Christmas & The Beads Of Sweat	LP	CBS	64157	1970	**£10**	**£4**	
Eli & The Thirteenth Confession	LP	CBS	63346	1968	**£12**	**£5**	
First Songs	LP	Verve	SVLP6022	1969	**£15**	**£6**	
First Songs	LP	CBS	64991	1973	**£10**	**£4**	
Gonna Take A Miracle	LP	CBS	64770	1971	**£10**	**£4**	
More Than A New Discovery	LP	Verve	FTS3020	1966	**£20**	**£8**	*US*
New York Tendaberry	LP	CBS	63510	1969	**£10**	**£4**	

O

O LEVEL

East Sheen	7"	Psycho	PSYCHO1	1978	**£15**	**£7.50**	*2 picture sleeves*
Malcolm McLaren	7"	King's Road	KR002	1978	**£8**	**£4**	*2 picture sleeves*

O'BRIAN, HUGH

TV's Wyatt Earp Sings	10" LP	HMV	DLP1189	1958	**£15**	**£6**	

O'BRIEN, ANNE

Anne O'Brien	LP	Spin			**£60**	**£30**	

O'BRIEN, HUGH

Wyatt Earp Sings	LP	ABC	203	1957	**£25**	**£10**	*US*

O'CONNOR, DES

Moonlight Swim	7"	Columbia	DB4011	1957	**£4**	**£1.50**	

O'CONNOR, HAZEL

Compact Hits	CD-s	A&M	AMCD902	1988	**£5**	**£2**	

O'CONNOR, SINEAD

Emperor's New Clothes	CD-s	Ensign	ENYCD633	1990	**£5**	**£2**	
I Do Not Want What I Have Not Got	CD	Chrysalis	CCD1759	1994	**£12**	**£5**	*Chrysalis 25 pack*
I Want Your Hands On Me	CD-s	Ensign	ENYCD613	1988	**£5**	**£2**	
Jump In The River	CD-s	Ensign	ENYCD618	1988	**£5**	**£2**	
Mandinka	CD-s	Ensign	ENYCD611	1987	**£8**	**£4**	
My Special Child	CD-s	Ensign	ENYCD646	1991	**£5**	**£2**	
Nothing Compares 2U	CD-s	Ensign	ENYCD630	1990	**£5**	**£2**	
Silent Night	CD-s	Ensign	ENYCD652	1991	**£5**	**£2**	
Three Babies	CD-s	Ensign	ENYCD635	1990	**£5**	**£2**	

O'CONNOR, SINEAD & THE EDGE

Heroine	12"	Virgin	VS89712	1986	**£6**	**£2.50**	

O'DAY, ANITA

And Billy May Swing Rodgers And Hart	LP	HMV	CLP1436/ CSD1354	1961	**£15**	**£6**	
Anita	LP	HMV	CLP1085	1956	**£15**	**£6**	
Anita O'Day Collates	10" LP	Columbia	33C9020	1956	**£30**	**£15**	
Anita Sings Jazz	LP	World Record Club	T244	196–	**£10**	**£4**	*with Oscar Peterson*
Anita Sings The Most	LP	Columbia	33CX10125	1958	**£15**	**£6**	
At Mister Kelly's	10" LP	HMV	DLP1203	1959	**£15**	**£6**	
Evening With Anita O'Day	LP	Columbia	33CX10068	1957	**£25**	**£10**	
Pick Yourself Up	10" LP	HMV	DLP1169	1958	**£15**	**£6**	
Swings Cole Porter With Billy May	LP	HMV	CLP1332	1960	**£15**	**£6**	

O'DAY, PAT

Earth Angel	7"	MGM	SP1129	1955	**£10**	**£5**	
Soldier Boy	7"	MGM	SP1142	1955	**£6**	**£2.50**	

O'DELL, MAC

Hymns For The Country Folk	LP	Audio Lab	AL1544	1960	**£25**	**£10**	*US*
Stone Has Rolled Away	7"	Parlophone	CMSP25	1954	**£15**	**£7.50**	*export*

O'DELL, RONNIE

Melody Of Napoli	7"	London	HLD8439	1957	**£8**	**£4**	

O'DONNELL, AL

Al O'Donnell	LP	Trailer	LER2073	1972	**£25**	**£10**	
Al O'Donnell 2	LP	Transatlantic	LTRA501	1978	**£10**	**£4**	

O'DONNELL, JOE

Gaodhal's Vision	LP	Polydor	2383465	1977	**£20**	**£8**	

O'DOORS, PATTI

World Turned Upside Down	LP	MEK	MEK002	1985	**£15**	**£6**	

O'HALLORAN BROTHERS

Men Of The Island	LP	Topic	12TS305	1976	**£12**	**£5**	

O'HARA'S PLAYBOYS

Get Ready	LP	Fontana	(S)TL5461	1968	**£25**	**£10**	
Party No. 1	LP	Decca	SKL16295P	1964	**£50**	**£25**	*German*

O'JAYS

Back On Top	LP	Bell	6014	1968	**£20**	**£8**	*US*
Backstabbers	LP	CBS	65257	1972	**£10**	**£4**	
Comin' Through	LP	Imperial	LP9290/12290	1965	**£20**	**£8**	*US*
Full Of Soul	LP	Sunset	SLS50038	1969	**£10**	**£4**	
I'll Be Sweeter Tomorrow	7"	Stateside	SS2073	1967	**£40**	**£20**	
In Philadelphia	LP	Epic	EPC65469	1973	**£10**	**£4**	
Lipstick Traces	7"	Liberty	LIB66102	1965	**£25**	**£12.50**	
Look Over Your Shoulder	7"	Bell	BLL1020	1968	**£6**	**£2.50**	
Soul Sounds	LP	Minit	LP40008	1967	**£20**	**£8**	*US*
Stand In For Love	7"	Liberty	LIB66197	1966	**£10**	**£5**	

O'KEEFE, JOHNNY

Real Wild Child	7"	Coral	Q72330	1958	**£100**	**£50**	
Tell the Blues So Long	7"	Zodiac	ZR0016	196–	**£15**	**£7.50**	

O'KEEFE, PADRAIG, DENIS MURPHY, JULIA CLIFFORD

Kerry Fiddles	LP	Topic	12T309	1977	**£10**	**£4**	

O'LEARY, JOHN

Music For The Set	LP	Topic	12TS357	1977	**£10**	**£4**	

O'NEIL, MATTY

Don't Sell Daddy Any More Whisky	7"	London	L1037	1954	**£20**	**£10**	*gold label*

O'NEILL, JOHNNY

Wagon Train	7"	RCA	RCA1114	1959	**£4**	**£1.50**	

O'QUIN, GENE

Boogie Woogie Fever	78	Capitol	CL13600	1951	**£6**	**£2.50**	

O'RIADA, SEAN

Ceol Na Nuasal	LP	Gael-Linn	CEF015	1967	**£12**	**£5**	*Irish*
O'Riada's Farewell	LP	Claddagh	CC12	1972	**£10**	**£4**	*Irish*
Reacaireacht An Riadaigh	LP	Gael-Linn	CEF010	1965	**£12**	**£5**	*Irish*

O'SULLIVAN, BERNARD & TOMMY McMAHON

Play Irish Traditional Music From County Clare	LP	Free Reed	FRS505	1976	**£10**	**£4**	

OAK

Welcome To Our Fair	LP	Topic	12TS212	1971	**£75**	**£37.50**	

OAKENSHIELD

Across The Narrow Seas	LP	Acorn	OAK1	1983	**£15**	**£6**	
Against The Grain	LP	Acorn	OAK2	1985	**£15**	**£6**	

OASIS

Oasis have achieved far greater success than predecessors like the Stone Roses or the Charlatans, partly because the Gallagher brothers have proved themselves to be experts at handling the media. On the premise that no publicity is bad publicity, they have ensured their continual presence in the public notice through real or contrived drug escapades, public squabbling and generally loutish behaviour. By the end of 1996, the group's hold on the popular media was so secure that Liam Gallagher managed to get himself front page coverage by the simple device of getting his hair cut! The actual music struggles to be worthy of the resultant attention, but it is suitably robust – if not at all innovative – and many of the tunes are genuinely memorable.

Acquiesce	12"	Creation	CTP204	1995	**£60**	**£30**	*promo*
Acquiesce	CD-s	Creation	CCD204P	1995	**£100**	**£50**	*promo*
All Around The World	12"	Creation	CTP282	1997	**£20**	**£10**	*promo*
All Around The World	CD-s	Creation	CCD282X	1997	**£15**	**£7.50**	*2 track promo*
All Around The World	CD-s	Creation	CRESCD282P	1997	**£10**	**£5**	*promo*
All Around The World	CD-s	Creation	CCD282	1997	**£10**	**£5**	*1 track promo*
Be Here Now	CD	Creation	CCD219	1997	**£25**	**£10**	*promo*
Be Here Now	CD	Creation	no number	1997	**£40**	**£20**	*12" boxed set*
Be Here Now	CD-s	Creation	CCD219PL	1997	**£25**	**£12.50**	*promo*
Be Here Now	LP	Creation		1997	**£50**	**£25**	*double album boxed set*
Cigarettes And Alcohol	12"	Creation	CRE190TP	1994	**£40**	**£20**	*promo*
Cigarettes And Alcohol	12"	Creation	CTP190CL	1994	**£60**	**£30**	*1 sided promo*
Cigarettes And Alcohol	7"	Creation	CRE190	1994	**£5**	**£2**	*in polythene bag*
Cigarettes And Alcohol	CD-s	Creation	CRESCD190P	1994	**£12**	**£6**	*1 sided promo*
Columbia	12"	Creation	CTP8	1993	**£250**	**£150**	*1 sided promo only*
Cum On Feel The Noize	12"	Creation	CTP221X	1996	**£50**	**£25**	*promo*
Cum On Feel The Noize	CD-s	Creation	CCD221	1996	**£60**	**£30**	*promo*
D'You Know What I Mean	12"	Creation	CTP256	1997	**£20**	**£10**	*promo*
D'You Know What I Mean	CD-s	Creation	CCD256	1997	**£15**	**£7.50**	*1 track promo*
D'You Know What I Mean	CD-s	Creation	CCD256X	1997	**£15**	**£7.50**	*2 track promo*
D'You Know What I Mean	CD-s	Creation	CRESCD256P	1997	**£8**	**£4**	*promo*
Definitely, Maybe	CD	Creation	CRECD169P	1994	**£50**	**£25**	
Definitely, Maybe	CD	Sony	SAMP369	1994	**£20**	**£8**	*French or Australian, with bonus CD-s*
Don't Look Back In Anger	CD-s	Creation	CRESCD221P	1996	**£8**	**£4**	*promo*
I Am The Walrus	12"	Creation	CTP190	1994	**£300**	**£180**	*promo only*

Title	Format	Label	Number	Year	Mint	Value	Notes
It's Good To Be Free	12"	Creation	CTP195	1994	£60	£30	promo
Live At The Metro, Chicago	CD	Sony	ESK6805	1995	£50	£25	US promo only
Live Forever	12"	Creation	CRE185TP	1994	£40	£20	promo
Live Forever	7"	Creation	CRE185	1994	£10	£5	in polythene bag
Live Forever	CD-s	Creation	CRESCD185P	1994	£10	£5	promo
Masterplan	LP	Creation	CRELX241	1998	£50	£25	boxed set of 7 × 10" singles
Oasis	CD-s	Creation	P961	1996	£25	£12.50	promo sampler
Roll With It	12"	Creation	CTP212	1996	£40	£20	promo
Roll With It	CD-s	Creation	CRESCD212P	1995	£8	£4	promo
Round Are Way	12"	Creation	CTP215	1995	£50	£25	promo
Shakermaker	12"	Creation	CRE182TP	1994	£40	£20	promo
Shakermaker	7"	Creation	CRE182	1994	£8	£4	
Shakermaker	CD-s	Creation	CRESCD182P	1994	£10	£5	promo
Singles Collection	CD-s	Sony	HES6611112	1995	£75	£37.50	French 5 disc set
Slide Away	CD-s	Creation	CCD169	1995	£30	£15	promo
Some Might Say	CD-s	Creation	CCD204	1995	£50	£25	1 track promo
Some Might Say	CD-s	Creation	CCD204P	1995	£8	£4	promo
Stand By Me	12"	Creation	CTP278	1997	£20	£10	promo
Stand By Me	CD-s	Creation	CCD278	1997	£15	£7.50	1 track promo
Stand By Me	CD-s	Creation	CRESCD278P	1997	£8	£4	promo
Stand By Me	CD-s	Creation	CCD278X	1997	£15	£7.50	2 track promo
Supersonic	12"	Creation	CRE176TP	1994	£40	£20	promo
Supersonic	7"	Creation	CRE176	1994	£10	£5	
Supersonic	CD-s	Creation	CRESCD176P	1994	£15	£7.50	promo
Vox Box	CD-s	Creation	no number	1997	£400	£250	9 CD set in amplifier box
What's The Story Morning Glory?	CD	Creation	CRECD189P	1995	£40	£20	promo with extra track
What's The Story Morning Glory?	CD	Sony		1995	£20	£8	Australian, with bonus CD-s
Whatever	12"	Creation	CRE195TP	1994	£40	£20	promo
Whatever	CD-s	Creation	CRESCD195P	1994	£8	£4	promo
Wibbling Rivalry	CD-s	Fierce Panda	CDNING12	1995	£5	£2	
Wonderwall	CD-s	Creation	CRESCD215P	1995	£8	£4	promo

OBELISQUE

Title	Format	Label	Number	Year	Mint	Value	Notes
How Time Flies	LP	Ultimate Record Label		1978	£200	£100	Dutch

OBERON

Title	Format	Label	Number	Year	Mint	Value	Notes
Midsummer Night's Dream	LP	Acorn		1971	£750	£500	

OBSERVERS

Title	Format	Label	Number	Year	Mint	Value	Notes
Brimstone And Fire	7"	Big Shot	BI575	1971	£5	£2	
Keep Pushing	7"	Big Shot	BI588	1971	£5	£2	

OBTAINERS

Title	Format	Label	Number	Year	Mint	Value	Notes
Yeh Yeh Yeh	7"	Dance Fools Dance		1979	£75	£37.50	Mag-Spys B side

OCCASIONAL WORD ENSEMBLE

Title	Format	Label	Number	Year	Mint	Value	Notes
Year Of The Great Leap Sideways	LP	Dandelion	63753	1969	£15	£6	

OCCASIONALLY DAVID

Title	Format	Label	Number	Year	Mint	Value	Notes
Twist And Shout	7"	Oven Ready	OD77901	1979	£5	£2	

OCCULT CHEMISTRY

Title	Format	Label	Number	Year	Mint	Value	Notes
Water Earth Fire Air	7"	Bikini Girl		1980	£6	£2.50	clear flexi
Water Earth Fire Air	7"	Dining Out	TUX4	1981	£5	£2	

OCEAN COLOUR SCENE

Ocean Colour Scene's reinvention of themselves, encouraged by the experience gained by two of their members playing in Paul Weller's backing group, resulted in their second album being a near perfect re-creation of the early seventies progressive hard rock style, and a massive commercial success. *Moseley Shoals* files easily alongside such overlooked classics as *Andromeda* and T2's *It'll All Work Out In Boomland* and proves that there is still much that can be done with the progressive guitar formula. Inevitably, the acclaim generated by *Moseley Shoals* has caused considerable interest in the group's earlier releases.

Title	Format	Label	Number	Year	Mint	Value	Notes
Do Yourself A Favour	12"	Fontana	OCS312	1992	£6	£2.50	
Do Yourself A Favour	12"	Fontana	OCS312	1992	£6	£2.50	
Do Yourself A Favour	CD-s	Fontana	OCSCD3	1992	£10	£5	
Giving It All Away	CD-s	Fontana	OCSCD2	1992	£5	£2	
One Of Those Days	12"	Phffft	WAVE1	1990	£50	£25	promo only
Sway	12"	Phffft	FITX001	1990	£6	£2.50	
Sway	CD-s	Fontana	OCSCD1	1992	£6	£2.50	
Sway	CD-s	Phffft	FITCD1	1990	£25	£12.50	
Yesterday Today	CD-s	Phffft	FITCD2	1991	£15	£7.50	
You've Got It Bad	7"	MCA	OCS1	1995	£6	£2.50	promo
You've Got It Bad	7"	MCA	OCS2	1995	£10	£5	mail order issue

OCHS, PHIL

Title	Format	Label	Number	Year	Mint	Value	Notes
All The News That's Fit To Sing	LP	Elektra	EKL269	1964	£25	£10	
Chords Of Fame	LP	A&M	AMLM64599	1974	£15	£6	double
Greatest Hits	LP	A&M	AMLS973	1970	£15	£6	
Gunfight At Carnegie Hall	LP	A&M	SP9010	1971	£15	£6	Canadian
I Ain't Marchin' Anymore	LP	Elektra	EKL287	1965	£25	£10	
I Ain't Marchin' Anymore	7"	Elektra	EKSN45002	1965	£5	£2	

In Concert .... LP .... Elektra .... EKL310 .... 1966 £**20** .... £**8** ....
Interviews With Phil Ochs .... LP .... Folkways .... FB5321 .... 1971 £**15** .... £**6** .... US
Pleasures Of The Harbour .... LP .... A&M .... AML(S)913 .... 1967 £**15** .... £**6** ....
Rehearsals For Retirement .... LP .... A&M .... AMLS934 .... 1969 £**15** .... £**6** ....
Small Circle Of Friends .... 7" .... A&M .... AMS716 .... 1968 £**4** .... £**1.50** ....
Tape From California .... LP .... A&M .... AMLS919 .... 1968 £**15** .... £**6** ....

OCTOBER, JOHNNY

Growin' Prettier .... 7" .... Capitol .... CL15070 .... 1959 £**4** .... £**1.50** ....
There'll Always Be A Feeling .... 7" .... Capitol .... CL15121 .... 1960 £**4** .... £**1.50** ....

OCTOBRE

Octobre .... LP .... PGP .... 13001 .... 1973 £**40** .... £**20** .... *Canadian*

OCTOPUS

Hey Na Na .... 7" .... Mooncrest .... MOON7 .... 1973 £**4** .... £**1.50** ....
Laugh At The Poor Man .... 7" .... Penny Farthing .... PEN705 .... 1969 £**12** .... £**6** ....
Restless Nights .... LP .... Penny Farthing .... PELS508 .... 1970 £**150** .... £**75** ....
River .... 7" .... Penny Farthing .... PEN716 .... 1970 £**10** .... £**5** ....

OCTOPUS (2)

Octopus .... LP .... ESP-Disk .... 2000 .... 1969 £**30** .... £**15** .... US

OCTOPUS (3)

Keep Smiling .... 7" EP .. Vogue .... EPL8167 .... 1963 £**8** .... £**4** .... *French*

ODA

Oda .... LP .... Loud .... 80011 .... 1973 £**100** .... £**50** .... US

ODD PERSONS

Odd Persons .... LP .... Somerset .... 658 .... 1966 £**30** .... £**15** .... *German*

ODDS

Dread In My Bed .... 7" .... JSO .... EAT7 .... 1981 £**5** .... £**2** ....

ODDSOCKS

Gerald Claridge, whose tape-only *Staggering* album from 1990 is well worth investigating as a set of intriguing contemporary folk songs, is also central to the one album made by Oddsocks. Also in the group is Nick Saloman, later to issue a series of albums under the name of Bevis Frond.

Men Of The Moment .... LP .... Sweet Folk & Country .... SFA030 .... 1975 £**50** .... £**25** ....

ODELL, ANN

A Little Taste .... LP .... DJM .... DJLPS434 .... 1973 £**25** .... £**10** ....

ODETTA

Odetta Sings Dylan .... LP .... RCA .... RD7703 .... 1965 £**10** .... £**4** ....

ODIN

Odin .... LP .... Vertigo .... 6360608 .... 1972 £**20** .... £**8** .... *German*

ODYSSEY

Setting Forth .... LP .... Trip .... T1000 .... 1990 £**12** .... £**5** .... US
Setting Forth .... LP .... private .... £**1500** .. £**1000** .... US

ODYSSEY (2)

Beware .... 7" EP .. Jag .... 232001 .... 1967 £**12** .... £**6** .... *French, B side by Jimmy Powell*

ODYSSEY (3)

Odyssey .... LP .... Mowest .... MWS7002 .... 1973 £**20** .... £**8** ....

ODYSSEY (4)

How Long Is Time .... 7" .... Strike .... JH312 .... 1966 £**4** .... £**1.50** ....

OHIO EXPRESS

Beg Borrow & Steal .... LP .... Cameo .... CS20000 .... 1968 £**12** .... £**5** .... US
Chewy Chewy .... LP .... Buddah .... 203015 .... 1969 £**10** .... £**4** ....
Ohio Express .... LP .... Pye .... NSPL28117 .... 1969 £**10** .... £**4** ....

OHIO PLAYERS

Skin Tight .... LP .... Mercury .... 6338497 .... 1974 £**10** .... £**4** ....

OISIN

Bealoideas .... LP .... ID .... IDLP2011 .... 1979 £**10** .... £**4** .... *Irish*
Jeannie C .... LP .... Tara .... 2013 .... 1982 £**10** .... £**4** .... *Irish*
Oisin .... LP .... ID .... IDLP2006 .... 1976 £**10** .... £**4** .... *Irish*
Over The Moor To Maggie .... LP .... Tara .... 2012 .... 1980 £**10** .... £**4** .... *Irish*

OKAYSIONS

Girl Watcher .... 7" .... Stateside .... SS2126 .... 1969 £**15** .... £**7.50** ....

OKEEFENOKEE JUG BAND

Okeefenokee Jug Band	7" EP	Vogue	EPV1188	1958	£5	£2	

OKIN, EARL

Stop And You'll Become Aware	7"	CBS	4495	1968	£5	£2	

OKKO

Sitar And Electronics	LP	BASF	20211177	1971	£15	£6	*German*

OKTOBER

Uhrsprung	LP	Trikont	US0024	1976	£10	£4	*German*

OLA & THE JANGLERS

Alex Is The Man	7" EP	Pathe	EGF975	1966	£20	£10	*French*
Happily Together	LP	Sonet	GMG1217	1969	£20	£8	*Swedish*
I Can Wait	7"	Decca	F12646	1967	£5	£2	
Let's Dance	LP	Sonet	GMG1214	1968	£20	£8	*Swedish*
Limelight	LP	Sonet	GMG1205	1967	£20	£8	*Swedish*
Patterns	LP	Sonet	GMG1204	1967	£20	£8	*Swedish*
Pictures And Sounds	LP	Sonet	GMG1208	1967	£20	£8	*Swedish*
Surprise Surprise	LP	Sonet	GP9928	1968	£20	£8	*Swedish*
That's When	7" EP	Pathe	EGF924	1966	£20	£10	*French*
Twelve Big Hits	LP	Sonet	GP9939	1969	£15	£6	*Swedish*
Underground	LP	Sonet	GMG1211	1968	£20	£8	*Swedish*
What A Way To Die	7"	Transatlantic	BIG108	1968	£4	£1.50	

OLD MAN & THE SEA

Old Man & The Sea	LP	Sonet	SLPS1539	1972	£250	£150	*Danish*

OLD PULL & PUSH

Velocipede	LP	Druid	DR1A	1980	£10	£4	

OLD SWAN BAND

Gamesters, Pickpockets And Harlots	LP	Dingles	DIN322	1981	£12	£5	
No Reels	LP	Free Reed	FRR011	1976	£12	£5	
Old Swan Band	LP	Free Reed	FRR028	1980	£15	£6	

OLDFIELD, MIKE

Interesting variations exist with regard to the quadrophonic version of Mike Oldfield's *Tubular Bells*. All copies of the picture disc are a stereo remix of the quadrophonic version, the same as first appeared in the four-album *Boxed* compilation. The first 40,000 copies of the black vinyl edition are not a true quadrophonic recording at all, but merely a doctored version of the stereo issue. Thereafter, the records are a true quadrophonic mix, but there is no indication on the cover or label of the record that the substitution has been made.

Alright Now Theme Tune	7"	Tyne Tees	TT362	1980	£40	£20	*flexi*
Amarok	CD	Virgin	CDVG2640	1991	£15	£6	*Australian gold CD*
Amarok X-Trax	CD-s	Virgin	AMACD1	1990	£15	£7.50	*3" single*
Boxed	LP	Virgin	VBOX1	1976	£20	£8	*4 LP boxed set*
Don Alfonso	7"	Virgin	VS117	1975	£8	£4	*with David Bedford*
Don Alfonso	7"	Virgin	VS117	1975	£75	£37.50	*picture sleeve*
Earth Moving	CD-s	Virgin	VSCD1189	1989	£10	£5	
Etude	7"	Virgin	SWALLOW1	1984	£25	£12.50	*promo*
Family Man	7"	Virgin	VSY489	1982	£4	£1.50	*picture disc*
Five Miles Out	7"	Virgin	VSY464	1982	£4	£1.50	*picture disc*
Guilty	12"	Virgin	VS24512	1979	£6	£2.50	*blue vinyl*
Heaven's Open	CD-s	Virgin	VSCDT1341	1991	£5	£2	
Hergest Ridge	LP	Virgin	QV2013	1975	£15	£6	*quad*
Impressions	cass	Tellydisc	TEL4	1979	£15	£6	
Impressions	LP	Tellydisc	TELLY4	1980	£20	£8	
Innocent	CD-s	Virgin	VSCD1214	1989	£8	£4	
Islands	CD-s	Virgin	CDEP6	1988	£5	£2	
Mike Oldfield's Single	7"	Virgin	VS101	1974	£15	£7.50	*picture sleeve*
Mistake	7"	Virgin	VSY541	1982	£4	£1.50	*picture disc*
Moonlight Shadow	7"	Virgin	VSY586	1983	£5	£2	*picture disc*
Moonlight Shadow	CD-s	Virgin	CDT7	1988	£6	£2.50	*3" single*
Ommadawn	12"	Virgin	VDJ9	1975	£20	£10	*promo sampler*
Ommadawn	LP	Virgin	QV2043	1976	£15	£6	*quad*
Orchestral Tubular Bells	7"	Virgin	VDJ1	1975	£8	£4	*promo sampler*
Pictures In The Dark	7"	Virgin	VSD836	1985	£6	£2.50	*double*
Platinum	LP	Virgin	V2141	1979	£50	£25	*with 'Sally'*
Shine	7"	Virgin	VSS863	1986	£8	£4	*shaped picture disc*
Songs Of Distant Earth	CD	WEA	SAM1477	1995	£40	£20	*promo in tin box*
Spanish Tune	7"	Virgin	VS112	1974	£40	£20	*promo*
Take Four	12"	Virgin	VS23812	1978	£8	£4	*white vinyl*
Take Four	7"	Virgin	VS238	1978	£5	£2	
Tubular Bells	CD	Virgin	CDVG2001	1991	£15	£6	*Australian gold CD*
Tubular Bells	LP	Virgin	QV2001	1974	£15	£6	*quad*
Tubular Bells	LP	Virgin	VP2001	1978	£10	£4	*picture disc*
Virgin Compilation	CD	Virgin	PRCD2113	1987	£40	£20	*US promo*
Women Of Ireland	12"	WEA	SAM3096	1997	£8	£4	*promo*
Wonderful Land	7"	Virgin	VS389	1980	£4	£1.50	

OLDHAM, ANDREW ORCHESTRA

16 Hip Hits	LP	Ace Of Clubs	ACL1180	1964	£30	£15	
365 Rolling Stones	7"	Decca	F11878	1964	£15	£7.50	
East Meets West	LP	Parrot	PA6/PAS71003	1965	£30	£15	*US*

Title	Format	Label	Cat. No.	Year	Price	Price	Notes
Funky And Fleopatra	7"	Decca	F11829	1964	**£20**	**£10**	*B side by Jeannie & Her Redheads*
Maggie May	LP	Decca	LK4636	1964	**£20**	**£8**	
Right Of Way	7"	Decca	F11987	1964	**£15**	**£7.50**	
Rolling Stones Songbook	LP	Decca	LK/SKL4796	1966	**£40**	**£20**	
There Are But Five Rolling Stones	7"	Decca	F11817	1964	**£12**	**£6**	*B side by Cleo*

OLDHAM TINKERS

Title	Format	Label	Cat. No.	Year	Price	Price	Notes
Best O'T Bunch	LP	Topic	12TS237	1974	**£10**	**£4**	
For Old Time's Sake	LP	Topic	12TS276	1975	**£12**	**£5**	
Oldham's Burning Sands	LP	Topic	12TS206	1971	**£12**	**£5**	
Sit Thee Down	LP	Topic	12TS323	1977	**£12**	**£5**	
That Lancashire Band	LP	Topic	[illegible]	1979	**£1[illegible]**	**£[illegible]**	

OLENN, JOHNNY

Title	Format	Label	Cat. No.	Year	Price	Price	Notes
Born Reckless	7"	Mercury	AMT1050	1959	**£50**	**£25**	
Just Rollin'	LP	LIberty	LRP3029	1958	**£150**	**£75**	*US*
My Idea Of Love	7"	London	HLU8388	1957	**£250**	**£150**	*best auctioned*

OLIVER

Title	Format	Label	Cat. No.	Year	Price	Price	Notes
Standing Stone	LP	private	OL1	1974	**£200**	**£100**	

OLIVER, JOHNNY

Title	Format	Label	Cat. No.	Year	Price	Price	Notes
Chain Gang	7"	MGM	SP1165	1956	**£8**	**£4**	
What A Kiss Won't Do	7"	Mercury	AMT1095	1960	**£4**	**£1.50**	

OLIVER, KING

Title	Format	Label	Cat. No.	Year	Price	Price	Notes
Creole Jazz Band	10" LP	London	AL3504	1954	**£25**	**£10**	
In Harlem	10" LP	HMV	DLP1609	1955	**£25**	**£10**	
King Oliver	LP	Philips	BBL7181	1957	**£15**	**£6**	
King Oliver Jazz Band	10" LP	Columbia	33S1065	1955	**£25**	**£10**	
Louis Armstrong 1923	LP	Riverside	RLP12122	1961	**£10**	**£4**	
Oliver Dixie Syncopators	10" LP	Vogue Coral	LRA10020	1955	**£25**	**£10**	
Plays The Blues	10" LP	London	AL3510	1954	**£25**	**£10**	

OLIVER, PAUL

Title	Format	Label	Cat. No.	Year	Price	Price	Notes
Conversation With The Blues	LP	Decca	LK4664	1965	**£40**	**£20**	

OLIVER & THE TWISTERS

Title	Format	Label	Cat. No.	Year	Price	Price	Notes
Look Who's Twistin' Everybody	LP	Pye	NPL28018	1964	**£20**	**£8**	

OLLIE & THE NIGHTINGALES

Title	Format	Label	Cat. No.	Year	Price	Price	Notes
You're Leaving Me	7"	Stax	STAX109	1969	**£6**	**£2.50**	

OLSSON, NIGEL

Title	Format	Label	Cat. No.	Year	Price	Price	Notes
Drum Orchestra And Chorus	LP	DJM	DJLPS417	1972	**£10**	**£4**	

OLYMPICS

Title	Format	Label	Cat. No.	Year	Price	Price	Notes
Baby Do The Philly Dog	7"	Action	ACT4539	1969	**£5**	**£2**	
Baby Do The Philly Dog	7"	Fontana	TF778	1966	**£8**	**£4**	
Baby It's Hot	7"	Vogue	V9204	1962	**£8**	**£4**	
Dance By The Light Of The Moon	LP	Vocalion	VAH8059	1961	**£30**	**£15**	
Dance With A Dolly	7"	Vogue	V9181	1961	**£8**	**£4**	
Dance With The Teacher	7"	HMV	POP564	1958	**£10**	**£5**	
Do The Bounce	LP	Tri-Disc	1001	1963	**£30**	**£15**	*US*
Doin' The Hully Gully	LP	Arvee	A423	1960	**£75**	**£37.50**	*US*
Good Lovin'	7"	Warner Bros	WB157	1965	**£8**	**£4**	
I Wish I Could Shimmy	7"	Vogue	V9174	1960	**£8**	**£4**	
I'll Do A Little Bit More	7"	Action	ACT4556	1969	**£5**	**£2**	
Little Pedro	7"	Vogue	V9184	1961	**£12**	**£6**	*B side Cappy Lewis*
Nothing	7"	HMV	POP1155	1963	**£5**	**£2**	
Party Time	LP	Arvee	A429	1961	**£60**	**£30**	*US*
Private Eye	7"	Columbia	DB4346	1959	**£12**	**£6**	
Something Old, Something New	LP	Fontana	TL5407	1967	**£25**	**£10**	
Stomp	7"	Vogue	V9198	1962	**£8**	**£4**	
The Bounce	7"	Sue	WI348	1964	**£12**	**£6**	
Twist	7"	Vogue	V9196	1962	**£8**	**£4**	
We Go Together	7"	Fontana	TF678	1966	**£8**	**£4**	
Western Movies	7"	HMV	POP528	1958	**£8**	**£4**	

O.M.D.

The rarest Orchestral Manoeuvres in the Dark record is not one that a collector of the group's music is ever likely to find. As a mispressing, however, it is arguably only of interest to the completist in any case – the song 'Souvenir' replaces 'Love Action' as the A side on forty copies of the Human League single. Thirty-five of these were destroyed, which leaves a grand total of five copies available for collectors. In the circumstances, it is not realistic to quote a price for these.

Title	Format	Label	Cat. No.	Year	Price	Price	Notes
Call My Name	CD-s	Virgin	VSCDG1380	1991	**£6**	**£2.50**	*digipak*
Constructive Conversation With OMD	LP	Epic	AS1408	1982	**£12**	**£5**	*US promo*
Dreaming	CD-s	Virgin	VSCD987	1988	**£5**	**£2**	
Dreaming	CD-s	Virgin	VSCDX987	1988	**£10**	**£5**	
Dreaming	CD-s	Virgin	TRICD4	1988	**£6**	**£2.50**	*3" single*
Electricity	7"	Factory	FAC6	1979	**£10**	**£5**	
La Femme Accident	12"	Virgin	VSD81112	1985	**£6**	**£2.50**	*double*
La Femme Accident	7"	Virgin	VSS811	1985	**£5**	**£2**	*square picture disc*
Locomotion	7"	Virgin	VSX660	1984	**£20**	**£10**	*'competition' sleeve*
Locomotion	7"	Virgin	VSY660	1984	**£6**	**£2.50**	*shaped picture disc*
Locomotion	CD-s	Virgin	CDT12	1988	**£8**	**£4**	*3" single*
Maid Of Orleans	12"	Din Disc	DIN4012	1982	**£8**	**£4**	*'coin' cover*
Maid Of Orleans	CD-s	Virgin	CDT27	1988	**£8**	**£4**	*3" single*

Pandora's Box	CD-s	Virgin	VSCDX1331	1991	£10	£5	in black wooden box
Red Flame – White Light	12"	Din Disc	DIN612	1980	£6	£2.50	
Sailing On The Seven Seas	CD-s	Virgin	VSCDT1310	1991	£8	£4	
Secret	12"	Virgin	VS79612	1985	£6	£2.50	double
Shame	CD-s	Virgin	MIKE93812	1987	£8	£4	
Telegraph	12"	Virgin	VS58012	1983	£10	£5	
Then You Turn Away	CD-s	Virgin	VSCDG1368	1991	£8	£4	in felt box
We Love You	7"	Virgin	VSC911	1986	£6	£2.50	with cassette

OMEGA

Csillagok Utjaa	LP	Pepita	SLPX17570	1978	£15	£6	Hungarian
Elo	LP	Pepita	SLPX17447	1972	£15	£6	Hungarian
Five	LP	Pepita	SLPX17457	1974	£15	£6	Hungarian
Hall Of Floaters In The Sky	LP	Decca	SKL5219	1976	£10	£4	
Idorablo	LP	Pepita	SLPX17523	1977	£15	£6	Hungarian
Omega	LP	Bellaphon	BLPS19147	1973	£15	£6	German
Omega III	LP	Bellaphon	BLPS19191	1974	£15	£6	German
Red Star	LP	Decca	SKL/LK4974	1968	£40	£20	
Time Robbers	LP	Decca	SKL5243	1976	£10	£4	
Trombitas Fredi	LP	Pepita	SLPX17390	1968	£30	£15	Hungarian
Two Hundred Years After The Last War	LP	Bellaphon	BLPS19175	1974	£15	£6	German

OMEGA (2)

Prophet	LP	Rock Machine	MACH1	1985	£15	£6	

OMEN SEARCHER

Teacher Of Sin	7"	OCS	002	1982	£25	£12.50	
Too Much	7"	OCS	001	1982	£25	£12.50	

ON THE SEVENTH DAY

On The Seventh Day	LP	Mercury	SR61248	1972	£15	£6	US

ONE

One	LP	Fontana	STL5539	1969	£60	£30	

ONE (2)

St Stephen	LP	private	710	197–	£50	£25	

ONE EYED JACKS

Take Away	LP	Pennine	PSS154	1978	£20	£8	

ONE HUNDRED PER CENT PROOF

100% Proof	LP	Myrrh	MYR1107	1981	£15	£6	
New Way Of Livin'	7"	Smile	SR929	1980	£15	£7.50	

ONE HUNDRED PER CENT PROOF AGED IN SOUL

Somebody's Been Sleeping In My Bed	LP	Hot Wax	SHW5003	1971	£12	£5	

ONE HUNDRED PER CENT PURE POISON

Coming Right At You	LP	EMI	INS3001	1977	£25	£10	

ONE IN A MILLION

Guitarist Jimmy McCulloch must have been no more than fourteen when recording for the first time with One in a Million. He later played with Thunderclap Newman, Stone the Crows and Paul McCartney's Wings.

Fredereek Hernando	7"	MGM	MGM1370	1968	£400	£250	best auctioned
Use Your Imagination	7"	CBS	202513	1967	£75	£37.50	

ONE-O-ONERS

Elgin Avenue Breakdown	LP	Andalucia	AND101	1981	£10	£4	
Key To Your Heart	7"	Chiswick	S3	1976	£10	£5	picture sleeve

ONE THOUSAND MEXICANS

Art Of Love	7"	Whaam!	WHAAM12	1983	£4	£1.50	

ONE THOUSAND VIOLINS

Halcyon Days	12"	Dreamworld	DREAM2	1985	£6	£2.50	

ONE TWO & THREE

Black Pearl	7"	Decca	F12093	1965	£5	£2	
Black Pearls And Green Diamonds	LP	Decca	LK4682	1965	£75	£37.50	

ONE-TWO-SIX

Curtains Falling	LP	RCA	10156	1967	£25	£10	German

ONE WAY SYSTEM

Stab The Judge	7"	Lightbeat	WAY1	1982	£5	£2	

ONE WAY TICKET

Time Is Right	LP	President	PTLS1069	1978	£60	£30	

ONES

The lead guitarist with the Ones was Edgar Froese, later to play in an entirely different style as leader of Tangerine Dream.

Lady Greengrass	7"	Star Club	148593STF	1966	£200	£100	German, best auctioned

ONES (2)

Title	Format	Label	Cat. No.	Year	Price	Price	Notes
Ones	LP	Ashwood House	1105	1966	**£400**	**£250**	*US*

ONLOOKERS

Title	Format	Label	Cat. No.	Year	Price	Price	Notes
You And I	7"	Demon	D1012	1982	**£10**	**£5**	

ONLY ONES

Many of the punk musicians to emerge in the late seventies were far from being the brash youngsters they were painted. Skulking at the back of the Only Ones' line-up was the familiar face of Mike Kellie, formerly the drummer with Spooky Tooth. The pedigree of the group's bass player went back even further – he was a member of Scottish beat group, the Beatstalkers. This experience was no doubt the reason the Only Ones were able to deliver such convincing interpretations of Peter Perrett's material. *Another Girl, Another Planet* in particular is a classic rock recording by any standard.

Title	Format	Label	Cat. No.	Year	Price	Price	Notes
Another Girl, Another Planet	CD-s	CBS	6577502	1992	**£5**	**£2**	*with track by Psychedelic Furs*
Another Girl, Another Planet	12"	CBS	126576	1978	**£6**	**£2.50**	
Another Girl, Another Planet	7"	CBS	6228	1978	**£6**	**£2.50**	*picture sleeve*
Another Girl, Another Planet	7"	CBS	6576	1978	**£6**	**£2.50**	*demo*
Lovers Of Today	12"	Vengeance	VEN001	1977	**£8**	**£4**	
Lovers Of Today	7"	Vengeance	VEN001	1977	**£6**	**£2.50**	
Trouble In The World	7"	CBS	7963	1979	**£75**	**£37.50**	*black & red picture sleeve*

ONO, YOKO

Title	Format	Label	Cat. No.	Year	Price	Price	Notes
Approximately Infinite Universe	LP	Apple	SAPDO1001	1973	**£12**	**£5**	*double*
Death Of Samantha	7"	Apple	47	1973	**£10**	**£5**	
Feeling The Space	LP	Apple	SAPCOR26	1973	**£25**	**£10**	
Fly	LP	Apple	SPTU101/2	1971	**£30**	**£15**	*double*
Mind Train	7"	Apple	41	1972	**£12**	**£6**	*picture sleeve*
Mind Train	7"	Apple	41	1972	**£5**	**£2**	
Mrs Lennon	7"	Apple	38	1971	**£8**	**£4**	
Plastic Ono Band	LP	Apple	SAPCOR17	1970	**£30**	**£15**	
Run Run Run	7"	Apple	48	1973	**£12**	**£6**	
Walking On Thin Ice	12"	WEA	PROA934	1981	**£15**	**£7.50**	*promo*
Welcome (The Many Sides Of Yoko Ono)	LP	Apple	PRP18026	1974	**£250**	**£150**	*Japanese promo*

ONSLAUGHT

Title	Format	Label	Cat. No.	Year	Price	Price	Notes
First Strike	7"	Complete Control	TROL1	1983	**£5**	**£2**	

ONYX

Title	Format	Label	Cat. No.	Year	Price	Price	Notes
Air	7"	Parlophone	R5888	1971	**£5**	**£2**	
My Son John	7"	Pye	7N17622	1968	**£8**	**£4**	
Next Stop Is Mine	7"	Parlophone	R5906	1971	**£5**	**£2**	
Tamaris Khan	7"	Pye	7N17668	1969	**£30**	**£15**	
Time Off	7"	CBS	4635	1969	**£10**	**£5**	
You've Gotta Be With Me	7"	Pye	7N17477	1968	**£8**	**£4**	

004s

Title	Format	Label	Cat. No.	Year	Price	Price	Notes
It's Alright	LP	CBS	ALD6911	1966	**£100**	**£50**	*South African*

OPAL BUTTERFLY

Ian 'Lemmy' Kilminster was the guitarist on the third Opal Butterfly single, while his colleague in Hawkwind, Simon King, was the group's drummer.

Title	Format	Label	Cat. No.	Year	Price	Price	Notes
Beautiful Beige	7"	CBS	3576	1968	**£25**	**£12.50**	
Mary Anne With The Shakey Hand	7"	CBS	3921	1969	**£50**	**£25**	
You're A Groupie Girl	7"	Polydor	2058041	1970	**£10**	**£5**	

OPEL, JACKIE

Title	Format	Label	Cat. No.	Year	Price	Price	Notes
Cry Me A River	7"	King	KG1011	1965	**£10**	**£5**	
Done With A Friend	7"	Ska Beat	JB190	1965	**£10**	**£5**	
Go Whey	7"	Island	WI209	1965	**£10**	**£5**	
I Am What I Am	7"	Rio	R117	1966	**£8**	**£4**	*Jackie Mittoo B side*
Little More	7"	Ska Beat	JB227	1965	**£10**	**£5**	
Old Rockin' Chair	7"	Island	WI227	1965	**£10**	**£5**	*Skatalites B side*
Pity The Fool	7"	R&B	JB160	1964	**£10**	**£5**	
Solid Rock	7"	R&B	JB138	1964	**£10**	**£5**	
TV In Jamaica	7"	Jump Up	JU512	1967	**£6**	**£2.50**	
Wipe Those Tears	7"	Island	WI203	1965	**£10**	**£5**	
You're No Good	7"	Black Swan	WI421	1964	**£10**	**£5**	

OPEN MIND

Title	Format	Label	Cat. No.	Year	Price	Price	Notes
Horses And Chariots	7"	Philips	BF1790	1969	**£40**	**£20**	
Magic Potion	7"	Philips	BF1805	1969	**£150**	**£75**	
Open Mind	LP	Philips	SBL7893	1969	**£500**	**£330**	
Open Mind	LP	Antar	ANTAR2	1986	**£12**	**£5**	

OPEN ROAD

Title	Format	Label	Cat. No.	Year	Price	Price	Notes
Swamp Fever	7"	Greenwich	GSS102	1972	**£4**	**£1.50**	
Windy Daze	LP	Greenwich	GSLP1001	1971	**£25**	**£10**	

OPEN SKY

Title	Format	Label	Cat. No.	Year	Price	Price	Notes
Open Sky	LP	P.M.Records	PMR001	1975	**£15**	**£6**	*US*

Spirit In The Sky	LP	P.M.Records	PMR003	1975	£15	£6	US

O.P.M.C.

Amalgamation	LP	Pink Elephant	PE877001	1970	£20	£8	Dutch
Product Of Pisces And Capricorn	LP	Pink Elephant	PEL877006	1970	£25	£10	Dutch

OPO

Fallen Asleep Just Like Papa	LP	Spoof		1975	£75	£37.50	Dutch
Opo 2	LP	Spoof		1977	£60	£30	Dutch

OPPRESSED

Never Say Die	7"	Firm	NICK1	1983	£8	£4	
Work Together	7"	Oppressed	OPPO1	1983	£8	£4	

OPUS

Baby Come On	7"	Columbia	DB8675	1970	£10	£5	

OPUS 5

Contre Courant	LP	Celebration	1929	1976	£25	£10	Canadian

ORA

The rare album by Ora contains one decent piece of psychedelia, surrounded by attractive folky songs that provide a striking contrast. A couple of the group members subsequently joined Byzantium, but guitarist Mark Barakan has done better for himself. He appeared on several US albums during the eighties and toured with Bruce Springsteen in the early nineties, under the name of Shane Fontayne.

Ora	LP	Tangerine	DPLP002S	1969	£200	£100	

ORANG UTAN

Orang Utan	LP	Bell	6054	1971	£30	£15	US

ORANGE & BLUE

English Dancing Master	LP	EFDSS	PLA1	1976	£10	£4	

ORANGE BICYCLE

Carry That Weight	7"	Parlophone	R5811	1969	£5	£2	
Early Pearly Morning	7"	Columbia	DB8352	1968	£10	£5	
Goodbye Stranger	7"	Regal Zonophone	RZ3029	1971	£6	£2.50	
Hyacinth Threads	7"	Columbia	DB8259	1967	£10	£5	
Hyacinth Threads	7" EP	Impact	200013	1967	£50	£25	French
Jelly On The Bread	7"	Parlophone	R5854	1970	£5	£2	
Jenskadajka	7"	Columbia	DB8413	1968	£10	£5	
Laura's Garden	7"	Columbia	DB8311	1967	£10	£5	
Let's Take A Trip On An Orange Bicycle	LP	Morgan Blue Town	MBT5003	1988	£10	£4	
Orange Bicycle	LP	Parlophone	PCS7108	1970	£60	£30	
Sing This All Together	7"	Columbia	DB8483	1968	£10	£5	
Take Me To The Pilot	7"	Parlophone	R5827	1970	£5	£2	
Tonight I'll Be Staying Here	7"	Parlophone	R5789	1969	£5	£2	

ORANGE JUICE

One feature of the punk explosion was the emergence of a number of independently run record labels. Only a lucky few have survived, but one of the most fondly regarded of those that have not is Postcard records. Much of this regard has to do with the label's sponsoring of Orange Juice. The group's series of sparkling singles are amongst the delights of the immediate post-punk years and they possess a drive and a liveliness somewhat lacking in the new versions of the same songs recorded for the first Polydor LP. These singles are rightly highly prized.

Blue Boy	7"	Postcard	80-2	1980	£5	£2	*white or brown sleeve*
Blue Boy	7"	Postcard	80-2	1980	£15	£7.50	*hand coloured sleeve*
Falling And Laughing	7"	Postcard	80-0	1980	£40	£20	*picture in bag, Felicity flexi*
Falling And Laughing	7"	Postcard	80-0	1980	£50	£25	*picture in bag, Felicity flexi, postcard*
Poor Old Soul	7"	Postcard	81-2	1981	£6	£2.50	*with postcard*
Poor Old Soul	7"	Postcard	81-2	1981	£4	£1.50	
Simply Thrilled Honey	7"	Postcard	80-6	1980	£12	£6	*colour insert in bag*
Simply Thrilled Honey	7"	Postcard	80-6	1980	£4	£1.50	

ORANGE MACHINE

Three Jolly Little Dwarfs	7"	Pye	7N17559	1968	£40	£20	
You Can All Join In	7"	Pye	7N17680	1969	£40	£20	

ORANGE PEEL

I Got No Time	7"	Reflection	R55	1970	£6	£2.50	
Orange Peel	LP	Bellaphon	BLPS19036	1972	£100	£50	German

ORANGE SEAWEED

Stay Awhile	7"	Pye	7N17515	1968	£25	£12.50	

ORANGE WEDGE

No One Left But Me	LP	private		1974	£500	£330	US
Wedge	LP	private		1972	£500	£330	US

ORB

The success of the Orb was achieved despite (or because of?) breaking so many of the rules governing the methods of most rock artists that it becomes impossible not to be fascinated by their career. Within a critical climate that still reviled the progressive rock of the seventies, the Orb nevertheless managed to achieve acclaim by working within an approach that is indistinguishable from one of the major progressive strands (emphasized by the Orb's use of Pink Floyd quotes and imagery, and the collaborations with Steve Hillage). At the same time, the Orb managed to persuade people that a music based on texture and sound-sculpture – music that seems to call for its listeners to be sitting or lying down in a blissed-out condition – is actually a kind of dance music. Along the way, the Orb have sold a large number of records, including several multiple-album sets and singles playing for vastly longer than the norm. One of the group's biggest hits is 'Blue Room', a single playing at just two seconds under the forty-minute time-span ruled by Gallup to be the maximum length for an item to qualify for inclusion in the singles charts.

Adventures Beyond The Underworld	LP	Big Life	BLRDLP5	1991	£**15**	£**7.50**	*double*
Assassin	CD-s	Big Life	ORBPROMOCD5	1992	£**5**	£**2**	*promo*
Aubrey Mixes: The Ultraworld Excursions	CD	Big Life	BLRCD14	1991	£**12**	£**5**	
Aubrey Mixes: The Ultraworld Excursions	LP	Big Life	BLRLP14	1991	£**12**	£**5**	
Blue Room	CD-s	Big Life	BLRDA75	1992	£**5**	£**2**	*with postcard*
Huge Ever Growing Pulsating Brain	12"	Big Life	BLR27T	1990	£**8**	£**4**	
Huge Ever Growing Pulsating Brain	12"	Wau! Mr Modo	MWS017T	1990	£**10**	£**5**	
Huge Ever Growing Pulsating Brain	CD-s	Big Life	BLR27CD	1990	£**10**	£**5**	
Huge Ever Growing Pulsating Brain (remixes)	12"	Big Life	BLR27T	1990	£**8**	£**4**	
Huge Ever Growing Pulsating Brain (remixes)	CD-s	Big Life	BLR27CD	1990	£**10**	£**5**	
Huge Ever Growing Pulsating Remix	12"	Big Life	ORBPROMO1	1990	£**8**	£**4**	*promo*
Huge Ever Growing Pulsating Brain	12"	Wau! Mr Modo	MWS017R	1990	£**20**	£**10**	*promo*
Huge Ever Growing Pulsating Remix	12"	Wau! Mr Modo	MWS017T	1990	£**30**	£**15**	*promo*
Kiss	12"	Wau! Mr Modo	MWS010T	1989	£**15**	£**7.50**	
Little Fluffy Clouds	CD-s	Big Life	BLR33CD	1990	£**5**	£**2**	
Little Fluffy Clouds (Dance Mix)	12"	Big Life	ORBPROMO2	1990	£**6**	£**2.50**	*promo*
Little Fluffy Clouds (Drums And Vox Version)	12"	Big Life	BLR33R	1990	£**6**	£**2.50**	
Orb In Dub	12"	Big Life	BLRR46	1991	£**6**	£**2.50**	
Orbis Terrarum	CD	Island	CID8037	1995	£**12**	£**5**	*card sleeve in plastic wallet*
Perpetual Dawn	CD-s	Big Life	BLR46CD	1991	£**5**	£**2**	
Perpetual Dawn: Ultrabass II	12"	Big Life	ORBPICTURE3	1991	£**15**	£**7.50**	*promo picture disc – plays Towers Of Dub*
Perpetual Dawn: Ultrabass II	12"	Big Life	ORBPICTURE3	1991	£**8**	£**4**	*promo picture disc*
U.F.Orb	LP	Big Life	BLRLA18	1992	£**15**	£**6**	*triple*

ORBIDOIG

Nocturnal Operation	7"	Situation 2	SIT15	1981	£**5**	£**2**	

ORBISON, ROY

Although the thousands of fans who bought the hits for which Roy Orbison is best known would doubtless disagree, the aching purity of Orbison's high tenor voice was seldom displayed to best advantage on his sixties material. The pathos of 'It's Over', the tranquillity of 'Blue Bayou', even the raunch of 'Pretty Woman' are all undermined by trite, poppy arrangements, conceived without any long-term view of the singer's art. Collectors, it would seem, are inclined to agree, for the values of the sixties records remain stubbornly unspectacular. The recordings made near the end of Roy Orbison's life are another matter altogether – the robust country-rock of both the Traveling Wilburys and Orbison's own *Mystery Girl* album sounds like the music that Orbison had waited all his life to make.

At The Rockhouse	LP	Sun	LP1260	1961	£**100**	£**50**	*US*
Big O	LP	London	HAU/SHU8406	1970	£**12**	£**5**	
Black And White Night	CD	Virgin	PRCDPOLAROY	1989	£**20**	£**8**	*US promo*
Blue Angel	7"	London	HLU9207	1960	£**4**	£**1.50**	
Born To Be Loved By You	7"	London	HLU10176	1968	£**4**	£**1.50**	
Break My Mind	7"	London	HLU10294	1969	£**4**	£**1.50**	
California Blue	12"	Virgin	VST1193	1989	£**6**	£**2.50**	
California Blue	7"	Virgin	VS1193	1989	£**4**	£**1.50**	
California Blue	CD-s	Virgin	VSCD1193	1989	£**10**	£**5**	
Classic	LP	London	HAU/SHU8297	1966	£**15**	£**6**	
Cry Softly Lonely One	7"	London	HLU10143	1967	£**4**	£**1.50**	
Cry Softly Lonely One	LP	London	HAU/SHU8357	1968	£**15**	£**6**	
Crying	CD-s	Virgin	VUSCX63	1992	£**6**	£**2.50**	*with k. d. lang*
Crying	CD-s	Virgin	VUSCD63	1992	£**5**	£**2**	*with k. d. lang*
Crying	LP	London	HAU2437/ SHU6229	1962	£**20**	£**8**	
Devil Doll	7" EP	Ember	EMBEP4570	1965	£**30**	£**15**	
Early Orbison	LP	Monument	LMO/SMO5013	1967	£**12**	£**5**	
Exciting Sounds	LP	Ember	NR5013	1964	£**12**	£**5**	
Fastest Guitar Alive	LP	London	HAU/SHU8358	1968	£**20**	£**8**	
God Loves You	7"	London	HLU10358	1972	£**4**	£**1.50**	
Hank Williams The Roy Orbison Way	LP	MGM	SE4683	1970	£**10**	£**4**	*US*
Heartache	7"	London	HLU10222	1968	£**4**	£**1.50**	
Hillbilly Rock	7" EP	London	RES1089	1957	£**100**	£**50**	*tri centre*
Hillbilly Rock	7" EP	London	RES1089	1963	£**40**	£**20**	*yellow sleeve*
I'm Hurtin'	7"	London	HLU9307	1961	£**4**	£**1.50**	
I'm Hurtin'	7"	London	HLU7108	1961	£**10**	£**5**	*export*
In Dreams	7" EP	London	REU1373	1963	£**12**	£**6**	
In Dreams	CD	Virgin	VDGCD3514	1991	£**15**	£**6**	*Australian gold CD*
In Dreams	LP	London	HAU/SHU8108	1963	£**20**	£**8**	
It's Over	7" EP	London	REU1435	1964	£**12**	£**6**	
Last Night	7"	London	HLU10339	1971	£**4**	£**1.50**	
Lonely And Blue	LP	London	HAU2342	1961	£**25**	£**10**	
Love Hurts	7" EP	London	REU1440	1965	£**15**	£**7.50**	

Memphis	LP	London	SHU8445	1973	£20	£8	
Memphis Tennessee	7"	London	HLU10388	1972	£6	£2.50	
Memphis Tennessee	7"	London	HLU10388	1972	£12	£6	*alternate A side take (matrix MSC8474T21L)*
My Friend	7"	London	HLU10261	1969	£4	£1.50	
Mystery Girl	CD	Virgin	PROCDROY	1989	£20	£8	*US promo in cloth cover*
Mystery Girl	CD	Virgin	CDVG2576	1991	£15	£6	*Australian gold CD*
Oh Pretty Woman	7" EP	London	REU1437	1964	£10	£5	
Oh Pretty Woman	CD-s	Virgin	VSCD1224	1989	£5	£2	*3" single*
Oh Pretty Woman	LP	London	HAU8207	1964	£15	£6	
Only The Lonely	7"	London	HLU9149	1960	£4	£1.50	
Only The Lonely	7" EP	London	REU1274	1960	£12	£6	
Only The Lonely	78	London	HLU9149	1960	£100	£50	
Orbison Way	LP	London	HAU/SHU8279	1966	£15	£6	
Orbisongs	LP	Monument	LMO/SMO5004	1966	£12	£5	
Penny Arcade	7"	London	HLU10285	1969	£10	£5	
Roy Orbison Sings	LP	London	SHU8435	1972	£12	£5	
Roy Orbison's Stage Show Hits	7" EP	London	REU1439	1965	£15	£7.50	
She	7"	London	HLU10159	1967	£4	£1.50	
She's A Mystery To Me	12"	Virgin	VST1173	1989	£6	£2.50	
She's A Mystery To Me	7"	Virgin	VS1173	1989	£4	£1.50	
She's A Mystery To Me	CD-s	Virgin	VSCD1173	1989	£10	£5	
Sings Don Gibson	LP	London	HAU/SHU8318	1967	£15	£6	
So Young	7"	London	HLU10310	1970	£4	£1.50	
Special Delivery	LP	Camden	CAL820	1964	£12	£5	*US*
Sweet And Easy To Love	7"	Ember	EMBS209	1965	£4	£1.50	
Sweet And Easy To Love	7"	Ember	EMBS209	1965	£10	£5	*picture sleeve*
Sweet And Easy To Love	7" EP	Ember	EMBEP4546	1964	£40	£20	
There Is Only One	LP	London	HAU/SHU8252	1965	£15	£6	
This Kind Of Love	7"	Ember	EMBS200	1964	£4	£1.50	
This Kind Of Love	7"	Ember	EMBS200	1964	£10	£5	*picture sleeve*
Trying To Get To You	7" EP	Ember	EMBEP4563	1964	£40	£20	
Uptown	7" EP	London	REU1354	1963	£12	£6	
Walk On	7"	London	HLU10206	1968	£4	£1.50	
Wild Hearts	7"	ZTT	DZTAS9	1985	£15	£7.50	*double*
Workin' For The Man	7"	London	HLU9607	1962	£4	£1.50	
You Got It	12"	Virgin	VST1166	1989	£10	£5	
You Got It	CD-s	Virgin	VSCD1166	1989	£15	£7.50	
You're My Baby	7"	Ember	EMBS197	1964	£6	£2.50	

ORBIT FIVE

I Wanna Go To Heaven	7"	Decca	F12799	1968	£6	£2.50	
I Wanna Go To Heaven	7"	Decca	F12799	1968	£20	£10	*picture sleeve*

ORBITAL

Box	CD-s	Internal	LICDP30	1996	£5	£2	
Chariot	12"	ffrr	FRRXR145	1990	£10	£5	
Chime	12"	Oh Zone	ZONE1	1989	£25	£12.50	
Chime	12"	ffrr	FRRFXR135	1990	£10	£5	
Chime	12"	ffrr	FRRFX135	1990	£10	£5	
Chime	7"	ffrr	FRRF135	1990	£4	£1.50	
Chime	CD-s	FFRR	FCD135	1990	£15	£7.50	
Halcyon	CD-s	Internal	LIECD1	1992	£6	£2.50	
Lush 3-1	CD-s	Internal	LIECD7	1993	£5	£2	
Midnight	CD-s	FFRR	FCD163	1991	£5	£2	
Midnight	CD-s	Internal	LIECD26	1996	£5	£2	
Mutations	CD-s	ffrr	FRRCD181	1992	£6	£2.50	
Omen	12"	ffrr	FRRX145	1990	£10	£5	
Omen	7"	ffrr	FRR145	1990	£4	£1.50	
Omen	CD-s	FFRR	FCD145	1990	£10	£5	
Orbital	CD	ffrr	FRR8282482	1991	£15	£6	
Orbital	LP	ffrr	FRR8282481	1991	£12	£5	*double*
Peel Sessions	CD-s	Internal	LIECD12	1994	£6	£2.50	
Satan	12"	ffrr	FRRX147	1991	£10	£5	
Satan	12"	ffrr	FRRXR147	1991	£10	£5	
Satan	7"	ffrr	FRR147	1991	£4	£1.50	
Satan	CD-s	FFRR	FCD149	1991	£10	£5	
Satan	CD-s	Internal	LIECD25	1995	£5	£2	
Times Fly (Slow)	CD-s	Internal	LICDP23	1995	£5	£2	

ORCHIDS

Gonna Make Him Mine	7"	Decca	F11743	1963	£10	£5	
I've Got That Feeling	7"	Decca	F11861	1964	£10	£5	
Love Hit Me	7"	Decca	F11785	1963	£10	£5	

ORCHIDS (2)

From This Day	7"	Sha La La	005	1988	£5	£2	*flexi, B side by Sea Urchins*
I've Got A Habit	7"	Sarah	002	1988	£10	£5	*with poster*

ORE

Halcyon Days	LP	Akashic		1979	£25	£10	*US picture disc*
Your Time Will Come	7"	Bandit	BR003	1982	£12	£6	

OREGON

Distant Hills	LP	Vanguard	VSD79341	1974	£12	£5	

Title	Format	Label	Cat. No.	Year	Mint	Good	Notes
In Concert	LP	Vanguard	VSD79358	1976	**£12**	**£5**	*US*
Music Of Another Present Era	LP	Vanguard	VSD79326	1974	**£12**	**£5**	
Winter Light	LP	Vanguard	VSD79350	1975	**£12**	**£5**	

ORGANAIRE, CHARLES

Title	Format	Label	Cat. No.	Year	Mint	Good	Notes
Little Village	7"	R&B	JB149	1964	**£10**	**£5**	
Little Village	7"	Rio	R28	1964	**£10**	**£5**	

ORGANGRINDERS

Title	Format	Label	Cat. No.	Year	Mint	Good	Notes
Out Of The Egg	LP	Mercury	SR61282	1970	**£30**	**£15**	*US*

ORGANISATION

Ralf Hutter and Florian Schneider-Esleban, the creative centre of Kraftwerk, recorded an earlier album as Organisation. Like Tangerine Dream's *Electronic Meditation*, *Tone Float* is the work of a unit trying to create an electronic soundscape with acoustic instruments and essentially biding time until the invention of a usable synthesizer. Objectively, the music is not really very impressive, although its historical importance is undeniable.

Title	Format	Label	Cat. No.	Year	Mint	Good	Notes
Tone Float	LP	RCA	SF8111	1970	**£150**	**£75**	

ORGANISERS

Title	Format	Label	Cat. No.	Year	Mint	Good	Notes
Lonesome Road	7"	Pye	7N17022	1966	**£75**	**£37.50**	

ORGANUM

Title	Format	Label	Cat. No.	Year	Mint	Good	Notes
Pulp	7"	Aeroplane	AR7	198–	**£20**	**£10**	

ORIENT EXPRESS

Title	Format	Label	Cat. No.	Year	Mint	Good	Notes
Orient Express	LP	Mainstream	S6117	1969	**£75**	**£37.50**	*US*

ORIENTAL SUNSHINE

Title	Format	Label	Cat. No.	Year	Mint	Good	Notes
Dedicated To The Bird We Love	LP	Fontana		1971	**£300**	**£180**	*Swedish*

ORIGINAL BARNSTORMERS SPASM BAND

Title	Format	Label	Cat. No.	Year	Mint	Good	Notes
That's All There Is	7"	Tempo	A168	195–	**£4**	**£1.50**	

ORIGINAL BLIND BOYS OF ALABAMA

Title	Format	Label	Cat. No.	Year	Mint	Good	Notes
Old Time Religion	LP	Fontana	688520ZL	1965	**£10**	**£4**	

ORIGINAL CHECKMATES

Title	Format	Label	Cat. No.	Year	Mint	Good	Notes
Checkmate Twist	7"	Pye	7N15442	1962	**£8**	**£4**	
Hot Toddy	7"	Pye	7N15428	1962	**£6**	**£2.50**	
Union Pacific	7"	Decca	F11688	1963	**£20**	**£10**	

ORIGINAL DIXIELAND JAZZ BAND

Title	Format	Label	Cat. No.	Year	Mint	Good	Notes
Historic Records Of The First Recorded Jazz Music	10" LP	HMV	DLP1065	1955	**£20**	**£8**	
In England	10" LP	Columbia	33S1087	1956	**£20**	**£8**	
In England No. 2	10" LP	Columbia	33S1133	1957	**£20**	**£8**	

ORIGINAL DOWNTOWN SYNCOPATORS

Title	Format	Label	Cat. No.	Year	Mint	Good	Notes
It's Jass	7" EP	Columbia	SEG8293	1964	**£5**	**£2**	
Original Downtown Syncopators	10" LP	J.R.T.Davies	DAVLP301/2	1963	**£20**	**£8**	
Original Downtown Syncopators	7" EP	VJM	VEP14	1962	**£5**	**£2**	

ORIGINAL DYAKS

Title	Format	Label	Cat. No.	Year	Mint	Good	Notes
Gotta Get A Good Thing Going	7"	Columbia	DB8184	1967	**£5**	**£2**	

ORIGINAL FIVE BLIND BOYS

Title	Format	Label	Cat. No.	Year	Mint	Good	Notes
Original Five Blind Boys	7" EP	Vogue	EPV1159	1957	**£8**	**£4**	

ORIGINAL NEW ORLEANS RHYTHM KINGS

Title	Format	Label	Cat. No.	Year	Mint	Good	Notes
Golden Leaf Strut	7"	Columbia	SCM5113	1954	**£4**	**£1.50**	

ORIGINAL TORNADOES

Title	Format	Label	Cat. No.	Year	Mint	Good	Notes
Telstar	7"	SRT	SRTS75350	1975	**£5**	**£2**	

ORIGINALS

Title	Format	Label	Cat. No.	Year	Mint	Good	Notes
Baby I'm For Real	7"	Tamla Motown	TMG733	1970	**£5**	**£2**	
Good Night Irene	7"	Tamla Motown	TMG592	1967	**£40**	**£20**	
Green Grow The Lilacs	7"	Tamla Motown	TMG702	1969	**£6**	**£2.50**	
Green Grow The Lilacs	LP	Tamla Motown	(S)TML11116	1969	**£20**	**£8**	

ORIGINALS (2)

Title	Format	Label	Cat. No.	Year	Mint	Good	Notes
Gimme A Little Kiss Will Ya	7"	Top Rank	JAR600	1962	**£10**	**£5**	

ORIGINELLS

Title	Format	Label	Cat. No.	Year	Mint	Good	Notes
My Girl	7"	Columbia	DB7259	1964	**£8**	**£4**	
Nights	7"	Columbia	DB7388	1964	**£6**	**£2.50**	

ORIOLES

Title	Format	Label	Cat. No.	Year	Mint	Good	Notes
Crying In The Chapel	78	London	L1201	1953	**£50**	**£25**	
Hold Me, Thrill Me, Kiss Me	78	London	L1180	1953	**£50**	**£25**	
In The Mission Of St Augustine	78	London	HL8001	1954	**£50**	**£25**	

ORION

Title	Format	Label	Cat. No.	Year	Value	Value	Notes
Insane In Another World	7"	Lost Moment	LM02	1984	£8	£4	

ORION, P. J. & THE MAGNATES

Title	Format	Label	Cat. No.	Year	Value	Value	Notes
P. J. Orion & The Magnates	LP	Magnate	122459	1961	£30	£15	US

ORION THE HUNTER

Title	Format	Label	Cat. No.	Year	Value	Value	Notes
Orion The Hunter	CD	Portrait	PRT25906	1984	£25	£10	

ORLANDO

Title	Format	Label	Cat. No.	Year	Value	Value	Notes
Am I The Same Guy	7"	NEMS	564159	1969	£4	£1.50	

ORLANDO, TONY

Title	Format	Label	Cat. No.	Year	Value	Value	Notes
Beautiful Dreamer	7"	Columbia	DB4954	1963	£4	£1.50	
Bless You	7"	Fontana	H330	1961	£4	£1.50	
Bless You	7" EP	Columbia	SEG8238	1963	£50	£25	
Bless You	LP	Fontana	STFL582	1963	£40	£20	*stereo*
Bless You	LP	Fontana	TFL5167	1963	£30	£15	*mono*
Chills	7"	Columbia	DB4871	1962	£4	£1.50	
Halfway To Paradise	7"	Fontana	H308	1961	£8	£4	
Happy Times	7"	Fontana	H350	1961	£5	£2	
Joannie	7"	Columbia	DB4991	1963	£4	£1.50	
Talking About You	7"	Fontana	H366	1962	£4	£1.50	
Tell Me What I Can Do	7"	Columbia	DB7288	1964	£4	£1.50	

ORLONS

Title	Format	Label	Cat. No.	Year	Value	Value	Notes
All The Hits	LP	Cameo Parkway	C1033	1962	£30	£15	
Biggest Hits	LP	Cameo Parkway	C1061	1963	£25	£10	
Bon Doo Wah	7"	Cameo Parkway	C287	1963	£6	£2.50	
Cameo Parkway Sessions	LP	London	HAU8504	1978	£10	£4	
Crossfire	7"	Cameo Parkway	C273	1963	£5	£2	
Don't Hang Up	7"	Cameo Parkway	C231	1962	£5	£2	
Down Memory Lane	LP	Cameo	C1073	1963	£25	£10	US
Knock Knock	7"	Cameo Parkway	C332	1964	£6	£2.50	
Not Me	7"	Cameo Parkway	C257	1963	£4	£1.50	
Not Me	LP	Cameo	C1054	1963	£25	£10	US
Rules Of Love	7"	Cameo Parkway	C319	1964	£6	£2.50	
Shimmy Shimmy	7"	Cameo Parkway	C295	1963	£4	£1.50	
South Street	7"	Cameo Parkway	C243	1963	£6	£2.50	
South Street	LP	Cameo	C1041	1963	£30	£15	US
Spinning Top	7"	Planet	PLF117	1966	£40	£20	
Spinning Top	7"	Mojo	2092029	1972	£4	£1.50	
Wah Watusi	7"	Columbia	DB4865	1962	£8	£4	
Wah Watusi	LP	Cameo	C1020	1962	£30	£15	US

ORLONS & DOVELLS

Title	Format	Label	Cat. No.	Year	Value	Value	Notes
Golden Hits	LP	Cameo	C1067	1963	£25	£10	US

ORNANDEL, CYRIL

Title	Format	Label	Cat. No.	Year	Value	Value	Notes
King Of Kings	7"	MGM	SP 1141	1955	£4	£1.50	

ORPHAN

Title	Format	Label	Cat. No.	Year	Value	Value	Notes
Nervous	7"	Swoop	RTLS013	1986	£8	£4	

ORPHAN EGG

Title	Format	Label	Cat. No.	Year	Value	Value	Notes
Orphan Egg	LP	Carole	CARS8004	1968	£30	£15	US

ORPHEUS

Title	Format	Label	Cat. No.	Year	Value	Value	Notes
My Life	7"	Red Bird	RB10041	1966	£10	£5	

ORPHEUS (2)

Title	Format	Label	Cat. No.	Year	Value	Value	Notes
Orpheus	LP	Bell	6061	1968	£15	£6	*US, different tracks*
Orpheus	LP	MGM	C(S)8072	1968	£15	£6	

ORY, KID

Title	Format	Label	Cat. No.	Year	Value	Value	Notes
Dance With Kid Ory – Or Just Listen	LP	HMV	CLP1395/ CSD1325	1960	£12	£5	
In The Beginning	7" EP	Collector	JE117	1960	£5	£2	
In The Mood	LP	HMV	CLP1329	1960	£12	£5	
Kid From New Orleans	LP	HMV	CLP1303	1959	£15	£6	
Kid Ory	7" EP	Philips	BBE12275	1959	£5	£2	
Kid Ory	7" EP	Storyville	SEP317	195–	£5	£2	
Kid Ory In Europe	LP	Columbia	33CX10116	1958	£15	£6	
Kid Ory Plays W. C. Handy	LP	HMV	CLP1364	1960	£12	£5	
Kid Ory's Creole Jazz Band	10" LP	Philips	BBR8088	1956	£12	£5	
Kid Ory's Creole Jazz Band	7" EP	Tempo	EXA5	1955	£5	£2	
Kid Ory's Creole Jazz Band	7" EP	Vogue	EPV1035	1955	£5	£2	

Title	Format	Label	Cat. No.	Year			Notes
Kid Ory's Creole Jazz Band	7" EP	Good Time Jazz	EPG1006	195–	£**5**	£**2**	
Kid Ory's Creole Jazz Band	LP	Good Time Jazz	LAG12064	1957	£**15**	£**6**	
Kid Ory's Creole Jazz Band	LP	Good Time Jazz	LAG12104	1958	£**12**	£**5**	
Kid Ory's Creole Jazz Band 1944–1945	10" LP	Good Time Jazz	LDG055	1954	£**15**	£**6**	
Kid Ory's Creole Jazz Band 1944–1945 Vol. 2	10" LP	Good Time Jazz	LDG093	1954	£**15**	£**6**	
Kid Ory's Creole Jazz Band 1944–1945 Vol. 3	10" LP	Good Time Jazz	LDG184	1956	£**15**	£**6**	
Kid Ory's Creole Jazz Band 1954	LP	Good Time Jazz	LAG12004	1955	£**12**	£**5**	
Legendary Kid 1956	LP	Good Time Jazz	LAG12084	1958	£**12**	£**5**	
Song Of The Wanderer	LP	Columbia	33CX10134	1959	£**15**	£**6**	
We've Got Rhythm	LP	HMV	CLP1422/ CSD1342	1961	£**15**	£**6**	*with Henry Allen*

OS MUNDI

Title	Format	Label	Cat. No.	Year			Notes
43 Minuten	LP	Brain	1015	1972	£**25**	£**10**	*German*
Latin Mass	LP	Metronome	15381	1970	£**25**	£**10**	*German*

OSAMU

Title	Format	Label	Cat. No.	Year			Notes
Banzaiten	LP	Island	ILPS80580	1976	£**20**	£**8**	*Japanese*

OSANNA

Title	Format	Label	Cat. No.	Year			Notes
L'Uomo	LP	Fonit	LPX10	1971	£**20**	£**8**	*Italian*
Landscape Of Life	LP	Fonit	LPX32	1974	£**15**	£**6**	*Italian*
Milano Calibro 9	LP	Fonit	LPX14	1972	£**15**	£**6**	*Italian*
Palepoli	LP	Fonit	LPX19	1972	£**15**	£**6**	*Italian*
Uno	LP	Fonit	LPX26	1974	£**15**	£**6**	*Italian*

OSBORNE, MIKE

Title	Format	Label	Cat. No.	Year			Notes
All Night Long	LP	Ogun	OG700	1975	£**20**	£**8**	
Border Crossing	LP	Ogun	OG300	1974	£**20**	£**8**	
Marcel's Muse	LP	Ogun	OG810	1977	£**20**	£**8**	
Original	LP	Cadillac	SGC1002	1974	£**20**	£**8**	*with Stan Tracy*
Outback	LP	Turtle	TUR300	1971	£**50**	£**25**	
Tandem	LP	Ogun	OG210	1976	£**20**	£**8**	*with Stan Tracy*

OSBORNE BROTHERS

Title	Format	Label	Cat. No.	Year			Notes
Banjo Boys	7"	MGM	MGM1184	1962	£**5**	£**2**	
Bluegrass Music	LP	MGM	C914	1962	£**10**	£**4**	
Country Picking & Hillside Singing	7" EP	MGM	MGMEP691	1959	£**20**	£**10**	

OSBOURNE, JOHNNY

Title	Format	Label	Cat. No.	Year			Notes
Come Back Darling	LP	Trojan	TTL29	1970	£**15**	£**6**	
See And Blind	7"	Big Shot	BI549	1970	£**4**	£**1.50**	*Techniques B side*

OSBOURNE, OZZY

Title	Format	Label	Cat. No.	Year			Notes
Bark At The Moon	12"	Epic	TA3915	1983	£**12**	£**6**	*silver vinyl*
Crazy Train	7"	Jet	JET197	1980	£**4**	£**1.50**	
Diary Of A Madman	LP	Jet		1981	£**30**	£**15**	*US promo picture disc*
Just Say Ozzy	CD	Epic	4659402	1993	£**12**	£**5**	
Mama I'm Coming Home	CD-s	Epic	6576179	1991	£**5**	£**2**	
Miracle Man	7"	Epic	6530639	1988	£**5**	£**2**	*shaped picture disc*
Miracle Man	CD-s	Epic	6530632	1988	£**5**	£**2**	
Mr Crowley	12"	Jet	JETP12003	1980	£**12**	£**6**	*picture disc*
Mr Crowley	7"	Jet	JET7003	1980	£**5**	£**2**	
No More Tears	CD-s	Epic	6574402	1991	£**5**	£**2**	*wallet sleeve*
Shot In The Dark	7"	Epic	QA6859	1986	£**4**	£**1.50**	*poster sleeve*
So Tired	12"	Epic	WA4452	1984	£**8**	£**4**	*gold vinyl*
Symptom Of The Universe	7"	Jet	JETP7030	1982	£**6**	£**2.50**	*picture disc*
Tribute	CD	Columbia	ASK2695	1987	£**25**	£**10**	*US promo sampler*
Ultimate Sin	CD-s	Epic	6528752	1988	£**5**	£**2**	
Ultimate Sin	LP	Epic	1126404	1986	£**10**	£**4**	*picture disc*

OSBURN, BOB

Title	Format	Label	Cat. No.	Year			Notes
Bound To Happen	7"	London	HLD9869	1964	£**10**	£**5**	

OSCAR

Oscar (Beuselinck) is the real name of the singer and actor who has found far greater success under the name of Paul Nicholas. 'Over The Wall We Go' has the extra attraction of being an early David Bowie production (with Bowie himself making a cameo appearance), while 'Join My Gang' is a Pete Townshend song that the Who never recorded themselves.

Title	Format	Label	Cat. No.	Year			Notes
Club Of Lights	7"	Reaction	591003	1966	£**12**	£**6**	
Holiday	7"	Reaction	591016	1967	£**12**	£**6**	
Join My Gang	7"	Reaction	591006	1966	£**15**	£**7.50**	
Open Up The Skies	7"	Polydor	56257	1968	£**12**	£**6**	
Over The Wall We Go	7"	Reaction	591012	1967	£**15**	£**7.50**	

OSCAR BICYCLE

Title	Format	Label	Cat. No.	Year			Notes
On A Quiet Night	7"	CBS	3237	1968	£**25**	£**12.50**	

OSIBISA

Osibisa	LP	MCA	MDKS8001	1971	**£10**	**£4**	
Woyaya	LP	MCA	MDKS8005	1971	**£10**	**£4**	

OSMOND, DONNY

If It's Love That You Want	CD-s	Virgin	VSCD1140	1988	**£5**	**£2**	*3" single*

OSMOND BROTHERS

Be My Little Baby Bumble Bee	7"	MGM	MGM1208	1963	**£10**	**£5**	
New Sound Of The Brothers	LP	MGM	C1011	1963	**£20**	**£8**	
Travels Of Jamie McPheeters	7"	MGM	MGM1245	1963	**£10**	**£5**	

OSMOSIS

Osmosis	LP	RCA	LSA3010	1970	**£30**	**£15**	

OSSIAN

Ossian	LP	Spring Thyme	SPR1004	1977	**£10**	**£4**	
Seal Song	LP	Iona	IR002	1981	**£10**	**£4**	
St Kilda Wedding	LP	Iona	IR001	1979	**£10**	**£4**	

OSWALD, JOHN

Plunderphonic is constructed entirely from other people's records, which John Oswald manipulates, chops and changes with all the skill of a surgeon. The result is a masterpiece to be filed alongside Christian Marclay's *More Encores* and the KLF's *1987*. Unfortunately, like the KLF album, *Plunderphonic* managed to offend one of the original copyright holders. Despite being conceived as a totally non-profit making album – original copies were given away rather than sold – Michael Jackson's management objected to the unauthorized sampling of 'Bad' and were able to order the destruction of all remaining copies of the CD. One suspects, however, that the real source of outrage was the cover picture, created as a visual parallel to the sound aesthetics inside, and showing Jackson in half-naked 'Bad' pose, the body clearly revealed as being female.

Plunderphonic	CD	Mystery Lab	no number	1989	**£50**	**£25**	*Canadian*

OSWALD, LEE HARVEY

Self Portrait In Red	LP	Inca	1001	1967	**£20**	**£8**	*US*
Speaks	LP	Truth	2265	1967	**£20**	**£8**	*US*

OTHER BROTHERS

Let's Get Together	7"	Pama	PM785	1969	**£4**	**£1.50**	

OTHER HALF

Guitarist with the Other Half was Randy Holden, who subsequently became a member of Blue Cheer.

Mr Pharmacist	7" EP	Vogue	INT18112	1966	**£100**	**£50**	*French*
Other Half	LP	Acta	A38004	1968	**£40**	**£20**	*US*

OTHER HALF (2)

Other Half	LP	Resurrection	CX1266	1984	**£12**	**£5**	*US*
Other Half	LP	7/2 Records	HS12	1966	**£1250**	**£875**	*US*

OTHER TWO

Don't You Wanna Love Me	7"	RCA	RCA1465	1965	**£4**	**£1.50**	
I Wanna Be With You	7"	Decca	F11911	1964	**£5**	**£2**	
I'll Never Let You Go	7"	RCA	RCA1531	1966	**£5**	**£2**	

OTHERS

Oh Yeah	7"	Fontana	TF501	1964	**£50**	**£25**	

OTIS, JOHNNY

All I Want Is Your Love	7"	Capitol	CL14837	1958	**£6**	**£2.50**	
Bye Bye Baby	7"	Capitol	CL14817	1958	**£8**	**£4**	
Casting My Spell	7"	Capitol	CL15018	1959	**£8**	**£4**	
Crazy Country Hop	7"	Capitol	CL14941	1958	**£10**	**£5**	
Cuttin' Up	LP	Epic	BN26524	1970	**£12**	**£5**	*US*
Formidable	LP	Ember	SPE6604	1972	**£12**	**£5**	
Hand Jive	7"	Ember	EMBS192	1964	**£5**	**£2**	
Harlem Nocturne	78	Parlophone	R3291	1950	**£20**	**£10**	*B side Slim Gaillard*
Johnny Otis	7" EP	Vocalion	VEP170162	1965	**£75**	**£37.50**	
Johnny Otis Show	7" EP	Capitol	EAP11134	1959	**£50**	**£25**	
Johnny Otis Show	LP	Capitol	T940	1958	**£40**	**£20**	
Ma He's Making Eyes At Me	7"	Capitol	CL14794	1957	**£5**	**£2**	
Mumbling Mosie	7"	Capitol	CL15112	1960	**£5**	**£2**	
Pioneers Of Rock Vol. 3	LP	Starline	SRS5129	1973	**£10**	**£4**	
Ring A Ling	7"	Capitol	CL14875	1958	**£10**	**£5**	
Rock And Roll Hit Parade Vol. 1	LP	Dig	104	1957	**£100**	**£50**	*US*
Three Girls Named Molly	7"	Capitol	CL15057	1959	**£5**	**£2**	
Well Well Well Well	7"	Capitol	CL14854	1958	**£6**	**£2.50**	
You	7"	Capitol	CL15008	1959	**£6**	**£2.50**	

OTIS, SHUGGIE

Here Comes Shuggie Otis	LP	CBS	63996	1970	**£10**	**£4**	

OTWAY, JOHN

Beware Of The Flowers	7"	Viking	no number	1975	**£15**	**£7.50**	
Deep And Meaningless	LP	Polydor	2383501	1978	**£10**	**£4**	*with 7" (OT1)*
Gypsy	7"	County	COUN215	1972	**£15**	**£7.50**	
John Otway & Wild Willie Barrett	LP	Extracted	ELP1	1977	**£10**	**£4**	*with Wild Willy Barrett*

Title	Format	Label	Number	Year	Mint	VG	Notes
Live At The Roundhouse	LP	private	OBL1	1977	**£40**	**£20**	*with Wild Willy Barrett*
Murder Man	7"	Track	2094111	1973	**£4**	**£1.50**	*with Wild Willy Barrett*
New Jerusalem	7"	Warner Bros	OTWEAY1	1986	**£15**	**£7.50**	*actually a private pressing*

OUGENWEIDE

Title	Format	Label	Number	Year	Mint	VG	Notes
All Die Weill Ich Mag	LP	Polydor	2371517	1974	**£15**	**£6**	*German*
Eulenspiegel	LP	Polydor	2371714	1976	**£12**	**£5**	*German*
Fryheit	LP	Polydor	2437576	1978	**£12**	**£5**	*German*
Ohrenschmaus	LP	Polydor	2371700	1975	**£12**	**£5**	*German*
Ougenweide	LP	Zebra	2949009	1973	**£15**	**£6**	*German*
Ougenweide	LP	Polydor	2371678	1974	**£15**	**£6**	*German*
Ungezwungen	LP	Polydor	2634091	1977	**£15**	**£6**	*German double*

OUR PLASTIC DREAM

Title	Format	Label	Number	Year	Mint	VG	Notes
Little Bit Of Shangrila	7"	Go	AJ11411	1967	**£75**	**£37.50**	

OUT

Title	Format	Label	Number	Year	Mint	VG	Notes
Who Is Innocent	7"	Rabid	TOSH113	1979	**£4**	**£1.50**	

OUT OF DARKNESS

Title	Format	Label	Number	Year	Mint	VG	Notes
Out Of Darkness	LP	Key	KL006	1970	**£200**	**£100**	

OUT OF FOCUS

Title	Format	Label	Number	Year	Mint	VG	Notes
Four Letter Monday Afternoon	LP	Kuckuck	2640101	1972	**£40**	**£20**	*German double*
Out Of Focus	LP	Kuckuck	2375010	1972	**£30**	**£15**	*German*
Wake Up	LP	Kuckuck	2375006	1971	**£30**	**£15**	*German*

OUTCASTS

Title	Format	Label	Number	Year	Mint	VG	Notes
Frustration	7"	It	IT4	1978	**£6**	**£2.50**	
Just Another Teenage Rebel	7"	Good Vibrations	GOT3	1978	**£5**	**£2**	*2 different picture sleeves*
Self Conscious Over You	LP	Good Vibrations	BIG1	1979	**£10**	**£4**	

OUTER LIMITS

Title	Format	Label	Number	Year	Mint	VG	Notes
Dark Side Of The Moon	7"	Decca	F13176	1971	**£5**	**£2**	
Great Train Robbery	7"	Instant	IN001	1968	**£15**	**£7.50**	
Great Train Robbery	7"	Immediate	IM067	1968	**£50**	**£25**	*demo*
Just One More Chance	7"	Deram	DM125	1967	**£10**	**£5**	
When The Work Is Thru'	7"	Elephant	LUR100	1967	**£30**	**£15**	*5 Man Cargo B side*

OUTER LIMITS (2)

Title	Format	Label	Number	Year	Mint	VG	Notes
Paradise For Two	7"	Teldisc	TD154	196–	**£15**	**£7.50**	

OUTER LIMITS (3)

Title	Format	Label	Number	Year	Mint	VG	Notes
Your Stepping Stone	7"	Deroy	1049	197–	**£15**	**£7.50**	

OUTLAW BLUES BAND

Title	Format	Label	Number	Year	Mint	VG	Notes
Breaking In	LP	Stateside	SSL10290	1969	**£12**	**£5**	
Outlaw Blues Band	LP	Bluesway	BLS6021	1968	**£12**	**£5**	*US*

OUTLAWS

The Outlaws were employed as session men by producer Joe Meek and therefore appear on records by the likes of Mike Berry, John Leyton and Heinz. Between October 1962 and April 1964 the lead guitarist was Ritchie Blackmore. He can be heard on the four Outlaws singles issued in 1963–4, but not on the Outlaws album. This record, which contains cowboy-oriented instrumentals, has been highly sought-after since the early days of record collecting.

Title	Format	Label	Number	Year	Mint	VG	Notes
Ambush	7"	HMV	POP877	1961	**£8**	**£4**	
Dream Of The West	LP	HMV	CLP1484	1961	**£100**	**£50**	
Dream Of The West	LP	HMV	CLP1489	1961	**£60**	**£30**	*black label*
Keep A Knocking	7"	HMV	POP1277	1964	**£30**	**£15**	
Last Stage West	7"	HMV	POP990	1962	**£10**	**£5**	
Law And Order	7"	HMV	POP1241	1963	**£10**	**£5**	
Return Of The Outlaws	7"	HMV	POP1124	1963	**£8**	**£4**	
Sioux Serenade	7"	HMV	POP1074	1962	**£10**	**£5**	
Swinging Low	7"	HMV	POP844	1961	**£8**	**£4**	
That Set The Wild West Free	7"	HMV	POP1195	1963	**£10**	**£5**	
Valley Of The Sioux	7"	HMV	POP927	1961	**£10**	**£5**	

OUTRIGGERS

Title	Format	Label	Number	Year	Mint	VG	Notes
Surrender	7" EP	Warner Bros	WSEP2027	1961	**£5**	**£2**	*stereo*

OUTSIDERS

Title	Format	Label	Number	Year	Mint	VG	Notes
Album No. 2	LP	Capitol	(S)T2568	1966	**£25**	**£10**	*US*
Girl In Love	7"	Capitol	CL15450	1966	**£10**	**£5**	
Happening Live	LP	Capitol	(S)T2745	1967	**£25**	**£10**	*US*
Help Me Girl	7"	Capitol	CL15480	1966	**£6**	**£2.50**	
Help Me Girl	7" EP	Capitol	EAP120879	1966	**£30**	**£15**	*French*
I'll Give You Time	7"	Capitol	CL15495	1967	**£8**	**£4**	
I'll Give You Time	7" EP	Capitol	EAP120948	1967	**£30**	**£15**	*French*
Outsiders In	LP	Capitol	(S)T2636	1967	**£25**	**£10**	*US*
Respectable	7"	Capitol	CL15468	1966	**£10**	**£5**	
Time Won't Let Me	7"	Capitol	CL15435	1966	**£12**	**£6**	

Time Won't Let Me	7" EP	Capitol	EAP120804	1966	£30	£15	French
Time Won't Let Me	LP	Capitol	(S)T2501	1966	£25	£10	US

OUTSIDERS (2)

Calling On Youth	LP	Raw Edge	RER001	1977	£20	£8	
Close Up	LP	Raw Edge	RER003	1978	£20	£8	
One To Infinity	7"	Raw Edge	RER002	1977	£12	£6	
Vital Hours	7"	Xciting Plastic		1978	£15	£7.50	

OUTSIDERS (3)

CQ	LP	Polydor	236803	1972	£100	£50	Dutch
Outsiders	LP	Relax	30007	1964	£75	£37.50	Dutch
Outsiders Or Insiders	LP	CNR	GA5501	1966	£75	£37.50	Dutch

OUTSIDERS (4)

Keep On Doing It	7"	Decca	F12213	1965	£8	£4	

OUTSKIRTS OF INFINITY

Lord Of The Dark Skies	LP	Woronzow	WOO7	1987	£10	£4	

OVALTINEES

British Justice	7"	none	BAA021	1983	£20	£10	

OVARY LODGE

Ovary Lodge	LP	RCA	SF8372	1973	£30	£15	
Ovary Lodge	LP	Ogun	OG600	1976	£12	£5	

OVERLANDERS

Don't It Make You Feel Good	7" EP	Pye	PNV24124	1964	£15	£7.50	French
Michelle	7" EP	Pye	NEP24245	1966	£15	£7.50	
Michelle	7" EP	Pye	PNV24161	1966	£15	£7.50	French
Michelle	LP	Pye	NPL18138	1966	£25	£10	

OVERLORD

Lucy	7"	Airebeat	ABT3	1978	£15	£7.50	

OVERMAN, RUNE

Big Bass Boogie	7"	Decca	F11605	1963	£4	£1.50	

OVERTAKERS

That's The Way You Like It	7"	Amalgamated	AMG803	1968	£8	£4	

OWEN, RAY

Ray Owen's Moon	LP	Polydor	2325061	1971	£15	£6	

OWEN, REG

Manhattan Spiritual	7"	Pye	7N25009	1959	£4	£1.50	
Manhattan Spiritual	LP	Pye	NSPL93000	1959	£15	£6	stereo
Manhattan Spiritual	LP	Pye	NPL28000	1959	£10	£4	
Swing Me High	10" LP	Parlophone	PMD1045	1956	£10	£4	

OWEN & LEON

Fits Is On Me	7"	Island	WI164	1964	£10	£5	Skatalites B side
My Love For You	7"	Island	WI163	1964	£10	£5	
Running Around	7"	Island	WI165	1964	£10	£5	Skatalites B side

OWEN-B

Owen-B	LP	Musicol	101209/10	1970	£75	£37.50	US

OWENS, BUCK

Act Naturally	7" EP	Capitol	EAP120602	1964	£10	£5	
Before You Go	LP	Capitol	(S)T2353	1966	£10	£4	
Best Of Buck Owens	LP	Capitol	(S)T2105	1964	£10	£4	
Buck Owens Sings Harlan Howard	LP	Capitol	(S)T1482	1961	£12	£5	US
Carnegie Hall Concert	LP	Capitol	(S)T2556	1967	£10	£4	
Everlasting Love	7"	Capitol	CL15009	1959	£4	£1.50	
Fabulous Country Music Sound	LP	Starday	SLP172	1962	£10	£4	US
Foolin' Around	7" EP	Capitol	EAP11550	1961	£10	£5	
I've Got A Tiger By The Tail	LP	Capitol	(S)T2283	1966	£10	£4	
It Takes People Like You To Make People Like Me	LP	Capitol	(S)T2841	1968	£10	£4	
Roll Out The Red Carpet	LP	Capitol	(S)T2443	1966	£10	£4	
Together Again	LP	Capitol	T2135	1965	£10	£4	
Under Your Spell Again	LP	Capitol	(D)T1489	1961	£12	£5	US
Your Tender Loving Care	LP	Capitol	(S)T2760	1968	£10	£4	
Yours, Country Style	LP	Capitol	(S)T20861	1966	£10	£4	

OWENS, DONNIE

Need You	7"	London	HL8747	1958	£15	£7.50	

OWL

Run To The Sun	7"	United Artists	UP2240	1968	£15	£7.50	

OXFORDS

Flying Up Through The Sky	LP	Union Jac	LH6497	1970	£30	£15	US

OXLEY, TONY

Title	Format	Label	Cat. No.	Year	Mint	VG	Notes
Ach Was?	LP	FMP	0871	1981	£**12**	£**5**	*German*
Baptised Traveller	LP	CBS	52664	1969	£**40**	£**20**	
Duo	LP	ADMW	005	197–	£**15**	£**6**	*with Davie Alan*
February Papers	LP	Incus	INCUS18	1976	£**15**	£**6**	
Four Compositions For Sextet	LP	CBS	64071	1970	£**40**	£**20**	
Ichnos	LP	RCA	SF8215	1971	£**40**	£**20**	
Quartet – Dedications	LP	Knonnex	ST5002	1983	£**12**	£**5**	
Ronnie's Lament	LP	View	VS0018	1981	£**12**	£**5**	*German*
SOH	LP	Ego	4011	1979	£**15**	£**6**	
Tomorrow Is Here	LP	Dossier	ST7507	1986	£**12**	£**5**	
Tony Oxley	LP	Incus	INCUS8	1975	£**20**	£**8**	

OXYM

Title	Format	Label	Cat. No.	Year	Mint	VG	Notes
Music Power	7"	Cargo	CRS3	1981	£**20**	£**10**	

OYSTER BAND

Title	Format	Label	Cat. No.	Year	Mint	VG	Notes
English Rock And Roll The Early Years (1800–1850)	LP	Pukka	YOP01	1982	£**40**	£**20**	
Jack's Alive	LP	Dingles	DIN309	1980	£**30**	£**15**	*credited to Oyster Ceilidh Band*
Liberty Hall	LP	Pukka	YOP07	1985	£**40**	£**20**	
Lie Back And Think Of England	LP	Pukka	YOP04	1985	£**40**	£**20**	
Twenty Golden Tie Slackeners	LP	Pukka	YOP06	1984	£**40**	£**20**	

OZ KNOZZ

Title	Format	Label	Cat. No.	Year	Mint	VG	Notes
Ruff Mix	LP	Ozone	OZ1000	1975	£**300**	£**180**	*US*

OZO

Title	Format	Label	Cat. No.	Year	Mint	VG	Notes
Listen To The Buddah	LP	DJM	DJF20488	1970	£**20**	£**8**	

OZZ II

Title	Format	Label	Cat. No.	Year	Mint	VG	Notes
Assassin	LP	Zebra	ZEB2	1984	£**15**	£**6**	

PABLO, AUGUSTUS

Title	Format	Label	Cat. No.	Year	Mint	VG	Notes
405	7"	Creole	CR1004	1971	£5	£2	
Bedroom Mazurka	7"	Randys	RAN536	1973	£5	£2	
East Of The River Nile	7"	Big Shot	BI579	1971	£10	£5	*Herman B side*
Ital Dub	LP	Trojan	TRLS115	1976	£15	£6	
King Tubby Meets Rockers Uptown	LP	Yard Music	DSR8225	197–	£15	£6	
Original Rockers	LP	Greensleeves	GREL8	1979	£12	£5	
Reggae In The Fields	7"	Duke	DU122	1971	£4	£1.50	*Tommy McCook B side*
Snowball And Pudding	7"	Ackee	ACK138	1971	£10	£5	*Aquarians B side*
Still Yet	7"	Ackee	ACK134	1971	£10	£5	*Aquarians B side*
This Is Augustus Pablo	LP	Tropical	TROPS101	1974	£15	£6	

PACIFIC DRIFT

Title	Format	Label	Cat. No.	Year	Mint	VG	Notes
Feelin' Free	LP	Nova	(S)DN13	1970	£25	£10	
Water Woman	7"	Deram	DM304	1970	£4	£1.50	

PACIFIC GAS & ELECTRIC

Title	Format	Label	Cat. No.	Year	Mint	VG	Notes
Are You Ready	LP	CBS	64026	1970	£10	£4	
Get It On	LP	B&C	CAS1003	1969	£12	£5	
Hard Burn	LP	CBS	64295	1971	£10	£4	
Pacific Gas & Electric	LP	CBS	63822	1969	£10	£4	

PACIFIC SOUND

Title	Format	Label	Cat. No.	Year	Mint	VG	Notes
Forget Your Dream	LP	Splendid	50104	1972	£400	£250	*Swiss*

PACK

Title	Format	Label	Cat. No.	Year	Mint	VG	Notes
Do You Believe In Magic	7"	Columbia	DB7702	1965	£20	£10	

PACK *(2)*

Title	Format	Label	Cat. No.	Year	Mint	VG	Notes
Brave New Soldiers	7"	SS	PAK1	1979	£8	£4	
King Of Kings	7"	Rough Trade	RT025	1979	£6	£2.50	
Kirk Brandon And The Pack Of Lies	7"	SS	SS1N2/SS2N1	1980	£10	£5	
Long Live The Past	7"	Cyclops	CYCLOPS1	1982	£4	£1.50	

PACKABEATS

Title	Format	Label	Cat. No.	Year	Mint	VG	Notes
Dream Lover	7"	Pye	7N15549	1963	£12	£6	
Evening In Paris	7"	Pye	7N15480	1962	£12	£6	
Gypsy Beat	7"	Parlophone	R4729	1961	£8	£4	

PACKERS

Title	Format	Label	Cat. No.	Year	Mint	VG	Notes
Hole In The Wall	7"	Pye	7N25343	1966	£8	£4	
Hole In The Wall	7"	Soul City	SC111	1969	£5	£2	
Hole In The Wall	LP	Soul City	SCM003	1970	£20	£8	

PAC-KEYS

Title	Format	Label	Cat. No.	Year	Mint	VG	Notes
Stone Fox	7"	Speciality	SPE1003	1967	£5	£2	

PADDY, KLAUS & GIBSON

Title	Format	Label	Cat. No.	Year	Mint	VG	Notes
I Wanna Know	7"	Pye	7N15906	1965	£10	£5	
No Good Without You Baby	7"	Pye	7N17060	1966	£20	£10	
Teresa	7"	Pye	7N17112	1966	£10	£5	

PAESE DEI BOLOCCHI

Title	Format	Label	Cat. No.	Year	Mint	VG	Notes
Paese Dei Bolocchi	LP	CGD	FGL5115	1972	£40	£20	*Italian*

PAGE, HAL & THE WHALERS

Title	Format	Label	Cat. No.	Year	Mint	VG	Notes
Going Back To My Home Town	7"	Melodisc	1553	1960	£20	£10	

PAGE, HOT LIPS

Title	Format	Label	Cat. No.	Year	Mint	VG	Notes
Ain't Nothing Wrong With That Page	7"	Parlophone	MSP6172	1955	£15	£7.50	

PAGE, JIMMY

Title	Format	Label	Cat. No.	Year	Mint	VG	Notes
Interview With Jimmy Page	CD	Geffen	PROCD3099	1988	£25	£10	*US promo*
Outrider	CD	Geffen	9241882	1988	£40	£20	*promo box set, with cassette, interview CD, video, photo*
Outrider	CD	Geffen		1988	£25	£10	*US promo sampler with interview*
She Just Satisfies	7"	Fontana	TF533	1965	£300	£180	*best auctioned*
She Just Satisfies	CD-s	Fontana	TFCD533	1991	£6	£2.50	*Led Zeppelin pack*

Wasting My Time	7"	Geffen	GEF41	1988	£**5**	£**2**	

PAGE, JIMMY & ROBERT PLANT

Conversations With Jimmy Page And Robert Plant	CD	Atlantic	PRCD59872	1994	£**25**	£**10**	*US promo*
Gallows Pole	CD-s	Fontana	PPDD2	1994	£**6**	£**2.50**	
No Quarter – Unledded Radio Special	CD	Fontana	PPID1	1995	£**75**	£**37.50**	*interview promo*
Songwriting Legacy	CD	Atlantic	PRCD60952	1995	£**40**	£**20**	*US promo only 'Greatest Hits'*

PAGE, LARRY

Big Blon' Baby	7"	Saga	SAG452902	1959	£**15**	£**7.50**	
Cool Shake	7"	Columbia	DB3965	1957	£**10**	£**5**	
How Am I Doing, Hey, Hey	7"	Saga	SAG452903	1959	£**5**	£**2**	
Kinky Music	LP	Decca	LK4692	1965	£**50**	£**25**	
Sings His Personal Choice	7" EP	Saga	STP1024	1963	£**5**	£**2**	
That'll Be The Day	7"	Columbia	DB4012	1957	£**10**	£**5**	
Under Control	7"	Columbia	DB4080	1958	£**8**	£**4**	

PAGE, MALLY

Life And Soul Of The Party	7"	Pye	7N17105	1966	£**4**	£**1.50**	

PAGE, PATTI

Bring Us Together	7"	Mercury	7MT200	1958	£**4**	£**1.50**	
Christmas With Patti Page	10" LP	Mercury	MPT7510	1956	£**15**	£**6**	
Folk Song Favourites	10" LP	Mercury	MG25101	1954	£**15**	£**6**	
I'll Remember Today	7"	Mercury	7MT184	1958	£**4**	£**1.50**	
I'm Getting Sentimental Over You	10" LP	Mercury	MPT7531	1957	£**12**	£**5**	
In The Land Of Hi-Fi	LP	Emarcy	EJL1252	1957	£**10**	£**4**	
Lady Is A Tramp	7" EP	Mercury	SEZ19008	1961	£**5**	£**2**	*stereo*
Left Right Out Of Your Heart	7"	Mercury	7MT223	1958	£**5**	£**2**	
My Kinda Love	7" EP	Mercury	SEZ19020	1961	£**5**	£**2**	*stereo*
Patti Page	7" EP	Mercury	MEP9502	1956	£**6**	£**2.50**	
Patti Page No. 1	7" EP	Mercury	ZEP10006	1959	£**6**	£**2.50**	
Patti Page No. 2	7" EP	Mercury	ZEP10017	1959	£**6**	£**2.50**	
Patti Page No. 3	7" EP	Mercury	ZEP10032	1959	£**6**	£**2.50**	
Patti Page No. 4	7" EP	Mercury	ZEP10045	1959	£**6**	£**2.50**	
Patti's Songs	10" LP	Mercury	MG25197	1955	£**15**	£**6**	
Patti's Songs	10" LP	Mercury	MPT7535	1957	£**10**	£**4**	
These Worldly Wonders	7"	Mercury	7MT206	1958	£**4**	£**1.50**	

PAGE BOYS

You're My Kind Of Girl	7"	Whaam!	WHAAM10	1983	£**5**	£**2**	

PAGE FIVE

Let Sleeping Dogs Lie	7"	Parlophone	R5426	1966	£**15**	£**7.50**	

PAGE TEN

Boutique	7"	Decca	F12248	1965	£**4**	£**1.50**	

PAICH, MARTY

Marty Paich Quartet	10" LP	London	LZU14040	1957	£**20**	£**8**	

PAIGE, ELAINE

Radio Ga Ga	CD-s	Siren	SRNCD110	1989	£**5**	£**2**	*3" single*

PAIGE, JOEY

Cause I'm In Love With You	7"	Fontana	TF554	1965	£**10**	£**5**	

PAIGE, ROSALIND

Love, Oh Careless Love	7"	MGM	MGM937	1957	£**4**	£**1.50**	
When The Saints	7"	London	HL8120	1955	£**10**	£**5**	

PAINTED SHIP

Frustration	7"	Mercury	MF988	1967	£**40**	£**20**	

PAISLEYS

Cosmic Mind At Play	LP	Audio City	94452809	1968	£**100**	£**50**	*US*
Cosmic Mind At Play	LP	Peace	70P1	1970	£**60**	£**30**	*US*
Cosmic Mind At Play	LP	Psycho	PSYCHO7	1983	£**10**	£**4**	

PALADIN

Charge	LP	Bronze	ILPS9190	1972	£**20**	£**8**	
Paladin	LP	Bronze	ILPS9150	1971	£**15**	£**6**	

PALE FOUNTAINS

Just A Girl	7"	Operation Twilight	OPT09	1982	£**8**	£**4**	

PALE SAINTS

Children Break	7"	Panic	PANICFIRST	198–	£**4**	£**1.50**	*flexi, B side by Savlons & Kerry Fiddles*
Extracts From In Ribbons	CD-s	4AD	PS2CD	1992	£**6**	£**2.50**	

PALEY, TOM

Sue Cow	LP	Argo	ZFB3	1969	£**12**	£**5**	

Title	Format	Label	Number	Year	Mint	VG+	Notes
Who's Going To Shoe Your Pretty Little Foot?	LP	Topic	12T113	1964	£25	£10	*with Peggy Seeger*

PALEY BROTHERS

Come On Let's Go	7"	Sire	SRE4005	1978	£5	£2	

PALI GAP

Under The Sun	7"	Sinister	SYN001	1982	£20	£10	

PALLAS

Arrive Alive	7"	Granite Wax	GWS1	1982	£25	£12.50	
Arrive Alive	LP	Cool King	CKLP002	1983	£10	£4	
Knightmoves	12"	Harvest	12PLSD3	1985	£15	£7.50	*with Mad Machine 7"*
Pallas	7"	Sueicide	PAL101	1978	£40	£20	
Paris Is Burning	12"	Cool King	12CK010	1983	£6	£2.50	

PALMEIRA

Palmeira	LP	ANS		1983	£12	£5	*Dutch*

PALMER, BRUCE

Cycle Is Complete	LP	Verve	VRF3086	1971	£25	£10	*US*

PALMER, CLIVE

Just Me	LP	Autogram	ALLP258	1979	£50	£25	*German*

PALMER, EARL

Drum Village	7"	Capitol	CL14859	1958	£5	£2	
Drumsville	LP	Liberty	LBY1008	1961	£12	£5	
Swingin' Drums	7" EP	Capitol	EAP11026	1958	£5	£2	*with Billy May*

PALMER, ROBERT

Bad Case Of Lovin' You	CD-s	Island	CID438	1989	£5	£2	
Change His Ways	CD-s	EMI	CDEM85	1989	£5	£2	
I Didn't Mean To Turn You On	CD-s	Island	CID283	1986	£15	£7.50	
It Could Happen To You	CD-s	EMI	CDEM99	1989	£5	£2	
Live In Boston	LP	Warner Bros	WBMS111	1979	£20	£8	*US promo*
Secrets	LP	Island	PROA819	1979	£20	£8	*US promo picture disc*
She Makes My Day	CD-s	EMI	CDEM65	1988	£5	£2	
Simply Irresistible	CD-s	EMI	CDEM61	1988	£5	£2	

PALMER, ROY & THE STATE STREET RAMBLERS

Chicago Skiffle Session	10" LP	London	AL3518	1954	£25	£10	

PALMETTO KINGS

Ten Rum Bottles	7"	Starlite	ST45021	1960	£4	£1.50	

PAMA DICE

Bongo Man	7"	Jackpot	JP715	1969	£5	£2	
Brixton Fight	7"	Reggae	REG3001	1970	£4	£1.50	*Opening B side*
Sin, Sun And Sex	7"	Jackpot	JP716	1969	£5	£2	

PAN

Pan	LP	Sonet	SLPS1518	1970	£200	£100	

PAN (2)

Pan	LP	Columbia	KC32062	1973	£20	£8	*US*

PANAMA LTD JUG BAND

Indian Summer	LP	Harvest	SHVL779	1970	£40	£20	
Lady Of Shallott	7"	Harvest	HAR5010	1969	£5	£2	
Panama Ltd Jug Band	LP	Harvest	SHVL753	1969	£30	£15	
Round And Round	7"	Harvest	HAR5022	1970	£5	£2	

PANCAKE

Roxy Elephant	LP	Offers	OMP7602	1975	£10	£4	*German*

PANCHO, GENE

I Like Sweet Music	7"	Giant	GN21	1968	£4	£1.50	

PANDAMONIUM

Chocolate Buster Dan	7"	CBS	3451	1968	£40	£20	
No Presents For Me	7"	CBS	2664	1967	£60	£30	
Season Of The Witch	7"	CBS	202462	1967	£40	£20	

PANDORRA ENSEMBLE

III	LP	Disaster Electronics		1978	£100	£50	*Dutch*

PANHANDLE

Panhandle	LP	Decca	SKL5105	1972	£15	£6	

PANIC, JOHNNY & THE BIBLE OF DREAMS

Johnny Panic	CD-s	Fontana	PANCD1	1991	£8	£4	

PANIK

It Won't Sell	7"	Rainy City	SHOT1	1977	£10	£5	

PANTA RHEI

Title	Format	Label	Cat. No.	Year	Mint	VG	Notes
Panta Rhei	LP	Amiga	855318	1973	**£40**	**£20**	*East German*

PANTER, JAN

Title	Format	Label	Cat. No.	Year	Mint	VG	Notes
Let It Be Now	7"	CBS	201810	1965	**£6**	**£2.50**	
My Two Arms Minus You Equals Tears	7"	Oriole	CB1938	1965	**£8**	**£4**	
Scratch My Back	7"	Pye	7N17097	1966	**£10**	**£5**	

PANTHEON

Title	Format	Label	Cat. No.	Year	Mint	VG	Notes
Orion	LP	Vertigo	6360850	1973	**£60**	**£30**	*Dutch*

PANTHER

Title	Format	Label	Cat. No.	Year	Mint	VG	Notes
Wir Wollen Alles	LP	Panther	2667	1974	**£30**	**£15**	*German*

PANTHERS

Title	Format	Label	Cat. No.	Year	Mint	VG	Notes
Baby	7" EP	Polydor	60118	196–	**£50**	**£25**	*French*

PANTON, DAVE

Title	Format	Label	Cat. No.	Year	Mint	VG	Notes
One Music	LP	Nondo	HTLP1370	1973	**£25**	**£10**	

PANTON, ROY

Title	Format	Label	Cat. No.	Year	Mint	VG	Notes
Cherita	7"	Rio	R19	1964	**£10**	**£5**	
Forty Four	7"	Blue Beat	BB117	1962	**£12**	**£6**	*Leon & Owen B side*
Hell Gate	7"	Blue Beat	BB219	1964	**£12**	**£6**	
Mighty Ruler	7"	Blue Beat	BB182	1963	**£12**	**£6**	
You Don't Know Me	7"	Rio	R33	1964	**£10**	**£5**	*Edward's Allstars B side*

PANTRY, JOHN

Title	Format	Label	Cat. No.	Year	Mint	VG	Notes
John Pantry	LP	Philips	6308129	1972	**£10**	**£4**	
Long White Trail	LP	Philips	6308138	1973	**£10**	**£4**	

PANZA DIVISION

Title	Format	Label	Cat. No.	Year	Mint	VG	Notes
We'll Rock The World	7"	Panza Trax	PTO1	1982	**£12**	**£6**	

PAOLA

Title	Format	Label	Cat. No.	Year	Mint	VG	Notes
Bonjour Bonjour	7"	Decca	F22916	1969	**£4**	**£1.50**	

PAPAS, NIKKI

Title	Format	Label	Cat. No.	Year	Mint	VG	Notes
By The River	7"	Parlophone	R4652	1960	**£6**	**£2.50**	
Forty-Nine State Rock	7"	Parlophone	R4590	1959	**£10**	**£5**	

PAPER BLITZ TISSUE

Title	Format	Label	Cat. No.	Year	Mint	VG	Notes
Boy Meets Girl	7"	RCA	RCA1652	1967	**£125**	**£62.50**	

PAPER BUBBLE

Title	Format	Label	Cat. No.	Year	Mint	VG	Notes
Scenery	LP	Deram	DML/SML1059	1970	**£20**	**£8**	

PAPER DOLLS

Title	Format	Label	Cat. No.	Year	Mint	VG	Notes
Paper Doll's House	LP	Pye	N(S)PL18226	1968	**£12**	**£5**	

PAPER GARDEN

Title	Format	Label	Cat. No.	Year	Mint	VG	Notes
Paper Garden	LP	Musicor	MS3175	1968	**£40**	**£20**	*US*

PAPER TOYS

Title	Format	Label	Cat. No.	Year	Mint	VG	Notes
Cold Surrender	7"	Armada	ARMAP003	1990	**£6**	**£2.50**	

PAPER WINGED DREAMS

Title	Format	Label	Cat. No.	Year	Mint	VG	Notes
Paper Winged Dreams	LP	Brimstone		1970	**£40**	**£20**	*US*

PARADIS, VANESSA

Title	Format	Label	Cat. No.	Year	Mint	VG	Notes
Be My Baby	CD-s	Polydor	PZCDD235	1992	**£5**	**£2**	*picture insert*
Coup Coup	CD-s	Polydor	0813122	1988	**£30**	**£15**	*CD video*
Coupe Coupe	7"	Polydor	8719427	1989	**£8**	**£4**	*French*
Joe Le Taxi	7"	Polydor	POSPG902	1988	**£20**	**£10**	*poster picture sleeve*
Joe Le Taxi	CD-s	Polydor	0804662	1987	**£40**	**£20**	*CD video*
Just As Long As You Are There	CD-s	Polydor	PZCDD272	1993	**£5**	**£2**	*with 2 pics*
La Magie Des Surprises Parties	7"	Polydor		1985	**£150**	**£75**	*French*
Manolo Manolete	12"	Polydor	8872651	1988	**£30**	**£15**	*French*
Manolo Manolete	7"	Polydor	8872657	1988	**£15**	**£7.50**	*French*
Manolo Manolete	CD-s	Polydor	8873082	1988	**£40**	**£20**	*French*
Marilyn And John	12"	Polydor	PZ16	1988	**£8**	**£4**	
Marilyn And John	7"	Polydor	PO16	1988	**£4**	**£1.50**	
Marilyn And John	CD-s	Polygram		1988	**£30**	**£15**	*CD video*
Maxou	12"	Polydor	PZ38	1988	**£10**	**£5**	
Maxou	7"	Polydor	PO38	1988	**£4**	**£1.50**	
Maxou	CD-s	Polydor	8712252	1989	**£12**	**£6**	
Mosquito	7"	Polydor	8730747	1989	**£8**	**£4**	*French*
Sunday Mondays	CD-s	Polydor	PZCDD251	1992	**£5**	**£2**	*with poster*
Tandem	12"	Polydor	8773022	1990	**£15**	**£7.50**	*French*
Tandem	7"	Polydor	8773027	1990	**£8**	**£4**	*French*
Tandem (remix)	12"	Polydor	8773031	1990	**£25**	**£12.50**	*French*
Tandem (remix)	CD-s	Polydor		1990	**£50**	**£25**	*French*
Variations Sur Le Même T'aime	LP	Polydor		1990	**£20**	**£8**	*French*

Title	Format	Label	Cat. No.	Year	Mint	VG+	Notes
Works	CD	Polydor	DCI3106	1994	£100	£50	*Japanese promo compilation*

PARADONS

Title	Format	Label	Cat. No.	Year	Mint	VG+	Notes
Diamonds And Pearls	7"	Top Rank	JAR514	1960	£100	£50	

PARADOX

Title	Format	Label	Cat. No.	Year	Mint	VG+	Notes
Ring The Changes	7"	Polydor	56275	1968	£60	£30	

PARAGON

Title	Format	Label	Cat. No.	Year	Mint	VG+	Notes
Looking For You	LP	Delta Music Corporat.		1982	£30	£15	*Dutch*

PARAGONS

Title	Format	Label	Cat. No.	Year	Mint	VG+	Notes
Paragons Meet The Jesters	LP	Jubilee	JLP1098	1959	£75	£37.50	*US*
Paragons Meet The Jesters	LP	Jubilee	JLP1098	1959	£125	£62.50	*US, coloured vinyl*
Paragons Vs The Harptones	LP	Musicnote	M8001	1964	£30	£15	*US*

PARAGONS (2)

Title	Format	Label	Cat. No.	Year	Mint	VG+	Notes
Happy Go Lucky Girl	7"	Doctor Bird	DB1060	1966	£10	£5	
Have You Ever Been In Love	7"	Studio One	SO2081	1969	£12	£6	
Left With A Broken Heart	7"	Duke	DU7	1968	£8	£4	
Memories By The Score	7"	Island	WI3138	1968	£10	£5	
Mercy Mercy Mercy	7"	Treasure Isle	TI7011	1967	£10	£5	
On The Beach	7"	Island	WI3045	1967	£10	£5	*Tommy McCook B side*
On The Beach	LP	Doctor Bird	DLM5010	1967	£100	£50	
Same Song	7"	Treasure Isle	TI7013	1967	£10	£5	*Tommy McCook B side*
Silver Bird	7"	Treasure Isle	TI7034	1968	£10	£5	
So Depressed	7"	Island	WI3093	1967	£10	£5	
Talking Love	7"	Island	WI3067	1967	£10	£5	
Tide Is High	7"	Treasure Isle	TI7009	1967	£10	£5	
Wear You To The Ball	7"	Treasure Isle	TI7025	1967	£10	£5	

PARALEX

Title	Format	Label	Cat. No.	Year	Mint	VG+	Notes
Travelling Man, Black Widow, White Lightning	12"	Reddingtons	DAN4	1980	£25	£12.50	*green vinyl*

PARAMETER

Title	Format	Label	Cat. No.	Year	Mint	VG+	Notes
Galactic Ramble	LP	Deroy	DER696	1970	£400	£250	

PARAMOR, NORRIE ORCHESTRA

Title	Format	Label	Cat. No.	Year	Mint	VG+	Notes
Dance Of The Warriors	7"	Columbia	DB7446	1965	£4	£1.50	
Randall And Hopkirk (Deceased)	7"	Polydor	56375	1970	£20	£10	
Shads In Latin	LP	Columbia	TWO107	1966	£10	£4	*stereo*
Z Cars	7"	Columbia	DB4789	1962	£4	£1.50	

PARAMOUNTS

The Paramounts were yet another R&B group who gigged hard through the sixties without ever gaining very much success and who made several singles that essentially serve to emphasize why this was. Arguably, however, the group was capable of very much more, for the handful of unreleased tracks included on the Edsel compilation of the Paramounts singles are easily the most impressive. And later, the original line-up of the group made two LPs which do much more to realize its potential – but these, *Home* and *Broken Barricades*, came out under a different name – that of Procol Harum.

Title	Format	Label	Cat. No.	Year	Mint	VG+	Notes
Bad Blood	7"	Parlophone	R5187	1964	£8	£4	
Blue Ribbons	7"	Parlophone	R5272	1965	£10	£5	
Draw Me Closer	7" EP	Odeon	SOE3774	1965	£250	£150	*French*
I'm The One Who Loves You	7"	Parlophone	R5155	1964	£10	£5	
Little Bitty Pretty One	7"	Parlophone	R5107	1964	£10	£5	
Paramounts	7" EP	Parlophone	GEP8908	1964	£250	£150	*best auctioned*
Poison Ivy	7"	Parlophone	R5093	1963	£8	£4	
You've Never Had It So Good	7"	Parlophone	R5351	1965	£10	£5	

PARCEL OF ROGUES AND THE VILLAGERS

Title	Format	Label	Cat. No.	Year	Mint	VG+	Notes
Parcel Of Folk	LP	Deroy		1973	£200	£100	*insert, no sleeve*

PARCHMENT

Title	Format	Label	Cat. No.	Year	Mint	VG+	Notes
Hollywood Sunset	LP	Pye	NSPL18409	1973	£15	£6	
Light Up The Fire	LP	Pye	NSPL18388	1972	£12	£5	
Rehearsal For A Reunion	LP	Pilgrim	106	1977	£15	£6	
Shamblejam	LP	Myrrh	MYR1028	1975	£20	£8	

PARENTI, TONY

Title	Format	Label	Cat. No.	Year	Mint	VG+	Notes
Ragtime	7" EP	London	EZV19022	1957	£6	£2.50	
Ragtime	LP	London	LTZU15072	1957	£15	£6	

PARFITT, PAULA

Title	Format	Label	Cat. No.	Year	Mint	VG+	Notes
I'm Gonna Give Back Your Ring	7"	Beacon	BEA135	1969	£50	£25	

PARIS, BOBBY

Title	Format	Label	Cat. No.	Year	Mint	VG+	Notes
Personally	7"	Polydor	56747	1968	£40	£20	

PARIS, MICA

After 4th & Broadway had sent out 200 promotional copies of Mica Paris's *A Stand 4 Love* EP, they discovered that they had inadvertently included Prince's original demo of 'If I Love U 2 Nite' on the record. The DJs who had received it were asked to return the offending article, but one wonders how many actually did.

If I Love U 2 Nite ... 12" ... 4th & Broadway ... 12BRWDJ207 ... 1991 **£60** ... **£30** ... *promo*

PARIS, PRISCILLA

I Love How You Love Me ... 7" ... RAK ... RAK184 ... 1974 **£4** ... **£1.50**

PARIS SISTERS

Dream Lover ... 7" ... MGM ... MGM1240 ... 1964 **£20** ... **£10**
I Love How You Love Me ... 7" ... Top Rank ... JAR588 ... 1961 **£60** ... **£30**

PARISH HALL

Parish Hall ... LP ... Liberty ... LBS83374 ... 1970 **£10** ... **£4**

PARKER, ALAN

Guitar Fantasy ... LP ... Aristocrat ... AR1022 ... 1970 **£10** ... **£4**

PARKER, BENNY & THE DYNAMICS

Boys And Girls ... 7" ... Decca ... F11944 ... 1964 **£25** ... **£12.50**

PARKER, BOBBY

It's Hard But It's Fair ... 7" ... Blue Horizon ... 573151 ... 1969 **£20** ... **£10**
Watch Your Step ... 7" ... Sue ... WI340 ... 1964 **£15** ... **£7.50**
Watch Your Step ... 7" ... London ... HLU9393 ... 1961 **£20** ... **£10**

PARKER, CHARLIE

All Star Quintet/Sextet ... 7" EP ... Vogue ... EPV1264 ... 1960 **£5** ... **£2**
April In Paris ... LP ... Columbia ... 33CX10081 ... 1957 **£50** ... **£25**
Bird And Diz ... 10" LP ... Columbia ... 33C9026 ... 1956 **£75** ... **£37.50** ... *with Dizzy Gillespie*
Bird At St Nick's ... LP ... Melodisc ... MLP12105 ... 1955 **£40** ... **£20**
Bird Is Free ... LP ... Esquire ... 32157 ... 1962 **£15** ... **£6**
Charlie Parker Big Band ... 7" EP ... HMV ... 7EG8626 ... 1960 **£5** ... **£2**
Charlie Parker Big Band ... LP ... Columbia ... 33CX10004 ... 1955 **£75** ... **£37.50**
Charlie Parker Plays ... 7" EP ... Vogue ... EPV1011 ... 1955 **£5** ... **£2**
Charlie Parker Plays Cole Porter ... LP ... Columbia ... 33CX10090 ... 1957 **£40** ... **£20**
Charlie Parker Quintet ... 7" EP ... Esquire ... EP57 ... 1955 **£5** ... **£2**
Charlie Parker Vol. 1 ... 10" LP ... Vogue ... LDE004 ... 1952 **£100** ... **£50**
Charlie Parker Vol. 2 ... 10" LP ... Vogue ... LDE016 ... 1953 **£100** ... **£50**
Essential Charlie Parker ... LP ... HMV ... CLP1538 ... 1961 **£12** ... **£5**
Immortal Charlie Parker Vol. 1 ... LP ... London ... LTZC15104 ... 1958 **£25** ... **£10**
Immortal Charlie Parker Vol. 2 ... LP ... London ... LTZC15105 ... 1958 **£25** ... **£10**
Immortal Charlie Parker Vol. 3 ... LP ... London ... LTZC15106 ... 1958 **£25** ... **£10**
Immortal Charlie Parker Vol. 4 ... LP ... London ... LTZC15107 ... 1958 **£25** ... **£10**
Immortal Charlie Parker Vol. 5 ... LP ... London ... LTZC15108 ... 1958 **£25** ... **£10**
In Sweden ... LP ... Collector ... JGN1002 ... 1960 **£15** ... **£6**
In Sweden 1950 ... LP ... Storyville ... SLP27 ... 1962 **£12** ... **£5**
Jazz Perennial ... LP ... Columbia ... 33CX10117 ... 1958 **£25** ... **£10**
Magnificent Charlie Parker No. 1 ... 7" EP ... Columbia ... SEB10002 ... 1955 **£5** ... **£2**
Magnificent Charlie Parker No. 2 ... 7" EP ... Columbia ... SEB10038 ... 1956 **£5** ... **£2**
Magnificent Charlie Parker No. 3 ... 7" EP ... Columbia ... SEB10053 ... 1957 **£5** ... **£2**
Now's The Time ... 7" EP ... Columbia ... SEB10026 ... 1956 **£5** ... **£2**
Parker Panorama ... LP ... Verve ... VLP9138 ... 1966 **£10** ... **£4**
Parker's Mood ... 7" EP ... Realm ... REP4008 ... 1964 **£5** ... **£2**
Pick Of Parker ... LP ... Verve ... VLP9078 ... 1964 **£10** ... **£4**
Plays South Of The Border ... 7" EP ... Columbia ... SEB10032 ... 1956 **£5** ... **£2**
Portrait Of The Bird ... LP ... Columbia ... 33SX1555 ... 1963 **£10** ... **£4**

PARKER, CHET

Hammer Dulcimer ... LP ... Folkways ... FA2381 ... 1966 **£10** ... **£4** ... *US*

PARKER, DAVID

David Parker ... LP ... Polydor ... 2460101 ... 1971 **£25** ... **£10**

PARKER, DEAN & THE REDCAPS

Stormy Evening ... 7" ... Decca ... F11555 ... 1962 **£25** ... **£12.50**

PARKER, DYON

Out On The Highway ... LP ... Marble Arch ... MAL787 ... 1968 **£10** ... **£4**

PARKER, EULA

Silhouettes ... 7" ... Oriole ... CB1411 ... 1957 **£10** ... **£5**

PARKER, EVAN

At The Unity Theatre ... LP ... Incus ... INCUS14 ... 197– **£12** ... **£5** ... *with Paul Lytton*
Circadian Rhythm ... LP ... Incus ... INCUS33 ... 1979 **£12** ... **£5** ... *with other artists*
Collective Calls ... LP ... Incus ... INCUS5 ... 197– **£25** ... **£10** ... *with Paul Lytton*
From Saxophone And Trombone ... LP ... Incus ... INCUS35 ... 1980 **£12** ... **£5** ... *with George Lewis*
Hook, Line And Shuffle ... LP ... Incus ... INCUS45 ... 1985 **£12** ... **£5**
Monoceros ... LP ... Incus ... INCUS27 ... 1978 **£12** ... **£5**
Saxophone Solos ... LP ... Incus ... INCUS19 ... 1976 **£12** ... **£5**
Six Of One ... LP ... Incus ... INCUS39 ... 1982 **£12** ... **£5**
Snake Decides ... LP ... Incus ... INCUS49 ... 1986 **£12** ... **£5**

Topography Of The Lungs	LP	Incus	INCUS1	1970	**£30**	**£15**	*with Derek Bailey & Han Bennink*
Tracks	LP	Incus	INCUS42	1983	**£12**	**£5**	*with Barry Guy & Paul Lytton*

PARKER, FESS

Wringle Wrangle	7"	Oriole	CB1378	1957	**£5**	**£2**	

PARKER, GRAHAM

Live At Marble Arch	LP	Vertigo	GP1	1977	**£10**	**£4**	*promo*
Live Sparks	LP	Arista	SP63	1979	**£10**	**£4**	*US promo*

PARKER, JIMMY

We Gonna	7"	Top Rank	JAR608	1962	**£6**	**£2.50**	

PARKER, JOHNNY

Barrelhouse	7" EP	Pye	NJE1000	1955	**£5**	**£2**	

PARKER, JUNIOR

Annie Get Your Yo Yo	7"	Vogue	V9193	1962	**£12**	**£6**	
Blue Shadows Falling	LP	Groove Merchant	GM502	1972	**£10**	**£4**	
Driving Wheel	LP	Duke	DLP76	1962	**£40**	**£20**	*US*
Good Things Don't Happen Every Day	LP	Groove Merchant	GM2205	1973	**£10**	**£4**	
Goodbye Little Girl	7"	Vocalion	VP9275	1966	**£6**	**£2.50**	
Like It Is	LP	Mercury	SMCL20097	1967	**£15**	**£6**	
Memorial	LP	Vogue	LDM30163	1973	**£10**	**£4**	
Stand By Me	7"	Vogue	V9179	1961	**£15**	**£7.50**	
These Kind Of Blues	7"	Vocalion	VP9256	1966	**£10**	**£5**	
You Don't Have To Be Black To Love The Blues	LP	People	PLEO4	1974	**£10**	**£4**	

PARKER, KEN

Change Is Gonna Come	7"	Giant	GN34	1968	**£8**	**£4**	*Val Bennett B side*
Down Low	7"	Island	WI3096	1967	**£10**	**£5**	
Help Me Make It Through The Night	7"	Treasure Isle	TI7073	1972	**£4**	**£1.50**	*Tommy McCook B side*
I Can't Hide	7"	Duke	DU79	1970	**£5**	**£2**	*Tommy McCook B side*
It's Alright	7"	Amalgamated	AMG847	1969	**£6**	**£2.50**	*Cobbs B side*
Jimmy Brown	7"	Duke Reid	DR2521	1971	**£4**	**£1.50**	
Jimmy Brown	LP	Trojan	TRLS80	1974	**£10**	**£4**	
Lonely Man	7"	Island	WI3105	1967	**£10**	**£5**	*Errol Dunkley B side*
My Whole World Is Falling Down	7"	Bamboo	BAM1	1969	**£5**	**£2**	
Only Yesterday	7"	Amalgamated	AMG853	1969	**£6**	**£2.50**	*Cobbs B side*
See Them A Come	7"	Studio One	SO2001	1967	**£12**	**£6**	*Mr Foundation B side*
Sugar Pantie	7"	Duke Reid	DR2504	1971	**£5**	**£2**	*Tommy McCook B side*

PARKER, KNOCKY

Knocky Parker	LP	London	HAU2008	1956	**£12**	**£5**	
Knocky Parker Trio	10" LP	London	HBU1044	1956	**£12**	**£5**	

PARKER, LEO

Let Me Tell You 'Bout It	LP	Blue Note	BLP/BST84087	1961	**£40**	**£20**	

PARKER, RAY

Ghostbusters	12"	Arista	ARIPD12580	1984	**£6**	**£2.50**	*luminous picture disc*

PARKER, RAYMOND

Ring Around The Roses	7"	Sue	WI4024	1966	**£12**	**£6**	

PARKER, ROBERT

Barefootin'	7"	Island	WI286	1966	**£5**	**£2**	
Barefootin'	LP	Island	ILP942	1966	**£25**	**£10**	
Happy Feet	7"	Island	WI3008	1966	**£8**	**£4**	

PARKER, SONNY

My Soul's On Fire	7"	Vogue	V2392	1956	**£200**	**£100**	*best auctioned*

PARKING LOT

World Spinning Sadly	7"	Parlophone	R5779	1969	**£25**	**£12.50**	

PARKINSON, JIMMY

But You	7"	Columbia	DB3876	1957	**£4**	**£1.50**	
Great Pretender	7"	Columbia	SCM5236	1956	**£20**	**£10**	
In The Middle Of The House	7"	Columbia	DB3833	1956	**£10**	**£5**	
Lover's Quarrel	7"	Columbia	DB3808	1956	**£8**	**£4**	
Round And Round	7"	Columbia	DB3912	1957	**£5**	**£2**	
Solo	10" LP	Columbia	33S1109	1957	**£25**	**£10**	
Walk Hand In Hand	7"	Columbia	SCM5267	1956	**£10**	**£5**	

PARKS, BERNICE

Only Love Me	7"	Vogue Coral	Q72056	1955	**£6**	**£2.50**	

PARKS, SONNY

New Boy In Town	7"	Warner Bros	WB100	1963	£4	**£1.50**	

PARKS, VAN DYKE

Number Nine	7"	MGM	MGM1301	1966	£5	**£2**	
Song Cycle	LP	Warner Bros	WS1727	1968	£12	**£5**	*US*

PARLAN, HORACE

Headin' South	LP	Blue Note	BLP/BST84062	1961	£40	**£20**	
Movin' & Groovin'	LP	Blue Note	BLP/BST84028	196–	£50	**£25**	
On The Spur Of The Moment	LP	Blue Note	BLP/BST840[illegible]	1961	£40	**£20**	
Speakin' My Piece	LP	Blue Note	BLP/BST84043	196–	£40	**£20**	
Up And Down	LP	Blue Note	BLP/BST84082	1961	£30	**£15**	
Us Three	LP	Blue Note	BLP/BST84037	196–	£40	**£20**	

PARLET

The album credited to Parlet is one of several spin-off projects undertaken by George Clinton of Parliament and Funkadelic fame – this time his female backing singers are given the star billing.

Invasion Of The Booty Snatchers	LP	Casablanca	CAL2052	1979	£15	**£6**	

PARLIAMENT

George Clinton takes the uncompromising stance of James Brown, the ultra-hip posing of Sly Stewart, and the electric-warrior/sky-gypsy combination that was Jimi Hendrix and reaches wider still. He pulls in the most colourful black dialect, with his own variations; comic book science fiction; updated psychedelia; and a considerable amount of pure lunacy. Above all, he is obsessed with funk, reminding us, though with tongue firmly in cheek, that the term has a euphemistic meaning that goes hand in hand with its musical one. All this becomes apparent from Clinton's album covers alone. Songs are given titles like 'Dr Funkenstein', 'The Landing Of The Holy Mothership' and 'Lunchmeataphobia'; there are credits for 'extra-singing clones' and 'bass thumpasaurians'; and the artwork incorporates underground-style cartoons or else photographs of band members in fantastic costumes. There are, in fact, several different, overlapping recording outlets used by George Clinton – Parliament, ostensibly a vocal group, with roots in the more conventional sixties approach of Clinton's Parliaments; Funkadelic, a band devoted more to instrumental prowess; and Bootsy's Rubber Band, led by Clinton's bass guitarist, Bootsy Collins – as well as more recent recordings in Clinton's own name and minor projects like Parlet, the Brides of Funkenstein, and the Horny Horns – all united under the banner of P-Funk.

Chocolate City	LP	Casablanca	NBLP7014	1975	£15	**£6**	
Chocolate City	LP	Casablanca	CAL2012	1976	£12	**£5**	
Clones Of Dr Funkenstein	LP	Casablanca	CAL2003	1976	£12	**£5**	
Come In Out Of The Rain	7"	Invictus	INV522	1972	£5	**£2**	
Funkentelechy Vs The Placebo Syndrome	LP	Casablanca	CALH2021	1978	£12	**£5**	
Gloryhallastoopid	LP	Casablanca	NBLP7195	1979	£10	**£4**	*US*
Live/Funk Earth Tour	LP	Casablanca	CALD5002	1977	£15	**£6**	*double*
Mothership Connection	LP	Casablanca	CBC4009	1976	£12	**£5**	
Mothership Connection	LP	Casablanca	CAL2013	1977	£10	**£4**	
Motor Booty Affair	LP	Casablanca	NBPIX7125	1978	£12	**£5**	*US picture disc*
Motor Booty Affair	LP	Casablanca	CALN2044	1979	£12	**£5**	
Osmium	LP	Invictus	SVT1004	1971	£50	**£25**	
Silent Boatman	7"	Invictus	INV513	1971	£5	**£2**	
Trombipulation	LP	Casablanca	NBLP7294	1981	£10	**£4**	*US*
Up For The Down Stroke	LP	Casablanca	NBLP7002	1974	£20	**£8**	
Up For The Down Stroke	LP	Casablanca	CAL2011	1976	£12	**£5**	

PARLIAMENTS

I Wanna Testify	7"	Track	604013	1967	£10	**£5**	
I Wanna Testify	7"	Track	604032	1969	£4	**£1.50**	

PARLOPHONE POPS ORCHESTRA

Rock Around The Clock	7"	Parlophone	R4250	1956	£5	**£2**	

PARLOUR BAND

Is A Friend	LP	Deram	SDL10	1972	£150	**£75**	

PARNELL, JACK

Jack Parnell And His Orchestra	7" EP	Parlophone	GEP8532	1955	£5	**£2**	
Jack Parnell Quartet	10" LP	Decca	LF1065	1952	£10	**£4**	
Kansas City	7"	HMV	POP630	1959	£4	**£1.50**	
Night Train	7"	Parlophone	MSP6031	1953	£4	**£1.50**	
Skin Deep	7"	Parlophone	MSP6078	1954	£15	**£7.50**	
Trip To Mars	10" LP	Parlophone	PMD1053	1958	£40	**£20**	
Waltzing The Blues	7"	Parlophone	MSP6009	1953	£4	**£1.50**	

PARR, CATHERINE

You Belong To Me	7"	Decca	F12210	1965	£5	**£2**	

PARRALELE

Parralele	LP	Barclay	920389	1971	£20	**£8**	*French*

PARRISH, DEAN

Determination	7"	Stateside	SS550	1966	£30	**£15**	
Skate	7"	Stateside	SS580	1967	£15	**£7.50**	
Tell Her	7"	Stateside	SS531	1966	£20	**£10**	

PARRISH & GURVITZ

Parrish & Gurvitz	LP	Regal Zonophone	SRZA8506	1971	£10	**£4**	

PARRY, SAM

If Sadness Could Sing	LP	Argo	ZDA155	1972	**£50**	**£25**	

PARSONS, ALAN PROJECT

Best Of The Alan Parsons Project	LP	Mobile Fidelity	MFSL1175	1984	**£10**	**£4**	*US audiophile*
I, Robot	LP	Mobile Fidelity	MFSL1084	1982	**£12**	**£5**	*US audiophile (UHQR)*
I, Robot	LP	Mobile Fidelity	MFSL1084	1982	**£10**	**£4**	*US audiophile*
Turn Of A Friendly Card	LP	Arista		1980	**£10**	**£4**	*audiophile*
Vulture Culture	LP	Arista		1984	**£12**	**£5**	*US promo picture disc*

PARSONS, BILL

All American Boy	7"	London	HL8798	1959	**£8**	**£4**	

PARSONS, GRAM

G.P.	LP	Reprise	K44228	1973	**£10**	**£4**	
Grievous Angel	LP	Reprise	K54018	1974	**£10**	**£4**	
Sleepless Nights	LP	A&M	AMLH65478	1976	**£10**	**£4**	*with Emmylou Harris*

PARTISANS

Partisans	7" EP	Eaglestone Recording	EP6333	1963	**£100**	**£50**	

PARTISANS (2)

Partisans	LP	No Future	PUNK4	1983	**£10**	**£4**	
Police Story	7"	No Future	OI2	1982	**£5**	**£2**	
Seventeen Years Of Hell	7"	No Future	OI12	1982	**£5**	**£2**	
Time Was Right	LP	Cloak & Dagger	PARTLP1	1984	**£10**	**£4**	

PARTISANS (3)

Open Your Eyes	7"	Hotwire	HWS863	1988	**£5**	**£2**	

PARTON, DOLLY

Dolly Parton And George Jones	LP	Starday	SLP429	1968	**£10**	**£4**	*US, with George Jones*
Hello I'm Dolly	LP	Monument	MLP8085/ SLP18085	1967	**£12**	**£5**	*US*

PARTRIDGE, DON

Don Partridge	LP	Columbia	SX/SCX6280	1968	**£12**	**£5**	
Singing Soho Style	7" EP	CFP	CFP001/002	196–	**£8**	**£4**	

PARTY BOYS

He's Gonna Step On You Again	7"	Epic	6512300	1987	**£8**	**£4**	*shaped picture disc*

PARZIVAL

Barock	LP	Telefunken	SLE14685	1972	**£50**	**£25**	*German*
Legend	LP	Teldec	14635	1971	**£15**	**£6**	*German*

PASCAL, JEAN CLAUDE

Nous Les Amoureux	7"	HMV	POP861	1961	**£4**	**£1.50**	

PASCALIS, MARIANNA, ROBERT & BESSY

Music Lesson	7"	Power Exchange	PX254	1977	**£5**	**£2**	

PASHA

Although suggestions of this kind are often proved to be misplaced, the rumour that Pasha was actually the Searchers in disguise has yet to be refuted.

Someone Shot The Lollipop Man	7"	Liberty	LBF15199	1968	**£75**	**£37.50**	

PASSENGERS

Miss Sarajevo	CD-s	Island	CID625	1995	**£25**	**£12.50**	*with poster*
Original Soundchat	CD	Island	OST2	1995	**£100**	**£50**	*promo double*
Your Blue Room	CD-s	Island	OST3	1996	**£30**	**£15**	*1 track promo*

PASSING FANCY

Passing Fancy	LP	Boo	6801	196–	**£75**	**£37.50**	*US*

PASSIONS

I Only Want You	7"	Top Rank	JAR313	1960	**£30**	**£15**	
Jackie Brown	7"	Capitol	CL14874	1958	**£25**	**£12.50**	
Just To Be With You	7"	Top Rank	JAR224	1959	**£30**	**£15**	

PASSPORT

Passport	LP	Reprise	K44243	1973	**£12**	**£5**	

PAST SEVEN DAYS

Raindance	7"	4AD	AD102	1981	**£6**	**£2.50**	

PASTEL SIX

Title	Format	Label	Cat. No.	Year	Mint	VG	Notes
Cinnamon Cinder	7"	London	HLU9651	1963	**£5**	**£2**	
Cinnamon Cinder	LP	Zen	1001	1963	**£25**	**£10**	*US*
Golden Oldies	LP	Mark56	MLP511	1963	**£20**	**£8**	*US*

PASTELS

Title	Format	Label	Cat. No.	Year	Mint	VG	Notes
Heavens Above	7"	Whaam!	WHAAM5	1982	**£15**	**£7.50**	
Heavens Above	7"	Villa 21	VILLA3	1985	**£20**	**£10**	
I Wonder Why	7"	Rough Trade	RT137	1983	**£12**	**£6**	
Million Tears	12"	Creation	CRE011T	1984	**£6**	**£2.50**	
Something Going On	7"	Creation	CRE005	1984	**£1[illegible]**	**£[illegible]**	
Truck Train Tractor	12"	Glass	PASTEL001	1987	**£6**	**£2.50**	*double*

PASTIES & CREAM

Title	Format	Label	Cat. No.	Year	Mint	VG	Notes
Pasties & Cream	LP	Sentinel		1971	**£12**	**£5**	

PASTORAL SYMPHONY

Title	Format	Label	Cat. No.	Year	Mint	VG	Notes
Love Machine	7"	President	PT202	1968	**£4**	**£1.50**	

PASTORIUS, JACO

Title	Format	Label	Cat. No.	Year	Mint	VG	Notes
Jaco Pastorius	LP	Epic	PE33949	1976	**£15**	**£6**	*US*

PAT & MARIE

Title	Format	Label	Cat. No.	Year	Mint	VG	Notes
I Try Not To Tell You	7"	Ska Beat	JB234	1966	**£10**	**£5**	
You're Really Leaving	7"	Ska Beat	JB235	1966	**£10**	**£5**	

PAT & ROXIE

Title	Format	Label	Cat. No.	Year	Mint	VG	Notes
Sing To Me	7"	Caribou	CRC2	1965	**£4**	**£1.50**	

PATCHES

Title	Format	Label	Cat. No.	Year	Mint	VG	Notes
Living In America	7"	Warner Bros	K16201	1972	**£5**	**£2**	

PATCHWORK

Title	Format	Label	Cat. No.	Year	Mint	VG	Notes
Patchwork	LP	Great Western	DM1027	197–	**£100**	**£50**	

PATE, JOHNNY

Title	Format	Label	Cat. No.	Year	Mint	VG	Notes
Jazz Goes Ivy League	10" LP	Parlophone	PMD1057	1958	**£25**	**£10**	
Shaft In Africa	LP	ABC	ABCL5035	1974	**£15**	**£6**	
Shaft In Africa	LP	Probe	SPB1077	1973	**£20**	**£8**	*with the Four Tops*
Swingin' Flute	10" LP	Parlophone	PMD1072	1959	**£25**	**£10**	

PATERNOSTER

Title	Format	Label	Cat. No.	Year	Mint	VG	Notes
Paternoster	LP	CBS	64958	1972	**£50**	**£25**	*Austrian*

PATERSON, BOBBY & THE CAMP CREEK BOYS

Title	Format	Label	Cat. No.	Year	Mint	VG	Notes
Virginia Reel	LP	Leader	LED2053	1973	**£10**	**£4**	

PATHETIX

Title	Format	Label	Cat. No.	Year	Mint	VG	Notes
Aleister Crowley	7"	No Records	001	1978	**£12**	**£6**	
Pathetix	7"	TJM	TJM12	1979	**£15**	**£7.50**	

PATHFINDERS

Title	Format	Label	Cat. No.	Year	Mint	VG	Notes
I Love You Caroline	7"	Decca	F12038	1964	**£6**	**£2.50**	

PATHFINDERS (2)

Title	Format	Label	Cat. No.	Year	Mint	VG	Notes
Don't You Believe It	7"	Parlophone	R5372	1965	**£6**	**£2.50**	

PATHFINDERS (3)

Title	Format	Label	Cat. No.	Year	Mint	VG	Notes
What'd I Say	7"	Hayton	SP138/9	1964	**£20**	**£10**	

PATHWAY TO YOUR MIND

Title	Format	Label	Cat. No.	Year	Mint	VG	Notes
Preparing The Mind And Body For Meditation	LP	Major Minor	MM/SMLP19	1968	**£25**	**£10**	

PATIENCE & PRUDENCE

Title	Format	Label	Cat. No.	Year	Mint	VG	Notes
Dreamers' Bay	7"	London	HLU8425	1957	**£8**	**£4**	
Gonna Get Along Without Ya Now	7"	London	HL7017	1957	**£8**	**£4**	*export*
Gonna Get Along Without Ya Now	7"	London	HLU8369	1957	**£12**	**£6**	
Smile And A Song	7" EP	London	REU1087	1957	**£30**	**£15**	
Tom Thumb's Tune	7"	London	HLU8773	1958	**£6**	**£2.50**	
Tonight You Belong To Me	7"	London	HLU8321	1956	**£15**	**£7.50**	
You Tattletale	7"	London	HLU8493	1957	**£6**	**£2.50**	

PATRICK, BOBBY BIG SIX

Title	Format	Label	Cat. No.	Year	Mint	VG	Notes
Monkey Time	7"	Decca	F12030	1964	**£12**	**£6**	
Shake It Easy Baby	7"	Decca	F11898	1964	**£15**	**£7.50**	
Tenbeat From Star Club Hamburg	7" EP	Decca	DFE8570	1964	**£75**	**£37.50**	

PATRICK, DAN

Title	Format	Label	Cat. No.	Year	Mint	VG	Notes
Tiger Lee	7"	Stateside	SS2004	1967	**£5**	**£2**	

PATRICK, KENTRICK

Title	Format	Label	Cat. No.	Year	Mint	VG	Notes
Don't Stay Out Late	7"	Island	WI079	1963	**£10**	**£5**	
End Of The World	7"	Island	WI104	1963	**£10**	**£5**	
Golden Love	7"	Island	WI119	1963	**£10**	**£5**	
Goodbye Peggy Darling	7"	Island	WI137	1964	**£10**	**£5**	*Baba Brooks B side*

I Am Wasting Time	7"	Island	WI140	1964	**£10**	**£5**	
Man To Man	7"	Island	WI066	1963	**£10**	**£5**	
Take Me To The Party	7"	Island	WI132	1963	**£10**	**£5**	

PATRIOTS

Prophet	7"	Fontana	TF650	1966	**£5**	**£2**	

PATRON OF THE ARTS

Eleanor Rigby	7"	Page One	POF012	1966	**£15**	**£7.50**	

PATSY

Little Flea	7"	Doctor Bird	DB1122	1968	**£10**	**£5**	

PATTEN, BRIAN

Brian Patten	LP	Caedmon	TC1300	1970	**£25**	**£10**	
Sly Cormorant	LP	Argo	ZSW607	1977	**£15**	**£6**	
Vanishing Trick	LP	Tangent	TGS116	1971	**£40**	**£20**	

PATTERN PEOPLE

Take A Walk In The Sun	7"	MGM	MGM1429	1968	**£4**	**£1.50**	

PATTERSON, BOBBY

Broadway Ain't Funky No More	7"	Pama	PM735	1968	**£4**	**£1.50**	
I'm In Love With You	7"	Action	ACT4604	1972	**£6**	**£2.50**	
T.C.B. Or T.Y.A.	7"	Pama	PM763	1969	**£5**	**£2**	

PATTERSON, OTTILIE

3000 Years With Ottilie	LP	Marmalade	608011	1969	**£15**	**£6**	
Baby Please Don't Go	7"	Columbia	DB7208	1964	**£15**	**£7.50**	
Blueberry Hill	7"	Columbia	DB4760	1961	**£15**	**£7.50**	
Blues	7" EP	Decca	DFE6303	1956	**£12**	**£6**	
Jailhouse Blues	7"	Pye	7NJ2015	1958	**£5**	**£2**	
Ottilie	7" EP	Columbia	SEG7915	1959	**£10**	**£5**	
Ottilie's Irish Night	LP	Pye	NPL18028	1959	**£10**	**£4**	
That Patterson Girl	7" EP	Polygon	JTE102	1956	**£10**	**£5**	
That Patterson Girl	7" EP	Pye	NJE1012	1956	**£10**	**£5**	
That Patterson Girl Vol. 2	7" EP	Pye	NJE1023	1956	**£10**	**£5**	

PATTERSON'S PEOPLE

Shake Hands With The Devil	7"	Mercury	MF913	1966	**£8**	**£4**	

PATTISON, LITTLE JOHN

Needles And Pins	7"	Giv-A-Disc	LYN510	1964	**£6**	**£2.50**	*flexi*

PATTO

Patto's original take on jazz-rock never quite managed to achieve the wide acclaim that it deserved, despite the band having a singer (Mike Patto) possessing one of the classic rock voices and a guitarist (Ollie Halsall) whose blend of technical expertise and imagination made him into the kind of player that other guitarists looked up to. The album *Hold Your Fire* is an oddity in that it exists with two different versions of the A side. The songs are the same, but on one they have a much rougher, rawer sound than on the other. There do not appear to be any visual differences between the two versions of the album, unfortunately.

Hold Your Fire	LP	Vertigo	6360032	1971	**£100**	**£50**	*spiral label*
Patto	LP	Vertigo	6360016	1970	**£30**	**£15**	*spiral label*
Roll Em Smoke Em	LP	Island	ILPS9210	1972	**£20**	**£8**	

PATTO, MIKE

Can't Stop Talking About My Baby	7"	Columbia	DB8091	1966	**£60**	**£30**	

PATTON, ALEXANDER

Li'l Lovin' Sometimes	7"	Capitol	CL15461	1966	**£60**	**£30**	

PATTON, CHARLIE

Charlie Patton	7" EP	Heritage	REU4	195–	**£15**	**£7.50**	

PATTON, JIMMY

Blue Darlin'	LP	Sims	127	1965	**£20**	**£8**	*US*
Make Room For The Blues	LP	Moon	101	196–	**£20**	**£8**	*US*

PATTON, JOHN

Accent On The Blues	LP	Blue Note	BST84340	1969	**£25**	**£10**	
Along Came John	LP	Blue Note	BLP/BST84130	1963	**£40**	**£20**	
Got A Good Thing Goin'	LP	Blue Note	BLP/BST84229	1966	**£30**	**£15**	
I'll Never Be Free	7"	Blue Note	451889	1964	**£5**	**£2**	
Let 'Em Roll	LP	Blue Note	BLP/BST84239	1966	**£30**	**£15**	
Oh Baby!	LP	Blue Note	BLP/BST84192	1964	**£50**	**£25**	
That Certain Feeling	LP	Blue Note	BST84281	1968	**£25**	**£10**	
Understanding	LP	Blue Note	BST84306	1968	**£25**	**£10**	
Way I Feel	LP	Blue Note	BLP/BST84174	1964	**£30**	**£15**	

PATTY & THE EMBLEMS

Mixed Up Shook Up Girl	7"	Stateside	SS322	1964	**£25**	**£12.50**	

PAUL

Will You Follow Me	7"	Polydor	BM56045	1965	**£75**	**£37.50**	

PAUL, BILLY

360 Degrees Of Billy Paul	LP	Epic	EPC65351	1973	**£10**	**£4**	

Ebony Woman	LP	Epic	EPC65456	1973	**£10**	**£4**	
War Of The Gods	LP	Philadelphia	PIR65861	1974	**£10**	**£4**	

PAUL, BUNNY

Lovey Dovey	7"	Columbia	SCM5131	1954	**£10**	**£5**	
New Love	7"	Columbia	SCM5102	1954	**£5**	**£2**	
Please Have Mercy	7"	Capitol	CL14279	1955	**£5**	**£2**	
Song Of The Dreamer	7"	Capitol	CL14368	1955	**£4**	**£1.50**	
Such A Night	7"	Columbia	SCM5112	1954	**£6**	**£2.50**	
Two Castanets	7"	Capitol	CL14304	1955	**£4**	**£1.50**	
You Came A Long Way From St Louis	7"	Columbia	SCM5151	1954	**£5**	**£2**	

PAUL, DARLENE

Act Like Nothing Happened	7"	Capitol	CL15344	1964	**£8**	**£4**	

PAUL, JOHN E.

I Wanna Know	7"	Decca	F12685	1967	**£20**	**£10**	

PAUL, LES & MARY FORD

Although guitarist Les Paul gained his many hits by playing a bouncy, light pop with his singer wife, Mary Ford, he has an importance in the history of rock that entirely transcends the actual sound of his music. He was a fearless experimentalist in the studio, pioneering the use of multiple over-dubbing and speeded-up tape effects and building the first eight-track tape recorder as early as 1954. And if that was not enough, he also designed the electric guitar that still bears his name and which has played such a major role in the development of blues and heavy rock – persuading the Gibson company to begin mass production of the instrument at a time when the only other commercially available electric guitar was the Fender Telecaster.

Amukiriki	7"	Capitol	CL14521	1956	**£5**	**£2**	
At The Save A Penny Super Store	7"	Philips	PB906	1959	**£4**	**£1.50**	
Bewitched	7"	Capitol	CL14839	1958	**£4**	**£1.50**	
Bye Bye Blues	10" LP	Capitol	LC6806	1956	**£15**	**£6**	
Bye Bye Blues	LP	Capitol	T356	1953	**£20**	**£8**	*US*
Cimarron	7"	Capitol	CL14593	1956	**£4**	**£1.50**	
Cinco Robles	7"	Capitol	CL14710	1957	**£4**	**£1.50**	
Genuine Love	7"	Capitol	CL14300	1955	**£8**	**£4**	
Hitmakers	LP	Capitol	T416	195–	**£12**	**£5**	
Hits Of Les And Mary	LP	Capitol	T1476	1960	**£10**	**£4**	
Hummin' And Waltzin'	7"	Capitol	CL14738	1957	**£4**	**£1.50**	
Hummingbird	7"	Capitol	CL14342	1955	**£8**	**£4**	
Jazz Me Blues	7" EP	Capitol	EAP120740	1965	**£6**	**£2.50**	
Jealous Heart	7"	Philips	PB882	1959	**£4**	**£1.50**	
Les And Mary	10" LP	Capitol	LC6704	1955	**£20**	**£8**	
Les And Mary	LP	Capitol	T577	195–	**£12**	**£5**	*US*
Les Paul And Mary Ford	10" LP	Capitol	LC6701	1955	**£20**	**£8**	
Lover	LP	Capitol	T1276	1959	**£10**	**£4**	
Lover's Luau	LP	Philips	BBL7306	1959	**£10**	**£4**	
Mandolino	7"	Capitol	CL14185	1954	**£8**	**£4**	
Mister Sandman	7"	Capitol	CL14212	1954	**£12**	**£6**	
Mr And Mrs Music	7" EP	Capitol	EAP20048	1959	**£8**	**£4**	
New Sound Vol. 1	10" LP	Capitol	LC6514	1951	**£20**	**£8**	
New Sound Vol. 1	LP	Capitol	T226	195–	**£20**	**£8**	*US*
New Sound Vol. 2	10" LP	Capitol	LC6581	1953	**£20**	**£8**	
New Sound Vol. 2	LP	Capitol	T286	195–	**£20**	**£8**	*US*
Nola	7" EP	Capitol	EAP120145	1961	**£5**	**£2**	
Pair Of Fools	7"	Capitol	CL14809	1957	**£5**	**£2**	
Presenting Les Paul And Mary Ford	7" EP	Capitol	EAP19121	1955	**£6**	**£2.50**	
Put A Ring On My Finger	7"	Philips	PB873	1958	**£6**	**£2.50**	
Runnin' Wild	7"	Capitol	CL14665	1956	**£5**	**£2**	
Say The Words I Love To Hear	7"	Capitol	CL14577	1956	**£4**	**£1.50**	
Sitting On Top Of The World	7" EP	Capitol	EAP1540	1955	**£8**	**£4**	
Small Island	7"	Capitol	CL14858	1958	**£4**	**£1.50**	
Song In Blue	7"	Capitol	CL14233	1955	**£8**	**£4**	
Strollin' Blues	7"	Capitol	CL14776	1957	**£5**	**£2**	
Texas Lady	7"	Capitol	CL14502	1956	**£5**	**£2**	
Theme From The Threepenny Opera	7"	Capitol	CL14534	1956	**£5**	**£2**	
Time To Dream	LP	Capitol	T802	1957	**£12**	**£5**	

PAUL & PAULA

First Day Back At School	7"	Philips	BF1281	1963	**£4**	**£1.50**	
First Quarrel	7"	Philips	BF1256	1963	**£4**	**£1.50**	
Hey Paula	7"	Philips	304012BF	1963	**£4**	**£1.50**	
Holiday For Teens	LP	Philips	BL7587	1964	**£20**	**£10**	
No Other Baby	7"	Philips	BF1380	1964	**£4**	**£1.50**	
Sing For Young Lovers	LP	Philips	652026BL	1963	**£25**	**£10**	
Something Old Something New	7"	Philips	BF1269	1963	**£4**	**£1.50**	
We Go Together	LP	Philips	BL7573	1963	**£20**	**£10**	
Young Lovers	7"	Philips	304016BF	1963	**£4**	**£1.50**	
Young Lovers	7" EP	Philips	BBE12539	1963	**£20**	**£10**	

PAUL & RITCHIE & THE CRYIN' SHAMES

C'mon Back	7"	Decca	F12483	1966	**£125**	**£62.50**	

PAUL & THE JETLINERS

Great Pretender	7"	Rainbow	RAI102	1966	**£5**	**£2**	
Something On My Mind	7"	Rainbow	RAI105	1966	**£4**	**£1.50**	

PAUL'S DISCIPLES

See That My Grave Is Kept Clean	7"	Decca	F12081	1965	**£15**	**£7.50**	

PAULETTE & DELROY

Little Lover	7"	Island	WI120	1963	**£10**	**£5**	

PAULETTE SISTERS

Dream Boat	7"	Capitol	CL14294	1955	**£8**	**£4**	
Ring-A-Dang-A-Do	7"	Capitol	CL14310	1955	**£8**	**£4**	
You Win Again	7"	Capitol	CL14347	1955	**£8**	**£4**	

PAUL'S TROUBLES

You'll Find Out	7"	Ember	EMBS233	1967	**£15**	**£7.50**	

PAUPERS

The sleeve notes to *Magic People* refer to the Paupers as being a Canadian Beatles but they are actually far more like the Byrds, if not quite in the same league. Nevertheless, the combination of harmony vocals with folky material, spiced with innovative modal guitar solos, should have given the band a considerable cult following. Yet, remarkably, Vernon Joynson's exhaustive guide to the garage and psychedelic music of the era makes no mention of them. Drummer Skip Prokop was borrowed by Al Kooper and Mike Bloomfield for their *Live Adventures* set and he subsequently formed the jazz-rock group Lighthouse, who recorded several albums in the early seventies.

Ellis Island	LP	Verve	SVLP6017	1968	**£12**	**£5**	
Magic People	LP	Verve	3026	1967	**£15**	**£6**	*US*

PAVILION, PERCY (CAPTAIN SENSIBLE)

Cricket EP	7"	Pavilioned In Splendour	PIS1	1983	**£4**	**£1.50**	

PAVLOV'S DOG

Pampered Menial	LP	CBS	80872	1975	**£10**	**£4**	
Sound Of The Bell	LP	CBS	81163	1976	**£10**	**£4**	
St Louis Hounds	LP	private		197–	**£75**	**£37.50**	*US*

PAX ETERNAL

Second Chance Mr Jones	7"	Decca	F13167	1971	**£4**	**£1.50**	

PAXTON, GARY

Stop Twistin' Baby	7"	Liberty	LIB55485	1962	**£5**	**£2**	

PAXTON, TOM

Ain't That News	LP	Elektra	EKL/EKS7289	1965	**£15**	**£6**	
Jennifer's Rabbit	7"	Elektra	EKSN45021	1967	**£4**	**£1.50**	
Last Thing On My Mind	7"	Elektra	EKSN45001	1965	**£4**	**£1.50**	
Leaving London	7"	Elektra	EKSN45006	1967	**£4**	**£1.50**	
Morning Again	LP	Elektra	EKL/EKS74019	1968	**£12**	**£5**	
Number Six	LP	Elektra	EKS74066	1970	**£10**	**£4**	
One Time And One Time Only	7"	Elektra	EKSN45003	1967	**£4**	**£1.50**	
Outward Bound	LP	Elektra	EKL/EKS7317	1966	**£12**	**£5**	
Ramblin' Boy	LP	Elektra	EKL/EKS7277	1965	**£15**	**£6**	
Things I Notice Now	LP	Elektra	EKS74043	1969	**£12**	**£5**	
Tom Paxton	7" EP	Elektra	EPK802	1967	**£10**	**£5**	

PAYNE, BENNY

Sunny Side Up	LP	London	LTZR15103	1957	**£25**	**£10**	

PAYNE, CECIL

Connection	LP	Summit	AJS16	1962	**£20**	**£8**	

PAYNE, FREDA

Band Of Gold	7"	Invictus	INV533	1973	**£5**	**£2**	
Band Of Gold	7"	Invictus	INV502	1970	**£4**	**£1.50**	
Band Of Gold	LP	Invictus	SVT1001	1971	**£12**	**£5**	
Best Of Freda Payne	LP	Invictus	SVT1007	1972	**£10**	**£4**	
Contact	LP	Invictus	SVT1005	1972	**£12**	**£5**	
He Who Laughs Last	7"	HMV	POP1091	1962	**£6**	**£2.50**	

PAYNE, GORDON

Gordon Payne	LP	A&M	SP4725	1978	**£20**	**£8**	*US*

PAYNE, LEON

Americana	LP	London	HAB8136	1964	**£10**	**£4**	
Leon Payne	LP	Starday	SLP231	1963	**£12**	**£5**	*US*

PAZ

Kandeen Love Song	LP	Spotlight	SPJ507	1983	**£12**	**£5**	
Live At Chichester	LP	Magnus	2	1978	**£15**	**£6**	
Look Inside	LP	Paradin	PALP001	1983	**£12**	**£5**	
Paz Are Back	LP	Spotlight	SPJ518	1980	**£12**	**£5**	

PEABODY, DAVE

Peabody Hotel	LP	Village Thing	VTS22	1973	**£12**	**£5**	

PEABODY, EDDIE

Man With The Banjo	7" EP	London	RED1034	1955	**£5**	**£2**	

PEACE, DAVE QUARTET

Good Morning Mr Blues	LP	Saga	FID2155	1969	**£15**	**£6**	

PEACE, JOE

Finding Peace Of Mind	LP	Rite	29917	1972	**£150**	**£75**	*US*

PEACEFUL COMPANY

Title	Format	Label	Number	Year	Mint	VG	Notes
Peaceful Company	LP	Sovereign	SVNA7252	1973	**£20**	**£8**	

PEACHES & HERB

Title	Format	Label	Number	Year	Mint	VG	Notes
Close Your Eyes	7"	CBS	2711	1967	**£4**	**£1.50**	
For Your Love	7"	CBS	2866	1967	**£6**	**£2.50**	
For Your Love	LP	CBS	63119	1967	**£10**	**£4**	
Golden Duets	LP	Direction	863263	1968	**£10**	**£4**	
Let's Fall In Love	7"	CBS	202509	1967	**£6**	**£2.50**	
Let's Fall In Love	LP	CBS	62966	1967	**£10**	**£4**	
Soothe Me With Your Love	7"	Direction	585249	1970	**£5**	**£2**	

PEACOCK, ANNETTE

Singer Annette Peacock was championed by jazz pianist Paul Bley, who recorded many of her compositions on his albums from the late sixties. In the seventies they toured together, pioneering the use of synthesizers as live improvising tools – the collectable albums they made in the style are listed under Bley's name in this guide. *I'm The One*, however, is Peacock's masterpiece. As much a rock album as jazz, the record demonstrates her impressive ability to direct electronic technology towards her own creative ends, using her voice as a sound-source to be shaped by the synthesizers.

Title	Format	Label	Number	Year	Mint	VG	Notes
I'm The One	LP	RCA	SF8255	1972	**£10**	**£4**	
I'm The One	LP	RCA	LSP4578	1972	**£12**	**£5**	*US, metallic cover*
Live In Paris	LP	Aura	0060476	1981	**£25**	**£10**	
Perfect Release	LP	Aura	AUL707	1978	**£10**	**£4**	

PEACOCK, TREVOR

Title	Format	Label	Number	Year	Mint	VG	Notes
I Didn't Figure On Him To Come Back	7"	Decca	F11414	1961	**£5**	**£2**	

PEAK FOLK

Title	Format	Label	Number	Year	Mint	VG	Notes
Peak Folk	LP	Folk Heritage		197–	**£15**	**£6**	

PEANUT

Peanut was a teenage American girl singer (at least she sounds like a teenager – she features in no rock reference books) whose version of 'Home Of The Brave' was played on the radio a few times without becoming a chart hit. Nevertheless, her singing conveys such a sense of angst, of youthful hopes and wishes and love – and frustration in the face of blind adult unreason – that the song is an absolute classic, even if an unheralded one. (It has since been suggested elsewhere that Peanut is Katie Kissoon, who has appeared on numerous recordings as a backing singer, including some by Van Morrison, as well as scoring a number of seventies chart hits as half of the duo Mac and Katie Kissoon.)

Title	Format	Label	Number	Year	Mint	VG	Notes
Home Of The Brave	7"	Pye	7N15963	1965	**£6**	**£2.50**	
I Didn't Love Him Anyway	7"	Columbia	DB8104	1967	**£6**	**£2.50**	
I'm Waiting For The Day	7"	Columbia	DB8032	1966	**£6**	**£2.50**	
Thank You For The Rain	7"	Pye	7N15901	1965	**£4**	**£1.50**	

PEANUT BUTTER CONSPIRACY

The Peanut Butter Conspiracy added Mamas-and-Papas-style harmony vocals on to the instrumental sound of Jefferson Airplane. The combination works brilliantly and the group's best songs are quite delightful, although somehow the group failed to find the success that they should have.

Title	Format	Label	Number	Year	Mint	VG	Notes
Back In L.A.	7"	London	HLH10290	1969	**£5**	**£2**	
For Children Of All Ages	LP	Challenge	2000	1968	**£25**	**£10**	*US*
Great Conspiracy	LP	CBS	63277	1968	**£25**	**£10**	
Is Spreading	LP	Columbia	CL2654/CS9495	1967	**£30**	**£15**	*US*
It's A Happening Thing	7"	CBS	2981	1967	**£5**	**£2**	
Turn On A Friend	7"	CBS	3543	1968	**£5**	**£2**	

PEARCE, BOB BLUES BAND

Title	Format	Label	Number	Year	Mint	VG	Notes
Blues Crusade	LP	Avenue	BEV1054	1968	**£10**	**£4**	
Colour Blind	LP	Forest Tracks	FT3015	1979	**£10**	**£4**	
Let's Get Drunk Again	LP	Westwood	WRS040	1974	**£12**	**£5**	

PEARL JAM

Title	Format	Label	Number	Year	Mint	VG	Notes
Alive	12"	Epic	6575726	1992	**£6**	**£2.50**	*poster sleeve*
Even Flow	12"	Epic	6578578	1992	**£6**	**£2.50**	*white vinyl*
Jeremy	12"	Epic	6582586	1992	**£6**	**£2.50**	*picture disc*
Jeremy	CD-s	Epic	6582582	1992	**£5**	**£2**	*picture disc*
Pearl Jam Live – KROQ	CD	private	no number	1994	**£50**	**£25**	*US promo*
Rarified And Live	CD	Epic	SAMP656	1995	**£300**	**£180**	*Australian double promo*
Ten	CD	Epic	4688845	1992	**£15**	**£6**	*metallic yellow pack*
Ten	LP	Epic	4688840	1992	**£20**	**£8**	*picture disc*

PEARLS BEFORE SWINE

Title	Format	Label	Number	Year	Mint	VG	Notes
Balaklava	LP	Fontana	STL5503	1968	**£20**	**£8**	
Beautiful Lies You Could Live	LP	Reprise	RSLP6467	1971	**£10**	**£4**	
City Of Gold	LP	Reprise	RSLP6442	1971	**£12**	**£5**	
One Nation Underground	LP	Fontana	STL5505	1967	**£20**	**£8**	
These Things Too	LP	Reprise	RSLP6364	1969	**£12**	**£5**	
Use Of Ashes	LP	Reprise	RSLP6405	1970	**£12**	**£5**	

PEARSE, JOHN

Title	Format	Label	Number	Year	Mint	VG	Notes
John Pearse	LP	XTRA	XTRA1056	1968	**£10**	**£4**	
Teach Yourself Folk Guitar	LP	Saga	XID5503	1963	**£10**	**£4**	

PEARSON, DUKE

Title	Format	Label	Number	Year	Mint	VG	Notes
How Insensitive	LP	Blue Note	BST84344	1969	**£12**	**£5**	
Introducing Duke Pearson's Big Band	LP	Blue Note	BST84276	1968	**£15**	**£6**	
Merry Ole Soul	LP	Blue Note	BST84323	1969	**£15**	**£6**	

Now Hear This	LP	Blue Note	BST84308	1969	**£12**	**£5**	
Phantom	LP	Blue Note	BST84293	1968	**£12**	**£5**	
Right Touch	LP	Blue Note	BST84267	1968	**£15**	**£6**	
Sweet Honey Bee	LP	Blue Note	BLP/BST84252	1967	**£25**	**£10**	
Tender Feelin's	LP	Blue Note	BLP/BST84035	196–	**£40**	**£20**	
Wahoo	LP	Blue Note	BLP/BST84191	1965	**£25**	**£10**	

PEARSON, JOHNNY

Rat Catcher's Theme	7"	Columbia	DB7851	1966	**£8**	**£4**	

PEARSON, RONNIE

Teenage Fancy	7"	HMV	POP489	1958	**£500**	**£330**	*best auctioned*

PEASANTS

Got Some Lovin' For You Baby	7"	Columbia	DB7642	1965	**£200**	**£100**	*best auctioned*

PEBBLES

Incredible George	7"	Decca	F22944	1969	**£4**	**£1.50**	

PEBBLES (2)

Huma La La La La	7" EP	President	PRC512	196–	**£8**	**£4**	*French*

PEDDLERS

Birthday	LP	CBS	63682	1969	**£10**	**£4**	
Fantastic Peddlers	LP	Fontana	SFL13016	1968	**£10**	**£4**	
Freewheelers	LP	CBS	(S)BPG63183	1968	**£10**	**£4**	
Georgia On My Mind	LP	Philips	6386066	1971	**£10**	**£4**	
Live At The Pickwick	LP	Philips	(S)BL7768	1967	**£15**	**£6**	
Suite London	LP	Philips	6308102	1972	**£10**	**£4**	
Three For All	LP	Philips	6308028	1970	**£10**	**£4**	
Three In A Cell	LP	CBS	63411	1968	**£10**	**£4**	

PEDECIN, MIKE QUINTET

Musical Medicine	LP	Apollo	LP484	1957	**£50**	**£25**	*US*

PEDRICKS, BOBBY

White Bucks And Saddle Shoes	7"	London	HLX8740	1958	**£25**	**£12.50**	

PEEBLES, ANN

I Can't Stand The Rain	LP	London	SHU8468	1974	**£10**	**£4**	
Part Time Love	LP	Hi	HL32059	1971	**£12**	**£5**	*US*
Straight From The Heart	LP	London	SHU8434	1972	**£10**	**£4**	
Tellin' It	LP	London	SHU8490	1976	**£10**	**£4**	
This Is	LP	Hi	HL32053	1969	**£12**	**£5**	*US*

PEEK, PAUL

Brother In Law	7"	Pye	7N25102	1961	**£6**	**£2.50**	
Pin The Tail On The Donkey	7"	CBS	202073	1966	**£5**	**£2**	

PEEL, DAVID & LOWER EAST SIDE

American Revolution	LP	Elektra	EKS74069	1970	**£12**	**£5**	
American Revolution	LP	Elektra	K42074	1972	**£10**	**£4**	
Have A Marijuana	LP	Elektra	EKL/EKS74032	1968	**£15**	**£6**	
Pope Smokes Dope	LP	Apple	SW3391	1972	**£15**	**£6**	*US*

PEEL, JOHN

John Peel has made many cameo appearances on other people's records – the odd spoken line, the occasional burst of jew's harp – but *Archive Things*, which is credited to him, contains not a single sound of Peel. Instead, the record is a compilation of short world music extracts that were included in John Peel's wide-ranging *Night Ride* radio programme. There are some fascinating noises to be heard here and, as a sixties artefact, the record is almost as essential as *Sgt Pepper*, if rather less celebrated.

Archive Things	LP	BBC	REC68M	1970	**£20**	**£8**	

PEELERS

Banished Misfortune	LP	Polydor	2460165	1972	**£200**	**£100**	

PEELS

Juanita Banana	LP	Karate	5402	1966	**£20**	**£8**	*US*
Time Marches On	7"	Audio Fidelity	AFSP527	1966	**£8**	**£4**	

PEENUTS

Theme From The Monkees	7"	Ember	EMBS242	1967	**£4**	**£1.50**	
Theme From The Monkees	7"	Ember	EMBS242	1967	**£8**	**£4**	*picture sleeve*

PEEP SHOW

Esprit De Corps	7"	Polydor	BM52226	1968	**£10**	**£5**	
Mazy	7"	Polydor	56196	1967	**£100**	**£50**	

PEEPS

Gotta Get A Move On	7"	Philips	BF1478	1966	**£4**	**£1.50**	
Now Is The Time	7"	Philips	BF1421	1965	**£5**	**£2**	
Tra La La	7"	Philips	BF1509	1966	**£4**	**£1.50**	
What Can I Say	7"	Philips	BF1443	1965	**£6**	**£2.50**	

PEG LEG SAM

Last Medicine Show	LP	Flyright	LP507/8	1974	**£12**	**£5**	*double*

PEGASUS

Seems A Long Time Gone	LP	private	CPK175	1975	£**20**	£**8**	*German*

PEGASUS (2)

Pegasus	LP	Univers		1979	£**30**	£**15**	*Dutch*

PEGG, BEV

Foundry Ditty And The Industrial Air	LP	Beaujangle	DB008	197–	£**40**	£**20**	
Nostalgia Is A Thing Of The Past	LP	Beaujangle	DB007	197–	£**75**	£**37.50**	

PEGG, BOB

Ancient Maps	LP	Transatlantic	TRA299	1975	£**12**	£**5**	
And Now It Is So Early	LP	Galliard	GAL4017	1972	£**75**	£**37.50**	*with Carolanne Pegg*
Bob Pegg & Nick Strutt	LP	Transatlantic	TRA265	1973	£**12**	£**5**	
He Came From The Mountains	LP	Trailer	LER3016	1971	£**15**	£**6**	*with Carolanne Pegg*
Shipbuilder	LP	Transatlantic	TRA280	1974	£**12**	£**5**	

PEGG, CAROLANNE

Carolanne Pegg	LP	Transatlantic	TRA266	1973	£**60**	£**30**	

PEGGY & JIMMY

Remember Easter Monday	7"	Hot Rod	HR101	1970	£**5**	£**2**	*Carl Levy B side*

PEGGY'S LEG

Grinilla	LP	Bunch	BAN2001	1973	£**300**	£**180**	
William Tell Overture	7"	Bunch	no number	1973	£**20**	£**10**	

PEIFFER, BERNARD

Bernard Peiffer	LP	Felsted	PDL85022	1956	£**12**	£**5**	
Bernard Peiffer Trio	10" LP	Felsted	EDL87016	1955	£**25**	£**10**	
Bernard Peiffer Trio	LP	Top Rank	30025	1960	£**10**	£**4**	
Orchestra	10" LP	Felsted	EDL87011	1955	£**25**	£**10**	
Piano A La Mood	LP	Brunswick	LAT8262	1958	£**12**	£**5**	
Trio	10" LP	Felsted	EDL87013	1955	£**25**	£**10**	

PELL, DAVE

Dave Pell Octet	LP	London	HAK2021	1957	£**12**	£**5**	
I Had The Craziest Dream	LP	Capitol	T925	1958	£**10**	£**4**	
Irving Berlin Gallery	10" LP	London	HAPB1020	1954	£**40**	£**20**	
Irving Berlin Gallery Vol. 1	7" EP	London	REP1008	1954	£**6**	£**2.50**	
Love Story	LP	London	LTZK15082	1957	£**25**	£**10**	
Rodgers And Hart	7" EP	London	REP1018	1955	£**6**	£**2.50**	
Rodgers And Hart Gallery	10" LP	London	HAPB1034	1955	£**30**	£**15**	

PELL MELL

From The New World	LP	Philips	6305193	1975	£**10**	£**4**	*German*
Marburg	LP	Bacillus	BLPS19090	1972	£**12**	£**5**	*German*
Rhapsody	LP	Venus	VB761PMAB	1976	£**10**	£**4**	*German*

PEMBROKE, JIM

Corporal Cauliflower's Mental Functions	LP	Love	LRLP214	1977	£**15**	£**6**	*Swedish*
Hot Thumbs O'Riley	LP	Charisma	CAS1071	1973	£**15**	£**6**	
Pigworm	LP	Love	LRLP103	1974	£**15**	£**6**	*Swedish*
Wicked Ivory	LP	Love	LRLP52	1972	£**15**	£**6**	*Swedish*

PENDARVIS, TRACY

South Bound Line	7"	London	HLS9213	1960	£**15**	£**7.50**	
Thousand Guitars	7"	London	HLS9059	1960	£**15**	£**7.50**	

PENDLEFOLK

Pendlefolk	LP	Folk Heritage	FHR007	1970	£**15**	£**6**	

PENDRAGON

Saved By You	7"	Toff	PENDS7S	1989	£**5**	£**2**	

PENETRATION

Aquarian Symphony	LP	Higher Key	33071	1974	£**60**	£**30**	*US*

PENGUIN CAFE ORCHESTRA

Broadcasting From Home	LP	Editions EG	EGED38	1984	£**12**	£**5**	
Mini Album	LP	Editions EG	EGMLP2	1983	£**20**	£**8**	
Music From The Penguin Café	LP	Obscure	OBS7	1976	£**20**	£**8**	
Music From The Penguin Café	LP	Editions EG	EGED27	1984	£**10**	£**4**	
Penguin Café Orchestra	LP	Editions EG	EGED11	1983	£**15**	£**6**	

PENGUINS

The Penguins' 'Earth Angel' is arguably the definitive doo-wop performance, although the UK sales of the original issue were minimal. In consequence, this is now one of the most valuable London recordings of all. The later 'Memories Of El Monte' is collectable largely on account of its having been written by Frank Zappa and Ray Collins.

Best Vocal Groups: Rhythm And Blues	LP	DooTone	DTL204	195–	£**1500**	£**1000**	*US, with other artists, red vinyl*
Best Vocal Groups: Rhythm And Blues	LP	DooTone	DTL204	195–	£**250**	£**150**	*US, with other artists*
Cool Cool Penguins	LP	DooTone	DTL242	1959	£**300**	£**180**	*US*
Earth Angel	7"	London	HL8114	1955	£**1,000**	£**700**	*gold label, best auctioned*

Memories Of El Monte	7"	Original Sound	27	1962	**£150**	**£75**	*US*

PENN, DAWN

Long Days, Short Nights	7"	Rio	R113	1967	**£15**	**£7.50**	
You Don't Love Me	7"	Studio One	SO2030	1967	**£15**	**£7.50**	

PENN, TONY

That's What I Like	7"	Starlite	ST45083	1962	**£20**	**£10**	

PENNINES

Manchester Morning	LP	Penny Farthing	PELS514	1971	**£100**	**£50**	

PENNY, HANK

Bloodshot Eyes	7"	Parlophone	MSP6202	1956	**£40**	**£20**	

PENNY & JEAN

Two For The Road	LP	RCA	SF5119	1961	**£25**	**£10**	

PENNY PEEPS

I See The Morning	7"	Liberty	LBF15114	1968	**£6**	**£2.50**	
Model Village	7"	Liberty	LBF15053	1968	**£30**	**£15**	

PENROSE, CHARLES

Adventures Of A Laughing Policeman	7" EP	Columbia	SEG7743	1957	**£5**	**£2**	
Laughing Policeman	7"	Columbia	DB8959	1972	**£4**	**£1.50**	

PENTAD

Don't Throw It All Away	7"	Parlophone	R5368	1965	**£5**	**£2**	
It Better Be Me	7"	Parlophone	R5424	1966	**£5**	**£2**	
Silver Dagger	7"	Parlophone	R5288	1965	**£10**	**£5**	

PENTAGONS

To Be Loved	7"	London	HLU9333	1961	**£50**	**£25**	

PENTANGLE

The Pentangle were a kind of folk super-group, formed when the influential solo guitarists Bert Jansch and John Renbourn decided to join forces with the current rhythm section from Alexis Korner's Blues Incorporated and with folk singer Jacqui McShee. The group's approach was more of a folk-jazz synthesis than anything to do with what is normally conceived as rock music, but it proved to be enormously popular. 'Light Flight', a television theme (for *Take Three Girls*) that is probably better known than the series it was designed to introduce, is included on the group's best-known album, *Basket Of Light*.

Basket Of Light	LP	Transatlantic	TRA205	1969	**£10**	**£4**	*gatefold sleeve*
Cruel Sister	LP	Transatlantic	TRA228	1970	**£12**	**£5**	*gatefold sleeve*
Pentangle	LP	Transatlantic	TRA162	1968	**£12**	**£5**	
Reflection	LP	Transatlantic	TRA240	1971	**£10**	**£4**	*gatefold sleeve*
Solomon's Seal	LP	Reprise	K44197	1972	**£25**	**£10**	
Sweet Child	LP	Transatlantic	TRA178	1968	**£20**	**£8**	*double*
Travellin' Song	7"	Transatlantic	BIG109	1968	**£4**	**£1.50**	

PEOPLE

Both Sides Of People	LP	Capitol	ST151	1969	**£25**	**£10**	*US*
I Love You	LP	Capitol	ST2924	1968	**£25**	**£10**	*US*
Somebody Tell Me My Name	7"	Capitol	CL15553	1968	**£5**	**£2**	
There Are People And There Are People	LP	Paramount	PAS5013	1970	**£15**	**£6**	*US*
Ulla	7"	Capitol	CL15599	1969	**£4**	**£1.50**	

PEOPLE (2)

In Ancient Times	7"	Deram	DM346	1971	**£4**	**£1.50**	

PEOPLE BAND

People Band	LP	Transatlantic	TRA214	1970	**£40**	**£20**	

PEOPLES, TOMMY

Tommy Peoples	LP	Eireann	CL13	1976	**£15**	**£6**	

PEOPLES, TOMMY & DAITHI SPROULE

Iron Man	LP	Shanachie	79044	1985	**£10**	**£4**	*US*

PEOPLES, TOMMY & PAUL BRADY

High Part Of The Road	LP	Shanachie	29003	1976	**£10**	**£4**	*US*

PEOPLE'S CHOICE

I Like To Do It	7"	Mojo	2092024	1971	**£5**	**£2**	

PEPPER

We'll Make It Together	7"	Pye	7N17569	1968	**£5**	**£2**	

PEPPER, ART

Art Pepper Quartet	10" LP	Vogue	LDE067	1954	**£50**	**£25**	
Art Pepper Quartet	10" LP	London	HLZV14038	195–	**£50**	**£25**	
Art Pepper Quartet	LP	London	LZU14038	1956	**£30**	**£15**	
Gettin' Together	LP	Contemporary	LAC12262	1961	**£20**	**£8**	
Meets The Rhythm Section	LP	Contemporary	LAC12066	1958	**£20**	**£8**	
Modern Jazz Classics	LP	Contemporary	LAC12229	1960	**£20**	**£8**	

PEPPER, JIM

Pepper's Pow Wow	LP	Atlantic	2400149	1971	£15	£6	

PEPPERMINT, DANNY

Maybe Tomorrow	7"	London	HLL9614	1962	£4	£1.50	
One More Time	7"	London	HLL9516	1962	£4	£1.50	
Peppermint Twist	7"	London	HLL9478	1961	£4	£1.50	
Twist With Danny Peppermint	LP	London	HAL2438	1962	£25	£10	

PEPPERMINT CIRCUS

All The King's Horses	7"	Olga	OLE007	1967	£4	£1.50	

PEPPERMINT TROLLEY COMPANY

Peppermint Trolley Company	LP	Acta	A38007	1968	£25	£10	US

PEPPI

I Never Danced Before	7"	Decca	F11638	1963	£4	£1.50	
Pistol Packin' Mama	7"	Decca	F11991	1964	£4	£1.50	
Skip	7"	Decca	F12055	1965	£4	£1.50	

PERCELLS

Cheek To Cheek	7"	HMV	POP1154	1963	£5	£2	

PERCEWOOD'S ONAGRAM

Ameurope	LP	Onagram	PO1004	1974	£15	£6	*German*
Lessons For Virgins	LP	Virgin	AR6601	1971	£15	£6	*German*
Percewood's Onagram	LP	Virgin	PO1	1970	£15	£6	*German*
Tropical Brainforest	LP	Virgin	AR6602	1972	£15	£6	*German*

PERE UBU

Breath	CD-s	Fontana	UBUCD4	1989	£5	£2	
Fabulous Sequel	7"	Chrysalis	CHS2372	1979	£5	£2	
I Hear They Smoke The Barbeque	CD-s	Fontana	UBUCD5	1990	£5	£2	
Love Love Love	CD-s	Fontana	UBUCD3	1989	£5	£2	
Love Love Love	CD-s	Fontana	UBUCD33	1989	£5	£2	
Modern Dance	CD	Fontana	8342672	1988	£12	£5	*numbered limited edition*
Modern Dance	LP	Fontana	SFLP3	1988	£10	£4	
Modern Dance	LP	Mercury	9100052	1978	£10	£4	
Tenement Year	CD	Fontana	8345372	1988	£12	£5	
Waiting For Mary	CD-s	Fontana	UBUCD2	1989	£5	£2	
We Have The Technology	CD-s	Fontana	UBUCD1	1988	£5	£2	

PEREGRINE

Songs Of Mine	LP	Westwood	WRS016	1972	£75	£37.50	

PERERIN

Haul Ar Yr Eira	LP	Gwerin	SYWM215	1980	£100	£50	

PERFECT, CHRISTINE

Christine Perfect was pianist and vocalist with Chicken Shack and since the songs that she led were always the best that the group produced, it is not surprising that her solo LP is a particularly good example of British blues. When Peter Green left Fleetwood Mac, Christine Perfect was drafted in as his replacement, when she began to use her married name, Christine McVie.

Christine Perfect	LP	Blue Horizon	763860	1970	£40	£20	
I'm Too Far Gone	7"	Blue Horizon	573172	1970	£8	£4	
When You Say	7"	Blue Horizon	573165	1969	£6	£2.50	

PERFECT PEOPLE

House In The Country	7"	MCA	MU1079	1969	£6	£2.50	

PERFORMERS

I Can't Stop You	7"	Action	ACT4552	1969	£5	£2	

PERIGEO

Abbiamo Tutti Un Blues Da Piangere	LP	RCA	DPSL10609	1973	£15	£6	*Italian*
Attraverso Il Parigeo	LP	RCA	NL33039	1977	£12	£5	*Italian*
Azimut	LP	RCA	DPSL10555	1972	£15	£6	*Italian*
Genealogia	LP	RCA	TPL11080	1974	£15	£6	*Italian*
La Valle Del Tepli	LP	RCA	TPL11175	1975	£15	£6	*Italian*
Non E Poi Cosi Lontano	LP	RCA		1976	£15	£6	*Italian*

PERISHERS

How Does It Feel	7"	Fontana	TF965	1968	£15	£7.50	

PERKINS, BILL

Just Friends	LP	Vogue	LAE12088	1958	£25	£10	
On Stage	LP	Vogue	LAE12078	1958	£20	£8	

PERKINS, CARL

Any Way The Wind Blows	7"	Philips	PB1179	1961	£8	£4	
Big Bad Blues	7"	Brunswick	05909	1964	£5	£2	*with the Nashville Teens*
Blue Suede Shoes	7"	London	HLU8271	1956	£150	£75	
Blue Suede Shoes	7"	London	HLS10192	1968	£4	£1.50	
Boppin' The Blues	LP	CBS	63826	1970	£10	£4	*with NRBQ*
Country Boy's Dream	7"	London	HLP7125	1968	£10	£5	*export*

Country Boy's Dream	7"	Stateside	SS599	1967	£5	£2	
Country Boy's Dream	LP	London	HAP/SHP8366	1968	£15	£6	
Dance Album	LP	Sun	LP1225	1957	£250	£150	US
Dance Album (Teen Beat)	LP	London	HAS2202	1959	£75	£37.50	
Dixie Fried	7"	London	HLS10192	1968	£60	£30	demo
Glad All Over	7"	London	HLS8527	1957	£75	£37.50	
Gone, Gone, Sone	7"	Sun	224	1955	£50	£25	US
Greatest Hits	LP	CBS	63676	1969	£10	£4	
Help Me Find My Baby	7"	Brunswick	05905	1964	£5	£2	
King Of Rock	LP	CBS	63309	1968	£10	£4	
Lake County Cotton Country	7"	Spark	SRL1009	1968	£5	£2	
Matchbox	7"	London	HLS8408	1957	£100	£50	
Monkeyshine	7"	Brunswick	05923	1964	£6	£2.50	
Movie Magg	7"	Flip	501	1955	£250	£150	US, best auctioned
One Ticket To Loneliness	7"	Philips	PB983	1959	£8	£4	
Restless	7"	CBS	3932	1969	£4	£1.50	
Teen Beat	LP	Sun	LP1225	1961	£150	£75	US
That's Right	7"	London	HLS8608	1958	£75	£37.50	
Whole Lotta Carl Perkins	LP	CBS Realm	52305	1966	£12	£5	
Whole Lotta Shakin'	LP	Columbia	CL1234	1958	£100	£50	US

PERKINS, LASCELLES

Creation	7"	Blue Beat	BB41	1961	£12	£6	
I'm So Grateful	7"	Ska Beat	JB175	1964	£10	£5	
Tango Lips	7"	Island	WI038	1963	£10	£5	
Tell It All Brothers	7"	Banana	BA317	1970	£5	£2	Sound Dimension B side

PERKINS, POLLY

Falling In Love Again	7"	Oriole	CB1979	1963	£4	£1.50	
Girls Are At It Again	7"	Decca	F11583	1963	£4	£1.50	
Liberated Woman	LP	Chapter One	CMS1018	1973	£10	£4	
Sweet As Honey	7"	Oriole	CB1869	1963	£4	£1.50	
Young Lover	7"	Oriole	CB1929	1963	£4	£1.50	

PERKINS, TONY

Moonlight Swim	7"	RCA	RCA1018	1957	£4	£1.50	

PERLINPINPIN FOLO

Al Biule	LP	Auvidis	AV4520	1985	£20	£8	French

PERMANENTS

Oh Dear, What Can The Matter Be	7"	London	HLU9803	1983	£4	£1.50	

PERREY, JEAN-JACQUES

Amazing New Electronic Pop Sound	LP	Vanguard	VSD79286	1973	£20	£8	
Best Of The Moog	LP	Vanguard	DPS2051	1974	£25	£10	double
Gossipo Perpetuo	7"	Vanguard	VAN1005	1972	£4	£1.50	
In Sound From Way Out	LP	Vanguard	VSD79222	1973	£20	£8	with Gershon Kingsley
Kaleidoscopic Vibrations	LP	Vanguard	VSD6525	1971	£20	£8	with Gershon Kingsley
Minuet Of The Robots	7"	Vanguard	VAN1008	1973	£4	£1.50	
Moog Indigo	LP	Vanguard	VSD6549	1972	£25	£10	
Moog Indigo	LP	Beat Goes Public	BGPZ1103	1996	£10	£4	

PERRIN, PAT

Over You	7"	Island	WI3115	1968	£10	£5	Lloyd Terrell B side

PERRINE, PEP

Live And In Person	LP	Hideout	1004	1968	£100	£50	US

PERRI'S

Jerri-Lee	7"	Oriole	CB1481	1959	£6	£2.50	

PERRY, BARBARA

Say You Need Me	7"	Pama	PM795	1970	£4	£1.50	

PERRY, JEFF

Love Don't Come No Stronger	7"	Arista	ARIST51	1976	£4	£1.50	

PERRY, LEE

Africa's Blood	LP	Trojan	TBL166	1980	£15	£6	
All Combine	7"	Bullet	BU461	1971	£8	£4	
Back Biter	7"	Upsetter	US389	1972	£6	£2.50	
Bad Minded People	7"	Port-O-Jam	PJ4003	1964	£10	£5	Tommy McCook B side
Bucky Skank	7"	Downtown	DT513	1973	£8	£4	
Chatty Chatty Woman	7"	Port-O-Jam	PJ4010	1964	£10	£5	Tommy McCook B side
Country Girl	7"	Island	WI223	1965	£10	£5	
Cow Thief Skank	7"	Upsetter	US398	1973	£5	£2	
Doctor Dick	7"	Island	WI292	1966	£12	£6	Soul Brothers B side
Dreader Locks	7"	Dip	DL5060	1974	£4	£1.50	
Dub A Pum Pum	7"	Dip	DL5037	1974	£4	£1.50	
French Connection	7"	Upsetter	US385	1972	£6	£2.50	
Jungle Lion	7"	Upsetter	US397	1973	£5	£2	

Title	Format	Label	Cat. No.	Year	Mint	VG	Notes
Just Keep It Up	7"	Island	WI259	1965	£12	£6	*Roland Alphonso B side*
Justice To The People	7"	Jackpot	JP812	1973	£8	£4	
Kill Them All	7"	Upsetter	US325	1970	£4	£1.50	
King Tubby Meets The Upsetter	LP	Fay	FMLP304	1975	£20	£8	
Man And Wife	7"	R&B	JB106	1963	£12	£6	
Never Get Weary	7"	Island	WI118	1963	£12	£6	*Tommy McCook B side*
Old For New	7"	R&B	JB104	1963	£12	£6	
Open The Gate	LP	Trojan	PERRY2	1989	£25	£10	*3 LP boxed set*
Open Up	7"	Ska Beat	JB215	1965	£10	£5	*Roland Alphonso B side*
People Funny Boy	7"	Doctor Bird	DB1146	1968	£10	£5	*Burt Walters B side*
Please Don't Go	7"	Island	WI210	1965	£10	£5	
Prince In The Dark	7"	R&B	JB102	1963	£12	£6	
Reggae Greats	LP	Island	IRG12	1985	£10	£4	
Revolution Dub	LP	Cactus	CTLP112	1979	£12	£5	
Roast Duck	7"	Ska Beat	JB201	1965	£10	£5	
Roast Fish Collie Weed & Corn Bread	LP	Upsetter	LPIR0000	1978	£12	£5	*Jamaican*
Royalty	7"	R&B	JB135	1964	£12	£6	
Rub And Squeeze	7"	Island	WI298	1966	£10	£5	*Soul Brothers B side*
Run For Cover	7"	Doctor Bird	DB1073	1967	£10	£5	
Scratch On The Wire	LP	Island	ILPS9583	1979	£12	£5	
Station Underground	7"	Bread	BR1111	1973	£8	£4	*Carlton & The Shoes B side*
Super Ape	LP	Island	ILPS9417	1976	£20	£8	*orange label*
Trial And Crosses	7"	Ska Beat	JB203	1965	£10	£5	
Uncle Desmond	7"	Trojan	TR644	1968	£8	£4	
Upsetter	7"	Amalgamated	AMG808	1968	£8	£4	
Upsetter	LP	Trojan	TTL13	1969	£20	£8	
Upsetter Again	LP	Trojan	TTL28	1970	£25	£10	
Whop Whop Man	7"	Doctor Bird	DB1098	1967	£10	£5	
Wishes Of The Wicked	7"	Ska Beat	JB212	1965	£10	£5	
Woodman	7"	Ska Beat	JB251	1966	£10	£5	
Yakety Yak	7"	Upsetter	US324	1969	£4	£1.50	

PERRY, MAL

Title	Format	Label	Cat. No.	Year	Mint	VG	Notes
Richer Than I	7"	Fontana	H172	1959	£5	£2	
That's When Your Heartaches Begin	7"	Fontana	H133	1958	£5	£2	
Things I Didn't Say	7"	Fontana	H157	1958	£5	£2	
Too Young To Love	7"	Fontana	H149	1958	£5	£2	

PERRY, STEVE

Title	Format	Label	Cat. No.	Year	Mint	VG	Notes
Ginny Come Lately	7"	Decca	F11462	1962	£4	£1.50	
Step By Step	7"	HMV	POP745	1960	£4	£1.50	

PERRY SISTERS

Title	Format	Label	Cat. No.	Year	Mint	VG	Notes
Willie Boy	7"	Brunswick	05802	1959	£15	£7.50	

PERSEPHONE, BILLY

Title	Format	Label	Cat. No.	Year	Mint	VG	Notes
Billy Persephone	LP	Orion		1972	£25	£10	*US*

PERSEPHONY

Title	Format	Label	Cat. No.	Year	Mint	VG	Notes
To Those Who Loved Us	LP	Unidentified Artist	UAP3	1979	£75	£37.50	*Dutch*

PERSIAN RISK

Title	Format	Label	Cat. No.	Year	Mint	VG	Notes
Calling For You	7"	SRT	SRTS81CUS1146	1981	£100	£50	
Ridin' High	7"	Neat	NEAT24	1983	£6	£2.50	

PERSIMMON'S PECULIAR SHADES

Title	Format	Label	Cat. No.	Year	Mint	VG	Notes
Watchmaker	7"	Major Minor	MM554	1968	£12	£6	

PERSONALITIES

Title	Format	Label	Cat. No.	Year	Mint	VG	Notes
Hey Little Girl	7"	Ska Beat	JB222	1965	£10	£5	
Push It Down	7"	Blue Beat	BB354	1966	£12	£6	
Suffering	7"	Dice	CC30	1965	£10	£5	

PERSUADERS

Title	Format	Label	Cat. No.	Year	Mint	VG	Notes
Surfer's Nightmare	LP	Saturn	SAT(S)5000	1963	£50	£25	*US*

PERSUADERS (2)

Title	Format	Label	Cat. No.	Year	Mint	VG	Notes
Persuaders	LP	Atlantic	K40476	1973	£10	£4	
Thin Line Between Love And Hate	LP	Atlantic	K40370	1972	£12	£5	

PERSUASIONS

Title	Format	Label	Cat. No.	Year	Mint	VG	Notes
Acappella	LP	Straight	STS1062	1970	£25	£10	
Party In The Woods	7"	Minit	MLF11017	1969	£5	£2	
Street Corner Symphony	LP	Island	ILPS9201	1972	£15	£6	
We Came To Play	LP	Capitol	ST791	1971	£15	£6	*US*

PERSUASIONS (2)

Title	Format	Label	Cat. No.	Year	Mint	VG	Notes
Big Brother	7"	Columbia	DB7700	1965	£15	£7.50	
I'll Go Crazy	7"	Columbia	DB7560	1965	£10	£5	
La La La La La	7"	Columbia	DB7859	1966	£15	£7.50	

PERT, MORRIS

Title	Format	Label	Cat. No.	Year	Mint	Excellent	Notes
Book Of Love/ Fragmenti I/ Ultimate Decay	LP	Chantry	CHT007	1982	£25	£10	
Contemporary Clarinet Vol. 2	LP	Chantry	CHT005	198–	£20	£8	*with Georgina Dobree & works by John Mayer & Elisabeth Lutyens*
Contemporary Clarinet Vol. 2	LP	Chantry	ABM25	1978	£25	£10	*with Georgina Dobree & works by John Mayer & Elisabeth Lutyens*
Luminos/ Chromosphere/ 4 Japanese Verses	LP	Chantry	ABM21	1975	£25	£10	*with Georgina Dobree, Veronica Hayward & Suntreader*
Luminos/ Chromosphere/ 4 Japanese Verses	LP	Chantry	CHT001	198–	£20	£8	*with Georgina Dobree, Veronica Hayward & Suntreader*

PERTH COUNTY CONSPIRACY

Title	Format	Label	Cat. No.	Year	Mint	Excellent	Notes
Does Not Exist	LP	Columbia	ELS375	1969	£25	£10	*Canadian*

PERTWEE, JON

Title	Format	Label	Cat. No.	Year	Mint	Excellent	Notes
Who Is The Doctor?	7"	Purple	PUR111	1972	£8	£4	

PESKY GEE

Title	Format	Label	Cat. No.	Year	Mint	Excellent	Notes
Exclamation Mark	LP	Pye	NSPL18293	1969	£40	£20	
Where Is My Mind	7"	Pye	7N17708	1969	£10	£5	

PET SHOP BOYS

Title	Format	Label	Cat. No.	Year	Mint	Excellent	Notes
Actually	CD	Parlophone	CDPCSDX104	1987	£15	£6	*with US CD-s 'Always On My Mind'*
Actually	LP	Parlophone	PCSD104	1987	£50	£25	*blue vinyl*
Actually	LP	Parlophone	PCSD104	1987	£40	£20	*clear vinyl*
Always On My Mind	CD-s	Parlophone	CDR6171	1987	£8	£4	
Always On My Mind (Dance Mix)	12"	Parlophone	12RS6171	1987	£10	£5	*gatefold picture sleeve*
Always On My Mind (Phil Harding Remix)	12"	Parlophone	12RX6171	1987	£10	£5	
Before	12"	Parlophone	12RJD6431	1996	£20	£10	*promo*
Before	12"	Parlophone	12RDJD6431	1996	£25	£12.50	*promo double*
Before	7"	Parlophone	RLH6431	1996	£6	£2.50	*jukebox issue*
Behaviour	CD	Parlophone	CDPCSD113	1990	£75	£37.50	*promo pack with cassette*
Being Boring	CD-s	Parlophone	CDR6275	1990	£5	£2	
Bilingual	CD	Parlophone	BILING1	1996	£75	£37.50	*promo pack*
Bilingual	CD	Parlophone	PSBCDDJ1	1996	£150	£75	*promo box set*
Boy Who Couldn't Keep His Clothes On	12"	Parlophone	12BOYDJ101	1997	£30	£15	*promo*
Can You Forgive Her?	12"	Parlophone	12RXDJ6348	1993	£25	£12.50	*promo*
Can You Forgive Her?	7"	Parlophone	R6348	1993	£300	£180	*red vinyl, best auctioned*
Disco 2	CD	EMI	E230852	1994	£25	£10	*US double pack – bonus 5 track CD including 'Euroboy'*
Discography	CD	Parlophone	CDPSBDJ1	1991	£20	£8	*promo with spoken intros*
DJ Culturemix	CD-s	Parlophone	CDRX6301	1991	£12	£6	
Domino Dancing	CD-s	Parlophone	CDR6190	1988	£10	£5	
Domino Dancing (Remix)	12"	Parlophone	12RX6190	1988	£10	£5	
Heart	CD-s	Parlophone	CDR6177	1988	£10	£5	
Heart (Julian Mendelsohn Remix)	12"	Parlophone	12RX6177	1988	£10	£5	
Hit Music	CD	Parlophone		1991	£50	£25	*French promo of original version of Discography*
Introspective	cass	Parlophone	no number	1988	£30	£15	*promo in video case*
Introspective	LP	Parlophone	PCSX7325	1988	£400	£250	*3 × clear vinyl 12"*
It's A Sin	12"	Parlophone	12R6158	1987	£8	£4	*double sleeve*
It's A Sin	cass-s	Parlophone	TCR6158	1987	£6	£2.50	
It's A Sin	CD-s	Parlophone	CDR6158	1987	£10	£5	
It's A Sin (Ian Levine Remix)	12"	Parlophone	12RX6158	1987	£10	£5	
It's Alright	10"	Parlophone	10R6220	1989	£6	£2.50	*with poster*
It's Alright	CD-s	Parlophone	CDR6220	1989	£10	£5	
Jealousy	CD-s	Parlophone	CDR6283	1991	£5	£2	
Jealousy	CD-s	Parlophone	CDRS6283	1991	£12	£6	*digipak*
Left To My Own Devices	12"	Parlophone	12RDJ6198	1988	£15	£7.50	*promo*
Left To My Own Devices	CD-s	Parlophone	CDR6198	1988	£10	£5	
Love Comes Quickly	10"	Parlophone	10R6116	1986	£50	£25	*with poster*
Love Comes Quickly	7"	Parlophone	R6116	1986	£50	£25	*1 sided promo*
Love Comes Quickly (Dance Mix)	12"	Parlophone	12R6116	1986	£6	£2.50	
Love Comes Quickly (Dance Mix)	12"	Parlophone	12R6116	1986	£10	£5	*cut out sleeve*
Megamix	CD-s	ZYX	ZYX95995	1988	£5	£2	
Music For Boys	12"	Parlophone	12MFBX1	1991	£15	£7.50	*promo*
Music For Boys	12"	Parlophone	MFB1	1991	£30	£15	*promo*
Opportunities	12"	Parlophone	12R6129	1986	£40	£20	*autographed promo with press release*

Opportunities	12"	Parlophone	12R6097	1985	**£20**	**£10**	
Opportunities	7"	Parlophone	R6097	1985	**£15**	**£7.50**	*2 different mixes*
Opportunities	7"	Parlophone	R6097	1985	**£75**	**£37.50**	*different mix – matrix A1U111*
Opportunities (Version Latina)	12"	Parlophone	12RA6097	1985	**£30**	**£15**	
Paninaro	12"	Parlophone	2015626	1987	**£30**	**£15**	*Italian*
Paninaro '95	7"	Parlophone	RLH6414	1995	**£6**	**£2.50**	*jukebox issue*
Pet Shop Boys Compiled	CD	Abbey Road		1993	**£250**	**£150**	*promo CD-R, autographed*
Relentless	LP	Parlophone	DF118	1993	**£60**	**£30**	*promo 3 × coloured vinyl 12"*
Rent	CD-s	Parlophone	CDR6168	1987	**£8**	**£4**	
So Hard	CD-s	Parlophone	CDR6269	1990	**£8**	**£4**	
Somewhere	12"	Parlophone	12RDJD6470	1997	**£15**	**£7.50**	*promo double*
Suburbia	12"	Parlophone	12R6140	1986	**£8**	**£4**	*double sleeve*
Suburbia	7"	Parlophone	RD6140	1986	**£8**	**£4**	*double*
Suburbia	cass-s	Parlophone	TCR6140	1986	**£6**	**£2.50**	*2 versions*
Truck Driver And His Mate	12"	Parlophone	12BARDJ2	1996	**£100**	**£50**	*promo*
Very Relentless	CD	Parlophone	CDPCSDX143	1993	**£15**	**£6**	*with 6 track bonus CD*
Was It Worth It	CD-s	Parlophone	CDR6306	1991	**£5**	**£2**	
West End – Sunglasses	CD-s	ZYX	ZYX85196	1988	**£5**	**£2**	
West End Girls	12"	Epic	TA4292	1984	**£40**	**£20**	
West End Girls	7"	Epic	A4292	1984	**£25**	**£12.50**	
West End Girls (Dance Mix)	12"	Parlophone	12R6115	1985	**£8**	**£4**	*cut-out sleeve, picture labels*
West End Girls (Shep Pettibone Mastermix)	12"	Parlophone	12RA6115	1986	**£10**	**£5**	*2 sleeves*
West End Girls (Untitled Remix)	10"	Parlophone	10R6115	1985	**£30**	**£15**	*round sleeve*
What Have I Done To Deserve This	CD-s	Parlophone	CDR6163	1987	**£8**	**£4**	*with Dusty Springfield*
Where The Streets Have No Name	CD-s	Parlophone	CDR6285	1991	**£5**	**£2**	
Yesterday When I Was Mad	12"	Parlophone	12RDJ6386	1994	**£20**	**£10**	*promo double*

PETARDS

Deeper Blue	LP	Europa	E313	1968	**£25**	**£10**	*German*
Hits	LP	Sunset	SLS50143	1971	**£20**	**£8**	*German*
Hitshock	LP	Liberty	LBS83325	1969	**£25**	**£10**	*German*
Pet Arts	LP	Liberty	LBS83481/2	1971	**£25**	**£10**	*German double*
Petards	LP	Liberty	LBS83204	1969	**£25**	**£10**	*German*

PETER & GORDON

Chantent En Français	7" EP	Columbia	ESRF1726	1965	**£20**	**£10**	*French*
Hits Of Nashville	LP	Capitol	(S)T2430	1966	**£15**	**£6**	*US*
Hot, Cold & Custard	LP	Capitol	(S)T2882	1968	**£15**	**£6**	*US*
Hurtin' 'n' Lovin'	LP	Columbia	33SX1761/ SCX3565	1965	**£15**	**£6**	
I Don't Want To See You Again	LP	Capitol	(S)T2220	1964	**£15**	**£6**	*US*
I Don't Want To See You Again (Cilla Black B side)	7"	Capitol	PRO2720	1964	**£30**	**£15**	*US promo – Paul McCartney & John Lennon intros*
I Go To Pieces	7" EP	Columbia	ESRF1677	1965	**£10**	**£5**	*French*
I Go To Pieces	LP	Capitol	(S)T2324	1965	**£15**	**£6**	*US*
I Go To Pieces	LP	Columbia	SCXC25	1965	**£30**	**£15**	*export*
In London For Tea	LP	Capitol	(S)T2747	1967	**£15**	**£6**	*US*
In Touch	LP	Columbia	33SX1660/ SCX3532	1964	**£15**	**£6**	
Knight In Rusty Armour	LP	Capitol	(S)T2729	1967	**£15**	**£6**	*US*
Lady Godiva	7" EP	Columbia	ESRF1824	1966	**£10**	**£5**	*French*
Lady Godiva	LP	Capitol	(S)T2664	1967	**£15**	**£6**	*US*
Lady Godiva	LP	Columbia	SCXC33	1966	**£30**	**£15**	*export*
Nobody I Know	7" EP	Columbia	SEG8348	1964	**£15**	**£7.50**	
Nobody I Know	7" EP	Columbia	ESRF1566	1964	**£10**	**£5**	*French*
Peter & Gordon	LP	Columbia	33SX1630/ SCX3518	1964	**£15**	**£6**	
Peter & Gordon	LP	Columbia	SX/SCX6045	1966	**£20**	**£8**	
Somewhere	LP	Columbia	SX/SCX6097	1966	**£15**	**£6**	
Sunday For Tea	7" EP	Columbia	ESRF1858	1967	**£10**	**£5**	*French*
True Love Ways	LP	Capitol	(S)T2368	1965	**£15**	**£6**	*US*
Woman	LP	Columbia	SCXC29	1965	**£30**	**£15**	*export*
Woman	LP	Capitol	(S)T2477	1966	**£15**	**£6**	*US*
World Without Love	7" EP	Columbia	ESRF1533	1964	**£10**	**£5**	*French*
World Without Love	LP	Capitol	(S)T2115	1964	**£15**	**£6**	*US*

PETER & PAUL

Schoolgirl	7"	Blue Beat	BB364	1966	**£12**	**£6**	

PETER & THE HEADLINES

Don't Cry Little Girl	7"	Decca	F11980	1964	**£8**	**£4**	
I've Got My Reasons	7"	Decca	F12035	1964	**£8**	**£4**	

PETER & THE PERSUADERS

Wanderer	7" EP	Oak	RGJ197	1965	**£25**	**£12.50**	

PETER & THE TEST TUBE BABIES

Banned From The Pubs	7"	No Future	OI14	1982	**£6**	**£2.50**	
Rotting In The Fart-Sack	12"	Jungle	JUNG21T	1985	**£6**	**£2.50**	*white vinyl*

Run Like Hell	7"	No Future	OI15	1982	**£6**	**£2.50**	

PETER & THE WOLVES

Julie	7"	MGM	MGM1397	1968	**£5**	**£2**	
Lanternlight	7"	MGM	MGM1374	1968	**£6**	**£2.50**	
Little Girl Lost And Found	7"	MGM	MGM1352	1967	**£6**	**£2.50**	

PETER Bs

Each member of this instrumental group went on to further success. Initially, they all formed the backing group for Shotgun Express; later bassist Dave Ambrose joined the Brian Auger Trinity, organist Peter Bardens formed Camel, while guitarist Peter Green and drummer Mick Fleetwood became half of Fleetwood Mac.

If You Wanna Be Happy	7"	Columbia	DB7862	1966	**£40**	**£20**	

PETER, PAUL & MARY

In Concert	LP	Warner Bros	(W)W21555	1964	**£12**	**£5**	*double*
In The Wind	LP	Warner Bros	(W)W1507	1963	**£10**	**£4**	
In The Wind Vol. 1	7" EP	Warner Bros	WEP6135	1964	**£5**	**£2**	
In The Wind Vol. 2	7" EP	Warner Bros	WEP6137	1964	**£5**	**£2**	
Moving	7" EP	Warner Bros	WEP6119	1964	**£5**	**£2**	
Moving	LP	Warner Bros	(W)W1473	1962	**£10**	**£4**	
Peter, Paul & Mary	7" EP	Warner Bros	WEP6114	1963	**£5**	**£2**	
Peter, Paul & Mary	7" EP	Warner Bros	WEP6122	1964	**£5**	**£2**	
Peter, Paul & Mary	LP	Warner Bros	(W)W1449	1962	**£10**	**£4**	

PETERS, JANICE

This Little Girl's Gone Rocking	7"	Columbia	DB4222	1958	**£20**	**£10**	
You're The One	7"	Columbia	DB4276	1959	**£15**	**£7.50**	

PETERS, JENNY

This Is Jenny Peters	LP	Redball	RR031	1980	**£50**	**£25**	

PETERS, MARK

Cindy's Gonna Cry	7"	Oriole	CB1909	1964	**£10**	**£5**	
Don't Cry For Me	7"	Piccadilly	7N35207	1964	**£5**	**£2**	
Janie	7"	Oriole	CB1836	1963	**£10**	**£5**	

PETERS, WENDY

Morning Dew	7"	Saga	OPP1	1968	**£8**	**£4**	

PETER'S FACES

Try A Little Love My Friend	7"	Piccadilly	7N35196	1964	**£4**	**£1.50**	
Wait	7"	Piccadilly	7N35205	1964	**£6**	**£2.50**	
Why Did You Bring Him To The Dance	7"	Piccadilly	7N35178	1964	**£4**	**£1.50**	

PETERSEN, PAUL

She Can't Find Her Keys	7"	Pye	7N25133	1962	**£4**	**£1.50**	*with Shelley Fabares*

PETERSON, BOBBY

Hunch	7"	Top Rank	JAR232	1959	**£10**	**£5**	
Piano Rock	7"	Sue	WI346	1965	**£10**	**£5**	
Rocking Charlie	7"	Sue	WI342	1964	**£10**	**£5**	

PETERSON, OSCAR

Affinity	LP	Verve	VLP9035	1962	**£10**	**£4**	
At The Cocertgebouw	LP	HMV	CLP1317	1959	**£15**	**£6**	
In Romantic Mood	LP	HMV	CLP1086	1956	**£15**	**£6**	
Jazz Portrait Of Frank Sinatra	LP	HMV	CLP1355	1960	**£10**	**£4**	
Jazz Soul	LP	HMV	CLP1429	1961	**£15**	**£6**	
Keyboard	LP	Columbia	33CX10062	1957	**£15**	**£6**	
My Fair Lady	LP	HMV	CLP1278	1959	**£15**	**£6**	
Newport Jazz Frestival 1957	LP	Columbia	33CX10109	1958	**£15**	**£6**	
Night On The Town	LP	Columbia	33CX10135	1959	**£15**	**£6**	
Night Train	LP	Verve	VLP9052	1963	**£10**	**£4**	
O Lady Be Good	10" LP	Columbia	33C9025	1956	**£25**	**£10**	
Oscar Peterson	7" EP	Columbia	SEB10005	1955	**£5**	**£2**	
Oscar Peterson	LP	Columbia	33CX10024	1956	**£20**	**£8**	
Oscar Peterson No. 2	7" EP	Columbia	SEB10022	1956	**£5**	**£2**	
Oscar Peterson Quartet	10" LP	Columbia	33C1038	1955	**£40**	**£20**	
Oscar Peterson Quartet	10" LP	Columbia	33C9013	1955	**£30**	**£15**	
Oscar Peterson Sings	10" LP	Columbia	33C1039	1955	**£40**	**£20**	
Oscar Peterson Sings	10" LP	Columbia	33C9014	1955	**£30**	**£15**	
Plays Cole Porter	LP	Columbia	33CX10016	1955	**£25**	**£10**	
Plays Count Basie	LP	Columbia	33CX10039	1956	**£25**	**£10**	
Plays Duke Ellington	LP	Columbia	33CX10012	1955	**£25**	**£10**	
Plays Harold Arlen	LP	Columbia	33CX10073	1957	**£15**	**£6**	
Plays Pretty	10" LP	Columbia	33C9012	1955	**£30**	**£15**	
Plays Pretty	10" LP	Columbia	33C1037	1955	**£40**	**£20**	
Plays Richard Rogers	LP	Columbia	33CX10028	1956	**£25**	**£10**	
Stratford Shakespearean Festival	LP	Columbia	33CX10096	1958	**£15**	**£6**	
Swinging Brass	LP	HMV	CLP1403/ CSD1326	1960	**£15**	**£6**	

PETERSON, PAUL

Little Bit Of Sandy	7"	Tamla Motown	TMG670	1968	**£15**	**£7.50**	

PETERSON, RAY

Answer Me	7"	RCA	RCA1175	1960	£6	£2.50	
Corrine Corrina	7"	London	HLX9246	1960	£6	£2.50	
Corrine Corrina	7" EP	London	REX1293	1961	£50	£25	
Give Us Your Blessing	7"	London	HLX9746	1963	£5	£2	
I Could Have Loved You So Well	7"	London	HLX9489	1962	£6	£2.50	
Other Side Of Ray Peterson	LP	MGM	(S)E4277	1965	£20	£8	US
Shirley Purly	7"	RCA	RCA1154	1959	£10	£5	
Sweet Little Kathy	7"	London	HLX9332	1961	£5	£2	
Tell Laura I Love Her	7"	RCA	RCA1195	1960	£5	£2	
Tell Laura I Love Her	LP	RCA	LPM/LSP2297	1960	£50	£25	US
Very Best Of Ray Peterson	LP	MGM	(S)E4250	1964	£30	£15	US
Wonder Of You	7"	RCA	RCA1131	1959	£6	£2.50	
You Didn't Care	7"	London	HLX9569	1962	£4	£1.50	
You Thrill Me	7"	London	HLX9379	1961	£4	£1.50	

PETITES

Get Your Daddy's Car Tonight	7"	Philips	PB1035	1960	£4	£1.50	

PETS

Beyond The Sea	7"	Pye	7N25004	1959	£4	£1.50	
Cha Hua Hua	7"	London	HL8652	1958	£15	£7.50	

PETTI, MARY

Hey Lawdy Lawdy	7"	RCA	RCA1239	1961	£25	£12.50	

PETTIFORD, OSCAR

In Hi Fi No. 2	10" LP	HMV	DLP1197	1958	£30	£15	
Oscar Pettiford Group	10" LP	London	LZN14023	1956	£40	£20	
Oscar Pettiford Group	LP	London	LTZN15035	1957	£30	£15	
Oscar Pettiford Orchestra	LP	HMV	CLP1171	1958	£30	£15	
Oscar Pettiford Sextet	10" LP	Vogue	LDE098	1954	£75	£37.50	

PETTY, FRANK

St Louis Blues	7"	MGM	SP1010	1953	£8	£4	

PETTY, NORMAN

Corsage	LP	Vik	1073	1959	£30	£15	US
Mood Indigo	7"	HMV	7M274	1954	£8	£4	
Moondreams	LP	Columbia	CL1092	1958	£75	£37.50	US
Petty For Your Thoughts	LP	Top Rank	RS639	1960	£25	£10	US

PETTY, TOM

1991 Into The Great Wide Open	CD	MCA		1991	£20	£8	US interview promo
American Girl	12"	Shelter	WIP126403	1977	£6	£2.50	
Anything That's Rock'n'Roll	12"	Shelter	WIP126396	1977	£6	£2.50	
Damn The Torpedoes	LP	MCA	MCA5105	1980	£10	£4	Canadian audiophile
Free Fallin'	CD-s	MCA	DMCAX1381	1989	£5	£2	boxed with biography
Full Moon Fever	CD	MCA	6253P	1990	£20	£8	US promo with bonus live track
Gone Gator Sampler	CD	Gone Gator	CD331478	1991	£20	£8	US promo
Hard Promises	CD	Mobile Fidelity	UDCD565	1991	£15	£6	US audiophile
Hard Promises	LP	MCA	BSR5162	1981	£10	£4	Canadian audiophile
I Won't Back Down	CD-s	MCA	DMCAT1334	1989	£5	£2	
I Won't Back Down	CD-s	MCA	DMCAX1334	1989	£6	£2.50	black plastic case
Official Bootleg	LP	Shelter	IDJ24	1977	£20	£8	promo
Refugee	12"	MCA	MCAT1047	1985	£6	£2.50	
Runnin' Down A Dream	CD-s	MCA	DMCAX1359	1989	£5	£2	
Tom Petty Interview	CD	MCA	TOM1	1989	£20	£8	German promo

PFM

Per Un Amico	LP	Numero Uno	ZSLN55155	1972	£10	£4	Italian
Storia Di Un Minoto	LP	Numero Uno	ZSLN55055	1972	£10	£4	Italian

PHAFNER

Overdrive	LP	Dragon	no number	1971	£1500	£1000	US

PHANTOM

Phantom's Divine Comedy Part One	LP	Capitol	ST11313	1974	£75	£37.50	US

PHANTOMS

Great Guitar Hits	LP	Arc	655	1964	£30	£15	
Ken Levy And The Phantoms	LP	Nashville	NSPL30102	1964	£60	£30	Swedish
Phantom Guitar	7"	Palette	PG9014	1961	£8	£4	
Phantoms	LP	Metronome	MLP10057	1965	£30	£15	German

PHARE, RORY

Laughing Inside	7"	Parlophone	RP1	1988	£4	£1.50	promo, actually Roy Harper

PHAROAHS

Pharoahs	7" EP	Decca	DFE6522	1958	£500	£330	best auctioned

PHASE FOUR

Man Am I Worried?	7"	Fab	FAB6	1967	£25	£12.50	
What Do You Say About That	7"	Decca	F12327	1966	£6	£2.50	

Title	Format	Label	Number	Year	Mint	VG	Notes
What Do You Say About That	7"	Fab	FAB1	1966	£6	£2.50	

PHASE 5

Title	Format	Label	Number	Year	Mint	VG	Notes
Star Trek	7"	Polydor	2058063	1970	£15	£7.50	

PHEASANT PLUCKERS

Title	Format	Label	Number	Year	Mint	VG	Notes
Live At The Plume Of Feathers	LP	Sentinel	SENP506	1973	£25	£10	

PHELPS, JAMES

Title	Format	Label	Number	Year	Mint	VG	Notes
Check Yourself	7"	Paramount	3019	1971	£5	£2	

PHENOMENA

Title	Format	Label	Number	Year	Mint	VG	Notes
Dance With The Devil	12"	Bronze	BROX193	1985	£6	£2.50	*with poster*
Dance With The Devil	7"	Bronze	BRO193	1985	£4	£1.50	

PHEW

Title	Format	Label	Number	Year	Mint	VG	Notes
Phew	LP	Pass	3F28002	1981	£15	£6	*Japanese*

PHIL & THE FLINTSTONES

Title	Format	Label	Number	Year	Mint	VG	Notes
Love Potion No. 9	7"	Bedrock	PR5371	1964	£30	£15	

PHILLIPS, ANTHONY

Anthony Phillips was an original member of Genesis, playing guitar on both the debut album and its follow-up, *Trespass* – his successor was Steve Hackett.

Title	Format	Label	Number	Year	Mint	VG	Notes
Anthem From Tarka	7"	PRT	PYS18	1988	£6	£2.50	
Anthem From Tarka	CD-s	PRT	PYD18	1988	£10	£5	
Collections	7"	Philips	6837406	1977	£15	£7.50	*picture sleeve*
Prelude '84	7"	RCA	RCA102	1981	£5	£2	*picture sleeve*
Private Parts And Pieces	LP	Arista	AFLP1	1979	£10	£4	
Um And Aargh	7"	Arista	ARIST252	1978	£5	£2	*picture sleeve*
We're All As We Lie	7"	Arista	ARIST192	1978	£6	£2.50	
Wise After The Event	LP	Passport	PB9828	1978	£10	£4	*US picture disc*

PHILLIPS, BARRE

Title	Format	Label	Number	Year	Mint	VG	Notes
For All It Is	LP	Japo	60003	1973	£15	£6	
Unaccompanied Barre	LP	Music Man	SMLS601	1970	£15	£6	

PHILLIPS, CONFREY

Title	Format	Label	Number	Year	Mint	VG	Notes
Shotgun Rock And Roll	7"	Decca	F10866	1957	£6	£2.50	

PHILLIPS, ESTHER

Title	Format	Label	Number	Year	Mint	VG	Notes
Alone Again, Naturally	LP	Kudu	KUL6	1973	£10	£4	
Am I That Easy To Forget	7"	Ember	EMBS174	1963	£4	£1.50	
And I Love Him	7"	Atlantic	AT4028	1965	£5	£2	
And I Love Him	LP	Atlantic	ATL5030	1965	£25	£10	
Chains	7"	Sue	WI395	1965	£12	£6	
Confessin' The Blues	LP	Atlantic	K50521	1976	£10	£4	
Country Side Of Esther Phillips	LP	Atlantic	(SD)8130	1966	£15	£6	*US*
Esther	LP	Atlantic	(SD)8122	1966	£15	£6	*US*
From A Whisper To A Scream	LP	Kudu	KUL2	1973	£15	£6	
Home Is Where The Hatred Is	7"	Kudu	KUS4000	1973	£5	£2	
I Could Have Told You	7"	Atlantic	AT4077	1966	£25	£12.50	
Let Me Know When It's Over	7"	Atlantic	AT4048	1965	£5	£2	
Memory Lane	LP	King	LP622	1956	£600	£400	*US*
Performance	LP	Kudu	KU18	1975	£10	£4	
Reflections Of Great Country And Western Standards	LP	Ember	CW103	1963	£15	£6	
Release Me	7"	Stateside	SS140	1962	£4	£1.50	
Release Me	7"	Ember	EMBS221	1966	£4	£1.50	
Release Me	LP	Lenox	227	1962	£25	£10	*US*
Sings	LP	Atlantic	587/588010	1966	£15	£6	

PHILLIPS, FLIP

Title	Format	Label	Number	Year	Mint	VG	Notes
Flip Phillips	10" LP	Columbia	33C9003	1955	£50	£25	

PHILLIPS, GREGORY

Title	Format	Label	Number	Year	Mint	VG	Notes
Angie	7"	Pye	7N15546	1963	£4	£1.50	
Down In The Boondocks	7"	Immediate	IM004	1965	£8	£4	

PHILLIPS, JOHN

Title	Format	Label	Number	Year	Mint	VG	Notes
Wolfking Of L.A.	LP	Stateside	SSL5027	1970	£10	£4	

PHILLIPS, PHIL

Title	Format	Label	Number	Year	Mint	VG	Notes
I Love To Love You	7"	Mercury	AMT1139	1961	£10	£5	
Sea Of Love	7"	Mercury	AMT1059	1959	£25	£12.50	
Take This Heart	7"	Mercury	AMT1072	1960	£6	£2.50	
Your True Love Once More	7"	Mercury	AMT1093	1960	£8	£4	

PHILLIPS, SHAWN

Title	Format	Label	Number	Year	Mint	VG	Notes
I'm A Loner	LP	Columbia	33SX1748	1965	£75	£37.50	
Little Tin Soldier	7"	Columbia	DB7789	1965	£4	£1.50	
Nobody Listens	7"	Columbia	DB7699	1965	£5	£2	
Shawn	LP	Columbia	SCX6006	1966	£60	£30	
Solitude	7"	Columbia	DB7611	1965	£5	£2	
Stargazer	7"	Parlophone	R5606	1967	£20	£10	
Summer Came	7"	Columbia	DB7956	1966	£4	£1.50	

PHILLIPS, SID

Cruising Down To Dixie	10" LP	HMV	DLP1194	1958	£10	£4	
Dixieland Express	10" LP	HMV	DLP1206	1960	£10	£4	
Down Dixieland Highway	10" LP	HMV	DLP1164	1957	£12	£5	
Flying Down To Dixie	10" LP	HMV	DLP1212	1960	£10	£4	
Hors D'Oeuvres	10" LP	HMV	DLP1102	1955	£15	£6	

PHILLIPS, STU

Champlain & St Lawrence Line	7"	London	HL8673	1958	£6	£2.50	
Strangers When We Meet	7"	Pye	7N25062	1960	£4	£1.50	*Bob Mersey Orchestra B side*
Stu Phillips	7" EP	Pye	NEP44001	1959	£5	£2	

PHILLIPS, TEDDY

Down Boy	7"	Parlophone	CMSP4	1954	£6	£2.50	*export*
Life Is Like A Slice Of Cake	7"	Parlophone	CMSP28	1954	£6	£2.50	*export*
Old Red Barn	7"	Parlophone	CMSP12	1954	£6	£2.50	*export, Jimmy Blue Crew B side*
Ridin' To Tennessee	7"	London	HL8032	1954	£25	£12.50	

PHILLIPS, TOM, GAVIN BRYARS & FRED ORTON

Irma	LP	Obscure	OBS9	1978	£10	£4	

PHILLIPS, WARREN & THE ROCKETS (SAVOY BROWN)

World Of Rock And Roll	LP	Decca	(S)PA43	1969	£10	£4	

PHILOSOPHERS

After Sundown	LP	PS	1001	1969	£100	£50	*US*

PHILPOTT, VINCE & THE DRAGS

Cramp	7"	Decca	F11997	1964	£10	£5	

PHILWIT & PEGASUS

Philwit & Pegasus	LP	Chapter One	CHS805	1970	£25	£10	

PHLUPH

Phluph	LP	Verve	V65054	1968	£15	£6	*US*

PHOENIX, PAT

Rovers Chorus	7"	HMV	POP1030	1962	£6	£2.50	

PHONES SPORTSMAN BAND

I Really Like You	7"	Rather	GEAR9	1981	£6	£2.50	

PHOTOGRAPHED BY LIGHTNING

Sleeps Terminator	7"	Fierce	FRIGHT008	1986	£20	£10	

PIAF, EDITH

At The Paris Olympia	LP	Columbia	33SX1330	1961	£10	£4	
Great Piaf	7" EP	Columbia	SEG8220	1963	£5	£2	
Mea Culpa	LP	Columbia	SCX5	1957	£12	£5	
Non Je Ne Regrette Rien	7" EP	Columbia	SEG8308	1964	£5	£2	
Qu'il Etait Triste	7" EP	Columbia	SEG8387	1965	£5	£2	
Sincerely	LP	Columbia	33SX1276	1960	£10	£4	

PIANO RED

Bouncin' With Red	78	HMV	B10316	1952	£10	£5	
Hey Good Lookin'	78	HMV	B10246	1952	£10	£5	
In Concert	LP	Groove	1002	1964	£100	£50	*US*
Jump Man Jump	LP	Groove	1001	1964	£100	£50	*US*
Rhythm & Blues Vol. 2	7" EP	RCA	RCX7138	1964	£25	£12.50	
Rocking With Red	7"	HMV	7M108	1953	£150	£75	

PIC & BILL

All I Want Is You	7"	Page One	POF024	1967	£5	£2	
Sad World Without You	7"	Page One	POF052	1968	£5	£2	

PICCADILLY LINE

At The Third Stroke	7"	CBS	2785	1967	£5	£2	
Emily Small	7"	CBS	2958	1967	£5	£2	
Evenings With Corrina	7"	CBS	3743	1968	£4	£1.50	
Huge World Of Emily Small	LP	CBS	(S)BPG63129	1967	£40	£20	
Yellow Rainbow	7"	CBS	3595	1968	£4	£1.50	
Yellow Rainbow/I Know, She Believes	7"	CBS	3595	1968	£8	£4	*demo*

PICKENS, BUSTER

Texas Piano	LP	Heritage	HLP1008	196–	£30	£15	

PICKETT, BOBBY & THE CRYPT KICKERS

Monster Mash	7"	London	HLU9597	1962	£6	£2.50	
Monster Mash	LP	London	ZGU133	1973	£10	£4	
Monster Mash	LP	Garpax	(S)GP67001	1962	£25	£10	*US*

PICKETT, DAN

Dan Pickett	7" EP	XX	MIN710	196–	£8	£4	

PICKETT, KENNY

Got A Gun	7"	F-Beat	PRO2	1980	£6	£2.50	promo

PICKETT, NICK

Silversleeves	LP	Reprise	K44172	1972	£15	£6	

PICKETT, WILSON

634-5789	7"	Atlantic	AT4072	1966	£4	£1.50	
99 & A Half Won't Do	7"	Atlantic	584023	1966	£4	£1.50	
Best Of Wilson Pickett	LP	Atlantic	587/588092	1968	£10	£4	
Don't Fight It	7"	Atlantic	AT4052	1965	£4	£1.50	
Engine No. 9	7"	Atlantic	2091032	1970	£4	£1.50	
Engine No. 9	LP	Atlantic	2400026	1971	£10	£4	
Everybody Needs Somebody To Love	7"	Atlantic	584101	1967	£4	£1.50	
Exciting Wilson Pickett	LP	Atlantic	587/588029	1966	£15	£6	
Funky Broadway	7"	Atlantic	584130	1967	£4	£1.50	
Hey Joe	7"	Atlantic	584281	1969	£4	£1.50	
Hey Jude	7"	Atlantic	584236	1969	£4	£1.50	
Hey Jude	LP	Atlantic	588170	1969	£10	£4	
I Found A True Love	7"	Atlantic	584221	1968	£4	£1.50	
I'm A Midnight Mover	7"	Atlantic	584203	1968	£4	£1.50	
I'm In Love	LP	Atlantic	587/588107	1968	£10	£4	
In The Midnight Hour	7"	Atlantic	584150	1968	£4	£1.50	
In The Midnight Hour	7"	Atlantic	AT4036	1965	£5	£2	
In The Midnight Hour	LP	Atlantic	ATL5037	1965	£25	£10	
In The Midnight Hour	LP	Atlantic	587032	1966	£12	£5	
It's Too Late	7"	Liberty	LIB10115	1963	£10	£5	
It's Too Late	LP	Double-L	DL2300/SDL8300	1963	£30	£15	US
Land Of 1000 Dances	7"	Atlantic	584039	1966	£4	£1.50	
Midnight Mover	LP	Atlantic	587/588111	1968	£10	£4	
Mini-Skirt Minnie	7"	Atlantic	584261	1969	£4	£1.50	
Mustang Sally	7"	Atlantic	584066	1966	£4	£1.50	
My Heart Belongs To You	7"	MGM	MGM1286	1965	£30	£15	
New Orleans	7"	Atlantic	584107	1967	£4	£1.50	
She's Looking Good	7"	Atlantic	584183	1968	£4	£1.50	
Sound Of Wilson Pickett	LP	Atlantic	587/588080	1967	£12	£5	
Stag-o-lee	7"	Atlantic	584142	1967	£4	£1.50	
Sugar Sugar	7"	Atlantic	2091005	1970	£4	£1.50	
That Kind Of Love	7"	Atlantic	584173	1968	£4	£1.50	
Wicked Pickett	LP	Atlantic	587/588057	1967	£12	£5	
You Keep Me Hanging On	7"	Atlantic	584313	1970	£4	£1.50	

PICKFORD, ED

Facing The Crowd	LP	Rip Off	ROF002	1982	£10	£4	
Songwriter	LP	Rip Off	ROF001	1976	£12	£5	

PICKFORD-HOPKINS, GARY

Why?	12"	Spartan	SP143T	1983	£6	£2.50	
Why?	7"	Spartan	SP143	1983	£5	£2	

PICKUPS

Keep On Dancing	LP	Metronome	MLP10058	1967	£20	£8	German
Keep On Dancing Vol. 2	LP	Metronome	MLP10084	1967	£15	£6	German

PICKWICKS

Apple Blossom Time	7"	Decca	F11901	1964	£5	£2	
Little By Little	7"	Warner Bros	WB151	1965	£40	£20	
You're Old Enough	7"	Decca	F11957	1964	£5	£2	

PIED PIPERS

Kissin' Drive Rock	7"	Parlophone	CMSP21	1954	£10	£5	export
Ragamuffin	7"	Columbia	DB7883	1966	£4	£1.50	

PIERCE, BILLY & DEDE

Jazz At Preservation Hall Vol. 2	LP	London	HAK/SHK8163	1964	£12	£5	

PIERCE, NAT

Chamber Music For Moderns	LP	Vogue Coral	LVA9060	1957	£12	£5	
Kansas City Memories	LP	Vogue Coral	LVA9050	1957	£12	£5	

PIERCE, WEBB

Bound For The Kingdom	LP	Decca	DL(7)8889	1959	£15	£6	US
Bye Bye Love	7"	Brunswick	05682	1957	£25	£12.50	
Country & Western Favourites Vol. 1	7" EP	Ember	EMBEP4520	1962	£10	£5	
Country Round Up	7" EP	Parlophone	GEP8792	1959	£20	£10	
Cross Country	LP	Brunswick	LAT8551	1965	£10	£4	
Drifting Texas Sands	7"	Brunswick	05842	1960	£5	£2	
Hideaway Heart	LP	Brunswick	LAT8540	1965	£15	£6	
I Ain't Never	7"	Brunswick	05809	1959	£8	£4	
In The Jailhouse Now	LP	MCA	MUPS364	1969	£10	£4	
Just Imagination	LP	Decca	DL8728	1957	£20	£8	US
No Love Have I	7"	Brunswick	05820	1960	£5	£2	
One And Only Webb Pierce	LP	King	648	1959	£15	£6	US
Teenage Boogie	7"	Brunswick	05630	1956	£125	£62.50	
That Wondering Boy	10" LP	Brunswick	LA8716	1955	£30	£15	
That Wondering Boy	LP	Decca	DL8295	1956	£20	£8	US
Webb	LP	Brunswick	LAT8324	1959	£15	£6	

Title	Format	Label	Cat. No.	Year	Value	Value	Notes
Webb Pierce	LP	Decca	DL8129	1955	£20	£8	US
Webb Pierce Pt 1	7" EP	Brunswick	OE9253	1956	£10	£5	
Webb Pierce Pt 2	7" EP	Brunswick	OE9254	1956	£10	£5	
Webb Pierce Pt 3	7" EP	Brunswick	OE9255	1956	£10	£5	
Webb Pierce Story	LP	Decca	DX(S)B(7)181	1964	£15	£6	US, with booklet

PIERROT LUNAIRE

Title	Format	Label	Cat. No.	Year	Value	Value	Notes
Patrice	LP	RCA	NL74114	1984	£20	£8	Italian

PIGG, BILLY

Title	Format	Label	Cat. No.	Year	Value	Value	Notes
Border Minstrel	LP	Leader	LEA4006	1971	£12	£5	

PIGGLESWICK FOLK

Title	Format	Label	Cat. No.	Year	Value	Value	Notes
Pig In The Middle	LP	Acorn	CF256	1977	£15	£6	

PIGS

Title	Format	Label	Cat. No.	Year	Value	Value	Notes
Youthenasia	7"	Bristol Recorder	NBR01	1977	£4	£1.50	

PIGSTY HILL LIGHT ORCHESTRA

Title	Format	Label	Cat. No.	Year	Value	Value	Notes
Cushion Foot Stomp	LP	Village Thing	VTS1	1970	£20	£8	
Piggery Jokery	LP	Village Thing	VTS8	1971	£20	£8	
Pigsty Hill Light Orchestra	LP	PHLO	001	1976	£25	£10	

PIIRPAUKE

Title	Format	Label	Cat. No.	Year	Value	Value	Notes
Live	LP	Love	LRLP251	1977	£15	£6	Swedish
Piirpauke I	LP	Love	LRLP148	1975	£20	£8	Swedish
Piirpauke II	LP	Love	LRLP192	1976	£20	£8	Swedish

PIKEMEN

Title	Format	Label	Cat. No.	Year	Value	Value	Notes
Lonesome Boatmen	LP	Emerald	GES1185	1978	£20	£8	

PILGRIM, RAY

Title	Format	Label	Cat. No.	Year	Value	Value	Notes
Baby Doll	7"	Oriole	CB1557	1960	£5	£2	
Kissin' Cousins	7"	Embassy	WB645	1964	£5	£2	Jaybirds B side
Little Miss Makebelieve	7"	Oriole	CB1616	1961	£5	£2	

PILTDOWN MEN

Title	Format	Label	Cat. No.	Year	Value	Value	Notes
Gargantua	7"	Capitol	CL15211	1961	£6	£2.50	
Goodnight Mrs Flintstone	7"	Capitol	CL15186	1961	£4	£1.50	
Goodnight Mrs Flintstone/Piltdown Rides Again	7" EP	Capitol	EAP120155	1961	£25	£12.50	
McDonald's Cave	7"	Capitol	CL15149	1960	£4	£1.50	
Piltdown Rides Again	7"	Capitol	CL15175	1961	£4	£1.50	
Pretty Girl Is Like A Melody	7"	Capitol	CL15245	1962	£6	£2.50	

PIMM, SIR HUBERT

Title	Format	Label	Cat. No.	Year	Value	Value	Notes
Goodnight And Cheerio	7"	London	HL8155	1955	£20	£10	
Pimm's Party	7" EP	London	REU1032	1955	£15	£7.50	

PINDER, MICHAEL

Title	Format	Label	Cat. No.	Year	Value	Value	Notes
Promise	CD	Threshold	8207762	1989	£12	£5	

PINEAPPLE BOYS

Title	Format	Label	Cat. No.	Year	Value	Value	Notes
Fabulous	LP	Moon	23001	1983	£40	£20	Japanese

PINEAPPLE CHUNKS

Title	Format	Label	Cat. No.	Year	Value	Value	Notes
Drive My Car	7"	Mercury	MF922	1965	£5	£2	

PINEWOOD TOM & TALL TOM

Title	Format	Label	Cat. No.	Year	Value	Value	Notes
Male Blues Vol. 4	7" EP	Collector	JEL5	1959	£10	£5	

PINGUIN

Title	Format	Label	Cat. No.	Year	Value	Value	Notes
Der Grosse Rote Vogel	LP	Zebra	2949001	1971	£20	£8	German

PINHAS, RICHARD

Title	Format	Label	Cat. No.	Year	Value	Value	Notes
Chronolyse	LP	Cobra	COB37015	1978	£10	£4	French
East West	LP	Pulse	003	1980	£10	£4	
Iceland	LP	Polydor	2393254	1979	£10	£4	French
L'Ethique	LP	Pulse	006	1982	£10	£4	
Rhizosphere	LP	Cobra	COB37005	1977	£10	£4	French

PINK FAIRIES

Title	Format	Label	Cat. No.	Year	Value	Value	Notes
Kings Of Oblivion	LP	Polydor	2383212	1973	£15	£6	with cardboard poster
Never Never Land	LP	Polydor	2383045	1971	£40	£20	plastic cover
Never Never Land	LP	Polydor	2383045	1971	£12	£5	
Never Never Land	LP	Polydor	2383045	1971	£300	£180	red vinyl
Snake	7"	Polydor	2058089	1970	£10	£5	
Well Well Well	7"	Polydor	2058302	1972	£6	£2.50	

PINK FLOYD

In their early days, Pink Floyd epitomized what British psychedelic music was all about and their first two albums are rightly prized as crucially important documents of the period. Like many LPs recorded in the second half of the sixties, there are many differences between the mono and stereo versions, this being particularly noticeable on the often densely arranged *Saucerful Of Secrets* record. The Columbia singles are also much in demand, especially since the only vinyl reissue of the last three consists of a German compilation LP. Promotional copies of the 1967 singles were issued in picture sleeves, which are extremely scarce today.

Title	Format	Label	Cat. No.	Year			Notes
Animals	LP	Columbia	PCQ34474	1977	£25	£10	*US quad*
Another Brick In The Wall Pt 2 (live)	12"	EMI	12PF1	1988	£15	£7.50	*promo only*
Apples And Oranges	7"	Columbia	DB8310	1967	£500	£330	*promo, picture sleeve, best auctioned*
Apples And Oranges	7"	Columbia	DB8310	1967	£30	£15	
Arnold Layne	7"	Columbia	DB8156	1967	£500	£330	*promo, picture sleeve, best auctioned*
Arnold Layne	7"	Columbia	DB8156	1967	£25	£12.50	
Arnold Layne	7" EP	Columbia	ESRF1857	1967	£300	£180	*French, best auctioned*
Atom Heart Mother	CD	Mobile Fidelity	UDCD584	1993	£15	£6	*US audiophile*
Atom Heart Mother	LP	Harvest	Q4SHVL781	1973	£25	£10	*quad*
Atom Heart Mother	LP	Harvest	SHVL781	1970	£10	£4	
Collection Of Great Dance Songs	LP	Columbia	HC47680	1983	£20	£8	*US audiophile*
Dark Side Of The Moon	CD	EMI	PCDDSOM20	1993	£40	£20	*promo with slides, photos, biog*
Dark Side Of The Moon	CD	EMI	077778147923	1993	£15	£6	*20th Anniversary Edition, in cardboard box with 5 cards*
Dark Side Of The Moon	CD	Mobile Fidelity	UDCD517	1988	£15	£6	*US audiophile*
Dark Side Of The Moon	LP	Harvest	Q4SHVL804	1973	£25	£10	*quad*
Dark Side Of The Moon	LP	Mobile Fidelity	MFSL1017	1978	£20	£8	*US audiophile*
Dark Side Of The Moon	LP	Capitol	SEAX11902	1978	£20	£8	*US picture disc*
Dark Side Of The Moon	LP	Mobile Fidelity	UHQR1017	1982	£150	£75	*US audiophile, numbered box set*
Dark Side Of The Moon	LP	Harvest	SHVL804	1973	£10	£4	*2 posters, 2 stickers, stickered sleeve*
Delicate Sound Of Thunder	CD	PMI	PMCD4912752	1995	£25	£10	*double CD video, initial pressings gave black lines across the screen*
Division Bell	CD	EMI	8289842	1994	£100	£50	*French promo box set with cassette, booklet*
First XI	LP	Harvest	PF11	1979	£200	£100	*9 LPs plus 2 picture discs, boxed*
High Hopes	CD-s	EMI	CDEMS342	1994	£5	£2	*card packet with 7 cards*
In Europe '88	12"	EMI	PSLP1026	1988	£15	£7.50	*promo*
It Would Be So Nice	7"	Columbia	DB8401	1968	£30	£15	
Learning To Fly	7"	EMI	EMDJ26	1987	£8	£4	*pink vinyl promo*
Learning To Fly	7"	EMI	EMDJ26	1987	£20	£10	*black vinyl promo*
Learning To Fly	CD-s	EMI	CDEM26	1987	£10	£5	
Meddle	CD	Harvest	CDP7460342	1987	£50	£25	*mispressing – plays With The Beatles*
Meddle	CD	Mobile Fidelity	UDCD518	1989	£15	£6	*US audiophile*
Meddle	LP	Harvest	SHVL795	1971	£10	£4	
Momentary Lapse Of Reason Official Tour CD	CD	Columbia	CSK1100	1987	£30	£15	*US promo*
Money	7"	Harvest	HAR5217	1981	£40	£20	*1 sided promo with B side label*
Money	7"	Harvest	HAR5217	1981	£25	£12.50	*1 sided promo, pink vinyl*
More	LP	Columbia	SCX6346	1969	£15	£6	*green rear sleeve*
More	LP	Columbia	SCX6346	197–	£10	£4	*grey rear sleeve*
More	LP	Columbia	SCX6346	197–	£20	£8	*reversed grey rear sleeve (couple face east)*
Nice Pair	LP	Harvest	SHDW403	1973	£12	£5	*double, Mr Phang sleeve*
Obscured By Clouds	LP	Harvest	SHSP4020	1972	£12	£5	*rounded sleeve*
Off The Wall	LP	Columbia	AS756	1979	£20	£8	*US promo sampler*
On The Turning Away	12"	EMI	12EMP34	1987	£8	£4	*poster sleeve*
On The Turning Away	7"	EMI	EMP34	1987	£5	£2	*pink vinyl*
On The Turning Away	CD-s	EMI	CDEM34	1987	£10	£5	
One Slip	7"	EMI	EMG52	1988	£5	£2	*pink vinyl*
One Slip	CD-s	EMI	CDEM52	1988	£8	£4	
Pink Floyd	LP	EMI	SIGMA630	1997	£75	£37.50	*7 LP boxed set*
Piper At The Gates Of Dawn	LP	Columbia	SX6157	1967	£150	£75	*mono*
Piper At The Gates Of Dawn	LP	Columbia	SCX6157	1967	£75	£37.50	*stereo*
Piper At The Gates Of Dawn	LP	Columbia	SCX6157	1970	£15	£6	*silver & black label*
Point Me At The Sky	7"	Columbia	DB8511	1968	£40	£20	
Pulse	LP	EMI	EMD578	1995	£30	£15	*4 LP boxed set*
Saucerful Of Secrets	LP	Columbia	SX6258	1968	£150	£75	*mono*
Saucerful Of Secrets	LP	Columbia	SCX6258	1968	£60	£30	*stereo*
Saucerful Of Secrets	LP	Columbia	SCX6258	1970	£15	£6	*silver & black label*
See Emily Play	7"	Columbia	DB8214	1967	£500	£330	*promo, picture sleeve, best auctioned*
See Emily Play	7"	Columbia	DB8214	1967	£25	£12.50	
Selected Tracks From Shine On	CD-s	EMI	SHINE1	1992	£12	£6	*promo*
Take It Back	7"	EMI	EM309	1994	£4	£1.50	*red vinyl*
Take It Back	7"	EMI	EM309	1994	£5	£2	*jukebox issue*
Take It Back	CD-s	EMI	CDEMS309	1994	£5	£2	*with poster*
Tonite Let's All Make Love In London	CD	See For Miles	SFM2	1993	£10	£4	*promo sampler*
Tonite Let's All Make Love In London	CD-s	See For Miles	SEACD4	1991	£5	£2	

Title	Format	Label	Cat. No.	Year	Mint	VG	Notes
Tonite Let's All Make Love In London	LP	Instant	INLP002	1968	**£75**	**£37.50**	*with other artists*
Tour '75	LP	Capitol	SPRO8116/7	1975	**£30**	**£15**	*US promo compilation*
Ummagumma	LP	Harvest	SHDW1/2	1969	**£15**	**£6**	*double, laminated sleeve*
Wall	CD	Harvest	CDS7460368	1988	**£50**	**£25**	*mispressing – plays Beatles Past Masters I on 1 disc*
Wall	CD	Mobile Fidelity	UDCD2537	1990	**£25**	**£10**	*US audiophile*
Wall	LP	Columbia	H2C46183	1983	**£50**	**£25**	*US audiophile*
Wall In Store	LP	Columbia	XDAP93012	1979	**£60**	**£30**	*US promo*
When The Tigers Broke Free	7"	Harvest	HAR5222	1982	**£4**	**£1.50**	*2 sleeves*
Wish You Were Here	CD-s	EMI	CDPINK1	1988	**£15**	**£7.50**	*promo*
Wish You Were Here	LP	Columbia	HC43453	1982	**£20**	**£8**	*US audiophile*
Wish You Were Here	LP	Harvest	Q4SHVL814	1976	**£30**	**£15**	*quad*
Wish You Were Here	LP	Harvest	SHVL814	1976	**£10**	**£4**	*black polythene wrapper*
Zabriskie Point	LP	MGM	2315002	1970	**£15**	**£6**	*with other artists*
Zabriskie Point	LP	MGM	CS8120	1970	**£20**	**£8**	*with other artists*
Zabriskie Point	LP	MGM	2354040	197–	**£10**	**£4**	*with other artists*

PINK MICE

Title	Format	Label	Cat. No.	Year	Mint	VG	Notes
In Action	LP	Europa	E456	1971	**£10**	**£4**	*German*
In Synthesizer	LP	Europa	E1011	1973	**£10**	**£4**	*German*

PINK MILITARY

Title	Format	Label	Cat. No.	Year	Mint	VG	Notes
Buddha Waking Disney Sleeping	7"	Last Trumpet	LT001	1979	**£5**	**£2**	

PINK PEOPLE

Title	Format	Label	Cat. No.	Year	Mint	VG	Notes
Indian Hate Call	7"	Philips	BF1356	1964	**£10**	**£5**	
Psychologically Unsound	7"	Philips	BF1355	1964	**£20**	**£10**	

PINKERTON'S ASSORTED COLOURS

Title	Format	Label	Cat. No.	Year	Mint	VG	Notes
Don't Stop Loving Me Baby	7"	Decca	F12377	1966	**£4**	**£1.50**	
Kentucky Woman	7"	Pye	7N17574	1968	**£4**	**£1.50**	
Magic Rocking Horse	7"	Decca	F12493	1966	**£10**	**£5**	
Mirror Mirror	7"	Decca	F12307	1966	**£4**	**£1.50**	
Mirror Mirror	7" EP	Decca	457113	1966	**£20**	**£10**	*French*
Mum And Dad	7"	Pye	7N17327	1967	**£4**	**£1.50**	
There's Nobody I'd Sooner Love	7"	Pye	7N17414	1967	**£4**	**£1.50**	

PINKY

Title	Format	Label	Cat. No.	Year	Mint	VG	Notes
All Cried Out	7"	Polydor	BM56009	1965	**£4**	**£1.50**	

PINNACLE

Title	Format	Label	Cat. No.	Year	Mint	VG	Notes
Assassin	LP	Stag	HP125	1974	**£100**	**£50**	

PIONEERS

Title	Format	Label	Cat. No.	Year	Mint	VG	Notes
Alli Button	7"	Amalgamated	AMG850	1969	**£8**	**£4**	*Hippy Boys B side*
Bad To Be Good	7"	Trojan	TR7897	1973	**£4**	**£1.50**	
Battle Of The Giants	LP	Trojan	TBL139	1970	**£12**	**£5**	
Black Bud	7"	Trojan	TR685	1969	**£4**	**£1.50**	
Catch The Beat	7"	Amalgamated	AMG828	1968	**£8**	**£4**	*Sir Gibbs' Allstars B side*
Don't You Know	7"	Amalgamated	AMG833	1969	**£8**	**£4**	
Easy Come Easy Go	7"	Pyramid	PYR6062	1969	**£6**	**£2.50**	*Beverley's Allstars B side*
Freedom Feeling	LP	Trojan	TRLS64	1973	**£10**	**£4**	
Give And Take	7"	Trojan	TR7846	1972	**£4**	**£1.50**	
Give It To Me	7"	Blue Cat	BS103	1968	**£8**	**£4**	*Leaders B side*
Give Me A Little Loving	7"	Amalgamated	AMG811	1968	**£8**	**£4**	
Give Up	7"	Rio	R106	1966	**£8**	**£4**	
Good Nannie	7"	Rio	R102	1966	**£8**	**£4**	
Greetings From The Pioneers	LP	Amalgamated	AMGLP2003	1968	**£60**	**£30**	
Honey Bee	7"	Trojan	TR7923	1974	**£4**	**£1.50**	
I Believe In Love	LP	Trojan	TRLS48	1972	**£10**	**£4**	
I Love No Other Girl	7"	Caltone	TONE119	1968	**£8**	**£4**	*Milton Boothe B side*
Jackpot	7"	Amalgamated	AMG821	1968	**£8**	**£4**	*Creators B side*
Let Your Yeah Be Yeah	7"	Trojan	TR7825	1971	**£4**	**£1.50**	
Long Shot	7"	Amalgamated	AMG814	1968	**£8**	**£4**	
Long Shot Kick The Bucket	7"	Trojan	TR672	1969	**£4**	**£1.50**	*Rico B side*
Longshot	LP	Trojan	TBL103	1969	**£12**	**£5**	
Love Love Every Day	7"	Amalgamated	AMG846	1969	**£8**	**£4**	*Moon Boys B side*
Mama Look Deh	7"	Amalgamated	AMG835	1969	**£8**	**£4**	*Blenders B side*
No Dope Me Pony	7"	Amalgamated	AMG823	1968	**£8**	**£4**	*Lord Salmons B side*
Pee Pee Cluck Cluck	7"	Pyramid	PYR6065	1969	**£6**	**£2.50**	*Beverley's Allstars B side*
Poor Rameses	7"	Trojan	TR698	1969	**£4**	**£1.50**	*Beverley's Allstars B side*
Reggae Beat	7"	Blue Cat	BS139	1968	**£8**	**£4**	
Shake It Up	7"	Blue Cat	BS100	1968	**£8**	**£4**	
Sweet Dreams	7"	Amalgamated	AMG830	1968	**£8**	**£4**	*Don Drummond Jr B side*
Tickle Me For Days	7"	Amalgamated	AMG826	1968	**£8**	**£4**	*Versatiles B side*
Whip Them	7"	Blue Cat	BS105	1968	**£8**	**£4**	
Who The Cap Fits	7"	Amalgamated	AMG840	1969	**£8**	**£4**	
Yeah	LP	Trojan	TRL24	1971	**£10**	**£4**	

PIPS

Every Beat Of My Heart	7"	Top Rank	JAR574	1961	**£20**	**£10**	

PIRANHAS

Somethin' Fishy	LP	Custom Fidelity	1452	1969	**£75**	**£37.50**	*US*

PIRATES

My Babe	7"	HMV	POP1250	1964	**£12**	**£6**	
Shades Of Blue	7"	Polydor	56712	1966	**£15**	**£7.50**	

PISCES

Pisces	LP	Trailer	LER2025	1971	**£20**	**£8**	

PITNEY, GENE

Backstage	7" EP	Stateside	SE1040	1966	**£8**	**£4**	
Being Together	LP	Stateside	(S)SL10181	1966	**£10**	**£4**	*with Melba Montgomery*
Big Sixteen	LP	United Artists	ULP1073	1964	**£15**	**£6**	
Big Sixteen Vol. 2	LP	Stateside	SL10132	1965	**£10**	**£4**	
Big Sixteen Vol. 3	LP	Stateside	(S)SL10199	1967	**£10**	**£4**	
Blue Gene	LP	United Artists	ULP1061	1964	**£12**	**£5**	
Every Breath I Take	7"	HMV	POP933	1961	**£10**	**£5**	
Gene Italiano	7" EP	Stateside	SE1032	1965	**£10**	**£5**	
Gene Pitney Sings Just For You	7" EP	Stateside	SE1036	1966	**£6**	**£2.50**	
George Jones And Gene Pitney	LP	Stateside	SL10147	1965	**£10**	**£4**	*with George Jones*
I Must Be Seeing Things	7" EP	Stateside	SE1030	1965	**£8**	**£4**	
I Wanna Love My Life Away	7"	London	HL9270	1961	**£8**	**£4**	
I'm Gonna Be Strong	LP	Stateside	SL10120	1965	**£10**	**£4**	
I'm Gonna Find Myself A Girl	7"	United Artists	UP1055	1964	**£5**	**£2**	
It's Country Time Again	LP	Stateside	SL10173	1966	**£10**	**£4**	*with George Jones*
Just One Smile	LP	Stateside	(S)SL10212	1967	**£10**	**£4**	
Looking Thru The Eyes Of Love	LP	Stateside	SL10148	1965	**£10**	**£4**	
Man Who Shot Liberty Valance	7"	HMV	POP1018	1962	**£6**	**£2.50**	
Many Sides Of Gene Pitney	LP	HMV	CLP1566	1961	**£25**	**£10**	
Meets The Fair Young Ladies Of Folkland	LP	United Artists	ULP1064	1964	**£12**	**£5**	
Nobody Needs Your Love	LP	Stateside	(S)SL10183	1966	**£10**	**£4**	
Only Love Can Break A Heart	LP	United Artists	(S)ULP1028	1963	**£15**	**£6**	
Pitney Sings Just For You	LP	United Artists	ULP1043	1963	**£12**	**£5**	
Pitney Today	LP	Stateside	(S)SL10242	1968	**£10**	**£4**	
San Remo Winners And Others	7" EP	Stateside	SE1041	1967	**£8**	**£4**	
Sings The Great Songs Of Our Time	LP	Stateside	SL10156	1965	**£10**	**£4**	
That Girl Belongs To Yesterday	7" EP	Stateside	SE1028	1965	**£6**	**£2.50**	
That Girl Belongs To Yesterday	7" EP	United Artists	UEP1002	1964	**£6**	**£2.50**	
There's No Living Without Your Love	7" EP	Stateside	SE1045	1967	**£6**	**£2.50**	
Town Without Pity	7"	HMV	POP952	1962	**£8**	**£4**	
Town Without Pity	7" EP	HMV	7EG8832	1963	**£40**	**£20**	
Twenty Four Hours From Tulsa	7" EP	Stateside	SE1027	1965	**£8**	**£4**	
Twenty Four Hours From Tulsa	7" EP	United Artists	UEP1001	1964	**£6**	**£2.50**	
Young, Warm And Wonderful	LP	Stateside	(S)SL10194	1967	**£10**	**£4**	
Yours Until Tomorrow	7"	Stateside	SS2131	1968	**£5**	**£2**	

PIXIES

Dig For Fire	CD-s	4AD	BAD0014CD	1990	**£5**	**£2**	
Doolittle	LP	4AD	CAD905	1989	**£10**	**£4**	*in carrier bag*
Gigantic	CD-s	4AD	BAD805CD	1988	**£5**	**£2**	
Here Comes Your Man	CD-s	4AD	BAD909CD	1989	**£5**	**£2**	
Live	LP	4AD		1989	**£30**	**£15**	*promo*
Planet Of Sound	CD-s	4AD	BAD1008CD	1991	**£5**	**£2**	
This Monkey's Gone To Heaven	CD-s	4AD	BAD904CD	1989	**£5**	**£2**	
Velouria	CD-s	4AD	BADCD0009	1990	**£5**	**£2**	

PIXIES THREE

Birthday Party	7"	Mercury	AMT1214	1963	**£4**	**£1.50**	
Party With The Pixies Three	LP	Mercury	MG2/SR60912	1964	**£40**	**£20**	*US*

PLACEBO

Bruise Pristine	7"	Fierce Panda	NING13	1995	**£10**	**£5**	*Soup B side*
Come Home	7"	Deceptive	BLUFF024	1996	**£6**	**£2.50**	

PLAGUE

Looking For The Sun	7"	Decca	F12730	1968	**£50**	**£25**	

PLAIN JANE

Plain Jane	LP	Hobbit	HB5000	1969	**£30**	**£15**	*US*

PLAINSONG

In Search Of Amelia Earhart	LP	Elektra	K42120	1972	**£12**	**£5**	
Plainsong II	LP	Elektra	K42136	1973	**£100**	**£50**	*demo only*

PLANETARIUM

Infinity	LP	Victory	RCA10051	1971	**£150**	**£75**	*Italian*

PLANETEN SIT IN

Planeten Sit In	LP	Kosmische	KM58011	1974	**£20**	**£8**	*German*

PLANETS

Chunky	7"	HMV	POP818	1960	**£5**	**£2**	
Jam Roll	7"	HMV	POP832	1961	**£8**	**£4**	
Jungle Street	7"	HMV	POP895	1961	**£10**	**£5**	
Like Party	7"	Palette	PG9008	1960	**£6**	**£2.50**	
Like Party	7"	Palette	PG9008	1960	**£10**	**£5**	*picture sleeve*

PLANT, RICHARD

Better Be Sane	LP	Tradition	TSR022	1975	**£10**	**£4**	

PLANT, ROBERT

Heaven Knows	CD-s	Es Paranza	A9373CD	[illegible]	**£[illegible]**	**£[illegible]**	*3" single*
Long Time Coming	7"	CBS	202858	1966	**£125**	**£62.50**	
Manic Nirvana	CD	Es Paranza	WX339CD	1990	**£40**	**£20**	*promo box set*
Our Song	7"	CBS	202656	1966	**£125**	**£62.50**	
Pictures At Eleven	LP	Swan Song	SAM154	1982	**£10**	**£4**	*interview promo*
Principal Of Moments	LP	Es Paranza	SAM169	1983	**£10**	**£4**	*interview promo*
Profiled!	CD	Es Paranza	PRCD32972	1990	**£25**	**£10**	*US promo*
Ship Of Fools	CD-s	Es Paranza	A9281CDB	1988	**£5**	**£2**	*3" single, inserts*
Tall Cool One	CD-s	Es Paranza	A9348CD	1988	**£5**	**£2**	*3" single*
Your Ma Said You Cried In Your Sleep Last Night	CD-s	East West	A8945CD	1990	**£5**	**£2**	

PLANXTY

After The Break	LP	Tara	3001	1979	**£10**	**£4**	*Irish*
Aris	LP	Polydor	8152291	1984	**£10**	**£4**	*Irish*
Cold Blow And Rainy Night	LP	Polydor	2383301	1974	**£12**	**£5**	
Planxty	LP	Polydor	2383186	1973	**£12**	**£5**	
Planxty Collection	LP	Polydor	2383397	1974	**£10**	**£4**	
Time Dance	12"	WEA	IR28207	1981	**£25**	**£10**	*Irish*
Well Below The Valley	LP	Polydor	2383232	1973	**£12**	**£5**	
Woman I Loved So Well	LP	Tara	3005	1980	**£10**	**£4**	*Irish*
Words And Music	LP	WEA	2401011	1983	**£10**	**£4**	*Irish*

PLASTIC CLOUD

Plastic Cloud	LP	Allied	10	1968	**£150**	**£75**	*Canadian*

PLASTIC GANGSTERS

Plastic Gangsters	7"	Secret	SHH144	1983	**£50**	**£25**	*promo*

PLASTIC PENNY

Currency	LP	Page One	POLS014	1969	**£40**	**£20**	
Heads I Win, Tails You Lose	LP	Page One	POLS611	1970	**£40**	**£20**	
Two Sides Of Plastic Penny	LP	Page One	POL(S)005	1968	**£40**	**£20**	
Your Way To Tell Me Go	7"	Page One	POF079	1968	**£6**	**£2.50**	

PLASTIC PEOPLE OF THE UNIVERSE

Egon Bondy's Happy Hearts Club Banned	LP	Invisible	SCOPA10001	1979	**£12**	**£5**	*French*

PLATFORM SIX

Girl Down Town	7"	Piccadilly	7N35255	1965	**£10**	**£5**	

PLATT, EDDIE

Tequila	7"	Columbia	DB4101	1958	**£4**	**£1.50**	

PLATTERS

Are You Sincere	7"	Mercury	7MT205	1958	**£15**	**£7.50**	
Around The World	LP	Mercury	MMC14009	1959	**£25**	**£10**	
Ebb Tide	7"	Mercury	AMT1098	1960	**£4**	**£1.50**	
Enchanted	7"	Mercury	AMT1039	1959	**£4**	**£1.50**	
Fabulous Platters	7" EP	Mercury	MEP9504	1956	**£10**	**£5**	
Fabulous Platters Vol. 2	7" EP	Mercury	MEP9514	1957	**£12**	**£6**	
Fabulous Platters Vol. 3	7" EP	Mercury	MEP9524	1957	**£12**	**£6**	
Flying Platters	7" EP	Mercury	MEP9526	1958	**£12**	**£6**	
Flying Platters	LP	Mercury	MPL6528	1957	**£25**	**£10**	
Flying Platters No. 2	7" EP	Mercury	MEP9528	1958	**£12**	**£6**	
Golden Hits	LP	Mercury	MMC14091	1962	**£10**	**£4**	
Great Pretender	7"	Mercury	MT117	1956	**£20**	**£10**	*export*
Harbour Lights	7"	Mercury	AMT1081	1960	**£4**	**£1.50**	
Harbour Lights	7" EP	Mercury	ZEP10112	1961	**£12**	**£6**	
Helpless	7"	Mercury	7MT197	1958	**£25**	**£12.50**	
I Love You A Thousand Times	7"	Stateside	SS511	1966	**£10**	**£5**	
I Wish	7"	Mercury	AMT1001	1958	**£8**	**£4**	
I'll Be Home	7"	Stateside	SS568	1966	**£4**	**£1.50**	
I'll Never Smile	7"	Mercury	AMT1154	1961	**£4**	**£1.50**	
If I Didn't Care	7"	Mercury	AMT1128	1961	**£4**	**£1.50**	
Life Is Just A Bowl Of Cherries	LP	Mercury	MMC14072	1961	**£15**	**£6**	
Magic Touch	78	Mercury	MT107	1956	**£8**	**£3**	
My Blue Heaven	7"	Mercury	AMT1066	1959	**£4**	**£1.50**	
My Secret	7"	Mercury	AMT1076	1960	**£4**	**£1.50**	
Only You	7"	Ember	JBS701	1962	**£125**	**£62.50**	
Pick Of The Platters No. 1	7" EP	Mercury	ZEP10000	1959	**£12**	**£6**	
Pick Of The Platters No. 2	7" EP	Mercury	ZEP10008	1959	**£12**	**£6**	
Pick Of The Platters No. 3	7" EP	Mercury	ZEP10025	1959	**£12**	**£6**	
Pick Of The Platters No. 4	7" EP	Mercury	ZEP10031	1959	**£12**	**£6**	
Pick Of The Platters No. 5	7" EP	Mercury	ZEP10042	1959	**£12**	**£6**	

Title	Format	Label	Cat. No.	Year	Mint	VG+	Notes
Pick Of The Platters No. 6	7" EP	Mercury	ZEP10056	1960	**£15**	**£7.50**	
Pick Of The Platters No. 7	7" EP	Mercury	ZEP10070	1960	**£15**	**£7.50**	
Platters	10" LP	Parlophone	PMD1058	1958	**£250**	**£150**	
Platters	7" EP	Mercury	MEP9537	1958	**£12**	**£6**	
Platters	LP	Mercury	MPL6504	1956	**£30**	**£15**	
Platters	LP	King	LP549	1956	**£200**	**£100**	*US*
Platters	LP	Federal	395549	1955	**£300**	**£180**	*US*
Platters On A Platter	7" EP	Mercury	ZEP10126	1962	**£15**	**£7.50**	
Platters On Parade	LP	Mercury	MMC14010	1959	**£25**	**£10**	
Platters Vol. 2	LP	Mercury	MPL6511	1957	**£30**	**£15**	
Red Sails In The Sunset	7"	Mercury	AMT1106	1960	**£4**	**£1.50**	
Reflections	LP	Mercury	MMC14045	1960	**£15**	**£6**	
Remember When	7"	Mercury	AMT1053	1959	**£4**	**£1.50**	
Remember When	LP	Mercury	MMC14014	1959	**£20**	**£8**	
Smoke Gets In Your Eyes	7"	Mercury	AMT1016	1958	**£5**	**£2**	
Sweet Sweet Lovin'	7"	Stateside	SS2067	1967	**£6**	**£2.50**	
To Each His Own	7"	Mercury	AMT1118	1960	**£4**	**£1.50**	
Twilight Time	7"	Mercury	7MT214	1958	**£8**	**£4**	
Washed Ashore	7"	Stateside	SS2042	1967	**£5**	**£2**	
With This Ring	7"	Stateside	SS2007	1967	**£5**	**£2**	
You're Making A Mistake	7"	Mercury	7MT227	1958	**£10**	**£5**	

PLAY DEAD

Title	Format	Label	Cat. No.	Year	Mint	VG+	Notes
Poison Takes A Hold	7"	Fresh	FRESH29	1981	**£4**	**£1.50**	
This Side Of Heaven	7"	Tanz	TANZ1	1985	**£4**	**£1.50**	*promo only*
TV Eye	7"	Fresh	FRESH38	1981	**£4**	**£1.50**	

PLAYBOYS

Title	Format	Label	Cat. No.	Year	Mint	VG+	Notes
Over The Weekend	7"	London	HLU8681	1958	**£25**	**£12.50**	

PLAYBOYS (2)

Title	Format	Label	Cat. No.	Year	Mint	VG+	Notes
Playboys	10" LP	Electrocord	EDD1115	1965	**£100**	**£50**	*Romanian*

PLAYBOYS (3)

Title	Format	Label	Cat. No.	Year	Mint	VG+	Notes
For Charity	7"	Lyntone	LYN549/550	196–	**£10**	**£5**	*flexi*

PLAYBOYS OF EDINBURGH

Title	Format	Label	Cat. No.	Year	Mint	VG+	Notes
Up Through The Spiral	LP	Uni	73099	1971	**£15**	**£6**	*US*

PLAYERS

Title	Format	Label	Cat. No.	Year	Mint	VG+	Notes
Mockingbird	7"	Oriole	CB1861	1963	**£8**	**£4**	

PLAYGIRLS

Title	Format	Label	Cat. No.	Year	Mint	VG+	Notes
Hey Sport	7"	RCA	RCA1133	1959	**£10**	**£5**	

PLAYGIRLS (2)

Title	Format	Label	Cat. No.	Year	Mint	VG+	Notes
Looks Are Deceiving	7"	Black Swan	WI456	1965	**£10**	**£5**	

PLAYGROUND

Title	Format	Label	Cat. No.	Year	Mint	VG+	Notes
At The Zoo	7"	MGM	MGM1351	1967	**£4**	**£1.50**	

PLAYMATES

Title	Format	Label	Cat. No.	Year	Mint	VG+	Notes
At Play With The Playmates	7" EP	Columbia	SEG7864	1958	**£5**	**£2**	
Barefoot Girl	7"	Columbia	DB3941	1957	**£5**	**£2**	
Beep Beep	7"	Columbia	DB4224	1958	**£4**	**£1.50**	
Darling It's Wonderful	7"	Columbia	DB4033	1957	**£5**	**£2**	
Day I Died	7"	Columbia	DB4207	1958	**£4**	**£1.50**	
Don't Go Home	7"	Columbia	DB4151	1958	**£4**	**£1.50**	
Jo-Ann	7"	Columbia	DB4084	1958	**£4**	**£1.50**	
Let's Be Lovers	7"	Columbia	DB4127	1958	**£4**	**£1.50**	
Party Playmates	7" EP	Columbia	SEG7949	1959	**£5**	**£2**	
Party Playmates No. 2	7" EP	Columbia	SEG7966	1960	**£5**	**£2**	
Star Love	7"	Columbia	DB4288	1959	**£4**	**£1.50**	
What Is Love	7"	Columbia	DB4338	1959	**£5**	**£2**	

PLEASE, BOBBY

Title	Format	Label	Cat. No.	Year	Mint	VG+	Notes
Your Driver's License Please	7"	London	HLB8507	1957	**£200**	**£100**	*demo*

PLEASURE, KING

Title	Format	Label	Cat. No.	Year	Mint	VG+	Notes
Golden Days	LP	Vogue	LAE12258	1961	**£12**	**£5**	
King Pleasure	10" LP	Esquire	20066	1956	**£50**	**£25**	
King Pleasure	7" EP	Vocalion	EPVH1285	1964	**£5**	**£2**	

PLEASURE GARDEN

Title	Format	Label	Cat. No.	Year	Mint	VG+	Notes
Permissive Paradise	7"	Sound For Industry	SFI31H/32H	196–	**£25**	**£12.50**	*flexi, Emperor Rosko & Jonathan King B side*

PLEASURE SEEKERS

Suzi Quatro was just fifteen when she formed the Pleasure Seekers – an all-girl group that also included her sister Patti, who later turned up as a member of Fanny.

Title	Format	Label	Cat. No.	Year	Mint	VG+	Notes
Good Kind Of Hurt	7"	Mercury	72800	1968	**£15**	**£7.50**	*US*
Never Thought You'd Leave Me	7"	Hideout	1006	1967	**£60**	**£30**	*US*

PLEASURES

Title	Format	Label	Cat. No.	Year	Mint	VG+	Notes
Music City	7"	Sue	WI357	1965	**£12**	**£6**	

PLEBS

Title	Format	Label	Cat. No.	Year	Mint	VG	Notes
Bad Blood	7"	Decca	F12006	1964	**£25**	**£12.50**	
Plebs	LP	Oak		196–	**£500**	**£330**	*1 sided*

PLETHYN

Title	Format	Label	Cat. No.	Year	Mint	VG	Notes
Blas Y Pridd	LP	Sain	SAIN1145M	1979	**£15**	**£6**	

PLEXUS

Title	Format	Label	Cat. No.	Year	Mint	VG	Notes
Life Up The Creek	LP	Hill And Dale	HD4004	1979	**£50**	**£25**	
Plexus	LP	Look	LKLP6175	1978	**£50**	**£25**	

PLUM, JON

Title	Format	Label	Cat. No.	Year	Mint	VG	Notes
Alice	7"	SNB	SS3971	1969	**£4**	**£1.50**	

PLUM NELLY

Title	Format	Label	Cat. No.	Year	Mint	VG	Notes
Deceptive Lines	LP	Capitol	ST692	1971	**£30**	**£15**	*US*

PLUMMERS

Title	Format	Label	Cat. No.	Year	Mint	VG	Notes
Litle Stars	7"	Blue Beat	BB260	1964	**£12**	**£6**	

PLUS

Title	Format	Label	Cat. No.	Year	Mint	VG	Notes
Seven Deadly Sins	LP	Probe	SPB1009	1970	**£50**	**£25**	

PLUTO

Title	Format	Label	Cat. No.	Year	Mint	VG	Notes
I Really Want It	7"	Dawn	DNS1026	1972	**£10**	**£5**	
Pluto	LP	Dawn	DNLS3030	1972	**£75**	**£37.50**	
Rag A Bone Joe	7"	Dawn	DNS1017	1971	**£10**	**£5**	

PNEUMONIA

Title	Format	Label	Cat. No.	Year	Mint	VG	Notes
I Can See Your Face	7"	Oak	RGJ625	1968	**£100**	**£50**	

POACHER, CYRIL

Title	Format	Label	Cat. No.	Year	Mint	VG	Notes
Broomfield Wager	LP	Topic	12TS252	1975	**£10**	**£4**	

POCHETTE NOIRE

Title	Format	Label	Cat. No.	Year	Mint	VG	Notes
Fais Que Ton Rêve Soit Plus Long	LP	Reprise	540009	1971	**£50**	**£25**	*French*

POCO

Title	Format	Label	Cat. No.	Year	Mint	VG	Notes
Cantamos	LP	Epic	PEQ33192	1974	**£10**	**£4**	*US quad*
Crazy Eyes	LP	Epic	EQ32354	1973	**£10**	**£4**	*US quad*
Deliverin'	LP	Epic	EQ30209	1971	**£10**	**£4**	*US quad*
Legend	LP	Mobile Fidelity	MFSL1020	1978	**£10**	**£4**	*US audiophile*

POEMS

Title	Format	Label	Cat. No.	Year	Mint	VG	Notes
Achieving Unity	7"	Polka	DOT1	1981	**£5**	**£2**	*with booklet*

POET & THE ONE MAN BAND

Poet and the One Man Band featured neither a poet nor a one-man band, but instead was the home for some subsequently well-known musicians – notably guitarists Albert Lee and Jerry Donahue and bass player Pat Donaldson. The group was not able to survive the collapse of its record company, but eventually metamorphosed into Heads, Hands and Feet.

Title	Format	Label	Cat. No.	Year	Mint	VG	Notes
Poet & The One Man Band	LP	Verve	SVLP6012	1969	**£30**	**£15**	

POETS

Title	Format	Label	Cat. No.	Year	Mint	VG	Notes
Baby Don't You Do It	7"	Immediate	IM024	1966	**£75**	**£37.50**	
Call Again	7"	Immediate	IM006	1965	**£75**	**£37.50**	
Heyla Hola	7"	Strike Cola	RSA1	1971	**£30**	**£15**	
I Am So Blue	7"	Decca	F12195	1965	**£30**	**£15**	
Now We're Thru	7"	Decca	F11995	1964	**£30**	**£15**	
That's The Way It's Got To Be	7"	Decca	F12074	1965	**£50**	**£25**	
Wooden Spoon	7"	Decca	F12569	1967	**£125**	**£62.50**	

POETS (2)

Title	Format	Label	Cat. No.	Year	Mint	VG	Notes
Alone Am I	7"	Pye	7N17668	1968	**£125**	**£62.50**	

POGUE MAHONE

Title	Format	Label	Cat. No.	Year	Mint	VG	Notes
Dark Streets Of London	7"	Rough Trade	PM1	1984	**£5**	**£2**	*no picture sleeve*
Dark Streets Of London	7"	Pogue Mahone	PM1	1984	**£40**	**£20**	*tour copy with harp sticker*

POGUES

Title	Format	Label	Cat. No.	Year	Mint	VG	Notes
Boys From The County Hell	7"	Stiff	BUY212	1984	**£8**	**£4**	
Dark Streets Of London	7"	Stiff	BUY207	1984	**£5**	**£2**	*no picture sleeve*
Dirty Old Town	12"	Stiff	BUYIT229	1985	**£15**	**£7.50**	*with poster*
Dirty Old Town	12"	Stiff	BUYIT229	1985	**£10**	**£5**	
Dirty Old Town	12"	Stiff	MAIL3	1985	**£10**	**£5**	*mail order*
Dirty Old Town	7"	Stiff	PBUY229	1985	**£10**	**£5**	*picture disc*
Fairytale Of New York	CD-s	Pogue Mahone	CDNY1	1987	**£5**	**£2**	*with Kirsty MacColl*
Haunted	12"	MCA	MCAT1084	1986	**£6**	**£2.50**	*with poster*
If I Should Fall From Grace With God	CD-s	Stiff	CDFG1	1988	**£5**	**£2**	
Jack's Heroes	CD-s	WEA	YZ500CD	1990	**£5**	**£2**	*with the Dubliners*
Miss Otis Regrets	CD-s	Chrysalis	CHSCD3629	1990	**£5**	**£2**	*with Kirsty MacColl*
Misty Morning	CD-s	WEA	YZ407CD	1989	**£12**	**£6**	*3" single*
Pair Of Brown Eyes	12"	Stiff	BUYIT220	1985	**£10**	**£5**	
Pair Of Brown Eyes	7"	Stiff	DBUY220	1985	**£15**	**£7.50**	*picture disc*

Pair Of Brown Eyes	7"	Stiff	BUY220	1985	£4	**£1.50**	
Poguetry In Motion	7"	Stiff	PBUY243	1986	£4	**£1.50**	*picture disc*
Sally MacLennane	12"	Stiff	BUYIT224	1985	£8	**£4**	
Sally MacLennane	7"	Stiff	DBUY224	1985	£10	**£5**	*shaped picture disc*
Sally MacLennane	7"	Stiff	BUY224	1985	£6	**£2.50**	*green vinyl, wraparound picture sleeve*
White City	CD-s	WEA	YZ409CD	1989	£5	**£2**	*3" single*

POHJOLA, PEKKA

Group	LP	Dig It	LP1	1978	£12	**£5**	*Finnish*
Katkavaaran Lohikaarme	LP	Dig It	LP12	1980	£12	**£5**	*Finnish*
Mathematician's Air Display	LP	Virgin	V2084	1977	£12	**£5**	
Pihkasilma Kaarnakorva	LP	Love	LRLP71	1972	£20	**£8**	*Swedish*
Visitation	LP	Dig It	LP4	1980	£12	**£5**	*Finnish*

POISON

Every Rose Has Its Thorn	CD-s	Capitol	CDCL520	1989	£5	**£2**	
Nothin' But A Good Time	CD-s	Capitol	CDCL539	1989	£5	**£2**	
Your Mama Don't Dance	CD-s	Capitol	CDCL523	1989	£5	**£2**	

POISON IVY

Clinging Memories	7" EP	Granta	GR7EP1011	1964	£75	**£37.50**	

POLECATS

John I'm Only Dancing	10"	Mercury	POLE10	1981	£8	**£4**	*pink vinyl*
Rockabilly Guy	7"	Nervous	NER001	1981	£10	**£5**	

POLICE

In addition to the various coloured vinyl releases, picture discs, and other limited edition rarities issued by the Police, there is an American version of *Ghost In The Machine* too rare to be given a realistic value. This is a picture disc, with red LED lights set into the vinyl, along with the (small!) batteries to operate them. Whether it was ever intended to issue this commercially is not clear, but in the event only ten copies were actually produced.

Can't Stand Losing You	7"	A&M	AMS7381	1978	£8	**£4**	*red, yellow, or green vinyl*
Can't Stand Losing You	7"	A&M	AMS7381	1979	£6	**£2.50**	*white vinyl*
Can't Stand Losing You	7"	A&M	AM214	1979	£15	**£7.50**	*US badge shaped picture disc*
Compact Hits	CD-s	A&M	AMCD905	1988	£5	**£2**	
Don't Stand So Close To Me	7"	A&M	SP3720	1981	£15	**£7.50**	*US star shaped picture disc*
Every Breath You Take	7"	A&M	AM117	1983	£8	**£4**	*double*
Every Breath You Take	7"	A&M	AMSP117	1983	£5	**£2**	*picture disc*
Fall Out	7"	Illegal	IL001	1977	£8	**£4**	*black & white picture sleeve*
Ghost In The Machine	LP	Nautilus	NR40	1981	£12	**£5**	*US audiophile*
Message In A Bottle	7"	A&M	PR4400	1980	£15	**£7.50**	*US star shaped picture disc*
Message In A Bottle	7"	A&M		1979	£15	**£7.50**	*US badge shaped picture disc*
Outlandos D'Amour	LP	A&M	AMLH68502	1978	£12	**£5**	*blue vinyl*
Police Enquiry	LP	A&M	SAMP13	1981	£10	**£4**	*interview promo*
Police Pack	7"	A&M	AMPP6001	1980	£15	**£7.50**	*6 × 7", blue vinyl*
Regatta De Blanc	10" LP	A&M	AMLT64792	1979	£12	**£5**	*double*
Roxanne	12"	A&M	AMS7348	1978	£10	**£5**	*telephone picture sleeve*
Roxanne	7"	A&M	AMS7348	1978	£4	**£1.50**	*telephone picture sleeve*
Roxanne	7"	A&M	AM2096/2147	1979	£15	**£7.50**	*US badge shaped picture disc*
Selections From Message In A Box	CD	A&M	8044	1993	£25	**£10**	*US promo*
Spirits In The Material World	7"	A&M	AMS8194	1981	£5	**£2**	*poster sleeve, badge*
Syncronicity	CD	Mobile Fidelity	UDCD511	1988	£15	**£6**	*US audiophile*
Wrapped Around Your Finger	7"	A&M	AMP127	1983	£6	**£2.50**	*picture disc (Stewart or Andy)*
Wrapped Around Your Finger	7"	A&M	AMP127	1983	£4	**£1.50**	*picture disc (Sting)*
Zenyatta Mondatta	LP	Nautilus	NR19	1981	£12	**£5**	*US audiophile*

POLITICIANS

Politicians	LP	Hot Wax	SHW5007	1972	£12	**£5**	

POLK, FRANK

Trying To Keep Up With The Joneses	7"	Capitol	CL15389	1965	£20	**£10**	

POLKA DOTS

Nice Work And You Can Buy It	LP	Philips	BL7576	1963	£10	**£4**	
Polka Dots	7" EP	Philips	BBE12487	1961	£5	**£2**	
Polka Dots	7" EP	Philips	SBBE9074	1961	£8	**£4**	*stereo*
Relax Awhile	7" EP	Philips	BE12534	1962	£5	**£2**	
Singin' And Swingin'	7" EP	Columbia	SEG7894	1959	£5	**£2**	
Strictly For Kicks	7" EP	Philips	BBE12528	1962	£5	**£2**	
Vocal Spectacular	7" EP	Philips	433625BE	1962	£5	**£2**	

POLLACK, BEN

Dixieland	LP	London	LTZC15081	1957	£12	**£5**	

Title	Format	Label	Cat. No.	Year	Mint	VG	Notes
Dixieland	LP	Realm	RM183	1964	**£10**	**£4**	

POLLARD, RAY

Title	Format	Label	Cat. No.	Year	Mint	VG	Notes
Drifter	7"	United Artists	UP1111	1965	**£100**	**£50**	
It's A Sad Thing	7"	United Artists	UP1133	1966	**£50**	**£25**	

POLLCATS

Title	Format	Label	Cat. No.	Year	Mint	VG	Notes
Poll Tax Blues	7"	Community Charge	AXT1	1990	**£6**	**£2.50**	

POLLEN

Title	Format	Label	Cat. No.	Year	Mint	VG	Notes
Pollen	LP	Kebec	908	1976	**£15**	**£6**	*Canadian*

POLYGON WINDOW

Title	Format	Label	Cat. No.	Year	Mint	VG	Notes
Surfing On The Sine Waves	LP	Warp	WARPLP7	1992	**£15**	**£6**	*clear vinyl*

POLYPHONY

Title	Format	Label	Cat. No.	Year	Mint	VG	Notes
Polyphony	LP	Zella	JHLPS136	1973	**£150**	**£75**	

POLYROCK

Polyrock's attractively brittle songs – exploring a similar territory to that of Talking Heads on its first albums – have yet to be discovered by serious collectors. It is interesting, however, to find composer Philip Glass taking the Brian Eno role here and establishing an early, yet generally unremarked connection with rock music.

Title	Format	Label	Cat. No.	Year	Mint	VG	Notes
Polyrock	LP	RCA	PL43502	1980	**£10**	**£4**	

POMEROY, HERB

Title	Format	Label	Cat. No.	Year	Mint	VG	Notes
Life Is A Many-Splendoured Gig	LP	Columbia	33SX1091	1958	**£25**	**£10**	

PONI-TAILS

Title	Format	Label	Cat. No.	Year	Mint	VG	Notes
Born Too Late	7"	HMV	POP516	1958	**£6**	**£2.50**	
Close Friends	7"	HMV	POP558	1958	**£5**	**£2**	
Early To Bed	7"	HMV	POP596	1959	**£5**	**£2**	
I'll Be Seeing You	7"	HMV	POP663	1959	**£5**	**£2**	
Moody	7"	HMV	POP644	1959	**£5**	**£2**	
Poni-Tails	7" EP	HMV	7EG8427	1957	**£75**	**£37.50**	

PONTY, JEAN-LUC

Ponty is a rather fine jazz violinist, who during the course of a long career has played with both Frank Zappa and John McLaughlin (and managed to annoy both of them, apparently). The *King Kong* album is effectively part of Frank Zappa's oeuvre – he produced the record and plays guitar on the one track he did not actually write.

Title	Format	Label	Cat. No.	Year	Mint	VG	Notes
Astrorama	LP	Far East	65016	1970	**£10**	**£4**	
Electric Connection	LP	Liberty	LBL/LBS83262	1969	**£12**	**£5**	
Experience	LP	Pacific Jazz	PJ20168	1969	**£12**	**£5**	*US*
King Kong	LP	Liberty	LBS83375	1970	**£10**	**£4**	
Open Strings	LP	BASF	21288	1972	**£10**	**£4**	*German*
Sunday Walk	LP	MPS	15045	1967	**£12**	**£5**	*German*
Sunday Walk	LP	BASF	BAP5070	197–	**£10**	**£4**	

POOGY

Title	Format	Label	Cat. No.	Year	Mint	VG	Notes
She Looked Me In The Eye	7"	EMI	EMI2136	1974	**£10**	**£5**	

POOH STICKS

Title	Format	Label	Cat. No.	Year	Mint	VG	Notes
1-2-3 Red Light	7"	Fierce	FRIGHT021	1988	**£12**	**£6**	
Alan McGee	CD-s	Fierce	FRIGHT026	1988	**£15**	**£7.50**	*boxed, booklet*
Alan McGee	CD-s	Fierce	FRIGHT026	1988	**£6**	**£2.50**	
Dying For It	7"	Fierce	FRIGHT034	1989	**£10**	**£5**	
Dying For It	7"	Fierce	FRIGHT034	1989	**£10**	**£5**	*1 sided*
Dying For It	7"	Fierce	FRIGHT034	1989	**£15**	**£7.50**	*autographed*
Encores	7"	Anonymous	ANON2	1989	**£5**	**£2**	*box set*
Fierce Box Set	7"	Fierce	FRIGHT021-025	1988	**£40**	**£20**	*5 one-sided singles*
Go Go Girl	7"	Cheree	3	1989	**£4**	**£1.50**	*flexi*
Hard On Love	7"	Woosh	WOOSH7	1989	**£8**	**£4**	*yellow flexi with fanzine*
Million Seller	7"	Fierce	FRIGHT42	1992	**£6**	**£2.50**	*1 sided*
On Tape	7"	Fierce	FRIGHT011	1988	**£30**	**£15**	
Orgasm	LP	53rd & 3rd	AGAMC5	1989	**£15**	**£6**	*pink vinyl*
Pooh Sticks	LP	Fierce	FRIGHT025	1989	**£10**	**£4**	
Trade Mark Of Quality	LP	Fierce	FRIGHT035	1990	**£15**	**£6**	

POOLE, BRIAN

Title	Format	Label	Cat. No.	Year	Mint	VG	Notes
Everything I Touch Turns To Tears	7"	CBS	202349	1966	**£5**	**£2**	
Just How Loud	7"	CBS	3005	1967	**£5**	**£2**	

POOLE, BRIAN & THE TREMELOES

This was the group that Decca elected to sign rather than the Beatles, a decision that might not have appeared too disastrous at first, as Poole and his group managed to achieve eight chart hits, including a number one with 'Do You Love Me'. When Poole decided to go solo in 1966, it must have been rather galling to see his former backing group go on to achieve considerably greater success without him. In the long run, moreover, he risks being known merely as the father of Karen and Shellie, who have recorded, with considerable success, as Alisha's Attic.

Title	Format	Label	Cat. No.	Year	Mint	VG	Notes
After A While	7"	Decca	F12124	1965	**£4**	**£1.50**	
Big Hits Of 1962	LP	Ace Of Clubs	ACL1146	1963	**£30**	**£15**	
Brian Poole & The Tremeloes	7" EP	Decca	DFE8566	1964	**£20**	**£10**	
Brian Poole & The Tremeloes Vol. 2	7" EP	Decca	DFE8610	1965	**£20**	**£10**	
Brian Poole Is Here	LP	Audio Fidelity	2151/6151	1966	**£30**	**£15**	*US*

Title	Format	Label	Number	Year	Mint	VG	Notes
Candy Man	7" EP	Decca	457027	1964	£20	£10	French
Do You Love Me	7" EP	Decca	457017	1963	£20	£10	French
Good Lovin'	7"	Decca	F12274	1965	£4	£1.50	
I Can Dance	7"	Decca	F11771	1963	£4	£1.50	
I Want Candy	7"	Decca	F12197	1965	£4	£1.50	
It's About Time	LP	Decca	LK4685	1965	£30	£15	
Keep On Dancing	7"	Decca	F11616	1963	£4	£1.50	
Meet Me Where We Used To Meet	7"	Decca	F11567	1963	£4	£1.50	
That Ain't Right	7"	Decca	F11515	1962	£5	£2	
Time Is On My Side	7" EP	Decca	457064	1965	£20	£10	French
Tremeloes Are Here	LP	Audio Fidelity	2177/6177	1967	£25	£10	US
Twelve Steps To Love	7"	Decca	F11951	1964	£4	£1.50	
Twenty Miles	7" EP	Decca	457034	1964	£20	£10	French
Twist And Shout	LP	Decca	LK4550	1963	£30	£15	
Twist Little Sister	7"	Decca	F11455	1962	£6	£2.50	

POOLE, LOU & LAURA

Title	Format	Label	Number	Year	Mint	VG	Notes
Only You And I Know	7"	Jay Boy	BOY63	1972	£4	£1.50	

POOR SOULS

Title	Format	Label	Number	Year	Mint	VG	Notes
Love Me	7"	Alp	595004	1966	£25	£12.50	
When My Baby Cries	7"	Decca	F12183	1965	£6	£2.50	

POOVEY, GROOVY JOE

Title	Format	Label	Number	Year	Mint	VG	Notes
Ten Long Fingers On The 88 Keys	7"	Injun	100	1970	£5	£2	

POP, IGGY

Title	Format	Label	Number	Year	Mint	VG	Notes
Candy	CD-s	Virgin	VUSCD29	1990	£5	£2	with Kate Pierson
Compact Hits	CD-s	A&M	AMCD909	1988	£5	£2	
Five Foot One	7"	Arista	ARIST274	1979	£4	£1.50	picture disc
Fun House	LP	Elektra	EKS74071	1970	£40	£20	with the Stooges
Fun House	LP	Elektra	K42051	1971	£12	£5	with the Stooges
Fun House	LP	Elektra	2410009	1970	£15	£6	with the Stooges
Home	CD-s	Virgin	VUSCD22	1990	£5	£2	
I Got Nothing	CD-s	Skydog	622332	1990	£5	£2	with the Stooges
Live At The Channel 7-19-88	CD	A&M	SP17641	1988	£30	£15	US promo
Livin' On The Edge Of The Night	CD-s	Virgin	VUSCD18	1990	£5	£2	3" single
Metallic K.O.	LP	Skydog	SGIS008	1976	£10	£4	French, with the Stooges
Raw Power	LP	CBS	65586	1973	£20	£8	inner sleeve, with the Stooges
Raw Trax	CD	Virgin	PRCD3365	1991	£30	£15	US demos compilation
Stooges	LP	Elektra	EKS74051	1969	£40	£20	with the Stooges
Stooges	LP	Elektra	K42032	1971	£12	£5	with the Stooges

POP GROUP

Title	Format	Label	Number	Year	Mint	VG	Notes
Y	LP	Radar	RAD20	1979	£10	£4	with poster

POP RIVITS

Title	Format	Label	Number	Year	Mint	VG	Notes
Empty Sounds From Anarchy Ranch	LP	Hypocrite	HIP0	1979	£15	£6	
Fun In The UK	7"	Hypocrite	JIM1	1979	£12	£6	double
Greatest Hits	LP	Hyppocrite	HIP007	1979	£10	£4	
Pop Rivits	7"	Hypocrite	HEP002	1979	£6	£2.50	
Pop Rivits EP	7"	Hypocrite	HEP001	1979	£6	£2.50	

POP TOPS

Title	Format	Label	Number	Year	Mint	VG	Notes
Oh Lord, Why Lord	7" EP	Princess	745001	196–	£8	£4	French

POP WILL EAT ITSELF

Title	Format	Label	Number	Year	Mint	VG	Notes
Beaver Patrol	7"	Chapter 22	LCHAP16	1987	£5	£2	pink vinyl
Can U Dig It	CD-s	RCA	PD42620	1989	£5	£2	
Def Con One	CD-s	RCA	PD42884	1989	£5	£2	
Def Con One	CD-s	Chapter 22	PWEICD001	1988	£6	£2.50	
Poppies Say Grrr	7"	Desperate	SRT1	1986	£5	£2	brown paper sleeve
Wise Up Sucker	CD-s	RCA	PD42762	1989	£5	£2	

POPCORN BLIZZARD

The 'Once Upon A Time' single marks the recording debut of Marvin Aday, better known by his stage name, Meat Loaf.

Title	Format	Label	Number	Year	Mint	VG	Notes
Once Upon A Time	7"	Magenta		1967	£30	£15	US

POPCORNS

Title	Format	Label	Number	Year	Mint	VG	Notes
Zero Zero	7"	Columbia	DB4968	1963	£5	£2	

POPE, TIM

Title	Format	Label	Number	Year	Mint	VG	Notes
I Want To Be A Tree	12"	Fiction	FICSX21	1984	£20	£10	
I Want To Be A Tree	7"	Fiction	FICS21	1984	£10	£5	

POPOL VUH

Title	Format	Label	Number	Year	Mint	VG	Notes
Affenstunde	LP	Liberty	LBS83460	1971	£25	£10	German
Aguirre	LP	Barclay	840103	1975	£15	£6	French
Bruder Des Schattens	LP	Brain	0060167	1978	£12	£5	German
Coeur De Verre	LP	Egg	900536	1977	£15	£6	French
Das Hohelied Salomos	LP	United Artists	UAS29781	1975	£15	£6	German
Discover Cosmic	LP	Ohr	940119/20	1976	£25	£10	French double
Einsjager Und Siebenjager	LP	Komische	KM58017	1975	£20	£8	German

Herz Aus Glas	LP	Brain	0060079	1977	£12	£5	German
Hosianna Mantra	LP	Pilz	20291431	1973	£25	£10	German
In Den Gärten Pharaos	LP	Pilz	20212769	1971	£25	£10	German
Letzte Tage Letzte Nächte	LP	United Artists	UAS29916	1976	£15	£6	German
Nosferatu	LP	Egg	900573	1978	£12	£5	French
Perlenklanged	LP	PDU	6073	1977	£12	£5	Italian
Seligpreisung	LP	Komische	KM58009	1974	£20	£8	German
Tantric Songs	LP	Brain	0060242	1979	£12	£5	German
Yoga	LP	PDU	6060	1976	£20	£8	Italian

POPOL VUH (2)

Popol Vuh	LP	Polydor	2923009	1972	£20	£8	Norwegian
Quiche Maya	LP	Polydor	2382038	1973	£20	£8	Norwegian

POPPIES

Lullaby Of Love	7"	Columbia	DB7879	1966	£10	£5	

POPPYHEADS

Cremation Town	7"	Sarah	006	1988	£5	£2	with poster
Postcard For Flossy	7"	Sha La La	004	1988	£5	£2	flexi

POPSICLES

I Don't Want To Be Your Baby Anymore	7"	Vogue	V9243	1965	£8	£4	

POPULAR FIVE

I'm A Lovemaker	7"	Minit	MLF11011	1968	£6	£2.50	

PORCUPINE TREE

Nostalgia Factory	cass	Delerium	DELC0003	1991	£15	£6	
On The Sunday Of Life	CD	Delerium	DELECCD008	1992	£15	£6	
On The Sunday Of Life	LP	Delerium	DELEC008	1992	£15	£6	double
Radioactive EP	CD-s	Delerium	DELEC-PROMOCD1	1993	£20	£10	promo
Tarquin's Seaweed Farm	cass	Delerium	DELC0002	1991	£15	£6	
Voyage 34 Phase 1	12"	Delerium	DELECEP010	1992	£10	£4	
Voyage 34 Phase 1	CD-s	Delerium	DELECCDEP010	1992	£10	£5	
Voyage 34 Remix Phase 3	12"	Delerium	DELECEP007	1993	£6	£2.50	
Yellow Hedgerow Dreamscape	CD	Magic Gnome	MG4299325	1994	£40	£20	

PORK DUKES

Pig In A Poke	LP	Butt	PORK1	1982	£10	£4	
Pig Out Of Hell	LP	Wood	PORK2	1980	£10	£4	
Pork Dukes	LP	Wood	PORK001	1978	£10	£4	pink vinyl

PORTER, DAVID

Gritty, Groovy And Gettin' It	LP	Stax	SXATS1034	1970	£10	£4	
Into A Real Thing	LP	Stax	2362006	1971	£10	£4	

PORTER, NOLAN

If I Could Only Be Sure	7"	Probe	PRO580	1972	£6	£2.50	

PORTION CONTROL

Great Divide	12"	Rhythmic	12RMICX7	1985	£8	£4	
Hit The Pulse	LP	In Phaze	EZ2	1983	£10	£4	
Raise The Pulse	12"	Illuminated	ILL2612	1984	£6	£2.50	
Simulate Sensual	LP	In Phaze	PHA5	1985	£15	£6	clear vinyl
Surface And Be Seen	12"	In Phaze	PORCON006	1982	£10	£5	

PORTOBELLO EXPLOSION

We Can Fly	7"	Carnaby	CNS4001	1969	£20	£10	

PORTSMOUTH SINFONIA

20 Classic Rock Classics	LP	Philips	9109231	1979	£12	£5	

POSEIDON

Found My Way	LP	private	Z33010	1975	£20	£8	German

POSEY, SANDY

Best Of Sandy Posey	LP	MGM	CS8060	1968	£10	£4	
Born A Woman	LP	MGM	C(S)8035	1967	£12	£5	
Looking At You	LP	MGM	C(S)8073	1968	£10	£4	
Sandy Posey	LP	MGM	C(S)8051	1968	£12	£5	
Single Girl	LP	MGM	C(S)8042	1967	£12	£5	

POSITIVELY THIRTEEN O'CLOCK

Psychotic Reaction	7" EP	Vogue	INT18099	1966	£60	£30	French, B side by TV & The Tribesmen

POST, HOWIE & THE SWIFTIES

Tom Swift	7"	Fontana	TF421	1963	£5	£2	

POSTER, ADRIENNE

He Doesn't Love Me	7"	Decca	F12079	1965	£8	£4	
Only Fifteen	7"	Decca	F11797	1963	£8	£4	
Only Fifteen	7"	Oriole	CB1890	1963	£10	£5	
Shang A Doo Lang	7"	Decca	F11864	1964	£10	£5	
Something Beautiful	7"	Decca	F12329	1966	£5	£2	

Winds That Blow	7"	Decca	F12181	1965	£6	£2.50	

POTEMKINE

Foetus	LP	Tapioca	TP10008	1976	£15	£6	*French*
Nicolas II	LP	Phaeton	7801	1978	£10	£4	*French*
Triton	LP	Phaeton	VST7162	1977	£10	£4	*French*

POTGER, KEITH

World Would Never Turn Again	7"	Mercury	MF1073	1969	£6	£2.50	*picture sleeve*

POTLIQUOR

First Taste	LP	Dawn	DNLS3016	1971	£60	£30	
Levee Blues	LP	Janus	JLS3033	1971	£20	£8	*US*
Louisiana Rock'n'Roll	LP	Janus	JLS3036	1971	£20	£8	*US*

POTTER, PHIL

My Song Is Love Unknown	LP	Genesis	GEN10	197–	£20	£8	
Restorer	LP	Dove	DOVE61	1979	£10	£4	

POUND

Odd Man Out	LP	AMS	74840	1974	£60	£30	*US*

POUND HOUNDS

Home Sweet Home	7"	Brunswick	05484	1955	£4	£1.50	*Mellomen B side*

POUNDS, ALAN GET RICH

Searching In The Wilderness	7"	Parlophone	R5532	1966	£300	£180	*best auctioned*

POWELL, BOBBY

Peace Begins Within	7"	Mojo	2092034	1972	£5	£2	

POWELL, BUD

Amazing Bud Powell Vol. 1	LP	Blue Note	BLP/BST81503	1963	£25	£10	
Amazing Bud Powell Vol. 2	LP	Blue Note	BLP/BST81504	1964	£25	£10	
At The Blue Note Café	LP	Fontana	SFJL924	1969	£10	£4	
Blues For Bouffemont	LP	Fontana	SFJL901	1968	£20	£8	
Blues For Bud	LP	Columbia	33CX10123	1958	£25	£10	
Bouncing With Bud	LP	XTRA	XTRA1011	1965	£10	£4	
Bud Powell	7" EP	Columbia	SEB10013	1955	£10	£5	
Bud Powell Trio	10" LP	Vogue	LDE010	1952	£60	£30	
Bud Powell Trio	10" LP	Columbia	33C9016	1956	£40	£20	
Bud Powell Trio	7" EP	Vogue	EPV1036	1955	£10	£5	
Bud Powell Trio	7" EP	Vogue	EPV1030	1955	£10	£5	
Bud Powell Trio Featuring Max Roach	LP	Columbia	33SX1575	1963	£20	£8	
Bud Powell's Modernists	7" EP	Vogue	EPV1033	1955	£10	£5	
Genius Of Bud Powell	7" EP	Columbia	SEB10074	1957	£10	£5	
Genius Of Bud Powell No. 2	7" EP	Columbia	SEB10094	1958	£10	£5	
Hot House	LP	Fontana	FJL903	1967	£20	£8	
Jazz At Massey Hall	LP	Vogue	LAE558	1964	£15	£6	
Jazz Original	LP	Columbia	33CX10069	1957	£40	£20	
Lonely One	LP	HMV	CLP1294	1959	£20	£8	
Return Of Bud Powell	LP	Columbia	33SX1700	1965	£12	£5	
Scene Changes	LP	Blue Note	BLP/BST84009	196–	£25	£10	
Time Waits	LP	Blue Note	BLP/BST81598	196–	£25	£10	
Vintage Years	LP	Verve	VLP9075	1964	£10	£4	

POWELL, JANE

Jane Powell	LP	HMV	CLP1131	1957	£12	£5	
Jane Powell Sings	7" EP	MGM	MGMEP701	1959	£10	£5	
King And I	7" EP	MGM	MGMEP584	1957	£5	£2	
Three Sailors And A Girl	10" LP	Capitol	LC6665	1954	£12	£5	
True Love	7"	HMV	POP267	1956	£4	£1.50	

POWELL, JIMMY

I Can Go Down	7"	Strike	JH309	1966	£5	£2	
I Just Can't Get Over You	7"	Decca	F12751	1968	£4	£1.50	
Remember Then	7"	Decca	F11570	1963	£4	£1.50	
Sugar Babe	7"	Decca	F11447	1962	£4	£1.50	
Sugar Babe	7"	Pye	7N15735	1964	£10	£5	
Sugar Babe	7"	Decca	F12793	1968	£4	£1.50	
That's Alright	7"	Pye	7N15663	1964	£25	£12.50	
Tom Hark	7"	Decca	F11544	1962	£4	£1.50	
Unexpected Mirrors	7"	Decca	F12664	1967	£4	£1.50	

POWELL, KEITH

Answer Is No	7"	Columbia	DB7116	1963	£5	£2	
I Should Know Better	7"	Columbia	DB7366	1964	£15	£7.50	
It Keeps Rainin'	7"	Piccadilly	7N35353	1966	£4	£1.50	
Tore Up	7"	Columbia	DB7229	1964	£6	£2.50	
When You Move, You Lose	7"	Piccadilly	7N35288	1966	£4	£1.50	*with Billie Davis*
You Don't Know Like I Know	7"	Piccadilly	7N35321	1966	£5	£2	*with Billie Davis*

POWELL, MARILYN

All My Loving	7"	Fontana	TF448	1964	£4	£1.50	
As Long As You Come Back To Me	7"	Fontana	TF557	1965	£4	£1.50	
Please Go Away	7"	Fontana	TF526	1965	£4	£1.50	
Showdown	7"	Fontana	TF687	1965	£4	£1.50	
Something To Hold On To	7"	CBS	2331	1968	£5	£2	

POWELL, MEL

Borderline	LP	Vanguard	PPL11001	1956	**£15**	**£6**	
Thingamagig	LP	Vanguard	PPL11000	1956	**£15**	**£6**	

POWELL, SELDON

Seldon Powell Plays	LP	Vogue	LAE12184	1959	**£15**	**£6**	
Seldon Powell Sextet	LP	Vogue	LAE12201	1959	**£20**	**£8**	

POWELL, SPECS

Movin' In	LP	Columbia	33SX1083	1958	**£12**	**£5**	

POWER, DUFFY

Davy O'Brien	7"	Parlophone	R5631	1967	**£10**	**£5**	
Dream Lover	7"	Fontana	H194	1959	**£8**	**£4**	
Duffy Power	LP	Spark	SRLM2005	1973	**£15**	**£6**	
Duffy Power	LP	GSF	GS502	1973	**£12**	**£5**	
Hell Hound	7"	CBS	5176	1970	**£6**	**£2.50**	
Hey Girl	7"	Parlophone	R5059	1963	**£6**	**£2.50**	
I Saw Her Standing There	7"	Parlophone	R5024	1963	**£20**	**£10**	
I've Got Nobody	7"	Fontana	H302	1961	**£10**	**£5**	
Innovations	LP	Transatlantic	TRA229	1971	**£25**	**£10**	
It Ain't Necessarily So	7"	Parlophone	R4992	1963	**£8**	**£4**	
Kissin' Time	7"	Fontana	H214	1959	**£8**	**£4**	
No Other Love	7"	Fontana	H344	1961	**£6**	**£2.50**	
Powerhouse	LP	Buk	BULP2010	1976	**£10**	**£4**	
Starry Eyed	7"	Fontana	H230	1959	**£6**	**£2.50**	
Tired Broke And Busted	7"	Parlophone	R5111	1964	**£8**	**£4**	
Where Am I	7"	Parlophone	R5169	1964	**£6**	**£2.50**	
Whole Lotta Shaking Going On	7"	Fontana	H279	1960	**£10**	**£5**	

POWER, JIMMY

Irish Fiddle Player	LP	Topic	12TS306	1976	**£10**	**£4**	

POWERHOUSE

Chain Gang	7"	Decca	F12471	1966	**£8**	**£4**	
Raindrops	7"	Decca	F12507	1966	**£4**	**£1.50**	

POWERPACK

Hannibal Brooks	7"	Polydor	56311	1969	**£4**	**£1.50**	
I'll Be Anything For You	7"	CBS	202551	1967	**£6**	**£2.50**	
It Hurts Me So	7"	CBS	202335	1966	**£15**	**£7.50**	
Oh Calcutta	7"	Polydor	2001077	1970	**£4**	**£1.50**	
Soul Cure	LP	Polydor	583057	1969	**£10**	**£4**	

POWERS, JOEY

Midnight Mary	7"	Stateside	SS236	1963	**£4**	**£1.50**	

PRADO, PEREZ

Cherry Pink And Apple Blossom White	7"	HMV	7M295	1955	**£6**	**£2.50**	
Guaglione	7"	RCA	RCA1082	1958	**£5**	**£2**	
Patricia	7"	RCA	RCA1067	1958	**£4**	**£1.50**	
Skokoiaan	7"	HMV	7M255	1954	**£4**	**£1.50**	

PRAISE

Blessed Quietness	LP	No Seven	001	1976	**£25**	**£10**	

PRALINS

Beat Beat Beat	LP	Popular	21003	1966	**£30**	**£15**	*German*
Beat With The Pralins	LP	Popular	21004	1966	**£25**	**£10**	*German*

PRAMS

Nowhere's Safe	7"	Product	TAKE3	1981	**£8**	**£4**	*TV Product B side*

PRANNATH, PANDIT

Earth Groove	LP	Transatlantic	TRA193	1969	**£15**	**£6**	

PRATT, GRAHAM & EILEEN

Clear Air Of The Day	LP	Cottage	811	1977	**£20**	**£8**	

PRATT, PHIL

Sweet Song	7"	Jolly	JY008	1968	**£8**	**£4**	*Thrillers B side*

PRAYING MANTIS

All Day And All Of The Night	7"	Arista	ARIST397	1981	**£5**	**£2**	
Cheated	7"	Arista	ARIST378	1980	**£5**	**£2**	*double*
Praying Mantis	7"	Gem	GEMS36	1980	**£5**	**£2**	*with transfer*
Soundhouse Tapes	12"	Ripper	12HAR5201	1979	**£10**	**£5**	
Soundhouse Tapes	7"	Ripper	HAR5201	1979	**£50**	**£25**	*picture sleeve*
Soundhouse Tapes	7"	Ripper	HAR5201	1980	**£6**	**£2.50**	
Tell Me The Nightmare's Wrong	7"	Jet	JET7026	1982	**£12**	**£6**	
Time Tells No Lies	LP	Arista	SPART1153	1981	**£15**	**£6**	

PREACHERS

Hole In My Soul	7"	Columbia	DB7680	1965	**£30**	**£15**	
Zeke	7" EP	Barclay	70890	1965	**£100**	**£50**	*French*

PRECISIONS

If This Is Love	7"	Track	604014	1967	**£6**	**£2.50**	

PREDATOR

Punk Man	7"	Bust	SOL2	1978	**£25**	**£12.50**	

PREDATOR (2)

Don't Stop	7"	CTM	C001	1985	**£8**	**£4**	
Don't Stop	7"	CTM	C001	1985	**£40**	**£20**	*picture sleeve*

PREDATUR

Take A Walk	7"	Quicksilver	QUICK5	1982	**£40**	**£20**	

PREFAB SPROUT

Cars And Girls	CD-s	Kitchenware	CDDSK35	1988	**£5**	**£2**	*picture disc*
Golden Calf	CD-s	Kitchenware	CDSK41	1989	**£5**	**£2**	
Hey Manhattan	CD-s	Kitchenware	CDSK38	1988	**£5**	**£2**	
King Of Rock And Roll	CD-s	Kitchenware	CDSK37	1988	**£5**	**£2**	
Lions In My Own Garden	7"	Candle	1	1982	**£15**	**£7.50**	*no picture sleeve*
Looking For Atlantis	CD-s	Kitchenware	SKQ47	1990	**£5**	**£2**	
Nightingales	CD-s	Kitchenware	CDSK39	1988	**£5**	**£2**	

PREGNANT INSOMNIA

Wallpaper	7"	Direction	583132	1967	**£30**	**£15**	

PRELUDE

Prelude	LP	Crochet	no number	197–	**£50**	**£25**	

PREMIERS

Farmer John	7"	Warner Bros	WB134	1964	**£6**	**£2.50**	
Farmer John	7" EP	Warner Bros	WEP1437	1964	**£40**	**£20**	*French*
Farmer John	LP	Warner Bros	W(S)1565	1964	**£75**	**£37.50**	*US*

PREMIERS (2)

Tears Tears	7"	Silver Phoenix	1002	1964	**£20**	**£10**	

PREMO & HOPETON

Your Safekeep	7"	Rio	R139	1967	**£8**	**£4**	

PRENOSILOVA, YVONNE

When My Baby Cries	7"	Pye	7N15775	1965	**£4**	**£1.50**	

PRESELI FOLK

Preseli Folk	LP	private	PRE001	1979	**£40**	**£20**	

PRESENCE

In Wonder	CD-s	Reality	LOLCD1	1991	**£5**	**£2**	
Presence	LP	NC	SLCW1031	1976	**£25**	**£10**	

PRESIDENTS

Candy Man	7"	Decca	F11826	1964	**£25**	**£12.50**	

PRESIDENTS (2)

5-10-15-20-25-30	LP	Sussex	AMLS65001		**£10**	**£4**	

PRESLEY, ELVIS

Elvis Presley's position as the most popular rock solo artist ever is indisputable and the list of collectable records made by him is correspondingly long. Although American singles are generally outside the scope of the present volume, Presley's Sun singles were felt to be of such historical importance that they have been included. For the same reason, the legendary *Elvis And Janis* South African release is also included. As far as Presley's earliest records in the UK are concerned, the HMV issues are not that rare: they were all enormous sellers at the time of their release. What are rare, however, are copies in anything like mint condition. The values quoted are for these rarities. For records in less than mint condition, the drop in value with deteriorating condition is dramatic – one of the HMV albums, with its cover torn and repaired with Selotape and with its playing surface displaying an impressive network of scratches and scars, would be worth a nominal few pounds only, if anything at all. Meanwhile, it should be noted that, with the exception of the last issued records whose sales were quite small in the format, 78 rpm releases are worth considerably less than their 45 rpm equivalents. Of course, not everything by Elvis Presley is automatically valuable – one example that is not, despite appearances to the contrary, is the double hits compilation, *Elvis's 40 Greatest*, pressed on pink vinyl. The record cover proclaims 'special pink pressing', but in fact most copies are like this, and the set is very common. Other non-rarities include the picture disc versions of the *Legendary Performer* albums, which are attractive items but not valuable, and any of the vast number of Elvis repackages on RCA's cheap Camden label.

All Shook Up	78	HMV	POP359	1957	**£12**	**£6**	
All Shook Up	78	RCA	RCA1088	1958	**£75**	**£37.50**	
All Shook Up	7"	HMV	JO473	1957	**£175**	**£87.50**	*export*
All Shook Up	7"	HMV	POP359	1957	**£75**	**£37.50**	*gold label*
All Shook Up	7"	HMV	POP359	1957	**£20**	**£10**	*silver label*
All Shook Up	7"	RCA	RCA1088	1969	**£40**	**£20**	*orange label*
All Shook Up	7"	RCA	RCA1088	1958	**£25**	**£12.50**	*tri-centre*
All That I Am	7"	RCA	RCA1545	1966	**£4**	**£1.50**	
Aloha From Hawaii Via Satellite	LP	RCA	VPSX6089	1973	**£750**	**£500**	*US, with 'Chicken of the Sea' sticker*
Aloha From Hawaii Via Satellite	LP	RCA	DPS2040	1973	**£12**	**£5**	*double*
Aloha From Hawaii Via Satellite	LP	RCA	R4P5035	1973	**£20**	**£8**	*quad double*
Always On My Mind	12"	RCA	PT49944	1988	**£15**	**£7.50**	
Always On My Mind	7"	RCA	PB49943	1988	**£5**	**£2**	
Always On My Mind	CD	BMG	ELVISDJ197	1997	**£100**	**£50**	*promo*
Amazing Grace	CD	RCA	RDJ66512	1994	**£30**	**£15**	*US promo sampler*
American Trilogy	LP	Imperial	DR1124	1984	**£20**	**£8**	*3 LP box set*

Title	Format	Label	Cat. No.	Year	Mint	VG	Notes
Are You Lonesome Tonight	7"	RCA	RCA1216	1969	**£40**	**£20**	*orange label*
Are You Lonesome Tonight (Laughing Version)	CD-s	RCA	PD49178	1991	**£5**	**£2**	
Baby I Don't Care	7"	RCA	RCAP332	1983	**£4**	**£1.50**	*picture disc*
Best Of Elvis	10" LP	HMV	DLP1159	1956	**£250**	**£150**	
Big Boss Man	7"	RCA	RCA1642	1967	**£5**	**£2**	
Big Hunk Of Love	7"	RCA	RCA1136	1959	**£6**	**£2.50**	*tri-centre*
Big Hunk Of Love	78	RCA	RCA1136	1959	**£75**	**£37.50**	
Blue Hawaii	LP	RCA	LPM2426	1961	**£20**	**£8**	*US, black label, 'Long 33 1/3 Play'*
Blue Hawaii	LP	RCA	LPM2426	1961	**£40**	**£20**	*US, black label, 'Long 33 1/3 Play', 'Contains The Twist Special'*
Blue Hawaii	LP	RCA	LSP2426	1961	**£30**	**£15**	*US, black label, 'Living Stereo'*
Blue Hawaii	LP	RCA	LSP2426	1961	**£50**	**£25**	*US, black label, 'Living Stereo', 'Contains The Twist Special'*
Blue Hawaii	LP	RCA	RD27238	1969	**£20**	**£8**	*orange label*
Blue Hawaii	LP	RCA	RD27238	1961	**£10**	**£4**	*mono*
Blue Hawaii	LP	RCA	SF5115	1961	**£25**	**£10**	*stereo*
Blue Moon	78	HMV	POP272	1956	**£20**	**£10**	
Blue Moon	7"	HMV	POP272	1956	**£150**	**£75**	*gold label*
Blue Moon	7"	HMV	POP272	1956	**£100**	**£50**	*silver label*
Blue Moon	7"	RCA	RCA2601	1975	**£5**	**£2**	
Blue River	7"	RCA	RCA1504	1966	**£4**	**£1.50**	
Blue Suede Shoes	78	HMV	POP213	1956	**£20**	**£10**	
Blue Suede Shoes	7"	HMV	7M405	1956	**£200**	**£100**	*gold label*
Blue Suede Shoes	7"	HMV	7M405	1956	**£200**	**£100**	*silver label*
Bossa Nova Baby	12"	RCA	ARONT1	1987	**£10**	**£5**	
Bossa Nova Baby	7"	RCA	RCA1374	1963	**£4**	**£1.50**	
Burning Love And Hits From His Movies	LP	RCA	INTS1414	1972	**£20**	**£8**	*UK issue*
Californian Holiday	LP	RCA	SF7820	1966	**£15**	**£6**	*stereo*
Californian Holiday	LP	RCA	RD7820	1966	**£12**	**£5**	*mono*
Canadian Tribute	LP	RCA	KKL17065	1978	**£10**	**£4**	*US, yellow vinyl*
Christmas Album	LP	RCA	LOC1035	1957	**£250**	**£150**	*US, black label, 'Long 33 1/3 Play'*
Christmas Album	LP	RCA	LPM1951	1958	**£50**	**£25**	*US, black label, 'Long 33 1/3 Play'*
Christmas Album	LP	RCA	RD27052	1957	**£60**	**£30**	*glossy cover*
Christmas Album	LP	RCA	RD27052	1958	**£40**	**£20**	*matt cover*
Christmas Album	LP	RCA	RD27052	1969	**£25**	**£10**	*orange label*
Clambake	LP	RCA	LPM3893	1967	**£75**	**£37.50**	*US, black label, 'Monaural'*
Clambake	LP	RCA	LPM3893	1967	**£100**	**£50**	*US, black label, 'Monaural', with photo*
Clambake	LP	RCA	LSP3893	1967	**£20**	**£8**	*US, black label, 'Stereo'*
Clambake	LP	RCA	LSP3893	1967	**£40**	**£20**	*US, black label, 'Stereo', with photo*
Clambake	LP	RCA	RD7917	1967	**£15**	**£6**	*mono*
Clambake	LP	RCA	RD7917	1969	**£20**	**£8**	*orange label*
Clambake	LP	RCA	SF7917	1967	**£20**	**£8**	*stereo*
Collectors' Gold	7" EP	RCA	RCX3	1983	**£6**	**£2.50**	
Date With Elvis	LP	RCA	LPM2011	1959	**£50**	**£25**	*US, black label, 'Long 33 1/3 Play'*
Date With Elvis	LP	RCA	LPM2011	1959	**£100**	**£50**	*US, black label, 'Long 33 1/3 Play', titles on sticker*
Date With Elvis	LP	RCA	RD27128	1959	**£40**	**£20**	
Date With Elvis	LP	RCA	RD27128	1969	**£20**	**£8**	*orange label*
Do The Clam	7"	RCA	RCA1443	1965	**£4**	**£1.50**	
Don't	7"	RCA	RCA1043	1958	**£6**	**£2.50**	*tri-centre*
Don't	78	RCA	RCA1043	1958	**£25**	**£12.50**	
Don't Be Cruel	CD-s	RCA	74321110612	1992	**£5**	**£2**	
Don't Cry Daddy	7"	RCA	RCA1916	1970	**£4**	**£1.50**	*picture sleeve*
Double Trouble	LP	RCA	LPM3787	1967	**£25**	**£10**	*US, black label, 'Monaural'*
Double Trouble	LP	RCA	LPM/LSP3787	1967	**£40**	**£20**	*US, black label, with photo*
Double Trouble	LP	RCA	LSP3787	1967	**£20**	**£8**	*US, black label, 'Stereo'*
Double Trouble	LP	RCA	RD7892	1967	**£12**	**£5**	*mono*
Double Trouble	LP	RCA	SF7892	1967	**£15**	**£6**	*stereo*
Easy Come Easy Go	7" EP	RCA	RCX7187	1967	**£30**	**£15**	
Elvis	LP	RCA	SF8378	1973	**£25**	**£10**	
Elvis	LP	RCA	LPM1382	1957	**£200**	**£100**	*US mispress – unbanded*
Elvis	LP	RCA	LPM1382	1957	**£200**	**£100**	*US mispress – same song 6 times on one side*
Elvis	LP	RCA	LPM1382	1956	**£750**	**£500**	*US, black label, 'Long 33 1/3 Play', alternate 'Old Shep'*

Title	Format	Label	Cat. No.	Year	Mint	VG+	Notes
Elvis	LP	RCA	LPM1382	1956	£75	£37.50	US, black label, 'Long 33 1/3 Play', album ads on cover
Elvis	LP	RCA	LPM1382	1956	£50	£25	US, black label, 'Long 33 1/3 Play'
Elvis	LP	RCA	LPM1382	1956	£150	£75	US, black label, 'Long 33 1/3 Play', tracks listed as 'band'
Elvis	LP	RCA	RD8011	1968	£10	£4	mono
Elvis	LP	RCA	RD27120	1969	£20	£8	orange label
Elvis – A Golden Celebration	LP	RCA	PL85172	1985	£25	£10	6 LPs, boxed
Elvis – For LP Fans Only	LP	RCA	RD27120	1959	£50	£25	
Elvis And Janis	10" LP	Teal	T31077	1958	£1500	£1000	South African, with Janis Martin
Elvis Aron Presley	LP	RCA	CPL83699	1980	£50	£25	8 LPs, booklet, boxed
Elvis Aron Presley Radio Station Sampler	LP	RCA	DJL13781	1980	£20	£8	promo
Elvis Aron Presley Sampler	LP	RCA	DJL13729	1980	£20	£8	promo
Elvis For Everyone	LP	RCA	LPM3450	1965	£20	£8	US, black label, 'Monaural'
Elvis For Everyone	LP	RCA	LSP3450	1965	£25	£10	US, black label, 'Stereo'
Elvis For Everyone	LP	RCA	RD7752	1965	£15	£6	mono
Elvis For Everyone	LP	RCA	SF7752	1965	£25	£10	stereo
Elvis For Everyone	LP	RCA	SF8232	1972	£25	£10	TV Special sleeve
Elvis For You Vol. 1	7" EP	RCA	RCX7142	1964	£40	£20	
Elvis For You Vol. 2	7" EP	RCA	RCX7143	1964	£40	£20	
Elvis In Concert	LP	RCA	PL02587	1977	£12	£5	double
Elvis In Demand	LP	RCA	PL42003	1977	£10	£4	
Elvis In Tender Mood	7" EP	RCA	RCX135	1959	£25	£12.50	tri-centre
Elvis In Tender Mood	7" EP	RCA	RCX135	1969	£10	£5	orange label
Elvis Is Back	LP	RCA	LPM2231	1960	£40	£20	US, black label, 'Long 33 1/3 Play'
Elvis Is Back	LP	RCA	LPM2231	1960	£60	£30	US, black label, 'Long 33 1/3 Play', titles on sticker
Elvis Is Back	LP	RCA	LSP2231	1960	£50	£25	US, black label, 'Living Stereo'
Elvis Is Back	LP	RCA	LSP2231	1960	£75	£37.50	US, black label, 'Living Stereo', song titles on sticker
Elvis Is Back	LP	RCA	RD27171	1960	£25	£10	gatefold mono
Elvis Is Back	LP	RCA	RD27171	1969	£20	£8	orange label
Elvis Is Back	LP	RCA	SF5060	1960	£30	£15	gatefold stereo
Elvis Now	LP	RCA	SF8266	1972	£15	£6	
Elvis Presley	LP	RCA	LPM1254	1956	£50	£25	US, black label, 'Long 33 1/3 Play', dark pink 'Elvis' on cover
Elvis Presley	LP	RCA	LPM1254	1956	£75	£37.50	US, black label, 'Long 33 1/3 Play', light pink 'Elvis' on cover
Elvis Presley	LP	St Michael	IMP113	1978	£30	£15	
Elvis Presley	7" EP	RCA	RCX104	1969	£8	£4	orange label
Elvis Presley	7" EP	RCA	RCX104	1957	£15	£7.50	tri-centre
Elvis Presley Interview Record	LP	RCA	PL80835		£20	£8	promo
Elvis Presley Story	LP	Watermark Inc	EPS1A13B	1977	£500	£330	promo 13 LP boxed set
Elvis Sails	7" EP	RCA	RCX131	1959	£30	£15	tri-centre
Elvis Sails	7" EP	RCA	RCX131	1969	£10	£5	orange label
Elvis Sings Christmas Songs	7" EP	RCA	RCX121	1958	£30	£15	tri-centre
Elvis Sings Christmas Songs	7" EP	RCA	RCX121	1958	£60	£30	round centre, gatefold sleeve
Elvis Today	LP	RCA	APD11039	1975	£75	£37.50	US quad (orange label)
Elvis Today	LP	RCA	APD11039	1975	£40	£20	US quad (black label)
EP Collection	7" EP	RCA	EP1	1982	£60	£30	11 EP set
EP Collection Vol. 2	7" EP	RCA	EP2	1983	£75	£37.50	11 EP set
Flaming Star And Summer Kisses	LP	RCA	RD7723	1965	£50	£25	
Flaming Star And Summer Kisses	LP	RCA	RD7723	1969	£300	£180	orange label
Follow That Dream	7" EP	RCA	RCX211	1962	£75	£37.50	mispressed 2nd side
Follow That Dream	7" EP	RCA	RCX211	1962	£8	£4	
Fool Such As I	7"	RCA	RCA1113	1959	£6	£2.50	tri-centre
Fool Such As I	78	RCA	RCA1113	1959	£60	£30	
For LP Fans Only	LP	RCA	LPM1990	1959	£75	£37.50	US, black label, 'Long 33 1/3 Play'
For The Asking	CD	RCA	ND90513	1990	£12	£5	
Four Double Features	CD	RCA		1993	£75	£37.50	US 4 picture disc set in film cannister
Frankie And Johnny	7"	RCA	RCA1509	1966	£4	£1.50	
Frankie And Johnny	LP	RCA	RD7793	1966	£12	£5	mono
Frankie And Johnny	LP	RCA	SF7793	1966	£15	£6	stereo
Frankie And Johnny	LP	RCA	LPM/LSP3553	1966	£40	£20	US, black label, with photo
Frankie And Johnny	LP	RCA	LPM3553	1966	£20	£8	US, black label, 'Monaural'

Title	Format	Label	Number	Year	Mint	VG+	Notes
Frankie And Johnny	LP	RCA	LSP3553	1966	**£20**	**£8**	*US, black label, 'Stereo'*
From Elvis In Memphis	LP	Mobile Fidelity	MFSL1059	1980	**£10**	**£4**	*US audiophile*
From Elvis In Memphis	LP	RCA	RD8029	1969	**£12**	**£5**	*mono*
From Elvis In Memphis	LP	RCA	SF8029	1969	**£10**	**£4**	*stereo*
From Memphis To Vegas – From Vegas To Memphis	LP	RCA	SF8080/1	1970	**£20**	**£8**	*double*
Fun In Acapulco	LP	RCA	LPM2756	1963	**£20**	**£8**	*US, black label, 'Mono'*
Fun In Acapulco	LP	RCA	LSP2756	1963	**£25**	**£10**	*US, black label, 'Living Stereo'*
Fun In Acapulco	LP	RCA	RD7609	1963	**£12**	**£5**	*mono*
Fun In Acapulco	LP	RCA	SF7609	1963	**£15**	**£6**	*stereo*
G.I. Blues	LP	RCA	LPM2256	1960	**£20**	**£8**	*US, black label, 'Long 33 1/3 Play'*
G.I. Blues	LP	RCA	LSP2256	1960	**£30**	**£15**	*US, black label, 'Living Stereo'*
G.I. Blues	LP	RCA	RD27192	1960	**£10**	**£4**	*mono*
G.I. Blues	LP	RCA	RD27192	1969	**£20**	**£8**	*orange label*
G.I. Blues	LP	RCA	SF5078	1960	**£25**	**£10**	*stereo*
G.I. Blues: The Alternate Takes	7" EP	RCA	RCX1	1982	**£8**	**£4**	
G.I. Blues: The Alternate Takes Vol. 2	7" EP	RCA	RCX2	1982	**£6**	**£2.50**	
Girl Happy	LP	RCA	LPM3338	1965	**£20**	**£8**	*US, black label, 'Monaural'*
Girl Happy	LP	RCA	LSP3338	1965	**£25**	**£10**	*US, black label, 'Stereo'*
Girl Happy	LP	RCA	RD7714	1965	**£12**	**£5**	*mono*
Girl Happy	LP	RCA	SF7714	1965	**£20**	**£8**	*stereo*
Girl Of My Best Friend	7"	RCA	RCA1194	1960	**£4**	**£1.50**	
Girl Of My Best Friend	78	RCA	RCA1194	1960	**£500**	**£330**	*best auctioned*
Girls Girls Girls	LP	RCA	LPM2621	1962	**£20**	**£8**	*US, black label, 'Long 33 1/3 Play'*
Girls Girls Girls	LP	RCA	LPM2621	1962	**£60**	**£30**	*US, black label, 'Long 33 1/3 Play', with calendar*
Girls Girls Girls	LP	RCA	LSP2621	1962	**£30**	**£15**	*US, black label, 'Living Stereo'*
Girls Girls Girls	LP	RCA	LSP2621	1962	**£75**	**£37.50**	*US, black label, 'Living Stereo', with calendar*
Girls Girls Girls	LP	RCA	RD7534	1963	**£12**	**£5**	*mono*
Girls Girls Girls	LP	RCA	SF7534	1963	**£15**	**£6**	*stereo*
Gold 16 Series	7"	RCA	RCA2694-2709	1977	**£40**	**£20**	*16 × 7" in cardboard carrier*
Gold Records Volume Two	CD	RCA	PCD15197	1984	**£150**	**£75**	*US promo picture disc*
Golden Boy Elvis	LP	Hör Zu	SHZT521	1965	**£125**	**£62.50**	*German*
Golden Boy Elvis	LP	RCA	25037	1965	**£750**	**£500**	*Swiss*
Golden Records	LP	RCA	LPM1707	1958	**£60**	**£30**	*US, black label, 'Long 33 1/3 Play', title in blue print*
Golden Records	LP	RCA	RB16069	1958	**£75**	**£37.50**	*gatefold sleeve, 4 photo pages*
Golden Records	LP	RCA	RB16069	1960	**£25**	**£10**	*gatefold sleeve, 2 photo pages*
Golden Records	LP	RCA	RB16069	1963	**£20**	**£8**	*no photo pages*
Golden Records	LP	RCA	RB16069	1967	**£12**	**£5**	*single sleeve*
Golden Records Vol. 2	LP	RCA	LPM2075	1960	**£50**	**£25**	*US, black label, 'Long 33 1/3 Play'*
Golden Records Vol. 2	LP	RCA	RD27159	1959	**£25**	**£10**	
Golden Records Vol. 2	LP	RCA	RD27159	1969	**£20**	**£8**	*orange label*
Golden Records Vol. 3	LP	RCA	LPM2765	1963	**£20**	**£8**	*US, black label, 'Mono'*
Golden Records Vol. 3	LP	RCA	LPM/LSP2765	1963	**£50**	**£25**	*US, black label, with book*
Golden Records Vol. 3	LP	RCA	LSP2765	1963	**£25**	**£10**	*US, black label, 'Living Stereo'*
Golden Records Vol. 3	LP	RCA	RD7630	1964	**£12**	**£5**	*mono*
Golden Records Vol. 3	LP	RCA	RD7630	1969	**£20**	**£8**	*orange label*
Golden Records Vol. 3	LP	RCA	SF7630	1964	**£15**	**£6**	*stereo*
Golden Records Vol. 4	LP	RCA	LPM3921	1968	**£300**	**£180**	*US, black label, 'Monaural'*
Golden Records Vol. 4	LP	RCA	LPM3921	1968	**£350**	**£210**	*US, black label, 'Monaural', with photo*
Golden Records Vol. 4	LP	RCA	LSP3921	1968	**£20**	**£8**	*US, black label, 'Stereo'*
Golden Records Vol. 4	LP	RCA	LSP3921	1968	**£75**	**£37.50**	*US, black label, 'Stereo', with photo*
Golden Records Vol. 4	LP	RCA	RD7924	1969	**£20**	**£8**	*orange label*
Golden Records Vol. 4	LP	RCA	RD/SF7924	1968	**£15**	**£6**	
Golden Records Vol. 4	LP	RCA	RD/SF7924	1968	**£25**	**£10**	*Never Ending listed on sleeve*
Golden Records Vol. 5	CD	RCA	PD84941	1986	**£12**	**£5**	
Good Rockin' Tonight	7"	Sun	210	1954	**£500**	**£330**	*US, best auctioned*
Good Rockin' Tonight	7" EP	HMV	7EG8256	1957	**£100**	**£50**	
Good Rockin' Tonight	78	Sun	210	1954	**£200**	**£100**	*US, best auctioned*

Title	Format	Label	Number	Year	Mint	VG	Notes
Good Times	LP	RCA	APL10475	1974	**£10**	**£4**	
Got A Lot Of Living To Do	7"	RCA	RCA1020	1957	**£10**	**£5**	*tri-centre*
Got A Lot Of Living To Do	78	RCA	RCA1020	1957	**£20**	**£10**	
Greatest Hits	LP	RCA/Readers Digest	GELV6A	1975	**£25**	**£10**	*7 LPs, booklet, boxed*
Green Green Grass Of Home	7"	RCA	RCA405	1984	**£15**	**£7.50**	*with poster*
Guitar Man	7"	RCA	RCA1663	1968	**£10**	**£5**	
Guitar Man	7"	RCA	RCA43	1981	**£25**	**£12.50**	*UK picture sleeve*
Hard Headed Woman	7"	RCA	RCA1070	1958	**£6**	**£2.50**	*tri-centre*
Hard Headed Woman	78	RCA	RCA1070	1958	**£30**	**£15**	
Harem Holiday	LP	RCA	RD7767	1965	**£12**	**£5**	*mono*
Harem Holiday	LP	RCA	SF7767	1965	**£15**	**£6**	*stereo*
Harum Scarum	LP	RCA	LPM3468	1965	**£20**	**£8**	*US, black label, 'Monaural'*
Harum Scarum	LP	RCA	LSP3468	1965	**£20**	**£8**	*US, black label, 'Stereo'*
Harum Scarum	LP	RCA	LPM/LSP3468	1965	**£40**	**£20**	*US, black label, with photo*
Having Fun On Stage	LP	RCA	APM10818	1974	**£20**	**£8**	
Having Fun On Stage	LP	Boxcar		1974	**£75**	**£37.50**	*US*
He Touched Me	LP	RCA	SF8275	1972	**£15**	**£6**	
Heartbreak Hotel	78	HMV	POP182	1956	**£15**	**£7.50**	
Heartbreak Hotel	7"	HMV	7M385	1956	**£200**	**£100**	*gold label*
Heartbreak Hotel	7"	HMV	7M385	1956	**£150**	**£75**	*silver label*
Heartbreak Hotel	CD-s	RCA	PD49467	1989	**£5**	**£2**	
His Hand In Mine	LP	RCA	LPM2328	1961	**£25**	**£10**	*US, black label, 'Long 33 1/3 Play'*
His Hand In Mine	LP	RCA	LSP2328	1961	**£40**	**£20**	*US, black label, 'Living Stereo'*
His Hand In Mine	LP	RCA	RD27211	1960	**£20**	**£8**	*mono*
His Hand In Mine	LP	RCA	RD27211	1969	**£20**	**£8**	*orange label*
His Hand In Mine	LP	RCA	SF5094	1960	**£25**	**£10**	*stereo*
Honeymoon Companion	CD	RCA	RDJ661242	1992	**£40**	**£20**	*US promo*
Hound Dog	78	HMV	POP249	1956	**£15**	**£7.50**	
Hound Dog	78	RCA	RCA1095	1958	**£75**	**£37.50**	
Hound Dog	7"	HMV	7MC50	1957	**£200**	**£100**	*export*
Hound Dog	7"	HMV	POP249	1956	**£100**	**£50**	*gold label*
Hound Dog	7"	HMV	POP249	1956	**£100**	**£50**	*silver label*
Hound Dog	7"	RCA	RCA1095	1969	**£40**	**£20**	*orange label*
Hound Dog	7"	RCA	RCA1095	1958	**£25**	**£12.50**	*tri-centre*
How Great Thou Art	LP	RCA	LPM3758	1967	**£25**	**£10**	*US, black label, 'Monaural'*
How Great Thou Art	LP	RCA	LSP3758	1967	**£20**	**£8**	*US, black label, 'Stereo'*
How Great Thou Art	LP	RCA	RD7867	1969	**£20**	**£8**	*orange label*
How Great Thou Art	LP	RCA	RD/SF7867	1967	**£20**	**£8**	
I Can Help	10"	RCA	RCAP369	1983	**£10**	**£5**	*picture disc*
I Can Help	10"	RCA	RCAT369	1983	**£8**	**£4**	
I Just Can't Help Believin'	7"	RCA	RCA2158	1971	**£4**	**£1.50**	
I Want You I Need You I Love You	78	HMV	POP235	1956	**£20**	**£10**	
I Want You I Need You I Love You	7"	HMV	7M424	1956	**£150**	**£75**	*gold label*
I Want You I Need You I Love You	7"	HMV	7M424	1956	**£100**	**£50**	*silver label*
I Want You I Need You I Love You	7"	HMV	7MC45	1957	**£200**	**£100**	*export*
I'm 10,000 Years Old – Elvis Country	LP	RCA	SF8172	1971	**£10**	**£4**	*glossy cover, with print*
I'm Left You're Right She's Gone	78	HMV	POP428	1958	**£25**	**£12.50**	
I'm Left You're Right She's Gone	78	Sun	217	1955	**£200**	**£100**	*US, best auctioned*
I'm Left You're Right She's Gone	7"	HMV	POP428	1957	**£50**	**£25**	
I'm Left You're Right She's Gone	7"	Sun	217	1955	**£500**	**£330**	*US, best auctioned*
If I Can Dream	7"	RCA	RCA1795	1969	**£4**	**£1.50**	
Indescribably Blue	7"	RCA	RCA1565	1967	**£4**	**£1.50**	
International Hotel, Las Vegas, Presents Elvis Presley	LP	RCA	LSP6020	1970	**£500**	**£330**	*US double LP, 7", various inserts, boxed*
It Happened At The World's Fair	LP	RCA	LPM2697	1963	**£25**	**£10**	*US, black label, 'Long 33 1/3 Play'*
It Happened At The World's Fair	LP	RCA	LPM2697	1963	**£100**	**£50**	*US, black label, 'Long 33 1/3 Play', with photo*
It Happened At The World's Fair	LP	RCA	LSP2697	1963	**£30**	**£15**	*US, black label, 'Living Stereo'*
It Happened At The World's Fair	LP	RCA	LSP2697	1963	**£125**	**£62.50**	*US, black label, 'Living Stereo', with photo*
It Happened At The World's Fair	LP	RCA	RD7565	1963	**£12**	**£5**	*mono*
It Happened At The World's Fair	LP	RCA	SF7565	1963	**£15**	**£6**	*stereo*
It's Now Or Never	7"	RCA	RCA1207	1969	**£40**	**£20**	*orange label*
Jailhouse Rock	7"	RCA	RCA1028	1958	**£6**	**£2.50**	*tri-centre*
Jailhouse Rock	7"	RCA	RCAMAXI2153	1971	**£4**	**£1.50**	
Jailhouse Rock	7"	RCA	RCAP1028	1983	**£20**	**£10**	*picture disc, B side credits 'Hound Dog'*
Jailhouse Rock	7"	RCA	RCAP1028	1983	**£4**	**£1.50**	*picture disc*
Jailhouse Rock	7" EP	RCA	RCX106	1958	**£15**	**£7.50**	*tri-centre*
Jailhouse Rock	7" EP	RCA	RCX106	1969	**£8**	**£4**	*orange label*
Jailhouse Rock	78	RCA	RCA1028	1958	**£15**	**£7.50**	
Jailhouse Rock	LP	MGM		1957	**£100**	**£50**	*US red vinyl promo with Leiber & Stoller interview*

Title	Format	Label	Cat. No.	Year	Mint	VG	Notes
Jailhouse Rock (B side not Elvis)	78	Decca		1958	**£75**	**£37.50**	*promo*
Kentucky Rain	7"	RCA	RCA1949	1970	**£4**	**£1.50**	*picture sleeve*
Kid Galahad	7" EP	RCA	RCX7106	1963	**£10**	**£5**	
King Creole	78	RCA	RCA1081	1958	**£30**	**£15**	
King Creole	LP	RCA	LPM1884	1958	**£60**	**£30**	*US, black label, 'Long 33 1/3 Play'*
King Creole	LP	RCA	LPM1884	1958	**£125**	**£62.50**	*US, black label, 'Long 33 1/3 Play', with bonus photo*
King Creole	LP	RCA	RD27088	1958	**£30**	**£15**	*mono*
King Creole	LP	RCA	RD27088	1969	**£20**	**£8**	*orange label*
King Creole	7"	RCA	RCA1081	1958	**£6**	**£2.50**	*tri-centre*
King Creole Vol. 1	7" EP	RCA	RCX117	1958	**£20**	**£10**	*tri-centre, black label*
King Creole Vol. 1	7" EP	RCA	RCX117	1969	**£8**	**£4**	*orange label*
King Creole Vol. 2	7" EP	RCA	RCX118	1958	**£15**	**£7.50**	*tri-centre*
King Creole Vol. 2	7" EP	RCA	RCX118	1969	**£8**	**£4**	*orange label*
King Of Rock And Roll – Instore Sampler	CD	RCA	KCDP51096	1992	**£40**	**£20**	*Canadian promo*
King Speaks	LP	Hammer	HMR6002	1979	**£20**	**£8**	
Kiss Me Quick	7"	RCA	RCA1375	1963	**£4**	**£1.50**	
Kissin' Cousins	LP	RCA	LPM/LSP2894	1964	**£50**	**£25**	*US, black label, no photo on cover*
Kissin' Cousins	LP	RCA	LPM2894	1964	**£20**	**£8**	*US, black label, 'Mono', with photo on cover*
Kissin' Cousins	LP	RCA	LSP2894	1964	**£25**	**£10**	*US, black label, 'Living Stereo', photo on cover*
Kissin' Cousins	LP	RCA	RD7645	1964	**£12**	**£5**	*mono*
Kissin' Cousins	LP	RCA	SF7645	1964	**£15**	**£6**	*stereo*
Last Farewell	10"	RCA	RCAT459	1984	**£10**	**£5**	
Lawdy Miss Clawdy	7"	HMV	POP408	1957	**£50**	**£25**	
Lawdy Miss Clawdy	78	HMV	POP408	1957	**£25**	**£12.50**	
Legend	CD	RCA	PD89000	1983	**£250**	**£150**	*3 gold discs, boxed*
Legend	CD	RCA	PD89000	1983	**£250**	**£150**	*3 silver discs, boxed*
Legendary Performer Vol. 1	LP	RCA	CPL10341	1974	**£10**	**£4**	
Legendary Performer Vol. 2	LP	RCA	CPL11349	1976	**£15**	**£6**	
Little Less Conversation	7"	RCA	RCA1768	1968	**£10**	**£5**	
Long Legged Girl	7"	RCA	RCA1616	1967	**£10**	**£5**	
Love In Las Vegas	7" EP	RCA	RCX7141	1964	**£10**	**£5**	
Love Letters	7"	RCA	RCA1526	1966	**£4**	**£1.50**	
Love Letters	CD	BMG	ELVIS58	1992	**£100**	**£50**	*1 track promo*
Love Letters From Elvis	LP	RCA	SF8202	1971	**£10**	**£4**	
Love Machine	7"	RCA	RCA1593	1967	**£10**	**£5**	
Love Me Tender	12"	RCA	ARONT2	1987	**£10**	**£5**	
Love Me Tender	7"	HMV	POP253	1956	**£100**	**£75**	*gold label*
Love Me Tender	7"	HMV	POP253	1956	**£100**	**£50**	*silver label*
Love Me Tender	7"	HMV	JO465	1957	**£250**	**£150**	*export*
Love Me Tender	7" EP	HMV	7EG8199	1957	**£75**	**£37.50**	
Love Me Tender	78	HMV	POP253	1956	**£20**	**£10**	
Loving You	10" LP	RCA	RC24001	1957	**£75**	**£37.50**	
Loving You	7"	RCA	RCA1013	1957	**£12**	**£6**	*tri-centre*
Loving You	78	RCA	RCA1013	1957	**£15**	**£7.50**	
Loving You	LP	RCA	LPM1515	1957	**£60**	**£30**	*US, black label, 'Long 33 1/3 Play'*
Mean Woman Blues	CD-s	RCA	PD49474	1989	**£5**	**£2**	
Milkcow Blues Boogie	7"	Sun	215	1955	**£500**	**£330**	*US, best auctioned*
Milkcow Blues Boogie	78	Sun	215	1955	**£200**	**£100**	*US, best auctioned*
Moody Blue	LP	RCA	AFL12428	1977	**£100**	**£50**	*US, black vinyl*
Mystery Train	7"	HMV	POP295	1957	**£200**	**£100**	*gold label*
Mystery Train	7"	HMV	POP295	1957	**£200**	**£100**	*silver label*
Mystery Train	7"	Sun	223	1955	**£400**	**£250**	*US, best auctioned*
Mystery Train	7"	HMV	7MC42	1957	**£200**	**£100**	*export*
Mystery Train	78	Sun	223	1955	**£200**	**£100**	*US, best auctioned*
Mystery Train	78	HMV	POP295	1957	**£25**	**£12.50**	
O Sole Mio	7"	RCA	479314	1961	**£15**	**£7.50**	*sung in Italian*
Off Camera	CD	BMG	74321466582	1997	**£40**	**£20**	*promo compilation*
On Stage February 1970	LP	RCA	SF8128	1970	**£10**	**£4**	
One Broken Heart For Sale	7"	RCA	RCA1337	1963	**£4**	**£1.50**	
One Night	7"	RCA	RCA1100	1959	**£5**	**£2**	*tri-centre*
One Night	78	RCA	RCA1100	1959	**£50**	**£25**	
Paradise Hawaiian Style	LP	RCA	LPM3643	1966	**£20**	**£8**	*US, black label, 'Monaural'*
Paradise Hawaiian Style	LP	RCA	LSP3643	1966	**£20**	**£8**	*US, black label, 'Stereo'*
Paradise Hawaiian Style	LP	RCA	RD7810	1966	**£15**	**£6**	*mono*
Paradise Hawaiian Style	LP	RCA	RD7810	1969	**£20**	**£8**	*orange label*
Paradise Hawaiian Style	LP	RCA	SF7810	1966	**£30**	**£15**	*stereo*
Paralyzed	78	HMV	POP378	1957	**£20**	**£10**	
Paralyzed	7"	HMV	POP378	1957	**£60**	**£30**	*gold label*
Paralyzed	7"	HMV	POP378	1957	**£60**	**£30**	*silver label*
Peace In The Valley	7" EP	RCA	RCX101	1957	**£25**	**£12.50**	*tri-centre*
Peace In The Valley	7" EP	RCA	RCX101	1969	**£10**	**£5**	*orange label*
Pot Luck	LP	RCA	RD27265	1962	**£10**	**£4**	*mono*
Pot Luck	LP	RCA	SF5135	1962	**£25**	**£10**	*stereo*
Pot Luck With Elvis	LP	RCA	LPM2523	1962	**£30**	**£15**	*US, black label, 'Long 33 1/3 Play'*

Title	Format	Label	Number	Year	Mint	VG	Notes
Pot Luck With Elvis	LP	RCA	LSP2523	1962	**£40**	**£20**	*US, black label, 'Living Stereo'*
Presley Gold – 16 Number Ones	7"	RCA	no number	1977	**£25**	**£12.50**	*boxed set, 16 singles*
Promised Land	LP	RCA	APD10873	1974	**£40**	**£20**	*US quad (black label)*
Promised Land	LP	RCA	APD10873	1974	**£75**	**£37.50**	*US quad (orange label)*
Promised Land	LP	RCA	APL10873	1975	**£10**	**£4**	
Promised Land/It's Midnight And I Miss You	7"	RCA	PB10074	1974	**£10**	**£5**	
Pure Elvis	LP	RCA	DJL13455	1980	**£200**	**£100**	*US promo*
Radio Special	CD	RCA	RDJ661212	1992	**£40**	**£20**	*US promo*
Rags To Riches	7"	RCA	RCA2084	1971	**£4**	**£1.50**	*picture sleeve*
Raised On Rock	LP	RCA	APL10388	1973	**£150**	**£75**	*UK pressing in US sleeve*
Recorded Live On Stage In Memphis	LP	RCA	APD10606	1974	**£125**	**£62.50**	*US quad*
Rip It Up	7"	HMV	POP305	1957	**£150**	**£75**	*gold label*
Rip It Up	7"	HMV	POP305	1957	**£125**	**£62.50**	*silver label*
Rip It Up	78	HMV	POP305	1957	**£25**	**£12.50**	
Rock'n'Roll	LP	HMV	CLP1093	1956	**£250**	**£150**	
Rock'n'Roll No. 2	LP	HMV	CLP1105	1956	**£300**	**£180**	
Rock'n'Roll No. 2	LP	RCA	RD7528	1962	**£12**	**£5**	*mono*
Rock'n'Roll No. 2	LP	RCA	RD7528	1969	**£20**	**£8**	*orange label*
Rock'n'Roll No. 2	LP	RCA	SF7528	1962	**£20**	**£8**	*stereo*
Rocker Elvis	CD	RCA	PD85182	1985	**£12**	**£5**	
Roustabout	LP	RCA	LPM/LSP2999	1964	**£25**	**£10**	*US, black label*
Roustabout	LP	RCA	LSP2999	1964	**£250**	**£150**	*US, black label, 'Living Stereo'*
Roustabout	LP	RCA	RD7678	1965	**£12**	**£5**	*mono*
Roustabout	LP	RCA	SF7678	1965	**£15**	**£6**	*stereo*
Santa Bring My Baby Back	7"	RCA	RCA1025	1957	**£15**	**£7.50**	*tri-centre*
Santa Bring My Baby Back	78	RCA	RCA1025	1957	**£25**	**£12.50**	
Selections From Amazing Grace	CD	BMG	74321240792	1994	**£75**	**£37.50**	*promo sampler*
Shake Rattle And Roll – 18 Number One Hits	CD	RCA	6382RDJ	1992	**£40**	**£20**	*US promo*
Singer Presents Elvis	LP	RCA	PRS279	1968	**£15**	**£6**	*US promo*
Singer Presents Elvis	LP	RCA	PRS279	1968	**£20**	**£8**	*US, with photo*
Sings The Wonderful World Of Christmas	CD	RCA	ND81936	1990	**£12**	**£5**	
Sings The Wonderful World Of Christmas	LP	RCA	SF8221	1971	**£20**	**£8**	
Something For Everybody	LP	RCA	LPM2370	1961	**£25**	**£10**	*US, black label, 'Long 33 1/3 Play'*
Something For Everybody	LP	RCA	LSP2370	1961	**£40**	**£20**	*US, black label, 'Living Stereo'*
Something For Everybody	LP	RCA	RD27244	1961	**£12**	**£5**	*mono*
Something For Everybody	LP	RCA	RD27224	1969	**£20**	**£8**	*orange label*
Something For Everybody	LP	RCA	SF5106	1961	**£20**	**£8**	*stereo*
Sound Of Your Cry	7"	RCA	RCAP232	1982	**£4**	**£1.50**	*picture disc*
Special Palm Sunday Programme	LP	RCA	SP33461	1967	**£600**	**£400**	*US promo*
Speedway	LP	RCA	LPM3989	1968	**£400**	**£250**	*US, black label, 'Monaural'*
Speedway	LP	RCA	LSP3989	1968	**£20**	**£8**	*US, black label, 'Stereo'*
Speedway	LP	RCA	LSP3989	1968	**£50**	**£25**	*US, black label, 'Stereo', with photo*
Speedway	LP	RCA	RD7957	1968	**£15**	**£6**	*mono*
Speedway	LP	RCA	RD7957	1969	**£20**	**£8**	*orange label*
Speedway	LP	RCA	SF7957	1968	**£20**	**£8**	*stereo*
Spinout	LP	RCA	LSP3702	1966	**£20**	**£8**	*US, black label, 'Stereo'*
Spinout	LP	RCA	LPM3702	1966	**£20**	**£8**	*US, black label, 'Monaural'*
Spinout	LP	RCA	LPM/LSP3702	1966	**£40**	**£20**	*US, black label, with photo*
Strictly Elvis	7" EP	RCA	RCX175	1959	**£30**	**£15**	*tri-centre*
Strictly Elvis	7" EP	RCA	RCX175	1969	**£10**	**£5**	*orange label*
Stuck On You	7"	RCA	RCA1187	1960	**£4**	**£1.50**	
Stuck On You	78	RCA	RCA1187	1960	**£250**	**£150**	*best auctioned*
Stuck On You	CD-s	RCA	PD49596	1989	**£5**	**£2**	
Such A Night	7"	RCA	RCA1411	1964	**£5**	**£2**	
Such A Night	7" EP	RCA	RCX190	1960	**£20**	**£10**	
Such A Night	7" EP	RCA	RCX190	1969	**£10**	**£5**	*orange label*
Sun Sessions	CD	RCA	C8812	1988	**£20**	**£8**	*box set*
Suspicious Minds	7"	RCA	RCA1900	1969	**£4**	**£1.50**	*picture sleeve*
Take Good Care Of Her	7"	RCA	APBO0196	1974	**£150**	**£75**	*UK pressing*
Take Good Care Of Her	7"	RCA	APBO0196	1974	**£10**	**£5**	*US import*
Tell Me Why	7"	RCA	RCA1489	1965	**£5**	**£2**	
That's All Right	7"	Sun	209	1954	**£500**	**£330**	*US, best auctioned*
That's All Right	78	Sun	209	1954	**£250**	**£150**	*US*
That's The Way It Is	CD	Mobile Fidelity	UDCD560	1993	**£15**	**£6**	*US audiophile*
That's The Way It Is	LP	RCA	SF8162	1971	**£10**	**£4**	*glossy cover*
There Goes My Everything	7"	RCA	RCA2060	1971	**£4**	**£1.50**	*picture sleeve*
There's Always Me	7"	RCA	RCA1628	1967	**£40**	**£20**	
Tickle Me Vol. 1	7" EP	RCA	RCX7173	1965	**£30**	**£15**	
Tickle Me Vol. 2	7" EP	RCA	RCX7174	1965	**£40**	**£20**	
Today	LP	RCA	RS1011	1975	**£10**	**£4**	

Too Much	7"	HMV	POP330	1957	£100	£50	gold label
Too Much	7"	HMV	POP330	1957	£100	£50	silver label
Too Much	7"	HMV	JO466	1957	£200	£100	export
Too Much	78	HMV	POP330	1957	£20	£10	
Torna A Surrento	7"	RCA	1160	1960	£15	£7.50	sung in Italian
Touch Of Gold	7" EP	RCA	RCX1045	1959	£30	£15	tri-centre
Touch Of Gold	7" EP	RCA	RCX1045	1969	£10	£5	orange label
Touch Of Gold Vol. 2	7" EP	RCA	RCX1048	1960	£100	£50	tri-centre
Touch Of Gold Vol. 2	7" EP	RCA	RCX1048	1969	£10	£5	orange label
Truth About Me	78	Weekend Mail		1957	£100	£50	cardboard folder
TV Guide Presents Elvis Presley	7"	RCA	GBMW8705	1956	£4000	£2500	promo, best auctioned
Twelfth Of Never	CD	BMG	74321365702	1996	£40	£20	promo
U.S. Male	7"	RCA	RCA1688	1968	£6	£2.50	
U.S. Male	7"	RCA	RCA1688	1969	£60	£30	orange label
Until It's Time For You To Go	7"	RCA	RCA2188	1972	£4	£1.50	picture sleeve
Viva Las Vegas	7"	RCA	RCA1390	1964	£4	£1.50	
Wear My Ring Around Your Neck	7"	RCA	RCA1058	1958	£6	£2.50	tri-centre
Wear My Ring Around Your Neck	78	RCA	RCA1058	1958	£30	£15	
Wonder Of You	7"	RCA	LB1	1979	£8	£4	
Wonderful World Of Elvis Presley	LP	St Michael	IMP204	1978	£50	£25	double
Wooden Heart	7"	RCA	RCA1226	1969	£40	£20	orange label
Worldwide Gold Award Hits Vol. 1	LP	RCA	LPM6401	1970	£25	£10	4 LPs, booklet, boxed
Worldwide Gold Award Hits Vol. 2	LP	RCA	LPM6402	1971	£30	£15	4 LPs, piece of cloth, boxed
You'll Never Walk Alone	7"	RCA	RCA1747	1968	£15	£7.50	
Your Time Hasn't Come Yet Baby	7"	RCA	RCA1714	1968	£10	£5	

PRESLEY, REG

It's Down To You Marianne	7"	CBS	1478	1973	£6	£2.50	
Lucinda Lee	7"	Page One	POF131	1969	£6	£2.50	

PRESS GANG

Press Gang	LP	Hawk	HALP135	1976	£12	£5	Irish

PRESTIGE BLUES SWINGERS

Outskirts Of Town	LP	Esquire	32110	1961	£20	£8	

PRESTON, BILLY

All That I've Got	7"	Apple	21	1970	£10	£5	picture sleeve
Billy's Bag	7"	Sue	WI4012	1966	£8	£4	
Billy's Bag	7"	President	PT263	1969	£4	£1.50	
Encouraging Words	LP	Apple	SAPCOR14	1969	£20	£8	
Greazee	7"	Soul City	SC107	1969	£6	£2.50	
Greazee Soul	LP	Soul City	SCM002	1970	£15	£6	
I Wrote A Simple Song	LP	A&M	AMLH63507	1972	£10	£4	
In The Midnight Hour	7"	Capitol	CL15458	1966	£4	£1.50	
Most Exciting Organ Ever	LP	Sue	ILP935	1966	£30	£15	
Sunny	7"	Capitol	CL15471	1966	£4	£1.50	
That's The Way God Planned It	7"	Apple	12	1969	£6	£2.50	picture sleeve
That's The Way God Planned It	7"	Apple	12	1969	£4	£1.50	
That's The Way God Planned It	LP	Apple	ST3359	1969	£10	£4	US, multiple Prestons on cover
That's The Way God Planned It	LP	Apple	ST3359	1969	£25	£10	US, face close-up on cover
That's The Way God Planned It	LP	Apple	SAPCOR9	1969	£15	£6	
Wildest Organ In Town	LP	Capitol	(S)T2532	1966	£10	£4	

PRESTON, DON

Bluse	LP	A&M	SP4155	1969	£15	£6	US

PRESTON, EARL

That's For Sure	7"	Fontana	TF481	1964	£10	£5	
Watch Your Step	7"	Fontana	TF406	1963	£10	£5	

PRESTON, JOHNNY

Big Chief Heartache	7"	Mercury	AMT1145	1961	£6	£2.50	
Charming Billy	7"	Mercury	AMT1114	1960	£6	£2.50	
Come Rock With Me	LP	Mercury	MG2/SR60609	1961	£40	£20	US
Cradle Of Love	7"	Mercury	AMT1092	1960	£4	£1.50	
Cradle Of Love	7"	Mercury	AMT1092	1960	£10	£4	picture sleeve
Free Me	7"	Mercury	AMT1167	1961	£6	£2.50	
I'm Starting To Go Steady	7"	Mercury	AMT1104	1960	£5	£2	
Leave My Kitten Alone	7"	Mercury	AMT1129	1961	£8	£4	
Ring Tail Tooter	7" EP	Mercury	ZEP10098	1960	£60	£30	
Rock And Roll Guitar	7"	Mercury	AMT1164	1961	£6	£2.50	
Running Bear	7"	Mercury	AMT1079	1960	£4	£1.50	
Running Bear	7" EP	Mercury	ZEP10078	1960	£40	£20	
Running Bear	LP	Mercury	MMC14051	1960	£60	£30	
Token Of Love	7" EP	Mercury	ZEP10116	1961	£75	£37.50	

PRESTON, MIKE

Four Songs By Ray Noble	7" EP	Decca	DFE6635	1960	£10	£5	
Girl Like You	7"	Decca	F11222	1960	£4	£1.50	
I'd Do Anything	7"	Decca	F11255	1960	£4	£1.50	
In Surabaya	7"	Decca	F11120	1959	£5	£2	
Marry Me	7" EP	Decca	DFE6679	1961	£10	£5	

Mr Blue	7"	Decca	F11167	1959	£4	£1.50	
My Lucky Love	7"	Decca	F11053	1958	£6	£2.50	
Togetherness	7"	Decca	F11287	1960	£4	£1.50	
Why Why Why	7"	Decca	F11087	1958	£5	£2	

PRETENDERS

Adultress	7"	Real		1981	£5	£2	*promo only*
Packed!	CD	WEA	WX346CD	1990	£40	£20	*promo with cassette in attaché case*
Packed!	CD	Sire	262192	1990	£30	£15	*US promo in mini-crate*
Pretenders	LP	Real	RAL3	1980	£25	£10	*autographed*
Pretenders	LP	Nautilus	NR38	1981	£12	£5	*US audiophile*
Windows Of The World	CD-s	Polydor	PRECD69	1989	£5	£2	*3" single*

PRETTY THINGS

The Pretty Things always seemed to suffer from too much labouring in the shadow of the Rolling Stones (Dick Taylor had, of course, been an early member of the Stones), but they nevertheless achieved a fair degree of success and, despite numerous comings and goings on the part of various of the group's members, they are still around and playing. *S.F. Sorrow* has received a fair amount of acclaim for being a kind of rock opera pre-dating the Who's *Tommy*, but the group's best work has always been found on their singles. The early Fontana singles are tough, gritty R&B that easily stand comparison with the likes of Them, or even the Rolling Stones. Later, the Columbia singles 'Defecting Grey' and 'Talkin' About The Good Times' are superb pieces of psychedelia and should definitely be included on any list of the essential recordings of the period.

Best Of The Pretty Things	LP	Wing	WL1164	1967	£20	£8	
Children	7"	Fontana	TF829	1967	£6	£2.50	
Come See Me	7"	Fontana	TF688	1966	£5	£2	
Cry To Me	7"	Fontana	TF585	1965	£5	£2	
Defecting Grey	7"	Columbia	DB8300	1967	£30	£15	
Don't Bring Me Down	7"	Fontana	TF503	1964	£5	£2	
Don't Bring Me Down	7" EP	Fontana	465253	1964	£40	£20	*French*
Emotions	LP	Fontana	(S)TL5425	1967	£30	£15	
Emotions	LP	Fontana	SFL13140	1969	£12	£5	
Get The Picture	LP	Fontana	TL5280	1965	£50	£25	
Good Mr Square	7"	Harvest	HAR5016	1970	£4	£1.50	
Honey I Need	7"	Fontana	TF537	1965	£5	£2	
House In The Country	7"	Fontana	TF722	1966	£5	£2	
I Can Never Say	7" EP	Fontana	465296	1965	£40	£20	*French*
Midnight To Six Man	7"	Fontana	TF647	1965	£5	£2	
Midnight To Six Man	7" EP	Fontana	465310	1966	£40	£20	*French*
October 26	7"	Harvest	HAR5031	1970	£4	£1.50	
On Film	7" EP	Fontana	TE17472	1966	£75	£37.50	
Parachute	LP	Harvest	SHVL774	1970	£15	£6	
Pretty Things	7" EP	Fontana	TE17434	1964	£25	£12.50	
Pretty Things	LP	Wing	WL1167	1967	£12	£5	
Pretty Things	LP	Fontana	TL5239	1965	£40	£20	
Private Sorrow	7"	Columbia	DB8494	1968	£15	£7.50	
Progress	7"	Fontana	TF773	1966	£6	£2.50	
Progress	7" EP	Fontana	465353	1966	£40	£20	*French*
Raining In My Heart	7" EP	Fontana	TE17442	1965	£25	£12.50	
Rosalyn	7"	Fontana	TF469	1964	£8	£4	
S.F. Sorrow	LP	Rare Earth	RS506	1969	£30	£15	*US, tombstone shaped cover*
S.F. Sorrow	LP	Columbia	SCX6306	1968	£40	£20	
S.F. Sorrow	LP	Columbia	SCX6306	1970	£20	£8	*silver & black label*
S.F. Sorrow/Parachute	LP	Harvest	SHDW406	1975	£12	£5	*double*
Stone Hearted Mama	7"	Harvest	HAR5037	1971	£4	£1.50	
Talkin' About The Good Times	7"	Columbia	DB8353	1968	£20	£10	
We'll Be Together	LP	Fontana	QL626000	1966	£40	£20	*Dutch*

PREVIN, ANDRE

André Previn	LP	Brunswick	LAT8093	1956	£15	£6	
Double Play	LP	Contemporary	LAC12142/ SCA5004	1959	£15	£6	*with Russ Freeman*
Modern Jazz Performances Of Songs From Gigi	LP	Contemporary	LAC12144	1959	£10	£4	
Pal Joey	LP	Contemporary	LAC12126	1958	£10	£4	

PREVIN, DORY

Dory Previn	LP	Warner Bros	K56066	1974	£10	£4	
Live At Carnegie Hall	LP	United Artists	UAD60045	1973	£12	£5	*double*
Mary C. Brown And The Hollywood Sign	LP	United Artists	UAG29435	1972	£10	£4	
On My Way To Where	LP	United Artists	UAG29176	1973	£10	£4	
Reflections In A Mud Puddle	LP	United Artists	UAG29346	1972	£10	£4	
We're Children Of Coincidence	LP	Warner Bros	K56213	1976	£10	£4	

PREVOST, EDDIE

Live Vol. 1	LP	Matchless	MR1	1978	£12	£5	
Live Vol. 2	LP	Matchless	MR2	197–	£12	£5	

PREVOST, JOEL

Somewhere Sometime	7"	CBS	6300	1978	£5	£2	

PRICE, ALAN

Amazing Alan Price	7" EP	Decca	DFE8677	1967	£20	£10	
Barefootin'	7" EP	Decca	457129	1966	£12	£6	*French*

Title	Format	Label	Cat. No.	Year	Mint	VG	Notes
I Put A Spell On You	7" EP	Decca	457109	1966	**£12**	**£6**	*French*
O Lucky Man	LP	Warner Bros	K46227	1973	**£10**	**£4**	
Price Is Right	LP	Parrot	PAS71018	1968	**£10**	**£4**	*US*
Price On His Head	LP	Decca	LK/SKL4907	1967	**£10**	**£4**	
Price To Pay	LP	Decca	LK4839	1966	**£15**	**£6**	
Simon Smith And The Amazing Dancing Bear	7" EP	Decca	457143	1967	**£12**	**£6**	*French*

PRICE, LLOYD

Title	Format	Label	Cat. No.	Year	Mint	VG	Notes
Another Fairy Tale	7"	HMV	POP983	1962	**£4**	**£1.50**	
Boo-Hoo	7"	HMV	POP926	1961	**£4**	**£1.50**	
Come Into My Heart	7"	HMV	POP672	1959	**£4**	**£1.50**	
Cookin'	LP	HMV	CSD1413	1962	**£40**	**£20**	*stereo*
Cookin'	LP	HMV	CLP1519	1962	**£30**	**£15**	*mono*
Exciting Lloyd Price	7" EP	HMV	GES5784	1959	**£40**	**£20**	*stereo*
Exciting Lloyd Price	7" EP	HMV	7EG8538	1959	**£30**	**£15**	
Exciting Lloyd Price	LP	HMV	CLP1285	1959	**£40**	**£20**	
Fantastic Lloyd Price	LP	HMV	CSD1323	1960	**£40**	**£20**	*stereo*
Fantastic Lloyd Price	LP	HMV	CLP1393	1960	**£30**	**£15**	*mono*
I'm Gonna Get Married	7"	HMV	POP650	1959	**£4**	**£1.50**	
Just Because	7"	London	HL8438	1957	**£75**	**£37.50**	
Just Call Me	7"	HMV	POP799	1960	**£4**	**£1.50**	
Know What You're Doing	7"	HMV	POP826	1961	**£4**	**£1.50**	
Lady Luck	7"	HMV	POP712	1960	**£4**	**£1.50**	
Lloyd Price	LP	London	HAU2213	1960	**£40**	**£20**	
Lloyd Price Now	LP	Major Minor	SMLP57	1969	**£10**	**£4**	
Lloyd Price Orchestra	LP	Double-L	D2301/SDL8301	1963	**£25**	**£10**	*US*
Lloyd Swings For Sammy	LP	Monument	MLP8032/ SMP18032	1965	**£15**	**£6**	*US*
Love Music	7"	GSF	GSZ5	1973	**£4**	**£1.50**	
Misty	LP	Double-L	D2303/SDL8303	1963	**£25**	**£10**	*US*
Mr Personality	LP	HMV	CLP1314	1959	**£30**	**£15**	
Mr Personality Sings The Blues	LP	HMV	CLP1361	1960	**£30**	**£15**	
Mr Personality's Big 15	LP	ABC	(S)324	1960	**£25**	**£10**	*US*
No Ifs No Ands	7"	HMV	POP741	1960	**£4**	**£1.50**	
Personality	7"	HMV	POP626	1959	**£4**	**£1.50**	
Question	7"	HMV	POP772	1960	**£4**	**£1.50**	
Sings The Million Dollar Sellers	LP	Encore	ENC2004	1963	**£12**	**£5**	
Stagger Lee	7"	HMV	POP580	1959	**£5**	**£2**	
Under Your Spell Again	7"	HMV	POP1100	1962	**£4**	**£1.50**	
Where Were You On Our Wedding Day	7"	HMV	POP598	1959	**£4**	**£1.50**	

PRICE, MALCOLM

Title	Format	Label	Cat. No.	Year	Mint	VG	Notes
Country Session	LP	Decca	LK4627	1964	**£10**	**£4**	
Pickin' On The Country Strings	7" EP	Oak	RGJ106	196–	**£15**	**£7.50**	
Then We All Got Up And Walked Away	LP	Sweet Folk And Count	SFA017	1975	**£10**	**£4**	
Way Down Town	LP	Decca	LK4665	1965	**£10**	**£4**	

PRICE, RAY

Title	Format	Label	Cat. No.	Year	Mint	VG	Notes
Greatest Hits	LP	Columbia	CL1566	1961	**£15**	**£6**	*US*
Ray Price	7" EP	Philips	BBE12137	1957	**£10**	**£5**	
Ray Price Sings Heart Songs	LP	Columbia	CL1015	1957	**£20**	**£8**	*US*
Talk To Your Heart	LP	Columbia	CL1148	1958	**£15**	**£6**	*US*

PRICE, RED

Title	Format	Label	Cat. No.	Year	Mint	VG	Notes
Danger Man	7"	Parlophone	R4789	1961	**£10**	**£5**	
Rocky Mountain Gal	7"	Decca	F10822	1956	**£6**	**£2.50**	
Weekend	7"	Pye	7N15169	1958	**£5**	**£2**	
Wow	7"	Pye	7N15262	1960	**£5**	**£2**	

PRICE, RED (2)

Title	Format	Label	Cat. No.	Year	Mint	VG	Notes
Blue Beat's Over	7"	Blue Beat	BB209	1964	**£12**	**£6**	

PRICE, RICK

Title	Format	Label	Cat. No.	Year	Mint	VG	Notes
Talking To The Flowers	LP	Gemini	GME1017	1971	**£10**	**£4**	

PRICE, RIKKI

Title	Format	Label	Cat. No.	Year	Mint	VG	Notes
Rikki Price	7" EP	Fontana	TFE17100	1958	**£10**	**£5**	

PRICE, SAMMY

Title	Format	Label	Cat. No.	Year	Mint	VG	Notes
Blues Ain't Nothin'	LP	London	LTZR15240/ SAHR6234	1962	**£30**	**£15**	
Boogieing With Big Sid	7"	Storyville	A45068	1963	**£25**	**£12.50**	*picture sleeve*
Boogieing With Big Sid	7"	Storyville	A45068	1963	**£15**	**£7.50**	
Original Sammy Blues	7" EP	Columbia	SEG7679	1957	**£10**	**£5**	
Sammy Price	7" EP	Vogue	EPV1146	1956	**£40**	**£20**	
Sammy Price's Bluesicians	7" EP	Vogue	EPV1151	1956	**£40**	**£20**	
Swingin' Paris Style	LP	Vogue	LAE12027	1957	**£20**	**£8**	

PRICE, VINCENT

Title	Format	Label	Cat. No.	Year	Mint	VG	Notes
Vincent Price	LP	Columbia	33SX1141	1959	**£25**	**£10**	

PRIDE

Title	Format	Label	Cat. No.	Year	Mint	VG	Notes
Pride	LP	Warner Bros	1848	1970	**£30**	**£15**	*US*

PRIDE, DICKIE

Betty Betty	7"	Columbia	DB4403	1960	£8	£4	
Midnight Oil	7"	Columbia	DB4296	1959	£15	£7.50	
Pride Without Prejudice	LP	Columbia	33SX1307	1960	£75	£37.50	
Pride Without Prejudice	LP	Columbia	SCX3369	1961	£100	£50	*stereo*
Primrose Lane	7"	Columbia	DB4340	1959	£15	£7.50	
Sheik Of Shake	7" EP	Columbia	SEG7937	1959	£150	£75	
Slipping And Sliding	7"	Columbia	DB4283	1959	£20	£10	
You're Singing Our Love Song	7"	Columbia	DB4451	1960	£4	£1.50	

PRIESTER, JULIAN

Love, Love	LP	ECM	ECM1044ST	1974	£15	£6	

PRIMA, LOUIS

Bei Mir Bist Du Schon	7"	London	HLD8923	1959	£4	£1.50	*with Keely Smith*
Buona Sera	7"	Capitol	CL14821	1958	£8	£4	
Call Of The Wildest	LP	Capitol	T836	1958	£15	£6	
Doin' The Twist	LP	Dot	DLP3410/25410	1961	£12	£5	*US*
Five Months, Two Weeks, Two Days	7"	Capitol	CL14669	1956	£20	£10	
Fun With Louis Prima	7" EP	Philips	BBE12290	1959	£5	£2	
I'm Confessin'	7"	London	HLD9084	1960	£4	£1.50	*with Keely Smith*
Las Vegas Prima Style	LP	Capitol	T1010	1958	£10	£4	
Louis And Keely	LP	London	HAD2243	1960	£10	£4	*with Keely Smith*
Louis Prima	LP	Rondo	842	1959	£20	£8	*US*
Ol' Man Moses	7"	London	HLD9230	1960	£5	£2	
On Stage	LP	London	HAD2350/ SAHD6149	1961	£10	£4	*with Keely Smith*
Strictly Prima	7" EP	Capitol	EAP11132	1959	£6	£2.50	
Strictly Prima	LP	Capitol	T1132	1959	£15	£6	
Take A Little Walk Around The Block	7"	Columbia	SCM5092	1954	£8	£4	*with Keely Smith*
Wildest	LP	Capitol	T755	1957	£20	£8	
Wildest Comes Home	LP	Capitol	(S)T1723	1962	£12	£5	*US*
Wonderland By Night	LP	Dot	DLP3352/25352	1960	£12	£5	*US*

PRIMAL SCREAM

All Fall Down	7"	Creation	CRE17	1985	£12	£6	
Crystal Crescent	12"	Creation	CRE016T	1986	£6	£2.50	
Crystal Crescent	7"	Creation	CRE26	1986	£5	£2	
Gentle Tuesday	12"	Elevation	ACID3T	1987	£6	£2.50	
Gentle Tuesday	7"	Elevation	ACID3	1987	£4	£1.50	
Gentle Tuesday/Imperial	7"	Elevation		1987	£10	£5	*promo*
Higher Than The Sun	CD-s	Creation	CRESCD096	1991	£5	£2	
Imperial	12"	Elevation	ACID5T	1987	£8	£4	*poster sleeve*
Ivy Ivy Ivy	CD-s	Creation	CRE067CD	1989	£5	£2	
Loaded	CD-s	Creation	CRESCD070	1990	£5	£2	
Primal Scream	LP	Creation	CRELP054	1989	£10	£4	*with 7" (Split Wide Open)*

PRIMARY INDUSTRY

At Gunpoint	7"	Temps Modernes	CSBTVV	1986	£8	£4	

PRIMETTES

Looking Back With The Primettes consists of early material recorded by the Supremes under their original name. Only one US single was actually released prior to the group signing with Tamla records.

Looking Back With The Primettes	LP	Ember	EMB3398	1968	£40	£20	
Roots Of Diana Ross	LP	Windmill	WMD192	1973	£15	£6	
Tears Of Sorrow	7"	Lupine	120	1960	£100	£50	*US*

PRIMEVIL

Smokin' Bats At Campton's	LP	700 West	740105	1974	£75	£37.50	*US*

PRIMITIVES

Blow Up	LP	Arc	SA22	1967	£150	£75	*Italian*
Help Me	7"	Pye	7N15721	1964	£150	£75	
Ho Mary	7" EP	Vogue	INT18093	1966	£150	£75	*French*
You Said	7"	Pye	7N15755	1965	£175	£87.50	

PRIMITIVES (2)

Ocean Blue	7"	Lazy	LAZY5	1987	£6	£2.50	*no picture sleeve*
Out Of Reach	CD-s	RCA	PD42012	1988	£5	£2	
Really Stupid	12"	Lazy	LAZYT2	1986	£6	£2.50	
Really Stupid	7"	Lazy	LAZY2	1986	£4	£1.50	
Secrets	CD-s	RCA	PD43174	1989	£5	£2	
Sick Of It	CD-s	RCA	PD42948	1989	£5	£2	
Stop Killing Me	7"	Lazy	LAZY3	1986	£4	£1.50	*with badge*
Thru The Flowers	12"	Lazy	LAZY1	1986	£8	£4	
Thru The Flowers	12"	Head	HEAD010	1986	£25	£12.50	*test pressing*

PRIMITIVES (3)

During 1964, Lou Reed was employed as a songwriter and performer by a company specializing in quick cash-in records. 'The Ostrich' was one of these, but it managed to gain sufficient attention for an invitation to be made to appear on Dick Clark's TV show. The group put together for the purpose was almost a prototype Velvet Underground, consisting of Lou Reed, John Cale and fellow avant-garde enthusiast Tony Conrad.

Ostrich	7"	Pickwick	1001	1964	£60	£30	US

PRINCE

All the major stars of the eighties have had their recording careers boosted by a proliferation of picture disc and other limited edition releases, and Prince is no exception. Most critics would have it that the legendary *Black Album* contains music of unparalleled splendour and that its last-minute withdrawal was an act of typically idiosyncratic and wilful behaviour on the part of its maker. Original copies are rare (though not as rare as to justify some of the extreme prices that are quoted on occasion – the thousand pound figure quoted here is a maximum), but bootleg versions, with a variety of cover designs, are in common circulation, while an official release was finally made in 1994 (effectively, this is a reissue). These enable anyone not overawed by the record's reputation to hear that the *Black Album* lacks entirely the sense of surprise that is present in the best of Prince's work. These days, of course, Prince is more frequently known as TAFKAP (The Artist Formerly Known As Talented, it has been suggested elsewhere). Whatever the truth of the matter, collectors' interest in him is certainly falling.

Title	Format	Label	Cat. No.	Year	Price	Price	Notes
1999	12"	WEA	W9896T	1983	£15	£7.50	
1999	7"	WEA	W9896C	1983	£15	£7.50	*with cassette*
1999	7"	WEA	W9896	1983	£5	£2	
1999	LP	WEA	9238091	1983	£15	£6	*single LP*
Alphabet Street	CD-s	WEA	W7900CD	1988	£12	£6	*3" single*
Anotherloverholenyohead	7"	WEA	W8521W	1986	£5	£2	*poster sleeve*
Anotherloverholenyohead	12"	WEA	W8521T	1986	£10	£5	*poster sleeve*
Anotherloverholenyohead	7"	WEA	W8521F	1986	£8	£4	*double*
Arms Of Orion	CD-s	WEA	W2757CDX	1989	£6	£2.50	*tri-fold sleeve*
Batdance	12"	WEA	W2924TP	1989	£8	£4	*picture disc*
Batdance	CD-s	WEA	W2924CDX	1989	£8	£4	*batpack box, 3" single*
Batdance	CD-s	WEA	W2924CD	1989	£5	£2	
Batman	CD	Paisley Park	9259782	1989	£15	£6	*in tin*
Batman	LP	WEA	WX281P	1989	£15	£6	*picture disc*
Black Album	LP	Warner Bros	145793	1995	£100	£50	*US promo, white or multicoloured vinyl*
Black Album	LP or CD	Paisley Park	WX147	1988	£1000	£700	*promo only*
Controversy	12"	WEA	K17866T	1981	£30	£15	
Controversy	7"	WEA	K17866	1981	£20	£10	
Crown Jewels	CD	WEA	SAM1037	1992	£50	£25	*promo*
D.M.S.R.	12"	WEA	SAM172	1983	£40	£20	*promo*
Diamonds And Pearls	CD	Paisley Park	7599253792	1991	£15	£6	*hologram cover*
Diamonds And Pearls	CD	Paisley Park	253792DJ	1991	£25	£10	*US promo picture disc*
Diamonds And Pearls	CD-s	Warner Bros	W0075CDX	1991	£5	£2	*holographic disc*
Do It All Night	12"	WEA	K17768T	1981	£40	£20	*no picture sleeve*
Do It All Night	7"	WEA	K17768	1981	£15	£7.50	*no picture sleeve*
Girls And Boys	12"	WEA	W8586T	1986	£10	£5	*with poster*
Girls And Boys	7"	WEA	W8586F	1986	£8	£4	*double*
Girls And Boys	7"	WEA	W8586P	1986	£40	£20	*shaped picture disc*
Glam Slam	CD-s	WEA	W7806CD	1988	£12	£6	*3" single*
Gotta Stop Messin' About	12"	WEA	LV47	1981	£100	£50	*2 different B sides*
Gotta Stop Messin' About	7"	WEA	K17819	1981	£60	£30	*2 different B sides*
Graffiti Bridge	CD	Paisley Park	274932DJ	1990	£25	£10	*US promo picture disc*
Hits Sampler	CD	Warner Bros	PRCD2	1993	£30	£15	*promo*
I Could Never Take The Place Of Your Man	12"	WEA	W8288TP	1987	£15	£7.50	*picture disc*
I Wanna Be Your Lover	12"	WEA	K17537T	1979	£12	£6	*no picture sleeve*
I Wanna Be Your Lover	7"	WEA	K17537	1979	£6	£2.50	*no picture sleeve*
I Wish U Heaven	12"	Paisley Park	W7745TE	1988	£40	£20	*purple vinyl*
I Wish U Heaven	12"	Paisley Park	W7745TW	1988	£10	£5	*with poster*
I Wish U Heaven	7"	WEA	W7745	1988	£5	£2	*poster sleeve*
I Wish U Heaven	CD-s	WEA	W7745CD	1988	£12	£6	*3" single*
I Would Die 4 U (US Remix)	12"	WEA	W9121TE	1984	£25	£12.50	
If I Was Your Girlfriend	12"	WEA	W8334TP	1987	£20	£10	*picture disc*
If I Was Your Girlfriend	7"	WEA	W8334E	1987	£8	£4	*peach vinyl, cards & stickers*
If I Was Your Girlfriend	7"	WEA	W8334W	1987	£5	£2	*poster sleeve*
Kiss	12"	WEA	W8751T	1986	£10	£5	*with poster*
Kiss	7"	WEA	W8751TP	1986	£20	£10	*shaped picture disc, plinth*
Kiss	7"	WEA	W8751TP	1986	£10	£5	*shaped picture disc*
Let's Go Crazy	12"	WEA	W2000T	1985	£6	£2.50	*with poster & sticker*
Let's Work	12"	WEA	K17922T	1982	£100	£50	
Let's Work	7"	WEA	K17922	1982	£25	£12.50	
Little Red Corvette	12"	WEA	W9436T	1983	£50	£25	*with poster*
Little Red Corvette	12"	WEA	W9688T	1983	£30	£15	*with poster & sticker*
Little Red Corvette	12"	WEA	W9436T	1983	£30	£15	
Little Red Corvette	12"	WEA	W9436T	1983	£75	£37.50	*with calendar*
Little Red Corvette	12"	WEA	W9688T	1983	£20	£10	
Little Red Corvette	7"	WEA	W9436	1983	£25	£12.50	*poster sleeve*
Little Red Corvette	7"	WEA	W9688	1983	£6	£2.50	
Little Red Corvette/1999	7"	Warner Bros	201290	1983	£15	£7.50	*US picture disc*
Mountains	10"	WEA	W8711TW	1986	£30	£15	*white vinyl*
Mountains	12"	WEA	W8711T	1986	£10	£5	*with poster*
New Power Generation	CD-s	Paisley Park	W9525CD	1990	£5	£2	
Paisley Park	12"	WEA	W9052T	1985	£6	£2.50	
Paisley Park	12"	WEA	W9052TP	1985	£10	£5	*with poster*
Paisley Park	7"	WEA	W9052P	1985	£25	£12.50	*shaped picture disc*
Parade	LP	WEA	WX39P	1986	£25	£10	*picture disc*
Partyman	12"	WEA	W2814TP	1989	£10	£5	*picture disc*

Partyman	CD-s	Paisley Park	W2814CDX	1989	£5	£2	hexagonal sleeve
Pop Life	12"	WEA	W8858T	1985	£8	£4	
Purple Rain	12"	WEA	W9174T	1984	£10	£5	with poster
Purple Rain	12"	WEA	W9174T	1984	£6	£2.50	
Purple Rain	7"	WEA	W9174P	1984	£40	£20	shaped picture disc
Purple Rain	CD	Warner Bros	251102	1984	£25	£10	US, special cardboard cover
Purple Rain	LP	WEA	9251101	1984	£25	£10	purple vinyl, poster
Raspberry Beret	12"	WEA	W8929T	1985	£6	£2.50	
Sexy Dancer	12"	WEA	K17590T	1980	£40	£20	no picture sleeve
Sexy Dancer	7"	WEA	K17590	1980	£15	£7.50	no picture sleeve
Sexy MF	12"	Paisley Park	W0123P	1992	£6	£2.50	picture disc
Sign O The Times	12"	WEA	W8399TP	1987	£25	£12.50	picture disc
Symbol	CD	Paisley Park	9451212	1992	£20	£8	gold cardboard box
Thieves In The Temple	12"	Paisley Park	W9751TP	1990	£8	£4	picture disc
Thieves In The Temple	CD-s	WEA	W9751CD	1990	£5	£2	
U Got The Look	12"	WEA	W8289TP	1987	£15	£7.50	picture disc
Undertaker	CD	no label	930902H	1995	£200	£100	no cover
When Doves Cry/1999	12"	WEA	W9296T	1984	£20	£10	shrinkwrapped double

PRINCE, VIV

Light Of The Charge Brigade	7"	Columbia	DB7960	1966	£20	£10	

PRINCE & PRINCESS

Ready Steady Go	7"	Island	WI609	1965	£10	£5	

PRINCE BUSTER

Aguar Fumar	7"	Blue Beat	BB293	1965	£12	£6	
Al Capone	7"	Blue Beat	BB324	1965	£12	£6	
All My Loving	7"	Fab	FAB35	1968	£8	£4	
All On My Mind	7"	Blue Beat	BB400	1967	£12	£6	
Ambition	7"	Blue Beat	BB328	1965	£12	£6	Ivanhoe Martin B side
Baldhead Pum Pum	7"	Prince Buster	PB47	1972	£4	£1.50	
Big Fight	7"	Blue Beat	BB338	1966	£12	£6	
Big Fight	7"	Blue Beat	BB282	1965	£12	£6	
Big Five	7"	Prince Buster	PB1	1970	£5	£2	
Big Five	7"	Fab	FAB150	1970	£4	£1.50	
Big Five	LP	Melodisc	MLP12157	1972	£15	£6	
Big Sister Stuff	7"	Prince Buster	PB14	1972	£4	£1.50	
Black Organ	7"	Fab	FAB141	1970	£4	£1.50	
Black Soul	7"	Fab	FAB102	1969	£6	£2.50	Caledonians B side
Blackhead Chinaman	7"	Dice	CC11	1963	£10	£5	
Blood Pressure	7"	Blue Beat	BB278	1965	£12	£6	
Blue Beat Spirit	7"	Blue Beat	BB211	1964	£12	£6	
Bonanza	7"	Blue Beat	BB307	1965	£12	£6	
Bull Buck	7"	Fab	FAB118	1969	£6	£2.50	Roland Alphonso B side
Burning Creation	7"	Blue Beat	BB173	1963	£12	£6	
Bye Bye Baby	7"	Fab	FAB16	1967	£8	£4	
Captain Burke	7"	Blue Beat	BB333	1965	£12	£6	
Cincinatti Kid	7"	Blue Beat	BB342	1966	£12	£6	
Come And Do It With Me	7"	Fab	FAB32	1968	£8	£4	
Come Home	7"	Blue Beat	BB317	1965	£12	£6	
Congo Revolution	7"	Blue Beat	BB325	1965	£12	£6	Little Darling B side
Dallas Texas	7"	Fab	FAB37	1968	£8	£4	
Dallas, Texas	7"	Blue Beat	BB266	1964	£12	£6	
Dance Cleopatra	7"	Blue Beat	BB388	1967	£12	£6	
Dark End Of The Street	7"	Blue Beat	BB377	1967	£12	£6	
Doctor Rodney	7"	Fab	FAB82	1969	£6	£2.50	
Don't Throw Stones	7"	Blue Beat	BB343	1966	£12	£6	
Drunkard's Psalm	7"	Blue Beat	BB378	1967	£12	£6	
Everybody Ska	7"	Stateside	SS335	1964	£10	£5	
Everybody Yeah Yeah	7"	Blue Beat	BB313	1965	£12	£6	
Eye For An Eye	7"	Blue Beat	BB294	1965	£12	£6	
Fabulous Greatest Hits	LP	Melodisc	MS1	1968	£10	£4	
Fishey	7"	Prince Buster	PB4	1971	£4	£1.50	
Float Like A Butterfly	7"	Blue Beat	BB314	1965	£12	£6	
Fowl Thief	7"	Blue Beat	BB186	1963	£12	£6	
Free Love	7"	Fab	FAB38	1968	£8	£4	Daltons B side
Ganja Plant	7"	Fab	FAB132	1970	£4	£1.50	
Glory Of Love	7"	Fab	FAB49	1968	£8	£4	
Glory Of Love	7"	Fab	FAB36	1968	£8	£4	
Going To Ethiopia	7"	Fab	FAB47	1968	£8	£4	
Going To The River	7"	Fab	FAB26	1967	£8	£4	
Going West	7"	Blue Beat	BB277	1965	£12	£6	
Green Green Grass Of Home	7"	Fab	FAB57	1968	£8	£4	Soul Makers B side
Here Comes The Bride	7"	Blue Beat	BB309	1965	£12	£6	
Hey Jude	7"	Fab	FAB94	1969	£6	£2.50	
Hit Me Back	7"	Fab	FAB140	1970	£4	£1.50	
Hypocrite	7"	Fab	FAB80	1968	£8	£4	
I Feel The Spirit	LP	Blue Beat	BBLP802	1963	£100	£50	
I Feel The Spirit	LP	Fab	MS2	1970	£40	£20	
I May Never Love You Again	7"	Blue Beat	BB274	1964	£12	£6	
I Wish Your Picture Was You	7"	Prince Buster	PB7	1971	£4	£1.50	
I Won't Let You Cry	7"	Blue Beat	BB357	1966	£12	£6	
Independence Day	7"	Blue Beat	BB116	1962	£12	£6	

Intensified Dirt	7″	Fab	FAB56	1968	£8	£4	
It's Burke's Law	LP	Blue Beat	BBLP806	1965	£100	£50	
It's Too Late	7″	Blue Beat	BB352	1966	£12	£6	
Jealous	7″	Blue Beat	BB243	1964	£12	£6	
Johnny Cool	7″	Fab	FAB11	1967	£10	£5	
Johnny Dark	7″	Blue Beat	BB290	1965	£12	£6	*Owen Gray B side*
Johnny Dollar	7″	Blue Beat	BB326	1965	£12	£6	*Terry Nelson B side*
Judge Dread	7″	Blue Beat	BB387	1967	£12	£6	*Fitzroy Campbell B side*
Judge Dread	LP	Blue Beat	BBLP809	1967	£75	£37.50	
King Duke Sir	7″	Blue Beat	BB163	1963	£12	£6	
Kings Of Old	7″	Fab	FAB31	1968	£8	£4	
Knock On Wood	7″	Blue Beat	BB373	1967	£12	£6	
Land Of Imagination	7″	Blue Beat	BB391	1967	£12	£6	
Ling Ting Tang	7″	Blue Beat	BB302	1965	£12	£6	
Love Each Other	7″	Rainbow	RAI110	1966	£8	£4	
Madness	7″	Blue Beat	BB170	1963	£15	£7.50	
Medley	7″	Prince Buster	PB19	1972	£4	£1.50	
Money	7″	Blue Beat	BB162	1963	£12	£6	*School Boys B side*
Mules Mules Mules	7″	Blue Beat	BB279	1965	£12	£6	*Charmers B side*
My Girl	7″	Blue Beat	BB321	1965	£12	£6	
My Happiness	7″	Prince Buster	PB9	1971	£4	£1.50	
My Heart Is Gone	7″	Prince Buster	PB16	1972	£4	£1.50	
Nice Nice	7″	Fab	FAB64	1968	£8	£4	
No Knowledge In College	7″	Blue Beat	BB271	1964	£12	£6	
Ob La Di Ob La Da	7″	Fab	FAB93	1969	£6	£2.50	
Old Lady	7″	Blue Beat	BB262	1964	£12	£6	
One Hand Washes The Other	7″	Blue Beat	BB138	1962	£12	£6	
Open Up Bartender	7″	Blue Beat	BB158	1963	£12	£6	
Original Golden Oldies Vol. 1	LP	Prince Buster	PB9	1973	£10	£4	
Outlaw	LP	Blue Beat	BBLP822	1969	£40	£20	
Pharaoh House Crash	7″	Fab	FAB92	1969	£6	£2.50	
Picket Line	7″	Blue Beat	BB349	1966	£12	£6	*Eric Morris B side*
Police Trim Rasta	7″	Fab	FAB176	1971	£4	£1.50	
Prince Buster On Tour	LP	Blue Beat	BBLP808	1967	£75	£37.50	
Prince Royal	7″	Blue Beat	BB244	1964	£12	£6	*Cosmo B side*
Prophet	7″	Blue Beat	BB359	1966	£12	£6	
Protection	7″	Prince Buster	PB15	1972	£4	£1.50	
Pum Pum A Go Kill You	7″	Fab	FAB101	1969	£6	£2.50	
Quiet Place	7″	Blue Beat	BB393	1967	£12	£6	
Rat Trap	7″	Prince Buster	PB2	1971	£4	£1.50	
Rat Trap	7″	Fab	FAB142	1970	£4	£1.50	
Rebel	7″	Fab	FAB124	1969	£4	£1.50	
Repect	7″	Blue Beat	BB335	1965	£12	£6	
Rock And Shake	7″	Fab	FAB20	1967	£8	£4	*Hortense Ellis B side*
Rolling Stones	7″	Blue Beat	BB192	1963	£12	£6	*Rico B side*
Rough Rider	7″	Fab	FAB40	1968	£8	£4	
Rum And Coca Cola	7″	Blue Beat	BB330	1965	£12	£6	
Run Man Run	7″	Blue Beat	BB150	1963	£12	£6	
Shakin' Up Orange Street	7″	Fab	FAB10	1967	£10	£5	
Shanty Town Get Scanty	7″	Blue Beat	BB370	1967	£12	£6	
She Loves You	7″	Blue Beat	BB234	1964	£12	£6	
She Pon Top	7″	Blue Beat	BB232	1964	£12	£6	
She Was A Rough Rider	LP	Blue Beat	BBLP820	1969	£50	£25	
Shepherd Beng	7″	Fab	FAB41	1968	£8	£4	*with Teddy King*
Sister's Big Stuff	LP	Melodisc	MLP12156	1972	£15	£6	
Sit And Wonder	7″	Blue Beat	BB382	1967	£12	£6	*Roland Alphonso B side*
Sit Down And Cry	7″	Blue Beat	BB389	1967	£12	£6	
Ska-Lip-Soul	LP	Blue Beat	BBLP805	1965	£100	£50	
Sons Of Zion	7″	Prince Buster	PB8	1971	£4	£1.50	*Ansell Collins B side*
Soul Dance	7″	Blue Beat	BB398	1967	£12	£6	
Soul Serenade	7″	Blue Beat	BB390	1967	£12	£6	
Sounds And Pressure	7″	Blue Beat	BB372	1967	£12	£6	
South Of The Border	7″	Prince Buster	PB36	1972	£4	£1.50	
Spider And The Fly	7″	Blue Beat	BB199	1963	£12	£6	
Stand Up	7″	Fab	FAB122	1969	£4	£1.50	
Still	7″	Prince Buster	PB32	1972	£4	£1.50	
Sugar Pop	7″	Blue Beat	BB316	1965	£12	£6	
Take It Easy	7″	Blue Beat	BB384	1967	£12	£6	
Talkin' 'Bout My Girl	7″	Blue Beat	BB355	1966	£12	£6	
Ten Commandments	7″	Blue Beat	BB167	1963	£12	£6	
Ten Commandments	7″	Philips	BF1552	1967	£10	£5	
Ten Commandments	7″	Blue Beat	BB334	1965	£12	£6	
Ten Commandments	LP	RCA	LPM/LSP3792	1967	£30	£15	*US*
That's All	7″	Fab	FAB131	1970	£4	£1.50	
They Got To Come	7″	Dice	CC6	1962	£10	£5	
They Got To Go	7″	Blue Beat	BB101	1962	£12	£6	
Thirty Pieces Of Silver	7″	Blue Beat	BB248	1964	£12	£6	
Thirty Pieces Of Silver	7″	Unity	UN522	1969	£5	£2	
This Gun For Hire	7″	Blue Beat	BB395	1967	£12	£6	
Three Blind Mice	7″	Blue Beat	BB225	1964	£12	£6	
Three More Rivers To Cross	7″	Blue Beat	BB180	1963	£12	£6	*Raymond Harper B side*
Tickler	7″	Blue Beat	BB269	1964	£12	£6	*Cosmo B side*
Tie The Donkey's Tail	7″	Fab	FAB119	1969	£6	£2.50	
Time Longer Than Rope	7″	Blue Beat	BB133	1962	£12	£6	
To Be Loved	7″	Blue Beat	BB362	1966	£12	£6	

Train To Girls Town	7"	Fab	FAB25	1967	£8	£4	
Tutti Frutti	LP	Fab	MS6	1970	£20	£8	
Under Arrest	7"	Blue Beat	BB339	1966	£12	£6	
Vagabond	7"	Blue Beat	BB402	1967	£12	£6	
Wash All Your Troubles Away	7"	Blue Beat	BB200	1963	£12	£6	*Rico B side*
Wash All Your Troubles Away	7"	Blue Beat	BB210	1964	£12	£6	*Rico B side*
Watch It Blackhead	7"	Blue Beat	BB189	1963	£12	£6	
We Shall Overcome	7"	Fab	FAB58	1968	£8	£4	
Welcome To Jamaica	LP	Blue Beat	BBLP821	1969	£30	£15	
What A Hard Man Fe Dead	LP	Blue Beat	BBLP807	1967	£100	£50	
What A World	7"	Blue Beat	BB144	1962	£12	£6	
Window Shopping	7"	Blue Beat	BB197	1963	£12	£6	
Wine And Grind	7"	Fab	FAB108	1969	£6	£2.50	
Wine And Grind	7"	Fab	FAB81	1968	£8	£4	
Wings Of A Dove	7"	Blue Beat	BB254	1964	£12	£6	*Maytals B side*
World Peace	7"	Dice	CC18	1963	£10	£5	
You'll Be Lonely And Blue	7"	Blue Beat	BB383	1967	£12	£6	
You're Mine	7"	Blue Beat	BB216	1964	£12	£6	
Young Gifted And Black	7"	Fab	FAB127	1970	£4	£1.50	
Your Turn	7"	Rainbow	RAI107	1966	£8	£4	

PRINCE CHARLIE

Hit And Run	7"	Coxsone	CS7101	1969	£10	£5	

PRINCE FAR I

Cry Tuff Dub Encounter Part Two	LP	Front Line	FLX4002	1979	£12	£5	
Free From Sin	LP	Trojan	TRLS175	1979	£10	£4	
Long Life	LP	Front Line	FL1021	1978	£12	£5	
Message From The King	LP	Front Line	FL1013	1978	£12	£5	

PRINCE HAROLD

Forget About Me	7"	Mercury	MF952	1966	£6	£2.50	

PRINCE JAZZBO

Free From Chains	7"	Grape	GR3047	1973	£4	£1.50	*Lloyd & Patsy B side*
Kick Boy	7"	Ackee	ACK532	1974	£4	£1.50	
Mr Harry Skank	7"	Technique	TE921	1973	£4	£1.50	*Glen Brown B side*
Penny Reel	7"	Dip	DL5036	1974	£4	£1.50	

PRINCE MOHAMMED

African Roots	LP	Burning Sounds	BR1005	1979	£10	£4	
People Are You Ready	LP	Ballistic	UAS30192	1978	£10	£4	

PRINCE OF DARKNESS

Burial Of Longshot	7"	Down Town	DT441	1969	£5	£2	
Meeting Over Yonder	7"	Downtown	DT448	1969	£5	£2	*Music Doctors B side*
Sound Of Today	7"	Downtown	DT467	1971	£5	£2	*Music Doctors B side*

PRINCE PATO EXPEDITION

Firebird	LP	Beacon	BEAS18	197–	£20	£8	

PRINCESS & THE SWINEHERD

Princess And The Swineherd	LP	Oak	RGJ633	1968	£25	£10	

PRINCIPAL EDWARD'S MAGIC THEATRE

Principal Edward's Magic Theatre was the first, and perhaps the only group ever to receive an Arts Council Grant. It was a large organization, incorporating dancers and light-show operators as well as musicians, so that the records do not entirely succeed in conveying what the group did. *Soundtrack*, however, is an interesting record, crossing folk with rock and poetry so well that one is never quite sure what is coming next. The music also features a cameo appearance from John Peel, who delivers one spoken line (in the role of a child). The second album, meanwhile, includes a welcome antidote to all those hymns of praise to various American cities, in the form of a song dedicated to the town of Kettering.

Asmoto Running Band	LP	Dandelion	DAN8002	1971	£12	£5	
Ballad Of The Big Girl Now	7"	Dandelion	K4405	1970	£4	£1.50	
Round One	LP	Deram	SML1108	1974	£12	£5	
Soundtrack	LP	Dandelion	63752	1969	£15	£6	

PRINE, JOHN

Diamonds In The Rough	LP	Atlantic	K40427	1972	£10	£4	
John Prine	LP	Atlantic	K40357	1972	£10	£4	

PRIOR, MADDY

Changing Winds	LP	Chrysalis	CHR1203	1978	£12	£5	
Hooked On Winning	LP	Plant Life	PLR036	1982	£10	£4	
I Saw Three Ships	CD-s	Park	PRKCD16	1992	£5	£2	
Silly Sisters	LP	Chrysalis	CHR1101	1976	£10	£4	*with June Tabor*
Woman In The Wings	LP	Chrysalis	CHR1185	1978	£12	£5	

PRISMA

Prisma	LP	Prisma		1983	£25	£10	*Dutch*

PRISONAIRES

Just Walkin' In The Rain	7"	Sun	186	1953	£60	£30	*US*
My God Is Real	7"	Sun	189	1953	£100	£50	*US*
Prisoner's Prayer	7"	Sun	191	1953	£60	£30	*US*

Title	Format	Label	Cat. No.	Year	Mint	VG	Notes
There Is Love In You	7"	Sun	207	1954	**£3000**	**£2100**	*US, best auctioned*

PRISONERS

Title	Format	Label	Cat. No.	Year	Mint	VG	Notes
Electric Fit	7"	Big Beat	SW98	1984	**£5**	**£2**	
Hurricane	7"	Big Beat	NS90	1983	**£5**	**£2**	
Last Fourfathers	LP	Own Up	OWNUPU3	1985	**£10**	**£4**	
Last Night At The Mic Club	LP	Empire	MIC001	1986	**£10**	**£4**	*with the Milkshakes*
Taste Of Pink	LP	Own Up	OWNUPU2	1985	**£20**	**£8**	*pink vinyl*
Taste Of Pink	LP	Own Up	OWNUPU2	1982	**£15**	**£6**	

PROBY, P. J.

All four members of Led Zeppelin appear on one track of the P. J. Proby album *Three Week Hero*, and the record has long been a collector's item for this reason. Proby's career is dotted with moments like this: he was the lucky recipient of an unreleased Beatles song (although his mannered voice is not actually ideal for making the best of 'That Means A Lot'); he managed to land the starring role in the *Elvis* stage show (and is accordingly central in the collectable album that was only ever available at the theatre); and was later to be found recording in an unlikely partnership with the group Focus. (The resulting album is listed within their entry. Cynics should resist making too much of its title, however, for *Focus Con Proby* is Italian in origin!)

Title	Format	Label	Cat. No.	Year	Mint	VG	Notes
Believe It Or Not	LP	Liberty	LBL/LBS83087	1968	**£15**	**£6**	
California License	LP	Liberty	LBL83320	1969	**£40**	**£20**	*credited to Jet Powers*
Christmas With P. J. Proby	7" EP	Liberty	LEP2239	1965	**£10**	**£5**	
Day That Lorraine Came Down	7"	Liberty	LIB15152	1968	**£6**	**£2.50**	
Elvis	LP	Astoria	1	1978	**£25**	**£10**	*with other artists*
Enigma	LP	Liberty	LBL/LBS83032	1967	**£10**	**£4**	
Enigma	LP	Liberty	LBY1361	1966	**£15**	**£6**	
Go Go P. J. Proby	LP	Liberty	LRP3406/ LST7406	1965	**£15**	**£6**	*US*
Hanging From Your Loving Tree	7"	Liberty	LIB15245	1969	**£6**	**£2.50**	
Hero	LP	Palm	7007	1981	**£15**	**£6**	*with other artists*
Hold Me	7" EP	Decca	457044	1964	**£15**	**£7.50**	*French*
I Am P. J. Proby	LP	Liberty	LBY1235	1964	**£15**	**£6**	
I Can't Make It Alone	7" EP	Liberty	LEP2274	1967	**£15**	**£7.50**	*French*
I'm Yours	LP	Ember	NR5069	1973	**£10**	**£4**	
It's Goodbye	7"	Liberty	LIB15386	1970	**£6**	**£2.50**	
Let The Water Run Down	7"	Liberty	LIB10206	1965	**£4**	**£1.50**	
My Prayer	7" EP	Liberty	LEP2253	1966	**£12**	**£6**	*French*
Niki Hoeky	7"	Liberty	LIB55936	1967	**£4**	**£1.50**	
P. J. Proby	7" EP	Liberty	LEP2192	1965	**£8**	**£4**	
P. J. Proby	LP	Liberty	LBY1264	1965	**£15**	**£6**	
P. J. Proby . . . In Town	LP	Liberty	LBY1291	1965	**£12**	**£5**	
P. J. Proby . . . In Town	LP	Liberty	LBL/LBS83018	1967	**£10**	**£4**	
P. J. Proby Again	7" EP	Liberty	LEP2267	1966	**£20**	**£10**	
P. J. Proby Hits	7" EP	Liberty	LEP2251	1966	**£15**	**£7.50**	
Phenomenon	LP	Liberty	LBL/LBS83045	1967	**£15**	**£6**	
Somewhere	7" EP	Liberty	LEP2229	1965	**£8**	**£4**	
Somewhere	7" EP	Liberty	LEP2220	1965	**£10**	**£5**	*French*
That Means A Lot	7"	Liberty	LIB10215	1965	**£5**	**£2**	
That Means A Lot	7" EP	Liberty	LEP2240	1965	**£20**	**£10**	*French*
Three Week Hero	LP	Liberty	LBS83219	1969	**£40**	**£20**	
Today I Killed A Man	7"	Liberty	LIB15280	1970	**£6**	**£2.50**	
Try To Forget Her	7"	Liberty	LIB55367	1964	**£5**	**£2**	
What's Wrong With My World	7"	Liberty	LIB15085	1968	**£4**	**£1.50**	
What's Wrong With My World	LP	Liberty	LST7561	1968	**£10**	**£4**	*US*
Work With Me Annie	7"	Liberty	LIB55974	1967	**£8**	**£4**	
You Got Me Cryin'	7"	Melodisc	FAB2	1966	**£4**	**£1.50**	
You Got Me Cryin'	7"	Melodisc	FAB2	1966	**£6**	**£2.50**	*picture sleeve*

PROCESSION

Title	Format	Label	Cat. No.	Year	Mint	VG	Notes
Every American Citizen	7"	Mercury	MF1053	1968	**£4**	**£1.50**	

PROCLAIMERS

Title	Format	Label	Cat. No.	Year	Mint	VG	Notes
I'm On My Way	CD-s	Chrysalis	CLAMCD4	1989	**£5**	**£2**	
Sunshine On Leith	CD-s	Chrysalis	CLAMCD3	1988	**£5**	**£2**	

PROCOL HARUM

When R&B veterans the Paramounts changed their name to Procol Harum and started wearing brightly coloured kaftans, they were almost ahead of their time. The music press berated the group for choosing to stand still on stage and simply play – an approach that became standard not long afterwards as the progressive rock movement developed. 'A Whiter Shade Of Pale' was one of those records destined to shoot to the top of the charts as soon as it was heard on the radio, but to some extent it became a millstone for the band, which never managed to make quite as much impact again. There is nevertheless much fine music to be found on the group's albums, particularly on *Shine On Brightly* and *A Salty Dog*, where Robin Trower's Hendrix-inspired guitar collides with Gary Brooker's dead-pan vocals and lyricist Keith Reid's finely crafted sense of the absurd. The hit single is not listed below – the record sold so many copies that it is quite common today.

Title	Format	Label	Cat. No.	Year	Mint	VG	Notes
Broken Barricades	LP	Chrysalis	ILPS9158	1971	**£10**	**£4**	
Home	CD	Mobile Fidelity	MFCD793	1989	**£15**	**£6**	*US audiophile*
Home	LP	Regal Zonophone	SLRZ1014	1970	**£12**	**£5**	
Il Tuo Diamente	7"	IL	IL9005	1969	**£8**	**£4**	*sung in Italian*
Live With The Edmonton Symphony Orchestra	CD	Mobile Fidelity	MFCD788	1989	**£15**	**£6**	*US audiophile*
Lives	LP	A&M	SP8053	1972	**£15**	**£6**	*US interview promo*
Procol Harum	LP	Regal Zonophone	LRZ1001	1967	**£15**	**£6**	
Prodigal Stranger	CD	Zoo		1991	**£40**	**£20**	*US promo double in cloth cover*

Title	Format	Label	Cat. No.	Year	Mint	VG	Notes
Salty Dog	CD	Mobile Fidelity	MFCD823	1985	£15	£6	US audiophile
Salty Dog	LP	Regal Zonophone	SLRZ1009	1969	£15	£6	
Shine On Brightly	LP	Regal Zonophone	(S)LRZ1004	1968	£15	£6	

PROCOPE, RUSSELL

Title	Format	Label	Cat. No.	Year	Mint	VG	Notes
Persuasive Sax	LP	London	HAD2013	1956	£12	£5	

PROCTOR, JUDD

Title	Format	Label	Cat. No.	Year	Mint	VG	Notes
Better Late	7"	Parlophone	R5126	1964	£5	£2	
Guitars Galore	LP	Morgan	MR103P	196–	£12	£5	
It's Bluesy	7"	Parlophone	R4920	1962	£5	£2	
Nola	7"	Parlophone	R4809	1961	£5	£2	
Plainsman	7"	Parlophone	R4769	1961	£5	£2	
Speakeasy	7"	Parlophone	R4841	1961	£5	£2	
Turk	7"	Parlophone	R4885	1962	£5	£2	

PROCTOR, MIKE

Title	Format	Label	Cat. No.	Year	Mint	VG	Notes
Mr Commuter	7"	Columbia	DB8254	1967	£25	£12.50	

PRODIGY

Title	Format	Label	Cat. No.	Year	Mint	VG	Notes
Breathe	7"	XL	XLS80LC	1997	£5	£2	jukebox issue
Charly	CD-s	XL	XLS21	1991	£8	£4	
Firestarter	12"	XL	XLT70P	1996	£10	£5	promo
Firestarter	7"	XL	XLT70LC	1996	£5	£2	jukebox issue
Firestarter	CD	XL	XLS70CDP	1996	£20	£8	promo sampler
Minefields	12"	XL	XLT76	1996	£200	£100	test pressing only
Minefields	cass	XL	XLS76	1996	£40	£20	promo only
Minefields	CD-s	XL	XLS76CD	1996	£60	£30	
Scienide	12"	XL	SC1	1995	£15	£7.50	promo
Smack My Bitch Up	12"	XL	XLT98	1998	£20	£10	promo
What Evil Lurks	12"	XL	XLT17	1991	£75	£37.50	

PROFESSIONALS

Title	Format	Label	Cat. No.	Year	Mint	VG	Notes
1-2-3	7"	Virgin	VS376	1980	£12	£6	signed by Cook & Jones
I Didn't See It Coming	LP	Virgin	V2220	1981	£10	£4	

PROFESSOR LONGHAIR

Title	Format	Label	Cat. No.	Year	Mint	VG	Notes
Baby Let Me Hold Your Hand	7"	Sue	WI397	1965	£15	£7.50	
Live On The Queen Mary	LP	Harvest	SHSP4086	1978	£10	£4	
New Orleans 88	10" LP	Speakeasy	1078	1972	£30	£15	
New Orleans Piano	LP	Atlantic	K40402	1972	£15	£6	
Professor Longhair	7" EP	XX	MIN708	196–	£8	£4	

PROFESSOR WOLFF

Title	Format	Label	Cat. No.	Year	Mint	VG	Notes
Professor Wolff	LP	Metronome	MLP15422	1972	£100	£50	German

PROFIL

Title	Format	Label	Cat. No.	Year	Mint	VG	Notes
Hey Music Man	7"	CBS	8574	1980	£5	£2	

PROFILE

Title	Format	Label	Cat. No.	Year	Mint	VG	Notes
Got To Find A Way	7"	Mercury	MF891	1965	£4	£1.50	
Haven't They Got Better Things To Do	7"	Mercury	MF875	1965	£4	£1.50	

PROJECTION COMPANY

Title	Format	Label	Cat. No.	Year	Mint	VG	Notes
Give Me Some Lovin'	LP	Custom		1966	£30	£15	US

PROLES

Title	Format	Label	Cat. No.	Year	Mint	VG	Notes
Proles Go To The Seaside	7"	Can't Play		1978	£12	£6	
Stereo Love	7"	Rock Against Racism	RAR1	1979	£5	£2	Condemned B side

PROPAGANDA

Title	Format	Label	Cat. No.	Year	Mint	VG	Notes
13th Life Of Dr Mabuse	12"	ZTT	12ZTAS2 (2A2U)	1985	£12	£5	
Bejewelled Duel	12"	ZTT	12ZTAS8	1985	£6	£2.50	white label promo
Complete Machinery	cass-s	ZTT	CTIS12	1985	£10	£4	
Das Testaments Des Mabuse	12"	ZTT	12ZTAS2	1985	£8	£4	2 different picture sleeves
Das Testaments Des Mabuse	cass-s	ZTT	CTIS101	1985	£8	£3	
Dr Mabuse (Remix)	12"	ZTT	12ZTAS2DJ	1985	£10	£5	promo
Duel	7"	ZTT	DUAL1	1985	£5	£2	double
Duel	7"	ZTT	PZTAS8	1985	£5	£2	shaped picture disc
Duel	CD-s	ZTT	CTIS108	1985	£10	£5	
Heaven Give Me Words	CD-s	Virgin	VSCDX1245	1990	£5	£2	boxed
Only One Word	CD-s	Virgin	CSCDT1271	1990	£5	£2	
P Machinery (Beta)	12"	ZTT	12ZTAST12	1985	£6	£2.50	double
P Machinery (Beta)	12"	ZTT	12XZTAS12	1985	£10	£5	
P Machinery (Polish)	12"	ZTT	12PZTAS12	1985	£6	£2.50	clear vinyl
Secret Wish	CD	ZTT	CID126	1985	£12	£5	
Wishful Thinking	CD	ZTT	ZCIDQ20	1985	£30	£15	

PROPAGATION

Title	Format	Label	Cat. No.	Year	Mint	VG	Notes
By Means Of Music	LP	Road		1983	£15	£6	Dutch

PROPELLER

Let Us Live Together	LP	Philips	6305114	1971	**£12**	**£5**	*German*

PROPHET, ORVAL

Run Run Run	7"	London	HLL9729	1963	**£5**	**£2**	

PROPHET, REX

Canadian Plowboy	7" EP	Brunswick	OE9144	1955	**£8**	**£4**	

PROPHETS

I Got The Fever	7"	Mercury	MF10[illegible]	1969	**£15**	**£7.50**	

PROTEX

Don't Ring Me Up	7"	Good Vibrations	GOT6	1978	**£5**	**£2**	
I Can Only Dream	7"	Polydor	2059167	1979	**£5**	**£2**	
I Can't Cope	7"	Polydor	2059124	1979	**£5**	**£2**	
Place In Your Heart	7"	Polydor	2059245	1980	**£5**	**£2**	

PROTOS

One Day A New Horizon	LP	Airship	AP391	1982	**£100**	**£50**	

PROVIDENCE

Ever Sense The Dawn	LP	Threshold	THS9	1972	**£20**	**£8**	

PROVINE, DOROTHY

Don't Bring Lulu	7"	Warner Bros	WB53	1961	**£4**	**£1.50**	

PROWLER

Alcatraz	7"	SRT	SRT5KS368	1985	**£20**	**£10**	

PROX

At Last	LP	Polydor	2413122	1979	**£20**	**£8**	*German*

PRUDENCE

Drunk And Happy	LP	Polydor	2382031	1973	**£15**	**£6**	*Norwegian*

PRYOR, SNOOKY

Snooky Pryor	LP	Flyright	LP100	1970	**£12**	**£5**	

PRYSOCK, ARTHUR

Again	7" EP	CBS	EP6076	1966	**£10**	**£5**	
Does It Again	LP	Polydor	2383481	1978	**£10**	**£4**	
I Worry About You	LP	Old Town	LP102	1962	**£20**	**£8**	*US*
It's Too Late Baby Too Late	7"	CBS	201820	1965	**£5**	**£2**	

PRYSOCK, RED

Battle Royal	LP	Mercury	MG20106	1956	**£40**	**£20**	*US*
Beat	LP	Mercury	MPL6535	1958	**£30**	**£15**	
Blow Your Horn	78	Mercury	MB3158	1954	**£15**	**£7.50**	
Chop Suey	7"	Mercury	AMT1028	1959	**£6**	**£2.50**	
First Rock'n'Roll Party	10" LP	Mercury	MPT7512	1957	**£40**	**£20**	
Fruit Boots	LP	Mercury	MPL6550	1958	**£30**	**£15**	
Jump Red, Jump	10" LP	Mercury	MPT7517	1957	**£40**	**£20**	
Rock'n'Roll	LP	Mercury	MG20088	1955	**£50**	**£25**	*US*
Swing Softly Red	LP	Mercury	MG20188	1956	**£40**	**£20**	*US*
Teen Age Rock	78	Mercury	MT154	1957	**£10**	**£5**	

PSEUDO EXISTERS

Pseudo Existence	7"	Dead Good	DEAD2	1980	**£20**	**£10**	

PSYCHEDELIC FURS

All That Money Wants	CD-s	CBS	CDFURS4	1988	**£5**	**£2**	
House	CD-s	CBS	CDFURS5	1990	**£5**	**£2**	
Interchords	LP	Columbia	AS1296	1981	**£15**	**£6**	*US interview promo*
We Love You	7"	Epic	8005DJ	1979	**£5**	**£2**	*censored promo*

PSYCHEDELIC PSOUL

Freak Scene	LP	Columbia	CS9456	1968	**£15**	**£6**	*US*

PSYCHIC TV

When Throbbing Gristle split, the pieces flew off into three directions, one of which led to the group Psychic TV. Genesis P. Orridge retained a similar record release policy to that of Throbbing Gristle, with a plethora of limited-edition issues that were inevitably destined to rise in value. The music is considerably more commercial on the whole, but with a sardonic streak reminiscent of Frank Zappa's irreverent approach.

Album Ten	LP	Temple	TOPY032	1988	**£15**	**£6**	*picture disc*
Allegory And Self	LP	Temple	TOPY038	1988	**£10**	**£4**	*picture disc*
Beyond The Infinite Beat	CD-s	Temple	TOPCD051	1990	**£5**	**£2**	
Dreams Less Sweet	LP	CBS	25737	1983	**£10**	**£4**	*with 12"*
Force The Hand Of Chance	LP	Some Bizarre	PSY1	1982	**£15**	**£6**	*double, with insert*
Godstar	12"	Temple	TOPIC009	1986	**£6**	**£2.50**	*picture disc*
Jack The Tab	12"	DC	DC23	1988	**£6**	**£2.50**	
Just Drifting	12"	Some Bizarre	PTV1T	1982	**£10**	**£5**	
Just Drifting	7"	Some Bizarre	PTV1	1982	**£5**	**£2**	
Live At Thee Pyramid NYC 1988	LP	Temple	TOPY047	1989	**£10**	**£4**	*picture disc*

Title	Format	Label	Cat. No.	Year	Mint	VG	Notes
Mouth Of The Night	LP	Temple	TOPY010	1985	£10	£4	*picture disc*
Pagan Day	LP	Temple	TOPY003	1984	£15	£6	*picture disc*
Psychick TV Themes Vol. 2	LP	Temple	TOPY004	1985	£10	£4	
Psychick TV Themes Vol. 3	LP	Temple	TOPY008	1985	£10	£4	
Rev. Jim Jones	LP				£20	£8	*US picture disc*
Roman P	7"	Sordide Sentimental	SS33009	1984	£8	£4	
Unclean	12"	Temple	TOPY001	1984	£6	£2.50	

PSYKYK VOLTS

Title	Format	Label	Cat. No.	Year	Mint	VG	Notes
Totally Useless	7"	Ellie Jay	EJPS9262	1979	£25	£12.50	

PTOLOMY PSYCON

Title	Format	Label	Cat. No.	Year	Mint	VG	Notes
Loose Capacitor	7" EP	private		197–	£400	£250	*best auctioned*

PUBLIC ENEMY

Title	Format	Label	Cat. No.	Year	Mint	VG	Notes
Rebel Without A Pause	7"	Def Jam	6512450	1987	£5	£2	*picture disc*

PUBLIC FOOT THE ROMAN

Title	Format	Label	Cat. No.	Year	Mint	VG	Notes
Public Foot The Roman	LP	Sovereign	SVNA7259	1973	£25	£10	

PUBLIC IMAGE LTD

Title	Format	Label	Cat. No.	Year	Mint	VG	Notes
Disappointed	CD-s	Virgin	VSCD1181	1989	£5	£2	*3" single*
Metal Box	LP	Virgin	METAL1	1979	£20	£8	*3 × 12" in can*
Public Image	7"	Virgin	VS228	1978	£4	£1.50	*newspaper sleeve*
This Is Not A Love Song	CD-s	Virgin	CDT14	1988	£5	£2	*3" single*
Warrior	CD-s	Virgin	VSCD1195	1989	£5	£2	*3" single*

PUCKETT, GARY & THE UNION GAP

Title	Format	Label	Cat. No.	Year	Mint	VG	Notes
Incredible	LP	CBS	63429	1968	£12	£5	
New Gary Puckett & The Union Gap Album	LP	CBS	63794	1970	£12	£5	
Woman Woman	LP	Columbia	CS9612	1968	£12	£5	*US*
Young Girl	LP	CBS	63342	1968	£12	£5	

PUDDING

Title	Format	Label	Cat. No.	Year	Mint	VG	Notes
Magic Bus	7"	Decca	F12603	1967	£25	£12.50	

PUGSLEY MUNION

Title	Format	Label	Cat. No.	Year	Mint	VG	Notes
Just Like You	LP	J&S	SLP0001	1969	£75	£37.50	*US*

PUKWANA, DUDU

Title	Format	Label	Cat. No.	Year	Mint	VG	Notes
Flute Music	LP	Caroline	CA2005	1975	£12	£5	
In The Townships	LP	Caroline	C1504	1974	£12	£5	*with Spear*

PULLINS, LEROY

Title	Format	Label	Cat. No.	Year	Mint	VG	Notes
I'm A Nut	7"	London	HLR10056	1966	£8	£4	
I'm A Nut	LP	Kapp	1488	1969	£60	£30	*US*

PULP

Pulp's *His 'n' Hers* was one of the highlights of 1994, the confident swagger and sleaze of Jarvis Cocker's songwriting being matched by a scintillating performance from the whole group and recalling some of the best moments of an imaginary meeting between Soft Cell and David Bowie. An album as fresh as this might have been expected to be the group's debut but, in fact, Pulp had been around for nearly a dozen years, so that there are numerous early recordings for collectors to seek out (although none is in the same league as *His 'n' Hers* or its follow-up, *Different Class*). Unless Jarvis Cocker once performed under the name of Ann Bean, who is the singer on 'Low Flying Aircraft', then the 1979 Pulp is a different group.

Title	Format	Label	Cat. No.	Year	Mint	VG	Notes
Babies	12"	Gift	GIF3	1992	£6	£2.50	
Babies	CD-s	Gift	GIF3CD	1992	£10	£5	
Countdown	CD-s	Fire	BLAZE51CD	1991	£5	£2	
Dogs Are Everywhere	12"	Fire	BLAZE10S	1986	£15	£7.50	
Everybody's Problem	7"	Red Rhino	RED37	1983	£20	£10	
Freaks	LP	Fire	FIRELP5	1987	£15	£6	
It	CD	Cherry Red	CDMRED112	1994	£20	£8	
It	LP	Red Rhino	REDLP29	1984	£10	£4	
Lipgloss	CD-s	Island	CID567	1993	£10	£5	
Little Girl With Blue Eyes	12"	Fire	BLAZE5	1985	£15	£7.50	
Master Of The Universe	12"	Fire	BLAZE21T	1987	£10	£5	
Master Of The Universe	7"	Fire	BLAZE21S	1987	£10	£5	
My Legendary Girlfriend	12"	Fire	BLAZE44T	1991	£8	£4	
My Legendary Girlfriend	7"	Caff	CAFF17	1992	£30	£15	
My Lighthouse	7"	Red Rhino	RED32	1983	£30	£15	
O.U.	12"	Gift	GIF1	1992	£8	£4	
O.U.	CD-s	Gift	GIF1CD	1992	£10	£5	
Razzmatazz	12"	Gift	GIF6	1993	£6	£2.50	
Razzmatazz	7"	Gift	7GIF6	1993	£5	£2	
Razzmatazz	CD-s	Gift	GIF6CD	1993	£10	£5	
Sisters	12"	Island	12IS595	1994	£6	£2.50	
Sisters	7"	Island	IS595	1994	£4	£1.50	
They Suffocate At Night	12"	Fire	BLAZE17T	1987	£12	£6	
They Suffocate At Night	7"	Fire	BLAZE17S	1987	£8	£4	

PULP (2)

Title	Format	Label	Cat. No.	Year	Mint	VG	Notes
Low Flying Aircraft	7"	Pulp	PB1	1979	£12	£6	

PULSAR

Title	Format	Label	Cat. No.	Year	Mint	VG	Notes
Halloween	LP	CBS	82477	1977	£15	£6	*French*

Pollen | LP | Decca | SKLR5228 | 1976 | **£15** | **£6**
Strands Of The Future | LP | Decca | TXS119 | 1976 | **£15** | **£6**

PULSE

Pulse | LP | Major Minor | SMLP64 | 1970 | **£50** | **£25**

PUMA, JOE

Joe Puma Quintet | 10" LP | London | LZN14033 | 1956 | **£50** | **£25**

PUMPKIN, PETER

Would You Believe A March | 7" | Page One | POF048 | 1968 | **£4** | **£1.50**

PUMPKIN PIE

Down The Cut | LP | Saydisc | SDL272 | 1976 | **£20** | **£8**

PUMPKINHEAD

Pumpkinhead | LP | Mulligan | LUN001 | 1976 | **£12** | **£5** | *Irish*

PUNCHERS

Sons Of Thunder | 7" | Punch | PH46 | 1970 | **£4** | **£1.50**

PUNCHIN' JUDY

Punchin' Judy | LP | Transatlantic | TRA272 | 1973 | **£12** | **£5**

PUNKETTES

Going Out Wiv A Punk | 7" | Response | SR511 | 1977 | **£5** | **£2**

PUPILS

Cheaply made cover version LPs like *Tribute To The Rolling Stones* seldom attract much collectors' interest. The reason for this album being one of the few exceptions is that the group masquerading as the Pupils was actually the cult freakbeat band, the Eyes.

Tribute To The Rolling Stones | LP | Wing | WL1150 | 1966 | **£75** | **£37.50**
Tribute To The Rolling Stones | LP | Fontana | SFL13087 | 1969 | **£40** | **£20**

PUPPETS

Baby Don't Cry | 7" | Pye | 7N15634 | 1964 | **£25** | **£12.50**
Everybody's Talking | 7" | Pye | 7N15556 | 1963 | **£25** | **£12.50**
Shake With Me | 7" | Pye | 7N15625 | 1964 | **£15** | **£7.50**

PURCELL, FRANK

James Bond's Greatest Hits | LP | Paramount | PAS6064 | 1973 | **£10** | **£4**

PURCHES, DANNY

Mama | 7" | Columbia | SCM5183 | 1955 | **£6** | **£2.50**
Shrine On The Second Floor | 7" | Columbia | DB4129 | 1958 | **£5** | **£2**

PURDIE, BERNARD 'PRETTY'

Soul Drums | LP | Direction | 863290 | 1968 | **£30** | **£15**
Soul Is | LP | Philips | 6369421 | 1971 | **£10** | **£4**

PURE HELL

These Boots Are Made For Walking | 7" | Golden Sphinx | GSX002 | 1978 | **£12** | **£6**

PURGE

Mayor Of Simpleton Hall | 7" | Corn | CP101 | 1969 | **£100** | **£50**

PURIFY, JAMES & BOBBY

Do Unto Me | 7" | Stateside | SS2093 | 1968 | **£5** | **£2**
Help Yourself To All My Lovin' | 7" | Bell | BLL1024 | 1968 | **£4** | **£1.50**
I Can't Remember | 7" | Bell | BLL1008 | 1968 | **£4** | **£1.50**
I Take What I Want | 7" | Stateside | SS2039 | 1967 | **£5** | **£2**
I'm Your Puppet | 7" | Stateside | SS547 | 1966 | **£5** | **£2**
James And Bobby Purify | LP | Stateside | SL10206 | 1967 | **£15** | **£6**
Let Love Come Between Us | 7" | Stateside | SS2049 | 1967 | **£5** | **£2**
Pure Sound Of James And Bobby Purify | LP | Bell | MBLL/SBLL101 | 1967 | **£12** | **£5**
Shake A Tail Feather | 7" | Stateside | SS2016 | 1967 | **£6** | **£2.50**
Shake A Tail Feather | 7" | Bell | BLL1056 | 1969 | **£4** | **£1.50**
Untie Me | 7" | Bell | BLL1043 | 1969 | **£4** | **£1.50**
Wish You Didn't Have To Go | 7" | Stateside | SS595 | 1967 | **£5** | **£2**

PURIM, FLORA

Butterfly Dreams | LP | Milestone | M9052 | 1973 | **£12** | **£5** | *US*
Five Hundred Miles High At Montreux | LP | Milestone | M9070 | 1976 | **£12** | **£5** | *US*
Open Your Eyes You Can Fly | LP | Milestone | M9065 | 1976 | **£12** | **£5** | *US*
Stories To Tell | LP | Milestone | M9058 | 1974 | **£12** | **£5** | *US*

PURNELL, ALTON

Travelling Light | LP | Dixie | DIX4 | 1970 | **£12** | **£5**

PURPLE BARRIER

Shapes And Sounds | 7" | Eyemark | EMS1011 | 1968 | **£50** | **£25**

PURPLE FOX

Tribute To Jimi Hendrix | LP | Stereo Gold Award | MER340 | 1971 | **£10** | **£4**

PURPLE GANG

'Granny Takes A Trip' became a theme tune for the hippy movement in Britain – the title being adopted too by a Carnaby Street clothes shop – although the song is a good-time folk jugband performance and not at all psychedelic.

Granny Takes A Trip	7"	Transatlantic	BIG101	1967	£4	£1.50	
Purple Gang Strikes	LP	Transatlantic		1968	£30	£15	

PURPLE HAZE

Hear It On The Radio	7"	SRS	SRS6	1985	£20	£10	

PURPLE HEARTS

My Life's A Jigsaw	7"	Safari	SAFE30	1980	£5	£2	*foldout sleeve*
Plane Crash	7"	Road Runner	RR1	1982	£8	£4	

PUSSY

Plays	LP	Morgan Blue Town	BT5002	1969	£300	£180	

PUSSY (2)

Feline Woman	7"	Deram	DM368	1972	£10	£5	

PUSSYCATS

Mrrr Mrrr	LP	Polydor	623020	1966	£25	£10	*Swedish*
Psst Psst	LP	Polydor	623013	1966	£25	£10	*German*

PUSSYFOOT

Freeloader	7"	Decca	F12474	1966	£6	£2.50	
Good Times	7"	Pye	7N17520	1968	£6	£2.50	
Mr Hyde	7"	Decca	F12561	1967	£6	£2.50	

PUTHLI, ASHA

Asha Puthli	LP	CBS	65804	1973	£20	£8	
Devil Is Loose	LP	CBS	81443	1976	£20	£8	
She Loves To Hear The Music	LP	CBS	80978	1975	£15	£6	

PUZZLE

Puzzle	LP	Stateside	SSL10285	1969	£20	£8	

PVC2

Put You In The Picture	7"	Zoom	ZUM2	1977	£4	£1.50	

PYNE, NATASHA

It's All In Your Head	7"	Polydor	56713	1966	£4	£1.50	

PYRAMID

The lead singer on the Pyramid's impressive Deram single was Ian Matthews, subsequently a member of Fairport Convention before embarking on a solo career.

Summer Of Last Year	7"	Deram	DM111	1966	£10	£5	

PYRAMIDS

Penetration	7"	London	HLU9847	1964	£20	£10	
Penetration	LP	Best	LPM1001/ BRS36501	1964	£40	£20	*US*

PYRAMIDS (2)

Pyramids	LP	President	PTL1021	1968	£15	£6	

PYRAMIDS (3)

Stay With Him	7"	Doctor Bird	DB1307	1969	£10	£5	

PYTHAGORAS

After The Silence	LP	WEA	58465	1981	£12	£5	*Dutch*
Journey To The Vast Unknown	LP	Syntone		1981	£25	£10	*Dutch*

q

Q65

Title	Format	Label	Cat. No.	Year	Mint	VG	Notes
Afghanistan	LP	Negram	NELP075	1969	**£100**	**£50**	*Dutch*
Greatest Hits	LP	Decca	6454409	1969	**£50**	**£25**	*Dutch*
Revival	LP	Decca	XBY846515	1969	**£125**	**£62.50**	*Dutch*
Revolution	LP	Decca	QL625363	1966	**£60**	**£30**	*Dutch*
We're Gonna Make It	LP	Negram	ELS914	1969	**£50**	**£25**	*Dutch*

Q-CHASTIC

Title	Format	Label	Cat. No.	Year	Mint	VG	Notes
Q-Chastic	7"	Rephlex	002EP	1992	**£30**	**£15**	*double*

QUAITE, CHRISTINE

Title	Format	Label	Cat. No.	Year	Mint	VG	Notes
Guilty Eyes	7"	Oriole	CB1739	1962	**£6**	**£2.50**	
Here She Comes	7"	Oriole	CB1921	1963	**£6**	**£2.50**	
If You've Got A Heart	7"	Stateside	SS435	1965	**£5**	**£2**	
In The Middle Of The Floor	7"	Oriole	CB1876	1963	**£6**	**£2.50**	
Long After Tonight Is All Over	7"	Stateside	SS482	1966	**£20**	**£10**	
Mister Heartache	7"	Oriole	CB1845	1963	**£6**	**£2.50**	
Will You Be The Same Tomorrow	7"	Oriole	CB1945	1964	**£6**	**£2.50**	
Your Nose Is Gonna Grow	7"	Oriole	CB1772	1962	**£6**	**£2.50**	

QUAKER CITY BOYS

Title	Format	Label	Cat. No.	Year	Mint	VG	Notes
Teasin'	7"	London	HLU8796	1959	**£6**	**£2.50**	

QUAKERS

Title	Format	Label	Cat. No.	Year	Mint	VG	Notes
I'm Ready	7"	Oriole	CB1992	1965	**£125**	**£62.50**	
She's Alright	7"	Studio 36	KSP109/110	1965	**£250**	**£150**	*best auctioned*

QUARRYMEN

Any value placed on the privately pressed copies of 'In Spite Of All The Danger' is necessarily speculative as no copy has yet been offered for sale. It seems reasonable, however, to place the record in line with the equally rare low-numbered first copies of the Beatles' *White Album*. The original acetate which was the source of this limited reissue (pressed by Paul McCartney for distribution to his family and friends) was recorded in 1958 by the Quarrymen, who included John Lennon, Paul McCartney and George Harrison among their number at the time. The acetate itself is a historical artefact of (probably) great value, but it is the property of Paul McCartney and never likely to be sold. It is interesting that the reissue was made, of course, but it is not historically significant in itself, while the actual music (both sides of the single) has been made available on the *Anthology I* compilation.

Title	Format	Label	Cat. No.	Year	Mint	VG	Notes
In Spite Of All The Danger	7"	Percy Phillips	no number	1981	**£5000**	**£3500**	*best auctioned*
In Spite Of All The Danger	78	Percy Phillips	no number	1981	**£5000**	**£3500**	*best auctioned*

QUARTER NOTES

Title	Format	Label	Cat. No.	Year	Mint	VG	Notes
Ten Minutes To Midnight	7"	Parlophone	R4365	1957	**£4**	**£1.50**	

QUARTERMAN, JOE & FREE SOUL

Title	Format	Label	Cat. No.	Year	Mint	VG	Notes
Joe Quarterman And Free Soul	LP	GSF	GS504	1973	**£50**	**£25**	
So Much Trouble In My Mind	7"	GSF	GSZ3	1973	**£4**	**£1.50**	

QUARTZ

Title	Format	Label	Cat. No.	Year	Mint	VG	Notes
Against All Odds	LP	Heavy Metal	HMRPD9	1983	**£10**	**£4**	*picture disc*
Nantucket Sleighride	7"	Reddingtons	DAN1	1980	**£5**	**£2**	*white vinyl*
Quartz	LP	Jet	UAG30081	1977	**£20**	**£8**	
Quartz Live – Count Dracula	LP	Reddingtons	REDD001	1980	**£10**	**£4**	*live sleeve*
Satan's Serenade	12"	Logo	GOT387	1980	**£8**	**£4**	*red vinyl*
Satan's Serenade	12"	Logo	GOT387	1980	**£15**	**£7.50**	*blue vinyl*
Satan's Serenade	7"	Sound For Industry	SFI549	1980	**£4**	**£1.50**	*flexi*
Stand Up And Fight	7"	MCA	MCA661	1981	**£5**	**£2**	
Stoking The Fires Of Hell	7"	MCA	MCA642	1980	**£4**	**£1.50**	
Street Fighting Lady	7"	Jet	UP36317	1977	**£6**	**£2.50**	
Street Fighting Lady	7"	Jet	SJET189	1980	**£4**	**£1.50**	
Sugar Rain	7"	Jet	UP36290	1977	**£8**	**£4**	
Tell Me Why	7"	Heavy Metal	HEAVY17	1983	**£4**	**£1.50**	

QUATERMASS

Title	Format	Label	Cat. No.	Year	Mint	VG	Notes
Quatermass	LP	Harvest	SHVL775	1970	**£40**	**£20**	

QUATRAIN

Title	Format	Label	Cat. No.	Year	Mint	VG	Notes
Quatrain	LP	Polydor	583743	1969	**£20**	**£8**	

QUATRO, SUZI

Title	Format	Label	Cat. No.	Year			Notes
Am I Dreaming	7"	Hackenbacker	HACK101	1987	£6	£2.50	
Greatest Hits	LP	RAK	GMTV24	1980	£15	£6	*test pressing*
Primitive Love	7"	RAK	PSR355	1973	£25	£12.50	*promo*
Quatro	LP	RAK	SRAK509	1974	£15	£6	*test pressing*
Rolling Stone	7"	RAK	RAK134	1972	£15	£7.50	

QUEBEC, IKE

Title	Format	Label	Cat. No.	Year			Notes
Blue And Sentimental	LP	Blue Note	BLP/BST84098	1963	£25	£10	
Bossa Nova – Soul Samba	LP	Blue Note	BLP/BST84114	1964	£25	£10	
Buzzard Lope	7"	Blue Note	451749	1964	£4	£1.50	
Heavy Soul	LP	Blue Note	BLP/BST84093	1961	£30	£15	
It Might As Well Be Spring	LP	Blue Note	BLP/BST84105	1964	£25	£10	

QUEEN

When EMI were given the Queen's Award to Industry, they were in a position to make an appropriate memento of the occasion and, accordingly, they pressed up a small number of copies of the group Queen's 'Bohemian Rhapsody' on royal blue vinyl. The choice has become doubly appropriate since then, for Queen went on to become one of EMI's bestselling acts. Since Freddie Mercury's death in November 1991, the values of Queen rarities have inevitably increased rapidly, as indeed have the solo records made by all four members. In addition to those items listed below, there have been coloured vinyl pressings of several Queen LPs issued in various countries and selling for £40–£50. The red vinyl UK pressing of *Sheer Heart Attack* that appears on several dealers' and collectors' want lists, however, would appear never to have been released.

Title	Format	Label	Cat. No.	Year			Notes
Another One Bites The Dust	7"	EMI	EMI5102	1980	£4	£1.50	*picture sleeve*
Another One Bites The Dust	CD-s	Parlophone	QUECD8	1988	£10	£5	*3" single*
Back Chat	12"	EMI	12EMI5325	1982	£20	£10	
Back Chat	7"	EMI	EMI5325	1982	£5	£2	*picture sleeve*
Bicycle Race	7"	EMI	EMI2870	1978	£4	£1.50	*picture sleeve*
Bicycle Race	7"	EMI	EMI2870	1978	£8	£4	*mispressed B side – plays Crystal Gale or Dollar*
Bicycle Race	7"	EMI	EMI2870	1978	£100	£50	*export picture sleeve*
Body Language	12"	EMI	12EMI5293	1982	£15	£7.50	
Bohemian Rhapsody	7"	EMI	EMI2375	1978	£2500	£1750	*blue vinyl, EMI envelope*
Bohemian Rhapsody	7"	EMI	EMI2375	1978	£3000	£2000	*blue vinyl, envelope, box of goblets & other goodies*
Bohemian Rhapsody	7"	EMI	EMI2375	1975	£2000	£1400	*blue vinyl, picture sleeve*
Bohemian Rhapsody	7"	EMI	EMI2375	1975	£25	£12.50	*picture sleeve*
Bohemian Rhapsody	7"	EMI	EMI2378	1975	£10	£5	*misprinted number*
Bohemian Rhapsody	7"	EMI	QUEENDJ95	1995	£150	£75	*purple vinyl*
Bohemian Rhapsody	CD-s	Parlophone	QUECD3	1988	£10	£5	*3" single*
Breakthru'	7"	EMI	QUEENPD11	1989	£25	£12.50	*shaped picture disc*
Breakthru'	CD-s	EMI	CDQUEEN11	1989	£20	£10	
Breakthru'	12"	Parlophone	12QUEEN11	1989	£6	£2.50	
Classic Queen	CD	Capitol	DPRO79591	1989	£30	£15	*US promo compilation*
Complete Works	LP	EMI	QB1	1985	£125	£62.50	*14 LP boxed set*
Complete Works	LP	EMI	QB1	1985	£400	£250	*14 LP boxed set, autographed*
Crazy Little Thing Called Love	7"	EMI	EMI5001	1979	£10	£5	*mispressed with 2 B sides*
Crazy Little Thing Called Love	CD-s	Parlophone	QUECD7	1988	£10	£5	*3" single*
Digital Master Sampler	CD	EMI	CDDIG1	1994	£75	£37.50	*promo compilation*
Don't Stop Me Now	7"	EMI	EMI2910	1979	£4	£1.50	*picture sleeve*
Eight Good Reasons To Buy Greatest Hits 2	cass	Parlophone		1991	£20	£8	*promo*
Five Live EP	CD-s	Parlophone	CDR6340	1993	£6	£2.50	
Friends Will Be Friends	12"	EMI	12QUEEN8	1986	£6	£2.50	
Friends Will Be Friends	7"	EMI	QUEENP8	1986	£30	£15	*picture disc*
Game	CD	Mobile Fidelity	UDCD610	1994	£15	£6	*US audiophile*
Greatest Hits	LP	EMI	EMTV30	1981	£12	£5	*mispress – side 2 plays Anne Murray*
Greatest Hits 2	LP	Parlophone	PMTV2	1991	£15	£6	*double*
Greatest Hits Volume Two	CD	Parlophone	CDPCSD161	1991	£100	£50	*promo box set, with video, photos, booklet*
Hammer To Fall	7"	EMI	QUEEN4	1984	£100	£50	*live picture sleeve*
Hammer To Fall (Headbangers Mix)	12"	EMI	12QUEEN4	1984	£8	£4	*red picture sleeve*
Hammer To Fall (Headbangers Mix)	12"	EMI	12QUEEN4	1984	£125	£62.50	*live picture sleeve*
Headlong	12"	Parlophone	12QUEENPD18	1991	£15	£7.50	*picture disc*
Headlong	CD-s	EMI	CDQUEEN18	1991	£10	£5	
Heaven For Everyone	12"	Parlophone	VIRGIN2	1996	£500	£330	*1 sided Virgin Radio prize*
Heaven For Everyone	7"	Parlophone	QUEENLHDJ21	1995	£15	£7.50	*jukebox issue with poster*
Highlander	CDV	EMI	EMCDV2	1986	£400	£250	
Hints Of Innuendo	cass	Parlophone		1991	£25	£10	*promo*
I Want It All	12"	Parlophone	12QUEEN10	1989	£8	£4	
I Want It All	CD-s	Parlophone	CDQUEEN10	1989	£20	£10	*picture disc*
I Want To Break Free	12"	EMI	12QUEEN2	1984	£8	£4	
I Want To Break Free	7"	EMI	QUEEN2	1984	£10	£5	*4 different picture sleeves, gold lettering*
I Want To Break Free	CD-s	Parlophone	QUECD11	1988	£10	£5	*3" single*

I Was Born To Love You	12"	Parlophone	VIRGIN8	1996	**£500**	**£330**	*1 sided Virgin Radio prize*
I'm Going Slightly Mad	12"	Parlophone	12QUEENG17	1991	**£10**	**£5**	*gatefold picture sleeve*
I'm Going Slightly Mad	7"	Parlophone	QUEENPD17	1991	**£15**	**£7.50**	*shaped picture disc*
I'm Going Slightly Mad	7"	Parlophone	QUEEN17	1991	**£4**	**£1.50**	
I'm Going Slightly Mad	CD-s	Parlophone	CDQUEEN17	1991	**£10**	**£5**	
Innuendo	12"	Parlophone	12QUEENPD16	1991	**£20**	**£10**	*picture disc*
Innuendo	CD	Parlophone	CDPCSD115	1991	**£100**	**£50**	*promo box set, with cassette, single and calendar*
Innuendo	CD	EMI	CDP7958870	1991	**£20**	**£8**	*German, with calendar*
Innuendo	CD-s	Parlophone	CDQUEEN16	1991	**£5**	**£2**	
Invisible Man	12"	EMI	12QUEENX12	1989	**£15**	**£7.50**	*clear vinyl*
Invisible Man	12"	Parlophone	12QUEEN12	1989	**£6**	**£2.50**	
Invisible Man	7"	Parlophone	QUEENX12	1989	**£8**	**£4**	*clear vinyl*
Invisible Man	7"	Parlophone	QUEEN12	1989	**£5**	**£2**	
Invisible Man	CD-s	Parlophone	CDQUEEN12	1989	**£25**	**£12.50**	
It's A Beautiful Day	12"	Parlophone	VIRGIN7	1996	**£500**	**£330**	*1 sided Virgin Radio prize*
It's A Hard Life	12"	EMI	12QUEENP3	1984	**£20**	**£10**	*picture disc*
It's A Hard Life	12"	EMI	12QUEEN3	1984	**£20**	**£10**	*no picture sleeve*
It's A Hard Life	7"	EMI	QUEEN3	1984	**£50**	**£25**	*John Taylor's head superimposed on cover pic*
Jazz	LP	EMI	PIC3	1978	**£200**	**£100**	*French picture disc*
Jealousy	7"	EMI		1979	**£25**	**£12.50**	*promo*
Keep Yourself Alive	7"	EMI	EMI2036	1973	**£20**	**£10**	
Killer Queen	CD-s	Parlophone	QUECD2	1988	**£10**	**£5**	*3" single*
Kind Of Magic	12"	EMI	12QUEEN7	1986	**£8**	**£4**	
Kind Of Magic	12"	EMI	12QUEENP7	1986	**£50**	**£25**	*picture disc*
Kind Of Magic	CD-s	Parlophone	QUECD12	1988	**£10**	**£5**	*3" single*
Let Me Live	12"	Parlophone	VIRGIN5	1996	**£500**	**£330**	*1 sided Virgin Radio prize*
Live At The BBC	LP	Hollywood	SPRO62005	1995	**£100**	**£50**	*US promo picture disc*
Live At Wembley	LP	Parlophone	PCSP725	1992	**£20**	**£8**	*double*
Love Of My Life	7"	EMI	EMI2959	1979	**£15**	**£7.50**	
Man On The Prowl	7"	EMI	QUEENDJ5	1984	**£100**	**£50**	*promo*
Message From Queen	7"	fan club		1989	**£20**	**£10**	*flexi*
Message From Queen	cass	fan club		1986	**£15**	**£7.50**	
Miracle	12"	Parlophone	12QUEEN15	1989	**£10**	**£5**	*yellow picture sleeve*
Miracle	12"	Parlophone	12QUEENP15	1989	**£15**	**£7.50**	*turquoise picture sleeve, insert*
Miracle	7"	Parlophone	QUEEN15	1989	**£4**	**£1.50**	
Miracle	7"	Parlophone	QUEENH15	1989	**£10**	**£5**	*hologram picture sleeve*
Miracle	CD	Parlophone	CDPCSD107	1989	**£75**	**£37.50**	*promo box set, with cassette sampler and booklet*
Miracle	CD-s	Parlophone	CDQUEEN15	1989	**£20**	**£10**	
Mother Love	12"	Parlophone	VIRGIN4	1996	**£500**	**£330**	*1 sided Virgin Radio prize*
News Of The World	LP	EMI	EMA784	1977	**£150**	**£75**	*promo, boxed*
News Of The World	LP	EMI		1977	**£250**	**£150**	*promo box set*
Night At The Opera	CD	Mobile Fidelity	UDCD568	1992	**£15**	**£6**	*US audiophile*
Night At The Opera	LP	Mobile Fidelity	MFSL1067	1980	**£20**	**£8**	*US audiophile*
Now I'm Here	7"	EMI	EMI2256	1975	**£5**	**£2**	
One Vision	12"	EMI	12QUEEN6	1985	**£25**	**£12.50**	*PVC cover, red inner*
One Vision	12"	EMI	12QUEEN6	1985	**£6**	**£2.50**	*with inner sleeve*
Play The Game	7"	EMI	EMI5076	1980	**£4**	**£1.50**	*picture sleeve*
Play The Game	7"	EMI	EMI5076	1980	**£10**	**£5**	*mispressed with 2 B sides*
Queen	LP	EMI	EMC3006	1973	**£50**	**£25**	*EMI conference copy, unfinished sleeve*
Queen	LP	Elektra	EQ5064	1973	**£20**	**£8**	*US quad*
Queen	LP	EMI		1973	**£200**	**£100**	*EMI conference promo*
Queen	LP	EMI		1973	**£300**	**£180**	*EMI conference promo, envelope*
Queen At The Beeb	LP	Band Of Joy	BOJLP001	1989	**£10**	**£4**	
Queen Rocks	CD	Hollywood		1991	**£150**	**£75**	*US promo 4 CD boxed set*
Queen Rocks	CD	Parlophone	CDQT1	1997	**£60**	**£30**	*interview promo*
Queen Rocks Volume Four	CD	Hollywood	PRCD82982	1991	**£30**	**£15**	*US promo sampler*
Queen Rocks Volume One	CD	Hollywood	PRCD82632	1991	**£30**	**£15**	*US promo sampler*
Queen Rocks Volume Three	CD	Hollywood	PRCD82972	1991	**£30**	**£15**	*US promo sampler*
Queen Rocks Volume Two	CD	Hollywood	PRCD82962	1991	**£30**	**£15**	*US promo sampler*
Queen Talks	CD	Hollywood	PRCD8674	1992	**£30**	**£15**	*US promo*
Queen's First EP	7" EP	EMI	EMI2623	1977	**£8**	**£4**	
Queen's First EP	CD-s	Parlophone	QUECD5	1988	**£10**	**£5**	*3" single*
Radio Ga Ga	12"	EMI	12QUEEN1	1984	**£6**	**£2.50**	
Radio Ga Ga	7"	EMI	QUEEN1	1984	**£400**	**£250**	*video shoot proof sleeve*
Radio Ga Ga	CD-s	Parlophone	QUECD10	1988	**£10**	**£5**	*3" single*
Sample Of Magic	CD	Parlophone		1991	**£75**	**£37.50**	*promo*

Scandal	12"	Parlophone	12QUEENS14	1989	£20	£10	*1 side etched with signatures*
Scandal	12"	Parlophone	12QUEEN14	1989	£6	£2.50	
Scandal	7"	Parlophone	QUEENP14	1989	£12	£6	*poster sleeve*
Scandal	7"	Parlophone	QUEEN14	1989	£5	£2	
Scandal	CD-s	Parlophone	CDQUEEN14	1989	£25	£12.50	
Seven Seas Of Rhye	7"	EMI	EMI2121	1974	£5	£2	
Seven Seas Of Rhye	CD-s	Parlophone	QUECD1	1988	£10	£5	*3" single*
Show Must Go On	12"	Parlophone	12QUEENSG19	1991	£15	£7.50	*1 side etched with signatures*
Show Must Go On	CD-s	Parlophone	CDQUEEN19	1991	£8	£4	
Show Must Go On	CD-s	Parlophone	CDQUEENS19	1991	£25	£12.50	*boxed with poster*
Show Must Go On/Bohemian Rhapsody	7"	Parlophone	QUEEN19/20	1991	£250	£150	*no picture sleeve*
Somebody To Love	7"	EMI	EMI2565	1976	£8	£4	*picture sleeve*
Somebody To Love	CD-s	Parlophone	QUECD4	1988	£10	£5	*3" single*
Spread Your Wings	7"	EMI	EMI2757	1978	£5	£2	*picture sleeve*
Teaser Tape	cass	Parlophone	TEASER1	1989	£10	£4	*promo*
Thank God It's Christmas	12"	EMI	12QUEEN5	1984	£10	£5	
Thank God It's Christmas	7"	EMI	QUEEN5	1984	£5	£2	
These Are The Days Of Our Lives	CD-s	Parlophone	CDQUEEN20	1991	£5	£2	
Tie Your Mother Down	7"	EMI	EMI2593	1977	£5	£2	
Too Much Love Will Kill You	7"	Parlophone	QUEENDJ23	1996	£5	£2	*jukebox issue*
Twelve Inch Collection (Box Of Trix)	cass	Parlophone	CQTEL0001	1992	£30	£15	*boxed set*
Twelve Inch Collection (Box Of Trix)	CD	Parlophone	CDQTEL0001	1992	£100	£50	*boxed set with video, badge, patch, T-shirt, booklet, poster*
Under Pressure	CD-s	Parlophone	QUECD9	1988	£12	£6	*3" single, with David Bowie*
Under Pressure (Live)	7"	EMI		1986	£25	£12.50	*promo*
We Are The Champions	7"	EMI	EMI2708	1977	£4	£1.50	*picture sleeve*
We Are The Champions	CD-s	Parlophone	QUECD6	1988	£10	£5	*3" single*
We Will Rock You	12"	EMI	SLP241A1U	1977	£150	£75	*1 sided test pressing*
Who Wants To Live Forever	12"	EMI	12QUEEN9	1986	£12	£6	
Who Wants To Live Forever	7"	EMI	QUEEN9	1986	£5	£2	
Winter's Tale	12"	Parlophone	VIRGIN3	1996	£500	£330	*1 sided Virgin Radio prize*
Winter's Tale	7"	Parlophone	QUEENDJ22	1995	£6	£2.50	*jukebox issue*
Works	7"	EMI	no number	1984	£8	£4	*promo flexi*
You Don't Fool Me	12"	Parlophone	VIRGIN6	1996	£500	£330	*1 sided Virgin Radio prize*
You Don't Fool Me (remixes)	12"	Parlophone	12RDJ6446	1996	£40	£20	*orange vinyl promo*
You're My Best Friend	7"	EMI	EMI2494	1976	£25	£12.50	*picture sleeve*

QUEEN'S NECTARINE MACHINE

Mystical Powers Of Roving Tarot Gamble	LP	ABC	ABCS666	1969	£30	£15	*US*

QUEENSRYCHE

Best I Can	CD-s	EMI	CDMT97	1991	£5	£2	
Empire	7"	EMI	MTPD90	1990	£6	£2.50	*shaped picture disc*
Empire	CD-s	EMI	CDMT90	1990	£5	£2	
Eyes Of A Stranger	12"	EMI	12MT65	1989	£6	£2.50	
Eyes Of A Stranger	12"	EMI	12MTG65	1989	£10	£5	*gatefold picture sleeve*
Eyes Of A Stranger	CD-s	EMI	CDMT65	1989	£8	£4	
Eyes Of A Stranger	CD-s	EMI	2033492	1989	£20	£10	
Gonna Get Close To You	12"	EMI	12EA22	1986	£10	£5	
Gonna Get Close To You	7"	EMI	EA22	1986	£10	£5	
Gonna Get Close To You	7"	EMI	EAD22	1986	£10	£5	*double*
Jet City Woman	CD-s	EMI	CDMT98	1991	£5	£2	
Operation Mindcrime	LP	EMI	SPRO04137	1988	£25	£10	*US promo picture disc*
Overseeing The Operation	10"	EMI	10QR1	1988	£10	£5	
Queen Of The Reich	12"	EMI	12EA162	1983	£10	£4	
Silent Lucidity	CD-s	EMI	CDMT94	1991	£5	£2	
Take Hold Of The Flame	7"	EMI	EA183	1984	£10	£5	

QUESTION MARK & THE MYSTERIANS

96 Tears	7"	Cameo Parkway	C428	1966	£12	£6	
96 Tears	7" EP	Columbia	ESRF1825	1966	£40	£20	*French*
96 Tears	LP	Cameo	C(S)2004	1966	£75	£37.50	*US*
Action	LP	Cameo	C(S)2006	1966	£75	£37.50	*US*
Can't Get Enough Of You Baby	7"	Cameo Parkway	C467	1967	£6	£2.50	
Can't Get Enough Of You Baby	7" EP	Stateside	FSE105	1967	£30	£15	*French*
Do Something To Me	7"	Cameo Parkway	C496	1967	£6	£2.50	
Girl	7" EP	Stateside	FSE1006	1967	£30	£15	*French*
I Need Somebody	7"	Cameo Parkway	C441	1966	£10	£5	
You Captivate Me	7"	Cameo Parkway	C479	1967	£6	£2.50	

QUESTIONS

We Got Love	7"	Decca	F22740	1968	£12	£6	

QUICK, BENNY & TWEN BAND

Title	Format	Label	Cat. No.	Year	Mint	VG	Notes
Twens Top	LP	Columbia	83874	1964	£25	£10	German

QUICKLY, TOMMY

Title	Format	Label	Cat. No.	Year	Mint	VG	Notes
Humpty Dumpty	7"	Pye	7N15748	1964	£8	£4	
Kiss Me Now	7"	Piccadilly	7N35151	1963	£4	£1.50	
Prove It	7"	Piccadilly	7N35167	1964	£4	£1.50	
Tip Of My Tongue	7"	Piccadilly	7N35137	1963	£20	£10	
Wild Side Of Life	7"	Pye	7N15708	1964	£4	£1.50	
You Might As Well Forget Him	7"	Piccadilly	7N35183	1964	£4	£1.50	

QUICKSAND

Title	Format	Label	Cat. No.	Year	Mint	VG	Notes
Home Is Where I Belong	LP	Dawn	DNLS3056	1974	£40	£20	
Passing By	7"	Carnaby	CNS4015	1970	£4	£1.50	
Time To Live	7"	Dawn	DNS1046	1973	£4	£1.50	

QUICKSILVER MESSENGER SERVICE

Title	Format	Label	Cat. No.	Year	Mint	VG	Notes
Comin' Thru'	LP	Capitol	ST11002	1972	£10	£4	
Happy Trails	LP	Capitol	E(S)T120	1969	£15	£6	
Just For Love	LP	Capitol	EAST498	1970	£10	£4	
Maiden Of The Cancer Moon	LP	Psycho	PSYCHO10	1983	£40	£20	double
Quicksilver	LP	Capitol	SW819	1972	£10	£4	
Quicksilver Messenger Service	LP	Capitol	(S)T2904	1968	£20	£8	
Shady Grove	LP	Capitol	EST391	1969	£10	£4	
What About Me	LP	Capitol	EAST630	1971	£10	£4	

QUIET FIVE

Title	Format	Label	Cat. No.	Year	Mint	VG	Notes
Homeward Bound	7"	Parlophone	R5421	1966	£4	£1.50	
Honeysuckle Rose	7"	Parlophone	R5302	1965	£4	£1.50	
I Am Waiting	7"	Parlophone	R5470	1966	£4	£1.50	
When The Morning Sun Dries The Dew	7"	Parlophone	R5273	1965	£10	£5	picture sleeve
When The Morning Sun Dries The Dew	7"	Parlophone	R5273	1965	£4	£1.50	

QUIET WORLD

Guitarist with Quiet World, prior to his joining Genesis, was the young Steve Hackett.

Title	Format	Label	Cat. No.	Year	Mint	VG	Notes
Love Is Walking	7"	Dawn	DNS1005	1970	£20	£10	
Miss Whittington	7"	Dawn	DNS1001	1969	£20	£10	
Rest Comfortably	7"	Pye	7N45005	1970	£8	£4	
Road	LP	Dawn	DNLS3007	1970	£50	£25	
Visitor	7"	Pye	7N45074	1971	£5	£2	

QUIK

Title	Format	Label	Cat. No.	Year	Mint	VG	Notes
I Can't Sleep	7"	Deram	DM155	1967	£50	£25	
King Of The World	7"	Deram	DM139	1967	£50	£25	
Love Is A Beautiful Thing	7"	Deram	DM121	1967	£50	£25	

QUILL, GENE

Title	Format	Label	Cat. No.	Year	Mint	VG	Notes
Three Bones And A Quill	LP	Vogue	LAE12204	1959	£20	£8	

QUINCICASM

Title	Format	Label	Cat. No.	Year	Mint	VG	Notes
Quincicasm	LP	Saydisc	SDL249	1973	£15	£6	

QUINICHETTE, PAUL

Title	Format	Label	Cat. No.	Year	Mint	VG	Notes
Basie Reunion	LP	Esquire	32087	1960	£20	£8	
For Basie	LP	Esquire	32067	1959	£25	£10	

QUINTESSENCE

Quintessence seemed to epitomize hippiedom – living communally, radiating peace and love, and above all being obsessed with Eastern religion and music. The group's albums are a smooth blend of Indian chanting and English electric guitar, the two being held together by Raja Ram's fluid, melodic flute playing. They are among the most successful attempts to fuse Eastern and Western musics, although the hippy context will inevitably make the music sound rather dated to modern listeners.

Title	Format	Label	Cat. No.	Year	Mint	VG	Notes
Dive Deep	LP	Island	ILPS9143	1970	£12	£5	
In Blissful Company	LP	Island	ILPS9110	1969	£25	£10	pink label
Indweller	LP	RCA	SF8317	1972	£10	£4	
Notting Hill Gate	7"	Island	WIP6075	1970	£4	£1.50	
Quintessence	LP	Island	ILPS9128	1970	£25	£10	pink label
Self	LP	RCA	SF8273	1971	£10	£4	
Sweet Jesus	7"	Neon	NE1003	1971	£10	£5	picture sleeve
Sweet Jesus	7"	Neon	NE1003	1971	£4	£1.50	

QUINTET OF THE YEAR

Title	Format	Label	Cat. No.	Year	Mint	VG	Notes
Jazz At Massey Hall	LP	Vogue	LAE12031	1957	£100	£50	
Jazz At Massey Hall Vol. 1	10" LP	Vogue	LDE040	1954	£100	£50	
Jazz At Massey Hall Vol. 2	10" LP	Vogue	LDE053	1954	£100	£50	
Jazz At Massey Hall Vol. 3	10" LP	Vogue	LDE087	1954	£100	£50	

QUIREBOYS

Title	Format	Label	Cat. No.	Year	Mint	VG	Notes
Hey You	CD-s	Parlophone	CDR6241	1989	£5	£2	
I Don't Love You Anymore	CD-s	Parlophone	CDR6248	1989	£5	£2	
Seven O'Clock	CD-s	Parlophone	CDR6230	1989	£5	£2	

QUIST, DARYL

Title	Format	Label	Cat. No.	Year	Mint	VG	Notes
Above And Beyond	7"	Pye	7N15605	1964	£4	£1.50	
Thanks To You	7"	Pye	7N15538	1963	£5	£2	picture sleeve

QUO VARDIS

100 mph .... 7" .... Redball .... RB001 .... 1979 £**10** .... £**5** ....

QUODLING'S DELIGHT

Among The Leaves So Green .... LP .... Volta .... Q121 .... 197– £**20** .... £**8** ....
Among The Leaves So Green .... LP .... Fanfare .... FR2179 .... 197– £**20** .... £**8** ....

QUOTATIONS

Imagination .... 7" .... HMV .... POP975 .... 1962 £**30** .... £**15** ....

QUOTATIONS *(2)*

Alright Baby .... 7" .... Decca .... F11907 .... 1964 £**8** .... £**4** ....
Cool It .... 7" .... CBS .... 3710 .... 1968 £**5** .... £**2** ....
Hello Memories .... 7" .... CBS .... 4378 .... 1969 £**4** .... £**1.50** ....

RA CAN ROW

Acid Rock For The Eighties ... LP ... Eye ... 8107 ... 1982 **£20** ... **£8** ... *US*

RABBLE

Rabble ... LP ... Roulette ... SR42010 ... 1969 **£100** ... **£50** ... *US*
Rabble Album ... LP ... Transworld ... 6700 ... 1966 **£100** ... **£50** ... *US*

RABIN, MIKE

Head Over Heels ... 7" ... Columbia ... DB7350 ... 1964 **£25** ... **£12.50** ...
If I Were You ... 7" ... Polydor ... BM56007 ... 1965 **£10** ... **£5** ...

RACAILLE, JOSEPH

Six Petites Chansons ... 7" ... Recommended ... RR16.5 ... 1983 **£8** ... **£4** ... *clear vinyl*

RACHELL, YANK TENNESSEE JUG BUSTERS

Mandolin Blues ... LP ... 77 ... LA1223 ... 1964 **£15** ... **£6** ...

RACHEL & THE REVOLVERS

'The Revo-Lution' is one of several early Brian Wilson productions.

Revo-Lution ... 7" ... Dot ... 16392 ... 1962 **£250** ... **£150** ... *US, best auctioned*

RADAR

Leave Her Alone ... 7" ... House Of Wax ... WAX1 ... 1983 **£15** ... **£7.50** ...

RADAVIQUE

B Sides ... LP ... Radavique ... ... 1984 **£150** ... **£75** ... *Dutch*

RADCLIFFE, JIMMY

Long After Tonight Is All Over ... 7" ... Stateside ... SS374 ... 1965 **£25** ... **£12.50** ...

RADHA KRISHNA TEMPLE

Govinda ... 7" ... Apple ... 25 ... 1970 **£10** ... **£5** ... *picture sleeve*
Hare Krishna Mantra ... 7" ... Apple ... 15 ... 1969 **£5** ... **£2** ...
Hare Krishna Mantra ... 7" ... Apple ... 15 ... 1969 **£12** ... **£6** ... *picture sleeve, insert*
Radha Krishna Temple ... LP ... Apple ... SAPCOR18 ... 1971 **£30** ... **£15** ...

RADIANTS

Hold On ... 7" ... Chess ... CRS8073 ... 1968 **£6** ... **£2.50** ...
Voice Your Choice ... 7" ... Chess ... CRS8002 ... 1965 **£10** ... **£5** ...

RADIATORS FROM SPACE

Song Of The Faithful Departed ... 7" ... Chiswick ... CHIS144 ... 1979 **£5** ... **£2** ... *Irish*
Sunday World ... 7" ... CBS ... 5572 ... 1977 **£15** ... **£7.50** ... *Irish*
Teenager In Love ... 7" ... Chiswick ... NS24 ... 1978 **£15** ... **£7.50** ... *test pressing*
Walkin' Home Alone Again ... 7" ... Chiswick ... NS45 ... 1979 **£15** ... **£7.50** ... *test presing*

RADIO ACTORS

Nuclear Waste ... 7" ... DB ... DBS5 ... 1979 **£4** ... **£1.50** ... *picture sleeve*
Nuclear Waste ... 7" ... Charly ... CYS1058 ... 1979 **£4** ... **£1.50** ... *picture sleeve*

RADIO BIRDMAN

Aloha Steve And Danno ... 7" ... Trafalgar ... TRS12 ... 1978 **£6** ... **£2.50** ...
Alone In The Endzone ... 7" ... WEA ... 100160 ... 1981 **£50** ... **£25** ...
Burn My Eye ... 7" ... Trafalgar ... ME109 ... 1976 **£100** ... **£50** ...
New Race ... 7" ... Trafalgar ... TRS11 ... 1977 **£50** ... **£25** ...
Radios Appear ... LP ... Sire ... 9103332 ... 1978 **£15** ... **£6** ...
Radios Appear (Second Version) ... LP ... Sire ... SRK6050 ... 1978 **£10** ... **£4** ...
What Gives? ... 7" ... Sire ... 6078617 ... 1978 **£6** ... **£2.50** ...

RADIO HEART

All Across The Nation ... CD-s ... NBR ... CDNBR1 ... 1987 **£6** ... **£2.50** ...
Radio Heart ... CD ... NBR ... ... 1987 **£40** ... **£20** ... *European*

RADIOHEAD

Anyone Can Play Guitar ... 12" ... Parlophone ... 12R6333 ... 1993 **£15** ... **£7.50** ...
Anyone Can Play Guitar ... CD-s ... EMI ... CDR6333 ... 1993 **£25** ... **£12.50** ...
Bends ... CD-s ... Parlophone ... 8831152 ... 1995 **£15** ... **£7.50** ... *export*
Creep ... 12" ... Parlophone ... 12R6078 ... 1992 **£25** ... **£12.50** ...

Title	Format	Label	Cat. No.	Year	Mint	VG	Notes
Creep	12"	Parlophone	12RG6359	1993	£15	£7.50	
Creep	7"	Parlophone	RS6359	1993	£12	£6	*clear vinyl*
Creep	CD-s	Parlophone	CDR6359	1993	£15	£7.50	*digipak*
Creep	CD-s	Parlophone	CDR6078	1992	£30	£15	
Fake Plastic Trees	CD-s	Parlophone	CDR6411	1995	£15	£7.50	*with poster*
Fake Plastic Trees	CD-s	Parlophone	CDRS6411	1995	£6	£2.50	
Just	CD-s	Parlophone	CDR6415	1995	£10	£5	*boxed with 2 prints*
My Iron Lung	12"	Parlophone	12R6394	1994	£8	£4	
My Iron Lung	CD-s	Parlophone	CDRS6394	1994	£10	£5	
My Iron Lung	CD-s	Parlophone	CDR6394	1994	£10	£5	
Pop Is Dead	12"	Parlophone	12R6345	1993	£12	£6	
Pop Is Dead	CD-s	EMI	CDR6345	1993	£25	£12.50	
Prove Yourself (Drill EP)	12"	Parlophone	12R6312	1992	£40	£20	
Prove Yourself (Drill EP)	CD-s	Parlophone	CDR6312	1992	£75	£37.50	
Ripcord	12"	Parlophone	12RDJ6369	1993	£20	£10	*promo*
Stop Whispering	CD-s	Parlophone	CDRDJ6369	1993	£10	£5	*promo*
Street Spirit (Fade Out)	7"	Parlophone	R6419	1996	£5	£2	*white vinyl*
Street Spirit (Fade Out)	CD-s	Parlophone	CDR6419	1996	£6	£2.50	*with poster*

RAEBURN, BOYD

Title	Format	Label	Cat. No.	Year	Mint	VG	Notes
Teen Rock	LP	Columbia	CL1073	1957	£30	£15	*US*

RAELETS

Title	Format	Label	Cat. No.	Year	Mint	VG	Notes
One Hurt Deserves Another	7"	HMV	POP1591	1967	£5	£2	

RAFFERTY, GERRY

Title	Format	Label	Cat. No.	Year	Mint	VG	Notes
Baker Street (remix)	CD-s	EMI	CDEM132	1990	£5	£2	

RAG DOLLS

Title	Format	Label	Cat. No.	Year	Mint	VG	Notes
Dusty	7"	Stateside	SS398	1965	£5	£2	
Society Girl	7"	Cameo Parkway	P921	1964	£5	£2	

RAG DOLLS (2)

Title	Format	Label	Cat. No.	Year	Mint	VG	Notes
My Old Man's A Groovy Old Man	7"	Columbia	DB8378	1968	£4	£1.50	
Never Had So Much Loving	7"	Columbia	DB8289	1967	£4	£1.50	

RAGE

Title	Format	Label	Cat. No.	Year	Mint	VG	Notes
Cry From A Hill	7"	Carrere	CAR304	1983	£6	£2.50	
Money	10"	Carrere	CAR159CT	1980	£6	£2.50	*red vinyl*
Out Of Control	12"	Carrere	CAR182CT	1981	£6	£2.50	*yellow vinyl*

RAGE (2)

Title	Format	Label	Cat. No.	Year	Mint	VG	Notes
Looking For You	12"	Diamond	RAGE112	1986	£50	£25	*test pressing*

RAGGED HEROES

Title	Format	Label	Cat. No.	Year	Mint	VG	Notes
Ragged Heroes Annual	LP	Celtic Music	CM013	1983	£200	£100	

RAGING STORMS

Title	Format	Label	Cat. No.	Year	Mint	VG	Notes
Dribble	7"	London	HLU9556	1962	£15	£7.50	

RAGLAND, LOU

Title	Format	Label	Cat. No.	Year	Mint	VG	Notes
Since You Said You'd Be Mine	7"	Warner Bros	K16312	1973	£5	£2	

RAGNAROK

Title	Format	Label	Cat. No.	Year	Mint	VG	Notes
Fata Morgana	LP	Silence	SRS4666	1981	£12	£5	*Swedish*
Fjarliar I Magen	LP	Silence	SRS4655	1980	£12	£5	*Swedish*
Ragnarok	LP	Silence	SRS4633	1977	£15	£6	*Swedish*
Three Signs	LP	Silence	SRS126704	1984	£10	£4	*Swedish*
Undertakers Circus	LP	Polydor	2382025	1973	£20	£8	*Swedish*

RAHMANN

Title	Format	Label	Cat. No.	Year	Mint	VG	Notes
Rahmann	LP	Polydor	2393252	1979	£30	£15	*French*

RAILWAY CHILDREN

Title	Format	Label	Cat. No.	Year	Mint	VG	Notes
Music From The East Zone	7"	Gross Product	OBCT1	1983	£5	£2	*with tracks by other artists*

RAIN

Title	Format	Label	Cat. No.	Year	Mint	VG	Notes
Album	LP	Axe	501	1976	£20	£8	*Canadian*

RAIN (2)

Title	Format	Label	Cat. No.	Year	Mint	VG	Notes
Live Xmas Night	LP	Whazoo!	USR3046	1968	£100	£50	*US*

RAIN (3)

Title	Format	Label	Cat. No.	Year	Mint	VG	Notes
Rain	LP	Project	3	1972	£15	£6	*US*

RAIN (4)

Title	Format	Label	Cat. No.	Year	Mint	VG	Notes
Once	7"	Jive Alive	JA002	1985	£4	£1.50	

RAINBEAUS

Title	Format	Label	Cat. No.	Year	Mint	VG	Notes
That's All I'm Asking Of You	7"	Vogue	V9161	1960	£75	£37.50	

RAINBOW

Title	Format	Label	Cat. No.	Year	Mint	VG	Notes
Can't Let You Go	7"	Polydor	POSPP654	1983	£6	£2.50	*shaped picture disc*
L.A. Connection	7"	Polydor	2066968	1978	£5	£2	*red vinyl*
On Stage	LP	Polydor	2808010	1977	£30	£15	
Street Of Dreams	7"	Polydor	POSPP631	1983	£15	£7.50	*picture disc*

RAINBOW *(2)*

After The Storm	LP	Crescendo	GNPS2049	1968	**£40**	**£20**	US

RAINBOW FFOLLY

Sallies Fforth is one of the more interesting post-*Sgt Pepper* albums, and should be filed next to the first Blossom Toes LP by all those with any interest in the musical delights of the best of late sixties music. The tracks were apparently recorded as demos, but it was felt that the group would not be able to improve on them, so that they were released just as they were. It was originally intended that the album should have a round sleeve, but the group was beaten at the starting gate by the Small Faces. I am informed by Mary Payne, whose husband was a founder member of Wycombe Hospital Radio, that the group also recorded a number of jingles for the station, although these never made it beyond the tape stage.

Drive My Car	7"	Parlophone	R5701	1968	**£25**	**£12.50**	
Sallies Fforth	LP	Parlophone	PMC/PCS7050	1967	**£200**	**£100**	

RAINBOW PEOPLE

Dream Time	7"	Pye	7N17582	1968	**£6**	**£2.50**	
Living In A Dream World	7"	Pye	7N17759	1969	**£4**	**£1.50**	

RAINBOW PRESS

Sunday Funnies	LP	Mr.G	9004	1969	**£75**	**£37.50**	US
There's A War On	LP	Mr.G	9003	1968	**£75**	**£37.50**	US

RAINBOW PROMISE

Rainbow Promise	LP	Wine Press	LPS25901	1970	**£400**	**£250**	US

RAINBOWS

Rainbows	LP	CBS	62625	1966	**£100**	**£50**	German

RAINBOWS *(2)*

Rainbows	7"	CBS	3995	1969	**£5**	**£2**	

RAINCHECKS

How Are You Baby	7"	R&B	MRB5002	1965	**£20**	**£10**	
Something About You	7"	Solar	SRP104	1964	**£6**	**£2.50**	

RAINDROPS

Book Of Love	7"	Fontana	TF463	1964	**£6**	**£2.50**	
Kind Of Boy You Can't Forget	7"	London	HL9769	1963	**£8**	**£4**	
Raindrops	LP	London	HA8140	1964	**£40**	**£20**	
That Boy John	7"	London	HL9825	1964	**£6**	**£2.50**	
What A Guy	7"	London	HL9718	1963	**£8**	**£4**	
What A Guy	7" EP	London	RE1415	1964	**£50**	**£25**	

RAINDROPS *(2)*

Along Came Jones	7"	Parlophone	R4559	1959	**£4**	**£1.50**	
Let's Make A Foursome	7"	Oriole	CB1544	1960	**£4**	**£1.50**	
Will You Love Me Tomorrow	7"	Oriole	CB1595	1961	**£4**	**£1.50**	

RAINE, LORRY

Love Me Tonight	7"	London	HL8132	1955	**£20**	**£10**	
You Broke My Broken Heart	7"	London	HL8043	1954	**£20**	**£10**	

RAINEY, MA

Female Blues Vol. 3	7" EP	Collector	JEL22	1964	**£10**	**£5**	*with Trixie Smith*
Ma Rainey	10" LP	Ristic	LP13	195–	**£25**	**£10**	
Ma Rainey	10" LP	Ristic	LP19	195–	**£25**	**£10**	
Mother Of The Blues	LP	Riverside	RLP8807	1964	**£12**	**£5**	
Sings The Blues	LP	Riverside	RL12108	1962	**£15**	**£6**	
Vol. 1	10" LP	London	AL3502	1953	**£25**	**£10**	
Vol. 2	10" LP	London	AL3538	1955	**£25**	**£10**	
Vol. 3	10" LP	London	AL3558	1956	**£25**	**£10**	

RAINMAN

Rainman	LP	Negram	NQ20038	1971	**£75**	**£37.50**	Dutch

RAINWATER, MARVIN

Country & Western Favourites Vol. 2	7" EP	Ember	EMBEP4521	1962	**£12**	**£6**	
Dance Me Daddy	7"	MGM	MGM988	1958	**£6**	**£2.50**	
Gonna Find Me A Bluebird	7"	MGM	MGM961	1957	**£15**	**£7.50**	
Gonna Find Me A Bluebird	LP	MGM	E4046	1962	**£30**	**£15**	US
Half Breed	7"	MGM	MGM1030	1959	**£6**	**£2.50**	
I Can't Forget	7"	London	HLU9447	1961	**£75**	**£37.50**	
I Dig You Baby	7"	MGM	MGM980	1958	**£5**	**£2**	
Marvin Rainwater	7" EP	MGM	MGMEP685	1958	**£40**	**£30**	
Meet Marvin Rainwater	7" EP	MGM	MGMEP647	1958	**£30**	**£15**	
Nothin' Needs Nothin'	7"	MGM	MGM1052	1960	**£6**	**£2.50**	
Songs By Marvin Rainwater	10" LP	MGM	D152	1957	**£60**	**£30**	
Songs By Marvin Rainwater	LP	MGM	E3534	1957	**£60**	**£30**	US
Tennessee Hound Dog Yodel	7"	MGM	SP1150	1955	**£30**	**£15**	
What Am I Supposed To Do	7"	MGM	MGM929	1956	**£15**	**£7.50**	
Whole Lotta Marvin	7" EP	MGM	MGMEP662	1958	**£40**	**£20**	
Whole Lotta Woman	7"	MGM	MGM974	1958	**£5**	**£2**	
With A Heart, With A Beat	LP	MGM	E3721	1958	**£40**	**£20**	US

RAINY DAY

Painting Pictures	7"	EMI	EMI5472	1984	**£8**	**£4**	

RAINY DAZE

Title	Format	Label	Cat. No.	Year	Mint	VG	Notes
Blood Of Oblivion	7"	Polydor	BM56737	1968	**£15**	**£7.50**	
That Acapulco Gold	7"	Polydor	56731	1968	**£25**	**£12.50**	
That Acapulco Gold	LP	Uni	(7)3002	1967	**£50**	**£25**	*US*
What Do You Think	7"	CBS	3200	1967	**£15**	**£7.50**	

RAISINS

Title	Format	Label	Cat. No.	Year	Mint	VG	Notes
Ain't That Lovin' You Baby	7"	Major Minor	MM540	1968	**£4**	**£1.50**	

RAITT, BONNIE

Title	Format	Label	Cat. No.	Year	Mint	VG	Notes
I Can't Make You Love Me	CD-s	Capitol	CDCLS639	1991	**£5**	**£2**	*boxed*
Nick Of Time	CD-s	Capitol	CDCL530	1990	**£5**	**£2**	
Thing Called Love	CD-s	Capitol	CDCL576	1990	**£5**	**£2**	

RALLY ROUNDERS

'Bike Beat' is actually the work of the Outlaws, with Ritchie Blackmore on guitar.

Title	Format	Label	Cat. No.	Year	Mint	VG	Notes
Bike Beat	7"	Lyntone	LYN574	1964	**£50**	**£25**	*flexi*

RAM

Title	Format	Label	Cat. No.	Year	Mint	VG	Notes
Where? In Conclusion	LP	Polydor	POLD5013	1972	**£30**	**£15**	*US*

RAM, BUCK

Title	Format	Label	Cat. No.	Year	Mint	VG	Notes
Benfica	7"	London	HLU9677	1963	**£6**	**£2.50**	
Magic Touch	LP	Mercury	MG2/SR60392	1960	**£12**	**£5**	*US*

RAM JAM BAND

Title	Format	Label	Cat. No.	Year	Mint	VG	Notes
Shake Shake Senora	7"	Columbia	DB7621	1965	**£5**	**£2**	

RAMASES

Title	Format	Label	Cat. No.	Year	Mint	VG	Notes
Ballroom	7"	Philips	6113001	1971	**£4**	**£1.50**	
Crazy One	7"	CBS	3717	1968	**£60**	**£30**	*with Selket*
Glass Top Coffin	LP	Vertigo	6360115	1975	**£12**	**£5**	
Jesus Come Back	7"	Philips	6113003	1972	**£4**	**£1.50**	
Love You	7"	Major Minor	MM704	1970	**£12**	**£6**	*with Seleka*
Space Hymns	LP	Vertigo	6360046	1973	**£12**	**£5**	
Space Hymns	LP	Vertigo	6360046	1971	**£25**	**£10**	*spiral label*

RAMATAM

Title	Format	Label	Cat. No.	Year	Mint	VG	Notes
In April Came The Dawning	LP	Atlantic	SD7261	1973	**£10**	**£4**	*US*

RAMBLERS

Title	Format	Label	Cat. No.	Year	Mint	VG	Notes
Dodge City	7"	Decca	F11775	1963	**£20**	**£10**	

RAMBLETTES

Title	Format	Label	Cat. No.	Year	Mint	VG	Notes
Thinking Of You	7"	Brunswick	05932	1965	**£5**	**£2**	

RAMON & THE CRYSTALITES

Title	Format	Label	Cat. No.	Year	Mint	VG	Notes
Golden Chickens	7"	Songbird	SB1053	1971	**£5**	**£2**	

RAMONES

Title	Format	Label	Cat. No.	Year	Mint	VG	Notes
Blitzkrieg Bop	7"	Sire	6078601	1976	**£75**	**£37.50**	*picture sleeve*
Chasing The Night	12"	Beggars Banquet	BEGTP128	1985	**£6**	**£2.50**	
Chasing The Night	7"	Beggars Banquet	BEG128D	1985	**£5**	**£2**	*double*
Don't Come Close	12"	Sire	SRE1031	1978	**£8**	**£4**	*yellow or red vinyl*
Don't Come Close	7"	Sire	SRE1031	1978	**£5**	**£2**	*picture sleeve*
I Remember You	7"	Sire	6078603	1977	**£15**	**£7.50**	*picture sleeve*
I Wanna Be Sedated	7"	RSO	RSO70	1981	**£5**	**£2**	
Meltdown With The Ramones	7"	Sire	SREP1	1980	**£6**	**£2.50**	
Poison Heart	CD-s	Chrysalis	CDCHSS3917	1992	**£5**	**£2**	
Ramones	LP	Sire	9103253	1976	**£10**	**£4**	*with insert*
Ramones Leave Home	LP	Sire	9103254	1977	**£15**	**£6**	*with 'Carbona Not Glue'*
Rock'n'Roll High School	7"	Sire	SIR4021	1979	**£5**	**£2**	*picture sleeve*
Rockaway Beach	12"	Sire	6078611	1977	**£15**	**£7.50**	*with poster*
Rockaway Beach	7"	Sire	6078611	1977	**£5**	**£2**	*picture sleeve*
She's A Sensation	7"	Sire	SIR4052	1981	**£10**	**£5**	
She's The One	7"	Sire	SIR4009	1979	**£5**	**£2**	
Sheena Is A Punk Rocker	12"	Sire	6078606	1977	**£10**	**£5**	*with T-shirt offer*
Sheena Is A Punk Rocker	12"	Sire	6078606	1977	**£6**	**£2.50**	
Sheena Is A Punk Rocker	7"	Sire	6078606	1977	**£10**	**£5**	*picture sleeve*
Sheena Is A Punk Rocker	7"	Sire	6078606	1977	**£5**	**£2**	
Somebody Put Something In My Drink	12"	Beggars Banquet	BEG157T	1986	**£10**	**£5**	*with poster*
Swallow My Pride	7"	Sire	6078607	1977	**£5**	**£2**	
Time Has Come Today	12"	Sire	WT9606	1983	**£15**	**£7.50**	
Time Has Come Today	7"	Sire	W9606	1983	**£8**	**£4**	
We Want The Airwaves	7"	Sire	SIR4051	1981	**£6**	**£2.50**	

RAMPART STREET PARADERS

Title	Format	Label	Cat. No.	Year	Mint	VG	Notes
Rampart And Vine	LP	Philips	BBL7194	1958	**£15**	**£6**	
Rampart Street Paraders	LP	Philips	BBL7112	1957	**£15**	**£6**	

RAMRODS

Title	Format	Label	Cat. No.	Year	Mint	VG	Notes
Loch Lomond Rock	7"	London	HLU9355	1961	**£6**	**£2.50**	

Riders In The Sky 7" London HLU9282 1961 £**4** £**1.50**
Riders In The Sky 7" EP London REU1292 1961 £**60** £**30**

RAMRODS (2)

Overdrive 7" United Artists UP1113 1965 £**5** £**2**

RAMSEY, BILL

Go Man Go 7" Polydor NH66812 1962 £**5** £**2**

RANALDO, LEE

From Here To Infinity 12" Blast First BFFP9 1987 £**6** £**2.50** *clear vinyl*

RANCHERS

American Sailor At The Cavern 7" Cavern Sound IMSTL2 1965 £**15** £**7.50**

RANDALL, FREDDY

Chicago Jazz 7" EP Parlophone GEP8715 1958 £**8** £**4**
Dr Jazz 10" LP Parlophone PMD1046 1957 £**10** £**4**

RANDAZZO, TEDDY

Big Wide World LP Colpix CP445 1963 £**40** £**20** *US*
Dance To The Locomotion 7" HMV POP1062 1962 £**4** £**1.50**
Hey, Let's Twist LP Roulette R25168 1962 £**40** £**20** *US*
I'm Confessin' LP Vik LX1121 1960 £**40** £**20** *US*
Journey To Love LP HMV CLP1527/CSD1421 1962 £**40** £**20**
Twists LP HMV CLP1601 1963 £**50** £**25**

RANDELL, LYNNE

Ciao Baby 7" CBS 2847 1967 £**100** £**50**
That's A Hoe Down 7" CBS 2927 1967 £**6** £**2.50**

RANDELLS

Martian Hop 7" London HLU9760 1963 £**15** £**7.50**

RANDI, DON

Live At The Discotheque 7" EP Reprise RVEP6102 1967 £**6** £**2.50** *French*

RANDOLPH, BARBARA

I Got A Feeling 7" Tamla Motown TMG628 1967 £**25** £**12.50**
I Got A Feeling 7" Tamla Motown TMG788 1971 £**4** £**1.50**

RANDOLPH, BOOTS

Hey Mr Sax Man 7" London HLU9891 1964 £**4** £**1.50**
More Yakety Sax LP London HAU8280 1966 £**15** £**6**
Yakety Sax 7" London HLU9685 1963 £**5** £**2**
Yakety Sax LP London HAU8106 1963 £**15** £**6**
Yakety Sax Of Boots Randolph 7" EP London REU1365 1963 £**15** £**7.50**

RANDOM BLUES BAND

Winchester Cathedral 7" EP Vogue INT18103 1966 £**6** £**2.50** *French*

RANDY & THE RAINBOWS

Denise 7" Stateside SS214 1963 £**25** £**12.50**

RANEE & RAJ

Don't Tell Me I Must Go 7" Fontana TF941 1968 £**4** £**1.50**
Feel Like A Clown 7" Fontana TF920 1968 £**5** £**2**

RANEY, JIMMY

In Three Attitudes LP HMV CLP1264 1959 £**20** £**8**
Jimmy Raney 1955 10" LP Esquire 20054 1955 £**40** £**20**
Visits Paris 10" LP Vogue LDE071 1954 £**40** £**20**
Visits Paris Vol. 2 10" LP Vogue LDE097 1955 £**40** £**20**

RANEY, SUE

When Your Lover Has Gone 7" EP Capitol EAP1964 1958 £**8** £**4**

RANEY, WAYNE

Adam 7" Parlophone CSMP20 1954 £**20** £**10** *export*
Country And Western 7" EP Parlophone GEP8746 1958 £**25** £**12.50**

RANGLERS

You Never Said Goodbye 7" Trend TRE1007 1968 £**10** £**5**

RANGLIN, ERNEST

Harmonica Twist 7" Island WI015 1962 £**10** £**5**
Reflections LP Island ILP915 1964 £**40** £**20**
Soho 7" EP Black Swan IEP704 1966 £**25** £**12.50**
Swing-A-Ling 7" Black Swan WI417 1964 £**10** £**5**
Wranglin' LP Island ILP909 1964 £**50** £**25**

RANIERI, MASSIMO

Goodbye My Love 7" CBS 7207 1971 £**6** £**2.50**

RANKIN, KENNY

Mind Dusters	LP	Mercury	20145SMCL	1968	£10	£4	

RANKIN FILE

Rankin File	LP	Circle		1971	£50	£25	

RANSOME, PETER

Peter Ransome	LP	York	FYK402	1972	£10	£4	

RAPED

Philes And Smiles	LP	Iguana	PILLAGED1	1984	£10	£4	

RAPEMAN

Hated Chinee	7"	Fierce	FRIGHT031	1988	£10	£5	

RAPHAEL

Please Speak To Me Of Love	7"	Hispavox	HXS303	1966	£10	£5	

RAPHAEL, JOHNNY

We're Only Young Once	7"	Vogue	V9104	1958	£60	£30	

RAPIERS

1961	LP	Off Beat	WIK67	1987	£15	£6	
Closing Theme	7"	Off Beat	NS112A	1986	£6	£2.50	
Rapiers Vol. 4	7"	Twang	RA004	1986	£8	£4	
Straight To The Point	LP	Off Beat	WIK40	1985	£15	£6	
Vol. 1	7"	Red Door	RA001	1983	£15	£7.50	
Vol. 2	7"	Twang	RA002	1984	£10	£5	
Vol. 3	7"	Twang	RA003	1985	£10	£5	

RAPIERS (2)

Phantom Stage	7"	Ilford Sound	ILF272	196–	£6	£2.50	

RAPKIN, BRIAN & KELVIN JONES

Dreams Of The Blue Beast	LP	MSR		197–	£15	£6	

RAPP, TOM

Stardancer	LP	Blue Thumb	BTS44	1972	£15	£6	US
Sunforest	LP	Blue Thumb	BTS56	1973	£12	£5	US
Tom Rapp	LP	Reprise	MS2069	1972	£15	£6	US

RARE AMBER

The group's satanic image fitted in with the Black Sabbath-led fashion of the time, but the B. B. King and Muddy Waters covers are more indicative of where Rare Amber's true interest lay.

Malfunction Of The Engine	7"	Polydor	56309	1969	£6	£2.50	
Rare Amber	LP	Polydor	583046	1969	£100	£50	

RARE BIRD

As Your Mind Flies By	LP	Charisma	CAS1011	1970	£12	£5	
Epic Forest	LP	Polydor	2442101	1972	£20	£8	*with 7" (2814011)*
Rare Bird	LP	Charisma	CAS1005	1969	£12	£5	
Sympathy	7"	Charisma	CB179	1972	£4	£1.50	*picture sleeve*

RARE BREED

Beg Borrow And Steal	7"	Strike	JH316	1966	£15	£7.50	

RARE EARTH

Ecology	LP	Tamla Motown	STML11180	1971	£10	£4	
Get Ready	7"	Tamla Motown	TMG742	1970	£5	£2	
Get Ready	LP	Tamla Motown	STML11165	1970	£12	£5	
In Concert	LP	Rare Earth	SRESP301	1972	£12	£5	*double*
Ma	LP	Rare Earth	SRE3010	1973	£10	£4	
One World	LP	Rare Earth	SREA4001	1971	£10	£4	
Willie Remembers	LP	Rare Earth	SRE3008	1973	£10	£4	

RAS MICHAEL & THE SONS OF NEGUS

Dadawah	LP	Trojan	TRLS103	1975	£15	£6	
Nyahbinghi	LP	Trojan	TRS113	1975	£12	£5	
Rastafari	LP	Grounation	GROL505	1976	£15	£6	
Tribute To The Emperor	LP	Trojan	TRS132	1976	£12	£5	

RASCALS

Beautiful Morning	7"	Atlantic	584182	1968	£4	£1.50	
Collection	LP	Atlantic	587060	1967	£15	£6	
Come On Up	7"	Atlantic	584050	1966	£6	£2.50	
Freedom Suite	LP	Atlantic	588183	1969	£10	£4	
Freedom Suite Narration	LP	Atlantic		1969	£12	£5	*US promo*
Girl Like You	7"	Atlantic	584128	1967	£4	£1.50	
Good Lovin'	7"	Atlantic	AT4082	1966	£4	£1.50	
Good Lovin'	7" EP	Atlantic	750011	1966	£12	£6	*French*
Greatest Hits	LP	Atlantic	587/588120	1968	£10	£4	
Groovin'	7"	Atlantic	584111	1967	£4	£1.50	

Groovin'	LP	Atlantic	587/588074	1967	**£15**	**£6**	
How Can I Be Sure	7"	Atlantic	584138	1967	**£4**	**£1.50**	
I Ain't Gonna Eat Out My Heart	7"	Atlantic	AT4059	1965	**£5**	**£2**	
I Ain't Gonna Eat Out My Heart	7"	Atlantic	584085	1967	**£4**	**£1.50**	
I've Been Lonely Too Long	7"	Atlantic	584081	1967	**£6**	**£2.50**	
I've Been Lonely Too Long	7" EP	Atlantic	750021	1967	**£12**	**£6**	*French*
It's Wonderful	7"	Atlantic	584161	1968	**£4**	**£1.50**	
Love Is A Beautiful Thing	7"	Atlantic	584024	1966	**£6**	**£2.50**	
Once Upon A Dream	LP	Atlantic	587/588098	1968	**£10**	**£4**	
Search And Nearness	LP	Atlantic	2400113	1971	**£10**	**£4**	
See	LP	Atlantic	588210	1969	**£10**	**£4**	
Sentirai La Pioggla	7"	Atlantic	NP3124	1968	**£8**	**£4**	*sung in Italian*
Suona	7" EP	Atlantic	750027	1967	**£12**	**£6**	*French*
Too Many Fish In The Sea	7"	Atlantic	584067	1966	**£4**	**£1.50**	
Young Rascals	LP	Atlantic	587012	1966	**£20**	**£8**	

RASCEL, RENATO

Romantica	7"	RCA	RCA1177	1960	**£5**	**£2**	

RASPUT & THE SEPOY MUTINY

Flower Power Sitar	LP	Design	SDLP280	1967	**£25**	**£10**	*US*

RASPUTIN & THE MONKS

Rasputin & The Monks	LP	Resurrection	CX1227	198–	**£15**	**£6**	*US, one sided*
Sum Of My Soul	LP	Trans Radio	200836	1965	**£400**	**£250**	*US, B side by the Octet*

RAT, MIKE & THE RUNAWAYS

Live Recording From The Kaskade Beat Club	LP	Ariola	72659IT	1963	**£100**	**£50**	*German*

RATHBONE, BASIL

Edgar Allan Poe	LP	Caedmon	TC1028	196–	**£10**	**£4**	

RATIONALS

Rationals	LP	Crewe	1334	1969	**£20**	**£8**	*US*

RATIP, ARMAN

Introducing	LP	Columbia	SCX6432	1970	**£20**	**£8**	
Spy From Istanbul	LP	Regal Zonophone	SLRZ1038	1973	**£30**	**£15**	

RATS

The Rats, whose recording career had begun and ended a little earlier, were the group taken on by David Bowie and renamed the Spiders From Mars. The assumption is that Mick Ronson is to be heard playing on the singles, but in fact he did not join the Rats until the late sixties. His recording debut is therefore not to be found on any of the singles by the Rats, but on the 1969 album by Michael Chapman, *Fully Qualified Survivor*.

I Gotta See My Baby	7"	Columbia	DB7607	1965	**£50**	**£25**	
Spoonful	7"	Columbia	DB7483	1965	**£75**	**£37.50**	
Spoonful	7"	Oak	RGJ145	1964	**£150**	**£75**	*1 sided*
Spoonful	7"	Oak	RGJ145	1964	**£250**	**£150**	*1 sided, picture sleeve*

RATS (2)

Parchman Farm	7"	Oriole	CB1967	1964	**£60**	**£30**	
Sack Of Woe	7"	CBS	201740	1965	**£40**	**£20**	

RATS (3)

First	LP	Goodear	EARLH5003	1974	**£10**	**£4**	

RATT

Lay It Down	7"	Atlantic	A9546P	1985	**£4**	**£1.50**	*shaped picture disc*
You're In Love	7"	Atlantic	A9502P	1986	**£5**	**£2**	*shaped picture disc*

RATTLES

Au Star Club De Hambourg	7" EP	Barclay	70656	1964	**£60**	**£30**	*French*
Bye Bye Johnny	7"	Decca	F11873	1964	**£8**	**£4**	
Come On And Sing	7"	Fontana	TF618	1965	**£5**	**£2**	
Gin Mill	LP	RCA	PPL14016	1974	**£12**	**£5**	*German*
Greatest Hits	LP	Mercury	MG1127	1967	**£25**	**£10**	
Hurra, Die Rattles Kommen	LP	Star Club	STY158013	1966	**£60**	**£30**	*German*
Liverpool Beat Vol. 2	LP	Ariola	71741IT	1965	**£50**	**£25**	*German*
Rattles	LP	Decca	SKL5088	1971	**£20**	**£8**	
Rattles Production	LP	Fontana	885445ZY	1968	**£25**	**£10**	*German*
Remember Finale Ligure	LP	Star Club	STY158031	1967	**£75**	**£37.50**	*German*
Say All Right	7"	Fontana	TF724	1966	**£5**	**£2**	
Sha-La-La-La-Lee	7" EP	Fontana	466030	1967	**£60**	**£30**	*French*
Star Club Show 1	LP	Starclub	STY158000	1965	**£60**	**£30**	*German*
Stomp	7"	Philips	BF1277	1963	**£5**	**£2**	
Teenbeat From The Star Club Hamburg	7" EP	Decca	DFE8568	1964	**£75**	**£37.50**	
Tell Me What Can I Do	7"	Decca	F11936	1964	**£5**	**£2**	
Tonight Starring Edna	LP	Philips	6305176	1972	**£10**	**£4**	*German*
Twist At The Star Club	LP	Philips	BL7614	1964	**£75**	**£37.50**	
Witch	LP	Philips	6305072	1971	**£20**	**£8**	*German*

RAVA, ENRICO

Pilgrim And The Stars	LP	ECM	ECM1063ST	1975	**£10**	**£4**	

RAVE ONS

She's A Spoon	7"	Sounds Good	MT103	196–	**£60**	**£30**	

RAVEL, CHRIS & THE RAVERS

Chris Ravel was Chris Andrews, later a moderately successful solo artist and a more successful songwriter and producer – most notably for Sandie Shaw.

I Do	7"	Decca	F11696	1963	**£8**	**£4**	

RAVEN

Live At The Inferno	LP	Discovery	36133	1967	**£15**	**£6**	*US*
Raven	LP	Columbia	CS9903	1969	**£12**	**£5**	*US*

RAVEN (2)

Crash Bang Wallop	12"	Neat	NEAT15	1982	**£6**	**£2.50**	*mauve vinyl*
Don't Need Your Money	7"	Neat	NEAT06	1980	**£5**	**£2**	

RAVEN, JON

Ballad Of The Black Country	LP	Broadside	BRO116	1975	**£12**	**£5**	
English Canals	LP	Broadside	BRO118	1976	**£12**	**£5**	*with John Kirkpatrick & Sue Harris*
Harvest	LP	Broadside	BRO117	1976	**£12**	**£5**	
Kate Of Coalbrookdale	LP	Argo	ZFB29	1971	**£20**	**£8**	*with Mike Raven, Pete Sage, Jean Ward*
Songs Of A Changing World	LP	Trailer	LER2083	1973	**£25**	**£10**	*with Nic Jones & Tony Rose*

RAVEN, MIKE

Mike Raven was a disc jockey on pirate radio and then on Radio One. He used to present a specialist programme of soul and blues and the two LPs listed here are to some extent re-creations of the blues part. The *Blues Show* provides a necessarily brief, but effective, history of the blues. Mike Raven introduces each track and his comments are relevant enough – and his voice soothing enough – to prevent the introductions becoming irritating on successive hearings. The *Blues Sampler* is similar, but attempts to show the range of blues styles rather than following a historical approach.

Mike Raven Blues Sampler	LP	Transatlantic	TRASAM5	1969	**£10**	**£4**	
Mike Raven Blues Show	LP	XTRA	XTRA1047	1966	**£12**	**£5**	

RAVEN, PAUL

It is astonishing to realize that the earliest record made by Gary Glitter dates from as early as 1960! The man who was born Paul Gadd adopted the Raven surname for most of the sixties, and has a starring role on the original *Jesus Christ Superstar* album under this name.

Musical Man	7"	MCA	MU1024	1968	**£6**	**£2.50**	
Soul Thing	7"	MCA	MU1035	1968	**£6**	**£2.50**	
Stand	7"	MCA	MKS5053	1970	**£5**	**£2**	
Too Proud	7"	Decca	F11202	1960	**£20**	**£10**	
Tower Of Strength	7"	Parlophone	R4842	1961	**£10**	**£5**	
Walk On Boy	7"	Parlophone	R4812	1961	**£10**	**£5**	

RAVEN, SIMON

I Wonder If She Remembers Me	7"	Piccadilly	7N35301	1966	**£20**	**£10**	

RAVENS

Begin The Beguine	78	Oriole	CB1149	1953	**£20**	**£10**	
I Just Wanna Hear You Say	7"	Oriole	CB1910	1964	**£6**	**£2.50**	
Rock Me All Night Long	78	Oriole	CB1148	1953	**£20**	**£10**	
Who'll Be The Fool?	78	Oriole	CB1258	1954	**£20**	**£10**	
Write Me A Letter	LP	Regent	MG6062	195–	**£75**	**£37.50**	*US*

RAVENS ROCK GROUP

Ghoul Friend	7"	Pye	7N25077	1961	**£6**	**£2.50**	

RAVERS

Badam Bam	7"	Upsetter	US312	1969	**£5**	**£2**	*Upsetters B side*

RAW DEAL

Out Of My Head	7"	White Witch	WIT701	1981	**£60**	**£30**	*no picture sleeve*

RAW HERBS

Old Joe	7"	Medium Cool	MC002	1986	**£4**	**£1.50**	*flexi*

RAW HOLLY

Raw Holly	LP	MCA	MAPS4067	1971	**£20**	**£8**	*German*

RAW MATERIAL

Hi There Allelujah	7"	Evolution	E2445	1970	**£15**	**£7.50**	
Raw Material Album	LP	Evolution	Z1006	1970	**£150**	**£75**	
Ride On Pony	7"	Neon	NE1002	1972	**£15**	**£7.50**	
Time And Illusion	7"	Evolution	E2441	1969	**£20**	**£10**	
Time Is	LP	Neon	NE8	1971	**£250**	**£150**	
Traveller Man	7"	Evolution	E24495	1970	**£20**	**£10**	

RAWLS, LOU

Black And Blue	LP	Capitol	T1824	1965	**£12**	**£5**	
Carryin' On	LP	Capitol	(S)T2632	1967	**£10**	**£4**	
Feelin' Good	LP	Capitol	(S)T2864	1968	**£10**	**£4**	
I Don't Love You Anymore	7"	Capitol	CL15515	1967	**£4**	**£1.50**	
Live	LP	Capitol	(S)T2459	1966	**£12**	**£5**	

Lost And Looking	7" EP	Capitol	EAP120646	1964	£25	£12.50	
Love Is A Hurting Thing	7"	Capitol	CL15465	1966	£4	£1.50	
Soul Serenade	7"	Capitol	CL15548	1968	£4	£1.50	
Soulin'	LP	Capitol	(S)T2566	1967	£12	£5	
Yes It Hurts Doesn't It	7"	Capitol	CL15499	1967	£4	£1.50	
You Can Bring Me All Your Heartaches	7"	Capitol	CL15488	1967	£4	£1.50	
You're Good For Me	LP	Capitol	ST2927	1969	£10	£4	

RAY, FROGGIE

Uncle Charlie	7"	Big	BG313	1971	£5	£2	

RAY, JAMES

If You Gotta Make A Fool Of Somebody	7"	Pye	7N25126	1962	£8	£4	
If You Gotta Make A Fool Of Somebody	LP	Caprice	(S)LP1002	1962	£40	£20	US
Itty Bitty Pieces	7"	Pye	7N25147	1962	£6	£2.50	

RAY, JAMES (2)

Another Million Dollars	CD-s	Merciful Release	MRAY99CD	1989	£5	£2	
Mexican Sundown Blues	7"	Merciful Release	MRAY52	1986	£4	£1.50	
New Kind Of Assassin	CD-s	Merciful Release	MRAY89CD	1989	£5	£2	
Without Conscience	CD-s	Merciful Release	MRAY101CD	1990	£5	£2	

RAY, JOHNNIE

At The London Palladium	10" LP	Philips	BBR8001	1953	£25	£10	
Best Of Johnnie Ray	LP	Realm	RM52317	1966	£10	£4	
Big Beat	LP	Philips	BBL7148	1957	£25	£10	
Build Your Love	7"	Philips	JK1025	1957	£12	£6	
How Many Nights How Many Days	7"	HMV	POP902	1961	£5	£2	
I Believe	7"	London	HLG9484	1962	£5	£2	*Timi Yuro B side*
I'll Never Fall In Love Again	7"	Philips	PB952	1959	£4	£1.50	
I'm Just A Shadow Of Myself	7"	Columbia	SCM5122	1954	£15	£7.50	
In Las Vegas	LP	Philips	BBL7254	1958	£25	£10	
In The Heart Of A Fool	7"	London	HLA9216	1960	£4	£1.50	
Johnnie Ray	7" EP	Philips	BBE12217	1958	£8	£4	
Johnnie Ray	7" EP	Columbia	SEG7511	1954	£10	£5	
Johnnie Ray	7" EP	Philips	BBE12006	1955	£10	£5	
Johnnie Ray	LP	Liberty	LBY1020	1962	£15	£6	
Lonely For A Letter	7"	Philips	PB829	1958	£4	£1.50	
Look Homeward Angel	7"	Philips	JK1004	1957	£20	£10	
Mama Says, Pa Says	7"	Columbia	SCM5033	1953	£15	£7.50	
Miss Me Just A Little	7"	Philips	PB785	1958	£4	£1.50	
Nobody's Sweetheart	7"	Columbia	SCM5111	1954	£15	£7.50	
On The Trail	7" EP	Philips	BBE12460	1961	£10	£5	
On The Trail	LP	Philips	BBL7363	1961	£20	£8	
Pink Sweater Angel	7"	Philips	JK1033	1957	£15	£7.50	
Please Don't Talk About Me	7"	Columbia	SCM5074	1953	£25	£12.50	
Showcase Of Hits	LP	Philips	BBL7264	1959	£20	£8	
Sinner Man Am I	LP	Philips	BBL7348	1960	£20	£8	
So Long	7"	Philips	JK1011	1957	£15	£7.50	
Tales From The Vienna Woods	LP	Ace Of Clubs	ACL1059	1961	£10	£4	
Tell The Lady I Said Goodbye	7"	Columbia	SCM5041	1953	£30	£15	
Till Morning	LP	Philips	BBL7285/ SBBL555	1959	£20	£8	
Up Until Now	7"	Philips	PB849	1958	£4	£1.50	
Voice Of Your Choice	10" LP	Philips	BBR8062	1955	£25	£10	
Walkin' My Baby Back Home	7"	Columbia	SCM5015	1953	£25	£12.50	
Walking And Crying	7" EP	Philips	BBE12115	1957	£10	£5	
What More Can I Say	7"	Philips	PB884	1958	£4	£1.50	
When's Your Birthday Baby	7"	Philips	PB901	1959	£4	£1.50	
Yes Tonight Josephine	7"	Philips	JK1016	1957	£20	£10	
Yes Tonight Josephine	7" EP	Philips	BBE12192	1958	£10	£5	

RAY, RICARDO

Nitty Gritty	7"	Roulette	RO501	1967	£4	£1.50	

RAY, WADE

Burning Desire	7"	London	HL9700	1963	£6	£2.50	

RAY & COLLUNEY

Tyrants Of England	LP	Westwood	WRS001	1971	£30	£15	

RAYBURN, MARGIE

I Would	7"	London	HLU8648	1958	£10	£5	
I'm Available	7"	London	HLU8515	1957	£10	£5	
Wedding Song	7"	Capitol	CL14532	1956	£4	£1.50	

RAYMOND, LEE & THE COSTELLO SISTERS

Foolishly Yours	7"	Brunswick	05438	1955	£6	£2.50	

RAYMOND, TONY

Infant King	7"	Oriole	CB1777	1962	£4	£1.50	

RAYNE, JULIE

Title	Format	Label	Cat. No.	Year	Mint	VG	Notes
Bim Bam Bom	7"	HMV	POP785	1960	£4	£1.50	
Faithfully	7"	Windsor	WPS123	196–	£4	£1.50	
Green With Envy Purple With Passion	7"	HMV	POP868	1961	£4	£1.50	
Waltz Me Around	7"	HMV	POP665	1959	£4	£1.50	
You Can't Come Back	7"	Windsor	WPS128	196–	£4	£1.50	

RAYNOR, MARTIN & THE SECRETS

Title	Format	Label	Cat. No.	Year	Mint	VG	Notes
Candy To Me	7"	Columbia	DB7563	1965	£15	£7.50	

RAYNOR, MIKE

Title	Format	Label	Cat. No.	Year	Mint	VG	Notes
Ob La Di Ob La Da	7"	Decca	F22864	1969	£4	£1.50	

RAYS

Title	Format	Label	Cat. No.	Year	Mint	VG	Notes
Silhouettes	7"	London	HLU8505	1957	£25	£12.50	

RAZORCUTS

Title	Format	Label	Cat. No.	Year	Mint	VG	Notes
Big Pink Cake	7"	Subway Organisation	SUBWAY5	1986	£5	£2	
Sometimes I Worry About You	7"	Caff	CAFF10	198–	£8	£4	

REA, CHRIS

Title	Format	Label	Cat. No.	Year	Mint	VG	Notes
Driving Home For Christmas	CD-s	WEA	YZ325CD	1988	£5	£2	*3" single*
I Can Hear Your Heart Beat	CD-s	WEA	YZ320CD	1988	£5	£2	
Joys Of Christmas	CD-s	Magnet	CDMAG314	1987	£5	£2	
Let's Dance	CD-s	Magnet	CDMAG299	1987	£5	£2	
On The Beach	CD-s	WEA	YZ195CD	1988	£5	£2	
Que Sera	CD-s	Magnet	CDMAG318	1988	£5	£2	
Road To Hell	CD	Geffen	224276DJ	1989	£20	£8	*US promo picture disc*
Road To Hell	CD	Magnet	K2462852	1989	£40	£20	*promo box set, with cassette and booklet*
Road To Hell	CD-s	WEA	YZ431CD	1989	£5	£2	
So Much Love	7"	Magnet	MAG10	1974	£25	£12.50	
That's What They Always Say	CD-s	WEA	YZ448CD	1989	£5	£2	
Working On It	CD-s	WEA	YZ350CD	1989	£5	£2	

REA, JOHN

Title	Format	Label	Cat. No.	Year	Mint	VG	Notes
Traditional Music On The Hammer Dulcimer	LP	Topic	12TS373	1978	£10	£4	

REACTA

Title	Format	Label	Cat. No.	Year	Mint	VG	Notes
Stop The World	7"	Battery Operated	WAC1	1979	£25	£12.50	

REACTION

Title	Format	Label	Cat. No.	Year	Mint	VG	Notes
Oh Me Oh My	7"	Columbia	DB119	1970	£5	£2	*Rico B side*

REACTION (2)

Title	Format	Label	Cat. No.	Year	Mint	VG	Notes
Reaction	LP	Polydor	2371251	1972	£75	£37.50	*German*

REACTION (3)

Title	Format	Label	Cat. No.	Year	Mint	VG	Notes
I Can't Resist	7"	Island	WIP6437	1978	£5	£2	

READER, PAT

Title	Format	Label	Cat. No.	Year	Mint	VG	Notes
Cha Cha On The Moon	7"	Piccadilly	7N35077	1962	£30	£15	
Helpless	7"	Oriole	CB1903	1963	£6	£2.50	
Ricky	7"	Triumph	RGM1024	1960	£20	£10	

READING, BERTICE

Title	Format	Label	Cat. No.	Year	Mint	VG	Notes
Jazz Train Girl	7" EP	Parlophone	GEP8537	1955	£5	£2	
My Big Best Shoes	7"	Parlophone	R4487	1958	£15	£7.50	
No Flowers By Request	7"	Decca	F10965	1957	£5	£2	
Rock Baby Rock	7"	Parlophone	R4462	1958	£25	£12.50	

REAL McCOY

Title	Format	Label	Cat. No.	Year	Mint	VG	Notes
This Is The Real McCoy	LP	Marble Arch	MAL1251	1970	£20	£8	

REALITY FOLK

Title	Format	Label	Cat. No.	Year	Mint	VG	Notes
Light Up My Life	LP	Profile			£125	£62.50	

REALITY FROM DREAM

Title	Format	Label	Cat. No.	Year	Mint	VG	Notes
Reality From Dream	LP	private		1975	£250	£150	

REALIZATION OF ETERNITY

Title	Format	Label	Cat. No.	Year	Mint	VG	Notes
Beyond The End	LP	Narco		197–	£40	£20	*US*

REALLY RED

Title	Format	Label	Cat. No.	Year	Mint	VG	Notes
Teaching You The Fear	LP	CIA	CIA006	1981	£30	£15	

REALM

Title	Format	Label	Cat. No.	Year	Mint	VG	Notes
Hard Time Loving You	7"	CBS	202044	1966	£10	£5	

REAPERS

Title	Format	Label	Cat. No.	Year	Mint	VG	Notes
No Greater Love	LP	Agra	BSS388	1979	£25	£10	

REBECCA & THE SUNNYBROOK FARMERS

Title	Format	Label	Number	Year	Mint	Ex	Notes
Birth	LP	Musicor	MS3176	1967	£40	£20	US

REBEL

Title	Format	Label	Number	Year	Mint	Ex	Notes
Beat Hits Vol. 3	LP	Bellaphon	MWS308	1965	£20	£8	German

REBEL (2)

Title	Format	Label	Number	Year	Mint	Ex	Notes
Rocka Shocka	7"	Bridge House	BHS2	1981	£8	£4	
Valentino	7"	Flying Pig	REBS1	1986	£8	£4	double

REBEL ROUSERS

Title	Format	Label	Number	Year	Mint	Ex	Notes
Should I	7"	Fontana	TF973	1968	£10	£5	

REBELS

Title	Format	Label	Number	Year	Mint	Ex	Notes
Hard To Love You	7"	Page One	POF017	1967	£15	£7.50	

REBELS (2)

Title	Format	Label	Number	Year	Mint	Ex	Notes
It's All In The Game	7"	Trojan	TR7779	1970	£5	£2	

REBENNACK, MAC

Mac Rebennack achieved early notoriety as the only white musician to find employment on R&B sessions in New Orleans. Later he re-invented himself as the voodoo singer Dr John, although it is as Rebennack that he continues to play as a highly respected boogie pianist.

Title	Format	Label	Number	Year	Mint	Ex	Notes
Good Times	7"	Ace	611	1961	£15	£7.50	US
Storm Warning	7"	Rex	1008	196–	£15	£7.50	US

REBIRTH

Title	Format	Label	Number	Year	Mint	Ex	Notes
Rebirth	LP	Avantgarde	135	1968	£50	£25	US

REBOUNDS

Title	Format	Label	Number	Year	Mint	Ex	Notes
Help Me	7"	Fontana	TF461	1964	£10	£5	

REBS

Title	Format	Label	Number	Year	Mint	Ex	Notes
Bunky	7"	Capitol	CL14932	1958	£5	£2	

REBS (2)

Title	Format	Label	Number	Year	Mint	Ex	Notes
1968 A.D. Break Through	LP	Fredlo	6830	1968	£300	£180	US

RECO, EZO & THE LAUNCHERS

Rico Rodriguez, the legendary (and still recording) Rastafarian trombone player, had records issued under the names Reco, Ezo Reco and Ezz Reco, with and without the Launchers. Apart from the records below, all are listed under Rico in this guide.

Title	Format	Label	Number	Year	Mint	Ex	Notes
Jamaica Blue Beat	7" EP	Columbia	SEG8326	1964	£25	£12.50	
King Of Kings	7"	Columbia	DB7217	1964	£6	£2.50	
Little Girl	7"	Columbia	DB7222	1964	£6	£2.50	
Memory Of Don Drummond	7"	Jackpot	JP710	1969	£4	£1.50	
Please Come Back	7"	Columbia	DB7290	1964	£6	£2.50	

RECREATION

Title	Format	Label	Number	Year	Mint	Ex	Notes
Recreation	LP	Bellaphon	BLPS19006	1970	£10	£4	German

RED

Title	Format	Label	Number	Year	Mint	Ex	Notes
Red	LP	Jigsaw	SAW2	1983	£20	£8	

RED, SONNY

Title	Format	Label	Number	Year	Mint	Ex	Notes
Out Of The Blue	LP	Blue Note	BLP/BST84032	196–	£40	£20	

RED ALERT

Title	Format	Label	Number	Year	Mint	Ex	Notes
Border Guards	7"	Guardian	GMRAB61	1980	£40	£20	
City Invasion	7"	No Future	OI20	1983	£5	£2	
In Britain	7"	No Future	OI5	1982	£5	£2	
Take No Prisoners	7"	No Future	OI13	1982	£5	£2	
There's A Guitar Burning	12"	No Future	OI27	1983	£8	£4	
We've Got The Power	LP	No Future	PUNK5	1983	£10	£4	

RED ALERT (2)

Title	Format	Label	Number	Year	Mint	Ex	Notes
Run To Ground	7"	Steel City	AJS7R	1982	£5	£2	

RED BOX

Title	Format	Label	Number	Year	Mint	Ex	Notes
Circle And The Square	CD	WEA	K2420372	1986	£25	£10	
Motive	CD	East West	9031726142	1990	£25	£10	
Train	CD-s	East West	YZ531CD	1990	£5	£2	

RED CHAIR FADEAWAY

Any group choosing to name itself after a Bee Gees song is either impossibly naive or else uncaringly knowing – for the original 'Red Chair Fadeaway' is a classy piece of psychedelic pop, but from a group that is terminally unfashionable. Red Chair Fadeaway's music is proving to be unfashionable too. Despite being recorded in the nineties, the sound is that of a progressive folk group *circa* 1970, and for the album *Curiouser And Curiouser* there is packaging to match. Issued in a limited edition of a thousand copies, this is likely to be a very expensive collectors' item in the future.

Title	Format	Label	Number	Year	Mint	Ex	Notes
Curiouser And Curiouser	LP	Tangerine	MM10	1991	£25	£10	
Let It Happen	12"	Cosmic English Music	CTA103	1989	£10	£5	
Mesmerised	LP	Aural	AUR102	1993	£15	£6	

Mr Jones	12"	Cosmic English Music	CTA105	1989	**£10**	**£5**	

RED CRAYOLA

God Bless The Red Crayola	LP	International Artist	IALP7	1968	**£50**	**£25**	*US*
God Bless The Red Crayola	LP	Radar	RAD16	1978	**£10**	**£4**	
Parable Of Arable Land	LP	Radar	RAD12	1978	**£10**	**£4**	
Parable Of Arable Land	LP	International Artist	IALP2	1967	**£50**	**£25**	*US stereo*
Parable Of Arable Land	LP	International Artist	IALP2	1967	**£60**	**£30**	*US mono*
Soldier Talk	LP	Radar	RAD18	1979	**£10**	**£4**	

RED DIRT

Red Dirt	LP	Fontana	STL5540	1970	**£500**	**£330**	

RED HASH

Red Hash	LP	Nufusmoon	3673	1973	**£30**	**£15**	*US*

RED HOT CHILI PEPPERS

Abbey Road EP	12"	EMI	12MTPD41	1988	**£6**	**£2.50**	*picture disc*
Fight Like A Brave	12"	EMI	12EAP241	1988	**£6**	**£2.50**	*picture disc*
Higher Ground	CD-s	EMI	CDMT88	1990	**£5**	**£2**	
Higher Ground	CD-s	EMI	CDMT75	1989	**£5**	**£2**	
Knock Me Down	7"	EMI	MTPD70	1989	**£4**	**£1.50**	*picture disc*
Knock Me Down	CD-s	EMI	CDMT70	1989	**£5**	**£2**	
Taste The Pain	CD-s	EMI	CDMT85	1990	**£5**	**£2**	

RED HOUSE PAINTERS

I Am A Rock	CD-s	4AD	RHP1CD	1993	**£6**	**£2.50**	*promo*

RED LETTERS

Sacred Voices	7"	Burning Bing	CPS025	197–	**£40**	**£20**	

RED LIGHTS

Never Wanna Leave	7"	Free Range	PF5	1978	**£5**	**£2**	

RED LONDON

Sten Guns In Sunderland	7"	Razor	RZS105	1983	**£5**	**£2**	

RED LORRY YELLOW LORRY

Beating My Head	7"	Red Rhino	RED20	1982	**£8**	**£4**	
He's Read	7"	Red Rhino	RED39	1983	**£5**	**£2**	
Take It All	7"	Red Rhino	RED28	1983	**£6**	**£2.50**	

RED ONION JAZZ BABIES

Dance Off Both Your Shoes	LP	London	LTZU15138	1958	**£15**	**£6**	
New Orleans Encore	10" LP	London	HAPB1025	1954	**£15**	**£6**	
Red Onion Jazz Babies	7" EP	Collector	JE19	1960	**£5**	**£2**	

RED RAGE

Total Control	7"	Flicknife	FLS203	1980	**£25**	**£12.50**	

RED RIVER BAND

I'm Gonna Use What I've Got	7"	Banana	BA35	1970	**£4**	**£1.50**	

RED SQUARES

It's Happening	LP	Columbia	KSX6	1967	**£25**	**£10**	*Danish*
Mountain's High	7"	Columbia	DB8160	1967	**£4**	**£1.50**	
Red Squares	LP	Columbia	KSX5	1966	**£25**	**£10**	*Danish*
True Love Story	7"	Columbia	DB8247	1967	**£4**	**£1.50**	

RED TELEVISION

Red Television	LP	Brecht Times		1971	**£200**	**£100**	

REDCAPS

Mighty Fine Girl	7"	Decca	F11903	1964	**£5**	**£2**	
Shout	7"	Decca	F11716	1963	**£5**	**£2**	
Talking About You	7"	Decca	F11789	1963	**£6**	**£2.50**	

REDD, FREDDIE

Get Happy	LP	Nixa	NJL19	1958	**£20**	**£8**	
Music From The Connection	LP	Blue Note	BLP/BST84027	196–	**£30**	**£15**	
Shades Of Redd	LP	Blue Note	BLP/BST84045	196–	**£40**	**£20**	

REDD, GENE & THE GLOBE TROTTERS

Red River Valley Rock	7"	Parlophone	R4584	1959	**£10**	**£5**	

REDDING, OTIS

Champagne And Wine	7"	Atlantic	584220	1968	**£4**	**£1.50**	
Come To Me	7"	London	HLK9876	1964	**£10**	**£5**	
Day Tripper	7"	Stax	601005	1967	**£4**	**£1.50**	
Dictionary Of Soul	LP	Atlantic	587/588050	1967	**£15**	**£6**	
Dock Of The Bay	7"	Stax	601031	1968	**£4**	**£1.50**	
Dock Of The Bay	7"	Atlantic	2091112	1971	**£4**	**£1.50**	
Dock Of The Bay	LP	Atco	228022	1969	**£10**	**£4**	
Dock Of The Bay	LP	Stax	230/231001	1968	**£15**	**£6**	

Early Otis Redding	7" EP	Sue	IEP710	1966	**£50**	**£25**	
Fa Fa Fa Fa Fa Song	7"	Atlantic	584049	1966	**£5**	**£2**	
Free Me	7"	Atco	226002	1969	**£4**	**£1.50**	
Glory Of Love	7"	Stax	601017	1967	**£5**	**£2**	
Happy Song	7"	Stax	601040	1968	**£4**	**£1.50**	
Hard To Handle	7"	Atlantic	584199	1968	**£4**	**£1.50**	
History Of Otis Redding	LP	Volt	418	1968	**£15**	**£6**	
History Of Otis Redding	LP	Atco	228001	1969	**£10**	**£4**	
I Can't Turn You Loose	7"	Atlantic	584030	1966	**£5**	**£2**	
I've Been Loving You Too Long	7"	Atlantic	AT4029	1965	**£40**	**£20**	*demo only*
I've Been Loving You Too Long	7"	Atlantic	2091062	1971	**£4**	**£1.50**	
Immortal Otis Redding	LP	Atlantic	587/588113	1968	**£15**	**£6**	
In Person At The Whiskey	LP	Atlantic	587/588148	1968	**£15**	**£6**	
Let Me Come On Home	7"	Stax	601007	1967	**£4**	**£1.50**	
Live In Europe	LP	Stax	589016	1968	**£15**	**£6**	
Live In Europe	LP	Atco	228017	1969	**£10**	**£4**	
Look At The Girl	7"	Atco	226012	1970	**£4**	**£1.50**	
Love Man	7"	Atco	226001	1969	**£4**	**£1.50**	
Love Man	LP	Atco	228025	1969	**£12**	**£5**	
Lover's Question	7"	Atlantic	584249	1969	**£4**	**£1.50**	
Mr Pitiful	7"	Atlantic	AT4024	1965	**£8**	**£4**	
My Girl	7"	Atlantic	AT4050	1965	**£6**	**£2.50**	
My Girl	7"	Atlantic	584092	1967	**£5**	**£2**	
My Lover's Prayer	7"	Atlantic	584019	1966	**£5**	**£2**	
Otis Blue	CD	Mobile Fidelity	EUCD575	1992	**£15**	**£6**	*US audiophile*
Otis Blue	LP	Atlantic	ATL5041	1966	**£25**	**£10**	
Otis Blue	LP	Atlantic	587/588036	1966	**£15**	**£6**	
Pain In My Heart	7"	London	HLK9833	1964	**£10**	**£5**	
Pain In My Heart	LP	Atlantic	587042	1967	**£15**	**£6**	
Papa's Got A Brand New Bag	7"	Atlantic	584234	1968	**£4**	**£1.50**	
Remembering	LP	Atlantic	2464003	1970	**£10**	**£4**	
Respect	7"	Atlantic	AT4039	1965	**£6**	**£2.50**	
Respect	7"	Atlantic	584091	1967	**£5**	**£2**	
Satisfaction	7"	Stax	601027	1967	**£4**	**£1.50**	
Satisfaction	7"	Atlantic	AT4080	1966	**£5**	**£2**	
Shake	7"	Stax	601011	1967	**£4**	**£1.50**	
She's Alright	7"	Pye	7N25463	1968	**£5**	**£2**	
She's Alright	7"	Evolution	E2442	1969	**£5**	**£2**	
Shout Bamalama	7"	Sue	WI362	1965	**£15**	**£7.50**	
Sings Soul Ballads	LP	Atlantic	ATL5029	1965	**£30**	**£15**	
Sings Soul Ballads	LP	Atlantic	587035	1966	**£15**	**£6**	
Soul Album	LP	Atlantic	587011	1966	**£20**	**£8**	
Tell The Truth	LP	Atco	2400018	1971	**£10**	**£4**	
Try A Little Tenderness	7"	Atlantic	584070	1967	**£5**	**£2**	
Wonderful World	7"	Atlantic	2091020	1970	**£4**	**£1.50**	

REDDING, OTIS & CARLA THOMAS

King And Queen	LP	Atlantic	589007	1967	**£15**	**£6**	
Knock On Wood	7"	Stax	601021	1967	**£4**	**£1.50**	
Lovey Dovey	7"	Stax	601033	1968	**£4**	**£1.50**	
Tramp	7"	Stax	601012	1967	**£4**	**£1.50**	

REDDING, OTIS & JIMI HENDRIX

Historic Performances Recorded At Monterey	LP	Reprise	MS2029	1970	**£15**	**£6**	*US, 1 side each artist*

REDE, EMMA

Just Like A Man	7"	Columbia	DB8136	1967	**£8**	**£4**	

REDELL, TEDDY

Judy	7"	London	HLK9140	1960	**£50**	**£25**	

REDMAN, GEORGE

George Redman Group	10" LP	London	HAPB1036	1955	**£25**	**£10**	

REDMOND, ROY

Good Day Sunshine	7"	Warner Bros	WB2075	1967	**£4**	**£1.50**	

REDPATH, JEAN

Ballad Folk	LP	BBC	REC293	1977	**£12**	**£5**	
Love, Life And Laughter	LP	Clan Special	233004	1969	**£12**	**£5**	
Love, Lilt And Laughter	LP	Bounty	BY6004	1966	**£15**	**£6**	
There Were Minstrels	LP	Trailer	LER2106	1977	**£10**	**£4**	

REDSKINS

Lean On Me	7"	CNT	CNT016	1983	**£5**	**£2**	
Lev Bronstein	7"	CNT	CNT007	1982	**£12**	**£6**	

REDUCERS

Man With A Gun	7"	Vibes	VR003	1979	**£12**	**£6**	
Things Go Wrong	7"	Vibes	VR001	1978	**£20**	**£10**	

REDWAY, MIKE

Darling Take Me Back	7"	CBS	201755	1965	**£4**	**£1.50**	
Have No Fear, Bond Is Here	7"	Deram	DM124	1967	**£5**	**£2**	

REDWOODS

Please Mister Scientist	7"	Columbia	DB4859	1962	£8	£4	

REECE, DIZZY

Asia Minor	LP	Esquire	32185	1958	£50	£25	
Dizzy/Deuchar	LP	Tempo	TAP4	1956	£100	£50	*with Jimmy Deuchar*
New Star	10" LP	Tempo	LAP3	1955	£100	£50	
Nowhere To Go	7" EP	Tempo	EXA86	1957	£100	£50	
On The Scene	7" EP	Tempo	EXA89	1957	£25	£12.50	
Progress Report	LP	Tempo	TAP9	1957	£200	£100	
Soundin' Off	LP	Blue Note	BLP/BST84033	196–	£30	£15	
Variation On Monk	7" EP	Tempo	EXA84	1957	£100	£50	

REED, CHUCK

Just Plain Hurt	7"	Stateside	SS108	1962	£5	£2	
Let's Put Our Hearts Together	7"	Columbia	DB4113	1958	£8	£4	
Whispering Heart	7"	Brunswick	05646	1957	£5	£2	

REED, DENNY

Teenager Feels It Too	7"	London	HLK9274	1961	£10	£5	

REED, FRED

Northumbrian Voice	LP	White Meadow	01	1978	£10	£4	

REED, JERRY

Bessie Baby	7"	Capitol	CL14851	1958	£150	£75	

REED, JIMMY

At Carnegie Hall	LP	Stateside	SL10012	1962	£25	£10	
At Soul City	LP	Vee Jay	LP1095	1964	£20	£8	*US*
Baby What You Want Me To Do	7"	Top Rank	JAR333	1960	£10	£5	
Best Of Jimmy Reed	LP	Vee Jay	LP/SR1039	1962	£20	£8	*US*
Big Boss Man	LP	BluesWay	BLS6013	1968	£12	£5	*US*
Blues Of Jimmy Reed	7" EP	Stateside	SE1016	1964	£12	£6	
Boss Man Of The Blues	LP	Stateside	SL10091	1964	£15	£6	
Down In Virginia	LP	Action	ACLP6011	1969	£20	£8	
Found Love	7"	Top Rank	JAR394	1960	£8	£4	
Found Love	LP	Vee Jay	LP1022	1960	£25	£10	*US*
Hush Hush	7"	Top Rank	JAR533	1961	£8	£4	
I'm Jimmy Reed	7" EP	Stateside	SE1026	1964	£12	£6	
I'm Jimmy Reed	LP	Vee Jay	LP1004	1958	£50	£25	*US*
Jimmy Reed & Eddie Taylor	7" EP	XX	MIN704	196–	£6	£2.50	*with Eddie Taylor*
Just Jimmy Reed	LP	Stateside	SL10055	1963	£25	£10	
Legend, The Man	LP	Vee Jay	VJ(S)8501	1965	£15	£6	*US*
More Of The Best Of Jimmy Reed	LP	Vee Jay	LP/SR1080	1964	£15	£6	*US*
New Jimmy Reed	LP	HMV	CLP/CSD3611	1967	£12	£5	
Now Appearing	LP	Vee Jay	LP1025	1960	£25	£10	*US*
Odds And Ends	7"	Sue	WI4004	1966	£12	£6	
Plays 12 String Guitar Blues	LP	Stateside	SL10086	1964	£15	£6	
Rockin' With Reed	LP	Vee Jay	LP1008	1959	£40	£20	*US*
Shame Shame Shame	7"	Stateside	SS330	1964	£4	£1.50	
Shame Shame Shame	7"	Stateside	SS205	1963	£6	£2.50	
Sings The Best Of The Blues	LP	Stateside	SL10069	1964	£15	£6	
Soulin'	LP	Stateside	(S)SL10221	1968	£12	£5	
T'Ain't No Big Thing	LP	Vee Jay	LP1067	1963	£20	£8	*US*
Things Ain't What They Used To Be	LP	Fontana	688514ZL	1965	£12	£5	
Two Ways To Skin A Cat	7"	HMV	POP1579	1967	£5	£2	

REED, LOU

The battle of the formats was won by the compact disc the moment that a reissue of Lou Reed's *Metal Machine Music* was released on CD. The disturbing electronic hubbub that the album contains may be an interesting insight into Reed's early association with minimalist avant-garde composer La Monte Young, but it does not make for a listening experience that many Reed fans would wish to endure even once. It has been suggested that the album was Reed's ironic way of fulfilling a contract, but tapes exist of the Velvet Underground playing music not very dissimilar to this. More indicative of cynicism are the live recordings of the Velvet Underground's 1993 tour, which show Reed to be performing some of the old material with an alarming lack of enthusiasm. (The shame of this being heightened all the more by the knowledge that much of Reed's solo material from recent years has been rather fine.)

Blue Mask	LP	RCA	DJL14266	1981	£10	£4	*US interview promo*
Candy Says	7"	MGM	2006283	1973	£5	£2	
Dirty Boulevard	CD-s	Sire	W7547CD	1989	£5	£2	*3" single*
Magic And Loss	CD	Sire		1992	£40	£20	*US promo in metal box*
Metal Machine Music	LP	RCA	CPL21101	1975	£25	£10	
Metal Machine Music	LP	RCA	CPD21101	1975	£40	£20	*US quad*
New York	CD	Sire		1988	£20	£8	*US promo in metal box*
No Money Down	12"	RCA		1986	£6	£2.50	*promo, green vinyl*
Rock'n'Roll Life	CD	Sire	PROCD3358	1989	£30	£15	*US promo double*
Selections From Between Thought And Expression	CD	RCA	62284RDJ	1992	£20	£8	*US promo*
Songs For Drella	CD	Sire	9262052	1990	£20	£8	*US promo in velvet cover, with John Cale*
Transformer	CD	RCA	C8819	1988	£15	£6	*box set*
Walk And Talk It	7"	RCA	RCA2240	1972	£5	£2	
Walk On The Wild Side	CD-s	RCA	PD49453	1989	£5	£2	

REED, LULA

Title	Format	Label	Number	Year	Mint	VG	Notes
Blue And Moody	LP	King	604	1959	£200	£100	US
Lula Reed & Freddie King	7" EP	Ember	EMBEP4536	1963	£25	£12.50	with Freddie King
Lula Reed & Syl Johnson	7" EP	Ember	EMBEP4535	1963	£25	£12.50	with Syl Johnson
Troubles On Your Mind	7"	Parlophone	CMSP34	1955	£25	£10	export

REED, NEHEMIAH

Title	Format	Label	Number	Year	Mint	VG	Notes
Family War	7"	Island	WI3102	1968	£10	£5	

REED, OLIVER

Title	Format	Label	Number	Year	Mint	VG	Notes
Sometimes	7"	Piccadilly	7N35037	1962	£5	£2	
Wild One	7"	Decca	F11390	1961	£8	£4	

REED, TAWNY

Title	Format	Label	Number	Year	Mint	VG	Notes
Needle In A Haystack	7"	Pye	7N15935	1965	£4	£1.50	
You Can't Take It Away	7"	Pye	7N17078	1966	£4	£1.50	

REEGAN, VALA & THE VALARONS

Title	Format	Label	Number	Year	Mint	VG	Notes
Fireman	7"	Atlantic	584009	1966	£100	£50	

REESE, DELLA

Title	Format	Label	Number	Year	Mint	VG	Notes
Della	LP	RCA	RD27167/SF5057	1960	£10	£4	
Della Della Cha-Cha-Cha	LP	RCA	RD27208/SF5091	1961	£10	£4	
I Cried For You	7"	London	HL7024	1957	£6	£2.50	export
On Stage	LP	RCA	RD/SF7508	1963	£10	£4	
Sermonette	7"	London	HLJ8814	1959	£5	£2	
Special Delivery	LP	RCA	RD27234/SF5112	1962	£10	£4	
Story Of The Blues	LP	London	LTZJ15163/ SAHJ6021	1959	£15	£6	
You Gotta Love Everybody	7"	London	HLJ8687	1958	£6	£2.50	

REESE, PETER & THE PAGES

Title	Format	Label	Number	Year	Mint	VG	Notes
Hippy Hippy Shake	LP	Philips	P48075L	1964	£25	£10	German

REESE, TONY

Title	Format	Label	Number	Year	Mint	VG	Notes
Just About This Time Tomorrow	7"	London	HLJ8987	1959	£5	£2	

REEVES, EDDIE

Title	Format	Label	Number	Year	Mint	VG	Notes
Cry Baby	7"	London	HL9548	1962	£6	£2.50	

REEVES, JIM

Title	Format	Label	Number	Year	Mint	VG	Notes
Bimbo	7"	London	HL8014	1954	£125	£62.50	
Bimbo	LP	London	HAU8015	1962	£15	£6	
Bimbo Boy	7" EP	London	REP1015	1954	£60	£30	
Bimbo Vol. 2	7" EP	London	REP1033	1955	£60	£30	
Blue Boy	7"	RCA	RCA1074	1958	£10	£5	
Butterfly Love	7"	London	HL8055	1954	£125	£62.50	
Drinking Tequila	7"	London	HL8159	1955	£150	£75	
Echo Bonita	7"	London	HL8064	1954	£125	£62.50	
Four Walls	7"	RCA	RCA1005	1957	£20	£10	
Girls I Have Known	LP	RCA	LPM1685	1958	£20	£8	US
God Be With You	LP	RCA	LPM/LSP1950	1958	£12	£5	US
He'll Have To Go	LP	RCA	RD27176	1960	£10	£4	
Intimate Jim Reeves	LP	RCA	RD27193/SF5079	1961	£10	£4	
Jim Reeves	LP	RCA	LPM1576	1957	£25	£10	US
Jim Reeves Sings	LP	Abbott	LP5001	1956	£350	£210	US
Jimbo	LP	RCA	LPM1410	1957	£30	£15	US
Mexican Joe	7"	London	HL8030	1954	£125	£62.50	
Padre Of Old San Antone	7"	London	HL8105	1954	£75	£37.50	
Partners	7"	RCA	RCA1144	1959	£10	£2	tri-centre
Penny Candy	7"	London	HL8118	1955	£100	£50	
Singing Down The Lane	LP	RCA	LPM1256	1956	£50	£25	US
Songs To Warm Your Heart	LP	RCA	LPM/LSP2001	1959	£12	£5	US
Tahiti	7"	London	HLU8185	1955	£100	£50	
Talkin' To Your Heart	LP	RCA	LPM/LSP2339	1961	£12	£5	US
Tall Tales And Short Tempers	LP	RCA	LPM/LSP2284	1961	£12	£5	US
Wilder Your Heart Beats	7"	London	HLU8351	1956	£100	£50	

REFLECTION

Title	Format	Label	Number	Year	Mint	VG	Notes
Present Tense	LP	Reflection	RL301	1968	£25	£10	

REFLECTIONS

Title	Format	Label	Number	Year	Mint	VG	Notes
Just Like Romeo And Juliet	7"	Stateside	SS294	1964	£15	£7.50	
Just Like Romeo And Juliet	LP	Golden World	LPM300	1964	£50	£25	US
Poor Man's Son	7"	Stateside	SS406	1965	£5	£2	
Poor Man's Son	7" EP	Stateside	SE1034	1965	£30	£15	

REFLECTIONS (2)

Title	Format	Label	Number	Year	Mint	VG	Notes
Love And Affection	7"	Purple	PUR124	1974	£4	£1.50	
Moon Power	7"	Purple	PUR127	1975	£4	£1.50	

REFUGEE

Title	Format	Label	Number	Year	Mint	VG	Notes
Refugee	LP	Charisma	CAS1087	1974	£10	£4	

REGAN, JOAN

Title	Format	Label	Number	Year	Mint	VG	Notes
Cross Of Gold	7"	Decca	F10659	1956	£8	£4	

Title	Format	Label	Cat. No.	Year	Mint	VG+	Notes
Danger Heartbreak Ahead	7"	Decca	F10505	1955	£5	£2	
Don't Take Me For Granted	7"	Decca	F10710	1956	£4	£1.50	
Don't Talk To Me About Love	7"	CBS	202100	1966	£25	£12.50	
Girl Next Door	10" LP	Decca	LF1182	1954	£20	£8	
Gone	7"	Decca	F10801	1956	£4	£1.50	
Honestly	7"	Decca	F10742	1956	£4	£1.50	
If I Give My Heart To You	7"	Decca	F10373	1954	£10	£5	
Just Joan	LP	Decca	LK4153	1956	£10	£4	
Just Say You Love Her	7"	Decca	F10521	1955	£5	£2	
No One Beside You	7"	CBS	2657	1967	£10	£5	
Open Up Your Heart	7"	Decca	F10474	1955	£10	£5	
Prize Of Gold	7"	Decca	F10432	1955	£10	£5	
Shepherd Boy	7"	Decca	F10598	1955	£5	£2	
Successes	7" EP	Decca	DFE6235	1955	£10	£5	
Successes Vol. 2	7" EP	Decca	DFE6278	1956	£10	£5	
Sweet Heartaches	7"	Decca	F10757	1956	£4	£1.50	
This Ole House	7"	Decca	F10397	1954	£10	£5	
Wait For Me Darling	7"	Decca	F10362	1954	£15	£7.50	

REGENTS

Title	Format	Label	Cat. No.	Year	Mint	VG+	Notes
Barbara Ann	7"	Columbia	DB4666	1961	£10	£5	
Barbara Ann	LP	Gee	(S)GLP708	1961	£50	£25	*US*
Live At The Am/Pm Discotheque	LP	Capitol	(S)KAO2153	1964	£30	£15	*US*
Runaround	7"	Columbia	DB4694	1961	£10	£5	

REGENTS (2)

Title	Format	Label	Cat. No.	Year	Mint	VG+	Notes
Bye Bye Johnny	7"	Oriole	CB1912	1964	£15	£7.50	

REGENTS (3)

Title	Format	Label	Cat. No.	Year	Mint	VG+	Notes
Words	7"	CBS	202247	1966	£12	£6	

REGENTS (4)

Title	Format	Label	Cat. No.	Year	Mint	VG+	Notes
Seventeen	7"	Rialto	TREB111	1979	£5	£2	

REGGAE BOYS

Title	Format	Label	Cat. No.	Year	Mint	VG+	Notes
Hurry Up	7"	Upsetter	US339	1970	£6	£2.50	
Me No Born Ya	7"	Amalgamated	AMG841	1969	£6	£2.50	
Pupa Live On Eye Top	7"	Bullet	BU431	1970	£4	£1.50	
Reggae Train	7"	Amalgamated	AMG843	1969	£6	£2.50	
Walk By Day Fly By Night	7"	Pressure Beat	PB5503	1970	£4	£1.50	*Joe Gibbs B side*

REICH, STEVE

Title	Format	Label	Cat. No.	Year	Mint	VG+	Notes
Four Organs	LP	Shandar	83511		£12	£5	
Four Organs	LP	Angel	S36059		£12	£5	
Live/Electronic Music	LP	Columbia	MS7265		£12	£5	*US*
New Sounds In Electronic Music	LP	Odyssey	32160160		£12	£5	

REICHEL, ACHIM

Title	Format	Label	Cat. No.	Year	Mint	VG+	Notes
A.R.3	LP	Zebra	2949006	1973	£15	£6	*German*
A.R.4	LP	Zebra	2949008	1973	£15	£6	*German*
Autovision	LP	Zebra	2949016	1974	£15	£6	*German*
Die Grüne Reise	LP	Polydor	2371128	1971	£20	£8	*German*
Echo	LP	Polydor	2633003	1972	£25	£10	*German double*
Erholung	LP	Brain	1068	1975	£12	£5	*German*

REID, CARLTON

Title	Format	Label	Cat. No.	Year	Mint	VG+	Notes
Leave Me To Cry	7"	Blue Cat	BS162	1969	£6	£2.50	
Turn On The Lights	7"	Ska Beat	JB254	1966	£10	£5	

REID, DANNY

Title	Format	Label	Cat. No.	Year	Mint	VG+	Notes
Teenager Feels It Too	7"	London	HLK9274	1961	£4	£1.50	

REID, DUKE

Title	Format	Label	Cat. No.	Year	Mint	VG+	Notes
Duke's Cookies	7"	Blue Beat	BB24	1960	£12	£6	*Jiving Juniors B side*
Hurt	7"	Duke Reid	DR2522	1971	£4	£1.50	
Mood I Am In	7"	Blue Beat	BB165	1963	£12	£6	*Stranger Cole B side*
Religious Service At Bond Street Gospel Hall	7"	Master's Time	MT003	1967	£4	£1.50	
True Confession	7"	Doctor Bird	DB1028	1966	£10	£5	*Tommy McCook B side*

REID, LEROY

Title	Format	Label	Cat. No.	Year	Mint	VG+	Notes
Fiddler	7"	Blue Cat	BS125	1968	£6	£2.50	*Lovelettes B side*

REID, P.

Title	Format	Label	Cat. No.	Year	Mint	VG+	Notes
Redeemed	7"	Ska Beat	JB197	1965	£10	£5	

REID, TERRY

Title	Format	Label	Cat. No.	Year	Mint	VG+	Notes
Bang Bang, You're Terry Reid	LP	Epic	BN26427	1968	£15	£6	*US*
Better By Far	7"	Columbia	DB8409	1968	£8	£4	
Hand Don't Fit The Glove	7"	Columbia	DB8166	1967	£6	£2.50	
River	LP	Warner Bros	K40340	1973	£10	£4	
Superlungs	7"	Columbia	PSRS323	1969	£10	£5	*1 sided demo*
Terry Reid	LP	Columbia	SCX6370	1969	£15	£6	

REIGN

Title	Format	Label	Cat. No.	Year	Mint	VG+	Notes
Line Of Least Resistance	7"	Regal Zonophone	RZ3028	1970	£40	£20	

REIGN GHOST

Allied	LP				**£200**	**£100**	*Canadian*

REILLY, JOHN

Bonny Green Tree	LP	Topic	12T359	1978	**£12**	**£5**	

REILLY, PADDY

At Home	LP	Dolphin	DOLM5006	1975	**£15**	**£6**	*Irish*
Fields Of Athenry	LP	Dolphin	DLX9002		**£15**	**£6**	
Life Of Paddy Reilly	LP	Dolphin	DOLM5001	1975	**£15**	**£6**	*Irish*
Town I Loved So Well	LP	Dolphin	DOLM5010	1975	**£15**	**£6**	*Irish*

REILLY, VINI

Vini Reilly	7"	Factory	FACT244+	1989	**£12**	**£5**	*with 7" by Reilly & Morrissey*
Vini Reilly	CD	Factory	FACD244	1988	**£20**	**£8**	*with 3" CD by Reilly & Morrissey*

REINHARDT, DJANGO

Art Of Django	LP	HMV	CLP1340	1960	**£15**	**£6**	
Django	10" LP	Mercury	MG10019	1957	**£40**	**£20**	
Django	LP	HMV	CLP1249	1959	**£20**	**£8**	
Django – The Unforgettable	LP	HMV	CLP1389	1960	**£15**	**£6**	
Django Reinhardt	10" LP	HMV	DLP1045	1954	**£40**	**£20**	
Django Reinhardt	7" EP	HMV	7EG8132	1955	**£5**	**£2**	
Django Reinhardt Vol. 1	10" LP	Vogue	LDE049	1954	**£40**	**£20**	
Django Reinhardt Vol. 2	10" LP	Vogue	LDE084	1954	**£40**	**£20**	
Django Reinhardt Vol. 3	10" LP	Vogue	LDE106	1954	**£40**	**£20**	
Improvisation	7" EP	Collector	JEN8	1962	**£5**	**£2**	
Memorial	LP	Vogue	LAE12251	1961	**£10**	**£4**	
Nuages	10" LP	Felsted	EDL87005	1954	**£40**	**£20**	
Requiem For A Jazzman	LP	Ember	CJS810	196–	**£12**	**£5**	
Swing From Paris	10" LP	Decca	LF1139	1953	**£40**	**£20**	
Swing Guitars	7" EP	Collector	JEN6	1961	**£5**	**£2**	

REIVERS

Work Of The Reivers Vol. 2	7" EP	Top Rank	JKP2062	1960	**£5**	**£2**	

RELEASE MUSIC ORCHESTRA

Garuda	LP	Brain	1072	1975	**£10**	**£4**	*German*
Get The Ball	LP	Brain	1083	1975	**£10**	**£4**	*German*
Life	LP	Brain	1056	1974	**£12**	**£5**	*German*

RELF, JANE

Without A Song From You	7"	Decca	F13231	1971	**£15**	**£7.50**	

RELF, KEITH

Mr Zero	7"	Columbia	DB7920	1966	**£20**	**£10**	
Shapes In My Mind	7"	Columbia	DB8084	1966	**£30**	**£15**	

RELOAD

Auto Reload	12"	Evolution	EVO02	1992	**£12**	**£6**	
Reload	12"	Evolution	EVO01	1992	**£12**	**£6**	
Reload	12"	Evolution	EVO03	1992	**£10**	**£5**	

R.E.M.

R.E.M. stand in the odd position of having signed a record-breaking 1996 contract with Warner Bros, making them in one sense the biggest rock group in the world, yet have achieved such little chart success in the UK that the casual listener is likely to be largely unaware of their music. Arguably, the group's eighties version of a Byrds–Band hybrid is a little too restrained, a little too dignified to be inspirational in the way that those sixties bands were. For this listener, R.E.M. never sounded so convincing as when they borrowed the vocal chords of Kate Pierson from the B52's, while Michael Stipe has produced his best work in a side-project, as a member of the Golden Palominos.

Academy Fight Song	7"	fan club	122589	1989	**£75**	**£37.50**	
AOR Staple	CD	IRS	IRSDSEVEN	1987	**£30**	**£15**	*US promo compilation*
Automatic For The People	CD	Warner Bros	9362450552	1992	**£25**	**£10**	*boxed with cards*
Baby Baby	7"	fan club	122591	1991	**£50**	**£25**	
Can't Get There From Here	12"	IRS	IRT102	1985	**£10**	**£5**	
Can't Get There From Here	7"	IRS	IRM102	1985	**£6**	**£2.50**	
Chronic Town	LP	IRS	SP70502	1982	**£20**	**£8**	*US, gargoyle label*
Dead Letter Office	CD	IRS	CDA70054	1987	**£12**	**£5**	
Document	CD	IRS	DMIRG1025	1987	**£12**	**£5**	
Fables Of The Reconstruction	CD	IRS	DMIRF1003	1987	**£12**	**£5**	
Fall On Me	12"	IRS	IRMT121	1986	**£10**	**£5**	
Fall On Me	7"	IRS	IRM121	1986	**£5**	**£2**	
Femme Fatale	7"	Evatone	REAL005	1986	**£15**	**£7.50**	*US flexi, picture sleeve*
Finest Worksong	12"	IRS	IRMT161	1988	**£8**	**£4**	
Finest Worksong	CD-s	IRS	DIRM161	1988	**£15**	**£7.50**	*6" box*
Ghost Reindeer In The Sky	7"	fan club	122590	1990	**£50**	**£25**	
Green	CD	Warner Bros	PROCD3292	1988	**£25**	**£10**	*US promo, cloth cover*
It's The End Of The World As We Know It	12"	IRS	IRMT145	1987	**£8**	**£4**	
It's The End Of The World As We Know It	7"	IRS	IRM145	1987	**£4**	**£1.50**	

Title	Format	Label	Cat. No.	Year	Price	Price	Notes
It's The End Of The World As We Know It	CD-s	IRS	DIRMX180	1992	**£10**	**£5**	
It's The End Of The World As We Know It	CD-s	MCA	DMIRT180	1991	**£5**	**£2**	
It's The End Of The World As We Know It	CD-s	IRS	DIRM145	1987	**£20**	**£10**	
Losing My Religion	CD-s	Warner Bros	W0015CDX	1991	**£20**	**£10**	*with poster*
Losing My Religion	CD-s	Warner Bros	W0015CD	1991	**£6**	**£2.50**	
Murmur	CD	A&M	CDA7014	1988	**£12**	**£5**	
Near Wild Heaven	CD-s	Warner Bros	W0055CDX	1991	**£5**	**£2**	
One I Love	12"	IRS	IRMT146	1987	**£8**	**£4**	
One I Love	7"	IRS	IRM146	1987	**£4**	**£1.50**	
One I Love	CD-s	IRS	DIRM146	1987	**£15**	**£7.50**	
One I Love	CD-s	MCA	DIRM178	1991	**£5**	**£2**	
One I Love	CD-s	IRS	DIRM173	1988	**£10**	**£5**	
One I Love	CD-s	IRS	DIRMX178	1991	**£5**	**£2**	
Orange Crush	7"	Warner Bros	W2960B	1989	**£8**	**£4**	*boxed with poster*
Orange Crush	CD-s	Warner Bros	W2960CD	1989	**£10**	**£5**	*3" single*
Our Price New Releases	CD	Our Price	no number	1995	**£75**	**£37.50**	*promo*
Out Of Time	CD	Warner Bros	7599264962	1991	**£20**	**£8**	*black 'leather' cover, with 10 cards*
Parade Of The Wooden Soldiers	7"	fan club	U23528M	1988	**£100**	**£50**	*green vinyl*
Pop Songs 89–95	CD	Warner Bros	SAM1558	1995	**£40**	**£20**	*promo compilation*
Pop Songs 89–95	CD	Warner Bros	SAM1558	1995	**£20**	**£8**	*promo*
Radio Free Europe	7"	Hibtone	HT0001	1981	**£100**	**£50**	*US*
Radio Free Europe	7"	IRS	PFP1017	1983	**£30**	**£15**	
Radio Song	CD-s	Warner Bros	W0072CDX	1991	**£8**	**£4**	*in case for CD set*
Rockville	12"	IRS	IRSX107	1984	**£15**	**£7.50**	
Rockville	7"	IRS	IRS107	1984	**£12**	**£6**	
Sampler From The Best Of R.E.M.	CD	Warner Bros	REM1	1994	**£40**	**£20**	*promo*
Shall We Talk About The Weather	CD	Warner Bros	PROCD3377	1988	**£25**	**£10**	*US promo*
Shiny Happy People	CD-s	Warner Bros	W0027CDX	1991	**£8**	**£4**	
Shiny Happy People	CD-s	Warner Bros	W0027CD	1991	**£5**	**£2**	
Silver Bells	7"	fan club	L41936X	1993	**£25**	**£10**	
Songs That Are Live	CD	Warner Bros	PROCD7888	1995	**£25**	**£10**	*promo*
South Central Rain	12"	IRS	IRSX105	1984	**£12**	**£6**	
South Central Rain	7"	IRS	IRS105	1984	**£8**	**£4**	
Stand	12"	Warner Bros	W2833T	1989	**£8**	**£4**	
Stand	7"	Warner Bros	W2833	1989	**£4**	**£1.50**	
Stand	7"	Warner Bros	W2833W	1989	**£8**	**£4**	
Stand	CD-s	Warner Bros	W2833CDX	1989	**£15**	**£7.50**	*black sleeve in envelope*
Stand	CD-s	Warner Bros	W2833CD	1989	**£10**	**£5**	
Stand	CD-s	Warner Bros	W7577CD	1989	**£8**	**£4**	*3" single*
Stand	CD-s	Warner Bros	W7577CDX	1989	**£20**	**£10**	*3" single, maple leaf pack*
Superman	12"	IRS	IRMT128	1986	**£8**	**£4**	
Superman	7"	IRS	IRM128	1986	**£5**	**£2**	
Talk About The Passion	12"	IRS	PFSX1026	1983	**£20**	**£10**	
Talk About The Passion	7"	IRS	PFP1026	1983	**£25**	**£12.50**	*promo only*
Tighten Up	7"	Bucketfull Of Brains	BOB5	1985	**£6**	**£2.50**	*flexi*
Wendell Gee	12"	IRS	IRT105	1985	**£10**	**£5**	
Wendell Gee	7"	IRS	IRMD105	1985	**£10**	**£5**	*double*
Wendell Gee	7"	IRS	IRM105	1985	**£8**	**£4**	
Where's Captain Kirk?	7"	fan club	REM92	1992	**£40**	**£20**	
Wolves Lower	7"	Trouser Press	FLEXI12	1982	**£20**	**£10**	*US, flexi*

REMAINS

Title	Format	Label	Cat. No.	Year	Price	Price	Notes
Remains	LP	Epic	LN24214/ BN26214	1967	**£75**	**£37.50**	*US*
Remains	LP	Spoonfed	3305	1978	**£15**	**£6**	*US*

REMA-REMA

Title	Format	Label	Cat. No.	Year	Price	Price	Notes
Wheel In The Roses	12"	4AD	BAD5	1980	**£6**	**£2.50**	

REMO FOUR

Title	Format	Label	Cat. No.	Year	Price	Price	Notes
Attention	LP	Phonogram	6434158	1973	**£20**	**£8**	*German*
Live Like A Lady	7"	Fontana	TF787	1967	**£50**	**£25**	
Peter Gunn	7"	Piccadilly	7N35175	1964	**£10**	**£5**	
Sally Go Round The Roses	7"	Piccadilly	7N35186	1964	**£10**	**£5**	
Smile	LP	Starclub	STY158034	1967	**£100**	**£50**	*German*

RENAISSANCE

The history of Renaissance is complicated by the fact that the name covers what, in effect, are two entirely different groups. The first eponymous LP was made by ex-Yardbirds Keith Relf and Jim McCarty and represented the results of a conscious attempt to broaden their music beyond the Yardbirds' blues-based material. It is Beethoven, rather than Jimmy Reed, who is the major influence here. While making the second LP, however (eventually given a limited release as *Illusion*), the group fell apart, with only pianist John Hawken prepared to carry on. He found a new group of musicians to complete the line-up, then decided to leave himself. The immediate result was a stage set consisting of songs from the first LP played by a set of musicians, none of whom had played on the record. Somewhat later, most of the original members got back together, but now had to issue their records under the name Illusion, as the second Renaissance had become quite successful in their own right during the intervening years.

Title	Format	Label	Cat. No.	Year	Price	Price	Notes
Illusion	LP	Island	6339017	1972	**£20**	**£8**	*German*
Illusion	LP	Island	HELP27	1976	**£40**	**£20**	*test pressing only*
Jekyll And Hyde	7"	Sire	SIR4019	1979	**£10**	**£5**	
Northern Lights	7"	Sire	SRE1022	1978	**£10**	**£5**	*export picture disc*

Title	Format	Label	Cat. No.	Year	Mint	VG	Notes
Prologue/Ashes Are Burning	LP	Sovereign	CAPACK3	1979	**£12**	**£5**	*double*
Renaissance	LP	Island	ILPS9114	1969	**£20**	**£8**	*pink label*
Scheherazade	LP	Mobile Fidelity	MFSL1099	1982	**£10**	**£4**	*US audiophile*
Sea	7"	Island	WIP6079	1970	**£4**	**£1.50**	

RENAUD

Title	Format	Label	Cat. No.	Year	Mint	VG	Notes
Renaud	LP	Disjuncta	000003	1975	**£15**	**£6**	*French*

RENAUD, HENRI

Title	Format	Label	Cat. No.	Year	Mint	VG	Notes
Henri Renaud All Stars	10" LP	Vogue	LDE088	1955	**£30**	**£15**	
Henri Renaud Band	10" LP	Vogue	LDE111	1955	**£30**	**£15**	
Henri Renaud–Al Cohn Quartet	10" LP	Vogue	LDE103	1954	**£30**	**£15**	
Henri Renaud–Bobby Jaspar Quintet	10" LP	Vogue	LDE096	1955	**£30**	**£15**	

RENAUD, LINE

Title	Format	Label	Cat. No.	Year	Mint	VG	Notes
If I Love You	7"	Capitol	CL14230	1955	**£8**	**£4**	
Line And Dino	7" EP	Capitol	EAP120060	1961	**£8**	**£4**	*with Dean Martin*

RENAY, DIANE

Title	Format	Label	Cat. No.	Year	Mint	VG	Notes
Kiss Me Sailor	7"	Stateside	SS290	1964	**£4**	**£1.50**	
Navy Blue	LP	Twentieth Century	TF(S)3133	1964	**£12**	**£5**	*US*
Troublemaker	7"	MGM	MGM1274	1965	**£5**	**£2**	
Unbelievable Guy	7"	Stateside	SS270	1964	**£5**	**£2**	
Watch Out Sally	7"	MGM	MGM1262	1964	**£5**	**£2**	

RENBOURN, JOHN

Title	Format	Label	Cat. No.	Year	Mint	VG	Notes
Another Monday	LP	Transatlantic	TRA149	1966	**£15**	**£6**	
Enchanted Garden	LP	Transatlantic	TRA356	1980	**£10**	**£4**	
Faro Annie	LP	Transatlantic	TRA247	1971	**£10**	**£4**	
Hermit	LP	Transatlantic	TRA336	1976	**£15**	**£6**	
John Renbourn	LP	Transatlantic	TRA135	1965	**£15**	**£6**	
Lady & The Unicorn	LP	Transatlantic	TRA224	1970	**£12**	**£5**	
Maid In Bedlam	LP	Transatlantic	TRA348	1977	**£10**	**£4**	
Sir John Alot Of Merrie England	LP	Transatlantic	TRA167	1968	**£12**	**£5**	

RENBOURN, JOHN & STEFAN GROSSMAN

Title	Format	Label	Cat. No.	Year	Mint	VG	Notes
John Renbourn And Stefan Grossman	LP	Sonet	SNTF139	1978	**£10**	**£4**	

RENDELL, DON

As one of the British jazz musicians to emerge after the War, saxophonist Don Rendell's earliest records are not especially remarkable. Unlike the majority of his contemporaries, however, Rendell was interested in the way jazz in America was moving forwards. *Roarin'* is a good hard bop recording which stands up well against the American competition. It also features the playing of a young Graham Bond on alto saxophone. Later Don Rendell formed a quintet with trumpeter Ian Carr and the pair proceeded to create an English version of what Miles Davis was doing in America. When Davis went electric, Ian Carr did the same, founding the group Nucleus. For Rendell, however, this was a step too far. His contribution to rock-influenced jazz is limited to membership of the jazz orchestra used on Neil Ardley's *Symphony Of Amaranths*.

Title	Format	Label	Cat. No.	Year	Mint	VG	Notes
Don Rendell Jazz Six	7" EP	Pye	NJE1044	1957	**£25**	**£12.50**	
Don Rendell Presents The Jazz Six	LP	Nixa	NJL7	1957	**£150**	**£75**	
Don Rendell Quartet	7" EP	Tempo	EXA11	1955	**£50**	**£25**	
Don Rendell Quintet	7" EP	Tempo	EXA20	1956	**£15**	**£7.50**	
Don Rendell Sextet	7" EP	Tempo	EXA16	1955	**£15**	**£7.50**	*2 tracks by Damian Robinson*
Don Rendell Sextet	7" EP	Tempo	EXA12	1955	**£50**	**£25**	
In Paris	10" LP	Vogue	LDE144	1955	**£100**	**£50**	
Jazz At The Festival Hall	LP	Decca	LK4087	1954	**£100**	**£50**	
Jazz Britannia	7" EP	MGM	MGMEP615	1957	**£15**	**£7.50**	*2 tracks by Joe Harriott*
Jazz Committee	7" EP	Decca	DFE6587	1959	**£15**	**£7.50**	
Meet Don Rendell	10" LP	Tempo	LAP1	1955	**£200**	**£100**	
Music In The Making	10" LP	Vogue	LDE050	1954	**£100**	**£50**	
Packet Of Blues	7" EP	Decca	DFE6501	1958	**£15**	**£7.50**	
Playtime	LP	Decca	LK4265	1958	**£100**	**£50**	
Roarin'	LP	Jazzland	JLP51	1962	**£100**	**£50**	
Spacewalk	LP	Columbia	SCX6491	1971	**£60**	**£30**	
Tenorama	LP	Nixa	NJL4	1956	**£100**	**£50**	

RENDELL, DON & IAN CARR QUINTET

Title	Format	Label	Cat. No.	Year	Mint	VG	Notes
Change Is	LP	Columbia	SCX6368	1969	**£200**	**£100**	
Dusk Fire	LP	Columbia	SX6064	1966	**£200**	**£100**	
Live	LP	Columbia	SX/SCX6316	1969	**£150**	**£75**	
Phase III	LP	Columbia	SX/SCX6214	1968	**£150**	**£75**	
Shades Of Blue	LP	Columbia	33SX1733	1965	**£250**	**£150**	

RENE, GOOGIE

Title	Format	Label	Cat. No.	Year	Mint	VG	Notes
Chica Boo	7"	Atlantic	584015	1966	**£4**	**£1.50**	
Forever	7"	London	HLY9056	1960	**£8**	**£4**	
Smokey Joe's Lala	7"	Atlantic	AT4076	1966	**£15**	**£7.50**	

RENE & RENE

Title	Format	Label	Cat. No.	Year	Mint	VG	Notes
Loving You Could Hurt Me So	7"	Island	WIP6001	1967	**£4**	**£1.50**	

RENE & THE ALLIGATORS

Title	Format	Label	Cat. No.	Year	Mint	VG	Notes
Guitar Boogie	LP	Fontana	826401	1967	**£30**	**£15**	*Dutch*
She Broke My Heart	7"	Decca	F22324	1966	**£6**	**£2.50**	

RENEGADE

Title	Format	Label	Cat. No.	Year	Mint	VG	Notes
Lonely Road	12"	White Witch	WIT1	1980	£50	£25	

RENEGADE SOUNDWAVE

Title	Format	Label	Cat. No.	Year	Mint	VG	Notes
Cocaine Sex	12"	Rhythm King	LEFT20T	1988	£20	£10	
Kray Twins	12"	Rhythm King	LEFT8T	1987	£6	£2.50	

RENEGADES

Title	Format	Label	Cat. No.	Year	Mint	VG	Notes
Cadillac	7"	Polydor	56508	1970	£15	£7.50	
Cadillac	7" EP	Riviera	231113	1965	£75	£37.50	*French*
Cadillac	LP	Artone	PSM041	1965	£40	£20	*Dutch*
Cadillac	LP	Ariola	73368	1965	£75	£37.50	*German*
Half And Half	LP	Ariston	AR0162	1967	£60	£30	*Italian*
Have Beat, Will Travel	LP	Artone	PSM034	1965	£40	£20	*Dutch*
No Man's Land	7"	Columbia	DB8383	1968	£10	£5	
Pop	LP	Artone	PSM007	1965	£40	£20	*Dutch*
Take A Heart	LP	Ariola	73956	1966	£75	£37.50	*German*
Take A Message	7"	Parlophone	R5592	1967	£10	£5	
Thirteen Women	7"	President	PT106	1968	£50	£25	

RENIA

Title	Format	Label	Cat. No.	Year	Mint	VG	Notes
First Offenders	LP	Transatlantic	TRA261	1973	£15	£6	

RENNARD, JON

Title	Format	Label	Cat. No.	Year	Mint	VG	Notes
Brimbledon Fair	LP	Tradition	TSR003	1970	£12	£5	
Parting Glass	LP	Tradition	TSR010	1971	£12	£5	

RENO, DON & RED SMILEY

Title	Format	Label	Cat. No.	Year	Mint	VG	Notes
Country And Western	7" EP	Parlophone	GEP8777	1958	£15	£7.50	

RENTAL, ROBERT

Title	Format	Label	Cat. No.	Year	Mint	VG	Notes
Bridge	LP	Industrial	IR0007	1979	£10	£4	*with Thomas Leer*
Paralysis	7"	Regular	ER102	1978	£5	£2	

REO SPEEDWAGON

Title	Format	Label	Cat. No.	Year	Mint	VG	Notes
Life As We Know It	LP	Epic	E2S2640	1987	£20	£8	*US double promo*

REPARATA & THE DELRONS

Title	Format	Label	Cat. No.	Year	Mint	VG	Notes
Captain Of Your Ship	7"	Bell	BLL1002	1968	£4	£1.50	
I Can Hear The Rain	7"	RCA	RCA1691	1968	£5	£2	
Saturday Night It Didn't Happen	7"	Bell	BLL1014	1968	£15	£7.50	
Tommy	7"	Stateside	SS414	1965	£6	£2.50	
Whenever A Teenager Cries	7"	Stateside	SS382	1965	£10	£5	
Whenever A Teenager Cries	LP	World Artists	2/3006	1965	£30	£15	*US*

RESEARCH 1-6-12

Title	Format	Label	Cat. No.	Year	Mint	VG	Notes
1-6-12 In Research	LP	Flick City	FC5001	1967	£60	£30	*US*

RESIDENTS

The Residents' gimmick of keeping the individual members' identities completely secret has, amazingly, been successfully maintained since the early seventies. Their music is extremely eccentric, a quality that is emphasized by their record release policy. The proliferation of limited-edition cover designs, coloured vinyls and so forth listed here does not include such ultra-rarities as a one-sided clear vinyl 'Duck Stab' 12", of which just six copies were made.

Title	Format	Label	Cat. No.	Year	Mint	VG	Notes
Big Bubble	LP	Ralph	RZ8552	1985	£50	£25	*US pink marbled vinyl*
Blorp Esette	LP	LAFMS	005	1975	£50	£25	*US*
Census Taker	LP	Episode	ED21	1985	£30	£15	*US*
Commercial Album	LP	Pre	PREX2	1980	£10	£4	
Commercial Single	7"	Pre	PRE009	1980	£8	£4	
Diskomo	CD-s	Torso	CD421	1990	£5	£2	
Double Shot	CD-s	Torso	TORSOCD355	1989	£5	£2	*3" single*
Duck Stab/Buster And Glen	LP	Ralph	RR0278	1978	£10	£4	*US*
Eskimo	LP	Ralph	ESK7906	1983	£20	£8	*US picture disc*
Eskimo	LP	Ralph	ESK7906	1979	£10	£4	*US*
Eskimo	LP	Ralph	ESK7906	1979	£25	£10	*US, white vinyl*
Fingerprince	LP	Ralph	RR1276	1977	£50	£25	*US, brown sleeve*
Fingerprince	LP	Ralph	RR1276	1978	£20	£8	*US, sienna sleeve*
Fingerprince	LP	Ralph	RR1276	1979	£10	£4	*US, black & pink sleeve*
George And James	LP	Korova	KODE9	1984	£10	£4	
George And James	LP	Ralph	RZ8402	1984	£50	£25	*US, clear vinyl*
George And James	LP	Ralph	RZ8402	1984	£15	£6	*US*
Hit The Road Jack	7"	Torso	70032	1987	£4	£1.50	*picture disc*
Intermission	12"	London	RALPH1	1983	£6	£2.50	
Intermission	LP	Ralph	RZ8522	1982	£10	£4	*US*
It's A Man's Man's Man's World	7"	Korova	KOW36	1984	£4	£1.50	
Kaw-Liga	CD-s	Torso	CD322	1988	£5	£2	
Mark Of The Mole	LP	Ralph	RZ8152	1981	£25	£10	*US, brown vinyl*
Mark Of The Mole	LP	Ralph	RZ8152	1981	£10	£4	*US*
Meet The Residents	LP	Ralph	RR0677	1985	£20	£8	*US picture disc*
Meet The Residents	LP	Ralph	RR0274	1974	£75	£37.50	*US*
Meet The Residents (remixed)	LP	Ralph	RR0677	1977	£10	£4	*US*
Mole Show	LP	Ralph	MOLESHOW001	1983	£25	£10	*US picture disc*
Mole Show	LP	Ralph	MOLESHOW001	1983	£15	£6	*US*
Nibbles	LP	Virgin	VR3	1979	£10	£4	
Not Available	LP	Ralph	RR1174	1978	£50	£25	*US, purple label*

Not Available	LP	Ralph	RR1174	1978	**£10**	**£4**	*US*
Pal TV LP	LP	Doublevision	DVR17	1985	**£10**	**£4**	*red vinyl*
Please Do Not Steal It	LP	Ralph	DJ7901	1979	**£15**	**£6**	*US*
Ralph Before '84 Vol. 1	LP	Korova	KODE10	1984	**£10**	**£4**	
Ralph Before '84 Vol. 2	LP	Korova	KODE12	1985	**£10**	**£4**	
Residents Radio Special	LP	Ralph	173	1977	**£25**	**£10**	*US promo*
Residue Of The Residents	LP	Ralph	RZ8302	1983	**£10**	**£4**	*US*
Stars And Hank Forever	LP	Ralph		1986	**£50**	**£25**	*US green vinyl*
Subterranean Modern	LP	Ralph	SM7908	1979	**£10**	**£4**	*US*
Ten Years In Twenty Minutes	LP	Ralph	RR8205D	198–	**£50**	**£25**	*US clear vinyl, 1 sided, no sleeve*
Third Reich And Roll	LP	Ralph	RR1075	1975	**£50**	**£25**	*US, orange & green carrot on sleeve*
Third Reich And Roll	LP	Ralph	RR1075	1977	**£20**	**£8**	*US, censored sleeve*
Third Reich And Roll	LP	Ralph	RR1075	1979	**£10**	**£4**	*US*
Thirteenth Anniversary Edition	LP	Ralph	RZ8602	1986	**£15**	**£6**	*US picture disc*
Title In Limbo	LP	Ralph	RR8351	1983	**£10**	**£4**	*with Renaldo & The Loaf*
Tunes Of Two Cities	LP	Ralph	RR8202	1982	**£10**	**£4**	*US*
Whatever Happened To Vileness Fats?	LP	Ralph	RZ8452	1984	**£50**	**£25**	*US, red vinyl*
Whatever Happened To Vileness Fats?	LP	Ralph	RZ8452	1984	**£10**	**£4**	*US*

RESTIVO, JOHNNY

'The Shape I'm In' is something of a rock 'n' roll classic – made by a singer who was just sixteen years old at the time – although it somehow managed to avoid the charts. The song is not the one recorded a few years later by the Band!

I Like Girls	7"	RCA	RCA1159	1959	**£8**	**£4**	
Oh Johnny	LP	RCA	LPM/LSP2149	1959	**£50**	**£25**	*US*
Shape I'm In	7"	RCA	RCA1143	1959	**£20**	**£10**	*tri-centre*
Sweet Sweet Loving	7"	Ember	EMBS135	1961	**£6**	**£2.50**	

RESTLESS ONES

Restless Ones	7"	Herald	HSR2521	1965	**£6**	**£2.50**	*picture sleeve*

RESTRICTED HOURS

Getting Thimgs Done	7"	Stevenage		1979	**£5**	**£2**	*Syndicate B side*

RETREADS

Would You Listen Girl	7"	Eddi Cosmo	EO101	1980	**£20**	**£10**	

REVALONS

Discotheque A Go Go	LP	Fantastic	1410	1964	**£25**	**£10**	*Canadian*

REVELL, DIGGER & THE DENVER MEN

Surfside	7"	Decca	F11657	1963	**£8**	**£4**	

REVELLERS

Revellers Again	LP	Spin	LP1703	1967	**£25**	**£10**	

REVELLS

Mind Party	7"	CBS	7050	1971	**£5**	**£2**	

REVELS

Midnight Stroll	7"	Top Rank	JAR235	1959	**£20**	**£10**	

REVELS (2)

Revels On A Rampage	LP	Impact	LPM1	1964	**£50**	**£25**	*US*

REVENGE

Don't Tell Me Lies	7"	Blood	CUS614	197–	**£5**	**£2**	
Go Away	7"	Normal	QS000	1976	**£8**	**£4**	

REVENGE (2)

Seven Reasons	CD-s	Factory	FACD247	1989	**£5**	**£2**	

REVERE, PAUL & THE RAIDERS

Alias Pink Puzz	LP	Columbia	CS9905	1969	**£12**	**£5**	*US*
Christmas Past And Present	LP	Columbia	CL2755/CS9555	1967	**£30**	**£15**	*US*
Cinderella Sunshine	7"	CBS	3757	1968	**£4**	**£1.50**	
Don't Take It So Hard	7"	CBS	3586	1968	**£4**	**£1.50**	
Goin' To Memphis	LP	CBS	63265	1968	**£10**	**£4**	
Good Thing	7"	CBS	202502	1967	**£5**	**£2**	
Good Thing	LP	CBS	(S)BPG62963	1969	**£10**	**£4**	
Great Airplane Strike	7"	CBS	202411	1966	**£5**	**£2**	
Greatest Hits	LP	Columbia	KCL2662/ KCS9462	1967	**£10**	**£4**	*US*
Hard 'n' Heavy	LP	CBS	63649	1969	**£10**	**£4**	
Here They Come	LP	Columbia	CL2307/CS9107	1965	**£20**	**£8**	*US*
Him Or Me – Who's It Gonna Be?	7"	CBS	2737	1967	**£5**	**£2**	
Hungry	7"	CBS	202253	1966	**£5**	**£2**	
In The Beginning	LP	Jerden	JRL/JRS7004	1966	**£75**	**£37.50**	*US*
Indian Reservation	LP	Columbia	CQ30768	1973	**£10**	**£4**	*US quad*
Just Like Me	7"	CBS	202027	1966	**£6**	**£2.50**	
Just Like Us	LP	CBS	(S)BPG62406	1966	**£15**	**£6**	
Kicks	7"	CBS	202205	1966	**£5**	**£2**	
Let Me	7"	CBS	4260	1969	**£4**	**£1.50**	
Like Long Hair	7"	Top Rank	JAR557	1961	**£10**	**£5**	

Like Long Hair — 7" — Sue — WI344 — 1966 — £10 — £5
Like Long Hair — LP — Gardena — G1000 — 1961 — £150 — £75 — US
Midnight Ride — LP — CBS — (S)BPG62797 — 1966 — £15 — £6
Moreen — 7" — CBS — 3186 — 1967 — £4 — £1.50
Paul Revere & The Raiders — LP — Sears — SPS439 — 1970 — £50 — £25 — US
Paul Revere & The Raiders — LP — Sande — 1001 — 1962 — £200 — £100 — US
Revolution — LP — CBS — (S)BPG63095 — 1967 — £10 — £4
Something Happening — LP — Columbia — CS9665 — 1968 — £12 — £5 — US
Spirit Of '67 — LP — Columbia — CL2595/CS9395 — 1967 — £12 — £5 — US
Steppin' Out — 7" — CBS — 202003 — 1965 — £4 — £1.50
Steppin' Out — 7" EP — CBS — 5930 — 1966 — £30 — £15 — *French*
Ups And Downs — 7" — CBS — 202610 — 1967 — £5 — £2

REVEREND BLACK & THE ROCKIN' VICARS

Zing Went The Strings Of My Heart — 7" — Decca — — 1963 — £50 — £25 — *Irish*

REVILLOS

Attack — LP — Superville — SV4001 — 1982 — £40 — £20
Rev Up — LP — Dindisc — DIDX3 — 1980 — £10 — £4

REVOLUTION

Hallelujah — 7" — Piccadilly — 7N35289 — 1966 — £25 — £12.50

REVOLUTIONARIES

Black Ash — LP — Trojan — TRLS186 — 1980 — £10 — £4
Goldmine Dub — LP — Greensleeves — GREL4 — 1979 — £12 — £5
Jonkanoo Dub — LP — Cha Cha — CHALP005 — 1978 — £12 — £5
Negrea Love Dub — LP — Trojan — TRLS153 — 1979 — £12 — £5
Outlaw Dub — LP — Trojan — TRLS169 — 1979 — £12 — £5
Reaction In Dub — LP — Cha Cha — CHALP002 — 1978 — £12 — £5
Revolutionary Sounds Vol. 2 — LP — Ballistic — UAS30237 — 1978 — £12 — £5

REVOLUTIONARY BLUES BAND

Revolutionary Blues Band — LP — MCA — MUPS402 — 1970 — £10 — £4

REVOLVER

Frisco Annie — 7" — Youngblood — YB1006 — 1969 — £10 — £5

REVOLVING PAINT DREAM

Flowers In The Sky — 7" — Creation — CRE2 — 1984 — £10 — £5

REX & THE MINORS

Chicken Sax — 7" — Triumph — RGM1023 — 1960 — £25 — £12.50

REXROTH, KENNETH

Poetry And Jazz At The Blackhawk — LP — Fantasy — 7008 — 1958 — £25 — £10 — US

REY, ALVINO

Greatest Hits — LP — London — HAD2414 — 1961 — £12 — £5
Original Mama Blues — 7" — London — HLD9431 — 1961 — £5 — £2

REY, LITTLE BOBBY

Rockin' J Bells — 7" — Top Rank — JAR525 — 1960 — £4 — £1.50

REYNARD

Fresh From The Earth — LP — Pilgrim — GRA102 — 1976 — £50 — £25

REYNOLDS, DEBBIE

Am I That Easy To Forget? — LP — London — HAD2294/SAHD6106 — 1960 — £15 — £6
Athena — LP — Mercury — MG25202 — 1954 — £50 — £25 — US
Bundle Of Joy — LP — RCA — LPM1339 — 1956 — £30 — £15 — US
Carolina In The Morning — 7" — MGM — SP1127 — 1955 — £6 — £2.50
Debbie — LP — London — HAD2200/SHD6051 — 1959 — £15 — £6
Debbie Reynolds — 7" EP — MGM — MGMEP670 — 1958 — £8 — £4
Delightful — 7" EP — MGM — MGMEP694 — 1959 — £8 — £4
Fine And Dandy — LP — London — HAD2326 — 1961 — £15 — £6
From Debbie With Love — 7" EP — MGM — MGMEP725 — 1960 — £8 — £4
Great Folk Hits — LP — London — HAD/SHD8075 — 1963 — £15 — £6
I Love Melvin — 10" LP — MGM — D114 — 1953 — £30 — £15
Love Is The Tender Trap — 7" — MGM — SP1155 — 1956 — £4 — £1.50
Say One For Me — LP — Columbia — CL1337/CS8137 — 1959 — £15 — £6 — US
Tammy — 7" — Vogue Coral — Q72274 — 1957 — £5 — £2
Tammy — LP — Vogue Coral — LVA9070 — 1957 — £30 — £15
This Happy Feeling — 7" — Coral — Q72324 — 1958 — £4 — £1.50
Two Weeks With Love — 10" LP — MGM — E530 — 1950 — £25 — £10 — US
Two Weeks With Love — LP — MGM — E3233 — 1955 — £15 — £6 — US

REYNOLDS, DONN

Songbag — 7" EP — Pye — NEP24098 — 1959 — £10 — £5

REYNOLDS, JODY

Endless Sleep — 7" — London — HL8651 — 1958 — £15 — £7.50

REYNOLDS, TIMMY

Lullaby Of Love — 7" — Ember — EMBS133 — 1962 — £4 — £1.50 — *B side Jeff Mills*

REYS, RITA

Title	Format	Label	Cat. No.	Year	Mint	VG	Notes
Cool Voice Of Rita Reys	10″ LP	Philips	BBR8120	1958	**£20**	**£8**	

REZILLOS

Title	Format	Label	Cat. No.	Year	Mint	VG	Notes
Can't Stand My Baby	7″	Sensible	FAB1	1977	**£4**	**£1.50**	*picture sleeve*
Can't Stand My Baby	7″	Sensible	FAB1	1977	**£8**	**£4**	*numbered*
Can't Stand The Rezillos	LP	Sire	K56530	1978	**£12**	**£5**	*inner and card insert*
Cold Wars	7″	Sire	SIR4014	1979	**£4**	**£1.50**	*picture sleeve*
Flying Saucer Attack	7″	Sire	6078612	1977	**£4**	**£1.50**	*picture sleeve*
Flying Saucer Attack	7″	Sensible	FAB2	1977	**£25**	**£12.50**	
Mission Accomplished	LP	Sire	SRK6060	1978	**£10**	**£4**	
Top Of The Pops	7″	Sire	SIR4001	1978	**£4**	**£1.50**	*picture sleeve*

RHABSTALLION

Title	Format	Label	Cat. No.	Year	Mint	VG	Notes
Day To Day	7″	Rhab	RHAB001	1981	**£20**	**£10**	*with badge*
Day To Day	7″	Rhab	RHAB001	1981	**£15**	**£7.50**	

RHESUS

Title	Format	Label	Cat. No.	Year	Mint	VG	Notes
O-	LP	Epic	EPC64560	1971	**£25**	**£10**	*French*

RHINOCEROS

Title	Format	Label	Cat. No.	Year	Mint	VG	Notes
Apricot Brandy	7″	Elektra	EKSN45051	1968	**£4**	**£1.50**	
Better Times Are Coming	LP	Elektra	2469006	1970	**£10**	**£4**	
Rhinoceros	LP	Elektra	EKL/EKS74030	1968	**£12**	**£5**	
Satin Chickens	LP	Elektra	EKL/EKS74056	1969	**£10**	**£4**	

RHODEN, PAT

Title	Format	Label	Cat. No.	Year	Mint	VG	Notes
Time is Tight	7″	Mary Lyn	ML101	1970	**£4**	**£1.50**	
Jezebel	7″	Ska Beat	JB195	1965	**£10**	**£5**	
Woman Is Greedy	7″	Trojan	TR606	1968	**£4**	**£1.50**	

RHODEN, WINSTON

Title	Format	Label	Cat. No.	Year	Mint	VG	Notes
Make Believe	7″	Blue Beat	BB360	1966	**£12**	**£6**	

RHODES, TODD

Title	Format	Label	Cat. No.	Year	Mint	VG	Notes
Specks	7″	Parlophone	MSP6171	1955	**£20**	**£10**	

RHUBARB RHUBARB

Title	Format	Label	Cat. No.	Year	Mint	VG	Notes
Rainmaker	7″	President	PT229	1968	**£20**	**£10**	

RHYTHM ACES

Title	Format	Label	Cat. No.	Year	Mint	VG	Notes
Christmas	7″	Island	WI032	1962	**£10**	**£5**	
I'll Be There	7″	Blue Beat	BB134	1962	**£12**	**£6**	
Please Don't Go Away	7″	Starlite	ST45066	1961	**£10**	**£5**	
Thousand Teardrops	7″	Starlite	ST45061	1961	**£10**	**£5**	

RHYTHM & BLUES INC.

Title	Format	Label	Cat. No.	Year	Mint	VG	Notes
Honey Don't	7″	Fontana	TF524	1965	**£30**	**£15**	

RHYTHM KINGS

Title	Format	Label	Cat. No.	Year	Mint	VG	Notes
Blue Soul	7″	Vogue	V9212	1963	**£8**	**£4**	

RHYTHM OF LIFE

Title	Format	Label	Cat. No.	Year	Mint	VG	Notes
Soon	7″	Rhythm Of Life	RHYTHM001	1982	**£4**	**£1.50**	

RHYTHM ROCKERS

Title	Format	Label	Cat. No.	Year	Mint	VG	Notes
Soul Surfin'	LP	Challenge	CHL617	1963	**£20**	**£8**	*US*

RHYTHMETTES

Title	Format	Label	Cat. No.	Year	Mint	VG	Notes
I'll Be With You In Apple Blossom Time	7″	Coral	Q72358	1959	**£4**	**£1.50**	

RIBA, PAU

Title	Format	Label	Cat. No.	Year	Mint	VG	Notes
Jo, La Donya I El Gripau	LP	Edigsa		1971	**£60**	**£30**	*US*

RIBEIRO, CATHERINE & ALPES

Title	Format	Label	Cat. No.	Year	Mint	VG	Notes
Le Rat Débile Et L'Homme Des Champs	LP	Philips	9101003	1974	**£15**	**£6**	*French*
Libertes?	LP	Fontana	9101501	1975	**£15**	**£6**	*French*
Paix	LP	Philips	6325019	1974	**£15**	**£6**	*French*
Passions	LP	Philips	9101270	1979	**£10**	**£4**	*French*

RIBS

Title	Format	Label	Cat. No.	Year	Mint	VG	Notes
Man With No Brain	7″	Aerco	AERS101	1978	**£6**	**£2.50**	

RICE, BOYD

Title	Format	Label	Cat. No.	Year	Mint	VG	Notes
Music, Martinis And Misanthropy	LP	New European	BADVC1969	1990	**£15**	**£6**	

RICE, TIM & THE WEBBER GROUP

Title	Format	Label	Cat. No.	Year	Mint	VG	Notes
Come Back Richard Your Country Needs You	7″	RCA	RCA1895	1969	**£5**	**£2**	

RICE-DAVIES, MANDY

Title	Format	Label	Cat. No.	Year	Mint	VG	Notes
Introducing Mandy	7″ EP	Ember	EMBEP4537	1963	**£25**	**£12.50**	

RICH, BUDDY

Big Swing Face	LP	Fontana	STL5435	1967	£12	£5	
Buddy And Sweets	LP	Columbia	33CX10080	1957	£15	£6	*with Harry Edison*
Buddy Rich	7" EP	Columbia	SEB10024	195–	£5	£2	
In Miami	LP	Columbia	33CX10138	1959	£15	£6	
Just Sings	LP	HMV	CLP1185	1958	£15	£6	
Rich Versus Roach	LP	Mercury	MMC14031	1960	£15	£6	*with Max Roach*
Sings Johnny Mercer	LP	HMV	CLP1092	1956	£15	£6	
Swingin' New Big Band	LP	Fontana	STL5408	1966	£12	£5	
Swinging Buddy Rich	7" EP	Columbia	SEB10071	1957	£5	£2	
Take It Away	LP	Liberty	LBL/LBS83090	1968	£12	£5	
This One's For Basie	LP	Columbia	33CX10071	1957	£15	£6	
Very Alive At Ronnie Scotts	LP	RCA	DPS2031	1972	£15	£6	*double*
Wailing Buddy Rich	LP	Columbia	33CX10052	1956	£15	£6	

RICH, CHARLIE

Big Boss Man	LP	RCA	LPM/LSP3537	1966	£20	£8	*US*
Charlie Rich	LP	Groove	G(S)1000	1964	£20	£8	*US*
Just A Little Bit Sweet	7"	London	HLS9482	1962	£20	£10	
Lonely Weekends	7"	London	HLU9107	1960	£25	£12.50	
Lonely Weekends	LP	Philips	1970	1960	£250	£150	*US*
Love Is After Me	7"	London	HLU10104	1967	£10	£5	
Many New Sides Of Charlie Rich	LP	Philips	BL7695	1966	£15	£6	
Mohair Sam	7"	Philips	BF1432	1965	£5	£2	
That's Rich	LP	RCA	RD7719	1965	£25	£10	
Too Many Teardrops	7"	RCA	RCA1433	1965	£5	£2	

RICH, DAVE

City Lights	7"	RCA	RCA1092	1958	£10	£5	

RICH, LEWIS

Everybody But Me	7"	Parlophone	R5283	1965	£4	£1.50	
I Don't Want To Hear It Anymore	7"	Parlophone	R5434	1966	£5	£2	

RICH, RICHIE

Salsa House	12"	ffrr	FX113	1989	£10	£5	
You Used To Salsa	12"	ffrr	FXR156	1989	£10	£5	

RICH MOUNTAIN TOWER

Rich Mountain Tower	LP	London	SHO8427	1972	£10	£4	

RICHARD, CLIFF

Cliff Richard's first two LPs were issued in mono only and yet stereo mixes of some the tracks can be found on EPs. These are consequently much sought after. Cliff's 78 rpm releases are also scarce and break the usual maxim that 78s are much less valuable than their 45 rpm equivalents. Few of the religious records he has made over the years have sold particularly well and many of these now fetch quite high prices. Becoming increasingly hard to find, too, is the single 'Honky Tonk Angel', which was withdrawn at Cliff Richard's insistence, despite being a likely chart hit, after someone told him what a honky tonk angel actually was (a prostitute). The most desirable Cliff Richard collectors' item of all, however (apart from unreleased acetates which are too scarce to be a realistic collectors' goal for most people), is likely to be one of the complete film soundtrack albums that were presented to all the people involved in the making of *Summer Holiday* and *Wonderful Life*.

21 Today	LP	Columbia	33SX1368	1961	£20	£8	*mono*
21 Today	LP	Columbia	SCX3409	1961	£50	£25	*stereo*
31st Of February Street	LP	EMI	EMC3048	1974	£25	£10	
32 Minutes 17 Seconds	LP	Columbia	33SX1431	1962	£20	£8	*mono*
32 Minutes 17 Seconds	LP	Columbia	SCX3436	1962	£50	£25	*stereo*
About That Man	LP	Columbia	SCX6408	1970	£100	£50	
Aladdin & His Wonderful Lamp	LP	Columbia	33SX1676	1964	£12	£5	*mono*
Aladdin & His Wonderful Lamp	LP	Columbia	SCX3522	1964	£20	£8	*stereo*
All I Have To Do Is Dream	CD-s	EMI	CDEMS359	1994	£5	£2	*with Phil Everly*
All I Have To Do Is Dream	CD-s	EMI	CDEM359	1994	£5	£2	*with Phil Everly*
Always Guaranteed	LP	EMI	EMDB1004	1987	£10	£4	*boxed with 7"*
Angel	7"	Columbia	DC762	1965	£75	£37.50	*export*
Angel	7" EP	Columbia	SEG8444	1965	£25	£12.50	
Best Of Cliff Richard	LP	Columbia	SX/SCX6343	1969	£10	£4	
Best Of Cliff Richard And The Shadows	7"	Lyntone	LYN14745	197–	£6	£2.50	*flexi*
Best Of Cliff Richard And The Shadows	LP	Readers Digest	GRICA140	1984	£50	£25	*8 LPs, boxed*
Best Of Cliff Vol. 2	LP	Columbia	SCX6519	1972	£10	£4	
Best Of Me	CD-s	EMI	CDEM(S)92	1989	£5	£2	*2 versions*
Big Ship	7"	Columbia	DB8581	1969	£5	£2	
Bin Verliebt	7"	Columbia	C21703	1961	£15	£7.50	*Sung In German*
Blue Turns To Grey	7"	Columbia	DB7866	1966	£4	£1.50	
Boyfriend flexi	7"	Boyfriend		196–	£15	£7.50	*flexi*
Brand New Song	7"	Columbia	DB8957	1972	£5	£2	
Carnival	7"	Columbia	23060	1965	£15	£7.50	*German import*
Carol Singers	7" EP	Columbia	SEG8533	1967	£25	£12.50	
Carols	LP	Word	WRDR3034	1988	£25	£10	
Cinderella	7" EP	Columbia	SEG8527	1967	£75	£37.50	
Cinderella	LP	Columbia	SX/SCX6103	1967	£25	£10	
Cliff	CD	EMI	CZ1	1987	£12	£5	
Cliff	LP	Columbia	33SX1147	1959	£40	£20	*green label*
Cliff	LP	Columbia	33SX1147	1959	£25	£10	*blue & black label*
Cliff En España	7" EP	HMV	7EPL13979	1963	£30	£15	*sung in Spanish*
Cliff In Japan	LP	Columbia	SX/SCX6244	1968	£25	£10	*blue & black label*
Cliff In Japan	LP	Columbia	SX/SCX6244	1968	£15	£6	*white & black label*
Cliff No. 1	7" EP	Columbia	ESG7754	1959	£50	£25	*stereo*

Title	Format	Label	Number	Year	Price	Price	Notes
Cliff No. 1	7" EP	Columbia	SEG7903	1959	£25	£12.50	
Cliff No. 2	7" EP	Columbia	ESG7769	1959	£50	£25	*stereo*
Cliff No. 2	7" EP	Columbia	SEG7910	1959	£25	£12.50	
Cliff Richard	7" EP	Columbia	SEG8151	1962	£25	£12.50	
Cliff Richard	LP	Columbia	33SX1709	1965	£25	£10	*mono*
Cliff Richard	LP	Columbia	SCX3546	1965	£30	£15	*stereo*
Cliff Richard	LP	World Record Club	STP1051	1972	£50	£25	
Cliff Richard In Spain	LP	Epic	LN24115/ BN26115	1964	£25	£10	*US*
Cliff Richard No. 2	7" EP	Columbia	SEG8168	1962	£25	£12.50	
Cliff Richard Singles Sampler	LP	EMI	PSLP350	1982	£30	£15	*promo*
Cliff Richard Songbook	LP	World Record Club	ALBUM26	1980	£30	£15	*6 LPs, boxed*
Cliff Richard Story	7"	Lyntone	LYNSF1218	1973	£4	£1.50	*sampler flexi with interview*
Cliff Richard Story	LP	World Record Club	SM255-260	1972	£30	£15	*6 LPs, boxed*
Cliff Sings	LP	Columbia	33SX1192	1959	£30	£15	*green label*
Cliff Sings	LP	ABC	(S)321	1960	£30	£15	*US*
Cliff Sings	LP	Columbia	33SX1192	1959	£25	£10	*blue & black label*
Cliff Sings No. 1	7" EP	Columbia	ESG7788	1960	£40	£20	*stereo*
Cliff Sings No. 1	7" EP	Columbia	SEG7979	1960	£20	£10	
Cliff Sings No. 2	7" EP	Columbia	ESG7794	1960	£40	£20	*stereo*
Cliff Sings No. 2	7" EP	Columbia	SEG7987	1960	£20	£10	
Cliff Sings No. 3	7" EP	Columbia	ESG7808	1960	£40	£20	*stereo*
Cliff Sings No. 3	7" EP	Columbia	SEG8005	1960	£20	£10	
Cliff Sings No. 4	7" EP	Columbia	ESG7816	1960	£40	£20	*stereo*
Cliff Sings No. 4	7" EP	Columbia	SEG8021	1960	£20	£10	
Cliff's Hit Parade	7" EP	Columbia	SEG8133	1962	£12	£6	
Cliff's Hits	7" EP	Columbia	SEG8203	1962	£12	£6	
Cliff's Hits From Aladdin	7" EP	Columbia	SEG8395	1965	£12	£6	
Cliff's Lucky Lips	7" EP	Columbia	SEG8269	1963	£12	£6	
Cliff's Palladium Successes	7" EP	Columbia	SEG8320	1964	£25	£12.50	
Cliff's Rock Party	7"	Serenade		196–	£15	£7.50	*flexi*
Cliff's Silver Discs	7" EP	Columbia	SEG8050	1960	£10	£5	
Congratulations	7" EP	Columbia	SEG8540	1968	£20	£10	
Das Gluck Ist Rosarot	7"	Columbia	C23371	1966	£15	£7.50	*German import*
Das Ist Die Frage Aller Fragen	7"	Columbia	C22811	1964	£15	£7.50	*German import*
Don't Forget To Catch Me	7"	Columbia	DB8503	1968	£4	£1.50	
Don't Stop Me Now	LP	Columbia	SX/SCX6133	1967	£25	£10	
Don't Talk To Him	7" EP	Columbia	SEG8299	1964	£15	£7.50	
Dream	7" EP	Columbia	ESG7867	1961	£40	£20	*stereo*
Dream	7" EP	Columbia	SEG8119	1961	£12	£6	
Du Bist Mein Erster Gedanke	7"	Columbia	C23211	1967	£15	£7.50	*sung in German*
Ein Girl Wiedu	7"	Columbia	C23510	196–	£15	£7.50	*sung in German*
Es War Keine So Wunderbar Wie Du	7"	Columbia	22962	1964	£15	£7.50	*German import*
Established 1958	LP	Columbia	SX/SCX6282	1968	£12	£5	
Every Face Tells A Story	7"	EMI	PSR410	1977	£20	£10	*promo sampler*
Expresso Bongo	7" EP	Columbia	ESG7783	1960	£30	£15	*stereo*
Expresso Bongo	7" EP	Columbia	SEG7971	1960	£15	£7.50	
Fall In Love With You	7"	Columbia	DB4431	1960	£4	£1.50	
Fall In Love With You	7"	Columbia	DB4431	1960	£8	£4	*black label*
Finders Keepers	7"	EMI	PSR304	1967	£10	£5	*1 sided promo*
Finders Keepers	LP	Columbia	SX/SCX6079	1966	£12	£5	
Flying Machine	7"	Columbia	DB8797	1971	£5	£1.50	
Forever Kind Of Love	7" EP	Columbia	SEG8347	1964	£20	£10	
Forty Greatest Hits	7"	EMI	PSR414/5	1977	£15	£7.50	*double promo sampler*
Forty Years Of Hits	CD	EMI	CDCRDJ40	1998	£50	£25	*promo with book*
From A Distance	7"	EMI	EMPD155	1990	£4	£1.50	*picture disc*
From A Distance	CD-s	EMI	CDEM155	1990	£5	£2	
From A Distance – The Event	CD	EMI	CDCRTV31	1990	£30	£15	*promo with bonus single*
From A Distance – The Event	LP	EMI	CRTVB31	1990	£10	£4	*box set with 7", poster, prints*
From The Heart	LP	Tellydisc	TELLY28	1985	£20	£8	*double*
Gee Whiz It's You	7"	Columbia	DC756	1961	£5	£2	*export*
Girl Like You	7"	Columbia	DB4667	1961	£6	£2.50	*black label*
Girl Like You	7"	Columbia	DB4667	1961	£4	£1.50	
Good News	7"	Spree	no number	1973	£15	£7.50	*flexi, Johnny Cash B side*
Good News	LP	Columbia	JSX6167	1967	£30	£15	*export*
Good News	LP	Columbia	SX/SCX6167	1967	£15	£6	
Good Times (Better Times)	7"	Columbia	DB8548	1969	£4	£1.50	
Green Light	7"	EMI	EMI2920	1979	£20	£10	*picture sleeve*
Gut Das Es Freunde Gibt	7"	EMI	1C00605315	196–	£15	£7.50	*sung in German*
Healing Love	CD-s	EMI	CDEM294	1993	£5	£2	*boxed with badge & print*
Healing Love	CD-s	EMI	CDEMS294	1993	£5	£2	
Heart User	12"	EMI	12RICH2	1985	£6	£2.50	*poster picture sleeve*
Help It Along	7"	EMI	EMI2022	1973	£6	£2.50	*picture sleeve*
Help It Along	LP	EMI	EMA768	1974	£20	£8	
High Class Baby	7"	Columbia	DB4203	1958	£10	£5	
High Class Baby	7"	Columbia	DB4203	1958	£25	£12.50	*black label*
High Class Baby	78	Columbia	DB4203	1958	£30	£15	
His Land	LP	Columbia	SCX6443	1970	£50	£25	
Hit Album	LP	Columbia	33SX1512	1963	£10	£4	
Hits From Summer Holiday	7" EP	Columbia	ESG7896	1963	£30	£15	*stereo*

Hits From Summer Holiday	7" EP	Columbia	SEG8250	1963	£10	£5	
Hits From The Young Ones	7" EP	Columbia	SEG8159	1962	£10	£5	*different mixes*
Hits From When In Rome	7" EP	Columbia	SEG8478	1966	£50	£25	
Hits From Wonderful Life	7" EP	Columbia	ESG7906	1964	£40	£20	*stereo*
Hits From Wonderful Life	7" EP	Columbia	SEG8376	1964	£15	£7.50	
Holiday Carnival	7" EP	Columbia	ESG7892	1963	£30	£15	*stereo*
Holiday Carnival	7" EP	Columbia	SEG8246	1963	£12	£6	
Honky Tonk Angel	7"	EMI	EMI2344	1975	£20	£10	
How Wonderful To Know	LP	World Record Club	(S)T643	1964	£20	£8	
Human Work Of Art	CD-s	EMI	CDEMS267	1993	£5	£2	
Human Work Of Art	CD-s	EMI	CDEM267	1993	£5	£2	
Hymns And Inspirational Songs	LP	Word	WRDR3017	1986	£25	£10	
I Ain't Got Time Anymore	7"	Columbia	DB8708	1970	£4	£1.50	
I Just Don't Have The Heart	12"	EMI	12EMX101	1989	£6	£2.50	
I Just Don't Have The Heart	CD-s	EMI	CDEM101	1989	£6	£2.50	
I Love You	7"	Columbia	DB4547	1960	£4	£1.50	
I Love You	7"	Columbia	DB4547	1960	£8	£4	*black label*
I Still Believe In You	CD-s	EMI	CDEMS255	1992	£5	£2	
I Still Believe In You	CD-s	EMI	CDEM255	1992	£6	£2.50	
I'll Come Running	7"	Columbia	DB8210	1967	£4	£1.50	
I'll Love You Forever Today	7"	Columbia	DB8437	1968	£5	£2	
I'm Lookin' Out The Window	7"	Columbia	DB4828	1962	£4	£1.50	
I'm Lookin' Out The Window	7"	Columbia	DB4828	1962	£6	£2.50	*black label*
Ich Traume Deine Träume	7"	Columbia	1C00604706	1971	£15	£7.50	*sung in German*
In The Country	7"	Columbia	DB8094	1966	£4	£1.50	
It'll Be Me	7"	Columbia	DB4886	1962	£4	£1.50	
It'll Be Me	7"	Columbia	DB4886	1962	£6	£2.50	*black label*
It's A Small World	LP	Myrrh	MYRR1209	1988	£30	£15	
It's All In The Game	LP	Epic	LN24089/ BN26089	1964	£25	£10	*US*
It's All Over	7"	Columbia	DB8150	1967	£4	£1.50	
It's Only Me You've Left Behind	7"	EMI	EMI2279	1975	£8	£4	
Japan Tour 1974	LP	EMI	EMS67037	1975	£100	£50	*Japanese*
Jesus	7"	Columbia	DB8864	1972	£5	£2	
Kinda Latin	LP	Columbia	SCX6039	1966	£30	£15	*stereo*
Kinda Latin	LP	Columbia	SX6039	1966	£25	£10	*mono*
La La La La La	7" EP	Columbia	SEG8517	1966	£25	£12.50	
Lean On You	7"	EMI	EMP105	1989	£5	£2	*picture disc*
Lean On You	CD-s	EMI	CDEM105	1989	£6	£2.50	
Leave My Woman Alone	7"	Columbia	DB8657	1970	£4	£1.50	*with Hank Marvin*
Listen To Cliff	LP	ABC	(S)391	1961	£25	£10	*US*
Listen To Cliff	LP	Columbia	33SX1320	1961	£20	£8	*mono*
Listen To Cliff	LP	Columbia	SCX3375	1961	£50	£25	*stereo*
Listen To Cliff No. 1	7" EP	Columbia	ESG7858	1961	£40	£20	*stereo*
Listen To Cliff No. 1	7" EP	Columbia	SEG8105	1961	£20	£10	
Listen To Cliff No. 2	7" EP	Columbia	ESG7870	1961	£40	£20	*stereo*
Listen To Cliff No. 2	7" EP	Columbia	SEG8126	1961	£20	£10	
Little Town	7"	EMI	EMIP5348	1982	£4	£1.50	*picture disc*
Live In Japan '72	LP	EMI	EOP930773B	1972	£125	£62.50	*Japanese*
Livin' Lovin' Doll	7"	Columbia	DB4249	1959	£30	£15	*black label*
Livin' Lovin' Doll	7"	Columbia	DB4249	1959	£15	£7.50	
Livin' Lovin' Doll	78	Columbia	DB4249	1959	£75	£37.50	
Living Doll	7"	Columbia	DB4306	1959	£4	£1.50	
Living Doll	7"	Columbia	DB4306	1959	£20	£10	*black label*
Living Doll	7"	WEA	YZ65P	1986	£5	£2	*picture disc, with The Young Ones*
Living Doll	78	Columbia	DB4306	1959	£30	£15	
Look In My Eyes Maria	7" EP	Columbia	SEG8405	1965	£20	£10	
Love Is Forever	7" EP	Columbia	SEG8488	1966	£30	£15	
Love Is Forever	LP	Columbia	SX1769/SCX3569	1965	£20	£8	
Love Songs	7" EP	Columbia	ESG7900	1963	£40	£20	*stereo*
Love Songs	7" EP	Columbia	SEG8272	1963	£12	£6	
Man Gratuliert Mir	7"	Columbia	C23776	1968	£15	£7.50	*sung in German*
Maria No Mas	7"	Columbia	C22667	1964	£15	£7.50	*sung in Spanish*
Marianne	7"	Columbia	DB8476	1968	£4	£1.50	
Me And My Shadows	LP	Columbia	33SX1261	1960	£25	£10	*mono*
Me And My Shadows	LP	Columbia	SCX3330	1960	£50	£25	*stereo*
Me And My Shadows	LP	Regal	SREG1120	1960	£60	£30	*export*
Me And My Shadows No. 1	7" EP	Columbia	ESG7837	1961	£40	£20	*stereo*
Me And My Shadows No. 1	7" EP	Columbia	SEG8065	1961	£20	£10	
Me And My Shadows No. 2	7" EP	Columbia	ESG7841	1961	£40	£20	*stereo*
Me And My Shadows No. 2	7" EP	Columbia	SEG8071	1961	£20	£10	
Me And My Shadows No. 3	7" EP	Columbia	ESG7843	1961	£40	£20	*stereo*
Me And My Shadows No. 3	7" EP	Columbia	SEG8078	1961	£20	£10	
Mean Streak	7"	Columbia	DB4290	1959	£8	£4	
Mean Streak	7"	Columbia	DB4290	1959	£25	£12.50	*black label*
Mean Streak	78	Columbia	DB4290	1959	£75	£37.50	
Mistletoe And Wine	12"	EMI	12EMX78	1988	£6	£2.50	*with Advent calendar*
Mistletoe And Wine	CD-s	EMI	CDEM78	1988	£6	£2.50	*with Christmas card*
More Hits	LP	Columbia	SCX3555	1965	£12	£5	*stereo*
More Hits	LP	Columbia	SX1737	1965	£10	£4	*mono*
More Hits From Summer Holiday	7" EP	Columbia	ESG7898	1963	£30	£15	*stereo*
More Hits From Summer Holiday	7" EP	Columbia	SEG8263	1963	£20	£10	
More To Life	CD-s	EMI	CDEM205	1991	£5	£2	
Move It	7"	Columbia	DB4178	1958	£10	£5	
Move It	7"	Columbia	DB4178	1958	£25	£12.50	*black label*
Move It	78	Columbia	DB4178	1958	£30	£15	

Music And Life Of Cliff Richard	cass	EMI	TCEXSP1601	1974	**£20**	**£8**	*6 tapes, boxed*
Music From America	7"	Rainbow		196–	**£15**	**£7.50**	*flexi*
Never Let Go	CD-s	EMI	CDEMS281	1993	**£5**	**£2**	*boxed with 3 prints*
Never Say Die	12"	EMI	12EMI5415	1983	**£6**	**£2.50**	
Nine Times Out Of Ten	7"	Columbia	DB4506	1960	**£4**	**£1.50**	
Nine Times Out Of Ten	7"	Columbia	DB4506	1960	**£8**	**£4**	*black label*
Non Dimenticare Chi Ti Ama	7"	Columbia	SCMQ	1968	**£15**	**£7.50**	*sung in Italian*
Non L'Ascoltare	7"	Columbia	SCMQ1860	196–	**£15**	**£7.50**	*sung in Italian*
Nothing To Remind Me	7"	EMI	PSR368	1967	**£30**	**£15**	*promo*
O Mio Signore	7" EP	Columbia	SLEM2221	196–	**£30**	**£15**	*sung in Italian*
Ocean Deep	7"	EMI	EMI5457	1984	**£10**	**£[illegible]**	
Original	10" LP	Columbia	C00891	1959	**£125**	**£62.50**	*German*
Peace In Our Time	CD-s	EMI	CDEMS265	1993	**£5**	**£2**	
Peace In Our Time	CD-s	EMI	CDEM265	1993	**£5**	**£2**	
Per Un Bacio Di Amour	LP	Columbia	QPX8081	196–	**£50**	**£25**	*sung in Italian*
Personal Message To You	7"	Serenade		1960	**£15**	**£7.50**	*blue flexi*
Please Don't Tease	7"	Columbia	DB4479	1960	**£4**	**£1.50**	
Please Don't Tease	7"	Columbia	DB4479	1960	**£8**	**£4**	*black label*
Please Remember Me	7"	EMI	EMI2832	1978	**£5**	**£2**	
Power To All Our Friends	7"	EMI	1J00605340	196–	**£15**	**£7.50**	*sung in Spanish*
Presentation	CD	EMI	CDP7913702	199–	**£75**	**£37.50**	*promo only commemorative picture CD*
Remember Me	12"	EMI	12EMP31	1987	**£6**	**£2.50**	
Remember Me	CD-s	EMI	CDEM31	1987	**£6**	**£2.50**	
Rote Lippen Soll Man Küssen	7"	Columbia	C22563	196–	**£15**	**£7.50**	*sung in German*
Saviour's Day	7"	EMI	XMASP90	1990	**£4**	**£1.50**	*envelope with 5 photos*
Saviour's Day	CD-s	EMI	CDXMAS90	1990	**£6**	**£2.50**	
Schon Wie Ein Traume	7"	Columbia	C21843	196–	**£15**	**£7.50**	*sung in German*
Serious Charge	7" EP	Columbia	SEG7895	1959	**£25**	**£12.50**	
Shooting From The Heart	7"	EMI	RICHP1	1984	**£8**	**£4**	*shaped picture disc*
Silhouettes	CD-s	EMI	CDEM152	1990	**£5**	**£2**	
Silver	CD	EMI	CDP7460082	1983	**£12**	**£5**	
Silver	LP	EMI	EMC1077871/881	1983	**£15**	**£6**	*boxed double*
Silvery Rain	7"	Columbia	DB8774	1971	**£5**	**£2**	
Sincerely	LP	Columbia	SCX6357	1969	**£15**	**£6**	*stereo*
Sincerely	LP	Columbia	SX6357	1969	**£20**	**£8**	*mono*
Small Corners	LP	Word	WRDR3036	1988	**£25**	**£10**	
Some People	7"	EMI	EMP18	1987	**£6**	**£2.50**	*shaped picture disc*
Star Souvenir Greetings	7"	New Spotlight		196–	**£15**	**£7.50**	*flexi*
Stronger Than That	7"	EMI	EM129	1989	**£4**	**£1.50**	*with 3 postcards*
Stronger Than That	CD-s	EMI	CDEM129	1990	**£6**	**£2.50**	
Summer Holiday	LP	Columbia	33SX1472	1963	**£10**	**£4**	*mono*
Summer Holiday	LP	Columbia	SCX3462	1963	**£15**	**£6**	*blue & black label*
Summer Holiday	LP	Columbia	SCX3462	1963	**£25**	**£10**	*stereo, green label*
Summer Holiday	LP	Elstree Studios	EMS1009	1963	**£500**	**£330**	*original soundtrack, double*
Summer Holiday	LP	Epic	LN24063/ BN26063	1963	**£25**	**£10**	*US*
Sunny Honey Girl	7"	Columbia	DB8747	1971	**£5**	**£2**	
Swinger's Paradise	LP	Epic	LN24145/ BN26145	1965	**£25**	**£10**	*US*
Take Four	7" EP	Columbia	SEG8450	1965	**£25**	**£12.50**	
Take Me High	LP	EMI	EMC3016	1973	**£10**	**£4**	
Take Me High	LP	EMI	EMC3016	1973	**£20**	**£8**	*with poster*
Theme for A Dream	7"	Columbia	DB4593	1961	**£4**	**£1.50**	
Theme For A Dream	7"	Columbia	DB4593	1961	**£8**	**£4**	*black label*
Thirtieth Anniversary Picture Record Collection	LP	EMI	CR1	1989	**£40**	**£20**	*double picture disc*
This Was My Special Day	7"	Columbia	DB7435	1964	**£25**	**£12.50**	*demo only*
Throw Down A Line	7"	Columbia	DB8615	1969	**£4**	**£1.50**	*with Hank Marvin*
Thunderbirds Are Go	7" EP	Columbia	SEG8510	1966	**£40**	**£20**	
Time For Cliff And The Shadows	7" EP	Columbia	ESG7887	1963	**£40**	**£20**	*stereo*
Time For Cliff And The Shadows	7" EP	Columbia	SEG8228	1963	**£15**	**£7.50**	
Time In Between	7"	Columbia	DB7660	1965	**£4**	**£1.50**	
To My Italian Friends	LP	Columbia	QPX8024	196–	**£50**	**£25**	
Tracks And Grooves	LP	Columbia	SCX6435	1970	**£20**	**£8**	
Travellin' Light	7"	Columbia	DB4351	1959	**£4**	**£1.50**	
Travellin' Light	7"	Columbia	DB4351	1959	**£8**	**£4**	*black label*
Travellin' Light	78	Columbia	DB4351	1959	**£40**	**£20**	
Two A Penny	LP	Columbia	SX/SCX6262	1968	**£20**	**£8**	*blue & black label*
Two A Penny	LP	Columbia	SX/SCX6262	1968	**£15**	**£6**	*white & black label*
Two Hearts	7"	EMI	EMP42	1987	**£6**	**£2.50**	*shaped picture disc*
Two Hearts	CD-s	EMI	CDEM42	1988	**£6**	**£2.50**	
Un Saludo De Cliff	7" EP	HMV	13955	196–	**£30**	**£15**	*sung in Spanish*
Voice In The Wilderness	7"	Columbia	DB4398	1960	**£8**	**£4**	*black label*
Voice In The Wilderness	7"	Columbia	DB4398	1960	**£4**	**£1.50**	
Voice In The Wilderness	78	Columbia	DB4398	1960	**£60**	**£30**	
Walking In The Light	CD	Myrrh	MYRCD1176	1985	**£15**	**£6**	
Walking In The Light	LP	Myrrh	MYR1176	1985	**£25**	**£10**	
We Don't Talk Anymore	7"	EMI	EMI2975	1979	**£8**	**£4**	*mispress – plays Queen's 'Bohemian Rhapsody'*
We Don't Talk Anymore (2 versions)	12"	EMI	SPRO9252	1979	**£10**	**£5**	*US promo*
We Should Be Together	CD-s	EMI	CDXMAS91	1991	**£5**	**£2**	
What'd I Say	7"	Columbia	DC758	1963	**£250**	**£150**	*export, best auctioned*

When In France	7" EP	Columbia	SEG8290	1964	£15	£7.50	
When In France	LP	EMI	4C06206234	1977	£20	£8	Belgian
When In Rome	LP	Columbia	SX1762	1965	£25	£10	
When In Spain	LP	Columbia	33SX1541	1963	£15	£6	mono
When In Spain	LP	Columbia	SCX3488	1963	£25	£10	stereo
When The Girl In Your Arms	7"	Columbia	DB4716	1961	£4	£1.50	
When The Girl In Your Arms	7"	Columbia	DB4716	1961	£6	£2.50	black label
Why Don't They Understand	7" EP	Columbia	SEG8384	1965	£20	£10	
Wind Me Up	7" EP	Columbia	SEG8474	1966	£20	£10	
With The Eyes Of A Child	7"	Columbia	DB8641	1969	£4	£1.50	
Wonderful Life	LP	Columbia	33SX1628	1964	£10	£4	mono
Wonderful Life	LP	Elstree Studios		1963	£500	£330	original soundtrack, double
Wonderful Life	LP	Columbia	SCX3515	1964	£20	£8	stereo
Wonderful Life No. 1	7" EP	Columbia	SEG8338	1964	£12	£6	
Wonderful Life No. 1	7" EP	Columbia	ESG7902	1964	£30	£15	stereo
Wonderful Life No. 2	7" EP	Columbia	SEG8354	1964	£15	£7.50	
Wonderful Life No. 2	7" EP	Columbia	ESG7903	1964	£30	£15	stereo
Wonderful To Be Young	LP	Dot	DLP3474/25474	1962	£25	£10	US
Yes He Lives	7"	EMI	EMI2730	1978	£5	£2	
Young Ones	7"	Columbia	DB4761	1962	£4	£1.50	
Young Ones	LP	Columbia	33SX1384	1961	£12	£5	mono
Young Ones	LP	Columbia	SCX3397	1961	£25	£10	stereo
Zuviel Allein	7"	Columbia	C22707	1964	£15	£7.50	sung in German

RICHARD & THE YOUNG LIONS

Open Up Your Door	7"	Philips	BF1520	1966	£40	£20	

RICHARD BROTHERS

I Need A Girl	7"	Island	WI060	1963	£8	£4	
I Shall Wear A Crown	7"	Island	WI109	1963	£10	£5	Baba Brooks B side

RICHARDS, CYNTHIA

Can't Wait	7"	Clandisc	CLA216	1970	£5	£2	
Conversation	7"	Clandisc	CLA210	1970	£4	£1.50	Dynamites B side
Foolish Fool	7"	Clandisc	CLA220	1970	£5	£2	Clancy & Stitt B side
Foolish Fool	LP	Trojan	TBL123	1970	£12	£5	
Place In My Heart	7"	G.G.	GG4528	1971	£5	£2	
Stand By Your Man	7"	Clandisc	CLA229	1971	£4	£1.50	Dynamites B side

RICHARDS, JOHNNY

Experiments In Sound	LP	Capitol	T981	1959	£10	£4	
Rites Of Diablo	LP	Esquire	32076	1959	£10	£4	
Something Else	LP	London	LTZN1511	1958	£12	£5	
Walk Softly – Run Wild	LP	Coral	LVA9122	1960	£10	£4	
Wide Range	LP	Capitol	T885	1958	£12	£5	

RICHARDS, KEITH

Before They Make Me Run	7"	Rolling Stones		1979	£6	£2.50	promo
Jumping Jack Flash	7"	Arista	ARIST678P	1986	£8	£4	shaped picture disc & plinth
Make No Mistake	CD-s	Virgin	VSCD1179	1989	£5	£2	3" single
Run Rudolph Run	7"	Rolling Stones	RSR102	1979	£10	£5	picture sleeve
Take It So Hard	CD-s	Virgin	VSCD1125	1988	£5	£2	3" single
Talk Is Cheap	CD	Virgin	291047	1988	£30	£15	3 × 3" discs in tin
Talk Is Cheap	CD	Mobile Fidelity	UDCD557	1992	£15	£6	US audiophile
Talk Is Cheap	CD	Virgin		1988	£30	£15	US interview promo
Talk Is Cheap	LP	Virgin	KEITH1234	1988	£75	£37.50	promo album on 4 × 7"

RICHARDS, LISA

Mean Old World	7"	Vocalion	VP9244	1965	£15	£7.50	

RICHARDS, LLOYD

Be Good	7"	Port-O-Jam	PJ4004	1964	£10	£5	

RICHARDS, ROY

Contact	7"	Doctor Bird	DB1012	1966	£10	£5	
Double Trouble	7"	Island	WI283	1966	£10	£5	Fitzy & Freddy B side
Hopeful Village	7"	Island	WI3037	1967	£10	£5	Delroy Wilson B side
Rub-A-Dub	7"	Island	WI3027	1967	£10	£5	
South Vietnam	7"	Island	WI3000	1966	£10	£5	
Summertime	7"	Coxsone	CS7061	1968	£10	£5	Righteous Flames B side
Western Standard Time	7"	Island	WI299	1966	£10	£5	Eagles B side

RICHARDS, TRUDY

Crazy In Love!	LP	Capitol	T838	1957	£10	£4	
Wishbone	7"	Capitol	CL14728	1957	£4	£1.50	

RICHARDS, WENDY & DIANA BERRY

We Had A Dream	7"	Decca	F11680	1963	**£10**	**£5**	

RICHARDS, WINSTON

Green Coolie	7"	Island	WI297	1966	**£10**	**£5**	*Marcia Griffiths B side*
Studio Blitz	7"	Rio	R124	1967	**£8**	**£4**	

RICHARDSON, WARREN S.

Warren S. Richardson	LP	Cotillion	SD9013	1969	**£20**	**£8**	German

RICHMAN, JONATHAN

Road Runner	7"	United Artists	UP36006	1975	**£4**	**£1.50**	

RICHMOND

Frightened	LP	Dart	ARTS65371	1973	**£20**	**£8**	

RICK & THE KEENS

Peanuts	7"	Mercury	AMT1150	1961	**£25**	**£12.50**	

RICKETTS, BERESFORD

Baby Baby	7"	Starlite	ST45029	1960	**£5**	**£2**	
Cherry Baby	7"	Starlite	ST45025	1960	**£10**	**£5**	
I'm Going To Cry	7"	Starlite	ST45079	1962	**£10**	**£5**	
Jailer Bring Me Water	7"	Blue Beat	BB350	1966	**£12**	**£6**	
O Jean	7"	Dice	CC12	1963	**£10**	**£5**	
You Better Be Gone	7"	Blue Beat	BB107	1962	**£12**	**£6**	

RICKETTS & ROWE

Hold Me Tight	7"	Starlite	ST45048	1961	**£10**	**£5**	

RICO

Baby Face	7"	Doctor Bird	DB1302	1969	**£10**	**£5**	*Rudies B side*
Blow Your Horn	LP	Trojan	TTL12	1969	**£20**	**£8**	
Blues From The Hills	7"	Blue Beat	BB195	1963	**£12**	**£6**	*Stranger Cole B side*
Bullet	7"	Blue Cat	BS160	1969	**£6**	**£2.50**	
In Reggae Land	LP	Pama	ECO14	1969	**£25**	**£10**	
Jama	LP	Two Tone	TT5006	1982	**£10**	**£4**	
Jingle Bells	7"	Fab	FAB12	1967	**£6**	**£2.50**	
Lion Speaks	7"	Treasure Isle	TI7052	1969	**£6**	**£2.50**	*Andy Capp B side*
Luke Lane Shuffle	7"	Blue Beat	BB56	1961	**£12**	**£6**	*Prince Buster B side*
Man From Wareika	LP	Island	ILPS9485	1977	**£12**	**£5**	
Midnight In Ethiopia	LP	Island	ILPS9516	1978	**£12**	**£5**	
Planet Rock	7"	Planetone	RC4	197–	**£4**	**£1.50**	
Quando Quando	7"	Downtown	DT417	1969	**£5**	**£2**	
Reco's Farewell	7"	Island	WI022	1962	**£10**	**£5**	*Bunny & Skitter B side*
Soul Man	7"	Pama	PM706	1968	**£6**	**£2.50**	
Tender Foot Ska	7"	Pama	PM715	1968	**£6**	**£2.50**	
That Man Is Forward	LP	Two Tone	TT5005	1981	**£10**	**£4**	
Tribute To Don Drummond	7"	Bullet	BU407	1969	**£4**	**£1.50**	
Warreika Dub	LP	Ghetto Rockers	PRE1	197–	**£12**	**£5**	
Youth Boogie	7"	Planetone	RC5	197–	**£4**	**£1.50**	

RICOTTI, FRANK

Our Point Of View	LP	CBS	52668	1969	**£25**	**£10**	
Ricotti And Albuquerque	LP	Pegasus	PEG2	1971	**£12**	**£5**	

RIDDLE, NELSON

Batman	LP	Stateside	(S)SL10179	1966	**£40**	**£20**	
El Dorado	LP	Columbia	SX/SCX6155	1967	**£15**	**£6**	
Route 66 And Other Great TV Themes	LP	Capitol	T1771	1962	**£10**	**£4**	
Route Sixty-Six	7" EP	Capitol	EAP41771	1961	**£6**	**£2.50**	
Run For Cover	7"	Capitol	CL14305	1955	**£4**	**£1.50**	
Supercar	7"	Capitol	CL15309	1963	**£6**	**£2.50**	
Vera Cruz	7"	Capitol	CL14241	1955	**£4**	**£1.50**	

RIDDLERS

Batman Theme	7"	Polydor	56716	1966	**£8**	**£4**	

RIDE

Fall EP	CD-s	Creation	CRE087CD	1990	**£5**	**£2**	
Play EP	CD-s	Creation	CRE075CD	1990	**£5**	**£2**	
Ride EP	CD-s	Creation	CRESCD072	1990	**£5**	**£2**	
Taste	7"	Creation	CRE087P	1990	**£5**	**£2**	*1 sided promo*
Today Forever	CD-s	Creation	CRECD100T	1991	**£5**	**£2**	

RIEU, NICOLE

Live For Love	7"	Barclay	BAR31	1975	**£5**	**£2**	

RIFF RAFF

Original Man	LP	RCA	LPL15023	1974	**£25**	**£10**	
Riff Raff	LP	RCA	SF8351	1973	**£25**	**£10**	

RIFFS

Oh What A Feeling	7"	Blue Beat	BB242	1964	**£12**	**£6**	

RIFKIN

Title	Format	Label	Cat. No.	Year	Price	Price	Notes
Continental Hesitation	7"	Page One	POF071	1968	£50	£25	

RIFKIN, JOSHUA

Title	Format	Label	Cat. No.	Year	Price	Price	Notes
Baroque Beatles Book	LP	Nonesuch	H7306	1965	£25	£10	

RIGBY, ELEANOR

Title	Format	Label	Cat. No.	Year	Price	Price	Notes
I Want To Sleep With You	7"	Waterloo Sunset	RUSS101	1985	£8	£4	with condom & sticker
Take Another Shot Of My Heart	7"	Waterloo Sunset	RUSS102	1985	£6	£2.50	with signed story

RIGG, BRAM SET

Title	Format	Label	Cat. No.	Year	Price	Price	Notes
Take The Time To Be Yourself	7"	Stateside	SS2020	1967	£75	£37.50	

RIGG, DIANA

Title	Format	Label	Cat. No.	Year	Price	Price	Notes
Sentimental Journey	7"	RCA	RCA2179	1972	£5	£2	

RIGGS, JACKIE

Title	Format	Label	Cat. No.	Year	Price	Price	Notes
Great Pretender	7"	London	HLF8244	1956	£20	£10	

RIGHTEOUS BROTHERS

Title	Format	Label	Cat. No.	Year	Price	Price	Notes
Back To Back	LP	London	HA8278	1966	£15	£6	
Ebb Tide	7"	London	HL10011	1965	£4	£1.50	
Ebb Tide	7" EP	Barclay	070915	1965	£12	£6	French
In Action	LP	Sue	ILP937	1966	£25	£10	
Just Once In My Life	7"	London	HL9962	1965	£40	£20	demo only
Just Once In My Life	LP	London	HA8245	1965	£20	£8	
Little Latin Lupe Lu	7"	London	HL9743	1963	£4	£1.50	
My Babe	7"	London	HL9814	1963	£4	£1.50	
One For The Road	LP	Verve	(S)VLP9228	1968	£10	£4	
Right Now	LP	Pye	NPL28059	1965	£15	£6	
Righteous Brothers	7" EP	Verve	VEP5025	1966	£10	£5	
Righteous Brothers	7" EP	Pye	NEP44043	1965	£15	£7.50	
Righteous Brothers	7" EP	Verve	VEP5024	1966	£12	£6	
Some Blue Eyed Soul	LP	Pye	NPL28056	1965	£20	£8	
Soul And Inspiration	7"	Verve	VS535	1966	£4	£1.50	
Soul And Inspiration	7" EP	Verve	26501	1966	£12	£6	French
Soul And Inspiration	LP	Verve	(S)VLP9131	1966	£15	£6	
Souled Out	LP	Verve	(S)VLP9190	1967	£10	£4	
Unchained Melody	7"	London	HL9975	1965	£4	£1.50	
Unchained Melody	7" EP	Barclay	70860	1965	£12	£6	French
You Can Have Her	7"	Sue	WI4018	1966	£10	£5	
You've Lost That Lovin' Feelin'	7"	London	HL9943	1965	£4	£1.50	
You've Lost That Lovin' Feelin'	LP	London	HA8226	1965	£20	£8	
You've Lost That Lovin' Feelin'	7" EP	Barclay	70766	1965	£12	£6	French

RIGHTEOUS FLAMES

Title	Format	Label	Cat. No.	Year	Price	Price	Notes
Gimme Some Sign Girl	7"	Fab	FAB18	1967	£8	£4	
Run To The Rock	7"	High Note	HS052	1971	£4	£1.50	Gaytones B side

RIGHTEOUS TWINS

Title	Format	Label	Cat. No.	Year	Price	Price	Notes
If I Could Hear My Master	7"	Blue Cat	BS174	1969	£4	£1.50	

RIKKI & THE LAST DAYS OF EARTH

Title	Format	Label	Cat. No.	Year	Price	Price	Notes
City Of The Damned	7"	DJM	DJS10814	1977	£5	£2	
Oundle 29/5/77	7"	private		1977	£20	£10	

RILEY, BILLY LEE

Title	Format	Label	Cat. No.	Year	Price	Price	Notes
Going Back To Memphis	7"	Stax	STAX120	1969	£5	£2	
Harmonica Beatlemania	LP	Mercury	SR60974	1964	£20	£8	US
I've Been Searchin'	7"	King	KG1015	1965	£6	£2.50	

RILEY, BOB

Title	Format	Label	Cat. No.	Year	Price	Price	Notes
Midnight Line	7"	MGM	MGM977	1958	£40	£20	

RILEY, DESMOND

Title	Format	Label	Cat. No.	Year	Price	Price	Notes
Skinhead, A Message To You	7"	Downtown	DT450	1969	£5	£2	Music Doctors B side

RILEY, HOWARD

Title	Format	Label	Cat. No.	Year	Price	Price	Notes
Angle	LP	CBS	52669	1969	£25	£10	
Day Will Come	LP	CBS	64077	1970	£20	£8	
Discussions	LP	Opportunity	CP2500	1967	£250	£150	
Duality	LP	View	VS0020	1982	£12	£5	German
Facets	LP	Impetus	38002	1981	£25	£10	3 LP box set
Flight	LP	Turtle	TUR301	1970	£40	£20	
For Four On Two Two	LP	Affinity	AFF110	1983	£10	£4	
In Focus	LP	Affinity	AFF137	1985	£10	£4	with Keith Tippett
Intertwine	LP	Mosaic	GCM771	1977	£12	£5	
Other Side	LP	Spotlight	SPJ511	1979	£12	£5	
Shaped	LP	Mosaic	GCM781	1977	£12	£5	
Singleness	LP	Canon		197–	£15	£6	
Solo Imprints	cass	Jaguar	JS3	1974	£12	£5	
Synopsis	LP	Incus	INCUS13	1973	£15	£6	
Turin Concert	LP	Vinyl	VS112	1977	£12	£5	

RILEY, ILLMAN

Gambler .... LP .... Tradition .... TSR009 .... 1971 **£20** ....**£8** ....

RILEY, JIMMY

Mount Zion .... 7" .... Supreme .... SUP217 .... 1971 **£4** .... **£1.50** .. *Eccle & Nevil B side*

RILEY, TERRY

Composer Terry Riley pioneered the use of tape-loops to create a dense, meditational sound, and was a direct influence on the Soft Machine school of rock music. His *Church Of Anthrax* is co-credited to John Cale, and the well-known ex-member of the Velvet Underground gets the star billing. However, the music is all Riley's, with Cale essentially sitting at the feet of the master and following as best as he can.

Church Of Anthrax .... LP .... CBS .... 64259 .... 1971 **£12** ....**£5** .... *with John Cale*
Happy Ending .... LP .... Warner Bros .... WB46125 .... 1972 **£15** ....**£6** ....*French*
In 'C' .... LP .... CBS .... 64565 .... 1970 **£10** ....**£4** ....
Keyboard Studies .... LP .... Byg .... 1969 **£30** ....**£15** ....*French*
Le Secret De La Vie .... LP .... Philips .... 9120037 .... 1975 **£10** ....**£4** ....
Persian Surgery Dervishes .... LP .... Shandar .... 83501 .... 1972 **£25** ....**£10** .... *French double*
Rainbow In Curved Air .... LP .... CBS .... 64564 .... 1971 **£10** ....**£4** ....
Reed Streams .... LP .... Mass Art Inc .... M131 .... 1967 **£30** ....**£15** .... *US*

RIMMER, SHANE

Three Bells .... 7" .... Columbia .... DB4343 .... 1959 **£4** .... **£1.50** ....

RINGS & THINGS

Strange Things Are Happening .... 7" .... Fontana .... TF987 .... 1968 **£50** ....**£25** ....

RINKY DINKS

Choo Choo Cha Cha .... 7" .... Capitol .... CL14999 .... 1959 **£5** ....**£2** ....

RIO, BOBBY

Angelica .... 7" .... Piccadilly .... 7N35337 .... 1966 **£4** .... **£1.50** ....
Ask The Lonely .... 7" .... Piccadilly .... 7N35303 .... 1966 **£4** .... **£1.50** ....
Boy Meets Girl .... 7" .... Pye .... 7N15790 .... 1965 **£25** .... **£12.50** ....
Don Diddley .... 7" .... Stateside .... SS211 .... 1963 **£6** .... **£2.50** ....
Everything In The Garden .... 7" .... Pye .... 7N15897 .... 1965 **£25** .... **£12.50** ....
Value For Love .... 7" .... Pye .... 7N15958 .... 1965 **£25** .... **£12.50** ....

RIO GRANDES

Soldiers Take Over .... 7" .... Pyramid .... PYR6001 .... 1966 **£6** .... **£2.50** ....

RIOT SQUAD

Any Time .... 7" .... Pye .... 7N15752 .... 1965 **£15** .... **£7.50** ....
Cry Cry Cry .... 7" .... Pye .... 7N17041 .... 1966 **£25** .... **£12.50** ....
Gotta Be A First Time .... 7" .... Pye .... 7N17237 .... 1967 **£25** .... **£12.50** ....
I Take It We're Through .... 7" .... Pye .... 7N17092 .... 1966 **£25** .... **£12.50** ....
I Wanna Talk About My Baby .... 7" .... Pye .... 7N15817 .... 1965 **£25** .... **£12.50** ....
I Wanna Talk About My Baby .... 7" EP .. Pye .... PNV24134 .... 1965 **£175** .. **£87.50** ....*French*
It's Never Too Late to Forgive .... 7" .... Pye .... 7N17130 .... 1966 **£25** .... **£12.50** ....
Not A Great Talker .... 7" .... Pye .... 7N15869 .... 1965 **£20** ....**£10** ....

RIOTS

I Am In Love .... 7" .... Island .... WI197 .... 1965 **£10** ....**£5** ....
Telling Lies .... 7" .... Island .... WI176 .... 1965 **£10** ....**£5** ....

RIPCHORDS

Gone .... 7" .... CBS .... AAG162 .... 1963 **£6** .... **£2.50** ....
Here I Stand .... 7" .... CBS .... AAG143 .... 1963 **£6** .... **£2.50** ....
Hey Little Cobra .... 7" .... CBS .... AAG181 .... 1964 **£10** ....**£5** ....
Hey Little Cobra .... 7" EP .. CBS .... 5682 .... 1964 **£20** ....**£10** ....*French*
Hey Little Cobra .... LP .... CBS .... BPG62228 .... 1964 **£30** ....**£15** ....
Three Window Coupe .... 7" .... CBS .... AAG202 .... 1964 **£10** ....**£5** ....
Three Window Coupe .... LP .... CBS .... CL2216/CS9016 ..... 1965 **£30** ....**£15** .... *US*

RIPPERS

Honestly .... LP .... Saga .... FID2142 .... 1968 **£15** ....**£6** ....

RIPPERTON, MINNIE

Adventures In Paradise .... LP .... Epic .... EPC69142 .... 1975 **£10** ....**£4** ....
Perfect Angel .... LP .... Epic .... EPC80426 .... 1974 **£10** ....**£4** ....

RISING MOON

Rising Moon .... LP .... Theatre Projects .... 1974 **£25** ....**£10** ....

RISING SONS

The bright blues-based music of the Rising Sons was gathered together on to CD in 1992. The result shows the band to be one of the great lost sixties units, with a timeless quality that allows the music to easily transcend its decade. The Rising Sons were driven by the combined talents of Taj Mahal and Ry Cooder, both of whose careers can be seen to proceed logically from this starting point.

Candy Man .... 7" .... Columbia .... 43534 .... 1966 **£20** ....**£10** .... *US*
Rising Sons .... LP .... Groucho .... MARX48501 .... **£40** ....**£20** .... *Italian*
You're My Girl .... 7" .... Stateside .... SS426 .... 1965 **£10** ....**£5** ....

RISING STORM

Alive Again At Andover .... LP .... ARF .... 007 .... 1983 **£20** ....**£8** .... *US*

Calm Before The Rising Storm ... LP ... Remnant ... BBA3571 ... 1966 £**1000** ... £**700** ... *US*

RITA

Erotica ... 7" ... Major Minor ... MM6533 ... 1969 £**10** ... £**5**

RITCHIE, JEAN

Child Ballads Vol. 1 ... LP ... Folkways ... FA2301 ... 1960 £**12** ... £**5** ... *US*
Child Ballads Vol. 2 ... LP ... Folkways ... FA2302 ... 1961 £**12** ... £**5** ... *US*
Jean Ritchie ... LP ... XTRA ... XTRA1030 ... 1966 £**10** ... £**4**
Songs From Kentucky ... 10" LP ... Argo ... ARS1009 ... 1953 £**20** ... £**8**

RITTER, TEX

Blood On The Saddle ... LP ... Capitol ... (S)T1292 ... 1960 £**10** ... £**4**
Cowboy Favourites ... 10" LP ... Capitol ... LC6552 ... 1952 £**15** ... £**6**
Deck Of Cards ... 7" EP .. Capitol ... EAP11323 ... 1960 £**6** ... £**2.50**
Hillbilly Heaven ... LP ... Capitol ... (S)T1623 ... 1961 £**10** ... £**4** ... *US*
Is There A Santa Claus? ... 7" ... Capitol ... CL14175 ... 1954 £**6** ... £**2.50**
Last Frontier ... 7" ... Capitol ... CL14536 ... 1956 £**4** ... £**1.50**
Last Wagon ... 7" ... Capitol ... CL14660 ... 1956 £**4** ... £**1.50**
Lincoln Hymns ... LP ... Capitol ... (S)W1562 ... 1961 £**10** ... £**4** ... *US*
Marshall Of Wichita ... 7" ... Capitol ... CL14335 ... 1955 £**6** ... £**2.50**
Psalms ... LP ... Capitol ... T1100 ... 1959 £**10** ... £**4**
Searchers ... 7" ... Capitol ... CL14605 ... 1956 £**5** ... £**2**
Songs From The Western Screen ... LP ... Capitol ... T971 ... 1958 £**25** ... £**10** ... *US*
Wayward Wind ... 7" ... Capitol ... CL14581 ... 1956 £**8** ... £**4**
Whale Of A Tale ... 7" ... Capitol ... CL14277 ... 1955 £**6** ... £**2.50**

RIVALS

Skateboarding In The UK ... 7" ... Sound On Sound ... SOS100 ... 1978 £**5** ... £**2**

RIVALS (2)

Future Rights ... 7" ... Ace ... ACE007 ... 1980 £**12** ... £**6**
Here Comes The Night ... 7" ... Ace ... ACE011 ... 1980 £**8** ... £**4**

RIVERA, HECTOR

At The Party ... 7" ... Polydor ... 65728 ... 1967 £**15** ... £**7.50**

RIVERS, BLUE & THE MAROONS

Blue Beat In My Soul ... LP ... Columbia ... SX6192 ... 1967 £**25** ... £**10**
Witchcraft Man ... 7" ... Columbia ... DB103 ... 1967 £**4** ... £**1.50**

RIVERS, BOYD & CLIFF AUNGIER

Wanderin' ... LP ... Decca ... LK4696 ... 1965 £**15** ... £**6**

RIVERS, CLIFF

True Lips ... 7" ... London ... HLU9739 ... 1963 £**15** ... £**7.50**

RIVERS, DANNY

Can't You Hear My Heart ... 7" ... Decca ... F11294 ... 1960 £**10** ... £**5**
Hawk ... 7" ... Top Rank ... JAR408 ... 1960 £**12** ... £**6**
Moving In ... 7" ... HMV ... POP1000 ... 1962 £**25** ... £**12.50**
My Baby's Gone Away ... 7" ... Decca ... F11357 ... 1961 £**15** ... £**7.50**
There Will Never Be Anyone ... 7" ... Decca ... F11865 ... 1964 £**5** ... £**2**

RIVERS, DEKE

Outsider ... 7" ... Oriole ... CB1735 ... 1962 £**6** ... £**2.50**

RIVERS, JOHNNY

And I Know You Wanna Dance ... LP ... Imperial ... LP9307/12307 ... 1966 £**10** ... £**4** ... *US*
At The Whisky A Go-Go ... LP ... Liberty ... LBY3031 ... 1964 £**15** ... £**6**
Back At The Whisky ... LP ... Imperial ... LP9284/12284 ... 1965 £**10** ... £**4** ... *US*
Blue Skies ... 7" ... Pye ... 7N25118 ... 1962 £**4** ... £**1.50**
Changes ... LP ... Liberty ... (S)LBY3087 ... 1967 £**10** ... £**4**
Go Johnny Go ... LP ... United Artists .. UAL3386/UAS6386 ... 1964 £**10** ... £**4** ... *US*
Golden Hits ... LP ... Imperial ... LP9324/12324 ... 1966 £**10** ... £**4** ... *US*
Here We A Go-Go Again ... LP ... Liberty ... LBY3036 ... 1964 £**12** ... £**5**
I Washed My Hands In Muddy Water ... 7" ... Liberty ... LIB66175 ... 1966 £**4** ... £**1.50**
In Action ... LP ... Imperial ... LP9280/12280 ... 1965 £**10** ... £**4** ... *US*
Maybellene ... 7" ... Liberty ... LIB66056 ... 1964 £**4** ... £**1.50**
Meanwhile Back At The Whisky A Go-Go ... LP ... Liberty ... LBY3056 ... 1965 £**10** ... £**4**
Memphis ... 7" ... Liberty ... LIB66032 ... 1964 £**4** ... £**1.50**
Midnight Special ... 7" ... Liberty ... LIB66087 ... 1965 £**4** ... £**1.50**
More Johnny Rivers ... 7" EP .. Liberty ... LEP4049 ... 1966 £**10** ... £**5**
Mountain Of Love ... 7" ... Liberty ... LIB66075 ... 1964 £**4** ... £**1.50**
Rocks The Folk ... LP ... Liberty ... LBY3064 ... 1965 £**10** ... £**4**
Sensational Johnny Rivers ... LP ... Capitol ... (S)T2161 ... 1964 £**12** ... £**5** ... *US*
Tom Dooley ... 7" ... Liberty ... LIB12023 ... 1965 £**4** ... £**1.50**
Tracks Of My Tears ... 7" ... Liberty ... LIB66244 ... 1966 £**4** ... £**1.50**

RIVERS, SAM

Contours ... LP ... Blue Note ... BLP/BST84206 ... 1965 £**20** ... £**8**
Fuchsia Swing Song ... LP ... Blue Note ... BLP/BST84184 ... 1964 £**20** ... £**8**
New Conception ... LP ... Blue Note ... BLP/BST84249 ... 1966 £**20** ... £**8**
Streams ... LP ... Impulse ... AS9251 ... 1973 £**15** ... £**6** ... *US*

RIVERS, TONY & THE CASTAWAYS

Come Back	7"	Columbia	DB7536	1965	£5	£2	
Girl Don't Tell Me	7"	Immediate	IM027	1966	£10	£5	
God Only Knows	7"	Columbia	DB7971	1966	£5	£2	
I Can Guarantee Your Love	7"	Polydor	56245	1968	£4	£1.50	
I Love The Way You Walk	7"	Columbia	DB7224	1964	£5	£2	
Life's Too Short	7"	Columbia	DB7336	1964	£5	£2	
Nowhere Man	7"	Parlophone	R5400	1966	£4	£1.50	
Shake Shake Shake	7"	Columbia	DB7135	1963	£8	£4	
She	7"	Columbia	DB7448	1965	£5	£2	

RIVETS

Yes It's Time	LP	Starclub	158019STY	1966	£50	£25	*German*

RIVIERAS

California Sun	7"	Pye	7N25237	1964	£10	£5	
California Sun	7" EP	Columbia	ESRF1523	1964	£25	£12.50	*French*
California Sun	LP	USA	102	1967	£25	£10	*US*
Campus Party	LP	Riviera	701	1964	£40	£20	*US*
Let's Have A Party	LP	USA	102	1964	£30	£15	*US*

RIVIERAS (2)

Blessings Of Love	7"	HMV	POP773	1960	£25	£12.50	

RIVINGTONS

Bird's The Word	7"	Liberty	LIB55553	1963	£20	£10	
Doin' The Bird	LP	Liberty	LRP3282/ LST7282	1963	£40	£20	*US*
Pappa Oom Mow Mow	7"	Liberty	LIB55427	1962	£20	£10	
Rose Growing In The Ruins	7"	CBS	202088	1966	£25	£12.50	

RO RO

Blackbird	7"	Regal Zonophone	RZ3076	1973	£8	£4	
Down On The Road	7"	Regal Zonophone	RZ3056	1972	£8	£4	
Here I Go Again	7"	Parlophone	R5920	1971	£8	£4	
Meet At The Water	LP	Regal Zonophone	SRZA8510	1972	£150	£75	

ROACH, FREDDIE

All That's Good	LP	Blue Note	BLP/BST84190	1965	£30	£15	
Brown Sugar	LP	Blue Note	BLP/BST84168	1964	£30	£15	
Down To Earth	LP	Blue Note	BLP/BST84113	1962	£30	£15	
Good Move	LP	Blue Note	BLP/BST84158	1964	£30	£15	
Mo' Greens Please	LP	Blue Note	BLP/BST84128	1963	£30	£15	
Soul Book	LP	Transatlantic	PR7490	1967	£12	£5	

ROACH, MAX

At Newport	LP	Emarcy	MMB12005	1959	£20	£8	
Best Of Max Roach & Clifford Brown In Concert	LP	Vocalion	LAE12036	1957	£30	£15	
Jazz In 3/4 Time	LP	Emarcy	EJL1282	1958	£30	£15	
Max Roach And Clifford Brown	7" EP	Vogue	EPV1074	1956	£5	£2	
Max Roach And Clifford Brown	7" EP	Vogue	EPV1083	1956	£5	£2	
Max Roach And Clifford Brown	7" EP	Vogue	EPV1091	1956	£5	£2	
Max Roach And Clifford Brown In Concert Vol. 1	10" LP	Vogue	LDE117	1955	£40	£20	
Max Roach And Clifford Brown In Concert Vol. 2	10" LP	Vogue	LDE128	1955	£40	£20	
Max Roach Plus Four	LP	Emarcy	MMB12009	1959	£25	£10	
Percussion Bitter Suite	LP	HMV	CLP1522	1962	£12	£5	
Quiet As It's Kept	LP	Mercury	MMC14054	1961	£20	£8	

ROAD

Road	LP	Rare Earth	SRE3006	1972	£10	£4	

ROADRUNNERS

Pantomania	7" EP	Cavern Sound	2BSNL7	1965	£40	£20	
Star Club Show 2	LP	Starclub	158001STY	1965	£75	£37.50	*German, with Shorty & Them*
Twist Time Im Star Club Hamburg 4	LP	Ariola	71224IT	1964	£100	£50	*German*

ROADSTER

Fantasy	7"	Mayhem	SRTS81	1981	£15	£7.50	

ROADSTERS

Joy Ride	7"	Stateside	SS293	1964	£10	£5	

ROARING JELLY

Golden Greats	LP	Free Reed	FRR013	1976	£10	£4	

ROARING SIXTIES

Confusion as to the identity of the group who made this single in defence of the pirate radio stations has arisen from the fact that the Leicester band the Farinas used the 'Roaring Sixties' name before changing to Family. In fact, the single was made by a completely different

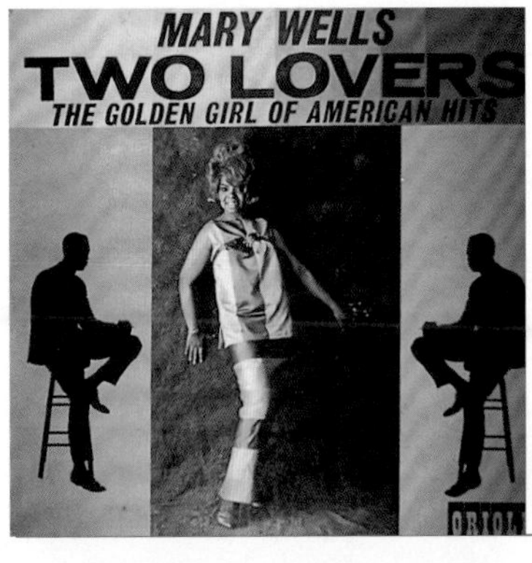

MARY WELLS
Two Lovers
£50

DIANA ROSS & THE SUPREMES
Love Child
£10

VARIOUS
Hitsville USA
£20

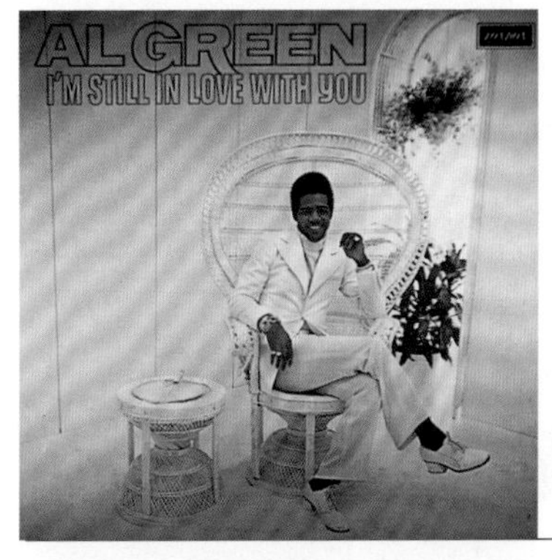

AL GREEN
I'm Still In Love With You
£10

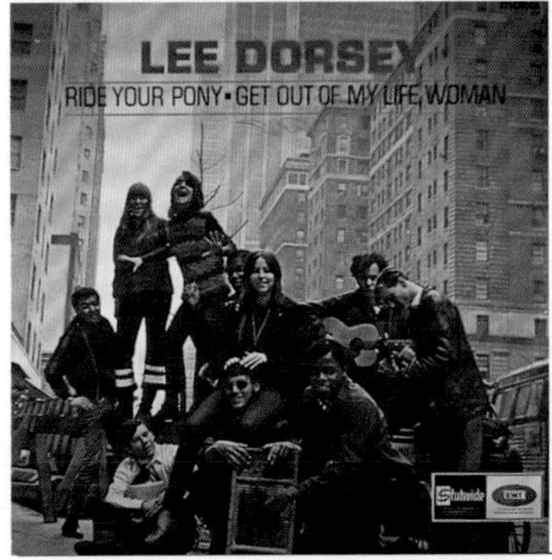

LEE DORSEY
Lee Dorsey
£15

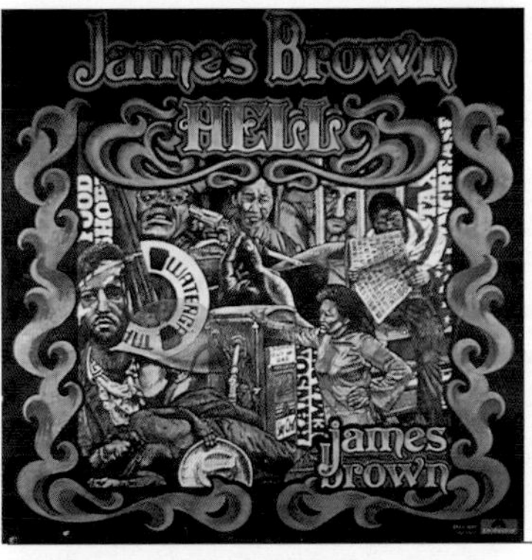

JAMES BROWN
Hell
£40

OTIS REDDING
The Dock Of The Bay
£15

PARLIAMENT
Chocolate City
£15

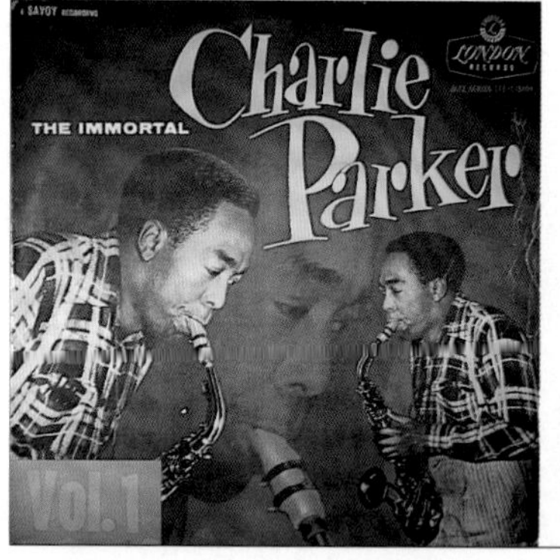

CHARLIE PARKER
The Immortal Charlie Parker Vol. 1
£25

DAVE PELL
I Had The Craziest Dream
£10

SHORTY ROGERS
Cool And Crazy
10" LP £50

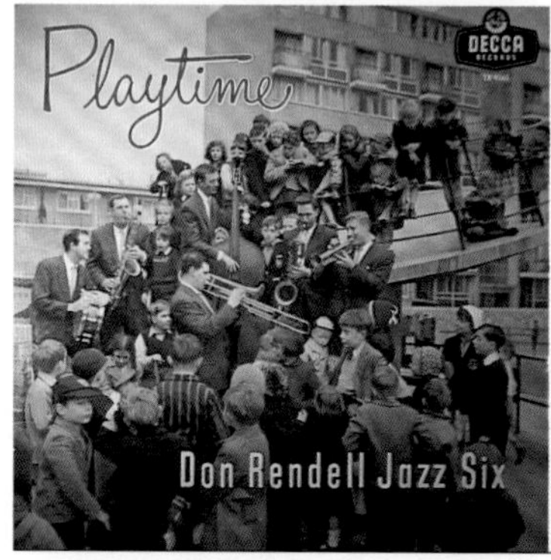

DON RENDELL
Playtime
£100

CECIL TAYLOR
Looking Ahead!
£25

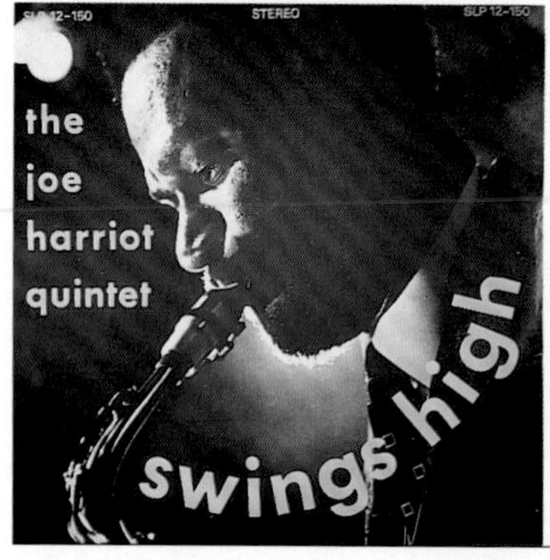

JOE HARRIOTT
Swings High
£75

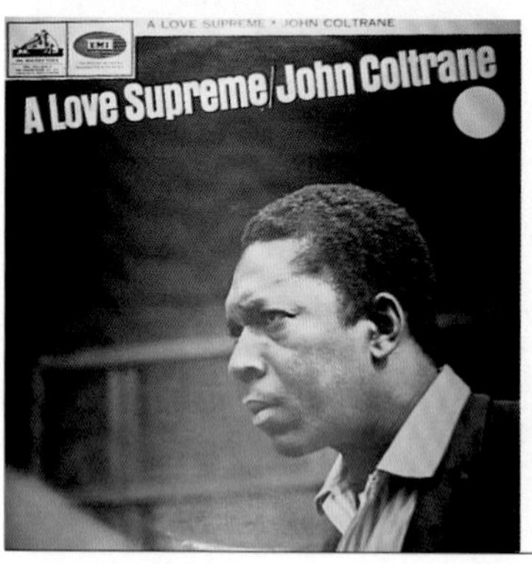

JOHN COLTRANE
A Love Supreme
£20

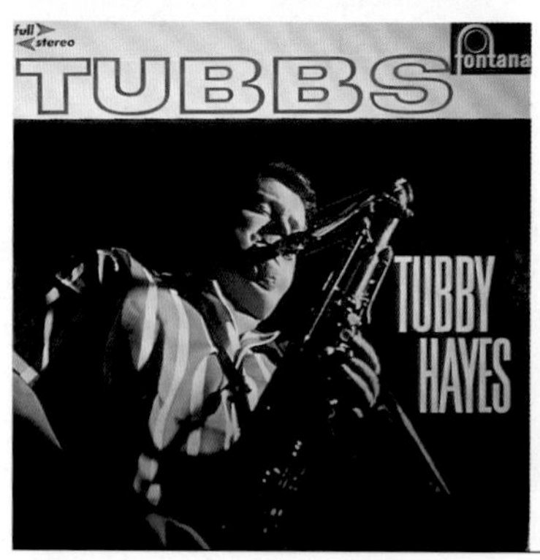

TUBBY HAYES
Tubbs
£100

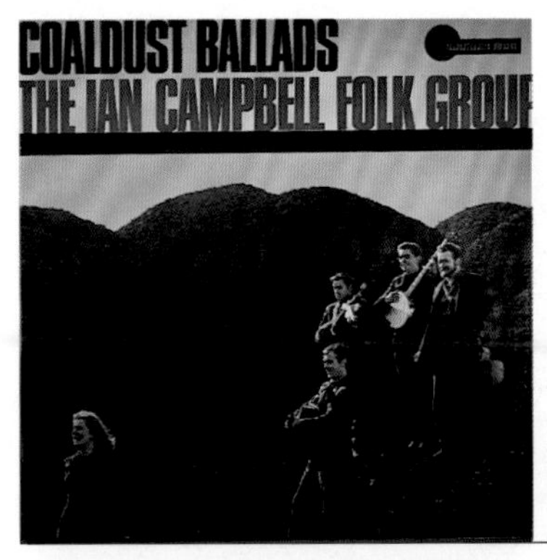

IAN CAMPBELL FOLK GROUP
Coaldust Ballads
£25

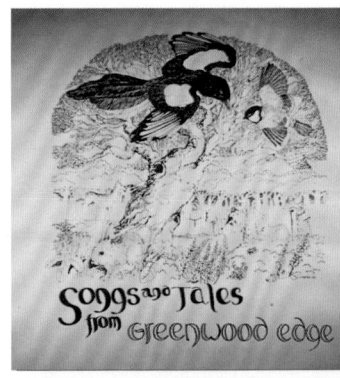

CELEBRATED RATLIFFE STOUT BAND
Songs And Tales From Greenwood Edge
£150

TIM HART & MADDY PRIOR
Folk Songs of Old England Vol. 1
£25

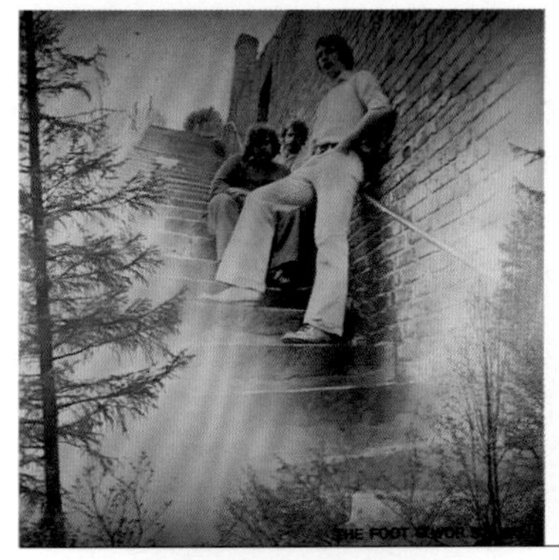

CROOKED OAK
The Foot O'Wor Stairs
£30

BARRY DRANSFIELD
Barry Dransfield
£250

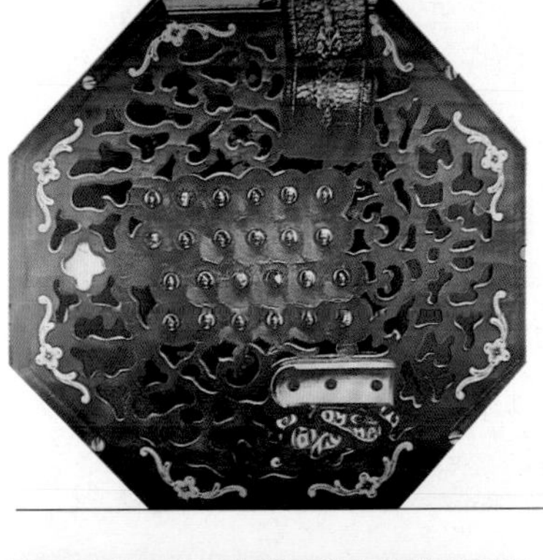

HORSLIPS
Happy To Meet Sorry To Part
£20

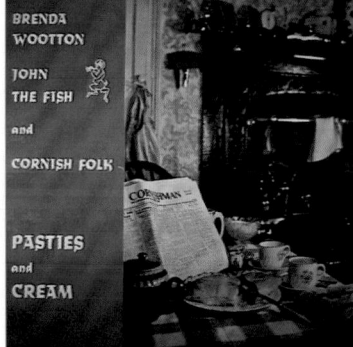

BRENDA WOOTTON & JOHN THE FISH
Pasties And Cream
£75

OYSTER BAND
English Rock And Roll – The Early Years (1800–1850)
£40

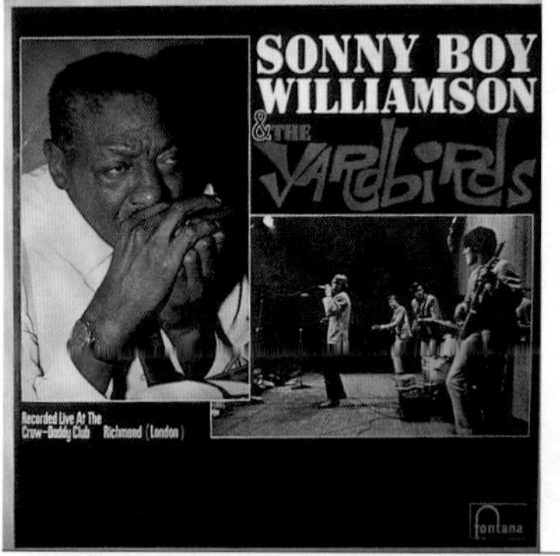

SONNY BOY WILLIAMSON
Sonny Boy Williamson And The Yardbirds
£75

STAGECOACH
Soundtrack
£25

TAJ MAHAL
Taj Mahal
£15

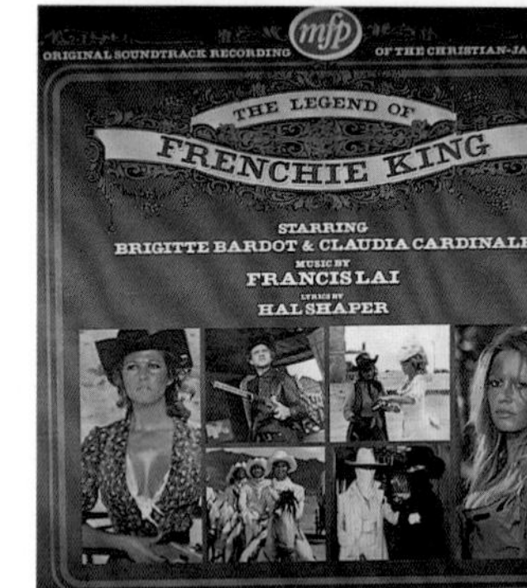

THE LEGEND OF FRENCHIE KING
Soundtrack
£25

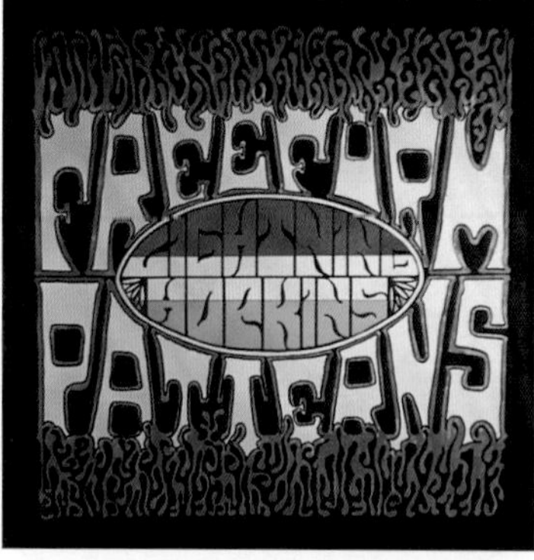

LIGHTNING HOPKINS
Freeform Patterns
£75

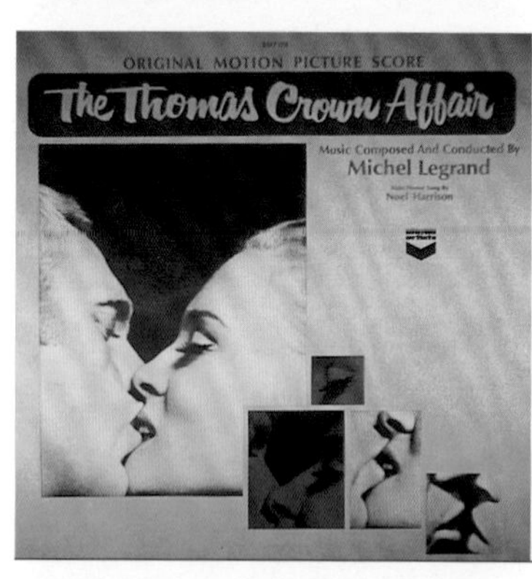

MICHEL LEGRAND
The Thomas Crown Affair
£20

B. B. KING
The B. B. King Story Chapter One
£40

JOHN BARRY
Deadfall
£30

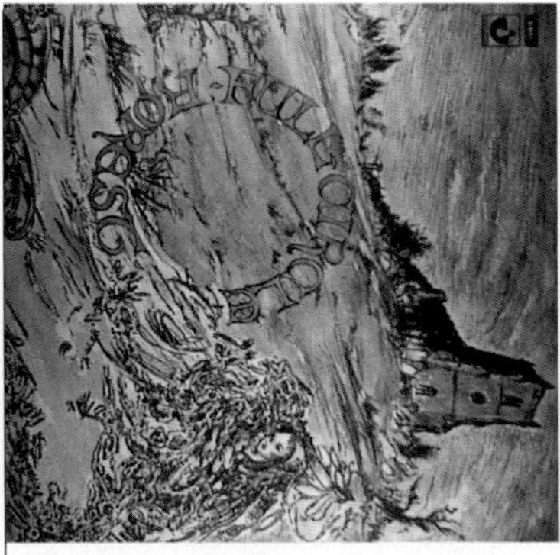

FOREST
Full Circle
£75

AARDVARK
Aardvark
£75

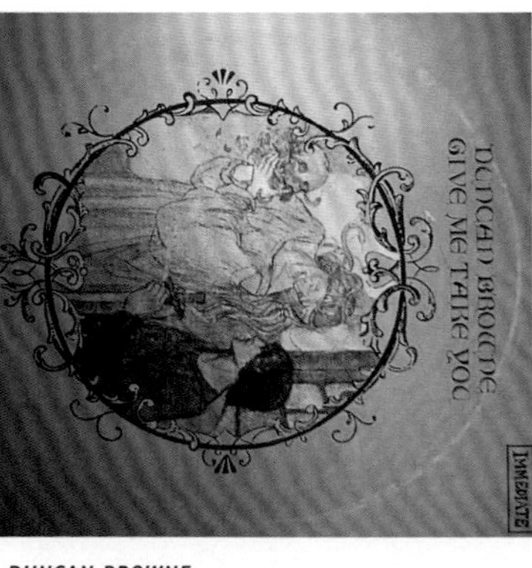

DUNCAN BROWNE
Give Me Take You
£150

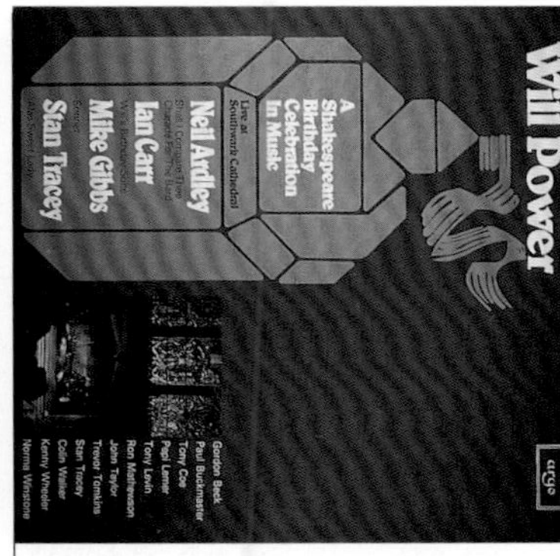

NEIL ARDLEY & OTHER ARTISTS
Will Power
£150

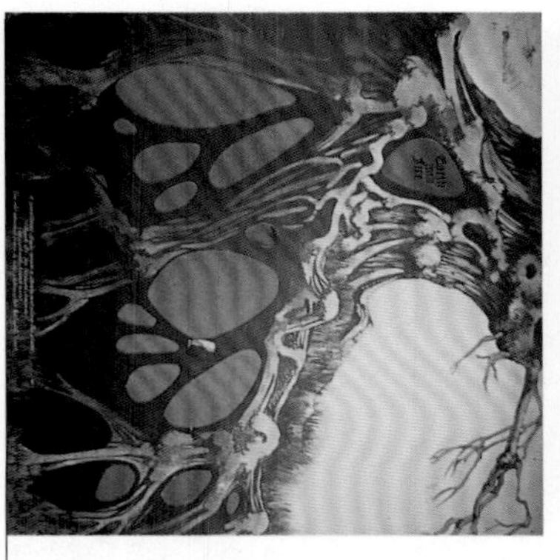

EARTH AND FIRE
Earth And Fire (Nepentha)
£150

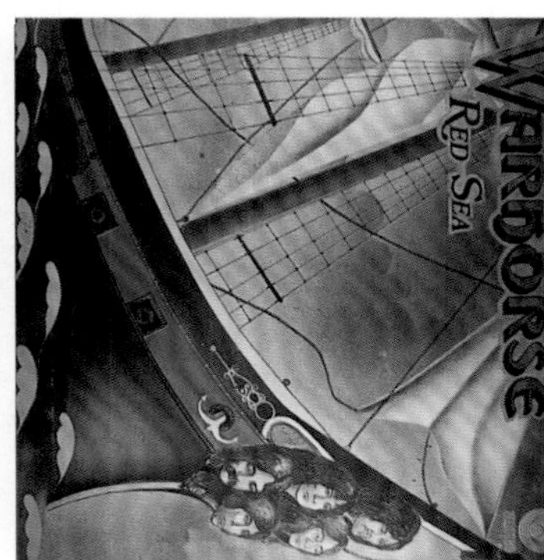

WARHORSE
Red Sea
£50

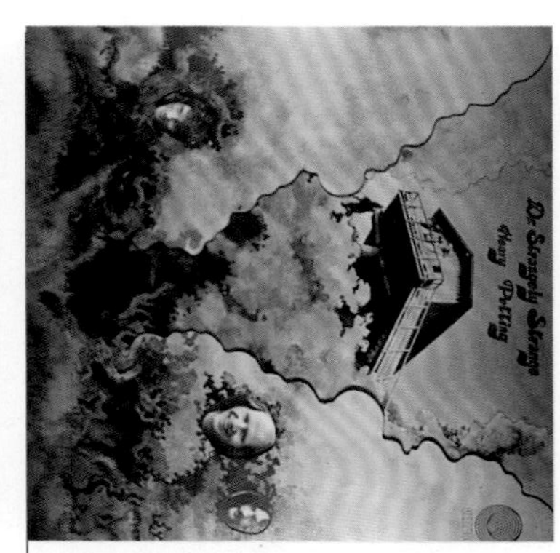

DR STRANGELY STRANGE
Heavy Petting
£60

QUINTESSENCE
In Blissful Company
£25

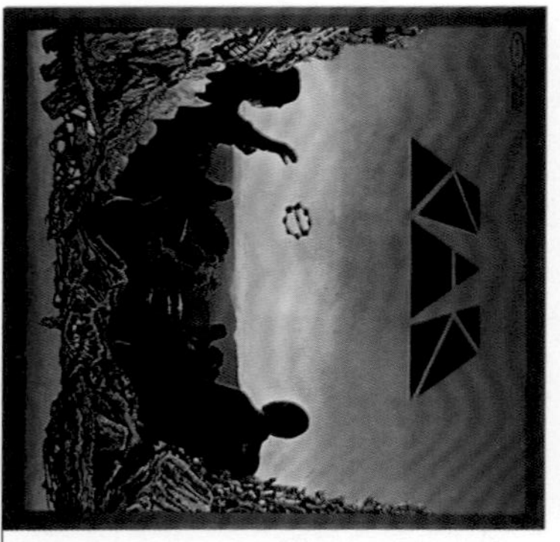

KAK
Kak
£100

CULPEPER'S ORCHARD
Culpeper's Orchard
£100

SAM GOPAL
Escalator
£75

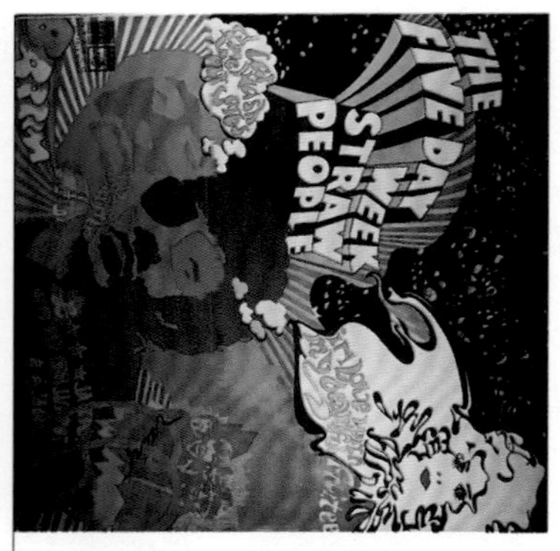

FIVE DAY WEEK STRAW PEOPLE
Five Day Week Straw People
£60

SLAPP HAPPY
Sort Of
£100

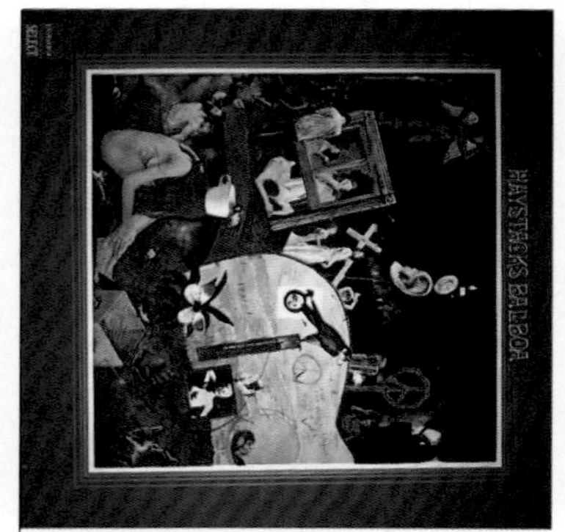

HAYSTACKS BALBOA
Haystacks Balboa
£100

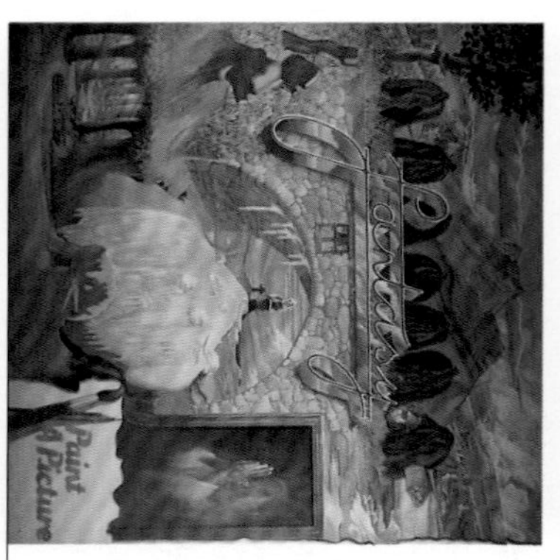

FANTASY
Paint A Picture
£200

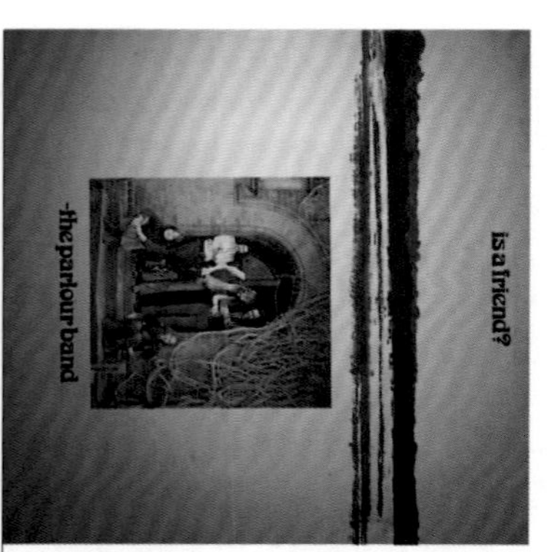

PARLOUR BAND
Is A Friend?
£150

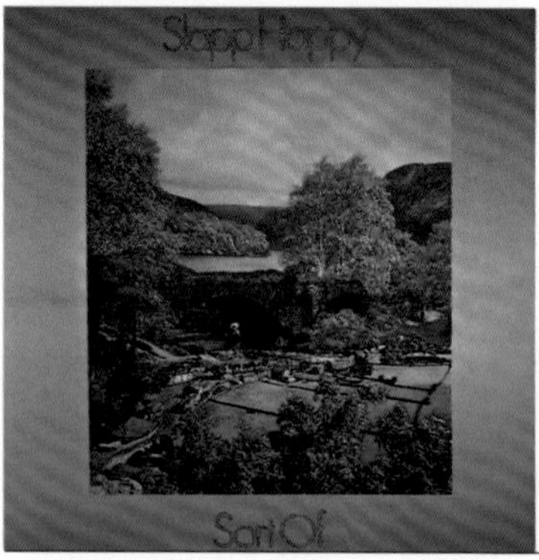

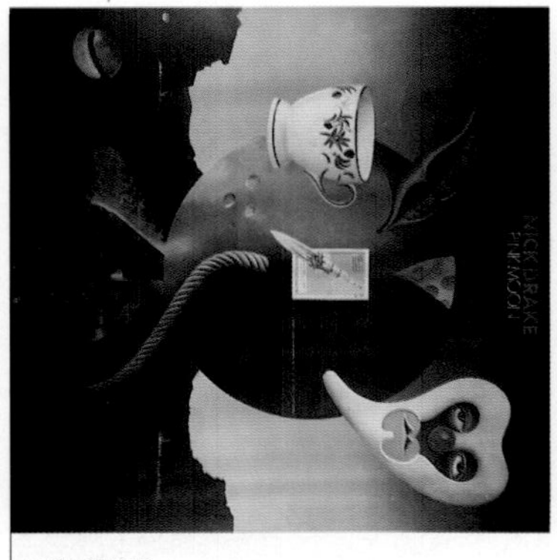

NICK DRAKE
Pink Moon
£50

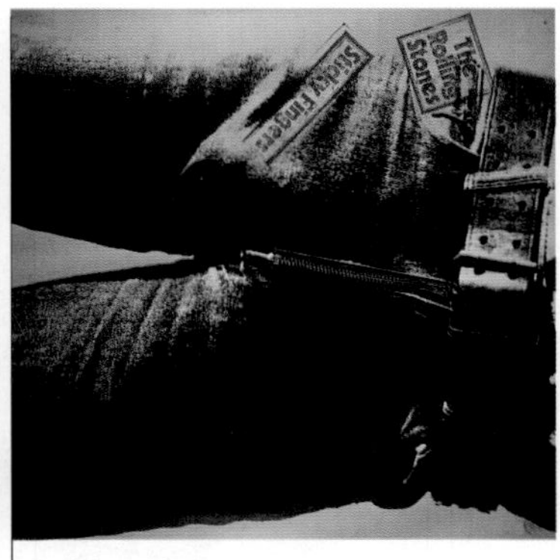

ROLLING STONES
Sticky Fingers
£15

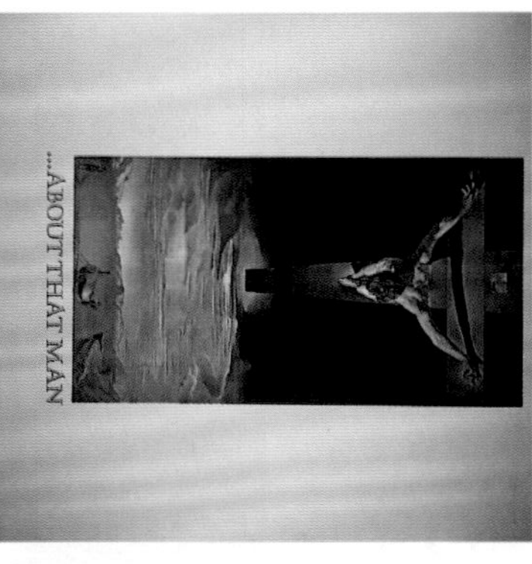

CLIFF RICHARD
About That Man
£100

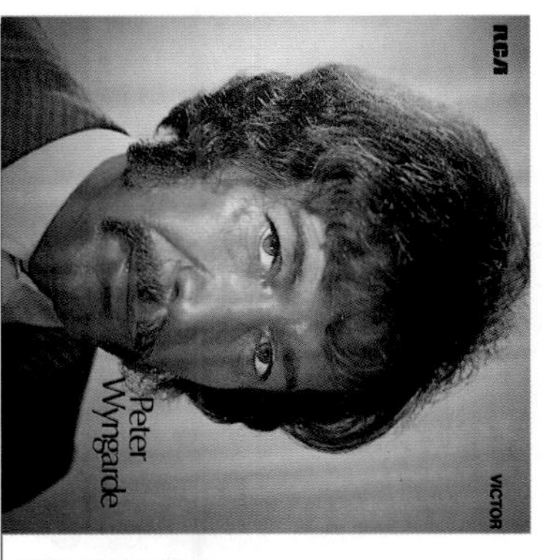

PETER WYNGARDE
Peter Wyngarde
£200

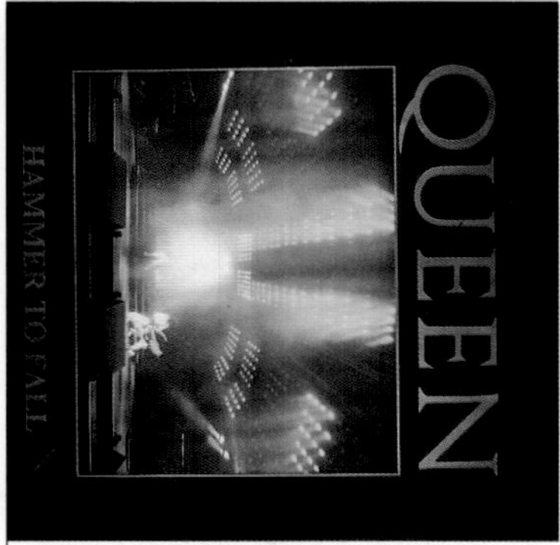

QUEEN
Hammer To Fall
12" single £125

SEX PISTOLS
Never Mind The Bollocks
picture disc £20

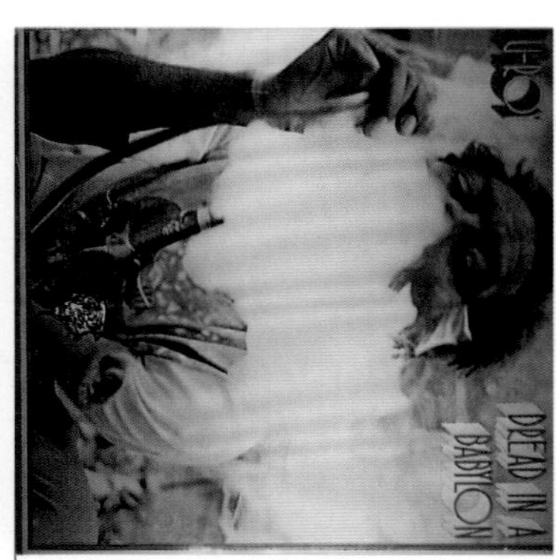

U ROY
Dread In A Babylon
£12

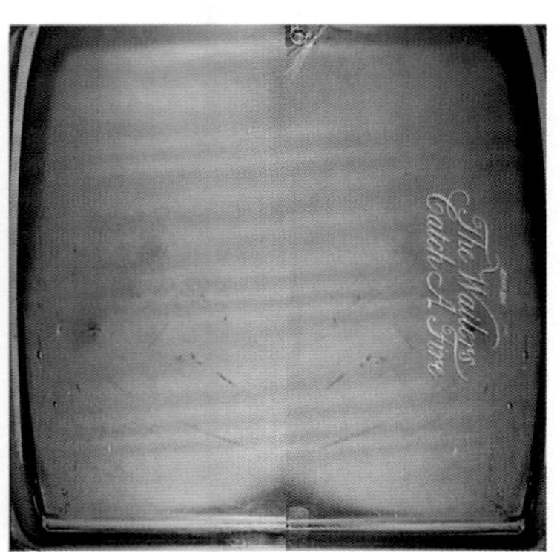

BOB MARLEY & THE WAILERS
Catch A Fire
£25

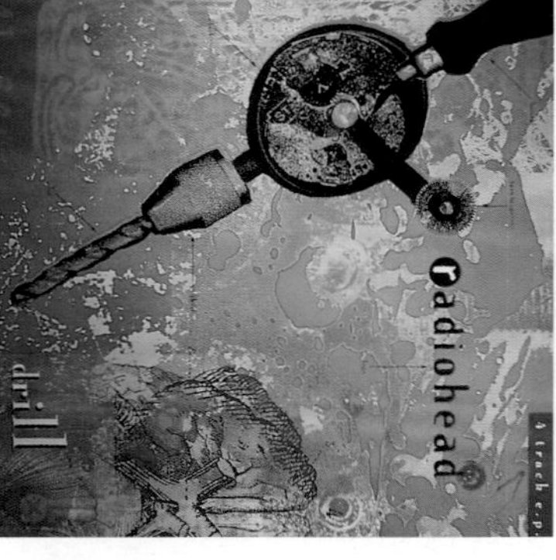

RADIOHEAD
Prove Yourself (Drill EP)
12″ single £40

GEORGE MICHAEL
Careless Whisper
12″ picture disc single £25

JUSTIFIED ANCIENTS OF MU MU
Justified Ancients Of Mu Mu
1987 £60

CURE
A Forest
12″ single £20

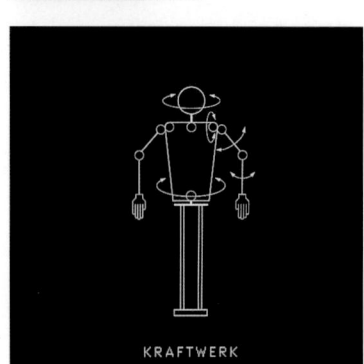

KRAFTWERK
Klang Box 101
12″ boxed set with t-shirt £400

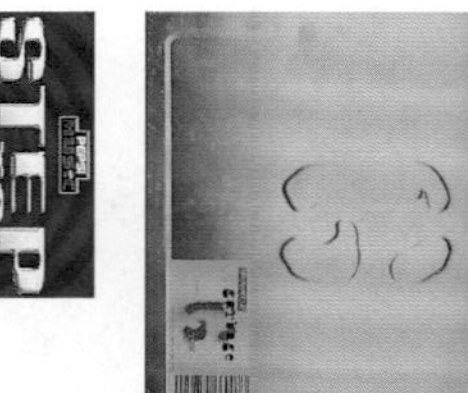

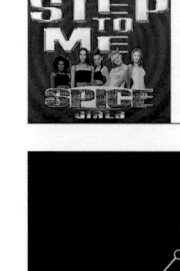

SPICE GIRLS
Step To Me
CD single £12

GARBAGE
Vow
7″ single £50

ALANIS MORISSETTE
Alanis
CD £40

R.E.M.
Stand
CD single £50

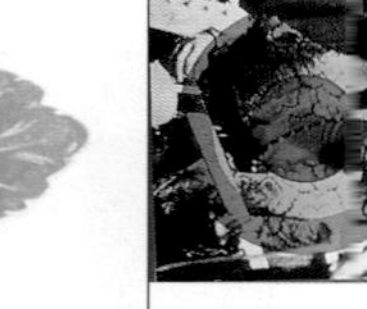

PAUL WELLER
Into Tomorrow
CD single £?0

U2
Lemon
promo CD single

group, and one that subsequently changed its name to one that brought success – Ten Years After. (Information supplied by Harry Overnall, drummer with the Farinas and Family.)

Title	Format	Label	Number	Year	Mint	VG	Notes
We Love The Pirates	7"	Marmalade	598001	1966	**£25**	**£12.50**	

ROBAN'S SKIFFLE GROUP

Title	Format	Label	Number	Year	Mint	VG	Notes
Careless Love	7"	Storyville	A45062	1961	**£20**	**£10**	*picture sleeve*
Careless Love	7"	Storyville	A45062	1962	**£8**	**£4**	
Roban's Skiffle Group	7" EP	Storyville	SEP507	195–	**£60**	**£30**	
Roban's Skiffle Group	7" EP	Storyville	SEP511	195–	**£60**	**£30**	
Roban's Skiffle Group	7" EP	Storyville	SEP509	195–	**£60**	**£30**	

ROBB, E. G.

Title	Format	Label	Number	Year	Mint	VG	Notes
Stage To Cimarron	7"	Columbia	DB7100	1963	**£5**	**£2**	

ROBBINS, MARTY

Title	Format	Label	Number	Year	Mint	VG	Notes
Ballad Of The Alamo	7"	Fontana	H270	1960	**£6**	**£2.50**	*picture sleeve*
Big Iron	7"	Fontana	H229	1959	**£4**	**£1.50**	
Carl, Lefty, & Marty	10" LP	Columbia	CL2544	1956	**£100**	**£50**	US
Devil Woman	7"	CBS	AAG114	1962	**£4**	**£1.50**	
Devil Woman	LP	CBS	(S)BPG62113	1963	**£10**	**£4**	
El Paso	7"	Fontana	H233	1959	**£4**	**£1.50**	
Greatest Hits	LP	Fontana	TFL5086	1960	**£15**	**£6**	
Gunfighter	7" EP	Fontana	TFE17224	1960	**£10**	**£5**	
Gunfighter Ballads And Trail Songs	LP	Fontana	TFL5063	1959	**£20**	**£8**	
Hanging Tree	7"	Fontana	H184	1959	**£4**	**£1.50**	
Hawaii's Calling Me	LP	CBS	(S)BPG62169	1963	**£10**	**£4**	
Heart Of Marty Robbins	LP	Columbia	STS2016	1969	**£15**	**£6**	US
Island Woman	LP	CBS	(S)BPG62297	1964	**£10**	**£4**	
Just A Little Sentimental	7" EP	CBS	AGG20004	1962	**£6**	**£2.50**	
Just A Little Sentimental	LP	Fontana	TFL5162/ STFL579	1961	**£15**	**£6**	
Just A Little Sentimental Vol. 2	7" EP	CBS	AGG20013	1962	**£6**	**£2.50**	
Long Tall Sally	78	Philips	PB590	1956	**£10**	**£5**	
Marty After Midnight	LP	CBS	(S)BPG62041	1962	**£12**	**£5**	
Marty Robbins	7" EP	CBS	AGG20049	1964	**£6**	**£2.50**	
Marty Robbins	LP	Columbia	CL1189	1958	**£20**	**£8**	US
Marty's Big Hits	7" EP	Fontana	TFE17161	1959	**£25**	**£12.50**	
More Greatest Hits	LP	Fontana	TFL5145/ STFL565	1961	**£12**	**£5**	
More Gunfighter Ballads And Trail Songs	LP	Fontana	TFL5113/ STFL541	1961	**£20**	**£8**	
Portrait Of Marty	LP	Columbia	CL1855/CS8655	1962	**£12**	**£5**	US
R.F.D.	LP	CBS	(S)BPG62437	1965	**£10**	**£4**	
Rock'n'Roll 'n' Robbins	10" LP	Columbia	CL2601	1956	**£350**	**£210**	US
Sittin' In A Tree House	7"	Fontana	H150	1958	**£6**	**£2.50**	
Song Of Robbins	LP	Columbia	CL976	1957	**£25**	**£10**	US
Song Of Robbins	LP	Columbia	CL2621/CS9421	1967	**£10**	**£4**	US
Song Of The Islands	7" EP	Fontana	TFE17167	1959	**£6**	**£2.50**	
Song Of The Islands	LP	Columbia	CL2625	1967	**£10**	**£4**	US
Song Of The Islands	LP	Columbia	CL1087	1957	**£25**	**£10**	US
Stairway Of Love	7"	Fontana	H128	1958	**£12**	**£6**	
Wedding Bells	7" EP	Fontana	TFE17168	1959	**£8**	**£4**	
White Sports Coat	7"	Philips	JK1019	1957	**£25**	**£12.50**	

ROBBINS, MEL

Title	Format	Label	Number	Year	Mint	VG	Notes
Save It	7"	London	HLM8966	1959	**£300**	**£180**	*tri-centre, best auctioned*

ROBBINS, SYLVIA

Title	Format	Label	Number	Year	Mint	VG	Notes
Frankie And Johnny	7"	London	HLJ9118	1960	**£10**	**£5**	

ROBBS

Title	Format	Label	Number	Year	Mint	VG	Notes
Robbs	LP	Mercury	MG2/SR61130	1966	**£25**	**£10**	US

ROBERTS, ANDY

Title	Format	Label	Number	Year	Mint	VG	Notes
Andy Roberts & The Great Stampede	LP	Elektra	K42151	1973	**£10**	**£4**	
Home Grown	LP	RCA	SF8086	1970	**£12**	**£5**	
Nina And The Dream Tree	LP	Pegasus	PEG5	1971	**£12**	**£5**	
Urban Cowboy	LP	Elektra	K42139	1973	**£10**	**£4**	

ROBERTS, BOB

Title	Format	Label	Number	Year	Mint	VG	Notes
Songs From The Sailing Barges	LP	Topic	12TS361	1978	**£10**	**£4**	
Stormy Weather Boys	7" EP	Collector	JEB6	1961	**£5**	**£2**	

ROBERTS, HOWARD

Title	Format	Label	Number	Year	Mint	VG	Notes
Mr Roberts Plays Guitar	10" LP	Columbia	33C9038	1957	**£15**	**£6**	

ROBERTS, HUGH

Title	Format	Label	Number	Year	Mint	VG	Notes
California Dreaming	7"	Explosion	EX2041	1970	**£4**	**£1.50**	

ROBERTS, JOHN

Title	Format	Label	Number	Year	Mint	VG	Notes
I'll Forget About You	7"	Action	ACT4511	1968	**£6**	**£2.50**	
Sockin' 1, 2, 3, 4	7"	Sue	WI4042	1967	**£10**	**£5**	

ROBERTS, KEITH

Title	Format	Label	Number	Year	Mint	VG	Notes
Pier Of The Realm	LP	Trailer	LER3031	1972	**£12**	**£5**	

ROBERTS, KENNY

Run Like The Devil	7"	Pye	7N17054	1966	£10	£5	

ROBERTS, KENNY (2)

I'm Looking For The Bully Of The Town	7"	Brunswick	05638	1957	£6	£2.50	

ROBERTS, KIM

I'll Prove It	7"	Decca	F11813	1964	£50	£25	

ROBERTS, LUCKEY

Harlem Piano Solos	LP	Good Time Jazz	LAG12256	1960	£10	£4	*with Willie 'The Lion' Smith*

ROBERTSON, DON

Happy Whistler	7"	Capitol	CL14575	1956	£5	£2	

ROBERTSON, JEANNIE

Cuckoo's Nest & Other Scottish Folk Songs	LP	XTRA	XTRA5037	1968	£10	£4	
Gallowa' Hills	7" EP	Collector	JES1	1960	£5	£2	
I Ken Where I'm Going	7" EP	Collector	JES8	1960	£5	£2	
Jeannie Robertson	10" LP	Topic	10T52	1960	£20	£8	
Jeannie Robertson	LP	Topic	12T96	1963	£15	£6	
Jeannie's Merry Muse	7" EP	HMV	7EG8534	1960	£5	£2	
Lord Donald	LP	Collector	JFS4001	1960	£15	£6	
Twa Brothers	7" EP	Collector	JES4	1960	£5	£2	

ROBERTSON, JIM

Pride Of My Heart	7"	MGM	SPC7	1955	£6	£2.50	*export*

ROBERTSON, ROBBIE

Fallen Angel	CD-s	Geffen	GEF46CD	1988	£5	£2	*3" single*
Robbie Robertson	CD	Mobile Fidelity	UDCD618	1994	£15	£6	*US audiophile*

ROBIC, IVO

Morgen	7"	Polydor	NH23923	1959	£4	£1.50	

ROBIN, TINA

Everyday	7"	Vogue Coral	Q72309	1958	£6	£2.50	
Get Out Of My Life	7"	Mercury	AMT1199	1962	£4	£1.50	
Lady Fair	7"	Vogue Coral	Q72284	1957	£8	£4	
Never In A Million Years	7"	Vogue Coral	Q72294	1957	£5	£2	
No School Tomorrow	7"	Coral	Q72323	1958	£6	£2.50	

ROBINS

Cherry Lips	7"	Vogue	V9168	1960	£100	£50	
Just Like That	7"	Vogue	V9173	1960	£75	£37.50	
Rock'n'Roll With The Robins	LP	Whippet	WLP703	195–	£200	£100	*US*

ROBINS, JIMMY

I Can't Please You	7"	President	PT118	1968	£25	£12.50	

ROBINSON, ALVIN

Down Home Girl	7"	Red Bird	RB10010	1964	£8	£4	
Something You Got	7"	Pye	7N25248	1964	£8	£4	
You Brought My Heart Right Down	7"	Strike	JH307	1966	£8	£4	

ROBINSON, BROTHER CLEOPHUS

Negro Spirituals	7" EP	Vogue	EPV1196	1958	£15	£7.50	

ROBINSON, FLOYD

Floyd Robinson	LP	RCA	RD27166	1960	£30	£15	
Makin' Love	7"	RCA	RCA1146	1959	£5	£2	

ROBINSON, FREDDY

At The Drive-In	LP	Stax	2325085	1972	£12	£5	

ROBINSON, JACKEY

Heart Made Of Stone	7"	Punch	PH50	1970	£8	£4	*Bob Taylor B side*

ROBINSON, JACKIE

Let The Little Girl Dance	7"	Amalgamated	AMG824	1968	£6	£2.50	*Derrick Morgan B side*
Over And Over	7"	Amalgamated	AMG819	1968	£8	£4	

ROBINSON, JIM NEW ORLEANS BAND

Living Legends	LP	Riverside	RLP369	1961	£15	£6	
Plays Sprituals And Blues	LP	Riverside	RLP393	1964	£15	£6	

ROBINSON, LLOYD

Cuss Cuss	7"	Duke	DU5	1968	£6	£2.50	
When You Walk	7"	Blue Beat	BB122	1962	£12	£6	
Worm	7"	Camel	CA41	1970	£4	£1.50	
You Told Me	7"	Blue Beat	BB159	1963	£12	£6	

ROBINSON, M.

Title	Format	Label	Cat. No.	Year	Mint	VG	Notes
Who Are You	7"	Port-O-Jam	PJ4114	1964	**£10**	**£5**	

ROBINSON, ROSCOE

Title	Format	Label	Cat. No.	Year	Mint	VG	Notes
That's Enough	7"	Pye	7N25385	1966	**£15**	**£7.50**	

ROBINSON, SMOKEY & THE MIRACLES

Title	Format	Label	Cat. No.	Year	Mint	VG	Notes
Baby Baby Don't Cry	7"	Tamla Motown	TMG687	1969	**£4**	**£1.50**	
Four In Blue	LP	Tamla Motown	STML11151	1970	**£10**	**£4**	
Greatest Hits	LP	Tamla Motown	(S)TML11072	1968	**£10**	**£4**	
I Second That Emotion	7"	Tamla Motown	TMG631	1967	**£4**	**£1.50**	
If You Can Want	7"	Tamla Motown	TMG648	1968	**£5**	**£2**	
Live!	LP	Tamla Motown	(S)TML11107	1969	**£10**	**£4**	
Love I Saw In You Was Just A Mirage	7"	Tamla Motown	TMG598	1967	**£8**	**£4**	
Make It Happen	LP	Tamla Motown	(S)TML11067	1968	**£20**	**£8**	
More Love/Come Spy With Me	7"	Tamla Motown	TMG614	1967	**£60**	**£30**	
More Love/Swept For You Baby	7"	Tamla Motown	TMG614	1967	**£10**	**£5**	
Pocketful Of Miracles	LP	Tamla Motown	STML11172	1971	**£10**	**£4**	
Special Occasion	7"	Tamla Motown	TMG673	1968	**£4**	**£1.50**	
Special Occasion	LP	Tamla Motown	(S)TML11089	1969	**£10**	**£4**	
Tears Of A Clown/Who's Gonna Take The Blame	7"	Tamla Motown	TMG745	1970	**£4**	**£1.50**	
Tears Of A Clown/You Must Be Love	7"	Tamla Motown	TMG745	1970	**£25**	**£12.50**	
Time Out	LP	Tamla Motown	(S)TML11129	1970	**£10**	**£4**	
Tracks Of My Tears	7"	Tamla Motown	TMG696	1969	**£4**	**£1.50**	
Yester-Love	7"	Tamla Motown	TMG661	1968	**£4**	**£1.50**	

ROBINSON, SUGAR CHILE

Title	Format	Label	Cat. No.	Year	Mint	VG	Notes
Capitol Presents	10" LP	Capitol	LC6586	1953	**£30**	**£15**	

ROBINSON, TOM

Title	Format	Label	Cat. No.	Year	Mint	VG	Notes
All Right All Night	7"	EMI	EMI2946	1978	**£6**	**£2.50**	*demo*
Glad To Be Gay	7"	Chebel	SRT/CUS015	1975	**£20**	**£10**	
Pre-Album Sampler	LP	Harvest	SPRO8791	1978	**£12**	**£5**	*US*
Stand Together	7"	Deviant	DEVIANT1	1979	**£4**	**£1.50**	

ROBISON, CARSON

Title	Format	Label	Cat. No.	Year	Mint	VG	Notes
Eight Square Dances	10" LP	MGM	D101	1952	**£10**	**£4**	
Jitterbug	7"	MGM	SP1024	1953	**£8**	**£4**	
Lady Round	7"	MGM	SP1004	1953	**£5**	**£2**	
Life Gets Teejus	7" EP	MGM	MGMEP669	1958	**£8**	**£4**	
Square Dance – With Calls	7" EP	MGM	MGMEP755	1961	**£6**	**£2.50**	

ROBSON, NICKY

Title	Format	Label	Cat. No.	Year	Mint	VG	Notes
Stars	12"	Scratch	SCRT6	1980	**£30**	**£15**	
Stars	7"	Scratch	SCR6	1980	**£12**	**£6**	

ROCCO, TONY

Title	Format	Label	Cat. No.	Year	Mint	VG	Notes
Keep A Walking	7"	Parlophone	R4886	1962	**£6**	**£2.50**	
Torture	7"	Parlophone	R4946	1962	**£4**	**£1.50**	

ROCHE, HARRY CONSTELLATION

Title	Format	Label	Cat. No.	Year	Mint	VG	Notes
Spiral	LP	Pye	NSPL41024	1973	**£40**	**£20**	

ROCK, DICKIE

Title	Format	Label	Cat. No.	Year	Mint	VG	Notes
Come Back To Stay	7"	Pye	7N17063	1965	**£8**	**£4**	
Come Back To Stay	7"	Pye	NEP24251	1965	**£6**	**£2.50**	

ROCK, JOHNNY

Title	Format	Label	Cat. No.	Year	Mint	VG	Notes
Johnny Rock	7" EP	Vogue	VE170112	1958	**£5**	**£2**	

ROCK AID ARMENIA

Title	Format	Label	Cat. No.	Year	Mint	VG	Notes
Smoke On The Water	CD-s	Life Aid Armenia	ARMEDCD01	1989	**£6**	**£2.50**	*Black Sabbath B side*

ROCK BROTHERS

Title	Format	Label	Cat. No.	Year	Mint	VG	Notes
Dungaree Doll	7"	Parlophone	MSP6201	1956	**£50**	**£25**	

ROCK ISLAND

Rock island	LP	Total Sound Stereo	PR4005	1970	**£15**	**£6**	*US*

ROCK MACHINE

Themes	LP	T.I.M.		1973	**£40**	**£20**	

ROCK SHOP

Rock Shop	LP	Lee	1	1969	**£75**	**£37.50**	*US*

ROCK WORKSHOP

Rock Workshop	LP	CBS	64075	1970	**£15**	**£6**	
Very Last Time	LP	CBS	64394	1971	**£15**	**£6**	

ROCK-A-TEENS

Woo Hoo	7"	Columbia	DB4361	1959	**£20**	**£10**	
Woo Hoo	LP	Roulette	(S)R25109	1960	**£60**	**£30**	*US*

ROCKERS

Get Cracking	7"	Oriole	CB1501	1959	**£8**	**£4**	

ROCKERS (2)

We Are The Boys	12"	CBS	TA3929	1983	**£8**	**£4**	
We Are The Boys	7"	CBS	A3929	1983	**£5**	**£2**	

ROCKET 88

Rocket 88	LP	Atlantic	K50776	1981	**£10**	**£4**	

ROCKETS

Gibraltar Rock	7"	Philips	PB982	1959	**£8**	**£4**	
Warrior	7"	Zodiac	ZR0010	196–	**£10**	**£5**	

ROCKETS (2)

Neil Young became friendly with the Rockets while still a member of Buffalo Springfield. When later he was looking for a permanent backing band, the Rockets were an obvious choice. Young renamed the group Crazy Horse, recording a 'Requiem For The Rockets' on the first album they made together (*Everybody Knows This Is Nowhere*).

Hole In My Pocket	7"	White Whale	270	1967	**£12**	**£6**	*US*
Rockets	LP	White Whale	S7116	1968	**£20**	**£8**	*US*

ROCKETS (3)

Plasteroid	LP	Rockland	RKL20137	1977	**£10**	**£4**	*French picture disc*

ROCKIN' BERRIES

Dawn Go Away	7"	Pye	7N17411	1967	**£5**	**£2**	
Happy To Be Blue	7" EP	Piccadilly	NEP34045	1965	**£25**	**£12.50**	
He's In Town	7" EP	Pye	PNV24128	1964	**£20**	**£10**	*French*
I Could Make You Fall In Love	7"	Piccadilly	7N35304	1966	**£4**	**£1.50**	
I Didn't Mean To Hurt You	7"	Piccadilly	7N35197	1964	**£4**	**£1.50**	
I Didn't Mean To Hurt You	7" EP	Piccadilly	NEP34039	1965	**£15**	**£7.50**	
In Town	LP	Piccadilly	NPL38013	1964	**£50**	**£25**	
Itty Bitty Pieces	7"	Decca	F11760	1963	**£10**	**£5**	
Life Is Just A Bowl Of Berries	LP	Piccadilly	NPL38022	1964	**£50**	**£25**	
Midnight Mary	7"	Piccadilly	7N35327	1966	**£4**	**£1.50**	
Mr Blue	7"	Pye	7N17589	1968	**£4**	**£1.50**	
New From The Berries	7" EP	Piccadilly	NEP34043	1965	**£20**	**£10**	
Smiles	7"	Piccadilly	7N35400	1967	**£5**	**£2**	
Sometimes	7"	Piccadilly	7N35373	1967	**£4**	**£1.50**	
Wah Wah Woo	7"	Decca	F11698	1963	**£15**	**£7.50**	
Water Is Over My Head	7"	Piccadilly	7N35270	1965	**£4**	**£1.50**	
When I Reach The Top	7"	Pye	7N17519	1968	**£5**	**£2**	
You're My Girl	7"	Piccadilly	7N35254	1965	**£4**	**£1.50**	

ROCKIN' FOO

Rockin' Foo	LP	Stateside	SSL10303	1970	**£10**	**£4**	

ROCKIN' HORSE

Biggest Gossip In Town	7"	Philips	6006156	1971	**£4**	**£1.50**	
Julian The Hooligan	7"	Philips	6006200	1972	**£4**	**£1.50**	
Yes It Is	LP	Philips	6308075	1970	**£40**	**£20**	

ROCKIN' RAMRODS

Don't Fool With Fu Manchu	7"	Polydor	56512	1970	**£10**	**£5**	

ROCKIN' REBELS

Rockin' Crickets	7"	Stateside	SS187	1963	**£6**	**£2.50**	
Wild Weekend	7"	Stateside	SS162	1963	**£6**	**£2.50**	
Wild Weekend	LP	Swan	SLP509	1962	**£50**	**£25**	*US*

ROCKIN' Rs

Crazy Baby	7"	London	HL8872	1959	**£25**	**£12.50**	

ROCKIN' SAINTS

Cheat On Me Baby	7"	Brunswick	05843	1960	**£75**	**£37.50**	

ROCKIN' VICKERS

Dandy	7"	CBS	202241	1966	£20	£10	
I Go Ape	7"	Decca	F11993	1964	£12	£6	
It's Alright	7"	CBS	202051	1966	£30	£15	

ROCKING GHOSTS

For Ghosts Only	LP	Metronome	MLP15230	1966	£30	£15	*German*
Golden Pigtrad	LP	Metronome	HLP10559	1975	£25	£10	*Danish*
Keep Rocking	LP	Metronome	MLP15192	1967	£40	£20	*German*
Rocking Ghosts	LP	Metronome	MLP15166	1966	£30	£15	*German*
Rocking Ghosts	LP	Metronome	MLP10052	1965	£30	£15	*German*
Two Band Party	LP	Metronome	HLP10066	1965	£30	£15	*German, with the Matadors*

ROCK'N'ROLL REVIVAL SHOW

Midnight Train	7"	Decca	F12752	1968	£4	£1.50	

ROCK-OLGA

Red Sails In The Sunset	7"	Ember	EMBS105	1960	£5	£2	*picture sleeve*

ROCKSTEADYS

Squeeze And Freeze	7"	Giant	GN2	1967	£5	£2	

ROCKSTONES

A.B.C. Reggae	7"	Trojan	TR7762	1970	£5	£2	*Beverley's All Stars B side*
Everything Is Beautiful	7"	Summit	SUM8501	1970	£5	£2	*Beverley's All Stars B side*

ROCKY HORROR SHOW

Rocky Horror Box Set	LP	Pacific	RHBX1	1983	£25	£10	*2 LPs, 1 double LP, poster, badge, confetti, boxed*
Rocky Horror Picture Show	CD	Ode	RHBXCD1	1990	£40	£20	*4 CD boxed set*
Rocky Horror Picture Show	LP	Ode	ODE78332	1975	£10	£4	
Rocky Horror Show	LP	UK	UKAL1015	1973	£10	£4	
Rocky Horror Show (US Roxy Cast)	LP	Ode	ODE77026	1974	£10	£4	
Rocky Horror Show (US Roxy Cast)	LP	Ode	OSVP77026	1983	£10	£4	*picture disc*
Time Warp	7"	Ode	ODS66305	1975	£5	£2	

ROCKYFELLERS

Ching A Ling Baby	7"	Pye	7N25225	1963	£4	£1.50	
Killer Joe	7"	Stateside	SS175	1963	£4	£1.50	
Killer Joe	LP	Scepter	SP(S)512	1963	£20	£8	*US*
Like The Big Guys Do	7"	Stateside	SS212	1963	£4	£1.50	

ROCOMARS

All In Black Woman	7"	King	KG1031	1965	£10	£5	

ROD, KEN & THE CAVALIERS

Magic Wheel	7"	Triumph	RGM1001	1960	£25	£12.50	

ROD & THE COBRAS

At A Drag Race At Surf City	LP	Somerset	20500	1963	£15	£6	*US*

RODDENBERRY, GENE

Star Trek Theme	7"	CBS	4692	1976	£6	£2.50	

RODGERS, EILEEN

Careful, Careful	7"	Fontana	H136	1958	£5	£2	
Sailor	7"	London	HLR9271	1961	£6	£2.50	
Treasure Of Your Love	7"	Fontana	H156	1958	£5	£2	

RODGERS, IKE

Ike Rodgers	10" LP	London	AL3512	1954	£12	£5	

RODGERS, JIMMIE

Best Of Jimmie Rodgers	LP	RCA	LPM3315	1965	£12	£5	*US*
Country Music Hall Of Fame	LP	RCA	RD7505	1962	£12	£5	*US*
Honeycomb	LP	London	HAD/SHD8116	1965	£15	£6	
Jimmie Rodgers	7" EP	HMV	7EG8163	1956	£12	£6	
Jimmie The Kid	LP	RCA	RD27241	1961	£10	£4	
Legendary Jimmie Rodgers	7" EP	RCA	RCX1058	1960	£10	£5	
Memorial Album Vol. 1	10" LP	RCA	LPT3037	1952	£25	£10	*US*
Memorial Album Vol. 2	10" LP	RCA	LPT3038	1952	£25	£10	*US*
Memorial Album Vol. 3	10" LP	RCA	LPT3039	1952	£25	£10	*US*
My Rough And Rowdy Ways	LP	RCA	RD27203	1961	£10	£4	
My Time Ain't Long	LP	RCA	RD7644	1964	£10	£4	
Never No Mo' Blues	LP	RCA	RD27138	1960	£12	£5	
No One Will Ever Know	LP	London	HAD8040	1963	£15	£6	
Short But Brilliant Life Of Jimmie Rodgers	LP	RCA	RD7562	1963	£10	£4	
Train Whistle Blues	LP	RCA	RD27110	1959	£12	£5	
Travellin' Blues	10" LP	RCA	LPT3073	1952	£25	£10	*US*

RODGERS, JIMMIE (2)

Title	Format	Label	Cat. No.	Year	Mint	VG	Notes
At Home With Jimmie Rodgers	LP	Columbia	33SX1292/ SCX3355	1961	**£10**	**£4**	
English Country Garden	7" EP	Dot	DEP20002	1965	**£5**	**£2**	
English Country Garden	7" EP	Columbia	SEG8253	1963	**£5**	**£2**	
Favourites	LP	Columbia	33SX1176	1959	**£10**	**£4**	
Folk Songs And Readings	LP	Roulette	R25020	1958	**£10**	**£4**	*US*
Folk Song World Of Jimmie Rodgers	LP	Columbia	33SX1393/ SCX3425	1961	**£10**	**£4**	
His Golden Year	LP	Roulette	R25057	1959	**£10**	**£4**	*US*
Honeycomb	7"	Columbia	DB3986	1957	**£8**	**£4**	
It's Christmas Once Again	LP	Columbia	33SX1206	1959	**£10**	**£4**	
Jimmie Rodgers	7" EP	Columbia	SEG7770	1958	**£1[illegible]**	**£[illegible]**	
Jimmie Rodgers	LP	Columbia	33SX1082	1958	**£20**	**£8**	
Jimmie Rodgers Favourites	7" EP	Dot	DEP20007	1965	**£6**	**£2.50**	
Jimmie Rodgers No. 2	7" EP	Columbia	SEG7911	1959	**£10**	**£5**	
Jimmie Rodgers Sings	7" EP	Columbia	SEG7811	1958	**£10**	**£5**	
Kisses Sweeter Than Wine	7"	Columbia	DB4052	1957	**£4**	**£1.50**	
Long Hot Summer	LP	Roulette	R25026	1958	**£15**	**£6**	*US*
Number One Ballads	LP	Columbia	33SX1097	1958	**£15**	**£6**	
Oh Oh, I'm Falling In Love Again	7"	Columbia	DB4078	1958	**£4**	**£1.50**	
Secretly	7"	Columbia	DB4130	1958	**£4**	**£1.50**	
Sings Folk Songs	LP	Columbia	33SX1144	1959	**£10**	**£4**	
Twilight On The Trail	LP	Columbia	33SX1217/ SCX3302	1960	**£10**	**£4**	
When The Spirit Moves You	LP	Columbia	33SX1236/ SCX3313	1960	**£10**	**£4**	
Wizard	7"	Columbia	DB4175	1958	**£4**	**£1.50**	
Woman From Liberia	7"	Columbia	DB4206	1958	**£4**	**£1.50**	

RODYS

Title	Format	Label	Cat. No.	Year	Mint	VG	Notes
Earnest Vocation	LP	Philips	855075XPY	1968	**£20**	**£8**	*Dutch*
Just Fancy	LP	Philips	855034XPY	1967	**£20**	**£8**	*Dutch*

ROE, TOMMY

Title	Format	Label	Cat. No.	Year	Mint	VG	Notes
Ballads And Beat	LP	HMV	CLP1860	1965	**£20**	**£8**	
Dizzy	LP	Stateside	(S)SL10282	1969	**£10**	**£4**	
Everybody Likes Tommy Roe	LP	HMV	CLP1074	1965	**£25**	**£10**	
Folk Singer	7" EP	HMV	7EG8806	1963	**£25**	**£12.50**	
Greatest Hits	LP	Stateside	SSL10296	1970	**£10**	**£4**	
Sheila	7"	HMV	POP1060	1962	**£4**	**£1.50**	
Sheila	LP	HMV	CLP1614	1963	**£30**	**£15**	
Something For Everybody	LP	ABC	(S)467	1964	**£20**	**£8**	*US*
Sweet Pea	LP	ABC	(S)575	1966	**£20**	**£8**	*US*
Town Crier	7"	HMV	POP1116	1963	**£8**	**£4**	*demo only*

ROGERS, CE CE

Title	Format	Label	Cat. No.	Year	Mint	VG	Notes
Forever	12"	WEA	A8852T	1989	**£15**	**£7.50**	

ROGERS, DEAN

Title	Format	Label	Cat. No.	Year	Mint	VG	Notes
Keep The Miracle Going	7"	Parlophone	R4732	1961	**£4**	**£1.50**	
Timber	7"	Parlophone	R4835	1961	**£4**	**£1.50**	

ROGERS, JULIE

Title	Format	Label	Cat. No.	Year	Mint	VG	Notes
Contrasts	LP	Mercury	20086(S)MCL	1966	**£15**	**£6**	
Julie Rogers	7" EP	Mercury	10023MCE	1964	**£8**	**£4**	
Songs Of Inspiration	LP	Mercury	20100(S)MCL	1967	**£12**	**£5**	
Sound Of Julie	7" EP	Mercury	10028MCE	1965	**£8**	**£4**	
Sound Of Julie	LP	Mercury	20048(S)MCL	1965	**£15**	**£6**	

ROGERS, LINCOLN

Title	Format	Label	Cat. No.	Year	Mint	VG	Notes
Let Love Come Between Us	7"	Phoenix	NIX137	1973	**£5**	**£2**	

ROGERS, MARK & THE MARKSMEN

Title	Format	Label	Cat. No.	Year	Mint	VG	Notes
Hold It	7"	Parlophone	R5045	1963	**£6**	**£2.50**	

ROGERS, PAULINE

Title	Format	Label	Cat. No.	Year	Mint	VG	Notes
Spinning The Blues	7"	Columbia	SCM5106	1954	**£4**	**£1.50**	

ROGERS, PIERCE & THE OVERLANDERS

Title	Format	Label	Cat. No.	Year	Mint	VG	Notes
Do You Still Love Me?	7"	Parlophone	R4838	1961	**£5**	**£2**	

ROGERS, ROY

Title	Format	Label	Cat. No.	Year	Mint	VG	Notes
Bible Tells Me So	LP	Capitol	(S)T1745	1962	**£12**	**£5**	*US*
Christmas Is Always	LP	Capitol	(S)T2818	1967	**£10**	**£4**	*US*
Happy Trails	7" EP	HMV	7EG8182	1956	**£10**	**£5**	
Hymns Of Faith	10" LP	RCA	LPT3168	1954	**£20**	**£8**	*US*
Jesus Loves Me	LP	Bluebird	LBY1022	1959	**£12**	**£5**	*US*
Roy Rogers	7" EP	HMV	7EG8145	1955	**£10**	**£5**	
Souvenir Album	10" LP	RCA	LPT3041	1952	**£25**	**£10**	*US*
Sweet Hour Of Prayer	LP	RCA	LPM1439	1957	**£15**	**£6**	*US*

ROGERS, SHORTY

Title	Format	Label	Cat. No.	Year	Mint	VG	Notes
Chances Are It Swings	LP	RCA	RD27149/SF5048	1960	**£12**	**£5**	
Cool And Crazy	10" LP	HMV	DLP1030	1954	**£50**	**£25**	
Courts The Count	LP	HMV	CLP1041	1955	**£25**	**£10**	
Eight Shorty Rogers Numbers	10" LP	HMV	DLP1058	1954	**£50**	**£25**	

Modern Sounds	10" LP	Capitol	LC6549	1952	**£50**	**£25**	
Modern Sounds	LP	Capitol	T2025	1963	**£12**	**£5**	*with Gerry Mulligan*
Shorty Rogers And His Giants	LP	London	LTZK15056	1957	**£25**	**£10**	
Shorty Rogers And His Giants	LP	London	LTZK15023	1957	**£25**	**£10**	
Shorty Rogers And His Orchestra	7" EP	HMV	7EG8044	1954	**£5**	**£2**	
Shorty Rogers And His Orchestra	LP	MGM	C820	1960	**£10**	**£4**	
Shorty Rogers Plays Richard Rodgers	LP	RCA	RD27018	1958	**£20**	**£8**	
Swingin' Nutcracker	LP	RCA	RD27199/SF5084	1961	**£12**	**£5**	
Way Up There	LP	London	LTZK15179	1960	**£15**	**£6**	
Wherever The Five Winds Blow	LPL	HMV	CLP1129	1957	**£25**	**£10**	

ROGERS, TIMMIE

Back To School Again	7"	London	HLU8510	1957	**£50**	**£25**
Take Me To Your Leader	7"	London	HLU8601	1958	**£60**	**£30**

ROGERS, TRACY

Back With You Baby	7"	Polydor	56197	1967	**£5**	**£2**

ROGERS, VERN & THE HI-FIS

I Will	7"	Oriole	CB1885	1963	**£5**	**£2**
That Ain't Right	7"	Oriole	CB1785	1962	**£5**	**£2**

ROGUES

Rogue's Reef	7"	CBS	201731	1965	**£5**	**£2**

ROHDE, JAN

Come Back Baby	7"	Qualiton	PSP7128	1960	**£4**	**£1.50**	
Play Let Kiss	LP	Metronome	MLP15194	1965	**£15**	**£6**	*German, with the Wild Ones*

ROKES

The fact that the majority of the collectable Rokes albums are Italian reflects their considerable popularity in that country during the sixties. Actually, the Rokes were British but, despite some of their recordings being fine pieces of psychedelia, they were unable to make any commercial headway at home.

Che Mondo Strano	LP	RCA	FPM185	1967	**£30**	**£15**	*US*
Hold My Hand	7"	RCA	RCA1646	1967	**£25**	**£12.50**	
Let's Live For Today	7"	RCA	RCA1587	1967	**£10**	**£5**	
Let's Live For Today	7" EP	RCA	86577	1967	**£30**	**£15**	*French*
Rokes	LP	ARC	SA4	1965	**£50**	**£25**	*Italian*
Rokes	LP	ARC	ALP11002	1965	**£50**	**£25**	*Italian*
Rokes	LP	ARC	ALP11006	1968	**£30**	**£15**	*Italian*
Rokes Vol. 2	LP	ARC	SA8	1966	**£50**	**£25**	*Italian*
These Were Beat	LP	RCA	33037	1967	**£25**	**£10**	*Italian*
When The Wind Arises	7"	RCA	RCA1694	1968	**£40**	**£20**	

ROKKA

Come Back	7"	Rock Trax	RT01	1980	**£5**	**£2**

ROLAND, CHERRY

Boys	7"	Fontana	TF420	1963	**£4**	**£1.50**	*as Cherry Rowland*
Handy Sandy	7"	Decca	F11579	1963	**£4**	**£1.50**	
Here Is Where The Love Is	7"	Decca	F13491	1974	**£5**	**£2**	*as Cherry Rowland*
Just For Fun	7"	Decca	F11648	1963	**£4**	**£1.50**	

ROLAND, JOE

Joe Roland Quintet	LP	London	LTZN15005	1956	**£20**	**£8**

ROLAND, PAUL

Alice's House	7"	Bam Caruso	PABL094	1987	**£5**	**£2**
Blades Of Battenburg	12"	Aftermath	AEP12011	1983	**£6**	**£2.50**
Demon In A Glass Case	7"	Imaginary	MIRAGE002	1986	**£4**	**£1.50**
Doctor Strange	7"	Aristocrat	ARC1389	1982	**£5**	**£2**
Gabrielle	7"	Aftermath	AEP12013	1986	**£5**	**£2**
Werewolf Of London	LP	Ace	ACE013	1980	**£12**	**£5**

ROLAND, WALTER & GEORGIA SLIM

Male Blues Vol. 1	7" EP	Collector	JEL2	1959	**£10**	**£5**

ROLL MOVEMENT

I'm Out On My Own	7"	Go	AJ11410	1967	**£8**	**£4**

ROLL-UPS

Low Dives For Highballs	LP	Bridgehouse	BHLP004	1979	**£10**	**£4**

ROLLERS

Continental Walk	7"	London	HLG9340	1961	**£8**	**£4**

ROLLING STONES

It is easily forgotten how the Rolling Stones had the role of tougher alter egos for the Beatles during the sixties. As the Beatles started to become more and more experimental in their approach, so the Rolling Stones did the same. When the Beatles eventually came up with *Sgt Pepper* and 'Strawberry Fields For Ever', the Rolling Stones responded with *Their Satanic Majesties Request* and 'We Love You'. Critics do not like these records very much, seeing them as being apart from what the Rolling Stones are all about, but they quite clearly achieve everything that psychedelic music tried to do. The death of Brian Jones, who loved to experiment with different instruments, apparently robbed the Rolling Stones of their ambition, for little of what the group has played since has extended much beyond a diet of the blues and Chuck Berry. The mono pressing of *Satanic Majesties* attracts a premium, especially in America, but for once, the mix does not actually sound any different in detail to the stereo version. The LP *Sticky Fingers*, with its Andy Warhol zip cover, just scrapes into the collectors' list – this was not a limited edition and is very much more common than some people believe. Bootleg copies of the notorious 'Cocksucker Blues', recorded to fulfil the Stones' Decca contract, have long been available. The German Teldec boxed set is remarkable, however, for including a copy of the single as a bonus, issued for the first and only time as an official release.

Title	Format	Label	Cat. No.	Year	Mint	VG	Notes
12 × 5	LP	London	LL3402	1964	**£1000**	**£700**	*US, blue vinyl*
12 × 5	LP	London	LL3402	1964	**£25**	**£10**	*US*
1963–1971 – A Selection Of No. 1 Singles	CD	London	ROLCD1	1995	**£30**	**£15**	*US promo compilation*
19th Nervous Breakdown	7"	Decca	F12331	1966	**£4**	**£1.50**	
19th Nervous Breakdown	7"	Decca	F12331	1966	**£25**	**£12.50**	*export, Dutch picture sleeve*
19th Nervous Breakdown	7" EP	Decca	450206	1966	**£150**	**£75**	*French*
2000 Light Years From Home	7"	Decca	F22706	1967	**£25**	**£12.50**	*export*
Aftermath	LP	Decca	LK4786	1966	**£25**	**£10**	*mono*
Aftermath	LP	London	LL3476	1966	**£25**	**£10**	*US*
Aftermath	LP	Decca	SKL4786	1966	**£40**	**£20**	*stereo*
Aftermath	LP	Decca	SKL4786	1970	**£12**	**£5**	*black print on white label*
Aftermath And Out Of Time	LP	Decca	H220	1967	**£100**	**£50**	*German Club pressing*
Almost Hear You Sigh	CD-s	CBS	6560655	1990	**£25**	**£12.50**	*in tin*
Almost Hear You Sigh	CD-s	CBS	6560652	1990	**£15**	**£7.50**	*gold disc*
Around And Around	LP	Decca	SLK16315P	1965	**£30**	**£15**	*German*
As Tears Go By	7" EP	Decca	457104	1966	**£20**	**£10**	*French*
Beat Beat Beat	10" LP	Decca	60368	1964	**£100**	**£50**	*German Club pressing*
Beggar's Banquet	LP	Decca	LK4955	1968	**£30**	**£15**	*mono, insert*
Beggars Banquet	LP	Decca	LK4955	1968	**£25**	**£10**	*no insert*
Beggar's Banquet	LP	Decca	SKL4955	1968	**£20**	**£8**	*stereo, insert*
Beggars Banquet	LP	Decca	SKL4955	1968	**£15**	**£6**	*no insert*
Best Of Beat	LP	Decca	25035	1966	**£100**	**£50**	*Swiss Club pressing*
Between The Buttons	LP	Decca	LK/SKL4852	1967	**£30**	**£15**	
Between The Buttons	LP	London	LL3499	1967	**£25**	**£10**	*US*
Between The Buttons	LP	Decca	6835207		**£20**	**£8**	*Dutch, yellow vinyl*
Big Hits	LP	Decca	78299	1969	**£50**	**£25**	*German Club pressing*
Big Hits (High Tide And Green Grass)	LP	London	NP1	1966	**£25**	**£10**	*US*
Big Hits (High Tide And Green Grass)	LP	Decca	TXL/TXS101	1966	**£25**	**£10**	*picture booklet*
Bravo	LP	Hör Zu	SHZT531	1965	**£50**	**£25**	*German*
Bridges To Babylon	CD	Virgin	CDVDJ2840	1997	**£40**	**£20**	*promo*
Bridges To Babylon Interview	CD	Virgin	IVDG2840	1997	**£50**	**£25**	*promo double*
Brown Sugar	7"	Atlantic	K19107	1974	**£75**	**£37.50**	
Brown Sugar	7"	Rolling Stones	SUGARP1	1984	**£15**	**£7.50**	*shaped picture disc*
Brown Sugar	7"	Rolling Stones	RS19100	1971	**£15**	**£7.50**	*picture sleeve*
Brown Sugar	7"	Rolling Stones	RSLH1	1993	**£10**	**£5**	*jukebox issue*
Carol	7" EP	Decca	457036	1964	**£20**	**£10**	*French*
Come On	7"	Decca	F11675	1963	**£8**	**£4**	
Complete Singles Collection – sampler	CD	ABKCO	121831	1989	**£25**	**£10**	*US promo*
Con Le Mie La Crime	7"	Decca	F22270	1965	**£30**	**£15**	*sung in Italian*
Could You Walk On The Waters	LP	Decca		1966	**£250**	**£150**	
December's Children	LP	London	LL3451	1965	**£25**	**£10**	*US*
Desert Island Survival Kit	CD	ABKCO		1994	**£40**	**£20**	*US promo compilation*
Ed Rudy Interview Album	LP	INS Radio	1003	1965	**£50**	**£25**	*US*
Emotional Rescue	7"	Rolling Stones		1980	**£5**	**£2**	*interview promo, blue flexi*
Emotional Rescue	LP	Rolling Stones	CUN39111	1980	**£10**	**£4**	*with poster & inner*
Empty Heart	7"	Decca	AT15035	1964	**£75**	**£37.50**	*export*
Exile On Main Street	LP	Rolling Stones	COC69100	1972	**£20**	**£8**	*double, with postcards*
Fan Club Single	7"	Rolling Stones	R8370/1	1983	**£5**	**£2**	*interview disc*
First Eight Studio Albums	LP	Decca	ROLL1	1983	**£200**	**£100**	*8 LPs, book, boxed*
Five By Five	12"	Decca	DFEX8590	1983	**£6**	**£2.50**	
Five By Five	7" EP	Decca	DFE8590	1964	**£10**	**£5**	
Flashpoint/Interview 1990	CD	Sony	4681359/4681352	1991	**£40**	**£20**	*double pack*
Flowers	LP	Decca	LK/SKL4888	1967	**£100**	**£50**	*export*
Flowers	LP	Decca	SKL4888	197–	**£30**	**£15**	*boxed Decca logo*
Flowers	LP	Decca	25084	1967	**£100**	**£50**	*Swiss Club pressing*
Flowers	LP	London	LL3509	1967	**£25**	**£10**	*US*
Get Off My Cloud	7"	Decca	F22265	1965	**£15**	**£7.50**	*export*
Get Off My Cloud	7"	Decca	F12263	1965	**£4**	**£1.50**	
Get Off My Cloud	7"	Decca	F22265	1965	**£40**	**£20**	*export, picture sleeve*
Get Off My Cloud	7" EP	Decca	457092	1965	**£20**	**£10**	*French*
Get Off My Cloud	7" EP	Decca	457092	1965	**£75**	**£37.50**	*French, picture sleeve on stage at Olympia*
Get Yer Ya-Ya's Out	LP	Decca	SKL5065	1970	**£12**	**£5**	
Get Yer Ya-Ya's Out	LP	Decca	SKL5065	1970	**£12**	**£5**	*black print on white label*
Gimme Shelter	7"	Rolling Stones	ORDERLH1	1993	**£10**	**£5**	*jukebox issue, Tom Jones B side*
Gimme Shelter	LP	Decca	SKL5101	1971	**£10**	**£4**	

Title	Format	Label	Cat. No.	Year	Mint	VG	Notes
Golden B Sides	LP	Decca	SKL5165	1973	£500	£330	test pressing only
Got Live If You Want It	12"	Decca	DFEX8620	1983	£6	£2.50	
Got Live If You Want It	7" EP	Decca	DFE8620	1965	£60	£30	export, red label
Got Live If You Want It	7" EP	Decca	SDE7502	1965	£50	£25	export
Got Live If You Want It	7" EP	Decca	457081	1965	£12	£6	French
Got Live If You Want It	7" EP	Decca	DFE8620	1965	£10	£5	
Got Live If You Want It	LP	London	LL3493	1966	£25	£10	US
Great Years	LP	Reader's Digest	GROLA119	1983	£30	£15	4 LPs, boxed
Greatest Hits	LP	RCA	SP0268	1972	£30	£15	US
Happy	7"	Rolling Stones	SAM4	1971	£20	£10	promo
Harlem Shuffle	12"	CBS	QTA6864	1986	£10	£5	
Harlem Shuffle	12"	CBS	TA6864	1986	£6	£2.50	
Harlem Shuffle	7"	CBS	QA6864	1986	£5	£2	poster sleeve
Have You Seen Your Mother Baby	7"	Decca	F12497	1966	£4	£1.50	
Have You Seen Your Mother Live!	LP	Decca	LK/SKL4838	1966	£100	£50	export
Have You Seen Your Mother Live!	LP	Decca	SKL4838	197–	£30	£15	boxed Decca logo
Heart Of Stone	7"	Decca	F22180	1965	£40	£20	export, picture sleeve
Heart Of Stone	7"	Decca	F22180	1965	£20	£10	export
Heart Of Stone	7" EP	Decca	457066	1965	£20	£10	French
Highwire	12"	CBS	6567561	1990	£6	£2.50	
Highwire	CD-s	CBS	6567565	1991	£12	£6	gatefold card sleeve
Highwire	CD-s	CBS	6567562	1991	£6	£2.50	
History Of The Rolling Stones	LP	Decca	ZAL12996-13001	1975	£750	£500	3 LP test pressings
Hits Live	LP	Decca	SKL4495	1965	£150	£75	export promo
Honky Tonk Women	7"	Decca	F12952	1969	£30	£15	export, picture sleeve
Honky Tonk Women	7"	Decca	F12952	1969	£4	£1.50	
Hot Rocks	CD	Decca	8000832	1984	£25	£10	
Hot Stuff	12"	Rolling Stones		1976	£25	£10	promo, clear vinyl
Hot Stuff	12"	Rolling Stones		1976	£20	£10	promo, black & blue vinyl
I Don't Know Why	7"	Decca	F13584	1975	£8	£4	Jagger/Richard writing credit
I Don't Know Why	7"	Decca	F13584	1975	£5	£2	Stevie Wonder writing credit
I Go Wild	7"	Virgin	VSP1539	1994	£5	£2	picture disc
I Go Wild	CD-s	Virgin	VSCDX1539	1994	£5	£2	with 4 cards
I Wanna Be Your Man	7"	Decca	AT15005	1963	£60	£30	export
I Wanna Be Your Man	7"	Decca	F11764	1963	£6	£2.50	
I Wanna Be Your Man	7"	Decca	F11764	1963	£8	£4	'Stones' B side
I Wanna Be Your Man	7" EP	Decca	457026	1963	£50	£25	French, picture sleeve with 4 titles listed
I Wanna Be Your Man	7" EP	Decca	457026	1963	£30	£15	French, picture sleeve with main title only
If You Need Me	7" EP	Decca	457043	1964	£20	£10	French
In Action	LP	S*R International	74307	1966	£150	£75	German Club pressing
Interview	CD	Rolling Stones	CSK1910	1989	£40	£20	US promo
Interview With Mick Jagger By Tom Donahue	LP	Rolling Stones	PR164	1971	£30	£15	US promo
It's All Over Now	7"	Decca	F11934	1964	£4	£1.50	
It's All Over Now	7"	Decca	F13517	1974	£100	£50	demo only
It's All Over Now	7" EP	Decca	457039	1964	£20	£10	French
Jumpin' Jack Flash	7"	Decca	F12782	1968	£50	£25	export, picture sleeve
Jumpin' Jack Flash	7"	Decca	F12782	1968	£4	£1.50	
Last Time	7"	Decca	F12104	1965	£4	£1.50	
Last Time	7"	Decca	F12104	1965	£30	£15	export, Dutch picture sleeve
Let It Bleed	LP	Decca	LK5025	1969	£25	£10	mono
Let It Bleed	LP	Decca	LK5025	1969	£30	£15	mono, with sticker and poster
Let It Bleed	LP	Decca	SKL5025	1969	£15	£6	with inner sleeve
Let It Bleed	LP	Decca	SKL5025	1969	£25	£10	with sticker, inner sleeve and poster
Let It Bleed	LP	Decca	6835204		£20	£8	Dutch, red vinyl
Let's Spend The Night Together	7"	Decca	F12546	1967	£30	£15	export, picture sleeve
Let's Spend The Night Together	7"	Decca	F12546	1967	£4	£1.50	
Let's Spend The Night Together (live)	7"	Rolling Stones	RSR112DJ	1983	£12	£6	promo only
Little Queenie	7"	Decca	F13126	1971	£10	£5	export
Little Queenie	7"	Decca	F13126	1971	£25	£12.50	export, picture sleeve
Little Red Rooster	7"	Decca	F12014	1964	£4	£1.50	
Little Red Rooster	7"	Decca	AT15040	1965	£75	£37.50	export
Live Stones	LP	Decca	ROST3/4	1975	£500	£330	test pressing double
Love Is Strong	7"	Virgin	VS1503	1994	£6	£2.50	
Love Is Strong	CD-s	Virgin	VSCDX1503	1994	£5	£2	
Mick Jagger Introduces Exile On Main Street	7"	Sound For Industry	SFI107	1972	£4	£1.50	flexi
Miss You	12"	Rolling Stones	12EMI2802	1978	£6	£2.50	pink vinyl
Mixed Emotions	CD-s	CBS	6552142	1989	£30	£15	in tin
Mixed Emotions	CD-s	CBS	6551935	1989	£30	£15	in tin
Mixed Emotions	CD-s	CBS	6551932	1989	£6	£2.50	

Title	Format	Label	Cat. No.	Year	Mint	VG	Notes
Mother's Little Helper	7" EP	Decca	457122	1966	**£20**	**£10**	*French*
No Security	CD	Virgin	CDIDJ2880	1999	**£50**	**£25**	*promo 3 CD set*
Not Fade Away	7"	Decca	F11845	1964	**£4**	**£1.50**	
Not Fade Away	7"	Decca	AT15008	1964	**£60**	**£30**	*export*
Not Fade Away	7" EP	Decca	457031	1964	**£30**	**£15**	*French*
Original Master Records	LP	Mobile Fidelity	01657	1984	**£175**	**£87.50**	*US 10 LP boxed set*
Out Of Our Heads	LP	Decca	LK4733	1965	**£25**	**£10**	
Out Of Our Heads	LP	Decca	LK/SKL4725	1965	**£75**	**£37.50**	*export, US format*
Out Of Our Heads	LP	Decca	SKL4733	1965	**£250**	**£150**	*stereo*
Out Of Our Heads	LP	Decca	SKL4733	196–	**£15**	**£6**	*boxed Decca logo*
Out Of Our Heads	LP	London	LL3429	1965	**£25**	**£10**	*US*
Out Of Tears	7"	Virgin	VS1524	1994	**£5**	**£2**	
Out Of Tears	CD-s	Virgin	VSCDX1524	1994	**£10**	**£5**	
Out Of Tears	CD-s	Virgin	VSCDG1524	1994	**£250**	**£150**	
Paint It Black	7"	Decca	F12395	1966	**£4**	**£1.50**	
Paint It Black	7"	Decca	F12395	1966	**£30**	**£15**	*export, picture sleeve*
Pleasure Of Pain	CD	Rolling Stones	XDDP930823	1990	**£500**	**£330**	*Japanese promo double*
Poison Ivy	7"	Decca	F11742	1963	**£400**	**£250**	*best auctioned*
Promotional LP	LP	Decca	RSM1	1969	**£600**	**£400**	*promo compilation*
Radio Sampler	CD	London	RSCD1	1990	**£30**	**£15**	*promo*
Rest Of The Best Of The Rolling Stones	LP	Teldec	630125FX	1984	**£100**	**£50**	*4 LPs, boxed, with 7", German*
Rock And A Hard Place	CD-s	CBS	6554485	1989	**£20**	**£10**	*tongue-shaped sleeve*
Rock And A Hard Place	CD-s	CBS	6554222	1989	**£10**	**£5**	
Rock And A Hard Place	CD-s	CBS	6554482	1989	**£25**	**£12.50**	*boxed with poster*
Rock And Roll Circus	CD	Abkco	12112	1996	**£30**	**£15**	*US promo*
Rocks Off	7"	Rolling Stones	SAM3	1971	**£20**	**£10**	*promo*
Rolling Stones	LP	Decca	LK4605	1964	**£30**	**£15**	
Rolling Stones	LP	Decca	LK4605	1964	**£75**	**£37.50**	*with 2.52 version of 'Tell Me', side 2 matrix XARL6272-1A*
Rolling Stones	12"	Decca	DFEX8560	1983	**£6**	**£2.50**	
Rolling Stones	7" EP	Decca	DFE8560	1964	**£10**	**£5**	
Rolling Stones	7" EP	Decca	SDE7260	1964	**£60**	**£30**	*export*
Rolling Stones	7" EP	Decca	SDE7503	1966	**£75**	**£37.50**	*export*
Rolling Stones	LP	Decca	25014	1965	**£200**	**£100**	*Swiss Club pressing*
Rolling Stones	LP	London	LL3375	1964	**£25**	**£10**	*US*
Rolling Stones	LP	London	LL3375	1964	**£100**	**£50**	*US, maroon label, 'London/ffrr' in box, bonus photo – advertised*
Rolling Stones	CD	Rolling Stones		1986	**£40**	**£20**	*US promo compilation*
Rolling Stones No. 2	LP	Decca	LK4661	1965	**£30**	**£15**	
Rolling Stones Now!	LP	London	LL3420	1965	**£25**	**£10**	*US*
Rolling Stones Story	LP	Decca	630120	1980	**£75**	**£37.50**	*German 12 LP boxed set*
Rolling Stones Vol. 2	7" EP	Decca	SDE7501	1964	**£50**	**£25**	*export*
Rolling Stones/ Living Colour	CD	Columbia		1989	**£30**	**£15**	*US promo*
Ruby Tuesday	12"	CBS	6568926	1990	**£8**	**£4**	
Ruby Tuesday	CD-s	CBS	6568925	1990	**£6**	**£2.50**	
Ruby Tuesday (live)	CD-s	CBS	6568922	1991	**£6**	**£2.50**	
Sad Day	7"	Decca	F13404	1973	**£4**	**£1.50**	
Saint Of Me	12"	Virgin	VSTDJ1667	1998	**£10**	**£5**	*promo double*
Saint Of Me	CD-s	Virgin	VSCDJX1667	1998	**£5**	**£2**	*1 track promo*
Satisfaction	7"	Decca	AT15043	1965	**£75**	**£37.50**	*export, picture sleeve*
Satisfaction	7"	Decca	F12220	1965	**£4**	**£1.50**	
Satisfaction	7" EP	Decca	457086	1965	**£75**	**£37.50**	*French, K. Richard in centre of group pic*
Satisfaction	7" EP	Decca	457086	1965	**£20**	**£10**	*French, B. Jones in centre of group pic*
Satisfaction/Under Assistant West Coast . . .	7"	Decca	F12220	1965	**£25**	**£12.50**	*export, picture sleeve*
Satisfaction/Under Assistant West Coast . . .	7"	Decca	F12220	1965	**£10**	**£5**	*export*
Say Ahhh!	CD	Rolling Stones	CSK1827	1989	**£40**	**£20**	*US promo compilation*
She Was Hot	7"	Rolling Stones	RSRP114	1984	**£15**	**£7.50**	*shaped picture disc*
Single Stones	7"	Decca	STONE1-12	1981	**£50**	**£25**	*mail order box set with poster & badge*
Singles Collection – The London Years	LP	ABKCO	8209001	1989	**£40**	**£20**	*4 LP set*
Some Girls	LP	Decca	DC2	1978	**£20**	**£8**	*French, red vinyl*
Some Girls	LP	Mobile Fidelity	MFSL1087	1982	**£15**	**£6**	*US audiophile*
Songs Of The Rolling Stones	LP	ABKCO	MPD1	1973	**£100**	**£50**	*US promo*
Songs Of The Rolling Stones Vol. 2	LP	ABKCO		197–	**£100**	**£50**	*US promo*
Steel Wheels	CD	Rolling Stones	4657522	1990	**£125**	**£62.50**	*promo box set, with LP, cassette, T-shirt, 12", book*

Title	Format	Label	Cat. No.	Year	Mint	VG	Notes
Steel Wheels	CD	Rolling Stones	CK46009	1989	**£25**	**£10**	*US, in steel case*
Sticky Fingers	CD	Rolling Stones	4501959	1990	**£20**	**£8**	*German, zip sleeve*
Sticky Fingers	LP	Rolling Stones	HRSS59101	1971	**£60**	**£30**	*Spanish, treacle tin sleeve*
Sticky Fingers	LP	Rolling Stones	COC59100	1971	**£15**	**£6**	*zip sleeve, insert*
Sticky Fingers	LP	Mobile Fidelity	MFSL1060	1980	**£20**	**£8**	*US audiophile*
Still Life	LP	Rolling Stones	CUNP39115	1982	**£10**	**£4**	*picture disc*
Stones In The Park	CD	BMG	781223	1992	**£25**	**£10**	*Laser disc*
Stones On CD	CD	CBS	SAMP1103	1987	**£75**	**£37.50**	*promo*
Street Fighting Man	7"	Decca	F13195	1971	**£4**	**£1.50**	
Street Fighting Man	7"	Decca	F13204	1971	**£25**	**£12.50**	*export, picture sleeve*
Street Fighting Man	7"	Decca	F13195	1971	**£20**	**£10**	*export, picture sleeve*
Street Fighting Man	7"	Decca	F13203	1971	**£10**	**£5**	
Street Fighting Man	7"	Decca	F22825	1968	**£75**	**£37.50**	*export, picture sleeve*
Street Fighting Man	7"	Decca	F13204	1971	**£10**	**£5**	*export*
Street Fighting Man	7"	Decca	F22825	1968	**£20**	**£10**	*export*
Stripped	CD	Virgin	IVDG2801	1996	**£100**	**£50**	*promo with bonus interview disc*
Tell Me	7"	Decca	AT15032	1964	**£75**	**£37.50**	*export*
Terrifying	CD-s	CBS	6551225	1990	**£10**	**£5**	*card sleeve*
Terrifying	CD-s	CBS	6561222	1990	**£5**	**£2**	
Their Satanic Majesties Request	LP	Decca	6835208		**£20**	**£8**	*Dutch, white vinyl*
Their Satanic Majesties Request	LP	Decca	TXL103	1967	**£50**	**£25**	*3D cover, mono*
Their Satanic Majesties Request	LP	Decca	TXL/TXS103	1967	**£1000**	**£700**	*promo with padded silk sleeve*
Their Satanic Majesties Request	LP	Decca	TXS103	1970	**£12**	**£5**	*black print on white label*
Their Satanic Majesties Request	LP	Decca	TXS103	1967	**£40**	**£20**	*3D cover*
Their Satanic Majesties Request	LP	Decca	TXS103	198–	**£15**	**£6**	*reissue with 3D sleeve*
Their Satanic Majesties Request	LP	London	NP2	1967	**£75**	**£37.50**	*US, mono*
Through The Past Darkly	LP	Decca	LK5019	1969	**£25**	**£10**	*octagonal cover, mono*
Through The Past Darkly	LP	Decca	SKL5019	1969	**£20**	**£8**	*octagonal cover*
Time Is On My Side	12"	Rolling Stones	12RSR111	1982	**£6**	**£2.50**	
Time Is On My Side	7"	Decca	AT15039	1965	**£75**	**£37.50**	*export*
Time Is On My Side	7" EP	Decca	457050	1964	**£20**	**£10**	*French*
Trident Mixes	LP	ABKCO	PR164	1971	**£500**	**£330**	*US promo double*
Under Cover	CD	Rolling Stones	CDP7460242	1984	**£15**	**£6**	
Urban Jungle Tour Special	CD	Rolling Stones		1990	**£100**	**£50**	*promo box set, with cassette, 12", biog*
Voodoo Lounge	CD	Rolling Stones		1994	**£25**	**£10**	*Australian, in slipcase*
We Love You	7"	Decca	F12654	1967	**£4**	**£1.50**	
We Love You	7"	Decca	F12654	1967	**£30**	**£15**	*export, picture sleeve*
Wild Horses	CD-s	Virgin	VSCDJ1578	1996	**£20**	**£10**	*1 track promo*
You Got Me Rocking	7"	Virgin	VS1518	1994	**£5**	**£2**	
You Got Me Rocking	CD-s	Virgin	VSCDG1518	1994	**£5**	**£2**	

ROLLINS, HENRY

Title	Format	Label	Cat. No.	Year	Mint	VG	Notes
Let There Be Rock	CD-s	Vinyl Solution	VS30CD	1991	**£5**	**£2**	

ROLLINS, SONNY

Title	Format	Label	Cat. No.	Year	Mint	VG	Notes
Alfie	LP	HMV	CLP/CSD3529	1967	**£25**	**£10**	
Alfie	LP	Impulse	AS9111	1973	**£20**	**£8**	
Alfie	LP	Impulse	IMPL8050	1976	**£15**	**£6**	
At Music Inn	LP	MGM	C818	1960	**£20**	**£8**	*side 2 by Teddy Edwards*
Blow!	LP	Fontana	FJL124	1965	**£12**	**£5**	
Bridge	LP	RCA	RD/SF7504	1962	**£15**	**£6**	
East Broadway Rundown	LP	HMV	CLP/CSD3610	1967	**£15**	**£6**	
Freedom Suite	LP	Riverside	RLP12258	1962	**£20**	**£8**	
Horn Culture	LP	Milestone	M9051	1973	**£15**	**£6**	*US*
Movin' Out	LP	Esquire	32155	1962	**£20**	**£8**	
Newk's Time	LP	Blue Note	BLP/BST84001	1964	**£25**	**£10**	
Next Album	LP	Milestone	MSP9042	1972	**£15**	**£6**	*US*
Night At The Village Vanguard	LP	Blue Note	BLP/BST81581	1964	**£25**	**£10**	
Now's The Time	LP	RCA	RD7670	1965	**£15**	**£6**	
Nucleus	LP	Milestone	M9064	1975	**£15**	**£6**	*US*
On Impulse	LP	HMV	CLP1915	1966	**£15**	**£6**	
Our Man In Jazz	LP	RCA	RD/SF7546	1963	**£15**	**£6**	
Perspectives	LP	Esquire	32035	1957	**£25**	**£10**	*with MJQ*
Rollins And Brownie	7" EP	Esquire	EP238	1961	**£5**	**£2**	*with Clifford Brown*
Saint Thomas	7" EP	Esquire	EP248	1962	**£5**	**£2**	
Saxophone Colossus	LP	Stateside	SL10164	1966	**£12**	**£5**	
Saxophone Colossus	LP	Esquire	32045	1958	**£25**	**£10**	
Sonny Boy	LP	Esquire	32175	1963	**£15**	**£6**	
Sonny Meets Hawk	LP	RCA	RD/SF7593	1964	**£20**	**£8**	*with Coleman Hawkins*

Sonny Rollins	LP	Blue Note	BLP/BST81542	1961	£25	£10	
Sonny Rollins & Co.	LP	RCA	RD/SF7626	1964	£15	£6	
Sonny Rollins And The Big Brass	LP	MGM	C776	1959	£20	£8	
Sonny Rollins And The Contemporary Leaders	LP	Contemporary	LAC12213	1960	£20	£8	
Sonny Rollins And The Contemporary Leaders	LP	Contemporary	SCA5013	1960	£20	£8	
Sonny Rollins And The Modern Jazz Quartet	7" EP	Esquire	EP94	1956	£5	£2	
Sonny Rollins Plus Four	LP	Esquire	32025	1957	£25	£10	
Sonny Rollins Quartet	10" LP	Esquire	20050	1955	£50	£25	
Sonny Rollins Quartet	LP	Esquire	32038	1958	£25	£10	
Sonny Rollins Quintet	10" LP	Esquire	20080	1957	£50	£25	
Sonny Rollins Quintet	LP	Esquire	32075	1959	£25	£10	
Sonny Rollins Vol. 2	LP	Blue Note	BLP/BST81558	1961	£25	£10	
Sonny Rollins With Thelonious Monk	7" EP	Esquire	EP148	1957	£5	£2	
Sound Of Sonny	LP	Riverside	RLP12241	1961	£20	£8	
Standard Sonny Rollins	LP	RCA	RD/SF7736	1967	£15	£6	
Tenor Madness	LP	Esquire	32058	1958	£25	£10	
Tour De Force	LP	Esquire	32085	1959	£25	£10	
Valse Hot	7" EP	Esquire	EP228	1960	£5	£2	
Wailing Mr Rollins	7" EP	Esquire	EP198	1958	£5	£2	
Way I Feel	LP	Milestone	M9074	1976	£12	£5	*US*
Way Out West	LP	Contemporary	LAC12118	1958	£20	£8	
What's New	LP	RCA	RD/SF7524	1963	£15	£6	

ROMAN, MURRAY

Blind Man's Movie	LP	Track	613015	1969	£10	£4	
You Can't Beat People Up . . .	LP	Track	613007	1969	£12	£5	

ROMAN, RON

'Love Of My Life' was written by Frank Zappa and was later recorded by him on the LP *Cruising With Ruben And The Jets*.

Love Of My Life	7"	Daani	101	1963	£150	£75	*US*

ROMAN, TONY

Shadows On A Foggy Day	7" EP	Festival	CEP19101	196–	£8	£4	*French*

ROMEO, MAX

Belly Woman	7"	Unity	UN507	1969	£4	£1.50	*Paulett & The Lovers B side*
Blowing In The Wind	7"	Nu Beat	NB022	1969	£6	£2.50	*Larry Marshall B side*
Clap Clap	7"	Unity	UN545	1969	£4	£1.50	
Don't Want To Let You Go	7"	Caltone	TONE106	1967	£8	£4	
Dream	LP	Pama	PMLP11	1969	£20	£8	
It's Not The Way	7"	Blue Cat	BS163	1969	£6	£2.50	*Al Reid B side*
Let The Power Fall	LP	Pama	PMP2010	1971	£20	£8	
Me Want Man	7"	Blue Cat	BS161	1969	£6	£2.50	
Put Me In The Mood	7"	Island	WI3104	1968	£10	£5	
Sweet Chariot	7"	Trojan	TR656	1969	£4	£1.50	
Twelfth Of Never	7"	Island	WI3124	1967	£10	£5	*Val Bennett B side*
Twelfth Of Never	7"	Unity	UN511	1969	£4	£1.50	*Tartons B side*
Walk Into The Room	7"	Island	WI3111	1968	£10	£5	*Dawn Penn B side*
War In A Babylon	7"	Island	WIP6283	1976	£4	£1.50	
Wet Dream	7"	Unity	UN503	1969	£4	£1.50	
Wine Her Goosie	7"	Unity	UN516	1969	£4	£1.50	*King Cannon B side*

ROMEOS

Precious Memories	LP	Mark II	1001	1967	£15	£6	*US*

ROMERO, CHAN

Hippy Hippy Shake	7"	Columbia	DB4341	1959	£60	£30	
My Little Ruby	7"	Columbia	DB4405	1960	£75	£37.50	

ROMNEY, HUGH 'WAVY GRAVY'

Third Stream Humor	LP	World Pacific	WP1805	1962	£15	£6	*US*

RONALD, TONY

Tony Ronald	LP	Ariola	86447IT	1972	£15	£6	*German*
Tony Ronald And His Kroners	LP	Imperial	NCLP1001	1966	£60	£30	*Dutch*

RONALD & RUBY

Lollipop	7"	RCA	RCA1053	1958	£20	£10	

RONALDE, RONNIE

Ballad Of Davy Crockett	7"	Columbia	SCM5214	1956	£6	£2.50	
Beautiful Dreamer	7" EP	Columbia	SEG7678	1957	£5	£2	
In A Monastery Garden	7"	Columbia	SCM5007	1953	£6	£2.50	
Robin Hood	7"	Columbia	SCM5241	1956	£6	£2.50	
Ronnie	7" EP	Columbia	SEG7945	1959	£5	£2	
Ronnie Ronalde	7" EP	Columbia	SEG7512	1955	£5	£2	
Song Of The Mountains	7"	Columbia	SCM5006	1953	£6	£2.50	
Story Of Christmas	7" EP	Columbia	SEG7838	1958	£5	£2	
TV Top Four	7" EP	Columbia	SEG7784	1958	£5	£2	
Yarmouth Song	7"	Columbia	SCM5262	1956	£4	£1.50	
Yodelling, Whistling And Singing	7" EP	Columbia	SEG7651	1956	£5	£2	

RONDELLS

Title	Format	Label	Cat. No.	Year	Mint	VG+	Notes
Backbeat Number One	7"	London	HLU9404	1961	£10	£5	
Good Good	7"	London	HLU8716	1958	£75	£37.50	

RONDO, DON

Title	Format	Label	Cat. No.	Year	Mint	VG+	Notes
Blonde Bombshell	7"	London	HLJ8641	1958	£8	£4	
I've Got Bells On My Heart	7"	London	HLJ8610	1958	£5	£2	
Rondo Part One	7" EP	London	REJ1154	1958	£12	£6	
Rondo Part Two	7" EP	London	REJ1155	1958	£12	£6	
What A Shame	7"	London	HLJ8567	1958	£6	£2.50	
White Silver Sands	7"	London	HLJ8466	1957	£5	£2	

RONDO, GENE

Title	Format	Label	Cat. No.	Year	Mint	VG+	Notes
Ben Nevis	7"	Giant	GN39	1968	£4	£1.50	

RONETTES

Title	Format	Label	Cat. No.	Year	Mint	VG+	Notes
Baby I Love You	7"	London	HLU9826	1964	£4	£1.50	
Be My Baby	7"	London	HLU9793	1963	£4	£1.50	
Best Part Of Breaking Up	7"	London	HLU9905	1964	£6	£2.50	
Born To Be Together	7"	London	HLU9952	1965	£8	£4	
Do I Love You	7"	London	HLU9922	1964	£5	£2	
I Can Hear Music	7"	London	HLU10087	1966	£40	£20	
I'm Gonna Quit While I'm Ahead	7"	Colpix	646	1962	£15	£7.50	*US*
Is This What I Get For Loving You	7"	London	HLU9976	1965	£8	£4	
Presenting The Fabulous Ronettes	LP	London	HAU8212	196–	£30	£15	*black label*
Presenting The Fabulous Ronettes	LP	London	HAU8212	1964	£75	£37.50	*plum label*
Presenting The Fabulous Ronettes	LP	Philles	PHLP4006	1964	£75	£37.50	*US, mono*
Presenting The Fabulous Ronettes	LP	Philles	PHLPST4006	1964	£100	£50	*US, stereo*
Ronettes	LP	Colpix	PXL486	1965	£60	£30	
Walking In The Rain	7"	London	HLU9931	1964	£5	£2	
You Came You Saw You Conquered	7"	A&M	AMS748	1969	£4	£1.50	

RONNIE & ROY

Title	Format	Label	Cat. No.	Year	Mint	VG+	Notes
Big Fat Sally	7"	Capitol	CL15028	1959	£75	£37.50	

RONNIE & THE DEL AIRES

Title	Format	Label	Cat. No.	Year	Mint	VG+	Notes
Drag	7"	Coral	Q72473	1964	£10	£5	

RONNIE & THE HI-LITES

Title	Format	Label	Cat. No.	Year	Mint	VG+	Notes
Twistin' And Kissin'	7"	Pye	7N25140	1962	£10	£5	

RONNIE & THE POMONA CASUALS

Interest in this group revolves around the fact that Arthur Lee sang lead vocal on the track 'Slow Jerk', which was also written by him. The music, however, bears no resemblance to that of any of the incarnations of Lee's better-known group, Love.

Title	Format	Label	Cat. No.	Year	Mint	VG+	Notes
Everybody Jerk	LP	Donna	2112	1965	£100	£50	*US*

RONNIE & THE RAINBOWS

Title	Format	Label	Cat. No.	Year	Mint	VG+	Notes
Loose Ends	7"	London	HL9345	1961	£6	£2.50	

RONNO

The single credited to Ronno was recorded by the musicians who featured on David Bowie's *Ziggy Stardust* album (led by much-missed guitarist Mick Ronson), with the former singer from the Rats, Benny Marshall.

Title	Format	Label	Cat. No.	Year	Mint	VG+	Notes
Fourth Hour Of My Sleep	7"	Vertigo	6059029	1970	£15	£7.50	

RONNY & THE DAYTONAS

Title	Format	Label	Cat. No.	Year	Mint	VG+	Notes
Beach Boy	7"	Stateside	SS432	1965	£8	£4	
Bucket T	7"	Stateside	SS391	1965	£8	£4	
Bucket T	7" EP	Columbia	ESRF1641	1964	£20	£10	*French*
California Bound	7"	Stateside	SS367	1964	£5	£2	
GTO	7"	Stateside	SS333	1964	£6	£2.50	
GTO	LP	Mala	4001	1964	£40	£20	*US*
Sandy	7"	Stateside	SS484	1966	£6	£2.50	
Sandy	LP	Mala	4002(S)	1964	£30	£15	*US*

RONSON, MICK

Title	Format	Label	Cat. No.	Year	Mint	VG+	Notes
Heaven And Hull	LP	Epic	EPC4747421	1994	£12	£5	*picture disc*
Love Me Tender	7"	RCA	11474XSP	1974	£6	£2.50	*flexi*
Mick Ronson Primer	CD	Epic	ESK6076	1994	£20	£8	*US promo compilation*
Mick Ronson Story – Heaven And Hull	CD	Epic	ESK6143	1994	£20	£8	*US promo*

RONSTADT, LINDA

Title	Format	Label	Cat. No.	Year	Mint	VG+	Notes
Cry Like A Rainstorm, Howl Like The Wind	CD	Elektra	9608722	1989	£40	£20	*promo box set, with cassette*
Home Sown, Home Grown	LP	Capitol	EST208	1969	£10	£4	
Silk Purse	LP	Capitol	EST407	1970	£10	£4	

ROOFTOP SINGERS

Title	Format	Label	Cat. No.	Year	Mint	VG+	Notes
Walk Right In	7"	Fontana	271700TF	1963	£4	£1.50	
Walk Right In	LP	Fontana	680999TL	1963	£10	£4	

ROOM

Title	Format	Label	Cat. No.	Year	Mint	VG+	Notes
Pre-Flight	LP	Deram	SML1073	1970	£300	£180	

ROOM 13

Title	Format	Label	Cat. No.	Year	Mint	VG	Notes
Murder Mystery	12"	Woronzow	WOO2	1982	**£20**	**£10**	

ROONEY, MICKEY

Title	Format	Label	Cat. No.	Year	Mint	VG	Notes
Sings George M. Cohan	LP	RCA	RD27038	1957	**£12**	**£5**	

ROOT BOYS

Title	Format	Label	Cat. No.	Year	Mint	VG	Notes
Please Don't Stop The Wedding	7"	Columbia	DB115	1970	**£6**	**£2.50**	

ROPE, HARRY

Title	Format	Label	Cat. No.	Year	Mint	VG	Notes
Laughing Inside	7"	Regal Zonophone	HR1	1988	**£4**	**£1.50**	*promo by Roy Harper*

ROSA, LISA

Title	Format	Label	Cat. No.	Year	Mint	VG	Notes
Mama He Treats Your Daughter Mean	7"	Ember	EMBS168	1963	**£5**	**£2**	

ROSANO, ROSITA

Title	Format	Label	Cat. No.	Year	Mint	VG	Notes
Queer Things	7"	Melodisc	1436	1957	**£4**	**£1.50**	

ROSANOVA, JOE & THE VINEYARD

Title	Format	Label	Cat. No.	Year	Mint	VG	Notes
In Dedication To The Ones We Love	LP	Astro Sonic	DAP4000	1968	**£60**	**£30**	*US*

ROSE, ANDY

Title	Format	Label	Cat. No.	Year	Mint	VG	Notes
Just Young	7"	London	HLU8761	1958	**£15**	**£7.50**	

ROSE, DUSTY

Title	Format	Label	Cat. No.	Year	Mint	VG	Notes
Birds And The Bees	7"	London	HLU8162	1955	**£30**	**£15**	
Country Songs	7" EP	London	REU1078	1957	**£40**	**£20**	

ROSE, JOHNNY

Title	Format	Label	Cat. No.	Year	Mint	VG	Notes
Linda Lea	7"	Capitol	CL15166	1960	**£4**	**£1.50**	

ROSE, TIM

Title	Format	Label	Cat. No.	Year	Mint	VG	Notes
I Got A Loneliness	7"	CBS	3277	1968	**£15**	**£7.50**	
Love – A Kind Of Hate Story	LP	Capitol	ST673	1970	**£12**	**£5**	*US*
Morning Dew	7"	CBS	202631	1967	**£4**	**£1.50**	
Through Rose Coloured Glasses	LP	CBS	63636	1969	**£12**	**£5**	
Tim Rose	LP	CBS	(S)BPG63168	1967	**£15**	**£6**	
Tim Rose	LP	Dawn	DNLS3062	1974	**£10**	**£4**	
Tim Rose	LP	Playboy	PB101	1972	**£12**	**£5**	*US*

ROSE, TONY

Title	Format	Label	Cat. No.	Year	Mint	VG	Notes
On Banks Of Green Willow	LP	Trailer	LER2101	1976	**£10**	**£4**	
Under The Greenwood Tree	LP	Trailer	LER2024	1971	**£10**	**£4**	
Young Hunting	LP	Trailer	LER2013	1970	**£12**	**£5**	

ROSE GARDEN

Title	Format	Label	Cat. No.	Year	Mint	VG	Notes
Next Plane To London	7"	Atlantic	584163	1968	**£4**	**£1.50**	
Rose Garden	LP	Atco	SD33225	1968	**£20**	**£8**	*US*

ROSE TATTOO

Title	Format	Label	Cat. No.	Year	Mint	VG	Notes
Born To Be Wild	12"	Mushroom	K9837	1985	**£8**	**£4**	*promo*
Release Legalise	7"	Repeal	PRS2724	1980	**£30**	**£15**	*Col Paterson B side*
Rock'n'Roll Is King	12"	Mirage	PR405	1981	**£6**	**£2.50**	*promo*

ROSENMAN, LEONARD

Title	Format	Label	Cat. No.	Year	Mint	VG	Notes
Lord Of The Rings	LP	Fantasy	LORPD2	1978	**£20**	**£8**	*US double picture disc*
Tribute To James Dean	LP	London	HAP2040	1957	**£10**	**£4**	

ROSIE

Title	Format	Label	Cat. No.	Year	Mint	VG	Notes
Angel Baby	7"	London	HLU9266	1961	**£25**	**£10**	*with the Originals*
Lonely Blue Nights	7"	Coral	Q72426	1961	**£10**	**£5**	

ROSOLINO, FRANK

Title	Format	Label	Cat. No.	Year	Mint	VG	Notes
I Play Trombone	LP	London	LTZN15067	1957	**£20**	**£8**	
That Old Black Magic	7"	Capitol	KC65001	1954	**£4**	**£1.50**	

ROSS, ANNIE

Title	Format	Label	Cat. No.	Year	Mint	VG	Notes
Annie By Candlelight	10" LP	Nixa	NJT504	1957	**£100**	**£50**	
Annie By Candlelight	LP	Golden Guinea	GGL0316	1965	**£50**	**£25**	
Annie Ross And Pony Poindexter	LP	Polydor	583711	1968	**£10**	**£4**	*with Pony Poindexter*
Fish	7"	Decca	F10514	1955	**£6**	**£2.50**	
Gasser	LP	Vogue	LAE12233	1960	**£20**	**£8**	*with Zoot Sims*
Go To The Wall	7" EP	Transatlantic	TRAEP112	1964	**£5**	**£2**	
Handful Of Songs	LP	Ember	NR5008	1963	**£50**	**£25**	
Nocturne For Vocalist	7" EP	Pye	NJE1035	1957	**£5**	**£2**	
Only You	7"	Decca	F10680	1956	**£5**	**£2**	
Sings A Song With Mulligan	LP	Vogue	LAE12203	1959	**£20**	**£8**	*with Gerry Mulligan*
With The Teacho Wiltshire Group	7" EP	Esquire	EP1	1954	**£8**	**£4**	
With The Tony Crombie Fourtet	7" EP	Pieces Of Eight	PEP604	195–	**£8**	**£4**	
With The Tony Kinsey Quintet	LP	XTRA	XTRA1049	1966	**£40**	**£20**	

ROSS, DAVE

Title	Format	Label	Cat. No.	Year	Mint	VG	Notes
Pit-A-Patter Boom Boom	7"	Oriole	CB1416	1958	£5	£2	

ROSS, DIANA

Diana Ross's decision to continue as a solo singer at the beginning of 1970 was hardly surprising, given the fact that she had always dominated the Supremes. That she has managed to sustain – and even increase – the level of stardom that she had achieved by that time is due, in part, to careful and expert career management, and also to the fact that she has been able to produce a long succession of memorable singles. These have given her a continually high chart profile that has made her one of the most successful female singers of all time.

Title	Format	Label	Cat. No.	Year	Mint	VG	Notes
Best Years Of My Life	CD	EMI	MIDEM94	1994	£30	£15	*promo picture disc*
Ease On Down The Road	12"	MCA	MCAT12396	1978	£10	£5	*with Michael Jackson*
Ease On Down The Road	12"	MCA	MCAT12898	1978	£8	£4	*with Michael Jackson*
Ease On Down The Road	7"	MCA	MCA396	1978	£5	£2	*with Michael Jackson*
Theme From Mahogany	7"	Tamla Motown	TMG1010	1976	£6	£2.50	*demo, picture sleeve*
Workin' Overtime	CD	Motown		1989	£50	£25	*US promo lunchbox, with cassette, video, biog*

ROSS, DIANA & THE SUPREMES

Title	Format	Label	Cat. No.	Year	Mint	VG	Notes
Forever Came Today	7"	Tamla Motown	TMG650	1968	£4	£1.50	
I'm Gonna Make You Love Me	7"	Tamla Motown	TMG685	1969	£4	£1.50	
I'm Living In Shame	7"	Tamla Motown	TMG695	1969	£4	£1.50	
In And Out of Love	7"	Tamla Motown	TMG632	1967	£4	£1.50	
Live At The Talk Of The Town	LP	Tamla Motown	(S)TML11070	1968	£10	£4	
Love Child	7"	Tamla Motown	TMG677	1968	£4	£1.50	
Love Child	LP	Tamla Motown	TML11095	1969	£10	£4	*mono*
No Matter What Sign You Are	7"	Tamla Motown	TMG704	1969	£4	£1.50	
Reflections	7"	Tamla Motown	TMG616	1967	£4	£1.50	
Reflections	LP	Tamla Motown	(S)TML11073	1968	£10	£4	
Sing And Perform Funny Girl	LP	Tamla Motown	TML11088	1969	£10	£4	*mono*
Some Things You Never Get Used To	7"	Tamla Motown	TMG662	1968	£4	£1.50	

ROSS, DR ISAIAH

Title	Format	Label	Cat. No.	Year	Mint	VG	Notes
Call The Doctor	LP	Bounty	BY6020	1966	£15	£6	
Doctor Ross	LP	XTRA	XTRA1038	1966	£25	£10	
Flying Eagle	LP	Blue Horizon	LP1	1966	£600	£400	
Live At Montreux	LP	Polydor	2460169	1972	£12	£5	

ROSS, GENE

Title	Format	Label	Cat. No.	Year	Mint	VG	Notes
Endless Sleep	7"	Parlophone	R4434	1958	£15	£7.50	

ROSS, JACKIE

Title	Format	Label	Cat. No.	Year	Mint	VG	Notes
Jerk And Twine	7"	Chess	CRS8003	1965	£10	£5	
Selfish One	7"	Pye	7N25259	1964	£25	£12.50	

ROSS, RICKY

Title	Format	Label	Cat. No.	Year	Mint	VG	Notes
So Long Ago	CD	Sticky Music	GUM8CD	1993	£20	£8	

ROSS, RONNIE

Title	Format	Label	Cat. No.	Year	Mint	VG	Notes
Cleopatra's Needle	LP	Fontana	SFJL915	1968	£50	£25	
Double Event	LP	Parlophone	PMC1079	1959	£25	£10	
Stompin' With Ronnie Ross	LP	Ember	EMB3323	1961	£40	£20	

ROSSELSON, LEON

Title	Format	Label	Cat. No.	Year	Mint	VG	Notes
Laugh, A Song, And A Hand Grenade	LP	Transatlantic	TRA171	1968	£20	£8	*with Adrian Mitchell*
Palaces Of Gold	LP	Acorn	CF249	1975	£15	£6	
Songs For Sceptical Circles	LP	Acorn	CF206	1970	£15	£6	
That's Not The Way It's Got To Be	LP	Acorn	CF251	1975	£10	£4	*with Roy Bailey*
Word Is Hugga Mugga Chugga Humbugga Boom Chit	LP	Trailer	LER3015	1971	£10	£4	*with Roy Bailey & Martin Carthy*

ROSSI, NITA

Title	Format	Label	Cat. No.	Year	Mint	VG	Notes
Here I Go Again	7"	Piccadilly	7N35307	1966	£10	£5	
Misty Blue	7"	Piccadilly	7N35384	1967	£4	£1.50	
Untrue Unfaithful	7"	Piccadilly	7N35258	1965	£6	£2.50	

ROSSI & FROST

Title	Format	Label	Cat. No.	Year	Mint	VG	Notes
Jealousy	12"	Vertigo	VERX24	1985	£6	£2.50	
Modern Romance	12"	Vertigo	VERX17	1985	£8	£4	

ROSTILL, JOHN

Title	Format	Label	Cat. No.	Year	Mint	VG	Notes
Funny Old World	7"	Columbia	DB8794	1971	£50	£25	

ROTARY CONNECTION

Aladdin	LP	Chess	CRLS4547	1969	**£25**	**£10**	
Rotary Connection	LP	Chess	CRL4538	1968	**£25**	**£10**	
Songs	LP	Chess	CRLS4551	1969	**£25**	**£10**	

ROTATIONS

'Heavies' is one of several early Frank Zappa productions.

Heavies	7"	Original Sound	41	1964	**£150**	**£75**	*US*

ROTH, DAVID LEE

California Girls	CD-s	Warner Bros	W7650CD	1988	**£5**	**£2**	
Just Like Paradise	CD-s	Warner Bros	W8119CD	1988	**£5**	**£2**	*3" single*
Sensible Shoes	5"	Warner Bros	W0016P	1991	**£6**	**£2.50**	*shaped picture disc*
Skyscraper	CD	Warner Bros		1988	**£20**	**£8**	*US promo picture disc*
Yankee Rose	7"	Warner Bros	W8656	1986	**£8**	**£4**	*shaped picture disc*

ROTHCHILDS

Artificial City	7"	Decca	F12488	1966	**£6**	**£2.50**	
You've Made Your Choice	7"	Decca	F12411	1966	**£5**	**£2**	

ROULETTES

The Roulettes were formed as a backing group for Adam Faith, when the singer attempted to meet the challenge of the Beatles head-on by adopting the beat style himself. The Roulettes tried very hard to establish an independent career for themselves as well, but little of the group's material was sufficiently distinctive. The closest they came to a hit was with 'Long Cigarette', which is a memorable song for all that it is closely modelled on a John Lennon performance, but a BBC ban put a stop to its progress up the charts. Guitarist Russ Ballard and drummer Bob Henrit were subsequently members of Argent.

Bad Time	7"	Parlophone	R5110	1964	**£5**	**£2**	
Help Me Help Myself	7"	Fontana	TF876	1967	**£6**	**£2.50**	
Hully Gully Slip And Slide	7"	Pye	7N15467	1962	**£6**	**£2.50**	
I Can't Stop	7"	Parlophone	R5461	1966	**£5**	**£2**	
I Can't Stop	7"	Oak	RGJ205	1965	**£50**	**£25**	*1 sided*
I Can't Stop	7"	Oak	RGJ205	1966	**£100**	**£50**	*picture sleeve*
I Hope He Breaks Your Heart	7"	Parlophone	R5278	1965	**£5**	**£2**	
I'll Remember Tonight	7"	Parlophone	R5148	1964	**£5**	**£2**	
Long Cigarette	7"	Parlophone	R5382	1965	**£5**	**£2**	
Rhyme Boy Rhyme	7"	Fontana	TF822	1967	**£6**	**£2.50**	
Soon You'll Be Leaving	7"	Parlophone	R5072	1963	**£5**	**£2**	
Stakes And Chips	LP	Parlophone	PMC1257	1965	**£400**	**£250**	
Stubborn Kind Of Fellow	7"	Parlophone	R5218	1964	**£5**	**£2**	
Tracks Of My Tears	7"	Parlophone	R5419	1966	**£6**	**£2.50**	

ROUND ROBIN

Kick That Little Foot Sally Ann	7"	London	HLU9908	1964	**£25**	**£12.50**	

ROUNDTABLE

Spinning Wheel	LP	Jay Boy	JSL2	1969	**£15**	**£6**	

ROUSE, CHARLIE

Bossa Nova Bacchanal	LP	Blue Note	BLP/BST84119	1962	**£25**	**£10**	
Chase Is On	LP	Parlophone	PMC1090	1959	**£15**	**£6**	*with Paul Quinichette*
Takin' Care Of Business	LP	Jazzland	JLP19	1960	**£20**	**£8**	

ROUTERS

A Ooga	7"	Warner Bros	WB108	1963	**£4**	**£1.50**	
Charge!	LP	Warner Bros	WM/WS8162	1964	**£20**	**£8**	
Let's Go	7"	Warner Bros	WB77	1962	**£4**	**£1.50**	
Let's Go	7" EP	Warner Bros	WEP1418	1962	**£15**	**£7.50**	*French*
Let's Go With The Routers	LP	Warner Bros	WM/WS8126	1963	**£30**	**£15**	
Make It Snappy	7"	Warner Bros	WB91	1963	**£4**	**£1.50**	
Play 1963's Great Instrumentals	LP	Warner Bros	WM/WS8144	1964	**£20**	**£8**	
Stamp And Shake	7"	Warner Bros	WB139	1964	**£4**	**£1.50**	
Stingray	7"	Warner Bros	WB97	1963	**£5**	**£2**	

ROUTH, JONATHAN

Candid Mike	10" LP	Nixa	NPT19016	1957	**£10**	**£4**	
Candid Mike	7" EP	Pye	NEP24128	1960	**£5**	**£2**	

ROVERS

Ichi Bon Tami Dachi	7"	Capitol	CL14283	1955	**£75**	**£37.50**	

ROWAN & MARTIN

Rowan & Martin At Work	LP	Atlantic	588151	1969	**£10**	**£4**	
Rowan & Martin's Laugh-In	LP	CBS	63490	1969	**£10**	**£4**	

ROWDIES

She's No Angel	7"	Teenage Depression	TD1/2	1979	**£4**	**£1.50**	

ROWE, NORMIE

Going Home	7"	Polydor	56159	1967	**£5**	**£2**	*picture sleeve*
So Much Love	LP	Sunshine Festival	L32144	1966	**£20**	**£8**	*Australian*

ROWELY, MAJOR

There's A Riot Going On	7"	Stateside	SS438	1965	£5	£2	

ROWLAND, JACKIE

Indian Reservation	7"	Sioux	SI015	1972	£5	£2	Junior Smith B side

ROWLAND, KEVIN

Tonight	CD-s	Mercury	ROWCD1	1988	£5	£2	
Walk Away	CD-s	Mercury	DEXCD14	1988	£5	£2	
Young Man	CD-s	Mercury	ROWCD2	1988	£5	£2	

ROWLAND, STEVE

So Sad	7"	Fontana	TF844	1967	£5	£2	

ROWSOME, LEO

Classics Of Irish Piping Vol. 1	LP	Topic	12T259	1976	£10	£4	
Classics Of Irish Piping Vol. 3	LP	Topic	12T322	1977	£10	£4	
Ri Na Bpiobari	LP	Claddagh	CC1	1969	£25	£10	Irish

ROX

Hot Love In The City	7"	Teenteeze	ROX100	1982	£15	£7.50	

ROXETTE

Big L	CD-s	EMI	CDEM204	1991	£6	£2.50	
Church Of Your Heart	CD-s	EMI	CDEM(S)227	1992	£5	£2	2 versions
Dance Passion	LP	EMI	1362611	1987	£50	£25	Swedish
Dressed For Success	12"	EMI	12EM96	1989	£6	£2.50	
Dressed For Success	CD-s	EMI	CDEM162	1990	£15	£7.50	
Dressed For Success	CD-s	EMI	CDEM96	1989	£15	£7.50	
Fading Like A Flower	CD-s	EMI	CDEM190	1991	£6	£2.50	
How Do You Do	CD-s	EMI	CDEM241	1992	£5	£2	
It Must Have Been Love	CD-s	EMI	CDEM285	1993	£5	£2	
It Must Have Been Love	CD-s	EMI	CDEM141	1990	£12	£6	
Joyride	CD-s	EMI	CDEM177	1991	£5	£2	
Listen To Your Heart	CD-s	EMI	CDEM108	1990	£12	£6	
Listen To Your Heart	CD-s	EMI	CDEM149	1990	£10	£5	
Look	12"	EMI	12EM87	1989	£50	£25	red vinyl
Look	7"	EMI	EM87	1989	£30	£15	red vinyl
Look	CD-s	EMI	CDEM87	1989	£15	£7.50	
Look '95	12"	EMI	12EMDJ406	1995	£8	£4	promo
Look Sharp	CD	EMI	CDEMC3557	1989	£100	£50	picture disc, special cover
Look Sharp	LP	EMI		1989	£100	£50	European picture disc
Pearls Of Passion	CD	EMI	7464592	1986	£75	£37.50	Swedish
Pearls Of Passion	LP	EMI	1362451	1986	£40	£20	Swedish
Queen Of Rain	CD-s	EMI	CDEM(S)253	1992	£5	£2	2 versions
Spending My Time	CD-s	EMI	CDEM215	1991	£5	£2	

ROXY MUSIC

Jealous Guy	CD-s	Virgin	CDT8	1988	£5	£2	3" single
Love Is The Drug	12"	Editions EG	EGOX26	1986	£8	£4	promo
Love Is The Drug	CD-s	Editions EG	EGOCD55	1990	£5	£2	
Over You/Eight Miles High	12"	Polydor	POSPX93	1980	£8	£4	promo
Trash	12"	Polydor	POSPX32	1978	£8	£4	promo
Virginia Plain	7"	Island	WIP6144	1972	£10	£5	picture sleeve

ROY, DEREK

All-Star Party	7"	Oriole	CB1415	1957	£5	£2	

ROY, I

Blackman Time	7"	Downtown	DT503	1973	£5	£2	
Buck And The Preacher	7"	Duke	DU156	1973	£5	£2	Pete Weston B side
Can't Conquer Rasta	LP	Justice	JUSTLP008	1977	£12	£5	
Cancer	LP	Front Line	4001	1979	£12	£5	
Clapper's Tail	7"	Downtown	DT519	1973	£5	£2	
Cowtown Skank	7"	Pama	PM854	1973	£4	£1.50	Augustus Pablo B side
Crisus Time	LP	Caroline	CA2011	1976	£12	£5	
Dread Baldhead	LP	Klik	KLP9020	1976	£12	£5	
Drifter	7"	Moodisc	HM104	1971	£4	£1.50	Jo Jo Bennett B side
General	LP	Front Line	FLD6002	1978	£15	£6	double
Godfather	LP	Third World	930	1978	£10	£4	
Great Great Great	7"	Ackee	ACK503	1973	£4	£1.50	Rupie Edwards B side
Heart Don't Leap	7"	Moodisc	MU3510	1971	£5	£2	Dennis Walks B side
Heart Of A Lion	LP	Front Line	FL1001	1978	£12	£5	
Hell And Sorrow	LP	Trojan	TRLS71	1973	£15	£6	
Hot Bomb	7"	Green Door	GD4030	1972	£4	£1.50	Jumpers B side
I Man Time	7"	Lucky	DL5098	1975	£4	£1.50	
I Roy	LP	Trojan	TRLS91	1974	£15	£6	
Let Me Tell You Boy	7"	Moodisc	MU3512	1971	£4	£1.50	Mudie's All Stars B side
Magnificent Seven	7"	Smash	SMA2337	1973	£5	£2	
Make Love	7"	Green Door	GD4044	1972	£4	£1.50	Stage B side
Monkey Fashion	7"	Technique	TE930	1973	£5	£2	
Mood For Love	7"	Ashanti	ASH412	1974	£5	£2	
Musical Drum Sound	7"	Harry J	HJ6655	1973	£4	£1.50	

Title	Format	Label	Number	Year	Price	Price	Notes
Musical Pleasure	7"	Moodisc	MU3509	1971	£5	£2	*Jo Jo Bennett B side*
Musical Shark Attack	LP	Virgin	V2075	1977	£12	£5	
Outformer Parker	7"	Attack	ATT8102	1975	£4	£1.50	
Padlock	7"	Dip	DL5107	1976	£4	£1.50	
Pauper And The King	7"	Technique	TE926	1973	£5	£2	*Gregory Isaacs B side*
Presenting I Roy	LP	Trojan	TRLS63	1973	£15	£6	
Rose Of Sheron	7"	Smash	SMA2338	1973	£5	£2	
Sound Education	7"	Ackee	ACK510	1973	£5	£2	*Augustus Pablo B side*
Space Flight	7"	Attack	ATT8050	1973	£5	£2	*Jerry Lewis B side*
Step Right Up	7"	Bullet	BU551	1975	£4	£1.50	*Andy's All Stars B side*
Ten Commandments	LP	Front Line	FL1028	1978	£12	£5	
Tip From The Prince	7"	Pyramid	PYR7001	1973	£4	£1.50	
Welding	7"	Philips	6006479	1975	£4	£1.50	
Whap'n Bap'n	LP	Virgin	V2164	1980	£10	£4	
World On Fire	LP	Front Line	FL1033	1978	£12	£5	
Yaha Ma Ride	7"	Atra	ATRA17	1974	£4	£1.50	

ROY, LEE

Title	Format	Label	Number	Year	Price	Price	Notes
Oh Ee Baby	7"	Island	WI251	1965	£10	£5	

ROY, U

U Roy is the major pioneer where the art of Jamaican DJ music is concerned. It was U Roy who first scored a series of successes with singles that used the stripped-down backing tracks from other people's hits as a springboard for his spoken rants. This 'toasting' style rapidly became all-pervasive in reggae and was undoubtedly a significant influence on the later American rapping scene.

Title	Format	Label	Number	Year	Price	Price	Notes
Aunt Kereba	7"	Technique	TE928	1973	£4	£1.50	*Don Reco B side*
Behold	7"	Treasure Isle	TI7062	1971	£5	£2	
Double Attack	7"	Supreme	SUP211	1970	£4	£1.50	
Dread In A Babylon	LP	Virgin	V2048	1976	£12	£5	
Dreadlocks In Jamaica	LP	Love And Live	LALP05	1978	£10	£4	*with other artists*
Drive Her Home	7"	Treasure Isle	TI7059	1971	£5	£2	
Earthquake	7"	Upsetter	US375	1971	£5	£2	
Everybody Bawlin'	7"	Treasure Isle	TI7064	1971	£5	£2	
Festival Wise	7"	Dynamic	DYN448	1972	£4	£1.50	
Flashing My Whip	7"	Duke Reid	DR2519	1971	£6	£2.50	
Froggie	7"	Randys	RAN532	1973	£4	£1.50	*Rhythm Rulers B side*
Hard Feeling	7"	Gay Feet	GS210	1973	£4	£1.50	
Higher The Mountain	7"	Duke	DU157	1973	£4	£1.50	*Old Boys Inc B side*
Hudson Affair	7"	Green Door	GD4034	1972	£4	£1.50	*Keith Hudson B side*
Jah Son Of Africa	LP	Live And Love	LALP08	1977	£12	£5	
Keep On Running	7"	Banana	BA367	1972	£4	£1.50	*Larry's All Stars*
King Of The Road	7"	Ashanti	ASH405	1972	£4	£1.50	*Roosevelt All Stars*
King Tubbys Special	7"	Green Door	GD4052	1973	£4	£1.50	
Live It Up	7"	Duke	DU137	1972	£4	£1.50	*Dennis Brown B side*
Love I Tender	7"	Duke	DU105	1970	£5	£2	*Joya Landis B side*
Nannyscrank	7"	Punch	PH104	1972	£4	£1.50	*Pittsburg All Stars*
Natty Rebel	LP	Virgin	V2059	1976	£12	£5	
On Top The Peak	7"	Grape	GR3026	1972	£4	£1.50	*Typhoon All Stars*
Papacito	7"	Big	BG329	1971	£4	£1.50	
Rasta Ambassador	LP	Virgin	V2092	1977	£12	£5	
Rock To The Beat	7"	Duke Reid	DR2520	1972	£4	£1.50	
Rule The Nation	7"	Duke Reid	DR2510	1970	£6	£2.50	*Nora Dean B side*
Scandal	7"	Punch	PH34	1970	£5	£2	
This Is A Pepper	7"	Attack	ATT8030	1972	£4	£1.50	*John Holt B side*
Tom Drunk	7"	Duke Reid	DR2517	1971	£6	£2.50	
Tom Drunk	7"	Duke Reid	DR2517	1971	£5	£2	
Treasure Isle Skank	7"	Harry J	HJ6651	1973	£4	£1.50	
True True	7"	Duke Reid	DR2518	1971	£6	£2.50	
Two Ton Guletto	7"	Jackpot	JP806	1972	£4	£1.50	
U Roy	LP	Attack	ATLP1006	1973	£15	£6	
Version Galore	7"	Duke Reid	DR2515	1970	£6	£2.50	*Tommy McCook B side*
Version Galore	LP	Trojan	TBL161	1971	£15	£6	*with other artists*
Version Galore	LP	Front Line	FL1018	1978	£12	£5	
Wake The Town	7"	Duke Reid	DR2509	1970	£6	£2.50	
Way Down South	7"	Pama	PM835	1972	£4	£1.50	*Billy Dyce B side*
Wear You To The Ball	7"	Duke Reid	DR2513	1970	£6	£2.50	*Earl Lindo B side*
Wedding	7"	Sioux	Si024	1972	£4	£1.50	*Lloyd's All Stars*
Whisper A Little Prayer	7"	Explosion	EX2040	1970	£4	£1.50	
You'll Never Get Away	7"	Duke Reid	DR2514	1970	£6	£2.50	*Tommy McCook B side*

ROY & ANNETTE

Title	Format	Label	Number	Year	Price	Price	Notes
My Baby	7"	R&B	JB107	1963	£10	£5	

ROY & ENID

Title	Format	Label	Number	Year	Price	Price	Notes
He'll Have To Go	7"	Coxsone	CS7069	1968	£10	£5	
Reggae For Days	7"	Coxsone	CS7088	1969	£10	£5	
Rockin' Time	7"	Coxsone	CS7063	1968	£10	£5	

ROY & MILLIE

Title	Format	Label	Number	Year	Price	Price	Notes
Cherry I Love You	7"	Black Swan	WI409	1964	£10	£5	

Oh Merna	7"	Black Swan	WI410	1964	£10	£5	*Don Drummond B side*
Oh Shirley	7"	Black Swan	WI427	1964	£10	£5	
Over And Over	7"	Blue Beat	BB154	1963	£12	£6	
There'll Come A Day	7"	Island	WI090	1963	£10	£5	
We'll Meet	7"	Island	WI005	1962	£10	£5	*Roland Alphonso B side*

ROY & PATSY

In Your Arms Dear	7"	Blue Beat	BB118	1962	£12	£6	

ROY & PAULINE

Have You Seen My Baby	7"	Island	WI067	1963	£10	£5	

ROY & THE DUKE ALL STARS

Pretty Blue Eyes	7"	Blue Cat	BS113	1968	£8	£4	
Train	7"	Blue Cat	BS117	1968	£8	£4	

ROY & YVONNE

Little Girl	7"	Blue Beat	BB258	1964	£12	£6	
Two Roads	7"	Black Swan	WI436	1964	£10	£5	

ROYAL, BILLY JOE

Down In The Boondocks	7"	CBS	201802	1965	£4	£1.50	
Down In The Boondocks	7" EP	CBS	6206	1965	£10	£5	*French*
Heart's Desire	7"	CBS	202087	1966	£20	£10	
Introducing Billy Joe Royal	LP	CBS	BPG62590	1966	£10	£4	
Never In A Hundred Years	7"	Oriole	CB1751	1962	£6	£2.50	
Yo Yo	7"	CBS	202548	1967	£4	£1.50	

ROYAL, JAMES

Call My Name	LP	CBS	63780	1967	£10	£4	
Hey Little Boy	7"	CBS	3450	1968	£6	£2.50	
Light And Shade	LP	Carnaby	CNLS6008	1971	£15	£6	
One Way	LP	Carnaby	CNLS6008	1970	£20	£8	
Send Out Love	7"	CBS	4463	1969	£5	£2	
She's About A Mover	7"	Parlophone	R5290	1965	£6	£2.50	
Woman Called Sorrow	7"	CBS	3624	1968	£6	£2.50	
Work Song	7"	Parlophone	R5383	1965	£8	£4	

ROYAL, ROBBIE

Only Me	7"	Mercury	MF923	1965	£4	£1.50	

ROYAL FLAIRS

Rare Recordings	LP	Unlimited Production	UPLP1007	1988	£12	£5	*US*

ROYAL GUARDSMEN

Return Of The Red Baron	LP	London	HAP/SHP8351	1968	£15	£6	
Snoopy And His Friends	LP	Laurie	(S)LLP2042	1967	£15	£6	*US*
Snoopy For President	LP	Laurie	SLLP2046	1968	£15	£6	*US*
Snoopy Vs The Red Baron	7"	Stateside	SS574	1967	£4	£1.50	
Snoopy Vs The Red Baron	7" EP	Vogue	INT18118	1967	£20	£10	*French*
Snoopy Vs The Red Baron	LP	Stateside	(S)SL10202	1967	£15	£6	
Wednesday	7"	Stateside	SS2051	1967	£4	£1.50	

ROYAL HOLIDAYS

Margaret	7"	London	HLU8722	1958	£60	£30	

ROYAL JOKERS

Rock And Roll Spectacular	LP	Dawn	1119	195–	£25	£10	*US*

ROYAL PLAYBOYS

Spirituals And Jubilees	10" LP	Waldorf	33136	195–	£20	£8	*US*

ROYAL ROCKERS

Jet II	7"	Top Rank	JAR329	1960	£6	£2.50	

ROYAL SERVANTS

We	LP	Elite	PLPS30130	1969	£25	£10	*German*

ROYAL TEENS

Little Cricket	7"	Capitol	CL15068	1959	£12	£6	
Music Gems	LP	Tru-Gems	TG1001	1966	£25	£10	*US*
Newies But Oldies	LP	Musicor	MS3186	1969	£25	£10	*US*
Short Shorts	7"	HMV	POP454	1958	£25	£12.50	

ROYALETTES

Elegant Sound Of The Royalettes	LP	MGM	C8028	1966	£40	£20	
I Want To Meet Him	7"	MGM	MGM1292	1965	£10	£5	
It's A Big Mistake	7"	MGM	MGM1324	1966	£6	£2.50	
It's Gonna Take A Miracle	7"	MGM	MGM1279	1965	£15	£7.50	
It's Gonna Take A Miracle	LP	MGM	(S)E4332	1965	£40	£20	*US*
Poor Boy	7"	MGM	MGM1272	1965	£6	£2.50	
River Of Tears	7"	Transatlantic	BIG106	1968	£6	£2.50	
You Bring Me Down	7"	MGM	MGM1302	1966	£10	£5	

ROYALS

Israel Be Wise	LP	Ballistic	UAG30206	1978	**£12**	**£5**	
Never Gonna Give You Up	7"	Duke	DU29	1969	**£5**	**£2**	
Never See Come See	7"	Amalgamated	AMG831	1968	**£8**	**£4**	*Cannonball Bryan B side*
Pick Out Me Eye	7"	Trojan	TR662	1969	**£6**	**£2.50**	
Pick Up The Pieces	LP	Magnum	DEAD1004	1977	**£12**	**£5**	
Save Mama	7"	Blue Beat	BB259	1964	**£12**	**£6**	
Ten Years After	LP	United Artists	UAS30189	1978	**£12**	**£5**	

ROYALTONES

Flamingo Express	7"	London	HLU9296	1961	**£8**	**£4**	
Holy Smokes	7"	Stateside	SS309	1964	**£6**	**£2.50**	
Poor Boy	7"	London	HLJ8744	1958	**£10**	**£5**	

ROYCE, EARL & THE OLYMPICS

Guess Things Happen That Way	7"	Parlophone	R5261	1965	**£10**	**£5**	
Que Sera Sera	7"	Columbia	DB7433	1964	**£10**	**£5**	

ROZA, LITA

Bell Bottom Blues	7"	Decca	F10269	1954	**£6**	**£2.50**	
Between The Devil And The Deep Blue Sea	7" EP	Decca	DFE6443	1957	**£15**	**£7.50**	
Between The Devil And The Deep Blue Sea	LP	Decca	LK4218	1957	**£25**	**£10**	
But Love Me	7"	Decca	F10761	1956	**£4**	**£1.50**	
Changing Partners	7"	Decca	F10240	1954	**£5**	**£2**	
Drinka Lita Roza Day	LP	Pye	NPL18047	1960	**£20**	**£8**	
Heartbeat	7"	Decca	F10427	1954	**£5**	**£2**	
Hey There	7"	Decca	F10611	1955	**£8**	**£4**	
How Much Is That Doggie In The Window	7"	Decca	F75082	1953	**£25**	**£12.50**	*export*
Innismore	7"	Decca	F10792	1956	**£4**	**£1.50**	
Jimmy Unknown	7"	Decca	F10679	1956	**£8**	**£4**	
Julie	7"	Decca	F10830	1956	**£4**	**£1.50**	
Let Me Go Lover	7"	Decca	F10431	1955	**£5**	**£2**	
Listening In The After Hours	10" LP	Decca	LF1243	1956	**£30**	**£15**	
Lita Roza	7" EP	Decca	DFE6399	1957	**£15**	**£7.50**	
Love Is The Answer	LP	Decca	LK4171	1957	**£25**	**£10**	
Love Songs For Night People	LP	Ember	NR5009	1964	**£10**	**£4**	
Lucky Lips	7"	Decca	F10861	1957	**£5**	**£2**	
Mama Doll Song	7"	Decca	F10393	1954	**£4**	**£1.50**	
Man In The Raincoat	7"	Decca	F10541	1955	**£4**	**£1.50**	
Me On A Carousel	LP	Pye	NPL18020/ NSPL83003	1958	**£15**	**£6**	
Presenting	10" LP	Decca	LF1187	1954	**£30**	**£15**	
Secret Love	7"	Decca	F10277	1954	**£5**	**£2**	
Selection	7" EP	Decca	DFE6386	1956	**£20**	**£10**	
Tomorrow	7"	Decca	F10479	1955	**£5**	**£2**	
Tonight My Heart She Is Crying	7"	Decca	F10884	1957	**£4**	**£1.50**	
Too Young To Go Steady	7"	Decca	F10728	1956	**£4**	**£1.50**	
Two Hearts, Two Kisses	7"	Decca	F10536	1955	**£5**	**£2**	

R.U.1.2.

She's Gone	7"	SRT	SRTS78CUS131	1978	**£5**	**£2**	

RUB-A-DUBS

Without Love	7"	Blue Beat	BB304	1965	**£12**	**£6**	

RUBAIYATS

Omar Khayam	7"	Action	ACT4516	1968	**£5**	**£2**	

RUBBER BAND

Cream Song Book	LP	Major Minor	SMLP5045	1969	**£10**	**£4**	
Hendrix Song Book	LP	Major Minor	SMLP5048	1969	**£10**	**£4**	

RUBBER BOOTZ

Joy Ride	7"	Deram	DM134	1967	**£5**	**£2**	

RUBBER BUCKET

The Rubber Bucket single is actually the work of Gary Glitter.

We Are Living In One Place	7"	MCA	MK5006	1969	**£8**	**£4**	

RUBBER MEMORY

Welcome	LP	RPC	69401	1966	**£25**	**£10**	*US*

RUBEN & THE JETS

Con Safos	LP	Mercury	SRM1694	1973	**£12**	**£5**	*US*
For Real	LP	Mercury	SRM1659	1973	**£15**	**£6**	*US*

RUBY & THE ROMANTICS

Baby Come Home	7"	London	HLR9916	1964	**£6**	**£2.50**	
Greatest Hits	LP	London	HAR8282	1966	**£30**	**£15**	
Hey There Lonely Boy	7"	London	HLR9771	1963	**£8**	**£4**	
Hey There Lonely Boy	7" EP	London	RER1427	1964	**£50**	**£25**	

Title	Format	Label	Cat. No.	Year	Mint	VG	Notes
More Than Yesterday	LP	ABC	S638	1968	**£25**	**£10**	*US*
My Summer Love	7"	London	HLR9734	1963	**£6**	**£2.50**	
Our Day Will Come	7"	London	HLR9679	1963	**£5**	**£2**	
Our Day Will Come	7" EP	London	RER1389	1963	**£50**	**£25**	
Our Day Will Come	LP	London	HAR8078	1963	**£40**	**£20**	
Our Everlasting Love	7"	London	HLR9881	1964	**£5**	**£2**	
Ruby And The Romantics	LP	Kapp	KL1526/KS3526	1967	**£25**	**£10**	*US*
Till Then	LP	Kapp	KL1341/KS3341	1963	**£40**	**£20**	*US*
When You're Young And In Love	7"	London	HLR9935	1964	**£6**	**£2.50**	
Young Wings Can Fly	7"	London	HLR9801	1963	**£6**	**£2.50**	
Your Baby Doesn't Love You Anymore	7"	London	HLR9972	1965	**£8**	**£4**	

RUDE BOYS

Title	Format	Label	Cat. No.	Year	Mint	VG	Notes
Rock Steady Massachusetts	7"	Island	WI3088	1967	**£10**	**£5**	

RUDIES

Title	Format	Label	Cat. No.	Year	Mint	VG	Notes
7-11	7"	Blue Cat	BS107	1968	**£8**	**£4**	
Brixton Market	7"	Fab	FAB104	1969	**£4**	**£1.50**	
Cupid	7"	Blue Cat	BS109	1968	**£8**	**£4**	*Rico B side*
Engine 59	7"	Nu Beat	NB005	1968	**£4**	**£1.50**	
Give Me The Rights	7"	Fab	FAB70	1968	**£4**	**£1.50**	
I Wanna Go Home	7"	Fab	FAB46	1968	**£5**	**£2**	
Mighty Meaty	7"	Fab	FAB71	1968	**£4**	**£1.50**	
Train To Vietnam	7"	Nu Beat	NB001	1968	**£5**	**£2**	

RUDIMENTARY PENI

Title	Format	Label	Cat. No.	Year	Mint	VG	Notes
Farce	7"	Crass	2119842	1982	**£5**	**£2**	
Media Person	7"	Outer Himalayan	OH003	1981	**£6**	**£2.50**	

RUDY & SKETTO

Title	Format	Label	Cat. No.	Year	Mint	VG	Notes
ABC Boogie	7"	Dice	CC2	1962	**£10**	**£5**	
Hold The Fire	7"	Dice	CC16	1963	**£10**	**£5**	
Little Schoolgirl	7"	Dice	CC7	1962	**£10**	**£5**	
Minna	7"	Blue Beat	BB252	1964	**£12**	**£6**	
Mr Postman	7"	Dice	CC10	1963	**£10**	**£5**	
Oh Dolly	7"	Blue Beat	BB310	1965	**£12**	**£6**	
See What You Done	7"	Blue Beat	BB297	1965	**£12**	**£6**	
Show Me The Way To Go Home	7"	Blue Beat	BB208	1964	**£12**	**£6**	
Summer Is Just Around The Corner	7"	Dice	CC5	1962	**£10**	**£5**	
Ten Thousand Miles From Home	7"	Blue Beat	BB230	1964	**£12**	**£6**	
Was It Me	7"	Blue Beat	BB198	1963	**£12**	**£6**	
We Are So Happy	7"	Dice	CC19	1963	**£10**	**£5**	

RUFF, RAY & THE CHECKMATES

Title	Format	Label	Cat. No.	Year	Mint	VG	Notes
I Took A Liking To You	7"	London	HLU9889	1964	**£12**	**£6**	

RUFFIANS

Title	Format	Label	Cat. No.	Year	Mint	VG	Notes
Room Full Of Tears	7"	Banana	BA369	1971	**£5**	**£2**	

RUFFIN, BRUCE

Title	Format	Label	Cat. No.	Year	Mint	VG	Notes
Bruce Ruffin	LP	Rhino	SRNO8001	1972	**£10**	**£4**	
Candida	7"	Summit	SUM8516	1971	**£4**	**£1.50**	
Cecilia	7"	Trojan	TR7776	1970	**£4**	**£1.50**	*Beverley All Stars B side*
Dry Up Your Tears	7"	Trojan	TR7704	1969	**£4**	**£1.50**	*Beverley All Stars B side*
I'm The One	7"	Trojan	TR7737	1970	**£4**	**£1.50**	
Long About Now	7"	Songbird	SB1002	1969	**£4**	**£1.50**	
O-o-h Child	7"	Summit	SUM8509	1970	**£4**	**£1.50**	
Rain	LP	Trojan	TRL23	1971	**£12**	**£5**	

RUFFIN, DAVID

Title	Format	Label	Cat. No.	Year	Mint	VG	Notes
Feelin' Good	LP	Tamla Motown	(S)TML11139	1970	**£15**	**£6**	
I've Lost Everything I Ever Loved	7"	Tamla Motown	TMG711	1969	**£4**	**£1.50**	
My Whole World Ended	7"	Tamla Motown	TMG689	1969	**£4**	**£1.50**	
My Whole World Ended	LP	Tamla Motown	(S)TML11118	1969	**£20**	**£8**	

RUFFIN, JIMMY

Title	Format	Label	Cat. No.	Year	Mint	VG	Notes
Don't Let Him Take Your Love From Me	7"	Tamla Motown	TMG664	1968	**£4**	**£1.50**	
Don't You Miss Me A Little Bit Baby	7"	Tamla Motown	TMG617	1967	**£5**	**£2**	
Forever	LP	Tamla Motown	STML11161	1970	**£15**	**£6**	
Gonna Give Her All The Love I Got	7"	Tamla Motown	TMG603	1967	**£4**	**£1.50**	
I Am My Brother's Keeper	LP	Tamla Motown	STML11176	1971	**£12**	**£5**	*with David Ruffin*
I'll Say Forever My Love	7"	Tamla Motown	TMG649	1968	**£4**	**£1.50**	
I've Passed This Way Before	7"	Tamla Motown	TMG593	1967	**£5**	**£2**	

Title	Format	Label	Cat. No.	Year	Mint	VG	Notes
Jimmy Ruffin Way	LP	Tamla Motown	(S)TML11048	1967	£**20**	£**8**	
Ruff 'n' Ready	LP	Tamla Motown	(S)TML11106	1969	£**15**	£**6**	
What Becomes Of The Broken Hearted	7"	Tamla Motown	TMG577	1966	£**4**	£**1.50**	

RUFUS

Title	Format	Label	Cat. No.	Year	Mint	VG	Notes
Rufus With Chaka Khan	LP	ABC	ABCL5151	1975	£**10**	£**4**	

RUFUS ZUPHALL

Title	Format	Label	Cat. No.	Year	Mint	VG	Notes
Phallobst	LP	Pilz	20210995	1971	£**30**	£**15**	*German*
Weiss Der Teufel	LP	Good Will	GLS10001	1969	£**150**	£**75**	*German*

RUGBYS

Title	Format	Label	Cat. No.	Year	Mint	VG	Notes
Hot Cargo	LP	Amazon	1000	1969	£**30**	£**15**	*US*
Wendegahl The Warlock	7"	Polydor	56789	1970	£**6**	£**2.50**	
You And I	7"	Polydor	56781	1969	£**30**	£**15**	

RUGOLO, PETE

Title	Format	Label	Cat. No.	Year	Mint	VG	Notes
Adventures In Rhythm	LP	Philips	BBL7035	1955	£**12**	£**5**	
Behind Brigitte Bardot	LP	Warner Bros	WM4001/ WS8001	1960	£**10**	£**4**	
Music From Richard Diamond	LP	Mercury	MMC14034/ CMS18025	1960	£**12**	£**5**	
Out On A Limb	LP	Emarcy	EJL1274	1958	£**10**	£**4**	
Percussion At Work	LP	Mercury	MMB12004	1959	£**10**	£**4**	
Pete Rugolo	LP	Philips	BBL7069	1956	£**12**	£**5**	
Pete Rugolo And His Orchestra	10" LP	Philips	BBR8024	1954	£**10**	£**4**	
Pete Rugolo Orchestra	LP	Emarcy	EJL1254	1957	£**12**	£**5**	
Reeds In Hi Fi	LP	Mercury	MMC14012	1959	£**10**	£**4**	
Rugolo Plays Kenton	LP	Mercury	BMS17000	1959	£**15**	£**6**	
Rugolo Plays Kenton	LP	Mercury	MMB12011	1959	£**10**	£**4**	

RULERS

Title	Format	Label	Cat. No.	Year	Mint	VG	Notes
Copasetic	7"	Rio	R107	1966	£**10**	£**5**	
Don't Be A Rude Boy	7"	Rio	R105	1966	£**8**	£**4**	
Got To Be Free	7"	Trojan	TR696	1969	£**4**	£**1.50**	
Well Covered	7"	Rio	R135	1967	£**8**	£**4**	*Carl Dawkins B side*
Wrong Embryo	7"	Rio	R132	1967	£**8**	£**4**	

RUMBLERS

Title	Format	Label	Cat. No.	Year	Mint	VG	Notes
Boss	7"	London	HLD9684	1963	£**12**	£**6**	
Bossounds	7" EP	London	RED1396	1963	£**100**	£**50**	
Bossounds	LP	London	HAD/SHD8081	1963	£**75**	£**37.50**	
Soulful Jerk	7"	King	KG1021	1965	£**25**	£**12.50**	

RUMPLESTILTSKIN

Title	Format	Label	Cat. No.	Year	Mint	VG	Notes
Rumplestiltskin	LP	Bell	SBLL130	1970	£**30**	£**15**	

RUMPO, SID

Title	Format	Label	Cat. No.	Year	Mint	VG	Notes
First Offence	LP	Mushroom	35109	1971	£**25**	£**10**	*Australian*

RUMSEY, HOWARD

Title	Format	Label	Cat. No.	Year	Mint	VG	Notes
Howard Rumsey's Lighthouse All Stars	10" LP	Contemporary	LDC187	1956	£**25**	£**10**	
Howard Rumsey's Lighthouse All Stars	LP	Contemporary	LAC12055	1957	£**20**	£**8**	
Howard Rumsey's Lighthouse All-Stars	10" LP	Vogue	EPC1175	1953	£**25**	£**10**	
Jazz Rolls Royce	LP	Colrich	XSD5	1959	£**10**	£**4**	
Lighthouse All Stars	10" LP	Contemporary	LDC152	1955	£**25**	£**10**	
Lighthouse All Stars	10" LP	Contemporary	LDC146	1955	£**25**	£**10**	
Lighthouse All Stars Vol. 3	LP	Contemporary	LAC12182	1960	£**12**	£**5**	
Lighthouse At Laguna	LP	Contemporary	LAC12125	1959	£**15**	£**6**	
Music For Lighthousekeeping	LP	Contemporary	LAC12086	1958	£**15**	£**6**	
Oboe – Flute	LP	Contemporary	LAC12146	1959	£**15**	£**6**	
Sunday Jazz A La Lighthouse Vol. 1	LP	Contemporary	LAC12120	1958	£**15**	£**6**	

RUN 229

Title	Format	Label	Cat. No.	Year	Mint	VG	Notes
Soho	7"	MM	JR7040S	1980	£**15**	£**7.50**	

RUNAWAYS

Title	Format	Label	Cat. No.	Year	Mint	VG	Notes
And Now . . . The Runaways	LP	Cherry Red	ARED38	1979	£**12**	£**5**	*blue, orange, red, or yellow vinyl*
Little Lost Girls	LP	Rhino	RNDF250	1981	£**10**	£**4**	*US picture disc*
Right Now	7"	Cherry Red	CHERRY8	1979	£**6**	£**2.50**	*picture sleeve*
Runaways	LP	Mercury	9100029	1976	£**10**	£**4**	*orange vinyl*
School Days	7"	Mercury	6167587	1977	£**4**	£**1.50**	

RUNDGREN, TODD

Title	Format	Label	Cat. No.	Year	Mint	VG	Notes
Back To The Bars	LP	Bearsville	PROA788	1978	£**25**	£**10**	*US promo, with Patti Smith*
Ballad Of Todd Rundgren	LP	Bearsville	K45506	1971	£**10**	£**4**	
Oops! Wrong Planet	CD	Mobile Fidelity		1995	£**15**	£**6**	*US audiophile*
Runt	LP	Bearsville	K45505	1970	£**10**	£**4**	
Something/Anything	LP	Bearsville	2BR2066	1972	£**75**	£**37.50**	*US double promo, 1 red, 1 blue vinyl*
Something/Anything	CD	Mobile Fidelity	UDCD2591	1994	£**15**	£**6**	*US audiophile*

Todd Rundgren Radio Show	LP	Bearsville	PRO524	1972	**£30**	**£15**	*US promo*
Todd Rundgren Radio Show	LP	Bearsville	PRO597	1974	**£25**	**£10**	*US promo*
Wizard A True Star	LP	Bearsville	K45513	1973	**£10**	**£4**	

RUNNING MAN

Running Man	LP	Neon	NE11	1972	**£125**	**£62.50**	

RUNRIG

Alba	7"	Ridge	RRS007	1987	**£10**	**£5**	
Capture The Heart	10"	Chrysalis	CHS103594	1990	**£8**	**£4**	
Capture The Heart	CD-s	Chrysalis	CHSCD3594	1990	**£6**	**£2.50**	
Cutter And The Clan	CD	Chrysalis	CD25CR17	1994	**£12**	**£5**	*Chrysalis 25 pack*
Dance Called America	12"	Simple	12SIM4	1987	**£15**	**£7.50**	
Dance Called America	7"	Simple	SIM4	1987	**£8**	**£4**	
Every River	12"	Chrysalis	CHS123451	1989	**£10**	**£5**	
Every River	CD-s	Chrysalis	CHSCD3451	1989	**£15**	**£7.50**	
Flower Of The West	CD-s	Chrysalis	CHSCD3805	1991	**£8**	**£4**	
Hearthammer	CD-s	Chrysalis	CHSGCD3754	1991	**£6**	**£2.50**	
Highland Connection	LP	Ridge	RR001	1979	**£10**	**£4**	
Loch Lomond	7"	Ridge	RRS003	1982	**£12**	**£6**	
News From Heaven	12"	Chrysalis	CHS123404	1989	**£12**	**£6**	*picture disc*
News From Heaven	12"	Chrysalis	CHS123404	1989	**£8**	**£4**	
News From Heaven	CD-s	Chrysalis	CHSCD3404	1989	**£15**	**£7.50**	
Protect And Survive	12"	Chrysalis	CHS123284	1988	**£10**	**£5**	
Protect And Survive	7"	Chrysalis	CHS3284	1988	**£8**	**£4**	
Protect And Survive	CD-s	Chrysalis	CHSCD3284	1990	**£15**	**£7.50**	
Runrig Play Gaelic	LP	Neptune	NA105	1978	**£15**	**£6**	
Skye	7"	Simple	SIM8	1984	**£15**	**£7.50**	
Work Song	7"	Ridge	RRS006	1986	**£15**	**£7.50**	

RUPERT'S PEOPLE

I Can Show You	7"	Columbia	DB8362	1968	**£60**	**£30**	
Prologue To A Magic World	7"	Columbia	DB8278	1967	**£60**	**£30**	
Reflections Of Charles Brown	7"	Columbia	DB8226	1967	**£20**	**£10**	

RUSH

2112	CD	Mobile Fidelity	UDCD590	1993	**£15**	**£6**	*US audiophile*
All The World's A Stage	LP	Mercury	6672015	1977	**£15**	**£6**	*double with photo page*
Big Money	12"	Vertigo	RUSHG12	1985	**£6**	**£2.50**	
Big Money	CD-s	Polygram	0800842	1989	**£40**	**£20**	*CD video*
Body Electric	10"	Mercury	RUSH1110	1984	**£10**	**£5**	*red vinyl*
Body Electric	12"	Vertigo	RUSH1112	1984	**£30**	**£15**	
Closer To The Heart	12"	Mercury	RUSH12	1978	**£8**	**£4**	
Countdown	7"	Mercury	RUSHP10	1982	**£20**	**£10**	*shaped picture disc*
Everything You Always Wanted To Hear	LP	Mercury	MK32	1975	**£15**	**£6**	*US promo*
Ghost Of A Chance	CD-s	Atlantic	A7491CD	1992	**£5**	**£2**	
Hemispheres	LP	Mercury	9100059	1978	**£12**	**£5**	*picture disc*
Moving Pictures	CD	Mobile Fidelity	UDCD569	1992	**£15**	**£6**	*US audiophile*
Not Fade Away	7"	Moon	MN001	1973	**£200**	**£100**	*Canadian, best auctioned*
Power Windows	LP	Vertigo	VERHP31	1985	**£15**	**£6**	*picture disc*
Prime Mover	CD-s	Vertigo	RUSHCD14	1988	**£6**	**£2.50**	
Profiled!	CD	Atlantic		1990	**£20**	**£8**	*US promo*
Rush	LP	Moon			**£125**	**£62.50**	*Canadian*
Rush 'n' Roulette	12"	Mercury		1982	**£20**	**£10**	*US promo, 6 tracks running simultaneously*
Rush Through Time	LP	Mercury	001	1978	**£25**	**£10**	*US promo picture disc*
Signals	CD	Mobile Fidelity	UDCD614	1994	**£15**	**£6**	*US audiophile*
Spirit Of Radio	12"	Mercury	RADIO12	1980	**£6**	**£2.50**	
Subdivisions	7"	Mercury	RUSHP9	1982	**£6**	**£2.50**	*picture disc*
Time Stand Still	CD-s	Vertigo	RUSHCD13	1987	**£6**	**£2.50**	

RUSH (2)

Make Mine Music	7"	Decca	F12635	1967	**£4**	**£1.50**	

RUSH, OTIS

All Your Love	7"	Blue Horizon	573159	1969	**£10**	**£5**	
Groaning The Blues	LP	Python	KM3	1970	**£25**	**£10**	
Homework	7"	Vocalion	VP9260	1966	**£15**	**£7.50**	
Mourning In The Morning	LP	Atlantic	588188	1969	**£25**	**£10**	
This One's A Good Un	LP	Blue Horizon	763222	1968	**£50**	**£25**	

RUSH, TOM

At The Unicorn	LP	Ly Cornu	SA702	1962	**£50**	**£25**	*US*
Blues And Folk	LP	XTRA	XTRA5024	1966	**£15**	**£6**	
Circle Game	LP	Elektra	EKL/EKS74018	1968	**£12**	**£5**	
Classic Rush	LP	Elektra	EKL/EKS74062	1969	**£10**	**£4**	
I Got A Mind To Ramble	LP	XTRA	XTRA5053	1968	**£15**	**£6**	
Long John	7" EP	Vogue	INT18040	1965	**£10**	**£5**	*French*
Mind Ramblin'	LP	Prestige	14003	1963	**£15**	**£6**	*US*
No Regrets	7"	Elektra	EKSN45025	1968	**£4**	**£1.50**	
On The Road Again	7"	Elektra	EKSN45015	1967	**£4**	**£1.50**	

Something In The Way She Moves Me	7"	Elektra	EKSN45032	1968	£4	£1.50	
Take A Little Walk With Me	LP	Elektra	EKL/EKS7308	1966	£20	£8	
Tom Rush	LP	Elektra	EKL288	1965	£12	£5	
Who Do You Love	7"	Elektra	EKSN45005	1967	£4	£1.50	

RUSHING, JIMMY

And The Big Brass	LP	Philips	BBL7252/ SBBL524	1958	£15	£6	
Blues I Love To Sing	LP	Ace Of Hearts	AH119	1966	£10	£4	
Cat Meets Chick	7" EP	Philips	BBE12150	1957	£8	£4	*with Ada Moore*
Cat Meets Chick	LP	Philips	BBL7105	1957	£15	£6	*with Ada Moore*
Every Day I Have The Blues	LP	HMV	CLP/CSD3632	1967	£10	£4	
If This Ain't The Blues	LP	Vanguard	PPL11008	1958	£15	£6	
Jazz Odyssey	LP	Philips	BBL7166	1957	£15	£6	
Jimmy Rushing	7" EP	Ember	EMBEP4523	1962	£5	£2	
Jimmy Rushing	7" EP	Parlophone	GEP8597	1957	£6	£2.50	
Listen To The Blues	LP	Fontana	FJL405	1967	£10	£4	
Little Jimmy All Star Band	7" EP	Vanguard	EPP14003	1957	£6	£2.50	
Rushing Lullabies	LP	Philips	BBL7360	1960	£15	£6	
Showcase	10" LP	Vanguard	PPT12016	1957	£20	£8	
Sings The Blues	10" LP	Vanguard	PPT12002	1955	£25	£10	
Smith Girls – Bessie, Clara	LP	Philips	BBL7484/ SBBL631	1961	£15	£6	
Way I Feel	7" EP	Parlophone	GEP8695	1958	£6	£2.50	

RUSKIN, BARBARA

Come Into My Arms Again	7"	Parlophone	R5642	1967	£4	£1.50	
Euston Station	7"	Parlophone	R5593	1967	£4	£1.50	
Halfway To Paradise	7"	Piccadilly	7N35224	1965	£4	£1.50	
Light Of Love	7"	Piccadilly	7N35328	1966	£4	£1.50	
Song Without End	7"	Piccadilly	7N35296	1966	£4	£1.50	
Take It Easy	7"	Parlophone	R5571	1967	£4	£1.50	
Well How Does It Feel	7"	Piccadilly	7N35274	1966	£4	£1.50	
You Can't Blame A Girl For Trying	7"	Piccadilly	7N35246	1965	£4	£1.50	

RUSSAL, THANE

Drop Everything And Run	7"	CBS	202403	1966	£60	£30	
Security	7"	CBS	202049	1966	£125	£62.50	*picture sleeve*
Security	7"	CBS	202049	1966	£60	£30	

RUSSELL, CONNIE

Ayuh Ayuh	7"	Capitol	CL14236	1955	£6	£2.50	
Farewell Farewell	7"	Capitol	CL14268	1955	£4	£1.50	
Foggy Night In San Francisco	7"	Capitol	CL14214	1955	£4	£1.50	
Green Fire	7"	Capitol	CL14246	1955	£4	£1.50	
Love Me	7"	Capitol	CL14197	1954	£4	£1.50	
No One But You	7"	Capitol	CL14171	1954	£5	£2	

RUSSELL, DOROTHY

You're The One I Love	7"	Duke Reid	DR2524	1971	£4	£1.50	

RUSSELL, GEORGE

At Beethoven Hall	LP	Polydor	583706	1965	£12	£5	
Ezz-thetics	LP	Riverside	RLP375	1961	£15	£6	
Jazz Workshop	LP	RCA	RD7511	1962	£15	£6	
New York, N.Y.	LP	Brunswick	LAT8333	1960	£20	£8	
Outer View	LP	Fontana	688705ZL	1964	£12	£5	
Stratus Seekers	LP	Riverside	RLP(9)412	1962	£12	£5	

RUSSELL, JANE

If You Wanna See Mamie Tonight	7"	Capitol	CL14590	1956	£6	£2.50	
Jane Russell	7" EP	MGM	MGMEP702	1959	£15	£7.50	
Please Do It Again	7"	Columbia	SCM5043	1953	£8	£4	

RUSSELL, JOHNNY

Lonesome Boy	7"	MGM	MGM1074	1960	£4	£1.50	

RUSSELL, LEON

Everybody's Talkin' 'Bout The Young	7"	Pye	7N16771	1965	£6	£2.50	
Leon Russell	LP	Shelter	SHE1001	1968	£10	£4	*US, extra track*

RUSSELL, MICHO

Traditional Country Music Of County Clare	LP	Free Reed	FRR004	1976	£10	£4	

RUSSELL, PEE WEE & RUBY BRAFF

Jazz At Storyville Vol. 2	LP	London	LTZC15061	1957	£15	£6	

RUSSELL, RAY

Dragon Hill	LP	CBS	52663	1969	£25	£10	
Illusions	LP	Music House	MHA4	197–	£15	£6	
June 11th 1971	LP	RCA	SF8214	1971	£20	£8	
Master Format	LP	JW Music Library		197–	£15	£6	
Rites And Rituals	LP	CBS	64271	1971	£25	£10	
Secret Asylum	LP	Black Lion	2460207	1973	£15	£6	
Turn Circle	LP	CBS	52586	1968	£25	£10	

RUSSELL, ROLAND

Rhythm Hips ... 7" ... Nu Beat ... NB019 ... 1968 **£5** ... **£2**

RUSSELL FAMILY

Of Doolin County Clare ... LP ... Topic ... 12TS251 ... 1975 **£10** ... **£4**

RUSSO, WILLIAM

Three Pieces For Blues Band & Symphony Orchestra ... LP ... Deutsche Grammophon ... 2530309 ... 197– **£15** ... **£6** ... *with Siegel–Schwall Band*

RUST

Come With Me ... LP ... Hör Zu ... SHZEL59 ... 1969 **£20** ... **£8** ... *German*

RUSTIKS

What A Memory Can Do ... 7" ... Decca ... F11960 ... 1964 **£4** ... **£1.50**

RUSTLERS

High Strung ... 7" ... Pye ... 7N15398 ... 1961 **£4** ... **£1.50**

RUSTY & DOUG

Cajun Joe ... 7" ... Fontana ... 267238TF ... 1962 **£8** ... **£4**
Hey Mae ... 7" ... Oriole ... CB1510 ... 1959 **£125** .. **£62.50**
Hey Mae ... 7" ... Polydor ... NH66970 ... 1962 **£30** ... **£15**
I Like You ... 7" ... London ... HL8972 ... 1959 **£20** ... **£10**

RUSTY HARNESS

Ain't Gonna Get Married ... 7" ... Ember ... EMBS283 ... 1970 **£6** ... **£2.50** ... *picture sleeve*

RUTLES

The Rutles album and its accompanying television programme is an affectionate parody by Neil Innes and Eric Idle of the career of the Beatles. The cover of the LP is almost better than the music inside – it displays numerous photographs of album sleeves and group portraits that exactly mirror originals featuring the Beatles. The music is cleverly constructed to be reminiscent of key songs by the Beatles, although ultimately Neil Innes's re-creations are rather less skilful than those put together by XTC on their Dukes of Stratosfear albums.

Rutles ... LP ... Warner Bros ... K56459 ... 1978 **£10** ... **£4**
Rutles Sampler ... 12" ... Warner Bros ... PROA723 ... 1978 **£10** ... **£5** ... *US promo, yellow vinyl*

RUTS

In A Rut ... 7" ... People Unite ... SJP795 ... 1979 **£15** ... **£7.50**
Stepping Bondage ... 7" ... Bohemian ... BO4 ... 1983 **£8** ... **£4**
Weak Heart ... 7" ... Bohemian ... BO3 ... 1983 **£10** ... **£5** ... *promo*
Whatever We Do ... 7" ... Bohemian ... BO2 ... 1982 **£8** ... **£4**

RYAN, BARRY

Barry Ryan ... LP ... Polydor ... 583067 ... 1969 **£10** ... **£4**
Sings Paul Ryan ... LP ... MGM ... CS8106 ... 1968 **£15** ... **£6**

RYAN, CHARLIE

Hot Rod ... LP ... King ... 751 ... 1961 **£20** ... **£8** ... *US*

RYAN, KRIS

Don't Play That Song ... 7" ... Mercury ... MF832 ... 1964 **£4** ... **£1.50**

RYAN, KRIS & THE QUESTIONS

On The Right Track ... 7" EP .. Mercury ... 10024MCE ... 1965 **£25** ... **£10**

RYAN, MARION

Better Use Your Head ... 7" ... Philips ... BF1721 ... 1968 **£5** ... **£2**
Hit Parade ... 7" EP .. Pye ... NEP24079 ... 1958 **£15** ... **£7.50**
Jo-Jo The Dog Faced Boy ... 7" ... Pye ... 7N15200 ... 1959 **£4** ... **£1.50**
Lady Loves ... LP ... Pye ... NPL18030 ... 1959 **£30** ... **£15** ... *mono*
Lady Loves ... LP ... Pye ... NSPL18030 ... 1959 **£40** ... **£20** ... *stereo*
Love Me Forever ... 7" ... Pye ... 7N15121 ... 1958 **£5** ... **£2**
Oh Oh I'm Falling In Love Again ... 7" ... Pye ... 7N15130 ... 1958 **£4** ... **£1.50**
Stairway Of Love ... 7" ... Pye ... 7N15138 ... 1958 **£4** ... **£1.50**
That Ryan Gal ... 7" EP .. Pye ... NEP24041 ... 1957 **£20** ... **£10**
World Goes Around And Around ... 7" ... Pye ... 7NSR15157 ... 1958 **£6** ... **£2.50** ... *stereo*

RYAN, PAT

Lea Boy's Lassie ... LP ... Folk Heritage ... FHR094 ... 1977 **£12** ... **£5**

RYAN, PAUL & BARRY

Claire ... 7" ... Decca ... F12633 ... 1967 **£4** ... **£1.50**
Paul And Barry Ryan ... LP ... MGM ... C(S)8081 ... 1968 **£15** ... **£6**
Two Of A Kind ... LP ... Decca ... LK4878 ... 1967 **£20** ... **£8**

RYAN, PHIL & THE CRESCENTS

Gypsy Woman ... 7" ... Columbia ... DB7574 ... 1965 **£8** ... **£4**
Mary Don't You Weep ... 7" ... Columbia ... DB7406 ... 1964 **£4** ... **£1.50**

RYDELL, BOBBY

All The Hits ... LP ... Cameo Parkway ... C1019 ... 1962 **£15** ... **£6**
All The Hits Vol. 2 ... LP ... Cameo Parkway ... C1040 ... 1963 **£15** ... **£6**

At The Copa	LP	Columbia	33SX1425	1962	**£40**	**£20**	
Best Of Bobby Rydell	7″ EP	Summit	LSE2036	1963	**£6**	**£2.50**	
Biggest Hits	LP	Cameo	C1009	1961	**£15**	**£6**	*US, gatefold*
Biggest Hits Vol. 2	LP	Cameo	C1028	1962	**£15**	**£6**	*US*
Bobby Rydell	7″ EP	Cameo Parkway	CPE553	1963	**£15**	**£7.50**	
Bye Bye Birdie	LP	Cameo Parkway	C1043	1963	**£10**	**£4**	
Forget Him	7″	Cameo Parkway	C108	1963	**£5**	**£2**	*picture sleeve*
Kissin' Time	7″	Top Rank	JAR181	1959	**£6**	**£2.50**	
Lovingest	7″ EP	Top Rank	JKP2059	1960	**£25**	**£12.50**	
Salutes The Great Ones	LP	Columbia	33SX1352	1961	**£12**	**£5**	
Sings And Swings	LP	Columbia	33SX1308	1960	**£15**	**£6**	
Somebody Loves You	LP	Capitol	T2281	1965	**£10**	**£4**	
Sway With Bobby Rydell	7″ EP	Cameo Parkway	CPE551	1963	**£15**	**£7.50**	
Swinging School	7″	Columbia	DB4471	1960	**£4**	**£1.50**	
Volare	7″	Columbia	DB4495	1960	**£4**	**£1.50**	
We Got Love	7″	Top Rank	JAR227	1959	**£5**	**£2**	
We Got Love	LP	Cameo	C1006	1959	**£25**	**£10**	*US*
When I See That Girl Of Mine	7″	Capitol	CL15424	1965	**£4**	**£1.50**	
Wild (Wood) Days	LP	Cameo	C1055	1963	**£15**	**£6**	
Wild One	7″	Columbia	DB4429	1960	**£4**	**£1.50**	
Wild One	LP	Columbia	33SX1243	1960	**£30**	**£15**	

RYDER, FREDDIE

Some Kind Of Wonderful	7″	Mercury	MF879	1965	**£6**	**£2.50**	

RYDER, MAL

Cry Baby	7″	Decca	F11669	1963	**£8**	**£4**	
Lonely Room	7″	Piccadilly	7N35234	1965	**£10**	**£5**	
See The Funny Little Clown	7″	Vocalion	V9219	1964	**£50**	**£25**	
Your Friend	7″	Piccadilly	7N35209	1964	**£15**	**£7.50**	

RYDER, MITCH

All Mitch Ryder Hits!	LP	Bell	MBLL/SBLL114	1968	**£10**	**£4**	
Breakout	7″	Stateside	SS521	1966	**£10**	**£5**	
Breakout	LP	Stateside	(S)SL10189	1967	**£20**	**£8**	
Devil With A Blue Dress On	7″	Stateside	SS549	1966	**£4**	**£1.50**	
Jenny Take A Ride	7″	Stateside	SS481	1966	**£4**	**£1.50**	
Jenny Take A Ride	7″ EP	Columbia	ESRF1745	1966	**£15**	**£7.50**	*French*
Little Latin Lupe Lu	7″	Stateside	SS498	1966	**£4**	**£1.50**	
Little Latin Lupe Lu	7″ EP	Columbia	ESRF1804	1966	**£15**	**£7.50**	*French*
Mitch Ryder Sings The Hits	LP	New Voice	S2005	1968	**£10**	**£4**	*US*
Personality	7″	Stateside	SS2096	1968	**£4**	**£1.50**	
Ridin'	7″ EP	Stateside	SE1039	1966	**£20**	**£10**	
Sock It To Me	LP	Stateside	(S)SL10204	1967	**£15**	**£6**	
Sock It To Me Baby	7″	Stateside	SS596	1967	**£4**	**£1.50**	
Sock It To Me Baby	7″ EP	Columbia	ESRF1849	1967	**£15**	**£7.50**	*French*
Take A Ride	LP	Stateside	(S)SL10178	1966	**£15**	**£6**	
Too Many Fish In The Sea	7″	Stateside	SS2023	1967	**£5**	**£2**	
Too Many Fish In The Sea	7″ EP	Stateside	FSE1005	1967	**£15**	**£7.50**	*French*
What Now My Love	7″	Stateside	SS2063	1967	**£10**	**£5**	
What Now My Love	LP	Stateside	(S)SL10229	1967	**£10**	**£4**	

RYLES & DALLAS

Blowin' In The Wind	7″ EP	Riviera	231125	1965	**£8**	**£4**	*French*

RYPDAL, TERJE

Terje Rypdal is one of the stars of the ECM label, having made a large number of albums in both the jazz and orchestral categories. As a guitarist, Rypdal is without question one of the great players, with an instantly recognizable sound based on the use of long sustain, frequently with no initial plectrum attack, and combined with a cavernous echo.

After The Rain	LP	ECM	ECM1083ST	1976	**£12**	**£5**	
Bleak House	LP	Polydor	2915053	1968	**£100**	**£50**	*Swedish*
Odyssey	LP	ECM	ECM1067/8ST	1975	**£20**	**£8**	*double*
Rolling Stone	LP	Polydor	2371618	1975	**£40**	**£20**	*German*
Terje Rypdal	LP	ECM	ECM1016ST	1971	**£20**	**£8**	
Ved Soerevatn	LP	BASF	15269	1969	**£75**	**£37.50**	*German*
What Comes After	LP	ECM	ECM1031ST	1974	**£12**	**£5**	
Whenever I Seem To Be Far Away	LP	ECM	ECM1045ST	1974	**£12**	**£5**	

S

SABLE, PARK & THE JUNGLE 'N' BEATS

Title	Format	Label	Cat. No.	Year	Mint	VG	Notes
Rave On	7"	Fontana	TF457	1964	**£20**	**£10**	

SABLES, BILL

Title	Format	Label	Cat. No.	Year	Mint	VG	Notes
Bill Sables	LP	Westwood	WRS027	1973	**£30**	**£15**	

SABRES

Title	Format	Label	Cat. No.	Year	Mint	VG	Notes
Roly Poly	7"	Decca	F12528	1966	**£10**	**£5**	

SABRES OF PARADISE

Title	Format	Label	Cat. No.	Year	Mint	VG	Notes
Smokebelch II	12"	Sabres Of Paradise	PT009R	1994	**£10**	**£5**	
Smokebelch II	12"	Sabres Of Paradise	PT009	1994	**£6**	**£2.50**	
United	12"	Sabres Of Paradise	PT001	1993	**£15**	**£7.50**	

SACRED ALIEN

Title	Format	Label	Cat. No.	Year	Mint	VG	Notes
Legends	7"	Neon	SADX1	1984	**£15**	**£7.50**	
Spiritual Planet	7"	Greenwood	GW1	1981	**£20**	**£10**	*picture sleeve*

SACRED MUSHROOMS

Title	Format	Label	Cat. No.	Year	Mint	VG	Notes
Sacred Mushrooms	LP	Parallax	P4001	1969	**£60**	**£30**	*US*

SACROS

Title	Format	Label	Cat. No.	Year	Mint	VG	Notes
Sacros	LP	IRT	ILS136	1973	**£30**	**£15**	*Chilean*

SAD LOVERS & GIANTS

Title	Format	Label	Cat. No.	Year	Mint	VG	Notes
Colourless Dream	7"	Last Movement	LM005	1981	**£6**	**£2.50**	
Imagination	7"	Last Movement	LM003	1981	**£10**	**£5**	
Lost In A Moment	7"	Midnight Music	DING1	1982	**£4**	**£1.50**	

SADI, FATS

Title	Format	Label	Cat. No.	Year	Mint	VG	Notes
Fats Sadi	10" LP	Vogue	LDE133	1955	**£75**	**£37.50**	
Fats Sadi–Martial Solal Quartet	LP	Vogue	LAE12043	1957	**£25**	**£10**	

SAFARIS

Title	Format	Label	Cat. No.	Year	Mint	VG	Notes
Image Of A Girl	7"	Top Rank	JAR424	1960	**£30**	**£15**	
Summer Nights	7"	Top Rank	JAR528	1961	**£15**	**£7.50**	

SAFT

Title	Format	Label	Cat. No.	Year	Mint	VG	Notes
Horn	LP	Polydor	2923005	1971	**£20**	**£8**	*Norwegian*

SAGA

Title	Format	Label	Cat. No.	Year	Mint	VG	Notes
To Whom It Concerns	LP	Unidentified Artist	UAP4	1979	**£50**	**£25**	*Dutch*

SAGA (2)

Title	Format	Label	Cat. No.	Year	Mint	VG	Notes
Saga	LP	Westwood	WRS017	1972	**£60**	**£30**	
Sweet Peg O'Derby	LP	Westwood	WRS036	1973	**£75**	**£37.50**	

SAGAR, MIKE

Title	Format	Label	Cat. No.	Year	Mint	VG	Notes
Brothers Three	7"	HMV	POP988	1961	**£8**	**£4**	
Deep Feeling	7"	HMV	POP819	1960	**£10**	**£5**	*with the Cresters*

SAGE

Title	Format	Label	Cat. No.	Year	Mint	VG	Notes
Going Strong	LP	Redball	RR032	1980	**£75**	**£37.50**	

SAGITTARIUS

Title	Format	Label	Cat. No.	Year	Mint	VG	Notes
Another Time	7"	CBS	3276	1968	**£6**	**£2.50**	
Blue Marble	LP	Together	STT1002	1969	**£50**	**£25**	*US*
My World Fell Down	7"	CBS	2867	1967	**£8**	**£4**	
Present Tense	LP	Columbia	CS9644	1968	**£50**	**£25**	*US*

SAGRAM

Title	Format	Label	Cat. No.	Year	Mint	VG	Notes
Pop Explosion Sitar Style	LP	Windmill	WMD118	1972	**£25**	**£10**	

SAHARA

Sunrise ... LP ... Dawn ... DNLS3068 ... 1973 **£10** ... **£4**

SAHM, DOUG

Return Of Doug Saldana ... LP ... Philips ... PHS600353 ... 1971 **£30** ... **£15** ... *US*
Rough Edges ... LP ... Mercury ... SRM1655 ... 1973 **£12** ... **£5** ... *US*

SAINT ETIENNE

I Love To Paint ... CD ... Heavenly ... HVNCD9 ... 1995 **£40** ... **£20**
Kiss And Make Up ... 12" ... Heavenly ... HVN412R ... 1990 **£8** ... **£4**
Kiss And Make Up ... 12" ... Heavenly ... HVN412 ... 1990 **£6** ... **£2.50**
Kiss And Make Up ... CD-s ... Heavenly ... HVN4CD ... 1990 **£8** ... **£4**
Live – Paris '92 ... 7" ... Heavenly ... HVN22 ... 1992 **£6** ... **£2.50** ... *clear flexi*
Nothing Can Stop Us ... CD-s ... Heavenly ... HVN9CD ... 1991 **£6** ... **£2.50**
Only Love Can Break Your Heart ... 12" ... Heavenly ... HVN212R ... 1990 **£8** ... **£4**
Only Love Can Break Your Heart ... 12" ... Heavenly ... HVN212 ... 1990 **£6** ... **£2.50**
Only Love Can Break Your Heart ... CD-s ... Creation ... HVN12CD ... 1991 **£5** ... **£2**
Too Young To Die ... CD ... Heavenly ... HVNCD10 ... 1995 **£15** ... **£6** ... *with bonus remix CD*
Xmas '95 ... CD-s ... Heavenly ... HVN41 ... 1995 **£20** ... **£10** ... *autographed*

SAINT JUST

La Casa Del Lago ... LP ... Harvest ... 1974 **£100** ... **£50** ... *Italian*
Saint Just ... LP ... Harvest ... 1973 **£100** ... **£50** ... *Italian*

SAINT ORCHESTRA

Return Of The Saint ... 7" ... Pye ... 7N46127 ... 1978 **£8** ... **£4**

SAINT STEVEN

Over The Hills ... LP ... Probe ... SPB1005 ... 1969 **£75** ... **£37.50**

SAINTE ANTHONY'S FYRE

Sainte Anthony's Fyre ... LP ... Zonk ... ZP001 ... 1971 **£100** ... **£50** ... *US*

SAINTE-MARIE, BUFFY

Fire, Fleet & Candle Light ... LP ... Vanguard ... VSD79250 ... 1967 **£10** ... **£4**
I'm Gonna Be A Country Girl Again ... LP ... Vanguard ... VSD79280 ... 1968 **£10** ... **£4**
Illuminations ... LP ... Vanguard ... VSD79300 ... 1969 **£10** ... **£4**
It's My Way ... LP ... Fontana ... TFL6040 ... 1964 **£12** ... **£5**
It's My Way ... LP ... Vanguard ... VSD79142 ... 1969 **£10** ... **£4**
Little Wheel Spin And Spin ... LP ... Fontana ... (S)TFL6071 ... 1966 **£12** ... **£5**
Little Wheel Spin And Spin ... LP ... Vanguard ... SVRL19023 ... 1969 **£10** ... **£4**
Many A Mile ... LP ... Fontana ... TFL6047 ... 1965 **£12** ... **£5**
Many A Mile ... LP ... Vanguard ... SVRL19031 ... 1969 **£10** ... **£4**
Sweet America ... LP ... ABC ... ABCL5168 ... 1976 **£10** ... **£4**

SAINTS

I'm Stranded ... 7" ... Power Exchange ... PX242 ... 1976 **£4** ... **£1.50**

SAINTS (2)

Husky Team ... 7" ... Pye ... 7N15582 ... 1963 **£15** ... **£7.50**
Wipe Out ... 7" ... Pye ... 7N15548 ... 1963 **£15** ... **£7.50**

SAINTS (3)

Alive ... LP ... MJB ... BEVLP127/8 ... 1964 **£500** ... **£330**
Saints ... 10" LP ... MJB ... BEV73/4 ... 1964 **£300** ... **£180**

SAINTS JAZZ BAND

Hey Lawdy Papa ... 7" ... Parlophone ... MSP6042 ... 1953 **£4** ... **£1.50**
Saints Jazz Band ... 7" EP ... Parlophone ... GEP8577 ... 1956 **£10** ... **£5**
Saints Play Jazz ... 7" EP ... Parlophone ... GEP8560 ... 1956 **£15** ... **£7.50**

SAINTY, RUSS

Genius Of Lennon And McCartney ... LP ... Society ... SOC1035 ... 196– **£10** ... **£4**
Happy Go Lucky Me ... 7" ... Top Rank ... JAR381 ... 1960 **£5** ... **£2**
Race With The Devil ... 7" ... Decca ... F11270 ... 1960 **£5** ... **£2**

SAKAMOTO, KYU

Sukiyaki ... LP ... HMV ... CLP1674 ... 1962 **£12** ... **£5**

SAKER

Foggy Tuesday ... 7" ... Parlophone ... R5740 ... 1968 **£5** ... **£2** ... *credited to Bob Saker*
Hey Joe ... 7" ... Parlophone ... R5752 ... 1969 **£5** ... **£2**

SALAD

Drink Me ... CD ... Island ... CIRDX1002 ... 1995 **£12** ... **£5** ... *boxed with book*

SALAMANDER

Crystal Ball ... 7" ... CBS ... 5102 ... 1970 **£10** ... **£5**
Ten Commandments ... LP ... Youngblood ... SSYB14 ... 1972 **£125** ... **£62.50**

SALEM

Cold As Steel ... 7" ... Hilton ... FMR056 ... 1982 **£40** ... **£20**

SALEM MASS

Witch Burning ... LP ... Salem Mass ... SLP101 ... 197– **£150** ... **£75** ... *US*

SALES, SOUPY

Title	Format	Label	Cat. No.	Year	Mint	Ex	Notes
Mouse	7"	HMV	POP1432	1965	£4	£1.50	

SALLOOM, SINCLAIR & THE MOTHER BEAR

Title	Format	Label	Cat. No.	Year	Mint	Ex	Notes
Salloom, Sinclair & The Mother Bear	LP	Cadet	LPS316	1968	£15	£6	US

SALLY & THE ALLEYCATS

Title	Format	Label	Cat. No.	Year	Mint	Ex	Notes
Is It Something I Said	7"	Parlophone	R5183	1964	£5	£2	

SALLYANGIE

The Sallyangie was a folky duo comprising Sally Oldfield and her young brother Michael. Their one LP was re-released in the seventies, in a vain attempt on the part of Transatlantic records to gain some spin-off benefit from the success of *Tubular Bells* and its successors. The new cover, however, is completely different to the original, which shows a close-up of the two Oldfields, so distinguishing the two versions is no problem.

Title	Format	Label	Cat. No.	Year	Mint	Ex	Notes
Child Of Allah	7"	Philips	6006259	1972	£10	£5	
Children Of The Sun	LP	Transatlantic	TRA176	1968	£40	£20	
Children Of The Sun	LP	Transatlantic	TRA176	1973	£12	£5	*reissue, different sleeve*
Two Ships	7"	Transatlantic	BIG126	1969	£10	£5	

SALLY'S FRIENDS

Title	Format	Label	Cat. No.	Year	Mint	Ex	Notes
Boys Of The Town	LP	Cottage	COT231	1980	£30	£15	

SALMONTAILS

Title	Format	Label	Cat. No.	Year	Mint	Ex	Notes
Salmontails	LP	Oblivion	OBL001	1980	£20	£8	

SALT

Title	Format	Label	Cat. No.	Year	Mint	Ex	Notes
Beyond A Song	LP	Grapevine	GRA111	1978	£12	£5	

SALT & PEPPER

Title	Format	Label	Cat. No.	Year	Mint	Ex	Notes
High Noon	7"	London	HLU9338	1961	£4	£1.50	

SALVADOR, SAL

Title	Format	Label	Cat. No.	Year	Mint	Ex	Notes
Sal Salvador Quartet	10" LP	Capitol	KPL105	1955	£30	£15	

SALVATION

Title	Format	Label	Cat. No.	Year	Mint	Ex	Notes
Salvation	LP	United Artists	UAS29062	1969	£15	£6	

SALVATION (2)

Title	Format	Label	Cat. No.	Year	Mint	Ex	Notes
Girlsoul	12"	Merciful Release	MRX025	1983	£8	£4	
Girlsoul	7"	Merciful Release	MR025	1983	£6	£2.50	

SALVO, SAMMY

Title	Format	Label	Cat. No.	Year	Mint	Ex	Notes
Afraid	7"	London	HLP8997	1959	£6	£2.50	
Billy Blue	7"	Polydor	NH66974	1962	£5	£2	
Say Yeah	7"	RCA	RCA1032	1958	£15	£7.50	

SAM & BILL

Title	Format	Label	Cat. No.	Year	Mint	Ex	Notes
Fly Me To The Moon	7"	Pye	7N25355	1966	£10	£5	
I Feel Like Tryin'	7"	Brunswick	05973	1967	£15	£7.50	

SAM & DAVE

Title	Format	Label	Cat. No.	Year	Mint	Ex	Notes
Baby Baby Don't Stop Now	7"	Atlantic	584324	1970	£4	£1.50	
Best Of Sam And Dave	LP	Atlantic	587/588155	1969	£10	£4	
Can't You Find Another Way	7"	Atlantic	584211	1968	£4	£1.50	
Double Dynamite	LP	Atlantic	588181	1969	£12	£5	
Double Dynamite	LP	Stax	589003	1967	£15	£6	
Everybody Got To Believe	7"	Atlantic	584228	1968	£4	£1.50	
Hold On I'm Comin'	7"	Atlantic	584003	1966	£4	£1.50	
Hold On I'm Comin'	LP	Atlantic	587/588045	1966	£15	£6	
I Thank You	7"	Stax	601030	1968	£4	£1.50	
I Thank You	LP	Atlantic	587/588154	1968	£10	£4	
If You Got The Loving	7"	Atlantic	584047	1966	£4	£1.50	
No More Pain	7"	King	KG1041	1966	£5	£2	
Ooh Ooh Ooh	7"	Atlantic	584303	1969	£4	£1.50	
Sam And Dave	LP	King	KGL4001	1966	£20	£8	
Sam And Dave	LP	Major Minor	MCP5000	1968	£10	£4	
Soothe Me	7"	Stax	601004	1967	£4	£1.50	
Soul Man	7"	Stax	601023	1967	£4	£1.50	
Soul Men	LP	Stax	589015	1967	£15	£6	
Soul Men	LP	Atlantic	588185	1969	£10	£4	
Soul Sister Brown Sugar	7"	Atlantic	584237	1969	£4	£1.50	
When Something Is Wrong With My Baby	7"	Stax	601006	1967	£4	£1.50	
You Don't Know Like I Know	7"	Atlantic	AT4066	1966	£5	£2	
You Don't Know Like I Know	7"	Atlantic	584086	1967	£4	£1.50	
You Don't Know Like I Know	7"	Atlantic	584247	1969	£4	£1.50	
You Don't Know What You Mean To Me	7"	Atlantic	584192	1968	£4	£1.50	
You Got Me Hummin'	7"	Atlantic	584064	1967	£4	£1.50	

SAM APPLE PIE

Title	Format	Label	Cat. No.	Year	Mint	Ex	Notes
East 17	LP	DJM	DJLPS429	1973	£15	£6	

Sam Apple Pie	LP	Decca	LKR/SKLR5005	1969	£75	£37.50	
Sometime Girl	7"	Decca	F22932	1969	£6	£2.50	

SAM THE SHAM & THE PHARAOHS

Best Of Sam The Sham	LP	MGM	(S)E4422	1967	£20	£8	*US*
Black Sheep	7"	MGM	MGM1343	1967	£5	£2	
Hair On My Chinny Chin Chin	7" EP	MGM	63639	1966	£20	£10	*French*
Ju Ju Hand	7"	MGM	MGM1278	1965	£4	£1.50	
Ju Ju Hand	7" EP	MGM	63624	1965	£20	£10	*French*
Li'l Red Riding Hood	7"	MGM	MGM1315	1966	£4	£1.50	
Li'l Red Riding Hood	LP	MGM	C(S)8032	1966	£20	£8	
Lil' Red Riding Hood	7" EP	MGM	63637	1966	£20	£10	*French*
Nefertiti	LP	MGM	(S)E4479	1967	£15	£6	*US*
On Tour	LP	MGM	(S)E4347	1966	£20	£8	*US*
Red Hot	7"	MGM	MGM1298	1966	£5	£2	
Red Hot	7" EP	MGM	MGMEP794	1966	£25	£12.50	
Red Hot	7" EP	MGM	63631	1966	£20	£10	*French*
Ring Dang Doo	7"	MGM	MGM1285	1965	£4	£1.50	
Ring Dang Doo	7" EP	MGM	63626	1965	£20	£10	*French*
Ten Of Pentacles	LP	MGM	SE4526	1968	£15	£6	*US*
Their Second Album	LP	MGM	(S)E4314	1965	£20	£8	*US*
Wooly Bully	7"	MGM	MGM1269	1965	£4	£1.50	
Wooly Bully	7" EP	MGM	63623	1965	£25	£12.50	*French, group picture sleeve*
Wooly Bully	7" EP	MGM	63623	1965	£20	£10	*French, sphinx picture sleeve*
Wooly Bully	LP	MGM	C1007	1965	£20	£8	
Yakety Yak	7"	MGM	MGM1379	1968	£4	£1.50	

SAMAIN

Vibrations Of Doom	LP	Roadrunner			£75	£37.50	*Canada*

SAME

Wild About You	7"	Wessex	WEX267	1979	£4	£1.50	

SAMETI

Hungry For Love	LP	Warner Bros	56074	1974	£10	£4	*German*
Sameti	LP	Brain	1020	1972	£15	£6	*German*

SAMLA MAMMAS MANNA

Klossa Knapitatet	LP	Silence	SRS4627	1974	£10	£4	*Swedish*
Maltid	LP	Silence	SRS4621	1973	£12	£5	*Swedish*
Samla Mammas Manna	LP	Silence	SRS4604	1971	£15	£6	*Swedish*
Schlagerns Mystik/For Aldre Nybegynnare	LP	Silence	SRS4640	1978	£15	£6	*Swedish double*
Snorungarnas Symfoni	LP	Musiknatet Waxholm	MNW70	1976	£10	£4	*Swedish*

SAMMY

1, 2, 3, 4	7"	Harvest	HAR5137	1977	£5	£2	*double*
Sammy	LP	Philips	6308136	1972	£20	£8	

SAMPSON, DAVE & THE HUNTERS

Dave	7" EP	Columbia	SEG8095	1961	£60	£30	
Dave	7" EP	Columbia	ESG7853	1961	£100	£50	*stereo*
Easy To Dream	7"	Columbia	DB4625	1961	£6	£2.50	
If You Need Me	7"	Columbia	DB4502	1960	£8	£4	
Sweet Dreams	7"	Columbia	DB4449	1960	£8	£4	
Why The Chicken	7"	Columbia	DB4597	1961	£5	£2	
Wide Wide World	7"	Fontana	H361	1962	£5	£2	

SAMPSON, EDGAR

Swing Softly Sweet Sampson	LP	Vogue Coral	LVA9039	1957	£15	£6	

SAMPSON, TOMMY & HIS STRONGMEN

Rockin'	7"	Melodisc	1411	1958	£10	£5	

SAMSON

Are You Ready?	7"	Polydor	POSPP670	1984	£5	£2	*picture disc*
Are You Samson	LP	Instant	INSP004	1969	£30	£15	
Head On	LP	Gem	GEMLP108	1980	£10	£4	*2 different mixes, with patch*
Losing My Grip	7"	Polydor	POSPP471	1982	£5	£2	*picture disc*
Mr Rock'n'Roll	7"	Lightning	GIL553	1979	£25	£12.50	
Mr Rock'n'Roll	7"	Laser	LAS6	1979	£4	£1.50	
Red Skies	7"	Polydor	SAM2	1982	£10	£5	*promo*
Red Skies	7"	Polydor	PODJ554	1983	£6	£2.50	*1 sided promo*
Vice Versa	7"	Gem	GEMS34	1980	£4	£1.50	*with sticker*

SAMSON (2)

Riding With The Angels	7"	RCA	RCA67	1981	£10	£5	*picture disc*
Telephone	7"	Lightning	GIL547	1978	£25	£12.50	
Vice Versa	7"	EMI	EMI5061	1980	£20	£10	*promo only*

SAMSON (3)

Venus	7"	Parlophone	R5867	1970	£4	£1.50	

SAMUEL PRODY

Samuel Prody	LP	Global	6306906	1974	**£150**	**£75**	*German*

SAMUEL THE FIRST

Sounds Of Babylon	7"	Summit	SUM8515	1971	**£5**	**£2**	*Beverley All Stars B side*

SAMUELS, JERRY

Puppy Love	7"	HMV	7M411	1956	**£6**	**£2.50**	

SAMUELS, WINSTON

Be Prepared	7"	Ska Beat	JB196	1965	**£10**	**£5**	
Follow	7"	Rio	R26	1964	**£10**	**£5**	
Greatest	7"	Island	WI3051	1967	**£10**	**£5**	
I Won't Be Discouraged	7"	Island	WI3053	1967	**£10**	**£5**	
Luck Will Come My Way	7"	Black Swan	WI419	1964	**£10**	**£5**	*Lloyd Brevitt B side*
My Angel	7"	Ska Beat	JB214	1965	**£10**	**£5**	
Time Will Tell	7"	Ska Beat	JB244	1966	**£10**	**£5**	
Up And Down	7"	Ska Beat	JB241	1966	**£10**	**£5**	
What Have I Done	7"	Ska Beat	JB238	1966	**£10**	**£5**	
You Are The One	7"	Black Swan	WI426	1964	**£10**	**£5**	
You Are The One	7"	Columbia	DB7405	1964	**£6**	**£2.50**	

SAMURAI

Samurai	LP	Greenwich	GSLP1003	1971	**£75**	**£37.50**	

SAMURAI (2)

Fires Of Hell	7"	Ebony	EBON25	1984	**£6**	**£2.50**	

SAN FRANCISCO EARTHQUAKE

Fairy Tales Can Come True	7"	Mercury	MF1036	1968	**£5**	**£2**	

SAN REMO STRINGS

Festival Time	7"	Tamla Motown	TMG795	1971	**£4**	**£1.50**	

SANCTUS

Sound Of Celebration	LP	Focus	F3326	1975	**£50**	**£25**	

SAND

Sand	LP	Barnaby	BR15006	1973	**£15**	**£6**	*US double*

SANDELLS

Scramblers	LP	World Pacific	(ST)1818	1964	**£15**	**£6**	*US*
Scramblers	LP	World Pacific	ST1818	1964	**£25**	**£10**	*US red vinyl*

SANDERS, ALEX

Witch Is Born	LP	A&M	AMLS984	1970	**£30**	**£15**	

SANDERS, GARY

Ain't No Beatle	7"	Warner Bros	WB5676	1966	**£5**	**£2**	

SANDERS, PHAROAH

These days, Pharoah Sanders has matured into a tranquil elder statesman of jazz. Originally, however, he was the angry young saxophonist with the flame-thrower technique, who was brought in by John Coltrane to help push his own playing towards a new peak of intensity. Sanders's own first album on ESP has become very scarce, although the music represents the uneasy compromise that results when a fiery, avant-garde player is provided with a rhythm section whose idea of an appropriate support derives from a politer, earlier time.

Best Of Pharoah Sanders	LP	Impulse	AS92292	1973	**£25**	**£10**	
Black Unity	LP	Impulse	AS9219	1972	**£30**	**£15**	
Deaf, Dumb And Blind	LP	Probe	SPB1019	1971	**£30**	**£15**	
Elevation	LP	Impulse	AS9261	1974	**£25**	**£10**	*US*
Izipho Zau	LP	Strata East		197–	**£50**	**£25**	
Jewels Of Thought	LP	Impulse	AS9190	1969	**£25**	**£10**	*US*
Karma	LP	Impulse	AS9181	1969	**£25**	**£10**	*US*
Live At The East	LP	Impulse	AS9227	1973	**£25**	**£10**	
Love In Us All	LP	Impulse	AS9280	1974	**£20**	**£8**	*US*
Pharoah	LP	ESP-Disk	1003	1965	**£60**	**£30**	
Pharoah	LP	India Navigation	IN1027	1977	**£50**	**£25**	
Summun Bukmun Umyun	LP	Impulse	AS9199	1971	**£30**	**£15**	*US*
Tauhid	LP	Impulse	AS9138	1967	**£30**	**£15**	*US*
Thembi	LP	Impulse	AS9206	1971	**£20**	**£8**	*US*
Village Of The Pharoahs	LP	Impulse	AS9254	1973	**£30**	**£15**	*US*
Wisdom Through Music	LP	Impulse	AS9238	1973	**£30**	**£15**	*US*

SANDERS, RAY

World So Full Of Love	7"	London	HLG7106	1960	**£8**	**£4**	*export*

SANDERSON, TOMMY & THE SANDMEN

Deadline	7"	Ember	EMB131	1961	**£4**	**£1.50**	
Ding Dong Rag	7"	Ember	EMB152	1962	**£4**	**£1.50**	

SANDON, JOHNNY

Blizzard	7"	Pye	7N15717	1964	**£4**	**£1.50**	
Donna Means Heartbreak	7"	Pye	7N15665	1964	**£4**	**£1.50**	

Title	Format	Label	Cat. No.	Year	Mint	Good	Notes
Lies	7"	Pye	7N15542	1963	£5	£2	
Magic Potion	7"	Pye	7N15559	1963	£5	£2	
Sixteen Tons	7"	Pye	7N15602	1964	£4	£1.50	

SANDPEBBLES

Title	Format	Label	Cat. No.	Year	Mint	Good	Notes
Love Power	7"	Track	604028	1969	£4	£1.50	
Love Power	7"	Track	604015	1967	£5	£2	

SANDPIPERS

Title	Format	Label	Cat. No.	Year	Mint	Good	Notes
Guantanamera	7" EP	Pye	NEP44081	1966	£5	£2	

SANDRA

Title	Format	Label	Cat. No.	Year	Mint	Good	Notes
Everlasting Love	CD-s	Siren	SRNCD85	1989	£12	£6	
Heaven Can Wait	CD-s	Siren	SRNCD104	1989	£15	£7.50	3" single
I'll Never Be Maria Magdalena	12"	10	TENY7812	1986	£10	£5	picture disc

SANDROSE

The music on the one album made by Sandrose is superior progressive rock, occupying similar territory to that of Yes. Rose Podwojny is a terrific singer, with a voice like a slightly more fragile Grace Slick, while guitarist Jean-Pierre Alarcen, who is the leader of the group, manages to deliver a number of impressive solos without ever outstaying his welcome. The album was one of the first rare progressive records to cross the £100 barrier (although its value has remained static since due to the availability of a vinyl reissue) and, for once, the music is worth it.

Title	Format	Label	Cat. No.	Year	Mint	Good	Notes
Sandrose	LP	Polydor	2480137	1972	£125	£62.50	

SANDS

The Sands evolved out of an R&B group called the Others, who began playing while at grammar school in Middlesex. The single, 'Mrs Gillespie's Refrigerator', however, is not R&B but a novelty Bee Gees song that the Gibb brothers wisely decided not to record themselves. The single is very collectable, but for the sake of its B side, 'Listen To The Sky'. This starts fairly unpromisingly too, but then, without warning, the song gives way to the sounds of an air attack, simulated by multiple overdriven guitars. The song then ends with a section of Gustav Holst's 'Mars', played on guitars.

Title	Format	Label	Cat. No.	Year	Mint	Good	Notes
Mrs Gillespie's Refrigerator	7"	Reaction	591017	1967	£125	£62.50	
Venus	7"	Major Minor	MM681	1970	£10	£5	

SANDS (2)

Title	Format	Label	Cat. No.	Year	Mint	Good	Notes
Dance Dance Dance	7"	Tribune	TRS122	1969	£5	£2	
Sand Doin's	LP	Tribune	TRLP1009	1969	£30	£15	

SANDS, CLIVE

Title	Format	Label	Cat. No.	Year	Mint	Good	Notes
Witchi Tai To	7"	SNB	554431	1969	£6	£2.50	

SANDS, DAVEY & THE ESSEX

Title	Format	Label	Cat. No.	Year	Mint	Good	Notes
Advertising Girl	7"	CBS	202620	1967	£6	£2.50	
Please Be Mine	7"	Decca	F12170	1965	£8	£4	

SANDS, EVIE

Title	Format	Label	Cat. No.	Year	Mint	Good	Notes
Picture Me Gone	7"	Cameo Parkway	C413	1966	£50	£25	
Take Me For A Little While	7"	Red Bird	BC118	1965	£20	£10	

SANDS, JODIE

Title	Format	Label	Cat. No.	Year	Mint	Good	Notes
All I Ask Of You	7"	Starlite	ST45005	1958	£5	£2	
Please Don't Tell Me	7"	London	HL8530	1957	£8	£4	
Someday	7"	HMV	POP533	1958	£4	£1.50	
With All My Heart	7"	London	HL8456	1957	£6	£2.50	

SANDS, TOMMY

Title	Format	Label	Cat. No.	Year	Mint	Good	Notes
Big Date	7"	Capitol	CL14889	1958	£5	£2	
Blue Ribbon Baby	7"	Capitol	CL14925	1958	£10	£5	
Connie	7"	HMV	POP1193	1963	£4	£1.50	
Dream With Me	LP	Capitol	T1426	1961	£20	£8	
Going Steady	7"	Capitol	CL14745	1957	£6	£2.50	
Hawaiian Rock	7"	Capitol	CL14872	1958	£10	£5	
Is It Ever Gonna Happen	7"	Capitol	CL15013	1959	£10	£5	
Let Me Be Loved	7"	Capitol	CL14781	1957	£5	£2	
Love In A Goldfish Bowl	7"	Capitol	CL15219	1961	£4	£1.50	
Man Like Wow	7"	Capitol	CL14811	1957	£8	£4	
Old Oaken Bucket	7"	Capitol	CL15143	1960	£5	£2	
Only 'Cos I'm Lonely	7"	HMV	POP1247	1963	£4	£1.50	
Ring A Ding Ding	7"	Capitol	CL14724	1957	£8	£4	
Sands At The Sands	LP	Capitol	(S)T1364	1960	£25	£10	US
Sands Storm	LP	Capitol	T1081	1959	£25	£10	
Sands Storm Part 1	7" EP	Capitol	EAP11081	1959	£25	£12.50	
Sands Storm Part 2	7" EP	Capitol	EAP21081	1959	£25	£12.50	
Sands Storm Part 3	7" EP	Capitol	EAP31081	1959	£25	£12.50	
Sing Boy Sing	7"	Capitol	CL14834	1958	£6	£2.50	
Sing Boy Sing	LP	Capitol	T929	1958	£30	£15	
Sinner Man	7"	Capitol	CL15047	1959	£4	£1.50	
Statue	7"	Liberty	LIB55842	1966	£15	£7.50	
Steady Date	LP	Capitol	T848	1957	£30	£15	
Steady Date Part 1	7" EP	Capitol	EAP1848	1957	£25	£12.50	
Steady Date Part 2	7" EP	Capitol	EAP2848	1957	£20	£10	
Steady Date Part 3	7" EP	Capitol	EAP3848	1957	£20	£10	
Teenage Crush	7"	Capitol	CL14695	1957	£10	£5	
Teenage Crush	7" EP	Capitol	EAP1851	1957	£25	£12.50	
Teenage Rock	LP	Capitol	T1109	1959	£25	£10	US

That's The Way I Am	7"	Capitol	CL15071	1959	£4	£1.50	
This Thing Called Love	7" EP	Capitol	EAP11123	1959	£15	£7.50	
This Thing Called Love	LP	Capitol	T1123	1959	£15	£6	
When I'm Thinking Of You	LP	Capitol	(S)T1239	1960	£15	£6	
Worrying Kind	7"	Capitol	CL14971	1959	£15	£7.50	
You Hold The Future	7"	Capitol	CL15109	1960	£4	£1.50	

SANDS, TONY & THE DRUMBEATS

Shame Shame Shame	7"	Studio 36	NSRSEP1/2	1964	£200	£100	

SANDS, WES

There's Lots More Where This Came From	7"	Columbia	DB4996	1963	£25	£12.50	

SANDS FAMILY

First Day And Second Day	LP	Autogram	FLLP501	1974	£12	£5	*German*
Folk From The Mournes	LP	Outlet	OAS3004	1968	£12	£5	*Irish*
Real Irish Folk	LP	Emerald	GES1201	1979	£12	£5	
Third Day	LP	Autogram	ALLP233	1974	£12	£5	*German*
You'll Be Well Looked After	LP	Leaf	7005	1975	£10	£4	*Irish*

SANDY, PAT

Gentle On My Mind	7"	Attack	ATT8000	1969	£5	£2	*Big L B side*

SANDY & JEANIE

Sandy And Jeanie	LP	XTRA	XTRA1015	1965	£10	£4	

SANDY COAST

Blackboard Jungle Lady	7"	Polydor	2001457	1973	£10	£5	
From The Stereo Workshop	LP	Page One	POLS020	1969	£125	£62.50	
Shipwreck	LP	Page One	MORS201	1969	£125	£62.50	
Stone Wall	LP	Polydor	2310277	1973	£20	£8	
True Love	7"	Polydor	2121046	1971	£8	£4	

SANG, CLAUDE

World Of Reggae Vol. 1	LP	Sugar	SUM1	1970	£10	£4	

SANSOM, BOBBY

There's A Place	7"	Oriole	CB1837	1963	£6	£2.50	
Where Have You Been	7"	Oriole	CB1888	1963	£5	£2	

SANSON, VERONIQUE

French singer-songwriter Véronique Sanson composed 'Amoureuse', which was a big hit for Kiki Dee. Her own version is the lead track of an excellent album which was released in two versions, one with French lyrics and one with English. One would not have thought that it would make much difference, but the French version is far superior. The way in which Ms Sanson's voice takes on an attractive soft vibrato at the end of the lines is ideally matched to the soft endings of the French words. In English she sounds a little ordinary, but in French the record stands revealed as a superb example of the singer-songwriting genre. Véronique Sanson is a considerable star in France these days, but 'Amoureuse' remains her only success outside that country.

Amoureuse	LP	Elektra	K42106	1972	£15	£6	*English vocals*
Véronique Sanson	LP	Elektra	K42106	1972	£15	£6	*French vocals*

SANTAMARIA, MONGO

25 Miles	7"	Direction	584430	1969	£4	£1.50	
Cloud Nine	7"	Direction	584086	1969	£4	£1.50	
El Pussycat	7"	CBS	201766	1965	£4	£1.50	
Hey! Let's Party	LP	CBS	62723	1966	£15	£6	
Mongo's Way	LP	Atlantic	2400140	1971	£15	£6	
Mongo's Way	LP	Atlantic	K40210	1973	£12	£5	
Sherry	7"	Oriole		1963	£15	£7.50	
Watermelon Man	7"	Riverside	RIF106909	1963	£6	£2.50	
Working On A Groovy Thing	LP	CBS	63904	1971	£15	£6	

SANTANA

Abraxas	CD	Mobile Fidelity	UDCD552	1991	£15	£6	*US audiophile*
Abraxas	LP	CBS	Q64087	1974	£10	£4	*quad*
Abraxas	LP	Columbia	HC40130	1981	£10	£4	*US audiophile*
Amigos	LP	Columbia	PCQ33576	1975	£10	£4	*US quad*
Barboletta	LP	CBS	Q69084	1974	£10	£4	*quad*
Caravanserai	LP	CBS	Q65299	1974	£10	£4	*quad*
Carlos Santana & Buddy Miles	LP	CBS	CQ31308	1973	£10	£4	*quad*
Festival	LP	Columbia	PCQ34423	1977	£10	£4	*US quad*
Greatest Hits	LP	CBS	Q69081	1974	£10	£4	*quad*
Gypsy Woman	CD-s	CBS	6560272	1990	£5	£2	
Illuminations	LP	Columbia	PCQ32900	1974	£10	£4	*US quad*
Lotus	LP	CBS	66325	1975	£15	£6	*triple*
Mother Earth Tour	CD	Columbia	CSK2099	1990	£25	£10	*US promo*
Santana	LP	Columbia	PCQ32964	1974	£10	£4	*US quad*
Santana	LP	CBS	63815	1970	£10	£4	*laminated cover*
Santana III	LP	CBS	Q69015	1974	£10	£4	*quad*
Solid Gold	CD-s	CBS	6545683	1989	£5	£2	*3" single*
Solo Guitar Of Devadip Carlos Santana	LP	Columbia	AS573	1979	£20	£8	*US promo*
Viva Santana – sampler	CD	Columbia	CSK1264	1988	£20	£8	*US promo*
Welcome	LP	CBS	Q69040	1974	£10	£4	*quad*
Zebop	LP	Columbia	HC47158	1981	£10	£4	*US audiophile*

SANTELLS

Title	Format	Label	Cat. No.	Year	Price	Price	Notes
So Fine	7"	Sue	WI4020	1966	**£12**	**£6**	

SANTO & JOHNNY

Title	Format	Label	Cat. No.	Year	Price	Price	Notes
Beatles' Greatest Hits	LP	Canadian American	(S)1017	1964	**£25**	**£10**	US
Birmingham	7"	Parlophone	R4865	1962	**£4**	**£1.50**	
Brilliant Guitar Sounds	LP	Imperial	LP9363/12363	1967	**£12**	**£5**	US
Bullseye	7"	Parlophone	R4844	1961	**£4**	**£1.50**	
Caravan	7"	Parlophone	R4644	1960	**£4**	**£1.50**	
Come On In	LP	Canadian American	(S)1006	1962	**£20**	**£8**	US
Come September	7"	Pye	7N25111	1961	**£4**	**£1.50**	
Encore	LP	Canadian American	(S)1002	1960	**£20**	**£8**	US
Golden Guitars	LP	Imperial	LP12366	1968	**£12**	**£5**	US
Hawaii	LP	Stateside	(S)SL1008	1964	**£15**	**£6**	
In The Still Of The Night	LP	Canadian American	(S)1014	1963	**£20**	**£8**	US
Mona Lisa	LP	Philips	(S)BL7760	1967	**£10**	**£4**	
Mucho	LP	Canadian American	(S)1018	1965	**£15**	**£6**	US
Off Shore	LP	Canadian American	(S)1011	1963	**£20**	**£8**	US
On The Road Again	LP	Imperial	LP12418	1968	**£12**	**£5**	US
Pulcinella	LP	Philips	(S)BL7759	1967	**£10**	**£4**	
Santo & Johnny No. 1	7" EP	Parlophone	GEP8806	1960	**£15**	**£7.50**	
Santo & Johnny No. 2	7" EP	Parlophone	GEP8813	1960	**£15**	**£7.50**	
Santo And Johnny	LP	Canadian American	1001	1959	**£30**	**£15**	US
Sleepwalk	7"	Pye	7N25037	1959	**£5**	**£2**	
Spanish Harlem	7"	Stateside	SS110	1962	**£4**	**£1.50**	
Teardrop	7"	Parlophone	R4619	1960	**£4**	**£1.50**	
Wish You Were Here	LP	Canadian American	(S)1016	1964	**£20**	**£8**	US

SANTORO, ANGELO NOCE

Title	Format	Label	Cat. No.	Year	Price	Price	Notes
For You	LP	ANS		1979	**£15**	**£6**	*Dutch*
Land Of The Pharao	LP	ANS		1981	**£15**	**£6**	*Dutch*

SAPPHIRE THINKERS

Title	Format	Label	Cat. No.	Year	Price	Price	Notes
From Within	LP	Hobbit	5003	1969	**£40**	**£20**	US

SAPPHIRES

Title	Format	Label	Cat. No.	Year	Price	Price	Notes
Evil One	7"	HMV	POP1461	1965	**£100**	**£50**	
Gotta Have Your Love	7"	HMV	POP1441	1965	**£75**	**£37.50**	
Who Do You Love	7"	Stateside	SS267	1964	**£20**	**£10**	
Who Do You Love	LP	Swan	LP513	1964	**£50**	**£25**	US
Your True Love	7"	Stateside	SS223	1963	**£20**	**£10**	

SARABAND

Title	Format	Label	Cat. No.	Year	Price	Price	Notes
Close To It All	LP	Folk Heritage	FHR050	1973	**£25**	**£10**	

SARACEN

Title	Format	Label	Cat. No.	Year	Price	Price	Notes
Heroes Saints And Fools	LP	Nucleus	NEAT492	1982	**£15**	**£6**	
No More Lonely Nights	7"	Nucleus	SAR1	1982	**£5**	**£2**	*with patch*
We Have Arrived	7"	Nucleus	NEAT30	1983	**£4**	**£1.50**	

SARGEANT, DEREK & HAZEL KING

Title	Format	Label	Cat. No.	Year	Price	Price	Notes
Folk Matters	LP	Assembly	JP3012	1973	**£50**	**£25**	
Sings English Folk	LP	Joy	JS5001	1970	**£25**	**£10**	

SARGENT, DON

Title	Format	Label	Cat. No.	Year	Price	Price	Notes
Gypsy Boots	7"	Vogue	V9160	1960	**£250**	**£150**	

SARI & THE SHALIMARS

Title	Format	Label	Cat. No.	Year	Price	Price	Notes
It's So Lonely Being Together	7"	United Artists	UP2235	1968	**£8**	**£4**	

SARJEANT, DEREK

Title	Format	Label	Cat. No.	Year	Price	Price	Notes
Derek Sarjeant Folk Trio	LP	Assembly	JP3001	1971	**£30**	**£15**	
Folk Songs	7" EP	Oak	RGJ101	1961	**£20**	**£10**	
Folk Songs Vol. 2	7" EP	Oak	RGJ105	1961	**£20**	**£10**	
Man Of Kent	7" EP	Oak	RGJ117	1963	**£20**	**£10**	
Songs We Like To Sing	7" EP	Oak	RGJ103	1961	**£15**	**£7.50**	

SARNE, MIKE

Title	Format	Label	Cat. No.	Year	Price	Price	Notes
Come Outside	LP	Parlophone	PMC1187	1962	**£30**	**£15**	
Just Like Eddie	7"	Parlophone	DP558	1963	**£60**	**£30**	*export*
Love Me Please	7"	Parlophone	R5170	1964	**£4**	**£1.50**	
Mike Sarne Hit Parade	7" EP	Parlophone	GEP8879	1963	**£25**	**£12.50**	
Out And About	7"	Parlophone	R5129	1964	**£4**	**£1.50**	

SAROFEEN & SMOKE

Title	Format	Label	Cat. No.	Year	Price	Price	Notes
Do It	LP	Pye	NSPL28153	1971	**£10**	**£4**	

SASSAFRAS

Title	Format	Label	Cat. No.	Year	Price	Price	Notes
Expecting Company	LP	Polydor	2383245	1973	**£10**	**£4**	

SASSENACHS

That Don't Worry Me .... 7" .... Fontana .... TF518 .... 1964 **£15** ...... **£7.50** ....

SATAN

Court In The Act .... LP .... Neat .... NEAT1012 .... 1985 **£15** .... **£6** ....
Kiss Of Death .... 7" .... Guardian .... GRC145 .... 1982 **£75** .... **£37.50** .... *picture sleeve*
Kiss Of Death .... 7" .... Guardian .... GRC145 .... 1982 **£15** ...... **£7.50** ....

SATAN & THE DE-CIPLES

Underground .... LP .... Goldband .... 7750 .... 1969 **£100** .... **£50** .... *US*

SATANIC RITES

Live To Ride .... 7" .... Heavy Metal .... HEAVY8 .... 1981 **£8** .... **£4** ....
No Use Crying .... LP .... Chub .... CHUBLP002 .... 1987 **£12** .... **£5** ....
Which Way The Wind Blows .... LP .... Chub .... CHUBLP001 .... 1985 **£10** .... **£4** ....

SATAN'S RATS

In My Love For You .... 7" .... DJM .... DJS10819 .... 1977 **£10** .... **£5** ....
In My Love For You .... 7" .... Overground ..... OVER02 .... 1989 **£10** .... **£5** .... *gold vinyl*
In My Love For You .... 7" .... Overground ..... OVER02 .... 1989 **£4** .... **£1.50** ... *yellow or white vinyl*
Year Of The Rats .... 7" .... DJM .... DJS10821 .... 1978 **£8** .... **£4** ....
Year Of The Rats .... 7" .... Overground ..... OVER01 .... 1989 **£10** .... **£5** .... *gold vinyl*
Year Of The Rats .... 7" .... Overground ..... OVER01 .... 1989 **£4** .... **£1.50** ... *yellow or white vinyl*
You Make Me Sick .... 7" .... DJM .... DJS10840 .... 1978 **£8** .... **£4** ....
You Make Me Sick .... 7" .... Overground ..... OVER14 .... 1991 **£4** .... **£1.50** .... *clear vinyl*

SATCHMO, PAT

Hello Dolly .... 7" .... Upsetter .... US316 .... 1969 **£4** .... **£1.50** ....
Hello Dolly .... 7" .... Punch .... PH9 .... 1969 **£4** .... **£1.50** .... *Eric Donaldson B side*
What's Going On .... 7" .... Attack .... ATT8024 .... 1972 **£5** .... **£2** .... *Lloyd & Carey B side*
Wonderful World .... 7" .... Punch .... PH24 .... 1970 **£4** .... **£1.50** .... *Meditators B side*

SATIN BELLS

I Stand Accused .... 7" .... Decca .... F22937 .... 1969 **£5** .... **£2** ....

SATIN WHALE

Desert Places .... LP .... Brain .... 0001049 .... 1974 **£10** .... **£4** .... *German*

SATINS FOUR & THE CINNAMON ANGELS

Mixed Soul .... LP .... B.T.Puppy .... S1010 .... 1970 **£15** .... **£6** .... *US*

SATISFACTION

Satisfaction .... LP .... Decca .... SKL5075 .... 1971 **£12** .... **£5** ....

SATISFIERS

Satisfiers .... LP .... Vogue Coral .... LVA9068 .... 1957 **£12** .... **£5** ....
Where'll I Be Tomorrow Tonight? .... 7" .... Vogue Coral .... Q72247 .... 1957 **£8** .... **£4** ....

SATRIANI, JOE

Joe Satriani's records, which consist for the most part of furiously delivered guitar instrumentals, are very highly rated by those who have never heard the work of a top-flight contemporary jazz guitarist like John Scofield or Bill Frisell.

Satch EP .... CD-s ... Relativity .... 6589532 .... 1991 **£5** .... **£2** ....
Surfing With The Alien .... LP .... Food For Thought .... GRUB8P .... 1987 **£10** .... **£4** .... *picture disc*

SATTIN, LONNIE

Trapped .... 7" .... Capitol .... CL14552 .... 1956 **£4** .... **£1.50** ....

SATURNALIA

Like the other early rock LP picture disc (Curved Air's *Airconditioning*), *Magical Love* looks rather better than it sounds, for only a few playings are enough to make the sound quality begin to deteriorate seriously. And unlike the situation with Curved Air, Saturnalia's record was never issued in the more conventional form. As a result, it is hard to be fair to the music: it sounds like third-division progressive fare – a bit like Principal Edward's Magic Theatre on an off day – but listening through the welter of background hiss one cannot be sure. To be complete, by the way, the record should come with a booklet, although few copies of this seem to have survived.

Magical Love .... LP .... Matrix .... TRIX1 .... 1969 **£25** .... **£10** .... *picture disc with centre pattern & booklet*
Magical Love .... LP .... Matrix .... TRIX1 .... 1969 **£50** .... **£25** ...... *test pressing, black vinyl*

SAUNDERS, JACK

Mike Todd's Broadway .... LP .... Top Rank .... 35021 .... 1959 **£10** .... **£4** .... *with the Robert Farnon Orchestra*

SAUNDERS, LARRY

On The Real Side .... 7" .... London .... HLU10469 .... 1974 **£5** .... **£2** ....

SAUNDERS, MAHALIA

Pieces Of My Heart .... 7" .... Upsetter .... US374 .... 1971 **£5** .... **£2** .... *Upsetters B side*

SAUTER, JIM & DON DIETRICH

Bells Together .... LP .... Agaric .... AG1985 .... 1985 **£20** .... **£8** .... *US*

SAUTER–FINEGAN ORCHESTRA

Inside Sauter–Finegan	LP	HMV	CLP1027	1955	**£25**	**£10**	
Memories Of Goodman And Miller	LP	RCA	RD27093/SF5029	1959	**£12**	**£5**	

SAUTERELLES

Heavenly Club	7"	Decca	F22824	1968	**£30**	**£15**	
Les Sauterelles	LP	Columbia	10108	1968	**£30**	**£15**	*Swiss*
View To Heaven	LP	Decca	SLK16561	1968	**£40**	**£20**	*German*

SAVAGE, EDNA

Arrivederci Darling	7"	Parlophone	MSP6189	1955	**£8**	**£4**	
Candlelight	7"	Parlophone	MSP6181	1955	**£6**	**£2.50**	
Let Me Be Loved	7"	Parlophone	R4360	1957	**£4**	**£1.50**	
Me Head's In De Barrel	7"	Parlophone	R4301	1957	**£4**	**£1.50**	
My Prayer	7"	Parlophone	R4226	1956	**£5**	**£2**	
Never Leave Me	7"	Parlophone	R4253	1957	**£4**	**£1.50**	
Please Hurry Home	7"	Parlophone	MSP6217	1956	**£5**	**£2**	
Stars Shine In Your Eyes	7"	Parlophone	MSP6175	1955	**£6**	**£2.50**	

SAVAGE, JOAN

Five Oranges, Four Apples	7"	Columbia	DB3929	1957	**£4**	**£1.50**	
Left Right Out Of My Heart	7"	Columbia	DB4159	1958	**£4**	**£1.50**	
Love Letters In The Sand	7"	Columbia	DB3968	1957	**£4**	**£1.50**	
Shake Me I Rattle	7"	Columbia	DB4039	1957	**£8**	**£4**	

SAVAGE GRACE

Savage Grace	LP	Reprise	RS6399	1970	**£15**	**£6**	*US*
Savage Grace 2	LP	Reprise	RS6434	1971	**£12**	**£5**	*US*

SAVAGE RESURRECTION

Savage Resurrection	LP	Mercury	SMCL20123	1968	**£60**	**£30**	
Thing In E	7"	Mercury	MF1027	1968	**£10**	**£5**	

SAVAGE ROSE

In The Plain	LP	Polydor	46292	1968	**£10**	**£4**	
Savage Rose	LP	Polydor	184144	1968	**£10**	**£4**	
Travellin'	LP	Polydor	184316	1969	**£10**	**£4**	

SAVAGES

Everybody Surf	7" EP	Decca	DFE8546	1963	**£200**	**£100**	
Surfin' USA	7" EP	Decca	457020	1963	**£200**	**£100**	*French*

SAVAGES (2)

Live 'n' Wild	LP	Resurrection	CX1330	1984	**£12**	**£5**	*US*
Live 'n' Wild	LP	Duane	1047	1966	**£300**	**£180**	*US*

SAVARIN, JULIAN JAY

I Am You	7"	Lyntone	LYN3426	197–	**£6**	**£2.50**	
Waiters On The Dance	LP	Birth	RAB2	1971	**£100**	**£50**	

SAVILLE, JIMMY

Ahab The Arab	7"	Decca	F11493	1962	**£4**	**£1.50**	

SAVOY BROWN

Savoy Brown passed through numerous line-ups, in which the presence of guitarist Kim Simmonds was the only constant factor. Simmonds and his companions lacked the imagination to break very far out of the constraints of playing the blues, although they tried hardest on *Blue Matter*, which includes the memorable 'Train To Nowhere'.

Blue Matter	LP	Decca	LK/SKL4994	1968	**£20**	**£8**	
Boogie Brothers	LP	Decca	SKL5186	1974	**£10**	**£4**	
Getting To The Point	LP	Decca	LK/SKL4925	1968	**£30**	**£15**	
Hard Way To Go	7"	Decca	F13019	1970	**£5**	**£2**	
Hellbound Train	LP	Decca	TXS107	1972	**£10**	**£4**	
I Tried	7"	Purdah	453503	1966	**£100**	**£50**	
I'm Tired	7"	Decca	F12978	1969	**£5**	**£2**	
Jack The Toad	LP	Decca	TXS112	1973	**£10**	**£4**	
Lion's Share	LP	Decca	SKL5152	1973	**£10**	**£4**	
Looking In	LP	Decca	SKL5066	1970	**£15**	**£6**	
Poor Girl	7"	Decca	F13098	1970	**£5**	**£2**	
Raw Sienna	LP	Decca	LK/SKL5030	1970	**£15**	**£6**	
Shake Down	LP	Decca	LK/SKL4883	1967	**£30**	**£15**	
Skin 'n' Bone	LP	London	PS670	1976	**£12**	**£5**	*US*
Step Further	LP	Decca	LK/SKL5013	1969	**£15**	**£6**	
Street Corner Talking	LP	Decca	TXS104	1970	**£12**	**£5**	
Taste And Try Before You Buy	7"	Decca	F12702	1967	**£8**	**£4**	
Tell Mama	7"	Decca	F13247	1971	**£4**	**£1.50**	
Train To Nowhere	7"	Decca	F12843	1969	**£5**	**£2**	
Walking By Myself	7"	Decca	F12797	1968	**£5**	**£2**	
Wire Fire	LP	London	PS659	1975	**£12**	**£5**	*US*

SAX, ACE DINNING

Mulholland Drive	7"	Top Rank	JAR184	1959	**£5**	**£2**	

SAXON

And The Bands Played On	7"	Carrere	CAR180P	1981	**£4**	**£1.50**	*picture disc*
Back On The Streets	7"	Parlophone	RP6103	1985	**£4**	**£1.50**	*shaped picture disc*
Power And The Glory	7"	RCA	SAXONP1	1983	**£4**	**£1.50**	*signed picture disc*

Ride Like The Wind	CD-s	EMI	CDEM43	1988	£5	£2	
Rock The Nations	7"	EMI	EMIP5587	1986	£4	£1.50	shaped picture disc

SAXON, AL

Battle Of The Sexes	7" EP	Fontana	TFE17271	1960	£8	£4	
Big Deal	7" EP	Fontana	TFE17202	1959	£8	£4	
Only Sixteen	7"	Fontana	H205	1959	£4	£1.50	
Those You've Never Heard	7" EP	Fontana	TFE17014	1958	£8	£4	
You're The Top Cha	7"	Fontana	H164	1958	£4	£1.50	

SAXON, SKY

Dog=God	7"	Fierce	FRIGHT029	1987	£8	£4	various inserts
They Say	7"	Conquest	777	196–	£20	£10	US

SAXONE, LINDA

Love Is A Many Splendoured Thing	7"	Pye	7N15624	1964	£4	£1.50	

SAXONS

Meet The Saxons	LP	Ace Of Clubs	ACL1173	1963	£75	£37.50	
Saxon War Cry	7"	Decca	F12179	1965	£30	£15	

SAXONS (2)

Love Minus Zero	LP	Mirrosonic	AS1017	1966	£25	£10	US

SAYLES, JOHNNY

Deep Down In Your Heart	7"	Liberty	LIB12042	1966	£10	£5	

SCAFFOLD

2 Day's Monday	7"	Parlophone	R5443	1966	£4	£1.50	
Do You Remember?	7"	Parlophone	R5679	1968	£4	£1.50	
Evening With The Scaffold	LP	Parlophone	PMC/PCS7051	1968	£12	£5	
Fresh Liver	LP	Island	ILPS9234	1973	£10	£4	
Goodbat Nightman	7"	Parlophone	R5548	1966	£5	£2	
L The P	LP	Parlophone	PMC/PCS7077	1969	£10	£4	

SCAGGS, BOZ

Boz	LP	Polydor	LPHM46253	1965	£40	£20	Swedish
Boz Scaggs	LP	Columbia	AS203	1974	£15	£6	US promo sampler
Boz Scaggs	LP	Atlantic	588205	1969	£10	£4	
Heart Of Mine	CD-s	CBS	6515592	1988	£5	£2	
Silk Degrees	LP	Columbia	HC43920	1980	£10	£4	US audiophile
Still Falling For You	LP	Columbia		1978	£15	£6	US early version of 'Two Down Then Left'

SCALA

Theme From Brond	CD-s	Cocteau	COQCD21	1988	£5	£2	3" single

SCALES, HARVEY & THE SOUND

Get Down	7"	Atlantic	584146	1967	£4	£1.50	

SCAMPS

Petite Fleur	7"	London	HLW8827	1959	£5	£2	

SCAPA FLOW

Uuteen Aikaan	LP		KOLP22	1980	£75	£37.50	Finnish

SCARECROW

Scarecrow	LP	Spilt Milk	SMFM11278	1978	£60	£30	numbered

SCENE

Hey Girl	7"	Hole In The Wall	HS1	1980	£5	£2	

SCHAEFER, HAL ORCHESTRA

March Of The Vikings	7"	London	HLT8692	1958	£4	£1.50	

SCHAUBROECK, ARMAND STEALS

I Came To Visit	LP	Mirror	3	1977	£12	£5	US
Live At Holiday Inn	LP	Mirror	4	1977	£15	£6	US, with 12"
Lot Of People Would Like To See A.S. Dead	LP	Mirror	FPV42202/3/4	1977	£20	£8	US triple
Ratfucker	LP	Mirror	7	1978	£12	£5	US
Shakin' Shakin'	LP	Mirror	5	1978	£12	£5	US

SCHICKE, FUHRS, FROHLING

Symphonic Pictures	LP	Brain	60010	1976	£10	£4	

SCHICKERT, GUNTER

Samtvogel	LP	Brain	1080	1975	£15	£6	German
Samtvogel	LP	SCH	33003	1974	£30	£15	German

SCHIFRIN, LALO

Ape Shuffle	7"	20th Century	BTC2150	1974	£5	£2	
Mission Impossible	7"	Dot	DOT103	1968	£5	£2	
Mission Impossible	LP	Dot	(S)LPD503	1968	£30	£15	
More Mission: Impossible	LP	Paramount	SPFL252	1969	£30	£15	

SCHMETTERLINGE

Boom Boom Boomerang	7"	Pye	7N25743	1977	**£6**	**£2.50**	

SCHMIDT, ZAPPATA

It's Gonna Get You	LP	President	PTLS1041	1971	**£10**	**£4**	

SCHMITT, OLIVER LINDSEY

Graffenstadden	LP	private		1972	**£40**	**£20**	

SCHNITZLER, CONRAD

Auf Dem Schwarzen Kanal	LP	RCA	5908	1980	**£10**	**£4**	*German*
Black Cassette	cass	private		1974	**£15**	**£6**	*German*
Blau	LP	Block	KS1003	1972	**£20**	**£8**	*German*
Con	LP	Paragon	66052	1978	**£10**	**£4**	*German*
Con 3	LP	Sky	SKY061	1981	**£10**	**£4**	*German*
Conal	LP	Uniton	U002	1981	**£10**	**£4**	*Norwegian*
Conrad Und Sohn	LP	private	GS1001	1981	**£10**	**£4**	*German*
Contempora	LP	private	CT1001	1981	**£10**	**£4**	*German*
Control	LP	Dys	DYS04	1981	**£10**	**£4**	*US*
Convex	LP	private	GS1002	1982	**£10**	**£4**	*German*
Conzequenz	LP	Block	KS1004	1980	**£10**	**£4**	*German*
Gelb	LP	Block	EB110	1983	**£10**	**£4**	*German*
Grun	LP	Block	EB111	1983	**£10**	**£4**	*German*
Red Cassette	cass	private		1974	**£15**	**£6**	*German*
Rot	LP	Block	KS1002	1971	**£20**	**£8**	*German*
Schwarz	LP	Block	KS1001	1971	**£20**	**£8**	*German*

SCHOENER, EBERHARD

Bali Agung	LP	Hör Zu	29647	1976	**£10**	**£4**	*German*
Bastien Und Bastienne	LP	EMI	30231	1977	**£10**	**£4**	*German*
Book	LP	Ariola	28706	1978	**£10**	**£4**	*German*
Day's Lullaby	LP	Reprise	REP44143	1971	**£10**	**£4**	*German*
Der Schauspieldirektor	LP	EMI	30230	1977	**£10**	**£4**	*German*
Destruction Of Harmony	LP	Ariola	808471U	1971	**£12**	**£5**	*German*
Die Schachtel	LP	Reprise		1971	**£25**	**£10**	*German*
Events	LP	Harvest	45879	1980	**£10**	**£4**	*German*
Flash Back	LP	Harvest	32839	1978	**£10**	**£4**	*German*
Meditation	LP	Ariola	87131	1974	**£10**	**£4**	*German*
Spurensicherung	LP	Phonogram	814167	1983	**£10**	**£4**	*German*
Trance Formation	LP	Harvest	32526	1977	**£10**	**£4**	*German*
Video Flashback	LP	Harvest	SHSM2030	1979	**£10**	**£4**	
Video Magic	7"	Harvest	HAR5196	1979	**£4**	**£1.50**	
Video Magic	LP	Harvest	45234	1978	**£10**	**£4**	*German*
Windows	LP	EMI	95634	1974	**£10**	**£4**	*German*

SCHOLARS

Scholars	7" EP	Stagesound	SDE29370/1	1964	**£10**	**£5**	

SCHOOL BOYS

Dream Lover	7"	Port-O-Jam	PJ4000	1964	**£10**	**£5**	
Little Dilly	7"	Blue Beat	BB174	1963	**£12**	**£6**	*Prince Buster B side*

SCHOOL GIRLS

Last Time	7"	Blue Beat	BB214	1964	**£12**	**£6**	
Live Up To Justice	7"	Blue Beat	BB185	1963	**£12**	**£6**	
Love Another Love	7"	Blue Beat	BB168	1963	**£12**	**£6**	
Never Let You Go	7"	Blue Beat	BB263	1964	**£12**	**£6**	*Skatalites B side*

SCHOOLBOYS

Beatle Mania	LP	Palace	778	1964	**£20**	**£8**	*US*

SCHOOLGIRL BITCH

Abusing The Rules	7"	Garage	AERS102	1978	**£25**	**£12.50**	

SCHROEDER, JOHN ORCHESTRA

Agent OO Soul	7"	Piccadilly	7N35271	1965	**£6**	**£2.50**	
Dolly Catcher	LP	Piccadilly	N(S)PL38036	1967	**£10**	**£4**	
Fugitive Theme	7"	Piccadilly	7N35240	1965	**£4**	**£1.50**	*picture sleeve*
Hungry For Love	7"	Piccadilly	7N35285	1966	**£5**	**£2**	
Soul For Sale	7"	Piccadilly	7N35362	1967	**£8**	**£4**	
Themes From Television	LP	Polydor	2460188	1973	**£10**	**£4**	
TV Vibrations	LP	Polydor	2460149	1972	**£10**	**£4**	
Virgin Soldiers March	7"	Pye	7N17862	1969	**£4**	**£1.50**	
Working In The Soulmine	LP	Piccadilly	N(S)PL38025	1966	**£15**	**£6**	
You've Lost That Lovin' Feeling	7"	Piccadilly	7N35253	1965	**£4**	**£1.50**	

SCHULLER, GUNTHER

Jazz Abstractions	LP	Atlantic	587/588043	1966	**£15**	**£6**	

SCHULMAN, IVY & THE BOWTIES

Rock Pretty Baby	7"	London	HLN8372	1957	**£40**	**£20**	

SCHULTZ, ERNST

Paranoia Picknick	LP	Kuckuck	2375014	1972	**£25**	**£10**	*German*

SCHULZE, KLAUS

Although Schulze started his recording career as a drummer with Tangerine Dream (he appears on the group's debut, *Electronic Meditation*), all his own albums, of which there are a large number, contain music performed by a bank of synthesizers. Schulze's music, which has a kinship with that of Tangerine Dream, tends nevertheless to sound starker and more experimental. His records vary considerably in their effectiveness, but at their best, they show Schulze to be the finest synthesizer artist of all. *Irrlicht* is available in two different versions – the one listed here has the added benefit of a real orchestra blended with the electronics.

Black Dance	LP	Brain	1051	1974	**£15**	**£6**	*German*
Cyborg	LP	Komische	KM258005	1973	**£20**	**£8**	*German double*
Irrlicht	LP	Ohr	OMM556022	1972	**£15**	**£6**	*German*
Picture Music	LP	Brain	1067	1974	**£10**	**£4**	*German*

SCHUMANN, WALTER

Haunted House	7"	HMV	7M229	1954	**£4**	**£1.50**	
Man From Laramie	7"	HMV	7M323	1955	**£4**	**£1.50**	

SCHUNGE

Ballad Of A Simple Love	7"	Regal Zonophone	RZ3077	1973	**£4**	**£1.50**	
Ballad Of A Simple Love	LP	Regal Zonophone	SLRZ1033	1972	**£15**	**£6**	
Misty	7"	Regal Zonophone	RZ3066	1972	**£4**	**£1.50**	

SCIENCE POPTION

You've Got Me High	7"	Columbia	DB8106	1967	**£30**	**£15**	

SCIENTIST

Professor In Action	7"	Amalgamated	AMG848	1969	**£6**	**£2.50**	

SCI-FI SEX STARS

Rock It Miss USA	7"	Who Am I	WMI0017	1986	**£5**	**£2**	

SCOBEY, BOB

Bob Scobey Band	10" LP	Good Time Jazz	LDG155	1955	**£15**	**£6**	
Bob Scobey Band	LP	Columbia	33CX10058	1956	**£12**	**£5**	
Bob Scobey's Frisco Band	LP	Good Time Jazz	LAG12116	1958	**£15**	**£6**	
Bob Scobey's Frisco Band	LP	Good Time Jazz	LAG12180	1959	**£12**	**£5**	
Bob Scobey's Frisco Jazz Band	10" LP	HMV	DLP1146	1957	**£12**	**£5**	
Scobey And Clancy	LP	Good Time Jazz	LAG12145	1959	**£12**	**£5**	*with Clancy Hayes*
Swingin' On The Golden Gate	LP	RCA	RD27031	1958	**£12**	**£5**	

SCORCHED EARTH

Tomorrow Never Comes	12"	Carrere	CART342	1985	**£25**	**£12.50**	
Tomorrow Never Comes	7"	Carrere	CAR342	1985	**£20**	**£10**	

SCORCHERS

Ugly Man	7"	Doctor Bird	DB1170	1968	**£10**	**£5**	

SCORE

Please Please Me	7"	Decca	F12527	1966	**£100**	**£50**	

SCORPIONS

Lonesome Crow	LP	Heavy Metal	MHIPD2	1982	**£10**	**£4**	*picture disc*
Lonesome Crow	LP	Brain	1001	1972	**£10**	**£4**	*German*
Passion Rules The Game	CD-s	Harvest	CDHAR5242	1989	**£5**	**£2**	

SCORPIONS (2)

Riders In The Sky	7"	Parlophone	R4740	1961	**£8**	**£4**	
Scorpio	7"	Parlophone	R4768	1961	**£8**	**£4**	

SCORPIONS (3)

Scorpions	LP	Tower	ST5171	1969	**£20**	**£8**	*US*

SCORPIONS (4)

Climbing The Charts	LP	CNR	LPT35023	1965	**£100**	**£50**	*Dutch*
Hello Josephine	LP	CNR	GA5000	1965	**£50**	**£25**	*Dutch*
Keep In Touch	LP	CNR	SKLP4240	1966	**£100**	**£50**	*Dutch*
Scorpions	LP	CNR	385250	1965	**£50**	**£25**	*Dutch*
Sweet And Lovely	LP	CNR	GA5027	1968	**£50**	**£25**	*Dutch*

SCOTCH

Scotch	LP	R.T.Club	LP25002	1966	**£250**	**£150**	*Italian*

SCOTS OF ST JAMES

Gypsy	7"	Go	AJ111404	1966	**£100**	**£50**	
Timothy	7"	Spot	JW1	1967	**£100**	**£50**	

SCOTT, ANDY

Invisible	12"	Static	TAK3112	1984	**£6**	**£2.50**	*clear vinyl*
Invisible	7"	Static	TAK31	1984	**£4**	**£1.50**	*clear vinyl*
Krugerrands	7"	Static	TAK10	1983	**£5**	**£2**	

Title	Format	Label	Number	Year	Mint	Excellent	Note
Lady Starlight	7"	RCA	RCA2629	1975	**£8**	**£4**	
Let Her Dance	12"	Static	TAK2412	1984	**£6**	**£2.50**	
Let Her Dance	7"	Static	TAK24	1984	**£6**	**£2.50**	

SCOTT, ARTIE ORCHESTRA

Title	Format	Label	Number	Year	Mint	Excellent	Note
March Of The Skinheads	7"	Major Minor	MM670	1970	**£5**	**£2**	

SCOTT, BILLY

Title	Format	Label	Number	Year	Mint	Excellent	Note
You're The Greatest	7"	London	HLU8565	1958	**£10**	**£5**	

SCOTT, BOBBY

Title	Format	Label	Number	Year	Mint	Excellent	Note
Bobby Scott Trio	10" LP	London	LZN14001	1955	**£25**	**£10**	
Bobby Scott Trio	7" EP	London	EZC19008	1956	**£5**	**£2**	
Chain Gang	7"	London	HL8254	1956	**£[illegible]**	**£[illegible]**	
Compositions	10" LP	London	LZN14018	1956	**£25**	**£10**	
Great Scott	10" LP	Bethlehem	1004	1954	**£20**	**£8**	*US*

SCOTT, BRUCE

Title	Format	Label	Number	Year	Mint	Excellent	Note
I Made An Angel Cry	7"	Mercury	MF857	1965	**£10**	**£5**	

SCOTT, CECIL

Title	Format	Label	Number	Year	Mint	Excellent	Note
Harlem Washboard	LP	Columbia	33SX1232	1960	**£10**	**£4**	

SCOTT, DANA & THE CROWN FOLK

Title	Format	Label	Number	Year	Mint	Excellent	Note
Folk In Worship	LP	BBC	REC58M	1969	**£15**	**£6**	

SCOTT, FREDDIE

Title	Format	Label	Number	Year	Mint	Excellent	Note
Am I Grooving You	7"	London	HLZ10139	1967	**£4**	**£1.50**	
Are You Lonely For Me	7"	London	HLZ10103	1967	**£5**	**£2**	
Are You Lonely For Me	LP	Shout	SLP(S)501	1967	**£15**	**£6**	*US*
Are You Lonely For Me	LP	Joy	JOYS215	1971	**£10**	**£4**	
Cry To Me	7"	London	HLZ10123	1967	**£4**	**£1.50**	
Everything I Have Is Yours	LP	Columbia	CL2258/CS9058	1964	**£20**	**£8**	*US*
Freddie Scott Sings	LP	Colpix	(S)CP461	1964	**£20**	**£8**	*US*
Hey Girl	7"	Colpix	PX692	1963	**£10**	**£5**	
I Got A Woman	7"	Colpix	PX709	1963	**£10**	**£5**	
Lonely Man	LP	Columbia	CL2660/CS9460	1967	**£15**	**£6**	*US*

SCOTT, HAZEL

Title	Format	Label	Number	Year	Mint	Excellent	Note
Late Show	10" LP	Capitol	LC6607	1953	**£15**	**£6**	

SCOTT, JACK

Title	Format	Label	Number	Year	Mint	Excellent	Note
All I See Is Blue	7"	Capitol	CL15302	1963	**£8**	**£4**	
Burning Bridges	7"	Top Rank	JAR375	1960	**£4**	**£1.50**	
Burning Bridges	7" EP	Capitol	EAP20035	1959	**£100**	**£50**	*demo*
Burning Bridges	LP	Capitol	(S)T2035	1964	**£40**	**£20**	
Cool Water	7"	Top Rank	JAR419	1960	**£6**	**£2.50**	
Goodbye Baby	7"	London	HLU8804	1959	**£8**	**£4**	
Goodbye Baby	7"	London	HL7069	1959	**£5**	**£2**	*export*
I Can't Hold Your Letters In My Arms	7"	Capitol	CL15261	1962	**£8**	**£4**	
I Never Felt Like This	7"	London	HLL8851	1959	**£8**	**£4**	
I Remember Hank Williams	7" EP	Top Rank	JKP3011	1961	**£30**	**£15**	
I Remember Hank Williams	LP	Top Rank	BUY034	1960	**£30**	**£15**	
Is There Something On Your Mind	7"	Top Rank	JAR547	1961	**£5**	**£2**	
Jack Scott	LP	London	HAL2156	1958	**£75**	**£37.50**	
Little Feeling	7"	Capitol	CL15200	1961	**£5**	**£2**	
My Dream Come True	7"	Capitol	CL15216	1961	**£6**	**£2.50**	
My True Love	7"	London	HLU8626	1958	**£5**	**£2**	
My True Love	7" EP	London	REI1205	1959	**£75**	**£37.50**	*tri-centre*
Patsy	7"	Top Rank	JAR524	1960	**£5**	**£2**	
Spirit Moves Me	LP	Top Rank	35109	1961	**£40**	**£20**	
Steps One And Two	7"	Capitol	CL15236	1962	**£6**	**£2.50**	
There Comes A Time	7"	London	HLL8970	1959	**£10**	**£5**	*tri-centre*
Way I Walk	7"	London	HLL8912	1959	**£15**	**£7.50**	*tri-centre*
What Am I Living For	LP	Carlton	(ST)LP12122	1958	**£75**	**£37.50**	*US*
What In The World's Come Over You	7"	Top Rank	JAR280	1960	**£4**	**£1.50**	
What In The World's Come Over You	7" EP	Top Rank	JKP3002	1961	**£40**	**£20**	
What In The World's Come Over You	LP	Top Rank	25024	1960	**£50**	**£25**	
With Your Love	7"	London	HLU8765	1958	**£8**	**£4**	

SCOTT, JOHNNY

Title	Format	Label	Number	Year	Mint	Excellent	Note
Communication	LP	Columbia	SX/SCX6149	1967	**£15**	**£6**	
Purcell Variations For Five	LP	Fontana	6383002	1970	**£15**	**£6**	

SCOTT, JUDI

Title	Format	Label	Number	Year	Mint	Excellent	Note
Billy Sunshine	7"	Page One	POF066	1968	**£6**	**£2.50**	

SCOTT, LINDA

Title	Format	Label	Number	Year	Mint	Excellent	Note
Count Every Star	7"	Columbia	DB4829	1961	**£4**	**£1.50**	
Great Scott	LP	Columbia		1961	**£40**	**£20**	
Greatest Hits	LP	Canadian American	(S)1007	1962	**£40**	**£20**	*US*
Hey Look At Me Now	LP	Kapp	KL1424/KS3424	1965	**£25**	**£10**	*US*
I've Told Every Little Star	7"	Columbia	DB4638	1960	**£4**	**£1.50**	
It's All Because	7"	Columbia	DB4748	1961	**£4**	**£1.50**	
Let's Fall In Love	7"	London	HLR9802	1963	**£4**	**£1.50**	
Linda	LP	Congress	(S)3001	1962	**£40**	**£20**	*US*
Never In A Million Years	7"	Pye	7N25146	1962	**£4**	**£1.50**	

Starlight, Starbright	LP	Columbia	33SX1386	1961	**£50**	**£25**	

SCOTT, LINDA (2)

Composer	7"	CBS	4528	1969	**£4**	**£1.50**	

SCOTT, MIKE

I Am A Rock	7"	Mercury	MF906	1965	**£4**	**£1.50**	

SCOTT, NICKY

Back Street Girl	7"	Immediate	IM045	1967	**£10**	**£5**	
Big City	7"	Immediate	IM044	1967	**£15**	**£7.50**	

SCOTT, PETE

Don't Panic	LP	Rubber	RUB003	1971	**£25**	**£10**	
Jimmy The Moonlight	LP	Rubber	RUB020	1976	**£25**	**£10**	

SCOTT, RAMBLIN' TOMMY

Ain't Love Grand	7"	Parlophone	CMSP15	1954	**£10**	**£5**	*export*

SCOTT, ROBIN

Sailor	7"	Head	HEAD4003	1969	**£20**	**£10**	
Woman From The Warm Grass	LP	Head	HDLS6003	1969	**£100**	**£50**	

SCOTT, RONNIE

At The Royal Festival Hall	10" LP	Decca	LF1261	1956	**£30**	**£15**	
Basie Talks	7"	Decca	FJ10712	1956	**£4**	**£1.50**	
Live At Ronnie Scott's	LP	CBS	52661	1969	**£25**	**£10**	
Night Is Scott And You're So Swingable	LP	Fontana	TL5332	1966	**£40**	**£20**	
Presenting The Ronnie Scott Sextet	LP	Philips	BBL7153	1957	**£20**	**£8**	
Ronnie Scott Blows	7" EP	Tempo	EXA45	1956	**£50**	**£25**	
Ronnie Scott Jazz Club Vol. 1	LP	Esquire	32001	1954	**£40**	**£20**	
Ronnie Scott Jazz Club Vol. 2	LP	Esquire	32002	1954	**£40**	**£20**	
Ronnie Scott Jazz Club Vol. 3	LP	Esquire	32003	1954	**£40**	**£20**	
Ronnie Scott Jazz Club Vol. 4	LP	Esquire	32006	1954	**£40**	**£20**	
Ronnie Scott Orchestra	7" EP	Esquire	EP85	1956	**£15**	**£7.50**	
Ronnie Scott Orchestra	7" EP	Esquire	EP81	1956	**£10**	**£5**	
Ronnie Scott Orchestra	7" EP	Esquire	EP95	1956	**£10**	**£5**	
Ronnie Scott Orchestra	7" EP	Esquire	EP31	1955	**£10**	**£5.50**	
Ronnie Scott Orchestra	7" EP	Esquire	EP61	1955	**£10**	**£5**	
Ronnie Scott Quartet	10" LP	Esquire	20006	1953	**£40**	**£20**	
Ronnie Scott Quartet	7" EP	Esquire	EP51	1955	**£10**	**£5**	
Ronnie Scott Quintet	7" EP	Esquire	EP65	1955	**£10**	**£5**	
Scott At Ronnie's	LP	RCA	LPL1	1974	**£20**	**£8**	
Serious Gold	LP	Pye	NSPL18542	1977	**£12**	**£5**	

SCOTT, SHIRLEY

And The Soul Saxes	LP	Atlantic	SD1532	1970	**£12**	**£5**	*US*
Hip Soul	LP	Transatlantic	PR7205	1966	**£15**	**£6**	
Mystical Lady	LP	Chess	6310109	1971	**£10**	**£4**	
Soul Song	LP	Atlantic	588175	1969	**£12**	**£5**	

SCOTT, SIMON

Move It Baby	7"	Parlophone	R5164	1964	**£4**	**£1.50**	*with Le Roys*
My Baby's Got Soul	7"	Parlophone	R5207	1964	**£4**	**£1.50**	*with Le Roys*
Tell Him I'm Not Home	7"	Parlophone	R5298	1965	**£8**	**£4**	

SCOTT, TERRY

My Brother	7"	Parlophone	R4967	1962	**£6**	**£2.50**	

SCOTT, TONY

Fifty-Second Street Scene	LP	Coral	LVA9109	1959	**£20**	**£8**	
South Pacific Jazz	LP	HMV	CLP1190	1958	**£12**	**£5**	
Tony Scott Quartet	10" LP	Vogue Coral	LRA10037	1955	**£30**	**£15**	
Tony Scott Quartet	10" LP	Vogue Coral	LRA10034	1955	**£30**	**£15**	

SCOTT, WILLIE

Shepherd's Song – Border Ballads	LP	Topic	12T183	1968	**£15**	**£6**	

SCOTT-HERON, GIL

Gil Scott-Heron's blending of street poetry with music that straddles the divide between funk and jazz has a crucial role in the development of rap. Indeed, when Scott-Heron took on the rap approach directly, on his savage attack against Ronald Reagan, 'B Movie', he managed to create one of the most powerful performances of all. All his records, with the possible exception of the hit single, 'Johannesburg', are now keenly sought after, especially the early albums issued only in the US.

1980	LP	Arista	AL9514	1980	**£15**	**£6**	*US*
B Movie	12"	Arista	ARIST573	1984	**£6**	**£2.50**	
B Movie	7"	Arista	ARIST452	1981	**£4**	**£1.50**	
B Movie	7"	Arista	ARIST573	1984	**£4**	**£1.50**	
Best Of Gil Scott-Heron	LP	Arista	206618	1984	**£10**	**£4**	
Bottle	12"	Arista	ARIST169	1978	**£6**	**£2.50**	
Bottle	12"	Inferno	HEAT2312	1979	**£6**	**£2.50**	
Bottle	7"	Arista	ARIST169	1978	**£4**	**£1.50**	
Bottle	7"	Inferno	HEAT23	1979	**£4**	**£1.50**	
Bottle	LP	Audio Fidelity	AFEMP1017	1981	**£15**	**£6**	
Bridges	LP	Arista	SPARTY1031	1977	**£15**	**£6**	
First Minute Of A New Day	LP	Arista	ARTY106	1975	**£25**	**£10**	

Title	Format	Label	Number	Year	Mint	VG	Notes
Free Will	LP	Flying Dutchman	10153	1972	£40	£20	US
From South Africa To South Carolina	LP	Arista	ARTY121	1976	£15	£6	
It's Your World	LP	Arista	DARTY1	1976	£30	£15	double
Lady Day And John Coltrane	7"	Philips	6073705	1971	£4	£1.50	
Moving Targets	LP	Arista	204921	1982	£12	£5	
Pieces Of a Man	LP	Philips	6369415	1973	£30	£15	
Real Eyes	LP	Arista	AL9540	1980	£15	£6	US
Reflections	LP	Arista	SPARTY1180	1981	£12	£5	
Revolution Will Not Be Televised	LP	RCA	SF8428	1975	£20	£8	
Secrets	LP	Arista	SPARTY1073	1978	£15	£6	
Small Talk At 125th And Lennox	LP	Flying Dutchman	FDS131	1972	£40	£20	US
Winter In America	LP	Strata East	19742	1975	£30	£15	US

SCOTTI, MICHELLE

Title	Format	Label	Number	Year	Mint	VG	Notes
Little Drummer Boy	7"	Philips	BF1384	1964	£4	£1.50	

SCOTTY

Title	Format	Label	Number	Year	Mint	VG	Notes
Donkey Skank	7"	Duke	DU106	1971	£4	£1.50	Murphy's All Stars B side
Jam Rock Style	7"	Songbird	SB1051	1971	£4	£1.50	
Riddle I This	7"	Songbird	SB1049	1971	£4	£1.50	
Schooldays	LP	Trojan	TRL33	1971	£30	£15	
Sesame Street	7"	Songbird	SB1044	1970	£5	£2	Crystalites B side

SCRAMBLERS

Title	Format	Label	Number	Year	Mint	VG	Notes
Cycle Psychos	LP	Crown	384	1964	£20	£8	US

SCREAMING GYPSY BANDITS

Title	Format	Label	Number	Year	Mint	VG	Notes
In The Eye	LP	BRBQ	BRBQ3	1973	£60	£30	US

SCRITTI POLITTI

Title	Format	Label	Number	Year	Mint	VG	Notes
Absolute	12"	Virgin	VSY68012	1984	£6	£2.50	picture disc
First Boy In This Town	CD-s	Virgin	VSCD1082	1988	£5	£2	
Oh Patti	CD-s	Virgin	CDEP17	1988	£5	£2	
Skank Bloc	7"	St Pancras	SCRIT1	1978	£4	£1.50	
Wood Beez	CD-s	Virgin	CDT34	1988	£5	£2	3" single
Word Girl	CD-s	Virgin	CDT13	1988	£5	£2	3" single

SCROTUM POLES

Title	Format	Label	Number	Year	Mint	VG	Notes
Revelation	7"	Scrotum Poles	ERECT1	1980	£20	£10	

SCRUGG

Title	Format	Label	Number	Year	Mint	VG	Notes
I Wish I Was Five	7"	Pye	7N17451	1968	£20	£10	
Lavender Popcorn	7"	Pye	7N17551	1968	£30	£15	
Will The Real Geraldine Please Stand Up	7"	Pye	7N17656	1969	£20	£10	

SEA URCHINS

Title	Format	Label	Number	Year	Mint	VG	Notes
30.10.88	7"	Fierce	FRIGHT032	1989	£6	£2.50	
Pristine Christine	7"	Sarah	001	1987	£15	£7.50	with poster
Solace	7"	Sarah	008	1988	£5	£2	

SEA-DERS

Title	Format	Label	Number	Year	Mint	VG	Notes
Sea-ders	7" EP	Decca	DFER8674	1968	£175	£87.50	export
Thanks A Lot	7"	Decca	F22576	1967	£25	£12.50	

SEAMEN, PHIL

Title	Format	Label	Number	Year	Mint	VG	Notes
Meets Eddie Gomez	LP	Saga	OPP102	1968	£60	£30	
Phil On Drums	LP	77	SEU1253	1974	£30	£15	
Phil Seamen Now . . . Live!	LP	Verve	(S)VLP9220	1968	£100	£50	
Phil Seamen Story	LP	Decibel	BSN103	1973	£40	£20	

SEARCH PARTY

Title	Format	Label	Number	Year	Mint	VG	Notes
Montgomery's Chapel	LP	private		1969	£2000	£1400	US

SEARCHERS

The Searchers filtered the R&B material of the day through vocal harmonies derived from the Everly Brothers and a noticeable country influence, emerging as the second most successful of the Merseybeat groups. Although the group's run of hit singles ran out towards the end of the sixties, they continued to tour with new material despite having no record contract for much of the seventies. They came close to managing a come-back in 1980 with a critically acclaimed album for Sire, but these days they are finally forced to ply the nostalgia circuit – sadly split by internal disagreement into two separate sets of Searchers. The group's collectable items from the sixties include their own privately pressed demo album and a live album recorded in Germany, neither of which turns up very often.

Title	Format	Label	Number	Year	Mint	VG	Notes
Ain't Gonna Kiss Ya	7" EP	Pye	NEP24177	1963	£6	£2.50	
Another Night	7"	Sire	SIR4049	1981	£5	£2	
Bumble Bee	7" EP	Pye	NEP24218	1965	£8	£4	
Bumble Bee	7" EP	Pye	PNV24137	1965	£20	£10	French
Chantent En Français	7" EP	Pye	PNV24121	1964	£100	£50	French
Desdemona	7"	RCA	RCA2057	1971	£10	£5	
Don't Make Promises	7"	private		197–	£6	£2.50	
Don't Throw Your Love Away	7" EP	Pye	PNV24120	1964	£20	£10	French
Four By Four	7" EP	Pye	NEP24228	1965	£10	£5	
Four Strong Winds	7"	private		197–	£6	£2.50	
He's Got No Love	7"	Pye	7N15878	1965	£4	£1.50	
Hear Hear	LP	Mercury	MG2/SR60914	1964	£25	£10	US

Title	Format	Label	Cat. No.	Year	Mint	VG	Notes
Hearts In Her Eyes	7"	Sire	SIR4029	1979	**£5**	**£2**	
Hungry For Love	7" EP	Pye	NEP24184	1964	**£6**	**£2.50**	
It's The Searchers	LP	Pye	NPL18092	1964	**£15**	**£6**	
It's Too Late	7"	Sire	SIR4036	1980	**£4**	**£1.50**	
Kinky Kathy Abernathy	7"	Liberty	LBF15340	1969	**£25**	**£12.50**	
Love Is Everywhere	7"	RCA	RCA2139	1971	**£5**	**£2**	
Love's Melody	7"	Sire	SIR4046	1981	**£6**	**£2.50**	
Meet The Searchers	LP	Pye	NPL18086	1963	**£15**	**£6**	
Meet The Searchers	LP	Kapp	KL1363/KS3363	1964	**£15**	**£6**	*US*
Needles And Pins	7"	Ariola		1964	**£20**	**£10**	*sung in German*
Needles And Pins	7"	Pye		1964	**£20**	**£10**	*sung in French*
Needles And Pins	7"	RCA	RCA2248	1972	**£5**	**£2**	
Needles And Pins	7" EP	Pye	PNV24118	1964	**£20**	**£10**	*French*
New Searchers LP	LP	Kapp	KL1412/KS3412	1965	**£15**	**£6**	*US*
Play The System	7" EP	Pye	NEP24201	1964	**£8**	**£4**	
Popcorn Double Feature	7"	Pye	7N17225	1967	**£6**	**£2.50**	
Searchers	LP	private		1962	**£150**	**£75**	
Searchers '65	7" EP	Pye	NEP24222	1965	**£10**	**£5**	
Searchers Meet The Rattles	LP	Mercury	MG2/SR60994	1965	**£30**	**£15**	*US*
Searchers No. 4	LP	Kapp	KL1449/KS3449	1965	**£15**	**£6**	*US*
Secondhand Dealer	7"	Pye	7N17424	1967	**£15**	**£7.50**	
Sing Singer Sing	7"	RCA	RCA2231	1972	**£5**	**£2**	
Someday We're Gonna Love Again	7" EP	Pye	PNV24123	1964	**£20**	**£10**	*French*
Sounds Like The Searchers	LP	Pye	NPL18111	1964	**£15**	**£6**	
Sub Ist Sie	7"	Vogue	14116	1963	**£20**	**£10**	*sung in German*
Sugar And Spice	LP	Pye	NPL18089	1963	**£15**	**£6**	
Surf Encore	7" EP	Pye	PNV24114	1963	**£20**	**£10**	*French*
Surfin' With The Searchers	7" EP	Pye	PNV24112	1963	**£20**	**£10**	*French*
Sweet Nothings	7"	Philips	BF1274	1963	**£5**	**£2**	
Sweets For My Sweet	7" EP	Pye	NEP24183	1963	**£5**	**£2**	
Sweets For My Sweet	7" EP	Pye	PNV24108	1963	**£15**	**£7.50**	*French*
Sweets For My Sweet – At The Starclub Hamburg	LP	Philips	48052L	1963	**£75**	**£37.50**	*German*
Take It Or Leave It	7"	Pye	7N17094	1966	**£4**	**£1.50**	
Take Me For What I'm Worth	7"	Pye	7N15992	1965	**£20**	**£10**	*export picture sleeve*
Take Me For What I'm Worth	7" EP	Pye	NEP24263	1966	**£60**	**£30**	
Take Me For What I'm Worth	LP	Pye	NPL18120	1965	**£15**	**£6**	
Tausend Nadelstiche	7"	Vogue	14130	1963	**£20**	**£10**	*sung in German*
Umbrella Man	7"	Liberty	LBF15159	1968	**£20**	**£10**	
Vahevala	7"	RCA	RCA2288	1972	**£8**	**£4**	
Verzeih My Love	7"	Vogue	14338	1965	**£20**	**£10**	*sung in German*
Western Union	7"	Pye	7N17308	1967	**£8**	**£4**	
When You Walk In The Room	7"	Pye	7N15694	1964	**£4**	**£1.50**	
When You Walk In The Room	7" EP	Pye	NEP24204	1964	**£10**	**£5**	

SEASTONE

Title	Format	Label	Cat. No.	Year	Mint	VG	Notes
Mirrored Dreams	LP	Plankton	PKN101	1978	**£100**	**£50**	

SEATHROUGH

Title	Format	Label	Cat. No.	Year	Mint	VG	Notes
Lala Lapla	LP	private		197–	**£40**	**£20**	

SEATON, B. B.

Title	Format	Label	Cat. No.	Year	Mint	VG	Notes
Hold On	7"	R&B	JB143	1964	**£10**	**£5**	*Lester Sterling B side*
I'm So Glad	7"	Island	WI123	1963	**£10**	**£5**	
Thin Line Between Love And Hate	LP	Trojan	TRLS59	1973	**£12**	**£5**	

SEATRAIN

Seatrain evolved out of the Blues Project, following the departure of founder members Danny Kalb, Steve Katz and Al Kooper. The new sounds of violin and saxophone acquired a dominant role and for the first Seatrain LP the musicians are clearly inspired by the novelty of their new line-up. Unfortunately, this inspiration was short-lived and the two LPs that followed are rather ordinary.

Title	Format	Label	Cat. No.	Year	Mint	VG	Notes
Seatrain	LP	A&M	AMLS941	1969	**£15**	**£6**	

SEAWIND

Title	Format	Label	Cat. No.	Year	Mint	VG	Notes
One Sweet Night	7"	CTI	CTSP13	1978	**£5**	**£2**	

SEBASTIAN, JOHN

Title	Format	Label	Cat. No.	Year	Mint	VG	Notes
John B. Sebastian	LP	Reprise	RSLP6379	1970	**£10**	**£4**	
Live	LP	MGM	SE4720	1970	**£12**	**£5**	*US*

SEBASTIAN, JOHN (2)

Title	Format	Label	Cat. No.	Year	Mint	VG	Notes
Inca Dance	7"	London	HL8029	1954	**£15**	**£7.50**	
Stranger In Paradise	7"	London	HL8131	1955	**£12**	**£6**	

SECOND CITY JAZZMEN

Title	Format	Label	Cat. No.	Year	Mint	VG	Notes
Tribute To Madge	LP	Esquire	32053	1958	**£10**	**£4**	

SECOND COMING

Title	Format	Label	Cat. No.	Year	Mint	VG	Notes
Second Coming	LP	Mercury	6338030	1970	**£10**	**£4**	

SECOND HAND

Second Hand revolved around keyboard virtuoso Ken Elliott and drummer Kieran O'Connor, who subsequently recorded as Seventh Wave. Their music is an interesting blend of classical and avant-garde influences within a sound that is nevertheless rock-based – rather like the better-known Egg, in fact. *Death May Be Your Santa Claus* is that rare thing, an expensive progressive album that is actually something of a forgotten masterpiece.

Title	Format	Label	Cat. No.	Year	Mint	VG	Notes
Death May Be Your Santa Claus	LP	Mushroom	200MR6	1972	**£100**	**£50**	

Fairy Tale	7"	Polydor	56308	1969	£10	£5	
Reality	LP	Polydor	583045	1968	£60	£30	

SECOND LAYER

Flesh As Property	7"	Tortch	TOR001	1979	£8	£4	
Flesh As Property	7"	Fresh	FRESH5	1979	£6	£2.50	
State Of Emergency	7"	Tortch	TOR006	1980	£5	£2	

SECOND LIFE

Second Life	LP	Metronome	MLP15409	1971	£30	£15	*German*

SECOND MOVEMENT

Blind Man's Mirror	LP	Castle	1003	1976	£12	£5	*German*

SECOND VISION

First Steps	LP	Chrysalis	CHR1289	1980	£10	£4	

SECRET OYSTER

Sea Son	LP	SBS80489	1974		£12	£5	
Secret Oyster	LP	CBS	65769	1973	£15	£6	*Danish*
Vidunderlige Kalling	LP	CBS	81044	1975	£15	£6	*Danish*

SECRETS

Boy Next Door	7"	Philips	BF1298	1964	£6	£2.50	
Other Side Of Town	7"	Philips	BF1318	1964	£6	£2.50	

SECRETS (2)

I Intend To Please	7"	CBS	2818	1967	£12	£6	
Infatuation	7"	CBS	202585	1967	£12	£6	
Such A Pity	7"	CBS	202466	1967	£12	£6	

SEDAKA, NEIL

Circulate	LP	RCA	RD27207/SF5090	1960	£30	£15	
Greatest Hits	LP	RCA	LPM/LSP2627	1962	£20	£8	*US*
I Go Ape	7"	RCA	RCA1115	1959	£6	£2.50	
Little Devil And His Other Hits	LP	RCA	LPM/LSP2421	1961	£25	£10	*US*
Neil Sedaka	7" EP	RCA	RCX166	1959	£25	£12.50	
Neil Sedaka	LP	RCA	RD27140	1959	£60	£30	
Neil Sedaka No. 2	7" EP	RCA	RCX186	1960	£20	£10	
Neil Sedaka No. 3	7" EP	RCA	RCX212	1962	£20	£10	
No Vacancy	7"	RCA	RCA1099	1959	£10	£5	
Oh Carol	7"	RCA	RCA1152	1959	£6	£2.50	*tri-centre*
Oh Delilah	7"	Stateside	SS105	1962	£6	£2.50	*Marvels B side*
Ring A Rocking	7"	London	HLW8961	1959	£25	£12.50	
Rock With Sedaka	LP	RCA	LPM/LSP2035	1959	£50	£25	*US*
With The Tokens	LP	Vernon	518	1963	£20	£8	*US*
World Through A Tear	7"	RCA	RCA1475	1965	£4	£1.50	
You've Got To Learn Your Rhythm And Blues	7"	RCA	RCA1130	1959	£10	£5	

SEDUCER

Call Your Name	7"	Sticky	SSR0017	1983	£30	£15	

SEEDORF, RUDY

One Million Stars	7"	Island	WI189	1965	£10	£5	

SEEDS

The Seeds, led by the eccentric Sky Saxon, were a garage punk band who achieved considerable success in their native California before being rendered obsolete by the more adventurous West Coast bands like Jefferson Airplane and Quicksilver Messenger Service. Some of their titles and visual imagery suggested that the group was heavily into psychedelia, but they are not really very convincing in this role.

Can't Seem To Make You Mine	7"	Vocalion	VN9287	1967	£20	£10	
Farmer	7" EP	Vogue	INT18125	1967	£50	£25	*French*
Full Spoon Of Seedy Blues	LP	GNP Crescendo	(S)2040	1967	£30	£15	*US red label*
Future	LP	Vocalion	VAN/SAVN8070	1967	£30	£15	
Lover's Cosmic Voyage	LP	private		1977	£150	£75	*US*
Merlin's Music Box	LP	GNP Crescendo	(S)2043	1967	£30	£15	*US red label*
No Escape	7" EP	Vogue	INT18022	1966	£75	£37.50	*French*
Psych-Out	LP	Sidewalk	ST5913	1968	£25	£10	*US, with other artists*
Pushin' Too Hard	7"	Vocalion	VN9277	1966	£20	£10	
Seeds	LP	GNP Crescendo	(S)2023	1966	£40	£20	*US red label*
Try To Understand	7" EP	Vogue	INT18077	1966	£50	£25	*French*
Web Of Sound	LP	Vocalion	VAN8062	1966	£30	£15	

SEEGER, MIKE

Mike Seeger	LP	Fontana	TFL6039	1965	£20	£8	

SEEGER, PEGGY

America At Play	LP	HMV	CLP1174	1958	£20	£8	*with Guy Carawan*
Best Of Peggy Seeger	LP	Pre	PRE13005	1961	£20	£8	
Different Therefore Equal	LP	Blackthorne	BR1061	1979	£15	£6	
Early In The Spring	7" EP	Topic	TOP73	1962	£8	£4	
Female Frolic	LP	Argo	ZFB64	1972	£10	£4	*with Frankie Armstrong & Sandra Kerr*

Origins Of Skiffle	7" EP	Pye	NJE1043	1957	£15	£7.50	
Peggy 'n' Mike	LP	Argo	(Z)DA80	1968	£20	£8	*with Mike Seeger*
Peggy 'n' Mike	LP	Argo	ZFB62	1972	£10	£4	*with Mike Seeger*
Peggy Alone	LP	Argo	ZFB63	1972	£10	£4	
Peggy Alone	LP	Argo	(Z)DA81	1968	£20	£8	
Pretty Little Baby	7"	Decca	F12282	1965	£4	£1.50	
Shine Like A Star	7" EP	Topic	TOP38	1960	£10	£5	
Troubled Love	7" EP	Topic	TOP72	1962	£8	£4	

SEEGER, PETE

Careless Love	7"	Top Rank	TR5020	1960	£4	£1.50	*B side by Leon Bibb*
D-Day Dodgers	7" EP	Ember	EP4560	1966	£5	£2	
Guitar Guide For Folksingers	LP	Topic	12T20	1958	£20	£8	*with booklet*
Healing River	7" EP	CBS	EP6065	1965	£5	£2	
In Concert	7" EP	CBS	AGG20055	1964	£5	£2	
Pete And Five Strings	7" EP	Topic	TOP33	1959	£8	£4	
Tribute To Leadbelly	7" EP	Melodisc	EPM778	1958	£8	£4	
We Shall Overcome	LP	CBS	(S)BPG62209	1963	£12	£5	

SEEKERS

With A Swag On My Shoulder	7"	Oriole	CB1935	1965	£5	£2	

SEEMON & MARIJKE

Son Of America	LP	A&M	SP4309	1970	£20	£8	*US*

SEFTONES

I Can See Through You	7"	CBS	202491	1966	£15	£7.50	

SEGAL, MARTIN & SILVER JADE

Fly On Strange Wings	LP	DJM	DJM9100	1970	£25	£10	

SEGER, BOB

Against The Wind	LP	Mobile Fidelity	MFSL1127	1983	£10	£4	*US audiophile*
Bob Seger Story	LP	Capitol		1981	£15	£6	*US promo*
Brand New Morning	LP	Capitol	ST731	1971	£15	£6	*US*
Fire Inside	CD	Capitol	DPRO79227	1991	£20	£8	*US interview promo*
Lucifer	7"	Capitol	CL15642	1970	£5	£2	
Mongrel	LP	Capitol	SKAO499	1970	£10	£4	*US gatefold*
Night Moves	LP	Mobile Fidelity	MFSL1034	1979	£12	£5	*US audiophile*
Night Moves	LP	Capitol	PST11557	1977	£25	£10	*US picture disc*
Noah	LP	Capitol	ST236	1969	£15	£6	*US*
Ramblin' Gamblin' Man	7"	Capitol	CL15574	1968	£4	£1.50	
Ramblin' Gamblin' Man	LP	Capitol	ST172	1969	£12	£5	*US*
Seger Classics	LP	Capitol	PSLP271/2	1977	£25	£10	*promo double*
Silver Seger Sampler	CD	Capitol	DPRO79622	1993	£20	£8	*US promo*
Smokin' OP's	LP	Reprise	K44214	1972	£10	£4	
Stranger In Town	CD	DCC		1995	£15	£6	*US audiophile*
Stranger In Town	LP	Capitol	SEAX11904	1978	£10	£4	*US picture disc*

SEIZE

Everybody Dies	7"	Why Not	NOT002	1982	£8	£4	
Grovelands Road	7"	Why Not	NOT001	1981	£8	£4	

SELAH JUBILEE QUARTET

Spirituals	10" LP	Remington	1023	195–	£25	£10	*US*

SELECTED FOUR

Selection Train	7"	Banana	BA351	1971	£5	£2	*Sound Dimension B side*

SELF, RONNIE

Bop-A-Lena	78	Philips	PB810	1958	£50	£25	

SELLERS, BROTHER JOHN

Big Beat Up The River	LP	Monitor	505		£20	£8	*US*
Blues & Spirituals	7" EP	Vanguard	EPP14002	1956	£8	£4	
Blues & Spirituals	7" EP	Columbia	SEG7740	1957	£8	£4	
In London	7" EP	Decca	DFE6457	1957	£6	£2.50	
In London	LP	Decca	LK4197	1957	£15	£6	
Jack Of Diamonds	10" LP	Vanguard	PPT12017	1957	£12	£5	
Sings Blues And Folk Songs	10" LP	Vanguard	PPT12008	1956	£12	£5	

SELLERS, PETER

Any Old Iron	7"	Parlophone	R4337	1957	£4	£1.50	
Best Of Sellers	10" LP	Parlophone	PMD1069	1958	£10	£4	
Best Of Sellers	7" EP	Parlophone	GEP8770	1958	£5	£2	
Drop Of The Hard Stuff	7"	Parlophone	R4491	1958	£4	£1.50	
How To Win An Election	LP	Philips	AL3464	1964	£10	£4	*with Spike Milligan & Harry Secombe*
Peter And Sophia	LP	Parlophone	PMC1131/ PCS3012	1960	£10	£4	*with Sophia Loren*
Peter And Sophia No. 1	7" EP	Parlophone	GEP8843/ SGE2021	1961	£5	£2	*with Sophia Loren*
Peter And Sophia No. 2	7" EP	Parlophone	GEP8845/ SGE2022	1961	£5	£2	*with Sophia Loren*

Peter And Sophia No. 3	7" EP	Parlophone	GEP8848/ SGE2023	1961	£5	£2	with Sophia Loren
Putting on The Smile	7"	Parlophone	R4605	1959	£4	£1.50	
Songs For Swingin' Sellers	7" EP	Parlophone	GEP8822/ SGE2013	1960	£5	£2	
Songs For Swingin' Sellers No. 2	7" EP	Parlophone	GEP8827/ SGE2016	1960	£5	£2	
Songs For Swingin' Sellers No. 3	7" EP	Parlophone	GEP8832/ SGE2019	1961	£5	£2	
Songs For Swingin' Sellers No. 4	7" EP	Parlophone	GEP8835/ SGE2020	1961	£5	£2	
Unchained Melody	CD-s	EMI	CDEM146	1990	£5	£2	with Spike Milligan

SEMA FOUR

Four From Sema Four	7"	Pollen	PBM022	1979	£20	£10	
Up And Down	7"	Pollen	PBM024	1979	£12	£6	

SEMIRAMIS

Dedicato A Frazzo	LP	Trident	TRI1004		£20	£8	Italian

SEMOOL

Essais	LP	Futura	005	1972	£25	£10	French

SEMPLE, ARCHIE

Easy Living	LP	Columbia	33SX1450	1962	£30	£15	

SENATE

I Can't Stop	7"	Columbia	DB8110	1967	£10	£5	
Sock It To You One More Time	LP	United Artists	(S)ULP1180	1968	£12	£5	

SENATOR BOBBY

Wild Thing	7"	Cameo Parkway	P127	1962	£4	£1.50	

SENATORS

Breakdown	7"	Oriole	CB1957	1964	£15	£7.50	
She's A Mod	7"	Dial	DSP7001	1964	£30	£15	
Tables Are Turning	7"	CBS	201768	1965	£15	£7.50	

SENDIT, RAY & HIS ROCKY TEAM

Rocket 0869	7"	Felsted	SD80052	1957	£4	£1.50	

SENSATION FIX

Boxes Paradise	LP	Polydor	2448068	1977	£12	£5	Italian
Finest Finger	LP	Polydor	2448048	1976	£15	£6	Italian
Flying Tapes	LP	Polydor	2448074	1978	£12	£5	Italian
Fragment Of Light	LP	Polydor	2448023	1974	£15	£6	Italian
Portable Madness	LP	Polydor	2448034	1974	£15	£6	Italian
Vision's Fugitives	LP	All Ears	SF11478	1977	£12	£5	US

SENSATIONAL CREED

Nocturnal Operations	12"	Beggars Banquet	BEG125T	1984	£6	£2.50	
Nocturnal Operations	7"	Beggars Banquet	BEG125	1984	£5	£2	

SENSATIONS

Let Me In	7"	Pye	7N25128	1962	£6	£2.50	
Let Me In	LP	Argo	LP4022	1963	£30	£15	US
Music Music Music	7"	Pye	7N25110	1961	£6	£2.50	

SENSATIONS (2)

Born To Love You	7"	Doctor Bird	DB1102	1967	£10	£5	
Right On Time	7"	Doctor Bird	DB1100	1967	£10	£5	
Thing Called Soul	7"	Doctor Bird	DB1074	1967	£10	£5	
Those Guys	7"	Duke	DU2	1968	£8	£4	
War Boat	7"	Technique	TE902	1970	£4	£1.50	
Warrior	7"	Camel	CA31	1969	£4	£1.50	Johnny Organ B side

SENSATIONS (3)

Look At My Baby	7"	Decca	F12392	1966	£4	£1.50	

SENSELESS THINGS

Andi In A Karma	12"	What Goes On	GOESON37	1990	£15	£7.50	test pressing
Everybody's Gone	CD-s	Epic	6569802	1991	£5	£2	
Got It At The Delmar	CD-s	Epic	6574492	1991	£5	£2	
I'm Moving	7"	Yo Jo Jo	3	1988	£8	£4	flexi
Up And Coming	12"	Red	RED001T	1988	£15	£7.50	2 versions
Up And Coming	12"	Way Cool	WC006	1991	£8	£4	
Up And Coming	CD-s	Way Cool	WC006CD	1991	£10	£5	

SENSORY SYSTEM

Sensory System	LP	Hookfarm	HKS1	1973	£25	£10	Danish

SENTINELS

Big Surf	LP	Del-Fi	LP/ST1232	1963	£15	£6	US

Surfer Girl	LP	Del-Fi	LP/ST1241	1963	**£15**	**£6**	*US*
Vegas Go-Go	LP	Sutton	SU338	1964	**£25**	**£10**	*US*

SEPULTURA

Arise	LP	Roadracer	RO93288	1991	**£10**	**£4**	*picture disc*
Bestial Devastation	LP	Gogumelo	803248	1985	**£40**	**£20**	*Brazilian, B side by Overdose*
Chaos A.D.	CD	Roadrunner	RR900000	1994	**£20**	**£8**	*in tin*

SERENADE

Serenade	LP	Negram	NQ20019	1972	**£25**	**£10**	*Dutch*

SERENDIPITY

Castles	7"	CBS	4428	1969	**£50**	**£25**	
Through With You	7"	CBS	3733	1968	**£75**	**£37.50**	

SERFS

Early Bird Café	LP	Capitol	SKAO207	1969	**£25**	**£10**	*US*

SERGEANT, WILL

Favourite Branches	7"	WEA	K19238	1982	**£15**	**£7.50**	*Ravi Shankar & Bill Loveday B side*

SERGIO & ESTIBALIZ

Love Come Home	7"	Epic	SEPC3187	1975	**£5**	**£2**	

SERPENT POWER

Serpent Power	LP	Vanguard	VSD79252	1967	**£60**	**£30**	*US*

SESSION MEN

Beatle Music	LP	World Record Club	T758	1967	**£10**	**£4**	

SETTERS

Paint Your Wagon	7"	Duke	DU65	1970	**£4**	**£1.50**	

SETTLERS

Alive	LP	Columbia	SCX6381	1969	**£15**	**£6**	
Call Again	LP	Marble Arch	MAL1226	1969	**£10**	**£4**	
Early Settlers	LP	Island	ILP947	1967	**£20**	**£8**	
Lightning Tree	LP	York	FYK405	1972	**£15**	**£6**	
Sing A New Song	LP	Myrrh	MST6507	1972	**£10**	**£4**	
Sing Out	LP	Decca	LK4645	1964	**£15**	**£6**	

SEVEN LETTERS

Bam Bam Baji	7"	Doctor Bird	DB1209	1969	**£10**	**£5**	
Flour Dumpling	7"	Doctor Bird	DB1195	1969	**£10**	**£5**	
Fung Sure	7"	Doctor Bird	DB1306	1969	**£10**	**£5**	
Mama Me Want Girl	7"	Doctor Bird	DB1206	1969	**£10**	**£5**	
People Get Ready	7"	Doctor Bird	DB1189	1969	**£10**	**£5**	
Please Stay	7"	Doctor Bird	DB1194	1969	**£10**	**£5**	
Soul Crash	7"	Doctor Bird	DB1207	1969	**£10**	**£5**	
There Goes My Heart	7"	Doctor Bird	DB1208	1969	**£10**	**£5**	

SEVEN SECONDS

Skins, Brains, And Guts	7"	Alternative Tentacle	VIRUS15	1982	**£8**	**£4**	

SEVENTEEN

Don't Let Go	7"	Vendetta	VD001	1980	**£30**	**£15**	

SEVENTEEN-SEVENTY-SIX

1776	LP	Palladium	1005	1971	**£25**	**£10**	*US*

SEVENTH SON

Man In The Street	7"	Rising Son	FMR067	1982	**£30**	**£15**	*picture sleeve*
Man In The Street	7"	Rising Son	FMR067	1982	**£8**	**£4**	
Metal To The Moon	7"	Rising Son	SRT4KS282	1984	**£10**	**£5**	
Northern Boots	7"	Music Factory	MF0043	1987	**£10**	**£5**	
What More Do You Want	12"	Rising Son	SRT9KLS	1989	**£6**	**£2.50**	

SEVENTH SONS

4.00am At Franks	LP	ESP-Disk	1078	1968	**£25**	**£10**	*US*

SEVERIN

Chance In Time	7"	CBS	7280	1971	**£5**	**£2**	

SEVILLE, DAVID

Armen's Theme	7"	London	HLU8359	1957	**£6**	**£2.50**	*gold label*
Bird On My Head	7"	London	HLU8659	1958	**£4**	**£1.50**	
Bonjour Tristesse	7"	London	HLU8582	1958	**£4**	**£1.50**	
David Seville & His Orchestra	7" EP	London	REU1085	1957	**£15**	**£7.50**	
Gift	7"	London	HLU8411	1957	**£5**	**£2**	
Got To Get To Your House	7"	London	HLU8485	1957	**£5**	**£2**	
Witch Doctor	7"	London	HLU8619	1958	**£4**	**£1.50**	
Witch Doctor	LP	London	HAU2153	1959	**£12**	**£5**	
Witch Doctor & His Friends	7" EP	London	REU1219	1959	**£12**	**£6**	

SEWARD, ALEX

City Blues	10" LP	Vogue	LDE165	1956	**£20**	**£8**	

SEX

End Of My Life	LP	Trans-Canada	785	1972	**£15**	**£6**	*Canadian*
Sex	LP	Trans-Canada	775	1971	**£30**	**£15**	*Canadian*

SEX PISTOLS

What was revolutionary about the Sex Pistols was not so much their music or their image, but the way in which they (or rather their manager, Malcolm McLaren) saw rock music as an institution out of which it was possible to make a considerable amount of money. The strategy of signing to a label for a large advance, which was retained when the record company became too outraged by the group's behaviour to honour its side of the contract, worked supremely well. The Sex Pistols found themselves wealthy almost before they had recorded anything. Curiously, when Sigue Sigue Sputnik demonstrated a similarly mercenary attitude to music making, they found themselves vilified, rather than lauded as the Sex Pistols had been. Meanwhile, the Sex Pistols' early carryings-on have left us with one of the most valuable of modern collectors' items: the version of 'God Save The Queen' that was very briefly available on the A&M label.

Anarchie Pour L'UK	7"	Barclay	640162	1979	**£5**	**£2**	*French, picture sleeve*
Anarchy In The UK	12"	Barclay	740501	1977	**£6**	**£2.50**	*French*
Anarchy In The UK	7"	Barclay	640112	1977	**£5**	**£2**	*French, picture sleeve*
Anarchy In The UK	7"	EMI	EMI2566	1976	**£20**	**£10**	*Chris Thomas production credit on B side*
Anarchy In The UK	7"	EMI	EMI2566	1976	**£10**	**£5**	*Dave Goodman production credit on B side*
Anarchy In The UK	CD-s	Virgin	CDT3	1988	**£5**	**£2**	*3" single*
Biggest Blow	12"	Virgin	VS22012	1978	**£6**	**£2.50**	*with Interview*
Filth And The Fury	LP	McDonald Brothers	JOCKBOX	1987	**£25**	**£10**	*6 LP boxed set*
Frigging In The Rigging	7"	Barclay	640159	1979	**£8**	**£4**	*French, picture sleeve*
Frigging In The Rigging	7"	Virgin	VS240	1979	**£10**	**£5**	*mispress, A side plays 'Silly Thing'*
God Save The Queen	7"	A&M	AMS7284	1977	**£1500**	**£1000**	
God Save The Queen	7"	Barclay	640106	1977	**£6**	**£2.50**	*French, picture sleeve*
God Save The Queen	CD-s	Virgin	CDT37	1988	**£5**	**£2**	*3" single*
Great Rock'n'Roll Swindle	7"	Virgin	VS290	1979	**£8**	**£4**	*with bonus 'telephone call' track*
Heyday	cass	Factory	FACT30	1980	**£10**	**£4**	*satin pouch, Xmas card*
Holidays In The Sun	7"	Virgin	VS191	1977	**£4**	**£1.50**	*picture sleeve*
Holidays In The Sun	7"	Barclay	640116	1977	**£5**	**£2**	*French, picture sleeve*
Kiss This	CD	Virgin	CDVX2702	1992	**£20**	**£8**	*double, with Live In Trondheim disc*
My Way	12"	Barclay	740509	1979	**£8**	**£4**	*French*
My Way	7"	Barclay	640154	1978	**£6**	**£2.50**	*French, picture sleeve*
My Way	7"	Virgin	VS220	1978	**£10**	**£5**	*mispress, other side plays The Motors*
Never Mind The Bollocks	LP	Virgin	V2086	1977	**£50**	**£25**	*with poster & 1 sided 7" (VDJ24)*
Never Mind The Bollocks	LP	Virgin	V2086	1977	**£10**	**£4**	*no track listing on sleeve*
Never Mind The Bollocks	LP	Virgin	VP2086	1978	**£20**	**£8**	*picture disc*
Never Mind The Bollocks, Here's The Sex Pistols	CD	Virgin	CDV2086	1986	**£15**	**£6**	*mispress – plays country music*
Pistols Pack	7"	Virgin	SEX1	1980	**£15**	**£7.50**	*6 × 7", plastic wallet*
Pretty Vacant	7"	Barclay	640109	1977	**£5**	**£2**	*French, picture sleeve*
Stepping Stone	7"	Virgin	VS339	1980	**£8**	**£4**	*mispress, plays Gillan*
Submission	7"	Chaos	DICK1	1985	**£6**	**£2.50**	*blue, pink, or yellow vinyl*
Submission	7"	Barclay	640137	1977	**£5**	**£2**	*French, picture sleeve*
Who Killed Bambi	7"	Barclay	640160	1979	**£8**	**£4**	*French, picture sleeve*
You Need Hands	7"	Barclay	640161	1979	**£5**	**£2**	*French, picture sleeve*

SEXY GIRLS

Pom-Pom Song	7"	Fab	FAB100	1969	**£4**	**£1.50**	*Little Joe B side*

SEYTON, DENNY & THE SABRES

It's The Gear (14 Hits)	LP	Wing	WL1032	1965	**£25**	**£10**	
Just A Kiss	7"	Parlophone	R5363	1965	**£20**	**£10**	
Short Fat Fanny	7"	Mercury	MF814	1964	**£10**	**£5**	
Tricky Dicky	7"	Mercury	MF800	1964	**£8**	**£4**	
Way You Look Tonight	7"	Mercury	MF824	1964	**£20**	**£10**	

SHACK

Emergency	CD-s	Ghetto	GTGCD1	1988	**£6**	**£2.50**	
High Rise Low Life	CD-s	Ghetto	GTGCD2	1989	**£6**	**£2.50**	
I Know You Well	CD-s	Ghetto	GTGCD11	1990	**£6**	**£2.50**	

SHACKLEFORDS

Shacklefords	LP	Capitol	SMK74129	1966	**£15**	**£6**	*German*

SHADE JOEY & THE NIGHT OWLS

Blue Birds Over The Mountain	7"	Parlophone	R5180	1964	**£40**	**£20**	

SHADES

Title	Format	Label	Cat. No.	Year	Mint	VG	Notes
Sun Glasses	7"	London	HLX8713	1958	**£25**	**£12.50**	*B side Knott Sisters*

SHADES (2)

Title	Format	Label	Cat. No.	Year	Mint	VG	Notes
Weird Walk	7"	Starlite	ST45074	1962	**£12**	**£6**	

SHADES (3)

Title	Format	Label	Cat. No.	Year	Mint	VG	Notes
Never Gonna Give You Up	7"	Gas	GAS119	1969	**£4**	**£1.50**	

SHADES OF BLACK LIGHTNING SOUL

Title	Format	Label	Cat. No.	Year	Mint	VG	Notes
Shades Of Black Lightning Soul	LP	Tower		1968	**£15**	**£6**	*US*

SHADES OF BLUE

Title	Format	Label	Cat. No.	Year	Mint	VG	Notes
Happiness Is The Shades Of Blue	LP	Impact	IM101/1001	1966	**£15**	**£6**	*US*
Oh How Happy	7"	Sue	WI4022	1966	**£10**	**£5**	

SHADES OF BLUE (2)

Title	Format	Label	Cat. No.	Year	Mint	VG	Notes
Voodoo Blues	7"	Parlophone	R5270	1965	**£20**	**£10**	
Where Did All The Good Times Go	7"	Pye	7N15988	1965	**£6**	**£2.50**	

SHADES OF JOY

Title	Format	Label	Cat. No.	Year	Mint	VG	Notes
Shades Of Joy	LP	Fontana	STL5498	1969	**£10**	**£4**	

SHADOW, JOHNNY

Title	Format	Label	Cat. No.	Year	Mint	VG	Notes
Golli Golli	7"	Pye	7N15506	1963	**£5**	**£2**	*picture sleeve*

SHADOWS

The Shadows came together as a backing group for Cliff Richard (initially as the Drifters), but started to gain considerable success in their own right as soon as they realized that their strength lay in playing guitar instrumentals. Although only gaining very limited recognition in America (where the Ventures had an equivalent role), as far as UK listeners are concerned, when it comes to instrumental rock, the Shadows wrote the book. Several other groups attempted to copy the Shadows sound, but only the originals managed to achieve a string of chart hits – not least because their instrumental skills were probably unequalled in rock music during the early sixties.

Title	Format	Label	Cat. No.	Year	Mint	VG	Notes
Alice In Sunderland	7" EP	Columbia	SEG8445	1965	**£15**	**£7.50**	
Atlantis	7" EP	Columbia	ESDF1480	1963	**£12**	**£6**	*French*
Be Bop A Lula	7" EP	Columbia	ESRF20002	196–	**£12**	**£6**	*French*
Boys	7" EP	Columbia	SEG8193	1962	**£6**	**£2.50**	
Boys	7" EP	Columbia	ESG7881	1962	**£25**	**£12.50**	*stereo*
Brilliant Shadows – Brilliant Songs	LP	Columbia	C83609	1963	**£20**	**£8**	*German mono*
Brilliant Shadows – Brilliant Songs	LP	Columbia	SMC83609	1966	**£25**	**£10**	*German stereo*
Chelsea Boot	7"	Columbia	PSR310	1967	**£40**	**£20**	*promo*
Dance On	7" EP	Columbia	ESDF1457	1963	**£12**	**£6**	*French*
Dance On With The Shadows	7" EP	Columbia	SEG8233	1963	**£10**	**£5**	
Dance With The Shadows	LP	Columbia	33SX1619	1964	**£10**	**£4**	
Dance With The Shadows	LP	Columbia	SCX3511	1964	**£15**	**£6**	*stereo*
Dance With The Shadows No. 1	7" EP	Columbia	SEG8342	1964	**£10**	**£5**	
Dance With The Shadows No. 2	7" EP	Columbia	SEG8375	1964	**£10**	**£5**	
Dance With The Shadows No. 3	7" EP	Columbia	SEG8408	1965	**£12**	**£6**	
Dancing In The Dark	12"	Polydor	POSPX808	1986	**£10**	**£5**	
Dear Old Mrs Bell	7"	Columbia	DB8372	1968	**£5**	**£2**	
Don't Cry For Me Argentina	12"	EMI	12EMI2890	1978	**£6**	**£2.50**	*double groove*
Don't Make My Baby Blue	7"	Columbia	DB7650	1965	**£15**	**£7.50**	*export picture sleeve*
Dreams I Dream	7"	Columbia	DB8034	1966	**£4**	**£1.50**	
F.B.I.	7"	Columbia	DB4580	196–	**£8**	**£4**	*black label*
Foot Tapping With The Shadows	7" EP	Columbia	SEG8268	1963	**£10**	**£5**	
Frightened City	7"	Columbia	DB4637	196–	**£8**	**£4**	*black label*
From Hank, Bruce, Brian, & John	LP	Columbia	SX/SCX6199	1967	**£10**	**£4**	
Greatest Hits	LP	Columbia	33SX1522	1963	**£10**	**£4**	
Guitar Tango	7"	Columbia	DB4870	196–	**£8**	**£4**	*black label*
Guitar Tango	7" EP	Columbia	ESDF1437	1963	**£12**	**£6**	*French*
I Met A Girl	7"	Columbia	DB7853	1966	**£4**	**£1.50**	
In Japan	LP	Odeon	8259	1967	**£175**	**£87.50**	*Japanese, red vinyl*
It'll Be Me Babe	7"	EMI	EMI2461	1976	**£4**	**£1.50**	
Jigsaw	LP	Columbia	SX/SCX6148	1967	**£10**	**£4**	
Kon-Tiki	7"	Columbia	DB4698	196–	**£8**	**£4**	*black label*
Little B	7" EP	Columbia	ESDF1447	1963	**£12**	**£6**	*French*
Los Shadows	7" EP	Columbia	SEG8278	1963	**£10**	**£5**	*2 different sleeves*
Los Shadows	7" EP	Columbia		1964	**£20**	**£10**	*export*
Magical Mrs Clamps	7"	EMI	PSR316	1968	**£10**	**£5**	*promo, B side by Cliff Richard*
Man Of Mystery	7"	Columbia	DB4530	196–	**£8**	**£4**	*black label*
Maroc 7	7"	Columbia	PSR304	1967	**£30**	**£15**	*promo, spoken intro*
More Hits	LP	Columbia	33SX1791/ SCX3578	1965	**£10**	**£4**	
Mountains Of The Moon	CD-s	Polydor	PZCD47	1989	**£5**	**£2**	
Naughty Nippon Nights	7"	Columbia	PSR313	1967	**£60**	**£30**	*promo*
On Stage And Screen	7" EP	Columbia	SEG8528	1967	**£20**	**£10**	
Out Of The Shadows	10" LP	Columbia	FP1143	1962	**£40**	**£20**	*French*
Out Of The Shadows	7" EP	Columbia	ESG7883	1963	**£25**	**£12.50**	*stereo*
Out Of The Shadows	7" EP	Columbia	SEG8218	1963	**£10**	**£5**	
Out Of The Shadows	LP	Columbia	33SX1458	1962	**£10**	**£4**	
Out Of The Shadows	LP	Columbia	SCX3449	1962	**£20**	**£8**	*stereo*
Out Of The Shadows No. 2	7" EP	Columbia	ESG7895	1963	**£25**	**£12.50**	*stereo*
Out Of The Shadows No. 2	7" EP	Columbia	SEG8249	1963	**£10**	**£5**	
Place In The Sun	7"	Columbia	DB7952	1966	**£4**	**£1.50**	
Rhythm And Greens	7" EP	Columbia	ESG7904	1964	**£25**	**£12.50**	*stereo*

Title	Format	Label	Cat. No.	Year	Mint	VG	Notes
Rhythm And Greens	7" EP	Columbia	SEG8362	1964	£10	£5	
Rise And Fall Of Flingel Bunt	7"	Columbia	DB7261	1964	£6	£2.50	*mispress, 2 A sides*
Rockin' With Curly Leads	LP	EMI	EMA762	1973	£10	£4	
Saturday Dance	7"	Columbia	DB4387	1959	£25	£12.50	
Savage	7"	Columbia	DB4726	196–	£8	£4	*black label*
Shadow Music	LP	Columbia	33SX/SCX6041	1966	£10	£4	
Shadowmix	CD-s	Polydor	PZCD61	1989	£5	£2	
Shadows	7" EP	Columbia	ESG7834	1961	£25	£12.50	*stereo*
Shadows	7" EP	Columbia	SEG8061	1961	£8	£4	
Shadows	LP	Columbia	SCX3414	1962	£25	£10	*stereo*
Shadows	LP	World Record Club	ALBUM72	1972	£30	£15	*6 LPs, boxed*
Shadows	LP	Columbia	33SX1374	1962	£10	£4	
Shadows Know	LP	Atlantic	(SD)8007	1964	£25	£10	*US*
Shadows No. 2	7" EP	Columbia	SEG8148	1962	£10	£5	
Shadows No. 3	7" EP	Columbia	SEG8166	1962	£10	£5	
Shadows To The Fore	7" EP	Columbia	SEG8094	1961	£6	£2.50	
Shazam	7" EP	Columbia	ESRF1402	1963	£12	£6	*French*
Shindig With The Shadows	7" EP	Columbia	SEG8286	1963	£10	£5	
Sleepwalk	7" EP	Columbia	ESDF1434	1963	£12	£6	*French*
Sound Of The Shadows	LP	Columbia	33SX1736	1965	£10	£4	
Sound Of The Shadows	LP	Columbia	SCX3554	1965	£15	£6	*stereo*
Sound Of The Shadows No. 1	7" EP	Columbia	SEG8459	1965	£15	£7.50	
Sound Of The Shadows No. 2	7" EP	Columbia	SEG8473	1966	£15	£7.50	
Sound Of The Shadows No. 3	7" EP	Columbia	SEG8494	1966	£15	£7.50	
Spotlight On The Shadows	7" EP	Columbia	SEG8135	1962	£8	£4	
Stingray	7"	Columbia	DB7588	1965	£15	£7.50	*export picture sleeve*
Surfing With The Shadows	LP	Atlantic	(SD)8089	1963	£25	£10	*US*
Themes From Aladdin	7" EP	Columbia	SEG8396	1965	£10	£5	
Those Brilliant Shadows	7" EP	Columbia	SEG8321	1964	£10	£5	
Those Talented Shadows	7" EP	Columbia	SEG8500	1966	£15	£7.50	
Thunderbirds Are Go	7"	EMI	PSR305	1967	£40	£20	*1 sided promo*
Tomorrow's Cancelled	7"	Columbia	DB8264	1967	£6	£2.50	
Twenty Golden Greats	7"	EMI		1977	£4	£1.50	*promo sampler*
Wonderful Land	7"	Columbia	DB4790	196–	£6	£2.50	*black label*
Wonderful Land Of The Shadows	7" EP	Columbia	SEG8171	1962	£8	£4	

SHADOWS (2)

Title	Format	Label	Cat. No.	Year	Mint	VG	Notes
Under Stars Of Love	7"	HMV	POP563	1958	£60	£30	

SHADOWS OF KNIGHT

Title	Format	Label	Cat. No.	Year	Mint	VG	Notes
Back Door Men	LP	Dunwich	(S)667	1966	£60	£30	*US*
Bad Little Woman	7"	Atlantic	584045	1966	£15	£7.50	
Gloria	7"	Atlantic	AT4085	1966	£15	£7.50	
Gloria	LP	Radar	ADA11	1979	£12	£5	
Gloria	LP	Dunwich	(S)666	1966	£60	£30	*US*
Oh Yeah	7"	Atlantic	584021	1966	£15	£7.50	
Oh Yeah	7" EP	Atco	113	1966	£60	£30	*French*
Shadows Of Knight	LP	Super K	SKS6002	1969	£30	£15	*US*
Shake	7"	Buddah	201024	1968	£10	£5	
Someone Like Me	7"	Atlantic	584136	1967	£15	£7.50	

SHADRACK CHAMELEON

Title	Format	Label	Cat. No.	Year	Mint	VG	Notes
Shadrack Chameleon	LP	Iglus	40515	1971	£300	£180	*US*

SHADROCKS

Title	Format	Label	Cat. No.	Year	Mint	VG	Notes
Go Go Special	7"	Island	WI3061	1967	£8	£4	

SHAFTESBURY

Title	Format	Label	Cat. No.	Year	Mint	VG	Notes
Lull Before The Storm	LP	OK Records	OKA001	1980	£15	£6	

SHAFTO, BOBBY

Title	Format	Label	Cat. No.	Year	Mint	VG	Notes
Feel So Blue	7"	Parlophone	R4958	1962	£4	£1.50	
How Could You Do A Thing Like That To Me	7"	Parlophone	R5252	1965	£4	£1.50	
Little Like You	7"	Parlophone	R5481	1966	£4	£1.50	
Lonely Is As Lonely Does	7"	Parlophone	R5403	1966	£4	£1.50	
Love, Love, Love	7"	Parlophone	R5167	1964	£4	£1.50	
Over And Over	7"	Parlophone	R4870	1962	£4	£1.50	
She's My Girl	7"	Parlophone	R5130	1964	£4	£1.50	
Who Wouldn't Love A Girl Like That	7"	Parlophone	R5184	1964	£4	£1.50	

SHAG NASTY

Title	Format	Label	Cat. No.	Year	Mint	VG	Notes
No Bullshit Just Rock'n'Roll	7"	Shag Nasty	SN1	1979	£8	£4	

SHAGGS

Title	Format	Label	Cat. No.	Year	Mint	VG	Notes
Philosophy Of The World	LP	Third World	3001	1972	£500	£330	*US*

SHAGGS (2)

Title	Format	Label	Cat. No.	Year	Mint	VG	Notes
Wink	LP	Resurrection	CX1295	1984	£15	£6	*US*
Wink	LP	MCM	6311	1967	£1000	£700	*US*

SHAKEOUTS

Title	Format	Label	Cat. No.	Year	Mint	VG	Notes
Every Little Once In A While	7"	Columbia	DB7613	1965	£25	£12.50	

SHAKERS (KINGSIZE TAYLOR & THE DOMINOES)

Title	Format	Label	Cat. No.	Year	Mint	VG	Notes
Hippy Hippy Shake	7"	Polydor	NH66991	1963	£10	£5	
Hippy Hippy Shake	7"	Polydor	NH52213	1963	£10	£5	

Let's Do The Madison, Twist, Locomotion . . .	LP	Polydor	46639/237139	1963	£60	£30	German
Memphis Tennessee	7" EP	Polydor	50025	1963	£40	£20	French
Money	7"	Polydor	NH52158	1963	£10	£5	
Money	7"	Polydor	NH52258	1963	£10	£5	
Whole Lotta Loving	7"	Polydor	NH52272	1964	£10	£5	

SHAKERS (2)

Break It All	LP	Audio Fidelity	(S)2155	1966	£20	£8	US

SHAKESPEAR

Stay	LP	Real	RR2001	1975	£30	£15	

SHAKESPEARE, CHRIS GLOBE SHOW

Ob La Di, Ob La Da	7"	Page One	POF113	1969	£10	£5	

SHAKESPEARES

Something To Believe In	7"	RCA	RCA1695	1968	£40	£20	

SHAKESPEARS

Give It To Me	LP	Philips	QU625276	196–	£250	£150	Dutch
Saint	7" EP	Barclay	070981	1966	£25	£12.50	French
Summertime	7" EP	Barclay	071036	1966	£25	£12.50	French

SHAKESPEAR'S SISTER

Break My Heart	CD-s	London	LONCD200	1988	£15	£7.50	
Run Silent	CD-s	ffrr	FBCD119	1989	£10	£5	

SHAKEY JAKE

Further On Up The Road	LP	Liberty	LBL83217E	1969	£15	£6	

SHAKEY VICK

Little Woman You're So Sweet	LP	Pye	NSPL18276	1969	£30	£15	

SHAM, SAM

Drumbago's Dead	7"	Blue Cat	BS157	1969	£5	£2	Sparters B side

SHAM 69

I Don't Wanna	12"	Step Forward	SF4	1977	£6	£2.50	
I Don't Wanna	7"	Step Forward	SF4	1977	£5	£2	
Sons Of The Streets	7"	Polydor	no number	1977	£5	£2	1 sided, red label

SHAME

Don't Go Away Little Girl	7"	MGM	MGM1349	1967	£60	£30	

SHAME (2)

Real Tears	7"	Fierce	FRIGHT003	1985	£20	£10	test pressing

SHAMEN

Jesus Loves Amerika	CD-s	Ediesta	CALCCD069	1988	£5	£2	
Omega Amigo	CD-s	One Little Indian	7TP30CD	1989	£5	£2	
Phorward	CD	Moksha	SOMACD3	1989	£15	£6	
You, Me And Everything	CD-s	Moksha	SOMA6CD	1989	£5	£2	

SHAMES

Greenburg Glickstein Charles	7"	CBS	3820	1968	£4	£1.50	
I Wanna Meet You	7"	CBS	202450	1966	£4	£1.50	
Mr Unreliable	7"	CBS	2704	1967	£4	£1.50	
Sugar And Spice	7"	CBS	202344	1966	£15	£7.50	

SHAMPOO

Vol. One	LP	Motor	MT44009	1972	£15	£6	French

SHAMROCKS

Cadillac	7" EP	Polydor	60122	196–	£20	£10	French
Don't Say	7" EP	Polydor	60124	196–	£25	£12.50	French
In Paris	LP	Polydor	658032	1966	£75	£37.50	French
La La La La La	7"	Polydor	BM56503	1965	£5	£2	
Shamrocks	LP	Ariola	72151	1965	£75	£37.50	German
Smoke Rings	LP	Polydor	623015	1966	£75	£37.50	German

SHANE, VALERIE

One Billion Seven Million Thirty-Three	7"	Philips	PB879	1958	£5	£2	

SHANE & THE SHANE GANG

Whistle Stop	7"	Pye	7N15662	1964	£6	£2.50	

SHANES

I Don't Want Your Love	7"	Columbia	DB7601	1965	£40	£20	
SSS-Shanes	LP	Columbia	1026	1967	£25	£10	Swedish

SHANGAANS

Jungle Drums	LP	Columbia	SMC74113	1965	£15	£6	German

SHANGRI-LAS

Give Him A Great Big Kiss	7"	Red Bird	RB10018	1965	£5	£2	
Give Him A Great Big Kiss	7" EP	Red Bird	RBEV28007	1965	£30	£15	French

Give Us Your Blessings	7"	Red Bird	RB10030	1965	**£6**	**£2.50**	
Golden Hits	LP	Mercury	MCL20096	1966	**£12**	**£5**	
He Cried	7"	Red Bird	RB10053	1966	**£6**	**£2.50**	
I Can Never Go Home Any More	7"	Red Bird	RB10043	1966	**£5**	**£2**	
I Can Never Go Home Any More	7" EP	Red Bird	RB40004	1966	**£60**	**£30**	*demo*
I Can Never Go Home Any More	7" EP	Red Bird	RBEV28009	1966	**£30**	**£15**	*French*
I Can Never Go Home Anymore	LP	Red Bird	RB20104	1965	**£50**	**£25**	*US*
Leader Of The Pack	7"	Red Bird	RB10014	1964	**£4**	**£1.50**	
Leader Of The Pack	7" EP	Red Bird	RBEV28005	1964	**£25**	**£12.50**	*French, B side by the Jelly Beans*
Leader Of The Pack	LP	Red Bird	RB20101	1964	**£40**	**£20**	
Long Live Our Love	7"	Red Bird	RB10048	1966	**£6**	**£2.50**	
Maybe	7"	Red Bird	RB10019	1965	**£12**	**£6**	
Out In The Streets	7"	Red Bird	RB10025	1965	**£5**	**£2**	
Past Present And Future	7"	Red Bird	RB10068	1966	**£10**	**£5**	
Remember	7" EP	Red Bird	RBEV28004	1964	**£25**	**£12.50**	*French, B side by the Butterflies*
Remember Walking In The Sand	7"	Red Bird	RB10008	1964	**£4**	**£1.50**	
Remember Walking In The Sand	CD-s	Charly	CDS3	1989	**£5**	**£2**	
Right Now And Not Later	7"	Red Bird	RB10036	1965	**£12**	**£6**	
Shangri-Las	7" EP	Red Bird	RB40002	1965	**£40**	**£20**	
Shangri-Las '65	LP	Red Bird	RB20104	1965	**£40**	**£20**	*US*
Shangri-Las Sing	LP	Post	4000		**£12**	**£5**	*US*
Sweet Sound Of Summer	7"	Mercury	MF962	1967	**£5**	**£2**	
Take Your Time	7"	Mercury	MF979	1967	**£5**	**£2**	

SHANK, BUD

Bud Shank Group	10" LP	Vogue	LDE157	1955	**£30**	**£15**	
Bud Shank Quartet	LP	Vogue	LAE12113	1958	**£25**	**£10**	
Bud Shank Quintet	LP	Vogue	LAE12020	1956	**£25**	**£10**	
Bud Shank–Bob Brookmeyer Group	10" LP	Vogue	LDE181	1956	**£30**	**£15**	
California Dreamin'	LP	Fontana	STL5371	1966	**£12**	**£5**	*with Chet Baker*
Evening With The Bud Shank Quartet	LP	Ember	EMB3322	1961	**£10**	**£4**	
Flute 'n' Oboe	LP	Vogue	VA160124	1958	**£15**	**£6**	*with Bob Cooper*
Holiday In Brazil	LP	Vogue	LAE12215	1960	**£15**	**£6**	
Jazz At Cal-Tech	LP	Vogue	LAE12095	1958	**£20**	**£8**	
Michelle	LP	Fontana	TL5326	1966	**£12**	**£4**	*with Chet Baker*
New Groove	LP	Vogue	LAE12288	1961	**£12**	**£5**	
Swing's To TV	LP	Vogue	VA160134	1959	**£20**	**£8**	*with Bob Cooper*

SHANKAR, ANANDA

Although George Harrison, Brian Jones, and other rock musicians in the late sixties tried adding sitar to their music, the album made by trained sitar virtuoso Ananda Shankar is a unique attempt from that time to forge a link from the other side of the East–West divide. His version of 'Jumpin' Jack Flash', which is on the album, was a considerable club success in recent years, which is the main reason for the rise in the album's value – although this value is already starting to fall back down. Before his death in 1999, Shankar gave a few concerts in the UK as a natural response to his unexpected, and belated, acclaim.

Ananda Shankar	LP	Reprise	K44082	1971	**£40**	**£20**	
Ananda Shankar	LP	Reprise	RSLP6398	1969	**£50**	**£25**	

SHANKAR, L.

Touch Me There	LP	Zappa	SRZ11602	1979	**£10**	**£4**	*US*

SHANKAR, RAVI

At The Woodstock Festival	LP	United Artists	UAG29379	1970	**£12**	**£5**	
Four Raga Moods	LP	Melodisc	300ML8	1971	**£20**	**£8**	*double*
Improvisations	LP	Liberty	LBS83076	1968	**£12**	**£5**	
In Concert	LP	Liberty	LBS83077	1968	**£12**	**£5**	
In Concert 1972	LP	Apple	SAPDO1002	1973	**£100**	**£50**	*double*
In New York	LP	Fontana	TL5424	1967	**£15**	**£6**	
In San Francisco	LP	Columbia	SCX6382	1970	**£12**	**£5**	
India's Master Musician	LP	Fontana	TL5253	1965	**£15**	**£6**	
India's Master Musician	LP	Vogue	VA160156	1959	**£15**	**£6**	
Joi Bangla	7"	Apple	37	1971	**£8**	**£4**	*picture sleeve*
Live At The Monterey Pop Festival	LP	Columbia	SX/SCX6273	1968	**£12**	**£5**	
Music Of India	LP	HMV	ASD463	1962	**£15**	**£6**	
Portrait Of Genius	LP	Fontana	TL5285	1966	**£15**	**£6**	
Raga	LP	Apple	SWAO3384	1971	**£20**	**£8**	*US*
Sitar Recital	LP	Transatlantic	TRA182	1968	**£12**	**£5**	
Song From The Hills	7"	Fontana	TF712	1966	**£5**	**£2**	
Sound Of The Sitar	LP	Fontana	TL5357	1966	**£15**	**£6**	

SHANNON, DEAN

Jezebel	7"	HMV	POP820	1960	**£10**	**£5**	
Ubangi Stomp	7"	HMV	POP1103	1962	**£15**	**£7.50**	

SHANNON, DEL

The years between the decline of rock'n'roll at the end of the fifties and the rise of the Beatles in 1963 are generally viewed as holding comparatively few delights for the rock historian. One definite exception, however, is the work of Del Shannon, whose powerful, ragged voice was linked to incisive material, much of it written by himself. When the Beatles did arrive, Shannon was one of the first people to see which way things were going and his version of 'From Me To You' was the first Beatles cover version to be issued in America. In the long term, however, Shannon found the decline in his fortunes too hard to take – sadly, he took his own life in 1990.

1,661 Seconds	LP	Stateside	SL10140	1965	**£25**	**£10**	
1,661 Seconds	LP	Amy	S8006	1965	**£40**	**£20**	*US, stereo*
Best Of Del Shannon	LP	Dot	DLP3834	1967	**£10**	**£4**	*US*
Big Hurt	7"	Liberty	LIB55866	1966	**£5**	**£2**	

Title	Format	Label	Cat. No.	Year	Mint	VG	Notes
Break Up	7"	Stateside	SS430	1965	£4	£1.50	
Comin' Back To Me	7"	Stateside	SS8025	1969	£5	£2	
Cry Myself To Sleep	7"	London	HLX9587	1962	£4	£1.50	
Del Shannon	7" EP	London	REX1332	1962	£15	£7.50	
Del Shannon No. 2	7" EP	London	REX1346	1963	£15	£7.50	
Del Shannon's Hits	7" EP	Stateside	SE1029	1965	£15	£7.50	
Del's Own Favourites	7" EP	London	REX1383	1963	£15	£7.50	
Do You Want To Dance	7"	Stateside	SS349	1964	£4	£1.50	
For A Little While	7"	Liberty	LIB55889	1966	£5	£2	
From Del To You	7" EP	London	REX1387	1963	£20	£10	
Further Adventures Of Charles Westover	LP	Liberty	LBL/LBS83114	1968	£40	£20	
Gemini	7"	Liberty	LBF15079	1968	£5	£2	
Handy Man	7"	Stateside	SS317	1964	£4	£1.50	
Handy Man	LP	Stateside	SL10115	1965	£25	£10	
Hats Off To Del Shannon	LP	London	HAX8071	1963	£25	£10	
Hats Off To Larry	7"	London	HLX9402	1961	£4	£1.50	
I Can't Believe My Ears	7"	Stateside	SS494	1966	£5	£2	
Little Town Flirt	7"	London	HLX9653	1963	£4	£1.50	
Little Town Flirt	LP	Big Top	S121308	1963	£50	£25	*US, stereo*
Little Town Flirt	LP	London	HAX8091	1963	£25	£10	
Live In England	LP	United Artists	UAS29474	1973	£10	£4	
Mary Jane	7"	Stateside	SS269	1964	£4	£1.50	
Mind Over Matter	7"	Liberty	LIB10277	1967	£4	£1.50	
Move It On Over	7"	Stateside	SS452	1965	£6	£2.50	
New Del Shannon	7" EP	Liberty	LEP2272	1967	£25	£12.50	
Runaway	7"	London	HLX9317	1961	£4	£1.50	
Runaway	7"	London	HLX9317	1961	£10	£5	*B side mispress – plays 'Snake'*
Runaway	LP	London	HAX2402	1961	£25	£10	
Runaway	LP	Big Top	S123003	1961	£250	£150	*US, stereo*
Runaway	LP	Big Top	123003	1961	£40	£20	*US, mono*
Runaway '67	7"	Liberty	LBF15020	1967	£4	£1.50	
She	7"	Liberty	LIB55939	1967	£5	£2	
Sings Hank Williams	LP	Stateside	SL10130	1965	£25	£10	
Sister Isabelle	7"	Stateside	SS8040	1970	£5	£2	
Stranger In Town	7"	Stateside	SS395	1965	£4	£1.50	
Sue's Gonna Be Mine	7"	London	HLX9800	1963	£4	£1.50	
Swiss Maid	7"	London	HLX9609	1962	£4	£1.50	
That's The Way Love Is	7"	London	HLX9858	1964	£4	£1.50	
Thinkin' It Over	7"	Liberty	LBF15061	1968	£5	£2	
This Is My Bag	LP	Liberty	(S)LBY1320	1966	£20	£8	
Total Commitment	LP	Liberty	(S)LBY1335	1966	£20	£8	
Two Kinds Of Teardrops	7"	London	HLX9719	1963	£4	£1.50	
Two Silhouettes	7"	London	HLX9761	1963	£4	£1.50	
What's A Matter Baby	7"	United Artists	UP35460	1972	£4	£1.50	

SHANNON, HUGH

Title	Format	Label	Cat. No.	Year	Mint	VG	Notes
Hugh Shannon Sings	10" LP	Atlantic	406		£20	£8	US

SHAPE OF THE RAIN

Title	Format	Label	Cat. No.	Year	Mint	VG	Notes
Riley, Riley, Wood & Waggett	LP	Neon	NE7	1971	£25	£10	
Woman	7"	Neon	NE1001	1971	£4	£1.50	

SHAPES

Title	Format	Label	Cat. No.	Year	Mint	VG	Notes
Blast Off	7"	Good Vibrations	GOT13	1979	£10	£5	
Shapes	7"	Sofa	SEAT1	1979	£10	£5	

SHAPIRO, HELEN

Helen's first hit, 'Don't Treat Me Like A Child' (which sold far too many copies to be particularly collectable now) was achieved when she was just fourteen years old. Even at that age, she always maintained that what she really wanted to do was sing jazz, and these days that is exactly what she does – and she has a number of jazz albums to her name, mostly recorded with Humphrey Lyttelton. The two rare singles are fruitful forays into the world of soul music – 'He Knows How To Love Me' has a good version of the Miracles' 'Shop Around' on its B side, while the terrific 'Stop And You'll Become Aware' has long been a Northern soul favourite.

Title	Format	Label	Cat. No.	Year	Mint	VG	Notes
Even More Hits From Helen	7" EP	Columbia	SEG8209	1962	£8	£4	
Fever	7"	Columbia	DB7190	1964	£6	£2.50	
Forget About The Bad Things	7"	Columbia	DB7810	1966	£5	£2	
He Knows How To Love Me	7"	Columbia	DB7340	1964	£50	£25	
Helen	7" EP	Columbia	ESG7872	1961	£10	£5	*stereo, 2 sleeves*
Helen	7" EP	Columbia	SEG8128	1961	£6	£2.50	*2 different sleeves*
Helen Hits Out	LP	Columbia	33SX1661	1964	£20	£8	
Helen Hits Out	LP	Columbia	SCX3533	1964	£30	£15	*stereo*
Helen In Nashville	LP	Columbia	33SX1561	1963	£25	£10	
Helen's Hit Parade	7" EP	Columbia	SEG8136	1961	£6	£2.50	
Helen's Sixteen	LP	Columbia	33SX1494	1963	£20	£8	
Helen's Sixteen	LP	Columbia	SCX3470	1963	£30	£15	*stereo*
Here In Your Arms	7"	Columbia	DB7587	1965	£5	£2	
I Wish I'd Never Loved You	7"	Columbia	DB7395	1964	£5	£2	
In My Calendar	7"	Columbia	DB8073	1966	£5	£2	
Look Over Your Shoulder	7"	Columbia	DB7266	1964	£5	£2	
Look Who It Is	7"	Columbia	DB7130	1963	£5	£2	
Make Me Belong To You	7"	Columbia	DB8148	1967	£5	£3	
More Hits From Helen	7" EP	Columbia	SEG8174	1962	£6	£2.50	
Not Responsible	7"	Columbia	DB7072	1963	£5	£2	
Queen For Tonight	7"	Columbia	DB4966	1963	£5	£2	
Something Wonderful	7"	Columbia	DB7690	1965	£5	£2	

Stop & You'll Become Aware	7"	Columbia	DB8256	1967	**£50**	**£25**	
Take Down A Note Miss Smith	7"	Pye	7N17893	1970	**£5**	**£2**	
Teenager In Love	LP	Epic	LN24/BN26075	1963	**£20**	**£8**	*US*
Teenager Sings The Blues	7" EP	Columbia	ESG7880	1962	**£15**	**£7.50**	*stereo*
Teenager Sings The Blues	7" EP	Columbia	SEG8170	1962	**£10**	**£5**	
Today Has Been Cancelled	7"	Pye	7N17714	1969	**£5**	**£2**	
Tomorrow Is Another Day	7"	Columbia	DB7517	1965	**£5**	**£2**	
Tops With Me	LP	Columbia	33SX1397	1962	**£12**	**£5**	
Tops With Me	LP	Columbia	SCX3428	1962	**£25**	**£10**	*stereo*
Tops With Me No. 1	7" EP	Columbia	ESG7888	1962	**£25**	**£12.50**	*stereo*
Tops With Me No. 1	7" EP	Columbia	SEG8229	1963	**£15**	**£7.50**	
Tops With Me No. 2	7" EP	Columbia	ESG7891	1962	**£25**	**£12.50**	*stereo*
Tops With Me No. 2	7" EP	Columbia	SEG8243	1963	**£15**	**£7.50**	
Twelve Hits And A Miss	LP	Encore	ENC209	1967	**£12**	**£5**	
Very Best Of Helen Shapiro	LP	Columbia	SCX6565	1974	**£10**	**£4**	
Waiting On The Shores Of Nowhere	7"	Pye	7N17975	1970	**£5**	**£2**	
Woe Is Me	7"	Columbia	DB7026	1963	**£5**	**£2**	
You'll Get Me Loving You	7"	Pye	7N17600	1968	**£5**	**£2**	
You've Guessed It	7"	Pye	7N17785	1969	**£6**	**£2.50**	

SHARADES

Dumbhead	7"	Decca	F11811	1964	**£75**	**£37.50**	

SHARAE, BILLY

Do It	7"	Action	ACT4602	1971	**£4**	**£1.50**	

SHARKEY & HIS KINGS OF DIXIELAND

Midnight On Bourbon Street	10" LP	Capitol	LC6600	1953	**£12**	**£5**	
Sharkey's Kings Of Dixieland	10" LP	Melodisc	MLP503	1954	**£12**	**£5**	
Sharkey's Southern Comfort	10" LP	Capitol	LC6531	1951	**£12**	**£5**	

SHARKS

Goodbye Lorene	7"	RCA	RCA1776	1968	**£4**	**£1.50**	

SHARON, RALPH

Around The World In Jazz	LP	Columbia	33SX1090	1958	**£15**	**£6**	
Autumn Leaves	10" LP	Decca	LF1138	1953	**£20**	**£8**	
Cocktail Time	10" LP	Lyragon	AF1	1953	**£20**	**£8**	
Mr And Mrs Jazz	LP	London	LTZN15102	1958	**£12**	**£5**	*with Sue Sharon*
Spring Fever	10" LP	Decca	LF1107	1953	**£20**	**£8**	

SHARON MARIE

These songs were produced by Brian Wilson, who used the same tune for 'Thinkin' 'Bout You Baby' as for the later Beach Boys' song 'Darlin''.

Run-Around Lover	7"	Capitol	5064	1963	**£60**	**£30**	*US*
Thinkin' 'Bout You Baby	7"	Capitol	5195	1964	**£60**	**£30**	*US*

SHARON PEOPLE

Inside Looking Out	LP	Indigo	IRS5510	1974	**£200**	**£100**	*Irish*

SHARONS

Someone To Turn To	LP	Emblem	JDR325	1970	**£75**	**£37.50**	

SHARP, DEE DEE

All The Hits	LP	Cameo	(S)C1032	1962	**£25**	**£10**	*US*
Biggest Hits	LP	Cameo	C1062	1963	**£20**	**£8**	*US*
Do The Bird	7"	Cameo Parkway	C244	1963	**£6**	**£2.50**	
Do The Bird	LP	Cameo	(S)C1050	1963	**£25**	**£10**	*US*
Down Memory Lane	LP	Cameo	C1074	1963	**£20**	**£8**	*US*
Eighteen Golden Hits	LP	Cameo	(S)C2002	1966	**£20**	**£8**	*US*
Gravy For My Mashed Potatoes	7"	Columbia	DB4874	1962	**£5**	**£2**	
I Really Love You	7"	Cameo Parkway	C375	1965	**£40**	**£20**	
It's A Funny Situation	7"	Cameo Parkway	C382	1965	**£75**	**£37.50**	*demo*
It's Mashed Potato Time	LP	Cameo	C1018	1962	**£25**	**£10**	*US*
Mashed Potato Time	7"	Columbia	DB4818	1962	**£5**	**£2**	
My Best Friend's Man	7"	Atlantic	584056	1966	**£6**	**£2.50**	
Ride	7"	Cameo Parkway	C230	1962	**£4**	**£1.50**	
Rock Me In The Cradle Of Love	7"	Cameo Parkway	C260	1963	**£5**	**£2**	
Songs Of Faith	LP	Cameo	C1022	1962	**£20**	**£8**	*US*
What Kinda Lady	7"	Action	ACT4522	1969	**£20**	**£10**	
Wild	7"	Cameo Parkway	C274	1963	**£4**	**£1.50**	

SHARP, STEVIE & CLEANCUTS

We Are The Mods	7"	Happy Face	MM122	1980	**£50**	**£25**	*no picture sleeve*

SHARPE, BILL

Change Your Mind	12"	Polydor	POPX722	1985	**£10**	**£5**	*picture disc*
Change Your Mind	7"	Polydor	POSPP722	1985	**£6**	**£2.50**	*picture disc*
Famous People	CD	Polydor	8254972	1985	**£12**	**£5**	

SHARPE, RAY

Title	Format	Label	Cat. No.	Year	Mint	VG	Notes
Hey Little Girl	7"	United Artists	UP1032	1963	**£10**	**£5**	
Linda Lu	7"	London	HLW8932	1959	**£25**	**£12.50**	*tri-centre*

SHARPE, ROCKY & THE REPLAYS

Title	Format	Label	Cat. No.	Year	Mint	VG	Notes
Heart	7"	Chiswick	DICE9	1982	**£8**	**£4**	

SHARPE & NUMAN

Title	Format	Label	Cat. No.	Year	Mint	VG	Notes
Automatic	CD	Polydor	8395202	1989	**£12**	**£5**	
I'm On Automatic	CD-s	Polydor	PVCD43	1989	**£5**	**£2**	
No More Lies	CD-s	Polydor	POCD894	1988	**£5**	**£2**	

SHARPEES

Title	Format	Label	Cat. No.	Year	Mint	VG	Notes
Tired Of Being Lonely	7"	Stateside	SS495	1966	**£40**	**£20**	

SHARPS

Title	Format	Label	Cat. No.	Year	Mint	VG	Notes
Lock My Heart	7"	Vogue	V9086	1957	**£400**	**£250**	*best auctioned*
Shuffling	7"	Vogue	V9096	1958	**£350**	**£210**	*best auctioned*

SHARROCK, SONNY

Title	Format	Label	Cat. No.	Year	Mint	VG	Notes
Paradise	LP	Atco	SD36121	1975	**£15**	**£6**	*US, with Linda Sharrock*

SHATNER, WILLIAM

Title	Format	Label	Cat. No.	Year	Mint	VG	Notes
Transformed Man	LP	Decca	DL75043	1968	**£25**	**£10**	*US*

SHAVERS, CHARLIE

Title	Format	Label	Cat. No.	Year	Mint	VG	Notes
Charlie Shavers Quintet	10" LP	London	LZN14009	1956	**£25**	**£10**	
Gershwin, Shavers And Strings	10" LP	London	HBU1053	1956	**£20**	**£8**	
With The Sy Oliver Orchestra	10" LP	London	HBN1047	1956	**£25**	**£10**	

SHAW, ARTIE

Title	Format	Label	Cat. No.	Year	Mint	VG	Notes
Any Old Time	LP	RCA	RD27065	1958	**£15**	**£6**	
Artie Shaw And His Gramercy Five	10" LP	Columbia	33C9006	1955	**£20**	**£8**	
Speak To Me Of Love	10" LP	Brunswick	LA8677	1954	**£20**	**£8**	

SHAW, ARVELL

Title	Format	Label	Cat. No.	Year	Mint	VG	Notes
Skin Tight And Cymbal Wise	LP	Columbia	33SX1076	1958	**£10**	**£4**	

SHAW, GEORGIE

Title	Format	Label	Cat. No.	Year	Mint	VG	Notes
Banjo Woogie	7"	Brunswick	05476	1955	**£4**	**£1.50**	

SHAW, MARLENA

Title	Format	Label	Cat. No.	Year	Mint	VG	Notes
Mercy, Mercy, Mercy	7"	Chess	CRS8054	1967	**£5**	**£2**	

SHAW, NINA

Title	Format	Label	Cat. No.	Year	Mint	VG	Notes
Woven In My Soul	7"	CBS	3239	1968	**£4**	**£1.50**	

SHAW, RICKY

Title	Format	Label	Cat. No.	Year	Mint	VG	Notes
No Love But Your Love	7"	London	HLU9606	1962	**£4**	**£1.50**	

SHAW, ROLAND ORCHESTRA

Title	Format	Label	Cat. No.	Year	Mint	VG	Notes
I Spy	7" EP	Decca	DFE8670	1966	**£12**	**£6**	
James Bond In Action	LP	Decca	LK4730	1965	**£15**	**£6**	
Themes For Secret Agents	LP	Decca	LK4765/PFS4094	1966	**£10**	**£4**	

SHAW, SANDIE

Title	Format	Label	Cat. No.	Year	Mint	VG	Notes
Always Something There To Remind Me	7" EP	Pye	NEP24208	1964	**£8**	**£4**	
Anyone Who Had A Heart	7"	Virgin	VS484	1982	**£6**	**£2.50**	
As Long As You're Happy Baby	7"	Pye	7N15671	1964	**£20**	**£10**	
Hand In Glove	12"	Rough Trade	RTT130	1984	**£6**	**£2.50**	*with the Smiths*
Hello Angel	CD-s	Rough Trade	ROUGHCD110	1988	**£5**	**£2**	
Long Live Love	7" EP	Pye	NEP24220	1965	**£8**	**£4**	
Love Me, Please Love Me	LP	Pye	N(S)PL18205	1967	**£10**	**£4**	
Me	LP	Pye	NPL18121	1965	**£15**	**£6**	
Message Understood	7" EP	Pye	NEP24236	1966	**£8**	**£4**	
Nothing Comes Easy	7" EP	Pye	NEP24254	1966	**£12**	**£6**	
Nothing Less Than Brilliant	CD-s	Rough Trade	RTT230CD	1988	**£5**	**£2**	
Please Help The Cause Against Loneliness	CD-s	Rough Trade	RTT220CD	1988	**£8**	**£4**	
Puppet On A String	LP	Pye	N(S)PL18182	1967	**£10**	**£4**	
Reviewing The Situation	LP	Pye	N(S)PL18323	1970	**£15**	**£6**	
Run With Sandie Shaw	7" EP	Pye	NEP24264	1966	**£12**	**£6**	
Sandie	7" EP	Pye	NEP24232	1965	**£8**	**£4**	
Sandie	LP	Pye	NPL18110	1965	**£12**	**£5**	
Sandie Shaw In French	7" EP	Pye	NEP24271	1967	**£25**	**£12.50**	
Sandie Shaw In Italian	7" EP	Pye	NEP24273	1967	**£25**	**£12.50**	
Sandie Shaw Supplement	LP	Pye	N(S)PL18232	1968	**£10**	**£4**	
Tell The Boys	7" EP	Pye	NEP24281	1967	**£12**	**£6**	
Tomorrow	7" EP	Pye	NEP24247	1966	**£12**	**£6**	

SHAW, THOMAS

Title	Format	Label	Cat. No.	Year	Mint	VG	Notes
Thomas Shaw	LP	XTRA	XTRA1132	1972	**£10**	**£4**	

SHAW, TIMMY & THE STERNPHONES

Title	Format	Label	Cat. No.	Year	Mint	VG	Notes
Gonna Send You Back To Georgia	7"	Pye	7N25239	1964	**£6**	**£2.50**	

SHE TRINITY

Across The Street	7"	CBS	2819	1967	**£4**	**£1.50**	
Hair	7"	President	PT283	1969	**£4**	**£1.50**	
Have I Sinned	7"	Columbia	DB7943	1966	**£4**	**£1.50**	
He Fought The Law	7"	Columbia	DB7874	1966	**£5**	**£2**	
Wild Flower	7"	Columbia	DB7959	1966	**£4**	**£1.50**	
Yellow Submarine	7"	Columbia	DB7992	1966	**£6**	**£2.50**	

SHEARING, GEORGE

Black Satin	LP	Capitol	(S)T858	1958	**£10**	**£4**	
Blue Chiffon	LP	Capitol	T1124	1959	**£10**	**£4**	
Burnished Brass	LP	Capitol	T1038	1959	**£10**	**£4**	
George Shearing And The Montgomery Brothers	LP	Jazzland	JLP55	1961	**£15**	**£6**	
I Hear Music	10" LP	MGM	D118	1953	**£15**	**£6**	
In The Night	LP	Capitol	T1003	1959	**£12**	**£5**	*with Dakota Staton*
Jazz Conceptions	LP	MGM	C769	1958	**£10**	**£4**	
Latin Escapade	LP	Capitol	T737	1957	**£10**	**£4**	
Latin Lace	LP	Capitol	(S)T1082	1959	**£10**	**£4**	
Nearness Of You	10" LP	Decca	LF1036	1951	**£15**	**£6**	
On Stage	LP	Capitol	(S)T1187	1960	**£10**	**£4**	
Shearing Caravan	LP	MGM	C767	1958	**£10**	**£4**	
Shearing Piano	LP	Capitol	T909	1958	**£10**	**£4**	
Shearing Spell	10" LP	Capitol	LC6803	1956	**£15**	**£6**	
Touch Of Genius	10" LP	MGM	D129	1954	**£15**	**£6**	
Velvet Carpet	LP	Capitol	T720	1956	**£10**	**£4**	
Very First Session	10" LP	Vogue	LDE188	1956	**£15**	**£6**	
White Satin	LP	Capitol	T1334	1960	**£10**	**£4**	
You're Hearing George Shearing	10" LP	MGM	D103	1952	**£15**	**£6**	

SHED SEVEN

There are those who maintain that Shed Seven have never really amounted to any more than a second division Britpop band, performing in a style that is fast becoming terminally unfashionable. The fact is, however, that *Going For Gold*, the greatest hits album, contains a body of work of which the band has every right to feel proud. The earlier collectable singles are eclipsed by the later stronger songs but they are, nevertheless, well worth seeking out.

Dolphin	CD-s	Polydor	YORKCD2	1994	**£8**	**£4**	
Going For Gold	7"	Polydor	5762147	1996	**£15**	**£7.50**	*'nude' sleeve*
Mark	12"	Polydor	YORKX1	1994	**£8**	**£4**	
Mark	7"	Polydor	YORK1	1994	**£8**	**£4**	
Mark	CD-s	Polydor	YORKCD1	1994	**£10**	**£5**	
Maximum High	CD	Polydor	5333772	1996	**£15**	**£6**	*double*

SHEEN, BOBBY

Dr Love	7"	Capitol	CL15455	1966	**£50**	**£25**	

SHEEP

Hide And Seek	7"	Stateside	SS493	1966	**£8**	**£4**	

SHEEP (2)

Sheep	LP	Myrrh	MYR1000	1973	**£20**	**£8**	

SHEFFIELDS

Bag's Groove	7"	Pye	7N15767	1965	**£60**	**£30**	
Got My Mojo Working	7"	Pye	7N15627	1964	**£50**	**£25**	
It Must Be Love	7"	Pye	7N15600	1964	**£50**	**£25**	

SHEIKS

Missing You	7"	Parlophone	R5500	1966	**£5**	**£2**	
Missing You	7" EP	Odeon	MEO123	1966	**£12**	**£6**	*French*
Tears Are Coming	7" EP	Odeon	MEO131	1966	**£12**	**£6**	*French*

SHEIKS (2)

Très Chic	7"	London	HLW9012	1959	**£6**	**£2.50**	

SHEILA & JENNY

When The Boy's Happy	7"	Ember	EMBS202	1964	**£5**	**£2**	*picture sleeve*

SHELDON, DOUG

Here I Stand	7" EP	Decca	DFE8527	1963	**£40**	**£20**	
Mickey's Monkey	7"	Decca	F11790	1963	**£4**	**£1.50**	
Take It Like A Man	7"	Sue	WI332	1965	**£8**	**£4**	

SHELL

Goodbye Little Girl	7"	Columbia	DB8082	1966	**£5**	**£2**	

SHELLEY

I Will Be Wishing	7"	Pye	7N15711	1964	**£6**	**£2.50**	

SHELLEY, LIZ

Make Me Your Baby	7"	Brunswick	05940	1965	**£4**	**£1.50**	
No More Love	7"	Brunswick	05953	1966	**£4**	**£1.50**	

SHELLEY, PETE

Qu'est-ce que c'est?	7"	Lyntone	10952/3	1982	**£8**	**£4**	*hard vinyl test pressing*
Sky Yen	12"	Groovy	STP2	1980	**£8**	**£4**	

SHELLS

Baby Oh Baby	7"	London	HLU9288	1961	**£25**	**£12.50**	
It's A Happy Holiday	7"	London	HLU9644	1962	**£25**	**£12.50**	

SHELLY, ALAN

Lady Black Wife	7"	Philips	BF1709	1969	**£8**	**£4**	

SHELTON, ANNE

Absent Friends	7"	Philips	JK1012	1957	**£8**	**£4**	
Anne Shelton	7" EP	Philips	BBE12090	1956	**£12**	**£6**	
Anne Shelton	7" EP	Philips	BBE12218	1958	**£5**	**£2**	
Answer Me	7"	HMV	7M164	1953	**£6**	**£2.50**	
Book	7"	HMV	7M186	1954	**£6**	**£2.50**	
Cross Over The Bridge	7"	HMV	7M197	1954	**£6**	**£2.50**	
Favourites	10" LP	Decca	LF1023	1952	**£20**	**£8**	
Favourites	7" EP	Philips	BBE12430	1961	**£5**	**£2**	
Favourites Vol. 2	10" LP	Decca	LF1106	1953	**£20**	**£8**	
Four Standards	7" EP	Decca	DFE6321	1956	**£6**	**£2.50**	
Goodnight, Well It's Time To Go	7"	HMV	7M240	1954	**£6**	**£2.50**	
Italian Touch	7" EP	Philips	BBE12205	1958	**£5**	**£2**	
Just Love Me	7" EP	Philips	BBE12292	1959	**£5**	**£2**	
My Gypsy Heart	7"	HMV	7M279	1954	**£6**	**£2.50**	
My Yiddishe Momma	7" EP	Philips	BBE12347	1960	**£5**	**£2**	
My Yiddishe Momma	7" EP	Philips	SBBE9003	1960	**£6**	**£2.50**	*stereo*
Sailor	7"	Philips	PB1096	1961	**£5**	**£2**	*picture sleeve*
Shelton Sound	7" EP	Philips	BBE12169	1958	**£5**	**£2**	
Shelton Sound	LP	Philips	BBL7188	1957	**£12**	**£5**	
Showcase	LP	Philips	BBL7393	1960	**£10**	**£4**	
Songs From The Heart	LP	Philips	BBL7291	1959	**£10**	**£4**	
Songs Of Faith	7" EP	Philips	BBE12344	1960	**£5**	**£2**	
Souvenir Of Ireland	LP	Philips	SBBL664	1962	**£10**	**£4**	*stereo*
Spring Fever	7" EP	Philips	BBE12526	1962	**£5**	**£2**	

SHELTON, ROSCOE

Question	7"	Sue	WI354	1965	**£12**	**£6**	
Roscoe Shelton	LP	Excello	8002	1961	**£40**	**£20**	US

SHENDERY, DEANNA

Comin' Home Baby	7"	Decca	F12090	1965	**£4**	**£1.50**	

SHENLEY & ANNETTE

Million Dollar Baby	7"	Blue Beat	BB72	1961	**£12**	**£6**	

SHENLEY & HYACINTH

World Is On A Wheel	7"	Rio	R80	1966	**£8**	**£4**	

SHEP & THE LIMELITES

Daddy's Home	7"	Pye	7N25090	1961	**£60**	**£30**	
Our Anniversary	LP	Hull	1001	1962	**£200**	**£100**	US
Our Anniversary	LP	Roulette	R25350	1967	**£25**	**£10**	US
Ready For Your Love	7"	Pye	7N25112	1961	**£40**	**£20**	

SHEPARD, JEAN

Lonesome Love	LP	Capitol	T1126	1959	**£10**	**£4**	US
Songs Of A Love Affair	LP	Capitol	T728	1956	**£20**	**£8**	US
Songs Of A Love Affair No. 1	7" EP	Capitol	EAP1030	1956	**£5**	**£2**	
Songs Of A Love Affair No. 2	7" EP	Capitol	EAP2728	1956	**£5**	**£2**	

SHEPARD, TOMMY

Shepard's Flock	LP	Vogue Coral	LVA9046	1957	**£25**	**£10**	

SHEPHERD, BILL

Big Guitar	7"	Pye	7N15137	1958	**£4**	**£1.50**	
Whistling Sailor	7"	Island	WIP6013	1967	**£4**	**£1.50**	

SHEPHERD, PAULINE

Love Me To Pieces	7"	Columbia	DB4010	1957	**£5**	**£2**	

SHEPHERD BOYS

Teenage Love	7"	Columbia	SCM5282	1956	**£4**	**£1.50**	

SHEPHERD SISTERS

Alone	7"	HMV	POP411	1957	**£5**	**£2**	
Dancing Baby	7"	Mercury	AMT1005	1958	**£4**	**£1.50**	
Eating Pizza	7"	Mercury	7MT218	1958	**£4**	**£1.50**	
Gettin' Ready For Freddy	7"	Mercury	7MT196	1958	**£6**	**£2.50**	
Talk Is Cheap	7"	London	HLK9758	1963	**£8**	**£4**	
What Makes Little Girls Cry	7"	London	HLK9681	1963	**£10**	**£5**	

SHEPLEY, TOM

How Do You Do?	LP	Tradition	TSR031	1978	**£10**	**£4**	

SHEPP, ARCHIE

And The New York Contemporary Five	LP	Polydor	623235	1967	**£20**	**£8**	
And The New York Contemporary Five	LP	Sonet	SLP36	1973	**£12**	**£5**	
And The New York Contemporary Five	LP	Delmark	DL409/DS9409	1967	**£20**	**£8**	

And The New York Contemporary Five Vol. 2	LP	Polydor	623267	1968	**£20**	**£8**	
And The New York Contemporary Five Vol. 2	LP	Delmark	DS412	1968	**£20**	**£8**	
Archie Shepp	LP	Impulse	AS71	1964	**£30**	**£15**	*US*
Attica Blues	LP	Impulse	AS9222	1972	**£20**	**£8**	*US*
Black Gypsy	LP	America	30AM6099	1970	**£20**	**£8**	*French*
Cry Of My People	LP	Impulse	AS9231	1973	**£15**	**£6**	*US*
Fire Music	LP	Impulse	AS86	1965	**£25**	**£10**	*US*
For Losers	LP	Impulse	AS9188	1969	**£20**	**£8**	*US*
Four For Trane	LP	HMV	CLP/CSD3524	1966	**£20**	**£8**	
Live In San Francisco	LP	HMV	CLP/CSD3600	1967	**£20**	**£8**	
Magic Of Ju-Ju	LP	Impulse	MIPL/SIPL512	1969	**£20**	**£8**	
Mama Too Tight	LP	Impulse	MIPL/SIPL500	1968	**£20**	**£8**	
New Africa	LP	Impulse	AS9262	1974	**£15**	**£6**	*US*
On This Night	LP	HMV	CLP/CSD3561	1966	**£20**	**£8**	
One For The Trane	LP	Atlantic	583732	1969	**£20**	**£8**	
Rufus	LP	Fontana	681014ZL	1967	**£20**	**£8**	
Three For A Quarter, One For A Dime	LP	Impulse	SIPL520	1969	**£20**	**£8**	
Way Ahead	LP	Impulse	MIPL/SIPL516	1969	**£20**	**£8**	

SHEPPARDS

How Do You Like It	7"	Jay Boy	BOY30	1971	**£6**	**£2.50**	
Sheppards	LP	Constellation	CS4	1964	**£25**	**£10**	*US*

SHEPPERD, VIC & JOHN BOWDEN

Motty Down	LP	Burlington	BURL015	1982	**£20**	**£8**	

SHEPPERTON FLAMES

Take Me For What I Am	7"	Deram	DM257	1969	**£5**	**£2**	

SHERIDAN, DANI

Guess I'm Dumb	7"	Planet	PLF106	1966	**£10**	**£5**	

SHERIDAN, MIKE

Don't Turn Your Back On Me	7"	Columbia	DB7798	1966	**£25**	**£12.50**	*with the Lot*
Follow Me Follow	7"	Gemini	GMS001	1970	**£6**	**£2.50**	
Here I Stand	7"	Columbia	DB7462	1965	**£20**	**£10**	*with the Night Riders*
No Other Guy	7"	Columbia	DB7141	1963	**£25**	**£12.50**	*with the Night Riders*
Please Mister Postman	7"	Columbia	DB7183	1963	**£20**	**£10**	*with the Night Riders*
Take My Hand	7"	Columbia	DB7677	1965	**£25**	**£12.50**	*with the Lot*
What A Sweet Thing That Was	7"	Columbia	DB7302	1964	**£20**	**£10**	*with the Night Riders*

SHERIDAN, TONY

Best Of Tony Sheridan	LP	Polydor	237640	1964	**£125**	**£62.50**	*German*
Foolish Little Girl	LP	Scepter	511	1964	**£30**	**£15**	*US*
Little Bit Of Tony Sheridan	LP	Polydor	237629	1964	**£40**	**£20**	*German*
Live In Der Deutschlandhalle	LP	Metronome	MLP15489	1973	**£60**	**£30**	*German*
Skinnie Minnie	7"	Polydor	NH52927	1964	**£8**	**£4**	
Skinnie Minnie	7" EP	Polydor	21978	1964	**£40**	**£20**	*French*
Tony Sheridan	LP	Polydor	46612/237112	1963	**£40**	**£20**	*German*
Will You Still Love Me Tomorrow	7"	Polydor	NH52315	1964	**£8**	**£4**	

SHERIDAN-PRICE

Sometimes I Wonder	7"	Gemini	GMS009	1979	**£4**	**£1.50**	
This Is To Certify That	LP	Gemini	GME1002	1970	**£12**	**£5**	

SHERLOCK, ROGER

Memories Of Sligo	LP	Inchecronin	INC7419	1978	**£12**	**£5**	

SHERMAN, ALLAN

My Son The Nut Vol. 1	7" EP	Warner Bros	WSEP6120	1964	**£5**	**£2**	*stereo*

SHERRYS

At The Hop With The Sherrys	LP	Guyden	GLP503	1962	**£50**	**£25**	*US*
Do The Popeye	7" EP	London	RE1363	1963	**£60**	**£30**	
Pop Pop Popeye	7"	London	HLW9625	1962	**£6**	**£2.50**	
Slop Time	7"	London	HL9686	1963	**£8**	**£4**	

SHERWOOD

Riding The Rainbow	12"	Sherwood	SRT6KL901	1986	**£25**	**£12.50**	

SHERWOOD, BOBBY

Bobby Sherwood Orchestra	10" LP	Capitol	LC6632	1954	**£15**	**£6**	

SHERWOOD, ROBERTA

On Stage	LP	Stateside	SL10039	1963	**£10**	**£4**	

SHERWOOD, TONY

Piano Boogie Twist	7"	Zodiac	ZR010	196–	**£6**	**£2.50**	

SHERWOODS

El Scorpion	7"	Pye	7N25097	1961	**£5**	**£2**	

SHERWOODS (2)

Memories .... 7" .... Solar .... SRP105 .... 1964 £**5** .... £**2**

SHEVELLS

Big City Lights .... 7" .... Polydor .... 56239 .... 1968 £**10** .... £**5**
Come On Home .... 7" .... United Artists .... UP1125 .... 1966 £**40** .... £**20**
I Could Conquer The World .... 7" .... United Artists .... UP1059 .... 1964 £**10** .... £**5**
Walking On The Edge .... 7" .... United Artists .... UP1076 .... 1965 £**10** .... £**5**
Watermelon Man .... 7" .... United Artists .... UP1081 .... 1965 £**10** .... £**5**

SHEVELLS (2)

Ooh Poo Pah Do .... 7" .... Oriole .... CB1915 .... 1963 £**6** .... £**2.50**

SHEVETON, TONY

Excuses .... 7" .... Oriole .... CB1975 .... 1964 £**6** .... £**2.50**
Hey Little Girl .... 7" .... Oriole .... CB1766 .... 1962 £**15** .... £**7.50**
Lonely Heart .... 7" .... Oriole .... CB1726 .... 1962 £**6** .... £**2.50**
Lullaby Of Love .... 7" .... Oriole .... CB1705 .... 1962 £**6** .... £**2.50**
Million Drums .... 7" .... Oriole .... CB1895 .... 1963 £**4** .... £**1.50**
Runaround Sue Is Getting Married .... 7" .... Oriole .... CB1788 .... 1963 £**15** .... £**7.50**

SHIDE & ACORN

Under The Tree .... LP .... Acme .... AC8006LP .... 1994 £**10** .... £**4**
Under The Tree .... LP .... private .... 1973 £**500** .... £**330**

SHIELD, TREVOR

Moon is Playing A Trick .... 7" .... Trojan .... TR664 .... 1969 £**5** .... £**2**

SHIELDS

You Cheated .... 7" .... London .... HLD8706 .... 1958 £**30** .... £**15**

SHIELDS, KEITH

Hey Gyp .... 7" .... Decca .... F12572 .... 1967 £**25** .... £**12.50**
So Hard Living Without You .... 7" .... Decca .... F12666 .... 1967 £**8** .... £**4**
Wonder Of You .... 7" .... Decca .... F12609 .... 1967 £**6** .... £**2.50**

SHIHAB, SAHIB

Seeds .... LP .... Youngblood .... SSYB12 .... 1970 £**10** .... £**4**

SHILOH

Shiloh was an early country-rock band and included several members who achieved later success. Pedal steel guitarist Al Perkins played with Stephen Stills and the Flying Burrito Brothers, keyboard player Jim Norman became string arranger for the Eagles, while drummer Don Henley followed his years as a member of the Eagles with a flourishing solo career.

Shiloh .... LP .... Amos .... AAS7015 .... 1970 £**30** .... £**15** .... *US*

SHINDIGS

Little While Back .... 7" .... Parlophone .... R5377 .... 1965 £**20** .... £**10**
One Little Letter .... 7" .... Parlophone .... R5316 .... 1965 £**20** .... £**10**

SHINDOGS

Who Do You Think You Are .... 7" .... Fontana .... TF790 .... 1967 £**5** .... £**2**

SHINES, JOHNNY

Country Blues .... LP .... XTRA .... XTRA1142 .... 1974 £**12** .... £**5**
Last Night's Dream .... LP .... Blue Horizon .... 763212 .... 1969 £**50** .... £**25**

SHINN, DON

Departures .... LP .... Columbia .... SCX6355 .... 1969 £**15** .... £**6**
Minor Explosion .... 7" .... Polydor .... BM56075 .... 1966 £**30** .... £**15** .. *with the Soul Agents*
Temples With Prophets .... LP .... Columbia .... SX/SCX6319 .... 1969 £**25** .... £**10**

SHIP

Contemporary Folk Music Journey .... LP .... Elektra .... K42122 .... 1972 £**15** .... £**6**

SHIRALEE

I'll Stay By Your Side .... 7" .... Fontana .... TF855 .... 1967 £**6** .... £**2.50**

SHIRELLES

Are You Still My Baby .... 7" .... Pye .... 7N25288 .... 1965 £**4** .... £**1.50**
Baby It's You .... 7" .... Top Rank .... JAR601 .... 1962 £**6** .... £**2.50**
Baby It's You .... LP .... Stateside .... SL10006 .... 1962 £**40** .... £**20**
Big John .... 7" .... Top Rank .... JAR590 .... 1961 £**5** .... £**2**
Dedicated To The One I Love .... 7" .... Top Rank .... JAR549 .... 1961 £**5** .... £**2**
Don't Say Goodnight .... 7" .... Stateside .... SS213 .... 1963 £**5** .... £**2**
Everybody Loves A Lover .... 7" .... Stateside .... SS152 .... 1963 £**5** .... £**2**
Foolish Little Girl .... 7" .... Stateside .... SS181 .... 1963 £**5** .... £**2**
Foolish Little Girl .... LP .... Scepter .... S(PS)511 .... 1963 £**40** .... £**20** .... *US*
Greatest Hits .... LP .... Stateside .... SL10041 .... 1963 £**30** .... £**15**
Greatest Hits Vol. 2 .... LP .... Scepter .... S(PS)560 .... 1967 £**20** .... £**8** .... *US*
Here And Now .... LP .... Pricewise .... P4002 .... 197– £**12** .... £**5** .... *US*
I Met Him On A Sunday .... 7" .... Brunswick .... 05746 .... 1958 £**40** .... £**20**
It's A Mad, Mad, Mad, Mad World .... 7" .... Pye .... 7N25229 .... 1963 £**4** .... £**1.50**
It's A Mad, Mad, Mad, Mad World .... LP .... Scepter .... S(PS)514 .... 1963 £**30** .... £**15** .... *US*
It's Love That Really Counts .... 7" .... Stateside .... SS129 .... 1962 £**6** .... £**2.50**
Mama Said .... 7" .... Top Rank .... JAR567 .... 1961 £**5** .... £**2**
Maybe Tonight .... 7" .... Pye .... 7N25279 .... 1964 £**8** .... £**4**

Sha La La	7"	Pye	7N25240	1964	**£4**	**£1.50**	
Shades of Blue	7"	Pye	7N25386	1966	**£4**	**£1.50**	
Shirelles Sing The Golden Oldies	LP	Scepter	S(PS)516	1964	**£25**	**£10**	*US*
Shirelles Sound	7" EP	Top Rank	JKP3012	1961	**£50**	**£25**	
Sing To Trumpet & Strings	LP	Top Rank	35115	1961	**£60**	**£30**	
Soldier Boy	7"	HMV	POP1019	1962	**£5**	**£2**	
Spontaneous Combustion	LP	Scepter	S(PS)562	1967	**£20**	**£8**	*US*
Swing The Most	LP	Pricewise	P4001	197–	**£12**	**£5**	*US*
There's A Storm Going On In My Heart	7"	Mercury	MF1093	1969	**£8**	**£4**	
Tonight You're Gonna Fall In Love	7"	Pye	7N25233	1964	**£4**	**£1.50**	
Tonight's The Night	7"	London	HL9233	1960	**£10**	**£5**	
Tonight's The Night	LP	Scepter	S(PS)501	1961	**£50**	**£25**	*US*
Too Much Of A Good Thing	7"	Pye	7N25425	1967	**£6**	**£2.50**	
Twist Party	LP	Scepter	S(PS)505	1962	**£30**	**£15**	*US, with King Curtis*
Welcome Home Baby	7"	Stateside	SS119	1962	**£6**	**£2.50**	
What A Sweet Thing That Was	7"	Top Rank	JAR578	1961	**£4**	**£1.50**	
What Does A Girl Do	7"	Stateside	SS232	1963	**£5**	**£2**	
Will You Still Love Me Tomorrow	7"	Top Rank	JAR540	1960	**£5**	**£2**	

SHIRLEY, DON

Improvisations	LP	London	HAA2046	1957	**£10**	**£4**	*with Richard Davis*
Piano Perspectives	LP	London	HAA2003	1956	**£10**	**£4**	
Tonal Expressions	LP	London	HAA2004	1956	**£10**	**£4**	

SHIRLEY, ROY

Dance Arena	7"	Giant	GN32	1968	**£8**	**£4**	
Dance The Reggae	7"	Doctor Bird	DB1168	1968	**£10**	**£5**	
Facts Of Life	7"	Island	WI3119	1968	**£10**	**£5**	
Get On The Ball	7"	Caltone	TONE101	1967	**£8**	**£4**	*Johnny Moore B side*
Good Is Better Than Bad	7"	Island	WI3118	1967	**£10**	**£5**	
Hold Them	7"	Doctor Bird	DB1068	1966	**£10**	**£5**	
Hush A Bye	7"	Doctor Bird	DB1165	1968	**£10**	**£5**	
I'm The Winner	7"	Doctor Bird	DB1079	1967	**£10**	**£5**	
If I Did Know	7"	Island	WI3125	1967	**£10**	**£5**	
Life	7"	Duke	DU18	1969	**£4**	**£1.50**	
Million Dollar Baby	7"	Island	WI3110	1967	**£10**	**£5**	*Sensations B side*
Move All Day	7"	Island	WI3108	1967	**£10**	**£5**	
Musical Field	7"	Doctor Bird	DB1093	1967	**£10**	**£5**	*Lee Perry B side*
Musical War	7"	Island	WI3071	1967	**£10**	**£5**	
Paradise	7"	Ska Beat	JB253	1966	**£10**	**£5**	
Prophet	7"	Doctor Bird	DB1088	1967	**£10**	**£5**	
Thank You	7"	Doctor Bird	DB1108	1967	**£10**	**£5**	
Thank You	7"	Island	WI3098	1967	**£10**	**£5**	
Think About The Future	7"	Fab	FAB54	1968	**£8**	**£4**	
Warming Up The Scene	7"	Giant	GN33	1968	**£8**	**£4**	*Glen Adams B side*
World Needs Love	7"	Amalgamated	AMG815	1968	**£8**	**£4**	

SHIRLEY, SUSAN

Really Into Something Good	7"	Philips	6006037	1970	**£10**	**£5**	

SHIRLEY & LEE

Come On And Have Your Fun	7"	Vogue	V9129	1959	**£60**	**£30**	*tri-centre*
Everybody's Rocking	7"	Vogue	V9118	1958	**£75**	**£37.50**	*tri-centre*
I Feel Good	7"	Vogue	V9063	1957	**£60**	**£30**	*tri-centre*
I Want To Dance	7"	Vogue	V9088	1957	**£60**	**£30**	*tri-centre*
I'll Do It	7"	Vogue	V9137	1959	**£60**	**£30**	*tri-centre*
I'll Thrill You	7"	Vogue	V9103	1958	**£60**	**£30**	*tri-centre*
I've Been Loved Before	7"	London	HLI9186	1960	**£15**	**£7.50**	
Legendary Masters	LP	United Artists	LA026G2	1974	**£15**	**£6**	*US*
Let The Good Times Roll	7"	London	HLI9209	1960	**£12**	**£6**	
Let The Good Times Roll	7"	Vogue	V9059	1956	**£100**	**£50**	*tri-centre*
Let The Good Times Roll	7"	Island	WI257	1965	**£10**	**£5**	
Let The Good Times Roll	LP	Imperial	A9179	1962	**£60**	**£30**	*US*
Let The Good Times Roll	LP	Warwick	(WST)2028	1961	**£75**	**£37.50**	*US*
Let The Good Times Roll	LP	Aladdin	807	1956	**£200**	**£100**	*US*
Let The Good Times Roll	LP	Score	SLP4023	1957	**£100**	**£50**	*US*
Let The Good Times Roll	LP	Jay Boy	JSX2005	1971	**£15**	**£6**	
Little Word	7"	Vogue	V9135	1959	**£60**	**£30**	*tri-centre*
Rock All Nite	7"	Vogue	V9072	1957	**£75**	**£37.50**	*tri-centre*
Rock'n'Roll	7" EP	Vogue	VE170101	1957	**£200**	**£100**	*tri-centre*
Rocking With The Clock	7"	Vogue	V9084	1957	**£75**	**£37.50**	*tri-centre*
Shirley And Lee	7" EP	Vogue	VE170145	1960	**£175**	**£87.50**	
That's What I Wanna Do	7"	Vogue	V9067	1957	**£60**	**£30**	*tri-centre*
True Love	7"	Vogue	V9156	1959	**£50**	**£25**	
You'd Be Thinking Of Me	7"	Vogue	V9094	1957	**£60**	**£30**	*tri-centre*

SHIRLEY & THE RUDE BOYS

Gently Set Me Free	7"	Blue Beat	BB375	1967	**£12**	**£6**	

SHIRLEY & THE SHIRELLES

Look What You've Done	7"	Bell	BLL1049	1969	**£5**	**£2**	

SHIVA

Angel Of Mons	7"	Heavy Metal	HEAVY16	1982	**£5**	**£2**	
Firedance	LP	Heavy Metal	HMRLP6	1982	**£12**	**£5**	
Rock Lives On	7"	Heavy Metal	HEAVY13	1982	**£5**	**£2**	

SHIVA'S HEADBAND

Coming To A Head	LP	Armadillo	NO001	1972	£75	£37.50	US
Psychedelic Yesterday	LP	Ape	1001	1977	£20	£8	US
Take Me To The Mountains	LP	Capitol	ST538	1970	£50	£25	US

SHIVEL, BUNNY

You'll Never Find Another Love Like Mine	7"	Capitol	CL15487	1967	£5	£2	

SHIVER

Walpurgis	LP	Maris	20501	1969	£125	£62.50	German

SHIVOO

Shivoo	LP	private		1983	£100	£50	Dutch

SHOCK, JOYCE

Take Your Foot From The Door	7"	Philips	PB824	1958	£4	£1.50	

SHOCKING BLUE

With a lead singer who sounded not unlike Grace Slick, Shocking Blue would have loved to have been taken seriously as the Dutch Jefferson Airplane. Unfortunately, their material was cast a little too firmly in the light-weight pop mould, but this stood the group in good stead in the case of their hit single 'Venus', whose absurdly catchy melody and rhythm have made the song into a perennial favourite.

At Home	LP	Penny Farthing	PELS500	1969	£15	£6	
Scorpio's Dance	LP	Penny Farthing	PELS510	1970	£15	£6	
Send Me A Postcard	7"	Olga	OLE015	1969	£30	£15	demo

SHOES

Un Dans Versailles	LP	private		1974	£100	£50	US

SHOGUN

High In The Sky	7"	Attack	ATA913	1986	£12	£6	
Shogun	LP	Attack	ATA006	1986	£25	£10	

SHONDELL, TROY

I Got A Woman	7"	London	HL9668	1963	£6	£2.50	
Many Sides Of Troy Shondell	LP	London	HAY8128	1964	£50	£25	
Tears From An Angel	7"	Liberty	LIB55398	1962	£4	£1.50	
This Time	7"	London	HLG9432	1961	£4	£1.50	

SHONDELLS

At The Saturday Hop	LP	La Louisianne	109	1964	£50	£25	US
Don't Cry My Soldier Boy	7"	Ember	EMBS191	1964	£6	£2.50	

SHONEN KNIFE

Get The Wow	CD-s	August	CAUG003CD	1993	£5	£2	2 versions
Riding On The Rocket	CD-s	August	CAUG001CD	1992	£5	£2	
We Are Very Happy You Came	CD-s	August	RUST004CD	1993	£5	£2	

SHOOT

On The Frontier	LP	EMI	EMA73	1973	£20	£8	

SHOP ASSISTANTS

All Day Long	7"	Subway Organisation	SUBWAY1	1985	£8	£4	red picture sleeve
Something To Do	7"	Villa 21	002	1985	£25	£12.50	with Buba

SHORE, DINAH

Buttons And Bows	LP	Fontana	Z4026	1960	£10	£4	
Cattle Call	7"	RCA	RCA1003	1957	£4	£1.50	
Changing Partners	7"	HMV	7M183	1954	£6	£2.50	
Come Back To My Arms	7"	HMV	7M221	1954	£6	£2.50	
Dinah Sings Some Blues With Red	LP	Capitol	(S)T1354	1960	£10	£4	with Red Norvo
Dinah, Yes Indeed	LP	Capitol	(S)T1247	1959	£10	£4	
Holding Hands At Midnight	LP	RCA	RD27072	1958	£10	£4	
If I Give My Heart To You	7"	HMV	7M250	1954	£8	£4	
Keep It A Secret	7"	HMV	7M119	1953	£8	£4	
Love And Marriage	7"	HMV	7M352	1956	£5	£2	
Somebody Loves Me	LP	Capitol	(S)T1296	1960	£10	£4	
Sweet Thing	7"	HMV	7M139	1953	£6	£2.50	
Three Coins In The Fountain	7"	HMV	7M236	1954	£8	£4	

SHORT, BOBBY

Bobby Short	LP	London	HAK2123	1958	£10	£4	

SHORT, BRIAN

Anything For A Laugh	LP	Transatlantic	TRA245	1971	£20	£8	

SHORT CROSS

Arising	LP	Grizly	16013	1970	£200	£100	US

SHORTER, WAYNE

Adam's Apple	LP	Blue Note	BLP/BST84232	1966	£20	£8	
All Seeing Eye	LP	Blue Note	BLP/BST84219	1965	£20	£8	
Ju Ju	LP	Blue Note	BLP/BST84182	1964	£25	£10	

Title	Format	Label	Cat. No.	Year	Mint	Value	Notes
Moto Grosso Feio	LP	Blue Note	LA014G	1974	**£15**	**£6**	*US*
Native Dancer	LP	CBS	80721	1975	**£12**	**£5**	
Night Dreamer	LP	Blue Note	BLP/BST84173	1964	**£25**	**£10**	
Schizophrenia	LP	Blue Note	BST84297	1968	**£20**	**£8**	
Speak No Evil	LP	Blue Note	BLP/BST84194	1965	**£20**	**£8**	
Super Nova	LP	Blue Note	BST84332	1969	**£15**	**£6**	

SHORTKUTS

Title	Format	Label	Cat. No.	Year	Mint	Value	Notes
Your Eyes May Shine	7"	United Artists	UP2233	1968	**£10**	**£5**	

SHORTWAVE

Title	Format	Label	Cat. No.	Year	Mint	Value	Notes
Greatest Hats	LP	Crescent	ARS111	1977	**£12**	**£5**	

SHORTY

Title	Format	Label	Cat. No.	Year	Mint	Value	Notes
Aquarius Pressure	7"	Ackee	ACK509	1973	**£5**	**£2**	

SHORTY & THEM

Title	Format	Label	Cat. No.	Year	Mint	Value	Notes
Pills	7"	Fontana	TF460	1964	**£15**	**£7.50**	

SHOTGUN EXPRESS

Title	Format	Label	Cat. No.	Year	Mint	Value	Notes
Funny 'Cos Neither Could I	7"	Columbia	DB8178	1967	**£30**	**£15**	
I Could Feel The Whole World	7"	Columbia	DB8025	1966	**£30**	**£15**	
I Could Feel The Whole World Turn Round	7" EP	Columbia	ESRF1864	1967	**£200**	**£100**	*French*

SHOTGUN LTD

Title	Format	Label	Cat. No.	Year	Mint	Value	Notes
Shotgun Ltd	LP	Prophesy	SD6050	1971	**£15**	**£6**	*US*

SHOTS

Title	Format	Label	Cat. No.	Year	Mint	Value	Notes
Keep A Hold Of What You've Got	7"	Columbia	DB7713	1965	**£25**	**£12.50**	

SHOUTERS

Title	Format	Label	Cat. No.	Year	Mint	Value	Notes
Beat Party	LP	Eurocord	H997	1966	**£30**	**£15**	*German*

SHOUTS

Title	Format	Label	Cat. No.	Year	Mint	Value	Notes
She Was My Baby	7"	React	EA101	1964	**£6**	**£2.50**	

SHOWBIZ KIDS

Title	Format	Label	Cat. No.	Year	Mint	Value	Notes
I Don't Want To Discuss That	7"	Top Secret	CON1	198–	**£20**	**£10**	

SHOWMEN

Title	Format	Label	Cat. No.	Year	Mint	Value	Notes
It Will Stand	7"	London	HLP9481	1962	**£50**	**£25**	
Wrong Girl	7"	London	HLP9571	1962	**£75**	**£37.50**	

SHOWSTOPPERS

Title	Format	Label	Cat. No.	Year	Mint	Value	Notes
Ain't Nothing But A House Party	7"	Beacon	3100	1968	**£5**	**£2**	
Ain't Nothing But A House Party	7"	Beacon	BEA100	1970	**£4**	**£1.50**	

SHOX

Title	Format	Label	Cat. No.	Year	Mint	Value	Notes
No Turning Back	7"	Beggars Banquet	BEG33	1980	**£5**	**£2**	
No Turning Back	7"	Axis	AXIS4	1980	**£8**	**£4**	

SHREEVE, MARK

Title	Format	Label	Cat. No.	Year	Mint	Value	Notes
Assassin	LP	Uniton	U021	1983	**£10**	**£4**	
Thoughts Of War	LP	Uniton	U001	1981	**£10**	**£4**	

SHRIEVE, MICHAEL

Title	Format	Label	Cat. No.	Year	Mint	Value	Notes
Transfer Station Blue	LP	Fortuna	FOR023	1984	**£40**	**£20**	*US*

SHUBERT

Title	Format	Label	Cat. No.	Year	Mint	Value	Notes
Until The Rains Come	7"	Fontana	TF942	1968	**£8**	**£4**	

SHUMAN, MORT

Title	Format	Label	Cat. No.	Year	Mint	Value	Notes
I'm A Man	7"	Decca	F11184	1959	**£40**	**£20**	*tri-centre*
Monday Monday	7"	Immediate	IM048	1967	**£8**	**£4**	

SHUSHA

Title	Format	Label	Cat. No.	Year	Mint	Value	Notes
From East To West	LP	Tangent	TGS138	1978	**£10**	**£4**	
Persian Love Songs And Mystic Chants	LP	Tangent	TGS108	1970	**£15**	**£6**	
Shusha	LP	United Artists	UAS29575	1974	**£10**	**£4**	
Song Of Long Time Lovers	LP	Tangent	TGS114	1972	**£10**	**£4**	

SHUTDOWN DOUGLAS

Title	Format	Label	Cat. No.	Year	Mint	Value	Notes
Twin Cut Outs	7" EP	Capitol	EAP41997	1964	**£8**	**£4**	*French*

SHUTDOWNS

Title	Format	Label	Cat. No.	Year	Mint	Value	Notes
Four In The Floor	7"	Colpix	PX11016	1963	**£12**	**£6**	

SHY

Title	Format	Label	Cat. No.	Year	Mint	Value	Notes
Once Bitten Twice Shy	LP	Ebony	EBON15	1983	**£20**	**£8**	

SHY LIMBS

Title	Format	Label	Cat. No.	Year	Mint	Value	Notes
Lady In Black	7"	CBS	4624	1969	**£50**	**£25**	
Reputation	7"	CBS	4190	1969	**£50**	**£25**	

SHY ONES

La Route	7"	Oriole	CB1924	1964	£6	£2.50	
Nightcap	7"	Oriole	CB1848	1963	£8	£4	

SHYLOCK

Ile De Fievre	LP	CBS	82862	1978	£15	£6	*French*

SHYSTER

The name Shyster conceals the identity of sixties cult group, the Fleur De Lys.

Tick Tock	7"	Polydor	56202	1968	£100	£50	

SIBLEY, DUDLEY

Gun Man	7"	Island	WI3034	1967	£10	£5	
Run Boy Run	7"	Coxsone	CS7010	1967	£10	£5	

SICK THINGS

Legendary Sick Things	7"	Chaos	CH3	1983	£6	£2.50	

SIDEKICKS

The Sidekicks evolved into the highly rated British progressive pop band, Kaleidoscope.

Suspicions	7"	RCA	RCA1538	1966	£10	£4	

SIDEKICKS (2)

Fifi The Flea	LP	RCA	3712	1966	£15	£6	US

SIDEWINDERS

Sidewinders	LP	RCA	LSP4696	1972	£15	£6	US

SIEGEL–SCHWALL BAND

The Siegel–Schwall Band so accurately epitomizes the worst aspects of the late-sixties fascination with the blues on the part of white rock performers, that it is amazing how the group managed to make such a large number of albums. Each is characterized by an entirely routine approach to the blues in which the form is reproduced without any understanding or feeling. Composer William Russo was able to use this to interesting effect, however, when he incorporated the group within his 'Three Pieces For Blues Band And Symphony Orchestra'. Here it is vital that the blues group play clichés, so that they can be subverted by the oblique lines superimposed by the orchestra. It is an unusual approach to the combination of rock and classical styles, but it works superbly well.

Say Siegel–Schwall	LP	Vanguard	VRS/VSD79249	1967	£10	£4	US
Shake	LP	Vanguard	SVRL19044	1968	£10	£4	
Siegel–Schwall '70	LP	Vanguard	VSD6562	1970	£10	£4	US
Siegel–Schwall Band	LP	Vanguard	VRS/VSD79235	1966	£10	£4	US
Siegel–Schwall Band	LP	RCA	SF8246	1971	£10	£4	
Sleepy Hollow	LP	RCA	LSP10394	1972	£10	£4	

SIFFRE, LABI

Remember My Song	LP	EMI	EMC3065	1975	£40	£20	
Singer And The Song	LP	Pye	NSPL28147	1971	£15	£6	

SIGHT & SOUND

Alley Alley	7"	Fontana	TF982	1968	£8	£4	
Our Love Is In The Pocket	7"	Fontana	TF927	1968	£8	£4	

SIGLER, BUNNY

Let The Good Times Roll	7"	Cameo Parkway	P153	1967	£10	£5	
Let The Good Times Roll	LP	Parkway	P(S)50000	1967	£20	£8	US

SIGNATURES

Prepare To Flip	LP	Warner Bros	W1353	1959	£12	£5	US
Sing In	LP	Warner Bros	W1250	1959	£12	£5	US
Their Voices And Instruments	LP	Whippet	702	1957	£15	£6	US

SIGNS

Ain't You Got A Heart	7"	Decca	F12522	1966	£6	£2.50	

SILBERBART

Four Times Sound Razing	LP	Philips	6305095	1971	£40	£20	*German*

SILENT NOISE

I've Been Hurt	7"	Silent Noise	ER02	1979	£5	£2	

SILENT PARTNER

Hung By A Thread	LP	Lucky Boy			£150	£75	US

SILHOUETTES

Get A Job	7"	Parlophone	R4407	1958	£30	£15	
Get A Job	LP	Goodway	GLP100	195–	£150	£75	US
Heading For The Poorhouse	7"	Parlophone	R4425	1958	£60	£30	

SILK

Smooth As Raw Silk	LP	ABC	ABCS694	1969	£20	£8	US

SILK, ERIC

Silken Touch	10" LP	Esquire	20095	1958	£15	£6	

SILKIE

Born To Be With You	7" EP	Fontana	465306	1966	£12	£6	*French*
Sing Dylan	LP	Fontana	TL5256	1965	£12	£5	
You've Got To Hide Your Love Away	7"	Fontana	TF603	1965	£4	£1.50	
You've Got To Hide Your Love Away	7" EP	Fontana	465294	1965	£20	£10	*French*
You've Got To Hide Your Love Away	LP	Fontana	MGF2/SRF67548	1965	£20	£8	*US*

SILL, JUDEE

Heart Food	LP	Asylum	SYL9006	1973	£10	£4	
Judee Sill	LP	Asylum	SYLA8751	1971	£10	£4	

SILLY SURFERS

Sounds Of The Silly Surfers	LP	Mercury	MG2/SR60977	1965	£20	£8	*US*

SILLY WIZARD

Caledonia's Hardy Sons	LP	Highway	SHY7004	1979	£10	£4	
Silly Wizard	LP	XTRA	XTRA1158	1976	£12	£5	
So Many Partings	LP	Highway	SHY7010	1980	£10	£4	

SILOAH

Saureadler	LP	Car	1558015	1970	£200	£100	*German*
Sukram Gurk	LP	German Blues	1558025	1972	£200	£100	*German*

SILVER

Baby Oh Yeah	7"	Jolly	JY006	1968	£4	£1.50	
I Need A Girl	7"	Jolly	JY017	1968	£4	£1.50	
Love Me Forever	7"	Columbia	DB117	1970	£4	£1.50	
Things	7"	Jolly	JY012	1968	£4	£1.50	

SILVER, ANDEE

Boy I Used To Know	7"	HMV	POP1344	1964	£4	£1.50	
Handful Of Silver	LP	Decca	SKL5059	1970	£15	£6	
Love Me	7"	Decca	F23071	1970	£5	£2	
Only Your Love Can Save Me	7"	Fontana	TF666	1966	£4	£1.50	
Too Young To Go Steady	7"	HMV	POP1297	1964	£4	£1.50	

SILVER, EDDIE

Rockin' Robin	7"	Parlophone	R4483	1958	£6	£2.50	
Seven Steps To Love	7"	Parlophone	R4439	1958	£8	£4	

SILVER, HORACE

Best Of Horace Silver	LP	Blue Note	BST84325	1969	£12	£5	
Blowin' The Blues Away	LP	Blue Note	BLP/BST84017	196–	£30	£15	
Cape Verdean Blues	LP	Blue Note	BLP/BST84220	1965	£25	£10	
Doin' The Thing At The Village Gate	LP	Blue Note	BLP/BST84076	196–	£30	£15	
Finger Poppin'	LP	Blue Note	BLP/BST84008	196–	£30	£15	
Horace Silver And The Jazz Messengers	LP	Blue Note	BLP/BST81518	196–	£25	£10	
Horace Silver Trio	10" LP	Vogue	LDE065	1954	£50	£25	
Horace-Scope	LP	Blue Note	BLP/BST84042	196–	£30	£15	
Jody Grind	LP	Blue Note	BLP/BST84250	1966	£20	£8	
Let's Get To The Nitty Gritty	7"	Blue Note	451902	1963	£5	£2	
Serenade To A Soul Sister	LP	Blue Note	BST84277	1968	£20	£8	
Silver's Blue	LP	Philips	BBL7183	1957	£25	£10	
Silver's Serenade	LP	Blue Note	BLP/BST84131	1963	£30	£15	
Sister Sadie	7"	Blue Note	451750	1961	£5	£2	
Six Pieces Of Silver	LP	Blue Note	BLP/BST81539	196–	£40	£20	
Song For My Father	LP	Blue Note	BLP/BST84185	1964	£25	£10	
Stylings Of Silver	LP	Blue Note	BLP/BST81562	196–	£30	£15	
Sweet Sweetie Dee	7"	Blue Note	451903	1964	£5	£2	
That Healin' Feelin'	LP	Blue Note	BST84352	1970	£12	£5	
Tokyo Blues	LP	Blue Note	BLP/BST84110	1962	£30	£15	
Too Much Sake	7"	Blue Note	451873	1963	£5	£2	
United States Of Mind	LP	Blue Note	BST84368	1970	£12	£5	
You Gotta Take A Little Love	LP	Blue Note	BST84309	1969	£15	£6	

SILVER, LORRAINE

Happy Faces	7"	Pye	7N17055	1966	£25	£12.50	
Lost Summer Love	7"	Pye	7N15922	1965	£50	£25	

SILVER APPLES

Musician credits suggesting a line-up of banjo and drums give no clue that the Silver Apples were actually one of the first electronic groups, exploring similar territory to that of Suicide ten years later. Banjo and drums do feature, but less prominently than the tone generators and ring modulators that the group wields in these pre-synthesizer days. The duo was recently persuaded to reform for a tour with Sonic Boom and Pete Bassman – which would be the least likely of all sixties revivals were it not for the fact that the Silver Apples' music carries far more resonance in the late nineties than it ever did the first time round.

Contact	LP	Kapp	KS3584	1969	£50	£25	*US*
Silver Apples	LP	Kapp	KL/KS3562	1968	£50	£25	*US*

SILVER BIRCH

Silver Birch	LP	Brayford	BR02	1974	£200	£100	

SILVER EAGLE

Theodore	7"	MGM	MGM1345	1967	£10	£5	

SILVER METRE

Silver Metre	LP	National General	NG2000	1969	**£10**	**£4**	*US*

SILVER MOUNTAIN

Shakin' Brains	LP	Road Runner	RR9884	1983	**£10**	**£4**	

SILVER SISTERS

Waiting For The Stars To Shine	7"	Parlophone	R4669	1960	**£4**	**£1.50**	

SILVER STARS STEEL BAND

Silver Stars Steel Band	LP	Island	ILP904	1963	**£25**	**£10**	
Silver Stars Steel Band	LP	Trojan	TTI39	1970	**£10**	**£4**	

SILVERHEAD

Ace Supreme	7"	Purple	PUR104	1972	**£4**	**£1.50**	
Rolling With My Baby	7"	Purple	PUR110	1972	**£4**	**£1.50**	

SILVERS, PHIL

Bugle Calls For Big Band	LP	Fontana	Z4040	1957	**£10**	**£4**	

SILVERSTARS

Old Man Say	7"	Trojan	TR646	1968	**£6**	**£2.50**	

SILVERSTEIN, SHEL

Hairy Jazz	LP	Elektra	EKL/EKS7176	1959	**£15**	**£6**	*US*
Inside Folk Songs	LP	Atlantic	(SD)8072	1963	**£12**	**£5**	*US*

SILVERTONES

Cool Down	7"	Treasure Isle	TI7020	1967	**£10**	**£5**	*Tommy McCook B side*
Intensified Change	7"	Trojan	TR7705	1969	**£4**	**£1.50**	
It's Real	7"	Doctor Bird	DB1041	1966	**£10**	**£5**	*Lyn Taitt B side*
Midnight Hour	7"	Treasure Isle	TI7027	1968	**£10**	**£5**	*Tommy McCook B side*
Silver Bullets	LP	Trojan	TRLS69	1971	**£15**	**£6**	

SILVERWING

Alive And Kicking	LP	Bullet	BULP1	1983	**£10**	**£4**	
Rock And Roll Are Four Letter Words	7"	Mayhem	SILVER1	1980	**£4**	**£1.50**	
Sittin' Pretty	12"	Mayhem	SILV212	1982	**£6**	**£2.50**	
Sittin' Pretty	7"	Mayhem	SILV02	1982	**£5**	**£2**	

SILVESTER, VICTOR

Alligator Roll	7"	Columbia	DB3907	1957	**£5**	**£2**	
Rockin' Rhythm Roll	7"	Columbia	DB3888	1957	**£5**	**£2**	

SILVO, JOHNNY & DAVE MOSES

Live From London	LP	Bus Stop	BUSLP5001	1973	**£10**	**£4**	

SIMEON, OMER

Omer Simeon	10" LP	Vogue	LDE174	1956	**£50**	**£25**	

SIMMONS, BEVERLEY

Mr Pitiful	7"	Pama	PM716	1968	**£4**	**£1.50**	
Remember Otis	LP	Pama	PMLP/PMSP9	1969	**£15**	**£6**	

SIMMONS, JEFF

Simmons's brief membership of the Mothers of Invention and his ambitions to achieve solo success are described within Frank Zappa's film *200 Motels*. Zappa produced *Lucille Has Messed Up My Mind* and subsequently recorded the title track himself, but Simmons did not achieve the stardom he craved.

Lucille Has Messed Up My Mind	LP	Reprise	RS6391	1969	**£40**	**£20**	
Lucille Has Messed Up My Mind	LP	Straight	STS1057	1969	**£40**	**£20**	
Naked Angels Soundtrack	LP	Straight	STS1056	1969	**£30**	**£15**	*US*

SIMMONS, JUMPIN' GENE

Haunted House	7"	London	HLU9913	1964	**£8**	**£4**	
Jump	7"	London	HLU9933	1964	**£8**	**£4**	
Jumpin' Gene Simmons	LP	Hi	(S)HL12018	1964	**£25**	**£10**	*US*

SIMMONS, LITTLE MAC

Blues From Chicago	7" EP	Outasite	OSEP1	1966	**£100**	**£50**	

SIMMS, JASON & MUSIC THROUGH SIX

It's Got To Be Mellow	7"	Domain	D5	1968	**£5**	**£2**	

SIMOLA, SEIJA

Give Love A Chance	7"	Sonet	SON2145	1978	**£8**	**£4**	

SIMON

Mrs Lillyco	7"	Plum	PLS002	1969	**£20**	**£10**	

SIMON, CARLY

Coming Round Again	CD	Polygram	0803781	1988	**£10**	**£4**	*CD video*
Coming Round Again	CD-s	Arista	ARISTCD687	1987	**£5**	**£2**	
Let The River Run	CD-s	Arista	162124	1989	**£5**	**£2**	

Nobody Does It Better (live)	CD-s	Arista	661807	1988	£5	£2	
You're So Vain	CD-s	Elektra	EKR123CD	1991	£5	£2	

SIMON, JOE

My Special Prayer	7"	Monument	MON1004	1967	£4	£1.50	
Nine Pound Steel	7"	Monument	MON1010	1968	£4	£1.50	
Simon Pure Soul	LP	Monument	L/SMO5005	1967	£10	£4	
Teenager's Prayer	7"	London	HLU10057	1966	£15	£7.50	
That's The Way I Want Our Love	7"	Monument	MON1051	1970	£5	£2	

SIMON, PAUL

Early Songs	LP	Crest	EBM7172	196–	£30	£15	*US promo*
Greatest Hits, Etc.	LP	Columbia	HC45032	1981	£12	£5	*US audiophile*
I Am A Rock	7"	CBS	201797	1965	£10	£5	
I Am A Rock	7" EP	CBS	6211	1965	£12	£6	*French, no picture sleeve*
Kodachrome	7"	CBS	1545	1973	£10	£5	
Mother And Child Reunion	CD-s	WEA	W7655CD	1988	£5	£2	
Obvious Child	CD-s	WEA	W9549CD	1990	£5	£2	
Paul Simon	LP	CBS	Q69007	1972	£10	£4	*quad*
Paul Simon 1964–1993 Box Set Sampler	CD	Warner Bros		1993	£25	£10	*US promo*
Paul Simon Plus	LP	MCP	8027	1966	£20	£8	*US, with Neil Sedaka & 4 Seasons*
Paul Simon Songbook	LP	CBS	(S)BPG62579	1965	£12	£5	
Proof	CD-s	WEA	W0003CD	1991	£5	£2	
Rhythm Of The Saints	CD	Warner Bros	9260982	1990	£25	£10	*US promo with ribbon, bead, feather, cloth cover*
Still Crazy After All These Years	LP	Columbia	HC43540	1981	£12	£5	*US audiophile*
Still Crazy After All These Years	LP	CBS	Q86001	1975	£10	£4	*quad*
There Goes Rhymin' Simon	LP	CBS	Q69035	1973	£10	£4	*quad*

SIMON, PLUG & GRIMES

Is This A Dream?	7"	Deram	DM296	1970	£5	£2	

SIMON, TONY

Gimme A Little Sign	7"	Track	604012	1967	£4	£1.50	

SIMON & GARFUNKEL

At The Zoo	7"	CBS	202608	1967	£5	£2	
At The Zoo	7" EP	CBS	6339	1967	£8	£4	*French*
Bridge Over Troubled Water	LP	CBS	Q63699	1973	£12	£5	*quad*
Bridge Over Troubled Waters	LP	Columbia	HC49914	1981	£12	£5	*US audiophile*
Bridge Over Troubled Waters	LP	Mobile Fidelity	MFSL1173	1981	£12	£5	*US audiophile*
Dangling Conversation	7"	CBS	202285	1966	£8	£4	
Fakin' It	7"	CBS	2911	1967	£5	£2	
Feelin' Groovy	7" EP	CBS	EP6360	1967	£10	£5	
Graduate	LP	CBS	70042	1968	£10	£4	*mono*
Greatest Hits	LP	Columbia	HC41350	1981	£12	£5	*US audiophile*
Hazy Shade Of Winter	7"	CBS	202378	1966	£4	£1.50	
Hit Sounds Of Simon And Garfunkel	LP	Pickwick	SPC3059	1966	£15	£6	*US*
Homeward Bound	7"	CBS	202045	1966	£4	£1.50	
I Am A Rock	7"	CBS	202303	1966	£4	£1.50	
I Am A Rock	7" EP	CBS	EP6074	1966	£10	£5	
Mrs Robinson	7" EP	CBS	EP6400	1968	£6	£2.50	
Seven O'Clock News	CD-s	CBS	6576535	1991	£5	£2	
Simon & Garfunkel	LP	Sears	SP435	1969	£15	£6	*US*
Simon And Garfunkel	LP	Allegro	ALL836	1967	£15	£6	
Sound Of Silence	7"	CBS	201977	1965	£4	£1.50	
Sound Of Silence	LP	CBS	(S)BPG62690	1966	£10	£4	
Sounds Of Silence	7" EP	CBS	5655	1965	£8	£4	*French*
Wednesday Morning 3am	7" EP	CBS	EP6053	1965	£10	£5	
Wednesday Morning 3am	LP	CBS	63370	1968	£10	£4	*mono*

SIMON SISTERS

The Simon Sisters made a number of records of mainly children's songs, before sister Lucy got married and decided to leave the music business. Younger sister Carly carried on by herself and eventually became rather successful.

Cuddlebug	7"	London	HLR9984	1965	£5	£2	
Cuddlebug	LP	Kapp	KL1397/KS3397	1964	£15	£6	*US*
Lobster Quadrille	LP	Columbia	CS24506	1969	£12	£5	*US*
Simon Sisters	LP	Kapp	KL1359/KS3359	1964	£15	£6	*US*
Winkin' Blinkin' And Nod	7"	London	HLR9893	1964	£6	£2.50	

SIMONE, NINA

Amazing	LP	Colpix	(S)CP407	1959	£10	£4	*US*
And Her Friends	LP	Bethlehem	BCP6041	1959	£10	£4	*US*
At Carnegie Hall	LP	Colpix	(S)CP455	1963	£10	£4	*US*
At Newport	LP	Colpix	(S)CP412	1960	£10	£4	*US*
At The Town Hall	LP	Pye	NPL28014	1962	£12	£5	
At The Village Gate	LP	Colpix	PXL421	1965	£10	£4	
Best Of Nina Simone	LP	Philips	SBL7895	1969	£10	£4	
Broadway, Blues, Ballads	LP	Philips	BL7662	1965	£10	£4	
Don't Let Me Be Misunderstood	7"	Philips	BF1388	1965	£4	£1.50	
Don't Let Me Be Misunderstood	7" EP	Philips	BE12585	1965	£6	£2.50	
Either Way I Lose	7"	Philips	BF1465	1966	£5	£2	

Exactly Like You	7"	Colpix	PX799	1964	£4	£1.50	
Fine And Mellow	7" EP	Colpix	PXE303	1964	£8	£4	
Folksy Nina	LP	Colpix	PXL465	1964	£10	£4	
Forbidden Fruit	LP	Colpix	PXL419	1965	£10	£4	
Forbidden Fruit	LP	Pye	NJL36	1961	£12	£5	
High Priestess Of Soul	LP	Philips	BL7764	1967	£10	£4	
I Love To Love	7" EP	Colpix	PXE307	1966	£8	£4	
I Loves You Porgy	7"	Parlophone	R4583	1959	£4	£1.50	
I Put A Spell On You	7"	Philips	BF1415	1965	£4	£1.50	
I Put A Spell On You	LP	Philips	BL7671	1965	£10	£4	
In Concert	LP	Philips	BL7678	1965	£10	£4	
Intimate Nina Simone	7" EP	Parlophone	GEP8864	1962	£8	£4	
Just Say I Love Him	7" EP	Colpix	PXE306	1966	£8	£4	
Let It All Out	LP	Philips	(S)BL7722	1966	£10	£4	
Little Girl Blue	LP	Bethlehem	BCP6028	1959	£15	£6	US
My Baby Just Cares For Me	7" EP	Parlophone	GEP8844	1961	£10	£5	
My Baby Just Cares For Me	CD-s	Charly	CDS1	1987	£5	£2	
Nina Simone	LP	Polydor	623214	1969	£10	£4	
Nina With Strings	LP	Colpix	(S)CP496	1966	£10	£4	US
Nina's Choice	LP	Colpix	(S)CP443	1963	£10	£4	US
Nuff Said	LP	RCA	SF7979	1969	£10	£4	
Original	LP	Bethlehem	BCP(S)6028	1961	£10	£4	US
Pastel Blues	LP	Philips	BL7683	1966	£10	£4	
Silk And Soul	LP	RCA	RD/SF7967	1968	£10	£4	
Sings Ellington	LP	Colpix	(S)CP425	1962	£10	£4	US
Sings The Blues	LP	RCA	RD/SF7883	1967	£10	£4	
Solitaire	7"	Pye	7N25029	1959	£4	£1.50	
Strange Fruit	7" EP	Philips	BE12589	1965	£6	£2.50	
Tell Me More	LP	Fontana	SFJL954	1968	£10	£4	
Wild Is The Wind	LP	Philips	BL7726	1966	£10	£4	
You Can Have Him	7"	Colpix	PX200	1963	£4	£1.50	

SIMONE, SUGAR

Black Is Gold	7"	Doctor Bird	DB1192	1969	£10	£5	
Boom Biddy Boom	7"	Fab	FAB106	1969	£4	£1.50	Rudies B side
Come And Try	7"	Doctor Bird	DB1201	1969	£10	£5	
I Love My Baby	7"	Rainbow	RAI114	1967	£8	£4	
I Need A Witness	7"	Fab	FAB107	1969	£4	£1.50	
Is It Because	7"	Rainbow	RAI103	1966	£8	£4	
It's Alright	7"	Go	AJ11409	1967	£5	£2	
Squeeze Is On	7"	Doctor Bird	DB1193	1969	£10	£5	
Suddenly	7"	Sue	WI4029	1967	£10	£5	
Vow	7"	CBS	3250	1968	£4	£1.50	

SIMON'S SECRETS

I Know What Her Name Is	7"	CBS	3056	1967	£15	£7.50	
Naughty Boy	7"	CBS	3406	1968	£15	£7.50	

SIMPER, NIC FANDANGO

Slipstreaming	LP	Gull	GULP1033	1979	£12	£5	

SIMPLE MINDS

Amsterdam EP	CD-s	Virgin	SMXCD6	1989	£5	£2	3" single
Amsterdam EP	CD-s	Virgin	SMXX6	1989	£5	£2	
Ballad Of The Streets	CD-s	Virgin	SMXCD3	1989	£5	£2	3" single
Celebrate	12"	Arista	ARIST12394	1981	£6	£2.50	
Celebrate	7"	Arista	ARIST394	1981	£4	£1.50	
Changeling	7"	Zoom	ARIST325	1980	£6	£2.50	
Chelsea Girl	7"	Zoom	ZUM11	1979	£4	£1.50	
Don't You Forget About Me	7"	Virgin	VSS749	1985	£15	£7.50	shaped picture disc
Don't You Forget About Me	CD-s	Virgin	CDT2	1988	£5	£2	3" single
Ghostdancing	CD-s	Virgin	MIKE90712	1986	£6	£2.50	
I Travel	7"	Arista	ARIST372	1980	£8	£4	with blue flexi 7"
Kick It In	CD-s	Virgin	SMXCD5	1989	£5	£2	
Let There Be Love	CD-s	Virgin	VSCDT1332	1991	£5	£2	
Life In A Day	7"	Zoom	ZUM10	1979	£5	£2	
Live In The City Of Light	CD	Virgin	CDSM1	1987	£40	£20	promo box set, with LP and cassette
Live In The City Of Light	LP	Virgin	SMDL1	1987	£12	£5	double, booklet, gold embossed sleeve
Once Upon A Time	LP	Virgin	V2364	1985	£10	£4	picture disc
Real Life	CD	A&M		1991	£25	£10	US promo with 2 CD singles
Real Life	CD-s	Virgin	VSCDG1382	1991	£5	£2	
Real Life Tour	CD	Virgin		1991	£25	£10	Australian double
See The Lights	CD-s	Virgin	VSCDT1343	1991	£5	£2	
Someone Somewhere In Summertime	7"	Virgin	VSY538	1982	£5	£2	picture disc
Someone Somewhere In Summertime	7"	Virgin	VS538	1982	£5	£2	poster sleeve
Sons And Fascination/Sister Feelings Call	LP	Virgin	V2207	1981	£15	£6	double
Sparkle In The Rain	LP	Virgin	V2300	1984	£10	£4	white vinyl
Speed Your Love To Me	7"	Virgin	VSY649	1984	£6	£2.50	picture disc
Street Fighting Years	cass	Virgin	SMBXC1	1989	£12	£5	boxed with book & interview cassettes
Street Fighting Years	CD	Virgin	SMBXD1	1989	£25	£10	boxed with book & interview cassettes
Themes Vol. 1	CD-s	Virgin	SMTCD1	1990	£20	£10	5 CD set
Themes Vol. 2	CD-s	Virgin	SMTCD2	1990	£20	£10	5 CD set
Themes Vol. 3	CD-s	Virgin	SMTCD3	1990	£20	£10	5 CD set

Themes Vol. 4	CD-s	Virgin	SMTCD4	1990	**£20**	**£10**	*5 CD set*
This Is Your Land	CD-s	Virgin	SMXCD4	1989	**£5**	**£2**	*3" single*
Up On The Catwalk	7"	Virgin	VSY661	1984	**£6**	**£2.50**	*picture disc*

SIMPLY RED

Come To My Aid	12"	Elektra	EKR19TX	1985	**£6**	**£2.50**	
Every Time We Say Goodbye	10"	WEA	YZ161TE	1987	**£6**	**£2.50**	
Every Time We Say Goodbye	12"	WEA	YZ161TW	1987	**£12**	**£6**	*with sheet music & 4 cards*
Every Time We Say Goodbye	CD-s	WEA	YZ161CD	1987	**£8**	**£4**	
For Your Babies	CD-s	East West	YZ642CDX	1992	**£5**	**£2**	*holographic*
Holding Back The Years	12"	Elektra	EKR29T	1985	**£8**	**£4**	
Holding Back The Years	7"	Elektra	EKR29P	1985	**£15**	**£7.50**	*shaped picture disc*
Holding Back The Years	7"	Elektra	EKR29F	1985	**£6**	**£2.50**	*gatefold picture sleeve, poster*
I Won't Feel Bad	CD-s	WEA	YZ172CD	1988	**£10**	**£5**	*3" single*
If You Don't Know Me By Now	10"	WEA	YZ377TE	1989	**£6**	**£2.50**	
If You Don't Know Me By Now	CD-s	WEA	YZ377CDX	1989	**£8**	**£4**	
If You Don't Know Me By Now	CD-s	WEA	YZ377CD	1989	**£5**	**£2**	*3" single*
Infidelity	12"	Elektra	YZ114TP	1987	**£8**	**£4**	*picture disc*
It's Only Love	10"	WEA	YZ349TE	1989	**£6**	**£2.50**	
It's Only Love	CD-s	WEA	YZ349CDX	1989	**£12**	**£6**	*3" single*
It's Only Love	CD-s	WEA	YZ349CD	1989	**£6**	**£2.50**	
Jericho	7"	WEA	YZ63R	1986	**£4**	**£1.50**	*red vinyl*
Let Me Take You Home	CD-s	Warner Bros	9031728296	1990	**£10**	**£5**	*CD video*
Life	CD	East West	0630120692	1995	**£25**	**£10**	*promo in ring-binder*
Maybe Someday	12"	WEA	YZ141T	1987	**£6**	**£2.50**	
Money's Too Tight To Mention	12"	Elektra	EKR9TX	1985	**£6**	**£2.50**	
Money's Too Tight To Mention	7"	Elektra	EKR9P	1985	**£5**	**£2**	*picture disc*
Montreux EP	CD-s	East West	YZ716CDX	1992	**£5**	**£2**	*digipak with booklet*
New Flame	10"	WEA	YZ404TE	1989	**£6**	**£2.50**	
New Flame	CD-s	WEA	YZ404CD	1989	**£6**	**£2.50**	
Open Up The Red Box	7"	WEA	YZ75B	1986	**£5**	**£2**	*box sleeve*
Open Up The Red Box	7"	WEA	YZ75F	1986	**£5**	**£2**	*double*
Open Up The Red Box – Remix	12"	WEA	YZ75TF	1986	**£8**	**£4**	*double*
Picture Book	LP	Elektra	EKT27P	1985	**£15**	**£6**	*picture disc*
Right Thing	12"	WEA	YZ103TP	1987	**£6**	**£2.50**	*picture disc*
Right Thing	7"	WEA	YZ103F	1987	**£5**	**£2**	*double*
Something Got Me Started	CD-s	East West	YZ614CD	1991	**£5**	**£2**	
Something's Burning	7"	Lyntone	LYN15914	1985	**£4**	**£1.50**	*flexi, 10,000 Maniacs B side*
Stars	CD-s	East West	YZ626CD	1991	**£5**	**£2**	
You've Got It	CD-s	WEA	YZ424CD	1989	**£5**	**£2**	
Your Mirror	CD-s	East West	YZ689CD	1992	**£5**	**£2**	*holographic*

SIMPSON, DANNY

Outa Sight	7"	Trojan	TR653	1969	**£4**	**£1.50**	

SIMPSON, DUDLEY ORCHESTRA

Blake Seven	7"	BBC	RESL58	1978	**£5**	**£2**	

SIMPSON, FRANK

Four Star Hits	LP	Audio Lab	1552	1960	**£25**	**£10**	*US*

SIMPSON, HOKE

I Finally Found You	7"	HMV	POP442	1958	**£4**	**£1.50**	

SIMPSON, JEANETTE

My Baby Just Cares For Me	7"	Giant	GN29	1968	**£6**	**£2.50**	
Rain	7"	Giant	GN16	1967	**£6**	**£2.50**	
Through Loving You	7"	Giant	GN35	1968	**£6**	**£2.50**	

SIMPSON, LEO

I Love Her So	7"	Blue Beat	BB351	1966	**£12**	**£6**	
Waxy Doodle	7"	Pyramid	PYR7004	1973	**£4**	**£1.50**	

SIMPSON, LIONEL

Eight People	7"	Ska Beat	JB221	1965	**£10**	**£5**	
Give Over	7"	Ska Beat	JB233	1966	**£10**	**£5**	
Love Is A Game	7"	Ska Beat	JB205	1965	**£10**	**£5**	

SIMPSON, MARTIN

Golden Vanity	LP	Trailer	LER2099	1976	**£20**	**£8**	

SIMPSON, VALERIE

Exposed	LP	Tamla Motown	STML11194	1972	**£12**	**£5**	

SIMS, CHUCK

Little Pigeon	7"	London	HLR8577	1958	**£250**	**£150**	*best auctioned*

SIMS, ZOOT

At Ronnie Scott's	LP	Fontana	TFL5176	1961	**£25**	**£10**	
Choice	LP	Vogue	LAE12309	1961	**£25**	**£10**	
Cookin!	LP	Fontana	FJL123	1965	**£12**	**£5**	
Down Home	LP	Parlophone	PMC1169	1961	**£25**	**£10**	
George Handy Compositions	LP	HMV	CLP1165	1958	**£30**	**£15**	
Goes To Town	10" LP	Vogue	LDE056	1954	**£50**	**£25**	

Plays Four Altos	LP	HMV	CLP1188	1958	£30	£15	
Solo For Zoot	LP	Phillips	680982	196–	£25	£10	
Trotting	LP	XTRA	XTRA5001	1966	£12	£5	
Waiting Game	LP	Impulse	MIPL/SIPL501	1968	£12	£5	
You 'n' Me	LP	Mercury	MMC14071	1961	£25	£10	*with Al Cohn*
Zoot Sims Allstars	10" LP	Esquire	20010	1953	£50	£25	
Zoot Sims Quartet	LP	Jazzland	JLP2	195–	£50	£25	
Zoot Sims Quartet/Quintet	10" LP	Esquire	20040	1955	£50	£25	
Zoot Sims Quartet/Quintet	10" LP	Esquire	20018	1953	£50	£25	
Zoot Sims Quartet/Quintet	10" LP	Esquire	20002	1952	£50	£25	
Zoot!	LP	London	LTZU15135	1958	£30	£15	
Zoot!	LP	Riverside	RLP12228	196–	£15	£6	

SIMS, ZOOT (2)

Please Don't Do It	7"	Port-O-Jam	PJ4007	1964	£10	£5	*with Lloyd Robinson*
Press Along	7"	Blue Beat	BB183	1963	£12	£6	*Prince Buster B side*
Searching	7"	Blue Beat	BB143	1962	£12	£6	*with Lloyd Robinson*
Tit For Tat	7"	Coxsone	CS7095	1969	£10	£5	

SIN SAY SHUNS

I'll Be There	LP	Venett	VS940	1966	£30	£15	*US*

SINATRA, FRANK

The biggest singing star before Elvis Presley has a large number of collectable records to his name, but the great majority of them have values that only just qualify them for inclusion in this guide. Often the death of an artist leads to a general rise in value of their original record releases, but despite various media reports to the contrary in the aftermath of Sinatra's death, fan interest in his back catalogue has primarily been confined to the purchase of CD reissues.

Adventures Of The Heart	LP	Fontana	TFL5006	1958	£15	£6	
All The Way	LP	Capitol	W(S)1538	1962	£10	£4	
Among My Souvenirs	7" EP	Fontana	TFE17272	1960	£5	£2	
Anchors Aweigh	7" EP	Fontana	TFE17043	1958	£5	£2	
Birth Of The Blues	7"	Columbia	SCM5052	1953	£10	£5	
Broadway Kick	LP	Fontana	TFL5054	1959	£15	£6	
Bye Baby	7" EP	Fontana	TFE17273	1960	£5	£2	
Capitol Years	CD	Capitol	DPRO79375	1990	£20	£8	*US promo*
Christmas Dreaming	10" LP	Philips	BBR8114	1957	£15	£6	
Christmas Songs	10" LP	Columbia	CL6019	195–	£15	£6	*US*
Christmas Waltz	7"	Capitol	CL14174	1954	£8	£4	
Close To You	LP	Capitol	LCT6130	1957	£10	£4	
Come Back To Sorrento	LP	Fontana	TFL5082	1960	£10	£4	
Come Dance With Me	LP	Capitol	(S)LCT6179	1959	£10	£4	
Come Swing With Me	LP	Capitol	W(S)1594	1962	£10	£4	
Complete Frank Sinatra Sampler	CD	Columbia		1993	£20	£8	*US promo*
Conducts The Music Of Alex Wilder	10" LP	Columbia	ML4271	195–	£15	£6	*US*
Conducts Tone Poems Of Colour	LP	Capitol	LCT6111	1956	£10	£4	
Dedicated To You	10" LP	Columbia	CL6096	195–	£15	£6	*US*
Don't Change Your Mind About Me	7"	Capitol	CL14270	1955	£8	£4	
Dream	7" EP	Fontana	TFE17158	1959	£5	£2	
Duets	CD	DCC	GZS1053	1994	£15	£6	*US audiophile*
Duets II	CD	DCC	GZS1073	1994	£15	£6	*US audiophile*
Embraceable You	7" EP	Fontana	TFE17286	1960	£5	£2	
Fabulous Frank	10" LP	Philips	BBR8038	1955	£15	£6	
Fairy Tale	7"	Capitol	CL14373	1955	£6	£2.50	
Five Minutes More	7" EP	Fontana	TFE17280	1960	£5	£2	
Flowers Mean Forgiveness	7"	Capitol	CL14564	1956	£4	£1.50	
Fools Rush In	7" EP	Fontana	TFE17037	1958	£5	£2	
Francis A. Sinatra And Edward K. Ellington	LP	Reprise	R(S)LP1024	1968	£10	£4	
Frank Sinatra	7" EP	Columbia	SEG7565	1955	£6	£2.50	
Frank Sinatra	7" EP	HMV	7EG8070	1954	£5	£2	
Frankie	7" EP	Fontana	TFE17182	1959	£5	£2	
Frankie	LP	Philips	BBL7168	1957	£15	£6	
Frankie And Tommy (with Tommy Dorsey)	LP	RCA	RD27069	1958	£15	£6	
Frankie's Favourites	7" EP	Columbia	SEG7597	1955	£6	£2.50	
Frankly Sentimental	10" LP	Columbia	CL6059	195–	£15	£6	*US*
Gal That Got Away	7"	Capitol	CL14221	1955	£8	£4	
Great Years	LP	Capitol	W1/2/31762	1963	£15	£6	*triple*
High Hopes	7" EP	Capitol	EAP11224	1959	£5	£2	
I Am Loved	7" EP	Fontana	TFE17038	1958	£5	£2	
I Dream Of You	7" EP	Fontana	TFE17284	1960	£5	£2	
I've Got A Crush On You	10" LP	Columbia	CL6290	195–	£15	£6	*US*
I've Got A Crush On You	7" EP	Fontana	TFE17254	1960	£5	£2	
I've Got You Under My Skin	CD-s	Capitol	DUETS1	1993	£10	£5	*promo, with Bono*
If I Forget You	7"	Fontana	H140	1958	£4	£1.50	
In The Wee Small Hours Of The Morning	7"	Capitol	CL14360	1955	£6	£2.50	
In The Wee Small Hours Vol. 1	10" LP	Capitol	LC6702	1955	£12	£5	
In The Wee Small Hours Vol. 2	10" LP	Capitol	LC6705	1955	£12	£5	
It MIght As Well Be Swing	LP	Reprise	R1012	1964	£10	£4	*with Count Basie*
It's D-Lovely	10" LP	HMV	DLP1123	1956	£20	£8	*with Tommy Dorsey*
Jolly Christmas	LP	Capitol	LCT6144	1957	£10	£4	
Learnin' The Blues	7"	Capitol	CL14296	1955	£8	£4	
London By Night	LP	Capitol	T20389	1962	£10	£4	
Look To Your Heart	LP	Capitol	LCT6181	1959	£10	£4	
Love And Marriage	7"	Capitol	CL14503	1956	£5	£2	

Love Is A Kick	LP	Fontana	TFL5074	1960	£10	£4	
Lover	7" EP	Fontana	TFE17012	1958	£5	£2	
Mad About You	7" EP	Fontana	TFE17023	1958	£5	£2	
Man And His Music	LP	Reprise	R(9)1016	1966	£12	£5	*double*
Melancholy Baby	7" EP	Fontana	TFE17274	1960	£5	£2	
Melody Of Love	7"	Capitol	CL14238	1955	£8	£4	
Melody Of Love	7" EP	Capitol	EAP1590	1956	£5	£2	
Moonlight Sinatra	7" EP	HMV	7EG8128	1955	£6	£2.50	
Moonlight Sinatra	LP	Reprise	R(9)1018	1966	£10	£4	
My Funny Valentine	7"	Capitol	CL14352	1955	£6	£2.50	
My Funny Valentine	LP	Capitol	T20577	1964	£10	£4	
Nearness Of You	7" EP	Philips	BBE12182	1958	£5	£2	
New Orleans (with Jo Stafford)	10" LP	Columbia	CL6268	195–	£15	£6	*US*
Nice 'n' Easy	LP	Capitol	W(S)1417	1961	£10	£4	
No One Cares	7" EP	Capitol	SEP11221	1961	£8	£4	*stereo*
No One Cares	LP	Capitol	(S)LCT6185	1959	£10	£4	
No One Cares No. 2	7" EP	Capitol	SEP21221	1961	£8	£4	*stereo*
No One Cares No. 3	7" EP	Capitol	SEP31221	1961	£8	£4	*stereo*
Not As A Stranger	7"	Capitol	CL14326	1955	£8	£4	
Out Town	7" EP	Capitol	EAP1025	1956	£5	£2	
Pal Joey	LP	Capitol	LCT6148	1958	£10	£4	
Point Of No Return	LP	Capitol	W(S)1676	1962	£10	£4	
Put Your Dreams Away	LP	Fontana	TFL5048	1959	£20	£8	
Reflections	LP	Fontana	TFL5107	1960	£10	£4	
Reprise Collection	CD	Reprise	PROCD4540	1990	£20	£8	*US promo*
Ring-A-Ding-Ding	LP	Reprise	R1001	1961	£10	£4	
Robin And The Seven Hoods	LP	Reprise	R2021	1964	£50	£25	
S'posin'	7"	Columbia	SCM5167	1955	£10	£5	
Santa Claus Is Comin' To Town	7"	Columbia	SCM5076	1953	£10	£5	
Session With Sinatra	7" EP	Capitol	EAP1629	1956	£5	£2	
Sinatra '65	LP	Reprise	R(9)6167	1965	£10	£4	
Sinatra And Strings	LP	Reprise	R(9)1004	1962	£10	£4	
Sinatra Family Wish You A Happy Christmas	LP	Reprise	R(S)LP1026	1969	£12	£5	*with Nancy Sinatra*
Sinatra Plus	LP	Fontana	SET303	1961	£12	£5	*double*
Sinatra Serenade	7" EP	Columbia	SEG7582	1955	£6	£2.50	
Sinatra Souvenir	LP	Fontana	TFL5138	1961	£10	£4	
Sinatra, Bailey & James (with Pearl Bailey & Harry James)	7" EP	Fontana	TFE17028	1958	£5	£2	
Sing And Dance	10" LP	Philips	BBR8003	1954	£20	£8	
Sing And Dance No. 1	7" EP	Philips	BBE12016	1956	£5	£2	
Sing And Dance No. 2	7" EP	Philips	BBE12058	1956	£5	£2	
Sings For Only The Lonely	LP	Capitol	(S)LCT6168	1958	£10	£4	
Sings Great Songs From Great Britain	LP	Reprise	R1006	1962	£20	£8	
Sings Great Songs From Great Britain	LP	Reprise	R91006	1962	£30	£15	*stereo*
Sings Of Love And Things	LP	Capitol	W(S)1729	1963	£10	£4	
Sings Rodgers And Hart	LP	Capitol	W1825	1963	£10	£4	
Sings Songs From Carousel	7" EP	Philips	BBE12152	1957	£5	£2	
Song Is You	7" EP	Fontana	TFE17253	1960	£5	£2	
Songs By Sinatra Vol. 1	10" LP	Columbia	CL6087	195–	£15	£6	*US*
Songs For Swingin' Lovers	LP	Capitol	LCT6106	1956	£10	£4	
Songs For Swinging Lovers	CD	Mobile Fidelity	UDCD538	1990	£15	£6	*US audiophile*
Songs For Young Lovers	10" LP	Capitol	LC6654	1954	£15	£6	
Songs For Young Lovers No. 1	7" EP	Capitol	EAP1488	1955	£5	£2	
Songs For Young Lovers No. 2	7" EP	Capitol	EAP2488	1955	£5	£2	
Songs From Young At Heart	7" EP	Capitol	EAP1571	1955	£5	£2	
Story	LP	Fontana	TFL5030	1958	£15	£6	
Summit	LP	Reprise	R5031	1966	£50	£25	*with Crosby, Davis Jr, Martin*
Swing Easy	10" LP	Capitol	LC6689	1954	£15	£6	
Swing Easy	LP	Capitol	W587	1960	£10	£4	
Swingin' Affair	LP	Capitol	LCT6135	1957	£10	£4	
Swingin' Session	LP	Capitol	W(S)1491	1961	£10	£4	
Tender Trap	7"	Capitol	CL14511	1956	£5	£2	
That Old Feeling	LP	Philips	BBL7180	1957	£15	£6	
They Say It's Wonderful	7" EP	Fontana	TFE17255	1960	£5	£2	
This Is Sinatra	LP	Capitol	LCT6123	1957	£10	£4	
This Is Sinatra Vol. 2	LP	Capitol	LCT6155	1958	£10	£4	
Three Coins In The Fountain	7"	Capitol	CL14120	1954	£10	£5	
Two Hearts, Two Kisses	7"	Capitol	CL14292	1955	£8	£4	
Voice	LP	Fontana	TFL5000	1958	£15	£6	
Voice No. 1 – Four Star	7" EP	Fontana	TFE17181	1959	£5	£2	
Voice Of Sinatra	10" LP	Columbia	CL6001	195–	£15	£6	*US*
Watertown	LP	Reprise	RSLP1031	1970	£10	£4	
We're In Love	7" EP	Fontana	TFE17042	1958	£5	£2	
When I Stop Loving You	7"	Capitol	CL14188	1954	£8	£4	
Where Are You?	LP	Capitol	(S)LCT6152	1958	£10	£4	
Who Wants To Be A Millionaire	7"	Capitol	CL14644	1956	£4	£1.50	
You Do Something To Me	7"	Columbia	SCM5060	1953	£10	£5	
You Go To My Head	7" EP	Fontana	TFE17256	1960	£5	£2	
You My Love	7"	Capitol	CL14240	1955	£8	£4	
Young At Heart	7"	Capitol	CL14064	1954	£12	£6	

SINATRA, NANCY

Boots	LP	Reprise	R(S)LP6202	1966	£10	£4	
Country My Way	LP	Reprise	R(S)LP6251	1967	£10	£4	
Cuff Links And A Tie Clip	7"	Reprise	R20017	1961	£6	£2.50	

Title	Format	Label	Number	Year	Mint	VG+	Notes
Greatest Hits	LP	Reprise	RSLP6409	1970	**£10**	**£4**	
How Does That Grab You?	LP	Reprise	R6207	1966	**£10**	**£4**	
I Move Around	7" EP	Reprise	REP30072	1966	**£8**	**£4**	
Movin' With Nancy	LP	Reprise	R(S)LP6277	1968	**£10**	**£4**	
Nancy	LP	Reprise	RSLP6333	1969	**£10**	**£4**	
Nancy In London	LP	Reprise	R(S)LP6221	1966	**£10**	**£4**	
Nashville Nancy	7" EP	Reprise	REP30086	1967	**£5**	**£2**	
Run For Your Life	7" EP	Reprise	REP30069	1966	**£8**	**£4**	
Something Stupid	7" EP	Reprise	REP30082	1967	**£5**	**£2**	*with Frank Sinatra*
Sorry 'Bout That	7" EP	Reprise	REP30080	1967	**£8**	**£4**	
Sugar	LP	Reprise	RLP6239	1966	**£10**	**£4**	
To Know Him Is To Love Him	7"	Reprise	R20045	1962	**£5**	**£2**	
Woman	LP	RCA	SF8331	1972	**£10**	**£4**	
You Only Live Twice	7"	Reprise	RS20595	1967	**£4**	**£1.50**	

SINATRA, NANCY & LEE HAZELWOOD

Title	Format	Label	Number	Year	Mint	VG+	Notes
Did You Ever?	LP	RCA	SF8240	1972	**£10**	**£4**	
Jackson	7" EP	Reprise	REP30083	1967	**£10**	**£5**	
Nancy And Lee	LP	Reprise	R(S)LP6273	1968	**£10**	**£4**	
Nancy And Lee Again	LP	RCA	LSP4645	1972	**£10**	**£4**	*US*

SINCLAIR, JIMMY

Title	Format	Label	Number	Year	Mint	VG+	Notes
Verona	7"	Blue Beat	BB47	1961	**£12**	**£6**	

SINCLAIR, WINSTON

Title	Format	Label	Number	Year	Mint	VG+	Notes
Another Heartache	7"	Nu Beat	NB026	1969	**£4**	**£1.50**	

SINDELFINGEN

Title	Format	Label	Number	Year	Mint	VG+	Notes
Odgipig	LP	Medway	no number	1973	**£500**	**£330**	
Odgipig/Triangle	LP	Cenotaph	CEN111	1990	**£25**	**£10**	*double*

SINEWAVE

Title	Format	Label	Number	Year	Mint	VG+	Notes
Star Trek	7"	Chapter One	CH172	1972	**£5**	**£2**	

SINFIELD, PETE

Title	Format	Label	Number	Year	Mint	VG+	Notes
Still	LP	Manticore	K43501	1973	**£12**	**£5**	

SINGAROUND

Title	Format	Label	Number	Year	Mint	VG+	Notes
Singaround	LP	Golden Guinea	GSGL10436	1969	**£10**	**£4**	

SINGER, RAY

Title	Format	Label	Number	Year	Mint	VG+	Notes
I'm The Richest Man Alive	7"	Ember	EMBS215	1965	**£5**	**£2**	*picture sleeve*
What's Been Done	7"	Ember	EMBS231	1967	**£5**	**£2**	

SINGER, SUSAN

Title	Format	Label	Number	Year	Mint	VG+	Notes
Autumn Leaves	7"	Oriole	CB1778	1962	**£6**	**£2.50**	
Hello First Love	7"	Oriole	CB1703	1962	**£6**	**£2.50**	
I Know	7"	Oriole	CB1882	1963	**£6**	**£2.50**	
Johnny Summertime	7"	Oriole	CB1741	1962	**£12**	**£6**	
Lock Your Heart Away	7"	Oriole	CB1802	1963	**£6**	**£2.50**	

SINGING BELLES

Title	Format	Label	Number	Year	Mint	VG+	Notes
Someone Loves You Joe	7"	Top Rank	JAR350	1960	**£4**	**£1.50**	

SINGING DOGS

Title	Format	Label	Number	Year	Mint	VG+	Notes
Singing Dogs	7" EP	Pye	NEP24029	1957	**£10**	**£5**	

SINGING FOLK

Title	Format	Label	Number	Year	Mint	VG+	Notes
I Was Wrong	7"	Polydor	BM56018	1965	**£4**	**£1.50**	

SINGING POSTMAN

Title	Format	Label	Number	Year	Mint	VG+	Notes
First Delivery	7" EP	Parlophone	GEP8956	1966	**£5**	**£2**	

SINGLETON, MARGIE

Title	Format	Label	Number	Year	Mint	VG+	Notes
Eyes Of Love	7"	Melodisc	1544	1960	**£5**	**£2**	
Magic Star	7"	Mercury	AMT1197	1962	**£8**	**£4**	

SINGLETON, VALERIE

Title	Format	Label	Number	Year	Mint	VG+	Notes
Solomon Centipede	7"	Pye	7N17800	1969	**£4**	**£1.50**	

SINISTER DUCKS

Title	Format	Label	Number	Year	Mint	VG+	Notes
March Of The Sinister Ducks	7"	Situation 2	SIT25	1983	**£6**	**£2.50**	

SINK, EARL

Title	Format	Label	Number	Year	Mint	VG+	Notes
Little Suzie Parker	7"	Warner Bros	WB51	1961	**£10**	**£5**	
Looking For Love	7"	Capitol	CL15310	1963	**£8**	**£4**	
Supermarket	7"	Warner Bros	WB38	1961	**£6**	**£2.50**	

SINNERS

Title	Format	Label	Number	Year	Mint	VG+	Notes
I Can't Stand It	7"	Columbia	DB7158	1963	**£5**	**£2**	
It's So Exciting	7"	Columbia	DB7295	1964	**£6**	**£2.50**	

SINNERS (2)

Title	Format	Label	Number	Year	Mint	VG+	Notes
Sinnerisme	LP	Jupiter	JDY7009	1974	**£100**	**£50**	*Canadian*
Sinners	LP	Transworld	TW6801	1968	**£50**	**£25**	*Canadian*
Vox Populi	LP			197–	**£40**	**£20**	*Canadian*

SIOUXSIE & THE BANSHEES

Candyman	7"	Wonderland	SHEDP10	1986	£5	£2	*double, gatefold picture sleeve*
Head Cut	7"	Fan Club	FILE1	1983	£30	£15	
Hong Kong Garden	7"	Polydor	2059052	1978	£8	£4	*gatefold sleeve*
Israel	12"	Polydor	POSPX205	1980	£6	£2.50	*no picture sleeve*
Killing Jar	CD-s	Wonderland	SHECD15	1988	£5	£2	
Kiss Them For Me	CD-s	Wonderland	SHECD19	1991	£5	£2	
Last Beat Of My Heart	CD-s	Wonderland	SHECD16	1988	£5	£2	
Mittageisen	7"	Polydor	2059151	1979	£5	£2	*picture sleeve*
Peek-A-Boo	CD-s	Polygram	0803982	1988	£10	£5	*CD video*
Peek-A-Boo	CD-s	Wonderland	SHECD14	1988	£5	£2	
Peel Sessions	CD-s	Strange Fruit	SFPSCD012	1988	£5	£2	
Peel Sessions II	CD-s	Strange Fruit	SFPSCD066	1989	£5	£2	
Playground Twist	7"	Polydor	POSP59	1979	£4	£1.50	*red paper label*
Shadowtime	CD-s	Polydor	SHECD20	1991	£5	£2	
Superstition	CD	Geffen	PROCD4260	1991	£25	£10	*US promo, round box set with cracked mirror front*
This Wheel's On Fire	7"	Wonderland	SHEG11	1987	£5	£2	*double, gatefold picture sleeve, numbered*
Through The Looking Glass	7"	Wonderland		1987	£12	£6	*3 × 7" in plastic wallet, promo*
Through The Looking Glass	LP	Wonderland	SHELP4	1987	£12	£5	*mispress, 1 side plays Jimi Hendrix*
Voices	7"	Wonderland		1984	£5	£2	*promo*

SIR COLLINS BAND

Black Diamonds	7"	Duke	DU47	1969	£5	£2	*Diamonds B side*
Black Panther	7"	Duke	DU46	1969	£5	£2	
Brother Moses	7"	Duke	DU55	1969	£5	£2	
Collins And The Boys	7"	Collins Downbeat	CR0011	1968	£10	£5	
Sock It Softly	7"	Collins Downbeat	CR005	1968	£10	£5	
Soul Feelings	7"	Collins Downbeat	CR0017	1968	£10	£5	

SIR DOUGLAS QUINTET

1+1+1=4	LP	Philips	PHS600344	1970	£10	£4	*US*
Best Of The Sir Douglas Quintet	LP	London	HAU8311	1965	£50	£25	
Best Of The Sir Douglas Quintet	LP	Tribe	37001	1966	£75	£37.50	*US*
Dynamite Woman	7"	Mercury	MF1129	1969	£4	£1.50	
Honky Blues	LP	Smash	SRS67108	1968	£20	£8	*US*
Mendocino	7"	Mercury	MF1079	1969	£4	£1.50	
Mendocino	LP	Mercury	SMCL20160	1969	£10	£4	
Rains Came	7"	London	HLU10019	1966	£4	£1.50	
She's About A Mover	7"	London	HLU9964	1965	£4	£1.50	
She's About A Mover	7" EP	London	REU10171	1965	£25	£12.50	*French*
Story Of John Hardy	7"	London	HLU10001	1965	£4	£1.50	
Together After Five	LP	Mercury	SMCL20186	1970	£10	£4	
Tracker	7"	London	HLU9982	1965	£4	£1.50	

SIR HENRY & HIS BUTLERS

Camp	LP	Columbia	SMC74562	1968	£20	£8	*German*
H2O	LP	Columbia	73006	1967	£20	£8	*German*
Let's Go	7" EP	Polydor	60101	196–	£25	£12.50	*French*
Let's Go	LP	Polydor	623003	1965	£40	£20	*German*
Portrait	LP	Columbia	KSX4	1966	£25	£10	*Danish*
Pretty Style	7"	Columbia	DB8497	1968	£8	£4	
Pretty Style	7"	Columbia	DB8351	1968	£8	£4	
Sir Henry & His Butlers Are Serving You	LP	Sonet	SLPS1211	1964	£30	£15	*Danish*
Sir Henry And His Butlers	LP	Columbia	KSX2	1965	£30	£15	*Danish*

SIR HORATIO

Abracadubra	12"	Rock Steady	MIX1T	1982	£8	£4	

SIR LORD COMIC

Great Wuga Wuga	7"	Doctor Bird	DB1070	1967	£10	£5	
Jack Of My Trade	7"	Pressure Beat	PB5506	1969	£8	£4	*Cynthia Richards B side*
Rhythm Rebellion	7"	Bamboo	BAM66	1970	£8	£4	*Roy Richards B side*
Ska-ing West	7"	Doctor Bird	DB1019	1966	£10	£5	*Maytals B side*

SIREN

Originally named Coyne–Clague after the lead singer and guitarist, the group had settled on the rather more wieldy Siren by the time of their first recording for John Peel's Dandelion label. Kevin Coyne has made Siren's bluesy style into the basis of a still continuing solo career, gaining a considerable cult following, while Dave Clague has opted to temper his music-making with the financial security of being a teacher.

Siren	LP	Dandelion	63755	1969	£15	£6	
Strange Locomotion	LP	Dandelion	DAN8001	1971	£15	£6	

SISTER MARY GERTRUDE

My Auld Killarney Hat	7"	Pye	7N15787	1965	£4	£1.50	

SISTERS OF MERCY

Title	Format	Label	Cat. No.	Year	Mint	VG	Notes
Alice	7"	Merciful Release	MR015	1982	£10	£5	*white background*
Body And Soul	7"	Merciful Release	MR029	1984	£5	£2	
Body Electric	7"	CNT	002	1982	£40	£20	
Damage Done	7"	Merciful Release	MR7	1980	£75	£37.50	
Doctor Jeep	12"	Merciful Release	MR51TX	1990	£6	£2.50	*3 tracks*
Doctor Jeep	CD-s	Merciful Release	MR51CD	1990	£5	£2	
Dominion	CD-s	Merciful Release	MR43CD	1988	£5	£2	*3" single*
First And Last And Always	LP	Merciful Release	MR337L	1985	£10	£4	*gatefold sleeve*
Floodland	CD	Merciful Release	2422462	1987	£40	£20	*promo bag set, with video and T-shirt*
Lucretia My Reflection	CD-s	Merciful Release	MR44CD	1988	£5	£2	
More	CD-s	Merciful Release	MR47CDX	1990	£6	£2.50	*12" sleeve*
More	CD-s	Merciful Release	MR47CD	1990	£5	£2	
No Time To Cry	12"	Merciful Release	MR035T	1985	£6	£2.50	
No Time To Cry	7"	Merciful Release	MR035	1985	£5	£2	
Reptile House	12"	Merciful Release	MR023	1983	£6	£2.50	*with lyric sheet*
Temple Of Love	CD-s	Merciful Release	MR53CD	1992	£5	£2	*boxed*
This Corrosion	12"	Merciful Release	MR039T	1987	£25	£10	*promo with video*
This Corrosion	7"	Merciful Release	MR039	1987	£6	£2.50	*boxed with 3 postcards*
This Corrosion	CD-s	Merciful Release	MR039CD	1987	£8	£4	
Tour Thing	CD	Elektra		1991	£25	£10	*US promo sampler*
Walk Away	12"	Merciful Release	MR033T	1984	£8	£4	*with flexi (SAM218)*
Walk Away	7"	Merciful Release	MR033	1984	£8	£4	*with flexi*
Walk Away	7"	Merciful Release	MR033	1984	£5	£2	

SITTING BULL

Title	Format	Label	Cat. No.	Year	Mint	VG	Notes
Trip Away	LP	CBS	64697	1971	£12	£5	*German*

SITUATION

Title	Format	Label	Cat. No.	Year	Mint	VG	Notes
Situation	7"	CBS	202392	1966	£5	£2	

SIX

Title	Format	Label	Cat. No.	Year	Mint	VG	Notes
Six	10" LP	Columbia	33C9028	1956	£25	£10	
Six	LP	London	LTZN15042	1957	£25	£10	
View From Jazzbo's Head	LP	London	LTZN15066	1957	£25	£10	

SIX TEENS

Title	Format	Label	Cat. No.	Year	Mint	VG	Notes
Casual Look	7"	London	HLU8345	1956	£300	£180	*best auctioned*

SIXTY FOOT DOLLS

Title	Format	Label	Cat. No.	Year	Mint	VG	Notes
Happy Shopper	7"	Townhill	TIDY001	1994	£10	£5	
White Knuckle Ride	7"	Rough Trade	R3797	1995	£5	£2	*clear or white vinyl*

SIXTY-NINE

Title	Format	Label	Cat. No.	Year	Mint	VG	Notes
Circle Of The Crayfish	LP	Philips	6305164	1972	£12	£5	*German*
Live	LP	Philips	6623046	1974	£15	£6	*German double*

SIZE SEVEN GROUP

Title	Format	Label	Cat. No.	Year	Mint	VG	Notes
Where Do We Go From Here	7"	Mercury	MF845	1965	£5	£2	

SKA CHAMPIONS

Title	Format	Label	Cat. No.	Year	Mint	VG	Notes
My Tears	7"	Blue Beat	BB305	1965	£12	£6	

SKA KINGS

Title	Format	Label	Cat. No.	Year	Mint	VG	Notes
Oil In My Lamp	7"	Atlantic	AT4003	1964	£8	£4	
Skasville	7"	Parlophone	R5338	1965	£5	£2	

SKA-DOWS

Title	Format	Label	Cat. No.	Year	Mint	VG	Notes
Ska'd For Life	LP	Cheapskate	SKATE3	1982	£10	£4	
Ska's On 45	12"	Penthouse	PENT127	1981	£6	£2.50	

SKATALITES

Title	Format	Label	Cat. No.	Year	Mint	VG	Notes
Ball O' Fire	7"	Island	WI207	1965	£10	£5	*Linval Sparker B side*

Title	Format	Label	Cat. No.	Year	Mint	VG	Notes
Beardman Ska	7"	Island	WI228	1965	**£10**	**£5**	*Bonnie & Rita B side*
Confucius	LP	Doctor Bird	DLM5000	1966	**£100**	**£50**	
Dick Tracy	7"	Island	WI226	1965	**£10**	**£5**	*Soulettes B side*
Dr Kildare	7"	Island	WI191	1965	**£10**	**£5**	
Dragon Weapon	7"	Island	WI175	1965	**£10**	**£5**	*Desmond Dekker B side*
Guns Of Navarone	7"	Island	WI168	1965	**£10**	**£5**	
Latin Goes Ska	7"	Ska Beat	JB177	1965	**£10**	**£5**	*Lord Tanamo B side*
Ska Authentic	LP	Studio One	SOL9006	1967	**£100**	**£50**	
Timothy	7"	Ska Beat	JB206	1965	**£10**	**£5**	*King Scratch B side*

SKATALITES (2)

Title	Format	Label	Cat. No.	Year	Mint	VG	Notes
Cos You're The One I Love	7"	Spark	SRL1034	1971	**£5**	**£2**	
Don't Knock It	7"	Decca	F12743	1968	**£4**	**£1.50**	

SKEL, BOBBY

Title	Format	Label	Cat. No.	Year	Mint	VG	Notes
Kiss And Run	7"	London	HLU9942	1964	**£5**	**£2**	

SKELETAL FAMILY

Title	Format	Label	Cat. No.	Year	Mint	VG	Notes
Night	7"	Red Rhino	RED36	1983	**£5**	**£2**	
Trees	7"	Luggage	RRP00724	1983	**£8**	**£4**	

SKERNE

Title	Format	Label	Cat. No.	Year	Mint	VG	Notes
Better Late Than Never	LP	Guardian	GRC81	1981	**£10**	**£4**	

SKI PATROL

Title	Format	Label	Cat. No.	Year	Mint	VG	Notes
Agent Orange	7"	Malicious Damage	MD2	1980	**£5**	**£2**	

SKID ROW

A modern band calling itself Skid Row cannot detract from the fact that the name truly belongs to the Irish band with whom the seventeen-year-old Gary Moore made his first recordings.

Title	Format	Label	Cat. No.	Year	Mint	VG	Notes
34 Hours	LP	CBS	64411	1971	**£12**	**£5**	
New Places, Old Faces	7"	Song	SO0002	1969	**£30**	**£15**	*Irish*
Night Of The Warm Witch	7"	CBS	7181	1971	**£6**	**£2.50**	
Sandie's Gone	7"	CBS	4893	1970	**£6**	**£2.50**	
Saturday Morning Man	7"	Song	SO0003	1969	**£30**	**£15**	*Irish*
Skid	LP	CBS	63965	1970	**£12**	**£5**	

SKID ROW (2)

Title	Format	Label	Cat. No.	Year	Mint	VG	Notes
Eighteen And Life	7"	Atlantic	A8883P	1990	**£4**	**£1.50**	*shaped picture disc*
Eighteen And Life	CD-s	Atlantic	A8883CD	1990	**£5**	**£2**	
I Remember You	CD-s	Atlantic	A8886CD	1990	**£5**	**£2**	
Monkey Business	CD-s	Atlantic	A7673CD	1991	**£5**	**£2**	
Slave To The Grind	CD-s	Atlantic	A7603CD	1991	**£5**	**£2**	
Wasted Time	CD-s	Atlantic	A7570CD	1991	**£5**	**£2**	
Youth Gone Wild	CD-s	Atlantic	A7444CD	1992	**£5**	**£2**	*hologram cover*

SKIDMORE, ALAN

Title	Format	Label	Cat. No.	Year	Mint	VG	Notes
Jazz In Britain 1968–69	LP	Decca	ECS2114	1972	**£25**	**£10**	*with other artists*
Morning Rise	LP	Ego	4006	1977	**£15**	**£6**	
Once Upon A Time	LP	Nova	SDN11	1969	**£40**	**£20**	
TCB	LP	Philips	6308041	1970	**£40**	**£20**	

SKIDMORE, JIMMY

Title	Format	Label	Cat. No.	Year	Mint	VG	Notes
Skid Marks	LP	DJM	DJSL026	1972	**£10**	**£4**	

SKIDS

Title	Format	Label	Cat. No.	Year	Mint	VG	Notes
Scared To Dance	LP	Virgin	V2116	1979	**£25**	**£10**	*blue vinyl*
Skids Vs The Ruts	7"	Virgin	VSCDT1411	1992	**£6**	**£2.50**	

SKIFS, BJORN

Title	Format	Label	Cat. No.	Year	Mint	VG	Notes
Haunted By A Dream	7"	EMI	EMI5172	1981	**£5**	**£2**	

SKILLETS

Title	Format	Label	Cat. No.	Year	Mint	VG	Notes
Both Sides Now	LP	Panatonic	PAN6303	1970	**£30**	**£15**	

SKIN ALLEY

Title	Format	Label	Cat. No.	Year	Mint	VG	Notes
Skin Alley	LP	CBS	63847	1969	**£50**	**£25**	
Skintight	LP	Transatlantic	TRA273	1973	**£12**	**£5**	
To Pagham & Beyond	LP	CBS	64140	1970	**£20**	**£8**	
Two Quid Deal	LP	Transatlantic	TRA260	1972	**£12**	**£5**	

SKIN, FLESH & BONES

Title	Format	Label	Cat. No.	Year	Mint	VG	Notes
Butter Te Fish	7"	Pyramid	PYR7014	1974	**£4**	**£1.50**	

SKINNER, J. SCOTT

Title	Format	Label	Cat. No.	Year	Mint	VG	Notes
Strathspey King	LP	Topic	12T280	1975	**£10**	**£4**	

SKINNER, JIMMIE

Title	Format	Label	Cat. No.	Year	Mint	VG	Notes
Country Singer	LP	Decca	DL(7)4132	1961	**£15**	**£6**	*US*
John Wesley Hardin	7"	Mercury	AMT1062	1959	**£4**	**£1.50**	
Kentucky Colonel Vol. 1	7" EP	London	REB1421	1964	**£10**	**£5**	
Kentucky Colonel Vol. 2	7" EP	London	REB1422	1964	**£10**	**£5**	
Kentucky Colonel Vol. 3	7" EP	London	REB1423	1964	**£10**	**£5**	
Songs That Make The Juke Box Play	LP	Mercury	MG20352	1957	**£20**	**£8**	*US*

Walking My Blues Away	7"	Mercury	AMT1030	1959	**£4**	**£1.50**	

SKIP & FLIP

Cherry Pie	7"	Top Rank	JAR358	1960	**£5**	**£2**	
Fancy Nancy	7"	Top Rank	JAR248	1959	**£4**	**£1.50**	
It Was I	7"	Top Rank	JAR156	1959	**£5**	**£2**	

SKIP & THE CREATIONS

Mobam	LP	Justice		196–	**£200**	**£100**	*US*

SKIP BIFFERTY

The album made by Skip Bifferty is something of a forgotten sixties classic, to file next to the debut albums by Family and Traffic. The group never managed to build on its encouraging start, however. Four years later, the follow-up was finally made and issued under the name of Bell and Arc. Sadly, by this time, much of the group's inspiration seemed to have evaporated.

Happy Land	7"	RCA	RCA1648	1967	**£15**	**£7.50**	
Man In Black	7"	RCA	RCA1720	1968	**£15**	**£7.50**	
On Love	7"	RCA	RCA1621	1967	**£15**	**£7.50**	
Skip Bifferty	LP	RCA	RD/SF7941	1968	**£75**	**£37.50**	*black label*
Skip Bifferty	LP	RCA	RD/SF7941	1968	**£50**	**£25**	*orange label*

SKREWDRIVER

All Skrewed Up	LP	Chiswick	CH3	1977	**£20**	**£8**	*plays at 45 rpm*
Anti-Social	7"	Chiswick	NS18	1977	**£6**	**£2.50**	*picture sleeve*
Back With A Bang	12"	Skrewdriver	SKREW1T	1982	**£20**	**£10**	
Built Up	7"	TJM	TJM4	1980	**£12**	**£6**	
Streetfight	7"	Chiswick	NS28	1978	**£75**	**£37.50**	*test pressing*
Voice Of Britain	7"	White Noise	WN2	1983	**£20**	**£10**	
White Power	7"	White Noise	WN1	1983	**£20**	**£10**	
You're So Dumb	7"	Chiswick	S11	1977	**£10**	**£5**	*picture sleeve*

SKULLSNAPS

My Hang Up Is You	7"	GSF	GSZ7	1973	**£8**	**£4**	

SKUNK ANANSIE

Little Baby Swastikkka	7"	One Little Indian	TPLP55PROMO	1994	**£15**	**£7.50**	*promo*

SKUNKS

Gettin' Started	LP	Teen Town	101	1967	**£20**	**£8**	*US*

SKY, PATRICK

Harvest Of Gentle Clang	LP	Vanguard	SVRL19054	1970	**£12**	**£5**	
Patrick Sky	LP	Vanguard	VSD79179	1965	**£15**	**£6**	
Photographs	LP	Verve	FTS3079	1969	**£12**	**£5**	*US*
Reality Is Bad Enough	LP	Verve	FTS3052	1968	**£15**	**£6**	*US*

SKYBIRD

Summer Of '73	LP	Holyground	HGS118	1973	**£40**	**£20**	

SKYLINERS

I'll Close My Eyes	7"	Pye	7N25091	1961	**£8**	**£4**	
It Happened Today	7"	London	HLU8971	1959	**£25**	**£12.50**	
Pennies From Heaven	7"	Polydor	NH66951	1960	**£8**	**£4**	
Since I Don't Have You	7"	London	HLB8829	1959	**£150**	**£75**	
Since I Don't Have You	LP	Original Sound	(S)8873	1963	**£40**	**£20**	*US*
Skyliners	LP	Calico	LP3000	1959	**£200**	**£100**	*US*
This I Swear	7"	London	HLU8924	1959	**£50**	**£25**	

SKYLINERS (2)

	7"	Studio 36		1964	**£100**	**£50**	

SLACK, FREDDIE

Boogie Woogie	10" LP	Capitol	LC6529	1951	**£25**	**£10**	
Boogie Woogie On The 88	10" LP	Wing	MGW60003	195–	**£25**	**£10**	*US*

SLADE

Alive At Reading '80	7"	Cheapskate	CHEAP5	1980	**£4**	**£1.50**	
Alive Vol. 2	LP	Barn	2314106	1978	**£15**	**£6**	
All Join Hands	12"	RCA	RCAT455	1984	**£10**	**£5**	
Bangin' Man	7"	Polydor	2058492	1974	**£20**	**£10**	*picture sleeve*
Burning In The Heat Of Love	7"	Barn	2014106	1977	**£10**	**£5**	
Cum On Feel The Noize	12"	Polydor	POSPX399	1981	**£6**	**£2.50**	
Do You Believe In Miracles	12"	RCA	RCAPT40449D	1985	**£8**	**£4**	*double*
Do You Believe In Miracles	12"	RCA	PT40450D	1985	**£10**	**£5**	*double*
Do You Believe In Miracles	7"	RCA	PB40449	1985	**£8**	**£4**	*double*
Far Far Away	7"	Lyntone	LYN3156/7	1975	**£6**	**£2.50**	*flexi*
Get Down And Get With It	7"	Polydor	2058112	1971	**£5**	**£2**	
Ginny Ginny	7"	Barn	002	1979	**£8**	**£4**	*yellow vinyl*
Ginny Ginny	7"	Barn	002	1979	**£20**	**£10**	*black vinyl promo*
Hear Me Calling	7"	Polydor	2814008	1970	**£75**	**£37.50**	*promo*
Hokey Cokey	7"	Speed	SPEED201P	1982	**£5**	**£2**	*picture disc*
How Does It Feel	CD-s	Counterpoint	CDEP12C	1988	**£5**	**£2**	*with tracks by Wizzard*
In For A Penny	7"	Polydor	2058663	1975	**£5**	**£2**	*picture sleeve*
Know Who You Are	7"	Polydor	2058054	1970	**£50**	**£25**	
Knuckle Sandwich	7"	Cheapskate	CHEAP24	1981	**£4**	**£1.50**	
Let's Dance (1988 Remix)	CD-s	Cheapskate	BOYZCD3	1988	**£5**	**£2**	*3" single*

Merry Xmas Everybody	7"	Cheapskate	CHEAP11	1980	£5	£2	*picture sleeve*
Merry Xmas Everybody	7"	Polydor	2058422	1973	£20	£10	*picture sleeve*
Merry Xmas Everybody	CD-s	Receiver	CDBOYZ4	1989	£5	£2	
My Baby Left Me/That's Alright Mama	7"	Barn	2014114	1977	£6	£2.50	*picture sleeve*
Myzsterious Mizster Jones	7"	RCA	PB40027	1985	£5	£2	*picture disc*
Night Starvation	7"	S.O.T.B.	SUPER3	1980	£20	£10	*demo*
Okey Cokey	7"	Barn	011	1979	£6	£2.50	
Okey Cokey	7"	Speed	SPEED201	1982	£6	£2.50	*no picture sleeve*
Return To Base	LP	Barn	NARB003	1979	£25	£10	
Rock'n'Roll	7"	Barn	2014127	1978	£8	£4	
Rogues Gallery	CD	RCA	PD70604	1985	£15	£6	
Ruby Red	7"	RCA	RCAD191	1982	£5	£2	*double*
Ruby Red	7"	RCA	RCA191	1982	£6	£2.50	
Shape Of Things To Come	7"	Fontana	TF1079	1970	£40	£20	
Sign Of The Times	7"	Barn	010	1979	£10	£5	
Six Of The Best	12"	S.O.T.B.	SUPER453	1980	£8	£4	
Slade Talk To 19 Readers	7"	Lyntone	LYN2797	1973	£5	£2	*flexi*
Slade Talk To Melanie Readers	7"	Lyntone	LYN2645	1973	£5	£2	*flexi*
Slade Talk To Melanie/19 Readers	7"	Lyntone	LYN2645/2797	1975	£8	£4	*flexi*
Still The Same	7"	RCA	PB41147	1987	£6	£2.50	*double*
Thanks For The Memory	7"	Polydor	2058585	1975	£20	£10	*promo, different lyrics*
We'll Bring The House Down	7"	Cheapskate	CHEAP16	1981	£4	£1.50	
Whatever Happened To Slade	LP	Barn	2314103	1977	£15	£6	
Wheels Ain't Comin' Down	7"	Cheapskate	CHEAP21	1981	£4	£1.50	
Whole World's Going Crazy	7"	Polydor	SFI122	1972	£5	£2	*flexi, Mike Hugg B side*
Wild Winds Are Blowing	7"	Fontana	TF1056	1969	£40	£20	
You Boyz Make Big Noize	7"	Cheapskate	BOYZ1	1987	£5	£2	

SLADE, PRENTIS

I Can Tell	7"	Parlophone	R4850	1961	£4	£1.50	

SLAM CREEPERS

Saturday	7"	Olga	OLE009	1968	£10	£5	

SLAM SLAM

Move	CD-s	MCA	DMCA1346	1989	£5	£2	*3" single*

SLANEY, IVOR ORCHESTRA

High Wire	7"	HMV	POP1347	1964	£5	£2	

SLAPP HAPPY

Acnalbasac Noom	LP	Recommended	RRFIVE	1980	£12	£5	*2 different covers*
Casablanca Moon	7"	Virgin	VS105	1974	£4	£1.50	
Desperate Straights	LP	Virgin	V2024	1974	£10	£4	*with Henry Cow*
Johnny's Dead	7"	Virgin	VS124	1975	£5	£2	*picture sleeve*
Slapp Happy	LP	Virgin	V2014	1974	£10	£4	
Sort Of	LP	Polydor	2310204	1972	£100	£50	*with insert*
Sort Of	LP	Recommended	RRS5	1986	£10	£4	

SLAUGHTER & THE DOGS

Cranked Up Really High	7"	Rabid	TOSH101	1977	£4	£1.50	
Do It Dog Style	LP	Decca	SKL5292	1978	£15	£6	
It's Alright	12"	TJM	TJM3	1979	£8	£4	
Where Have All The Boot Boys Gone	12"	Decca	LF13723	1977	£6	£2.50	
Where Have All The Boot Boys Gone	7"	Decca	FR13723	1977	£4	£1.50	

SLAY, FRANK ORCHESTRA

Flying Circle	7"	Top Rank	JAR599	1962	£4	£1.50	

SLAYER

Criminally Insane	7"	London	LON133	1987	£10	£5	*cross sleeve, red vinyl*
Decade Of Agression	CD-s	Def American	226792	1991	£40	£20	*US metal pack*
Haunting The Chapel	CD-s	Road Runner	RR24442	1989	£5	£2	
Seasons In The Abyss	CD-s	Def American	DEFAC9	1991	£5	£2	

SLEDGE, F.

Red Eye Girl	7"	Blue Beat	BB386	1967	£12	£6	

SLEDGE, PERCY

Any Day Now	7"	Atlantic	584264	1969	£4	£1.50	
Baby Help Me	7"	Atlantic	584080	1967	£4	£1.50	
Best Of Percy Sledge	LP	Atlantic	587/588153	1969	£10	£4	
Come Softly To Me	7"	Atlantic	584225	1968	£4	£1.50	
Heart Of A Child	7"	Atlantic	584055	1966	£4	£1.50	
It Tears Me Up	7"	Atlantic	584071	1967	£4	£1.50	
Kind Woman	7"	Atlantic	584286	1969	£4	£1.50	
Out Of Left Field	7"	Atlantic	584108	1967	£4	£1.50	
Percy Sledge Way	LP	Atlantic	587/588081	1967	£15	£6	
Pledging My Love	7"	Atlantic	584140	1967	£4	£1.50	
Take Time To Know Her	LP	Atlantic	SD8180	1968	£15	£6	*US*
Take Time To Love Her	7"	Atlantic	584177	1968	£4	£1.50	
True Love Travels On A Gravel Road	7"	Atlantic	584300	1969	£4	£1.50	
Warm And Tender Love	7"	Atlantic	584034	1966	£4	£1.50	
Warm And Tender Soul	LP	Atlantic	587/588048	1967	£15	£6	
When A Man Loves A Woman	7"	Atlantic	584001	1966	£4	£1.50	
When A Man Loves A Woman	CD-s	Intertape	500068	1987	£5	£2	
When A Man Loves A Woman	LP	Atlantic	587/588105	1968	£15	£6	

SLEDGEHAMMER

Title	Format	Label	Cat. No.	Year	Mint	VG+	Notes
Blood On Their Hands	LP	Illuminated	JAMS32	1985	£20	£8	
In The Middle Of The Night	7"	Slammer	MRSB2	198–	£5	£2	
In The Queue	7"	Illuminated	ILL33	1985	£8	£4	shaped picture disc
Living In Dreams	7"	Slammer	CELL2	1980	£5	£2	
Sledgehammer	7"	Slammer	SRTS79/CUS395	1979	£5	£2	
Sledgehammer	7"	Valiant	ROUND2	1980	£4	£1.50	
Sledgehammer	7"	Valiant	STRONG1	1980	£4	£1.50	

SLEEPER

Title	Format	Label	Cat. No.	Year	Mint	VG+	Notes
Alice In Vain	CD-s	Indolent	SLEEP001CD	1993	£6	£2.50	
Bucket And Spade	7"	Indolent	SLEEP004	1994	£10	£5	green vinyl
Bucket And Spade	7"	Indolent	SLEEP004CD	1994	£6	£2.50	

SLEEPWALKERS

Title	Format	Label	Cat. No.	Year	Mint	VG+	Notes
Sleepwalk	7"	Parlophone	R4580	1959	£6	£2.50	

SLEEPY

Title	Format	Label	Cat. No.	Year	Mint	VG+	Notes
Love's Immortal Fire	7"	CBS	3592	1968	£25	£12.50	
Rosie Can't Fly	7"	CBS	3838	1968	£25	£12.50	

SLENDER PLENTY

Title	Format	Label	Cat. No.	Year	Mint	VG+	Notes
Silver Tree Top School For Boys	7"	Polydor	56189	1967	£20	£10	

SLEVIN, JIMI

Title	Format	Label	Cat. No.	Year	Mint	VG+	Notes
Freeflight	LP	Claddagh	CCF7	1982	£75	£37.50	

SLICK, GRACE

Title	Format	Label	Cat. No.	Year	Mint	VG+	Notes
And Through The Hoop	LP	RCA	DJL13544	1979	£12	£5	US interview promo
Welcome To The Wrecking Ball	LP	RCA	DJL13922	1981	£12	£5	US interview promo

SLICKEE BOYS

Title	Format	Label	Cat. No.	Year	Mint	VG+	Notes
Separated Vegetables	LP	Dacoit	1001	1977	£100	£50	US
Separated Vegetables	LP	Limp	10003	1980	£75	£37.50	US

SLICKERS

Title	Format	Label	Cat. No.	Year	Mint	VG+	Notes
Frying Pan	7"	Blue Cat	BS154	1969	£6	£2.50	Rarfield Williams B side
Johnny Too Bad	7"	Dynamic	DYN406	1970	£4	£1.50	Roland Alphonso B side
Man Beware	7"	Amalgamated	AMG852	1969	£6	£2.50	
Money Reaper	7"	Amalgamated	AMG866	1969	£6	£2.50	
Nana	7"	Blue Cat	BS134	1968	£8	£4	Martin Riley B side
Run Fattie	7"	Trojan	TR7719	1969	£4	£1.50	
Wala Wala	7"	Blue Cat	BS133	1968	£8	£4	Lester Sterling B side

SLIM & THE FREEDOM SINGERS

Title	Format	Label	Cat. No.	Year	Mint	VG+	Notes
Do Dang Do	7"	Banana	BA304	1970	£5	£2	Jackie Mittoo B side

SLIME

Title	Format	Label	Cat. No.	Year	Mint	VG+	Notes
Controversial	7"	Toadstool	GOOD1	1978	£4	£1.50	

SLITS

Title	Format	Label	Cat. No.	Year	Mint	VG+	Notes
Peel Sessions	CD-s	Strange Fruit	SFPMACD207	1989	£5	£2	
Return Of The Giant Slits	LP	CBS	85269	1981	£10	£4	with 7" (XPS125)

SLOAN, P. F.

Title	Format	Label	Cat. No.	Year	Mint	VG+	Notes
12 More Times	LP	Dunhill	D50007	1966	£12	£5	US
Man Behind The Red Balloon	7" EP	RCA	86903	1966	£6	£2.50	French
Sins Of The Family	7" EP	RCA	86901	1965	£6	£2.50	French
Songs Of Our Times	LP	Dunhill	D50004	1965	£12	£5	US

SLOAN, SAMMI

Title	Format	Label	Cat. No.	Year	Mint	VG+	Notes
Yes I Would	7"	Columbia	DB8480	1968	£5	£2	

SLOWDIVE

Title	Format	Label	Cat. No.	Year	Mint	VG+	Notes
Catch The Breeze	CD-s	Creation	CRESCD112	1991	£5	£2	
Morningrise	CD-s	Creation	CRESCD098	1991	£5	£2	
Slowdive	CD-s	Creation	CRESCD93	1990	£5	£2	
Souvlaki	CD	Creation	CRECD139/ CRECDX101	1993	£15	£6	double

SLY & THE FAMILY STONE

Title	Format	Label	Cat. No.	Year	Mint	VG+	Notes
Dance To The Music	7"	Columbia	DB8369	1968	£25	£12.50	
Dance To The Music	7"	Direction	583568	1968	£4	£1.50	
Dance To The Music	LP	Direction	863412	1968	£15	£6	
Everyday People	7"	Direction	583938	1969	£4	£1.50	
Family Affair	7"	Epic	EPC7632	1971	£4	£1.50	
Family Affair	7"	Epic	EPC1148	1973	£5	£2	picture sleeve
Fresh	LP	Epic	EPC69039	1973	£10	£4	
Greatest Hits	LP	CBS	Q69002	1973	£12	£5	quad
Greatest Hits	LP	Epic	EPC69002	1970	£10	£4	
High Energy	LP	Epic	EPC22004	1975	£15	£6	double
High On You	LP	Epic	PEQ33835	1975	£10	£4	US quad
Hot Fun In The Summertime	7"	Direction	584471	1969	£4	£1.50	
I Want To Take You Higher	7"	CBS	5054	1970	£4	£1.50	
Life	LP	Epic	BN26397	1968	£15	£6	US

M'Lady	7"	Direction	583707	1968	**£4**	**£1.50**	
M'Lady	LP	Direction	863461	1968	**£15**	**£6**	
Running Away	7"	Epic	EPC7810	1972	**£4**	**£1.50**	
Small Talk	LP	Epic	EPC69070	1974	**£10**	**£4**	
Small Talk	LP	Epic	PEQ32930	1974	**£10**	**£4**	*US quad*
Stand	7"	Direction	584279	1969	**£4**	**£1.50**	
Stand	LP	Direction	863655	1969	**£15**	**£6**	
Thank You	7"	Direction	584782	1970	**£4**	**£1.50**	
There's A Riot Going On	LP	Epic	EPC64613	1971	**£12**	**£5**	
Whole New Thing	LP	Epic	LN24/BN26324	1967	**£15**	**£6**	*US*

SMACK

Smack	LP	Audio House	no number	1967	**£1000**	**£700**	*US*

SMALL, JOAN

Afraid	7"	Parlophone	R4431	1958	**£10**	**£5**	
Big Hurt	7"	Parlophone	R4622	1960	**£10**	**£5**	
You Can't Say I Love You	7"	Parlophone	R4269	1957	**£6**	**£2.50**	

SMALL, KAREN

To Get You Back Again	7"	Vocalion	VP9281	1966	**£6**	**£2.50**	

SMALL FACES

The music of the Small Faces seems to have grown in stature over the years, a fact that is reflected amongst collectors by substantial recent gains in value of the group's albums. As the only genuine mods to achieve success with their own music, the Small Faces stayed slightly apart from the rock mainstream in the sixties – a factor which stood them in good stead when British beat evolved into psychedelia. 'Itchycoo Park' is a great psychedelic single (with the first recorded use of phasing), at least in part because the Small Faces were making fun of the style, even while delivering a masterful example of it. The chaotic state of the group's reissue catalogue is a reflection of the fact that the Small Faces switched from Decca to Immediate half way through their career. Though too late to benefit the sadly missed Steve Marriott (who died in a house fire in 1991) or Ronnie Lane (who finally succumbed to multiple sclerosis in 1997), drummer Kenny Jones won a lengthy legal battle in 1996 to retrieve substantial unpaid royalties.

Afterglow Of Your Love	7"	Immediate	IM077	1969	**£4**	**£1.50**	
Afterglow Of Your Love	7"	Immediate	IM077	1969	**£30**	**£15**	*demo with demo mix B side*
All Or Nothing	7"	Decca	F12470	1966	**£6**	**£2.50**	
All Or Nothing	7" EP	Decca	457123	1966	**£50**	**£25**	*French*
Autumn Stone	LP	Immediate	IMA101/2	1969	**£75**	**£37.50**	*double*
Darlings Of Wapping Wharf Launderette	LP	Virgin	V2178	1980	**£10**	**£4**	
From The Beginning	LP	Decca	LK4879	1967	**£75**	**£37.50**	
From The Beginning	LP	Decca	LK4879	1969	**£25**	**£10**	*boxed Decca label*
Here Come The Nice	7" EP	Columbia	ESRF1876	1967	**£50**	**£25**	*French*
Here Comes The Nice	7"	Immediate	IM050	1967	**£5**	**£2**	
Hey Girl	7"	Decca	F12393	1966	**£6**	**£2.50**	
I Can't Make It	7"	Decca	F12565	1967	**£10**	**£5**	
I Can't Make It	7" EP	Decca	457144	1967	**£50**	**£25**	*French*
I've Got Mine	7"	Decca	F12276	1965	**£10**	**£5**	
In Memoriam	LP	Immediate	IMSP022	1970	**£40**	**£20**	*German*
In Memoriam	LP	Immediate	IMSP022	1969	**£250**	**£150**	
Itchycoo Park	7"	Immediate	IM057	1967	**£5**	**£2**	
Itchycoo Park	7" EP	Columbia	ESRF1882	1967	**£50**	**£25**	*French*
Lazy Sunday	7"	Immediate	IM064	1968	**£5**	**£2**	
My Mind's Eye	7"	Decca	F12500	1966	**£40**	**£20**	*demo mix, matrix ... T1-1C*
My Mind's Eye	7"	Decca	F12500	1967	**£4**	**£1.50**	
My Mind's Eye	7" EP	Decca	457133	1967	**£50**	**£25**	*French*
Ogden's Nut Gone Flake	CD	Castle	CLACT016	1991	**£20**	**£8**	*round tin*
Ogden's Nut Gone Flake	LP	NEMS	IML1001	1975	**£10**	**£4**	*round sleeve*
Ogden's Nut Gone Flake	LP	Immediate	IMLP/IMSP012	1967	**£75**	**£37.50**	*round cover*
Patterns	7"	Decca	F12619	1967	**£30**	**£15**	
Sha-La-La-La-Lee	7"	Decca	F12317	1966	**£6**	**£2.50**	
Sha-La-La-La-Lee	7" EP	Decca	457106	1966	**£50**	**£25**	*French*
Small Faces	7"	Immediate	AS1	1967	**£75**	**£37.50**	*promo*
Small Faces	LP	Immediate	IMLP/IMSP008	1967	**£100**	**£50**	
Small Faces	LP	Decca	LK4790	1966	**£60**	**£30**	
Small Faces	LP	Decca	LK4790	1969	**£25**	**£10**	*boxed Decca label*
Small Faces EP	CD-s	Special Edition	CD39	1988	**£5**	**£2**	
There Are But Four Small Faces	LP	Immediate	Z1252002	1968	**£60**	**£30**	*US*
Tin Soldier	7"	Immediate	IM062	1967	**£20**	**£10**	*picture sleeve*
Tin Soldier	7"	Immediate	IM062	1967	**£6**	**£2.50**	
Universal	7"	Immediate	IM069	1968	**£6**	**£2.50**	*lilac label*
Whatcha Gonna Do About it	7"	Decca	F12208	1965	**£6**	**£2.50**	
Whatcha Gonna Do About It	7" EP	Decca	457091	1965	**£50**	**£25**	*French*

SMALL HOURS

Kid	10"	Automatic	K17708X	1980	**£15**	**£6**	
Kid	7"	Automatic	K17708	1980	**£20**	**£10**	

SMALL WORLD

First Impressions	7"	Valid	VC001	1983	**£25**	**£12.50**	
Love Is Dead	7"	Whaam!	WHAAM3	1982	**£25**	**£12.50**	

SMART ALEC

Scooter Boys	7"	B&C	BCS20	1980	**£12**	**£6**	

SMASH

Vanguardia Y Pureza Del Flamenco	LP	Serdisco	30112047	1989	**£25**	**£10**	*Spanish*

We Come To Smash	LP	Philips	4328044	1973	**£125**	**£62.50**	*Spanish*

SMASHING PUMPKINS

Cherub Rock	7"	Hut	HUT31	1993	**£15**	**£7.50**	*clear vinyl*
I Am One	10"	Hut	HUTEN018	1992	**£15**	**£7.50**	
I Am One	12"	Hut	HUTT18	1992	**£8**	**£4**	
Lull EP	12"	Hut	HUTT10	1992	**£6**	**£2.50**	
Lull EP	CD-s	Hut	CDHUT10	1992	**£5**	**£2**	
Peel Sessions	12"	Hut	HUTT017	1992	**£8**	**£4**	
Rocket	7"	Hut	HUTL48	1994	**£25**	**£12.50**	*boxed, pink vinyl*
Screen Raver	CD			1995	**£25**	**£10**	*promo only Apple Mac CD-ROM*
Siamese Singles	7"	Hut	SPBOX1	1994	**£30**	**£15**	*4 × 7" boxed set*
Siva	12"	Hut	HUTT6	1991	**£25**	**£12.50**	
Siva	7"	Caroline	SMASH1	1991	**£30**	**£15**	*promo*
Smile	7"	Hut	HUT43	1994	**£6**	**£2.50**	*purple vinyl*
Today	7"	Hut	HUT37	1993	**£10**	**£5**	*red vinyl*
Tristessa	12"	Sub Pop	SP90	1993	**£25**	**£12.50**	
Zero	12"	Hut	HUTTDJ73	1994	**£8**	**£4**	*promo*

SMECK, ROY

Songs Of The Range	10" LP	Brunswick	LA8649	1954	**£10**	**£4**	

SMILE

Smile included Brian May and Roger Taylor who, not long after the release of the group's only single, left in order to help found Queen. Red vinyl copies of the single, incidentally, are counterfeits.

Earth	7"	Mercury	72977	1969	**£100**	**£50**	*US, promo only (stamped matrix no.)*
Smile	LP	Mercury	18PP1	1982	**£40**	**£20**	*Japanese*

SMILIN' JOE

ABC's	78	London	HL8106	1954	**£50**	**£25**	

SMITH, ADAM

I Wonder Why	7"	Island	WI057	1962	**£10**	**£5**	

SMITH, ARTHUR 'GUITAR BOOGIE'

Arthur 'Guitar Boogie' Smith And His Crackerjacks	7" EP	MGM	MGMEP695	1959	**£15**	**£7.50**	
Arthur 'Guitar Boogie' Smith And His Crackerjacks	7" EP	MGM	MGMEP510	1954	**£12**	**£6**	
Express Boogie	7"	MGM	SP1039	1953	**£12**	**£6**	
Fingers On Fire	10" LP	MGM	D111	1953	**£25**	**£10**	
Fingers On Fire	LP	MGM	E3525	1958	**£20**	**£8**	*US*
Five String Banjo Boogie	7"	MGM	SP1021	1953	**£12**	**£6**	
Foolish Questions	10" LP	MGM	D131	1954	**£25**	**£10**	
Guitar Boogie	7"	MGM	SP1008	1953	**£20**	**£10**	
Hi Lo Boogie	7"	MGM	SP1122	1955	**£12**	**£6**	
I Get So Lonely	7"	MGM	SP1096	1954	**£12**	**£6**	
Mister Guitar	7" EP	Stateside	SE1005	1963	**£10**	**£5**	
Original Guitar Boogie	LP	Dot	DLP5600	1964	**£10**	**£4**	*US*
Red Headed Stranger	7"	MGM	SP1110	1954	**£12**	**£6**	
Specials	10" LP	MGM	E3301	195–	**£25**	**£10**	*US*

SMITH, BARRY

Hold On To It	7"	People	PEO119	1975	**£10**	**£5**	

SMITH, BEASLEY

Goodnight Sweet Dreams	7"	London	HLD8235	1956	**£15**	**£7.50**	
My Foolish Heart	7"	London	HLD8273	1956	**£15**	**£7.50**	

SMITH, BESSIE

Any Woman's Blues	LP	CBS	66262	1971	**£12**	**£5**	*double*
Bessie Smith	7" EP	Philips	BBE12360	1960	**£8**	**£4**	
Bessie Smith Story Vol. 1	LP	Philips	BBL7019	1955	**£20**	**£8**	
Bessie Smith Story Vol. 1	LP	CBS	BPG62377	1966	**£12**	**£5**	
Bessie Smith Story Vol. 2	LP	CBS	BPG62378	1966	**£12**	**£5**	
Bessie Smith Story Vol. 2	LP	Philips	BBL7020	1955	**£20**	**£8**	
Bessie Smith Story Vol. 3	LP	Philips	BBL7042	1955	**£20**	**£8**	
Bessie Smith Story Vol. 3	LP	CBS	BPG62379	1966	**£12**	**£5**	
Bessie Smith Story Vol. 4	LP	CBS	BPG62380	1966	**£12**	**£5**	
Bessie Smith Story Vol. 4	LP	Philips	BBL7049	1955	**£20**	**£8**	
Bessie's Blues	LP	Philips	BBL7513	1962	**£15**	**£6**	
Empress	LP	CBS	66264	1971	**£12**	**£5**	*double*
Empress Of The Blues	7" EP	Philips	BBE12202	1958	**£8**	**£4**	
Empress Of The Blues No. 2	7" EP	Philips	BBE12231	1959	**£8**	**£4**	
Empress Of The Blues No. 3	7" EP	Philips	BBE12233	1959	**£8**	**£4**	
Empty Bed Blues	LP	CBS	66273	1971	**£12**	**£5**	*double*
Nobody's Blues But Mine	LP	CBS	67232	1972	**£12**	**£5**	*double*
World's Greatest Blues Singer	LP	CBS	66258	1971	**£12**	**£5**	*double*

SMITH, BETTY

Begin The Beguine	7"	Decca	F11071	1958	**£4**	**£1.50**	
Betty Smith Quintet	7" EP	Decca	DFE6446	1957	**£15**	**£7.50**	
Betty's Blues	7"	Decca	F11031	1958	**£5**	**£2**	
Bewitched	7"	Decca	F10986	1958	**£5**	**£2**	

Song Of India	7"	Decca	F11124	1959	**£4**	**£1.50**	
Sweet Georgia Brown	7"	Tempo	A163	1957	**£15**	**£7.50**	
There's A Blue Ridge Mountain	7"	Tempo	A162	1957	**£8**	**£4**	

SMITH, BOB

Visit	LP	Kent	KST551	1969	**£75**	**£37.50**	*US*

SMITH, BUSTER

Legendary Buster Smith	LP	London	LTZK15206	1960	**£10**	**£4**	

SMITH, CARL

Carl Smith	10" LP	Columbia	HL2579	1956	**£20**	**£8**	*US*
Carl Smith Touch	LP	Philips	BBL7437	1960	**£10**	**£4**	
Let's Live A Little	LP	Columbia	CL1172	1958	**£15**	**£6**	*US*
Sentimental Songs	10" LP	Columbia	HL9023	195–	**£20**	**£8**	*US*
Smith's The Name	LP	Columbia	CL1022	1957	**£15**	**£6**	*US*
Softly And Tenderly	10" LP	Columbia	HL9026	195–	**£20**	**£8**	*US*
Sunday Down South	LP	Columbia	CL959	1957	**£15**	**£6**	*US*
Ten Thousand Drums	7"	Philips	PB943	1959	**£5**	**£2**	

SMITH, CLARA

Blues	7" EP	Philips	BBE12491	1961	**£8**	**£4**	
Volume 1	LP	VJM	VLP15	1969	**£10**	**£4**	
Volume 2	LP	VJM	VLP16	1969	**£10**	**£4**	
Volume 3	LP	VJM	VLP17	1969	**£10**	**£4**	

SMITH, CONNIE

Cute And Country	LP	RCA	RD7785	1966	**£10**	**£4**	

SMITH, D.

Ball Of Confusion	7"	Smash	SMA2311	1970	**£5**	**£2**	*Keith Hudson B side*

SMITH, DAVE & THE ASTRONAUTS

Lover Like You	7"	Columbia	DB104	1967	**£5**	**£2**	

SMITH, EDDIE

Silver Star Stomp	7"	Parlophone	MSP6186	1955	**£8**	**£4**	
Upturn	7"	Top Rank	JAR285	1960	**£6**	**£2.50**	

SMITH, EDGEWOOD & FABULOUS TAILFEATHERS

Ain't That Lovin' You	7"	Sue	WI4037	1967	**£10**	**£5**	

SMITH, EFFIE

Dial That Phone	7"	Sue	WI4010	1966	**£10**	**£5**	

SMITH, ELSON

Flip Flop	7"	Fontana	H291	1961	**£10**	**£5**	

SMITH, GEORGE HARMONICA

Arkansas Trap	LP	Deram	SML1082	1971	**£30**	**£15**	
Blues In The Dark	7"	Blue Horizon	451002	1966	**£100**	**£50**	
Blues With A Feeling	LP	Liberty	LBS83218	1970	**£20**	**£8**	
No Time To Jive	LP	Blue Horizon	763856	1970	**£60**	**£30**	
Someday You're Gonna Learn	7"	Blue Horizon	573170	1970	**£10**	**£5**	

SMITH, GLORIA

Playmates	7"	London	HLU8903	1959	**£6**	**£2.50**	

SMITH, GORDON

Long Overdue	LP	Blue Horizon	763211	1968	**£40**	**£20**	
Too Long	7"	Blue Horizon	573156	1969	**£8**	**£4**	

SMITH, HOBART

Hobart Smith	LP	Topic	12T187	1969	**£15**	**£6**	

SMITH, HUEY 'PIANO'

Don't You Know Yokomo	7"	Top Rank	JAR282	1960	**£15**	**£7.50**	
For Dancing	LP	Ace	LP1015	1961	**£60**	**£30**	*US*
Having A Good Time	LP	Ace	LP1004	1959	**£75**	**£37.50**	*US*
High Blood Pressure	7"	Columbia	DB4138	1958	**£40**	**£20**	
If It Ain't One Thing It's Another	7"	Sue	WI364	1965	**£12**	**£6**	
Popeye	7"	Top Rank	JAR614	1962	**£10**	**£5**	
Rock'n'Roll Revival	LP	Ace	LP2021	196–	**£50**	**£25**	*US*
Rockin' Pneumonia	7"	Sue	WI380	1965	**£12**	**£6**	
Rockin' Pneumonia And Boogie Woogie Flu	LP	Sue	ILP917	1965	**£30**	**£15**	
Twas The Night Before Christmas	LP	Ace	LP1027	1962	**£50**	**£25**	*US*

SMITH, JIMMY

Any Number Can Win	LP	Verve	VLP9057	1963	**£10**	**£4**	
At Club Baby Grand, Wilmington, Delaware Vol. 1	LP	Blue Note	BLP/BST81528	1966	**£25**	**£10**	
At Club Baby Grand, Wilmington, Delaware Vol. 2	LP	Blue Note	BLP/BST81529	1966	**£25**	**£10**	
At Small's Paradise Vol. 1	LP	Blue Note	BLP/BST81585	196–	**£25**	**£10**	
At Small's Paradise Vol. 2	LP	Blue Note	BLP/BST81586	196–	**£25**	**£10**	
At The Organ Vol. 1	LP	Blue Note	BLP/BST81512	196–	**£25**	**£10**	
At The Organ Vol. 2	LP	Blue Note	BLP/BST81514	196–	**£25**	**£10**	

Title	Format	Label	Cat. No.	Year	Mint	VG	Notes
Back At The Chicken Shack	LP	Blue Note	BLP/BST84117	1964	**£25**	**£10**	
Bashin'	LP	Verve	CLP1596/ CSD1462	1962	**£10**	**£4**	
Boss	LP	Verve	SVLP9247	1970	**£10**	**£4**	
Bucket	LP	Blue Note	BLP/BST84235	1966	**£15**	**£6**	
Can Heat	7"	Blue Note	451905	1964	**£5**	**£2**	
Cat	LP	Verve	(S)VLP9079	1964	**£10**	**£4**	
Christmas Cookin'	LP	Verve	(S)VLP9231	1968	**£10**	**£4**	
Crazy Baby	LP	Blue Note	BLP/BST84030	1961	**£25**	**£10**	
Creeper	7" EP	Verve	VEP5021	1965	**£8**	**£4**	
Date With Jimmy Smith Vol. 1	LP	Blue Note	BLP/BST81547	196–	**£25**	**£10**	
Date With Jimmy Smith Vol. 2	LP	Blue Note	BLP/BST81548	196–	**£25**	**£10**	
Dynamic Duo	LP	Verve	(S)VLP9160	1967	**£10**	**£4**	*with Wes Montgomery*
Further Adventures Of Jimmy And Wes	LP	Verve	(S)VLP9241	1969	**£10**	**£4**	*with Wes Montgomery*
Got My Mojo Working	LP	Verve	(S)VLP9123	1966	**£10**	**£4**	
Greatest Hits	LP	Verve	VLP9164	1967	**£10**	**£4**	
Greatest Hits	LP	Blue Note	BST89901	1970	**£10**	**£4**	
Groove Drops	LP	Verve	SVLP9253	1970	**£10**	**£4**	
Hobo Flats	LP	Verve	(S)VLP9039	1963	**£10**	**£4**	
Home Cookin'	LP	Blue Note	BLP/BST84050	1961	**£25**	**£10**	
Hoochie Coochie Man	LP	Verve	(S)VLP9142	1966	**£10**	**£4**	
House Party	LP	Blue Note	BLP/BST84002	1964	**£25**	**£10**	
I'm Movin' On	LP	Blue Note	BLP/BST84255	1967	**£15**	**£6**	
Incredible Jimmy Smith Vol. 1	LP	Blue Note	BLP/BST81551	1964	**£25**	**£10**	
Incredible Jimmy Smith Vol. 2	LP	Blue Note	BLP/BST81552	1965	**£25**	**£10**	
Jimmy Smith Vol. 3	LP	Blue Note	BLP/BST81525	196–	**£25**	**£10**	
Livin' It Up	LP	Verve	(S)VLP9227	1968	**£10**	**£4**	
Midnight Special	LP	Blue Note	BLP/BST84078	1962	**£25**	**£10**	
Monster	LP	Verve	(S)VLP9093	1965	**£10**	**£4**	
Open House	LP	Blue Note	BST84269	1968	**£15**	**£6**	
Organ Grinder Swing	LP	Verve	(S)VLP9108	1966	**£10**	**£4**	
Peter And The Wolf	LP	Verve	(S)VLP9159	1966	**£10**	**£4**	
Plain Talk	LP	Blue Note	BST84296	1968	**£12**	**£5**	
Plays Fats Waller	LP	Blue Note	BLP/BST84100	1964	**£20**	**£8**	
Plays Pretty For You	LP	Blue Note	BLP/BST81563	196–	**£25**	**£10**	
Plays The Blues	7" EP	Verve	VEP5016	1965	**£8**	**£4**	
Prayer Meetin'	LP	Blue Note	BLP/BST84164	1964	**£25**	**£10**	
Respect	LP	Verve	(S)VLP9182	1967	**£10**	**£4**	
Rockin' The Boat	LP	Blue Note	BLP/BST84141	1964	**£20**	**£8**	
Sermon	7"	Blue Note	451879	1964	**£5**	**£2**	
Sermon	LP	Blue Note	BLP/BST84011	1966	**£25**	**£10**	
Softly As A Summer Breeze	LP	Blue Note	BLP/BST84200	1966	**£20**	**£8**	
Sounds Of Jimmy Smith	LP	Blue Note	BLP/BST81556	196–	**£25**	**£10**	
Stay Loose	LP	Verve	(S)VLP9218	1968	**£10**	**£4**	
Swinging With The Incredible Jimmy Smith	7" EP	Verve	VEP5022	1965	**£8**	**£4**	
Walk On The Wild Side	7" EP	Verve	VEP5008	1964	**£8**	**£4**	
When My Dreamboat Comes Home	7"	Blue Note	451904	1963	**£5**	**£2**	
Who's Afraid Of Virginia Woolf	LP	Verve	VLP9068	1964	**£10**	**£4**	

SMITH, JOEY & BABA BROOKS

Title	Format	Label	Cat. No.	Year	Mint	VG	Notes
Maybe Once	7"	R&B	JB131	1964	**£10**	**£5**	

SMITH, JOHN

Title	Format	Label	Cat. No.	Year	Mint	VG	Notes
Rock'n'Roll Again	LP	Vogue	10160	1968	**£15**	**£6**	*German*
Rockin' With John Smith	LP	Pop	ZS10169	1968	**£15**	**£6**	*German*

SMITH, JOHNNY

Title	Format	Label	Cat. No.	Year	Mint	VG	Notes
Johnny Smith And His New Quartet	LP	Vogue	LAE12202	1960	**£10**	**£4**	
Johnny Smith Quartet	LP	Vogue	LAE12221	1960	**£10**	**£4**	
Moods	LP	Vogue	LAE12198	1961	**£15**	**£6**	
Moonlight In Vermont	LP	Vogue	LAE12189	1959	**£20**	**£8**	
Plays Jimmy Van Heusen	LP	Vogue	LAE12169	1959	**£20**	**£8**	

SMITH, JOHNNY 'HAMMOND'

Title	Format	Label	Cat. No.	Year	Mint	VG	Notes
Rufus Toofus	LP	Riverside	673017	1969	**£10**	**£4**	

SMITH, JUDI

Title	Format	Label	Cat. No.	Year	Mint	VG	Notes
Leaves Come Tumbling Down	7"	Decca	F12132	1965	**£6**	**£2.50**	

SMITH, JUNIOR

Title	Format	Label	Cat. No.	Year	Mint	VG	Notes
Come Cure Me	7"	Giant	GN25	1968	**£5**	**£2**	
Cool Down Your Temper	7"	Giant	GN1	1967	**£5**	**£2**	
I'm Gonna Leave You Girl	7"	Giant	GN18	1968	**£5**	**£2**	

SMITH, KATHY

Title	Format	Label	Cat. No.	Year	Mint	VG	Notes
Some Songs I've Saved	LP	Polydor	2310081	1970	**£50**	**£25**	

SMITH, KEELY

Title	Format	Label	Cat. No.	Year	Mint	VG	Notes
Autumn Leaves	7"	Capitol	CL14803	1957	**£4**	**£1.50**	
Don't Take Your Love From Me	7"	Capitol	CL14994	1959	**£4**	**£1.50**	
Good Behaviour	7"	Capitol	CL14754	1957	**£4**	**£1.50**	
Here In My Heart	7"	London	HLD9240	1960	**£5**	**£2**	
Hey Boy! Hey Girl!	LP	Capitol	T1160	1959	**£15**	**£6**	*with Louis Prima*
Hurt Me	7"	Capitol	CL14717	1957	**£4**	**£1.50**	
I Wish You Love	LP	Capitol	(S)T914	1958	**£12**	**£5**	

I've Got The World On A String	7" EP	Reprise	R30062	1966	£5	£2	
If I Knew I'd Find You	7"	London	HLD8984	1959	£6	£2.50	
Intimate Smith	LP	Reprise	R6132	1965	£10	£4	
It's Magic	7" EP	Capitol	EAP120629	1965	£5	£2	
Lennon & McCartney Songbook Vol. 1	7" EP	Reprise	R30042	1965	£6	£2.50	
Lennon & McCartney Songbook Vol. 2	7" EP	Reprise	R30046	1965	£6	£2.50	
Little Girl Blue, Little Girl New	LP	Reprise	R6086	1964	£10	£4	
Politely	LP	Capitol	T1073	1959	£10	£4	
Sings The John Lennon–Paul McCartney Songbook	LP	Reprise	R6142	1965	£10	£4	
Somebody Loves Me	7" EP	Reprise	R30053	1966	£5	£2	
Success Of Keely Smith	7" EP	Reprise	R30045	1965	£5	£2	
Swingin' Pretty	LP	Capitol	T1145	1959	£10	£4	
That Old Black Magic	7"	Capitol	CL14948	1958	£4	£1.50	
You Lovers	7" EP	London	RED1269	1961	£20	£10	
You're Breaking My Heart	LP	Reprise	R5012	1965	£10	£4	
Young And In Love	7"	Capitol	CL14739	1957	£4	£1.50	

SMITH, LONNIE

Drives	LP	Blue Note	BST84351	1970	£15	£6	
Finger Lickin' Good	LP	CBS	63146	1967	£15	£6	
Move Your Hand	LP	Blue Note	BST84326	1969	£15	£6	
Think	LP	Blue Note	BST84290	1968	£15	£6	
Turning Point	LP	Blue Note	BST84313	1969	£15	£6	

SMITH, LONNIE LISTON

Lonnie Liston Smith is a jazz keyboard player who was briefly a part of the Miles Davis band during the time in the early seventies when the trumpeter was engaged in some of his most experimental work with densely constructed rhythms. Smith's own records contain a very much more commercial form of jazz-funk, the track 'Expansions' having acquired something of the status of a disco classic.

Expansions	12"	RCA	PC9450	1979	£8	£4	
Expansions	LP	RCA	SF8434	1975	£15	£6	
Reflections Of A Golden Dream	LP	RCA	RS1053	1976	£10	£4	
Renaissance	LP	RCA	PL11822	1977	£10	£4	
Visions Of A New World	LP	RCA	SF8461	1976	£10	£4	

SMITH, LORENZO

Firewater	7"	Outasite	45503	1966	£50	£25	

SMITH, LOU

Cruel Love	7"	Top Rank	JAR520	1960	£4	£1.50	

SMITH, MARVIN

Time Stopped	7"	Coral	Q72486	1966	£20	£10	

SMITH, MEL

Mel Smith's Greatest Hits	7"	Mercury	MEL1	1981	£15	£7.50	

SMITH, MICHAEL

Mi Cyaan Believe It	LP	Island	ILPS9717	1982	£10	£4	

SMITH, MICK

Somebody Nobody Knows	LP	Midas	MFHR078	1976	£60	£30	
Unlucky Me	7" EP	Keri	KE802	1980	£10	£5	
Words And Music	LP	Alida Star	AS771	1977	£30	£15	

SMITH, MIKE

Raindance	LP	Repercussion	RR1000	1979	£15	£6	

SMITH, O. C.

At Home	LP	CBS	63805	1969	£10	£4	
Dynamic O. C. Smith	LP	CBS	63147	1968	£10	£4	
Hickory Holler Revisited	LP	CBS	(S)63362	1968	£10	£4	
Lighthouse	7"	London	HLA8480	1957	£50	£25	*credited to Ocie Smith*

SMITH, OTELLO & THE TOBAGO BAD BOYS

Big Ones Go Ska	LP	Direction	863242	1968	£10	£4	

SMITH, PATTI

Brian Jones	7"	Fierce	FRIGHT017	1988	£10	£5	
Hey Joe	7"	Sire	6078614	1978	£10	£5	
Hey Joe	7"	Mer	601	1974	£75	£37.50	*US*
Horses	LP	Arista	S4066	1975	£15	£6	*US grey vinyl*
People Have The Power	CD-s	Arista	659877	1988	£5	£2	
Privilege	12"	Arista	ARIST12197	1978	£6	£2.50	

SMITH, PAUL

Big Men	LP	HMV	CLP1356	1960	£12	£5	
Delicate Jazz	LP	Capitol	T1017	1959	£12	£5	
Paul Smith	10" LP	Capitol	LC6820	1956	£20	£8	
Paul Smith Quartet	10" LP	Vogue	LDE168	1956	£20	£8	

SMITH, PETER & THE JOHNSONS

Faith, Folk And Nativity	LP	Pilgrim	JLP168	1970	£25	£10	

SMITH, PHOEBE

Once I Had A True Love	LP	Topic	12T93	1970	£15	£6	
Travelling Songster	LP	Topic	12TS304	1976	£15	£6	

SMITH, RAY

Best Of Ray Smith	LP	T	56062	196–	£20	£8	US
Greatest Hits	LP	Columbia	CL1937/CS8737	1963	£15	£6	US
Rocking Little Angel	7"	London	HL9051	1960	£50	£25	
Travellin' With Ray	LP	Judd	JLPA701	1960	£100	£50	US

SMITH, SLIM

Blessed Are The Meek	7"	Unity	UN527	1969	£4	£1.50	
Everybody Needs Love	7"	Unity	UN504	1969	£4	£1.50	*Junior Smith B side*
Everybody Needs Love	LP	Pama	ECO9	1969	£25	£10	
For Once In My Life	7"	Unity	UN508	1969	£4	£1.50	
Greatest Hits	LP	Trojan	TBL198	1973	£10	£4	
Honey	7"	Unity	UN542	1969	£4	£1.50	
I Need Your Loving	7"	Jackpot	JP786	1972	£4	£1.50	
I've Got Your Number	7"	Island	WI3023	1966	£10	£5	
If It Don't Work Out	7"	Jackpot	JP703	1969	£4	£1.50	
Jenny	7"	Unity	UN570	1970	£4	£1.50	
Just A Dream	7"	Dynamic	DYN428	1972	£4	£1.50	
Just A Dream	LP	Trojan	TBL186	1972	£12	£5	
Keep That Light Shining On Me	7"	Unity	UN537	1969	£4	£1.50	
Keep Walking	7"	Jackpot	JP779	1971	£4	£1.50	
Let It Be Me	7"	Unity	UN513	1969	£4	£1.50	
Let Me Love You	7"	Green Door	GD4058	1973	£4	£1.50	
Love Me Tender	7"	Unity	UN539	1969	£4	£1.50	
Rougher Yet	7"	Coxsone	CS7034	1968	£10	£5	
Send Me Some Loving	7"	Pama	PS334	1971	£4	£1.50	
Slim Smith	LP	Lord Koos	KLP1	197–	£20	£8	
Slip Away	7"	Unity	UN520	1969	£4	£1.50	
Somebody To Love	7"	Unity	UN515	1969	£4	£1.50	
Stay	7"	Supreme	SUP219	1971	£4	£1.50	
Sunny Side Of The Sea	7"	Unity	UN524	1969	£4	£1.50	
Vow	7"	Gas	GAS132	1969	£4	£1.50	*James Nephew B side*
Watch This Sound	7"	Trojan	TR619	1968	£4	£1.50	
What Kind Of Life	7"	Gas	GAS150	1970	£4	£1.50	*Martin Riley B side*
Zip A Dee Doo Dah	7"	Unity	UN510	1969	£4	£1.50	

SMITH, SOMETHIN' & THE REDHEADS

I Don't Want To Set The World On Fire	7"	Fontana	H154	1958	£4	£1.50	
Put The Blame On Me	10" LP	Fontana	TFR6005	1958	£10	£4	

SMITH, STUFF

Stuff Smith	LP	Columbia	33CX10093	1957	£15	£6	

SMITH, TAB

All My Life	7"	Vogue	V2299	1962	£4	£1.50	
Jump Time	7"	Vogue	V2410	1956	£8	£4	
Music Styled By Tab Smith	10" LP	United	LP001	195–	£50	£25	US
My Happiness Cha-Cha	7"	London	HLM8801	1959	£5	£2	
My Mother's Eyes	7"	Vogue	V2416	1960	£4	£1.50	
Red Hot And Cool Blues	10" LP	United	LP003	195–	£50	£25	US

SMITH, TED

Requiem For A Nobody	LP	Light	LS7003	1973	£20	£8	

SMITH, TERRY

Fall Out	LP	Philips	SBL7871	1969	£40	£20	
Terry Smith	LP	Lambert	LAM002	1977	£30	£15	

SMITH, TRIXIE

Freight Train Blues	78	Vocalion	V1006	1952	£10	£5	
He Likes It Slow	78	Tempo	R42	1951	£10	£5	
My Daddy Rocks Me	78	Vocalion	V1017	1952	£10	£5	
Trixie Smith	10" EP	Ristic	12	195–	£10	£4	
Trixie Smith	10" EP	Poydras	101	195–	£10	£4	
Trixie Smith	10" LP	Audubon		195–	£20	£8	

SMITH, TRULY

I Wanna Go Back There Again	7"	Decca	F12645	1967	£5	£2	
Love Is Me Love Is You	7" EP	Decca	457115	1966	£10	£5	*French*
My Smile Is Just A Frown Turned Upside Down	7"	Decca	F12373	1966	£15	£7.50	
This Is The First Time	7"	MGM	MGM1431	1968	£5	£2	

SMITH, T.V. EXPLORERS

Servant	cass-s	Kaleidoscope	KRLA401162	1981	£20	£10	

SMITH, VERDELLE

I Don't Need Anything	7"	Capitol	CL15481	1966	£6	£2.50	
Tar And Cement	7"	Capitol	CL15456	1966	£4	£1.50	
There's So Much Love Around Me	7"	Capitol	CL15514	1967	£4	£1.50	

SMITH, WARREN

First Country Collection	LP	Liberty	LRP3199/ LST7199	1961	**£25**	**£10**	US
I Don't Believe I'll Fall In Love	7"	London	HL7101	1960	**£20**	**£10**	export
Judge And Jury	7"	Liberty	LIB55699	1964	**£8**	**£4**	
Odds And Ends	7"	London	HLG7110	1961	**£20**	**£10**	

SMITH, WHISPERING

Over Easy	LP	Blue Horizon	2431015	1971	**£40**	**£20**	

SMITH, WHISTLING JACK

Billy Moeller, brother of the Unit Four Plus Two singer, appeared on television miming to the novelty hit, 'I Was Kaiser Bill's Batman', although he had not been part of the studio team that put the record together. Dressed in an antique military costume to match the title of the tune, he became the unlikely inspiration for a Carnaby Street shop, selling exotic uniforms as fashion items from premises called I Was Kaiser Bill's Batman.

Around The World	LP	Deram	DML1009	1967	**£10**	**£4**	
Hey There Little Miss Mary	7" EP	Deram	15005	1967	**£8**	**£4**	*French*
I Was Kaiser Bill's Batman	7"	Deram	DM112	1967	**£4**	**£1.50**	
I Was Kaiser Bill's Batman	7" EP	Deram	15001	1967	**£6**	**£2.50**	*French*

SMITH, WILLIE

And His Friends	10" LP	Mercury	MG26000	1954	**£40**	**£20**	

SMITH, WILLIE 'THE LION'

Legend Of Willie 'The Lion' Smith	LP	Top Rank	RX3015	1959	**£15**	**£6**	
Willie 'The Lion' Smith	10" LP	London	HAPB1017	1954	**£25**	**£10**	
Willie 'The Lion' Smith	10" LP	Vogue	LDE177	1956	**£20**	**£8**	

SMITH & JONES

Pete And Ben	7"	Alias	ALE02	1989	**£5**	**£2**	

SMITHEREENS

Beauty And Sadness	LP	Little Ricky	LR103	1983	**£15**	**£6**	*US*
Blue Period	CD-s	Enigma	UNVCD21	1990	**£8**	**£4**	*with Belinda Carlisle*
House We Used To Live In	CD-s	Enigma	ENVCD2	1988	**£5**	**£2**	*3" single*

SMITHFIELD MARKET

After Shakespeare	LP	Gloucester	GLS0443	1974	**£400**	**£250**	
London In 1665	LP	Gloucester	GLS0435	1973	**£500**	**£330**	

SMITHS

The Smiths remained with Rough Trade for the major part of their career and saw the record company's fortunes rise along with their own, so that there are no obscure early singles for the Smiths collector to seek out. The single 'This Charming Man', available in three versions, has, however, become quite scarce, despite gaining a respectable position in the lower reaches of the charts. The original cover of 'What Difference Does It Make', showing a film still of Terence Stamp in *The Collector*, is not particularly rare. One suspects that its withdrawal in favour of a cover with Morrissey in identical pose was designed solely to illustrate the song's title.

Ask	12"	Rough Trade	RTT194	1986	**£10**	**£5**	*clear vinyl*
Ask	cass-s	Rough Trade	RT194C	1986	**£6**	**£2.50**	
Ask	CD-s	Rough Trade	RT194CD	1988	**£15**	**£7.50**	
Barbarism Begins At Home	12"	Rough Trade	RTT171	198	**£20**	**£10**	*1 sided promo*
Barbarism Begins At Home	CD-s	Rough Trade	RT171CD	1988	**£20**	**£10**	
Boy With The Thorn In His Side	CD-s	Rough Trade	RT191CD	1988	**£15**	**£7.50**	
Girlfriend In A Coma	cass-s	Rough Trade	RTT197C	1987	**£6**	**£2.50**	
Hand In Glove	7"	Rough Trade	RT131	1983	**£250**	**£150**	*blue sleeve, silver photo*
Hand In Glove	7"	Rough Trade	RT131	1983	**£6**	**£2.50**	*Rough Trade logo on label*
Hatful Of Hollow	CD	Rough Trade	ROUGHCD76	1988	**£15**	**£6**	
Headmaster Ritual	CD-s	Rough Trade	RTT215CD	1988	**£30**	**£15**	
Heaven Knows I'm Miserable Now	CD-s	Rough Trade	RTT156CD	1988	**£15**	**£7.50**	
How Soon Is Now?	CD-s	WEA	YZ0002CD1/CD2	1992	**£12**	**£6**	*2 single set*
I Started Something I Couldn't Finish	cass	Rough Trade	RTT198C	1987	**£6**	**£2.50**	
Last Night I Dreamt Somebody Loved Me	CD-s	Rough Trade	RT200CD	1988	**£12**	**£6**	
Louder Than Bombs	CD	Rough Trade	ROUGHCD255	1987	**£15**	**£6**	
Meat Is Murder	12"	Rough Trade	RTT186	1985	**£100**	**£50**	*test pressing*
Meat Is Murder	7"	Rough Trade	RT186	1985	**£100**	**£50**	*test pressing*
Meat Is Murder	CD	Rough Trade	ROUGHCD81	1985	**£15**	**£6**	
Panic	12"	Rough Trade	RTT193	1986	**£8**	**£4**	*blue vinyl*
Panic	12"	Rough Trade	RTT193	1986	**£8**	**£4**	*'Hang the DJ' stickers*
Panic	7"	Rough Trade	RT193	1986	**£6**	**£2.50**	*'Hang the DJ' stickers*
Panic	CD-s	Rough Trade	RT193CD	1988	**£15**	**£7.50**	
Peel Sessions	CD-s	Strange Fruit	SFPSCD055	1988	**£5**	**£2**	
Queen Is Dead	CD	Rough Trade	ROUGHCD96	1986	**£15**	**£6**	
Queen Is Dead	LP	Rough Trade	RTD36	1986	**£20**	**£8**	*German, green vinyl*
Rank	DAT	Rough Trade	ROUGH126D	1988	**£25**	**£10**	
Reel Around The Fountain	7"	Rough Trade	RT136	1983	**£250**	**£150**	*test pressing*
Shoplifters Of The World Unite	12"	Rough Trade	RTT195	1987	**£6**	**£2.50**	*with carrier bag*
Smiths	CD	Rough Trade	ROUGHCD61	1986	**£15**	**£6**	
Smiths	LP	Rough Trade	RTD25	1984	**£100**	**£50**	*German, multi-coloured vinyl*
Still Ill	7"	Rough Trade	RT161DJ	1984	**£20**	**£10**	*promo*

Title	Format	Label	Number	Year	Mint	VG+	Notes
Strangeways Here We Come	CD	Rough Trade	ROUGHCD106	1987	£15	£6	
Strangeways Here We Come	LP	Rough Trade	RTD60	1987	£15	£6	*German, blue-grey vinyl*
This Charming Man	12"	Rough Trade	RTT136	1983	£8	£4	
This Charming Man	7"	Rough Trade	RT136	1983	£4	£1.50	
This Charming Man (New York remix)	12"	Rough Trade	RTT136NY	1983	£10	£5	
What Difference Does It Make	12"	Rough Trade	RTT146	1984	£8	£4	
What Difference Does It Make?	7"	Rough Trade	RT146	1984	£4	£1.50	
What Difference Does It Make?	CD-s	Rough Trade	RT146CD	1988	£20	£10	
William, It Was Really Nothing	CD-s	Rough Trade	RT166CD	1988	£15	£7.50	
World Won't Listen	CD	Rough Trade	ROUGHCD101	1987	£15	£6	
You Just Haven't Earned It Yet Baby	12"	Rough Trade	RTT195	1987	£50	£25	*mispressing*

SMOKE

The English Smoke managed to maintain a surprisingly long career (including making records under the name of Chords Five) for a group that was essentially a one-hit wonder. That one hit, however, 'My Friend Jack', is something of a psychedelic classic, driven by viciously reverbed and fuzzed guitars.

Title	Format	Label	Number	Year	Mint	VG+	Notes
Dreams Of Dreams	7"	Revolution	REVP1002	1970	£20	£10	
If The Weather's Sunny	7"	Columbia	DB8252	1967	£20	£10	
It Could Be Wonderful	7"	Island	WIP6023	1967	£50	£25	
It's Just Your Way Of Lovin'	7" EP	Impact	200012	1967	£50	£25	*French*
It's Smoke Time	LP	Metronome	MLP15279	1967	£60	£30	*German*
My Friend Jack	7"	Columbia	DB8115	1966	£20	£10	
My Friend Jack	7" EP	Impact	200010	1967	£50	£25	*French*
My Friend Jack	LP	Morgan Blue Town	MBT5001	1988	£12	£5	
Ride Ride Ride	7"	Pageant	SAM101	1971	£20	£10	
Sugar Man	7"	Regal Zonophone	RZ3071	1972	£20	£10	
Utterly Simple	7"	Island	WIP6031	1968	£200	£100	*demo, best auctioned*

SMOKE (2)

Title	Format	Label	Number	Year	Mint	VG+	Notes
Smoke	LP	Sidewalk	ST5912	1968	£30	£15	*US*

SMOKE (3)

Title	Format	Label	Number	Year	Mint	VG+	Notes
At George's Coffee Shop	LP	Uni	73065	1970	£15	£6	*US*
Carry On Your Idea	LP	Uni	73052	1969	£15	£6	*US*

SMOKESTACK LIGHTNIN'

Although the name would suggest a blues group, Smokestack Lightnin' actually played blue-eyed soul, though without very much ambition or even very much soulfulness. The long version of the song after which the group was named is used as a climax to the *Off The Wall* album. The piece becomes stretched out as each member delivers a solo on his instrument – but none is in the least memorable.

Title	Format	Label	Number	Year	Mint	VG+	Notes
Off The Wall	LP	Bell	MBLL/SBLL116	1969	£20	£8	

SMOKEY BABE

Title	Format	Label	Number	Year	Mint	VG+	Notes
Smokey Babe And His Friends	LP	77	LA1212	1962	£20	£8	

SMOKEY CIRCLES

Title	Format	Label	Number	Year	Mint	VG+	Notes
Long, Long, Love	7"	Carnaby	CNS4011	1970	£4	£1.50	
Smokey Circles' Album	LP	Carnaby	CNLS6006	1970	£50	£25	

SMOTHERS, SMOKEY

Title	Format	Label	Number	Year	Mint	VG+	Notes
Backporch Blues	LP	King	779	1962	£100	£50	*US*
Driving Blues Of Smokey Smothers	LP	Polydor	623239	1966	£40	£20	

SMYTH, GILLI & MOTHER GONG

Title	Format	Label	Number	Year	Mint	VG+	Notes
Mother	LP	Charly	CRL5007	1978	£10	£4	

SMYTHE, DONALD

Title	Format	Label	Number	Year	Mint	VG+	Notes
Where Love Goes	7"	Punch	PH83	1971	£5	£2	*Hurricanes B side*

SMYTHE, GLORIA

Title	Format	Label	Number	Year	Mint	VG+	Notes
I'll Be Over After A While	7"	Vogue	V9159	1960	£6	£2.50	

SNAKEFINGER

Title	Format	Label	Number	Year	Mint	VG+	Notes
Chewing Hides The Sound	LP	Ralph	V2140	1980	£10	£4	*with the Residents*
Greener Postures	LP	Ralph	SN8053L	1980	£10	£4	*US, with the Residents*

SNAKEHIPS

Title	Format	Label	Number	Year	Mint	VG+	Notes
Snakehips Arnold And The King Of Boogie	LP	Spaceward	3S2/EDENLP75	1975	£15	£6	

SNAPPERS

Title	Format	Label	Number	Year	Mint	VG+	Notes
If There Were	7"	Top Rank	JAR167	1959	£6	£2.50	

SNAPPERS (2)

Title	Format	Label	Number	Year	Mint	VG+	Notes
Snappers	LP	Elite	PLPS30110	1967	£25	£10	*German*
Upside Down Inside Out	7"	CBS	2719	1967	£6	£2.50	

SNEAKERS

Title	Format	Label	Number	Year	Mint	VG+	Notes
In The Red	LP	Car	0398	1978	£15	£6	*US*

SNEAKY PETES

Title	Format	Label	Number	Year	Mint	VG+	Notes
Savage	7"	Decca	F11199	1960	£5	£2	

SNEEKERS

I Just Can't Get To Sleep	7"	Columbia	DB7385	1964	**£60**	**£30**	

SNIFF 'N' THE TEARS

Driver's Seat	7"	Chiswick	NS40	1979	**£6**	**£2.50**	*test pressing*

SNIVELLING SHITS

Isgodaman?	7"	Damaged Goods	FNARR4B	1989	**£4**	**£1.50**	*box set, pink vinyl*
Terminal Stupid	7"	Ghetto Rockers	PRE2	1977	**£8**	**£4**	

SNODS

Buckle Shoe Stomp	7"	Decca	F11867	1964	**£15**	**£7.50**	

SNOOKY & MOODY

Snooky And Moody's Blues	7"	Blue Horizon	451003	1966	**£100**	**£50**	

SNOW, HANK

Big Country Hits	LP	RCA	LPM/LSP2458	1961	**£15**	**£6**	*US*
Country & Western Jamboree	LP	RCA	LPM1419	1957	**£25**	**£10**	*US*
Country Classics	10" LP	RCA	LPT3026	1952	**£30**	**£15**	*US*
Country Classics	LP	RCA	LPM1233	1955	**£25**	**£10**	*US*
Country Guitar No. 4	7" EP	RCA	RCX116	1958	**£6**	**£2.50**	
Country Guitar No. 7	7" EP	RCA	RCX142	1959	**£8**	**£4**	
Hank Snow Salutes Jimmie Rodgers	10" LP	RCA	LPT3131	1953	**£30**	**£15**	*US*
Hank Snow Sings	10" LP	RCA	LPT3070	1952	**£30**	**£15**	*US*
Hank Snow Sings Jimmie Rodgers Songs	LP	RCA	LPM/LSP2043	1959	**£15**	**£6**	*US*
Hank Snow Sings Sacred Songs	LP	RCA	LPM1638	1958	**£20**	**£8**	*US*
Hank Snow's Country Guitar	10" LP	RCA	LPT3267	1954	**£30**	**£15**	*US*
Hank Snow's Country Guitar	LP	RCA	LPM1435	1957	**£25**	**£10**	*US*
Hits, Hits And More Hits	LP	RCA	LPM/LSP3965	1968	**£10**	**£4**	*US*
I've Been Everywhere	LP	RCA	RD/SF7607	1964	**£10**	**£4**	
Just Keep A-Movin'	LP	RCA	LPM1113	1955	**£25**	**£10**	*US*
My Arabian Baby	7"	HMV	7MC24	1954	**£10**	**£5**	*export*
My Religion's Not Old-Fashioned	7"	HMV	7MC25	1954	**£10**	**£5**	*export*
Old Doc Brown	LP	RCA	LPM1156	1955	**£30**	**£15**	*US*
Poor Little Jimmie	7"	RCA	RCA1248	1961	**£4**	**£1.50**	
Railroad Man	LP	RCA	RD/SF7579	1963	**£10**	**£4**	
Sings Your Favourite Country Hits	LP	RCA	RD7741	1966	**£10**	**£4**	
Songs Of Tragedy	LP	RCA	RD7658	1964	**£10**	**£4**	
Souvenirs	LP	RCA	LPM/LSP2285	1961	**£15**	**£6**	*US*
Spanish Fireball	7"	HMV	7MC15	1954	**£10**	**£5**	*export*
That Country Gentleman	7" EP	RCA	RCX7154	1964	**£8**	**£4**	
Together Again	LP	RCA	LPM/LSP2580	1962	**£12**	**£5**	*US*
When Tragedy Struck	7" EP	RCA	RCX7125	1963	**£6**	**£2.50**	
When Tragedy Struck	LP	RCA	RD27115	1959	**£12**	**£5**	
Why Do You Punish Me	7"	HMV	7MC7	1954	**£10**	**£5**	*export*
Yellow Roses	7"	HMV	7MC31	1954	**£10**	**£5**	*export*

SNYDER, BILL

Bewitched	10" LP	London	HAPB1004	1951	**£10**	**£4**	
Bewitched	7" EP	London	REP1011	1954	**£8**	**£4**	

SOAR, MIKE

Our Side Of The Bridge	LP	Westwood	WRS014	1972	**£25**	**£10**	

SOCIAL SECURITY

I Don't Want My Heart To Rule My Head	7"	Heartbeat	PULSE1	1978	**£5**	**£2**	

SOCIALITES

Jive Jimmy	7"	Warner Bros	WB148	1964	**£10**	**£5**	

SOCIETIE

Bird Has Flown	7"	Deram	DM162	1967	**£20**	**£10**	

SOCOLOW, FRANK

Sounds By Socolow	LP	London	LTZN15090	1957	**£25**	**£10**	

SOCRATES

On The Wings	LP	Peters	PILPS9002	1976	**£12**	**£5**	*US*
Phos	LP	Peters	PILPS9013	1977	**£12**	**£5**	*US*

SODS

Moby Grape	7"	Tap	TAP1	1979	**£8**	**£4**	

SOFT BOYS

Anglepoise Lamp	7"	Radar	ADA8	1978	**£6**	**£2.50**	*picture sleeve*
Can Of Bees	LP	Two Crabs	CLAW1001	1979	**£15**	**£6**	*white & black labels*
Face Of Death	7"	Overground	OVER4	1989	**£4**	**£1.50**	*yellow or white vinyl*
Face Of Death	7"	Overground	OVER4	1989	**£10**	**£5**	*gold vinyl*
Give It To The Soft Boys	7"	Raw	RAW5	1977	**£12**	**£6**	
Give It To The Soft Boys	7"	Raw	RAW5	1977	**£100**	**£50**	*test pressing with 'Vyma Knowl'*
He's A Reptile	7"	Midnight Music	DING4	1983	**£5**	**£2**	

I Wanna Destroy You	7"	Armageddon	AS005	1980	£6	£2.50	
Love Poisoning	7"	Bucketfull Of Brains	BOB1	1982	£5	£2	
Near The Soft Boys	7"	Armageddon	AEP002	1980	£8	£4	
Only The Stones Remain	7"	Armageddon	AS029	1981	£5	£2	
Two Halves For The Price Of One	LP	Armageddon	BYE1	1982	£10	£4	
Wading Through The Ventilator	12"	Delorean	SOFT1P	1985	£6	£2.50	*picture disc*

SOFT CELL

The combination of a singer with a limited, rather tuneless voice and a keyboard player still struggling with the opening chapter of his synthesizer instruction manual was an unlikely recipe for the creation of some of the finest single releases of the eighties. Soft Cell proved that rock music's perennial reliance on the inspired amateur can sometimes strike gold.

12" Singles	12"	Some Bizarre	CELBX1	1982	£40	£20	*6 × 12", boxed*
A Man Can Get Lost	7"	Some Bizarre	HARD1	1981	£6	£2.50	
Down In The Subway (Remix)	12"	Some Bizarre	BZSR2212	1984	£12	£6	
Ghostrider (live)	7"	fan club	no number	1984	£8	£4	*flexi*
Megamix '91	12"	Some Bizarre	no number	1991	£8	£4	*promo*
Memorabilia	12"	Some Bizarre	HARD12	1981	£6	£2.50	
Mutant Moments	7"	Big Frock	ABF1	1980	£50	£25	*with insert*
Say Hello Wave Goodbye (live)	7"	fan club	no number	1983	£10	£5	*flexi*
Say Hello Wave Goodbye '91	CD-s	Mercury	SOFCD1	1991	£5	£2	
Say Hello Wave Goodbye '91	CD-s	Mercury	SOFCP1	1991	£6	£2.50	*picture disc*
Soul Inside	7"	Some Bizarre	BZS2020	1983	£5	£2	*double*
Tainted Love	CD-s	Mercury	SOFCP2	1991	£6	£2.50	*picture disc*
Tainted Love	CD-s	Mercury	SOFCD2	1991	£5	£2	
Tainted Love	CD-s	Mercury	SOFCD2	1991	£10	£5	*leather pouch*

SOFT MACHINE

Alive And Well	LP	Harvest	SHSP4083	1978	£10	£4	
Bundles	LP	Harvest	SHSP4044	1975	£10	£4	
Fifth	LP	CBS	64806	1972	£10	£4	
Fourth	LP	CBS	64280	1971	£10	£4	
Love Makes Sweet Music	7"	Polydor	56151	1967	£75	£37.50	
Seven	LP	CBS	65799	1973	£10	£4	
Six	LP	CBS	68214	1973	£15	£6	*double*
Soft Machine	LP	Probe	4500	1968	£25	£10	*US, wheel cover*
Soft Space	7"	Harvest	HAR5155	1978	£5	£2	*picture sleeve*
Softs	LP	Harvest	SHSP4056	1976	£10	£4	
Third	LP	CBS	66246	1970	£15	£6	*double*
Triple Echo	LP	Harvest	SHTW800	1977	£30	£15	*triple*
Volume 2	LP	Probe	SPB1002	1969	£25	£10	
Volumes 1 & 2	LP	ABC	ABCL5004	1974	£12	£5	*double*

SOFT SHOE

For Those Alone	LP	Aardvark	AARD1	1978	£75	£37.50	

SOFTLEY, MICK

Am I The Red One	7"	CBS	202469	1967	£25	£12.50	
Any Mother Doesn't Grumble	LP	CBS	64841	1972	£25	£10	
I'm So Confused	7"	Immediate	IM014	1965	£10	£5	
Songs For Swingin' Survivors	LP	Columbia	33SX1781	1965	£100	£50	
Street Singer	LP	CBS	64395	1971	£25	£10	
Sunrise	LP	CBS	64098	1970	£25	£10	

SOHO SKIFFLE GROUP

Soho Skiffle Group	7" EP	Melodisc	EPM772	1957	£60	£30	

SOL INVICTUS

Looking For Europe	7"	World Serpent	WS7002	1991	£5	£2	*1 sided*
See The Dove Fall	7"	Shock	SX016	1991	£5	£2	

SOLAL, MARTIAL

At Newport '63	LP	RCA	RD/SF7614	1963	£15	£6	
Martial Solal Trio	10" LP	Vogue	LDE105	1954	£25	£10	

SOLAR PLEXUS

Concerto Grosso (English)	LP	Odeon	E15434684/5	1972	£15	£6	*Swedish double*
Concerto Grosso (Swedish)	LP	Odeon	34573/4	1972	£15	£6	*Swedish double*
Det Er Inte Baten	LP	Harvest	06234975	1974	£10	£4	*European*
Hellrre Gycklare An Hycklare	LP	Harvest	06235166	1975	£10	£4	*European*
Solar Plexus	LP	Polydor	2383222	1973	£12	£5	
Solar Plexus 2	LP	Odeon	34797	1973	£12	£5	*Swedish*

SOLDIER

Sheralee	7"	Heavy Metal	HEAVY12	1982	£8	£4	

SOLEN SKINER

Solen Skiner	LP	Silence	MNW60P	1976	£20	£8	*Swedish*

SOLID GOLD CADILLAC

In common with most British jazz musicians of the time, Mike Westbrook incorporated many elements of rock music within his compositions, while many of the members of his band were equally at home whether playing jazz, rock or somewhere in between. Solid Gold Cadillac was the closest that Westbrook came to leading a straight rock group, although the music is inevitably suffused with a jazz sensibility.

Brain Damage	LP	RCA	SF8365	1973	£15	£6	

Solid Gold Cadillac ... LP ... RCA ... SF8311 ... 1972 **£15** ... **£6** ...

SOLID ROCK BAND

Footprints On The Water ... LP ... Chapel Lane ... RWA1 ... 1978 **£20** ... **£8** ...

SOLITAIRES

Walking Along ... 7" ... London ... HLM8745 ... 1958 **£100** ... **£50** ...

SOLO

Solo ... LP ... ... 197– **£50** ... **£25** ... *US*

SOLO, BOBBY

Una Lacrima Sul Viso ... 7" ... Fontana ... TF[illegible] ... 196[illegible] **£[illegible]** ... **£[illegible]** ... *picture sleeve*

SOLSTICE

Marillion pulled off a considerable feat when they managed to get progressive rock into the album and singles charts at a time when the music was supposed to be deeply unfashionable. A number of other bands were actually working in the same area at the time, one of the best being Solstice – for all that they sounded strongly reminiscent of mid-seventies Yes. Bass player Mark Hawkins was invited to join Marillion in the early days – sadly, he turned the offer down on the grounds that Solstice were more likely to be successful.

Silent Dance ... LP ... Equinox ... EQRLP001 ... 1984 **£25** ... **£10** ...

SOME CHICKEN

Arabian Daze ... 7" ... Raw ... RAW13 ... 1978 **£50** ... **£25** ... *picture sleeve, coloured vinyl*
Arabian Daze ... 7" ... Raw ... RAW13 ... 1978 **£5** ... **£2** ... *picture sleeve*
New Religion ... 7" ... Raw ... RAW7 ... 1977 **£6** ... **£2.50** ... *picture sleeve*

SOMEONE'S BAND

Someone's Band ... LP ... Deram ... SML1068 ... 1970 **£150** ... **£75** ...
Story ... 7" ... Deram ... DM313 ... 1970 **£6** ... **£2.50** ...

SOMERS, GORDON

Sound Of The Beatles ... 7" EP .. Top Ten ... TPSX101 ... 1964 **£5** ... **£2** ...

SOMERS, VIRGINIA

Lovin' Spree ... 7" ... Decca ... F10301 ... 1954 **£4** ... **£1.50** ...

SOMETHING HAPPENS!

Burn Clear ... 7" ... Cooking Vinyl ... WILD001 ... 1986 **£5** ... **£2** ...
Two Chances ... 7" ... Prophet ... PRS002 ... 1986 **£8** ... **£4** ...

SOMMERS, JOANNIE

Behind Closed Doors ... LP ... Warner Bros ... B1348 ... 1960 **£15** ... **£6** ... *US, boxed with booklet*
Come Alive ... LP ... Columbia ... CL2495/CS9295 ... 1966 **£10** ... **£4** ... *US*
For Those Who Think Young ... LP ... Warner Bros ... WM4062/WS8062 ... 1962 **£15** ... **£6** ...
Goodbye Joey ... 7" ... Warner Bros ... WB85 ... 1963 **£4** ... **£1.50** ...
If You Love Him ... 7" ... Warner Bros ... WB150 ... 1965 **£4** ... **£1.50** ...
Johnny Get Angry ... 7" ... Warner Bros ... WB71 ... 1962 **£4** ... **£1.50** ...
Johnny Get Angry ... LP ... Warner Bros ... WM/WS8107 ... 1963 **£15** ... **£6** ...
Johnny Get Angry Vol. 1 ... 7" EP .. Warner Bros ... WEP6121 ... 1964 **£8** ... **£4** ...
Johnny Get Angry Vol. 1 ... 7" EP .. Warner Bros ... WSEP6121 ... 1964 **£15** ... **£7.50** ... *stereo*
Johnny Get Angry Vol. 2 ... 7" EP .. Warner Bros ... WEP6123 ... 1964 **£8** ... **£4** ...
Johnny Get Angry Vol. 2 ... 7" EP .. Warner Bros ... WSEP6123 ... 1964 **£15** ... **£7.50** ... *stereo*
Let's Talk About Love ... LP ... Warner Bros ... WM/WS8119 ... 1964 **£12** ... **£5** ...
Little Girl Bad ... 7" ... Warner Bros ... WB105 ... 1963 **£4** ... **£1.50** ...
Lively Set ... LP ... Decca ... DL(7)9119 ... 1964 **£12** ... **£5** ... *US*
Positively The Most ... 7" EP .. Warner Bros ... WEP6013 ... 1960 **£8** ... **£4** ...
Positively The Most ... 7" EP .. Warner Bros ... WSEP2013 ... 1960 **£15** ... **£7.50** ... *stereo*
Positively The Most ... LP ... Warner Bros ... W(S)1346 ... 1960 **£15** ... **£6** ... *US*
Softly, The Brazilian Sound ... LP ... Warner Bros ... W(S)1575 ... 1965 **£12** ... **£5** ... *US*
Sommers' Seasons ... LP ... Warner Bros ... W(S)1504 ... 1964 **£15** ... **£6** ... *US*
Voice Of The Sixties ... 7" EP .. Warner Bros ... WEP6047 ... 1961 **£8** ... **£4** ...
Voice Of The Sixties ... 7" EP .. Warner Bros ... WSEP2047 ... 1961 **£15** ... **£7.50** ... *stereo*
Voice Of The Sixties ... LP ... Warner Bros ... WM4045/WS8045 ... 1961 **£15** ... **£6** ...

SONG PEDDLERS

Rose Marie ... 7" ... Philips ... BF1352 ... 1964 **£4** ... **£1.50** ...

SONGSTERS

Bahama Buggy Ride ... 7" ... London ... HL8100 ... 1954 **£12** ... **£6** ...

SONIC BOOM

Since the acrimonious split between Pete Kember and Jason Pierce put an end to the career of cult favourites Spacemen 3, Kember has worked under his solo identity, Sonic Boom. Sadly, his continuation of Spacemen 3's characteristic drone style seems very pedestrian in comparison with the flights of fancy created by Pierce's group, Spiritualized. Meanwhile, his attempts to forge a more avant-garde version of the approach lack the sense of excitement and power of the group that should be a major influence – Sonic Youth. (The impact of the guitar drones on 'Octaves' compares very poorly with Lee Ranaldo's earlier 'From Here To Infinity' experimental creation.)

Angel ... CD-s ... Silvertone ... ORECD11 ... 1989 **£5** ... **£2** ...
Octaves ... 10" ... Silvertone ... SONIC1 ... 1990 **£8** ... **£3** ... *orange vinyl*
Soul Kiss (Glide Divine) ... LP ... Silvertone ... OREZLP518 ... 1992 **£15** ... **£6** ... *oil filled cover*
Spectrum ... LP ... Silvertone ... OREZLP506 ... 1990 **£10** ... **£4** ... *rotating disc sleeve*

To The Moon And Back	7"	Silvertone	SONIC2	1991	£8	£4	picture sleeve
To The Moon And Back	7"	Silvertone	SONIC2	1991	£5	£2	

SONIC YOUTH

Sonic Youth have never seemed able to make up their minds whether they want to be a rock group or an avant-garde assembly of noise explorers, with the result that they are frequently both. Guitarists Lee Ranaldo and Thurston Moore have both taken part in side-projects of an extremely listener unfriendly nature. Their love of extreme sound abrasion spills over too into their rock work, giving Sonic Youth a cutting-edge quality that has made them into one of the key shapers of modern rock.

Daydream Nation	LP	Blast First	BFFP34	1988	£12	£5	double, with signed poster
Dirty Boots EP	CD-s	Geffen	DGCD21634	1991	£5	£2	
Flower	12"	Blast First	BFFP3	1986	£10	£5	yellow vinyl
Flower	7"	Blast First	BFFP3	1985	£10	£5	promo
Flower (censored version)/Rewolf	12"	Blast First	BFFP3	1985	£15	£7.50	promo
Into The Groove(y)	CD-s	Blast First	BFUS28CD	1988	£8	£4	credited to Ciccone Youth
Kool Thing	CD-s	Geffen	GEF81CD	1990	£5	£2	
Savage Pencil	12"	Blast First	BFFP3P	1986	£30	£15	signed by S. Pencil
Savage Pencil	12"	Blast First	BFFP3P	1986	£10	£5	
Screaming Fields Of Sonic Love	CD	Geffen	PROCD4577	1994	£20	£8	US promo compilation
Sonic Death	cass	Ecstatic Peace		1984	£15	£6	US
Sonic Youth	LP	Neutral	ND01	1982	£10	£4	US
Starpower	7"	Blast First	BFFP7	1986	£8	£4	with badge & poster
Stick Me Donna Magick Momma	7"	Fierce	FRIGHT015/6	1988	£10	£5	
Stick Me Donna Magick Momma	7"	Fierce	FRIGHT015/6	1988	£20	£10	2 × 1 sided 7"
Teen Age Riot (Edit)	CD-s	Blast First	BFUS34CD	1988	£8	£4	
Walls Have Ears	LP	NOT	NOT1	1986	£50	£25	double

SONICS

Explosives	LP	Buckshot	BSR001	1973	£125	£62.50	US
Here Are The Sonics	LP	Etiquette	LP024	1965	£100	£50	US
Introducing The Sonics	LP	Jerden	JRL7007	1967	£100	£50	US
Merry Christmas	LP	Etiquette	ALB025	1965	£125	£62.50	US, with the Wailers & the Galaxies
Sonics Boom	LP	Etiquette	LP(S)027	1966	£100	£50	US

SONLIGHT

Sonlight	LP	Light			£60	£30	

SONN, LARRY

Larry Sonn Orchestra	LP	Vogue Coral	LVA9040	1957	£15	£6	

SONNY

Inner Views	LP	Atco	SD33329	1967	£20	£8	US
Laugh At Me	7" EP	Atco	107	1965	£8	£4	French

SONNY (2)

Love And Peace	7"	Ackee	ACK127	1971	£5	£2	Larry & Alvin B side

SONNY & CHER

Baby Don't Go	7"	Reprise	R20309	1964	£4	£1.50	
Baby Don't Go	7" EP	Reprise	RVEP60076	1965	£8	£4	French, B side by Jerry Keller
Beat Goes On	7" EP	Atco	118	1967	£8	£4	French
I Got You Babe	7" EP	Atco	101	1965	£10	£5	French
Je M'En Balance Car Je L'Aime	7" EP	Atco	108	1965	£8	£4	French
Just You	7" EP	Atco	102	1965	£8	£4	French
Look At Us	LP	Atlantic	ATL/STL5036	1964	£10	£4	
Petit Homme	7" EP	Atco	117	1966	£8	£4	French
Plastic Man	7" EP	Atco	125	1967	£8	£4	French
Sonny And Cher And Caesar And Cleo	7" EP	Reprise	R30056	1965	£10	£5	
What Now My Love	7" EP	Atco	112	1966	£8	£4	French

SONNY & THE CASCADES

Exciting New Liverpool Sound	LP	Columbia	CL2172	1964	£25	£10	US

SONNY & THE DAFFODILS

Sonny And The Daffodils	7" EP	Ember	EMBEP4538	1963	£25	£10	

SONS & LOVERS

Matters	7"	Camp	602002	1967	£4	£1.50	

SONS OF CHAMPLIN

Follow Your Heart	LP	Capitol	ST675	1971	£15	£6	US
Loosen Up Naturally	LP	Capitol	SWBB200	1969	£30	£15	US double
Minus Stems And Seeds	LP	private		1971	£100	£50	US
Sons	LP	Capitol	SKAO322	1969	£20	£8	US
Welcome To The Dance	LP	CBS	65663	1973	£12	£5	

SONS OF FRED

I, I, I	7"	Parlophone	R5391	1965	£40	£20	
Sweet Love	7"	Columbia	DB7605	1965	£75	£37.50	
You Told Me	7"	Parlophone	R5415	1966	£50	£25	

SONS OF MAN

Sons Of Man	7" EP	Oak	RGJ612	1967	**£250**	**£150**	*best auctioned*

SONS OF PILTDOWN MEN

Mad Goose	7"	Pye	7N25206	1963	**£10**	**£5**	

SONS OF SOUL

Yea Yea Baby	7"	Doctor Bird	DB1037	1966	**£10**	**£5**	

SONS OF THE PIONEERS

Cowboy Classics	10" LP	RCA	LPM3032	1952	**£30**	**£15**	*US*
Cowboy Hymns And Spirituals	10" LP	RCA	LPM3095	1952	**£30**	**£15**	*US*
Favorite Cowboy Songs	LP	RCA	LPM1130	1955	**£15**	**£6**	*US*
Favourite Cowboy Songs	LP	RCA	RD27016	1957	**£12**	**£5**	
How Great Thou Art	LP	RCA	LPM1431	1957	**£12**	**£5**	*US*
One Man's Songs	LP	RCA	LPM1483	1957	**£15**	**£6**	*US*
Sons Of The Pioneers	7" EP	HMV	7EG8069	1954	**£8**	**£4**	
Sons Of The Pioneers	LP	RCA	RD27016	1957	**£15**	**£6**	
Western Classics	10" LP	RCA	LPM3162	1953	**£30**	**£15**	*US*

SONSONG

Sonsong	LP	Zebra	ZM5761	1976	**£20**	**£8**	

SOPWITH CAMEL

Hello Hello	7"	Kama Sutra	KAS205	1966	**£4**	**£1.50**	
Hello Hello	LP	Kama Sutra	KSBS2063	1973	**£15**	**£6**	*US*
Miraculous Hump Returns From The Moon	LP	Reprise	K44251	1973	**£15**	**£6**	
Postcard From Jamaica	7" EP	Kama Sutra	617109	1967	**£30**	**£15**	*French*
Sopwith Camel	LP	Kama Sutra	KLP(S)8060	1967	**£25**	**£10**	*US*

SORCERERS

The German single by the Sorcerers is the first recording to feature drummer Cozy Powell. The group subsequently changed its name to Young Blood and released several singles in the UK.

Love Is A Beautiful Thing	7"	Paletten	667711	1967	**£200**	**£100**	*German, best auctioned*

SORROWS

The Sorrows only had one hit, but their powerful sound makes them one of the great forgotten sixties groups. Lead singer Don Fardon later scored a big hit with 'Indian Reservation'.

Baby	7"	Piccadilly	7N35230	1965	**£25**	**£12.50**	
I Don't Wanna Be Free	7"	Piccadilly	7N35219	1965	**£30**	**£15**	
Let Me In	7"	Piccadilly	7N35336	1966	**£25**	**£12.50**	
Let Me In	7" EP	Pye	PNV24168	1966	**£75**	**£37.50**	*French*
Let The Love Live	7"	Piccadilly	7N35309	1966	**£25**	**£12.50**	
Old Songs New Songs	LP	Miura	10011	1968	**£100**	**£50**	*Italian*
Pink, Purple, Yellow, Red	7"	Piccadilly	7N35385	1967	**£75**	**£37.50**	
Take A Heart	7"	Piccadilly	7N35260	1965	**£12**	**£6**	
Take A Heart	7" EP	Pye	PNV24150	1965	**£75**	**£37.50**	*French*
Take A Heart	LP	Pye	NPL38023	1965	**£100**	**£50**	
Take A Heart	LP	Pye	NSPL38023	1966	**£200**	**£100**	*stereo*
You've Got What I Want	7"	Piccadilly	7N35277	1966	**£25**	**£12.50**	*export picture sleeve*
You've Got What I Want	7"	Piccadilly	7N35277	1966	**£12**	**£6**	

SORT SOL

Marble Station	7"	4AD	AD101	1981	**£6**	**£2.50**	

S.O.S.

Skidmore–Osborne–Surman	LP	Ogun	OG400	1974	**£20**	**£8**	

S.O.U.L.

Can You Feel It	LP	Pye	NSPL28162	1972	**£25**	**£10**	

SOUL, HORATIO

Ten White Horses	7"	Island	WI3132	1968	**£5**	**£2**	

SOUL, JIMMY

I Hate You Baby	7"	Stateside	SS274	1964	**£5**	**£2**	
If You Wanna Be Happy	7"	Stateside	SS178	1963	**£6**	**£2.50**	
If You Wanna Be Happy	7" EP	Stateside	SE1010	1964	**£20**	**£10**	
If You Wanna Be Happy	LP	SPQR	E16001	1963	**£25**	**£10**	*US*
Jimmy Soul And The Belmonts	LP	Spinorama	123	1963	**£20**	**£8**	*US*
Twisting Mathilda	7"	Stateside	SS103	1962	**£5**	**£2**	

SOUL, JUNIOR

Chattie Chattie	7"	Big Shot	BI503	1968	**£6**	**£2.50**	
Hustler	7"	Big Shot	BI527	1969	**£4**	**£1.50**	
Jennifer	7"	Gayfeet	GS205	1970	**£4**	**£1.50**	
Miss Cushie	7"	Doctor Bird	DB1112	1967	**£10**	**£5**	*Lyn Taitt B side*

SOUL, SHARON

How Can I Get To You?	7"	Stateside	SS411	1965	**£40**	**£20**	

SOUL AGENTS

Don't Break It Up	7"	Pye	7N15768	1965	£30	£15	
I Just Want To Make Love To You	7"	Pye	7N15660	1964	£30	£15	
Seventh Son	7"	Pye	7N15707	1964	£30	£15	

SOUL AGENTS (2)

For Your Education	7"	Coxsone	CS7018	1967	£10	£5	*Summertaires B side*
Lecture	7"	Coxsone	CS7027	1967	£10	£5	*Soul Boys B side*

SOUL BROTHERS

Carib Soul	LP	Coxsone	CSL8002	1967	£75	£37.50	
Green Moon	7"	Island	WI282	1966	£10	£5	
Hi Life	7"	Island	WI3039	1967	£10	£5	*Delroy Wilson B side*
Hot Shot Ska	LP	Coxsone	CSL8001	1967	£100	£50	
James Bond Girl	7"	Ska Beat	JB258	1967	£10	£5	*Summertaires B side*
Our Man Flint	7"	Island	WI3016	1967	£10	£5	
Ska Shuffle	7"	Rio	R119	1966	£8	£4	*Hortense & Delroy B side*
Sound One	7"	Island	WI296	1966	£10	£5	*Emillo Straker B side*

SOUL BROTHERS (2)

Good Lovin' Never Hurt	7"	Mercury	MF916	1965	£4	£1.50	
I Can't Believe It	7"	Parlophone	R5321	1965	£8	£4	
I Keep Ringing My Baby	7"	Decca	F12116	1965	£5	£2	

SOUL BROTHERS SIX

Some Kind Of Wonderful	7"	Atlantic	584118	1967	£20	£10	

SOUL CARAVAN

Gettin' High	LP	CBS	63268	1967	£20	£8	*German*

SOUL CHILDREN

Friction	LP	Stax	STX1005	1974	£10	£4	
Genesis	LP	Stax	2325076	1972	£10	£4	

SOUL CITY

Everybody Dance Now	7"	Cameo Parkway	C103	1962	£25	£12.50	

SOUL CITY EXECUTIVES

Happy Chatter	7"	Soul City	SC109	1969	£4	£1.50	

SOUL CLAN

Soul Meeting	7"	Atlantic	584202	1968	£6	£2.50	*picture sleeve*
Soul Meeting	7"	Atlantic	584202	1968	£4	£1.50	

SOUL DEFENDERS

Sound Almighty	7"	Ackee	ACK147	1972	£5	£2	*Count Ossie B side*
Way Back Home	7"	Banana	BA354	1971	£4	£1.50	*Soul Rebels B side*

SOUL DIRECTIONS

Su Su Su	7"	Attack	ATT8011	1970	£4	£1.50	

SOUL EXPLOSION

My Mother's Eyes	7"	J-Dan	JDN4405	1970	£4	£1.50	

SOUL KINGS

Magnificent Seven	7"	Blue Cat	BS169	1969	£6	£2.50	*Rupie Edwards B side*

SOUL LEADERS

Pour On The Sauce	7"	Rio	R134	1967	£8	£4	

SOUL PROPRIETORS

All	7"	Concord	CONSTD74	1965	£150	£75	

SOUL PURPOSE

Hummin'	7"	Island	WIP6040	1968	£10	£5	

SOUL REBELS

Listen And Observe	7"	Banana	BA374	1972	£5	£2	

SOUL RHYTHMS

National Lottery	7"	High Note	HS013	1969	£5	£2	

SOUL RUNNERS

Grits 'n' Cornbread	7"	Polydor	56732	1967	£5	£2	

SOUL SEARCHERS

Salt Of The Earth	LP	Sussex	LPSX4	1974	£15	£6	

SOUL SISTERS

Good Time Tonight	7"	London	HLC9970	1965	£15	£7.50	
I Can't Stand It	7"	Sue	WI312	1964	£20	£10	
Loop De Loop	7"	Sue	WI336	1964	£20	£10	
Soul Sisters	LP	Sue	ILP913	1964	£60	£30	

SOUL SISTERS (2)

Title	Format	Label	Catalogue no.	Year	Mint value	Value	Notes
Wreck A Buddy	7"	Amalgamated	AMG839	1969	**£5**	**£2**	

SOUL SOUNDS

Soul Survival is an album of R&B instrumentals played by various ex-Savages and Rebel Rousers. Soul Sounds was not a working group, but the musicians could play this kind of music with one arm tied behind their backs and the record is a convincing addition to the genre, if a little out of date for 1967.

Title	Format	Label	Catalogue no.	Year	Mint value	Value	Notes
Soul Survival	LP	Columbia	SX6158	1967	**£10**	**£4**	

SOUL STIRRERS

Title	Format	Label	Catalogue no.	Year	Mint value	Value	Notes
Soul Stirrers Featuring Sam Cooke	LP	London	HAU8232	1965	**£25**	**£10**	

SOUL SURVIVORS

Title	Format	Label	Catalogue no.	Year	Mint value	Value	Notes
Explosion	7"	Stateside	SS2094	1968	**£4**	**£1.50**	
Expressway To Your Heart	7"	Stateside	SS2057	1967	**£8**	**£4**	
When The Whistle Blows Anything Goes	LP	Crimson	LP502	1967	**£30**	**£15**	*US*

SOUL SYNDICATE

Title	Format	Label	Catalogue no.	Year	Mint value	Value	Notes
Riot	7"	Green Door	GD4021	1972	**£5**	**£2**	

SOUL TWINS

Title	Format	Label	Catalogue no.	Year	Mint value	Value	Notes
Little Suzie	7"	High Note	HS043	1970	**£5**	**£2**	

SOUL VENDORS

Title	Format	Label	Catalogue no.	Year	Mint value	Value	Notes
Captain Cojoe	7"	Studio One	SO2070	1968	**£12**	**£6**	*Jackie Mittoo B side*
Drum Song	7"	Coxsone	CS7031	1967	**£10**	**£5**	*Cool Spoon B side*
Evening Time	7"	Studio One	SO2048	1968	**£12**	**£6**	*Righteous Flames*
Fat Fish	7"	Coxsone	CS7029	1967	**£10**	**£5**	*Marcia Griffiths B side*
Grooving Steady	7"	Coxsone	CS7037	1968	**£10**	**£5**	*Roy Richards B side*
Hot Rod	7"	Studio One	SO2034	1967	**£12**	**£6**	*Gaylads B side*
On Tour	LP	Coxsone	CSL8010	1967	**£100**	**£50**	
Real Rock	7"	Coxsone	CS7057	1968	**£10**	**£5**	*Al Campbell B side*
Rocking Sweet Pea	7"	Studio One	SO2018	1967	**£12**	**£6**	*Joe Higgs B side*
Sixth Figure	7"	Coxsone	CS7084	1969	**£10**	**£5**	*Denzil Laing B side*
Soul Joint	7"	Studio One	SO2066	1968	**£12**	**£6**	
To Sir With Love	7"	Blue Cat	BS112	1968	**£8**	**£4**	*Righteous Flames B side*
You Troubled Me	7"	Coxsone	CS7028	1967	**£10**	**£5**	*Bop & The Beltones B side*

SOULE, GEORGE

Title	Format	Label	Catalogue no.	Year	Mint value	Value	Notes
Get Involved	7"	United Artists	UP35771	1975	**£6**	**£2.50**	

SOULETTES

Title	Format	Label	Catalogue no.	Year	Mint value	Value	Notes
All Of Your Loving	7"	Jackpot	JP767	1971	**£5**	**£2**	*LLoyd Clarke B side*
Let It Be	7"	Upsetter	US337	1970	**£5**	**£2**	*Upsetters B side*
My Desire	7"	Jackpot	JP766	1971	**£4**	**£1.50**	

SOULFUL STRINGS

Title	Format	Label	Catalogue no.	Year	Mint value	Value	Notes
Burning Spear	7"	Chess	CRS8068	1967	**£10**	**£5**	
Groovin' With The Soulful Strings	LP	Chess	CRLS4534	1969	**£12**	**£5**	

SOULMATES

Title	Format	Label	Catalogue no.	Year	Mint value	Value	Notes
Bring Your Love Back Home	7"	Parlophone	R5407	1966	**£5**	**£2**	
Is That You	7"	Parlophone	R5601	1967	**£4**	**£1.50**	
Mood Melancholy	7"	Parlophone	R5506	1966	**£4**	**£1.50**	
Too Late To Say You're Sorry	7"	Parlophone	R5334	1965	**£5**	**£2**	

SOULMATES (2)

Title	Format	Label	Catalogue no.	Year	Mint value	Value	Notes
On The Move	7"	Amalgamated	AMG842	1969	**£6**	**£2.50**	
Them A Laugh And A Ki Ki	7"	Amalgamated	AMG836	1969	**£6**	**£2.50**	

SOUND

Title	Format	Label	Catalogue no.	Year	Mint value	Value	Notes
Physical World	7"	Tortch	TOR003	1979	**£12**	**£6**	
Sound	LP	Tortch	TOR008	1979	**£15**	**£6**	

SOUND BARRIER

Title	Format	Label	Catalogue no.	Year	Mint value	Value	Notes
She Always Comes Back To Me	7"	Beacon	BEA109	1968	**£6**	**£2.50**	

SOUND DIMENSION

Title	Format	Label	Catalogue no.	Year	Mint value	Value	Notes
Baby Face	7"	Bamboo	BAM7	1969	**£4**	**£1.50**	*Gladiators B side*
Black Onion	7"	Bamboo	BAM14	1969	**£4**	**£1.50**	
Doctor Sappa Too	7"	Bamboo	BAM5	1969	**£4**	**£1.50**	
In The Summertime	7"	Banana	BA313	1970	**£4**	**£1.50**	
Jamaica Rag	7"	Bamboo	BAM9	1969	**£4**	**£1.50**	*C. Marshall B side*
More Games	7"	Supreme	SUP202	1970	**£5**	**£2**	*Mr Foundation B side*
More Scorcia	7"	Coxsone	CS7093	1969	**£10**	**£5**	*Lennie Hibbert B side*
My Sweet Lord	7"	Banana	BA338	1970	**£4**	**£1.50**	*Dennis Brown B side*
Poison Ivy	7"	Bamboo	BAM18	1970	**£4**	**£1.50**	
Scorcia	7"	Coxsone	CS7083	1969	**£10**	**£5**	*Cecil & Jackie B side*
Soulful Strut	7"	Coxsone	CS7090	1969	**£10**	**£5**	

Title	Format	Label	Cat. No.	Year	Mint	VG+	Notes
Time Is Tight	7"	Coxsone	CS7097	1969	£10	£5	Barry Llewellyn B side
Whoopee	7"	Bamboo	BAM13	1969	£4	£1.50	Norma Fraser B side

SOUND NETWORK

Watching	7"	Mercury	MF944	1965	£15	£7.50	

SOUND OF REFLECTION

Brave New World	7"	Reflection	RS6001	1968	£5	£2	

SOUND RIDERS

Sound Riders	LP	Ariola	72657IT	1964	£100	£50	German

SOUND SIXTY-SIX

Flight 4864	7"	Decca	F12323	1966	£4	£1.50	

SOUNDGARDEN

Flower	CD-s	SST	SST231CD	1989	£5	£2	
Hands All Over	10"	A&M	AMX560	1990	£6	£2.50	
Hands All Over	CD-s	A&M	AMCD560	1990	£6	£2.50	
Jesus Christ Pose	CD-s	A&M	AMCD691	1991	£5	£2	
Louder Than Love	12"	A&M	AMY574	1989	£6	£2.50	1 side etched
Rusty Cage	CD-s	A&M	AMCD723	1992	£5	£2	

SOUNDS AROUND

Red White And You	7"	Piccadilly	7N35396	1967	£6	£2.50	
What Does She Do?	7"	Piccadilly	7N35345	1966	£6	£2.50	

SOUNDS GALACTIC

Astronomical Odyssey	LP	Decca	PFS4208	1970	£10	£4	

SOUNDS INCORPORATED

Emily	7"	Parlophone	R4815	1961	£6	£2.50	
Go	7"	Decca	F11590	1963	£4	£1.50	
I'm Coming Through	7"	Columbia	DB7737	1965	£10	£5	
Keep Moving	7"	Decca	F11723	1963	£12	£6	
Rinky Dink	LP	Regal	SREG1071	1965	£10	£4	
Sounds Incorporated	LP	Columbia	SX/SCX3531	1964	£15	£6	
Sounds Incorporated	LP	Studio Two	TWO1449	1966	£10	£4	
Top Gear	7" EP	Columbia	SEG8360	1964	£10	£5	
Twist At The Star Club Hamburg	LP	Philips	P48036L	1964	£20	£8	German

SOUNDS NICE

Love At First Sight	LP	Parlophone	PMC/PCS7089	1969	£20	£8	

SOUNDS OF MODIFICATION

Sounds Of Modification	LP	London	SHAU111	1967	£20	£8	German

SOUNDS OF SALVATION

Sounds Of Salvation	LP	Reflection	RL310	1974	£60	£30	

SOUNDS ORCHESTRAL

Thunderball	7"	Piccadilly	7N35284	1966	£5	£2	
Thunderball	LP	Pye	NPL38016	1965	£25	£10	gatefold sleeve
Thunderball	LP	Pye	NPL38016	1965	£15	£6	

SOUNDS PROGRESSIVE

Kid Jensen Introduces Sounds Progressive	LP	Eyemark	EMCL1009	1970	£50	£25	

SOUNDS SENSATIONAL

Love In The Open Air	7"	HMV	POP1584	1967	£6	£2.50	

SOUNDSVILLE

Soundsville	LP	Spectrum	187	1962	£50	£25	US

SOUNDTRACK

Addams Family	LP	RCA	LPM/LSP3421	1964	£20	£8	US, by Vic Muzzy
Adventurers	LP	Paramount	SPFL260	1970	£10	£4	by Antonio Carlos Jobim
Advise And Consent	LP	RCA	RD7512	1962	£10	£4	by Jerry Fielding
Africa	LP	MGM	(S)E4462	1967	£20	£8	US, by Alex North
Africa Addio	LP	United Artists	(S)ULP1172	1967	£15	£6	by Riz Ortolani
After The Fox	LP	United Artists	(S)ULP1151	1966	£25	£10	by Burt Bacharach
Agony And The Ecstasy	LP	Capitol	(S)MAS2427	1965	£30	£15	US, by Alex North
Alakazam The Great	LP	Vee Jay	LP6000	1961	£25	£10	US, by Les Baxter
Alamo	LP	Philips	BBL7429/ SBBL599	1960	£10	£4	by Dimitri Tiomkin
Alexander The Great	10" LP	Nixa	NPT19010	1956	£150	£75	by Mario Nascimbene
Alfred The Great	LP	MGM	CS8112	1969	£100	£50	by Raymond Leppard
Alice In Wonderland	LP	Argo	ZTA501/2	1970	£15	£6	double
All Night Long	LP	Fontana	STFL591	1961	£20	£8	by Ira Newborn & Richard Hazard
Ambassador	LP	RCA	SER5618	1971	£15	£6	
Americanization Of Emily	LP	Reprise	R6151	1965	£15	£6	by Johnny Mandel
Amorous Adventures Of Moll Flanders	LP	RCA	RD7732	1965	£25	£10	by John Addison

Title	Format	Label	Cat. No.	Year	Mint	Price	Notes
Anastasia	LP	Brunswick	LAT8175	1957	**£10**	**£4**	*by Alfred Newman*
Anne Of Green Gables	LP	CBS	70053	1970	**£10**	**£4**	
Anthony And Cleopatra	LP	Polydor	2383109	1972	**£25**	**£10**	*by John Scott*
Apartment	LP	London	HAT2287	1960	**£20**	**£8**	*by Adolph Deutsch*
April Fools	LP	CBS	70054	1969	**£10**	**£4**	*by Marvin Hamlisch*
As Long As They're Happy	10" LP	HMV	DLPC1	1954	**£40**	**£20**	*by Jack Buchanan*
Barabbas	LP	Pye	NPL28020	1962	**£25**	**£10**	*by Mario Nascimbene*
Barbarella	LP	Stateside	(S)SL10260	1968	**£60**	**£30**	*by Bob Crewe*
Barefoot In The Park	LP	London	HAD8337	1967	**£20**	**£8**	*by Neal Hefti*
Battle Of The Bulge	LP	Warner Bros	W1617	1966	**£20**	**£8**	*by Benjamin Frankel*
Beau James	LP	London	HAP2056	1957	**£10**	**£4**	*by Joseph Lilley*
Becket	LP	RCA	RD7679	1964	**£10**	**£4**	
Behold A Pale Horse	LP	Colpix	(S)CP519	1964	**£30**	**£15**	*US, by Maurice Jarre*
Belle – Or The Ballad Of Doctor Crippen	LP	Decca	SKL4136	1961	**£10**	**£4**	
Bells Are Ringing	LP	Capitol	(S)W1435	1960	**£10**	**£4**	*by André Previn*
Ben Hur	LP	MGM	C802	1960	**£10**	**£4**	*by Miklos Rozsa, mono*
Ben Hur	LP	MGM	CS802	1960	**£15**	**£6**	*by Miklos Rozsa, stereo*
Ben Hur – More Music	LP	MGM	C857	1960	**£10**	**£4**	*by Miklos Rozsa, mono*
Ben Hur – More Music	LP	MGM	CS857	1960	**£15**	**£6**	*by Miklos Rozsa, stereo*
Beyond The Valley Of The Dolls	LP	Stateside	SSL10311	1970	**£60**	**£30**	*by Stu Phillips*
Bible	LP	Stateside	(S)SL10188	1966	**£10**	**£4**	*by Toshiro Mayuzumi*
Big Country	LP	London	HAT2142	1958	**£15**	**£6**	
Biggest Bundle Of Them All	LP	MGM	C(S)8066	1968	**£15**	**£6**	*by Riz Ortolani*
Biggles	LP	MCA	MCF3328	1986	**£10**	**£4**	*by Stanilas*
Billion Dollar Brain	LP	United Artists	(S)ULP1183	1967	**£20**	**£8**	*by Richard Rodney Bennett*
Billy Jack	LP	Warner Bros	WS1926	1971	**£10**	**£4**	
Bittersweet	LP	MFP	MFP1091	1970	**£10**	**£4**	
Blitz!	LP	HMV	CLP1569/CSD1441	1962	**£10**	**£4**	
Blue	LP	Dot	(S)LPD508	1968	**£25**	**£10**	*by Manos Hadjidakis*
Blue Max	LP	Mainstream	5/S6081	1966	**£20**	**£8**	*US, by Jerry Goldsmith*
Boccaccio '70	LP	RCA	FOC/FSO5	1962	**£30**	**£15**	*US*
Bonnie And Clyde	LP	Warner Bros	W1742	1968	**£15**	**£6**	*by Charles Strouse*
Borsalino	LP	Paramount	SPFL263	1970	**£15**	**£6**	*by Claude Bolling*
Boy On A Dolphin	LP	Brunswick	LAT8193	1957	**£30**	**£15**	*by Hugo Friedhoffer*
Bullitt	LP	Warner Bros	WS1777	1968	**£30**	**£15**	*US, by Lalo Schifrin*
Burke's Law	LP	Liberty	LBY1246	1964	**£20**	**£8**	*by Herschel Burke Gilbert*
Candy	LP	Stateside	(S)SL10276	1969	**£10**	**£4**	
Captain Horatio Hornblower	LP	Delyse	D3057/DS6057	1960	**£60**	**£30**	*by Robert Farnon*
Card	LP	Pye	NPL/NSPL18408	1965	**£20**	**£8**	
Carmen Jones	LP	Brunswick	LAT8057	1955	**£15**	**£6**	
Cat Ballou	LP	Capitol	T2340	1965	**£10**	**£4**	
Chapman Report	LP	Warner Bros	WS8177	1962	**£10**	**£4**	*by Leonard Rosenman*
Charade	LP	RCA	SF7620	1963	**£20**	**£8**	*by Henry Mancini*
Che!	LP	Polydor	583736	1969	**£10**	**£4**	*by Lalo Schifrin*
Checkmate	LP	Columbia	CL1591/CS8391	1960	**£30**	**£15**	*US, by John Williams*
Cherry And Harry And Raquel	LP	Beverly Hills	BHS23	1968	**£50**	**£25**	*US, by Bill Loose*
Chimes At Midnight	LP	Fontana	TL5417	1967	**£40**	**£20**	*by Angelo Lavagnino*
Chinatown	LP	ABC	ABCL5068	1974	**£15**	**£6**	*by Jerry Goldsmith*
Chitty Chitty Bang Bang	LP	United Artists	(S)ULP1200	1968	**£10**	**£4**	
Circus Of Horrors	LP	Imperial	9132	1960	**£75**	**£37.50**	*US, by Muir Mathieson*
Cleopatra	LP	Stateside	(S)SL10044	1963	**£10**	**£4**	*by Alex North*
Collector	LP	Fontana	(S)TL5259	1965	**£20**	**£8**	*by Maurice Jarre*
Cool Mikado	LP	Parlophone	PMC1194	1962	**£60**	**£30**	
Countess From Hong Kong	LP	Brunswick	AXA4544	1967	**£10**	**£4**	
Cromwell	LP	Capitol	EST640	1970	**£10**	**£4**	*by Frank Cordell*
Cross And The Switchblade	LP	Word	WST5550	1970	**£20**	**£8**	*by Ralph Carmichael*
Cross Of Iron	LP	EMI	EMA782	1977	**£10**	**£4**	*by Ernest Gold*
Custer Of The West	LP	Stateside	(S)SL10222	1968	**£30**	**£15**	*by Bernardo Segall*
Dames At Sea	LP	CBS	70063	1970	**£15**	**£6**	
Dangerous Friendships	LP	Fontana	TFL5184	1962	**£12**	**£5**	
Decline And Fall Of A Birdwatcher	LP	Stateside	(S)SL10259	1968	**£75**	**£37.50**	*by Ron Goodwin*
Diamond Head	LP	Colpix	PXL440	1963	**£12**	**£5**	*by John Williams*
Diary Of Anne Frank	LP	Top Rank	RX3016	1959	**£50**	**£25**	*by Alfred Newman*
Dick Powell Presents	LP	Dot	DLP3421/25421	1962	**£25**	**£10**	*US*
Dirty Dozen	LP	MGM	C(S)8048	1968	**£10**	**£4**	*by Frank De Vol*
Do Re Mi	LP	RCA	RD27228/SF5107	1961	**£10**	**£4**	
Doctor Dolittle	LP	Stateside	(S)SL10214	1967	**£15**	**£6**	*by Lionel Newman*
Doctor Who Collector's Edition	LP	BBC	2LP22001	1982	**£25**	**£10**	*double with poster*
Dr Faustus	LP	CBS	63189	1967	**£75**	**£37.50**	*by Mario Nascimbene*
Drum Crazy (The Gene Krupa Story)	LP	HMV	CLP1352/CSD1296	1960	**£10**	**£4**	
Earthquake	LP	MCA	MCF2580	1975	**£10**	**£4**	*by John Williams*

Title	Format	Label	Number	Year	Mint	VG	Notes
Easter Parade/Singin' In The Rain	10" LP	MGM	D140	1956	£20	£8	*with Judy Garland & Gene Kelly*
Egyptian	LP	Brunswick		1954	£30	£15	*by Alfred Newman*
El Cid	LP	MGM	C(S)6048	1961	£10	£4	*by Miklos Rosza*
Electra Glide In Blue	LP	United Artists	UAS29486	1973	£10	£4	*by James William Guercio*
Emmanuelle 2	LP	Warner Bros	K56231	1974	£10	£4	*by Francis Lai*
Enter The Dragon	LP	Warner Bros	K46275	1973	£15	£6	*by Lalo Schifrin*
Exorcist	LP	Warner Bros	K56071	1974	£15	£6	
Experiment In Terror	LP	RCA	LPM/LSP2442	1962	£30	£15	*US, by Henry Mancini, Lee Remick sleeve*
Expresso Bongo	LP	Pye	NPL18016	1958	£12	£5	
Face In The Crowd	10" LP	Capitol	LCT6139	1957	£15	£6	*by Tom Glazer*
Fall Of The Roman Empire	LP	CBS	(S)BPG62277	1964	£10	£4	*by Dimitri Tiomkin*
Fantasia	LP	Top Rank	30003/4/5	1960	£25	£10	*triple*
Far From The Madding Crowd	LP	MGM	C(S)8053	1967	£15	£6	*by Richard Rodney Bennett*
Farewell To Arms	LP	Capitol	LCT6162	1958	£10	£4	*by Mario Nascimbene*
Fathom	LP	Stateside	(S)SL10213	1967	£25	£10	*by John Dankworth*
Fifty-Five Days At Peking	LP	CBS	SBPG62148	1963	£10	£4	*by Dimitri Tiomkin*
Finian's Rainbow	LP	Reprise	F(S)2015	1964	£10	£4	
Fire Down Below	LP	Brunswick	LAT8194	1957	£30	£15	*by Arthur Benjamin*
Fistful Of Dynamite	LP	United Artists	UAS29345	1972	£10	£4	*by Ennio Morricone*
Flash Fearless Vs The Zorg Women Parts 5 & 6	LP	Chrysalis	CHR1081	1975	£10	£4	
Flintstones	LP	Golden Guinea	GGL0092	1961	£10	£4	
Flintstones In SASFATPOGOBSQALT	LP	Hanna Barbera	HLP8	1966	£10	£4	
Flower Drum Song	LP	Brunswick	STA3054	1962	£12	£5	*stereo*
Flying Clipper	LP	Ace Of Clubs	ACL1166	1964	£20	£8	*by Riz Ortolani*
Follow That Girl	LP	HMV	CLP1366	1960	£20	£8	
Fox	LP	Warner Bros	WS1738	1968	£25	£10	*US, by Lalo Schifrin*
Francis Of Assisi	LP	Twentieth Century Fox	FOX/SFX3053	1961	£60	£30	*US, by Mario Nascimbene & Franco Ferrara*
Free As Air	LP	Oriole	MG20016	1957	£10	£4	
Freedom Road	LP	Fontana	TL5208	1964	£10	£4	
Fritz The Cat	LP	Fantasy	FAN9406	1972	£25	£10	
Fugitive Kind	LP	London	HAT2257	1960	£10	£4	*by Kenyon Hopkins*
Genesis Of The Daleks	LP	BBC	REH364	1979	£15	£6	
Genghis Khan	LP	Liberty	(S)LBY1261	1965	£15	£6	*by Dusan Radic*
Gentle Rain	LP	Mercury	20061MCL	1965	£10	£4	*by Luis Bonfa & Deodato*
Gentlemen Marry Brunettes	LP	Vogue Coral	LVA9003	1956	£20	£8	*by Robert Farnon*
Get Smart	LP	United Artists	UAL3533/UAS6533	1965	£20	£8	*US, by Don Adams*
Giant	LP	Capitol	LCT6122	1957	£10	£4	*by Dimitri Tiomkin*
Girl From UNCLE	LP	MGM	C(S)8034	1966	£30	£15	*by Jerry Goldsmith & Teddy Randazzo*
Girl On A Motorcycle	LP	Polydor	583714	1968	£40	£20	*by Les Reed*
Glory Guys	LP	United Artists	SULP1120	1966	£10	£4	*by Riz Ortolani*
Golden Boy	LP	Capitol	(S)W2124	1964	£10	£4	
Golden Voyage Of Sinbad	LP	United Artists	UAS29576	1973	£10	£4	*by Miklos Rozsa*
Goliath And The Barbarians	LP	American International	1001M/S	1960	£20	£8	*US, by Les Baxter*
Gone With The Wave	LP	Colpix	(S)CP492	1965	£20	£8	*US, by Lalo Schifrin*
Gospel According To St Matthew	LP	Mainstream	(S)54000	1966	£25	£10	*US*
Great Race	LP	RCA	RD7759	1965	£25	£10	*by Henry Mancini*
Greatest Story Ever Told	LP	United Artists	SULP1093	1965	£10	£4	*by Alfred Newman*
Green Hornet	LP	Twentieth Century Fox	TF/S3186	1966	£40	£20	*US, by Billy May*
Groupie Girl	LP	Polydor	2384021	1970	£15	£6	
Guns Of Navarone	LP	Philips	SBBL646	1963	£10	£4	*by Dimitri Tiomkin, stereo*
Guys And Dolls	LP	Reprise	F(S)2016	1964	£10	£4	
Gypsy	LP	Warner Bros	WM/WS8120	1962	£20	£8	*by Jule Styne*
Gypsy	LP	RCA	SER5686	197–	£10	£4	
Hallelujah Trail	LP	United Artists	SULP1106	1967	£10	£4	*by Elmer Berstein*
Hang 'Em High	LP	United Artists	SULP1240	1968	£10	£4	*by Dominic Frontiere*
Harmony Close	LP	Oriole	MG20014	1957	£10	£4	
Harper	LP	Mainstream	(5)6078	1966	£20	£8	*US, by Johnny Mandel*
Heavy Traffic	LP	Fantasy	FT516	1973	£10	£4	
Heidi	LP	Capitol	SKA02995	1968	£40	£20	*US, by John Williams*
Hell To Eternity	LP	Warwick	W(ST)2030	1960	£25	£10	*US, by Leith Stevens*
Hell's Bells	LP	Sidewalk	5919	1969	£30	£15	*US, by Les Baxter*
Hello Dolly	LP	RCA	RD/SF7768	1965	£15	£6	
Hemingway's Adventures Of A Young Man	LP	RCA	MOC1074	1962	£25	£10	*US, by Franz Waxman*
High Spirits	LP	Pye	NPL18100/NSPL83022	1964	£20	£8	
Honey Pot	LP	United Artists	ULP1161	1967	£10	£4	*by John Addison*

Title	Format	Label	Cat. No.	Year	Price	Price	Notes
Hong Kong	LP	ABC	(S)367	1961	**£20**	**£8**	*US*
Horse Soldiers	LP	London	HAT2197	1959	**£25**	**£10**	*by David Buttolph*
Houdini – Man Of Magic	LP	CBS	BRG70027	1970	**£15**	**£6**	
How To Murder Your Wife	LP	United Artists	(S)ULP1098	1964	**£20**	**£8**	*by Neal Hefti*
How To Save A Marriage And Ruin Your Life	LP	CBS	(S)BPG63276	1968	**£10**	**£4**	*by Michel Legrand*
How To Steal A Million	LP	Stateside	(S)SL10187	1966	**£30**	**£15**	*by John Williams*
How To Succeed In Business Without Really Trying	LP	RCA	RD/SF7564	1963	**£15**	**£6**	
Hustler	LP	Kapp	KL/KS1264	1961	**£30**	**£15**	*US, by Kenyon Hopkins*
I Do! I Do!	LP	RCA	RD/SF7938	1968	**£12**	**£5**	
I Want To Live	LP	London	LTZT15160	1959	**£25**	**£10**	*by Johnny Mandel*
Ice Station Zebra	LP	MGM	C(S)8101	1969	**£10**	**£4**	*by Michel Legrand*
In Harm's Way	LP	RCA	LOC/LSO1100	1965	**£20**	**£8**	*US, by Jerry Goldsmith*
In Like Flint	LP	Stateside	(S)SL10207	1967	**£30**	**£15**	*by Jerry Goldsmith*
Inspector Clouseau	LP	United Artists	ULP1201	1968	**£20**	**£8**	*by Ken Thorne*
Instant Marriage	LP	Oriole	PS40062	1965	**£20**	**£8**	
Interlude	LP	RCA	RD/SF7990	1968	**£20**	**£8**	*by Georges Delarue*
Interns	LP	Colpix	PXL427	1962	**£15**	**£6**	*by Leith Stevens*
Is Paris Burning?	LP	CBS	(S)BPG62843	1966	**£10**	**£4**	*by Maurice Jarre*
It Started In Naples	LP	Dot	DLP3324/25324	1960	**£30**	**£15**	*US, by Alessandro Cicognini*
It's A Mad Mad Mad Mad World	LP	United Artists	(S)ULP1053	1963	**£15**	**£6**	*by Ernest Gold*
Italian Job	LP	Paramount	SPFL256	1969	**£50**	**£25**	*by Quincy Jones*
Jack And The Beanstalk	LP	HBR	HLP8511	1967	**£25**	**£10**	*US, by James Van Heusen*
Jack The Ripper	LP	RCA	CAL590	1960	**£40**	**£20**	*US, by Stanley Black*
James Dean Story	LP	Capitol	LCT6140	1957	**£25**	**£10**	*by Leith Stevens*
Jazz Themes From The Wild One	10" LP	Brunswick	LA8671	1954	**£25**	**£10**	*by Leith Stevens*
Jeeves	LP	MCA	MCF2726	1975	**£40**	**£20**	
Jesus Of Nazareth	LP	Pye	NSPH28504	1977	**£10**	**£4**	*by Maurice Jarre*
Jorrocks	LP	HMV	CLP/CSD3591	1966	**£10**	**£4**	
Juliet Of The Spirits	LP	Fontana	(S)TL5317	1967	**£30**	**£15**	*by Nino Rota*
Just For You	LP	Decca	LK4620	1964	**£30**	**£15**	
Justine	LP	Monument	L/SMO5031	1969	**£20**	**£8**	*by Jerry Goldsmith*
Kaleidoscope	LP	Warner Bros	W(S)1663	1966	**£30**	**£15**	*US, by Stanley Myers*
Khartoum	LP	United Artists	(S)ULP1139	1966	**£30**	**£15**	*by Frank Cordell*
King Of Kings	LP	MGM	CS6043	1961	**£15**	**£6**	*by Miklos Rozsa*
Kiss Me Kate	LP	MGM	C753	1954	**£15**	**£6**	
Krakatoa – East Of Java	LP	Stateside	(S)SL10227	1968	**£10**	**£4**	*by Frank De Vol*
La Dolce Vita	LP	RCA	RD27202	1961	**£60**	**£30**	*by Nino Rota*
Lady In Cement	LP	Stateside	(S)SL10267	1969	**£25**	**£10**	*by Hugo Montenegro*
Last Run	LP	MGM	2315072	1972	**£10**	**£4**	*by Jerry Goldsmith*
Legend	LP	United Artists	86002	1985	**£20**	**£8**	*by Jerry Goldsmith*
Legend Of Frenchie King	LP	MFP	MFP50034	1971	**£25**	**£10**	*by Francis Lai*
Leopard	LP	Stateside	(S)SL10058	1964	**£25**	**£10**	*by Nino Rota*
Lilies Of The Field	LP	Columbia	SX1626	1964	**£15**	**£6**	*by Jerry Goldsmith*
Lion	LP	London	M76001	1962	**£100**	**£50**	*US, by Malcolm Arnold*
Liquidator	LP	MGM	CS8029	1966	**£20**	**£8**	*by Lalo Schifrin*
Logan's Run	LP	MGM	2315376	1976	**£10**	**£4**	*by Jerry Goldsmith*
Lolita	LP	MGM	C896	1962	**£20**	**£8**	*by Nelson Riddle*
Long Duel	LP	Polydor	583014	1967	**£15**	**£6**	*by Patrick John Scott*
Long Good Friday	LP	CES	CES1001	1983	**£12**	**£5**	*by Francis Monkman, blue label print*
Long Good Friday	LP	CES	CES1001	1983	**£25**	**£10**	*by Francis Monkman, black label print*
Long Ships	LP	Colpix	(S)CP517	1964	**£50**	**£25**	*US, by Dusan Radic*
Lord Jim	LP	Colpix	PXL521	1965	**£15**	**£6**	*by Bronislau Kaper*
Loss Of Innocence	LP	Colpix	CP508	1962	**£30**	**£15**	*US, by Richard Addinsell*
Lost Command	LP	Cinema	LP8017	1966	**£25**	**£10**	*US, by Franz Waxman*
Madwoman Of Chaillot	LP	Warner Bros	WS1805	1969	**£15**	**£6**	*by Michael Lewis*
Maggie May	LP	Decca	LK/SKL4643	1964	**£10**	**£4**	
Magic Christian	LP	Pye	NSPL28133	1970	**£30**	**£15**	
Major Dundee	LP	CBS	SBPG62525	1966	**£10**	**£4**	*by Daniele Amfitheatrof*
Man For All Seasons	LP	RCA	RB6712/3	1966	**£25**	**£10**	*by Georges Delarue, double*
Man In The Wilderness	LP	Warner Bros	K46126	1972	**£10**	**£4**	*by Johnny Harris*
Man With The Golden Arm	LP	Brunswick	LAT8101	1956	**£20**	**£8**	*by Elmer Bernstein*
Mayerling	LP	Philips	SBL7876	1969	**£50**	**£25**	*by Francis Lai*
McLintock	LP	United Artists	SULP1059	1963	**£20**	**£8**	*by Frank DeVol*
Merry Andrew	LP	Capitol	T1016	1958	**£25**	**£10**	*with Danny Kaye*
Merry Widow	LP	Columbia	TWO234	1968	**£10**	**£4**	
Midas Run	LP	Citadel	CT6016	1968	**£60**	**£30**	*US, by Elmer Bernstein*
Midnight Cowboy	LP	United Artists	UAS29043	1969	**£10**	**£4**	
Mine Fair Sadie	LP	Oriole	MG20054	1961	**£15**	**£6**	
Misfits	LP	United Artists	CLP1481	1961	**£20**	**£8**	*by Alex North*
Mission: Impossible	LP	Dot	(S)LPD503	1968	**£30**	**£15**	*by Lalo Schifrin*
Modesty Blaise	LP	Fontana	TL5347	1966	**£30**	**£15**	*by John Dankworth*
Monte Carlo Or Bust!	LP	Paramount	SPFL255	1969	**£30**	**£15**	*by Ron Goodwin*

Title	Format	Label	Cat. No.	Year	Price	Price	Notes
More Than A Miracle	LP	MGM	C(S)8063	1968	**£10**	**£4**	by *Piero Piccioni*
Most Happy Fella	LP	HMV	CLP1365	1960	**£15**	**£6**	
Mr And Mrs	LP	CBS	70048	1968	**£12**	**£5**	
Munsters	LP	Decca	DL(7)4588	1964	**£25**	**£10**	*US*
Murder Inc.	LP	Canadian American	CALP1003	1960	**£30**	**£15**	*US, by Frank DeVol*
Murderer's Row	LP	RCA	RD7847	1967	**£40**	**£20**	*by Lalo Schifrin*
Mutiny On The Bounty	LP	MGM	CS6060	1962	**£15**	**£6**	*by Bronislau Kaper*
My Geisha	LP	RCA	LOC/LSO1070	1962	**£25**	**£10**	*US, by Franz Waxman*
Mysterious Island	LP	Cloud Nine	CN4002	1985	**£20**	**£8**	*by Bernard Herrman*
Nevada Smith	LP	Dot	DLP3718/25718	1966	**£20**	**£8**	*US, by Alfred Newman*
Nicholas And Alexandra	LP	Bell	BELLS202	1972	**£10**	**£4**	*by Richard Rodney Bennett*
Night Of Music Hall	LP	Ace Of Clubs	ACL1238	1972	**£15**	**£6**	
Night Of The Generals	LP	RCA	RD7848	1967	**£20**	**£8**	*by Maurice Jarre*
Night Of The Iguana	LP	MGM	C994	1965	**£10**	**£4**	*by Benjamin Frankel*
Night They Raided Minsky's	LP	United Artists	(S)ULP1235	1969	**£10**	**£4**	*by Charles Strouse*
Nine Hours To Rama	LP	Decca	LK4527	1962	**£75**	**£37.50**	*by Malcolm Arnold*
No Strings	LP	Decca	LK/SKL4576	1963	**£15**	**£6**	
Obsession	LP	Decca	PFS4381	1976	**£10**	**£4**	*by Bernard Herrman*
Octopussy	CD	A&M	3949672	1983	**£75**	**£37.50**	*by John Barry*
Odessa File	LP	MCA	MCF2591	1975	**£10**	**£4**	*by Andrew Lloyd Webber*
Oh! What A Lovely War	LP	Paramount	SPFL251	1969	**£10**	**£4**	
Oliver	LP	HMV	CLP1459/ CSD1370	1961	**£25**	**£10**	
Oliver	LP	Decca	LK4359/SKL4105	1960	**£10**	**£4**	
Oliver	LP	World Record Club	TP151	1960	**£15**	**£6**	
On The Beach	LP	Columbia	33SX1208	1959	**£30**	**£15**	*by Ernest Gold*
On The Town	LP	CBS	60005	1963	**£30**	**£15**	
One Flew Over The Cuckoo's Nest	LP	Fantasy	FTA3004	1975	**£10**	**£4**	*by Jack Nitzsche*
One Over The Eight	LP	Decca	LK4393/SKL4133	1961	**£15**	**£6**	
Orfeu Negro	LP	Fontana	SFJL950	1970	**£10**	**£4**	*by Luis Bonfa & Antonio Carlos Jobim*
Oscar	LP	CBS	(S)BPG62684	1966	**£10**	**£4**	*by Percy Faith*
Our Man Flint	LP	Stateside	(S)SL10174	1966	**£30**	**£15**	*by Jerry Goldsmith*
Our Mother's House	LP	MGM	(S)E4495	1967	**£20**	**£8**	*US, by Georges Delarue*
Owl And The Pussycat	LP	CBS	70081	1971	**£10**	**£4**	*with Blood, Sweat & Tears*
Panic Button	LP	Musicor	MM2026/MS3026	1964	**£25**	**£10**	*US, by Georges Garavarentz*
Papillon	LP	EMI	EMC3020	1974	**£10**	**£4**	*by Jerry Goldsmith*
Paris Blues	LP	HMV	CLP1499	1961	**£10**	**£4**	*by Duke Ellington*
Parrish	LP	Warner Bros	WS8044	1961	**£20**	**£8**	*by Max Steiner & George Creeley*
Passion Flower Hotel	LP	CBS	BPG62598	1965	**£20**	**£8**	
Patton	LP	Stateside	SSL10302	1970	**£10**	**£4**	*by Jerry Goldsmith*
Peking Medallion	LP	Philips	(S)BL7782	1966	**£25**	**£10**	
Penthouse	LP	Ember	NR5040	1967	**£40**	**£20**	*by John Hawksworth*
Perchance To Dream	LP	Ace Of Clubs	ACL1112	1962	**£10**	**£4**	
Phil The Fluter	LP	Philips	SBL7916	1969	**£25**	**£10**	
Pickwick	LP	Philips	(S)AL3431	196–	**£12**	**£5**	
Picnic	LP	Brunswick	LAT8120	1956	**£20**	**£8**	
Play Time/Les Vacances De M. Hulot . . . etc.	LP	Philips	SBL7858	1968	**£25**	**£10**	*by Jacques Tati*
Point	LP	MCA	MCF2826	1977	**£10**	**£4**	
Preachin', Prayin', Singin' And Shoutin' Gospel	LP	Melodisc	MLP12117	1960	**£10**	**£4**	
Pretty Boy Floyd	LP	Audio Fidelity	AFLP1936/ SD5936	1960	**£20**	**£8**	*US, by William Sandford*
Prisoner	LP	Bam Caruso	WEBA066	1986	**£25**	**£10**	*with booklet, map, poster*
Privates On Parade	LP	EMI	EMC3233	1978	**£20**	**£8**	
Professional Gun	LP	United Artists	UAS29005	1969	**£10**	**£4**	*by Ennio Morricone*
Professionals	LP	RCA	RD/SF7876	1976	**£30**	**£15**	*by Maurice Jarre*
Promises Promises	LP	United Artists	UAS29075	1969	**£10**	**£4**	
Prudence And The Pill	LP	Stateside	(S)SL10248	1968	**£10**	**£4**	*by Bernard Ebbinghouse*
Pulp Fiction	CD	MCA	MCD11103	1994	**£25**	**£10**	*with bonus CD featuring Tarantino interview*
Raggedy Rawney	LP	Silva Screen	FILM033	1988	**£10**	**£4**	*by Michael Kamen*
Ransom	LP	Dart	ARTS65376	1975	**£40**	**£20**	*by Jerry Goldsmith*
Red And Blue	LP	United Artists	(S)ULP1184	1967	**£30**	**£15**	*with Vanessa Redgrave*
Reivers	LP	CBS	70068	1970	**£10**	**£4**	*by John Williams*
Return Of The Seven	LP	United Artists	(S)ULP1156	1967	**£10**	**£4**	*by Elmer Bernstein*
Rise And Fall Of The Third Reich	LP	MGM	C(S)8079	1968	**£15**	**£6**	*by Lalo Schifrin*
Road To Bali	10" LP	Brunswick	LA8578	1953	**£25**	**£10**	*with Bob Hope & Bing Crosby*
Robbery	LP	Decca	LK/SKL4892	1967	**£10**	**£4**	*by Johnny Keating*
Robe	LP	Brunswick	LAT8031	1954	**£15**	**£6**	*by Alfred Newman*

Robert And Elizabeth	LP	HMV	CLP1820/ CSD1575	1965	£10	£4	
Rock Pretty Baby	LP	Brunswick	LAT8162	1957	£60	£30	by Henry Mancini
Rocket To The Moon	LP	Polydor	583013	1967	£60	£30	by John Scott
Rosemary's Baby	LP	Dot	(S)LPD519	1968	£20	£8	by Christopher Komeda
Salome	10" LP	Brunswick	LA8604	1953	£40	£20	by George Duning
Sand Pebbles	LP	Stateside	(S)SL10198	1967	£10	£4	by Jerry Goldsmith
Sandpiper	LP	Mercury	MCL20065	1965	£15	£6	by Johnny Mandel
Scalphunters	LP	United Artists	(S)ULP1190	1968	£10	£4	by Elmer Bernstein
Sergeants Three	LP	Reprise	R2013	1962	£25	£10	by Billy May
Serpico	LP	Paramount	SPFL296	1973	£15	£6	by Mikis Theodorakis
Seventh Voyage Of Sinbad	LP	United Artists	UAS29763	1974	£20	£8	by Bernard Herrman
Shaft's Big Score	LP	MGM	2315115	1972	£10	£4	
Shakespeare Wallah	LP	CBS	BPG62755	1966	£10	£4	by Satyajit Ray
Shalako	LP	Philips	SBL7867	1968	£20	£8	by Robert Farnon
Sicilian Clan	LP	Stateside	SSL10307	1970	£10	£4	by Ennio Morricone
Silencers	LP	RCA	RD7792	1966	£25	£10	by Elmer Berstein
Six Three Three Squadron	LP	United Artists	ULP1071	1964	£10	£4	by Ron Goodwin
Ski On The Wild Side	LP	MGM	(S)E4439	1967	£20	£8	US, by Billy Allen
Smashing Bird I Used To Know	LP	NEMS	670059	1969	£10	£4	by Bobby Richards
Sodom And Gomorrah	LP	RCA	LOC/LSO1076	1963	£60	£30	US, by Miklos Rozsa
Some Came Running	LP	Capitol	LCT6180	1959	£20	£8	by Elmer Bernstein
Sons Of Katie Elder	LP	CBS	BPG62558	1965	£25	£10	by Elmer Bernstein, with Johnny Cash
Space Is So Startling	LP	Philips	632303BL	196–	£15	£6	
Spanish Affair	LP	London	HAD2079	1958	£40	£20	by Daniele Amfitheatrof
Spartacus	LP	Brunswick	LAT8393	1961	£20	£8	by Alex North
Spy Who Came In From The Cold	LP	RCA	RD7787	1966	£15	£6	by Sol Kaplan
Stagecoach	LP	Fontana	(S)TL5354	1966	£25	£10	by Jerry Goldsmith
Subterraneans	LP	MGM	C864	1961	£10	£4	by André Previn
Summer And Smoke	LP	RCA	LOC/LSO1067	1961	£30	£15	US, by Elmer Bernstein
Summer Song	LP	Wing	WL1172	1967	£15	£6	
Sun Also Rises	LP	London	HAR2077	1957	£15	£6	by Hugo Friedhofer
Sweet Charity	LP	CBS	(S)BRG70035	196–	£10	£4	
Sweet Charity	LP	MCA	MUCS133	1969	£20	£8	by Cy Coleman and Dorothy Fields
Sweet Smell Of Success	LP	Brunswick	LAT8195	1957	£20	£8	by Elmer Bernstein
Swimmer	LP	CBS	70043	1968	£10	£4	by Marvin Hamlisch
Sylvia	LP	Mercury	20057SMCL	1966	£10	£4	by David Raksin
Take A Girl Like You	LP	Pye	NSPL18353	1970	£10	£4	with the Foundations
Take It From Here	LP	Fontana	TFL5103/ STFL534	1960	£10	£4	
Taming Of The Shrew	LP	RCA	VDM117	1967	£30	£15	US, by Nino Rota
Taras Bulba	LP	United Artists	ULP1025	1963	£15	£6	by Franz Waxman
Taxi Driver	LP	Arista	ARTY12	1976	£25	£10	by Bernard Herrman
Tender Is The Night	LP	Twentieth Century Fox	FOX/SFX3054	1962	£75	£37.50	US, by Sammy Fain & Bernard Herrmann
That Riviera Touch	LP	Parlophone	PMC1112	1960	£15	£6	by Ron Goodwin
There's No Business Like Show Business	LP	Brunswick	LAT8059	1955	£10	£4	with Marilyn Monroe
They Came To Rob Las Vegas	LP	Philips	SBL7898	1969	£40	£20	by Georges Gavarentz
They Shoot Horses, Don't They?	LP	Stateside	SSL10305	1970	£15	£6	by John Green
Thoroughly Modern Millie	LP	World Record Club	SH849	1967	£10	£4	
Those Magnificent Men In Their Flying Machines	LP	Stateside	SL10136	1965	£25	£10	by Ron Goodwin
Three Musketeers	LP	Bell	BELLS235	1973	£10	£4	by Michel Legrand
Three Worlds Of Gulliver	LP	Cloud Nine	CN4003	1985	£20	£8	by Bernard Herrman
Three Worlds Of Gulliver	LP	Colpix	CP414	1961	£40	£20	US, by Bernard Herrmann
To Kill A Mockingbird	LP	MGM	MGMC934	1964	£20	£8	by Elmer Bernstein
Tom Browne's Schooldays	LP	Decca	SKL5137	1972	£10	£4	
Tom Jones	LP	United Artists	SULP1062	1964	£10	£4	by John Addison
Tom Thumb	LP	MGM	C772	1959	£10	£4	by Russ Tamblyn
Touchables	LP	Stateside	(S)SL10271	1969	£25	£10	
Trap	LP	Polydor	582004	1966	£25	£10	by Ron Goodwin
Trouble With Angels	LP	Mainstream	5/S6073	1966	£30	£15	US, by Jerry Goldsmith
Tunes Of Glory	LP	United Artists	UAL4086/ UAS5086	1961	£20	£8	US, by Malcolm Arnold
Twisted Nerve/Les Bicyclettes De Belsize	LP	Polydor	583728	1968	£100	£50	by Bernard Herrmann/Reed and Mason
Twister	LP	Decca	SKL5345	1976	£15	£6	
Two For The Seesaw	LP	United Artists	ULP1027	1963	£10	£4	by André Previn
Unforgiven	LP	London	HAT2258	1960	£25	£10	by Dmitri Tiomkin
Valley Of The Dolls	LP	Stateside	(S)SL10228	1968	£25	£10	by André & Dory Previn & John Williams
Vanishing Point	LP	London	SHU8420	1971	£10	£4	
Victors	LP	Colpix	PXL516	1963	£10	£4	by Sol Kaplan

Vikings	LP	London	HAT2118	1958	£50	£25	by Mario Nascimbene
VIPs	LP	MGM	C951/CS6074	1963	£15	£6	by Miklos Rozsa
Viva Maria!	LP	United Artists	(S)ULP1126	1966	£25	£10	by Georges Delarue
Vixen	LP	Beverly Hills	BHS22	1968	£50	£25	US, by Bill Loose
Walk With Love And Death	LP	Citadel	CT6025	1969	£40	£20	US, by Georges Delarue
War Lord	LP	Brunswick	STA8636	1966	£30	£15	by Jerome Moross
Water	LP	London	YEAR2	1985	£15	£6	
Welles Raises Kane	LP	Virtuoso	TPLS13010	1967	£30	£15	by Bernard Herman
What A Crazy World	LP	Piccadilly	NPL/NSPL38011	1964	£12	£5	
What's New Pussycat?	LP	United Artists	ULP1096	1965	£10	£4	
Whiplash Willie	LP	United Artists	(S)ULP1166	1966	£10	£4	by André Previn
Who's Afraid Of Virginia Woolf?	LP	Warner Bros	W1656	1966	£30	£15	by Alex North
Wild Bill Hickock And Jingles On The Santa Fe Trail	LP	London	HAN2023	1957	£12	£5	
Wild Bunch	LP	Warner Bros	WS1814	1969	£30	£15	by Jerry Fielding
Wild In The Streets	LP	Capitol	(S)T5099	1968	£12	£5	
Wind And The Lion	LP	Arista	ARTY111	1975	£10	£4	by Jerry Goldsmith
Withnail And I	LP	Filmtrax	MOMENT110	1987	£20	£8	
Wiz	LP	MCA	MCSP287	1978	£10	£4	
Wizard Of Oz	LP	MGM	C757	1957	£30	£15	
Woman Times Seven	LP	Capitol	(S)T2800	1967	£25	£10	by Riz Ortolani
World Of Suzie Wong	LP	RCA	RD27198	1960	£10	£4	by George Duning
Yellow Rolls Royce	LP	MGM	C997	1965	£10	£4	by Riz Ortolani
Yojimbo	LP	MGM	(S)E4096	1962	£50	£25	US, by Masaru Sato
Young Lions	LP	Brunswick	LAT8252	1957	£20	£8	by Hugo Friedhofer
Young Visitors	LP	RCA	SB6792	1968	£15	£6	
Your Cheatin' Heart	LP	MGM	CS6081	1965	£12	£5	with Hank Williams Jr
Zita	LP	Philips	600287	1969	£40	£20	

SOUP

Soup	LP	Arf Arm	1	1970	£25	£10	US, insert but no cover

SOUP DRAGONS

Deep Trash (Lovegod)	cass	Raw TV Products		1989	£10	£4	
I'm Free	CD-s	Raw TV Products	RTV9CD	1990	£5	£2	
Mother Universe	CD-s	Raw TV Products	RTV8CD	1990	£5	£2	
Sun Is In The Sky	7"	Subway	SUBWAY2	1986	£10	£5	

SOUP GREENS

Like A Rolling Stone	7"	Stateside	SS457	1965	£40	£20	

SOUPHERBS

Soupherbs	LP	Oak	RGJ601	1965	£200	£100	

SOUTH, HARRY ORCHESTRA

Presenting Harry South	LP	Mercury	20081MCL	1967	£15	£6	
Sweeney	7"	EMI	EMI2252	1975	£15	£7.50	

SOUTH, JOE

Introspect	LP	Capitol	E(S)T108	1969	£10	£4	
Masquerade	7"	Oriole	CB1752	1962	£5	£2	

SOUTH COAST SKA STARS

South Coast Rumble	7"	Safari	SAFE27	1980	£5	£2	

SOUTH FORTY

Live At The Someplace Else	LP	Metrobeat	MBS1000	1964	£20	£8	US

SOUTHERN, JERI

At The Crescendo	LP	Capitol	(S)T1278	1960	£10	£4	
Caresses	7" EP	Brunswick	OE9438	1959	£8	£4	
Coffee, Cigarettes And Memories	LP	Columbia	33SX1134	1958	£12	£5	
Fire Down Below	7"	Brunswick	05665	1957	£4	£1.50	
Jeri Gently Jumps	LP	Brunswick	LAT8209	1957	£15	£6	
Man That Got Away	7"	Brunswick	05367	1955	£6	£2.50	
Meets Cole Porter	LP	Capitol	(S)T1173	1959	£10	£4	
Meets Johnny Smith	LP	Columbia	33SX1155	1959	£10	£4	
Occasional Man	7"	Brunswick	05490	1955	£6	£2.50	
Prelude To A Kiss	LP	Decca	DL8745	1958	£12	£5	US
Remind Me	7"	Brunswick	05343	1954	£6	£2.50	
Ridin' High	7" EP	Columbia	SEG7935	1959	£8	£4	
Southern Breeze	LP	Columbia	33SX1110	1958	£12	£5	
Southern Hospitality	LP	Decca	DL8761	1958	£12	£5	US
Southern Style	LP	Brunswick	LAT8100	1956	£15	£6	
Warm	10" LP	Brunswick	LA8699	1955	£20	£8	
When Your Heart's On Fire	LP	Decca	DL8394	1957	£15	£6	US
Where Walks My True Love	7"	Brunswick	05529	1956	£5	£2	
You Better Go Now	LP	Decca	DL8214	1956	£15	£6	US

SOUTHERN, JOHNNY

She's Long, She's Tall	7"	Melodisc	1434	1957	£4	£1.50	

We Will Make Love	7"	Melodisc	1413	1958	**£4**	**£1.50**	

SOUTHERN SOUND

Just The Same As You	7"	Columbia	DB7982	1966	**£250**	**£150**	*best auctioned*

SOUTHERN TONES

Waiting On The Lord	7" EP	Collector	JEN10	1962	**£6**	**£2.50**	

SOUTHLANDERS

Ain't That A Shame	7"	Parlophone	MSP6182	1955	**£12**	**£6**	
Alone	7"	Decca	F10946	1957	**£4**	**£1.50**	
Choo-Choo-Choo Cha-Cha-Cha	7"	Decca	F11067	1958	**£4**	**£1.50**	
Down Deep	7"	Decca	F11014	1958	**£4**	**£1.50**	
Hush A Bye Rock	7"	Parlophone	MSP6236	1956	**£8**	**£4**	
Peanuts	7"	Decca	F10958	1957	**£4**	**£1.50**	
Put A Light In The Window	7"	Decca	F10982	1958	**£10**	**£5**	
Southlanders No. 1	7" EP	Decca	DFE6508	1958	**£20**	**£10**	
Torero	7"	Decca	F11032	1958	**£8**	**£4**	

SOUTHSIDE JOHNNY & THE ASBURY DUKES

Juke Up Album Network	CD	Impact		1992	**£20**	**£8**	*US promo*
Little Girl So Fine	7"	Epic	EPC5230	1977	**£10**	**£5**	
Live At The Bottom Line	LP	Epic	AS275	1976	**£15**	**£6**	*US promo*

SOUTHWEST F.O.B.

Smell Of Incense	7"	Stax	STAX107	1968	**£4**	**£1.50**	
Smell Of Incense	LP	Hip	HIS7001	1969	**£30**	**£15**	*US*

SOVEREIGNS

Bring Me Home Love	7"	King	KG1050	1966	**£4**	**£1.50**	

SOVIET FRANCE

Garista	CD	Charrm	CHARRMCD001	1988	**£12**	**£5**	
Hessian	CD	Charrm	CHARRMCD002	1989	**£12**	**£5**	
Look Into Me	CD	Charrm	CHARRMCD014	1990	**£12**	**£5**	
Norsche	CD	Charrm	CHARRMCD003	1984	**£12**	**£5**	
Soviet France	12"	Red Rhino	RED12	1982	**£10**	**£5**	*hessian sleeve*

SOVINE, RED

Country Music	7" EP	Top Rank	JKP3015	1962	**£8**	**£4**	
Giddy-Up Go	LP	London	HAB8288	1966	**£10**	**£4**	
I Didn't Jump The Fence	LP	London	HAB8343	1967	**£10**	**£4**	
One And Only Red Sovine	LP	Starday	SLP132	1961	**£15**	**£6**	*US*
Red Sovine	LP	MGM	E3465	1957	**£20**	**£8**	*US*
Sixteen Tons	7"	Brunswick	05513	1956	**£30**	**£15**	

SOXX, BOB B. & THE BLUE JEANS

Not Too Young To Get Married	7"	London	HLU9754	1963	**£10**	**£5**	
Why Do Lovers Break Each Others' Hearts	7"	London	HLU9694	1963	**£8**	**£4**	
Zip A Dee Doo Dah	7"	London	HLU9646	1963	**£6**	**£2.50**	
Zip A Dee Doo Dah	LP	Philles	PHLP4002	1963	**£75**	**£37.50**	*US*
Zip A Dee Doo Dah	LP	London	HAU8121	1963	**£60**	**£30**	

SPACE

If It's Real	12"	Hug	HUGG1T	1993	**£20**	**£10**	

SPACE (2)

Space	CD	KLF	SPACECD1	1990	**£30**	**£15**	
Space	LP	KLF	SPACELP1	1990	**£20**	**£8**	

SPACE (3)

Space	LP	Hand	ST5167	1968	**£20**	**£8**	*US*

SPACE (4)

Just Blue	LP	Pye	NSPH28275	1979	**£15**	**£6**	*picture disc*

SPACE ART

Space Art	LP	Ariola Hansa	AHAL8001	1977	**£10**	**£4**	

SPACE OPERA

Space Opera	LP	Epic	32117	1973	**£15**	**£6**	*US*

SPACEMEN

Clouds	7"	Top Rank	JAR228	1959	**£10**	**£5**	
Music For Batman And Robin	LP	Roulette	MG/SR25322	1966	**£20**	**£8**	*US*
Rockin' In The 25th Century	LP	Roulette	MG/SR25275	1964	**£20**	**£8**	*US*

SPACEMEN 3

First Genesis and then Spacemen 3 emerged to prove public schools as an effective, if unlikely, breeding ground for innovative rock music. Spacemen 3 developed rapidly from the first album catalogue of their sixties influences, finding a variety of imaginative ways of texturing electric guitar drones. Though not all of the songs are equally successful, at their best (such as on the album length 12" single 'Transparent Radiation' and on all of the records of the group's main successor, Spiritualized) the result is music that is both moving and magisterial. The demise of the Glass label has ensured that original pressings of the group's records are rising in value, even though album reissues on the Fire label are readily available.

Big City	CD-s	Fire	BLAZE41CD	1991	**£5**	**£2**	

Big City (remix)/I Love You	12"	Fire	BLAZE41TR	1991	**£50**	**£25**	*test pressing*
Dreamweapon	CD	Fierce	FRIGHT042CD	1990	**£15**	**£6**	
Dreamweapon	LP	Fierce	FRIGHT042	1990	**£10**	**£4**	
Extract From A Contemporary Sitar Evening	7"	Cheree	CHEREE5	1989	**£8**	**£4**	*flexi, B side by Bark Psychosis & Fury Things*
Hypnotized	CD-s	Fire	BLAZE36CD	1989	**£5**	**£2**	
Perfect Precription	LP	Glass	GLALP026	1987	**£15**	**£6**	
Performance	CD	Glass	GLACD030	1988	**£15**	**£6**	
Performance	LP	Glass	GLALP030	1988	**£15**	**£6**	
Revolution	12"	Fire	THREEBIE3	1989	**£20**	**£10**	
Revolution	CD-s	Fire	BLAZE29CD	1988	**£5**	**£2**	
Sound Of Confusion	LP	Glass	GLALP018	1986	**£15**	**£6**	
Take Me To The Other Side	12"	Glass	GLASS12054	1988	**£15**	**£7.50**	
Taking Drugs	LP	private	FYPL25	1986	**£10**	**£4**	
Transparent Radiation	12"	Glass	GLAEP108	1987	**£60**	**£30**	
Walkin' With Jesus	12"	Glass	GLAEP105	1986	**£40**	**£20**	*lyric insert*
When Tomorrow Hits	7"	Sniffin' Rock	SR008A7	1990	**£10**	**£5**	*with magazine*

SPADES

Subsequent issues of 'You're Gonna Miss Me' were credited to the group's new name – the Thirteenth Floor Elevators.

You're Gonna Miss Me	7"	Zero	10002	1966	**£150**	**£75**	*US*

SPAGHETTI JUNCTION

Work's Nice – If You Can Get It	7"	Columbia	DB8935	1972	**£6**	**£2.50**	

SPANDAU BALLET

Be Free With Your Love	CD-s	CBS	SPANSP4	1989	**£5**	**£2**	*picture disc*
Be Free With Your Love	CD-s	CBS	SPANSC4	1989	**£5**	**£2**	
Crashed Into Love	CD-s	CBS	SPANSC6	1990	**£5**	**£2**	
Crashed Into Love	CD-s	CBS	SPANSD6	1990	**£5**	**£2**	
Diamond	LP	Chrysalis	CBOX1353	1982	**£10**	**£4**	*boxed set of 4 × 12"*
Empty Spaces	CD-s	CBS	SPANSD5	1989	**£5**	**£2**	
Empty Spaces	CD-s	CBS	SPANSC5	1989	**£5**	**£2**	
Raw	CD-s	CBS	SPANSD3	1988	**£5**	**£2**	
Raw	CD-s	CBS	SPANSC3	1988	**£5**	**£2**	

SPANIELS

Goodnite, It's Time To Go	LP	Vee Jay	LP1002	1958	**£300**	**£180**	*US*
Spaniels	LP	Joy	JOYS197	1971	**£10**	**£4**	
Spaniels	LP	Vee Jay	LP1024	1960	**£150**	**£75**	*US*

SPANIER, MUGGSY

Broadcasts This Is Is Jazz	10" LP	Vogue	LDE015	1953	**£20**	**£8**	
Gem Of The Ocean	LP	MGM	C936	1963	**£10**	**£4**	
Great Sixteen	LP	RCA	RD27132	1959	**£20**	**£8**	
Muggsy Spanier And His Band	10" LP	Brunswick	LA8722	1955	**£20**	**£8**	
Muggsy Spanier And His Dixieland Band	LP	Mercury	MPL6516	1957	**£15**	**£6**	
Muggsy Spanier And His Ragtime Band	10" LP	HMV	DLP1031	1954	**£20**	**£8**	
Muggsy Spanier And The Bucktown Five	10" LP	London	AL3528	1954	**£20**	**£8**	

SPANISH BOYS

I Am Alone	7"	Blue Beat	BB331	1965	**£12**	**£6**	

SPANISHTOWN SKABEATS

Solomon	7"	Blue Beat	BB320	1965	**£12**	**£6**	

SPANKY & OUR GANG

Like To Get To Know You	LP	Mercury	SMCL20121	1968	**£10**	**£4**	
Spank's Greatest Hits	LP	Mercury	SR61227	1970	**£10**	**£4**	*US*
Spanky & Our Gang	LP	Mercury	(S)MCL20114	1967	**£10**	**£4**	
Without Rhyme Or Reason	LP	Mercury	SR61183	1968	**£10**	**£4**	*US*

SPANN, OTIS

Biggest Thing Since Colossus	LP	Blue Horizon	763217	1969	**£60**	**£30**	*with Fleetwood Mac*
Blues Are Where It's At	LP	HMV	CLP/CSD3609	1963	**£20**	**£8**	
Blues Never Die	LP	Stateside	SL10169	1966	**£20**	**£8**	
Blues Of Otis Spann	LP	Decca	LK4615	1964	**£60**	**£30**	
Bottom Of The Blues	LP	Stateside	(S)SL10255	1968	**£20**	**£8**	
Can't Do Me No Good	7"	Blue Horizon	573142	1968	**£6**	**£2.50**	
Cracked Spanner Head	LP	Deram	DML/SML1036	1969	**£30**	**£15**	
Cryin' Time	LP	Vanguard	VSD6514	1970	**£10**	**£4**	
Good Morning Mr Blues	LP	Storyville	SLP157	1964	**£20**	**£8**	
Nobody Knows My Troubles	LP	Bounty	BY6037	1967	**£20**	**£8**	
Nobody Knows My Troubles	LP	Polydor	545030	1967	**£20**	**£8**	
Otis Spann Is The Blues	LP	Candid	CJS9001	1960	**£40**	**£20**	*US*
Piano Blues	LP	Storyville	SLP168	1965	**£20**	**£8**	*with Memphis Slim*
Portraits In Blues Vol. 3	LP	Storyville	670157	1967	**£10**	**£4**	
Raised In Mississippi	LP	Python	KM4	1969	**£40**	**£20**	
Stirs Me Up	7"	Decca	F11972	1964	**£6**	**£2.50**	
Walkin'	7"	Blue Horizon	573155	1969	**£10**	**£5**	*with Fleetwood Mac*

SPARKERS

Dip It Up	7"	Blue Cat	BS155	1969	**£8**	**£4**	

SPARKES, LOU

By The Time I Get To Phoenix	7"	Gayfeet	GS203	1969	£5	£2	
We Will Make Love	7"	Gayfeet	GS208	1970	£5	£2	*Roland Alphonso B side*

SPARKLES

Tell Me	7" EP	DMF		196–	£12	£6	*French*

SPARKS

Beat The Clock	12"	Virgin	VS27012	1979	£6	£2.50	*various coloured vinyls*
Girl From Germany	7"	Bearsville	K15516	1974	£4	£1.50	
Gratuitous Sax And Senseless Violins	CD	Logic	74321243022	1994	£60	£30	*promo sampler*
I Like Girls	7"	Island	WIP6377	1976	£4	£1.50	
I Want To Hold Your Hand	7"	Island	WIP6282	1976	£12	£6	
Introducing Sparks	LP	Columbia	PC34901	1976	£30	£15	*US red vinyl promo*
National Crime Awareness Week	12"	Finiflex	FF1004	1994	£6	£2.50	
National Crime Awareness Week	CD-s	Finiflex	FFCD1004	1994	£15	£7.50	
Never Turn Your Back On Mother Earth	7"	Island	WIP6211	1974	£4	£1.50	
Number One Song In Heaven	12"	Virgin	VS24412	1979	£6	£2.50	*blue or red vinyl*
Number One Song In Heaven	7"	Virgin	VS244	1979	£5	£2	*green vinyl*
Number One Song In Heaven	CD-s	Roadrunner	RR22629	1997	£5	£2	
Tips For Teens	12"	Why	WHYT1	1981	£6	£2.50	
Tryouts For The Human Race	12"	Virgin	VS28912	1979	£6	£2.50	*various coloured vinyls*
Wonder Girl	7"	Bearsville	K15505	1972	£8	£4	
Young Girls	12"	Virgin	VS34312	1980	£6	£2.50	

SPARKS, RANDY

Birmingham Train	7"	HMV	POP683	1959	£4	£1.50	

SPARLING, CANDY

Can You Keep A Secret	7"	Piccadilly	7N35096	1963	£4	£1.50	
When's He Gonna Kiss Me?	7"	Piccadilly	7N35046	1962	£4	£1.50	

SPARROW

Carnival Boycott	7"	Kalypso	XX10	1960	£4	£1.50	
Clara Honey Bunch	7"	Melodisc	CAL17	1964	£4	£1.50	
Goaty	7"	Melodisc	CAL18	1964	£4	£1.50	
Greetings From Sparrow	7" EP	Kalypso	XXEP5	1961	£6	£2.50	
Hotter Than Ever	LP	Trojan	TRL49	1972	£10	£4	
Leading Calypsonians	7"	Melodisc	CAL15	1964	£4	£1.50	
Man, Dig This Sparrow	7" EP	Kalypso	XXEP2	1960	£6	£2.50	
Mighty Sparrow	7" EP	Kalypso	XXEP1	1960	£6	£2.50	
Mr Herbert	7"	Kalypso	XX22	1960	£4	£1.50	
Mr Walker	7"	Nems	3558	1968	£4	£1.50	
Party With The Sparrow	7" EP	Kalypso	XXEP3	1960	£6	£2.50	
Sack	7"	Kalypso	XX17	1960	£4	£1.50	
Slave	LP	Island	ILP902	1963	£40	£20	
Sparrow Come Back	LP	RCA	SF7516	1962	£25	£10	
Sparrow Meets The Dragon	LP	Trojan	TRL8	1969	£10	£4	*with Byron Lee*
Sparrow The Conqueror	7" EP	Kalypso	XXEP6	1962	£6	£2.50	
This Is The Sparrow Again	7" EP	Kalypso	XXEP4	1961	£6	£2.50	
Village Ram	7"	Jump Up	JU523	1967	£4	£1.50	

SPARROW (2)

This is the first recording of the group that became better known as Steppenwolf.

Tomorrow's Ship	7"	CBS	202342	1966	£30	£15	

SPARROW, JACK

Ice Water	7"	Doctor Bird	DB1005	1966	£10	£5	
More Ice Water	7"	Doctor Bird	DB1027	1966	£10	£5	

SPARROWS

Mersey Sound	LP	Elkay	3009	1964	£20	£8	*US*

SPEAR, ROGER RUSKIN

Electric Shocks	LP	United Artists	UAS29381	1972	£12	£5	
Rebel Trouser	7"	United Artists	UP35221	1971	£4	£1.50	
Unusual	LP	United Artists	UAG29508	1972	£12	£5	

SPEAR OF DESTINY

Flying Scotsman	12"	Epic	SPEAR131	1983	£6	£2.50	*autographed*
Never Take Me Alive	CD-s	Virgin	CDT17	1988	£5	£2	*3" single*
Radio Radio	CD-s	Virgin	VSCD1144	1988	£5	£2	*3" single in metal can*
So In Love With You	CD-s	Virgin	VSCD1123	1988	£5	£2	
Was That You	CD-s	10	TENZ173	1987	£6	£2.50	

SPECIAL DUTIES

Violent Society	7"	Sarcophagi	2	1981	£4	£1.50	

SPECIALS

Specials	CD	Chrysalis	CD25CR02	1994	£12	£5	*Chrysalis 25 pack*

SPECKLED RED

Dirty Dozens	LP	Esquire	32190	1963	£25	£10	
Dirty Dozens	LP	Storyville	SLP117	1964	£12	£5	

Oh Red	LP	VJM	LC11	1971	**£12**	**£5**	
Storyville Blues Anthology Vol. 4	7" EP	Storyville	SEP384	1962	**£10**	**£5**	

SPECTOR, PHIL

Despite the growing importance in the late eighties of record producers as artists, Phil Spector is still the only producer with the status of a star. His Christmas album, released a number of times over the years, is the perfect seasonal recording. Various artists associated with Spector are given traditional songs to perform (none of them carols, interestingly) and surrounded by dense arrangements that stay just on the right side of mawkishness.

Christmas Album	LP	Warner Bros	K59010	1974	**£10**	**£4**	*with poster*
Christmas Album	LP	Apple	APCOR24	1972	**£15**	**£6**	
Christmas Gift For You	LP	Philles	PHLP4005	1964	**£25**	**£10**	*US yellow label*
Christmas Gift For You	LP	London	HAU8141	1963	**£30**	**£15**	*plum label*
Christmas Gift For You	LP	Philles	PHLP4005	1963	**£50**	**£25**	*US blue label*
Presents Today's Hits	LP	Philles	PHLP4004	1963	**£60**	**£30**	*US*
Rare Masters Vol. 1	LP	Phil Spector	2307008	1976	**£12**	**£5**	
Wall Of Sound	LP	Phil Spector	WOS001	1981	**£40**	**£20**	*9 LP box set*

SPECTOR, RONNIE

Try Some Buy Some	7"	Apple	33	1971	**£20**	**£10**	*picture sleeve*

SPECTRES

The three singles recorded by the Spectres are the first releases by the group that was eventually to gain international success as Status Quo.

Hurdy Gurdy Man	7"	Piccadilly	7N35352	1966	**£200**	**£100**	*best auctioned*
I Who Have Nothing	7"	Piccadilly	7N35339	1966	**£200**	**£100**	*best auctioned*
We Ain't Got Nothin' Yet	7"	Piccadilly	7N35368	1967	**£200**	**£100**	*best auctioned*

SPECTRES (2)

Facts Of Life	7"	Lloyd Sound	UEDQU1	1965	**£150**	**£75**	

SPECTRES (3)

This Strange Effect	7"	Direct Hit	DH1	1980	**£10**	**£5**	

SPECTRUM

I'll Be Gone	7"	Parlophone	R5908	1971	**£4**	**£1.50**	
Light Is Dark Enough	LP	RCA	INTS1118	1970	**£30**	**£15**	
Portobello Road	7"	RCA	RCA1619	1967	**£4**	**£1.50**	

SPEDDING, CHRIS

Backwoods Progression	LP	Harvest	SHSP4004	1970	**£15**	**£6**	
Only Lick I Know	LP	Harvest	SHSP4017	1972	**£15**	**£6**	
Rock And Roll Band	7"	Harvest	HAR5013	1970	**£8**	**£4**	*B side by Battered Ornaments*

SPEED

Big City	7"	It	IT1	1978	**£25**	**£12.50**	*picture sleeve*
Big City	7"	It	IT1	1978	**£10**	**£5**	

SPEED GLUE SHINKI

	LP				**£500**	**£330**	*Japanese*

SPEEDBALL

No Survivor	7"	Dirty Dick	DD1/2	1980	**£15**	**£7.50**	*printed sleeve*
No Survivor	7"	Dirty Dick	DD1/2	1980	**£10**	**£5**	

SPEIRS, DAVID

David Speirs	LP	Beltona	LBA/LBS61	1969	**£12**	**£5**	

SPELLBINDERS

Chain Reaction	7"	Direction	583970	1969	**£4**	**£1.50**	
Chain Reaction	7"	CBS	202622	1967	**£10**	**£5**	
Help Me	7"	CBS	202453	1966	**£10**	**£5**	
Since I Don't Have You	7"	CBS	2776	1967	**£4**	**£1.50**	
Sweet Sweet Lovin'	7"	CBS	202435	1967	**£8**	**£4**	

SPELLMAN, BENNY

Fortune Teller	7"	London	HLP9570	1962	**£30**	**£15**	

SPELMAN, BRUCE

You Don't Know What You're Paddling In	LP	Montagu		1972	**£25**	**£10**	

SPENCE, JOSEPH

Bahaman Folk Guitar	LP	Folkways	FS3844	1965	**£10**	**£4**	*US*

SPENCE, SKIP

Although a guitarist, Skip Spence was recruited to play drums with Jefferson Airplane because Marty Balin thought that he looked like a drummer! He reverted back to his natural instrument when he helped to form Moby Grape, but was soon following the Syd Barrett route to drug-derived eccentricity. The solo album made by Skip Spence after his departure from Moby Grape is actually rather less weird and a lot less impressive than some critics would have us believe – although with Spence now having suffered a premature death, it seems likely that *Oar* is set to acquire legendary status regardless. The album was not released in the UK until it was reissued in the eighties, but US copies do turn up from time to time.

Oar	LP	Columbia	CS9831	1968	**£40**	**£20**	*US*

SPENCER, DON

Fireball	7"	HMV	POP1087	1962	**£10**	**£5**	*blue label*
Fireball	7"	HMV	POP1087	196–	**£6**	**£2.50**	*black label*
Fireball & Other Titles	7" EP	HMV	7EG8802	1963	**£25**	**£12.50**	

SPENCER, JEREMY

Jeremy Spencer	LP	Reprise	K44105	1971	**£25**	**£10**	
Jeremy Spencer	LP	Reprise	RSLP9002	1970	**£30**	**£15**	
Linda	7"	Reprise	RS27002	1970	**£4**	**£1.50**	

SPENCER, SONNY

Oh Boy	7"	Parlophone	R4611	1959	**£12**	**£6**	

SPERRMULL

Sperrmull	LP	Brain	1026	1973	**£75**	**£37.50**	*German*

SPHYNKTA

Death And Violence	7"	Sultanic	SUL999	1983	**£25**	**£12.50**	*red vinyl*
In The Shade Of The Gods	7"	Sultanic	SUL666	1983	**£30**	**£15**	*red vinyl*
Spike Up My Sphynkta	7"	Sultanic	SUL000	1984	**£50**	**£25**	

SPICE

Union Jack	7"	Olga	OLE013	1968	**£50**	**£25**	

SPICE (2)

What About The Music	7"	United Artists	UP2246	1968	**£50**	**£25**	

SPICE GIRLS

The Spice Girls achieved so much, and so quickly, that it comes as a surprise to find a version of their first number one hit – even a limited edition second CD issue – already acquiring the status of a £30 collectors' item. It seems likely that the list of Spice Girls items will become longer in the future.

Five Go Mad In Cyberspace	CD-ROM	Virgin	SGCDR1	1996	**£40**	**£20**	*promo*
Move Over Generation Next	CD-s	Virgin	CDLIC116	1998	**£8**	**£4**	
Say You'll Be There	12"	Virgin	VSTDJ1601	1996	**£6**	**£2.50**	*promo*
Say You'll Be There	CD-s	Virgin	VSCDG1601	1996	**£10**	**£5**	
Spice	CD	Virgin	CDVDJ2812	1996	**£25**	**£10**	*promo*
Step To Me	CD-s	Virgin	SGPC97	1997	**£12**	**£6**	*Pepsi promo*
Stop	12"	Virgin	VSTDJ1679	1998	**£10**	**£5**	*promo double*
Two Become One	12"	Virgin	VSTDJ1607	1996	**£6**	**£2.50**	*promo*
Wannabe	12"	Virgin	VSTDJ1588	1996	**£8**	**£4**	*promo*
Wannabe	7"	Virgin	VSLH1588	1996	**£5**	**£2**	*jukebox issue*
Wannabe	CD-s	Virgin	VSCXD1588	1996	**£30**	**£15**	

SPICER, GEORGE

Blackberry Fold	LP	Topic	12T235	1974	**£10**	**£4**	

SPIDELLS

Find Out What's Happening	7"	Sue	WI4019	1966	**£15**	**£7.50**	

SPIDER

All The Time	7"	City	NIK7	1981	**£5**	**£2**	
Children Of The Street	7"	Alien	ALIEN14	1980	**£20**	**£10**	*picture sleeve*
College Luv	7"	Alien	ALIEN16	1980	**£12**	**£6**	
Comedown Song	7"	Decca	F12430	1966	**£10**	**£5**	

SPIDER (2)

Children Of The Street	7"	Alien	ALIEN14	1980	**£4**	**£1.50**	

SPIDER-MAN

From Beyond The Grave	LP	Buddah	2318075	1973	**£10**	**£4**	

SPIDERS

I Didn't Wanna Do It	LP	Imperial	LP9140	1961	**£100**	**£50**	*US*
I'm Slippin' In	78	London	HL8086	1954	**£30**	**£15**	

SPIDERS (2)

The Spiders were led by Vincent Furnier – later to adopt the stage name of Alice Cooper.

Don't Blow Your Mind	7"	Santa Cruz	003	1966	**£400**	**£250**	*US, best auctioned*
Why Don't You Love Me?	7"	Nascot	112	1965	**£750**	**£500**	*US, best auctioned*

SPIDERS (3)

Sad Sunset	7"	Philips	BF1531	1966	**£30**	**£15**	

SPIN

Let's Pretend	CD-s	Foundation	TFL9CD	1991	**£12**	**£6**	
Scratches In The Sand	CD-s	Foundation	TFL7CD	1990	**£12**	**£6**	

SPINNERS

Heebie Jeebies	7"	Columbia	DB4693	1961	**£100**	**£50**	
Original Spinners	LP	Motown	639	1967	**£20**	**£8**	*US*
Party My Pad	LP	Time	52092	1963	**£50**	**£25**	*US*
Sweet Thing	7"	Tamla Motown	TMG514	1965	**£100**	**£50**	*demo only*

SPINNERS (2)

Title	Format	Label	Cat. No.	Year	Mint	VG	Notes
Songs Spun In Liverpool	7" EP	Topic	TOP69	1961	**£8**	**£4**	*as the Liverpool Spinners*
Spinners	LP	Fontana	TL5201	1963	**£10**	**£4**	

SPINNING WHEEL

Title	Format	Label	Cat. No.	Year	Mint	VG	Notes
Jacob's Fleece	LP	private		1979	**£20**	**£8**	

SPIRAL STAIRCASE

Title	Format	Label	Cat. No.	Year	Mint	VG	Notes
Baby What I Mean	7"	CBS	3507	1968	**£6**	**£2.50**	
More Today Than Yesterday	7"	CBS	4187	1969	**£20**	**£10**	
No One For Me To Turn To	7"	CBS	4524	1969	**£10**	**£5**	

SPIRALS

Title	Format	Label	Cat. No.	Year	Mint	VG	Notes
Rocking Cow	7"	Capitol	CL14958	1958	**£10**	**£5**	

SPIRIT

Listening to any of the recordings made by the original line-up of Spirit (the first four albums) makes it impossible to avoid the claim that the group was one of the great bands of the sixties. Like the Byrds (although Spirit's music is not at all similar), the group created a body of work that has hardly dated at all, because it failed to take on the fashionable trappings of its own time in the first place. Fans of intelligent, slightly jazz-inflected rock songs, with distinctive melodies linked to imaginative and incisive playing, can safely purchase any of the recordings made before 1971. Personnel changes at this point rendered the subsequent albums considerably less than essential, although versions of Spirit including guitarist Randy California and drummer Ed Cassidy (proudly wearing his status as one of the oldest working musicians in rock) managed to recapture much of the fire of the original group whenever they played versions of the original material.

Title	Format	Label	Cat. No.	Year	Mint	VG	Notes
12 Dreams Of Dr Sardonicus	LP	Epic	EPC64191	1970	**£12**	**£5**	
1984	7"	CBS	4773	1970	**£4**	**£1.50**	
Animal Zoo	7"	CBS	5149	1970	**£4**	**£1.50**	
Clear	LP	CBS	63729	1969	**£12**	**£5**	
Dark Eyed Woman	7"	CBS	4511	1969	**£4**	**£1.50**	
Dark Eyed Woman	7"	CBS	4565	1969	**£4**	**£1.50**	
Family That Plays Together	LP	CBS	63523	1968	**£12**	**£5**	
Highlights Of Spirit Of '76	LP	Mercury	001	1976	**£10**	**£4**	*promo*
I Got A Line On You	7"	CBS	3880	1969	**£4**	**£1.50**	
Potatoland	LP	Beggars Banquet	BEGA23	1981	**£10**	**£4**	*with cartoon book*
Spirit	LP	CBS	63278	1968	**£15**	**£6**	
Uncle Jack	7"	CBS	3523	1968	**£4**	**£1.50**	

SPIRIT OF JOHN MORGAN

Title	Format	Label	Cat. No.	Year	Mint	VG	Notes
Age Machine	7"	Carnaby	CNS4019	1970	**£5**	**£2**	
Age Machine	LP	Carnaby	CNLS6007	1970	**£50**	**£25**	
Kaleidoscope	LP	Carnaby	6302010	1972	**£50**	**£25**	
Live At Durrant House	LP	SWP	1007	197–	**£100**	**£50**	
Spirit Of John Morgan	LP	Carnaby	CNLS6002	1969	**£50**	**£25**	
Spirit Of John Morgan	LP	Carnaby	6437503	1971	**£15**	**£6**	
Train For All Reasons	7"	Carnaby	CNS4005	1969	**£5**	**£2**	

SPIRIT OF MEMPHIS QUARTET

Title	Format	Label	Cat. No.	Year	Mint	VG	Notes
Negro Spirituals	10" LP	Parlophone	PMD1070	1958	**£15**	**£6**	
Negro Spirituals	LP	Vogue	LAE1033	1965	**£10**	**£4**	

SPIRITS AND WORM

Title	Format	Label	Cat. No.	Year	Mint	VG	Notes
Spirits And Worm	LP	A&M	SP4229	1969	**£250**	**£150**	*US*

SPIRITUALIZED

Title	Format	Label	Cat. No.	Year	Mint	VG	Notes
Anyway That You Want Me	7"	Dedicated	ZB43783	1990	**£5**	**£2**	
Anyway That You Want Me	CD-s	Dedicated	ZD43784	1990	**£20**	**£10**	
Anyway That You Want Me (Remix)	12"	Dedicated	ZT43780	1990	**£15**	**£7.50**	
Anyway That You Want Me (Remix)	12"	Dedicated	ZT43784	1990	**£12**	**£6**	
Electric Mainline	CD	Dedicated	DEDCD0175	1995	**£15**	**£6**	*glow-in-the-dark case*
Feel So Sad	7"	Fierce	FRIGHT053	1991	**£20**	**£10**	
Feel So Sad	CD-s	Dedicated	SPIRT001CD	1991	**£5**	**£2**	
Fucked Up Inside	CD	Dedicated	DEDCD008	1993	**£20**	**£8**	*mail order only*
Fucked Up Inside	LP	Decicated	DEDLP008	1993	**£12**	**£5**	
Ladies And Gentlemen We Are Floating In Space	CD	Dedicated	DEDCD034	1997	**£75**	**£37.50**	*with 'wise men say . . .' lyric*
Ladies And Gentlemen We Are Floating In Space	CD	Dedicated	DEDCD034S	1997	**£75**	**£37.50**	*pack of 12 × 3" singles*
Lay Back In The Sun	CD-s	Dedicated	74321311782	1996	**£5**	**£2**	
Lazer Guided Melodies	CD-s	Dedicated	SPIRT004CD	1992	**£8**	**£4**	*mail order sampler*
Run	CD-s	Dedicated	SPIRIT002CD	1991	**£5**	**£2**	
Smile	CD-s	Dedicated	SPIRIT003CD	1991	**£5**	**£2**	

SPIROGYRA

Having as manager a university professor of chemistry (the father of the band's violinist) was perhaps not the best way of ensuring stardom, and although Spirogyra's brand of folk-rock managed to see the group through three albums, none sold well and all are very scarce today. Lead singer Barbara Gaskin subsequently worked with ex-Hatfield and the North keyboard player Dave Stewart, gaining a number one hit in 1981 with a high-tech cover of 'It's My Party'.

Title	Format	Label	Cat. No.	Year	Mint	VG	Notes
Bells Boots & Shambles	LP	Polydor	2310246	1973	**£200**	**£100**	
Dangerous Dave	7"	Pegasus	PGS3	1972	**£6**	**£2.50**	*picture sleeve*
Old Boot Wine	LP	Pegasus	PEG13	1972	**£60**	**£30**	
St Radigunds	LP	B&C	CAS1042	1971	**£60**	**£30**	

SPITFIRE & THE BLACKFIRE BARMIES

Title	Format	Label	Cat. No.	Year	Mint	VG	Notes
So You Want To Be A Rock'n'Roll Star	7"	Carrere	CAR253	1982	**£15**	**£7.50**	*no picture sleeve*

SPITFIRE BOYS

Title	Format	Label	Cat. No.	Year	Mint	VG	Notes
British Refugee	7"	RK	RK1001	1977	**£15**	**£7.50**	

SPITZBROOK

Title	Format	Label	Cat. No.	Year	Mint	VG	Notes
Stranger	7"	Ace	SPIT1	197–	**£25**	**£12.50**	

SPIVAK, CHARLIE

Title	Format	Label	Cat. No.	Year	Mint	VG	Notes
Red Lilacs	7"	Parlophone	CMSP14	1954	**£5**	**£2**	*export*

SPIVEY, VICTORIA

Title	Format	Label	Cat. No.	Year	Mint	VG	Notes
Treasures Of North American Negro Music No. 5	7" EP	Fontana	TFE17264	1960	**£8**	**£4**	
Victoria Spivey	7" EP	HMV	7EG8190	1956	**£12**	**£6**	
Victoria Spivey	LP	XTRA	XTRA1022	1965	**£20**	**£8**	

S.P.K.

Title	Format	Label	Cat. No.	Year	Mint	VG	Notes
Dekompositiones	12"	Side Effekts	SER003	1983	**£10**	**£5**	
Information Overload Unit	LP	Side Effekts	SER01	1981	**£20**	**£8**	*with booklet & poster*
Information Overload Unit	LP	Side Effekts	SER01	1981	**£12**	**£5**	
Leichenschrei	LP	Side Effekts	SER002	198–	**£10**	**£4**	
Meat Processing Section	7"	Industrial	IR0011	1980	**£10**	**£5**	

SPLASH

Title	Format	Label	Cat. No.	Year	Mint	VG	Notes
Splash	LP	Polydor	PLA3001	1974	**£25**	**£10**	*Norwegian*
Ut Pa Vischan	LP	Polydor	2379036	1972	**£25**	**£10**	*Swedish*

SPLINTER

Title	Format	Label	Cat. No.	Year	Mint	VG	Notes
untitled – known as The White Album	LP	Dark Horse	DH2	1975	**£50**	**£25**	*demo*

SPLIT BEAVER

Title	Format	Label	Cat. No.	Year	Mint	VG	Notes
Savage	7"	Heavy Metal	HEAVY7	1981	**£10**	**£5**	*picture sleeve*

SPLIT ENZ

Title	Format	Label	Cat. No.	Year	Mint	VG	Notes
I See Red	7"	Illegal	ILS19	1979	**£4**	**£1.50**	
My Mistake	12"	Chrysalis	CHS217012	1977	**£6**	**£2.50**	

SPLIT KNEE LOONS

Title	Format	Label	Cat. No.	Year	Mint	VG	Notes
Special Collectors EP	7"	Avatar	AAA111	1981	**£5**	**£2**	

SPOELSTRA, MARK

Title	Format	Label	Cat. No.	Year	Mint	VG	Notes
5 & 20 Questions	LP	Elektra	EKL283	1965	**£20**	**£8**	*US*
Mark Spoelstra	LP	Columbia	CS9793	1969	**£15**	**£6**	*US*
State Of Mind	LP	Elektra	EKL307	1966	**£20**	**£8**	*US*

SPOILT BRATZ

Title	Format	Label	Cat. No.	Year	Mint	VG	Notes
Be My Guest	cass	Spoilt Bratz	BRAT3	1989	**£25**	**£10**	
Gasoline And Suicide	cass	Spoilt Bratz	SB2	1988	**£25**	**£10**	
Spoilt Bratz	cass	Spoilt Bratz	SB1	1988	**£25**	**£10**	

SPOKESMEN

Title	Format	Label	Cat. No.	Year	Mint	VG	Notes
Dawn Of Correction	LP	Decca	DL(7)4712	1965	**£15**	**£6**	*US*
Michelle	7" EP	Decca	60003	1966	**£10**	**£5**	*French*

SPONTANEOUS COMBUSTION

Title	Format	Label	Cat. No.	Year	Mint	VG	Notes
Gay Time Night	7"	Harvest	HAR5060	1972	**£4**	**£1.50**	
Leaving	7"	Harvest	HAR5046	1971	**£4**	**£1.50**	
Sabre Dance	7"	Harvest	HAR5066	1973	**£4**	**£1.50**	
Spontaneous Combustion	LP	Harvest	SHVL801	1972	**£25**	**£10**	
Triad	LP	Harvest	SHVL805	1972	**£25**	**£10**	

SPONTANEOUS MUSIC ENSEMBLE

The name of the group formed by drummer John Stevens describes exactly what the group was about and although Stevens led and played with many other groups (including that of John Martyn in the mid-seventies), it is the S.M.E. for which he will be best remembered. The group, with a variable personnel, but including at various times many of the best-known names in British jazz, was the first to record free improvisation in the UK and has proved to be enormously influential.

Title	Format	Label	Cat. No.	Year	Mint	VG	Notes
Biosystem	LP	Incus	INCUS24	1977	**£12**	**£5**	
Birds Of A Feather	LP	Byg	529023	1972	**£20**	**£8**	*French*
Bobby Bradford And The SME	LP	Freedom	SLP40111	1974	**£20**	**£8**	
Bobby Bradford, John Surman & S.M.E.	LP	Nessa	17	1971	**£20**	**£8**	
Challenge	LP	Eyemark	EMPL1002	1966	**£75**	**£37.50**	
Face To Face	LP	Emanen	303	1973	**£15**	**£6**	
For CND For Peace And You To Share	LP	A Records		1970	**£30**	**£15**	
How Ya Doin?	LP	Nondo	003	1973	**£15**	**£6**	
Karyobin	LP	Island	ILPS9079	1968	**£50**	**£25**	*pink label*
Live Big Band And Quartet	LP	Vinyl	VS0015	1971	**£20**	**£8**	
S.M.E. + = S.M.O.	LP	A Records		1975	**£15**	**£6**	
S.M.E./S.M.O. In Concert	LP	Sweet Folk And Count	SFA112	1981	**£15**	**£6**	
So What Do You Think?	LP	Tangent	TGS118	1971	**£15**	**£6**	
Source – From & Towards	LP	Tangent	TNGS107	1971	**£15**	**£6**	
Spontaneous Music Ensemble	LP	Polydor	2384009	1972	**£10**	**£4**	
Spontaneous Music Ensemble	LP	Marmalade	608008	1969	**£25**	**£10**	*credited to John Stevens*

SPOOKY TOOTH

Spooky Tooth's frequent personnel changes prevented the group from ever achieving stardom. The best material, however (which includes the first two albums and much of *The Last Puff*, although this is as much the work of the Grease Band as of the original Spooky Tooth), provides a distinctive approach to blue-eyed soul that has worn very much better than some of its trendier companions from the time. All the original group members subsequently turned up elsewhere. Singer/keyboard players Gary Wright and Mike Harrison made solo albums; guitarist Luther Grosvenor joined Mott the Hoople and became Ariel Bender; bass player Greg Ridley joined Humble Pie; while drummer Mike Kellie became a member of Three Man Army and then the Only Ones. The album *Ceremony* sees Spooky Tooth cast as session musicians for a project by avant-garde composer Pierre Henry and is not generally liked by fans of the group!

Ceremony	LP	Island	ILPS9107	1969	**£15**	**£6**	*with Pierre Henry, pink label*
It's All About	LP	Island	ILP980/ILPS9080	1968	**£30**	**£15**	*pink label*
Last Puff	LP	Island	ILPS9117	1970	**£15**	**£6**	*pink label*
Love Really Changed Me	7"	Island	WIP6037	1968	**£4**	**£1.50**	
Mirror	LP	Island	ILPS9292	1974	**£10**	**£4**	*export*
Nobody There At All	7"	Island	WIP6048	1969	**£30**	**£15**	*demo only, Art B side*
Son Of Your Father	7"	Island	WIP6060	1969	**£4**	**£1.50**	
Spooky Two	LP	Island	ILPS9098	1969	**£20**	**£8**	*pink label*
Sunshine Help Me	7"	Island	WIP6022	1967	**£4**	**£1.50**	
Weight	7"	Island	WIP6046	1968	**£4**	**£1.50**	
Witness	LP	Island	ILPS9255	1973	**£10**	**£4**	
You Broke My Heart	LP	Island	ILPS9227	1973	**£15**	**£6**	

SPOTLIGHTERS

Please Be My Girlfriend	7"	Vogue	V9130	1959	**£300**	**£180**	*best auctioned*

SPOTLIGHTS

Batman And Robin	7"	Philips	BF1485	1966	**£4**	**£1.50**	

SPOTNICKS

The Spotnicks were Sweden's answer to the Shadows (and are still playing in fact). The lead guitarist was impressive in a Hank Marvinish sort of way, and the two singles 'Orange Blossom Special' and 'Rocket Man' (which also turn up on the EP *On The Air* and the LP *Out-a Space*) are as good as anything produced by the English group. The Spotnicks also had two gimmicks – they performed wearing rather unserviceable-looking space suits, and they used radio-controlled guitars rather than electric leads, although the equipment tended to be somewhat temperamental!

Anna	7"	Oriole	CB1886	1963	**£6**	**£2.50**	
Around The World	LP	Swedisc	SWELP42	1966	**£20**	**£8**	*Swedish*
At Home In Gothenberg	LP	Swedisc	SWELP33	1965	**£20**	**£8**	*Swedish*
Back In The Race	LP	Polydor	2379005	1971	**£12**	**£5**	*Swedish*
Bo Winberg And The Spotnicks Today	LP	Polydor	2379060	1973	**£10**	**£4**	*Swedish*
By Request	LP	Swedisc	SWELP67	1968	**£15**	**£6**	*Swedish*
Donner Wetter	7"	Oriole	CB1981	1964	**£6**	**£2.50**	
Hava Nagila	7"	Oriole	CB1790	1963	**£4**	**£1.50**	
In Acapulco	LP	Swedisc	SWELP60	1967	**£20**	**£8**	*Swedish*
In Paris	LP	Oriole	PS40040	1963	**£15**	**£6**	
In Spain	LP	Oriole	PS40054	1964	**£20**	**£8**	
In Stockholm	LP	Swedisc	SWELP20	1964	**£20**	**£8**	*Swedish*
In The Groove	LP	Swedisc	SWELP63	1968	**£15**	**£6**	*Swedish*
In Tokyo	LP	Swedisc	SWELP38	1966	**£20**	**£8**	*Swedish*
In Winterland	LP	Swedisc	SWELP48	1966	**£20**	**£8**	*Swedish*
Just Listen To My Heart	7"	Oriole	CB1818	1963	**£4**	**£1.50**	
Live In Berlin '74	LP	Polydor	2480201	1974	**£10**	**£4**	*German*
Live In Japan	LP	Swedisc	SWELP53	1966	**£20**	**£8**	*Swedish*
Lovesick Blues	7"	Oriole	CB1953	1964	**£6**	**£2.50**	
On The Air	7" EP	Oriole	EP7075	1963	**£10**	**£5**	
Orange Blossom Special	7"	Oriole	CB1724	1962	**£4**	**£1.50**	
Out-a Space: The Spotnicks In London	LP	Oriole	PS40036	1962	**£15**	**£6**	
Out-a Space: The Spotnicks In London	LP	Oriole	SPS40037	1963	**£30**	**£15**	*stereo*
Rocket Man	7"	Oriole	CB1755	1962	**£4**	**£1.50**	
Something Like Country	LP	Polydor	2379032	1972	**£10**	**£4**	*Swedish*
Spotnicks At The Olympia Paris	7" EP	Oriole	EP7079	1964	**£12**	**£6**	
Spotnicks In Berlin	LP	Oriole	PS40064	1965	**£25**	**£10**	
Spotnicks In Paris	7" EP	Oriole	EP7078	1964	**£10**	**£5**	
Valentina	7"	Oriole	CB1844	1963	**£4**	**£1.50**	
Very Best Of The Spotnicks	LP	Air	CHM1171	1977	**£10**	**£4**	
Volume 1	LP	Swedisc	SWELP50001	1967	**£15**	**£6**	*Swedish*
Volume 2	LP	Swedisc	SWELP50002	1967	**£15**	**£6**	*Swedish*

SPRATT, JACK

Give Me Your Love	7"	Coxsone	CS7100	1969	**£10**	**£5**	

SPREDTHICK

Spredthick	LP	An Actual	ACT003	1978	**£15**	**£6**	

SPRIGUNS

Nothing Else To Do	7"	Decca	F13676	1976	**£5**	**£2**	
Revel Weird And Wild	LP	Decca	SKL5262	1976	**£100**	**£50**	
Rowdy Dowdy Day	cass	private		1974	**£20**	**£8**	
Rowdy Dowdy Day	LP	Kissing Spell	KSLP002	1992	**£10**	**£4**	
Time Will Pass	LP	Decca	SKL5286	1977	**£100**	**£50**	
White Witch	7"	Decca	F13739	1977	**£5**	**£2**	

SPRIGUNS OF TOLGUS

Jack With A Feather	LP	Alida Star Cottage	ASC7755A	1975	**£1000**	**£700**	

SPRING

Title	Format	Label	Cat. No.	Year	Mint	VG	Notes
Spring	LP	Neon	NE6	1971	**£100**	**£50**	

SPRINGFIELD, DUSTY

Title	Format	Label	Cat. No.	Year	Mint	VG	Notes
All I See Is You	7"	Philips	BF1510	1966	**£5**	**£2**	*picture sleeve*
Arrested By You	CD-s	Parlophone	CDR6266	1990	**£5**	**£2**	
Cameo	LP	Philips	6308152	1973	**£10**	**£4**	
Demain Tu Peux Changer	7" EP	Philips	433570	1963	**£20**	**£10**	*French*
Dusty	7" EP	Philips	BE12564	1964	**£10**	**£5**	
Dusty Definitely	LP	Philips	(S)BL7864	1968	**£12**	**£5**	
Dusty In Memphis	LP	Philips	SBL7889	1969	**£12**	**£5**	
Dusty In New York	7" EP	Philips	BE12572	1965	**£10**	**£5**	
Dusty Springfield	LP	World Record Club	ST848	1968	**£10**	**£4**	
Everything Is Coming Up Dusty	LP	Philips	(S)BL1002	1965	**£12**	**£5**	
From Dusty With Love	LP	Philips	SBL7927	1970	**£10**	**£4**	
Girl Called Dusty	LP	Philips	(S)BL7594	1964	**£12**	**£5**	
Give Me Time	7"	Philips	BF1577	1967	**£4**	**£1.50**	
Goin' Back	CD-s	Philips	SPRCD1	1994	**£5**	**£2**	
Heart And Soul	CD-s	Columbia	6598562	1993	**£5**	**£2**	*with Cilla Black*
Hits Of Dusty Springfield	cass-s	Philips	MCP100	1968	**£8**	**£3**	
Hits Of The Walker Brothers & Dusty Springfield	cass-s	Philips	MCP1004	1968	**£8**	**£3**	
I Only Want To Be With You	7" EP	Philips	BE12560	1964	**£8**	**£4**	
I Only Want To Be With You	7" EP	Philips	433664	1963	**£10**	**£5**	*French*
I'll Try Anything	7"	Philips	BF1553	1967	**£4**	**£1.50**	
If You Go Away	7" EP	Philips	BE12605	1968	**£10**	**£5**	
In Private	CD-s	Parlophone	CDR6234	1989	**£6**	**£2.50**	
Legend Of Dusty Springfield	CD	Philips	5222542	1994	**£60**	**£30**	*4 CD boxed set*
Mademoiselle Dusty	7" EP	Philips	BE12579	1965	**£15**	**£7.50**	
Nothing Has Been Proved	CD-s	Parlophone	CDR6207	1989	**£10**	**£5**	
Oh Holy Child	7"	Philips	BF1381	1964	**£5**	**£2**	*picture sleeve, Springfields B side*
Reputation	CD-s	Parlophone	CDR6253	1990	**£5**	**£2**	
See All Her Faces	LP	Philips	6308117	1972	**£10**	**£4**	
Sometimes Like Butterflies	12"	Hippodrome	12HIPPO103	1985	**£8**	**£4**	
Sometimes Like Butterflies	7"	Hippodrome	HIPPO103	1985	**£5**	**£2**	
Star Dusty	7" EP	Philips	6850751	1968	**£6**	**£2.50**	
Warten Und Hoffen	7"	Philips		1964	**£12**	**£6**	*German*
What's It Gonna Be	7"	Philips	BF1608	1967	**£8**	**£4**	
Where Am I Going	LP	Philips	(S)BL7820	1967	**£12**	**£5**	
Your Love Still Brings Me To My Knees	7"	Mercury	DUSTY5	1980	**£5**	**£2**	

SPRINGFIELD, TOM

Title	Format	Label	Cat. No.	Year	Mint	VG	Notes
Love's Philosophy	LP	Decca	LK/SKL5003	1969	**£20**	**£8**	

SPRINGFIELDS

Title	Format	Label	Cat. No.	Year	Mint	VG	Notes
Christmas With The Springfields	7" EP	Woman's Own	P125	1962	**£6**	**£2.50**	
Folk Songs From The Hills	LP	Philips	632304BL	1963	**£10**	**£4**	
Hit Sounds	7" EP	Philips	BE12538	1963	**£5**	**£2**	
Kinda Folksy	LP	Philips	BBL7551/ SBBL674	1962	**£10**	**£4**	
Kinda Folksy No. 1	7" EP	Philips	433622BE	1962	**£10**	**£5**	
Kinda Folksy No. 2	7" EP	Philips	433623BE	1962	**£10**	**£5**	
Kinda Folksy No. 3	7" EP	Philips	433624BE	1962	**£10**	**£5**	
Springfields	7" EP	Philips	BBE12476	1961	**£8**	**£4**	
Springfields	7" EP	Philips	SBBE9068	1961	**£12**	**£6**	*stereo*
Springfields Story	LP	Philips	BET606	1964	**£12**	**£5**	*double*
Swahili Papa	7"	Philips	326536BF	1962	**£4**	**£1.50**	

SPRINGFIELDS (2)

Title	Format	Label	Cat. No.	Year	Mint	VG	Notes
Sunflower	7"	Sarah	010	1988	**£8**	**£4**	*with poster*

SPRINGSTEEN, BRUCE

Jon Landau's accolade, in which he described Bruce Springsteen as the future of rock 'n' roll, was proved to be not too far from the mark by Springsteen's subsequent rise to the ranks of megastardom. The corresponding simplification in the man's material, however, is much to be regretted by those who thrilled to the narrative adventures of the songs on his first four great albums. Like Bob Dylan, Bruce Springsteen is an artist for whom a full appreciation depends on the collector obtaining some of his many bootleg recordings – both for the discarded out-takes, which include many songs easily the equal of those chosen for release (a fact which can be belatedly appreciated by a larger number of fans than previously, following the compilation of the official boxed set of out-takes), and for a sampling of Springsteen's magisterial live performances, whose impact is sadly diluted in the official live recordings.

Title	Format	Label	Cat. No.	Year	Mint	VG	Notes
57 Channels (And Nothin' On)	CD-s	Sony	6581385	1992	**£15**	**£7.50**	*picture disc*
As Requested Around The World	LP	Columbia	AS978	1981	**£20**	**£8**	*US promo sampler*
Atlantic City	7"	CBS	A2794	1982	**£12**	**£6**	*picture sleeve*
Badlands	7"	CBS	A6532	1978	**£5**	**£2**	
Blinded By The Light	7" EP	Columbia	AS45	1973	**£150**	**£75**	*US, with special sleeve, questionnaire, booklet*
Born In The USA	7"	CBS			**£25**	**£12.50**	*5 track promo*
Born In The USA	LP	CBS	86304	1984	**£20**	**£8**	*picture disc*
Born In The USA – The 12" Collection	12"	CBS	BRUCE1	1985	**£15**	**£7.50**	*4 × 12", 1 × 7", poster, boxed*
Born To Run	48"	CBS		1975	**£75**	**£37.50**	*US unplayable promo!*
Born To Run	7"	CBS	A3661	1975	**£4**	**£1.50**	

Title	Format	Label	Cat. No.	Year	Mint	VG	Notes
Born To Run	7"	CBS	A3661	1975	**£15**	**£7.50**	*picture sleeve*
Born To Run	7"	CBS	A7077	1985	**£15**	**£7.50**	
Born To Run	7"	CBS	BRUCEB2	1987	**£8**	**£4**	*2 × 7", boxed*
Born To Run	7"	CBS	BRUCEBP2	1987	**£4**	**£1.50**	*with badge*
Born To Run	LP	Columbia	HC43795	1980	**£20**	**£8**	*US audiophile*
Born To Run	LP	Columbia	PC33795	1975	**£200**	**£100**	*US, cover titles in script*
Born To Run (live)	CD-s	CBS	BRUCEC2	1987	**£8**	**£4**	
Bruce Springsteen	LP	CBS	66353	1979	**£25**	**£10**	*3 LPs, boxed*
Cadillac Ranch	7"	CBS	A1557	1981	**£12**	**£6**	
Circus Song	7" EP	Columbia	AS52	1973	**£250**	**£150**	*US, with special sleeve, questionnaire, booklet*
Cover Me	7"	CBS	WA4662	1984	**£12**	**£6**	*shaped picture disc, stand*
Cover Me	7"	CBS	DA4662	1984	**£6**	**£2.50**	*double*
Cover Me	7"	CBS	A4662	1984	**£6**	**£2.50**	*poster picture sleeve*
Dancing In The Dark	7"	CBS	WA4436	1984	**£15**	**£7.50**	*shaped picture disc*
Darkness On The Edge Of Town	LP	Columbia	HC45318	1981	**£20**	**£8**	*US audiophile*
Darkness On The Edge Of Town	LP	Columbia	PAL35318	1978	**£125**	**£62.50**	*US promo picture disc*
Ghost Of Tom Joad	CD	Sony	SAMPCD3006	1995	**£40**	**£20**	*promo with lyric booklet*
Greetings From Asbury Park, N.J.	LP	CBS	65480	1973	**£10**	**£4**	*gatefold sleeve, orange label*
Hungry Heart	7"	CBS	A9309	1980	**£12**	**£6**	*picture sleeve*
I'm On Fire	12"	CBS	TA6342	1985	**£6**	**£2.50**	
I'm On Fire	7"	CBS	WA6342	1985	**£8**	**£4**	*shaped picture disc*
I'm On Fire	7"	CBS	A6342	1985	**£4**	**£1.50**	*with card*
Interviews	7"	CBS		1986	**£10**	**£5**	*2 × 7", boxed*
Joe Grushecky and Bruce Springsteen In Conversation	CD	Pinnacle	PLR003	1995	**£40**	**£20**	*promo*
Leap Of Faith	CD-s	Sony	6583692	1992	**£5**	**£2**	
Live 1975–'85	LP	CBS	SAMP1104	1986	**£10**	**£4**	*promo*
Nebraska	CD	Columbia	CK38358	1983	**£20**	**£8**	*US, early copy with different mix*
Open All Night	7"	CBS	A2969	1982	**£12**	**£6**	
Prodigal Son	cass	Dare International		1984	**£30**	**£15**	*demo*
Prodigal Son	CD	Dare International		1994	**£50**	**£25**	
Promised Land	7"	CBS	A6720	1978	**£5**	**£2**	
Prove It All Night	7"	CBS	A6424	1978	**£8**	**£4**	
River	12"	CBS	A121179	1981	**£8**	**£4**	
River	7"	CBS	A1179	1981	**£8**	**£4**	
Rosalita	7" EP	Columbia	AS66	1973	**£150**	**£75**	*US, with special sleeve, questionnaire, booklet*
Sherry Darling	7"	CBS	A9568	1980	**£8**	**£4**	
Sherry Darling/Independence Day	7"	CBS	A9568	1980	**£50**	**£25**	*promo*
Sherry Darling/Independence Day	7"	CBS	A9568	1980	**£125**	**£62.50**	*promo, picture sleeve*
Spare Parts	CD-s	CBS	BRUCEC4	1988	**£5**	**£2**	
Spare Parts	CD-s	CBS	BRUCEB4	1988	**£15**	**£7.50**	*in tin*
Tenth Avenue Freeze-Out	7"	CBS	A3940	1976	**£5**	**£2**	
Tougher Than The Rest	CD-s	CBS	BRUCEC3	1988	**£10**	**£5**	
Tunnel Of Love	12"	CBS	6512955	1987	**£8**	**£4**	*shaped picture disc*
Tunnel Of Love	12"	CBS	6512956	1987	**£6**	**£2.50**	*with poster*
Tunnel Of Love	CD	CBS	CDCBS4602709	1987	**£15**	**£6**	*picture disc*
Tunnel Of Love	CD-s	CBS	6512952	1987	**£30**	**£15**	
Viva Las Vegas	10"	NME	PRO101990	1990	**£30**	**£15**	*promo, Paul McCartney B side*
Viva Las Vegas	CD-s	NME	CDPRO1990	1990	**£40**	**£20**	*promo, Paul McCartney B side*
Wild, The Innocent & E Street Shuffle	LP	CBS	65780	1973	**£10**	**£4**	*yellow sleeve lettering, Ashbury label*

SPRONG & NYAH SHUFFLE

Title	Format	Label	Cat. No.	Year	Mint	VG	Notes
Moonwalk	7"	Grape	GR3001	1969	**£4**	**£1.50**	

SPROUD, BILLY & THE ROCK & ROLL SIX

Title	Format	Label	Cat. No.	Year	Mint	VG	Notes
Rock Mister Piper	7"	Columbia	DB3893	1957	**£30**	**£15**	

SPROUTS

Title	Format	Label	Cat. No.	Year	Mint	VG	Notes
Teen Billy Baby	7"	RCA	RCA1031	1958	**£60**	**£30**	

SPUD

Title	Format	Label	Cat. No.	Year	Mint	VG	Notes
Happy Handful	LP	Philips	9108003	1975	**£12**	**£5**	
Silk Purse	LP	Philips	9108002	1975	**£12**	**£5**	
Smoking In The Bog	LP	Sonet	SNTF742	1977	**£10**	**£4**	

SPUR

Title	Format	Label	Cat. No.	Year	Mint	VG	Notes
Spur Of The Moment	LP	Cinema	CSLP1500		**£60**	**£30**	*US*

SPUTNIKS

Title	Format	Label	Cat. No.	Year	Mint	VG	Notes
Die Frühen Jahre	LP	Amiga	850872	1981	**£20**	**£8**	*East German*

SPYROGYRA

Title	Format	Label	Cat. No.	Year	Mint	VG	Notes
Morning Dance	LP	MCA	INF9004	1979	**£15**	**£6**	*US picture disc, 2 B-side designs*

SQUADRONAIRES

Title	Format	Label	Cat. No.	Year	Mint	VG	Notes
Coach Call Boogie	7"	Decca	F10248	1954	£5	£2	
Contrasts In Jazz	10" LP	Decca	LF1141	1953	£12	£5	
Rock And Roll Boogie	7"	Columbia	DB3882	1957	£6	£2.50	
Wolf On The Prowl	7"	Decca	F10274	1954	£5	£2	

SQUEEZE

Title	Format	Label	Cat. No.	Year	Mint	VG	Notes
Cool For Cats	12"	A&M	AMSP7426	1979	£6	£2.50	*pink vinyl*
Cool For Cats	7"	A&M	AMS7426	1979	£5	£2	*red vinyl*
Cool For Cats	7"	A&M	AMS7426	1979	£4	£1.50	*brilliant pink vinyl*
Labelled With Love	7"	A&M	AMS8166	1981	£10	£5	*picture sleeve*
Packet Of Three	12"	Deptford Fun City	01	1977	£6	£2.50	*pink sleeve*
Play	CD	Reprise		1991	£25	£10	*US promo picture disc, plant pot*
Singles 45s And Under	CD	A&M	394922	1984	£12	£5	*American track listing*
Six Squeeze Songs Crammed On To One Ten Inch Record	10" LP	A&M	SP3719	1980	£10	£4	*US*
UK Squeeze	LP	A&M	SP4687	1978	£10	£4	*US red vinyl*

SQUIER, BILLY

Title	Format	Label	Cat. No.	Year	Mint	VG	Notes
Emotions In Motion	7"	Capitol	CL261	1982	£10	£5	*picture disc*
Emotions In Motion	7"	Capitol	CL261	1982	£8	£4	
Love Is The Hero	12"	Capitol	12CL433	1986	£50	£25	*with Freddie Mercury intro*

SQUIRE

Title	Format	Label	Cat. No.	Year	Mint	VG	Notes
Does Stephanie Know	7"	Hi Lo	LOX1	1985	£5	£2	*flexi*
Get Ready To Go	7"	Rok	ROKI/II	1979	£8	£4	*B side by Coming Shortly*
Something Old, Something New, Something Borrowed	LP	fan club	L0004	1984	£10	£4	
Young Idea	7"	Squire Fan Club	SFC2	1984	£6	£2.50	

SQUIRES

The scarce single by the Squires marks the recording debut of Neil Young, who was a member of the group.

Title	Format	Label	Cat. No.	Year	Mint	VG	Notes
Sultan	7"	V	109	1961	£150	£75	*US, best auctioned*

SQUIRES, DOROTHY

Title	Format	Label	Cat. No.	Year	Mint	VG	Notes
Dorothy Squires	7" EP	Pye	NEP24036	1957	£10	£5	
Sings Billy Reid	LP	Pye	NPL18015	1958	£12	£5	

SQUIRES, ROSEMARY

Title	Format	Label	Cat. No.	Year	Mint	VG	Notes
My Love Is A Wanderer	7" EP	MGM	MGMEP640	1956	£8	£4	
Rosemary	7" EP	HMV	7EG8588	1960	£6	£2.50	

SRC

SRC (short for Scott Richard Case, after the lead singer) made three albums, with limited commercial success, before quitting in 1970. Led by the delightfully named Quackenbush brothers, the group is in many ways the quintessential American psychedelic band. Scott Richardson's earnest, slightly fragile vocals are the first word in cool glamour, while the piercing sustain of Gary Quackenbush's lead guitar lines is the sound that the likes of Bevis Frond and Screaming Trees have been trying to emulate for years. The single 'Black Sheep', taken from the first album, is a genuine sixties classic. An extremely rare album made by an earlier version of the group is listed under the name of the Fugitives.

Title	Format	Label	Cat. No.	Year	Mint	VG	Notes
Black Sheep	7"	Capitol	CL15576	1969	£10	£5	
Milestones	LP	Capitol	(S)T134	1969	£40	£20	
SRC	LP	Capitol	(S)T2991	1968	£40	£20	
Traveller's Tale	LP	Capitol	(S)T273	1970	£40	£20	

ST CHRISTOPHER

Title	Format	Label	Cat. No.	Year	Mint	VG	Notes
Crystal Clear	7"	Bluegrass	GM001	1984	£6	£2.50	
Forevermore Starts Here	7"	Veston	VOD001	1987	£4	£1.50	*flexi*
Go Ahead Cry	7"	Bluegrass	GM003	1986	£5	£2	

ST CLAIR, CHERYL

Title	Format	Label	Cat. No.	Year	Mint	VG	Notes
My Heart's Not In It	7"	CBS	202041	1966	£6	£2.50	
What About Me	7"	Columbia	DB8077	1966	£5	£2	

ST JOHN, BARRY

Title	Format	Label	Cat. No.	Year	Mint	VG	Notes
According To St John	LP	Major Minor	MMLP/SMLP43	1969	£20	£8	
Bread And Butter	7"	Decca	F11975	1964	£5	£2	
Come Away Melinda	7"	Columbia	DB7783	1965	£4	£1.50	
Everything I Touch Turns To Tears	7"	Columbia	DB7868	1966	£30	£15	
Hey Boy	7"	Decca	F12145	1965	£5	£2	
Little Bit Of Soap	7"	Decca	F11933	1964	£5	£2	
Mind How You Go	7"	Decca	F12111	1965	£6	£2.50	

ST JOHN, BRIDGET

Title	Format	Label	Cat. No.	Year	Mint	VG	Notes
Ask Me No Questions	LP	Dandelion	63750	1969	£25	£10	
Fly High	7"	Polydor	2001280	1972	£5	£2	*picture sleeve*
If You've Got Money	7"	Warner Bros	WB8019	1970	£5	£2	
Jumble Queen	LP	Chrysalis	CHR1062	1974	£12	£5	
Nice	7"	Polydor	2001361	1972	£4	£1.50	

Passing Thru	7"	MCA	MUS1203	1973	£4	£1.50	
Songs For The Gentle Man	LP	Dandelion	DAN8007	1971	£25	£10	
Thank You For	LP	Dandelion	2310193	1972	£25	£10	
To B Without A Hitch	7"	Dandelion	K4404	1969	£4	£1.50	

ST JOHN, JEFF COPPERWINE

Joint Effort	LP	Spin	SEL933742	1970	£20	£8	*New Zealand*

ST JOHN, RICH

Thru' His Eyes	LP	Polydor	623034	1966	£20	£8	*German*

ST JOHN, ROY

Immigration Declaration	LP	Caroline	CA2008	1975	£10	£4	

ST JOHN, TAMMY

Boys	7"	Pye	7N15682	1964	£4	£1.50	
Concerning Love	7"	Tangerine	DP0007	1969	£4	£1.50	
Dark Shadows And Empty Hallways	7"	Pye	7N15948	1965	£4	£1.50	
He's The One For Me	7"	Pye	7N15762	1965	£4	£1.50	
Nobody Knows What's Goin' On	7"	Pye	7N17042	1966	£30	£15	

ST LOUIS JIMMY

Goin' Down Slow	LP	Bluesville	BV1028	1961	£15	£6	*US*

ST LOUIS UNION

Behind The Door	7"	Decca	F12386	1966	£15	£7.50	
East Side Story	7"	Decca	F12508	1966	£40	£20	
Girl	7"	Decca	F12318	1966	£12	£6	

ST PATRICK, OLIVER

I Want To Be Loved By You	7"	Trojan	TR005	1967	£10	£5	

ST PETERS, CRISPIAN

Almost Persuaded	7" EP	Decca	DFE8678	1967	£30	£15	
At This Moment	7"	Decca	F12080	1965	£5	£2	
Changes	7" EP	Decca	457126	1966	£12	£6	*French*
Follow Me	LP	Decca	LK4805	1966	£25	£10	
No No No	7"	Decca	F12207	1965	£5	£2	
Simply	LP	Square	SQA102	1970	£10	£4	
So Long	7"	Decca	F13055	1970	£8	£4	
You Were On My Mind	7" EP	Decca	457110	1966	£12	£6	*French*

ST VALENTINE'S DAY MASSACRE

The Artwoods changed their name for this one single, but it caused no improvement in their fortunes and they split up soon afterwards.

Brother Can You Spare A Dime	7"	Fontana	TF883	1967	£75	£37.50	
Brother Can You Spare A Dime	7"	Fontana	TF883	1967	£100	£50	*picture sleeve*

STACCATOS

Butchers And Bakers	7"	Fontana	TF966	1968	£10	£5	

STACCATOS (2)

Half Past Midnight	7"	Capitol	CL15505	1967	£5	£2	
Let's Run Away	7"	Capitol	CL15478	1966	£5	£2	

STACCATOS (3)

Main Line	7"	Parlophone	R4828	1961	£6	£2.50	

STACEY, CLARENCE

Just Your Love	7"	Pye	7N25025	1959	£5	£2	

STACEY, GWEN

Introducing Gwen Stacey	7" EP	RCA	RCX7166	1965	£50	£25	

STACKIE, BOB

Bob Stackie In Soho	7"	Collins Downbeat	CRC0017	1968	£10	£5	
Grab It Hold It Feel It	7"	Collins Downbeat	CR009	1968	£10	£5	

STACKRIDGE

Stackridge	LP	MCA	MDKS8002	1971	£20	£8	

STACKWADDY

Bugger Off	LP	Dandelion	2310231	1972	£50	£25	
Roadrunner	7"	Dandelion	5119	1970	£6	£2.50	
Stackwaddy	LP	Dandelion	2310154/ DAN8003	1971	£40	£20	
You Really Got Me	7"	Dandelion	2001331	1972	£5	£2	

STACY, JESS

Jess Stacy	10" LP	Brunswick	LA8737	1956	£15	£6	
Jess Stacy And The Famous Sidemen	LP	London	LTZK15012	1957	£15	£6	

STAEHELY BROTHERS

Sta-Hay-Lee	LP	Epic	32385	1973	£25	£10	*US*

STAFFORD, JO

Title	Format	Label	Cat. No.	Year	Mint	VG	Notes
American Folk Songs	10" LP	Capitol	LC6500	1950	**£15**	**£6**	
As You Desire Me	10" LP	Columbia	33S1024	1954	**£20**	**£8**	
Autumn In New York	10" LP	Capitol	H197	195–	**£20**	**£8**	*US*
Ballad Of The Blues	LP	Philips	BBL7327	1959	**£10**	**£4**	
Capitol Presents	10" LP	Capitol	LC6575	1953	**£15**	**£6**	
Capitol Presents Vol. 2	10" LP	Capitol	LC6635	1954	**£15**	**£6**	
Chow, Willy	7"	Columbia	SCM5064	1953	**£12**	**£6**	*with Frankie Laine*
Floatin' Down To Cotton Town	10" LP	Philips	BBR8075	1956	**£25**	**£10**	*with Frankie Laine*
Greatest Hits	LP	Columbia	CL1228	1959	**£20**	**£8**	*US*
Happy Holiday	LP	Philips	BBL7100	1956	**£12**	**£5**	
I'll Be Seeing You	LP	Philips	BBL7290	1959	**£10**	**£4**	
It Is No Secret	7"	Columbia	SCM5012	1953	**£8**	**£4**	
Jo + Jazz	7" EP	Philips	BBE12459	1961	**£6**	**£2.50**	
Jo + Jazz	LP	Philips	BBL7428/ SBBL595	1960	**£10**	**£4**	
Jo Stafford	7" EP	Philips	BBE12014	1955	**£10**	**£5**	
Jo Stafford And Nelson Eddy	7" EP	Columbia	SEG7516	1954	**£5**	**£2**	*with Nelson Eddy*
Jo Stafford No. 2	7" EP	Philips	BBE12138	1957	**£6**	**£2.50**	
Jo Stafford Touch	7" EP	Capitol	EAP20049	1960	**£5**	**£2**	
Jo Stafford With Art Van Damme Quintet	7" EP	Philips	BBE12141	1957	**£6**	**£2.50**	
Keep It A Secret	7"	Columbia	SCM5026	1953	**£8**	**£4**	
Kiss Me Kate	10" LP	Capitol	LC6515	1951	**£12**	**£5**	*with Gordon MacRae*
Musical Portrait Of New Orleans	LP	Columbia	CL578	195–	**£20**	**£8**	*US, with Frankie Laine*
My Heart's In The Highlands	10" LP	Philips	BBR8011	1954	**£15**	**£6**	
On London Bridge	7"	Philips	JK1003	1957	**£8**	**£4**	
Once Over Lightly	LP	Philips	BBL7169	1957	**£12**	**£5**	
Pine Top's Boogie	7"	Philips	PB935	1959	**£5**	**£2**	
Settin' The Woods On Fire	7"	Columbia	SCM5014	1953	**£15**	**£7.50**	*with Frankie Laine*
Show Songs	7" EP	Columbia	SEG7548	1954	**£5**	**£2**	
Showcase	LP	Philips	BBL7395	1960	**£10**	**£4**	
Simple Melody	7" EP	Capitol	EAP20154	1961	**£5**	**£2**	
Sings Sacred Songs	7" EP	Philips	BBE12147	1957	**£5**	**£2**	
Sings Sacred Songs No. 2	7" EP	Philips	BBE12198	1958	**£5**	**£2**	
Sings Sacred Songs No. 3	7" EP	Philips	BBE12378	1960	**£5**	**£2**	
Sings Songs Of Scotland	7" EP	Philips	BBE12163	1958	**£5**	**£2**	
Ski Trails	LP	Philips	BBL7187	1957	**£12**	**£5**	
Something To Remember You By	7"	Columbia	SCM5046	1953	**£6**	**£2.50**	
Songs Of Scotland	LP	Columbia	CL1043	1957	**£20**	**£8**	*US*
Star Of Hope	7"	Columbia	SCM5011	1953	**£8**	**£4**	
Sunday Evening Songs	10" LP	Capitol	LC6611	1953	**£15**	**£6**	*with Gordon MacRae*
Swingin' Down Broadway	LP	Philips	BBL7243	1958	**£10**	**£4**	
TV Series	7" EP	Philips	BBE12214	1958	**£8**	**£4**	
Voice Of Your Choice	10" LP	Philips	BBR8076	1956	**£15**	**£6**	
With A Little Bit Of Luck	7"	Philips	PB818	1958	**£4**	**£1.50**	
You Belong To Me	7"	Columbia	SCM5013	1953	**£15**	**£7.50**	

STAFFORD, TERRY

Title	Format	Label	Cat. No.	Year	Mint	VG	Notes
Follow The Rainbow	7"	London	HLU9923	1964	**£5**	**£2**	
Heartache On The Way	7"	Stateside	SS225	1963	**£5**	**£2**	
I'll Touch A Star	7"	London	HLU9902	1964	**£5**	**£2**	
Suspicion	7"	London	HLU9871	1964	**£4**	**£1.50**	
Suspicion	7" EP	London	REU1436	1964	**£30**	**£15**	
Suspicion	LP	London	HAU8200	1964	**£50**	**£25**	

STAINED GLASS

Title	Format	Label	Cat. No.	Year	Mint	VG	Notes
Aurora	LP	Capitol	ST242	1971	**£25**	**£10**	*US*
Crazy Horse Roads	LP	Capitol	ST154	1969	**£25**	**£10**	*US*

STAINED GLASS (2)

Title	Format	Label	Cat. No.	Year	Mint	VG	Notes
Open Road	LP	Sweet Folk And Country	SFA019	1975	**£200**	**£100**	

STAIRWAY

Title	Format	Label	Cat. No.	Year	Mint	VG	Notes
Moonstone	CD	New World	NWCD168	1986	**£15**	**£6**	

STAKKER

Title	Format	Label	Cat. No.	Year	Mint	VG	Notes
Humanoid	12"	Westside	WSRT12	1988	**£6**	**£2.50**	
Humanoid	CD-s	Westside	WSRCD12	1988	**£6**	**£2.50**	*3" single*

STAMFORD BRIDGE & FRIENDS

Title	Format	Label	Cat. No.	Year	Mint	VG	Notes
Come Up And See Us Some Time	LP	Penny Farthing	PELS507	1970	**£50**	**£25**	

STAMP, TERRY

Title	Format	Label	Cat. No.	Year	Mint	VG	Notes
Fat Sticks	LP	A&M	AMLH63329	1975	**£15**	**£6**	

STAMPEDE

Title	Format	Label	Cat. No.	Year	Mint	VG	Notes
Days Of Wine And Roses	12"	Polydor	POSPX507	1982	**£20**	**£10**	
Days Of Wine And Roses	7"	Polydor	POSP507	1982	**£6**	**£2.50**	
Other Side	7"	Polydor	POSP592	1983	**£5**	**£2**	

STAMPEDERS

Title	Format	Label	Cat. No.	Year	Price	Price	Notes
From The Fire	LP	Regal Zonophone	SLRZ1039	1974	£15	£6	
Stampeders	LP	Regal Zonophone	SLRZ1032	1972	£15	£6	

STAMPLEY, JOE

Title	Format	Label	Cat. No.	Year	Price	Price	Notes
Soul Song	7"	Dot	DOT145	1973	£5	£2	

STANBACK, JEAN

Title	Format	Label	Cat. No.	Year	Price	Price	Notes
I Still Love You	7"	Deep Soul	DS9101	1970	£10	£5	

STANDELLS

The Standells were responsible for a definitive garage punk performance in the single 'Dirty Water'. Much of the group's other material is in the same league, apart from the *Hot Ones* album, which is an ill-advised collection of cover versions. Gary Leeds, who was subsequently one of the Walker Brothers, is the drummer on the first LP, *In Person At P.J.'s.*

Title	Format	Label	Cat. No.	Year	Price	Price	Notes
Dirty Water	7"	Capitol	CL15446	1966	£15	£7.50	
Dirty Water	7" EP	Capitol	EAP122009	1966	£150	£75	*French*
Dirty Water	LP	Tower	(S)T5027	1966	£40	£20	*US*
Help Yourself	7"	Liberty	LIB55722	1964	£15	£7.50	
Hot Ones	LP	Tower	(S)T5049	1966	£40	£20	*US*
In Person At P.J.'s	LP	Liberty	LBY1243	1965	£40	£20	
In Person At P.J.'s	7" EP	Liberty	LEP2211	1964	£100	£50	*French*
Live & Out Of Sight	LP	Sunset	SUM1186/ SUS5186	1966	£40	£20	*US*
Try It	LP	Tower	(S)T5098	1967	£40	£20	*US*
Why Pick On Me	LP	Tower	(S)T5044	1966	£40	£20	*US*

STANDLEY, JOHNNY

Title	Format	Label	Cat. No.	Year	Price	Price	Notes
It's In The Book	7" EP	Capitol	EAP1020	1956	£6	£2.50	

STANG, ARNOLD

Title	Format	Label	Cat. No.	Year	Price	Price	Notes
Where Ya' Calling From, Charlie	7"	Fontana	H226	1959	£4	£1.50	

STANSFIELD, LISA

Title	Format	Label	Cat. No.	Year	Price	Price	Notes
Your Alibis	7"	Devil	DEV2	1981	£4	£1.50	*picture sleeve*

STANSHALL, VIV

The former lead singer of the Bonzo Dog Band made a number of eccentric records after the demise of that group. One recording not listed here is the alternative ending to Mike Oldfield's *Tubular Bells* (included in the four-album boxed set of Oldfield's first Virgin recordings) in which Stanshall is the commentator for a drunken guided tour of the Manor recording-studio complex. This favourite caricature of a vacuous aristocrat was the inspiration behind Stanshall's classic comedy recording *Sir Henry At Rawlinson End*, versions of which were first broadcast on the radio. 'Labio-Dental Fricative' would be an unlikely title for a single by anyone but Stanshall – it is one for Eric Clapton completists, as the guitarist lends his support to the musical proceedings.

Title	Format	Label	Cat. No.	Year	Price	Price	Notes
Labio-Dental Fricative	7"	Liberty	LBS15309	1970	£12	£6	*with Eric Clapton*
Lakanga	7"	Warner Bros	K16424	1974	£4	£1.50	
Men Opening Umbrellas Ahead	LP	Warner Bros	K56052	1974	£20	£8	
Question	7"	Harvest	HAR5114	1976	£4	£1.50	
Sir Henry At Rawlinson End	LP	Charisma	CAS1139	1978	£12	£5	
Suspicion	7"	Fly	BUG4	1970	£6	£2.50	
Teddy Boys Don't Knit	LP	Charisma	CAS1153	1981	£10	£4	
Terry Keeps His Clips On	7"	Charisma	CB373	1980	£4	£1.50	

STAPLE SINGERS

Title	Format	Label	Cat. No.	Year	Price	Price	Notes
Beatitude/Respect Yourself	LP	Stax	2325069	1972	£10	£4	
City In The Sky	LP	Stax	STX1001	1972	£10	£4	
City In The Sky	LP	Stax	STX1001	1972	£10	£4	
For What It's Worth	7"	Soul City	SC117	1969	£5	£2	
For What It's Worth	7"	Columbia	DB8292	1967	£6	£2.50	
Freedom Highway	LP	Columbia	SX6023	1966	£20	£8	
Hammer And Nails	7"	Riverside	106902	1963	£6	£2.50	
Hammer And Nails	LP	Riverside	RLP3501	1963	£25	£10	
Saviour Is Born	7" EP	Riverside	REP3220	1962	£6	£2.50	
Soul Folk In Action	LP	Stax	2363011	1971	£10	£4	
Staple Singers	LP	Stax	2362005	1971	£10	£4	
Swing Low	LP	Stateside	SL10015	1963	£20	£8	
Uncloudy Day	LP	Fontana	688515ZL	1965	£15	£6	
We'll Get Over	LP	Stax	SXATS1018	1969	£10	£4	

STAPLETON, CYRIL

Title	Format	Label	Cat. No.	Year	Price	Price	Notes
Blue Star	7"	Decca	F10559	1955	£5	£2	
Come Twistin'	LP	Ace Of Clubs	ACL1114	1962	£15	£6	
Department S	7"	Pye	7N17807	1969	£20	£10	*picture sleeve*
Department S	7"	Pye	7N17807	1969	£10	£5	
Elephant Tango	7"	Decca	F10488	1955	£5	£2	
Fanfare Boogie	7"	Decca	F10470	1955	£4	£1.50	
Forgotten Dreams	7"	Decca	F10912	1957	£4	£1.50	
Happy Whistler	7"	Decca	F10735	1956	£5	£2	
Italian Theme	7"	Decca	F10703	1956	£5	£2	
Presenting	7" EP	Decca	DFE6288	1956	£5	£2	
Presenting No. 2	7" EP	Decca	DFE6340	1956	£5	£2	
Theme From The Power Game	7"	Pye	7N17040	1966	£5	£2	*picture sleeve*

STAPREST

| Schooldays | 7" | Avatar | AAA103 | 1981 | **£10** | **£5** | |

STARCASTLE

| Citadel | LP | Epic | 34935 | 1978 | **£10** | **£4** | *US picture disc* |

STARCHER, BUDDY

And His Mountain Guitar Vol. 1	7" EP	London	REB1424	1964	**£8**	**£4**	
And His Mountain Guitar Vol. 2	7" EP	London	REB1425	1964	**£8**	**£4**	
And His Mountain Guitar Vol. 3	7" EP	London	REB1426	1964	**£8**	**£4**	

STARFIGHTERS

| I'm Calling | 7" | Motor City | MCR105 | 1980 | **£20** | **£10** | *picture sleeve* |

STARFIRES

| Starfires Play | LP | Ohio Recording Service | 34 | 1964 | **£40** | **£20** | *US* |
| Teenbeat A Go-Go | LP | La Brea | LS8018 | 1965 | **£40** | **£20** | *US* |

STARGAZERS

365 Kisses	7"	Decca	F10379	1954	**£4**	**£1.50**	
Close The Door	7"	Decca	F10594	1955	**£8**	**£4**	
Crazy Otto Rag	7"	Decca	F10523	1955	**£8**	**£4**	
Happy Wanderer	7"	Decca	F10259	1954	**£10**	**£5**	
Honky Tonk Song	7"	Decca	F10898	1957	**£4**	**£1.50**	
I See The Moon	7"	Decca	F10213	1953	**£15**	**£7.50**	
Presenting The Stargazers	10" LP	Decca	LF1186	1954	**£30**	**£15**	
Rocking And Rolling	7"	Decca	F10731	1956	**£8**	**£4**	
Rocking And Rolling	7" EP	Decca	DFE6362	1956	**£15**	**£7.50**	
Rose Of The Wildwood	7"	Decca	F10412	1954	**£4**	**£1.50**	
She Loves To Rock	7"	Decca	F10775	1956	**£8**	**£4**	
Skiffling Dogs	7"	Decca	F10969	1957	**£4**	**£1.50**	
Somebody	7"	Decca	F10437	1955	**£8**	**£4**	
South Of The Border	LP	Decca	LK4309	1959	**£25**	**£10**	
Stargazers	7" EP	Decca	DFE6341	1956	**£15**	**£7.50**	
Tender Trap	7"	Decca	F10668	1956	**£4**	**£1.50**	
Twenty Tiny Fingers	7"	Decca	F10626	1955	**£8**	**£4**	
Who Is It?	7"	Decca	F10916	1957	**£4**	**£1.50**	
You Won't Be Around	7"	Decca	F10867	1957	**£4**	**£1.50**	
Zambesi	7"	Decca	F10696	1956	**£5**	**£2**	

STARK, PETER

| Mushroom Country | LP | Montage | | 1976 | **£50** | **£25** | *US* |

STARK NAKED

| Stark Naked | LP | RCA | SP4592 | 1971 | **£25** | **£10** | *US* |

STARR, CINDY

| Pain Of Love | 7" | Columbia | DB107 | 1968 | **£4** | **£1.50** | *with the Rude Boys* |
| Way I Do | 7" | Columbia | DB110 | 1968 | **£4** | **£1.50** | *with the Mopeds* |

STARR, EDWIN

25 Miles	7"	Tamla Motown	TMG672	1968	**£4**	**£1.50**	
25 Miles	LP	Tamla Motown	(S)TML11115	1969	**£15**	**£6**	
Agent OO-Soul	7"	Tamla Motown	TMG790	1971	**£4**	**£1.50**	
Headline News	7"	Polydor	56717	1966	**£6**	**£2.50**	
Hell Up In Harlem	LP	Tamla Motown	STML11260	1974	**£12**	**£5**	
Hits Of Edwin Starr	LP	Tamla Motown	STML11209	1972	**£12**	**£5**	
I Am The Man For You Baby	7"	Tamla Motown	TMG646	1968	**£10**	**£5**	
I Want My Baby Back	7"	Tamla Motown	TMG630	1967	**£10**	**£5**	
Involved	LP	Tamla Motown	STML11199	1972	**£10**	**£4**	
It's My Turn Now	7"	Polydor	56726	1967	**£10**	**£5**	
Just We Two	LP	Tamla Motown	(S)TML11131	1970	**£12**	**£5**	*with Blinky*
Oh How Happy	7"	Tamla Motown	TMG720	1969	**£100**	**£50**	*demo only, with Blinky*
Oh How Happy	7"	Tamla Motown	TMG748	1970	**£4**	**£1.50**	*with Blinky*
Soul Master	LP	Tamla Motown	(S)TML11094	1969	**£25**	**£10**	
Stop Her On Sight	7"	Polydor	56702	1966	**£8**	**£4**	
Stop Her On Sight	7"	Polydor	56753	1968	**£4**	**£1.50**	
Time	7"	Tamla Motown	TMG725	1970	**£4**	**£1.50**	
War	7"	Tamla Motown	TMG754	1970	**£4**	**£1.50**	
Way Over There	7"	Tamla Motown	TMG692	1969	**£5**	**£2**	

STARR, FRANK

Title	Format	Label	Cat. No.	Year	Mint	Good	Notes
Little Bitty Feeling	7"	London	HLU9545	1962	**£8**	**£4**	

STARR, FREDDIE

Comedian Freddie Starr's inspired impersonations of Elvis Presley are made slightly poignant by the knowledge that Starr is a failed rock singer made good. His group, the Midnighters, was one of the many Merseybeat outfits to emerge in the wake of the Beatles, but none of its singles managed to enter the charts. Starr's drummer was Keef Hartley, who subsequently played with the Artwoods and John Mayall before leading his own band.

Title	Format	Label	Cat. No.	Year	Mint	Good	Notes
Baby Blue	7"	Decca	F11786	1963	**£25**	**£12.50**	
Never Cry On Someone's Shoulder	7"	Decca	F12009	1964	**£25**	**£12.50**	
This Is Liverpool Beat	LP	Vogue	LDVS17006	1964	**£60**	**£30**	*German*
Who Told You	7"	Decca	F11663	1963	**£25**	**£12.50**	

STARR, JIMMY

Title	Format	Label	Cat. No.	Year	Mint	Good	Notes
It's Only Make Believe	7"	London	HL8731	1958	**£25**	**£12.50**	

STARR, KAY

Title	Format	Label	Cat. No.	Year	Mint	Good	Notes
Am I A Toy Or A Treasure?	7"	Capitol	CL14151	1955	**£10**	**£5**	
Blue Starr	LP	RCA	RD27056	1958	**£10**	**£4**	
Capitol Presents	10" LP	Capitol	LC6574	1953	**£15**	**£6**	
Fool Fool Fool	7"	Capitol	CL14167	1954	**£10**	**£5**	
Foolin' Around	7"	Capitol	CL15194	1961	**£4**	**£1.50**	
Foolishly Yours	7"	HMV	7M307	1955	**£6**	**£2.50**	
Heavenly Kay Starr	7" EP	Top Rank	JKP2042	1960	**£8**	**£4**	
Hits Of Kay Starr	10" LP	Capitol	LC6835	1956	**£15**	**£6**	
If Anyone Finds This, I Love You	7"	HMV	7M300	1955	**£6**	**£2.50**	
In A Blue Mood	LP	Capitol	T580	1957	**£10**	**£4**	
Jamie Boy	7"	HMV	POP357	1957	**£5**	**£2**	
Kay Starr	7" EP	Vogue	EPV1014	1955	**£10**	**£5**	
Kay Starr Style	10" LP	Capitol	LC6630	1954	**£15**	**£6**	
Kay Stars Again	7" EP	HMV	7EG8184	1956	**£6**	**£2.50**	
Little Loneliness	7"	HMV	POP345	1957	**£5**	**£2**	
Moving Pt 1	7" EP	Capitol	EAP11254	1960	**£5**	**£2**	
Moving Pt 2	7" EP	Capitol	EAP21254	1960	**£5**	**£2**	
Moving Pt 3	7" EP	Capitol	EAP31254	1960	**£10**	**£5**	
Riders In The Sky	7"	Capitol	CL15105	1959	**£4**	**£1.50**	
Rock And Roll Waltz	7"	HMV	7M371	1956	**£10**	**£5**	
Rockin' With Kay	LP	RCA	LPM1720	1958	**£20**	**£8**	*US*
Second Fiddle	7"	HMV	7M420	1956	**£8**	**£4**	
Stroll Me	7"	RCA	RCA1065	1958	**£4**	**£1.50**	
Swinging With The Starr	LP	London	HAU2039	1957	**£20**	**£8**	
Well I Ask You	7" EP	Capitol	EAP120210	1962	**£5**	**£2**	
What A Star Is Kay	7" EP	HMV	7EG8165	1956	**£6**	**£2.50**	
Wheel Of Fortune	7"	Capitol	CL15137	1960	**£4**	**£1.50**	
Wheel Of Fortune	7" EP	Capitol	EAP120063	1961	**£8**	**£4**	
Where, What Or When?	7"	HMV	7M315	1955	**£6**	**£2.50**	

STARR, MAXINE

Title	Format	Label	Cat. No.	Year	Mint	Good	Notes
Wishing Star	7"	London	HLU9712	1963	**£4**	**£1.50**	

STARR, RANDY

Title	Format	Label	Cat. No.	Year	Mint	Good	Notes
After School	7"	London	HL8443	1957	**£25**	**£12.50**	
Count On Me	7"	Felsted	AF106	1958	**£8**	**£4**	
Workin' On The Santa Fe	7"	Top Rank	JAR264	1960	**£4**	**£1.50**	

STARR, RINGO

The rarest Ringo Starr record typifies the variety of work that Starr has undertaken since the break-up of the Beatles. *Scouse The Mouse* is a children's story produced by Donald Pleasence and dramatized with Ringo Starr playing the title role (and singing eight songs). A projected TV version never happened so that the album failed to attract any attention at the time of its release.

Title	Format	Label	Cat. No.	Year	Mint	Good	Notes
Beaucoups Of Blues	LP	Apple	PAS10002	1970	**£15**	**£6**	
Dose Of Rock'n'Roll	7"	Polydor	2001694	1976	**£4**	**£1.50**	
Drowning In A Sea Of Love	7"	Polydor	2001734	1977	**£40**	**£20**	
Hey Baby	7"	Polydor	2001699	1976	**£4**	**£1.50**	
Lipstick Traces	7"	Polydor	2001782	1978	**£60**	**£30**	*demo*
Oh My My	7"	Apple	R6011	1976	**£6**	**£2.50**	
Old Wave	LP	Bellaphon	26016029	1983	**£40**	**£20**	*German*
Old Wave/Stop And Smell The Roses	CD	Right Stuff	DPRO66732	1994	**£100**	**£50**	*US promo sampler with bonus track*
Only You	7"	Apple	PSR374	1974	**£150**	**£75**	*interview promo*
Ringo	CD	DCC	GZS1066	1994	**£15**	**£6**	*US audiophile*
Ringo	LP	Apple	SWAL3413	1973	**£12**	**£5**	*US, with long version of 'Six O' Clock'*
Ringo Starr And His All Starr Band	CD	Ryko		1990	**£20**	**£8**	*US, with bonus CD-s*
Scouse The Mouse	cass	Polydor	3194429	1978	**£15**	**£6**	*with other artists*
Scouse The Mouse	LP	Polydor	2480429	1978	**£75**	**£37.50**	*with other artists*
Sentimental Journey	LP	Apple	PCS7101	1970	**£15**	**£6**	
Sentimental Journey	r-reel	Apple	TAPMC7101	1970	**£20**	**£8**	*mono*
Sentimental Journey	r-reel	Apple	TDPCS7101	1970	**£15**	**£6**	*stereo*
Steel	7"	R.O.R.	ROR2001	1972	**£200**	**£100**	*1 sided interview promo*
Tonight	7"	Polydor	2001795	1978	**£30**	**£15**	

STARR, STELLA

Title	Format	Label	Cat. No.	Year	Mint	Median	Notes
Bring Him Back	7"	Piccadilly	7N35366	1967	£25	£12.50	

STARR, TONY

Title	Format	Label	Cat. No.	Year	Mint	Median	Notes
Rocket To The Moon	7"	Decca	F11847	1964	£30	£15	

STARRY EYED AND LAUGHING

Title	Format	Label	Cat. No.	Year	Mint	Median	Notes
Starry Eyed And Laughing	LP	CBS	80450	1974	£10	£4	
Thought Talk	LP	CBS	80907	1975	£10	£4	

STARS OF HEAVEN

Title	Format	Label	Cat. No.	Year	Mint	Median	Notes
Clothes Of Pride	7"	Hotwire	HWS855	1985	£8	£4	

STATE OF MICKY & TOMMY

Title	Format	Label	Cat. No.	Year	Mint	Median	Notes
Frisco Bay	7"	Mercury	MF1009	1967	£50	£25	
Frisco Bay	7" EP	Mercury	152102	196–	£60	£30	*French*
With Love From	7" EP	Mercury	152095	196–	£60	£30	*French*
With Love From One To Five	7"	Mercury	MF996	1967	£50	£25	

STATESMEN

Title	Format	Label	Cat. No.	Year	Mint	Median	Notes
I've Just Fallen In Love	7"	Fontana	TF432	1964	£4	£1.50	
Look Around	7"	Decca	F11687	1963	£4	£1.50	

STATESMEN (2)

Title	Format	Label	Cat. No.	Year	Mint	Median	Notes
Five Plus One	LP	Studio Republic		1963	£100	£50	

STATIC

Title	Format	Label	Cat. No.	Year	Mint	Median	Notes
When You Went Away	7"	Page One	POF039	1967	£5	£2	

STATION SKIFFLE GROUP

Title	Format	Label	Cat. No.	Year	Mint	Median	Notes
Station Skiffle Group	7" EP	Esquire	EP161	1958	£40	£20	

STATON, DAKOTA

Title	Format	Label	Cat. No.	Year	Mint	Median	Notes
Ballads And The Blues	LP	Capitol	(S)T1387	1960	£10	£4	
Confessin' The Blues	7"	Capitol	CL14917	1959	£5	£2	
Crazy He Calls Me	LP	Capitol	T1170	1959	£10	£4	
Don't Leave Me Now	7"	Capitol	CL14314	1955	£6	£2.50	
Dynamic Dakota Staton	7" EP	Capitol	EAP11054	1959	£6	£2.50	
Dynamic Dakota Staton	LP	Capitol	(S)T1054	1959	£10	£4	
Dynamic Dakota Staton Pt 2	7" EP	Capitol	EAP21054	1959	£6	£2.50	
Dynamic Dakota Staton Pt 3	7" EP	Capitol	EAP31054	1959	£6	£2.50	
I Never Dreamt	7"	Capitol	CL14339	1955	£4	£1.50	
Invitation	LP	World Record Club	T387	196–	£10	£4	
Late, Late Show	LP	Capitol	T876	1958	£10	£4	
More Than The Mood	LP	Capitol	(S)T1325	1960	£10	£4	
Party's Over	7"	Capitol	CL14870	1958	£4	£1.50	
Time To Swing	LP	Capitol	(S)T1421	1961	£10	£4	

STATUES

Title	Format	Label	Cat. No.	Year	Mint	Median	Notes
Blue Velvet	7"	London	HLG9192	1960	£30	£15	

STATUS QUO

Status Quo are one of the more unlikely success stories of rock music, having stuck with the same Chuck Berry and boogie style ever since first deciding on it some time around 1970. The group's earlier recordings – as the Spectres and Traffic Jam before becoming Status Quo – are more varied in style, but perhaps not very expertly performed. The slightly psychedelic 'Pictures Of Matchstick Men' was a considerable hit, of course, but no one bought the accompanying album, which is now extremely scarce. Its awkward title probably did not help its sales when released: *Picturesque Matchstickable Messages*. The succeeding *Spare Parts* is also highly sought-after today, as is the Marble Arch release *Status Quotations*, even though this is only a compilation of singles and tracks from the first LP.

Title	Format	Label	Cat. No.	Year	Mint	Median	Notes
1+9+8+2	CD	Vertigo	8000352	1983	£25	£10	
Ain't Complainin'	CD-s	Vertigo	QUOCD22	1988	£8	£4	
Ain't Complaining	CD-s	Vertigo	0803222	1988	£30	£15	*CD video*
Anniversary Waltz	CD-s	Vertigo	QUOCD28	1990	£5	£2	
Anniversary Waltz Part 2	CD-s	Vertigo	QUOCD29	1990	£5	£2	
Anniversary Waltz Part One	7"	Vertigo	QUOG28	1990	£5	£2	*silver vinyl*
Anniversary Waltz Parts 1 & 2	12"	Vertigo	QUO2812	1990	£25	£12.50	*B side plays Little Lady & Paper Plane*
Anniversary Waltz Parts 1 & 2	7"	Vertigo	QUODJ28	1990	£12	£6	*promo*
Are You Growing Tired Of My Love	7"	Pye	7N17728	1969	£15	£7.50	
Back To Back	CD	Vertigo	814662	1983	£12	£5	
Black Veils Of Melancholy	7"	Pye	7N17497	1968	£12	£6	
Burning Bridges	CD-s	Vertigo	QUOCD25	1988	£6	£2.50	
Burning Bridges	CD-s	Vertigo	0806202	1988	£20	£10	*CD video*
Can't Give You More	7"	Vertigo	STATUS30	1991	£12	£6	*promo*
Can't Give You More	CD-s	Vertigo	QUOCD30	1991	£12	£6	
Caroline	7"	Vertigo	QUOP10	1982	£6	£2.50	*picture disc*
Caroline (Live)	12"	Vertigo	QUO1012	1982	£6	£2.50	
Down Down Down	7"	Lyntone	LYN3154/5	1976	£6	£2.50	*flexi, picture sleeve*
Dreamin'	7"	Vertigo	QUOP21	1986	£6	£2.50	*with poster*
Fakin' The Blues	12"	Vertigo	QUO3112	1991	£150	£75	
Fakin' The Blues	7"	Vertigo	QUO31	1991	£150	£75	
Fakin' The Blues	CD-s	Vertigo	QUOCD31	1993	£20	£10	*no inlay*
File Series	LP	Pye	FILD005	1977	£15	£6	*double*
From The Beginning	LP	PRT	PYX4007	1988	£12	£5	*picture disc*

Title	Format	Label	Cat. No.	Year	Mint	VG	Notes
From The Makers Of	LP	Vertigo	PROBX1	1982	**£15**	**£6**	*3 LPs in metal box*
From The Makers Of	LP	Phonogram	PROBX1	1982	**£300**	**£180**	*promo bronze tin*
Gerdundula	7"	Pye	7N45253	1973	**£5**	**£2**	
Hello	LP	Vertigo	6360098	1973	**£10**	**£4**	*with inner sleeve & poster*
In My Chair	7"	Pye	7P103	1979	**£5**	**£2**	*picture sleeve*
In My Chair	7"	Pye	7N17998	1970	**£40**	**£20**	*picture sleeve*
In My Chair	7"	Pye	QUO1	1979	**£4**	**£1.50**	*flexi*
In The Army Now	12"	Vertigo	QUO2012	1986	**£15**	**£7.50**	*with poster*
In The Army Now	7"	Vertigo	QUODP20	1986	**£6**	**£2.50**	*double*
In The Army Now	7"	Vertigo	QUOPD20	1986	**£20**	**£10**	*picture disc*
In The Army Now	7"	Vertigo	QUO20	1986	**£5**	**£2**	*with patch*
Jealousy	7"	Vertigo	QUO9	1982	**£100**	**£50**	*Irish promo*
Just For The Record	LP	Pye	NSPL18607	1979	**£10**	**£4**	*red vinyl*
Lies	7"	Vertigo	QUO4	1980	**£5**	**£2**	*misspelt B side*
Little Dreamer	CD-s	Vertigo	QUOCD27	1989	**£6**	**£2.50**	
Ma Kelly's Greasy Spoon	LP	Pye	NSPL18344	1970	**£15**	**£6**	*with poster*
Make Me Stay A Bit Longer	7"	Pye	7N17665	1969	**£15**	**£7.50**	
Marguerita Time	7"	Vertigo	QUOP14	1983	**£10**	**£5**	*picture disc*
Marguerita Time	7"	Vertigo	QUOP1414	1983	**£12**	**£6**	*double Xmas gift pack*
Marguerita Time	7"	Vertigo	QUO1414	1983	**£15**	**£7.50**	*double*
Mess Of Blues	12"	Vertigo	QUO1212	1983	**£6**	**£2.50**	
Mess Of Blues	7"	Vertigo	QUO12	1983	**£10**	**£5**	*reversed sleeve, rear table picture*
Never Too Late	CD	Vertigo	8000532	1983	**£25**	**£10**	
Not At All	CD-s	Vertigo	QUOCD26	1989	**£6**	**£2.50**	
Ol' Rag Blues	12"	Vertigo	QUO1112	1983	**£6**	**£2.50**	
Paper Plane	7"	Vertigo	6059071	1972	**£5**	**£2**	
Pictures Of Matchstick Men	7"	Pye	FBS2	1979	**£5**	**£2**	*yellow vinyl*
Pictures Of Matchstick Men	7"	Pye	7N17449	1968	**£5**	**£2**	
Picturesque Matchstickable Messages	LP	Pye	N(S)PL18220	1968	**£100**	**£25**	
Price Of Love	7"	Pye	7N17825	1969	**£15**	**£7.50**	
Quo	LP	Vertigo	ACB00217	1974	**£15**	**£6**	*record club issue*
Red Sky	12"	Vertigo	QUO1912	1986	**£12**	**£6**	*poster sleeve*
Red Sky	7"	Vertigo	QUOD19	1986	**£6**	**£2.50**	*double*
Rock 'Til You Drop	CD-s	Vertigo	QUOCD32	1991	**£5**	**£2**	
Rock Till You Drop	12"	Vertigo	QUO3212	1992	**£6**	**£2.50**	*2 tracks*
Rock'n'Roll	7"	Vertigo	QUOJB6	1981	**£5**	**£2**	*jukebox issue, no picture sleeve*
Rockin' All Over The World	7"	Vertigo	6059184	1977	**£6**	**£2.50**	*picture sleeve*
Rockin' All Over The World	7"	Vertigo	6059184	1977	**£15**	**£7.50**	*picture sleeve, poster*
Rollin' Home	7"	Vertigo	QUOP18	1986	**£10**	**£5**	*shaped picture disc*
Running All Over The World	CD-s	Vertigo	QUACD1	1988	**£8**	**£4**	
Spare Parts	LP	Pye	N(S)PL18301	1968	**£100**	**£25**	
Status Quotations	LP	Marble Arch	MAL(S)1193	1969	**£40**	**£20**	
Technicolour Dreams	7"	Pye	7N17650	1968	**£1000**	**£700**	*best auctioned*
Technicolour Dreams	7"	Pye	7N17650	1968	**£500**	**£330**	*demo, best auctioned*
Tune To The Music	7"	Pye	7N45077	1971	**£12**	**£6**	
Wanderer	12"	Vertigo	QUOP16	1984	**£15**	**£7.50**	*clear vinyl, picture disc centre*
Who Gets The Love?	CD-s	Vertigo	QUOCD23	1988	**£8**	**£4**	

STAVELY MAKEPEACE

Title	Format	Label	Cat. No.	Year	Mint	VG	Notes
Tarzan Harvey	7"	Pyramid	PYR6082	1969	**£6**	**£2.50**	*test pressing only*

STAVERTON BRIDGE

Title	Format	Label	Cat. No.	Year	Mint	VG	Notes
Staverton Bridge	LP	Saydisc	SDL266	1975	**£25**	**£10**	

STEAMHAMMER

Steamhammer arrived at the tail end of the British blues boom amidst publicity that spoke of them being a next-generation group who would find ways of going beyond the blues. For once, this was no hype, the second LP in particular being a fine example of jazz-rock, in which Martin Pugh's fluid guitar playing is ably complemented by Steve Joliffe's flute and saxophone. The long 'Another Travelling Tune' shows how improvised rock can be entirely successful when the musicians are as inspired as these.

Title	Format	Label	Cat. No.	Year	Mint	VG	Notes
Autumn Song	7"	CBS	4496	1969	**£5**	**£2**	
Junior's Wailing	7"	CBS	4141	1969	**£5**	**£2**	
Mountains	LP	B&C	CAS1024	1970	**£25**	**£10**	
Speech	LP	Brain	1009	1972	**£25**	**£10**	*German*
Steamhammer	LP	Reflection	REFL1	1970	**£25**	**£10**	
Steamhammer	LP	CBS	63611	1968	**£30**	**£15**	
Steamhammer Mark 2	LP	CBS	63694	1969	**£25**	**£10**	
Steamhammer Mark 2	LP	Reflection	REFL12	1971	**£15**	**£6**	

STEAM-SHOVEL

Title	Format	Label	Cat. No.	Year	Mint	VG	Notes
Rudi The Red-Nosed Reindeer	7"	Decca	F22863	1968	**£6**	**£2.50**	
Rudi The Red-Nosed Reindeer	7"	Trojan	TR635	1968	**£4**	**£1.50**	

STEEL

Title	Format	Label	Cat. No.	Year	Mint	VG	Notes
Rock Out	7"	Neat	NEAT14	1981	**£6**	**£2.50**	

STEEL MILL

Bruce Springsteen once led a group called Steel Mill, but the hard rock group who recorded the scarce *Green Eyed God* album has no connection with this.

Title	Format	Label	Cat. No.	Year	Mint	VG	Notes
Get On The Line	7"	Penny Farthing	PEN783	1971	**£8**	**£4**	

Green Eyed God	7"	Penny Farthing	PEN770	1971	£8	£4	
Green Eyed God	7"	Penny Farthing	PEN894	1975	£4	£1.50	
Green Eyed God	LP	Penny Farthing	PELS549	1975	£200	£100	

STEEL RIVER

Better Road	LP	Evolution	Z3006	1971	£12	£5	
Weighing Heavy	LP	Evolution	E2018	1970	£12	£5	

STEELE, BETTE ANN

Barricade	7"	Capitol	CL14315	1955	£5	£2	

STEELE, DAVY

Long Time Getting	LP	Bracken	BKN1001	1983	£20	£8	

STEELE, DORIS

Why Must I?	7"	Oriole	CB1468	1959	£4	£1.50	

STEELE, JAN & JOHN CAGE

Voices & Instruments	LP	Obscure	OBS5	1976	£12	£5	

STEELE, SANDRA & JON

I'm Crazy With Love	7"	Parlophone	MSP6166	1955	£4	£1.50	

STEELE, TOMMY

Butterfingers	7"	Decca	F10877	1957	£5	£2	
Come On Let's Go	7"	Decca	F11072	1958	£4	£1.50	
Come On Let's Go	7" EP	Decca	DFE6551	1958	£8	£4	
Doomsday Rock	7"	Decca	F10808	1956	£20	£10	
Dream Maker	7"	Columbia	DB7070	1963	£4	£1.50	
Duke Wore Jeans	10" LP	Decca	LF1308	1958	£12	£5	
Duke Wore Jeans	7" EP	Decca	DFE6472	1958	£8	£4	
Get Happy	LP	Decca	LK4351	1960	£10	£4	
Half A Sixpence	LP	RCA	RB/SB6735	196–	£10	£4	
Happy Guitar	7"	Decca	F10976	1958	£4	£1.50	
Hey You	7"	Decca	F10941	1957	£5	£2	
Knee Deep In The Blues	7"	Decca	F10849	1957	£8	£4	
Little White Bull	7"	Decca	F11177	1959	£5	£2	*picture sleeve*
Nairobi	7"	Decca	F10991	1958	£4	£1.50	
Only Man On The Island	7"	Decca	F11041	1958	£4	£1.50	
Rock With The Caveman	7"	Decca	F10795	1956	£25	£12.50	
Shiralee	7"	Decca	F10896	1957	£6	£2.50	
Singing The Blues	7"	Decca	F10819	1956	£10	£5	
Singing The Blues	7" EP	Decca	DFE6389	1956	£10	£5	
Tallahassie Lassie	7"	Decca	F11152	1959	£5	£2	
Tommy Steele	7" EP	Decca	DFE6592	1959	£6	£2.50	
Tommy Steele Stage Show	10" LP	Decca	LF1287	1957	£20	£8	
Tommy Steele Story	10" LP	Decca	LF1288	1957	£15	£6	
Tommy Steele Story Vol. 1	7" EP	Decca	DFE6398	1957	£10	£5	
Tommy Steele Story Vol. 2	7" EP	Decca	DFE6424	1957	£10	£5	
Tommy The Toreador	7" EP	Decca	DFE6607	1959	£5	£2	
Trial	7"	Decca	F11117	1959	£4	£1.50	
Truth About Me	78	Weekend	14056	1957	£15	£7.50	
Water Water	7"	Decca	F10923	1957	£4	£1.50	
What A Mouth	7" EP	Decca	DFE6660	1960	£5	£2	
Young Love	7" EP	Decca	DFE6388	1956	£10	£5	

STEELEYE SPAN

Adam Catched Eve	LP	Boulevard	BD3004	1979	£12	£5	
All Around My Hat	LP	Mobile Fidelity	MFSL1027	1978	£12	£5	*US audiophile*
Hark The Village Wait	LP	RCA	SF8113	1970	£15	£6	
Jigs And Reels	7"	Pegasus	PGS6	1972	£6	£2.50	*picture sleeve*
Please To See The King	LP	B&C	CAS1029	1971	£15	£6	*textured sleeve*
Rave On	7"	B&C	CB164	1971	£4	£1.50	*picture sleeve*
Ten Man Mop	LP	Pegasus	PEG9	1971	£10	£4	*with booklet*

STEELY DAN

Aja	CD	Mobile Fidelity	UDCD515	1988	£15	£6	*US audiophile*
Aja	LP	Mobile Fidelity	MFSL1033	1979	£15	£6	*US audiophile*
Can't Buy A Thrill	LP	Command	QD40009	1974	£10	£4	*US quad*
Countdown To Ecstasy	LP	Command	QD40010	1974	£10	£4	*US quad*
Gaucho	CD	Mobile Fidelity	UDCD545	1991	£15	£6	*US audiophile*
Katy Lied	LP	Mobile Fidelity	MFSL1007	1978	£15	£6	*US audiophile*
Pretzel Logic	LP	Command	QD40015	1974	£10	£4	*US quad*

STEEPLECHASE

Lady Bright	LP	Polydor	2489001	1970	£20	£8	

STEERPIKE

Steerpike	LP	private	ADM417	1968	£400	£250	

STEGMEYER, BILL

Title	Format	Label	Cat. No.	Year	Mint	VG	Notes
On The Waterfront	7"	London	HL8078	1954	£20	£10	

STEIG, JEREMY

Title	Format	Label	Cat. No.	Year	Mint	VG	Notes
Wayfaring Stranger	LP	Blue Note	BST84354	1970	£10	£4	

STEIN, LOU

Title	Format	Label	Cat. No.	Year	Mint	VG	Notes
Almost Paradise	7"	London	HLZ8419	1957	£10	£5	
Who Slammed The Door	7"	Mercury	7MT226	1958	£4	£1.50	

STEINMAN, JIM

Title	Format	Label	Cat. No.	Year	Mint	VG	Notes
Dance In My Pants	7"	Epic	EPCA1707	1981	£5	£2	*promo*
Tonight Is What It Means To Be Young	12"	MCA	MCAT889	1984	£8	£4	

STEINWAYS

Title	Format	Label	Cat. No.	Year	Mint	VG	Notes
You've Been Leading Me On	7"	Kent	TOWN106	1985	£5	£2	*Johnny Caswell B side*

STELLA

Title	Format	Label	Cat. No.	Year	Mint	VG	Notes
Si Tu Aimes Ma Musique	7"	President	PT504	1982	£4	£1.50	

STENSON, BOBO

Title	Format	Label	Cat. No.	Year	Mint	VG	Notes
Underwear	LP	ECM	ECM1012ST	1971	£15	£6	

STEPHENS, LEIGH

Title	Format	Label	Cat. No.	Year	Mint	VG	Notes
Cast Of Thousands	LP	Charisma	CAS1040	1971	£15	£6	
Red Weather	LP	Philips	SBL7897	1969	£20	£8	

STEPPENWOLF

Although their recorded output is quite large, John Kay's Steppenwolf is quite adequately summed up by three great songs – 'Magic Carpet Ride', 'The Pusher' and especially 'Born To Be Wild'. Apart from being a glorious rocker, the last song also contains the first use of the phrase 'heavy metal'. The album *Early Steppenwolf*, recorded live at the Matrix, San Francisco in 1967, is best avoided. Long improvisations clearly did not really suit the group, who tend to use random noise as a substitute for genuine inspiration.

Title	Format	Label	Cat. No.	Year	Mint	VG	Notes
At Your Birthday Party	LP	Stateside	(S)SL5011	1969	£10	£4	
Born To Be Wild	7"	RCA	RCA1735	1968	£4	£1.50	
Early Steppenwolf	LP	Stateside	(S)SL5015	1969	£10	£4	
Live	LP	Stateside	SSL5029	1970	£10	£4	
Magic Carpet Ride	7"	Stateside	SS8003	1968	£4	£1.50	
Monster	LP	Stateside	SSL5021	1970	£10	£4	
Second	LP	Stateside	(S)SL5003	1968	£10	£4	
Sookie Sookie	7"	RCA	RCA1679	1968	£4	£1.50	
Steppenwolf	LP	RCA	RD/SF7974	1968	£12	£5	

STEREOLAB

Title	Format	Label	Cat. No.	Year	Mint	VG	Notes
Crumb Duck	10"	Clawfist	20	1993	£30	£15	*Nurse With Wound B side*
Crumb Duck	10"	Clawfist	20	1993	£40	£20	*hand made sleeve, B side by Nurse With Wound*
Crumb Duck	LP	United Dairies	UD059	1993	£20	£8	*yellow vinyl, with Nurse With Wound*
Crumb Duck	LP	United Dairies	UD059	1993	£40	£20	*pink vinyl, with Nurse With Wound*
Cybele's Reverie	10"	Duophonic	DUHFD10	1996	£10	£5	
Eclipse	7"	Wurlitzer Jukebox	WJ3	1995	£10	£5	*flexi*
French Disko	7"	Duophonic	DUHFD01P	1993	£10	£5	
French Disko	CD-s	Duophonic	DUHFD03	1993	£10	£5	
French Disko	CD-s	Flying Nun	STEREO1	1995	£6	£2.50	
Harmonium	7"	Duophonic	DS4504	1992	£20	£10	*amber vinyl*
Iron Man	7"	Duophonic	DUHFD18	1997	£6	£2.50	*red vinyl*
Jenny Ondioline	10"	Duophonic	DUHFD01	1993	£60	£30	*clear vinyl*
Jenny Ondioline	CD-s	Duophonic	DUHFCD01	1993	£6	£2.50	
Light (That Will Cease To Fail)	7"	Big Money Inc	BMI025	1992	£6	£2.50	*pink vinyl*
Long Hair Of Death	7"	Duophonic	DS4510	1995	£8	£4	*yellow vinyl*
Low Fi	10"	Too Pure	PURE14	1992	£15	£7.50	*clear vinyl*
Mars Audiac Quintet	CD	Duophonic	DUHFCD05	1995	£25	£10	*with bonus CD-s*
Mars Audiac Quintet	LP	Duophonic	DUHFD05X	1995	£20	£8	*double with bonus 7"*
Metronomic Underground	12"	Duophonic	DUHFD15	1997	£6	£2.50	
Music For The Amorphous Body Study Center	CD	Duophonic	DUHFCD08	1995	£25	£10	*soundtrack to sound and sculpture exhibition, white cover*
Music For The Amorphous Body Study Centre	10" LP	Duophonic	DUHFD08	1995	£25	£10	
Ping Pong	7"	Duophonic	DUHFD04S	1994	£5	£2	*pink or green vinyl*
Refried Ectoplasm	LP	Duophonic	DUHFD09	1995	£12	£5	*amber vinyl double*
Ronco Symphony	7"	Spacewatch	FLX2107	1993	£10	£5	*clear flexi*
Simple Headphone Mind	12"	Duophonic	DS3311	1997	£6	£2.50	*yellow vinyl, Nurse With Wound B side*
Speedy Car	7"	Duophonic	DUHFD12	1996	£12	£6	*blue vinyl, Tortoise B side*
Stunning Debut Album	7"	Duophonic	DS4502	1991	£150	£75	*multi-coloured vinyl*

Title	Format	Label	Cat. No.	Year	Mint	Value	Notes
Stunning Debut Album	7"	Duophonic	DS4502	1991	£40	£20	*clear vinyl*
Super 45	10"	Duophonic	DS4501	1991	£50	£25	
Super 45	10"	Duophonic	DS4501	1991	£75	£37.50	*hand painted picture sleeve*
Tone Burst	7"	Silvertone		1994	£60	£30	*test pressing, picture sleeve*
Transient Random Noise-Bursts With Announcements	LP	Duophonic	DUHFD02	1993	£25	£10	*gold vinyl double*
Wow And Flutter	7"	Duophonic	DUHF07	1994	£8	£4	*hand-painted sleeve*
You Used To Call Me Sadness	7"	Lissys	LISS15	1996	£10	£5	*white vinyl*

STEREOPHONICS

Title	Format	Label	Cat. No.	Year	Mint	Value	Notes
Looks Like Chaplin	7"	V2	SPH1	1996	£10	£5	
Looks Like Chaplin	CD-s	V2	SPHD1	1996	£8	£4	

STEREOS

Title	Format	Label	Cat. No.	Year	Mint	Value	Notes
Big Knock	7"	MGM	MGM1149	1961	£20	£10	
Big Knock	7"	MGM	MGM1328	1966	£10	£5	
Please Come Back To Me	7"	MGM	MGM1143	1961	£20	£10	

STERLING, LESTER

Title	Format	Label	Cat. No.	Year	Mint	Value	Notes
Africkaan Beat	7"	Coxsone	CS7080	1968	£10	£5	*Paragons B side*
Air Raid Shelter	7"	R&B	JB111	1963	£10	£5	*Roy & Annette B side*
Bangarang	7"	Unity	UN502	1968	£4	£1.50	*with Stranger Cole*
Bangarang	LP	Pama	SECO15	1969	£30	£15	
Clean The City	7"	Island	WI121	1963	£10	£5	
Forest Gate Rock	7"	Big Shot	BI507	1968	£5	£2	
Gravy Cool	7"	R&B	JB115	1963	£10	£5	*Winston & Bibby B side*
Indian Summer	7"	R&B	JB172	1964	£10	£5	*Stranger & Patsy B side*
Lonesome Feeling	7"	Unity	UN531	1969	£4	£1.50	
Man About Town	7"	Unity	UN518	1969	£4	£1.50	
One Thousand Tons Of Megaton	7"	Unity	UN517	1969	£4	£1.50	*King Cannon B side*
Reggae In The Wind	7"	Gas	GAS103	1969	£4	£1.50	*Soul Set B side*
Regina	7"	Unity	UN512	1969	£4	£1.50	
Sir Collins Special	7"	Collins Downbeat	CR001	1967	£8	£4	
Soul Voyage	7"	Doctor Bird	DB1107	1967	£10	£5	*Alva Lewis B side*
Spoogy	7"	Unity	UN509	1969	£4	£1.50	*Tommy McCook B side*
Zigaloo	7"	Blue Cat	BS116	1968	£8	£4	

STEVE & STEVIE

Title	Format	Label	Cat. No.	Year	Mint	Value	Notes
Steve And Stevie	LP	Toast	TLP2	1968	£40	£20	

STEVENS, APRIL

Title	Format	Label	Cat. No.	Year	Mint	Value	Notes
Falling In Love Again	7"	MGM	MGM1366	1967	£50	£25	
How Could Red Riding Hood	7"	Parlophone	MSP6088	1954	£5	£2	
Soft Warm Lips	7"	Parlophone	MSP6060	1953	£5	£2	
Teach Me Tiger	LP	Imperial	LP9055/12055	1961	£15	£6	*US*
Torrid Tunes	LP	Audio Lab	AL1534	1959	£25	£10	*US*

STEVENS, CAT

Title	Format	Label	Cat. No.	Year	Mint	Value	Notes
Bad Night	7" EP	Deram	15006	1967	£10	£5	*French*
Buddha And The Chocolate Box	LP	A&M	QU53623	1974	£10	£4	*US quad*
Catch Bull At Four	LP	A&M	QU54365	1972	£10	£4	*US quad*
Cats And Dogs	LP	Deram		1967	£30	£15	*test pressing*
Foreigner	LP	A&M	QU54391	1974	£10	£4	*US quad*
Greatest Hits	LP	A&M	QU54519	1975	£10	£4	*US quad*
I Love My Dog	7" EP	Deram	15000	1966	£10	£5	*French*
I'm Gonna Get Me A Gun	7" EP	Deram	15003	1967	£10	£5	*French*
Lady D'Arbanville	7"	Island	WIP6086	1970	£4	£1.50	*picture sleeve*
Matthew And Son	LP	Deram	DML/SML1004	1967	£10	£4	
Mona Bone Jakon	LP	Island	ILPS9118	1970	£10	£4	*pink label*
New Masters	LP	Deram	DML/SML1018	1967	£10	£4	
Saturday Night Live	LP	A&M		1975	£15	£6	*US promo*
Tea For The Tillerman	LP	A&M	QU54280	1972	£12	£5	*US quad*
Tea For The Tillerman	LP	Mobile Fidelity	MFSL1035	1984	£100	£50	*US audiophile (UHQR)*
Tea For The Tillerman	LP	Mobile Fidelity	MFSL1035	1979	£12	£5	*US audiophile*
Tea For The Tillerman	LP	Island	ILPS9135	1970	£20	£8	*pink label*
Teaser And The Firecat	LP	A&M	QU54313	1972	£10	£4	*US quad*

STEVENS, CONNIE

Title	Format	Label	Cat. No.	Year	Mint	Value	Notes
As Cricket	7" EP	Warner Bros	WEP6007	1960	£8	£4	
As Cricket	7" EP	Warner Bros	WSEP2007	1962	£12	£6	*stereo*
As Cricket No. 2	7" EP	Warner Bros	WEP6105	1963	£8	£4	
As Cricket No. 2	7" EP	Warner Bros	WSE6105	1963	£12	£6	*stereo*
As Cricket No. 3	7" EP	Warner Bros	WEP6112	1963	£8	£4	
As Cricket No. 3	7" EP	Warner Bros	WSE6112	1963	£12	£6	*stereo*
Conchetta	LP	Warner Bros	W1208	1958	£15	£6	*US*
Connie	LP	Warner Bros	WM4061/WS8061	1962	£15	£6	
Connie Stevens From Hawaiian Eye	LP	Warner Bros	W(S)1382	1960	£15	£6	*US*

Hank Williams Song Book	LP	Warner Bros	WM/WS8111	1963	£10	£4	
Hawaiian Eye	LP	Warner Bros	W(S)1335	1959	£15	£6	US
They're Jealous Of Me	7"	Warner Bros	WB128	1964	£5	£2	

STEVENS, DODIE

Dodie Stevens	LP	Dot	DLP3212/25212	1960	£15	£6	US
I Wore Out The Record	7"	Liberty	LIB83	1964	£4	£1.50	
Over The Rainbow	LP	Dot	DLP3323/25323	1960	£15	£6	US
Pink Shoe Laces	7"	London	HLD8834	1959	£12	£6	
Pink Shoelaces	LP	Dot	DLP3371/25371	1961	£15	£6	US
Yes I'm Lonesome Tonight	7"	London	HLD9280	1961	£5	£2	

STEVENS, JOHN

John Stevens, the erstwhile motivator behind the Spontaneous Music Ensemble, began to move into more commercial areas during the seventies. He is the drummer on John Martyn's *Live At Leeds*, and for the single 'Anni', John Martyn returned the favour – playing guitar and singing on a version of the piece that is quite different from the one found on the LP *John Stevens Away*.

Anni	7"	Vertigo	6059140	1976	£8	£4	*with John Martyn*
Longest Night Vol. 2	LP	Ogun	OG420	1978	£12	£5	*with Evan Parker*

STEVENS, KIRK

Once	7"	Decca	F10863	1957	£4	£1.50	

STEVENS, MEIC

Meic Stevens is a major folk-rock artist, whose career is unknown to most collectors apart from the solitary cult favourite album, *Outlander*. The obscurity that is Stevens's lot has nothing to do with his output, which is large, but everything to do with the fact that he has chosen to stay true to his Celtic roots and performs almost exclusively in the Welsh language. Most of his early records are much harder to find than their values might suggest – 'Did I Dream' will prove near-impossible, although it is an essential item for Led Zeppelin completists, being produced by John Paul Jones. Further Stevens items are listed under Bara Menyn, a folk band of which he was a member. The discographical information included here (together with the other Welsh language items to be found in this guide) was provided by dealer Andrew Hawkey, who operates a thriving mail order company in Lampeter.

Ballad Of Old Joe Blind	7"	Warner Bros	WB8007	1970	£15	£7.50	
Byw Yn Y Wlad	7" EP	Wren	WRE1107	1971	£15	£7.50	
Can Nana	7"	Theatr Yr Ymylon	YMSP01	1978	£8	£4	
Caneuon Cynnar	LP	TicToc	TTL001	1979	£150	£75	
Did I Dream	7"	Decca	F12174	1965	£50	£25	
Diolch Yn Fawr	7" EP	Sain	SAIN13	1971	£15	£7.50	
Gog	LP	Sain	1065M	1977	£50	£25	
Gwymon	LP	Wren	WRL536	1972	£75	£37.50	
Lapis Lazuli	LP	Sain	1312M	1983	£15	£6	
Meic Stevens	7" EP	Wren	WRE1045	1968	£20	£10	
Meic Stevens	7" EP	Newyddion Da	ND1	1970	£30	£15	
Mwg	7" EP	Wren	WRE1073	1969	£20	£10	
Nid Oes Un Gwydr Ffenestr	7"	Wren	WSP2005	1970	£15	£7.50	
Nos Du Nos Da	LP	Sain	1239M	1982	£20	£8	
Outlander	LP	Warner Bros	WS3005	1970	£125	£62.50	
Pe Medrwn	7"	Theatr Yr Ymylon	YMSP02	1978	£8	£4	
Rhif 2	7" EP	Wren	WRE1053	1968	£20	£10	
Y Brawd Houdini	7" EP	Sain	SAIN4	1970	£15	£7.50	

STEVENS, MICK

No Savage Word	LP	Deroy	no number	1975	£75	£37.50	
See The Morning	LP	Deroy	no number	1971	£100	£50	

STEVENS, RAY

1,837 Seconds Of Humor	LP	Mercury	MG2/SR60732	1962	£12	£5	US
Ahab The Arab	7"	Mercury	AMT1184	1962	£4	£1.50	
Crying Goodbye	7"	Capitol	CL14881	1958	£6	£2.50	
Harry The Hairy Ape	7"	Mercury	AMT1207	1963	£4	£1.50	
Jeremiah Peabody	7"	Mercury	AMT1158	1961	£4	£1.50	

STEVENS, RICKY

I Cried For You	7" EP	Columbia	SEG8172	1962	£30	£15	

STEVENS, SHAKIN'

Because I Love You	7"	Epic	SHAKY2	1986	£5	£2	*2 sleeves with autograph*
Bop Won't Stop	LP	Epic	BX86301	1983	£15	£6	*LP, cassette, autograph book, boxed*
Cry Just A Little Bit	7"	Epic	WA3774	1983	£5	£2	*picture disc*
Down On The Farm	7"	Parlophone	R5860	1970	£30	£15	
Endless Sleep	7"	Epic	SEPC6845	1979	£8	£4	
Feel The Need In Me	CD-s	Epic	SHAKYC6	1988	£5	£2	
Hey Mae	7"	Epic	SEPC8573	1980	£8	£4	*picture sleeve*
Honey Honey	7"	Emerald	MD1176	1974	£15	£7.50	
Hot Dog	7"	Epic	SEPC8090	1980	£8	£4	*picture sleeve*
How Many Tears Can You Hide	CD-s	Epic	SHAKYC7	1988	£5	£2	
I'm No J.D.	LP	CBS	52901	1971	£40	£20	
It's Late	7"	Epic	WA3565	1983	£8	£4	*shaped picture disc*
It's Raining	7"	Epic	EPCA1643	1981	£5	£2	*picture disc*
Jezebel	CD-s	Epic	SHAKYC9	1989	£5	£2	
Jungle Rock	7"	Battle Of The Bands	BOB2	1981	£4	£1.50	

Jungle Rock	7"	Mooncrest	MOON51	1976	**£10**	**£5**	
Justine	7"	Track	2094141	1978	**£15**	**£7.50**	
Legend	LP	Parlophone	PCS7112	1970	**£50**	**£25**	
Love Attack	CD-s	Epic	SHAKYC10	1989	**£5**	**£2**	
Love Waiting For You	7"	Epic	A4291	1984	**£6**	**£2.50**	*poster sleeve*
Marie Marie	LP	Epic	EPC84547	1980	**£10**	**£4**	
Never	7"	Track	2094134	1977	**£8**	**£4**	
Rockin' And Shakin'	LP	Contour	2870152	1972	**£10**	**£4**	
Shakin' Stevens	LP	Track	2406011	1978	**£10**	**£4**	
Shaky Sings Elvis	7"	Solid Gold	SGR107	1981	**£8**	**£4**	
Shooting Gallery	7"	Epic	SEPC9064	1980	**£8**	**£4**	*picture sleeve*
Somebody Touched Me	7"	Track	2094136	1977	**£5**	**£2**	
Somebody Touched Me	7"	Track	2094136	1977	**£10**	**£5**	*picture sleeve*
Special Christmas CD	CD-s	Epic	SHAKYC8	1988	**£5**	**£2**	
Spooky	7"	Epic	SEPC7235	1979	**£8**	**£4**	
Sweet Little Rock'n'Roller	7"	Polydor	2058213	1972	**£20**	**£10**	
Teardrops	7"	Epic	DA4882	1984	**£6**	**£2.50**	*double*
Tiger	7"	Everest	EV10000	1983	**£5**	**£2**	*picture disc*
Tiger	7"	Everest	RAY1	1982	**£4**	**£1.50**	
Treat Her Right	7"	Epic	SEPC6567	1978	**£8**	**£4**	

STEVENS, TERRI

My Wish Tonight	7"	Felsted	AF112	1959	**£4**	**£1.50**	

STEVENSEN, RICHARD

Faces Of Me	LP	Pye	NSPL18358	1970	**£10**	**£4**	

STEWART, AL

As soon as he achieved a small measure of success, Al Stewart decided that his first LP was not as he would have liked it to be, and managed to persuade CBS to issue a new version, with a slightly different track selection and with the whole album re-mixed. The original *Bedsitter Images* is now quite scarce. As for the even scarcer 'Elf' single, Al Stewart would probably prefer to forget about it altogether.

Al Stewart Concert	LP	Arista	SP40	1977	**£12**	**£5**	*US promo*
Bedsitter Images	7"	CBS	3034	1967	**£5**	**£2**	
Bedsitter Images	LP	CBS	(S)BPG63087	1967	**£60**	**£30**	
Electric Los Angeles Sunset	7"	CBS	4843	1970	**£4**	**£1.50**	
Elf	7"	Decca	F12467	1966	**£75**	**£37.50**	
First Album (Bedsitter Images)	LP	CBS	64023	1970	**£20**	**£8**	
King Of Portugal	CD-s	Enigma	ENVCD4	1988	**£5**	**£2**	*3" single*
Love Chronicles	LP	CBS	63460	1969	**£15**	**£6**	
Orange	LP	CBS	64739	1972	**£10**	**£4**	
Year Of The Cat	CD	Mobile Fidelity	MFCD8039	1986	**£15**	**£6**	*US audiophile*
Year Of The Cat	LP	Mobile Fidelity	MFSL1009	1978	**£12**	**£5**	*US audiophile*
Zero She Flies	LP	CBS	63848	1970	**£15**	**£6**	

STEWART, ANDY

Donald, Where's Your Troosers?	7"	Top Rank	JAR427	1960	**£4**	**£1.50**	

STEWART, BILLY

Because I Love You	7"	Chess	CRS8028	1966	**£8**	**£4**	
Billy Stewart Remembered	LP	Chess	LPS1547	1968	**£12**	**£5**	*US*
I Do Love You	7"	Chess	CRS8009	1965	**£5**	**£2**	
I Do Love You	7" EP	Chess	CRE6024	1966	**£12**	**£6**	
I Do Love You	LP	Chess	LP(S)1496	1965	**£20**	**£8**	*US*
In Crowd	7" EP	Chess	CRE6010	1966	**£15**	**£7.50**	
Love Me	7"	Chess	CRS8038	1966	**£4**	**£1.50**	
Ol' Man River	7"	Chess	CRS8050	1966	**£4**	**£1.50**	
Reap What You Sow	7"	Pye	7N25164	1962	**£4**	**£1.50**	
Secret Love	7"	Chess	CRS8045	1966	**£5**	**£2**	
Sitting In The Park	7"	Chess	CRS8017	1965	**£5**	**£2**	
Strange Feeling	7"	Pye	7N25222	1963	**£4**	**£1.50**	
Summertime	7"	Chess	CRS8040	1966	**£4**	**£1.50**	
Teaches Old Standards New Tricks	LP	Chess	LP(S)1513	1967	**£15**	**£6**	*US*
Unbelievable	LP	Chess	CRL4523	1966	**£15**	**£6**	

STEWART, BOB

Unique Sound Of The Psaltery	LP	Argo	ZDA207	1975	**£10**	**£4**	
Up Like The Swallow	LP	Broadside	BRO131	1978	**£10**	**£4**	
Wraggle Taggle Gypsies O	LP	Crescent	ARS105	1976	**£10**	**£4**	

STEWART, DAVE & BRIAN HARRISON

Deep December	7"	Multicord		197–	**£12**	**£6**	
Girl	7" EP	Multicord	MULTSH1	1971	**£12**	**£6**	

STEWART, DAVIE

Davie Stewart	LP	Topic	12T293	1978	**£10**	**£4**	

STEWART, DELANO

Got To Come Back	7"	High Note	HS027	1969	**£4**	**£1.50**	
Hallelujah	7"	High Note	HS034	1969	**£4**	**£1.50**	
Let's Have Some Fun	7"	High Note	HS004	1968	**£6**	**£2.50**	
Rocking Sensation	7"	High Note	HS014	1969	**£6**	**£2.50**	*Gaytones B side*
Stay A Little Bit Longer	LP	Trojan	TBL138	1970	**£12**	**£5**	
That's Life	7"	Doctor Bird	DB1138	1968	**£10**	**£5**	
Wherever I Lay My Hat	7"	High Note	HS039	1970	**£5**	**£2**	

STEWART, IAN

Title	Format	Label	Number	Year	Mint	VG	Notes
Plays The Million Sellers	LP	Fontana	886105TY	1968	£20	£8	Dutch

STEWART, JAMES

Title	Format	Label	Number	Year	Mint	VG	Notes
Legend Of Shenendoah	7"	Brunswick	05938	1965	£5	£2	

STEWART, JOHN

Title	Format	Label	Number	Year	Mint	VG	Notes
Signals Through The Glass	LP	Capitol	(S)T2975	1968	£12	£5	US

STEWART, PAUL

Title	Format	Label	Number	Year	Mint	VG	Notes
Saturday Morning Man	7"	Decca	F12577	1967	£6	£2.50	

STEWART, RED

Title	Format	Label	Number	Year	Mint	VG	Notes
Favorite Old Songs	LP	Audio Lab	AL1528	1959	£25	£10	US

STEWART, REX

Title	Format	Label	Number	Year	Mint	VG	Notes
Rendezvous With Rex	LP	Felsted	FAJ7001	1959	£12	£5	
Rex Stewart Orchestra	10" LP	Felsted	EDL87017	1955	£25	£10	

STEWART, ROD

The fact that Rod Stewart often performs indifferent material should not be allowed to obscure the fact that he is one of the great rock singers. His early Vertigo LPs are fine records that successfully blend acoustic and electric styles into a very satisfying whole. Even better is Stewart's powerful blues singing on Jeff Beck's two sixties albums, *Truth* and *Beckola*. Before this, Rod Stewart learnt his craft as a member of Long John Baldry's Hoochie Coochie Men and of Steampacket – his first singles come from this period and still hold up well, especially a version of 'Shake', backed by Brian Auger's Trinity (who were also a part of Steampacket), which is actually more dynamic than Sam Cooke's original.

Title	Format	Label	Number	Year	Mint	VG	Notes
Blondes Have More Fun	LP	Mobile Fidelity	MFSL1054	1981	£10	£4	US audiophile
Day Will Come	7"	Columbia	DB7766	1965	£50	£25	
Do Ya Think I'm Sexy	12"	Riva	SAM92	1978	£15	£7.50	promo, green or blue vinyl
Every Picture Tells A Story	CD	Mobile Fidelity	UDCD532	1990	£15	£6	US audiophile
Forever Young	CD-s	WEA	W7796CD	1988	£5	£2	3" single
Gasoline Alley	LP	Vertigo	6360500	1970	£10	£4	spiral label
Good Morning Little Schoolgirl	7"	Decca	F11996	1982	£5	£2	reissue
Good Morning Little Schoolgirl	7"	Decca	F11996	1964	£50	£25	
Infatuation	7"	Warner Bros	SAM194	1984	£10	£5	1 sided picture disc, interview tape
It's All Over Now	7"	Vertigo	6086002	1970	£6	£2.50	
Little Miss Understood	7"	Immediate	IM060	1967	£50	£25	
Lost In You	CD-s	WEA	W7927CD	1988	£5	£2	
Old Raincoat Won't Ever Let You Down	LP	Vertigo	VO4	1970	£10	£4	spiral label
Old Raincoat Won't Let You Down	CD	Mercury	8305722	1987	£12	£5	
Reason To Believe	LP	St Michael	21020102	1978	£15	£6	
Sailing	7"	Riva	RIVA9	1977	£60	£30	blue vinyl, picture sleeve
Shake	7"	Columbia	DB7892	1966	£50	£25	
Sing It Again Rod	CD	Mercury	8248822	1985	£12	£5	
This Old Heart Of Mine	CD-s	WEA	W2686CD	1989	£5	£2	3" single
Tonight's The Night/First Cut Is The Deepest	7"	Riva	RIVA3	1977	£6	£2.50	
You're Insane	12"	Riva	DISCO1A	1980	£12	£6	promo
You're Insane	7"	Riva	RIVA1	1977	£15	£7.50	promo

STEWART, ROMAN

Title	Format	Label	Number	Year	Mint	VG	Notes
Changing Times	7"	Songbird	SB1075	1972	£5	£2	Crystalites B side
Try Me	7"	Downtown	DT518	1973	£5	£2	Big Youth B side

STEWART, SANDY

Title	Format	Label	Number	Year	Mint	VG	Notes
Certain Smile	7"	London	HLE8683	1958	£10	£5	

STEWART, TINGA

Title	Format	Label	Number	Year	Mint	VG	Notes
Brand New Me	7"	Tropical	AL0018	1972	£5	£2	Browns All Stars B side
Message	7"	Dragon	DRA1025	1974	£5	£2	

STEWART, WINSTON

Title	Format	Label	Number	Year	Mint	VG	Notes
All Of My Life	7"	Port-O-Jam	PJ4002	1964	£10	£5	
But I Do	7"	R&B	JB147	1964	£10	£5	

STEWART, WYNN

Title	Format	Label	Number	Year	Mint	VG	Notes
Wishful Thinking	7"	London	HL7087	1960	£20	£10	export

STEWART & HARRISON

Title	Format	Label	Number	Year	Mint	VG	Notes
Girl	7"	Multicord	MULTSH1	1970	£10	£5	

STEWARTS OF BLAIR

Title	Format	Label	Number	Year	Mint	VG	Notes
Stewarts Of Blair	LP	Topic	12T138	1966	£20	£8	

STIDHAM, ARBEE

Title	Format	Label	Number	Year	Mint	VG	Notes
Tired Of Wandering	LP	Bluesville	BV1021	1961	£20	£8	US

STIFF LITTLE FINGERS

Title	Format	Label	Number	Year	Mint	VG	Notes
Listen	7"	Chrysalis	CHSDJ2580	1982	£5	£2	juke box issue

Peel Sessions	CD-s	Strange Fruit	SFPSCD004	1988	£5	£2	
Suspect Device	7"	Rigid Digits	SRD1	1978	£6	£2.50	*yellow label*
Suspect Device	7"	Rigid Digits	SRD1	1978	£10	£5	*red label, hand-made picture sleeve*

STILETTOS

This Is The Way	7"	Ariola	ARO200	1980	£5	£2	

STILL LIFE

Still Life	LP	Vertigo	6360026	1971	£75	£37.50	*spiral label*
What Did We Miss	7"	Columbia	DB8345	1968	£20	£10	

STILLS, STEPHEN

Stephen Stills	LP	Atlantic	2401004	1970	£10	£4	
Stephen Stills 2	LP	Atlantic	2401013	1971	£10	£4	

STING

Acoustic Live In Newcastle	CD	A&M	3971712	1991	£25	£10	*boxed with book*
All This Time	CD-s	A&M	AMCD713	1991	£5	£2	*with 12" print*
Compact Hits	CD-s	A&M	AMCD911	1988	£5	£2	
Dream Of The Blue Turtles	LP	A&M	DREMP1	1985	£10	£4	*picture disc*
Englishman In New York	CD-s	A&M	AMCD431	1987	£5	£2	
Englishman In New York	CD-s	A&M	AMCDR580	1988	£5	£2	*picture disc*
Fragile	CD-s	A&M	AMCD439	1988	£5	£2	
It's Probably Me	CD-s	A&M	AMCD883	1992	£5	£2	*with Eric Clapton*
Mad About You	CD-s	A&M	AMCDR721	1991	£5	£2	
Nado Como El Sol	CD	A&M		1988	£20	£8	*German, songs in Spanish*
Someone To Watch Over Me	CD-s	A&M	AMC911	1988	£5	£2	
Soul Cages	CD	A&M		1991	£25	£10	*US promo box set*
Soul Cages	CD-s	A&M	AMCD759	1991	£5	£2	
Soul Cages Interview Disc	CD	A&M		1991	£25	£10	*Canadian promo*
Ten Summoners' Tales	CD	A&M		1993	£25	£10	*Australian double, with live disc*
Ten Summoners' Tales – Interview Disc	CD	A&M	8029	1993	£25	£10	*US promo*
They Dance Alone	10"	A&M	AMX458	1988	£6	£2.50	*promo*
They Dance Alone	CD-s	A&M	AMCD458	1988	£5	£2	
We'll Be Together	CD-s	A&M	AMCD410	1987	£5	£2	*3" single, boxed*

STINGERS

Preacher Man	7"	Upsetter	US395	1972	£5	£2	*Upsetters B side*

STING-RAYS

Dinosaurs	7"	Big Beat	SW82	1982	£15	£7.50	*test pressing*
Goodbye To All That – Live Vol. 2	LP	Media Burn	MB18	1988	£10	£4	*red vinyl*
Live Retaliation	LP	Media Burn	MB1	1984	£10	£4	*white vinyl*

STINKY TOYS

Stinky Toys	LP	Polydor	2393174	1977	£10	£4	

STIRLING, PETER LEE

This answer record to John Barry's Bond song 'You Only Live Twice' is the sole entry by a singer who actually turns up on a large number of sixties records. In addition to recording several singles under his own name, he also worked as a session singer, particularly when anything of a budget nature was being produced. He finally scored a couple of small hits in the seventies, under the name of Daniel Boone, although as a songwriter he had already been successful with the Merseybeats.

You Don't Live Twice	7"	Decca	F12628	1967	£4	£1.50	

STITES, GARY

Lawdy Miss Clawdy	7"	London	HLL9082	1960	£10	£5	
Lonely For You	7"	London	HLL8881	1959	£15	£7.50	
Lonely For You	LP	Carlton	(ST)LP120	1960	£20	£8	*US*
Starry Eyed	7"	London	HLL9003	1959	£6	£2.50	

STITT, SONNY

37 Minutes And 48 Seconds	LP	Vogue	LAE12208	1960	£20	£8	
Blows The Blues	LP	HMV	CLP1420/ CSD1341	1961	£20	£8	
Deuces Wild	LP	Atlantic	3008	1968	£15	£6	
Kaleidoscope	LP	Esquire	32112	1961	£25	£10	
New York Jazz	LP	Columbia	33CX10114	1958	£40	£20	
Only The Blues	LP	HMV	CLP1280	1959	£20	£8	
Personal Appearance	LP	HMV	CLP1363	1960	£20	£8	
Quartet/Quintet	LP	Vogue	LAE12196	1960	£20	£8	
S.P.J. Jazz	LP	Esquire	32049	1958	£40	£20	*with Bud Powell & J. J. Johnson*
Sonny Side Up	LP	Columbia	33CX10140	1959	£15	£6	*with Dizzy Gillespie & Sonny Rollins*
Sonny Stitt–Bud Powell Quartet	10" LP	Esquire	20013	1953	£75	£37.50	
Stitt Plays Bird	LP	Atlantic	ATL5011	1964	£15	£6	
Stitt's Bits	LP	Esquire	32078	1959	£40	£20	
With The New Yorkers	LP	Vogue	LAE12191	1959	£20	£8	
With The Oscar Peterson Trio	LP	HMV	CLP1384	1960	£20	£8	

STIVELL, ALAN

A L'Olympia	LP	Fontana	6399005	1972	£10	£4	
E Langonned	LP	Fontana	9101500	1975	£10	£4	

From Celtic Roots	LP	Fontana	6325304	1974	£10	£4	
In Dublin	LP	Fontana	9299547	1975	£10	£4	
Reflections	LP	Fontana	6399008	1974	£10	£4	
Renaissance Of The Celtic Harp	LP	Philips	6414406	1971	£10	£4	

STOCKER, GREENWOOD & FRIENDS

Billy Plus Nine	LP	Changes	CR1400	1979	£50	£25	

STOCKHAUSEN, KARLHEINZ

Stockhausen has always tended to be the first port of call for those wishing to investigate the classical avant-garde, and with good reason, for he pioneered most of it. Amongst his vast output are to be found purely electronic works (try *Telemusik* and *Kontakte* for starters); works that mix electronics with voices and acoustic instruments (*Gesang der Jünglinge* and *Mixtur*); works that experiment with spatial effects (*Carre*); essentially mantric exercises (*Stimmung*); orchestral freak-outs (*Trans*); and free improvisation (*Aus den Sieben Tagen*). None of it is rock music and yet his ideas have been a considerable influence on many of the more open rock musicians.

Aus Den Sieben Tagen	LP	Deutsche Grammophon	2720073	1971	£75	£37.50	*7 LP boxed set*
Ceylon/Bird Of Passage	LP	Chrysalis	CHR1110	1976	£10	£4	
Elektronische Studie I & II	LP	Deutsche Grammophon	LP16133		£12	£5	
Gesang Der Jünglinge/Kontakte	LP	Deutsche Grammophon	138811	1962	£12	£5	*also a later remixed issue*
Gruppen/Carre	LP	Deutsche Grammophon	137002	1968	£12	£5	
Hymnen	LP	Deutsche Grammophon	2707039	1969	£20	£8	*double*
Klavierstücke 8	LP	Vox	STGBY637	1971	£10	£4	
Klavierstücke 9, 11	LP	Philips	6500101	1971	£10	£4	
Klavierstücke	LP	CBS	72591/2		£15	£6	*double*
Kontakte (piano version)/Refrain	LP	Vox	STGBY638	1970	£10	£4	
Kurzwellen	LP	Deutsche Grammophon	2707045	1971	£20	£8	*double*
Mantra	LP	Deutsche Grammophon	2530208	1972	£12	£5	
Mikrophonie I and II	LP	Deutsche Grammophon	2530583	197–	£10	£4	
Momente	LP	Deutsche Grammophon	2709055	1976	£25	£10	*triple*
Momente	LP	Nonesuch	H71157	196–	£12	£5	
Opus 1970	LP	Deutsche Grammophon	139461	197–	£12	£5	
Prozession	LP	Deutsche Grammophon	2530582	197–	£12	£5	
Prozession	LP	Vox	STGBY615	1969	£12	£5	
Solo	LP	Deutsche Grammophon	137005	196–	£10	£4	
Stimmung	LP	Deutsche Grammophon	2543003	1970	£12	£5	
Stop/Ylem	LP	Deutsche Grammophon	2530442	1974	£12	£5	
Telemusik/Mixtur	LP	Deutsche Grammophon	137012	1970	£12	£5	
Trans	LP	Deutsche Grammophon	2530726	1976	£12	£5	
Zyklus	LP	Erato	STU70603		£12	£5	

STOCKTON'S WING

Stockton's Wing	LP	Tara	2004	1978	£10	£4	*Irish*
Take A Chance	LP	Tara	30041980	1980	£10	£4	*Irish*

STOEBER, ORVILLE

Songs	LP	UNI	6369611	1970	£15	£6	*German*

STOKES

Whipped Cream	7"	London	HLU9955	1965	£5	£2	

STOLLER, RHET

Bandit	7"	Windsor	PS118	1964	£15	£7.50	*demo*
Caravan	7"	Windsor	PS119	1964	£10	£5	
Chariot	7"	Decca	F11302	1960	£5	£2	
Countdown	7"	Decca	F11738	1963	£5	£2	
Incredible Rhet Stoller	LP	Coronet	EC101	1967	£20	£8	
Ricochet	7"	Windsor	PS130	1964	£10	£5	
Sunshine Anytime	7" EP	Mosaic	MOSAIC1	1969	£5	£2	
Treble Gold + One	7"	Melodisc	1595	1964	£10	£5	
Uncrowned King	7"	Columbia	DB8013	1966	£15	£7.50	*demo*
Walk Don't Run	7"	Decca	F11271	1960	£8	£4	

STOMPERS

Foolish Idea	7"	Fontana	H385	1962	£8	£4	

STONE, CLIFFIE

Cool Cowboy	LP	Capitol	(S)T1230	1959	£12	£5	*US*
Popcorn Song	7"	Capitol	CL14330	1955	£75	£37.50	

STONE, GEORGE

Hole In The Wall	7"	Stateside	SS479	1965	£5	£2	

STONE, KIRBY FOUR

Honey Hush	7"	Vogue Coral	Q72129	1956	£6	£2.50	
Man, I Flipped	LP	London	HAA2164	1959	£10	£4	

STONE, MARK

Stroll	7"	London	HLR8543	1958	£60	£30	

STONE, ROLAND

Just A Moment	LP	Ace	LP1018	1961	£15	£6	US

STONE ANGEL

Stone Angel	LP	Acme	AC8008LP	1994	£10	£4	
Stone Angel	LP	private	SSLP04	1975	£200	£100	

STONE CIRCUS

Stone Circus	LP	Mainstream	S6119	1969	£75	£37.50	US

STONE HARBOUR

Emerges	LP	private		1974	£500	£330	US

STONE PONEYS

Lead singer with the Stone Poneys was Linda Ronstadt – these are her first recordings.

Different Drum	7"	Capitol	CL15523	1967	£4	£1.50	
Evergreen	LP	Capitol	ST2763	1967	£12	£5	US
Stone Poneys	LP	Capitol	ST2666	1967	£12	£5	US
Stone Poneys & Friends	LP	Capitol	ST2863	1968	£12	£5	US

STONE ROSES

Begging You	CD-s	Geffen	WGFTD22060	1995	£5	£2	*promo*
CD Singles Collection	CD-s	Silvertone	SRBX1	1992	£50	£25	*8 singles box set*
Complete Stone Roses	CD	Silvertone	ORECD535	1995	£12	£5	*with bonus CD single*
Elephant Stone	12"	Silvertone	ORE1T	1988	£8	£4	*black catalogue number*
Elephant Stone	7"	Silvertone	ORE1	1988	£4	£1.50	*black catalogue number*
Elephant Stone	CD-s	Silvertone	ORECD1	1990	£5	£2	
Fools Gold	12"	Silvertone	OREZ13	1990	£12	£6	*promo*
Fools Gold	12"	Silvertone	OREDJ71	1995	£6	£2.50	*promo*
Fools Gold	12"	Silvertone	STONEONE	1990	£12	£6	*promo*
Fools Gold	CD-s	Silvertone	ORECD13	1990	£5	£2	
Fools Gold	CD-s	Silvertone	OREZCD13	1990	£8	£4	*promo*
I Want To Be Adored	CD-s	Silvertone	ORECD31	1991	£5	£2	
Made Of Stone	CD-s	Silvertone	ORECD2	1990	£5	£2	
One Love	CD-s	Silvertone	ORECD17	1990	£5	£2	
Sally Cinnamon	12"	Black	12REV36	1987	£15	£7.50	*'printed in England' on rear sleeve*
She Bangs The Drum	CD-s	Silvertone	ORECD6	1989	£5	£2	
She Bangs The Drums	12"	Silvertone	OREZ6	1989	£8	£4	*with print*
She Bangs The Drums	7"	Silvertone	OREX6	1989	£4	£1.50	*with postcard*
So Young	12"	Thin Line	THIN001	1985	£60	£30	
So Young	CD-s	Silvertone	ORECD37	1993	£8	£4	
Spike Island EP	7"	Fierce	FRIGHT044	1990	£10	£5	*with assorted goodies*
Twelve Inch Singles Collection	12"	Silvertone	SRBX2	1992	£50	£25	*10 singles box set*
What The World Is Waiting For	12"	Silvertone	ORET13	1989	£6	£2.50	*with print*

STONE THE CROWS

Continuous Performance	LP	Polydor	2391043	1972	£10	£4	
Ode To John Law	LP	Polydor	2425042	1970	£15	£6	
Stone The Crows	LP	Polydor	2425017	1970	£20	£8	
Teenage Licks	LP	Polydor	2425071	1971	£12	£5	

STONEFIELD TRAMP

Dreaming Again	LP	Acorn	CF247	1974	£150	£75	

STONEGROUND

Family Album	LP	Warner Bros	K53999	1971	£10	£4	
Stoneground	LP	Warner Bros	K46087	1971	£10	£4	

STONEGROUND BAND

Sunstruck	LP	Nut		197–	£25	£10	

STONEHENGE MEN

Big Feet	7"	HMV	POP981	1962	£30	£15	

STONEHOUSE

Stonehouse Creek	LP	RCA	SF8197	1971	£100	£50	

STONE'S MASONRY

The recorded evidence is that Martin Stone was one of the great sixties guitarists, even if he seems to have long ago vanished from rock music. The blues instrumental 'Flapjacks', which was released on Mike Vernon's pre-Blue Horizon Purdah label, is a good demonstration of his talents. The group folded, before it could record anything else, when Stone joined Savoy Brown – moving from there to Mighty Baby and on to Chilli Willi and the Red Hot Peppers.

Flapjacks	7"	Purdah	453504	1966	£100	£50	

STONEWALL

Stonewall .... LP .... private .... 1974 **£1000**.... **£700** .... *US*

STOREY SISTERS

Bad Motorcycle .... 7" .... London .... HLU8571 .... 1958 **£75**.... **£37.50** ....

STORM

Storm .... LP .... Vamp .... 25004 .... 1974 **£125**.. **£62.50** .... *Swiss*

STORM (2)

At The Top .... LP .... Harvest .... 7C06435179 .... 1975 **£15** .... **£6** .... *Swedish*
Stormvarning .... LP .... Harvest .... 7C06435010 .... 1974 **£30** .... **£15** .... *Swedish*

STORM, BILLY

Billy Storm .... LP .... Buena Vista ..... BV3315 .... 1963 **£30** .... **£15** .... *US*
Sure As You're Born .... 7" .... London .... HLK9236 .... 1960 **£5** .... **£2** ....
This Is The Night .... LP .... Famous .... F504 .... 1969 **£15** .... **£6** .... *US*

STORM, DANNY

Honest I Do .... 7" .... Piccadilly .... 7N35025 .... 1962 **£6** .... **£2.50** .... *picture sleeve*
I Just Can't Fool My Heart .... 7" .... Piccadilly .... 7N35091 .... 1962 **£6** .... **£2.50** ....
Just You .... 7" .... Piccadilly .... 7N35053 .... 1962 **£5** .... **£2** ....
Say You Do .... 7" .... Piccadilly .... 7N35143 .... 1963 **£6** .... **£2.50** ....

STORM, GALE

Dark Moon .... 7" .... London .... HLD8424 .... 1957 **£10** .... **£5** ....
Don't Be That Way .... 7" .... London .... HLD8311 .... 1956 **£20** .... **£10** ....
Farewell To Arms .... 7" .... London .... HLD8570 .... 1958 **£8** .... **£4** ....
Gale Storm .... LP .... Dot .... DLP3011 .... 1956 **£30** .... **£15** .... *US*
Heart Without A Sweetheart .... 7" .... London .... HLD8329 .... 1956 **£15** ...... **£7.50** ....
Hits .... LP .... Dot .... DLP3098 .... 1958 **£30** .... **£15** .... *US*
I Hear You Knocking .... 7" .... London .... HLD8222 .... 1956 **£25**.... **£12.50** ....
Ivory Tower .... 7" .... London .... HLD8283 .... 1956 **£25**.... **£12.50** ....
Lucky Lips .... 7" .... London .... HLD8393 .... 1957 **£25**.... **£12.50** ....
Memories Are Made Of This .... 7" .... London .... HLD8232 .... 1956 **£25**.... **£12.50** ....
Orange Blossoms .... 7" .... London .... HLD8413 .... 1957 **£10** .... **£5** ....
Presenting Gale Storm .... 10" LP London .... HBD1056 .... 1956 **£50** .... **£25** ....
Sentimental Me .... LP .... London .... HAD2104 .... 1958 **£30** .... **£15** ....
Why Do Fools Fall In Love .... 7" .... London .... HLD8286 .... 1956 **£25**.... **£12.50** ....
Why Do Fools Fall In Love .... 7" .... London .... HL7008 .... 1956 **£10** .... **£5** .... *export*
You .... 7" .... London .... HLD8632 .... 1958 **£8** .... **£4** ....

STORM, RORY & THE HURRICANES

America .... 7" .... Parlophone ...... R5197 .... 1964 **£10** .... **£5** ....
Doctor Feelgood .... 7" .... Oriole .... CB1858 .... 1963 **£20** .... **£10** ....

STORME, ROBB

Earth Angel .... 7" .... Decca .... F11388 .... 1961 **£6** .... **£2.50** ....
Here Today .... 7" .... Columbia .... DB7993 .... 1966 **£4** .... **£1.50** ....
I Don't Need Your Love Anymore .... 7" .... Decca .... F11282 .... 1960 **£6** .... **£2.50** ....
Pretty Hair And Angel Eyes .... 7" .... Decca .... F11432 .... 1962 **£5** .... **£2** ....
Wheels .... 7" EP .. Decca .... DFE6700 .... 1962 **£60** .... **£30** ....
Where Is My Girl .... 7" .... Columbia .... DB7756 .... 1965 **£4** .... **£1.50** ....

STORMER

My Home Town .... 7" .... Ring O' .... 2017113 .... 1978 **£6** .... **£2.50** .... *promo in picture sleeve*

STORMSVILLE SHAKERS

Number One .... 7" EP .. Odeon .... MEO148 .... 1967 **£20** .... **£10** .... *French*

STORMTROOPER

I'm A Mess .... 7" .... Solent .... SS047 .... 1978 **£8** .... **£4** ....
I'm A Mess .... 7" .... Solent .... SS047 .... 1978 **£20** .... **£10** .... *stamped sleeve with insert*

STORMTROOPER (2)

Pride Before A Fall .... 7" .... Heartbeat .... BEAT1 .... 1980 **£20** .... **£10** ....

STORYTELLER

Storyteller's blend of poetry and folk song was greeted with ecstatic reviews and the chance of a performance at the Royal Festival Hall while still very much an up-and-coming group. The first track on the *Storyteller* LP is a delightful piece of folk-rock, with a sparkling guitar solo from Peter Frampton, but its companion tracks are not often in the same league. Singer Caroline Attard married the group's producer, Andy Bown (who was formerly a member of the Herd and subsequently the keyboard player with Status Quo), but her attractive voice has not been heard on record since the early seventies. Poet and singer Terry Durham, the brother of the Seekers' Judith Durham, also has a solo album listed under his name.

More Pages .... LP .... Transatlantic .... TRA232 .... 1971 **£20** .... **£8** ....
Remarkable .... 7" .... CBS .... 7182 .... 1971 **£4** .... **£1.50** ....
Storyteller .... LP .... Transatlantic .... TRA220 .... 1970 **£25** .... **£10** ....

STOUGHTON, DAVID

Transformer .... LP .... Elektra .... EKL/EKS74034 ...... 1968 **£20** .... **£8** ....

STOWAWAYS

In Our Time .... LP .... Justice .... 148 .... 196– **£200** ...... **£100** .... *US*

STP23

Let Jimi Take Over	12"	Wau!Mr.Modo	WMS001R	1989	£6	£2.50	

STRAIGHT EIGHT

Modern Times	7"	Eel Pie	EPS003	1978	£8	£4	

STRAKER, PETER

Jackie	7"	EMI	EMI2758	1978	£6	£2.50	
Ragtime Piano Joe	7"	EMI	EMI2700	1977	£5	£2	
This One's On Me	LP	EMI	EMC3204	1977	£12	£5	

STRANGE, BILLY

Few Dollars More	7"	Vocalion	VP9209	1967	£5	£2	
Get Smart	7"	Vocalion	VP9259	1966	£8	£4	
Goldfinger	7"	Vocalion	VP9231	1964	£15	£7.50	
Goldfinger	LP	Vocalion	VAN/SAVN8038	1965	£10	£4	
Great Western Themes	LP	London	ZGL104	1970	£10	£4	
James Bond Theme	7"	Vocalion	VP9228	1964	£6	£2.50	
James Bond Theme	LP	Vocalion	VAN/SAVN8032	1964	£10	£4	
Thunderball	7"	Vocalion	VP9257	1966	£6	£2.50	
Where Your Arms Used To Be	7"	London	HLG9321	1961	£5	£2	

STRANGE, GILES

Watch The People Dance	7"	Stateside	SS570	1966	£40	£20	

STRANGE, STEVE

In The Year 2525	7"	Palace	1	1982	£60	£30	*test pressing, picture sleeve*
In The Year 2525	7"	Palace	1	1982	£30	£15	*test pressing only*

STRANGE DAYS

Nine Parts To The Wind	LP	Retreat	RTL6005	1975	£25	£10	

STRANGE FOX

Bring It On Home	7"	Parlophone	R5876	1970	£4	£1.50	

STRANGE FRUIT

Cut Across Shorty	7"	Village Thing	VTSX1001	1971	£8	£4	

STRANGELOVE

Hysteria	12"	Sermon	SERT002	1993	£10	£5	*picture sleeve*
Hysteria	CD-s	Sermon	SERT002CD	1993	£20	£10	
Time For The Rest Of Your Life	CD-s	Food	CDFOOD49	1994	£5	£2	
Visionary	12"	Sermon	SERT001	1992	£20	£10	
Zoo'd Out	7"	Rough Trade	45REV18	1993	£10	£5	

STRANGELOVES

Cara Lin	7"	Immediate	IM007	1965	£5	£2	
Cara-Lin	7"	Immediate	IM007	196–	£4	£1.50	*pink label*
Dansez Le Monkiss	7" EP	Atlantic	750006	1965	£25	£12.50	*French*
Hand Jive	7"	London	HLZ10063	1966	£5	£2	
Honey Do	7"	London	HLK10238	1969	£5	£2	
I Want Candy	7"	London	HLM10481	1975	£4	£1.50	
I Want Candy	7"	Stateside	SS446	1965	£10	£5	
I Want Candy	LP	Bang	BLP(S)211	1965	£50	£25	*US*
Night Time	7"	London	HLZ10020	1966	£15	£7.50	

STRANGERS

Do You Or Don't You	7"	Philips	BF1378	1964	£4	£1.50	
One And One Is Two	7"	Philips	BF1335	1964	£25	£12.50	*with Mike Shannon*
Ram-Bunk-Shush	7" EP	President	281	1964	£25	£12.50	*French*
Strangers With Mike Shannon	7" EP	Pathe	EGF795	1964	£30	£15	*French*

STRANGERS (2)

I'm On An Island	7"	Pye	7N17585	1968	£4	£1.50	
Look Out	7"	Pye	7N17240	1967	£10	£5	
You Didn't Have To Be So Nice	7"	Pye	7N17351	1967	£4	£1.50	

STRANGEWAYS

All The Sounds Of Fear	7"	Real	ARE7	1979	£5	£2	
Show Her You Care	7"	Real	ARE2	1978	£5	£2	

STRANGLERS

96 Tears	CD-s	Epic	TEARSC1/P1	1990	£5	£2	*2 versions*
All Day And All Of The Night	7"	Epic	VICE1	1988	£4	£1.50	*Monica Couglan sleeve*
All Day And All Of The Night	CD-s	Epic	CDVICE1	1988	£10	£5	
Always The Sun	CD-s	Epic	6564302	1990	£5	£2	*2 versions*
Bear Cage	12"	United Artists	12BP344	1980	£10	£5	*picture sleeve*
Black And White	LP	A&M	SP4706	1978	£15	£6	*US, black & white vinyl*
Don't Bring Harry	7"	United Artists	UASTR1DJ	1979	£15	£7.50	*promo*
Dreamtime	LP	Epic	EPC1126648	1986	£10	£4	*picture disc*
European Female	7"	Epic	EPCA112893	1983	£5	£2	*picture disc*
Golden Brown	7"	United Artists	BP407	1982	£10	£5	*mispressed B side*
Golden Brown	CD-s	Epic	6567612	1991	£5	£2	
Gospel According To The Men In Black	LP	Liberty	LBG30313	1981	£20	£8	*test pressing*

Title	Format	Label	Cat. No.	Year	Mint	VG	Notes
Greatest Hits	CD	Epic	4675419	1990	**£12**	**£5**	*picture disc*
Grip '89	CD-s	Liberty	CDEM84	1989	**£10**	**£5**	
Just Like Nothing On Earth	7"	Liberty	BP393	1981	**£10**	**£5**	*mispressed B side*
N'Emmenes Pas Harry	7"	United Artists		1979	**£8**	**£4**	*sung in French*
Nice 'n' Sleazy	7"	United Artists	UP36379	1978	**£10**	**£5**	*mispressed B side*
Nice In Nice	7"	Epic	EPC6500550	1986	**£4**	**£1.50**	*shaped picture disc*
Night Tracks	CD-s	Strange Fruit	SFNTCD020	1989	**£5**	**£2**	
No Mercy	7"	Epic	EPCGA4921	1984	**£5**	**£2**	*double*
No Mercy	7"	Epic	WA4921	1984	**£4**	**£1.50**	*shaped picture disc*
No More Heroes	7"	United Artists	FREE8	1977	**£20**	**£10**	*1 sided promo*
Peaches	7"	United Artists	FREE4	1977	**£50**	**£25**	*promo*
Peaches	7"	United Artists	UP36248	1978	**£10**	**£5**	*mispress, B side plays Buzzcocks*
Peaches	7"	United Artists	UP36248	1977	**£200**	**£100**	*picture sleeve, newspaper lettering & group picture*
Rattus Norvegicus	LP	United Artists	UAG30045	1977	**£10**	**£4**	*with 7" (FREE3)*
Raven	LP	United Artists	UAG30262	1979	**£12**	**£5**	*3D cover*
Shakin' Like A Leaf	7"	Epic	SHEIKP1	1987	**£4**	**£1.50**	*shaped picture disc*
Something Better Change	7"	A&M	AM1973	1977	**£5**	**£2**	*US, pink marbled vinyl*
Stranglers Singles Collection	LP	Liberty	LBG30353	1982	**£15**	**£6**	*with original dark cover*
Sverge	7"	United Artists	UP36459	1978	**£8**	**£4**	*sung in Swedish*
Sweet Smell Of Success	CD-s	Epic	TEARSC2	1990	**£5**	**£2**	
Walk On By	7"	United Artists	FREE9	1978	**£15**	**£7.50**	*blue or beige vinyl*

STRAPS

Title	Format	Label	Cat. No.	Year	Mint	VG	Notes
Brixton	7"	Donut	DONUT3	1982	**£5**	**£2**	
Straps Album	LP	Cyclops	CYC2	1983	**£10**	**£4**	

STRATEGY

Title	Format	Label	Cat. No.	Year	Mint	VG	Notes
Technical Overflow	7"	Ebony	EBON7	1982	**£5**	**£2**	

STRATUS

Title	Format	Label	Cat. No.	Year	Mint	VG	Notes
Throwing Shapes	LP	Steel Trax	STEEL31001	1985	**£10**	**£4**	

STRAW, SYD

Title	Format	Label	Cat. No.	Year	Mint	VG	Notes
Future 40's	CD-s	Virgin	VUSCD6	1989	**£5**	**£2**	*3" single, with Michael Stipe*

STRAWBERRY ALARM CLOCK

The Strawberry Alarm Clock recorded several American singles as the Sixpence, before adopting a suitably trippy name for their big pop-psychedelic hit, 'Incense And Peppermints'. Though the group made several more records, they remained peripheral to the real centre of rock innovation. Lead guitarist Ed King was later a member of Lynyrd Skynyrd.

Title	Format	Label	Cat. No.	Year	Mint	VG	Notes
Best Of The Strawberry Alarm Clock	LP	Uni	73074	1970	**£25**	**£10**	*US*
Changes	LP	Vocalion	73915	1971	**£25**	**£10**	*US*
Good Morning Starshine	7"	MCA	MU1080	1969	**£5**	**£2**	
Good Morning Starshine	LP	Uni	73054	1969	**£30**	**£15**	*US*
Incense & Peppermints	LP	Pye	N(S)PL28106	1968	**£25**	**£10**	
Incense And Peppermints	7"	Pye	7N25436	1967	**£10**	**£5**	
Sit With The Guru	7"	Pye	7N25456	1968	**£8**	**£4**	
Tomorrow	7"	Pye	7N25446	1968	**£8**	**£4**	
Wake Up It's Tomorrow	LP	Uni	73025	1967	**£40**	**£20**	*US*
World In A Sea Shell	LP	Uni	73035	1968	**£30**	**£15**	*US*

STRAWBERRY CHILDREN

Songwriter and producer Jimmy Webb made his first bid for stardom as a performer with the one single released by the Strawberry Children – a trio fronted by Webb himself.

Title	Format	Label	Cat. No.	Year	Mint	VG	Notes
Love Years Coming	7"	Liberty	LBF15012	1967	**£8**	**£4**	

STRAWBERRY JAM

Title	Format	Label	Cat. No.	Year	Mint	VG	Notes
Personally	7"	Pye	7N17711	1969	**£4**	**£1.50**	

STRAWBERRY SWITCHBLADE

Title	Format	Label	Cat. No.	Year	Mint	VG	Notes
Jolene	7"	Korova	KOW42	1985	**£5**	**£2**	*shaped picture disc*
Let Her Go	7"	Korova	KOW39	1985	**£5**	**£2**	*shaped picture disc*
Strawberry Switchblade LP Sampler	7"	Korova	FLX3881	1985	**£4**	**£1.50**	*clear square flexi, booklet*
Trees And Flowers	12"	92 Happy Customers	HAPT1	1983	**£6**	**£2.50**	
Trees And Flowers	7"	92 Happy Customers	HAP1	1983	**£4**	**£1.50**	

STRAWBS

The earlier editions of this guide list a Strawbs LP called *Heartbreak Hill*, which would be worth a tidy sum if it ever appeared on the market. Alas, the music was recorded in 1979 but never actually committed to vinyl – there are not even any test pressings for collectors to discover. During the eighties, however, Dave Cousins was selling cassettes of the actual music, so that a version of *Heartbreak Hill* does exist, albeit not in a form that is likely to reach any kind of high value.

Title	Format	Label	Cat. No.	Year	Mint	VG	Notes
Benedictus	7"	A&M	AM874	1971	**£4**	**£1.50**	
Burning For You	LP	Oyster	2391287	1977	**£10**	**£4**	
Bursting At The Seams	LP	A&M	AMLH68144	1973	**£10**	**£4**	
Dead Lines	LP	Arista	SPART1036	1978	**£10**	**£4**	
Deep Cuts	LP	Oyster	2391234	1976	**£10**	**£4**	

Dragonfly	LP	A&M	AMLS970	1970	**£20**	**£8**	
Forever	7"	A&M	AM791	1970	**£5**	**£2**	
From The Witchwood	LP	A&M	AMLS64304	1971	**£10**	**£4**	
Ghosts	LP	A&M	AMLH68277	1975	**£10**	**£4**	
Grave New World	LP	A&M	AMLS68078	1972	**£10**	**£4**	*with booklet*
Hero And Heroine	LP	A&M	AMLH63607	1974	**£10**	**£4**	
Just A Collection Of Antiques And Curios	LP	A&M	AMLS994	1970	**£12**	**£5**	
King	7"	LO	LO1	1980	**£6**	**£2.50**	*picture sleeve*
Man Who Called Himself Jesus	7"	A&M	AM738	1968	**£5**	**£2**	
Nomadness	LP	A&M	AMLH68331	1976	**£10**	**£4**	
Oh How She Changed	7"	A&M	AM725	1968	**£4**	**£1.50**	
Strawberry Music Sampler No. 1	LP	private		1969	**£500**	**£330**	
Strawbs	LP	A&M	AMLS936	1969	**£20**	**£8**	
Witchwood	7"	A&M	AM837	1971	**£6**	**£2.50**	*promo*

STRAWHEAD

Fortunes Of War	LP	Tradition	TSR032	1978	**£10**	**£4**	

STRAY

Mudanzas	LP	Transatlantic	TRA268	1973	**£10**	**£4**	
Only What You Make It	7"	Transatlantic	PROMO1	1970	**£5**	**£2**	*promo*
Saturday Morning Pictures	LP	Transatlantic	TRA248	1972	**£10**	**£4**	
Stray	LP	Transatlantic	TRA216	1970	**£25**	**£10**	
Suicide	LP	Transatlantic	TRA233	1971	**£15**	**£6**	

STRAY CATS

Bring It Back Again	CD-s	EMI	CDMT62	1989	**£5**	**£2**	
Gina	CD-s	EMI	CDMT67	1989	**£5**	**£2**	
She's Sexy And Seventeen	7"	Arista	SCAT6	1983	**£6**	**£2.50**	*shaped picture disc*

STRAYHORN, BILLY

Cue For Saxophone	LP	Felsted	FAJ7008/SJA2008	1960	**£25**	**£10**	

STREAMLINERS & JOANNE

Everybody's Doin' The Twist	7"	Columbia	DB4808	1962	**£4**	**£1.50**	
Frankfurter Sandwiches	7"	Columbia	DB4689	1961	**£4**	**£1.50**	

STREAPLERS

Times They Are A-Changin'	7" EP	Columbia	ESRF1786	1966	**£10**	**£5**	*French*

STREET

Street	LP	Verve	FT(S)3057	1969	**£25**	**£10**	*US*

STREET, HILLARD

River Love	7"	Capitol	CL14960	1958	**£4**	**£1.50**	

STREISAND, BARBRA

All I Ask Of You	CD-s	CBS	CPBARB3	1989	**£15**	**£7.50**	*picture disc*
All I Ask Of You	CD-s	CBS	CDBARB3	1989	**£5**	**£2**	
All I Ask Of You	12"	CBS	BARBQT3	1989	**£8**	**£4**	*with poster*
Barbra Joan Streisand	LP	Columbia	PCQ30792	1971	**£10**	**£4**	*US quad*
Barbra Streisand	7" EP	CBS	AGG20054	1964	**£5**	**£2**	
Butterfly	LP	Columbia	PCQ33005	1974	**£10**	**£4**	*US quad*
Color Me Barbra	LP	Columbia	CL2478	1966	**£40**	**£20**	*US, red vinyl*
Deluxe Box Set	LP	CBS	66349	1977	**£20**	**£8**	
En Français	7" EP	CBS	EP6048	1965	**£8**	**£4**	
Event Of The Decade – A Retrospective	CD	CBS	XPCD417	1994	**£150**	**£75**	*promo double*
Funny Girl	LP	Columbia	SQ30992	1972	**£10**	**£4**	*US quad*
Funny Lady	LP	Arista	ARTY101	1975	**£10**	**£4**	
Funny Lady	LP	Arista	AQ9004	1975	**£12**	**£5**	*US quad*
Greatest Hits Vol. 2	LP	Columbia	HC45679	1982	**£10**	**£4**	*US audiophile*
Guilty	LP	Columbia	HC46750	1982	**£10**	**£4**	*US audiophile*
Just For The Record – Selection One	CD	Columbia	CSK4196	1991	**£25**	**£10**	*US promo compilation*
Just For The Record – Selection Two	CD	Columbia	CSK4200	1991	**£25**	**£10**	*US promo compilation*
Just For The Record	CD	Columbia	4687342	1991	**£50**	**£25**	*4 CD box set*
Lazy Afternoon	LP	Columbia	PCQ33815	1975	**£10**	**£4**	*US quad*
Left In The Dark	12"	CBS	TA4754	1984	**£40**	**£20**	
Live In Concert At The Forum	LP	Columbia	PCQ31760	1972	**£10**	**£4**	*US quad*
Lover Come Back To Me	7" EP	CBS	AGG20042	1964	**£10**	**£5**	
Main Event	12"	CBS	127714	1979	**£6**	**£2.50**	*picture label*
Memories	LP	Columbia	HC47678	1982	**£10**	**£4**	*US audiophile*
Music Of The Night	CD-s	Columbia	6597382	1994	**£5**	**£2**	
My Man	7" EP	CBS	EP6068	1966	**£8**	**£4**	
Nuts	LP	CBS	6513796	1988	**£10**	**£4**	
On A Clear Day You Can See Forever	LP	CBS	70075	1970	**£10**	**£4**	*with Yves Montand*
Ordinary Miracles Tour CD	CD	Columbia	CSK6120	1994	**£40**	**£20**	*US promo compilation*
Owl And The Pussycat	LP	CBS	70081	1971	**£10**	**£4**	
People	7"	CBS	201543	1964	**£5**	**£2**	*picture sleeve*
Places That Belong To You	CD-s	CBS	6577945	1992	**£5**	**£2**	
Places That Belong To You	CD-s	CBS	6577949	1992	**£15**	**£7.50**	*picture disc*
Second Barbra Streisand Album	LP	Columbia	CS8854	1963	**£50**	**£25**	*US, blue vinyl*
Second Hand Rose	7" EP	CBS	EP6150	1967	**£5**	**£2**	
Stoney End	LP	Columbia	PCQ30378	1971	**£10**	**£4**	*US quad*
Till I Loved You	CD-s	CBS	CDBARB2	1988	**£5**	**£2**	*with Don Johnson*

Way We Were	LP	Columbia	PCQ32801	1974	£10	£4	US quad
We're Not Making Love Anymore	CD-s	CBS	CDBARB4	1989	£5	£2	
We're Not Making Love Anymore	CD-s	CBS	CPBARB4	1989	£12	£6	picture disc

STRENGTH, TEXAS BILL

Yellow Rose Of Texas	7"	Capitol	CL14357	1955	£10	£5	

STRETCH

Elastique	LP	Anchor	ANCL2014	1975	£12	£5	
Forget The Past	LP	Hot Wax	HW1	1978	£20	£8	
Life Blood	LP	Anchor	ANCL2023	1977	£12	£5	
You Can't Beat Your Brain For Entertainment	LP	Anchor	ANCL2016	1976	£10	£4	

STRICKLAND, WILLIAM R.

William Strickland was reputed to have made his songs up as he went along and certainly they sound ramshackle enough for him to have done so. At the time, the Deram label was willing to try anything, but in the end, all that can really be said about Mr Strickland is that he is no Syd Barrett.

Is Only The Name	LP	Deram	DML/SML1041	1969	£12	£5	

STRIDER

Exposed	LP	GM	GML1002	1973	£15	£6	
Misunderstanding	LP	GM	GML1012	1974	£15	£6	

STRIFE

Rush	LP	Chrysalis	CHR1063	1975	£12	£5	

STRING CHEESE

String Cheese	LP	RCA	SF8222	1971	£15	£6	

STRING DRIVEN THING

Another Night	7"	Concord	CON7	1970	£12	£6	
Machine That Cried	LP	Charisma	CAS1070	1973	£10	£4	
String Driven Thing	LP	Charisma	CAS1062	1972	£10	£4	
String Driven Thing	LP	Concord	CON1001	1970	£100	£50	

STRINGALONGS

Brass Buttons	7"	London	HLU9354	1961	£4	£1.50	
Matilda	7"	London	HLD9652	1963	£6	£2.50	
Mina Bird	7"	London	HLU9452	1961	£5	£2	
Spinnin' My Wheels	7"	London	HLD9588	1962	£5	£2	
String-Alongs	LP	London	HAD/SHD8054	1963	£25	£10	
Stringalong With The Stringalongs	7" EP	London	REU1398	1963	£20	£10	
Stringalongs	7" EP	London	REU1322	1961	£25	£12.50	
Stringalongs	7" EP	London	REU1350	1963	£25	£12.50	
Twistwatch	7"	London	HLD9535	1962	£5	£2	
Wide World Hits	LP	London	HAU/SHU8371	1969	£15	£6	

STRIPES OF GLORY

Denial	7"	Vogue	V9194	1962	£10	£5	

STROLLERS

Come On Over	7"	London	HLL9336	1961	£10	£5	
Jumping With Symphony Sid	7"	Vogue	V9113	1958	£25	£12.50	
Little Bitty Pretty One	7"	Vogue	V9124	1958	£25	£12.50	

STROLLERS (2)

Cuckoo	7"	Fontana	TF598	1965	£4	£1.50	

STRONG, BARRETT

Money	7"	London	HLU9088	1960	£100	£50	

STRONG, NOLAN & THE DIABLOS

Fortune Of Hits	LP	Fortune	LP8010	1961	£30	£15	US
Fortune Of Hits Vol. 2	LP	Fortune	LP8012	1962	£30	£15	US
Mind Over Matter	LP	Fortune	LP8015	1963	£30	£15	US

STRYPER

Always There For You	CD-s	Enigma	ENVCD1	1988	£5	£2	3" single

STUART, CHAD & JEREMY CLYDE

Before And After	7"	CBS	201769	1965	£6	£2.50	
Before And After	7" EP	CBS	6101	1965	£10	£5	French
Best Of Chad And Jeremy	LP	Ember	(ST)NR5036	1967	£10	£4	
Chad Stuart And Jeremy Clyde	7" EP	United Artists	UEP1008	1965	£8	£4	
Early In The Morning	7"	Ember	EMBS186	1964	£4	£1.50	
I Don't Want To Lose You	7"	CBS	201814	1965	£4	£1.50	
Like I Love You Today	7" EP	Pathe	EGF716	1963	£10	£5	French
Second Album	LP	Ember	NR5031	1966	£15	£6	
Sing For You	LP	Ember	NR5021	1965	£15	£6	
Summer Song	7" EP	Pathe	EGF775	1964	£10	£5	French
What Do You Want With Me	7" EP	Pathe	EGF850	1965	£10	£5	French
Yesterday's Gone	7"	Ember	EMBS180	1963	£4	£1.50	
Yesterday's Gone	7" EP	Ember	EMBEP4543	1964	£8	£4	
Yesterday's Gone	LP	World Artists	WAM2002/WAS3002	1964	£15	£6	US

STUART, GLEN

Make Me An Angel	7"	Honey Hit	TB126	196–	**£5**	**£2**	*picture sleeve*

STUART, MIKE SPAN

Children Of Tomorrow	7"	Jewel	JL01	1968	**£250**	**£150**	*best auctioned*
Come On Over To Our Place	7"	Columbia	DB8066	1966	**£15**	**£7.50**	
Dear	7"	Columbia	DB8206	1967	**£20**	**£10**	
Mike Stuart Span	LP	Tenth Planet	TP014	1995	**£15**	**£6**	
You Can Understand Me	7"	Fontana	TF959	1968	**£8**	**£4**	

STUD

Goodbye Live At Command	LP	BASF	2029117	1973	**£20**	**£8**	*German*
September	LP	BASF	2029054	1972	**£25**	**£10**	*German*
Stud	LP	Deram	SMLR1084	1971	**£25**	**£10**	

STUDIO Gs

Beta Group	LP	LPSG	100	1970	**£75**	**£37.50**	

STUDIO ONE ALL STARS

Sherry	7"	Island	WI3038	1967	**£10**	**£5**	

STUDIO SIX

Strawberry Window	7"	Polydor	BM56219	1967	**£15**	**£7.50**	
Times Were When	7"	Polydor	BM56189	1967	**£4**	**£1.50**	
When I See My Baby	7"	Polydor	BM56131	1966	**£4**	**£1.50**	

STUDIO SWEETHEARTS

I Believe	7"	DJM	DJS10915	1979	**£6**	**£2.50**	*picture sleeve*

STUPIDS

Violent Nun	7"	Children Of The Revo	COR3	1985	**£10**	**£5**	

STYLE COUNCIL

Agent 88 EP	CD-s	Polydor	TSCCD103	1987	**£5**	**£2**	
Angel	12"	Polydor	COST2	1987	**£6**	**£2.50**	*promo*
Birds And The B's EP	CD-s	Polydor	TSCCD102	1987	**£6**	**£2.50**	
Café Bleu	CD	Polydor	8175352	1984	**£12**	**£5**	
Café Bleu EP	CD-s	Polydor	TSCCD101	1987	**£6**	**£2.50**	
Confessions Of A Pop Group	CD	Polydor	8357852	1988	**£12**	**£5**	
Confessions Of A Pop Group	CD	Polydor	8357852	1988	**£40**	**£20**	*promo brief case set, with video, cassette, towel, biog*
Confessions Of A Pop Group	CD-s	Polygram	0803849	1988	**£10**	**£5**	*CD video*
Cost Of Loving	CD	Polydor	8314432	1987	**£12**	**£5**	
Cost Of Loving	CD-s	Polydor	TSCCD14	1987	**£6**	**£2.50**	
Have You Ever Had It Blue	CD-s	Polygram	0803362	1988	**£10**	**£5**	*CD video*
How She Threw It All Away	CD-s	Polygram	0804002	1988	**£10**	**£5**	*CD video*
How She Threw It All Away	CD-s	Polydor	TSCCD16	1988	**£5**	**£2**	
It Just Came To Pieces (live)	7"	Lyntone	LYN15344/5	1984	**£8**	**£4**	*flexi*
Life At A Top People's Health Club	CD-s	Polygram	0805602	1989	**£10**	**£5**	*CD video*
Life At A Top People's Health Farm	CD-s	Polydor	TSCCD15	1988	**£6**	**£2.50**	
Long Hot Summer	CD-s	Polygram	0802062	1988	**£10**	**£5**	*CD video*
Long Hot Summer – '89 remix	CD-s	Polydor	LHSCD1	1989	**£6**	**£2.50**	
Modernism: A New Decade	LP	Polydor	TSCLP6	1998	**£50**	**£25**	*promo LP or double 12"*
Promised Land	CD-s	Polydor	TSCCD17	1989	**£5**	**£2**	
Promised Land	CD-s	Polydor	TSCD17	1989	**£6**	**£2.50**	
Showbiz	CD-s	Polygram	0800381	1988	**£10**	**£5**	*CD video*
You're The Best Thing	CD-s	Polygram	0803302	1988	**£10**	**£5**	*CD video*

STYLOS

Head Over Heels	7"	Liberty	LIB10173	1964	**£75**	**£37.50**	

STYX

Best Of Styx	LP	RCA	3597	1979	**£10**	**£4**	*Canadian blue vinyl*
Collection Of Styx	LP	A&M	SAMP3	1979	**£20**	**£8**	*promo, 3 LPs, boxed*
Compact Hits	CD-s	A&M	AMCD904	1988	**£5**	**£2**	
Cornerstone	LP	Nautilus		198–	**£12**	**£5**	*US audiophile*
Cornerstone	LP	A&M	SP3711	1979	**£12**	**£5**	*US silver vinyl*
Grand Illusion	LP	Mobile Fidelity	MFSL1026	1978	**£12**	**£5**	*US audiophile*
Grand Illusion	LP	A&M	SP4637	1977	**£10**	**£4**	*Canadian gold vinyl*
Paradise Theatre	LP	Nautilus		198–	**£12**	**£5**	*US audiophile*
Pieces Of Eight	LP	A&M	PR4724	1978	**£12**	**£5**	*US picture disc*
Pieces Of Eight	LP	Nautilus		198–	**£12**	**£5**	*US audiophile*
Styx Radio Show	LP	A&M	SP8431	1976	**£15**	**£6**	*US promo*
Styx Radio Special	LP	A&M	SP17053	1977	**£20**	**£8**	*US promo*

SUB

In Concert	LP	Help		197–	**£300**	**£180**	

SUBHUMANS

Incorrect Thoughts	LP	Friends	FR008	1980	**£25**	**£10**	
No Wishes No Prayers	LP				**£15**	**£6**	*Canadian*

SUBJECT ESQ.

Subject Esq.	LP	Epic	EPC64998	1972	£15	£6	*German*

SUBOTNICK, MORTON

Silver Apples Of The Moon	LP	Nonesuch	H71174	1967	£20	£8	
The Wild Bull	LP	Nonesuch	H71208	1968	£20	£8	

SUBSTITUTE

One	7"	Ignition	IR2	1979	£10	£5	*picture sleeve*
One	7"	Ignition	IR2	1979	£4	£1.50	

SUBURBAN STUDS

No Faith	7"	Pogo	POG001	1977	£10	£5	*version with brass*
Slam	LP	Pogo	POW001	1978	£10	£4	

SUBWAY SECT

Ambition	7"	Rough Trade	RT007	1979	£4	£1.50	*yellow sleeve*
Nobody's Scared	7"	Braik	BRS01	1978	£8	£4	

SUDDEN SWAY

Jane's Third Party	7"	Chant	CHANT1	1980	£10	£5	
Spacemate	12"	WEA	BYN8B	1986	£8	£4	*double boxed set*
To You, With Regard	12"	Chant	CHANT2	1981	£6	£2.50	
Traffic Tax Scheme	12"	Chant	CHANT3	1984	£8	£4	

SUE & SUNNY

I Like Your Style	7"	Columbia	DB8099	1967	£4	£1.50	
Show Must Go On	7"	CBS	3874	1968	£4	£1.50	
Sue & Sunny	LP	CBS	63740	1970	£10	£4	
Sue And Sunny	LP	Reflection	REFL4	1972	£15	£6	

SUE & SUNSHINE

Little Love	7"	Columbia	DB7409	1964	£4	£1.50	

SUEDE

Be My God	12"	RML	RML001	1990	£100	£50	*test pressing*
Drowners	7"	Nude	NUD1S	1992	£10	£5	
Drowners	CD-s	Nude	NUD1CD	1992	£10	£5	*promo*
My Insatiable One	7"	Nude	SUEDE1	1993	£6	£2.50	*clear flexi*
New Generation	CD-s	Nude	NUD12CD2	1995	£10	£5	
Trash	7"	Nude	NUD21S	1996	£8	£4	
Wild Ones	CD-s	Nude	NUD11CD2	1994	£10	£5	

SUGAR

Beaster	CD	Ryko		1993	£20	£8	*US promo, leatherette sleeve*
Copper Blue	CD	Ryko	RCD10239	1992	£20	£8	*US promo, copper cover*
Life Before Sugar	CD	Ryko	VRCD0239	1992	£30	£15	*US promo double – Copper Blue plus compilation*

SUGAR & DANDY

I Want To Be Your Lover	7"	Carnival	CV7029	1965	£4	£1.50	
I'm Into Something Good	7"	Carnival	CV7024	1965	£4	£1.50	
I'm Not Crying Now	7"	Carnival	CV7016	1964	£4	£1.50	
Let's Ska	7"	Page One	POF23044	1967	£4	£1.50	
Let's Ska	7"	Carnival	CV7023	1965	£4	£1.50	
Meditation	7"	Blue Beat	BB367	1966	£12	£6	*Jetliners B side*
Oh Dear What Can The Matter Be	7"	Carnival	CV7009	1964	£4	£1.50	
One Man Went To Mow	7"	Carnival	CV7006	1963	£4	£1.50	
Ska's The Limit	LP	Page One	FOR006	1967	£15	£6	
Think Of The Good Times	7"	Carnival	CV7027	1965	£4	£1.50	
What A Life	7"	Carnival	CV7015	1964	£4	£1.50	

SUGAR & PEEWEE

One Two Let's Rock	7"	Vogue	V9112	1958	£400	£250	*best auctioned*

SUGAR CREEK

Please Tell A Friend	LP	Metromedia	MD1020	1969	£60	£30	*US*

SUGAR SHOPPE

Skip Along Sam	7"	Capitol	CL15555	1968	£4	£1.50	

SUGARBEATS

Alice Designs	7"	Polydor	56120	1966	£4	£1.50	
I Just Stand Here	7"	Polydor	56069	1966	£4	£1.50	

SUGARCUBES

The Sugarcubes gained a fair amount of success outside their native Iceland and were responsible for first unleashing the full splendour of the Björk singing voice on the indie classic 'Birthday'.

12.11	12"	One Little Indian	TPBOX1	1990	£40	£20	*11 × 12", boxed*
7.8	7"	One Little Indian	TPBOX2	1990	£30	£15	*8 × 7", boxed*

Title	Format	Label	Cat. No.	Year	Mint	VG	Notes
Birthday	CD-s	One Little Indian	7TP7CD	1987	**£10**	**£5**	
Birthday Christmas Mix	CD-s	One Little Indian	12TP11CD	1988	**£8**	**£4**	*with Jesus & Mary Chain*
CD.6	CD-s	One Little Indian	TPBOX3	1990	**£40**	**£20**	*6 × CD-s, boxed*
Cold Sweat	CD-s	One Little Indian	7TP9CD	1988	**£6**	**£2.50**	
Deus	CD-s	One Little Indian	7TP10CD	1988	**£6**	**£2.50**	
Finn Mol'a Mann	7"	Smekkleysa	SM3/86	1986	**£60**	**£30**	*Icelandic, as Sykurmolarnir*
Here Today, Tomorrow, Next Week	LP	One Little Indian	TPLP15SP	1989	**£10**	**£4**	*silver vinyl*
Life's Too Good	DAT	One Little Indian	DTPLP5	1988	**£20**	**£8**	
Luftgitar	12"	Smekkleysa	SM7	1987	**£25**	**£12.50**	*Icelandic, as Sykurmolarnir*
Planet	CD-s	One Little Indian	7TP32CD	1990	**£5**	**£2**	
Regina	CD-s	One Little Indian	7TP26CD	1989	**£5**	**£2**	
Skytturnar	12"	Gramm	GRAMM31	1986	**£25**	**£12.50**	*Icelandic, as Sykurmolarnir*
Sykurmolarnir Illur Arfur	LP	One Little Indian	TPLP15L	1989	**£10**	**£4**	*as Sykurmolarnir*

SUGARLOAF

Title	Format	Label	Cat. No.	Year	Mint	VG	Notes
Don't Call Us, We'll Call You	LP	Polydor	2310394	1975	**£10**	**£4**	
Sugarloaf	LP	Liberty	LBS83415	1971	**£10**	**£4**	

SUGARPLUMS

Title	Format	Label	Cat. No.	Year	Mint	VG	Notes
Red River Reggae	7"	Fab	FAB160	1970	**£4**	**£1.50**	

SUGGS

Title	Format	Label	Cat. No.	Year	Mint	VG	Notes
I'm Only Sleeping	7"	WEA	YZ975	1995	**£6**	**£2.50**	

SUICIDE

Title	Format	Label	Cat. No.	Year	Mint	VG	Notes
23 Minutes In Brussels	LP	Bronze	FRANKIE1	1978	**£20**	**£8**	
Alan Vega–Martin Rev	LP	Ze	ILPS7007	1980	**£10**	**£4**	
Cheree	12"	Bronze	12BRO57	1978	**£6**	**£2.50**	
Cheree	7"	Bronze	BRO57	1978	**£5**	**£2**	
Dream Baby Dream	12"	Island	12WIP6543	1979	**£6**	**£2.50**	
Johnny	7"	Sound For Industry	SFI323	1977	**£5**	**£2**	*flexi*
Suicide	LP	Bronze	BRON508	1977	**£10**	**£4**	

SUICIDE COMMANDOS

Title	Format	Label	Cat. No.	Year	Mint	VG	Notes
Commandos Commit Suicide Dance Concert	LP	Twintone	TTR7906	1979	**£15**	**£6**	*US*

SULLIVAN, BIG JIM

Title	Format	Label	Cat. No.	Year	Mint	VG	Notes
She Walks Through The Fair	7"	Mercury	MF928	1965	**£15**	**£7.50**	
Sitar A Go-Go	LP	Mercury	SML30001	1968	**£20**	**£8**	
You Don't Know What You've Got	7"	Decca	F11387	1961	**£4**	**£1.50**	

SULLIVAN, IRA

Title	Format	Label	Cat. No.	Year	Mint	VG	Notes
Billy Taylor Introduces Ira Sullivan	LP	HMV	CLP1236	1959	**£20**	**£8**	

SULLIVAN, JOE

Title	Format	Label	Cat. No.	Year	Mint	VG	Notes
Joe Sullivan	LP	Columbia	33CX10047	1956	**£15**	**£6**	
Joe Sullivan	LP	London	HAU2011	1956	**£15**	**£6**	
Joe Sullivan Plays Fats Waller	10" LP	Philips	BBR8091	1956	**£20**	**£8**	

SULLIVAN, MAXINE

Title	Format	Label	Cat. No.	Year	Mint	VG	Notes
Boogie Woogie Maxine	7"	Parlophone	MSP6086	1954	**£4**	**£1.50**	

SULLIVAN'S GYPSIES

Title	Format	Label	Cat. No.	Year	Mint	VG	Notes
Leprechaun	LP	Emerald	GES1032	1970	**£10**	**£4**	

SULTANS

Title	Format	Label	Cat. No.	Year	Mint	VG	Notes
Les Sultans	LP	Telediscs	356	1966	**£20**	**£8**	*Canadian*
Vol. 2	LP	Idole	306	1967	**£15**	**£6**	*Canadian*

SUM PEAR

Title	Format	Label	Cat. No.	Year	Mint	VG	Notes
Sum Pear	LP	Euphoria	EST1	1971	**£30**	**£15**	*US*

SUMAC, YMA

Title	Format	Label	Cat. No.	Year	Mint	VG	Notes
Legend Of Jivaro Part 1	7" EP	Capitol	EAP1770	1957	**£25**	**£12.50**	
Legend Of Jivaro Part 2	7" EP	Capitol	EAP2770	1957	**£25**	**£12.50**	
Legend Of Jivaro Part 3	7" EP	Capitol	EAP3770	1957	**£25**	**£12.50**	
Mambo Part 1	7" EP	Capitol	EAP1564	1955	**£25**	**£12.50**	
Mambo Part 2	7" EP	Capitol	EAP2564	1955	**£25**	**£12.50**	
Miracles	LP	London	SHU8431	1972	**£30**	**£15**	
Voice Of The Xtaby	10" LP	Capitol	LC6522	1953	**£40**	**£20**	

SUMLIN, HUBERT

Title	Format	Label	Cat. No.	Year	Mint	VG	Notes
Across The Board	7"	Blue Horizon	451000	1965	**£100**	**£50**	

SUMMER, DONNA

Hot Stuff	12"	Casablanca	CANL151	1979	**£10**	**£5**	*red vinyl*

SUMMER SET

Farmer's Daughter	7"	Columbia	DB8004	1966	**£10**	**£5**	*2 different B sides*
It's A Dream	7"	Columbia	DB8215	1967	**£40**	**£20**	

SUMMERFIELD, SAFFRON

Fancy Meeting You Here	LP	Mother Earth	MUM1202	1976	**£40**	**£20**	
Salisbury Plain	LP	Mother Earth	MUM1001	1974	**£40**	**£20**	

SUMMERHILL

Summerhill	LP	Polydor	583746	1969	**£30**	**£15**	

SUMMERS, BOB

Excitement	7"	Capitol	CL15063	1959	**£4**	**£1.50**	
Little Brown Jug	7"	Capitol	CL15130	1960	**£5**	**£2**	

SUMPIN' ELSE

I Can't Get Through To You	7" EP	Liberty	LEP2268	1967	**£8**	**£4**	*French*

SUN ALSO RISES

Sun Also Rises	LP	Village Thing	VTS2	1970	**£15**	**£6**	

SUN & MOON

Alive: Not Dead	CD-s	Midnight Music	DONG44CD	1989	**£8**	**£4**	

SUN DIAL

Exploding In Your Mind	12"	Tangerine	no number	1991	**£25**	**£12.50**	*test pressing*
Other Way Out	LP	Tangerine	MM07	1990	**£15**	**£6**	

SUN RA

Despite the lengthy list of records by avant-garde jazz eccentric Sun Ra, there are actually many more albums in existence, whose details have thus far remained obscure. Over the years Sun Ra issued a large number of albums on his own El Saturn label, with a minority being subsequently reissued on more widely distributed labels. Only in recent years has the man's enormous contribution to jazz begun to be widely appreciated (whether performing on electric piano or synthesizer, whether leading his band through free improvisation or world music chanting, he seemed to do most things before anyone else) and his albums are becoming increasingly collectable.

Angels And Demons At Play	LP	Impulse	AS9245	1973	**£20**	**£8**	*US*
Art Forms From Dimension Tomorrow	LP	El Saturn	404/9956	1965	**£30**	**£15**	*US*
Astro Black	LP	Impulse	AS9255	1973	**£20**	**£8**	*US*
Atlantis	LP	Impulse	AS9239	1973	**£20**	**£8**	*US*
Atlantis	LP	El Saturn			**£30**	**£15**	*US*
Continuation	LP	El Saturn	ESR29691/520		**£30**	**£15**	*US*
Cosmo Sun Connection	LP	El Saturn	SRRRD1	1985	**£30**	**£15**	*US*
Cosmos	LP	Inner City	IC1020	1977	**£20**	**£8**	*US*
Dance Of Innocent Passion	LP	El Saturn	1981	1981	**£30**	**£15**	*US*
Disco 3000	LP	El Saturn	CMIJ78	1978	**£30**	**£15**	*US*
Dreams Come True	LP	El Saturn	485	1984	**£30**	**£15**	*US*
Fate In A Pleasant Mood	LP	Cobra	COB37001	1979	**£12**	**£5**	
Fate In A Pleasant Mood	LP	El Saturn	202		**£30**	**£15**	*US*
Fate In A Pleasant Mood	LP	Impulse	AS9270	1974	**£20**	**£8**	*US*
Futuristic Sounds Of Sun Ra	LP	BYG	529111	197–	**£20**	**£8**	*French*
Futuristic Sounds Of Sun Ra	LP	Savoy	MG12169	1960	**£40**	**£20**	*US*
Heliocentric Worlds Vol. 1	LP	Fontana	STL5514	1965	**£25**	**£10**	
Heliocentric Worlds Vol. 2	LP	Fontana	STL5499	1966	**£20**	**£8**	
Hiroshima	LP	El Saturn	1183	1983	**£30**	**£15**	*US*
Horizon	LP	El Saturn	121771	1972	**£30**	**£15**	*US*
It's After The End Of The World	LP	MPS	MPS15047	1970	**£25**	**£10**	*French*
Jazz By Sun Ra	LP	Transition	TRLP10	1956	**£100**	**£50**	*US*
Jazz By Sun Ra	LP	Sonet	SLP23	196–	**£30**	**£15**	
Jazz In Silhouette	LP	El Saturn	205	1958	**£50**	**£25**	*US*
Jazz In Silhouette	LP	Impulse	ASD9265	1975	**£20**	**£8**	*US*
Live At Montreux	LP	Inner City	IC1039	1977	**£30**	**£15**	*US double*
Live At Praxis '84 Vol. 1	LP	Praxis	CM108	1984	**£15**	**£6**	*Greek*
Magic City	LP	Impulse	AS9243	1973	**£20**	**£8**	*US*
Magic City	LP	El Saturn	LPB711/403		**£30**	**£15**	*US*
My Brother The Wind	LP	El Saturn	ESR521		**£30**	**£15**	*US*
My Brother The Wind Vol. 2	LP	El Saturn	SRA2000/523/ SR1970		**£30**	**£15**	*US*
Nidhamu	LP	El Saturn	7771	1972	**£30**	**£15**	*US*
Nubians Of Plutonia	LP	El Saturn	LP406		**£30**	**£15**	*US*
Nubians Of Plutonia	LP	Impulse	AS9242	1974	**£20**	**£8**	*US*
Nuclear War	12"	Y	RA1	1982	**£20**	**£10**	
Nuits De La Fondation Maeght	LP	Recommended	RRELEVEN	1981	**£20**	**£8**	
Nuits De La Fondation Maeght Vol. 1	LP	Shandar	SR10001	1972	**£25**	**£10**	*French*
Nuits De La Fondation Maeght Vol. 2	LP	Shandar	SR10003	1972	**£25**	**£10**	*French*
Oblique Parallax	LP	El Saturn	SR72881	1981	**£30**	**£15**	*US*
Pathways To Unknown Worlds	LP	El Saturn	564	1973	**£30**	**£15**	*US*
Pathways To Unknown Worlds	LP	Impulse	ASD9298	1975	**£20**	**£8**	*US*
Pictures Of Infinity	LP	Black Lion	BLP30103	197–	**£15**	**£6**	
Pictures Of Infinity	LP	Polydor	2460106	1971	**£20**	**£8**	
Saturn Research	LP	El Saturn	1978	1978	**£30**	**£15**	*US*
Secrets Of The Sun	LP	El Saturn	9954	196–	**£40**	**£20**	
Sleeping Beauty	LP	El Saturn	11179	1979	**£30**	**£15**	*US*

Title	Format	Label	Cat. No.	Year	Mint	VG	Notes
Solar-Myth Approach Vol. 1	LP	Affinity	AFF10	1978	£15	£6	
Solar-Myth Approach Vol. 2	LP	Affinity	AFF76	1983	£15	£6	
Solo Piano Vol. 1	LP	Improvising Arts	IA1373850	1978	£15	£6	
Solo Piano Vol. 2	LP	Improvising Arts	IA1373858	1978	£15	£6	
Soul Vibrations Of Man	LP	El Saturn	771	1976	£30	£15	US
Sound Of Joy	LP	Delmark	DS414	1968	£25	£10	
Springtime Again	LP	El Saturn	11179	1979	£30	£15	US
Strange Celestial Road	LP	Y	Y19	1980	£15	£6	
Sun Ra	LP	Concert Hall	J1348	197–	£20	£8	French
Sun Song	LP	Delmark	DL411	1967	£25	£10	
Sunrise In Different Dimensions	LP	Hat Art	2017	198–	£20	£8	double
Sunrise In Different Dimensions	LP	Hat Hut	HH2R17	1981	£25	£10	double
Super-Sonic Sounds	LP	El Saturn	204		£30	£15	US
Super-Sonic Sounds	LP	Impulse	AS9271	1974	£20	£8	US
Supersonic Jazz	LP	El Saturn	LP0216	196–	£40	£20	
Unity	LP	Horo	HDP19/20	1978	£30	£15	Italian double
Universe In Blue	LP	El Saturn	ESR200/ESR5000		£30	£15	US
Visions	LP	Steeplechase	SCS1126	1979	£20	£8	US, with Walt Dickerson
Voice Of The Eternal Tomorrow	LP	El Saturn	91780	1980	£30	£15	US

SUNDAE TIMES

Title	Format	Label	Cat. No.	Year	Mint	VG	Notes
Us Coloured Kids	LP	Joy	JOYS159	1969	£12	£5	

SUNDANCE

Title	Format	Label	Cat. No.	Year	Mint	VG	Notes
Chuffer	LP	Decca	SKL5183	1974	£10	£4	
Rain Steam Speed	LP	Decca	TXS111	1973	£12	£5	

SUNDAY AFTERNOON

Title	Format	Label	Cat. No.	Year	Mint	VG	Notes
Sunday Afternoon	LP	Longman		197–	£75	£37.50	

SUNDAYS

Title	Format	Label	Cat. No.	Year	Mint	VG	Notes
Can't Be Sure	12"	Rough Trade	RTTX218	1989	£6	£2.50	export
Can't Be Sure	CD-s	Rough Trade	RT218CD	1989	£5	£2	3" single
Reading, Writing And Arithmetic	LP	Rough Trade	ROUGH148P	1990	£10	£4	picture disc

SUNDOWN PLAYBOYS

Title	Format	Label	Cat. No.	Year	Mint	VG	Notes
Saturday Night Special	7"	Apple	44	1972	£15	£7.50	picture sleeve
Saturday Night Special	78	Apple	44	1972	£200	£100	promo, best auctioned

SUNDOWNERS

Title	Format	Label	Cat. No.	Year	Mint	VG	Notes
Dr J. Wallace-Browne	7"	Columbia	DB8339	1968	£4	£1.50	
House Of The Rising Sun	7"	Piccadilly	7N35142	1963	£4	£1.50	
Shot Of Rhythm And Blues	7"	Piccadilly	7N35162	1964	£4	£1.50	
Where Am I	7"	Parlophone	R5243	1965	£4	£1.50	

SUNDRAGON

Title	Format	Label	Cat. No.	Year	Mint	VG	Notes
Blueberry Blue	7"	MGM	MGM1391	1968	£5	£2	
Five White Horses	7"	MGM	MGM1458	1968	£4	£1.50	
Green Tambourine	7"	MGM	MGM1380	1968	£5	£2	
Green Tambourine	LP	MGM	C(S)8090	1968	£40	£20	

SUNFOREST

Title	Format	Label	Cat. No.	Year	Mint	VG	Notes
Sound Of Sunforest	LP	Nova	SDN7	1969	£60	£30	

SUNNIES

Title	Format	Label	Cat. No.	Year	Mint	VG	Notes
Stimmung In Beat	LP	Philips	843941PY	1967	£15	£6	German

SUNNY & THE SUNGLOWS

Title	Format	Label	Cat. No.	Year	Mint	VG	Notes
All Night Worker	LP	Tear Drop	2019	196–	£15	£6	US
Peanuts	LP	Sunglow	SLP103	1965	£15	£6	US
Talk To Me	7"	London	HL9792	1963	£15	£7.50	
Talk To Me/Rags To Riches	LP	Tear Drop	2000	1963	£20	£8	US

SUNNYLAND SLIM

Title	Format	Label	Cat. No.	Year	Mint	VG	Notes
I Done You Wrong	LP	Storyville	SLP169	1965	£15	£6	
Midnight Jump	LP	Blue Horizon	763213	1969	£40	£20	
Portraits In Blues	LP	Storyville	670169	1968	£12	£5	
Slim's Got This Thing Goin' On	LP	Liberty	LBS83237	1969	£20	£8	
Slim's Shout	LP	Bluesville	BV1016	1961	£20	£8	US
Sunnyland Slim	LP	Storyville	616012	1970	£15	£6	

SUNNYSIDERS

Title	Format	Label	Cat. No.	Year	Mint	VG	Notes
Banjo Woogie	7"	London	HLU8180	1955	£25	£12.50	
Doesn't He Love Me	7"	London	HLU8246	1956	£25	£12.50	
Hey Mister Banjo	7"	London	HL8135	1955	£40	£20	
I Love You Fair Dinkum	7"	London	HLU8202	1955	£20	£10	
Oh Me Oh My	7"	London	HL8160	1955	£25	£12.50	

SUNRAYS

Title	Format	Label	Cat. No.	Year	Mint	VG	Notes
Andrea	7"	Capitol	CL15433	1966	£4	£1.50	
Andrea	LP	Tower	(S)T5017	1966	£20	£8	US
I Live For The Sun	7"	Capitol	CL15416	1965	£4	£1.50	

SUNRISE

Title	Format	Label	Cat. No.	Year	Mint	VG	Notes
Before My Eyes	LP	Grapevine	GRA105	1976	£25	£12.50	

SUNSCREEM

Perfect Motion	12"	Sony	XPR1825	1992	£20	£10	*promo*

SUNSET ALL STARS

Jammin' At Sunset Vol. 1	LP	Fontana	SFJL918	1969	£10	£4	

SUNSETS

Cry Of The Wild Goose	7"	Ember	EMBS125	1960	£10	£5	
Surfing With The Sunsets	LP	Palace	752	1963	£20	£8	*US*

SUNSHINE, MONTY

Black Moonlight And Sunshine	LP	London	SHR8158	1964	£15	£6	
Gonna Build A Mountain	7" EP	London	RER1368	1963	£5	£2	
Monty	7" EP	Columbia	SEG8059	1961	£5	£2	
Shades Of Sunshine	LP	Major Minor	SMCP5062	1969	£15	£6	
Showcase	7" EP	Pye	NJE1050	1957	£5	£2	
Sunshine	7" EP	Columbia	SEG8127	1961	£8	£4	
Taste Of Sunshine	LP	DJM	DJB26088	197–	£10	£4	

SUNSHINE COMPANY

Sunshine & Shadows	LP	Liberty	LBL/LBS83159	1968	£10	£4	
Sunshine Company	LP	Liberty	LBL/LBS83120	1968	£10	£4	

SUNTREADER

Zin-Zin	LP	Island	HELP13	1973	£10	£4	

SUPER FURRY ANIMALS

Hon Yw'r Gan Sy'n Mynd	7"	Debiel	SS01	1996	£10	£5	*1 sided*
Man Don't Give A Fuck	CD-s	Creation	CRESCD247	1996	£6	£2.50	

SUPERBOYS

Ain't That A Shame	7"	Giant	GN22	1968	£5	£2	
You're Hurtin' Me	7"	Giant	GN31	1968	£5	£2	

SUPERFINE DANDELION

Superfine Dandelion	LP	Mainstream	S6102	1968	£30	£15	*US*

SUPERGRASS

Caught By The Fuzz	12"	Parlophone	12R6396DJ	1994	£8	£4	*promo*
Caught By The Fuzz	7"	Backbeat	no number	1994	£10	£5	
Caught By The Fuzz	CD-s	Parlophone	CDR6396	1994	£5	£2	
Mansize Rooster	7"	Backbeat	no number	1994	£8	£4	*green vinyl*
Mansize Rooster	7"	Backbeat	no number	1994	£4	£1.50	*marbled green vinyl*
Mansize Rooster	CD-s	Parlophone	CDR6402	1995	£5	£2	
Singles 1994–1997	7"	Parlophone	GRASS9497	1997	£40	£20	*8 single promo box set*
Sofa (Of My Lethargy)	CD-s	Parlophone	GRASS2	1995	£5	£2	*promo*
Sun Hits The Sky	12"	Parlophone	12RDJ6469	1997	£8	£4	*promo*

SUPERSISTER

Iskander	LP	Polydor	2925021	1973	£15	£6	*Dutch*
Present From Nancy	LP	Polydor	2419061	1972	£12	£5	
Pudding And Gisteren	LP	Polydor	2419058	1972	£12	£5	
Super Starshine Vol. 3	LP	Polydor	2419030	1971	£15	£6	
Sweet Okay	LP	Polydor	2441048	1974	£10	£4	*Dutch*
To The Highest Bidder	LP	Dandelion	2310146	1971	£20	£8	

SUPERSONICS

Second Fiddle	LP	Trojan	TRL6	1968	£20	£8	

SUPERSTOCKS

School Is A Drag	LP	Capitol	(S)T2190	1964	£40	£20	*US*
Surf Route 101	LP	Capitol	(S)T2113	1964	£40	£20	*US*
Thunder Road	LP	Capitol	(S)T2060	1964	£40	£20	*US*

SUPERTONES

Freedom Blues	7"	Banana	BA312	1970	£5	£2	

SUPERTRAMP

Breakfast In America	LP	Mobile Fidelity	MFSL1045	1980	£10	£4	*US audiophile*
Compact Hits	CD-s	A&M	AMCD914	1988	£5	£2	
Crime Of The Century	LP	Mobile Fidelity	MFSL1005	1978	£10	£4	*US audiophile*
Crime Of The Century	LP	Mobile Fidelity	MFSL1005	1982	£40	£20	*US audiophile (UHQR)*
Crisis? What Crisis	LP	A&M			£10	£4	*audiophile*
Even In The Quietest Moments	LP	A&M			£10	£4	*audiophile*
Famous Last Words	LP	A&M			£10	£4	*audiophile*
Paris	LP	A&M			£15	£6	*audiophile double*

SUPREMES

A Go-Go	LP	Tamla Motown	(S)TML11039	1966	£12	£5	
At The Copa	LP	Tamla Motown	(S)TML11026	1966	£15	£6	

Title	Format	Label	Cat. No.	Year	Mint	Half	Notes
Baby Love	7"	Stateside	SS350	1964	£4	£1.50	
Back In My Arms Again	7"	Tamla Motown	TMG516	1965	£8	£4	
Breathtaking Guy	7"	Motown	1044	1963	£15	£7.50	*US*
Come See About Me	7"	Stateside	SS376	1965	£6	£2.50	
Country, Western & Pop	LP	Tamla Motown	TML11018	1965	£30	£15	
Happening	7"	Tamla Motown	TMG607	1967	£4	£1.50	
I Hear A Symphony	7"	Tamla Motown	TMG543	1965	£5	£2	
I Hear A Symphony	LP	Tamla Motown	(S)TML11028	1966	£10	£4	
I Want A Guy	7"	Tamla	154038	1961	£100	£50	*US*
I Want A Guy	7"	Tamla	1008	1961	£1000	£700	*US demo, best auctioned*
L'Amore Verra	7"	Tamla Motown	TM8004	1966	£75	£37.50	*sung in Italian*
Little Bit Of Liverpool	LP	Motown	M/S623	1964	£40	£20	*US*
Little Bit Of Liverpool	LP	Stateside	LES501	1965	£100	£50	*export*
Love Is Here And Now You're Gone	7"	Tamla Motown	TMG597	1967	£4	£1.50	
Love Is Like An Itching In My Heart	7"	Tamla Motown	TMG560	1966	£20	£10	
Meet The Supremes	LP	Motown	M606	1964	£150	£75	*US, group seated on stools on cover*
Meet The Supremes	LP	Motown	M/S606	1964	£50	£25	*US*
Meet The Supremes	LP	Stateside	SL10109	1964	£20	£8	
Merry Christmas	LP	Motown	M/S638	1965	£40	£20	*US*
Moonlight And Kisses	7"	Tamla Motown	GO42625	1967	£20	£10	*Dutch, B side sung in French*
More Hits	LP	Tamla Motown	TML11020	1965	£15	£6	
My Heart Can't Take It No More	7"	Motown	1040	1963	£15	£7.50	*US*
My World Is Empty Without You	7"	Tamla Motown	TMG548	1966	£10	£5	
Nothing But Heartaches	7"	Tamla Motown	TMG527	1965	£12	£6	
Shake	7" EP	Tamla Motown	TME2011	1966	£40	£20	
Sing Motown	LP	Tamla Motown	(S)TML11047	1967	£12	£5	
Sing Rodgers & Hart	LP	Tamla Motown	(S)TML11054	1967	£10	£4	
Stop In The Name Of Love	7"	Tamla Motown	TMG501	1965	£4	£1.50	
Supremes Hits	7" EP	Tamla Motown	TME2008	1965	£15	£7.50	
Supremes Hits	7" EP	Tamla Motown	TME2008	1965	£8	£4	*solid centre reissue*
Thank You Darling	7"	Tamla Motown	GO42609	1967	£20	£10	*Dutch, B side sung in French*
We Remember Sam Cooke	LP	Tamla Motown	TML11012	1965	£30	£15	
When The Lovelight Starts Shining	7"	Stateside	SS257	1964	£30	£15	
Where Did Our Love Go	7"	Stateside	SS327	1964	£4	£1.50	
Where Did Our Love Go	LP	Motown	M/S621	1964	£25	£10	*US*
Who's Loving You	7"	Tamla	T54045	1961	£100	£50	*US*
With Love From Us To You	LP	Tamla Motown	TML11002	1965	£30	£15	
You Can't Hurry Love	7"	Tamla Motown	TMG575	1966	£4	£1.50	
You Keep Me Hanging On	7"	Tamla Motown	TMG585	1966	£4	£1.50	
Your Heart Belongs To Me	7"	Motown	1027	1962	£200	£100	*US, picture sleeve*

SURF STOMPERS

Title	Format	Label	Cat. No.	Year	Mint	Half	Notes
Original Surfer Stomp	LP	Del Fi	DFS1236	1964	£25	£10	*US*

SURF TEENS

Title	Format	Label	Cat. No.	Year	Mint	Half	Notes
Surf Mania	LP	Sutton	339	1964	£30	£15	*US*

SURFARIS

Title	Format	Label	Cat. No.	Year	Mint	Half	Notes
Fun City	LP	Brunswick	LAT8582	1964	£25	£10	
Hit City '64	LP	Brunswick	LAT8567	1964	£20	£8	
Hit City '64	LP	Brunswick	STA8567	1964	£25	£10	*stereo*
Hit City '65	LP	Brunswick	LAT8605	1965	£25	£10	
It Ain't Me Babe	LP	Brunswick	LAT8631	1965	£20	£8	
It Ain't Me Babe	LP	Brunswick	STA8631	1965	£25	£10	*stereo*
Point Panic	7"	Brunswick	05894	1963	£4	£1.50	
Scatter Shield	7"	Brunswick	05902	1964	£5	£2	
Surfaris Play	LP	Brunswick	LAT8561	1963	£20	£8	
Surfaris Play	LP	Brunswick	STA8561	1963	£25	£10	*stereo*
Wipe Out	7"	London	HLD9751	1963	£4	£1.50	
Wipe Out	7" EP	London	RED1405	1963	£25	£12.50	
Wipe Out	7" EP	Dot	VDEP34019	1963	£25	£12.50	*French*

Title	Format	Label	Number	Year	Mint	VG	Notes
Wipe Out	LP	London	HAD8110	1963	**£30**	**£15**	*with the Challengers*
Wipe Out	LP	Dot	DLP3535	1966	**£15**	**£6**	

SURFERS

Mambo Jambo	7"	Vogue	V9147	1959	**£8**	**£4**	*Alan Kalani B side*

SURFRIDERS

Surfbeat	LP	Vault	V(S)105	1963	**£15**	**£6**	*US*

SURFSIDE FIVE

Recorded Live	LP	Intermountain	153	196–	**£75**	**£37.50**	*US*

SURGEONS

Sid Never Did It	7"	Surgery	S100	1979	**£8**	**£4**	

SURMAN, JOHN

Alors!	LP	Futura	GER12	1970	**£50**	**£25**	
How Many Clouds Can You See?	LP	Deram	DMLR/ SMLR1045	1969	**£75**	**£37.50**	
Jazz Double Vol. 1	LP	Vogue	VJD505/1	1974	**£25**	**£15**	*French*
Jazz Double Vol. 2	LP	Vogue	VJD505/2	1974	**£25**	**£15**	*French*
John Surman	LP	Deram	DML/SML1030	1968	**£50**	**£25**	
Live At Moers Festival	LP	Ring	1006	1975	**£15**	**£6**	
Live At Woodstock Town Hall	LP	Daw	DNLS3072	1975	**£10**	**£4**	*with Stu Martin*
Obeah Wedding	7"	Deram	DM224	1969	**£4**	**£1.50**	
Sonatinas	LP	Stream	SJ106	1978	**£15**	**£6**	
Tales Of The Algonquin	LP	Deram	SML1094	1971	**£75**	**£37.50**	*with John Warren*
Westering Home	LP	Island	HELP10	1972	**£12**	**£5**	

SURPLUS STOCK

Spiv	7"	Outatune	OUT7911	1979	**£8**	**£4**	

SURPRIEZE

Zeer Oude Klanken En Heel Nieuwe Geluiden	LP	private		1973	**£600**	**£400**	*Dutch*

SURPRISE PACKAGE

Free Up	LP	LHI	S12006	1968	**£40**	**£20**	*US*

SURPRISES

Jeremy Thorpe Is Innocent	7"	Dead Dog	DEAD01	1979	**£5**	**£2**	

SURPRIZE

Keep On Truckin'	LP	East Coast	EC1049	1974	**£75**	**£37.50**	*US*

SURVIVOR

Eye Of The Tiger	7"	Scotti Brothers	A2411P	1982	**£4**	**£1.50**	*picture disc*

SURVIVORS

Rawhide Ska	7"	Rio	R70	1965	**£10**	**£5**	*Owen Gray B side*
Take Charge	7"	Rio	R55	1965	**£10**	**£5**	

SURVIVORS (2)

Not only was the single by the Survivors written and produced by Brian Wilson, but the Survivors themselves were actually the Beach Boys. The group wanted to see if they could have a hit under another name – with the result that a typically classy performance has become the great lost Beach Boys track.

Pamela Jean	7"	Capitol	5102	1964	**£200**	**£100**	*US*

SUSTAIN

Sustain	LP	Unidentified Artist	UAP2	1978	**£100**	**£50**	*Dutch*

SUTCH, SCREAMING LORD

That a small-time rock 'n' roll singer who never had a hit record could still be a celebrity is a tribute to David Sutch's skills at self-publicity. Well-known as the leader of the Monster Raving Loony Party, Sutch never let it be forgotten that he was also a rock performer. His concerts, however, were always chaotic affairs. In the wake of his *Lord Sutch And Heavy Friends* LP, expectations were high that he would appear accompanied by some of those same heavy friends – Jeff Beck, Jimmy Page and the rest. People turned up in droves to watch Sutch chase members of an anonymous backing group around the stage with a mop!

Cause I Love You	7"	Atlantic	2091006	1970	**£5**	**£2**	
Cause I Love You	7"	Atlantic	584321	1970	**£6**	**£2.50**	
Cheat	7"	CBS	202080	1966	**£25**	**£12.50**	
Dracula's Daughter	7"	Oriole	CB1962	1964	**£25**	**£12.50**	
Election Fever	7"	Atlantic	2091017	1970	**£5**	**£2**	
Good Golly Miss Molly	7"	HMV	POP953	1961	**£10**	**£5**	
Gotta Keep A-Rockin'	7"	Atlantic	K10221	1972	**£5**	**£2**	
Hands Of Jack The Ripper	LP	Atlantic	K40313	1972	**£20**	**£8**	
Honey Hush	7"	CBS	201767	1965	**£30**	**£15**	
I'm A Hog For You	7"	Decca	F11747	1963	**£10**	**£5**	
Jack The Ripper	7"	Decca	F11598	1963	**£10**	**£5**	
Jack The Ripper	7" EP	Decca	457063	1965	**£30**	**£15**	*French*
Lord Sutch & Heavy Friends	LP	Atlantic	2400008	1970	**£20**	**£8**	
Screaming Lord Sutch Meets The Meteors	10" LP	Ace	MAD1	1981	**£75**	**£37.50**	
She's Fallen In Love With A Monster	7"	Oriole	CB1944	1964	**£25**	**£12.50**	

Train Kept A-Rollin'	7" EP	CBS	6104	1965	**£30**	**£15**	*French*

SUTCLIFFE, ROGER

Death Letter	LP	Look	LKLP6038RS	1976	**£50**	**£25**	

SUTHERLAND, ISABEL

Bank Of Red Roses	7" EP	Collector	JES11	1961	**£5**	**£2**	
Vagrant Songs Of Scotland	LP	Topic	12T151	1966	**£10**	**£4**	

SUTTON, RALPH

I Got Rhythm	10" LP	Brunswick	LA8719	1955	**£20**	**£8**	
Music Of Fats Waller	10" LP	Columbia	33S1025	1954	**£20**	**£8**	
Piano Moods	10" LP	Columbia	33S1018	1954	**£20**	**£8**	
Ralph Sutton Quartet	LP	Columbia	33CX10061	1956	**£12**	**£5**	
Stride Piano	10" LP	Audio Fidelity	AF2	1953	**£20**	**£8**	

SUZANNE

Born On Halloween	7"	Ring O'	2017108	1977	**£10**	**£5**	*promo in picture sleeve*

SUZI & BIG DEE IRWIN

Ain't That Lovin' You Baby	7"	Polydor	BM65715	1966	**£6**	**£2.50**	

SUZUKI, PAT

Daddy	7"	RCA	RCA1069	1958	**£4**	**£1.50**	
I Enjoy Being A Girl	7"	RCA	RCA1171	1960	**£5**	**£2**	

SUZY & THE RED STRIPES

Seaside Woman	12"	A&M	AMSP7548	1980	**£6**	**£2.50**	
Seaside Woman	12"	EMI	12EMI5572	1986	**£6**	**£2.50**	
Seaside Woman	7"	A&M	AMSP7461	1979	**£25**	**£12.50**	*yellow vinyl, boxed*
Seaside Woman	7"	EMI	EMI5572	1986	**£4**	**£1.50**	
Seaside Woman	7"	A&M	AMS7548	1980	**£4**	**£1.50**	
Seaside Woman	7"	A&M	AM7461	1979	**£5**	**£2**	*yellow vinyl*

SVANTE

Baby I Need Your Loving	7"	United Artists	UP2224	1968	**£4**	**£1.50**	

SVENSK

Dream Magazine	7"	Page One	POF036	1967	**£10**	**£5**	
You	7"	Page One	POF050	1967	**£10**	**£5**	

SVENSSON, REINHOLD

New Sounds From Sweden Vol. 4	10" LP	Esquire	20024	1954	**£75**	**£37.50**	*with Putte Wickman*
Reinhold Svensson Quintet	10" LP	Esquire	20004	1953	**£75**	**£37.50**	

SWALLOWS

Roll Roll Pretty Baby	78	Vogue	V2136	1952	**£15**	**£7.50**	

SWAMP DOGG

Total Destruction To Your Mind	LP	Polydor	2916014	1972	**£12**	**£5**	

SWAMP RATS

Disco Sucks	LP	Keystone	K11154139	1979	**£15**	**£6**	*US*

SWAN

From Swan With Love	LP	SLP		1981	**£50**	**£25**	*Dutch*

SWAN ARCADE

Matchless	LP	Stoof	MU7428	1976	**£10**	**£4**	
Swan Arcade	LP	Trailer	LER2032	1973	**£25**	**£10**	

SWANEE RIVER BOYS

Do You Believe	7"	Parlophone	CMSP7	1954	**£6**	**£2.50**	*export*
Was He Quiet Or Did He Cry	7"	Parlophone	DP385	1954	**£6**	**£2.50**	*export*

SWANN, BETTYE

Don't Touch Me	7"	Capitol	CL15586	1969	**£15**	**£7.50**	
Heading In The Right Direction	7"	Atlantic	K10851	1976	**£6**	**£2.50**	
Make Me Yours	7"	CBS	2942	1967	**£60**	**£30**	*demo in picture sleeve*
Make Me Yours	7"	CBS	2942	1967	**£25**	**£12.50**	
Today I Started Loving You Again	7"	Atlantic	K10273	1972	**£5**	**£2**	
Victim Of A Foolish Heart	7"	Atlantic	K10174	1972	**£6**	**£2.50**	

SWANS

Boy With The Beatle Hair	7"	Cameo Parkway	C302	1964	**£10**	**£5**	
He's Mine	7"	Stateside	SS224	1963	**£8**	**£4**	

SWANS (2)

Burning World	CD-s	MCA	DMCG6047	1989	**£5**	**£2**	
Can't Find My Way Home	CD-s	MCA	CDDMCAT1347	1989	**£5**	**£2**	
Filth	LP	Zensor	NDO3	1985	**£25**	**£10**	
Love Of Life/White Light From The Mouth Of Infinity	CD	Young God	YGCD3/5	1992	**£20**	**£8**	*boxed 2 CD set*
Love Will Tear Us Apart	CD-s	Product Inc	PROD23CD	1988	**£5**	**£2**	
Saved	CD-s	MCA	DMCAT1332	1989	**£5**	**£2**	

SWANSON, BERNICE

Baby I'm Yours	7"	Chess	CRS8008	1965	£20	£10	

SWARBRICK, DAVE

Ceilidh Album	LP	Sonet	SNTF764	1978	£10	£4	
Close To The Wind	LP	Woodworm	WR006	1984	£12	£5	*with Simon Nicol*
Live At The White Bear	LP	White Bear	WBR001	1982	£25	£10	*with Simon Nicol*
Rags, Reels And Airs	LP	Polydor	236514	1967	£60	£30	
Rags, Reels And Airs	LP	Bounty	BY6030	1967	£75	£37.50	
Smiddyburn	LP	Logo	LOGO1029	1981	£12	£5	
Swarbrick	LP	Transatlantic	TRA337	1976	£10	£4	
Swarbrick 2	LP	Transatlantic	TRA341	1977	£10	£4	

SWARBRIGGS

That's What Friends Are For	7"	MCA	MCA179	1975	£4	£1.50	

SWEAT, ROSALYN & THE PARAGONS

Blackbird Singing	LP	Horse	HRLP703	1973	£12	£5	

SWE-DANES

Skandinavian Shuffles	LP	Warner Bros	1388	1960	£25	£10	*German*
Swe-Danes	7" EP	Warner Bros	WEP6017	1961	£10	£5	
Swe-Danes	7" EP	Warner Bros	SWEP2017	1961	£15	£7.50	*stereo*

SWEDEN THROUGH THE AGES

It Helps To Cry	12"	Snappy	SW001	1986	£6	£2.50	

SWEENEY TODD

The claim to fame of this otherwise obscure Canadian rock band is that future megastar Bryan Adams was the lead singer.

If Wishes Were Horses	LP	London	PS694	1977	£100	£50	*Canadian*

SWEENEY'S MEN

Old Maid In The Garrett	7"	Pye	7N17312	1967	£6	£2.50	
Rattlin' & Roarin' Willy	LP	Transatlantic	TRA170	1968	£50	£25	
Sullivan's John	7"	Transatlantic	TRASP19	1968	£5	£2	
Sweeney's Men	LP	Transatlantic	TRASAM37	1976	£12	£5	
Tracks Of Sweeney	LP	Transatlantic	TRA200	1969	£75	£37.50	
Tracks Of Sweeney	LP	Transatlantic	TRASAM40	1977	£12	£5	
Waxies Dargle	7"	Pye	7N17459	1968	£6	£2.50	

SWEET

Beginning as a teeny-bopper group, the Sweet's music gradually became heavier as it progressed. At the same time, the group aligned itself with the glamour-rock movement, and as the only way for anyone to adopt the kind of extravagant image favoured by the likes of Gary Glitter was with his tongue placed firmly in his cheek, so the Sweet became high princes of camp, mocking themselves and their music even while playing it. In the end, of course, this rebounded on them, and the classy 'Love Is Like Oxygen' apart, the group failed to convince when they tried to become serious artists.

All You'll Ever Get From Me	7"	Parlophone	R5902	1971	£15	£7.50	
All You'll Ever Get From Me	7"	Parlophone	R5826	1970	£20	£10	
Ballroom Blitz	7"	RCA	GOLD551	1981	£5	£2	
Ballroom Blitz	7"	RCA	RCA2403	1973	£10	£5	*plays slow – matrix 2403-A-1E*
Big Apple	7"	Polydor	POSP73	1979	£25	£12.50	
Blockbuster	7"	RCA	GOLD524	1981	£5	£2	
California Nights	7"	Polydor	POSP5	1978	£20	£10	*demo*
Call Me	7"	Polydor	POSP36	1979	£4	£1.50	
Cut Above The Rest	LP	Polydor	POLD5022	1979	£12	£5	
Cut Above The Rest	LP	Capitol	SO11929	1979	£25	£10	*US, different 'Hold Me' & cover*
For AOR Radio Only	LP	Capitol	SPRO8371/73	1975	£30	£15	*US promo*
Fox On The Run	7"	RCA	PE5226	1980	£10	£5	
Funny How Sweet Coco Can Be	LP	RCA	SF8288	1971	£20	£8	
Get On The Line	7"	Parlophone	R5848	1970	£50	£25	
Give The Lady Some Respect	7"	Polydor	POSP131	1980	£4	£1.50	
Give Us A Wink	LP	RCA	RS1936	1976	£10	£4	
Identity Crisis	LP	Polydor	23111179	1982	£20	£8	
It's It's . . . The Sweet Mix	12"	Anagram	12ANA28	1984	£6	£2.50	
Lollipop Man	7"	Parlophone	R5803	1969	£100	£50	
Off The Record	LP	RCA	PL25072	1977	£10	£4	
Sixties Man/Oh Yeah	7"	Polydor	POSP160	1980	£15	£7.50	*B side plays 'Tall Girls'*
Sixties Man/Oh Yeah	7"	Polydor	POSP160	1980	£10	£5	
Slow Motion	7"	Fontana	TF958	1968	£500	£330	*best auctioned*
Stairway To The Stars	7"	RCA	PB5046	1977	£5	£2	
Strung Up	LP	RCA	SPC0001	1975	£12	£5	*double*
Sweet Sixteen	LP	Anagram	PGRAM16	1984	£30	£15	*picture disc*
Water's Edge	LP	Polydor	POLS1021	1980	£20	£8	
Wig Wam Bam	7"	RCA	PB43337	1989	£10	£5	

SWEET CHARIOT

Sweet Chariot And Friends	LP	De Wolfe		1972	£75	£37.50	

SWEET CHARLES

For Sweet People	LP	People	PE6603	1974	£25	£10	*US*
For Sweet People	LP	Urban	URBLP9	1988	£10	£4	
Yes It's You	12"	Urban	URBX15	1988	£6	£2.50	*Lyn Collins B side*

SWEET FEELING

All So Long Ago ...... 7" ...... Columbia ...... DB8195 ...... 1967 **£60** ...... **£30** ......

SWEET INSPIRATIONS

Let It Be Me ...... 7" ...... Atlantic ...... 584132 ...... 1967 **£4** ...... **£1.50** ......
Sweet Inspiration ...... 7" ...... Atlantic ...... 584167 ...... 1968 **£4** ...... **£1.50** ......
Sweet Inspirations ...... LP ...... Atlantic ...... 587/588090 ...... 1968 **£10** ...... **£4** ......
Sweet Sweet Soul ...... LP ...... Atlantic ...... 2465003 ...... 1970 **£10** ...... **£4** ......
Sweets For My Sweet ...... 7" ...... Atlantic ...... 584279 ...... 1969 **£4** ...... **£1.50** ......
Sweets For My Sweet ...... LP ...... Atlantic ...... 587/588194 ...... 1969 **£10** ...... **£4** ......
What The World Needs Now Is Love ...... 7" ...... Atlantic ...... 584233 ...... 1968 **£4** ...... **£1.50** ......
What The World Needs Now Is Love ...... LP ...... Atlantic ...... 587/588137 ...... 1969 **£10** ...... **£4** ......
Why Am I Treated So Bad ...... 7" ...... Atlantic ...... 584117 ...... 1967 **£4** ...... **£1.50** ......

SWEET JESUS

Cat Thing ...... 12" ...... Chapter 22 ...... CHAP63 ...... 1991 **£6** ...... **£2.50** ...... *test pressing*

SWEET MARIE

Stuck In Paradise ...... LP ...... Yardbird ...... YDBS771 ...... 1972 **£20** ...... **£8** ...... *US*

SWEET PAIN

Sweet Pain ...... LP ...... Mercury ...... SMCL20146 ...... 1969 **£40** ...... **£20** ......
Timber Gibbs ...... 7" ...... United Artists .. UP35268 ...... 1971 **£4** ...... **£1.50** ......

SWEET PANTS

Fat Peter Presents ...... LP ...... private ...... LP1141 ...... 1969 **£200** ...... **£100** ...... *US*

SWEET PLUM

Lazy Day ...... 7" ...... Middle Earth ... MDS103 ...... 1969 **£15** ...... **£7.50** ......
Set The Wheels In Motion ...... 7" ...... Middle Earth ... MDS105 ...... 1969 **£15** ...... **£7.50** ......

SWEET SAVAGE

Killing Time ...... 7" ...... Sweet Savage ... 1980 ...... 1981 **£50** ...... **£25** ......
Raid ...... 7" ...... private ...... 198– **£30** ...... **£15** ......
Straight Through The Heart ...... 7" ...... Crashed ...... CAR48 ...... 198– **£75** .... **£37.50** ......

SWEET SLAG

Tracking With Close Ups ...... LP ...... XTRA ...... XTRA1112 ...... 1971 **£25** ...... **£10** ......
Tracking With Close-Ups ...... LP ...... President ...... PTLS1042 ...... 1971 **£25** ...... **£10** ......

SWEET SMOKE

Just A Poke ...... LP ...... Catfish ...... 5C05424311 ...... 1972 **£12** ...... **£5** ...... *Dutch*

SWEET THURSDAY

Sweet Thursday ...... LP ...... Polydor ...... 2310051 ...... 1969 **£15** ...... **£6** ......
Sweet Thursday ...... LP ...... CBS ...... 65573 ...... 1973 **£10** ...... **£4** ......

SWEET TOOTHE

Testing ...... LP ...... Dominion ...... NR7360 ...... 1971 **£100** ...... **£50** ...... *US*

SWEETING, HARRY

From Jamaica With Love ...... 7" ...... Coxsone ...... CS7012 ...... 1967 **£10** ...... **£5** ......

SWEETSHOP

Barefoot And Tiptoe ...... 7" ...... Parlophone ...... R5707 ...... 1968 **£6** ...... **£2.50** ......

SWEGAS

Child Of Light ...... LP ...... Trend ...... 6480002 ...... 1971 **£20** ...... **£8** ......

SWELL MAPS

Read About Seymour ...... 7" ...... Rather ...... GEAR1 ...... 1977 **£10** ...... **£5** ......
Trip to Marineville ...... LP ...... Big Rather ...... TROY1 ...... 1979 **£10** ...... **£4** .... *with 7" (GEAR5)*
What A Nice Way To Turn Seventeen No. 2 ...... 7" ...... Rather ...... GEAR17 ...... 1984 **£6** ...... **£2.50** ...... *with other artists*
Whatever Happens Next ...... LP ...... Rough Trade... ROUGH21 ...... 1981 **£12** ...... **£5** ...... *double*

SWERVEDRIVER

Rave Down EP ...... CD-s ... Creation ...... CRESCD088 ...... 1990 **£5** ...... **£2** ......
Sandblasted EP ...... CD-s ... Creation ...... CRESCD102 ...... 1991 **£5** ...... **£2** ......
Swervedriver EP ...... CD-s ... Creation ...... CRESCD79 ...... 1990 **£5** ...... **£2** ......

SWIFT, T. & THE ELECTRIC BAG

Are You Experienced? ...... LP ...... Custom ...... 1115 ...... 1967 **£30** ...... **£15** ...... *US*

SWIFT, TUFTY

How To Make A Bakewell Tart ...... LP ...... Free Reed ...... FRR017 ...... 1977 **£15** ...... **£6** ......
You'll Never Die For Love ...... LP ...... Shark ...... 04 ...... 1985 **£10** ...... **£4** ......

SWINDELLS, STEVE

Messages ...... LP ...... RCA ...... LPL15057 ...... 1974 **£10** ...... **£4** ......

SWINDLEFOLK

Swindled ...... LP ...... Ace Of Clubs... ACL1273 ...... 1970 **£25** ...... **£10** ......

SWINFIELD, RAY

Pne For Ray ...... LP ...... Morgan Blue Town ...... 1969 **£75** .... **£37.50** ......

SWINGERS

Love Makes The World Go Round .... 7″........ Vogue .... V9158.................... 1960 £**10**...........£**5** ....

SWINGING BLUE JEANS

Blue Jeans A Swinging .... LP .... HMV .... CSD1570................ 1964 £**60**..........£**30** .... *stereo*
Blue Jeans A Swinging .... LP .... HMV .... CLP1802 .... 1964 £**40**..........£**20** .... *mono*
Brand New And Faded .... LP .... Dart .... BULL1001.............. 1974 £**10**..........£**4** ....
Crazy 'Bout My Baby .... 7″........ HMV .... POP1477 .... 1965 £**5**............£**2** ....
Do You Know .... 7″........ HMV .... POP1206 .... 1963 £**6**........ £**2.50** ....
Don't Go Out Into The Rain .... 7″........ HMV .... POP1605 .... 1967 £**5**............£**2** ....
Don't Make Me Over .... 7″........ HMV .... POP1501 .... 1966 £**5**............£**2** ....
Good Golly Miss Molly .... 7″........ HMV .... POP1273 .... 1964 £**4**........ £**1.50** ....
Good Golly Miss Molly .... 7″ EP .. Pathe .... EGF736 .... 1964 £**30**..........£**15** .... *French*
Hippy Hippy Shake .... 7″........ HMV .... POP1242 .... 1963 £**4**........ £**1.50** ....
Hippy Hippy Shake .... 7″ EP .. Pathe .... EGF707 .... 1963 £**30**..........£**15** .... *French*
Hippy Hippy Shake .... CD-s ... EMI .... CDEM83.................. 1989 £**5**............£**2** ....
Hippy Hippy Shake .... LP .... Imperial.......... LP9261/12261 .... 1964 £**50**..........£**25** .... *US*
It Isn't There .... 7″........ HMV .... POP1375 .... 1964 £**4**........ £**1.50** ....
It's So Right .... 7″ EP .. Pathe .... EGF782 .... 1964 £**30**..........£**15** .... *French*
It's Too Late Now .... 7″........ HMV .... POP1170 .... 1963 £**5**............£**2** ....
Make Me Know You're Mine .... 7″........ HMV .... POP1409 .... 1965 £**4**........ £**1.50** ....
Promise You'll Tell Her .... 7″........ HMV .... POP1327 .... 1964 £**4**........ £**1.50** ....
Rumours, Gossip, Words Untrue .... 7″........ HMV .... POP1564 .... 1966 £**5**............£**2** ....
Rumours, Gossip, Words Untrue .... 7″ EP .. Pathe .... EGF950 .... 1966 £**30**..........£**15** .... *French*
Sandy .... 7″........ HMV .... POP1533 .... 1966 £**5**............£**2** ....
Shake With The Swinging Blue Jeans .... 7″ EP .. HMV .... 7EG8850 .... 1964 £**25**..... £**12.50** ....
Swinging Blue Jeans .... LP .... MFP.............. MFP1163 .... 1967 £**10**..........£**4** ....
Tremblin' .... 7″........ HMV .... POP1596 .... 1967 £**5**............£**2** ....
Tutti Frutti .... LP .... Regal .... SREG1073 .... 1964 £**40**..........£**20** .... *export*
You're No Good .... 7″........ HMV .... POP1304 .... 1964 £**4**........ £**1.50** ....
You're No Good Miss Molly .... 7″ EP .. HMV .... 7EG8868 .... 1964 £**30**..........£**15** ....

SWINGING MEDALLIONS

Double Shot .... LP .... Smash............ MGS2/SRS67083 ... 1966 £**20**..........£**8** .... *US*
She Drives Me Out Of My Mind .... 7″........ Philips .... BF1515 .... 1966 £**4**........ £**1.50** ....

SWINGING SWEDES

Swinging Swedes .... LP .... Telefunken...... LGX66050.............. 1957 £**20**..........£**8** ....

SWINGTONES

Geraldine .... 7″........ HMV .... POP471 .... 1958 £**200**......£**100** .... *best auctioned*

SYDNEY ALL STARS

Return Of Batman .... 7″........ Bullet .... BU436.................... 1970 £**4**........ £**1.50** ....

SYKES, ERIC & HATTIE JACQUES

Eric, Hattie And Things .... LP .... Decca............ LK4507.................... 1963 £**15**..........£**6** ....

SYKES, JOHN

Please Don't Leave Me .... 7″........ MCA .... MCA792 .... 1982 £**25**..... £**12.50** .... *picture sleeve*
Please Don't Leave Me .... 7″........ MCA .... MCA792 .... 1982 £**6**........ £**2.50** ....

SYKES, ROOSEVELT

Back To The Blues .... 7″ EP .. Delmark .... DJB2 .... 1966 £**20**..........£**10** ....
Big Man Of The Blues .... LP .... Encore............ ENC183 .... 1959 £**12**..........£**5** ....
Blues From Bar Rooms .... LP .... 77 .... LEU1250 .... 1967 £**12**..........£**5** ....
Face To Face With The Blues .... LP .... Columbia .... 33SX1343 .... 1961 £**25**..........£**10** ....
Hard Drivin' Blues .... LP .... Delmark .... DS607 .... 1970 £**12**..........£**5** ....
Honeydripper .... LP .... Columbia .... 33SX1422 .... 1962 £**25**..........£**10** ....
Mr Sykes Blues 1929–1932 .... LP .... Riverside......... RLP8819 .... 1967 £**20**..........£**8** ....
Return Of Roosevelt Sykes .... LP .... Bluesville......... BV1006 .... 1960 £**25**..........£**10** .... *US*
Sings The Blues .... LP .... Ember .... EMB3391 .... 1968 £**12**..........£**5** ....
Too Hot To Hold .... 7″........ Vogue .... V2389.................... 1956 £**60**..........£**30** ....
Walking This Boogie .... 7″........ Vogue .... V2393.................... 1956 £**60**..........£**30** ....

SYKO & THE CARIBS

Do The Dog .... 7″........ Blue Beat......... BB213 .... 1964 £**12**..........£**6** ....
Sugar Baby .... 7″........ Blue Beat......... BB223 .... 1964 £**12**..........£**6** ....

SYLTE SISTERS

Summer Magic .... 7″........ London .... HLU9753 .... 1963 £**5**............£**2** ....

SYLVAN

We Don't Belong .... 7″........ Columbia .... DB7674 .... 1965 £**6**........ £**2.50** ....

SYLVESTER, C.

Going South .... 7″........ Blue Beat......... BB206 .... 1964 £**12**..........£**6** ....

SYLVIA

I Can't Help It .... 7″........ Soul City......... SC103.................... 1968 £**6**........ £**2.50** ....

SYLVIAN, DAVID

Damage .... CD ...... Virgin............ DAMAGE1 .... 1994 £**20**..........£**8** ......*gold disc, slip case, booklet, with Robert Fripp*

Forbidden Colours	CD-s	Virgin	CDT18	1988	**£10**	**£5**	*3" single, with Ryuichi Sakamoto*
God's Monkey, A Retrospective	CD	Virgin	DPRO12805	1994	**£20**	**£8**	*US promo, with Robert Fripp*
Heartbeat	CD-s	Virgin	VUSDG57	1992	**£6**	**£2.50**	*boxed with cards, with Ryuichi Sakamoto*
Pop Song	CD-s	Virgin	VSCDX1221	1989	**£15**	**£7.50**	
Pop Song	CD-s	Virgin	VSCD1211	1989	**£6**	**£2.50**	
Pulling Punches	7"	Virgin	VSY717	1984	**£4**	**£1.50**	*picture disc*
Red Guitar	7"	Virgin	VSY633	1984	**£4**	**£1.50**	*picture disc*
Secrets Of The Beehive	CD	Virgin	CDV2471	1987	**£12**	**£5**	
Taking The Veil	7"	Virgin	VSY815	1986	**£4**	**£1.50**	*square picture disc*
Weatherbox	CD-s	Virgin	DSCD1	1989	**£60**	**£30**	*5 CD boxed set*
Words With The Shaman	CD-s	Virgin	CDT23	1988	**£8**	**£4**	*3" single*

SYMARIP

I'm A Puppet	7"	Attack	ATT8013	1970	**£4**	**£1.50**	
La Bella Jig	7"	Treasure Isle	TI7055	1969	**£6**	**£2.50**	
Parsons Corner	7"	Treasure Isle	TI7054	1969	**£6**	**£2.50**	
Skinhead Moon Stomp	7"	Treasure Isle	TI7050	1969	**£4**	**£1.50**	
Skinhead Moon Stomp	LP	Trojan	TBL102	1968	**£20**	**£8**	

SYMBOLS

Best Part Of The Symbols	LP	President	PTL1018	1968	**£15**	**£6**	
Canadian Sunset	7"	President	PT113	1968	**£4**	**£1.50**	
One Fine Girl	7"	Columbia	DB7459	1965	**£4**	**£1.50**	
You're My Girl	7"	Columbia	DB7664	1965	**£4**	**£1.50**	

SYMON & PI

Got To See The Sunrise	7"	Parlophone	R5719	1968	**£5**	**£2**	
Sha La La La Lee	7"	Parlophone	R5662	1968	**£6**	**£2.50**	

SYMPHONIC SLAM

Symphonic Slam	LP	A&M	AMLH69023	1976	**£10**	**£4**	

SYMPHONICS

Heaven Must Have Sent You	7"	Polydor	2058341	1973	**£5**	**£2**	

SYN

The Syndicats eventually metamorphosed into the Syn, none of whose members had been in the original Syndicats line-up. The Yes connection continued, however, for the bass player and guitarist on the Syn's psychedelic singles were Chris Squire and Peter Banks.

Created By Clive	7"	Deram	DM130	1967	**£60**	**£30**	
Flowerman	7"	Deram	DM145	1967	**£60**	**£30**	

SYNANTHESIA

Synanthesia	LP	RCA	SF8058	1969	**£75**	**£37.50**	

SYNCHROMESH

October Friday	7"	Rok	ROKXI/XII	1980	**£15**	**£7.50**	*E.F. Band B side*

SYNDICATE

One Way Or Another	7"	Rock Against Racism		1979	**£5**	**£2**	*Restricted Hours B side*

SYNDICATE OF SOUND

Little Girl	7"	Stateside	SS523	1966	**£15**	**£7.50**	
Little Girl	7" EP	Columbia	ESRF1794	1966	**£30**	**£15**	*French*
Little Girl	LP	Stateside	(S)SL10185	1966	**£40**	**£20**	
Rumours	7"	Stateside	SS538	1966	**£8**	**£4**	

SYNDICATS

The singles made by the Syndicats are collectable on three counts. They are good examples of mid-sixties British R&B; they were produced by legendary producer Joe Meek; and the group's guitarist was Steve Howe, of later Yes fame.

Crawdaddy Simone	7"	Columbia	DB7686	1965	**£400**	**£250**	*best auctioned*
Howlin' For My Baby	7"	Columbia	DB7441	1965	**£100**	**£50**	
Maybelline	7"	Columbia	DB7238	1964	**£75**	**£37.50**	

SYNERGY

Audion	LP	Logo	LOGO1033	1982	**£12**	**£5**	
Chords	LP	Passport	PB6000	1979	**£12**	**£5**	*US*
Electronic Realizations	LP	Sire	9299752	1976	**£15**	**£6**	
Games	LP	Passport	PB6003	1979	**£12**	**£5**	*US*
Jupiter Menace	LP	Shanghai	HAI105	1984	**£10**	**£4**	
Semi-Conductor	LP	Passport	PB11002	1984	**£10**	**£4**	*US*
Sequencer	LP	Sire	9103326	1976	**£15**	**£6**	

SYRINX

Long Lost Relatives	LP	True North	TN5	1971	**£20**	**£8**	*Canadian*
Syrinx	LP	True North	TN2	1970	**£20**	**£8**	*Canadian*

SYSTEM

Other Side Of Time	LP	private		1977	**£100**	**£50**	

SYSTEM 7

Habibi	12"	10	TENX385	1991	£6	**£2.50**	
Habibi	12"	10	TENY385	1991	£8	**£4**	*clear vinyl*
Miracle	12"	Ten	TENDJ381	1990	£10	**£5**	*clear vinyl*
Sunburst	12"	10	TENX335	1990	£6	**£2.50**	

SYSTEME CRAPOUTCHIK

Aussi Loin Que Je Me Souvienne	LP	Flamophone	FL3301	1969	£200	**£100**	*French*
Flop	LP	Flamophone	FL3302	1971	£200	**£100**	*French double*

SYZYGY

Lady In Grey	LP	Taptag	TAP3	1985	£10	**£4**	

SZABO, GABOR

Jazz Raga	LP	HMV	CLP3614	1966	£20	**£8**	
Sorcerer	LP	Impulse	MIPL/SIPL506	1968	£12	**£5**	

t

T2

Title	Format	Label	Number	Year	Mint	Value	Notes
It'll All Work Out In Boomland	LP	Decca	SKL5050	1970	**£50**	**£25**	

TABLE

Title	Format	Label	Number	Year	Mint	Value	Notes
Do The Standing Still	7"	Virgin	VS176	1977	**£4**	**£1.50**	

TABLETOPPERS

Title	Format	Label	Number	Year	Mint	Value	Notes
Rocking Mountain Dew	7"	Starlite	ST45069	1962	**£8**	**£4**	

TABOR, CHARLIE

Title	Format	Label	Number	Year	Mint	Value	Notes
Blue Atlantic	7"	Island	WI061	1963	**£8**	**£4**	

TABOR, JUNE

Title	Format	Label	Number	Year	Mint	Value	Notes
Airs And Graces	LP	Topic	12TS298	1976	**£12**	**£5**	
Ashes And Diamonds	LP	Topic	12TS360	1977	**£12**	**£5**	

TAD & THE SMALL FRY

Title	Format	Label	Number	Year	Mint	Value	Notes
Checkered Continental Pants	7"	London	HLU9542	1962	**£5**	**£2**	

TAGES

Title	Format	Label	Number	Year	Mint	Value	Notes
Contrast	LP	Parlophone	PMCS313	1967	**£30**	**£15**	*Swedish*
Crazy 'Bout My Baby	7"	Columbia	DB8019	1966	**£5**	**£2**	
Extra Extra	LP	Platina		1966	**£30**	**£15**	*Swedish*
Halcyon Days	7"	MGM	MGM1443	1968	**£5**	**£2**	
In My Dreams	7" EP	Impact	200006	1967	**£20**	**£10**	*French*
Lilac Years	LP	Fontana		1969	**£25**	**£10**	*Swedish*
So Many Girls	7"	HMV	POP1515	1966	**£25**	**£12.50**	
Studio	LP	Parlophone		1967	**£30**	**£15**	*Swedish*
Tages	LP	Platina		1965	**£30**	**£15**	*Swedish*
There's A Blind Man Playing	7"	Parlophone	R5702	1968	**£5**	**£2**	
Treat Me Like A Lady	7"	Parlophone	R5640	1967	**£5**	**£2**	
Two	LP	Platina		1966	**£30**	**£15**	*Swedish*

TAGMEMICS

Title	Format	Label	Number	Year	Mint	Value	Notes
Chimneys	7"	Index	003	1980	**£8**	**£4**	

TAIEB, JACQUELINE

Title	Format	Label	Number	Year	Mint	Value	Notes
Tonight I'm Going Home	7"	Fontana	TF952	1968	**£30**	**£15**	

TAITT, LYN

Title	Format	Label	Number	Year	Mint	Value	Notes
Dial 609	7"	Ska Beat	JB264	1967	**£10**	**£5**	*Tommy McCook B side*
El Casino Royale	7"	Amalgamated	AMG810	1968	**£8**	**£4**	
Glad Sounds	LP	Big Shot	BBTL4002	1968	**£50**	**£25**	
I Don't Want To Make You Cry	7"	Island	WI3075	1967	**£10**	**£5**	
Napoleon Solo	7"	Island	WI3139	1968	**£10**	**£5**	
Something Stupid	7"	Island	WI3066	1967	**£10**	**£5**	
Soul Food	7"	Pama	PM723	1968	**£6**	**£2.50**	
Sounds Rock Steady	LP	Island	ILP969	1968	**£60**	**£30**	*pink label*
Spanish Eyes	7"	Doctor Bird	DB1047	1966	**£10**	**£5**	*with Tommy McCook, Stranger Cole B side*
Vilmas Jump Up	7"	Doctor Bird	DB1006	1966	**£10**	**£5**	*Glen Miller B side*

TAKE FIVE

Title	Format	Label	Number	Year	Mint	Value	Notes
My Girl	7" EP	D.S.C.A.	no number	196–	**£40**	**£20**	

TAKE THAT

Confounding the expectations of many observers (including those of the author of this *Price Guide*), Take That managed to maintain a high level of popularity for far longer than the couple of years that is the normal lot of groups of their type (predecessors the Bay City Rollers and New Kids on the Block were enormous in their day, but ceased to sell records as soon as their teenage fans grew old enough to want something different). It seems likely, therefore, that the collectors' items listed here will retain their values for quite a while to come.

Title	Format	Label	Number	Year	Mint	Value	Notes
Could It Be Magic	12"	RCA	743211123131	1992	**£10**	**£5**	*poster sleeve*
Could It Be Magic	CD-s	RCA	74321123132	1992	**£5**	**£2**	
Do What U Like	12"	Dance UK	12DUK2	1991	**£15**	**£7.50**	
Do What U Like	7"	Dance UK	DUK2	1991	**£15**	**£7.50**	
Do What U Like	cass-s	Dance UK	CADUK2	1991	**£10**	**£5**	
Every Guy	CD-s	RCA	no number	1995	**£15**	**£7.50**	*1 track promo*
I Found Heaven	7"	RCA	74321108147	1992	**£6**	**£2.50**	

Title	Format	Label	Number	Year	Mint	VG	Notes
I Found Heaven	7"	RCA	74321108137B	1992	**£10**	**£5**	*picture disc*
I Found Heaven	CD-s	RCA	74321108132	1992	**£5**	**£2**	
It Only Takes A Minute	7"	RCA	74321101007	1992	**£10**	**£5**	*frame pack with one of 2 sets of prints*
It Only Takes A Minute	CD-s	RCA	74321101002	1992	**£5**	**£2**	
Million Love Songs	CD-s	RCA	74321116002	1992	**£5**	**£2**	
Once You've Tasted Love	12"	RCA	PT45258	1992	**£15**	**£7.50**	*picture disc*
Once You've Tasted Love	7"	RCA	PB45265	1992	**£15**	**£7.50**	*with calendar*
Once You've Tasted Love	7"	RCA	PB45257	1992	**£5**	**£2**	
Once You've Tasted Love	cass-s	RCA	PK45257	1992	**£6**	**£2.50**	*with stencil*
Pray	CD-s	RCA	74321154502	1993	**£5**	**£2**	*2 versions*
Promises	12"	RCA	PT45086	1991	**£10**	**£5**	
Promises	7"	RCA	PB45085P	1991	**£10**	**£5**	*poster picture sleeve*
Promises	7"	RCA	PB45085	1991	**£6**	**£2.50**	
Promises	cass-s	RCA	PK45085	1991	**£5**	**£2**	
Take That Special	CD	Our Price	no number	1995	**£50**	**£25**	*promo*
Why Can't I Wake Up With You	CD-s	RCA	74321133102	1993	**£5**	**£2**	
Yellow Tape	cass	private		1990	**£250**	**£150**	

TAKERS

Title	Format	Label	Number	Year	Mint	VG	Notes
If You Don't Come Back	7"	Pye	7N15690	1964	**£8**	**£4**	

TALBOT BROTHERS

Title	Format	Label	Number	Year	Mint	VG	Notes
Bloodshot Eyes	7"	Melodisc	1507	1959	**£5**	**£2**	
Bloodshot Eyes	7"	Melodisc	CAL20	1964	**£4**	**£1.50**	

TALENT, ZIGGY

Title	Format	Label	Number	Year	Mint	VG	Notes
Cheek To Cheek	7"	Brunswick	05506	1955	**£4**	**£1.50**	

TALES OF JUSTINE

Tim Rice and Andrew Lloyd Webber made their first venture into pop music with Tales of Justine.

Title	Format	Label	Number	Year	Mint	VG	Notes
Albert	7"	HMV	POP1614	1967	**£20**	**£10**	
Albert	7"	HMV	POP1614	1967	**£60**	**£30**	*picture sleeve*

TALISMAN

Title	Format	Label	Number	Year	Mint	VG	Notes
Primrose Dreams	LP	Argo	ZFB33	1972	**£20**	**£8**	
Stepping Stones	LP	Argo	ZDA161	1973	**£20**	**£8**	

TALISMEN

Title	Format	Label	Number	Year	Mint	VG	Notes
Masters Of War	7"	Stateside	SS408	1965	**£20**	**£10**	
Talismen's Style	LP	RCA	S15	1965	**£100**	**£50**	*Italian*

TALIX

Title	Format	Label	Number	Year	Mint	VG	Notes
Spuren	LP	Vogue	LDVS17237	1971	**£20**	**£8**	*German*

TALK TALK

Title	Format	Label	Number	Year	Mint	VG	Notes
After The Flood	CD-s	Verve	TALKD1	1991	**£8**	**£4**	
Ascension Day	CD-s	Verve	TALKD3	1991	**£8**	**£4**	
Dum Dum Girl	12"	EMI	12EMI5480	1984	**£6**	**£2.50**	
I Believe In You	CD-s	Parlophone	CDR6189	1988	**£8**	**£4**	
It's My Life	CD-s	Parlophone	CDR6254	1990	**£5**	**£2**	
Laughing Stock	CD	Verve	8477172	1991	**£50**	**£25**	*promo in wooden box with stationery items*
Life's What You Make It	12"	EMI	12EMID5540	1986	**£6**	**£2.50**	*double*
Life's What You Make It	CD-s	Parlophone	CDR6264	1990	**£5**	**£2**	
Living In Another World	7"	EMI	EMIP5551	1986	**£6**	**£2.50**	*shaped picture disc*
My Foolish Friend	12"	EMI	12EMI5433	1984	**£6**	**£2.50**	
New Grass	CD-s	Verve	TALKD2	1991	**£5**	**£2**	
Such A Shame	CD-s	Parlophone	CDR6276	1990	**£5**	**£2**	
Talk Talk	12"	EMI	12EMI5352	1982	**£6**	**£2.50**	
Talk Talk	7"	EMI	EMIP5352	1982	**£4**	**£1.50**	*picture disc*
Talk Talk Demos	7"	EMI	EMID5433	1984	**£8**	**£4**	*double*
Today	12"	EMI	12EMI5314	1982	**£6**	**£2.50**	

TALKING HEADS

Title	Format	Label	Number	Year	Mint	VG	Notes
Blind	CD-s	EMI	CDEM68	1988	**£5**	**£2**	
Fear Of Music	LP	Sire	K56707	1979	**£10**	**£4**	*with 'Psycho Killer' 7"*
Live At The Roxy	LP	Warner Bros	WBMS104	1979	**£25**	**£10**	*promo*
Love Goes To Building On Fire	7"	Sire	6078604	1977	**£4**	**£1.50**	*picture sleeve*
Naked	CD	Sire		1988	**£25**	**£10**	*US promo with on-screen graphics*
Nothing But Flowers	CD-s	EMI	CDEM53	1988	**£5**	**£2**	
Psycho Killer	12"	Sire	6078610	1977	**£6**	**£2.50**	
Pulled Up	7"	Sire	6078620	1978	**£5**	**£2**	*picture sleeve*
Radio Head	CD-s	EMI	CDEM1	1987	**£5**	**£2**	
Road To Nowhere	7"	EMI	EMIP5530	1985	**£4**	**£1.50**	*picture disc*
Speaking In Tongues	LP	EMI	9238831	1983	**£10**	**£4**	*clear vinyl*
Storytelling Giant	CD	Polygram	0805061	1988	**£15**	**£6**	*CD video*
Take Me To The River	7"	Sire	SIR4004	1979	**£6**	**£2.50**	*double*

TALL, TOM

Title	Format	Label	Number	Year	Mint	VG	Notes
Are You Mine	7"	London	HL8150	1955	**£15**	**£7.50**	*with Ginny Wright*
Country Songs Vol. 2	7" EP	London	REU1035	1955	**£25**	**£12.50**	*with Ginny Wright*
Don't You Know	7"	London	HLU8429	1957	**£20**	**£10**	*with Ruckus Taylor*
Give Me A Chance	7"	London	HLU8216	1955	**£25**	**£12.50**	

Underway	7"	London	HLU8231	1956	**£25**	**£12.50**	

TALMY/STONE BAND

Roses Are Red & Other Hits	LP	Ace Of Clubs	ACL1134	1962	**£10**	**£4**	

TALULAH GOSH

Who Needs The Bloody Cartel Anyway	7"	Sha La La	002	1986	**£4**	**£1.50**	*flexi*

TAM, TIM & THE TURN ONS

Wait A Minute	7"	Island	WIP6007	1967	**£10**	**£5**	

TAMALONE

New Acres	LP	Crossroad	[illegible]	1979	**£25**	**£10**	*Dutch*

TAMLIN, JAMES

Is There Time	7"	Columbia	DB7438	1965	**£6**	**£2.50**	

TAMPA RED

Don't Jive With Me	LP	Bluesville	BV1043	1962	**£15**	**£6**	*US*
Don't Tampa With The Blues	LP	Bluesville	BV1030	1961	**£15**	**£6**	*US*
Male Blues Vol. 2	7" EP	Collector	JEL3	1959	**£10**	**£5**	*with Georgia Tom*
R&B Vol. 3	7" EP	RCA	RCX7160	1964	**£20**	**£10**	
Tampa Red	LP	Memory	TR1	196–	**£20**	**£8**	

TAMS

Be Young, Be Foolish, Be Happy	7"	Stateside	SS2123	1969	**£5**	**£2**	
Be Young, Be Foolish, Be Happy	LP	Stateside	SSL10304	1970	**£12**	**£5**	
Best Of The Tams	LP	Probe	SPB1044	1974	**£12**	**£5**	
Concrete Jungle	7"	HMV	POP1464	1965	**£6**	**£2.50**	
Hey Girl Don't Bother Me	7"	HMV	POP1331	1964	**£25**	**£12.50**	
Hey Girl Don't Bother Me	LP	ABC	(S)499	1964	**£20**	**£8**	*US*
It's All Right	7"	HMV	POP1298	1964	**£5**	**£2**	
Little More Soul	LP	Stateside	(S)SL10258	1968	**£15**	**£6**	
Presenting The Tams	LP	ABC	(S)481	1964	**£20**	**£8**	*US*
Too Much Foolin' Around	7"	Capitol	CL15650	1970	**£5**	**£2**	
Untie Me	7"	Stateside	SS146	1963	**£6**	**£2.50**	
What Kind Of Fool	7"	HMV	POP1254	1963	**£8**	**£4**	

TANDEM

Song Of My Life	7"	Chapter One	CH102	1968	**£4**	**£1.50**	

TANDOORI CASSETTE

Angel Talk	7"	IKA	IKA001	1983	**£10**	**£5**	

TANDY, SHARON

The reissue specialists, who have turned their attention on to some of the most obscure sixties artists, have nevertheless managed to ignore Sharon Tandy. Her numerous near-miss singles contain many impressive blue-eyed soul performances, which are made even more compelling in some cases by the fiery support of cult favourites, the Fleur De Lys. Tracks like 'Hold On' and 'Our Day Will Come' emerge as rather fine and distinctive pieces of psychedelic soul.

Fool On The Hill	7"	Atlantic	584166	1968	**£15**	**£7.50**	
Gotta Get Enough Time	7"	Atlantic	584242	1969	**£10**	**£5**	
Hold On	7"	Atlantic	584219	1968	**£30**	**£15**	
I've Found Love	7"	Pye	7N15939	1965	**£8**	**£4**	
Love Is Not A Simple Affair	7"	Atlantic	584181	1968	**£10**	**£5**	
Love Makes The World Go Round	7"	Mercury	MF898	1965	**£10**	**£5**	
Now That You've Gone	7"	Pye	7N15806	1965	**£8**	**£4**	
Our Day Will Come	7"	Atlantic	584137	1967	**£15**	**£7.50**	
Stay With Me	7"	Atlantic	584124	1967	**£20**	**£10**	
Toe-Hold	7"	Atlantic	584098	1967	**£12**	**£6**	
Way She Looks At You	7"	Atlantic	584214	1968	**£10**	**£5**	
You Gotta Believe It	7"	Atlantic	584194	1968	**£10**	**£5**	

TANEGA, NORMA

Walking My Cat Named Dog	LP	Stateside	(S)SL10182	1966	**£10**	**£4**	

TANGERINE DREAM

Perhaps it has something to do with the German character that the rock musicians in that country seized on the newly developed synthesizer, not as a device for creating previously unheard sounds, but as a means for performing mathematically precise patterns of notes. Such is the main approach of Tangerine Dream, as it is of Klaus Schulze and Kraftwerk. 'Ultima Thule' is a particularly rare non-album track, and is atypical in style.

Alpha Centauri	LP	Ohr	OMM556012	1971	**£10**	**£4**	*German*
Atem	LP	Ohr	OMM556031	1973	**£15**	**£6**	*German*
Betrayal	7"	MCA	PSR413	1977	**£15**	**£7.50**	*promo*
Chronozon	7"	Virgin	VS444	1981	**£5**	**£2**	
Das Madchen Auf Der Treppe	12"	Virgin	60065213	1982	**£6**	**£2.50**	*German*
Electronic Meditation	LP	Ohr	OMM56004	1970	**£25**	**£10**	*German*
Electronic Meditation	LP	Ohr	OMM556004	1971	**£20**	**£8**	*German*
Flashpoint	CD	Heavy Metal	HMXD29	1985	**£40**	**£20**	*non-faulty CD!*
Flashpoint	LP	Heavy Metal	HMIPD29	1984	**£10**	**£4**	*picture disc*
Le Parc	CD	Jive	CHIP26	1987	**£12**	**£5**	*UK pressing*
Oranges Don't Dance	CD-s	Private	663747	1989	**£25**	**£12.50**	*promo*
Phaedra	7"	Virgin	PR214	1974	**£15**	**£7.50**	*promo*
Stratosfear	7"	Virgin	VDJ17	1976	**£12**	**£6**	*promo*
Streethawk	12"	Jive Electro	T101	1985	**£6**	**£2.50**	
Tangerine Dream '70–'80	LP	Virgin	VBOX2	1980	**£25**	**£10**	*4 LP boxed set*

Thief	LP	Elektra	SE521	1981	**£10**	**£4**	*US promo picture disc*
Tyger	12"	Jive Electro	T143	1987	**£6**	**£2.50**	
Ultima Thule	7"	Ohr	OSS7006	1972	**£50**	**£25**	*German*
Warsaw Concert	LP	Jive Electro	HIPX22	1984	**£20**	**£8**	*double picture disc*
Warsaw In The Sun	7"	Jive Electro	JIVEP74	1984	**£6**	**£2.50**	*picture disc*
Zeit	LP	Ohr	OMM2/56021	1972	**£20**	**£8**	*German double*

TANGERINE PEEL

Every Christian Lion-Hearted Man Will Show You	7"	United Artists	UP1193	1967	**£10**	**£5**	
Soft Delights	LP	RCA	LSA3002	1970	**£20**	**£8**	*US*

TANGERINE ZOO

Outside Looking In	LP	Mainstream	S6116	1968	**£60**	**£30**	*US*
Tangerine Zoo	LP	Mainstream	S6107	1968	**£30**	**£15**	*US*

TANK

Don't Walk Away	7"	Kamaflage	KAM1	1981	**£4**	**£1.50**	*with patch*
Filth Hounds Of Hades	LP	Kamaflage	KAMLP1	1982	**£10**	**£4**	*with 7" (KAMF1)*
This Means War	LP	Music For Nations	MFN3P	1983	**£10**	**£4**	*picture disc*
Turn Your Head Around	7"	Kamaflage	KAM3	1982	**£10**	**£5**	

TANNAHILL WEAVERS

Are Ye Sleeping Maggie	LP	Plant Life	PLR001	1976	**£10**	**£4**	
Old Woman's Dance	LP	Plant Life	PLR010	1978	**£10**	**£4**	

TANNED LEATHER

Child Of Never Ending Love	LP	Harvest	1C06229440	1972	**£10**	**£4**	*German*

TANNED LEATHER (2)

Saddle Soap	LP	Response	RFSP013	1977	**£50**	**£25**	

TANNEN, HOLLY & PETE COOPER

Frosty Morning	LP	Plant Life	PLR015	1979	**£10**	**£4**	

TANSEY, SEAMUS

Masters Of Irish Music	LP	Leader	LEA2005	1970	**£10**	**£4**	*with Eddie Corcoran*
Traditional Music From Sligo	LP	Outlet	SDLP1022	1973	**£12**	**£5**	*Irish*

TANTONES

So Afraid	7"	Vogue	V9085	1957	**£400**	**£250**	*best auctioned*

TAPESTRY

Carnaby Street	7"	London	HLZ10138	1967	**£5**	**£2**	

TAPPI TIKARRASS

Tappi Tikarrass was a band playing in Iceland during 1981–3, whose lead singer was the very youthful Björk.

Bitid Fast I Vitid	LP	Spor	SPOR4	1981	**£50**	**£25**	*Icelandic*
Miranda	LP	Gramm	GRAMM16	1983	**£20**	**£8**	*Icelandic*

TARA

Happy	7"	Polydor	2066009	1971	**£5**	**£2**	

TARANTULA

Tarantula	LP	A&M	AMLS959	1970	**£10**	**£4**	

TARBUCK, JIMMY

Someday	7"	Immediate	IM018	1965	**£5**	**£2**	

TARDENSKJOLDS SOLDATER

Peace	LP	Spectator	SL1019	1970	**£30**	**£15**	*Danish*

TARGEL, JEM

Lucky Guy	LP	Sheany		1978	**£50**	**£25**	*US*

TARGUS

Somebody's Watching You	LP	Crossroad		1981	**£20**	**£8**	*Dutch*

TARHEEL SLIM & LITTLE ANN

You Make Me Feel So Good	7"	Sue	WI390	1965	**£12**	**£6**	

TARRA

Hard Nipples	LP	Platerie		1981	**£20**	**£8**	*Dutch*

TARRIERS

Banana Boat Song	7"	Columbia	DB3891	1957	**£4**	**£1.50**	
Dunya	7"	Columbia	DB4025	1957	**£4**	**£1.50**	
Hard Travellin'	LP	United Artists	UAL4033/UAS5033	1959	**£15**	**£6**	*US*
Hard Travellin' Vol. 1	7" EP	London	RET1236	1960	**£5**	**£2**	
Hard Travellin' Vol. 2	7" EP	London	RET1237	1960	**£5**	**£2**	
I Know Where I'm Going	7"	Columbia	DB4148	1958	**£4**	**£1.50**	
Lonesome Traveller	7"	London	HLU8600	1958	**£8**	**£4**	
Tarriers	10" LP	Columbia	33S1115	1957	**£15**	**£6**	

Tell The World About This	LP	Atlantic	(SD)8042	1960	£15	£6	US
Tom Dooley	7"	Columbia	DB3961	1957	£4	£1.50	

TARTAN HORDE

Bay City Rollers, We Love You	7"	United Artists	UP35891	1975	£8	£4	

TARTANS

Awake The Town	7"	Caltone	TONE115	1968	£8	£4	
Coming On Strong	7"	Caltone	TONE117	1968	£8	£4	
Dance All Night	7"	Island	WI3058	1967	£10	£5	

TASAVALLAN PRESIDENTTI

Hailing from Finland, Tasavallan Presidentti played top quality progressive jazz-rock, sounding like a cross between John McLaughlin's Mahavishnu Orchestra and Jethro Tull. Further albums by the group were issued under the name of guitarist Jukka Tolonen – a virtuoso and distinctive player who deserves to be much better known than he is, although the early, group-credited albums are inevitably the best.

Lambertland	LP	Sonet	SNTF636	1973	£12	£5	
Milky Way Moses	LP	Sonet	SNTF658	1974	£10	£4	
Tasavallan Presedentti	LP	Love	LRLP7	1969	£15	£6	Swedish

TASSELS

To A Soldier Boy	7"	London	HL8885	1959	£60	£30	
To A Young Lover	7"	Top Rank	JAR229	1959	£20	£10	

TASTE

Guitarist Rory Gallagher began his long career with this trio. The titles issued as singles can be found on the *Taste* LP, but these are re-recordings. The Major Minor originals sound significantly different.

Blister On The Moon	7"	Major Minor	MM560	1968	£10	£5	
Born On The Wrong Side Of Time	7"	Major Minor	MM718	1970	£6	£2.50	
Born On The Wrong Side Of Time	7"	Polydor	56313	1969	£4	£1.50	
Live At The Isle Of Wight	LP	Polydor	2383120	1972	£10	£4	
Live Taste	LP	Polydor	2310082	1971	£10	£4	
On The Boards	LP	Polydor	583083	1970	£12	£5	
Taste	LP	Polydor	583042	1969	£15	£6	

TATE, BUDDY

Swinging Like Tate	LP	Felsted	FAJ7004/SJA2004	1958	£15	£6	

TATE, ERIC QUINCY

Can't Keep A Good Band Down	LP	EQT		1977	£40	£20	US

TATE, HOWARD

Ain't Nobody Home	7"	Verve	VS541	1966	£5	£2	
Baby I Love You	7"	Verve	VS555	1967	£4	£1.50	
Get It While You Can	7"	Verve	VS552	1967	£4	£1.50	
Get It While You Can	LP	Verve	(S)VLP9179	1967	£15	£6	
I Learned It All The Hard Way	7"	Verve	VS556	1967	£4	£1.50	
Look At Granny Run Run	7"	Verve	VS584	1968	£4	£1.50	
Look At Granny Run Run	7"	Verve	VS549	1967	£6	£2.50	
Night Owl	7"	Verve	VS571	1968	£5	£2	
Stop	7"	Verve	VS565	1968	£4	£1.50	

TATE, PHIL

Party Dances	7" EP	Oriole	EP7052	1962	£5	£2	
Tunes For Twisters	7" EP	Oriole	EP7060	1962	£6	£2.50	

TATE, TOMMY

Big Blue Diamonds	7"	Columbia	DB8046	1966	£20	£10	

TATUM, ART

Art	LP	Fontana	FJL904	1967	£10	£4	
Art Of Tatum	LP	Brunswick	LAT8358	1961	£15	£6	
Art Tatum	10" LP	Capitol	LC6524	1951	£30	£15	
Art Tatum	7" EP	Columbia	SEB10003	1955	£5	£2	
Art Tatum	7" EP	Vogue	EPV1212	1957	£5	£2	
Art Tatum	7" EP	Vogue	EPV1008	1954	£5	£2	
Art Tatum	7" EP	Columbia	SEG7540	1955	£5	£2	
Art Tatum	LP	XTRA	XTRA1007	1965	£10	£4	
Art Tatum	LP	Columbia	33CX10115	1958	£20	£8	
Art Tatum No. 1	7" EP	Fontana	TFE17235	1960	£5	£2	
Art Tatum No. 2	7" EP	Fontana	TFE17236	1960	£5	£2	
Art Tatum No. 3	7" EP	Fontana	TFE17237	1960	£5	£2	
Art Tatum Trio	10" LP	Vogue Coral	LRA10011	1955	£25	£10	
Art Tatum Trio	7" EP	Melodisc	EPM7108	195–	£5	£2	
Art Tatum–Ben Webster Quartet	LP	Columbia	33CX10137	1959	£20	£8	
Art Tatum–Buddy De Franco Quartet	7" EP	HMV	7EG8619	1960	£5	£2	
Art Tatum–Buddy De Franco Quartet	7" EP	Columbia	SEB10101	1958	£5	£2	
Art Tatum–Roy Eldridge–Alvin Stoller–John Simmons Quartet	LP	Columbia	33CX10042	1956	£40	£20	
At Hollywood Bowl	7" EP	Columbia	SEB10084	1958	£5	£2	
Delicate Touch	7" EP	Columbia	SEB10116	1959	£5	£2	
Discoveries	LP	Top Rank	35067	1960	£12	£5	
Encores	10" LP	Capitol	LC6638	1954	£25	£10	
Genius Of Art Tatum	LP	Columbia	33CX10005	1955	£25	£10	
Genius Of Art Tatum No. 2	LP	Columbia	33CX10053	1956	£25	£10	

Title	Format	Label	Cat. No.	Year	Mint	VG	Notes
Genius Of Art Tatum No. 3	10" LP	Columbia	33C9033	1957	**£25**	**£10**	
Greatest Piano Of Them All	7" EP	HMV	7EG8604	1960	**£5**	**£2**	
Here's Art Tatum	LP	Vogue Coral	LVA9047	1957	**£25**	**£10**	
Incomparable Music	7" EP	HMV	7EG8684	1961	**£5**	**£2**	
Just Jazz	10" LP	Vogue	LDE081	1954	**£30**	**£15**	
Memories	7" EP	Ember	EMBEP4502	1962	**£5**	**£2**	
Memories	LP	Ember	EMB3314	1961	**£10**	**£4**	
Memories Vol. 2	LP	Ember	EMB3326	1961	**£10**	**£4**	
Out Of Nowhere	10" LP	Capitol	LC6625	1953	**£30**	**£15**	
Presenting The Art Tatum Trio	10" LP	Columbia	33C9039	1957	**£25**	**£10**	
Tatum–Carter–Bellson Trio	7" EP	Columbia	SEB10027	1956	**£5**	**£2**	
Tatum–Carter–Bellson Trio	7" EP	Columbia	SEB10062	1957	**£5**	**£2**	
Unforgettable Art	7" EP	Philips	BBE12136	1957	**£5**	**£2**	

TAUPIN, BERNIE

Title	Format	Label	Cat. No.	Year	Mint	VG	Notes
An Interview With Bernie Taupin	LP	RCA		1987	**£12**	**£5**	*US double promo*

TAVENER, JOHN

Of all the surprising records to have been issued on the Apple label, the pair of works composed by John Tavener are perhaps the most surprising of all. They have nothing to do with rock music at all in themselves, being prime examples of the classical avant-garde, but they were apparently included in the Beatles' release schedule because Ringo Starr liked them. Tavener's more recent work is inspired by his devout religious beliefs and is considerably less way-out than these early works. His tranquil *The Protecting Veil* gained considerable acclaim in some quarters and not a little commercial success during the nineties.

Title	Format	Label	Cat. No.	Year	Mint	VG	Notes
Celtic Requiem	LP	Apple	SAPCOR20	1971	**£125**	**£62.50**	
Whale	LP	Apple	SAPCOR15	1970	**£40**	**£20**	
Whale	LP	Ring O'	2320104	1977	**£20**	**£8**	

TAVERNERS

Title	Format	Label	Cat. No.	Year	Mint	VG	Notes
Blowing Sand	LP	Trailer	LER2080	1973	**£10**	**£4**	
Same Old Friends	LP	Folk Heritage	FHR101	1978	**£10**	**£4**	
Seldom Sober	LP	Saga	EROS8146	1969	**£15**	**£6**	
Times Of Old England	LP	Folk Heritage	FHR062	1974	**£10**	**£4**	

TAW FOLK

Title	Format	Label	Cat. No.	Year	Mint	VG	Notes
Devonshire Cream And Cider	LP	Sentinel	SENS1030	1975	**£12**	**£5**	

TAWNEY, CYRIL

Title	Format	Label	Cat. No.	Year	Mint	VG	Notes
Baby, Lie Easy	7" EP	HMV	7EG8738	1962	**£10**	**£5**	
Down Among The Barley Straw	LP	Trailer	LER2095	1976	**£10**	**£4**	
I Will Give My Love	LP	Argo	ZFB87	1973	**£10**	**£4**	
In Port	LP	Argo	ZFB28	1972	**£12**	**£5**	
Mayflower Garland	LP	Argo	ZFB9	1970	**£25**	**£10**	
Outlandish Knight	LP	Polydor	236577	1970	**£25**	**£10**	
Sings Children's Songs From Devon And Cornwall	LP	Argo	ZFB4	1970	**£25**	**£10**	

TAYLES

Title	Format	Label	Cat. No.	Year	Mint	VG	Notes
Who Are These Guys?	LP	Cineviste	CV1001	1972	**£100**	**£50**	*US*

TAYLOR, ALLAN

Title	Format	Label	Cat. No.	Year	Mint	VG	Notes
American Album	LP	United Artists	UAG29468	1973	**£15**	**£6**	
Lady	LP	United Artists	UAS29275	1972	**£15**	**£6**	
Roll On The Day	LP	Rubber	RUB040	1980	**£10**	**£4**	
Sometimes	LP	Liberty	LBG83483	1971	**£25**	**£10**	
Traveller	LP	Rubber	RUB026	1978	**£10**	**£4**	

TAYLOR, ART

Title	Format	Label	Cat. No.	Year	Mint	VG	Notes
A.T.'s Delight	LP	Blue Note	BLP/BST84047	196–	**£40**	**£20**	

TAYLOR, AUSTIN

Title	Format	Label	Cat. No.	Year	Mint	VG	Notes
Push Push	7"	Top Rank	JAR511	1960	**£10**	**£5**	

TAYLOR, BILLY

Title	Format	Label	Cat. No.	Year	Mint	VG	Notes
And His Rhythm	10" LP	Felsted	L87001	195–	**£40**	**£20**	
At The London House	LP	HMV	CLP1176	1958	**£10**	**£4**	
Billy Taylor	7" EP	Esquire	EP115	1956	**£5**	**£2**	
Billy Taylor Trio	10" LP	Esquire	20053	1955	**£50**	**£25**	
Billy Taylor Trio	7" EP	Esquire	EP169	1958	**£5**	**£2**	
Billy Taylor Trio	LP	Esquire	32010	1955	**£25**	**£10**	
Evergreens	10" LP	HMV	DLP1171	1958	**£10**	**£4**	
Jazz At Storyville	10" LP	Felsted	EDL87009	1954	**£40**	**£20**	
My Fair Lady Loves Jazz	10" LP	HMV	DLP1181	1958	**£10**	**£4**	*with Quincy Jones*
New Billy Taylor Trio	LP	HMV	CLP1231	1959	**£10**	**£4**	
Taylor Made	10" LP	Esquire	20020	1953	**£40**	**£20**	
Taylor Made Piano	LP	Vogue	LAE12192	1960	**£10**	**£4**	

TAYLOR, BOBBY

Title	Format	Label	Cat. No.	Year	Mint	VG	Notes
Bobby Taylor & The Vancouvers	LP	Tamla Motown	(S)TML11093	1969	**£30**	**£15**	*with the Vancouvers*
Does Your Mama Know About Me	7"	Tamla Motown	TMG654	1968	**£25**	**£12.50**	*with the Vancouvers*
Taylor Made Soul	LP	Tamla Motown	(S)TML11125	1970	**£50**	**£25**	

TAYLOR, BRYAN

Taylor's 'The Donkey's Tale' is listed elsewhere as a considerable collectors' item. The author of this guide finds this to be rather mysterious, as, in his experience, the market for children's Christmas songs performed by a boy soprano with no subsequent claim to fame is rather limited.

Title	Format	Label	Cat. No.	Year	Mint	VG	Notes
Donkey's Tale	7"	Piccadilly	7N35018	1961	**£4**	**£1.50**	

TAYLOR, CECIL

Title	Format	Label	Cat. No.	Year	Mint	VG	Notes
At The Café Montmartre	LP	Fontana	SFJL928	1969	**£20**	**£8**	
Conquistador	LP	Blue Note	BLP/BST84260	1967	**£25**	**£10**	
Hard Driving Jazz/Stereo Drive	LP	United Artists	UAL4014/ UAS5011	1959	**£40**	**£20**	*US*
Innovations	LP	Polydor	2383094	1972	**£15**	**£6**	
Jazz Advance	LP	Transition	TRLP19	1956	**£75**	**£37.50**	*US*
Looking Ahead	LP	Contemporary	LAC12216	1959	**£25**	**£10**	
Love For Sale	LP	United Artists	UAL4046/ UAS5046	1959	**£40**	**£20**	*US*
Nefertiti, The Beautiful One Has Come	LP	Fontana	SFJL926	1969	**£20**	**£8**	
Newport Jazz Festival 1957	LP	Columbia	33CX10102	1958	**£25**	**£10**	*side 2 by Gigi Gryce & Donald Byrd*
Nuits De La Fondation Maeght Vol. 1	LP	Shandar	83507	1969	**£20**	**£8**	*French*
Nuits De La Fondation Maeght Vol. 2	LP	Shandar	SR10011	1969	**£20**	**£8**	*French*
Unit Structures	LP	Blue Note	BLP/BST84237	1966	**£25**	**£10**	
World Of Cecil Taylor	LP	Candid	8/9006	1960	**£40**	**£20**	*US*

TAYLOR, EARL

Title	Format	Label	Cat. No.	Year	Mint	VG	Notes
Bluegrass Taylor Made	LP	Capitol	(S)T2090	1963	**£12**	**£5**	*US*

TAYLOR, EDDIE & FLOYD JONES

Title	Format	Label	Cat. No.	Year	Mint	VG	Notes
Eddie Taylor & Floyd Jones	7" EP	XX	MIN712	196–	**£8**	**£4**	

TAYLOR, ELIZABETH

Title	Format	Label	Cat. No.	Year	Mint	VG	Notes
In London	LP	Colpix	PXL459	1963	**£40**	**£20**	*with John Barry*

TAYLOR, FELICE

Title	Format	Label	Cat. No.	Year	Mint	VG	Notes
I Can Feel Your Love	7"	President	PT193	1968	**£4**	**£1.50**	
I Feel Love Comin' On	7"	President	PT155	1967	**£4**	**£1.50**	

TAYLOR, GEOFF

Title	Format	Label	Cat. No.	Year	Mint	VG	Notes
Geoff Taylor All Stars	7" EP	Esquire	EP105	1956	**£5**	**£2**	
Geoff Taylor Sextet	7" EP	Esquire	EP55	1955	**£5**	**£2**	

TAYLOR, GLORIA

Title	Format	Label	Cat. No.	Year	Mint	VG	Notes
You Gotta Pay The Price	7"	Polydor	56788	1970	**£4**	**£1.50**	

TAYLOR, HOUND DOG

Title	Format	Label	Cat. No.	Year	Mint	VG	Notes
Christine	7"	Outasite	45504	1966	**£50**	**£25**	

TAYLOR, JAMES

Title	Format	Label	Cat. No.	Year	Mint	VG	Notes
Carolina In My Mind	7"	Apple	32	1970	**£5**	**£2**	
Gorilla	LP	Warner Bros	BS42866	1975	**£10**	**£4**	*US quad*
James Taylor	LP	Apple	SAPCOR3	1968	**£12**	**£5**	*stereo*
James Taylor	LP	Apple	APCOR3	1968	**£30**	**£15**	*mono*
Live	CD	Columbia	CSK5342	1994	**£20**	**£8**	*US promo*
Never Die Young	CD-s	CBS	6512042	1988	**£5**	**£2**	
One Man Dog	LP	Warner Bros	BS42660	1974	**£10**	**£4**	*US quad*

TAYLOR, JAMES QUARTET

Title	Format	Label	Cat. No.	Year	Mint	VG	Notes
Blow Up	7"	Re-Elect President	FORD1	1987	**£4**	**£1.50**	
Breakout	CD-s	Urban	URCD38	1989	**£5**	**£2**	
It Doesn't Matter	CD-s	Urban	URCD43	1989	**£5**	**£2**	
Killing Time	CD-s	Urban	URBCD61	1990	**£5**	**£2**	
Love The Life	CD-s	Urban	URBCD57	1990	**£5**	**£2**	

TAYLOR, JEREMY

Title	Format	Label	Cat. No.	Year	Mint	VG	Notes
Always Something New	LP	Decca	LK4731	1966	**£20**	**£8**	
His Songs	LP	Fontana	STL5475	1968	**£12**	**£5**	
Jobsworth	LP	Canon	CPT3982	1973	**£10**	**£4**	
More Of His Songs	LP	Fontana	STL5523	1969	**£12**	**£5**	
Piece Of Ground	LP	Galliard	GAL4018	1972	**£15**	**£6**	
Wait A Minim Songs	7" EP	Decca	DFE8581	1964	**£6**	**£2.50**	

TAYLOR, JOHN

Title	Format	Label	Cat. No.	Year	Mint	VG	Notes
Pause And Think Again	LP	Turtle	TUR302	1971	**£50**	**£25**	

TAYLOR, JOHNNIE

Title	Format	Label	Cat. No.	Year	Mint	VG	Notes
Ain't That Loving You	7"	Stax	601003	1967	**£4**	**£1.50**	
Friday Night	7"	Stax	STX2025	1968	**£4**	**£1.50**	
Looking For Johnnie Taylor	LP	Atco	228008	1969	**£12**	**£5**	
Philosophy Continues	LP	Stax	SXATS1024	1969	**£12**	**£5**	
Raw Blues	LP	Stax	STS2008	1969	**£12**	**£5**	*US*
Roots Of Johnnie Taylor	LP	Soul City	SCB2	1970	**£20**	**£8**	
Steal Away	7"	Stax	STAX150	1970	**£5**	**£2**	
Wanted: One Soul Singer	LP	Stax	589008	1967	**£12**	**£5**	
Who's Making Love?	LP	Stax	(S)XATS1006	1969	**£12**	**£5**	

TAYLOR, JOSEPH

Unto Brigg Fair	LP	Leader	LEA4050	1972	**£25**	**£10**	*with other artists*

TAYLOR, KARL

Taylor Maid	LP	Polydor	2907023	1976	**£50**	**£25**	*Australian*

TAYLOR, KINGSIZE & THE DOMINOES

Hippy Hippy Shake	7"	Polydor	NH66991	1964	**£10**	**£5**	
Keep On Rockin'	LP	Brunswick	LP2911109	1973	**£20**	**£8**	*German*
Kingsize Taylor And The Dominoes	LP	Ariola	71765IT	1964	**£75**	**£37.50**	*German, with Bobby Patrick Big Six*
Memphis Tennessee	7"	Polydor	NH66990	1963	**£10**	**£5**	
Real Gonk Man	LP	Midnight	HLP/HST2101	1964	**£50**	**£25**	*US*
Somebody's Always Trying	7"	Decca	F11935	1964	**£10**	**£5**	
Star Club Time	LP	Ariola	71431	1964	**£100**	**£50**	*German*
Stupidity	7"	Decca	F11874	1964	**£10**	**£5**	
Teenbeat 2 – Teanbeat From The Star Club Hamburg	7" EP	Decca	DFE8569	1964	**£75**	**£37.50**	
Thinkin'	7"	Polydor	BM56152	1965	**£12**	**£6**	
Twist And Shake	7" EP	Polydor	EPH21628	1963	**£60**	**£30**	
Twist Time Im Star Club Hamburg	LP	Ariola	70953	1964	**£100**	**£50**	*German, with Bobby Patrick Big Six*

TAYLOR, KOKO

Koko Taylor	LP	Chess	LPS1532	1968	**£20**	**£8**	*US*
Wang Dang Doodle	7"	Chess	CRS8035	1966	**£6**	**£2.50**	

TAYLOR, LITTLE JOHNNY

Little Johnny Taylor	LP	Vocalion	VAF8031	1965	**£25**	**£10**	
Little Johnny Taylor	LP	Vocalion	VAP8031	1965	**£25**	**£10**	
Little Johnny Taylor	LP	Galaxy	(8)203	1963	**£25**	**£10**	*US*
One More Chance	7"	Vocalion	VF9264	1966	**£6**	**£2.50**	
Part Time Love	7"	Vocalion	VP9234	1965	**£6**	**£2.50**	

TAYLOR, MICK

If the single by Mick Taylor has acquired any value by reason of its authorship by the future Bluesbreaker and Rolling Stone, then the justification for this is a little dubious. The Mick Taylor who joined John Mayall in 1967 was only seventeen at the time and a confirmed blues guitarist. It is not at all likely that he would have had a single released two years earlier under the title of 'London Town/Hoboin''.

London Town/Hoboin'	7"	CBS	201770	1965	**£10**	**£5**	

TAYLOR, MIKE

Mike Taylor showed every sign of developing into a major talent before his premature death in the late sixties. He co-wrote songs for Cream ('Those Were The Days', 'Passing The Time') and for Colosseum ('Jumping Off The Sun') and was also a fine jazz pianist. The two rare albums he made have Jack Bruce, Tony Reeves and Jon Hiseman among the small supporting cast.

Pendulum	LP	Columbia	SX6042	1965	**£200**	**£100**	
Trio	LP	Columbia	SX6137	1966	**£200**	**£100**	

TAYLOR, NEVILLE

Baby Lay Sleeping	7"	Parlophone	R4493	1958	**£5**	**£2**	
Dance With A Dolly	7"	Oriole	CB1546	1960	**£5**	**£2**	
First Words Of Love	7"	Parlophone	R4524	1959	**£10**	**£5**	
Joshua Fit The Battle Of Jericho	7"	Honey Hit	TB127	196–	**£5**	**£2**	*picture sleeve*
Mercy Mercy Percy	7"	Parlophone	R4447	1958	**£10**	**£5**	
Tears On My Pillow	7"	Parlophone	R4476	1958	**£8**	**£4**	

TAYLOR, PADDY

Boy In The Gap	LP	Claddagh	CC8	1969	**£10**	**£4**	*Irish*

TAYLOR, R. DEAN

Ain't It A Sad Thing	7"	Tamla Motown	TMG786	1971	**£40**	**£20**	*demo only*
Ain't It A Sad Thing	7"	Rare Earth	RES101	1971	**£10**	**£5**	*TMG786 matrix*
Gotta See Jane	7"	Tamla Motown	TMG656	1968	**£4**	**£1.50**	
Indiana Wants Me	LP	Tamla Motown	STML11185	1971	**£15**	**£6**	

TAYLOR, ROGER

Fun In Space	LP	EMI	EMC3369	1981	**£10**	**£4**	
Future Management	7"	EMI	EMI5157	1981	**£10**	**£5**	
Happiness?	LP	Parlophone	PCSD157	1993	**£30**	**£15**	
I Wanna Testify	7"	EMI	EMI2679	1977	**£40**	**£20**	
Man On Fire	12"	EMI	EMI125478	1984	**£30**	**£15**	
Man On Fire	7"	EMI	EMI5478	1984	**£10**	**£5**	
My Country	7"	EMI	EMI5200	1981	**£20**	**£10**	
Nazis 1994	12"	Parlophone	NAZIS1	1994	**£15**	**£7.50**	*promo*
Nazis 1994	12"	Parlophone	NAZIS4	1994	**£15**	**£7.50**	*promo*
Nazis 1994	12"	Parlophone	NAZIS3	1994	**£15**	**£7.50**	*promo*
Nazis 1994	CD-s	Parlophone	CDR6379	1994	**£5**	**£2**	
Strange Frontier	12"	EMI	EMI125490	1984	**£30**	**£15**	
Strange Frontier	7"	EMI	EMI5490	1984	**£10**	**£5**	
Strange Frontier	LP	EMI	EJ2401371	1984	**£10**	**£4**	

TAYLOR, ROSEMARY

Taylormaid	LP	private	JD2009	1975	**£150**	**£75**	

TAYLOR, SAM

Please Be Kind	7"	MGM	SP1106	1954	**£15**	**£7.50**	
Sam Taylor Orchestra	7" EP	MGM	MGMEP531	1956	**£20**	**£10**	

TAYLOR, TED

Cat's Eyes	7"	Oriole	CB1628	1961	**£4**	**£1.50**	
Fried Onions	7"	Oriole	CB1574	1961	**£5**	**£2**	
Haunted Pad	7"	Oriole	CB1630	1961	**£6**	**£2.50**	
Jericho	7"	Oriole	CB1713	1962	**£6**	**£2.50**	
M1	7"	Oriole	CB1573	1961	**£5**	**£2**	
Son Of Honky Tonk	7"	Oriole	CB1464	1958	**£5**	**£2**	
Surfrider	7"	Oriole	CB1767	1962	**£10**	**£5**	

TAYLOR, TRUE

True Taylor is one of several names tried by Paul Simon during the early years of his recording career.

True Or False	7"	Big	614	1958	**£40**	**£20**	*US*

TAYLOR, VERNON

Mystery Train	7"	London	HLS9025	1960	**£50**	**£25**	

TAYLOR, VIC

Does It His Way	LP	Trojan	TRLS38	1971	**£10**	**£4**	
Heartaches	7"	Treasure Isle	TI7021	1967	**£10**	**£5**	

TAYLOR, VINCE

Brand New Cadillac	7"	Parlophone	R4539	1959	**£25**	**£12.50**	
Jet Black Machine	7"	Palette	PG9001	1960	**£12**	**£6**	
Luv	10" LP	Big Beat	BBR0004	1962	**£75**	**£37.50**	*French*
Right Behind You Baby	7"	Parlophone	R4505	1958	**£30**	**£15**	
Sweet Little Sixeen	7" EP	Barclay	70394	1961	**£30**	**£15**	*French*
Whatcha Gonna Do	7"	Palette	PG9020	1961	**£15**	**£7.50**	

TAYLOR MAIDS

Theme From I Am A Camera	7"	Capitol	CL14322	1955	**£5**	**£2**	

T-BONES

I Am Louisiana Red	7" EP	Riviera	231075	1965	**£100**	**£50**	*French*
I'm A Lover	7"	Columbia	DB7401	1964	**£25**	**£12.50**	
Won't You Give Me One More Chance	7"	Columbia	DB7489	1965	**£20**	**£10**	

T-BONES (2)

No Matter What Shape	7" EP	Liberty	LEP2248	1965	**£8**	**£4**	*French*

T.C. ATLANTIC

Live At Bel-Rae Ballroom	LP	Dove	LP4459	1967	**£100**	**£50**	*US*

TEA & SYMPHONY

Asylum For The Musically Insane	LP	Harvest	SHVL761	1969	**£60**	**£30**	
Boredom	7"	Harvest	HAR5005	1969	**£6**	**£2.50**	
Jo Sago	LP	Harvest	SHVL785	1970	**£60**	**£30**	

TEA COMPANY

Come & Have Some Tea	LP	Mercury	SMCL20127	1968	**£30**	**£15**	

TEA SET

Join The Tea Set	7"	King	KG1048	1966	**£6**	**£2.50**	

TEACHO & THE STUDENTS

Rocket	7"	Felsted	AF104	1958	**£30**	**£15**	

TEAGARDEN, JACK

At The Round Table	LP	Columbia	33SX1235/ SCX3312	1960	**£10**	**£4**	
Big T's Jazz	LP	Brunswick	LAT8229	1958	**£15**	**£6**	
Jack Teagarden's Dixieland Band	LP	Capitol	T1095	1959	**£12**	**£5**	
Jazz Great	LP	London	LTZN15077	1957	**£20**	**£8**	
This Is Teagarden	LP	Capitol	T721	1956	**£12**	**£5**	

TEAL, J. BAND

Cooks	LP	Mother Cleo		1977	**£25**	**£10**	*US*

TEAM-BEATS

It's Liverpool Time	LP	Vogue	LDV17003	1964	**£30**	**£15**	*German*

TEAR GAS

Tear Gas was a Scottish heavy rock group, whose *Piggy Go Getter* LP received a considerable publicity campaign to little avail. The members' fortunes gained a considerable boost, however, when Tear Gas was taken on entire by singer Alex Harvey, to become the Sensational Alex Harvey Band.

Piggy Go Getter	LP	Famous	SFMA5751	1971	**£25**	**£10**	
Tear Gas	LP	Regal Zonophone	SLRZ1021	1971	**£125**	**£62.50**	

TEARDROP EXPLODES

Bouncing Babies	7"	Zoo	CAGE005	1979	**£6**	**£2.50**	*picture sleeve*
Count To Ten And Run For Cover	CD-s	Mercury	DROCD2	1990	**£5**	**£2**	

Ha Ha I'm Drowning 7" Mercury TEAR44 1981 **£5** **£2** *double*
Ha Ha I'm Drowning 7" Mercury TEAR4 1981 **£20** **£10** *picture sleeve*
Serious Danger CD-s Fontana DROCD1 1990 **£5** **£2**
Sleeping Gas 7" Zoo CAGE003 1979 **£8** **£4** *red picture sleeve*
Sleeping Gas 7" Zoo CAGE003 1979 **£6** **£2.50** *blue picture sleeve*
Treason 7" Zoo CAGE008 1980 **£5** **£2**

TEARS

It's So Easy LP Spectator SL1031 1972 **£20** **£8** *Danish*
Tears LP Spectator SL1011 1971 **£50** **£25** *Danish*

TEARS FOR FEARS

Advice For The Young At Heart CD-s Fontana IDCD14 1990 **£5** **£2**
Everybody Wants To Rule The World CD-s Polygram 0800322 1988 **£10** **£5** *CD video*
Famous Last Words CD-s Fontana IDCD15 1990 **£5** **£2**
Head Over Heels CD-s Polygram 0800622 1988 **£10** **£5** *CD video*
I Believe CD-s Polygram 0800682 1988 **£10** **£5** *CD video*
Raoul And The Kings Of Spain CD-s Mercury FFFCJ1 1995 **£15** **£7.50** *promo*
Scenes From The Big Chair CD-s Polygram 0801721 1988 **£10** **£5** *CD video*
Shout CD-s Polygram 0800642 1988 **£10** **£5** *CD video*
Sowing The Seeds Of Love CD-s Mercury IDCD12 1989 **£5** **£2**
Suffer The Children 12" Mercury IDEA12 1981 **£6** **£2.50**
Woman In Chains CD-s Mercury IDCD13 1989 **£5** **£2** *2 versions*

TEARS ON THE CONSOLE

Tears On The Console LP Holyground HG120 1975 **£200** **£100** *actually by Chick Shannon*

TEATIME

Teatime LP Incus INCUS15 1975 **£15** **£6**

TEAZE

Live In Japan LP Aquarius AQR520 1978 **£10** **£4** *Canadian*
One Night Stands LP Capitol 11919 1979 **£10** **£4** *US*

TECHNIQUES

Hey Little Girl 7" Columbia DB4072 1958 **£25** **£12.50**

TECHNIQUES (2)

Come Back Darling 7" Big Shot BI543 1970 **£4** **£1.50**
Devoted 7" Treasure Isle TI7038 1968 **£10** **£5** *with Tommy McCook*
Feel A Little Better 7" Technique TE906 1970 **£4** **£1.50**
He Who Keepeth His Mouth 7" Treasure Isle TI7054 1970 **£4** **£1.50**
I Wish It Would Rain 7" Duke DU1 1968 **£8** **£4**
It's You I Love 7" Treasure Isle TI7040 1968 **£10** **£5**
Lonely Man 7" Technique TE904 1970 **£4** **£1.50**
Love Is Not A Gamble 7" Treasure Isle TI7026 1967 **£10** **£5**
Man Of My Word 7" Duke DU6 1968 **£8** **£4**
My Girl 7" Treasure Isle TI7031 1968 **£10** **£5** *with Tommy McCook*
Queen Majesty 7" Treasure Isle TI7019 1967 **£10** **£5**
Since I Lost You 7" Banana BA350 1971 **£4** **£1.50** *Riley's All Stars B side*
What Am I To Do 7" Duke DU22 1969 **£4** **£1.50**
Where Were You 7" Duke DU60 1969 **£4** **£1.50**
Who You Gonna Run To 7" Camel CA10 1969 **£4** **£1.50**
You Don't Care 7" Treasure Isle TI7001 1967 **£10** **£5** *Tommy McCook B side*

TEDDY

Elusion 7" Upsetter US353 1971 **£8** **£4** *Upsetters B side*

TEDDY & THE PANDAS

Basic Magnetism LP Tower ST5125 1968 **£15** **£6** *US*

TEDDY & THE TIGERS

Hold On I'm Coming 7" Spin SP2004 1967 **£15** **£7.50**

TEDDY & THE TWILIGHTS

I'm Just Your Clown 7" Stateside SS167 1963 **£6** **£2.50**

TEDDY BEARS

Although Phil Spector is famous as a producer – indeed he was the first such to attain fame independently of the artists he produced – he started his career as a singer. He was one-third of a group, the Teddy Bears, whose best-known song is remembered as a particularly golden oldie – 'To Know Him Is To Love Him'.

If Only You Knew 7" London HLP8889 1959 **£20** **£10**
Oh Why 7" London HLP8836 1959 **£10** **£5**
Teddy Bears Sing LP London HAP2183 1959 **£125** **£62.50**
Teddy Bears Sing LP Imperial LP9067 1959 **£200** **£100** *US, mono*
Teddy Bears Sing LP Imperial SLP12067 1959 **£300** **£180** *US, stereo*
To Know Him Is To Love Him 7" London HLN8733 1958 **£5** **£2**

TEE, WILLIE

Thank You John 7" Atlantic 584116 1967 **£12** **£6**
Walkin' Up A One Way Street 7" Mojo 2092025 1971 **£4** **£1.50**

TEE SET

In The Morning Of My Days	LP	Negram	ELS963	1972	**£12**	**£5**	*Dutch*
Ma Belle Amie	LP	Columbia	SCX6419	1970	**£12**	**£5**	

TEEMATES

Jet Set Dance Discotheque	LP	Audio Fidelity	DFS7042	1964	**£40**	**£20**	*US*

TEEN BEATS

Slop Beat	7"	Top Rank	JAR342	1960	**£10**	**£5**	

TEEN KINGS

When reissued as the more common Sun label recording, 'Ooby Dooby' was credited to the Teen Kings' lead singer, Roy Orbison.

Ooby Dooby	7"	Jewel	101	1956	**£500**	**£330**	*US, best auctioned*
Ooby Dooby	7"	Jewel	102	1956	**£400**	**£250**	*US, best auctioned*

TEEN QUEENS

Eddie My Love	7"	R&B	MRB5000	1965	**£30**	**£15**	
Eddie My Love	LP	Crown	CLP5022	1957	**£60**	**£30**	*US*
Teen Queens	LP	Crown	CLP5373	1963	**£25**	**£10**	*US*

TEENAGE FANCLUB

Ballad Of John And Yoko	7"	Paperhouse	PAPER005	1990	**£8**	**£4**	*1 side etched*
Everything Flows	7"	Paperhouse	PAPER003	1990	**£10**	**£5**	
King	CD	Creation	CD096	1991	**£15**	**£6**	*sprayed paint cover*
King	LP	Creation	LP096	1991	**£10**	**£4**	*sprayed paint cover*

TEENAGE FILMSTARS

Cloud Over Liverpool	7"	Clockwork	COR002	1979	**£6**	**£2.50**	
Cloud Over Liverpool	7"	Clockwork	COR002	1979	**£50**	**£25**	*picture sleeve*
I Helped Patrick McGoohan Escape	7"	Fab Listening	FL1	1980	**£6**	**£2.50**	
Odd Man Out	7"	Blueprint	BLU2013	1980	**£6**	**£2.50**	*picture sleeve*
Odd Man Out	7"	Wessex	WEX275	1980	**£8**	**£4**	*no picture sleeve*

TEENAGERS

Teenagers	7" EP	RCA	RCX102	1957	**£25**	**£12.50**	

TEENMAKERS

Teenmakers	LP	Triola	TLD216	1966	**£15**	**£6**	*Danish*

TEESIDE FETTLERS

Ring Of Iron	LP	Tradition	TSR016	1974	**£10**	**£4**	

TELESCOPES

Ever So	CD-s	Creation	CRESCD092	1990	**£5**	**£2**	
Precious Little	CD-s	Creation	CRECD81	1990	**£5**	**£2**	
Trade Mark of Quality	CD	Fierce	FRIGHTCD039	1990	**£12**	**£5**	

TELEVISION

It is curious how the music of Television, which was conceived as a vehicle for the lengthy display of lead guitar expertise, managed to become considered as part of the seventies punk movement, which generally had no time for such excesses. There was, of course, no denying the freshness and sheer excitement of the *Marquee Moon* album, whose status as a classic recording is never likely to be undermined.

Little Johnny Jewel	12"	Ork	NYC1	1979	**£8**	**£4**	*US*
Little Johnny Jewel	7"	Ork	81975	1975	**£8**	**£4**	*US*

TELEVISION PERSONALITIES

14th Floor	7"	Teen	CUS77089	1978	**£30**	**£15**	*3 picture sleeves*
And Don't The Kids Just Love It	LP	Rough Trade	RT24	1981	**£25**	**£10**	*with insert*
Biff Bang Pow!	7"	Creation/ Lyntone	LYN13546	1982	**£12**	**£6**	*flexi*
How I Learned To Love The Bomb	12"	Dreamworld	DREAM4	1986	**£8**	**£4**	
How I Learned To Love The Bomb	7"	Dreamworld	DREAM10	1986	**£10**	**£5**	
I Know Where Syd Barrett Lives	7"	Rough Trade	RT063	1981	**£12**	**£6**	
I Still Believe In Magic	7"	Caff	CAFF5	1989	**£15**	**£7.50**	
Mummy You're Not Watching Me	LP	Whaam!	BIG1	1982	**£25**	**£10**	*with insert*
Mummy You're Not Watching Me	LP	Dreamworld	BIGDREAM4	1986	**£10**	**£4**	
Painted Word	LP	Illuminated	JAMS37	1984	**£25**	**£10**	
Sense Of Belonging	7"	Rough Trade	RT109	1983	**£8**	**£4**	
Smashing Time	7"	Rough Trade	RT051	1980	**£10**	**£5**	
They Could Have Been Bigger Than The Beatles	LP	Whaam!	BIG5	1982	**£25**	**£10**	
They Could Have Been Bigger Than The Beatles	LP	Dreamworld	BIGDREAM2	1986	**£10**	**£4**	
Three Wishes	7"	Whaam!	WHAAM4	1982	**£8**	**£4**	*2 sleeves*
Where's Bill Grundy Now	7"	King's Road	LYN5976/7	1978	**£10**	**£5**	*4 picture sleeves*
Where's Bill Grundy Now	7"	Rough Trade	RT033	1979	**£6**	**£2.50**	

TELEX

Haven't We Met Somewhere Before	12"	Interdisc	IN1X12	1982	**£6**	**£2.50**	
L'Amour Toujours	12"	Interdisc	IN2X12	1982	**£6**	**£2.50**	
Moskow Diskow	12"	Sire	SIR4017T	1979	**£6**	**£2.50**	
Soul Waves	12"	Sire	SIR4047T	1980	**£8**	**£4**	

TELHAM TINKERS

Hot In Alice Springs	LP	Eron	031	1984	**£10**	**£4**	

TELSTARS

Eurovision Team	LP	Nashville	30107	1966	£25	£10	Swedish
I Went A Walkin'	7"	Oriole	CB1754	1962	£5	£2	

TEMPERANCE SEVEN

Temperance Seven 1961	LP	Parlophone	PMC1152/ PCS3021	1961	£12	£5	
Temperance Seven Plus One	LP	Argo	RG11	1961	£12	£5	

TEMPEST

Living In Fear	LP	Bronze	ILPS9267	1974	£15	£6	
Tempest	LP	Bronze	ILPS9220	1973	£20	£8	

TEMPEST, BOBBY

Love Or Leave	7"	Decca	F11125	1959	£5	£2	

TEMPLE, BOB

Vim Vam Vamoose	7"	Parlophone	R4264	1957	£75	£37.50	

TEMPLE, GERRY

Angel Face	7"	HMV	POP1114	1963	£20	£10	
Lovin' Up A Storm	7"	RCA	RCA1670	1968	£6	£2.50	
No More Tomorrows	7"	HMV	POP823	1961	£20	£10	
Seventeen Come Sunday	7"	HMV	POP939	1961	£15	£7.50	

TEMPLE, SHIRLEY

I Remember	7" EP	Top Rank	JKR8003	1959	£10	£5	

TEMPLE ROW

King And Queen	7"	Polydor	2058254	1972	£5	£2	
Walk The World Away	7"	Polydor	2058329	1973	£4	£1.50	

TEMPLEAIRES

He Spoke	7"	Vogue	V2421	1970	£5	£2	

TEMPO, NINO

Rock'n'Roll Beach Party	10" LP	London	HBU1075	1957	£100	£50	
Tempo's Tempo	7"	London	HLU8387	1957	£200	£100	best auctioned

TEMPO, NINO & APRIL STEVENS

All Strung Out	7"	London	HLU10084	1966	£4	£1.50	
All Strung Out	LP	London	HAU/SHU8314	1967	£15	£6	
Deep Purple	7"	London	HLK9782	1963	£4	£1.50	
Deep Purple	7" EP	London	REK1412	1964	£10	£5	
Deep Purple	LP	London	HAK8168	1964	£25	£10	
Great Songs	LP	Atlantic	ATL/STL5006	1964	£15	£6	
Habit Of Lovin' You Baby	7"	London	HLU10106	1967	£4	£1.50	
I'm Confessing	7"	London	HLK9890	1964	£4	£1.50	
Stardust	7"	London	HLK9859	1964	£4	£1.50	
Sweet And Lovely	7"	London	HLK9580	1962	£5	£2	Top Notes B side
Whispering	7"	London	HLK9829	1964	£4	£1.50	

TEMPOS

See You In September	7"	Pye	7N25026	1959	£40	£20	

TEMPOS (2)

Speaking Of The Tempos	LP	Justice	104	1966	£250	£150	US

TEMPREES

Love Men	LP	Stax	2325083	1972	£10	£4	
Three	LP	Stax	STX1040	1974	£15	£6	

TEMPTATIONS

Ain't Too Proud To Beg	7"	Tamla Motown	TMG699	1969	£4	£1.50	
Ain't Too Proud To Beg	7"	Tamla Motown	TMG565	1966	£8	£4	
All I Need	7"	Tamla Motown	TMG610	1967	£6	£2.50	
Ball Of Confusion	7"	Tamla Motown	TMG749	1970	£4	£1.50	
Beauty is Only Skin Deep	7"	Tamla Motown	TMG578	1966	£6	£2.50	
Cloud Nine	7"	Tamla Motown	TMG707	1969	£4	£1.50	
Cloud Nine	LP	Tamla Motown	(S)TML11109	1969	£10	£4	
Get Ready	7"	Tamla Motown	TMG557	1966	£12	£6	
Get Ready	7"	Tamla Motown	TMG688	1969	£4	£1.50	
Gettin' Ready	LP	Tamla Motown	(S)TML11035	1966	£25	£10	
Greatest Hits	LP	Tamla Motown	(S)TML11042	1967	£10	£4	
I Can't Get Next To You	7"	Tamla Motown	TMG722	1970	£4	£1.50	

I Could Never Love Another	7"	Tamla Motown	TMG658	1968	**£4**	**£1.50**	
I Wish It Would Rain	7"	Tamla Motown	TMG641	1968	**£5**	**£2**	
I'll Be In Trouble	7"	Stateside	SS319	1964	**£30**	**£15**	
I'm Losing You	7"	Tamla Motown	TMG587	1966	**£5**	**£2**	
In A Mellow Mood	LP	Tamla Motown	(S)TML11068	1968	**£15**	**£6**	
It's Growing	7"	Tamla Motown	TMG504	1965	**£20**	**£10**	
It's The Temptations	7" EP	Tamla Motown	TME2010	1966	**£20**	**£10**	
It's You That I Need	7"	Tamla Motown	TMG633	1967	**£20**	**£10**	
Just My Imagination	7"	Tamla Motown	TMG773	1971	**£4**	**£1.50**	
Live	LP	Tamla Motown	(S)TML11053	1967	**£10**	**£4**	
Live At The Copa	LP	Tamla Motown	(S)TML11104	1969	**£10**	**£4**	
Live At The Talk Of The Town	LP	Tamla Motown	(S)TML11141	1970	**£10**	**£4**	
Meet The Temptations	LP	Tamla Motown	TML11009	1965	**£75**	**£37.50**	
Memories	7"	Tamla Motown	TMG948	1975	**£6**	**£2.50**	*demo, picture sleeve*
My Baby	7"	Tamla Motown	TMG541	1965	**£15**	**£7.50**	
My Girl	7"	Stateside	SS378	1965	**£25**	**£12.50**	
Papa Was A Rolling Stone	7"	Tamla Motown	TMG839	1973	**£4**	**£1.50**	
Psychedelic Shack	7"	Tamla Motown	TMG741	1970	**£4**	**£1.50**	
Psychedelic Shack	LP	Tamla Motown	(S)TML11147	1970	**£15**	**£6**	
Puzzle People	LP	Tamla Motown	(S)TML11133	1970	**£10**	**£4**	
Runaway Child Running Wild	7"	Tamla Motown	TMG716	1969	**£4**	**£1.50**	
Since I Lost My Baby	7"	Tamla Motown	TMG526	1965	**£15**	**£7.50**	
Sing Smokey	LP	Tamla Motown	TML11016	1965	**£30**	**£15**	
Temptations	7" EP	Tamla Motown	TME2004	1965	**£25**	**£12.50**	
Temptations Show	LP	Gordy	GS933	1969	**£15**	**£6**	*US*
Temptations Wish It Would Rain	LP	Tamla Motown	(S)TML11079	1968	**£15**	**£6**	
Temptin' Temptations	LP	Tamla Motown	TML11023	1966	**£25**	**£10**	
Way You Do The Things You Do	7"	Stateside	SS278	1964	**£30**	**£15**	
Why Did You Leave Me Darling	7"	Tamla Motown	TMG671	1968	**£4**	**£1.50**	
Why You Wanna Make Me Blue	7"	Stateside	SS348	1964	**£40**	**£20**	
With A Lot O'Soul	LP	Tamla Motown	(S)TML11057	1967	**£12**	**£5**	
You're My Everything	7"	Tamla Motown	TMG620	1967	**£4**	**£1.50**	

TEMPTATIONS (2)

Barbara	7"	Top Rank	JAR384	1960	**£25**	**£10**	

TEMPUS FUGIT

Come Alive	7"	Philips	BF1802	1969	**£15**	**£7.50**	

TEN CC

Greatest Hits	LP	Mercury	HS9102504	1982	**£10**	**£4**	*audiophile*
Original Soundtrack	LP	Mercury	HS9102500	1982	**£10**	**£4**	*audiophile*

TEN FEET

Got Everything But Love	7"	RCA	RCA1544	1966	**£15**	**£7.50**	
Shot On Sight	7"	CBS	3045	1966	**£15**	**£7.50**	

TEN FEET FIVE

Two members of Ten Feet Five left to join the Troggs soon after the release of the group's only single – guitarist Chris Britton and bass player Pete Staples.

Baby's Back In Town	7"	Fontana	TF578	1965	**£20**	**£10**	

TEN FOOT BONELESS

Powerslide	12"	Fierce	FRIGHT027	1988	**£8**	**£4**	

TEN THOUSAND MANIACS

Can't Ignore The Train	12"	Elektra	EKR11T	1985	**£8**	**£4**	
Eat For Two	CD-s	Elektra	EKR100CD	1989	**£5**	**£2**	*3" single*

Grey Victory	7"	Lyntone	LYN15914	1985	£4	**£1.50**	*flexi, Simply Red B side*
Human Conflict 5	12"	Press	P2010	1984	£20	**£10**	
Just As The Tide Was A-Flowin'	7"	Elektra	EKR19	1985	£6	**£2.50**	
My Mother The War	12"	Reflex	12RE1	1984	£15	**£7.50**	
Secrets Of The I Ching	LP	Press	P3001LP	1984	£40	**£20**	*US*
Trouble Me	CD-s	Elektra	EKR93CDX	1989	£6	**£2.50**	*3" single in elephant-shaped pack*
Trouble Me	CD-s	Elektra	EKR93CD	1989	£5	**£2**	

TEN YEARS AFTER

Before Woodstock showed Alvin Lee the mileage he could get from guitar excess, Ten Years After had a light, jazzy sound that made them stand out from the mass of blues bands emerging at the time. *Undead* shows off this quality well – it even includes a lengthy jam on 'Woodchopper's Ball', which succeeds in dragging the Woody Herman original into the rock age with its dignity intact. *Stonedhenge* is still impressive too as the work of a band thinking hard and imaginatively of ways in which to break free of the constraints of playing the blues, even if that imagination was largely placed on hold for subsequent recordings.

Cricklewood Green	LP	Deram	SML1065	1970	£10	**£4**	
Hear Me Calling	7"	Deram	DM221	1968	£4	**£1.50**	
Love Like A Man	7"	Deram	DM299	1970	£4	**£1.50**	
Portable People	7"	Deram	DM176	1967	£4	**£1.50**	
Recorded Live	LP	Chrysalis	CHR1049	1973	£10	**£4**	
Rock'n'Roll To The World	LP	Chrysalis	CHR1009	1972	£10	**£4**	
She Lies In The Morning	7"	Deram	XDR48532	1971	£8	**£4**	*demo*
Space In Time	LP	Columbia	CQ30801	1972	£10	**£4**	*US quad*
Space In Time	LP	Chrysalis	CHR1001	1972	£10	**£4**	
Ssssh!	CD	Chrysalis	CD25CR05	1994	£12	**£5**	*Chrysalis 25 pack*
Ssssh!	LP	Deram	DML1052	1969	£20	**£8**	*mono*
Ssssh!	LP	Deram	SML1052	1969	£15	**£6**	
Stonedhenge	LP	Deram	SML1029	1968	£15	**£6**	
Stonedhenge	LP	Deram	DML1029	1968	£20	**£8**	*mono*
Ten Years After	LP	Deram	SML1015	1967	£20	**£8**	
Ten Years After	LP	Deram	DML1015	1967	£25	**£10**	*mono*
Undead	LP	Deram	SML1023	1968	£15	**£6**	
Undead	LP	Deram	DML1023	1968	£20	**£8**	*mono*
Watt	LP	Deram	SML1078	1970	£10	**£4**	

TENDER SLIM & COUSIN LEROY

Tender Slim & Cousin Leroy	7" EP	XX	MIN702	196–	£5	**£2**	

TENNORS

Another Scorcher	7"	Big Shot	BI517	1969	£4	**£1.50**	
Copy Me Donkey	7"	Island	WI3140	1968	£10	**£5**	*Romeo Stewart B side*
Grampa	7"	Island	WI3156	1968	£10	**£5**	*Romeo Stewart B side*
Hopeful Village	7"	Duke Reid	DR2502	1969	£6	**£2.50**	*Tommy McCook B side*
Khaki	7"	Blue Cat	BS127	1968	£8	**£4**	*Leroy Reid B side*
Let Go Yah Donkey	7"	Fab	FAB50	1968	£8	**£4**	*Romeo Stewart B side*
Massie Massa	7"	Doctor Bird	DB1152	1968	£10	**£5**	*Clive Allstars B side*
Pressure And Slide	7"	Coxsone	CS7024	1967	£10	**£5**	*Soul Brothers B side*
Ride Your Donkey	7"	Fab	FAB41	1968	£8	**£4**	
Ride Your Donkey	7"	Island	WI3133	1968	£10	**£5**	
Sufferer	7"	Doctor Bird	DB1175	1968	£10	**£5**	
Weather Report	7"	Explosion	EX2079	1973	£5	**£2**	
You're No Good	7"	Big Shot	BI514	1969	£4	**£1.50**	

TERJE, JESPER OG JOACHIM

Jesper Og Joachim Terje	LP	Spectator	1037	1970	£150	**£75**	*Danish*

TERMITES

Tell Me	7"	Oriole	CB1989	1965	£15	**£7.50**	

TERMITES (2)

Do It Right Now	7"	Coxsone	CS7025	1967	£10	**£5**	*Summertaires B side*
Do The Rock Steady	LP	Studio One	SOL9003	1967	£100	**£50**	
It Takes Two To Make Love	7"	Studio One	SO2029	1967	£12	**£6**	
Mama Didn't Know	7"	Coxsone	CS7039	1968	£10	**£5**	
Mercy Mr Percy	7"	Studio One	SO2006	1967	£12	**£6**	*Soul Brothers B side*
Mr DJ	7"	Studio One	SO2040	1968	£12	**£6**	
Push It Up	7"	Pama	PM729	1968	£6	**£2.50**	
Push Push	7"	Nu Beat	NB017	1968	£6	**£2.50**	
Show Me The Way	7"	Pama	PM738	1968	£6	**£2.50**	
Sign Up	7"	Coxsone	CS7008	1967	£10	**£5**	*Delroy Wilson B side*

TERRA COTTA

To Be Near You	7"	Terra Cotta	TC001	1978	£12	**£6**	

TERRACE, PETE

At The Party	7"	Pye	7N25427	1967	£6	**£2.50**	
Boogaloo	LP	Pye	NPL28102	1967	£15	**£6**	
Shotgun Boogaloo	7"	Pye	7N25440	1967	£10	**£5**	

TERRAPLANE

If That's What It Takes	12"	Epic	TERRAQ4	1987	£8	£4	*with poster*
Moving Target	12"	Epic	TERRAG3	1987	£8	£4	
Moving Target	CD	Epic	4601572	1987	£15	£6	

TERRELL, LLOYD

Bang Bang Lulu	7"	Pama	PM710	1968	£4	£1.50	*Mrs Miller B side*
Birth Control	7"	Pama	PM792	1969	£6	£2.50	
How Come	7"	Pama	PM740	1968	£4	£1.50	*Mrs Miller B side*
Lulu Returns	7"	Pama	PM752	1968	£4	£1.50	*Mrs Miller B side*
Mr Rhya	7"	Nu Beat	NB023	1969	£4	£1.50	

TERRELL, TAMMI

Come On And See Me	7"	Tamla Motown	TMG561	1966	£50	£25	
Irresistible Tammi Terrell	LP	Tamla Motown	(S)TML11103	1969	£40	£20	

TERRORVISION

American TV	CD-s	Total Vegas	CDPVEGAS3	1993	£5	£2	
Blackbird	cass	private		1991	£30	£15	
Brand New Toy	cass	private		1990	£30	£15	
Formaldehyde	CD	Total Vegas	VEGASCDS1	1993	£15	£6	*with 12 page booklet*
Formaldehyde	CD	Total Vegas	ATVRCD1	1992	£25	£10	*14 tracks*
Formaldehyde	LP	Total Vegas	ATVRLP1	1992	£20	£8	*14 tracks, green vinyl*
Live At Don Valley Stadium	CD	Total Vegas	BOOT1	1993	£30	£15	*promo*
Middle Man	CD-s	Total Vegas	CDVEGASS7	1995	£5	£2	
My House	12"	Total Vegas	12VEGAS2	1992	£6	£2.50	
My House	7"	Total Vegas	VEGAS2	1992	£6	£2.50	
My House	CD-s	Total Vegas	CDVEGAS2	1992	£10	£5	
New Policy One	CD-s	Total Vegas	CDVEGASSP4	1993	£5	£2	
Oblivion	CD-s	Total Vegas	CDVEGASS6	1993	£5	£2	
Prime Time Terrorvision	CD	Total Vegas	CDPRIMEDJ1	1994	£20	£8	*promo*
Problem Solved	CD-s	Total Vegas	CDATVR1	1993	£8	£4	
Pump Action Sunshine	cass	private		1991	£30	£15	
Thrive EP	12"	Total Vegas	12VEGAS1	1992	£20	£10	
Thrive EP	CD-s	Total Vegas	CDVEGAS1	1992	£20	£10	

TERRY, BLAIR & ANOUCHKA

Ultra Modern Nursery Rhyme	CD-s	Chrysalis	CHSCD3478	1989	£6	£2.50	
Ultra Modern Nursery Rhymes	CD	Chrysalis	CCD1701	1989	£15	£6	

TERRY, CARL & DERRICK

True Love	7"	Grape	GR3012	1969	£4	£1.50	*Roy Smith B side*

TERRY, CLARK

Clark Terry	LP	Emarcy	EJL1256	1957	£20	£8	
Duke With A Difference	LP	Riverside	RLP12246	1961	£15	£6	
Gingerbread Men	LP	Fontana	(S)TL5394	1967	£10	£4	*with Bob Brookmeyer*
It's What's Happenin'	LP	Impulse	MIPL/SIPL507	1968	£10	£4	
Mumbles	LP	Fontana	TL5373	1966	£10	£4	
Power Of Positive Swinging	LP	Fontana	TL5290	1966	£10	£4	*with Bob Brookmeyer*
Serenade To A Bus Seat	LP	Riverside	RLP12237	196–	£15	£6	
Tonight	LP	Fontana	TL5265	1965	£10	£4	*with Bob Brookmeyer*

TERRY, GORDON

Country Clambake	7" EP	London	REA1098	1957	£20	£10	

TERRY, SONNY

Blues	10" LP	Stinson	55		£20	£8	US
Blues And Folk Songs	10" LP	Folkways	2327		£20	£8	US
Blues From Everywhere	LP	XTRA	XTRA1099	1970	£10	£4	
City Blues	10" LP	Vogue	LDE165	1955	£20	£8	
Folk Blues	10" LP	Vogue	LDE137	1955	£20	£8	
Folk Blues	7" EP	Vogue	EPV1095	1956	£25	£12.50	*with Alec Stewart*
Fox Chase	78	Vogue	V2326	1955	£6	£2.50	
Harmonica	10" LP	Folkways	35		£20	£8	US
Harmonica	10" LP	Folkways	2035		£20	£8	US
Harmonica Blues	10" LP	Topic	10T30	1958	£25	£10	
Harmonica Blues	LP	Topic	12T30	1965	£15	£6	
Hooting Blues	7"	Parlophone	MSP6017	1953	£20	£10	
On The Road	LP	XTRA	XTRA1110	1971	£10	£4	
Sonny Is King	LP	Bluesville	BV1059	1963	£15	£6	US
Sonny Terry	LP	XTRA	XTRA1064	1969	£10	£4	
Sonny Terry	LP	Everest	206	196–	£15	£6	US
Sonny Terry And His Mouth Harp	LP	Riverside	12644		£15	£6	US
Sonny's Story	LP	XTRA	XTRA5025	1966	£12	£5	
Sonny's Story	LP	Bluesville	BV1025	1961	£15	£6	US
Talkin' 'Bout The Blues	LP	Washington	W702	1961	£20	£8	US
Washboard Band	10" LP	Folkways	2006		£20	£8	US
Whoopin' The Blues	10" LP	Melodisc	MLP516	1958	£20	£8	

TERRY, SONNY & BROWNIE MCGHEE

At The Bunk House	LP	Philips	BL7675	1966	£12	£5	
At The Second Fret	LP	Bluesville	BV1058	1962	£15	£6	US
Back Country Blues	LP	Savoy	MG14019	195–	£30	£15	US
Back Country Blues	LP	CBS	52165	1963	£15	£6	

Title	Format	Label	Number	Year	Price	Price	Notes
Blues	LP	Folkways	F63557	1959	**£20**	**£8**	*US*
Blues All Around My Head	LP	Bluesville	BV(S)1020	1961	**£15**	**£6**	*US*
Blues And Folk	LP	Bluesville	BV(S)1005	1960	**£15**	**£6**	*US*
Blues And Shouts	LP	Fantasy	F3317	1962	**£15**	**£6**	*US*
Blues And Shouts	LP	Fantasy	F3317	1962	**£30**	**£15**	*US, red vinyl*
Blues In My Soul	LP	Bluesville	BV(S)1033	1961	**£15**	**£6**	*US*
Blues Is A Story	LP	Vogue	SAE5014	1961	**£25**	**£10**	*stereo*
Blues Is A Story	LP	Vogue	LAE12247	1961	**£20**	**£8**	*mono*
Blues Is My Companion	LP	Columbia	33SX1223	1960	**£25**	**£10**	
Brownie McGhee And Sonny Terry	LP	Vogue	LAE552	1964	**£20**	**£8**	
Brownie's Blues	LP	Bluesville	BV(S)1042	1962	**£15**	**£6**	*US*
Down Home Blues	LP	Bluesville	BV(S)1002	1960	**£15**	**£6**	*US*
Down South Summit Meeting	LP	Vogue	LAE12266	1961	**£15**	**£6**	
Folk Songs Of Sonny And Brownie	LP	Roulette	R25074	1959	**£20**	**£8**	*US*
Going Down Slow	7"	Oriole	CBA1946	1964	**£10**	**£5**	
Guitar Highway	LP	Verve	(S)VLP5010	1966	**£15**	**£6**	
Hometown Blues	LP	Fontana	TL5289	1966	**£12**	**£5**	
In London	LP	Nixa	NJL18	1958	**£20**	**£8**	
Just A Closer Walk With Thee	LP	Fantasy	F3296	1962	**£30**	**£15**	*US, red vinyl*
Just A Closer Walk With Thee	LP	Fantasy	F3296	1962	**£15**	**£6**	*US*
Key To The Highway	LP	XTRA	XTRA1004	1965	**£15**	**£6**	*with Big Bill Broonzy*
Livin' With The Blues	LP	Fontana	688006ZL	1965	**£15**	**£6**	
Me And Sonny	7" EP	Melodisc	EPM783	1958	**£12**	**£6**	
Pawn Shop Blues	7" EP	Realm	REP4002	1964	**£12**	**£6**	
Penetentiary Blues	LP	Fontana	688007ZL	1965	**£12**	**£5**	
R And B From S And B	7" EP	Topic	TOP121	1964	**£12**	**£6**	
Rocking And Whooping	7"	Columbia	DB4433	1960	**£10**	**£5**	
Simply Heavenly	LP	Columbia	OL5240	1957	**£20**	**£8**	*US*
Sonny & Brownie At Sugar Hill	LP	Fantasy	F8091	1962	**£15**	**£6**	*US*
Sonny & Brownie At Sugar Hill	LP	Fantasy	F8091	1962	**£30**	**£15**	*US, blue vinyl*
Sonny Terry & Brownie McGhee	7" EP	Ember	EMBEP4562	1964	**£12**	**£6**	
Sonny Terry & Brownie McGhee	LP	Fantasy	F3254	1961	**£15**	**£6**	*US*
Sonny Terry & Brownie McGhee	LP	Fantasy	F3254	1961	**£30**	**£15**	*US, red vinyl*
Sonny Terry & Brownie McGhee & Chris Barber	7" EP	Pye	NJE1073	1957	**£8**	**£4**	
Sonny Terry And Brownie McGhee	7" EP	Vocalion	EPVF1279	1964	**£12**	**£6**	
Sonny Terry And Brownie McGhee	7" EP	Vocalion	EPV1274	1963	**£12**	**£6**	
Sonny Terry And Brownie McGhee	LP	Topic	12T29	1958	**£20**	**£8**	
Sonny Terry And Brownie McGhee	LP	World Record Club	T7379	1961	**£10**	**£4**	
Sonny, Brownie And Chris	10" LP	Pye	NJT515	1958	**£20**	**£8**	*with Chris Barber*
Terry & McGhee In London	7" EP	Pye	NJE1074	1957	**£12**	**£6**	
Traditional Blues Vol. 1	LP	Folkways	F2421	1961	**£15**	**£6**	*US*
Traditional Blues Vol. 2	LP	Folkways	F2422	1961	**£15**	**£6**	*US*
Way Down South Summit Meeting	LP	World Pacific	WP(S)1296	1960	**£15**	**£6**	*US*
Where The Blues Began	LP	Fontana	SFJL979	1968	**£10**	**£4**	
Whoopin' The Blues	LP	Capitol	T20906	1967	**£10**	**£4**	
Work-Play-Faith-Fun Songs	7" EP	Top Rank	JKP3007	1961	**£12**	**£6**	

TERRY & JERRY

Title	Format	Label	Number	Year	Price	Price	Notes
People Are Doing It Every Day	7"	R&B	MRB5009	1965	**£8**	**£4**	

TERRY & THE BLUE JEANS

Title	Format	Label	Number	Year	Price	Price	Notes
Black And Beach	LP	King	SKD390	1976	**£30**	**£15**	*Japanese*
Blue Star	LP	King	SKA106	1975	**£30**	**£15**	*Japanese*
Electric Guitar Folk	LP	King	SKA96	1974	**£30**	**£15**	*Japanese*
Great Tracks	LP	King	SKM1297/98	1974	**£30**	**£15**	*Japanese double*
Pealing Shells	LP	Toshiba	7071	1965	**£125**	**£62.50**	*Japanese*
Samba Pa Ti	LP	King	SKA87	1973	**£30**	**£15**	*Japanese*
Surfin'	LP	Toshiba	7031	1964	**£150**	**£75**	*Japanese red vinyl*

TERRY SISTERS

Title	Format	Label	Number	Year	Price	Price	Notes
It's The Same Old Jazz	7"	Parlophone	R4364	1957	**£6**	**£2.50**	

TERRY-THOMAS

Title	Format	Label	Number	Year	Price	Price	Notes
Strictly T T	LP	Decca	LK4398	1961	**£15**	**£6**	
Sweet Old Fashioned Boy	7"	Decca	F10804	1956	**£6**	**£2.50**	

TEST DEPARTMENT

Title	Format	Label	Number	Year	Price	Price	Notes
Beating The Retreat	12"	Some Bizarre	TEST2/3	1984	**£8**	**£4**	*boxed double with inserts*
Compulsion	12"	Test	TEST112	1983	**£6**	**£2.50**	
Ecstasy Under Duress	cass	Pleasantly Surprised	PS5	198–	**£12**	**£5**	*in bag with inserts*
Godaddin	12"	Media City	CMC1	1988	**£10**	**£5**	
History	cass	Test	TESTONE	1982	**£15**	**£6**	
Pax Americana	CD-s	Ministry Of Power	MOP5CD	1990	**£5**	**£2**	

TETRAGON

Title	Format	Label	Number	Year	Price	Price	Notes
Nature	LP	Soma	SM1	1971	**£150**	**£75**	*German*

TEX, JOE

Title	Format	Label	Number	Year	Price	Price	Notes
Best Of Joe Tex	LP	London	HAU8334	1967	**£25**	**£10**	
Buying A Book	LP	Atlantic	588193	1969	**£10**	**£4**	
From The Roots Came The Rapper	LP	Atlantic	K40239	1972	**£10**	**£4**	
Go Home And Do It	7"	Atlantic	584212	1968	**£4**	**£1.50**	

Greatest Hits	LP	Atlantic	587/588089	1967	£12	£5	
Hold On	LP	Checker	2993	1964	£30	£15	US
Hold On To What You've Got	7"	Atlantic	584096	1967	£4	£1.50	
Hold On To What You've Got	7"	Atlantic	AT4015	1965	£4	£1.50	
Hold On To What You've Got	LP	Atlantic	(SD)8106	1965	£25	£10	US
I Gotcha	LP	Mercury	6338093	1972	£10	£4	
I Want To Do Everything	7"	Atlantic	AT4045	1965	£4	£1.50	
I've Got To Do A Little Better	LP	Atlantic	587053	1967	£15	£6	
Live And Lively	LP	Atlantic	587/588104	1968	£12	£5	
Love You Save	7"	Atlantic	AT4081	1966	£4	£1.50	
Love You Save	LP	Atlantic	(SD)8124	1966	£15	£6	US
Men Are Getting Scarce	7"	Atlantic	584171	1968	£4	£1.50	
New Boss	LP	Atlantic	587/588059	1967	£12	£5	
New Boss	LP	Atlantic	ATL5043	1965	£30	£15	
Papa Was Too	7"	Atlantic	584068	1967	£4	£1.50	
S.Y.S.L.J.F.M.	7"	Atlantic	584016	1966	£4	£1.50	
Show Me	7"	Atlantic	584102	1967	£4	£1.50	
Skinny Legs And All	7"	Atlantic	584144	1967	£4	£1.50	
Soul Country	LP	Atlantic	587/588118	1968	£12	£5	
Sweet Woman Like You	7"	Atlantic	AT4058	1965	£4	£1.50	
We Can't Sit Down Now	7"	Atlantic	584296	1969	£4	£1.50	
Woman Can Change A Man	7"	Atlantic	AT4027	1965	£4	£1.50	
Woman Like That, Yeah	7"	Atlantic	584119	1967	£4	£1.50	
You Better Believe It Baby	7"	Atlantic	584035	1966	£4	£1.50	
You Better Get It	7"	Atlantic	AT4021	1965	£6	£2.50	
You Better Get It	LP	Atlantic	587/588130	1968	£12	£5	
Yum Yum Yum	7"	Sue	WI370	1965	£12	£6	

TEXAS

Everyday Now	CD-s	Mercury	TEXCD3	1989	£5	£2	
I Don't Want A Lover	CD-s	Mercury	TEXCD1	1989	£6	£2.50	
Prayer For You	CD-s	Mercury	TEXCD4	1989	£5	£2	
Thrill Has Gone	CD-s	Mercury	TEXCD2	1989	£5	£2	
Tired Of Being Alone	CD-s	Mercury	TEXCD8	1992	£5	£2	
You Owe It All To Me	CD-s	Mercury	TEXCL10	1993	£6	£2.50	*with 3 cards*

TEXAS ALEXANDER

Treasures Of North American Negro Music Vol. 7	7" EP	Fontana	467136TE	1961	£10	£5	

TEXAS RANGERS

Way Out West	7" EP	HMV	7EG8387	1957	£6	£2.50	

TEXTOR SINGERS

Sobbin' Women	7"	Capitol	CL14211	1954	£4	£1.50	

THACKER, RUDY & THE STRINGBEANS

Ballad Of Johnny Horton	7"	Starlite	ST45087	1962	£8	£4	

THACKRAY, JAKE

Jake's Progress	LP	Columbia	SCX6345	1969	£10	£4	
Last Will And Testament	LP	Columbia	SX/SCX6178	1967	£10	£4	
Live Performance	LP	Columbia	SCX6453	1971	£10	£4	

THARPE, SISTER ROSETTA

Gospel Singer	7" EP	Mercury	ZEP10127	1962	£6	£2.50	
Gospel Songs No. 2	7" EP	Brunswick	OE9284	1958	£6	£2.50	
Gospel Train	LP	Mercury	MPL6529	1957	£12	£5	
Gospel Train	LP	Brunswick	LAT8290	1959	£10	£4	
Gospel Truth	LP	Mercury	MMC14057	1961	£10	£4	
If I Can Help Somebody	7"	MGM	MGM1072	1960	£4	£1.50	
Sister Rosetta Tharpe	7" EP	Mercury	10000MCE	1964	£6	£2.50	
Sister Rosetta Tharpe	7" EP	MGM	MGMEP746	1962	£6	£2.50	
Sister Rosetta Tharpe	LP	Brunswick	LAT8290	1959	£10	£4	

THAT PETROL EMOTION

Cellophane	CD-s	Virgin	VSCD1116	1988	£5	£2	
Genius Move	CD-s	Virgin	CDEP13	1988	£5	£2	
Groove Check	CD-s	Virgin	VSCD1159	1989	£5	£2	

THE THE

Alive	CD	Epic	ESK1867	1989	£25	£10	*US promo*
Armageddon Days Are Here Again	CD-s	Epic	CDEMU10	1989	£5	£2	
Beaten Generation	CD-s	Epic	CDEMU8	1989	£5	£2	*2 versions*
Cold Spell Ahead	7"	Some Bizarre	BZS4	1981	£20	£10	
Controversial Subject	7"	4AD	AD10	1980	£20	£10	
Flesh And Bones	7"	Some Bizarre		1985	£8	£4	*1 sided promo*
Gravitate To Me	CD-s	Epic	CDEMU9	1989	£5	£2	
Infected	12"	Epic	TRUTHQ3	1986	£8	£4	*uncensored picture sleeve*
Infected	12"	Epic	TRUTHD3	1986	£6	£2.50	*double*
Live In New York	CD	Epic	ESK5300	1993	£25	£10	*US promo*
Perfect	12"	Epic	EPCA133119	1983	£8	£4	
Soul Mining	LP	Epic	25525	1983	£10	£4	*with 12"*
Sweet Bird Of Truth	CD-s	Epic	CDTHE2	1987	£5	£2	
This Is The Day	7"	Epic	A3710	1983	£6	£2.50	*double*
Uncertain Smile	12"	Epic	EPC132787	1982	£6	£2.50	*insert*
Uncertain Smile	12"	Epic	EPC132787	1982	£15	£7.50	*yellow vinyl, insert*

Title	Format	Label	Cat. No.	Year	Mint	VG+	Notes
Uncertain Smile	7"	Epic	EPCA2787	1982	**£5**	**£2**	*with insert*

THEATRE OF HATE

Title	Format	Label	Cat. No.	Year	Mint	VG+	Notes
He Who Dares Wins – Live At The Warehouse Leeds	LP	S.S.	SSSSS1P	1981	**£12**	**£5**	*autographed*
Wake	7"	Bliss	TOH1EP	1981	**£8**	**£4**	*with T-shirt in 12" pack*

THEE

Title	Format	Label	Cat. No.	Year	Mint	VG+	Notes
Each And Every Day	7"	Decca	F12163	1965	**£30**	**£15**	

THEE MIDNIGHTERS

Title	Format	Label	Cat. No.	Year	Mint	VG+	Notes
Bring You Love Special Delivery	LP	Whittier	W5000	1966	**£20**	**£8**	*US*
Giants	LP	Whittier	WS5002	1967	**£20**	**£8**	*US*
Land Of A Thousand Dances	7" EP	Vogue	EPL8314	1966	**£15**	**£7.50**	*French*
Thee Midnighters	LP	Chattahoochee.	CS1001	1965	**£20**	**£8**	*US*
Unlimited	LP	Whittier	W5001	1966	**£20**	**£8**	*US*

THEE MUFFINS

Title	Format	Label	Cat. No.	Year	Mint	VG+	Notes
Pop Up	LP	Fan Club		1966	**£300**	**£180**	*US*

THELWALL, LLANS & THE CELESTIALS

Title	Format	Label	Cat. No.	Year	Mint	VG+	Notes
Choo Choo Ska	7"	Island	WI262	1966	**£10**	**£5**	

THEM

Despite being continually plagued by management and record company problems, Them managed to produce some of the toughest and most enduring of British R&B. Much of the credit for this inevitably goes to the group's lead singer – Van Morrison – already a distinctive and commanding vocalist.

Title	Format	Label	Cat. No.	Year	Mint	VG+	Notes
Angry Young Them	LP	Decca	LK4700	1965	**£60**	**£30**	
Angry Young Them	LP	Decca	LK4700	1969	**£15**	**£6**	*boxed Decca logo*
Baby Please Don't Go	7"	Decca	F12018	1964	**£4**	**£1.50**	
Baby Please Don't Go	CD-s	London	LONCD292	1991	**£5**	**£2**	
Being Em On In	7" EP	Decca	457108	1966	**£60**	**£30**	*French*
Call My Name	7"	Decca	F12355	1966	**£6**	**£2.50**	
Don't Start Crying Now	7"	Decca	F11973	1964	**£30**	**£15**	
Don't Start Crying Now	7" EP	Decca	457069	1965	**£60**	**£30**	*French*
Gloria	7"	Major Minor	MM509	1967	**£6**	**£2.50**	
Gloria	7" EP	Decca	457073	1965	**£60**	**£30**	*French*
Gloria's Dream	7" EP	Vogue	INT18079	1966	**£75**	**£37.50**	*French*
Here Comes The Night	7"	Decca	F12094	1965	**£4**	**£1.50**	
In Reality	LP	Happy Tiger	HT1012	1971	**£25**	**£10**	*US*
It Won't Hurt Half As Much	7"	Decca	F12215	1965	**£5**	**£2**	
Mystic Eyes	7"	Decca	F12281	1965	**£5**	**£2**	
Now & Them	LP	Tower	ST5104	1968	**£40**	**£20**	*US*
One More Time	7"	Decca	F12175	1965	**£5**	**£2**	
Portland Town	7" EP	Vogue	INT18135	1967	**£75**	**£37.50**	*French*
Richard Cory	7"	Decca	F12403	1966	**£6**	**£2.50**	
Story Of Them	7"	Major Minor	MM513	1967	**£8**	**£4**	
Them	7" EP	Decca	DFE8612	1965	**£60**	**£30**	
Them	7" EP	Decca	DFE8612	1965	**£300**	**£180**	*export*
Them	LP	Happy Tiger	HT1004	1970	**£30**	**£25**	*US*
Them Again	LP	Decca	LK4751	1969	**£15**	**£6**	*boxed Decca logo*
Them Again	LP	Decca	LK4751	1966	**£60**	**£30**	
Time Out, Time In For Them	LP	Tower	ST5116	1968	**£40**	**£20**	*US*
World Of Them	LP	Decca	(S)PA86	1970	**£10**	**£4**	

THEN JERICHO

Title	Format	Label	Cat. No.	Year	Mint	VG+	Notes
Prairie Rose	CD-s	London	LONCD131	1987	**£5**	**£2**	

THERAPY

Title	Format	Label	Cat. No.	Year	Mint	VG+	Notes
One Night Stand	LP	Indigo	IRS5124	1973	**£15**	**£6**	*Irish*

THERAPY?

Title	Format	Label	Cat. No.	Year	Mint	VG+	Notes
Have A Merry Fucking Christmas	7"	A&M	THX1	1992	**£10**	**£5**	
Meat Abstract	7"	Multifucking-national	MFN1	1990	**£10**	**£5**	
Meat Abstract	cass	private		1990	**£10**	**£4**	
Pleasure Death	LP	Wiija	WIJ11	1992	**£75**	**£37.50**	*test pressing*
Teethgrinder	12"	A&M		1992	**£40**	**£20**	*double promo*
Thirty Seconds Of Silence	cass	private		1989	**£10**	**£4**	

THESE TRAILS

Title	Format	Label	Cat. No.	Year	Mint	VG+	Notes
These Trails	LP	Sinergia		1973	**£100**	**£50**	*US*

THIELMANS, JEAN 'TOOTS'

Title	Format	Label	Cat. No.	Year	Mint	VG+	Notes
Sound	LP	Philips	BBL7058	1956	**£15**	**£6**	

THIN END OF THE WEDGE

Title	Format	Label	Cat. No.	Year	Mint	VG+	Notes
Lights Are On Green	7"	Jungle	JR051S	1981	**£20**	**£10**	

THIN LIZZY

Title	Format	Label	Cat. No.	Year	Mint	VG+	Notes
Boys Are Back In Town	CD-s	Vertigo	LIZCD15	1991	**£5**	**£2**	
Dedication	CD-s	Vertigo	LIZCD14	1991	**£5**	**£2**	
Farmer	7"	Parlophone	DIP513	1970	**£750**	**£500**	*Irish, best auctioned*
Hollywood	10"	Vertigo	LIZZY10	1982	**£10**	**£5**	*1 sided*
Jailbreak	7"	Vertigo	6059150	1976	**£6**	**£2.50**	

Little Darling	7"	Decca	F13507	1974	£5	£2	
New Day EP	7"	Decca	F13208	1972	£200	£100	
Philomena	7"	Vertigo	6059111	1974	£5	£2	
Randolph's Tango	7"	Decca	F13402	1973	£10	£5	2 versions
Rocker	7"	Decca	F13467	1973	£5	£2	
Rocker	CD	Castle Collector	CCSCD117	1987	£20	£8	box set with 20 track CD The Collection plus biography, in 6" × 9" box
Shades Of A Blue Orphanage	LP	Decca	TXS108	1972	£20	£8	
Thin Lizzy	LP	Decca	SKL5082	1971	£20	£8	
Thunder And Lightning	12"	Vertigo	LIZZY1212	1983	£10	£5	with poster
Thunder And Lightning	LP	Vertigo	VERL3	1983	£10	£4	with 12"
Vagabonds Of The Western World	LP	Decca	SKL5170	1973	£20	£8	with insert

THIRD EAR BAND

Alchemy	LP	Harvest	SHVL756	1969	£20	£8	
Experiences	LP	Harvest	SHSM2007	1976	£10	£4	
Music From Macbeth	LP	Harvest	SHSP4019	1972	£12	£5	
Third Ear Band	LP	Harvest	SHVL773	1970	£15	£6	

THIRD ESTATE

Years Before The Wine	LP	private		1976	£500	£330	US

THIRD POWER

Believe	LP	Vanguard	VSD6554	1970	£30	£15	US

THIRD QUADRANT

Seeing Yourself As You Really Are	LP	Rock Cottage	no number	1982	£100	£50	

THIRD RAIL

Id Music	LP	Epic	LN24327/ BN26327	1967	£40	£20	US
Run Run Run	7"	Columbia	DB8274	1967	£20	£10	

THIRD WORLD

Third World	LP	RCA	SF8185	1971	£12	£5	

THIRD WORLD WAR

Ascension Day	7"	Fly	BUG7	1971	£4	£1.50	picture sleeve
Third World War	LP	Fly	FLY4	1971	£15	£6	
Third World War II	LP	Track	2406108	1972	£40	£20	

THIRSTY MOON

Blitz	LP	Brain	1079	1975	£10	£4	German
Thirsty Moon	LP	Brain	1021	1973	£10	£4	German
You'll Never Come Back	LP	Brain	1041	1974	£10	£4	German

THIRTEENTH FLOOR ELEVATORS

The group led by Roky Erickson were apparently the first to describe themselves as psychedelic and the first LP has a suitably colourful cover. Musically, however, the group pales next to more celebrated artists like Jefferson Airplane and the Grateful Dead. The Elevators' brand of garage punk is further undermined by the inclusion of an 'electric jug' player, who sounds for the most part like a slightly demented chicken.

Bull Of The Woods	LP	International Artist	IA9	1969	£60	£30	US
Easter Everywhere	LP	International Artist	IA5	1968	£175	£87.50	US
Easter Everywhere	LP	Radar	RAD15	1979	£12	£5	
Fire In My Bones	LP	Texas Archive	TAR4	1985	£10	£4	US
Live	LP	International Artist	IA8	1968	£60	£30	US
Psychedelic Sounds	LP	International Artist	LP1	1966	£75	£37.50	US
Psychedelic Sounds	LP	Radar	RAD13	1978	£12	£5	
Reverberation	7" EP	Riviera	231240	1966	£750	£500	French, best auctioned

THIRTY SECOND TURN OFF

Thirty Second Turn Off	LP	Jay Boy	JSL1	1969	£40	£20	

THIRTY-FIRST OF FEBRUARY

Butch Trucks, one of the two drummers in the Allman Brothers Band, played in this band previously, while guitarist Scott Boyer went on to play with the sub-Allmans group, Cowboy.

Thirty-First Of February	LP	Vanguard	(S)VRL19045	1969	£30	£15	

THIS DRIFTIN'S GOTTA STOP

This Driftin's Gotta Stop	LP	private		197–	£30	£15	

THIS HEAT

Deceit	LP	Rough Trade	ROUGH26	1981	£10	£4	
Health And Efficiency	12"	Piano	THIS1201	1980	£10	£5	
This Heat	LP	Piano	THIS1	1979	£12	£5	

THIS MORTAL COIL

Come Here My Love	10"	4AD	BAD608	1986	£6	£2.50	

Extracts From Blood	CD-s	4AD	TMC1CD	1991	**£20**	**£10**	*promo*

THIS 'N' THAT

Someday	7"	Mercury	MF938	1966	**£10**	**£5**	

THOLLOT, JACQUES

Quand Le Son Devient Trop Aigu	LP	Futura	24	1971	**£10**	**£4**	*French*

THOMAS, B. J.

B. J. Thomas And The Triumphs	LP	Pacemaker	PLP3001	196–	**£20**	**£8**	*US*
Very Best Of B. J. Thomas	LP	Hickory	LP(S)133	1966	**£12**	**£5**	*US*

THOMAS, CARLA

B-a-b-y	7"	Atlantic	584042	1966	**£4**	**£1.50**	
Best Of Carla Thomas	LP	Atlantic	SD8232	1969	**£15**	**£6**	*US*
Carla	LP	Stax	589004	1967	**£15**	**£6**	
Comfort Me	7"	Atlantic	AT4074	1966	**£4**	**£1.50**	
Comfort Me	LP	Stax	ST(S)706	1966	**£20**	**£8**	*US*
Gee Whiz	7"	London	HLK9310	1961	**£10**	**£5**	
Gee Whiz	LP	Atlantic	8057	1961	**£40**	**£20**	*US*
I Like What You're Doing To Me	7"	Stax	STAX112	1969	**£4**	**£1.50**	
I'll Bring It On Home To You	7"	London	HLK9618	1962	**£8**	**£4**	
I'll Never Stop Loving	7"	Kent	6T7	1991	**£10**	**£5**	
I've Got No Time To Lose	7"	Atlantic	AT4005	1964	**£5**	**£2**	
Let Me Be Good To You	7"	Atlantic	584011	1966	**£4**	**£1.50**	
Love Means	LP	Stax	2363023	1972	**£10**	**£4**	
Love Of My Own	7"	London	HLK9359	1961	**£8**	**£4**	
Memphis Queen	LP	Stax	SXATS2019	1969	**£15**	**£6**	
Memphis Queen	LP	Stax	2363004	1971	**£10**	**£4**	
Pick Up The Pieces	7"	Stax	601032	1968	**£4**	**£1.50**	
Queen Alone	LP	Stax	589012	1967	**£15**	**£6**	
Something Good	7"	Stax	601002	1967	**£4**	**£1.50**	
When Tomorrow Comes	7"	Stax	601008	1967	**£4**	**£1.50**	
Where Do I Go	7"	Stax	STAX103	1968	**£4**	**£1.50**	

THOMAS, CHARLIE

I'm Gonna Take You Home	7"	EMI	INT506	1975	**£5**	**£2**	

THOMAS, CLAUDETTE

Roses Are Red My Love	7"	Caltone	TONE116	1968	**£8**	**£4**	

THOMAS, CREEPY JOHN

Creepy John Thomas	LP	RCA	SF8061	1969	**£40**	**£20**	
Ride A Rainbow	7"	RCA	RCA1912	1970	**£6**	**£2.50**	

THOMAS, DAVID

Didn't Have A Very Good Time	7"	Recommended	REDT7	1983	**£8**	**£4**	*1 side painted*

THOMAS, DOC GROUP

The rare LP recorded in Italy by the British Doc Thomas Group achieves its high value by virtue of its connection with Mott the Hoople, whose guitarist Mick Ralphs and bassist Pete (Overend) Watts played in the earlier band. There was, incidentally, no Mr Thomas.

Doc Thomas Group	LP	Interrecord	ILP280	1966	**£125**	**£62.50**	*Italian*

THOMAS, GENE

Baby's Gone	7"	United Artists	UP1047	1964	**£10**	**£5**	

THOMAS, IRMA

Don't Mess With My Man	7"	Sue	WI372	1965	**£15**	**£7.50**	
I'm Gonna Cry Till My Tears Run Dry	7"	Liberty	LIB66106	1965	**£12**	**£6**	
It's A Man's Woman's World	7"	Liberty	LIB66178	1966	**£5**	**£2**	
Live	LP	Island	HELP29	1976	**£10**	**£4**	
Some Things You Never Get Used To	7"	Liberty	LIB66095	1965	**£10**	**£5**	
Take A Look	7"	Liberty	LIB66137	1966	**£15**	**£7.50**	
Take A Look	LP	Minit	MLL/MLS40004	1966	**£30**	**£15**	
Time Is On My Side	7"	Liberty	LIB66041	1964	**£15**	**£7.50**	
Time Is On My Side	7" EP	Liberty	LEP4035	1965	**£30**	**£15**	
True True Love	7"	Liberty	LIB66080	1965	**£6**	**£2.50**	
Wish Someone Would Care	7"	Liberty	LIB66013	1964	**£10**	**£5**	
Wish Someone Would Care	LP	Imperial	LP9266/12266	1964	**£30**	**£15**	*US*

THOMAS, JAMO

I Spy (For The FBI)	7"	Polydor	56709	1966	**£5**	**£2**	
I Spy (For The FBI)	7"	Polydor	56755	1969	**£4**	**£1.50**	
I'll Be Your Fool	7"	Chess	CRS8098	1969	**£5**	**£2**	

THOMAS, JIMMY

Beautiful Night	7"	Parlophone	R5773	1969	**£75**	**£37.50**	*demo*
Beautiful Night	7"	Parlophone	R5773	1969	**£100**	**£50**	

THOMAS, KID

Victory Walk	LP	77	LA1226	1964	**£10**	**£4**	

THOMAS, LEON

Blues And Soulful Truth	LP	Philips	6369417	1973	**£12**	**£5**	
Facets – The Legend Of Leon Thomas	LP	Flying Dutchman	FD10164	1973	**£10**	**£4**	*US*

THOMAS, NICKY

If I Had A Hammer	7"	Trojan	TR7807	1970	£4	£1.50	
Love Of The Common People	LP	Trojan	TBL143	1970	£10	£4	

THOMAS, RUFUS

Can Your Monkey Do The Dog	7"	London	HLK9850	1964	£6	£2.50	
Crown Prince Of Dance	LP	Stax	STX1004	1974	£10	£4	
Did You Hear Me?	LP	Stax	2362028	1972	£15	£6	
Do The Dog	7" EP	Atlantic	AET6001	1964	£20	£10	
Doing The Push And Pull	LP	Stax	2362010	1971	£15	£6	
Down To My House	7"	Stax	601020	1968	£4	£1.50	
Funky Chicken	LP	Stax	SXATS1033	1970	£12	£5	
Funky Chicken	LP	Stax	2363001	1971	£10	£4	
Greasy Spoon	7"	Stax	601013	1967	£4	£1.50	
Jump Back	7"	Atlantic	AT4009	1964	£5	£2	
Jump Back	7"	Atlantic	584089	1967	£4	£1.50	
Jump Back With Rufus Thomas	7" EP	Atlantic	AET6011	1965	£25	£12.50	
Memphis Train	7"	Stax	601037	1968	£4	£1.50	
Somebody Stole My Dog	7"	London	HLK9884	1964	£6	£2.50	
Walking The Dog	7"	London	HLK9799	1963	£10	£5	
Walking The Dog	LP	London	HAK8183	1964	£30	£15	
Willy Nilly	7"	Atlantic	584029	1966	£4	£1.50	

THOMAS, TIMMY

Why Can't We Live Together	LP	Mojo	2956002	1973	£10	£4	

THOMAS, VAUGHAN

Vaughan Thomas	LP	Jam	JAL101	1972	£15	£6	

THOMOPOULOUS, ANDREAS

Born Out Of The Tears Of The Sun	LP	Mushroom	150MR4	1971	£75	£37.50	
So Long Suzanne	7"	Mushroom		1970	£40	£20	
Songs Of The Street	LP	Mushroom	100MR1	1970	£75	£37.50	

THOMPSON, BOBBY

That's How Strong My Love Is	7"	Jolly	JY001	1968	£5	£2	
That's How Strong My Love Is	7"	Columbia	DB113	1969	£4	£1.50	

THOMPSON, CHRIS

Chris Thompson	LP	Village Thing	VTS21	1973	£15	£6	

THOMPSON, DON

Don Thompson	LP	Sunday		1975	£125	£62.50	US

THOMPSON, EDDIE

His Master's Jazz	LP	Tempo	TAP24	1960	£25	£10	
Piano Moods	LP	Ember	EMB3303	1960	£10	£4	

THOMPSON, ERIC

Magic Roundabout No. 1	7" EP	CBS	EP6398	1968	£5	£2	
Magic Roundabout No. 2	7" EP	CBS	EP6399	1968	£5	£2	

THOMPSON, HANK

Anybody's Girl	7"	Capitol	CL15014	1959	£4	£1.50	
At The Golden Nugget	LP	Capitol	(S)T1632	1962	£10	£4	
Dance Ranch	LP	Capitol	T975	1958	£15	£6	US
Favorite Waltzes	LP	Capitol	T1111	1959	£12	£5	US
Favorites	LP	Capitol	T911	1957	£15	£6	US
Favourite Waltzes	7" EP	Capitol	EAP11111	1959	£6	£2.50	
Gathering Flowers	7"	Capitol	CL14945	1958	£5	£2	
Hank	7" EP	Capitol	EAP1826	1957	£8	£4	
Hank	LP	Capitol	T826	1957	£15	£6	US
Hank Thompson Favorites	10" LP	Capitol	H911	1956	£25	£10	US
Honey, Honey Bee Ball	7"	Capitol	CL14517	1956	£8	£4	
I Guess I'm Getting Over You	7"	Capitol	CL15074	1959	£4	£1.50	
I'm Not Mad, Just Hurt	7"	Capitol	CL14668	1956	£6	£2.50	
I've Run Out Of Tomorrows	7"	Capitol	CL14961	1958	£4	£1.50	
Li'l Liza Jane	7"	Capitol	CL14869	1958	£6	£2.50	
Most Of All	LP	Capitol	(S)T1360	1960	£12	£5	US
New Recordings Of Hank's All-Time Hits	10" LP	Capitol	H729	1956	£25	£10	US
New Recordings Of Hank's All-Time Hits	LP	Capitol	T729	1956	£20	£8	US
North Of The Rio Grande	10" LP	Capitol	H618	1955	£25	£10	US
North Of The Rio Grande	LP	Capitol	T618	1956	£20	£8	US
Six Pack To Go	7"	Capitol	CL15114	1960	£8	£4	
Songs For Rounders	LP	Capitol	(S)T1246	1959	£10	£4	
Songs Of The Brazos Valley	10" LP	Capitol	H418	1953	£25	£10	US
Songs Of The Brazos Valley	LP	Capitol	T418	1956	£20	£8	US
Songs Of The Brazos Valley No. 1	7" EP	Capitol	EAP1028	1956	£8	£4	
This Broken Heart Of Mine	LP	Capitol	(S)T1469	1960	£10	£4	

THOMPSON, HAYDEN

Title	Format	Label	Cat. No.	Year	Mint	VG	Notes
Here's Hayden Thompson	LP	Kapp	KL1507/KS3507	1966	**£12**	**£5**	*US*

THOMPSON, JOHNNY & THE ONE-EYED JACKS

Title	Format	Label	Cat. No.	Year	Mint	VG	Notes
For Us There'll Be No Tomorrow	7"	Ember	EMBS206	1965	**£5**	**£2**	*picture sleeve*

THOMPSON, KAY

Title	Format	Label	Cat. No.	Year	Mint	VG	Notes
Eloise	7"	London	HLA8268	1956	**£15**	**£7.50**	
Kay Thompson	LP	MGM	E3146	195–	**£15**	**£6**	*US*

THOMPSON, LUCKY

Title	Format	Label	Cat. No.	Year	Mint	VG	Notes
But Not For Me	7"	Vogue	V2388	1956	**£5**	**£2**	
Lucky Thompson	LP	HMV	CLP1237	1958	**£25**	**£10**	
Recorded In Paris '56	10" LP	Ducretet-Thomson	D93098	1956	**£20**	**£8**	
With The Gerard Pochonet Orchestra	LP	Vogue	LAE12022	1956	**£20**	**£8**	

THOMPSON, MAYO

Title	Format	Label	Cat. No.	Year	Mint	VG	Notes
Corky's Debt To His Father	LP	Texas Revolution	CFS2270	1970	**£40**	**£20**	*US*

THOMPSON, MIKE

Title	Format	Label	Cat. No.	Year	Mint	VG	Notes
Rocksteady Wedding	7"	Island	WI3090	1967	**£10**	**£5**	

THOMPSON, MOLLIE

Title	Format	Label	Cat. No.	Year	Mint	VG	Notes
Song Notes Sing From Worlds Afar	LP	Asteroid	JH101	1966	**£30**	**£15**	

THOMPSON, RICHARD

Since leaving Fairport Convention, Richard Thompson has matured, not only into a songwriter of particularly fine material, but also into a brilliant and highly individual guitarist. Inevitably, a man who is a major but not especially fashionable talent had trouble in the eighties in finding suitable recording contracts. The relative scarcity of the *Strict Tempo* album is an immediate consequence of this. Happily, Thompson's fortunes have risen in recent years, and following a run of superb albums for Capitol (it is remarkable enough that any rock musician should make the best music of his career over twenty years after starting it) his profile is higher than it has ever been.

Title	Format	Label	Cat. No.	Year	Mint	VG	Notes
First Light	LP	Chrysalis	CHR1177	1978	**£10**	**£4**	*with Linda Thompson*
Guitar, Vocal	LP	Island	ICD8	1976	**£15**	**£6**	*double*
Henry The Human Fly	LP	Island	ILPS9197	1972	**£12**	**£5**	
Hokey Pokey	LP	Island	ILPS9305	1974	**£10**	**£4**	*with Linda Thompson*
I Feel So Good	CD-s	Capitol	CDCL617	1991	**£5**	**£2**	
I Want To See The Bright Lights Tonight	LP	Island	ILPS9266	1974	**£10**	**£4**	*with Linda Thompson*
Live	CD	Capitol		1992	**£25**	**£10**	*US promo*
Official Live Tour 1975	LP	Island		1975	**£100**	**£50**	*test pressing*
Pour Down Like Silver	LP	Island	ILPS9348	1975	**£10**	**£4**	*with Linda Thompson*
Read About Love	CD-s	Capitol	CDCL638	1991	**£5**	**£2**	
Reckless Kind	CD-s	Capitol	CDCL550	1989	**£5**	**£2**	
Strict Tempo	LP	Elixir	LP1	1981	**£10**	**£4**	
Sunny Vista	LP	Chrysalis	CHR1247	1979	**£10**	**£4**	*with Linda Thompson*
Watching The Dark	CD	Ryko	VRCD5303	1991	**£20**	**£8**	*US promo sampler*

THOMPSON, ROY

Title	Format	Label	Cat. No.	Year	Mint	VG	Notes
Sookie Sookie	7"	Columbia	DB8108	1967	**£5**	**£2**	

THOMPSON, SIR CHARLES

Title	Format	Label	Cat. No.	Year	Mint	VG	Notes
Allstars With Charlie Parker	10" LP	Vogue	LDE032	1953	**£60**	**£30**	
And His Band Featuring Coleman Hawkins	10" LP	Vanguard	PPT12011	1956	**£40**	**£20**	
Sir Charles Thompson Quartet	10" LP	Vanguard	PPT12007	1956	**£30**	**£15**	
Sir Charles Thompson Trio	10" LP	Vanguard	PPT12020	1958	**£30**	**£15**	

THOMPSON, SONNY

Title	Format	Label	Cat. No.	Year	Mint	VG	Notes
Houseful Of Blues	78	Esquire	10320	1953	**£12**	**£6**	
Mellow Blues For The Late Hours	LP	King	655	1959	**£40**	**£20**	*US*
Moody Blues	LP	King	568	1956	**£50**	**£25**	*US*
Real Real Fine	78	Vogue	V2143	1952	**£12**	**£6**	
Screamin' Boogie	78	Esquire	10339	1953	**£12**	**£6**	
Screaming Boogie	7"	Starlite	ST45008	1960	**£150**	**£75**	

THOMPSON, SUE

Title	Format	Label	Cat. No.	Year	Mint	VG	Notes
Bad Boy	7"	Hickory	451255	1964	**£5**	**£2**	
Big Daddy	7"	Hickory	451240	1964	**£4**	**£1.50**	
Have A Good Time	7"	Polydor	NH66979	1962	**£4**	**£1.50**	
I Like Your Kind Of Love	7"	Polydor	NH66989	1963	**£5**	**£2**	*with Bob Luman*
I'm Looking For A World	7"	Hickory	451359	1965	**£4**	**£1.50**	
It's Break-Up Time	7"	Hickory	451328	1965	**£5**	**£2**	
James	7"	Fontana	267244TF	1962	**£5**	**£2**	
Norman	7"	Polydor	NH66973	1962	**£5**	**£2**	
Paper Tiger	7"	Hickory	451284	1965	**£4**	**£1.50**	
Paper Tiger	LP	Hickory	LPM102	1964	**£20**	**£8**	
Sad Movies	7"	Polydor	NH66967	1961	**£5**	**£2**	
Sue Thompson Story	LP	DJM	DJD28024	1976	**£12**	**£5**	*double*
Two Of A Kind	7"	Polydor	NH66976	1962	**£4**	**£1.50**	

What's Wrong Billy	7"	Polydor	NH66987	1963	£4	£1.50	
Willie Can	7"	Fontana	267262TF	1963	£4	£1.50	

THOMPSON TWINS

Into The Gap	CD	Arista	610106	1984	£15	£6	
Live	LP	fan club		1986	£25	£10	*autographed*
Quickstep And Sidekick	CD	Arista	610183	1984	£25	£10	
Roll Over	12"	Arista	TWINS128	1985	£30	£15	
Roll Over	7"	Arista	TWIN8	1985	£25	£12.50	
She's In Love With Mystery	7"	Latent	LATE1	1980	£5	£2	
Squares And Triangles	7"	Dirty Discs	RANK1	1980	£5	£2	

THORN, GUNILLA

Merry Go Round	7"	HMV	POP1239	1963	£60	£30	

THORNE, DAVID

Alley Cat Songster	LP	Stateside	SL10036	1963	£20	£8	
What Will I Tell My Heart	7" EP	Stateside	SE1020	1964	£5	£2	

THORNE, WOODY

Sadie Lou	7"	Vogue	V9202	1962	£250	£150	

THORNHILL, CLAUDE

Claude On A Cloud	LP	Brunswick	LAT827-/ STA3003	1959	£10	£4	
Dream Music	10" LP	London	HAPB1021	1954	£25	£10	
Goes Modern	10" LP	London	HAPB1019	1954	£25	£10	
Goes Modern	7" EP	London	REP1009	1954	£10	£5	
Pussyfooting	7"	London	HL8042	1954	£20	£10	

THORNTON, EDDIE

Baby Be My Gal	7"	Instant	IN003	1969	£5	£2	

THORNTON, FRADKIN & UNGER

Pass On This Side	LP	ESP-Disk	63019	1968	£25	£10	*US*

THORNTON, WILLIE MAE (BIG MAMA)

Hound Dog	78	Vogue	V2284	1954	£25	£12.50	
Stronger Than Dirt	LP	Mercury	SMCL20176	1969	£12	£5	
Tom Cat	7"	Sue	WI345	1964	£75	£37.50	
Way It Is	LP	Mercury	SRM161249	1970	£12	£5	*US*

THOR'S HAMMER

If You Knew	7"	Parlophone	DP567	1966	£100	£50	*export*
Once	7"	Parlophone	DP565	1966	£100	£50	*export*
Thor's Hammer	7" EP	Parlophone	CGEP62	1966	£600	£400	*export, with bonus 7", best auctioned*
Thor's Hammer	LP	Metronome	MLP15412	1971	£125	£62.50	*Danish*

THORSON, LINDA

Here I Am	7"	Ember	EMBS257	1968	£12	£6	
Here I Am	7"	Ember	EMBS257	1968	£25	£12.50	*picture sleeve*

THORUP, PETER

Thin Slices	LP	Metronome	MLP15635	1978	£10	£4	*German*

THOUGHTS

All Night Stand	7"	Planet	PLF118	1966	£50	£25	

THOUGHTS AND WORDS

Thoughts And Words	LP	Liberty	LBL83224	1969	£10	£4	

THOUSAND YARD STARE

Strange	12"	Stifled Aardvark	AARD6T	1991	£6	£2.50	*1 sided*
Weatherwatching	12"	Stifled Aardvark	AARD003	1990	£6	£2.50	*with insert*

THRASHING DOVES

Angel Visit	CD-s	A&M	CDEE497	1989	£5	£2	
Another Deadly Sunset	CD-s	A&M	CDEE523	1989	£5	£2	
Lorelei	CD-s	A&M	CDEE511	1989	£5	£2	
Reprobate's Hymn	CD-s	A&M	CDEE479	1989	£5	£2	

THREADS OF LIFE

Threads Of Life	LP	Alco	ALC530	1972	£400	£250	

THREE BARRY SISTERS

Jo Jo The Dog Faced Boy	7"	Decca	F11141	1959	£4	£1.50	
Little Boy Blue	7"	Decca	F11099	1959	£4	£1.50	
Tall Paul	7"	Decca	F11118	1959	£4	£1.50	

THREE BELLS

Cry No More	7"	Columbia	DB7980	1966	£4	£1.50	
Softly In The Night	7"	Columbia	DB7399	1964	£5	£2	

THREE CHUCKLES

Runaround	7"	HMV	7M292	1955	£20	£10	

Three Chuckles	LP	Vik	LX1067	1956	**£60**	**£30**	*US*
Times Two, I Love You	7"	HMV	7M333	1955	**£15**	**£7.50**	
We're Gonna Rock Tonight	7"	HMV	POP292	1957	**£100**	**£50**	

THREE CITY FOUR

Smoke And Dust	LP	CBS	63039	1967	**£100**	**£50**	
Three City Four	LP	Decca	LK4705	1965	**£125**	**£62.50**	

THREE CROWS

At The Junction	LP	private	JNC1	1973	**£25**	**£10**	

THREE D

Never	7"	RAK	RAKH377	1984	**£5**	**£2**	*1 sided hologram disc*

THREE DEGREES

Close Your Eyes	7"	Stateside	SS459	1965	**£25**	**£12.50**	
Gee Baby I'm Sorry	7"	Stateside	SS413	1965	**£10**	**£5**	
Three Degrees	LP	Mojo	2916002	1971	**£10**	**£4**	

THREE DOG NIGHT

It Ain't Easy	LP	Dunhill	DS50078	1970	**£15**	**£6**	*US, nude group on cover*

THREE DOLLS

Living End	7"	MGM	MGM958	1957	**£4**	**£1.50**	

THREE FLAMES

At The Bon Soir	LP	Mercury	MG20239	1957	**£15**	**£6**	*US*

THREE GOOD REASONS

Nowhere Man	7"	Mercury	MF899	1966	**£4**	**£1.50**	

THREE JOHNS

English White Boy Engineer	7"	CNT	CNT003	1982	**£5**	**£2**	
Pink Headed Bug	7"	CNT	CNT011	1983	**£4**	**£1.50**	

THREE MAN ARMY

Mahesha	LP	Polydor	2310241	1974	**£30**	**£15**	*German*
Third Of A Lifetime	LP	Pegasus	PEG3	1971	**£25**	**£10**	
Three Man Army	LP	Reprise	K44254	1973	**£20**	**£8**	
Three Man Army 2	LP	Reprise	K54015	1974	**£25**	**£10**	

THREE SOUNDS

Black Orchid	LP	Blue Note	BLP/BST84155	1963	**£20**	**£8**	
Coldwater Flat	LP	Blue Note	BST84285	1968	**£10**	**£4**	
Elegant Soul	LP	Blue Note	BST84301	1968	**£10**	**£4**	
Feelin' Good	LP	Blue Note	BLP/BST84072	1961	**£30**	**£15**	
Gene Harris And The Three Sounds	LP	Blue Note	BST84378	1970	**£10**	**£4**	
Here We Come	LP	Blue Note	BLP/BST84088	1961	**£25**	**£10**	
Hey There!	LP	Blue Note	BLP/BST84102	1962	**£25**	**£10**	
It Just Got To Be	LP	Blue Note	BLP/BST84120	1963	**£25**	**£10**	
Live At The Lighthouse	LP	Blue Note	BLP/BST84265	1967	**£15**	**£6**	
Moods	LP	Blue Note	BLP/BST84044	196–	**£25**	**£10**	
Out Of This World	LP	Blue Note	BLP/BST84197	1965	**£20**	**£8**	
Soul Symphony	LP	Blue Note	BST84341	1969	**£10**	**£4**	
Vibrations	LP	Blue Note	BLP/BST84248	1966	**£20**	**£8**	

THREE SOUNDS (2)

Makin' Bread Again	7"	Liberty	LBF15062	1968	**£4**	**£1.50**	

THREE STOOGES

Sing For Kids	LP	Vocalion	VL73823	1968	**£15**	**£6**	*US*

THREE SUNS

High Fi And Wide	LP	RCA	LPM1249	1956	**£15**	**£6**	*US*
Midnight For Two	LP	RCA	LPM1333	1957	**£15**	**£6**	*US*
Soft And Sweet	LP	RCA	LPM1041	1955	**£15**	**£6**	*US*

THREE TOPS

Do It Right	7"	Treasure Isle	TI7008	1967	**£10**	**£5**	
Great Train In '68	7"	Coxsone	CS7051	1968	**£10**	**£5**	
It's Raining	7"	Trojan	TR003	1967	**£10**	**£5**	
Moving To Progress	7"	Studio One	SO2023	1967	**£12**	**£6**	

THREE WISE MEN

Thanks For Christmas	7"	Virgin	VS642	1983	**£6**	**£2.50**	

THREE'S A CROWD

Look Around The Corner	7"	Fontana	TF673	1966	**£8**	**£4**	

THRESHOLD OF PLEASURE

Rain, Rain, Rain	7"	Decca	F12785	1968	**£4**	**£1.50**	

THRICE MICE

Thrice Mice	LP	Philips	6305104	1970	**£20**	**£8**	*German*

THRILLINGTON, PERCY 'THRILLS'

Title	Format	Label	Cat. No.	Year	Price	Price	Notes
Thrillington	LP	Regal Zonophone	EMC3175	1975	**£150**	**£75**	
Uncle Albert, Admiral Halsey	7"	EMI	EMI2594	1977	**£40**	**£20**	

THRILLS

Title	Format	Label	Cat. No.	Year	Price	Price	Notes
No One	7"	Capitol	CL15469	1966	**£30**	**£15**	

THROBBING GRISTLE

Throbbing Gristle emerged at about the same time as punk, yet their music was more profoundly revolutionary than anything produced by the Sex Pistols or their colleagues. Designed to counterpoint the squalor and cruelty that the group saw in late twentieth century city life, Throbbing Gristle's music consisted of ugly and angry sound, with none of the melodic or rhythmic landmarks that are normally taken for granted. Due to the group's habit of taping all their live performances, the amount of available Throbbing Gristle material is vast and much of it has become very collectable.

Title	Format	Label	Cat. No.	Year	Price	Price	Notes
24 Hours	cass	Industrial	IRC1-24	198–	**£175**	**£87.50**	*26 tapes in case with inserts*
Adrenalin	7"	Industrial	IR0015	1980	**£6**	**£2.50**	*polythene bag, picture sleeve*
Assume Power Focus	LP	Cause For Concern	POWER FOCUS001	1982	**£40**	**£20**	
Best Of Vol. 2	cass	Industrial	IR0001	1975	**£50**	**£25**	
Boxed Set	LP	Fetish	FX001	1981	**£75**	**£37.50**	*5 LPs, booklet, badge*
D.o.A. The Third And Final Report	LP	Industrial	IR0004	1978	**£15**	**£6**	*with calendar and postcard*
D.o.A. The Third And Final Report	LP	Industrial	IR0004	1979	**£10**	**£4**	*16 equal length tracks*
Discipline	12"	Fetish	FET006	1981	**£10**	**£5**	
Editions Frankfurt–Berlin	LP	Svensk Illuminated	SJAMS31	1983	**£15**	**£6**	
Führer Der Menscheit	10"	American Phonogram	1JAPSO36	1983	**£12**	**£5**	
Führer Der Menscheit	10"	Bundestag-rücksache	29681	1982	**£15**	**£6**	*some orange vinyl*
Funeral In Berlin	LP	Zensor	ZENSOR01	1981	**£15**	**£6**	*German*
Greatest Hits – Entertainment Through Pain	LP	Rough Trade	ROUGHUS23	1981	**£10**	**£4**	
Heathen Earth	LP	Industrial	IR0009	1980	**£10**	**£4**	
Heathen Earth	LP	Industrial	IR0009	1980	**£50**	**£25**	*blue vinyl*
Journey Through A Body	LP	Walter Ulbricht	ST3382	1982	**£20**	**£8**	
Mission Is Terminated	LP + 12"	Nice	EX39LY2	1983	**£15**	**£6**	*with booklet*
Music From The Death Factory	LP	Death	01	1982	**£75**	**£37.50**	
Once Upon A Time	LP	Casual Abandon	CAS1J	1984	**£10**	**£4**	
Second Annual Report	LP	Industrial	IR0002	1977	**£50**	**£25**	*with questionnaire*
Second Annual Report	LP	Fetish	FET2001	1979	**£10**	**£4**	*glossy sleeve*
Second Annual Report	LP	Fetish	FET2001	1981	**£15**	**£6**	*backwards version, 2 sleeves*
Second Annual Report	LP	Fetish	FET2001	1978	**£15**	**£6**	*with questionnaire, insert*
Subhuman	7"	Industrial	IR0013	1980	**£6**	**£2.50**	*polythene bag, picture sleeve*
Thee Psychick Sacrifice	LP	Karnage	KILL1	1982	**£15**	**£6**	*double*
Twenty Jazz Funk Greats	LP	Industrial	IR0008	1979	**£15**	**£6**	*with poster*
Twenty Jazz Funk Greats	LP	Industrial	IR0008	1979	**£10**	**£4**	
United	7"	Industrial	IR0003	1978	**£5**	**£2**	
United	7"	Industrial	IR0003	1980	**£10**	**£5**	*extended B side, white or clear vinyl*
We Hate You Little Girls	7"	Sordide Sentimentale	SS45001	1979	**£50**	**£25**	*A4 sleeve, numbered*

THROWING MUSES

Title	Format	Label	Cat. No.	Year	Price	Price	Notes
Dizzy	CD-s	4AD	BAD903CD	1989	**£5**	**£2**	
Firepile	12"	4AD	MUSETWO	1992	**£6**	**£2.50**	*promo*
Red Heaven	CD	4AD	CADD2013	1992	**£15**	**£6**	*double*
Red Heaven	LP	4AD	CADD2013	1993	**£12**	**£5**	*with live Kristin Hersh LP*
University	CD	4AD	CADD5002CD	1995	**£15**	**£6**	*with postcards*

THUNDER, JOHNNY

Title	Format	Label	Cat. No.	Year	Price	Price	Notes
Loop De Loop	LP	Stateside	SL10029	1963	**£20**	**£8**	

THUNDER

Title	Format	Label	Cat. No.	Year	Price	Price	Notes
Backstreet Symphony	CD-s	EMI	CDEM137	1990	**£5**	**£2**	
Better Man	CD-s	EMI	CDBETTER1	1993	**£5**	**£2**	
Dirty Love	7"	EMI	EMPD126	1990	**£5**	**£2**	*shaped picture disc*
Dirty Love	CD-s	EMI	CDEM126	1990	**£5**	**£2**	
Gimme Some Lovin'	CD-s	EMI	CDEM148	1990	**£5**	**£2**	
She's So Fine	7"	EMI	EMS11	1989	**£4**	**£1.50**	*with patch*
She's So Fine	CD-s	EMI	CDEM158	1990	**£5**	**£2**	
She's So Fine	CD-s	EMI	CDEM111	1989	**£5**	**£2**	

THUNDER AND ROSES

King Of The Black Sunrise	LP	United Artists	UAS6709	1969	**£30**	**£15**	*US*

THUNDER COMPANY (BRIAN BENNETT)

Riding On The Gravy Train	7"	Columbia	DB8706	1970	**£20**	**£10**	

THUNDERBIRDS

Ayuh Ayuh	7"	London	HL8146	1955	**£60**	**£30**	

THUNDERBIRDS (2)

New Orleans Beat	7"	Oriole	CB1625	1961	**£8**	**£4**	
Wild Weekend	7"	Oriole	CB1610	1961	**£8**	**£4**	

THUNDERBIRDS (3)

Your Ma Said You Cried	7"	Polydor	56710	1966	**£30**	**£15**	

THUNDERBIRDS (4)

Meet The Fabulous Thunderbirds	LP	Red Feather	TH1	1964	**£200**	**£100**	*US*

THUNDERBOLTS

Fugitive	7"	Decca	F11522	1962	**£5**	**£2**	

THUNDERBOYS

Fashion	7"	Recent	EJSP9339	1980	**£5**	**£2**	

THUNDERCLAP NEWMAN

For a group not particularly intended to be a novelty outfit, Thunderclap Newman was one of the oddest ever to top the charts. Andy Newman, after whom the group was named, was a middle-aged pianist, whose passion was the traditional jazz of Bix Beiderbecke rather than anything to do with rock. Guitarist Jimmy McCulloch, on the other hand, was just sixteen years old. In between came John 'Speedy' Keene, a moderately talented singer-songwriter, with one dynamite song to his name, 'Something In The Air'. The song was a well-deserved number one hit (and was revived in 1996 for a telephone company advert on television). Sadly, nothing else by the group was in the same league and even the sponsorship of the Who's Pete Townshend, who played bass on the record, could not keep the group together for more than one album.

Hollywood Dream	LP	Track	2406003	1970	**£15**	**£6**	
Peter Townshend Talks To, And About, Thunderclap Newman	LP	Track	PR160	1969	**£15**	**£6**	*US interview promo*
Something In The Air	7"	Track	604301	1969	**£4**	**£1.50**	

THUNDERPUSSY

Documents Of Captivity	LP	MRT	RL31748	1973	**£100**	**£50**	*US*

THUNDERS, JOHNNY

Dead Or Alive	7"	Real	ARE1	1978	**£8**	**£4**	*picture sleeve*
Vintage '77	12"	Jungle	JUNG5	1983	**£6**	**£2.50**	
You Can't Put Your Arms Around A Memory	7"	Real	ARE3	1978	**£6**	**£2.50**	*picture sleeve*

THUNDERTHUMBS & TOETSENMAN

Freedom	12"	Polydor	POSPX480	1982	**£12**	**£6**	
Freedom	7"	Polydor	POSP480	1982	**£10**	**£5**	

THUNDERTRAIN

Teenage Suicide	LP	Jelly	JPLP1	1977	**£12**	**£5**	

THUNDERTREE

Thundertree	LP	Roulette	SR42038	1970	**£40**	**£20**	*US*

THURSDAY'S CHILDREN

Just You	7"	Piccadilly	7N35276	1966	**£6**	**£2.50**	

THYRDS

The Thyrds did well in the *Ready Steady Go* beat group competition won by the Bo Street Runners, but were no more able than the winners to launch any kind of successful career from the exposure. The two issues of 'Hide 'n' Seek' are different recordings, with different songs on the two B sides.

Hide 'n' Seek	7"	Decca	F12010	1964	**£25**	**£12.50**	
Hide 'n' Seek	7"	Oak	RGJ133	1964	**£150**	**£75**	

TIARAS

You Told Me	7"	Warner Bros	WB92	1963	**£5**	**£2**	

TIBET

Tibet	LP	Bellaphon	BBS2581	1978	**£25**	**£10**	*German*

TICH & QUACKERS

Santa Bring Me Ringo	7"	Oriole	CB1980	1965	**£4**	**£1.50**	

TICKAWINDA

With scarce folk albums attracting increasing collectors' interest these days, the private pressing made by Tickawinda earns its high value through a combination of real rarity with easily likeable songwriting and performance. That the group also contained the talents of Clive Gregson – later to be heard with Any Trouble, Richard Thompson and the Clive Gregson-Christine Collister duo – comes as a bonus.

Rosemary Lane	LP	Pennine	PSS153	1975	**£300**	**£180**	

TICKET

Awake	LP	Atlantic	SD1008	1972	**£125**	**£62.50**	*Australian*

TICKLE

Subway	7"	Regal Zonophone	RZ3004	1967	**£125**	**£62.50**	

TICO & THE TRIUMPHS

The group name hides the identity of the young Paul Simon.

Cards Of Love	7"	Amy	876	1963	**£30**	**£15**	*US*
Cry, Little Boy, Cry	7"	Amy	860	1962	**£20**	**£10**	*US*
Express Train	7"	Amy	845	1962	**£20**	**£10**	*US*
Motorcycle	7"	Amy	835	1962	**£20**	**£10**	*US*
Motorcycle	7"	Madison	169	1961	**£20**	**£10**	*US*

TIDAL WAVE

Spider Spider	7"	Storm	PD9616	1969	**£10**	**£5**	
With Tears In My Eyes	7"	Decca	F22973	1969	**£5**	**£2**	

TIDE

Almost Live	LP	Mouth	7237	1971	**£60**	**£30**	*US*

TIEKIN, FREDDIE & THE ROCKERS

By Popular Demand	LP	IT	2301	1957	**£20**	**£8**	*US*
Freddie Tiekin & The Rockers	LP	IT	2304	1958	**£20**	**£8**	*US*

TIELMAN BROTHERS

East–West	LP	Ariola	IHLP1	1965	**£50**	**£25**	*Dutch*
Little Bird	LP	Negram	ELS895	1969	**£20**	**£8**	*Dutch*
Live	LP	Ariola	72129	1964	**£50**	**£25**	*German*
Tielman Brothers	LP	Imperial	1015	1964	**£60**	**£30**	*Dutch*

TIERNEY, ROY

Cupid	7"	Philips	BF1159	1961	**£5**	**£2**	*picture sleeve*

TIERNEY'S FUGITIVES

Did You Want To Run Away	7"	Decca	F12247	1965	**£6**	**£2.50**	

TIETCHENS, ASMUS

Nachtstücke	LP	Egg	91040	1977	**£20**	**£8**	*French*

TIFFANIES

It's Got To Be A Great Song	7"	Chess	CRS8059	1967	**£30**	**£15**	

TIFFANY

I Know	7"	Parlophone	R5311	1965	**£4**	**£1.50**	

TIFFANY SHADE

Tiffany Shade	LP	Fontana	(S)TL5469	1968	**£40**	**£20**	

TIFFANY'S THOUGHTS

Find Out What's Happening	7"	Parlophone	R5439	1966	**£20**	**£10**	

TIGER

Souls Of Africa	7"	New Beat	NB052	1970	**£4**	**£1.50**	

TIGER (2)

Tiger	LP	Retreat	RTL6006	1976	**£25**	**£10**	

TIGER B. SMITH

Tigerrock	LP	Vertigo	6360610	1972	**£25**	**£10**	*German*
We're The Tiger Bunch	LP	Bacillus	BLPS19176Q	1974	**£15**	**£6**	*German*

TIGER LILY

The single by Tiger Lily was the first release by the group that issued all its subsequent records as Ultravox.

Monkey Jive	7"	Gull	GULS54	1977	**£6**	**£2.50**	*picture sleeve*
Monkey Jive	7"	Gull	GULS12	1975	**£20**	**£10**	*picture sleeve*
Monkey Jive	7"	Gull	GULS12	1975	**£8**	**£4**	

TIGG, JIMMY & LOUIS

Who Can I Turn To	7"	Deep Soul	DS9105	1970	**£6**	**£2.50**	

TIGHT LIKE THAT

Hokum	LP	Village Thing	VTS12	1972	**£15**	**£6**	

TIKARAM, TANITA

Cathedral Song	CD-s	WEA	YZ331CD	1989	**£5**	**£2**	
Good Tradition	CD-s	WEA	YZ196CD	1988	**£5**	**£2**	
Little Sister Leaving Town	CD-s	WEA	YZ459CDP	1990	**£5**	**£2**	*picture disc*
Twist In My Sobriety	CD-s	WEA	YZ321CD	1988	**£5**	**£2**	
World Outside Your Window	CD-s	WEA	YZ363CDX	1989	**£5**	**£2**	*boxed*

TIL TUESDAY

Believed You Were Lucky	CD-s	Epic	6530642	1989	**£5**	**£2**	

TILLIS, MEL

Mr Mel	LP	London	HAR8345	1968	**£15**	**£6**	

TILLMAN, BERTHA

Oh My Angel	7"	Oriole	CB1746	1962	**£25**	**£12.50**	

TILLOTSON, JOHNNY

Alone With You	LP	MGM	C972	1964	**£20**	**£8**	
Angel	7"	MGM	MGM1266	1964	**£4**	**£1.50**	
Cabaret	7"	MGM	MGM1393	1968	**£4**	**£1.50**	
Dreamy Eyes	7"	London	HLA9514	1962	**£4**	**£1.50**	
Earth Angel	7"	London	HLA9101	1960	**£20**	**£10**	
Funny How Time Slips Away	7"	London	HLA9811	1963	**£4**	**£1.50**	
Heartaches By The Number	7"	MGM	MGM1281	1965	**£4**	**£1.50**	
Hello Enemy	7"	MGM	MGM1300	1966	**£4**	**£1.50**	
I Can't Help It	7"	London	HLA9642	1962	**£4**	**£1.50**	
I'm Watching My Watch	7"	MGM	MGM1235	1963	**£4**	**£1.50**	
It Keeps Right On A-Hurtin'	7"	London	HLA9550	1962	**£4**	**£1.50**	
It Keeps Right On A-Hurtin'	LP	London	HAA8019	1962	**£40**	**£20**	
J.T.	7" EP	London	REA1388	1963	**£25**	**£12.50**	
Jimmy's Girl	7"	London	HLA9275	1961	**£4**	**£1.50**	
Johnny Tillotson	7" EP	London	REA1345	1962	**£20**	**£10**	
Johnny Tillotson	7" EP	MGM	MGMEP788	1963	**£20**	**£10**	
Johnny Tillotson's Best	LP	London	HAA2431	1961	**£40**	**£20**	
Johnny Tillotson's Hit Parade	7" EP	MGM	MGMEP790	1964	**£20**	**£10**	
Me Myself And I	7"	MGM	MGM1311	1966	**£4**	**£1.50**	
No Love At All	7"	MGM	MGM1319	1966	**£4**	**£1.50**	
No Love At All	LP	MGM	C(S)8025	1966	**£15**	**£6**	
Our World	7"	MGM	MGM1290	1965	**£4**	**£1.50**	
Out Of My Mind	7"	London	HLA9695	1963	**£4**	**£1.50**	
Poetry In Motion	7"	London	HLA9231	1960	**£4**	**£1.50**	
Send Me The Pillow You Dream On	7"	London	HLA9598	1962	**£4**	**£1.50**	
She Understands Me	7"	MGM	MGM1252	1964	**£4**	**£1.50**	
Sings Our World	LP	MGM	C(S)8005	1965	**£15**	**£6**	
Suffering From A Heartache	7"	MGM	MGM1247	1964	**£4**	**£1.50**	
Talk Back Trembling Lips	7"	MGM	MGM1214	1963	**£4**	**£1.50**	
Then I'll Count Again	7"	MGM	MGM1275	1965	**£4**	**£1.50**	
True True Happiness	7"	London	HLA8930	1959	**£40**	**£20**	
Why Do I Love You So	7"	London	HLA9048	1960	**£20**	**£10**	
Without You	7"	London	HLA9412	1961	**£4**	**£1.50**	
Worried Guy	7"	MGM	MGM1225	1963	**£4**	**£1.50**	
You Can Never Stop Me Loving You	LP	Cadence	CLP3067/25067	1963	**£30**	**£15**	*US*

TILSLEY ORCHESTRA

Thunderbirds Theme	7"	Fontana	TF783	1966	**£8**	**£4**	
Top TV Themes	LP	Fontana	(S)TL5411	1967	**£10**	**£4**	

TILSTON, STEVE

Acoustic Confusion	LP	Village Thing	VTS5	1971	**£25**	**£10**	
Collection	LP	Transatlantic	TRA252	1972	**£10**	**£4**	
In For A Penny In For A Pound	LP	TM	PROP4	1983	**£10**	**£4**	
Songs From The Dress Rehearsal	LP	Cornucopia	CR1	1977	**£15**	**£6**	

TIME

First Time I Saw The Sunshine	7"	Pye	7N17146	1966	**£10**	**£5**	
Take A Bit Of Notice	7"	Pye	7N17019	1965	**£30**	**£15**	

TIME (2)

Time	LP	Buk	BULP2005	1975	**£75**	**£37.50**	

T.I.M.E.

Smooth Ball	LP	Liberty	LBS83232	1969	**£25**	**£10**	
Take Me Along	7"	Liberty	LBF15082	1969	**£4**	**£1.50**	
Trust In Men Everywhere	LP	Liberty	LBS83144E	1968	**£30**	**£15**	

TIME ZONE

World Destruction	CD-s	Virgin	CDT29	1988	**£5**	**£2**	*3" single*

TIMEBOX

Timebox were an interesting soul-inflected group, several of whose songs employ touches of psychedelia to worthwhile effect. In the seventies, the group became Patto.

Baked Jam Roll In Your Eye	7"	Deram	DM246	1969	**£6**	**£2.50**	
Beggin'	7"	Deram	DM194	1968	**£6**	**£2.50**	
Don't Make Promises	7"	Deram	DM153	1967	**£6**	**£2.50**	
Girl Don't You Make Me Wait	7"	Deram	DM219	1968	**£6**	**£2.50**	
I'll Always Love You	7"	Piccadilly	7N35369	1967	**£15**	**£7.50**	
Original Moose On The Loose	LP	Cosmos	CCLPS9016	1977	**£30**	**£15**	*US*
Soul Sauce	7"	Piccadilly	7N35379	1967	**£30**	**£15**	
Yellow Van	7"	Deram	DM271	1969	**£6**	**£2.50**	

TIMELORDS

Doctorin' The Tardis	7"	KLF	KLF003P	1988	**£10**	**£5**	*shaped picture disc*
Doctorin' The Tardis	CD-s	KLF	KLFCD003	1988	**£30**	**£15**	*CD video*
Gary Glitter Joins The Jams	12"	KLF	KLF003R	1988	**£25**	**£12.50**	*picture sleeve*
Gary In The Tardis	7"	KLF	KLF003GG	1988	**£15**	**£7.50**	*promo with Gary Glitter*

TIMERS

Brian Wilson performs on the A side of this single by the Timers.

No-Go Showboat 7″ Reprise 231 1963 £**50** £**25** *US*

TIMES

Boys About Town 7″ Artpop 43DOZ 1985 £**6** £**2.50**
Boys Brigade 7″ Artpop POP46 1984 £**4** £**1.50**
Here Comes The Holidays 7″ Artpop POP50 1982 £**8** £**4**
I Helped Patrick McGoohan Escape 12″ Artpop No1 1983 £**8** £**4**
I Helped Patrick McGoohan Escape 7″ Artpop POP49 1983 £**8** £**4**
Pop Goes Art LP Artpop ART20 1981 £**10** £**4**
Pop Goes Art LP Whaam! WHAAMLP1 1982 £**20** £**8**
Red With Purple Flashes 7″ Whaam! WHAAM002 1981 £**20** £**10**

TIMES (2)

Love We Knew 7″ Columbia DB7904 1966 £**10** £**5**
Ooh Wee 7″ EP Columbia 7ES24 1965 £**50** £**25** *demo, no picture sleeve*
Think About The Times 7″ Columbia DB7804 1966 £**15** £**7.50**

TIMMONS, BOBBY

Easy Does It LP Riverside RLP363 1961 £**15** £**6**
In Person LP Riverside RLP(9)391 1961 £**15** £**6**
Moanin' 7″ Riverside 3204 1967 £**4** £**1.50**
Soul Time LP Riverside RLP(9)334 1960 £**15** £**6**
This Here Is Bobby Timmons LP Riverside RLP12317 1960 £**15** £**6**

TIMMS, SALLY & THE DRIFTING COWGIRLS

This House Is A House Of Trouble 12″ T.I.M. 12MOT6 1987 £**8** £**4**

TIMON

Bitter Thoughts Of Little Jane 7″ Pye 7N17451 1968 £**40** £**20**

TIMONEERS

Roasted Live LP WHM WHM1919 1976 £**15** £**6**

TIN HOUSE

Tin House LP Epic BN26291 1971 £**15** £**6** *Dutch*

TIN MACHINE

Prisoner Of Love 7″ EMI MTPD76 1989 £**4** £**1.50** *shaped picture disc*
Prisoner Of Love CD-s EMI CDMT76 1989 £**5** £**2**
Tin Machine CD EMI 1989 £**60** £**30** *US promo boxed set with video, cassette, biography*
Tin Machine CD-s EMI CDMT73 1989 £**5** £**2**
Under The God CD-s EMI CDMT68 1989 £**5** £**2**
You Belong In Rock'n'Roll CD-s London LOCDT305 1991 £**5** £**2** *round pack*

TIN TIN

Hold It 12″ WEA X9763T 1983 £**10** £**5** *double*
Kiss Me 12″ WEA TIN1T 1982 £**6** £**2.50**

TIN TIN (2)

Astral Taxi LP Polydor 2382080 1972 £**10** £**4**
Tin Tin LP Polydor 2384011 1969 £**10** £**4**
Toast And Marmalade 7″ Polydor 2058023 1970 £**5** £**2**

TINDERSTICKS

City Sickness CD-s This Way Up WAY1899 1993 £**8** £**4**
Kathleen CD-s This Way Up WAY2833 1994 £**8** £**4**
Live In Amsterdam 10″ LP This Way Up WAY3288 1994 £**15** £**6**
Live In Amsterdam CD This Way Up WAY3299 1994 £**20** £**8**
Live In Berlin 7″ Tippy Toe 003 1993 £**20** £**10**
Marbles 10″ Tippy Toe TIPPY-CHE2 1993 £**15** £**7.50**
Marriage Made In Heaven 7″ Rough Trade 45REV16 1993 £**15** £**7.50**
Patchwork 7″ Tippy Toe 1 1992 £**30** £**15**
Smooth Sound Of Tindersticks 7″ Sub Pop SP297 1995 £**5** £**2**
Unwired EP 7″ Domino RUG006 1993 £**10** £**5**
We Have All The Time In The World 7″ Clawfist XPIG21 1993 £**15** £**7.50** *Gallon Drunk B side*

TINGA & ERNIE

She's Gone 7″ Explosion EX2009 1969 £**5** £**2**

TINGLING MOTHER'S CIRCUS

Circus Of The Mind LP Musicor MS3167 1968 £**30** £**15** *US*

TINKERBELL'S FAIRYDUST

The records made by this obscure group are typical of the slightly psychedelic late-sixties pop that is still sought after by enthusiasts looking for that elusive lost 'masterpiece' of the period. The album is a recent discovery – at the time of writing only one copy of a demo in a finished sleeve is known to have surfaced, but others must presumably exist.

In My Magic Garden 7″ Decca F12705 1967 £**20** £**10**
Sheila's Back In Town 7″ Decca F12865 1969 £**25** £**12.50**
Tinkerbell's Fairydust LP Decca LK/SKL5028 1969 £**1000** £**700** *demo only*
Twenty Ten 7″ Decca F12778 1968 £**20** £**10**

TINKERS

Title	Format	Label	Cat. No.	Year	Mint	VG	Notes
Spring Rain	LP	Argo	ZFB35	1970	**£15**	**£6**	
Til The Wild Birds	LP	Fontana	6438020	1970	**£12**	**£5**	

TINO, BABS

Title	Format	Label	Cat. No.	Year	Mint	VG	Notes
Forgive Me	7"	London	HLR9589	1962	**£10**	**£5**	
Forgive Me	7" EP	London	RER1377	1963	**£50**	**£25**	

TINO & THE REVLONS

Title	Format	Label	Cat. No.	Year	Mint	VG	Notes
By Request At The Sway-Zee	LP	Dearborn		1966	**£60**	**£30**	*US*

TINTERN ABBEY

Title	Format	Label	Cat. No.	Year	Mint	VG	Notes
Beeside	7"	Deram	DM164	1967	**£175**	**£87.50**	

TINY TIM

Title	Format	Label	Cat. No.	Year	Mint	VG	Notes
For All My Little Friends	LP	Reprise	RS6351	1969	**£15**	**£6**	*US*
God Bless Tiny Tim	LP	Reprise	RSLP6292	1968	**£15**	**£6**	
Great Balls Of Fire	7"	Reprise	R20802	1968	**£4**	**£1.50**	
Second Album	LP	Reprise	RSLP6323	1968	**£15**	**£6**	
There'll Always Be An England	78	Reprise	RS27004	1969	**£10**	**£5**	
Tip Toe Thru The Tulips	7"	Reprise	R23258	1968	**£4**	**£1.50**	

TIP TOPS

Title	Format	Label	Cat. No.	Year	Mint	VG	Notes
Oo-Kook-A-Boo	7"	Cameo Parkway	P868	1963	**£12**	**£6**	

TIPPETT, KEITH

Title	Format	Label	Cat. No.	Year	Mint	VG	Notes
Blueprint	LP	RCA	SF8290	1972	**£30**	**£15**	
Dedicated To You But You Weren't Listening	LP	Vertigo	6360024	1971	**£25**	**£10**	*spiral label*
Frames	LP	Ogun	OGD003/4	1978	**£15**	**£6**	*double*
T 'n' T	LP	Steam	SJ104	1976	**£12**	**£5**	*with Stan Tracey*
Warm Spirits Cool Spirits	LP	Vinyl	VS101	1977	**£12**	**£5**	
You Are Here I Am There	LP	Polydor	2384004	1969	**£50**	**£25**	

TIPPETTS, JULIE

Title	Format	Label	Cat. No.	Year	Mint	VG	Notes
Sunset Glow	LP	Utopia	UTS601	1975	**£12**	**£5**	
Voice	LP	Ogun	OG110	1977	**£15**	**£6**	*with Maggie Nichols, Phil Minton, Brian Eley*

TIPPI & THE CLOVERS

Title	Format	Label	Cat. No.	Year	Mint	VG	Notes
My Heart Said	7"	Stateside	SS160	1963	**£8**	**£4**	

TIPTON, LESTER

Title	Format	Label	Cat. No.	Year	Mint	VG	Notes
This Won't Change	7"	Grapevine	GRP138	1979	**£8**	**£4**	*Masqueraders B side*

TIR NA NOG

Title	Format	Label	Cat. No.	Year	Mint	VG	Notes
Strong In The Sun	LP	Chrysalis	CHR1047	1973	**£10**	**£4**	
Tear And A Smile	LP	Chrysalis	CHR1006	1972	**£15**	**£6**	
Tir Na Nog	LP	Chrysalis	ILPS9153	1971	**£15**	**£6**	

TITANIC

Title	Format	Label	Cat. No.	Year	Mint	VG	Notes
Titanic	LP	CBS	64104	1971	**£10**	**£4**	

TITANS

Title	Format	Label	Cat. No.	Year	Mint	VG	Notes
Don't You Just Know It	7"	London	HLU8609	1958	**£60**	**£30**	
Today's Teen Beat	LP	MGM	(S)E3992	1961	**£20**	**£8**	*US*

TITUS GROAN

Title	Format	Label	Cat. No.	Year	Mint	VG	Notes
Open The Door Homer	7"	Dawn	DNX2053	1970	**£20**	**£10**	*picture sleeve*
Titus Groan	LP	Dawn	DNLS3012	1970	**£50**	**£25**	

TITUS OATS

Title	Format	Label	Cat. No.	Year	Mint	VG	Notes
Jungle Lady	LP	Lips		1974	**£150**	**£75**	*US*

TJADER, CAL

Title	Format	Label	Cat. No.	Year	Mint	VG	Notes
Best Of Cal Tjader	LP	Verve	(S)VLP9192	1968	**£15**	**£6**	
Cal Tjader Group/Don Elliott Group	LP	London	LTZC15050	1957	**£15**	**£6**	
Greatest Hits	LP	Vocalion	LAEF599	1965	**£25**	**£10**	
Hip Vibrations	LP	Verve	(S)VLP9215	1968	**£15**	**£6**	
Solar Heat	LP	Fontana	STL5527	1969	**£12**	**£5**	
Soul Sauce	7"	Verve	VS529	1965	**£15**	**£7.50**	

TOAD

Title	Format	Label	Cat. No.	Year	Mint	VG	Notes
Dreams	LP	Frog		1975	**£75**	**£37.50**	*Italian*
Toad	LP	RCA	SF8241	1972	**£125**	**£62.50**	
Tomorrow Blue	LP	Hallelujah	X626	1973	**£100**	**£50**	*Swiss*

TOAD THE WET SPROCKET

Title	Format	Label	Cat. No.	Year	Mint	VG	Notes
Pete's Punk Song	7"	Sprocket		1979	**£40**	**£20**	
Reaching For The Sky	7"	Sprockets	BRS008	1980	**£30**	**£15**	

TOADS

Title	Format	Label	Cat. No.	Year	Mint	VG	Notes
Toads	LP	Wiggins	64021	1964	**£100**	**£50**	*US*

TOBY JUG

Greasy Quiff	LP	private		1969	**£500**	**£330**	

TOBY TWIRL

Harry Faversham	7"	Decca	F12728	1968	**£15**	**£7.50**	
Movin' In	7"	Decca	F12867	1969	**£10**	**£5**	
Toffee Apple Sunday	7"	Decca	F12804	1968	**£40**	**£20**	

TODAY'S WITNESS

Today's Witness	LP	Emblem	TDR345	1972	**£30**	**£15**	

TODD, ART & DOTTIE

Chanson D'Amour	7"	London	HLB8620	1958	**£10**	**£5**	
Straight As An Arrow	7"	London	HLN8838	1959	**£10**	**£5**	

TODD, GARRY & ROGER TURNER

Sunday Best	LP	Incus	INCUS32	1979	**£10**	**£4**	

TODD, NICK

At The Hop	7"	London	HLD8537	1958	**£12**	**£6**	
Plaything	7"	London	HLD8500	1957	**£25**	**£12.50**	
Tiger	7"	London	HLD8902	1959	**£20**	**£10**	

TODD, PATSY

We Were Lovers	7"	High Note	HS012	1968	**£4**	**£1.50**	

TODD, SHARKEY & THE MONSTERS

Cool Ghoul	7"	Parlophone	R4536	1959	**£10**	**£5**	

TODD, WILF

He Took Her Away	7"	Blue Beat	BB240	1964	**£12**	**£6**	

TODD, WILF (2)

Wilf Todd's album is undoubtedly rare and it is on the collectable Oak label, but it contains quite the wrong kind of music to interest all but the most ardent of completist collectors.

Wilf Todd And His Music	LP	Oak	WT101	1966	**£12**	**£5**	

TODOROW, CAMY

Bursting At The Seams	12"	Virgin	VS81612	1985	**£20**	**£10**	
Bursting At The Seams	7"	Virgin	VS816	1985	**£10**	**£5**	

TOEFAT

Toefat's LP is most notable for its unsettling cover, showing human figures with enormous toes replacing their heads. The group was one of Cliff Bennett's attempts to revive his career after the demise of the Rebel Rousers – on this occasion he effectively took over a pre-existing band, the Gods.

Bad Side Of The Road	7"	Parlophone	R5829	1970	**£4**	**£1.50**	
Brand New Band	7"	Chapter One	CH175	1972	**£4**	**£1.50**	
Toefat	LP	Parlophone	PCS7097	1970	**£30**	**£15**	
Toefat II	LP	Regal Zonophone	SLRZ1015	1971	**£40**	**£20**	

TOGETHER

Henry's Coming Home	7"	Columbia	DB8491	1968	**£40**	**£20**	

TOGGERY FIVE

I'd Much Rather Be With The Boys	7"	Parlophone	R5249	1965	**£25**	**£12.50**	
I'm Gonna Jump	7"	Parlophone	R5175	1964	**£20**	**£10**	

TOKENS

B'wa Nina	7" EP	RCA	75701	1962	**£8**	**£4**	*French*
December 5th	LP	B.T.Puppy	BTPS1014	1971	**£12**	**£5**	*US*
Greatest Moments	LP	B.T.Puppy	BTPS1012	1970	**£12**	**£5**	*US*
He's In Town	7"	Fontana	TF500	1964	**£4**	**£1.50**	
I Hear Trumpets Blow	LP	B.T.Puppy	BTLP(S)1000	1966	**£12**	**£5**	*US*
It's A Happening World	7" EP	Warner Bros	WEP1457	1967	**£8**	**£4**	*French*
Lion Sleeps Tonight	7" EP	RCA	75688	1962	**£12**	**£6**	*French*
Lion Sleeps Tonight	LP	RCA	RD27256/SF5128	1962	**£30**	**£15**	
Tokens Again	LP	RCA	LPM/LSP3685	1966	**£12**	**£5**	*US*
Tokens Of Gold	LP	B.T.Puppy	BTPS1006	1969	**£12**	**£5**	*US*
Tonight I Fell In Love	7"	Parlophone	R4790	1961	**£5**	**£2**	
We Sing Folk	LP	RCA	SF7535	1962	**£10**	**£4**	
Wheels	LP	RCA	LPM/LST2886	1964	**£12**	**£5**	*US*

TOKYO BLADE

Cave Sessions	12"	Powerstation	LEG1T	1985	**£10**	**£5**	
Powergame	7"	Powerstation	OHM2	1983	**£5**	**£2**	

TOKYO ROSE

Dry Your Eyes	7"	Guardian	GRC270	1983	**£40**	**£20**	

TOLONEN, JUKKA

Crossection	LP	Sonet	SNTF699	1975	**£10**	**£4**	
Hook	LP	Love	LRLP113	1974	**£10**	**£4**	*Finnish*
Hysterica	LP	Love	LRLP149	1975	**£10**	**£4**	*Finnish*

Summer Games	LP	Love	LRLP91	1973	£12	£5	*Finnish*
Tolonen	LP	Sonet	SNTF652	1974	£10	£4	

TOM & JERRY

The Tom and Jerry who made the single 'Baby Talk' were Tom Graph and Jerry Landis, otherwise known (in the reverse order) as Simon and Garfunkel.

Baby Talk	7"	Big	621	1958	£40	£20	*US*
Baby Talk	7"	Gala	GSP806	1959	£20	£10	
Hey Schoolgirl	7"	King	5167	1957	£30	£15	*US*
Hey Schoolgirl	7"	Big	613	1957	£30	£15	*US*
I'll Drown In My Tears	7"	Mercury	71930	1961	£20	£10	*US*
I'm Lonesome	7"	Pye	7N25202	1963	£60	£30	
I'm Lonesome	7"	Ember	1094	1959	£30	£15	*US*
Our Song	7"	Big	616	1958	£30	£15	*US*
Surrender, Please Surrender	7"	Paramount	10363	1962	£20	£10	*US*
That's My Story	7"	Big	618	1958	£30	£15	*US*
That's My Story	7"	Hunt	319	1958	£30	£15	*US*

TOM & JERRY (2)

Johann Mouse	7" EP	MGM	MGMEP688	1958	£8	£4	

TOM & JERRYO

Boogaloo	7"	HMV	POP1435	1965	£10	£5	

TOM CATS

Tom Tom Cat	7"	Starlite	ST45054	1961	£15	£7.50	

TOMCATS (2)

A Tu Vera	7" EP	Philips	436388PE	1966	£10	£5	*Spanish*
La Neurastenia	7" EP	Philips	436826PE	1966	£20	£10	*Spanish*
Somebody Help Me	7" EP	Philips	436849PE	1966	£20	£10	*Spanish*
Yesterday	7" EP	Philips	436387PE	1966	£20	£10	*Spanish*

TOMLIN, LEE

Sweet Sweet Lovin'	7"	CBS	202455	1966	£5	£2	

TOMLINSON, ALBERT

Don't Wait For Me	7"	Giant	GN28	1968	£10	£5	*Lloyd Evans B side*

TOMLINSON, ROY

I Stand For I	7"	Coxsone	CS7056	1968	£10	£5	*Martin B side*

TOMORROW

Tomorrow are usually held up as the classic psychedelic group, but this reputation derives less from their album, which is very uneven in quality, than from the two wonderful singles, 'My White Bicycle' and 'Revolution'. The chaotic, anarchist streak within the group (Twink) carried through into the Pink Fairies; the musically inventive part (Steve Howe) joined the group Yes.

My White Bicycle	7"	Parlophone	R5813	1969	£20	£10	
My White Bicycle	7"	Parlophone	R5597	1967	£20	£10	
Revolution	7"	Parlophone	R5627	1967	£20	£10	
Tomorrow	LP	Parlophone	PMC/PCS7042	1968	£100	£50	
Tomorrow	LP	Harvest	SHSM2010	1976	£15	£6	

TOMORROW COME SOMEDAY (ITHACA)

Tomorrow Come Someday	LP	private	SNP97	1969	£500	£330	

TOMORROW'S CHILDREN

Bang Bang Rock Steady	7"	Island	WI3073	1967	£10	£5	

TOMORROW'S GIFT

Goodbye Future	LP	Amok	28515	1973	£25	£10	*German*
Tomorrow's Gift	LP	Plus	1+2	1970	£75	£37.50	*German double*

TON STEINE SCHERBEN

Keine Macht Für Niemand	LP	Volksmund	TSS2	1972	£12	£5	*German double*
Warum Geht Es Mir So Dreckig	LP	Volksmund	TSS13	1971	£12	£5	*German*
Wenn Die Nacht Am Tiefsten	LP	Volksmund	TSS3	1975	£12	£5	*German double*

TONE DEAF & THE IDIOTS

Why Does Politics Turn Men Into Toads	7"	Angel	BL12	198–	£5	£2	*flexi*

TONER, ELEANOR

All Cried Out	7"	Decca	F12119	1965	£4	£1.50	
Will You Still Love Me Tomorrow	7"	Decca	F12192	1965	£4	£1.50	

TONETTES

Love That Is Real	7"	Island	WI064	1962	£10	£5	

TONEY JR, OSCAR

For Your Precious Love	7"	Stateside	SS2033	1967	£6	£2.50	
For Your Precious Love	LP	Stateside	(S)SL10211	1967	£15	£6	
No Sad Songs	7"	Bell	BLL1011	1968	£4	£1.50	
Turn On Your Lovelight	7"	Stateside	SS2046	1967	£5	£2	
You Can Lead Your Woman To The Altar	7"	Stateside	SS2061	1967	£5	£2	

TONGUE & GROOVE

Tongue & Groove .... LP .... Fontana .... STL5528 .... 1969 **£20** .... **£8** ....

TONIK, TERRY

Just A Little Mod .... 7" .... Posh .... TOFF1 .... 1980 **£15** ...... **£7.50** ....
Just A Little Mod .... 7" .... Posh .... TOFF1 .... 1980 **£50** .... **£25** ..... *promo with booklet*

TONTON MACOUTE

Tonton Macoute .... LP .... Neon .... NE4 .... 1971 **£50** .... **£25** ....

TONTO'S EXPANDING HEADBAND

Tonto is an instrument (The Original New Timbral Orchestra) – a huge synthesizer – played by Robert Margouleff and Malcolm Cecil. These two are among the more imaginative electronic keyboard performers and *Zero Time* is a good example of what can be achieved. They take advantage of the possibilities afforded to them, by such stratagems as using a ten-note, equally tempered scale (impossible on conventional instruments) and yet the music still manages to be as accessible as it is interesting. Margouleff and Cecil also worked as advisers to Stevie Wonder and their sounds can be heard on many of his records.

Zero Time .... LP .... Atlantic .... 2400150 .... 1971 **£15** .... **£6** ....

TONY, CARO & JOHN

All On The First Day .... LP .... private .... 1972 **£400** ...... **£250** ....

TONY & DENNIS

Folk Song .... 7" .... Trojan .... TR002 .... 1967 **£10** .... **£5** .... *Tommy McCook B side*

TONY & HOWARD WITH THE DICTATORS

Just In Case .... 7" .... Oriole .... CB307 .... 1965 **£8** .... **£4** ....

TONY & HOWIE

Fun It Up .... 7" .... Banana .... BA371 .... 1972 **£5** .... **£2** ....

TONY & JOE

Freeze .... 7" .... London .... HLN8694 .... 1958 **£30** .... **£15** ....

TONY & LOUISE

Ups And Downs .... 7" .... Island .... WI059 .... 1962 **£8** .... **£4** ....

TONY & TANDY

Two Can Make It Together .... 7" .... Atlantic .... 584262 .... 1969 **£8** .... **£4** ....
Two Can Make It Together .... 7" .... Atlantic .... 2091075 .... 1971 **£4** .... **£1.50** ....

TONY & THE GRADUATES

Statue .... 7" .... Hit .... HIT13 .... 196– **£40** .... **£20** ....

TONY'S DEFENDERS

Since I Lost My Baby .... 7" .... Columbia .... DB7996 .... 1966 **£15** ...... **£7.50** ....
Yes I Do .... 7" .... Columbia .... DB7850 .... 1966 **£15** ...... **£7.50** ....

TOO MUCH

Lick Me One More Time .... 7" .... Lightning .... GIL552 .... 1978 **£15** ...... **£7.50** ....
Who You Wanna Be .... 7" .... Lightning .... GIL513 .... 1978 **£15** ...... **£7.50** ....

TOOMORROW

Toomorrow was a group put together, Monkees-style, for the purpose of making a rather silly film. This was the flop it deserved to be, but the group's lead singer, Olivia Newton-John, persevered with her musical career.

I Could Never Live Without Your Love ... 7" .... Decca .... F13070 .... 1970 **£30** .... **£15** ....
Toomorrow .... LP .... RCA .... LSA3008 .... 1970 **£75** .... **£37.50** ....
You're My Baby Now .... 7" .... RCA .... RCA1978 .... 1970 **£30** .... **£15** ....

TOOP, DAVID

New And Rediscovered Musical Instruments .... LP .... Obscure .... OBS4 .... 1976 **£10** .... **£4** ....

TOOTS

Do You Like It .... 7" .... Upsetter .... US327 .... 1970 **£4** .... **£1.50** .... *Upsetters B side*

TOP DRAWER

Solid Oak .... LP .... Wishbon .... 83615 .... 1969 **£300** ...... **£180** .... *US*
Solid Oak .... LP .... Resurrection .... CX1185 .... 198– **£60** .... **£30** .... *US*

TOP TEN ALLSTARS

Beat Party .... LP .... Decca .... 16434 .... 1966 **£30** .... **£15** .... *German*
Three O'Clock In The Mornin' .... LP .... Decca .... SLK16387P .... 1965 **£50** .... **£25** .... *German*

TOPHAM, TOP

Top Topham was the original lead guitarist with the Yardbirds, but he was replaced by the young Eric Clapton before the group made any recordings. His later solo album consists of a set of blues guitar instrumentals, proving Topham to be a worthy first link in the Yardbirds' lead guitar chain.

Ascension Heights .... LP .... Blue Horizon ... 763857 .... 1970 **£75** .... **£37.50** ....
Christmas Cracker .... 7" .... Blue Horizon ... 573167 .... 1969 **£10** .... **£5** ....

TOPICS

The Topics shortly afterwards changed their name to the Four Seasons.

Girl In My Dreams	7"	Perri	1007	1961	£75	£37.50	US

TOPSY, TINY & THE CHARMS

After Marriage Blues	7"	Pye	7N25104	1961	£15	£7.50	
Come On Come On Come On	7"	Parlophone	R4397	1958	£40	£20	
You Shocked Me	7"	Parlophone	R4427	1958	£40	£20	

TORA TORA

Don't Want To Let You Go	7"	Tora	TT5001	1980	£25	£12.50	
Red Sun Setting	7"	Mancunian Metal	TT5000	1980	£6	£2.50	

TORME, BERNIE

All Day And All Of The Night	7"	Fresh	FRESH7	1981	£6	£2.50	
I'm Not Ready	7"	Jet	JET126	1978	£5	£2	*orange vinyl*

TORME, MEL

All Of You	7"	Vogue Coral	Q72202	1956	£4	£1.50	
And The Marty Paich Dektette	LP	London	LTZN15009	1956	£15	£6	
At The Crescendo	LP	Parlophone	PMC1096	1959	£10	£4	
At The Crescendo	LP	Vogue Coral	LVA9004	1955	£15	£6	
At The Red Hill	LP	London	HAK/SHK8021	1963	£10	£4	
Back In Town	LP	HMV	CLP1382	1960	£15	£6	
Blue Moon	7"	Vogue Coral	Q72159	1956	£5	£2	
California Suite	LP	Bethlehem	BCP6016	1958	£20	£8	US
Comin' Home Baby	7"	London	HLK9643	1962	£5	£2	
Comin' Home Baby	LP	London	HAK8065	1963	£10	£4	
I Can't Give You Anything But Love	7"	MGM	MGM922	1956	£4	£1.50	
It's A Blue World	LP	London	HAN2016	1956	£15	£6	
Love Is Here To Stay	7"	Vogue Coral	Q72185	1956	£4	£1.50	
Lullaby Of Birdland	7"	London	HLN8322	1956	£6	£2.50	
Lulu's Back In Town	7"	London	HLN8305	1956	£6	£2.50	
Magic Of Mel	7" EP	London	REK1372	1963	£8	£4	
Meets The British	7" EP	Philips	BBE12181	1958	£8	£4	
Meets The British	LP	Philips	BBL7205	1957	£30	£15	
Mel Tormé	LP	Bethlehem	BCP52	1956	£20	£8	US
Mel Tormé	LP	HMV	CLP1238	1958	£10	£4	
Mountain Greenery	7"	Vogue Coral	Q72150	1956	£6	£2.50	
Musical Sounds	LP	Coral	CRL57044	1954	£20	£8	US
Musical Sounds Are The Best Songs	LP	Vogue Coral	LVA9032	1956	£15	£6	
My Kind Of Music	LP	HMV	CLP1584/ CSD1442	1962	£10	£4	
My Rosemarie	7"	Vogue Coral	Q72217	1957	£4	£1.50	
Olé Tormé	LP	HMV	CLP1315	1960	£10	£4	
Sings At The Crescendo Pt 1	7" EP	Coral	FEP2026	1959	£6	£2.50	
Sings At The Crescendo Pt 2	7" EP	Coral	FEP2027	1959	£6	£2.50	
Sings At The Crescendo Pt 3	7" EP	Coral	FEP2028	1959	£6	£2.50	
Sings Fred Astaire	LP	London	LTZN15076	1957	£10	£4	
Sings Fred Astaire Pt 1	7" EP	London	EZN19027	1958	£6	£2.50	
Sings Fred Astaire Pt 2	7" EP	London	EZN19028	1958	£6	£2.50	
Sings Fred Astaire Pt 3	7" EP	London	EZN19039	1958	£6	£2.50	
Songs	10" LP	MGM	552	1952	£25	£10	US
Songs For Any Taste	LP	Parlophone	PMC1114	1959	£15	£6	
Sunday In New York	LP	Atlantic	(SD)8091	1963	£12	£5	US
Swingin' On The Moon	LP	HMV	CLP1449/ CSD1349	1961	£15	£6	
Swings Schubert Alley	LP	HMV	CLP1405/ CSD1330	1960	£15	£6	
Torme	LP	Verve	V2105	1958	£12	£5	US
Voice In Velvet	7" EP	MGM	MGMEP562	1956	£8	£4	
Voice In Velvet No. 2	7" EP	MGM	MGMEP591	1957	£8	£4	
Walkin' Shoes	7"	Decca	F10800	1956	£4	£1.50	
Walkin' Shoes	7" EP	Decca	DFE6384	1956	£6	£2.50	

TORMENTORS

Hanging Round	LP	Royal	RLP111	196–	£150	£75	US

TORNADOES

Bustin' Surfboards	LP	Josie	4005	1963	£50	£25	US

TORNADOS

Away From It All	LP	Decca	LK4552	1963	£30	£15	
Dragonfly	7"	Decca	F11745	1963	£5	£2	
Earlybird	7"	Columbia	DB7589	1965	£12	£6	
Exodus	7"	Decca	F11946	1964	£10	£5	
Globetrotter	7"	Decca	F11562	1963	£4	£1.50	
Granada	7"	Columbia	DB7455	1965	£12	£6	
Hot Pot	7"	Decca	F11838	1964	£5	£2	
Ice Cream Man	7"	Decca	F11662	1963	£5	£2	
Is That A Ship I Hear	7"	Columbia	DB7984	1966	£25	£12.50	
Love And Fury	7"	Decca	F11449	1962	£8	£4	
Monte Carlo	7"	Decca	F11889	1964	£10	£5	
More Sounds From The Tornados	7" EP	Decca	DFE8521	1963	£10	£5	

Pop Art Goes Mozart	7"	Columbia	DB7856	1966	**£20**	**£10**	
Robot	7"	Decca	F11606	1963	**£4**	**£1.50**	
Sounds Of The Tornados	7" EP	Decca	DFE8510	1962	**£10**	**£5**	
Sounds Of The Tornados	LP	London	LL3293	1963	**£30**	**£15**	*US*
Stingray	7"	Columbia	DB7687	1965	**£25**	**£12.50**	
Telstar	7" EP	Decca	DFE8511	1962	**£12**	**£6**	
Telstar	CD	Decca		1988	**£50**	**£25**	
Telstar	LP	London	LL3279	1962	**£30**	**£15**	*US*
Tornado Rock	7" EP	Decca	DFE8533	1963	**£15**	**£7.50**	
World Of The Tornados	LP	Decca	SPA253	1972	**£10**	**£4**	

TOROK, MITCHELL

Caribbean	7"	London	HL8001	1954	**£25**	**£12.50**	*tri-centre*
Caribbean	LP	London	HAW2279	1960	**£50**	**£25**	
Drink Up And Go Home	7"	Brunswick	05642	1957	**£8**	**£4**	
Haunting Waterfall	7"	London	HL8083	1954	**£25**	**£12.50**	
Havana Huddle	7"	Brunswick	05626	1956	**£15**	**£7.50**	
Hootchy Coochy	7"	London	HL8048	1954	**£25**	**£12.50**	
Louisiana Hayride	7" EP	London	REP1014	1954	**£30**	**£15**	
Pink Chiffon	7"	London	HLW9130	1960	**£6**	**£2.50**	
Pledge Of Love	7"	Brunswick	05657	1957	**£8**	**£4**	
Two Words	7"	Brunswick	05718	1957	**£6**	**£2.50**	
When Mexico Gave Up The Rhumba	7"	Brunswick	05586	1956	**£10**	**£5**	
World Keeps Turning Around	7"	Brunswick	05423	1955	**£10**	**£5**	

TORQUES

Live	LP	Lemco	604	196–	**£50**	**£25**	*US*
Zoom!	LP	Wiggins	64010	1964	**£75**	**£37.50**	*US*

TORR, MICHELLE

Only Tears Are Left For Me	7"	Fontana	TF676	1966	**£5**	**£2**	

TORRENCE, GEORGE & THE NATURALS

Lickin' Stick	7"	London	HLZ10181	1968	**£6**	**£2.50**	

TORRIANI, VICO

All The Big Italian Hits	LP	Decca	LF1589	1960	**£40**	**£20**	*German*

TORTILLA

Little Heroes	LP	Catfish	5C05624381	1971	**£40**	**£20**	*Dutch*

TORTILLA FLAT

Für Eine 3/4 Stunde	LP		TF0175	1974	**£125**	**£62.50**	*German*

TORTOISE

Rhythms, Resolutions And Clusters	LP	City Slang	EFA04971	1996	**£25**	**£10**	*clear vinyl*

TOSH, PETER

Bush Doctor	LP	Rolling Stones	CUN39109	1978	**£12**	**£5**	*with scratch & sniff sticker*
Crimson Pirate	7"	Jackpot	JP706	1969	**£10**	**£5**	
Equal Rights	LP	Virgin	V2081	1977	**£12**	**£5**	
Legalise It	LP	Virgin	V2061	1976	**£12**	**£5**	
Maga Dog	7"	Bullet	BU486	1971	**£10**	**£5**	*Third & Fourth Generation B side*
Return Of Al Capone	7"	Unity	UN525	1969	**£6**	**£2.50**	*Lennox Brown B side*
Rudies Medley	7"	Punch	PH91	1972	**£5**	**£2**	
Selassie Serenade	7"	Bullet	BU414	1971	**£4**	**£1.50**	*Glen Adams B side*
Sun Valley	7"	Unity	UN529	1969	**£6**	**£2.50**	*Hedley Bennett B side*
Them A Fi Get A Beatin'	7"	Pressure Beat	PB5509	1972	**£10**	**£5**	*Third & Fourth Generation B side*

TOTNAMITES

Danny Boy	7"	Oriole	CB1615	1961	**£4**	**£1.50**	

TOTO

Africa	7"	CBS	A2510	1982	**£4**	**£1.50**	*shaped picture disc*
Africa	CD-s	CBS	6562982	1990	**£5**	**£2**	
Pamela	CD-s	CBS	6516072	1988	**£5**	**£2**	
Rosanna	7"	CBS	A2079	1982	**£4**	**£1.50**	*shaped picture disc*
Solid Gold	CD-s	CBS	6545693	1989	**£5**	**£2**	*3" single*
Stop Loving You	CD-s	CBS	6514112	1988	**£5**	**£2**	
Toto	LP	Epic	PJC35317	1978	**£12**	**£5**	*French picture disc*

TOTTERDELL, DAVE

Whitby Bells	LP	Cottage	COT711	1977	**£10**	**£4**	

TOUCH

Miss Teach	7"	Deram	DM243	1969	**£5**	**£2**	
This Is Touch	LP	Deram	DML/SML1033	1969	**£30**	**£15**	*with poster*
This Is Touch	LP	Deram	DML/SML1033	1969	**£20**	**£8**	

TOUCH (2)

Don't You Know What Love Is	7"	Ariola	ARO243	1980	**£6**	**£2.50**	
Touch	LP	Ariola	ARL5036	1980	**£10**	**£4**	

When The Spirit Moves You	7"	Ariola	ARO209	1980	**£5**	**£2**	

TOUCH (3)

Street Suite	LP	Mainline	LP2001	1969	**£1250**	**£875**	*US*

TOUCH OF VELVET

Touch Of Velvet	LP	Statik	MADLP002		**£25**	**£10**	

TOUCHSTONE

Drummer Chicken Hirsh was previously a member of Country Joe and the Fish, while keyboard player Tom Constanten has managed to sustain a lengthy career following his membership of the Grateful Dead.

Tarot	LP	United Artists	UAS5563	1972	**£40**	**£20**	*US*

TOUFF, CY

Having A Ball	LP	Vogue	LAE12040	1957	**£15**	**£6**	

TOURISTS

Blind Among The Flowers	7"	Logo	GOD350	1979	**£4**	**£1.50**	*double*
Loneliest Man In The World	7"	Logo	GOP360	1979	**£5**	**£2**	*picture disc*

TOUSAN, AL

Naomi	7"	London	HLU9291	1961	**£5**	**£2**	

TOUSSAINT, ALLEN

Life, Love And Faith	LP	Reprise	K44202	1972	**£12**	**£5**	
Southern Nights	LP	Reprise	K54021	1975	**£10**	**£4**	
We The People	7"	Soul City	SC119	1969	**£6**	**£2.50**	
Wild Sound Of New Orleans	LP	RCA	LPM1767	1958	**£50**	**£25**	*US*

TOUSSAINT, CALINE & OLIVER

Gardens Of Monaco	7"	Epic	SEPC6334	1978	**£8**	**£4**	

TOVEY, ROBERTA

Who's Who	7"	Polydor	BM56021	1965	**£20**	**£10**	
Who's Who	7"	Polydor	BM56021	1965	**£30**	**£15**	*picture sleeve*

TOWER OF POWER

Back To Oakland	LP	Warner Bros	K46282	1974	**£10**	**£4**	
Bump City	LP	Warner Bros	K46167	1972	**£10**	**£4**	
East Bay Grease	LP	San Francisco	SD204	1970	**£15**	**£6**	*US*
Tower Of Power	LP	Warner Bros	K46223	1974	**£10**	**£4**	
Urban Renewal	LP	Warner Bros	K56093	1975	**£10**	**£4**	

TOWERS

To Know Him Is To Love Him	7"	Capitol	CL14944	1958	**£5**	**£2**	

TOWNER, RALPH

Diary	LP	ECM	ECM1032ST	1973	**£12**	**£5**	
Solstice	LP	ECM	ECM1060ST	1975	**£12**	**£5**	
Sound And Shadows	LP	ECM	ECM1095T	1976	**£10**	**£4**	
Trios Solos	LP	ECM	ECM1025ST	1972	**£12**	**£5**	*with Glen Moore*

TOWNES, COLIN

Breakdown	7"	MCA	MCA643	1980	**£5**	**£2**	

TOWNLEY, JOHN

Townley	LP	EMI	EMC3298	1979	**£15**	**£6**	

TOWNSEL SISTERS

Will I Ever	7"	Polydor	NH66954	1960	**£5**	**£2**	

TOWNSEND, ED

Ed Townsend	7" EP	Capitol	EAP11091	1959	**£5**	**£2**	
Stay With me	7"	Warner Bros	WB21	1960	**£5**	**£2**	

TOWNSEND, HENRY

Tired Of Bein' Mistreated	LP	Bluesville	BV1041	1962	**£12**	**£5**	*US*

TOWNSHEND, PETE

Friend Is A Friend	CD-s	Virgin	VSCD1198	1989	**£5**	**£2**	*3" single*
I Won't Run Anymore	CD-s	Virgin	VSCD1209	1989	**£5**	**£2**	*3" single*
Interview With A Psychoderelict	CD	Atlantic	PRCD51612	1993	**£20**	**£8**	*US promo*
Iron Man	CD	Atlantic		1989	**£30**	**£15**	*US promo pack, with CD-s, book, press kit*
Pete's Listening Time	LP	Atco	SAM150	1982	**£12**	**£5**	*interview promo*
Pete's Listening Time	LP	Atco	SAM150	1982	**£25**	**£10**	*interview promo, autographed*
Psychoderelict	CD	Atlantic	PRCD51032	1993	**£25**	**£10**	*US promo double*
Townshend Tapes	LP	Atco	SAM121/2	1980	**£30**	**£15**	*double interview promo, autographed*
Townshend Tapes	LP	Atco	SAM121/2	1980	**£25**	**£10**	*double interview promo*
Who Came First	LP	Track	2408201	1972	**£10**	**£4**	
Won't Get Fooled Again	7"	Island	SPB1	1981	**£6**	**£2.50**	*1 sided promo, with John Williams*

TOWNSHEND, PETE & MEHER BABA

Title	Format	Label	Cat. No.	Year	Mint	VG	Notes
All Time Star . . .	LP	Universal Spiritual	MBO1	1975	£60	£30	reissue of USL001
Happy Birthday	LP	Universal Spiritual	USL001	1970	£75	£37.50	
I Am	LP	Universal Spiritual	MBO2	1975	£60	£30	
I Am	LP	Universal Spiritual	USL002	1973	£75	£37.50	
With Love	LP	Universal Spiritual	USL003	1974	£75	£37.50	

TOWNSHEND, PETE & RONNIE LANE

Title	Format	Label	Cat. No.	Year	Mint	VG	Notes
Street In The City	12"	Polydor	2058944	1977	£8	£4	

TOY DOLLS

Title	Format	Label	Cat. No.	Year	Mint	VG	Notes
Alfie From The Bronx	7"	Volume	VOL7	1983	£6	£2.50	
Cheerio And Toodle Pip	7"	Volume	VOL5	1983	£6	£2.50	
Everybody Jitterbug	7"	Zonophone	Z31	1982	£10	£5	
Nellie The Elephant	7"	Volume	VOL3	1983	£10	£5	
Tommy Kowie's Car	7"	GBH	SSM005	1981	£25	£12.50	no picture sleeve
Tommy Kowie's Car	7"	GBH	GRC104	1981	£20	£10	
We're Mad	12"	Volume	VOLT10	1984	£8	£4	
We're Mad	7"	Volume	VOL10	1984	£5	£2	

TOY DOLLS (2)

Title	Format	Label	Cat. No.	Year	Mint	VG	Notes
Little Tin Soldier	7"	London	HLN9647	1963	£10	£5	

TOYS

Title	Format	Label	Cat. No.	Year	Mint	VG	Notes
Attack	7"	Stateside	SS483	1966	£5	£2	
Baby Toys	7"	Stateside	SS539	1966	£6	£2.50	
Ciao Baby	7"	Philips	BF1563	1967	£4	£1.50	
Lover's Concert/Attack	LP	Stateside	(S)SL10175	1966	£20	£8	
Lover's Concerto	7"	Stateside	SS460	1965	£4	£1.50	
Lover's Concerto	7"	Bell	BLL1053	1969	£4	£1.50	
May My Heart Be Cast To Stone	7"	Stateside	SS502	1966	£8	£4	
My Lover's Sonata	7"	Philips	BF1581	1967	£5	£2	
Silver Spoon	7"	Stateside	SS519	1966	£8	£4	

T.P. SMOKE

Title	Format	Label	Cat. No.	Year	Mint	VG	Notes
Smoke	LP	Telefunken	PT12033	1970	£30	£15	German

T'PAU

Title	Format	Label	Cat. No.	Year	Mint	VG	Notes
Bridge Of Spies	CD	Siren	CDPSRN8	1988	£12	£5	picture disc
China In Your Hand	CD-s	Siren	SRNCD64	1987	£5	£2	
I Will Be With You	CD-s	Siren	SRNCD87	1988	£5	£2	picture disc
Only The Lonely	CD-s	Siren	SRNCD107	1989	£5	£2	3" single
Road To Our Dream	CD-s	Siren	SRNCD100	1988	£5	£2	
Secret Garden	CD-s	Siren	SRNCD93	1988	£5	£2	picture disc
Sex Talk	CD-s	Siren	SRNCD80	1988	£5	£2	picture disc
Valentine	CD-s	Siren	SRNCD69	1988	£5	£2	
View From A Bridge	CD-s	Polygram	0804989	1988	£10	£5	CD video

TRACEY, GRANT & THE SUNSETS

Title	Format	Label	Cat. No.	Year	Mint	VG	Notes
Everybody Shake	7"	Decca	F11741	1963	£6	£2.50	
Love Me	7"	Ember	EMBS130	1961	£10	£5	
Please Baby Please	7"	Ember	EMBS126	1961	£12	£6	
Taming Tigers	7"	Ember	EMBS155	1962	£10	£5	
Tears Came Rolling Down	7"	Ember	EMBS148	1962	£10	£5	
Teenbeat	LP	Ember	EMB3352	1964	£30	£15	

TRACEY, MARK

Title	Format	Label	Cat. No.	Year	Mint	VG	Notes
Caravan Of Lonely Men	7"	Parlophone	R4944	1962	£5	£2	

TRACEY, STAN

Title	Format	Label	Cat. No.	Year	Mint	VG	Notes
Alice In Jazzland	LP	Columbia	SX/SCX6051	1966	£50	£25	
Alone At Wigmore Hall	LP	Cadillac	SGC1003	1974	£15	£6	
Captain Adventure	LP	Steam	SJ102	1975	£15	£6	
Crompton Suite	LP	Steam	SJ109	1981	£10	£4	
Free 'n' One	LP	Columbia	SCX6385	1970	£40	£20	
In Person	LP	Columbia	SX/SCX6124	1967	£40	£20	
Jazz Suite	LP	Columbia	33SX1774/ SCX3589	1965	£40	£20	
Latin American Caper	LP	Columbia	SCX6358	1969	£30	£15	
Little Klunk	LP	Vogue	VA160155	1959	£150	£75	
Little Klunk	LP	Ace Of Clubs	ACL1259	1969	£30	£15	
New Departures Quartet	LP	Transatlantic	TRA134	1964	£25	£10	
Perspectives	LP	Columbia	SCX6485	1971	£30	£15	
Seven Ages Of Man	LP	Columbia	SCX6413	1970	£30	£15	
Showcase	LP	Vogue	VA160130	1958	£60	£30	
Under Milk Wood	LP	Steam	SJ101	1975	£15	£6	
We Love You Madly	LP	Columbia	SX/SCX6320	1969	£40	£20	
With Love From Jazz	LP	Columbia	SX/SCX6205	1968	£30	£15	

TRACEY, WENDALL

Title	Format	Label	Cat. No.	Year	Mint	VG	Notes
Who's To Know	7"	London	HLM8664	1958	£20	£10	

TRACK

Why Do Fools Fall In Love	7"	Columbia	DB7987	1966	£6	£2.50	

TRACTOR

No More Rock And Roll	7"	Cargo	CRS002	1977	£6	£2.50	
Stone Glory	7"	Polydor	2001282	1972	£6	£2.50	
Tractor	LP	Dandelion	2310217	1972	£75	£37.50	

TRACY

Don't Hold It Against Me	7"	Columbia	DB7802	1966	£4	£1.50	

TRAD GRADS

Runnin' Shoes	7"	Decca	F11403	1961	£6	£2.50	

TRADE WINDS

Crossroads	7"	RCA	RCA1141	1959	£8	£4	

TRADE WINDS (2)

Excursions	LP	Kama Sutra	KLP(S)8057	1967	£15	£6	US
Mind Excursion	7"	Kama Sutra	KAS202	1966	£5	£2	
Mind Excursion	7" EP	Kama Sutra	617104	1966	£10	£5	French
New York's A Lonely Town	7"	Red Bird	RB10020	1965	£8	£4	

TRADER HORNE

Trader Horne was a folky group formed by Jackie McAuley, who had played keyboards with Them for a while, and Judy Dyble, who was the original lead singer with Fairport Convention. Their one album was followed by a Jackie McAuley solo LP in a similar style, but neither was sufficiently distinctive to make much headway in the market place.

Here Comes The Rain	7"	Dawn	DNS1003	1970	£4	£1.50	
Morning Way	LP	Dawn	DNLS3004	1970	£60	£30	
Sheena	7"	Pye	7N17846	1969	£5	£2	

TRAFFIC

The first two albums made by Traffic are near-perfect examples of why so many rock music collectors view the sixties through rose-coloured glasses. Presenting a blend of inspirational songwriting, ever-imaginative arranging, and skilful playing, these qualities emerging relatively undiminished by the passing of time, the albums are far more satisfying than any number of more expensive 'progressive' rarities. (Sadly, the reformed 1994 model of Traffic is not the same at all – some of the sound is the same, but the white heat of inspiration has cooled to charcoal.) The two versions of the group's first album provide a striking explanation of why collectors frequently distinguish between mono and stereo editions of sixties albums. Several of the tracks here are markedly different in mono and stereo, with completely different guitar solos being used on occasion.

Best Of Traffic	LP	Island	ILPS9112	1969	£15	£6	*pink label*
Far From Home	CD	Virgin	CDVDJ2727	1994	£15	£6	*promo, card sleeve*
Feelin' Alright	7"	Island	WIP6041	1968	£4	£1.50	
Gimme Some Lovin'	7"	Island		1971	£6	£2.50	*promo*
Heaven Is In Your Mind	LP	United Artists	UAS6651	1968	£12	£5	*US*
Here We Go Round The Mulberry Bush	7"	Island	WIP6025	1967	£5	£2	*picture sleeve*
Here We Go Round The Mulberry Bush	7"	Island	WIP6025	1967	£4	£1.50	
Hole In My Shoe	7"	Island	IEP7	1978	£5	£2	*picture disc*
Hole In My Shoe	7"	Island	WIP6017	1967	£5	£2	*picture sleeve*
John Barleycorn Must Die	LP	Island	ILPS9116	1970	£12	£5	*pink label*
Last Exit	CD	Island	CID9097	1988	£12	£5	
Last Exit	LP	Island	ILPS9097	1969	£15	£6	*pink label*
Live At The Fillmore	LP	Island	ILPS9124	1970	£100	£50	*demo only*
Low Spark Of High Heeled Boys	CD	Mobile Fidelity	UDCD609	1994	£15	£6	*US audiophile*
Low Spark Of High Heeled Boys	LP	Island	ILPS9180	1971	£10	£4	*cube cover*
Medicated Goo	7"	Island	WIP6050	1968	£4	£1.50	
Mr Fantasy	CD	Mobile Fidelity	UDCD572	1992	£15	£6	*US audiophile*
Mr Fantasy	LP	Island	ILP961	1967	£50	£25	*mono, pink label*
Mr Fantasy	LP	Island	ILPS9061	1967	£25	£10	*stereo, pink label*
No Face, No Name, No Number	7"	Island	WIP6030	1968	£4	£1.50	
On The Road	LP	Island	ILPSD2	1973	£12	£5	*double*
Paper Sun	7"	Island	WIP6002	1967	£4	£1.50	
Paper Sun	7"	Island	WIP6002	1967	£8	£4	*picture sleeve*
Shoot Out At The Fantasy Factory	LP	Island	ILPS9224	1973	£10	£4	*cube cover*
Traffic	LP	Island	ILP981	1968	£30	£15	*mono, pink label*
Traffic	LP	Island	ILPS9081	1968	£15	£6	*stereo, pink label*
Traffic	CD	Mobile Fidelity		1995	£15	£6	*US audiophile*
Traffic Control	CD	Island	PR2300	1989	£20	£8	*US promo compilation*
Traffic Report	CD	Island	PR2158	1988	£20	£8	*US promo compilation*
Walking In The Wind	7"	Island	WIP6207	1974	£4	£1.50	
Welcome To The Canteen	LP	Island	ILPS9166	1971	£10	£4	
When The Eagle Flies	LP	Island	ILPS9273	1974	£10	£4	*pink rim label*
You Can All Join In	7"	Island	WIP6041	1968	£10	£5	*demo only*

TRAFFIC JAM

The Spectres changed their name to Traffic Jam for one single, before deciding that the possible confusion with Stevie Winwood's new group, Traffic, was not helping their career. Accordingly, they changed names yet again, this time to Status Quo.

Almost But Not Quite There ... 7" ... Piccadilly ... 7N35386 ... 1967 **£150** ... **£75**

TRAGICIAN

Wild The Scared And The Timid ... 7" ... Look ... LKSP6411 ... 1979 **£20** ... **£10**

TRAIN

Costumed Cuties ... LP ... Vanguard ... 6542 ... 1970 **£20** ... **£8** ... *US*

TRAINER, PHIL

Trainer ... LP ... BASF ... 2029107 ... 1973 **£20** ... **£8** ... *German*

TRAITS

Harlem Shuffle ... 7" ... Pye ... 7N25404 ... 1967 **£6** ... **£2.50**

TRAJAN, ALAN

Firm Roots ... LP ... MCA ... MKPS2000 ... 1969 **£60** ... **£30**
Speak To Me, Clarissa ... 7" ... MCA ... MK5002 ... 1969 **£8** ... **£4**

TRAMLINE

Moves Of Vegetable Centuries ... LP ... Island ... ILPS9095 ... 1969 **£40** ... **£20** ... *pink label*
Somewhere Down The Line ... LP ... Island ... ILPS9088 ... 1968 **£40** ... **£20** ... *pink label*

TRAMMELL, BOBBY LEE

Arkansas Twist ... LP ... Atlantic ... LPM1503 ... 1962 **£30** ... **£15** ... *US*
New Dance In France ... 7" ... Sue ... WI326 ... 1964 **£15** ... **£7.50**

TRAMP

Each Day ... 7" ... Youngblood ... SBY4 ... 1969 **£5** ... **£2**
Put A Record On ... LP ... Spark ... SRLP112 ... 1974 **£30** ... **£15**
Tramp ... LP ... Spark ... SRLM2001 ... 1973 **£30** ... **£15**
Tramp ... LP ... Music Man ... SMLS603 ... 1969 **£100** ... **£50**

TRANSATLANTICS

Don't Fight It ... 7" ... Mercury ... MF948 ... 1965 **£15** ... **£7.50**
Louie Go Home ... 7" ... King ... KG1040 ... 1966 **£5** ... **£2**
Many Things From Your Window ... 7" ... Fontana ... TF593 ... 1965 **£5** ... **£2**
Run For Your Life ... 7" ... King ... KG1033 ... 1965 **£5** ... **£2**
Stand Up And Fight Like A Man ... 7" ... Fontana ... TF638 ... 1965 **£5** ... **£2**

TRANSPARENT ILLUSION

Chagrin Receiver ... LP ... Vortex ... VEX4 ... 1982 **£15** ... **£6**
Guilty Rich Men ... 7" ... Vortex ... VEX5 ... 1982 **£5** ... **£2**
Still Human ... LP ... Vortex ... VEX3 ... 1981 **£15** ... **£6**
Vortex ... 7" ... Vortex ... VEX001/2 ... 1981 **£5** ... **£2**

TRANSVISION VAMP

Baby I Don't Care ... CD-s ... MCA ... DTVVT6 ... 1989 **£5** ... **£2**
Born To Be Sold ... CD-s ... MCA ... DTVVT9 ... 1989 **£5** ... **£2**
I Want Your Love ... CD-s ... MCA ... DTVV3 ... 1988 **£15** ... **£7.50** ... *3" single*
Landslide Of Love ... CD-s ... MCA ... DTVVT8 ... 1989 **£5** ... **£2**
Only One ... CD-s ... MCA ... DTVVT7 ... 1989 **£5** ... **£2**
Revolution Baby ... CD-s ... MCA ... DTVVT4 ... 1988 **£5** ... **£2**
Sister Moon ... CD-s ... MCA ... DTVV5 ... 1988 **£8** ... **£4**
Tell That Girl To Shut Up ... CD-s ... MCA ... DVVT2 ... 1988 **£15** ... **£7.50** ... *picture disc*

TRAPEZE

Coast To Coast ... 7" ... Threshold ... TH11 ... 1972 **£4** ... **£1.50**
Don't Ask Me How I Know ... 7" ... Aura ... AUS114 ... 1979 **£6** ... **£2.50**
Final Swing ... LP ... Threshold ... THS11 ... 1974 **£15** ... **£6**
Medusa ... LP ... Threshold ... THS4 ... 1970 **£20** ... **£8**
Running Away ... 7" ... Aura ... AUS116 ... 1980 **£6** ... **£2.50**
Send Me No More Letters ... 7" ... Threshold ... TH2 ... 1969 **£4** ... **£1.50**
Trapeze ... LP ... Threshold ... THS2 ... 1970 **£20** ... **£8**
You Are The Music ... LP ... Threshold ... THS8 ... 1972 **£15** ... **£6**

TRASH

Golden Slumbers ... 7" ... Apple ... 17 ... 1969 **£8** ... **£4**

TRASHCAN SINATRAS

Cake ... LP ... Go!Discs ... 8282011 ... 1990 **£15** ... **£6**
Circling The Circumference ... 12" ... Go!Discs ... GODX46 ... 1990 **£8** ... **£4**
Circling The Circumference ... CD-s ... Go!Discs ... GODCD46 ... 1990 **£10** ... **£5**
Obscurity Knocks ... 12" ... Go!Discs ... GODX34 ... 1989 **£8** ... **£4**
Obscurity Knocks ... CD-s ... Go!Discs ... GODCD34 ... 1989 **£10** ... **£5**
Only Tongue ... 12" ... Go!Discs ... GODX41 ... 1990 **£6** ... **£2.50**
Only Tongue ... CD-s ... Go!Discs ... GODCD41 ... 1990 **£6** ... **£2.50**

TRASHMEN

Bad News ... 7" EP ... Columbia ... ESRF1564 ... 1964 **£40** ... **£20** ... *French*
Bird Dance Beat ... 7" ... Stateside ... SS276 ... 1964 **£15** ... **£7.50**
Surfin' Bird ... 7" ... Stateside ... SS255 ... 1964 **£25** ... **£12.50**
Surfin' Bird ... 7" EP ... Columbia ... ESRF1491 ... 1964 **£40** ... **£20** ... *French*
Surfin' Bird ... LP ... Garrett ... GA(S)200 ... 1964 **£100** ... **£50** ... *US*
Whoa Dad ... 7" EP ... Columbia ... ESRF1627 ... 1964 **£60** ... **£30** ... *French*

TRAUM, HAPPY & ARTIE

Doubleback ... LP ... Capitol ... ST799 ... 1971 **£10** ... **£4**
Happy & Artie Traum ... LP ... Capitol ... ST586 ... 1969 **£10** ... **£4**

Title	Format	Label	Cat. No.	Year	Price	Price	Notes
Mud Acres	LP	Matchbox	239	1972	**£10**	**£4**	

TRAVEL AGENCY

Title	Format	Label	Cat. No.	Year	Price	Price	Notes
Travel Agency	LP	Viva	36017	1968	**£20**	**£8**	*US*

TRAVELING WILBURYS

Title	Format	Label	Cat. No.	Year	Price	Price	Notes
End Of The Line	12"	Warner Bros	W7637T	1989	**£8**	**£4**	*with stickers*
End Of The Line	CD-s	WEA	W7637CD	1989	**£8**	**£4**	
Handle With Care	10"	Warner Bros	W7732TE	1988	**£6**	**£2.50**	
Handle With Care	7"	Warner Bros	W7732	1988	**£5**	**£2**	*gatefold picture sleeve*
Handle With Care	CD-s	WEA	W7732CD	1988	**£8**	**£4**	
Nodody's Child	CD-s	WEA	W9973CD	1990	**£6**	**£2.50**	
She's My Baby	CD-s	WEA	W9523CD	1990	**£8**	**£4**	
Traveling Wilburys	CD	Wilbury	9257962	1988	**£15**	**£6**	
Traveling Wilburys	CD	Wilbury		1988	**£25**	**£10**	*US promo picture disc*
Traveling Wilburys	LP	Wilbury	WX224	1988	**£15**	**£6**	
Traveling Wilburys Vol. 3	CD	Wilbury	9263242	1988	**£15**	**£6**	
Traveling Wilburys Vol. 3	CD	Wilbury	9263242DJ	1990	**£25**	**£10**	*US promo picture disc*
Traveling Wilburys Vol. 3	LP	Wilbury	WX384	1988	**£15**	**£6**	
Wilbury Twist	7"	Warner Bros	W0018W	1991	**£6**	**£2.50**	*with cards*
Wilbury Twist	CD-s	Warner Bros	W0018CD	1991	**£6**	**£2.50**	

TRAVELLING STEWARTS

Title	Format	Label	Cat. No.	Year	Price	Price	Notes
Travelling Stewarts	LP	Topic	12T179	1968	**£25**	**£10**	

TRAVERS, PAT

Title	Format	Label	Cat. No.	Year	Price	Price	Notes
Makes No Difference	7"	Polydor	2814040	1976	**£10**	**£5**	*1 sided promo flexi*

TRAVIS

Title	Format	Label	Cat. No.	Year	Price	Price	Notes
Shine On Me	LP	A&M	AMLS68120	1973	**£30**	**£15**	

TRAVIS (2)

Title	Format	Label	Cat. No.	Year	Price	Price	Notes
All I Wanna Do Is Rock	10"	Red Telephone Box	PHONE001	1996	**£25**	**£12.50**	
Good Feeling	CD-s	Independiente	SAMCD44992	1997	**£6**	**£2.50**	*promo*
Line Is Fine	12"	Independiente	GOODT1	1997	**£6**	**£2.50**	*promo*
Line Is Fine	CD-s	Independiente	GOOD1	1997	**£6**	**£2.50**	*promo*

TRAVIS, DAVE

Title	Format	Label	Cat. No.	Year	Price	Price	Notes
Dave Travis	LP	Polydor	236557	1969	**£15**	**£6**	*with Dave Cousins*

TRAVIS, MERLE

Title	Format	Label	Cat. No.	Year	Price	Price	Notes
Back Home	7" EP	Capitol	EAP1891	1957	**£10**	**£5**	
Back Home	LP	Capitol	T891	1957	**£15**	**£6**	
Merle Travis And Joe Maphis	LP	Capitol	T2102	1965	**£10**	**£4**	
Merle Travis Guitar	LP	Capitol	T650	1956	**£25**	**£10**	*US*
Merle Travis Guitar No. 1	7" EP	Capitol	EAP1032	1956	**£15**	**£7.50**	
Merle Travis Guitar No. 2	7" EP	Capitol	EAP2650	1956	**£10**	**£5**	
Travis	LP	Capitol	(S)T1664	1963	**£10**	**£4**	
Walkin' The Strings	7" EP	Capitol	EAP41391	1960	**£10**	**£5**	
Walkin' The Strings	LP	Capitol	T1391	1960	**£15**	**£6**	*US*

TRAVIS, NICK

Title	Format	Label	Cat. No.	Year	Price	Price	Notes
Panic Is On	LP	HMV	CLP1036	1955	**£25**	**£10**	

TRAVIS, PAUL

Title	Format	Label	Cat. No.	Year	Price	Price	Notes
Return Of The Native	LP	A&M	AMLS68290	1975	**£15**	**£6**	

TRAVIS & BOB

Title	Format	Label	Cat. No.	Year	Price	Price	Notes
Tell Him No	7"	Pye	7N25018	1959	**£6**	**£2.50**	

TREASURE ISLE BOYS

Title	Format	Label	Cat. No.	Year	Price	Price	Notes
Love Is A Treasure	7"	Trojan	TR010	1967	**£10**	**£5**	*Tommy McCook B side*

TREBLETONES

Title	Format	Label	Cat. No.	Year	Price	Price	Notes
Butlin Holiday	7"	Butlin	CP2424	1961	**£5**	**£2**	
In Real Life	7"	Oriole	CB1838	1963	**£5**	**£2**	

TREDEGAR

Title	Format	Label	Cat. No.	Year	Price	Price	Notes
Duma	7"	Aires	CEP0001	1986	**£15**	**£7.50**	
Tredegar	LP	Aires	CEPLP001	1986	**£15**	**£6**	*embossed sleeve*
Tredegar	LP	Aires	CEPLP001	1986	**£10**	**£4**	

TREDJE, ANNA SJALV

Title	Format	Label	Cat. No.	Year	Price	Price	Notes
Tussilago Fanfara	LP	Silence	SR4646	1979	**£20**	**£8**	*Swedish*

TREE

Title	Format	Label	Cat. No.	Year	Price	Price	Notes
Tree	LP	Goat Farm	580	1970	**£75**	**£37.50**	*US*

TREE, VIRGINIA (SHIRLEY KENT)

Title	Format	Label	Cat. No.	Year	Price	Price	Notes
Fresh Out	LP	Minstrel	0001	1975	**£30**	**£15**	

TREES

Despite the inclusion of tracks by Trees on two of the best-selling CBS rock album samplers, the group's albums sold poorly. They are, however, superior folk-rock and have been sought-after by collectors for a long time (without, however, changing very much in value over the years). Many of the same musicians formed the seventies band Casablanca, but for some reason their album is almost completely ignored by collectors.

Garden Of Jane Delawney	LP	CBS	63837	1970	**£60**	**£30**	
Garden Of Jane Delawney	LP	Decal	LIK15	1987	**£10**	**£4**	
Nothing Special	7"	CBS	5078	1970	**£10**	**£5**	
On The Shore	LP	Decal	LIK12	1987	**£10**	**£4**	
On The Shore	LP	CBS	64168	1970	**£60**	**£30**	

TREESE, JACK

Maitoo The Truffle Man	LP	Savanah		197–	**£15**	**£6**	*French*

TREETOPS

California My Way	7"	Parlophone	R5669	1968	**£4**	**£1.50**	
Don't Worry Baby	7"	Parlophone	R5628	1967	**£4**	**£1.50**	
Mississippi Valley	7"	Columbia	DB8727	1970	**£4**	**£1.50**	
Without The One You Love	7"	Columbia	DB8799	1971	**£4**	**£1.50**	

TREKKAS

Please Go	7"	Planet	PLF105	1965	**£30**	**£15**	

TREKKERS

Trekkers Go Uptown	10" LP	Advision		1963	**£75**	**£37.50**	

TREMELOES

58/68 World Explosion	LP	CBS	BN26388	1968	**£10**	**£4**	*US*
Blessed	7"	Decca	F12423	1966	**£6**	**£2.50**	
Chip, Rick, Alan And Dave	LP	CBS	(S)BPG63138	1967	**£10**	**£4**	
Here Come The Tremeloes	LP	CBS	(S)BPG63017	1967	**£10**	**£4**	
Live In Cabaret	LP	CBS	63547	1969	**£10**	**£4**	
Master	LP	CBS	64242	1970	**£10**	**£4**	
My Little Lady	7" EP	CBS	EP6402	1968	**£6**	**£2.50**	

TREMORS

Beaten An Knuller	LP	Elite	SOLPS246	1965	**£12**	**£5**	*German*

TREND

Shot On Sight	7"	Page One	POF004	1966	**£10**	**£5**	

TRENDS

All My Loving	7"	Piccadilly	7N35171	1964	**£5**	**£2**	
Way You Do The Things You Do	7"	Pye	7N15644	1964	**£5**	**£2**	

TRENDSETTERS

At The Hotel De France	7" EP	Oak	RGJ999	196–	**£20**	**£10**	
You Don't Care	7"	Silver Phoenix	1001	1964	**£30**	**£15**	

TRENDSETTERS LTD

The roots of King Crimson lie in the four unprepossessing singles made by Trendsetters Ltd, which feature the early work of Michael and Peter Giles.

Funny Way Of Showing Your Love	7"	Parlophone	R5324	1965	**£10**	**£5**	
Go Away	7"	Parlophone	R5191	1964	**£10**	**£5**	
Hello Josephine	7"	Parlophone	R5161	1964	**£10**	**£5**	
In A Big Way	7"	Parlophone	R5118	1964	**£10**	**£5**	

TRENIERS

Go Go Go	7"	Fontana	H137	1958	**£100**	**£50**	
Ooh La La	7"	Coral	Q72319	1958	**£25**	**£12.50**	
Rock'n'Roll With The Treniers	10" LP	Philips	B07746R	195–	**£150**	**£75**	
Souvenir Album	LP	Dot	DLP3257	1960	**£30**	**£15**	*US*
Treniers On TV	LP	Epic	LG3125	195–	**£60**	**£30**	*US*
When Your Hair Has Turned Silver	7"	London	HLD8858	1959	**£25**	**£12.50**	

TRENT, JACKIE

If You Love Me	7"	Piccadilly	7N35165	1964	**£6**	**£2.50**	
Magic Of Jackie Trent	LP	Pye	NPL18125	1965	**£12**	**£5**	
Once More With Feeling	LP	Pye	NPL18173	1967	**£10**	**£4**	
One Who Really Loves You	7"	Oriole	CB1749	1962	**£6**	**£2.50**	
Stop Me And Buy One	LP	Pye	NPL18201	1967	**£12**	**£5**	
Where Are You Now	7" EP	Pye	NEP24225	1965	**£6**	**£2.50**	
You Baby	7"	Pye	7N17047	1966	**£8**	**£4**	

TREPTE, ULI

Spacebox	LP	Spacebox	SP1	1981	**£10**	**£4**	*German, record mailer sleeve*

TRESPASS

Bright Lights	7"	Trial	CASE3	1982	**£15**	**£7.50**	
Jealousy	7"	Trial	CASE2	1980	**£10**	**£5**	
One Of These Days	7"	Trial	CASE1	1979	**£10**	**£5**	

TRETOW, MICHAEL B.
Michael B. Tretow .... LP .... CBS .... 81143 .... 1976 £20 .... £8 .... German

TREVOR
Down In Virginia .... 7" .... Blue Beat .... BB228 .... 1964 £12 .... £6 ....
Everyday Like A Holiday .... 7" .... Blue Cat .... BS153 .... 1969 £4 .... £1.50 .... with the Maytones

TRIADE
1998: La Storia Di Sabazio .... LP .... Derby .... DBR65801 .... 1973 £30 .... £15 .... Italian

TRIANA
Hyos Del Agobio .... LP .... Movie Play .... 1709079 .... 1977 £15 .... £6 .... Spanish
Sombra Y Luz .... LP .... Movie Play .... 1714394 .... 1979 £12 .... £5 .... Spanish
Triana .... LP .... Movie Play .... 1706787 .... 1975 £15 .... £6 .... Spanish
Un Encuentro .... LP .... Movie Play .... 5506785 .... 1980 £12 .... £5 .... Spanish

TRIANGLE
Vol. 1 .... LP .... Select .... 298193 .... 1970 £20 .... £8 .... Canadian

TRIANGLE (2)
How Now Blue Cow .... LP .... Capitol .... ST5001 .... 1969 £30 .... £15 .... US

TRIARCHY
Metal Messiah .... 7" .... Direct .... NEON2 .... 1980 £40 .... £20 ....
Save The Khan .... 7" .... SRT .... SRT79CUS599 .... 1979 £50 .... £25 ....
Save The Khan .... 7" .... Direct .... NEON1 .... 1979 £20 .... £10 ....

TRIBAN
Black Paper Roses .... 7" .... Decca .... F13115 .... 1970 £5 .... £2 ....
Leaving On A Jet Plane .... 7" .... CSP .... 707 .... 1969 £5 .... £2 ....
Rainmaker .... LP .... Cambrian .... MCT218 .... 1972 £30 .... £15 ....
Triban .... LP .... Cambrian .... MCT592 .... 1969 £30 .... £15 ....

TRIBE
Gamma Goochi .... 7" .... Planet .... PLF108 .... 1966 £40 .... £20 ....
Love Is A Beautiful Thing .... 7" .... RCA .... RCA1592 .... 1967 £10 .... £5 ....

TRIBE (2)
Dancin' To The Beat Of My Heart .... 7" .... Polydor .... 56510 .... 1970 £10 .... £5 ....

TRIBE, TONY
Gonna Give You All The Love .... 7" .... Downtown .... DT439 .... 1969 £5 .... £2 .... Herbie Grey B side
Red Red Wine .... 7" .... Down Town .... DT419 .... 1969 £4 .... £1.50 .... Rico B side

TRIBE OF TOFFS
John Kettley Is A Weatherman .... 7" .... Completely Different .... DAFT1 .... 1988 £4 .... £1.50 ....

TRIFFIDS
Bury Me Deep In Love .... CD-s ... Island .... CID424 .... 1989 £5 .... £2 ....
Falling Over You .... CD-s ... Island .... CID413 .... 1989 £5 .... £2 ....
Goodbye Little Boy .... CD-s ... Island .... CID420 .... 1989 £5 .... £2 ....
Holy Water .... CD-s ... Island .... CID367 .... 1988 £5 .... £2 ....

TRIFFIDS (2)
Are Really Folk .... LP .... Fontana .... TL5231 .... 1965 £10 .... £4 ....

TRIFFIDS (3)
Lookin' Around .... 7" .... Columbia .... DB7084 .... 1963 £4 .... £1.50

TRIFLE
First Meeting .... LP .... Dawn .... DNLS3017 .... 1971 £15 .... £6 ....

TRIKHA, PANDIT KANWAR SAIN
Three Sitar Pieces .... LP .... Mushroom .... 100MR7 .... 1970 £40 .... £20 ....

TRILOGY
I'm Beginning To Feel It .... LP .... Mercury .... 6338034 .... 1970 £10 .... £4 ....

TRINITY HOUSE
Flashback Through History .... LP .... Profile .... GMOR146 .... 1977 £40 .... £20 ....

TRIO
Trio .... LP .... London .... LTZC15017 .... 1956 £30 .... £15 ....
Trio With Guests .... LP .... London .... LTZC15046 .... 1957 £25 .... £10 ....

TRIO (2)
In the heady days of the early seventies, the Trio (John Surman, Barre Phillips, and Stu Martin) achieved the remarkable feat of playing uncompromising avant-garde jazz while gaining a record contract with one of the major record companies. The group even managed a tour of rock venues on the strength of this, yet actually managed to sell very few records, as their scarcity today testifies.

By Contract .... LP .... Ogun .... OG529 .... 1978 £12 .... £5 ....
Conflagration .... LP .... Dawn .... DNLS3022 .... 1971 £30 .... £15 ....
Trio .... LP .... Dawn .... DNLS3006 .... 1970 £40 .... £20 .... double

TRIOS, CHUCK & AMAZING MAZE

Call On You	7"	Action	ACT4517	1968	**£4**	**£1.50**	

TRIP

Atlantide	LP	RCA		1972	**£50**	**£25**	

TRIPPERS

Dance With Me	7"	Pye	7N25388	1966	**£10**	**£5**	

TRIPSICHORD MUSIC BOX

San Francisco Sound	LP	Janus	JLS3016	1971	**£150**	**£75**	*US*

TRISHA

Darkness Of My Night	7"	CBS	201800	1965	**£4**	**£1.50**	

TRISTANO, LENNIE

Bebop	LP	Mercury	SMWL21028	1969	**£10**	**£4**	*with tracks by Red Rodney*
Lennie Tristano	LP	London	LTZK15033	1957	**£30**	**£15**	
Lines	LP	Atlantic	590031	1969	**£10**	**£4**	
New Tristano	LP	Atlantic	590017	1968	**£12**	**£5**	

TRISTAR AIRBUS

Travellin' Man	7"	RCA	RCA2170	1972	**£4**	**£1.50**	

TRISTRAM SHANDY

Tristram Shandy	LP	Silvermore	SIL0001	1979	**£10**	**£4**	

TRIUMPH

Rock'n'Roll Machine	LP	Attic	LATX1036	1977	**£12**	**£5**	*Canadian, vinyl & metal*

TRIXIE'S BIG RED MOTORBIKE

Norman And Narcissus	7"	Lobby Ludd	L100001	1984	**£5**	**£2**	
Splash Of Red	7"	Chew	CH9271	1982	**£6**	**£2.50**	
Trixie's Big Red Motorbike EP	7"	Chew	RAM510	1982	**£4**	**£1.50**	

TRO, MARCUS

Introducing	LP	Ember	EMB3365	1965	**£15**	**£6**	
Tell Me	7"	Ember	EMBS203	1965	**£6**	**£2.50**	*picture sleeve*

TROGGS

When the Troggs' 'Wild Thing', with its novelty ocarina solo offsetting the Louie Louie riff, climbed to the top of the charts, Jonathan King offered to treat the group to a slap-up meal if they were still in the charts three years later. He lost his bet – but only just. The Troggs' simple hard(ish) rock bordered on the inept, but they have managed to create a considerable affection in the minds of the record-collecting public. All the Troggs' original recordings are becoming increasingly sought-after, especially the LP *Mixed Bag*, which includes the group's over-the-top attempts at psychedelia.

Anyway That You Want Me	7"	Page One	POF010	1966	**£4**	**£1.50**	
Anyway That You Want Me	7" EP	Fontana	460987	1966	**£25**	**£12.50**	*French*
Best Of Vol. 1	LP	Page One	FOR001	1967	**£20**	**£8**	
Best Of Vol. 2	LP	Page One	FOR002	1967	**£25**	**£10**	
Cellophane	LP	Page One	POL003	1967	**£40**	**£20**	
Contrasts	LP	DJM	DJML009	1970	**£15**	**£6**	
Easy Livin'	7"	Page One	POF164	1970	**£4**	**£1.50**	
Everything's Funny	7"	Pye	7N45147	1972	**£4**	**£1.50**	
Evil Woman	7"	Page One	POF114	1969	**£4**	**£1.50**	
From Nowhere	LP	Fontana	(S)TL5355	1966	**£30**	**£15**	
Give It To Me	7"	Page One	POF015	1967	**£4**	**£1.50**	
Give It To Me	7" EP	Fontana	460203	1967	**£25**	**£12.50**	*French*
Hi Hi Hazel	7"	Page One	POF030	1967	**£4**	**£1.50**	
Hip Hip Hooray	7"	Page One	POF092	1968	**£4**	**£1.50**	
I Can't Control Myself	7"	Page One	POF001	1966	**£4**	**£1.50**	
I Can't Control Myself	7" EP	Fontana	460981	1966	**£25**	**£12.50**	*French*
Lazy Weekend	7"	DJM	DJM248	1971	**£4**	**£1.50**	
Listen To The Man	7"	Pye	7N45244	1973	**£4**	**£1.50**	
Little Girl	7"	Page One	POF056	1968	**£4**	**£1.50**	
Lost Girl	7"	CBS	202038	1966	**£20**	**£10**	
Love Is All Around	7"	Page One	POF040	1967	**£4**	**£1.50**	
Lover	7"	Page One	POF171	1970	**£4**	**£1.50**	
Mixed Bag	LP	Page One	POLS012	1968	**£75**	**£37.50**	
My Lady	7"	Page One	POF022	1967	**£25**	**£12.50**	
Night Of The Long Grass	7"	Page One	POF022	1967	**£4**	**£1.50**	
Night Of The Long Grass	7" EP	Fontana	460212	1967	**£25**	**£12.50**	*French*
On Tour	LP	Page One	POL1	1968	**£150**	**£75**	*export*
Raver	7"	Page One	POF182	1970	**£4**	**£1.50**	
Strange Movies	7"	Pye	7N45295	1973	**£4**	**£1.50**	
Surprise Surprise	7"	Page One	POF064	1968	**£4**	**£1.50**	
Trogg Tops Vol. 1	7" EP	Page One	POE001	1967	**£12**	**£6**	
Trogg Tops Vol. 2	7" EP	Page One	POE002	1967	**£25**	**£12.50**	
Trogglodynamite	LP	Page One	POL001	1966	**£30**	**£15**	
Trogglomania	LP	Page One	POS602	1969	**£25**	**£10**	
Troggs Tapes	7"	DJM	DJS6	1981	**£5**	**£2**	*double*
Wild Thing	7"	Fontana	TF689	1966	**£4**	**£1.50**	
Wild Thing	7" EP	Fontana	460974	1966	**£25**	**£12.50**	*French*
Wild Thing	LP	Fontana	SRF27556	1966	**£40**	**£20**	*US*

With a Girl Like You	7"	Fontana	TF717	1966	**£4**	**£1.50**	
With A Girl Like You	7" EP	Fontana	465321	1966	**£25**	**£12.50**	*French*
You Can Cry If You Want To	7"	Page One	POF082	1968	**£4**	**£1.50**	

TROIS, CHUCK

Call On You	7"	Action	ACT4517	1968	**£5**	**£2**	

TROJAN

March Is On	LP	GI	GILP444	1988	**£10**	**£4**	

TROJANS

Man I'm Gonna Be	7"	Decca	F11065	1958	**£12**	**£6**	

TROLL

Animated Music	LP	Smash	SRS67114	1968	**£50**	**£25**	*US*

TROLL BROTHERS

You Turn Me On	7"	SRT	SRT733316	197–	**£6**	**£2.50**	

TROMBONES INC.

Trombones Inc.	LP	Warner Bros	WM4023/ WS8023	1961	**£12**	**£5**	

TRONICS

Cantina	7"	Fontana	H348	1961	**£6**	**£2.50**	

TRONICS (2)

Suzie	7"	Tronics	T001	1978	**£5**	**£2**	
Time Off	7"	Tronics	T002	1979	**£5**	**£2**	

TROOPERS

Get Out	7"	Vogue	V9087	1957	**£350**	**£210**	*best auctioned*

TROTT, ARCHIBALD

Get Together	7"	Black Swan	WI407	1964	**£10**	**£5**	

TROTTO

Trotto	LP	Free Reed	FRR005	1976	**£10**	**£4**	

TROUBADOURS

Fascination	7"	London	HLR8469	1957	**£8**	**£4**	
Lights Of Paris	7"	London	HLR8541	1958	**£8**	**£4**	
Troubadours	7" EP	London	RER1135	1958	**£5**	**£2**	

TROUBLE

After The War	LP	Sonet	SLPS1521	1970	**£20**	**£8**	*Danish*

TROUP, BOBBY

Bobby Troup	10" LP	Capitol	LC6660	1954	**£10**	**£4**	
Bobby Troup	7" EP	Capitol	EAP1484	1955	**£5**	**£2**	
Julie Is Her Name	7"	Capitol	CL14219	1954	**£4**	**£1.50**	

TROW, BOB

Soft Squeeze Baby	7"	London	HL8082	1954	**£15**	**£7.50**	

TROWER, ROBIN

The former guitarist with Procol Harum was never entirely happy with a group that provided limited opportunity for guitar excess. The albums made by his own power trio were a different matter. Heavily influenced by Jimi Hendrix, Trower was actually one of the few guitarists working in the seventies who was able to impose something of himself on to the Hendrix sound. Bass player Jimmy Dewar, who also proved himself to be a fine lead vocalist, had previously been a member of Stone the Crows – and earlier still was rhythm guitarist with Lulu and the Luvvers – while the drummer on the first two albums, Reg Isadore, played with Peter Bardens amongst other people, and was later to be found supporting Peter Green on a couple of his rare visits to the recording studio.

Bridge Of Sighs	CD	Chrysalis	CD25CR15	1994	**£12**	**£5**	*Chrysalis 25 pack*
Bridge Of Sighs	LP	Charisma	CHR1057	1974	**£10**	**£4**	
For Earth Below	LP	Charisma	CHR1073	1975	**£10**	**£4**	
Twice Removed From Yesterday	LP	Charisma	CHR1039	1973	**£10**	**£4**	

TROY, DORIS

Ain't That Cute	7"	Apple	24	1970	**£8**	**£4**	*picture sleeve*
Ain't That Cute	7"	Apple	24	1970	**£4**	**£1.50**	
Doris Troy	LP	Apple	SAPCOR13	1970	**£20**	**£8**	
Heartaches	7"	Atlantic	AT4032	1965	**£5**	**£2**	
I'll Do Anything	7"	Toast	TT507	1968	**£4**	**£1.50**	
I'll Do Anything	7"	Cameo Parkway	C101	1962	**£50**	**£25**	
Jacob's Ladder	7"	Apple	28	1970	**£5**	**£2**	
Just One Look	7"	London	HLK9749	1963	**£10**	**£5**	
Just One Look	7"	Atlantic	584148	1968	**£4**	**£1.50**	
Just One Look	LP	Atlantic	(SD)8088	1964	**£30**	**£15**	*US*
Just One Look	LP	Polydor	2464001	1974	**£12**	**£5**	
One More Chance	7"	Atlantic	AT4020	1965	**£5**	**£2**	
Rainbow Testament	LP	Polydor	2956001	1972	**£10**	**£4**	
Stretching Out	LP	People	PLEO12	1974	**£12**	**£5**	
Whatcha Gonna Do About It	7"	Atlantic	AT4011	1964	**£5**	**£2**	
Whatcha Gonna Do About It	7" EP	Atlantic	AET6007	1965	**£40**	**£20**	

TROY & THE T-BIRDS

Twistle	7"	London	HL9476	1961	£6	£2.50	

TRUBROT

Trubrot	LP	Parlophone	027	1969	£100	£50	*Danish*
Undir Ahrifum	LP	Parlophone	023	1970	£125	£62.50	*Danish*

TRUMPETEERS

Milky White Way	LP	Score	4021	1960	£50	£25	*US*

TRUTH

Baby Don't You Know	7"	Pye	7N15923	1965	£6	£2.50	
Girl	7"	Pye	7N17035	1966	£6	£2.50	
I Go To Sleep	7"	Pye	7N17095	1966	£15	£7.50	
Jingle Jangle	7"	Deram	DM105	1966	£30	£15	
Seuno	7"	Decca	F22764	1968	£10	£5	
Walk Away Renee	7"	Decca	F12582	1967	£8	£4	
Who's Wrong	7"	Pye	7N15998	1965	£8	£4	

TRUTH (2)

Truth	LP	People	PLP5002	1970	£40	£20	*US*

TRUTH & JANEY

Just A Little Bit Of Magic	LP	Bee Bel		1979	£12	£5	*US*
Live	LP	Rock And Bach		1988	£15	£6	*US double*
No Rest For The Wicked	LP	Montrose	MR376	1976	£75	£37.50	*US*

TRUTH OF TRUTHS

Truth Of Truths	LP	Oak	OR1001	1971	£25	£10	*double*

TSANAKLIDOU, TANIA

Charlie Chaplin	7"	EMI	EMI2797	1978	£5	£2	

TUBB, ERNEST

All Time Hits	LP	Decca	DL(7)4046	1961	£12	£5	*US*
Country Double Date	7" EP	Brunswick	OE9148	1955	£10	£5	
Daddy Of 'Em All	LP	Decca	DL8553	1956	£20	£8	*US*
Daddy Of 'Em All	LP	Brunswick	LAT8260	1958	£15	£6	
Daddy Of 'Em All Pt 1	7" EP	Brunswick	OE9372	1958	£10	£5	
Daddy Of 'Em All Pt 2	7" EP	Brunswick	OE9373	1958	£10	£5	
Daddy Of 'Em All Pt 3	7" EP	Brunswick	OE9374	1958	£10	£5	
Ernest Tubb Record Shop	LP	Brunswick	LAT8349	1960	£15	£6	
Ernest Tubb Story Vol. 1	LP	Brunswick	LAT8313	1959	£10	£4	
Ernest Tubb Story Vol. 2	LP	Brunswick	LAT8314	1960	£10	£4	
Favorites	10" LP	Decca	DL5301	1951	£25	£10	*US*
Favorites	LP	Decca	DL8291	1956	£20	£8	*US*
Favourites	LP	Brunswick	LAT8161	1957	£15	£6	
Golden Favorites	LP	Decca	DL(7)4118	1961	£12	£5	*US*
Importance Of Being Ernest	LP	Brunswick	LAT8292	1959	£15	£6	
Jimmie Rodgers Songs	10" LP	Decca	DL5336	1951	£25	£10	*US*
Jimmie Rodgers Songs	10" LP	Brunswick	LA8736	1956	£25	£10	
Just Call Me Lonesome	LP	Decca	DL(7)4385	1964	£12	£5	*US*
Midnight Jamboree	LP	Decca	DL(7)4045	1960	£12	£5	*US*
My Pick Of The Hits	LP	Brunswick	LAT8627	1966	£12	£5	
Old Rugged Cross	10" LP	Decca	DL5334	1951	£25	£10	*US*
On Tour	LP	Decca	DL(7)4321	1962	£12	£5	*US*
Sing A Song Of Christmas	10" LP	Decca	DL5497	1954	£25	£10	*US*
So Doggone Lonesome	7"	Brunswick	05587	1956	£10	£5	
Thirty Days	7"	Brunswick	05527	1956	£25	£12.50	
What Am I Living For	7"	Decca	BM31214	195–	£8	£4	*export*

TUBB, JUSTIN

Take A Letter Miss Gray	7" EP	RCA	RCX7133	1964	£20	£10	

TUBES

Prime Time	7"	A&M	AMS7423	1979	£25	£12.50	*7 × coloured vinyl 7" plus picture disc, boxed, promo*
Remote Control	LP	A&M	AMLH9964751	1979	£10	£4	*Dutch picture disc*
Tubes First Clean Album	LP	A&M	SP17012	1978	£12	£5	*US promo*

TUBEWAY ARMY

Are 'Friends' Electric?	12"	Intercord	INT126501	1979	£10	£5	*German*
Are 'Friends' Electric?	7"	Beggars Banquet	BEG18P	1979	£6	£2.50	*picture disc, insert*
Bombers	7"	Beggars Banquet	BEG8	1978	£5	£2	
Down In The Park	12"	Beggars Banquet	BEG17T	1979	£15	£7.50	
Replicas	LP	Beggars Banquet	BEGA7	1979	£15	£6	*with poster*
That's Too Bad	7"	Beggars Banquet	BEG5	1978	£5	£2	
This Is My Life	7"	Beggars Banquet	TUB1	1985	£25	£12.50	*promo*

Tubeway Army	LP	Beggars Banquet	BEGA4	1978	£30	£15	blue vinyl
Tubeway Army '78–'79 Vol. 2	12"	Beggars Banquet	BEG123E	1984	£6	£2.50	red or black vinyl
Tubeway Army '78–'79 Vol. 3	12"	Beggars Banquet	BEG124E	1984	£6	£2.50	blue or black vinyl
Tubeway Army Vol. 1	12"	Beggars Banquet	BEG92E	1985	£6	£2.50	yellow vinyl

TUCKER, BESSIE

Blues By Bessie	7" EP	HMV	7EG8085	1955	£20	£10	

TUCKER, BILLY JOE

Boogie Woogie Bill	7"	London	HLD9455	1961	£50	£25	

TUCKER, CY

I Apologise	7"	Fontana	TF470	1964	£5	£2	
My Friend	7"	Fontana	TF534	1965	£5	£2	
My Prayer	7"	Fontana	TF424	1963	£6	£2.50	

TUCKER, MAUREEN

Playin' Possum	LP	Trash	TLP1001	1981	£10	£4	US

TUCKER, SOPHIE

Cabaret Days	LP	Mercury	MG20046	1954	£10	£4	
Great Sophie Tucker	LP	Brunswick	LAT8144	1957	£10	£4	
My Dream	LP	Mercury	MG20035	1954	£10	£4	

TUCKER, TOMMY

Hi Heel Sneakers	7"	Pye	7N25238	1964	£8	£4	
Hi Heel Sneakers	7"	Chess	CRS8086	1969	£5	£2	
Hi Heel Sneakers	7" EP	Pye	NEP44027	1964	£25	£12.50	
Hi Heel Sneakers	LP	Checker	2990	1964	£30	£15	US
Long Tall Shorty	7"	Pye	7N25246	1964	£8	£4	
Oh What A Feeling	7"	London	HLU9932	1964	£20	£10	

TUCKY BUZZARD

Alright On The Night	LP	Purple	TPSA7510	1973	£15	£6	
Buzzard	LP	Purple	TPSA7512	1973	£15	£6	
Coming On Again	LP	Capitol	864	1971	£15	£6	US
Gold Medallions	7"	Purple	PUR113	1973	£4	£1.50	
Gold Medallions	7"	Purple	PUR134	1977	£4	£1.50	
Warm Slash	LP	Capitol	EST864	1969	£15	£6	

TUDOR LODGE

Lady's Changing Home	7"	Vertigo	6059044	1971	£10	£5	
Tudor Lodge	LP	Vertigo	6360043	1971	£150	£75	

TUDOR MINSTRELS

Family Way	7"	Decca	F12536	1966	£10	£5	

TUESDAY'S CHILDREN

Baby's Gone	7"	Pye	7N17406	1967	£5	£2	
High On A Hill	7"	Columbia	DB8018	1966	£6	£2.50	
In The Valley Of The Shadow Of Love	7"	Pye	7N17474	1968	£4	£1.50	
Strange Light From The East	7"	King	KG1051	1967	£8	£4	
When You Walk In The Sun	7"	Columbia	DB7978	1966	£6	£2.50	

T.U.F.F.

We've Got A Hot One	7"	SONO	001	198–	£12	£6	test pressing

TULLY

Loving Hard	LP	Harvest	SHVL607	1971	£50	£25	Australian
Sea Of Joy	LP	Harvest	SHVL605	1971	£50	£25	Australian
Tully	LP	Harvest	SRXO7926	1970	£50	£25	Australian

TULLY, LEE

Around The World With Elwood Pretzel	7"	London	HL8363	1957	£50	£25	gold label

TUNDRA

Kentish Garland	LP	Sweet Folk	SFA078	1978	£15	£6	
Kentish Songster	LP	Greenwich Village	GVR208	197–	£15	£6	

TUNEROCKERS

Green Mosquito	7"	London	HLT8717	1958	£20	£10	

TUNETOPPERS

At The Madison Dance Party	LP	Amy	A1	1960	£20	£8	US

TUNEWEAVERS

Happy Happy Birthday Baby	7"	London	HL8503	1957	£100	£50	B side by Paul Gayten

TUNNEY, PADDY

Flowery Vale	LP	Topic	12TS289	1976	£10	£4	
Ireland Her Own	LP	Topic	12T153	1966	£15	£6	with Arthur Kearney

Title	Format	Label	Cat. No.	Year	Mint	VG+	Notes
Irish Edge	LP	Topic	12T165	1966	**£15**	**£6**	
Wild Bees Nest	LP	Topic	12T139	1965	**£15**	**£6**	

TURNER, BRUCE

Title	Format	Label	Cat. No.	Year	Mint	VG+	Notes
Bruce Turner	10" LP	Polygon	JTL2	1955	**£30**	**£15**	

TURNER, DENNIS

Title	Format	Label	Cat. No.	Year	Mint	VG+	Notes
Lover Please	7"	London	HL9537	1962	**£6**	**£2.50**	

TURNER, GORDON

Title	Format	Label	Cat. No.	Year	Mint	VG+	Notes
Meditation	LP	Charisma	CAS1009	1969	**£30**	**£15**	

TURNER, IKE

Title	Format	Label	Cat. No.	Year	Mint	VG+	Notes
Ike Turner Rocks The Blues	LP	Ember	EMB3395	1968	**£15**	**£6**	

TURNER, IKE & TINA

Title	Format	Label	Cat. No.	Year	Mint	VG+	Notes
Anything I Wasn't Born With	7"	HMV	POP1544	1966	**£10**	**£5**	
Crazy 'Bout You Baby	7"	Liberty	LIB15233	1969	**£5**	**£2**	
Dance With Ike & Tina Turner	LP	Sue	LP2003	1962	**£40**	**£20**	US
Don't Play Me Cheap	LP	Sue	LP2005	1963	**£40**	**£20**	US
Dynamite	LP	Sue	LP2004	1963	**£40**	**£20**	US
Finger Poppin'	7"	Warner Bros	WB153	1965	**£8**	**£4**	
Fool In Love	7"	London	HLU9226	1960	**£6**	**£2.50**	
Goodbye So Long	7"	Stateside	SS551	1966	**£4**	**£1.50**	
Greatest Hits	LP	London	HAC8248	1965	**£25**	**£10**	
Greatest Hits	LP	Sue	LP1038	1965	**£25**	**£10**	US
Hunter	7"	Harvest	HAR5018	1970	**£5**	**£2**	
Hunter	LP	Harvest	SHSP4001	1970	**£25**	**£10**	
I Can't Believe What You Say	7"	Sue	WI350	1964	**£10**	**£5**	
I'll Never Need More Than This	7"	London	HLU10155	1967	**£5**	**£2**	
I'm Gonna Do All I Can	7"	Minit	MLF11016	1969	**£6**	**£2.50**	
I'm Hooked	7"	HMV	POP1583	1967	**£20**	**£10**	
Ike & Tina Turner Revue	LP	Ember	EMB3368	1966	**£12**	**£5**	
Ike & Tina Turner Show II	LP	Warner Bros	WB5904	1967	**£10**	**£4**	
Ike & Tina Turner Show Vol. 1	7" EP	Warner Bros	WEP619	1965	**£25**	**£12.50**	
Ike And Tina Turner Show	LP	Warner Bros	WM8170	1965	**£20**	**£8**	
Ike And Tina Turner Show	LP	Warner Bros	W1579	1966	**£10**	**£4**	
In Person	LP	Minit	MLS40014	1969	**£10**	**£4**	
It's Gonna Work Out Fine	7"	Sue	WI306	1964	**£10**	**£5**	
It's Gonna Work Out Fine	7"	London	HL9451	1961	**£10**	**£5**	
It's Gonna Work Out Fine	LP	Sue	LP2007	1963	**£40**	**£20**	US
Love Like Yours	7"	London	HLU10083	1966	**£4**	**£1.50**	
Make Em Wait	7"	A&M	AMS783	1970	**£6**	**£2.50**	
Outta Season	LP	Liberty	LBS83241	1969	**£10**	**£4**	
Please Please Please	7"	Sue	WI376	1965	**£10**	**£5**	
Poor Fool	7"	Sue	WI322	1964	**£10**	**£5**	
River Deep & Mountain High	LP	London	HAU/SHU8298	1966	**£20**	**£8**	
River Deep & Mountain High	LP	Philles	PHLP4011	1966	**£1250**	**£875**	*US, no cover*
River Deep Mountain High	7"	London	HLU10046	1966	**£4**	**£1.50**	
River Deep Mountain High	7"	A&M	AMS829	1971	**£4**	**£1.50**	
River Deep, Mountain HIgh	CD	Mobile Fidelity	MFCD849	1987	**£15**	**£6**	*US audiophile*
So Fine	7"	London	HLU10189	1968	**£4**	**£1.50**	
So Fine	LP	London	HAU/SHU8370	1969	**£10**	**£4**	
Somebody	7"	Warner Bros	WB5766	1966	**£10**	**£5**	
Somebody Needs You	7" EP	Warner Bros	WEP620	1966	**£25**	**£12.50**	
Soul Of Ike & Tina Turner	7" EP	Sue	IEP706	1966	**£75**	**£37.50**	
Sound Of Ike & Tina Turner	LP	Sue	LP2001	1961	**£50**	**£25**	US
Tell Her I'm Not At Home	7"	Warner Bros	WB5753	1966	**£4**	**£1.50**	
We Need An Understanding	7"	London	HLU10217	1968	**£4**	**£1.50**	

TURNER, JESSE LEE

Title	Format	Label	Cat. No.	Year	Mint	VG+	Notes
Do I Worry	7"	Top Rank	JAR516	1960	**£8**	**£4**	
I'm The Little Space Girl's Father	7"	London	HLP9108	1960	**£20**	**£10**	
Shake Baby Shake	7"	London	HLL8785	1959	**£40**	**£20**	
Teenage Misery	7"	Top Rank	JAR303	1960	**£10**	**£5**	
Voice Changing Song	7"	Vogue	V9201	1962	**£8**	**£4**	

TURNER, JOE

Title	Format	Label	Cat. No.	Year	Mint	VG+	Notes
Best Of Joe Turner	LP	Atlantic	8081	1963	**£30**	**£15**	US
Big Joe Is Here	LP	London	HAE2231	1960	**£60**	**£30**	
Big Joe Rides Again	LP	London	LTZK15205/ SAHK6123	1960	**£50**	**£25**	
Boogie Woogie Country Girl	7"	London	HLE8332	1956	**£500**	**£330**	*best auctioned*
Boss Of The Blues	LP	London	LTZK15053/ SAHK6019	1957	**£60**	**£30**	
Boss Of The Blues	LP	Atlantic	590006	1967	**£10**	**£4**	
Careless Love	LP	Savoy	MG14106	1963	**£25**	**£10**	US
Corrine Corrina	7"	London	HLE8301	1956	**£250**	**£150**	*tri-centre, best auctioned*
Honey Hush	7"	London	HLE9055	1960	**£30**	**£15**	
Joe Turner	LP	Atlantic	8005	1957	**£75**	**£37.50**	US
Joe Turner & Pete Johnson	LP	EmArcy	36014	1955	**£75**	**£37.50**	US
Joe Turner & Pete Johnson Group	7" EP	Emarcy	ERE1500	1956	**£25**	**£12.50**	
Joe Turner & The Blues	LP	Savoy	MG14012	1962	**£25**	**£10**	US
Jumpin' The Blues	LP	Fontana	688802ZL	1965	**£15**	**£6**	
Kansas City Jazz	LP	Atlantic	1243	1956	**£75**	**£37.50**	US
Lipstick Powder And Paint	7"	London	HLE8357	1957	**£300**	**£180**	*gold label, best auctioned*

Mardi Gras Boogie	78	MGM	MGM253	1949	**£12**	**£6**	
Midnight Cannonball	7"	Atlantic	AT4026	1965	**£8**	**£4**	
My Little Honeydripper	7"	London	HLK9119	1960	**£30**	**£15**	
Presenting Joe Turner	7" EP	London	REE1111	1957	**£100**	**£50**	*tri-centre*
Rockin' The Blues	LP	London	HAE2173	1959	**£75**	**£37.50**	
Singing The Blues	LP	Stateside	(S)SL10226	1967	**£12**	**£5**	
Sings The Blues Vol. 1	LP	Realm	RM207	1964	**£10**	**£4**	
Sings The Blues Vol. 2	LP	Realm	RM229	1964	**£10**	**£4**	
Stride By Stride	LP	77	LEU1232	1964	**£12**	**£5**	

TURNER, JOHN

Jewel	LP	private	SKL1016	1985	**£20**	**£8**	

TURNER, MEL

Let Me Hold Your Hand	7"	Melodisc	1580	1964	**£10**	**£5**	
Mohican Crawl	7"	Carnival	CV7003	1963	**£4**	**£1.50**	
Swing Low Sweet Chariot	7"	Columbia	DB4791	1962	**£6**	**£2.50**	
Welcome Home Little Darlin'	7"	Island	WI276	1966	**£5**	**£2**	
What's The Matter With Me	7"	Carnival	CV7005	1963	**£4**	**£1.50**	

TURNER, NIK

Pass Out	LP	Riddle	RID002	1980	**£10**	**£4**	
Sphynx – Xitintoday	LP	Charisma	CDS4011	1978	**£10**	**£4**	
Sphynx – Xitintoday	LP	Charisma	CDS4011	1978	**£20**	**£8**	*with booklet*

TURNER, NIK & ROBERT CALVERT

Ersatz	LP	Pompadour	POMP001	1982	**£30**	**£15**	

TURNER, SAMMY

Always	7"	London	HLX8963	1959	**£5**	**£2**	
Lavender Blue	7"	London	HLX8918	1959	**£8**	**£4**	
Lavender Blue Moods	LP	London	HAX2246	1960	**£50**	**£25**	
Paradise	7"	London	HLX9062	1960	**£5**	**£2**	
Raincoat In The River	7"	London	HLX9488	1962	**£10**	**£5**	

TURNER, SPYDER

Stand By Me	7"	MGM	MGM1332	1967	**£15**	**£7.50**	
Stand By Me	LP	MGM	(S)E4450	1967	**£20**	**£8**	*US*

TURNER, TINA

Addicted To Love	CD-s	Capitol	CDCL484	1988	**£5**	**£2**	
Ball Of Confusion	7"	Virgin	VS500	1982	**£5**	**£2**	*with B.E.F.*
Best	CD-s	Capitol	CDCL543	1989	**£5**	**£2**	
Better Be Good To Me	7"	Capitol	CLP338	1984	**£4**	**£1.50**	*picture disc*
Break Every Rule	7"	Capitol	CLP452	1987	**£4**	**£1.50**	*picture disc*
Collected Recordings – Sixties To Nineties	CD	Capitol	DPRO79449	1994	**£20**	**£8**	*US promo compilation*
Foreign Affair	CD	Capitol	CDP7931292	1989	**£12**	**£5**	*US passport package*
Help	7"	Capitol	CLP325	1984	**£4**	**£1.50**	*picture disc*
I Don't Wanna Lose You	CD-s	Capitol	CDCL553	1989	**£5**	**£2**	
Paradise Is Here	7"	Capitol	CLP459	1987	**£4**	**£1.50**	*picture disc*
Play This – In Store	CD	Capitol	DPRO79777	1993	**£20**	**£8**	*US promo compilation*
Rio '88	CD	Polygram	0803481	1988	**£15**	**£6**	*CD video*
Simply The Best	CD	Capitol	DPRO79963	1991	**£20**	**£8**	*US promo with CD-s*
Tina Live, Private Dancer Tour	CD	EMI		1994	**£30**	**£15**	*CD and video set*
We Don't Need Another Hero	7"	Capitol	CLP364	1985	**£5**	**£2**	*picture disc*
What You See Is What You Get	7"	Capitol	7CLD439	1987	**£4**	**£1.50**	*double*

TURNER, TITUS

Miss Rubberneck Jones	7"	Blue Beat	BB32	1961	**£12**	**£6**	
Pony Train	7"	Oriole	CB1611	1961	**£10**	**£5**	
Sound Off	7"	Parlophone	R4746	1961	**£15**	**£7.50**	
Sound Off	LP	Jamie	JLP(70)3018	1961	**£25**	**£10**	*US*
We Told You Not To Marry	7"	London	HLU9024	1960	**£15**	**£7.50**	

TURNQUIST REMEDY

Turnquist Remedy	LP	Pentagram	10004	1970	**£30**	**£15**	*US*

TURNSTYLE

Riding A Wave	7"	Pye	7N17653	1968	**£100**	**£50**	

TURQUOISE

53 Summer Street	7"	Decca	F12756	1968	**£25**	**£12.50**	
Woodstock	7"	Decca	F12842	1968	**£25**	**£12.50**	

TURRENTINE, STANLEY

Always Something There	LP	Blue Note	BST84298	1968	**£12**	**£5**	
Another Story	LP	Blue Note	BST84336	1970	**£12**	**£5**	
Blue Hour	LP	Blue Note	BLP/BST84057	1964	**£30**	**£15**	
Chip Off The Old Block	LP	Blue Note	BLP/BST84150	1965	**£25**	**£10**	
Common Touch	LP	Blue Note	BST84315	1969	**£12**	**£5**	
Dearly Beloved	LP	Blue Note	BLP/BST84081	1964	**£25**	**£10**	
Easy Walker	LP	Blue Note	BLP/BST84268	1967	**£20**	**£8**	
Flipped Out	LP	Polydor	2383111	1972	**£10**	**£4**	
Hustlin'	LP	Blue Note	BLP/BST84162	1965	**£25**	**£10**	

Title	Format	Label	Cat. No.	Year	Value	Value	Notes
Joyride	LP	Blue Note	BLP/BST84201	1966	**£20**	**£8**	
Look Of Love	LP	Blue Note	BST84286	1968	**£12**	**£5**	
Look Out!	LP	Blue Note	BLP/BST84039	1961	**£30**	**£15**	
Never Let Me Go	7"	Blue Note	451894	1964	**£5**	**£2**	
Never Let Me Go	LP	Blue Note	BLP/BST84129	1964	**£25**	**£10**	
Nightwings	LP	Fantasy	FT535	1977	**£10**	**£4**	
Rough 'n Tumble	LP	Blue Note	BLP/BST84240	1966	**£20**	**£8**	
Spoiler	LP	Blue Note	BLP/BST84256	1967	**£15**	**£6**	
Sugar	LP	CTI	CTL2	1972	**£10**	**£4**	
That's Where It's At	LP	Blue Note	BLP/BST84096	1962	**£25**	**£10**	
Tiger Tail	LP	Fontana	TL5300	1966	**£12**	**£5**	
Up At Minton's	LP	Blue Note	BLP/BST84069	1962	**£30**	**£15**	
Up At Minton's Part 2	LP	Blue Note	BLP/BST84070	1964	**£30**	**£15**	
What About You	LP	Fantasy	FT551	1978	**£10**	**£4**	

TURTLES

Title	Format	Label	Cat. No.	Year	Value	Value	Notes
Battle Of The Bands	LP	London	HAU/SHU8376	1968	**£15**	**£6**	
Can I Get To Know You Better	7"	London	HLU10095	1966	**£4**	**£1.50**	
Golden Hits	LP	White Whale	(S7)115	1967	**£15**	**£6**	*US*
Happy Together	7"	London	HLU10115	1967	**£4**	**£1.50**	
Happy Together	7" EP	London	REU10185	1967	**£15**	**£7.50**	*French*
Happy Together	LP	London	HAU8330	1967	**£20**	**£8**	
It Ain't Me Babe	7"	Pye	7N25320	1965	**£4**	**£1.50**	
It Ain't Me Babe	7" EP	Polydor	27770	1965	**£15**	**£7.50**	*French*
It Ain't Me Babe	7" EP	Pye	NEP44089	1967	**£25**	**£12.50**	
It Ain't Me Babe	LP	White Whale	(S7)111	1965	**£30**	**£15**	*US*
Let Me Be	7"	Pye	7N25341	1966	**£4**	**£1.50**	
Let Me Be	7" EP	Polydor	27780	1966	**£15**	**£7.50**	*French*
She'd Rather Be With Me	7"	London	HLU10135	1967	**£4**	**£1.50**	
She'd Rather Be With Me	7" EP	London	REU10189	1967	**£15**	**£7.50**	*French*
She's My Girl	7"	London	HLU10168	1967	**£4**	**£1.50**	
Sound Asleep	7"	London	HLU10184	1968	**£4**	**£1.50**	
Story Of Rock And Roll	7"	London	HLU10207	1968	**£4**	**£1.50**	
Turtle Soup	LP	White Whale	S7124	1969	**£15**	**£6**	*US*
Wooden Head	LP	White Whale	WW7133	1971	**£15**	**£6**	*US*
You Baby	7"	Immediate	IM031	1966	**£6**	**£2.50**	
You Baby	LP	White Whale	(S7)112	1966	**£30**	**£15**	*US*
You Know What I Mean	7"	London	HLU10153	1967	**£4**	**£1.50**	

TUSHINGHAM, RITA & LYNN REDGRAVE

Title	Format	Label	Cat. No.	Year	Value	Value	Notes
Smashing Time	7"	Stateside	SS2081	1968	**£4**	**£1.50**	

TU-TONES

Title	Format	Label	Cat. No.	Year	Value	Value	Notes
Still In Love With You	7"	London	HLW8904	1959	**£75**	**£37.50**	

TUTTLE, WESLEY & MARILYN

Title	Format	Label	Cat. No.	Year	Value	Value	Notes
Jim, Johnny And Jonas	7"	Capitol	CL14291	1955	**£4**	**£1.50**	

TV 21

Title	Format	Label	Cat. No.	Year	Value	Value	Notes
Ambition	7"	Powbeat	AAARGH!2	1980	**£10**	**£5**	
Playing With Fire	7"	Powbeat	AAARGH!1	1980	**£8**	**£4**	

T.V. & THE TRIBESMEN

Title	Format	Label	Cat. No.	Year	Value	Value	Notes
Barefootin'	7"	Pye	7N25375	1966	**£8**	**£4**	

TV PRODUCT

Title	Format	Label	Cat. No.	Year	Value	Value	Notes
Nowhere's Safe	7"	Limited Edition	TAKE3	1979	**£5**	**£2**	*B side by the Prams*

TWARDZIK, RICHARD

Title	Format	Label	Cat. No.	Year	Value	Value	Notes
Last Set	LP	Vogue	LAE12117	1959	**£20**	**£8**	*with tracks by Russ Freeman*

TWELFTH NIGHT

Title	Format	Label	Cat. No.	Year	Value	Value	Notes
First 7" Album	7"	Twelfth Night	TN001	1980	**£25**	**£12.50**	
Shame	12"	Charisma	CBY42412	1986	**£6**	**£2.50**	*picture disc*
Shame	7"	Charisma	CBY424	1986	**£5**	**£2**	*picture disc*

TWELFTH NIGHT (2)

Title	Format	Label	Cat. No.	Year	Value	Value	Notes
Twelfth Night	7"	Acorn	CF239	1973	**£4**	**£1.50**	

TWENTIETH CENTURY

Title	Format	Label	Cat. No.	Year	Value	Value	Notes
Folk Passion	LP	Reflection	RL305	1972	**£100**	**£50**	

TWENTIETH CENTURY ZOO

Title	Format	Label	Cat. No.	Year	Value	Value	Notes
Thunder On A Clear Day	LP	Vault	122	1965	**£30**	**£15**	*US*

TWENTY-FIVE RIFLES

Title	Format	Label	Cat. No.	Year	Value	Value	Notes
World War Three	12"	25 Rifles	TFR1	1979	**£8**	**£4**	

TWENTY SEVEN DOLLAR SNAP ON FACE

Title	Format	Label	Cat. No.	Year	Value	Value	Notes
Heterodyne State Hospital	LP	Heterodyne	00100200001	1977	**£60**	**£30**	*US, blue vinyl*

TWENTY SIXTY-SIX AND THEN

Title	Format	Label	Cat. No.	Year	Value	Value	Notes
Reflections Of The Future	LP	United Artists	UAS29314	1972	**£100**	**£50**	*German*

TWENTY-THIRD TURNOFF

Michael Angelo	7"	Deram	DM150	1967	£30	£15	

TWENTY-THREE SKIDOO

Ethics	7"	Pineapple	PULP23	1981	£5	£2	
Last Words	7"	Fetish	FE10	1981	£5	£2	*no picture sleeve*

TWICE AS MUCH

Crystal Ball	7"	Immediate	IM042	1967	£5	£2	
Own Up	LP	Immediate	IMLP/IMSP007	1966	£25	£10	
Sittin' On A Fence	7"	Immediate	IM033	1966	£4	£1.50	
Step Out Of Line	7"	Immediate	IM036	1966	£4	£1.50	
That's All	LP	Immediate	IMSP013	1968	£25	£10	
True Story	7"	Immediate	IM039	1966	£5	£2	
True Story	7" EP	Columbia	ESRF1818	1966	£15	£7.50	*French*

TWIGGY

Beautiful Dreams	7"	Ember	EMBS239	1966	£6	£2.50	
Beautiful Dreams	7"	Ember	EMBS239	1966	£10	£5	*picture sleeve*
Beautiful Dreams	7" EP	Pathe	EGF966	1966	£15	£7.50	*French*
Twiggy And The Girlfriends	LP	Ember	SE8012	1972	£10	£4	
When I Think Of You	7"	Ember	EMBS244	1967	£5	£2	

TWILIGHT ZONERZ

Zero Zero One EP	7"	Zip/Dining Out	ZEROZERO1	1979	£10	£5	*many different sleeves*

TWILIGHTS

Cathy Come Home	7"	Columbia	DB8396	1968	£10	£5	
Needle In A Haystack	7"	Columbia	DB8065	1966	£6	£2.50	
What's Wrong With The Way	7"	Columbia	DB8125	1967	£6	£2.50	

TWILIGHTS (2)

Take What I Got	7"	London	HLU9992	1965	£8	£4	

TWIN TONES

Jo Ann	7"	RCA	RCA1040	1958	£30	£15	

TWIN TUNES QUINTET

Baby Lover	7"	RCA	RCA1046	1958	£6	£2.50	

TWINK

Odds And Beginnings	LP	Twink	LP2	1991	£10	£4	*red vinyl*
Think Pink	LP	Polydor	2343032	1970	£250	£150	*pink vinyl*
Think Pink	LP	Polydor	2343032	1970	£60	£30	
Think Pink	LP	Polydor	2343032	1970	£100	£50	*with insert*

TWINKLE

End Of The World	7"	Decca	F12305	1965	£4	£1.50	
Golden Lights	7"	Decca	F12076	1965	£4	£1.50	
Golden Lights	7" EP	Decca	457059	1965	£20	£10	*French*
Lonely Singing Doll	7" EP	Decca	DFE8621	1965	£30	£15	
Lonely Singing Doll	7" EP	Decca	457077	1965	£20	£10	*French*
Micky	7"	Instant	IN005	1969	£4	£1.50	
Poor Old Johnny	7"	Decca	F12219	1965	£4	£1.50	
Terry	7"	Decca	F12013	1964	£4	£1.50	
Tommy	7"	Decca	F12139	1965	£5	£2	
What Am I Doing Here With You	7"	Decca	F12464	1966	£6	£2.50	

TWINKLE BROTHERS

Do Your Own Thing	LP	Carib Gems		1977	£12	£5	
Miss World	7"	Jackpot	JP740	1970	£4	£1.50	
Praise Jah	LP	Frontline	FL1041	1979	£10	£4	
She Be Du	7"	Jackpot	JP731	1970	£4	£1.50	
Sweet Young Thing	7"	Jackpot	JP741	1970	£4	£1.50	
You Took Me By Surprise	7"	Big Shot	BI593	1971	£5	£2	

TWINS

Teenagers Love The Twins	LP	RCA	LPM1708	1958	£25	£10	*US*

TWINSET

Tremblin'	7"	Decca	F12629	1967	£5	£2	

TWIST

This Is Your Life	LP	Polydor	2383552	1979	£15	£6	

TWISTED ACE

Firebird	7"	Heavy Metal	HEAVY9	1981	£8	£4	

TWISTED SISTER

Kids Are Back	7"	Atlantic	A9827P	1983	£5	£2	*shaped picture disc*
Ruff Cuts	12"	Secret	SHH13712	1982	£6	£2.50	

TWISTERS

Doin' The Twist	LP	Treasure	TLP890	1962	£20	£8	*US*

Peppermint Twist Time	7"	Windsor	PSA106	1962	£**6**	£**2.50**	
Turn The Page	7"	Capitol	CL15167	1960	£**5**	£**2**	

TWISTIN' KINGS

Twistin' The World Around	LP	Motown	MLP601	1960	£**100**	£**50**	*US*

TWITTY, CONWAY

C'Est Si Bon	7"	MGM	MGM1118	1961	£**4**	£**1.50**	
Comfy 'n' Cozy	7"	MGM	MGM1170	1962	£**4**	£**1.50**	
Conway Twitty Sings	LP	MGM	C781	1959	£**50**	£**25**	
Conway Twitty Touch	LP	MGM	(S)E3943	1961	£**40**	£**20**	*US*
Go On And Cry	7"	HMV	POP1258	1963	£**4**	£**1.50**	
Greatest Hits	LP	MGM	(S)E3849	1960	£**50**	£**25**	*US, with poster*
Greatest Hits	LP	MGM	(S)E3849	1960	£**30**	£**15**	*US*
Handy Man	7"	MGM	MGM1201	1963	£**5**	£**2**	
Here's Conway Twitty	LP	MCA	MUP(S)342	1968	£**10**	£**4**	
Hey Little Lucy	7"	MGM	MGM1016	1959	£**4**	£**1.50**	
Hey Little Lucy	7" EP	MGM	MGMEP698	1959	£**40**	£**20**	
Hit The Road	LP	MGM	(S)E4217	1964	£**20**	£**8**	*US*
Hurt In My Heart	7"	MGM	MGM1066	1960	£**4**	£**1.50**	
I Need Your Lovin'	7" EP	Mercury	ZEP10069	1960	£**100**	£**50**	
Is A Bluebird Blue	7"	MGM	MGM1082	1960	£**4**	£**1.50**	
Is A Bluebird Blue	7" EP	MGM	MGMEP738	1960	£**40**	£**20**	
It's Drivin' Me Wild	7"	MGM	MGM1137	1961	£**4**	£**1.50**	
It's Only Make Believe	7"	MGM	MGM992	1958	£**4**	£**1.50**	
It's Only Make Believe	7" EP	MGM	MGMEP684	1958	£**40**	£**20**	
Lonely Blue Boy	7"	MGM	MGM1056	1960	£**4**	£**1.50**	
Lonely Blue Boy	LP	MGM	C829	1960	£**50**	£**25**	
Mona Lisa	7"	MGM	MGM1029	1959	£**4**	£**1.50**	
Next In Line	LP	MCA	MUPS363	1969	£**10**	£**4**	
Next Kiss	7"	MGM	MGM1129	1961	£**4**	£**1.50**	
Pick-Up	7"	MGM	MGM1187	1962	£**5**	£**2**	
Portrait Of A Fool	LP	MGM	(S)E4019	1962	£**30**	£**15**	*US*
R&B '63	LP	MGM	C950	1963	£**40**	£**20**	
Rock And Roll Story	7" EP	MGM	MGMEP752	1961	£**50**	£**25**	
Rock And Roll Story	LP	MGM	(S)E3907	1961	£**40**	£**20**	*US*
Rock And Roll Story	LP	MGM	C(S)8100	1968	£**25**	£**10**	
Rosaleena	7"	MGM	MGM1047	1959	£**4**	£**1.50**	
Saturday Night With Conway	7" EP	MGM	MGMEP719	1960	£**40**	£**20**	
Saturday Night With Conway	LP	MGM	C801	1959	£**50**	£**25**	
Shake It Up	78	Mercury	MT173	1957	£**30**	£**15**	
She Ain't No Angel	7"	MGM	MGM1209	1963	£**5**	£**2**	
Story Of My Love	7"	MGM	MGM1003	1959	£**4**	£**1.50**	
Tell Me One More Time	7"	MGM	MGM1095	1960	£**4**	£**1.50**	
Tower Of Tears	7"	MGM	MGM1152	1962	£**4**	£**1.50**	
Whole Lotta Shakin' Goin' On	7"	MGM	MGM1108	1960	£**5**	£**2**	

TWO AND A HALF

I Don't Need To Tell You	7"	Decca	F22715	1967	£**6**	£**2.50**	
Midnight Swim	7"	CBS	202248	1966	£**4**	£**1.50**	
Questions	7"	CBS	202404	1966	£**4**	£**1.50**	
Suburban Early Morning Station	7"	Decca	F22672	1967	£**8**	£**4**	
Walls Are High	7"	CBS	202526	1967	£**4**	£**1.50**	

TWO FRIENDS

Two Friends	LP	Natural Resources	NR101L	1972	£**15**	£**6**	*US*

TWO KINGS

Hit You Let You Feel It	7"	Island	WI249	1965	£**10**	£**5**	
Rolling Stone	7"	Island	WI240	1965	£**10**	£**5**	

TWO MUCH

It's A Hip Hip Hippy World	7"	Fontana	TF900	1968	£**5**	£**2**	

TWO NINETEEN SKIFFLE GROUP

Two Nineteen Skiffle Group	7" EP	Esquire	EP126	1957	£**20**	£**10**	
Two Nineteen Skiffle Group	7" EP	Esquire	EP196	1958	£**30**	£**15**	
Two Nineteen Skiffle Group	7" EP	Esquire	EP176	1958	£**30**	£**15**	
Two Nineteen Skiffle Group	7" EP	Esquire	EP146	1957	£**25**	£**12.50**	

TWO OF CLUBS

Angels Must Have Made You	7"	Columbia	DB7371	1964	£**5**	£**2**	

TYE, ARLYNE

Universe	7"	London	HLL8825	1959	£**10**	£**5**	

TYGERS OF PAN TANG

Do It Good	7"	MCA	MCA759	1981	£**15**	£**7.50**	
Don't Touch Me There	7"	Neat	NEAT03	1979	£**6**	£**2.50**	
Don't Touch Me There	7"	MCA	MCA582	1980	£**5**	£**2**	

TYLER, BIG T

King Kong	7"	Vogue	V9079	1957	£**100**	£**50**	

TYLER, BONNIE

Best	CD-s	CBS	CDBEST1	1988	£**5**	£**2**	

Hide Your Heart	CD-s	CBS	6515168	1988	£5	£2	*3" single*

TYLER, FRANKIE

This was a pseudonym used by Frankie Valli, lead singer with the Four Lovers – later the Four Seasons.

I Go Ape	7"	OKeh	7103	1958	£60	£30	US

TYLER, JIMMY

Fool 'Em Devil	7"	Parlophone	MSP6215	1956	£8	£4	

TYLER, RED

Junk Village	7"	Top Rank	JAR306	1960	£6	£2.50	
Rockin' And Rollin'	LP	Ace	LP1006	1960	£30	£15	US

TYLER, T. TEXAS

Country Round Up	7" EP	Parlophone	GEP8788	1959	£20	£10	
Deck Of Cards	LP	Sound	607	1958	£25	£10	US
Great Texan	LP	King	686	1960	£20	£8	US
Man With A Million Friends	LP	London	HAB8322	1967	£12	£5	
Songs Along The Way	LP	King	734	1961	£20	£8	US
T. Texas Tyler	LP	King	664	1959	£20	£8	US
T. Texas Tyler	LP	King	721	1961	£20	£8	US

TYMES

Come With Me To The Sea	7"	Cameo Parkway	P884	1963	£4	£1.50	
Come With Me To The Sea	7"	Cameo Parkway	P884	1963	£10	£5	*picture sleeve*
Here She Comes	7"	Cameo Parkway	P924	1964	£60	£30	
Magic Of Our Summer Love	7"	Cameo Parkway	P919	1964	£4	£1.50	
People	LP	Direction	863558	1969	£15	£6	
So Much In Love	7"	Cameo Parkway	P871	1963	£4	£1.50	
So Much In Love	LP	Cameo Parkway	P7032	1963	£25	£10	
Somewhere	7"	Cameo Parkway	P891	1964	£4	£1.50	
Somewhere	LP	Parkway	P7039	1964	£20	£8	US
Sound Of Wonderful Tymes	LP	Parkway	P7038	1963	£20	£8	US
To Each His Own	7"	Cameo Parkway	P908	1964	£4	£1.50	
Twelfth Of Never	7"	Cameo Parkway	P933	1964	£60	£30	

TYNER, McCOY

The pianist who accompanied master saxophonist John Coltrane on his ground-breaking early-sixties records hit his stride as a band-leader in his own right some ten years later. The albums issued by McCoy Tyner through the seventies are masterpieces of modern jazz and include some inspired post-Coltrane playing from some of the same musicians as were employed by Miles Davis during the same period. In many ways, Tyner's music acted as an acoustic counterpoint to Davis's electric experiments, with records like *Sama Layuca, Song For My Lady* and the live *Enlightenment* emerging as absolutely essential documents.

Asante	LP	Blue Note	BNLA223G	1974	£15	£6	US
Atlantis	LP	Milestone	55002	1975	£20	£8	US double
Echoes Of A Friend	LP	Milestone	M9055	1973	£15	£6	US
Enlightenment	LP	Milestone	55001	1973	£20	£8	US double
Expansions	LP	Blue Note	BST84338	1969	£20	£8	
Extensions	LP	Blue Note	BNLA006F	1973	£15	£6	US
Fly With The Wind	LP	Milestone	M9067	1976	£12	£5	US
Focal Point	LP	Milestone	M9072	1976	£10	£4	US
Inception	LP	HMV	CLP1638	1962	£20	£8	
Live At Newport	LP	Impulse	A48	1963	£20	£8	US
Night Of Ballads	LP	Impulse	A39	1963	£20	£8	US
Plays Ellington	LP	Impulse	A79	1965	£20	£8	US
Reaching Fourth	LP	Impulse	A33	1963	£20	£8	US
Real McCoy	LP	Blue Note	BLP/BST84264	1967	£20	£8	
Sahara	LP	Milestone	MSP9039	1972	£15	£6	US
Sama Layuca	LP	Milestone	M9056	1974	£15	£6	US
Song For My Lady	LP	Milestone	MSP9044	1973	£15	£6	US
Song Of The New World	LP	Milestone	M9049	1973	£15	£6	US
Tender Moments	LP	Blue Note	BST84275	1968	£20	£8	
Time For Tyner	LP	Blue Note	BST84307	1969	£20	£8	
Today And Tomorrow	LP	Impulse	A63	1964	£20	£8	US
Trident	LP	Milestone	M9063	1975	£12	£5	US

TYPHOONS

Needles And Pins	7" EP	Festival	FX451384	196–	£20	£10	*French*
Presenting The Fabulous Typhoons	LP	Ray	50	1964	£50	£25	*South African*
Surf City	7"	Embassy	WB589	1963	£4	£1.50	

TYRANNOSAURUS REX

Tyrannosaurus Rex was originally a duo consisting of Marc Bolan on vocals and acoustic guitar, and Steve Peregrine-Took on bongos – the style of their acoustic music being determined less by a burning desire to create modern folk music than by the fact that they had all their electric equipment stolen just as they were starting out. The duo did have a very distinctive sound, although this became considerably diluted once they began to expand the line-up and switched the electricity back on.

Title	Format	Label	Cat. No.	Year	Price	Price	Notes
Beard Of Stars	LP	Regal Zonophone	SLRZ1013	1970	**£30**	**£15**	*with insert*
By The Light Of A Magical Moon	7"	Regal Zonophone	RZ3025	1970	**£30**	**£15**	
Debora	7"	Magnifly	ECHO102	1972	**£5**	**£2**	*picture sleeve*
Debora	7"	Regal Zonophone	RZ3008	1968	**£20**	**£10**	
Debora	7"	Regal Zonophone	RZ3008	1968	**£400**	**£250**	*picture sleeve, best auctioned*
King Of The Rumbling Spires	7"	Regal Zonophone	RZ3022	1969	**£30**	**£15**	
King Of The Rumbling Spires	7"	Regal Zonophone	RZ3022	1969	**£400**	**£250**	*picture sleeve, best auctioned*
My People Were Fair . . .	LP	Regal Zonophone	LRZ1003	1968	**£50**	**£25**	*with insert, mono*
My People Were Fair . . .	LP	Regal Zonophone	SLRZ1003	1968	**£25**	**£10**	*with insert*
My People Were Fair . . ./Prophets . . .	LP	Fly	TOOFA3/4	1972	**£12**	**£5**	*double*
One Inch Rock	7"	Regal Zonophone	RZ3011	1968	**£30**	**£15**	
One Inch Rock	7"	Regal Zonophone	RZ3011	1968	**£400**	**£250**	*picture sleeve, best auctioned*
Pewter Suitor	7"	Regal Zonophone	RZ3016	1969	**£30**	**£15**	
Prophets, Seers And Sages	LP	Regal Zonophone	LRZ1005	1968	**£40**	**£20**	*mono, with insert*
Prophets, Seers, and Sages	LP	Regal Zonophone	SLRZ1005	1968	**£25**	**£10**	*stereo, with insert*
Unicorn	LP	Regal Zonophone	LRZ1007	1969	**£40**	**£20**	*mono*
Unicorn	LP	Regal Zonophone	LRZ1007	1970	**£30**	**£15**	*red label, mono*
Unicorn	LP	Regal Zonophone	SLRZ1007	1969	**£25**	**£10**	*stereo*
Unicorn	LP	Regal Zonophone	SLRZ1007	1970	**£20**	**£8**	*red label, stereo*

TYSONDOG

Title	Format	Label	Cat. No.	Year	Price	Price	Notes
Eat The Rich	7"	Neat	NEAT33	1983	**£4**	**£1.50**	
School's Out	7"	Neat	NEAT56	1986	**£4**	**£1.50**	
Shoot To Kill	12"	Neat	NEAT4612	1985	**£6**	**£2.50**	

TYTAN

Title	Format	Label	Cat. No.	Year	Price	Price	Notes
Blind Men And Fools	12"	Kamaflage	KAMA6	1982	**£10**	**£5**	
Blind Men And Fools	7"	Kamaflage	KAM6	1982	**£10**	**£5**	
Rough Justice	LP	Metal Masters	METALP105	1985	**£12**	**£5**	

TZUKE, JUDIE

Title	Format	Label	Cat. No.	Year	Price	Price	Notes
God Only Knows	CD-s	CBS	TZUKEC1	1990	**£5**	**£2**	
Stay With Me Till Dawn	7"	Rocket	XPRES17	1979	**£6**	**£2.50**	*picture sleeve*
We'll Go Dreaming	CD-s	Polydor	PZCD31	1989	**£5**	**£2**	

TZUKE & PAXO

Tzuke and Paxo are Judie Tzuke and her writing partner, Mike Paxman.

Title	Format	Label	Cat. No.	Year	Price	Price	Notes
These Are The Laws	7"	Good Earth	GD12	1976	**£25**	**£12.50**	

U

U2

The transformation of U2 from punk camp-followers into international superstars was one of the highlights of rock music in the eighties. In fact, the growth in confidence and originality of the group was extremely rapid in the early days. Bootlegs of U2's very first efforts suggest the group's abilities to be very limited even by the dubious standards of punk. Yet the first album has a freshness and poise that might as well be the work of a different group, while by the time of the live *Under A Blood Red Sky*, U2 had managed to stockpile a considerable armoury of anthemic choruses and had developed a way with an audience that already marked them as great. The various coloured vinyl Irish versions of the early releases have long been collectable; they are joined today by fan-inspired issues appropriate to the group's station, like the limited edition 'Melon' remixes and the promotional sampler CD, *Previously*.

Title	Format	Label	Cat. No.	Year	Mint	VG	Notes
11 O'Clock Tick Tock	7"	CBS	8687	1980	**£30**	**£15**	*Irish, yellow vinyl*
11 O'Clock Tick Tock	7"	CBS	8687	1980	**£60**	**£30**	*orange vinyl*
11 O'Clock Tick Tock	7"	Island	WIP6601	1980	**£10**	**£5**	
4 U2 Play	7"	CBS	PAC1	1982	**£250**	**£150**	*Irish, 4-pack, yellow vinyl*
4 U2 Play	7"	CBS	PAC1	1982	**£50**	**£25**	*Irish, 4-pack*
Achtung Baby	CD	Island		1991	**£30**	**£15**	*Australian, first day cover*
Achtung Baby	CD	Island	U28	1991	**£300**	**£180**	*promo pack with cassette & goodies*
Achtung Baby	CD	Island	U28	1991	**£25**	**£10**	*with 12 prints*
Alex Descends Into Hell	7"	Island	IS500B	1991	**£25**	**£12.50**	*test pressing*
All I Want Is You	12"	Island	12ISB422	1989	**£6**	**£2.50**	*boxed with 4 prints*
All I Want Is You	7"	Island	ISB422	1989	**£10**	**£5**	*in tin box*
All I Want Is You	CD-s	Island	CIDP422	1989	**£8**	**£4**	*picture disc*
All I Want Is You	CD-s	Island	CID422	1989	**£5**	**£2**	
Angel Of Harlem	CD-s	Island	CIDP402	1988	**£6**	**£2.50**	*picture disc*
Angel Of Harlem	CD-s	Island	CIDX402	1988	**£10**	**£5**	*long box*
Another Day	7"	CBS	8306	1980	**£50**	**£25**	*Irish, yellow or orange vinyl*
Another Day	7"	CBS	8306	1980	**£100**	**£50**	*white vinyl*
Another Day	7"	CBS	8306	1980	**£25**	**£12.50**	*Irish*
Best Of 1980–1990	LP	Island		1998	**£200**	**£100**	*promo boxed set of 14 × 7" singles*
Boy	CD	Island	CID9646	1986	**£15**	**£6**	*ten tracks*
Celebration	7"	Island	WIP6770	1982	**£15**	**£7.50**	
Conversation With Larry, Bono, Adam & The Edge	LP	Island	U2CLP1	1987	**£30**	**£15**	*promo*
Day Without Me	7"	Island	WIP6630	1980	**£10**	**£5**	
Desire	12"	Island	12ISX400	1988	**£20**	**£10**	*promo*
Desire	CD-s	Island	CIDP400	1988	**£6**	**£2.50**	*picture disc*
Discotheque	12"	Island	ISDX649DJ	1997	**£20**	**£10**	*promo 3 single set*
Discotheque	7"	Island	ISJB649	1997	**£6**	**£2.50**	*jukebox issue*
Discotheque	CD-s	Island	CID649	1996	**£12**	**£6**	
Discotheque	CD-s	Island	DISCO1	1997	**£8**	**£4**	*1 track promo*
Discotheque	CD-s	Island	DISCO2	1997	**£15**	**£7.50**	*1 track promo*
Even Better Than The Real Thing	12"	Island	12IS525	1992	**£8**	**£4**	*with poster*
Even Better Than The Real Thing	12"	Island	REAL1	1992	**£20**	**£10**	*promo*
Even Better Than The Real Thing	7"	Island	REAL2DJ	1992	**£20**	**£10**	*promo with picture sleeve*
Even Better Than The Real Thing	7"	Island	REAL2DJ	1992	**£10**	**£5**	*promo*
Even Better Than The Real Thing	CD-s	Island	CID525	1992	**£5**	**£2**	
Even Better Than The Real Thing (Perfecto Remix)	CD-s	Island	CREAL2	1992	**£8**	**£4**	
Excerpts From Rattle And Hum	CD-s	Island	U2V7	1988	**£40**	**£20**	*promo*
Fire	7"	Island	WIP6679DJ	1981	**£25**	**£12.50**	*1 sided promo*
Fire	7"	Island	UWIP6679	1981	**£8**	**£4**	*double*
Fire	7"	Island	WIP6679	1981	**£6**	**£2.50**	
Fly	CD-s	Island	CID500	1991	**£5**	**£2**	
Gloria	7"	Island	WIP6733DJ	1981	**£25**	**£12.50**	*1 sided promo*
Gloria	7"	Island	WIP6733	1981	**£8**	**£4**	
Hold Me, Thrill Me, Kiss Me, Kill Me	7"	Atlantic	A7131	1995	**£5**	**£2**	*jukebox issue*
I Still Haven't Found What I'm Looking For	CD-s	Island	CID328	1987	**£25**	**£12.50**	
I Still Haven't Found What I'm Looking For	CD-s	Island	659152	1988	**£5**	**£2**	*Dutch import*
I Will Follow	7"	Island	WIP6656DJ	1980	**£30**	**£15**	*1 sided promo*
I Will Follow	7"	Island	WIP6656	1980	**£8**	**£4**	
I Will Follow	7"	CBS	9065	1980	**£30**	**£15**	*Irish, yellow vinyl*
I Will Follow	7"	Island	9065	1980	**£125**	**£62.50**	*Irish, white vinyl*
I Will Follow	7"	CBS	9065	1980	**£60**	**£30**	*orange vinyl*
If God Will Send His Angels	7"	Island	ISJB684	1997	**£5**	**£2**	*jukebox issue*

Joshua Tree	7"	Island		1987	£50	£25	box set, 5 × 7"
Joshua Tree	CD	Island	CIDU26	1987	£150	£75	promo box set, with cassette and LP
Joshua Tree	CD	Island	CIDU26	1987	£30	£15	promo picture disc
Joshua Tree Collection	7"	Island	U261-65	1987	£200	£100	promo 5 single set
Joshua Tree Singles	7"	Island	U2PK1	1988	£12	£6	4 single set
Lady With The Spinning Head	12"	Island	12IS515B	1992	£40	£20	test pressing
Last Night On Earth	12"	Island	IS664DJ	1997	£20	£10	promo
Last Night On Earth	7"	Island	ISJB664	1997	£5	£2	jukebox issue
Lemon	12"	Island	12LEMDJ1	1993	£60	£30	promo double
Lemon	CD-s	Island	LEMCD1	1993	£20	£10	promo only
Melon	12"	Island	12MELON1	1995	£10	£5	promo
Melon	CD	Island	MELONCD1	1995	£30	£15	9 track fan club remix CD with magazine
Mofo	12"	Island	12IS684	1997	£8	£4	
Mofo	12"	Island	12MOFO3	1997	£50	£25	1 sided promo
Mofo	12"	Island	12MOFO2	1997	£25	£12.50	promo
Mofo	12"	Island	12MOFO1	1997	£20	£10	promo
Mofo	CD-s	Island	MOFOCD1	1997	£25	£12.50	1 track promo
Mofo	CD-s	Island	MOFOCD2	1997	£25	£12.50	1 track promo
Mysterious Ways	CD-s	Island	CID509	1991	£5	£2	
New Year's Day	12"	Island	12WIP6848	1983	£6	£2.50	
New Year's Day	7"	Island	UWIP6848	1983	£8	£4	double
New Year's Day	7"	Island	WIP6848	1983	£20	£10	B side plays Martha Reeves
Night And Day	12"	Island	RHB1	1990	£40	£20	promo
Numb	7"	Island	NUMJB1	1993	£8	£4	jukebox issue
Numb	CD-s	Island	NUMCD1	1993	£40	£20	promo only
October	CD	Island	CID111	1986	£50	£25	
October 1991	CD-s	Island	U23	1991	£75	£37.50	promo
One	CD-s	Island	CID515	1992	£5	£2	
Out Of Control (U2:3)	12"	CBS	127951	1979	£100	£50	Irish, numbered
Out Of Control (U2:3)	12"	CBS	127951	1979	£25	£10	Irish
Out Of Control (U2:3)	7"	CBS	7951	1979	£200	£100	Irish, white vinyl
Out Of Control (U2:3)	7"	CBS	7951	1979	£400	£250	Irish, brown vinyl
Out Of Control (U2:3)	7"	CBS	7951	1979	£60	£30	Irish, yellow or orange vinyl
Out Of Control (U2:3)	7"	CBS	7951	1979	£20	£10	Irish
Out Of Control (U2:3)	cass	CBS	40-7951	1985	£10	£5	Irish
PAC2	7"	CBS	PAC2	198–	£30	£15	Irish, 4-pack
PAC3	7"	CBS	PAC3	198–	£30	£15	Irish, 4-pack
Please	7"	Island	ISJB673	1997	£5	£2	jukebox issue
Please	CD-s	Island	PLEASECD1	1997	£25	£12.50	1 track promo
Please	CD-s	Island	PLEASECD1	1997	£15	£7.50	2 track promo
Pop	CD	Island	CIDU210	1997	£150	£75	promo boxed set
Pop Muzik	CD-s	Island	MUZIK1	1997	£25	£12.50	1 track promo
Previously	CD-s	Island	PRECD1	1996	£25	£12.50	promo
Pride	12"	Island	ISX202	1984	£10	£5	5 tracks
Pride	7"	Island	ISD202	1984	£8	£4	double
Pride	7"	Island	ISP202	1984	£20	£10	picture disc
Pride	cass-s	Island	CIS202	1984	£8	£4	
Pride (In The Name Of Love)	12"	Island	12ISX202	1984	£10	£5	
Rattle And Hum	CD	Island	CIDU27	1988	£400	£200	promo set with CD, LP, cassette
Rattle And Hum	LP	Island	U27	1988	£100	£50	studio versions of 2 live tracks
Salome	12"	Island	12IS550DJ	1992	£50	£25	promo
Staring At The Sun	12"	Island	12IS658DJ	1997	£15	£7.50	promo
Staring At The Sun	7"	Island	ISJB658	1997	£5	£2	jukebox issue
Stay (Faraway, So Close)	CD-s	Island	CIDX578	1993	£10	£5	
Stay (Faraway, So Close)	CD-s	Island	CID578	1993	£10	£5	
Three D Dance Mixes	12"	Island	12ISX411	1989	£20	£10	promo
Two Hearts Beat As One	12"	Island	12IS109	1983	£6	£2.50	
Two Hearts Beat As One	7"	Island	ISD109	1983	£10	£5	double
Two Sides Live	LP	Warner Bros	BUG101	1981	£100	£50	US promo
U2 2 Date	LP	Island	U22D1	1989	£20	£8	promo
U2 Talk Pop	CD	Island	POP1	1997	£50	£25	promo
U2 Talk Pop	CD	Island	POP2	1997	£25	£10	promo
U2 Talk Pop	CD	Island	POP3	1997	£25	£10	promo
Under A Blood Red Sky	LP	Island	US1PR	1983	£30	£15	promo with interviews
Under A Blood Red Sky	LP	Island	IMA3	1983	£50	£25	red vinyl
Unforgettable Fire	7"	Island	ISD220	1985	£5	£2	double
Unforgettable Fire	7"	Island	ISP220	1985	£25	£12.50	shaped picture disc
Unforgettable Fire	CD	Mobile Fidelity	UDCD624	1995	£15	£6	US audiophile
Unforgettable Fire	CD-s	Island	664974	198–	£5	£2	Austrian import
War	CD	Mobile Fidelity	UDCD571	1992	£15	£6	US audiophile
War	LP	Island	PILPS9733	1983	£50	£25	picture disc
When Love Comes To Town	CD-s	Island	CIDP411	1989	£6	£2.50	picture disc
When Love Comes To Town	CD-s	Island	CIDX411	1989	£12	£6	imported US long box
Where The Streets Have No Name	12"	Island	12IS340	1987	£6	£2.50	
Where The Streets Have No Name	CD-s	Island	CID340	1987	£10	£5	
Who's Gonna Ride Your Wild Horses	CD-s	Island	CIDX550	1992	£12	£6	digipak with prints
Who's Gonna Ride Your Wild Horses	CD-s	Island	CID550	1992	£5	£2	
Wire	12"	Island	U22	1984	£25	£12.50	promo

With Or Without You	CD-s	Island	CID319	1987	**£10**	**£5**	
With Or Without You	CD-s	Island	IS319	1988	**£200**	**£100**	*CD video*

UB40

Breakfast In Bed	CD-s	DEP International	DEPX29	1988	**£5**	**£2**	*with Chrissie Hynde*
Come Out To Play	CD-s	DEP International	DEPX31	1989	**£5**	**£2**	*3" single*
Here I Am	CD-s	DEP International	DEPX34	1990	**£5**	**£2**	
Homely Girl	CD-s	DEP International	DEPX33	1989	**£5**	**£2**	*3" single*
I Would Do For You	CD-s	DEP International	DEPX32	1989	**£5**	**£2**	*3" single*
Impossible Love	CD-s	DEP International	DEPXT37	1990	**£5**	**£2**	
Kingston Town	CD-s	DEP International	DEPXT35	1990	**£5**	**£2**	
Promises And Lies	CD	Virgin	UBCDJ94	1994	**£20**	**£8**	*promo with calendar*
UB40	CD	DEP International	DEPCDP13	1988	**£12**	**£5**	*picture disc*
Wear You To The Ball	CD-s	DEP International	DEPXT36	1990	**£5**	**£2**	
Where Did I Go Wrong?	CD-s	DEP International	DEPX30	1988	**£5**	**£2**	

UFO

Alone Again Or	7"	Chrysalis	CHS2146	1977	**£4**	**£1.50**	
Back Into My Life	7"	Chrysalis	CHSP2607	1982	**£4**	**£1.50**	*picture disc*
Blinded By A Lie	7"	Lyntone	LYN12821	1983	**£4**	**£1.50**	*flexi*
Boogie For George	7"	Beacon	BEA172	1971	**£10**	**£5**	
Come Away Melinda	7"	Beacon	BEA165	1971	**£12**	**£6**	
Flying	LP	Beacon	BEAS19	1972	**£25**	**£10**	
One Of Those Nights	CD-s	Essential	ESSX2009	1991	**£5**	**£2**	
Prince Kajuki	7"	Beacon	BEA181	1971	**£10**	**£5**	
Shake It About	7"	Beacon	BEA161	1970	**£15**	**£7.50**	
This Time	7"	Chrysalis	UFOP1	1985	**£4**	**£1.50**	*shaped picture disc*
UFO	LP	Beacon	BEAS12	1971	**£25**	**£10**	

UGGAMS, LESLIE

Eyes Of God	LP	Philips	BBL7370	1960	**£10**	**£4**	

UGLY CUSTARD

Hardly a real group, the musicians recording this low-budget set of rock instrumentals were taking time out from their regular work as members of Blue Mink. The music is essentially workman-like rather than inspired, with Alan Parker demonstrating the proper overdriven tone for turn-of-the-decade 'progressive' guitar, yet without ever really breaking into a sweat.

Ugly Custard	LP	Kaleidoscope	KAL100	1971	**£50**	**£25**	

UGLY DUCKLINGS

Off The Wall	LP	Razor	003	1968	**£15**	**£6**	*Canadian*
Somewhere Outside	LP	Yorktown	50001	1966	**£75**	**£37.50**	*Canadian*

UGLYS

End Of The Season	7"	Pye	7N17178	1966	**£20**	**£10**	
Good Idea	7"	Pye	7N17027	1966	**£20**	**£10**	
I See The Light	7"	MGM	MGM1465	1969	**£400**	**£250**	*demo, best auctioned*
It's Alright	7"	Pye	7N15968	1965	**£10**	**£5**	
Squire Blew His Horn	7"	CBS	2933	1967	**£40**	**£20**	
Wake Up My Mind	7"	Pye	7N15858	1965	**£20**	**£10**	

UK

UK	CD	Editions EG	EGCD35	1988	**£12**	**£5**	

UK DECAY

UK Decay	7"	Plastic	PLAS001	1979	**£12**	**£6**	*B side by Pneumania*

UK SUBS

C.I.D.	7"	City	NIK5	1978	**£4**	**£1.50**	*various coloured vinyls*
Crash Course	LP	Gem	GEMLP111	1980	**£10**	**£4**	*purple vinyl, with 12" (GEMEP1)*
Party In Paris	7"	Ramkup	CAC2	1981	**£20**	**£10**	*1 sided, no picture sleeve*

U.K.s

Ever Faithful Ever True	7"	HMV	POP1310	1964	**£8**	**£4**	
I Will Never Let You Go	7"	HMV	POP1357	1964	**£8**	**£4**	

ULMER, JAMES 'BLOOD'

James 'Blood' Ulmer is a guitarist and occasional singer whose thrilling blend of harmolodic jazz (he was once a member of Ornette Coleman's group) and blues would be enough to make him into a Jimi Hendrix for the nineties if only his kind of cutting-edge music was not so marginalized these days.

Are You Glad To Be In America?	LP	Rough Trade	ROUGH16	1980	**£12**	**£5**	
Black Rock	LP	CBS	25064	1982	**£10**	**£4**	
Eye Level	12"	Rough Trade	RTT128	1984	**£6**	**£2.50**	

Freelancing	LP	CBS	85224	1981	£10	£4	
Part Time	LP	Rough Trade	ROUGH65	1984	£10	£4	
Tales Of Captain Black	LP	Artists House	AH7	1979	£12	£5	*US, credited to James Blood*

ULTIMATE SPINACH

Given a group name like Ultimate Spinach, any sixties collector will know exactly what to expect, especially with song titles like 'Gilded Lamp Of The Cosmos' and 'Mind Flowers'. If one is prepared to forgive the frequent preciousness of the lyrics, then the first two albums emerge as interesting and worthwhile bodies of music, although the female singer is given too little to do and the much weaker male singer too much (but he wrote the material). The third album is the work of an almost completely different line-up and is much less impressive.

Behold And See	LP	MGM	C(S)8094	1968	£50	£25	
Ultimate Spinach	LP	MGM	SE4600	1969	£25	£10	*US*
Ultimate Spinach	LP	MGM	C(S)8071	1968	£40	£20	

ULTRA VIVID SCENE

Mercy Seat	12"	4AD	BAD906	1989	£15	£7.50	
Mercy Seat	CD-s	4AD	BADCD906	1989	£5	£2	
She Screamed	CD-s	4AD	BAD806CD	1988	£5	£2	
Something To Eat	7"	4AD	AD908	1989	£5	£2	
Special One	CD-s	4AD	BAD0016CD	1990	£5	£2	
Staring At The Sun	CD-s	4AD	BADCD0004	1990	£5	£2	

ULTRAFUNK

Ultrafunk	LP	Contempo	CLP509	1975	£10	£4	

ULTRAVOX

Dangerous Rhythm	7"	Island	WIP6375	1977	£4	£1.50	*picture sleeve*
Quiet Men	12"	Island	12WIP6459	1978	£6	£2.50	*white vinyl*
Slow Motion	12"	Island	12WIP6454	1978	£6	£2.50	*clear vinyl*
U-Vox	CD	Chrysalis	CCD1545	1986	£15	£6	
Vienna	12"	Chrysalis	CHS122481	1980	£6	£2.50	
Vienna	7"	Chrysalis	CHS2481	1980	£5	£2	*clear vinyl*
Voice (live)	7"	fan club		1981	£6	£2.50	

ULVAEUS, BJÖRN & BENNY ANDERSSON

Lycka is the album made by the two male members of Abba immediately before forming the group.

Lycka	LP	Polar	POLL113	1970	£15	£6	*Swedish, mono*
Lycka	LP	Polar	POLS226	1970	£10	£4	*Swedish, stereo*

UMPS AND DUMPS

Moon's In A Fit	LP	Topic	12TS416	1980	£10	£4	

UNBEATABLES

Live At Palisades Park	LP	Fawn	LP5050	1964	£30	£15	*US*

UNCLE DOG

Old Hat	LP	Signpost	SG4253	1972	£10	£4	

UNCLE JOHN'S BAND

Different Circles	LP	private	EJSP9422	1980	£40	£20	

UNDER THE SUN

Under The Sun	LP	Redball	RR010	1979	£60	£30	

UNDERGROUND

Psychedelic Visions	LP	Wing	WC16337	1967	£20	£8	*US*
Psychedelic Visions	LP	Mercury	MG/SR16337	1967	£20	£8	*US*

UNDERGROUND SET

Underground Set	LP	Pan	PAN6302	1970	£25	£10	

UNDERGROUND SUNSHINE

Birthday	7"	Fontana	TF1049	1969	£4	£1.50	
Let There Be Light	LP	Intrepid	IT4003	1969	£15	£6	*US*

UNDERNEATH

Imp Of The Perverse	12"	El	GPO17T	1986	£6	£2.50	
Imp Of The Perverse	7"	El	GPO17	1986	£5	£2	
Lunatic Dawn Of The Dismantler	LP	Acme	ACME9	1986	£10	£4	

UNDERTAKERS

The Undertakers were rated as one of the most exciting of the Merseybeat groups, but like their rivals the Big Three they were not particularly successful in translating this reputation on to record. Of the group's four singles (the last credited to the Takers), only 'Just A Little Bit' managed to dent the charts, although this was a fine example of the genre. The group used to follow the implications of their name to the full, travelling in a hearse and dressing in black morning suits. Singer Jackie Lomax tried very hard to maintain a solo career after the group split up, but managed only limited success, despite the enthusiastic patronage of George Harrison. Sax player Brian Jones's name caused much confusion when a saxophone was credited to 'Brian Jones' on the Beatles' single 'You Know My Name', but, surprisingly, this was actually the Rolling Stone. The Undertakers' Jones did, however, join Gary Glitter's Glitter Band in the seventies.

Everybody Loves A Lover	7"	Pye	7N15543	1963	£8	£4	
Just A Little Bit	7"	Pye	7N15607	1964	£8	£4	
What About Us	7"	Pye	7N15562	1963	£8	£4	

UNDERTONES

Get Over You	7"	Sire	SIR4010	1979	£4	£1.50	

Title	Format	Label	Cat. No.	Year	Mint	VG	Notes
Peel Sessions	CD-s	Strange Fruit	SFPSCD016	1988	£5	£2	
Sin Of Pride	LP	Ardeck	ARD104	1983	£25	£10	*with tracks Bittersweet and Stand So Close*
Teenage Kicks	7"	Good Vibrations	GOT4	1978	£5	£2	*poster sleeve*

UNDERWORLD

Underworld's long career in rock music – two thirds of the trio were members of Freur in the early eighties – has given them a mastery of their musical resources to make the group into one of the prime innovators of electronic music in the nineties. Darren Emerson enjoys a parallel career as a successful working DJ, while Karl Hyde and Rick Smith are part of the highly regarded Tomato design team, responsible for a number of high profile advertising projects.

Title	Format	Label	Cat. No.	Year	Mint	VG	Notes
King Of Snake	12"	Junior Boys Own	JBO5005816P/26P	1999	£30	£15	*promo double*
Mmm . . . Skyscraper I Love You	12"	Boys Own	BOIX13	1993	£30	£15	
Mmm . . . Skyscraper I Love You	CD-s	Boys Own	BOIXCD13	1993	£15	£7.50	
Mother Earth	12"	Tomato	PLUM2001	1992	£40	£20	
Rez	12"	Boys Own	COLLECT002P	1993	£40	£20	*pink vinyl test pressing*
Rez	12"	Boys Own	COLLECT002	1993	£10	£5	

UNDISPUTED TRUTH

Title	Format	Label	Cat. No.	Year	Mint	VG	Notes
Best Of The Undisputed Truth	LP	Tamla Motown	STML8029	1977	£10	£4	
Cosmic Truth	LP	Tamla Motown	STMA8023	1975	£10	£4	
Down To Earth	LP	Tamla Motown	STML11277	1975	£10	£4	
Face To Face With The Truth	LP	Tamla Motown	STMA8004	1972	£10	£4	
Higher Than High	LP	Tamla Motown	STML12009	1975	£10	£4	
Law Of The Land	LP	Tamla Motown	STML11240	1973	£12	£5	
Save My Love For A Rainy Day	7"	Parlophone	TMG776	1971	£6	£2.50	*mispressed label*
Save My Love For A Rainy Day	7"	Tamla Motown	TMG776	1971	£4	£1.50	
Smiling Face Sometimes	7"	Tamla Motown	TMG789	1971	£4	£1.50	
Undisputed Truth	LP	Tamla Motown	STML11197	1972	£10	£4	

UNFOLDING

Title	Format	Label	Cat. No.	Year	Mint	VG	Notes
How To Blow Your Mind	LP	Audio Fidelity	6184	1967	£60	£30	*US*

UNFOLDING BOOK OF LIFE

Title	Format	Label	Cat. No.	Year	Mint	VG	Notes
Volume 1	LP	Island	ILPS9093	1969	£20	£8	*pink label*
Volume 2	LP	Island	ILPS9094	1969	£20	£8	*pink label*

UNICORN

Title	Format	Label	Cat. No.	Year	Mint	VG	Notes
Going Home	7"	Hollick & Taylor	HT1258	196–	£25	£12.50	

UNICORN (2)

Title	Format	Label	Cat. No.	Year	Mint	VG	Notes
Uphill All The Way	LP	Transatlantic	TRA238	1971	£12	£5	

UNIFICS

Title	Format	Label	Cat. No.	Year	Mint	VG	Notes
Court Of Love	7"	London	HLZ10231	1968	£5	£2	

UNIQUES

Title	Format	Label	Cat. No.	Year	Mint	VG	Notes
A-Yuh	7"	Trojan	TR645	1968	£8	£4	
Absolutely The Uniques	LP	Trojan	TRL15	1969	£40	£20	
Beatitude	7"	Unity	UN527	1969	£5	£2	
Beatitude	7"	Island	WI3123	1967	£10	£5	*Keith Blake B side*
Build My World Around You	7"	Island	WI3114	1967	£10	£5	*Lloyd Clarke B side*
Crimson And Clover	7"	Nu Beat	NB034	1969	£5	£2	
Dry The Water	7"	Collins Downbeat	CR002	1967	£8	£4	
Girl Of My Dreams	7"	Island	WI3145	1968	£10	£5	*Lester Stirling B side*
Gypsy Woman	7"	Island	WI3084	1967	£10	£5	*Ken Ross B side*
I'll Make You Love Me	7"	Nu Beat	NB037	1969	£5	£2	
Lesson Of Love	7"	Island	WI3107	1967	£10	£5	*Delroy Wilson B side*
Let Me Go Girl	7"	Island	WI3086	1967	£10	£5	*Soulettes B side*
More Love	7"	Trojan	TR610	1968	£8	£4	*Race Dans B side*
More Love	7"	Island	WI3117	1967	£10	£5	*Val Bennett B side*
My Conversation	7"	Island	WI3122	1967	£10	£5	*Slim Smith B side*
Never Let Me Go	7"	Island	WI3087	1967	£10	£5	*Don Tony Lee B side*
People Rock Steady	7"	Island	WI3070	1967	£10	£5	
Speak No Evil	7"	Island	WI3106	1967	£10	£5	*Glen Adams B side*
Too Proud To Beg	7"	Gas	GAS117	1969	£6	£2.50	

UNIQUES (2)

Title	Format	Label	Cat. No.	Year	Mint	VG	Notes
Fast Way Of Living	7"	Pye	7N25303	1965	£40	£20	
Uniquely Yours	LP	Pye	NPL28094	1966	£60	£30	

UNIT FOUR PLUS TWO

Title	Format	Label	Cat. No.	Year	Mint	VG	Notes
Baby Never Say Goodbye	7"	Decca	F2333	1966	**£4**	**£1.50**	
Butterfly	7"	Fontana	TF840	1967	**£6**	**£2.50**	
Concrete And Clay	7"	Decca	F12071	1965	**£4**	**£1.50**	
Concrete And Clay	7" EP	Decca	457070	1965	**£20**	**£10**	*French*
For A Moment	7"	Decca	F12398	1966	**£5**	**£2**	
Green Fields	7"	Decca	F11821	1964	**£8**	**£4**	
Hark	7"	Decca	F12211	1965	**£4**	**£1.50**	
I Was Only Playing Games	7"	Decca	F12509	1966	**£5**	**£2**	
Loving Takes A Little Understanding	7"	Fontana	TF891	1967	**£4**	**£1.50**	
Sorrow And Pain	7"	Decca	F11994	1964	**£6**	**£2.50**	
Three Thirty	7"	Fontana	TF990	1969	**£20**	**£10**	
Too Fast, Too Slow	7"	Fontana	TF834	1967	**£8**	**£4**	
Unit Four Plus Two	7" EP	Decca	DFE8619	1965	**£25**	**£12.50**	
Unit Four Plus Two	LP	Fontana	SFL13123	1969	**£50**	**£25**	
Unit Four Plus Two	LP	Decca	LK4697	1965	**£60**	**£30**	
You Ain't Goin' Nowhere	7"	Fontana	TF931	1968	**£6**	**£2.50**	
You've Got To Be Cruel To Be Kind	7"	Decca	F12299	1965	**£4**	**£1.50**	
You've Never Been In Love Like This Before	7"	Decca	F12144	1965	**£4**	**£1.50**	
You've Never Been In Love Like This Before	7" EP	Decca	457087	1965	**£20**	**£10**	*French*

UNITED ISLANDS

Title	Format	Label	Cat. No.	Year	Mint	VG	Notes
I Love This Day	LP	Audio Art		1986	**£20**	**£8**	*Dutch*

UNITED SONS OF AMERICA

Title	Format	Label	Cat. No.	Year	Mint	VG	Notes
Greetings From The U.S. of A.	LP	Mercury	SR61312	1970	**£15**	**£6**	*US*

UNITED STATES DOUBLE QUARTET

Title	Format	Label	Cat. No.	Year	Mint	VG	Notes
Life Is Groovy	LP	B.T.Puppy	BTPS1005	1969	**£20**	**£8**	*US*

UNITED STATES OF AMERICA

Title	Format	Label	Cat. No.	Year	Mint	VG	Notes
Garden Of Earthly Delights	7"	CBS	3745	1968	**£10**	**£5**	
United States Of America	LP	CBS	63340	1968	**£25**	**£10**	

UNIVERIA ZEKT

Title	Format	Label	Cat. No.	Year	Mint	VG	Notes
Unnamables	LP	Theleme	6332501	1972	**£40**	**£20**	*French*

UNIVERS ZERO

Title	Format	Label	Cat. No.	Year	Mint	VG	Notes
Ceux Du Dehors	LP	Recommended	RRTEN	1981	**£10**	**£4**	
Hérésie	LP	Recommended	RR4	1979	**£12**	**£5**	
Triomphe Des Mouches	7"	Recommended	RR10.5	1981	**£8**	**£4**	*1 side painted*
Univers Zéro	LP	Atem	7001	1978	**£12**	**£5**	*French*

UNIVERSALS

Title	Format	Label	Cat. No.	Year	Mint	VG	Notes
Green Veined Orchid	7"	Page One	POF049	1967	**£8**	**£4**	
I Can't Find You	7"	Page One	POF032	1967	**£25**	**£12.50**	

UNO

Title	Format	Label	Cat. No.	Year	Mint	VG	Notes
Uno	LP	Pan Ariola	88397	1974	**£20**	**£8**	*German*

UNREST WORK AND PLAY

Title	Format	Label	Cat. No.	Year	Mint	VG	Notes
Informs	LP	Recommended	RRC19	1984	**£10**	**£4**	

UNTAMED

Title	Format	Label	Cat. No.	Year	Mint	VG	Notes
Daddy Longlegs	7"	Planet	PLF113	1966	**£40**	**£20**	*as Lindsay Muir's Untamed*
I'll Go Crazy	7"	Stateside	SS431	1965	**£40**	**£20**	
It's Not True	7"	Planet	PLF103	1966	**£40**	**£20**	
Once Upon A Time	7"	Parlophone	R5258	1965	**£50**	**£25**	
So Long	7"	Decca	F12045	1964	**£40**	**£20**	

UNTAMED YOUTH

Title	Format	Label	Cat. No.	Year	Mint	VG	Notes
Untamed Youth	7"	Hardcore	HAR001	1979	**£10**	**£5**	

UNTOUCHABLES

Title	Format	Label	Cat. No.	Year	Mint	VG	Notes
Can't Reach You	7"	Bullet	BU460	1971	**£4**	**£1.50**	*Carl Dawkins B side*
Knock On Wood	7"	Upsetter	US350	1970	**£6**	**£2.50**	*Upsetters B side*
Prisoner In Love	7"	Blue Cat	BS137	1968	**£8**	**£4**	
Same Thing All Over	7"	Upsetter	US345	1970	**£6**	**£2.50**	*Upsetters B side*
Tighten Up	7"	Trojan	TR613	1968	**£6**	**£2.50**	

UNUSUAL WE

Title	Format	Label	Cat. No.	Year	Mint	VG	Notes
Unusual We	LP	Pulsar	10608	1969	**£15**	**£6**	*US*

UNWANTED

Title	Format	Label	Cat. No.	Year	Mint	VG	Notes
Memory Man	7"	Raw	RAW30	1978	**£8**	**£4**	
Secret Police	7"	Raw	RAW15	1978	**£5**	**£2**	
Withdrawal	12"	Raw	RAWT6	1978	**£8**	**£4**	
Withdrawal	7"	Raw	RAW6	1977	**£12**	**£6**	*picture sleeve*

UNWIN, STANLEY

Title	Format	Label	Cat. No.	Year	Mint	VG	Notes
Fairy Stories	7" EP	Golden Guinea	GGE00884	1961	**£8**	**£4**	
Rotatety Diskers	LP	Pye	NPL18062	1961	**£15**	**£6**	

UPBEATS

Keep Cool Crazy Heart	7"	Pye	7N25016	1959	**£5**	**£2**	
My Foolish Heart	7"	London	HLJ8688	1958	**£12**	**£6**	
Teeny Weeny Bikini	7"	Pye	7N25028	1959	**£5**	**£2**	

UPCHURCH, PHIL

Darkness Darkness	LP	Blue Thumb	ILPS9219	1972	**£10**	**£4**	
Feeling Blue	LP	Milestone	9010	1968	**£10**	**£4**	*US*
Nothing But Soul	7"	Sue	WI4017	1966	**£12**	**£6**	
Twist The Big Hit Dances	LP	United Artists	6175	1960	**£15**	**£6**	*US*
You Can't Sit Down	7"	HMV	POP899	1961	**£15**	**£7.50**	
You Can't Sit Down	7"	Sue	WI4005	1966	**£12**	**£6**	
You Can't Sit Down	LP	Boyd	398	1960	**£20**	**£8**	*US*
You Can't Sit Down II	LP	United Artists	6162	1960	**£15**	**£6**	*US*

UPSETTERS

The records credited to the Upsetters are all the work of star reggae producer Lee Perry, who has also made numerous records under his own name, as well as producing several other artists' records.

All Combine	7"	Bullet	BU461	1971	**£4**	**£1.50**	
Battle Axe	LP	Trojan	TBL167	1971	**£15**	**£6**	
Bigger Joke	7"	Upsetter	US346	1970	**£6**	**£2.50**	
Black Ipa	7"	Downtown	DT499	1973	**£5**	**£2**	
Bronco	7"	Upsetter	US326	1970	**£6**	**£2.50**	
Cane River Rock	7"	Dip	DL5054	1975	**£5**	**£2**	
Capasetic	7"	Upsetter	US361	1971	**£6**	**£2.50**	
Capo	7"	Trojan	TR7749	1970	**£4**	**£1.50**	
Chokin' Kind	7"	Spinning Wheel	SW102	1970	**£5**	**£2**	*Chuck Junior B side*
Clint Eastwood	7"	Punch	PH21	1969	**£5**	**£2**	
Clint Eastwood	LP	Pama	PSP1014	1969	**£30**	**£15**	
Cold Sweat	7"	Upsetter	US315	1969	**£6**	**£2.50**	
Cow Thief Skank	7"	Upsetter	US398	1973	**£5**	**£2**	
Crummy People	7"	Upsetter	US393	1972	**£5**	**£2**	*Big Youth B side*
Dark Moon	7"	Upsetter	US370	1971	**£6**	**£2.50**	*David Isaacs B side*
Double Seven	LP	Trojan	TRLS70	1974	**£15**	**£6**	
Dry Acid	7"	Punch	PH19	1970	**£5**	**£2**	*Reggae Boys B side*
Earthquake	7"	Upsetter	US365	1971	**£6**	**£2.50**	*Junior Byles B side*
Eastwood Rides Again	LP	Trojan	TBL125	1970	**£25**	**£10**	
Eight For Eight	7"	Upsetter	US300	1969	**£6**	**£2.50**	
Eight For Eight	7"	Duke	DU11	1969	**£6**	**£2.50**	
Enter The Dragon	7"	Dip	DL5031	1974	**£5**	**£2**	*Joy White*
Family Man	7"	Trojan	TR7748	1970	**£4**	**£1.50**	
Fire Fire	7"	Upsetter	US334	1970	**£6**	**£2.50**	
French Connection	7"	Upsetter	US385	1972	**£5**	**£2**	
Fresh Up	7"	Upsetter	US338	1970	**£6**	**£2.50**	
Good, The Bad And The Upsetters	LP	Trojan	TBL119	1970	**£25**	**£10**	
Granny Show	7"	Upsetter	US333	1970	**£6**	**£2.50**	
Haunted House	7"	Spinning Wheel	SW100	1970	**£5**	**£2**	
Heart And Soul	7"	Upsetter	US352	1970	**£6**	**£2.50**	
Illusion	7"	Upsetter	US353	1971	**£6**	**£2.50**	
Jungle Lion	7"	Upsetter	US397	1973	**£5**	**£2**	
Kiddyo	7"	Upsetter	US309	1969	**£6**	**£2.50**	
Kill Them All	7"	Upsetter	US325	1970	**£6**	**£2.50**	
Land Of Kinks	7"	Spinning Wheel	SW103	1970	**£5**	**£2**	*O'Neil Hall B side*
Live Injection	7"	Upsetter	US313	1969	**£6**	**£2.50**	*Bleechers B side*
Man From MI5	7"	Upsetter	US310	1969	**£6**	**£2.50**	*West Indians B side*
Many Moods Of The Upsetters	LP	Pama	SECO24	1970	**£30**	**£15**	
Miser	7"	Spinning Wheel	SW101	1970	**£5**	**£2**	*Chuck Junior B side*
Na Na Hey Hey	7"	Upsetter	US332	1970	**£6**	**£2.50**	
Night Doctor	7"	Upsetter	US307	1969	**£6**	**£2.50**	*Termites B side*
Pillow	7"	Upsetter	US335	1970	**£6**	**£2.50**	
Prisoner	LP	Trojan	TBL127	1970	**£15**	**£6**	
Puss Sea Hole	7"	Upsetter	US396	1973	**£5**	**£2**	*Winston Groovy B side*
Rebels Train	7"	Dip	DL5032	1974	**£5**	**£2**	
Result	7"	Punch	PH27	1970	**£4**	**£1.50**	
Return Of Django	7"	Upsetter	US301	1969	**£4**	**£1.50**	
Return Of Django	LP	Trojan	TRL19	1969	**£20**	**£8**	
Return Of The Super Ape	LP	Lion Of Judah	LPIR0001	1978	**£12**	**£5**	*Jamaican*
Return Of The Ugly	7"	Punch	PH18	1969	**£5**	**£2**	
San-San	7"	Count Shelly	CS052	1974	**£5**	**£2**	*Osbourne Graham B side*
Self Control	7"	Upsetter	US336	1970	**£6**	**£2.50**	
Sipreano	7"	Upsetter	US343	1970	**£6**	**£2.50**	
Stranger On The Shore	7"	Upsetter	US321	1969	**£6**	**£2.50**	
Sunshine Showdown	7"	Downtown	DT506	1973	**£5**	**£2**	
Taste Of Killing	7"	Camel	CA13	1969	**£4**	**£1.50**	
Ten To Twelve	7"	Upsetter	US303	1969	**£6**	**£2.50**	
Three In One	7"	Island	WIP6328	1976	**£4**	**£1.50**	
Tighten Up Skank	7"	Downtown	DT512	1973	**£5**	**£2**	
Upsetter Collection	LP	Trojan	TRLS195	1981	**£10**	**£4**	
Upsetting Station	7"	Upsetter	US349	1970	**£20**	**£10**	*plays Bob Marley track*

Vampire	7"	Upsetter	US317	1969	£6	£2.50	Bleechers B side
Walk Down The Aisle	7"	Rio	R70	1965	£10	£5	
Water Pump	7"	Upsetter	US394	1972	£5	£2	
Wildcat	7"	Doctor Bird	DB1034	1966	£10	£5	

URCHIN

Black Leather Fantasy	7"	DJM	DJS10776	1977	£60	£30	picture sleeve
She's A Roller	7"	DJM	DJS10850	1978	£50	£25	picture sleeve

URE, MIDGE

Dear God	CD-s	Chrysalis	URECD6	1988	£5	£2	in tin box

URIAH HEEP

Demons And Wizards	LP	Island	ILPS9193	1972	£10	£4	
One Way Or Another	7"	Bronze	BRODJ1	1976	£5	£2	promo, picture sleeve
Salisbury	LP	Vertigo	6360028	1971	£40	£20	spiral label
Salisbury	LP	Bronze	ILPS9152	1971	£10	£4	
Salisbury	LP	Island	ILPS9152	1971	£20	£8	
Very 'Umble, Very 'Eavy	LP	Vertigo	6360006	1970	£30	£15	spiral label
Very 'Umble, Very 'Eavy	LP	Bronze	ILPS9142	1971	£10	£4	

URSO, PHIL

Phil Urso	10" LP	London	LZC14016	1955	£30	£15	

URUSEI YATSURA

Pampered Adolescent	7"	Modern	MIR001	1995	£15	£7.50	dark red vinyl

US

You're OK With Us	7"	Jeff Wayne Music	SD015	197–	£6	£2.50	picture sleeve

U.S. T-BONES

No Matter What Shape	7"	Liberty	LIB55836	1965	£4	£1.50	
Proper Thing To Do	7"	Liberty	LIB55951	1967	£5	£2	
Sippin' And Chippin'	7"	Liberty	LIB55867	1966	£5	£2	

USE OF ASHES

Castle Of Fair Welcome	LP	Rosebud		1989	£75	£37.50	Dutch

USERS

Kicks In Style	7"	Warped	WARP1	1978	£5	£2	
Sick Of You	12"	Raw	RAWT1	1978	£6	£2.50	
Sick Of You	7"	Raw	RAW1	1977	£10	£5	numbered picture sleeve

USTINOV, PETER

Mock Mozart	7"	Parlophone	MSP6012	1953	£5	£2	

UTOPIA

Utopia	LP	United Artists	UAG29438	1973	£12	£5	

UTOPIA (2)

Utopia	LP	Kent	KST566	1967	£60	£30	US

UV POP

Anyone For Me	12"	Flowmotion	FM007	1985	£6	£2.50	
Just A Game	7"	Pax	PAX9	1982	£5	£2	

V

V2

Title	Format	Label	Cat. No.	Year	Mint	VG	Notes
Man In The Box	12"	TJM	TJM1	1979	£10	£5	
Speed Freak	7"	Bent	SMALLBENT1	1978	£5	£2	*red or black vinyl*

VACELS

Title	Format	Label	Cat. No.	Year	Mint	VG	Notes
Can You Please Crawl Out Of Your Window	7"	Pye	7N25330	1965	£6	£2.50	

VAGABONDS

Title	Format	Label	Cat. No.	Year	Mint	VG	Notes
Behold	7" EP	Decca	DFE8588	1964	£20	£10	
Presenting The Fabulous Vagabonds	LP	Island	ILP916	1964	£50	£25	
Ska Time	LP	Decca	LK4617	1964	£25	£10	

VAGINA DENTATA ORGAN

Title	Format	Label	Cat. No.	Year	Mint	VG	Notes
Cold Meat	12"	WSNS	004	198–	£15	£7.50	*picture disc*
Music For Hashasins	LP	Temple	TOPY012	1987	£20	£8	

VAGRANTS

Title	Format	Label	Cat. No.	Year	Mint	VG	Notes
Great Lost Album	LP	Arista	AL8459	1987	£25	£10	*US*
I Can't Make A Friend	7"	Fontana	TF703	1966	£40	£20	

VALADIERS

Title	Format	Label	Cat. No.	Year	Mint	VG	Notes
I Found A Girl	7"	Oriole	CBA1809	1963	£600	£400	*best auctioned*

VALANCE, RICKY

Title	Format	Label	Cat. No.	Year	Mint	VG	Notes
Bobby	7"	Columbia	DB4680	1961	£4	£1.50	
Don't Play Number Nine	7"	Columbia	DB4864	1962	£4	£1.50	
I Never Had A Chance	7"	Columbia	DB4725	1961	£4	£1.50	
Jimmy's Girl	7"	Columbia	DB4586	1961	£4	£1.50	
Lipstick On Your Lips	7"	Columbia	DB4543	1960	£4	£1.50	
Ricky Valance	7" EP	Valley	VLY001	1976	£12	£6	*no picture sleeve*
Six Boys	7"	Decca	F12129	1965	£5	£2	
Tell Laura I Love Her	7"	Columbia	DB4493	1960	£4	£1.50	
Try To Forget Her	7"	Columbia	DB4787	1962	£4	£1.50	
Why Can't We	7"	Columbia	DB4592	1961	£4	£1.50	

VALE, JERRY

Title	Format	Label	Cat. No.	Year	Mint	VG	Notes
Moon Is My Pillow	7"	Philips	PB963	1959	£8	£4	

VALE, RICKY & HIS SURFERS

Title	Format	Label	Cat. No.	Year	Mint	VG	Notes
Everybody's Surfin'	LP	Strand	SL(S)1104	1963	£20	£8	*US*

VALENS, RITCHIE

Title	Format	Label	Cat. No.	Year	Mint	VG	Notes
C'mon Let's Go	7"	Pye	7N25000	1958	£75	£37.50	
Donna	7"	London	HL8803	1959	£15	£7.50	
Donna	7"	President	PT126	1967	£4	£1.50	
Donna	7"	London	HL7068	1959	£15	£7.50	*export*
Greatest Hits	LP	London	HA8196	1964	£40	£20	
Greatest Hits Vol. 2	LP	Del-Fi	1247	1965	£40	£20	*US*
I Remember Ritchie Valens	LP	President	PTL1001	1967	£12	£5	
In Concert At Pacoima Jr High	LP	Del-Fi	1214	1960	£75	£37.50	*US*
La Bamba	7"	London	HL9494	1962	£12	£6	
La Bamba	7"	Sue	WI4011	1966	£30	£15	*demo*
Ritchie	LP	London	HA2390	1961	£60	£30	
Ritchie Valens	7" EP	London	RE1232	1959	£100	£50	*tri-centre*
Ritchie Valens	LP	Del-Fi	1201	1959	£100	£50	*US*
Ritchie Valens	LP	MGM	GAS117	1970	£12	£5	*US*
Ritchie Valens	LP	London	HAR8535	1979	£10	£4	
That's My Little Suzie	7"	London	HL8886	1959	£20	£10	*tri-centre*

VALENTE, CATERINA

Title	Format	Label	Cat. No.	Year	Mint	VG	Notes
A L'Olympia	10" LP	Decca	133893	1958	£40	£20	*French*
Arriba Caterina	LP	Polydor	46073	1962	£25	£10	*German*
Bravo Caterina	7" EP	Polydor	20605EPH	1957	£30	£15	*German*
Bravo Caterina	7" EP	Polydor	EPH20282	1963	£5	£2	
Breeze And I	7"	Polydor	NH66953	1960	£5	£2	
Caterina Cherie	LP	Polydor	LPHM46310	1961	£15	£6	
Caterina Valente	7" EP	Polydor	EPH21613	1963	£5	£2	
Caterina Valente	7" EP	Polydor	EPH20106	1963	£5	£2	
Caterina Valente	7" EP	Polydor	EPH20501	1963	£5	£2	
Caterina Valente No. 2	7" EP	Polydor	EPH20528	1963	£5	£2	

Caterina Valente No. 3	7" EP	Polydor	EPH20545	1963	£5	£2	
Caterina Valente Singers	LP	Decca	SLK16317	1965	£20	£8	German
Catrin	LP	Decca	T74036	1962	£40	£20	German
Classics With A Chaser	LP	RCA	RD27240	1960	£30	£15	
Cosmopolitan Lady	LP	Polydor	LPHM46065	1960	£15	£6	
Date With Caterina Valente	10" LP	Polydor	LPH45517	1955	£25	£10	German
De Paris A Grenade	7" EP	Polydor	EPH20547	1963	£5	£2	
Ein Gruss Von Caterina Valente	10" LP	Polydor	LPH45077	1953	£60	£30	German
Frenesi	7" EP	London	GEB7001	1962	£5	£2	
Great Continental Hits	LP	Decca	LK/SKL4508	1962	£12	£5	
Haiti Cherie	7" EP	Polydor	EPH20516	1963	£5	£2	
I Happen To Like New York	LP	Decca	LK/SKL4630	1964	£12	£5	
I Wish You Love	LP	London	PS275	1962	£40	£20	US
In Italia	LP	Decca	BLK16211P	1962	£50	£25	German
Intimate Valente	LP	Decca	SKL4756	1966	£20	£8	
Kleine Geschichten Von Grosser Liebe	7" EP	Polydor	EPH20231	1956	£20	£10	German
La Malagueña	7"	Polydor	NH66816	1960	£6	£2.50	
Latino	LP	London	GLB1013	1964	£10	£4	with Edmundo Ros
Many Voices Of Caterina Valente	LP	Decca	BLK16214	1963	£25	£10	German
My Hawaiian Melody	7" EP	Decca	DFE8544	1963	£5	£2	
Ole Caterina	LP	Polydor	46029	1961	£25	£10	German
On Tour	LP	Decca	BLK16213P	1962	£40	£20	German
Pariser Chic, Pariser Charme	LP	Decca	BLK16266P	1963	£20	£8	German
Plenty Caterina	7" EP	Polydor	20578EPH	1957	£25	£12.50	French
Rendezvous With Caterina	LP	Decca	LK4350	1960	£15	£6	
Serenata D'Amore	LP	Polydor	45529LPH	1958	£40	£20	German
Silk 'n' Latin	LP	London	SP44125	1969	£40	£20	US double
Sombreros Y Guitarras	7" EP	Polydor	EPH20596	1963	£5	£2	
Superfonics	LP	RCA	RD27216/SF5099	1961	£12	£5	
Third Deutsches Jazz Festival	7" EP	Brunswick	10021EPB	1955	£60	£30	German
Third Deutsches Jazz Festival 2	7" EP	Brunswick	10025EPB	1955	£60	£30	German
Toast To The Girls	7" EP	Polydor	20622EPH	1958	£10	£5	German
Toast To The Girls	LP	Decca	DL8755	1958	£25	£10	US
Valente And Violins	LP	Decca	LK/SKL4646	1965	£12	£5	
Valente In Swingtime	LP	Decca	LK/SKL4537	1963	£10	£4	
Valente On TV	LP	Decca	LK4604	1964	£10	£4	
Veel Liefs Van Caterina Valente	LP	Capri	CA1G	1972	£40	£20	Dutch

VALENTE, DINO

Dino	LP	CBS	65715	1968	£30	£15	
Dino Valente	LP	CBS	63443	1968	£30	£15	

VALENTINE, BILLY

It's A Sin	7"	Capitol	CL14320	1955	£40	£20	

VALENTINE, DICKIE

At The Talk Of The Town	LP	Philips	BL7831	1967	£15	£6	
Belonging To Someone	7" EP	Decca	DFE6549	1958	£6	£2.50	
Blossom Fell	7"	Decca	F10430	1955	£10	£5	
Chapel Of The Roses	7"	Decca	F10874	1957	£4	£1.50	
Christmas Alphabet	7"	Decca	F10628	1955	£20	£10	
Christmas Island	7"	Decca	F10798	1956	£8	£4	
Day Dreams	7"	Decca	F10766	1956	£5	£2	
Dickie Goes Dixie	7" EP	Decca	DFE6427	1957	£8	£4	
Dickie Valentine's Rock'n'Roll Party	7"	Decca	F10820	1956	£5	£2	
Dreams Can Tell A Lie	7"	Decca	F10667	1956	£5	£2	
Endless	7"	Decca	F10346	1954	£20	£10	
Finger Of Suspicion Points At You	7"	Decca	F10394	1954	£20	£10	
Hello Mrs Jones	7"	Decca	F10517	1955	£6	£2.50	
Here Is Dickie Valentine	10" LP	Decca	LF1211	1955	£15	£6	
Hit Parade	7" EP	Pye	NEP24120	1959	£6	£2.50	
I Wonder	7"	Decca	F10493	1955	£10	£5	
Long Before I Knew You	7"	Decca	F10949	1957	£4	£1.50	
Love Me Again	7"	Decca	F11005	1958	£4	£1.50	
Ma Cherie Amie	7"	Decca	F10484	1955	£8	£4	
Mister Sandman	7"	Decca	F10415	1954	£25	£12.50	
My Impossible Castle	7"	Decca	F10753	1956	£4	£1.50	
No Such Luck	7"	Decca	F10549	1955	£6	£2.50	
Old Pianna Rag	7"	Decca	F10645	1955	£8	£4	
Only For You	7" EP	Decca	DFE6363	1956	£8	£4	
Over My Shoulder	10" LP	Decca	LF1257	1956	£15	£6	
Presenting	7" EP	Decca	DFE6279	1956	£10	£5	
Presenting Dickie Valentine	10" LP	Decca	LF1163	1954	£20	£8	
Puttin' On The Style	7"	Decca	F10906	1957	£4	£1.50	
Snowbound For Christmas	7"	Decca	F10950	1957	£5	£2	
Standards	7" EP	Decca	DFE6429	1957	£6	£2.50	
Swing Along	7" EP	Decca	DFE6236	1955	£8	£4	
Venus	7"	Pye	7N15192	1959	£4	£1.50	
Voice	7"	Decca	F10714	1956	£5	£2	
With Vocal Refrain By . . .	7" EP	Decca	DFE6529	1958	£8	£4	
With Vocal Refrain By . . .	LP	Decca	LK4269	1958	£10	£4	

VALENTINE, HILTON

All In Your Head	LP	Capitol	ST330	1969	£50	£25	US

VALENTINE, JACK

Dressing Up My Heart	7"	MGM	SPC8	1955	£6	£2.50	export

VALENTINES

Title	Format	Label	Cat. No.	Year			Notes
Hey Baby	7"	Ember	EMBS123	1960	**£50**	**£25**	

VALENTINO, ANNA

Title	Format	Label	Cat. No.	Year			Notes
Calypso Joe	7"	London	HLD8421	1957	**£15**	**£7.50**	

VALENTINO, DANNY

Title	Format	Label	Cat. No.	Year			Notes
Biology	7"	MGM	MGM1067	1960	**£8**	**£4**	
Pictures	7"	MGM	MGM1109	1960	**£5**	**£2**	
Stampede	7"	MGM	MGM1049	1959	**£15**	**£7.50**	

VALENTINO, MARK

Title	Format	Label	Cat. No.	Year			Notes
Do It	7"	Stateside	SS186	1963	**£4**	**£1.50**	
Jiving At The Drive In	7"	Stateside	SS233	1963	**£10**	**£5**	
Mark Valentino	LP	Swan	LP508	1963	**£15**	**£6**	*US*
Push And Kick	7"	Stateside	SS148	1963	**£4**	**£1.50**	

VALENTINOS

Title	Format	Label	Cat. No.	Year			Notes
It's All Over Now	7"	Soul City	SC106	1968	**£6**	**£2.50**	
Tired Of Being Nobody	7"	Stateside	SS2137	1969	**£4**	**£1.50**	
Valentinos/The Sims Twins	LP	Soul City	SCM001	1969	**£15**	**£6**	*with the Sims Twins*

VALERIE & THE ROCK & ROLL YOUNGSTERS

Title	Format	Label	Cat. No.	Year			Notes
Tonight You Belong To Me	7"	Columbia	DB3832	1956	**£8**	**£4**	

VALINO, JOE

Title	Format	Label	Cat. No.	Year			Notes
Garden Of Eden	7"	HMV	POP283	1957	**£10**	**£5**	
God's Little Acre	7"	London	HLT8705	1958	**£8**	**£4**	

VALKYRIES

Title	Format	Label	Cat. No.	Year			Notes
Rip It Up	7"	Parlophone	R5123	1964	**£8**	**£4**	

VALLADARES, DIORIS

Title	Format	Label	Cat. No.	Year			Notes
Authentic Merengue	7" EP	Sue	IEP703	1966	**£10**	**£5**	
Let's Go Latin	LP	Island	ILP910	1964	**£25**	**£10**	

VALLEY, JIM

Title	Format	Label	Cat. No.	Year			Notes
Harpo	LP	Panorama	104	1969	**£15**	**£6**	*US*

VALLEY OF ACHOR

Title	Format	Label	Cat. No.	Year			Notes
Door Of Hope	LP	Dovetail	DOVE18	1975	**£15**	**£6**	

VALLI, FRANKIE

Title	Format	Label	Cat. No.	Year			Notes
My Mother's Eye	7"	Corona	1234	1953	**£500**	**£330**	*US, best auctioned*
Night	7"	Mowest	MW3002	1972	**£5**	**£2**	*with the Four Seasons*
Please Take A Chance	7"	Decca	30994	1959	**£75**	**£37.50**	*US*
Real	7"	Cindy	3012	1959	**£75**	**£37.50**	*US*
Somebody Else Took Her Home	7"	Mercury	70381	1954	**£75**	**£37.50**	*US*
You're Gonna Hurt Yourself	7"	Philips	BF1467	1966	**£4**	**£1.50**	
You're Ready Now	7"	Philips	BF1512	1966	**£6**	**£2.50**	

VALLI, JUNE

Title	Format	Label	Cat. No.	Year			Notes
Anonymous Letter	7"	Mercury	AMT1048	1959	**£4**	**£1.50**	
Answer To A Maiden's Prayer	7"	Mercury	AMT1034	1959	**£4**	**£1.50**	
Apple Green	7"	Mercury	AMT1091	1960	**£4**	**£1.50**	
I Understand	7"	HMV	7M245	1954	**£6**	**£2.50**	
Por Favor	7"	HMV	7M347	1956	**£5**	**£2**	
Tell Me, Tell Me	7"	HMV	7M259	1954	**£6**	**£2.50**	
Wrong, Wrong, Wrong	7"	HMV	7M284	1955	**£5**	**£2**	

VALLONS, JOHNNY & THE DEEJAYS

Title	Format	Label	Cat. No.	Year			Notes
Non-Stop Show At Kingside	LP	Swedisc	SWELP8	1966	**£100**	**£50**	*Swedish*

VALUES

Title	Format	Label	Cat. No.	Year			Notes
Return To Me	7"	Ember	EMBS211	1966	**£25**	**£12.50**	

VALVES

Title	Format	Label	Cat. No.	Year			Notes
I Don't Mean Nothing At All	7"	Albion	DEL3	1979	**£4**	**£1.50**	
Robot Love	7"	Zoom	ZUM1	1977	**£10**	**£5**	
Tarzan Of The Kings Road	7"	Zoom	ZUM3	1977	**£8**	**£4**	

VAMP

Andy Clark and Mick Hutchinson, who recorded three albums together in the early seventies, were previously members of the short-lived Vamp. The group's line-up was completed by the former drummer with the Pretty Things, Viv Prince, and by Pete Sears, who was later a member of Jefferson Starship.

Title	Format	Label	Cat. No.	Year			Notes
Floatin'	7"	Atlantic	584213	1968	**£50**	**£25**	
Green Pea	7"	Atlantic	584263	1969	**£50**	**£25**	*demo*

VAMPIRE'S SOUND INCORPORATED

Title	Format	Label	Cat. No.	Year			Notes
Psychedelic Dance Party	LP	Mercury	MCY134615	1969	**£40**	**£20**	*German*

VAMPIRES

Title	Format	Label	Cat. No.	Year			Notes
Do You Wanna Dance	7"	Pye	7N17553	1968	**£4**	**£1.50**	

VAMPIRES (2)

Title	Format	Label	Number	Year	Value	Value	Notes
Swinging Ghosts	7"	Parlophone	R4599	1959	**£8**	**£4**	

VAN DAMME, ART

Title	Format	Label	Number	Year	Value	Value	Notes
Art Van Damme Quintet	10" LP	Capitol	LC6622	1954	**£12**	**£5**	

VAN DER GRAAF GENERATOR

Peter Hammill's complicated songs, each incorporating several melodic themes and intricate instrumental passages, are well served by Van Der Graaf Generator's musicians. Hugh Banton, in particular, shines as one of the very few organ players in rock to have made a serious attempt to fully explore the potential of the electronic instrument. Peter Hammill's voice too has some of the characteristics of an instrument, as he varies its tonal qualities considerably from moment to moment sometimes with a little electronic assistance. It is the combination of instrumental bravado and compositional depth that arguably makes these albums, by a short head, the most durable of all the progressive rock canon. Two different mixes of the first Charisma album are listed – there are actually supposed to be three in existence, although details of the third have proved to be hard to come by. With regard to the group's rare singles, it should be noted that 'Refugees' is a different version to that found on *The Least We Can Do Is Wave To Each Other*. 'Firebrand' – the rarest Van Der Graaf release of all – is actually the B side of the single, but this is always the named title to appear on dealers' and collectors' wants lists, due to it being the more experimental and dynamic side.

Title	Format	Label	Number	Year	Value	Value	Notes
Aerosol Grey Machine	LP	Mercury	SR61238	1968	**£25**	**£10**	*US*
Aerosol Grey Machine	LP	Fontana	6430083	1975	**£10**	**£4**	
Firebrand	7"	Polydor	56758	1968	**£250**	**£150**	
H To He Who Am The Only One	LP	Charisma	CAS1027	1970	**£12**	**£5**	
Least We Can Do Is Wave To Each Other	LP	Charisma	CAS1007	1970	**£30**	**£15**	*with poster*
Least We Can Do Is Wave To Each Other	LP	Charisma	CAS1007	1969	**£12**	**£5**	
Least We Can Do Is Wave To Each Other	LP	Charisma	CAS1007	1970	**£50**	**£25**	*original mix, matrix CAS1007A/B, poster*
Long Hello	LP	no label	no number	1973	**£20**	**£8**	
Pawn Hearts	LP	Buddah		1971	**£15**	**£6**	*US, with 'Theme One'*
Pawn Hearts	LP	Charisma	CAS1051	1971	**£12**	**£5**	
Refugees	7"	Charisma	CB122	1970	**£30**	**£15**	
Theme One	7"	Charisma	CB175	1972	**£20**	**£10**	*picture sleeve*
Wondering	7"	Charisma	CB297	1976	**£5**	**£2**	

VAN DER REE, PAUL (THE HAPPIEST BAND THAT EVER PLAYED)

Title	Format	Label	Number	Year	Value	Value	Notes
In The Balancing Of Night And Day	LP	Goldfish	LP0001	1970	**£500**	**£250**	*Dutch*

VAN DOREN, MAMIE

Title	Format	Label	Number	Year	Value	Value	Notes
Something To Dream About	7"	Capitol	CL14850	1958	**£4**	**£1.50**	
Something To Dream About	7"	Capitol	CL14850	1958	**£15**	**£7.50**	*promo in picture sleeve*

VAN DYKE, EARL

Title	Format	Label	Number	Year	Value	Value	Notes
All For You	7"	Tamla Motown	TMG506	1965	**£50**	**£25**	
Earl Of Funk	LP	Soul	SS715	1970	**£25**	**£10**	*US*
Six By Six	7"	Tamla Motown	TMG759	1970	**£4**	**£1.50**	
Soul Stomp	7"	Stateside	SS357	1964	**£60**	**£30**	
That Motown Sound	LP	Tamla Motown	TML11014	1965	**£75**	**£37.50**	

VAN DYKE, LEROY

Title	Format	Label	Number	Year	Value	Value	Notes
Big Man In A Big House	7"	Mercury	AMT1173	1962	**£4**	**£1.50**	
Broken Promise	7"	Mercury	AMT1183	1962	**£4**	**£1.50**	
It's All Over Now, Baby Blue	7"	Warner Bros	WB5650	1965	**£4**	**£1.50**	
Movin'	LP	Mercury	MMC14118	1963	**£25**	**£10**	
Walk On By	7"	Mercury	AMT1166	1961	**£4**	**£1.50**	
Walk On By	LP	Mercury	MMC14101	1961	**£25**	**£10**	

VAN DYKE & THE BAMBIS

Title	Format	Label	Number	Year	Value	Value	Notes
Doin' The Mod	7"	Piccadilly	7N35180	1964	**£5**	**£2**	

VAN DYKES

Title	Format	Label	Number	Year	Value	Value	Notes
I've Gotta Go On Without You	7"	Stateside	SS530	1966	**£12**	**£6**	
No Man Is An Island	7"	Stateside	SS504	1966	**£8**	**£4**	
Tellin' It Like It Is	LP	Bell	6004	1967	**£15**	**£6**	*US*

VAN EATON, LON & DERREK

Title	Format	Label	Number	Year	Value	Value	Notes
Brother	LP	Apple	SAPCOR25	1973	**£25**	**£10**	*with insert*
Warm Woman	7"	Apple	46	1973	**£25**	**£12.50**	*picture sleeve*
Warm Woman	7"	Apple	46	1973	**£4**	**£1.50**	

VAN EEDE, NICK

Title	Format	Label	Number	Year	Value	Value	Notes
All Or Nothing	7"	Barn	BARN003	1979	**£4**	**£1.50**	
I Only Want	7"	Barn	BARN008	1979	**£4**	**£1.50**	

VAN HALEN

Title	Format	Label	Number	Year	Value	Value	Notes
Dance The Night Away	7"	Warner Bros	K17371	1979	**£6**	**£2.50**	*picture disc*
Dance The Night Away	7"	Warner Bros	K17371	1979	**£4**	**£1.50**	
Dreams	7"	Warner Bros	W8642P	1986	**£8**	**£4**	*shaped picture disc, plinth*
Feels So Good	CD-s	WEA	W7565CD	1989	**£5**	**£2**	

Jump	CD-s	Warner Bros	W0155CDX	1993	**£5**	**£2**	*in metal tin*
When It's Love	CD-s	WEA	W7816CD	1988	**£5**	**£2**	*3" single*
Why Can't This Be Love	7"	Warner Bros	W8740P	1986	**£6**	**£2.50**	*shaped picture disc, plinth*

VAN RONK, DAVE

Ballads And Blues And Spirituals	LP	Folkways	F3818	1959	**£20**	**£8**	*US*

VAN SPYK, ROB

Follow The Sun	LP	private		197–	**£40**	**£20**	

VAN ZANDT, TOWNES

For The Sake Of A Song	LP	Poppy	PYS40001	1968	**£12**	**£5**	*US*
Late Great Townes Van Zandt	LP	United Artists	UAS29442	1973	**£10**	**£4**	

VANCE

Epitaph For Mary	LP	VRL		1982	**£50**	**£25**	*Dutch*

VANCE, TOMMY

Off The Hook	7"	Columbia	DB8062	1966	**£4**	**£1.50**	
You Must Be The One	7"	Columbia	DB7999	1966	**£4**	**£1.50**	

VANDER, CHRISTIAN

Tristan Et Iseult	LP	Egg	90171	1978	**£10**	**£4**	*French*

VANGELIS

Apocalypse Des Animaux	LP	Polydor	2489113	1976	**£20**	**£8**	
Chariots Of Fire	LP	Polydor	POLS1026	1981	**£15**	**£6**	*gatefold sleeve*
Chariots Of Fire/China/Opera Sauvage	LP	Polydor	BOX1	1982	**£15**	**£6**	*3 LP boxed set*
Pulsar	7"	RCA	RCA2762	1976	**£5**	**£2**	
Will Of The Wind	CD-s	Arista	661767	1988	**£6**	**£2.50**	

VANILLA FUDGE

Beat Goes On	LP	Atlantic	587/588100	1968	**£10**	**£4**	
Eleanor Rigby	7"	Atlantic	584139	1967	**£4**	**£1.50**	
Near The Beginning	LP	Atco	228020	1969	**£10**	**£4**	
Renaissance	LP	Atlantic	587/588110	1968	**£10**	**£4**	
Rock'n'Roll	LP	Atco	228029	1970	**£10**	**£4**	
Shotgun	7"	Atlantic	584257	1969	**£4**	**£1.50**	
Some Velvet Morning	7"	Atlantic	584276	1969	**£4**	**£1.50**	
Vanilla Fudge	LP	Atlantic	587/588086	1967	**£12**	**£5**	
Where Is My Mind	7"	Atlantic	584179	1968	**£4**	**£1.50**	
You Keep Me Hanging On	7"	Atlantic	584123	1967	**£4**	**£1.50**	

VANITY FARE

Sun, The Wind And Other Things	LP	Page One	POLS010	1968	**£15**	**£6**	

VANN, TEDDY

Cindy	7"	London	HLU9097	1960	**£10**	**£5**	

VARDAS, PETER

He Threw A Stone	7"	Top Rank	JAR173	1959	**£4**	**£1.50**	

VARDIS

100 Mph	7"	Redball	RR017	1979	**£60**	**£30**	
If I Were King	7"	Castle	QUEL2/100	1980	**£5**	**£2**	
Quo Vardis	LP	Logo	LOGO1034	1982	**£10**	**£4**	*with 7" (VARFREE1)*

VARIATIONS

Man With All The Toys	7"	Immediate	IM019	1965	**£6**	**£2.50**	

VARICOSE VEINS

Geographical Problem	7"	Warped	WARP1	1978	**£40**	**£20**	

VARIOUS

Various artists albums can become collectable for a number of reasons. Some contain tracks that are only available on that particular record. One of the most valuable of this sort is the *Glastonbury Fayre* triple album, which within its extravagant packing and multiple inserts contains material by artists like David Bowie, Marc Bolan and the Grateful Dead, none of which has been released anywhere else. Other albums are on labels that are themselves collectable, like the various Tamla Motown anthologies, or the United Dairies compilation. Others simply seem to epitomize an area or era of music particularly well – the classic example here being the *Nuggets* double, which gathers together a number of the American groups whose music represents what was meant by 'punk rock' in the sixties. For jazz collectors, various artist compilations are not popular, and the large number of such albums from the fifties do not, in general, appear in these listings, even when they feature artists who do have substantial collectors' discographies to their names.

	LP	Treasure Isle	TI101	1966	**£60**	**£30**	
18 Original Hits Performed By 18 Unoriginal Artists	CD	Polygram	PMP011	1995	**£50**	**£25**	*US promo*
1968 Memphis Country Music Festival	LP	Blue Horizon	763210	1968	**£30**	**£15**	
1980 The First Fifteen Minutes	7"	Neutron	NT003	1980	**£10**	**£5**	
49 Greek Street	LP	RCA	SF8118	1970	**£10**	**£4**	
50 Minutes & 24 Seconds Of Recorded Dynamite	LP	Sue	ILP920	1965	**£30**	**£15**	
Abbey Tavern Traditional Music And Song	LP	Abbey Tavern	ATP101	1970	**£20**	**£8**	*Irish*
Acid Dreams	LP	Acid	5199	1980	**£100**	**£50**	*US*
Action Packed Soul	LP	Action	ACLP6005	1969	**£15**	**£6**	

Title	Format	Label	Number	Year	Mint	VG+	Notes
Afflicted Man's Musica Box	LP	United Dairies	UD012	1982	**£40**	**£20**	*gatefold sleeve*
Afflicted Man's Musica Box	LP	United Dairies	UD012	1982	**£15**	**£6**	
African Melody	LP	Pama	PMP2004	1970	**£10**	**£4**	
Album Full Of Soul	LP	Stateside	SL10172	1966	**£20**	**£8**	
Alive In The Living Room	LP	Creation	CRELP001	1984	**£10**	**£4**	
Alive!	LP	Key	KL002	1969	**£25**	**£10**	
All Cops In Delirium	LP	private	no number	1980	**£50**	**£25**	*US*
All Folk Together	LP	Talisman	STAL5013	1970	**£15**	**£6**	
All For Art . . . And Art For All	LP	Whaam!	BIG8	1984	**£20**	**£8**	
All Good Clean Fun	LP	United Artists	UDX201/2	1971	**£12**	**£5**	*double*
All Hell Let Loose	LP	Neat	NEAT102	1983	**£15**	**£6**	
All Star Hit Parade	7"	Decca	F10752	1956	**£6**	**£2.50**	
All Star Hit Parade	7" EP	Pye	NEP24168	1963	**£6**	**£2.50**	
All Star Hit Parade No. 2	7"	Decca	F10915	1957	**£5**	**£2**	
All Star Hit Parade No. 2	7"	Decca	F10915	1957	**£5**	**£2**	
All Star Hit Parade Vol. 2	7" EP	Pye	NEP24172	1964	**£6**	**£2.50**	
All Time Country And Western Hits	10" LP	Parlophone	PMD1064	1958	**£12**	**£5**	
American Country Jubilee No. 1	7" EP	Decca	DFE8571	1964	**£6**	**£2.50**	
American Folk Blues Festival	LP	Polydor	LPHM46397/ SLPHM237597	1963	**£10**	**£4**	
American Folk Blues Festival 1963	LP	Fontana	TL5204	1964	**£10**	**£4**	
American Folk Blues Festival 1964	LP	Fontana	TL5225	1965	**£10**	**£4**	
American Folk Blues Festival 1965	LP	Fontana	TL5286	1966	**£10**	**£4**	
American Folk Blues Festival 1966	LP	Fontana	(S)TL5389	1966	**£15**	**£6**	
Angels And Other BBC TV Themes	LP	BBC	REB236	197–	**£10**	**£4**	
Angola Prisoners' Blues	LP	Collector	JGN1003	1960	**£12**	**£5**	
Anniversary Issue	7"	Recommended	RRR&RE	1985	**£150**	**£75**	*15 single set*
Anthology Of British Blues Vol. 1	LP	Immediate	IMAL03/04	1969	**£15**	**£6**	*double*
Anthology Of British Blues Vol. 2	LP	Immediate	IMAL05/06	1969	**£15**	**£6**	*double*
Apollo Saturday Night	LP	London	HAK/SHK8174	1964	**£25**	**£10**	
At The Cavern	LP	Decca	LK4597	1964	**£40**	**£20**	
Atlantic Discotheque	LP	Atlantic	ATL5020	1965	**£15**	**£6**	
Atlantic Is Soul	LP	Atlantic	AP2	196–	**£10**	**£4**	
Atlanticlassics	LP	Atlantic	AC3	196–	**£25**	**£10**	
Attack Of The Jersey Teens	LP	Bona Fide	BFRNJ6601	1984	**£12**	**£5**	*US*
Authentic Chicago Blues	LP	Windmill	WMD124	1972	**£10**	**£4**	
Authentic Chicago Blues	LP	Beacon	SBEAB9	1970	**£10**	**£4**	
Authentic Rhythm And Blues	LP	Stateside	SL10068	1964	**£25**	**£10**	
Authentic Ska	LP	Stateside	SL10107	1964	**£25**	**£10**	
Avant Garde	LP	Deutsche Grammophon		196–	**£60**	**£30**	*6 LP boxed set*
Avant Garde Vol. 2	LP	Deutsche Grammophon	643541/46	196–	**£60**	**£30**	*6 LP boxed set*
Avant Garde Vol. 3	LP	Deutsche Grammophon	2561039/044	197–	**£60**	**£30**	*6 LP boxed set*
Ayrshire Folk	LP	Deroy	DER1052	1974	**£30**	**£15**	
Backtrack Six	LP	Track	2407006	1970	**£12**	**£5**	
Backwoods Blues	10" LP	London	AL3535	1954	**£30**	**£15**	
Badger A Go-Go	LP	Night Owl	KTV3	1968	**£15**	**£6**	*US*
Ballin'	LP	Fontana	688200ZL	1962	**£10**	**£4**	
Bang Bang Lulu	LP	Pama	PMLP4	1968	**£20**	**£8**	
Barrelhouse Blues And Boogie Woogie Vol. 1	LP	Storyville	670155	1964	**£10**	**£4**	
Barrelhouse Blues And Boogie Woogie Vol. 2	LP	Storyville	670183	1965	**£10**	**£4**	
Barrelhouse Blues And Boogie Woogie Vol. 3	LP	Storyville	SLP213	1965	**£10**	**£4**	
Barrelhouse Piano	10" LP	Vogue Coral	LRA10022	1955	**£15**	**£6**	
Barrelhouse Piano Vol. 2	10" LP	Vogue Coral	LRA10023	1955	**£15**	**£6**	
Barrelhouse, Boogie Woogie, And Blues	10" LP	Fontana	TFR6018	1959	**£12**	**£5**	
Battle Of Jazz – Hot Versus Cool	10" LP	MGM	D115	1953	**£10**	**£4**	
Battle Of The Bands	10" LP	Capitol	LC6510	1951	**£15**	**£6**	
Battle Of The Bands	LP	Onyx	ES80689	1966	**£100**	**£50**	*US*
Battle Of The Bands	LP	Onyx	ES80689	198–	**£25**	**£10**	*US*
Battle Of The Bands Vol. 1	LP	Panorama	103	1966	**£50**	**£25**	*US*
Battle Of The Bands Vol. 1	LP	Ren-Vell	317	196–	**£100**	**£50**	*US*
Battle Of The Bands Vol. 2	LP	Panorama	108	1967	**£50**	**£25**	*US*
Battle Of The Giants	LP	Melodisc	12192	1964	**£10**	**£4**	
Bay State Rock Vol. 1	LP	Star Rhythm	LP101	1980	**£12**	**£5**	*US*
Beat For You	LP	Polydor	94042	1964	**£40**	**£20**	*German*
Beat In Liverpool	10" LP	Europäische Verlage	101	1965	**£50**	**£25**	*German*
Beat Merchants	LP	United Artists	UDM101/2	1976	**£12**	**£5**	*double*
Beat Party	LP	CBS	52327	1966	**£25**	**£10**	*German*
Beat-Wettbewerb Der Stadt Frankfurt	LP	CBS	52330	1966	**£40**	**£20**	*German*
Beater's Hit Parade	LP	Philips	75283	1966	**£50**	**£25**	*German*
Bebop Era	LP	RCA	RD7909	1967	**£10**	**£4**	
Bee Jay Demo Record	LP	Tener	1014	1967	**£300**	**£180**	*US*
Belfast Rocks	LP	Rip Off	ROLP1	1978	**£15**	**£6**	
Bell's Cellar Of Soul Vol. 1	LP	Bell	MBLL102	1968	**£12**	**£5**	
Bell's Cellar Of Soul Vol. 2	LP	Bell	MBLL107	1969	**£12**	**£5**	
Bell's Cellar Of Soul Vol. 3	LP	Bell	MBLL117	1969	**£12**	**£5**	
Bells Are Ringing	7" EP	Philips	BBE12148	1957	**£6**	**£2.50**	
Best Of Bluegrass	7" EP	Melodisc	EPM7115	195–	**£6**	**£2.50**	
Best Of Camel	LP	Pama	SECO18	1969	**£15**	**£6**	

Title	Format	Label	Number	Year	Price	Price	Notes
Best Of Golden Guinea	7" EP	Golden Guinea	7GG3	1962	**£5**	**£2**	
Best Of The Hideouts	LP	Hideout	HLP1002	1965	**£100**	**£50**	*US*
Best Wishes For Christmas	7" EP	Philips	BBE12225	1958	**£5**	**£2**	
Big Bamboo	LP	Attack	ATLP1011	1973	**£20**	**£8**	
Big Beat	7" EP	Concert Hall	BPC717	1963	**£15**	**£7.50**	
Big Beat	LP	Fontana	TFL5080	1959	**£50**	**£25**	
Big D Jamboree	LP	London	HAB8199	1964	**£15**	**£6**	
Big Four	7" EP	Embassy	WT2011	1965	**£5**	**£2**	
Big Four	7" EP	Embassy	WT2008	1965	**£5**	**£2**	
Big Four	7" EP	Fontana	TE17469	1966	**£6**	**£2.50**	
Big Four	7" EP	Philips	BE12593	1966	**£6**	**£2.50**	
Big Four	7" EP	Philips	BBE12021	1956	**£8**	**£4**	
Big Four No. 2	7" EP	Philips	BBE12040	1956	**£8**	**£4**	
Big Four No. 3	7" EP	Philips	BBE12088	1956	**£5**	**£2**	
Big Four No. 4	7" EP	Philips	BBE12091	1956	**£8**	**£4**	
Big Four No. 5	7" EP	Philips	BBE12114	1957	**£5**	**£2**	
Big Four No. 6	7" EP	Philips	BBE12139	1957	**£5**	**£2**	
Big Four No. 7	7" EP	Philips	BBE12145	1957	**£8**	**£4**	
Big Four No. 8	7" EP	Philips	BBE12158	1957	**£5**	**£2**	
Big Four No. 9	7" EP	Philips	BBE12165	1957	**£6**	**£2.50**	
Big Four No. 10	7" EP	Philips	BBE12190	1958	**£6**	**£2.50**	
Big Four No. 11	7" EP	Philips	BBE12288	1959	**£6**	**£2.50**	
Big Four No. 12	7" EP	Philips	BBE12336	1959	**£8**	**£4**	
Big Hits Of Mid-America Vol. 1	LP	Soma	1245	1964	**£50**	**£25**	*US*
Big Hits Of Mid-America Vol. 2	LP	Soma	1246	1965	**£50**	**£25**	*US*
Big One	LP	Minit	MML40007E	1969	**£10**	**£4**	
Birth Control	LP	Pama	SECO32	1970	**£12**	**£5**	
Bitter End Years	LP	Roxbury	RX3300	1976	**£25**	**£10**	*US triple*
Black Country Night Out	LP	Broadside	BRO120	1976	**£10**	**£4**	
Black Country Night Out Vol. 2	LP	Broadside	BRO122	1977	**£10**	**£4**	
Black Diamond Express To Hell	LP	Matchbox	SDX207/8	1970	**£15**	**£6**	*double*
Black Slacks And Bobby Socks	LP	HMV	CLP1167	1958	**£150**	**£75**	
Black, Whites And Blues	LP	CBS	52796	1970	**£10**	**£4**	
Blackpool Nights	LP	Columbia	33SX1244	1960	**£15**	**£6**	
Blank Tapes Vol. 1	7"	Skeleton	SKL002	1979	**£15**	**£6**	
Blue Beat Special	LP	Coxsone	CSP1	1968	**£30**	**£15**	
Blue Note Gems Of Jazz	LP	Blue Note	BLP/BST82001	1966	**£10**	**£4**	
Blue Ridge Mountain Field Trip	LP	Leader	LEA4012	1970	**£10**	**£4**	
Blue Ridge Mountain Music	LP	London	LTZK15210	1961	**£12**	**£5**	
Bluebird Blues	LP	RCA	RD7786	1966	**£10**	**£4**	
Bluegrass	7" EP	Range	JRE7005	196–	**£5**	**£2**	
Blues	7" EP	Fontana	TFE17081	1959	**£5**	**£2**	
Blues	LP	Columbia	33SX1417	1962	**£25**	**£10**	
Blues Anytime Vol. 1	LP	Immediate	IMLP014	1968	**£12**	**£5**	
Blues Anytime Vol. 2	LP	Immediate	IMLP015	1968	**£12**	**£5**	
Blues Anytime Vol. 3	LP	Immediate	IMLP019	1968	**£12**	**£5**	
Blues At Newport	LP	Vanguard	VSD79145	1965	**£10**	**£4**	*US*
Blues At Newport 1964 Part 1	LP	Fontana	TFL6048	1965	**£15**	**£6**	
Blues Came Down From Memphis	LP	London	HAS8265	1966	**£25**	**£10**	
Blues Chicago Style	LP	Python	PLPKM17	1971	**£20**	**£8**	
Blues Fell This Morning	LP	Philips	BBL7369	1960	**£30**	**£15**	
Blues Festival	7" EP	Pye	NEP44038	1964	**£15**	**£7.50**	
Blues From Chicago	LP	Python	PLP6	1969	**£20**	**£8**	
Blues From Chicago Vol. 2	LP	Python	PLP9	1970	**£20**	**£8**	
Blues From Chicago Vol. 3	LP	Python	PLP15	1970	**£20**	**£8**	
Blues From Maxwell Street	LP	Heritage	1004	196–	**£25**	**£10**	
Blues From The Bayou	LP	Pye	NPL28142	1971	**£10**	**£4**	
Blues From The Delta	LP	Saydisc	SDM226	1972	**£15**	**£6**	
Blues From The Windy City	LP	Python	PLP21	1971	**£20**	**£8**	
Blues Is My Companion	LP	Sunflower	no number	196–	**£20**	**£8**	
Blues Keep Falling	LP	Sunflower	no number	196–	**£20**	**£8**	
Blues Like Showers Of Rain	LP	Matchbox	SDM142	1967	**£50**	**£25**	
Blues Like Showers Of Rain Vol. 2	LP	Saydisc	SDM167	1968	**£50**	**£25**	
Blues Now	LP	Decca	LK4681	1965	**£25**	**£10**	
Blues Obscurities Vol. 1	LP	London	HAU8454	1974	**£10**	**£4**	
Blues Obscurities Vol. 1	LP	Blues Obscurities		1972	**£20**	**£8**	
Blues Obscurities Vol. 2	LP	London	HAU8455	1974	**£10**	**£4**	
Blues Obscurities Vol. 2	LP	Blues Obscurities		1972	**£20**	**£8**	
Blues Obscurities Vol. 3	LP	London	HAU8456	1974	**£10**	**£4**	
Blues Obscurities Vol. 3	LP	Blues Obscurities		1972	**£20**	**£8**	
Blues Obscurities Vol. 4	LP	Blues Obscurities		1972	**£20**	**£8**	
Blues Obscurities Vol. 5	LP	Blues Obscurities		1972	**£20**	**£8**	
Blues Obscurities Vol. 6	LP	Blues Obscurities		1972	**£20**	**£8**	
Blues Obscurities Vol. 7	LP	Blues Obscurities		1972	**£20**	**£8**	
Blues Obscurities Vol. 8	LP	Blues Obscurities		1972	**£20**	**£8**	
Blues Obscurities Vol. 9	LP	Blues Obscurities		1972	**£20**	**£8**	
Blues Obscurities Vol. 10	LP	Blues Obscurities		1972	**£20**	**£8**	

Title	Format	Label	Cat. No.	Year			Notes
Blues On Parade No. 1	7" EP	Columbia	SEG8226	1963	£10	£5	
Blues Package '69	LP	Mercury	SMXL77	1969	£10	£4	
Blues People	LP	Highway 51	H102	1969	£40	£20	
Blues Piano – Chicago Plus	LP	Atlantic	K40404	1972	£12	£5	
Blues Potpourri	LP	Kokomo	K1001	1968	£40	£20	
Blues Rarities Vol. 1	LP	Rarities		1971	£15	£6	double
Blues Roll On	LP	London	LTZK15215	1961	£12	£5	
Blues Roots Vol. 1	LP	Poppy	PYM11001	1969	£12	£5	
Blues Southside Chicago	LP	Decca	LK4748	1966	£40	£20	
Blues Today – Southern Style	LP	Python	PLP16	1971	£20	£8	
Blues Vol. 1	7" EP	Pye	NEP44029	1964	£12	£6	
Blues Vol. 1	LP	Pye	NPL28030	1964	£10	£4	
Blues Vol. 1 Pt 2	7" EP	Pye	NEP44035	1964	£12	£6	
Blues Vol. 2	LP	Pye	NPL28035	1964	£10	£4	
Blues Vol. 2 Part 1	7" EP	Chess	CRE6011	1966	£12	£6	
Blues Vol. 3	LP	Pye	NPL28045	1964	£10	£4	
Blues Vol. 4	LP	Chess	CRL4003	1964	£12	£5	
Blues Vol. 5	LP	Chess	CRL4512	1965	£15	£6	
Bluescene USA Vol. 1	LP	Storyville	SLP176	1965	£10	£4	
Bluescene USA Vol. 2	LP	Storyville	SLP177	1965	£10	£4	
Bluescene USA Vol. 3	LP	Storyville	SLP181	1965	£10	£4	
Bluescene USA Vol. 4	LP	Storyville	SLP189	1967	£10	£4	
Bocastle Breakdown	LP	Topic	12TS240	1974	£10	£4	
Bolo Bash	LP	Bolo	BLP8002	1964	£25	£10	US
Bonnie Lass Come O'er The Burn	LP	Topic	12T128	1965	£20	£8	
Bonny North Tyne	LP	Topic	12TS239	1974	£10	£4	
Boogie Woogie Rarities	LP	Milestone	MLP2009	197–	£10	£4	
Boogie Woogie With The Blues	10" LP	London	AL3544	1955	£15	£6	
Boskoop Project	LP	private		1981	£30	£15	Dutch
Boss Reggae	LP	Pama	SECO17	1969	£50	£25	
Both Sides Of The Downs	LP	Eron	002	1974	£12	£5	
Bothy Ballads	LP	Tangent	TNGM109	1971	£10	£4	
Bouquet Of Steel	LP	Aardvark	STEAL2	1980	£10	£4	blue vinyl
Brave Plough Boy	LP	XTRA	XTRA1150	1975	£20	£8	
Breeze From Erin	LP	Topic	12T184	1969	£10	£4	
Bristol Recorder Vol. 2	LP	Bristol Recorder	BR002	1981	£12	£5	
British Blue-Eyed Soul	LP	Island	ILP966/ILPS9066	1968	£30	£15	pink label
Broadside Ballads Vol. 1	LP	Broadside	BR301	1964	£15	£6	US
Brum Beat – Live At The Barrel Organ	LP	Big Bear	BRUM1	1979	£12	£5	double
Brumbeat	LP	Dial	DLP1	1964	£50	£25	
Built To Blast	7"	Fierce Panda	NING04	1994	£6	£2.50	double
Bumper Bundle – 16 Hits	LP	Decca	LK4734	1965	£15	£6	
Burghers Vol. 1	LP	private	304083	1983	£12	£5	US
Buskers	LP	Columbia	SX/SCX6356	1969	£25	£10	
Busted At Oz	LP	Autumn	AU2	1981	£15	£6	
Buttons And Bows Vol. 1	LP	Dambusters	DAM003	1984	£15	£6	double
Buttons And Bows Vol. 2	LP	Dambusters	DAM006	1985	£15	£6	double
Bye Bye Birdie	7" EP	Pye	NEP24142	1961	£8	£4	
Cabaret Night In London	LP	Columbia	33SX1481	1963	£15	£6	
Cabaret Night In Paris	7" EP	Columbia	33S1083	1956	£5	£2	
Cabaret Night In Paris No. 4	7" EP	Columbia	33S1099	1957	£5	£2	
Cabaret Night In Paris No. 5	7" EP	Columbia	33S1105	1957	£5	£2	
California Acid Folk	LP	Penguin Egg	11/12	1985	£25	£10	US double
California Christmas	LP	Penguin Egg	6/7	1983	£25	£10	US double
California Christmas Vol. 2	LP	Penguin Egg	9/10	1983	£25	£10	US double
California Halloween	LP	Penguin Egg		198–	£25	£10	US double
California New Year	LP	Penguin Egg		198–	£25	£10	US double
Calypso Time	7" EP	Melodisc	EPM767	1956	£5	£2	
Cameo Big Four	7" EP	Cameo Parkway	CPE552	1963	£8	£4	
Can't Keep From Crying	LP	Bounty	BY6035	1967	£15	£6	
Canny Newcassel	LP	Topic	12TS219	1972	£20	£8	
Caribbean Dance Festival	LP	Trojan	TBL171	1971	£15	£6	
Carolina Country Blues	LP	Flyright	LP505	1973	£10	£4	
Castle Rock	LP	Nottingham Festival	FEST002	1974	£75	£37.50	
Cerne Box Set	LP	Cerne	CERNE123	1990	£50	£25	3 LPs, boxed
Changes	LP	Magistral	2000	1980	£100	£50	US
Chaplin Revue	LP	Brunswick	LAT8345	1960	£15	£6	
Charge Of The Light Brigade	LP	United Artists	SULP1189	1968	£10	£4	
Chess Story Vol. 1	LP	Chess	CRL4004	1964	£20	£8	
Chess Story Vol. 2	LP	Chess	CRL4516	1965	£20	£8	
Chicago – The Blues Today	LP	Fontana	TFL6068	1966	£15	£6	
Chicago – The Blues Today Vol. 1	LP	Vanguard	SVRL19020	1969	£15	£6	
Chicago – The Blues Today Vol. 2	LP	Vanguard	SVRL19021	1969	£15	£6	
Chicago – The Blues Today Vol. 2	LP	Fontana	TFL6069	1966	£15	£6	
Chicago – The Blues Today Vol. 3	LP	Vanguard	SVRL19022	1969	£15	£6	
Chicago – The Blues Today Vol. 3	LP	Fontana	TFL6070	1966	£15	£6	
Chicago House Bands	LP	Sunflower	ET1401	1968	£25	£10	
Chicago Sessions Vol. 1	LP	Kokomo	K1005	1969	£30	£15	
Chicken Stuff	LP	Flyright	LP4700	1970	£10	£4	
Chocolate Soup For Diabetics Vol. 1	LP	Relics	LSD1	1980	£25	£10	
Chocolate Soup For Diabetics Vol. 2	LP	Relics	ACID1	1981	£25	£10	
Chocolate Soup For Diabetics Vol. 3	LP	Relics	CSFD3	198–	£25	£10	
Chosen Few Vol. 1	LP	A-Go-Go	1966	1982	£50	£25	US
Chosen Few Vol. 2	LP	Tom-Tom	3752	1983	£50	£25	US
Christmas	10" LP	Philips	BBR8112	1957	£10	£4	

Title	Format	Label	Number	Year	Mint	VG+	Notes
Christmas Dedication	LP	Chess	CRLS4541	1968	£10	£4	
Christmas Reggae	7" EP	Coxsone	SCE1	1967	£40	£20	
Classic Jazz Piano	10" LP	London	AL3559	1955	£15	£6	
Classic Scots Ballads	LP	Tangent	TNGM199D	1975	£15	£6	*double*
Classics In Jazz – Cool And Quiet	10" LP	Capitol	LC6598	1953	£10	£4	
Classics In Jazz – Dixieland Style	10" LP	Capitol	LC6562	1952	£10	£4	
Classics In Jazz – Modern Idiom	10" LP	Capitol	LC6561	1952	£10	£4	
Classics In Jazz – Piano Items	10" LP	Capitol	LC6559	1952	£10	£4	
Classics In Jazz – Sax Stylists	10" LP	Capitol	LC6582	1953	£10	£4	
Classics In Jazz – Trumpet Stylists	10" LP	Capitol	LC6579	1953	£10	£4	
Classics Of Irish Traditional Music	LP	Morning Star	45001	1973	£12	£5	*US*
Club Rock Steady	LP	Trojan	TTL54	1970	£20	£8	
Club Rock Steady '68	LP	Island	ILP965	1968	£60	£30	*pink label*
Club Ska '67	LP	Island	ILP948	1967	£50	£25	
Club Ska '67 Vol. 2	LP	Island	ILP956	1967	£60	£30	
Club Ska Vol. 1	LP	Trojan	TTL48	1970	£20	£8	
Club Ska Vol. 2	LP	Trojan	TTL51	1970	£20	£8	
Club Soul	LP	Island	ILP964	1968	£25	£10	*pink label*
Club Spangle No. 1	7"	Fierce Panda	SPANG01	1994	£6	£2.50	
Coca Cola	LP	Coca Cola	PD2945	1980	£30	£15	*German picture disc*
Collection Of 16 Big Hits Vol. 6	LP	Tamla Motown	(S)TML11074	1968	£12	£5	
Collection Of 16 Original Big Hits Vol. 4	LP	Tamla Motown	TML11043	1967	£20	£8	
Collection Of 16 Original Big Hits Vol. 5	LP	Tamla Motown	TML11050	1967	£12	£5	
Collection Of 16 Tamla Motown Hits	LP	Tamla Motown	TML11001	1965	£25	£10	
Collection Of Big Hits Vol. 7	LP	Tamla Motown	(S)TML11092	1969	£10	£4	
Collectors Blues Series Vol. 1	LP	Chicago	202	1975	£15	£6	
Collectors Blues Series Vol. 2	LP	Chicago	205	1975	£15	£6	
Collectors Blues Series Vol. 3	LP	Chicago	210	1975	£15	£6	
Collectors Blues Series Vol. 4	LP	Chicago	212	1975	£15	£6	
Collectors Blues Series Vol. 5	LP	Chicago	213	1975	£15	£6	
Collectors Items Vol. 1	10" LP	London	AL3514	1954	£10	£4	
Collectors Items Vol. 2	10" LP	London	AL3533	1954	£10	£4	
Collectors Items Vol. 3	10" LP	London	AL3550	1956	£10	£4	
Come Fly With Me	LP	Blue Beat	BBLP803	1964	£200	£100	
Connecticut's Greatest Hits	LP	Co-op	CP101	1968	£25	£10	*US*
Cool Music For A Hot Night	LP	Tempo	TAP10	1957	£25	£10	
Country & Western Hits Vol. 1	7" EP	CBS	AGG20033	1963	£5	£2	
Country & Western Hits Vol. 2	7" EP	CBS	AGG20041	1964	£5	£2	
Country And Western	7" EP	Range	JRE7001	196–	£5	£2	
Country And Western	7" EP	Range	JRE7004	196–	£5	£2	
Country And Western Express Vol. 1	7" EP	Top Rank	JKP2055	1960	£5	£2	
Country And Western Express Vol. 4	7" EP	Top Rank	JKP2063	1960	£5	£2	
Country And Western Express Vol. 6	7" EP	Top Rank	JKP2065	1960	£10	£5	
Country And Western Golden Hit Parade Vol. 1	LP	London	HAB8145	1964	£10	£4	
Country And Western Golden Hit Parade Vol. 2	LP	London	HAB8146	1964	£10	£4	
Country And Western Showcase Vol. 2	7" EP	Hickory	LPE1505	1965	£5	£2	
Country And Western Spectacular	7" EP	Philips	BBE12149	1957	£8	£4	
Country And Western Trail Blazers No. 1	7" EP	Mercury	ZEP10038	1959	£6	£2.50	
Country Blues	7" EP	Heritage	105	196–	£15	£7.50	
Country Blues	LP	RBF	RF1	1961	£15	£6	
Country Blues	LP	Speciality	SNTF5014	1973	£25	£10	
Country Blues Vol. 2	LP	RBF	RBF9	1964	£15	£6	
Country Favourites Vol. 1	10" LP	Brunswick	LA8729	1956	£12	£5	
Country Guitar Hall Of Fame	LP	London	HAB8243	1965	£10	£4	
Country Guitar Vol. 1	7" EP	RCA	RCX107	1958	£5	£2	
Country Guitar Vol. 2	7" EP	RCA	RCX110	1958	£5	£2	
Country Guitar Vol. 5	7" EP	RCA	RCX127	1959	£5	£2	
Country Guitar Vol. 6	7" EP	RCA	RCX141	1959	£5	£2	
Country Guitar Vol. 8	7" EP	RCA	RCX147	1959	£5	£2	
Country Guitar Vol. 9	7" EP	RCA	RCX159	1959	£5	£2	
Country Guitar Vol. 10	7" EP	RCA	RCX176	1959	£5	£2	
Country Guitar Vol. 11	7" EP	RCA	RCX177	1959	£5	£2	
Country Guitar Vol. 12	7" EP	RCA	RCX185	1960	£5	£2	
Country Jubilee Vol. 1	7" EP	Decca	DFE8522	1963	£5	£2	
Country Jubilee Vol. 2	7" EP	Decca	DFE8523	1963	£5	£2	
Crab – Biggest Hits	LP	Pama	ECO2	1969	£20	£8	
Crazed And Confused	7"	Fierce Panda	NING02	1994	£12	£6	*double*
Damn Yankees	7" EP	Mercury	MEP9509	1956	£5	£2	
Dance Craze	7" EP	Capitol	EAP1518	1955	£6	£2.50	
Dancebusters Volume One	CD	Wau! Mr Modo	WAMCD002	1990	£12	£5	
Dancing Down Orange Street	LP	Big Shot	BSLP5002	1968	£50	£25	
Dandelion Sampler	7"	Dandelion	DS7001	1971	£4	£1.50	
Dark Horse Records '76	LP	Dark Horse	DH1	1976	£40	£20	*promo*
Dark Muddy Bottom	7" EP	XX	MIN706	196–	£8	£4	
Decade Of The Blues – The 1950s	LP	Highway 51	H100	1966	£40	£20	
Decade Of The Blues – The 1950s Vol. 2	LP	Highway 51	H104	1966	£30	£15	
Decca Showcase Vol. 5	10" LP	Decca	LF1265	1955	£10	£4	
Deep In My Heart	7" EP	MGM	MGMEP652	1958	£5	£2	

Deep Lancashire	LP	Topic	12T188	1969	**£10**	**£4**	
Demention Of Sound: British Beat And R&B From 1964–65	LP	Feedback	LESSON1	1983	**£20**	**£8**	
Depression Blues	7" EP	Poydras	102	195–	**£10**	**£5**	
Devastate To Liberate	LP	YANGKI	1	1985	**£10**	**£4**	
Diana's Rooten Tooten Rock And Roll Party	LP	Romulan	UFOX01	198–	**£25**	**£10**	*US*
Ding Dong Dollar Anti-Polaris And Scottish Republican Songs	LP	Folkways	FD5444	1962	**£20**	**£8**	*US*
Dingles Regatta	LP	Dingles	DIN301	1976	**£10**	**£4**	
Dirt Blues	LP	Minit	MLL/MLS40005	1969	**£15**	**£6**	
Dirty Water – The History Of Eastern Iowa Rock Vol. 2	LP	Unlimited Production	RRRLP003	1986	**£12**	**£5**	*US*
Disc A Dawn	LP	BBC	REC65M	1970	**£15**	**£6**	
Discs A Go Go	7" EP	Decca	DFE8520	1962	**£30**	**£15**	
Doctor Soul	LP	Island	ILP943	1967	**£30**	**£15**	
Down Home Blues – Sixties Style	7" EP	Jan & Dil	JR450	196–	**£10**	**£5**	
Down In Hogan's Alley	LP	Flyright	LP4703	1971	**£10**	**£4**	
Downhome Blues	LP	Python		1970	**£25**	**£10**	
Downhome Blues Vol. 2	LP	Python	PLP14	1970	**£25**	**£10**	
Downhome Blues Vol. 3	LP	Python	PLP22	1971	**£25**	**£10**	
Downhome Harp	7" EP	XX	MIN709	196–	**£6**	**£2.50**	
Dr Kitch	LP	Trojan	TTl41	1970	**£15**	**£6**	
Dr Kitch	LP	Island	ILP954	1967	**£40**	**£20**	
Drumbeat	7" EP	Fontana	TFE17146	1959	**£25**	**£12.50**	
Drumbeat	LP	Parlophone	PMC1101	1959	**£25**	**£10**	
Duke And The Peacock	LP	Island	ILP976	1968	**£50**	**£25**	*pink label*
Duke Reid's Golden Hits	LP	Trojan	TTL8	1969	**£20**	**£8**	
Duke Reid's Rock Steady	LP	Trojan	TTL53	1970	**£30**	**£15**	
Duke Reid's Rock Steady	LP	Island	ILP958	1967	**£100**	**£50**	*pink label*
Dulcimer Players	LP	Transatlantic	LTRA502	1978	**£10**	**£4**	
Dungeon Folk	LP	BBC	REC355	1969	**£12**	**£5**	
Ear-Piercing Punk	LP	Trash	0001	1983	**£25**	**£10**	*US*
Early Blues Vol. 1	LP	Saydisc	SDR199	1970	**£10**	**£4**	
Early Blues Vol. 2	LP	Saydisc	SDR206	1970	**£10**	**£4**	
Early Chicago	LP	Happy Tiger	HT1017	1972	**£15**	**£6**	*US*
Earthed	LP	Middle Earth	MDLS20	1970	**£40**	**£20**	
East	LP	Dead Good	GOOD1	1980	**£12**	**£5**	
East Vernon Blues	LP	Southern Sound	SD200	1973	**£20**	**£8**	
Easy Rider	LP	Stateside	SSL5018	1969	**£10**	**£4**	
Echoes In Time Vol. 1	LP	Solar	S000	1983	**£25**	**£10**	*US*
Echoes In Time Vol. 1	LP	Solar	SR2000	1983	**£25**	**£10**	*US*
Edinburgh Folk Festival	LP	Decca	LK4546	1963	**£50**	**£25**	
Edinburgh Folk Festival Vol. 2	LP	Decca	LK4563	1964	**£60**	**£30**	
Edinburgh Students Charity Appeal	7" EP	E.S.C.	ESC02	1965	**£30**	**£15**	
Edinburgh Students Charity Appeal	7" EP	E.S.C.	ESC03	1966	**£30**	**£15**	
El Pea	LP	Island	IDLP1	1971	**£10**	**£4**	*pink rim label*
Electric Blues	LP	Chess	109597/8/9	1969	**£30**	**£15**	*German, 3 LPs in metal box*
Electric Muse	LP	Island/ Transatlantic	FOLK1001	1975	**£40**	**£20**	*4 LP set*
Electric Newspaper	LP	ESP-Disk	1034	1966	**£50**	**£25**	*US*
Electric Sugar Cube Flashbacks	LP	Archive International	AIP10008	1983	**£15**	**£6**	
Electric Sugar Cube Flashbacks Vol. 2	LP	Archive International	AIP10010	1983	**£15**	**£6**	
Elegance, Charm And Deadly Danger	LP	Push	PUSH001	1985	**£15**	**£6**	
Endless Journey Phase 1	LP	Psycho	1	1982	**£25**	**£10**	*US*
Endless Journey Phase 2	LP	Psycho	3	1983	**£25**	**£10**	*US*
Endless Journey Phase 3	LP	Psycho	19	1983	**£15**	**£6**	*US*
England's Greatest Hitmakers	LP	London	LL3430	1968	**£40**	**£20**	*US*
English Country Music	LP	Topic	12T296	1976	**£10**	**£4**	
English Country Music From East Anglia	LP	Topic	12TS229	1973	**£10**	**£4**	
English Melodeon Players	LP	Plant Life	PLR073	1986	**£10**	**£4**	
Epitaph For A Legend	LP	International Artist	13	1980	**£25**	**£10**	*US double*
Esquire's Jazz	LP	RCA	RD7904	1967	**£10**	**£4**	
Eternity Project One	CD	Gee Street	GEEACD002	1989	**£20**	**£8**	
European Song Cup 1963	7" EP	Decca	DFE8534	1963	**£5**	**£2**	
Every Day I Have The Blues	LP	Speciality	SPE6601	1967	**£10**	**£4**	
Everything's Alright	LP	Decca	SLK16333P	1964	**£40**	**£20**	*German*
Everywhere Chainsaw Sound	LP	CSR	001	1982	**£100**	**£50**	*US*
Everywhere Interferences	LP	Chanesaw Sound	CSR002	1983	**£50**	**£25**	*US*
Excello Story	LP	Blue Horizon	2683007	1972	**£60**	**£30**	*double*
Explosive Rocksteady	LP	Amalgamated	AMGLP2002	1968	**£50**	**£25**	
Exquisite Form	7" EP	Philips	P160E	1967	**£6**	**£2.50**	
Extracts From Stiff's Greatest Hits	7"	Stiff	FREEBIE2	1978	**£6**	**£2.50**	
Ey Up Mi Duck! A Celebration Of Derbyshire	LP	RAM	1	1978	**£10**	**£4**	
Fantastic Folk	LP	Elektra	EUK259	1968	**£10**	**£4**	
Farewell Nancy	LP	Topic	12T110	1964	**£20**	**£8**	
Fashioned To A Device Behind A Tree	LP	Come Organisation	WDC881021	198–	**£50**	**£25**	
FCU (Folk Centrum Utrecht) '69	LP	private		1969	**£200**	**£100**	*Dutch*
Feast Of Irish Folk	LP	Polydor	2475605	1977	**£10**	**£4**	*Irish*

Title	Format	Label	Cat. No.	Year	Mint	VG	Notes
Festival At Towersey	LP	Zeus	CF201	1968	**£40**	**£20**	
Festival Of British Jazz	LP	Decca	LK4180	1957	**£15**	**£6**	
Festival Of The Blues Vol. 1	7" EP	Pye	NEP44030	1964	**£10**	**£5**	
Fifteen Flaming Groovies	CD	Fire	FIRECD19	1989	**£12**	**£5**	*promo only*
Fifteen Oldies But Goodies	LP	Melodisc	MS4	196–	**£10**	**£4**	
Fifth Pipe Dream	LP	San Francisco Sound	11680	1968	**£75**	**£37.50**	*US*
Filling The Gap	LP	Obscure World	001	1989	**£40**	**£20**	*US 4 LP boxed set*
Fillmore Last Days	LP	Warner Bros	K66013	1972	**£50**	**£25**	*promo boxed set with interview single*
Fillmore Last Days	LP	Warner Bros	K66013	1972	**£30**	**£15**	*boxed set, with booklet, ticket, poster*
Fingers On Fire	LP	London	HAB8205	1965	**£10**	**£4**	
Fings Ain't Wot They Used To Be	LP	HMV	CLP1358/ CSD1298	1960	**£15**	**£6**	
Firepoint	LP	Spark	SRLM2003	1969	**£20**	**£8**	
First Lame Bunny Album	LP	Spaceward	3S1/EDENLP53	1973	**£15**	**£6**	
First National Skiffle Contest	10" LP	Esquire	20089	1957	**£30**	**£15**	
First O T'Sort	LP	Transatlantic	LTRA505	1978	**£10**	**£4**	
First Rock'n'Roll Party	10" LP	Mercury	MPT7512	1956	**£60**	**£30**	
Flashback Vol. 1	LP	Flashback	1001	1980	**£25**	**£10**	*US*
Flashback Vol. 2	LP	Flashback	1002	1980	**£25**	**£10**	*US*
Flashback Vol. 3	LP	Flashback	1003	1981	**£50**	**£25**	*US*
Flashback Vol. 4	LP	Flashback	1004	1981	**£50**	**£25**	*US*
Flashback Vol. 5	LP	Flashback	1005	1982	**£50**	**£25**	*US*
Flashback Vol. 6	LP	Flashback	1006	1982	**£50**	**£25**	*US*
Fleadh Ceoil 1975	LP	Dolphin	DOLM5013	1975	**£12**	**£5**	*Irish*
Folk At The Black Horse	LP	Eron	012	1976	**£10**	**£4**	
Folk At The Wren	LP	private		1969	**£100**	**£50**	
Folk Blues Song Fest	LP	Ember	NR5015	1964	**£15**	**£6**	
Folk Box	LP	Elektra	EUK251/2	1966	**£12**	**£5**	*double*
Folk Centrum Utrecht 1970	LP	private		1970	**£200**	**£100**	*Dutch*
Folk Festival	LP	World Record Club	ST890	1964	**£20**	**£8**	
Folk Festival	LP	Transatlantic	TRA324	1976	**£15**	**£6**	*double*
Folk Festival At Newport 1959 Vol. 1	LP	Top Rank	35070	1960	**£15**	**£6**	
Folk Festival At Newport 1959 Vol. 2	LP	Top Rank	35071	1960	**£15**	**£6**	
Folk Festival At Newport 1959 Vol. 3	LP	Top Rank	35072	1960	**£15**	**£6**	
Folk Festival At Newport Vol. 1	LP	Fontana	TFL6000	1962	**£15**	**£6**	
Folk Festival At Newport Vol. 2	LP	Fontana	TFL6004	1962	**£15**	**£6**	
Folk Festival At Newport Vol. 3	LP	Fontana	TFL6009	1962	**£15**	**£6**	
Folk Festival Of The Blues	LP	Pye	NPL28033	1964	**£15**	**£6**	
Folk From McTavish's Kitchen	LP	Counterpoint	CPT3994	1973	**£12**	**£5**	
Folk Nottingham Style	LP	Nottingham Festival	FEST1	197–	**£100**	**£50**	
Folk Now	LP	Decca	LK4683	1965	**£25**	**£10**	
Folk On Friday	LP	BBC	REC955	1970	**£25**	**£10**	
Folk Philosophy	LP	Talisman	STAL5019	1971	**£15**	**£6**	
Folk Scene	LP	Folkscene	SSP001	1966	**£100**	**£50**	
Folk Song Today	10" LP	HMV	DLP1143	1957	**£40**	**£20**	
Folk Songs Of Britain Vol. 1	LP	Topic	12T157	1966	**£12**	**£5**	
Folk Songs Of Britain Vol. 2	LP	Topic	12T158	1966	**£12**	**£5**	
Folk Songs Of Britain Vol. 3	LP	Topic	12T159	1966	**£12**	**£5**	
Folk Songs Of Britain Vol. 4	LP	Topic	12T160	1966	**£12**	**£5**	
Folk Songs Of Britain Vol. 5	LP	Topic	12T161	1966	**£12**	**£5**	
Folk Songs Of Britain Vol. 6	LP	Topic	12T194	1969	**£12**	**£5**	
Folk Songs Of Britain Vol. 7	LP	Topic	12T195	1969	**£12**	**£5**	
Folk Songs Of Britain Vol. 8	LP	Topic	12T196	1969	**£12**	**£5**	
Folk Songs Of Britain Vol. 9	LP	Topic	12T197	1969	**£12**	**£5**	
Folk Songs Of Britain Vol. 10	LP	Topic	12T198	1969	**£12**	**£5**	
Folk Trailer	LP	Trailer	LER2019	1970	**£12**	**£5**	
Folk Upstairs	LP	Nicro	K220971	1971	**£75**	**£37.50**	
Folksound Of Britain	7" EP	HMV	7EG8911	1965	**£15**	**£7.50**	
Folksound Of Britain	LP	HMV	CLP1910	1965	**£20**	**£8**	
Fontana Singles Box Set Vol. 1	7"	Fontana	FONT1	1991	**£30**	**£15**	*12 single box set*
Fontana Singles Box Set Vol. 2	7"	Fontana	FONT2	1991	**£30**	**£15**	*12 single box set*
Four Bob Dylan Songs	7" EP	Riviera	231160	1966	**£20**	**£10**	*French*
Four Great Movie Themes	7" EP	Philips	BBE12140	1957	**£8**	**£4**	
Four Of The Tops	7" EP	Pye	NEP24300	1968	**£5**	**£2**	
Fourteen	LP	Decca	LK4695	1965	**£25**	**£10**	
Freak Out USA	LP	Sidewalk	5901	1967	**£15**	**£6**	*US*
Freedom Sounds	LP	Bamboo	BLP205	1970	**£40**	**£20**	
Fresh From The Can	LP	Polydor	2675004	1970	**£25**	**£10**	*German, 3 LPs in metal box*
From Bam Bam To Cherry Oh Baby	LP	Trojan	TRL51	1972	**£10**	**£4**	
From Greer To Eternity	7"	Fierce Panda	NING05	1994	**£5**	**£2**	*double*
From The Bayou	LP	Liberty	LBS83321	1970	**£10**	**£4**	
From The Vaults	LP	Liberty	LBS83278	1970	**£10**	**£4**	
From Torture To Conscience	LP	New European	BADVC666	198–	**£12**	**£5**	
Funky Chicken	LP	Trojan	TBL137	1970	**£15**	**£6**	
Funky Reggae	LP	Bamboo	BLP206	1970	**£30**	**£15**	
Fylde Acoustic	LP	Trailer	LER2105	1977	**£20**	**£8**	
Garage Punk Unknowns Vol. 1	LP	Stone Age		1985	**£25**	**£10**	*US, black and white sleeve*
Garage Punk Unknowns Vol. 2	LP	Stone Age		1985	**£25**	**£10**	*US, black and white sleeve*

Garage Punk Unknowns Vol. 3	LP	Stone Age		1985	**£25**	**£10**	*US, black and white sleeve*
Garage Punk Unknowns Vol. 4	LP	Stone Age		1985	**£25**	**£10**	*US, black and white sleeve*
Garage Punk Unknowns Vol. 5	LP	Stone Age	SA665	1986	**£25**	**£10**	*US, black and white sleeve*
Garage Punk Unknowns Vol. 6	LP	Stone Age	SA666	1986	**£25**	**£10**	*US, black and white sleeve*
Garage Punk Unknowns Vol. 7	LP	Stone Age	SA667	1986	**£25**	**£10**	*US, black and white sleeve*
Garage Zone Box Set	LP	Moxie	MLP16/17/20/21/ 1055	1990	**£40**	**£20**	*US, 4 LP plus 1 EP boxed set*
Gas – Greatest Hits	LP	Pama	ECO4	1969	**£20**	**£8**	
Gathering At The Depot	LP	Beta	S80471414S	1970	**£40**	**£20**	*US*
Gathering Of The Tribe	LP	Bona Fide	5913330001	1982	**£50**	**£25**	*US*
Gathering Of The Tribe 4	LP	Myst	001	1987	**£25**	**£10**	*US*
Gayfeet	LP	Doctor Bird	DLM5001	1966	**£75**	**£37.50**	
Gems Of Jazz Vol. 1	10″ LP	Brunswick	LA8544	1952	**£10**	**£4**	
Gems Of Jazz Vol. 2	10″ LP	Brunswick	LA8561	1952	**£10**	**£4**	
Gene Norman Presents Just Jazz	10″ LP	HMV	DLP1039	1955	**£15**	**£6**	
Gene Norman's Just Jazz	LP	Vogue	LAE12001	1955	**£20**	**£8**	
Genesis – Memphis To Chicago	LP	Chess	6641125	1973	**£40**	**£20**	*4 LPs, boxed*
Genesis – Sweet Home Chicago	LP	Chess	6641174	1975	**£40**	**£20**	*4 LPs, boxed*
Genesis – The Beginnings Of Rock	LP	Chess	6641047	1972	**£40**	**£20**	*4 LPs, boxed*
Georgia Guitars 1927–1938	LP	Kokomo	K1004	1969	**£30**	**£15**	
Get Ready Rock Steady	LP	Coxsone	CSL8007	1967	**£100**	**£50**	
Giants Of Modern Jazz	LP	Concert Hall	BJ1204	1955	**£12**	**£5**	
Gift From Pama	LP	Pama	SECO20	1970	**£20**	**£8**	
Girls And More Girls	7″ EP	MGM	MGMEP703	1959	**£5**	**£2**	
Glastonbury Fayre	LP	Revelation	REV1	1974	**£100**	**£50**	*triple, 4 inserts, printed polythene outer*
Glimpses Vol. 1	LP	Wellington	201085	1982	**£50**	**£25**	*US*
Glimpses Vol. 2	LP	Wellington		1982	**£50**	**£25**	*US*
Glimpses Vol. 3	LP	Wellington		1983	**£25**	**£10**	*US*
Glimpses Vol. 4	LP	Wellington	W1004	1989	**£15**	**£6**	*US*
Go	LP	Columbia	SX6062	1966	**£30**	**£15**	
God's Favourite Dog	LP	Touch & Go	TG11	198–	**£15**	**£6**	
Goin' Away Walkin'	LP	Flyright	LP103	1972	**£10**	**£4**	
Goin' Back To Chicago	LP	Python	LP1	1970	**£25**	**£10**	
Goin' Up The Country	LP	Decca	LK4931	1968	**£10**	**£4**	
Going To California	LP	Heritage	1003	196–	**£25**	**£10**	
Gold	LP	Mother	MO4001	1972	**£30**	**£15**	
Golden Age Of Hollywood Musicals	LP	United Artists	UAG29421	1972	**£10**	**£4**	
Golden Goodies Vol. 1	LP	Roulette	RCP1000	1969	**£15**	**£6**	
Golden Goodies Vol. 2	LP	Roulette	RCP1001	1969	**£15**	**£6**	
Golden Hits	LP	Philips	BBL7331	1959	**£12**	**£5**	
Golden Hits Vol. 2	LP	Philips	BBL7422	1960	**£10**	**£4**	
Golden Hits Vol. 3	LP	Philips	BBL7581	1961	**£12**	**£5**	
Golden Pops	LP	Deram	SML1027	1968	**£75**	**£37.50**	
Gonks Go Beat	LP	Decca	LK4673	1965	**£60**	**£30**	
Good Folk Of Kent	LP	Eron	004	1975	**£50**	**£25**	
Good Time Music	LP	Elektra	EUK/EUKS7260	1967	**£20**	**£8**	
Gospel Sound	LP	CBS	67234	1972	**£15**	**£6**	*double*
Gospel Train	LP	Brunswick	LAT8290	1959	**£10**	**£4**	
Grand Airs Of Connemara	LP	Topic	12T177	1968	**£10**	**£4**	
Grand Old Fifties	LP	Atlantic	ATL5004	1964	**£20**	**£8**	
Greasy Truckers Live At Dingwalls Dance Hall	LP	Greasy Truckers	GT4997	1973	**£15**	**£6**	*double*
Greasy Truckers Party	LP	United Artists	UDX203/4	1974	**£15**	**£6**	*double*
Great Blues Singers	10″ LP	London	AL3530	1954	**£20**	**£8**	
Great Blues Singers	LP	Riverside	RLP12121	1961	**£12**	**£5**	
Great Bluesmen	LP	Vanguard	VSD25/26	1972	**£12**	**£5**	*double*
Great Country And Western Hits	7″ EP	Philips	BBE12318	1959	**£6**	**£2.50**	
Great Trumpet Soloists	10″ LP	HMV	DLP1054	1954	**£15**	**£6**	
Great White Dap	7″ EP	Village Thing	VTSX1000	1970	**£20**	**£10**	
Greater Jamaica	LP	Trojan	TBL111	1970	**£20**	**£8**	
Greatest Jamaican Beat	LP	Doctor Bird	DLM5009	1967	**£75**	**£37.50**	
Greatest On Stage	7″ EP	Pye	NEP44054	1966	**£6**	**£2.50**	
Green Metal	LP	Crashed	METALPS107	1985	**£20**	**£8**	
Grooving With Bamboo	LP	Bamboo	BDLP215	1971	**£30**	**£15**	
Group Beat '63	LP	Realm	RM149	1963	**£25**	**£10**	
Group Of Goodies	7″ EP	London	REU1393	1963	**£15**	**£7.50**	
Group Of Goodies	LP	London	HAU8086	1963	**£15**	**£6**	
Groups Galore	7″ EP	Mercury	ZEP10010	1959	**£75**	**£37.50**	
Guitar Workshop	LP	Transatlantic	TRA271	1973	**£15**	**£6**	*double*
Gulf Coast Blues	LP	Sunnyland	KS102	1971	**£25**	**£10**	
Guns Of Navarone	LP	Trojan	TTL16	1969	**£20**	**£8**	
Gutbucket	LP	Liberty	LBX3	1969	**£10**	**£4**	
Guy Stevens' Testament Of Rock'n'Roll	LP	Island	ILP977	1968	**£20**	**£8**	*pink label*
Guys And Dolls	7″ EP	Philips	BBE12077	1956	**£5**	**£2**	
Hallucinations Off 2 – Psychedelic Underground	LP	Elektra/ Metronome	KMLP310	1969	**£25**	**£10**	*German picture disc*
Handmade Films Music – The Tenth Anniversary	CD	Handmade Films		1988	**£100**	**£50**	*promo only*
Hard Up Heroes 1963–68	LP	Decca	DPA3009/10	1974	**£12**	**£5**	*double*
Harlem Piano Roll	10″ LP	London	AL3553	1956	**£15**	**£6**	
Hart Rock	7″	Abreaction	ABR001	1971	**£25**	**£12.50**	

Title	Format	Label	Cat. No.	Year	Mint	VG	Notes
Harvest Sampler	LP	Harvest	HARSPSLP118	1969	**£60**	**£30**	*promo*
Havin' A Good Time – Chicago Blues Anthology	LP	Sunnyland	KS101	1971	**£25**	**£10**	
Headline News	LP	Polydor	582701	1966	**£10**	**£4**	
Heads And Tales	LP	Transatlantic	TRASAD18	1970	**£15**	**£6**	*double*
Heads Together, First Round	LP	Vertigo	6360045	1971	**£12**	**£5**	*double, spiral label*
Heather And Glen	LP	Tradition	TLP1047	1963	**£15**	**£6**	*US*
Heavy Christmas	LP	Pilz	15211142	1971	**£40**	**£20**	*German*
Heavy Metal Heroes	LP	Heavy Metal	HMRLP1	1981	**£20**	**£8**	
Heavy Metal Heroes Vol. 2	LP	Heavy Metal	HMRLP7	1982	**£20**	**£8**	
Here Come The Girls	LP	Pye	NPL18122	1965	**£10**	**£4**	
Here Comes The Duke	LP	Trojan	TRL6	1968	**£30**	**£15**	
Heures Sans Soleil	LP	Temps Modernes	LTMV:XI	198–	**£15**	**£6**	
Hey Boy Hey Girl	LP	Pama	PSP1002	1969	**£25**	**£10**	
Hickory Showcase Vol. 1	7" EP	Hickory	LPE1500	1964	**£5**	**£2**	
Highway To Heaven	LP	Parlophone	PMC1085	1959	**£12**	**£5**	
Hillside '66	LP	Hillside	2520961	1966	**£300**	**£180**	*US*
Hipsville 29 B.C.	LP	Kramden	KRANMAR101	1983	**£25**	**£10**	*US*
Hipsville 29 B.C. Vol. 2	LP	Kramden	KRANMAR102	1985	**£15**	**£6**	*US*
Hipsville Vol. 3	LP	Kramden	KRANMAR103	1986	**£15**	**£6**	*US*
History Of Jazz Part 1	10" LP	Capitol	LC6507	1951	**£15**	**£6**	
History Of Jazz Part 2	10" LP	Capitol	LC6508	1951	**£15**	**£6**	
History Of Northwest Rock Vol. 1	LP	Great Northwest	GNW4003	1976	**£15**	**£6**	*US*
History Of Northwest Rock Vol. 2	LP	Great Northwest	GNW4008	1977	**£15**	**£6**	*US*
History Of Northwest Rock Vol. 3	LP	Great Northwest	GNW4009	1981	**£15**	**£6**	*US*
History Of Northwest Rock Vol. 4	LP	Great Northwest	GNW4010	1983	**£15**	**£6**	*US*
History Of R&B Vol. 1	LP	Atlantic	587094	1968	**£10**	**£4**	
History Of R&B Vol. 2	LP	Atlantic	587095	1968	**£10**	**£4**	
History Of R&B Vol. 3	LP	Atlantic	587096	1968	**£10**	**£4**	
History Of R&B Vol. 4	LP	Atlantic	587097	1968	**£10**	**£4**	
History Of R&B Vol. 5	LP	Atlantic	587140	1968	**£10**	**£4**	
History Of R&B Vol. 6	LP	Atlantic	587141	1968	**£10**	**£4**	
History Of Ska Vol. 1	LP	Bamboo	BDLP203	1969	**£40**	**£20**	
Hit Factory – Best Of Stock, Aitken & Waterman Vol. 2	CD	PWL	HFCD4	1988	**£15**	**£6**	
Hit Parade	7" EP	Brunswick	OE9340	1957	**£5**	**£2**	
Hit Parade Of 1956	10" LP	Pye	NPT19015	1957	**£15**	**£6**	
Hit Parade Vol. 1	7" EP	Mercury	MEP9003	1956	**£10**	**£5**	
Hit Parade Vol. 2	7" EP	Mercury	MEP9510	1956	**£10**	**£5**	
Hit Parade Vol. 2	7" EP	Brunswick	OE9450	1959	**£5**	**£2**	
Hit The Road Stax	LP	Stax	589005	1967	**£12**	**£5**	
Hitmakers	7" EP	Piccadilly	NEP34100	1966	**£5**	**£2**	
Hitmakers	LP	Jerden	7005	1965	**£15**	**£6**	*US*
Hitmakers	LP	Pye	NPL18108	1964	**£15**	**£6**	
Hitmakers International	7" EP	Pye	NEP44065	1966	**£6**	**£2.50**	
Hitmakers No. 1	7" EP	Pye	NEP24213	1965	**£5**	**£2**	
Hitmakers No. 2	7" EP	Pye	NEP24214	1965	**£12**	**£6**	
Hitmakers No. 3	7" EP	Pye	NEP24215	1965	**£6**	**£2.50**	
Hitmakers Vol. 1	7" EP	Pye	NEP24241	1966	**£5**	**£2**	
Hitmakers Vol. 2	7" EP	Pye	NEP24242	1966	**£6**	**£2.50**	
Hitmakers Vol. 2	LP	Pye	NPL18115	1965	**£15**	**£6**	
Hitmakers Vol. 3	7" EP	Pye	NEP24243	1966	**£6**	**£2.50**	
Hits From Can Can	7" EP	Capitol	EAP1482	1955	**£5**	**£2**	
Hits Vol. 1	7" EP	Decca	DFE8648	1965	**£5**	**£2**	
Hits Vol. 2	7" EP	Decca	DFE8649	1965	**£5**	**£2**	
Hits Vol. 3	7" EP	Decca	DFE8653	1965	**£6**	**£2.50**	
Hits Vol. 4	7" EP	Decca	DFE8662	1966	**£5**	**£2**	
Hits Vol. 5	7" EP	Decca	DFE8663	1966	**£6**	**£2.50**	
Hits Vol. 6	7" EP	Decca	DFE8667	1966	**£6**	**£2.50**	
Hits Vol. 7	7" EP	Decca	DFER8675	1967	**£6**	**£2.50**	
Hitsville	7" EP	Mercury	ZEP10133	1962	**£15**	**£7.50**	
Hitsville USA	LP	Tamla Motown	TML11019	1965	**£20**	**£8**	
Hitsville USA No. 1	7" EP	Tamla Motown	TME2001	1965	**£40**	**£20**	
Hitsville Vol. 1	7" EP	Coral	FEP2034	1959	**£30**	**£15**	
Hitsville Vol. 2	7" EP	Coral	FEP2035	1959	**£20**	**£10**	
Hobos And Drifters	7" EP	Postwar Blues	100	1966	**£15**	**£7.50**	
Hoisting The Black Flag	LP	United Dairies	UD06	1981	**£50**	**£25**	
Honeys	LP	Melodisc	12216	196–	**£12**	**£5**	
Honky Tonk Train	LP	Riverside	RLP8806	1967	**£15**	**£6**	
Hoot'nanny Show Vol. 1	LP	Waverley	ZLP2025	1964	**£20**	**£8**	
Hoot'nanny Show Vol. 2	LP	Waverley	ZLP2032	1964	**£15**	**£6**	
Hootenanny At The Troubadour	LP	Stateside	SL10079	1964	**£10**	**£4**	
Hootenanny In London	LP	Decca	LK4544	1963	**£25**	**£10**	
Hootenanny New York City	7" EP	Topic	TOP37	1959	**£15**	**£7.50**	
Hootenanny Saturday Night	LP	Fontana	688009ZL	1965	**£15**	**£6**	
Hot Calypsos	7" EP	Capitol	EAP1852	1957	**£5**	**£2**	
Hot Numbers	LP	Pama	PMP2006	1971	**£15**	**£6**	
Hot Numbers Vol. 2	LP	Pama	PMP2009	1971	**£15**	**£6**	
Hot Shots Of Reggae	LP	Trojan	TBL128	1970	**£15**	**£6**	
House That Track Built	LP	Track	613016	1969	**£15**	**£6**	

Title	Format	Label	Cat. No.	Year	Mint	Half	Note
Houston Hallucinations	LP	Texas Archive	TAR2	1982	**£12**	**£5**	*US*
Houston Jump	7" EP	Solid Sender	SEP100	1975	**£5**	**£2**	
How Blue Can We Get?	LP	Blue Horizon	PR45/46	1970	**£20**	**£8**	*double*
I Love You Gorgo	LP	Suemi	1090	1969	**£25**	**£10**	*US*
I'm Your Country Man	LP	Highway 51	H104	1970	**£25**	**£10**	
In Crowd	7" EP	Chess	CRE6010	1966	**£10**	**£5**	
In Crowd	LP	CBS		1966	**£15**	**£6**	
In Fractured Silence	LP	United Dairies	UD015	198–	**£25**	**£10**	
In Loving Memory	LP	Tamla Motown	(S)TML11124	1969	**£40**	**£20**	
In Our Own Way/Oldies But Goodies	LP	Blue Horizon	PR37	1969	**£15**	**£6**	
Independent Jamaica	LP	Trojan	TTL15	1969	**£20**	**£8**	
Industrial Records Story	LP	Illuminated	JAMS39	1984	**£15**	**£6**	
Intensified! Original Ska 1962–66	LP	Mango	MLPS1006	1979	**£10**	**£4**	
International Artists	7"	Radar	SAM88	1978	**£5**	**£2**	
Ireland's Greatest Sounds	LP	Ember	FA2034	1966	**£40**	**£20**	
Irish Folk Night	LP	Decca	LK4633	1964	**£15**	**£6**	
Irish Music In London Pubs	LP	XTRA	XTRA1090	1969	**£12**	**£5**	
Irish Music In London Pubs	LP	Folkways	FG3575	1965	**£20**	**£8**	*US*
Irish Pipering	LP	Claddagh	CC11	1971	**£12**	**£5**	*Irish*
Irish Reels, Jigs, Hornpipes And Airs	LP	Kicking Mule	SNKF153	1979	**£10**	**£4**	
Irish Traditional Concertina Styles	LP	Free Reed	FRS506	1977	**£10**	**£4**	
Iron Muse	LP	Topic	12T86	1963	**£25**	**£10**	
Isle Of Wight/Atlanta Festival	LP	CBS	66311	1971	**£20**	**£8**	*triple*
It's All Happening	LP	Columbia	SCX3486	1963	**£15**	**£6**	
It's Beat Time In Liverpool	LP	Ariola	72756	1965	**£50**	**£25**	*German*
It's Cha Cha Time	7" EP	Mercury	ZEP10001	1959	**£5**	**£2**	
It's Great To Be Young	7" EP	Columbia	SEG7639	1956	**£6**	**£2.50**	
It's Trad Dad	LP	Columbia	33SX1412	1962	**£15**	**£6**	
Items From Guys And Dolls	7" EP	Mercury	MEP9503	1956	**£8**	**£4**	
Jack Good's Oh Boy!	LP	Parlophone	PMC1072	1958	**£30**	**£15**	
Jackpot Of Hits	LP	Amalgamated	CSP3	1969	**£40**	**£20**	
Jamaica Ska	LP	Atlantic	ATL5010	1964	**£75**	**£37.50**	
Jamaica Ska	LP	Atlantic	587075	1968	**£40**	**£20**	
Jamaica's Greatest Hits	LP	Melodisc	MLP12158	197–	**£12**	**£5**	
Jamaican Blues	LP	Blue Beat	BBLP801	1961	**£150**	**£75**	
Jamaican Memories	LP	Blue Cat	BCL1	1968	**£50**	**£25**	
Jambalaya On The Bayou Vol. 1	LP	Flyright	LP3502	1968	**£15**	**£6**	
Jambalaya On The Bayou Vol. 2	LP	Flyright	LP3503	1969	**£15**	**£6**	
James Bond Collection	LP	United Artists	UAD60027/8	1972	**£20**	**£8**	*double*
Jazz At The Fabulous Flamingo	LP	Ember	EMB3321	1961	**£20**	**£8**	
Jazz Explosion	LP	Columbia	SLJS1	1969	**£10**	**£4**	
Jazz Juice	LP	Streetsounds	SOUND1	1985	**£20**	**£8**	
Jazz Juice	LP	Streetsounds	MUSIC1	1984	**£25**	**£10**	
Jazz Juice 2	LP	Streetsounds	SOUND4	1986	**£15**	**£6**	
Jazz Juice 3	LP	Streetsounds	SOUND5	1986	**£15**	**£6**	
Jazz Juice 4	LP	Streetsounds	SOUND6	1986	**£15**	**£6**	
Jazz Juice 5	LP	Streetsounds	SOUND8	1987	**£12**	**£5**	
Jazz Juice 6	CD	Streetsounds	CDSND9	1987	**£12**	**£5**	
Jazz Juice 6	LP	Streetsounds	SOUND9	1987	**£12**	**£5**	
Jazz Juice 7	CD	Streetsounds	CDSND10	1988	**£12**	**£5**	
Jazz Juice 7	LP	Streetsounds	SOUND10	1988	**£12**	**£5**	
Jazz Juice 8	CD	Streetsounds	CDSND11	1988	**£12**	**£5**	
Jazz Juice 8	LP	Streetsounds	SOUND11	1988	**£10**	**£4**	
Jazz Juice 9	CD	Streetsounds	CDSND12	1988	**£12**	**£5**	
Jazz Juice 9	LP	Streetsounds	SOUND12	1988	**£10**	**£4**	
Jazz Of The Roaring Twenties Vol. 2	10" LP	London	AL3562	1957	**£10**	**£4**	
Jazz Piano Rarities	10" LP	London	AL3565	1957	**£12**	**£5**	
Jazz Scene	10" LP	Columbia	33C9007	1955	**£10**	**£4**	
Jazz Scene Vol. 2	10" LP	Columbia	33C9008	1955	**£10**	**£4**	
Jazz Sounds Of The Twenties Vol. 4	LP	Parlophone	PMC1177	1962	**£10**	**£4**	
Joe Meek Story	LP	Decca	DPA3035/6	1977	**£20**	**£8**	*double*
John Peel Presents Top Gear	LP	BBC	REC52S	1969	**£25**	**£10**	
Journey To Tyme Vol. 1	LP	Phantom	PRS1001	1982	**£15**	**£6**	*US*
Journey To Tyme Vol. 2	LP	Phantom	PRS1002	1985	**£15**	**£6**	*US*
Journey To Tyme Vol. 3	LP	Phantom	PRS1003	1985	**£15**	**£6**	*US*
Journey To Tyme Vol. 4	LP	Phantom	PRS1006	1986	**£15**	**£6**	*US*
Journey To Tyme Vol. 5	LP	Phantom	PRS1007	1986	**£15**	**£6**	*US*
Jug Bands Vol. 1	7" EP	Natchez	NEP701	1967	**£10**	**£5**	
Jug Of Punch	LP	HMV	XLP50003	1960	**£40**	**£20**	
Jug Of Punch	LP	HMV	CLP1327	1960	**£40**	**£20**	
Jugs And Washboards	LP	Ace Of Hearts	AH163	1967	**£10**	**£4**	
Jugs, Washboards And Kazoos	LP	RCA	RD7893	1967	**£10**	**£4**	
Jump Jamaica Jump	LP	R&B	JBL1111	1964	**£125**	**£62.50**	
Jumping At The Go Go	LP	RCA	RS1066	1976	**£12**	**£5**	
Just For Fun	LP	Decca	LK4524	1963	**£25**	**£10**	
Just For Kicks	LP	Kick	KK1	1979	**£15**	**£6**	
K.C. In The Thirties	LP	Capitol	T1057	1958	**£15**	**£6**	
KDWB Radio: 21 All Time Dream Hits Vol. 1	LP	Take Six	2033	1967	**£15**	**£6**	*US*
Keele Rag Record	7"	Lyntone	LYN347/8	1963	**£10**	**£5**	
Kent Rocks	LP	White Witch		1981	**£15**	**£6**	
Kerbside Entertainers	LP	Jayboy	JSX2009	1971	**£25**	**£10**	
Keyboard Kings Of Jazz	10" LP	HMV	DLP1048	1954	**£15**	**£6**	
Kicks And Chicks Vol. 1	LP	Eleventh Hour	EH5806	1990	**£12**	**£5**	*US*
King Size Reggae	LP	Trojan	TBL140	1970	**£20**	**£8**	

Kings Of Memphis Town 1927–1930	LP	Saydisc	RL333	196–	£10	£4	
Kings Of The Blues Vol. 2	7" EP	RCA	RCX203	1961	£8	£4	
Kings Of The Blues Vol. 3	7" EP	RCA	RCX204	1961	£8	£4	
Kings Of The Twelve String Guitar	LP	Gryphon	13159	196–	£12	£5	
Kings Of The Twelve String Guitar	LP	Flyright	LP101	1971	£10	£4	
Kinney Collection	LP	Kinney	KC1	1971	£10	£4	
Kosmische Musik	LP	Ohr	OMM256027	1973	£30	£15	German double
Kralingen	LP	Wild Thing	WC2001	1970	£60	£30	Dutch triple
Label – Sofa	LP	The Label	TRLP002S	1979	£30	£15	picture disc
Lark In The Morning	LP	Tradition	TLP1004	1955	£25	£10	US
Last Testament	LP	Fetish	FR2011	1983	£12	£5	
Last Thing On My Mind	7" EP	Holyground	HG111	1966	£25	£12.50	
Last Warrior	LP	Other	OTH10	1987	£20	£8	
Let Me Tell You About The Blues	LP	Blue Horizon	LP2	1966	£250	£150	
Let's Go	7" EP	Top Rank	JKR8008	1959	£8	£4	
Let's Go Down South	LP	Neshoba	N11	1966	£30	£15	
Let's Go Vol. 2	7" EP	Top Rank	JKR8012	1959	£10	£5	
Let's Have A Party	LP	Brunswick	LAT8271	1958	£10	£4	
Levi Commercials	10" LP	Levi Strauss	6720	1967	£100	£50	US
Liberty/United Artists Sampler	LP	United Artists	REP102	1971	£25	£10	promo
Life At The Top	LP	Third Mind		198–	£20	£8	
Live At Bunjies	LP	Bunjie	BUN01	1980	£25	£10	
Live At Spree	LP	Key	KL021	1974	£20	£8	
Live At The Cavern	LP	Decca	SLK16294	1965	£50	£25	German
Live At The Funny Farm	LP	Scene	200	1966	£100	£50	US
Live At The Liverpool Hoop Vol. 1	LP	Telefunken	SLE14395	1965	£75	£37.50	German
Live At The Liverpool Hoop Vol. 2	LP	Telefunken	SLE14411	1965	£75	£37.50	German
Live At The Vortex	LP	NEMS	NEL6013	1977	£10	£4	
Live It Up	LP	Big Shot	BBTL4000	1968	£60	£30	
Live Recording From The Top Ten Beat Club Vol. 1	LP	Decca	SLK16330P	1965	£50	£25	German
Liverpool And Blue Beat	LP	Eurocord	J022	1964	£50	£25	German
Liverpool Beat	LP	Embassy	WLP6065	1964	£12	£5	
Liverpool Beat Time	LP	Discoton	72351	1964	£75	£37.50	German
Liverpool Hoop	LP	Columbia	SMC83983	1964	£50	£25	German
Liverpool Today – Live At The Cavern	LP	Ember	NR5028	1965	£20	£8	
Lleisiau	LP	private	ADF1	1975	£60	£30	
Loch Ness Monster	LP	Trojan	TBL135	1970	£15	£6	
London Boys	7"	Decca	FR13864	1979	£4	£1.50	
London Hit Parade Vol. 1	7" EP	London	RED1075	1957	£10	£5	
London Hit Parade Vol. 2	7" EP	London	REP1096	1957	£40	£20	
London Hit Parade Vol. 3	7" EP	London	RED1097	1958	£10	£5	
London Hit Parade Vol. 4	7" EP	London	RED1130	1958	£10	£5	
London Hit Parade Vol. 5	7" EP	London	RED1145	1958	£8	£4	
London Really Swings	LP	Columbia	0301	1965	£75	£37.50	US triple
Lonely Is An Eyesore	CD/vid/cass	4AD	CADX703	1987	£150	£75	wooden box, etching, screen print
Lonely Is An Eyesore	LP	4AD	CAD703D	1987	£25	£10	
Loose Routes	LP	Holyground	HG121	1991	£20	£8	double
Louisville Scene	LP	Rod 'n' Custom	3001	196–	£300	£180	US
Lovely Dozen	LP	Pama	PSP1001	1969	£25	£10	
Made In Cornwall	LP	Cornish Legend	CLM1	1976	£60	£30	
Magic Carpet Ride	LP	TVAA	001	1986	£25	£10	US
Magic Cube	9" LP	Evatone	EVA116811	1982	£12	£5	US flexi
Male Blues Singers	LP	Collectors' Classics	CC3	196–	£10	£4	
Man From Carolina	LP	Trojan	TBL129	1970	£12	£5	
Matchbox Days	LP	Village Thing	VTSAM16	1972	£20	£8	
Maxi Track Record	7" EP	Track	2094011	1970	£75	£37.50	blue sleeve
Maxi Track Record	7" EP	Track	2094011	1970	£40	£20	red & white sleeve, press pack
Maxi Track Record	7" EP	Track	2094011	1970	£5	£4	maroon & gold sleeve
Meet The Beat	10" LP	Polydor	J73557	1965	£125	£62.50	German
Memories Are Made Of Hits Vol. 1	LP	London	HA8129	1964	£12	£5	
Memories Are Made Of Hits Vol. 2	LP	London	HA8130	1964	£12	£5	
Memories Are Made Of Hits Vol. 3	LP	London	HA8131	1964	£12	£5	
Memories Are Made Of Hits Vol. 4	LP	London	HA8138	1964	£12	£5	
Memories Are Made Of Hits Vol. 5	LP	London	HA8148	1964	£12	£5	
Memories Are Made Of Hits Vol. 6	LP	London	HA8171	1964	£12	£5	
Memories Are Made Of Hits Vol. 7	LP	London	HA8189	1964	£12	£5	
Memories Are Made Of Hits Vol. 8	LP	London	HA8213	1965	£12	£5	
Merry Christmas	10" LP	Vogue Coral	LVC10008	1954	£10	£4	
Merry Christmas	7" EP	Decca	DFE6408	1957	£5	£2	
Merry Christmas From Motown	LP	Tamla Motown	(S)TML11126	1969	£15	£6	
Metal Explosion	LP	BBC	REH397	1980	£15	£6	
Metal For Muthas	LP	EMI	EMC3318	1980	£10	£4	
MGM Evergreens	7" EP	MGM	MGMEP749	1960	£5	£2	
Midwest vs Canada Vol. 2	LP	Unlimited Production	UPLP1002	1984	£50	£25	US
Midwest vs The Rest Vol. 1	LP	Unlimited Production	UPLP1001	1983	£50	£25	US
Midwestern Jazz	10" LP	London	AL3554	1956	£10	£4	
Million-Airs	LP	Coral	LVA9126	1960	£12	£5	
Milwaukee Sentinel Rock'n'Roll Revue	LP	Century	23214	196–	£100	£50	US

Title	Format	Label	Number	Year	Mint	Good	Notes
Mind Blowers Vol. 1	LP	White Rabbit	WRLP001	1983	£25	£10	US
Miniatures	LP	Pipe	PIPE2	1980	£10	£4	
Miss Labba Labba Reggae	LP	Trojan	TBL174	1971	£15	£6	
Modern Chicago Blues	LP	Polydor	545031	1967	£10	£4	
Modern Chicago Blues	LP	Bounty	BY6025	1966	£20	£8	
Modern Jazz Piano	10" LP	HMV	DLP1022	1955	£12	£5	
Modern Jazz Scene 1956	LP	Tempo	TAP2	1956	£12	£5	
Modern Mixture Vol. 1	10" LP	Esquire	20011	1953	£10	£4	
Money Music	LP	August	100	1967	£300	£180	US
Monsters Of The Midwest Vol. 2	LP	Titan	1002	1985	£12	£5	US
Month's Best From The Country And West	7" EP	RCA	RCX7159	1964	£5	£2	
Month's Best From The Country And West Vol. 2	7" EP	RCA	RCX7162	1964	£5	£2	
Month's Best From The Country And West Vol. 3	7" EP	RCA	RCX7171	1964	£5	£2	
Month's Best From The Country And West Vol. 4	7" EP	RCA	RCX7172	1965	£5	£2	
Month's Best From The Country And West Vol. 5	7" EP	RCA	RCX7178	1965	£5	£2	
Month's Best From The Country And West Vol. 6	7" EP	RCA	RCX7181	1965	£5	£2	
Month's Best From The Country And West Vol. 7	7" EP	RCA	RCX7186	1967	£5	£2	
Moonlight Groover	LP	Trojan	TTL31	1970	£20	£8	
More American Graffiti	LP	MCA		1979	£15	£6	*US promo picture disc, 4 different B sides*
More Down Home Blues	7" EP	Jan & Dil	JR451	196–	£10	£5	
More Of Your Favourite TV And Radio Themes	LP	HMV	CLP1583	1962	£10	£4	
More Singing At The Count House	LP	private		1965	£150	£75	
Morpeth Rant Northumbrian Country Music	LP	Topic	12TS267	1975	£10	£4	
Most Happy Fella	7" EP	Philips	BBE12348	1960	£5	£2	
Motortown Revue	LP	Tamla Motown	TML11007	1965	£75	£37.50	
Motortown Revue Live In Paris	LP	Tamla Motown	TML11027	1966	£60	£30	
Motown Chartbusters Vol. 4	LP	Tamla Motown	STML11162	197–	£10	£4	*red vinyl*
Motown Magic	LP	Tamla Motown	TML11030	1966	£20	£8	
Motown Memories	LP	Tamla Motown	TML11064	1968	£25	£10	
Motown Memories Vol. 2	LP	Tamla Motown	TML11077	1968	£30	£15	
Motown Memories Vol. 3	LP	Tamla Motown	STML11143	1970	£25	£10	
Motown Story	LP	Tamla Motown	TMSP1130	1972	£20	£8	*boxed set*
Motown Story – The First 25 Years	LP	Tamla Motown	TMSP6019	1983	£15	£6	*boxed set*
Murderer's Home	LP	Golden Guinea	GGL0317	1964	£10	£4	
Murderer's Home	LP	Pye	NJL11	1957	£12	£5	
Murderer's Home Part 1	7" EP	Pye	NJE1062	1957	£6	£2.50	
Murderer's Home Part 2	7" EP	Pye	NJE1063	1957	£6	£2.50	
Murderer's Home Part 3	7" EP	Pye	NJE1064	1957	£6	£2.50	
Murderer's Home Part 4	7" EP	Pye	NJE1065	1957	£6	£2.50	
Murray The K Presents	LP	Brooklyn	302	1967	£30	£15	US
Murray The K's Greatest Holiday	LP	Brooklyn	301	1967	£30	£15	US
Mushroom Folk Sampler	LP	Mushroom	100MR16	1971	£50	£25	
Music For The Boy Friend	LP	Brunswick	LAT8201	1957	£20	£8	
Music From Free Creek	LP	Charisma	CADS101	1973	£12	£5	*double*
Music House	LP	Trojan	TBL170	1971	£12	£5	
Music House Vol. 2	LP	Trojan	TBL177	1971	£12	£5	
Mutha's Pride	12"	EMI	12EMI5074	1980	£15	£7.50	
Na Ceirnini 78	LP	Gael Linn	CEF075	1979	£10	£4	*Irish*
Napton Folk Club	LP	Eden	LP43	1971	£50	£25	
Natural Reggae Vol. 1	LP	Bamboo	BLP201	1969	£40	£20	
Natural Reggae Vol. 2	LP	Bamboo	BLP204	1970	£40	£20	
Natures Mortes – Still Lives	LP	4AD	CAD117	1981	£50	£25	*export*
Necropolis, Amphibians And Reptiles	LP	Musique Brut	BRV002	198–	£15	£6	
Nederbiet	LP	Decca	DQL662507	1967	£50	£25	*Dutch*
Negro Folklore From Texas State Prisons	LP	Polydor	236511	1966	£12	£5	
Negro Folklore From Texas State Prisons	LP	Bounty	BY(S7)6012	1966	£15	£6	
Negro Spirituals	7" EP	Vogue	EPV1276	1962	£8	£4	
Negro Spirituals	7" EP	Vogue	EPV1106	1956	£8	£4	
Negro Spirituals	7" EP	Vogue	EPV1271	1962	£8	£4	
Negro Spirituals	LP	Vogue	LAE12033	1957	£15	£6	
Neue Deutsche Volksmusik	LP	Pilz	20292262	1972	£25	£10	*German*
New Electric Warriors	LP	Logo	MOGO4011	1980	£15	£6	
New England Teen Scene	LP	Moulty	MLP101	1983	£25	£10	US
New England Teen Scene Vol. 2	LP	Moulty	MLP103	1984	£15	£6	US
New Faces From Hitsville	7" EP	Tamla Motown	TME2014	1966	£100	£50	
New Folks	LP	Fontana	TFL6012	1962	£20	£8	
New Hi: Dallas 1971 Part 1	LP	Tempo	2	1971	£25	£10	US

New Orleans Horns	10" LP	London	AL3509	1953	**£10**	**£4**	
New Orleans Horns Vol. 2	10" LP	London	AL3557	1956	**£10**	**£4**	
New Orleans R&B Vol. 1	LP	Flyright	LP4708	1974	**£10**	**£4**	
New Orleans R&B Vol. 2	LP	Flyright	LP4709	1974	**£10**	**£4**	
New Sounds In Folk	7" EP	Halcyon	HAL1	196–	**£50**	**£25**	
New Sounds In Folk	7" EP	Harlequin	HW349	1966	**£125**	**£62.50**	
New Voices From Scotland	LP	Topic	12T133	1965	**£25**	**£10**	
New York City Blues	LP	Flyright	LP4706	1972	**£10**	**£4**	
New York Jazz Of The Roaring Twenties	10" LP	London	AL3541	1955	**£10**	**£4**	
New York Rhythm And Blues	LP	Flyright	LP4707	1972	**£10**	**£4**	
Newport Broadside	LP	Fontana	TFL6038	1965	**£20**	**£8**	
Newport Folk Festival 1964 Evening Concerts Vol. 2	LP	Fontana	TFL6051	1965	**£10**	**£4**	
Newport Folk Festival 1964 Evening Concerts Vol. 3	LP	Fontana	TFL6052	1965	**£10**	**£4**	
Newport Folk Festival Evening Concerts Vol. 1	LP	Fontana	TFL6041	1965	**£20**	**£8**	
Newport Folk Festival Vol. 1	LP	Fontana	TFL6050	1965	**£10**	**£4**	
Newport Spiritual Stars	LP	London	LTZC15155	1959	**£12**	**£5**	
Night At The Apollo	LP	Vanguard	PPL11004	1957	**£10**	**£4**	
Nixa Hit Parade No. 1	7" EP	Pye	NEP24052	1957	**£6**	**£2.50**	
Nixa Hit Parade No. 2	7" EP	Pye	NEP24064	1958	**£10**	**£5**	
Nixa Hit Parade No. 3	7" EP	Pye	NEP24071	1958	**£5**	**£2**	
Nixa Hit Parade No. 4	7" EP	Pye	NEP24078	1958	**£5**	**£2**	
Nixa Hit Parade No. 5	7" EP	Pye	NEP24082	1958	**£5**	**£2**	
Nixa Hit Parade No. 6	7" EP	Pye	NEP24090	1958	**£5**	**£2**	
Nixa Hit Parade No. 7	7" EP	Pye	NEP24100	1959	**£5**	**£2**	
No Introduction	LP	Spark	SRLM107	1968	**£15**	**£6**	
No More Heartaches	LP	Trojan	TTL14	1969	**£12**	**£5**	
No One's Gonna Change My World	LP	Regal Starline	SRS5013	1969	**£12**	**£5**	
No Wave	LP	A&M	PR4738	1978	**£15**	**£6**	*US picture disc*
Non Stop Soul	LP	Polydor	545017	1970	**£20**	**£8**	
Norman Granz Jazz Concert No. 1	LP	Columbia	33CX10059	1956	**£20**	**£8**	
Norman Granz Jazz Concert No. 2	LP	Columbia	33CX10060	1956	**£20**	**£8**	
Northland Shopping Center 3rd Annual Battle Of The Bands	LP	Magna		1967	**£100**	**£50**	*US*
Northumbrian Minstrelry	LP	Concert Hall	AM2339	1964	**£30**	**£15**	
Northwest Collection Vol. 1	LP	Etiquette	1018	196–	**£50**	**£25**	*US*
Nothin' But The Blues	LP	Fontana	TFL5123	1960	**£12**	**£5**	
Nothing But The Blues	LP	CBS	66278	1971	**£20**	**£8**	*double*
Nova Sampler	LP	Nova/Decca	SPA72	1970	**£10**	**£4**	
Nubeat – Greatest Hits	LP	Pama	ECO6	1969	**£20**	**£8**	
Nuggets	LP	Elektra	K62012	1972	**£30**	**£15**	*double*
Nuggets	LP	Sire	SASH37162	1976	**£20**	**£8**	*US double*
Oakland Blues	LP	Liberty	LBS83234	1969	**£12**	**£5**	
Odd Bods, Mods And Sods	LP	Rok	TOKLP001	1979	**£20**	**£8**	
Off The Wall Vol. 1	LP	Wreckford Wrack	LP1025	1982	**£25**	**£10**	*US*
Off The Wall Vol. 2	LP	Wreckford Wrack	LP1301	1983	**£25**	**£10**	*US*
Oh No It's More From Raw	LP	Raw	RAWLP2	1978	**£10**	**£4**	
Oil Stains	LP	dB	DB101	1982	**£50**	**£25**	*US*
Oil Stanes Vol. 2	LP	Bone	1001	1988	**£12**	**£5**	*US*
Old British Ballads Of Donegal and Derry	LP	Leader	LEA4055	1975	**£10**	**£4**	
Oldies R&B	LP	Stateside	SL10094	1964	**£20**	**£8**	
On Stage	LP	Stateside	SL10065	1963	**£40**	**£20**	
On The Road Again	LP	XTRA	XTRA1133	1973	**£20**	**£8**	
On The Scene	7" EP	Columbia	SEG8413	1965	**£30**	**£15**	
On The Scene	LP	Columbia	33SX1662	1964	**£50**	**£25**	
Once A Week's Enough	LP	private	C2005	1977	**£20**	**£8**	
Once More	LP	Big Shot	BBTL4001	1968	**£60**	**£30**	
One Night Stand	LP	Columbia	33SX1536	1963	**£25**	**£10**	
Open Up Your Door	LP	Frog Death	GLP101	1984	**£15**	**£6**	*US*
Open Up Your Door Vol. 2	LP	Frog Death	GLP102	1987	**£15**	**£6**	*US*
Original American Folk Blues Festival	LP	Polydor	236216	1967	**£10**	**£4**	
Original Cool Jamaican Ska	LP	Rio	RLP1	1964	**£60**	**£30**	
Original Golden Oldies Vol. 2	LP	Prince Buster	PB10	1973	**£20**	**£8**	
Original Golden Rhythm And Blues Hits Vol. 1	LP	Mercury	SMCL20183	1970	**£10**	**£4**	
Original Great Northwest Hits Vol. 1	LP	Jerden	JRL7001	1964	**£25**	**£10**	*US*
Original Great Northwest Hits Vol. 2	LP	Jerden	JRL7002	1964	**£25**	**£10**	*US*
Original Hits	7" EP	London	REK1390	1963	**£15**	**£7.50**	
Original Hits	7" EP	MGM	MGMEP787	1963	**£15**	**£7.50**	
Original Hits	LP	London	HAG2308	1960	**£25**	**£10**	
Original Hits Vol. 2	7" EP	Atlantic	AET6006	1965	**£12**	**£6**	
Original Hits Vol. 2	LP	London	HAG2339	1961	**£25**	**£10**	
Original Liverpool Sound	LP	Decca	BD5526	1963	**£75**	**£37.50**	*German*
Original Motion Picture Hit Themes	LP	United Artists	ULP1012	1962	**£10**	**£4**	
Original Rhythm And Blues Hits	7" EP	Ember	EMBEP4522	1962	**£25**	**£12.50**	
Original Soundtracks Of Hits Music	LP	United Artists	ULP1182	1967	**£10**	**£4**	
Original Surfin' Hits	LP	Vocalion	VA8017	1964	**£30**	**£15**	
Original USA Hit Parade	LP	Heliodor	343001	1958	**£40**	**£20**	*German*
Ossiach Live	LP	BASF	49211193	1971	**£40**	**£20**	*German triple*
Our Choice	7" EP	Columbia	SEG7669	1957	**£6**	**£2.50**	
Our Significant Hits	LP	London	HAU2404	1962	**£30**	**£15**	
Out Came The Blues	LP	Ace Of Hearts	AH72	1964	**£10**	**£4**	

Title	Format	Label	Cat. No.	Year	Value	Value	Notes
Out Came The Blues Vol. 2	LP	Ace Of Hearts	AH158	1967	**£10**	**£4**	
Out Of Sight	LP	Design	DLP269	1968	**£20**	**£8**	*US*
Owdham Edge Popular Song And Verse From Lancashire	LP	Topic	12T204	1970	**£10**	**£4**	
Package Tour	LP	Golden Guinea	GGL0268	1963	**£15**	**£6**	
Paddy In The Smoke	LP	Topic	12T176	1968	**£10**	**£4**	
Pain In My Belly	LP	Blue Beat	BBLP804	1965	**£100**	**£50**	
Pajama Game	7" EP	London	REA1036	1955	**£5**	**£2**	
Pakistani Soul Session	LP	Island	ILP945	1967	**£20**	**£8**	
Parkside Steelworks	LP	LIL	LP2	1985	**£30**	**£25**	
Party Time In Jamaica	LP	Studio One	SOL9009	1968	**£100**	**£50**	
Pennsylvanian Unknowns	LP	Time Tunnel	TTR1217425	1982	**£25**	**£10**	*US*
Penthouse Magazine Presents The Bedside Bond	LP	Decca	LK4824	1966	**£20**	**£8**	
Perfumed Garden	LP	Psycho	6	1983	**£15**	**£6**	
Perfumed Garden II	LP	Psycho	15	1983	**£15**	**£6**	
Perspectives And Distortions	LP	Cherry Red	BRED15	1981	**£10**	**£4**	
Philadelphia Years	LP	Streetsounds	PHST1986	1986	**£75**	**£37.50**	*14 LP boxed set*
Piano Blues 1927–1933	LP	Riverside	RLP8809	1967	**£12**	**£5**	
Piano Jazz – Barrelhouse And Boogie Woogie	LP	Vogue Coral	LVA9069	1956	**£10**	**£4**	
Picnic	LP	Harvest	SHSS1/2	1970	**£12**	**£5**	*double*
Piedmont Blues	LP	Flyright	LP104	1972	**£10**	**£4**	
Pinch Of Salt	LP	HMV	CLP1362	1960	**£40**	**£20**	
Pinch Of Salt	LP	HMV	XLP50004	1960	**£40**	**£20**	
Pioneers Of Boogie Woogie	10" LP	London	AL3506	1953	**£25**	**£10**	
Pioneers Of Boogie Woogie Vol. 2	10" LP	London	AL3537	1954	**£25**	**£10**	
Pipeline	LP	Trojan	TBL203	1973	**£12**	**£5**	
Pop Parade Vol. 1	10" LP	Mercury		1956	**£10**	**£4**	
Pop Parade Vol. 2	10" LP	Mercury		1956	**£10**	**£4**	
Pop Parade Vol. 3	10" LP	Mercury	MPT7519	1957	**£10**	**£4**	
Pop Parade Vol. 4	10" LP	Mercury	MPT7523	1957	**£10**	**£4**	
Pop Parade Vol. 5	10" LP	Mercury	MPT7525	1957	**£15**	**£6**	
Pop Party	LP	Polydor	236517/8/9	1968	**£25**	**£10**	*triple*
Pops Go Stereo	7" EP	Pye	NSEP85000	1958	**£6**	**£2.50**	
Post War Blues: Chicago	LP	Post War Blues	PWB1	1965	**£20**	**£8**	
Post War Blues: Detroit	LP	Post War Blues	PWB5	1968	**£20**	**£8**	
Post War Blues: Eastern And Gulf Coast States	LP	Post War Blues	PWB3	1967	**£20**	**£8**	
Post War Blues: Memphis On Down	LP	Post War Blues	PWB2	1966	**£20**	**£8**	
Post War Blues: Texas	LP	Post War Blues	PWB4	1968	**£20**	**£8**	
Post War Blues: The Deep South	LP	Post War Blues	PWB7	1969	**£20**	**£8**	
Post War Blues: West Coast	LP	Post War Blues	PWB6	1969	**£20**	**£8**	
Post War Collector Series Vol. 1	LP	Python	PWBC1	1969	**£20**	**£8**	
Pot Of Flowers	LP	Mainstream	S6100	1967	**£15**	**£6**	*US*
Pre-War Texas Blues	LP	Kokomo	K1006	1970	**£30**	**£15**	
Preachin' The Blues	LP	Stateside	SL10046	1963	**£10**	**£4**	
Presages	LP	4AD	BAD11	1980	**£10**	**£4**	
Pride Of Cleveland Past	LP	private	NR15744	198–	**£12**	**£5**	*US*
Primitive Piano	LP	Jazz Collector	ABC1	1959	**£20**	**£8**	
Psilotripitaka	CD	United Dairies	UD134CD	198–	**£60**	**£30**	*4 CD set*
Psilotripitaka	CD	United Dairies	UD134CD	198–	**£300**	**£180**	*4 CD set, leather bag*
Psilotripitaka	LP	United Dairies	UD134	198–	**£60**	**£30**	*4 LP set*
Psilotripitaka	LP	United Dairies	UD134	198–	**£300**	**£180**	*4 LP set, leather bag*
Psychedelic Disaster Whirl	LP	Frantic	555777	1986	**£25**	**£10**	*US*
Psychedelic Dream	LP	Columbia	CS38025	1982	**£15**	**£6**	*US double*
Psychedelic Patchwork Vol. 1	LP	private	PP101	1986	**£25**	**£10**	*US*
Psychedelic Salvage Co. Vol. 1	LP	private	no number	1990	**£15**	**£6**	
Psychedelic Salvage Co. Vol. 2	LP	private	no number	1990	**£15**	**£6**	
Psychedelic Unknowns Vol. 1	7" EP	Calico	EP0001	1979	**£25**	**£10**	*US double*
Psychedelic Unknowns Vol. 2	7" EP	Calico	EP0002	1979	**£25**	**£10**	*US double*
Psychedelic Unknowns Vol. 3	LP	Calico	EP0003	1981	**£50**	**£25**	*US*
Psychedelic Unknowns Vol. 4	LP	Dayglow-Freon	DFLP001	1982	**£25**	**£10**	*US*
Psychedelic Unknowns Vol. 5	LP	Starglow-Neon	SN00001	1983	**£25**	**£10**	*US*
Psychedelic Unknowns Vol. 6	LP	Scrap	SCLP1	1985	**£12**	**£5**	*US*
Psychedelic Unknowns Vol. 7	LP	Scrap	SCLP2	1986	**£12**	**£5**	*US*
Psychedelic Unknowns Vol. 8	LP	Scrap	SCLP3	1986	**£12**	**£5**	*US*
Psychotic Moose And The Soul Searchers	LP	Psychotic Moose	PMS101	1982	**£50**	**£25**	*US*
Pure Blues Vol. 1	LP	Sue	ILP919	1965	**£25**	**£10**	
Purple Twilight	LP	Color Disc	COLORS2	1985	**£15**	**£6**	
Put It On, It's Rock Steady	LP	Island	ILP978	1968	**£50**	**£25**	*pink label*
Pye Sales Sampler	LP	Pye	PSA6	1971	**£15**	**£6**	*promo*
Queen Of The World	LP	Trojan	TBL136	1970	**£12**	**£5**	
Querschnitt Berlin	LP	private		1982	**£20**	**£8**	*German*

Title	Format	Label	Number	Year	Mint	Ex	Notes
R&B Chartmakers	7" EP	Stateside	SE1009	1964	£50	£25	
R&B Chartmakers No. 2	7" EP	Stateside	SE1018	1964	£50	£25	
R&B Chartmakers No. 3	7" EP	Stateside	SE1022	1964	£50	£25	
R&B Chartmakers No. 4	7" EP	Stateside	SE1025	1964	£50	£25	
R&B Greats Vol. 1	LP	Realm	RM101	1963	£15	£6	
R&B Greats Vol. 2	LP	Realm	RM175	1964	£15	£6	
R&B Party	LP	Mercury	MCL20019	1964	£12	£5	
Ragtime Piano Roll	10" LP	London	AL3515	1954	£15	£6	
Ragtime Piano Roll Vol. 2	10" LP	London	AL3523	1954	£15	£6	
Ragtime Piano Roll Vol. 3	10" LP	London	AL3542	1955	£15	£6	
Ragtime Piano Roll Vol. 4	10" LP	London	AL3563	1957	£15	£6	
Raptor Presents	12"	Raptor	RAP1	1993	£40	£20	
Rave	LP	United Artists	(S)UX1214	1969	£10	£4	
Raw Blues	LP	Ace Of Clubs	ACL/SCL1220	1967	£12	£5	
Reading Rock Vol. 1	LP	Mean	MNLP82	1983	£15	£6	*double*
Ready Steady Go	LP	Decca	LK4577	1964	£25	£10	
Ready Steady Go Rocksteady	LP	Pama	PMLP3	1968	£30	£15	
Ready Steady Win	LP	Decca	LK4634	1964	£50	£25	
Real R&B	LP	Stateside	SL10112	1965	£20	£8	
Recommended Records Sampler	7"	Recommended	RR8.9	1982	£8	£4	*clear vinyl, 1 side painted*
Recommended Sampler	LP	Recommended	104	1982	£10	£4	
Record Collector	LP	Destiny	DS10001	1979	£15	£6	
Recording The Blues	LP	CBS	52797	1970	£10	£4	
Red Bird Goldies	LP	Red Bird	RB20102	1965	£25	£10	
Red, Red Wine Vol. 1	LP	Trojan	TTL11	1969	£40	£20	*pink Island label*
Red, Red Wine Vol. 1	LP	Trojan/ Downtown	TTL11	1969	£12	£5	
Red, Red Wine Vol. 2	LP	Trojan	TBL116	1970	£12	£5	
Reggae Chartbusters	LP	Trojan	TBLS105	1970	£10	£4	
Reggae Chartbusters Vol. 2	LP	Trojan	TBL147	1970	£10	£4	
Reggae Chartbusters Vol. 3	LP	Trojan	TBL169	1971	£10	£4	
Reggae Flight 404	LP	Trojan	TBL115	1970	£12	£5	
Reggae Girl	LP	Big Shot	BIL3000	1968	£40	£20	
Reggae Hit The Town	LP	Pama	PTP1001	1969	£25	£10	
Reggae Hits '69 Vol. 1	LP	Pama	ECO3	1969	£20	£8	
Reggae Hits '69 Vol. 2	LP	Pama	ECO11	1969	£20	£8	
Reggae In The Grass	LP	Studio One	SOL9007	1968	£100	£50	
Reggae Jamaica	LP	Trojan	TBL181	1971	£10	£4	
Reggae Movement	LP	Trojan	TBL144	1970	£12	£5	
Reggae Power	LP	Trojan	TBL189	1972	£10	£4	
Reggae Reggae Reggae	LP	Trojan	TBL130	1970	£15	£6	
Reggae Reggae Reggae Vol. 2	LP	Trojan	TBL176	1971	£12	£5	
Reggae Revolution	LP	London	LGJ/ZGJ101	1970	£15	£6	
Reggae Special	LP	Coxsone	CSP2	1969	£25	£10	
Reggae Steady Go	LP	Trojan	TBL151	1970	£12	£5	
Reggae Time	LP	Coxsone	CSL8017	1968	£100	£50	
Reggae To Reggae	LP	Pama	PMP2012	1971	£25	£10	
Reggae To UK With Love	LP	Pama	PSP1004	1969	£20	£8	
Reggaematic Sounds	LP	Bamboo	BDLP208	1971	£40	£20	
Relics – Collectors' Obscurities From The First Psychedelic Era	LP	dB	DB102	1982	£25	£10	US
Return Of The Young Pennsylvanians	LP	Bona Fide	BFR1672466	1983	£12	£5	US
Return To Splendour	7"	Fierce Panda	NING03	1994	£25	£12.50	*double*
Revolution	LP	United Artists	UAS29069	1969	£12	£5	
Rhythm & Blues	LP	Decca	LK4616	1964	£30	£15	
Rhythm & Blues Showcase Vol. 1	7" EP	Pye	NEP44021	1964	£15	£7.50	
Rhythm & Blues Showcase Vol. 2	7" EP	Pye	NEP44022	1964	£15	£7.50	
Rhythm And Blues	LP	Golden Guinea	GGL0280	1964	£15	£6	
Rhythm And Blues Classics Vol. 1	LP	Minit	MLS40008	1969	£15	£6	
Rhythm And Blues Classics Vol. 2	LP	Minit	MLS40009	1969	£12	£5	
Rhythm And Blues Party	LP	Philips	6436028	1976	£10	£4	
Rhythm And Blues Party	LP	Mercury	MCL20019	1964	£25	£10	
Rhythm And Blues Vol. 1	LP	Liberty	LBL83216	1969	£10	£4	
Rhythm And Blues Vol. 2	LP	Liberty	LBL83328	1969	£10	£4	
Rhythm'n'Blues	LP	Decca	31031-2	1964	£30	£15	German double
Ric Tic Relics	LP	Tamla Motown	STML11232	1973	£15	£6	
Ride Me Donkey	LP	Coxsone	CSL8015	1968	£100	£50	
Ride Your Donkey	LP	Trojan	TTL18	1969	£20	£8	
Riot On Sunset Strip	LP	Tower	5065	1967	£25	£10	US
Riverboat Jazz	10" LP	Vogue Coral	LRA10023	1955	£10	£4	
Riverside – The Soul Of Jazz – 1961	LP	Riverside	(9)S5	1961	£10	£4	
Rivertown Blues	LP	London	SHU8245	1971	£12	£5	
Rock All Night	10" LP	Mercury	MPT7527	1957	£150	£75	
Rock And Dole	7"	Consett Music Project	RD1	1983	£15	£7.50	
Rock And Roll	7" EP	Vogue	VE170111	1958	£75	£37.50	
Rock On	LP	KPM	KPM1196	1977	£50	£25	
Rock Und Beat Im Star-Club Hamburg	LP	Ariola	70983	1964	£75	£37.50	German
Rock'n'Roll	10" LP	London	HBC1067	1956	£30	£15	
Rock'n'Roll Forever	LP	London	HAE2180	1959	£40	£20	
Rock'n'Roll Music	LP	Vogue	LDVS17198	1970	£25	£10	German
Rock, Rock, Rock	LP	Chess	LP1425	1957	£50	£25	US
Rock-A-Hits	LP	London	HAA2338	1961	£40	£20	
Rocket Along	10" LP	HMV	DLP1204	1960	£20	£8	
Rockin' At The 2 I's	10" LP	Decca	LF1300	1958	£30	£15	

Rockin' Together	LP	London	HAE2167	1959	**£40**	**£20**	
Rocksteady Cool	LP	Pama	PMLP7	1969	**£30**	**£15**	
Rocksteady Coxsone Style	LP	Coxsone	CSL8013	1968	**£100**	**£50**	
Roksnax	LP	Guardian	GRC80	1980	**£30**	**£15**	
Rollercoaster EP	CD-s	Warner Bros	SAM986	1982	**£5**	**£2**	*Melody Maker disc*
Roofgarden Jamboree	LP	Iglus	103	1967	**£200**	**£100**	*US*
Roots '66 Vol. 1	LP	Paraquat	TPLP84	1984	**£12**	**£5**	*US*
Roots Of The Blues	LP	London	LTZK15211	1961	**£12**	**£5**	
Round Up	7" EP	Capitol	EAP120197	1962	**£8**	**£4**	
Roxcalibur	LP	Guardian	GRC130	1982	**£25**	**£10**	
Rubble 1 – The Psychedelic Snarl	LP	Bam-Caruso	KIRI024	1984	**£25**	**£10**	
Rubble 2 – Pop-Sike Pipe-Dreams	LP	Bam-Caruso	KIRI025	1986	**£25**	**£10**	
Rubble 3 – Nightmares In Wonderland	LP	Bam-Caruso	KIRI026	1986	**£25**	**£10**	
Rubble 4 – 49 Minute Technicolour Dream	LP	Bam-Caruso	KIRI027	1984	**£25**	**£10**	
Rubble 5 – The Electric Crayon Set	LP	Bam-Caruso	KIRI044	1986	**£25**	**£10**	
Rubble 6 – The Clouds Have Groovy Faces	LP	Bam-Caruso	KIRI049	1986	**£25**	**£10**	
Rubble 7 – Pictures In The Sky	LP	Bam-Caruso	KIRI083	1988	**£25**	**£10**	
Rubble 8 – All The Colours Of Darkness	LP	Bam-Caruso	KIRI051	1991	**£25**	**£10**	
Rubble 9 – Plastic Wilderness	LP	Bam-Caruso	KIRI079	1991	**£25**	**£10**	
Rubble 10 – Professor Jordan's Magic Sound Show	LP	Bam-Caruso	KIRI098	1988	**£25**	**£10**	
Rubble 11 – Adventures In The Mist	LP	Bam-Caruso	KIRI069	1986	**£25**	**£10**	
Rubble 12 – Staircase To Nowhere	LP	Bam-Caruso	KIRI070	1986	**£25**	**£10**	
Rubble 13 – Freakbeat Fantoms	LP	Bam-Caruso	KIRI102	1989	**£25**	**£10**	
Rubble 14 – The Magic Rocking Horse	LP	Bam-Caruso	KIRI106	1988	**£25**	**£10**	
Rubble 15 – 5,000 Seconds Over Toyland	LP	Bam-Caruso	KIRI084	1991	**£25**	**£10**	
Rubble 16 – Glass Orchid Aftermath	LP	Bam-Caruso	KIRI096	1991	**£25**	**£10**	
Rubble 17 – A Trip In A Painted World	LP	Bam-Caruso	KIRI099	1991	**£25**	**£10**	
Rupert Preaching At A Picnic	LP	Naive	NAIVE2	1981	**£10**	**£4**	
Rural Blues	LP	XTRA	XTRA1035	1969	**£15**	**£6**	*double*
Rural Blues Vol. 1	LP	Liberty	LBL83213	1969	**£12**	**£5**	
Rural Blues Vol. 2	LP	Liberty	LBL83214	1969	**£12**	**£5**	
Rural Blues Vol. 3	LP	Liberty	LBL83329	1969	**£12**	**£5**	
Samantha Promotions	LP	Transworld	SPLP102	1970	**£750**	**£500**	
Samantha Promotions	LP	Transworld	SPLP101	1970	**£750**	**£500**	
San Francisco Interntional Pop Festival	LP	Colstar	5001	196–	**£300**	**£180**	*US*
San Francisco Roots	LP	Vault	SLP119	1969	**£15**	**£6**	*US*
Sandy Bell's Ceilidh	LP	Alba	MAR056	1979	**£12**	**£5**	
Saturday Club	LP	Decca	LK4583	1964	**£20**	**£8**	
Saturday Club	LP	Parlophone	PMC1130	1960	**£25**	**£10**	
Saturday Night At The Apollo	LP	Atlantic	590007	1966	**£10**	**£4**	
Saturday Night At The Uptown	LP	Atlantic	ATL5018	1964	**£15**	**£6**	
Savannah Syncopators	LP	CBS	52799	1970	**£10**	**£4**	
Scene '65	LP	Columbia	33SX1730	1965	**£50**	**£25**	
Scene Of The Crime	LP	Suspect	SUS3	1981	**£30**	**£15**	
Scorcha From Bamboo	LP	Bamboo	BDLP202	1969	**£40**	**£20**	
Scotia Folk	LP	Fontana	6438021	1970	**£20**	**£8**	
Screening The Blues	LP	CBS	66208	1968	**£15**	**£6**	*double*
Scum Of The Earth Part 1	LP	Killdozer	KILL001	1984	**£50**	**£25**	*US*
Scum Of The Earth Part 2	LP	Killdozer	KILL002	1984	**£100**	**£50**	*US*
Sea Shanties	LP	Topic	12TS234	1974	**£10**	**£4**	
Seaside Rock	LP	Airship	AP342	1981	**£15**	**£6**	*double*
Second Coming	LP	Come Organisation	WDC881008	1980	**£40**	**£20**	
Second Folk Review Record	LP	Folksound	FS107	1976	**£30**	**£15**	
Secret Liverpool	LP	Davies	LPD2VOR8	1984	**£15**	**£6**	
Secret Policeman's Other Ball	10"	Springtime	RARA1001	1981	**£10**	**£4**	*promo sampler*
Select Elektra	LP	Elektra	EUK261/ EUKS7261	1968	**£15**	**£6**	
Seoda Ceoil 2	LP	Gael-Linn	CEF002	1969	**£10**	**£4**	*Irish*
Shades Of Gospel Soul	LP	Motown	M/S701	1969	**£15**	**£6**	*US*
Shagging In The Streets	7"	Fierce Panda	NING01	1994	**£10**	**£5**	*double*
Shake It Baby	LP	Polydor	623002	1965	**£30**	**£15**	*German*
Shake, Rattle And Roll	LP	Atlantic	587109	1968	**£10**	**£4**	
Sheffield University Rag Record	7" EP	Lyntone	LYN738/9	1964	**£15**	**£7.50**	
Shepway Folk	LP	Eron	003	1974	**£25**	**£10**	
Shimmies In Super 8	7"	Duophonic	DS4505/06	1993	**£25**	**£12.50**	*double, green and white vinyls*
Short Circuit – Live At The Electric Circus	10" LP	Virgin	VCL5003	1978	**£25**	**£10**	*yellow vinyl*
Short Circuit – Live At The Electric Circus	10" LP	Virgin	VCL5003	1978	**£10**	**£4**	*blue vinyl*
Short Circuit – Live At The Electric Circus	10" LP	Virgin	VCL5003	1978	**£75**	**£37.50**	*orange vinyl*
Signed D.C.	LP	Satan	SR666	1984	**£12**	**£5**	*US*
Sing A Song Of Soul	LP	Chess	CRL4519	1966	**£10**	**£4**	
Singer Songwriter Project	LP	Elektra	EKL/EKS7299	1965	**£30**	**£15**	*US*
Singing In The Rain	7" EP	MGM	MGMEP671	1958	**£6**	**£2.50**	
Singing The Blues	7" EP	London	REP1403	1963	**£30**	**£15**	
Six Five Special	7" EP	Decca	DFE6485	1958	**£12**	**£6**	
Six Five Special	LP	Parlophone	PMC1047	1957	**£30**	**£15**	
Sixteen Beat Groups From The Hamburg Scene	LP	Polydor	237639	1964	**£75**	**£37.50**	*German*
Sixteen Dynamic Reggae Hits	LP	Pama	PMP2015	1971	**£12**	**£5**	
Sixteen Dynamic Reggae Hits	LP	Trojan	TBL191	1972	**£10**	**£4**	

Title	Format	Label	Number	Year	Mint	VG	Notes
Sixteen Original R&B Golden Hits	LP	Starclub	158011STY	1965	£100	£50	German
Ska at The Jamaican Playboy Club	LP	Island	ILP930	1966	£150	£75	
Ska To Rocksteady	LP	Studio One	SOL9000	1967	£100	£50	
Ska's The Limit	LP	Page One	FOR006	196–	£15	£6	
Skiffle	LP	Ace Of Clubs	ACL1250	1967	£25	£10	
Soft Beat '66	LP	Decca	H210	1966	£50	£25	German
Solid Gold	LP	Bamboo	BDLP212	1971	£40	£20	
Solid Gold Soul	LP	Atlantic	ATL5048	1966	£10	£4	
Solid Gold Soul Vol. 2	LP	Atlantic	587058	1967	£10	£4	
Solid On Soul	LP	United Artists	LBR1007	197–	£10	£4	
Some Cleveland And Dales Folk Vol. 1	LP	Pied Piper	MIK1001	1976	£12	£5	
Some Cold Rainy Day	LP	Southern Preservation	SPR1	1972	£15	£6	
Some Cold Rainy Day	LP	Flyright	LP114	1975	£10	£4	
Some Folk In Leicester	LP	Lestar	LLP101	1965	£50	£25	
Something Sweet From The Lady	LP	Pama	PMP2003	1970	£15	£6	
Son Of Gutbucket	LP	Liberty	LBX4	1969	£10	£4	
Son Of The Gathering Of The Tribe	LP	BF	20183	1983	£25	£10	US
Songs From Washington Davy Lamp Folksong Club	LP	DLFC	110	1974	£40	£20	
Soul '66	LP	Sue	ILP934	1966	£30	£15	
Soul Food	LP	Minit	MLL40011E	1968	£15	£6	
Soul From The City	LP	Soul City	SCB001	1969	£15	£6	
Soul Of Jamaica	LP	Trojan	TRL3	1968	£30	£15	
Soul Sauce From Pama	LP	Pama	PMLP8	1969	£15	£6	
Soul Seller	LP	Polydor	236554	1969	£10	£4	
Soul Sixteen	LP	Stateside	SL10186	1966	£20	£8	
Soul Sounds Of The Sixties	LP	HMV	CLP3617	1967	£20	£8	
Soul Supply	LP	Stateside	SL10203	1967	£20	£8	
Sound Of Bacharach	LP	Pye	NPL28061	1965	£12	£5	
Sound Of The Grapevine	LP	Grapevine	GRAL1001	197–	£12	£5	
Sound Of The R&B Hits	LP	Stateside	SL10077	1964	£30	£15	
Sound Of The Sixties	LP	Eva	12021/2	1983	£20	£8	French double
Sound Of The Sixties: San Francisco Part 1	LP	Phantom	PLP1004	1985	£12	£5	US
Sound Of The Sixties: San Francisco Part 2	LP	Phantom	PLP1005	1985	£12	£5	US
Sound Of The Stars	7"	Lyntone	LYN995	1966	£15	£7.50	Disc And Music Echo flexi, envelope
Sounds And Songs Of London	LP	Columbia	SAX9001	1968	£10	£4	
Sounds Of Savile	7" EP	Lyntone	LYN951/2	1965	£40	£20	
Sounds Of The South	LP	London	LTZK15209	1961	£12	£5	
Soundsville	LP	Design	DLP187	1965	£50	£25	US
Southern Comfort	LP	London	HAK8405	1969	£20	£8	
Southern Comfort	LP	Spectrum	ASPEC001	198–	£30	£15	
Southern Sanctified Singers	LP	Saydisc	RL328	196–	£10	£4	
Southside Chicago	LP	Python	PLP10	1971	£25	£10	
Southside Chicago Jazz	10" LP	London	AL3529	1954	£10	£4	
Speak Low – More Music In The Modern Manner	LP	Tempo	TAP17	1958	£25	£10	
Spin With The Stars No. 2	10" LP	Pye	NPT19019	1957	£12	£5	
Spin With The Stars No. 3	10" LP	Pye	NPT19021	1957	£12	£5	
Spirituals To Swing Vol. 1	LP	Top Rank	35064	1959	£15	£6	
Spirituals To Swing Vol. 2	LP	Top Rank	35065	1959	£15	£6	
Spree '73	LP	Key	KL021	1973	£10	£4	
St Andrews University Charities Campaign	7" EP	S.A.U.C.C.	PR5462	196–	£50	£25	
Star Club Center Of Beat	LP	Brunswick	2910502	1965	£50	£25	German
Star Club Information Record	LP	Starclub	111371L	1964	£175	£87.50	German
Star Parade	7" EP	Decca	DFE6147	1955	£6	£2.50	
Star Souvenir Greetings	7"	208 Radio Luxembourg		196–	£10	£5	flexi
Star-Club Scene '65	LP	Starclub	158018	1965	£60	£30	German
Star-Club Show 6	LP	Starclub	148005STL	1965	£60	£30	German
Stars Of Liberty	LP	Liberty	LBY1001	1960	£20	£8	
Stars Of the 6.5 Special	10" LP	Decca	LF1299	1957	£40	£20	
Statik Compilation One	LP	Statik	POL274	1985	£12	£5	
Stax/Volt Tour In London Vol. 1	LP	Stax	589010	1967	£15	£6	
Stax/Volt Tour In London Vol. 2	LP	Stax	589011	1967	£15	£6	
Steam Ballads	LP	Broadside	BRO121	1977	£12	£5	
Stiff Box Set No. 1	7"	Stiff	BUY1-10	1979	£30	£15	10 × 7", boxed
Story Of Oak Records	LP	Tenth Planet	TP010	1994	£20	£8	double
Story Of The Blues Vol. 2	LP	CBS	66232	1970	£15	£6	double
Straighten Up	LP	Pama	PMP2002	1970	£15	£6	
Straighten Up Vol. 2	LP	Pama	PMP2007	1971	£15	£6	
Straighten Up Vol. 3	LP	Pama	PMP2014	1971	£15	£6	
Straighten Up Vol. 4	LP	Pama	PMP2017	1972	£15	£6	
Strangers From A Strange Land	LP	private		1991	£15	£6	US
Street To Street – A Liverpool Compilation	LP	Open Eye	OELP501	1979	£12	£5	
Strictly Canadian	LP	Birchmont	BM523	1971	£30	£15	Canadian
Sue Sampler Record For Clubs	LP	Sue	ILP919	1965	£100	£50	promo only
Sue Story	LP	London	HAC8239	1965	£25	£10	different to Sue LP
Sue Story	LP	Sue	ILP925	1965	£30	£15	
Sue Story	LP	United Artists	UAS29028	1969	£12	£5	
Sue Story Vol. 2	LP	Sue	ILP933	1966	£30	£15	
Sue Story Vol. 3	LP	Sue	ILP938	1966	£40	£20	
Summer '75	LP	Island	ISS1	1975	£20	£8	

Title	Format	Label	Cat. No.	Year	Mint	VG	Notes
Super Black Blues	LP	Philips	6369416	1973	**£10**	**£4**	
Super Duper Blues	LP	Blue Horizon	PR31	1969	**£12**	**£5**	
Super Soul	LP	Pye	NPL28107	1968	**£10**	**£4**	
Surf Battle	LP	Vocalion	VA8018	1964	**£25**	**£10**	
Surf Party	LP	Ava	AVA28	1962	**£40**	**£20**	*US*
Swamp Blues	LP	Blue Horizon	766263	1970	**£40**	**£20**	*double*
Sweet Beat	7" EP	Top Rank	JKR8007	1959	**£20**	**£10**	
Sweet Beat	LP	Starclub	158022STY	1966	**£100**	**£50**	*German*
Sweet Home Chicago	LP	Delmark	DS618	1970	**£12**	**£5**	
Sweet Soul Sounds	LP	Stateside	(S)SL10243	1968	**£15**	**£6**	
Swing Easy	LP	Studio One	SOL0017	196–	**£100**	**£50**	
Swing Easy	LP	Coxsone	CSL8018	1968	**£100**	**£50**	
Swingin' Set	LP	MGM	C8012	1966	**£20**	**£8**	
Swingin' The Blues	LP	Tempo	TAP21	1958	**£25**	**£10**	
Syde Tryps Four	LP	Tenth Planet	TP008	1994	**£15**	**£6**	
Syde Tryps One	LP	Tenth Planet	TP002	1993	**£15**	**£6**	
Syde Tryps Three	LP	Tenth Planet	TP006	1993	**£15**	**£6**	
Syde Tryps Two	LP	Tenth Planet	TP004	1993	**£15**	**£6**	
Take Off Your Head And Listen	LP	Rubber	LP001	1971	**£15**	**£6**	
Take Six	7" EP	Oriole	EP7080	1964	**£30**	**£15**	
Tale Of Ale	LP	Free Reed	FRRD023/4	1978	**£15**	**£6**	*double*
Talk Of The Grapevine	LP	Grapevine	GRAL1000	1978	**£12**	**£5**	
Tamla Motown Box	7"	Tamla Motown	TMG956-975,1000	1975	**£100**	**£50**	*boxed set of demos*
Tear It Up	7" EP	Mercury	ZEP10015	1959	**£75**	**£37.50**	
Teen Scene '64	7" EP	Ember	EMBEP4540	1964	**£30**	**£15**	
Teenage Rock	7" EP	Mercury	MEP9522	1957	**£75**	**£37.50**	
Teenage Rock	LP	Capitol	T1009	1958	**£30**	**£15**	
Teenage Tops	7" EP	RCA	RCX111	1958	**£20**	**£10**	
Teenager Party '64	LP	Polydor	46840	1964	**£50**	**£25**	*German mono*
Teenager Party '64	LP	Polydor	237340	1964	**£60**	**£30**	*German stereo*
Texas Blues	LP	Fountain	FV205	197–	**£10**	**£4**	
Texas Reverberations	LP	Texas Archive	TAR1	1982	**£12**	**£5**	*US*
Texas–Louisiana Blues	LP	Highway 51	H103	1969	**£40**	**£20**	
Thank Your Lucky Stars	LP	Ace Of Clubs	ACL1108	1962	**£15**	**£6**	
Thank Your Lucky Stars Vol. 2	LP	Decca	LK4554	1963	**£25**	**£10**	
That's Underground	LP	CBS	SPR23	1970	**£15**	**£6**	*German, multi-coloured vinyl*
Themes From James Bond Films	7" EP	CBS	WEP1126	1967	**£5**	**£2**	
There Is Some Fun Going Forward	LP	Dandelion	2485021	1972	**£50**	**£25**	*with poster*
These Kind Of Blues Vol. 1	LP	Action	ACLP6009	1969	**£15**	**£6**	
They Sold A Million No. 4	7" EP	Brunswick	OE9420	1959	**£5**	**£2**	
They Sold A Million No. 9	7" EP	Brunswick	OE9425	1959	**£10**	**£5**	
They Sold A Million No. 10	7" EP	Brunswick	OE9426	1959	**£5**	**£2**	
They Sold A Million No. 11	7" EP	Brunswick	OE9427	1959	**£10**	**£5**	
They Sold A Million No. 12	7" EP	Brunswick	OE9428	1959	**£5**	**£2**	
They Sold A Million No. 13	7" EP	Brunswick	OE9429	1959	**£5**	**£2**	
Third Irish Folk Festival In Concert	LP	Intercord	INT181008	1976	**£25**	**£10**	*German double*
Thirteen Year Itch	CD	4AD	SHUFFLE	1993	**£20**	**£8**	
Thirty-Three Minits Of Blues And Soul	LP	Minit	MLL/S40002	1968	**£12**	**£5**	
This Is Blue Beat	LP	Island	ILP910	1964	**£150**	**£75**	*test pressing*
This Is Blues	LP	Island	IWP5	1970	**£20**	**£8**	*pink label*
This Is Chess	LP	Chess	CRL4540	1969	**£10**	**£4**	
This Is Merseybeat Vol. 1	LP	Oriole	PS40047	1963	**£50**	**£25**	
This Is Merseybeat Vol. 2	LP	Oriole	PS40048	1963	**£50**	**£25**	
This Is Northern Soul	LP	Grapevine	GRAL1002	1980	**£15**	**£6**	
This Is Reggae	LP	Pama	PSP1003	1969	**£20**	**£8**	
This Is Reggae Vol. 2	LP	Pama	PMP2005	1971	**£15**	**£6**	
This Is Reggae Vol. 3	LP	Pama	PMP2008	1971	**£15**	**£6**	
This Is Reggae Vol. 4	LP	Pama	PMP2016	1972	**£15**	**£6**	
This Is Sue!	LP	Island	IWP3	1969	**£12**	**£5**	*pink label*
This Is White Noise	7"	White Noise	WN3	1983	**£20**	**£10**	
Those Cakewalkin' Babies From Home	LP	Saydisc	SDR182	1970	**£12**	**£5**	
Three O'Clock Merrian Webster Time	LP	Cicadelic	CICLP999	1982	**£12**	**£5**	*US*
Tighten Up	LP	Trojan	TTL1	1969	**£12**	**£5**	
Tighten Up	LP	Trojan	TBL120	1969	**£10**	**£4**	
Tighten Up Vol. 2	LP	Trojan	TTL7	1969	**£40**	**£20**	*pink Island label*
Tighten Up Vol. 2	LP	Trojan	TTL7	1969	**£10**	**£4**	
Tighten Up Vol. 2	LP	Trojan	TBL131	1970	**£10**	**£4**	
Tighten Up Vol. 3	LP	Trojan	TBL145	1970	**£10**	**£4**	
Tighten Up Vol. 4	LP	Trojan	TBL163	1971	**£10**	**£4**	
Tighten Up Vol. 5	LP	Trojan	TBL165	1971	**£10**	**£4**	
Tighten Up Vol. 6	LP	Trojan	TBL185	1972	**£10**	**£4**	
Tijd For Teenagers 1	10" LP	Philips	600369	1965	**£40**	**£20**	*Dutch*
Tijd For Teenagers 2	10" LP	Philips	600701	1965	**£40**	**£20**	*Dutch*
To The Shores Of Lake Placid	LP	Zoo	ZOO4	1982	**£10**	**£4**	
Tobacco A-Go-Go	LP	Blue Mold	BMLP101	1984	**£12**	**£5**	*US*
Together Sound Of Reading	LP	Airport	MO70870	1970	**£25**	**£10**	*US*
Top Teen Bands Vol. 1	LP	Bud-Jet	311	1965	**£50**	**£25**	*US*
Top Teen Bands Vol. 2	LP	Bud-Jet	312	1965	**£50**	**£25**	*US*
Top Teen Bands Vol. 3	LP	Bud-Jet	313	1965	**£50**	**£25**	*US*
Top Teen Dances	7" EP	Stateside	SE1004	1963	**£10**	**£5**	
Top TV Themes	7" EP	Pye	NEP24276	1967	**£5**	**£2**	
Topic Sampler No. 1	LP	Topic	TPS114	1964	**£15**	**£6**	
Topic Sampler No. 2	LP	Topic	TPS145	1965	**£12**	**£5**	
Topic Sampler No. 3	LP	Topic	TPS166	1966	**£10**	**£4**	
Topic Sampler No. 4	LP	Topic	TPS168	1966	**£10**	**£4**	
Topic Sampler No. 5	LP	Topic	TPS169	1967	**£10**	**£4**	

Title	Format	Label	Number	Year	Mint	VG+	Notes
Topic Sampler No. 6	LP	Topic	TPS201	1968	£10	£4	
Topic Sampler No. 7	LP	Topic	TPS205	1969	£10	£4	
Topic Sampler No. 8	LP	Topic	TPSS221	1972	£12	£5	
Tops In Pops No. 1	7" EP	Decca	DFE6411	1957	£8	£4	
Tops In Pops No. 3	7" EP	Decca	DFE6467	1958	£6	£2.50	
Tops In Pops No. 7	7" EP	Decca	DFE6583	1959	£5	£2	
Traditional Jazz At The Royal Festival Hall	LP	Decca	LK4088	1955	£15	£6	
Traditional Jazz At The Royal Festival Hall Vol. 2	LP	Decca	LK4100	1955	£15	£6	
Traditional Music Of Ireland Vol. 1	LP	Folkways	FW8781	1963	£15	£6	*US*
Traditional Music Of Ireland Vol. 2	LP	Folkways	FW8782	1963	£15	£6	*US*
Travelling Folk	LP	Eron	006	1976	£20	£8	
Treasures Of North American Negro Music Vol. 6	7" EP	Fontana	TFE17265	1960	£6	£2.50	
Treasury Of Field Recordings	LP	77	LA122	1960	£15	£6	
Treasury Of Field Recordings Vol. 2	LP	77	LA123	1960	£15	£6	
Tribute To Michael Holliday	LP	Columbia	33SX1635	1964	£20	£8	
Tribute To Youth Praise	LP	Key	KL003	1969	£30	£15	
Triple Treat	LP	Parlophone	PMC1139	1961	£12	£5	
Trojan Reggae Party	LP	Trojan	TBL172	1971	£10	£4	
Trojan Story	LP	Trojan	TALL100	1980	£25	£10	*3 LP box set*
Trojan Story	LP	Trojan	TALL1	1972	£40	£20	*triple*
Trojan Story Vol. 2	LP	Trojan	TALL200	1982	£20	£8	*3 LP box set*
Trojan's Greatest Hits	LP	Trojan	TBL180	1971	£10	£4	
Trojan's Greatest Hits Vol. 2	LP	Trojan	TBL190	1972	£10	£4	
Troublemakers	LP	Warner Bros	PROA857	1981	£20	£8	*promo double*
Tub Jug Washboard Bands	LP	Riverside	RLP8802	1967	£15	£6	
TV Themes	7" EP	Decca	DFE8585	1964	£30	£15	
TV Themes 1966	7" EP	Pye	NEP24244	1966	£8	£4	
Twelve Big Hits	LP	Melodisc	12193	196–	£12	£5	
Twelve Carat Gold	LP	Melodisc	12217	196–	£12	£5	
Twelve-String Story – Guitar Solos	LP	London	HAF/SHF8285	1966	£10	£4	
Twenty-Five Years Of Rhythm And Blues Hits	LP	Ember	EMB3359	1965	£15	£6	
Twist At The Star Club	LP	Philips	BL7578	1963	£50	£25	
Twist Festival Live '64 In Berlin	LP	Metronome	HLP10020	1964	£40	£20	*German*
Twist Off	7" EP	Starlite	STEP31	1962	£60	£30	
Twist On	7" EP	Starlite	STEP29	1962	£60	£30	
Twist Time Im St C. Hamburg 3	LP	Ariola	70954IT	1964	£50	£25	*German*
Twrw Tanllyd	LP	Sain	1201M	1981	£12	£5	
Ulster's Flowery Vale	LP	BBC	REC28M	1968	£25	£10	
Unholy Montage	7"	Fierce	FRIGHT38	198–	£20	£10	
Unity's Great Reggae Hits	LP	Pama	ECO7	1969	£20	£8	
Urban Acid	LP	Urban	URBLP15	1988	£10	£4	
Urban Blues Vol. 1	LP	Liberty	LBL83215	1969	£10	£4	
Urban Blues Vol. 2	LP	Liberty	LBL83327	1969	£10	£4	
Valley Of Son Of Gathering Of The Tribe	LP	Gott	3	1984	£25	£10	*US*
Vaudeville Blues	LP	VJM	VLP30	1970	£10	£4	
Version Galore Vol. 2	LP	Trojan	TBL175	1971	£12	£5	
Version Galore Vol. 3	LP	Trojan	TBL200	1973	£12	£5	
Version To Version	LP	Trojan	TBL182	1972	£12	£5	
Version To Version Vol. 3	LP	Trojan	TBL206	1973	£12	£5	
Vertigo Annual 1970	LP	Vertigo	6499407/8	1970	£12	£5	*double*
Vile Vinyl Vol. 1	LP	High Noon	HINLP001	1985	£12	£5	*US*
Vile Vinyl Vol. 2	LP	High Noon	HINLP002	1985	£12	£5	*US*
Vogue Surprise Partie	7" EP	Vogue	VRE5002	1965	£5	£2	
Voices Record One	LP	Argo	PLP1112	1968	£30	£15	
Voices Record Two	LP	Argo	PLP1115	1968	£20	£8	
Wagon Train	7" EP	RCA	RCX128	1959	£5	£2	
Wakey Wakey	LP	Columbia	33SX1385	1962	£15	£6	
Walking By Myself	LP	Pye	NPL28041	1964	£20	£8	
Walking The Blues	LP	Pye	NPL28044	1964	£15	£6	
Walls Ice Cream Presents	7" EP	Apple	CT1	1969	£40	£20	
Washboard Rhythm	LP	Ace Of Hearts	AH55	1963	£10	£4	
We Like Girls	LP	Coral	LVA9096	1959	£12	£5	
We Like Guys	LP	Coral	LVA9098	1959	£12	£5	
We Love You Beatles	7" EP	CBS	5649	1965	£20	£10	*French*
We Sing The Blues	7" EP	Liberty	LEP4036	1965	£15	£7.50	
We Sing The Blues	LP	Sue	ILP921	1965	£25	£10	
We Sing The Blues	LP	Liberty	LBY3051	1965	£15	£6	
We Sing The Blues	LP	London	HAP8061	1963	£25	£10	
We Three Kings	LP	Syndicate Chapter	SC005	1972	£10	£4	
We've Moved	LP	MPL	MPL1	1977	£150	£75	*promo with press pack*
Weekend At The Bridgehouse	LP	Bridgehouse	BHLP001	1978	£20	£8	*with 12"*
West Coast Love In	LP	Vault	SLP113	1967	£15	£6	*US*
West Side Chicago	7" EP	Solid Sender	SEP101	1975	£6	£2.50	
What A Way To Die: 15 Forgotten Losers From The Mid-Sixties	LP	Satan	SR1313	1983	£12	£5	*US*
What Am I Do	LP	Trojan	TTL34	1970	£15	£6	
What's Shakin'	LP	Elektra	EKS7304	1968	£12	£5	
Where It's At – Live At The Cheetah	LP	Audio Fidelity	AFLP2168	1966	£25	£10	*US*
Whip	LP	Kamera	KAM14	1983	£15	£6	
Wholly Grail	LP	Grail		1972	£75	£37.50	
Wide Midlands	LP	Topic	12TS210	1971	£10	£4	

Wild Beach Weekend	7" EP	RCA	86466	1964	**£10**	**£5**	*French*
Wipe Out	LP	Dot	DLP3535	1966	**£10**	**£4**	
Wir Im Scheinwerfer	LP	Resono	13003	1970	**£20**	**£8**	*German*
Women Of The Blues	LP	RCA	RD7840	1967	**£15**	**£6**	
WONE: The Dayton Scene	LP	Prism		1966	**£100**	**£50**	*US*
Woodstock	LP	Atlantic	2663001	1970	**£15**	**£6**	*triple*
Woodstock 2	LP	Atlantic	2400130/1	1971	**£12**	**£5**	*double*
Woorden – Poetry And Experimental Music	LP	Omega	333023	1966	**£30**	**£15**	*Dutch*
World Of Blues	LP	London	HAP8099	1963	**£25**	**£10**	
World Of Blues Power Vol. 3	LP	Decca	SPA263	1973	**£10**	**£4**	
World Of Bullet	LP	Pama	SECO19	1969	**£12**	**£5**	
World Of Folk	LP	Argo	SPA132	1971	**£15**	**£6**	
Yes L.A.	LP	Dangerhouse	EW79	1979	**£15**	**£6**	*1 sided clear picture disc*
You Can't Wine	LP	Trojan	TBL142	1970	**£12**	**£5**	
You Left Me Standing	LP	Trojan	TTL9	1969	**£20**	**£8**	
You're Either On The Train . . .	LP	Stiff	DEAL1	1978	**£12**	**£5**	*promo*
Your Chess Requests	7" EP	Chess	CRE6026	1968	**£15**	**£7.50**	
Your Choice	7" EP	Mercury	MEP9525	1957	**£12**	**£6**	
Your Choice No. 2	7" EP	Mercury	MEP9532	1958	**£8**	**£4**	
Your Favourite TV And Radio Themes	LP	HMV	CLP1565	1962	**£10**	**£4**	
Your Jamaican Girl	LP	Bamboo	BDLP211	1971	**£40**	**£20**	
Your Secret's Safe With Us	LP	Statik	STATLP7	1982	**£15**	**£6**	*double*
Zebra Selection	LP	private		1968	**£50**	**£25**	*US*
Zulu Compilation	LP	Zulu	ZULU6	1984	**£15**	**£6**	

VARNEY, REG

This Is Reg Varney	LP	Columbia	SCX6518	1973	**£10**	**£4**	

VARTAN, SYLVIE

Another Heart	7"	RCA	RCA1495	1965	**£4**	**£1.50**	
Ihre Grossen Erfolge	LP	RCA	CAS10264	1974	**£25**	**£10**	*German*
L'Avventura E L'Avventura	LP	United Artists	UAS29296	1972	**£30**	**£15**	*Italian*
Le Locomotion	7" EP	RCA	76593	1963	**£40**	**£20**	*French*
One More Day	7"	RCA	RCA1490	1965	**£4**	**£1.50**	
Sylvie	LP	RCA	FSP225	1968	**£20**	**£8**	*US*
Sylvie	LP	RCA	440103	1963	**£25**	**£10**	*French*
Sylvie Vartan	7" EP	RCA	RCX7165	1965	**£40**	**£20**	

VARUKERS

Another Religion Another War	12"	Riot City	RIOT31	1983	**£6**	**£2.50**	
Die For Your Government	7"	Riot City	RIOT27	1983	**£4**	**£1.50**	
Led To The Slaughter	7"	Riot City	RIOT29	1983	**£4**	**£1.50**	
Massacred Millions	12"	Rot	ASS16	1984	**£8**	**£4**	
Prepare For The Attack	LP	Attack	ATTACK001	1984	**£10**	**£4**	

VASELINES

Dum Dum	LP	53rd And 3rd	AGAS7	1990	**£10**	**£4**	
Dying For It	12"	53rd And 3rd	AGARR17T	1988	**£8**	**£4**	
Dying For It	CD-s	53rd And 3rd	AGARR17CD	1988	**£5**	**£2**	
Son Of A Gun	7"	53rd And 3rd	AGARR10	1987	**£8**	**£4**	

VASHTI

Some Things Just Stick In Your Mind	7"	Decca	F12157	1965	**£30**	**£15**	
Train Song	7"	Columbia	DB7917	1966	**£30**	**£15**	

VATTEN

Tungt Vatten	LP	Prophone	PROP7756	1975	**£60**	**£30**	*Swedish*

VAUGHAN, FRANKIE

At The London Palladium	LP	Philips	BBL7330/ SBBL511	1959	**£10**	**£4**	
Cuff Of My Shirt	7"	HMV	7M182	1954	**£6**	**£2.50**	
Frankie Vaughan	7" EP	Philips	BBE12220	1958	**£5**	**£2**	
Frankie Vaughan	7" EP	Philips	BBE12071	1956	**£5**	**£2**	
Frankie Vaughan	7" EP	Philips	BBE12111	1957	**£5**	**£2**	
Frankie Vaughan	7" EP	Philips	BBE12022	1956	**£5**	**£2**	
Garden Of Eden	7"	Philips	JK1002	1957	**£15**	**£7.50**	
Give Me The Moonlight	7"	Philips	PB423	1955	**£6**	**£2.50**	
Gotta Have Something In The Bank, Frank	7"	Philips	JK1030	1957	**£6**	**£2.50**	
Happy Days And Lonely Nights	7"	HMV	7M270	1954	**£10**	**£5**	
Happy Go Lucky	7" EP	Philips	BBE12171	1958	**£5**	**£2**	
Happy Go Lucky	LP	Philips	BBL7198	1957	**£10**	**£4**	
Heart Of A Man	7" EP	Philips	BBE12299	1959	**£5**	**£2**	
Istanbul	7"	HMV	7M167	1953	**£15**	**£7.50**	
It's Frankie	7" EP	Philips	BBE12157	1957	**£5**	**£2**	
Kisses Sweeter Than Wine	7"	Philips	JK1035	1957	**£8**	**£4**	
Lady Is A Square	7" EP	Philips	BBE12247	1959	**£5**	**£2**	
Let Me Sing & I'm Happy	7" EP	Philips	BBE12484	1961	**£5**	**£2**	
Let Me Sing & I'm Happy	7" EP	Philips	SBBE9071	1961	**£6**	**£2.50**	*stereo*
Let Me Sing & I'm Happy No. 2	7" EP	Philips	BBE12485	1961	**£5**	**£2**	
Let Me Sing & I'm Happy No. 2	7" EP	Philips	SBBE9072	1961	**£6**	**£2.50**	*stereo*
Let Me Sing & I'm Happy No. 3	7" EP	Philips	BBE12486	1961	**£5**	**£2**	
Let Me Sing & I'm Happy No. 3	7" EP	Philips	SBBE9073	1961	**£6**	**£2.50**	*stereo*
Let Me Sing And I'm Happy	LP	Philips	BBL7482/ SBBL629	1961	**£10**	**£4**	

Title	Format	Label	Cat. No.	Year	Mint	VG	Notes
Mister Elegant	7" EP	HMV	7EG8245	1957	£5	£2	
My Son, My Son	7"	HMV	7M252	1954	£6	£2.50	
Showcase	LP	Philips	BBL7233	1958	£10	£4	
These Dangerous Years	7"	Philips	JK1022	1957	£6	£2.50	
Too Many Heartaches	7"	HMV	7M298	1955	£6	£2.50	
What's Behind That Strange Door	7"	Philips	JK1014	1957	£6	£2.50	

VAUGHAN, MALCOLM

Title	Format	Label	Cat. No.	Year	Mint	VG	Notes
Chapel Of The Roses	7"	HMV	POP325	1957	£4	£1.50	
Hello	LP	HMV	CLP1284	1959	£10	£4	
Hello No. 1	7" EP	HMV	GES5785	1959	£5	£2	*stereo*
Hello No. 2	7" EP	HMV	GES5793	1959	£5	£2	*stereo*
More Than A Millionaire	7"	HMV	7M317	1955	£5	£2	
Only You	7"	HMV	7M389	1956	£4	£1.50	
Requests	7" EP	HMV	GES5799	1959	£5	£2	*stereo*
Sincerity In Song	7" EP	HMV	7EG8272	1957	£6	£2.50	
Sincerity In Song No. 2	7" EP	HMV	7EG8377	1957	£5	£2	
Sincerity In Song No. 3	7" EP	HMV	7EG8453	1957	£5	£2	
St Therese Of The Roses	7"	HMV	POP250	1956	£4	£1.50	
With Your Love	7"	HMV	7M338	1955	£8	£4	
World Is Mine	7"	HMV	POP303	1957	£4	£1.50	

VAUGHAN, NORMAN

Title	Format	Label	Cat. No.	Year	Mint	VG	Notes
Swinging In The Rain	7"	Pye	7N15438	1962	£4	£1.50	*picture sleeve*

VAUGHAN, SARAH

Title	Format	Label	Cat. No.	Year	Mint	VG	Notes
After Hours At The London House	7" EP	Mercury	ZEP10030	1959	£5	£2	
After Hours At The London House	LP	Mercury	MMC14001	1959	£12	£5	
At Mister Kelly's	LP	Mercury	MPL6542	1958	£10	£4	
Best Of Berlin Vol. 1	7" EP	Mercury	SEZ19016	1961	£5	£2	*stereo*
Close To You	LP	Mercury	CMS18040	1961	£10	£4	*stereo*
Count Basie–Sarah Vaughan	LP	Columbia	SCX3403	1962	£10	£4	*stereo*
Divine One	LP	Columbia	SCX3390	1962	£10	£4	*stereo*
Dreamy	LP	Columbia	SCX3324	1960	£10	£4	*stereo*
Explosive Side Of Sarah Vaughan	LP	Columbia	SCX3479	1963	£10	£4	
Great Songs From Hit Shows Part 1	LP	Mercury	CMS18019	1960	£10	£4	*stereo*
Great Songs From Hit Shows Part 2	LP	Mercury	CMS18023	1960	£10	£4	*stereo*
Hit Parade	7" EP	Mercury	MEP9511	1956	£5	£2	
Hit Parade No. 2	7" EP	Mercury	MEP9519	1957	£5	£2	
Images	10" LP	Mercury	MG26005	1955	£12	£5	
Images	10" LP	Mercury	MPT7518	1957	£10	£4	
In Romantic Mood	LP	Mercury	MPL6540	1958	£10	£4	
In The Land Of Hi Fi	LP	Emarcy	EJL100	1956	£15	£6	
Linger Awhile	LP	Philips	BBL7165	1957	£10	£4	
Live For Love	7" EP	Mercury	ZEP10087	1960	£5	£2	
Live For Love	7" EP	Mercury	SEZ19006	1961	£8	£2.50	*stereo*
Make Yourself Comfortable	10" LP	Mercury	MPT7503	1956	£12	£5	
No Count Blues	7" EP	Mercury	ZEP10115	1962	£5	£2	
Sarah Vaughan	7" EP	Emarcy	YEP9507	1957	£5	£2	
Sarah Vaughan	7" EP	London	REU1065	1956	£8	£4	
Sarah Vaughan	LP	Philips	BBL7082	1956	£10	£4	
Sarah With Feeling	7" EP	Mercury	ZEP10041	1959	£5	£2	
Sassy	LP	Emarcy	EJL1258	1957	£10	£4	
Sings	10" LP	London	HBU1049	1956	£15	£6	
Sings George Gershwin Vol. 1	LP	Mercury	MPL6525	1957	£10	£4	
Sings George Gershwin Vol. 1	LP	Mercury	CMS18011	1959	£12	£5	*stereo*
Sings George Gershwin Vol. 2	LP	Mercury	MPL6527	1957	£10	£4	
Sings George Gershwin Vol. 2	LP	Mercury	CMS18012	1959	£12	£5	*stereo*
Sings Great Songs From Hit Shows Part 1	LP	Mercury	MPL6522	1957	£10	£4	
Sings Great Songs From Hit Shows Part 2	LP	Mercury	MPL6523	1957	£10	£4	
Smooth Sarah	7" EP	Mercury	ZEP10054	1960	£5	£2	
Songs From Sarah	7" EP	Mercury	ZEP10011	1959	£5	£2	
Swingin' Easy	LP	Emarcy	EJL1273	1958	£10	£4	
Vaughan And Violins	LP	Mercury	CMS18003	1959	£10	£4	*stereo*
Wonderful Sarah	LP	Mercury	MPL6532	1958	£10	£4	

VAUGHAN, STEVIE RAY

Title	Format	Label	Cat. No.	Year	Mint	VG	Notes
Tick Tock	CD-s	CBS	6563525	1990	£5	£2	

VAUGHN, BILLY

Title	Format	Label	Cat. No.	Year	Mint	VG	Notes
Billy Vaughn	7" EP	London	RED1285	1961	£5	£2	
Brazil	7"	London	HL7094	1960	£5	£2	*export*
Golden Instrumentals	LP	London	HAD2025	1957	£10	£4	
Golden Instrumentals	LP	London	SAHD6018	1959	£15	£6	*stereo*
Golden Instrumentals No. 1	7" EP	London	RED1083	1957	£6	£2.50	
Golden Instrumentals No. 2	7" EP	London	RED1084	1957	£6	£2.50	
Great Billy Vaughn	7" EP	Dot	DEP20004	1965	£5	£2	
Happy Cowboy	7" EP	London	RED1380	1963	£5	£2	
Johnny Tremain	7"	London	HLD8511	1957	£5	£2	
La Paloma	7"	London	HLD7107	1960	£5	£2	*export*
Melodies Of Love	10" LP	London	HBD1048	1956	£15	£6	
Melody Of Love	7"	London	HL8112	1955	£15	£7.50	*gold label*
Petticoats Of Portugal	7"	London	HLD8342	1956	£6	£2.50	*gold label*
Plays The Hits No. 1	7" EP	London	RED1329	1962	£5	£2	
Plays The Hits No. 2	7" EP	London	RED1330	1962	£5	£2	
Plays The Million Sellers	LP	London	SAHD6003	1958	£10	£4	*stereo*

Raunchy	7"	London	HLD8522	1957	£5	£2	
Red Sails In The Sunset	7"	London	HL7093	1960	£5	£2	*export*
Sail Along Silvery Moon	7" EP	London	RED1189	1959	£6	£2.50	
Sail Along Silvery Moon	LP	London	SAHD6037	1958	£10	£4	*stereo*
Sixty-Two's Greatest Hits	7" EP	London	RED1395	1963	£5	£2	
Swingin' Safari	7" EP	London	RED1352	1963	£6	£2.50	
Theme From The Threepenny Opera	7"	London	HLD8238	1956	£8	£4	*gold label*
Themes From Billy Vaughn	7" EP	London	RED1248	1960	£5	£2	
Tumbling Tumbleweeds	7"	London	HLD8612	1958	£5	£2	
When The Lilac Blooms Again	7"	London	HLD8319	1956	£6	£2.50	*gold label*

VAUGHN, MORRIS

My Love Keeps Growing	7"	Fontana	TF1031	1969	£10	£5	

VAUGHT, BOB & THE RENAGADES

Surf Crazy	LP	GNP-Crescendo	(S)83	1963	£20	£8	*US*

VEDDAR, CHUCK

Spanky Boy	7"	London	HLU8951	1959	£20	£10	

VEE, BOBBY

Bobby Tomorrow	7"	Liberty	LIB55530	1963	£4	£1.50	
Bobby Vee	LP	London	HAG2352/SAHG6152	1961	£40	£20	
Bobby Vee Meets The Crickets	7" EP	Liberty	LEP2116	1963	£20	£10	
Bobby Vee Meets The Crickets	7" EP	Liberty	SLEP2116	1963	£30	£15	*stereo*
Bobby Vee Meets The Crickets Vol. 2	7" EP	Liberty	LEP2149	1963	£20	£10	
Bobby Vee No. 1	7" EP	London	REG1278	1961	£20	£10	
Bobby Vee No. 2	7" EP	London	REG1299	1961	£20	£10	
Bobby Vee No. 3	7" EP	London	REG1308	1961	£20	£10	
Bobby Vee No. 4	7" EP	London	REG1323	1961	£25	£12.50	
Bobby Vee's Biggest Hits	7" EP	Liberty	LEP2102	1963	£15	£7.50	
Bobby Vee's Biggest Hits	7" EP	Liberty	SLEP2102	1963	£20	£10	*stereo*
Buddy's Song	7"	Liberty	LIB10141	1963	£5	£2	
Devil Or Angel	7"	London	HLG9179	1960	£15	£7.50	
Do What You Gotta Do	LP	Liberty	LBL/LBS83130	1968	£12	£5	
Forever Kind Of Love	7"	Liberty	LIB10046	1962	£4	£1.50	
Forever Kind Of Love	7" EP	Liberty	LEP2089	1963	£15	£7.50	
Golden Greats	LP	Liberty	(S)LBY1112	1962	£25	£10	
Hickory, Dick And Dock	7"	Liberty	LIB55700	1964	£4	£1.50	
Hits Of The Rockin' Fifties	7" EP	London	REG1324	1961	£25	£12.50	
Hits Of The Rockin' Fifties	LP	London	HAG2406/SAHG6206	1961	£40	£20	
How Many Tears	7"	London	HLG9389	1961	£4	£1.50	
I Remember Buddy Holly	LP	Liberty	(S)LBY1188	1963	£25	£10	
I'm Gonna Make It Up To You	7"	Liberty	LBF15234	1969	£4	£1.50	
Just For Fun	7" EP	Liberty	LEP2084	1963	£15	£7.50	*with the Crickets*
Just Today	LP	Liberty	LBL/LBS83112	1968	£12	£5	
Keep On Trying	7"	Liberty	LIB10197	1965	£4	£1.50	
Like You've Never Known Before	7"	Liberty	LIB10272	1967	£4	£1.50	
Live On Tour	LP	Liberty	(S)LBY1263	1965	£20	£8	
Look At Me Girl	7"	Liberty	LIB55877	1966	£4	£1.50	
Look At Me Girl	LP	Liberty	(S)LBY1341	1966	£15	£6	
Love's Made A Fool Of You	7"	London	HLG9459	1961	£8	£4	
Meets The Crickets	LP	Liberty	(S)LBY1086	1962	£15	£6	
Meets The Ventures	7" EP	Liberty	LEP2212	1965	£20	£10	
Meets The Ventures	LP	Liberty	(S)LBY1147	1963	£25	£10	
Merry Christmas From Bobby Vee	LP	Liberty	LRP3267/LST7267	1962	£25	£10	*US*
More Than I Can Say	7"	London	HLG9316	1961	£4	£1.50	
New Sound From England	LP	Liberty	LRP3352/LST7352	1964	£25	£10	*US*
New Sounds	7" EP	Liberty	LEP2181	1964	£20	£10	
Night Has A Thousand Eyes	7"	Liberty	LIB10069	1963	£4	£1.50	
Night Has A Thousand Eyes	LP	Liberty	(S)LBY1139	1963	£25	£10	
Please Don't Ask About Barbara	7"	Liberty	LIB55419	1962	£4	£1.50	
Recording Session	LP	Liberty	(S)LBY1084	1962	£25	£10	
Rubber Ball	7"	London	HLG9255	1961	£5	£2	
Run Like The Devil	7"	Liberty	LIB55828	1965	£5	£2	
Run To Him	7"	London	HLG9470	1961	£4	£1.50	
Run To Him	7"	Liberty	LIB55388	1962	£4	£1.50	
Sharing You	7"	Liberty	LIB55451	1962	£4	£1.50	
Sincerely	7" EP	Liberty	LEP2053	1962	£15	£7.50	
Sings Your Favourites	LP	London	HAG2320	1961	£50	£25	
Stranger In Your Arms	7"	Liberty	LIB10124	1963	£4	£1.50	
Take Good Care Of My Baby	7"	London	HLG7111	1961	£15	£7.50	*export*
Take Good Care Of My Baby	7"	London	HLG9438	1961	£4	£1.50	
Take Good Care Of My Baby	LP	London	HAG2428/SAHG6224	1961	£30	£15	
Take Good Care Of My Baby	LP	Liberty	(S)LBY1004	1961	£20	£8	
Thirty Big Hits From The 60s	LP	Liberty	LRP3385/LST7385	1964	£25	£10	*US*
True Love Never Runs Smooth	7"	Liberty	LIB10213	1965	£4	£1.50	
With Strings And Things	LP	London	HAG2374/SAHG6174	1961	£40	£20	

VEGA, SUZANNE

Book Of Dreams	CD-s	A&M	AMCDH559	1990	£5	£2	hologram sleeve
Compact Hits	CD-s	A&M	AMCD912	1988	£5	£2	
Left Of Center	CD-s	A&M	CDQ320	1986	£10	£5	
Small Blue Thing	7"	A&M	AM294	1985	£4	£1.50	double
Solitude Standing	CD-s	A&M	VEGCD3	1988	£8	£4	
Tom's Diner	CD-s	A&M	VEGCD2	1987	£8	£4	

VEGAS, PAT & LOLLY

At The Haunted House	LP	Mercury	MG2/SR61059	1966	£15	£6	US

VEJTABLES

I Still Love You	7"	Pye	7N25339	1965	£15	£7.50	
I Still Love You	7" EP	Vogue	INT18051	1965	£25	£12.50	French

VELEZ, MARTHA

It was a considerable coup when the previously unknown singer Martha Velez managed to persuade members of Cream, Chicken Shack, the Keef Hartley Band and Free to perform on her debut album and she almost manages to rise to the occasion. Her later *Escape From Babylon* is much less celebrated, but its music is actually provided by the Wailers, including that group's leader, Bob Marley.

Boogie Kitchen	7"	Blue Horizon	2096010	1972	£8	£4	
Escape From Babylon	LP	Sire	9103252	1976	£12	£5	with Bob Marley
Fiends And Angels	LP	London	HAK/SHK8395	1969	£15	£6	
Fiends And Angels Again	LP	Blue Horizon	763867	1970	£40	£20	
It Takes A Lot To Laugh	7"	London	HLK10266	1966	£4	£1.50	
Tell Mama	7"	London	HLK10280	1969	£4	£1.50	

VELVELETTES

He Was Really Sayin' Something	7"	Stateside	SS387	1965	£30	£15	
Lonely Lonely Girl Am I	7"	Tamla Motown	TMG521	1965	£75	£37.50	
Needle In A Haystack	7"	Tamla Motown	TMG595	1967	£8	£4	
Needle In A Haystack	7"	Stateside	SS361	1964	£20	£10	
These Things Keep Me Loving You	7"	Tamla Motown	TMG580	1966	£15	£7.50	

VELVET HUSH

Broken Heart	7"	Oak	RGJ648	1968	£75	£37.50	

VELVET OPERA

Anna Dance Square	7"	CBS	4189	1969	£4	£1.50	
Black Jack Davy	7"	CBS	4802	1970	£4	£1.50	
Ride A Hustler's Dream	LP	CBS	63692	1969	£40	£20	
She Keeps Giving Me These Feelings	7"	Spark	SRL1045	1970	£4	£1.50	

VELVET UNDERGROUND

The Velvet Underground's sponsorship by artist Andy Warhol on their first album derives from the group's early involvement with the New York avant-garde. Distinctive and innovative though their albums are, they are to some extent a commercial version of the music the group liked to play live. Bootleg recordings exist of extended performances of 'Sister Ray' and unnamed instrumental pieces, where the meditational drone music of La Monte Young is given a quasi-rock'n'roll setting to create a sound like no other of its time. The song 'Venus In Furs' from the first album found unlikely employment as music for a tyre advert in the nineties, but it remains a stunning performance. The late guitarist Sterling Morrison proudly referred to the song in a television interview as being totally unlike any other sixties track (by anybody) and he is right. Nico appears only on the first album – the inclusion of her songs giving the record an effectively schizophrenic feel. John Cale's departure after *White Light/White Heat* had a more serious effect, while Lou Reed's exit from the group he had created himself means that *Squeeze* is essentially the work of an entirely different group.

All Tomorrow's Parties	7"	Verve	10427	1966	£150	£75	US
Andy Warhol's Velvet Underground Featuring Nico	LP	MGM	2683006	1971	£15	£6	double
Candy Says	7"	MGM	2006283	1973	£5	£2	
Index Cardboard Picture Disc	7"	Index		1966	£200	£100	US
Live At Max's Kansas City	LP	Atlantic	K30022	1972	£10	£4	
Loaded	LP	Atlantic	2400111	1970	£15	£6	
Loop	7"	Aspen		1966	£200	£100	US flexi
Radio Spot	7"	MGM	VU1	1969	£250	£150	US promo, best auctioned
Squeeze	LP	Polydor	2383180	1972	£12	£5	
Sunday Morning	7"	Verve	10466	1966	£125	£62.50	US
Sweet Jane	7"	Atlantic	K10339	1973	£5	£2	
Velvet Underground	LP	Polydor	VUBOX1	1986	£40	£20	5 LP boxed set
Velvet Underground	LP	MGM	CS8108	1969	£30	£15	
Velvet Underground	LP	MGM	2353022	1971	£10	£4	
Velvet Underground And Nico	CD	Polydor	C88115	1988	£15	£6	box set
Velvet Underground And Nico	LP	Verve	VLP9184	1967	£60	£30	mono
Velvet Underground And Nico	LP	Verve	SVLP9184	1967	£40	£20	
Velvet Underground And Nico	LP	MGM	2315056	1971	£12	£5	
Velvet Underground And Nico	LP	MGM	2315056	1971	£50	£25	with US peelable banana cover
Velvet Underground And Nico	LP	Verve	V5008	1967	£100	£50	US, peelable banana cover, sticker covers group photo, mono
Velvet Underground And Nico	LP	Verve	V5008	1967	£150	£75	US, peelable banana cover, male torso frames group photo, mono

Title	Format	Label	Number	Year	Price	Price	Notes
Velvet Underground And Nico	LP	Verve	V5008	1967	£75	£37.50	US, peelable banana cover, male torso airbrushed out, mono
Velvet Underground And Nico	LP	Verve	V65008	1967	£75	£37.50	US, peelable banana cover, sticker covers group photo, stereo
Velvet Underground And Nico	LP	Verve	V65008	1967	£75	£37.50	US, peelable banana cover, male torso airbrushed out, stereo
Velvet Underground And Nico	LP	Verve	V65008	1967	£125	£62.50	US, peelable banana cover, male torso James group photo, stereo
What Goes On?	7"	MGM	14057	1969	£50	£25	US promo
White Light White Heat	LP	MGM	2353024	1971	£10	£4	
White Light, White Heat	7"	Verve	10560	1968	£50	£25	US promo, 2 different B sides
White Light/White Heat	LP	Verve	VLP9201	1967	£60	£30	mono
White Light/White Heat	LP	Verve	SVLP9201	1967	£40	£20	stereo
Who Loves The Sun	7"	Atlantic	2091088	1971	£10	£5	
Who Loves The Sun	7"	Cotillion	44107	1971	£30	£15	US promo

VELVETS

Title	Format	Label	Number	Year	Price	Price	Notes
Laugh	7"	London	HLU9444	1961	£15	£7.50	
That Lucky Old Sun	7"	London	HLU9328	1961	£15	£7.50	
Tonight	7"	London	HLU9372	1961	£15	£7.50	
Velvets	7" EP	London	REU1297	1961	£75	£37.50	

VELVETT FOGG

Title	Format	Label	Number	Year	Price	Price	Notes
Telstar '69	7"	Pye	7N17673	1969	£10	£5	
Velvet Fogg	LP	Pye	NSPL18272	1967	£75	£37.50	laminated sleeve

VELVETTES

Title	Format	Label	Number	Year	Price	Price	Notes
He's The One I Want	7"	Mercury	MF802	1964	£5	£2	
He's The One I Want	7"	Mercury	MF802	1964	£8	£4	picture sleeve

VENDORS

Title	Format	Label	Number	Year	Price	Price	Notes
Peace Pipe	7"	Domino Studios	no number	1964	£400	£250	demo, best auctioned

VENGERS

Title	Format	Label	Number	Year	Price	Price	Notes
Shake And Clap	7"	Oriole	CB1879	1963	£6	£2.50	

VENOM

Title	Format	Label	Number	Year	Price	Price	Notes
At War With Satan	LP	Neat	NEATP1015	1985	£20	£8	picture disc
Black Metal	LP	Neat	NEATP1005	1985	£20	£8	picture disc
Blood Lust	7"	Neat	NEAT13	1982	£5	£2	
Blood Lust	7"	Neat	NEAT13	1982	£25	£12.50	purple vinyl
Die Hard	7"	Neat	NEAT27	1983	£8	£4	export picture disc
Die Hard	7"	Neat	NEAT27	1983	£6	£2.50	with poster
In League With Satan	7"	Neat	NEAT08	1982	£5	£2	
Manitou	12"	Neat	NEAT4312	1985	£6	£2.50	
Manitou	7"	Neat	NEATSHAPE43	1985	£6	£2.50	shaped picture disc
Manitou	7"	Neat	NEATP43	1985	£5	£2	picture disc
Nightmare	12"	Neat	NEATSP4712	1985	£15	£7.50	picture disc
Nightmare	12"	Neat	NEAT4712	1985	£6	£2.50	
Nightmare	7"	Neat	NEATS47	1985	£10	£5	shaped picture disc
Prime Evil	LP	Under One Flag	FLAG36P	1989	£10	£4	picture disc
Warhead	7"	Neat	NEATP38	1984	£8	£4	purple vinyl
Welcome To Hell	LP	Neat	NEATP1002	1983	£25	£10	purple vinyl

VENTURA, CAROL

Title	Format	Label	Number	Year	Price	Price	Notes
Carol	LP	Stateside	SL10146	1965	£12	£5	
I Love To Sing	LP	Stateside	(S)SL10180	1966	£10	£4	

VENTURA, CHARLIE

Title	Format	Label	Number	Year	Price	Price	Notes
Concert	LP	Brunswick	LAT8023	1953	£30	£15	
Gene Norman Concert Recordings	10" LP	Vogue	LDE107	1954	£30	£15	

VENTURA, TOBY

Title	Format	Label	Number	Year	Price	Price	Notes
If My Heart Were A Story Book	7"	Decca	F11581	1963	£25	£12.50	

VENTURAS

Title	Format	Label	Number	Year	Price	Price	Notes
Here They Are	LP	Drum Boy	DB(S)1003	1964	£25	£10	US

VENTURES

The Ventures are the American equivalent of the Shadows, maintaining a long and still buoyant career by playing melodic guitar instrumentals with no more than a token regard for the prevailing musical fashions. The size of the Ventures' output is astonishing – they have released far more albums than are listed here, including many that have been issued only in Japan. Despite this, the group still found it necessary to issue an album on their own label in 1964, thereby producing the only real rarity in their catalogue.

Title	Format	Label	Number	Year	Price	Price	Notes
A Go-Go	LP	Liberty	(S)LBY1274	1965	£10	£4	
Another Smash	7" EP	London	REG1326	1961	£15	£7.50	
Another Smash	LP	London	HAG2376/ SAHG6176	1961	£20	£8	

Batman Theme	LP	Dolton	BLP2042/ BST8042	1966	**£15**	**£6**	*US*
Beach Party	LP	Dolton	BLP2016/ BST8016	1963	**£15**	**£6**	*US*
Best Of Pop Sounds	LP	United Artists	UAS29249	1971	**£10**	**£4**	
Blue Moon	7"	London	HLG9465	1961	**£6**	**£2.50**	
Christmas Album	LP	Liberty	(S)LBY1285	1965	**£15**	**£6**	
Colourful Ventures	7" EP	London	REG1328	1961	**£12**	**£6**	
Colourful Ventures	LP	London	HAG2409/ SAHG6209	1961	**£20**	**£8**	
Dance Party	LP	Liberty	(S)LBY1110	1962	**£15**	**£6**	
Dance With The Ventures	LP	Dolton	BLP2014/ BST8014	1963	**£15**	**£6**	*US*
Dance!	LP	Dolton	BLP2010/ BST8010	1963	**£15**	**£6**	*US*
Diamond Head	7"	Liberty	LIB303	1965	**£4**	**£1.50**	
El Cumbanchero	7"	Liberty	LIB68	1964	**£4**	**£1.50**	
Fabulous Ventures	LP	Dolton	BLP2029/ BST8029	1964	**£15**	**£6**	*US*
Flights Of Fantasy	7"	Liberty	LBF15075	1968	**£8**	**£4**	
Go With The Ventures	LP	Liberty	(S)LBY1323	1966	**£10**	**£4**	
Great Performances Vol. 1	LP	Liberty	LBL/LBS83085E	1968	**£10**	**£4**	
Guitar Freakout	LP	Liberty	(S)LBY1345	1967	**£10**	**£4**	
Hawaii Five-O	7"	Liberty	LBF15221	1969	**£4**	**£1.50**	
In Space	LP	Liberty	(S)LBY1189	1964	**£15**	**£6**	
Journey To The Stars	7"	Liberty	LIB91	1964	**£4**	**£1.50**	
Knock Me Out	LP	Liberty	(S)LBY1252	1965	**£12**	**£5**	
Lady Of Spain	7"	London	HLG7113	1961	**£20**	**£10**	*export*
Let's Go	LP	Liberty	(S)LBY1169	1963	**£10**	**£4**	
Lolita Ya Ya	7"	Liberty	LIB60	1964	**£4**	**£1.50**	
Lullaby Of The Leaves	7"	London	HLG9344	1961	**£4**	**£1.50**	
Mashed Potatoes And Gravy	LP	Dolton	BLP2016/ BST8016	1962	**£20**	**£8**	*US*
Ninth Wave	7"	Liberty	LIB78	1964	**£4**	**£1.50**	
On Stage	LP	Liberty	(S)LBY1270	1965	**£10**	**£4**	
Penetration	7"	Liberty	LIB10142	1964	**£4**	**£1.50**	
Perfidia	7"	London	HLG9232	1960	**£4**	**£1.50**	
Perfidia	7" EP	London	REG1279	1960	**£12**	**£6**	
Play Guitar With The Ventures	LP	Dolton	BLP16501	1965	**£15**	**£6**	*US*
Play Guitar With The Ventures Vol. 2	LP	Dolton	BLP16502	1966	**£15**	**£6**	*US*
Play Guitar With The Ventures Vol. 3	LP	Dolton	BLP16503	1966	**£15**	**£6**	*US*
Play Guitar With The Ventures Vol. 4	LP	Dolton	BLP16504	1966	**£15**	**£6**	*US*
Ram Bunk Shush	7"	London	HLG9292	1961	**£4**	**£1.50**	
Ram Bunk Shush	7" EP	London	REG1288	1961	**£15**	**£7.50**	
Secret Agent Man	7"	Liberty	LIB316	1966	**£4**	**£1.50**	
Secret Agent Man	7" EP	Liberty	LEP2250	1966	**£15**	**£7.50**	
Slaughter On Tenth Avenue	7"	Liberty	LIB300	1965	**£4**	**£1.50**	
Sleigh Ride	7"	Liberty	LIB10219	1965	**£4**	**£1.50**	
Smash Hits	7" EP	Liberty	LEP2131	1963	**£12**	**£6**	
Stranger	7"	Liberty	LIB308	1965	**£4**	**£1.50**	
Strawberry Fields Forever	7"	Liberty	LIB55967	1967	**£4**	**£1.50**	
Super Psychedelics	LP	Liberty	LBL/LBS83033	1968	**£10**	**£4**	
Super Psychedelics	LP	Liberty	(S)LBY1372	1967	**£12**	**£5**	
Surfing	LP	Liberty	(S)LBY1150	1963	**£15**	**£6**	
Swingin' Creeper	7"	Liberty	LIB306	1965	**£4**	**£1.50**	
Telstar, The Lonely Bull	LP	Dolton	BLP2019/ BST8019	1963	**£20**	**£8**	*US*
Tenth Anniversary Album	LP	Liberty	LST35000	1970	**£10**	**£4**	*US*
Theme From Silver City	7"	London	HLG9411	1961	**£4**	**£1.50**	
Theme From The Wild Angels	7"	Liberty	LIB10266	1967	**£4**	**£1.50**	
Twist Party	LP	Liberty	LBY1072	1962	**£15**	**£6**	
Twist With The Ventures	7" EP	Liberty	LEP2058	1962	**£12**	**£6**	
Twist With The Ventures	LP	London	HAG2429/ SAHG6225	1962	**£20**	**£8**	
Two Thousand Pound Bee	7"	Liberty	LIB67	1964	**£4**	**£1.50**	
Ventures	LP	London	HAG2340	1961	**£25**	**£10**	
Ventures	LP	London	SAHG6143	1961	**£30**	**£15**	*stereo*
Ventures	LP	Ventures	BG101	1964	**£50**	**£25**	*US*
Ventures	LP	Dolton	BLP2042/ BST8042	1966	**£15**	**£6**	*US*
Ventures Play Country Greats	7" EP	Liberty	LEP2174	1964	**£12**	**£6**	
Ventures Play Telstar & Lonely Bull	7" EP	Liberty	LEP2104	1963	**£12**	**£6**	
Ventures Play The Country Classics	LP	Dolton	BLP2023/ BST8023	1963	**£20**	**£8**	*US*
Versatile Ventures	LP	Liberty	SCR5	1966	**£15**	**£6**	*US*
Walk Don't Run	7"	Top Rank	JAR417	1960	**£4**	**£1.50**	
Walk Don't Run	LP	Liberty	LBY1002	1960	**£15**	**£6**	
Walk Don't Run '64	7"	Liberty	LIB96	1964	**£6**	**£2.50**	
Walk Don't Run Vol. 2	LP	Liberty	(S)LBY1228	1964	**£15**	**£6**	
Where The Action Is	LP	Liberty	(S)LBY1297	1966	**£10**	**£4**	
Wild Things	LP	Dolton	BLP2047/ BST8047	1966	**£15**	**£6**	*US*

VENUS IN FURS

Momento Mori	7"	Backs	PNCH105	1985	**£5**	**£2**	*picture disc*
Momento Mori	7"	Movement	MOO1	1984	**£5**	**£2**	

VENUTI, JOE

Joe Venuti ... 10" LP ... Brunswick ... LA8522 ... 1951 ... **£25** ... **£10**

VERA, BILLY & JUDY CLAY

Storybook Children ... LP ... Atlantic ... 588158 ... 1968 ... **£10** ... **£4**

VERLANDER, TIM

Tim Verlander ... LP ... Midas ... MR007 ... 1972 ... **£20** ... **£8**

VERMILION

Angry Young Women ... 7" ... Illegal ... ILM0010 ... 1978 ... **£5** ... **£2**
I Like Motorcycles ... 7" ... Illegal ... ILM0015 ... 1979 ... **£5** ... **£2**

VERN & ALVIN

Everybody Reggae ... 7" ... Blue Cat ... BS167 ... 1969 ... **£5** ... **£2**
Old Man Dead ... 7" ... Big Shot ... BI525 ... 1969 ... **£5** ... **£2** ... *G.G. Rhythm Section B side*

VERNE, LARRY

Mr Custer ... 7" ... London ... HLN9194 ... 1960 ... **£4** ... **£1.50**
Mr Larry Verne ... LP ... Era ... EL104 ... 1961 ... **£15** ... **£6** ... *US*
Mr Livingston ... 7" ... London ... HLN9263 ... 1961 ... **£4** ... **£1.50**

VERNON, MIKE

Although he has made the occasional record himself, both under his own name and as a member of the Olympic Runners, Mike Vernon is best known as a producer and as the proprietor of Blue Horizon records. As the producer of John Mayall's pivotal *Bluesbreakers* and *Hard Road* albums, Vernon was ideally placed to take a major role within the development of British blues, and he went on to work with most of the significant talents within the genre, including Fleetwood Mac, Chicken Shack, Savoy Brown and the Groundhogs. Every record on his Blue Horizon label is now a collectors' item, as indeed are the handful of singles issued by the label's predecessor, Purdah.

Bring It Back Home ... LP ... Blue Horizon ... 2931003 ... 1971 ... **£60** ... **£30**
Let's Try It Again ... 7" ... Blue Horizon ... 2096007 ... 1971 ... **£15** ... **£7.50**
Moment Of Madness ... LP ... Sire ... SAS7410 ... 1973 ... **£12** ... **£5** ... *US*

VERNONS GIRLS

Do The Bird ... 7" ... Decca ... F11629 ... 1963 ... **£4** ... **£1.50**
Don't Look Now ... 7" ... Parlophone ... R4596 ... 1959 ... **£8** ... **£4**
Funny All Over ... 7" ... Decca ... F11549 ... 1962 ... **£4** ... **£1.50**
He'll Never Come Back ... 7" ... Decca ... F11685 ... 1963 ... **£4** ... **£1.50**
It's A Sin To Tell A Lie ... 7" ... Decca ... F12021 ... 1964 ... **£4** ... **£1.50**
Jealous Heart ... 7" ... Parlophone ... R4532 ... 1959 ... **£8** ... **£4**
Let's Get Together ... 7" ... Parlophone ... R4832 ... 1961 ... **£4** ... **£1.50**
Locomotion ... 7" ... Decca ... F11495 ... 1962 ... **£4** ... **£1.50**
Lover Please ... 7" ... Decca ... F11450 ... 1962 ... **£4** ... **£1.50**
Madison Time ... 7" ... Parlophone ... R4654 ... 1960 ... **£5** ... **£2**
Only You Can Do It ... 7" ... Decca ... F11887 ... 1964 ... **£4** ... **£1.50**
Ten Little Lonely Boys ... 7" ... Parlophone ... R4734 ... 1961 ... **£4** ... **£1.50**
Tomorrow Is Another Day ... 7" ... Decca ... F11781 ... 1963 ... **£4** ... **£1.50**
Vernons Girls ... 7" EP ... Decca ... DFE8506 ... 1962 ... **£20** ... **£10**
Vernons Girls ... LP ... Parlophone ... PMC1052 ... 1958 ... **£60** ... **£30**
We Like Boys ... 7" ... Parlophone ... R4624 ... 1960 ... **£6** ... **£2.50**
We Love The Beatles ... 7" ... Decca ... F11807 ... 1964 ... **£6** ... **£2.50**
White Bucks And Saddle Shoes ... 7" ... Parlophone ... R4497 ... 1958 ... **£12** ... **£6**

VERONICA

Veronica Bennett was the lead singer of the Ronettes and, not long after these solo releases, became Mrs Phil Spector.

So Young ... 7" ... Phil Spector ... 1 ... 1964 ... **£40** ... **£20** ... *US*
Why Don't They Let Us Fall In Love? ... 7" ... Phil Spector ... 2 ... 1964 ... **£40** ... **£20** ... *US*

VERSATILE NEWTS

Newtrition ... 7" ... Shanghai ... No.2 ... 1980 ... **£15** ... **£7.50**

VERSATILES

Children Get Ready ... 7" ... Crab ... CRAB1 ... 1968 ... **£5** ... **£2**
Cutting Razor ... 7" ... Dip ... DL5039 ... 1974 ... **£5** ... **£2** ... *Upsetters B side*
Just Can't Win ... 7" ... Amalgamated ... AMG802 ... 1968 ... **£8** ... **£4** ... *Leaders B side*
Lu Lu Bell ... 7" ... Amalgamated ... AMG854 ... 1969 ... **£6** ... **£2.50**
Pick My Pocket ... 7" ... New Beat ... NB060 ... 1970 ... **£4** ... **£1.50** ... *Freedom Singers B side*
Spread Your Bed ... 7" ... Crab ... CRAB5 ... 1969 ... **£5** ... **£2**
Teardrops Falling ... 7" ... Island ... WI3142 ... 1968 ... **£10** ... **£5**
Worries A Yard ... 7" ... Big Shot ... BI520 ... 1969 ... **£5** ... **£2** ... *Val Bennett B side*

VERSATONES

Versatones ... LP ... RCA ... LPM1538 ... 1957 ... **£25** ... **£10** ... *US*

VERTO

Krig/Volubilis ... LP ... Tapioca ... 10007 ... 1976 ... **£10** ... **£4** ... *French*
Reel 19/36 ... LP ... Fleau ... FL7004 ... 1978 ... **£10** ... **£4** ... *French*

VERVE

Bitter Sweet Symphony ... 12" ... Hut ... HUTTR82 ... 1997 ... **£10** ... **£5** ... *promo*
Blue Twilight ... 10" ... Hut ... HUTEN29 ... 1993 ... **£8** ... **£4**
Gravity Grave ... 10" ... Hut ... HUTEN21 ... 1992 ... **£6** ... **£2.50**
Lucky Man ... 7" ... Hut ... HUTLH92 ... 1997 ... **£4** ... **£1.50** ... *jukebox issue*

Make It Till Monday	7"	none	FLEXI1	1993	£8	£4	*clear flexi*
Northern Soul	CD	Hut	DGHUT27	1995	£12	£5	*fold-out cover*
Peel Sessions	CD-s	Strange Fruit	SFMCD214	1992	£5	£2	
She's A Superstar	7"	Hut	HUT16	1992	£4	£1.50	
Urban Hymns	CD	Hut	CDPHUT45	1997	£30	£15	*promo*
Urban Hymns	LP	Hut	HUTLPX45	1997	£15	£6	*double*
Verve EP	CD-s	Hut	HUTUS1	1993	£5	£2	
Voyager	LP	Jolly Roger	JOLLYROGER2	1993	£75	£37.50	*blue vinyl*

VETERANS

Administration	LP		NO1406	1968	£25	£10	*US*

VETTES

Rev-up	LP	MGM	(S)E4193	1963	£12	£5	*US*

VIAN, PATRICK

Bruits Et Temps Analogues	LP	Egg	900541	1978	£10	£4	*French*

VIBRATIONS

Canadian Sunset	7"	Columbia	DB7895	1966	£8	£4	
Greatest Hits	LP	Direction	863644	1969	£15	£6	
Love In Them There Hills	7"	Direction	583511	1968	£5	£2	
Misty	LP	OKeh	OKM4112/ OKS14112	1966	£15	£6	*US*
My Girl Sloopy	7"	London	HLK9875	1964	£8	£4	
New Vibrations	LP	Columbia	SX6106	1966	£25	£10	
One Mint Julep	7"	Columbia	DB8319	1967	£5	£2	
Pick Me	7"	Columbia	DB8175	1967	£10	£5	
Shout	LP	OKeh	OKM4111/ OKS14111	1965	£20	£8	*US*
Talkin' 'Bout Love	7"	Columbia	DB8318	1967	£6	£2.50	
Watusi	7"	Pye	7N25107	1961	£10	£5	
Watusi	LP	Checker	2978	1961	£25	£10	*US*

VIBRATORS

Halfway To Paradise	CD-s	Revolver	REVXD52	1990	£5	£2	

VIBRATORS (2)

Sloop John B	7"	Doctor Bird	DB1036	1966	£10	£5	

VICE CREEMS

Danger Love	7"	Zig Zag	ZZ22001	1979	£4	£1.50	
Won't You Be My Girl	7"	Tiger	GRRRR1	1978	£5	£2	

VICE SQUAD

Evil	7"	fan club		198–	£8	£4	*flexi*
Last Rockers	7"	Riot City	RIOT1	1980	£5	£2	*with poster*

VICE VERSA

Music 4	7"	Neutron	NT001	1980	£8	£4	

VICEROYS

Fat Fish	7"	Blue Cat	BS121	1968	£8	£4	*Octaves B side*
Jump In A Fire	7"	Punch	PH3	1969	£4	£1.50	
Last Night	7"	Studio One	SO2064	1968	£12	£6	
Lips And Tongue	7"	Island	WI3095	1967	£10	£5	*Dawn Penn B side*
Lose And Gain	7"	Studio One	SO2016	1967	£12	£6	*Soul Brothers B side*
Try Hard To Leave	7"	Coxsone	CS7036	1968	£10	£5	
Work It	7"	Crab	CRAB12	1969	£4	£1.50	

VICEROYS (2)

At Granny's Pad	LP	Bolo	BLP8000	1963	£20	£8	*US*

VICIOUS PINK PHENOMENA

My Private Tokyo	12"	Mobile Suit Corp.	CORP12	1982	£8	£4	
My Private Tokyo	7"	Mobile Suit Corp.	CORP1	1982	£5	£2	

VICK, HAROLD

Steppin' Out	LP	Blue Note	BLP/BST84138	1963	£40	£20	

VICKERS, MIKE

Air On A String	7"	Columbia	DB8171	1967	£4	£1.50	
Captain Scarlet And The Mysterons	7"	Columbia	DB8281	1967	£10	£5	
Eleventy One	7"	Columbia	DB7825	1966	£4	£1.50	
I Wish I Were A Group Again	LP	Columbia	SX/SCX6180	1968	£15	£6	
Morgan	7"	Columbia	DB7906	1966	£5	£2	
Puff Adder	7"	Columbia	DB7657	1965	£15	£7.50	

VICKERY, MACK

Fantasy	7"	Top Rank	JAR420	1960	£4	£1.50	

VICKY

Colours Of Love	7"	Philips	B1565	1967	£6	£2.50	
Dance With Me Until Tomorrow	7"	Philips	BF1631	1968	£4	£1.50	
Sunshine Boy	7"	Philips	BF1599	1967	£5	£2	

VICKY & JERRY

Don't Cry	7"	HMV	POP715	1960	£6	£2.50	

VICTIMIZE

Baby Buyer	7"	I.M.E.	IME1	1979	£12	£6	
Where Did The Money Go	7"	I.M.E.	IME2	1980	£12	£6	

VICTIMS OF CHANCE

Victims Of Chance	LP	Crestview	CRS3052		£75	£37.50	US
Victims Of Chance	LP	Stable	SLE8004	1969	£30	£15	

VICTIMS OF PLEASURE

When You're Young	7"	PAM	VOP1	1980	£8	£4	

VICTOR, TONY

Dear One	7"	Decca	F11459	1962	£12	£6	
In The Still Of The Night	7"	Decca	F11708	1963	£4	£1.50	
Thinking Of You	7"	Decca	F11626	1963	£4	£1.50	

VICTORIA

Secret Of The Bloom	LP	Mojo	2466008	1971	£25	£10	
Victoria	LP	Atlantic	2400176	1971	£12	£5	

VICTORIANS

Oh What A Night For Love	7"	Liberty	LIB55693	1964	£6	£2.50	

VICTORS

Reggae Buddy	7"	High Note	HS019	1969	£5	£2	
Things Come Up To Bump	7"	Studio One	SO2077	1969	£12	£6	*Lyrics B side*

VIDELS

Mister Lonely	7"	London	HLI9153	1960	£30	£15	

VIGILANTES

Eclipse	7"	Pye	7N25082	1961	£10	£5	

VIKINGS

Come Into The Parlour	7"	Black Swan	WI430	1964	£10	£5	
Daddy	7"	Island	WI167	1965	£10	£5	
Down By The Riverside	7"	Black Swan	WI423	1964	£10	£5	
Fever	7"	Island	WI117	1963	£10	£5	
Get Ready	7"	Island	WI122	1963	£10	£5	*Don Drummond B side*
Hallelujah	7"	Island	WI065	1962	£10	£5	
Just Got To Be	7"	Island	WI107	1963	£10	£5	
Maggie Don't Leave Me	7"	Island	WI035	1962	£10	£5	
Never Grow Old	7"	Island	WI101	1963	£10	£5	
Six And Seven Books Of Moses	7"	Island	WI075	1963	£10	£5	
Treat Me Bad	7"	Black Swan	WI428	1964	£10	£5	

VIKINGS (2)

Bad News Feeling	7"	Alp	595011	1966	£10	£5	

VILLAGE

Man In The Moon	7"	Head	HDS4002	1969	£30	£15	

VILLAGE STOMPERS

Washington Square	7"	Columbia	DB7123	1963	£4	£1.50	

VINCENT, GENE

Anna Annabelle	7"	Capitol	CL15169	1960	£10	£5	
B I Bickey Bi Bo Bo Go	7"	Capitol	CL14722	1957	£60	£30	
B I Bickey Bi Bo Bo Go	7"	Capitol	CL14722	1957	£75	£37.50	*promo in picture sleeve*
Baby Blue	7"	Capitol	CL14868	1958	£20	£10	
Baby Don't Believe Him	7"	Capitol	CL15243	1962	£10	£5	
Be Bop A Lula	7"	Capitol	CL15264	1962	£10	£5	
Be Bop A Lula	7"	Capitol	CL14599	1956	£20	£10	
Be Bop A Lula	7"	Dandelion	4596	1969	£5	£2	
Best Of Gene Vincent	LP	Capitol	T20957	1967	£12	£5	
Best Of Gene Vincent Vol. 2	LP	Capitol	(S)T21144	1969	£15	£6	
Bird Doggin'	7"	London	HLH10079	1966	£20	£10	
Bluejean Bop	7"	Capitol	CL14637	1956	£40	£20	
Bluejean Bop	LP	Capitol	T764	1957	£60	£30	*turquoise label*
Bluejean Bop	LP	Capitol	T764	1956	£40	£20	*rainbow label*
Bluejean Bop	LP	Capitol	T764	1957	£200	£100	*US*
Capitol Years '56–'63	LP	Charly	BOX108	1987	£50	£25	*10 LP boxed set*
Crazy Beat	7"	Capitol	CL15307	1963	£20	£10	
Crazy Beat Of Gene Vincent	LP	Capitol	T20453	1963	£40	£20	
Crazy Beat Of Gene Vincent Pt 1	7" EP	Capitol	EAP120453	1963	£40	£20	
Crazy Beat Of Gene Vincent Pt 2	7" EP	Capitol	EAP220453	1964	£40	£20	
Crazy Beat Of Gene Vincent Pt 3	7" EP	Capitol	EAP320453	1964	£40	£20	
Crazy Legs	7"	Capitol	CL14693	1957	£60	£30	
Crazy Legs	7"	Capitol	CL14693	1957	£75	£37.50	*promo in picture sleeve*
Crazy Times	LP	MFP	MFP1053	1965	£10	£4	
Crazy Times	LP	Capitol	ST1342	1960	£60	£30	*stereo*

Crazy Times	LP	Capitol	T1342	1960	£150	£75	*US*
Crazy Times	LP	Capitol	T1342	1960	£40	£20	
Dance To The Bop	7"	Capitol	CL14808	1957	£30	£15	
Day The World Turned Blue	7"	Kama Sutra	2013018	1971	£5	£2	
Day The World Turned Blue	LP	Kama Sutra	2316005	1971	£12	£5	
Gene Vincent	LP	London	HAH8333	1967	£30	£15	
Gene Vincent & The Bluecaps	LP	Capitol	T811	1957	£40	£20	*rainbow label*
Gene Vincent & The Blue Caps	LP	Capitol	T811	1957	£60	£30	*turquoise label*
Gene Vincent & The Blue Caps	LP	Capitol	T811	1957	£200	£100	*US*
Gene Vincent Box Set	CD	EMI	CDGV1	1990	£50	£25	*6 CD set*
Gene Vincent Record Date	LP	Capitol	T1059	1958	£40	£20	
Gene Vincent Record Date	LP	Capitol	T1059	1958	£200	£100	*US*
Gene Vincent Record Date Pt 1	7" EP	Capitol	EAP11059	1959	£40	£20	
Gene Vincent Record Date Pt 2	7" EP	Capitol	EAP21059	1959	£60	£30	
Gene Vincent Record Date Pt 3	7" EP	Capitol	EAP31059	1960	£40	£20	
Gene Vincent Rocks & The Bluecaps Roll	LP	Capitol	T970	1958	£40	£20	*rainbow label*
Gene Vincent Rocks & The Blue Caps Roll	LP	Capitol	T970	1958	£60	£30	*turquoise label*
Gene Vincent Rocks & The Blue Caps Roll	LP	Capitol	T970	1958	£200	£100	*US*
Git It	7"	Capitol	CL14935	1958	£20	£10	
Held For Questioning	7"	Capitol	CL15290	1963	£10	£5	
Hot Rod Gang	7" EP	Capitol	EAP1985	1958	£40	£20	
Humpity Dumpity	7"	Columbia	DB7218	1964	£10	£5	
I Got A Baby	7"	Capitol	CL14830	1958	£20	£10	
I'm Back & I'm Proud	LP	Dandelion	63754	1969	£20	£8	
I'm Going Home	7"	Capitol	CL15215	1961	£8	£4	
If You Could Only See Me Today	LP	Kama Sutra	2316009	1972	£12	£5	
If You Want My Loving	7"	Capitol	CL15185	1961	£10	£5	
If You Want My Loving	7" EP	Capitol	EAP120173	1961	£40	£20	
Jumps Giggles And Shouts	7"	Capitol	CL14681	1957	£60	£30	
Jumps Giggles And Shouts	7"	Capitol	CL14681	1957	£75	£37.50	*promo in picture sleeve*
La Den Da Den Da Da	7"	Columbia	DB7293	1964	£10	£5	
Live And Rockin'	7" EP	Emidisc/fan club		1968	£150	£75	
Lonely Street	7"	London	HLH10099	1966	£15	£7.50	
Maybe	7"	Capitol	CL15179	1961	£10	£5	
My Heart	7"	Capitol	CL15115	1960	£8	£4	
Nighttracks	7"	Nighttracks	SFNT001	1987	£6	£2.50	*promo*
Over The Rainbow	7"	Capitol	CL15000	1959	£10	£5	
Pistol Packing Mama	7"	Capitol	CL15136	1960	£8	£4	
Private Detective	7"	Columbia	DB7343	1964	£10	£5	
Race With The Devil	7"	Capitol	CL14628	1956	£60	£30	
Race With The Devil	7" EP	Capitol	EAP120354	1962	£40	£20	
Rainy Day Sunshine	7" EP	Rollin' Danny	RD1	1979	£10	£5	
Rainy Day Sunshine	7" EP	Magnum Force	MFEP003	1981	£6	£2.50	
Right Now	7"	Capitol	CL15053	1959	£10	£5	
Rip It Up	7"	Capitol	CL15307	1963	£150	£75	*demo*
Rocky Road Blues	7"	Capitol	CL14908	1958	£20	£10	
Roll Over Beethoven	7"	BBC	BEEB001	1974	£4	£1.50	
Say Mama	7"	Capitol	CL15546	1968	£6	£2.50	
Say Mama	7"	Capitol	CL15906	1977	£4	£1.50	
Say Mama	7"	Capitol	CL14974	1959	£15	£7.50	
Shakin' Up A Storm	LP	Columbia	33SX1646	1964	£40	£20	
She She Little Sheila	7"	Capitol	CL15202	1961	£10	£5	
Sounds Like Gene Vincent	LP	Capitol	T1207	1959	£50	£25	
Sounds Like Gene Vincent	LP	Capitol	T1207	1959	£150	£75	*US*
Story Of The Rockers	7"	Spark	SRL1091	1973	£4	£1.50	
Summertime	7"	Capitol	CL15035	1959	£10	£5	
Temptation Baby	7"	Columbia	DB7174	1963	£10	£5	
True To You	7" EP	Capitol	EAP120461	1963	£40	£20	
Unchained Melody	7"	Capitol	CL15231	1961	£10	£5	
Walkin' Home From School	7"	Capitol	CL14830	1958	£40	£20	*promo in picture sleeve*
Wear My Ring	7"	Capitol	CL14763	1957	£25	£12.50	
White Lightning	7"	Dandelion	4974	1970	£6	£2.50	
Wild Cat	7"	Capitol	CL15099	1959	£8	£4	

VINCI, CAROLE

Vivre	7"	EMI	EMI2801	1978	£5	£2	

VINE, JOEY

Down And Out	7"	Immediate	IM017	1965	£10	£5	

VINEGAR

Vinegar	LP	Phonofoly	WP710101	1971	£150	£75	*German*

VINEGAR JOE

Rock'n'Roll Gypsies	LP	Island	ILPS9214	1972	£10	£4	
Six Star General	LP	Island	ILPS9262	1973	£10	£4	
Vinegar Joe	LP	Island	ILPS9183	1972	£12	£5	

VINNEGAR, LEROY

Leroy Walks	LP	Contemporary	LAC12136	1959	£20	£8	

VINSON, EDDIE 'CLEANHEAD'

Title	Format	Label	Number	Year	Mint	VG	Notes
Backdoor Blues	LP	Riverside	3502	196–	£20	£8	US
Cherry Red	LP	BluesWay	BL(S)6007	1967	£10	£4	US
Eddie Cleanhead Vinson Sings	LP	Bethlehem	BCP5005	196–	£15	£6	US
Eddie Cleanhead Vinson Sings	LP	Aamco	312	196–	£10	£4	US
Jump And Grunt	78	Vogue	V2023	1951	£10	£5	
Original Cleanhead	LP	Philips	6369406	1972	£10	£4	

VINSON, EDDIE 'CLEANHEAD' & JIMMY WITHERSPOON

Title	Format	Label	Number	Year	Mint	VG	Notes
Battle Of The Blues Vol. 3	LP	King	634	1959	£300	£180	US

VINSTRICK, V.

Title	Format	Label	Number	Year	Mint	VG	Notes
Love Is Not A Game	7"	Doctor Bird	DB1167	1968	£10	£5	Cinderella B side

VINTON, BOBBY

Title	Format	Label	Number	Year	Mint	VG	Notes
Blue On Blue	LP	Columbia	33SX1566	1963	£15	£6	
Blue Velvet	7"	Columbia	DB7110	1963	£6	£2.50	
Blue Velvet	CD-s	Epic	6505242	1990	£5	£2	
Corrine Corrina	7"	Fontana	H307	1961	£6	£2.50	
Dancing At The Hop	LP	Epic	LN3727/LN579	1960	£20	£8	US
Greatest Hits Of The Greatest Groups	LP	Epic	LN24049/ BN26049	1963	£20	£8	US
I Love The Way You Are	7"	London	HLU9592	1962	£6	£2.50	
Mr Lonely	7"	Columbia	DB7422	1964	£10	£5	
My Heart Belongs To Only You	LP	Columbia	33SX1611	1963	£15	£6	
Roses Are Red	CD-s	Epic	6564672	1990	£5	£2	
Sings The Big Ones	LP	Columbia	33SX1517	1963	£15	£6	
Songs Of Christmas	7" EP	Columbia	SEG8363	1964	£15	£7.50	
Tell Me Why	LP	Columbia	33SX1649	1965	£15	£6	
Young In Heart	7" EP	Columbia	SEG8212	1962	£12	£6	
Young Man With A Big Band	LP	Epic	LN3780/LN597	1961	£20	£8	US

VINYL, MATT

Title	Format	Label	Number	Year	Mint	VG	Notes
Useless Tasks	7"	Housewife's Choice		1977	£5	£2	

VIOLATORS

Title	Format	Label	Number	Year	Mint	VG	Notes
NY Ripper	7"	Violators	FRS0022	1980	£5	£2	

VIOLATORS (2)

Title	Format	Label	Number	Year	Mint	VG	Notes
Gangland	7"	No Future	OI9	1982	£5	£2	
Summer Of '81	7"	No Future	OI19	1982	£5	£2	

VIOLENTS

Title	Format	Label	Number	Year	Mint	VG	Notes
Alpens Ros	LP	Sonet	9926	1967	£10	£4	Swedish
Complete '61–'64	LP	Sonet	SLPD2643	1979	£20	£8	Swedish double
Ghia	7"	HMV	POP1130	1963	£6	£2.50	
Live At The Star-Club	LP	Sonet	9913	1966	£10	£4	Swedish
String Of Hits	LP	Philips	107400SNL	1966	£20	£8	Swedish

VIPERS

Title	Format	Label	Number	Year	Mint	VG	Notes
I've Got You	7"	Mulligan	LUNS718	1978	£5	£2	

VIPERS SKIFFLE GROUP

Title	Format	Label	Number	Year	Mint	VG	Notes
Coffee Bar Session	10" LP	Parlophone	PMD1050	1957	£30	£15	
Cumberland Gap	7"	Parlophone	R4289	1957	£8	£4	
Don't You Rock Me Daddyo	7"	Parlophone	R4261	1957	£10	£5	
Homing Bird	7"	Parlophone	R4351	1957	£6	£2.50	
Jim Dandy	7"	Parlophone	R4286	1957	£10	£5	
Make Ready For Love	7"	Parlophone	R4435	1958	£6	£2.50	
No Other Baby	7"	Parlophone	R4393	1958	£6	£2.50	
Pick A Bale Of Cotton	7"	Parlophone	R4238	1956	£10	£5	
Skiffle Music Vol. 1	7" EP	Parlophone	GEP8615	1957	£10	£5	
Skiffle Music Vol. 2	7" EP	Parlophone	GEP8626	1957	£10	£5	
Skiffle Party	7"	Parlophone	R4371	1957	£6	£2.50	
Skiffling Along With The Vipers	7" EP	Parlophone	GEP8655	1957	£15	£7.50	
Streamline Train	7"	Parlophone	R4308	1957	£6	£2.50	
Summertime Blues	7"	Parlophone	R4484	1958	£15	£7.50	

VIPPS

Title	Format	Label	Number	Year	Mint	VG	Notes
Wintertime	7"	CBS	202031	1966	£30	£15	

V.I.P.s

Title	Format	Label	Number	Year	Mint	VG	Notes
Don't Keep Shouting At Me	7"	RCA	RCA1427	1964	£40	£20	
I Wanna Be Free	7"	Island	WI3003	1966	£30	£15	
I Wanna Be Free	7" EP	Fontana	460982	1966	£75	£37.50	French
Mercy Mercy	7"	Philips	40387	1966	£30	£15	US
Stagger Lee	7" EP	Fontana	460219	1967	£75	£37.50	French
Straight Down To The Bottom	7"	Island	WIP6005	1967	£30	£15	
Straight Down To The Bottom	7" EP	Fontana	460996	1967	£75	£37.50	French
What's That Sound	7" EP	Fontana	460238	1968	£75	£37.50	French

V.I.P.s (2)

Title	Format	Label	Number	Year	Mint	VG	Notes
Music For Funsters	7"	Bust	SOL3	1978	£5	£2	

VIRGIL BROTHERS

Title	Format	Label	Number	Year	Mint	VG	Notes
Temptation 'Bout To Get Me	7"	Parlophone	R5787	1969	£4	£1.50	

VIRGIN PRUNES

Heresie	10"	Baby	BABY011	1987	£8	£3	double, clear vinyl
In The Grey Light	7"	Rough Trade	RT072	1981	£4	£1.50	blue picture sleeve
New Form Of Beauty	7"/ 10"/ 12"	Rough Trade	RT089-91	1981	£20	£10	3 records, boxed
Twenty Tens	7"	Baby	BABY001	1981	£6	£2.50	

VIRGIN SLEEP

Love	7"	Deram	DM146	1967	£25	£12.50	
Secret	7"	Deram	DM173	1968	£25	£12.50	

VIRGINIA WOLVES

Stay	7"	Stateside	SS563	1966	£15	£7.50	

VIRGINIANS

Limbo Baby	7"	Pye	7N25175	1963	£4	£1.50	

VIRTUES

Guitar Boogie Shuffle	7"	HMV	POP621	1959	£10	£5	
Guitar Boogie Shuffle	LP	Wynne	WLP111	1960	£25	£10	US
Guitar Boogie Shuffle	LP	Strand	SL1061	1960	£25	£10	US
Shuffling Along	7"	HMV	POP637	1959	£10	£5	

VIRTUES (2)

High Tide	7"	Doctor Bird	DB1164	1968	£10	£5	
Your Wife And Your Mother	7"	Island	WI196	1965	£10	£5	

VIRTUOSA, FRANK

Rollin' And Rockin'	7"	Melodisc	MEL1386	1958	£20	£10	red label
Rollin' And Rockin'	7"	Melodisc	MEL1386	1958	£8	£4	green label

VIRUS

Revelation	LP	BASF	CRC015	1971	£25	£10	German
Thoughts	LP	Pilz	20211029	1971	£25	£10	German

VISAGE

Der Amboss	12"	Polydor	POSPV523	1982	£10	£5	promo
Mind Of A Toy	CD-s	Polydor	0800122	1988	£15	£7.50	CD video
Pleasure Boys	12"	Polydor	POSPX523	1982	£10	£5	
Pleasure Boys	7"	Polydor	POSPP523	1982	£5	£2	picture disc

VISCOUNTS

Chug A Lug	7"	Top Rank	JAR388	1960	£8	£4	
Harlem Nocturne	7"	Top Rank	JAR254	1959	£8	£4	
Harlem Nocturne	7"	Stateside	SS468	1965	£6	£2.50	
Harlem Nocturne	LP	Amy	(S)8008	1965	£25	£10	US
Night Train	7"	Top Rank	JAR502	1960	£6	£2.50	
Viscounts	LP	Madison	1001	1960	£50	£25	US
Viscounts' Rock	7" EP	Top Rank	JKP3005	1961	£60	£30	

VISCOUNTS (2)

The Viscounts were a vocal trio, whose easy harmonies were typical of the kind of thing the Beatles blew away. One of the group, however, was Gordon Mills, who later made himself a very comfortable living as manager of both Tom Jones and Engelbert Humperdinck.

Money Is The Root Of All Evil	7"	Pye	7N15323	1961	£4	£1.50	
Rockin' Little Angel	7"	Pye	7N15249	1960	£5	£2	
Shortnin' Bread	7"	Pye	7N15287	1960	£4	£1.50	
Viscounts' Hit Parade	7" EP	Pye	NEP24132	1960	£20	£10	

VISION

Lucifer's Friend	7"	MVM	2885	1983	£5	£2	

VISITORS

Empty Rooms	7"	Departure	RAPTURE1	1980	£4	£1.50	

VISITORS (2)

Take It Or Leave It	7"	NRG	SRTSNRG002	1978	£12	£6	

VITA NOVA

Vita Nova	LP	Life	LS5010	1972	£75	£37.50	Austrian

VITOUS, MIROSLAV

Mountain In The Clouds	LP	Atlantic	SD1622	1973	£12	£5	US

VIXEN

Crying	7"	EMI	MTPD60	1988	£4	£1.50	shaped picture disc
Edge Of A Broken Heart	7"	EMI	MTPD48	1988	£4	£1.50	shaped picture disc
Love Made Me	7"	EMI	MTPD66	1991	£4	£1.50	shaped picture disc
Vixen's Debut Album	LP	EMI	MTL1028	1988	£15	£6	with 'Charmed Life'

VLADO & ISOLDA

Ciao Amore	7"	Ariola	106500	1984	£5	£2	

VOGUES

Younger Girl	7"	Columbia	DB7985	1966	£6	£2.50	

VOGUES (2)

Five O'Clock World	7"	London	HLU10014	1966	**£5**	**£2**	
Five O'Clock World	7"	London	HLG10247	1969	**£4**	**£1.50**	
Five O'Clock World	7" EP	London	RE10176	1966	**£10**	**£5**	*French*
Five O'Clock World	LP	Co&Ce	1230	1966	**£20**	**£8**	*US*
Magic Town	7"	King	KG1035	1966	**£4**	**£1.50**	
Meet The Vogues	LP	Co&Ce	1229	1965	**£20**	**£8**	*US*
Please Mr Sun	7" EP	Vogue	INT18104	1966	**£10**	**£5**	*French*
You're The One	7"	London	HLU9996	1965	**£5**	**£2**	
You're The One	LP	King	KGL4003	1966	**£15**	**£6**	

VOICE

Train To Disaster	7"	Mercury	MF905	1965	**£125**	**£62.50**	

VOICE OF THE BEEHIVE

Don't Call Me Baby	CD-s	London	LONCD175	1988	**£5**	**£2**	
Don't Call Me Baby	CD-s	Polygram	0804842	1988	**£10**	**£5**	*CD video*
Evening Show EP	CD-s	Strange Fruit	SFNTCD017	1989	**£5**	**£2**	
I Say Nothing	CD-s	London	LONCD190	1988	**£5**	**£2**	
I Walk The Earth	CD-s	London	LONCD169	1988	**£5**	**£2**	
I Walk The Earth	CD-s	London	LONCD206	1988	**£5**	**£2**	
Man In The Moon	CD-s	London	LONCD209	1988	**£5**	**£2**	

VOICES

Rock & Roll Hit Parade	7"	Beltona	BL2667	1956	**£5**	**£2**	

VOICES OF EAST HARLEM

Right On Be Free	LP	Elektra	2469007	1970	**£12**	**£5**	

VOIDS

Come On Out	7"	Polydor	BM56073	1966	**£50**	**£25**	

VOIGHT, WES

I'm Moving In	7"	Parlophone	R4586	1959	**£75**	**£37.50**	

VOIZ

Boanerges	LP	Grapevine	GRA110	1977	**£75**	**£37.50**	

VOKES, HOWARD COUNTRY BOYS

Howard Vokes Country Boys	7" EP	Starlite	STEP27	1962	**£12**	**£6**	
Howard Vokes Country Boys	7" EP	Starlite	GRK508	1966	**£8**	**£4**	
Mountain Guitar	7" EP	Starlite	STEP37	1963	**£10**	**£5**	

VOLCANOES

Polaris	7"	Philips	BF1246	1963	**£6**	**£2.50**	
Ruby Duby Du	7"	Philips	PB1098	1961	**£8**	**£4**	
Tightrope	7"	Philips	PB1113	1961	**£8**	**£4**	
Volcanoes	7" EP	Philips	BBE12432	1960	**£60**	**£30**	

VOLMAN, MARK & HOWARD KAYLAN

Phlorescent Leech And Eddie	LP	Reprise	K44201	1972	**£10**	**£4**	

VOLUMES

Dreams	7"	Fontana	270109TF	1962	**£25**	**£12.50**	
I Just Can't Help Myself	7"	Pama	PM755	1968	**£250**	**£150**	*test pressing, best auctioned*
Sandra	7"	London	HL9733	1963	**£30**	**£15**	

VON TRAPP FAMILY

Brand New Thrill	7"	Woronzow	WOO1	1980	**£30**	**£15**	

VONTASTICS

Day Tripper	7"	Chess	CRS8043	1966	**£8**	**£4**	
Lady Love	7"	Stateside	SS2002	1967	**£15**	**£7.50**	

VOOMINS

If You Don't Come Back	7"	Polydor	56001	1965	**£6**	**£2.50**	

VOXPOPPERS

Last Drag	7"	Mercury	7MT202	1958	**£25**	**£12.50**	
Voxpoppers	7" EP	Mercury	MEP9533	1958	**£75**	**£37.50**	

VULCANS

Star Trek	LP	Trojan	TRLS53	1971	**£12**	**£5**	

VULCAN'S HAMMER

True Hearts And Sound Bottoms	LP	Brown	BVH1	1973	**£600**	**£400**	

W

W. GIMMICS

Hot Rods	7" EP	Polydor	EPH27125	1965	**£20**	**£10**	

W12 SPOTS

Sid Never Did	7"	Shepherds Bush	SB1	197–	**£8**	**£4**	*Cosmic Punks B side*

WACHTOLZ, BARBEL

Ich Hab Musik Im Blut	LP	Amiga	850015	1964	**£25**	**£10**	*East German*

WACKERS

Girl Who Wanted Fame	7"	Piccadilly	7N35210	1964	**£4**	**£1.50**	
I Wonder Why	7"	Oriole	CB1902	1964	**£6**	**£2.50**	
Love Or Money	7"	Piccadilly	7N35195	1964	**£4**	**£1.50**	

WADE, ADAM

Adam And Evening	LP	HMV	CLP1451	1961	**£20**	**£8**	
And Then Came Adam	7" EP	HMV	7EG8620	1960	**£10**	**£5**	
And Then Came Adam	LP	Coed	LPC902	1960	**£20**	**£8**	*US*
Four Film Songs	7" EP	Columbia	SEG8316	1964	**£10**	**£5**	

WADE, CLIFF

You've Never Been To My House	7"	Morgan Bluetown	BT1S	1969	**£5**	**£2**	

WADE, WAYNE

Dancing Time	LP	Grove Music	GMCP3	1979	**£10**	**£4**	

WADE, WELLINGTON

Let's Turkey Trot	7"	Oriole	CB1857	1963	**£10**	**£5**	

WAGNER, ADRIAN

Distance Between Us	LP	Atlantic	K50082	1974	**£10**	**£4**	

WAGNER, ROBERT

Almost Eighteen	7"	London	HLU8491	1957	**£12**	**£6**	

WAGON, CHUCK

Rock'n'Roll Won't Go Away	7"	A&M	AMS7450	1979	**£5**	**£2**	*black or purple vinyl*

WAGONER, PORTER

Blue Grass Story	LP	RCA	RD7693	1965	**£15**	**£6**	
Little Slice Of Life	7" EP	RCA	RCX7157	1964	**£10**	**£5**	
Satisfied Mind	LP	RCA	LPM1358	1956	**£20**	**£8**	*US*
Y'All Come	7" EP	RCA	RCX7158	1964	**£10**	**£5**	

WAILER, BUNNY

Blackheart Man	LP	Island	ILPS9415	1976	**£12**	**£5**	
Protest	LP	Island	ILPS9512	1978	**£12**	**£5**	
Sings The Wailers	LP	Island	ILPS9629	1981	**£10**	**£4**	

WAILERS

At The Castle	LP	Etiquette	ALB01	1962	**£60**	**£30**	*US*
Mau Mau	7"	London	HL8994	1959	**£100**	**£50**	*tri-centre*
Out Of Our Tree	LP	Etiquette	ALB026	1966	**£25**	**£10**	*US*
Outburst	LP	United Artists	UAL3557/ UAS6557	1966	**£25**	**£10**	*US*
Tall Cool One	7"	London	HL9892	1964	**£6**	**£2.50**	
Tall Cool One	7"	London	HL8958	1959	**£12**	**£6**	
Tall Cool One	LP	Golden Crest	CR3075	1959	**£75**	**£37.50**	*US*
Tall Cool One	LP	Imperial	LP9262/12262	1964	**£30**	**£15**	*US*
Wailers And Company	LP	Etiquette	ALB022	1963	**£60**	**£30**	*US*
Wailers Wailers Everywhere	LP	Etiquette	ALB023	1965	**£30**	**£15**	*US*
Walkin' Through People	LP	Bell	6016	1968	**£20**	**£8**	*US*

WAILING SOULS

Back Out	7"	Banana	BA307	1970	**£6**	**£2.50**	
Dungeon	7"	Punch	PH106	1972	**£5**	**£2**	*Nora Dean B side*
Harbour Shark	7"	Green Door	GD4014	1971	**£5**	**£2**	
Row Fisherman Row	7"	Banana	BA305	1970	**£6**	**£2.50**	
Walk Walk Walk	7"	Banana	BA335	1971	**£6**	**£2.50**	*King Sporty B side*

WAINER, CHERRY

Cherry Wainer	7" EP	Pye	NEP24099	1959	£15	**£7.50**	
Happy Organ	7"	Pye	7N15197	1959	£4	**£1.50**	
I'll Walk The Line	7"	Top Rank	JAR253	1959	£4	**£1.50**	
Itchy Twitchy Feeling	7"	Pye	7N15161	1958	£6	**£2.50**	
Money	7"	Columbia	DB4528	1960	£15	**£7.50**	
Sleepwalk	7"	Honey Hit	TB128	1963	£5	**£2**	*picture sleeve*
Valencia	7"	Pye	7N15170	1958	£5	**£2**	
Waltzes In Springtime	LP	Top Rank	BUY042	1960	£10	**£4**	

WAINMAN, PHIL

Hear Me A Drummer Man	7"	Columbia	DB7615	1965	£6	**£2.50**	

WAINWRIGHT III, LOUDON

Album I	LP	Atlantic	2400103	1971	£10	**£4**	

WAITING FOR THE SUN

Waiting For The Sun	LP	Profile	GMOR167	1978	£100	**£50**	

WAITS, TOM

Bone Machine Operators' Manual	CD	Island		1992	£20	**£8**	*US interview promo*
Closing Time	LP	Asylum	SYL9007	1973	£10	**£4**	
Nighthawks At The Diner	LP	Asylum	SYSP903	1975	£12	**£5**	*double*

WAKE

23.59	LP	Carnaby	CNLS6005	1970	£100	**£50**	
Angelina	7"	Pye	7N17813	1969	£8	**£4**	
Boys In The Band	7"	Carnaby	CNS4014	1970	£8	**£4**	
Linda	7"	Carnaby	6151001	1971	£8	**£4**	
Live Today Little Girl	7"	Carnaby	CNS4010	1970	£8	**£4**	
Noah	7"	Carnaby	CNS4016	1971	£8	**£4**	

WAKE (2)

On Our Honeymoon	7"	Scanlist	SCN1	1982	£10	**£5**	

WAKELY, JIMMY

Are You Mine	7"	Vogue Coral	Q72125	1956	£8	**£4**	
Are You Satisfied	7"	Brunswick	05542	1956	£8	**£4**	
Christmas On The Range	10" LP	Capitol	H9004	195–	£20	**£8**	*US*
Country Million Sellers	LP	Shasta	SHLP501	1959	£12	**£5**	*US*
Enter And Rest And Pray	LP	Decca	DL8680	1957	£15	**£6**	*US*
Folsom Prison Blues	7"	Brunswick	05563	1956	£10	**£5**	
Jimmy Wakely Sings	LP	Shasta	SHLP505	1960	£12	**£5**	*US*
Merry Christmas	LP	Shasta	SHLP502	1959	£12	**£5**	*US*
Santa Fe Trail	LP	Brunswick	LAT8179	1957	£15	**£6**	
Songs Of The West	10" LP	Capitol	H4008	195–	£20	**£8**	*US*

WAKEMAN, RICK

Those critics who dismiss Rick Wakeman's music as no more than Muzak will be delighted if they hear the scarce *Piano Vibrations*, as this really is a Muzak LP. Nevertheless, the modest value achieved by this rarity reflects not its paucity of musical imagination, but Rick Wakeman's limited status as a collectable artist. Many records as bland as this do attain high values.

Journey To The Centre Of The Earth	CD	Mobile Fidelity	MFCD848	1987	£15	**£6**	*US audiophile*
Journey To The Centre Of The Earth	LP	A&M	QU53621	1975	£15	**£6**	*US quad*
Myths And Legends Of King Arthur	LP	A&M	QU54515	1975	£15	**£6**	*US quad*
Piano Vibrations	LP	Polydor	2460135	1971	£12	**£5**	
Six Wives Of Henry VIII	LP	A&M	QU54361	1973	£15	**£6**	*US quad*
Spider	7"	WEA	K18354	1980	£5	**£2**	*picture sleeve*
Twentieth Anniversary	CD	A&M	RWCD20	1989	£50	**£25**	*4 CD box set*

WALCOTT, COLLIN

Cloud Dance	LP	ECM	ECM1062ST	1975	£10	**£4**	

WALDRON, MAL

Free At Last	LP	ECM	ECM1001ST	1970	£12	**£5**	
Quest	LP	XTRA	XTRA5006	1966	£15	**£6**	

WALHAM GREEN EAST WAPPING C.C.R.B.E. ASSOCIATION

Sorry Mr Green	7"	Columbia	DB8426	1968	£40	**£20**	

WALKER, BILLY

Certain Girl	7"	Columbia	DB7724	1965	£4	**£1.50**	
Forever	7"	Philips	PB1001	1960	£4	**£1.50**	

WALKER, CLINT

Inspiration	7" EP	Warner Bros	WEP6006/ WSEP2006	1960	£6	**£2.50**	

WALKER, DAVID

Ring The Changes	7"	RCA	RCA1664	1968	£15	**£7.50**	

WALKER, GARY

Album No. 1	LP	Philips	SFX7133	1970	£100	**£50**	*Japanese, credited to Gary Walker & The Rain*

Come In You'll Get Pneumonia	7"	Philips	BF1740	1968	**£30**	**£15**	
Here's Gary	7" EP	CBS	EP5742	1966	**£25**	**£12.50**	
Spooky	7"	Polydor	56237	1968	**£6**	**£2.50**	
Twinkie Lee	7"	CBS	202081	1966	**£6**	**£2.50**	
You Don't Love Me	7"	CBS	202036	1966	**£6**	**£2.50**	

WALKER, JACKIE

Oh Lonesome Me	7"	London	HLP8588	1958	**£150**	**£75**	

WALKER, JERRY JEFF

Driftin' Way Of Life	LP	Vanguard	SVRL19049	1969	**£10**	**£4**	
Jerry Jeff Walker	LP	Atco	SD33297	1969	**£12**	**£5**	*US*
Mr Bojangles	7"	Atlantic	584200	1968	**£4**	**£1.50**	
Mr Bojangles	LP	Atco	SD33259	1968	**£12**	**£5**	*US*

WALKER, JOHN

Anabella	7"	Philips	BF1593	1967	**£10**	**£5**	
If You Go Away	LP	Philips	(S)BL7829	1967	**£25**	**£10**	
Solo John – Solo Scott	7" EP	Philips	BE12597	1966	**£10**	**£5**	*1 side by Scott Walker*
This Is John Walker	LP	Carnaby	CNLS6001	1969	**£20**	**£8**	

WALKER, JUNIOR & THE ALL STARS

Cleo's Mood	7"	Tamla Motown	TMG550	1966	**£12**	**£6**	
Come See About Me	7"	Tamla Motown	TMG637	1968	**£5**	**£2**	
Do The Boomerang	7"	Tamla Motown	TMG520	1965	**£40**	**£20**	
Gasssss	LP	Tamla Motown	STML11167	1970	**£10**	**£4**	
Greatest Hits	LP	Tamla Motown	(S)TML11120	1969	**£10**	**£4**	
Hip City	7"	Tamla Motown	TMG667	1968	**£6**	**£2.50**	
Home Cookin'	7"	Tamla Motown	TMG682	1969	**£5**	**£2**	
Home Cookin'	LP	Tamla Motown	(S)TML11097	1969	**£15**	**£6**	
How Sweet It Is	7"	Tamla Motown	TMG571	1966	**£6**	**£2.50**	
Live	LP	Tamla Motown	STML11152	1970	**£12**	**£5**	
Money	7"	Tamla Motown	TMG586	1966	**£8**	**£4**	
Moody Jr	LP	Tamla Motown	STML11211	1972	**£10**	**£4**	
Pucker Up Buttercup	7"	Tamla Motown	TMG596	1967	**£10**	**£5**	
Rainbow Funk	LP	Tamla Motown	STML11198	1972	**£10**	**£4**	
Road Runner	7"	Tamla Motown	TMG559	1966	**£6**	**£2.50**	
Road Runner	LP	Tamla Motown	(S)TML11038	1966	**£15**	**£6**	
Shake & Fingerpop	7" EP	Tamla Motown	TME2013	1966	**£25**	**£12.50**	
Shake And Fingerpop	7"	Tamla Motown	TMG529	1965	**£15**	**£7.50**	
Shotgun	7"	Tamla Motown	TMG509	1965	**£20**	**£10**	
Shotgun	LP	Tamla Motown	TML11017	1965	**£25**	**£10**	
Soul Session	LP	Tamla Motown	TML11029	1966	**£20**	**£8**	
These Eyes	7"	Tamla Motown	TMG727	1970	**£4**	**£1.50**	
These Eyes	LP	Tamla Motown	(S)TML11140	1970	**£15**	**£6**	
Way Back Home	7"	Tamla Motown	TMG857	1973	**£4**	**£1.50**	

WALKER, KARL & THE ALL STARS

One Minute To Zero	7"	Rymska	RA103	1966	**£12**	**£6**	

WALKER, LUCILLE

Best Of Lucille Walker	LP	Checker	1428	1957	**£20**	**£8**	*US*

WALKER, ROBERT

Excuse Me, It's My First LSD Trip	LP	GNP Crescendo	2027	1966	**£30**	**£15**	*US*

WALKER, RONNIE

It's A Good Feeling	7"	Stateside	SS2151	1969	**£5**	**£2**	

WALKER, SCOTT

Scott Walker has followed an unusual musical course. He has the voice and the musical inclinations of a cabaret singer, yet he writes much of his own material in a style which is too unsettling and too idiosyncratic to fit comfortably into a cabaret setting. His tendency towards hermit-like behaviour has added to his enigma and created a climate within which his cult following is steadily increasing. As a result, the LPs he made in the years after the demise of the Walker Brothers are becoming more and more collectable.

Any Day Now	LP	Philips	6308148	1973	**£30**	**£15**	
Best Of Scott Vol. 1	LP	Philips	SBL7910	1969	**£10**	**£4**	
Fire Escape In The Sky	LP	Zoo	ZOO2	1981	**£15**	**£6**	
Great Scott	cass	Philips	MCP1006	1967	**£15**	**£6**	
Jackie	7"	Philips	BF1628	1967	**£6**	**£2.50**	
Joanna	7"	Philips	BF1662	1968	**£6**	**£2.50**	
Looking Back With Scott Walker	LP	Ember	EMB3393	1968	**£15**	**£6**	
Mathilde	7" EP	Philips	438402	1967	**£20**	**£10**	*French*
Moviegoer	LP	Philips	6308127	1972	**£30**	**£15**	
Romantic Scott Walker	LP	Philips	6850013	1973	**£25**	**£10**	
Scott	LP	Philips	BL7816	1967	**£12**	**£5**	
Scott	LP	Philips	SBL7816	1967	**£15**	**£6**	*stereo*
Scott 2	LP	Philips	BL7840	1968	**£12**	**£5**	
Scott 2	LP	Philips	BL7840	1968	**£20**	**£8**	*with picture insert*
Scott 2	LP	Philips	SBL7840	1968	**£20**	**£8**	*stereo*
Scott 2	LP	Philips	SBL7840	1968	**£25**	**£10**	*with picture insert, stereo*
Scott 3	LP	Philips	SBL7882	1969	**£30**	**£15**	
Scott 4	LP	Philips	SBL7913	1969	**£50**	**£25**	
Sings Songs From His TV Series	LP	Philips	SBL7900	1969	**£10**	**£4**	
Spotlight On Scott Walker	LP	Philips	6625017	1976	**£15**	**£6**	*double*
Stretch	LP	CBS	65725	1973	**£20**	**£8**	
Sun Ain't Gonna Shine Anymore	CD-s	Fontana	WALKC1	1991	**£5**	**£2**	
Terrific	LP	Philips	6856022	197–	**£25**	**£10**	
Till The Band Comes In	LP	Philips	6308035	1970	**£50**	**£25**	
Tilt Interview CD	CD	Fontana	SWINT1	1995	**£30**	**£15**	*promo*
We Had It All	LP	CBS	80254	1974	**£15**	**£6**	

WALKER, T-BONE

Blues Of T-Bone Walker	LP	MFP	MFP1043	1965	**£15**	**£6**	
Classics In Jazz	10" LP	Capitol	LC6681	1954	**£40**	**£20**	
Classics In Jazz	10" LP	Capitol	H370	1953	**£75**	**£37.50**	*US*
Classics In Jazz	LP	Capitol	T370	1956	**£50**	**£25**	*US*
Funky Town	LP	Stateside	(S)SL10265	1969	**£15**	**£6**	
Hustle Is On	78	London	HL8087	1954	**£15**	**£7.50**	
I Get So Weary	LP	Imperial	9146	1961	**£25**	**£10**	*US*
Party Girl	7"	Liberty	LIB12018	1965	**£10**	**£5**	
Singing The Blues	LP	Imperial	9116	1960	**£25**	**£10**	*US*
Singing The Blues	LP	Liberty	LBY3057	1966	**£30**	**£15**	
Sings The Blues	LP	Imperial	9098	1959	**£25**	**£10**	*US*
Sings The Blues	LP	Liberty	LBY4047	1963	**£30**	**£15**	
Stormy Monday Blues	LP	Stateside	(S)SL10223	1968	**£15**	**£6**	
T B Walker	LP	Capitol	T1958	1963	**£25**	**£10**	
T-Bone Blues	LP	Atlantic	SD8020	196–	**£15**	**£6**	*US, red label*
T-Bone Blues	LP	Atlantic	SD8020	1959	**£30**	**£15**	*US, black label*
Travellin' Blues	7" EP	London	REP1404	1963	**£50**	**£25**	
Truth	LP	MCA	MUPS331	1968	**£12**	**£5**	

WALKER BROTHERS

Scott Engel, John Morse and Gary Leeds were not called Walker and were not brothers. Gary Leeds did not even seem to do very much – he had no voice to match the rich tones of the other two, and so he sat behind a drum kit and pretended (very unconvincingly) that drumming was a vital ingredient in the group's music. The cult interest in Scott Walker's solo music has extended only slightly towards the Walker Brothers, whose music was too popular to ever acquire the attraction of exclusivity and which has none of the disturbing quality of Scott's best work.

Another Tear Falls	7"	Philips	BF1514	1966	**£4**	**£1.50**	
But I Do	7" EP	Philips	434560	1965	**£10**	**£5**	*French*
Deadlier Than The Male	7"	Philips	BF1537	1966	**£4**	**£1.50**	
Fabulous Walker Brothers	LP	Wing	WL1188	1968	**£10**	**£4**	
I Need You	7" EP	Philips	BE12596	1966	**£8**	**£4**	
Images	LP	Philips	(S)BL7770	1967	**£10**	**£4**	
Love Her	7"	Philips	BF1409	1965	**£4**	**£1.50**	
My Ship Is Coming In	7" EP	Philips	434564	1965	**£10**	**£5**	*French*
Portrait	LP	Philips	(S)BL7732	1966	**£10**	**£4**	
Portrait	LP	Philips	(S)BL7732	1966	**£15**	**£6**	*with photo*
Pretty Girls Everywhere	7"	Philips	BF1401	1965	**£6**	**£2.50**	
Stay With Me Baby	7"	Philips	BF1548	1967	**£4**	**£1.50**	
Story	LP	Philips	DBL002	1967	**£12**	**£5**	*double*
Sun Ain't Gonna Shine Anymore	7" EP	Philips	434567	1966	**£10**	**£5**	*French*
Take It Easy	LP	Philips	BL7691	1965	**£10**	**£4**	
Walker Brothers	7" EP	Philips	BE12603	1967	**£25**	**£12.50**	*demo*
Walking In The Rain	7"	Philips	BF1576	1967	**£4**	**£1.50**	

WALKIE TALKIES

Rich And Nasty	7"	Sire	SIR4023	1979	**£4**	**£1.50**	

WALKS, DENNIS

Billy Lick	7"	Blue Cat	BS144	1968	**£8**	**£4**	*Drumbago B side*
Having A Party	7"	Amalgamated	AMG816	1968	**£8**	**£4**	*Groovers B side*
Heart Don't Leap	7"	Bullet	BU402	1969	**£4**	**£1.50**	*Clarendonians B side*
Love Of My Life	7"	Bullet	BU408	1969	**£4**	**£1.50**	

WALLACE, GIG

Rockin' On The Railroad	7"	Philips	PB981	1960	**£5**	**£2**	

WALLACE, JERRY

Title	Format	Label	Cat. No.	Year	Mint	VG	Notes
Little Coco Palm	7"	London	HLH9040	1960	£4	£1.50	
Primrose Lane	7"	London	HLH8943	1959	£4	£1.50	
With This Ring	7"	London	HL8719	1958	£10	£5	
With This Ring	7"	London	HL7062	1958	£5	£2	*export*
You're Singing Our Love Song	7"	London	HLH9110	1960	£4	£1.50	

WALLACE, SIPPIE

Title	Format	Label	Cat. No.	Year	Mint	VG	Notes
Sings The Blues	LP	Storyville	671198	1967	£10	£4	

WALLACE BROTHERS

Title	Format	Label	Cat. No.	Year	Mint	VG	Notes
I'll Step Aside	7"	Sue	WI4036	1967	£15	£7.50	
Lover's Prayer	7"	Sue	WI355	1965	£15	£7.50	
Precious Words	7"	Sue	WI334	1964	£12	£6	
Soul Connection	LP	Sue	ILP950	1967	£100	£50	

WALLACE COLLECTION

Title	Format	Label	Cat. No.	Year	Mint	VG	Notes
Daydream	7"	Parlophone	R5764	1969	£5	£2	
Fly Me To The Earth	7"	Parlophone	R5793	1969	£5	£2	
Laughing Cavalier	LP	Parlophone	PMC/PCS7076	1969	£10	£4	
Walk On Out	7"	Parlophone	R5844	1970	£5	£2	
Wallace Collection	LP	Parlophone	PMC/PCS7099	1970	£10	£4	

WALLENSTEIN

Title	Format	Label	Cat. No.	Year	Mint	VG	Notes
Blitzkrieg	LP	Pilz	20290646	1971	£30	£15	*German*
Blue Eyed Boys	LP	RCA	PL30061	1979	£12	£5	*German*
Charline	LP	RCA	PL30045	1978	£12	£5	*German*
Cosmic Century	LP	Komische	KM58006	1973	£20	£8	*German*
Frauleins	LP	Harvest	06445932	1980	£12	£5	*German*
Lunatics	LP	Clear Light Of Jupiter	CLOJ783	1981	£12	£5	*Australian*
Mother Universe	LP	Pilz	20291138	1972	£25	£10	*German*
No More Love	LP	RCA	PL30010	1977	£15	£6	*German*
SSSSS . . . Top	LP	RCA	06446307	1981	£10	£4	*German*
Stories, Songs And Symphonies	LP	Komische	KM58014	1975	£20	£8	*German*

WALLER, FATS

Title	Format	Label	Cat. No.	Year	Mint	VG	Notes
By The Light Of The Silvery Moon	7"	HMV	7M244	1954	£6	£2.50	
Fats 1935–1937	LP	RCA	RD27047	1957	£20	£8	
Fats 1938–1942	10" LP	RCA	RC24004	1958	£20	£8	
Fats At The Organ	10" LP	London	AL3521	1954	£40	£20	
Fats Waller	7" EP	RCA	RCX1010	1959	£5	£2	
Fats Waller	7" EP	HMV	7EG8212	1957	£5	£2	
Fats Waller	7" EP	HMV	7EG8098	1955	£5	£2	
Fats Waller And His Rhythm	7" EP	HMV	7EG8022	1954	£5	£2	
Fats Waller And His Rhythm	7" EP	HMV	7EG8042	1954	£5	£2	
Fats Waller And His Rhythm	7" EP	HMV	7EG8054	1954	£5	£2	
Fats Waller And His Rhythm	7" EP	HMV	7EG8078	1955	£5	£2	
Fats Waller And His Rhythm	7" EP	HMV	7EG8148	1956	£5	£2	
Fats Waller And His Rhythm	7" EP	HMV	7EG8242	1957	£5	£2	
Fats Waller And His Rhythm	7" EP	HMV	7EG8255	1957	£5	£2	
Favourites	10" LP	HMV	DLP1008	1953	£40	£20	
Favourites No. 2	10" LP	HMV	DLP1118	1956	£30	£15	
Fun With Fats	10" LP	HMV	DLP1082	1955	£40	£20	
Good Man Is Hard To Find	7"	HMV	7M157	1953	£4	£1.50	
Handful Of Keys	LP	RCA	RD27185	1960	£15	£6	
Honey Hush	7"	HMV	7M142	1953	£5	£2	
In London No. 1	7" EP	HMV	7EG8304	1958	£5	£2	
In London No. 2	7" EP	HMV	7EG8341	1958	£5	£2	
In London No. 3	7" EP	HMV	7EG8602	1960	£5	£2	
Jivin' With Fats	10" LP	London	AL3522	1954	£40	£20	
My Very Good Friend The Milkman	7"	HMV	7M128	1953	£5	£2	
Plays And Sings	10" LP	HMV	DLP1017	1953	£40	£20	
Real Fats Waller	LP	RCA	CDN131	1959	£12	£5	
Rediscovered Solos	10" LP	London	AL3507	1953	£40	£20	
Rhythm And Romance	10" LP	HMV	DLP1056	1954	£40	£20	
Spreadin' Rhythm Around	10" LP	HMV	DLP1138	1957	£30	£15	
Swinging At The Organ	7" EP	HMV	7EG8191	1956	£5	£2	
Thomas Fats Waller No. 1	LP	HMV	CLP1035	1955	£20	£8	
Thomas Fats Waller No. 2	LP	HMV	CLP1042	1955	£20	£8	
You've Been Taking Lessons In Love	7"	HMV	7M208	1954	£4	£1.50	
Young Fats Waller	10" LP	HMV	DLP1111	1956	£30	£15	
Your Feet's Too Big	7" EP	RCA	RCX1053	1959	£5	£2	

WALLER, GORDON

Title	Format	Label	Cat. No.	Year	Mint	VG	Notes
Gordon	LP	Vertigo	6360069	1972	£100	£50	*spiral label*
Rosecrans Boulevard	7"	Columbia	DB8337	1968	£4	£1.50	

WALLER, JIM & THE DELTAS

Title	Format	Label	Cat. No.	Year	Mint	VG	Notes
Surfin' Wild	LP	Arvee	A(S)432	1963	£25	£10	*US*

WALLINGTON, GEORGE

Title	Format	Label	Cat. No.	Year	Mint	VG	Notes
George Wallington	10" LP	Esquire	20025	1954	£50	£25	
George Wallington Trio	10" LP	Esquire	20076	1956	£30	£15	
Jazz For The Carriage Trade	LP	Esquire	32032	1957	£100	£50	
New Sounds From Europe Vol. 5	10" LP	Vogue	LDE059	1954	£50	£25	
Workshop	10" LP	Columbia	33C9035	1957	£30	£15	

WALLIS, BOB

Title	Format	Label	Cat. No.	Year	Mint	VG	Notes
Bob Wallis Plays	7" EP	Pye	NJE1085	1960	£5	£2	
Bob Wallis Storyville Jazzmen	7" EP	Pye	NJE1079	1960	£5	£2	
Bob Wallis Storyville Jazzmen	7" EP	Storyville	SEP368	1962	£5	£2	
Everybody Loves Saturday Night	LP	Top Rank	BUY023	1960	£15	£6	
Ole Man River	LP	Pye	NJL27	1961	£15	£6	
Raving Sounds Of Bob Wallis	LP	77	77LE122	1959	£30	£15	
Travellin' Blues	LP	Pye	NJL30	1961	£10	£4	
Wallis Collection	LP	Pye	NJL41	1962	£10	£4	

WALLIS, SHANI

Title	Format	Label	Cat. No.	Year	Mint	VG	Notes
I'm A Girl	LP	London	HAR8324	1967	£10	£4	
Look To Love	LP	London	HAR/SHR8338	1967	£10	£4	

WALPURGIS

Title	Format	Label	Cat. No.	Year	Mint	VG	Notes
Queen Of Sheba	LP	Ohr	OMM556023	1972	£20	£8	*German*

WALRUS

Title	Format	Label	Cat. No.	Year	Mint	VG	Notes
Walrus	LP	Deram	SML1072	1971	£20	£8	

WALSH, JOE

Title	Format	Label	Cat. No.	Year	Mint	VG	Notes
Smoker You Drink The Player You Get	LP	ABC	COQ40016	1974	£10	£4	*US quad*

WALSH, SHEILA & CLIFF RICHARD

Title	Format	Label	Cat. No.	Year	Mint	VG	Notes
Drifting	12"	DJM	SHEILT100	1983	£8	£4	*picture disc*
Drifting	7"	DJM	SHEIL100	1983	£6	£2.50	*picture disc*

WALTON, DAVE

Title	Format	Label	Cat. No.	Year	Mint	VG	Notes
After You There Can Be Nothing	7"	CBS	202508	1967	£4	£1.50	
Every Window In The City	7"	CBS	202098	1966	£4	£1.50	
Love Ain't What It Used To Be	7"	CBS	202057	1966	£5	£2	

WAMMACK, TRAVIS

Title	Format	Label	Cat. No.	Year	Mint	VG	Notes
Scratchy	7"	Atlantic	AT4017	1965	£15	£7.50	

WANDERERS

Title	Format	Label	Cat. No.	Year	Mint	VG	Notes
As Time Goes By	7"	MGM	MGM1169	1961	£10	£5	
I Could Make You Mine	7"	MGM	MGM1102	1960	£25	£12.50	
Run Run Señorita	7"	United Artists	UP1020	1964	£12	£6	

WANDERERS (2)

Title	Format	Label	Cat. No.	Year	Mint	VG	Notes
Wiggle Waggle	7"	Trojan	TR7721	1969	£4	£1.50	

WANSEL, DEXTER

Title	Format	Label	Cat. No.	Year	Mint	VG	Notes
Voyager	LP	Philadelphia	PIR82786	1978	£20	£8	

WAPASSOU

Title	Format	Label	Cat. No.	Year	Mint	VG	Notes
Wapassou	LP	Prodisc	PS37342	1974	£20	£8	*French*

WAR

Title	Format	Label	Cat. No.	Year	Mint	VG	Notes
All Day Music	LP	United Artists	UAS29269	1972	£10	£4	
Deliver The Word	LP	United Artists	UAG29521	1973	£10	£4	
Galaxy	LP	MCA	MCF2822	1978	£10	£4	
Greatest Hits	LP	Island	ILPS9413	1976	£10	£4	
Music Band	LP	MCA	MCG4001	1979	£10	£4	
Platinum Funk	LP	Island	ILPS9507	1977	£10	£4	
War	LP	Liberty	LBG83478	1971	£10	£4	
War Live	LP	United Artists	UAD60067/8	1974	£12	£5	*double*
Why Can't We Be Friends	LP	United Artists	UAG29843	1975	£10	£4	
World Is A Ghetto	LP	United Artists	UAS29400	1973	£10	£4	
Youngblood	LP	MCA	MCF2804	1978	£10	£4	

WARD, BILLY & THE DOMINOES

Title	Format	Label	Cat. No.	Year	Mint	VG	Notes
Billy Ward & His Dominoes	10" LP	Federal	29594	1954	£1000	£700	*US*
Billy Ward & His Dominoes	LP	Decca	DL8621	1958	£150	£75	*US*
Billy Ward & His Dominoes	LP	Federal	395548	1956	£500	£330	*US*
Billy Ward & His Dominoes	LP	King	LP548	1956	£250	£150	*US*
Billy Ward & His Dominoes Feat. Clyde McPhatter & Jackie Wilson	LP	King	LP733	1961	£200	£100	*US*
Billy Ward & The Dominoes	10" LP	Parlophone	PMD1061	1958	£500	£330	*best auctioned*
Billy Ward & The Dominoes	7" EP	London	REU1114	1958	£100	£50	
Clyde McPhatter With Billy Ward	LP	Federal	395559	1957	£500	£330	*US*
Clyde McPhatter With Billy Ward	LP	King	LP559	1956	£250	£150	*US*
Deep Purple	7"	London	HLU8502	1957	£15	£7.50	
Don't Thank Me	78	Parlophone	R3789	1953	£20	£10	
Evermore	7"	Brunswick	05656	1957	£15	£7.50	
Have Mercy Baby	78	Vogue	V2135	1952	£12	£6	
Jennie Lee	7"	London	HLU8634	1958	£20	£10	
Pagan Love Song	LP	Liberty	LRP3113/ LST7113	1959	£50	£25	*US*
Please Don't Say No	7"	London	HLU8883	1959	£10	£5	
Sea Of Glass	LP	Liberty	LRP3056	1959	£50	£25	*US*
Sixty Minute Man	78	Vogue	V9012	1951	£20	£10	
St Theresa Of The Roses	7"	Brunswick	05599	1956	£25	£12.50	
Stardust	7"	London	HLU8465	1957	£15	£7.50	
Three Coins In A Fountain	7"	Parlophone	MSP6112	1954	£100	£50	
Twenty-Four Songs	LP	King	LP952	1966	£40	£20	*US*

Yours Forever .... LP .... London .... HAU2116 .... 1958 **£50** .... **£25** ....

WARD, BURT

Burt Ward was the Boy Wonder (Robin in *Batman*), of course – this record is a Frank Zappa creation.

Boy Wonder, I Love You .... 7" .... MGM .... 13632 .... 1967 **£150** .... **£75** .... *US*

WARD, CHRISTINE

Face Of Empty Me .... 7" .... Decca .... F12339 .... 1966 **£6** .... **£2.50** ....

WARD, CLIFFORD T.

Both Of Us .... LP .... Philips .... 814777 .... 1984 **£10** .... **£4** ....
Carrie .... 7" .... Dandelion .... 2001327 .... 1972 **£5** .... **£2** ....
Coathanger .... 7" .... Dandelion .... 2001382 .... 1972 **£4** .... **£1.50** ....
Cricket .... 7" .... Tembo .... TML114 .... 1986 **£5** .... **£2** ....
Messenger .... 7" .... Philips .... 8805507 .... 1984 **£5** .... **£2** ....
Singer Songwriter .... LP .... Dandelion .... 2310216 .... 1972 **£10** .... **£4** ....
Someone I Know .... 7" .... Mercury .... LUV1 .... 1977 **£4** .... **£1.50** ....
Sometime Next Year .... 7" .... Tembo .... TML123 .... 1986 **£5** .... **£2** ....
Sometime Next Year .... LP .... Tembo .... TMB111 .... 1986 **£10** .... **£4** ....

WARD, DALE

Letter from Shirley .... 7" .... London .... HLD9835 .... 1964 **£8** .... **£4** ....

WARD, ROBIN

Wonderful Summer .... 7" .... London .... HLD9821 .... 1963 **£6** .... **£2.50** ....
Wonderful Summer .... LP .... Dot .... DLP3555/2555 .... 1963 **£20** .... **£8** .... *US*

WARDS OF COURT

All Night Girl .... 7" .... Deram .... DM127 .... 1967 **£10** .... **£5** ....

WARE, LEON

Musical Massage .... LP .... Tamla Motown .... STML12050 .... 1977 **£12** .... **£5** ....

WARHORSE

Red Sea .... LP .... Vertigo .... 6360066 .... 1972 **£50** .... **£25** .... *spiral label*
St Louis .... 7" .... Vertigo .... 6059027 .... 1970 **£6** .... **£2.50** ....
Warhorse .... LP .... Vertigo .... 6360015 .... 1970 **£30** .... **£15** .... *spiral label*

WARING, FRED & HIS PENNSYLVANIANS

Ballad Of Davy Crockett .... 7" EP .. Brunswick .... OE9194 .... 1955 **£6** .... **£2.50** ....

WARLEIGH, RAY

First Album .... LP .... Philips .... SBL7881 .... 1969 **£40** .... **£20** ....

WARLOCK, OZZIE & THE WIZARDS

Juke Box Fury .... 7" .... HMV .... POP635 .... 1959 **£6** .... **£2.50** ....

WARM

Demo Tapes .... 7" .... Warm .... SMS001 .... 1978 **£6** .... **£2.50** .... *double*

WARM DUST

And It Came To Pass .... LP .... Trend .... TNLS700 .... 1970 **£20** .... **£8** ....
It's A Beautiful Day .... 7" .... Trend .... 6099002 .... 1970 **£4** .... **£1.50** ....
Peace For Our Time .... LP .... Trend .... 6480001 .... 1971 **£12** .... **£5** ....

WARM EXPRESSION

Let No Man Put Asunder .... 7" .... Columbia .... DB8672 .... 1970 **£4** .... **£1.50** ....

WARM SOUNDS

Birds And Bees .... 7" .... Deram .... DM120 .... 1967 **£6** .... **£2.50** ....
Nite Is A-Comin' .... 7" .... Deram .... DM174 .... 1968 **£15** .... **£7.50** ....
Sticks And Stones .... 7" .... Immediate .... IM058 .... 1967 **£6** .... **£2.50** ....

WARMAN, JOHNNY

Head On Collision .... 7" .... Ring O' .... 2017112 .... 1978 **£8** .... **£4** .... *picture sleeve*

WARNER, FLORENCE

Florence Warner .... LP .... Epic .... EPC80077 .... 1973 **£10** .... **£4** ....

WARNER, MIKE & HIS NEW STARS

Mike Warner And His New Stars .... LP .... Ariola .... 72359 .... 1964 **£125** .. **£62.50** .... *German*

WARNING, GALE

Rock Those Crazy Skins .... 78 .... Oriole .... CB1349 .... 1956 **£5** .... **£2** ....

WARPIG

Warpig .... LP .... Fonthill .... NAS13528 .... 1971 **£75** .... **£37.50** .... *Canadian*

WARREN, ALMA

Stealin' .... 7" .... Parlophone .... MSP6200 .... 1956 **£4** .... **£1.50** ....

WARREN, ELLIE

Shattered Glass 7" PRT 7P263 1983 £10 £5

WARREN, PETER

Bass Is LP Enja 2018 1974 £25 £10

WARREN J. 5

Rhythm & Blues LP Vedette VRM36049 1967 £100 £50 *Italian*

WARREN OF GHANA, GUY

Africa Speaks America Answers LP Brunswick LAT8237 1958 £40 £20
African Soundz LP Regal Zonophone SLRZ1031 1972 £40 £20
Afro-Jazz LP Columbia SCX6340 1969 £40 £20
Monkeys And Butterflies 7" Brunswick 05791 1959 £5 £2

WARRIOR

Breakout 7" Warrior W002 1984 £20 £10
For Europe Only LP Warrior W001 1983 £12 £5

WARRIOR (2)

Invasion LP Eden LP27 1972 £500 £330

WARRIOR (3)

Trouble Maker LP Goodwood GM12326 1980 £100 £50

WARRIOR (4)

Let Battle Commence LP rainbow RSL132 1980 £40 £20

WARRIORS

The collectability of the Warriors' single derives from the fact that the group's singer was Jon Anderson. The drummer, meanwhile, was Ian Wallace, who has played on numerous records since, most notably LPs made by King Crimson and Bob Dylan.

You Came Along 7" Decca F11926 1964 £40 £20

WARSAW PAKT

Needletime LP Island ILPS9515 1977 £12 £5
Safe And Warm 7" Island PAKT1 1978 £6 £2.50
Safe And Warm 7" Island PAKT1 1978 £15 £7.50 *picture sleeve*

WARWICK, DEE DEE

Do It With All Your Heart 7" Mercury MF860 1965 £6 £2.50
Gotta Get A Hold Of Myself 7" Mercury MF890 1965 £5 £2
I Want To Be With You LP Mercury MG2/SR61100 1967 £15 £6 *US*
I'll Be Better Off 7" Mercury MF1061 1968 £8 £4
Lover's Chant 7" Mercury MF909 1966 £15 £7.50
We're Doin' Fine 7" Mercury MF867 1965 £6 £2.50
We're Doin' Fine 7" EP Mercury 10036MCE 1966 £12 £6
When Love Slips Away 7" Mercury MF974 1967 £6 £2.50

WARWICK, DIONNE

Dionne 7" EP Pye NEP44044 1965 £5 £2
Do You Know The Way To San Jose 7" EP Pye NEP44090 1968 £5 £2
Don't Make Me Over 7" Stateside SS157 1963 £6 £2.50
Don't Make Me Over 7" EP Pye NEP44026 1964 £5 £2
Forever My Love 7" EP Pye NEP44046 1965 £5 £2
Here I Am 7" EP Pye NEP44051 1966 £5 £2
I Just Don't Know What To Do With Myself 7" EP Pye NEP44077 1966 £5 £2
I Love Paris 7" EP Pye NEP44083 1967 £5 £2
It's Love That Really Counts 7" EP Pye NEP44024 1964 £5 £2
Make The Music Play 7" Stateside SS222 1963 £8 £4 *demo only*
Message To Michael 7" EP Pye NEP44067 1966 £5 £2
Presenting LP Pye NPL28037 1964 £10 £4
Who Can I Turn To 7" EP Pye NEP44049 1965 £5 £2
Window Wishing 7" EP Pye NEP44073 1966 £5 £2
Wishin' And Hopin' 7" Stateside SS191 1963 £6 £2.50
Wishin' And Hopin' 7" EP Pye NEP44039 1965 £5 £2

WAS (NOT WAS)

Anything Can Happen CD-s Polygram 0804542 1988 £8 £4 *CD video*
Out Come The Freaks CD-s Fontana WASCD4 1988 £5 £2
Spy In The House Of Love CD-s Fontana WASCD2 1987 £5 £2
Walk The Dinosaur CD-s Polygram 0804522 1988 £8 £4 *CD video*

WASA

Wasa LP Polar POLS261 1975 £20 £8 *Swedish*

WASHBOARD RHYTHM KINGS

Washboard Rhythm Kings 7" EP HMV 7EG8101 1955 £12 £6
Washboard Rhythm Kings 7" EP HMV 7EG8126 1955 £12 £6

WASHINGTON, ALBERT & THE KINGS

Turn On The Bright Lights 7" President PT242 1969 £4 £1.50
Woman Love 7" President PT227 1969 £4 £1.50

WASHINGTON, BABY

Breakfast In Bed	7"	Atlantic	584316	1970	£5	£2	
Get A Hold Of Yourself	7"	United Artists	UP2247	1968	£10	£5	
I Can't Wait Until I See My Baby	7"	Sue	WI321	1964	£20	£10	
I Don't Know	7"	Atlantic	584299	1969	£5	£2	
Lay A Little Lovin' On Me	LP	People	PLEO13	1974	£10	£4	*with Don Gardner*
Only Those In Love	7"	London	HLC9987	1965	£10	£5	
Only Those In Love	LP	London	HAC8292	1966	£25	£10	
That's How Heartaches Are Made	7"	Sue	WI302	1963	£20	£10	
That's How Heartaches Are Made	LP	London	HAC8260	1963	£25	£10	
With You In Mind	LP	United Artists	SULP1217	1968	£25	£10	

WASHINGTON, DELROY

I-Sus	LP	Virgin	V2060	1976	£12	£5	
Rasta	LP	Virgin	V2088	1977	£12	£5	

WASHINGTON, DINAH

After Hours With Miss D	10" LP	Emarcy	EJT501	1956	£20	£8	
Blues	LP	Top Rank	RX3006	1959	£10	£4	*with tracks by Betty Roche*
Dinah	LP	Emarcy	EJL1255	1957	£12	£5	
Dinah '63	LP	Columbia	33SX1608	1963	£10	£4	
For Lonely Lovers	LP	Mercury	MMC14085	1962	£10	£4	
I Concentrate On You	LP	Mercury	MMC14063/ CMS18043	1961	£10	£4	
September In The Rain	LP	Mercury	MMC14107	1961	£10	£4	
Sings The Best In Blues	LP	Mercury	MPL6519	1957	£10	£4	
Soulville	7"	Columbia	DB7049	1963	£5	£2	
Unforgettable	LP	Mercury	MMC14048	1960	£10	£4	
What A Difference A Day Made	7"	Mercury	AMT1051	1959	£4	£1.50	
What A Difference A Day Made	LP	Mercury	MMC14030	1960	£10	£4	

WASHINGTON, ELLA

He Called Me Baby	7"	Monument	MON1030	1969	£5	£2	

WASHINGTON, GENO & THE RAM JAM BAND

Different Strokes	7" EP	Pye	NEP24293	1968	£12	£6	
Hand Clappin', Foot Stompin'	LP	Piccadilly	NPL38026	1966	£15	£6	
Hi	7" EP	Piccadilly	NEP34054	1966	£10	£5	
Hipsters And Flipsters	LP	Piccadilly	N(S)PL38032	1967	£12	£5	
I Can't Let You Go	7"	Pye	7N17649	1968	£4	£1.50	
Running Wild	LP	Pye	N(S)PL18219	1968	£12	£5	
Shake A Tail Feather	LP	Piccadilly	N(S)PL38029	1968	£12	£5	
She Shot A Hole In My Soul	7"	Piccadilly	7N35392	1967	£4	£1.50	
Small Package Of Hipsters	7" EP	Pye	NEP24302	1968	£15	£7.50	
Tell It Like It Is	7"	Piccadilly	7N35403	1967	£4	£1.50	
Tell It Like It Is	7" EP	Pye	PNV24198	1967	£12	£6	*French*
Water	7"	Piccadilly	7N35312	1966	£4	£1.50	
Water	7" EP	Pye	PNV24178	1966	£12	£6	*French*

WASHINGTON, GROVER

All The King's Horses	LP	Kudu	KUL5	1973	£10	£4	
Feels So Good	LP	Kudu	KU24	1975	£10	£4	
Inner City Blues	LP	Kudu	KUL1	1973	£10	£4	
Mister Magic	LP	Kudu	KU20	1975	£10	£4	
Secret Place	LP	Kudu	KU32	1976	£10	£4	
Soul Box	LP	Kudu	KULD501	1973	£10	£4	

WASHINGTON, JUSTINE

Only Those In Love	LP	Sue	(S)1042	1965	£15	£6	*US*

WASHINGTON, KENNETH

If I Had A Ticket	7"	CBS	202494	1967	£6	£2.50	*with Chris Barber*

WASHINGTON, SHERI

I Got Plenty	7"	Vogue	V9070	1957	£300	£180	*best auctioned*

WASHINGTON, SISTER ERNESTINE

Sister Ernestine Washington	7" EP	Melodisc	EPM752	1955	£8	£4	

WASHINGTON, TONY

But I Do	7"	Black Swan	WI459	1965	£5	£2	
Crying Man	7"	React	EA002	1963	£8	£4	
Dilly Dilly	7"	Black Swan	WI460	1965	£5	£2	
Show Me How	7"	Sue	WI327	1964	£8	£4	
Surely You Love Me	7"	Fontana	TF478	1964	£4	£1.50	

WASHINGTON, TYRONE

Natural Essence	LP	Blue Note	BST84274	1968	£15	£6	

WASHINGTON DCs

I've Done It All Wrong	7"	Domain	D9	1969	£5	£2	
Kisses Sweeter Than Wine	7"	Ember	EMBS190	1964	£6	£2.50	
Kisses Sweeter Than Wine	7" EP	Pathe	EGF761	1964	£12	£6	*French*
Seek And Find	7"	CBS	202464	1967	£50	£25	*picture sleeve*
Seek And Find	7"	CBS	202464	1967	£25	£12.50	
Thirty-Second Floor	7"	CBS	202226	1966	£8	£4	

W.A.S.P.

Title	Format	Label	Cat. No.	Year	Mint	VG+	Notes
9.5 N.A.S.T.Y.	7"	Capitol	CLP432	1986	£4	£1.50	*picture disc*
9.5 N.A.S.T.Y.	7"	Capitol	CLP432	1986	£5	£2	*shaped picture disc*
Animal	12"	Music For Nations	12KUT109	1984	£10	£4	*white or clear vinyl*
Animal	12"	Music For Nations	12KUT109	1984	£8	£4	*red vinyl*
Animal	12"	Music For Nations	12KUT109	1984	£20	£10	*gold vinyl*
Animal	7"	Music For Nations	PKUT109	1984	£8	£4	*shaped picture disc, 2 different designs*
Blind In Texas	7"	Capitol	CLP374	1985	£6	£2.50	*shaped picture disc*
Forever Free	7"	Capitol	CLPD546	1989	£5	£2	*picture disc*
Forever Free	CD-s	Capitol	CDCL546	1989	£5	£2	
I Don't Need No Doctor	7"	Capitol	CLB469	1987	£4	£1.50	*with tour pass*
I Wanna Be Somebody	12"	Capitol	12CLP336	1984	£6	£2.50	*picture disc*
Mean Man	CD-s	Capitol	CDCL521	1989	£5	£2	
Real Me	CD-s	Capitol	CDCL534	1989	£5	£2	
Schooldaze	12"	Capitol	12CL344	1984	£6	£2.50	
Wild Child	12"	Capitol	12CL388	1986	£6	£2.50	

WASP (BRIAN BENNETT)

Title	Format	Label	Cat. No.	Year	Mint	VG+	Notes
Melissa	7"	EMI	EMI2253	1975	£15	£7.50	

WASPS

Title	Format	Label	Cat. No.	Year	Mint	VG+	Notes
Can't Wait Till '78	7"	NEMS	NES115	1977	£5	£2	*Mean Street B side*

WASTELAND

Title	Format	Label	Cat. No.	Year	Mint	VG+	Notes
Friends, Romans, Countrymen	7"	Invicta	INV014	1979	£15	£7.50	
Want Not	7"	Ellie Jay	EJSP9261	1979	£15	£7.50	

WATER FOR A THIRSTY LAND

Title	Format	Label	Cat. No.	Year	Mint	VG+	Notes
Water For A Thirsty Land	LP	MRA	P100	1974	£15	£6	

WATER INTO WINE BAND

Title	Format	Label	Cat. No.	Year	Mint	VG+	Notes
Harvest Time	LP	private	CJT002	1976	£200	£100	
Hill Climbing For Beginners	LP	Myrrh	MYR1004	1973	£50	£25	*brown cover*
Hill Climbing For Beginners	LP	Myrrh	MYR1004	1974	£75	£37.50	*white cover, re-recorded tracks*

WATER PISTOLS

Title	Format	Label	Cat. No.	Year	Mint	VG+	Notes
Gimme That Punk Junk	7"	State	STATE38	1976	£6	£2.50	

WATERBOYS

Title	Format	Label	Cat. No.	Year	Mint	VG+	Notes
And A Bang On The Ear	CD-s	Ensign	ENYCD624	1989	£5	£2	
Best Of The Waterboys	CD	Ensign	CCD1845	1991	£25	£10	*promo double*
Dream Harder – Interview Album	CD	Ensign	PROCD4522	1993	£20	£8	*US promo*
Kit Number One	CD	Ensign		1991	£40	£20	*promo box set, with Best Of CD, 2 × 12", CD-s, video, 7"*
Mike Scott Interview	CD	Ensign	DPRO23719	1991	£20	£8	*US promo*
Room To Roam	CD	Ensign		1991	£40	£20	*promo box set, with Best Of CD, 7", CD-s, interview CD*
This Is The Sea	CD	Chrysalis	CD25CR23	1994	£12	£5	*Chrysalis 25 pack*

WATERFALL

Title	Format	Label	Cat. No.	Year	Mint	VG+	Notes
Beneath The Stars	LP	Gun Dog	LP003	1981	£30	£15	
Flight Of The Day	LP	Bob	FRR001	198–	£40	£20	
Three Birds	LP	Avada	AVA104	1979	£30	£15	

WATERPROOF CANDLE

Title	Format	Label	Cat. No.	Year	Mint	VG+	Notes
Electronically Heated Child	7"	RCA	RCA1717	1968	£6	£2.50	

WATERS, MUDDY

Title	Format	Label	Cat. No.	Year	Mint	VG+	Notes
After The Rain	LP	Chess	CRL4553	1969	£30	£15	
At Newport	LP	Chess	CRL4513	1965	£15	£6	
At Newport	LP	Pye	NJL34	1961	£25	£10	
Back In The Good Old Days	LP	Syndicate	001	1970	£20	£8	*double*
Best Of Muddy Waters	LP	London	LTZM15152	1959	£50	£25	
Blues From Big Bill's Copacabana	LP	Chess	LP(S)1533	1968	£15	£6	*US*
Blues Man	LP	Polydor	236574	1969	£10	£4	
Country Boy	7"	Python	P04	1969	£25	£12.50	
Down On Stovall's Plantation	LP	Bounty	BY6031	1968	£12	£5	
Electric Mud	LP	Chess	CRL4542	1968	£40	£20	
Fathers And Sons	LP	Chess	CRL4556	1969	£15	£6	*with other artists*
Folk Singer	LP	Pye	NPL28038	1964	£20	£8	
Good News	LP	Syndicate	002	1970	£15	£6	
Honey Bee	78	Vogue	V2372	1956	£20	£10	
I Got A Rich Man's Woman	7"	Chess	CRS8019	1965	£6	£2.50	
I'm Ready	7" EP	Chess	CRE6006	1965	£30	£15	
Let's Spend The Night Together	7"	Chess	CRS8083	1969	£4	£1.50	
Long Distance Call	78	Vogue	V2273	1954	£20	£10	
McKinley Morganfield AKA Muddy Waters	LP	Chess	6671001	1971	£10	£4	
Mississippi Blues	7" EP	London	REU1060	1956	£75	£37.50	*gold label*

More Real Folk Blues	LP	Chess	LP(S)1511	1966	**£20**	**£8**	*US*
Muddy Waters	7" EP	Pye	NEP44010	1963	**£10**	**£5**	
Muddy Waters	LP	Pye	NPL28040	1964	**£20**	**£8**	
Muddy Waters	LP	Python	PLP12	1969	**£25**	**£10**	
Muddy Waters Vol. 2	LP	Python	PLP18	1969	**£25**	**£10**	
Muddy Waters Vol. 3	LP	Python	PLP19	1969	**£25**	**£10**	
Muddy Waters With Little Walter	7" EP	Vogue	EPV1046	1955	**£100**	**£50**	
Muddy, Brass, & The Blues	LP	Chess	CRL4525	1967	**£15**	**£6**	
My John The Conqueror Root	7"	Chess	CRS8001	1965	**£8**	**£4**	
Rare Live Recordings Vol. 1	LP	Black Bear	LP901	1972	**£15**	**£6**	
Rare Live Recordings Vol. 2	LP	Black Bear	LP902	1972	**£15**	**£6**	
Rare Live Recordings Vol. 3	LP	Black Bear	LP903	1972	**£15**	**£6**	
Real Folk Blues	LP	Chess	CRL4515	1966	**£15**	**£6**	
Real Folk Blues Vol. 4	7" EP	Chess	CRE6022	1966	**£15**	**£7.50**	
Rollin' Stone	78	Vogue	V2101	1952	**£20**	**£10**	
Sail On	LP	Chess	LPS1539	1969	**£12**	**£5**	*US*
Sings Big Bill Broonzy	LP	Pye	NPL28048	1964	**£15**	**£6**	
Super Blues	LP	Chess	CRL4529	1967	**£20**	**£8**	*with Bo Diddley and Little Walter*
Super Super Blues Band	LP	Chess	CRL4537	1968	**£25**	**£10**	*with Bo Diddley and Howlin' Wolf*
Vintage Mud	LP	Sunnyland	KS100	1969	**£15**	**£6**	

WATERS, ROGER

5:06 am (Every Stranger's Eyes)	7"	Harvest	HAR5230	1984	**£6**	**£2.50**	
Amused To Death	LP	Columbia	COL4687610	1992	**£12**	**£5**	*blue vinyl double*
Another Brick In The Wall Part 2	CD-s	Mercury	MERCD332	1990	**£5**	**£2**	*with Cyndi Lauper*
Bravery Of Being Out Of Range	CD-s	Columbia	6588192	1992	**£5**	**£2**	
Pieces From The Wall	CD-s	Mercury	8781472	1990	**£15**	**£7.50**	*promo*
Pros And Cons Of Hitch-Hiking	LP	Harvest	SHVL2401051	1984	**£10**	**£4**	*banded promo*
Radio K.A.O.S.	LP	EMI	KAOSDJ1	1987	**£20**	**£8**	*banded promo, no dialogue*
Radio Waves	CD-s	EMI	CDEM6	1987	**£6**	**£2.50**	
Sunset Strip	7"	EMI	EM20	1987	**£10**	**£5**	
Tide Is Turning	CD-s	EMI	CDEM37	1987	**£6**	**£2.50**	
Tide Is Turning	CD-s	Mercury	MERCD336	1990	**£5**	**£2**	
What God Wants Part 1	CD-s	Columbia	6581399	1992	**£5**	**£2**	*boxed set with 2 cards*
What God Wants Part I	CD-s	Columbia	6581395	1992	**£5**	**£2**	

WATERSON, MIKE

Mike Waterson	LP	Topic	12TS332	1977	**£10**	**£4**	

WATERSONS

Bright Phoebus	LP	Trailer	LES2076	1972	**£12**	**£5**	
Frost And Fire	LP	Topic	12T136	1965	**£15**	**£6**	
New Voices	LP	Topic	12T125	1965	**£25**	**£10**	*with Harry Boardman and Maureen Craik*
Watersons	LP	Topic	12T142	1966	**£15**	**£6**	
Yorkshire Garland	LP	Topic	12T167	1966	**£15**	**£6**	

WATKINS, LOVELACE

I Apologise Baby	7"	Fontana	TF879	1967	**£5**	**£2**	

WATSON, DOC

Doc Watson	LP	Fontana	TFL6045	1964	**£15**	**£6**	
Doc Watson And Son	LP	Fontana	TFL6055	1965	**£15**	**£6**	
Doc Watson Family	LP	XTRA	XTRA1082	1969	**£12**	**£5**	
Home Again!	LP	Fontana	(S)TFL6083	1968	**£15**	**£6**	

WATSON, JOHN L.

Mother's Love	7"	Deram	DM285	1970	**£4**	**£1.50**	
White Hot Blue Black	LP	Deram	SMLR1061	1970	**£20**	**£8**	

WATSON, JOHNNY GUITAR

Bad	LP	OKeh	OKM4118/ OKS14118	1967	**£20**	**£8**	*US*
Blues Soul	LP	Chess	1490	1965	**£30**	**£15**	*US*
I Cried For You	LP	Cadet	LP4056	1967	**£15**	**£6**	*US*
In The Fats Bag	LP	OKeh	OKM4124/ OKS14124	1967	**£20**	**£8**	*US*
Johnny Guitar Watson	LP	King	LP857	1963	**£50**	**£25**	*US*

WATSON, WAH WAH

Elementary	LP	CBS	81582	1976	**£10**	**£4**	

WATT, TOMMY

It Might As Well Be Swing	LP	Parlophone	PMC1068	1959	**£15**	**£6**	
Watt's Cooking	LP	Parlophone	PMC1107	1959	**£15**	**£6**	

WATTERS, LU

Dixieland Jamboree	10" LP	Columbia	33C9036	1957	**£15**	**£6**	
Lu Watters 1947	10" LP	London	HBU1061	1956	**£15**	**£6**	
Lu Watters And His Jazz Band	10" LP	Vogue	LDE009	1952	**£20**	**£8**	
Lu Watters And The Yerba Buena Jazz Band	LP	Good Time Jazz	LAG12030	1956	**£12**	**£5**	

Lu Watters Jazz Band — LP — Good Time Jazz — LAG12025 — 1956 — **£12** — **£5**

Lu Watters Jazz Band Vol. 1 — 10" LP — Good Time Jazz — LDG038 — 1954 — **£20** — **£8**

Lu Watters Yerba Buena Band — 10" LP — Columbia — 33C9004 — 1955 — **£20** — **£8**

Lu Watters Yerba Buena Band Vol. 1 — 10" LP — Good Time Jazz — LP8 — 1953 — **£20** — **£8**

Lu Watters' Yerba Buena Jazz Band — LP — Good Time Jazz — LAG12123 — 1958 — **£12** — **£5**

WATTS, CHARLIE

From One Charlie — 10" LP — UFO — UFO2LP — 1991 — **£15** — **£6** — *box set*

From One Charlie — 10" LP — UFO — UFO2LP — 1991 — **£[illegible]** — **£[illegible]** — *autographed box set*

My Ship — CD-s — Continuum — CDCTUM103 — 1993 — **£10** — **£5**

WATTS, NOBLE THIN MAN

Hard Times — 7" — London — HLU8627 — 1958 — **£40** — **£20**

Noble Thin Man Watts & Wild Jimmy Spurrill — 7" EP — XX — MIN717 — 196– — **£10** — **£5**

Noble's Theme — 7" — Sue — WI347 — 1964 — **£15** — **£7.50** — *June Bateman B side*

WATTS 103RD STREET RHYTHM BAND

Cornbread And Grits — LP — Warner Bros — WS1741 — 1967 — **£15** — **£6** — *US*

Express Yourself — 7" — Warner Bros — WB7417 — 1970 — **£4** — **£1.50**

Express Yourself — LP — Warner Bros — 1864 — 1970 — **£15** — **£6** — *US*

In The Jungle Babe — LP — Warner Bros — WS1801 — 1969 — **£15** — **£6** — *US*

Spreadin' Honey — 7" — Jay Boy — BOY71 — 1973 — **£5** — **£2**

You're So Beautiful — LP — Warner Bros — 1904 — 1970 — **£15** — **£6** — *US*

WATUSI WARRIORS

Wa-chi-bam-ba — 7" — London — HL8866 — 1959 — **£8** — **£4**

WAVE CRESTS

Surftime USA — LP — Viking — VKS6606 — 1963 — **£20** — **£8** — *US*

WAY, DARRYL & WOLF

Canis Lupus — LP — Deram — SDL14 — 1973 — **£15** — **£6**

Saturation Point — LP — Deram — SML1104 — 1973 — **£15** — **£6**

WAY WE LIVE

Candle For Judith — LP — Dandelion — DAN8004 — 1971 — **£100** — **£50**

WAYBURN, NANCY

World Goes On Without Me — 7" — Warner Bros — WB5646 — 1965 — **£5** — **£2**

WAYFARERS

Songs And Dance Tunes — LP — MWM — MWM1017 — 1978 — **£20** — **£8**

WAYNE, ALVIS

Don't Mean Maybe Baby — 7" — Starlite — ST45104 — 1963 — **£300** — **£180** — *best auctioned*

WAYNE, BOBBY

Ballad Of A Teenage Queen — 7" — Pye — 7N25315 — 1965 — **£5** — **£2**

WAYNE, CARL

Carl Wayne — LP — RCA — SF8239 — 1971 — **£10** — **£4**

This Is Love — 7" — Pye — 7N15824 — 1965 — **£25** — **£12.50** — *with the Vikings*

What's A Matter Baby — 7" — Pye — 7N15702 — 1964 — **£25** — **£12.50** — *with the Vikings*

WAYNE, CHRIS & THE ECHOES

Lonely — 7" — Decca — F11231 — 1960 — **£5** — **£2**

WAYNE, CHUCK

Chuck Wayne Quintet — 10" LP — London — LZC14014 — 1955 — **£40** — **£20**

WAYNE, FRANCES

Frances Wayne — LP — Brunswick — BL54022 — 1957 — **£12** — **£5** — *US*

Songs For My Man — LP — Epic — LN3222 — 195– — **£12** — **£5** — *US*

Warm Sound Of Frances Wayne — LP — Atlantic — 1263 — 1956 — **£15** — **£6** — *US*

WAYNE, JEFF

Two Cities — LP — Columbia — SX/SCX6330 — 1969 — **£20** — **£8**

War Of The Worlds — LP — CBS — WOW100 — 1979 — **£20** — **£8** — *double LP, 12", book, poster, boxed*

WAYNE, JERRY

Half Hearted Love — 7" — Vogue — V9169 — 1960 — **£15** — **£7.50**

WAYNE, PAT & THE BEACHCOMBERS

Brand New Man — 7" — Columbia — DB7417 — 1964 — **£6** — **£2.50**

Bye Bye Johnny — 7" — Columbia — DB7262 — 1964 — **£8** — **£4**

Jambalaya — 7" — Columbia — DB7121 — 1963 — **£8** — **£4**

Roll Over Beethoven — 7" — Columbia — DB7182 — 1963 — **£8** — **£4**

Roll Over Beethoven — 7" EP — Columbia — ESRF1502 — 1964 — **£30** — **£15** — *French*

WAYNE, RICKY

Chick A Roo — 7" — Triumph — RGM1009 — 1960 — **£30** — **£15**

Chick A Roo — 7" — Top Rank — JAR432 — 1960 — **£20** — **£10** — *demo*

Title	Format	Label	Cat. No.	Year	Mint	VG	Notes
In My Imagination	7"	CBS	201764	1965	£4	£1.50	
Make Way Baby	7"	Pye	7N15289	1960	£20	£10	
Say You're Gonna Be My Own	7"	Oriole	CB306	1965	£6	£2.50	

WAYNE, TERRY

Title	Format	Label	Cat. No.	Year	Mint	VG	Notes
All Mama's Children	7"	Columbia	DB4067	1958	£12	£6	
Matchbox	7"	Columbia	DB4002	1957	£15	£7.50	
Oh Lonesome Me	7"	Columbia	DB4112	1958	£8	£4	
She's Mine	7"	Columbia	DB4312	1959	£5	£2	
Slim Jim Tie	7"	Columbia	DB4035	1957	£12	£6	
Terrific	7" EP	Columbia	SEG7758	1958	£60	£30	
Where My Baby Goes	7"	Columbia	DB4205	1958	£6	£2.50	

WAYNE, THOMAS

Title	Format	Label	Cat. No.	Year	Mint	VG	Notes
Tragedy	7"	London	HLU8846	1959	£25	£12.50	
Tragedy	7"	London	HL7075	1959	£10	£5	*export*

WAYNE, WEE WILLIE

Title	Format	Label	Cat. No.	Year	Mint	VG	Notes
Travellin' Mood	LP	Imperial	LP9144	1961	£40	£20	*US*

WAYS AND MEANS

Title	Format	Label	Cat. No.	Year	Mint	VG	Notes
Breaking Up A Dream	7"	Trend	TRE1005	1968	£10	£5	
Little Deuce Coupe	7"	Columbia	DB7907	1966	£6	£2.50	
Sea Of Faces	7"	Pye	7N17217	1966	£10	£5	

WAZOO

Title	Format	Label	Cat. No.	Year	Mint	VG	Notes
Weird Freakout	LP	Zigzag	212	1969	£15	£6	*US*

WE FIVE

Title	Format	Label	Cat. No.	Year	Mint	VG	Notes
Let's Get Together	7"	Pye	7N25346	1966	£4	£1.50	
Let's Get Together	7" EP	Pye	NEP44056	1966	£15	£7.50	
You Were On My Mind	7"	Pye	7N25314	1965	£4	£1.50	
You Were On My Mind	LP	Pye	NPL28067	1965	£25	£10	

WE THE PEOPLE

Title	Format	Label	Cat. No.	Year	Mint	VG	Notes
He Doesn't Go About It Right	7"	London	HLH10089	1966	£75	£37.50	
St John's Shop	7" EP	London	RE10184	1966	£200	£100	*French*
You Burn Me Up And Down	7" EP	London	RE10191	1966	£200	£100	*French*

WEAPON

Title	Format	Label	Cat. No.	Year	Mint	VG	Notes
It's A Mad Mad World	12"	Weapon	WEAPONE	1981	£15	£7.50	
It's A Mad Mad World	7"	Weapon	WEAP1	1980	£20	£10	

WEASELS

Title	Format	Label	Cat. No.	Year	Mint	VG	Notes
Liverpool Beat	LP	Wing	MGW/SRW12282	1964	£15	£6	*US*

WEASELSNOUT

Title	Format	Label	Cat. No.	Year	Mint	VG	Notes
Unsung Lies	LP	Weaselsnout	WUS140	1972	£100	£50	

WEATHER REPORT

When the time comes to assess the major innovators of late-twentieth-century music, then the name of Weather Report is likely to loom large. Marketed as jazz, Weather Report's music is of equal appeal to progressive rock fans for the way in which it blends improvisation with composed passages, setting up frequently elaborate structures in which the textures and timbres available to electronic instruments are exploited to the full. Under Josef Zawinul's fingers, the synthesizer begins to achieve some of the potential of which it is obviously capable, but which is so seldom realized. The double Japan-only release *Live In Tokyo* contains the complete concert that was presented in excerpt on the UK album *I Sing The Body Electric*.

Title	Format	Label	Cat. No.	Year	Mint	VG	Notes
Black Market	CD	CBS	CD81325	1987	£12	£5	
Domino Theory	CD	CBS	CD25839	1984	£12	£5	
I Sing The Body Electric	LP	CBS	64943	1972	£10	£4	
Live In Tokyo	LP	CBS Sony	40AP942-3	1972	£30	£15	*Japanese double*
Mysterious Traveller	CD	CBS	CD80027	1984	£12	£5	
Mysterious Traveller	LP	CBS	80027	1974	£10	£4	
New Album	CD	CBS	CD26367	1988	£12	£5	
Night Passage	CD	CBS	CD84597	1983	£12	£5	
Sweetnighter	LP	CBS	65532	1973	£12	£5	
Tale Spinnin'	LP	CBS	80734	1975	£10	£4	
Weather Report	LP	CBS	64521	1971	£10	£4	

WEAVERS

Title	Format	Label	Cat. No.	Year	Mint	VG	Notes
At Home	LP	Top Rank	RX3008	1959	£10	£4	
At The Carnegie Hall	LP	Vanguard	PPL11006	1957	£10	£4	
Best Of The Weavers	LP	Decca	DL8893	1959	£10	£4	*US*
Best Of The Weavers	LP	Brunswick	LAT8357	1961	£10	£4	
Folk Songs Around The World	LP	Decca	DL8909	1959	£10	£4	*US*
On Tour	LP	Vanguard	PPL11011	1958	£10	£4	
Reunion At Carnegie Hall	LP	Fontana	TFL6032	1963	£10	£4	

WEB

Title	Format	Label	Cat. No.	Year	Mint	VG	Notes
Baby Won't You Leave Me Alone	7"	Deram	DM217	1968	£4	£1.50	
Fully Interlocking	LP	Deram	SML1025	1968	£20	£8	
Hatton Mill Morning	7"	Deram	DM201	1968	£5	£2	
I Spider	LP	Polydor	2383024	1970	£100	£50	
Monday To Friday	7"	Deram	DM253	1969	£4	£1.50	
Theraphosa Blondi	LP	Deram	SML1058	1970	£20	£8	

WEBB, DEAN

Title	Format	Label	Cat. No.	Year	Mint	VG	Notes
Hey Miss Fanny	7"	Parlophone	R4549	1959	**£15**	**£7.50**	
Streamline Baby	7"	Parlophone	R4587	1959	**£15**	**£7.50**	

WEBB, DON

Title	Format	Label	Cat. No.	Year	Mint	VG	Notes
Little Ditty Baby	7"	Coral	Q72385	1960	**£100**	**£50**	

WEBB, GEORGE

Title	Format	Label	Cat. No.	Year	Mint	VG	Notes
George Webb Dixielanders	7" EP	Melodisc	WPM770	195–	**£5**	**£2**	

WEBB, JIMMY

Jimmy Webb is a songwriter of genius – 'By The Time I Get To Phoenix', 'Didn't We', 'MacArthur Park' and 'Wichita Lineman' are early landmarks in his career. His own records reveal him to be a limited but effective singer, with *Land's End* containing some particularly fine material.

Title	Format	Label	Cat. No.	Year	Mint	VG	Notes
And So On	LP	Reprise	K44134	1971	**£10**	**£4**	
El Mirage	LP	Atlantic	K50370	1977	**£10**	**£4**	
I Keep It Hid	7"	CBS	3672	1968	**£6**	**£2.50**	*B side Shane Martin*
Jim Webb Sings Jim Webb	LP	CBS	63335	1968	**£15**	**£6**	
Land's End	LP	Asylum	SYL9014	1974	**£10**	**£4**	
Letters	LP	Reprise	K44173	1972	**£10**	**£4**	
Words And Music	LP	Reprise	RSLP6421	1970	**£12**	**£5**	
Words And Music	LP	Reprise	K44101	1971	**£10**	**£4**	

WEBB, JOHN

Title	Format	Label	Cat. No.	Year	Mint	VG	Notes
Experiment Of Love	12"	Numa	NUM14	1986	**£6**	**£2.50**	
Experiment Of Love	7"	Numa	NU14	1986	**£4**	**£1.50**	

WEBB, JOHNNY

Title	Format	Label	Cat. No.	Year	Mint	VG	Notes
Dig	7"	Columbia	DB3805	1956	**£5**	**£2**	
Song Of The Moon	7"	Columbia	DB3904	1957	**£5**	**£2**	
Travelin' Man	7"	Melodisc	MEL1617	196–	**£8**	**£4**	*picture sleeve*

WEBB, PETA

Title	Format	Label	Cat. No.	Year	Mint	VG	Notes
I Have Wandered In Exile	LP	Topic	12TS223	1973	**£25**	**£10**	

WEBB, PETA & PETE COOPER

Title	Format	Label	Cat. No.	Year	Mint	VG	Notes
Heart Is True	LP	Heart	HR001	1986	**£10**	**£4**	

WEBB, ROGER

Title	Format	Label	Cat. No.	Year	Mint	VG	Notes
John, Paul And All That Jazz	LP	Parlophone	PMC1233	1964	**£12**	**£5**	

WEBB, SKEETER

Title	Format	Label	Cat. No.	Year	Mint	VG	Notes
Was It A Bad Dream	7"	Parlophone	CMSP32	1955	**£8**	**£4**	*export*

WEBB, SONNY & THE CASCADES

Title	Format	Label	Cat. No.	Year	Mint	VG	Notes
You've Got Everything	7"	Oriole	CB1873	1963	**£25**	**£12.50**	
You've Got Everything	7"	Polydor	NH52158	1963	**£6**	**£2.50**	

WEBBER, MARLENE

Title	Format	Label	Cat. No.	Year	Mint	VG	Notes
My Baby	7"	Bamboo	BAM33	1970	**£5**	**£2**	*Brentford All Stars B side*

WEBBER SISTERS

Title	Format	Label	Cat. No.	Year	Mint	VG	Notes
My World	7"	Island	WI3109	1967	**£10**	**£5**	*Alva Lewis B side*

WEBER, EBERHARD

Title	Format	Label	Cat. No.	Year	Mint	VG	Notes
Colours Of Chloe	LP	ECM	ECM1042ST	1974	**£12**	**£5**	
Following Morning	LP	ECM	ECM1084ST	1976	**£10**	**£4**	
Yellow Fields	LP	ECM	ECM1066ST	1975	**£12**	**£5**	

WEBS

Title	Format	Label	Cat. No.	Year	Mint	VG	Notes
This Thing Called Love	7"	London	HLU10188	1968	**£5**	**£2**	

WEBSTER, BEN

Title	Format	Label	Cat. No.	Year	Mint	VG	Notes
Ben Webster	10" LP	Vogue Coral	LRA10021	1955	**£60**	**£30**	
Ben Webster And Associates	LP	HMV	CLP1336	1960	**£20**	**£8**	
Ben Webster Meets Oscar Peterson	LP	HMV	CLP1412/ CSD1336	1960	**£20**	**£8**	
Ben Webster With Strings	LP	Columbia	33CX10014	1955	**£25**	**£10**	
Big Sound	LP	Verve	VLP9100	1966	**£12**	**£5**	
See You At The Fair	LP	HMV	CLP1806	1964	**£20**	**£8**	
Soulville	LP	Columbia	33CX10122	1958	**£25**	**£10**	

WEBSTER, DEENA

Title	Format	Label	Cat. No.	Year	Mint	VG	Notes
Tuesday's Child	LP	Parlophone	PMC/PCS7052	1968	**£20**	**£8**	
You're Losing	7"	Parlophone	R5699	1968	**£5**	**£2**	

WEDDING PRESENT

Title	Format	Label	Cat. No.	Year	Mint	VG	Notes
Blue Eyes	7"	RCA	PB45185	1992	**£6**	**£2.50**	*no. 1 of 1992 singles*
Brassneck	7"	RCA	PB43403	1990	**£6**	**£2.50**	*handpainted cover*
Brassneck	CD-s	RCA	PD43404	1990	**£5**	**£2**	
Come Play With Me	7"	RCA	PB45313	1992	**£4**	**£1.50**	*no. 5 of 1992 singles*
Don't Try And Stop Me Mother	12"	Reception	REC002/12	1986	**£6**	**£2.50**	
Evening Show EP	CD-s	Strange Fruit	SFNTCD016	1988	**£5**	**£2**	
Go Go Dancer	7"	RCA	PB45183	1992	**£5**	**£2**	*no. 2 of 1992 singles*

Go Out And Get 'Em Boy!	7"	Reception	REC001	1985	£30	£15	
Go Out And Get 'Em Boy!	7"	City Slang	CSL001	1985	£20	£10	
Katrusyu	7"	RCA		1989	£8	£4	*promo only*
Kennedy	CD-s	RCA	PD43118	1989	£5	£2	
Make Me Smile	CD-s	RCA	PD44022	1990	£5	£2	
Million Miles	7"	Reception		1987	£8	£4	*promo only*
My Favourite Dress	7"	Reception	REC005	1987	£5	£2	*white vinyl*
Nobody's Twisting Your Arm	CD-s	Reception	REC009CD	1988	£5	£2	
Once More	7"	Reception	REC002	1986	£8	£4	
Peel Sessions	CD-s	Strange Fruit	SFPSCD009	1988	£5	£2	
Silver Shorts	7"	RCA	PB45311	1992	£4	£1.50	*no. 4 of 1992 singles*
This Boy Can Wait	12"	Reception	REC003/12	1986	£6	£2.50	
This Boy Can Wait	7"	Reception	REC003	1986	£5	£2	
Three	7"	RCA	PB45181	1992	£4	£1.50	*no. 3 of 1992 singles*
Tommy	LP	Reception	LEEDS2	1988	£15	£6	*signed, with poster*
Why Are You Being So Reasonable Now	CD-s	Reception	REC011CD	1988	£5	£2	

WEDGE

No One Left But Me	LP	private		197–	£40	£20	*US*

WEDGES

Hang Ten	LP	Time	(S)T2090	1963	£20	£8	*US*

WEE WILLIE & THE WINNERS

Get Some	7"	Action	ACT4624	1974	£5	£2	

WEED

Weed	LP	Philips	6305096	1971	£100	£50	*German*

WEED, BUDDY

Kent Song	7"	Vogue	V9075	1957	£15	£7.50	

WEEDON, BERT

$64,000 Question	7"	Parlophone	R4256	1957	£8	£4	
Big Note Blues	7"	Parlophone	R4446	1958	£5	£2	
Boy With The Magic Guitar	7"	Parlophone	MSP6242	1956	£10	£5	
Demonstration Record With David Gell	7" EP	Selmer		1959	£5	£2	
Fifi	7"	Saga	SAG2906	1959	£8	£4	
Guitar Boogie Shuffle	7"	Top Rank	JAR117	1959	£4	£1.50	
Guitar Man	7" EP	HMV	7EG8856	1964	£8	£4	
Honky Tonk Guitar	LP	Top Rank	35101	1961	£20	£8	
King Size Guitar	LP	Top Rank	BUY026	1960	£25	£10	
Night Cry	7"	HMV	POP1141	1963	£6	£2.50	
Play That Big Guitar	7"	Parlophone	R4381	1957	£5	£2	
Roulette	7" EP	Top Rank	TR5004	1959	£8	£4	*with other artists*
Soho Fair	7"	Parlophone	R4315	1957	£8	£4	
Teenage Guitar	7"	Top Rank	JAR136	1959	£4	£1.50	
Tune For Two	7"	HMV	POP1039	1962	£8	£4	*demo only*
Waxing The Winners	7" EP	Esquire	EP56	1955	£15	£7.50	
Weedon Winners	7" EP	Top Rank	JKP3008	1961	£10	£5	

WEGMULLER, WALTER

Tarot	LP	Kosmische	KK258003	1973	£150	£75	*German boxed double*

WEIR, BOB

Ace	LP	Warner Bros	K46165	1972	£10	£4	

WEIR, FRANK ORCHESTRA

Theme From Journey Into Space	7"	Decca	F10435	1955	£4	£1.50	

WEIRD STRINGS

Criminal Cage	7"	Ace	ACE009	1980	£5	£2	
Oscar Mobile	7"	Velvet Moon	VM1	1980	£6	£2.50	

WEIRDOS

We Got The Neutron Bomb	7"	Dangerhouse	SP1063	1978	£10	£5	

WELCH, BOB

French Kiss	LP	Capitol	EST11663	1977	£12	£5	*US picture disc*

WELCH, BRUCE

Please Mr Please	7"	EMI	EMI2141	1974	£60	£30	

WELCH, ELIZABETH

Stormy Weather	7"	Industrial	IR002	1980	£6	£2.50	

WELCH, KEN & MITZIE

Piano, Ice Box And Bed	7" EP	London	RER1275	1962	£5	£2	

WELCH, LENNY

Darling Take Me Back	7"	London	HLR9981	1965	£5	£2	
Rags To Riches	LP	London	HAR8290	1966	£10	£4	
Run To My Lovin' Arms	7"	London	HLR10010	1965	£6	£2.50	
Since I Fell For You	LP	Cadence	CLP5068/25068	1963	£12	£5	*US*
Two Different Worlds	LP	London	HAR/SHR8267	1966	£10	£4	

WELCH, TIM

Weak In The Knees	7"	Columbia	DB4529	1960	£4	£1.50	

WELDON, LIAM

Dark Horse On The Wind	LP	Mulligan	LUN066	1976	£25	£10	

WELFARE STATE

Welfare State Songs	LP	Look	LKLP6347	1978	£75	£37.50	

WELK, LAWRENCE ORCHESTRA

Addams Family Theme	7"	Dot	DS16607	1961	£15	£7.50	

WELLER, PAUL

Paul Weller's new status as one of the major rock figures of the nineties is an astonishing turn around for a man who floundered in a critical wilderness for most of the eighties. Despite the tremendous success of the Jam, Weller's Style Council seldom impressed, seeming for the most part like the work of a man whose creative inspiration was evaporated. Fortunately, his nineties recordings are something else again, the new influence of late-sixties groups like Traffic proving to be highly beneficial.

Above The Clouds	12"	Go! Discs	GODX91	1992	£8	£4	
Above The Clouds	CD-s	Go! Discs	GODCD91	1992	£12	£6	
Brushed	7"	Island	ISJB666	1997	£4	£1.50	*jukebox issue*
CD Sampler	CD	Go!Discs	no number	1995	£40	£20	*promo*
Conversation With Paul Weller	CD	London	PRCD70072	1995	£30	£15	*US promo*
Heavy Soul	CD	Island	PWICD1	1997	£50	£25	*boxed set*
Hung Up	12"	Go! Discs	GODX111	1994	£6	£2.50	
Hung Up	CD-s	Go! Discs	GODCD111	1994	£8	£4	
In Conversation	CD	Island	INTCD3	1999	£25	£10	*interview promo*
Into Tomorrow	12"	Freedom High	FHPT1	1991	£15	£7.50	
Into Tomorrow	7"	Freedom High	FHP1	1991	£10	£5	
Into Tomorrow	CD-s	Freedom High	FHPCD1	1991	£40	£20	
Kings Road	CD	Island	KINGS1	1997	£30	£15	*promo*
Live At The Hayward Gallery	LP	Southern Songs	WELLER1	1997	£60	£30	*promo*
Live Wood	CD	Pony Canyon	PCCY00601	1994	£30	£15	*Japanese with bonus CD single*
More Wood	CD	Pony Canyon	PCCY00509	1994	£20	£8	*Japanese*
Out Of The Sinking	CD-s	Go! Discs	GODCD121	1994	£6	£2.50	
Out Of The Sinking	CD-s	Go! Discs	GODCD143	1996	£5	£2	
Paul Weller Special	CD	Our Price		1995	£60	£30	*promo*
Peacock Suit	CD-s	Go! Discs	PWRT1	1996	£25	£12.50	*promo*
Sexy Sadie	CD-s	Go! Discs	PNPCD1	1994	£20	£10	*promo*
Songs Of Paul Weller 1982–1988	CD	EMI	CDWELLER3	1989	£100	£50	*promo sampler*
Stanley Road	CD	Go! Discs	8286192	1995	£20	£8	*in 12" box*
Stanley Road	LP	Go! Discs	8500707	1995	£30	£15	*as boxed set of 6 singles*
Sunflower	12"	Go! Discs	GODX102	1993	£10	£5	
Sunflower	7"	Go! Discs	GOD102	1993	£5	£2	
Sunflower	CD-s	Go! Discs	GODCD102	1993	£12	£6	
Uh Huh Oh Yeh	12"	Go! Discs	GODX86	1992	£8	£4	
Uh Huh Oh Yeh	7"	Go! Discs	GOD86	1992	£4	£1.50	
Uh Huh Oh Yeh	CD-s	Go! Discs	GODCD86	1992	£12	£6	
Walk On Gilded Splinters	12"	Go! Discs	SPLINT1	1995	£50	£25	*1 sided promo*
Weaver	10"	Go! Discs	GODT107	1994	£8	£4	
Weaver	CD-s	Go! Discs	GODCD107	1993	£15	£7.50	
Whirlpools End	12"	Go! Discs	LYNCH1	1995	£50	£25	*1 sided promo*
Wild Wood	10"	Go! Discs	GODT104	1993	£8	£4	*with poster*
Wild Wood	CD	London	8285132/ CDP1216	1993	£25	£10	*US with bonus 3 track CD*
Wild Wood	CD	Go! Discs	8284352	1993	£12	£5	*fold-out cover*
Wild Wood	CD-s	Go! Discs	GODCD104	1993	£12	£6	
Wild Wood	CD-s	Go! Discs	PWBCD1	1993	£10	£5	*promo*
Wild Wood To Heavy Soul	CD	Island	PAULCD1	1997	£30	£15	*promo*

WELLES, ORSON

Courtroom Scene From Compulsion	7"	Top Rank	TR5001	1959	£5	£2	*picture sleeve*
War Of The Worlds	LP	Charisma	DCS10	1969	£12	£5	*double*

WELLS, BOBBY

Let's Coppa Groove	7"	Beacon	3102	1968	£4	£1.50	*yellow label*

WELLS, DICKY

Bones For The King	LP	Felsted	FAJ7006	1959	£12	£5	
Trombone Four-In-Hand	LP	Felsted	FAJ7009/SJA2009	1960	£12	£5	

WELLS, HOUSTON

Anna Marie	7"	Parlophone	R5099	1964	£6	£2.50	
Blowing Wild	7"	Parlophone	R5069	1963	£6	£2.50	
Blue Of The Night	7"	Parlophone	R5226	1965	£4	£1.50	
Just For You	7" EP	Parlophone	GEP8878	1963	£40	£20	
Livin' Alone	7"	Parlophone	R5141	1964	£6	£2.50	
Only The Heartaches	7"	Parlophone	R5031	1963	£6	£2.50	
Ramona	7" EP	Parlophone	GEP8914	1964	£60	£30	
Shutters And Boards	7"	Parlophone	R4980	1962	£6	£2.50	

Title	Format	Label	Cat. No.	Year	Mint	VG	Notes
This Song Is Just For You	7"	Parlophone	R4955	1962	£6	£2.50	
Western Style	LP	Parlophone	PMC1215	1963	£40	£20	

WELLS, JEAN

Title	Format	Label	Cat. No.	Year	Mint	VG	Notes
World! Here Comes Jean Wells	LP	Sonet	SNTF606	1970	£20	£8	

WELLS, JOHNNY

Title	Format	Label	Cat. No.	Year	Mint	VG	Notes
Lonely Moon	7"	Columbia	DB4377	1959	£5	£2	

WELLS, JUNIOR

Title	Format	Label	Cat. No.	Year	Mint	VG	Notes
Blues With A Beat	7" EP	Delmark	DJB1	1966	£20	£10	
Coming At You	LP	Vanguard	SVRL19011	1968	£12	£5	
Hoodoo Man Blues	7"	Delmark	DS9612	1966	£15	£7.50	
Hoodoo Man Blues	LP	Delmark	DL612	1966	£15	£6	US
It's My Life Baby	LP	Fontana	(S)TFL6084	1966	£15	£6	
It's My Life Baby	LP	Vanguard	SVRL19028	1968	£10	£4	
Junior Wells	7" EP	XX	MIN715	196–	£10	£5	
On Tap	LP	Delmark	DS635	1975	£10	£4	
Southside Blues Jam	LP	Delmark	DS628	1971	£10	£4	
You're Tuff Enough	LP	Mercury	SMCL20130	1968	£10	£4	

WELLS, KITTY

Title	Format	Label	Cat. No.	Year	Mint	VG	Notes
After Dark	LP	Decca	DL8888	1959	£12	£5	US
Country Hit Parade	LP	Decca	DL8293	1956	£15	£6	US
Dust On The Bible	LP	Decca	DL8858	1959	£12	£5	US
I Gave My Wedding Dress Away	7"	Brunswick	05920	1964	£4	£1.50	
Kitty Sings	7" EP	Brunswick	OE9149	1955	£12	£6	
Kitty Wells Story	LP	Decca	DX(S)B(7)174	1963	£10	£4	*US, with booklet*
Kitty's Choice	LP	Brunswick	LAT8361	1961	£12	£5	
Winner Of Your Heart	LP	Decca	DL8552	1956	£15	£6	US

WELLS, MARY

Title	Format	Label	Cat. No.	Year	Mint	VG	Notes
Ain't It The Truth	7"	Stateside	SS372	1965	£8	£4	
Bye Bye Baby	LP	Oriole	PS40051	1963	£50	£25	
Dear Lover	7"	Atlantic	AT4067	1966	£10	£5	
Doctor	7"	Stateside	SS2111	1968	£4	£1.50	
Greatest Hits	LP	Tamla Motown	TML11032	1966	£20	£8	
Greatest Hits	LP	Motown	616	1964	£30	£15	US
He's A Lover	7"	Stateside	SS439	1965	£6	£2.50	
Laughing Boy	7"	Oriole	CBA1829	1963	£40	£20	
Live On Stage	LP	Motown	611	1963	£50	£25	US
Love Songs To The Beatles	LP	Stateside	(S)SL10171	1966	£20	£8	
Mary Wells	7" EP	Tamla Motown	TME2007	1965	£40	£20	
Mary Wells	LP	Stateside	SL10133	1965	£20	£8	
Me And My Baby	7"	Atlantic	584054	1966	£4	£1.50	
Me Without You	7"	Stateside	SS463	1965	£6	£2.50	
My Baby Just Cares For Me	LP	Tamla Motown	TML11006	1965	£25	£10	
My Guy	7"	Stateside	SS288	1964	£4	£1.50	
My Guy	LP	Stateside	SL10095	1964	£30	£15	
Never Never Leave Me	7"	Stateside	SS415	1965	£6	£2.50	
Nothing But A Man	LP	Motown	(MS)630	1965	£30	£15	US
One Who Really Loves You	LP	Motown	605	1962	£75	£37.50	US
Ooh	LP	Movietone	71010/72010	1966	£15	£6	US
Servin' Up Some Soul	LP	Stateside	(S)SL10266	1968	£12	£5	
Set My Soul On Fire	7"	Atlantic	584104	1967	£4	£1.50	
Two Lovers	7"	Oriole	CBA1796	1963	£30	£15	
Two Lovers	LP	Oriole	PS40045	1963	£50	£25	
Two Sides Of Mary Wells	LP	Atlantic	587049	1966	£12	£5	
Use Your Head	7"	Stateside	SS396	1965	£6	£2.50	
Vintage Stock	LP	Motown	653	1966	£30	£15	US
You Beat Me To The Punch	7"	Oriole	CBA1762	1962	£30	£15	
You Lost The Sweetest Boy	7"	Stateside	SS242	1963	£12	£6	
Your Old Standby	7"	Oriole	CBA1847	1963	£40	£20	

WELLSTOOD, DICK

Title	Format	Label	Cat. No.	Year	Mint	VG	Notes
Dick Wellstood	10" LP	London	HBU1059	1956	£15	£6	

WELSH, ALEX

Title	Format	Label	Cat. No.	Year	Mint	VG	Notes
Alex Welsh And His Band	10" LP	Nixa	NJT507	1957	£20	£8	
Alex Welsh And His Band '69	LP	Columbia	S(C)X6333	1969	£15	£6	
Alex Welsh Entertains	7" EP	Strike	JHE201	1966	£20	£10	
At Home With Alex Welsh	LP	Columbia	S(C)X6213	1968	£15	£6	
Band Showcase Vol. 1	LP	Black Lion	BLP12120	1975	£15	£6	
Band Showcase Vol. 2	LP	Black Lion	BLP12121	1976	£15	£6	
Dixieland Party	LP	Columbia	SCX6376	1970	£15	£6	
Echoes Of Chicago	LP	Columbia	33SX1429	1962	£20	£8	
Evening With . . . Vol. 1	LP	Black Lion	BLP12112	1972	£15	£6	
Evening With . . . Vol. 2	LP	Black Lion	BLP12113	1972	£15	£6	
If I Had A Talking Picture	LP	Black Lion	BLP12109	1972	£15	£6	
In Concert	LP	Black Lion	BLP12115/6	1972	£15	£6	*double*
It's Right Here For You	LP	Columbia	33SX1322/ SCX3377	1961	£20	£8	
Melrose Folio	10" LP	Nixa	NJT516	1958	£20	£8	
Music From Pete Kelly	7" EP	Decca	DFE6315	1955	£15	£7.50	
Music Of The Mauve Decade	LP	Columbia	33SX1219	1960	£20	£8	

Salute To Satchmo	LP	Black Lion	BLP12161/2	1976	£15	£6	double
Strike One	LP	Strike	JHL102	1967	£15	£6	
Tribute To Louis Armstrong Vol. 1	LP	Polydor	2460123	1971	£15	£6	
Tribute To Louis Armstrong Vol. 2	LP	Polydor	2460124	1971	£15	£6	
Tribute To Louis Armstrong Vol. 3	LP	Polydor	2460125	1971	£15	£6	
Welsh Wails	7" EP	Columbia	SEG8143	1962	£15	£7.50	

WENDY & LISA

Are You My Baby	CD-s	Virgin	VSCD1156	1989	£5	£2	3" single
Don't Try To Tell Me	CD-s	Virgin	VSCDX1337	1990	£5	£2	with 3 prints
Lolly Lolly	CD-s	Virgin	VSCD1175	1989	£5	£2	3" single
Satisfaction	CD-s	Virgin	VSCD1194	1989	£5	£2	3" single
Sideshow	CD-s	Virgin	CDEP16	1988	£5	£2	
Waterfall '89	CD-s	Virgin	VSCD1223	1989	£5	£2	3" single

WERKHOVEN, HENK

Orphical Positions	LP	VMU		1981	£60	£30	Dutch

WERLWINDS

Winding It Up	7"	Columbia	DB4650	1961	£10	£5	

WESKE, BRIAN

In The Midst Of The Crowd	7"	Oriole	CB1723	1962	£4	£1.50	
Twenty-four Hours In A Day	7"	Oriole	CB1776	1962	£4	£1.50	

WESLEY, FRED

House Party	12"	RSO	RSO67	1980	£12	£6	
House Party	7"	RSO	RSO67	1980	£5	£2	

WESS, FRANK

Frank Wess Quintet	10" LP	Atlantic	ATLLP1	195–	£40	£20	

WEST

Bridges	LP	Epic	26433	1969	£15	£6	US
West	LP	Epic	26380	1968	£15	£6	US

WEST, ADAM

Batman	LP	Twentieth Century	TF(S)4180	1966	£40	£20	US, with Burt Ward
Batman And Robin	7"	Target	TGT111	1976	£4	£1.50	

WEST, BRUCE & LAING

Live 'n' Kicking	LP	RSO	2394128	1974	£12	£5	
Whatever Turns You On	LP	RSO	2394107	1973	£10	£4	
Why Dontcha	LP	CBS	65314	1973	£10	£4	

WEST, DODIE

Going Out Of My Head	7"	Decca	F12046	1964	£4	£1.50	
In The Deep Of The Night	7"	Piccadilly	7N35239	1965	£6	£2.50	picture sleeve

WEST, HEDY

Ballads	LP	Topic	12T163	1967	£20	£8	
Getting Folk Out Of The Country	LP	Folk Variety	FV12008	1973	£15	£6	German, with Bill Clifton
Hedy West	LP	Vanguard	VRS9124	1963	£20	£8	US
Hedy West Vol. 2	LP	Vanguard	VRS/VSD79162	1964	£15	£6	US
Love, Hell And Biscuits	LP	Bear Family	BF15003	1976	£12	£5	German
Old Times And Hard Times	LP	Topic	12T117	1965	£20	£8	
Pretty Saro	LP	Topic	12T146	1966	£20	£8	
Serves 'Em Fine	LP	Fontana	STL5432	1967	£20	£8	

WEST, KEITH

Keith West was the singer with Tomorrow, and his solo singles featured at least some of the members of that group. Certainly guitarist Steve Howe can be heard on West's hit, 'Excerpt From A Teenage Opera'. The opera from which this song was supposedly taken never did appear, although a 1996 CD compilation of songs and out-takes made by Keith West and Mark Wirtz created a shadow of the work – the closest we are ever likely to get to the real thing. In any event, the single works brilliantly in isolation as a tantalizing glimpse of something much larger, but invisible.

Excerpt From A Teenage Opera	7"	Parlophone	R5623	1967	£4	£1.50	
On A Saturday	7"	Parlophone	R5713	1968	£25	£12.50	
Sam	7"	Parlophone	R5651	1967	£4	£1.50	
Sam	7"	Parlophone	R5651	1967	£10	£5	promo in picture sleeve
Smashing Time	LP	Stateside	(S)SL10224	1968	£20	£8	

WEST, LESLIE

Leslie West Band	LP	Phantom	701	1975	£10	£4	US
Mountain	LP	Bell	SBLL126	1969	£20	£8	

WEST, MAE

Fabulous Mae West	LP	Brunswick	LAT8082	1956	£15	£6	
Great Balls Of Fire	LP	Polydor	2315207	1973	£10	£4	
Twist And Shout	7"	Stateside	SS2021	1967	£8	£4	
Way Out West	LP	Stateside	(S)SL10197	1967	£10	£4	

WEST, SPEEDY

Capitol Presents	10" LP	Capitol	LC6619	1953	£20	£8	with Jimmy Bryant

Guitar Spectacular	LP	Capitol	(S)T1835	1962	**£15**	**£6**	*US*
Steel Guitar	LP	Capitol	(S)T1341	1960	**£20**	**£8**	*US*
Two Guitars Country Style	10" LP	Capitol	LC6694	1955	**£20**	**£8**	*with Jimmy Bryant*
Two Guitars Country Style	10" LP	Capitol	H520	1954	**£75**	**£37.50**	*US, with Jimmy Bryant*
Two Guitars Country Style	LP	Capitol	T520	1956	**£40**	**£20**	*US, with Jimmy Bryant*
Two Guitars Country Style Part 1	7" EP	Capitol	EAP1520	1955	**£12**	**£6**	*with Jimmy Bryant*
Two Guitars Country Style Part 2	7" EP	Capitol	EAP2520	1955	**£12**	**£6**	*with Jimmy Bryant*
West Of Hawaii	LP	Capitol	T956	1958	**£25**	**£10**	*US*

WEST COAST CONSORTIUM

Colour Sergeant Lillywhite	7"	Pye	7N17482	1968	**£10**	**£5**	
Some Other Someday	7"	Pye	7N17352	1967	**£4**	**£1.50**	

WEST COAST DELEGATION

Reach The Top	7"	Deram	DM113	1967	**£5**	**£2**	

WEST COAST KNACK

I'm Aware	7"	Capitol	CL15497	1967	**£8**	**£4**	

WEST COAST POP ART EXPERIMENTAL BAND

Child's Guide To Good & Evil	LP	Reprise	RSLP6298	1968	**£75**	**£37.50**	
Help I'm A Rock	7" EP	Reprise	RVEP60104	1966	**£125**	**£62.50**	*French*
Part One	LP	Reprise	R(S)6247	1967	**£75**	**£37.50**	*US*
Volume 2	LP	Reprise	R(S)6270	1967	**£75**	**£37.50**	*US*
West Coast Pop Art Experimental Band	LP	Fifo	M101	1966	**£1500**	**£1000**	*US*
Where's My Daddy	LP	Amos	AAS7004	1969	**£60**	**£30**	*US*

WEST COAST WORKSHOP

Wizard Of Oz And Other Trans Love Trips	LP	Capitol	ST2776	1967	**£30**	**£15**	*US*

WEST FIVE

But If It Doesn't Work Out	7"	HMV	POP1513	1966	**£4**	**£1.50**	
Congratulations	7"	HMV	POP1396	1965	**£20**	**£10**	
Just Like Romeo And Juliet	7"	HMV	POP1428	1965	**£8**	**£4**	

WEST INDIANS

Falling In Love	7"	Doctor Bird	DB1127	1968	**£10**	**£5**	
Never Gonna Give You Up	7"	Dynamic	DYN413	1971	**£4**	**£1.50**	*Rebellious Subjects B side*
Right On Time	7"	Doctor Bird	DB1121	1968	**£10**	**£5**	
Strange Whisperings	7"	Camel	CA16	1969	**£5**	**£2**	*Carl Dawkins B side*

WEST ONE

California '69	7"	Que	Q9	1988	**£5**	**£2**	*test pressing*

WEST POINT SUPERNATURAL

Time Will Tell	7"	Reaction	591013	1967	**£6**	**£2.50**	

WEST WON

Control	CD-s	Fun After All	CDFAA116D	1992	**£5**	**£2**	

WESTBROOK, MIKE

Celebration	LP	Deram	DML/SML1013	1967	**£50**	**£25**	
Citadel/Room 315	LP	RCA	SF8433	1975	**£15**	**£6**	
Cortege	LP	Original	ORA309	1982	**£25**	**£10**	*3 LP set*
Goose Sauce	LP	Original	ORA001	1978	**£15**	**£6**	
Life Of Its Own	7"	Deram	DM234	1969	**£5**	**£2**	
Little Westbrook Music	LP	Westbrook	LWN1	1983	**£15**	**£6**	
Live	LP	Cadillac	SGC1001	1974	**£20**	**£8**	
London Bridge Is Broken Down	LP	Venture	VEB13	1988	**£25**	**£10**	*3 LP boxed set*
Love Songs	LP	Deram	SML1069	1970	**£75**	**£37.50**	
Love, Dream And Variations	LP	Transatlantic	TRA323	1975	**£20**	**£8**	
Mama Chicago	LP	RCA	PL25252	1979	**£25**	**£10**	*double*
Marching Song Vol. 1	LP	Deram	DML/SML1047	1969	**£50**	**£25**	
Marching Song Vol. 2	LP	Deram	DML/SML1048	1969	**£50**	**£25**	
Metropolis	LP	Neon	NE10	1971	**£30**	**£15**	
Metropolis	LP	RCA	SF8396	1974	**£25**	**£10**	
Metropolis/Citadel/Room 315	LP	RCA		1979	**£20**	**£8**	*double*
On Duke's Birthday	LP	Hat Art	2021	1984	**£15**	**£6**	
Original Peter	7"	Deram	DM311	1970	**£50**	**£25**	*with Norma Winstone*
Piano	LP	Original	ORA002	1978	**£15**	**£6**	
Plays For The Record	LP	Transatlantic	TRA312	1976	**£20**	**£8**	
Release	LP	Deram	DML/SML1031	1968	**£50**	**£25**	
Requiem	7"	Deram	DM286	1970	**£5**	**£2**	
Tyger	LP	RCA	SER5612	1971	**£30**	**£15**	
Westbrook Blake	LP	Original	ORA203	1980	**£15**	**£6**	
Westbrook–Rossini	LP	Hat Art	2040	1987	**£12**	**£5**	

WESTFAUSTER

In A King's Dream	LP	Nasco	9008	1971	**£75**	**£37.50**	*US*

WESTLAKE, JILL

Sharin'	7"	Columbia	DB4132	1958	**£4**	**£1.50**	

WESTLAKE, KEVIN

Title	Format	Label	Number	Year	Price	Price	Notes
Stars Fade	LP	Utopia	1388	1976	**£12**	**£5**	*US*

WESTMINSTER FIVE

Title	Format	Label	Number	Year	Price	Price	Notes
Railroad Blues	7"	Carnival	CV7017	1964	**£6**	**£2.50**	
Sticks And Stones	7"	Carnival	CV7019	1965	**£6**	**£2.50**	

WESTON, KIM

Title	Format	Label	Number	Year	Price	Price	Notes
For The First Time	LP	MGM	C(S)8055	1967	**£30**	**£15**	
Helpless	7"	Tamla Motown	TMG554	1966	**£60**	**£30**	
I Got What You Need	7"	MGM	MGM1338	1967	**£6**	**£2.50**	
I'm Still Loving You	7"	Tamla Motown	TMG511	1965	**£60**	**£30**	
Kim Kim Kim	LP	Stax	2362021	1971	**£15**	**£6**	
Kim Weston	7" EP	Tamla Motown	TME2005	1965	**£60**	**£30**	
Little More Love	7"	Stateside	SS359	1964	**£60**	**£30**	
Nobody	7"	MGM	MGM1382	1968	**£10**	**£5**	
Rock Me A Little While	7" EP	Tamla Motown	TME2015	1966	**£150**	**£75**	
Take Me In Your Arms	7"	Tamla Motown	TMG538	1965	**£30**	**£15**	
That's Groovy	7"	MGM	MGM1357	1967	**£6**	**£2.50**	

WESTON, RANDY

Title	Format	Label	Number	Year	Price	Price	Notes
Cole Porter In Modern Mood	10" LP	London	HAPB1040	1955	**£30**	**£15**	
Randy Weston Trio	10" LP	London	HBU1046	1956	**£30**	**£15**	
Randy Weston Trio	LP	London	HAU2018	1956	**£20**	**£8**	
Trio And Solo	LP	Riverside	RLP12227	196–	**£15**	**£6**	

WESTWIND

Title	Format	Label	Number	Year	Price	Price	Notes
Love Is	LP	Penny Farthing	PELS505	1970	**£150**	**£75**	

WESTWOOD

Title	Format	Label	Number	Year	Price	Price	Notes
Winner Takes All	LP	Intercord	INT145610	1980	**£25**	**£10**	

WET WET WET

Title	Format	Label	Number	Year	Price	Price	Notes
Angel Eyes	7"	Precious	JEWEL6	1987	**£8**	**£4**	*boxed with calendar*
Angel Eyes	CD-s	Polygram	0802742	1988	**£15**	**£7.50**	*CD video*
Angel Eyes	CD-s	Precious	JWLCD6	1987	**£8**	**£4**	
Broke Away	CD-s	Mercury	JWLCD10	1989	**£5**	**£2**	
Hold Back The River	CD-s	Precious	JWLCD11	1990	**£5**	**£2**	
I Can Give You Everything	7"	Lyntone		1990	**£4**	**£1.50**	*flexi*
I Remember	12"	Precious	JEWEL512	1987	**£10**	**£5**	
I Remember	7"	Precious	JEWEL5	1987	**£6**	**£2.50**	
Stay With Me Heartache	CD-s	Precious	JWLCD13	1990	**£5**	**£2**	
Sweet Little Mystery	12"	Precious	JEWEL412	1987	**£12**	**£6**	*'wet' cover*
Sweet Little Mystery	7"	Precious	JWLS4	1987	**£8**	**£4**	*shaped picture disc*
Sweet Surrender	CD-s	Precious	JWLCD9	1989	**£5**	**£2**	
Temptation	CD-s	Precious	JWLCD7	1988	**£8**	**£4**	
Temptation	CD-s	Polygram	0804762	1988	**£15**	**£7.50**	*CD video*
Video Singles	CD-s	Polygram	0803389	1988	**£15**	**£7.50**	*CD video*
Wishing I Was Lucky	12"	Precious	JWLD3	1987	**£10**	**£5**	*double*
Wishing I Was Lucky	12"	Precious	JEWEL312	1987	**£6**	**£2.50**	

WETTLING, GEORGE

Title	Format	Label	Number	Year	Price	Price	Notes
George Wettling Jazz Band	10" LP	Columbia	33S1019	1954	**£12**	**£5**	

WHALEFEATHERS

Title	Format	Label	Number	Year	Price	Price	Notes
Declare	LP	Nasco	9003	1969	**£100**	**£50**	*US*
Whalefeathers	LP	Blue Horizon	2431009	1971	**£40**	**£20**	
Whalefeathers	LP	Nasco	9005	1970	**£75**	**£37.50**	*US*

WHALES

Title	Format	Label	Number	Year	Price	Price	Notes
Come Down Little Bird	7"	CBS	3766	1968	**£5**	**£2**	

WHAM!

Title	Format	Label	Number	Year	Price	Price	Notes
Bad Boys	7"	Innervision	IVLA3143	1983	**£5**	**£2**	*poster picture sleeve*
Bad Boys	7"	Innervision	IVLWA3143	1983	**£10**	**£5**	*picture disc*
Bad Boys	7"	Epic	no number	1983	**£4**	**£1.50**	*KP Crisps freebie*
Club Tropicana	7"	Innervision	IVLWA3613	1983	**£10**	**£5**	*picture disc*
Club Tropicana	7"	Epic	KELL4	1984	**£4**	**£1.50**	*Rice Krispies freebie*
Everything She Wants	12"	Epic	QTA4949	1985	**£8**	**£4**	*with calendar*
Fantastic	CD	Innervision	CDIVL25328	1983	**£50**	**£25**	
Final	LP	Epic	WHAM2	1986	**£40**	**£20**	*2 gold vinyl discs, inserts, boxed*
Freedom	7"	Epic	WA4743	1984	**£8**	**£4**	*shaped picture disc*
Freedom	7"	Epic	QA4743	1984	**£10**	**£5**	*shaped picture disc*
Last Christmas	7"	Epic	GA4949	1984	**£4**	**£1.50**	*gatefold sleeve*
Make It Big	CD	Epic	CDEPC86311	1984	**£50**	**£25**	
Merry Xmas From Wham!	7"	Epic	no number	1984	**£10**	**£5**	
Wake Me Up Before You Go-Go	12"	Epic	TA4440	1984	**£12**	**£6**	*poster sleeve*
Wake Me Up Before You Go-Go	CD-s	Epic	6549153	1989	**£10**	**£5**	*3" single*
Wham Rap!	12"	Innervision	IVLA122442	1982	**£8**	**£4**	*Panos/Ridgeley credit*

Wham Rap!	12"	Innervision	IVLA122442	1982	**£10**	**£5**	*picture sleeve*
Wham Rap!	7"	Innervision	IVLA2442	1982	**£4**	**£1.50**	*Panos/Ridgeley credit*

WHAT KEEPS US RUNNING

What Keeps Us Running	LP	Seagull		1979	**£25**	**£10**	*Dutch*

WHAT'S NEW

Early Morning Rain	7" EP	Number One	LOU2013	196–	**£8**	**£4**	*French*
Get Away	7" EP	Number One	LOU2014	196–	**£8**	**£4**	*French*

WHEATSTRAW, PEETIE

Devil's Son-In-Law	LP	Matchbox	SDR191	1969	**£12**	**£5**	
High Sheriff From Hell	LP	Matchbox	SDR192	1969	**£12**	**£5**	

WHEELER, KENNY

Gnu High	LP	ECM	ECM1069ST	1975	**£12**	**£5**	
Song For Someone	LP	Incus	INCUS10	197–	**£25**	**£10**	
Windmill Tilter	LP	Fontana	STL5494	1968	**£60**	**£30**	*with Johnny Dankworth*

WHEELS

Herbie Armstrong has enjoyed a lengthy and varied career – gaining chart hits as a member of Fox and of Yellow Dog, playing on several Van Morrison LPs and doing much other session work besides. His roots, however, go back to Belfast and an R&B group called Wheels. The group made two singles, then changed its name to Wheels-A-Way for a third.

Bad Little Woman/Call My Name	7"	Columbia	DB7827	1966	**£75**	**£37.50**	
Bad Little Woman/Road Block	7"	Columbia	DB7827	1966	**£250**	**£150**	*best auctioned*
Gloria	7"	Columbia	DB7682	1965	**£75**	**£37.50**	
Kicks	7"	Columbia	DB7981	1966	**£75**	**£37.50**	

WHEELS OF TIME

1984	7"	Spin	62008	1967	**£25**	**£12.50**	

WHICHWHAT

Whichwhat's First	LP	Beacon	BEAS14	1970	**£30**	**£15**	

WHIRLWIND

Midnight Blue	7"	Chiswick	PSR447	1980	**£5**	**£2**	*promo*

WHIRLWINDS

The Whirlwinds were led by Graham Gouldman, of later songwriting and 10cc fame.

Look At Me	7"	HMV	POP1301	1964	**£40**	**£20**	

WHISKERS

Beat Parade '65	LP	Ariola	73967	1965	**£30**	**£15**	*German*

WHISKEY, NANCY

Bowling Green	7"	Fontana	TF612	1965	**£4**	**£1.50**	
He's Solid Gone	7"	Oriole	CB1394	1957	**£10**	**£5**	
Hillside In Scotland	7"	Oriole	CB1452	1958	**£6**	**£2.50**	
Intoxicating Miss Whiskey	LP	Mercury	MG10018	1957	**£30**	**£15**	*with Chas McDevitt*
Nancy Whiskey	8" EP	Topic	T7	195–	**£20**	**£10**	
Old Grey Goose	7"	Oriole	CB1485	1959	**£5**	**£2**	

WHISPERS

Whispers	LP	Mojo	2916003	1971	**£12**	**£5**	
Whispers	LP	Contempo	CRM106	1974	**£12**	**£5**	
Whispers Gettin' Louder	LP	Janus	9104400	1974	**£10**	**£4**	

WHISPERS OF TRUTH

Whispers Of Truth	LP	Key			**£25**	**£10**	

WHISTLER

Ho-Hum	LP	Deram	SML1083	1971	**£20**	**£8**	

WHITBREAD, SHARON

Spice Of LIfe	LP	Ra			**£50**	**£25**	

WHITCOMB, IAN

Good Hard Rock	7"	Capitol	CL15431	1966	**£4**	**£1.50**	
Good Hard Rock	7" EP	Capitol	EAP122008	1966	**£8**	**£4**	*French*
Nervous	7" EP	Capitol	EAP122004	1965	**£10**	**£5**	*French*
Sporting Life	7" EP	Capitol	EAP160002	1965	**£8**	**£4**	*French*
You Turn Me On	7"	Capitol	CL15395	1965	**£5**	**£2**	
You Turn Me On	LP	Ember	NR5065	1967	**£30**	**£15**	

WHITE, BARRY

All In The Run Of A Day	7"	President	PT139	1967	**£5**	**£2**	

WHITE, BRIAN & THE MAGNA JAZZ BAND

Brian White And The Magna Jazz Band	LP	HMV	CLP1534	1962	**£50**	**£25**	

WHITE, BUKKA

Blues Masters Vol. 4	LP	Blue Horizon	4604	1972	**£12**	**£5**	*US*
Bukka White	LP	CBS	52629	1969	**£30**	**£15**	

Memphis Hot Shots	LP	Blue Horizon	763229	1969	£40	£20	
Sic 'Em Dogs	LP	Herwin	201	1965	£20	£8	US
Sky Songs	LP	Fontana	688804ZL	1966	£15	£6	

WHITE, DANNY

Keep My Woman Home	7"	Sue	WI4031	1967	£20	£10	

WHITE, DUKE

It's Over	7"	Island	WI084	1963	£10	£5	
Sow Good Seeds	7"	Black Swan	WI444	1965	£10	£5	

WHITE, GEORGIA

Was I Drunk?	78	Vocalion	V1038	1954	£12	£6	

WHITE, IAN

Ian White	LP	private		1970	£20	£8	

WHITE, JAY

Faraway Places	7" EP	London	REF1045	1956	£6	£2.50	

WHITE, JEANETTE

Music	7"	A&M	AMS761	1969	£15	£7.50	

WHITE, JOE

Baby I Care	7"	Big	BG309	1971	£4	£1.50	
Downtown Girl	7"	Island	WI166	1965	£10	£5	*Don Drummond B side*
Hog In A Coco	7"	Island	WI159	1964	£10	£5	*Roland Alphonso B side*
I Need A Woman	7"	Doctor Bird	DB1090	1967	£10	£5	
If It Don't Work Out	7"	Gayfeet	GS202	1973	£4	£1.50	
Irene	7"	Island	WI201	1965	£10	£5	
Kenyatta	7"	Dynamic	DYN440	1972	£4	£1.50	
Lonely Nights	7"	Doctor Bird	DB1080	1967	£10	£5	
My Guiding Star	7"	Sugar	ESS102	1969	£4	£1.50	
My Love For You	7"	Doctor Bird	DB1024	1966	£10	£5	*Sammy Ismay B side*
Punch You Down	7"	Ska Beat	JB180	1965	£10	£5	*Tommy McCook B side*
Rudies All Around	7"	Doctor Bird	DB1069	1966	£10	£5	
Since The Other Day	LP	Magnet	MGT006	197–	£12	£5	
Sinners	7"	R&B	JB137	1964	£10	£5	*Roland Alphonso B side*
This Is The Time	7"	Big	BG301	1970	£4	£1.50	
Trinity	7"	Songbird	SB1072	1972	£4	£1.50	*Scotty B side*
Try A Little Tenderness	7"	Blue Cat	BS119	1968	£8	£4	*Lyn Taitt B side*
Way Of Life	7"	Blue Cat	BS108	1968	£8	£4	
When You Are Young	7"	Island	WI145	1964	£10	£5	
Yesterday	7"	Sugar	SU103	1970	£4	£1.50	

WHITE, JOHN & GAVIN BRYARS

Machine Music	LP	Obscure	OBS8	1978	£10	£4	

WHITE, JOSH

Ballads And Blues	10" LP	Brunswick	LA8562	1953	£12	£5	
Ballads And Blues Vol. 2	10" LP	Brunswick	LA8653	1954	£12	£5	
Beginning	LP	Mercury	20039MCL	1964	£12	£5	
Beverly And Josh White Jnr	7" EP	Realm	REP4003	1964	£5	£2	*with Beverly White*
Blues And . . . Pt 1	7" EP	Pye	NJE1057	1957	£6	£2.50	
Blues And . . . Pt 2	7" EP	Pye	NJE1058	1957	£6	£2.50	
Blues And . . . Pt 3	7" EP	Pye	NJE1059	1957	£6	£2.50	
Blues And Josh White	LP	Nixa	NJL2	1957	£12	£5	
Blues Singer And Balladeer	LP	Storyville	SLP175	1965	£10	£4	
John Henry, Ballads, Blues And Other Songs	LP	Storyville	SLP123	1962	£10	£4	
Josh	LP	Elektra	EKL114	195–	£10	£4	US
Josh At Midnight	LP	Elektra	EKL102	195–	£10	£4	US
Josh Comes A-Visitin'	10" LP	London	HAPB1038	1955	£12	£5	
Josh White	10" LP	London	338	195–	£12	£5	US
Josh White	7" EP	Mercury	10006MCE	1964	£6	£2.50	
Josh White	LP	Decca	DL8665	1957	£12	£5	US
Josh White & Big Bill Broonzy	LP	Period	1209	196–	£12	£5	*US, with Big Bill Broonzy*
Josh White Program	10" LP	London	HAPB1005	1951	£15	£6	
Josh White's Blues	LP	Mercury	MG20203	1956	£12	£5	US
Live!	LP	HMV	CLP1588	1962	£10	£4	
Singer Supreme	LP	World Record Club	T298	196–	£10	£4	
Sings Vol. 2	10" LP	London	HAPB1032	1954	£12	£5	
Songs By Josh White	10" LP	Mercury	MG25014	1954	£12	£5	
Southern Blues	7" EP	Mercury	YEP9504	1956	£6	£2.50	
Stories Vol. 1	LP	HMV	CLP1159	1958	£10	£4	
Stories Vol. 2	LP	HMV	CLP1175	1958	£10	£4	
Storyville Blues Anthology Vol. 8	7" EP	Storyville	SEP388	1964	£6	£2.50	
Twenty-Fifth Anniversary Album	LP	Elektra	EKL123	195–	£10	£4	US

WHITE, KITTY & DAVID HOWARD

Jesse James .... 7" .... London .... HL8102 .... 1954 £**25** .... £**12.50** ....

WHITE, LENNY

Venusian Summer .... LP .... Atlantic .... K50213 .... 1975 £**10** .... £**4** ....

WHITE, LOUISA JANE

When the Battle Is Over .... 7" .... Philips .... BF1810 .... 1969 £**5** .... £**2** ....

WHITE, TAM

Lewis Carroll .... 7" .... Middle Earth ... MDS104 .... 1970 £**5** .... £**2** ....
Tam White .... LP .... Middle Earth ... MDLS304 .... 1970 £**25** .... £**10** ....
That Old Sweet Roll .... 7" .... Deram .... DM261 .... 1969 £**4** .... £**1.50** ....

WHITE, TERRY

Rock Around The Mailbag .... 7" .... Decca .... F11133 .... 1959 £**30** .... £**15** ....

WHITE, TONY JOE

Black And White .... LP .... Monument .... SMO5027 .... 1968 £**10** .... £**4** ....
Continued .... LP .... Monument .... SMO5035 .... 1969 £**10** .... £**4** ....
Tony Joe .... LP .... Monument .... SMO5043 .... 1970 £**10** .... £**4** ....

WHITE, TREVOR

Crazy Kids .... 7" .... Island .... WIP6291 .... 1976 £**6** .... £**2.50** .... *picture sleeve*

WHITE HART

In Search Of Reward .... LP .... Tradition .... TSR033 .... 1978 £**20** .... £**8** ....

WHITE HEAT

City Beat .... 7" .... Valium .... VAL03 .... 1981 £**5** .... £**2** ....
Finished With The Fashions .... 7" .... Valium .... VAL02 .... 1980 £**5** .... £**2** ....
In The Zero Hour .... LP .... Valium .... VALP101 .... 1982 £**12** .... £**5** ....
Nervous Breakdown .... 7" .... Valium .... VAL1 .... 1980 £**5** .... £**2** ....

WHITE LIGHT

White Light .... LP .... Century .... 39955 .... 1969 £**300** .... £**180** .... *US*

WHITE LIGHTNING

Midnight Approaches .... LP .... Workshop .... JOBLP2 .... 1990 £**10** .... £**4** ....
This Poison Fountain .... 7" .... Wild Party .... PP1000 .... 1984 £**25** .... £**12.50** ....

WHITE NOISE

Electric Storm .... LP .... Island .... ILPS9099 .... 1969 £**15** .... £**6** .... *pink label*

WHITE ON BLACK

White On Black .... LP .... Saydisc .... SDL251 .... 1974 £**30** .... £**15** ....

WHITE PLAINS

When You Are A King .... LP .... Deram .... SML1092 .... 1971 £**15** .... £**6** ....
White Plains .... LP .... Deram .... SML1067 .... 1970 £**15** .... £**6** ....

WHITE SPIRIT

High Upon High .... 7" .... MCA .... MCA652 .... 1981 £**10** .... £**5** .... *no picture sleeve*
Midnight Chaser .... 7" .... MCA .... MCA638 .... 1981 £**20** .... £**10** ....
White Spirit .... LP .... MCA .... MCF3079 .... 1980 £**15** .... £**6** ....

WHITE SS

Mercy Killing .... 7" .... White SS .... CIA72 .... 1978 £**15** .... £**7.50** ....

WHITE TRASH

Road To Nowhere .... 7" .... Apple .... 6 .... 1969 £**8** .... £**4** ....

WHITEFIRE

Suzanne .... 7" .... Whitefire .... 98DB001 .... 1978 £**30** .... £**15** ....

WHITEHORN, GEOFF

Whitehorn .... LP .... Stateside .... ISS80164 .... 1974 £**15** .... £**6** .... *Japanese*

WHITEHOUSE

The disturbing, aggressive industrial music made by Whitehouse was issued on a number of privately pressed LPs during the eighties. A distressing Fascist theme runs through much of it, which is apparently intended to be ironic, but within work that is not otherwise notable for any trace of humour it is easy to mistake the irony for the real thing.

Birthdeath Experience .... LP .... Come Organisation .... WDC881004 .... 1980 £**50** .... £**25** ....
Buchenwald .... LP .... Come Organisation .... WDC881013 .... 1981 £**30** .... £**15** ....
Dedicated To Peter Kurten .... LP .... Come Organisation .... WDC881010 .... 1981 £**40** .... £**20** ....
Erector .... LP .... Come Organisation .... WDC881007 .... 1980 £**40** .... £**20** ....
Great White Death .... LP .... Come Organisation .... WDC881069 .... 1981 £**30** .... £**15** ....
Live Action 1 .... cass .... Come Organisation .... WDC881020 .... 1982 £**12** .... £**5** ....
Live Action 2 .... cass .... Come Organisation .... WDC881022 .... 1982 £**12** .... £**5** ....

Title	Format	Label	Cat. No.	Year	Mint	VG	Notes
New Britain	LP	Come Organisation	WDC881017	1982	£50	£25	
One Hundred And Fifty Murderous Passions	LP	Come Organisation		198–	£30	£15	
Psychopathia Sexualis	LP	Come Organisation	WDC881027	198–	£60	£30	clear or black vinyl
Right To Kill	LP	Come Organisation	WDC881033	198–	£30	£15	
Total Sex	LP	Come Organisation	WDC881005	1980	£50	£25	

WHITESNAKE

Title	Format	Label	Cat. No.	Year	Mint	VG	Notes
Bloody Mary	7"	EMI	INEP751	1978	£6	£2.50	*picture sleeve, white vinyl*
Deeper The Love	CD-s	EMI	CDEM128	1990	£5	£2	
Fool For Your Loving	7"	United Artists	BP352	1980	£5	£2	*luminous sleeve*
Give Me All Your Love	12"	EMI	12EM23	1988	£6	£2.50	*white vinyl*
Give Me All Your Love	12"	EMI	12EMP23	1988	£6	£2.50	*picture disc*
Give Me All Your Love	CD-s	EMI	CDEM23	1988	£5	£2	
Guilty Of Love	7"	Liberty	BPP420	1983	£5	£2	*picture disc*
Here I Go Again	10"	EMI	10EMI35	1987	£6	£2.50	*white vinyl*
Here I Go Again	7"	Liberty	BPP416	1982	£5	£2	*picture disc*
Is This Love	7"	EMI	EMP3	1987	£5	£2	*shaped picture disc*
Is This Love	CD-s	EMI	CDEM3	1987	£5	£2	
Live At Hammersmith	LP	Polydor	MPF1288	1980	£12	£5	*Japanese*
Now You're Gone	7"	EMI	EMPD150	1990	£4	£1.50	*shaped picture disc, plinth*
Now You're Gone	CD-s	EMI	CDEM150	1990	£5	£2	
Slide It In	LP	Liberty	LBGP2400000	1984	£10	£4	*picture disc*
Standing In The Shadow	7"	Liberty	BPP423	1984	£4	£1.50	*picture disc*
Still Of The Night	12"	EMI	12EMIP5606	1987	£6	£2.50	*picture disc*
Still Of The Night	7"	EMI	EMIW5606	1987	£4	£1.50	*white vinyl, with poster*
Take Me With You	12"	Liberty		1982	£6	£2.50	*1 sided promo*
Victim Of Love	7"	Liberty	BP418	1982	£20	£10	
Whitesnake 1987	LP	EMI	EMC3528	1987	£10	£4	*picture disc*

WHITFIELD, DAVID

Title	Format	Label	Cat. No.	Year	Mint	VG	Notes
Adoration Waltz	7"	Decca	F10833	1957	£5	£2	
Alone	7" EP	Decca	STO158	1962	£6	£2.50	*stereo*
Beyond The Stars	7"	Decca	F10458	1955	£8	£4	
Book	7"	Decca	F10242	1954	£10	£5	
Cara Mia	7"	Decca	F10327	1954	£10	£5	
Cara Mia	7" EP	Decca	DFE6225	1955	£8	£4	
David Whitfield No. 1	7" EP	Decca	DFE6342	1956	£5	£2	
David Whitfield No. 2	7" EP	Decca	DFE6400	1957	£5	£2	
David Whitfield No. 3	7" EP	Decca	DFE6434	1957	£5	£2	
Everywhere	7"	Decca	F10515	1955	£8	£4	
From David With Love	LP	Decca	LK4270	1958	£10	£4	
I'll Find You	7"	Decca	F10864	1957	£5	£2	
I'll Never Stop Loving You	7"	Decca	F10596	1955	£4	£1.50	
Lady	7"	Decca	F10562	1955	£4	£1.50	
Land Of Hope And Glory	7"	Denman Discs	DD105	1977	£10	£5	
My September Love	7"	Decca	F10690	1956	£5	£2	
My Son John	7"	Decca	F10769	1956	£5	£2	
Santo Natale	7"	Decca	F10399	1954	£6	£2.50	
Scottish Soldier	7"	Decca	F11336	1961	£50	£25	
Smile	7"	Decca	F10355	1954	£5	£2	
When You Lose The One You Love	7"	Decca	F10627	1955	£5	£2	
Whitfield Favourites	LP	Decca	LK4242	1958	£10	£4	
You Belong In Someone Else's Arms	7"	HMV	POP1180	1963	£5	£2	
Yours From The Heart	10" LP	Decca	LF1165	1954	£15	£6	

WHITFIELD, WILBUR & THE PLEASERS

Title	Format	Label	Cat. No.	Year	Mint	VG	Notes
Heart To Heart	7"	Vogue	V9097	1958	£500	£330	*best auctioned*
P.B. Baby	7"	Vogue	V9078	1957	£250	£150	*best auctioned*
Plaything	7"	Vogue	V9091	1957	£300	£180	*best auctioned*

WHITING, LEONARD

Title	Format	Label	Cat. No.	Year	Mint	VG	Notes
Piper	7"	Pye	7N15943	1965	£15	£7.50	

WHITING, MARGARET

Title	Format	Label	Cat. No.	Year	Mint	VG	Notes
Capitol Presents	10" LP	Capitol	LC6585	1953	£15	£6	
Goin' Places	LP	London	HAD2109	1958	£20	£8	
Heat Wave	7"	Capitol	CL14242	1955	£8	£4	
Hot Spell	7"	London	HLD8662	1958	£8	£4	
I Can't Help It	7"	London	HLD8562	1958	£6	£2.50	
I Love A Mystery	7"	Capitol	CL14527	1956	£4	£1.50	
Just A Dream	LP	London	HAD2321	1961	£15	£6	
Just Like A Man	7"	London	HLD10114	1967	£4	£1.50	
Kill Me With Kisses	7"	London	HLD8451	1957	£8	£4	
Lover Lover	7"	Capitol	CL14375	1955	£8	£4	
Maggie Isn't Margaret Anymore	LP	London	HAU8332	1967	£10	£4	
Man	7"	Capitol	CL14348	1955	£8	£4	
Margaret Whiting	10" LP	Capitol	LC6811	1956	£15	£6	
My Own True Love	7"	Capitol	CL14213	1954	£8	£4	
Stowaway	7"	Capitol	CL14307	1955	£8	£4	
Wheel Of Hurt	LP	London	HAU/SHU8317	1967	£10	£4	

WHITLEY, RAY

Title	Format	Label	Cat. No.	Year	Mint	VG	Notes
I've Been Hurt	7"	HMV	POP1473	1965	£40	£20	

WHITMAN, SLIM

Title	Format	Label	Cat. No.	Year	Mint	VG	Notes
All Time Favorites	LP	Imperial	LP9252	1964	£10	£4	*US*
America's Favorite Folk Artist	10" LP	Imperial	LP3004	1954	£30	£15	*US*
And His Singing Guitar	10" LP	London	HAPB1015	1954	£40	£20	*gold label*
And His Singing Guitar	7" EP	London	REP1006	1954	£10	£5	*gold label*
And His Singing Guitar Vol. 2	LP	London	HAU2015	1956	£30	£15	
And His Singing Guitar Vol. 2 Pt 1	7" EP	London	REP1064	1956	£10	£5	*gold label*
And His Singing Guitar Vol. 2 Pt 2	7" EP	London	REP1070	1956	£10	£5	*gold label*
And His Singing Guitar Vol. 2 Pt 3	7" EP	London	REP1100	1957	£10	£5	*gold label*
Annie Laurie	LP	Imperial	LP9077	1959	£15	£6	*US*
Beautiful Dreamer	7"	London	HL8080	1954	£20	£10	*gold label*
Best Of Slim Whitman Vol. 2	LP	Liberty	LBY3060	1966	£10	£4	
Best Of Slim Whitman Vol. 3	LP	Liberty	LBY3092	1967	£10	£4	
Candy Kisses	7"	London	HLP8642	1958	£6	£2.50	
Country Songs, City Hits	LP	Liberty	LBY3034	1965	£10	£4	
Curtain Of Tears	7"	London	HLP8416	1957	£8	£4	
Dear Mary	7"	London	HLU8327	1956	£20	£10	*gold label*
Favorites	LP	Imperial	LP9003	1956	£25	£10	*US*
First Visit To Britain	LP	Imperial	LP9135	1960	£12	£5	*US*
Gone	7"	London	HLP8420	1957	£20	£10	*gold label*
Haunted Hungry Heart	7"	London	HL8141	1955	£20	£10	*gold label*
Heart Songs And Love Songs	LP	London	HAP8059	1963	£15	£6	
I Never See Maggie Alone	7"	London	HLP8835	1959	£5	£2	
I'll Never Stop Loving You	7"	London	HLU8167	1955	£20	£10	*gold label*
I'll Take You Home Again Kathleen	7"	London	HLP8403	1957	£10	£5	*gold label*
I'll Walk With God	LP	Imperial	LP9088	1960	£12	£5	*US*
I'm A Fool	7"	London	HLU8252	1956	£15	£7.50	*gold label*
I'm A Lonely Wanderer	LP	London	HAP8093	1963	£15	£6	
I'm Casting My Lasso	7"	London	HLU8350	1956	£15	£7.50	*gold label*
Indian Love Call	7"	London	L1149	1954	£15	£7.50	*gold label*
Irish Songs The Slim Whitman Way	7" EP	Liberty	LEP4018	1964	£8	£4	
Irish Songs The Whitman Way	LP	Imperial	LP9245	1963	£12	£5	*US*
Just Call Me Lonesome	LP	London	HAP2392	1961	£20	£8	
Lovesick Blues	7"	London	HLP8459	1957	£8	£4	
Many Times	7"	London	HLP8434	1957	£8	£4	
Million Record Hits	LP	Imperial	LP9102	1960	£12	£5	*US*
North Wind	7"	London	L1226	1954	£15	£7.50	*gold label*
Once In A Lifetime	LP	Imperial	LP9156	1961	£12	£5	*US*
Roll River Roll	7"	London	HLP9103	1960	£4	£1.50	
Rose Marie	7"	London	HL8061	1954	£10	£5	*gold label*
Satisfied Man	7" EP	Liberty	LEP4046	1966	£8	£4	
Secret Love	7"	London	HL8039	1954	£25	£12.50	*gold label*
Serenade	7"	London	HLU8287	1956	£15	£7.50	*gold label*
Singing Hills	7"	London	HL8091	1954	£20	£10	*gold label*
Sings	LP	Imperial	LP9064	1959	£15	£6	*US*
Slim Whitman	LP	London	HAP2343	1961	£20	£8	
Slim Whitman	LP	Imperial	LP9056	1958	£15	£6	*US*
Slim Whitman Sings	7" EP	London	REP1199	1959	£10	£5	*tri-centre*
Slim Whitman Sings	LP	London	HAP2139	1959	£20	£8	
Slim Whitman Sings	LP	Imperial	LP9026	1957	£25	£10	*US*
Slim Whitman Sings And Yodels	10" LP	RCA	LPM3217	1954	£30	£15	*US*
Slim Whitman Sings More Irish Songs	7" EP	Liberty	LEP4027	1965	£8	£4	
Slim Whitman Sings No. 2	7" EP	London	REP1258	1960	£10	£5	
Slim Whitman Sings Vol. 2	LP	London	HAP2199	1959	£20	£8	
Slim Whitman Sings Vol. 3	LP	London	SAHP6232	1962	£25	£10	*stereo*
Slim Whitman Sings Vol. 3	LP	London	HAP2443	1962	£20	£8	
Slim Whitman Sings Vol. 4	LP	London	HAP8013	1962	£15	£6	
Song Of The Wild	7"	London	HLU8196	1955	£20	£10	*gold label*
Song Of The Wild	7" EP	London	REP1042	1955	£10	£5	*gold label*
Stairway To Heaven	7"	London	HL8018	1954	£40	£20	*gold label*
There's A Rainbow In Every Teardrop	7"	London	L1214	1954	£15	£7.50	*gold label*
Tumbling Tumbleweeds	7"	London	HLU8230	1956	£15	£7.50	*gold label*
Unchain My Heart	7"	London	HLP8518	1957	£8	£4	
Vaya Con Dios	7"	London	HLP9302	1961	£4	£1.50	
Very Precious Love	7"	London	HLP8590	1958	£8	£4	
Wayward Wind	7" EP	London	REP1360	1963	£10	£5	
When I Grow Too Old To Dream	7"	London	HL8125	1955	£20	£10	*gold label*
Wherever You Are	7"	London	HLP8708	1958	£6	£2.50	
Yodelling	LP	Liberty	LBY3032	1964	£10	£4	

WHITNEY, MARVA

Title	Format	Label	Cat. No.	Year	Mint	VG	Notes
Daddy Don't Know About The Sugar Beat	7"	Mojo	2092041	1972	£5	£2	
I Sing Soul	LP	King	K1053	1969	£150	£75	*US*
It's My Thing	LP	Polydor	583767	1969	£100	£50	
Live And Lowdown At The Apollo	LP	King	K1079	1970	£100	£50	*US*
This Girl's In Love With You	7"	Polydor	2001036	1970	£10	£5	

WHITSETT, TIM

Title	Format	Label	Cat. No.	Year	Mint	VG	Notes
Macks By The Tracks	7"	Sue	WI318	1964	£12	£6	
Rhythm And Blues	7" EP	Range	JRE7002	196–	£12	£6	*with Sticks Herman*

WHITSUNTIDE EASTER

Title	Format	Label	Cat. No.	Year	Mint	VG	Notes
Next Time You Play A Wrong Note	LP	Grapevine	GRA109	1977	£200	£100	*at least 2 different covers*

WHITTLE, TOMMY

Title	Format	Label	Cat. No.	Year	Mint	Good	Notes
New Horizons	LP	Tempo	TAP27	1960	**£25**	**£10**	
Tommy Whittle	10" LP	Esquire	20048	1955	**£20**	**£8**	
Tommy Whittle Orchestra	10" LP	Esquire	20061	1956	**£10**	**£4**	
Tommy Whittle Quartet	10" LP	Esquire	20068	1956	**£10**	**£4**	
Waxing With Whittle	10" LP	Esquire	20028	1954	**£20**	**£8**	

WHIZZ KIDS

Title	Format	Label	Cat. No.	Year	Mint	Good	Notes
P.A.Y.E.	7"	Dead Good	DEADSIX	1979	**£5**	**£2**	
Suspect No. 1	7"	Quation	QYS1213	1980	**£5**	**£2**	

WHO

The Who's status as one of the world's most popular rock groups has inevitably led to a considerable interest in their early recordings, which fetch respectable prices even where they were chart hits. The three different B sides for the original issues of 'Substitute' are the result of a dispute between Brunswick and Reaction as to the ownership of the track 'Circles'. 'Instant Party' is the same track, whose change of title did not fool anyone, but 'Waltz For A Pig', credited to the Who Orchestra, is actually a Graham Bond Organisation instrumental. The 1976 reissue of 'Substitute' has the distinction of being the first twelve-inch single ever made, but stubbornly resists becoming a collectors' item. Meanwhile, the most expensive rarities include a withdrawn mail order compilation, *Who Did It*, and scarce picture sleeves for the singles 'Anyway, Anyhow, Anywhere' and 'My Generation'.

Title	Format	Label	Cat. No.	Year	Mint	Good	Notes
Acid Queen	7"	Track	PRO3	1969	**£30**	**£15**	*promo*
Anyway, Anyhow, Anywhere	7"	Brunswick	05935	1965	**£100**	**£50**	*picture sleeve*
Anyway, Anyhow, Anywhere	7"	Brunswick	05935	1965	**£12**	**£6**	
Athena/Why Did I Fall For That	12"	Polydor	WHOPX6	1982	**£10**	**£5**	*picture disc*
Christmas	7"	Track	PRO4	1969	**£30**	**£15**	*promo*
Circles	7"	Brunswick	05951	1966	**£100**	**£50**	*demo*
Direct Hits	LP	Track	612/613006	1969	**£15**	**£6**	
Dogs	7"	Track	604023	1968	**£6**	**£2.50**	
Excerpts From Tommy	7" EP	Track	2252001	1970	**£10**	**£5**	
Extracts From Thirty Years Of Maximum R&B	CD	Polydor	WHOBOX2	1994	**£20**	**£8**	*promo sampler*
Face Dances	LP	Mobile Fidelity	MFSL1115	1984	**£10**	**£4**	*US audiophile*
Filling In The Gaps	LP	Polydor	WHOT1	1981	**£60**	**£30**	*double interview promo*
Go To The Mirror	7"	Track	PRO2	1969	**£30**	**£15**	*promo*
Happy Jack	7"	Reaction	591010	1966	**£4**	**£1.50**	
Happy Jack	7" EP	Polydor	27799	1966	**£50**	**£25**	*French*
Happy Jack	LP	Decca	DL(7)4892	1967	**£25**	**£10**	*US*
I Can See For Miles	7"	Track	604011	1967	**£4**	**£1.50**	
I Can't Explain	7"	Brunswick	05926	1965	**£10**	**£5**	
I Can't Explain	7" EP	Brunswick	10668	1965	**£100**	**£50**	*French*
I'm A Boy	7"	Reaction	591004	1966	**£4**	**£1.50**	
I'm A Boy	7" EP	Polydor	27789	1966	**£50**	**£25**	*French*
I'm Free	7"	Track	PRO1	1969	**£30**	**£15**	*promo*
Instant Party	LP	Brunswick	BDV173269	1965	**£50**	**£25**	*Dutch*
It's Hard	LP	Warner Bros	237311	1982	**£20**	**£8**	*US audiophile promo*
Join Together	7"	Polydor	2094102	1972	**£10**	**£5**	*export, picture sleeve*
Join Together	CD-s	Virgin	VSCDT1259	1990	**£5**	**£2**	
Kids Are Alright	7"	Brunswick	05965	1966	**£20**	**£10**	
Kids Are Alright	7"	Brunswick	05956	1966	**£20**	**£10**	
Kids Are Alright	7" EP	Decca	60008	1966	**£50**	**£25**	*French*
Kids Are Alright	LP	Brunswick	177026	1967	**£50**	**£25**	*Dutch*
La La La Lies	7"	Brunswick	05968	1966	**£20**	**£10**	
Legal Matter	7"	Decca	AD1002	1968	**£40**	**£20**	*export*
Legal Matter	7"	Brunswick	05956	1966	**£15**	**£7.50**	
Legal Matter	7"	Brunswick	05956	1966	**£100**	**£50**	*export with Scandinavian picture sleeve*
Live At Leeds	CD	Polydor	5271692	1995	**£25**	**£10**	*boxed set*
Live At Leeds	LP	Track	2406001	1970	**£10**	**£4**	*12 inserts*
Long Live Rock	7"	MCA	41053	1979	**£15**	**£7.50**	*US picture disc, 6 different backs*
Magic Bus	7"	Track	604024	1968	**£4**	**£1.50**	
Magic Bus	LP	Decca	DL75064	1968	**£20**	**£8**	*US*
Making Of Tommy	LP	Polydor	SA010	1975	**£25**	**£10**	*US interview promo*
My Generation	7"	Brunswick	05944	1965	**£6**	**£2.50**	
My Generation	7"	Brunswick	05944	1965	**£150**	**£75**	*picture sleeve*
My Generation	7"	Decca	AD1001	1968	**£100**	**£50**	*export, picture sleeve*
My Generation	7"	Decca	AD1001	1968	**£50**	**£25**	*export*
My Generation	7" EP	Decca	60002	1965	**£50**	**£25**	*French*
My Generation	7" EP	Brunswick	10671	1965	**£50**	**£25**	*French*
My Generation	CD-s	Polydor	POCD907	1988	**£5**	**£2**	
My Generation	LP	Decca	DL(7)4664	1966	**£40**	**£20**	*US*
My Generation	LP	Brunswick	LAT8616	1965	**£75**	**£37.50**	
Out In The Street	7" EP	Decca	60004	1966	**£50**	**£25**	*French*
Phases	LP	Polydor	2675216	1981	**£75**	**£37.50**	*German 9 LP boxed set*
Pictures Of Lily	7"	Track	604002	1967	**£4**	**£1.50**	
Pictures Of Lily	7" EP	Polydor	27805	1967	**£50**	**£25**	*French*
Pinball Wizard	7"	Track	604027	1969	**£4**	**£1.50**	
Quadrophenia	CD	Mobile Fidelity	UDCD2550	1991	**£25**	**£10**	*US audiophile double*
Quadrophenia	LP	Track	2657013	1973	**£12**	**£5**	*double*

Quick One	LP	Reaction	593002	1966	**£40**	**£20**	
Ready Steady Who	7" EP	Reaction	592001	1966	**£25**	**£12.50**	
Ready Steady Who	7" EP	Polydor	27801	1966	**£40**	**£20**	*French*
Ready Steady Who	7" EP	Reaction	WHO7	1983	**£5**	**£2**	
Roger Daltrey & Pete Townshend Talk About Quadrophenia	LP	Polydor	PRO114	1979	**£20**	**£8**	*US interview promo*
See Me Feel Me	7"	Track	2094004	1970	**£10**	**£5**	
Seeker	7"	Track	604036	1970	**£4**	**£1.50**	
Substitute/Circles	7"	Reaction	591001	1966	**£10**	**£5**	
Substitute/Instant Party	7"	Reaction	591001	1966	**£10**	**£5**	
Substitute/Waltz For A Pig	7"	Reaction	591001	1966	**£6**	**£2.50**	
Summertime Blues	7"	Track	2094002	1970	**£4**	**£1.50**	
Thirty Years Of Maximum R&B	CD	Polydor	WHOBOX1	1994	**£20**	**£8**	*promo sampler*
Tommy	LP	Track	613013/014	1969	**£15**	**£6**	*double, book*
Tommy Part 1	LP	Track	2406007	1970	**£10**	**£4**	
Tommy Part 2	LP	Track	2406008	1970	**£10**	**£4**	
Under My Thumb	7"	Track	604006	1967	**£30**	**£15**	
Who	LP	Polydor	623025	1966	**£50**	**£25**	*German*
Who Are You	CD	Mobile Fidelity	UDCD561	1992	**£15**	**£6**	*US audiophile*
Who Are You	LP	MCA		1978	**£12**	**£5**	*US interview promo*
Who Are You	LP	MCA	P14950	1978	**£10**	**£4**	*US picture disc*
Who Are You	LP	Superdisk	SD166108	1981	**£12**	**£5**	*US audiophile*
Who Did It	LP	Track	2856001	1971	**£350**	**£210**	
Who Sell Out	LP	Track	613002	1967	**£30**	**£15**	*stereo*
Who Sell Out	LP	Track	612002	1967	**£40**	**£20**	*mono*
Who Sell Out	LP	Track	612002	1967	**£200**	**£100**	*with poster*
Who's Next	CD	Polydor	C88113	1988	**£15**	**£6**	*box set*
Who/Strawberry Alarm Clock	LP	Decca	DL734568	1969	**£30**	**£15**	*US, with Strawberry Alarm Clock*
Won't Get Fooled Again	7"	Track	2094009	1971	**£10**	**£5**	*picture sleeve*
Won't Get Fooled Again	7"	Track	A4112	1971	**£8**	**£4**	*1 sided promo*
Won't Get Fooled Again	CD-s	Polydor	POCD917	1988	**£5**	**£2**	

WHYTON, WALLY

All Over This World	7"	Parlophone	R4630	1960	**£4**	**£1.50**	
Don't Tell Me Your Troubles	7"	Parlophone	R4585	1959	**£5**	**£2**	
It's A Rat Race	7"	Pye	7N15304	1960	**£4**	**£1.50**	
Little Red Pony	7"	Piccadilly	7N35089	1961	**£4**	**£1.50**	

WIEBELFETZER

Live	LP	Bazillus	111-112	1971	**£30**	**£15**	*Swiss double*

WIEDLIN, JANE

Inside A Dream	CD-s	EMI	CDMT55	1988	**£5**	**£2**	
Rush Hour	CD-s	EMI	CDMT36	1988	**£5**	**£2**	

WIFFEN, DAVID

David Wiffen	LP	Fantasy	8411	1969	**£20**	**£8**	*US*

WIG

Live At The Jade Room	LP	Texas Archive	TAR3	1982	**£20**	**£8**	*US*

WIGGINS, GERALD

Music From Around The World In 80 Days	LP	London	LTZU15109	1958	**£15**	**£6**	

WIGGINS, PERCY

Book Of Memories	7"	Atlantic	584113	1967	**£6**	**£2.50**	

WIGGINS, SPENCER

I'm A Poor Man's Son	7"	Pama	PM794	1969	**£6**	**£2.50**	
Uptight Good Woman	7"	Stateside	SS2024	1967	**£5**	**£2**	

WIGGONS

Rock Baby	7"	Blue Beat	BB29	1961	**£12**	**£6**	

WIGWAM

Being	LP	Love	LRLP92	1974	**£20**	**£8**	*Swedish*
Dark Album	LP	Love	LRLP227	1978	**£15**	**£6**	*Swedish*
Fairyport	LP	Love	LRLP44/55	1971	**£30**	**£15**	*Swedish double*
Hard And Horny	LP	Love	LRLP9	1969	**£25**	**£10**	*Swedish*
Live From The Twilight Zone	LP	Love	LXPS517/8	1975	**£25**	**£10**	*Swedish double*
Lucky Golden Stripes And Starpose	LP	Virgin	V2051	1976	**£10**	**£4**	
Rumours On The Rebound	LP	Virgin	VD3503	1979	**£12**	**£5**	*double*
Tombstone Valentine	LP	Love	LRLP19	1970	**£30**	**£15**	*Swedish double*
Wicked Ivory	LP	Love	LRLP52	1972	**£20**	**£8**	*Swedish*
Wigwam	LP	Love	LRLP511	1972	**£20**	**£8**	*Swedish*

WILBURN BROTHERS

City Limits	LP	Brunswick	LAT8501	1961	**£10**	**£4**	
Cool Country	LP	Brunswick	LAT8686	1967	**£10**	**£4**	
Folk Songs	LP	Brunswick	LAT8507	1962	**£10**	**£4**	
Livin' In God's Country	LP	Decca	DL(7)8959	1959	**£10**	**£4**	*US*

Side By Side	LP	Brunswick	LAT8291	1959	**£12**	**£5**	
Silver Haired Daddy Of Mine	7"	Brunswick	05799	1959	**£5**	**£2**	
Wilburn Brothers	LP	Decca	DL8576	1957	**£12**	**£5**	*US*
Wonderful Wilburn Brothers	LP	King	746	1961	**£20**	**£8**	*US*

WILD & WANDERING

2000 Light Ales From Home	12"	Iguana	VYK14	1986	**£30**	**£15**	

WILD ANGELS

Buzz Buzz	7"	B&C	CB114	1970	**£5**	**£2**	
Nervous Breakdown	7"	Major Minor	MM569	1968	**£10**	**£5**	
Sally Ann	7"	B&C	CB123	1970	**£4**	**£1.50**	

WILD COUNTRY

Silent Country	7"	Trafalgar	TRAF01	1970	**£5**	**£2**	

WILD FLOWERS

Melt Like Ice	7"	No Future	FS11	1984	**£5**	**£2**	
Things Have Changed	7"	Reflex	RE2	1984	**£4**	**£1.50**	

WILD GEESE

Flight Two	LP	Joke	JLP207	1979	**£15**	**£6**	*German*

WILD HAVANA

Wild Havana	LP	private		1977	**£50**	**£25**	*Dutch*

WILD MAGNOLIAS

They Call Us Wild	7"	Barclay	BAR34	1975	**£5**	**£2**	
They Call Us Wild	LP	Barclay	XBLY90033	1975	**£15**	**£6**	*French*
Wild Magnolias	LP	Barclay	80529	1975	**£15**	**£6**	*French*

WILD OATS

Wild Oats	7" EP	Oak	RGJ117	1963	**£750**	**£500**	*best auctioned*

WILD ONES

Bowie Man	7"	Fontana	TF468	1964	**£25**	**£12.50**	

WILD SILK

Help Me	7"	Columbia	DB8611	1969	**£5**	**£2**	
Plaster Sky	7"	Columbia	DB8534	1969	**£6**	**£2.50**	

WILD SWANS

Revolutionary Spirit	12"	Zoo	CAGE009	1982	**£6**	**£2.50**	
Revolutionary Spirit	12"	Zoo	CAGE009	1981	**£15**	**£7.50**	*'Lament For Icarus' picture sleeve*
Revolutionary Spirit	7"	Zoo	CAGE009	1982	**£15**	**£7.50**	*test pressing*

WILD THING

Partyin'	LP	Polydor	2410003	1971	**£15**	**£6**	

WILD THYME

Plays Fallibroome	LP	Saydisc	SDL339	1983	**£10**	**£4**	

WILD TURKEY

Battle Hymn	LP	Chrysalis	CHR1002	1971	**£10**	**£4**	
Turkey	LP	Chrysalis	CHR1010	1972	**£10**	**£4**	

WILD UNCERTAINTY

Man With Money	7"	Planet	PLF120	1966	**£25**	**£12.50**	

WILD WALLY

I Go Ape	LP	Concord	CON1003	1970	**£10**	**£4**	

WILDCATS

Bandstand Record Hop	LP	United Artists	UAL3031	1958	**£25**	**£10**	*US*
Gazachstahagen	7"	London	HLT8787	1959	**£10**	**£5**	

WILDE, KIM

Another Step	CD	MCA	DMCF3339	1987	**£12**	**£5**	
Dancing In The Dark	12"	Rak	12RAK365	1983	**£6**	**£2.50**	*with poster*
Four Letter Word	CD-s	MCA	DKIM10	1988	**£5**	**£2**	
Heart Over Mind	CD-s	MCA	KIMTD16/ KIMXD16	1992	**£15**	**£7.50**	*2 single pack*
Hey Mr Heartache	CD-s	MCA	DKIM7	1988	**£5**	**£2**	
I Can't Say Goodbye	CD-s	MCA	DKIMT14	1990	**£5**	**£2**	
It's Here	CD-s	MCA	DKIMT12	1990	**£5**	**£2**	
Love In The Natural Way	CD-s	MCA	DKIM11	1989	**£5**	**£2**	*picture disc*
Never Trust A Stranger	CD-s	MCA	DKIM9	1988	**£5**	**£2**	
Rage To Love	7"	MCA	KIMP3	1985	**£6**	**£2.50**	*shaped picture disc*
Second Time	7"	MCA	KIMP1	1984	**£8**	**£4**	*picture disc*
Time (7" Version)	CD-s	MCA	DKIMT13	1990	**£5**	**£2**	
Time (Extended)	CD-s	MCA	DKIM13	1990	**£5**	**£2**	
Touch	7"	MCA	KIMP2	1984	**£6**	**£2.50**	*shaped picture disc*
You Came	CD-s	MCA	DKIM8	1988	**£6**	**£2.50**	*3" single*

WILDE, MARTY

Bad Boy	7"	Philips	PB972	1959	**£4**	**£1.50**	
Bad Boy	LP	Epic	LN3686	1960	**£30**	**£15**	*US*

Title	Format	Label	Number	Year	Mint	VG	Notes
Bye Bye Birdie	7" EP	Philips	BBE12472	1961	£6	£2.50	
Bye Bye Birdie	LP	Philips	ABL3383	1961	£12	£5	
Bye Bye Birdie No. 2	7" EP	Philips	BBE12473	1961	£6	£2.50	
Bye Bye Birdie No. 3	7" EP	Philips	BBE12474	1961	£6	£2.50	
Bye Bye Birdie No. 4	7" EP	Philips	BBE12475	1961	£6	£2.50	
Come Running	7"	Philips	PB1206	1961	£4	£1.50	
Come Running	7" EP	Philips	BBE12517	1962	£20	£10	
Diversions	LP	Philips	SBL7877	1969	£10	£4	
Donna	7"	Philips	PB902	1959	£5	£2	
Endless Sleep	7"	Philips	PB835	1958	£6	£2.50	
Ever Since You Said Goodbye	7"	Philips	326546BF	1962	£4	£1.50	
Fight	7"	Philips	PB1022	1960	£5	£2	
Hide And Seek	7"	Philips	PB1161	1961	£4	£1.50	
Honeycomb	7"	Philips	JK1028	1958	£30	£15	
I Wanna Be Loved By You	7"	Philips	PB1037	1960	£4	£1.50	
I've Got So Used To Loving You	7"	Philips	BF1490	1966	£4	£1.50	
Jezebel	7"	Philips	PB1240	1962	£4	£1.50	
Johnny Rocco	7"	Philips	PB1002	1960	£4	£1.50	
Kiss Me	7"	Columbia	DB7285	1964	£4	£1.50	
Little Girl	7"	Philips	PB1078	1960	£4	£1.50	
Lonely Avenue	7"	Columbia	DB4980	1963	£4	£1.50	
Love Bug Crawl	78	Philips	PB781	1958	£5	£2	
Marty	7" EP	Philips	433638BE	1963	£20	£10	
Marty Wilde Favourites	7" EP	Philips	BBE12422	1960	£20	£10	
Mexican Boy	7"	Decca	F11979	1964	£4	£1.50	
More Of Marty	7" EP	Philips	BBE12200	1958	£25	£12.50	
My Lucky Love	7"	Philips	PB850	1958	£4	£1.50	
No One Knows	7"	Philips	PB875	1958	£5	£2	
No! Dance With Me	7"	Philips	326579BF	1963	£4	£1.50	
Oh Oh I'm Falling In Love Again	7"	Philips	PB804	1958	£25	£12.50	
Presenting Marty Wilde	7" EP	Philips	BBE12164	1957	£30	£15	
Rock'n'Roll	LP	Philips	6308010	1970	£10	£4	
Rubber Ball	7"	Philips	PB1101	1961	£4	£1.50	
Save Your Love For Me	7"	Columbia	DB7145	1963	£4	£1.50	
Sea Of Love	7"	Philips	PB959	1959	£4	£1.50	
Sea Of Love	7" EP	Philips	BBE12327	1959	£25	£12.50	
Showcase	LP	Philips	BBL7380	1960	£25	£10	
Teenager In Love	7"	Philips	PB926	1959	£4	£1.50	
Tomorrow's Clown	7"	Philips	PB1191	1961	£4	£1.50	
Versatile Mr Wilde	7" EP	Philips	BBE12385	1960	£25	£12.50	
Versatile Mr Wilde	LP	Philips	BBL7385	1960	£25	£10	
Versatile Mr Wilde	LP	Philips	SBBL570	1960	£30	£15	*stereo*
When Does It Get To Be Love	7"	Philips	PB1121	1961	£4	£1.50	
Wilde About Marty	LP	Philips	BBL7342	1960	£30	£15	

WILDE THREE

Title	Format	Label	Number	Year	Mint	VG	Notes
I Cried	7"	Decca	F12232	1965	£40	£20	
Since You've Gone	7"	Decca	F12131	1965	£30	£15	

WILDER BROTHERS

Title	Format	Label	Number	Year	Mint	VG	Notes
I Want You	7"	HMV	POP365	1957	£125	£62.50	

WILDER, JOE

Title	Format	Label	Number	Year	Mint	VG	Notes
Jazz From Peter Gunn	LP	Philips	BBL7321	1959	£15	£6	
Joe Wilder	LP	London	LTZC15027	1957	£15	£6	

WILDFIRE

Title	Format	Label	Number	Year	Mint	VG	Notes
Brute Force And Ignorance	LP	Mausoleum	SKUL8307	1983	£15	£6	
Summer Lightning	LP	Mausoleum	SKUL8338	1983	£10	£4	

WILDHEARTS

Title	Format	Label	Number	Year	Mint	VG	Notes
Caffeine Bomb	12"	East West	YZ794T	1994	£15	£7.50	
Caffeine Bomb	7"	East West	YZ794	1994	£5	£2	*green vinyl*
Caffeine Bomb	CD-s	East West	YZ794CD	1994	£15	£7.50	
Don't Be Happy . . . Just Worry	CD	East West	509912022	1992	£20	£8	*double*
Don't Be Happy . . . Just Worry	LP	East West	509912021	1992	£20	£8	*double*
Fishing For Luckies	CD	East West	509990392	1994	£40	£20	
Fishing For More Luckies	LP	East West	0630128501	1995	£60	£30	
Greetings From Shitsville	7"	East West	YZ773	1993	£5	£2	*brown vinyl, insert*
If Life Is Like A Lovebank	CD-s	East West	YZ874CD	1996	£5	£2	
Living On A Landmine	CD	East West	SAM1582	1995	£20	£8	*promo sampler*
Mondo Akimbo A-Go-Go EP	12"	East West	YZ669T	1992	£25	£12.50	
Mondo Akimbo A-Go-Go EP	12"	East West	YZ669TX	1992	£40	£20	*white vinyl*
Mondo Akimbo A-Go-Go EP	CD-s	East West	YZ669CD	1992	£30	£15	
Naivety Play	CD	East West	SAM1555	1995	£20	£10	*promo*
Suckerpunch	10"	East West	YZ828TE	1994	£6	£2.50	*1 side etched*
Suckerpunch	7"	East West	SAM1262	1993	£25	£12.50	*Clawfinger B side*
Suckerpunch	CD-s	East West	YZ828CD	1994	£6	£2.50	
Suckerpunch	CD-s	East West	YZ828CDDJ	1994	£15	£7.50	*promo*
TV Tan	12"	East West	YZ784T	1993	£6	£2.50	
TV Tan	7"	East West	YZ784P	1993	£5	£2	*1 sided picture disc*
TV Tan	CD-s	East West	YZ784CD	1993	£8	£4	

WILDWEEDS

Title	Format	Label	Number	Year	Mint	VG	Notes
It Was Fun While It Lasted	7"	Chess	CRS8065	1967	£4	£1.50	
Wildweeds	LP	Vanguard	VSD6552	1970	£15	£6	*US*

WILEY, LEE

Title	Format	Label	Number	Year	Value 1	Value 2	Notes
Touch Of The Blues	LP	RCA	SF5003	1958	**£10**	**£4**	*stereo*

WILFRED & MILLIE

Title	Format	Label	Number	Year	Value 1	Value 2	Notes
Vow	7"	Island	WI190	1965	**£10**	**£5**	

WILHELM, MIKE

Title	Format	Label	Number	Year	Value 1	Value 2	Notes
Mike Wilhelm	LP	United Artists	ZZ1	1976	**£20**	**£8**	

WILKERSON, DON

Title	Format	Label	Number	Year	Value 1	Value 2	Notes
Elder Don	LP	Blue Note	BLP/BST84121	1963	**£40**	**£20**	
Preach, Brother!	LP	Blue Note	BLP/BST84107	1962	**£40**	**£20**	
Shoutin'	LP	Blue Note	BLP/BST84145	1963	**£40**	**£20**	

WILKINS, ERNIE

Title	Format	Label	Number	Year	Value 1	Value 2	Notes
Top Brass	LP	London	LTZC15013	1956	**£15**	**£6**	
Trumpets All Out	LP	London	LTZC15093	1957	**£15**	**£6**	

WILKINS, ROBERT

Title	Format	Label	Number	Year	Value 1	Value 2	Notes
Rev. Robert Wilkins	LP	Piedmont	PLP13162	196–	**£20**	**£8**	

WILKINS, ROGER

Title	Format	Label	Number	Year	Value 1	Value 2	Notes
Before The Reverence	LP	Spokane	SPL1002	1970	**£30**	**£15**	

WILKINSON, ARTHUR

Title	Format	Label	Number	Year	Value 1	Value 2	Notes
Beatle Cracker Suite	7" EP	HMV	7EG8919	1965	**£5**	**£2**	

WILKINSON TRI-CYCLE

Title	Format	Label	Number	Year	Value 1	Value 2	Notes
Wilkinson Tri-Cycle	LP	Date	TES4016	1969	**£30**	**£15**	*US*

WILLETT, SLIM

Title	Format	Label	Number	Year	Value 1	Value 2	Notes
Slim Willett	LP	Audio Lab	AL1542	1961	**£25**	**£10**	*US*

WILLETT FAMILY

Title	Format	Label	Number	Year	Value 1	Value 2	Notes
Roving Journeyman	LP	Topic	12T84	1962	**£20**	**£8**	

WILLETTE, BABY FACE

Title	Format	Label	Number	Year	Value 1	Value 2	Notes
Face To Face	LP	Blue Note	BLP/BST84068	1961	**£60**	**£30**	
Stop And Listen	LP	Blue Note	BLP/BST84084	1961	**£50**	**£25**	

WILLIAMS, AL

Title	Format	Label	Number	Year	Value 1	Value 2	Notes
I Am Nothing	7"	Grapevine	GRP136	1979	**£8**	**£4**	

WILLIAMS, ANDY

Title	Format	Label	Number	Year	Value 1	Value 2	Notes
Are You Sincere	7"	London	HLA8587	1958	**£8**	**£4**	
Baby Doll	7"	London	HLA8360	1956	**£20**	**£10**	*gold label*
Best	7" EP	London	REA1394	1963	**£10**	**£5**	
Best	LP	London	HAA8005	1962	**£10**	**£4**	
Big Hits	7" EP	London	REA1088	1957	**£12**	**£6**	
Big Hits No. 2	7" EP	London	REA1102	1957	**£12**	**£6**	
Butterfly	7"	London	HLA8399	1957	**£12**	**£6**	
Canadian Sunset	7"	London	HL7013	1956	**£4**	**£1.50**	*export*
Canadian Sunset	7"	London	HLA8315	1956	**£20**	**£10**	*gold label*
House Of Bamboo	7"	London	HLA8784	1959	**£5**	**£2**	
I Like Your Kind Of Love	7"	London	HLA8437	1957	**£10**	**£5**	
Lips Of Wine	7"	London	HLA8487	1957	**£10**	**£5**	
Lonely Street	7"	London	HLA8957	1959	**£4**	**£1.50**	
Lonely Street	LP	London	HAA2238	1960	**£12**	**£5**	
Promise Me, Love	7"	London	HLA8710	1958	**£8**	**£4**	
Sings Rodgers And Hammerstein	LP	London	HAA2113	1958	**£20**	**£8**	
Sings Steve Allen	LP	London	HAA2054	1957	**£20**	**£8**	
Two Time Winners	LP	London	HAA2203	1959	**£20**	**£8**	
Under Paris Skies	LP	London	HAA8090	1963	**£10**	**£4**	
Village Of St Bernadette	7"	London	HLA9018	1959	**£4**	**£1.50**	
Wake Me When It's Over	7"	London	HLA9099	1960	**£4**	**£1.50**	
Walk Hand In Hand	7"	London	HLA8284	1956	**£20**	**£10**	*gold label*

WILLIAMS, AUDREY

Title	Format	Label	Number	Year	Value 1	Value 2	Notes
Living It Up	7"	MGM	SP1179	1956	**£8**	**£4**	

WILLIAMS, BIG JOE

Title	Format	Label	Number	Year	Value 1	Value 2	Notes
Back To The Country	LP	Bounty	BY6018	1966	**£15**	**£6**	
Big Joe Williams	7" EP	XX	MIN700	196–	**£6**	**£2.50**	
Big Joe Williams	LP	XTRA	XTRA1033	1966	**£15**	**£6**	
Big Joe Williams	LP	Storyville	616011	1970	**£10**	**£4**	
Blues For Nine Strings	LP	Bluesville	BV1056	1963	**£15**	**£6**	*US*
Blues On Highway 49	LP	Delmark	DL604	1962	**£15**	**£6**	*US*
Blues On Highway 51	LP	Esquire	32191	1963	**£25**	**£10**	
Classic Delta Blues	LP	CBS	BPG63813	1964	**£10**	**£4**	
Crawlin' King Snake	LP	RCA	INTS1087	1970	**£10**	**£4**	
Hand Me Down My Old Walking Stick	LP	Liberty	LBL/LBS83207	1968	**£15**	**£6**	
Hell Bound And Heaven Sent	LP	Folkways	31004	1967	**£10**	**£4**	*US*
Mississippi's Big Joe Williams	LP	Folkways	F(S)3820	1962	**£15**	**£6**	*US*
On The Highway	7" EP	Delmark	DJB4	1966	**£8**	**£4**	
Piney Woods Blues	LP	77	LA1219	1963	**£20**	**£8**	
Portraits In Blues Vol. 4	LP	Storyville	SLP158	1964	**£12**	**£5**	
Portraits In Blues Vol. 7	LP	Storyville	SLP163	1964	**£12**	**£5**	

Title	Format	Label	Cat. No.	Year	Mint	VG	Notes
Starvin' Chain Blues	LP	Delmark	DL/DSD609	1966	£10	£4	US
Studio Blues	LP	Bluesville	BV1083	1964	£15	£6	US
Tough Times	LP	Fontana	688800ZL	1965	£10	£4	

WILLIAMS, BILLY

Title	Format	Label	Cat. No.	Year	Mint	VG	Notes
Begin The Beguine	7"	Coral	Q72414	1960	£4	£1.50	
Billy Williams	LP	Coral	LVA9092	1958	£20	£8	
Billy Williams Quartet	LP	MGM	E3400	1957	£20	£8	US
Billy Williams Revue	LP	Coral	LVA9139	1961	£15	£6	
Billy Williams Singing Oh Yeah	LP	Mercury	MG20317	1958	£20	£8	US
Butterfly	7"	Vogue Coral	Q72241	1957	£15	£7.50	
Crazy Little Palace	7"	Vogue Coral	Q72149	1956	£25	£12.50	
Don't Let Go	7"	Coral	Q72303	1958	£15	£7.50	
Follow Me	7"	Vogue Coral	Q72222	1957	£15	£7.50	
Goodnight Irene	7"	Coral	Q72369	1959	£15	£7.50	
Got A Date With An Angel	7"	Vogue Coral	Q72295	1957	£15	£7.50	
Half Sweet Half Beat	LP	Coral	LVA9120	1960	£15	£6	
I Cried For You	7"	Coral	Q72402	1960	£8	£4	
I'll Get By	7"	Coral	Q72331	1958	£8	£4	
I'm Gonna Sit Right Down	7"	Vogue Coral	Q72266	1957	£12	£6	
Love Me	7"	Vogue Coral	Q2039	1954	£25	£12.50	
Nola	7"	Coral	Q72359	1959	£5	£2	
Pray	7"	Vogue Coral	Q72180	1956	£10	£5	
Steppin' Out Tonight	7"	Coral	Q72316	1958	£30	£15	
Telephone Conversation	7"	Coral	Q72377	1959	£10	£5	
Vote For Billy Williams	LP	Wing	MGW12131	1959	£20	£8	US

WILLIAMS, BOBBY

Title	Format	Label	Cat. No.	Year	Mint	VG	Notes
Baby I Need Your Love	7"	Action	ACT4509	1968	£15	£7.50	
Let's Jam	7"	Contempo	C17	1973	£4	£1.50	

WILLIAMS, CHRIS & HIS MONSTERS

Title	Format	Label	Cat. No.	Year	Mint	VG	Notes
Kicking Around	7"	Triumph	RGM1003	1960	£200	£100	*demo, best auctioned*
Monster	7"	Columbia	DB4383	1959	£15	£7.50	

WILLIAMS, CLARENCE

Title	Format	Label	Cat. No.	Year	Mint	VG	Notes
Back Room Special	10" LP	Columbia	33S1067	1955	£25	£10	
Clarence Williams And His Orchestra	10" LP	London	AL3526	1954	£25	£10	
Clarence Williams And His Orchestra Vol. 2	10" LP	London	AL3561	1957	£25	£10	
Clarence Williams Vol. 1	LP	Philips	BBL7521	1962	£15	£6	
Clarence Williams' Washboard Band	7" EP	Parlophone	GEP8733	1959	£8	£4	
High Society	7"	Columbia	SCM5134	1954	£10	£5	
Jazz Originators	7" EP	Collector	JEL18	1964	£8	£4	
Sidney Bechet Memorial	LP	Fontana	TFL5087	1960	£15	£6	
Treasures Of North American Music Vol. 3	7" EP	Fontana	TFE17053	1958	£8	£4	

WILLIAMS, DAN

Title	Format	Label	Cat. No.	Year	Mint	VG	Notes
Donkey City	7"	London	CAY110	1955	£6	£2.50	

WILLIAMS, DANNY

Title	Format	Label	Cat. No.	Year	Mint	VG	Notes
Danny Williams	LP	HMV	CLP1458/ CSD1369	1961	£12	£5	
Danny Williams	LP	Deram	DML1017	1967	£10	£4	
Days Of Wine And Roses	7" EP	HMV	7EG8800	1963	£8	£4	
Forget Her, Forget Her	7"	HMV	POP1372	1964	£4	£1.50	
Go Away	7"	HMV	POP1410	1965	£4	£1.50	
Hits	7" EP	HMV	7EG8748	1962	£8	£4	
I've Got To Find That Girl Again	7"	HMV	POP1506	1966	£4	£1.50	
Moon River	LP	HMV	CLP1521	1961	£15	£6	
Only Love	LP	HMV	CLP/CSD3523	1966	£15	£6	
Rain	7"	HMV	POP1560	1966	£4	£1.50	
Romance With Danny Williams	LP	Woman's Privilege	AZ3	1966	£12	£5	
So High – So Low	7"	HMV	POP655	1959	£4	£1.50	
Swinging For You	LP	HMV	CLP1605/ CSD1471	1962	£15	£6	
Swings With Tony Osborne	7" EP	HMV	7EG8763	1962	£8	£4	
Tall Tree	7"	HMV	POP624	1959	£4	£1.50	
White On White	7"	HMV	POP1263	1963	£4	£1.50	
Youthful Years	7"	HMV	POP703	1959	£4	£1.50	

WILLIAMS, EDDIE & LITTLE SONNY WILLIS

Title	Format	Label	Cat. No.	Year	Mint	VG	Notes
Going To California	7" EP	XX	MIN707	196–	£6	£2.50	

WILLIAMS, GEORGE

Title	Format	Label	Cat. No.	Year	Mint	VG	Notes
No Business Of Yours	7"	Bullet	BU405	1969	£4	£1.50	

WILLIAMS, GRANVILLE ORCHESTRA

Title	Format	Label	Cat. No.	Year	Mint	VG	Notes
Hi-Life	7"	Island	WI3062	1967	£5	£2	
Hi-Life	LP	Island	ILP971	1968	£40	£20	*pink label*

WILLIAMS, HANK

Hank Williams's status as one of the architects of rock'n'roll, for all that he died, of a heart attack at the age of 29, a year before Elvis Presley made his first recordings, ensures that he is one of the few country artists with some seriously collectable records. The fact that the great majority of them were issued after Williams's death and should properly be regarded as reissues does not seem to bother collectors unduly.

Authentic Sound Of The Country Hits	7" EP	MGM	MGMEP770	1963	**£12**	**£6**	
Beyond The Sunset	LP	MGM	E4138	1961	**£12**	**£5**	*US*
Blue Love	7"	MGM	MGM931	1956	**£15**	**£7.50**	
Cold Cold Heart	78	MGM	MGM459	1951	**£8**	**£3**	
Crazy Heart	7"	MGM	SP1085	1954	**£25**	**£12.50**	
Dear John	78	MGM	MGM405	1951	**£8**	**£3**	
First, Last And Always	LP	MGM	E3928	1961	**£15**	**£6**	*US*
Greatest Hits	LP	MGM	E3918	1961	**£12**	**£5**	*US*
Half As Much	78	MGM	MGM527	1952	**£8**	**£3**	
Hank Williams	7" EP	MGM	MGMEP551	1956	**£25**	**£12.50**	*picture sleeve*
Hank Williams & His Drifting Cowboys	7" EP	MGM	MGMEP512	1954	**£20**	**£10**	
Hank Williams Favorites	7" EP	MGM	MGMEP757	1961	**£12**	**£6**	
Hank Williams Sings	10" LP	MGM	D105	1952	**£30**	**£15**	*company sleeve*
Hank Williams Sings	10" LP	MGM	D105	1952	**£50**	**£25**	*picture sleeve*
Hank Williams Story	LP	MGM	E4267	1966	**£20**	**£8**	*US*
Hank's Laments	7" EP	MGM	MGMEP675	1958	**£15**	**£7.50**	
Hey Good Lookin'	78	MGM	MGM454	1951	**£8**	**£3**	
Honky Tonk Blues	7" EP	MGM	MGMEP614	1957	**£15**	**£7.50**	
Honky Tonk Blues	78	MGM	MGM505	1952	**£8**	**£3**	
Honky Tonkin'	10" LP	MGM	E242	1954	**£40**	**£20**	*US*
Honky Tonkin'	7" EP	MGM	MGMEP582	1957	**£15**	**£7.50**	
Honky Tonkin'	LP	MGM	E3412	1957	**£30**	**£15**	*US*
I Ain't Got Nothing But Time	7"	MGM	SP1102	1954	**£25**	**£12.50**	
I Can't Help It	78	MGM	MGM471	1952	**£8**	**£3**	
I Saw The Light	10" LP	MGM	E243	1954	**£40**	**£20**	*US*
I Saw The Light	78	MGM	MGM630	1953	**£8**	**£3**	
I Saw The Light	LP	MGM	E3331	1956	**£30**	**£15**	*US*
I Saw The Light No. 1	7" EP	MGM	MGMEP569	1956	**£15**	**£7.50**	*picture sleeve*
I Saw The Light No. 1	7" EP	MGM	MGMEP569	1956	**£10**	**£5**	*company sleeve*
I Saw The Light No. 2	7" EP	MGM	MGMEP608	1957	**£15**	**£7.50**	
I Wish I Had A Nickel	7"	MGM	MGM921	1956	**£15**	**£7.50**	
I'll Never Get Out Of This World Alive	7"	MGM	SP1016	1953	**£30**	**£15**	
I'm Blue Inside	LP	MGM	C8021	1966	**£12**	**£5**	
I'm Blue Inside	LP	MGM	E3926	1961	**£12**	**£5**	*US*
I'm Gonna Sing	78	MGM	MGM799	1955	**£8**	**£3**	
I'm So Lonesome I Could Cry	7"	MGM	MGM1309	1966	**£5**	**£2**	
Immortal Hank Williams	10" LP	MGM	D154	1958	**£30**	**£15**	
Immortal Hank Williams	LP	MGM	E3605	1958	**£20**	**£8**	*US*
In Memory Of Hank Williams	LP	MGM	C8020	1966	**£10**	**£4**	
Jambalaya	78	MGM	MGM566	1952	**£8**	**£3**	
Just Waitin'	7" EP	MGM	MGMEP551	1955	**£15**	**£7.50**	*company sleeve*
Kaw Liga	7"	MGM	SP1034	1953	**£25**	**£12.50**	
Kaw-Liga	7"	MGM	MGM1322	1966	**£5**	**£2**	
Leave Me Alone With The Blues	7"	MGM	MGM966	1957	**£12**	**£6**	
Let Me Sing A Blue Song	LP	MGM	E3924	1961	**£12**	**£5**	*US*
Lives Again	LP	MGM	E3923	1961	**£12**	**£5**	*US*
Lonesome Sound Of Hank Williams	LP	MGM	C811	1960	**£20**	**£8**	
Love Songs, Comedy & Hymns	LP	MGM	C8040	1967	**£12**	**£5**	
Lovesick Blues	78	MGM	MGM269	1950	**£8**	**£3**	
Low Down Blues	7"	MGM	MGM942	1957	**£15**	**£7.50**	
Luke The Drifter	10" LP	MGM	D119	1953	**£30**	**£15**	*company sleeve*
Luke The Drifter	10" LP	MGM	D119	1953	**£40**	**£20**	*picture sleeve*
Luke The Drifter	LP	MGM	E3267	1955	**£40**	**£20**	*US*
Luke The Drifter	LP	MGM	C8022	1966	**£10**	**£4**	
Many Moods Of Hank Williams	LP	MGM	C8023	1966	**£10**	**£4**	
May You Never Be Alone	LP	MGM	C8019	1966	**£12**	**£5**	
Memorial Album	10" LP	MGM	D137	1955	**£25**	**£10**	
Memorial Album	LP	MGM	E3272	1955	**£30**	**£15**	*US*
Mind Your Own Business	78	MGM	MGM553	1952	**£8**	**£3**	
Moanin' The Blues	10" LP	MGM	D144	1956	**£30**	**£15**	
Moanin' The Blues	78	MGM	MGM381	1951	**£8**	**£3**	
Moanin' The Blues	LP	MGM	E3330	1956	**£30**	**£15**	*US*
More Greatest Hits	LP	MGM	E4040	1961	**£12**	**£5**	*US*
More Greatest Hits Vol. 3	LP	MGM	E4140	1962	**£12**	**£5**	*US*
My Bucket's Got A Hole In It	7"	MGM	SP1048	1953	**£25**	**£12.50**	
On Stage Recorded Live	LP	MGM	C893	1962	**£15**	**£6**	
Ramblin' Man	10" LP	MGM	E291	1954	**£40**	**£20**	*US*
Ramblin' Man	7"	MGM	SP1049	1954	**£25**	**£12.50**	
Ramblin' Man	LP	MGM	E3219	1955	**£30**	**£15**	*US*
Rootie Tootie	7"	MGM	MGM957	1957	**£12**	**£6**	
Sing Me A Blue Song	10" LP	MGM	D150	1958	**£30**	**£15**	
Sing Me A Blue Song	LP	MGM	E3560	1958	**£20**	**£8**	*US*
Songs For A Broken Heart	7" EP	MGM	MGMEP639	1958	**£15**	**£7.50**	
Songs For A Broken Heart No. 2	7" EP	MGM	MGMEP649	1958	**£15**	**£7.50**	
Spirit Of Hank Williams	LP	MGM	C956	1963	**£15**	**£6**	
Thirty-Six Greatest Hits	LP	MGM	3E2	1957	**£50**	**£25**	*US, triple*
Thirty-Six More Greatest Hits	LP	MGM	3E4	1958	**£50**	**£25**	*US, triple*
Unforgettable Hank Williams	7" EP	MGM	MGMEP710	1960	**£12**	**£6**	
Unforgettable Hank Williams	LP	MGM	C784	1959	**£20**	**£8**	
Unforgettable Hank Williams No. 2	7" EP	MGM	MGMEP726	1960	**£12**	**£6**	
Unforgettable Hank Williams No. 3	7" EP	MGM	MGMEP732	1960	**£12**	**£6**	
Wait For The Light To Shine	LP	MGM	C834	1960	**£15**	**£6**	
Wanderin' Around	LP	MGM	E3925	1961	**£12**	**£5**	*US*
Weary Blues	7"	MGM	SP1067	1954	**£25**	**£12.50**	
Why Don't You Love Me	78	MGM	MGM483	1952	**£8**	**£3**	
Window Shopping	78	MGM	MGM678	1953	**£8**	**£3**	
Your Cheatin' Heart	78	MGM	MGM896	1956	**£8**	**£3**	

WILLIAMS, HANK & HANK WILLIAMS JR

Singing Together	LP	MGM	C1008	1965	£**10**	£**4**	

WILLIAMS, HANK JR

Long Gone Lonesome Blues	7"	MGM	MGM1223	1963	£**4**	£**1.50**	

WILLIAMS, JEANETTE

Hound Dog	7"	Action	ACT4557	1969	£**8**	£**4**	
Stuff	7"	Action	ACT4534	1969	£**8**	£**4**	

WILLIAMS, JERRY & THE VIOLENTS

Jerry Williams And The Violents	LP	Grand Prix	GP9938	1968	£**25**	£**10**	*Swedish*
Rock And Roll Time	LP	Clan	7012	1968	£**40**	£**20**	*Italian*
Star Club Show 5	LP	Starclub	148004STL	1965	£**75**	£**37.50**	*German*

WILLIAMS, JIMMY

Walking On Air	7"	Atlantic	AT4042	1965	£**6**	£**2.50**	

WILLIAMS, JOE

Ballad And Blues	7" EP	Columbia	SEG7984	1960	£**5**	£**2**	
Everyday I Have The Blues	7" EP	Columbia	SEG8001	1960	£**8**	£**4**	
Greatest	LP	HMV	CLP1109	1957	£**15**	£**6**	
Groovy Joe Williams	7" EP	Columbia	SEB10110	1959	£**5**	£**2**	
Joe Sings The Blues	7" EP	Columbia	SEG8016	1960	£**8**	£**4**	
Joe Williams & Count Basie's Orchestra	7" EP	Columbia	SEG7810	1958	£**5**	£**2**	
Man Ain't Supposed To Cry	LP	Columbia	33SX1087	1958	£**15**	£**6**	
Memories Ad-Lib	LP	Columbia	33SX1175/ SCX3280	1959	£**15**	£**6**	*with Count Basie*
Sings	10" LP	London	HBC1065	1956	£**12**	£**5**	
Sings About You	LP	Columbia	33SX1229/ SCX3308	1960	£**12**	£**5**	
That Kind Of Woman	LP	Columbia	33SX1253/ SCX3325	1960	£**10**	£**4**	

WILLIAMS, JOHN

Can't Find Time For Anything Now	7"	Columbia	DB8251	1967	£**6**	£**2.50**	
John Williams	LP	Columbia	SX6169	1967	£**100**	£**50**	
She's That Kind Of Woman	7"	Columbia	DB8128	1967	£**6**	£**2.50**	

WILLIAMS, JOHN (2)

Paul McCartney's Theme From The Honorary Consul	7"	Island	IS155	1984	£**8**	£**4**	

WILLIAMS, KENNETH

Extracts From Pieces Of Eight	7" EP	Decca	DFE8548	1963	£**6**	£**2.50**	
In Season	7" EP	Decca	DFE8671	1966	£**6**	£**2.50**	
On Pleasure Bent	LP	Decca	LK4856	1967	£**12**	£**5**	
Rambling Syd Rumpo In Concert No. 1	7" EP	Parlophone	GEP8965	1967	£**8**	£**4**	
Rambling Syd Rumpo In Concert No. 2	7" EP	Parlophone	GEP8966	1967	£**8**	£**4**	

WILLIAMS, LARRY

Baby Baby	7"	London	HLM9053	1960	£**15**	£**7.50**	
Bony Moronie	7"	London	HLU8532	1958	£**20**	£**10**	
Dizzy Miss Lizzy	7"	London	HLU8604	1958	£**30**	£**15**	
Greatest Hits	LP	OKeh	OKM2123/ OKS12123	1967	£**15**	£**6**	*US*
Here's Larry Williams	LP	Speciality	SP2109	1959	£**75**	£**37.50**	*US*
I Can't Stop Loving You	7"	London	HLU8911	1960	£**15**	£**7.50**	
Larry Williams	7" EP	London	REU1213	1959	£**75**	£**37.50**	
Larry Williams Show	LP	Decca	LK4691	1965	£**40**	£**20**	*with Johnny Guitar Watson*
Mercy Mercy Mercy	7"	Columbia	DB8140	1967	£**25**	£**12.50**	*with Johnny Guitar Watson*
On Stage	LP	Sue	ILP922	1965	£**40**	£**20**	
Shake Your Body Girl	7"	MGM	MGM1447	1968	£**5**	£**2**	
She Said Yeah	7"	London	HLU8844	1959	£**15**	£**7.50**	
Short Fat Fannie	7"	London	HLN8472	1957	£**25**	£**12.50**	
Strange	7"	Sue	WI371	1965	£**10**	£**5**	
Sweet Little Baby	7"	Decca	F12151	1965	£**10**	£**5**	*with Johnny Guitar Watson*
Too Late	7"	Epic	EPC4421	1976	£**4**	£**1.50**	*with Johnny Guitar Watson*
Turn On Your Lovelight	7"	Sue	WI381	1965	£**12**	£**6**	
Two For The Price Of One	LP	OKeh	OKM4122/ OKS14122	1967	£**20**	£**8**	*US, with Johnny Guitar Watson*

WILLIAMS, LEW

Cat Walk	7"	London	no number	195–	£**30**	£**15**	*1 sided demo*

WILLIAMS, LITTLE JERRY

Baby You're My Everything	7"	Cameo Parkway	C100	1962	£**20**	£**10**	

WILLIAMS, LLOYD

Funky Beat	7"	Treasure Isle	TI7029	1968	£**10**	£**5**	
I'm In Love With You	7"	Bamboo	BAM41	1970	£**5**	£**2**	

Title	Format	Label	Cat. No.	Year	Mint	VG+	Notes
Sad World	7"	Doctor Bird	DB1051	1966	£10	£5	Tommy McCook B side
Wonderful World	7"	Doctor Bird	DB1135	1968	£10	£5	Tommy McCook B side

WILLIAMS, LORETTA

Title	Format	Label	Cat. No.	Year	Mint	VG+	Notes
Baby Cakes	7"	Atlantic	584032	1966	£15	£7.50	

WILLIAMS, LUTHER

Title	Format	Label	Cat. No.	Year	Mint	VG+	Notes
Tropical Rhythms Of Jamaica	LP	Melodisc	MLP12125	1961	£10	£4	

WILLIAMS, MARY LOU

Title	Format	Label	Cat. No.	Year	Mint	VG+	Notes
At The Piano	7" EP	Parlophone	GEP8567	1956	£5	£2	
Chug A Lug Jug	7"	Sue	WI311	1964	£12	£6	
Don Carlos Meets Mary Lou Williams	7" EP	Vogue	EPV1042	1955	£5	£2	
In Paris	10" LP	Felsted	EDL87012	1955	£30	£15	
Mary Lou Williams	7" EP	Columbia	SEG7608	1956	£5	£2	
Mary Lou Williams Quartet	7" EP	Esquire	EP66	1955	£5	£2	
Piano Panorama	10" LP	Esquire	20026	1954	£40	£20	
Plays In London	10" LP	Vogue	LDE022	1953	£40	£20	

WILLIAMS, MAURICE & THE ZODIACS

Title	Format	Label	Cat. No.	Year	Mint	VG+	Notes
At The Beach	LP	Snyder	5586	196–	£30	£15	US
Come Along	7"	Top Rank	JAR563	1961	£10	£5	
I Remember	7"	Top Rank	JAR550	1961	£6	£2.50	
Stay	7"	Top Rank	JAR526	1960	£6	£2.50	
Stay	7" EP	Top Rank	JKP3006	1961	£75	£37.50	
Stay	LP	Sphere Sound	SSR7007	1964	£30	£15	US
Stay	LP	Herald	HLP1014	1961	£75	£37.50	US

WILLIAMS, MEL & JOHNNY OTIS

Title	Format	Label	Cat. No.	Year	Mint	VG+	Notes
All Through The Night	LP	Dig	103	1955	£50	£25	US

WILLIAMS, MIKE

Title	Format	Label	Cat. No.	Year	Mint	VG+	Notes
Lonely Soldier	7"	Atlantic	584027	1966	£5	£2	

WILLIAMS, OTIS & THE CHARMS

Title	Format	Label	Cat. No.	Year	Mint	VG+	Notes
Hearts Of Stone	7"	Parlophone	MSP6155	1955	£400	£250	best auctioned
I'm Waiting Just For You	7"	Parlophone	R4293	1957	£300	£180	best auctioned
It's All Over Now	7"	Parlophone	R4210	1956	£250	£150	best auctioned
Ivory Tower	7"	Parlophone	MSP6239	1956	£300	£180	best auctioned
Ivory Tower	7"	Parlophone	CMSP36	1955	£200	£100	export, best auctioned
Secret	7"	Parlophone	R4495	1958	£50	£25	
Their All Time Hits	LP	Deluxe	750	1957	£250	£150	US
Their All Time Hits	LP	King	560	1957	£100	£50	US
This Is Otis Williams And The Charms	LP	King	614	1959	£100	£50	US
Two Hearts	7"	Parlophone	DP423	1955	£300	£180	export, best auctioned
Two Hearts	7"	Parlophone	R4860	1961	£40	£20	

WILLIAMS, PAUL

Title	Format	Label	Cat. No.	Year	Mint	VG+	Notes
Gin House	7"	Columbia	DB7421	1964	£10	£5	
Many Faces Of Love	7"	Columbia	DB7768	1965	£10	£5	with Zoot Money
My Sly Sadie	7"	Decca	F12844	1968	£4	£1.50	

WILLIAMS, PAUL (2)

Title	Format	Label	Cat. No.	Year	Mint	VG+	Notes
Delta Blues Singer	LP	Sonet	SNTF654	1973	£10	£4	
In Memory Of Robert Johnson	LP	Intercord	28754	1973	£12	£5	German

WILLIAMS, POOR JOE

Title	Format	Label	Cat. No.	Year	Mint	VG+	Notes
Man Sings The Blues	7" EP	Collector	JEN3	1960	£8	£4	
Man Sings The Blues Vol. 2	7" EP	Collector	JEN4	1960	£8	£4	

WILLIAMS, REEK & THE FIGHTING CATS

Title	Format	Label	Cat. No.	Year	Mint	VG+	Notes
Favourites	LP	Delta	210	1967	£20	£8	Dutch

WILLIAMS, RITA

Title	Format	Label	Cat. No.	Year	Mint	VG+	Notes
Looking For Someone To Love	7"	Oriole	CB1417	1958	£4	£1.50	

WILLIAMS, ROBBIE

Title	Format	Label	Cat. No.	Year	Mint	VG+	Notes
I've Been Expecting You	CD	Chrysalis	CDPP080	1998	£150	£75	promo pack with 2 CDs, video, photos

WILLIAMS, ROBERT PETE

Title	Format	Label	Cat. No.	Year	Mint	VG+	Notes
Robert Pete Williams	LP	Saydisc	AMS2002	1972	£10	£4	
Sugar Farm	LP	Blues Beacon	1932101ST	197–	£10	£4	
Those Prison Blues	LP	77	LA1217	1963	£15	£6	

WILLIAMS, ROGER

Title	Format	Label	Cat. No.	Year	Mint	VG+	Notes
Almost Paradise	7"	London	HLR8422	1957	£4	£1.50	
Anastasia	7"	London	HLU8379	1957	£5	£2	
Arrivederci Roma	7"	London	HLR8572	1958	£4	£1.50	
Autumn Leaves	7"	London	HLU8214	1955	£8	£4	
Till	7"	London	HLR8516	1957	£4	£1.50	
Two Different Worlds	7"	London	HLU8341	1956	£10	£5	with Jane Morgan

WILLIAMS, SMITTY

Title	Format	Label	Cat. No.	Year	Mint	VG+	Notes
Cure	7"	MGM	MGM1167	1962	£4	£1.50	

WILLIAMS, SONNY

Bye Bye Baby Goodbye	7"	London	HLD8931	1959	**£15**	**£7.50**	

WILLIAMS, TEX

All Time Greats	7" EP	Brunswick	OE9147	1955	**£6**	**£2.50**	
Be Sure You're Right	7"	Brunswick	05516	1956	**£4**	**£1.50**	
Country Music Time	LP	Decca	DL4295	1962	**£10**	**£4**	*US*
Dance-O-Rama	LP	Decca	DL5565	1955	**£30**	**£15**	*US*
Keeper Of Boot Hill	7"	Top Rank	JAR330	1960	**£5**	**£2**	
Money	7"	Brunswick	05393	1955	**£6**	**£2.50**	
River Of No Return	7"	Brunswick	05327	1954	**£8**	**£4**	
Smoke! Smoke! Smoke!	LP	Capitol	(S)T1463	1960	**£10**	**£4**	
Talking To The Blues	7"	Brunswick	05684	1957	**£8**	**£4**	
Tex Williams' Best	LP	Camden	CAL363	1958	**£12**	**£5**	*US*
This Ole House	7"	Brunswick	05341	1954	**£8**	**£4**	*with Rex Allen*

WILLIAMS, TOMMY

Springtime In Battersea	LP	Free Reed	FRR008	1976	**£10**	**£4**	

WILLIAMS, TONY

Life Time	LP	Blue Note	BLP/BST84180	1964	**£20**	**£8**	
Spring	LP	Blue Note	BLP/BST84216	1965	**£20**	**£8**	

WILLIAMS, TONY (2)

Girl Is A Girl Is A Girl	LP	Mercury	MMC14027	1960	**£20**	**£10**	
How Come	7"	Philips	BF1282	1962	**£20**	**£10**	
My Prayer	7"	Reprise	RS20030	1961	**£4**	**£1.50**	
Sleepless Nights	7"	Reprise	RS20019	1961	**£4**	**£1.50**	

WILLIAMS, TONY LIFETIME

Emergency and *Turn It Over* are densely electric albums like no others. Tony Williams, the group's leader, was the drummer with Miles Davis during the sixties. Lifetime was his idea of a rock group but, filtered through his jazz background, it did not sound very much like anyone else's. Larry Young makes the organ sound like a banshee, pressing adjacent treble keys down all at the same time; John McLaughlin, who has just discovered the delights of high amplification, employs a ferocious fuzz-tone; while Tony Williams plays his customary churning, multi-layered rhythms. Unfortunately, the group was plagued by management problems and when Jack Bruce joined during the recording of *Turn It Over* these only became worse. Later Lifetime recordings are much more routine affairs, although *Believe It*, with Allan Holdsworth in fine form on guitar, has its moments.

Believe It	LP	CBS	69201	1976	**£10**	**£4**	
Emergency	LP	Polydor	583574	1969	**£30**	**£15**	*double*
Lifetime	LP	Polydor	2482179	1975	**£10**	**£4**	
Million Dollar Legs	LP	CBS	81510	1976	**£10**	**£4**	
One Word	7"	Polydor	2066050	1970	**£8**	**£4**	
Turn It Over	LP	Polydor	2425019	1970	**£20**	**£8**	

WILLIAMS, WINSTON

D.J.'s Choice	7"	Jackpot	JP733	1970	**£5**	**£2**	*Slim Smith B side*
Love Version	7"	Jackpot	JP757	1971	**£5**	**£2**	*Slim Smith B side*
People's Choice	7"	Jackpot	JP743	1970	**£5**	**£2**	*Bobby James B side*

WILLIAMSON, CLAUDE

Claude Williamson Trio	10" LP	Capitol	LC6804	1956	**£20**	**£8**	
Claude Williamson Trio	10" LP	Capitol	KPL103	1955	**£20**	**£8**	

WILLIAMSON, DUDLEY

Coming On The Scene	7"	Doctor Bird	DB1117	1967	**£10**	**£5**	

WILLIAMSON, ROBIN

American Stonehenge	LP	Criminal	STEAL4	1978	**£12**	**£5**	
Glint At The Kindling	LP	Criminal	STEAL6	1979	**£12**	**£5**	
Journey Edge	LP	Flying Fish	FF033	1977	**£12**	**£5**	*US*
Myrrh	LP	Island	HELP2	1972	**£12**	**£5**	
Songs Of Love And Parting	LP	Flying Fish	FF257	1981	**£12**	**£5**	*US*

WILLIAMSON, SONNY BOY

It has long been a matter of some confusion that there were two Sonny Boy Williamsons. John Lee 'Sonny Boy' Williamson was a successful blues harmonica player who recorded in the thirties and forties, but who was murdered in 1948 at the age of thirty-four. Sonny Boy Williamson II was christened Alec Ford, but later adopted the surname of his stepfather and the nickname Rice. At the beginning of the forties, Rice Miller began calling himself Sonny Boy Williamson in a deliberate attempt to gain some success on the back of the man who was, at the time, the better-known artist. Ironically, Miller, who was actually the older man by some seventeen years, went on to achieve considerably more success than his namesake – and not because of the name confusion, but because he was himself a fine and innovative harmonica player. During the early sixties, he spent some time in the UK, touring and recording with several of the up-and-coming British R&B groups.

Blues Of Sonny Boy Williamson	LP	Storyville	SLP170	1965	**£15**	**£6**	
Bring It On Home	7"	Chess	CRS8030	1966	**£5**	**£2**	
Bummer Road	LP	Chess	1536	1969	**£10**	**£4**	*US*
Down And Out Blues	LP	Pye	NPL28036	1964	**£20**	**£8**	
From The Bottom	7"	Blue Horizon	451008	1966	**£100**	**£50**	
Help Me	7"	Pye	7N25191	1963	**£6**	**£2.50**	
Help Me	7" EP	Chess	CRE6001	1965	**£15**	**£7.50**	
In Memoriam	7" EP	Chess	CRE6013	1966	**£15**	**£7.50**	
In Memoriam	LP	Chess	CRL4510	1965	**£15**	**£6**	
Last Sessions	LP	Rarity	RLP1	1974	**£20**	**£8**	
Lonesome Cabin	7"	Pye	7N25268	1964	**£6**	**£2.50**	
More Real Folk Blues	LP	Chess	1509	1966	**£20**	**£8**	*US*

No Nights By Myself	7"	Sue	WI365	1965	**£10**	**£5**	
Portraits In Blues	LP	Fontana	670158	1966	**£12**	**£5**	
Real Folk Blues	LP	Chess	1503	1966	**£20**	**£8**	*US*
Real Folk Blues Vol. 2	7" EP	Chess	CRE6018	1966	**£12**	**£6**	
Sonny Boy Williamson	7" EP	Pye	NEP44037	1964	**£12**	**£6**	
Sonny Boy Williamson	LP	Checker	1437	1959	**£50**	**£25**	*US*

WILLIAMSON, SONNY BOY I

Bluebird Blues	LP	RCA	INTS1088	1970	**£10**	**£4**	
Sonny Boy And His Pals	LP	Saydisc	SDR169	1969	**£15**	**£6**	

WILLIAMSON, STU

Sapphire	10" LP	London	LZN14030	1956	**£40**	**£20**	
Stu Williamson	LP	London	LTZN15123	1958	**£20**	**£8**	

WILLIE & LLOYD

Marcus Is Alive	7"	Camel	CA80	1971	**£4**	**£1.50**	*Gladiators B side*

WILLIE & THE RED RUBBER BAND

We're Coming Up	LP	RCA	LSP4193	1969	**£15**	**£6**	*US*
Willie & The Red Rubber Band	LP	RCA	LSP4074	1968	**£15**	**£6**	*US*

WILLIE & THE WHEELS

Skateboard Craze	7"	ABC	ABC4184	1977	**£4**	**£1.50**	

WILLING, FOY & THE RIDERS OF THE PURPLE SAGE

Cowboy	LP	Roulette	R25035	1958	**£12**	**£5**	*US*
Cowboy No. 1	7" EP	Columbia	SEG7834	1958	**£5**	**£2**	
Cowboy No. 2	7" EP	Columbia	SEG7855	1958	**£5**	**£2**	

WILLINGHAM, DORIS

You Can't Do That	7"	Jay Boy	BOY1	1969	**£6**	**£2.50**	

WILLIS, CHUCK

Betty And Dupree	7"	London	HLE8595	1958	**£40**	**£20**	
C.C. Rider	7"	London	HLE8444	1957	**£50**	**£25**	
Chuck Willis Wails The Blues	LP	Epic	LN3425	1958	**£100**	**£50**	*US*
I Remember Chuck Willis	LP	Atlantic	588145	1968	**£10**	**£4**	
I Remember Chuck Willis	LP	Atlantic	ATL5003	1965	**£30**	**£15**	
King Of The Stroll	LP	Atlantic	8018	1958	**£100**	**£50**	*US, black label*
King Of The Stroll	LP	Atlantic	8018	1959	**£50**	**£25**	*US, red label*
My Life	7"	London	HLE8818	1959	**£25**	**£12.50**	
That Train Has Gone	7"	London	HLE8489	1957	**£40**	**£20**	
Tribute To Chuck Willis	LP	Epic	LN3728	1960	**£60**	**£30**	*US*
What Am I Living For	7"	London	HLE8635	1958	**£25**	**£12.50**	
What Am I Living For	7"	London	HL7039	1958	**£10**	**£5**	*export*
Willis Wails The Blues	7" EP	Fontana	TFE17138	1959	**£175**	**£87.50**	

WILLIS, HAL

Lumberjack	7"	President	PT197	1968	**£6**	**£2.50**	

WILLIS, LLOYD

Mad Rooster	7"	Pressure Beat	PR5502	1970	**£5**	**£2**	

WILLIS, RALPH

Goodbye Blues	78	Esquire	10370	1954	**£12**	**£6**	
Old Home Blues	78	Esquire	10380	1954	**£12**	**£6**	
Ralph Willis	7" EP	XX	MIN703	196–	**£6**	**£2.50**	
Ralph Willis	7" EP	Esquire	EP241	1961	**£15**	**£7.50**	
Ralph Willis	7" EP	XX	MIN711	196–	**£6**	**£2.50**	

WILLIS, SLIM

Running Around	7"	R&B	MRB5004	1965	**£10**	**£5**	

WILLOWS

Church Bells May Ring	7"	London	HLL8290	1956	**£600**	**£400**	*best auctioned*

WILLS, BOB

Best Of Bob Wills	LP	Harmony	HL7304	1963	**£15**	**£6**	*US*
Bob Wills And His Texas Playboys	LP	Decca	DL8727	1957	**£40**	**£20**	*US*
Bob Wills And Tommy Duncan	LP	Liberty	LRX/LSX1912	1961	**£15**	**£6**	*US*
Bob Wills Sings And Plays	LP	Liberty	LRP3303/ LST7303	1963	**£15**	**£6**	*US*
Bob Wills Special	LP	Harmony	HL7036	1957	**£20**	**£8**	*US*
Dance-O-Rama	10" LP	Decca	DL5562	1955	**£60**	**£30**	*US*
Great Bob Wills	LP	Harmony	HL7345	1965	**£15**	**£6**	*US*
Heart To Heart Talk	7"	London	HL7102	1960	**£8**	**£4**	*export, with Tommy Duncan*
Keepsake Album 1	LP	Longhorn	LP001	1965	**£30**	**£15**	*US*
Living Legend	LP	Liberty	LRP3182/ LST7182	1961	**£15**	**£6**	*US*
Mr Words And Music	LP	Liberty	LRP3194/ LST7194	1961	**£15**	**£6**	*US*
Old Time Favorites	10" LP	Antones	LP6010	195–	**£60**	**£30**	*US*
Old Time Favorites	10" LP	Antones	LP6000	195–	**£60**	**£30**	*US*
Ranch House Favorites	10" LP	MGM	E91	1951	**£60**	**£30**	*US*
Ranch House Favorites	LP	MGM	E3352	1956	**£60**	**£30**	*US*
Round Up	10" LP	Columbia	HL9003	195–	**£60**	**£30**	*US*

San Antonio Rose	LP	Starday	SLP375	1965	£15	£6	US
Together Again	LP	Liberty	LRP3173/ LST7173	1960	£12	£5	US, with Tommy Duncan
Western Swing Band	LP	Vocalion	VL(7)3735	1965	£15	£6	US

WILLS, MICK

Fern Hill	LP	Woronzow	WOO9	1988	£25	£10	

WILLS, TOMMY & HARRY LEWIS

Rhythm And Blues	7" EP	Range	JRE7006	196–	£5	£2	

WILLS, VIOLA

Lost Without The Love Of My Guy	7"	President	PT108	1968	£4	£1.50	
Soft Centres	LP	Goodear	EARLH5002	1974	£10	£4	

WILMER & THE DUKES

Give Me One More Chance	7"	Action	ACT4500	1968	£4	£1.50	
Wilmer & The Dukes	LP	Aphrodisiac	6001	1969	£15	£6	US

WILSON, ADA

In The Quiet Of My Room	7"	Ellie Jay	EJSP9288	1979	£6	£2.50	

WILSON, AL

Do What You Gotta Do	7"	Liberty	LBF15044	1968	£10	£5	
Searching For The Dolphins	LP	Liberty	LBS83173	1969	£15	£6	
Searching For The Dolphins	LP	Soul City	SCS92006	1970	£15	£6	
Snake	7"	Liberty	LIB15121	1968	£10	£5	

WILSON, ANN & THE DAYBREAKS

This is the same Ann Wilson as the later co-leader of Heart.

Standin' Watchin' You	7"	Topaz	1311	1967	£50	£25	US
Through Eyes And Glass	7"	Topaz	1312	1967	£50	£25	US

WILSON, BRIAN

Brian Wilson	CD	WEA	9256692	1988	£12	£5	
Caroline No	7"	Capitol	CL15438	1966	£8	£4	
Gettin' Hungry	7"	Capitol	CL15513	1967	£10	£5	with Mike Love
I Just Wasn't Made For These Times	CD	MCA	MCA5P3575	1996	£20	£8	US interview promo
Love And Mercy	CD-s	Sire	W7814CD	1988	£5	£2	
Night Time	CD-s	Sire	W7787CD	1988	£5	£2	
Words And Music	LP	Warner Bros	WBWM154	1988	£12	£5	US promo

WILSON, CLIVE

Mango Tree	7"	R&B	JB144	1964	£10	£5	

WILSON, COLIN

Cloudburst	LP	Tabitha		1975	£75	£37.50	

WILSON, DELROY

1-2-3	7"	Island	WI103	1963	£10	£5	
Adis Ababa	7"	Spur	SP2	1972	£5	£2	Keith Hudson B side
Ain't That Peculiar	7"	Green Door	GD4060	1973	£4	£1.50	
Better Must Come	7"	Jackpot	JP763	1971	£4	£1.50	Bunny Lee's All Stars B side
Better Must Come	LP	Trojan	TRLS44	1972	£12	£5	
Captivity	LP	Big Shot	BILP102	197–	£12	£5	
Come Down From Your Palms And Pray	7"	R&B	JB132	1963	£10	£5	
Dancing Mood	7"	Island	WI3013	1966	£10	£5	Soul Brothers B side
Dancing Mood	7"	Fab	FAB266	1975	£4	£1.50	
Don't Play That Song	7"	Joe	JRS11	1970	£4	£1.50	Boss All Stars
Easy Snappin'	7"	Studio One	SO2074	1969	£12	£6	Webber Sisters B side
Feel Good All Over	7"	Studio One	SO2057	1968	£12	£6	
Get Ready	7"	Island	WI3050	1967	£10	£5	Roy Richards B side
Give Me A Chance	7"	Doctor Bird	DB1022	1966	£10	£5	
Good All Over	LP	Coxsone	CSL8016	1968	£100	£50	
Goodbye	7"	Black Swan	WI420	1964	£10	£5	
I Am Not A King	7"	Studio One	SO2031	1967	£12	£6	Heptones B side
I Shall Not Remove	7"	Island	WI097	1963	£10	£5	
I Shall Not Remove	LP	R&B	JBL1112	1964	£100	£50	
I'm The One Who Loves You	7"	High Note	HS015	1969	£4	£1.50	Afrotones B side
Just Because Of You	7"	Banana	BA333	1971	£4	£1.50	
Lion Of Judah	7"	R&B	JB108	1963	£10	£5	
Lover Mouth	7"	R&B	JB148	1964	£10	£5	
Mr Cool Operator	LP	Eji	EJI1001	1977	£12	£5	
Never Conquer	7"	Studio One	SO2019	1967	£12	£6	
Once Upon A Time	7"	Island	WI3127	1967	£10	£5	
Pick Up The Pieces	7"	Island	WI205	1965	£10	£5	
Pretty Girl	7"	Downtown	DT501	1973	£5	£2	Joe Gibbs B side
Prince Pharoah	7"	R&B	JB128	1963	£10	£5	
Put Yourself In My Place	7"	High Note	HS011	1968	£4	£1.50	
Rain From The Skies	7"	Studio One	SO2046	1968	£12	£6	
Riding For A Fall	7"	Island	WI3033	1967	£10	£5	
Sad Mood	7"	Camel	CA15	1969	£4	£1.50	Stranger Cole B side

Sammy Dead .... 7" .... R&B .... JB168 .... 1964 **£10** .... **£5** ...... *Cynthia & Archie B side*
Satisfaction .... 7" .... Smash .... SMA2318 .... 1971 **£4** .... **£1.50** ....
Show Me The Way .... 7" .... Trojan .... TR7740 .... 1970 **£4** .... **£1.50** .... *Beverley's All Stars B side*
Spit In The Sky .... 7" .... Blue Beat .... BB172 .... 1963 **£12** .... **£6** ....
Spit In The Sky .... 7" .... Black Swan .... WI405 .... 1964 **£10** .... **£5** ....
This Heart Of Mine .... 7" .... Island .... WI3099 .... 1967 **£10** .... **£5** .... *Glen Adams B side*
True Believer .... 7" .... Coxsone .... CS7064 .... 1968 **£10** .... **£5** ..... *Marshall Williams B side*
What It Was .... 7" .... Smash .... SMA2323 .... 1971 **£4** .... **£1.50** ... *Lloyd Clarke B side*
Won't You Come Home Baby .... 7" .... Studio One .... SO2009 .... 1967 **£12** .... **£6** ...... *Peter & Hortense B side*
You Bend My Love .... 7" .... Island .... WI116 .... 1963 **£10** .... **£5** ....
Your Number One .... 7" .... High Note .... HS022 .... 1969 **£4** .... **£1.50** ....

WILSON, DENNIS

Pacific Ocean Blue .... LP .... Caribou .... CRB81672 .... 1977 **£15** .... **£6** .... *blue vinyl*
Pacific Ocean Blue .... LP .... Caribou .... CRB81672 .... 1977 **£10** .... **£4** ....
Sound Of Free .... 7" .... Stateside .... SS2184 .... 1970 **£25** .... **£12.50** ....

WILSON, DOYLE

Hey Hey .... 7" .... Vogue .... V9117 .... 1958 **£250** ...... **£150** .... *best auctioned*

WILSON, EDDIE

Get Out On The Street .... 7" .... Action .... ACT4555 .... 1969 **£4** .... **£1.50** ....
Shing A Ling A Stroll .... 7" .... Action .... ACT4536 .... 1969 **£6** .... **£2.50** ....

WILSON, EDDIE (2)

Dankeschoen Bitteschoen Wiederschoen ... 7" .... Oriole .... CB1780 .... 1962 **£4** .... **£1.50** ....

WILSON, EDITH

With Johnny Dunn's Jazzhounds .... LP .... Fountain .... FB302 .... 196– **£15** .... **£6** ....

WILSON, ERNEST

Freedom Train .... 7" .... Crab .... CRAB17 .... 1969 **£4** .... **£1.50** ... *Stranger Cole B side*
If I Were A Carpenter .... 7" .... Studio One .... SO2058 .... 1968 **£12** .... **£6** ... *Soul Vendors B side*
Money Worries .... 7" .... Studio One .... SO2032 .... 1967 **£12** .... **£6** ... *Soul Vendors B side*
Storybook Children .... 7" .... Coxsone .... CS7044 .... 1968 **£10** .... **£5** ... *Little Freddie B side*
Storybook Children .... 7" .... Fab .... FAB280 .... 1976 **£4** .... **£1.50** ...... *Sound Dimension B side*
Undying Love .... 7" .... Coxsone .... CS7059 .... 1968 **£10** .... **£5** ... *Soul Vendors B side*

WILSON, FRANK

Last Kiss .... 7" .... Fontana .... TF505 .... 1964 **£6** .... **£2.50** ....
Last Kiss .... LP .... Josie .... JS4006 .... 1964 **£25** .... **£10** .... *US*

WILSON, FRANK (2)

Do I Love You .... 7" .... Motown .... TMG1170 .... 1979 **£20** .... **£10** .... *demo, picture sleeve*

WILSON, JACK

Easterly Winds .... LP .... Blue Note .... BST84270 .... 1968 **£30** .... **£15** ....
Jack Wilson Quartet .... LP .... London .... HAK/SHK8170 .... 1964 **£25** .... **£10** ....
Ramblin' .... LP .... Vocalion .... LAEL603 .... 1966 **£25** .... **£10** ....
Something Personal .... LP .... Blue Note .... BLP/BST84251 .... 1967 **£25** .... **£10** ....
Song For My Daughter .... LP .... Blue Note .... BST84328 .... 1969 **£12** .... **£5** ....

WILSON, JACKIE

The dynamic singer with big hits in four decades (the *tour de force* vocal gymnastics of 'Reet Petite' in the fifties; 'Higher And Higher' in the sixties; 'I Get The Sweetest Feeling' in the seventies; and a reissued 'Reet Petite' in the eighties – when a memorable animated video helped propel the song to number one in the UK) is sadly perhaps best remembered for having died in 1984 after spending nearly nine years in a coma. Apart from some of his joyous performances, he should be remembered as the man who indirectly got the Tamla Motown company going. For Wilson's earliest hits were written by the young Berry Gordy, who was able to use the resulting windfall to start his own label.

All My Love .... 7" .... Coral .... Q72407 .... 1960 **£5** .... **£2** ....
Alone At Last .... 7" .... Coral .... Q72412 .... 1960 **£5** .... **£2** ....
At The Copa .... LP .... Coral .... SVL9209 .... 1962 **£40** .... **£20** .... *stereo*
At The Copa .... LP .... Coral .... LVA9209 .... 1962 **£30** .... **£15** .... *mono*
Baby Workout .... 7" .... Coral .... Q72460 .... 1963 **£5** .... **£2** ....
Baby Workout .... LP .... Brunswick .... BL(7)54110 .... 1963 **£30** .... **£15** .... *US*
Big Boss Line .... 7" .... Coral .... Q72474 .... 1964 **£5** .... **£2** ....
Body And Soul .... LP .... Coral .... LVA9202 .... 1962 **£30** .... **£15** ....
By Special Request .... LP .... Coral .... LVA9151 .... 1962 **£40** .... **£20** .... *mono*
By Special Request .... LP .... Coral .... SVL3018 .... 1962 **£50** .... **£25** .... *stereo*
Do Your Thing .... LP .... MCA .... MUPS405 .... 1970 **£15** .... **£6** ....
Dogging Around .... 7" .... Coral .... Q72393 .... 1960 **£6** .... **£2.50** ....
Dynamic Jackie Wilson .... 7" EP .. Coral .... FEP2043 .... 1960 **£60** .... **£30** .... *tri-centre*
For Your Precious Love .... 7" .... Decca .... AD1008 .... 1968 **£10** .... **£5** .... *export*
Greatest Hurt .... 7" .... Coral .... Q72450 .... 1962 **£5** .... **£2** ....
He's So Fine .... LP .... Coral .... LVA9087 .... 1958 **£75** .... **£37.50** ....
Higher And Higher .... 7" .... Coral .... Q72493 .... 1967 **£6** .... **£2.50** ....
Higher And Higher .... LP .... MCA .... MUP(S)304 .... 1967 **£10** .... **£4** ....
I Get The Sweetest Feeling .... LP .... MCA .... MUPS361 .... 1969 **£10** .... **£4** ....
I Just Can't Help It .... 7" .... Coral .... Q72454 .... 1962 **£5** .... **£2** ....
I'll Be Satisfied .... 7" .... Coral .... Q72372 .... 1959 **£6** .... **£2.50** ....
I'm Comin' On Back To You .... 7" .... Coral .... Q72434 .... 1961 **£5** .... **£2** ....
I'm Wandering .... 7" .... Coral .... Q72332 .... 1958 **£10** .... **£5** ....

Jackie Sings The Blues	LP	Coral	LVA9130	1960	**£60**	**£30**	
Lonely Teardrops	7"	Coral	Q72482	1965	**£6**	**£2.50**	
Lonely Teardrops	7"	Coral	Q72347	1958	**£10**	**£5**	
Lonely Teardrops	7" EP	Coral	FEP2016	1959	**£60**	**£30**	*tri-centre*
Lonely Teardrops	LP	Coral	LVA9108	1959	**£75**	**£37.50**	
Merry Christmas	LP	Brunswick	BL(7)54112	1963	**£30**	**£15**	*US*
My Golden Favourites	LP	Coral	LVA9135	1960	**£40**	**£20**	
My Golden Favorites Vol. 2	LP	Brunswick	BL(7)54115	1964	**£30**	**£15**	*US*
My Heart Belongs To Only You	7"	Coral	Q72444	1961	**£5**	**£2**	
New Breed	7"	Coral	Q72467	1963	**£5**	**£2**	
No Pity In The Naked City	7"	Coral	Q72481	1965	**£6**	**£2.50**	
Please Tell Me Why	7"	Coral	Q72430	1961	**£5**	**£2**	
Reet Petite	7"	Vogue Coral	Q72290	1957	**£12**	**£6**	
Reet Petite	7"	Coral	Q72290	1957	**£6**	**£2.50**	
Shake A Hand	7"	Coral	Q72464	1963	**£5**	**£2**	*with Linda Hopkins*
Shake A Hand	LP	Brunswick	BL(7)54113	1963	**£30**	**£15**	*US*
Shake Shake Shake	7"	Coral	Q72465	1963	**£5**	**£2**	
Since You Showed Me How To Be Happy	7"	Coral	Q72496	1967	**£8**	**£4**	
Sing	7"	Coral	Q72453	1962	**£5**	**£2**	
So Much	LP	Coral	LVA9121	1960	**£60**	**£30**	
Somethin' Else	LP	Brunswick	BL(7)54117	1964	**£30**	**£15**	*US*
Soul Galore	LP	Coral	LVA9232	1966	**£30**	**£15**	*mono*
Soul Galore	LP	Coral	SVL9232	1966	**£40**	**£20**	*stereo*
Soul Time	LP	Brunswick	BL(7)54118	1965	**£30**	**£15**	*US*
Spotlight On Jackie Wilson	LP	Coral	LVA9231	1965	**£30**	**£15**	
Squeeze Her, Tease Her	7"	Coral	Q72476	1964	**£5**	**£2**	
Talk That Talk	7"	Coral	Q72384	1959	**£6**	**£2.50**	
Tear Of The Year	7"	Coral	Q72421	1961	**£25**	**£12.50**	*demo*
Tear Of The Year	7"	Coral	Q72424	1961	**£5**	**£2**	
Tenderly	7"	Ember	JBS705	1962	**£175**	**£87.50**	*Clyde McPhatter B side*
That's Why	7"	Coral	Q72366	1959	**£8**	**£4**	
To Be Loved	7"	Coral	Q72306	1958	**£10**	**£5**	
To Make A Big Man Cry	7"	Coral	Q72484	1966	**£6**	**£2.50**	
We Have Love	7"	Coral	Q72338	1958	**£10**	**£5**	
Whispers	LP	Coral	LVA9235	1967	**£25**	**£10**	
Whispers Gettin' Louder	7"	Coral	Q72487	1966	**£6**	**£2.50**	
Woman, A Lover, A Friend	LP	Coral	LVA9144	1961	**£60**	**£30**	
World's Greatest Melodies	LP	Coral	LVA9214	1962	**£30**	**£15**	*mono*
World's Greatest Melodies	LP	Coral	SVL9214	1962	**£40**	**£20**	*stereo*
Years From Now	7"	Coral	Q72439	1961	**£5**	**£2**	
Yes Indeed	7"	Coral	Q72480	1965	**£6**	**£2.50**	*with Linda Hopkins*
You Ain't Heard Nothing Yet	LP	Coral	LVA9148	1961	**£40**	**£20**	
You Better Know	7"	Coral	Q72380	1959	**£6**	**£2.50**	

WILSON, MARTY & THE STRATOLITES

Hey Eula	7"	Brunswick	05750	1958	**£8**	**£4**	

WILSON, MURRY

At least John Lennon's father only got to make a single: they let the father of the Beach Boys make a whole album! The result consists of light instrumental music that would be of marginal interest were it not for Mr Wilson's superstar connections.

Many Moods Of Murry Wilson	LP	Capitol	(S)T2819	1967	**£12**	**£5**	

WILSON, NANCY

Broadway My Love	LP	Capitol	(S)T1828	1963	**£10**	**£4**	
Don't Look Over Your Shoulder	7"	Capitol	CL15508	1967	**£5**	**£2**	
Face It Girl It's Over	7"	Capitol	CL15547	1968	**£15**	**£7.50**	
Hello Young Lovers	LP	Capitol	(S)T1767	1962	**£10**	**£4**	
Hollywood My Way	LP	Capitol	(S)T1934	1963	**£10**	**£4**	
How Glad I Am	7"	Capitol	CL15352	1964	**£4**	**£1.50**	
Nancy Wilson & Cannonball Adderley	7" EP	Capitol	EAP41657	1963	**£6**	**£2.50**	
Nancy Wilson & Cannonball Adderley	LP	Capitol	(S)T1657	1962	**£15**	**£6**	
Second Time Around	7" EP	Capitol	EAP120604	1962	**£5**	**£2**	
Today, Tomorrow, Forever	7" EP	Capitol	EAP42082	1964	**£5**	**£2**	
Uptight	7"	Capitol	CL15466	1966	**£8**	**£4**	
Where Does That Leave Me	7"	Capitol	CL15412	1965	**£5**	**£2**	
Yesterday's Love Songs	LP	Capitol	(S)T2012	1963	**£10**	**£4**	

WILSON, PEANUTS

Cast Iron Arm	7"	Coral	Q72302	1958	**£300**	**£180**	*best auctioned*

WILSON, PHIL

Better Days	7"	Caff	CAFF3	1989	**£6**	**£2.50**	

WILSON, REUBEN

Blue Mode	LP	Blue Note	BST84343	1970	**£10**	**£4**	
Cisco Kid	LP	People	PLEO1	1973	**£10**	**£4**	
Got To Get Your Own	7"	Chess	6078700	1976	**£6**	**£2.50**	
Groovy Situation	LP	Blue Note	BST84365	1970	**£10**	**£4**	
I'll Take You There	7"	People	PEO109	1974	**£4**	**£1.50**	
Love Bug	LP	Blue Note	BST84317	1969	**£10**	**£4**	
On Broadway	LP	Blue Note	BST84295	1968	**£10**	**£4**	
Set Us Free	LP	Blue Note	BST84377	1970	**£10**	**£4**	
Sweet Life	LP	People	PLEO20	1974	**£10**	**£4**	

WILSON, SMILEY

Title	Format	Label	Cat. No.	Year	Price	Price	Notes
Running Bear	7"	London	HLG9066	1960	**£30**	**£15**	

WILSON, TEDDY

Title	Format	Label	Cat. No.	Year	Price	Price	Notes
For Quiet Lovers	10" LP	HMV	DLP1162	1957	**£25**	**£10**	
I Got Rhythm	LP	HMV	CLP1230	1958	**£20**	**£8**	
Mr Wilson And Mr Gershwin	LP	Philips	BBL7344	1960	**£10**	**£4**	
Newport Jazz Festival 1957	LP	Columbia	33CX10107	1958	**£15**	**£6**	*with Gerry Mulligan*
Teddy Wilson	10" LP	Columbia	33C9019	1956	**£30**	**£15**	
Teddy Wilson	10" LP	Columbia	33S1066	1955	**£40**	**£20**	
Teddy Wilson	10" LP	Philips	BBR8065	1955	**£40**	**£20**	
Teddy Wilson Orchestra With Billie Holiday	10" LP	Philips	BBR8061	1955	**£40**	**£20**	
Teddy Wilson Trio	10" LP	Esquire	20009	1953	**£50**	**£25**	

WILSON, TONY

Title	Format	Label	Cat. No.	Year	Price	Price	Notes
Tony Wilson	LP	Bearsville	K55513	1976	**£25**	**£10**	

WILSON, TREVOR

Title	Format	Label	Cat. No.	Year	Price	Price	Notes
You Couldn't Believe	7"	Ska Beat	JB207	1965	**£10**	**£5**	

WILTSHIRE, JOHNNY

Title	Format	Label	Cat. No.	Year	Price	Price	Notes
If The Shoe Fits	7"	Oriole	CB1494	1959	**£20**	**£10**	

WIMPLE WINCH

The expensive singles recorded by Wimple Winch are over-rated, third-division examples of the genre that has come to be called 'freakbeat'. The newly invented fuzzbox – ubiquitous on British beat records from 1966–7 – is much in evidence, as are the influences from the Yardbirds, the Who, and the other true innovators of the time. The group evolved out of Just Four Men, whose singles are also very collectable, but which have even less relevance to the creative mainstream.

Title	Format	Label	Cat. No.	Year	Price	Price	Notes
Rumble On Mersey Square South	7"	Fontana	TF781	1967	**£100**	**£50**	
Rumble On Mersey Square South/ Atmospheres	7"	Fontana	TF781	1967	**£350**	**£210**	*best auctioned*
Save My Soul	7"	Fontana	TF718	1966	**£150**	**£75**	
What's Been Done	7"	Fontana	TF686	1966	**£100**	**£50**	

WINCHESTER, JESSE

Title	Format	Label	Cat. No.	Year	Price	Price	Notes
Jesse Winchester	LP	Ampex	A10104	1970	**£10**	**£4**	*US*

WIND

Title	Format	Label	Cat. No.	Year	Price	Price	Notes
Morning	LP	CBS	65007	1972	**£60**	**£30**	*German*
Seasons	LP	Plus	3	1971	**£60**	**£30**	*German*

WIND IN THE WILLOWS

Lead singer with the Wind in the Willows was Debbie Harry. The folky music played by the group is as different from that of Blondie as is Debbie Harry's own hippy appearance from that of the blonde bombshell she decided to become.

Title	Format	Label	Cat. No.	Year	Price	Price	Notes
Moments Spent	7"	Capitol	CL15561	1968	**£10**	**£5**	
Wind In The Willows	LP	Capitol	SKAO2956	1968	**£40**	**£20**	*US, gatefold*

WINDING, KAI

Title	Format	Label	Cat. No.	Year	Price	Price	Notes
Comin' Home Baby	7"	Verve	VS512	1965	**£4**	**£1.50**	
East Coast Jazz No. 7	LP	London	LTZN15003	1956	**£20**	**£8**	
Slide Rule	LP	Parlophone	PMC1138	1961	**£12**	**£5**	*with Jay Jay Johnson*
Swingin' States	LP	Philips	BBL7316/ SBBL509	1959	**£20**	**£8**	
Trombone Panorama	LP	Philips	BBL7275	1959	**£20**	**£8**	
Trombone Sound	LP	Philips	BBL7150	1957	**£20**	**£8**	

WINDOWS

Title	Format	Label	Cat. No.	Year	Price	Price	Notes
Uppers On Downers	LP	Skeleton	SKULP2	1981	**£10**	**£4**	

WINDSOR, BARBARA

Title	Format	Label	Cat. No.	Year	Price	Price	Notes
Don't Dig Twiggy	7"	Parlophone	R5629	1967	**£4**	**£1.50**	
Grin And Bare It	7"	Decca	F13323	1972	**£4**	**£1.50**	
Sparrows Can't Sing	7"	HMV	POP1128	1963	**£4**	**£1.50**	
When I Was A Child	7"	UPC	UPC101	1970	**£4**	**£1.50**	

WINDY CORNER

Title	Format	Label	Cat. No.	Year	Price	Price	Notes
House At Windy Corner	LP	Deroy	DER977	1973	**£400**	**£200**	

WINE OF LEBANON

Title	Format	Label	Cat. No.	Year	Price	Price	Notes
Wine Of Lebanon	LP	Dovetail	DOVE46	1976	**£30**	**£15**	

WINSOR, MARTIN & REDD SULLIVAN

Title	Format	Label	Cat. No.	Year	Price	Price	Notes
Hosts Of The Troubadour	LP	Deacon	DEA1045	1971	**£10**	**£4**	

WINSTON, JIMMY & HIS REFLECTIONS

Jimmy Winston was the original organist with the Small Faces and plays on their first single. His own singles, however, recorded as Winston's Fumbs and as Jimmy Winston and His Reflections, were not at all successful.

Title	Format	Label	Cat. No.	Year	Price	Price	Notes
Sorry She's Mine	7"	Decca	F12410	1966	**£100**	**£50**	

WINSTON & CECIL

Title	Format	Label	Cat. No.	Year	Price	Price	Notes
United We Stand	7"	Banana	BA306	1970	**£5**	**£2**	*Sound Dimension B side*

WINSTON & ERROL

Title	Format	Label	Cat. No.	Year	Price		Notes
Fay Is Gone	7"	Blue Beat	BB272	1964	**£12**	**£6**	

WINSTON & GEORGE

Title	Format	Label	Cat. No.	Year	Price		Notes
Keep The Pressure On	7"	Pyramid	PYR6002	1966	**£8**	**£4**	

WINSTON & PAT

Title	Format	Label	Cat. No.	Year	Price		Notes
Pony Ride	7"	Trojan	TR605	1968	**£5**	**£2**	

WINSTON & ROY

Title	Format	Label	Cat. No.	Year	Price		Notes
Babylon Gone	7"	Blue Beat	BB80	1962	**£12**	**£6**	

WINSTONE, ERIC

Title	Format	Label	Cat. No.	Year	Price		Notes
Dr Who Theme	7"	Pye	7N15603	1964	**£6**	**£2.50**	
Plays 007	LP	Avenue	AVINT1005	1973	**£10**	**£4**	

WINSTONE, NORMA

Title	Format	Label	Cat. No.	Year	Price		Notes
Edge Of Time	LP	Argo	ZDA148	1971	**£60**	**£30**	
Let's Make Love	LP	BBC Radioplay	TSRP7568	197–	**£25**	**£10**	

WINSTONS

Title	Format	Label	Cat. No.	Year	Price		Notes
Colour Him Father	7"	Pye	7N25493	1969	**£6**	**£2.50**	

WINSTON'S FUMBS

Title	Format	Label	Cat. No.	Year	Price		Notes
Real Crazy Appartment	7"	RCA	RCA1612	1967	**£200**	**£100**	

WINTER, JOHNNY

Title	Format	Label	Cat. No.	Year	Price		Notes
First Winter	LP	Buddah	2359011	1970	**£10**	**£4**	
John Dawson Winter III	LP	Blue Sky	PZQ33292	1974	**£10**	**£4**	*US quad*
Johnny Winter	LP	CBS	63619	1969	**£20**	**£8**	
Johnny Winter And . . .	LP	CBS	64117	1971	**£10**	**£4**	
Johnny Winter And . . . Live	LP	CBS	64289	1971	**£10**	**£4**	
Johnny Winter And/Live	LP	Columbia	CG33651	1971	**£15**	**£6**	*US double*
Progressive Blues Experiment	LP	Liberty	LBS83240	1969	**£12**	**£5**	
Saints And Sinners	LP	Columbia	CQ32715	1974	**£10**	**£4**	*US quad*
Second Winter	LP	CBS	66231	1970	**£15**	**£6**	*3 sides*
Still Alive And Well	LP	Columbia	CQ32188	1973	**£10**	**£4**	*US quad*

WINTER, PAUL

Title	Format	Label	Cat. No.	Year	Price		Notes
Winter Consort	LP	A&M	AMLS942	1969	**£10**	**£4**	

WINTERHALTER, HUGO ORCHESTRA

Title	Format	Label	Cat. No.	Year	Price		Notes
Canadian Sunset	7"	HMV	POP241	1956	**£4**	**£1.50**	

WINTERS, DON

Title	Format	Label	Cat. No.	Year	Price		Notes
Someday Baby	7"	Brunswick	05827	1960	**£8**	**£4**	

WINTERS, LIZ & BOB CORT

Title	Format	Label	Cat. No.	Year	Price		Notes
Liz Winters & Bob Cort	7" EP	Decca	DFE6409	1957	**£12**	**£6**	
Love Is Strange	7"	Decca	F10878	1957	**£8**	**£4**	
Maggie May	7"	Decca	F10899	1957	**£6**	**£2.50**	

WINTERS, LOIS

Title	Format	Label	Cat. No.	Year	Price		Notes
Japanese Farewell Song	7"	London	HLD8266	1956	**£15**	**£7.50**	

WINTERS, MIKE & BERNIE

Title	Format	Label	Cat. No.	Year	Price		Notes
How Do You Do?	7"	Parlophone	R4384	1957	**£6**	**£2.50**	
That Man Batman	7"	CBS	202458	1966	**£8**	**£4**	*picture sleeve*

WINTERS, RUBY

Title	Format	Label	Cat. No.	Year	Price		Notes
Baby Lay Down	7"	Creole	CR171	1979	**£4**	**£1.50**	
Back To Love	7"	Creole	CR174	1979	**£4**	**£1.50**	
I Want Action	7"	Stateside	SS2090	1968	**£15**	**£7.50**	

WINWOOD, STEVE

Steve Winwood is surely one of rock music's great lost talents. His early recordings with the Spencer Davis Group and Traffic were remarkable for their energy and their imagination, especially when one realizes how young he was. By the age of twenty he had already produced two of the most interesting albums of the sixties, in *Dear Mr Fantasy* and *Traffic*. It is all the more tragic, therefore, that his recordings of the last two decades should have been such bland, unexciting affairs. Even a Traffic reunion could do little to halt his creative decline, the resulting album being a wasted opportunity to add to a growing list.

Title	Format	Label	Cat. No.	Year	Price		Notes
Arc Of A Diver	CD	Mobile Fidelity	UDCD579	1993	**£15**	**£6**	*US audiophile*
Back In The High Life	CD	Mobile Fidelity	UDCD611	1994	**£15**	**£6**	*US audiophile*
Back In The High Life	LP	Island	SW1/2/3	1987	**£15**	**£6**	*promo 3 × 7" box set*
Chronicles	LP	Island		1987	**£25**	**£10**	*promo 5 × 7" box set*
Conversation With Steve Winwood	LP	Island	SWCLP1	1986	**£12**	**£5**	*promo*
Don't You Know What The Night Can Do?	CD-s	Virgin	VSCD1107	1988	**£5**	**£2**	
Freedom Overspill	12"	Island	12ISD294	1986	**£6**	**£2.50**	
Holding On	CD-s	Virgin	VSCD1135	1988	**£5**	**£2**	
In Conversation	LP	Island	SWWLP1	1987	**£10**	**£4**	*promo*

Title	Format	Label	Cat. No.	Year	Mint	VG	Notes
One And Only Man	CD-s	Virgin	VSCDT1299	1990	£5	£2	
Refugee Of The Heart	CD	Virgin		1990	£20	£8	US gold promo in black velvet bag
Roll With It	CD	Virgin	CDVP2532	1988	£12	£5	picture disc
Roll With It	CD	Virgin	CDV2532	1988	£15	£6	Virgin Megastore 1st day issue, red inner tray
Roll With It	CD-s	Virgin	VSCD1085	1988	£5	£2	
Valerie	CD-s	Island	CID336	1987	£5	£2	
Winwood	LP	United Artists	UAS9950	1971	£10	£4	US, with booklet

WIPEOUT

Title	Format	Label	Cat. No.	Year	Mint	VG	Notes
No Sweat	LP	Out	OUT1	1983	£10	£4	

WIRE

Title	Format	Label	Cat. No.	Year	Mint	VG	Notes
154	12"	Harvest	SPSLP299	1979	£20	£10	promo sampler with press pack
154	LP	Harvest	SHSP4105	1979	£10	£4	with 7" (PSR444)
Crazy About Love	12"	Rough Trade	RTT123	1983	£6	£2.50	2 different coloured sleeves
Document And Eyewitness	LP	Rough Trade	ROUGH29	1984	£10	£4	with 12" (ROUGH2912)
Dot Dash	7"	Harvest	HAR5161	1978	£5	£2	picture sleeve
Eardrum Buzz	7"	Mute	MUTE87	1989	£8	£4	picture sleeve, clear vinyl
Eardrum Buzz	CD-s	Mute	CDMUTE87	1989	£5	£2	
I Am The Fly	7"	Harvest	HAR5151	1978	£5	£2	picture sleeve
Ibtaba	LP	Mute	STUMM66	1989	£12	£5	with signed print & 4 cards
In Vivo	CD-s	Mute	CDMUTE98	1989	£5	£2	
Mannequin	7"	Harvest	HAR5144	1977	£8	£4	picture sleeve
Our Swimmer	7"	Rough Trade	RT079	1981	£4	£1.50	
Outdoor Miner	7"	Harvest	HAR5172	1979	£5	£2	picture sleeve, white vinyl
Question Of Degree	7"	Harvest	HAR5187	1979	£4	£1.50	picture sleeve

WIRELESS

Title	Format	Label	Cat. No.	Year	Mint	VG	Notes
No Static	LP	Anthem	ANR11025	1980	£25	£10	Canadian

WIRTZ, MARK

Title	Format	Label	Cat. No.	Year	Mint	VG	Notes
He's Our Dear Old Weatherman	7"	Parlophone	R5668	1968	£10	£5	
Mrs Raven	7"	Parlophone	R5683	1968	£4	£1.50	
Ten Again	LP	World Record Club	T452	1964	£20	£8	with Belle Gonzalez & Russ Loader

WISDOM

Title	Format	Label	Cat. No.	Year	Mint	VG	Notes
Nefertiti	7"	Crystal	CR026	1976	£5	£2	

WISDOM, NORMAN

Title	Format	Label	Cat. No.	Year	Mint	VG	Notes
Follow A Star	7"	Top Rank	JAR246	1959	£4	£1.50	
Follow A Star	7" EP	Top Rank	JKP2052	1960	£10	£5	
Narcissus	7"	Columbia	SCD2160	1961	£5	£2	
Norman And Ruby	7" EP	Columbia	SEG7687	1957	£8	£4	with Ruby Murray
Norman Wisdom	7" EP	Columbia	SEG7612	1956	£10	£5	
Two Rivers	7"	Columbia	SCM5222	1956	£8	£4	with Ruby Murray
Up In The World	7"	Columbia	DB3864	1957	£4	£1.50	
Where's Charly?	LP	Columbia	33SX1085	1958	£12	£5	
Wisdom Of A Fool	7"	Columbia	DB3903	1957	£5	£2	

WISE BOYS

Title	Format	Label	Cat. No.	Year	Mint	VG	Notes
Why Why Why	7"	Parlophone	R4693	1960	£5	£2	

WISE GUYS

Title	Format	Label	Cat. No.	Year	Mint	VG	Notes
Big Noise	7"	Top Rank	JAR271	1960	£8	£4	

WISEMAN, MAC

Title	Format	Label	Cat. No.	Year	Mint	VG	Notes
Beside The Still Waters	LP	Dot	DLP3135/ DLP25135	1959	£20	£8	US
Fireball Mail	7"	London	HLD8259	1956	£40	£20	
Fireball Mail	LP	Dot	DLP3408	1961	£20	£8	US
Great Folk Ballads	LP	London	HAD2217	1960	£30	£15	
Jimmy Brown The Newsboy	7"	London	HL7084	1959	£25	£12.50	export
Keep On The Sunny Side	LP	Dot	DLP3336	1960	£20	£8	US
Kentuckian Song	7"	London	HLD8174	1955	£40	£20	
My Little Home In Tennessee	7"	London	HLD8226	1956	£30	£15	
Songs From The Hills	10" LP	London	HBD1052	1956	£40	£20	
Songs From The Hills	7" EP	London	RED1056	1956	£25	£12.50	
Songs From The Hills Vol. 2	7" EP	London	RED1147	1958	£25	£12.50	
Songs From The Hills Vol. 3	7" EP	London	RED1242	1960	£25	£12.50	
Step It Up And Go	7"	London	HLD8412	1957	£250	£150	best auctioned
Tis Sweet To Be Remembered	LP	Dot	DLP3084	1958	£20	£8	US

WISHART, TREVOR

Title	Format	Label	Cat. No.	Year	Mint	VG	Notes
Beach Singularity And Menagerie	LP	private		1979	£40	£20	
Journey Into Space Parts One And Two	LP	private	YU3-6	1973	£100	£50	double
Red Bird – A Political Prisoner's Dream	LP	private		1978	£40	£20	

WISHBONE ASH

Cosmic Jazz	12"	I.R.S.	EIRST104	1989	**£6**	**£2.50**	
Evening Program With Wishbone Ash	LP	Decca		1972	**£12**	**£5**	*US promo*
Get Ready	7"	MCA	MCA726	1981	**£4**	**£1.50**	*with patch*
Live Dates Vol. 2	LP	MCA	MCG4012	1980	**£12**	**£5**	*with bonus LP*
LIve From Memphis	LP	MCA	L331922	1974	**£20**	**£8**	*US promo*
Pilgrimage	LP	MCA	MDKS8004	1971	**£10**	**£4**	
Raw To The Bone	LP	Neat	NEAT1027	1985	**£12**	**£5**	
Wishbone Ash	LP	MCA	MKPS2014	1970	**£10**	**£4**	

WISHFUL THINKING

Alone	7"	Decca	F22742	1968	**£4**	**£1.50**	
Hiroshima	LP	B&C	CAS1038	1971	**£15**	**£6**	
Live Vol. 1	LP	Decca	SKL4900	1967	**£20**	**£8**	
Meet The Sun	7"	Decca	F22673	1967	**£4**	**£1.50**	
Turning Round	7"	Decca	F12438	1966	**£4**	**£1.50**	

WITCHFINDER GENERAL

Burning A Sinner	7"	Heavy Metal	HEAVY6	1981	**£20**	**£10**	
Music	7"	Heavy Metal	HMPD21	1983	**£5**	**£2**	*picture disc*
Music	7"	Heavy Metal	HEAVY21	1983	**£6**	**£2.50**	
Soviet Invasion	12"	Heavy Metal	12HM17	1982	**£25**	**£12.50**	

WITCHFYNDE

Cloak And Dagger	LP	Expulsion	PEXIT5	1983	**£10**	**£4**	*picture disc*
I'd Rather Go Wild	7"	Expulsion	OUT3	1983	**£10**	**£5**	

WITHERS, BILL

+Justments	LP	A&M	AMLH68230	1974	**£10**	**£4**	
Ain't No Sunshine	CD-s	CBS	6531982	1988	**£5**	**£2**	
Best Of Bill Withers	LP	Sussex	LPSX10	1975	**£10**	**£4**	
Just As I Am	LP	A&M	AMLS65002	1971	**£10**	**£4**	
Live At Carnegie Hall	LP	A&M	AMLD3001	1973	**£12**	**£5**	*double*
Lovely Day	CD-s	CBS	6530012	1988	**£5**	**£2**	
Still Bill	LP	A&M	AMLH68107	1972	**£10**	**£4**	

WITHERSPOON, JIMMY

All That's Good	7"	Vogue	V2420	1964	**£25**	**£12.50**	
At The Monterey Jazz Festival	LP	Hi Fi	421	1959	**£20**	**£8**	*US*
At The Renaissance	LP	Vogue	LAE12253	1961	**£12**	**£5**	
Back Door Blues	LP	Polydor	623256	1969	**£12**	**£5**	
Blue Point Of View	LP	Verve	(S)VLP9156	1967	**£12**	**£5**	
Blue Spoon	LP	Stateside	SL10139	1965	**£15**	**£6**	
Blues Around The Clock	LP	Stateside	SL10105	1965	**£20**	**£8**	
Blues For Easy Livers	LP	Transatlantic	PR7475	1968	**£10**	**£4**	
Blues Is Now	LP	Verve	(S)VLP9181	1968	**£15**	**£6**	*with Brother Jack McDuff*
Blues Singer	LP	Stateside	(S)SL10289	1969	**£10**	**£4**	
Come And Walk With Me	7"	Stateside	SS429	1965	**£6**	**£2.50**	
Evenin' Blues	LP	Stateside	SL10088	1964	**£15**	**£6**	
Evenin' Blues	LP	Transatlantic	PR7300	1967	**£10**	**£4**	
Falling By Degrees	78	Vogue	V2261	1955	**£12**	**£6**	
Feelin' The Spirit	LP	Hi Fi	422	1959	**£20**	**£8**	*US*
Feeling The Spirit Vol. 1	7" EP	Vocalion	VEH170158	1964	**£12**	**£6**	
Feeling The Spirit Vol. 2	7" EP	Vocalion	VEH170159	1964	**£12**	**£6**	
Goin' To Kansas City Blues	LP	RCA	LPM1639	1958	**£20**	**£8**	*US*
Hey Mrs Jones	LP	Reprise	R(9)6012	1962	**£15**	**£6**	*US*
Highway To Happiness	7"	Parlophone	MSP6125	1954	**£30**	**£15**	
I Done Told You	7"	Parlophone	MSP6142	1954	**£30**	**£15**	
I Never Will Marry	7"	Stateside	SS325	1964	**£6**	**£2.50**	
If There Wasn't Any You	7"	Stateside	SS503	1966	**£6**	**£2.50**	
In Person	LP	Vogue	VRL3005	1965	**£15**	**£6**	
It's All Over But The Crying	7"	Verve	VS538	1966	**£4**	**£1.50**	
Jimmy Witherspoon	7" EP	Vocalion	EPVH1278	1964	**£12**	**£6**	
Jimmy Witherspoon	LP	Ember	EMB3369	1966	**£12**	**£5**	
Jimmy Witherspoon At Monterey No. 1	7" EP	Vocalion	EPV1269	1962	**£25**	**£12.50**	
Jimmy Witherspoon At Monterey No. 2	7" EP	Vocalion	EPV1270	1962	**£25**	**£12.50**	
Jump Children	78	Vogue	V2356	1956	**£12**	**£6**	
Live	LP	Stateside	(S)SL10232	1968	**£15**	**£6**	
Love Me Right	7"	Stateside	SS461	1965	**£6**	**£2.50**	
Money Is Getting Cheaper	7"	Stateside	SS304	1964	**£6**	**£2.50**	
New Orleans Blues	LP	Atlantic	1266	1956	**£30**	**£15**	*US*
New Orleans Blues	LP	London	LTZK15150	1959	**£20**	**£8**	
No Rolling Blues	7"	Vogue	V2060	1956	**£25**	**£12.50**	
Outskirts Of Town	7" EP	Vocalion	EPVH1284	1965	**£12**	**£6**	
Rhythm & Blues Concert	7" EP	Vogue	EPV1198	1958	**£40**	**£20**	*with Helen Humes*
Roots	LP	Reprise	R(9)6059	1962	**£15**	**£6**	*US*
Singin' The Blues	LP	Vogue	LAE12218	1960	**£12**	**£5**	
Some Of My Best Friends Are The Blues	LP	Stateside	SL10114	1965	**£20**	**£8**	
Some Of My Best Friends Are The Blues	LP	Transatlantic	PR7356	1968	**£10**	**£4**	
Spoon	LP	Reprise	R(9)2008	1961	**£15**	**£6**	*US*
Spoon In London	LP	Transatlantic	PR7418	1968	**£12**	**£5**	
Spoon Sings And Swings	LP	Fontana	(S)TL5382	1967	**£20**	**£8**	
Spoonful Of Soul	LP	Verve	(S)VLP9216	1968	**£12**	**£5**	
Take This Hammer	LP	Constellation	M1422	1964	**£15**	**£6**	*US*
There's Good Rockin' Tonight	LP	Fontana	688005ZL	1965	**£12**	**£5**	
Who's Been Jivin' With You	78	Vogue	V2295	1954	**£12**	**£6**	

Title	Format	Label	Cat. No.	Year	Mint	VG+	Notes
You're Next	7"	Stateside	SS362	1964	£6	£2.50	

WITNESSES

Title	Format	Label	Cat. No.	Year	Mint	VG+	Notes
Witnesses	7" EP	Herald	ELR1076	196–	£50	£25	

WITTHUSER & WESTRUPP

Title	Format	Label	Cat. No.	Year	Mint	VG+	Notes
Bauer Plath	LP	Pilz	20291154	1972	£15	£6	German
Der Jesuspilz	LP	Pilz	20210987	1971	£15	£6	German
Lieder Von Vampiren, Nonnen Und Toten	LP	Ohr	OMM56002	1970	£20	£8	German
Live 68–73	LP	Kosmische	KM258004	1973	£20	£8	German double
Trips Und Traume	LP	Ohr	OMM56016	1971	£15	£6	German

WIZARD

Title	Format	Label	Cat. No.	Year	Mint	VG+	Notes
Original Wizard	LP	Peon	1069	1971	£200	£100	US

WIZARD'S CONVENTION

Title	Format	Label	Cat. No.	Year	Mint	VG+	Notes
Wizard's Convention	LP	RCA	RS1085	1976	£10	£4	

WIZARDS FROM KANSAS

Title	Format	Label	Cat. No.	Year	Mint	VG+	Notes
Wizards From Kansas	LP	Mercury	SR61309	1970	£75	£37.50	US

WIZZARD

Title	Format	Label	Cat. No.	Year	Mint	VG+	Notes
Are You Ready To Rock	CD-s	Counterpoint	CDEP12	1988	£5	£2	Slade B side
I Wish It Could Be Christmas Every Day	7"	Warner Bros	K16336	1973	£6	£2.50	gatefold picture sleeve
I Wish It Could Be Christmas Every Day	7"	Harvest	HAR5079	1973	£6	£2.50	picture sleeve
Indiana Rainbow	7"	Jet	JET768	1976	£6	£2.50	picture sleeve

WOLF

Title	Format	Label	Cat. No.	Year	Mint	VG+	Notes
Head Contact	12"	Chrysalis	CHS122592	1982	£8	£4	
Head Contact	7"	Chrysalis	CHS2592	1982	£6	£2.50	clear vinyl

WOLF, VIRGINIA

Title	Format	Label	Cat. No.	Year	Mint	VG+	Notes
Waiting For Your Love	7"	Atlantic	A9459	1986	£5	£2	

WOLFE, CHARLES

Title	Format	Label	Cat. No.	Year	Mint	VG+	Notes
Dance Dance Dance	7"	NEMS	563675	1968	£8	£4	

WOLFETONES

Title	Format	Label	Cat. No.	Year	Mint	VG+	Notes
Across The Broad Atlantic	LP	Triskel	TRL1002	1976	£10	£4	Irish
Belt Of The Celts	LP	Triskel	TRL1003	1978	£10	£4	Irish
Foggy Dew	LP	Fontana	STL5244	1965	£15	£6	
Irish To The Core	LP	Triskel	TRL1001	1976	£10	£4	Irish
Let The People Sing	LP	Dolphin	DOL1004	1972	£10	£4	Irish
Live Alive Oh!	LP	Triskel	TRL1005	1980	£12	£5	Irish double
Rifles Of The I.R.A.	LP	Dolphin	DOL1002	1976	£10	£4	Irish
Rights Of Man	LP	Fontana	STL5462	1968	£15	£6	
Teddy Bear's Head	LP	Dolphin	DOLM5005	1976	£10	£4	Irish
Till Ireland's A Nation	LP	Dolphin	DOL1006	1974	£10	£4	Irish
Up The Rebels	LP	Fontana		196–	£15	£6	
Up The Rebels	LP	Dolphin	DOLM5003	1976	£10	£4	Irish

WOLFF, HENRY & NANCY HENNINGS

Title	Format	Label	Cat. No.	Year	Mint	VG+	Notes
Tibetan Bells	LP	Island	HELP3	1972	£10	£4	

WOLFGANG PRESS

Title	Format	Label	Cat. No.	Year	Mint	VG+	Notes
Funky Little Demons	CD	4AD	CADD4016CD	1994	£15	£6	double
King Of Soul	12"	4AD	no number	1983	£10	£5	promo
King Of Soul	CD-s	4AD	BAD804CD	1988	£5	£2	
Raintime	CD-s	4AD	BAD907CD	1989	£5	£2	
Scarecrow	12"	4AD	BAD409	1984	£8	£4	
Water	12"	4AD	BAD502	1985	£6	£2.50	

WOLFMAN JACK

Title	Format	Label	Cat. No.	Year	Mint	VG+	Notes
And The Wolf Pack	LP	Bread	BD0170	1963	£30	£15	US
Fun And Romance	LP	Columbia	KC33501	1975	£12	£5	US

WOLFRILLA

Title	Format	Label	Cat. No.	Year	Mint	VG+	Notes
Song For Jimi	7"	Concord	CON015	1970	£8	£4	

WOLVENLEI

Title	Format	Label	Cat. No.	Year	Mint	VG+	Notes
Wolvenlei	LP	Spoof		1978	£25	£10	Dutch

WOLVES

Title	Format	Label	Cat. No.	Year	Mint	VG+	Notes
At The Club	7"	Pye	7N17013	1965	£10	£5	
Journey Into Dreams	7"	Pye	7N15676	1964	£5	£2	
Lust For Life	7"	Parlophone	R5511	1966	£40	£20	
Now	7"	Pye	7N15733	1964	£15	£7.50	

WOMACK, BOBBY

Title	Format	Label	Cat. No.	Year	Mint	VG+	Notes
Across 110th Street	LP	United Artists	UAS29451	1973	£10	£4	
Broadway Talk	7"	Minit	MLF11001	1968	£8	£4	
Communication	LP	United Artists	UAS29306	1973	£10	£4	
Facts Of Life	LP	United Artists	UAG29456	1973	£10	£4	
Harry Hippie	7"	United Artists	UP35456	1973	£6	£2.50	picture sleeve
I Can Understand It	LP	United Artists	UAS29715	1975	£10	£4	
I Don't Know What The World Is Coming To	LP	United Artists	UAG29762	1975	£10	£4	

Lookin' For A Love Again	LP	United Artists	UAS29574	1974	£10	£4	
Roads Of Life	LP	Arista	ARTY165	1979	£15	£6	
Safety Zone	LP	United Artists	UAG29907	1976	£10	£4	
Understanding	LP	United Artists	UAS29365	1972	£10	£4	
What Is This	7"	Jayboy	BOY75	1974	£4	£1.50	
What Is This	7"	Minit	MLF11005	1968	£5	£2	

WOMB

Overdub	LP	Dot	DLP25959	1969	£15	£6	US
Womb	LP	Dot	DLP25933	1969	£15	£6	US

WOMEGA

Quick Step	LP	Skruup	162210751	1975	£12	£5	*Belgian*

WOMENFOLK

At The Hungry I	LP	RCA	RD7704	1965	£10	£4	

WONDER, ALISON

Once More With Feeling	7"	Columbia	DB8667	1970	£5	£2	

WONDER, STEVIE

Blowin' In The Wind	7"	Tamla Motown	TMG570	1966	£8	£4	
Castles In The Sand	7"	Stateside	SS285	1964	£25	£12.50	
Down To Earth	LP	Tamla Motown	(S)TML11045	1967	£20	£8	
Eivets Rednow	LP	Gordy	GS932	1968	£15	£6	US
Fingertips	7"	Oriole	CBA1853	1963	£20	£10	
For Once In My Life	7"	Tamla Motown	TMG679	1968	£4	£1.50	
For Once In My Life	LP	Tamla Motown	(S)TML11098	1969	£10	£4	
Greatest Hits	LP	Tamla Motown	(S)TML11075	1968	£10	£4	
Hey Harmonica Man	7"	Stateside	SS323	1964	£25	£12.50	
Hey Harmonica Man	LP	Stateside	SL10108	1965	£60	£30	
Hi Heel Sneakers	7"	Tamla Motown	TMG532	1965	£25	£12.50	
I Call It Pretty Music	7" EP	Stateside	SE1014	1964	£60	£30	
I Was Made To Love Her	7"	Tamla Motown	TMG613	1967	£4	£1.50	
I Was Made To Love Her	LP	Tamla Motown	(S)TML11059	1968	£15	£6	
I'm Wondering	7"	Tamla Motown	TMG626	1967	£4	£1.50	
Innervisions	CD	Mobile Fidelity	UDCD554	1991	£15	£6	*US audiophile*
Jazz Soul Of Little Stevie	LP	Stateside	SL10078	1964	£60	£30	
Kiss Me Baby	7"	Tamla Motown	TMG505	1965	£25	£12.50	
Live	LP	Tamla Motown	(S)TML11150	1970	£10	£4	
Live At The Talk Of The Town	LP	Tamla Motown	STML11164	1970	£10	£4	
My Cherie Amour	7"	Tamla Motown	TMG690	1969	£4	£1.50	
My Cherie Amour	LP	Tamla Motown	(S)TML11128	1969	£10	£4	
Nothing's Too Good For My Baby	7"	Tamla Motown	TMG558	1966	£15	£7.50	
Place In The Sun	7"	Tamla Motown	TMG588	1966	£8	£4	
Shoo-Be-Doo-Be-Doo-Da-Day	7"	Tamla Motown	TMG653	1968	£4	£1.50	
Someday At Christmas	LP	Tamla Motown	(S)TML11085	1969	£20	£8	
Stevie Wonder	7" EP	Tamla Motown	TME2006	1965	£50	£25	
Talking Book	CD	Motown	C88114	1988	£15	£6	*box set*
Talking Book	LP	EMI	5CP06293880	1979	£15	£6	*Dutch picture disc*
Travelling Man	7"	Tamla Motown	TMG602	1967	£4	£1.50	
Tribute To Uncle Ray	LP	Oriole	PS40049	1963	£75	£37.50	
Twelve Year Old Genius	LP	Oriole	PS40050	1963	£50	£25	
Uptight	7"	Tamla Motown	TMG545	1966	£6	£2.50	
Uptight	LP	Tamla Motown	(S)TML11036	1966	£15	£6	
We Can Work It Out	7"	Tamla Motown	TMG772	1971	£15	£7.50	*picture sleeve*
Where I'm Coming From	LP	Tamla Motown	STML11183	1971	£10	£4	
With A Song In My Heart	LP	Tamla	T250	1964	£60	£30	US
Workout Stevie Workout	7"	Stateside	SS238	1963	£25	£12.50	
Workout Stevie, Workout	LP	Tamla	TS248	1963	£60	£30	US
You Met Your Match	7"	Tamla Motown	TMG666	1968	£4	£1.50	

WONDER BOY

Just For A Day	7"	Concord	CON015	1971	£4	£1.50	
Love Power	7"	Jackpot	JP705	1969	£4	£1.50	*Pat Kelly B side*
Sweeten My Coffee	7"	Jackpot	JP703	1969	£4	£1.50	*Mister Miller B side*

WONDER STUFF

Don't Let Me Down Gently	CD-s	Polydor	GONECD7	1989	£5	£2	
Eight-Legged Groove Machine	CD	Polydor	GONECD1	1988	£20	£8	*with 'Wish Away' printed on front cover*
Give Give Give Me More More More	12"	Polydor	GONEX3	1988	£6	£2.50	
Give Give Give Me More More More	CD-s	Polydor	GONECD3	1988	£10	£5	
Give Give Give Me More More More	CD-s	Polygram	0805822	1989	£10	£5	*CD video*
Golden Green	CD-s	Polydor	GONCD8	1989	£5	£2	
It's Yer Money I'm After Baby	CD-s	Polydor	GONCD5	1988	£8	£4	
Unbearable	7"	Farout	GONE002	1987	£15	£7.50	
Unbearable	7"	Far Out	GONE002	1987	£5	£2	*no picture sleeve*
Waffle And Maple Syrup	LP	Polydor	STUFF1	198–	£20	£8	*promo*
Who Wants To Be The Disco King?	CD-s	Polydor	GONECD6	1989	£5	£2	
Wish Away	CD-s	Polydor	GONECD4	1988	£8	£4	
Wonderful Day	7"	Farout	GONE ONE	1987	£40	£20	

WONDER WHO

The Wonder Who were the Four Seasons, recording under a pseudonym to see if they could still sell records. With a voice as distinctive as Frankie Valli's, however, they did not succeed in fooling anyone for very long.

Don't Think Twice It's Alright	7"	Philips	BF1440	1965	£4	£1.50	
Lonesome Road	7"	Philips	BF1600	1967	£4	£1.50	
On The Good Ship Lollipop	7"	Philips	BF1504	1966	£4	£1.50	

WONDERLAND

Poochy	7"	Polydor	56539	1968	£6	£2.50	

WONDERLAND, ALICE

He's Mine	7"	London	HLU9783	1963	£4	£1.50	

WONDERLAND BAND

Best Of The Wonderland Band	LP	Karussell	2415078	1973	£25	£10	*German*
No. 1	LP	Polydor	2371125	1971	£30	£15	*German*

WONG, ROYCE

Everything's Gonna Be Alright	7"	Blue Beat	BB301	1965	£12	£6	

WOOD, ANITA

Dream Baby	7"	Sue	WI328	1964	£10	£5	
I'll Wait Forever	7"	London	HLS9585	1962	£15	£7.50	

WOOD, BOBBY

I'm A Fool For Loving You	7"	Pye	7N25264	1964	£4	£1.50	

WOOD, BRENTON

Baby You Got It	LP	Double Shot	1003/5003	1967	£12	£5	*US*
Gimme Little Sign	7"	Liberty	LBF15021	1967	£4	£1.50	
Gimme Little Sign	LP	Liberty	LBL/LBS83088E	1967	£10	£4	
Great Big Bundle Of Love	7"	Pye	7N25522	1970	£5	£2	

WOOD, CHUCK

Seven Days Too Long	7"	Transatlantic	BIG104	1967	£5	£2	

WOOD, DEL

Ragtime Annie	7"	London	HL8036	1954	£25	£12.50	
Ragtime Piano	7" EP	London	REP1007	1954	£8	£4	

WOOD, ROBERT

Sonabular	LP	Edici	ED6103	1973	£10	£4	*French*
Tarot And Tombac	LP	Edici	ED6102	1972	£12	£5	*French*
Vibrarock	LP	Polydor	2393137	1976	£10	£4	*French*

WOOD, RONNIE

Big Bayou	7"	Warner Bros	K16679	1976	£4	£1.50	
I Can Feel The Fire	7"	Warner Bros	K16463	1974	£4	£1.50	
If You Don't Want Me Love	7"	Warner Bros	K16618	1975	£4	£1.50	
Seven Days	7"	CBS	7785	1979	£4	£1.50	
Show Me	CD-s	Continuum	122102	1992	£40	£20	*with signed print*

WOOD, ROY

I Never Believed In Love	7"	Warner Bros	K17028	1977	£4	£1.50	*with Annie Haslam*
Roy Wood Story	LP	Harvest	SHDW408	1976	£12	£5	*double*

WOOD, ROYSTON & HEATHER

No Relation	LP	Transatlantic	TRA342	1977	£50	£25	

WOOD, TED

Am I Blue	7"	Penny Farthing	PEN891	1976	£5	£2	

WOODBINE LIZZIE

By Numbers	LP	Fellside	FE019	1979	£20	£8	

WOODEN HORSE

Pick Up The Pieces 7" York SYK526 1972 **£5** **£2**
Wooden Horse LP York FYK403 1972 **£100** **£50**
Wooden Horse II LP York FYK413 1973 **£300** **£180**
Wooden Horses 7" York SYK543 1973 **£5** **£2**

WOODEN O

Handful Of Pleasant Delites LP Middle Earth MDLS301 1969 **£75** **£37.50**

WOODMAN, KEN & HIS PICCADILLY BRASS

That's Nice LP Strike JLH101 1966 **£15** **£6**

WOODPECKERS

Hey Little Girl 7" Oriole CB311 1965 **£8** **£4**
Woodpecker 7" Decca F11835 1964 **£4** **£1.50**

WOODS, CAROL

Out Of The Woods LP Ember NR5059 1972 **£10** **£4**

WOODS, DONALD

Memories Of An Angel 7" Vogue V9107 1958 **£300** **£180** *best auctioned*

WOODS, GAY & TERRY

Backwoods LP Polydor 2383322 1975 **£40** **£20**
Renowned LP Polydor 2383406 1976 **£40** **£20**
Tenderhooks LP Rockburgh ROC104 1978 **£15** **£6**
Time Is Right LP Polydor 2383375 1976 **£30** **£15**
Woods Band LP Greenwich GSLP1004 1971 **£60** **£30**
Woods Band LP Rockburgh CREST29 1977 **£20** **£8**
Woods Band LP Mulligan LUN015 1977 **£15** **£6** *different cover to 1971 issue*

WOODS, NICK

Ballad Of Billy Bud 7" London HLU9621 1962 **£4** **£1.50**

WOODS, PHIL

New Jazz Quintet 10" LP Esquire 20055 1955 **£50** **£25**
Phil Woods Quartet LP Esquire 32020 1957 **£30** **£15**
Phil Woods Septet LP Esquire 32026 1957 **£30** **£15**

WOODWARD, MAGGIE

Ali Bama 7" Vogue V9148 1959 **£6** **£2.50**

WOODY'S TRUCK STOP

Woody's Truck Stop LP Smash SRS67111 1969 **£15** **£6** *US*

WOOFERS

Dragsville LP Wyncote 9001 196– **£20** **£8** *US*

WOOLEY, SHEB

Hill Billy Mambo 7" MGM SPC5 1955 **£15** **£7.50** *export*
Hootenanny Hoot 7" MGM MGM1257 1965 **£4** **£1.50**
I Flipped 7" MGM SP1130 1955 **£12** **£6**
Jest Plain, Wild And Wooley 7" EP MGM MGMEP540 1956 **£25** **£12.50**
Laughing The Blues 7" MGM MGM1162 1962 **£5** **£2**
Luke The Spook 7" MGM MGM1081 1960 **£5** **£2**
Meet Mr Lonely 7" MGM MGM1147 1961 **£6** **£2.50**
More 7" MGM MGM1017 1959 **£4** **£1.50**
Purple People Eater/I Can't Believe You're Mine 7" MGM MGM981 1958 **£12** **£6**
Purple People Eater/Recipe For Love 7" MGM MGM981 1958 **£5** **£2**
Santa & The Purple People Eater 7" MGM MGM997 1958 **£4** **£1.50**
Sheb Wooley LP MGM E3299 1956 **£25** **£10** *US*
Songs From The Day Of Rawhide LP MGM C859 1961 **£10** **£4**
Spoofing The Big Ones LP MGM C945 1963 **£10** **£4**
Tales Of How The West Was Won LP MGM C955 1963 **£10** **£4**
That's My Ma & That's My Pa LP MGM C903 1962 **£10** **£4**
Wayward Wind 7" MGM MGM1132 1961 **£4** **£1.50**

WOOLIES

Basic Rock LP Split 96452001 1970 **£40** **£20** *US*
Live At Lizard's LP Spirit 2005 1973 **£40** **£20** *US*
Who Do You Love? 7" RCA RCA1602 1967 **£25** **£12.50**

WOOTTON, BRENDA

Crowdy Crawn LP Sentinel SENS1016 1973 **£75** **£37.50** *with Richard Gendall*
No Song To Sing? LP Sentinel SENS1021 1974 **£75** **£37.50** *with Robert Bartlett*
Pasties And Cream LP Sentinel SENS1006 1971 **£75** **£37.50** *with John The Fish*
Pipers Folk LP private VRC1 1968 **£75** **£37.50** *with John The Fish*
Starry Gazey Pie LP Sentinel SENS1031 1976 **£75** **£37.50** *with Robert Bartlett*

WORK, JIMMY

Country Songs 7" EP London RED1039 1955 **£30** **£15**
When She Said You All 7" London HLD8270 1956 **£50** **£25**
You've Got A Heart Like A Merry-Go-Round 7" London HLD8308 1956 **£30** **£15**

WORLD

Angelina	7"	Liberty	LBF15402	1970	**£4**	**£1.50**	
Lucky Planet	LP	Liberty	LBS83419	1970	**£15**	**£6**	

WORLD DOMINATION ENTERPRISES

Asbestos Lead Asbestos	7"	Karbon	KAR008	1985	**£5**	**£2**	

WORLD OF OZ

King Croesus	7"	Deram	DM205	1968	**£4**	**£1.50**	
Muffin Man	7"	Deram	DM187	1968	**£6**	**£2.50**	
Willow's Harp	7"	Deram	DM233	1969	**£6**	**£2.50**	
World Of Oz	LP	Deram	DML/SML1034	1969	**£40**	**£20**	

WORLD OF TWIST

Sausage	7"	Caff	CAFF16	1992	**£5**	**£2**	

WORLD PARTY

Brief History Of The World Party	CD-s	Ensign	WPCDDJ001	1997	**£8**	**£4**	*3 track promo compilation*
Message In The Box	CD-s	Ensign	ENYCD631	1990	**£5**	**£2**	
Ship Of Fools	CD-s	Ensign	ENYCD606	1987	**£5**	**£2**	
Way Down Now	CD-s	Ensign	ENYCD634	1990	**£5**	**£2**	

WORRYING KYNDE

Call Out The Name	7"	Piccadilly	7N35370	1967	**£30**	**£15**	

WORTH, JOHNNY

Just Because	7"	Columbia	DB3962	1957	**£4**	**£1.50**	
Nightmare	7"	Oriole	CB1545	1960	**£4**	**£1.50**	

WORTH, MARION

Are You Willing, Willie	7"	London	HL7089	1960	**£10**	**£5**	*export*
That's My Kind Of Love	7"	London	HL7097	1960	**£10**	**£5**	*export*

WRANGLERS

Liza Jane	7"	Parlophone	R5163	1964	**£40**	**£20**	

WRAY, LINK

Batman Theme	7"	Chiswick	NS32	1978	**£10**	**£5**	*demo*
Be What You Want To	LP	Polydor	2391063	1973	**£10**	**£4**	
Beans And Fatback	LP	Virgin	V2006	1973	**£10**	**£4**	
Good Rockin' Tonight	7"	Stateside	SS397	1965	**£10**	**£5**	
Great Guitar Hits	LP	Vermillion	1924	1966	**£25**	**£10**	*US*
Jack The Ripper	7"	Stateside	SS217	1963	**£10**	**£5**	
Jack The Ripper	LP	Swan	SLP510	1963	**£30**	**£15**	*US*
Link Wray	LP	Polydor	2489029	1971	**£10**	**£4**	
Link Wray And The Wraymen	LP	Epic	LN3661	1960	**£40**	**£20**	*US*
Link Wray Rumble	LP	Polydor	2391128	1974	**£10**	**£4**	
Link Wray Sings And Plays Guitar	LP	Vermillion	1925	1966	**£25**	**£10**	*US*
Mr Guitar	7" EP	Stateside	SE1015	1964	**£50**	**£25**	
Rumble	7"	London	HLA8623	1958	**£15**	**£7.50**	
Sweeper	7"	Stateside	SS256	1964	**£8**	**£4**	
There's Good Rockin' Tonight	LP	Union Pacific	UP002	1971	**£12**	**£5**	
Yesterday And Today	LP	Record Factory	1929	196–	**£15**	**£6**	*US*

WRAY, RAY QUARTET

When Your Lover Has Gone	7"	Salvo	SLO1808	1962	**£10**	**£5**	

WRAY, VERNON & LINK WRAY

Wasted	LP	Vermillion	1972	196–	**£15**	**£6**	*US*

WRECKERS

Wreckers' Sound	7" EP	Granta	GR7EP1010	1964	**£100**	**£50**	

WREN, JENNY

Chasing My Dreams All Over Town	7"	Fontana	TF672	1966	**£25**	**£12.50**	

WRIGGLERS

Cooler	7"	Giant	GN26	1968	**£8**	**£4**	
Get Right	7"	Blue Cat	BS106	1968	**£8**	**£4**	

WRIGHT, BETTY

I Love The Way You Love	LP	Atlantic	K540364	1972	**£10**	**£4**	

WRIGHT, DALE

She's Neat	7"	London	HLH8573	1958	**£125**	**£62.50**	
That's Show Biz	7"	Pye	7N25022	1959	**£30**	**£15**	

WRIGHT, GARY

Extraction	LP	A&M	AMLS2004	1970	**£10**	**£4**	
Foot Print	LP	A&M	AMLS64296	1971	**£10**	**£4**	
Ring Of Changes	LP	A&M	AMLH64362	1972	**£40**	**£20**	*test pressing*

WRIGHT, GEORGE

Heart Of My Heart	7"	Parlophone	MSP13	1954	**£8**	**£4**	*export*

WRIGHT, GINNY

Indian Moon	7"	London	HL8119	1955	£25	£12.50	
Wonderful World	7"	London	HL8093	1954	£25	£12.50	*with Tommy Cutrer*

WRIGHT, NAT

Anything	7"	HMV	POP629	1959	£40	£20	

WRIGHT, O. V.

8 Men, 4 Women	7"	London	HLZ10137	1967	£4	£1.50	
8 Men, 4 Women	LP	Island	ILP975	1968	£30	£15	*pink label*
Gone For Good	7"	Vocalion	VP9272	1966	£5	£2	
I Want Everyone To Know	7"	Action	ACT4527	1969	£5	£2	
If It's Only For Tonight	LP	Back Beat	61	1965	£20	£8	*US*
O. V. Wright	7" EP	Vocalion	VEP170165	1965	£40	£20	
Oh Baby Mine	7"	Action	ACT4505	1968	£8	£4	
Poor Boy	7"	Vocalion	VP9255	1966	£5	£2	
What About You	7"	Sue	WI4043	1968	£12	£6	
You're Gonna Make Me Cry	7"	Vocalion	VP9249	1965	£6	£2.50	

WRIGHT, OTIS

It Will Soon Be Done	LP	Doctor Bird	DLM5006	1967	£75	£37.50	
Over In Gloryland	LP	Coxsone	TLP1001	196–	£75	£37.50	
Peace Perfect Peace	LP	Doctor Bird	DLM5005	1967	£75	£37.50	

WRIGHT, OWEN

Wala Wala	7"	Banana	BA310	1970	£5	£2	*Freedom Singers B side*

WRIGHT, RITA

I Can't Give Back The Love	7"	Tamla Motown	TMG643	1968	£15	£7.50	
I Can't Give Back The Love I Feel For You	7"	Tamla Motown	TMG791	1971	£4	£1.50	
Love Is All You Need	7"	Jet	UP36382	1978	£8	£4	

WRIGHT, RUBEN

Hey Girl	7"	Capitol	CL15460	1966	£15	£7.50	

WRIGHT, RUBY

Bimbo	7"	Parlophone	MSP6073	1954	£20	£10	
I Fall In Love With You Every Day	7"	Parlophone	MSP6209	1956	£10	£5	
Santa's Little Sleigh Bells	7"	Parlophone	MSP6133	1954	£10	£5	
Three Stars	7"	Parlophone	R4556	1959	£8	£4	
Three Stars Girl	7" EP	Parlophone	GEP8785	1959	£30	£15	
Till I Waltz Again With You	7"	Parlophone	MSP6025	1953	£20	£10	
What Have They Told You?	7"	Parlophone	MSP6150	1955	£10	£5	
You're Just A Flower From An Old Bouquet	7"	Parlophone	R4589	1959	£4	£1.50	

WRIGHT, STEVE

Wild Wild Women	7"	London	HLW8991	1959	£125	£62.50	

WRIGHT, WINSTON

Example	7"	Upsetter	US378	1971	£5	£2	*Upsetters B side*
Five Miles High	7"	Doctor Bird	DB1308	1969	£10	£5	
Flight 404	7"	Explosion	EX2011	1970	£4	£1.50	*Lloyd & Robin B side*
Funny Girl	7"	Explosion	EX2015	1970	£4	£1.50	
Grass Roots	LP	Third World	TWS922	1977	£12	£5	
Meshwire	7"	Trojan	TR7775	1970	£4	£1.50	*Barons B side*
Moon Invader	7"	Trojan	TR7715	1970	£4	£1.50	*Radcliff Ruffin B side*
Moonlight	7"	Trojan	TR7701	1969	£4	£1.50	*Sensations B side*
Musically Red	7"	Moodisc	MU3501	1970	£4	£1.50	*Rhythm Rulers B side*
Poppy Cock	7"	Duke	DU62	1970	£4	£1.50	*Carl Dawkins B side*
Reggae Feet	7"	Bamboo	BAM60	1970	£5	£2	*Don Drummond B side*
Silhouettes	7"	Duke	DU111	1971	£4	£1.50	
Soul Pressure	7"	High Note	HS040	1970	£4	£1.50	

WRIGHT, ZACHARIAH

Lumumba Limbo	7"	Bamboo	BAM403	197–	£5	£2	

WRITING ON THE WALL

Aries	7"	Middle Earth	MDE201	1969	£30	£15	*promo, with tracks by Wooden O & Arcadium*
Child On A Crossing	7"	Middle Earth	MDS101	1969	£15	£7.50	
Man Of Renown	7"	Pye	7N45251	1973	£10	£5	
Power Of The Picts	LP	Middle Earth	MDLS303	1969	£125	£62.50	

WURZEL

Bess	12"	GWR	GWT4	1987	£6	£2.50	
Bess	7"	GWR	GWR4	1987	£4	£1.50	

WYATT, JOHNNY

This Thing Called Love ..... 7" ..... President ..... PT109 ..... 1968 **£4** ..... **£1.50** .....

WYATT, ROBERT

End Of An Ear ..... LP ..... CBS ..... 64189 ..... 1970 **£12** ..... **£5** .....
Las Vegas Fandango ..... LP ..... Pinguin ..... 4 ..... 1974 **£40** ..... **£20** ..... *Italian*
Rock Bottom ..... LP ..... Virgin ..... V2017 ..... 1974 **£10** ..... **£4** .....
Ruth Is Stranger Than Richard ..... LP ..... Virgin ..... V2034 ..... 1975 **£10** ..... **£4** .....

WYLIE, PETE

Foureleventortytour ..... CD-s ..... Siren ..... SRNCD59 ..... 1987 **£5** ..... **£2** .....

WYLIE, RICHARD

Brand New Man ..... 7" ..... Columbia ..... DB7012 ..... 1963 **£15** ..... **£7.50** .....

WYMAN, BILL

Apache Woman ..... 7" ..... Rolling Stones ..... RS19120 ..... 1976 **£4** ..... **£1.50** .....
Digital Dreams ..... LP ..... Ripple ..... no number ..... 1983 **£75** ..... **£37.50** ..... *promo*
Green Ice Theme ..... 7" ..... Polydor ..... POSP297 ..... 1981 **£8** ..... **£4** .....
Monkey Grip ..... LP ..... Rolling Stones ..... QD79100 ..... 1974 **£10** ..... **£4** ..... *US quad*
Stone Alone ..... LP ..... Rolling Stones ..... QD79103 ..... 1976 **£10** ..... **£4** ..... *US quad*
Tenderness ..... 7" ..... Polydor ..... POSP229 ..... 1981 **£4** ..... **£1.50** .....
White Lightning ..... 7" ..... Rolling Stones ..... RS19115 ..... 1974 **£4** ..... **£1.50** .....

WYNDHAM-READ, MARTYN

Andy's Gone ..... LP ..... Broadside ..... BRO134 ..... 1979 **£20** ..... **£8** .....
Ballad Singer ..... LP ..... Autogram ..... ALLP218 ..... 1977 **£20** ..... **£8** ..... *German*
Harry The Hawker Is Dead ..... LP ..... Argo ..... ZFB82 ..... 1973 **£30** ..... **£15** .....
Martyn Wyndham-Read ..... LP ..... Trailer ..... LER2028 ..... 1971 **£25** ..... **£10** .....
Maypoles To Mistletoe ..... LP ..... Trailer ..... LER2092 ..... 1975 **£20** ..... **£8** ..... *with Geoff and Pennie Harris*
Ned Kelly And That Gang ..... LP ..... Trailer ..... LER2009 ..... 1970 **£20** ..... **£8** .....
Rose From The Bush ..... LP ..... Greenwich Village ..... GVR222 ..... 1984 **£12** ..... **£5** .....
Songs And Music Of The Redcoats ..... LP ..... Argo ..... ZDA147 ..... 1971 **£50** ..... **£25** ..... *with the Druids*

WYNDRUSH

Let It Shine ..... LP ..... Wealden .... 1972 **£150** ..... **£75** .....

WYNGARDE, PETER

Commits Rape ..... 7" ..... RCA ..... PW1 ..... 1970 **£30** ..... **£15** ..... *promo*
La Ronde De L'Amour ..... 7" ..... RCA ..... RCA1967 ..... 1970 **£15** ..... **£7.50** .....
Peter Wyngarde ..... LP ..... RCA ..... SF8087 ..... 1970 **£200** ..... **£100** .....

WYNNS, SANDY

Touch Of Venus ..... 7" ..... Fontana ..... TF550 ..... 1965 **£150** ..... **£75** .....

WYNTER, MARK

Can I Get To Know You Better ..... 7" ..... Pye ..... 7N15771 ..... 1965 **£4** ..... **£1.50** .....
Dream Girl ..... 7" ..... Decca ..... F11323 ..... 1961 **£4** ..... **£1.50** .....
Exclusively Yours ..... 7" ..... Decca ..... F11354 ..... 1961 **£4** ..... **£1.50** .....
Girl For Everyday ..... 7" ..... Decca ..... F11380 ..... 1961 **£4** ..... **£1.50** .....
Heaven's Plan ..... 7" ..... Decca ..... F11434 ..... 1962 **£4** ..... **£1.50** .....
I Love Her Still ..... 7" ..... Decca ..... F11467 ..... 1962 **£4** ..... **£1.50** .....
Image Of A Girl ..... 7" ..... Decca ..... F11263 ..... 1960 **£4** ..... **£1.50** .....
It's Mark Time ..... 7" EP ..... Pye ..... NEP24176 ..... 1962 **£15** ..... **£7.50** .....
Kickin' Up The Leaves ..... 7" ..... Decca ..... F11279 ..... 1960 **£4** ..... **£1.50** .....
Mark Time ..... 7" EP ..... Decca ..... DFE6674 ..... 1960 **£25** ..... **£12.50** .....
Mark Wynter ..... LP ..... Golden Guinea ..... GGL0250 ..... 1963 **£10** ..... **£4** .....
Mark Wynter ..... LP ..... Ace Of Clubs ..... ACL1141 ..... 1962 **£25** ..... **£10** .....
Mark Wynter ..... LP ..... Marble Arch ..... MAL647 ..... 1967 **£10** ..... **£4** .....
Warmth Of Wynter ..... LP ..... Decca ..... LK4409 ..... 1961 **£30** ..... **£15** .....
Wynter Time ..... 7" EP ..... Pye ..... NEP24185 ..... 1964 **£15** ..... **£7.50** .....

X
Wild Thing CD-s RCA ZD49338 1989 £5 £2

X, JOHNNY & SINGIN' SWINGIN' EIGHT
Lemonade 7" Fontana TF408 1963 £5 £2

X MEN
Ghosts 7" Creation CRE006 1984 £6 £2.50
Spiral Girl 7" Creation CRE014 1985 £5 £2

XERO
Oh Baby 12" Brickyard XERO1T 1983 £10 £5
Oh Baby 7" Brickyard XERO1 1983 £6 £2.50 *3 tracks*
Oh Baby 7" Brickyard XERO1 1983 £15 £7.50 *2 tracks*

XHOL
Electrip LP Hansa 80099 1969 £30 £15 *German*
Hauruk LP Ohr OMM56014 1970 £25 £10 *German*
Motherfuckers GmbH And Co Kg LP Ohr OMM556024 1972 £25 £10 *German*

XILES
Our Love Will Never End 7" Xiles XIL004 1965 £15 £7.50

XIT
Entrance LP Canyon C7114 1974 £75 £37.50 *US*
Plight Of The Red Man LP Rare Earth SREA4002 1972 £12 £5
Relocation LP Canyon C721 1978 £15 £6 *US*

XL5
XL5 7" HMV POP1148 1963 £8 £4

XL5s
Fireball 7" Fourplay FOUR004 1980 £5 £2

XMAL DEUTSCHLAND
Incubus Succubus II 7" 4AD AD311 1983 £4 £1.50

X-O-DUS
English Black Boys 12" Factory FAC11 1979 £6 £2.50 *dark grey sleeve*

X-RAY SPEX
Day The World Turned Day-Glo 7" EMI INT553 1978 £4 £1.50 *orange vinyl*
Germ Free Adolescents LP EMI INS3023 1978 £12 £5
Highly Inflammable 7" EMI INT583 1979 £5 £2 *red vinyl*
Identity 7" EMI INT563 1978 £5 £2 *pink vinyl*
Oh Bondage Up Yours 12" Virgin VS18912 1977 £8 £4
Oh Bondage, Up Yours 7" Virgin VS189 1977 £10 £5 *picture sleeve*

X-RAYS
Out Of Control 7" London HLR8805 1959 £25 £12.50

XS DISCHARGE
Across The Border 7" Groucho Marxist COMMINIQUE3 1980 £8 £4
Life's A Wank 7" Groucho Marxist WH3 1980 £8 £4

XS ENERGY
Eighteen 7" World WRECK1 1978 £10 £5
Eighteen 7" Dead Good DEAD1 1979 £5 £2
Use You 7" Dead Good DEAD3 1979 £4 £1.50

XTC
3D EP (Science Friction) 12" Virgin VS18812 1977 £6 £2.50
3D EP (Science Friction) 7" Virgin VS188 1977 £50 £25 *without picture sleeve*
3D EP (Science Friction) 7" Virgin VS188 1977 £750 £500 *picture sleeve*
Ballad Of Peter Pumpkinhead CD-s Virgin VSCDG1415 1992 £5 £2
Dear God CD-s Virgin CDEP3 1987 £6 £2.50
Drums And Wires LP Virgin V2129 1979 £10 £4 *with 7" (VDJ30)*
Go 2 LP Virgin V2108 1978 £10 £4 *with Go +12"*
King For A Day CD-s Virgin VSCD1177 1988 £8 £4 *3" single*

Title	Format	Label	Cat. No.	Year	Mint	Good	Notes
Love On A Farmboy's Wages	7"	Virgin	VS613	1983	£4	**£1.50**	*double*
Loving	CD-s	Virgin	VSCD1201	1989	**£5**	**£2**	*3" single*
Mayor Of Simpleton	CD-s	Virgin	VSCD1158	1989	**£8**	**£4**	*3" single*
Oranges And Lemons	CD-s	Virgin	CDVT2581	1988	**£12**	**£6**	*album on 3 CD single boxed set*
Radios In Motion, A History Of XTC	CD	Geffen	PROCD4397	1992	**£20**	**£8**	*US promo*
Senses Working Overtime	CD-s	Virgin	CDT9	1988	**£5**	**£2**	*3" single*
Sgt Rock Is Going To Help Me	CD-s	Virgin	VVCS9	1990	**£5**	**£2**	
Skylarking	CD	Mobile Fidelity	UDCD625	1994	**£15**	**£6**	*US audiophile*
Wrapped In Grey	7"	Virgin	[illegible]	[illegible]	[illegible]	[illegible]	

XTRAVERTS

Title	Format	Label	Cat. No.	Year	Mint	Good	Notes
Blank Generation	7"	Spike	SRTSSP001	1979	**£50**	**£25**	*no picture sleeve*
Police State	7"	Rising Sun	RS1	1978	**£30**	**£15**	*multicoloured vinyl*
So Much Hate	LP	Bin Liner	RUBBISHLP001	1997	**£10**	**£4**	*:in carrier bag*
Speed	7"	Xtraverts	XTRA001	1981	**£25**	**£12.50**	

XXX

Title	Format	Label	Cat. No.	Year	Mint	Good	Notes
Live	LP	private			**£75**	**£37.50**	*US*

XYMOX

Title	Format	Label	Cat. No.	Year	Mint	Good	Notes
Day	12"	4AD	BAD504	1985	**£8**	**£4**	

Y BLEW

Title	Format	Label	Number	Year	Mint	VG	Notes
Maes B	7"	Qualiton	QSP7001	1967	£8	£4	picture sleeve

Y TRWYNAU COCH

Title	Format	Label	Number	Year	Mint	VG	Notes
Merched Dan 15	7"	Recordian Sqwar	RSROC002	1978	£15	£7.50	
Rhedeg Rhag Y Torpidos	LP	Recordian Coch	OCHR2198	198–	£15	£6	
Wastod Ar Y Tu Fas	7"	Recordian Sqwar	RSROC1	197–	£5	£2	

YA HO WA 13

A complete list of the albums made by hippy band Ya Ho Wa 13 finally appeared in the fourth edition of this guide. All apart from *Golden Sunrise* (which includes collaborations with the former leader of the Seeds, Sky Saxon) were issued on the group's own Higher Key label. They have long been sought after, but are so seldom seen that information on them continues to be somewhat sketchy. Prices, nevertheless, have started to fall – a recent CD boxed set of the group's work makes it clear that the stoned jams in which Ya Wo Ha 13 specialized are primarily interesting for the embarrassing ineptitude of their delivery.

Title	Format	Label	Number	Year	Mint	VG	Notes
All Or Nothing At All	LP	Higher Key	3304	1974	£200	£100	US
Father Yod And The Spirit Of '76 – Kohoutek	LP	Higher Key	3301	1973	£200	£100	US
Golden Sunrise	LP	Psycho	PSYCHO2	1982	£25	£10	
I'm Gonna Take You Home	LP	Higher Key	3309	1975	£200	£100	US
Penetration – An Aquarian Symphony	LP	Higher Key		1974	£200	£100	US
Principles Of The Children	LP	Higher Key		1978	£200	£100	US
Savage Sons Of Ya Ho Wa	LP	Higher Key	3306	1974	£200	£100	US
Spirit Of 76 – Contraction	LP	Higher Key		1976	£200	£100	US
Spirit Of 76 – Expansion	LP	Higher Key		1976	£200	£100	US
Ya Ho Wa 13	LP	Higher Key		1974	£75	£37.50	US
Ya Ho Wa 13	LP	Higher Key		1974	£200	£100	US, sheep shag cover, double

YAKS

Title	Format	Label	Number	Year	Mint	VG	Notes
Yakety Yak	7"	Decca	F12115	1965	£8	£4	

YAMA & THE KARMA DUSTERS

Title	Format	Label	Number	Year	Mint	VG	Notes
Up From The Sewers	LP	Manhole	no number	1970	£250	£150	US

YAMASH'TA, STOMU

Japanese percussionist Stomu Yamash'ta came to Britain during the early seventies and amazed the classical music world with his virtuosity. The last two LPs listed here contain works by some of the leading contemporary classical composers which allow Yamash'ta to show off his formidable technique – the L'Oiseau Lyre record has percussion as the only instrumentation. Interestingly, Yamash'ta discovered progressive rock and completely changed his musical policy with a number of jazz-rock albums. Perhaps he realized that this was where the most vital musical developments were taking place, although the cynic might argue that he merely realized that there was more money to be made out of rock music.

Title	Format	Label	Number	Year	Mint	VG	Notes
Come To The Edge/Floating Music	LP	Island	HELP12	1972	£10	£4	
Henze/Takemitsu/Maxwell Davies	LP	L'Oiseau Lyre	DSLO1	1972	£12	£5	
Takemitsu Ishii	LP	EMI	EMD5508	1973	£12	£5	

YANA

Title	Format	Label	Number	Year	Mint	VG	Notes
Climb Up The Wall	7"	HMV	POP252	1956	£8	£4	
I Miss You Mama	7"	HMV	POP481	1958	£5	£2	
Mr Wonderful	7"	HMV	POP340	1957	£6	£2.50	
Papa And Mama	7"	HMV	POP546	1958	£4	£1.50	

YANCEY, JIMMY

Title	Format	Label	Number	Year	Mint	VG	Notes
Jimmy And Mama Yancey	10" LP	Atlantic	130	195–	£30	£15	US
Jimmy And Mama Yancey	10" LP	Atlantic	134	195–	£30	£15	US
Jimmy Yancey	10" LP	Vogue	LDE166	1956	£20	£8	
Jimmy Yancey	7" EP	Vogue	EPV1203	1958	£12	£6	
Jimmy Yancey	7" EP	HMV	7EG8062	1954	£12	£6	
Lost Recording Date	10" LP	London	AL3525	1954	£20	£8	
Lowdown Dirty Blues	LP	Atlantic	590018	1968	£10	£4	
Pure Blues	LP	Atlantic	1231	1956	£25	£10	US
Yancey Special	10" LP	Atlantic	103	195–	£30	£15	US
Yancey's Piano	7" EP	HMV	7EG8083	1955	£12	£6	

YANCEY, MAMA & DON EWELL

Title	Format	Label	Number	Year	Mint	VG	Notes
Mama Yancey And Don Ewell	10" LP	Tempo	LAP7	1957	£30	£15	

YANKEE DOLLAR

Yankee Dollar	LP	Dot	DLP25874	1968	**£12**	**£5**	US

YANOVSKY, ZALMAN

Alive & Well In Argentina	LP	Buddah	BDS5019	1968	**£12**	**£5**	US
Alive And Well In Argentina	LP	Kama Sutra	2316003	1971	**£10**	**£4**	
As Long As You're Here	7"	Pye	7N25438	1967	**£4**	**£1.50**	

YARDBIRDS

All of the Yardbirds' innovative original records are now collectable – even the chart hits – although the rarest come from right at the start of the group's career, and right at the end. The single 'Goodnight Sweet Josephine' definitely does exist, despite occasional murmurings to the contrary, although possibly only as a demo. Meanwhile, the LP *Live Yardbirds*, ruined, according to the group, by the engineers miking Jimmy Page's monitor speaker rather than the real thing, and also by its extravagant over-dubbed applause, was given two releases and rapidly withdrawn each time. Counterfeits exist, but these have black and white covers, rather than the colour of the originals.

Evil Hearted You	7"	Columbia	DB7706	1965	**£4**	**£1.50**	
Face And Place	LP	Direction		1964	**£50**	**£25**	*New Zealand*
Five Live Yardbirds	LP	Columbia	33SX1677	1964	**£40**	**£20**	
Five Live Yardbirds	LP	Columbia	33SX1677	1969	**£10**	**£4**	*black and white label*
Five Yardbirds	7" EP	Columbia	SEG8421	1965	**£50**	**£25**	
For Your Love	7"	Columbia	DB7499	1965	**£4**	**£1.50**	
For Your Love	7" EP	Riviera	231074	1965	**£50**	**£25**	*French*
For Your Love	CD-s	Charly	CDS4	1989	**£5**	**£2**	
For Your Love	LP	Epic	LN24167/ BN26167	1965	**£30**	**£15**	*US*
Good Morning Little Schoolgirl	7"	Columbia	DB7391	1964	**£10**	**£5**	
Goodnight Sweet Josephine	7"	Columbia	DB8368	1968	**£200**	**£100**	*demo, best auctioned*
Greatest Hits	LP	Epic	LN24246/ BN26246	1966	**£25**	**£10**	*US*
Happening Ten Years Time Ago	7"	Columbia	DB8024	1966	**£20**	**£10**	
Happening Ten Years Time Ago	7" EP	Riviera	231220	1966	**£50**	**£25**	*French*
Having A Rave Up	LP	Columbia	SCXC28	1966	**£75**	**£37.50**	*export*
Having A Rave Up	LP	Epic	LN24177/ BN26177	1965	**£25**	**£10**	*US*
Heart Full Of Soul	7"	Columbia	DB7594	1965	**£4**	**£1.50**	
Heart Full Of Soul	7" EP	Riviera	231099	1965	**£50**	**£25**	*French*
I Wish You Would	7"	Columbia	DB7283	1964	**£10**	**£5**	
Little Games	7"	Columbia	DB8165	1967	**£20**	**£10**	
Little Games	7" EP	Riviera	231242	1967	**£75**	**£37.50**	*French*
Little Games	LP	Epic	LN24313/ BN26313	1967	**£40**	**£20**	*US*
Live Featuring Jimmy Page	LP	Columbia	P13311	1972	**£40**	**£20**	*US, colour cover*
Live Featuring Jimmy Page	LP	Epic	KE30615	1971	**£50**	**£25**	*US, colour cover*
Our Own Sound	LP	Riviera	4210305	1972	**£125**	**£62.50**	*French*
Over Under Sideways Down	7"	Columbia	DB7928	1966	**£8**	**£4**	
Over Under Sideways Down	7" EP	Riviera	231196	1966	**£50**	**£25**	*French*
Over Under Sideways Down	LP	Epic	LN24210/ BN26210	1966	**£25**	**£10**	*US*
Paf Bum	7"	Ricordi Internationa	SIR20010	1966	**£20**	**£10**	*Italian*
Shapes Of Things	7"	Columbia	DB7848	1966	**£4**	**£1.50**	
Shapes Of Things	7" EP	Riviera	231170	1966	**£50**	**£25**	*French*
Still I'm Sad	7" EP	Riviera	231131	1965	**£50**	**£25**	*French*
With Sonny Boy Williamson	LP	Fontana	TL5277	1964	**£75**	**£37.50**	
With Sonny Boy Williamson	LP	Fontana	SFJL960	1968	**£20**	**£8**	
With Sonny Boy Williamson	LP	Philips	6435011	1971	**£10**	**£4**	
Yardbirds	7" EP	Columbia	SEG8521	1966	**£200**	**£100**	
Yardbirds	LP	Columbia	SSX1018	1965	**£100**	**£50**	*Swedish, different cover*
Yardbirds	LP	Columbia	SX/SCX6063	1966	**£40**	**£20**	
Yardbirds	LP	Columbia	SX/SCX6063	1969	**£10**	**£4**	*black & silver label, flapped sleeve*
Yardbirds	LP	Epic	EG30135	1970	**£20**	**£8**	*US*
Yardbirds	LP	Epic	HE38455	1983	**£20**	**£8**	*US audiophile*

YARROH, PER

Laughing Inside	7"	HMV	PY1	198–	**£4**	**£1.50**	*promo, really Roy Harper*

YATES, CHRIS

New Born	LP	ILSM		1977	**£50**	**£25**	*US*

YATES, TOM

Love Comes Well Armed	LP	President	PTLS1053	1973	**£30**	**£15**	
Second City Spiritual	LP	CBS	BPG63094	1967	**£50**	**£25**	
Song Of The Shimmering Way	LP	Satril	SATL4007	1977	**£20**	**£8**	

YATHA SIDHRA

Meditation Mass	LP	Brain	1045	1974	**£50**	**£25**	*German*

YAZOO

Situation	CD-s	Mute	YAZ4CD	1990	**£5**	**£2**	

YELLO

Bimbo	7"	Do It	DUN11	1981	**£5**	**£2**	
Blazing Saddles	CD-s	Mercury	YELCD4	1989	**£5**	**£2**	
Bostich	12"	Do It	DUNIT13	1982	**£8**	**£4**	

Bostich	7"	Do It	DUN13	1982	**£4**	**£1.50**	
Call It Love	CD-s	Mercury	8883112	1988	**£5**	**£2**	
Desire	12"	Elektra	EKR17T	1985	**£12**	**£6**	*double*
Flag	LP	Mercury	8367781	1988	**£60**	**£30**	
Goldrush	12"	Mercury	MERXD218	1986	**£6**	**£2.50**	*double*
Hands On Yello – The Updates	CD	Urban	5277282	1995	**£40**	**£20**	*double*
I Love You	7"	Stiff	PBUY176	1983	**£4**	**£1.50**	*picture disc, with 3D glasses*
Lost Again	7"	Stiff	DBUY191	1983	**£5**	**£2**	*double*
Lost Again	7"	Stiff	BUY191	1983	**£5**	**£2**	
Of Course I'm Lying	CD-s	Mercury	YELCD3/32	1989	**£5**	**£2**	*2 versions*
One Second	LP	Mercury	MERH100	1987	**£12**	**£5**	*with 12"*
Pinball Cha Cha	12"	Do It	DUNIT23	1982	**£10**	**£5**	
Race	CD-s	Polygram	0805282	1989	**£10**	**£5**	*CD video*
Race	CD-s	Mercury	YELCD1	1988	**£5**	**£2**	
Rhythm Divine	12"	Mercury	MERXR253	1987	**£30**	**£15**	
Rubberbandman	CD-s	Mercury	YELCD5	1990	**£5**	**£2**	*with rubber face*
She's Got A Gun	12"	Do It	DUNIT18	1982	**£6**	**£2.50**	
Third Of June	CD-s	Mercury	0808322	1989	**£10**	**£5**	*CD video*
Tied Up	CD-s	Polygram	0806442	1989	**£10**	**£5**	*CD video*
Tied Up	CD-s	Mercury	YELCD2	1988	**£5**	**£2**	
Tied Up In Life	12"	Mercury	YELLR212	1988	**£6**	**£2.50**	
Video Race	CD-s	Polygram	0807202	1988	**£12**	**£6**	*CD video*
You Gotta Say Yes To Another Excess	LP	Stiff	SEEZ48	1983	**£15**	**£6**	*with 12"*

YELLOW

Roll It Down The Hill	7"	CBS	4869	1970	**£10**	**£5**	

YELLOW BALLOON

Yellow Balloon	7"	Stateside	SS2008	1967	**£8**	**£4**	
Yellow Balloon	LP	Canterbury	CLPM/CLPS1502	1967	**£40**	**£20**	*US*

YELLOW BELLOW ROOM BOOM

Seeing Things Green	7"	CBS	3205	1968	**£8**	**£4**	

YELLOW MAGIC ORCHESTRA

Behind The Mask	7"	A&M	AMS7559	1980	**£4**	**£1.50**	*yellow vinyl*
Computer Game	7"	A&M	AMS7502	1980	**£4**	**£1.50**	*yellow vinyl*
Nice Age	7"	A&M	JAPAN2	1980	**£4**	**£1.50**	*yellow vinyl*
Rydeen	7"	Alfa	ALF2145	1979	**£4**	**£1.50**	*white vinyl*
Tong Poo	12"	A&M	AMSP7447	1979	**£6**	**£2.50**	*yellow vinyl*

YELLOW PAYGES

Little Woman	7"	UNI	UNS516	1970	**£5**	**£2**	
Volume One	LP	Uni	73045	1969	**£12**	**£5**	*US*

YELLOWSTONE & VOICE

Yellowstone & Voice	LP	Regal Zonophone	SRZA8511	1972	**£10**	**£4**	

YEMM AND YEMEN

Black Is The Night	7"	Columbia	DB8022	1966	**£8**	**£4**	

YES

Sometimes the extended compositions for which Yes are best known have sounded a little forced, as though the group has initially written quite short pop songs and then cast around for ways of stretching them out. Indeed, over the first few albums one can hear this process being developed. *Yes* and *Time And A Word* and the associated singles contain a variety of intelligent harmony pop, in which the songs are carefully arranged, but fairly straightforward in structure. With *The Yes Album*, however, a process begins where the melodies are expanded and chopped about – which works well here because the melodies are strong enough to withstand the treatment, but which is much less successful on *Fragile*. Nevertheless, there are sufficient high points across Yes's catalogue to demonstrate that the symphonic approach to rock is an entirely valid one.

Classic Yes	LP	Atlantic	K50842	1980	**£25**	**£10**	*test pressing, different sleeve*
Close To The Edge	LP	Mobile Fidelity	MFSL1077	1980	**£15**	**£6**	*US audiophile*
Fragile	LP	Atlantic	2401019	1971	**£12**	**£5**	
Going For The One	12"	Atlantic	K10985T	1977	**£40**	**£20**	
Going For The One	7"	Atlantic	K10985	1977	**£40**	**£20**	
Going For The One	LP	Atlantic	DSK50379	1977	**£40**	**£20**	*3 × 12", boxed*
I've Seen All Good People	7"	Atlantic	2814003	1971	**£75**	**£37.50**	*promo*
Interview	7"	Atlantic	SAM7	1972	**£6**	**£2.50**	*promo*
Interview/Five Songs	7"	Lyntone	LYN2536	197–	**£5**	**£2**	
Looking Around	7"	Atlantic	584298	1969	**£75**	**£37.50**	*demo only*
Owner Of A Lonely Heart	7"	Atco	B9817P	1983	**£6**	**£2.50**	*shaped picture disc*
Sweet Dreams	7"	Atlantic	2091004	1970	**£20**	**£10**	
Sweetness	7"	Atlantic	584280	1969	**£25**	**£12.50**	
Time And A Word	7"	Atlantic	584323	1970	**£25**	**£12.50**	
Time And A Word	LP	Atlantic	2400006	1970	**£12**	**£5**	*lyric sheet*
Union	CD	Arista		1991	**£20**	**£8**	*US promo picture disc*
Wondrous Stories	12"	Atlantic	K10999	1977	**£6**	**£2.50**	*blue vinyl*
Yes	LP	Atlantic	588190	1969	**£15**	**£6**	*lyric sheet*
Yes Album	LP	Atlantic	2400101	1971	**£12**	**£5**	
Yes Solos	LP	Atlantic	PR260	1976	**£20**	**£8**	*US promo compilation*

Yesyears ... CD ... Atco ... PRCD4009 ... 1991 **£20** ... **£8** ... *US promo sampler*

YESTERDAY'S CHILDREN
To Be Or Not To Be ... 7" EP ... DiscAZ ... 1101 ... 1967 **£30** ... **£15** ... *French*

YETTI-MEN
Yetti-Men ... LP ... LAK ... KB4348 ... 1963 **£500** ... **£330** ... *US*

YETTIES
Dorset Is Beautiful ... LP ... Argo ... ZFB38 ... 1972 **£10** ... **£4**
Fifty Stone Of Loveliness ... LP ... Acorn ... CF203 ... 1969 **£20** ... **£8**
Our Friends ... LP ... Argo ... ZFB32 ... 1971 **£10** ... **£4**

YO LA TENGO
Blue-Green Arrow ... 7" ... Earworm ... WORM4 ... 1996 **£6** ... **£2.50** ... *handmade sleeve*

YOBS
Christmas Album ... LP ... Safari ... RUDE1 ... 1980 **£10** ... **£4**
Run Rudolph Run ... 7" ... NEMS ... NES114 ... 1977 **£4** ... **£1.50**
Silent Night ... 7" ... Yob ... YOB79 ... 1978 **£4** ... **£1.50**

YOGI, MAHARISHI MAHESH
Maharishi Mahesh Yogi ... LP ... Liberty ... LBS83075E ... 1967 **£15** ... **£6**

YOLANDA
With This Kiss ... 7" ... Triumph ... RGM1007 ... 1960 **£25** ... **£12.50**

YORK, PETE
Pete York Percussion Band ... LP ... Decca ... TXS109 ... 1972 **£15** ... **£6**

YORK, RUSTY
Peggy Sue ... 7" ... Parlophone ... R4398 ... 1958 **£300** ... **£180** ... *demo only, best auctioned*

YORK BROTHERS
Country And Western ... 7" EP ... Parlophone ... GEP8736 ... 1958 **£20** ... **£10**
Country And Western No. 2 ... 7" EP ... Parlophone ... GEP8753 ... 1958 **£20** ... **£10**
Sixteen Great Country & Western Hits ... LP ... King ... 820 ... 1963 **£12** ... **£5** ... *US*
Strange Town ... 7" ... Parlophone ... CMSP22 ... 1954 **£8** ... **£4** ... *export*
Why Don't You Open The Door ... 7" ... Parlophone ... CMSP5 ... 1954 **£8** ... **£4** ... *export*
York Brothers ... LP ... King ... 586 ... 1958 **£15** ... **£6** ... *US*
York Brothers Vol. 2 ... LP ... King ... 591 ... 1958 **£15** ... **£6** ... *US*

YORK POP MUSIC PROJECT
All Day ... LP ... private ... ... 1973 **£100** ... **£50**

YOU, YABBY
Deliver Me From My Enemies ... LP ... Grove Music ... GMLP001 ... 1978 **£12** ... **£5**

YOU KNOW WHO GROUP
My Love ... 7" EP ... Kapp ... KEV13016 ... 1965 **£12** ... **£6** ... *French, B side by Angelo & Initials*
Roses Are Red My Love ... 7" ... London ... HLR9947 ... 1965 **£8** ... **£4**
You Know Who Group ... LP ... International Allied ... 420 ... 1965 **£30** ... **£15** ... *US*

YOULDEN, CHRIS
City Child ... LP ... Deram ... SML1112 ... 1974 **£15** ... **£6**
Nowhere Road ... LP ... Deram ... SML1099 ... 1973 **£15** ... **£6**

YOUNG, BARBARA
No Game At All ... LP ... Corridor ... 020 ... ... **£40** ... **£20**

YOUNG, BRETT
Guess What ... 7" ... Pye ... 7N15578 ... 1963 **£4** ... **£1.50**
Never Again ... 7" ... Pye ... 7N15641 ... 1964 **£4** ... **£1.50**

YOUNG, CECIL
Cool Jazz ... 10" LP ... Vogue ... LDE003 ... 1953 **£20** ... **£8**

YOUNG, DARREN
My Tears Will Turn To Laughter ... 7" ... Parlophone ... R4919 ... 1963 **£10** ... **£5**

YOUNG, FARON
Country Dance Favourites ... LP ... Mercury ... 20025MCL ... 1964 **£10** ... **£4**
Every Time I'm Kissing You ... 7" ... Capitol ... CL14891 ... 1958 **£5** ... **£2**
Five Dollars And It's Saturday Night ... 7" ... Capitol ... CL14655 ... 1956 **£15** ... **£7.50**
Hello Walls ... 7" EP ... Capitol ... EAP11549 ... 1961 **£10** ... **£5**
I Can't Dance ... 7" ... Capitol ... CL14860 ... 1958 **£8** ... **£4**
I Hate Myself ... 7" ... Capitol ... CL14930 ... 1958 **£4** ... **£1.50**
I Hear You Talkin' ... 7" ... Capitol ... CL15050 ... 1959 **£4** ... **£1.50**
If You Ain't Lovin' ... 7" ... Capitol ... CL14574 ... 1956 **£15** ... **£7.50**
Live Fast, Love Hard, Die Young ... 7" ... Capitol ... CL14336 ... 1955 **£20** ... **£10**
Long Time Ago ... 7" ... Capitol ... CL14975 ... 1959 **£4** ... **£1.50**
Moonlight Mountain ... 7" ... Capitol ... CL14762 ... 1957 **£5** ... **£2**
Object Of My Affection ... LP ... Capitol ... T1004 ... 1958 **£12** ... **£5**
Shrine Of St Cecilia ... 7" ... Capitol ... CL14735 ... 1957 **£6** ... **£2.50**
Snowball ... 7" ... Capitol ... CL14822 ... 1958 **£5** ... **£2**

Story Songs For Country Folk	LP	Mercury	20026MCL	1964	**£10**	**£4**	
Sweethearts Or Strangers	LP	Capitol	T778	1957	**£15**	**£6**	*US*
Sweethearts Or Strangers Pt 1	7" EP	Capitol	EAP1778	1957	**£10**	**£5**	
Sweethearts Or Strangers Pt 2	7" EP	Capitol	EAP2778	1957	**£10**	**£5**	
Sweethearts Or Strangers Pt 3	7" EP	Capitol	EAP3778	1957	**£10**	**£5**	
That's The Way It's Gotta Be	7"	Capitol	CL15004	1959	**£4**	**£1.50**	
This Is Faron Young	LP	Capitol	T1096	1963	**£12**	**£5**	
Vacation's Over	7"	Capitol	CL14793	1957	**£8**	**£4**	

YOUNG, GEORGIE

Nine More Miles	7"	London	HLU8748	1958	**£6**	**£2.50**	

YOUNG, HARRY

Show Me The Way	7"	Dot	DS16756	1965	**£6**	**£2.50**	

YOUNG, JESSE COLIN

Soul Of A City Boy	LP	Capitol	(S)T2070	1964	**£15**	**£6**	*US*
Youngblood	LP	Mercury	MG2/SR61005	1965	**£15**	**£6**	*US*

YOUNG, JIM SAN FRANCISCO AVANTGARDE

Puzzle Box	LP	Polydor	623226	1966	**£25**	**£10**	*German*

YOUNG, JIMMY

Baby Cried	7"	Decca	F10232	1954	**£8**	**£4**	
Chain Gang	7"	Decca	F10694	1956	**£8**	**£4**	
Deep Blue Sea	7"	Decca	F10948	1957	**£4**	**£1.50**	
Give Me Your Word	7"	Decca	F10406	1954	**£8**	**£4**	
If Anyone Finds This	7"	Decca	F10483	1955	**£6**	**£2.50**	
Jimmy Young	7" EP	Decca	DFE6404	1957	**£8**	**£4**	
Jimmy Young Sings	7" EP	Pye	NEP24004	1955	**£8**	**£4**	
Lovin' Baby	7"	Decca	F10842	1957	**£4**	**£1.50**	
Man From Laramie	7"	Decca	F10597	1955	**£12**	**£6**	
Man On Fire	7"	Decca	F10925	1957	**£4**	**£1.50**	
More	7"	Decca	F10774	1956	**£6**	**£2.50**	
Night Is Young	LP	Decca	LK4219	1957	**£12**	**£5**	
Presenting Jimmy Young	10" LP	Decca	LF1200	1955	**£20**	**£8**	
Presenting Jimmy Young	7" EP	Decca	DFE6277	1956	**£8**	**£4**	
Rich Man Poor Man	7"	Decca	F10736	1956	**£6**	**£2.50**	
Round And Round	7"	Decca	F10875	1957	**£4**	**£1.50**	
Someone On Your Mind	7"	Decca	F10640	1955	**£8**	**£4**	
These Are The Things We'll Share	7"	Decca	F10444	1955	**£6**	**£2.50**	
Unchained Melody	7"	Decca	F10502	1955	**£12**	**£6**	

YOUNG, JOHNNY

Fat Mandolin	LP	Blue Horizon	763852	1970	**£50**	**£25**	

YOUNG, JOHNNY (2)

Step Back	7"	Decca	F22548	1967	**£5**	**£2**	

YOUNG, KAREN

Are You Kidding	7"	Mercury	MF943	1965	**£4**	**£1.50**	
Me And My Mini Skirt	7" EP	Fontana	460979	1966	**£10**	**£5**	*French*
Too Much Of A Good Thing	7"	Major Minor	MM584	1968	**£5**	**£2**	
We'll Start The Party Again	7"	Pye	7N15956	1965	**£5**	**£2**	

YOUNG, KATHY & THE INNOCENTS

Happy Birthday Blues	7"	Top Rank	JAR554	1961	**£12**	**£6**	
Innocently Yours	LP	Indigo	503	1961	**£60**	**£30**	*US*
Sound Of Kathy Young	LP	Indigo	504	1961	**£60**	**£30**	*US*
Thousand Stars	7"	Top Rank	JAR534	1961	**£20**	**£10**	

YOUNG, LA MONTE

Avant-garde composer La Monte Young is the founding father of minimalism. Much of his output consists of extracts from an ongoing work entitled *The Tortoise, His Dreams And Journeys*, whose electronic drones are intended to be a permanent feature of a special room, the Dream House.

La Monte Young Marian Zazeela	LP	Edition X	1079	1969	**£60**	**£30**	*German*
La Monte Young Marian Zazeela	LP	Edition X	1079	1969	**£100**	**£50**	*German, autographed*
Theatre Of Eternal Music	LP	Shandar	83510	1973	**£20**	**£8**	*French, with Marian Zazeela*

YOUNG, LARRY

Contrasts	LP	Blue Note	BLP/BST84266	1967	**£30**	**£15**	
Heaven On Earth	LP	Blue Note	BST84304	1968	**£25**	**£10**	
Into Somethin'	LP	Blue Note	BLP/BST84187	1964	**£50**	**£25**	
Of Love And Peace	LP	Blue Note	BLP/BST84242	1966	**£30**	**£15**	
Unity	LP	Blue Note	BLP/BST84221	1965	**£40**	**£20**	

YOUNG, LEON STRINGS

Glad All Over	7"	Pye	7N15646	1964	**£10**	**£5**	

YOUNG, LESTER

Battle Of The Saxes	10" LP	Felsted	EDL87014	1955	**£50**	**£25**	
Blue Lester	LP	London	LTZC15132	1958	**£30**	**£15**	
Greatest	LP	Vogue	LAE12194	1960	**£20**	**£8**	
Jazz Giants '56	LP	Columbia	33CX10054	1956	**£40**	**£20**	

Title	Format	Label	Cat. No.	Year	Mint	VG	Notes
Leaps Again	LP	Fontana	FJL128	1966	£10	£4	
Lester Young	10" LP	Columbia	33C9015	1956	£50	£25	
Lester Young	7" EP	Vogue	EPV1127	1956	£5	£2	
Lester Young	LP	Vogue	LAE12016	1956	£30	£15	
Lester Young And His Tenor Sax	LP	Liberty	LBY3048	1965	£10	£4	
Lester Young And The Kansas City Five	LP	Stateside	SL10002	1962	£12	£5	
Memorial Album Vol. 1	LP	Fontana	TFL5064	1959	£20	£8	
Memorial Album Vol. 2	LP	Fontana	TFL5065	1960	£20	£8	
Pres	LP	Columbia	33CX10070	1957	£40	£20	
Pres And Teddy	LP	HMV	CLP1302	1959	£25	£10	with Teddy Wilson
President	LP	Columbia	33CX10031	1956	£50	£25	
P[illegible]	LP	Fontana	TL5260	1965	£12	£5	
With The Oscar Peterson Trio	10" LP	Columbia	33C9001	1955	£50	£25	

YOUNG, MIGHTY JOE

Title	Format	Label	Cat. No.	Year	Mint	VG	Notes
Why Don't You Follow Me	7"	Parlophone	R5794	1969	£8	£4	

YOUNG, NEIL

Neil Young's blend of electric guitar overkill and acoustic folkiness was established quite early in his long career. It seems extraordinary, therefore, how his reputation among modern critics has become transformed in recent years. The man who was once dismissed as a 'boring old fart' is now extravagantly lauded for music that is hardly distinguishable from that which earned the condemnation. This critic finds Young's electric music to be frequently exhilarating, is bored by much of the acoustic stuff, but is glad that Neil Young is still around to show that a rock attitude and rock creativity do not have to be the exclusive preserve of youth.

Title	Format	Label	Cat. No.	Year	Mint	VG	Notes
After The Goldrush	CD	Reprise	C8817	1988	£15	£6	*box set*
After The Goldrush	LP	Reprise	RSLP6383	1970	£15	£6	
Ain't It The Truth	CD-s	Geffen	NYCD1	1993	£5	£2	*promo*
Complex Sessions	CD-s	Reprise	PROCD7342	1995	£20	£10	*US promo*
Conversation With Neil Young	LP	Warner Bros		1980	£20	£8	*US promo*
Don't Be Denied	7"	Reprise	SAM15	197–	£12	£6	*1 sided promo*
Down By The River	7"	Reprise	RS23462	1969	£5	£2	
Everybody Knows This Is Nowhere	7"	Reprise	0819	1969	£50	£25	*US promo, alternate version*
Everybody Knows This Is Nowhere	LP	Reprise	RSLP6349	1969	£20	£8	
Everybody's Rockin'	LP	Geffen		1983	£15	£6	*US audiophile promo*
For The Turntables	CD	WEA	SAM1310	1994	£30	£15	*promo compilation*
Freedom	CD	Reprise	258992	1989	£20	£8	*US promo picture disc*
Harvest	LP	Reprise	REP44131	1972	£15	£6	*Dutch, straw coloured vinyl*
Harvest	LP	Nautilus		1981	£12	£5	*US audiophile*
Journey Through The Past	LP	Reprise	K64015	1972	£20	£8	*double*
Loner	7"	Reprise	RS23405	1969	£5	£2	
My Back Pages	CD-s	Columbia	XPCD308	1993	£5	£2	*promo*
Needle And The Damage Done	CD-s	Reprise	PRO808	1993	£5	£2	*promo*
Neil Young	LP	Reprise	RSLP6317	1969	£40	£20	*no name on front cover*
Neil Young	LP	Reprise	RSLP6317	1969	£25	£10	
Neil Young	LP	Reprise	K44059	1971	£10	£4	
Oh Lonesome Me	7"	Reprise	RS20861	1970	£5	£2	
Old Ways	LP	Geffen	GEF26377	1985	£12	£5	
On The Beach	LP	Reprise	K54014	1974	£25	£10	
Only Love Can Break Your Heart	7"	Reprise	RS20958	1970	£4	£1.50	
Rockin' In The Free World	CD-s	Reprise	W2776CD	1990	£5	£2	
Sleeps With Angels – remastered	CD	Reprise	PROCD7136R	1994	£20	£8	*US promo*
Time Fades Away	LP	Reprise	K54010	1973	£15	£6	
Tonight's The Night	LP	Reprise	K54040	1975	£15	£6	
Trans	LP	Geffen	GHS2018	1982	£15	£6	*US audiophile promo*
When You Dance I Can Really Love	7"	Reprise	RS23488	1971	£4	£1.50	
Zuma	LP	Reprise	K54057	1975	£12	£5	

YOUNG, RALPH

Title	Format	Label	Cat. No.	Year	Mint	VG	Notes
Bible Tells Me So	7"	Brunswick	05466	1955	£8	£4	
Bring Me A Bluebird	7"	Brunswick	05500	1955	£5	£2	
Legend Of Wyatt Earp	7"	Brunswick	05605	1956	£5	£2	

YOUNG, ROGER

Title	Format	Label	Cat. No.	Year	Mint	VG	Notes
No Address	7"	Columbia	DB8092	1966	£25	£12.50	
Sweet Sweet Morning	7"	Columbia	DB7869	1966	£10	£5	

YOUNG, ROY

Title	Format	Label	Cat. No.	Year	Mint	VG	Notes
Big Fat Mamma	7"	Fontana	H200	1959	£10	£5	
Four And Twenty Thousand Kisses	7"	Ember	EMBS128	1961	£5	£2	
Hey Little Girl	7"	Fontana	H215	1959	£6	£2.50	
I Hardly Know It	7"	Fontana	H237	1960	£8	£4	
I'm In Love	7"	Fontana	H247	1960	£5	£2	
Plenty Of Love	7"	Fontana	H290	1961	£6	£2.50	
Roy Young Band	LP	RCA	SF8161	1971	£10	£4	

YOUNG, STEVE

Title	Format	Label	Cat. No.	Year	Mint	VG	Notes
Rock Salt And Nails	LP	A&M	4177	1969	£20	£8	*US*

YOUNG, VICKI

Title	Format	Label	Cat. No.	Year	Mint	VG	Notes
Bye Bye Just For A While	7"	Capitol	CL14528	1956	£5	£2	
Hearts Of Stone	7"	Capitol	CL14228	1955	£12	£6	
Live Fast Love Hard Die Young	7"	Capitol	CL14281	1955	£10	£5	
Spanish Main	7"	Capitol	CL14653	1956	£5	£2	

Vicki Young	7" EP	Capitol	EAP1593	1956	£25	£12.50	

YOUNG, VICTOR

Cherry Pink And Apple Blossom White	7"	Brunswick	05448	1955	£4	£1.50	

YOUNG BLOOD

Continuing Story Of Bungalow Bill	7"	Pye	7N17696	1969	£5	£2	
Green Light	7"	Pye	7N17495	1968	£10	£5	
I Can't Stop	7"	Pye	7N17627	1968	£5	£2	
Just How Loud	7"	Pye	7N17588	1968	£5	£2	

YOUNG BROTHERS

High Energy Rock	LP	GDM		1978	£25	£10	*US, gold vinyl*

YOUNG FLOWERS

Blomsterpistolen	LP	Sonet	1258	1968	£75	£37.50	*Danish*
No. 2	LP	Polydor	2444007	1969	£75	£37.50	

YOUNG FOLK

Ribble Valley Dream	LP	Midas	MR001	1972	£30	£15	

YOUNG GROWLER

V For Victory	7" EP	Columbia	SEG8502	1966	£5	£2	

YOUNG-HOLT TRIO

Wack Wack	7"	Coral	Q72489	1967	£12	£6	

YOUNG-HOLT UNLIMITED

Country Slicker Joe	7"	MCA	MU1053	1969	£5	£2	
Soulful Strut	LP	MCA	MUPS368	1969	£15	£6	

YOUNG IDEA

With A Little Help From My Friends	7"	Columbia	DB8205	1967	£4	£1.50	

YOUNG JESSIE

Shuffle In The Gravel	7"	London	HLE8544	1958	£200	£100	

YOUNG MC

Know How	12"	Delicious Vinyl	BRW120	1988	£15	£7.50	

YOUNG ONES

Baby That's It	7"	Decca	F11705	1963	£5	£2	

YOUNG RASCALS

The group that scored early hits with such songs as 'Groovin' ', 'Good Lovin' ' and 'Too Many Fish In The Sea', decided in 1967 that they could no longer credibly be described as 'young'. For the sake of continuity, all the group's collectable releases are listed in this guide under their adult name, the Rascals.

YOUNG SISTERS

Cassanova Brown	7"	London	HLU9610	1962	£5	£2	

YOUNG SOULS

Why Did You Leave	7"	Amalgamated	AMG844	1969	£6	£2.50	

YOUNG TRADITION

Boar's Head Carol	7"	Argo	AFW115	1974	£4	£1.50	
Chicken On A Raft	7" EP	Transatlantic	TRAEP164	1968	£15	£7.50	
Galleries	LP	Transatlantic	TRA172	1968	£20	£8	
Galleries Revisited	LP	Transatlantic	TRASAM30	1973	£10	£4	
So Cheerfully Round	LP	Transatlantic	TRA155	1967	£25	£10	
Young Tradition	LP	Transatlantic	TRA142	1966	£20	£8	
Young Tradition Sampler	LP	Transatlantic	TRASAM13	1969	£10	£4	

YOUNGBLOODS

Darkness Darkness	7"	RCA	RCA1821	1969	£4	£1.50	
Earth Music	LP	RCA	LPM/LSP3865	1967	£10	£4	*US*
Elephant Mountain	LP	RCA	SF8026	1969	£10	£4	
Get Together	7"	RCA	RCA1877	1969	£4	£1.50	
Jesse Colin Young & The Youngbloods	LP	Mercury	SR61005	1965	£12	£5	*US*
Ride The Wind	LP	Warner Bros	K46100	1971	£10	£4	
Rock Festival	LP	Warner Bros	WS1878	1970	£10	£4	
Sunlight	LP	RCA	SF8218	1972	£10	£4	
Two Trips	LP	Mercury	6338019	1970	£10	£4	
Youngbloods	LP	RCA	LPM/LSP3724	1967	£10	£4	*US*

YOUNGFOLK

Lonely Girl	7"	President	PT136	1968	£5	£2	

YOUTH

As Long As There Is Your Love	7"	Polydor	56121	1966	£6	£2.50	

YOUTH (2)

Empty Quarter	LP	Illuminated	JAMS36	1984	£12	£5	

YPER, LES SOUND

Too Fortiche	7"	Fontana	TF880	1967	£50	£25	

YR HWNTWS

Title	Format	Label	Cat. No.	Year	Mint	VG	Notes
Yr Hwntws	LP	Loco	LOCO1001	1982	**£10**	**£4**	

YURO, TIMI

Title	Format	Label	Cat. No.	Year	Mint	VG	Notes
Amazing Timi Yuro	LP	Mercury	20032MCL	1964	**£10**	**£4**	
As Long As There Is You	7″	Liberty	LIB15182	1969	**£150**	**£75**	
Best Of Timi Yuro	LP	Liberty	(S)LBY1290	1966	**£10**	**£4**	
Get Out Of My Life	7″	Mercury	MF859	1965	**£20**	**£10**	
Great Performances	LP	Liberty	LBL/LBS83115	1968	**£10**	**£4**	
Hurt	7″	Liberty	LIB10177	1964	**£4**	**£1.50**	
Hurt	7″	London	HLG9403	1961	**£[illegible]**	**£[illegible]**	
Hurt	LP	Liberty	LBY1247	1965	**£15**	**£6**	
I Ain't Gonna Cry No More	7″	Liberty	LIB55519	1963	**£10**	**£5**	
I Must Have Been Out Of My Mind	7″	Liberty	LBF15142	1968	**£10**	**£5**	
In The Beginning	LP	Liberty	LBL/LBS83128	1968	**£10**	**£4**	
Let Me Call You Sweetheart	LP	Liberty	(S)LBY1275	1966	**£10**	**£4**	
Make The World Go Away	7″	Liberty	LIB55587	1963	**£5**	**£2**	
Make The World Go Away	7″ EP	Liberty	LEP2252	1966	**£12**	**£6**	
Make The World Go Away	LP	Liberty	LBY1192	1963	**£10**	**£4**	
Satan Never Sleeps	7″	Liberty	LIB55410	1962	**£5**	**£2**	
Something Bad On My Mind	LP	Liberty	LBL/LBS83198	1968	**£15**	**£6**	
Soul	7″ EP	Liberty	LEP2214	1965	**£12**	**£6**	
Soul	LP	Liberty	LBY1042	1962	**£12**	**£5**	
Talented	LP	Mercury	SMWL21019	1969	**£10**	**£4**	
Timi Yuro	LP	London	HAG2415	1962	**£40**	**£20**	
What's A Matter Baby	7″	Liberty	LIB55469	1962	**£10**	**£5**	
What's A Matter Baby	LP	Liberty	(S)LBY1154	1963	**£10**	**£4**	
You Can Have Him	7″	Mercury	MF848	1965	**£4**	**£1.50**	

YWIS

Title	Format	Label	Cat. No.	Year	Mint	VG	Notes
Ywis	LP	Minirock	001	1983	**£20**	**£8**	*Dutch*

Z

ZACHERLEY, JOHN

Title	Format	Label	Cat. No.	Year	Mint	VG	Notes
Dinner With Drac	7"	London	HLU8599	1958	**£25**	**£12.50**	
Monster Mash	LP	Parkway	P7018	1962	**£20**	**£8**	*US*
Scary Tales	LP	Parkway	P7023	1963	**£20**	**£8**	*US*
Spook Along With Zacherley	LP	Elektra	EKL/EKS7190	1960	**£20**	**£8**	*US*
Zacherley's Monster Gallery	LP	Crestview	CR(S7)803	1963	**£20**	**£8**	*US*

ZAGER & EVANS

Title	Format	Label	Cat. No.	Year	Mint	VG	Notes
2525	LP	RCA	SF8056	1969	**£10**	**£4**	

ZAKARRIAS

Title	Format	Label	Cat. No.	Year	Mint	VG	Notes
Zakarrias	LP	Deram	SML1091	1971	**£350**	**£210**	

ZAKARY THAKS

Title	Format	Label	Cat. No.	Year	Mint	VG	Notes
Zakary Thaks	LP	Moxie	MLP2	1980	**£20**	**£8**	*US*

ZANG, TOMMY

Title	Format	Label	Cat. No.	Year	Mint	VG	Notes
Break The Chain	7"	HMV	POP611	1959	**£5**	**£2**	
Hey, Good Lookin'	7"	Polydor	NH66957	1962	**£8**	**£4**	
I Can't Hold Your Letters	7"	Polydor	NH66977	1962	**£4**	**£1.50**	
I'm Gonna Slip You Offa My Mind	7"	Polydor	NH66955	1962	**£4**	**£1.50**	
Just Call My Name	7"	Polydor	NH66980	1962	**£6**	**£2.50**	
Take These Chains From My Heart	7"	Polydor	NH66960	1962	**£4**	**£1.50**	

ZAPPA, FRANK

Critics have never known quite what to make of Frank Zappa. He was such a vastly talented musician and produced such a variety of material that they have tended to focus on just one of the things that he did (usually his satire) and then criticize the rest of his output for failing to measure up in this one area. The fact that Zappa was inclined to hide his art behind a smokescreen of vulgarity does not help, of course, nor does the fact that he was quite self-deprecating about works that are actually little short of being masterpieces. In ages past, many composers were virtuoso instrumentalists who wrote music which would enable them to display their prowess in public performance. Frank Zappa continued this tradition, and because he was working in the rock age and in America, his instrument was the electric guitar and the music he played is easily categorized as rock music. His best work, however (and much of his output qualifies), transcends all the usual categories, emerging as a classical music for our time that is far more relevant, and probably far more durable, than most of what is actually produced under that name. The proof is as close as a copy of *Studio Tan*, or *Uncle Meat*, or *Ship Arriving Too Late To Save A Drowning Witch*, or *The Perfect Stranger*, or *The Grand Wazoo*, or *Make A Jazz Noise Here*, or . . . Frank Zappa is much missed.

Title	Format	Label	Cat. No.	Year	Mint	VG	Notes
200 Motels	LP	United Artists	UDF50003	1971	**£25**	**£10**	*with booklet*
Absolutely Free	LP	Verve	VLP9174	1967	**£40**	**£20**	*mono*
Absolutely Free	LP	Verve	SVLP9174	1967	**£30**	**£15**	*stereo*
Absolutely Free	LP	Verve	2317035	1971	**£15**	**£6**	
Apostrophe	LP	Discreet	MS42175	1973	**£20**	**£8**	*US quad*
Apostrophe	LP	Discreet	K59201	1973	**£10**	**£4**	
Baby Snakes	LP	Barking Pumpkin	BPR1115	1983	**£20**	**£8**	*picture disc*
Big Leg Emma	7"	Verve	VS557	1967	**£30**	**£15**	
Bongo Fury	LP	Discreet	DS2234	1975	**£10**	**£4**	*US*
Bongo Fury	LP	Discreet	K59209	1975	**£75**	**£37.50**	*test pressing only*
Burnt Weeny Sandwich	LP	Reprise	K44083	1971	**£10**	**£4**	
Burnt Weeny Sandwich	LP	Reprise	RSLP6370	1969	**£15**	**£6**	
Burnt Weeny Sandwich/Weasels Ripped My Flesh	LP	Reprise	K64024	1979	**£12**	**£5**	*double*
Chunga's Revenge	LP	Reprise	K44020	1971	**£10**	**£4**	
Chunga's Revenge	LP	Reprise	RSLP2030	1970	**£10**	**£4**	*red cover*
Chunga's Revenge	LP	Reprise	RSLP2030	1970	**£12**	**£5**	*green cover*
Clean Cuts From Sheik Yerbouti	LP	Zappa	MK78	1980	**£20**	**£8**	*US promo*
Clean Cuts From Tinseltown Rebellion	LP	Barking Pumpkin	AS995	1981	**£20**	**£8**	*US promo*
Clean Cuts From You Are What You Is	LP	Barking Pumpkin	AS1294	1981	**£20**	**£8**	*US promo*
Cosmic Debris	7"	Discreet	K19201	1973	**£5**	**£2**	
Ditties And Beer	CD	Ryko	ZAP2	1996	**£40**	**£20**	*US promo compilation*
Don't Eat The Yellow Snow	7"	Discreet	K19205	1973	**£5**	**£2**	
Fillmore East 1971	LP	Reprise	K44150	1971	**£10**	**£4**	
Frank Zappa & The Mothers Of Invention	LP	Verve	2352057	1975	**£12**	**£5**	
Freak Out	LP	Verve	VLP9154	1966	**£50**	**£25**	*mono*
Freak Out	LP	Verve	SVLP9154	1966	**£40**	**£20**	*stereo*
Freak Out	LP	Verve	V(6)5005	1966	**£50**	**£25**	*US, with map insert*
Freak Out	LP	Verve	2683004	1971	**£25**	**£10**	*double*

Grand Wazoo	LP	Reprise	K44209	1972	**£10**	**£4**	
Hot Rats	LP	Reprise	K44078	1971	**£10**	**£4**	
Hot Rats	LP	Reprise	RSLP6356	1969	**£15**	**£6**	*pink, gold, & green label*
Hot Rats	LP	Reprise	RSLP6356	1970	**£10**	**£4**	*tan label*
Hot Rats	LP	Reprise	RSLP6356	1969	**£60**	**£30**	*with Zappa/ Beefheart argument*
Hot Rats	CD	Ryko		1992	**£20**	**£8**	*US gold picture disc*
It Can't Happen Here	7"	Verve	VS545	1966	**£60**	**£30**	
Joe's Garage	7"	CBS	7950	1980	**£15**	**£7.50**	*mispress with Bob Dylan B-side*
Joe's Garage Act 1	LP	CBS	86101	1979	**£10**	**£4**	*with lyric sheet*
Joe's Garage Acts 2/3	LP	CBS	88475	1979	**£12**	**£5**	*double, lyric sheets*
Just Another Band From L.A.	LP	Reprise	K44179	1972	**£10**	**£4**	
Lather	LP	Columbia	41500	1976	**£1000**	**£700**	*4 LPs, test pressings*
Lumpy Gravy	LP	Verve	VLP9223	1968	**£40**	**£20**	*mono*
Lumpy Gravy	LP	Verve	SVLP9223	1968	**£30**	**£15**	*stereo*
Lumpy Gravy	LP	Verve	2317046	1971	**£15**	**£6**	
Make A Jazz Noise Here	CD	Barking Pumpkin	CDDZAP41	1991	**£25**	**£10**	*original with Bartok & Stravinsky tracks*
Man From Utopia	7"	CBS	XPS180	1983	**£4**	**£1.50**	*promo only*
Mothermania	LP	Verve	VLP9239	1969	**£30**	**£15**	*mono*
Mothermania	LP	Verve	SVLP9239	1969	**£25**	**£10**	*stereo*
Mothermania	LP	Verve	2317047	1971	**£15**	**£6**	
Mothermania	LP	Verve	2352017	1972	**£15**	**£6**	
Mothers Of Invention	LP	MGM	GAS112	1970	**£20**	**£8**	*US*
No Commercial Potential	CD	Ryko	FZZAP1	1995	**£30**	**£15**	*promo compilation*
One Size Fits All	LP	Discreet	K59207	1974	**£10**	**£4**	
Orchestral Favourites	LP	Discreet	K59212	1978	**£10**	**£4**	
Overnight Sensation	LP	Discreet	K41000	1973	**£10**	**£4**	
Overnight Sensation	LP	Discreet	MS42149	1973	**£20**	**£8**	*US quad*
Roxy And Elsewhere	LP	Discreet	K69201	1974	**£12**	**£5**	*double*
Ruben And The Jets	LP	Verve	VLP9237	1969	**£40**	**£20**	*mono*
Ruben And The Jets	LP	Verve	SVLP9327	1968	**£30**	**£15**	*stereo*
Ruben And The Jets	LP	Verve	V65055	1968	**£50**	**£25**	*US, with 3 inserts*
Ruben And The Jets	LP	Verve	2317069	1971	**£15**	**£6**	
Ship Arriving Too Late . . . Sampler	LP	Barking Pumpkin	AS1569	1982	**£10**	**£4**	*US promo*
Shut Up And Play Your Guitar	LP	CBS	66368	1981	**£25**	**£10**	*triple*
Sleep Dirt	LP	Discreet	K59211	1978	**£10**	**£4**	
Specialised Digital Audio Gratification	CD	Barking Pumpkin	CDPROMO1111	1988	**£40**	**£20**	*promo*
Studio Tan	LP	Discreet	K59210	1978	**£10**	**£4**	
Tears Began To Fall	7"	Reprise	K14100	1971	**£20**	**£10**	
Thingfish	LP	EMI	2402943	1985	**£25**	**£10**	*with libretto*
Uncle Meat	LP	Bizarre	2MS2024	1969	**£15**	**£6**	*double*
Uncle Meat	LP	Transatlantic	TRA197	1969	**£25**	**£10**	*double*
Uncle Meat	LP	Transatlantic	TRA197	1969	**£30**	**£15**	*double, booklet*
Waka Jawaka	LP	Reprise	K44203	1972	**£10**	**£4**	
We're Only In It For The Money	LP	Verve	VLP9199	1968	**£40**	**£20**	*mono*
We're Only In It For The Money	LP	Verve	SVLP9199	1967	**£40**	**£20**	*stereo, with insert*
We're Only In It For The Money	LP	Verve	SVLP9199	1967	**£30**	**£15**	*stereo*
We're Only In It For The Money	LP	Verve	2317034	1971	**£15**	**£6**	
Weasels Ripped My Flesh	LP	Reprise	RSLP2028	1970	**£12**	**£5**	
Weasels Ripped My Flesh	LP	Reprise	K44019	1971	**£10**	**£4**	
Welcome To Joe's Garage	LP	Zappa	MK129	1981	**£20**	**£8**	*US promo*
What Will This Evening . . .	7"	United Artists	UP35319	1971	**£20**	**£10**	
Worst Of The Mothers	LP	MGM	SE4754	1971	**£20**	**£8**	*US*
XXXX Of The Mothers Of Invention	LP	Verve	V65074	1969	**£20**	**£8**	*US*
You Are What You Is	12"	CBS	A121622	1981	**£8**	**£4**	*picture disc*
You Can't Do That On The Radio Anymore	CD	Ryko	RCCPRO9003	1990	**£25**	**£10**	*US promo compilation*
Zappa In New York	LP	Discreet	K69204	1977	**£40**	**£20**	*double, with 'Punky's Whips'*
Zappa In New York	LP	Discreet	K69204	1977	**£12**	**£5**	*double*
Zapped	LP	Warner Bros	PRO368	1969	**£30**	**£15**	*US, collage cover*
Zapped	LP	Warner Bros	PRO368	1969	**£25**	**£10**	*US, photo cover*
Zoot Allures	LP	Warner Bros	K56298	1976	**£10**	**£4**	

ZARATHUSTRA

Zarathustra	LP	Metronome	MLP15421	1971	**£75**	**£37.50**	*German*

ZAWINUL, JOE

Zawinul	LP	Atlantic	2400151	1971	**£15**	**£6**	

ZEAR, PETE

Tomorrow's World	7"		22-1	1984	**£6**	**£2.50**	

ZEE

Confusion	12"	Harvest	HAR125277	1984	**£6**	**£2.50**	
Confusion	7"	Harvest	HAR5277	1984	**£5**	**£2**	
Identity	LP	Harvest	SHSP2401018	1984	**£10**	**£4**	

ZENITH SIX

At The Royal Festival Hall	7" EP	Decca	DFE6255	1956	**£6**	**£2.50**	
Zenith Six	7" EP	Tempo	EXA42	1957	**£6**	**£2.50**	

Zenith Six	7" EP	Tempo	EXA58	1957	£6	**£2.50**	

ZEPHYR

Going Back To Colorado	LP	Warner Bros	BS1897	1971	£20	**£8**	*US*
Sunset Ride	LP	Warner Bros	BS2603	1972	£20	**£8**	*US*
Zephyr	LP	Probe	SPB1006	1970	£25	**£10**	

ZEPHYRS

I Just Can't Take It	7"	Columbia	DB7571	1965	£15	**£7.50**	
Little Bit Of Soap	7"	Columbia	DB7324	1964	£15	**£7.50**	
She's Lost You	7"	Columbia	DB7481	1965	£15	**£7.50**	
Sweet Little Baby	7"	Columbia	DB7199	1964	£15	**£7.50**	
What's All That About	7"	Decca	F11647	1963	£20	**£10**	
Wonder What I'm Gonna Do	7"	Columbia	DB7410	1964	£15	**£7.50**	

ZERFAS

Zerfas	LP	700 West	LH730710	1973	£500	**£330**	*US*

ZETTERLINK, ZIPPO

In The Poor Sun	LP	Orschewski	OR001	1971	£20	**£8**	*German*

ZETTERLUND, MONICA

Make Mine Swedish Style	LP	Philips	BL7647	1964	£10	**£4**	

ZEVON, WARREN

Leave My Monkey Alone	CD-s	Virgin	CDEP2	1988	£5	**£2**	
Wanted Dead Or Alive	LP	Imperial	LP12456	1969	£15	**£6**	*US*
Werewolves Of London	12"	Asylum	AS11386	1978	£10	**£5**	*US picture disc*

ZIMMERMAN, TUCKER

Ten Songs By Tucker Zimmerman	LP	Regal Zonophone	SLRZ1010	1969	£12	**£5**	
Tucker Zimmerman	LP	Village Thing	VTS13	1972	£12	**£5**	

ZIOR

Cat's Eyes	7"	Nepentha	6129003	1973	£8	**£4**	
Every Inch A Man	LP	Global Intercord	26009U	1973	£100	**£50**	*German*
Za Za Za Zilda	7"	Nepentha	6129002	1971	£8	**£4**	
Zior	LP	Nepentha	6437005	1971	£40	**£20**	

ZIP CODES

Mustang	LP	Liberty	LRP3367/ LST7367	1964	£15	**£6**	*US*

ZIPPER

Zipper	LP	Whizeagle	W0001	1975	£50	**£25**	*US*

ZIPPERS

My Sailor Boy	7"	Hickory	451252	1964	£4	**£1.50**	

ZITRO

Zitro	LP	ESP-Disk	1052	1967	£25	**£10**	*US*

ZODIAC MOTEL

Story Of Roland Flagg	7"	Swordfish	SWF1	1987	£6	**£2.50**	*1 sided promo*
Sunshine Miner	7"	Swordfish	SWF004	1987	£5	**£2**	

ZOMBIES

With sixties rock music keenly seeking wider credibility within the arts generally, much used to be made of the Zombies' educational qualifications. In fact, the Zombies' brand of pop-R&B was particularly distinctive, but this had rather more to do with Rod Argent's skilful keyboard playing and Colin Blunstone's attractive, breathy singing than with any qualifications. *Odessey And Oracle* (the misspelling is on the record), recorded as the group was breaking up, is something of a pop masterpiece, inspired by the Beatles no doubt, but nevertheless retaining the Zombies' stamp.

Begin Here	LP	Decca	LK4679	1965	£125	**£62.50**	
Bunny Lake A Disparu	7" EP	RCA	86507	1965	£40	**£20**	*French*
Bunny Lake Is Missing	LP	RCA	RD7791	1965	£75	**£37.50**	
Care Of Cell 44	7"	CBS	3087	1967	£15	**£7.50**	
Friends Of Mine	7"	CBS	2960	1967	£15	**£7.50**	
Goin' Out Of My Head	7"	Decca	F12584	1967	£6	**£2.50**	
Gotta Get A Hold Of Myself	7"	Decca	F12495	1966	£6	**£2.50**	
I Love You	7"	Decca	F12798	1968	£6	**£2.50**	
Indication	7"	Decca	F12426	1966	£6	**£2.50**	
Is This The Dream	7"	Decca	F12296	1965	£5	**£2**	
Is This The Dream	7" EP	Decca	457100	1966	£40	**£20**	*French*
Kind Of Girl	7" EP	Decca	457083	1965	£40	**£20**	*French*
Leave Me Be	7"	Decca	F12004	1964	£4	**£1.50**	
Odessey And Oracle	LP	CBS	SBPG63280	1968	£40	**£20**	*stereo*
Odessey And Oracle	LP	CBS	BPG63280	1968	£75	**£37.50**	*mono*
Remember You	7"	Decca	F12322	1966	£6	**£2.50**	
She's Coming Home	7"	Decca	F12125	1965	£5	**£2**	
She's Not There	7"	Decca	F11940	1964	£4	**£1.50**	
She's Not There	7" EP	Decca	457051	1964	£40	**£20**	*French*
Tell Her No	7"	Decca	F12072	1965	£4	**£1.50**	
Time Of The Season	7"	CBS	3380	1968	£15	**£7.50**	
Time Of The Zombies	LP	Epic	EPC68262	1973	£20	**£8**	*double*

What More Can I Do	7" EP	Decca	457075	1965	**£40**	**£20**	*French*
Whenever You're Ready	7"	Decca	F12225	1965	**£5**	**£2**	
Zombies	7" EP	Decca	DFE8598	1965	**£40**	**£20**	
Zombies EP	CD-s	Special Edition	CD312	1988	**£5**	**£2**	*3" single*

ZOO

I Shall Be Free	LP	Riviera	521147	1971	**£15**	**£6**	*French*
Zoo	LP	Barclay	521172	1971	**£15**	**£6**	*French*
Zoo	LP	Major Minor	SMLP74	1970	**£15**	**£6**	

ZOO (2)

Though much less celebrated, the music played by the Zoo is lively sixties punk in the manner of the Seeds, only with superior instrumental work. Lead guitarist Howard Leese, in particular, impresses and it is he who later found successful employment elsewhere, as a member of Heart.

Presents Chocolate Moose	LP	Sunburst	7500	1968	**£40**	**£20**	*US*

ZOROASTER

Ahriman	LP				**£500**	**£330**	

ZORRO

'Arrods Don't Sell 'Em	7"	Bridgehouse	BHEP1	1979	**£40**	**£20**	*picture sleeve*
'Arrods Don't Sell 'Em	7"	Bridgehouse	BHEP1	1979	**£8**	**£4**	

ZOSKIA

Be Like Me	12"	Temple	TOPY005	1985	**£8**	**£4**	*clear vinyl*
J.G.	7"	Temple	TOPY021	1987	**£5**	**£2**	*test pressing*

ZOUNDS

Curse Of Zounds	LP	Rough Trade	ROUGH31	1984	**£12**	**£5**	
La Vache Qui Rit	7"	Not So Brave	NSB001	1982	**£4**	**£1.50**	

ZUIDERZEE

Peace Of Mind	7"	CBS	202235	1966	**£4**	**£1.50**	

ZUKIE, TAPPER

In Dub	LP	Front Line	FL1029	1978	**£12**	**£5**	
MPLA	LP	Front Line	FL1006	1978	**£12**	**£5**	
Peace In The Ghetto	LP	Front Line	FL1009	1978	**£12**	**£5**	
Tapper Roots	LP	Front Line	FL1032	1978	**£12**	**£5**	

ZWEISTEIN

Trip, Flipout, Meditation	LP	Philips	6630002	1970	**£50**	**£25**	*German triple*

ZZ & THE MASKERS

ZZ And The Maskers	LP	Artone	PDR138	1965	**£20**	**£8**	*Dutch*

ZZ TOP

Arrested For Driving While Blind	7"	London	HLU10547	1977	**£8**	**£4**	
Arrested For Driving While Blind	7"	London	HLU10547	1977	**£10**	**£5**	*mispress with Ray Charles B side*
Beer Drinkers And Hell Raisers	7"	London	HLU10458	1974	**£6**	**£2.50**	
Cheap Sunglasses	7"	Warner Bros	K17647	1979	**£5**	**£2**	
Cheap Sunglasses (Live)	12"	Warner Bros	PRO887	1980	**£10**	**£5**	*promo*
Double Back	CD-s	WEA	W9812CD	1990	**£5**	**£2**	
Eliminator	CD	Warner Bros	237742	1987	**£40**	**£20**	*mispressing – plays the Beatles' Revolver*
Eliminator	LP	Warner Bros	W3774	1983	**£12**	**£5**	*with 12"*
Eliminator	LP	Warner Bros	W3774P	1985	**£10**	**£4**	*picture disc*
First Album/Rio Grande . . .	CD	Warner Bros	9256612	1987	**£30**	**£15**	*1st 6 albums on 3 discs*
Francene	7"	London	HLU10376	1972	**£10**	**£5**	
Gimme All Your Lovin'	7"	Warner Bros	W9693P	1983	**£10**	**£5**	*shaped picture disc*
Give It Up	CD-s	WEA	W9509CD	1990	**£5**	**£2**	
I Thank You	7"	Warner Bros	K17576	1980	**£5**	**£2**	
It's Only Love	7"	London	HLU10538	1976	**£5**	**£2**	
La Grange	7"	London	HLU10475	1975	**£10**	**£5**	
Legs (Dance)	12"	Warner Bros	PRO2146	1983	**£8**	**£4**	*promo*
Legs (Extended)	12"	Warner Bros	PRO2127	1983	**£8**	**£4**	*promo*
Recycler	CD	Warner Bros		1990	**£25**	**£10**	*US promo with spoken intros*
Recycler	CD	Warner Bros	26458	1990	**£25**	**£10**	*US promo picture disc, metal case*
Rough Boy	7"	Warner Bros	W2003FP	1986	**£12**	**£6**	*interlocking shaped picture disc*
Sleeping Bag	12"	Warner Bros	W2001T	1985	**£6**	**£2.50**	
Sleeping Bag	7"	Warner Bros	W2001F	1985	**£6**	**£2.50**	*double*
Sleeping Bag	7"	Warner Bros	W2001P	1985	**£6**	**£2.50**	*shaped picture disc*
Sleeping Bag	7"	Warner Bros	W2001P	1985	**£15**	**£7.50**	*interlocking shaped picture disc*
Sleeping Bag	7"	Warner Bros	W2001DP	1985	**£6**	**£2.50**	*shaped picture disc*
Stages	7"	Warner Bros	W2002BP	1986	**£5**	**£2**	*interlocking shaped picture disc*
T.V. Dinners	12"	Warner Bros	W9334T	1984	**£6**	**£2.50**	*double*
Taste Of The Sixpack	CD	Warner Bros	PROCD2875	1987	**£25**	**£10**	*US promo sampler*
Tejas	LP	London	LDU1	1976	**£10**	**£4**	
Tush	7"	London	HLU10495	1975	**£6**	**£2.50**	

READ MORE IN PENGUIN

In every corner of the world, on every subject under the sun, Penguin represents quality and variety – the very best in publishing today.

For complete information about books available from Penguin – including [illegible] [illegible]

In the United Kingdom: [illegible]

In the United States: [illegible]

In Canada: [illegible]

In Australia: [illegible]

In New Zealand: [illegible]

In India: [illegible]

In the Netherlands: Please write to Penguin Books Netherlands [illegible]

In Germany: Please write to Penguin Books Deutschland GmbH, [illegible]

In Spain: [illegible]

In Italy: [illegible]

In France: [illegible]

In Japan: [illegible]

In South Africa: [illegible]

To be recommended without reservation ... a rich and rewarding online experience

READ MORE IN PENGUIN

PENGUIN AUDIOBOOKS

PENGUIN AUDIOBOOKS

PENGUIN AUDIOBOOKS

The Man in the Iron Mask by Alexandre Dumas, read by Simon Ward

Adam Bede by George Eliot, read by Paul Copley

Joseph Andrews by Henry Fielding, read by Sean Barrett

The Great Gatsby by F. Scott Fitzgerald, read by Marcus D'Amico

North and South by Elizabeth Gaskell, read by Diana Quick

The Diary of a Nobody by George Grossmith, read by Terrence Hardiman

Jude the Obscure by Thomas Hardy, read by Samuel West

The Go-Between by L. P. Hartley, read by Tony Britton

Les Misérables by Victor Hugo, read by Nigel Anthony

A Passage to India by E. M. Forster, read by Tim Pigott-Smith

The Odyssey by Homer, read by Alex Jennings

The Portrait of a Lady by Henry James, read by Claire Bloom

On the Road by Jack Kerouac, read by David Carradine

Women in Love by D. H. Lawrence, read by Michael Maloney

Nineteen Eighty-Four by George Orwell, read by Timothy West

Ivanhoe by Sir Walter Scott, read by Ciaran Hinds

Frankenstein by Mary Shelley, read by Richard Pasco

Of Mice and Men by John Steinbeck, read by Gary Sinise

Dracula by Bram Stoker, read by Richard E. Grant

Gulliver's Travels by Jonathan Swift, read by Hugh Laurie

Vanity Fair by William Makepeace Thackeray, read by Robert Hardy

War and Peace by Leo Tolstoy, read by Bill Nighy

Barchester Towers by Anthony Trollope, read by David Timson

Tao Te Ching by Lao Tzu, read by Carole Boyd and John Rowe

Ethan Frome by Edith Wharton, read by Nathan Osgood

The Picture of Dorian Gray by Oscar Wilde, read by John Moffatt

Orlando by Virginia Woolf, read by Tilda Swinton

READ MORE IN PENGUIN

READ MORE IN PENGUIN 

REFERENCE

The Penguin Dictionary of the Third Reich
James Taylor and Warren Shaw

This dictionary provides a full background to the rise of Nazism and the role of Germany in the Second World War. Among the areas covered are the major figures from Nazi politics, arts and industry, the German Resistance, the politics of race and the Nuremberg trials.

The Penguin Biographical Dictionary of Women

This stimulating, informative and entirely new Penguin dictionary of women from all over the world, through the ages, contains over 1,600 clear and concise biographies on major figures from politicians, saints and scientists to poets, film stars and writers.

Roget's Thesaurus of English Words and Phrases
Edited by Betty Kirkpatrick

This new edition of Roget's classic work, now brought up to date for the nineties, will increase anyone's command of the English language. Fully cross-referenced, it includes synonyms of every kind (formal or colloquial, idiomatic and figurative) for almost 900 headings. It is a must for writers and utterly fascinating for any English speaker.

The Penguin Dictionary of International Relations
Graham Evans and Jeffrey Newnham

International relations have undergone a revolution since the end of the Cold War. This new world disorder is fully reflected in this new Penguin dictionary, which is extensively cross-referenced with a select bibliography to aid further study.

The Penguin Guide to Synonyms and Related Words
S. I. Hayakawa

'More helpful than a thesaurus, more humane than a dictionary, the *Guide to Synonyms and Related Words* maps linguistic boundaries with precision, sensitivity to nuance and, on occasion, dry wit' *The Times Literary Supplement*

READ MORE IN PENGUIN

REFERENCE

The Penguin Dictionary of Troublesome Words Bill Bryson

Why should you avoid discussing the *weather conditions*? Can a married woman be celibate? Why is it eccentric to talk about the aroma of a cowshed? A straightforward guide to the pitfalls and hotly disputed issues in standard written English.

Swearing Geoffrey Hughes

'A deliciously filthy trawl among taboo words across the ages and the globe' Valentine Cunningham, *Observer*, Books of the Year. 'Erudite and entertaining' Penelope Lively, *Daily Telegraph*, Books of the Year.

Medicines: A Guide for Everybody Peter Parish

Now in its seventh edition and completely revised and updated, this bestselling guide is written in ordinary language for the ordinary reader yet will prove indispensable to anyone involved in health care: nurses, pharmacists, opticians, social workers and doctors.

Media Law Geoffrey Robertson QC and Andrew Nichol

Crisp and authoritative surveys explain the up-to-date position on defamation, obscenity, official secrecy, copyright and confidentiality, contempt of court, the protection of privacy and much more.

The Penguin Careers Guide
Anna Alston and Anne Daniel; Consultant Editor: Ruth Miller

As the concept of a 'job for life' wanes, this guide encourages you to think broadly about occupational areas as well as describing day-to-day work and detailing the latest developments and qualifications such as NVQs. Special features include possibilities for working part-time and job-sharing, returning to work after a break and an assessment of the current position of women.

READ MORE IN PENGUIN 

MUSIC REFERENCE

The Penguin Guide to Compact Discs
Ivan March, Edward Greenfield, Robert Layton

'Within the space of a few years *The Penguin Guide* has become something of an institution, its status earned largely through a cheerful, informative "plain speaking" style, copious entries, and attractive reader-friendly presentation' *CD Review*

The Penguin Encyclopedia of Popular Music Donald Clarke

'There has been a desperate need . . . for a quality reference book on popular music. Covering the huge terrain of "non-classical music this century" . . . this book goes a long way towards satisfying that need . . . the entries are well chosen, considered and informative' *Observer*. 'An indispensable companion' *Q Magazine*

All You Need to Know about the Music Business Donald S. Passman

Recommended by stars and top industry executives alike, *All You Need to Know about the Music Business* is the one essential reference for anyone involved with – or planning to get involved with – the multi-billion dollar music industry.

The Penguin Opera Guide
Edited by Amanda Holden with Nicholas Kenyon and Stephen Walsh

'Remarkably comprehensive . . . The criterion for any guide is whether it can be read not only for reference but for entertainment, and Amanda Holden and her contributors pass this test with first-class honours' *The Times*

The Penguin Guide to Jazz on CD
Richard Cook and Brian Morton

'An incisive account of available recordings, which cuts across the artificial boundaries by which jazz has been divided . . . each page has a revelation; everybody will find their own' *The Times*